CW00645573

The Form Book ®

FLAT ANNUAL FOR 2014

THE OFFICIAL FORM BOOK

ALL THE 2013 RETURNS

Complete record of Flat Racing
from 1 January to 31 December 2013

Associated Raceform products

The Form Book is updated weekly. Subscribers receive a binder, together with all the early racing. Weekly sections and a new index are threaded into the binder to keep it up to date.

The data contained in *The Form Book Flat Annual for 2014* is available in paper form or on computer disk. The disk service, Raceform Interactive, contains the same data as The Flat Form Book, and operates on any PC within a 'Windows' environment. The database is designed to allow access to the information in a number of different ways, and is extremely quick and easy to use.

Published in 2014 by Raceform Ltd
Compton, Newbury, Berkshire, RG20 6NL

A catalogue record for this book is available from the British Library,

ISBN 978-1-909471-25-2

Printed and bound by CPI Group (UK) Ltd, Croydon, CR0 4YY

Full details of all Raceform services and publications are available from:

Raceform Ltd, Compton, Newbury, Berkshire RG20 6NL
Tel: 01933 304858 • Fax: 01933 304796
Email: shop@racingpost.com
www.racingpost.com

Cover photo: Richard Hughes guiding Sky Lantern to victory in the Coronation Stakes at Royal Ascot. © Charlie Crowhurst/Getty Images

CONTENTS

Editor: Graham Dench

Production: Steffan Edwards

Key to racereaders' initials

WG ....Walter Glynn	JN ....Jonathan Neesom	JR ....Joe Rowntree
RL ....Richard Lowther	DO ....Darren Owen	AS ....Andrew Sheret
LM....................Lee McKenzie	SP ....Steve Payne	ST ....Steve Taylor
TM ....Tim Mitchell	CR ....Colin Roberts	RY ....Richard Young

The Official Scale of Weight, Age & Distance (Flat)

The following scale should only be used in conjunction with the Official ratings published in this book. Use of any other scale will introduce errors into calculations. The allowances are expressed as the number of pounds that is deemed the average horse in each group falls short of maturity at different dates and distances.

Dist		Jan		Feb		Mar		Apr		May		Jun		Jul		Aug		Sep		Oct		Nov		Dec	
(fur)	Age	1-15	16-31	1-14	15-28	1-15	16-31	1-15	16-30	1-15	16-31	1-15	16-30	1-15	16-31	1-15	16-31	1-15	16-30	1-15	16-31	1-15	16-30	1-15	16-31
5	2	-	-	-	-	-	47	44	41	38	36	34	32	30	28	26	24	22	20	19	18	17	17	16	16
	3	15	15	14	14	13	12	11	10	9	8	7	6	5	4	3	2	1	1	-	-	-	-	-	-
6	2	-	-	-	-	-	-	-	-	44	41	38	36	33	31	28	26	24	22	21	20	19	18	17	17
	3	16	16	15	15	14	13	12	11	10	9	8	7	6	5	4	3	2	2	1	1	-	-	-	-
7	2	-	-	-	-	-	-	-	-	-	-	-	-	38	35	32	30	27	25	23	22	21	20	19	19
	3	18	18	17	17	16	15	14	13	12	11	10	9	8	7	6	5	4	3	2	2	1	1	-	-
8	2	-	-	-	-	-	-	-	-	-	-	-	-	-	-	37	34	31	28	26	24	23	22	21	20
	3	20	20	19	19	18	17	15	14	13	12	11	10	9	8	7	6	5	4	3	3	2	2	1	1
9	3	22	22	21	21	20	19	17	15	14	13	12	11	10	9	8	7	6	5	4	4	3	3	2	2
	4	1	1	-	-	-	-	-	-	-	-	-	-	-	-	-	-	-	-	-	-	-	-	-	-
10	3	23	23	22	22	21	20	19	17	15	14	13	12	11	10	9	8	7	6	5	5	4	4	3	3
	4	2	2	1	1	-	-	-	-	-	-	-	-	-	-	-	-	-	-	-	-	-	-	-	-
11	3	24	24	23	23	22	21	20	19	17	15	14	13	12	11	10	9	8	7	6	6	5	5	4	4
	4	3	3	2	2	1	1	-	-	-	-	-	-	-	-	-	-	-	-	-	-	-	-	-	-
12	3	25	25	24	24	23	22	21	20	19	17	15	14	13	12	11	10	9	8	7	7	6	6	5	5
	4	4	4	3	3	2	2	1	1	-	-	-	-	-	-	-	-	-	-	-	-	-	-	-	-
13	3	26	26	25	25	24	23	22	21	20	19	17	15	14	13	12	11	10	9	8	8	7	7	6	6
	4	5	5	4	4	3	3	2	1	-	-	-	-	-	-	-	-	-	-	-	-	-	-	-	-
14	3	27	27	26	26	25	24	23	22	21	20	19	17	15	14	13	12	11	10	9	9	8	8	7	7
	4	6	6	5	5	4	4	3	2	1	-	-	-	-	-	-	-	-	-	-	-	-	-	-	-
15	3	28	28	27	27	26	25	24	23	22	21	20	19	17	15	14	13	12	11	10	9	8	8	7	7
	4	6	6	5	5	4	4	3	3	2	1	-	-	-	-	-	-	-	-	-	-	-	-	-	-
16	3	29	29	28	28	27	26	25	24	23	22	21	20	19	17	15	14	13	12	11	10	9	9	8	8
	4	7	7	6	6	5	5	4	4	3	2	1	-	-	-	-	-	-	-	-	-	-	-	-	-
18	3	31	31	30	30	29	28	27	26	25	24	23	22	21	20	18	16	14	13	12	11	10	10	9	9
	4	8	8	7	7	6	6	5	5	4	3	2	1	-	-	-	-	-	-	-	-	-	-	-	-
20	3	33	33	32	32	31	30	29	28	27	26	25	24	23	22	20	18	16	14	13	12	11	11	10	10
	4	9	9	8	8	7	7	6	6	5	4	3	2	1	-	-	-	-	-	-	-	-	-	-	-

The Form Book

Welcome to the 2014 edition of *The Form Book,* comprising the complete year's results from 2013.

Race details contain Racing Post Ratings assessing the merit of each individual performance, speed figures for every horse that clocks a worthwhile time, weight-for-age allowances, stall positions for every race and the starting price percentage, in addition to the traditional features.

Race Focus comments are printed below most races, along with the results of stewards' enquiries.

The official record

THE FORM BOOK records comprehensive race details of every domestic race, every major European Group race and every foreign event in which a British-trained runner participated.

MEETING BACK REFERENCE NUMBER is the Raceform number of the last meeting run at the track and is shown to the left of the course name. Abandoned meetings are signified by a dagger.

THE GOING, The Official going, shown at the head of each meeting, is recorded as follows: Turf: Hard; Firm; Good to firm; Good; Good to soft; Soft; Heavy. All-Weather: Fast; Standard to fast; Standard; Standard to slow; Slow. There may be variations for non-British meetings

Where appropriate, a note is included indicating track bias and any differences to the official going indicated by race times.

THE WEATHER is shown below the date for selected meetings.

THE WIND is given as a strength and direction at the Winning Post, classified as follows:
Strength: gale; v.str; str; fresh; mod; slt; almost nil; nil.
Direction: (half) against; (half) bhd; (half) across from or towards stands.

VISIBILITY is good unless otherwise stated.

RACE NUMBERS for foreign races carry the suffix 'a' in the race header and in the index.

RACE TITLE is the name of the race as shown in the Racing Calendar.

COMPETITIVE RACING CLASSIFICATIONS are shown on a scale from Class 1 to Class 7. All Pattern races are Class 1.

THE RACE DISTANCE is given for all races, and is accompanied by (s) for races run on straight courses and (r) for courses where there is a round track of comparable distance. On All-Weather courses (F) for Fibresand or (P) for Polytrack indicates the nature of the artificial surface on which the race is run.

OFFICIAL RACE TIME as published in the Racing Calendar is followed in parentheses by the time when the race actually started. This is followed by the race class, age restrictions, handicap restrictions and the official rating of the top weight.

PRIZE MONEY shows penalty values down to sixth place (where applicable).

THE POSITION OF THE STARTING STALLS is shown against each race, in the form of: High (H), Centre (C) or Low (L). In keeping with all other major racing nations, stalls are now numbered from the inside rail. If the stalls are placed adjacent to the inside rail they are described as low, if against the outside rail they are described as high. Otherwise they are central.

IN THE RACE RESULT, the figures to the far left of each horse (under FORM) show the most recent form figures. The figure in bold is the finishing position in this race as detailed below.

1...40 - finishing positions first to fortieth; **b** - brought down; **c** - carried out; **f** - fell; **p** - pulled up; **r** - refused; **ro** - ran out; **s** - slipped up; **u** - unseated rider; **v** - void race.

THE OFFICIAL DISTANCES between the horses are shown on the left-hand side immediately after their position at the finish.

NUMBER OF DAYS SINCE PREVIOUS RUN is the superscript figure immediately following the horse name and suffix.

PREVIOUS RACEFORM RACE NUMBER is the boxed figure to the right of the horse's name.

THE HORSE'S AGE is shown immediately before the weight carried.

WEIGHTS shown are actual weights carried.

OFFICIAL RATING is the figure in bold type directly after the horse's name in the race result. This figure indicates the Official BHA rating, at entry, after the following adjustments had been made:
(i) Overweight carried by the rider.
(ii) The number of pounds out of the handicap (if applicable).
(iii) Penalties incurred after the publication of the weights.
However, no adjustments have been made for:
(i) Weight-for-age.
(ii) Riders' claims.

HEADGEAR is shown immediately before the jockey's name and in parentheses and expressed as: **b** (blinkers); **v** (visor); **h** (hood); **e** (eyeshield); **c** (eyecover); **p** (sheepskin cheekpieces); **t** (tongue-tie).

THE JOCKEY is shown for every runner followed, in superscript, by apprentice allowances in parentheses.

APPRENTICE ALLOWANCES The holders of apprentice jockeys' licences under the provisions of Rule 60(iii) are permitted to claim the following allowances in Flat races:
7lb until they have won 20 Flat races run under the Rules of any recognised Turf Authority; thereafter 5lb until they have won 50 such Flat races; thereafter 3lb until they have won 95 such Flat races. These allowances can be claimed in the Flat races set out below, with the exception of races confined to apprentice jockeys:
(a) All handicap handicaps other than those Rated stakes which are classified as listed races.
(b) All selling and claiming races.
(b) All weight-for-age races classified 3, 4, 5, 6 and 7.

THE DRAW for places at the start is shown after each jockey's name.

RACING POST RATINGS, which record the level of performance attained in this race for each horse, appear in the end column after each horse. These are the work of handicappers Simon Turner, Sam Walker and Paul Curtis, who head a dedicated team dealing with Flat races for Raceform and sister publication, the *Racing Post*.

THE TRAINER is shown for every runner.

COMMENT-IN-RUNNING is shown for each horse in an abbreviated form. Details of abbreviations appear later in this section.

STARTING PRICES appear below the jockey in the race result. The favourite indicator appears to the right of the Starting Price; 1 for the favourite, 2 for the second-favourite and 3 for third-favourite. Joint favourites share the same number.

RACE TIMES in Great Britain are official times which are electronically recorded and shown to 100th of a second. Figures in parentheses following the time show the number of seconds faster or slower than the Raceform Median Time for the course and distance.

RACEFORM MEDIAN TIMES are compiled from all races run over the course and distance in the preceding five years. Times equal to the median are shown as (0.00). Times under the median are preceded by minus, for instance, 1.8 seconds under the median would be shown (-1.8). Record times are displayed either referring to the juvenile record (2y crse rec) or to the overall record (course record).

TRACK VARIANT appears against each race to allow for changing conditions of the track and ground. It is shown to a hundredth of a second and indicates the adjustment per furlong against the median time. The going based on the going correction is shown in parentheses and is recorded in the following stages:
Turf: HD (Hard); F (Firm); GF (Good to firm); G (Good); GS (Good to soft); S (Soft); HVY (Heavy). All-Weather: FST (Fast); SF (Standard to fast); STD (Standard); SS (Standard to slow); SLW (Slow)

WEIGHT-FOR-AGE allowances are given where applicable for mixed-age races.

STARTING PRICE PERCENTAGE follows the going correction and weight-for-age details, and gives the total SP percentage of all runners that competed. It precedes the number of runners taking part in the race.

SELLING DETAILS (where applicable) and details of any claim are given. Friendly claims are not detailed.

SPEED RATINGS appear below the race time and going correction. They are the work of time expert Dave Bellingham and differ from conventional ratings systems in that they are an expression of a horse's ability in terms of lengths-per-mile, as opposed to pounds in weight. They are not directly comparable with BHA and Racing Post Ratings.

The ratings take no account of the effect of weight, either historically or on the day, and this component is left completely to the user's discretion. What is shown is a speed rating represented in its purest form, rather than one that has been altered for weight using a mathematical formula that treats all types of horses as if they were the same.

A comparison of the rating achieved with the 'par' figure for the grade of race - the rating that should be achievable by an average winner in that class of race - will both provide an at-a-glance indication of whether or not a race was truly run and also highlight the value of the form from a time perspective.

In theory, if a horse has a best speed figure five points superior to another and both run to their best form in a race over a mile, the first horse should beat the second by five lengths. In a race run over two miles, the margin should be ten lengths and so on.

Before the speed figures can be calculated, it is necessary to establish a set of standard or median times for every distance at every track, and this is done by averaging the times of all winners over a particular trip going back several years. No speed ratings are produced when insufficient races have been run over a distance for a reliable median time to be calculated.

Once a meeting has taken place, a raw unadjusted speed rating is calculated for each winner by calculating how many lengths per mile the winning time was faster or slower than the median for the trip. A difference of 0.2 of a second equals one length. The raw speed ratings of all winners on the card are then compared with the 'par' figure for the class of race. The difference between the 'raw' speed rating and the 'par' figure for each race is then noted, and both the fastest and slowest races are discarded before the rest are averaged to produce the going allowance or track variant. This figure gives an idea as to how much the elements, of which the going is one, have affected the final times of each race.

The figure representing the going allowance is then used to adjust the raw speed figures and produce the final ratings, which represent how fast the winners would have run on a perfectly good surface with no external influences, including the weather. The ratings for beaten horses are worked out by taking the number of lengths they were behind the winner, adjusting that to take into account the distance of the race, and deducting that figure from the winner's rating. The reader is left with a rating which provides an instant impression of the value of a time performance.

The speed 'pars' below act as benchmark with which to compare the speed figures earned by each horse in each race. A horse that has already exceeded the 'par' for the class he is about to run in is of special interest, especially if he has done it more than once, as are horses that have consistently earned higher figures than their rivals.

Class 1 Group One	117
Class 1 Group Two	115
Class 1 Group Three	113
Class 1 Listed	111
Class 2	109
Class 3	107
Class 4	105
Class 5	103
Class 6	101
Class 7	99

Allowances need to be made for younger horses and for fillies. These allowances are as follows.

MONTH	2yo	3yo
Jan / Feb	n/a	-6
Mar / Apr	-11	-5
May / Jun	-10	-4
Jul / Aug	-9	-3
Sep / Oct	-8	-2
Nov / Dec	-7	-1
Races contested by fillies only		-3

Allowances are cumulative. For example, using a combination of the above pars and allowances, the par figure for the Epsom Oaks would be 110. The Group One par is 117, then deduct 4 because the race is confined to three year olds and run in June, then subtract another 3 because the race is confined to fillies.

TOTE prices include £1 stake. Exacta dividends are shown in parentheses. The Computer Straight Forecast dividend is preceded by the letters CSF, Computer Tricast is preceded by CT and Trifecta dividend is preceded by the word Trifecta. Jackpot, Placepot and Quadpot details appear at the end of the meeting to which they refer.

OWNER is followed by the breeder's name and the trainer's location.

STEWARDS' ENQUIRIES are included with the result, and any suspensions and/or fines incurred. Objections by jockeys and officials are included, where relevant.

HISTORICAL FOCUS details occasional points of historical significance.

FOCUS The Focus section helps readers distinguish good races from bad races and reliable form from unreliable form, by drawing together the opinions of handicapper, time expert and paddock watcher and interpreting their views in a punter-friendly manner.

Abbreviations and their meanings

Paddock comments

gd sort - well made, above average on looks
attr - attractive, but not as impressive as good sort
gd bodied - good bodied, well put together
h.d.w - has done well, improved in looks
wl grwn - well grown, has filled to its frame
lengthy - longer than average for its height
tall - tall
rangy - lengthy and tall but in proportion.
cl cpld - close coupled
scope - scope for physical development
str - strong, powerful looking
w'like - workmanlike, ordinary in looks
lt-f - light-framed, not much substance
cmpt - compact
neat - smallish, well put together
leggy - long legs compared with body
angular - unfurnished behind the saddle, not filled to frame
unf - unfurnished in the midriff, not filled to frame
narrow - not as wide as side appearance would suggest
small - lacks any physical scope
nt grwn - not grown
lw - looked fit and well
bkwd - backward in condition
t - tubed
swtg - sweating
b (off fore or nr fore) - bandaged in front
b.hind (off or nr) - bandaged behind

At the start

stdd s - jockey purposely reins back the horse
dwlt - missed the break and left for a short time
s.s - slow to start, left longer than a horse that dwelt
s.v.s - started very slowly
s.i.s - started on terms but took time to get going
ref to r - does not jump off, or travels a few yards then stops
rel to r - tries to pull itself up in mid-race
w.r.s - whipped round start

Position in the race

led - in lead on its own

disp ld - upsides the leader
w ldr - almost upsides the leader
w ldrs - in a line of three or more disputing the lead
prom - on the heels of the leaders, in front third of the field
trckd ldr(s) - just in behind the leaders giving impression that it could lead if asked
chsd ldr - horse in second place
chsd clr ldrs - horse heads main body of field behind two clear leaders
chsd ldrs - horse is in the first four or five but making more of an effort to stay close to the pace than if it were tracking the leaders.
clsd - closed
in tch - close enough to have a chance
hdwy - making ground on the leader
gd hdwy - making ground quickly on the leader, could be a deliberate move
sme hdwy - making some ground but no real impact on the race
w.w - waited with
stdy hdwy - gradually making ground
ev ch - upsides the leaders when the race starts in earnest
rr - at the back of main group but not detached
bhd - detached from the main body of runners
hld up - restrained as a deliberate tactical move
nt rcvr - lost all chance after interference, mistake etc.
wknd - stride shortened as it began to tire
lost tch - had been in the main body but a gap appeared as it tired
lost pl - remains in main body of runners but lost several positions quickly

Riding

effrt - short-lived effort
pushed along - received urgings with hands only, jockey not using legs
rdn - received urgings from saddle, including use of whip
hrd rdn - received maximum assistance from the saddle including use of whip
drvn - received forceful urgings, jockey putting in a lot of effort and using whip
hrd drvn - jockey very animated, plenty of kicking, pushing and reminders

Finishing comments

jst failed - closing rapidly on the winner and probably would have led a stride after the line
r.o - jockey's efforts usually involved to produce an increase in pace without finding an appreciable turn of speed
r.o wl - jockey's efforts usually involved to produce an obvious increase in pace without finding an appreciable turn of speed
unable qckn - not visibly tiring but does not possess a sufficient change of pace
one pce - not tiring but does not find a turn of speed, from a position further out than unable qckn
nt r.o. - did not consent to respond to pressure
styd on - going on well towards the end, utilising stamina
nvr able to chal - unable to produce sufficient to reach a challenging position
nvr nr to chal - in the opinion of the racereader, the horse was never in a suitable position to challenge.
nrst fin - nearer to the winner in distance beaten than at any time since the race had begun in earnest
nvr nrr - nearer to the winner position-wise than at any time since the race had begun in earnest
rallied - responded to pressure to come back with a chance having lost its place
no ex - unable to sustain its run
bttr for r - likely to improve for the run and experience
rn green - inclined to wander and falter through inexperience
too much to do - left with too much leeway to make up

Winning comments

v.easily - a great deal in hand
easily - plenty in hand
comf - something in hand, always holding the others
pushed out - kept up to its work with hands and heels without jockey resorting to whip or kicking along and wins fairly comfortably
rdn out - pushed and kicked out to the line, with the whip employed
drvn out - pushed and kicked out to the line, with considerable effort and the whip employed
all out - nothing to spare, could not have found any more
jst hld on - holding on to a rapidly diminishing lead, could not have found any more if passed
unchal - must either make all or a majority of the running and not be challenged from an early stage

Complete list of abbreviations

a - always
abt - about
a.p - always prominent
appr - approaching
awrdd - awarded
b.b.v - broke blood-vessel
b.d - brought down
bdly - badly
bef - before
bhd - behind
bk - back
blkd - baulked
blnd - blundered
bmpd - bumped
bnd - bend
btn- beaten
bttr - better
c - came
ch - chance
chal - challenged
chse - chase
chsd - chased
chsng - chasing
circ - circuit
cl - close
clr - clear
clsd - closed
comf - comfortably
cpld - coupled
crse - course
ct - caught
def - definite
dismntd - dismounted
disp - disputed
dist - distance
div - division
drvn - driven
dwlt - dwelt
edgd - edged
effrt - effort

ent - entering
ev ch - every chance
ex - extra
f - furlong
fin - finished
fnd - found
fnl - final
fr - from
gd - good
gng - going
gp - group
grad - gradually
grnd - ground
hd - head
hdd - headed
hdwy - headway
hld - held
hmpd - hampered
imp - impression
ins - inside
j.b - jumped badly
j.w - jumped well
jnd - joined
jst - just
kpt - kept
l - length
ld - lead
ldr - leader
lft - left
mod - moderate
m - mile
m.n.s - made no show
mde - made
mid div - mid division
mstke - mistake
n.d - never dangerous
n.g.t - not go through
n.m.r - not much room
nk - neck
no ex - no extra
nr - near
nrr - nearer
nrst fin - nearest finish
nt - not
nvr - never
one pce - one pace
out - from finish
outpcd - outpaced
p.u - pulled up
pce - pace
pckd - pecked
pl - place
plcd - placed
plld - pulled
press - pressure
prog - progress
prom - prominent
qckly - quickly
qckn - quicken
r - race
racd - raced
rch - reach
rcvr - recover
rdn - ridden
rdr - rider
reard - reared
ref - refused
rn - ran
rnd - round
r.o - ran on
rr - rear
rspnse - response
rt - right
s - start
sddle - saddle
shkn - shaken
slt - slight
sme - some
sn - soon
spd- speed
st - straight
stmbld - stumbled
stdd - steadied
stdy - steady
strly - strongly
styd - stayed
styng - staying
s. u - slipped up
swtchd - switched
swvd - swerved
tk - took
t.k.h - took keen hold
t.o - tailed off
tch - touch
thrght - throughout
trbld - troubled
trckd - tracked
u.p - under pressure
u.str.p- under strong pressure
w - with
w.r.s - whipped round start
wd - wide
whn - when
wknd - weakened
wl - well
wnr - winner
wnt - went
1/2-wy - halfway

Racing Post Ratings

Racing Post Ratings for each horse are shown in the right hand column, headed RPR, and indicate the actual level of performance attained in that race. The figure in the back index represents the BEST public form that Raceform's Handicappers still believe the horse capable of reproducing.

To use the ratings constructively in determining those horses best-in in future events, the following procedure should be followed:

(i) In races where all runners are the same age and are set to carry the same weight, no calculations are necessary. The horse with the highest rating is best-in.

(ii) In races where all runners are the same age but are set to carry different weights, add one point to the Racing Post Rating for every pound less than 10 stone to be carried; deduct one point for every pound more than 10 stone.

For example,

Horse	Age & wt	Adjustment from 10st	Base rating	Adjusted rating
Treclare	3-10-1	-1	78	77
Buchan	3-9-13	+1	80	81
Paper Money	3-9-7	+7	71	78
Archaic	3-8-11	+17	60	77

Therefore Buchan is top-rated (best-in)

(iii) In races concerning horses of different ages the procedure in (ii) should again be followed, but reference must also be made to the Official Scale of Weight-For-Age.

For example,

12 furlongs, July 20th

Horse	Age & wt	Adjustment from 10st	Base rating	Adjusted rating	W-F-A deduct	Final rating
Archaic	5-10-0	0	90	90	Nil	90
Orpheus	4-9-9	+5	88	93	Nil	93
Lemonora	3-9-4	+10	85	95	-12	83
Tamar	4-8-7	+21	73	94	Nil	94

Therefore Tamar is top-rated (best-in)

(A 3-y-o is deemed 12lb less mature than a 4-y-o or older horse on 20th July over 12f. Therefore, the deduction of 12 points is necessary.)

The following symbols are used in conjunction with the ratings:

++: almost certain to prove better

+: likely to prove better

d: disappointing (has run well below best recently)

?: form hard to evaluate

t: tentative rating based on race-time rating may prove unreliable

Weight adjusted ratings for every race are published daily in Raceform Private Handicap.

For subscription terms please contact the Subscription Department on 01933 304858.

Course descriptions

(R.H.) denotes right-hand and (L.H.) left-hand courses.

ASCOT (R.H)

Right-handed triangular track just under 1m 6f in length. The Round course descends from the 1m 4f start into Swinley Bottom, the lowest part of the track. It then turns right-handed and joins the Old Mile Course, which starts on a separate chute. The course then rises to the right-handed home turn over a new underpass to join the straight mile course. The run-in is about 3f, rising slightly to the winning post. The whole course is of a galloping nature with easy turns.

AYR (L.H)

A left-handed, galloping, flat oval track of 1m 4f with a 4f run-in. The straight 6f is essentially flat.

BATH (L.H)

Galloping, left-handed, level oval of 1m 4f 25y, with long, stiff run-in of about 4f which bends to the left. An extended chute provides for races over 5f 11y and 5f 161y.

BEVERLEY (R.H)

A right-handed oval of 1m 3f, generally galloping, with an uphill run-in of two and a half furlongs. The 5f course is very stiff.

BRIGHTON (L.H)

Left-handed, 1m 4f horseshoe with easy turns and a run-in of three and a half furlongs. Undulating and sharp, the track suits handy types.

CARLISLE (R.H)

Right-handed, 1m 4f pear-shaped track. Galloping and undulating with easy turns and a stiff uphill run-in of three and a half furlongs. 6f course begins on an extended chute.

CATTERICK (L.H)

A sharp, left-handed, undulating oval of 1m 180y with a downhill run-in of 3f.

CHEPSTOW (L.H)

A left-handed, undulating oval of about 2m, with easy turns, and a straight run-in of 5f. There is a straight track of 1m 14y.

CHESTER (L.H)

A level, sharp, left-handed, circular course of 1m 73y, with a short run-in of 230y. Chester is a specialists' track which generally suits the sharp-actioned horse.

DONCASTER (L.H)

A left-handed, flat, galloping course of 1m 7f 110y, with a long run-in which extends to a straight mile.

EPSOM (L.H)

Left-handed and undulating with easy turns, and a run-in of just under 4f. The straight 5f course is also undulating and downhill all the way, making it the fastest 5f in the world.

FFOS LAS (L.H)

The track is a 60m wide, basically flat, 1m4f oval with sweeping bends.

GOODWOOD (R.H)

A sharp, undulating, essentially right-handed track with a long run-in. There is also a straight 6f course.

HAMILTON PARK (R.H)

Sharp, undulating, right-handed course of 1m 5f with a five and a half furlong, uphill run-in. There is a straight track of 6f.

HAYDOCK PARK (L.H)

A galloping, almost flat, oval track, 1m 5f round, with a run-in of four and a half furlongs and a straight 6f course.

KEMPTON PARK (R.H)

A floodlit Polytrack circuit opened in March 2006. A 1m 2f outer track accommodates races over 6f, 7f, 1m, 1m 3f, 1m 4f and 2m. The 1m inner track caters for races over 5f and 1m 2f.

LEICESTER (R.H)

Stiff, galloping, right-handed oval of 1m 5f, with a 5f run-in. There is a straight course of 7f.

LINGFIELD PARK (L.H)

Turf Course: A sharp, undulating left-handed circuit, with a 7f 140y straight course.

Polytrack course: left-handed all-weather is 1m 2f round. It is a sharp, level track with a short run-in.

MUSSELBURGH (R.H)

A sharp, level, right-handed oval of 1m 2f, with a run-in of 4f. There is an additional 5f straight course.

NEWBURY (L.H)

Left-handed, oval track of about 1m 7f, with a slightly undulating straight mile. The round course is level and galloping with a four and a half furlong run-in. Races over the round mile and 7f 60y start on the adjoining chute.

NEWCASTLE (L.H)

Galloping, easy, left-handed oval of 1m 6f, with an uphill 4f run-in. There is a straight course of 1m 8y.

NEWMARKET (R.H)

Rowley Mile Course: There is a straight 1m2f course, which is wide and galloping. Races over 1m4f or more are right-handed. The Rowley course has a long run-in and a stiff finish.

July Course: Races up to a mile are run on the Bunbury course, which is straight. Races over 1m2f or more are right-handed, with a 7f run-in. Like the Rowley course, the July track is stiff.

NOTTINGHAM (L.H)

Left-handed, galloping, oval of about 1m 4f, and a run-in of four and a half furlongs. Flat with easy turns.

PONTEFRACT (L.H)

Left-handed oval, undulating course of 2m 133y, with a short run-in of 2f. It is a particularly stiff track with the last 3f uphill.

REDCAR (L.H)

Left-handed, level, galloping, oval course of 1m 6f with a straight run-in of 5f. There is also a straight 1m.

RIPON (R.H)

A sharp, undulating, right-handed oval of 1m 5f, with a 5f run-in. There is also a 6f straight course.

SALISBURY (R.H)

Right-handed and level, with a run-in of 4f. There is a straight 1m track. The last half mile is uphill, providing a stiff test of stamina.

SANDOWN PARK (R.H)

An easy right-handed oval course of 1m 5f with a stiff straight uphill run-in of 4f. Separate straight 5f track is also uphill. Galloping.

SOUTHWELL (L.H)

Left-handed oval, Fibresand course of 1m 2f with a 3f run-in. There is a straight 5f. Sharp and level, Southwell suits front-runners.

THIRSK (L.H)

Left-handed, oval of 1m 2f with sharp turns and an undulating run-in of 4f. There is a straight 6f track.

WARWICK (L.H)

Left-handed, sharp, level track of 1m 6f 32y in circumference, with a run-in of two and a half furlongs. There is also a 6f chute.

WINDSOR (Fig. 8)

Figure eight track of 1m 4f 110y. The course is level and sharp with a long run-in. The 6f course is essentially straight.

WOLVERHAMPTON (L.H)

Left-handed oval of 1m, with a run-in of 380y. A level track with sharp bends.

YARMOUTH (L.H)

Left-handed, level circuit of 1m 4f, with a run-in of 5f. The straight course is 1m long.

YORK (L.H)

Left-handed, level, galloping track, with a straight 6f. There is also an adjoining chute of 7f.

WOLVERHAMPTON (A.W) (L-H)

Tuesday, January 1

OFFICIAL GOING: Standard

Wind: Moderate half behind Weather: Fine and dry

1 CORAL.CO.UK CLAIMING STKS 1m 4f 50y(P)

1:15 (1:22) (Class 6) 4-Y-0+ **£1,940** (£577; £288; £144) **Stalls** Low

Form RPR

111- **1** **La Estrella (USA)**[15] 8148 10-9-9 89 AdamKirby 3 85
(Don Cantillon) *trckd ldng pair: pushed along 3f out: rdn over 2f out: drvn to chse ldr wl over 1f out: edgd lft and kpt on u.p fnl f to ld last stride* **1/12**[1]

245- **2** *shd* **Renegotiate**[14] 8153 4-8-9 65 DavidProbert 4 75
(Andrew Balding) *led and sn clr: pushed along 3f out: rdn wl over 1f out: drvn ins fnl f: hdd nr line* **8/1**[2]

466- **3** *7* **King Fingal (IRE)**[73] 7245 8-8-13 67 TomEaves 2 64
(John Quinn) *chsd clr ldr: rdn along 3f out: drvn 2f out and sn one pce* **16/1**[3]

00- **4** *14* **Father Shine (IRE)**[16] 6055 10-9-5 0 RobertWinston 1 47
(Shaun Harris) *trckd ldng pair: pushed along over 4f out: rdn over 3f out: sn wknd* **20/1**

\- **5** *67* **Silver Panther**[66] 5-9-0 0 MartinDwyer 5
(Aytach Sadik) *s.i.s and lost many l s: a bhd: t.o fnl 3f* **80/1**

2m 37.31s (-3.79) **Going Correction** -0.275s/f (Stan)
WFA 4 from 5yo+ 4lb **5** Ran SP% **115.3**
Speed ratings (Par 101): **101,100,96,86,42**
CSF £1.91 TOTE £1.10: £1.02, £2.20; EX 1.90 Trifecta £2.60 Pool: £1,359.13 - 389.62 winning units.Renegotiate was claimed by Dr R D P Newland for £6,000
Owner Don Cantillon **Bred** Five Horses Ltd And Theatrical Syndicate **Trained** Newmarket, Suffolk

FOCUS
This had looked another straightforward task for the red-hot favourite, but it proved anything but.

2 HORSE RACING FREE BETS WITH BOOKMAKERS.CO.UK H'CAP 1m 4f 50y(P)

1:50 (1:54) (Class 5) (0-70,75) 4-Y-0+ **£2,587** (£770; £384; £192) **Stalls** Low

Form RPR

031- **1** **Sir Boss (IRE)**[6] 8243 8-10-2 75 6ex TomEaves 1 78
(Michael Mullineaux) *hld up in rr: hdwy over 2f out: rdn jst over 1f out: qcknd to ld jst ins fnl f: styd on* **7/4**[1]

663- **2** *¾* **Stanley Rigby**[21] 8060 7-9-5 64 BarryMcHugh 3 65
(Richard Fahey) *trckd ldng pair on inner: hdwy 3f out: rdn to ld over 1f out: hdd jst ins fnl f: sn drvn and edgd rt: kpt on* **9/4**[2]

/00- **3** *2¼* **Blizzard Blues (USA)**[10] 8228 7-9-10 69 (b) IanMongan 4 67
(Aytach Sadik) *s.i.s: sn in tch: hdwy to chse ldrs 4f out: rdn along and outpcd wl over 2f out: kpt on u.p fnl f* **66/1**

212- **4** *½* **Resplendent Alpha**[2] 8297 9-8-13 63 LeonnaMayor(5) 2 60
(Jamie Osborne) *s.i.s and hld up in rr: in tch 1/2-way: rdn and qcknd arnd outer to chal 2f out: wd st: ev ch whn drvn and edgd lft ent fnl f: sn one pce* **9/2**[3]

034/ **5** *2¼* **Corres (IRE)**[45] 6079 6-8-10 60 (tp) WilliamTwiston-Davies(5) 5 53
(Paul Fitzsimons) *trckd ldr: hdwy and cl up 3f out: rdn along over 2f out: sn wknd* **20/1**

304- **6** *nk* **Elijah Pepper (USA)**[15] 8145 8-9-8 67 AdamKirby 6 60
(Conor Dore) *set stdy pce: qcknd over 3f out: rdn over 2f out: drvn and hdd over 1f out: sn wknd* **9/2**[3]

2m 43.36s (2.26) **Going Correction** -0.275s/f (Stan) **6** Ran SP% **109.8**
Speed ratings (Par 103): **81,80,79,78,77 76**
Tote swingers 1&2 £1.50, 1&3 £5.50, 2&3 £8.70 CSF £5.65 TOTE £2.50: £1.70, £1.10; EX 7.00 Trifecta £83.80 Pool: £1,290.49 - 11.54 winning units.
Owner Miss M Mullineaux, P Lawton, I Ross **Bred** Mrs E R Cantillon **Trained** Alpraham, Cheshire

FOCUS
A fair handicap, but they went no pace and it developed into a 3f sprint. The winning time was more than six seconds slower than the claimer.

3 BOOKMAKERS.CO.UK H'CAP 5f 20y(P)

2:25 (2:29) (Class 3) (0-95,93) 4-Y-0+ **£7,246** (£2,168; £1,084; £542; £270) **Stalls** Low

Form RPR

512- **1** **Woolfall Sovereign (IRE)**[4] 8272 7-9-7 93 IanMongan 3 102
(George Margarson) *hld up in rr: smooth hdwy 2f out: chal on inner ent fnl f: rdn and qcknd to ld last 100yds* **5/6**[1]

164- **2** *nk* **Dorback**[13] 8163 6-8-8 80 MartinDwyer 1 88
(David Nicholls) *trckd ldrs: hdwy 2f out: swtchd rt to outer and rdn to ld jst ins fnl f: hdd and nt qckn last 100yds* **8/1**[3]

522- **3** *3¼* **Moorhouse Lad**[13] 8163 10-9-0 86 DavidProbert 5 82
(Garry Moss) *slt ld 1 1/2f: cl up tl rdn to ld again over 1f out: drvn and hdd jst ins fnl f: sn one pce* **11/4**[2]

000- **4** *1* **Tango Sky (IRE)**[17] 8143 4-8-7 79 JoeFanning 2 72
(David Nicholls) *dwlt and in rr: hdwy 2f out: sn rdn and no imp fnl f* **14/1**

000- **5** *2¼* **Le Toreador**[48] 7704 8-9-1 87 (tp) AmyRyan 6 72
(Kevin Ryan) *chsd ldrs: rdn along over 2f out: sn drvn and wknd* **12/1**

160- **6** *3½* **Royal Bajan (USA)**[21] 8066 5-8-10 82 (b) JamesSullivan 4 54
(James Given) *cl up: led after 1 1/2f: rdn 2f out: sn hdd & wknd* **33/1**

59.79s (-2.51) **Going Correction** -0.275s/f (Stan) course record **6** Ran SP% **109.6**
Speed ratings (Par 107): **109,108,103,101,98 92**
Tote swingers 1&2 £1.90, 1&3 £1.20, 2&3 £1.80 CSF £7.96 TOTE £1.80: £1.10, £4.10; EX 5.90 Trifecta £10.10 Pool: £1,487.38 - 109.87 winning units.
Owner Wildcard Racing Syndicate **Bred** Saud Bin Saad **Trained** Newmarket, Suffolk

FOCUS
A decent sprint handicap, run at a true pace thanks to a contested lead, and they took 0.43 seconds off the track record.

4 CORAL.CO.UK MOBILE BETTING H'CAP 5f 216y(P)

3:00 (3:01) (Class 5) (0-75,75) 3-Y-0 **£2,587** (£770; £384; £192) **Stalls** Low

Form RPR

351- **1** **Archie Stevens**[11] 8204 3-9-7 75 RichardKingscote 4 86
(Tom Dascombe) *trckd ldr: smooth hdwy 2f out: rdn to ld ent fnl f: styd on* **10/11**[1]

21- **2** *2¼* **Golden Flower**[10] 8230 3-9-4 72 TomEaves 2 76
(David O'Meara) *plld hrd and set str pce: rdn along 2f out: drvn and hdd ent fnl f: sn one pce* **11/4**[2]

106- **3** *4½* **Be On The Bell**[11] 8211 3-9-4 72 GeorgeBaker 3 62
(Jamie Osborne) *trckd ldng pair: effrt over 2f out: sn rdn and no imp* **7/2**[3]

203- **4** *shd* **Clear Loch**[32] 7931 3-8-12 66 NickyMackay 1 55
(John Spearing) *dwlt: sn trcking ldng pair: rdn 2f out: sn drvn and one pce* **12/1**

1m 13.66s (-1.34) **Going Correction** -0.275s/f (Stan) **4** Ran SP% **109.0**
Speed ratings (Par 97): **97,94,88,87**
CSF £3.71 TOTE £1.70; EX 3.90 Trifecta £4.60 Pool: £841.34 - 136.36 winning units.
Owner L Bellman & Manor House Stables LLP **Bred** Howard Barton Stud **Trained** Malpas, Cheshire

FOCUS
An uncompetitive 3yo sprint handicap and the form looks straightforward.

5 NO DEPOSIT FREE BETS WITH BOOKMAKERS.CO.UK (S) STKS 1m 141y(P)

3:35 (3:36) (Class 6) 3-Y-0 **£2,045** (£603; £302) **Stalls** Low

Form RPR

454- **1** **Walter White (IRE)**[15] 8150 3-8-12 64 (v[1]) DavidProbert 2 65
(Andrew Balding) *hld up in midfield gng wl: smooth hdwy 3f out: n.m.r and swtchd to outer wl over 1f out: led ent fnl f: sn clr* **7/4**[1]

022- **2** *6* **Myzamour**[15] 8150 3-8-7 56 (b) JimmyQuinn 7 46
(J S Moore) *trckd ldrs on outer: effrt over 2f out: chsd ldr whn swtchd lft wl over 1f out: sn rdn and kpt on same pce fnl f* **9/2**[3]

3 *1* **Beau Sakhee**[109] 6220 3-8-12 54 (p) GrahamGibbons 4 49
(Adrian McGuinness, Ire) *trckd ldng pair: effrt and n.m.r wl over 1f out: sn swtchd rt and rdn: kpt on fnl f* **20/1**

004- **4** *shd* **Show More Faith**[11] 8207 3-8-12 56 NickyMackay 1 49
(Sylvester Kirk) *trckd ldrs on inner: effrt over 2f out: sn rdn and no imp* **14/1**

145- **5** *½* **Roland**[12] 8186 3-9-4 60 RobertWinston 3 54
(Kevin Ryan) *led: rdn along over 2f out: edgd wd on home turn: drvn and hdd ent fnl f: wknd* **3/1**[2]

544- **6** *8* **Squawk**[22] 8053 3-8-7 49 AndrewMullen 5 24
(Bill Turner) *hld up in rr: effrt and sme hdwy 3f out: sn rdn along and nvr a factor* **33/1**

34- **7** *2* **Doodles**[32] 7932 3-8-7 0 MartinDwyer 8 20
(David Nicholls) *hld up in rr: effrt 3f out: sn rdn along and nvr a factor* **12/1**

235- **8** *4½* **Don Eduardo**[5] 8258 3-8-12 57 (b) LiamKeniry 6 14
(J S Moore) *clsd up: rdn along wl over 2f out: sn wknd* **7/1**

1m 48.92s (-1.58) **Going Correction** -0.275s/f (Stan) **8** Ran SP% **114.1**
Speed ratings (Par 95): **96,90,89,89,89 82,80,76**
Tote swingers 1&2 £1.40, 1&3 £10.20, 2&3 £9.70 CSF £9.88 TOTE £2.90: £1.10, £1.50, £8.00; EX 9.90 Trifecta £61.90 Pool: £1,363.03 - 16.51 winning units.
Owner G A D Partnership **Bred** Catridge Farm Stud & S Von Schilcher **Trained** Kingsclere, Hants

FOCUS
A moderate 3yo seller and there was only one horse in it.

6 POKER AT CORAL.CO.UK H'CAP 1m 141y(P)

4:05 (4:05) (Class 3) (0-95,89) 4-Y-0+ **£7,246** (£2,168; £1,084; £542; £270) **Stalls** Low

Form RPR

201- **1** **Alfred Hutchinson**[5] 8259 5-9-0 87 6ex WilliamTwiston-Davies(5) 5 99
(Geoffrey Oldroyd) *hld up in tch: smooth hdwy 3f out: trckd ldrs 2f out: rdn to ld ins fnl f: kpt on strly* **7/2**[3]

211- **2** *2¼* **Aquilonius (IRE)**[5] 8250 4-9-1 84 6ex (t) GrahamGibbons 4 91
(Stuart Williams) *led: pushed along 2f out: rdn over 1f out: drvn and hdd ins fnl f: kpt on* **11/4**[1]

436- **3** *¾* **Kingscroft (IRE)**[19] 8098 5-9-7 89 JoeFanning 2 94
(Mark Johnston) *trckd ldr: effrt 3f out: rdn 2f out: drvn and kpt on same pce fnl f* **7/2**[3]

134- **4** *½* **Rakaan (IRE)**[6] 8242 6-9-5 87 GeorgeBaker 3 91
(Jamie Osborne) *dwlt: hld up and bhd: hdwy wl over 2f out: rdn to chse ldrs ent fnl f: hld whn n.m.r last 75yds* **3/1**[2]

053- **5** *hd* **Angelic Upstart (IRE)**[34] 7920 5-8-10 78 MichaelStainton 1 81
(Andrew Balding) *trckd ldrs on inner: hdwy over 2f out: rdn wl over 1f out: sn drvn and one pce* **15/2**

010- **6** *12* **Trois Vallees (USA)**[22] 8056 4-8-11 80 DavidProbert 6 56
(James Tate) *chsd ldr: rdn along 3f out: wknd 2f out: sn bhd and eased over 1f out* **14/1**

1m 46.07s (-4.43) **Going Correction** -0.275s/f (Stan) course record
WFA 4 from 5yo+ 1lb **6** Ran SP% **114.5**
Speed ratings (Par 107): **108,106,105,104,104 94**
Tote swingers 1&2 £4.60, 1&3 £2.00, 2&3 £1.90 CSF £13.94 TOTE £4.40: £2.10, £2.10; EX 19.00 Trifecta £84.70 Pool: £1,886.90 - 16.70 winning units.
Owner R C Bond **Bred** R C Bond **Trained** Brawby, N Yorks

FOCUS
A decent handicap and a true pace, which played into the hands of the winner. Another course record fell, this time by 0.41 seconds.

7 BEST HORSE RACING ODDS WITH BOOKMAKERS.CO.UK H'CAP 1m 141y(P)

4:35 (4:36) (Class 6) (0-55,55) 4-Y-0+ **£2,045** (£603; £302) **Stalls** Low

Form RPR

050- **1** **Rosie's Lady (IRE)**[65] 5330 4-9-2 51 GrahamGibbons 4 63+
(David O'Meara) *trckd ldng pair: tk clsr order 3f out: chal over 1f out: rdn to ld ins fnl f: sn clr* **11/2**[3]

000- **2** *2¾* **Justcallmehandsome**[11] 8212 11-8-7 48 (v) JoshBaudains(7) 9 52
(Dominic Ffrench Davis) *hld up: hdwy 3f out: rdn to chse ldrs over 1f out: styd on same pce fnl f* **20/1**

000- **3** *nk* **Spirit Of Gondree (IRE)**[13] 8167 5-9-7 55 (b) RobertWinston 13 58
(Milton Bradley) *stdd and swtchd lft s: hld up in rr: hdwy over 2f out: rdn over 1f out: styng on whn nt clr run and swtchd lft ins fnl f: fin wl* **12/1**

005- **4** *1* **Fleetwoodsands (IRE)**[12] 8180 6-9-4 52 (t) LiamKeniry 10 53
(Milton Bradley) *hld up towards rr: hdwy over 2f out: rdn to chse ldrs on wd outside over 1f out: kpt on u.p fnl f* **6/1**

600- **5** *¾* **Sairaam (IRE)**[46] 7747 7-8-13 47 MickyFenton 1 46
(Charles Smith) *led: rdn along 2f out: jnd over 1f out: drvn and hdd ins fnl f: grad wknd* **33/1**

000- **6** *½* **I'm Harry**[10] 8229 4-8-13 55 (tp) AaronJones(7) 5 53
(George Baker) *trckd ldrs on inner: hdwy 2f out: rdn over 1f out: kpt on same pce* **7/1**

003- **7** *shd* **Teth**[12] 8180 4-8-12 54 RobertTart(7) 11 52
(Anthony Carson) *in tch: hdwy 3f out: rdn 2f out: drvn and one pce appr fnl f* **5/1**[2]

44- **8** *nk* **Veyepea**[12] 8177 4-8-13 48 DavidProbert 6 45
(Sylvester Kirk) *nvr bttr than midfield* **9/1**

505- **9** *1* **Newington**[73] 7249 4-9-3 55 SimonPearce(3) 2 50
(Lydia Pearce) *s.i.s: a towards rr* **33/1**

/62- **10** *nk* **Romeo's On Fire (IRE)**[18] 8120 9-9-4 52 (p) AdamKirby 8 46
(Adrian McGuinness, Ire) *hld up towards rr: hdwy over 2f out: rdn and n.m.r ins fnl f: n.d* **4/1**[1]

200- 11 2 1/4 **Tukitinyasok (IRE)**[113] 6106 6-9-0 48..........(p) TomEaves 12 37
(Clive Mulhall) *chsd ldr: rdn along wl over 2f out: wknd wl over 1f out* **14/1**

440/ 12 3 **Caracal**[20] 8087 6-8-13 47..........(b) JamesSullivan 7 29
(Adrian McGuinness, Ire) *chsd ldrs: pushed along 3f out: rdn over 2f out: sn wknd* **8/1**

1m 48.73s (-1.77) **Going Correction** -0.275s/f (Stan)
WFA 4 from 5yo+ 1lb 12 Ran SP% **125.0**
Speed ratings (Par 101): **96,93,93,92,91 91,91,90,90,89 87,85**
Tote swingers 1&2 £18.00, 1&3 £22.10, 2&3 £76.30 CSF £117.64 TOTE £7.00: £2.20, £6.00, £5.70; EX 161.70 Trifecta £1039.90 Part won..
Owner Postracing Ltd The Charity Horse **Bred** Mrs Patricia Anne Vermeulen **Trained** Nawton, N Yorks

FOCUS
A poor 46-55 handicap and the form probably adds up to little.
T/Plt: £7.20 to a £1 stake. Pool: £42,629.06 - 4,296.34 winning units T/Qpdt: £5.50 to a £1 stake. Pool: £3,187.32 - 426.86 winning units JR

KEMPTON (A.W) (R-H)

Wednesday, January 2

OFFICIAL GOING: Standard
Wind: Moderate, across (away from stands) Weather: Dank, drizzly

8 BACK OR LAY AT BETDAQ.COM H'CAP 6f (P)
3:50 (3:50) (Class 5) (0-70,70) 3-Y-O **£2,587** (£770; £384) **Stalls** Low

Form RPR

001- 1 **Hazza The Jazza**[5] 8274 3-8-12 61 6ex..........(b) RobertWinston 2 62
(Richard Guest) *s.s and lost 4 l: sn in tch: rdn 2f out: chsd clr ldr jst over 1f out: styd on to ld last strides* **5/4**[1]

110- 2 nk **Seemenomore**[19] 8103 3-9-7 70..........(v) MartinLane 4 70
(Michael Bell) *pressed ldr: led over 2f out and hanging rt: continued to hang but drvn 3 l clr over 1f out: urged along fnl f: hdd last strides* **3/1**[3]

113- 3 3 3/4 **Sofi's Spirit (IRE)**[3] 8293 3-9-1 64.......... LiamKeniry 1 52
(J S Moore) *led to over 2f out: sn outpcd: lost 2nd jst over 1f out* **7/4**[2]

1m 13.48s (0.38) **Going Correction** +0.05s/f (Slow) 3 Ran SP% **105.8**
Speed ratings (Par 97): **99,98,93**
CSF £4.72 TOTE £1.90; EX 5.60 Trifecta £9.30 Pool: £1,188.20 - 95.68 winning tickets..
Owner Maze Rattan Limited **Bred** Aiden Murphy **Trained** Wetherby, W Yorks

FOCUS
Two non-runners left just three, and the form should be treated with caution.

9 BETDAQ MULTIPLES H'CAP 1m 4f (P)
4:20 (4:22) (Class 6) (0-60,60) 4-Y-O+ **£1,940** (£577; £288; £144) **Stalls** Centre

Form RPR

003- 1 **Irene Kennet**[20] 8097 6-8-10 46.......... JimmyQuinn 4 58
(Paul Burgoyne) *hld up in midfield: prog towards inner over 2f out: rdn to ld over 1f out: styd on wl* **25/1**

02- 2 1 3/4 **Cool Kid**[12] 8214 5-9-2 52.......... StevieDonohoe 8 61
(Ian Williams) *reluctant to enter stalls: led after 2f: drvn over 2f out: hdd and nt qckn over 1f out: kpt on* **4/1**[2]

301- 3 2 3/4 **El Bravo**[12] 8214 7-9-8 58.......... AdamKirby 9 63
(Shaun Harris) *trckd ldr 9f out to 7f out: styd prom: drvn over 2f out: kpt on one pce* **3/1**[1]

340- 4 1 **Here Comes Jeanie**[26] 7499 4-8-3 46 oh1.......... SimonPearce(3) 3 49
(Michael Madgwick) *dwlt: hld up wl in rr: urged along 3f out: prog over 1f out: styd on fnl f: nrst fin* **50/1**

350- 5 4 **Landesherr (GER)**[21] 8079 6-9-9 59..........(p) RobertWinston 6 56
(Steve Gollings) *hld up in midfield: drvn wl over 2f out: limited prog and no threat* **11/2**[3]

000- 6 nse **Shirataki (IRE)**[22] 8060 5-9-10 60.......... TomMcLaughlin 12 57
(Peter Hiatt) *trckd ldrs: prog to go 2nd over 3f out: chal over 2f out: wknd over 1f out* **8/1**

/00- 7 1/2 **Fromthestables Com (IRE)**[11] 8229 4-9-0 54.......... SebSanders 10 50
(Brendan Powell) *rrd s: hld up wl in rr: rdn and no prog wl over 2f out: kpt on fr over 1f out* **33/1**

401- 8 3 **Rodrigo De Freitas (IRE)**[28] 7991 6-9-10 60..........(v) EddieAhern 13 51
(Roger Ingram) *forced wd bnd 9f out: effrt fr rr 5f out: drvn and no great prog over 2f out: wl btn over 1f out* **7/1**

000- 9 4 **Nolecce**[4] 8288 6-9-4 54..........(p) LiamKeniry 7 39
(Richard Guest) *led 2f: styd handy: rdn over 3f out: wknd fnl 2f: eased last 100yds* **16/1**

440- 10 2 3/4 **Time Square (FR)**[30] 7960 6-9-6 56.......... MartinLane 11 36
(Tony Carroll) *hld up in rr: urged along wl over 2f out: hanging bdly and fnd nil: eased fnl f* **25/1**

004- 11 3 1/2 **Sir Dylan**[13] 8182 4-9-2 56.......... LukeMorris 1 31
(Ronald Harris) *hld up: plld way through to go 2nd 7f out to over 3f out: wknd qckly: eased over 1f out* **8/1**

430- 12 13 **Mayan Flight (IRE)**[119] 5939 5-8-13 52.......... RaulDaSilva(3) 2
(Tony Carroll) *a in rr: wknd 3f out and sn t.o* **25/1**

2m 34.78s (0.28) **Going Correction** +0.05s/f (Slow)
WFA 4 from 5yo+ 4lb 12 Ran SP% **117.4**
Speed ratings (Par 101): **101,99,98,97,94 94,94,92,89,87 85,76**
toteswingers 1&2 £10.20, 1&3 £11.00, 2&3 £3.00 CSF £116.77 CT £400.28 TOTE £23.70: £5.00, £1.40, £2.20; EX 126.10 Trifecta £1242.80 Part won..
Owner R W Floyd **Bred** Jim Duncan And Richard William Floyd **Trained** Shepton Montague, Somerset

FOCUS
This was routine Polytrack fare, but the first three had been in good form so it looks solid enough.

10 BETDAQ MOBILE APPS CONDITIONS STKS 7f (P)
4:50 (4:50) (Class 4) 4-Y-O+ **£5,038** (£1,744) **Stalls** Low

Form RPR

005- 1 **Spirit Of Sharjah (IRE)**[11] 8226 8-9-2 92.......... GeorgeBaker 2 93
(Julia Feilden) *mde all: set sedate pce tl past 1/2-way: kicked on and lft 4 l clr 2f out: unchal* **9/1**[3]

401- 2 2 **Chapter And Verse (IRE)**[20] 8098 7-9-2 87.......... EddieAhern 1 88
(Mike Murphy) *stdd s: t.k.h in last: lft 2nd jst over 2f out but 4 l bhd the wnr: nvr able to cl sufficiently* **7/2**[2]

204- P **Imperial Guest**[74] 7236 7-9-2 107.......... IanMongan 3
(George Margarson) *trckd wnr tl p.u jst over 2f out: fatally injured* **4/11**[1]

1m 34.29s (8.29) **Going Correction** +0.05s/f (Slow) 3 Ran SP% **105.5**
Speed ratings (Par 105): **54,51,**
CSF £28.05 TOTE £7.80; EX 10.20 Trifecta £16.50 Pool: £1089.79 - 49.29 winning tickets..
Owner A Dee **Bred** Mrs Kathleen Reynolds **Trained** Exning, Suffolk

FOCUS
A good-quality turnout, but only three started and the odds-on favourite failed to complete. The form means nothing.

11 FREE ENTRY FOR BETDAQ MEMBERS H'CAP 6f (P)
5:20 (5:20) (Class 5) (0-75,75) 4-Y-O+ **£2,587** (£770; £384; £192) **Stalls** Low

Form RPR

166- 1 **Alnoomaas (IRE)**[15] 8159 4-9-1 69.......... TomMcLaughlin 8 80
(Luke Dace) *pressed ldr: shkn up to ld wl over 1f out: drvn and hld on wl fnl f* **8/1**

221- 2 1/2 **Lastkingofscotland (IRE)**[11] 8236 7-9-7 75..........(b) GeorgeBaker 2 84
(Conor Dore) *trckd ldng pair: brought to chal on inner wl over 1f out: pressed wnr after: nt qckn ins fnl f* **3/1**[1]

314- 3 3/4 **Fortrose Academy (IRE)**[15] 8160 4-8-13 67.......... LiamKeniry 7 74
(Andrew Balding) *chsd ldng trio: drvn to take 3rd jst over 1f out: kpt on but nvr quite able to chal* **4/1**[2]

351- 4 1/2 **Belle Bayardo (IRE)**[18] 8144 5-9-1 69.......... LukeMorris 6 74
(Ronald Harris) *chsd ldng quartet: drvn over 2f out: kpt on fr over 1f out: nvr able to chal* **11/1**

000- 5 hd **Caldercruix (USA)**[18] 8143 6-9-4 75..........(v) RaulDaSilva(3) 9 79
(James Evans) *chsd ldrs disputing 5th: drvn over 2f out: no prog tl styd on fnl f: one pce nr fin* **16/1**

546- 6 1 **Gabbiano**[196] 3284 4-9-7 75..........[1] AdamKirby 1 76
(Jeremy Gask) *hld up disputing 7th: pushed along over 2f out: kpt on but nvr chal* **9/2**[3]

115- 7 1 1/4 **Gung Ho Jack**[23] 8058 4-9-1 69.......... RobertWinston 12 66
(John Best) *t.k.h: hld up disputing 7th fr wd draw: threatened to cl on ldrs fr 2f out: jst pushed along and nvr chal* **8/1**

440- 8 1 3/4 **Rambo Will**[23] 8058 5-9-1 69.......... JoeFanning 3 61
(J R Jenkins) *racd freely: led at gd pce: hdd & wknd wl over 1f out* **10/1**

660- 9 3 **Jake The Snake (IRE)**[53] 7685 12-8-13 72.......... GeorgeDowning(5) 4 54
(Tony Carroll) *s.v.s and lost several l: a detached in last trio: nvr a factor* **16/1**

320- 10 1/2 **Time Medicean**[34] 7928 7-9-6 74.......... StevieDonohoe 11 54
(Tony Carroll) *sn outpcd and detached in last trio: nvr a factor* **25/1**

422- 11 2 1/2 **Guest Book (IRE)**[149] 4872 6-8-11 68.......... MarkCoumbe(3) 10 40
(Michael Scudamore) *slowly away: nvr gng wl and a detached in last trio* **20/1**

1m 12.13s (-0.97) **Going Correction** +0.05s/f (Slow) 11 Ran SP% **123.2**
Speed ratings (Par 103): **108,107,106,105,105 104,102,100,96,95 92**
toteswingers 1&2 £9.20, 1&3 £9.80, 2&3 £4.10 CSF £33.81 CT £117.77 TOTE £7.40: £2.80, £1.70, £1.80; EX 52.90 Trifecta £209.50 Pool: £1,195.99 - 4.28 winning tickets..
Owner Mark Benton **Bred** Old Carhue & Graeng Bloodstock **Trained** Five Oaks, W Sussex

FOCUS
This was a competitive race featuring some decent performers on the surface.

12 KEMPTON.CO.UK H'CAP 2m (P)
5:50 (5:52) (Class 6) (0-60,60) 4-Y-O+ **£1,940** (£577; £288; £144) **Stalls** Low

Form RPR

055- 1 **Coup De Grace (IRE)**[13] 8189 4-9-1 56.......... IanMongan 4 68
(Pat Phelan) *hld up in midfield: rdn and gd prog over 2f out to ld over 1f out: sn clr: drvn out* **4/1**[2]

300- 2 3 3/4 **Bold Adventure**[22] 8067 9-9-4 52.......... JamieMackay 3 60
(Willie Musson) *hld up wl in rr: rdn and gd prog jst over 2f out: hanging sltly over 1f out: r.o to take 2nd last 100yds: no ch w wnr* **8/1**

4/3- 3 2 **If I Had Him (IRE)**[19] 8104 9-9-9 57..........(v) LukeMorris 6 62
(George Baker) *led: upped the pce fr 1/2-way: drvn and hdd over 1f out: one pce and lost 2nd fnl 100yds* **5/1**[3]

602- 4 3 **Perfect Shot (IRE)**[25] 8035 7-9-0 51.......... MarkCoumbe(3) 1 53
(Michael Attwater) *prom: chsd ldr over 3f out: drvn 2f out: lost 2nd and fdd over 1f out* **7/2**[1]

050- 5 3 1/4 **Rollin 'n Tumblin**[19] 8104 9-8-12 46 oh1.......... JimmyQuinn 2 44
(Michael Attwater) *trckd ldrs: rdn to chse ldng pair over 2f out: hld over 1f out: wknd fnl f* **14/1**

550/ 6 1 3/4 **Poppy Gregg**[492] 4951 8-8-12 46 oh1..........(b) RichardThomas 10 42
(Dr Jeremy Naylor) *hld up in last: pushed along 4f out: stl last over 2f out: styd on wl after: nrst fin* **50/1**

340- 7 3 1/2 **Big Time Billy (IRE)**[21] 8073 7-9-7 60.......(p) WilliamTwiston-Davies(5) 9 51
(Peter Bowen) *racd wd: chsd ldrs: drvn 3f out: steadily wknd: no ch over 1f out* **14/1**

060- 8 4 **Before Bruce**[19] 8104 6-9-2 50.......... SebSanders 8 37
(Brendan Powell) *hld up wl in rr: rdn and no prog over 3f out: no ch fnl 2f: modest late hdwy* **33/1**

0- 9 1 1/2 **Nadia Naes (IRE)**[24] 8048 4-8-5 46 oh1..........(e) MartinLane 14 31
(Roger Ingram) *trckd ldrs tl wknd wl over 2f out* **33/1**

060- 10 1 1/4 **Mariet**[26] 8023 4-9-3 58.......... GeorgeBaker 12 41
(Suzy Smith) *awkward s: t.k.h and hld up wl in rr: pushed along and no prog over 2f out: wl btn after and eased* **10/1**

500- 11 4 1/2 **Red Current**[22] 8067 9-9-6 54.......... JamieGoldstein 7 32
(Michael Scudamore) *awkward s and rousted along early: sn in midfield: gng wl enough over 3f out: hrd rdn over 2f out and wknd qckly* **33/1**

200- 12 16 **Caunay**[14] 8170 6-9-12 60..........(tp) AdamKirby 13 19
(Neil Mulholland) *mostly chsd ldr to over 6f out: drvn 4f out: wknd 3f out: eased over 1f out: t.o* **16/1**

324- 13 1 1/4 **Red Mystique (IRE)**[19] 8104 4-8-5 51..........(b) LeonnaMayor(5) 5 8
(Philip Hide) *hld up on outer: prog to go 2nd over 6f out: hanging lft bnd over 4f out: lost pl qckly whn v wd bnd 3f out: t.o* **4/1**[2]

3m 30.55s (0.45) **Going Correction** +0.05s/f (Slow)
WFA 4 from 5yo+ 7lb 13 Ran SP% **129.1**
Speed ratings (Par 101): **100,98,97,95,94 93,91,89,88,88 85,77,77**
toteswingers 1&2 £9.00, 1&3 £6.20, 2&3 £9.40 CSF £38.50 CT £173.06 TOTE £5.40: £2.20, £3.70, £1.10; EX 50.00 Trifecta £230.20 Pool: £1,777.18 - 5.79 winning tickets..
Owner Hugh J F Lang **Bred** Oliver Donlon **Trained** Epsom, Surrey

FOCUS
A modest stayers' race, but the placed horses are all solid at this level.

13 SKYSPORTS.COM H'CAP 1m (P)
6:20 (6:21) (Class 5) (0-70,70) 4-Y-O+ **£2,587** (£770; £384; £192) **Stalls** Low

Form RPR

102- 1 **Breakheart (IRE)**[14] 8167 6-8-3 59..........(p) JoeyHaynes(7) 12 64
(Andrew Balding) *hld up in midfield: drvn and prog fr 2f out: led ins fnl f: hld on wl* **12/1**

045- 2 nk **May's Boy**[14] 8162 5-8-6 60..........(p) RachealKneller(5) 4 65
(Mark Usher) *trckd ldng pair: pushed along to chal 2f out: narrow ld jst over 1f out to ins fnl f: styd on but jst hld* **8/1**

004- 3 nk **Ellie In The Pink (IRE)**[21] 8079 5-9-1 64 IanMongan 7 68
(Pat Phelan) *nt that wl away but pushed up into midfield: prog over 2f out: tried to chal fnl f: styd on but a jst hld* 11/2[2]

354- 4 1 1/4 **Rock Anthem (IRE)**[16] 8152 9-8-10 59 KieranO'Neill 11 60
(Mike Murphy) *t.k.h: hld up in rr: rdn and prog fr 2f out: styd on fnl f: nrst fin* 10/1

113- 5 nk **Crowning Star (IRE)**[253] 1582 4-9-7 70 (t) RobertWinston 8 70
(Gay Kelleway) *pressed ldr: narrow ld jst over 2f out to jst over 1f out: fdd fnl f* 11/1

000- 6 1/2 **Hip Hip Hooray**[71] 7310 7-8-12 61 TomMcLaughlin 9 60
(Luke Dace) *hld up in rr: rdn on outer wl over 2f out: no prog tl styd on wl fnl f: nrst fin* 10/1

125- 7 1 **Diplomatic (IRE)**[35] 7893 8-9-1 69 HarryPoulton(5) 10 66
(Michael Squance) *chsd ldrs on outer: rdn over 3f out: struggling over 2f out: kpt on but no threat* 6/1[3]

042- 8 nk **Zaheeb**[30] 7964 5-8-12 61 (b) LukeMorris 3 57
(Dave Morris) *led: narrowly hdd jst over 2f out: hanging lft over 1f out: wknd fnl f* 3/1[1]

000- 9 3/4 **Dream Prospector**[202] 3083 4-9-4 67 FergusSweeney 13 62
(James Evans) *hld up in last: jst pushed along fr 2f out: kpt on steadily fr over 1f out: nvr remotely involved* 50/1

000- 10 3 1/4 **Beauchamp Xerxes**[28] 7997 7-9-6 69 (t) RichardKingscote 5 56
(Hans Adielsson) *hld up in midfield: n.m.r on inner over 2f out: sn rdn and no prog* 25/1

060- 11 3 3/4 **Mullins Way (USA)**[28] 7998 5-9-3 66 J-PGuillambert 1 44
(Jo Hughes) *hld up in last pair: shkn up and no prog over 2f out* 10/1

050- 12 1 1/2 **Fluctuation (IRE)**[18] 8142 5-9-5 68 StevieDonohoe 2 43
(Ian Williams) *trckd ldng pair to over 2f out: wknd qckly* 25/1

1m 39.78s (-0.02) **Going Correction** +0.05s/f (Slow) **12** Ran SP% **118.7**
Speed ratings (Par 103): **102,101,101,100,99 99,98,98,97,94 90,88**
toteswingers 1&2 £18.70, 1&3 £19.40, 2&3 £8.30 CSF £103.02 CT £604.89 TOTE £13.50: £4.20, £3.20, £2.30; EX 125.30 Trifecta £208.00 Pool: £1,045.59 - 3.77 winning tickets..
Owner I A Balding **Bred** Littleton Stud **Trained** Kingsclere, Hants

FOCUS
Competitive stuff, with the first nine well-bunched at the finish.

14 BETDAQ MOBILE APPS MEDIAN AUCTION MAIDEN STKS 1m (P)
6:50 (6:50) (Class 6) 3-5-Y-O £1,940 (£577; £288; £144) **Stalls** Low

Form RPR

432- 1 **Captain Starlight (IRE)**[13] 8178 3-8-8 73 FergusSweeney 6 74
(Jo Crowley) *t.k.h: trckd ldr: led over 2f out: hd high but steadily asserted: edgd lft fnl f* 2/5[1]

665- 2 4 **Subtle Difference**[20] 8093 3-8-3 58 KirstyMilczarek 2 59
(Andrew Balding) *led: shkn up and hdd over 2f out: readily hld by wnr over 1f out: edgd lft fnl f* 4/1[2]

000- 3 9 **Automotive**[15] 8156 5-10-0 56 GeorgeBaker 3 42
(Julia Feilden) *hld up: chsd ldng pair over 2f out but already wl outpcd: no imp* 8/1[3]

500- 4 1 3/4 **Lea Valley**[13] 8187 4-9-2 45 ShelleyBirkett(7) 1 33
(Julia Feilden) *hld up in last: outpcd fr 3f out: tk v modest 4th over 1f out* 66/1

5 16 **Heroes Welcome (IRE)** 3-8-3 0 LukeMorris 4
(Hugo Palmer) *sn pushed along to chse ldng pair and rn green: wknd over 2f out: t.o* 12/1

1m 40.08s (0.28) **Going Correction** +0.05s/f (Slow)
WFA 3 from 4yo+ 20lb **5** Ran SP% **111.7**
Speed ratings (Par 101): **100,96,87,85,69**
CSF £2.46 TOTE £1.20: £1.10, £2.20; EX 2.60 Trifecta £5.40 Pool: £1,658.88 - 227.29 winning tickets..
Owner Kilstone Limited **Bred** David Bourke **Trained** Whitcombe, Dorset

FOCUS
An uncompetitive maiden in which the comfortable winner was the clear form pick.
T/Plt: £332.00 to a £1 stake. Pool: £54,863.51 - 120.62 winning tickets T/Qpdt: £61.40 to a £1 stake. Pool: £6,502.60 - 78.30 winning tickets JN

LINGFIELD (L-H)
Wednesday, January 2

OFFICIAL GOING: Standard
Wind: light, half behind Weather: dry

15 BET ON YOUR MOBILE AT BLUESQ.COM (S) STKS 1m 2f (P)
12:30 (12:30) (Class 6) 4-Y-0+ £2,045 (£603; £302) **Stalls** Low

Form RPR

005- 1 **Electrician**[13] 8177 4-8-12 63 (p) ShaneKelly 5 68
(Tim Pitt) *chsd ldr tl led over 2f out: rdn and qcknd 2f out: hrd pressed and edgd sltly rt ins fnl f: hld on wl: all out* 10/1

060- 2 shd **Paphos**[15] 8156 6-9-0 63 AdamKirby 7 68
(Stuart Williams) *in tch in midfield: chsd ldrs and rdn over 3f out: chsd clr wnr over 1f out: chal ent fnl f: carried sltly rt and ev ch fnl f: jst hld* 6/4[2]

262- 3 2 **One Way Or Another (AUS)**[24] 8047 10-9-0 66 (t) KirstyMilczarek 4 64
(David Evans) *stdd s: hld up in rr: effrt and chsd ldng pair 2f out: styd on same pce u.p fnl f* 5/4[1]

400- 4 3 1/4 **Formidable Guest**[118] 5974 9-8-9 51 FergusSweeney 3 52
(Jamie Poulton) *hld up in last pair: rdn and outpcd by ldng trio 2f out: plugged on but wl hld after* 25/1

016- 5 4 1/2 **Gay Gallivanter**[19] 8111 5-8-9 50 (p) TobyAtkinson(5) 2 48
(Mick Quinn) *led tl over 2f out: sn rdn and struggling: wknd wl over 1f out* 50/1

030- 6 2 3/4 **Parhelion**[34] 7819 6-8-7 59 (bt) NedCurtis(7) 1 43
(John Flint) *chsd ldrs tl over 4f out: dropped to rr and struggling 3f out: bhd fnl 2f* 9/2[3]

2m 6.1s (-0.50) **Going Correction** +0.10s/f (Slow)
WFA 4 from 5yo+ 2lb **6** Ran SP% **117.5**
Speed ratings (Par 101): **106,105,104,101,98 95**
toteswingers 1&2 £2.60, 1&3 £1.90, 2&3 £1.50 CSF £27.07 TOTE £17.60: £2.90, £1.20; EX 32.60 Trifecta £73.90 Pool: £760.06 - 7.71 winning tickets..There was no bid for the winner.
Owner Saintly Racing **Bred** Darley **Trained** Newmarket, Suffolk
■ Stewards' Enquiry : Shane Kelly one-day ban: careless riding (Jan 16)

FOCUS
Fair form from the principals in this seller.

16 COWDEN MAIDEN STKS 7f (P)
1:00 (1:00) (Class 5) 3-4-Y-O £2,726 (£805; £402) **Stalls** Low

Form RPR

522- 1 **Rangi**[21] 8070 3-8-9 76 RobertHavlin 1 71
(John Gosden) *mde all: pressed 3f out: drvn over 1f out: asserted ins fnl f: styd on wl* 4/6[1]

33- 2 2 1/4 **Lady Lunchalot (USA)**[5] 8262 3-8-4 0 LukeMorris 2 60
(J S Moore) *chsd wnr: rdn along to press wnr 3f out: drvn and ev ch wl over 1f out: no ex and btn fnl 100yds: wknd towards fin* 20/1[3]

5- 3 7 **Tanawar (IRE)**[53] 7686 3-8-9 0 AdamBeschizza 4 46
(William Haggas) *dwlt: in tch in 3rd: rdn and outpcd 2f out: wl hld and no imp fr over 1f out* 5/4[2]

0- 4 3 3/4 **Rectory Lane**[28] 7987 3-8-4 0 MartinLane 3 31
(Eve Johnson Houghton) *in tch in last: rdn and struggling whn hung rt bnd 2f out: sn wknd* 50/1

1m 25.08s (0.28) **Going Correction** +0.10s/f (Slow) **4** Ran SP% **111.2**
Speed ratings (Par 103): **102,99,91,87**
CSF £12.66 TOTE £2.10; EX 2.90 Trifecta £6.40 Pool: £230.51 - 37.17 winning tickets..
Owner RJH Geffen and Rachel Hood **Bred** Sheikh Abdulla Bin Isa Al Khalifa **Trained** Newmarket, Suffolk

FOCUS
Clearly a weak maiden.

17 LINGFIELDPARK.CO.UK H'CAP 7f (P)
1:30 (1:30) (Class 6) (0-65,65) 3-Y-O £2,045 (£603; £302) **Stalls** Low

Form RPR

532- 1 **Tilstarr (IRE)**[30] 7965 3-9-7 65 RobertWinston 1 68
(Roger Teal) *t.k.h: chsd ldrs: rdn and effrt over 1f out: r.o u.p to ld wl ins fnl f: r.o wl* 2/1[2]

046- 2 1/2 **Derwentwater (IRE)**[19] 8103 3-9-1 59 (b1) NickyMackay 3 60
(John Gosden) *jostled and squeezed for room sn after s: hld up in tch in rr: effrt on inner but then swtchd rt over 1f out: ev ch ins fnl f: r.o* 7/4[1]

014- 3 1/2 **Bay Laurel (IRE)**[20] 8096 3-9-5 63 RichardKingscote 2 63
(Mrs K Burke) *chsd ldr tl led 2f out: drvn over 1f out: hdd and no ex wl ins fnl f* 8/1

005- 4 1 1/4 **Man In The Arena**[19] 8103 3-9-1 59 LukeMorris 5 56
(Dr Jon Scargill) *in tch in last pair: rdn and effrt over 2f out: drvn and styd on same pce fr over 1f out* 8/1

025- 5 3/4 **Give Me High Five**[12] 8201 3-9-2 65 WilliamTwiston-Davies(5) 4 60
(Richard Hannon) *led: hdd 2f out: stl ev ch and drvn over 1f out: no ex and wknd wl ins fnl f* 7/2[3]

1m 26.54s (1.74) **Going Correction** +0.10s/f (Slow) **5** Ran SP% **114.1**
Speed ratings (Par 95): **94,93,92,91,90**
CSF £6.20 TOTE £3.30: £1.30, £1.40; EX 6.10 Trifecta £18.60 Pool: £755.07 - 30.30 winning tickets..
Owner H R Hunt **Bred** Ronnie Boland **Trained** Ashtead, Surrey

FOCUS
Hardly a competitive race for the grade. The gallop looked no better than a modest one for a long way.

18 BLUE SQUARE BET H'CAP 7f (P)
2:00 (2:00) (Class 4) (0-85,79) 3-Y-O £4,690 (£1,395; £697; £348) **Stalls** Low

Form RPR

014- 1 **Club House (IRE)**[2] 8302 3-8-2 67 RyanTate(7) 3 72
(Robert Mills) *hld up in 3rd: clsd and jnd ldr on bit over 1f out: rdn to ld ins fnl f: kpt on* 5/1[3]

512- 2 hd **Staffhoss**[12] 8211 3-9-7 79 JoeFanning 1 83+
(Mark Johnston) *led: rdn and edgd lft off bnd wl over 1f out: hdd ins fnl f: rallied u.p towards fin* 4/6[1]

025- 3 2 1/4 **Run It Twice (IRE)**[21] 8072 3-8-10 68 KirstyMilczarek 4 66
(David Evans) *hld up in tch in last: rdn and effrt to chse ldng pair jst over 1f out: edgd lft and no ex fnl 100yds* 3/1[2]

622- 4 6 **Ishigunnaeatit**[20] 8092 3-8-10 68 LukeMorris 2 50
(Mrs K Burke) *chsd ldr: rdn and unable qck 2f out: lost 2nd over 1f out: wknd fnl f* 7/1

1m 26.82s (2.02) **Going Correction** +0.10s/f (Slow) **4** Ran SP% **114.2**
Speed ratings (Par 99): **92,91,89,82**
CSF £9.55 TOTE £6.40; EX 11.80 Trifecta £19.30 Pool: £768.61 - 29.72 winning tickets..
Owner Trevor Jacobs & Mrs B B Mills **Bred** Val & Angela Leeson **Trained** Headley, Surrey

FOCUS
Another small-field handicap and predictably the pace wasn't strong.

19 TANDRIDGE MEDIAN AUCTION MAIDEN STKS 5f (P)
2:30 (2:31) (Class 6) 3-5-Y-O £2,045 (£603; £302) **Stalls** High

Form RPR

403- 1 **Outbid**[6] 8245 3-8-1 60 LeonnaMayor(5) 1 52
(Jamie Osborne) *hld up in tch in midfield: effrt on inner to chal over 1f out: led ins fnl f: in command whn edgd rt towards fin* 9/4[2]

432- 2 1 **Summer Sun**[6] 8251 4-9-7 50 LukeMorris 4 54
(Phil McEntee) *sn bustled along to press ldr on inner: jostling w rival over 3f out: led 1/2-way: rdn 2f out: hdd and one pce ins fnl f* 14/1

3 1/2 **Dangerous Age** 3-8-6 0 JoeFanning 5 46
(J W Hills) *awkward leaving stalls: t.k.h and sn chsng ldrs: rdn and sltly outpcd over 1f out: rallied to chse ldrs again 1f out: kpt on same pce* 5/1[3]

522- 4 1 3/4 **Jermatt**[32] 7952 4-9-12 60 ShaneKelly 6 51
(J R Jenkins) *led: jostling w rival over 3f out: hdd 1/2-way: w ldr after tl rdn and fnd little over 1f out: wknd ins fnl f* 4/5[1]

00- 5 1 1/2 **Woodland Fleur**[14] 8171 3-8-6 0 JimmyQuinn 7 35
(Tony Carroll) *racd off the pce in 5th: struggling 1/2-way: running green: edging rt but kpt on ins fnl f* 25/1

6 4 1/2 **It Ain't To Grand** 4-9-12 0 RobertHavlin 2 29
(Roger Ingram) *v.s.a: a detached in last* 40/1

59.36s (0.56) **Going Correction** +0.10s/f (Slow)
WFA 3 from 4yo 15lb **6** Ran SP% **115.9**
Speed ratings (Par 101): **99,97,96,93,91 84**
CSF £31.93 TOTE £2.20: £1.90, £2.70; EX 15.10 Trifecta £50.20 Pool: £1,958.95 - 29.25 winning tickets..
Owner Paul Hearn, Dean Margolis & Partners **Bred** Llety Stud **Trained** Upper Lambourn, Berks
■ Stewards' Enquiry : Shane Kelly two-day ban: careless riding (Jan 17-18)

FOCUS
An ordinary sprint maiden.

20 DRY HILL H'CAP — 1m 5f (P)
3:00 (3:00) (Class 6) (0-65,65) 4-Y-0+ — **£2,045** (£603; £302) **Stalls** Low

Form / RPR

500- **1** **Stentorian (IRE)**[43] 5908 5-9-7 **62**.....(v[1]) AdamKirby 5 — 70
(Gary Moore) *stdd s: hld up in tch in rr: rdn over 3f out: hdwy u.p over 1f out: styd on strly ins fnl f to ld last stride* **12/1**

331- **2** *shd* **Jacobs Son**[13] 8189 5-9-5 **65**..... WilliamTwiston-Davies(5) 3 — 73
(Robert Mills) *chsd ldr for 3f: chsd ldrs after tl rdn to chal over 1f out: drvn to ld jst ins fnl f: r.o u.p tl hdd last stride* **7/4**[1]

433- **3** *3/4* **La Belle Doyenne**[47] 7739 5-9-7 **62**..... FergusSweeney 8 — 69
(Alan King) *chsd ldrs: wnt 2nd 10f out tl led over 2f out: drvn and hrd pressed over 1f out: hdd jst ins fnl f: styd on same pce ins fnl f* **12/1**

606- **4** *2 1/2* **Shalambar (IRE)**[14] 8175 7-9-5 **65**..... GeorgeDowning(5) 1 — 68
(Tony Carroll) *dwlt: sn rcvrd and in tch in midfield: rdn and effrt whn swtchd rt over 1f out: no ex 1f out: styd on same pce ins fnl f* **8/1**[3]

031- **5** *hd* **Honest Strike (USA)**[22] 8067 6-8-12 **53**.....(b) ShaneKelly 6 — 56
(Daniel Mark Loughnane) *hld up in tch in midfield: effrt to chse ldrs 2f out: drvn and unable qck over 1f out: btn and one pce ins fnl f* **5/2**[2]

000- **6** *2 1/2* **One For Joules (IRE)**[84] 6981 6-9-7 **62**..... JamieGoldstein 4 — 61
(John Flint) *t.k.h: hld up in tch in last trio: rdn and hdwy jst over 2f out: no ex u.p over 1f out: wknd 1f out* **12/1**

0/4- **7** *nk* **Dynamic Idol (USA)**[43] 569 6-9-10 **65**.....(v[1]) GeorgeBaker 2 — 64
(Gary Moore) *led tl hdd and rdn over 2f out: btn jst over 1f out: wknd fnl f* **20/1**

432- **8** *1* **El Libertador (USA)**[13] 8189 7-8-7 **55**.....(b) JoeyHaynes(7) 7 — 52
(Eric Wheeler) *t.k.h: hld up in tch in last trio: rdn and effrt jst over 2f out: no prog over 1f out: wknd ins fnl f* **8/1**[3]

2m 47.08s (1.08) **Going Correction** +0.10s/f (Slow) — **8** Ran SP% **115.0**
Speed ratings (Par 101): **100,99,99,97,97 96,96,95**
toteswingers 1&2 £6.80, 1&3 £11.10, 2&3 £5.00 CSF £33.72 CT £267.30 TOTE £20.70: £3.10, £1.10, £3.00; EX 63.90 Trifecta £522.30 Pool: £1,490.32 - 2.14 winning tickets..
Owner B Homewood **Bred** Ceka Ireland Limited **Trained** Lower Beeding, W Sussex

FOCUS
Just a modest handicap. The pace wasn't strong, so the winner arguably deserves a little extra credit having still been at the back at the top of the straight.

21 GET STRAIGHT TO BET AT BLUESQ.COM H'CAP — 1m 2f (P)
3:30 (3:30) (Class 5) (0-70,69) 4-Y-0+ — **£2,726** (£805; £402) **Stalls** Low

Form / RPR

231- **1** **Ishikawa (IRE)**[46] 7768 5-9-7 **69**..... FergusSweeney 3 — 77+
(Alan King) *hld up in tch in midfield: rdn and effrt to chse ldrs over 1f out: chal ins fnl f: r.o wl u.p to ld nr fin* **5/4**[1]

005- **2** *hd* **Understory (USA)**[6] 8252 6-9-5 **67**..... RichardKingscote 5 — 74
(Tim McCarthy) *led and set stdy gallop: rdn and qcknd over 2f out: hrd pressed and drvn jst ins fnl f: kpt on wl tl hdd and no ex nr fin* **6/1**[2]

334- **3** *2* **Sail Home**[21] 8078 6-8-9 **64**..... ShelleyBirkett(7) 6 — 67
(Julia Feilden) *hld up in tch in last trio: rdn and effrt on outer bnd wl over 1f out: styng on whn edgd lft and nt clr run ins fnl f: swtchd lft fnl 100yds: styd on to snatch 3rd last stride* **12/1**

364- **4** *shd* **Silkee Supreme**[14] 8162 4-8-7 **57**.....(b) KieranO'Neill 9 — 60
(Richard Hannon) *chsd ldr: rdn 2f out: unable qck ent fnl f: styd on same pce after: lost 3rd last stride* **7/1**[3]

051- **5** *1* **Calypso Magic (IRE)**[21] 8078 5-8-9 **57**.....(t) KirstyMilczarek 2 — 58
(Olivia Maylam) *taken down early: hld up in last pair: rdn and effrt on inner over 1f out: styd on same pce and no imp fnl f* **6/1**[2]

060- **6** *1* **Broxbourne (IRE)**[71] 7303 4-8-5 **55**..... JoeFanning 1 — 54
(Mark Johnston) *chsd ldrs: rdn over 3f out: drvn and unable qck over 1f out: one pce after* **14/1**

0/4- **7** *2 1/4* **Deceptive**[48] 4875 5-9-2 **69**..... WilliamTwiston-Davies(5) 8 — 64
(Paul Webber) *chsd ldrs: rdn and unable qck 2f out: wknd u.p over 1f out* **10/1**

150- **8** *4 1/2* **Penbryn (USA)**[221] 2498 6-8-13 **61**.....(b) RobertHavlin 4 — 47
(Nick Littmoden) *stdd after s: hld up in tch in rr: rdn and no imp over 1f out: wknd fnl f* **8/1**

2m 5.16s (-1.44) **Going Correction** +0.10s/f (Slow)
WFA 4 from 5yo+ 2lb — **8** Ran SP% **120.1**
Speed ratings (Par 103): **109,108,107,107,106 105,102,99**
toteswingers 1&2 £2.90, 1&3 £4.40, 2&3 £11.20 CSF £9.85 CT £65.88 TOTE £2.40: £1.40, £2.20, £2.70; EX 12.20 Trifecta £95.90 Pool: £1,120.69 - 8.76 winning tickets..
Owner ROA Racing Partnership V **Bred** Ken Carroll **Trained** Barbury Castle, Wilts

FOCUS
Just another run-of-the-mill handicap. The pace was pretty sedate and it was an advantage to race handily.
T/Plt: £1,063.50 to a £1 stake. Pool: £43,417.54 - 29.80 winning tickets. T/Qpdt: £113.30 to a £1 stake. Pool: £4,838.59 - 31.6 winning tickets. SP

[1]WOLVERHAMPTON (A.W) (L-H)
Wednesday, January 2

OFFICIAL GOING: Standard
Wind: Light half behind Weather: Overcast

22 CORAL.CO.UK AMATEUR RIDERS' H'CAP — 2m 119y(P)
2:10 (2:10) (Class 6) (0-65,65) 4-Y-0+ — **£1,975** (£607; £303) **Stalls** Low

Form / RPR

232- **1** **Stormy Morning**[41] 7102 7-10-7 **61**.....(p) MissHBethell(3) 2 — 69
(Philip Kirby) *hld up in tch: smooth hdwy 4f out: trckd ldrs over 2f out: rdn to chal over 1f out: sn led and kpt on wl* **10/1**

023- **2** *1* **Baan (USA)**[28] 8001 10-9-11 **55**..... StevieSanders(7) 11 — 62
(James Eustace) *hld up in rr: hdwy 4f out: rdn to chse ldrs 2f out: styd on u.p fnl f: nrst fin* **12/1**

/12- **3** *hd* **Goldan Jess (IRE)**[23] 7862 9-10-1 **52**..... MrSWalker 8 — 59
(Philip Kirby) *trckd ldng pair: led 4f out: rdn along 2f out: jnd over 1f out: sn drvn and hdd: one pce ins fnl f* **15/8**[1]

040/ **4** *1 3/4* **Blazing Desert**[37] 3817 9-11-0 **65**..... MrWKinsey 9 — 70
(William Kinsey) *hld up: stdy hdwy 6f out: trckd ldrs 4f out: effrt over 2f out: sn rdn and kpt on same pce* **33/1**

512- **5** *3* **Roughlyn**[19] 8104 4-9-8 **52**.....(v) MissSBrotherton 4 — 53
(Lisa Williamson) *cl up: pushed along 3f out: rdn over 2f out: sn one pce* **4/1**[2]

0/0- **6** *1 1/2* **Dane Cottage**[28] 7991 6-9-8 **52** ow2..... MrTGreenwood(7) 13 — 51
(Richard Ford) *s.i.s and bhd: hdwy over 2f out: sn rdn and kpt on appr fnl f: nrst fin* **66/1**

350/ **7** *2 3/4* **Sparkaway**[121] 5898 7-9-13 **50**.....(b) MrSCrawford 10 — 46
(Ross O'Sullivan, Ire) *chsd ldrs: rdn along 3f out: wknd 2f out* **22/1**

131- **8** *6* **Passato (GER)**[32] 3216 9-10-7 **63**.....(t) MrJAPonting(5) 7 — 52
(Jo Davis) *chsd ldrs: rdn along 4f out: wknd over 2f out* **10/1**

0/0- **9** *1* **Sonara (IRE)**[17] 8035 9-10-9 **60**..... MrFWindsorClive 1 — 48
(David Evans) *led 7f: cl up and led again 7f out: rdn along and hdd 4f out: sn wknd* **50/1**

/00- **10** *6* **Augustus John (IRE)**[30] 7968 10-10-6 **57**..... MrTomDavid 3 — 37
(Roy Brotherton) *hld up: a towards rr* **33/1**

023- **11** *8* **Mcbirney (USA)**[12] 8214 6-10-9 **65**..... MrsRWilson(5) 6 — 36
(Paul D'Arcy) *dwlt and towards rr: t.k.h and hdwy on outer after 3f: sn cl up: led after 7f: hdd over 7f out: wknd over 4f out* **5/1**[3]

0/ **12** *31* **Daggers Bond (IRE)**[7] 2193 7-9-10 **52**..... JackSherwood(5) 12
(Aidan Anthony Howard, Ire) *a in rr: outpcd and bhd fnl 4f* **22/1**

3m 42.66s (0.86) **Going Correction** -0.15s/f (Stan)
WFA 4 from 6yo+ 7lb — **12** Ran SP% **115.4**
Speed ratings (Par 101): **91,90,90,89,88 87,86,83,82,80 76,61**
toteswingers 1&2 £9.70, 1&3 £4.20, 2&3 £5.80 CSF £109.53 CT £323.29 TOTE £14.40: £3.30, £3.80, £1.50; EX 65.20 Trifecta £291.00 Pool: £1,451.45 - 3.74 winning tickets..
Owner Colin Fletcher & Ownaracehorse **Bred** Wellsummers Stud **Trained** Middleham, N Yorks

FOCUS
This open handicap, confined to amateur riders, was run at steady gallop with few able to cope with the injection of pace at the 3f pole.

23 ONLINE BETTING OFFERS AT BOOKMAKERS.CO.UK CLAIMING STKS — 1m 141y(P)
2:40 (2:40) (Class 6) 4-Y-0+ — **£2,045** (£603; £302) **Stalls** Low

Form / RPR

136- **1** **Noble Jack (IRE)**[72] 7132 7-8-12 71.....(b[1]) J-PGuillambert 6 — 82
(Jo Hughes) *hld up towards rr: hdwy and in tch 1/2-way: pushed along 3f out: trckd ldrs and n.m.r 2f out: sn chsng ldr: rdn and edgd lft ins fnl f: sn led and styd on* **3/1**[2]

133- **2** *3* **Desert Vision**[7] 8242 9-9-10 83.....(vt) GrahamGibbons 7 — 88
(Michael Easterby) *hld up in tch: trckd ldrs 1/2-way: cl up 3f out: led 2f out: rdn over 1f out: hdd ins fnl f: one pce* **4/5**[1]

046- **3** *3* **Classic Colori (IRE)**[6] 8259 6-9-10 83..... TomEaves 1 — 80
(David O'Meara) *trckd ldrs: hdwy over 3f out: rdn 2f out: sn drvn and one pce appr fnl f* **7/1**[3]

044- **4** *3 1/2* **Sir George (IRE)**[24] 8047 8-8-6 62.....(p) BarryMcHugh 3 — 54
(Ollie Pears) *trckd ldrs on outer: hdwy over 2f out: rdn along and wd st: sn one pce* **20/1**

130- **5** *4 1/2* **Jordaura**[16] 8146 7-8-5 63..... JordanHibberd(7) 2 — 50
(Alan Berry) *dwlt: a in rr* **33/1**

000- **6** *4 1/2* **Pirate Chest (IRE)**[17] 6711 5-9-2 57.....(b[1]) DuranFentiman 5 — 43
(Patrick Holmes) *led: rdn along over 3f out: hdd 2f out: sn wknd* **66/1**

000- **7** *4 1/2* **Dunn'o (IRE)**[49] 7715 8-8-12 78.....(t) MartinDwyer 8 — 29
(David Nicholls) *trckd ldr: effrt and cl up 1/2-way: rdn along wl over 2f out: sn wknd* **11/1**

1m 47.93s (-2.57) **Going Correction** -0.15s/f (Stan) — **7** Ran SP% **110.6**
Speed ratings (Par 101): **105,102,99,96,92 88,84**
toteswingers 1&2 £1.40, 1&3 £2.10, 2&3 £1.70 CSF £5.34 TOTE £3.50: £1.60, £1.10; EX 7.10 Trifecta £23.60 Pool: £1,766.65 - 55.94 winning tickets..
Owner Darren & Annaley Yates **Bred** Team Hogdala Ab **Trained** Lambourn, Berks

FOCUS
This looked a fair contest for the grade, run at a sound pace with the field well strung out at the line.

24 DOWNLOAD CORAL.CO.UK MOBILE APP H'CAP — 7f 32y(P)
3:10 (3:10) (Class 6) (0-55,54) 4-Y-0+ — **£2,045** (£603; £302) **Stalls** High

Form / RPR

000- **1** **Boy The Bell**[35] 7917 6-8-13 **53**.....(b) JacobButterfield(7) 8 — 62
(Ollie Pears) *hld up: hdwy 3f out: chsd ldrs over 1f out: rdn and styd on ins fnl f: led last 75yds: kpt on* **16/1**

300- **2** *1 1/4* **Under Par**[6] 8257 5-9-2 **49**.....(t) GrahamGibbons 5 — 55
(Michael Easterby) *a.p: effrt 2f out: rdn to chal over 1f out and ev ch tl drvn and one pce wl ins fnl f* **8/1**

606- **3** *nk* **Kielty's Folly**[96] 6646 9-9-4 **51**..... WilliamCarson 4 — 56
(Brian Baugh) *hld up: stdy hdwy 1/2-way: trckd ldrs 3f out: effrt to chal on outer over 1f out: rdn and ev ch whn hmpd ins fnl f: kpt on same pce after* **20/1**

434- **4** *3/4* **Fortunate Bid (IRE)**[29] 7983 7-9-6 **53**.....(p) TomEaves 11 — 56
(Linda Stubbs) *s.i.s and bhd: hdwy 3f out: rdn 2f out: styd on u.p fnl f: nrst fin* **6/1**[2]

060- **5** *nk* **Calypso Cay**[48] 7733 5-9-7 **54**..... RenatoSouza 10 — 56
(Peter Salmon) *led: rdn along wl over 1f out: jnd and rdn whn hung rt ins fnl f and rdr dropped reins: sn hdd and nt rcvr* **16/1**

310- **6** *1 1/2* **Quan (IRE)**[21] 8075 4-9-7 **54**..... MartinDwyer 6 — 52
(Alan Swinbank) *sn trcking ldr: hdwy anbd cln up 2f out: rdn and ev ch over 1f out: hmpd ins fnl f: sn wknd* **9/4**[1]

220- **7** *1 1/2* **Forzarzi (IRE)**[75] 7225 9-8-12 **52**..... VictorSantos(7) 3 — 46
(H A McWilliams) *hld up in rr: hdwy over 2f out: sn rdn and no imp fnl f* **40/1**

62-0 **8** *1 1/4* **Romeo's On Fire (IRE)**[1] 7 9-9-5 **52**.....(p) JamesSullivan 2 — 43
(Adrian McGuinness, Ire) *nvr bttr than midfield* **14/1**

006- **9** *3 3/4* **Cadmium Loch**[18] 8131 5-9-0 **52**.....(p) JackDuern(5) 1 — 33
(Reg Hollinshead) *chsd ldrs on inner: rdn along 2f out: grad wknd* **11/1**

550- **10** *2* **Keys Of Cyprus**[58] 7593 11-9-0 **52**..... ShirleyTeasdale(5) 7 — 27
(David Nicholls) *hld up: a towards rr* **8/1**

104- **11** *6* **Star Kingdom (IRE)**[92] 6758 4-9-4 **51**..... DaleSwift 9 — 10
(Brian Ellison) *hld up: hdwy and in tch 1/2-way: rdn along to chse ldrs 3f out: wknd 2f out* **13/2**[3]

1m 28.29s (-1.31) **Going Correction** -0.15s/f (Stan) — **11** Ran SP% **114.6**
Speed ratings (Par 101): **101,99,99,98,98 96,94,93,88,86 79**
toteswingers 1&2 £12.10, 1&3 £40.30, 2&3 £22.20 CSF £134.87 CT £2565.07 TOTE £24.90: £5.50, £3.10, £5.10; EX 209.90 TRIFECTA Not won..
Owner K C West **Bred** D J P Turner **Trained** Norton, N Yorks

FOCUS
The pace was solid for this moderate contest with the complexion of the race changing inside the final furlong.

25 BOOKIE FREE BETS WITH BOOKMAKERS.CO.UK H'CAP 7f 32y(P)
3:40 (3:41) (Class 4) (0-85,85) 4-Y-0+ **£4,690** (£1,395; £697; £348) **Stalls** High

Form RPR

516- **1** **Kung Hei Fat Choy (USA)**[2] 8306 4-9-0 **78**........................(b) DaleSwift 7 89
(James Given) *t.k.h: trckd ldr: cl up 3f out: led wl over 1f out: rdn ins fnl f: kpt on wl* **7/2**[1]

261- **2** 1 1/2 **Atlantis Crossing (IRE)**[13] 8183 4-8-9 **78**.................. NathanAlison(5) 6 85
(Roger Ingram) *hld up in rr: effrt and n.m.r 2f out: chsng ldrs whn n.m.r and swtchd rt ent fnl f: sn rdn and styd on: nrst fin* **4/1**[2]

223- **3** 1 1/4 **Roy The Boy (USA)**[18] 8142 5-8-5 **76**..........................(v) RobertTart(7) 9 80
(Alan Bailey) *trckd ldrs: effrt over 2f out: sn rdn: kpt on same pce fnl f* **7/2**[1]

430- **4** hd **Copperwood**[80] 7083 8-8-13 **77**.. MartinDwyer 3 80
(Mark Johnston) *trckd ldrs on inner: effrt over 2f out: rdn wl over 1f out: kpt on same pce fnl f* **14/1**

611- **5** nk **Balti's Sister (IRE)**[30] 7975 4-8-5 **76**.......................... GeorgeBuckell(7) 1 78
(Terry Clement) *hld up: hdwy on inner 2f out: rdn to chse ldrs ent fnl f: sn drvn and no imp* **11/2**[3]

001- **6** 3 1/2 **Polar Kite (IRE)**[30] 7961 5-8-13 **77**................................. BarryMcHugh 5 70
(Richard Fahey) *t.k.h: led: rdn along 2f out: hdd wl over 1f out and sn wknd* **6/1**

405- **7** nk **Decent Fella (IRE)**[2] 8306 7-9-7 **85**...........................(tp) WilliamCarson 2 77
(Violet M Jordan) *in tch: rdn along wl over 2f out: sn btn* **9/1**

400- **8** 4 1/2 **Fantasy Gladiator**[23] 8057 7-8-8 **72** ow1..........................(p) TomEaves 8 52
(Robert Cowell) *stdd s and hld up in rr: hdwy on outer 1/2-way: cl up 3f out: rdn along 2f out: sn wknd* **20/1**

1m 26.98s (-2.62) **Going Correction** -0.15s/f (Stan) **8** Ran SP% **115.5**
Speed ratings (Par 105): **108,106,104,104,104 100,99,94**
toteswingers 1&2 £4.00, 1&3 £3.00, 2&3 £3.40 CSF £17.88 CT £51.89 TOTE £3.90: £1.40, £1.70, £1.10; EX 20.50 Trifecta £41.80 Pool: £2,391.20 - 42.88 winning tickets..
Owner Danethorpe Racing Partnership **Bred** Gilgai Farm **Trained** Willoughton, Lincs

FOCUS
A competitive handicap run at a steady pace with the winner benefiting by how the race unfolded.

26 MONEY BACK RACING SPECIALS AT BOOKMAKERS.CO.UK H'CAP 5f 20y(P)
4:10 (4:10) (Class 6) (0-60,60) 4-Y-0+ **£2,045** (£603; £302) **Stalls** Low

Form RPR

512- **1** **Miss Bunter**[6] 8253 4-9-5 **58**.. TomEaves 1 69
(David O'Meara) *trckd ldr: hdwy wl over 1f out: rdn to ld ins fnl f: kpt on* **11/10**[1]

020- **2** 1 **Ryedale Dancer (IRE)**[6] 8253 5-8-10 **54**......................... JasonHart(5) 2 61
(Richard Guest) *t.k.h: hld up in rr: hdwy on inner wl over 1f out: sn rdn and styd on strly fnl f: nrst fin* **8/1**

440- **3** 1/2 **Liberty Ship**[6] 8253 8-9-7 **60**... MartinDwyer 8 65
(Mark Buckley) *hld up: hdwy 2f out: sn rdn: drvn and styd on fnl f: nrst fin* **25/1**

101- **4** nk **M J Woodward**[11] 8231 4-9-7 **60**.................................... JamesSullivan 5 64
(Paul Green) *chsd ldng pair: hdwy on outer 2f out and sn rdn: drvn and ch ent fnl f: sn one pce* **3/1**[2]

003- **5** nk **Wreningham**[6] 8253 8-9-2 **60**..................................(b) CharlesBishop(5) 7 63
(Pat Eddery) *led: rdn along and edgd rt over 1f out: drvn and hdd ins fnl f: wknd* **5/1**[3]

450- **6** 1 1/2 **Steel City Boy (IRE)**[3] 8298 10-8-11 **55**......................... AnnStokell(5) 3 53
(Ann Stokell) *chsd ldrs: rdn along 2f out: kpt on same pce* **28/1**

240- **7** 7 **Absolute Fun (IRE)**[79] 7099 4-8-9 **48**......................... DuranFentiman 4 20
(Tim Easterby) *a in rr: rdn along 1/2-way: sn outpcd and bhd* **25/1**

1m 1.04s (-1.26) **Going Correction** -0.15s/f (Stan) **7** Ran SP% **111.5**
Speed ratings (Par 101): **104,102,101,101,100 98,87**
toteswingers 1&2 £2.60, 1&3 £4.80, 2&3 £11.80 CSF £10.13 CT £131.64 TOTE £1.70: £1.30, £2.10; EX 8.90 Trifecta £69.40 Pool: £2,848.63 - 30.75 winning tickets..
Owner D Fravigar Miss K Dixon & Mrs R Mitchell **Bred** Bumble Bloodstock Ltd **Trained** Nawton, N Yorks

FOCUS
An uncompetitive looking contest with the front five well grouped passing the post.

27 FREE SPORTS BETTING AT BOOKMAKERS.CO.UK H'CAP 5f 216y(P)
4:40 (4:40) (Class 5) (0-70,72) 4-Y-0+ **£2,587** (£770; £384; £192) **Stalls** Low

Form RPR

502- **1** **Colbyor**[11] 8236 4-9-1 **64**..(v[1]) BarryMcHugh 7 74
(Richard Fahey) *chsd ldng pair: pushed along 1/2-way: hdwy to chal over 1f out: rdn to ld ent fnl f: kpt on strly* **4/1**[1]

502- **2** 1 1/4 **Holy Angel (IRE)**[43] 7794 4-8-9 **63**.............................(e) AdamCarter(5) 5 69
(Tim Easterby) *chsd ldr: cl up 2f out: sn rdn and ev ch tl drvn and one pce ins fnl f* **5/1**[2]

000- **3** 1/2 **Cardinal**[47] 7741 8-9-6 **69**.. TomEaves 2 73
(Robert Cowell) *chsd ldrs on inner: hdwy 2f out: rdn over 1f out: drvn and kpt on fnl f* **14/1**

245- **4** 1/2 **Greenhead High**[4] 8285 5-8-11 **65**.......................... ShirleyTeasdale(5) 8 68
(David Nicholls) *led: pushed along wl over 1f out: sn rdn: hdd ent fnl f and kpt on same pce* **6/1**[3]

361- **5** 3/4 **Dark Lane**[3] 8294 7-9-2 **72** 6ex.. PhilipPrince(7) 3 72
(David Evans) *chsd ldrs: rdn along on inner 2f out: styd on u.p fnl f* **7/1**

602- **6** nk **Master Of Disguise**[18] 8144 7-9-2 **65**..............................(t) WilliamCarson 9 64
(Brian Baugh) *chsd ldrs: rdn along 2f out: sn no imp* **13/2**

406- **7** hd **Fenella Fudge**[58] 7590 5-9-0 **63**.......................................(v) MartinDwyer 4 62
(Derek Shaw) *t.k.h: hld up: hdwy 2f out: sn rdn and no imp fnl f* **16/1**

005- **8** nse **Celtic Sixpence (IRE)**[23] 8054 5-9-0 **70**.................... HannahNunn(7) 12 69+
(Peter Salmon) *hld up in rr: hdwy 2f out: effrt and n.m.r ins fnl f: sn no hdwy* **16/1**

461- **9** 1 3/4 **Dickie Le Davoir**[35] 7915 9-8-12 **66**...........................(b) JasonHart(5) 6 59
(Richard Guest) *s.i.s: a in rr* **8/1**

200- **10** nk **Green Mitas (ITY)**[5] 8271 4-8-10 **64**................................ AmyScott(5) 13 56
(Frank Sheridan) *s.i.s: a in rr* **20/1**

100- **11** 1 3/4 **Prince James**[18] 8144 6-9-0 **63**..................................... GrahamGibbons 11 49
(Michael Easterby) *a towards rr* **12/1**

1m 13.52s (-1.48) **Going Correction** -0.15s/f (Stan) **11** Ran SP% **118.8**
Speed ratings (Par 103): **103,101,100,100,99 98,98,98,95,95 93**
toteswingers 1&2 £4.10, 1&3 £12.30, 2&3 £10.60 CSF £23.69 CT £263.65 TOTE £3.30: £1.30, £2.40, £3.90; EX 15.70 Trifecta £457.50 Pool: £1,299.30 - 2.13 winning tickets..
Owner E Bruce **Bred** Mr And Mrs E Bruce **Trained** Musley Bank, N Yorks

FOCUS
This competitive handicap was run at a sound pace, with few able to close from behind.

28 CASINO AT CORAL.CO.UK MAIDEN FILLIES' STKS 1m 1f 103y(P)
5:10 (5:11) (Class 5) 4-Y-0+ **£2,587** (£770; £384; £192) **Stalls** Low

Form RPR

054- **1** **Malindi**[151] 4797 4-9-0 69.. JamesSullivan 4 53
(James Given) *trckd ldrs: green and pushed along 3f out: hdwy to chse ldng pair 2f out: rdn on inner to chal ent fnl f: sn rn green and edgd rt: styd on to ld last 75yds* **8/11**[1]

054- **2** nk **Merrjanah**[99] 6562 5-9-1 46.. PaddyAspell 1 52
(John Wainwright) *set stdy pce: pushed along and qcknd wl over 2f out: rdn over 1f out: edgd rt ins fnl f: hdd and no ex last 100yds* **12/1**

043- **3** 1 1/2 **Tijuca (IRE)**[13] 8187 4-9-0 57... MartinDwyer 9 49
(Ed de Giles) *hld up in tch: hdwy 3f out: rdn to chse ldrs wl over 1f out: kpt on u.p fnl f: nrst fin* **7/2**[2]

000- **4** 2 1/4 **Kuraanda**[7] 8239 4-9-0 35..(p) BarryMcHugh 8 44
(John Wainwright) *trckd ldr: cl up over 2f out: rdn along wl over 1f out: wknd fnl f* **150/1**

5 1 3/4 **Lil Sophella (IRE)** 4-9-0 0.. DuranFentiman 2 40
(Patrick Holmes) *in rr: hdwy 3f out: rdn along 2f out: kpt on u.p fnl f: n.d* **16/1**

6- **6** 4 1/2 **Dubai Story**[7] 8239 4-8-9 0... AmyScott(5) 6 31
(Alastair Lidderdale) *midfield: hdwy over 3f out: rdn along to chse ldrs over 2f out: sn no imp* **8/1**

U/0- **7** 4 1/2 **Supastarqueen (USA)**[18] 8133 5-9-1 0......................... WilliamCarson 5 22
(Brian Baugh) *chsd ldrs: rdn along 3f out: wknd 2f out* **100/1**

R00- **8** 3 **Idarose (IRE)**[131] 5549 4-8-7 15.................................(p) VictorSantos(7) 3 15
(H A McWilliams) *chsd ldng pair: rdn along 3f out: sn wknd* **150/1**

9 3 1/4 **Elusive**[31] 7-8-10 0.. AnnStokell(5) 11
(Ann Stokell) *awkward s and s.i.s: a bhd* **40/1**

10 3/4 **Princess Kheleyf** 4-9-0 0.. TomEaves 10
(Geoffrey Oldroyd) *s.i.s: green and a bhd* **7/1**[3]

2m 2.86s (1.16) **Going Correction** -0.15s/f (Stan)
WFA 4 from 5yo+ 1lb **10** Ran SP% **122.1**
Speed ratings (Par 100): **88,87,86,84,82 78,74,72,69,68**
toteswingers 1&2 £3.40, 1&3 £1.40, 2&3 £6.20 CSF £12.93 TOTE £1.80: £1.10, £2.80, £1.60; EX 13.10 Trifecta £22.30 Pool: £2,696.11 - 90.60 winning tickets..
Owner H J P Farr **Bred** H J P Farr **Trained** Willoughton, Lincs

FOCUS
A weak fillies´ maiden run at a fair pace, where it paid to race prominently.
T/Jkpt: Not won. T/Plt: £150.40 to a £1 stake. Pool: £91,018.16 - 441.77 winning tickets T/Qpdt: £52.30 to a £1 stake. Pool: £5,812.92 - 82.10 winning tickets JR

15 LINGFIELD (L-H)
Thursday, January 3

OFFICIAL GOING: Standard
Wind: Almost nil Weather: Cloudy, mild

29 BET AT BLUESQ.COM H'CAP 5f (P)
12:50 (12:55) (Class 5) (0-75,72) 4-Y-0+ **£2,726** (£805; £402) **Stalls** High

Form RPR

130- **1** **Roy's Legacy**[15] 8163 4-9-6 **71**..(t) AdamKirby 6 79
(Shaun Harris) *mde all: rdn 2f out: hrd pressed fnl f: jst hld on* **4/1**[3]

630- **2** nse **Billy Red**[12] 8225 9-9-2 **67**..(b) JoeFanning 5 75
(J R Jenkins) *chsd wnr: rdn 2f out: clsd steadily fnl f: needed one more stride* **14/1**

004- **3** 2 1/4 **Dancing Freddy (IRE)**[6] 8266 6-9-3 **68**....................(tp) WilliamCarson 2 68
(Violet M Jordan) *pushed along to chse ldng pair: rdn and kpt on same pce fnl 2f wout threatening* **7/1**

055- **4** 1 3/4 **Mother Jones**[16] 8157 5-9-2 **72**...................... WilliamTwiston-Davies(5) 3 66
(David Evans) *reluctant to go to post: dwlt: effrt on outside after 2f: no prog 2f out: wl hld after* **12/1**

325- **5** nse **Welease Bwian (IRE)**[12] 8225 4-8-11 **67**.................. NannaHansen(5) 1 60
(Stuart Williams) *dwlt: hld up in last pair: pushed along and effrt on inner 2f out: nt qckn over 1f out* **7/2**[2]

001- **6** 3 **Hot Sugar (USA)**[12] 8225 4-9-1 **66**...................................... IanMongan 4 49
(Michael Appleby) *chsd ldng trio: rdn and brief effrt 2f out: no prog over 1f out: sn wknd* **5/4**[1]

58.03s (-0.77) **Going Correction** -0.025s/f (Stan) **6** Ran SP% **113.5**
Speed ratings (Par 103): **105,104,101,98,98 93**
CSF £52.43 TOTE £3.90: £1.50, £4.80; EX 42.60 Trifecta £199.00 Pool: £1,459.78 - 5.50 winning tickets..
Owner Karl Blackwell Steve Mohammed S A Harris **Bred** A Christou **Trained** Carburton, Notts

FOCUS
A fair sprint handicap in which none could be confidently discounted. The first three held a similar order throughout and the winner produced a slight step up.

30 FOLLOW US ON TWITTER @LINGFIELDPARK (S) H'CAP 5f (P)
1:20 (1:21) (Class 6) (0-60,60) 4-Y-0+ **£2,045** (£603; £302) **Stalls** High

Form RPR

450- **1** **Johnny Splash (IRE)**[14] 8184 4-8-4 **48**.....................(b) NathanAlison(5) 9 55
(Roger Teal) *pressed ldr: clr of rest 1/2-way: chal 2f out: nt qckn and looked hld over 1f out: styd on fnl f to ld post* **8/1**

561- **2** hd **Liberal Lady**[14] 8190 5-9-7 **60**... JoeFanning 10 66
(Ralph Smith) *fast away fr wd draw: led: jnd 2f out: drvn ahd again over 1f out: tired last 100yds: hdd post* **4/1**[2]

066- **3** hd **Russian Bullet**[7] 8253 4-9-3 **56**...................................... FergusSweeney 1 61
(Jamie Osborne) *chsd ldng pair but nt on terms fr 1/2-way: clsd jst over 1f out: kpt on: nvr quite got there* **7/2**[1]

030- **4** 3/4 **Imaginary Diva**[14] 8190 7-9-4 **57**.. IanMongan 4 60
(George Margarson) *nt on terms w ldrs in midfield: rdn 2f out: styd on fr over 1f out: nrst fin* **5/1**[3]

044- **5** nk **Scommettitrice (IRE)**[12] 8231 5-8-13 **57**..(p) WilliamTwiston-Davies(5) 2 59
(David Evans) *awkward s: chsd ldng pair: rdn and nt on terms 2f out: kpt on fnl f: nvr able to chal* **5/1**[3]

65- **6** hd **Slatey Hen (IRE)**[216] 2647 5-8-11 **50**.........................(p) WilliamCarson 5 51
(Violet M Jordan) *sltly impeded s: towards rr and off the pce: urged along and styd on fr over 1f out: nrst fin* **8/1**

000- **7** hd **Thorpe Bay**[7] 8253 4-9-1 **54**...(b) AdamKirby 3 54
(Conor Dore) *sltly impeded s: off the pce in midfield: rdn and styd on fr over 1f out: nrst fin* **20/1**

6/5- **8** 4 1/2 **Spoof Master (IRE)**[288] 985 9-8-4 **46**............................ SimonPearce(3) 8 30
(Lydia Pearce) *dwlt: outpcd and a in last pair* **25/1**

360- **9** *3/4* **Mambo Spirit (IRE)**[16] [8159] 9-9-7 **60** LiamKeniry 6 41
(Tony Newcombe) *a in last trio and nvr on terms: no ch over 1f out* **6/1**

59.08s (0.28) **Going Correction** -0.025s/f (Stan) 9 Ran SP% **120.7**
Speed ratings (Par 101): **96,95,95,94,93 93,93,85,84**
CSF £41.94 CT £137.16 TOTE £11.40: £3.60, £1.20, £1.60; EX 72.30 Trifecta £803.80 Pool: £1,211.15 - 1.13 winning tickets..There was no bid for the winner.
Owner Epping Racing **Bred** J Connolly **Trained** Ashtead, Surrey

FOCUS
A typically moderate all-weather seller, but competitive on paper. Abunch finish and unconvincing form.

31 DOLLY LANGTON 80TH BIRTHDAY H'CAP 6f (P)
1:50 (1:51) (Class 6) (0-60,58) 3-Y-O **£2,045** (£603; £302) **Stalls** Low

Form RPR

406- **1** **Lager Time (IRE)**[25] [8044] 3-9-0 **51** AdamKirby 7 61+
(David Evans) *t.k.h: hld up: sweeping move and extremely wd bnd 4f out but led over 3f out: wd again bnd 2f out: pushed along and wl in command after* **9/2**[2]

031- **2** *1 1/2* **Katy Spirit (IRE)**[16] [8155] 3-9-7 **58** LiamKeniry 6 63
(Michael Blanshard) *pressed ldr to over 3f out: rdn to chse wnr 2f out: kpt on but no imp* **6/1**

024- **3** *1/2* **Devout (IRE)**[6] [8274] 3-9-0 **51** FergusSweeney 8 54
(Jamie Osborne) *pressed ldrs: rdn over 2f out: nt qckn over 1f out: kpt on again fnl f* **5/1**[3]

655- **4** *1 3/4* **Little Indian**[16] [8155] 3-9-2 **53** JoeFanning 3 51
(J R Jenkins) *hld up towards rr: rdn over 2f out: kpt on fr over 1f out to take 4th last strides* **9/2**[2]

433- **5** *hd* **Petite Georgia (IRE)**[168] [4239] 3-9-7 **58** JimCrowley 2 55
(George Baker) *hld up in midfield: effrt 2f out: shkn up and one pce over 1f out* **11/4**[1]

365- **6** *1 1/4* **Daisie Cutter**[68] [7410] 3-9-1 **55** SimonPearce(3) 4 48
(Lydia Pearce) *t.k.h: hld up and sn in last: pushed along 2f out: modest late hdwy: nvr in it* **8/1**

200- **7** *3 1/2* **Little Miss Zuri (IRE)**[6] [8274] 3-8-12 **49** NickyMackay 5 31
(Sylvester Kirk) *led to over 3f out: chsd wnr to 2f out: wknd fnl f* **16/1**

003- **8** *1 1/2* **Hats Off**[20] [8108] 3-8-11 **48** (b) StevieDonohoe 1 25
(John Best) *t.k.h: hld up and racd wd: no prog 2f out: no ch after* **16/1**

030- **9** *3 3/4* **Kalahari Breeze (IRE)**[16] [8155] 3-9-2 **53** WilliamCarson 9 18
(William Muir) *in tch over 2f: sn dropped to rr and struggling* **50/1**

1m 12.71s (0.81) **Going Correction** -0.025s/f (Stan) 9 Ran SP% **118.8**
Speed ratings (Par 95): **93,91,90,88,87 86,81,79,74**
toteswingers 1&2 £6.60, 1&3 £3.90, 2&3 £5.00 CSF £32.67 CT £142.12 TOTE £4.70: £1.40, £1.80, £1.90; EX 36.60 Trifecta £281.50 Pool: £1,291.25 - 3.44 winning tickets..
Owner Mrs E Evans **Bred** Polish Belle Partnership **Trained** Pandy, Monmouths

FOCUS
A low-grade handicap with a top weight rated just 58. The winner is worth more than the bare form.

32 BLUE SQUARE BET H'CAP 1m 2f (P)
2:20 (2:20) (Class 4) (0-85,84) 4-Y-O+ **£4,690** (£1,395; £697; £348) **Stalls** Low

Form RPR

221- **1** **Harry Buckle**[25] [8049] 4-8-7 **72** WilliamCarson 6 78
(Philip McBride) *trckd ldr: led over 2f out and kicked on: drvn and styd on wl fnl f* **3/1**[2]

553- **2** *1 1/4* **Ajeeb (USA)**[15] [8174] 5-9-4 **81** JamieSpencer 4 85
(David Simcock) *hld up in 4th: pushed along over 3f out: rdn to chse wnr over 1f out: kpt on but no imp* **7/2**[3]

510- **3** *hd* **Sheila's Buddy**[12] [8227] 4-8-13 **78** LiamKeniry 1 81
(J S Moore) *trckd ldng pair: nt clr run 2f out and lost momentum at vital stage: tried to cl on inner 1f out: styd on same pce* **10/1**

000- **4** *2* **Wilfred Pickles (IRE)**[15] [8174] 7-9-1 **78** FergusSweeney 2 77
(Jo Crowley) *hld up in last: stl there over 2f out as r unfolded: shkn up and nt qckn over 1f out: kpt on to take 4th ins fnl f* **33/1**

105/ **5** *2 3/4* **John Lightbody**[476] [6077] 4-8-10 **75** JoeFanning 3 69
(Mark Johnston) *led at reasonable pce: rdn and hdd over 2f out: wknd fnl f* **1/1**[1]

2m 4.33s (-2.27) **Going Correction** -0.025s/f (Stan)
WFA 4 from 5yo+ 2lb 5 Ran SP% **109.3**
Speed ratings (Par 105): **108,107,106,105,103**
CSF £13.34 TOTE £4.10: £3.30, £1.50; EX 7.00 Trifecta £13.50 Pool: £1,217.19 - 67.53 winning tickets..
Owner Four Winds Racing Partnership **Bred** Wood Farm Stud (Waresley) **Trained** Newmarket, Suffolk

FOCUS
A small field, but a fair handicap in which the top weight was rated 83. Muddling form, with the favourite disappointing.

33 LINGFIELDPARK.CO.UK MEDIAN AUCTION MAIDEN STKS 1m 2f (P)
2:50 (2:50) (Class 6) 4-6-Y-O **£1,940** (£577; £288; £144) **Stalls** Low

Form RPR

602- **1** **Sporting Gold (IRE)**[15] [8162] 4-9-3 65 JamieSpencer 6 63
(Roger Varian) *dwlt: rcvrd to trck ldr after 1f: led over 2f out but sn jnd and rdn: hrd pressed again fnl f: drvn rt out* **4/11**[1]

202- **2** *1* **Grand Theft Equine**[22] [8080] 5-9-5 66 JimCrowley 1 61
(Roger Ingram) *t.k.h: hld up in last trio: smooth prog to go 3rd over 2f out: rdn to chse wnr jst over 1f out and looked real threat: fnd little and hld last 100yds* **3/1**[2]

605- **3** *1 1/4* **Frosty Friday**[50] [7712] 5-9-0 57 (p) JoeFanning 2 54
(J R Jenkins) *hld up in last: stdy prog to go 4th over 1f out: light reminders and styd on encouragingly fnl f: nvr chal* **25/1**

460- **4** *1 3/4* **Delightful Sleep**[15] [8167] 5-9-5 44 AdamKirby 3 55
(David Evans) *hld up in last trio: prog on outer 3f out: jnd wnr and drvn 2f out: lost 2nd and fdd jst over 1f out* **20/1**[3]

6-6 **5** *14* **Dubai Story**[1] [28] 4-8-12 0 KirstyMilczarek 7 22
(Alastair Lidderdale) *dwlt: pushed up to ld after 1f and sn clr: c bk and hdd over 2f out: wknd and t.o* **50/1**

660- **6** *2 1/2* **Arbeejay**[6] [8265] 4-8-12 35 (t) WilliamCarson 4 17
(Simon Hodgson) *led 1f: in tch tl rdn and wknd 3f out: t.o* **100/1**

500- **6** *dht* **Tymismoni (IRE)**[6] [8265] 5-9-0 43 SebSanders 5 17
(Michael Attwater) *in tch tl rdn and wknd 3f out: t.o* **50/1**

2m 4.66s (-1.94) **Going Correction** -0.025s/f (Stan)
WFA 4 from 5yo 2lb 7 Ran SP% **111.8**
Speed ratings: **106,105,104,102,91 89,89**
toteswingers 1&2 £1.10, 1&3 £2.30, 2&3 £1.70 CSF £1.51 TOTE £1.40: £1.02, £1.60; EX 1.80 Trifecta £5.80 Pool: £1,866.35 - 238.24 winning tickets..
Owner A D Spence **Bred** J M Beever **Trained** Newmarket, Suffolk

FOCUS
An uncompetitive maiden in which two runners stood out on form. The winner may not have needed to improve, with the fourth close enough.

34 FOREST ROW H'CAP 7f (P)
3:20 (3:20) (Class 5) (0-75,75) 4-Y-O+ **£2,726** (£805; £402) **Stalls** Low

Form RPR

022- **1** **Al's Memory (IRE)**[19] [8142] 4-9-0 **68** AdamKirby 4 76
(David Evans) *trckd ldr: led over 2f out: brought wd in st: drvn over 1f out: hld on* **7/4**[1]

021- **2** *1/2* **Muhandis (IRE)**[28] [8005] 5-9-1 **69** (b) SebSanders 7 75
(Nick Littmoden) *s.s: hld up in last pair: prog wl over 1f out: drvn and styd on to take 2nd last strides* **4/1**[2]

552- **3** *hd* **Only Ten Per Cent (IRE)**[31] [7961] 5-9-5 **73** IanMongan 6 79
(J R Jenkins) *dwlt: hld up in last pair: prog wl over 1f out: drvn to chse wnr ins fnl f: kpt on but hld and lost 2nd last strides* **10/1**

066- **4** *1* **April Fool**[19] [8142] 9-8-12 **71** (b) WilliamTwiston-Davies(5) 1 74
(Ronald Harris) *led: set stdy pce to 1/2-way: rdn and hdd over 2f out: lost 2nd over 1f out: one pce* **5/1**[3]

402- **5** *nse* **Russian Ice**[16] [8158] 5-9-5 **73** (b) JimCrowley 3 76
(Dean Ivory) *in tch: pushed along 3f out: prog to chse wnr and drvn over 1f out: fdd and lost 2nd ins fnl f* **6/1**

032- **6** *1/2* **Masai Moon**[26] [8034] 9-8-13 **74** PatMillman(7) 2 76
(Rod Millman) *trckd ldng pair on inner: jst pushed along and lost pl steadily fr over 1f out* **8/1**

600- **7** *4 1/2* **The Guru Of Gloom (IRE)**[110] [6256] 5-9-7 **75** WilliamCarson 5 64
(William Muir) *t.k.h: trckd ldrs and racd wd: rdn over 2f out: wknd over 1f out* **10/1**

1m 24.24s (-0.56) **Going Correction** -0.025s/f (Stan) 7 Ran SP% **116.6**
Speed ratings (Par 103): **102,101,101,100,100 99,94**
toteswingers 1&2 £3.30, 1&3 £1.50, 2&3 £5.00 CSF £9.24 TOTE £3.00: £1.50, £2.50; EX 6.40 Trifecta £44.50 Pool: £1,233.05 - 20.77 winning tickets..
Owner Will Dawson **Bred** Brian Miller **Trained** Pandy, Monmouths

FOCUS
None could be confidently dismissed in this competitive-looking handicap. It wasn't that strong run. The winner built on his latter 2012 form.

35 ENOUGH SAID, JUST BET AT BLUESQ.COM APPRENTICE H'CAP 7f (P)
3:50 (3:50) (Class 6) (0-60,60) 4-Y-O+ **£2,045** (£603; £302) **Stalls** Low

Form RPR

411- **1** **Bussa**[4] [8298] 5-9-3 **59** 6ex (t) PhilipPrince(3) 3 69+
(David Evans) *trckd ldr: led wl over 2f out: rdn clr over 1f out: styd on wl* **4/6**[1]

060- **2** *1 1/2* **Cuthbert (IRE)**[4] [8298] 6-8-1 **47** oh1 ow1 (b) PaigeBolton(7) 1 54
(Michael Attwater) *trckd ldrs: outpcd over 2f out: pushed along and r.o to take 2nd ins fnl f: fin wl* **33/1**

023- **3** *3 1/2* **Spartic**[23] [8064] 5-9-2 **58** RufusVergette(3) 2 58
(Alan McCabe) *led: rdn and hdd wl over 2f out: outpcd wl over 1f out: lost 2nd ins fnl f* **8/1**[3]

510- **4** *nk* **Gallantry**[7] [8249] 11-9-4 **57** IanBurns 5 56
(Paul Howling) *chsd ldrs: rdn 3f out: sn outpcd: styd on again fnl f* **16/1**

512- **5** *shd* **Welsh Inlet (IRE)**[3] [8305] 5-9-3 **56** NedCurtis 11 55+
(John Bridger) *t.k.h: hld up in last trio: outpcd over 2f out: rdn on outer and styd on fr over 1f out: nrst fin* **5/1**[2]

000- **6** *nk* **Rise To Glory (IRE)**[29] [7993] 5-8-9 **53** (t) JordanNason(5) 4 52
(Shaun Harris) *t.k.h: hld up in 7th: sme prog 2f out: nt rch ldrs over 1f out: fdd* **25/1**

031- **7** *1* **Ishi**[16] [8154] 4-8-6 **48** (b) DanielMuscutt(3) 9 45
(Rod Millman) *t.k.h: prom: nt qckn 2f out: wknd fnl f* **20/1**

005- **8** *1 1/4* **Lady Mango (IRE)**[16] [8160] 5-9-7 **60** GeorgeDowning 6 54
(Ronald Harris) *t.k.h: trckd ldrs on outer: effrt over 2f out: no prog over 1f out: fdd* **8/1**[3]

060- **9** *1 1/4* **Sleepy Lucy**[12] [8236] 4-8-4 **46** oh1 (e) GemmaTutty(3) 10 38
(Richard Guest) *t.k.h: hld up in last trio: outpcd over 2f out: nvr on terms* **50/1**

000- **10** *3 1/4* **Kings 'n Dreams**[15] [8169] 6-8-6 **50** PaulBooth(5) 8 35
(Dean Ivory) *dwlt: t.k.h: hld up in last: lost tch by 1/2-way: sn wl bhd* **33/1**

1m 25.21s (0.41) **Going Correction** -0.025s/f (Stan) 10 Ran SP% **121.2**
Speed ratings (Par 101): **96,94,90,89,89 89,88,86,85,81**
toteswingers 1&2 £14.00, 1&3 £2.30, 2&3 £26.70 CSF £41.59 CT £123.80 TOTE £1.80: £1.20, £7.60, £1.10; EX 53.50 Trifecta £206.80 Pool: £1,801.22 - 6.53 winning tickets..
Owner Nick Shutts **Bred** Natton House Thoroughbreds & Mark Woodall **Trained** Pandy, Monmouths

FOCUS
A modest finale, with a top weight rated 60. The winner is on a high and rated in line with his recent form.

T/Jkpt: Part won. £20,323.30 to a £1 stake. Pool: £28,624.50 - 0.50 winning tickets. T/Plt: £63.30 to a £1 stake. Pool: £69,832.46 - 805.09 winning tickets. T/Qpdt: £4.40 to a £1 stake. Pool: £6,078.99 - 1,005.70 winning tickets. JN

[22]WOLVERHAMPTON (A.W) (L-H)
Thursday, January 3

OFFICIAL GOING: Standard
Wind: Light behind Weather: Overcast

36 CORAL.CO.UK H'CAP 5f 20y(P)
1:35 (1:41) (Class 6) (0-55,50) 3-Y-O **£1,940** (£577; £288; £144) **Stalls** Low

Form RPR

324- **1** **Prince Of Prophets (IRE)**[16] [8155] 3-9-7 **50** (t) ChrisCatlin 1 57
(Stuart Williams) *led 4f out: shkn up over 1f out: rdn out* **1/2**[1]

350- **2** *2 1/4* **Twinwood Star (IRE)**[6] [8274] 3-9-7 **50** LukeMorris 4 49
(John Weymes) *s.i.s: hld up: rdn and r.o ins fnl f: wnt 2nd towards fin: no ch w wnr* **12/1**

564- **3** *1 1/4* **Lexi's Beauty (IRE)**[20] [8108] 3-9-2 **45** TomEaves 5 40
(Patrick Morris) *chsd ldrs: rdn over 1f out: styd on same pce fnl f* **12/1**

335- **4** *3/4* **Scoobys Girl (IRE)**[122] [5873] 3-9-4 **47** (b[1]) ShaneKelly 3 39
(Daniel Mark Loughnane) *sn pushed along and prom: rdn 1/2-way: no ex fnl f* **17/2**[3]

503- **5** *1/2* **Her Royal Empress**[12] [8230] 3-9-2 **45** GrahamGibbons 2 35
(James Unett) *chsd ldrs: rdn over 1f out: wknd ins fnl f* **7/1**[2]

02- **6** 2 1/4 **Lady Calantha**[121] 5916 3-9-7 **50**................................ RobertWinston 6 32
(Alan Berry) *led 1f: chsd ldrs tl rdn and wknd over 1f out* **20/1**

1m 2.92s (0.62) **Going Correction** -0.10s/f (Stan) **6** Ran SP% **109.8**
Speed ratings (Par 95): **91,87,85,84,83 79**
toteswingers 1&2 £2.20, 1&3 £2.20, 2&3 £7.80 CSF £7.24 TOTE £1.20: £1.02, £5.90; EX 11.10 Trifecta £53.10 Pool: £1,394.81 - 19.68 winning tickets..
Owner Miss Emily Stevens & Paul Stevens **Bred** Barbara Prendergast **Trained** Newmarket, Suffolk

FOCUS
The going was standard with a slight tail wind in the straight. A very moderate handicap in which the odds-on favourite, a gelding, faced five fillies. Weak form, the race taking little winning.

37 CORAL.CO.UK MOBILE CASINO MEDIAN AUCTION MAIDEN STKS 5f 216y(P)
2:05 (2:11) (Class 6) 3-5-Y-O **£1,940** (£577; £288; £144) **Stalls** Low

Form RPR
254- **1** **Gaelic Wizard (IRE)**[49] 7719 5-9-5 67........................ JoshBaudains(7) 2 66
(Dominic Ffrench Davis) *mde all: rdn and edgd rt fr over 1f out: styd on* **5/2**[2]

563- **2** 2 **Clock Opera (IRE)**[13] 8208 3-8-5 69.................................. MartinLane 3 51
(Mrs K Burke) *chsd wnr: rdn over 1f out: sn hung lft: styd on same pce* **8/15**[1]

6- **3** 1/2 **Scarlet Strand**[13] 8208 3-8-7 0 ow2.................................... ChrisCatlin 1 51
(Reg Hollinshead) *chsd ldrs: pushed along 1/2-way: rdn over 1f out: styd on* **20/1**

00- **4** shd **Hidden Link**[83] 7020 3-8-10 0.. LukeMorris 6 54
(Ronald Harris) *s.i.s: sn prom: pushed along 1/2-way: rdn and r.o ins fnl f* **7/1**[3]

256- **5** 4 **Script**[103] 6477 4-9-0 47.. JordanHibberd(7) 5 40
(Alan Berry) *prom: hung rt over 2f out: edgd lft over 1f out: wknd fnl f* **125/1**

5- **6** 2 1/4 **Whiteflats**[12] 8230 3-8-10 0... MartinDwyer 4 34
(Derek Shaw) *hld up: rdn over 2f out: wknd over 1f out* **50/1**

1m 15.59s (0.59) **Going Correction** -0.10s/f (Stan)
WFA 3 from 4yo+ 16lb **6** Ran SP% **113.8**
Speed ratings (Par 101): **92,89,88,88,83 80**
toteswingers 1&2 £1.02, 1&3 £2.90, 2&3 £2.80 CSF £4.27 TOTE £2.40: £1.10, £1.10; EX 5.70 Trifecta £16.10 Pool: £1,445.39 - 67.02 winning tickets..
Owner D J Ffrench Davis **Bred** Mrs Mary Gallagher **Trained** Lambourn, Berks
■ Stewards' Enquiry : Chris Catlin three-day ban: weighed-in 2lb heavy (Jan 17-19)

FOCUS
A modest maiden and a two-horse race according to the market. The time was slow and it seems a case of the favourite being below par rather than the winner improving.

38 BOOKMAKERS.CO.UK CLASSIFIED CLAIMING STKS 5f 216y(P)
2:35 (2:41) (Class 5) 3-Y-O **£2,587** (£770; £384; £192) **Stalls** Low

Form RPR
136- **1** **Hiddon Coin (IRE)**[173] 4116 3-9-0 75......................... GrahamGibbons 3 71
(David O'Meara) *mde all: edgd lft over 5f out: rdn and hung rt fr over 1f out: styd on* **13/8**[2]

421- **2** 2 **Windforpower (IRE)**[7] 8247 3-8-6 66...........................(be) LukeMorris 5 57
(Ronald Harris) *sn pushed along and prom: chsd wnr over 1f out: rdn and hung rt ins fnl f: nt run on* **3/1**[3]

3 **3** 1 1/4 **Beau Sakhee**[2] 5 3-8-6 54......................................(p) JamesSullivan 4 53
(Adrian McGuinness, Ire) *broke wl: sn stdd and lost pl: hung rt over 3f out: outpcd over 2f out: r.o towards fin* **25/1**

352- **4** 1 **Hardy Red (IRE)**[7] 8258 3-9-2 73.................................. MartinDwyer 2 59
(Jamie Osborne) *chsd wnr: hmpd over 5f out: rdn and lost 2nd over 1f out: no ex ins fnl f* **5/4**[1]

1m 14.91s (-0.09) **Going Correction** -0.10s/f (Stan) **4** Ran SP% **111.4**
Speed ratings (Par 97): **96,93,91,90**
CSF £6.90 TOTE £2.10; EX 5.20.
Owner Hambleton Racing Ltd - Three In One **Bred** Noel & Anthony O'Callaghan **Trained** Nawton, N Yorks

FOCUS
A tight little 3yo claimer, and weak form with the favourite below par. The winner did not need to improve on his early 2yo form.

39 £50 FREE BET AT CORAL.CO.UK H'CAP 1m 4f 50y(P)
3:05 (3:10) (Class 5) (0-75,75) 4-Y-O+ **£2,587** (£770; £384; £192) **Stalls** Low

Form RPR
002- **1** **Illustrious Forest**[8] 8243 5-9-6 **71**.............................. GrahamGibbons 1 81
(John Mackie) *mde all: set stdy pce tl qcknd over 2f out: rdn and edgd rt over 1f out: styd on wl* **11/10**[1]

624- **2** 3 **Reflect (IRE)**[12] 8234 5-9-7 **72**......................................(t) MartinDwyer 3 77
(Derek Shaw) *hld up: hdwy over 2f out: rdn over 1f out: hung rt: styd on: nt trble wnr* **9/1**

346- **3** 1/2 **Standpoint**[14] 8191 7-9-9 **74**.. LukeMorris 2 78
(Conor Dore) *chsd ldrs: rdn over 2f out: styd on same pce ins fnl f* **6/1**[3]

140- **4** 1/2 **Epic Storm (IRE)**[20] 8110 5-9-10 **75**............................... AdamBeschizza 6 79
(Sean Curran) *s.i.s: hld up: styd on u.p fr over 1f out: nt rch ldrs* **7/2**[2]

423- **5** 2 **Minsky Mine (IRE)**[26] 7315 6-8-13 **64**.......................... AndrewMullen 5 64
(Michael Appleby) *chsd ldrs: rdn over 3f out: hung lft and no ex fnl f* **8/1**

000- **6** 13 **Mazij**[70] 7353 5-9-5 **70**... ChrisCatlin 7 50
(Peter Hiatt) *chsd wnr tl rdn over 2f out: wknd over 1f out* **33/1**

160- **7** 20 **Boston Blue**[35] 7927 6-9-7 **72**.. MartinLane 4 20
(Tony Carroll) *s.i.s: hld up: pushed along over 4f out: n.m.r 3f out: sn wknd* **33/1**

2m 37.15s (-3.95) **Going Correction** -0.10s/f (Stan) **7** Ran SP% **111.1**
Speed ratings (Par 103): **109,107,106,106,105 96,83**
toteswingers 1&2 £3.30, 1&3 £1.50, 2&3 £5.00 CSF £11.44 TOTE £2.10: £1.30, £5.80; EX 10.60 Trifecta £73.90 Pool: £1,249.61 - 12.67 winning tickets..
Owner Derbyshire Racing VII **Bred** Norman A Blyth **Trained** Church Broughton , Derbys

FOCUS
This moderate handicap was run at an average pace. The winner's best form since early last year.

40 HORSE RACING FREE BETS WITH BOOKMAKERS.CO.UK H'CAP 2m 119y(P)
3:35 (3:43) (Class 4) (0-85,81) 4-Y-O+ **£4,690** (£1,395; £697; £348) **Stalls** Low

Form RPR
341/ **1** **Murcar**[47] 7005 8-9-6 **74**...(b) LukeMorris 4 82
(Liam Corcoran) *chsd ldr: drvn along over 3f out: led over 1f out: styd on wl* **16/1**

421- **2** 4 **English Summer**[15] 8175 6-9-5 **73**.................................(t) TomEaves 1 76
(David Simcock) *set stdy pce tl qcknd over 3f out: rdn and hdd over 1f out: no ex ins fnl f* **9/4**[1]

021/ **3** shd **Harry Hunt**[48] 6504 6-9-13 **81**.. ChrisCatlin 5 84
(Graeme McPherson) *hld up: hdwy 5f out: rdn over 3f out: styd on same pce fr over 1f out* **5/1**[2]

100- **4** 5 **Lifetime (IRE)**[26] 7455 5-9-8 **76**.. DaleSwift 2 73
(Brian Ellison) *chsd ldrs: rdn over 4f out: wknd fnl f* **10/1**[3]

3m 40.54s (-1.26) **Going Correction** -0.10s/f (Stan)
WFA 4 from 5yo+ 7lb **4** Ran SP% **62.4**
Speed ratings (Par 105): **98,96,96,93**
CSF £16.49 TOTE £5.80; EX 8.90.
Owner Ray Antell **Bred** J Ford & Peter J Skinner **Trained** Lovington, Somerset

FOCUS
A staying handicap which completely changed its complexion when well-backed Somemothersdohavem refused to enter the stalls. It proved a tactical affair and the form is muddling. The winner is rated to his old Flat best.

41 BEST HORSE RACING ODDS WITH BOOKMAKERS.CO.UK H'CAP 1m 141y(P)
4:05 (4:10) (Class 7) (0-50,50) 4-Y-O+ **£1,940** (£577; £288; £144) **Stalls** Low

Form RPR
360- **1** **Kyllachykov (IRE)**[7] 6758 5-9-2 **45**............................... RobertWinston 8 56
(Robin Bastiman) *led: hdd over 6f out: chsd ldr tl led again over 2f out: rdn out* **6/1**[3]

/06- **2** 1 1/4 **Golan Heights (IRE)**[22] 8088 7-9-5 **48**...................(b) GrahamGibbons 7 56
(Adrian McGuinness, Ire) *hld up in tch: rdn to chse wnr over 1f out: styd on* **8/1**

344- **3** 4 **American Lover (FR)**[8] 8239 6-9-4 **47**............................. PaddyAspell 5 46
(John Wainwright) *hld up: hdwy over 1f out: styd on: nt rch ldrs* **7/1**

544- **4** 1 1/2 **May Boy**[8] 8241 7-9-4 **47**... ChrisCatlin 10 42
(Ron Hodges) *hld up: hdwy over 2f out: sn rdn: styd on same pce fnl f* **8/1**

44-0 **5** 3/4 **Veyepea**[2] 7 4-9-4 **48**.. MartinDwyer 4 42
(Sylvester Kirk) *hld up: hmpd over 2f out: styd on ins fnl f: nvr nrr* **9/1**

550- **6** shd **Meydan Style (USA)**[5] 8288 7-8-9 **45**......................... VictorSantos(7) 13 38
(Richard Ford) *chsd ldr tl led over 6f out: rdn and hdd over 2f out: wknd fnl f* **40/1**

502- **7** 1/2 **Stamp Duty (IRE)**[20] 8111 5-9-4 **47**...................................... TomEaves 1 39
(Suzzanne France) *chsd ldrs: rdn over 1f out: wknd ins fnl f* **5/1**[2]

000- **8** 3 1/4 **Sun Dream**[36] 7898 6-9-2 **45**... MartinLane 2 30
(Tony Carroll) *mid-div: hdwy u.p over 2f out: wknd over 1f out* **66/1**

40/0 **9** hd **Caracal**[2] 7 6-9-4 **47**..(b) JamesSullivan 9 31
(Adrian McGuinness, Ire) *hld up: hmpd over 2f out: n.d* **20/1**

00-2 **10** 5 **Justcallmehandsome**[2] 7 11-8-12 **48**..............(v) JoshBaudains(7) 3 21
(Dominic Ffrench Davis) *dwlt: bhd: nvr on terms* **4/1**[1]

660- **11** 6 **Titan Diamond (IRE)**[30] 7983 5-8-11 **45**................ RachealKneller(5) 12
(Mark Usher) *prom tl wknd wl over 2f out* **25/1**

025- **12** 4 **Mistress Shy**[8] 8239 6-9-2 **45**.......................................(t) AndrewMullen 11
(Michael Appleby) *hld up: rdn over 3f out: wknd over 2f out* **16/1**

500- **13** 15 **Fushicho**[25] 8050 4-9-6 **50**... LukeMorris 6
(Michael Wigham) *chsd ldrs: rdn over 3f out: wknd over 2f out: t.o* **12/1**

1m 48.85s (-1.65) **Going Correction** -0.10s/f (Stan)
WFA 4 from 5yo+ 1lb **13** Ran SP% **121.8**
Speed ratings (Par 97): **103,101,98,97,96 96,95,92,92,88 82,79,66**
CSF £52.62 CT £351.59 TOTE £6.20: £2.40, £3.00, £2.40; EX 67.50 Trifecta £731.10 Pool: £1,569.62 - 1.61 winning tickets..
Owner Ms M Austerfield **Bred** L K I Bloodstock Ltd **Trained** Cowthorpe, N Yorks

FOCUS
A weak handicap that looked wide open. There was no hanging about and few got involved. The winner is rated in line with last year's turf best.

42 NO DEPOSIT FREE BETS WITH BOOKMAKERS.CO.UK H'CAP 7f 32y(P)
4:35 (4:41) (Class 7) (0-50,56) 4-Y-O+ **£1,940** (£577; £288; £144) **Stalls** High

Form RPR
003- **1** **Dhhamaan (IRE)**[7] 8257 8-9-4 **48**..............................(b) JamesSullivan 11 59
(Ruth Carr) *mde all: rdn clr fr over 1f out: styd on* **11/1**

040- **2** 2 1/2 **Compton Target (IRE)**[118] 6000 4-9-3 **47**...............(t) RobertWinston 4 51
(Milton Bradley) *chsd ldrs: rdn over 1f out: styd on* **20/1**

625- **3** 1/2 **Monsieur Pontaven**[70] 7362 6-9-3 **47**....................(b) J-PGuillambert 10 50
(Robin Bastiman) *in rr: pushed along over 4f out: edgd lft and r.o u.p ins fnl f: nt rch ldrs* **8/1**[3]

1- **4** hd **Hittin'The Skids (IRE)**[7] 8257 5-9-12 **56** 6ex.................... PaddyAspell 3 58
(Kevin Ryan) *a.p: chsd wnr 2f out: sn rdn: styd on same pce ins fnl f* **5/4**[1]

002- **5** 1 **Lord Paget**[7] 8257 4-9-0 **49**..(p) JackDuern(5) 7 49
(Reg Hollinshead) *mid-div: rdn over 2f out: styd on: nt trble ldrs* **4/1**[2]

604- **6** 3/4 **Crucis Abbey (IRE)**[5] 8291 5-8-11 **46**..................(p) RachealKneller(5) 2 45
(Mark Brisbourne) *hld up: hdwy over 1f out: nt clr run ins fnl f: nvr nrr* **10/1**

00-5 **7** hd **Sairaam (IRE)**[2] 7 7-9-3 **47**... MartinLane 12 44
(Charles Smith) *chsd wnr tl rdn 2f out: no ex ins fnl f* **14/1**

040- **8** 1 **Bachelor Knight (IRE)**[7] 8256 5-8-10 **47**................ JacobButterfield(7) 8 41
(Suzzanne France) *hld up: racd keenly: hdwy over 2f out: rdn over 1f out: nt rch ldrs* **33/1**

004- **9** 1 3/4 **Athaakeel (IRE)**[15] 8169 7-9-2 **46**....................................... LukeMorris 1 36
(Ronald Harris) *prom: rdn over 1f out: wknd ins fnl f* **16/1**

460- **10** 8 **Very First Blade**[300] 845 4-9-5 **49**..................................... ShaneKelly 9 17
(Mark Brisbourne) *sn pushed along in rr: bhd fnl 3f* **50/1**

00- **11** 1 3/4 **Minty Jones**[118] 5994 4-9-5 **49**...(v) TomEaves 5 12
(Michael Mullineaux) *stdd s: hld up: nvr on terms* **28/1**

1m 28.21s (-1.39) **Going Correction** -0.10s/f (Stan) **11** Ran SP% **119.6**
Speed ratings (Par 97): **103,100,99,99,98 97,97,95,93,84 82**
toteswingers 1&2 £25.40, 1&3 £6.50, 2&3 £15.60 CSF £214.02 CT £1882.34 TOTE £10.40: £2.70, £4.90, £2.30; EX 239.50 Trifecta £2003.60 Part won. Pool: £2,671.58 - 0.72 winning tickets..
Owner S B Clark **Bred** D Veitch And Musagd Abo Salim **Trained** Huby, N Yorks

FOCUS
An ordinary handicap and another winner from the front, but the best time on the card. The form is rated around the winner.
T/Plt: £712.50 to a £1 stake. Pool: £51,372.70 - 52.63 winning tickets. T/Qpdt: £594.60 to a £1 stake. Pool: £4,178.82 - 5.20 winning tickets. CR

43 - 48a (Foreign Racing) - See Raceform Interactive

[36]WOLVERHAMPTON (A.W) (L-H)

Friday, January 4

OFFICIAL GOING: Standard

A record 15 races at the same track in one day , although technically two fixtures with the afternoon card moved from Southwell.

Wind: Light behind Weather: Cloudy

49 THE BLACK COUNTRY'S ONLY RACECOURSE H'CAP 1m 141y(P)

12:00 (12:00) (Class 5) (0-75,75) 4-Y-0+ £2,587 (£770; £384; £192) Stalls Low

Form RPR

003- 1 **Beautiful Day**[4] 8306 5-9-6 **74** JamieSpencer 1 84
(Kevin Ryan) *set stdy pce: qcknd over 3f out: rdn and edgd rt over 1f out: drvn out* 8/1[3]

000- 2 1 1/4 **California English (IRE)**[25] 8057 4-9-5 **74** (p) JimmyQuinn 9 81
(Marco Botti) *trckd ldrs: hdwy on outer 1/2-way: chsd wnr over 2f out: rdn to chal and ch whn carried sltly rt over 1f out: sn drvn and no imp* 16/1

662- 3 1 1/2 **Caledonia Prince**[20] 8137 5-8-13 **67** (v[1]) JoeFanning 5 71
(Jo Hughes) *t.k.h: trckd ldrs: effrt 3f out: rdn along 2f out: drvn and kpt on same pce fnl f* 4/1[2]

111- 4 2 **On The Hoof**[18] 8152 4-9-6 **75** GrahamGibbons 7 74
(Michael Easterby) *dwlt: sn trcking ldrs: hdwy on inner 3f out: rdn along 2f out: drvn and one pce appr fnl f* 1/1[1]

/10- 5 3/4 **Yeomanoftheguard**[42] 7843 4-8-11 **66** BarryMcHugh 8 63
(Richard Fahey) *hld up in midfield: hdwy on outer over 3f out: rdn along to chse ldrs 2f out: sn one pce* 16/1

010- 6 1 1/4 **Dream Win**[21] 8113 7-8-2 **63** (t) PaulBooth[(7)] 3 57
(Brian Ellison) *hld up in midfield: hdwy over 3f out: rdn to chse ldrs 2f out: sn one pce* 11/1

000- 7 2 3/4 **Final Drive (IRE)**[18] 8152 7-9-4 **72** (tp) StevieDonohoe 2 60
(John Butler) *dwlt: a in rr* 9/1

305- 8 10 **Mcconnell (USA)**[226] 2405 8-8-11 **65** (b) WilliamCarson 4 30
(Violet M Jordan) *a in rr* 40/1

140- 9 10 **Wicked Spirit (IRE)**[234] 2149 5-9-0 **68** RobertWinston 6 10
(Keith Dalgleish) *chsd wnr: pushed along 1/2-way: rdn over 3f out and sn wknd* 40/1

1m 48.09s (-2.41) **Going Correction** -0.15s/f (Stan)
WFA 4 from 5yo+ 1lb 9 Ran SP% **116.1**
Speed ratings (Par 103): **104,102,101,99,99 98,95,86,77**
toteswingers 1&2 £12.10, 2&3 £8.80, 1&3 £2.40 CSF £125.66 CT £588.11 TOTE £5.50: £2.30, £4.90, £1.10; EX 119.30 Trifecta £374.40 Pool: £748.85 - 1.50 winning units..
Owner Exors of The Late Guy Reed **Bred** G Reed **Trained** Hambleton, N Yorks

FOCUS
A fair handicap, run at a steady pace throughout with the winner getting an easy lead. The winner built on his Polytrack best latest but is still a few punds hort of his Fibresand best..

50 DOWNLOAD OUR IPHONE APP (S) H'CAP 7f 32y(P)

12:30 (12:30) (Class 6) (0-60,59) 4-Y-0+ £2,045 (£603; £302) Stalls High

Form RPR

561- 1 **Basle**[24] 8062 6-9-3 **57** (t) RichardKingscote 2 61
(Michael Blake) *trckd ldrs: hdwy 2f out: rdn to ld ins fnl f: sn drvn and kpt on wl towards fin* 11/4[1]

/34- 2 nk **Marshall Art**[7] 8267 4-9-4 **58** GrahamGibbons 7 61
(David Evans) *stdd and swtchd lft s: hld up in rr: hdwy on inner wl over 1f out: rdn ent fnl f: styd on wl* 9/2[3]

100- 3 2 1/4 **North Central (USA)**[13] 8236 6-9-4 **58** (e[1]) JamesSullivan 8 55
(Ruth Carr) *slt ld: pushed along and hdd briefly 3f out: rdn to ld again wl over 1f out: drvn and hdd ins fnl f: one pce* 33/1

000- 4 1/2 **Georgebernardshaw (IRE)**[6] 8288 8-9-2 **56** (e[1]) RobertWinston 5 52
(Richard Guest) *t.k.h: cl up: led 3f out: rdn and hdd wl over 1f out: sn edgd rt and carried hd awkwardly: could nt run on* 7/1

236- 5 1 1/4 **Lindoro**[8] 8248 8-9-3 **57** (p) ChrisCatlin 6 49
(Sean Curran) *dwlt and sltly hmpd s: t.k.h: hld up in rr: hdwy on outer 2f out: rdn and ev ch over 1f out: sn drvn and one pce* 7/2[2]

200- 6 hd **Katmai River (IRE)**[17] 8156 6-8-13 **58** RachealKneller[(5)] 3 50
(Mark Usher) *trckd ldrs: pushed along over 3f out: rdn over 2f out: sn btn* 7/2[2]

000- 7 2 3/4 **Hinton Admiral**[17] 8159 9-9-5 **59** (b) LiamKeniry 4 43
(Conor Dore) *t.k.h: chsd ldrs: cl up on outer 1/2-way: rdn along wl over 2f out: sn wknd* 14/1

1m 29.97s (0.37) **Going Correction** -0.15s/f (Stan) 7 Ran SP% **111.4**
Speed ratings (Par 101): **91,90,88,87,86 85,82**
toteswingers 1&2 £3.20, 2&3 £10.50, 1&3 £7.60 CSF £14.58 CT £313.25 TOTE £2.80: £1.30, £3.80; EX 15.10 Trifecta £63.70 Pool: £1116.89 - 13.15 winning units..There was no bid for the winner.
Owner West Wilts Hockey Lads **Bred** W H R John And Partners **Trained** Trowbridge, Wilts

FOCUS
There wasn't a great deal of early pace on in this seller and the time was slow. Unconvincing form.

51 WINNERS LOVE BOOKMAKERS.CO.UK MEDIAN AUCTION MAIDEN STKS 1m 141y(P)

1:00 (1:01) (Class 6) 4-6-Y-O £2,045 (£603; £302) Stalls Low

Form RPR

320- 1 **Charlcot**[45] 7799 5-9-6 64 JamieSpencer 4 66
(James Bethell) *mde all: rdn and hung rt wl over 1f out: drvn out: dismntd after line: fin lame* 1/2[1]

240- 2 1 3/4 **Gunner Will (IRE)**[14] 8213 4-9-5 60 FergusSweeney 5 62
(Jamie Osborne) *trckd wnr: effrt over 2f out: sn rdn and swtchd lft over 1f out: drvn and kpt on fnl f* 9/4[2]

5- 3 15 **Ches Jicaro (IRE)**[20] 8141 5-9-6 0 DavidProbert 3 28
(James Unett) *trckd wnr on inner: rdn along 3f out: outpcd fr over 2f out* 10/1[3]

-5 4 9 **Silver Panther**[3] 1 5-9-6 0 ChrisCatlin 2
(Aytach Sadik) *in rr: rdn along bef 1/2-way: outpcd and bhd fnl 3f* 200/1

1m 50.18s (-0.32) **Going Correction** -0.15s/f (Stan)
WFA 4 from 5yo 1lb 4 Ran SP% **107.0**
Speed ratings: **95,93,80,72**
CSF £1.83 TOTE £1.40; EX 1.80 Trifecta £2.60 Pool: £1206.38 - 344.00 winning units..
Owner Clarendon Thoroughbred Racing **Bred** Mrs James Bethell **Trained** Middleham Moor, N Yorks

FOCUS
A desperately weak maiden. The winner did not need to match his recent best.

52 HORSE RACING BEST BETS AT BOOKMAKERS.CO.UK H'CAP 1m 4f 50y(P)

1:30 (1:30) (Class 4) (0-80,81) 4-Y-0+ £4,690 (£1,395; £697; £348) Stalls Low

Form RPR

151- 1 **De Rigueur**[20] 8136 5-9-5 **75** (t) SebSanders 6 87+
(Marco Botti) *trckd ldrs: hdwy 4f out: led 3f out: rdn wl over 1f out: drvn and kpt on wl fnl f* 10/11[1]

012- 2 1 1/4 **Focail Maith**[23] 8082 5-9-10 **80** (p) JamieSpencer 2 87
(John Ryan) *hld up: hdwy 3f out: rdn to chse wnr over 1f out: drvn and kpt on fnl f* 8/1[3]

31-1 3 3 1/4 **Sir Boss (IRE)**[3] 2 8-9-11 **81** 12ex TomEaves 3 83
(Michael Mullineaux) *trckd ldrs on inner: hdwy over 2f out: rdn wl over 1f out: kpt on same pce fnl f* 9/1

500- 4 1 1/4 **White Diamond**[9] 8243 6-8-10 **66** oh1 AndrewMullen 8 66
(Michael Appleby) *chsd ldr: cl up 3f out: sn rdn: drvn wl over 1f out and grad wknd* 33/1

410- 5 21 **Zafranagar (IRE)**[14] 7132 8-8-13 **74** GeorgeDowning[(5)] 4 40
(Tony Carroll) *in tch: rdn along 3f out: sn wknd* 33/1

000- 6 1 **All The Winds (GER)**[7] 8275 8-9-5 **80** LeonnaMayor[(5)] 1 45
(Shaun Lycett) *a in rr: outpcd and bhd fnl 4f* 20/1

012- 7 59 **Alazan (IRE)**[7] 8275 7-9-2 **77** WilliamTwiston-Davies[(5)] 5
(Philip Hobbs) *led: rushed along 4f out: rdn and hdd 3f out: wknd qckly: sn eased and t.o fnl 2f: dismntd after line: lame* 5/2[2]

2m 36.34s (-4.76) **Going Correction** -0.15s/f (Stan)
WFA 4 from 5yo+ 4lb 7 Ran SP% **112.7**
Speed ratings (Par 105): **109,108,106,105,91 90,51**
toteswingers 1&2 £1.80, 2&3 £1.80, 1&3 £2.50 CSF £8.87 CT £39.61 TOTE £2.30: £2.70, £2.30; EX 9.00 Trifecta £34.40 Pool: £1295.43 - 28.20 winning units..
Owner K J P Gundlach **Bred** Cheveley Park Stud Ltd **Trained** Newmarket, Suffolk

FOCUS
A fair handicap and it saw a dominant display from the winner. He was value for extra and looks capable of better.

53 HOTEL & CONFERENCING AT WOLVERHAMPTON H'CAP 1m 4f 50y(P)

2:00 (2:00) (Class 6) (0-62,62) 4-Y-0+ £2,045 (£603; £302) Stalls Low

Form RPR

255- 1 **Kames Park (IRE)**[7] 8273 11-9-7 **62** JimmyQuinn 8 70
(Richard Guest) *dwlt and hld up in rr: stdy hdwy on inner wl over 2f out: swtchd rt and chsd ldrs over 1f out: styd on wl fnl f to ld last 75yds* 7/1

263- 2 3/4 **Annelko**[15] 8189 6-9-5 **60** RichardKingscote 2 67
(Michael Blake) *trckd ldrs: hdwy over 2f out: chal over 1f out: rdn to ld jst ins fnl f: drvn and hdd last 75yds: no ex* 3/1[1]

235- 3 2 **Viola Da Gamba (IRE)**[28] 8023 4-9-2 **61** JamieSpencer 11 65
(William Knight) *trckd ldrs: hdwy after 3f and sn cl up: effrt over 2f out: rdn to ld over 1f out: hdd and drvn ins fnl f: one pce* 9/2[3]

026- 4 nk **Daring Damsel (IRE)**[18] 8146 4-9-1 **60** GrahamGibbons 5 63
(Brian Baugh) *set stdy pce: pushed along and qcknd over 3f out: drvn 2f out: sn hdd: grad wknd ent fnl f* 12/1

040- 5 hd **The Ducking Stool**[73] 7315 6-9-0 **62** ShelleyBirkett[(7)] 4 65
(Julia Feilden) *trckd ldrs: rdn along 2f out: sn drvn and one pce fnl f* 33/1

344- 6 3/4 **Layla's Boy**[8] 8260 6-9-2 **60** (bt) RyanClark[(3)] 12 62
(John Mackie) *hld up: hdwy on wd outside over 4f out: rdn to chse ldrs 2f out: drvn and one pce ent fnl f* 8/1

512- 7 3/4 **Royal Sea (IRE)**[6] 8288 4-8-13 **58** 6ex TomEaves 1 59+
(Michael Mullineaux) *trckd ldrs: effrt over 2f out: rdn and n.m.r over 1f out: sn one pce* 4/1[2]

040- 8 1/2 **Maison Brillet (IRE)**[31] 7980 6-9-7 **62** (p) RobertHavlin 7 62
(Clive Drew) *midfield on inner: hdwy over 4f out: rdn along to chse ldrs over 2f out: sn no imp* 16/1

6/0- 9 2 3/4 **State Senator (USA)**[18] 8146 5-9-3 **58** JoeFanning 9 53
(Richard Ford) *a in rr* 25/1

366/ 10 1 **Hartforth**[49] 4151 5-8-10 **54** DeclanCannon[(3)] 6 48
(James Bethell) *trckd ldrs: pushed along over 3f out: rdn over 2f out: sn btn* 25/1

156- 11 3 1/2 **Arte Del Calcio**[26] 5810 4-9-2 **61** WilliamCarson 3 49
(Tony Carroll) *t.k.h: hld up: hdwy whn nt clr run 3f out: sn rdn along and nvr a factor* 14/1

2m 40.85s (-0.25) **Going Correction** -0.15s/f (Stan)
WFA 4 from 5yo+ 4lb 11 Ran SP% **117.7**
Speed ratings (Par 101): **94,93,92,91,91 91,90,90,88,88 85**
toteswingers 1&2 £4.90, 2&3 £4.30, 1&3 £6.80 CSF £27.68 CT £107.14 TOTE £9.40: £2.10, £1.90, £2.10; EX 29.10 Trifecta £223.50 Pool: £1052.23 - 3.53 winning units..
Owner Future Racing (Notts) Limited **Bred** Pat Beirne **Trained** Wetherby, W Yorks

FOCUS
Only a moderate handicap. Muddling form off a steady pace, with a bunch finish.

54 COMPARE BOOKIES WITH BOOKIES.CO.UK H'CAP 5f 216y(P)

2:30 (2:30) (Class 6) (0-58,64) 4-Y-0+ £2,045 (£603; £302) Stalls Low

Form RPR

12-1 1 **Miss Bunter**[2] 26 4-9-2 **64** 6ex DavidBergin[(7)] 1 78
(David O'Meara) *trckd ldrs: hdwy on inner 2f out: cl up over 1f out: rdn to chal ins fnl f: led last 100yds: kpt on* 9/4[2]

211- 2 hd **Sandy Lane (IRE)**[6] 8287 4-9-8 **63** 6ex RobertHavlin 3 77
(Amy Weaver) *trckd ldrs: hdwy on outer over 2f out: rdn to chal over 1f out: led ins fnl f: drvn: hdd and one pce last 100yds* 1/1[1]

504- 3 3 **Ace Master**[21] 8115 5-9-0 **58** (b[1]) MarkCoumbe[(3)] 9 62
(Roy Bowring) *trckd ldr: hdwy over 2f out and sn cl up: led wl over 1f out: rdn and hdd jst ins fnl f: kpt on same pce* 9/1

051- 4 1 1/4 **Methaaly (IRE)**[8] 8256 10-9-7 **62** 6ex (be) TomEaves 5 62
(Michael Mullineaux) *dwlt and towards rr: hdwy 2f out: sn rdn and kpt on fnl f: n.d* 14/1

440- 5 nk **Brown Volcano (IRE)**[56] 7667 4-9-2 **57** WilliamCarson 4 56
(John O'Shea) *dwlt and in rr: hdwy 2f out: sn rdn and one pce* 50/1

063- 6 1/2 **Bitaphon (IRE)**[8] 8255 4-9-3 **58** AndrewMullen 7 55
(Michael Appleby) *led: rdn along over 2f out: hdd wl over 1f out: sn wknd* 15/2[3]

1m 13.56s (-1.44) **Going Correction** -0.15s/f (Stan) 6 Ran SP% **111.2**
Speed ratings (Par 101): **103,102,98,97,96 96**
toteswingers 1&2 £1.70, 2&3 £3.00, 1&3 £3.40 CSF £4.75 CT £12.57 TOTE £2.40: £1.50, £1.30; EX 5.20 Trifecta £24.00 Pool: £1108.86 - 34.65 winning units..
Owner D Fravigar Miss K Dixon & Mrs R Mitchell **Bred** Bumble Bloodstock Ltd **Trained** Nawton, N Yorks

FOCUS
A small field sprint handicap, but a competitive race for the grade and it produced the closest finish of the afternoon. The time was decentr and a progressive pair finished 1-2.

55 GET FREE BETS WITH BOOKMAKERS.CO.UK H'CAP 1m 141y(P)
3:00 (3:01) (Class 6) (0-55,55) 3-Y-O **£2,045** (£603; £302) **Stalls** Low

Form RPR
024- **1** **Flying Tempo**[46] 7785 3-9-4 **52**....(b) StevieDonohoe 1 58
(Ed Dunlop) *s.i.s and hld up in rr: hdwy 3f out: swtchd wd off home turn: sn rdn and str run ent fnl f to ld last 100yds* **11/4**[1]
034- **2** 1 ¼ **Una Bella Cosa**[22] 8094 3-9-3 **51**....(p) SebSanders 9 54
(Alan McCabe) *sn led: rdn over 2f out: drvn ent fnl f: hdd and no ex last 100yds* **9/2**[2]
536- **3** ½ **Darkest Night (IRE)**[14] 8203 3-9-7 **55**.... FergusSweeney 8 57
(Jamie Osborne) *trckd ldrs: hdwy over 2f out: rdn to chse ldng pair over 1f out: ev ch ent fnl f: sn drvn and one pce* **9/2**[2]
300- **4** 1 **Shearian**[32] 7974 3-9-6 **54**.... KirstyMilczarek 2 54
(Tony Carroll) *chsd ldr: hdwy 3f out: rdn wl over 1f out: ev ch ent fnl f: sn drvn and one pce* **10/1**
603- **5** ½ **Schottische**[13] 8224 3-9-6 **54**....(p) WilliamCarson 4 52
(Derek Haydn Jones) *trckd ldrs: hdwy 3f out: rdn to chal wl over 1f out: ev ch ent fnl f: sn drvn and one pce* **25/1**
060- **6** 1 **Precision Strike**[6] 8289 3-9-4 **52**.... RobertWinston 6 48
(Richard Guest) *hld up in rr: stdy hdwy over 3f out: rdn to chse ldrs over 1f out: sn drvn and no imp* **7/1**
000- **7** 2 ¼ **Last Chance Ranch**[6] 8289 3-9-2 **50**....(t[1]) MartinDwyer 7 41
(Derek Shaw) *dwlt: a in rr* **40/1**
000- **8** ¾ **Chelsea Grey (IRE)**[22] 8094 3-9-1 **49**.... DavidProbert 5 38
(Ronald Harris) *hld up: a towards rr* **12/1**
33 **9** ½ **Beau Sakhee**[1] 38 3-9-6 **54**....(p) GrahamGibbons 3 42
(Adrian McGuinness, Ire) *chsd ldrs: rdn along 3f out: sn wknd* **5/1**[3]

1m 50.18s (-0.32) **Going Correction** -0.15s/f (Stan) 9 Ran SP% **115.3**
Speed ratings (Par 95): **95,93,93,92,92 91,89,88,88**toteswingers 1&2 £2.80, 2&3 £2.20, 1&3 £3.30. Placepot: £33.40 to a £1 stake. Pool of £39525.97 - 861.33 winning tickets. Quadpot: £5.80 to a £1 stake. Pool of £4165.85 - 529.61 winning tickets. CSF £15.01 CT £53.47 TOTE £2.30: £1.10, £1.90, £2.60; EX 12.40 Trifecta £28.70 Pool: £13227 Owner.

FOCUS
A weak handicap, run at a fierce pace and it served up a thrilling finish. The winner did not need to improve too much, with the second inside helping to set the standard.

56 BOOKIE FREE BETS WITH BOOKMAKERS.CO.UK CLAIMING STKS 5f 20y(P)
4:00 (4:00) (Class 5) 4-Y-O+ **£2,587** (£770; £384; £192) **Stalls** Low

Form RPR
311- **1** **Drawnfromthepast (IRE)**[8] 8246 8-9-2 83.... FergusSweeney 8 78
(Jamie Osborne) *chsd ldr: rdn over 1f out: r.o to ld post* **11/8**[1]
00-5 **2** shd **Le Toreador**[3] 3 8-9-7 87....(tp) JamieSpencer 4 83
(Kevin Ryan) *led: rdn ins fnl f: hdd post* **9/4**[2]
55-4 **3** hd **Mother Jones**[1] 29 5-7-13 72.... PhilipPrince[(7)] 6 67
(David Evans) *trckd ldrs: racd keenly: rdn over 1f out: r.o* **15/2**
112- **4** 1 ¼ **Majuro (IRE)**[9] 8238 9-9-2 79....(t) LeonnaMayor[(5)] 1 77
(Charles Smith) *s.i.s: hld up: r.o ins fnl f: nt rch ldrs* **5/1**[3]
003- **5** 2 **Blown It (USA)**[32] 7970 7-8-7 64.... JoeFanning 5 56
(Keith Dalgleish) *prom: rdn over 1f out: styd on same pce ins fnl f* **20/1**
533- **6** 1 ¼ **Amenable (IRE)**[5] 8294 6-8-11 74....(b[1]) WilliamCarson 2 56
(Violet M Jordan) *pushed along early in rr: styd on fnl f: nvr trbld ldrs* **20/1**
600- **7** 2 ¾ **Lesley's Choice**[30] 7995 7-9-1 68.... ChrisCatlin 3 50
(Sean Curran) *prom: pushed along 1/2-way: wknd over 1f out* **40/1**

1m 1.05s (-1.25) **Going Correction** -0.15s/f (Stan) 7 Ran SP% **113.3**
Speed ratings (Par 103): **104,103,103,101,98 96,91**
toteswingers 1&2 £2.30, 1&3 £2.50, 2&3 £5.10 CSF £4.50 TOTE £2.70: £1.50, £1.60; EX 7.00 Trifecta £26.00 Pool: £2,049.05 - 58.91 winning units..
Owner MCSD Racing & Mark Benton **Bred** D And Mrs D Veitch **Trained** Upper Lambourn, Berks

FOCUS
Straightforward claiming form. All eight runners had a chance at the weights if their official ratings were to be taken literally. The winner, runner-up and third filled the first three positions throughout

57 CORAL.CO.UK H'CAP 1m 5f 194y(P)
4:30 (4:30) (Class 5) (0-75,75) 4-Y-O+ **£2,587** (£770; £384; £192) **Stalls** Low

Form RPR
566- **1** **Sohcahtoa (IRE)**[96] 6706 7-9-1 **69**.... LMcNiff[(5)] 1 76
(David Barron) *hld up: hdwy over 2f out: rdn to ld wl ins fnl f: r.o* **4/1**[3]
266- **2** nk **Sherman McCoy**[16] 8170 7-9-5 **68**.... MartinDwyer 3 75
(Daniel Kubler) *chsd ldr tl rdn to ld 2f out: edgd rt over 1f out: hdd wl ins fnl f: styd on* **7/2**[2]
062- **3** 1 ¼ **Reaction**[7] 8273 7-8-11 **60**....(v) AndrewMullen 4 65
(Michael Appleby) *a.p: rdn 3f out: styd on u.p* **5/2**[1]
532- **4** 1 ½ **Mediterranean Sea (IRE)**[73] 7315 7-9-11 **74**.... JoeFanning 6 77
(J R Jenkins) *hld up: hdwy over 1f out: sn rdn: styd on same pce ins fnl f* **4/1**[3]
4- **5** 4 ½ **Adiynara (IRE)**[13] 8235 5-9-12 **75**.... LiamKeniry 2 71
(Neil Mulholland) *led: rdn and hdd 2f out: wknd ins fnl f* **7/1**
061- **6** 16 **Tram Express (FR)**[7] 8273 9-8-11 **60** 6ex....(t) KieranO'Neill 5 34
(Shaun Lycett) *prom: rdn over 3f out: wknd over 1f out* **12/1**

3m 0.5s (-5.50) **Going Correction** -0.15s/f (Stan) 6 Ran SP% **111.0**
Speed ratings (Par 103): **109,108,108,107,104 95**
toteswingers 1&2 £4.60, 1&3 £3.60, 2&3 £2.70 CSF £17.77 TOTE £5.80: £4.30, £3.20; EX 28.70 Trifecta £190.30 Pool: £1,966.52 -7.75 winning units..
Owner Douglas Pryde Jim Beaumont **Bred** Knockainey Stud **Trained** Maunby, N Yorks

FOCUS
A weak staying handicap.

58 MONEY BACK RACING SPECIALS AT BOOKMAKERS.CO.UK H'CAP 5f 216y(P)
5:00 (5:00) (Class 4) (0-85,83) 4-Y-O+ **£4,690** (£1,395; £697; £348) **Stalls** Low

Form RPR
200- **1** **Profile Star (IRE)**[37] 7918 4-9-4 **78**.... GrahamGibbons 1 90
(David Barron) *mde all: rdn over 1f out: jst hld on* **16/1**
231- **2** hd **Cut Across (IRE)**[4] 8306 5-9-9 **83** 6ex....(b) SebSanders 11 94
(Nick Littmoden) *a.p: chsd wnr over 2f out: rdn and hung lft ins fnl f: r.o* **5/2**[1]
106- **3** 2 ¼ **Lucky Dan (IRE)**[46] 7789 7-9-2 **76**.... JoeFanning 4 80
(Paul Green) *chsd ldrs: rdn over 1f out: styd on same pce fnl f* **16/1**
64-2 **4** nk **Dorback**[3] 3 6-9-6 **80**.... MartinDwyer 6 83
(David Nicholls) *a.p: rdn over 1f out: edgd lft and styd on same pce fnl f* **5/2**[1]
333- **5** ¾ **Waking Warrior**[13] 8232 5-9-4 **78**....(tp) JamieSpencer 9 79+
(Kevin Ryan) *hld up: hdwy over 1f out: nt clr run ins fnl f: nvr trbld ldrs* **11/2**[2]
226- **6** hd **Irish Heartbeat (IRE)**[7] 8269 8-9-3 **77**....(p) FergusSweeney 8 77+
(Jamie Osborne) *hld up: rdn and r.o ins fnl f: nrst fin* **17/2**[3]
416- **7** 1 ¼ **Bubbly Ballerina**[16] 8163 4-9-3 **77**.... NickyMackay 3 73
(Alan Bailey) *mid-div: sddle slipped 4f out: hdwy 2f out: styd on same pce fr over 1f out* **20/1**
000- **8** ½ **Little Garcon (USA)**[16] 8163 6-9-7 **81**....(p) JimmyQuinn 5 76
(Robert Cowell) *hld up: racd keenly: hdwy 2f out: sn rdn: styd on same pce* **10/1**
000- **9** 1 ½ **Lady Royale**[213] 2793 5-8-13 **78**.... AdamCarter[(5)] 7 68
(Geoffrey Oldroyd) *sn pushed along in rr: nvr on terms* **66/1**
500- **10** 1 ½ **Song Of Parkes**[20] 8143 6-9-3 **77**.... LiamKeniry 12 62
(Peter Grayson) *hld up: sme hdwy whn hmpd ins fnl f: eased* **50/1**
222- **11** 1 ¾ **Beauty Pageant (IRE)**[8] 8246 6-9-3 **77**.... WilliamCarson 2 56
(David Evans) *chsd wnr tl rdn over 2f out: wknd fnl f* **10/1**
520- **12** ½ **Bandstand**[66] 7464 7-9-4 **78**.... TomEaves 10 56
(Bryan Smart) *hld up: hdwy 2f out: sn rdn and wknd* **40/1**

1m 13.1s (-1.90) **Going Correction** -0.15s/f (Stan) **12** Ran SP% **123.7**
Speed ratings (Par 105): **106,105,102,102,101 101,99,98,96,94 92,91**
toteswingers 1&2 £11.00, 1&3 £39.30, 2&3 £12.60 CSF £57.25 CT £702.96 TOTE £28.70: £9.60, £1.60, £7.70; EX 25.60 TRIFECTA Not won..
Owner Profile Storage Ltd **Bred** Knocklong House Stud **Trained** Maunby, N Yorks
■ Stewards' Enquiry : Seb Sanders two-day ban; used whip above permitted level (18th-19th Jan).

FOCUS
A modest sprint handicap.

59 HORSE RACING BEST BETS AT BOOKMAKERS.CO.UK MEDIAN AUCTION MAIDEN STKS 7f 32y(P)
5:30 (5:31) (Class 6) 3-5-Y-O **£1,940** (£577; £288; £144) **Stalls** High

Form RPR
4- **1** **Testa Rossa (IRE)**[21] 8102 3-8-10 0.... SebSanders 5 64+
(J W Hills) *chsd ldrs: pushed along over 2f out: hmpd wl over 1f out: sn rdn and hung lft: r.o to ld wl ins fnl f* **7/4**[1]
2 ¾ **Iggy** 3-8-10 0.... JamesSullivan 7 62
(Michael Easterby) *hld up: hdwy 1/2-way: rdn to ld and edgd lft over 1f out: hdd wl ins fnl f* **5/1**[3]
6- **3** 1 ¾ **Exclusive Predator**[31] 7981 4-10-0 0.... TomEaves 3 61
(Geoffrey Oldroyd) *hld up: pushed along 3f out: hdwy over 1f out: r.o* **9/1**
533- **4** nk **Peak Storm**[56] 7670 4-10-0 59....(p) WilliamCarson 8 60
(John O'Shea) *prom: chsd ldr 1/2-way: rdn over 2f out: ev ch over 1f out: no ex ins fnl f* **15/8**[2]
000- **5** 3 ½ **Icanboogie**[113] 6156 3-8-3 41.... RyanTate[(7)] 6 47?
(Karen George) *s.s: nvr on terms* **20/1**
005- **6** ¾ **Findhornbay**[59] 7615 4-9-9 45.... JoeFanning 4 44
(Keith Dalgleish) *stmbld s: chsd ldr tl led 6f out: rdn and hdd over 1f out: wknd ins fnl f* **14/1**
50- **7** 3 ¼ **Imperial Bond**[67] 7445 4-10-0 0....(b[1]) SeanLevey 2 40
(Ricardo Lanfranco) *prom: rdn 1/2-way: wknd over 1f out* **28/1**
000- **8** 2 ¾ **Bellinda**[7] 8264 4-9-2 41.... RyanWhile[(7)] 1 28
(Martin Bosley) *led 1f: chsd ldr to 1/2-way: sn rdn: wknd over 1f out* **80/1**

1m 29.38s (-0.22) **Going Correction** -0.15s/f (Stan)
WFA 3 from 4yo 18lb 8 Ran SP% **113.9**
Speed ratings (Par 101): **95,94,92,91,87 86,83,80**
toteswingers 1&2 £5.40, 1&3 £5.60, 2&3 £8.80 CSF £10.78 TOTE £2.60: £1.10, £2.40, £2.30; EX 15.90 Trifecta £61.20 Pool: £13,582.79 - 166.42 winning units..
Owner Gary And Linnet Woodward **Bred** Hugo Merry And Khalid Al-Mudhaf **Trained** Upper Lambourn, Berks

FOCUS
A weak maiden.

60 POKER AT CORAL.CO.UK H'CAP 7f 32y(P)
6:00 (6:00) (Class 3) (0-95,92) 4-Y-O **£7,246** (£2,168; £1,084; £542; £270) **Stalls** High

Form RPR
560- **1** **Verse Of Love**[97] 6659 4-9-0 **85**.... GrahamGibbons 8 94
(David Evans) *mde all: rdn over 1f out: eased nr fin* **16/1**
01-2 **2** hd **Chapter And Verse (IRE)**[2] 10 7-9-2 **87**.... EddieAhern 3 95
(Mike Murphy) *hld up: shkn up and r.o wl ins fnl f: nt quite get up* **6/1**[3]
611- **3** 2 ¼ **Solar Deity (IRE)**[48] 7774 4-9-7 **92**.... SebSanders 5 94
(Marco Botti) *chsd ldrs: rdn over 2f out: styd on same pce fnl f* **10/11**[1]
160- **4** 1 ¾ **Outpost (IRE)**[22] 8098 5-9-1 **86**.... LiamKeniry 1 84
(Alan Bailey) *chsd ldrs: rdn over 1f out: no ex ins fnl f* **33/1**
130- **5** 3 ¾ **Corporal Maddox**[22] 8098 6-9-1 **86**.... WilliamCarson 7 74
(Ronald Harris) *s.s: hld up: hdwy and hung rt fr over 2f out: wknd fnl f* **20/1**
046- **6** ½ **Advanced**[35] 7934 10-8-11 **82**.... AmyRyan 4 68
(Kevin Ryan) *chsd wnr: pushed along 3f out: rdn and wknd over 1f out* **14/1**
101- **7** 5 **Cockney Dancer**[46] 7789 4-8-12 **83**.... RobertWinston 2 72
(Charles Hills) *s.i.s: hld up: pushed along 1/2-way: hdwy u.p and hung lft over 1f out: wknd and eased ins fnl f* **11/4**[2]

1m 26.89s (-2.71) **Going Correction** -0.15s/f (Stan) 7 Ran SP% **113.6**
Speed ratings (Par 107): **109,108,106,104,99 99,93**
toteswingers 1&2 £8.10, 1&3 £4.70, 2&3 £2.60 CSF £104.74 CT £177.10 TOTE £8.20: £4.00, £2.10; EX 43.10 Trifecta £122.20 Pool: £14,484.55 - 88.87 winning units..
Owner Wayne Clifford **Bred** Mrs S Clifford **Trained** Pandy, Monmouths

FOCUS
A fair handicap.

61 CORAL.CO.UK MOBILE BETTING H'CAP 1m 141y(P)
6:30 (6:30) (Class 6) (0-65,68) 4-Y-O+ **£1,940** (£577; £288; £144) **Stalls** Low

Form RPR
600- **1** **Berlusca (IRE)**[36] 7925 4-9-2 **61**.... GrahamGibbons 7 75+
(David O'Meara) *chsd ldrs: rdn to ld over 1f out: clr ins fnl f: comf* **7/2**[1]
441- **2** 2 ¼ **Big Sylv (IRE)**[21] 8111 4-8-11 **56**....(p) DavidProbert 9 65
(James Unett) *chsd ldrs: led wl over 1f out: sn rdn and hdd: styd on same pce* **7/1**
203- **3** 2 ½ **Aragorn Rouge**[18] 8145 5-9-4 **62**....(p) JoeFanning 1 65
(Keith Dalgleish) *hld up: hdwy 3f out: rdn over 1f out: styd on same pce* **7/2**[1]
400- **4** 1 **Moheebb (IRE)**[58] 7640 9-9-0 **58**....(e) RobertWinston 2 59
(Robert Johnson) *prom: rdn over 3f out: outpcd over 2f out: rdn and hung lft over 1f out: styd on u.p* **10/1**

311- **5** 3/4 **Outlaw Torn (IRE)**[7] 8271 4-9-4 **68** 6ex .... JasonHart(5) 3 67
(Richard Guest) *led: hdd over 7f out: chsd ldr tl led again over 2f out: rdn and hdd over 1f out: wknd ins fnl f* **9/2**[2]

/52- **6** 2 1/4 **Geronimo Chief (IRE)**[59] 7605 5-8-8 **52** ....(v) RobertHavlin 10 46
(Andrew Crook) *s.i.s: rcvrd to ld over 7f out: rdn and hdd over 2f out: wknd fnl f* **33/1**

203- **7** nk **Rogue Reporter (IRE)**[24] 8062 4-8-11 **56** ....(v) JamieSpencer 5 49
(Stuart Williams) *hld up: hdwy over 1f out: sn rdn: wknd fnl f* **6/1**[3]

005- **8** 1 1/4 **Sommersturm (GER)**[7] 8264 9-8-2 **53** .... PhilipPrince(7) 11 44
(David Evans) *hld up: hdwy 1/2-way: rdn and wknd over 2f out* **22/1**

200- **9** 8 **Edgware Road**[32] 7960 5-9-1 **59** .... ChrisCatlin 8 31
(Sean Curran) *hld up: hdwy 5f out: rdn and wknd over 3f out* **20/1**

065- **10** 3 3/4 **Spinning Ridge (IRE)**[121] 5941 8-9-7 **65** ....(b) WilliamCarson 4 29
(Ronald Harris) *hld up: drvn along over 2f out: sn wknd* **20/1**

1m 47.79s (-2.71) **Going Correction** -0.15s/f (Stan)
WFA 4 from 5yo+ 1lb **10** Ran SP% **115.3**
Speed ratings (Par 101): **106,104,101,100,100 98,97,96,89,86**
toteswingers 1&2 £6.60, 1&3 £3.70, 2&3 £3.80 CSF £26.31 CT £93.88 TOTE £9.00: £2.90, £2.30, £1.90; EX 55.30 Trifecta £241.30 Pool: £4,026.25 - 12.51 winning units..
Owner Peter R Ball **Bred** Value Bloodstock **Trained** Nawton, N Yorks
FOCUS
A moderate handicap.

62 FREE SPORTS BETTING AT BOOKMAKERS.CO.UK H'CAP 1m 1f 103y(P)
7:00 (7:00) (Class 7) (0-50,50) 4-Y-O+ **£1,940** (£577; £288; £144) **Stalls** Low

Form RPR

006- **1** **Sinchiroka (FR)**[30] 7991 7-9-6 **50** ....(t) JamieGoldstein 3 62
(Ralph Smith) *led: hdd over 7f out: chsd ldrs: rdn over 1f out: r.o to ld wl ins fnl f: sn clr* **9/1**

06-2 **2** 3 3/4 **Golan Heights (IRE)**[1] 41 7-9-4 **48** ....(b) GrahamGibbons 5 54
(Adrian McGuinness, Ire) *chsd ldrs: wnt 2nd over 3f out: led over 2f out: rdn and hung lft over 1f out: hdd wl ins fnl f: eased whn btn* **5/4**[1]

500- **3** 3 **Cairanne**[59] 7620 5-9-0 **47** .... RyanClark(3) 4 45
(Tom Keddy) *s.i.s: hld up: hdwy to go 3rd over 1f out: nvr trbld ldrs* **12/1**

060- **4** 4 **Thank You Joy**[74] 3794 5-9-4 **48** .... JoeFanning 6 37
(J R Jenkins) *hld up in tch: rdn over 2f out: wknd over 1f out* **8/1**[3]

065- **5** 11 **Carpentras**[15] 8179 5-9-5 **49** ....(b) RobertHavlin 8 15
(Dr Jon Scargill) *chsd ldr tl led over 7f out: rdn and hdd over 2f out: sn wknd* **10/1**

550- **6** 1 1/4 **Merchants Return**[26] 8048 4-9-0 **48** ....(v) SimonPearce(3) 7 12
(Lydia Pearce) *hld up: hdwy 1/2-way: rdn over 2f out: sn wknd* **7/2**[2]

300- **7** 1 3/4 **Venetias Dream (IRE)**[24] 8061 4-9-5 **50** ....(t) ChrisCatlin 1 10
(Stuart Williams) *prom tl rdn and wknd 3f out* **14/1**

000- **P** **High Five Society**[97] 6690 9-8-13 **46** ....(b) MarkCoumbe(3) 2
(Roy Bowring) *dwlt: hld up: rdn over 3f out: sn wknd: bhd whn p.u over 1f out* **25/1**

1m 59.27s (-2.43) **Going Correction** -0.15s/f (Stan)
WFA 4 from 5yo+ 1lb **8** Ran SP% **115.1**
Speed ratings (Par 97): **104,100,98,94,84 83,82,**
toteswingers 1&2 £6.20, 1&3 £13.60, 2&3 £10.10 CSF £20.89 CT £140.67 TOTE £14.50: £4.70, £1.10, £4.00; EX 52.80 Trifecta £226.40 Pool: £7,528.49 - 24.93 winning units..
Owner Kevin Old **Bred** Gfa Haras Du Hoguenet And Searching Sarl **Trained** Epsom, Surrey
FOCUS
A dire event.

63 HORIZONS RESTAURANT MEDIAN AUCTION MAIDEN STKS 1m 4f 50y(P)
7:30 (7:32) (Class 6) 4-6-Y-O **£1,940** (£577; £288; £144) **Stalls** Low

Form RPR

344- **1** **Rano Pano (USA)**[46] 6210 4-9-0 48 ....(p) DaleSwift 7 52
(Brian Ellison) *s.s: hld up: hdwy over 3f out: rdn over 1f out: hung lft and styd on to ld wl ins fnl f* **3/1**[2]

2 1 1/2 **Story Writer** 4-9-5 0 .... JamieSpencer 6 55
(William Knight) *s.i.s: hld up: hdwy over 4f out: shkn up to ld wl over 1f out: rdn: hung lft and hdd wl ins fnl f* **8/11**[1]

6/0- **3** 2 **Pobs Trophy**[9] 446 6-9-4 43 ....(b) JasonHart(5) 8 51
(Richard Guest) *chsd ldr: rdn over 3f out: ev ch over 1f out: styd on same pce ins fnl f* **40/1**

200- **4** 4 **Bygones For Coins (IRE)**[70] 6783 5-8-13 51[1] WilliamTwiston-Davies(5) 2 40
(Robert Johnson) *led: clr 7f out: rdn and hdd wl over 1f out: wknd ins fnl f* **11/2**[3]

0- **5** 25 **Johns Porridge**[23] 8080 4-9-0 0 .... WilliamCarson 1
(Peter Hiatt) *prom: pushed along over 6f out: rdn and wknd 3f out: t.o* **40/1**

6 6 **Reggie Rabbit**[42] 4-8-12 0 .... VictorSantos(7) 3
(Richard Ford) *hld up: rdn and wknd 3f out: t.o* **16/1**

06- **7** 58 **Nova Nimph**[20] 8135 4-9-0 0 ....(t) GrahamGibbons 5
(Mark Brisbourne) *chsd ldrs: rdn over 4f out: wknd over 3f out: t.o* **10/1**

2m 39.3s (-1.80) **Going Correction** -0.15s/f (Stan)
WFA 4 from 5yo+ 4lb **7** Ran SP% **118.1**
Speed ratings: **100,99,97,95,78 74,35**
toteswingers 1&2 £1.80, 1&3 £3.90, 2&3 £6.30 CSF £5.82 TOTE £4.20: £1.70, £1.80; EX 6.80 Trifecta £50.90 Pool: £9,682.97 - 142.63 winning units..
Owner Dan Gilbert **Bred** Castle Park Farm Llc & John Osborne **Trained** Norton, N Yorks
FOCUS
A very weak maiden.
T/Plt: £262.60 to a £1 stake. Pool of £66,724.75 - 185.47 winning units. T/Qpdt: £57.20 to a £1 stake. Pool of £8,778.54 - 113.50 winning units. CR

64 - 71a (Foreign Racing) - See Raceform Interactive

DEAUVILLE (R-H)
Friday, January 4
OFFICIAL GOING: Fibresand: standard

72a PRIX DE MERLERAULT (MAIDEN) (3YO COLTS & GELDINGS) (FIBRESAND) 7f 110y
11:00 (12:00) 3-Y-O **£9,756** (£3,414; £1,951; £975)

RPR

1 **Atomic Bere (FR)**[21] 3-9-2 0 ....(p) JeromeCabre 14 80
(Mlle C Cardenne, France) **47/1**

2 nk **Ellusivance (IRE)**[88] 3-9-2 0 .... MaximeGuyon 8 79
(E J O'Neill, France) **13/1**

2 dht **Avanzini (USA)**[16] 8176 3-9-2 0 .... StephanePasquier 7 79
(G Botti, France) **6/1**[3]

4 snk **Tianjin City (FR)**[30] 3-9-2 0 .... ThierryThulliez 2 79
(N Clement, France) **5/1**[2]

5 nse **Habeshia**[16] 8176 3-9-2 0 .... Pierre-CharlesBoudot 1 79
(John Best) *played up at s: broke wl on ins: sn led: rdn bef st: hdd 1 1/2f out: r.o wl u.p fnl f* **26/1**

6 1/2 **Chika Dream (FR)**[31] 7984 3-9-2 0 .... MorganDelalande 16 77
(Y Barberot, France) **14/5**[1]

7 3/4 **Artplace (IRE)** 3-9-2 0 ....(b) JulienAuge 13 75
(C Ferland, France) **12/1**

8 1 1/4 **Chene Boppe (FR)**[15] 8192 3-9-2 0 .... AlexisBadel 9 72
(F-X De Chevigny, France) **26/1**

9 3/4 **Epegard (IRE)** 3-8-11 0 .... StephaneBreux 15 65
(M Delzangles, France) **19/1**

10 hd **Gorki Park (FR)**[21] 3-9-2 0 .... AntoineHamelin 4 70
(Mme G Rarick, France) **27/1**

0 **Sparks Fly (FR)**[15] 8193 3-9-2 0 .... FabriceVeron 10
(S Kobayashi, France) **41/1**

0 **Tiberio (SPA)**[95] 3-8-10 0 .... AlexisAchard(6) 11
(M Delzangles, France) **18/1**

0 **Heintassin (FR)**[15] 8192 3-8-8 0 .... StephaneLaurent(8) 12
(Mlle B Renk, France) **88/1**

0 **Jo De Vati (FR)**[30] 3-9-2 0 .... TheoBachelot 5
(S Wattel, France) **50/1**

0 **Proposal (FR)**[10] 3-9-2 0 .... WilliamsSaraiva 3
(Mme J Bidgood, France) **68/10**

1m 32.0s (92.00) **15** Ran SP% **113.7**
WIN (incl. 1 euro stake): 48.40. PLACES: 12.60, 5.20 (Ellusivance), 2.50 (Avanzini). DF: 138.30 (Atomic Bere - Ellusivance), 95.10 (Atomic Bere-Avanzini). SF: 229.30 (Atomic Bere-Ellusivance), 189.40 (Atomic Bere-Avanzini)..
Owner R-J Philippe & Mlle C Cardenne **Bred** Snc Regnier, T Regnier & F Regnier **Trained** France

[29]LINGFIELD (L-H)
Saturday, January 5
OFFICIAL GOING: Standard
Wind: Light; half behind Weather: Dry; overcast

73 BET ON TODAY'S FOOTBALL AT BLUESQ.COM CLASSIFIED CLAIMING STKS 1m 2f (P)
11:50 (11:51) (Class 6) 4-Y-O+ **£2,045** (£603; £302) **Stalls** Low

Form RPR

526- **1** **Conducting**[15] 8214 5-8-6 65 .... JimmyQuinn 6 64
(Gay Kelleway) *chsd ldrs: effrt to ld over 1f out: drvn and hld on wl ins fnl f* **5/1**[2]

12-4 **2** 1/2 **Resplendent Alpha**[4] 2 9-8-3 63 .... MartinLane 1 60
(Jamie Osborne) *hld up in tch in last trio: rdn and effrt to chse ldrs whn pushed lft over 1f out: hdwy between horses 1f out: ev ch wl ins fnl f: hld towards fin* **7/1**

000- **3** 1 **Carter**[21] 8136 7-8-1 70 ....(b[1]) RyanPowell(3) 8 59
(Ian Williams) *led briefly: chsd ldr tl led again over 2f out: rdn and hdd over 1f out: outpcd 1f out: styd on again u.p fnl 100yds* **3/1**[1]

335- **4** nse **Handheld**[19] 8152 6-8-1 66 .... ShelleyBirkett(7) 7 63
(Julia Feilden) *chsd ldr: rdn and pressed wnr ent fnl f: no ex and one pce fnl 100yds* **6/1**[3]

040- **5** 3/4 **Aviso (GER)**[17] 8162 9-7-11 63 .... PhilipPrince(7) 5 57
(David Evans) *in tch in midfield: effrt and wdst bnd wl over 1f out: edgd lft and unable qck over 1f out: styd on same pce ins fnl f* **14/1**

230- **6** 1/2 **Officer In Command (USA)**[31] 7997 7-8-6 67 ow1 ......(p) ChrisCatlin 2 58
(Paul Rich) *in tch in midfield: effrt to chse ldrs over 1f out: drvn 1f out: styd on same pce fnl f* **3/1**[1]

500- **7** nse **Legal Legacy**[29] 8019 7-8-13 61 .... AmirQuinn 3 65
(Richard Rowe) *s.i.s: hld up in rr: grad clsd fr 5f out: effrt to chse ldrs u.p 1f out: one pce fnl f* **66/1**

001- **8** 1/2 **Daniel Thomas (IRE)**[8] 8261 11-8-4 61 ....(tp) WilliamCarson 9 55
(Violet M Jordan) *s.i.s: hld up in last trio: hdwy over 2f out: effrt u.p on inner over 1f out: one pce fnl f* **7/1**

130/ **9** 12 **Castle Myth (USA)**[10] 4177 7-8-4 60 ....(bt) JoeFanning 4 31
(Jim Best) *sn led: rdn and hdd over 2f out: wknd and bhd 1f out* **33/1**

2m 4.85s (-1.75) **Going Correction** -0.10s/f (Stan) **9** Ran SP% **117.1**
Speed ratings (Par 101): **103,102,101,101,101 100,100,100,90**
Tote swingers 1&2 £4.00, 1&3 £3.70, 2&3 £3.20 CSF £40.38 TOTE £4.10: £2.30, £2.10, £1.40; EX 24.20 Trifecta £98.20 Pool: £808.26 - 6.17 winning units..
Owner J Farley, M Brunner & M Whatley **Bred** David J Brown **Trained** Exning, Suffolk
■ Stewards' Enquiry : Amir Quinn two-day ban; used whip above permitted level (19th-20th Jan).
FOCUS
A modest claimer, run at an ordinary pace, and the front eight finished in a heap. It paid to race handily.

74 HARTFIELD MAIDEN STKS 1m 2f (P)
12:20 (12:20) (Class 5) 3-Y-O **£2,726** (£805; £402) **Stalls** Low

Form RPR

65- **1** **Little Buxted (USA)**[24] 8070 3-9-5 0 .... DavidProbert 2 75
(Robert Mills) *in tch in midfield: rdn and wnt between horses to chse ldr 2f out: led over 1f out: drvn and hdd ins fnl f: styd on to ld again last stride* **4/1**[2]

53- **2** shd **Gertrude Versed**[15] 8200 3-9-0 0 .... MarcHalford 4 70
(John Gosden) *chsd ldrs: nt clr run briefly on inner 2f out: rdn and ev ch over 1f out: drvn to ld ins fnl f: styd on u.p tl hdd last stride* **5/1**[3]

3 hd **Aryal** 3-9-5 0 .... JoeFanning 3 74+
(Mark Johnston) *s.i.s: niggled along and rn green in last trio: hdwy and swtchd rt wl over 1f out: ev ch over 1f out: unable qck ins fnl f* **3/1**[1]

2- **4** 3 1/4 **Too Difficult (IRE)**[92] 6844 3-9-0 0 .... JamieSpencer 5 63
(Andrew Balding) *in tch in midfield: effrt and rdn 2f out: no ex u.p over 1f out: no ch w ldrs and one pce fnl f* **4/1**[2]

5 1 3/4 **El Massivo (IRE)** 3-9-5 0 .... JimmyQuinn 7 64
(William Jarvis) *s.i.s: t.k.h: hld up in rr: rdn and hdwy on inner over 1f out: no imp 1f out* **33/1**

0- **6** shd **True Spirit**[244] 1886 3-9-5 0 .... SebSanders 6 64
(Paul D'Arcy) *t.k.h: mde most tl rdn and hdd over 1f out: wknd fnl f* **5/1**[3]

00- **7** 5 **Thought And Memory (IRE)**[24] 8071 3-9-5 0 .... GeorgeBaker 8 54
(Mick Channon) *chsd ldrs: rdn 4f out: unable qck u.p 2f out: wknd over 1f out* **14/1**

8 4 ½ **Kia Royale** 3-9-0 0 .... JimCrowley 9 40
(Ralph Beckett) *s.i.s: in tch towards rr: rdn and struggling whn carried rt bnd 2f out: no ch after* **16/1**

00- 9 24 **Upper Echelon**[24] 8070 3-9-0 0 .... RobertWinston 1
(Mark Johnston) *mostly chsd ldr tl over 2f out: wkng whn hung rt bnd 2f out: wl bhd and eased ins fnl f: t.o* **25/1**

2m 6.33s (-0.27) **Going Correction** -0.10s/f (Stan) 9 Ran SP% **117.7**
Speed ratings (Par 97): **97,96,96,94,92 92,88,85,65**
Tote swingers 1&2 £4.20, 1&3 £4.00, 2&3 £3.90 CSF £24.89 TOTE £4.50: £1.10, £1.80, £2.00; EX 25.70 Trifecta £117.90 Pool: £1,090.77 - 6.93 winning units.
Owner Buxted Partnership **Bred** S F Bloodstock LLC **Trained** Headley, Surrey

FOCUS
Quite an interesting 3yo maiden and a thrilling finish between the front three.

75 HOLTYE H'CAP 5f (P)
12:50 (12:50) (Class 5) (0-75,81) 3-Y-0 **£2,726** (£805; £402) **Stalls** High

Form RPR
21-2 1 **Golden Flower**[4] 4 3-8-11 **72** .... DavidBergin(7) 2 78
(David O'Meara) *t.k.h: chsd ldr tl led 1/2-way: rdn and kpt on wl fr over 1f out: eased cl home* **4/5**[1]

144- 2 1 ¼ **Layla's Oasis**[25] 8065 3-9-5 **73** .... JamieSpencer 5 74
(Jamie Osborne) *taken down early: stdd s: hdwy 2f out: rdn to chse wnr 1f out: hung lft and no imp fnl 100yds* **6/1**[3]

323- 3 5 **Modern Lady**[17] 8161 3-8-10 **64** .... J-PGuillambert 1 47
(Richard Guest) *led tl 1/2-way: rdn and no ex over 1f out: lost 2nd 1f out and wknd ins fnl f* **8/1**

042- 4 1 **Pixilated**[9] 8245 3-9-1 **69** .... RobertWinston 4 48
(Gay Kelleway) *chsd ldrs: rdn and pressed ldrs 2f out: no ex over 1f out: wknd fnl f* **11/4**[2]

58.48s (-0.32) **Going Correction** -0.10s/f (Stan) 4 Ran SP% **107.6**
Speed ratings (Par 97): **98,96,88,86**
CSF £5.82 TOTE £1.70; EX 5.10 Trifecta £20.10 Pool: £469.08 - 17.45 winning units.
Owner Middleham Park Racing XLII **Bred** Whitley Stud **Trained** Nawton, N Yorks

FOCUS
Just the four runners for this ordinary 3yo sprint and the form looks straightforward.

76 BLUE SQUARE BET SPRINT SERIES (ROUND 1) H'CAP (QUALIFIER) (DIV I) 6f (P)
1:25 (1:26) (Class 6) (0-65,65) 4-Y-0+ **£3,067** (£905; £453) **Stalls** Low

Form RPR
004- 1 **Desert Strike**[5] 8307 7-9-7 **65** .... (p) JimCrowley 7 73
(Conor Dore) *mde all: rdn and fnd ex over 1f out: styd on wl fnl f: rdn out* **5/1**[3]

004- 2 ¾ **My Own Way Home**[14] 8236 5-8-11 **60** ..... WilliamTwiston-Davies(5) 6 66
(David Evans) *hld up in tch towards rr: hdwy 2f out: n.m.r ent fnl f: squeezed between horses and styd on to chse wnr wl ins fnl f: nvr gng to rch wnr* **4/1**[1]

663- 3 nk **Frognal (IRE)**[25] 8063 7-9-0 **63** .... (bt) CharlesBishop(5) 12 68
(Violet M Jordan) *pushed sltly rt leaving s: sn swtchd lft: t.k.h: hld up in rr: rdn and hdwy ent fnl f: r.o: nvr gng to rch wnr* **8/1**

662- 4 ¾ **Colourbearer (IRE)**[9] 8255 6-9-2 **60** .... (t) RobertWinston 2 63
(Milton Bradley) *chsd ldrs: rdn and unable qck over 1f out: chsd wnr ins fnl f: lost 2 pls fnl f but kpt on* **4/1**[1]

65-6 5 1 **Slatey Hen (IRE)**[2] 30 5-8-7 **51** oh1 .... (p) WilliamCarson 4 50
(Violet M Jordan) *hld up in tch: rdn and effrt over 1f out: styd on same pce ins fnl f* **20/1**

531- 6 nk **Jonnie Skull (IRE)**[5] 8305 7-8-6 **57** 6ex .... (vt) RyanTate(7) 5 55
(Phil McEntee) *chsd ldrs tl hdwy to chse ldr 4f out tl jst ins fnl f: no ex and wknd wl ins fnl f* **8/1**

043- 7 1 **Speak The Truth (IRE)**[18] 8159 7-9-2 **65** .... (p) NathanAlison(5) 11 60
(Roger Ingram) *wnt sltly rt s: hld up in tch but stuck wd: effrt and stl wd on bnd 2f out: styd on same pce fr over 1f out* **9/2**[2]

410- 8 ½ **Lord Buffhead**[9] 8255 4-8-11 **55** .... (v) J-PGuillambert 1 49
(Richard Guest) *chsd ldr for 2f: styd chsng ldrs: rdn and unable qck over 1f out: wknd ins fnl f* **20/1**

404- 9 5 **Fantasy Fighter (IRE)**[37] 7929 8-8-7 **51** oh2 .... ChrisCatlin 8 29
(Ronald Harris) *chsd ldrs on outer: rdn and unable qck wl over 1f out: wknd fnl f* **12/1**

050- 10 2 ¾ **Dvinsky (USA)**[18] 8160 12-9-1 **59** .... (b) JimmyQuinn 3 28
(Paul Howling) *chsd ldrs: sn bustled along: hmpd after 1f and again 2f out: wknd wl over 1f out* **25/1**

050- 11 4 ½ **Waterloo Dock**[25] 8063 8-8-11 **60** .... (b) TobyAtkinson(5) 10 14
(Mick Quinn) *sn rdn along and struggling in rr: lost tch 2f out* **66/1**

1m 11.44s (-0.46) **Going Correction** -0.10s/f (Stan) 11 Ran SP% **119.6**
Speed ratings (Par 101): **99,98,97,96,95 94,93,92,86,82 76**
Tote swingers 1&2 £5.70, 1&3 £9.80, 2&3 £7.20 CSF £24.61 CT £164.35 TOTE £6.00: £2.00, £1.80, £3.50; EX 27.40 Trifecta £209.90 Pool: £1,242.95 - 4.44 winning units.
Owner Andrew Page **Bred** Mrs Mary Rowlands **Trained** Hubbert's Bridge, Lincs

FOCUS
A typically tight first qualifier of this series, but a dominant display from the winner.

77 BLUE SQUARE BET SPRINT SERIES (ROUND 1) H'CAP (QUALIFIER) (DIV II) 6f (P)
2:00 (2:01) (Class 6) (0-65,65) 4-Y-0+ **£3,067** (£905; £453) **Stalls** Low

Form RPR
235- 1 **Putin (IRE)**[5] 8304 5-8-7 **51** oh3 .... (bt) DavidProbert 3 60
(Phil McEntee) *chsd ldr: rdn to chal over 1f out: led ins fnl f: kpt on wl u.p* **10/1**

305- 2 ½ **Waabel**[25] 8063 6-9-1 **64** .... (t) CharlesBishop(5) 11 71
(Violet M Jordan) *sn bustled along to ld and crossed to rail: mde most: rdn over 1f out: hdd ins fnl f: kpt on wl but a hld* **7/1**[3]

101- 3 ¾ **Pharoh Jake**[16] 8184 5-8-9 **58** ow1 .... WilliamTwiston-Davies(5) 6 63
(John Bridger) *chsd ldrs: swtchd lft and rdn over 1f out: styd on same pce u.p ins fnl f* **10/1**

632- 4 nk **Catalinas Diamond (IRE)**[5] 8304 5-9-7 **65** .... (t) SebSanders 4 69
(Pat Murphy) *hld up in tch in midfield: effrt on inner over 1f out: drvn and nt qckn jst ins fnl f: styd on same pce after* **7/2**[1]

023- 5 ½ **Do More Business (IRE)**[5] 8305 6-8-4 **51** oh1 ..... (b[1]) RyanPowell(3) 12 53
(Alison Batchelor) *stdd s: t.k.h: hld up in rr: effrt on outer but stl plenty to do over 1f out: styd on wl ins fnl f: nt rch ldrs* **16/1**

004- 6 nk **Cornus**[5] 8305 11-9-2 **60** .... (be) SeanLevey 5 61
(Alan McCabe) *hld up in tch in midfield: rdn and effrt 2f out: chsd ldrs ins fnl f: kpt on same pce fnl 100yds* **20/1**

114- 7 1 ½ **George Fenton**[18] 8159 4-9-1 **59** .... (p) J-PGuillambert 2 55
(Richard Guest) *chsd ldrs: hung lft 3f out: effrt u.p and styd on inner over 1f out: no ex and btn ins fnl f: hld and eased clsd home* **5/1**[2]

020- 8 2 ¼ **Volcanic Dust (IRE)**[9] 8253 5-9-2 **60** .... (b) RobertWinston 10 49
(Milton Bradley) *in tch towards rr: rdn and no hdwy wl over 1f out: no threat to ldrs after* **25/1**

000- 9 1 **Cut The Cackle (IRE)**[22] 8107 7-8-7 **51** oh1 .... (bt) WilliamCarson 8 37
(Violet M Jordan) *hld up in tch towards rr: rdn and no hdwy over 1f out: wl hld and one pce fnl f* **12/1**

34-2 10 1 **Marshall Art**[1] 50 4-8-13 **57** .... ChrisCatlin 1 40
(David Evans) *sn niggled along in last pair: rdn and no imp over 1f out: n.d* **7/1**[3]

100- 11 ½ **Ace Of Spies (IRE)**[8] 8268 8-8-10 **57** .... SimonPearce(3) 9 38
(Conor Dore) *in tch in midfield: rdn and unable qck over 2f out: wknd over 1f out* **66/1**

1m 11.26s (-0.64) **Going Correction** -0.10s/f (Stan) 11 Ran SP% **105.7**
Speed ratings (Par 101): **100,99,98,97,97 96,94,91,90,89 88**
Tote swingers 1&2 £10.40, 1&3 £12.70, 2&3 £9.40 CSF £62.22 CT £537.68 TOTE £10.50: £3.10, £3.70, £2.30; EX 79.10 Trifecta £537.80 Part won. Pool:.
Owner Steve Jakes **Bred** D Llewelyn & J Runeckles **Trained** Newmarket, Suffolk
■ Haadeeth was withdrawn (6/1, unruly in stalls). Deduct 10p in the £ under R4.

FOCUS
The winning time was 0.18 seconds faster than the first division. This leg was totally dominated by those that raced on the pace with the first three up there from the off.

78 LINGFIELDPARK.CO.UK H'CAP 6f (P)
2:35 (2:35) (Class 2) (0-100,103) 4-Y-0+ **£12,291** (£3,657; £1,827; £913) **Stalls** Low

Form RPR
1/0- 1 **Farmleigh House (IRE)**[22] 8119 6-9-7 **100** .... NGMcCullagh 7 109
(W J Martin, Ire) *chsd clr ldng pair: rdn and clsd over 1f out: led ins fnl f: styd on and a gng to hold on* **5/2**[1]

051- 2 nk **Whaileyy (IRE)**[38] 7897 5-9-9 **102** .... (b) AdamBeschizza 5 110+
(Marco Botti) *hld up in last pair: effrt on outer wl over 1f out: hdwy 1f out: chsd wnr wl ins fnl f: r.o but nvr quite getting to wnr* **5/2**[1]

001- 3 1 **Piscean (USA)**[8] 8272 8-9-2 **98** .... RyanClark(3) 2 103
(Tom Keddy) *hld up in last pair: effrt on inner over 1f out: swtchd rt 1f out: styd in wl ins fnl f to go 3rd wl ins fnl f* **12/1**

043- 4 ¾ **Sulis Minerva (IRE)**[8] 8272 6-8-4 **86** .... RaulDaSilva(3) 3 89
(Jeremy Gask) *prom in main gp: clsd on ldng pair and nt clr run jst over 1f out: sltly outpcd and swtchd rt 1f out: styd on same pce fnl 100yds* **10/1**

000- 5 ½ **Fratellino**[49] 7772 6-9-4 **102** .... (t) WilliamTwiston-Davies(5) 6 103
(Alan McCabe) *led and sn clr w rival: rdn over 1f out: hdd ins fnl f: no ex and lost 3 pls wl ins fnl f* **14/1**

124- 6 ½ **Swiss Cross**[8] 8272 6-9-10 **103** .... (t) DavidProbert 4 102
(Phil McEntee) *hld up in midfield: rdn and effrt wl over 1f out: hdwy u.p 1f out: no imp and one pce ins fnl f* **7/1**[2]

110- 7 1 ¼ **Forest Edge (IRE)**[17] 8163 4-8-1 **87** .... (b) PhilipPrince(7) 8 82
(David Evans) *sn w ldr and clr of field: rdn and stl ev ch over 1f out: wknd ins fnl f* **12/1**

105- 8 1 ¾ **Mezzotint (IRE)**[8] 8272 4-8-10 **89** .... JimmyQuinn 9 79
(Marco Botti) *racd in midfield: rdn and no imp 2f out: wknd ent fnl f* **8/1**[3]

05-0 U **Decent Fella (IRE)**[3] 25 7-8-7 **86** oh1 .... (bt[1]) WilliamCarson 1
(Violet M Jordan) *rrd and uns rdr as stalls opened* **25/1**

1m 10.13s (-1.77) **Going Correction** -0.10s/f (Stan) 9 Ran SP% **115.7**
Speed ratings (Par 109): **107,106,105,104,103 102,101,98,**
Tote swingers 1&2 £2.20, 1&3 £8.90, 2&3 £7.50 CSF £8.03 CT £61.14 TOTE £3.10: £1.20, £1.30, £4.00; EX 8.70 Trifecta £60.10 Pool: £1,498.76 - 18.68 winning units.
Owner W J Martin **Bred** Mrs E Fitzsimons **Trained** Enniscorthy, Co Wexford

FOCUS
A decent sprint handicap and run at a scorching pace with Fratellino and Forest Edge taking each other on from the start and setting it up for the closers.

79 FOREST ROW H'CAP 1m (P)
3:10 (3:11) (Class 4) (0-85,83) 4-Y-0+ **£4,942** (£1,459; £730) **Stalls** High

Form RPR
000- 1 **Loyalty**[36] 7934 6-9-2 **78** .... (v) MartinDwyer 7 88
(Derek Shaw) *mde virtually all: grad crossed to rail: rdn over 1f out: styd on wl and asserted fnl 100yds* **12/1**

021- 2 1 ½ **Lowther**[22] 8105 8-9-2 **78** .... (b) WilliamCarson 4 85
(Lee Carter) *t.k.h: chsd ldrs: rdn and ev ch 2f out: forged ahd w wnr 1f out: no ex and btn fnl 100yds* **7/4**[1]

001- 3 1 ¼ **Kickingthelilly**[16] 8188 4-9-7 **83** .... ChrisCatlin 5 87
(Rae Guest) *sn rdn along in rr: hdwy u.p 1f out: styd on wl to go 3rd wl ins fnl f: nt rch ldrs* **6/1**

613- 4 ½ **Ancient Greece**[31] 7986 6-9-1 **77** .... (t) JimCrowley 1 80
(George Baker) *chsd ldrs: rdn and effrt over 1f out: styd on same pce ins fnl f* **3/1**[2]

30-4 5 hd **Copperwood**[3] 25 8-9-1 **77** .... JoeFanning 6 79
(Mark Johnston) *t.k.h: chsd ldr: ev ch and rdn 2f out: no ex ent fnl f: one pce and lost 2 pls ins fnl f* **8/1**

010- 6 3 ½ **The Happy Hammer (IRE)**[98] 6687 7-8-7 **69** .... DavidProbert 2 63
(Eugene Stanford) *awkward leaving stalls: hld up in tch towards rr: rdn and effrt 2f out: no hdwy over 1f out: wknd ins fnl f* **20/1**

232- 7 7 **Rugosa**[42] 7858 4-9-2 **78** .... RobertWinston 3 56
(Charles Hills) *hld up in tch towards rr: hdwy and rdn to chse ldrs 2f out: btn over 1f out: wknd 1f out* **5/1**[3]

1m 36.32s (-1.88) **Going Correction** -0.10s/f (Stan) 7 Ran SP% **115.9**
Speed ratings (Par 105): **105,103,102,101,101 98,91**
Tote swingers 1&2 £5.20, 1&3 £7.70, 2&3 £2.90 CSF £34.46 TOTE £16.70: £6.10, £1.50; EX 43.90 Trifecta £121.10 Pool: £1,814.09 - 11.23 winning units.
Owner Brian Johnson (Northamptonshire) **Bred** Ecoutila Partnership **Trained** Sproxton, Leics

FOCUS
A good handicap and another all-the-way winner.

80 GET STRAIGHT TO THE BET AT BLUESQ.COM H'CAP 7f (P)
3:45 (3:45) (Class 5) (0-70,74) 4-Y-0+ **£2,726** (£805; £402) **Stalls** Low

Form RPR
22-1 1 **Al's Memory (IRE)**[2] 34 4-9-4 **74** 6ex .... PhilipPrince(7) 1 82
(David Evans) *chsd ldrs: rdn 2f out: led over 1f out: hrd pressed and hld on gamely fnl 100yds: all out* **7/2**[1]

542- 2 hd **Paperetto**[8] 8268 5-8-9 **63** .... WilliamTwiston-Davies(5) 5 70
(Robert Mills) *chsd ldrs: clsd over 2f out: rdn and effrt over 1f out: str chal ins fnl f: r.o wl but jst hld* **7/2**[1]

312- 3 1 ¼ **Sunshine Always (IRE)**[5] 8306 7-9-7 **70** .... SebSanders 8 74
(Michael Attwater) *racd off the pce in last quartet: clsd over 2f out: rdn and hdwy on inner over 1f out: drvn and styd on same pce ins fnl f* **9/2**[2]

051- **4** nk **Flavius Victor (IRE)**[29] 8021 4-9-5 **68** .... GeorgeBaker 9 72
(Patrick Chamings) *stdd s: hld up off the pce in rr: clsd over 2f out: hdwy but hanging lft over 1f out: swtchd rt 1f out: chsng ldrs and nt clr run ins fnl f: kpt on fnl 50yds* **9/2**[2]
603- **5** 3/4 **Cyflymder (IRE)**[5] 8308 7-9-6 **69** .... KirstyMilczarek 2 70
(David C Griffiths) *led: rdn wl over 1f out: hdd over 1f out: no ex jst ins fnl f: wknd wl ins fnl f* **10/1**
031- **6** 2 1/4 **Stepturn**[18] 8160 4-9-2 **65** ....(p) ChrisCatlin 3 60
(Michael Wigham) *chsd ldr tl over 1f out: sn struggling u.p: wknd ins fnl f* **8/1**
05- **7** 1 1/4 **Wordismybond**[26] 8057 4-9-2 **65** .... JimCrowley 4 57
(Peter Makin) *racd off the pce in last quartet: clsd and n.m.r jst over 2f out: rdn and no prog over 1f out: wknd fnl f* **7/1**[3]
050- **8** 2 1/4 **Buxton**[8] 8268 9-8-8 **57** ....(t) AdamBeschizza 10 42
(Roger Ingram) *racd in last quartet on outer: rdn and lost pl wl over 1f out: wknd over 1f out* **33/1**

1m 23.85s (-0.95) **Going Correction** -0.10s/f (Stan) **8** Ran SP% **116.5**
Speed ratings (Par 103): **101,100,99,99,98 95,94,91**
Tote swingers 1&2 £3.40, 1&3 £3.60, 2&3 £3.30 CSF £16.08 CT £56.18 TOTE £5.00: £1.50, £1.80, £1.50; EX 19.10 Trifecta £80.90 Pool: £968.91 - 8.98 winning units..
Owner Will Dawson **Bred** Brian Miller **Trained** Pandy, Monmouths

FOCUS
An ordinary handicap in which the front pair may have gone off too quick.
T/Plt: £97.40 to a £1 stake. Pool: £54,738.92 - 410.03 winning units T/Qpdt: £34.70 to a £1 stake. Pool: £3,036.50 - 64.70 winning units SP

[49]WOLVERHAMPTON (A.W) (L-H)
Sunday, January 6

OFFICIAL GOING: Standard
Wind: almost nil Weather: overcast

81 CORAL.CO.UK "HANDS AND HEELS" APPRENTICE SERIES H'CAP (PART OF THE RACING EXCELLENCE INITIATIVE) 5f 20y(P)
1:45 (1:45) (Class 6) (0-55,55) 4-Y-0+ **£2,045** (£603; £302) **Stalls** Low

Form RPR
350- **1** **Hab Reeh**[10] 8256 5-9-1 **49** ....(bt) GemmaTutty 4 60
(Ruth Carr) *mde all: pushed clr appr fnl f: readily* **9/4**[1]
054- **2** 2 1/4 **Deveze (IRE)**[16] 8210 5-8-12 **46** oh1 ....(b) RyanTate 2 49
(Milton Bradley) *chsd ldrs: kpt on to take 2nd ins fnl f: no imp* **6/1**[3]
000- **3** 4 **Prigsnov Dancer (IRE)**[10] 8255 8-8-7 **46** ....(t) DanaZamecnikova(5) 1 35
(Frank Sheridan) *chsd ldrs: outpcd over 2f out: kpt on appr fnl f: tk 3rd nr fin* **33/1**
053- **4** 3/4 **Nafa (IRE)**[51] 7746 5-9-5 **53** .... DanielMuscutt 5 39
(Daniel Mark Loughnane) *chsd wnr: one pce over 1f out* **11/4**[2]
600- **5** 3/4 **Sophie's Beau (USA)**[15] 8231 6-8-9 **46** oh1 ....(bt) AaronJones(3) 6 29
(Michael Chapman) *s.i.s: hld up in rr: kpt on fnl f: nvr a threat* **8/1**
324- **6** nse **Chateau Lola**[10] 8253 4-8-13 **52** .... AdamMcLean(5) 3 35
(Derek Shaw) *dwlt: in rr: kpt on fnl f: nvr a factor* **6/1**[3]
000- **7** 1/2 **The Jailer**[113] 6233 10-8-10 **47** ....(p) RobertTart(3) 8 28
(John O'Shea) *rr-div: sme hdwy on outside 1f out: nvr on terms* **9/1**

1m 1.71s (-0.59) **Going Correction** -0.15s/f (Stan) **7** Ran SP% **110.1**
Speed ratings (Par 101): **98,94,88,86,85 85,84**
toteswingers 1&2 £3.40, 1&3 £11.80, 2&3 £15.70 CSF £14.87 CT £312.01 TOTE £2.50: £1.40, £3.90; EX 17.80 Trifecta £773.90 Part won. Pool: £1,031.96 - 0.90 winning units..
Owner Mrs B Taylor, A Dickman, Mrs R Carr **Bred** The Anglo Irish Choral Society **Trained** Huby, N Yorks

82 CORAL.CO.UK MOBILE CASINO H'CAP 1m 1f 103y(P)
2:15 (2:15) (Class 5) (0-70,72) 4-Y-0+ **£2,587** (£770; £384; £192) **Stalls** Low

Form RPR
115- **1** **Lean On Pete (IRE)**[52] 7722 4-9-6 **70** .... ShaneKelly 4 78
(Ollie Pears) *hld up in rr: n.m.r and edgd rt over 1f out: str run on outside ins fnl f: led post* **2/1**[1]
604- **2** shd **Follow The Flag (IRE)**[10] 8259 9-9-7 **70** ....(v) RobertWinston 3 77
(Alan McCabe) *in rr: drvn over 3f out: hdwy over 2f out: swtchd rt over 1f out: styd on to ld nr fin: hdd post* **14/1**
310- **3** 3/4 **One Scoop Or Two**[33] 7976 7-9-2 **70** ....(p) JackDuern(5) 2 76
(Reg Hollinshead) *trckd ldrs: led over 1f out: hdd and no ex towards fin* **10/1**
611- **4** 1 **Idol Deputy (FR)**[22] 8137 7-9-0 **68** ....(p) RachealKneller(5) 10 72
(Mark Usher) *hld up in mid-div: smooth hdwy to trck ldrs over 1f out: kpt on same pce last 100yds* **8/1**
402- **5** 1 1/4 **Dakota Canyon (IRE)**[10] 8259 4-9-8 **72** ....(b) DavidNolan 1 73
(Richard Fahey) *drvn to ld: hdd after 4f: rallied and upsides 2f out: one pce* **11/4**[2]
600- **6** 3 1/4 **John Potts**[22] 8137 8-8-11 **60** .... KellyHarrison 7 54
(Brian Baugh) *in rr: drvn over 3f out: nvr a factor* **40/1**
336- **7** 1 **Dazzling Valentine**[22] 8136 5-9-5 **68** .... AdamKirby 9 60
(Alan Bailey) *mid-div: reminders over 4f out: wknd 2f out* **9/2**[3]
403- **8** 3 3/4 **Elizabeth Coffee (IRE)**[15] 8234 5-9-5 **68** .... LukeMorris 8 52
(John Weymes) *t.k.h: sn trcking ldrs: drvn over 3f out: lost pl 2f out* **28/1**
640- **9** 3/4 **West End Lad**[22] 8136 10-9-2 **68** ....(b) MarkCoumbe(3) 6 51
(Roy Bowring) *sn chsng ldrs: led after 4f: hdd and lost pl over 1f out: eased nr fin* **20/1**

1m 58.96s (-2.74) **Going Correction** -0.15c/f (Stan)
WFA 4 from 5yo+ 1lb **9** Ran SP% **115.7**
Speed ratings (Par 103): **106,105,105,104,103 100,99,96,95**
toteswingers 1&2 £7.40, 1&3 £5.80, 2&3 £13.10 CSF £31.16 CT £230.38 TOTE £2.70: £1.80, £2.50, £2.90; EX 28.20 Trifecta £322.70 Pool: £1,222.02 - 2.84 winning units..
Owner Charles Wentworth **Bred** Mrs T Mahon **Trained** Norton, N Yorks

FOCUS
Fair form for the grade.

83 COMPARE ONLINE BOOKIES AT BOOKMAKERS.CO.UK H'CAP 1m 1f 103y(P)
2:45 (2:45) (Class 6) (0-65,67) 4-Y-0+ **£1,940** (£577; £288; £144) **Stalls** Low

Form RPR
00-1 **1** **Berlusca (IRE)**[2] 61 4-9-8 **67** 6ex .... GrahamGibbons 6 75+
(David O'Meara) *trckd ldrs: t.k.h: effrt over 1f out: led narrowly jst ins fnl f: drvn out* **8/13**[1]
560- **2** 1/2 **Scamperdale**[88] 6981 11-9-3 **61** ....(p) KellyHarrison 9 68
(Brian Baugh) *hld up in rr: gd hdwy on ins wl over 1f out: upsides jst ins fnl f: no ex nr fin* **25/1**
544- **3** 2 1/4 **Maz**[9] 8261 5-9-1 **59** ....(p) NickyMackay 5 61
(Alan Bailey) *led: hdd jst ins fnl f: kpt on same pce* **25/1**
144- **4** 1 **Mr Chocolate Drop (IRE)**[120] 6057 9-9-4 **62** ....(t) AdamKirby 2 62
(Mandy Rowland) *in rr: hdwy over 2f out: one pce appr fnl f* **16/1**
005- **5** 1/2 **Cabal**[20] 8145 6-8-12 **56** ....(b) RobertHavlin 1 55
(Andrew Crook) *chsd ldrs: kpt on same pce fnl f* **33/1**
003- **6** 1 3/4 **Flying Applause**[23] 8113 8-8-11 **58** ....(b) MarkCoumbe(3) 12 53
(Roy Bowring) *hdwy to chse ldrs after 1f: drvn 3f out: one pce over 1f out* **25/1**
111- **7** 3 1/4 **Brown Pete (IRE)**[9] 8264 5-9-9 **67** .... WilliamCarson 11 56
(Violet M Jordan) *w ldr: t.k.h: wknd over 1f out* **7/2**[2]
036- **8** 1 3/4 **Poetic Power (IRE)**[22] 8137 4-9-4 **63** .... StevieDonohoe 3 48
(Ian Williams) *hld up in rr: hdwy on outer over 2f out: wknd over 1f out* **8/1**[3]
305- **9** 1 3/4 **Glass Mountain (IRE)**[9] 8271 5-9-2 **63** ....(v) RyanClark(3) 8 44
(John Mackie) *mid-div: chsng ldrs over 2f out: one pce whn nt clr run appr fnl f: sn wknd: b.b.v* **16/1**

2m 0.7s (-1.00) **Going Correction** -0.15s/f (Stan)
WFA 4 from 5yo+ 1lb **9** Ran SP% **121.5**
Speed ratings (Par 101): **98,97,95,94,94 92,89,88,86**
toteswingers 1&2 £11.50, 1&3 £7.70, 2&3 £35.00 CSF £28.10 CT £245.53 TOTE £1.50: £1.10, £5.40, £6.40; EX 27.80 Trifecta £175.80 Pool: £825.23 - 3.52 winning units..
Owner Peter R Ball **Bred** Value Bloodstock **Trained** Nawton, N Yorks

FOCUS
The early pace wasn't that strong.

84 BOOKMAKERS.CO.UK GIVES YOU FREE BETS (S) STKS 1m 4f 50y(P)
3:20 (3:20) (Class 6) 4-Y-0+ **£2,045** (£603; £302) **Stalls** Low

Form RPR
035- **1** **Activate**[15] 8235 6-9-4 70 ....(b[1]) GrahamGibbons 3 62
(David O'Meara) *mde all: clr over 1f out: v easily* **4/7**[1]
005- **2** 3 3/4 **Turjuman (USA)**[20] 8148 8-9-4 55 ....(p) AdamKirby 5 56
(Alan Bailey) *s.i.s: chsd ldrs 4f out: sn rdn and outpcd: wnt 2nd ins fnl f: one pce* **8/1**[3]
000- **3** 2 1/4 **Yourinthewill (USA)**[20] 8145 5-9-4 61 .... ShaneKelly 1 52
(Daniel Mark Loughnane) *hld up in rr: t.k.h: chsd wnr over 4f out: hung lft and one pce fnl 2f* **14/1**
30-5 **4** nk **Jordaura**[4] 23 7-9-10 63 .... RobertWinston 2 58
(Alan Berry) *rn in snatches: hdwy and modest 3rd 4f out: one pce fnl 2f* **11/4**[2]
600- **5** 30 **Amber Moon**[9] 8265 8-8-8 39 .... AnnStokell(5) 4
(Ann Stokell) *t.k.h: sn trcking wnr: wknd over 4f out: sn bhd: t.o 2f out* **66/1**

2m 38.55s (-2.55) **Going Correction** -0.15s/f (Stan) **5** Ran SP% **109.6**
Speed ratings (Par 101): **102,99,98,97,77**
CSF £5.95 TOTE £1.40: £1.10, £2.10; EX 5.60 Trifecta £13.90 Pool: £1,310.45 - 70.64 winning units..Activate was bought by Steve Jakes for 5,000gns.
Owner W O'Brien **Bred** Card Bloodstock **Trained** Nawton, N Yorks

FOCUS
A weak race.

85 £50 FREE BET AT CORAL.CO.UK H'CAP 5f 216y(P)
3:50 (3:50) (Class 4) (0-85,89) 3-Y-O **£4,690** (£1,046; £1,046; £348) **Stalls** Low

Form RPR
01- **1** **Rene Mathis (GER)**[15] 8233 3-9-1 **79** .... JamieSpencer 6 84
(Richard Fahey) *dwlt: hld up in rr: hdwy on outside to chse ldrs over 3f out: edgd lft and led jst ins fnl f: drvn out* **11/2**[3]
215- **2** 1 **Midnight Dream (FR)**[18] 8161 3-8-13 **77** .... ShaneKelly 4 79
(Linda Stubbs) *trckd ldrs: edgd rt over 1f out: kpt on ins fnl f: dht 2nd* **25/1**
51-1 **2** dht **Archie Stevens**[5] 4 3-8-12 **81** 6ex .... WilliamTwiston-Davies(5) 3 83
(Tom Dascombe) *trckd ldrs: kpt on same pce fnl f* **15/8**[2]
131- **4** nk **Equitania**[24] 8096 3-9-11 **89** .... AdamKirby 5 90
(Alan Bailey) *led: hdd 1f out: kpt on same pce* **8/1**
122- **5** 1 1/4 **Fortinbrass (IRE)**[7] 8293 3-9-0 **78** .... JimCrowley 2 75
(Ralph Beckett) *hld up in rr: drvn 3f out: sn outpcd: edgd rt and kpt on fnl f: nvr a threat* **7/4**[1]
321- **6** 4 1/2 **Boxing Shadows**[11] 8237 3-8-8 **72** .... TomEaves 1 55
(Bryan Smart) *hld up in rr: drvn over 2f out: lost pl over 1f out* **12/1**

1m 13.64s (-1.36) **Going Correction** -0.15s/f (Stan) **6** Ran SP% **109.2**
Speed ratings (Par 99): **103,101,101,101,99 93**PL AS £0.70, MD £3.70, EX RM/AS £7.40, RM/MD £44.20, CSF RM/AS £7.69, RM/MD £0.00 TRIF RM/AS/MD £83.90, RM/MD/AS £159.90. toteswingers RM&AS £2.30, RM&MD £7.10, AS&MD £6.80 TOTE £5.30: £2.10 TRIFECTA Pool: £1,932.15 - 8.63 winning units. 27.

FOCUS
There wasn't much pace on early here.

86 GET INSIDE TRACK AT BOOKMAKERS.CO.UK H'CAP 5f 216y(P)
4:20 (4:20) (Class 5) (0-75,75) 4-Y-0+ **£2,587** (£770; £384; £192) **Stalls** Low

Form RPR
000- **1** **Khawatim**[19] 8157 5-9-3 **71** .... StevieDonohoe 7 80
(Noel Quinlan) *s.i.s: hld up towards rr: hdwy and n.m.r over 1f out: squeezed through jst ins fnl f: fin strly to ld fnl strides* **5/4**[1]
601- **2** nk **Strong Man**[23] 8115 5-8-12 **66** ....(b) GrahamGibbons 6 74
(Michael Easterby) *trckd ldrs: led 2f out: drvn 3 l clr over 1f out: hdd last strides* **6/1**
014- **3** 3/4 **Gabrial's Gift (IRE)**[17] 8183 4-9-7 **75** .... JamieSpencer 11 81
(Ian Williams) *trckd ldrs: keeping on same pce whn edgd lft jst ins fnl f: styd on towards fin* **12/1**
411- **4** shd **Invigilator**[10] 8255 5-8-7 **61** ....(t) MartinDwyer 1 67
(Derek Shaw) *mid-div: outpcd over 3f out: hdwy on ins wl over 1f out: swtchd rt appr fnl f: styd on* **11/2**[3]
51-4 **5** 1/2 **Belle Bayardo (IRE)**[4] 11 5-9-1 **69** .... LukeMorris 5 73
(Ronald Harris) *chsd ldrs: kpt on same pce fnl f* **6/1**
360- **6** 2 3/4 **Dancing Welcome**[15] 8232 7-9-3 **71** ....(b) RobertWinston 2 66
(Milton Bradley) *chsd ldrs: one pce over 1f out* **40/1**
043- **7** hd **Dancing Maite**[60] 7633 8-9-1 **72** ....(b) MarkCoumbe(3) 4 67
(Roy Bowring) *dwlt: hdwy on outer over 2f out: kpt on fnl f: nvr a factor* **50/1**
506- **8** shd **Fred Willetts (IRE)**[22] 8143 5-9-2 **75** ....(v) WilliamTwiston-Davies(5) 8 69
(Mark Brisbourne) *mid-div: outpcd over 3f out: kpt on fnl f* **5/1**[2]
536- **9** shd **Key Ambition**[17] 8183 4-9-4 **72** ....(vt) AdamKirby 10 66
(Garry Moss) *chsd ldrs: wkng whn hmpd jst ins fnl f* **20/1**
000- **10** 4 **Alive And Kicking**[8] 8285 5-8-10 **64** .... BarryMcHugh 3 45
(Richard Fahey) *led: hdd 2f out: wknd appr fnl f* **66/1**

230- **11** *nse* **Shawkantango**[27] 8058 6-9-0 **68**..(v) DaleSwift 9 49
(Derek Shaw) *s.i.s: a in rr* **50/1**
1m 13.47s (-1.53) **Going Correction** -0.15s/f (Stan) 11 Ran SP% **125.4**
Speed ratings (Par 103): **104,103,102,102,101 98,97,97,97,92 92**
toteswingers 1&2 £3.40, 1&3 £6.60, 2&3 £9.50 CSF £9.78 CT £71.99 TOTE £2.80: £1.30, £2.10, £3.60; EX 15.80 Trifecta £98.40 Pool: £2,049.58 - 15.62 winning units..
Owner The Unique Partnership **Bred** Baroness Bloodstock **Trained** Newmarket, Suffolk
FOCUS
There were two well-backed horses in this race and they finished first and second.

87 WIN MORE ON BETTING AT BOOKMAKERS.CO.UK H'CAP (DIV I) 5f 216y(P)
4:50 (4:50) (Class 6) (0-55,57) 4-Y-0+ **£1,940** (£577; £288; £144) **Stalls** Low

Form RPR
065- **1** **Glennten**[61] 7616 4-9-7 **53**.. AdamKirby 6 60
(Sylvester Kirk) *led: narrowly hdd over 1f out: hrd rdn and led again cl home* **3/1**[1]
045- **2** *hd* **Kai**[8] 8287 4-9-2 **53**...(b) WilliamTwiston-Davies(5) 7 59
(Alan McCabe) *w ldrs: narrow ld over 1f out: hdd and no ex nr fin* **4/1**[3]
050- **3** *hd* **John Coffey (IRE)**[73] 7354 4-9-6 **52**............................ RobertWinston 5 57
(David Nicholls) *chsd ldrs: upsides ins fnl f: no ex nr fin* **7/2**[2]
000- **4** *shd* **Vhujon (IRE)**[16] 8210 8-8-13 **45**... TomEaves 3 50
(Peter Grayson) *in rr: hdwy over 2f out: swtchd rt and styd on ins fnl f: keeping on at fin* **12/1**
604- **5** *2 ¼* **Lisselton Cross**[10] 8255 5-9-3 **49**......................................(v) AmyRyan 2 47
(Martin Bosley) *mid-div: effrt over 2f out: kpt on one pce fnl f* **11/2**
305- **6** *nk* **Media Jury**[68] 7465 6-9-2 **48**..(v) BarryMcHugh 4 45
(John Wainwright) *in rr: hdwy over 2f out: styd on fnl f: nt rch ldrs* **10/1**
31-6 **7** *1* **Jonnie Skull (IRE)**[1] 76 7-9-4 **57** 6ex.......................(vt) RyanTate(7) 10 51
(Phil McEntee) *chsd ldrs: drvn over 2f out: one pce fnl f* **4/1**[3]
000- **8** *5* **Spoken Words**[16] 8210 4-8-6 **45**..............................(p) VictorSantos(7) 9 23
(H A McWilliams) *s.s: mid-div on outer: effrt over 2f out: wknd appr fnl f* **100/1**
600- **9** *2 ½* **Takajan (IRE)**[295] 939 6-8-13 **45**................................ GrahamGibbons 1 15
(Mark Brisbourne) *trckd ldrs: effrt over 2f out: wknd over 1f out* **50/1**
400- **10** *17* **Valdemar**[28] 8045 7-8-13 **45**...(be) LukeMorris 8
(John Weymes) *mid-div: lost pl wl over 1f out: bhd whn eased towards fin: t.o* **40/1**
1m 14.59s (-0.41) **Going Correction** -0.15s/f (Stan) 10 Ran SP% **124.8**
Speed ratings (Par 101): **96,95,95,95,92 91,90,83,80,57**
toteswingers 1&2 £3.90, 1&3 £4.60, 2&3 £4.40 CSF £16.50 CT £46.01 TOTE £3.70: £1.40, £1.90, £1.90; EX 18.80 Trifecta £98.20 Pool: £ 1,733.12 - 13.23 winning units..
Owner S Glenn **Bred** The Hon Mrs R Pease **Trained** Upper Lambourn, Berks
FOCUS
Once getting to the front the first two slowed things down, and nothing else really got into it as the pair fought out the race up the straight.

88 WIN MORE ON BETTING AT BOOKMAKERS.CO.UK H'CAP (DIV II) 5f 216y(P)
5:20 (5:20) (Class 6) (0-55,55) 4-Y-0+ **£1,940** (£577; £288; £144) **Stalls** Low

Form RPR
04-0 **1** **Athaakeel (IRE)**[3] 42 7-8-12 **46**..................................(b) LukeMorris 5 54
(Ronald Harris) *dwlt: hdwy wl over 1f out: n.m.r 1f out: styd on wl to ld towards fin* **9/2**[2]
35-1 **2** *¾* **Putin (IRE)**[1] 77 5-8-13 **54** 6ex...................................(bt) RyanTate(7) 3 60
(Phil McEntee) *trckd ldrs: led narrowly 1f out: no ex and hdd nr fin* **5/4**[1]
000- **3** *½* **Onceaponatime (IRE)**[7] 8299 8-9-5 **53**........................... JimmyQuinn 4 57
(Michael Squance) *mid-div: effrt over 2f out: styd on fnl f: no ex clsng stages* **17/2**[3]
000- **4** *1 ¼* **Blue Noodles**[89] 6958 7-8-12 **46** oh1...........................(p) BarryMcHugh 8 46
(John Wainwright) *rr-div: hdwy on outer over 2f out: kpt on wl fnl f* **11/1**
000- **5** *nk* **Ishetoo**[10] 8255 9-9-4 **52**.. AdamKirby 2 51
(Peter Grayson) *blind removed late: s.i.s: effrt on inner over 1f out: sn chsng ldrs: kpt on ins fnl f* **10/1**
500- **6** *1 ¾* **Hold The Star**[7] 8299 7-8-11 **50**.. AnnStokell(5) 1 43
(Ann Stokell) *chsd ldrs: one pce fnl 2f* **16/1**
003- **7** *1* **Divertimenti (IRE)**[16] 8209 9-8-9 **46** oh1................(b) MarkCoumbe(3) 10 36
(Roy Bowring) *w ldrs: led wl over 1f out: sn hdd & wknd* **12/1**
050- **8** *¾* **Colamandis**[16] 8209 6-8-5 **46** oh1..............................(b) VictorSantos(7) 7 34
(H A McWilliams) *rr-div: n.m.r over 2f out: hdwy on ins wl over 1f out: nvr a factor* **100/1**
000- **9** *3* **Cape Of Storms**[47] 7794 10-9-7 **55**...............................(vt) TomEaves 6 33
(Roy Brotherton) *led: hdd wl over 1f out: sn wknd* **12/1**
000- **10** *20* **Johnson's Cat (IRE)**[39] 7903 4-8-12 **46** oh1............. GrahamGibbons 9
(Mandy Rowland) *w ldrs: wkng whn hmpd over 2f out: bhd and eased over 1f out: virtually p.u: t.o* **66/1**
1m 14.57s (-0.43) **Going Correction** -0.15s/f (Stan) 10 Ran SP% **114.3**
Speed ratings (Par 101): **96,95,94,92,92 89,88,87,83,56**
toteswingers 1&2 £2.30, 1&3 £4.40, 2&3 £3.70 CSF £10.20 CT £44.70 TOTE £5.60: £1.40, £1.40, £2.80; EX 11.40 Trifecta £70.50 Pool: £1,796.92 - 19.10 winning units..
Owner Drag Star On Swan **Bred** Shadwell Estate Company Limited **Trained** Earlswood, Monmouths
FOCUS
Although the final time was similar to the first division there was a good pace on.
T/Plt: £54.60 to a £1 stake. Pool of £79,184.87 - 1,057.65 winning tickets. T/Qpdt: £14.80 to a £1 stake. Pool of £6,334.36 - 315.00 winning tickets. WG

8 KEMPTON (A.W) (R-H)
Monday, January 7

OFFICIAL GOING: Standard
Wind: virtually nil Weather: dry, overcast

89 32RED APPRENTICE H'CAP 1m (P)
1:25 (1:25) (Class 6) (0-65,65) 4-Y-0+ **£1,940** (£577; £288; £144) **Stalls** Low

Form RPR
020- **1** **Travelling**[18] 8183 4-9-4 **65**.. RyanTate(3) 7 73
(Tony Carroll) *hld up in tch towards rr: stl travelling wl 2f out: rdn and effrt over 1f out: str run to ld wl ins fnl f: gng away at fin* **16/1**
662- **2** *1 ¼* **Hierarch (IRE)**[26] 8083 6-9-0 **65**.................................. SiobhanMiller(7) 3 70
(David Simcock) *hld up in tch: hdwy to chse ldrs 5f out: rdn and styng on to press ldr whn sltly hmpd 1f out: led fnl 100yds: sn hdd and one pce* **6/1**
262- **3** *nk* **Divine Rule (IRE)**[10] 8261 5-8-11 **55**..........................(v) ThomasBrown 1 59
(Laura Mongan) *stdd s: hld up in tch in rr: swtchd lft and effrt over 1f out: r.o strly to go 3rd wl ins fnl f* **8/1**
02-1 **4** *1* **Breakheart (IRE)**[5] 13 6-9-2 **65** 6ex.........................(p) JoeyHaynes(5) 4 67
(Andrew Balding) *hld up in tch in midfield: rdn and effrt to chse ldng trio over 1f out: kpt on ins fnl f* **4/1**[2]
054- **5** *hd* **Bloodsweatandtears**[17] 8199 5-9-4 **62**................................ NedCurtis 5 64
(William Knight) *t.k.h: led for 2f: chsd ldr after: rdn over 1f out: styd on to chal whn hung rt 1f out: no ex and one pce fnl 100yds* **3/1**[1]
45-2 **6** *hd* **May's Boy**[5] 13 5-8-9 **60**...(p) EmilyMelbourn(7) 9 61
(Mark Usher) *chsd ldr tl led after 2f: clr 1/2-way: stl clr and rdn 2f out: kpt on tl hdd fnl 100yds: no ex* **11/2**
000- **7** *7* **Da Ponte**[20] 8156 5-8-13 **57**...(v) IanBurns 8 42
(Michael Scudamore) *chsd ldrs tl over 2f out: wknd u.p 2f out* **25/1**
233- **8** *nk* **Sudden Wish (IRE)**[11] 8248 4-8-8 **55**........................... PhilipPrince(3) 6 39
(David Evans) *in tch in midfield: unable qck u.p over 2f out: wknd over 1f out* **5/1**[3]
000- **9** *nk* **Qeethaara (USA)**[39] 7925 9-9-4 **62**...........................(p) JoshBaudains 2 46
(Mark Brisbourne) *hld up in tch in last trio: rdn and effrt on inner 2f out: no prog: wknd over 1f out* **33/1**
1m 39.41s (-0.39) **Going Correction** +0.025s/f (Slow) 9 Ran SP% **115.1**
Speed ratings (Par 101): **102,100,100,99,99 99,92,91,91**
toteswingers 1&2 £11.00, 1&3 £14.80, 2&3 £7.20 CSF £108.23 CT £842.82 TOTE £23.10: £4.60, £2.60, £2.40; EX 134.10 TRIFECTA Not won..
Owner Longview Stud & Bloodstock Ltd **Bred** Longview Stud & Bloodstock Ltd **Trained** Cropthorne, Worcs
FOCUS
A modest but competitive apprentice handicap in which the gallop was strong and this set it up for the closers. The winner came down the centre in the straight and the third helps with the standard.

90 32RED CASINO MEDIAN AUCTION MAIDEN FILLIES' STKS 1m (P)
1:55 (1:57) (Class 5) 3-5-Y-O **£2,587** (£770; £384; £192) **Stalls** Low

Form RPR
003- **1** **Compton Rainbow**[26] 8074 4-9-7 61...............................(t) RyanTate(7) 5 75
(Hans Adielsson) *mde all: gng clr and travelling best ent fnl 2f: rdn over 1f out: kpt on and in n.d after* **9/2**[3]
042- **2** *3 ½* **Easy Life**[17] 8201 3-8-8 67... MartinDwyer 3 63
(Marcus Tregoning) *chsd wnr: rdn and outpcd ent fnl 2f: 3rd and wl hld over 1f out: chsd wnr again ins fnl f: no imp* **6/1**
422- **3** *1 ¾* **Liliana (IRE)**[7] 8303 3-8-8 0.. LukeMorris 6 59
(Peter Chapple-Hyam) *t.k.h: hld up in tch: rdn and effrt between horses ent fnl 2f: chsd clr wnr over 1f out: no imp: lost 2nd ins fnl f* **7/2**[2]
03- **4** *4* **Big Moza**[28] 8052 3-8-8 0... RobertWinston 4 50
(John Best) *chsd ldrs: rdn and outpcd over 2f out: 4th and wl btn over 1f out* **11/4**[1]
00- **5** *¾* **Impertinent**[72] 7403 3-8-8 0.. JohnFahy 2 48
(Jonathan Portman) *hld up in tch in last pair: rdn and outpcd over 2f out: wl btn fnl 2f* **14/1**
66- **6** *nse* **Lucilla**[19] 8171 3-8-8 0.. KieranO'Neill 1 48
(Paul Howling) *hld up in tch: rdn and outpcd jst over 2f out: wl btn whn hung lft over 1f out: bhd fnl f* **7/2**[2]
1m 39.99s (0.19) **Going Correction** +0.025s/f (Slow)
WFA 3 from 4yo 20lb 6 Ran SP% **110.2**
Speed ratings (Par 100): **100,96,94,90,90 89**
toteswingers 1&2 £3.60, 1&3 £2.80, 2&3 £2.50 CSF £28.71 TOTE £4.20: £1.30, £3.70; EX 29.20 Trifecta £53.50 Pool: £1,186.61 - 16.61 winning units..
Owner Erik Penser **Bred** Pegasus Racing Ltd **Trained** Kingston Lisle, Oxon
FOCUS
An open maiden but not form to get carried away with. An improved effort from the winner at face value though.

91 32RED.COM H'CAP (LONDON MILE QUALIFIER) 1m (P)
2:30 (2:30) (Class 5) (0-75,74) 3-Y-O **£2,587** (£770; £384) **Stalls** Low

Form RPR
01- **1** **Smileswithhiseyes (IRE)**[39] 7923 3-9-3 **70**................ RobertWinston 1 76
(Gay Kelleway) *t.k.h: trckd ldr: rdn over 2f out: ev ch over 1f out: led 1f out: wnt rt but r.o wl and drew clr fnl 100yds* **9/4**[2]
51- **2** *2 ½* **Ningara**[26] 8071 3-9-7 **74**... DavidProbert 4 74
(Andrew Balding) *led and set stdy gallop: rdn and qcknd but hanging lft fr 2f out: hdd 1f out: stl gng lft and outpcd fnl 100yds* **4/5**[1]
300- **3** *nk* **First Sargeant**[30] 8033 3-9-3 **70**.. AdamKirby 2 69
(Marco Botti) *sn chsng ldr: rdn wl over 2f out: ev ch over 1f out: carried lft and bmpd ins fnl f: outpcd fnl 100yds* **3/1**[3]
1m 40.86s (1.06) **Going Correction** +0.025s/f (Slow) 3 Ran SP% **111.3**
Speed ratings (Par 97): **95,92,92**
CSF £4.67 TOTE £3.80; EX 3.90 Trifecta £4.40 Pool: £607.90 - 102.71 winning units..
Owner Robert Ng **Bred** B Walsh **Trained** Exning, Suffolk
FOCUS
Only three runners. They went a steady early pace and the race developed into a 2f sprint. Muddling form, the winner building on his C&D win.

92 32REDPOKER.COM CLASSIFIED CLAIMING STKS 6f (P)
3:00 (3:00) (Class 6) 4-Y-0+ **£1,940** (£577; £288; £144) **Stalls** Low

Form RPR
61-5 **1** **Dark Lane**[5] 27 7-8-9 66.. LukeMorris 3 69
(David Evans) *chsd ldng trio: rdn and chal wl over 1f out: led over 1f out: clr ins fnl f: drvn fnl 100yds: a jst holding on* **9/4**[2]
536- **2** *nk* **Dixie Gwalia**[9] 8287 5-8-3 50.. MartinLane 6 62
(David Simcock) *t.k.h: hld up in tch: rdn and effrt 2f out: chsd wnr fnl 100yds: styd on wl towards fin: nvr quite getting to wnr* **33/1**
242- **3** *2 ½* **Beat The Bell**[8] 8294 8-8-4 73 ow1...............................(p) MartinDwyer 7 55
(Jamie Osborne) *pressed ldr on outer: ev ch and rdn wl over 1f out: drvn and no ex 1f out: wknd fnl 100yds* **13/8**[1]
604- **4** *3 ¼* **Where's Reiley (USA)**[9] 8285 7-8-4 72.................(p) LeonnaMayor(5) 1 50
(Alastair Lidderdale) *led on inner: rdn over 2f out: hdd over 1f out: edgd rt and fdd ins fnl f* **11/4**[3]
565- **5** *1 ¾* **Fairy Wing (IRE)**[7] 8308 6-9-1 70.....................................(p) AdamKirby 5 50
(Conor Dore) *sn bustled along: in tch in last pair: struggling u.p 1/2-way: bhd and swtchd rt 2f out: plugged on* **8/1**
00-0 **6** *4* **The Jailer**[1] 81 10-8-2 47..(p) AaronJones(7) 4 31
(John O'Shea) *w ldrs tl over 2f out: wkng whn edgd lft 2f out: sn bhd* **66/1**
1m 12.61s (-0.49) **Going Correction** +0.025s/f (Slow) 6 Ran SP% **111.1**
Speed ratings (Par 101): **104,103,100,95,93 88**
toteswingers 1&2 £6.50, 1&3 £1.70, 2&3 £4.90 CSF £55.12 TOTE £3.70: £1.40, £14.90; EX 44.00 Trifecta £217.20 Pool: £1,529.17 - 5.28 winning units..Beat The Bell was claimed by Mr Declan Carroll for £3,000. Dixie Gwalia was claimed by Mr P. D. Evans for £3,000. Fairy Wing was claimed by Mr S. Arnold for £9,000.
Owner Jason Tucker **Bred** David Jamison Bloodstock **Trained** Pandy, Monmouths

FOCUS
A fair claimer in which the pace was strong, and this set it up for those ridden in behind. The runner-up is the key to the form, which has been rated cautiously.

93 32RED H'CAP 1m 4f (P)
3:30 (3:30) (Class 4) (0-85,85) 4-Y-0+ £4,690 (£1,395; £697; £348) Stalls Centre

Form RPR

122- 1 **Noble Silk**[18] 8191 4-9-2 **81**....(p) LukeMorris 3 86
(Lucy Wadham) *in tch in last trio: rdn and effrt jst over 2f out: hdwy u.p 1f out: chsd ldr fnl 100yds: r.o wl to ld cl home* **7/2**[1]

061- 2 ½ **Wildomar**[18] 8191 4-9-1 **80**.... AdamKirby 6 84
(John Ryan) *hld up in tch in last trio: hdwy to chse ldr 7f out: rdn and qcknd to ld over 2f out: kpt on wl u.p tl hdd and no ex cl home* **7/2**[1]

/26- 3 nk **Noguchi (IRE)**[19] 8174 8-9-2 **77**.... TomMcLaughlin 2 80
(Michael Murphy) *t.k.h: chsd ldrs: rdn and effrt over 2f out: chsd wnr 2f out: kpt on u.p ins fnl f* **14/1**

155- 4 nk **Odin (IRE)**[19] 8174 5-9-4 **79**.... EddieAhern 4 82
(Don Cantillon) *hld up in tch in midfield: rdn and effrt on inner 2f out: chsd ldrs ins fnl f: kpt on* **7/1**[2]

250- 5 ¾ **Solfilia**[16] 8227 4-9-3 **82**.... GeorgeBaker 1 84
(Hughie Morrison) *t.k.h: hld up in tch in last trio: rdn and gd hdwy over 1f out: styd on same pce u.p ins fnl f* **7/1**[2]

021- 6 nk **Roberto Pegasus (USA)**[53] 2887 7-9-10 **85**.... FergusSweeney 8 86
(Alan King) *hld up in midfield: rdn and effrt over 2f out: hdwy over 1f out: kpt on ins fnl f but no real threat to ldrs* **9/1**[3]

254- 7 1 ½ **Moderator**[33] 7999 4-8-7 **79**.... NedCurtis(7) 7 78
(Gary Moore) *chsd ldrs: rdn and lost pl whn pce qcknd jst over 2f out: kpt on again fnl f but no threat to ldrs* **7/2**[1]

200/ 8 10 **King Olav (UAE)**[471] 2604 8-9-7 **82**.... JimCrowley 5 65
(Tony Carroll) *led tl hdd and rdn over 2f out: wknd over 1f out: bhd ins fnl f* **25/1**

2m 38.44s (3.94) **Going Correction** +0.025s/f (Slow)
WFA 4 from 5yo+ 4lb 8 Ran SP% **112.2**
Speed ratings (Par 105): **87,86,86,86,85 85,84,77**
toteswingers 1&2 £10.50, 1&3 £2.10, 2&3 £9.80 CSF £14.66 CT £147.01 TOTE £3.60: £1.60, £1.50, £5.30; EX 10.30 Trifecta £237.00 Pool: £1,185.33 - 3.75 winning units..
Owner The FOPS **Bred** Mr & Mrs A E Pakenham **Trained** Newmarket, Suffolk

FOCUS
A wide-open and competitive handicap but the pace was steady and they finished well bunched. The winner came up the centre. The first two are rated to their Lingfield latest.

94 32REDBET.COM H'CAP 1m 3f (P)
4:00 (4:02) (Class 6) (0-60,60) 4-Y-0+ £1,940 (£577; £288; £144) Stalls Low

Form RPR

033- 1 **Sweet Liberta (IRE)**[16] 8229 4-8-11 **53**.... DavidProbert 7 63
(Andrew Balding) *hld up in tch in midfield: rdn and hdwy 2f out: led ins fnl f: r.o strly* **9/2**[3]

300- 2 1 ¾ **Tinkerbell Will**[68] 7479 6-8-6 **48**.... NataliaGemelova(3) 6 55
(John E Long) *t.k.h: hld up in midfield: rdn and hdwy over 2f out: styng on whn swtchd lft over 1f out: r.o wl to go 2nd towards fin* **14/1**

200- 3 ½ **Missionaire (USA)**[11] 8260 6-9-0 **53**.... JimCrowley 3 59
(Tony Carroll) *chsd ldrs: rdn to ld over 1f out: drvn and hdd ins fnl f: one pce after and lost 2nd towards fin* **25/1**

220- 4 ¾ **Roman Senate (IRE)**[93] 6892 4-8-10 **52**....(tp) MartinLane 13 57
(Martin Bosley) *chsd ldr tl over 5f out: chsd ldr again over 4f out tl jst ins fnl f: styd on same pce fnl 150yds* **16/1**

51-5 5 nk **Calypso Magic (IRE)**[5] 21 5-9-4 **57**....(t) KirstyMilczarek 14 61
(Olivia Maylam) *hld up in midfield: swtchd lft and hdwy to ld over 5f out: rdn and hdd over 1f out: stl pressing ldr tl no ex ins fnl f* **8/1**

012- 6 ¾ **Bridge That Gap**[10] 8265 5-9-2 **55**.... FergusSweeney 10 58
(Roger Ingram) *hld up towards rr: hdwy into midfield 1/2-way: rdn and chsd ldrs 2f out: unable qck and styd on same pce fr over 1f out* **7/2**[1]

054- 7 ¾ **Menadati (USA)**[11] 8249 5-9-7 **60**.... AdamKirby 9 61
(Peter Hiatt) *hld up in tch in last trio: n.m.r over 2f out: hdwy over 1f out: kpt on ins fnl f but no threat to ldrs* **4/1**[2]

240- 8 1 **Awesome Rock (IRE)**[11] 8260 4-8-8 **50**.... RobertWinston 8 50
(Louise Best) *hld up in tch in last quartet: rdn and hdwy over 1f out: styd on ins fnl f: no threat to ldrs* **14/1**

500- 9 nk **Archelao (IRE)**[11] 8248 5-9-5 **58**.... AmirQuinn 2 57
(Richard Rowe) *chsd ldrs: rdn and effrt ent fnl 2f: unable qck over 1f out: styd on same pce fnl f* **14/1**

006- 10 3 ¼ **Prince Of Thebes (IRE)**[10] 8264 12-8-7 **46** oh1....(v) JohnFahy 1 39
(Michael Attwater) *dwlt: hld up in tch in rr: rdn and no hdwy over 2f out: plugged on fnl f but no threat to ldrs* **66/1**

604- 11 nk **Beggers Belief**[35] 7960 5-9-3 **56**....(b) LukeMorris 5 49
(Eric Wheeler) *in tch in midfield: rdn over 4f out: drvn and unable qck over 2f out: wknd over 1f out* **10/1**

000- 12 3 **Gower Rules (IRE)**[18] 8180 5-8-12 **51**.... KieranO'Neill 11 38
(John Bridger) *led tl over 5f out: styd chsng ldrs tl wknd u.p over 1f out* **25/1**

400- 13 6 **Nowdoro**[61] 7632 4-8-5 **47** oh1 ow1....(t) MartinDwyer 4 23
(Julie Camacho) *in tch in midfield: rdn and lost pl over 4f out: no ch over 1f out* **20/1**

530- 14 3 ¾ **Herschel (IRE)**[33] 7991 7-8-5 **51**.... NedCurtis(7) 12 21
(Gary Moore) *chsd ldrs tl lost pl over 2f out: sn wknd and bhd fnl f* **33/1**

2m 21.15s (-0.75) **Going Correction** +0.025s/f (Slow)
WFA 4 from 5yo+ 3lb 14 Ran SP% **123.4**
Speed ratings (Par 101): **103,101,101,100,100 100,99,98,98,96 95,93,89,86**
toteswingers 1&2 £13.90, 1&3 £13.60, 2&3 £70.70 CSF £63.62 CT £1450.52 TOTE £3.10: £1.10, £6.20, £7.40; EX 93.80 Trifecta £843.80 Pool: £1,125.17 - 0.10 winning units..
Owner Mick and Janice Mariscotti **Bred** W Maxwell Ervine **Trained** Kingsclere, Hants

FOCUS
A modest handicap, but quite competitive for the grade. The form makes a fair bit of sense.

95 £32 FREE AT 32RED.COM H'CAP 6f (P)
4:30 (4:31) (Class 5) (0-75,75) 4-Y-0+ £2,587 (£770; £384; £192) Stalls Low

Form RPR

21-2 1 **Lastkingofscotland (IRE)**[5] 11 7-9-7 **75**....(b) GeorgeBaker 2 85
(Conor Dore) *mde all: shkn and readily wnt clr wl over 1f out: r.o wl and in command fnl f* **4/6**[1]

000- 2 1 ½ **Dominium (USA)**[107] 6495 6-9-3 **71**....(b) RenatoSouza 4 75
(Jeremy Gask) *hld up in tch in last pair: rdn and effrt on inner 2f out: chsd clr wnr over 1f out: styd on but no imp* **7/1**

061- 3 4 ½ **Belinsky (IRE)**[20] 8159 6-8-12 **66**.... JimCrowley 1 56
(Julie Camacho) *chsd ldrs: rdn and chsd clr wnr wl over 1f out tl ent fnl f: sn outpcd and wl btn ins fnl f* **3/1**[2]

500- 4 ½ **Swendab (IRE)**[59] 7666 5-8-10 **64**....(v) FergusSweeney 6 52
(John O'Shea) *chsd ldr tl wl over 1f out: sn outpcd and wl btn 1f out: plugged on* **16/1**

600- 5 2 ¾ **Perlachy**[95] 6824 9-8-12 **66**....(v) LukeMorris 5 45
(Ronald Harris) *in tch in midfield: rdn and unable qck over 2f out: outpcd and no ch over 1f out* **25/1**

050- 6 5 **Monsieur Jamie**[53] 7726 5-9-5 **73**.... IanMongan 3 36
(J R Jenkins) *t.k.h: chsd ldrs tl over 2f out: sn rdn and lost pl: bhd 1f out* **20/1**

200- 7 10 **Black Cadillac (IRE)**[180] 3960 5-9-4 **72**.... DavidProbert 8
(Andrew Balding) *stdd s: hld up in last pair: wknd 2f out: bhd and eased wl ins fnl f* **7/2**[3]

1m 12.46s (-0.64) **Going Correction** +0.025s/f (Slow) 7 Ran SP% **134.2**
Speed ratings (Par 103): **105,103,97,96,92 86,72**
toteswingers 1&2 £3.00, 1&3 £1.70, 2&3 £4.80 CSF £8.84 CT £13.56 TOTE £1.70: £1.20, £4.40; EX 13.80 Trifecta £53.50 Pool: £1,930.20 - 27.04 winning units..
Owner Mrs Jennifer Marsh **Bred** Baronrath Stud **Trained** Hubbert's Bridge, Lincs

FOCUS
The winner was well in on last week's good effort here, and is rated close to his best form.
T/Plt: £1,129.40 to a £1 stake. Pool: £4,7421.26 - 30.65 winning tickets T/Qpdt: £60.60 to a £1 stake. Pool: £4,622.07 - 56.40 winning tickets SP

[81] WOLVERHAMPTON (A.W) (L-H)
Monday, January 7

OFFICIAL GOING: Standard
Wind: Light behind Weather: Overcast

96 ONLINE BETTING OFFERS AT BOOKMAKERS.CO.UK APPRENTICE H'CAP 7f 32y(P)
2:20 (2:20) (Class 6) (0-65,65) 4-Y-0+ £1,940 (£577; £288; £144) Stalls High

Form RPR

421- 1 **Spark Of Genius**[34] 7978 4-9-2 **63**.... WilliamTwiston-Davies(3) 5 74+
(Alan McCabe) *trckd ldrs: led over 1f out: edgd lft ins fnl f: rdn out* **13/8**[1]

001- 2 1 ¾ **Bang Tidy (IRE)**[24] 8114 4-8-12 **56**....(t) AshleyMorgan 4 62
(Brian Ellison) *hld up: hdwy 1/2-way: rdn over 1f out: r.o* **11/2**[2]

060- 3 ¾ **Mataajir (USA)**[10] 8271 5-8-4 **55**.... AdamMcLean(7) 2 59
(Derek Shaw) *led: rdn and hdd over 1f out: edgd lft ins fnl f: styd on same pce* **12/1**

663- 4 nk **Piccolo Express**[24] 8115 7-8-11 **58**.... AdamCarter(3) 9 62
(Brian Baugh) *hld up: hdwy over 1f out: sn rdn: r.o* **8/1**

314- 5 hd **Tidal's Baby**[26] 8074 4-9-6 **64**.... RyanClark 10 67
(Tony Carroll) *hld up: hdwy over 1f out: rdn and nt clr run ins fnl f: r.o* **6/1**[3]

616- 6 3 ¼ **Lucky Mark (IRE)**[20] 8156 4-8-11 **60**.... GeorgeChaloner(5) 8 54
(Garry Moss) *chsd ldr tl rdn over 1f out: wknd ins fnl f* **6/1**[3]

063- 7 1 ¼ **Sir Bruno (FR)**[24] 8114 6-9-7 **65**....(p) DeclanCannon 7 56
(Bryn Palling) *chsd ldrs: rdn over 2f out: edgd lft over 1f out: wknd fnl f* **8/1**

250- 8 ½ **Unlimited**[10] 8269 11-9-0 **65**.... AidenBlakemore(7) 1 55
(Tony Carroll) *hld up: rdn over 1f out: n.d* **50/1**

400- 9 7 **Upper Lambourn (IRE)**[16] 8236 5-9-3 **64**.... NathanAlison(3) 3 35
(Christopher Kellett) *prom: pushed along over 4f out: wknd over 1f out* **100/1**

000- 10 nse **Hellbender (IRE)**[95] 6812 7-9-4 **65**....[1] LMcNiff(3) 6 35
(George Foster) *hld up: a in rr: wknd 2f out* **28/1**

1m 27.96s (-1.64) **Going Correction** -0.15s/f (Stan) 10 Ran SP% **118.4**
Speed ratings (Par 101): **103,101,100,99,99 95,94,93,85,85**
toteswingers 1&2 £2.50, 1&3 £7.40, 2&3 £13.40 CSF £10.81 CT £82.44 TOTE £1.80: £1.10, £1.60, £5.90; EX 8.70 Trifecta £57.00 Pool: £984.39 - 12.94 winning units..
Owner Shropshire Wolves 4 **Bred** Elsdon Farms **Trained** Averham Park, Notts

FOCUS
A fair race for the grade with several in decent form. The second and fourth help with the level.

97 COMPARE BOOKIES WITH BOOKMAKERS.CO.UK (S) STKS 1m 141y(P)
2:50 (2:50) (Class 6) 4-Y-0+ £1,940 (£577; £288; £144) Stalls Low

Form RPR

62-3 1 **One Way Or Another (AUS)**[5] 15 10-8-13 66....(t) GrahamGibbons 1 69
(David Evans) *chsd ldr tl over 5f out: remained handy: led over 1f out: sn rdn: r.o* **7/4**[1]

200- 2 nk **Violent Velocity (IRE)**[134] 5618 10-8-13 70.... MichaelO'Connell 3 68
(John Quinn) *a.p: chsd ldr over 5f out tl rdn over 1f out: r.o* **9/4**[2]

030- 3 3 ¼ **Abhaath (USA)**[18] 8183 4-8-12 66.... WilliamCarson 2 61
(Ronald Harris) *dwlt: hld up: pushed along over 3f out: rdn over 1f out: styd on same pce fnl f* **3/1**[3]

143- 4 nse **Bold Marc (IRE)**[10] 8261 11-9-4 64....(p) SeanLevey 4 66
(Mrs K Burke) *led: rdn and hdd over 1f out: no ex ins fnl f* **5/1**

1m 49.71s (-0.79) **Going Correction** -0.15s/f (Stan)
WFA 4 from 10yo+ 1lb 4 Ran SP% **108.8**
Speed ratings (Par 101): **97,96,93,93**
CSF £5.96 TOTE £1.40; EX 5.70 Trifecta £7.80 Pool: £713.82 - 68.53 winning units..There was no bid for the winner.
Owner Mrs E Evans **Bred** Segenho Stud **Trained** Pandy, Monmouths
■ Stewards' Enquiry : Michael O'Connell two-day ban: used whip above permitted level (Jan 21-22)

FOCUS
Just four runners and the pace in this seller was fairly steady. The winner is rated to his autumn form.

98 CORAL.CO.UK H'CAP 1m 1f 103y(P)
3:20 (3:20) (Class 6) (0-58,58) 4-Y-0+ £1,940 (£577; £288; £144) Stalls Low

Form RPR

004- 1 **Flag Of Glory**[21] 8146 6-9-3 **54**.... WilliamCarson 10 65
(Peter Hiatt) *mde all: rdn over 1f out: edgd lft ins fnl f: styd on* **5/1**[3]

053- 2 2 ¾ **Arabian Flight**[9] 8288 4-9-6 **58**.... AndrewMullen 1 63
(Michael Appleby) *a.p: chsd wnr over 3f out: rdn over 1f out: styd on same pce ins fnl f* **4/1**[2]

00-4 3 2 ½ **Moheebb (IRE)**[3] 61 9-9-7 **58**.... RobbieFitzpatrick 7 58+
(Robert Johnson) *hld up: hmpd wl over 2f out: sn pushed along: r.o ins fnl f: nt rch ldrs* **11/2**

003- 4 nk **Petersboden**[18] 8179 4-8-8 **46**.... NickyMackay 13 45
(Michael Blanshard) *mid-div: hdwy over 5f out: rdn over 2f out: edgd lft and no ex fnl f* **14/1**

006- 5 1 **Justine Time (IRE)**[134] 5623 4-8-8 **46**....[1] BarryMcHugh 2 43
(Julie Camacho) *hld up: hdwy over 3f out: rdn over 1f out: no ex whn nt clr run ins fnl f* **40/1**

645- **6** *1* **Koo And The Gang (IRE)**^{40} 7917 6-9-4 **55**............ GrahamGibbons 6 50
(Brian Ellison) *prom: rdn over 2f out: styd on same pce fr over 1f out* **3/1**^{1}

033- **7** *3¼* **Corrib (IRE)**^{12} 8241 10-8-6 **46** oh1..........(p) DeclanCannon(3) 5 34
(Bryn Palling) *s.i.s: hld up: rdn and hung lft over 1f out: n.d* **20/1**

060- **8** *3* **Bonnie Prince Blue**^{17} 8214 10-9-4 **55**..........(b) DaleSwift 11 37
(Ian McInnes) *hld up: drvn along over 2f out: n.d* **66/1**

060- **9** *3¼* **Master Of Song**^{23} 8137 6-9-4 **58**..........(p) MarkCoumbe(3) 3 33
(Roy Bowring) *s.s: hld up: hdwy on outer over 2f out: rdn and wknd over 1f out* **22/1**

421- **10** *4½* **Spin A Wish**^{62} 7599 5-8-12 **49**.......... PaulQuinn 4 15
(Richard Whitaker) *prom: pushed along whn hmpd and wknd wl over 2f out* **10/1**

000- **11** *1½* **Pipers Piping (IRE)**^{33} 7993 7-9-7 **58**.......... ChrisCatlin 9 21
(John Butler) *chsd ldrs: lost pl over 4f out: rdn and wknd over 2f out* **10/1**

060/ **12** *18* **Hurricane Spear**^{562} 3393 5-8-9 **46** oh1..........(b^{1}) SeanLevey 8
(Ricardo Lanfranco) *chsd wnr 6f: rdn and wknd over 2f out: t.o* **20/1**

1m 59.97s (-1.73) **Going Correction** -0.15s/f (Stan)
WFA 4 from 5yo+ 1lb **12** Ran SP% **119.7**
Speed ratings (Par 101): **101,98,96,96,95 94,91,88,85,81 80,64**
toteswingers 1&2 £4.80, 1&3 £7.70, 2&3 £4.70 CSF £23.86 CT £116.39 TOTE £5.60: £2.00, £1.60, £2.00; EX 25.30 Trifecta £137.80 Pool: £895.41 - 4.87 winning units..
Owner N D Edden **Bred** Follow The Flag Partnership **Trained** Hook Norton, Oxon
■ Stewards' Enquiry : William Carson one-day ban: careless riding (Jan 21)

FOCUS
This low-grade handicap was a tactical affair, with the winner receiving a well-judged ride from the front. He built on his latest C&D run.

99 GET FREE BETS WITH BOOKMAKERS.CO.UK H'CAP (DIV I) 1m 4f 50y(P)
3:50 (3:50) (Class 6) (0-52,57) 4-Y-O+ **£1,940** (£577; £288; £144) **Stalls** Low

Form RPR

50-1 **1** **Rosie's Lady (IRE)**^{6} 7 4-9-8 **57** 6ex.......... DanielTudhope 10 69
(David O'Meara) *a.p: chsd ldr over 3f out: led on bit over 2f out: sn shkn up and clr: eased nr fin* **5/4**^{1}

600- **2** *5* **Seawood**^{220} 2670 7-8-12 **46** oh1.......... MarkCoumbe(3) 12 49
(Roy Bowring) *hld up: hdwy over 2f out: rdn over 1f out: styd on: no ch w wnr* **20/1**

044- **3** *¾* **Landown Littlerock**^{17} 8213 4-8-11 **51**..........(p) JackDuern(5) 5 53
(Reg Hollinshead) *a.p: rdn to go 2nd over 1f out: styd on same pce* **7/2**^{2}

635/ **4** *½* **Seaquel**^{855} 3290 7-9-1 **46** oh1.......... JimmyQuinn 4 47
(Tony Carroll) *hld up: hdwy u.p and hung lft over 1f out: nt trble ldrs* **25/1**

645- **5** *1¼* **Spring Secret**^{48} 7800 7-9-2 **50**.......... DeclanCannon(3) 1 49
(Bryn Palling) *hld up in tch: rdn and edgd lft wl over 1f out: styd on same pce* **9/1**

566- **6** *2¼* **Waldsee (GER)**^{24} 8104 8-9-4 **49**.......... AdamBeschizza 9 44
(Sean Curran) *s.i.s: hld up: rdn over 3f out: nvr nrr* **6/1**^{3}

00-4 **7** *3½* **Bygones For Coins (IRE)**^{3} 63 5-9-1 **51**. WilliamTwiston-Davies(5) 8 41
(Robert Johnson) *led: rdn and hdd over 2f out: wknd over 1f out* **12/1**

000- **8** *5* **Ivan The Engine**^{28} 8055 5-9-1 **46** oh1..........(t) SebSanders 6 28
(Paul Fitzsimons) *s.i.s: hld up: rdn whn hmpd wl over 2f out: nvr on terms* **25/1**

000- **9** *3¼* **Chik's Dream**^{30} 8038 6-9-1 **46** oh1.......... WilliamCarson 11 23
(Derek Haydn Jones) *chsd ldr tl pushed along over 3f out: wknd 2f out* **25/1**

/00- **10** *5* **Hector Spectre (IRE)**^{51} 7781 7-9-1 **46** oh1..........(p) FrankieMcDonald 2 15
(Nikki Evans) *chsd ldrs: pushed along over 4f out: wknd over 2f out* **100/1**

2m 38.54s (-2.56) **Going Correction** -0.15s/f (Stan)
WFA 4 from 5yo+ 4lb **10** Ran SP% **115.9**
Speed ratings (Par 101): **102,98,98,97,97 95,93,89,87,84**
toteswingers 1&2 £8.20, 1&3 £2.20, 2&3 £11.40 CSF £35.16 CT £75.45 TOTE £2.30: £1.10, £7.80, £1.10; EX 30.50 Trifecta £134.30 Pool: £902.57 - 5.04 winning units..
Owner Postracing Ltd The Charity Horse **Bred** Mrs Patricia Anne Vermeulen **Trained** Nawton, N Yorks

FOCUS
Division one of a low-grade 1m4f handicap. The pace was sound and the winner travelled easily the best, but she beat little.

100 GET FREE BETS WITH BOOKMAKERS.CO.UK H'CAP (DIV II) 1m 4f 50y(P)
4:20 (4:20) (Class 6) (0-52,52) 4-Y-O+ **£1,940** (£577; £288; £144) **Stalls** Low

Form RPR

/22- **1** **Easydoesit (IRE)**^{11} 8260 5-9-5 **50**.......... JimmyQuinn 1 58
(Tony Carroll) *s.i.s: hld up: hdwy and nt clr run over 2f out: chsd ldr over 1f out: shkn up to ld ins fnl f: r.o* **6/1**

15- **2** *1¼* **Liberty Love (IRE)**^{87} 7046 8-9-7 **52**..........(bt) WilliamCarson 5 58
(Shaun Harley, Ire) *s.i.s: hld up: hdwy over 2f out: rdn over 1f out: r.o 3/1*^{2}

005- **3** *shd* **Icy Quiet**^{17} 8214 5-9-4 **49**.......... DanielTudhope 3 55
(David O'Meara) *led 5f: chsd ldr tl led again 3f out: rdn and hdd ins fnl f: styd on same pce* **11/4**^{1}

00-0 **4** *nk* **Nolecce**^{5} 9 6-9-0 **50**..........(p) JasonHart(5) 9 55+
(Richard Guest) *s.i.s: hld up: nt clr run over 2f out: rdn and r.o ins fnl f: nt rch ldrs* **14/1**

00U- **5** *1½* **Crimson Monarch (USA)**^{27} 8067 9-8-12 **46** oh1..........(b) RyanClark(3) 6 49
(Peter Hiatt) *hld up: nt clr run over 2f out: rnm on u.p ins fnl f: nvr nrr* **33/1**

004- **6** *1½* **Gangsterbanksters (FR)**^{70} 7443 4-8-11 **49**..........(v) DeclanCannon(3) 7 50
(Mrs K Burke) *chsd ldrs: rdn over 2f out: hung lft ins fnl f: styd on same pce* **7/1**

051- **7** *1* **Scribe (IRE)**^{11} 8260 5-9-7 **52**..........(t) GrahamGibbons 10 51
(David Evans) *hld up: hdwy on outer over 2f out: sn rdn: styd on same pce fr over 1f out* **4/1**^{3}

310- **8** *1* **Pass The Time**^{12} 7148 4-8-11 **49**..........(p) AmyBaker(3) 11 46
(Neil Mulholland) *chsd ldr tl led 7f out: pushed along and hdd 3f out: no ex fnl f* **20/1**

060- **9** *5* **Dubai Emerald (USA)**^{29} 8049 4-8-10 **50**.......... JackDuern(5) 8 39
(Chris Dwyer) *hld up: a in rr: outpcd fr over 3f out* **40/1**

050- **10** *3¼* **Sacco D'Oro**^{11} 8260 7-9-1 **46** oh1..........(tp) TomEaves 4 30
(Michael Mullineaux) *chsd ldrs: pushed along whn hmpd and wknd over 2f out* **40/1**

000- **11** *13* **Prince Freddie**^{67} 6230 5-9-5 **50**..........(p) ChrisCatlin 12 13
(Roy Brotherton) *chsd ldrs tl rdn and wknd over 2f out* **28/1**

2m 40.44s (-0.66) **Going Correction** -0.15s/f (Stan)
WFA 4 from 5yo+ 4lb **11** Ran SP% **121.1**
Speed ratings (Par 101): **96,95,95,94,93 92,92,91,88,86 77**
toteswingers 1&2 £3.70, 1&3 £3.70, 2&3 £5.70 CSF £23.85 CT £61.79 TOTE £5.50: £1.90, £2.10, £1.40; EX 24.20 Trifecta £172.60 Pool: £701.93 - 3.05 winning units..
Owner T R Pearson **Bred** Tinnakill Bloodstock & Alan Byrne **Trained** Cropthorne, Worcs
■ Stewards' Enquiry : Amy Baker one-day ban: careless riding (Jan 21)

FOCUS
Part two and the gallop this time was very steady until the final 4f. It was the slower division. The winner stepped up on his latest C&D form, reversing it with the seventh.

101 COMPARE ONLINE BOOKIES AT BOOKMAKERS.CO.UK FILLIES' H'CAP 5f 216y(P)
4:50 (4:50) (Class 5) (0-70,70) 4-Y-O+ **£2,587** (£770; £384; £192) **Stalls** Low

Form RPR

106- **1** **Aubrietia**^{16} 8225 4-9-0 **68**..........(b) WilliamTwiston-Davies(5) 2 86
(Alan McCabe) *mde all: qcknd clr 2f out: rdn out* **4/1**^{2}

003- **2** *5* **Climaxfortackle (IRE)**^{11} 8256 5-8-13 **62**.......... JoeFanning 3 64+
(Derek Shaw) *s.i.s: hld up: hdwy over 1f out: r.o to go 2nd wl ins fnl f: no ch w wnr* **7/2**^{1}

363- **3** *¾* **Above The Stars**^{9} 8285 5-9-1 **64**.......... BarryMcHugh 7 64
(Richard Fahey) *hld up: hdwy over 2f out: rdn to chse wnr who was clr over 1f out: no imp and lost 2nd wl ins fnl f* **4/1**^{2}

500- **4** *2½* **Code Six (IRE)**^{115} 6211 4-8-13 **62**.......... TomEaves 1 54
(Bryan Smart) *chsd ldrs: rdn over 2f out: sn outpcd* **14/1**

220- **5** *nk* **Avonvalley**^{38} 7937 6-9-6 **69**.......... LiamKeniry 8 60
(Peter Grayson) *hld up: rdn and r.o ins fnl f: nvr nrr* **10/1**

00R- **6** *nse* **Blodwen Abbey**^{177} 4081 4-8-12 **68**.......... RobertTart(7) 5 58
(Michael Mullineaux) *s.s: bhd tl r.o ins fnl f: nvr on terms* **33/1**

040- **7** *nk* **Little China**^{187} 3762 4-9-7 **70**.......... WilliamCarson 6 60
(William Muir) *mid-div: hdwy over 1f out: no ex fnl f* **11/1**

036- **8** *nk* **Button Moon (IRE)**^{20} 8160 5-9-4 **67**.......... SebSanders 4 56
(Paul Fitzsimons) *chsd wnr: pushed along over 2f out: lost 2nd over 1f out: wknd fnl f* **5/1**^{3}

122- **9** *4* **Mey Blossom**^{27} 8064 8-8-11 **60**..........(p) GrahamGibbons 9 36
(Richard Whitaker) *chsd ldrs: rdn over 2f out: wkng whn n.m.r over 1f out* **8/1**

1m 12.92s (-2.08) **Going Correction** -0.15s/f (Stan) **9** Ran SP% **117.0**
Speed ratings (Par 100): **107,100,99,96,95 95,95,94,89**
toteswingers 1&2 £5.60, 1&3 £5.10, 2&3 £3.80 CSF £18.72 CT £59.86 TOTE £5.50: £1.70, £1.20, £1.50; EX 28.40 Trifecta £98.30 Pool: £2,067.32 - 15.77 winning units..
Owner Shropshire Wolves 4 **Bred** C J Murfitt **Trained** Averham Park, Notts

FOCUS
The winner had an uncontested lead and scored in a fair time. This has to rate a personal best.

102 CORAL.CO.UK MOBILE CASINO MAIDEN STKS 7f 32y(P)
5:20 (5:21) (Class 5) 3-Y-O **£2,587** (£770; £384; £192) **Stalls** High

Form RPR

\- **1** **Little Dolly** 3-9-0 0.......... SebSanders 8 61
(Alan McCabe) *sn prom: rdn to ld ins fnl f: r.o* **11/1**^{3}

4- **2** *½* **Rapscallion Deep (IRE)**^{30} 8033 3-9-5 0.......... BarryMcHugh 3 65
(Kevin Ryan) *chsd ldr tl led over 5f out: hung rt over 2f out: rdn and hdd ins fnl f: styd on same pce* **4/7**^{1}

050- **3** *4½* **Armada Bay (IRE)**^{17} 8203 3-9-5 40.......... TomEaves 7 53
(Bryan Smart) *chsd ldr: ev ch over 1f out: sn rdn: no ex fnl f* **50/1**

4 *1½* **Petra** 3-9-0 0.......... AndrewMullen 6 43
(Michael Appleby) *s.i.s: hld up: pushed along over 2f out: nvr trbld ldrs* **28/1**

0- **5** *1½* **So Vain (IRE)**^{10} 8262 3-9-5 0.......... GrahamGibbons 1 44
(David Brown) *led: hdd over 5f out: chsd ldrs: rdn over 1f out: wknd fnl f* **12/1**

6 *1¼* **Always Fabulous** 3-9-0 0.......... JoeFanning 4 36
(Mark Johnston) *stmbld s and s.i.s: hdwy over 5f out: rdn over 2f out: wknd over 1f out* **4/1**^{2}

5- **7** *4* **Arabougg**^{17} 8207 3-9-5 0.......... FrankieMcDonald 2 30
(Nikki Evans) *prom: racd keenly: rdn and wknd over 1f out* **80/1**

0- **8** *¾* **Sarahs Pal**^{68} 7491 3-9-0 0.......... JimmyQuinn 5 23
(Mandy Rowland) *s.i.s: hld up: rdn and wknd over 1f out* **150/1**

1m 29.62s (0.02) **Going Correction** -0.15s/f (Stan) **8** Ran SP% **107.0**
Speed ratings (Par 97): **93,92,87,85,83 82,77,77**
toteswingers 1&2 £1.90, 1&3 £19.60, 2&3 £4.70 CSF £15.77 TOTE £15.10: £2.60, £1.02, £9.20; EX 20.90 Trifecta £316.30 Pool: £2,282.28 - 5.41 winning units..
Owner C J Murfitt **Bred** C J Murfitt **Trained** Averham Park, Notts

FOCUS
A weak maiden lacking any strength in depth and the first two finished clear. It's doubtful that the favourite ran to his debut form and the level is shaky.

103 £50 FREE BET AT CORAL.CO.UK H'CAP 1m 1f 103y(P)
5:50 (5:50) (Class 6) (0-60,57) 3-Y-O **£1,259** (£1,259; £288; £144) **Stalls** Low

Form RPR

006- **1** **Salute To Seville (IRE)**^{17} 8200 3-9-7 **57**..........(b^{1}) LiamKeniry 5 59
(J S Moore) *chsd ldr: rdn over 1f out: r.o to dead-heat on line* **12/1**

164- **1** *dht* **Amelia Hull**^{18} 8186 3-9-5 **55**..........(p) JimmyQuinn 8 57
(J S Moore) *chsd ldrs: rdn to ld ins fnl f: jnd on line* **16/1**

60-6 **3** *1* **Precision Strike**^{3} 55 3-8-8 **49**.......... JasonHart(5) 7 49
(Richard Guest) *s.i.s: hld up: hdwy over 1f out: fin wl* **12/1**

432- **4** *2¼* **Dream About You (IRE)**^{18} 8186 3-9-7 **57**..........(p) RobertHavlin 4 52
(Robert Mills) *led: rdn over 1f out: hdd and no ex ins fnl f* **5/1**^{3}

005- **5** *3* **Rosie Future (IRE)**^{130} 5763 3-9-4 **54**.......... ChrisCatlin 2 43
(Rae Guest) *hld up: plld hrd early: pushed along over 3f out: rdn over 2f out: styd on ins fnl f: nvr nrr* **2/1**^{1}

404- **6** *1* **Poetic Verse**^{24} 8112 3-9-6 **56**.......... WilliamCarson 10 43
(Rod Millman) *chsd ldrs: rdn over 2f out: wknd over 1f out* **10/1**

650- **7** *shd* **Gabrial The Duke (IRE)**^{40} 7919 3-9-7 **57**.......... JoeFanning 3 44
(Patrick Morris) *s.s: hld up: rdn over 1f out: nvr on terms* **9/2**^{2}

002- **8** *hd* **Great Ormond (IRE)**^{24} 8112 3-9-3 **53**.......... TomEaves 9 39
(David Simcock) *hld up: shkn up over 1f out: n.d* **6/1**

000- **9** *6* **Positive Parenting (IRE)**^{111} 6330 3-8-9 **45**.......... NickyMackay 6 19
(Stuart Williams) *mid-div: pushed along over 3f out: wknd over 2f out* **20/1**

050- **10** *7* **Crafty Wonder (IRE)**^{107} 6501 3-9-1 **51**.......... GrahamGibbons 1 10
(David Evans) *chsd ldrs: rdn over 3f out: wknd over 1f out* **25/1**

2m 1.17s (-0.53) **Going Correction** -0.15s/f (Stan) **10** Ran SP% **121.4**
: £027, £Owner, £Dr Dean Harron & J S Moore, £BredDr Dean Harron & Ederidge Ltd Trained Trifecta £Upper Lambourn, Berks.
Owner Ron Hull **Bred** New Hall Stud **Trained** Upper Lambourn, Berks
■ Stewards' Enquiry : Jimmy Quinn two-day ban: used whip above permitted level (Jan 21-22)

FOCUS
A low-grade 3yo handicap and the two dead-heaters were both trained by Stan Moore. Few got involved off an ordinary pace.

T/Jkpt: £1,823.80 to a £1 stake. Pool: £35,963.31 - 14.00 winning tickets T/Plt: £9.40 to a £1 stake. Pool: £64,984.74 - 5021.19 winning tickets T/Qpdt: £3.50 to a £1 stake. Pool: £5,671.80 - 1171.20 winning tickets CR

[96]WOLVERHAMPTON (A.W) (L-H)
Tuesday, January 8

OFFICIAL GOING: Standard
Wind: Moderate half behind Weather: Overcast

104 CLAIM FREE BETS TODAY AT BOOKMAKERS.CO.UK H'CAP 7f 32y(P)
2:20 (2:20) (Class 5) (0-75,75) 4-Y-O+ **£2,587** (£770; £384; £192) **Stalls** High

Form RPR
115- 1 **Toga Tiger (IRE)**[165] 4541 6-9-2 **70** RobertWinston 1 79
(Jeremy Gask) *hld up towards rr: smooth hdwy wl over 1f out: rdn ins fnl f: styd on wl to ld last 50yds* **9/1**
005- 2 *hd* **Summerinthecity (IRE)**[17] 8232 6-9-5 **73** MartinDwyer 5 81
(David Nicholls) *trckd ldrs on inner: hdwy 2f out: chsd ldng pair over 1f out: rdn to ld jst ins fnl f: drvn and hdd last 50yds: no ex nr line* **14/1**
652- 3 *¾* **Azrael**[11] 8269 5-9-4 **72** (p) SebSanders 4 78
(Alan McCabe) *cl up: led after 1f: rdn 2f out: drvn ent fnl f: sn hdd and kpt on same pce* **4/1**[2]
150- 4 *nk* **Smalljohn**[50] 7790 7-9-7 **75** (v) TomEaves 3 80
(Bryan Smart) *led 1f: cl up: chsd ldr 2f out and sn rdn: drvn and ev ch ent fnl f: kpt on same pce* **14/1**
534- 5 *3* **Thereabouts (USA)**[140] 5454 4-8-12 **66** AndrewMullen 7 63
(Michael Appleby) *dwlt and in rr tl styd on fnl 2f: nrst fin* **22/1**
06-0 6 *shd* **Fred Willetts (IRE)**[2] 86 5-9-2 **75** (v) WilliamTwiston-Davies[(5)] 6 72
(Mark Brisbourne) *trckd ldrs: hdwy 3f out: rdn along on outer 2f out: sn drvn and no imp appr fnl f* **5/1**[3]
211- 7 *nk* **Mr Knightley (IRE)**[19] 8177 4-9-7 **75** (b) JimCrowley 9 71
(Roger Ingram) *hld up in tch: sme hdwy over 2f out: sn rdn and no imp fr over 1f out* **7/2**[1]
00-5 8 *6* **Caldercruix (USA)**[6] 11 6-9-4 **75** (v) RaulDaSilva[(3)] 8 55
(James Evans) *trckd ldr: effrt over 2f out: sn rdn and wknd wl over 1f out* **13/2**
245- 9 *1 ¾* **Rossetti**[12] 8259 5-9-4 **72** StevieDonohoe 10 47
(Ian Williams) *hld up: a in rr* **4/1**[2]

1m 27.09s (-2.51) **Going Correction** -0.175s/f (Stan) **9 Ran SP% 119.9**
Speed ratings (Par 103): **107,106,105,105,102 102,101,94,92**
toteswingers 1&2 £15.90, 2&3 £12.10, 1&3 £8.30 CSF £129.76 CT £590.44 TOTE £11.70: £3.40, £5.70, £1.80; EX 228.20 Trifecta £1425.80 Pool: £2558.16 - 1.34 winning units..
Owner For Sale **Bred** Daniel Spaight **Trained** Sutton Veny, Wilts

FOCUS
Track GallopMastered after race four. A competitive handicap for the grade and run at a true gallop throughout. Fair form for the grade, rated around the fourth.

105 HORSE RACING FREE BETS AT BOOKMAKERS.CO.UK H'CAP 7f 32y(P)
2:50 (2:50) (Class 6) (0-52,53) 4-Y-O+ **£2,045** (£603; £302) **Stalls** High

Form RPR
002- 1 **Coastal Passage**[10] 8291 5-9-5 **50** AdamKirby 2 60
(Charles Smith) *trckd ldr: hdwy 2f out: rdn to ld ent fnl f: drvn last 100yds and hld on wl* **3/1**[2]
06-3 2 *nk* **Kielty's Folly**[6] 24 9-9-6 **51** WilliamCarson 10 60
(Brian Baugh) *trckd ldrs on inner: smooth hdwy over 2f out: cl up and swtchd rt 1 1/2f out: effrt and ev ch ins fnl f: sn drvn and kpt on* **9/2**[3]
500- 3 *2 ½* **Flumps**[38] 7952 4-9-1 **46** oh1 (b[1]) JohnFahy 6 48
(John Stimpson) *dwlt and towards rr: hdwy wl over 2f out: sn rdn: styd on appr fnl f: nrst fin* **33/1**
60-0 4 *¾* **Sleepy Lucy**[5] 35 4-8-10 **46** oh1 (e) JasonHart[(5)] 1 46
(Richard Guest) *bhd: hdwy on wd outside 2f out: sn rdn and kpt on fnl f: nrst fin* **16/1**
03-1 5 *¾* **Dhhamaan (IRE)**[5] 42 8-9-8 **53** 6ex (b) JamesSullivan 8 51
(Ruth Carr) *led: rdn along 2f out: hdd ent fnl f: sn wknd* **2/1**[1]
430- 6 *2 ½* **Essell**[25] 8113 4-9-1 **51** CharlesBishop[(5)] 7 42
(Mick Channon) *hld up towards rr: hdwy over 2f out: sn rdn and no imp* **11/2**
000- 7 *1* **Forever Janey**[18] 8209 4-9-1 **46** oh1 LukeMorris 9 35
(Paul Green) *chsd ldrs: rdn along over 2f out: grad wknd* **66/1**
60- 8 *1* **Son Of May**[177] 2748 4-9-7 **52** (b) J-PGuillambert 5 38
(Jo Hughes) *midfield: rdn along over 3f out: wknd over 2f out* **13/2**
6/0- 9 *nk* **Chorister Girl**[34] 7993 4-8-10 **46** oh1 RachealKneller[(5)] 3 31
(Richard Ford) *prom: rdn along over 2f out: wknd wl over 1f out* **33/1**

1m 28.66s (-0.94) **Going Correction** -0.175s/f (Stan) **9 Ran SP% 118.5**
Speed ratings (Par 101): **98,97,94,93,93 90,89,87,87**
toteswingers 1&2 £2.80, 2&3 £10.60, 1&3 £21.50 CSF £17.31 CT £376.27 TOTE £2.70: £1.10, £1.40, £7.70; EX 15.10 Trifecta £207.70 Pool: £2057.21 - 7.42 winning units..
Owner Willie McKay **Bred** D J P Turner **Trained** Temple Bruer, Lincs

FOCUS
A weak handicap, with little strength in depth. The pace was good though, and the form makes sense among the front pair.

106 CORAL.CO.UK H'CAP 5f 216y(P)
3:25 (3:27) (Class 5) (0-70,68) 3-Y-O **£2,587** (£770; £384; £192) **Stalls** Low

Form RPR
434- 1 **Groove On (IRE)**[20] 8165 3-9-7 **68** (t) AdamKirby 9 74+
(Marco Botti) *trckd ldrs gng wl: pushed along and sltly outpcd wl over 1f out: rdn and hdwy ent fnl f: sn edgd lft: led last 100yds: sn clr* **11/4**[1]
21-2 2 *1 ¾* **Windforpower (IRE)**[5] 38 3-9-7 **68** (be) LukeMorris 4 68
(Ronald Harris) *trckd ldr: hdwy on inner over 1f out: effrt and ev ch ins fnl f: sn rdn: kpt on* **7/1**[3]
205- 3 *shd* **Sewn Up**[13] 8240 3-9-6 **67** (t) ChrisCatlin 5 67
(Reg Hollinshead) *hld up: hdwy 1/2-way: chsd ldrs on outer 2f out: rdn and cl up over 1f out: led briefly ins fnl f: hdd and one pce last 100yds* **7/1**[3]
225- 4 *¾* **Marvelino**[19] 8178 3-9-7 **68** RobertWinston 1 65
(Pat Eddery) *led: rdn along 2f out: drvn and jnd ent fnl f: sn hdd and one pce* **11/4**[1]
063- 5 *2 ½* **Duchess Of Dreams**[12] 8254 3-8-12 **59** RobbieFitzpatrick 8 48
(Richard Guest) *in rr: hdwy on wd outside 2f out: rdn wl over 1f out: sn no imp* **22/1**
643- 6 *2 ¼* **Loulou Vuitton**[11] 8274 3-8-13 **60** WilliamCarson 2 42
(Brian Baugh) *dwlt and towards rr: rdn along wl over 2f out: sn outpcd* **5/1**[2]

354- 7 *1* **We Are City**[74] 7379 3-8-9 **61** WilliamTwiston-Davies[(5)] 6 40
(Michael Bell) *trckd ldr: cl up 3f out: rdn along 2f out: sn wknd* **5/1**[2]

1m 14.36s (-0.64) **Going Correction** -0.175s/f (Stan) **7 Ran SP% 116.0**
Speed ratings (Par 97): **97,94,94,93,90 87,85**
toteswingers 1&2 £3.00, 2&3 £5.70, 1&3 £5.00 CSF £23.50 CT £122.39 TOTE £3.40: £1.40, £2.70; EX 19.60 Trifecta £109.70 Pool: £2529.72 - 17.29 winning units..
Owner Mrs Lucie Botti **Bred** L K I Bloodstock Ltd **Trained** Newmarket, Suffolk

FOCUS
A competitive handicap for the grade, and the form has a fairly solid look to it, based around the runner-up.

107 £50 FREE BET AT CORAL.CO.UK H'CAP 1m 4f 50y(P)
3:55 (3:55) (Class 5) (0-70,70) 4-Y-O+ **£2,726** (£805; £402) **Stalls** Low

Form RPR
45-2 1 **Renegotiate**[7] 1 4-9-1 **65** AdamKirby 7 76
(Dr Richard Newland) *mde all: rdn 2f out: drvn ins fnl f and kpt on strly* **3/1**[1]
453- 2 *1 ¼* **Cosmic Halo**[13] 8243 4-9-1 **65** BarryMcHugh 8 74
(Richard Fahey) *trckd ldrs: hdwy over 2f out: rdn to chse wnr ins fnl f: sn drvn and kpt on same pce* **10/3**[2]
423- 3 *½* **Strike Force**[9] 8297 9-9-4 **69** (t) TobyAtkinson[(5)] 1 77
(Alison Hutchinson) *trckd ldrs: effrt over 2f out: rdn and ev ch ent fnl f: kpt on same pce* **16/1**
015- 4 *2 ¼* **Honoured (IRE)**[13] 8243 6-9-4 **64** (t) AndrewMullen 4 68
(Michael Appleby) *hld up in tch: hdwy on outer 4f out: rdn to chse ldrs 2f out: drvn and no imp fnl f* **6/1**
326- 5 *2* **Bradbury (IRE)**[73] 6493 5-9-10 **70** (p) TomEaves 2 71
(Donald McCain) *dwlt and pushed along early: towards rr: hdwy 4f out: rdn along wl over 2f out: n.d* **4/1**[3]
030- 6 *16* **Jeer (IRE)**[13] 8243 9-9-5 **65** (bt) JamesSullivan 3 41
(Michael Easterby) *chsd wnr: rdn along 3f out: drvn 2f out and sn wknd* **12/1**
620- 7 *12* **Sweet Lavender (IRE)**[25] 8106 5-9-4 **64** GeorgeBaker 6 20
(Michael Wigham) *chsd ldrs: pushed along 1/2-way: rdn over 4f out: sn wknd* **5/1**
000- 8 *6* **Trip Switch**[20] 8162 7-9-6 **66** LiamKeniry 5 13
(John Butler) *hld up: a in rr: outpcd and bhd fnl 3f* **40/1**

2m 36.86s (-4.24) **Going Correction** -0.175s/f (Stan)
WFA 4 from 5yo+ 4lb **8 Ran SP% 115.0**
Speed ratings (Par 103): **107,106,105,104,103 92,84,80**
toteswingers 1&2 £2.40, 2&3 £4.60, 1&3 £3.80 CSF £13.32 CT £134.20 TOTE £4.10: £1.20, £1.60, £3.20; EX 14.60 Trifecta £102.30 Pool: £2674.23 - 19.59 winning units..
Owner Dr R D P And Mrs L J Newland **Bred** Hillen, Galvin, Hatta Bs & Tweenhills **Trained** Claines, Worcs

FOCUS
Another well-contested handicap, and a truly run race resulted. The third and fourth help set the standard.

108 BEST RACING ODDS GUARANTEED AT BOOKMAKERS.CO.UK MAIDEN STKS 1m 141y(P)
4:25 (4:27) (Class 5) 4-Y-O+ **£2,726** (£805; £402) **Stalls** Low

Form RPR
2- 1 **Frontier Fighter**[13] 8239 5-9-6 0 DanielTudhope 1 67+
(David O'Meara) *sn led: mde most: pushed clr wl over 1f out: easily* **10/11**[1]
0/4- 2 *3 ½* **Cape Crossing**[19] 8187 4-9-0 0 LiamKeniry 4 54
(Andrew Balding) *trckd ldng pair: rdn along 3f out: drvn wl over 1f: kpt on same pce u.p fnl f* **12/1**
054- 3 *½* **Harvest Mist (IRE)**[257] 1635 5-8-10 46 WilliamTwiston-Davies[(5)] 2 53
(Shaun Lycett) *chsd wnr: rdn along 3f out: drvn wl over 1f out: sn one pce* **33/1**
02- 4 *nk* **Fly Haaf (IRE)**[11] 8267 4-9-5 0 JimCrowley 6 57
(William Knight) *hld up in tch: hdwy 3f out: rdn to chse ldrs over 1f out: sn drvn and one pce* **5/2**[2]
5 *nk* **He's No Angel (IRE)** 4-9-5 0 AdamKirby 5 57+
(Clive Cox) *dwlt: green and sn pushed along in rr: hdwy 1/2-way: rdn to chse ldrs 2f out: sn one pce* **4/1**[3]
0- 6 *27* **Fountain Girl**[35] 7978 4-8-11 0 MarkCoumbe[(3)] 3
(Edward Bevan) *a in rr: rdn along 1/2-way: sn outpcd and bhd* **250/1**

1m 49.7s (-0.80) **Going Correction** -0.175s/f (Stan)
WFA 4 from 5yo 1lb **6 Ran SP% 112.0**
Speed ratings (Par 103): **96,92,92,91 67**
toteswingers 1&2 £2.10, 2&3 £9.70, 1&3 £3.30 CSF £13.64 TOTE £2.40: £1.80, £4.00; EX 9.40 Trifecta £51.80 Pool: £3539.13 - 51.21 winning units..
Owner Archibald Nichol **Bred** Darley **Trained** Nawton, N Yorks

FOCUS
A weak and steadily run maiden. The third limits the form but the winner is potentially better than this.

109 CORAL.CO.UK MOBILE CASINO H'CAP 2m 119y(P)
4:55 (4:55) (Class 6) (0-60,60) 4-Y-O+ **£2,045** (£603; £302) **Stalls** Low

Form RPR
00-2 1 **Bold Adventure**[6] 12 9-9-4 **52** JamieMackay 5 60+
(Willie Musson) *hld up in rr: smooth hdwy 3f out: chsd ldr wl over 1f out: rdn to ld ins fnl f: comf* **1/1**[1]
454- 2 *1 ¼* **Destiny Awaits (IRE)**[49] 7800 4-8-11 **52** (p) TomEaves 8 57
(George Foster) *trckd ldng pair: hdwy 3f out: rdn to ld 2f out: drvn and hdd ins fnl f: kpt on* **6/4**[2]
440- 3 *4* **David's Folly (IRE)**[11] 8273 4-8-5 **46** oh1 LukeMorris 3 46
(Bryn Palling) *led: rdn along 3f out: hdd 2f out and sn wknd* **14/1**
6/0- 4 *3 ¾* **Nouailhas**[39] 7933 7-8-10 **49** JackDuern[(5)] 6 45
(Reg Hollinshead) *trckd ldr: rdn along 3f out: drvn 2f out and sn wknd* **10/1**[3]
/20- 5 *6* **Iron Duke**[34] 7629 7-8-5 **46** oh1 (tp) PhilipPrince[(7)] 2 35
(Liam Corcoran) *trckd ldng pair on inner: rdn along over 3f out: wknd over 2f out* **10/1**[3]

3m 41.98s (0.18) **Going Correction** -0.175s/f (Stan)
WFA 4 from 5yo+ 7lb **5 Ran SP% 114.8**
Speed ratings (Par 101): **92,91,89,87,84**
CSF £2.94 TOTE £1.40: £1.10, £1.10; EX 2.40 Trifecta £10.60 Pool: £1943.95 - 137.15 winning units..
Owner W J Musson **Bred** Bricklow Ltd **Trained** Newmarket, Suffolk

FOCUS
A low-grade and weakly contested stayers' handicap that was decimated by the non-runners. The time was slow and the winner didn't need to improve on his Kempton run.

110 FREE BET BONANZA NOW AT BOOKMAKERS.CO.UK H'CAP 1m 141y(P)
5:25 (5:25) (Class 6) (0-52,63) 4-Y-O+ **£2,045** (£603; £302) **Stalls** Low

Form RPR

60-1 **1** **Kyllachykov (IRE)**^{5} [41] 5-9-6 **51** 6ex DanielTudhope 9 62
(Robin Bastiman) *in tch: hdwy to trck ldrs 1/2-way: effrt to chse ldrs over 2f out: rdn to chse ldr over 1f out: carried sltly rt ins fnl f: sn drvn to ld last 100yds: hung rt nr fin: kpt on* **11/4**^{2}

013- **2** *hd* **Bertie Blu Boy**^{12} [8249] 5-9-7 **52** (b) GrahamGibbons 10 63
(Lisa Williamson) *trckd ldng pair: hdwy to ld 2f out: rdn over 1f out: drvn and edgd rt ins fnl f: hdd last 100yds: ch whn bmpd nr fin: kpt on* **10/1**

60-0 **3** *3* **Titan Diamond (IRE)**^{5} [41] 5-8-10 **46** oh1 RachealKneller(5) 12 50
(Mark Usher) *in rr: hdwy on wd outside 2f out: sn rdn and kpt on strly fnl f to take 3rd nr fin* **66/1**

05-4 **4** *hd* **Fleetwoodsands (IRE)**^{7} [7] 6-9-7 **52** (t) RobertWinston 7 56
(Milton Bradley) *midfield: hdwy and in tch 1/2-way: rdn to chse ldrs over 2f out: sn drvn and one pce fnl f* **11/1**

02-5 **5** *1 ½* **Lord Paget**^{5} [42] 4-8-13 **50** (p) JackDuern(5) 6 50
(Reg Hollinshead) *hld up towards rr: hdwy on outer over 2f out: rdn to chse ldrs over 1f out: sn no imp* **20/1**

001- **6** *¾* **Aegean King**^{19} [8180] 7-9-7 **52** JimCrowley 13 50
(Michael Wigham) *dwlt: swtchd lft s and in rr tl styd on fnl 2f* **8/1**^{3}

015- **7** *1* **Count Ceprano (IRE)**^{13} [8241] 9-9-4 **52** SimonPearce(3) 8 48
(Lydia Pearce) *in rr tl styd on fnl 2f* **14/1**

0-11 **8** *hd* **Rosie's Lady (IRE)**^{1} [99] 4-9-10 **63** 12ex DavidBergin(7) 5 59
(David O'Meara) *trckd ldrs: hdwy to chse ldr 3f out: rdn 2f out: sn wknd* **10/11**^{1}

440- **9** *½* **Rigid**^{134} [3317] 6-9-6 **51** MichaelO'Connell 11 46
(Tony Carroll) *nvr nr ldrs* **33/1**

000- **10** *1* **Silver Marizah (IRE)**^{19} [8187] 4-9-6 **52** (e1) RobertHavlin 4 44
(Roger Ingram) *midfield: hdwy and in tch over 3f out: sn rdn and wknd* **50/1**

300- **11** *5* **Bidable**^{13} [8241] 9-9-1 **46** oh1 LukeMorris 2 27
(Bryn Palling) *a towards rr* **33/1**

00-4 **12** *2 ¼* **Georgebernardshaw (IRE)**^{4} [50] 8-9-2 **52** (p) JasonHart(5) 3 28
(Richard Guest) *cl up: led over 3f out: rdn along wl over 2f out: sn hdd & wknd* **25/1**

600- **13** *22* **Smirfy's Silver**^{19} [8180] 9-9-6 **51** (p) TomEaves 1
(Michael Mullineaux) *led: rdn along and hdd over 3f out: sn wknd* **66/1**

1m 48.24s (-2.26) **Going Correction** -0.175s/f (Stan)
WFA 4 from 5yo+ 1lb 13 Ran SP% **133.7**
Speed ratings (Par 101): **103,102,100,99,98 97,97,96,96,95 91,89,69**
toteswingers 1&2 £7.50, 2&3 £51.90, 1&3 £73.90 CSF £32.97 CT £1248.42 TOTE £4.10: £1.30, £2.60, £14.00; EX 37.30 Trifecta £2745.00 Part won. Pool: £3660.04 - 0.53 winning units..
Owner Ms M Austerfield **Bred** L K I Bloodstock Ltd **Trained** Cowthorpe, N Yorks
■ Stewards' Enquiry : Daniel Tudhope one-day ban: careless riding (Jan 22)

FOCUS
A fairly competitive handicap, and run a strong pace throughout, so the form has been given a chance.
T/Plt: £37.30 to a £1 stake. Pool of £73157.82 - 1429.55 winning tickets. T/Qpdt: £3.80 to a £1 stake. Pool of £8570.66 - 1645.30 winning tickets. JR

89 KEMPTON (A.W) (R-H)
Wednesday, January 9

OFFICIAL GOING: Standard
Wind: Moderate, across Weather: Clear

111 FREE ENTRY EVERY WEDNESDAY FOR BETDAQ MEMBERS H'CAP 5f (P)
4:10 (4:10) (Class 7) (0-50,50) 4-Y-O+ **£1,455** (£433; £216; £108) **Stalls** Low

Form RPR

00- **1** **Beach Candy (IRE)**^{9} [8307] 4-9-7 **50** (vt) DavidProbert 2 60
(Phil McEntee) *mde virtually all: rdn clr over 1f out: in control after: r.o wl* **10/1**

06- **2** *1 ¼* **Miserere Mei (IRE)**^{19} [8209] 4-9-2 **45** RobbieFitzpatrick 7 51
(Richard Guest) *mid-div: rdn and hdwy over 1f out: r.o to take 2nd ins fnl f: nt rch wnr* **33/1**

5-65 **3** *1* **Slatey Hen (IRE)**^{4} [76] 5-9-7 **50** (p) WilliamCarson 3 52
(Violet M Jordan) *prom: rdn 2f out: one pce appr fnl f* **5/1**^{2}

605- **4** *shd* **Burnt Cream**^{20} [8184] 6-9-3 **46** (t) StevieDonohoe 11 48
(Martin Bosley) *bhd: rdn and styd on fnl 2f: nvr nrr* **33/1**

000- **5** *shd* **Mr Optimistic**^{21} [8169] 5-9-6 **49** ^{1} KieranO'Neill 9 50
(Paul Howling) *towards rr: drvn along 2f out: r.o fnl f: nrst fin* **12/1**

00-4 **6** *½* **Vhujon (IRE)**^{3} [87] 8-9-2 **45** TomEaves 12 44
(Peter Grayson) *bhd: effrt and n.m.r ent fnl f: swtchd rt: r.o wl fnl 100yds* **8/1**

000- **7** *¾* **Fast Samurai (USA)**^{21} [8169] 5-8-12 **48** (t) JoeyHaynes(7) 1 45
(Tony Carroll) *chsd ldrs: hrd rdn over 1f out: sn wknd* **8/1**

04-5 **8** *½* **Lisselton Cross**^{3} [87] 5-9-6 **49** (v) JimCrowley 4 44
(Martin Bosley) *prom tl wknd over 1f out* **3/1**^{1}

356- **9** *¾* **Bobbyow**^{20} [8184] 5-9-3 **49** MarkCoumbe(3) 8 41
(Terry Clement) *in tch: pushed along over 2f out: wknd wl over 1f out* **7/1**^{3}

54-2 **10** *½* **Deveze (IRE)**^{3} [81] 5-9-2 **45** (b) JimmyQuinn 6 35
(Milton Bradley) *in tch tl rdn and wknd wl over 1f out* **5/1**^{2}

(-0.50) **Going Correction** -0.10s/f (Stan) 10 Ran SP% **115.7**
Speed ratings (Par 97): **100,98,96,96,96 95,94,93,92,91**
toteswingers 1&2 £24.60, 1&3 £5.40, 2&3 £16.30 CSF £282.52 CT £1828.84 TOTE £14.30: £3.60, £5.40, £1.50; EX 241.00 Trifecta £755.70 Part won. Pool: £1007.60 - 0.33 winning units..
Owner Steve Jakes **Bred** Lynn Lodge Stud **Trained** Newmarket, Suffolk
■ Stewards' Enquiry : Stevie Donohoe two-day ban: careless riding (23-24 January)

FOCUS
Little to dwell on in a very moderate handicap. The gallop was an ordinary one and the winner was another over this C&D to make all against the inside rail. She is rated in line with the balance of her 3yo form.

112 WIN BIG WITH BETDAQ MULTIPLES H'CAP 1m 2f (P)
4:40 (4:41) (Class 5) (0-75,75) 4-Y-O+ **£2,587** (£770; £384; £192) **Stalls** Low

Form RPR

613- **1** **Purple 'n Gold (IRE)**^{20} [8182] 4-8-13 **69** (v) JimCrowley 7 78
(David Pipe) *s.i.s and rdn s: sn in midfield: hdwy over 2f out: led wl over 1f out: hung rt: rdn out* **3/1**^{2}

246- **2** *1 ¼* **Presburg (IRE)**^{79} [7300] 4-9-5 **75** LiamKeniry 5 82
(Joseph Tuite) *in tch: rdn 2f out: styd on to take 2nd ent fnl f* **7/2**^{3}

451- **3** *1 ½* **Whitby Jet (IRE)**^{21} [8162] 5-9-6 **74** WilliamCarson 4 78+
(Ed Vaughan) *hld up towards rr: effrt on outer 2f out: styd on fr over 1f out* **7/4**^{1}

163- **4** *1 ½* **Having A Ball**^{21} [8162] 9-8-8 **62** JohnFahy 3 65+
(Peter Cundell) *hld up towards rr: hdwy and nt clr run over 1f out: swtchd lft and shkn up: styd on* **8/1**

650- **5** *nk* **St Ignatius**^{33} [8020] 6-8-12 **73** (p) RobertTart(7) 1 73
(Alan Bailey) *chsd ldrs tl wknd over 1f out* **20/1**

335- **6** *¾* **Hurricane Hymnbook (USA)**^{49} [7805] 8-8-13 **67** StevieDonohoe 8 65
(Willie Musson) *rdn early and sn bhd: pushed along and hung rt over 1f out: styd on fnl f* **12/1**

006- **7** *hd* **L'Hirondelle (IRE)**^{9} [8308] 9-9-1 **69** SebSanders 2 67
(Michael Attwater) *led 1f: chsd ldr: led briefly 2f out: wknd jst ins fnl f* **33/1**

000- **8** *2* **Six Silver Lane**^{21} [8174] 5-9-4 **72** MartinDwyer 6 66
(Derek Shaw) *led after 1f tl 2f out: wknd over 1f out* **33/1**

2m 7.3s (-0.70) **Going Correction** -0.10s/f (Stan)
WFA 4 from 5yo+ 2lb 8 Ran SP% **113.0**
Speed ratings (Par 103): **98,97,95,94,94 93,93,92**
toteswingers 1&2 £2.70, 1&3 £2.00, 2&3 £2.10 CSF £13.42 CT £22.24 TOTE £4.50: £1.50, £1.20, £1.30; EX 15.10 Trifecta £38.10 Pool: £2919.22 - 57.45 winning units..
Owner Mrs Lynne Webb **Bred** Stonethorn Stud Farms Ltd **Trained** Nicholashayne, Devon

FOCUS
A fair handicap but one in which a reasonable early gallop steadied around halfway. The winner edged towards the far rail in the straight. The form is not entirely convincing but has been taken at face value.

113 BACK AND LAY AT BETDAQ.COM H'CAP 5f (P)
5:10 (5:10) (Class 4) (0-85,82) 4-Y-O+ **£4,690** (£1,395; £697; £348) **Stalls** Low

Form RPR

060- **1** **Diamond Charlie (IRE)**^{130} [5832] 5-9-2 **77** SebSanders 6 93
(Simon Dow) *dwlt: sn in midfield: hdwy to ld ent fnl f: rdn clr: comf* **7/4**^{1}

604- **2** *3 ½* **Triple Dream**^{105} [6578] 8-9-1 **76** (tp) JimmyQuinn 3 79
(Milton Bradley) *chsd ldrs: hmpd and swtchd rt over 1f out: kpt on to take 2nd ins fnl f* **16/1**

30-1 **3** *1* **Roy's Legacy**^{6} [29] 4-9-2 **77** 6ex (t) AdamKirby 2 77
(Shaun Harris) *chsd ldr: led wl over 1f out tl ent fnl f: one pce* **4/1**^{2}

004- **4** *1 ¾* **Al Khan (IRE)**^{14} [8238] 4-8-11 **72** WilliamCarson 1 66
(Violet M Jordan) *s.s: sn rdn along towards rr: sme late hdwy* **14/1**

000- **5** *shd* **Quality Art (USA)**^{18} [8232] 5-8-11 **72** J-PGuillambert 4 65
(Richard Guest) *chsd ldrs tl no ex over 1f out* **12/1**

010- **6** *nse* **Rocket Rob (IRE)**^{21} [8163] 7-9-0 **75** StevieDonohoe 7 68
(Willie Musson) *dwlt: sn wl bhd: shkn up and sme hdwy over 1f out: styd on fnl f* **6/1**^{3}

60-6 **7** *2* **Royal Bajan (USA)**^{8} [3] 5-9-7 **82** DaleSwift 8 68
(James Given) *outpcd: sn wl bhd: nvr trbld ldrs* **12/1**

001- **8** *¾* **Island Legend (IRE)**^{21} [8163] 7-9-6 **81** (p) RobertWinston 5 64
(Milton Bradley) *led and set str pce: hdd wl over 1f out: edgd lft: sn wknd: fin lame* **7/1**

58.77s (-1.73) **Going Correction** -0.10s/f (Stan) 8 Ran SP% **111.1**
Speed ratings (Par 105): **109,103,101,99,98 98,95,94**
toteswingers 1&2 £7.40, 1&3 £9.00, 2&3 £5.20 CSF £30.62 CT £95.63 TOTE £3.40: £1.10, £4.20, £1.90; EX 36.00 Trifecta £191.70 Pool: £2361.68 - 9.23 winning units..
Owner David & Stanley Adams **Bred** John Malone **Trained** Epsom, Surrey

FOCUS
A useful handicap but a strong pace teed things up for the well-backed winner, who made his ground in the centre in the straight. The first two both have a good record over C&D.

114 BETDAQ GAMES £50 HARD CASH BONUS MEDIAN AUCTION MAIDEN STKS 6f (P)
5:40 (5:44) (Class 6) 3-5-Y-O **£1,940** (£577; £288; £144) **Stalls** Low

Form RPR

43- **1** **Two In The Pink (IRE)**^{21} [8165] 3-8-7 0 MartinLane 8 64+
(Hugo Palmer) *wnt lft s: towards rr: hdwy 2f out: styd on to ld 1f out: edgd rt: rdn clr* **4/7**^{1}

0- **2** *1 ¾* **Batchworth Lady**^{28} [8068] 3-8-7 0 JimmyQuinn 1 56
(Dean Ivory) *chsd ldrs: led 2f out tl 1f out: kpt on same pce* **9/2**^{2}

560- **3** *1 ¾* **Hanga Roa (IRE)**^{22} [8155] 3-8-12 35 FergusSweeney 6 55?
(Gary Moore) *mid-div: rdn over 2f out: styd on fr over 1f out* **33/1**

32-2 **4** *1 ¾* **Summer Sun**^{7} [19] 4-9-9 48 LukeMorris 3 48
(Phil McEntee) *trckd ldr: chal on bit over 2f out: wknd over 1f out* **6/1**^{3}

5 *6* **Visual Aspect** 3-8-12 0 WilliamCarson 4 30
(Dean Ivory) *dwlt: rn green: bhd and rdn along: nvr rchd ldrs* **8/1**

440- **6** *nse* **Back For Tea (IRE)**^{13} [8249] 5-10-0 45 (b) AdamKirby 7 34
(Phil McEntee) *chsd ldrs tl wknd 2f out* **14/1**

500- **7** *3* **Dancing Ellie Mae**^{26} [8109] 4-9-2 0 AdamMcLean(7) 5 19
(Derek Shaw) *led tl 2f out: sn wknd* **66/1**

0- **8** *7* **I Need A Dollar**^{71} [7466] 3-8-5 0 PhilipPrince(7) 2
(J R Jenkins) *towards rr: rdn 1/2-way: bhd and struggling after* **33/1**

1m 13.06s (-0.04) **Going Correction** -0.10s/f (Stan)
WFA 3 from 4yo+ 16lb 8 Ran SP% **121.3**
Speed ratings (Par 101): **96,93,91,89,81 80,76,67**
toteswingers 1&2 £1.90, 1&3 £9.00, 2&3 £5.60 CSF £3.92 TOTE £1.70: £1.02, £2.10, £9.50; EX 3.90 Trifecta £45.80 Pool: £2357.00 - 38.54 winning units..
Owner K J P Gundlach **Bred** Rathasker Stud **Trained** Newmarket, Suffolk

FOCUS
A low-grade and uncompetitive maiden run at a fair gallop. The first four finished clear. It's doubtful the winner needed to improve.

115 BOOK NOW FOR SATURDAY H'CAP 6f (P)
6:10 (6:10) (Class 6) (0-65,65) 4-Y-O+ **£1,940** (£577; £288; £144) **Stalls** Low

Form RPR

301- **1** **Captain Kendall (IRE)**^{13} [8251] 4-9-3 **61** LukeMorris 6 75+
(David Evans) *chsd ldrs: rdn to ld over 1f out: sn clr: comf* **3/1**^{2}

154- **2** *2* **Blue Deer (IRE)**^{9} [8304] 5-9-4 **62** (p) MickyFenton 9 69
(Lee Carter) *mid-div: rdn and hdwy 2f out: styd on to chse wnr ins fnl f* **7/1**

020- **3** *¾* **Steelcut**^{11} [8285] 9-9-6 **64** RobertWinston 3 69
(Mark Buckley) *s.s: bhd: rdn over 2f out: styd on fr over 1f out: nvr nrr* **16/1**

000- **4** *½* **Prince Of Passion (CAN)**^{18} [8232] 5-9-4 **62** (v) MartinDwyer 1 65
(Derek Shaw) *led: rdn and hdd over 1f out: one pce* **8/1**

14-0 **5** *½* **George Fenton**^{4} [77] 4-9-1 **59** (p) J-PGuillambert 5 61
(Richard Guest) *in tch: rdn over 2f out: styd on same pce* **6/1**^{3}

416- **6** *shd* **Efistorm**^{12} [8268] 12-9-7 **65** GeorgeBaker 8 66
(Conor Dore) *chsd ldrs: rdn over 2f out: one pce* **6/1**^{3}

000- **7** *2* **Justbookies Dotnet**[42] 7917 4-9-0 **58**......................(v) JimmyQuinn 12 53
(Louise Best) *chsd ldr: rdn over 2f out: wknd over 1f out* **33/1**

524- **8** *½* **Running Mate (IRE)**[78] 7308 6-9-5 **63**.............................. IanMongan 2 56
(Jo Crowley) *towards rr: sme hdwy on inner 2f out: wknd jst over 1f out* **11/4**[1]

600- **9** *12* **Mary's Pet**[12] 8268 6-8-11 **55** ow1..............................(p) StevieDonohoe 10 10
(Lee Carter) *towards rr on outer: rdn over 2f out: sn struggling* **25/1**

1m 12.44s (-0.66) **Going Correction** -0.10s/f (Stan) 9 Ran SP% **116.5**
Speed ratings (Par 101): **100,97,96,95,95 94,92,91,75**
toteswingers 1&2 £5.20, 1&3 £11.90, 2&3 £11.20 CSF £24.68 CT £291.70 TOTE £4.00: £2.20, £1.70, £3.00; EX 21.70 Trifecta £94.20 Pool: £1045.22 - 8.31 winning units..
Owner J G White **Bred** Pier House Stud **Trained** Pandy, Monmouths

FOCUS
A modest handicap run at a reasonable pace. The winner raced close to the inside rail throughout. The form is set around the second and third.

116 HOSPITALITY THIS SATURDAY STILL AVAILABLE FILLIES' H'CAP 7f (P)
6:40 (6:40) (Class 5) (0-70,70) 4-Y-0+ **£2,587** (£770; £384; £192) **Stalls** Low

Form RPR

103- **1** **Shaunas Spirit (IRE)**[34] 8004 5-9-1 **64**..........................(p) AdamKirby 3 76
(Dean Ivory) *trckd ldrs: led over 1f out: drvn clr: comf* **5/1**[2]

321- **2** *3¾* **Glastonberry**[12] 8268 5-9-6 **69**.. GeorgeBaker 6 71
(Geoffrey Deacon) *hld up in midfield: effrt 2f out: chsd wnr 1f out: no imp* **1/1**[1]

340- **3** *2* **Avonrose**[12] 8269 6-9-6 **69**..(v) DaleSwift 1 66
(Derek Shaw) *chsd ldr: led 3f out tl over 1f out: one pce* **10/1**[3]

640- **4** *1¾* **Roedean (IRE)**[131] 5803 4-9-7 **70**..............................(tp) JimCrowley 8 62
(William Stone) *travelling wl in rr of midfield: effrt and rdn 2f out: no imp* **12/1**

463- **5** *hd* **Chambles**[14] 8238 4-9-2 **65**... MartinDwyer 10 56
(Alan McCabe) *s.s: bhd: hdwy on inner 2f out: one pce appr fnl f* **12/1**

60- **6** *5* **Purley Queen (IRE)**[26] 8114 4-8-7 **61**.......................... LeeNewnes(5) 5 39
(Sylvester Kirk) *dwlt: sn in rr of midfield: rdn and no hdwy fnl 2f* **20/1**

000- **7** *shd* **Yurituni**[22] 8157 6-8-11 **65**... AmyScott(5) 4 43
(Eve Johnson Houghton) *chsd ldrs on outer: outpcd 3f out: sn btn* **33/1**

000- **8** *2* **Leelu**[35] 7990 7-8-7 **56**..[1] DavidProbert 7 28
(David Arbuthnot) *prom tl wknd over 2f out* **12/1**

102- **9** *1½* **Flamborough Breeze**[32] 8039 4-8-7 **56**......................(t) LukeMorris 9 24
(Ed Vaughan) *hld up towards rr: rdn over 2f out: nvr trbld ldrs* **10/1**[3]

000- **10** *½* **Tenbridge**[37] 7975 4-9-1 **64**.......................................(p) WilliamCarson 11 31
(Derek Haydn Jones) *towards rr: rdn over 3f out: n.d* **33/1**

300- **11** *12* **Ziefhd**[20] 8183 4-8-13 **69**..(p) PhilipPrince(7) 2
(Tim McCarthy) *led tl 3f out: sn rdn and lost pl* **10/1**[3]

1m 24.21s (-1.79) **Going Correction** -0.10s/f (Stan) 11 Ran SP% **127.7**
Speed ratings (Par 100): **106,101,99,97,97 91,91,89,87,86 73**
toteswingers 1&2 £2.50, 1&3 £7.20, 2&3 £6.80 CSF £11.07 CT £54.39 TOTE £7.20: £2.20, £1.02, £4.20; EX 16.00 Trifecta £156.00 Pool: £1537.82 - 7.39 winning units..
Owner Cynthia Smith & Dean Ivory **Bred** Miss Breda Wright **Trained** Radlett, Herts

FOCUS
A modest handicap run at a fair gallop. The winner came down the centre and the first five came clear. The form is taken at face value.

117 GET YOUR TICKETS FOR THE RACING PLUS CHASE H'CAP 7f (P)
7:10 (7:10) (Class 7) (0-50,55) 4-Y-0+ **£1,455** (£433; £216; £108) **Stalls** Low

Form RPR

564- **1** **Teen Ager (FR)**[247] 1908 9-9-4 **49**.................................... JimmyQuinn 6 55
(Paul Burgoyne) *plld hrd in midfield: rdn and hdwy over 1f out: styd on to ld wl ins fnl f* **16/1**

000- **2** *nk* **Invincible Beauty (IRE)**[111] 6395 4-9-3 **48**..................(t) MickyFenton 4 53
(Seamus Durack) *hld up towards rr: gd hdwy over 1f out: r.o to take 2nd fnl 75yds* **33/1**

40-2 **3** *hd* **Compton Target (IRE)**[6] 42 4-9-2 **47**.....................(t) RobertWinston 8 52
(Milton Bradley) *t.k.h: chsd ldrs: rdn over 2f out: kpt on fnl f* **7/1**

005- **4** *1* **Play The Blues (IRE)**[10] 8299 6-8-12 **50**......................(t) NedCurtis(7) 11 52
(Roger Curtis) *prom: led over 2f out: rdn and 2 l ahd over 1f out: no ex and hdd wl ins fnl f* **25/1**

005- **5** *1* **Northern Spy (USA)**[27] 8099 9-9-4 **49**.............................. LukeMorris 3 48
(Simon Dow) *in tch: effrt over 2f out: kpt on fnl f* **16/1**

035- **6** *shd* **Vale Of Lingfield (IRE)**[10] 8298 4-9-2 **47**.......................... AdamKirby 7 46
(John Best) *t.k.h: prom: hrd rdn over 1f out: one pce fnl f* **3/1**[1]

021- **7** *1¼* **Jackie Love (IRE)**[10] 8299 5-9-5 **55** 6ex................(v) NathanAlison(5) 12 51
(Olivia Maylam) *towards rr: rdn 3f out: styd on fr over 1f out: nvr nrr* **14/1**

205- **8** *½* **Dingaan (IRE)**[114] 6321 10-9-2 **47**................................... TomEaves 13 41
(Peter Grayson) *s.s: bhd: rdn over 2f out: nvr rchd ldrs* **33/1**

00-0 **9** *nk* **Cut The Cackle (IRE)**[4] 77 7-9-5 **50**...................(bt) WilliamCarson 14 43
(Violet M Jordan) *a abt same pl: drvn along over 2f out: nvr able to chal* **25/1**

060- **10** *¾* **Olynard (IRE)**[118] 6158 7-8-9 **47**........................... RobertTart(7) 2 38
(Michael Mullineaux) *hld up in midfield: rdn over 2f out: sn btn* **16/1**

000- **11** *½* **Vermeyen**[77] 7326 4-9-5 **50**.. GeorgeBaker 5 40
(Geoffrey Deacon) *stdd s: hld up off the pce in last: rdn 2f out: styng on at fin* **9/2**[3]

003- **12** *¾* **Greek Islands (IRE)**[19] 8205 5-9-4 **49**.............................. LiamKeniry 9 37
(Ed de Giles) *t.k.h: chsd ldrs tl wknd 2f out* **14/1**

426- **13** *3* **Royal Acclamation (IRE)**[328] 572 8-9-3 **48**...........(p) JamieGoldstein 1 28
(Michael Scudamore) *in tch: effrt over 2f out: wknd wl over 1f out* **20/1**

5-12 **14** *4* **Putin (IRE)**[3] 88 5-9-9 **54** 6ex..................................(bt) DavidProbert 10 23
(Phil McEntee) *led tl over 2f out: sn lost pl* **7/2**[2]

1m 25.72s (-0.28) **Going Correction** -0.10s/f (Stan) 14 Ran SP% **127.2**
Speed ratings (Par 97): **97,96,96,95,94 94,92,92,91,90 90,89,85,81**
toteswingers 1&2 £80.00, 1&3 £11.00, 2&3 £49.00 CSF £488.19 CT £4007.95 TOTE £17.00: £4.00, £11.70, £3.30; EX 443.20 Trifecta £1292.50 Part won. Pool: £1723.40 - 0.33 winning units..
Owner Mrs C Leigh-Turner **Bred** Haras De Beauvoir **Trained** Shepton Montague, Somerset

FOCUS
A low-grade handicap run at an ordinary gallop. The winner raced centre-to-far side in the straight. Typical ordinary form.
T/Plt: £24.30 to a £1 stake. Pool of £60,654.08 - 1816.12 winning tickets. T/Qpdt: £5.70 to a £1 stake. Pool of £8520.59 - 1091.02 winning tickets. LM

[73]LINGFIELD (L-H)
Wednesday, January 9

OFFICIAL GOING: Standard
Wind: virtually nil Weather: dry, overcast

118 BET ON YOUR TABLET AT BLUESQ.COM (S) STKS 1m (P)
12:30 (12:30) (Class 6) 4-Y-0+ **£2,045** (£603; £302) **Stalls** High

Form RPR

2-31 **1** **One Way Or Another (AUS)**[2] 97 10-8-12 66.......(t) PhilipPrince(7) 1 73
(David Evans) *hld up in tch in last pair: rdn and effrt to chal 1f out: led ins fnl f: r.o strly: readily* **2/1**[2]

050- **2** *2¼* **Miami Gator (IRE)**[30] 8057 6-8-12 71.......................(v) RobertWinston 3 61
(Mrs K Burke) *led: rdn over 2f out: battled on wl u.p tl hdd ins fnl f: no ex and sn outpcd* **1/1**[1]

320- **3** *shd* **Barachiel**[29] 8067 5-8-13 60 ow1.. IanMongan 4 62
(Luke Dace) *chsd ldr: rdn to chal wl over 2f out: drvn and stl ev ch over 1f out: no ex and outpcd ins fnl f* **5/1**[3]

65-0 **4** *7* **Spinning Ridge (IRE)**[5] 61 8-8-12 65.........................(v) LukeMorris 2 44
(Ronald Harris) *chsd ldr: rdn and fnd little wl over 1f out: wknd ins fnl f* **10/1**

/00- **5** *25* **Roe Valley (IRE)**[12] 8264 6-8-12 41..........................(p) FergusSweeney 5
(Linda Jewell) *s.i.s: in tch in last pair: sn niggled: rdn 4f out: lost tch over 2f out: t.o* **100/1**

1m 37.26s (-0.94) **Going Correction** +0.075s/f (Slow) 5 Ran SP% **110.1**
Speed ratings (Par 101): **107,104,104,97,72**
CSF £4.37 TOTE £4.50: £1.70, £1.10; EX 5.30 Trifecta £10.80 Pool: £1,304.17 - 89.91 winning units..There was no bid for the winner.
Owner Mrs E Evans **Bred** Segenho Stud **Trained** Pandy, Monmouths

FOCUS
An ordinary seller, run at a fair pace. The form is rated around the winner.

119 LINGFIELD PARK OWNERS GROUP H'CAP 2m (P)
1:00 (1:02) (Class 5) (0-75,72) 4-Y-0+ **£2,726** (£805; £402) **Stalls** Low

Form RPR

020- **1** **Honourable Knight (IRE)**[28] 8073 5-9-2 **68**..................... DavidProbert 1 73
(Mark Usher) *chsd ldrs: rdn over 2f out: led and edgd lft u.p over 1f out: kpt on wl: rdn out* **9/2**[3]

000- **2** *¾* **Where's Susie**[41] 7927 8-9-6 **72**...................................... GeorgeBaker 7 76
(Michael Madgwick) *chsd ldrs: nt clr run wl over 1f out tl 1f out: r.o u.p to go 2nd wl ins fnl f* **8/1**

005- **3** *hd* **Beat Route**[20] 8191 6-9-6 **72**.. SebSanders 8 77
(Michael Attwater) *stdd s: hld up in rr: clsd and nt clr run over 2f out: swtchd lft over 1f out: nvr enough room on inner fr 1f out: hmpd and swtchd rt wl ins fnl f: r.o to press for 2nd cl home* **5/1**

511- **4** *hd* **Six Of Clubs**[11] 8290 7-9-5 **71**......................................(b) LukeMorris 5 75
(Bill Turner) *s.i.s: hld up in tch in last trio: hdwy 4f out: rdn and chsd ldrs 2f out: styd on u.p fnl 100yds* **7/2**[2]

2/6- **5** *nk* **Ya Hafed**[25] 733 5-9-4 **70**... ChrisCatlin 4 74
(Sheena West) *chsd ldr: rdn over 2f out: no ex and styd on same pce fnl f* **7/1**

642- **6** *hd* **Squad**[21] 8170 7-9-6 **72**...(v) EddieAhern 3 77+
(Simon Dow) *s.i.s: hld up in tch in last trio: clsd and chsng ldrs whn nt clr run over 1f out tl swtchd rt jst ins fnl f: styd on wl fnl 75yds: nt rch ldrs* **11/4**[1]

/54- **7** *2¼* **Low Key (IRE)**[23] 8148 6-9-3 **69**......................................[1] MickyFenton 6 70?
(John Butler) *chsd ldrs: swtchd rt and rdn to ld over 3f out: hung lft and hdd over 1f out: wknd ins fnl f* **25/1**

302/ **8** *5* **Watergate (IRE)**[21] 6594 7-9-4 **70**...................................... AmirQuinn 2 67?
(Richard Rowe) *led and set stdy gallop: hdd and rdn over 3f out: stl chsng ldrs but styng on same pce whn nt clr run and hmpd jst ins fnl f: eased wl ins fnl f* **33/1**

3m 28.39s (2.69) **Going Correction** +0.075s/f (Slow) 8 Ran SP% **114.1**
Speed ratings (Par 103): **96,95,95,95,95 95,94,91**
Tote Swingers 1&2 £7.30, 2&3 £6.70, 1&3 £5.40 CSF £39.67 CT £185.49 TOTE £6.30: £2.30, £2.10, £2.70; EX 44.60 Trifecta £217.70 Pool: £2,027.64 - 6.98 winning units..
Owner Bryan Fry **Bred** Mohammed Al Sulaim **Trained** Upper Lambourn, Berks
■ Stewards' Enquiry : David Probert three day ban: careless riding (Jan 23-25)

FOCUS
A fair staying handicap, run at a muddling gallop with a bunch finish. The form is worth little.

120 LINGFIELDPARK.CO.UK (S) H'CAP 1m 2f (P)
1:30 (1:31) (Class 6) (0-60,60) 4-Y-0+ **£2,045** (£603; £302) **Stalls** Low

Form RPR

000- **1** **Temuco (IRE)**[13] 8249 4-9-1 **56**.......................................(v) AdamKirby 12 63
(David Evans) *hld up in tch in last pair: rdn and hdwy on outer to chse ldrs 2f out: styd on u.p to ld wl ins fnl f: rdn out* **9/2**[2]

354- **2** *¾* **Fairy Mist (IRE)**[10] 8298 6-8-7 **46** oh1.......................... WilliamCarson 2 52
(John Bridger) *chsd ldrs: rdn and effrt over 2f out: chsd ldr wl over 1f out: ev ch wl ins fnl f: styd on same pce towards fin* **12/1**

500- **3** *hd* **Young Jackie**[35] 8001 5-8-0 **46** oh1.....................(b[1]) JordanVaughan(7) 5 51
(George Margarson) *hld up in tch towards rr: hdwy into midfield on outer 4f out: nt clr run ent fnl 2f: hdwy to chse ldng trio 1f out: styd on strly ins fnl f: nt rch ldrs* **10/1**

040- **4** *1½* **Litmus (USA)**[12] 8264 4-8-0 **46** oh1.......................(b[1]) NathanAlison(5) 8 48
(Simon Dow) *t.k.h: sn led: rdn and clr 2f out: drvn over 1f out: hdd wl ins fnl f: wknd towards fin* **33/1**

453- **5** *2¾* **The Noble Ord**[20] 8177 4-8-11 **59**..............................(t) LouisSteward(7) 1 56
(Sylvester Kirk) *in tch in midfield: hdwy u.p on inner over 1f out: no imp fnl f* **6/1**[3]

066- **6** *nk* **Skyblue**[124] 5989 4-8-5 **46** oh1......................................(bt) MartinLane 9 42
(Tobias B P Coles) *in tch in midfield: rdn and unable qck over 2f out: styd on same pce fr over 1f out* **25/1**

510- **7** *nse* **Percythepinto (IRE)**[28] 8074 4-9-5 **60**..........................(t) LukeMorris 3 56
(George Baker) *hld up in tch towards rr: rdn over 3f out: nt clr run ent fnl 2f: no real imp tl swtchd rt 1f out: kpt on: nvr trbld ldrs* **2/1**[1]

530- **8** *1½* **King's Road**[14] 6940 8-9-2 **55**.....................................(t) RobertWinston 7 48
(Anabel K Murphy) *restless in stalls: awkward leaving stalls: t.k.h: hmpd after 1f and hld up towards rr after: rdn and effrt over 2f out: kpt on fnl f: nvr trbld ldrs* **9/2**[2]

000- **9** *8* **Flying Kitty**[10] 8299 4-8-5 **46** oh1.................................... KieranO'Neill 6 23
(John Bridger) *in tch in midfield: rdn and lost pl over 2f out: bhd over 1f out* **33/1**

545- **10** 1/2 **Rainbow Riches (IRE)**[93] 6935 4-8-2 **46** oh1 SimonPearce(3) 13 22
(Roger Curtis) *t.k.h: chsd ldrs: rdn 4f out: wknd over 2f out* **50/1**

000- **11** 3/4 **Ececheira**[31] 8048 4-8-5 **46** oh1 AndreaAtzeni 11 20
(Dean Ivory) *t.k.h: chsd ldr: rdn over 2f out: lost 2nd 2f out: 4th and btn over 1f out: wknd and eased ins fnl f* **50/1**

500- **12** 7 **Pose (IRE)**[13] 8248 6-8-8 **46** oh1 ow1 (t) AdamBeschizza 10
(Roger Ingram) *in tch towards rr: rdn and struggling over 2f out: bhd over 1f out* **33/1**

2m 5.67s (-0.93) **Going Correction** +0.075s/f (Slow)
WFA 4 from 5yo+ 2lb **12** Ran SP% **117.4**
Speed ratings (Par 101): **106,105,105,104,101 101,101,100,93,93 92,87**
Tote Swingers 1&2 £7.40, 2&3 £7.90, 1&3 £6.50 CSF £52.00 TOTE £6.00: £1.90, £3.00, £3.90; EX 45.10 Trifecta £306.30 Pool: £1,174.70 - 2.87 winning units..There was no bid for the winner.
Owner Ms S Howell & Mrs E Evans **Bred** Thomas McDonogh **Trained** Pandy, Monmouths

FOCUS
An ordinary selling handicap, run at an even pace. The form looks sound enough.

121 BLUE SQUARE BET H'CAP 7f (P)
2:05 (2:05) (Class 4) (0-85,84) 4-Y-O+ **£4,690** (£1,395; £697; £348) **Stalls** Low

Form RPR

1U3- **1** **Haaf A Sixpence**[37] 7966 4-9-3 **80** JimCrowley 7 89+
(Ralph Beckett) *mde all: set stdy gallop: rdn and qcknd 2f out: edgd rt but kpt on wl ins fnl f: rdn out* **4/5**[1]

122- **2** 1/2 **Fast Finian (IRE)**[99] 6768 4-9-7 **84** SebSanders 5 91+
(Paul D'Arcy) *t.k.h: chsd wnr over 5f out: rdn 2f out: drvn and edgd lft over 1f out: kpt on u.p but a hld ins fnl f* **9/4**[2]

044- **3** 1 1/4 **Patriotic (IRE)**[30] 8057 5-9-0 **77** AdamKirby 3 81
(Chris Dwyer) *chsd wnr tl over 5f out: chsd ldrs after: rdn 2f out: styd on same pce u.p over 1f out* **8/1**[3]

044- **4** shd **Crew Cut (IRE)**[20] 8188 5-9-1 **78** (p) LukeMorris 4 82
(Jeremy Gask) *t.k.h: chsd ldrs: rdn and effrt 2f out: drvn and styd on same pce fr over 1f out* **20/1**

006- **5** 1 **Bayleyf (IRE)**[20] 8188 4-9-6 **83** (t) GeorgeBaker 1 84?
(John Best) *led to post: s.i.s: t.k.h: hld up in rr: clsd 1/2-way: rdn and no real imp fr over 1f out* **10/1**

1m 24.4s (-0.40) **Going Correction** +0.075s/f (Slow) **5** Ran SP% **111.3**
Speed ratings (Par 105): **105,104,103,102,101**
Tote Swinger 1&2 £1.70 CSF £2.87 TOTE £1.70: £1.10, £1.40; EX 3.10 Trifecta £6.20 Pool: £1,461.00 - 175.51 winning units..
Owner Melody Racing **Bred** Melody Bloodstock **Trained** Kimpton, Hants

FOCUS
A fair little handicap and it was dominated throughout by the market principals. The form makes sense at face value but the first two could be better than they were able to show, as the pace wasn't strong.

122 FOREST ROW H'CAP 7f (P)
2:40 (2:40) (Class 6) (0-60,60) 3-Y-O **£2,045** (£603; £302) **Stalls** Low

Form RPR

006- **1** **Sweet Force**[23] 8147 3-8-9 **48** (b1) AndreaAtzeni 8 60+
(Marco Botti) *in tch tl hdwy to chse ldr over 2f out: led wl over 1f out: sn rdn and wnt clr: in command and edgd lft 1f out: r.o wl: rdn out* **9/2**[3]

46-2 **2** 3 1/4 **Derwentwater (IRE)**[7] 17 3-9-6 **59** (b) NickyMackay 5 60
(John Gosden) *hld up in last quartet: stl plenty to do and rdn over 1f out: hdwy 1f out: r.o wl to snatch 2nd last stride: no ch w wnr* **9/4**[1]

036- **3** shd **Black Truffle (FR)**[12] 8274 3-8-4 **48** RachealKneller(5) 4 49
(Mark Usher) *t.k.h: chsd ldr tl over 2f out: rdn and outpcd over 1f out: no ch w wnr but plugged on to chse wnr again ins fnl f: lost 2nd last stride* **8/1**

633- **4** 3/4 **Lincolnrose (IRE)**[19] 8203 3-8-13 **52** (p) SebSanders 3 51
(Alan McCabe) *sn bustled along to ld: rdn and hdd wl over 1f out: sn outpcd by wnr: plugged on tl lost 2 pls wl ins fnl f* **7/1**

033- **5** 1/2 **Sweet Vintage (IRE)**[42] 7916 3-9-7 **60** MartinLane 2 58
(J W Hills) *in tch in midfield: rdn and effrt jst over 2f out: no ch w wnr and kpt on same pce ins fnl f* **6/1**

004- **6** 1 **Handsome Stranger (IRE)**[18] 8233 3-9-7 **60** AdamKirby 1 55
(David Evans) *chsd ldrs: drvn and unable qck over 2f out: no ch w wnr and one pce fr over 1f out* **7/2**[2]

060- **7** 1 1/2 **Ocean Power (IRE)**[20] 8178 3-9-1 **54** FergusSweeney 6 45
(Richard Phillips) *a in rr: rdn and struggling 3f out: no ch w wnr but plugged on fr over 1f out* **33/1**

004- **8** 1/2 **Vergality Ridge (IRE)**[48] 7821 3-9-7 **60** LukeMorris 7 50
(Ronald Harris) *in tch towards rr: rdn and effrt wl over 2f out: struggling 2f out: sn wknd* **16/1**

000- **9** 6 **Sylvia's Diamond**[11] 8289 3-8-7 **46** oh1 (p) JohnFahy 9 19
(Richard Guest) *a in rr: rdn and struggling 3f out: bhd over 1f out* **100/1**

1m 25.12s (0.32) **Going Correction** +0.075s/f (Slow) **9** Ran SP% **118.9**
Speed ratings (Par 95): **101,97,97,96,95 94,92,92,85**
Tote Swingers 1&2 £6.10, 2&3 £3.90, 1&3 £11.00 CSF £15.54 CT £80.64 TOTE £8.70: £1.90, £1.50, £2.90; EX 19.00 Trifecta £149.10 Pool: £1,512.83 - 7.60 winning units..
Owner Dachel Stud **Bred** Dachel Stud **Trained** Newmarket, Suffolk

FOCUS
A moderate handicap, run at a generous pace. The second and third help set the standard.

123 SURREY MAIDEN STKS 6f (P)
3:15 (3:15) (Class 5) 3-Y-O+ **£2,726** (£805; £402) **Stalls** Low

Form RPR

02- **1** **Red Valerian (IRE)**[69] 7498 3-8-10 0 RobertWinston 4 66+
(Charles Hills) *chsd ldr: rdn and ev ch wl over 1f out: rn green and led ent fnl f: rdn and drew clr ins fnl f: comf* **4/11**[1]

2 2 1/4 **Perfect Muse** 3-8-5 LukeMorris 2 54+
(Clive Cox) *dwlt: sn chsng ldrs: rdn over 2f out: drvn and styd on to chse wnr ins fnl f: kpt on* **10/1**[3]

523- **3** 1 3/4 **Island Express (IRE)**[13] 8251 6-9-7 48 (tp) AnnStokell(5) 3 57
(Ann Stokell) *t.k.h: chsd ldrs: rdn and unable qck over 1f out: styd on same pce fnl f: wnt 3rd towards fin* **33/1**

0- **4** 3/4 **Dubai Applause**[42] 7894 3-8-5 0 AndreaAtzeni 6 46+
(Charles Hills) *in tch in last trio: rdn and outpcd over 2f out: no threat to wnr but styd on again ins fnl f* **33/1**

0- **5** nse **Thrasos (IRE)**[284] 1138 4-9-12 0 IanMongan 1 54
(Jo Crowley) *led: rdn 2f out: hdd ent fnl f: lost 2nd ins fnl f and fdd towards fin* **4/1**[2]

00- **6** 2 3/4 **Gold Weight**[63] 7628 3-8-10 0 FergusSweeney 7 42
(Michael Madgwick) *in tch towards rr on outer: sme hdwy over 2f out: rdn and unable qck over 1f out: wknd 1f out* **100/1**

6 **7** 1 1/4 **It Ain't To Grand**[7] 19 4-9-12 0 RobertHavlin 5 42
(Roger Ingram) *in tch in last trio: effrt on inner wl over 1f out: no imp: wknd 1f out* **66/1**

1m 12.81s (0.91) **Going Correction** +0.075s/f (Slow)
WFA 3 from 4yo+ 16lb **7** Ran SP% **110.8**
Speed ratings (Par 103): **96,93,90,89,89 85,84**
Tote Swingers 1&2 £1.30, 2&3 £4.90, 1&3 £3.10 CSF £4.51 TOTE £1.90: £1.10, £5.30; EX 5.80 Trifecta £21.30 Pool: £2,386.92 - 83.91 winning units..
Owner B W Hills **Bred** John Fallon **Trained** Lambourn, Berks

FOCUS
A dire maiden, lacking any depth and run in a slow time. The winner did not need to match his latest form.

124 ENOUGH SAID, JUST BET AT BLUESQ.COM MOBILE H'CAP 5f (P)
3:45 (3:46) (Class 6) (0-65,70) 4-Y-O+ **£2,045** (£603; £302) **Stalls** High

Form RPR

002- **1** **Charming (IRE)**[9] 8307 4-9-4 **62** (e) IanMongan 4 69
(Olivia Maylam) *taken down early: chsd ldrs: rdn over 1f out: styd on wl u.p to ld wl ins fnl f: hld on wl cl home* **3/1**[2]

055- **2** 1/2 **Sherjawy (IRE)**[13] 8246 9-8-7 **51** oh6 KirstyMilczarek 3 57
(Zoe Davison) *hld up in rr: rdn and hdwy on inner over 1f out: ev ch ins fnl f: r.o but hld by wnr cl home* **33/1**

245- **3** 1 **Molly Jones**[9] 8307 4-8-10 **54** LukeMorris 1 56
(Derek Haydn Jones) *chsd ldrs: swtchd out rt and effrt u.p wl over 1f out: kpt on ins fnl f to snatch 3rd cl home* **7/1**

341- **4** nk **Novabridge**[9] 8307 5-9-12 **70** 6ex (b) AdamKirby 8 71
(Neil Mulholland) *chsd ldr: rdn to ld over 1f out: drvn 1f out: hdd wl ins fnl f: no ex and wknd towards fin* **6/4**[1]

144- **5** nse **Brandywell Boy (IRE)**[26] 8107 10-8-8 **52** AdamBeschizza 5 53
(Dominic Ffrench Davis) *restless in stalls: sn pushed along in last pair: hdwy u.p 1f out: styd on wl fnl 100yds: nt rch ldrs* **20/1**

655- **6** 3/4 **Fathom Five (IRE)**[30] 8054 9-9-7 **65** (v1) GeorgeBaker 7 63
(Gary Moore) *led tl rdn and hdd over 1f out: wknd ins fnl f* **7/2**[3]

50-6 **7** 1/2 **Steel City Boy (IRE)**[7] 26 10-8-7 **56** ow1 AnnStokell(5) 2 52
(Ann Stokell) *chsd ldrs: rdn and unable qck over 1f out: wknd ins fnl f* **50/1**

3/0- **8** 8 **Lady Prodee**[130] 5815 5-8-13 **64** JakePayne(7) 6 31
(Bill Turner) *racd wd: in tch in midfield: rdn and lost pl whn rn wd bnd 2f out: sn bhd* **14/1**

59.47s (0.67) **Going Correction** +0.075s/f (Slow) **8** Ran SP% **116.1**
Speed ratings (Par 101): **97,96,94,94,94 92,92,79**
Tote Swingers 1&2 £10.10, 2&3 £7.50, 1&3 £3.50 CSF £94.64 CT £646.52 TOTE £2.80: £1.60, £5.60, £2.00; EX 105.30 Trifecta £403.80 Pool: £3,150.87 - 5.85 winning units..
Owner Mrs V A Ward **Bred** Rabbah Bloodstock Limited **Trained** Epsom, Surrey

FOCUS
A low-grade sprint handicap, run at a fierce pace. The winner was entitled to beat the favourite on their C&D latest.
T/Plt: £66.40 to a £1 stake. Pool: £39,067.33 - 429.33 winning tickets. T/Qpdt: £7.90 to a £1 stake. Pool: £4,387.27 - 406.76 winning tickets. SP

[72]DEAUVILLE (R-H)
Wednesday, January 9

OFFICIAL GOING: Fibresand: standard

125a PRIX DE LA VILLIERE (CONDITIONS) (5YO+) (FIBRESAND) 1m 1f 110y
10:20 (10:20) 5-Y-O+ **£8,536** (£3,414; £2,560; £1,707; £853)

RPR

1 **Anaxis (FR)**[12] 6-9-0 0 JeromeCabre 3 93
(S Wattel, France) **9/10**[1]

2 1 **Keep Cool**[20] 6-9-3 0 StephaneLaurent(5) 5 99
(Mme C Janssen, Belgium) **46/1**

3 hd **Tepmokea (IRE)**[14] 8242 7-9-4 0 ShaneKelly 2 95
(Mrs K Burke) *rdn to ld: travelled easily: 1 1/2 l clr ent st: r.o u.p ent fnl f: hdd 25yds out: lost 2nd fnl strides* **17/2**

4 1 1/2 **Mariage Tardif (FR)**[84] 5-9-4 0 MaximeGuyon 6 92
(Mme Pia Brandt, France) **4/1**[3]

5 3 **Appleby (GER)**[20] 5-9-6 0 (p) EddyHardouin 7 87
(S Smrczek, Germany) **17/1**

6 nk **Saltas (GER)**[237] 2223 5-8-11 0 FilipMinarik 1 78
(P Schiergen, Germany) **3/1**[2]

7 2 1/2 **Hail To The Chief (FR)**[12] 5-9-0 0 AdrienFouassier 4 76
(L Viel, France) **36/1**

1m 59.3s (119.30) **7** Ran SP% **118.5**
WIN (incl. 1 euro stake): 1.90. PLACES: 1.40, 8.30. SF: 38.80.
Owner Mathieu Offenstadt **Bred** Scea Haras De La Perelle **Trained** France

126a PRIX DES CHAUMES (MAIDEN) (3YO) (FIBRESAND) 6f 110y
12:00 (12:00) 3-Y-O **£9,756** (£3,902; £2,926; £1,951; £975)

RPR

1 **So Oops (IRE)**[15] 3-8-13 0 TheoBachelot 13 76
(S Wattel, France) **2/1**[1]

2 hd **Lewamy (IRE)**[20] 8193 3-9-2 0 Pierre-CharlesBoudot 3 78
(John Best) *broke fast to ld: rdn 1 1/2f out: r.o wl u.p fnl f: ct and hdd on line* **16/1**

3 1 1/4 **Kukurun (FR)**[15] 3-9-2 0 AlexisBadel 11 74
(Mme M Bollack-Badel, France) **11/2**[3]

4 hd **Mirror Image**[15] 3-8-13 0 StephanePasquier 4 71
(S Wattel, France) **10/1**

5 snk **Medeleck (FR)**[16] 3-9-2 0 MaximeGuyon 1 73
(Mme C De La Soudiere-Niault, France) **4/1**[2]

6 shd **Hubris (FR)**[21] 8176 3-9-2 0 DavidMichaux 2 73
(J-L Pelletan, France) **40/1**

7 1/2 **Aolida (FR)**[89] 3-8-13 0 (p) AnthonyCrastus 12 69
(F Chappet, France) **11/1**

8 1 **Ighraa (IRE)**[15] 3-8-13 0 RonanThomas 5 66
(F-H Graffard, France) **15/2**

9 snk **Ahfir (IRE)** 3-8-3 0 JeremyBonin(5) 7 60
(S Wattel, France) **53/1**

10 1 3/4 **Primadonna Girl (IRE)**[113] 6343 3-8-13 0 TonyPiccone 6 60
(C Boutin, France) **42/1**

0 **Kalevala (FR)**[58] 7699 3-8-13 0 LouisBeuzelin 14
(R Pritchard-Gordon, France) **65/1**

0 **Passage Du Caire (FR)**[21] 3-8-13 0 .... FabriceVeron 10
(H-A Pantall, France) **25/1**

0 **Blacksou (FR)**[21] 8176 3-8-10 0 .... NicolasLarenaudie(6) 9
(P Adda, France) **122/1**

0 **Jezlay (FR)** 3-8-13 0 .... FilipMinarik 8
(W Hickst, Germany) **34/1**

1m 19.1s (79.10) **14** Ran SP% **119.4**
WIN (incl. 1 euro stake): 3.00. PLACES: 1.50, 3.50, 2.00. DF: 24.10. SF: 41.50.
Owner Stephane Mathieu **Bred** A Collins **Trained** France

127a PRIX DE BEAUFOSSE (CLAIMER) (4YO+) (FIBRESAND) 6f 110y
2:05 (2:05) 4-Y-O+ **£6,097** (£2,439; £1,829; £1,219; £609)

RPR

1 **Birthday Sun (GER)**[227] 5-8-13 0 .... NJeanpierre 7 76
(W Hickst, Germany) **41/5**

2 2 ½ **Sky Skipper (IRE)**[20] 6-8-11 0 ....(b) TristanNormand 14 67
(G Doleuze, France) **44/5**

3 snk **Anton (IRE)**[573] 5-9-6 0 .... SoufyaneMoulin 13 76
(Mme Pia Brandt, France) **13/2**[2]

4 1 ¼ **Grand Archer (IRE)**[111] 9-9-2 0 .... LouisBeuzelin 2 68
(J D Hillis, Germany) **16/1**

5 hd **Opera Moon (GER)**[216] 6-9-2 0 ....(p) YannickLetondeur 6 67
(W Hickst, Germany) **15/1**

6 2 ½ **Elpais (ITY)**[580] 2867 6-9-2 0 .... GiacomoTemperini 4 60
(G Botti, France) **9/1**

7 1 ½ **Ertikaan**[20] 8188 6-9-6 0 ....(p) YohannBourgois 11 60
(Brendan Powell) *racd midfield on wd outside: no ex whn rdn 1 1/2f out: r.o wl fnl f: nrest at fin* **73/10**[3]

8 ¾ **Tag's Book (IRE)**[20] 6-8-11 0 ....(b) DavidMichaux 9 49
(U Suter, France) **9/1**

9 nk **Sumaro (GER)**[111] 6-9-2 0 ....(b) AlexandreChampenois 3 53
(W Hickst, Germany) **10/1**

10 1 **Asulaman (GER)**[224] 6-9-2 0 ....(b) TonyFarina 8 50
(S Cerulis, France) **4/1**[1]

0 **I Am That (IRE)**[10] 6-9-6 0 ....(b) StephaneLaurent 1
(Braem Horse Racing Sprl, Belgium) **53/1**

0 **Bad Mistone (FR)**[20] 6-9-2 0 .... SebastienMartino 10
(E Nicoleau, France) **29/1**

0 **Le Gamin (FR)**[10] 6-8-11 0 .... BenjaminHubert 16
(N Leenders, France) **32/1**

0 **Little Power (FR)**[12] 4-9-6 0 .... VivienAmiot 12
(J-P Carvalho, France) **154/1**

0 **So Grateful (FR)**[79] 4-8-8 0 .... EmmanuelEtienne 5
(F Pedrono, France) **200/1**

0 **Warned (FR)**[10] 4-8-8 0 ....(p) DavidFournier 15
(Mme A Blanchard, France) **156/1**

1m 17.9s (77.90) **16** Ran SP% **117.7**
WIN (incl. 1 euro stake): 9.20. PLACES: 3.10, 3.00, 2.60. DF: 57.00. SF: 92.70.
Owner Stall Von Hoegen **Bred** Frau Marlene Haller **Trained** Germany

[111]KEMPTON (A.W) (R-H)
Thursday, January 10

OFFICIAL GOING: Standard
Wind: Light; half against Weather: Very overcast

128 32REDPOKER.COM H'CAP 6f (P)
4:15 (4:15) (Class 7) (0-50,56) 4-Y-O+ **£1,455** (£433; £216; £108) **Stalls** Low

Form RPR

00-1 1 **Beach Candy (IRE)**[1] 111 4-9-13 **56** 6ex ....(vt) MickyFenton 5 64
(Phil McEntee) *mde all: hrd pressed and drvn over 1f out: hld on gamely* **6/1**[3]

235- 2 nk **First Rebellion**[14] 8253 4-9-0 **46** .... RaulDaSilva(3) 9 53
(Tony Carroll) *trckd wnr to over 1f out: drvn and kpt on to take 2nd again ins fnl f: nt qckn nr fin* **12/1**

23-5 3 nk **Do More Business (IRE)**[5] 77 6-9-0 **50** ....(b) NedCurtis(7) 2 56
(Alison Batchelor) *hld up bhd ldrs: prog over 2f out: chsd wnr over 1f out and sn chalng: fnd nil and lost 2nd ins fnl f: kpt on nr fin* **5/2**[1]

020- 4 nk **Kaylee**[11] 8298 4-9-7 **50** ....[1] GeorgeBaker 8 55
(Gary Moore) *hld up in midfield: effrt on outer 2f out: tried to mount a chal fnl f: nt qckn* **6/1**[3]

005- 5 2 ¾ **Rightcar**[20] 8209 6-9-4 **47** .... DaleSwift 7 43
(Peter Grayson) *awkward s: pushed along in last trio after 2f: effrt u.p 2f out: no imp fnl f* **10/1**

005- 6 1 ¼ **Cheyenne Red (IRE)**[108] 6530 7-9-3 **46** .... TomEaves 1 38
(Michael Herrington) *chsd ldng pair to 2f out: sn btn* **20/1**

04-0 7 nk **Fantasy Fighter (IRE)**[5] 76 8-9-6 **49** .... JimmyQuinn 4 40
(Ronald Harris) *s.s: hld up in last: effrt on inner over 2f out: no prog over 1f out* **8/1**

31-0 8 ¾ **Ishi**[7] 35 4-8-12 **48** ....(b) DanielMuscutt(7) 11 37
(Rod Millman) *dwlt: racd wd in rr: no prog fnl 2f* **16/1**

002- 9 4 ½ **Mucky Molly**[21] 8184 5-9-7 **50** ....(v) SebSanders 10 25
(Alison Hutchinson) *dwlt: sn in midfield: wknd over 2f out* **4/1**[2]

1m 12.58s (-0.52) **Going Correction** -0.10s/f (Stan) **9** Ran SP% **115.7**
Speed ratings (Par 97): **99,98,98,97,94 92,92,91,85**
Tote swingers 1&2 £15.50, 1&3 £9.20, 2&3 £3.20 CSF £74.76 CT £227.25 TOTE £13.10: £3.30, £2.90, £1.50; EX 140.40 Trifecta £583.70 Pool: £1,055.54 - 1.35 winning units.
Owner Steve Jakes **Bred** Lynn Lodge Stud **Trained** Newmarket, Suffolk
■ Spellmaker was withdrawn on vet's advice (9/2, deduct 15p in the £ under R4). New market formed.

FOCUS
Just a low-grade sprint, but the pace was solid and the winner is in fine form. The winner backed up the previous day's win.

129 32RED.COM H'CAP 7f (P)
4:45 (4:45) (Class 5) (0-75,75) 3-Y-O **£2,587** (£770; £384; £192) **Stalls** Low

Form RPR

1- 1 **Mystical Sapphire**[42] 7926 3-9-7 **73** .... LiamKeniry 2 82
(Jo Crowley) *dwlt: t.k.h: hld up in 4th: smooth prog over 2f out: led over 1f out: pushed out: comf* **11/2**[3]

651- 2 2 **Ashamaly**[10] 8302 3-9-9 **75** 6ex .... DavidProbert 6 79
(James Tate) *trckd ldr: rdn to chal wl over 1f out: no answer as wnr swept by sn after: kpt on same pce* **4/7**[1]

023- 3 1 ½ **Go Far**[21] 8185 3-9-2 **68** .... NickyMackay 5 68
(Alan Bailey) *hld up in 5th: rdn 3f out: no prog tl styd on fr over 1f out to take 3rd last strides* **9/2**[2]

254- 4 nk **Makinson Lane (IRE)**[29] 8072 3-9-0 **66** .... TomEaves 4 65
(Richard Fahey) *led: rdn and hdd over 1f out: fdd fnl f* **14/1**

325- 5 2 **Roman Order (IRE)**[10] 8302 3-9-5 **71** .... MartinLane 3 65
(Brian Meehan) *chsd ldng pair on outer: rdn 3f out: sn struggling: steadily outpcd* **16/1**

500- 6 10 **Compton Silver**[49] 7821 3-8-11 **63** .... WilliamCarson 1 30
(Hans Adielsson) *awkward s: plld hrd in last: rdn 1/2-way: sn wknd: t.o* **50/1**

1m 26.07s (0.07) **Going Correction** -0.10s/f (Stan) **6** Ran SP% **111.7**
Speed ratings (Par 97): **95,92,91,90,88 76**
Tote swingers 1&2 £1.40, 1&3 £1.70, 2&3 £1.20 CSF £9.04 TOTE £4.60: £1.90, £1.10; EX 11.20 Trifecta £29.20 Pool: £2,211.96 - 56.79 winning units.
Owner Mrs Liz Nelson **Bred** Mrs R I Nelson **Trained** Whitcombe, Dorset

FOCUS
A decent contest of its type with the first two rated in the mid-70s. The time was ordinary and the favourite disappointed, but the form is rated at face value.

130 32RED CASINO H'CAP 7f (P)
5:15 (5:15) (Class 5) (0-70,69) 4-Y-O+ **£2,587** (£770; £384; £192) **Stalls** Low

Form RPR

103- 1 **Golden Desert (IRE)**[27] 8105 9-9-4 **66** .... GeorgeBaker 1 75
(Simon Dow) *stdd s: hld up in detached last: plenty to do whn prog 2f out: r.o fnl f to ld last 50yds* **3/1**[2]

035- 2 ¾ **West Leake (IRE)**[13] 8268 7-8-9 **57** .... JimmyQuinn 6 64
(Paul Burgoyne) *hld up in last pair: prog to chse ldr over 2f out: clsd fnl f but wnr sn wnt by: tk 2nd post* **7/2**[3]

42-0 3 hd **Zaheeb**[8] 13 5-8-13 **61** ....(b) WilliamCarson 7 68
(Dave Morris) *led at gd pce: at least 2 l clr fr 2f out tl tired fnl f: hdd last 50yds: lost 2nd post* **7/2**[3]

215- 4 4 **The Mongoose**[19] 8234 5-9-5 **67** ....(vt[1]) AdamKirby 3 65
(David Evans) *chsd ldrs: hrd rdn over 2f out: no prog and wl btn over 1f out* **9/4**[1]

50-0 5 5 **Dvinsky (USA)**[5] 76 12-8-11 **59** ....(b) KieranO'Neill 2 45
(Paul Howling) *rousted along but unable to ld: chsd ldrs: disp 2nd briefly over 2f out: wknd qckly over 1f out* **25/1**

400- 6 1 **Standing Strong (IRE)**[168] 4517 5-9-6 **68** ....(p) JamieGoldstein 8 52
(Zoe Davison) *dwlt: rcvrd on outer and prom after 2f: wknd qckly over 2f out* **14/1**

00-0 7 1 ¼ **Ziefhd**[1] 116 4-9-0 **69** ....(p) PhilipPrince(7) 5 50
(Tim McCarthy) *tk fierce hold: chsd ldr to over 2f out: wknd qckly* **25/1**

1m 24.94s (-1.06) **Going Correction** -0.10s/f (Stan) **7** Ran SP% **114.6**
Speed ratings (Par 103): **102,101,100,96,90 89,88**
Tote swingers 1&2 £2.20, 1&3 £3.10, 2&3 £2.50 CSF £14.01 CT £36.39 TOTE £3.10: £1.30, £2.80; EX 10.60 Trifecta £35.00 Pool: £2,838.37 - 60.66 winning units.
Owner T G Parker **Bred** Mervyn Stewkesbury **Trained** Epsom, Surrey
■ Stewards' Enquiry : Jimmy Quinn four-day ban: use of whip (24-26, 28 Jan)

FOCUS
Standard Polytrack fare, but the winner was a class act a few years ago. The pace was good.

131 £32 FREE AT 32RED.COM H'CAP 2m (P)
5:45 (5:45) (Class 6) (0-65,65) 4-Y-O+ **£1,940** (£577; £288; £144) **Stalls** Low

Form RPR

043- 1 **Entitlement**[47] 7862 4-9-1 **59** .... MartinLane 2 66+
(James Fanshawe) *hld up in 5th: dropped bk to 7th 5f out: plld out and prog over 2f out: drvn to chal 1f out: disp ld after w hd at awkward angle: jst prevailed* **7/4**[1]

345/ 2 nse **Experimentalist**[163] 4691 5-9-12 **63** ....(t) DavidProbert 7 70
(Tim Vaughan) *hld up in 7th: prog 5f out: trckd ldrs over 2f out: drvn to chal and disp ld ins fnl f: jst pipped* **6/1**

001- 3 ¾ **Llamadas**[27] 8104 11-9-6 **57** .... IanMongan 1 63+
(Olivia Maylam) *trckd ldng pair to 5f out: styd cl up on inner: nt clr run and lost grnd over 2f out: hrd rdn and prog after: led briefly 1f out: styd on* **11/2**[3]

00-0 4 4 ½ **Fromthestables Com (IRE)**[8] 9 4-8-11 **55** ow1 .... SebSanders 9 56
(Brendan Powell) *hld up in last pair: drvn on outer over 2f out: kpt on fr over 1f out to take 4th last strides: no ch* **14/1**

/46- 5 shd **Ministry**[27] 8106 5-9-12 **63** .... GeorgeBaker 4 64
(Gary Moore) *trckd ldng trio: moved up to dispute ld over 2f out gng strly: hdd & wknd 1f out* **11/4**[2]

000- 6 hd **Rocky Rebel**[37] 7980 5-10-0 **65** ....(b) LiamKeniry 8 66
(Chris Bealby) *hld up in 8th: dropped to last 6f out: stl there 2f out and jst pushed along: reminders over 1f out: styd on but no ch* **33/1**

5/2- 7 ¾ **Now What**[56] 2167 6-9-4 **62** .... JoeyHaynes(7) 5 62
(Jonathan Portman) *hld up in 6th: prog on wd outside fr 5f out all way rnd bnd 4f out to 3f out: drvn to dispute ld over 2f out: hdd & wknd 1f out* **10/1**

500- 8 7 **Za'Lan (USA)**[11] 8297 4-9-2 **60** ....(v) FergusSweeney 3 51
(Chris Gordon) *led: upped the tempo 6f out: hdd over 2f out: wknd qckly* **33/1**

000- 9 4 **Burnbrake**[33] 8035 8-8-9 **46** oh1 .... RobertHavlin 6 33
(Richard Rowe) *chsd ldr to wl over 2f out: wknd rapidly* **50/1**

3m 35.03s (4.93) **Going Correction** -0.10s/f (Stan)
WFA 4 from 5yo+ 7lb **9** Ran SP% **116.3**
Speed ratings (Par 101): **83,82,82,80,80 80,79,76,74**
Tote swingers 1&2 £2.60, 1&3 £2.70, 2&3 £5.70 CSF £12.85 CT £48.54 TOTE £3.00: £1.10, £1.70, £2.10; EX 13.30 Trifecta £63.20 Pool: £1,607.43 - 19.06 winning units.
Owner Dr Catherine Wills **Bred** St Clare Hall Stud **Trained** Newmarket, Suffolk

FOCUS
An ordinary staying event, run at a pedestrian tempo, but the first two in particular are of interest despite the doubts over the bare form.

132 32REDBET.COM H'CAP 1m 4f (P)
6:15 (6:17) (Class 6) (0-58,58) 4-Y-O+ **£1,940** (£577; £288; £144) **Stalls** Centre

Form RPR

114- 1 **Pahente**[30] 5967 5-9-9 **57** ....(p) DavidProbert 7 71
(Tony Carroll) *hld up towards rr: prog over 4f out: rdn over 2f out: clsd to ld over 1f out: drew rt away as others wknd* **6/1**

002- 2 7 **Highly Likely (IRE)**[28] 8097 4-9-2 **54** .... AdamKirby 10 56
(Steve Woodman) *trckd ldng pair: wnt 2nd 1/2-way: clsd to ld jst over 4f out: drvn over 2f out: hdd over 1f out: fdd and no ch w wnr after* **5/1**[2]

065- 3 2 ¾ **Ice Apple**[28] 8097 5-8-9 **46** oh1 .... NataliaGemelova(3) 3 44
(John E Long) *chsd ldrs: rdn 1/2-way: sn lost pl: struggling bdly in last quartet over 3f out: styd on again fr 2f out to take 3rd last 75yds* **100/1**

P30- **4** *1 ¾* **Five Hearts**[14] 8260 5-9-2 **50** MartinLane 11 45
(Mark H Tompkins) *v s.i.s: hld up in rr: rdn and prog fr 3f out: n.d over 1f out: fdd fnl f* **20/1**

00-0 **5** *nse* **Gower Rules (IRE)**[3] 94 5-9-3 **51** KieranO'Neill 1 46
(John Bridger) *led 1f: chsd clr ldr to 1/2-way: rdn 4f out: stl disputing 3rd over 1f out: wknd* **20/1**

64-4 **6** *1 ¼* **Silkee Supreme**[8] 21 4-8-12 **57** (b) RufusVergette(7) 12 50
(Richard Hannon) *hld up in rr: prog on wd outside fr 7f out to chal 4f out: urged along over 2f out: wknd over 1f out* **4/1**[1]

500/ **7** *1 ¼* **Share Option**[42] 771 11-8-12 **46** oh1 JimmyQuinn 4 37
(Tony Carroll) *free to post: s.s: hld up wl in rr: no prog and adrift over 3f out: modest late hdwy* **50/1**

040- **8** *¾* **Bennelong**[21] 8189 7-9-9 **57** (p) AmirQuinn 6 47
(Richard Rowe) *hld up in midfield: prog 4f out: rdn to chse ldng pair over 2f out and tried to cl: wknd over 1f out* **8/1**

005- **9** *1 ¼* **Made Of More**[19] 8229 4-9-3 **55** RobertHavlin 9 43
(Roger Ingram) *in tch in midfield: rdn 5f out: last of main gp and u.p over 3f out: sn btn* **11/2**[3]

0/0- **10** *2 ½* **Bet Noir (IRE)**[127] 5935 8-8-9 **46** oh1 RaulDaSilva(3) 8 30
(Tony Carroll) *awkward s: tk fierce hold and restrained into last: no prog and struggling 4f out* **50/1**

600/ **11** *18* **Kambis**[53] 3518 5-9-10 **58** GeorgeBaker 5 13
(Gary Moore) *dwlt: a wl in rr: shoved along and struggling over 4f out: t.o* **4/1**[1]

04-0 **12** *4* **Sir Dylan**[8] 9 4-9-4 **56** (be) WilliamCarson 2
(Ronald Harris) *s.i.s: rousted along to ld over 10f out and sn clr: hdd & wknd jst over 4f out: t.o* **8/1**

2m 33.72s (-0.78) **Going Correction** -0.10s/f (Stan)
WFA 4 from 5yo+ 4lb 12 Ran SP% **123.0**
Speed ratings (Par 101): **98,93,91,90,90 89,88,88,87,85 73,70**
Tote swingers 1&2 £4.20, 1&3 £36.70, 2&3 £26.90 CSF £35.87 CT £2770.37 TOTE £8.30: £2.70, £2.10, £8.90; EX 36.70 Trifecta £1005.50 Part won. Pool: £1,340.75 - 0.80 winning units..

Owner Mayden Stud **Bred** Mayden Stud, J A And D S Dewhurst **Trained** Cropthorne, Worcs

FOCUS
A moderate race with no depth, in which the relative proximity of the third gives cause for concern. The winner confirmed that he was on a fair Flat mark.

133 32RED H'CAP 1m (P)
6:45 (6:46) (Class 4) (0-85,82) 4-Y-0+ **£4,690** (£1,395; £697; £348) **Stalls** Low

Form RPR

21-2 **1** **Lowther**[5] 79 8-8-12 **78** (b) NathanAlison(5) 4 87
(Lee Carter) *tk fierce hold: sn trckd ldrs: prog over 3f out: led 2f out: urged along and kpt on wl fr over 1f out* **3/1**[2]

101- **2** *¾* **Stir Trader (IRE)**[29] 8081 4-9-1 **76** TomEaves 5 83
(Philip Hide) *hld up in last pair: rdn over 2f out: prog over 1f out: tk 2nd last 100yds: styd on but nvr quite able to chal* **16/1**

112- **3** *1* **Haftohaf**[21] 8183 4-9-0 **75** AdamKirby 2 80
(Marco Botti) *t.k.h: trckd ldr to over 2f out: pressed wnr after: nt qckn over 1f out: kpt on same pce and lost 2nd last 100yds* **10/11**[1]

603- **4** *½* **Buckland (IRE)**[21] 8181 5-8-5 **71** NicoleNordblad(5) 3 75
(Hans Adielsson) *t.k.h: cl up: lost grnd and pls on outer bnd 4f out to 3f out: renewed effrt 2f out: kpt on but nvr chal* **16/1**

214- **5** *½* **Hometown Glory**[11] 8296 4-9-7 **82** (t) MartinLane 1 84
(Brian Meehan) *trckd ldrs: rdn on inner over 2f out: nt qckn wl over 1f out: one pce after* **6/1**[3]

122- **6** *¾* **Red Somerset (USA)**[14] 8250 10-9-4 **79** KieranO'Neill 7 80
(Mike Murphy) *dwlt: t.k.h: hld up in last: shkn up over 2f out: kpt on fnl f: nvr in it* **14/1**

253- **7** *2* **Jack Who's He (IRE)**[14] 8250 4-9-4 **79** (vt) WilliamCarson 6 75
(David Evans) *led: jinked lft after 2f: hdd 2f out: steadily wknd* **25/1**

1m 38.0s (-1.80) **Going Correction** -0.10s/f (Stan) 7 Ran SP% **113.9**
Speed ratings (Par 105): **105,104,103,102,102 101,99**
Tote swingers 1&2 £3.50, 1&3 £1.60, 2&3 £2.30 CSF £46.40 TOTE £3.00: £1.70, £7.60; EX 59.50 Trifecta £98.70 Pool: £1,658.84 - 12.79 winning units.

Owner P G Marsh **Bred** L J Barratt **Trained** Epsom, Surrey

FOCUS
A good race, with plenty of solid form on show, but the pace was slack. The winner remains on a good mark on his old form.

134 32REDBINGO.COM H'CAP 1m (P)
7:15 (7:15) (Class 6) (0-60,60) 3-Y-O **£1,940** (£577; £288; £144) **Stalls** Low

Form RPR

005- **1** **Taxiformissbyron**[20] 8203 3-8-9 **48** TomEaves 3 56
(Michael Herrington) *chsd clr ldng pair: clsd over 2f out: shkn up to ld over 1f out: drvn and kpt on fnl f* **7/2**[2]

65-2 **2** *1 ½* **Subtle Difference**[8] 14 3-9-5 **58** DavidProbert 8 62
(Andrew Balding) *chsd clr ld and clr of rest: clsd to ld jst over 2f out: hdd and one pce over 1f out* **3/1**[1]

153- **3** *hd* **Crystal Peaks**[12] 8289 3-9-7 **60** DaleSwift 6 63
(James Given) *w.w off the pce disputing 4th: rdn 3f out: kpt on u.p to take 3rd 1f out: clsd on runner-up nr fin* **4/1**[3]

566- **4** *5* **Entrapping**[36] 7989 3-9-6 **59** SeanLevey 7 52
(Richard Hannon) *led at gd pce: hdd jst over 2f out: sn wknd* **7/2**[2]

04-6 **5** *4 ½* **Handsome Stranger (IRE)**[1] 122 3-9-7 **60** AdamKirby 4 42
(David Evans) *w.w off the pce disputing 4th: rdn 3f out: no prog and wl btn fnl 2f* **4/1**[3]

400- **6** *6* **Silk Scarf (IRE)**[130] 5851 3-9-1 **54** MartinLane 5 22
(Mark H Tompkins) *awkward s and then snatched up sn after: a in last pair: rdn 1/2-way: struggling after* **25/1**

030- **7** *¾* **Cerys**[38] 7971 3-8-7 **46** oh1 (p) WilliamCarson 1 13
(Derek Haydn Jones) *dwlt: a in last pair: rdn 1/2-way: struggling after* **33/1**

1m 39.1s (-0.70) **Going Correction** -0.10s/f (Stan) 7 Ran SP% **116.2**
Speed ratings (Par 95): **99,97,97,92,87 81,81**
Tote swingers 1&2 £2.10, 1&3 £4.40, 2&3 £1.30 CSF £14.92 CT £43.21 TOTE £4.10: £1.40, £2.70; EX 11.60 Trifecta £50.00 Pool: £1,425.61 - 21.35 winning units.

Owner H Hurst **Bred** Hugh M Hurst **Trained** Cold Kirby, N Yorks

FOCUS
A modest line-up, but the pace tested them. Fillies filled the first three places. The form is rated around the second and third.
T/Plt: £40.20 to a £1 stake. Pool: £54,990.16 - 998.16 winning units T/Qpdt: £17.00 to a £1 stake. Pool: £7,239.20 - 314.60 winning units JN

[118]LINGFIELD (L-H)
Thursday, January 10

OFFICIAL GOING: Standard
Wind: Light; across Weather: Dry; overcast

135 LINGFIELDPARK.CO.UK APPRENTICE CLASSIFIED CLAIMING STKS 5f (P)
12:55 (12:55) (Class 6) 4-Y-0+ **£2,045** (£603; £302) **Stalls** High

Form RPR

320- **1** **Love You Louis**[115] 6314 7-9-0 70 PatrickHills 5 69
(J R Jenkins) *dwlt: sn rcvrd to chse ldr: rdn and ev ch 2f out: led 1f out: styd on wl and asserted fnl 75yds* **3/1**[2]

63-3 **2** *dht* **Above The Stars**[3] 101 5-8-6 64 ow1 GeorgeChaloner(5) 3 63
(Richard Fahey) *chsd ldng pair: rdn over 2f out: wnt for run on inner but n.m.r over 1f out: barging match w rival ins fnl f: kpt on to join 2nd cl home: fin dead-heat 2nd: promoted to outright 2nd* **1/2**[1]

50-1 **3** *¾* **Johnny Splash (IRE)**[7] 30 4-8-6 48 (b) NathanAlison(3) 4 61
(Roger Teal) *racd keenly: led: hrd pressed and rdn over 1f out: leaning in on rival ent fnl f: barging match w rival ins fnl f: jnd for 2nd on post: fin dead-heat 2nd: disqualified and plcd 3rd* **8/1**[3]

400- **4** *hd* **Atlantic Beach**[10] 8307 8-8-5 63 (p) PhilipPrince(5) 2 61
(Milton Bradley) *stdd after s: hld up in detached last: rdn over 1f out: no imp tl styd on strly fnl 100yds: nt quite rch ldrs* **10/1**

59.03s (0.23) **Going Correction** +0.10s/f (Slow) 4 Ran SP% **111.9**
Speed ratings (Par 101): **102,100,100,100**
CSF £10.72 TOTE £3.00; EX 7.10 Trifecta £10.80 Pool: £833.80 - 57.67 winning units.

Owner J Pepper **Bred** Mrs Wendy Jenkins **Trained** Royston, Herts
■ Stewards' Enquiry : Nathan Alison one-day ban: careless riding (24 Jan)

FOCUS
A weak claimer run at an honest pace with the field well grouped passing the post. Shaky form, rated around the third.

136 BECOME AN OWNER WITH LPOG MAIDEN STKS 5f (P)
1:25 (1:25) (Class 5) 3-Y-0+ **£2,726** (£805; £402) **Stalls** High

Form RPR

23- **1** **Tanghan (IRE)**[142] 5449 3-8-12 0 TomEaves 5 60+
(Richard Fahey) *racd keenly: mde all: rdn and r.o strly and drew clr ins fnl f: readily* **4/11**[1]

22-4 **2** *3 ¼* **Jermatt**[8] 19 4-9-13 60 IanMongan 6 54
(J R Jenkins) *t.k.h: chsd wnr: rdn: outpcd and lost 2nd over 1f out: kpt on again u.p to chse clr wnr again wl ins fnl f: no imp* **7/2**[2]

23-3 **3** *nk* **Island Express (IRE)**[1] 123 6-9-8 48 (tp) AnnStokell(5) 3 53
(Ann Stokell) *awkward leaving stalls: sn rcvrd to chse ldrs: rdn and effrt over 1f out: chsd wnr over 1f out: no imp: lost 2nd wl ins fnl f* **20/1**

005- **4** *½* **Desert Red (IRE)**[14] 8251 4-9-8 40 (vt) DavidProbert 2 46
(Phil McEntee) *wnt rt s and s.i.s: hld up wl in tch: rdn and effrt whn hung lft and hmpd over 1f out: swtchd rt 1f out: kpt on fnl 100yds: no ch w wnr* **50/1**

306- **5** *1* **Proventi**[19] 8224 3-8-12 50 (b) SebSanders 1 43
(Alan McCabe) *chsd ldrs: rdn and effrt on inner over 1f out: no ex and btn jst ins fnl f: wl hld and plugged on same pce after* **25/1**

000- **6** *2 ¾* **Actonetaketwo**[19] 8233 3-8-0 0 PhilipPrince(7) 8 27
(Ron Hodges) *in tch on outer: hung rt ent fnl 2f and lost pl: no prog fr over 1f out* **100/1**

7 *34* **Carbas (ITY)** 3-8-5 0 RyanWhile(7) 4
(Bill Turner) *restless in stalls: s.i.s: sn totally outpcd: t.o whn hung rt over 1f out* **12/1**[3]

59.79s (0.99) **Going Correction** +0.10s/f (Slow)
WFA 3 from 4yo+ 15lb 7 Ran SP% **114.8**
Speed ratings (Par 103): **96,90,90,89,87 83,29**
Tote swingers 1&2 £1.30, 1&3 £2.60, 2&3 £2.60 CSF £1.88 TOTE £1.30: £1.10, £1.90; EX 2.00 Trifecta £8.80 Pool: £2,804.69 - 237.25 winning units.

Owner Mrs H Steel **Bred** Irish National Stud **Trained** Musley Bank, N Yorks

FOCUS
A weak maiden. It was run at a steady pace, with the favourite making all to win well enough. The winner didn't need to get anywhere near last year's debut effort.

137 BREATHE SPA AT LINGFIELD MARRIOTT H'CAP 5f (P)
1:55 (1:55) (Class 6) (0-60,57) 3-Y-O **£2,045** (£603; £302) **Stalls** High

Form RPR

06-1 **1** **Lager Time (IRE)**[7] 31 3-9-8 **57** 6ex WilliamCarson 4 67+
(David Evans) *mde all: rdn and asserted jst over 1f out: styd on: rdn out* **1/3**[1]

235- **2** *2* **Holding Fast (IRE)**[26] 8132 3-9-2 **51** MartinLane 1 51
(Tobias B P Coles) *pressed wnr on inner: rdn 2f out: no ex and btn ent fnl f: kpt on but a hld fnl f* **5/1**[2]

104- **3** *2 ¼* **Tartan Blue**[14] 8245 3-9-0 **56** HannahNunn(7) 3 48
(Robert Cowell) *sn outpcd in rr: wl bhd 1/2-way: wnt modest 3rd and rdn wl over 1f out: styd on fnl f: nvr trbld ldrs* **6/1**[3]

650- **4** *10* **Jubilini**[116] 6276 3-8-10 **45** DavidProbert 2
(Brett Johnson) *chsd ldng pair: outpcd and rdn along after 1f: last and wl bhd over 1f out: eased wl ins fnl f* **20/1**

59.45s (0.65) **Going Correction** +0.10s/f (Slow) 4 Ran SP% **110.7**
Speed ratings (Par 95): **98,94,91,75**
CSF £2.58 TOTE £1.80; EX 2.00 Trifecta £3.60 Pool: £1,215.65 - 252.92 winning units.

Owner Mrs E Evans **Bred** Polish Belle Partnership **Trained** Pandy, Monmouths

FOCUS
An uncompetitive handicap run at a sound pace, and the short-price favourite won in convincing style. There is some doubt over the worth of the form.

138 FOLLOW US ON TWITTER @LINGFIELDPARK H'CAP 1m (P)
2:25 (2:25) (Class 5) (0-70,70) 4-Y-0+ **£2,587** (£770; £384; £192) **Stalls** High

Form RPR

521- **1** **Avertis**[20] 8199 8-9-2 **70** AmyScott(5) 7 77
(Alastair Lidderdale) *chsd ldr tl rdn to ld over 1f out: edgd lft u.p 1f out: kpt on wl: rdn out* **6/1**[2]

534- **2** *½* **Stormbound (IRE)**[50] 7818 4-9-4 **70** (b[1]) RaulDaSilva(3) 5 76
(Paul Cole) *dwlt: sn swtchd lft and rcvrd to chse ldrs: edgd rt 2f out: rdn and press wnr 1f out: kpt on fnl f: a jst hld* **7/4**[1]

211- **3** *1* **Storm Runner (IRE)**[10] 8308 5-9-2 **65** 6ex IanMongan 2 69
(George Margarson) *hld up in tch in last pair: rdn and effrt on outer wl over 1f out: hdwy u.p 1f out: chsd ldrs ins fnl f: styd on* **7/4**[1]

11-0 **4** ½ **Brown Pete (IRE)**[4] 83 5-9-4 67 WilliamCarson 4 70
(Violet M Jordan) *stdd after s: hld up in tch in last pair: rdn and effrt over 1f out: swtchd rt 1f out: styd on u.p fnl 100yds* **8/1**[3]

005- **5** 1¼ **Everybody Knows**[27] 8105 8-9-3 66 FergusSweeney 3 66
(Jo Crowley) *taken down early: led: rdn and hdd over 1f out: no ex 1f out: wknd fnl 100yds* **14/1**

400- **6** 1 **Shared Moment (IRE)**[14] 8248 7-8-9 58 DavidProbert 1 55
(Luke Dace) *wl in tch in midfield: rdn and effrt whn short of room and hmpd ent fnl 2f: styd on same pce fr over 1f out* **20/1**

13-5 **7** 2 **Crowning Star (IRE)**[8] 13 4-9-7 70 (t) GeorgeBaker 6 63
(Gay Kelleway) *chsd ldrs on outer: rdn and unable qck 2f out: wknd ent fnl f* **8/1**[3]

1m 37.97s (-0.23) **Going Correction** +0.10s/f (Slow) 7 Ran SP% **120.7**
Speed ratings (Par 103): **105,104,103,103,101 100,98**
Tote swingers 1&2 £2.80, 1&3 £2.40, 2&3 £1.80 CSF £18.25 TOTE £6.60: £3.30, £2.30; EX 24.50 Trifecta £45.40 Pool: £1,882.63 - 31.07 winning units.
Owner Chris Beek & Sally Doyle **Bred** Mrs Sally Doyle **Trained** Lambourn, Berks

FOCUS
A steady gallop for this ordinary handicap, which suited those racing close to the pace. A slight step up from the winner on his C&D latest.

139 REHOME FROM WORLD HORSE WELFARE H'CAP 6f (P)
2:55 (2:55) (Class 6) (0-60,60) 4-Y-O+ **£2,045** (£603; £302) **Stalls** Low

Form RPR

401- **1** **Reginald Claude**[22] 8169 5-9-1 59 RachealKneller(5) 3 69
(Mark Usher) *hld up in rr: swtchd rt and gd hdwy over 1f out: urged along hands and heels and r.o strly ins fnl f to ld last strides* **5/1**[2]

11-1 **2** hd **Bussa**[7] 35 5-9-6 59 6ex (t) AdamKirby 8 68
(David Evans) *short of room leaving stalls: hld up in tch in last trio: hdwy 1/2-way: rdn and effrt 2f out: chsd clr ldr 1f out: styd on wl u.p to ld cl home: hdd last strides* **4/6**[1]

23-3 **3** ½ **Spartic**[7] 35 5-9-5 58 (p) SeanLevey 6 66
(Alan McCabe) *led: rdn and wnt clr wl over 1f out: drvn 1f out: hdd and lost 2 pls cl home* **6/1**[3]

000- **4** 2 **Exkaliber**[21] 8190 4-8-10 49 (t) FergusSweeney 2 50
(Jeremy Gask) *chsd ldrs: hmpd jst over 2f out: hdwy u.p over 1f out: kpt on same pce ins fnl f* **50/1**

05-0 **5** 1¼ **Lady Mango (IRE)**[7] 35 5-9-7 60 WilliamCarson 1 57
(Ronald Harris) *hld up in tch towards rr: rdn and swtchd rt over 1f out: styd on ins fnl f: no threat to ldrs* **20/1**

404- **6** nk **Sannibel**[36] 7990 5-9-6 59 DavidProbert 9 55
(Graeme McPherson) *chsd ldr: rdn and unable qck 2f out: lost 2nd 1f out: wknd ins fnl f* **12/1**

30-4 **7** shd **Imaginary Diva**[7] 30 7-9-4 57 IanMongan 4 53
(George Margarson) *hld up wl in tch in midfield: nt clr run 2f out: rdn and effrt between horses over 1f out: no prog 1f out: wknd ins fnl f* **20/1**

303- **8** 3 **Christopher Chua (IRE)**[12] 8287 4-9-1 54 SebSanders 7 40
(Simon Dow) *sn bustled along to chse ldrs: rdn and unable qck 2f out: wknd ent fnl f* **12/1**

005- **9** 1¼ **Le King Beau (USA)**[11] 8294 4-9-4 57 (v) KieranO'Neill 5 39
(John Bridger) *hld up in tch towards rr: rdn and no hdwy wl over 1f out: wknd ent fnl f* **33/1**

1m 11.47s (-0.43) **Going Correction** +0.10s/f (Slow) 9 Ran SP% **120.8**
Speed ratings (Par 101): **106,105,105,102,100 100,100,96,94**
Tote swingers 1&2 £2.30, 1&3 £3.40, 2&3 £2.60 CSF £8.81 CT £22.14 TOTE £5.20: £1.60, £1.10, £1.60; EX 11.90 Trifecta £33.40 Pool: £1,919.54 - 43.10 winning units.
Owner High Five Racing **Bred** Whitsbury Manor Stud **Trained** Upper Lambourn, Berks

FOCUS
This moderate handicap was run at a fair pace, with the first two home coming late to fight out a thrilling finish. The winner backed up his C&D latest and the time was fair for the grade.

140 HALF PRICE GOLF/RACING AT LINGFIELD MARRIOTT MAIDEN STKS 1m 2f (P)
3:25 (3:26) (Class 5) 4-Y-O+ **£2,726** (£805; £402) **Stalls** Low

Form RPR

232- **1** **Srinagar Girl**[27] 8105 4-9-0 71 IanMongan 6 70+
(Sir Henry Cecil) *stdd s: hld up in last pair: hdwy to press ldrs 2f out: rdn and ev ch ent fnl f: led ins fnl f: kpt on: rdn out* **6/4**[1]

32- **2** hd **Suffice (IRE)**[204] 3273 4-9-5 0 DavidNolan 5 75+
(Richard Fahey) *chsd ldrs: rdn and effrt on inner to ld jst over 1f out: drvn and hdd ins fnl f: kpt on but hld towards fin* **6/4**[1]

060- **3** 6 **Who's That Chick (IRE)**[132] 5795 4-9-0 55 SeanLevey 1 58
(Ralph Smith) *led: rdn over 2f out: hdd jst over 1f out: sn outpcd and btn: plugged on to hold 3rd fnl f* **25/1**

54- **4** 1½ **Handsome Molly**[29] 8080 4-9-0 0 LiamKeniry 4 55
(David Elsworth) *pressed ldr: rdn and ev ch over 2f out: wknd u.p over 1f out* **20/1**[3]

52- **5** 8 **Minority Interest**[105] 6615 4-9-5 0 KieranO'Neill 2 44
(Brett Johnson) *t.k.h: hld up in last pair: rdn and struggling 3f out: bhd and rn wd bnd 2f out: sn lost tch* **11/4**[2]

2m 7.14s (0.54) **Going Correction** +0.10s/f (Slow) 5 Ran SP% **115.3**
Speed ratings (Par 103): **101,100,96,94,88**
CSF £4.27 TOTE £1.80: £1.20, £1.10; EX 4.50 Trifecta £39.30 Pool: £2,604.60 - 49.65 winning units.
Owner A Parker (London) **Bred** Allan Munnis & Laurance Walwin **Trained** Newmarket, Suffolk

FOCUS
Not a strong maiden. It wa run at a steady pace and the front two pulled clear up the straight to give Sir Henry Cecil a winner with his first runner of 2013. The winner did not have to find her best.

141 WEDDINGS AT LINGFIELD PARK H'CAP 1m 2f (P)
3:55 (3:55) (Class 5) (0-75,69) 3-Y-O **£2,587** (£770; £384; £192) **Stalls** Low

Form RPR

502- **1** **Grendisar (IRE)**[33] 8032 3-9-4 66 AdamKirby 2 71+
(Marco Botti) *led for 2f: chsd ldr after tl rdn to ld over 2f out: edgd lft u.p and hdd 2f out: led again over 1f out: rn green and veered rt ins fnl f: stened and kpt on fnl 75yds* **1/2**[1]

225- **2** ½ **Rakticate (IRE)**[12] 8289 3-8-5 60 CharlotteJenner(7) 7 62
(J S Moore) *racd keenly: chsd ldrs tl led 8f out: hdd over 2f out: short of room and hmpd bnd 2f out: rallied and pressed ldr again ins fnl f: edgd rt and one pce towards fin* **20/1**

003- **3** shd **Candyman Can (IRE)**[26] 8134 3-8-11 64 RachealKneller(5) 6 65
(Dominic Ffrench Davis) *hld up in midfield: lost pl over 2f out: rdn and effrt over 1f out: str run ins fnl f to go 3rd cl home: nt quite rch ldrs* **14/1**

255- **4** 1 **Inessa Armand (IRE)**[42] 7923 3-8-12 60 FergusSweeney 3 59
(J S Moore) *chsd ldrs: rdn and effrt to chal over 2f out: led 2f out: hdd and unable qck over 1f out: lft pressing wnr again ins fnl f: no ex and btn whn carried rt towards fin* **14/1**

646- **5** ½ **Abraq**[29] 8072 3-9-7 69 (b[1]) StevieDonohoe 5 67
(Ed Dunlop) *hld up in rr: hdwy on outer to press ldrs over 2f out: rdn and outpcd over 1f out: rallied u.p 1f out: chsng ldrs but hld whn nt clr run wl ins fnl f* **7/1**[3]

25-3 **6** 1 **Run It Twice (IRE)**[8] 18 3-9-6 68 SeanLevey 4 64
(David Evans) *hld up in last pair: hdwy 3f out: effrt u.p and swtchd lft 1f out: kpt on same pce ins fnl f* **6/1**[2]

010- **7** 11 **Bubbly Bailey**[20] 8203 3-9-0 62 (p) IanMongan 1 42
(Alan Bailey) *hld up in last trio: rdn and effrt jst over 2f out: wknd over 1f out: bhd and eased ins fnl f* **16/1**

2m 10.37s (3.77) **Going Correction** +0.10s/f (Slow) 7 Ran SP% **117.4**
Speed ratings (Par 97): **88,87,87,86,86 85,76**
Tote swingers 1&2 £4.80, 1&3 £3.80, 2&3 £5.30 CSF £14.66 TOTE £1.20: £1.40, £5.20; EX 9.60 Trifecta £58.30 Pool: £3,215.31 - 41.33 winning units.
Owner Mohamed Albousi Alghufli **Bred** Old Carhue & Graeng Bloodstock **Trained** Newmarket, Suffolk

FOCUS
A moderate contest. The pace was not strong and several had a chance inside the final furlong. It was a messy race and the form is a bit shaky.
T/Plt: £34.00 to a £1 stake. Pool: £41,222.31 - 884.75 winning units T/Qpdt: £5.20 to a £1 stake. Pool: £3,363.66 - 474.90 winning units SP

104 WOLVERHAMPTON (A.W) (L-H)
Thursday, January 10

OFFICIAL GOING: Standard
Wind: Light; behind Weather: Foggy

142 CORAL.CO.UK H'CAP 5f 20y(P)
1:35 (1:35) (Class 6) (0-58,58) 4-Y-O+ **£1,940** (£577; £288; £144) **Stalls** Low

Form RPR

40-3 **1** **Liberty Ship**[8] 26 8-9-7 58 MartinDwyer 3 66
(Mark Buckley) *trckd ldrs: racd keenly: shkn up to ld ins fnl f: r.o* **9/1**[3]

246- **2** nk **Loyal Royal (IRE)**[19] 8231 10-9-6 57 (bt) RobertWinston 5 64
(Milton Bradley) *hld up: hmpd sn after s: hdwy over 1f out: r.o to go 2nd nr fin: nt quite rch wnr* **14/1**

122- **3** ½ **Rose Garnet (IRE)**[14] 8256 5-9-6 57 JimCrowley 2 62
(Tony Carroll) *sn pushed along and prom: rdn and ev ch ins fnl f: styd on same pce: lost 2nd nr fin* **6/5**[1]

500- **4** 1½ **Sally's Swansong**[14] 8253 7-9-4 55 (b) LukeMorris 1 55
(Eric Alston) *led: rdn over 1f out: hdd and unable qck ins fnl f* **25/1**

24-6 **5** 1¾ **Chateau Lola**[4] 81 4-9-1 52 JoeFanning 4 45
(Derek Shaw) *chsd ldr: rdn and ev ch ins fnl f: styd on same pce* **20/1**

50-1 **6** ½ **Hab Reeh**[4] 81 5-8-5 49 (bt) GemmaTutty(7) 8 41
(Ruth Carr) *s.i.s: plld hrd and sn prom: rdn over 1f out: edgd lft and no ex fnl f* **7/4**[2]

53-4 **7** 2 **Nafa (IRE)**[4] 81 5-9-2 53 (p) ShaneKelly 7 37
(Daniel Mark Loughnane) *s.i.s: hld up: rdn over 1f out: nvr on terms* **25/1**

00-0 **8** nse **Thorpe Bay**[7] 30 4-9-1 52 (b) JamesSullivan 9 36
(Conor Dore) *chsd ldrs: rdn over 1f out: wknd ins fnl f* **33/1**

1m 2.22s (-0.08) **Going Correction** +0.05s/f (Slow) 8 Ran SP% **113.9**
Speed ratings (Par 101): **102,101,100,98,95 94,91,91**
Tote swingers 1&2 £4.10, 1&3 £2.60, 2&3 £3.20 CSF £106.03 CT £256.80 TOTE £10.30: £2.30, £5.70, £1.70; EX 44.40 Trifecta £152.60 Pool: £2,171.05 - 10.66 winning units.
Owner David Lockwood & Fred Lockwood **Bred** Mrs R D Peacock **Trained** Castle Bytham, Lincs
■ Stewards' Enquiry : Gemma Tutty one-day ban: careless riding (24 Jan)

FOCUS
Weak sprinting form, but the time was fair. The winner built on his better C&D latest.

143 CORAL.CO.UK MOBILE CASINO (S) H'CAP 5f 216y(P)
2:05 (2:05) (Class 6) (0-60,60) 4-Y-O+ **£1,940** (£577; £216; £216) **Stalls** Low

Form RPR

336- **1** **Ivestar (IRE)**[12] 8285 8-9-7 60 (vt) JamesSullivan 10 69
(Michael Easterby) *a.p: rdn over 1f out: styd on to ld wl ins fnl f* **11/2**[3]

054- **2** ½ **Adaeze (IRE)**[22] 8168 5-8-7 46 oh1 (v) JohnFahy 9 53
(Jonathan Portman) *trckd ldr tl led over 1f out: rdn and hdd wl ins fnl f* **22/1**

505- **3** 2¼ **Whipphound**[14] 8256 5-9-3 56 JimCrowley 3 56+
(Mark Brisbourne) *hld up: hdwy over 1f out: nt clr run and swtchd rt ins fnl f: r.o: nt rch ldrs* **4/1**[2]

200- **3** dht **Gypsy Rider**[55] 7747 4-9-1 54 LukeMorris 8 54
(Bryn Palling) *hld up: hdwy over 1f out: r.o: nt rch ldrs* **11/1**

005- **5** nse **Imjin River (IRE)**[14] 8255 6-9-3 56 (t) KirstyMilczarek 2 56
(William Stone) *chsd ldrs: rdn over 1f out: styd on* **8/1**

065- **6** 1¼ **Sir Nod**[26] 8144 11-9-7 60 PaddyAspell 1 56
(Julie Camacho) *hld up: racd keenly: nt clr run over 2f out: hdwy over 1f out: nt trble ldrs* **6/1**

/5-0 **7** 1 **Spoof Master (IRE)**[7] 30 9-8-4 46 (t) SimonPearce(3) 7 38
(Lydia Pearce) *prom: rdn over 1f out: styd on same pce* **50/1**

034- **8** ½ **Silver Wind**[14] 8256 8-9-5 58 (b) RobertWinston 5 49
(Alan McCabe) *s.i.s: sn drvn along in rr: reminders 4f out: nvr on terms* **2/1**[1]

006- **9** nk **Replicator**[20] 8210 8-8-7 46 oh1 (e) JamieMackay 6 36
(Patrick Gilligan) *led: rdn and hdd over 1f out: wknd ins fnl f* **40/1**

00-0 **10** ½ **Hinton Admiral**[6] 50 9-9-6 59 (b) BarryMcHugh 4 47
(Conor Dore) *broke wl: sn pushed along and lost pl: rdn over 2f out: sn lost tch* **11/1**

1m 14.91s (-0.09) **Going Correction** +0.05s/f (Slow) 10 Ran SP% **119.5**
Speed ratings (Par 101): **102,101,98,98,98 96,95,94,94,93**
CSF £119.96 TOTE £4.60: £2.10, £3.80; EX 90.20.There was no bid for the winner.
Owner Mrs Krista Brown **Bred** Grenane House Stud & Hatta International Bloodstoc **Trained** Sheriff Hutton, N Yorks

The Form Book Flat, Raceform Ltd, Compton, RG20 6NL.

FOCUS
Those who raced near the pace were seen to an advantage in this weak handicap. The winner's best form since his early days.

144 BOOKMAKER REVIEWS AT BOOKMAKERS.CO.UK H'CAP 1m 4f 50y(P)
2:35 (2:36) (Class 5) (0-75,80) 4-Y-0+ **£2,587** (£770; £384; £192) **Stalls** Low

Form RPR
311- **1** **Cool Sky**[19] 8229 4-9-6 **75**........ JimCrowley 4 84+
(William Knight) *chsd ldr 4f: remained handy: rdn to ld over 1f out: styd on* **1/1**[1]
1-13 **2** *1 ½* **Sir Boss (IRE)**[6] 52 8-9-8 **80** 6ex........ RobertTart(7) 6 86
(Michael Mullineaux) *a.p: chsd ldr 8f out: rdn over 1f out: styd on u.p* **7/1**[3]
420- **3** *nk* **Honest Deal**[15] 8243 5-9-5 **70**........ RobertWinston 7 76
(Alan Swinbank) *led at stdy pce tl qcknd over 2f out: shkn up: edgd rt and hdd over 1f out: styd on* **6/1**[2]
001- **4** *1 ¼* **Tingo In The Tale (IRE)**[20] 8206 4-9-2 **71**........ JoeFanning 5 75
(David Arbuthnot) *chsd ldrs: rdn over 1f out: styd on* **10/1**
24-2 **5** *nse* **Reflect (IRE)**[7] 39 5-9-7 **72**........(t) MartinDwyer 8 75
(Derek Shaw) *hld up: styd on u.p ins fnl f: nvr nrr* **8/1**
006- **6** *shd* **Brunston**[15] 8243 7-9-8 **73**........ LukeMorris 3 76
(Anthony Middleton) *hld up in tch: rdn over 2f out: styd on* **8/1**
63-2 **7** *2* **Stanley Rigby**[9] 2 7-8-13 **64**........ BarryMcHugh 2 64
(Richard Fahey) *prom: rdn over 2f out: no ex fnl f* **12/1**
215- **8** *8* **King Zeal (IRE)**[223] 2661 9-9-7 **72**........(t) KirstyMilczarek 9 59
(Barry Leavy) *s.i.s: hld up: rdn over 2f out: sn wknd* **66/1**

2m 41.78s (0.68) **Going Correction** +0.05s/f (Slow)
WFA 4 from 5yo+ 4lb **8** Ran SP% **117.3**
Speed ratings (Par 103): **99,98,97,96,96 96,95,90**
Tote swingers 1&2 £3.20, 1&3 £4.00, 2&3 £4.40 CSF £9.03 CT £30.01 TOTE £1.80: £1.10, £1.70, £1.80; EX 8.50 Trifecta £27.30 Pool: £2,258.52 - 61.97 winning units.
Owner No Quarter Partnership **Bred** Miss K J Keir **Trained** Patching, W Sussex

FOCUS
This was steadily run and the form may not be the most solid, but it's been taken at face value for now. The winner was value for a bit extra.

145 BOOKMAKERS.CO.UK GIVES YOU FREE BETS H'CAP 1m 1f 103y(P)
3:05 (3:05) (Class 6) (0-65,65) 4-Y-0+ **£1,940** (£577; £288; £144) **Stalls** Low

Form RPR
12-0 **1** **Royal Sea (IRE)**[6] 53 4-8-8 **60**........ RobertTart(7) 7 66
(Michael Mullineaux) *sn pushed along in rr: rdn over 2f out: hdwy over 1f out: hung lft ins fnl f: r.o to ld post* **4/1**[3]
221- **2** *nse* **Neige D'Antan**[20] 8213 4-9-6 **65**........ LukeMorris 8 71
(Sir Mark Prescott Bt) *chsd ldrs: led over 1f out: rdn and edgd lft ins fnl f: hdd post* **13/8**[1]
000- **3** *¾* **Going Grey (IRE)**[13] 8269 4-9-0 **59**........ BarryMcHugh 3 63
(Richard Fahey) *chsd ldrs: nt clr run wl over 1f out: sn rdn: styd on* **7/1**
/00- **4** *2* **Shelovestobougie**[13] 8271 5-8-13 **57**........(t) ShaneKelly 5 57
(Mark Brisbourne) *hld up: hdwy over 1f out: sn rdn: edgd lft and styd on same pce ins fnl f* **40/1**
450- **5** *4* **Olney Lass**[20] 8199 6-8-9 **56**........ SimonPearce(3) 2 48
(Lydia Pearce) *led 2f: chsd ldr: rdn and ev ch over 1f out: wknd ins fnl f* **25/1**
630- **6** *hd* **Sygnature**[225] 2604 4-9-1 **60**........ RobertWinston 1 51
(Alan Swinbank) *racd keenly: w ldr tl led over 7f out: rdn and hdd over 1f out: wknd ins fnl f* **6/1**
060- **7** *9* **Lyric Poet (USA)**[79] 7315 6-9-7 **65**........(t) ChrisCatlin 6 38
(Charlie Longsdon) *sn pushed along in rr: rdn and wknd over 2f out* **3/1**[2]

2m 1.97s (0.27) **Going Correction** +0.05s/f (Slow)
WFA 4 from 5yo+ 1lb **7** Ran SP% **116.2**
Speed ratings (Par 101): **100,99,99,97,93 93,85**
Tote swingers 1&2 £2.30, 1&3 £4.80, 2&3 £2.70 CSF £11.30 CT £43.45 TOTE £3.00: £1.10, £1.40; EX 9.40 Trifecta £59.90 Pool: £1,971.48 - 24.64 winning units.
Owner P Currey **Bred** Rabbah Bloodstock Limited **Trained** Alpraham, Cheshire

FOCUS
A steadily run handicap and the picture of the race changed dramatically in the straight. Reasonable form for the grade, rated around the third and fourth.

146 CORAL.CO.UK MOBILE BETTING H'CAP 1m 1f 103y(P)
3:35 (3:36) (Class 4) (0-80,80) 4-Y-0+ **£4,690** (£1,395; £697; £348) **Stalls** Low

Form RPR
031- **1** **Saoi (USA)**[14] 8252 6-9-7 **80**........ JimCrowley 3 89
(William Knight) *a.p: rdn over 1f out: r.o to ld post* **7/4**[1]
521- **2** *hd* **Knowe Head (NZ)**[19] 8234 6-8-13 **72**........(v) AdamBeschizza 4 80
(James Unett) *dwlt: hld up: hdwy over 1f out: rdn to ld ins fnl f: hdd post* **5/1**
213- **3** *½* **Fame Again**[13] 7685 5-8-12 **71**........ JamesSullivan 2 78
(Michael Easterby) *led: rdn and hdd ins fnl f: styd on* **3/1**[2]
100- **4** *2 ¼* **Canary Wharf (IRE)**[36] 7999 4-9-1 **75**........(p) LukeMorris 1 77
(Marco Botti) *chsd ldrs: rdn over 1f out: styd on same pce ins fnl f* **9/2**[3]
004- **5** *½* **Availed Speaker (IRE)**[13] 8269 4-8-8 **68**........ BarryMcHugh 5 69
(Richard Fahey) *chsd ldr: rdn over 2f out: no ex ins fnl f* **8/1**
000- **6** *1* **Spanish Plume**[48] 7842 5-8-8 **72**........ JackDuern(5) 7 71
(Reg Hollinshead) *hld up: rdn over 1f out: nvr trbld ldrs* **16/1**
050- **7** *14* **Chosen Forever**[48] 7842 8-8-13 **77**........ AdamCarter(5) 6 47
(Geoffrey Oldroyd) *prom: rdn over 3f out: wknd over 1f out* **16/1**

2m 1.12s (-0.58) **Going Correction** +0.05s/f (Slow)
WFA 4 from 5yo+ 1lb **7** Ran SP% **119.1**
Speed ratings (Par 105): **104,103,103,101,100 100,87**
Tote swingers 1&2 £2.30, 1&3 £2.50, 2&3 £2.80 CSF £11.81 TOTE £1.90: £1.10, £3.20; EX 10.40 Trifecta £25.50 Pool: £2,757.87 - 80.81 winning units.
Owner Surrey Horseracing Limited **Bred** Kilboy Estate Inc **Trained** Patching, W Sussex

FOCUS
Fair form for the grade, even if the pace wasn't strong. The winner built on his latest form.

147 EXCLUSIVE FREE BETS AT BOOKMAKERS.CO.UK H'CAP 1m 141y(P)
4:05 (4:05) (Class 6) (0-62,62) 4-Y-0+ **£1,940** (£577; £288; £144) **Stalls** Low

Form RPR
6- **1** **Jumbo Prado (USA)**[14] 8249 4-9-1 **57**........ ShaneKelly 7 67+
(Daniel Mark Loughnane) *hld up: hdwy over 1f out: led ins fnl f: comf* **15/2**
140- **2** *½* **Dubai Celebration**[66] 7593 5-9-2 **57**........ PaddyAspell 3 66
(Julie Camacho) *led: hdd over 6f out: led again over 1f out: hdd ins fnl f: styd on* **9/2**[3]
003- **3** *3* **Apache Glory (USA)**[13] 8271 5-9-7 **62**........ JoeFanning 4 64
(John Stimpson) *hld up: hdwy over 1f out: styd on same pce ins fnl f* **6/1**
214- **4** *1 ¼* **Nant Saeson (IRE)**[13] 8271 4-9-2 **58**........(p) MichaelO'Connell 1 57
(John Quinn) *chsd ldrs: rdn over 2f out: no ex ins fnl f* **7/2**[2]
15-0 **5** *1 ½* **Count Ceprano (IRE)**[2] 110 9-8-8 **52**........ SimonPearce(3) 8 48
(Lydia Pearce) *hld up: nt clr run over 2f out: r.o ins fnl f: nvr nrr* **12/1**
100- **6** *1 ½* **Rapid Water**[22] 8167 7-9-2 **57**........ JamesSullivan 2 49
(Pat Eddery) *mid-div: pushed along over 2f out: wknd ins fnl f* **25/1**
006- **7** *1 ¾* **Moral Issue**[13] 8271 5-9-7 **62**........ LukeMorris 5 50
(Ian McInnes) *chsd ldrs: rdn over 1f out: wknd ins fnl f* **8/1**
10-6 **8** *1* **Quan (IRE)**[8] 24 4-8-12 **54**........ RobertWinston 6 40
(Alan Swinbank) *racd keenly prom: led over 6f out: rdn and hdd over 1f out: wknd fnl f* **11/4**[1]

1m 49.25s (-1.25) **Going Correction** +0.05s/f (Slow)
WFA 4 from 5yo+ 1lb **8** Ran SP% **115.8**
Speed ratings (Par 101): **107,106,103,102,101 100,98,97**
Tote swingers 1&2 £7.50, 1&3 £6.20, 2&3 £5.50 CSF £41.63 CT £219.16 TOTE £12.40: £3.20, £2.00, £2.30; EX 53.00 Trifecta £449.60 Pool: £2,358.88 - 3.93 winning units.
Owner Mrs C Loughnane **Bred** Mr & Mrs Foreman Hardy **Trained** Baldwin's Gate, Staffs

FOCUS
An open handicap run at a fair pace, and the form looks sound. The winner will still be on a good mark after this.

148 GET THE INSIDE TRACK AT BOOKMAKERS.CO.UK MEDIAN AUCTION MAIDEN FILLIES' STKS 7f 32y(P)
4:35 (4:36) (Class 6) 3-4-Y-O **£1,940** (£577; £288; £144) **Stalls** High

Form RPR
23- **1** **Dutch Mistress**[15] 8239 4-9-12 0........ AdamBeschizza 5 65
(James Unett) *mde all: rdn over 1f out: jst hld on* **8/1**
2- **2** *½* **Rosie Rebel**[20] 8207 3-8-8 0........ ChrisCatlin 6 60+
(Rae Guest) *chsd ldrs: rdn over 2f out: r.o wl towards fin* **9/2**[3]
45- **3** *1 ½* **Gebayl**[22] 8171 3-8-8 0........ JoeFanning 7 56
(James Tate) *chsd wnr: shkn up over 2f out: styd on same pce ins fnl f* **15/8**[2]
4 *1 ¼* **Poet's Prospect (IRE)** 3-8-8 0........ AndreaAtzeni 4 52
(Marco Botti) *chsd ldrs: pushed along 1/2-way rdn over 1f out: styd on same pce fnl f* **11/8**[1]
000- **5** *2* **Charmel's Delight**[154] 5014 4-9-7 50........ AdamCarter(5) 2 51
(Geoffrey Oldroyd) *hld up: rdn over 1f out: nt trble ldrs* **66/1**
6 *8* **Combustible (IRE)** 3-8-8 0........ JamesSullivan 3 25
(Daniel Mark Loughnane) *hld up: plld hrd: wknd over 2f out* **33/1**
7 *21* **Bella Cinderella** 3-8-8 0........ DuranFentiman 1
(George Moore) *s.s: outpcd: t.o* **20/1**

1m 29.72s (0.12) **Going Correction** +0.05s/f (Slow)
WFA 3 from 4yo 18lb **7** Ran SP% **115.4**
Speed ratings (Par 98): **101,100,98,97,95 85,61**
Tote swingers 1&2 £2.00, 1&3 £1.90, 2&3 £1.30 CSF £43.08 TOTE £9.50: £4.70, £3.10; EX 21.40 Trifecta £64.20 Pool: £3,426.97 - 40.00 winning units.
Owner Gordon Kendrick **Bred** P And Mrs Venner And Trickledown Stud **Trained** Tedsmore Hall, Shropshire

FOCUS
A weak fillies' maiden in which the winner set an ordinary pace. This was a step up on her previous efforts.
T/Jkpt: Not won. T/Plt: £42.40 to a £1 stake. Pool: £60,317.44 - 1,037.80 winning units T/Qpdt: £10.00 to a £1 stake. Pool: £4,935.98 - 364.72 winning tickets CR

43 MEYDAN (L-H)
Thursday, January 10
OFFICIAL GOING: Tapeta: standard; turf: good

149a LONGINES SAINT IMIER (H'CAP) (TAPETA) 7f
3:05 (3:05) (95-105,104) 3-Y-0+
£40,490 (£13,496; £6,748; £3,374; £2,024; £1,349)

RPR
1 **Lily's Angel (IRE)**[62] 7680 4-8-11 **102**........ GaryCarroll 1 109
(G M Lyons, Ire) *trckd ldrs: smooth prog to ld 1 1/2f out: r.o wl: comf* **9/2**[2]
2 *1 ¾* **Ariete Arrollador**[90] 6-8-11 **102**........ ChristopheSoumillon 2 104
(G Arizkorreta Elosegui, Spain) *n.m.r after 2f: in rr of mid-div: r.o fnl 1 1/2f: nrst fin* **7/1**
3 *nk* **Yaa Wayl (IRE)**[91] 7010 6-8-11 **102**........(vt) SilvestreDeSousa 8 103
(Saeed bin Suroor) *mid-div: smooth prog 2f out: one pce fnl f* **7/1**
4 *1 ¼* **Spirit Of Battle (USA)**[21] 8198 5-8-11 **102**........(b) TadhgO'Shea 12 100+
(A bin Huzaim, UAE) *s.i.s: settled in rr: r.o fnl 1 1/2f: nrst fin* **16/1**
5 *¾* **Montmorency (IRE)**[18] 7-8-10 **101**........(vt) RichardMullen 6 97
(S Seemar, UAE) *sn led: kicked clr 2 1/2f out: hdd 1 1/2f out: kpt on same pce* **20/1**
6 *¾* **Iver Bridge Lad**[43] 7897 6-8-11 **102**........ DaraghO'Donohoe 14 96+
(John Ryan) *settled in rr: nvr nr to chal but r.o fnl 1 1/2f* **11/1**
7 *¾* **Tertio Bloom (SWE)**[123] 8-8-11 **102**........(t) Per-AndersGraberg 13 94
(Fabricio Borges, Sweden) *trckd ldrs: ev ch 1 1/2f out: wknd fnl 110yds* **20/1**
8 *1* **Canwinn (IRE)**[35] 8014 7-8-11 **102**........ JamesDoyle 11 91
(D Selvaratnam, UAE) *nvr bttr than mid-div* **20/1**
9 *4* **Oasis Dancer**[91] 7010 6-8-11 **102**........ KierenFallon 3 81
(Kevin Ryan) *nvr bttr than mid-div* **16/1**
10 *nk* **Belgian Bill**[50] 7809 5-8-13 **104**........(t) RyanMoore 7 82
(George Baker) *trckd ldrs tl outpcd 1 1/2f out* **6/1**[3]
11 *1 ¼* **Laa Rayb (USA)**[21] 8198 9-8-8 **102**........(t) SamJames(3) 9 76
(D Selvaratnam, UAE) *nvr bttr than mid-div* **33/1**
12 *½* **Akeed Wafi (IRE)**[203] 3322 4-8-11 **102**........ RoystonFfrench 4 75
(A Al Raihe, UAE) *slowly away: nvr nr to chal* **10/1**
13 *2* **Final Button (SAF)**[228] 5-8-11 **102**........ PatCosgrave 10 70
(M F De Kock, South Africa) *mid-div: chsd ldrs 3f out: one pce fnl 1 1/2f* **7/2**[1]
14 *1 ¼* **Il Grande Maurizio (IRE)**[350] 315 9-8-11 **102**........ PaulHanagan 5 66
(A Al Raihe, UAE) *trckd ldrs: ev ch 2 1/2f out: wknd fnl f* **25/1**

1m 24.48s (-0.72) **14** Ran SP% **130.0**
WIN: 4.30. PL: 2.00, 2.50, 2.30. EX: 25.60. CSF: 36.22. TRICAST: 231.04. TRIFECTA: 214.30..
Owner Clodagh Mitchell **Bred** N And Mrs N Nugent **Trained** Dunsany, Co. Meath

FOCUS
Rail moved out 4m on turf course. The sectionals for each quarter were 25.74, 48.78 and 1:12.37, and that proved a fair pace with the winner tracking the leaders while the next three finishers all raced well back. This had looked a competitive handicap - just 3lb separated the field - but it was won decisively by Lily's Angel.

150a LONGINES DOLCE VITA (H'CAP) (TURF) 5f
3:40 (3:40) (100-110,110) 3-Y-0+

£44,171 (£14,723; £7,361; £3,680; £2,208; £1,472)

RPR

1 **Fityaan**[18] 5-8-7 **100** PaulHanagan 16 105
(M Al Muhairi, UAE) *mid-div: rdn 2 1/2f out: r.o wl fnl 1 1/2f: led 55yds out: comf* **50/1**

2 1 1/4 **Temple Meads**[121] 6116 5-8-11 **105** (v) RichardMullen 9 105
(David Brown) *trckd ldrs: led 1 1/2f out: hdd fnl 55yds* **8/1**[3]

3 shd **Bear Behind (IRE)**[222] 2704 4-8-10 **104** RichardKingscote 8 104
(Tom Dascombe) *sn led: hdd 1 1/2f out wknd fnl 110yds* **16/1**

4 1 **Lui Rei (ITY)**[94] 6943 7-8-9 **102** KierenFallon 3 99
(Fawzi Abdulla Nass, Bahrain) *s.i.s: mid-div: r.o same pce fnl 2f* **12/1**

5 nse **Happy Dubai (IRE)**[21] 8197 6-9-3 **110** (t) DaneO'Neill 5 107
(A Al Raihe, UAE) *chsd ldrs: kpt on same pce fnl 110yds* **11/1**

6 shd **Inxile (IRE)**[95] 6908 8-9-1 **108** (p) DaraghO'Donohoe 12 104
(David Nicholls) *mid-div: kpt on same pce fnl f* **14/1**

7 shd **Smooth Operator (GER)**[27] 8130 7-9-0 **107** (v) ADeVries 15 103
(Mario Hofer, Germany) *nvr able to chal* **33/1**

8 hd **Invincible Ash (IRE)**[139] 5561 8-9-1 **108** (p) JamieSpencer 10 103
(M Halford, Ire) *nvr bttr than mid-div* **16/1**

9 1 **Pabusar**[81] 7288 5-8-9 **102** JamesDoyle 14 94
(Jamie Osborne) *nvr bttr than mid-div* **25/1**

10 hd **Balmont Mast (IRE)**[76] 7390 5-9-1 **108** GaryCarroll 2 99
(Edward Lynam, Ire) *a in mid-div* **6/1**[1]

11 shd **Confessional**[96] 6867 6-8-13 **106** (b) TedDurcan 7 97
(Tim Easterby) *fractious in stalls: nvr bttr than mid-div* **12/1**

12 1 1/4 **Cheviot (USA)**[75] 7397 7-8-10 **104** (p) RyanMoore 11 89
(Kevin Ryan) *trckd ldrs: one pce fnl 1 1/2f* **10/1**

13 1/2 **Desert Law (IRE)**[110] 6485 5-8-10 **104** SilvestreDeSousa 6 87
(Saeed bin Suroor) *chsd ldrs: one pce fnl f* **7/1**[2]

14 1 3/4 **Benji's Empire (AUS)**[48] 7-8-8 **101** StephenBaster 13 79
(S Burridge, Singapore) *nvr bttr than mid-div* **7/1**[2]

15 6 3/4 **Addictive Dream (IRE)**[225] 2602 6-9-0 **107** AdrianNicholls 4 61
(David Nicholls) *s.i.s: nvr bttr than mid-div* **6/1**[1]

16 2 1/2 **Govinda (USA)**[81] 7288 6-9-2 **109** Per-AndersGraberg 1 54
(Vanja Sandrup, Sweden) *led far side tl outpcd 3f out* **16/1**

57.1s (57.10) **16** Ran SP% **130.6**
WIN: 54.50. PL: EX:2685.60. CSF:438.54. TRICAST: 6659.25. TRIFECTA: 24755.40.
Owner Hamdan Al Maktoum **Bred** Usk Valley Stud **Trained** UAE

FOCUS
Hard to know what to make of this form. It looked a decent race beforehand, but the winner couldn't be fancied. The time, however, was the quickest of ten races to be run over C&D, lowering the record by over half a second.

151a LONGINES PRIMA LUNA (H'CAP) (TAPETA) 1m 1f 110y
4:15 (4:15) (95-105,104) 3-Y-0+

£40,490 (£13,496; £6,748; £3,374; £2,024; £1,349)

RPR

1 **Royal Empire (IRE)**[113] 6374 4-8-10 **100** SilvestreDeSousa 10 107
(Saeed bin Suroor) *trckd ldrs: led 1 1/2f out: r.o wl: comf* **7/2**[1]

2 1 1/2 **Kassiano (GER)**[102] 4-8-7 **97** TedDurcan 8 101
(Saeed bin Suroor) *trckd ldrs: rdn 1 1/2f out: one pce fnl 110yds* **8/1**[3]

3 1 **Start Right**[103] 6674 6-8-9 **97** (p) PatDobbs 12 99+
(Saeed bin Suroor) *settled in rr: r.o wl fnl 2f: nrst fin* **20/1**

4 hd **Plantagenet (SPA)**[81] 6-9-1 **102** J-LMartinez 16 105
(G Arizkorreta Elosegui, Spain) *trckd ldrs: ev ch 2 1/2f out: one pce fnl 110yds* **20/1**

5 3/4 **Arthur's Tale (USA)**[140] 5-8-10 **98** MickaelBarzalona 4 98
(Mahmood Al Zarooni) *mid-div: chsd ldrs 2f out: nt qckn fnl f* **10/1**

6 1 **Farrier (USA)**[27] 8124 5-8-8 **96** RichardMullen 2 94
(S Seemar, UAE) *trckd ldrs: ev ch 2f out: n.m.r 1 1/2f out: kpt on same pce* **6/1**[2]

7 3/4 **Rocks Off**[286] 5-8-11 **99** KierenFallon 5 95+
(Fawzi Abdulla Nass, Bahrain) *in rr of mid-div: kpt on one pce fnl 1 1/2f* **12/1**

8 1/2 **Ottoman Empire (FR)**[110] 6484 7-8-10 **98** HarryBentley 6 93
(David Simcock) *mid-div: kpt on same pce fnl 1 1/2f* **12/1**

9 2 **Tanfeeth**[21] 8195 5-9-1 **102** (t) WayneSmith 3 94+
(M Al Muhairi, UAE) *settled in rr: nvr able to chal* **20/1**

10 1/2 **Mushreq (AUS)**[285] 5-9-2 **104** PaulHanagan 7 94
(M F De Kock, South Africa) *sn led: hdd 3f out: wknd 1 1/2f out* **9/1**

11 1 1/2 **Marching Time**[18] 7-8-13 **100** (v) DaneO'Neill 13 88
(Doug Watson, UAE) *settled in rr: rdn 2 1/2f out: nt qckn fnl 1 1/2f* **25/1**

12 1/2 **Rochdale**[21] 8195 10-9-2 **104** (t) RoystonFfrench 1 90
(A Al Raihe, UAE) *settled in rr: nvr nr to chal* **33/1**

13 1 1/2 **Universal (IRE)**[103] 6661 4-8-9 **99** AdrianNicholls 9 82
(Mark Johnston) *slowly away: a in rr* **10/1**

14 1/4 **Topclas (FR)**[21] 8195 7-9-1 **102** (v) ADeVries 14 86
(M bin Shafya, UAE) *s.i.s: settled in last: n.d* **14/1**

15 4 1/4 **Muck 'N' Brass (IRE)**[55] 7759 4-8-8 **98** ow1 (t) PatCosgrave 11 72
(Edward Lynam, Ire) *nvr nr to chal* **14/1**

16 17 **Trois Rois (FR)**[298] 8-9-0 **101** (b) AntiocoMurgia 15 41
(Ismail Mohammed) *in rr of mid-div: v wde: rdn and struggling 3f out* **33/1**

1m 57.67s (-1.33)
WFA 4 from 5yo+ 1lb **16** Ran SP% **128.5**
WIN: 3.80. PL: EX:31.10. CSF: 28.93 TRICAST: 513.07 TRIFECTA: 1054.60.
Owner Godolphin **Bred** Twelve Oaks Stud **Trained** Newmarket, Suffolk

FOCUS
Not a bad race and Mushreq took them along at an even enough pace, setting splits of 26.80, 51.54, 1:16.09, before dropping away as though the run was needed. The winner is rated to the pick of his British form.

152a AL RASHIDIYA TRIAL PRESENTED BY LONGINES (CONDITIONS RACE) (TURF) 1m 1f
4:50 (4:50) 3-Y-0+

£46,012 (£15,337; £7,668; £3,834; £2,300; £1,533)

RPR

1 **Sharestan (IRE)**[194] 3646 5-9-0 111 SilvestreDeSousa 9 116+
(Saeed bin Suroor) *trckd ldng pair: led 2f out: r.o wl: comf* **10/11**[1]

2 4 **So Beautiful (FR)**[194] 3656 4-8-13 115 PaulHanagan 2 108+
(Doug Watson, UAE) *in rr of mid-div: n.m.r 4f out: r.o fnl 1 1/2f: nrst fin* **7/2**[2]

3 1/2 **Rerouted (USA)**[313] 792 5-9-0 108 ChristopheSoumillon 6 107
(M F De Kock, South Africa) *mid-div: chsd ldrs 2f out: outpcd 1 1/2f out but kpt on fnl f* **13/2**[3]

4 2 1/2 **Sham Sheer**[251] 7-9-0 100 KierenFallon 4 102?
(Fawzi Abdulla Nass, Bahrain) *trckd ldrs: ev ch tl outpcd 2 1/2f out: kpt on same pce* **33/1**

5 hd **Naseem Alyasmeen (IRE)**[117] 6236 4-8-8 91 DaneO'Neill 5 96
(A Al Raihe, UAE) *settled rr: nvr able to chal but kpt on fnl 1 1/2f* **33/1**

6 1 1/4 **Energia Dust (BRZ)**[18] 5-9-0 102 (t) TadhgO'Shea 1 99
(Fabricio Borges, Sweden) *led tl hdd 7f out: dropped to mid-div: one pce fnl 1 1/2f* **25/1**

7 nse **Theo Danon (GER)**[116] 6291 5-9-0 106 ADeVries 8 99
(Mario Hofer, Germany) *mid-div: smooth prog 3f out: nt qckn fnl f* **14/1**

8 nk **Al Shemali**[21] 8195 9-9-0 104 (t) RoystonFfrench 3 98
(A Al Raihe, UAE) *s.i.s: settled in rr: rdn 4 1/2f out: kpt on same pce fnl 1 1/2f* **16/1**

9 2 1/4 **Red Duke (USA)**[130] 5869 4-8-13 107 JamieSpencer 7 93
(David Simcock) *s.i.s: led 7f out: hdd & wknd 2f out* **7/1**

1m 49.72s (109.72)
WFA 4 from 5yo+ 1lb **9** Ran SP% **122.7**
WIN: 1.90. PL: 1.10, 1.20, 2.10. EX: 6.60. CSF: 4.51. TRIFECTA: 24.60..
Owner Godolphin **Bred** His Highness The Aga Khan's Studs S C **Trained** Newmarket, Suffolk

FOCUS
This trial for the Group 2 Al Rashidiya (to be run on January 31) didn't look a particularly strong race beforehand. Sound form, rated around the fifth.

153a AL MAKTOUM CHALLENGE R1 PRESENTED BY LONGINES (GROUP 2) (TAPETA) 1m
5:25 (5:25) 3-Y-0+

£92,024 (£30,674; £11,503; £11,503; £4,601; £3,067)

RPR

1 **Barbecue Eddie (USA)**[35] 8014 9-9-0 111 (b) DaneO'Neill 3 113+
(Doug Watson, UAE) *trckd ldng trio: rdn 2 1/2f out: led 1 1/2f out: comf* **4/1**[3]

2 1 1/2 **Out Of Bounds (USA)**[369] 4-9-0 110 SilvestreDeSousa 1 110
(Saeed bin Suroor) *sn led: rdn 2f out: hdd 1 1/2f out: kpt on gamely* **5/2**[1]

3 1/2 **Rutland Boy**[21] 8198 5-9-0 106 HarryBentley 9 109
(A Al Raihe, UAE) *trckd ldrs: ev ch 2f out: one pce fnl 110yds* **16/1**

3 dht **Fulbright**[89] 7048 4-9-0 113 (t) MickaelBarzalona 8 109+
(Mahmood Al Zarooni) *mid-div: chsd ldrs 2f out: nt qckn fnl f* **11/4**[2]

5 nse **Mufarrh (IRE)**[21] 8198 6-9-0 112 PaulHanagan 4 109+
(A Al Raihe, UAE) *slowly away: settled in rr: r.o fnl 2f: nrst fin* **7/1**

6 3 3/4 **Jamr**[322] 678 5-9-0 107 (v) ADeVries 7 100+
(M bin Shafya, UAE) *in rr of mid-div: nvr nr to chal* **12/1**

7 3 **Fanunalter**[104] 6634 7-9-0 113 RyanMoore 5 93+
(Marco Botti) *in rr of mid-div: nvr able to chal* **10/1**

8 nk **Tajaaweed (USA)**[322] 682 8-9-0 110 PatDobbs 6 93+
(Doug Watson, UAE) *settled in rr: nvr nr to chal* **20/1**

9 5 1/4 **Colliding Worlds (IRE)**[75] 7423 4-8-9 100 TadhgO'Shea 2 75+
(John Patrick Shanahan, Ire) *s.i.s: trckd ldng pair tl wknd fnl 1 1/2f* **33/1**

10 10 **Muraweg (IRE)**[21] 8197 7-9-0 97 (v) KierenFallon 10 57+
(Fawzi Abdulla Nass, Bahrain) *mid-div: n.m.r 3f out: sn btn* **20/1**

1m 37.24s (-0.26) **10** Ran SP% **122.9**
WIN: 4.60. PL: BE 1.60, OOB 1.30, F 1.20, RB 2.40. EX: 14.50. CSF: 14.92. TRIFECTA: BE/OOB/F 28.60, BE/OOB/RB 58.50..
Owner Hamdan Al Maktoum **Bred** Margaret Addis **Trained** United Arab Emirates

FOCUS
Usually the weakest of the three rounds, although in 2010 it went to subsequent Dubai World Cup winner Gloria De Campeao. This isn't form to be positive about, with Out Of Bounds hassled up front by Rutland Boy for most of the way (set fractions of 26.17, 48.85 and 1:12.23), and those two, involved in a bunch finish for the minor honours, were readily swept aside late on by the veteran winner.

154a LONGINES MASTER COLLECTION MOON PHASES (H'CAP) (TURF) 7f
6:00 (6:00) (100-110,109) 3-Y-0+

£44,171 (£14,723; £7,361; £3,680; £2,208; £1,472)

RPR

1 **Le Drakkar (AUS)**[306] 876 8-8-11 **105** (t) TadhgO'Shea 3 108
(A bin Huzaim, UAE) *s.i.s: settled in rr: smooth prog 2f out: led fnl 55yds* **25/1**

2 3/4 **Tamaathul**[21] 8198 6-9-2 **109** (t) DaneO'Neill 9 111
(A Al Raihe, UAE) *trckd ldrs: rdn to ld 2f out: hdd fnl 55yds: r.o wl* **16/1**

3 2 **Anaerobio (ARG)**[298] 6-8-8 **101** PatCosgrave 2 98
(M F De Kock, South Africa) *mid-div: chsd ldrs 3f out: one pce fnl f* **16/1**

4 nk **Lockwood**[123] 6088 4-9-2 **109** SilvestreDeSousa 14 105
(Saeed bin Suroor) *mid-div: chsd ldrs 1 1/2f out: one pce fnl 110yds* **8/1**[3]

5 3/4 **Don't Call Me (IRE)**[96] 6868 6-8-11 **105** (t) AdrianNicholls 6 98
(David Nicholls) *slowly away: nvr nr to chal but r.o fnl 1 1/2f* **10/1**

6 shd **Kenny Powers**[63] 7654 4-8-13 **106** (t) RichardKingscote 12 99
(Tom Dascombe) *settled in rr: kpt on fnl 2f but nvr nr to chal* **10/1**

7 nse **Disa Leader (SAF)**[315] 755 8-9-0 **107** JGeroudis 7 100
(M F De Kock, South Africa) *nvr bttr than mid-div* **20/1**

8 1 1/4 **Arnold Lane (IRE)**[89] 7048 4-8-11 **105** MartinHarley 8 94
(Mick Channon) *nvr bttr than mid-div* **9/1**

9 3/4 **Jaasoos (IRE)**[18] 9-9-0 **107** JamesDoyle 10 95
(D Selvaratnam, UAE) *trckd ldrs: ev ch 1f out: wknd fnl 110yds* **25/1**

10 nk **Dafeef**[21] 8197 6-9-0 **107** PaulHanagan 11 94
(Doug Watson, UAE) *s.i.s: nvr nr to chal* **25/1**

11 4 1/2 **Justineo**[61] 7690 4-8-7 **100** .... TedDurcan 15 75
(Roger Varian) *trckd ldrs tl wknd 1 1/2f out* **11/1**
12 1 **Fiscal**[306] 873 4-8-10 **104** .... HarryBentley 5 75
(M Al Jahouri, UAE) *nvr bttr than mid-div* **33/1**
13 3/4 **Amanee (AUS)**[250] 5-8-10 **103** ow1 .... ChristopheSoumillon 4 73
(M F De Kock, South Africa) *nvr bttr than mid-div* **5/1**[2]
14 shd **Firebeam**[96] 6882 5-9-1 **108** .... MickaelBarzalona 1 78
(Mahmood Al Zarooni) *nvr bttr than mid-div* **4/1**[1]
15 3/4 **Freezemaster (AUS)**[25] 6-8-7 **100** .... (t) StephenBaster 16 68
(S Burridge, Singapore) *sn led: hdd & wknd 2f out* **10/1**
16 2 **Captain Ramius (IRE)**[50] 7809 7-9-1 **108** .... JamieSpencer 13 71
(Kevin Ryan) *trckd ldrs: ev ch 2 1/2f out: wknd fnl 110yds* **16/1**

1m 23.14s (83.14) **16** Ran SP% **130.3**
WIN: 21.00. EX: 570.20. CSF: 384.65. TRIFECTA: 6586.00. TRICAST: 6496.29. PLACEPOT: £188.10. Pool £6276.80 - 24.35 winning units. QUADPOT: £19.40. Pool £356.90 - 13.60 winning units..
Owner Sheikh Hamdan Bin Mohammed Al Maktoum **Bred** Mrs J Hurst **Trained** United Arab Emirates

FOCUS
This looked a decent, competitive handicap beforehand, but a number of the fancied runners underperformed. The runner-up is the best guide. The pace was good thanks to Singapore raider Freezemaster, who did too much from his wide draw, setting fractions 24.83 and 47.66.

135 LINGFIELD (L-H)
Friday, January 11

OFFICIAL GOING: Standard
Wind: Almost nil, against Weather: Sunny, clouding over by race 5

155 BET AT BLUESQ.COM (S) STKS 7f (P)
12:30 (12:30) (Class 6) 4-Y-0+ **£2,045** (£603; £302) **Stalls** Low

Form RPR
5P1- 1 **Tarooq (USA)**[53] 7788 7-9-1 88 .... (t) DavidProbert 6 93
(Stuart Williams) *trckd ldr: led on bit 2f out: rdn clr 1f out: easily* **4/11**[1]
12-4 2 5 **Majuro (IRE)**[7] 56 9-9-1 77 .... (t) AdamKirby 1 80
(Charles Smith) *led after 1f tl 2f out: comf outpcd by wnr and btn 1f out* **5/2**[2]
623- 3 6 **Imprimis Tagula (IRE)**[20] 8236 9-8-10 69 .... (v) NickyMackay 4 58
(Alan Bailey) *broke wl and led 1f: settled in 3rd: rdn over 2f out: wknd wl over 1f out* **20/1**[3]
600- 4 23 **Buckley Boy**[14] 8264 4-8-10 44 .... JamieMackay 5
(K F Clutterbuck) *n.m.r and rdn in rr after 2f: drvn along and no ch fnl 4f* **100/1**

1m 22.66s (-2.14) **Going Correction** -0.025s/f (Stan) 4 Ran SP% **107.6**
Speed ratings (Par 101): **111,105,98,72**
CSF £1.52 TOTE £1.50; EX 1.30 Trifecta £1.90 Pool: £1,292.76 - 504.04 winning units.The winner was bought in for 15,200gns. Majuro was claimed by Mr S Arnold £6,000.
Owner H Chamberlain, I Pearce **Bred** Kirsten Rausing **Trained** Newmarket, Suffolk

FOCUS
The hot favourite had no trouble taking advantage of a good opportunity in this seller.

156 LINGFIELD PARK OWNERS GROUP H'CAP 5f (P)
1:00 (1:00) (Class 6) (0-65,68) 4-Y-0+ **£2,045** (£603; £302) **Stalls** High

Form RPR
411- 1 **Monumental Man**[21] 8209 4-9-7 **64** .... (p) DavidProbert 1 81
(James Unett) *mde all at str pce: rdn 2f out: drew clr of main pursuer 1f out: a in control* **9/4**[1]
323- 2 3 **Baby Dottie**[11] 8307 6-8-7 **57** .... (tp) SophieRalston(7) 8 63
(Pat Phelan) *mod 5th tl r.o fr over 1f out: clsng on wnr at fin: a wl hld* **12/1**
1-60 3 1 **Jonnie Skull (IRE)**[5] 87 7-9-0 **57** 6ex .... (vt) AdamKirby 4 59
(Phil McEntee) *chsd clr ldrs: rdn over 2f out: styd on fnl f* **16/1**
55-2 4 3/4 **Sherjawy (IRE)**[2] 124 9-8-7 **50** oh5 .... KirstyMilczarek 3 50
(Zoe Davison) *chsd clr ldrs: briefly wnt 2nd ins fnl f but nt trble wnr: one pce* **12/1**
01-3 5 1 1/4 **Pharoh Jake**[6] 77 5-9-0 **57** .... KieranO'Neill 6 52
(John Bridger) *s.i.s: outpcd and bhd: modest effrt on inner ent st: no imp* **5/1**[3]
61-2 6 3/4 **Liberal Lady**[8] 30 5-9-3 **60** .... (b[1]) GeorgeBaker 2 53
(Ralph Smith) *chsd wnr and clr of others: btn 1f out: wknd and lost 2nd ins fnl f* **7/1**
02-1 7 nk **Charming (IRE)**[2] 124 4-9-6 **68** 6ex .... (e) NathanAlison(5) 5 59
(Olivia Maylam) *outpcd towards rr: 6th and styng on whn squeezed out ins fnl f* **3/1**[2]
124- 8 2 1/4 **Illustrious Lad (IRE)**[72] 7482 4-8-13 **56** .... (p) JimCrowley 7 39
(Roger Ingram) *outpcd: sn bhd* **12/1**

58.48s (-0.32) **Going Correction** -0.025s/f (Stan) 8 Ran SP% **113.9**
Speed ratings (Par 101): **101,96,94,93,91 90,89,86**
toteswingers 1&2 £7.80, 1&3 £4.60, 2&3 £9.40 CSF £30.19 CT £349.53 TOTE £3.00: £1.10, £4.20, £3.20; EX 36.60 Trifecta £283.30 Pool: £840.09 - 2.22 winning units.
Owner P Fetherston-Godley **Bred** Christopher Chell **Trained** Tedsmore Hall, Shropshire
■ Stewards' Enquiry : Adam Kirby two-day ban; careless riding (25th-26th Jan).

FOCUS
This looked a competitive handicap for the grade but the favourite blitzed his rivals under an attacking ride.

157 LINGFIELDPARK.CO.UK MAIDEN STKS 1m 4f (P)
1:30 (1:30) (Class 5) 4-Y-0+ **£2,726** (£805; £402) **Stalls** Low

Form RPR
1 **Megastar**[265] 8-9-9 0 .... GeorgeBaker 7 73
(Gary Moore) *stdd s: hld up towards rr: gd hdwy to ld over 2f out: jnd by runner-up 1f out: hld on narrowly: rdn out nr fin* **9/2**[3]
042- 2 nk **Harlestone Wood**[127] 5982 4-9-5 80 .... AdamKirby 5 73
(Peter Hedger) *hld up in 4th: drew level w wnr 1f out: hrd rdn and r.o: jst hld nr fin* **4/5**[1]
54/ 3 8 **Polarity**[662] 930 7-8-11 0 .... NedCurtis(7) 3 55
(Gerry Enright) *dwlt: sn prom: one pce fnl 2f* **66/1**
4 3 1/4 **Chain Reactor**[69] 7-9-9 0 .... (b[1]) RobertHavlin 4 55
(Amy Weaver) *slowly away and rdn s: bhd: drvn along 3f out: passed btn rivals: nvr rchd ldrs* **20/1**
30- 5 2 1/4 **Faraway Land (USA)**[258] 1655 5-8-11 0 .... ShelleyBirkett(7) 1 46
(Julia Feilden) *towards rr: rdn 3f out: n.d after* **33/1**
6 2 **Big Kahuna**[382] 6-9-2 0 .... IanBurns(7) 6 48
(Jane Chapple-Hyam) *t.k.h in 5th: led briefly wl over 2f out: sn wknd* **33/1**
00- 7 18 **Lion's Maid**[268] 1443 4-9-0 0 .... (p) SebSanders 8 14
(Michael Attwater) *chsd ldr: led briefly 3f out: wknd over 2f out* **66/1**
202/ 8 nk **Lidar (FR)**[69] 5911 8-9-9 83 .... (b) FergusSweeney 2 18
(Alan King) *led: set sedate pce: hdd & wknd qckly 3f out: sn bhd and eased: lame* **7/4**[2]

2m 32.71s (-0.29) **Going Correction** -0.025s/f (Stan)
WFA 4 from 5yo+ 4lb 8 Ran SP% **123.7**
Speed ratings (Par 103): **99,98,93,91,89 88,76,76**
toteswingers 1&2 £2.10, 1&3 £18.70, 2&3 £6.70 CSF £9.19 TOTE £4.50: £1.10, £1.02, £14.90; EX 13.90 Trifecta £254.90 Pool: £3,053.84 - 8.98 winning units.
Owner Galloping On The South Downs Partnership **Bred** Pleasure Palace Racing **Trained** Lower Beeding, W Sussex

FOCUS
An interesting maiden. The favourite had achieved fair Flat form and there were a couple of useful jumps performers in the line-up. The pace was not very strong but the first two pulled clear and the form looks solid.

158 MARSH GREEN H'CAP 1m 2f (P)
2:00 (2:01) (Class 6) (0-55,55) 4-Y-0+ **£2,045** (£603; £302) **Stalls** Low

Form RPR
334- 1 **Precision Five**[22] 8180 4-9-1 **51** .... (p) JimCrowley 1 61
(Jeremy Gask) *in tch: effrt 2f out: slt ld over 1f out: jnd ent fnl f: jst on top nr fin* **3/1**[2]
151- 2 1/2 **Safwaan**[13] 8288 6-9-7 **55** .... StevieDonohoe 9 67+
(Willie Musson) *hld up towards rr: effrt and wd into st: str run fr over 1f out: hrd rdn and clsng at fin* **2/1**[1]
5/1- 3 shd **Reasons Unknown (IRE)**[28] 8113 5-9-4 **52** .... (v[1]) ShaneKelly 4 61
(Thomas McLaughlin, Ire) *hld up in rr of midfield: gd hdwy on inner over 1f out: jnd wnr ent fnl f: r.o* **6/1**[3]
340- 4 1 3/4 **Strategic Action (IRE)**[15] 8249 4-9-5 **55** .... (t) SebSanders 3 60
(Linda Jewell) *in tch: rdn to press ldrs over 1f out: n.m.r ins fnl f: one pce* **12/1**
405- 5 3 **Fonterutoli (IRE)**[15] 8249 6-9-7 **55** .... (e) RobertHavlin 10 54
(Roger Ingram) *bhd: rdn and styd on fnl 2f: nvr nrr* **14/1**
466- 6 2 **Connishka**[14] 8261 4-8-3 **48** oh1 .... ShelleyBirkett(7) 8 41
(Alan Bailey) *towards rr: rdn 3f out: sme late hdwy* **33/1**
002- 7 nk **High 'n Dry (IRE)**[11] 8301 9-8-10 **51** .... NedCurtis(7) 7 46
(Roger Curtis) *in tch: wnt 2nd 2f out: wknd over 1f out* **16/1**
/15- 8 1 1/4 **Brave Decision**[14] 8265 6-9-0 **48** .... JohnFahy 6 40
(Suzy Smith) *led tl wknd over 1f out* **25/1**
002- 9 hd **Signora Frasi (IRE)**[22] 8180 8-9-7 **55** .... FergusSweeney 12 47
(Tony Newcombe) *bhd: effrt and wd into st: nt rch ldrs* **6/1**[3]
036- 10 3/4 **Love Pegasus (USA)**[14] 8265 7-9-6 **54** .... MichaelO'Connell 5 44
(Paddy Butler) *chsd ldrs tl wknd 2f out* **25/1**
000- 11 1 1/4 **Sangrail**[22] 8187 4-9-3 **53** .... GeorgeBaker 2 41
(William Muir) *prom tl wknd 2f out: losing pl whn n.m.r over 1f out* **14/1**
500- 12 11 **Mutanaker**[22] 8179 6-9-5 **53** .... (b[1]) LiamKeniry 11 19
(Ed de Giles) *chsd ldr tl wknd over 2f out: sn lost pl* **33/1**

2m 5.2s (-1.40) **Going Correction** -0.025s/f (Stan)
WFA 4 from 5yo+ 2lb 12 Ran SP% **127.4**
Speed ratings (Par 101): **104,103,103,102,99 98,97,96,96,96 95,86**
toteswingers 1&2 £3.00, 1&3 £4.60, 2&3 £4.40 CSF £9.81 CT £35.66 TOTE £3.20: £1.10, £1.80, £3.40; EX 11.20 Trifecta £71.50 Pool: £2,429.12 - 25.45 winning units.
Owner Calne Engineering Ltd **Bred** Edward J G Young **Trained** Sutton Veny, Wilts

FOCUS
There was an exciting three-way finish to this modest handicap and the well-backed favourite just came up a bit short after finishing fast out wide from some way back.

159 BLUE SQUARE BET FILLIES' H'CAP 1m (P)
2:30 (2:30) (Class 5) (0-75,72) 4-Y-0+ **£2,726** (£805; £402) **Stalls** High

Form RPR
140- 1 **Al Freej (IRE)**[274] 1331 4-9-4 **72** .... RyanClark(3) 3 76
(Brian Ellison) *sn led: wnt 4 l clr and set gd pce: hrd rdn and tiring fnl f: jst lasted* **25/1**
003- 2 nk **Abigails Angel**[15] 8252 6-9-7 **72** .... DavidProbert 4 76
(Brett Johnson) *hld up in 4th: rdn and hdwy over 1f out: clsd on wnr fnl f: jst hld* **5/1**[3]
042- 3 nk **Chrissycross (IRE)**[11] 8308 4-9-0 **65** .... (v[1]) JimCrowley 6 68
(Roger Teal) *hld up in 5th: rdn and hdwy over 1f out: kpt on fnl f* **3/1**[2]
221- 4 1 **Fairyinthewind (IRE)**[24] 8158 4-9-7 **72** .... (p) SebSanders 7 73
(Paul D'Arcy) *hld up in 6th: effrt on outer 2f out: hrd rdn over 1f out: styd on* **5/4**[1]
060- 5 hd **Push Me (IRE)**[81] 7302 6-9-7 **72** .... MichaelO'Connell 1 72
(Jamie Poulton) *cl up: chsd wnr over 3f out tl no ex ins fnl f* **5/1**[3]
165- 6 1 3/4 **Caramelita**[48] 7858 6-9-6 **71** .... (v) GeorgeBaker 5 67
(J R Jenkins) *stdd s: t.k.h in rr: effrt 2f out: nvr able to chal* **12/1**
040- 7 10 **Ishiamiracle**[11] 8305 4-8-5 **63** .... (p) IanBurns(7) 2 36
(Phil McEntee) *broke wl and led briefly: chsd wnr tl over 3f out: hrd rdn and wknd over 2f out* **66/1**

1m 36.69s (-1.51) **Going Correction** -0.025s/f (Stan) 7 Ran SP% **115.8**
Speed ratings (Par 100): **106,105,105,104,104 102,92**
toteswingers 1&2 £11.20, 1&3 £5.60, 2&3 £2.70 CSF £146.12 TOTE £20.80: £8.50, £2.70; EX 60.80 Trifecta £404.30 Pool: £1,923.22 - 3.56 winning units.
Owner Kevin Corcoran Aaron Pierce Chris Weare **Bred** Mrs Sandra McCarthy **Trained** Norton, N Yorks

FOCUS
There was a surprise all-the-way winner of this fillies' handicap and she can be marked up because she set a strong pace.

160 FOREST ROW MAIDEN STKS 7f (P)
3:00 (3:07) (Class 5) 3-Y-0+ **£2,726** (£805; £402) **Stalls** Low

Form RPR
- 1 **Al Raqeeb (IRE)** 3-8-9 0 .... AndreaAtzeni 4 76+
(Marco Botti) *dwlt: sn in 3rd and travelling wl: led over 1f out: edgd rt: comf* **3/1**[2]
4- 2 2 1/4 **Pategonia**[72] 7477 4-9-13 0 .... RobertHavlin 7 73+
(John Gosden) *hld up in 4th: niggled along 4f out: rdn and hdwy over 1f out: wnt 2nd ins fnl f: unable qck* **4/5**[1]
5-3 3 1 1/4 **Tanawar (IRE)**[9] 16 3-8-9 0 .... AdamBeschizza 1 66+
(William Haggas) *led: shkn up and qcknd 3f out: hdd over 1f out: one pce* **9/2**[3]
344- 4 1 1/2 **The Black Jacobin**[62] 7687 3-8-9 65 .... LiamKeniry 3 62
(J S Moore) *chsd ldr tl wknd over 1f out* **9/2**[3]

565- 5 6 **King's Future**[14] 8261 4-9-6 49 ....(b) AaronChave(7) 5 50
(Lee Carter) *in tch in 5th: outpcd over 2f out: sn btn* 66/1

1m 24.63s (-0.17) **Going Correction** -0.025s/f (Stan)
WFA 3 from 4yo+ 18lb 5 Ran SP% **118.4**
Speed ratings (Par 103): **99,96,95,93,86**
CSF £6.38 TOTE £3.70: £2.30, £1.30; EX 8.70 Trifecta £15.00 Pool: £3,649.49 - 181.98 winning units.
Owner Mubarak Al Naemi **Bred** Ballylinch Stud **Trained** Newmarket, Suffolk

FOCUS
The odds-on favourite was turned over in this modest maiden. There was a nasty incident before the race when Boyzee (100/1, withdrawn) reared and fell over in the stalls.

161 GET STRAIGHT TO THE BET AT BLUESQ.COM APPRENTICE H'CAP 1m 4f (P)
3:30 (3:30) (Class 5) (0-70,76) 4-Y-0+ **£2,726** (£805; £402) **Stalls** Low

Form RPR
31-2 1 **Jacobs Son**[9] 20 5-9-3 **65** .... RobertTart(3) 1 71
(Robert Mills) *trckd ldr: rdn to ld 2f out: drvn to hold on fnl f* 1/1[1]
500- 2 ½ **Linkable**[37] 7998 4-8-13 **62** ....(t) RufusVergette 2 67
(Brendan Powell) *hld up in rr: rdn over 2f out: hdwy over 1f out: chsd wnr fnl f: r.o* 14/1
403- 3 1½ **Nave (USA)**[22] 8191 6-9-4 **70** .... SiobhanMiller(7) 3 73
(David Simcock) *t.k.h in 4th: effrt and hrd rdn over 1f out: styd on same pce* 6/4[2]
00-4 4 1¼ **Formidable Guest**[9] 15 9-8-6 **55** oh4 .... CharlotteJenner(5) 4 57
(Jamie Poulton) *trckd ldrs in 3rd: rdn over 2f out: no ex 1f out* 33/1
35-4 5 2 **Handheld**[6] 73 6-9-2 **66** .... ShelleyBirkett(5) 5 64
(Julia Feilden) *led: rdn 3f out: hdd 2f out: wknd 1f out* 7/1[3]

2m 34.26s (1.26) **Going Correction** -0.025s/f (Stan)
WFA 4 from 5yo+ 4lb 5 Ran SP% **112.1**
Speed ratings (Par 103): **94,93,92,91,90**
CSF £15.39 TOTE £1.70: £1.10, £6.90; EX 14.80 Trifecta £24.90 Pool: £2,338.48 - 70.43 winning units.
Owner Jacobs Construction (Holdings) Limited **Bred** Stowell Park Stud **Trained** Headley, Surrey

FOCUS
The favourite put in a willing display to deliver in this apprentice handicap which was run at an ordinary pace.
T/Plt: £79.80 to a £1 stake. Pool: £46,226.37 - 422.43 winning tickets T/Qpdt: £20.70 to a £1 stake. Pool: £4,299.15 - 153.00 winning tickets LM

[142]WOLVERHAMPTON (A.W) (L-H)
Friday, January 11

OFFICIAL GOING: Standard
Wind: Nil Weather: Cloudy

162 WINNERS LOVE BOOKMAKERS.CO.UK H'CAP 7f 32y(P)
4:00 (4:00) (Class 6) (0-60,60) 4-Y-0+ **£1,940** (£577; £288; £144) **Stalls** High

Form RPR
45-2 1 **Kai**[5] 87 4-9-0 **53** ....(b) SeanLevey 3 64
(Alan McCabe) *led 1f: chsd ldrs: rdn to ld ins fnl f: edgd lft: r.o* 10/3[1]
63-6 2 2 **Bitaphon (IRE)**[7] 54 4-9-4 **57** .... DanielTudhope 8 63
(Michael Appleby) *chsd ldr tl led 6f out: hdd over 4f out: led again over 1f out: rdn and hdd ins fnl f: styd on same pce* 8/1
4-20 3 1½ **Marshall Art**[6] 77 4-9-4 **57** .... FrannyNorton 5 59
(David Evans) *a.p: rdn over 1f out: styd on same pce ins fnl f* 4/1[2]
536- 4 shd **Amis Reunis**[22] 8177 4-9-5 **58** .... WilliamCarson 2 59
(Anthony Carson) *hld up: hdwy u.p 2f out: r.o: nt rch ldrs* 17/2
16-6 5 1 **Lucky Mark (IRE)**[4] 96 4-9-7 **60** .... JimmyQuinn 7 59
(Garry Moss) *plld hrd: trckd ldr over 5f out: led over 4f out: rdn and hdd over 1f out: no ex ins fnl f* 9/2[3]
400- 6 1½ **Bartley**[66] 7604 4-9-5 **58** .... TomEaves 12 53
(Bryan Smart) *sn outpcd: r.o ins fnl f: nrst fin* 28/1
134- 7 ½ **Renoir's Lady**[12] 8299 5-9-2 **55** .... LukeMorris 10 48
(Simon Dow) *mid-div: pushed along 1/2-way: rdn over 2f out: styd on same pce fr over 1f out* 11/2
205- 8 3½ **Red Shadow**[72] 7482 4-9-4 **57** ....(p) RobertWinston 6 41
(Alan Brown) *prom: rdn over 2f out: wknd over 1f out* 14/1
000- 9 2 **Chester'Slittlegem (IRE)**[15] 8255 4-8-11 **55** .... ShirleyTeasdale(5) 4 33
(Lisa Williamson) *s.i.s: a in rr* 33/1
346- 10 1¾ **Ridgeway Hawk**[15] 8256 5-8-13 **57** ....(v) LeeNewnes(5) 9 31
(Mark Usher) *s.i.s: hld up: a in rr* 25/1

1m 28.62s (-0.98) **Going Correction** -0.075s/f (Stan) 10 Ran SP% **115.2**
Speed ratings (Par 101): **102,99,98,97,96 95,94,90,88,86**
toteswingers 1&2 £8.00, 1&3 £3.90, 2&3 £6.20 CSF £29.45 CT £112.19 TOTE £4.00: £1.50, £2.70, £1.70; EX 43.30 Trifecta £276.30 Pool: £1,993.34 - 5.40 winning units.
Owner J R Atherton **Bred** Kirtlington Stud Ltd **Trained** Averham Park, Notts

FOCUS
A race weakened significantly by the late defection of the likely market leaders Ioannou and Bussa.

163 CORAL.CO.UK H'CAP 5f 216y(P)
4:30 (4:32) (Class 6) (0-55,55) 4-Y-0+ **£1,940** (£577; £288; £144) **Stalls** Low

Form RPR
006- 1 **Romanticize**[15] 8255 7-9-6 **54** .... DaleSwift 11 63
(Jason Ward) *chsd ldr to over 3f out: remained handy: rdn to ld over 1f out: edgd lft ins fnl f: styd on* 33/1
60-3 2 ¾ **Mataajir (USA)**[4] 96 5-9-7 **55** .... MartinDwyer 2 62+
(Derek Shaw) *hld up: hdwy over 1f out: edgd lft ins fnl f: r.o* 9/4[1]
026- 3 nk **Whiskey Junction**[23] 8169 9-9-7 **55** .... WilliamCarson 10 61
(Mick Quinn) *led: rdn and hdd over 1f out: styd on* 28/1
20-2 4 nk **Ryedale Dancer (IRE)**[9] 26 5-9-6 **54** .... RobbieFitzpatrick 12 59
(Richard Guest) *hld up: hung rt over 2f out: hdwy over 1f out: r.o: nt rch ldrs* 7/1
000- 5 ½ **Chester Deelyte (IRE)**[15] 8256 5-8-13 **52** ....(v) ShirleyTeasdale(5) 4 55
(Lisa Williamson) *hld up: r.o ins fnl f: nt rch ldrs* 20/1
400- 6 hd **Nine Before Ten (IRE)**[39] 7969 5-9-0 **55** .... ThomasBrown(7) 13 58
(Charles Smith) *broke wl: sn lost pl: r.o ins fnl f: nt rch ldrs* 50/1
442- 7 ½ **Red Ramesses (IRE)**[28] 8109 4-9-5 **53** .... LukeMorris 6 54
(John Best) *chsd ldrs: rdn over 1f out: styd on* 7/2[2]
66-3 8 1¼ **Russian Bullet**[8] 30 4-9-2 **55** .... LeonnaMayor(5) 9 52
(Jamie Osborne) *prom on outer: racd keenly: wnt 2nd over 2f out: rdn over 1f out: no ex ins fnl f* 11/2
00-2 9 ¾ **Under Par**[9] 24 5-9-0 **48** ....(t) JamesSullivan 1 43
(Michael Easterby) *chsd ldrs: rdn over 1f out: n.m.r ins fnl f: no ex* 5/1[3]
00-3 10 ½ **Onceaponatime (IRE)**[5] 88 8-9-5 **53** .... JimmyQuinn 8 46
(Michael Squance) *dwlt: outpcd: running on whn hmpd ins fnl f: nt rcvr* 14/1
00-5 11 1 **Ishetoo**[5] 88 9-9-4 **52** .... TomEaves 7 42
(Peter Grayson) *prom: drvn along 1/2-way: wknd over 1f out* 16/1

1m 14.93s (-0.07) **Going Correction** -0.075s/f (Stan) 11 Ran SP% **123.2**
Speed ratings (Par 101): **97,96,95,95,94 94,93,91,90,90 88**
toteswingers 1&2 £20.20, 1&3 £39.80, 2&3 £16.80 CSF £109.01 CT £2285.60 TOTE £39.70: £9.80, £1.60, £6.70; EX 155.70 Trifecta £2495.70 Part won. Pool: £3,327.62 - 0.59 winning units..
Owner Miss Vivian Pratt **Bred** Cheveley Park Stud Ltd **Trained** Middleham, N Yorks

FOCUS
A competitive albeit modest handicap this time over 6f which saw a gamble on the Derek Shaw-trained Mataajir.

164 CASINO AT CORAL.CO.UK H'CAP 5f 216y(P)
5:00 (5:00) (Class 4) (0-85,85) 4-Y-0+ **£4,690** (£1,395; £697; £348) **Stalls** Low

Form RPR
000- 1 **Seek The Fair Land**[29] 8098 7-9-7 **85** ....(b) WilliamCarson 5 93
(Jamie Osborne) *trckd ldrs: plld hrd: rdn to ld ins fnl f: edgd lft: r.o* 14/1
320- 2 nk **Sole Danser (IRE)**[128] 5933 5-8-9 **73** ow1 .... RobertWinston 2 80
(Milton Bradley) *hld up: racd keenly: nt clr run over 2f out: hdwy sn after: rdn and ev ch ins fnl f: r.o* 10/1
022- 3 ¾ **Clear Praise (USA)**[14] 8266 6-9-4 **82** .... LukeMorris 4 87
(Simon Dow) *hld up: hdwy over 1f out: sn rdn: r.o* 8/1
034- 4 ½ **Seeking Magic**[31] 8066 5-9-7 **85** ....(t) AdamKirby 1 88
(Clive Cox) *trckd ldrs: plld hrd: rdn over 1f out: styd on u.p* 13/8[1]
534- 5 ½ **Showboating (IRE)**[53] 7789 5-8-13 **77** ....(tp) SeanLevey 6 78+
(Alan McCabe) *s.i.s: hld up: rdn over 1f out: r.o: nt rch ldrs* 11/2[2]
000- 6 nk **Prince Of Burma (IRE)**[22] 8188 5-9-2 **80** ....(b) ChrisCatlin 8 80
(Jeremy Gask) *hld up: pushed along 1/2-way: hdwy over 1f out: sn rdn: styd on* 10/1
142- 7 nk **Speightowns Kid (USA)**[20] 8225 5-8-7 **71** .... FrannyNorton 3 70
(Jo Hughes) *sn led: rdn over 1f out: hdd and unable qck ins fnl f* 10/1
001- 8 nse **Kakatosi**[14] 8266 6-9-7 **85** .... EddieAhern 10 84
(Mike Murphy) *hld up: rdn over 1f out: r.o: nt rch ldrs* 7/1[3]
106- 9 14 **Da'Quonde (IRE)**[81] 7295 5-8-12 **76** .... TomEaves 7 31
(Bryan Smart) *chsd ldr tl rdn wl over 1f out: hmpd and wknd sn after: eased ins fnl f* 40/1

1m 13.91s (-1.09) **Going Correction** -0.075s/f (Stan) 9 Ran SP% **113.5**
Speed ratings (Par 105): **104,103,102,101,101 100,100,100,81**
toteswingers 1&2 £6.90, 1&3 £19.70, 2&3 £9.50 CSF £142.17 CT £1197.40 TOTE £18.70: £4.40, £3.70, £1.30; EX 216.20 Trifecta £8586.30 Part won. Pool: £11,448.44 - 0.18 winning units..
Owner Chris Watkins And David N Reynolds **Bred** Raimon Bloodstock **Trained** Upper Lambourn, Berks

FOCUS
A decent sprint handicapper, however it turned into a muddling affair with all bar the returning Da'Quonde in with a chance 1f out.

165 DOWNLOAD CORAL.CO.UK MOBILE APP H'CAP 1m 5f 194y(P)
5:30 (5:30) (Class 6) (0-65,65) 4-Y-0+ **£1,940** (£577; £288; £144) **Stalls** Low

Form RPR
000- 1 **Full Speed (GER)**[78] 7353 8-9-7 **60** .... DanielTudhope 6 69
(Philip Kirby) *hld up: hdwy over 2f out: led over 1f out: rdn and edgd lft ins fnl f: styd on* 5/1
51-0 2 1 **Scribe (IRE)**[4] 100 5-8-13 **52** ....(t) LukeMorris 1 60
(David Evans) *dwlt: sn pushed along: hdwy over 10f out: drvn along 6f out: styd on u.p* 7/1
063- 3 ½ **Party Palace**[4] 5811 9-8-7 **46** oh1 .... JimmyQuinn 4 53
(Stuart Howe) *chsd ldr after 2f: led over 2f out: rdn and hdd over 1f out: styd on* 66/1
424- 4 12 **Stetson**[14] 8273 7-9-5 **58** .... JoeFanning 5 48
(Ian Williams) *sn led: rdn and hdd over 2f out: wknd fnl f* 3/1[2]
022- 5 4 **Elegant Ophelia**[20] 8229 4-9-6 **65** .... AdamKirby 2 49
(Dean Ivory) *chsd ldrs: rdn over 2f out: wknd over 1f out* 2/1[1]
/33- 6 8 **Day Of Destiny (IRE)**[14] 8273 8-9-10 **63** .... JamesSullivan 7 36
(James Given) *trckd ldrs: plld hrd: rdn over 2f out: sn wknd* 4/1[3]
46/- 7 73 **Born To Perform**[983] 1803 8-9-1 **54** .... RobertWinston 3
(Alan Swinbank) *hld up: rdn and wknd over 3f out: eased: t.o* 14/1

3m 3.05s (-2.95) **Going Correction** -0.075s/f (Stan)
WFA 4 from 5yo+ 6lb 7 Ran SP% **115.7**
Speed ratings (Par 101): **105,104,104,97,95 90,48**
toteswingers 1&2 £21.50, 1&3 £12.50, 2&3 £11.20 CSF £39.80 TOTE £7.60: £4.50, £3.70; EX 42.00 Trifecta £369.30 Pool: £31,173.04 - 63.30 winning units.
Owner Ryan P Hadfield **Bred** Dr K Schulte **Trained** Middleham, N Yorks

FOCUS
A small field, competitive handicap for stayers.

166 FREE BETS GALORE AT BOOKMAKERS.CO.UK CLAIMING STKS 1m 4f 50y(P)
6:00 (6:00) (Class 5) 4-Y-0+ **£2,587** (£770; £384; £192) **Stalls** Low

Form RPR
115- 1 **Stand Guard**[20] 8228 9-9-7 87 .... AdamKirby 1 78
(John Butler) *chsd ldrs: shkn up to ld over 1f out: rdn and hung rt ins fnl f: styd on* 1/2[1]
4/3- 2 1 **Priors Gold**[39] 7972 6-8-10 75 .... JacobButterfield(7) 4 72
(Ollie Pears) *hld up: hdwy over 1f out: rdn ins fnl f: styd on* 11/4[2]
500- 3 2¼ **Wild Desert (FR)**[157] 4925 8-9-7 80 .... RobertWinston 5 73
(John Gallagher) *set stdy pce tl qcknd 3f out: rdn: edgd rt and hdd over 1f out: no ex ins fnl f* 8/1[3]
00-3 4 7 **Blizzard Blues (USA)**[10] 2 7-9-8 69 ....(b) RaulDaSilva(3) 3 67
(Aytach Sadik) *chsd ldr: rdn over 2f out: wknd and eased ins fnl f* 40/1
00-6 5 hd **Pirate Chest (IRE)**[9] 23 5-9-3 57 ....(bt) DuranFentiman 2 57?
(Patrick Holmes) *hld up: rdn over 1f out: wknd fnl f* 50/1

2m 41.21s (0.11) **Going Correction** -0.075s/f (Stan) 5 Ran SP% **108.8**
Speed ratings (Par 103): **96,95,93,89,89**
CSF £2.06 TOTE £1.80: £1.10, £1.50; EX 2.70 Trifecta £4.60 Pool: £36,804.39 - 5,877.64 winning units.
Owner J Butler **Bred** Juddmonte Farms Ltd **Trained** Newmarket, Suffolk

FOCUS
An uncompetitive claimer.

167 WIN MORE ON BETTING AT BOOKMAKERS.CO.UK H'CAP 1m 4f 50y(P)
6:30 (6:30) (Class 3) (0-95,88) 4-Y-O- £7,246 (£2,168; £1,084; £542; £270) Stalls Low

Form RPR
561- 1 **Mica Mika (IRE)**[14] 8275 5-9-3 81 BarryMcHugh 1 87
(Richard Fahey) *led 1f: chsd ldr tl led again over 2f out: rdn out* 10/3[2]
55-1 2 nk **Kames Park (IRE)**[7] 53 11-8-10 74 6ex oh1 JimmyQuinn 5 79
(Richard Guest) *hld up: shkn up over 1f out: r.o wl ins fnl f: jst failed* 25/1
311- 3 nk **Flying Power**[28] 8110 5-9-6 84 PaddyAspell 6 89
(John Norton) *hld up in tch: racd keenly: chsd wnr ins fnl f: r.o* 11/4[1]
023- 4 ½ **Ascendant**[14] 8275 7-9-4 82 MartinDwyer 3 86
(Alan McCabe) *hld up: hdwy over 1f out: sn rdn: r.o* 13/2
5-21 5 1 **Renegotiate**[3] 107 4-8-6 74 6ex (v) WilliamCarson 4 76
(Dr Richard Newland) *a.p: racd keenly: rdn over 1f out: edgd lft and styd on same pce ins fnl f* 7/2[3]
540- 6 1¼ **The Lock Master (IRE)**[14] 8275 6-9-4 82 LukeMorris 2 82
(Michael Appleby) *chsd ldrs: rdn over 2f out: hmpd over 1f out: styd on* 20/1
/00- 7 2¾ **Art History (IRE)**[62] 7689 5-9-10 88 DanielTudhope 7 84
(David O'Meara) *led after 1f: pushed along and hdd over 2f out: no ex fnl f* 9/2

2m 38.41s (-2.69) **Going Correction** -0.075s/f (Stan)
WFA 4 from 5yo+ 4lb 7 Ran SP% **112.1**
Speed ratings (Par 107): **105,104,104,104,103 102,100**
toteswingers 1&2 £5.00, 1&3 £3.30, 2&3 £6.10 CSF £69.85 TOTE £5.00: £2.80, £4.60; EX 96.40 Trifecta £513.90 Pool: £14,709.33 - 21.46 winning units.
Owner Mrs Una Towell **Bred** Yeomanstown Stud **Trained** Musley Bank, N Yorks

FOCUS
The feature on the card but it wasn't a strong race for the grade with top weight Art History rated 7lb below the ceiling. It featured mainly exposed performers.

168 WOLVERHAMPTON-RACECOURSE.CO.UK MEDIAN AUCTION MAIDEN STKS 1m 141y(P)
7:00 (7:00) (Class 6) 3-4-Y-O £1,940 (£577; £288; £144) Stalls Low

Form RPR
344- 1 **Tight Lipped (IRE)**[24] 7376 4-9-13 68 LukeMorris 2 76
(James Eustace) *sn pushed along to chse ldrs: wnt 2nd 3f out: rdn to ld 1f out: edgd rt: styd on* 9/2[3]
452- 2 ¾ **Solace (USA)**[25] 8147 3-8-1 65 NickyMackay 3 65
(John Gosden) *a.p: pushed along over 2f out: rdn over 1f out: r.o ins fnl f* 5/6[1]
432- 3 2¼ **Mosman**[14] 8270 3-8-6 67 ChrisCatlin 1 65
(Jamie Osborne) *led: rdn and hdd 1f out: no ex wl ins fnl f* 4/1[2]
64- 4 1¼ **Camachoice (IRE)**[22] 8178 3-8-3 0 (t) NataliaGemelova(3) 5 62
(Marco Botti) *s.i.s: hld up: hdwy over 2f out: rdn over 1f out: edgd lft and styd on same pce fnl f* 13/2
5 5 44 **Lil Sophella (IRE)**[9] 28 4-9-8 0 RobertWinston 4
(Patrick Holmes) *sn chsng ldr: rdn and lost 2nd 3f out: wknd 2f out: eased: t.o* 33/1

1m 49.73s (-0.77) **Going Correction** -0.075s/f (Stan)
WFA 3 from 4yo 22lb 5 Ran SP% **109.0**
Speed ratings (Par 101): **100,99,97,96,57**
CSF £8.62 TOTE £4.70: £2.00, £1.30; EX 12.80 Trifecta £31.30 Pool: £14,132.39 - 338.40 winning units.
Owner Blue Peter Racing 11 **Bred** P F Headon **Trained** Newmarket, Suffolk

FOCUS
A run-of-the-mill small-field median auction maiden.

169 PICK BEST BOOKIES AT BOOKMAKERS.CO.UK H'CAP 1m 4f 50y(P)
7:30 (7:40) (Class 7) (0-50,56) 4-Y-O+ £1,940 (£577; £288; £144) Stalls Low

Form RPR
22-1 1 **Easydoesit (IRE)**[4] 100 5-9-13 56 6ex JimmyQuinn 6 65
(Tony Carroll) *hld up in tch: shkn up to ld and hung lft ins fnl f: rdn out* 11/4[1]
663- 2 1¼ **Midnight Bahia (IRE)**[33] 8048 4-9-0 47 EddieAhern 4 54
(Dean Ivory) *chsd ldrs: rdn and ev ch whn carried lft ins fnl f: styd on same pce* 6/1
002- 3 shd **Peace In Our Time**[14] 8264 4-9-1 48 WilliamCarson 5 55
(Anthony Carson) *hld up: hdwy over 1f out: sn rdn: r.o* 3/1[2]
0-04 4 1½ **Nolecce**[4] 100 6-9-7 50 (p) RobbieFitzpatrick 12 55
(Richard Guest) *hld up: hdwy over 1f out: r.o: nt rch ldrs* 13/2
60-0 5 1 **Dubai Emerald (USA)**[4] 100 4-9-3 50 FrannyNorton 1 53
(Chris Dwyer) *prom: hmpd over 4f out: rdn over 1f out: styd on same pce fnl f* 50/1
156- 6 nk **Midnight Sequel**[31] 8067 4-9-1 48 AdamKirby 7 51
(Michael Blake) *hld up: rdn over 1f out: styd on ins fnl f: nvr nrr* 7/1
05-3 7 nse **Icy Quiet**[4] 100 5-9-6 49 DanielTudhope 8 51
(David O'Meara) *led 1f: chsd ldrs: led again over 2f out: rdn over 1f out: hdd ins fnl f: hmpd sn after: no ex* 4/1[3]
36- 8 1¼ **Revolving World (IRE)**[269] 1432 10-9-3 46 (t) LukeMorris 3 46
(Lee James) *mid-div: pushed along over 2f out: rdn over 1f out: no imp fnl f* 50/1
046- 9 2¼ **Corn Maiden**[33] 8049 4-8-7 45 (b) TobyAtkinson(5) 11 42
(Mark Rimmer) *led after 1f: clr 9f out tl 5f out: rdn and hdd over 2f out: wknd fnl f* 33/1
500- 10 54 **Trevose (IRE)**[22] 8179 4-9-3 50 TomEaves 9
(Roy Brotherton) *prom: racd keenly: wknd over 3f out: t.o* 100/1

2m 40.48s (-0.62) **Going Correction** -0.075s/f (Stan)
WFA 4 from 5yo+ 4lb 10 Ran SP% **119.6**
Speed ratings (Par 97): **99,98,98,97,96 96,96,95,93,57**
toteswingers 1&2 £4.10, 1&3 £3.20, 2&3 £4.20 CSF £20.17 CT £53.66 TOTE £4.10: £1.50, £2.30, £1.70; EX 25.20 Trifecta £82.10 Pool: £4,284.63 - 39.12 winning units.
Owner T R Pearson **Bred** Tinnakill Bloodstock & Alan Byrne **Trained** Cropthorne, Worcs
■ Sinchiroka was withdrawn (6/1, got loose and bolted bef s). Deduct 10p in the £ under R. New market formed.

FOCUS
The card closed with a 0-50 handicap, despite the lowly level it featured several in-form horses. Corn Maiden set a scorching gallop, however the pack left her alone.
T/Plt: £1,009.60 to a £1 stake. Pool: £74,839.20 - 54.11 winning units T/Qpdt: £148.30 to a £1 stake. Pool: £8,738.64 - 43.60 winning units CR

[155] LINGFIELD (L-H)
Saturday, January 12

OFFICIAL GOING: Standard
Wind: Moderate, across (away from stands) Weather: Very overcast

183 BET ON TODAY'S FOOTBALL AT BLUESQ.COM CLAIMING STKS 1m 2f (P)
11:45 (11:45) (Class 6) 4-Y-O+ £2,045 (£603; £302) Stalls Low

Form RPR
142- 1 **Honey Of A Kitten (USA)**[13] 8292 5-9-3 67 (v) AdamKirby 2 75
(David Evans) *hld up in last: reminder 1/2-way: travelled bttr after: clsd over 2f out: rdn to take 2nd wl over 1f out: led ins fnl f: pushed out* 8/1[3]
53-2 2 1½ **Ajeeb (USA)**[9] 32 5-9-7 81 JamieSpencer 5 76
(David Simcock) *trckd ldr: led over 2f out: sn rdn: hanging over 1f out: hdd and nt qckn ins fnl f* 2/9[1]
35-1 3 3¾ **Activate**[6] 84 6-9-3 70 (b) LukeMorris 4 65
(Phil McEntee) *led at decent pce: urged along over 3f out: hdd over 2f out: nt qckn and sn btn* 7/1[2]

2m 4.95s (-1.65) **Going Correction** -0.025s/f (Stan) 3 Ran SP% **105.4**
Speed ratings (Par 101): **105,103,100**
CSF £10.92 TOTE £4.00; EX 8.80 Trifecta £6.30 Pool: £1,520.18 - 178.38 winning units..Ajeeb claimed by Mr M. Scudamore for £12,000.
Owner Mrs E Evans **Bred** Kenneth L Ramsey And Sarah K Ramsey **Trained** Pandy, Monmouths

FOCUS
This was the quickest time of three races at the trip, including a Class 3 handicap.

184 BREATHE SPA AT MARRIOTT LINGFIELD MEDIAN AUCTION MAIDEN STKS 1m (P)
12:15 (12:16) (Class 6) 3-Y-O £2,045 (£603; £302) Stalls High

Form RPR
32- 1 **Emerging**[29] 8102 3-9-5 0 LiamKeniry 3 76
(David Elsworth) *t.k.h: sn pressed ldr: led briefly 3f out: shkn up over 2f out: styd on to ld again ins fnl f* 4/6[1]
3- 2 ¾ **Empowermentofwomen (IRE)**[22] 8201 3-9-0 0 JamieSpencer 2 69
(Michael Bell) *trckd ldrs: prog to ld wl over 2f out: urged along wl over 1f out: hdd and nt qckn ins fnl f* 5/1[2]
3 5 **Lady Who** 3-9-0 0 JimCrowley 6 58+
(Ralph Beckett) *dwlt: hld up in 8th: pushed along and stdy prog over 2f out: tk 3rd fnl f: styd on in encouraging style* 8/1[3]
03- 4 2¼ **Mystery Woman (IRE)**[44] 7923 3-9-0 0 LukeMorris 8 53
(Peter Chapple-Hyam) *trckd ldrs: shkn up to chse ldng pair over 2f out but sn wl outpcd: lost 3rd fnl f* 10/1
5 3 **Edwyn Ralph** 3-9-5 0 MartinLane 7 51+
(David Simcock) *s.i.s: rn green and pushed along in last: no prog tl styd on fr over 1f out* 10/1
5- 6 1¾ **Mastered (IRE)**[15] 8262 3-9-5 0 GeorgeBaker 1 47
(John Best) *prom: steadily lost pl fr 1/2-way: jst pushed along and no prog over 1f out* 33/1
00- 7 4 **Running Bull (IRE)**[23] 8185 3-9-5 0 RobertWinston 9 37
(Linda Jewell) *racd wd: in tch: outpcd fr 3f out: wknd over 1f out* 100/1
4- 8 7 **Roaring Rocks (FR)**[12] 8303 3-9-5 0 AdamKirby 4 21
(Heather Main) *led to 3f out: wknd rapidly: t.o* 14/1
0- 9 3 **High Lightning**[28] 8134 3-9-0 0 ShaneKelly 5
(Mrs K Burke) *in tch tl wknd wl over 2f out: t.o* 50/1

1m 38.87s (0.67) **Going Correction** -0.025s/f (Stan) 9 Ran SP% **118.5**
Speed ratings (Par 95): **95,94,89,87,84 82,78,71,68**
Tote Swingers: 1&2 £1.70, 1&3 £2.90, 2&3 £3.20 CSF £4.49 TOTE £2.10: £1.10, £1.10, £3.20; EX 5.00 Trifecta £22.50 Pool: £3,719.06 - 123.54 winning units..
Owner Ben CM Wong **Bred** D R Tucker **Trained** Newmarket, Suffolk

FOCUS
Probably just fair form, but this should produce some winners.

185 LINGFIELDPARK.CO.UK MAIDEN STKS 6f (P)
12:50 (12:50) (Class 5) 3-Y-O £2,726 (£805; £402) Stalls Low

Form RPR
3- 1 **Upavon**[31] 8068 3-9-5 0 LiamKeniry 7 81
(David Elsworth) *chsd ldr after 1f: shkn up over 2f out: 2 l down 1f out: pushed along and styd on to ld nr fin* 7/4[1]
2 nk **Hard Walnut (IRE)**[99] 6859 3-9-0 72 JamieSpencer 5 75
(Olly Stevens) *led: clr w wnr 2f out: hrd rdn over 1f out: edgd rt fnl f: hdd nr fin* 9/2[3]
0- 3 8 **Sand Boy (IRE)**[172] 4419 3-9-5 0 RobertWinston 3 54
(Charles Hills) *chsd ldrs: sltly hmpd after 1f: outpcd fr 1/2-way: styd on to take 3rd fnl f: no ch* 6/1
4 ¾ **Laudation** 3-9-5 0 JimmyQuinn 4 52
(William Jarvis) *s.i.s: rn green and pushed along in 6th: nvr on terms but styd on fnl f* 8/1
5-6 5 4 **Whiteflats**[9] 37 3-9-5 0 (v[1]) MartinDwyer 2 39
(Derek Shaw) *chsd ldr: hmpd and lost pl after 1f: outpcd over 2f out: hanging and wknd over 1f out* 100/1
6 7 **Irish Dream (IRE)** 3-9-0 0 JoeFanning 1
(Mark Johnston) *dwlt: nvr on terms w ldrs: no prog over 2f out: wknd* 9/4[2]
7 45 **Hester Street** 3-9-0 0 ChrisCatlin 6
(Rae Guest) *s.i.s: sn hopelessly t.o* 33/1

1m 12.01s (0.11) **Going Correction** -0.025s/f (Stan) 7 Ran SP% **114.6**
Speed ratings (Par 97): **98,97,86,85,80 71,11**
Tote Swingers: 1&2 £1.80, 1&3 £2.90, 2&3 £2.50 CSF £10.26 TOTE £2.80: £1.60, £2.10; EX 8.70 Trifecta £35.00 Pool: £2,737.98 - 58.56 winning units..
Owner McPabb Racing **Bred** Major-Gen Guy Watkins **Trained** Newmarket, Suffolk
■ Stewards' Enquiry : Jamie Spencer two-day ban; allowed mount to drift towards rails when not sufficiently clear (Jan 26, 28)

FOCUS
The front two, well clear of the others, probably ran to a fair level.

186 BLUE SQUARE BET SPRINT SERIES (ROUND 2) H'CAP (QUALIFIER) (DIV I) 6f (P)
1:25 (1:25) (Class 5) (0-70,76) 4-Y-O+ £3,067 (£905; £453) Stalls Low

Form RPR
423- 1 **Restless Bay (IRE)**[15] 8266 5-9-5 68 (v) LukeMorris 9 76
(Mrs K Burke) *chsd ldrs: cajoled along over 2f out: clsd to ld over 1f out: kpt on wl fnl f* 6/1
043- 2 ½ **Picansort**[21] 8225 6-9-3 66 ShaneKelly 5 72
(Peter Crate) *hld up in 5th: prog over 1f out: hrd rdn to press wnr ins fnl f: styd on but a hld* 8/1

411- **3** ¾ **Temple Road (IRE)**[24] 8168 5-9-4 **67** .... RobertWinston 6 71+
(Milton Bradley) *hld up in 6th: prog 2f out: burst through to chal and looked likely wnr 1f out: hung lft and nt qckn* **7/4**[1]

04-2 **4** *nk* **My Own Way Home**[7] 76 5-9-0 **63** ow1........................ AdamKirby 1 66
(David Evans) *anticipated s: chsd ldng pair: shkn up 2f out: tried to cl 1f out: styd on same pce* **9/2**[3]

061- **5** *4* **Danzoe (IRE)**[25] 8157 6-9-7 **70**................................... TomMcLaughlin 7 60
(Christine Dunnett) *t.k.h: w ldr to over 1f out: wknd qckly* **14/1**

150- **6** ¾ **Victorian Bounty**[32] 8063 8-9-4 **67**............................... FergusSweeney 8 55
(Tony Newcombe) *t.k.h: hld up in last: no prog 2f out: wknd over 1f out* **25/1**

05-2 **7** *nk* **Waabel**[7] 77 6-9-2 **65**...(t) WilliamCarson 2 52
(Violet M Jordan) *led to over 1f out: wknd rapidly fnl f* **3/1**[2]

1m 11.44s (-0.46) **Going Correction** -0.025s/f (Stan) **7** Ran SP% **115.5**
Speed ratings (Par 103): **102,101,100,99,94 93,93**
Tote Swingers: 1&2 £9.50, 1&3 £2.70, 2&3 £4.40 CSF £52.48 CT £118.38 TOTE £5.90: £2.50, £3.60; EX 51.50 Trifecta £197.50 Pool: £3,119.86 - 11.84 winning units..
Owner Mrs Elaine M Burke **Bred** Grangemore Stud **Trained** Middleham Moor, N Yorks

FOCUS
The second round of the Blue Square Bet Sprint Series.

187 BLUE SQUARE BET SPRINT SERIES (ROUND 2) H'CAP (QUALIFIER) (DIV II) 6f (P)
2:00 (2:00) (Class 5) (0-70,70) 4-Y-0+ **£3,067** (£905; £453) **Stalls** Low

Form RPR

315- **1** **Polar Venture**[23] 8183 4-9-3 **66**.................................. AdamBeschizza 9 75+
(William Haggas) *t.k.h: wd bnd over 4f out then hld up in last pair: prog over 1f out: squeezed through and drvn to ld last 100yds: hld on* **7/2**[2]

25-5 **2** *nk* **Welease Bwian (IRE)**[9] 29 4-9-2 **65**......................... AndreaAtzeni 2 73
(Stuart Williams) *hld up in midfield: gng strly 2f out: prog on outer over 1f out: str run to chal last 100yds: nt qckn nr fin* **8/1**

15-0 **3** ½ **Gung Ho Jack**[10] 11 4-9-6 **69**.. GeorgeBaker 4 75
(John Best) *trckd ldng pair: effrt on inner 2f out: rdn to ld over 1f out: hdd and one pce last 100yds* **11/4**[1]

023- **4** *1* **Exceedexpectations (IRE)**[23] 8183 4-9-4 **67**................. MartinLane 10 70
(Michael Bell) *chsd ldng pair on outer: rdn wl over 1f out: chal and upsides ins fnl f: no ex* **7/1**

504- **5** *hd* **Haadeeth**[16] 8246 6-8-11 **60**.. LukeMorris 1 64
(David Evans) *restless stalls: hld up in midfield: effrt on inner whn nt clr run jst over 1f out: squeezed through ins fnl f: kpt on same pce last 100yds* **12/1**

43-0 **6** 1¾ **Speak The Truth (IRE)**[7] 76 7-8-10 **64**...............(p) NathanAlison(5) 3 61
(Roger Ingram) *s.i.s: hld up in last: gng wl enough but nt clr run over 1f out: kpt on fnl f but nvr a threat* **5/1**[3]

04-1 **7** *1* **Desert Strike**[7] 76 7-9-7 **70**...(p) JimCrowley 5 64
(Conor Dore) *led to over 1f out: wknd fnl f* **10/1**

140- **8** 1¼ **New Decade**[169] 4534 4-9-5 **68**....................................... RobertWinston 8 58
(Milton Bradley) *t.k.h: pressed ldr: upsides over 1f out: sn wknd* **12/1**

04-3 **9** *1* **Dancing Freddy (IRE)**[9] 29 6-9-3 **66**....................(tp) WilliamCarson 7 53
(Violet M Jordan) *t.k.h: trckd ldrs: rdn and wknd jst over 1f out* **20/1**

-120 **10** 2½ **Putin (IRE)**[3] 117 5-8-7 **56** oh2...............................(bt) DavidProbert 6 35
(Phil McEntee) *racd wd: in tch: rdn over 2f out: wknd over 1f out* **20/1**

1m 11.7s (-0.20) **Going Correction** -0.025s/f (Stan) **10** Ran SP% **123.2**
Speed ratings (Par 103): **100,99,98,97,97 95,93,92,90,87**
Tote Swingers: 1&2 £8.20, 1&3 £3.20, 2&3 £7.40 CSF £33.89 CT £90.13 TOTE £5.10: £2.10, £2.80, £1.20; EX 43.20 Trifecta £157.80 Pool: £2,993.51 - 14.22 winning units..
Owner Cheveley Park Stud **Bred** F C T Wilson **Trained** Newmarket, Suffolk

FOCUS
The second division of a competitive handicap.

188 FOREST ROW H'CAP 1m (P)
2:35 (2:35) (Class 4) (0-85,83) 3-Y-0 **£4,690** (£1,395; £697; £348) **Stalls** High

Form RPR

14-1 **1** **Club House (IRE)**[10] 18 3-8-0 **69**.................................. RobertTart(7) 3 75
(Robert Mills) *hld up in last: prog 2f out: shkn up and decisive move to ld over 1f out: rdn out* **7/1**

311- **2** ½ **Jodies Jem**[31] 8072 3-9-4 **80**... JimCrowley 2 85
(William Jarvis) *trckd ldng pair after 2f: led over 2f out: hdd and nt qckn over 1f out: styd on to press wnr nr fin* **7/4**[2]

12-2 **3** 3¼ **Staffhoss**[10] 18 3-9-4 **80**.. JoeFanning 1 77
(Mark Johnston) *reluctant ldr 1f: sn bk in 4th: shkn up and effrt on inner 2f out: tk 3rd fnl f but outpcd after* **4/1**[3]

1- **4** ¾ **Azma (USA)**[36] 8017 3-8-10 **72**.. MartinDwyer 4 68
(Conrad Allen) *led after 1f and racd quite freely: rdn and hdd over 2f out: fdd fnl f* **6/4**[1]

020- **5** 4½ **Hillbilly Boy (IRE)**[169] 4526 3-9-0 **83**............................ RyanWhile(7) 5 68
(Bill Turner) *trckd ldr over 6f out: upsides on outer over 2f out: wknd over 1f out* **25/1**

1m 38.4s (0.20) **Going Correction** -0.025s/f (Stan) **5** Ran SP% **112.7**
Speed ratings (Par 99): **98,97,94,93,89**
CSF £20.22 TOTE £9.50: £3.60, £1.20; EX 13.70 Trifecta £51.60 Pool: £2,335.32 - 33.90 winning units..
Owner Trevor Jacobs & Mrs B B Mills **Bred** Val & Angela Leeson **Trained** Headley, Surrey

FOCUS
A small field and the pace seemed modest, but fair enough form.

189 MARSH GREEN H'CAP 1m 2f (P)
3:10 (3:10) (Class 3) (0-95,95) 4-Y-0+ **£7,439** (£2,213; £1,106; £553) **Stalls** Low

Form RPR

00-1 **1** **Loyalty**[7] 79 6-8-9 **83**...(v) MartinDwyer 5 91
(Derek Shaw) *mde all: set mod pce to over 3f out: kicked on wl over 1f out: edgd lft jst ins fnl f: jst lasted* **7/2**[2]

554- **2** *nk* **Hanoverian Baron**[51] 7825 8-8-11 **85**................................... SebSanders 2 93
(Tony Newcombe) *hld up in last: stl there and hanging over 1f out: plld out and hrd rdn fnl f: r.o to take 2nd post: too much to do* **6/1**

124- **3** *hd* **Robin Hoods Bay**[33] 8056 5-9-4 **92**................................... LukeMorris 3 99+
(Ed Vaughan) *trckd ldng pair: effrt 2f out: edgd lft and chsd wnr jst over 1f out: short or room briefly ins fnl f: r.o to cl but lost 2nd post* **7/2**[2]

015- **4** 1¾ **Mawaakef (IRE)**[21] 8227 5-9-3 **91**................................... JamieSpencer 4 94
(J R Jenkins) *hld up in last pair: prog on outer 3f out to press ldng pair 2f out: wknd fnl f* **5/1**[3]

322- **5** 1¼ **Emerald Wilderness (IRE)**[21] 8227 9-9-2 **95**............ TobyAtkinson(5) 1 98
(Mark Rimmer) *trckd ldrs: looking for room on inner 2f out: effrt whn hmpd jst over 1f out: nt rcvr* **5/1**[3]

301- **6** 1¼ **Kaafel (IRE)**[24] 8174 4-8-10 **86**... JimCrowley 7 84
(Peter Hedger) *pressed wnr: upsides 2f out: wknd over 1f out* **5/2**[1]

2m 4.97s (-1.63) **Going Correction** -0.025s/f (Stan)
WFA 4 from 5yo+ 2lb **6** Ran SP% **120.6**
Speed ratings (Par 107): **105,104,104,103,102 101**
Tote Swingers: 1&2 £5.10, 1&3 £3.20, 2&3 £4.70 CSF £26.08 TOTE £5.00: £3.00, £2.20; EX 42.60 Trifecta £155.40 Pool: £2,165.22 - 10.44 winning units..
Owner Brian Johnson (Northamptonshire) **Bred** Ecoutila Partnership **Trained** Sproxton, Leics
■ Stewards' Enquiry : Martin Dwyer two-day ban; careless riding (26th-28th Jan).
Luke Morris three-day ban; careless riding (26th,28th,29th Jan).

FOCUS
Not that strong a race for the class.

190 ENOUGH SAID, JUST BET AT BLUESQ.COM H'CAP 1m 2f (P)
3:40 (3:40) (Class 5) (0-75,75) 4-Y-0+ **£2,726** (£805; £402) **Stalls** Low

Form RPR

000- **1** **Destiny Of Dreams**[38] 7986 5-9-7 **75**................................... IanMongan 4 85
(Jo Crowley) *trckd ldrs: prog over 2f out: drvn and r.o to ld jst over 1f out: hld on wl* **8/1**

004- **2** *nk* **Flying Trader (USA)**[17] 8243 4-9-2 **72**.............................. GeorgeBaker 2 81
(Jane Chapple-Hyam) *trckd ldrs: prog on inner 2f out: rdn to chal jst over 1f out: pressed wnr after: styd on but a jst hld* **7/2**[1]

40-5 **3** 2¼ **Aviso (GER)**[7] 73 9-8-0 **61**... PhilipPrince(7) 3 66
(David Evans) *t.k.h: hld up inrr: prog wl over 1f out: styd on same pce to take 3rd nr fin* **16/1**

050- **4** *nk* **Parigino (FR)**[24] 8174 5-9-7 **75**.......................................(p) JimCrowley 7 79
(Nick Gifford) *hld up in last: taken wd over 2f out: drvn over 1f out: styd on to take 4th last strides: no ch* **9/2**[3]

05-2 **5** *hd* **Understory (USA)**[10] 21 6-9-1 **69**.................................... LukeMorris 9 73
(Tim McCarthy) *led: rdn over 2f out: hdd & wknd jst over 1f out* **10/1**

000- **6** ¾ **Ogaritmo**[194] 3711 4-9-0 **70**.. AdamKirby 1 72
(Marco Botti) *s.i.s: hld up in rr: drvn and sme prog on inner over 1f out: ch of a pl ins fnl f: eased nr fin* **4/1**[2]

46-3 **7** ¾ **Standpoint**[9] 39 7-9-6 **74**... LiamKeniry 5 75
(Conor Dore) *pressed ldr: rdn 2f out: wknd over 1f out* **5/1**

05/5 **8** *7* **John Lightbody**[9] 32 4-9-3 **73**.. JoeFanning 6 60
(Mark Johnston) *s.s: hld up in tch in rr: wknd over 2f out: t.o* **5/1**

05-1 **9** ½ **Electrician**[10] 15 4-8-9 **65** ow2....................................(p) ShaneKelly 8 51
(Tim Pitt) *trckd ldrs tl wknd qckly wl over 1f out: t.o* **7/1**

2m 5.44s (-1.16) **Going Correction** -0.025s/f (Stan)
WFA 4 from 5yo+ 2lb **9** Ran SP% **132.3**
Speed ratings (Par 103): **103,102,100,100,100 99,99,93,93**
Tote Swingers: 1&2 £11.70, 1&3 £24.70, 2&3 £11.30 CSF £41.74 CT £470.78 TOTE £12.50: £3.80, £1.50, £3.50; EX 62.70 Trifecta £972.00 Part won. Pool: £1,296.13 - 0.80 winning units..
Owner Kilstone Limited **Bred** Black Horse Farm **Trained** Whitcombe, Dorset

FOCUS
A modest handicap.
T/Plt: £502.00 to a £1 stake. Pool: £40,815.00 - 59.35 winning tickets. T/Qpdt: £29.70 to a £1 stake. Pool: £5,548.00 - 137.80 winning tickets. JN

125 DEAUVILLE (R-H)
Saturday, January 12
OFFICIAL GOING: Fibresand: standard

191a PRIX DE BELLOUET (MAIDEN) (3YO COLTS & GELDINGS) (FIBRESAND) 1m 1f 110y
10:45 (12:00) 3-Y-0 **£9,756** (£3,902; £2,926; £1,951; £975)

RPR

1 **Family Album (USA)** 3-8-11 0................................. MorganDelalande 3 73
(Y Barberot, France) **41/5**[3]

2 ¾ **Malki D'Aze (FR)** 3-8-11 0.. BenjaminHubert 8 72
(N Leenders, France) **22/1**

3 *1* **Tokum (FR)**[24] 8176 3-9-2 0.. TonyPiccone 10 75
(N Bertran De Balanda, France) **17/1**

4 ¾ **Azabitmour (FR)** 3-8-11 0... MaximeGuyon 13 68
(John Best) *racd in midfield towards outside: rdn 2f out: r.o wl u.p fnl f on wd outside: nrst at fin* **7/2**[2]

5 *shd* **Green Byron (FR)** 3-8-6 0............................... ChristopherGrosbois(5) 4 68
(D Allard, France) **41/1**

6 *snk* **El Nino (FR)**[38] 3-9-2 0... FlavienPrat 11 73
(M Nigge, France) **18/1**

7 ¾ **Caviar On Sunday (FR)** 3-9-2 0.................................... MickaelForest 7 71
(Mme A-M Poirier, France) **49/1**

8 *1* **Prince Gerard (FR)**[28] 3-9-2 0...................................... FranckBlondel 16 69
(Mlle S-V Tarrou, France) **3/1**[1]

9 *snk* **El Negrito (FR)**[24] 8176 3-9-2 0.................................... DavidMichaux 2 69
(J-L Pelletan, France) **39/1**

10 1½ **Abace (IRE)**[15] 3-9-2 0.. AdrienFouassier 1 66
(D Allard, France) **22/1**

0 **Vanistas (FR)**[28] 3-8-8 0... AurianeTeffaf(8) 12
(S Wattel, France) **15/1**

0 **Carlitoome (FR)**[28] 3-8-10 0.................................. EmmanuelEtienne(6) 9
(G Pannier, France) **33/1**

0 **Feed Me Rainbow (FR)**[28] 3-9-2 0.................................. LouisBeuzelin 15
(R Pritchard-Gordon, France) **12/1**

0 **Big Jones (FR)**[24] 8176 3-9-2 0...................................... ThomasMessina 6
(Mlle M-L Mortier, France) **19/1**

0 **Kytano (FR)**[15] 3-9-2 0..(p) FredericSpanu 14
(D Prod'Homme, France) **28/1**

0 **Ebulli (FR)** 3-8-11 0.. RonanThomas 5
(J Van Handenhove, France) **12/1**

2m 1.9s (121.90) **16** Ran SP% **117.5**
WIN (incl. 1 euro stake): 9.20. Places: 3.20, 7.60, 6.00. DF: 157.00. SF: 333.30..
Owner Mme Linda Cotti Brisebois **Bred** Gestut Ammerland **Trained** France

[162]WOLVERHAMPTON (A.W) (L-H)

Sunday, January 13

OFFICIAL GOING: Standard

Wind: Fine Weather: Light across

192 FIND THE BEST ODDS AT BOOKMAKERS.CO.UK APPRENTICE H'CAP 1m 1f 103y(P)

1:00 (1:00) (Class 6) (0-65,65) 4-Y-O+ **£1,940** (£577; £288; £144) **Stalls** Low

Form RPR

210- **1** **Refreshestheparts (USA)**[23] 8199 4-9-2 **65**..............(t) AaronJones(5) 7 74+
(George Baker) *a.p: swtchd lft over 1f out: led ins fnl f: r.o* **11/2**

03-3 **2** 1 3/4 **Aragorn Rouge**[9] 61 5-9-4 **61**.............. LMcNiff 5 67
(Keith Dalgleish) *chsd ldr tl rdn to ld over 1f out: hdd and unable qck ins fnl f* **11/4**[1]

10-6 **3** 2 1/4 **Dream Win**[9] 49 7-9-2 **62**..............(t) JacobButterfield(3) 1 63
(Brian Ellison) *set stdy pce tl qcknd over 2f out: rdn and hdd over 1f out: styd on same pce fnl f* **5/1**[3]

44-3 **4** 1/2 **American Lover (FR)**[10] 41 6-8-3 **51** oh1.............. KevinStott(5) 4 51
(John Wainwright) *chsd ldrs: rdn over 1f out: edgd lft and no ex ins fnl f* **20/1**

010- **5** 1 **Lord Of The Dance (IRE)**[18] 8241 7-9-3 **65**.............. RobertTart(5) 3 63
(Michael Mullineaux) *dwlt: hld up: rdn over 2f out: nvr trbld ldrs* **4/1**[2]

204- **6** nse **Songbird Blues**[17] 8248 4-8-13 **57**.............. RachealKneller 6 55
(Mark Usher) *prom: rdn over 1f out: styd on same pce* **9/1**

2-42 **7** hd **Resplendent Alpha**[8] 73 9-9-6 **63**.............. LeonnaMayor 8 60
(Jamie Osborne) *s.i.s: hld up: hdwy over 1f out: nt clr run and hmpd ins fnl f: n.d* **13/2**

600- **8** 1 **King Of Windsor (IRE)**[27] 8145 6-9-8 **65**.............. AdamCarter 2 60
(John Wainwright) *hld up: outpcd over 2f out: nvr on terms* **18/1**

2m 6.26s (4.56) **Going Correction** +0.025s/f (Slow)
WFA 4 from 5yo+ 1lb **8** Ran SP% **112.1**
Speed ratings (Par 101): **80,78,76,76,75 75,74,74**
toteswingers 1&2 £4.50, 1&3 £6.10, 2&3 £3.00 CSF £20.15 CT £78.82 TOTE £8.80: £2.90, £1.60, £1.70; EX 33.80 Trifecta £150.70 Pool: £1,134.43 - 5.64 winning tickets..
Owner Keith Jones & Family **Bred** Lazy Lane Farms Inc **Trained** Manton, Wilts

FOCUS
An open look to this modest apprentice handicap. The pace was very steady until the final half mile.

193 PICK TODAY'S WINNERS AT BOOKMAKERS.CO.UK H'CAP 1m 141y(P)

1:30 (1:30) (Class 6) (0-55,60) 4-Y-O+ **£1,940** (£577; £288; £144) **Stalls** Low

Form RPR

00-3 **1** **Spirit Of Gondree (IRE)**[12] 7 5-9-8 **56**..............(b) RobertWinston 10 65
(Milton Bradley) *hld up: hdwy over 1f out: shkn up to ld ins fnl f: r.o: eased nr fin* **7/1**[3]

000- **2** 1 1/4 **Meglio Ancora**[18] 8241 6-9-2 **55**.............. RachealKneller(5) 8 61
(Richard Ford) *hld up: hdwy over 1f out: rdn: edgd lft and wnt 2nd wl ins fnl f: nt rch wnr* **33/1**

050- **3** 1 1/4 **This Ones For Eddy**[80] 7348 8-9-5 **53**..............(b) DanielTudhope 4 56
(John Balding) *chsd ldrs: rdn over 2f out: styd on same pce fnl f* **33/1**

533- **4** 1 **Lieutenant Dan (IRE)**[15] 8291 6-9-6 **54**..............(v[1]) LukeMorris 6 55
(Michael Appleby) *chsd ldr tl over 5f out: wnt 2nd again over 2f out: sn rdn: ev ch 1f out: no ex ins fnl f* **10/1**

05-0 **5** hd **Sommersturm (GER)**[9] 61 9-8-10 **51**.............. PhilipPrince(7) 3 51
(David Evans) *hld up: r.o ins fnl f: nvr nrr* **25/1**

654- **6** nk **Raise The Rafters (IRE)**[16] 8264 8-9-5 **53**.............. AdamKirby 5 53
(John Butler) *trckd ldrs: rdn over 1f out: no ex ins fnl f* **9/4**[2]

0-04 **7** 1 1/4 **Sleepy Lucy**[5] 105 4-8-11 **46** oh1..............(e) RobbieFitzpatrick 1 43
(Richard Guest) *mid-div: hdwy over 1f out: no ex ins fnl f* **33/1**

003- **8** 1 1/4 **Youm Jamil (USA)**[16] 8264 6-9-0 **55**..............(t) RyanTate(7) 7 49
(Tony Carroll) *chsd ldrs: led over 5f out: rdn over 1f out: hdd ins fnl f: wknd towards fin* **8/1**

04-1 **9** 7 **Flag Of Glory**[6] 98 6-9-12 **60** 6ex.............. WilliamCarson 2 38
(Peter Hiatt) *led: hdd over 5f out: rdn over 2f out: wknd over 1f out: lame* **13/8**[1]

00-5 **10** 1/2 **Amber Moon**[7] 84 8-8-9 **48** oh1 ow2..............(be) AnnStokell(5) 9 25
(Ann Stokell) *hld up: racd keenly: pushed along 1/2-way: wknd wl over 2f out* **150/1**

1m 50.59s (0.09) **Going Correction** +0.025s/f (Slow)
WFA 4 from 5yo+ 1lb **10** Ran SP% **114.9**
Speed ratings (Par 101): **100,98,97,96,96 96,95,94,88,87**
toteswingers 1&2 £28.20, 1&3 £15.60, 2&3 £19.30 CSF £208.57 CT £7094.58 TOTE £10.20: £1.80, £6.00, £6.40; EX 314.30 Trifecta £797.40 Part won. Pool: £1,063.22 - 0.78 winning tickets..
Owner Paul & Ann de Weck & Partner **Bred** Windflower Overseas Holdings Inc **Trained** Sedbury, Gloucs

FOCUS
The gallop looked very generous and the two who took each other in finished well beaten in the end.

194 CLAIM FREE BETS TODAY AT BOOKMAKERS.CO.UK H'CAP 7f 32y(P)

2:00 (2:01) (Class 6) (0-65,65) 4-Y-O+ **£1,940** (£577; £288; £144) **Stalls** High

Form RPR

613- **1** **Bassett Road (IRE)**[50] 7857 5-9-7 **65**..............(p) JoeFanning 6 76
(Keith Dalgleish) *hld up: hdwy over 2f out: rdn to ld and edgd lft wl ins fnl f: r.o* **5/1**[3]

430- **2** nk **Jack My Boy (IRE)**[16] 8269 6-9-7 **65**..............(v) AdamKirby 4 75
(David Evans) *chsd ldrs: led 1f out: sn rdn and edgd rt: hdd wl ins fnl f: r.o* **7/1**

21-1 **3** 1 1/4 **Spark Of Genius**[6] 96 4-9-5 **63**.............. LukeMorris 10 70
(Alan McCabe) *s.i.s: hld up: hdwy over 1f out: edgd lft ins fnl f: r.o u.p* **6/4**[1]

112- **4** 1 1/4 **Royal Holiday (IRE)**[16] 8271 6-9-7 **65**..............(p) DanielTudhope 7 68
(Marjorie Fife) *chsd ldr: pushed along 1/2-way: rdn to ld over 2f out: hdd over 1f out: styd on same pce ins fnl f* **10/1**

061- **5** 3/4 **Ioannou**[15] 8291 4-9-2 **60**.............. StevieDonohoe 1 61
(Noel Quinlan) *hld up: hdwy over 1f out: rdn and no ex ins fnl f* **4/1**[2]

603- **6** 1 **File And Paint (IRE)**[29] 8137 5-9-4 **62**.............. EddieAhern 8 61
(Lawrence Mullaney) *chsd ldrs: led over 1f out: sn rdn and hdd: hmpd and no ex ins fnl f* **25/1**

50- **7** 11 **Reposer (IRE)**[23] 8218 5-9-7 **65**..............(t) RobertWinston 3 34
(Muredach Kelly, Ire) *led: rdn and hdd over 2f out: wknd over 1f out* **6/1**

00-3 **8** 2 **North Central (USA)**[9] 50 6-8-12 **56**..............(e) JamesSullivan 9 20
(Ruth Carr) *prom tl rdn and wknd over 1f out* **66/1**

0/0- **9** 30 **Rubenstar (IRE)**[22] 8236 10-9-4 **62**.............. ShaneKelly 2
(Daniel Mark Loughnane) *s.i.s: a in rr: bhd fr 1/2-way: t.o* **100/1**

1m 28.89s (-0.71) **Going Correction** +0.025s/f (Slow) **9** Ran SP% **118.9**
Speed ratings (Par 101): **105,104,103,101,100 99,87,84,50**
toteswingers 1&2 £5.80, 1&3 £2.70, 2&3 £3.80 CSF £40.48 CT £78.26 TOTE £5.60: £1.50, £2.00, £1.50; EX 32.20 Trifecta £167.20 Pool: £2,766.94 - 12.40 winning tickets..
Owner Keith Dalgleish **Bred** Michael Mullins **Trained** Carluke, S Lanarks

FOCUS
Again the pace was strong.

195 CORAL.CO.UK H'CAP 7f 32y(P)

2:30 (2:31) (Class 6) (0-65,63) 3-Y-O **£1,940** (£577; £288; £144) **Stalls** High

Form RPR

561- **1** **Red Dragon (IRE)**[41] 7974 3-9-7 **63**.............. RobertWinston 4 71
(Charles Hills) *chsd ldrs: shkn up over 2f out: r.o to ld nr fin* **7/2**[2]

000- **2** 1 **Rhyolite (IRE)**[50] 7868 3-9-5 **61**..............(tp) AndreaAtzeni 2 69+
(Marco Botti) *chsd ldr over 5f out tl led over 2f out: rdn and edgd lft 1f out: sn edgd rt: swvd lft wl ins fnl f: hdd nr fin* **9/2**[3]

6-11 **3** 1/2 **Lager Time (IRE)**[3] 137 3-9-7 **63** 6ex.............. WilliamCarson 5 67
(David Evans) *a.p: rdn over 1f out: styd on* **7/2**[2]

201- **4** 1 1/4 **It's Only Business**[17] 8258 3-9-4 **60**..............(p) JimmyQuinn 9 60
(Bill Turner) *hld up: hdwy over 1f out: sn rdn: r.o* **20/1**

10-0 **5** 1 **Bubbly Bailey**[3] 141 3-8-12 **61**..............(p) RobertTart(7) 7 58
(Alan Bailey) *a.p: rdn over 1f out: styd on same pce fnl f* **33/1**

621- **6** 1 1/2 **Blazeofenchantment (USA)**[23] 8203 3-9-7 **63**..............(p) AdamKirby 10 56
(Noel Quinlan) *s.i.s: pushed along in rr early: rdn over 1f out: styd on ins fnl f: nvr nrr* **5/4**[1]

14-3 **7** 2 3/4 **Bay Laurel (IRE)**[11] 17 3-9-7 **63**.............. LukeMorris 8 49
(Mrs K Burke) *hld up: hdwy over 2f out: rdn over 1f out: wknd fnl f* **25/1**

63-5 **8** 1 1/4 **Duchess Of Dreams**[5] 106 3-9-3 **59**.............. RobbieFitzpatrick 1 42
(Richard Guest) *hld up: rdn over 1f out: sn wknd* **40/1**

052- **9** 7 **Fat Bottom Girl**[30] 8108 3-8-7 **49** oh3.............. JamesSullivan 6 13
(Michael Easterby) *s.i.s and hmpd s: hld up: rdn and wknd over 2f out* **40/1**

00-0 **10** 11 **Sylvia's Diamond**[4] 122 3-8-7 **49** oh4..............(p) JohnFahy 3
(Richard Guest) *racd keenly: led and sn clr: rdn and hdd over 2f out: wknd over 1f out* **150/1**

1m 30.05s (0.45) **Going Correction** +0.025s/f (Slow) **10** Ran SP% **124.2**
Speed ratings (Par 95): **98,96,96,94,93 92,88,87,79,66**
toteswingers 1&2 £5.00, 1&3 £4.20, 2&3 £4.50 CSF £19.63 CT £61.67 TOTE £4.30: £1.50, £1.70, £2.80; EX 19.40 Trifecta £114.70 Pool: £2,348.31 - 15.34 winning tickets..
Owner The Hon R J Arculli & Des Anderson **Bred** N Hartery **Trained** Lambourn, Berks

FOCUS
The complexion of this 3yo handicap changed dramatically late on.

196 CORAL.CO.UK MOBILE CASINO H'CAP 5f 20y(P)

3:00 (3:00) (Class 4) (0-85,82) 4-Y-O+ **£4,690** (£1,395; £697; £348) **Stalls** Low

Form RPR

33-5 **1** **Waking Warrior**[9] 58 5-9-0 **78**..............(tp) JulieBurke(3) 4 87
(Kevin Ryan) *s.i.s and hmpd s: hld up: hdwy over 1f out: rdn: edgd lft and r.o wl to ld post* **7/1**[3]

06-1 **2** nse **Aubrietia**[6] 101 4-8-13 **74** 6ex..............(b) LukeMorris 3 83
(Alan McCabe) *chsd ldrs: rdn to ld 1f out: hdd post* **9/4**[1]

04-2 **3** 1/2 **Triple Dream**[4] 113 8-9-1 **76**..............(tp) RobertWinston 10 83
(Milton Bradley) *sn chsng ldrs: rdn over 1f out: r.o* **20/1**

4-24 **4** 1 1/4 **Dorback**[9] 58 6-9-7 **82**.............. MartinDwyer 2 85
(David Nicholls) *trckd ldrs: racd keenly: rdn over 1f out: styd on* **9/2**[2]

06-3 **5** 1/2 **Lucky Dan (IRE)**[9] 58 7-9-0 **75**.............. JoeFanning 5 76
(Paul Green) *hld up: hdwy over 1f out: r.o: nt rch ldrs* **16/1**

00-4 **6** 1/2 **Tango Sky (IRE)**[12] 3 4-9-2 **77**.............. FrannyNorton 1 76
(David Nicholls) *chsd ldr tl led 2f out: rdn and hdd 1f out: no ex ins fnl f* **16/1**

16-0 **7** nk **Bubbly Ballerina**[9] 58 4-8-8 **76**.............. RobertTart(7) 9 74
(Alan Bailey) *hld up: hdwy over 1f out: styd on same pce fnl f* **25/1**

006- **8** 2 3/4 **Verinco**[85] 7243 7-9-5 **80**..............(v) TomEaves 7 68
(Bryan Smart) *led: hdd 2f out: wknd ins fnl f* **11/1**

136- **9** 1 3/4 **Alaskan Bullet (IRE)**[38] 8009 4-9-4 **79**.............. AdamKirby 11 61
(Brian Ellison) *s.s: hld up: shkn up over 1f out: nvr on terms* **9/2**[2]

20-0 **10** 1 1/4 **Time Medicean**[11] 11 7-8-9 **70**.............. RobbieFitzpatrick 6 47
(Tony Carroll) *hld up: nvr on terms* **40/1**

22-0 **11** 2 1/4 **Beauty Pageant (IRE)**[9] 58 6-9-0 **75**.............. WilliamCarson 13 44
(David Evans) *chsd ldrs: pushed along 1/2-way: wknd over 1f out* **33/1**

043- **12** 3 **Sleepy Blue Ocean**[59] 7730 7-9-1 **76**..............(p) DanielTudhope 12 34
(John Balding) *mid-div: pushed along 1/2-way: wknd over 1f out* **20/1**

1m 1.22s (-1.08) **Going Correction** +0.025s/f (Slow) **12** Ran SP% **118.5**
Speed ratings (Par 105): **109,108,108,106,105 104,104,99,96,94 91,86**
toteswingers 1&2 £4.30, 1&3 £14.60, 2&3 £15.60 CSF £21.45 CT £312.94 TOTE £9.40: £2.30, £2.20, £4.60; EX 29.80 Trifecta £935.50 Pool: £1,493.66 - 1.19 winning tickets..
Owner Hambleton Racing Ltd XVII **Bred** Rosyground Stud **Trained** Hambleton, N Yorks

FOCUS
It was all change in the very last stride this time.

197 FREE BET BONANZA NOW AT BOOKMAKERS.CO.UK MAIDEN FILLIES' STKS 5f 216y(P)

3:30 (3:31) (Class 5) 3-Y-O+ **£2,587** (£770; £384; £192) **Stalls** Low

Form RPR

3- **1** **Lead Role**[29] 8138 3-8-8 0.............. AndreaAtzeni 1 66
(James Tate) *mde all: rdn and edgd rt over 1f out: r.o* **11/8**[1]

633- **2** 1 1/2 **Bouyrin (IRE)**[25] 8171 3-8-1 66.............. RyanTate(7) 11 60
(Michael Bell) *hld up: hdwy over 2f out: rdn over 1f out: r.o to go 2nd towards fin: nt rch wnr* **2/1**[2]

65- **3** 1/2 **First Serve (IRE)**[151] 5242 3-8-8 0.............. TomEaves 5 58
(David Barron) *chsd wnr: rdn over 1f out: styd on same pce ins fnl f: lost 2nd towards fin* **10/1**[3]

0- **4** 1 1/2 **Fire Fairy (USA)**[46] 7894 3-8-8 0.............. WilliamCarson 6 54
(Charles Hills) *broke wl: sn lost pl: hdwy over 1f out: r.o: nt trble ldrs* **16/1**

06- **5** 1 **Compton Albion (IRE)**[25] 8165 3-8-8 0.............. RenatoSouza 2 50
(Jeremy Gask) *prom: lost pl over 2f out: styd on ins fnl f* **100/1**

6 3/4 **Dutch Delight** 3-8-8 0.............. BarryMcHugh 7 48
(Tony Coyle) *in rr: rdn over 2f out: r.o ins fnl f: nvr nrr* **33/1**

0- **7** 3/4 **Club Electra (IRE)**[25] 8171 3-8-8 0.............. MartinLane 3 46
(Tobias B P Coles) *chsd ldrs: rdn over 2f out: wknd ins fnl f* **100/1**

8 3 **Lady Farah** 3-8-8 0 .... JoeFanning 9 36+
(Robert Cowell) *hld up: hdwy over 3f out: rdn over 1f out: wknd ins fnl f* **14/1**
9 3/4 **Is This Love (IRE)** 3-8-8 0 .... FergusSweeney 10 34
(Jamie Osborne) *s.s: a in rr* **14/1**
6-3 10 3 3/4 **Scarlet Strand**[10] 37 3-8-8 0 .... ChrisCatlin 12 22
(Reg Hollinshead) *prom tl rdn and wknd over 1f out* **28/1**
11 2 1/2 **Ivy Port** 3-8-8 0 .... LukeMorris 4 14
(Michael Appleby) *mid-div: pushed along 4f out: wknd over 2f out* **16/1**
0 12 3 3/4 **Elusive**[11] 28 7-9-5 0 .... AnnStokell(5) 8
(Ann Stokell) *in rr and pushed along 1/2-way: sn lost tch* **200/1**

1m 15.8s (0.80) **Going Correction** +0.025s/f (Slow)
WFA 3 from 7yo 16lb 12 Ran SP% **118.5**
Speed ratings (Par 100): **95,93,92,90,89 88,87,83,82,77 73,68**
toteswingers 1&2 £1.90, 1&3 £3.70, 2&3 £4.30 CSF £3.99 TOTE £2.20: £1.50, £1.40, £2.00; EX 4.60 Trifecta £27.80 Pool: £1,113.28 - 30.03 winning tickets..
Owner Saeed Manana **Bred** Genesis Green Stud Ltd **Trained** Newmarket, Suffolk
■ Stewards' Enquiry : Andrea Atzeni three-day ban; careless riding (28th-30th Jan).

FOCUS
Plenty of deadwood but a fair maiden fillies' race.

198 £50 FREE BET AT CORAL.CO.UK H'CAP 1m 4f 50y(P)
4:00 (4:00) (Class 6) (0-63,66) 4-Y-0+ **£1,940** (£577; £288; £144) **Stalls** Low

Form RPR
5-12 1 **Kames Park (IRE)**[2] 167 11-9-10 **66** .... JimmyQuinn 3 74+
(Richard Guest) *s.i.s: hld up: hdwy over 2f out: nt clr run over 1f out: shkn up to ld wl ins fnl f: r.o* **11/4**[1]
/1-3 2 1 1/4 **Reasons Unknown (IRE)**[2] 158 5-8-10 **52** ....(v) ShaneKelly 11 58
(Thomas McLaughlin, Ire) *hld up: hdwy 4f out: rdn to ld ins fnl f: sn hdd and unable qck* **9/2**[3]
26-4 3 nk **Daring Damsel (IRE)**[9] 53 4-8-13 **59** .... WilliamCarson 4 65
(Brian Baugh) *led: hdd over 5f out: led again over 2f out: rdn and hdd over 1f out: ev ch ins fnl f: unable qck towards fin* **20/1**
60-6 4 nk **Broxbourne (IRE)**[11] 21 4-8-7 **53** .... JoeFanning 1 59+
(Mark Johnston) *chsd ldrs: pushed along over 2f out: nt clr run over 1f out: swtchd rt: r.o wl* **14/1**
44-6 5 shd **Layla's Boy**[9] 53 6-9-3 **59** ....(bt) FrannyNorton 2 64
(John Mackie) *a.p: rdn and ev ch ins fnl f: no ex towards fin* **7/1**
601- 6 1/2 **Goldmadchen (GER)**[59] 7731 5-9-7 **63** .... TomEaves 8 67
(Keith Dalgleish) *hld up: hdwy over 2f out: rdn and ev ch ins fnl f: styd on same pce* **10/1**
240- 7 hd **Volcanic Jack (IRE)**[94] 7012 5-9-6 **62** .... BarryMcHugh 5 66
(Tony Coyle) *trckd ldrs: racd keenly: led over 1f out: rdn and hdd ins fnl f: styd on same pce* **16/1**
05-2 8 1 3/4 **Turjuman (USA)**[7] 84 8-8-6 **55** ....(p) RobertTart(7) 7 56
(Alan Bailey) *s.i.s: hld up: nt clr run over 1f out: r.o wl ins fnl f: nvr nrr* **14/1**
523- 9 1 1/4 **Gabrial's Hope (FR)**[23] 8206 4-9-0 **60** ....(t) StevieDonohoe 12 59
(Ian Williams) *hld up in tch: lost pl 4f out: hdwy over 1f out: rdn: hung lft and no ex ins fnl f* **4/1**[2]
360- 10 1 3/4 **Serjeant Buzfuz**[164] 4744 4-8-10 **56** .... LukeMorris 6 52
(Michael Appleby) *s.i.s: hld up: rdn over 3f out: nvr on terms* **33/1**
305- 11 8 **Maslak (IRE)**[271] 1429 9-9-4 **60** .... ChrisCatlin 9 43
(Peter Hiatt) *chsd ldr tl led over 5f out: hdd over 2f out: rdn and wknd over 1f out* **50/1**

2m 40.81s (-0.29) **Going Correction** +0.025s/f (Slow)
WFA 4 from 5yo+ 4lb 11 Ran SP% **115.3**
Speed ratings (Par 101): **101,100,99,99,99 99,99,98,97,96 90**
toteswingers 1&2 £4.00, 1&3 £14.80, 2&3 £20.80 CSF £14.14 CT £203.34 TOTE £3.70: £1.40, £2.70, £5.70; EX 21.70 Trifecta £479.00 Pool: £2,324.14 - 3.63 winning tickets..
Owner Future Racing (Notts) Limited **Bred** Pat Beirne **Trained** Wetherby, W Yorks

FOCUS
After a sound gallop six were almost in a line a furlong out.
T/Jkpt: Part won. £20,154.60 to a £1 stake. Pool: £28,386.87 - 0.50 winning tickets. T/Plt: £44.90 to a £1 stake. Pool: £81,028.17 - 1,314.87 winning tickets. T/Qpdt: £3.90 to a £1 stake. Pool: £8,047.26 - 1,525.83 winning tickets. CR

[183] LINGFIELD (L-H)
Monday, January 14

OFFICIAL GOING: Standard
Wind: Light; behind first four races, across last three races Weather: Light rain becoming more persistent; cold

199 BET AT BLUESQ.COM H'CAP 7f (P)
12:55 (12:55) (Class 5) (0-70,70) 4-Y-0+ **£2,726** (£805; £402) **Stalls** Low

Form RPR
60-2 1 **Paphos**[12] 15 6-9-1 **64** ....(v) DavidProbert 5 73
(Stuart Williams) *shkn up to ld: mde all at decent pce: kicked on over 2f out: styd on wl fr over 1f out: unchal* **4/1**[3]
21-2 2 1 1/2 **Muhandis (IRE)**[11] 34 5-9-7 **70** ....(b) SebSanders 2 75
(Nick Littmoden) *hld up in 4th: effrt 2f out: rdn to chse wnr fnl f: styd on same pce and nvr able to chal* **3/1**[2]
011- 3 1 1/4 **Commanche**[14] 8304 4-9-3 **66** .... AdamKirby 1 68
(Patrick Chamings) *cl up: chsd wnr 3f out: rdn and wl hld over 1f out: lost 2nd fnl f* **5/4**[1]
541- 4 2 3/4 **Spitfire**[55] 7794 8-9-4 **67** ....(t) IanMongan 4 61
(J R Jenkins) *awkward and stdd s: hld up in last: rdn 2f out: wnt 4th over 1f out: kpt on but nvr threatened* **12/1**
044- 5 7 **Yankee Storm**[14] 8308 8-9-5 **68** ....(b) JimCrowley 3 43
(Michael Wigham) *chsd wnr to 3f out: wknd 2f out* **7/1**

1m 23.55s (-1.25) **Going Correction** -0.025s/f (Stan) 5 Ran SP% **109.6**
Speed ratings (Par 103): **106,104,102,99,91**
CSF £15.93 TOTE £4.50: £1.50, £1.40; EX 18.10 Trifecta £31.70 Pool: £1,512.85 - 35.78 winning units..
Owner Stuart C Williams **Bred** L Ellinas And Old Mill Stud Ltd **Trained** Newmarket, Suffolk

FOCUS
A fair handicap that was run at a steady pace, with the winner making all on a pace-favouring track. The form is rated around the first two.

200 LINGFIELD PARK MARRIOTT HOTEL & COUNTRY CLUB H'CAP 1m 2f (P)
1:25 (1:25) (Class 6) (0-60,60) 4-Y-0+ **£2,045** (£603; £302) **Stalls** Low

Form RPR
501- 1 **Chella Thriller (SPA)**[36] 8050 4-9-3 **58** ....(b) GeorgeBaker 3 66+
(Alastair Lidderdale) *pressed ldr: chalng whn carried rt bnd 2f out but clr of rest: rdn to ld 1f out: styd on* **9/2**[3]
000- 2 1 **Dolly Colman (IRE)**[33] 8079 5-8-7 **46** .... ChrisCatlin 5 52
(Zoe Davison) *hld up in last: outpcd and pushed along 3f out: r.o fr over 1f out to take 2nd last 75yds: no ch to chal* **33/1**
01-0 3 1/2 **Daniel Thomas (IRE)**[9] 73 11-9-7 **60** ....(tp) WilliamCarson 1 65
(Violet M Jordan) *hld up in 5th: outpcd and pushed along 3f out: styd on fr over 1f out to take 3rd nr fin* **16/1**
613- 4 1/2 **Alezanna**[24] 8213 4-9-0 **55** .... AdamKirby 7 59
(James Toller) *led: kicked on strly 3f out: edgd rt bnd 2f out: hdd 1f out: wknd* **2/1**[2]
000- 5 1 3/4 **Bubbly Braveheart (IRE)**[275] 1379 6-9-0 **53** .... IanMongan 4 54
(Phil McEntee) *hld up in 4th: outpcd and pushed along 3f out: nvr on terms after: kpt on fnl f* **20/1**
006- 6 3/4 **Rasteau (IRE)**[42] 4966 5-8-2 **46** oh1 .... LeonnaMayor(5) 6 45
(Tom Keddy) *hld up in last pair: outpcd and pushed along 3f out: nvr on terms after* **50/1**
121- 7 2 1/4 **Norwegian Reward (IRE)**[17] 8265 5-9-4 **57** .... JimCrowley 2 52
(Michael Wigham) *trckd ldng pair: outpcd and pushed along 3f out: styd on inner and wknd over 1f out* **1/1**[1]

2m 6.0s (-0.60) **Going Correction** -0.025s/f (Stan)
WFA 4 from 5yo+ 2lb 7 Ran SP% **117.1**
Speed ratings (Par 101): **101,100,99,99,98 97,95**
Tote Swingers: 1&2 £12.10, 1&3 £3.30, 2&3 £14.90 CSF £123.46 TOTE £3.60: £1.70, £20.40; EX 118.40 Trifecta £473.60 Pool: £2,631.01 - 4.16 winning units..
Owner The Saucy Horse Partnership **Bred** John Patrick Duffy **Trained** Lambourn, Berks

FOCUS
An uncompetitive handicap, run at an honest pace. The winner built on her previous C&D win but the bare form is limited.

201 LINGFIELD PARK OWNERS GROUP H'CAP 1m 4f (P)
2:00 (2:00) (Class 6) (0-60,59) 4-Y-0+ **£2,045** (£603; £302) **Stalls** Low

Form RPR
33-1 1 **Sweet Liberta (IRE)**[7] 94 4-9-8 **59** 6ex .... DavidProbert 10 72+
(Andrew Balding) *hld up in rr but wl in tch: rdn and sweeping move on outer to ld jst over 1f out: sn clr* **1/1**[1]
306- 2 4 1/2 **Neil's Pride**[17] 8273 4-9-0 **51** ....(v[1]) BarryMcHugh 9 56
(Richard Fahey) *led 3f: trckd ldr: led 4f out: drvn and hdd jst over 1f out: wl outpcd after* **6/1**[3]
32-0 3 shd **El Libertador (USA)**[12] 20 7-9-1 **55** ....(b) JoeyHaynes(7) 3 60
(Eric Wheeler) *hld up in tch and gng wl: stl to be asked for effrt whn stmbld over 2f out: rdn and kpt on one pce fr over 1f out to press for 2nd nr fin* **8/1**
6-65 4 1 1/2 **Dubai Story**[11] 33 4-8-3 **45** ....(b[1]) LeonnaMayor(5) 2 48
(Alastair Lidderdale) *t.k.h: sn hld up in midfield: gng wl enough 3f out: rdn and outpcd jst over 1f out: one pce after* **16/1**
000- 5 nse **Asterales**[42] 7968 6-9-7 **54** .... FrannyNorton 4 57
(Jo Hughes) *dwlt: mostly in last: stl there 2f out: two reminders and sme prog 1f out: nvr in it* **10/1**
06-1 6 1 1/4 **Sinchiroka (FR)**[10] 62 7-9-10 **57** ....(t) JamieGoldstein 6 58
(Ralph Smith) *pressed ldr 3f: styd prom: wnt 2nd again u.p over 1f out: sn outpcd and btn* **4/1**[2]
00-3 7 8 **Cairanne**[10] 62 5-8-10 **46** .... RyanClark(3) 8 34
(Tom Keddy) *slowest away: quick move to ld after 3f: hdd 4f out: wknd rapidly over 1f out: eased* **14/1**
5/0- 8 1/2 **Rachael's Ruby**[62] 7169 6-8-7 **45** .... NatashaEaton(5) 7 32
(Roger Teal) *t.k.h: racd wd: in tch tl wknd over 2f out: sn bhd* **33/1**

2m 31.32s (-1.68) **Going Correction** -0.025s/f (Stan)
WFA 4 from 5yo+ 4lb 8 Ran SP% **120.0**
Speed ratings (Par 101): **104,101,100,99,99 99,93,93**
Tote Swingers: 1&2 £2.50, 1&3 £3.20, 2&3 £3.40 CSF £8.17 CT £34.11 TOTE £2.30: £2.40, £1.80, £1.20; EX 8.60 Trifecta £34.30 Pool: £2,605.74 - 56.84 winning units..
Owner Mick and Janice Mariscotti **Bred** W Maxwell Ervine **Trained** Kingsclere, Hants

FOCUS
There was little pace on for this modest contest and the heavily-supported favourite won easily. The form is rated around the runner-up.

202 WORLD HORSE WELFARE MEDIAN AUCTION MAIDEN STKS 5f (P)
2:30 (2:31) (Class 6) 3-5-Y-O **£2,045** (£603; £302) **Stalls** High

Form RPR
25-4 1 **Marvelino**[6] 106 3-8-11 68 ....(p) RobertWinston 5 65
(Pat Eddery) *mde all: clr fr 1/2-way: hrd rdn and pressed fnl f: fnd enough to hold on* **1/1**[1]
62- 2 1 **Princess Cammie (IRE)**[18] 8247 3-8-6 0 .... KieranO'Neill 6 56
(Mike Murphy) *chsd wnr and clr of rest 1/2-way: 3 l down whn sltly awkward bnd 2f out: clsd 1f out: rdn and nt qckn fnl f* **10/1**
0- 3 1 1/4 **Panther Patrol (IRE)**[201] 3506 3-8-11 0 .... JohnFahy 3 57+
(Eve Johnson Houghton) *hld up: lost pl after 2f and sn wl adrift of ldrs: pushed along and prog to take modest 3rd 1f out: r.o and clsng qckly at fin* **12/1**
500- 4 5 **Bonbon Bonnie**[31] 8109 5-9-0 38 ....(v) RyanTate(7) 2 40
(Phil McEntee) *chsd ldng pair 2f: outpcd and nvr on terms after* **50/1**
0- 5 3/4 **Big Storm Coming**[69] 7598 3-8-11 0 .... DaleSwift 1 36
(Brian Ellison) *s.i.s: a in rr: outpcd bef 1/2-way: no ch after* **10/1**
6 1 1/4 **Lasaraleen (IRE)** 3-8-6 0 .... BarryMcHugh 4 26
(Richard Fahey) *s.i.s: rn green on outer: nvr on terms w ldrs* **6/1**[3]
7 hd **Don't Be Scilly** 5-9-0 0 .... JoeyHaynes(7) 8 32
(Eric Wheeler) *dwlt: t.k.h and spd on outer: chsd ldng pair after 2f but nt on terms: wknd 1f out* **50/1**
354- 8 3/4 **Red Gift (IRE)**[158] 5010 3-8-11 69 .... TomEaves 7 28
(Brian Ellison) *dwlt: nvr on terms w ldrs: outpcd by 1/2-way: wknd fnl f* **11/4**[2]

59.08s (0.28) **Going Correction** -0.025s/f (Stan)
WFA 3 from 5yo 15lb 8 Ran SP% **120.7**
Speed ratings (Par 101): **96,94,92,84,83 81,80,79**
Tote Swingers: 1&2 £3.00, 1&3 £4.40, 2&3 £10.20 CSF £14.06 TOTE £1.50: £1.02, £2.30, £3.50; EX 9.10 Trifecta £65.50 Pool: £2,891.68 - 33.10 winning units..
Owner The Marvelino Partnership **Bred** Emma Thorman & Trickledown Stud **Trained** Nether Winchendon, Bucks

FOCUS
A weak maiden run at a sound pace, with the favourite making all. His main form rival was never going.

203 BLUE SQUARE BET H'CAP 5f (P)
3:00 (3:03) (Class 4) (0-85,88) 3-Y-O **£4,690** (£1,395; £697; £348) **Stalls High**

Form RPR
31-4 **1** **Equitania**[8] 85 3-9-3 **88** PhilipPrince(7) 2 91
(Alan Bailey) *w ldr: narrow ld 1/2-way: urged along over 1f out: hld on wl nr fin* **9/4**[2]
21-6 **2** *nk* **Boxing Shadows**[8] 85 3-8-8 **72** TomEaves 5 74
(Bryan Smart) *trckd other trio: wnt 3rd 1/2-way: trying to cl whn swtchd rt ins fnl f: drvn and r.o to take 2nd post: nt rch wnr* **5/1**[3]
1-21 **3** *nse* **Golden Flower**[9] 75 3-8-6 **77** DavidBergin(7) 1 79
(David O'Meara) *led: narrowly hdd 1/2-way: kpt pressing wnr after: jst hld nr fin and lost 2nd post* **4/5**[1]
162- **4** *17* **Multitask**[26] 8161 3-8-9 **73** LiamKeniry 4 42
(Michael Madgwick) *w ldng pair on outer 1f: dropped to last 1/2-way: sn wknd: t.o* **7/1**
58.44s (-0.36) **Going Correction** -0.025s/f (Stan) **4** Ran SP% **115.5**
Speed ratings (Par 99): **101,100,100,73**
CSF £13.09 TOTE £2.40; EX 12.20 Trifecta £19.50 Pool: £1,949.55 - 74.73 winning units..
Owner John Stocker **Bred** Longdon Stud **Trained** Newmarket, Suffolk

FOCUS
Only a small field but, the front three fought out an exciting finish. The runner-up helps set the level.

204 BREATHE SPA AT MARRIOTT LINGFIELD H'CAP 1m (P)
3:30 (3:30) (Class 5) (0-70,75) 3-Y-O **£2,726** (£805; £402) **Stalls High**

Form RPR
511- **1** **Pairumani Prince (IRE)**[16] 8289 3-9-7 **69** GeorgeBaker 5 72+
(Ed Dunlop) *t.k.h: pressed ldr: carried wd bnd 2f out but led over 1f out: drvn and styd on wl* **6/4**[1]
54-1 **2** *1/2* **Walter White (IRE)**[13] 5 3-9-4 **66** (v) DavidProbert 2 68
(Andrew Balding) *trckd ldng pair: rdn 2f out: styd on to take 2nd jst ins fnl f: nvr really able to chal* **5/2**[2]
32-1 **3** *1/2* **Tilstarr (IRE)**[12] 17 3-9-5 **67** RobertWinston 1 68
(Roger Teal) *hld up in last: shkn up once pce lifted over 2f out: prog to take 3rd ins fnl f: styd on but unable to chal* **4/1**[3]
44-4 **4** *1 1/2* **The Black Jacobin**[3] 160 3-9-3 **65** (b) LiamKeniry 3 62
(J S Moore) *racd freely: led at mod pce: upped the tempo over 2f out and steered wd bnd sn after: hdd over 1f out: fnd nil* **9/2**
540- **5** *2 1/4* **Whitford (IRE)**[14] 8302 3-9-1 **63** KirstyMilczarek 6 55
(Chris Dwyer) *hld up in 4th: rdn over 2f out: no prog and wl btn over 1f out* **14/1**
1m 39.79s (1.59) **Going Correction** -0.025s/f (Stan) **5** Ran SP% **113.4**
Speed ratings (Par 97): **91,90,90,88,86**
CSF £5.76 TOTE £2.20: £1.70, £1.40; EX 5.60 Trifecta £10.40 Pool: £1,955.88 - 139.85 winning units..
Owner Anamoine Limited **Bred** Windflower Overseas **Trained** Newmarket, Suffolk

FOCUS
A fair handicap run at a steady pace with the front four home well grouped entering the final furlong. The winner continues to progress.

205 GET STRAIGHT TO BET AT BLUESQ.COM APPRENTICE H'CAP 1m (P)
4:00 (4:00) (Class 6) (0-60,59) 4-Y-O+ **£2,045** (£603; £302) **Stalls High**

Form RPR
066- **1** **Mubtadi**[31] 8114 5-9-0 **57** ThomasBrown(5) 4 68
(Ismail Mohammed) *mde all: shkn up 2f out: styd on wl fr over 1f out: pushed out: comf* **9/2**[3]
660- **2** *2 1/4* **Mafi (IRE)**[33] 8078 5-9-2 **59** (bt) PhilipPrince(5) 3 65
(Mark Hoad) *trckd ldng pair: rdn to chse wnr wl over 1f out: styd on but no imp* **7/1**
342- **3** *2 3/4* **Silly Billy (IRE)**[15] 8299 5-8-11 **54** (v) JakePayne(5) 8 54
(Pat Phelan) *t.k.h: trckd ldng trio: rdn to go 3rd jst over 1f out: no imp after* **7/2**[2]
022- **4** *1/2* **My Scat Daddy (USA)**[15] 8298 4-8-6 **49** RyanTate(5) 5 48
(Brett Johnson) *hld up in midfield: gng wl whn n.m.r briefly over 2f out: rdn and hanging over 1f out: no ch after: kpt on nr fin* **9/4**[1]
352- **5** *shd* **Community (USA)**[18] 8249 5-9-3 **58** LeonnaMayor(3) 6 57
(Jamie Osborne) *broke wl: t.k.h: trckd wnr: shkn up and lost 2nd wl over 1f out: btn but ch of a pl whn eased ins fnl f* **9/2**[3]
50-0 **6** *nk* **Penbryn (USA)**[12] 21 6-9-7 **59** (b) RyanClark 7 57
(Nick Littmoden) *s.i.s: hld up in last: effrt 2f out: hd high and kpt on one pce fr over 1f out* **14/1**
400- **7** *1 1/2* **Salient**[33] 8079 9-8-6 **51** (b[1]) PaigeBolton(7) 1 45
(Michael Attwater) *hld up in last trio: pushed along and no prog on inner 2f out* **12/1**
10-4 **8** *2 3/4* **Gallantry**[11] 35 11-8-13 **56** IanBurns(5) 9 44
(Paul Howling) *hld up in last trio: urged along on wd outside to make sme grnd 3f out: wknd 2f out* **25/1**
1m 37.68s (-0.52) **Going Correction** -0.025s/f (Stan) **8** Ran SP% **120.1**
Speed ratings (Par 101): **101,98,96,95,95 95,93,90**
Tote Swingers: 1&2 £8.60, 1&3 £5.90, 2&3 £5.60 CSF £37.67 CT £126.34 TOTE £5.00: £1.80, £2.00, £1.40; EX 43.60 Trifecta £300.00 Pool: £2,715.97 - 6.78 winning units..
Owner Abdulla Al Mansoori **Bred** Whitsbury Manor Stud **Trained** Newmarket, Suffolk

FOCUS
A modest contest, run at a steady pace with the winner making all under a well-judged ride. It paid to race prominently. The form is rated around the second.
T/Plt: £233.80 to a £1 stake. Pool: £50,467.00 - 157.57 winning tickets. T/Qpdt: £13.70 to a £1 stake. Pool: £6,138.00 - 329.50 winning tickets. JN

[192] WOLVERHAMPTON (A.W) (L-H)
Monday, January 14

OFFICIAL GOING: Standard
Wind: Fresh behind changing to fresh across after race 3 Weather: Showers

206 CORAL.CO.UK CLAIMING STKS 7f 32y(P)
1:50 (1:50) (Class 6) 4-Y-O+ **£1,940** (£577; £288; £144) **Stalls High**

Form RPR
01-6 **1** **Polar Kite (IRE)**[12] 25 5-8-11 **73** TonyHamilton 8 80
(Richard Fahey) *hld up: hdwy over 2f out: shkn up to ld over 1f out: edgd rt: rdn out* **6/1**[2]
34-4 **2** *4 1/2* **Rakaan (IRE)**[13] 6 6-9-7 **87** FergusSweeney 5 78
(Jamie Osborne) *hld up: hdwy and hung lft fr over 1f out: sn rdn: styd on same pce ins fnl f* **4/7**[1]
00-0 **3** *1/2* **Dunn'o (IRE)**[12] 23 8-8-4 **68** (t) ShirleyTeasdale(5) 3 65
(David Nicholls) *chsd ldr tl led over 4f out: rdn and hdd over 1f out: styd on same pce ins fnl f* **16/1**
0/6- **4** *4 1/2* **Syrian**[311] 854 6-8-10 **73** ShaneKelly 9 53
(Thomas McLaughlin, Ire) *s.s: bhd tl r.o ins fnl f: nvr nrr* **15/2**[3]
003- **5** *1 1/2* **Frequency**[42] 7961 6-9-0 **75** (b) JoeFanning 4 53
(Keith Dalgleish) *chsd ldrs: ev ch over 1f out: wknd fnl f* **10/1**
160- **6** *1* **Needwood Ridge**[329] 639 6-8-9 **67** (bt) MarkCoumbe(3) 2 49
(Frank Sheridan) *prom tl rdn and wknd 2f out* **40/1**
000- **7** *9* **Point North (IRE)**[53] 7827 6-9-2 **72** DanielTudhope 7 28
(John Balding) *s.s: hdwy on outer 3f out: sn rdn and ev ch: wknd over 1f out* **20/1**
000- **8** *9* **Whitechapel**[73] 7530 6-8-2 **55** (bt[1]) DanielMuscutt(7) 1
(Keith Goldsworthy) *led: hdd over 4f out: rdn and wknd over 2f out* **100/1**
560- **9** *3 3/4* **Lexington Spirit (IRE)**[17] 8268 4-8-2 **57** PatrickMathers 6
(Richard Fahey) *chsd ldrs: pushed along 1/2-way: rdn and wknd over 2f out* **50/1**
1m 29.15s (-0.45) **Going Correction** +0.125s/f (Slow) **9** Ran SP% **114.8**
Speed ratings (Par 101): **107,101,101,96,94 93,83,72,68**
.Polar Kite claimed by Mr J. M. Curran for £8,000.\n\x\x
Owner Mr And Mrs J D Cotton **Bred** Holborn Trust Co **Trained** Musley Bank, N Yorks

FOCUS
A fair claimer in which the gallop was an ordinary one. The easy winner came down the centre in the straight. The form has been rated a bit cautiously.

207 CORAL.CO.UK MOBILE CASINO H'CAP 5f 216y(P)
2:20 (2:20) (Class 6) (0-55,55) 3-Y-O **£1,940** (£577; £288; £144) **Stalls Low**

Form RPR
302- **1** **Hazard Warning (IRE)**[17] 8274 3-9-0 **48** (b) DuranFentiman 2 54
(Tim Easterby) *in rr whn hmpd sn after s: sn pushed along: rdn over 1f out: edgd lft and str run ins fnl f: to ld post* **3/1**[1]
35-2 **2** *hd* **Holding Fast (IRE)**[4] 137 3-9-3 **51** MartinLane 11 56
(Tobias B P Coles) *sn led: rdn clr over 1f out: hdd post* **3/1**[1]
050- **3** *3* **Eyeline**[17] 8274 3-9-7 **55** (p) MartinDwyer 9 50
(Reg Hollinshead) *chsd ldr: rdn over 1f out: styd on same pce fnl f* **14/1**
65-6 **4** *3/4* **Daisie Cutter**[11] 31 3-9-3 **54** SimonPearce(3) 7 47
(Lydia Pearce) *chsd ldrs: rdn over 2f out: hung lft fnl f: styd on same pce* **8/1**[3]
03-5 **5** *1/2* **Her Royal Empress**[11] 36 3-8-12 **46** oh1 AdamBeschizza 3 37
(James Unett) *prom: pushed along 1/2-way: rdn over 1f out: styd on same pce fnl f* **25/1**
024- **6** *2 1/4* **Cromwell Rose (IRE)**[115] 6435 3-9-3 **51** (b) LukeMorris 8 35
(John Weymes) *chsd ldrs: rdn over 2f out: wknd fnl f* **20/1**
340- **7** *shd* **Persian Marvel (IRE)**[27] 8155 3-9-2 **50** (b) JoeFanning 5 34
(Roger Ingram) *dwlt: hld up: shkn up over 1f out: hung lft fnl f: nvr on terms* **9/2**[2]
000- **8** *1* **Jonny Wombat**[85] 7272 3-8-5 **46** oh1 VictorSantos(7) 6 27
(Richard Ford) *hld up: hmpd sn after s: rdn over 1f out: n.d* **100/1**
03-0 **9** *nk* **Hats Off**[11] 31 3-8-12 **46** (b) FergusSweeney 12 26
(John Best) *prom: racd keenly: rdn and wknd over 1f out* **14/1**
35-4 **10** *2 3/4* **Scoobys Girl (IRE)**[11] 36 3-8-13 **47** (b) ShaneKelly 4 18
(Daniel Mark Loughnane) *in rr whn hmpd sn after s: wknd over 2f out* **20/1**
00-5 **11** *3/4* **Woodland Fleur**[12] 19 3-9-7 **55** JimmyQuinn 1 24
(Tony Carroll) *hld up: rdn and wknd over 1f out* **12/1**
1m 16.44s (1.44) **Going Correction** +0.125s/f (Slow) **11** Ran SP% **114.7**
Speed ratings (Par 95): **95,94,90,89,89 86,85,84,84,80 79**
Tote Swingers: 1&2 £2.00, 1&3 £8.10, 2&3 £10.60 CSF £10.53 CT £107.67 TOTE £4.10: £1.80, £1.50, £4.00; EX 11.00 Trifecta £124.10 Pool: £1,973.03 - 11.91 winning units..
Owner Habton Farms **Bred** E O'Gorman **Trained** Great Habton, N Yorks

FOCUS
A moderate handicap in which the pace was sound throughout. The winner edged towards the far rail late on and the two market leaders pulled clear. The form has been given a bit of a chance.

208 BEST RACING ODDS GUARANTEED AT BOOKMAKERS.CO.UK H'CAP 1m 4f 50y(P)
2:50 (2:50) (Class 5) (0-75,81) 4-Y-O+ **£2,911** (£866; £432; £216) **Stalls Low**

Form RPR
21-2 **1** **English Summer**[11] 40 6-9-8 **73** (t) JamieSpencer 6 88
(David Simcock) *hld up: hdwy 1/2-way: chsd ldr 3f out: shkn up to ld over 1f out: sn hung lft: rdn clr* **5/2**[2]
11-1 **2** *5* **Cool Sky**[4] 144 4-9-5 **81** 6ex RobertTart(7) 3 88
(William Knight) *s.i.s: sn prom: chsd ldr over 6f out: led over 5f out: rdn and hdd over 1f out: styd on same pce* **8/11**[1]
510- **3** *4* **Cheers For Thea (IRE)**[17] 8271 8-9-6 **71** (t) DuranFentiman 1 72
(Tim Easterby) *chsd ldrs: lost pl 7f out: hdwy over 3f out: sn rdn: wknd over 1f out* **25/1**
000- **4** *8* **Admirable Duque (IRE)**[17] 8275 7-9-1 **73** (be) JoshBaudains(7) 4 61
(Dominic Ffrench Davis) *hld up: hdwy 7f out: chsd ldr over 4f out tl 3f out: rdn and wknd over 2f out* **9/1**[3]
/06- **5** *12* **Jezza**[41] 7980 7-8-11 **62** (p) JoeFanning 2 31
(Karen George) *led: hdd over 5f out: wknd 3f out* **14/1**
60-0 **6** *29* **Boston Blue**[11] 39 6-9-2 **67** JimmyQuinn 5
(Tony Carroll) *chsd ldr 5f: sn pushed along: wknd over 3f out: t.o* **66/1**
2m 40.37s (-0.73) **Going Correction** +0.125s/f (Slow)
WFA 4 from 6yo+ 4lb **6** Ran SP% **108.5**
Speed ratings (Par 103): **107,103,101,95,87 68**
Tote Swingers: 1&2 £1.60, 1&3 £3.20, 2&3 £4.00 CSF £4.30 TOTE £3.90: £3.10, £1.02; EX 4.60 Trifecta £17.20 Pool: £1,624.57 - 70.72 winning units..
Owner Dr Marwan Koukash **Bred** Juddmonte Farms Ltd **Trained** Newmarket, Suffolk

FOCUS
A fair handicap in which an ordinary gallop picked up leaving the back straight. The winner edged towards the far side in the closing stages. This rates his best form since last spring.

209 £50 FREE BET AT CORAL.CO.UK H'CAP 1m 141y(P)
3:20 (3:20) (Class 5) (0-75,75) 3-Y-O **£2,911** (£866; £432; £216) **Stalls Low**

Form RPR
011- **1** **Gabrial The Boss (USA)**[25] 8186 3-9-0 **68** JamieSpencer 2 73
(David Simcock) *a.p: pushed along to chse ldr 2f out: rdn to ld and hung lft wl ins fnl f* **4/1**[2]
514- **2** *1/2* **Tight Knit (USA)**[19] 8240 3-9-7 **75** LukeMorris 3 79
(James Tate) *led: rdn over 1f out: edgd lft and hdd wl ins fnl f* **10/11**[1]

00-3 **3** 1¾ **First Sargeant**[7] 91 3-9-2 **70**......(p) JimmyQuinn 4 70
(Marco Botti) *s.i.s: hld up: rdn over 2f out: hdwy over 1f out: nt rch ldrs* **11/2**[3]
003- **4** 7 **Rainford Glory (IRE)**[30] 8140 3-8-7 **61** oh1...... AndreaAtzeni 5 45
(Patrick Morris) *chsd ldrs: rdn over 2f out: wknd over 1f out* **12/1**
51- **5** 1 **Diletta Tommasa (IRE)**[56] 7786 3-9-0 **68**...... ShaneKelly 1 50
(John Stimpson) *prom: rdn over 2f out: wknd over 1f out* **16/1**
336- **6** ½ **Betzyoucan**[38] 8016 3-8-10 **64**...... JoeFanning 6 44
(Mark Johnston) *chsd ldr tl rdn 2f out: wknd over 1f out* **12/1**
100- **7** 24 **Firstkissoflove**[14] 8302 3-9-0 **68**...... MartinDwyer 7
(David C Griffiths) *hld up: pushed along 1/2-way: wknd over 2f out: t.o* **50/1**

1m 53.0s (2.50) **Going Correction** +0.125s/f (Slow) **7** Ran SP% **111.0**
Speed ratings (Par 97): **93,92,91,84,83 83,62**
Tote Swingers: 1&2 £1.90, 1&3 £2.00, 2&3 £3.10 CSF £7.52 TOTE £4.10: £2.10, £1.40; EX 8.30 Trifecta £28.40 Pool: £1,588.02 - 41.88 winning units..
Owner Dr Marwan Koukash **Bred** Hunter Valley Farm Et Al **Trained** Newmarket, Suffolk

FOCUS
A couple of unexposed sorts in a fair handicap. Although the gallop was just an ordinary one, the first three pulled clear and the winner edged from the centre towards the far side the last furlong. The time was slow and the form has not been rated too positively.

210 HORSE RACING FREE BETS AT BOOKMAKERS.CO.UK CLAIMING STKS 1m 141y(P)
3:50 (3:50) (Class 6) 3-Y-O **£1,940** (£577; £288) **Stalls** Low

Form RPR
5-36 **1** **Run It Twice (IRE)**[4] 141 3-9-5 67...... (b) LukeMorris 1 73
(David Evans) *chsd ldr: pushed along over 2f out: rdn to ld over 1f out: edgd lft: r.o* **13/8**[2]
034- **2** 1¼ **Mick Dundee (IRE)**[30] 8132 3-9-1 62...... (t) JamieSpencer 3 66
(J W Hills) *led: shkn up over 2f out: hdd over 1f out: nt clr run and swtchd rt sn after: styd on* **11/4**[3]
356- **3** ½ **Cheektocheek (IRE)**[46] 7922 3-8-7 72...... (b[1]) JimmyQuinn 2 57
(Marco Botti) *hld up in tch: rdn over 1f out: hung lft: styd on u.p: nt trble ldrs* **6/4**[1]

1m 52.77s (2.27) **Going Correction** +0.125s/f (Slow) **3** Ran SP% **104.8**
Speed ratings (Par 95): **94,92,92**
CSF £5.52 TOTE £2.60; EX 4.80 Trifecta £4.40 Pool: £1,041.85 - 177.32 winning units..
Owner Shropshire Wolves 4 **Bred** Yeomanstown Stud **Trained** Pandy, Monmouths

FOCUS
A modest, if uncompetitive claimer, in which the gallop was only fair. The winner edged towards the far rail in the straight. The form choice was again below his best.

211 HORSE RACING FREE BETS WITH BOOKMAKERS.CO.UK MAIDEN STKS 1m 1f 103y(P)
4:20 (4:22) (Class 5) 3-Y-O **£2,587** (£770; £384; £192) **Stalls** Low

Form RPR
0- **1** **Naru (IRE)**[140] 5668 3-9-5 0...... LukeMorris 7 71
(James Tate) *chsd ldrs: pushed along over 3f out: rdn over 1f out: r.o to ld last stride* **14/1**
6- **2** ½ **Good Evans**[51] 7868 3-9-5 0...... StephenCraine 1 70
(Tom Dascombe) *led: rdn and hdd over 1f out: rallied to ld nr fin: hdd last stride* **5/1**[3]
0- **3** ¾ **Passionate Diva (USA)**[37] 8033 3-9-0 0...... JimmyQuinn 2 63
(Ed Vaughan) *trckd ldrs: led over 1f out: rdn and hdd nr fin* **33/1**
04- **4** 1 **Masaadr**[25] 8185 3-9-5 0...... ShaneKelly 4 66
(James Tate) *hld up in tch: shkn up over 1f out: sn hung lft: styd on u.p* **9/1**
5- **5** 1½ **Ofcoursewecan (USA)**[30] 8134 3-9-5 0...... JoeFanning 3 63
(Mark Johnston) *chsd ldr tl rdn 2f out: styd on same pce ins fnl f* **7/1**
60- **6** 1¼ **Master Hamilton**[17] 8262 3-9-5 0...... MartinDwyer 6 61
(Tobias B P Coles) *chsd ldrs: pushed along over 5f out: outpcd over 2f out: styd on u.p ins fnl f* **100/1**
7 ½ **Moscow Circus (IRE)** 3-9-5 0...... DanielTudhope 8 59+
(Mark Johnston) *hld up: pushed along 1/2-way: rdn over 1f out: styd on: nt trble ldrs* **6/1**
0- **8** ½ **Pencombe (FR)**[33] 8070 3-9-5 0...... MartinLane 13 58+
(David Simcock) *prom: rdn over 2f out: hung lft over 1f out: no ex* **7/2**[1]
0- **9** 3¼ **Spirit Man**[67] 7641 3-9-5 0...... SebSanders 12 52
(Paul D'Arcy) *hld up: rdn over 1f out: n.d* **40/1**
10 1½ **Shockingdancer (IRE)** 3-9-5 0...... AndreaAtzeni 9 48+
(Marco Botti) *mid-div: hdwy over 2f out: wknd over 1f out* **9/2**[2]
11 4½ **Triple Aitch (USA)** 3-9-5 0...... JamieSpencer 10 39
(Peter Chapple-Hyam) *stdd s: hld up: a in rr* **16/1**
0- **12** 18 **How You Fixed (IRE)**[24] 8207 3-8-12 0...... TimClark(7) 11
(Denis Quinn) *a in rr: lost tch fnl 3f: t.o* **100/1**

2m 3.54s (1.84) **Going Correction** +0.125s/f (Slow) **12** Ran SP% **113.8**
Speed ratings (Par 97): **96,95,94,94,92 91,91,90,87,86 82,66**
Tote Swingers: 1&2 £4.60, 1&3 £2.70, 2&3 £4.60 CSF £78.46 TOTE £14.70: £3.50, £2.70, £6.90; EX 103.30 Trifecta £1805.30 Part won. Pool: £2,407.09 - 0.55 winning units..
Owner Saeed Manana **Bred** Rabbah Bloodstock Limited **Trained** Newmarket, Suffolk

FOCUS
No more than a modest maiden and a race run at just an ordinary gallop. The winner came down the centre in the straight. With little form to go on the winner has been rated in line with the race averages.

212 BOOKMAKERS.CO.UK H'CAP 1m 1f 103y(P)
4:50 (4:51) (Class 6) (0-60,60) 3-Y-O **£1,940** (£577; £288; £144) **Stalls** Low

Form RPR
00-4 **1** **Hidden Link**[11] 37 3-9-7 **60**...... LukeMorris 5 65+
(Ronald Harris) *chsd ldr: rdn over 1f out: styd on u.p to ld wl ins fnl f* **5/2**[1]
02-0 **2** 1 **Great Ormond (IRE)**[7] 103 3-9-0 **53**...... AndreaAtzeni 1 56+
(David Simcock) *hld up: hdwy over 1f out: sn rdn: r.o to go 2nd post: nt rch wnr* **6/1**[2]
34-2 **3** nk **Una Bella Cosa**[10] 55 3-8-13 **52**...... (p) SebSanders 8 54
(Alan McCabe) *led: rdn and hung rt fr over 1f out: hdd and unable qck wl ins fnl f* **5/2**[1]
0-63 **4** 2½ **Precision Strike**[7] 103 3-8-9 **48**...... RobbieFitzpatrick 3 45
(Richard Guest) *hld up: hdwy over 1f out: nt rch ldrs* **6/1**[2]
50-0 **5** 6 **Gabrial The Duke (IRE)**[7] 103 3-9-4 **57**...... (p) JamieSpencer 6 41
(Patrick Morris) *prom: pushed along over 3f out: rdn over 2f out: wknd over 1f out* **6/1**[2]
00-5 **6** shd **Icanboogie**[10] 59 3-8-0 **46**...... RobertTart(7) 2 30
(Karen George) *prom: rdn over 2f out: wknd over 1f out* **25/1**
00-0 **7** 24 **Last Chance Ranch**[10] 55 3-8-7 **46** oh1...... (t) MartinDwyer 4
(Derek Shaw) *s.i.s: sn pushed along and a bhd: lost tch fnl 3f: t.o* **20/1**

006- **P** **Charm Cry (USA)**[51] 7866 3-9-6 **59**...... JoeFanning 7
(Mark Johnston) *chsd ldrs: cl 3rd whn p.u and dismntd over 2f out* **12/1**[3]

2m 4.27s (2.57) **Going Correction** +0.125s/f (Slow) **8** Ran SP% **116.3**
Speed ratings (Par 95): **93,92,91,89,84 84,62,**
Tote Swingers: 1&2 £4.60, 1&3 £2.70, 2&3 £4.60 CSF £18.63 CT £40.84 TOTE £4.50: £1.10, £3.10, £1.40; EX 26.30 Trifecta £156.40 Pool: £3,480.38 - 16.68 winning units..
Owner Ridge House Stables Ltd **Bred** Mrs M Chaworth-Musters **Trained** Earlswood, Monmouths

FOCUS
A moderate handicap run at just an ordinary gallop to the home turn. The winner came down the centre and the form helps with the standard.
T/Jkpt: £24,325.40 to a £1 stake. Pool: £34,261.00 - 1.00 winning ticket. T/Plt: £30.80 to a £1 stake. Pool: £65,199.00 - 1,540.70 winning tickets. T/Qpdt: £15.10 to a £1 stake. Pool: £3,892.00 - 189.90 winning tickets. CR

206 WOLVERHAMPTON (A.W) (L-H)
Tuesday, January 15

OFFICIAL GOING: Standard
Wind: Viretually nil Weather: Fine

213 CORAL.CO.UK H'CAP 5f 20y(P)
2:20 (2:20) (Class 6) (0-60,66) 4-Y-O+ **£1,940** (£577; £288; £144) **Stalls** Low

Form RPR
01-4 **1** **M J Woodward**[13] 26 4-9-7 **60**...... JoeFanning 8 70
(Paul Green) *cl up: led wl over 1f out and sn rdn: drvn ins fnl f and kpt on wl* **9/2**[2]
0-16 **2** nk **Hab Reeh**[5] 142 5-8-3 **49**...... (t[1]) GemmaTutty(7) 9 58
(Ruth Carr) *trckd ldng pair: hdwy over 1f out: rdn to chal wl ins fnl f: carried hd high and ev ch tl no ex nr fin* **15/2**
06-2 **3** nk **Miserere Mei (IRE)**[6] 111 4-8-7 **46** oh1...... JimmyQuinn 4 54
(Richard Guest) *trckd ldrs: hdwy 2f out: rdn to chse wnr ins fnl f: ev ch tl drvn and no ex towards fin* **16/1**
0-24 **4** 1¼ **Ryedale Dancer (IRE)**[4] 163 5-9-2 **55**...... RobbieFitzpatrick 5 59
(Richard Guest) *dwlt and in rr: hdwy on wd outside over 1f out: sn rdn and styd on fnl f: nrst fin* **11/2**[3]
0-31 **5** ¾ **Liberty Ship**[5] 142 8-9-13 **66** 6ex...... MartinDwyer 1 67
(Mark Buckley) *in tch: hdwy 2f out: rdn to chse ldrs appr fnl f: kpt on same pce* **8/1**
50-3 **6** 1¼ **John Coffey (IRE)**[9] 87 4-8-13 **52**...... (vt[1]) RobertWinston 7 48
(David Nicholls) *dwlt and in rr: effrt 2f out: sn rdn along and edgd lft: nvr nr ldrs* **3/1**[1]
03-5 **7** 1½ **Wreningham**[13] 26 8-9-0 **58**...... CharlesBishop(5) 2 49
(Pat Eddery) *slt ld: rdn along 2f out: hdd wl over 1f out and grad wknd* **11/1**
410- **8** 1¼ **Dazzlin Bluebell (IRE)**[17] 8287 4-9-2 **55**...... (b) DuranFentiman 6 41
(Tim Easterby) *in tch: rdn along 2f out: sn wknd* **10/1**
45-3 **9** ¾ **Molly Jones**[6] 124 4-9-0 **53**...... WilliamCarson 3 37
(Derek Haydn Jones) *trckd ldng pair on inner: effrt wl over 1f out: rdn ent fnl f: sn wknd* **12/1**

1m 2.36s (0.06) **Going Correction** +0.05s/f (Slow) **9** Ran SP% **112.4**
Speed ratings (Par 101): **101,100,100,98,96 94,92,90,89**
toteswingers 1&2 £5.60, 2&3 £12.00, 1&3 £9.80 CSF £36.78 CT £490.39 TOTE £5.50: £2.60, £2.50, £3.90; EX 46.00 Trifecta £430.20 Pool: £1279.56 - 2.23 winning units..
Owner E Sciarrillo **Bred** Paul Green **Trained** Lydiate, Merseyside

FOCUS
It paid to race close to the pace in this 5f handicap which had an open look about it. A small personal best from the winner to beat the well-in second.

214 BEST RACING ODDS WITH BOOKMAKERS.CO.UK H'CAP 5f 216y(P)
2:55 (2:57) (Class 6) (0-65,65) 4-Y-O+ **£1,940** (£577; £288; £144) **Stalls** Low

Form RPR
62-4 **1** **Colourbearer (IRE)**[10] 76 6-9-2 **60**...... (t) SebSanders 9 71
(Milton Bradley) *in tch: hdwy 2f out: n.m.r over 1f out: squeezed through and rdn to ld jst ins fnl f: kpt on wl* **5/1**[3]
03-2 **2** 1¼ **Climaxfortackle (IRE)**[8] 101 5-9-4 **62**...... FrannyNorton 6 69+
(Derek Shaw) *s.i.s and bhd: hdwy over 2f out: swtchd rt to outer and rdn ent fnl f: styd on strly* **4/1**[1]
001- **3** 1 **Sunrise Dance**[19] 8253 4-9-6 **64**...... (p) RobertWinston 8 68
(Robert Johnson) *trckd ldrs: hdwy 2f out: rdn to chal ent fnl f: ev ch tl drvn and one pce last 100yds* **4/1**[1]
02-6 **4** ½ **Master Of Disguise**[13] 27 7-9-7 **65**...... (t) WilliamCarson 11 67
(Brian Baugh) *chsd ldrs: rdn along and hdwy 2f out: chal over 1f out and ev ch tl drvn and one pce wl ins fnl f* **11/1**
000- **5** ½ **Rafaaf (IRE)**[24] 8225 5-9-5 **63**...... FergusSweeney 7 64+
(Richard Phillips) *towards rr: hdwy over 1f out: sn rdn and kpt on fnl f: nrst fin* **25/1**
02-2 **6** ½ **Holy Angel (IRE)**[13] 27 4-9-6 **64**...... (e) DuranFentiman 4 63
(Tim Easterby) *trckd ldrs: hdwy on inner 2f out: rdn over 1f out: sn one pce* **9/2**[2]
545- **7** shd **Powerful Pierre**[71] 7589 6-9-4 **62**...... (v) DaleSwift 10 61
(Ian McInnes) *towards rr: sme hdwy over 1f out: rdn and kpt on fnl f:* **25/1**
51-4 **8** nk **Methaaly (IRE)**[11] 54 10-8-10 **61**...... (be) RobertTart(7) 12 59
(Michael Mullineaux) *dwlt and in rr tl sme late hdwy* **12/1**
45-4 **9** 1½ **Greenhead High**[13] 27 5-9-6 **64**...... MartinDwyer 5 57
(David Nicholls) *cl up: led 2f out: rdn over 1f out: hdd jst ins fnl f and sn wknd* **7/1**
304- **10** 7 **El Dececy (USA)**[34] 8077 9-9-0 **58**...... (p) AdamKirby 1 29
(Charles Smith) *slt ld on inner: pushed along and hdd 1/2-way: rdn and wknd wl over 1f out* **16/1**
000- **11** 1½ **Rowan Spirit (IRE)**[269] 1526 5-9-7 **65**...... ShaneKelly 3 31
(Mark Brisbourne) *cl up: slt ld 1/2-way: hdd 2f out: sn rdn and wknd fnl f* **66/1**
03-5 **12** 4½ **Blown It (USA)**[11] 56 7-9-6 **64**...... JoeFanning 2 15
(Keith Dalgleish) *dwlt: a in rr* **12/1**

1m 15.0s **Going Correction** +0.05s/f (Slow) **12** Ran SP% **126.1**
Speed ratings (Par 101): **102,100,99,98,97 97,96,96,94,85 83,77**
toteswingers 1&2 £5.20, 2&3 £6.10, 1&3 £7.20 CSF £26.69 CT £92.31 TOTE £5.00: £2.40, £1.30, £2.50; EX 39.40 Trifecta £209.10 Pool: £2080.72 - 7.46 winning units..
Owner E A Hayward **Bred** Corduff Stud & J Corcorcan **Trained** Sedbury, Gloucs

The Form Book Flat, Raceform Ltd, Compton, RG20 6NL.

FOCUS
No less than nine previous course winners in this wide-open sprint handicap. The pace held up well and the winner is rated slightly up on his recent form.

215 NO DEPOSIT FREE BETS WITH BOOKMAKERS.CO.UK MAIDEN STKS 1m 4f 50y(P)
3:25 (3:26) (Class 5) 4-Y-O+ £2,587 (£770; £384; £192) Stalls Low

Form RPR
1 **Biggins Boy (IRE)**[38] 4-9-5 0 .... RobertWinston 3 83+
(Alan Swinbank) *trckd ldrs: cl up 4f out: shkn up and qckd to ld wl over 1f out: sn clr: rdn out* 9/2[3]
2/2- 2 1 ¼ **Hepworth**[38] [8037] 4-9-0 0 .... (p) RobertHavlin 12 76+
(John Gosden) *prom: trckd ldr after 4f: effrt to ld over 2f out: sn rdn and hdd wl over 1f out: kpt on u.p fnl f* 6/4[1]
2/0- 3 9 **White Fusion**[45] [7954] 5-9-9 68 .... DanielTudhope 11 67
(David O'Meara) *led: rdn along and hdd over 2f out: sn drvn and kpt on same pce* 11/2
4 6 **Ice Tres**[11] 4-9-0 0 .... AndreaAtzeni 5 52
(Rod Millman) *bhd: hdwy 4f out: kpt on fnl 2f: nvr nr ldrs* 33/1
5 6 **Lacey** 4-9-5 0 .... LiamKeniry 1 47
(Reg Hollinshead) *t.k.h early: midfield: hdwy 4f out: rdn along 3f out: n.d* 50/1
- 6 11 **Shirazz** 4-8-9 0 .... AmyScott(5) 9 25
(Jeremy Noseda) *bhd: sme hdwy fnl 3f: nvr a factor* 10/1
5- 7 7 **Golden Share (USA)**[16] [8295] 4-9-5 0 .... AdamKirby 4 19
(Marco Botti) *in tch: hdwy over 4f out: rdn along over 3f out and sn outpcd* 11/4[2]
050- 8 ½ **One For The Girls**[27] [6948] 4-9-5 45 .... (t) LukeMorris 2 18
(Nicky Vaughan) *prom: rdn along over 4f out: sn outpcd* 66/1
9 ¾ **Wesleydale (IRE)**[30] 6-9-4 0 .... ShirleyTeasdale(5) 10 17
(Simon West) *midfield: rdn along 1/2-way: sn outpcd and bhd* 66/1
10 12 **Ultra Special**[36] 6-9-4 0 .... TomEaves 7
(Iain Jardine) *a in rr: bhd fnl 3f* 50/1
066- 11 26 **Tiny Thompson**[18] [8267] 4-8-11 36 .... SimonPearce(3) 6
(Lydia Pearce) *rn in snatches: chsd ldrs: rdn along and lost pl 1/2-way: sn bhd* 66/1

2m 39.5s (-1.60) **Going Correction** +0.05s/f (Slow)
WFA 4 from 5yo+ 4lb 11 Ran SP% **120.7**
Speed ratings (Par 103): **107,106,100,96,92 84,80,79,79,71 54**
toteswingers 1&2 £2.10, 2&3 £3.20, 1&3 £4.10 CSF £11.80 TOTE £7.60: £1.50, £1.30, £1.10; EX 15.10 Trifecta £123.30 Pool: £2421.32 - 14.72 winning units..
Owner G H Bell **Bred** Castlemartin Stud And Skymarc Farm **Trained** Melsonby, N Yorks

FOCUS
Plenty of dead wood in this maiden in which the pace was very steady until the final half-mile. There are doubts over the form.

216 BOOKIE FREE BETS WITH BOOKMAKERS.CO.UK (S) STKS 7f 32y(P)
4:00 (4:00) (Class 6) 3-Y-O £1,940 (£577; £288; £144) Stalls High

Form RPR
03-5 1 **Schottische**[11] [55] 3-8-7 53 .... (p) WilliamCarson 5 55
(Derek Haydn Jones) *cl up: rdn to ld wl over 1f out: drvn ins fnl f: kpt on strly towards fin* 11/2[3]
22-4 2 1 **Ishigunnaeatit**[13] [18] 3-8-13 66 .... (v[1]) LukeMorris 1 58
(Mrs K Burke) *trckd ldng pair: hdwy 2f out: effrt and n.m.r over 1f out: rdn to chal ins fnl f: sn drvn and ev ch: edgd lft and one pce last 100yds* 13/8[2]
553- 3 3 **Alfaisaliah (IRE)**[17] [8286] 3-8-7 52 .... DavidProbert 4 44
(J S Moore) *trckd ldng pair: rdn along and sltly outpcd over 3f out: kpt on u.p fnl f* 8/1
52-4 4 1 ¼ **Hardy Red (IRE)**[12] [38] 3-9-4 71 .... FergusSweeney 2 52
(Jamie Osborne) *t.k.h early: led: rdn along over 2f out: hdd wl over 1f out: drvn and wknd ent fnl f* 11/10[1]

1m 31.0s (1.40) **Going Correction** +0.05s/f (Slow) 4 Ran SP% **112.2**
Speed ratings (Par 95): **94,92,89,88**
CSF £15.19 TOTE £7.50; EX 16.30 Trifecta £63.30 Pool: £1189.57 - 14.07 winning units..There was no bid for the winner.
Owner Mrs E M Haydn Jones **Bred** Mrs M L Parry & P M Steele-Mortimer **Trained** Efail Isaf, Rhondda C Taff

FOCUS
The two market leaders had questions to answer and the winner had 7lb to find with both on official ratings. Dubious form which is worth more at face value.

217 CASINO AT CORAL.CO.UK H'CAP 7f 32y(P)
4:30 (4:30) (Class 4) (0-80,79) 4-Y-O+ £4,690 (£1,395; £697; £348) Stalls High

Form RPR
61-2 1 **Atlantis Crossing (IRE)**[13] [25] 4-9-7 79 .... AdamKirby 7 93+
(Roger Ingram) *hld up towards rr: smooth hdwy over 2f out: chal ins fnl f: rdn to ld last 100yds: comf* 3/1[1]
241- 2 1 **Light From Mars**[20] [8238] 8-9-5 77 .... LukeMorris 5 88
(Ronald Harris) *trckd ldrs: hdwy on bit over 2f out: led 1 1/2f out: rdn ent fnl f: hdd and could nt qckn last 100yds* 10/1
524- 3 3 **Chookie Avon**[48] [7901] 6-9-5 77 .... (p) RobertWinston 4 80
(Keith Dalgleish) *hld up in rr: hdwy on inner over 2f out: rdn wl over 1f out: kpt on fnl f: nrst fin* 11/1
4 nk **Creek Falcon (IRE)**[102] [6851] 4-8-8 69 .... RaulDaSilva(3) 8 71
(David O'Meara) *hld up in rr: hdwy wl over 2f out: rdn over 1f out: styd on fnl f: nrst fin* 7/1
26-6 5 ¾ **Irish Heartbeat (IRE)**[11] [58] 8-9-4 76 .... (p) FergusSweeney 3 76
(Jamie Osborne) *stdd s: hld up and bhd: hdwy on wd outside wl over 1f out: sn rdn and styd on: nrst fin* 12/1
11-4 6 hd **On The Hoof**[11] [49] 4-9-3 75 .... (b) JamesSullivan 6 75
(Michael Easterby) *trckd ldr: hdwy to ld wl over 2f out: rdn and hdd 1/2f out: grad wknd* 6/1[3]
05-2 7 3 **Summerinthecity (IRE)**[7] [104] 6-9-1 73 .... MartinDwyer 1 64
(David Nicholls) *in tch: effrt over 2f out: sn rdn and no imp* 11/2[2]
03-5 8 1 ¾ **Cyflymder (IRE)**[10] [80] 7-8-11 69 .... WilliamCarson 2 56
(David C Griffiths) *chsd ldrs on inner: rdn along wl over 2f out: sn wknd* 33/1
021- 9 hd **Silverware (USA)**[18] [8269] 5-9-6 78 .... ShaneKelly 9 64
(Linda Stubbs) *chsd ldng pair: rdn along wl over 1f out: edgd lft and wknd ent fnl f* 13/2
001- 10 1 ½ **Greyfriarschorista**[269] [1530] 6-9-3 78 .... RyanClark(3) 11 60
(Tom Keddy) *hld up towards rr: hdwy on outer wl over 2f out: rdn along wl over 1f out and n.d* 28/1
50-4 11 4 ½ **Smalljohn**[7] [104] 7-9-3 75 .... (v) TomEaves 12 45
(Bryan Smart) *led: hdd and rdn along wl over 2f out: sn wknd* 14/1
03-5 12 6 **Frequency**[1] [206] 6-9-3 75 .... (b) JoeFanning 10 29
(Keith Dalgleish) *midfield: rdn along wl over 2f out: sn wknd* 25/1

1m 27.99s (-1.61) **Going Correction** +0.05s/f (Slow) 12 Ran SP% **122.5**
Speed ratings (Par 105): **111,109,106,106,105 105,101,99,99,97 92,85**
toteswingers 1&2 £6.50, 2&3 £16.10, 1&3 £14.10 CSF £34.93 CT £302.96 TOTE £4.70: £2.70, £3.50, £4.30; EX 26.10 Trifecta £211.90 Pool: £1780.69 - 6.30 winning units..
Owner The 'In Recovery' Partnership **Bred** J K Thoroughbreds & P Doyle Bloodstock **Trained** Epsom, Surrey

FOCUS
A strongly-run decent-class 7f handicap. The winner continues on the upgrade.

218 MONEY BACK RACING SPECIALS AT BOOKMAKERS.CO.UK H'CAP 1m 141y(P)
5:00 (5:00) (Class 6) (0-65,65) 4-Y-O+ £1,940 (£577; £288; £144) Stalls Low

Form RPR
222- 1 **Goldstorm**[200] [3559] 5-9-4 62 .... (p) WilliamCarson 11 70+
(Brian Baugh) *hld up in tch: hdwy wl over 1f out: str run on outer ent fnl f: rdn to ld and edgd lft last 75yds: kpt on* 11/2[3]
330- 2 1 **Dundrum Dancer (IRE)**[56] [7684] 6-9-5 63 .... AndreaAtzeni 5 69
(Alex Hales) *trckd ldrs on inner: rdn along 2f out: styd on to chal and ev ch ins fnl f: sn drvn and kpt on* 40/1
3-32 3 1 **Aragorn Rouge**[2] [192] 5-9-3 61 .... JoeFanning 2 65
(Keith Dalgleish) *trckd ldng pair: hdwy over 1f out: rdn and ev ch ins fnl f: sn drvn and one pce* 3/1[1]
405- 4 ½ **Hawk Moth (IRE)**[32] [8115] 5-9-5 63 .... LukeMorris 6 66
(John Spearing) *midfield: hdwy on inner 2f out: rdn over 1f out: drvn and one pce ins fnl f* 11/2[3]
10-5 5 ½ **Yeomanoftheguard**[11] [49] 4-9-5 64 .... BarryMcHugh 3 65
(Richard Fahey) *led: rdn along 2f out: hdd appr fnl f: kpt on same pce* 7/1
350- 6 ½ **Imaginary World (IRE)**[47] [7925] 5-9-2 60 .... (p[1]) RobertWinston 7 61
(John Balding) *hld up in rr: hdwy 3f out: rdn to chse ldrs whn n.m.r ins fnl f: swtchd rt and styd on wl towards fin* 14/1
000- 7 hd **Minortransgression (USA)**[61] [7725] 6-9-6 64 .... AdamKirby 8 64
(Sean Curran) *in tch: effrt over 2f out: sn rdn and kpt on same pce fnl f* 4/1[2]
10-5 8 hd **Lord Of The Dance (IRE)**[2] [192] 7-9-0 65 .... RobertTart(7) 1 64
(Michael Mullineaux) *hld up in rr hdwy 2f out: sn rdn and kpt on fnl f: nrst fin* 10/1
06-0 9 ½ **Moral Issue**[5] [147] 5-9-4 62 .... DaleSwift 9 60
(Ian McInnes) *cl up: rdn 2f out: led appr fnl f: sn drvn: hdd and n.m.r last 100yds: wknd* 25/1
44-4 10 1 ¼ **Mr Chocolate Drop (IRE)**[9] [83] 9-9-4 62 .... (t) JimmyQuinn 10 57
(Mandy Rowland) *hld up: a in rr* 16/1
11 ½ **Joy For Life**[114] 4-9-4 63 .... MartinLane 12 57
(Tobias B P Coles) *chsd ldrs: rdn along 3f out: wknd fnl 2f* 20/1
140- 12 13 **Jericho (IRE)**[277] [1364] 4-9-4 63 .... FergusSweeney 13 27
(Jamie Osborne) *stdd s: hld up: a in rr* 33/1

1m 51.46s (0.96) **Going Correction** +0.05s/f (Slow)
WFA 4 from 5yo+ 1lb 12 Ran SP% **123.9**
Speed ratings (Par 101): **97,96,95,94,94 93,93,93,93,91 91,79**
toteswingers 1&2 £18.00, 2&3 £25.70, 1&3 £3.60 CSF £223.62 CT £807.71 TOTE £2.20: £2.70, £5.80, £2.50; EX 225.80 Trifecta £529.20 Pool: £2360.29 - 3.34 winning units..
Owner Magnate Racing **Bred** Andrew Bailey **Trained** Audley, Staffs

FOCUS
A true pace and many in with a chance in the home straight. The form is muddling and rather ordinary, but the winner can do better.

219 DOWNLOAD CORAL.CO.UK MOBILE APP H'CAP 1m 1f 103y(P)
5:30 (5:30) (Class 5) (0-70,70) 4-Y-O+ £2,587 (£770; £384; £192) Stalls Low

Form RPR
11-4 1 **Idol Deputy (FR)**[9] [82] 7-9-0 68 .... (p) RachealKneller(5) 7 75+
(Mark Usher) *trckd ldrs: hdwy over 1f out: effrt ins fnl f: styd on to ld nr line* 10/3[2]
10-3 2 hd **One Scoop Or Two**[9] [82] 7-9-2 70 .... (p) ShirleyTeasdale(5) 5 76
(Reg Hollinshead) *a.p: chsd ldr over 1f out: rdn to ld last 100yds: hdd and could nt qckn nr line* 9/4[1]
23-3 3 shd **Strike Force**[7] [107] 9-9-1 69 .... (t) NatashaEaton(5) 9 75
(Alison Hutchinson) *trckd ldr: hdwy to ld wl over 2f out: rdn over 1f out: drvn and hdd ins fnl f: kpt on* 7/1
400/ 4 2 ¾ **Ortea**[479] [6345] 4-9-6 70 .... StevieDonohoe 4 70
(Ian Williams) *in tch: hdwy 2f out: rdn to chse ldrs ins fnl f: kpt on same pce* 8/1
00-0 5 hd **Final Drive (IRE)**[11] [49] 7-9-6 69 .... (tp[1]) LiamKeniry 8 69
(John Butler) *hld up in rr: hdwy over 2f out: rdn to chse ldrs ins fnl f: no imp* 13/2[3]
600- 6 1 ½ **Kyle Of Bute**[71] [7593] 7-8-9 58 .... WilliamCarson 6 55
(Brian Baugh) *trckd ldrs: hdwy 2f out: rdn to chse ldng trio ins fnl f: sn drvn and btn* 16/1
04-6 7 ½ **Elijah Pepper (USA)**[14] [2] 8-8-10 66 .... RyanWhile(7) 3 62
(Conor Dore) *trckd ldrs on inner: rdn along 2f out: sn drvn and wknd* 14/1
040- 8 1 ¾ **Haywain**[230] [2604] 4-9-3 67 .... TomEaves 1 59
(Kevin Ryan) *set stdy pce: pushed along 4f out: hdd wl over 2f out and sn wknd* 8/1
/02- 9 5 **Amana (USA)**[235] [2454] 9-9-5 68 .... ShaneKelly 2 49
(Mark Brisbourne) *hld up: a in rr* 33/1

2m 5.8s (4.10) **Going Correction** +0.05s/f (Slow)
WFA 4 from 7yo+ 1lb 9 Ran SP% **117.4**
Speed ratings (Par 103): **83,82,82,80,80 78,78,76,72**
toteswingers 1&2 £2.40, 2&3 £1.60, 1&3 £4.20 CSF £11.47 CT £48.99 TOTE £3.50: £1.10, £1.60, £2.30; EX 12.30 Trifecta £35.10 Pool: £1805.45 - 38.50 winning units..
Owner Miss J C Blackwell **Bred** Sheikh Sultan Bin Khalifa Al Nayan **Trained** Upper Lambourn, Berks

FOCUS
Six course winners and the three ridden by lady jockeys fought out a very tight finish in a race run at a very steady pace until starting the home turn. The form has been rated at face value.

T/Jkpt: Not won. T/Plt: £352.20 to a £1 stake. Pool of £76135.12 - 157.79 winning tickets. T/Qpdt: £36.00 to a £1 stake. Pool of £7391.96 - 151.65 winning tickets. JR

[128]KEMPTON (A.W) (R-H)

Wednesday, January 16

OFFICIAL GOING: Standard

Wind: Light, against Weather: Fine, very cold

220 FREE ENTRY EVERY WEDNESDAY FOR BETDAQ MEMBERS H'CAP 1m (P)

4:15 (4:15) (Class 7) (0-50,50) 4-Y-O+ **£1,455** (£433; £216; £108) **Stalls** Low

Form RPR

600/ **1** **Commercial (IRE)**[592] 2722 5-9-7 **50**........................ FergusSweeney 10 57
(Jamie Osborne) *mde all at decent pce: kicked on wl over 2f out: drvn and 3 l clr over 1f out: jst lasted* **14/1**

60-4 **2** *nk* **Delightful Sleep**[13] 33 5-9-7 **50**................................ WilliamCarson 6 56
(David Evans) *hld up in tch: rdn and prog over 2f out: chsd wnr over 1f out: clsd nr fin* **7/2[1]**

000- **3** *hd* **Boris The Bold**[19] 8264 4-9-3 **46**...................................... GeorgeBaker 4 52
(John Best) *hld up towards rr: rdn and prog over 2f out: wnt 3rd fnl f: styd on and clsng at fin* **4/1[2]**

04-6 **4** *3/4* **Crucis Abbey (IRE)**[13] 42 5-9-2 **45**..........................(p) EddieAhern 11 49
(Mark Brisbourne) *hld up in midfield: rdn on outer 2f out: styd on fr over 1f out: nvr quite able to chal* **14/1**

00-0 **5** *2* **Sun Dream**[13] 41 6-9-2 **45**... MartinLane 3 45
(Tony Carroll) *dwlt: towards rr: rdn over 2f out: kpt on one pce fr over 1f out: nvr a threat* **50/1**

50-6 **6** *nk* **Meydan Style (USA)**[13] 41 7-8-9 **45**........................ VictorSantos(7) 9 44
(Richard Ford) *hld up in last trio: urged along over 2f out: kpt on fr over 1f out: nrst fin* **20/1**

45-0 **7** *nk* **Rainbow Riches (IRE)**[7] 120 4-8-9 **45**........................(p) NedCurtis(7) 5 43
(Roger Curtis) *chsd wnr 3f and again 3f out to over 1f out: wknd fnl f* **33/1**

/00- **8** *1 3/4* **West Side (IRE)**[20] 8248 5-9-7 **50**...........................(v) FrannyNorton 1 44
(Mick Quinn) *dwlt: hld up in last quartet: rdn over 2f out: no great prog over 1f out: n.d* **5/1**

000- **9** *1/2* **Prophet In A Dream**[35] 8077 5-9-2 **45**..........................(p) TomEaves 12 38
(Paddy Butler) *hld up in last: gng wl but stl there 3f out: repeatedly stuck bhd rivals jst over 2f out to 1f out: kpt on late* **66/1**

366- **10** *nse* **Querido (GER)**[17] 8298 9-9-6 **49**...............................(tp) IanMongan 2 42
(Paddy Butler) *dwlt: a wl in rr: rdn and no prog over 2f out* **9/2[3]**

65-5 **11** *3/4* **Carpentras**[12] 62 5-9-3 **46**...(b) JimmyQuinn 7 37
(Dr Jon Scargill) *plld hrd: chsd ldrs: effrt to go 3rd over 2f out to over 1f out: wknd qckly* **20/1**

05-5 **12** *3 3/4* **Northern Spy (USA)**[7] 117 9-9-6 **49**........................ LukeMorris 13 32
(Simon Dow) *chsd ldrs on outer: rdn 3f out: sn wknd* **7/1**

000/ **13** *2 1/4* **Catawollow**[21] 6049 6-9-2 **45**.......................................(e) JohnFahy 8 22
(Richard Guest) *chsd wnr after 3f to 3f out: wknd qckly* **33/1**

1m 39.44s (-0.36) **Going Correction** +0.075s/f (Slow) **13** Ran SP% **121.8**
Speed ratings (Par 97): **104,103,103,102,100 100,100,98,97,97 97,93,91**
toteswingers 1&2 £6.70, 1&3 £13.10, 2&3 £5.60 CSF £59.84 CT £250.84 TOTE £22.00: £4.70, £1.50, £2.40; EX 111.30 Trifecta £548.10 Pool: £1806.69 - 2.47 winning units..
Owner Mrs F Walwyn **Bred** Michael Keane **Trained** Upper Lambourn, Berks

FOCUS
Not the worst race for the class and a lively betting heat. There was no hanging about, but the winner nicked it from the front. Sound if limited form.

221 WIN BIG WITH BETDAQ MULTIPLES CLAIMING STKS 1m (P)

4:45 (4:45) (Class 6) 4-Y-O+ **£1,940** (£577; £288; £144) **Stalls** Low

Form RPR

001- **1** **Hurricane Spirit (IRE)**[38] 8047 9-8-4 71................. NicoleNordblad(5) 3 74
(Hans Adielsson) *cl up on inner: quick move to ld 2f out and sn pushed 3 l clr: shkn up and kpt on fnl f* **7/4[1]**

664- **2** *1 3/4* **Saharia (IRE)**[16] 8306 6-9-5 77...................................(v) ShaneKelly 4 80
(Daniel Mark Loughnane) *stdd s: hld up in last: followed wnr through on inner 2f out but nt qckn w him: tried to cl fnl f but little imp* **9/4[2]**

53-5 **3** *3 1/2* **The Noble Ord**[7] 120 4-8-7 59...(t) ChrisCatlin 5 59
(Sylvester Kirk) *hld up in 4th: pushed along after 3f: outpcd 2f out: tk 3rd 1f out: n.d* **10/1[3]**

66-4 **4** *3 1/2* **April Fool**[13] 34 9-9-1 69..(b) DavidProbert 1 59
(Ronald Harris) *led to 2f out: sn btn* **9/4[2]**

00-0 **5** *2* **Minortransgression (USA)**[1] 218 6-8-11 64................ LukeMorris 2 50
(Sean Curran) *racd in 2nd to over 2f out but u.p fr 1/2-way: sn btn* **25/1**

1m 38.14s (-1.66) **Going Correction** +0.075s/f (Slow) **5** Ran SP% **110.8**
Speed ratings (Par 101): **111,109,105,102,100**
CSF £6.07 TOTE £2.90: £1.20, £1.10; EX 5.50 Trifecta £12.60 Pool: £2026.67 - 119.75 winning units..Hurricane Spirit was the subject of a friendly claim.
Owner Hans Adielsson A B **Bred** Knocktoran Stud **Trained** Kingston Lisle, Oxon

FOCUS
This ordinary claimer went to script. Shaky form, and the winner did not need to match his best.

222 BACK AND LAY AT BETDAQ.COM H'CAP (LONDON MILE QUALIFIER) 1m (P)

5:15 (5:15) (Class 5) (0-75,75) 4-Y-O+ **£2,587** (£770; £384; £192) **Stalls** Low

Form RPR

061- **1** **Whispering Warrior (IRE)**[19] 8263 4-8-12 **66**................. JimCrowley 3 77+
(David Simcock) *trckd ldng pair: wnt 2nd after 3f: rdn to ld over 1f out but immediately pressed: styd on wl to assert last 100yds* **1/1[1]**

21-4 **2** *1* **Fairyinthewind (IRE)**[5] 159 4-9-4 **72**..........................(p) SebSanders 4 79
(Paul D'Arcy) *hld up bhd ldrs: clsd over 2f out: drvn to chal over 1f out: styd on but readily hld by wnr last 100yds* **5/1[3]**

03-4 **3** *1 1/2* **Buckland (IRE)**[6] 133 5-8-12 **71**..................... NicoleNordblad(5) 2 75
(Hans Adielsson) *trckd ldr 3f: styd cl up: chal on inner 2f out: outpcd over 1f out: n.m.r briefly sn after: kpt on* **10/1**

224- **4** *nse* **Warbond**[19] 8268 5-8-7 **61** oh1.. LukeMorris 1 64
(Michael Madgwick) *chsd ldrs: rdn over 3f out: kpt on u.p and in tch 2f out: outpcd over 1f out* **20/1**

2-14 **5** *1 3/4* **Breakheart (IRE)**[9] 89 6-8-1 **62**.........................(p) JoeyHaynes(7) 6 61
(Andrew Balding) *dwlt: hld up in last pair: pushed along and outpcd 2f out: no imp after* **16/1**

00-2 **6** *nse* **California English (IRE)**[12] 49 4-9-7 **75**..................(p) AdamKirby 5 74
(Marco Botti) *led: tried to kick on 2f out: hdd over 1f out: wknd* **3/1[2]**

25-0 **7** *nk* **Diplomatic (IRE)**[14] 13 8-9-0 **68**.................................... JimmyQuinn 7 67
(Michael Squance) *sn restrained into last pair: rdn over 3f out: outpcd 2f out: no imp after* **50/1**

1m 40.03s (0.23) **Going Correction** +0.075s/f (Slow) **7** Ran SP% **113.4**
Speed ratings (Par 103): **101,100,98,98,96 96,96**
toteswingers 1&2 £2.10, 1&3 £4.00, 2&3 £6.70 CSF £6.39 TOTE £1.90: £1.20, £2.60; EX 6.30 Trifecta £27.90 Pool: £2670.02 - 71.64 winning units..
Owner Daniel Pittack **Bred** Epona Bloodstock Ltd **Trained** Newmarket, Suffolk

FOCUS
This modest handicap was run at something of an uneven pace and two came well clear. The winner has more to offer.

223 BETDAQ GAMES £50 HARD CASH BONUS H'CAP 7f (P)

5:45 (5:45) (Class 6) (0-55,55) 4-Y-O+ **£1,940** (£577; £288; £144) **Stalls** Low

Form RPR

063- **1** **Vitznau (IRE)**[76] 7500 9-9-7 **55**...(t) AdamKirby 4 66+
(John Butler) *hld up in 5th: smooth prog to trck ldr over 1f out: pushed into ld 150yds out: decisively* **7/2[1]**

006- **2** *1 1/2* **Arachnophobia (IRE)**[28] 8167 7-9-7 **55**......................(b) GeorgeBaker 7 62
(Martin Bosley) *led: shkn up 2f out: kpt on wl but hdd and outpcd last 150yds* **8/1**

33-4 **3** *1 1/4* **Lieutenant Dan (IRE)**[3] 193 6-9-6 **54**.......................(v) LukeMorris 1 58
(Michael Appleby) *prom: chsd ldr 2f out to over 1f out: one pce after* **6/1**

000- **4** *nk* **Sextons House (IRE)**[16] 8304 5-9-4 **52**........................ WilliamCarson 2 55+
(Alan McCabe) *t.k.h: hld up towards rr: prog 2f out: rdn and kpt on fr over 1f out: nt pce to threaten* **5/1[3]**

3-53 **5** *1/2* **Do More Business (IRE)**[6] 128 6-9-2 **50**..................(b) JimCrowley 12 52
(Alison Batchelor) *dwlt: racd keenly on wd outside and sn prom: rdn over 2f out: kpt on tl fdd fnl f* **8/1**

62-3 **6** *1/2* **Divine Rule (IRE)**[9] 89 5-9-7 **55**..................................(v) AmirQuinn 10 55
(Laura Mongan) *hld up in last trio: pushed along 2f out: keeping on but no ch whn checked briefly 1f out: nvr in it* **14/1**

36-5 **7** *nk* **Lindoro**[12] 50 8-9-7 **55**.. JohnFahy 5 55
(Sean Curran) *hld up in last trio: effrt on inner over 2f out: rdn and no prog over 1f out: kpt on* **20/1**

0-32 **8** *2 1/4* **Mataajir (USA)**[5] 163 5-9-7 **55**...................................... MartinDwyer 9 49
(Derek Shaw) *chsd ldr to 2f out: sn wknd* **9/2[2]**

344- **9** *nk* **Littlecote Lady**[18] 8287 4-9-6 **54**.................................... DavidProbert 6 47
(Mark Usher) *hit stalls as they opened and v.s.a: mostly in last: effrt 2f out: plugging on but only pressing for 7th whn n.m.r ins fnl f* **14/1**

560- **10** *hd* **Doctor Hilary**[17] 8299 11-9-0 **48**.................................(v) RobertHavlin 8 40
(Mark Hoad) *dwlt: hld up towards rr: gng wl enough over 2f out: rdn and fnd nil wl over 1f out: wknd* **33/1**

045- **11** *2 3/4* **Rosa Lockwood**[18] 8291 4-8-12 **46** oh1............................ MartinLane 3 31
(Tony Carroll) *chsd ldrs but sn pushed along: wknd over 2f out* **50/1**

1m 25.89s (-0.11) **Going Correction** +0.075s/f (Slow) **11** Ran SP% **116.6**
Speed ratings (Par 101): **103,101,99,99,98 98,98,95,95,94 91**
toteswingers 1&2 £7.30, 1&3 £4.60, 2&3 £8.40 CSF £31.00 CT £166.26 TOTE £4.50: £1.90, £2.90, £2.20; EX 46.80 Trifecta £350.80 Pool: £1570.00 - 3.35 winning units..
Owner J Butler **Bred** John McLoughlin **Trained** Newmarket, Suffolk

FOCUS
A weak handicap, run at an average pace. The first three were all quite well in on their best form.

224 TIME ORDERED CARDS IN RACING PLUS H'CAP 2m (P)

6:15 (6:16) (Class 4) (0-85,85) 4-Y-O+ **£4,690** (£1,395; £697; £348) **Stalls** Low

Form RPR

P51- **1** **Woolfall Treasure**[25] 8235 8-9-13 **84**........................(v) GeorgeBaker 9 94
(Gary Moore) *mde all: stdy pce tl wound it up fr 6f out: edgd lft 2f out: pressed over 1f out: styd on wl to draw clr fnl f* **6/1[3]**

61-2 **2** *4* **Wildomar**[9] 93 4-9-2 **80**.. AdamKirby 1 85+
(John Ryan) *hld up in rr: prog over 3f out: chsd wnr jst over 2f out: tried to chal over 1f out: one pce u.p after* **9/4[1]**

00-2 **3** *1 1/2* **Where's Susie**[7] 119 8-9-1 **72**.. LukeMorris 3 75
(Michael Madgwick) *chsd ldrs: rdn 4f out: kpt on u.p to take 3rd fnl f: nt pce to threaten* **16/1**

42-6 **4** *3/4* **Squad**[7] 119 7-9-1 **72**...(v) EddieAhern 10 75+
(Simon Dow) *stdd s: hld up in last trio: plenty to do whn rdn wl over 2f out: styd on fr jst over 1f out: nrly snatched 3rd* **10/1**

5- **5** *1/2* **Private Equity (FR)**[19] 8275 5-9-13 **84**...................... FergusSweeney 11 86
(Nicky Henderson) *chsd wnr to jst over 2f out: wknd fnl f* **8/1**

/50- **6** *3/4* **Phoenix Flight (IRE)**[65] 7109 8-9-12 **83**.....................(p) JimCrowley 7 84
(James Evans) *stdd s: hld up in last: sme prog wl over 2f out: no imp on ldrs over 1f out* **8/1**

40-4 **7** *6* **Epic Storm (IRE)**[13] 39 5-9-3 **74**.................................... WilliamCarson 4 68
(Sean Curran) *t.k.h: chsd ldng pair to over 2f out: wknd qckly over 1f out* **6/1[3]**

022- **8** *2 1/4* **Vimiero (USA)**[18] 8290 6-9-6 **77**....................................... TomEaves 6 68
(Jonjo O'Neill) *stdd s: t.k.h: hld up in midfield: snatched up 7f out: rdn and no prog over 2f out: wl btn after* **16/1**

03- **9** *2 1/2* **First Avenue**[25] 6834 8-9-7 **85**................................. RobertTart(7) 8 73
(Laura Mongan) *wl in tch: wd bnd 3f out: sn rdn and wknd qckly* **5/1[2]**

120/ **P** **Excelsior Academy**[38] 4467 7-9-2 **73**.......................(p) RobertHavlin 5
(Richard Phillips) *chsd ldrs: drvn 4f out: wknd 3f out: broke down and p.u 2f out* **66/1**

3m 31.22s (1.12) **Going Correction** +0.075s/f (Slow)
WFA 4 from 5yo+ 7lb **10** Ran SP% **120.6**
Speed ratings (Par 105): **100,98,97,96,96 96,93,92,90,**
toteswingers 1&2 £2.00, 1&3 £9.70, 2&3 £9.60 CSF £20.60 CT £213.38 TOTE £7.70: £1.90, £1.60, £3.90; EX 18.10 Trifecta £343.90 Pool: £1524.52 - 3.32 winning units..
Owner Andrew Bradmore **Bred** Serpentine Bloodstock Et Al **Trained** Lower Beeding, W Sussex

FOCUS
This staying handicap proved another lively betting heat. It was a falsely run affair and those held up were at a disadvantage. The form has been rated at face value.

225 KEMPTON.CO.UK H'CAP 6f (P)

6:45 (6:48) (Class 5) (0-75,75) 3-Y-O **£2,587** (£770; £384; £192) **Stalls** Low

Form RPR

104- **1** **Blazing Knight (IRE)**[26] 8204 3-9-5 **73**........................ JimCrowley 5 75+
(Ralph Beckett) *hld up in last in slowly run r: prog 2f out: drvn to go 2nd ins fnl f: r.o to ld post* **3/1[2]**

512- **2** *nse* **Lucky Di**[16] 8302 3-9-7 **75**.. IanMongan 1 76
(Peter Hedger) *trckd ldr: led wl over 1f out and pressed on: styd on fnl f but hdd post* **3/1[2]**

01- **3** *1 1/4* **Al Gharrafa**[20] 8254 3-9-1 **69**.. AdamKirby 2 66
(Marco Botti) *hld up in 4th: drvn 2f out: tried to cl on ldr 1f out: kpt on one pce after* **5/1[3]**

10-2 **4** 3/4 **Seemenomore**[14] 8 3-8-10 **71**..........(b[1]) RobertTart[(7)] 4 66
(Michael Bell) *led at mod pce: urged along over 2f out but little rspnse: hdd wl over 1f out: one pce after* **7/4**[1]

104- **5** 1 1/2 **Girl At The Sands (IRE)**[104] 6809 3-9-1 **69**.......... JamesSullivan 3 59
(James Given) *chsd ldng pair to 2f out: sn outpcd and btn* **14/1**

1m 14.87s (1.77) **Going Correction** +0.075s/f (Slow) **5** Ran SP% **109.7**
Speed ratings (Par 97): **91,90,89,88,86**
CSF £12.12 TOTE £4.80: £1.50, £2.10; EX 13.00 Trifecta £70.00 Pool: £1087.44 - 11.64 winning units..
Owner Circuit Racing **Bred** Tally-Ho Stud **Trained** Kimpton, Hants
■ Stewards' Enquiry : Robert Tart two-day ban: used whip above permitted level (Jan 30-31)

FOCUS
A moderate sprint handicap, run at a fairly slow pace. The form is rated tentatively through the runner-up.

226 KEMPTON FOR WEDDINGS H'CAP 1m 4f (P)
7:15 (7:16) (Class 7) (0-50,62) 4-Y-0+ **£1,455** (£433; £216; £108) **Stalls** Low

Form RPR

-044 **1** **Nolecce**[5] 169 6-9-7 **50**..........(p) JimmyQuinn 12 58+
(Richard Guest) *t.k.h: trckd ldrs: quick move to ld over 2f out and dashed clr: edgd rt over 1f out: unchal* **5/1**[2]

02-3 **2** 1 1/4 **Peace In Our Time**[5] 169 4-8-8 **48**.......... RobertTart[(7)] 5 54+
(Anthony Carson) *trckd ldr after 2f to 8f out: styd cl up: nt clr run and swtchd lft over 2f out jst as wnr kicked on: drvn to go 2nd over 1f out: kpt on but nvr able to chal* **11/8**[1]

050- **3** 2 **Fire In Babylon (IRE)**[42] 7991 5-9-6 **49**..........(t) StevieDonohoe 8 52+
(Noel Quinlan) *hld up in last trio: pushed along and stl there over 2f out: gd prog over 1f out: r.o to take 3rd last 75yds: no ch to chal* **8/1**

240- **4** 1/2 **Hollywood All Star (IRE)**[176] 4440 4-9-3 **50**.......... MartinDwyer 7 52
(William Muir) *hld up in rr: prog on inner over 2f out: rdn to chse ldng pair over 1f out: no imp: lost 3rd last 75yds* **25/1**

40-0 **5** 1 **Awesome Rock (IRE)**[9] 94 4-9-3 **50**.......... FrannyNorton 10 50
(Louise Best) *t.k.h: hld up towards rr: rdn and prog over 2f out: chal for 3rd over 1f out: one pce after* **7/1**[3]

300- **6** 3 1/2 **Brandy Snapping**[7] 7921 4-9-2 **49**..........(t) TomMcLaughlin 4 46
(Mark Brisbourne) *t.k.h: hld up in midfield: u.p whn hmpd over 2f out and lost pl: kpt on fnl f* **50/1**

10-0 **7** 1/2 **Pass The Time**[9] 100 4-9-2 **49**..........(p) AdamKirby 3 43
(Neil Mulholland) *hld up in midfield: swtchd lft over 2f out and lost pl: rdn and kpt on fr over 1f out: n.d* **16/1**

040- **8** nk **Compton Crofter**[33] 8111 4-8-9 **47**..........(t) NicoleNordblad[(5)] 1 41
(Hans Adielsson) *t.k.h: led 2f: settled in midfield after: effrt on inner over 2f out but nt pce to make prog: wl hld over 1f out* **20/1**

00-0 **9** 1 **Ivan The Engine**[9] 99 5-9-2 **45**..........(t) FrankieMcDonald 2 37
(Paul Fitzsimons) *awkward s: t.k.h: hld up in last: shkn up over 2f out: modest late prog* **66/1**

44-4 **10** 1/2 **May Boy**[13] 41 7-8-10 **46**.......... PhilipPrince[(7)] 11 37
(Ron Hodges) *t.k.h early: racd wd: wl in tch tl wknd fr 2f out* **14/1**

/0-3 **11** 8 **Pobs Trophy**[12] 63 6-9-7 **50**..........(b) RobbieFitzpatrick 13 28
(Richard Guest) *led after 2f and set v mod pce: hdd over 2f out: sn wknd qckly* **25/1**

4-05 **12** 1 **Veyepea**[13] 41 4-9-0 **47**.......... LiamKeniry 9 24
(Sylvester Kirk) *trckd ldr after 4f: upsides over 2f out: wknd rapidly over 1f out* **16/1**

060/ **13** 22 **Jakeys Girl**[728] 207 6-9-2 **45**.......... IanMongan 6
(Pat Phelan) *racd wd towards rr: rdn 4f out: wknd wl over 2f out: t.o* **16/1**

2m 36.71s (2.21) **Going Correction** +0.075s/f (Slow)
WFA 4 from 5yo+ 4lb **13** Ran SP% **122.6**
Speed ratings (Par 97): **95,94,92,92,91 89,89,88,88,87 82,81,67**
toteswingers 1&2 £3.40, 2&3 £7.70, 1&3 £12.90 CSF £11.84 CT £57.69 TOTE £7.20: £1.90, £1.10, £3.00; EX 15.40 Trifecta £110.40 Pool: £1620.57 - 11.00 winning units..
Owner Future Racing (Notts) Limited **Bred** Hedsor Stud **Trained** Wetherby, W Yorks
■ Stewards' Enquiry : Robert Tart two-day ban: careless riding (Jan 1-2)

FOCUS
This ordinary handicap was run at an average pace. The winner was well in on old form, and the second was close to matching his recent level.
T/Plt: £57.60 to a £1 stake. Pool of £71,611.45 - 906.96 winning tickets. T/Qpdt: £21.10 to a £1 stake. Pool of £7,688.18 - 268.42 winning tickets. JN

[199]LINGFIELD (L-H)
Wednesday, January 16

OFFICIAL GOING: Standard
Wind: virtually nil Weather: foggy, cold

227 BET ON YOUR TABLET AT BLUESQ.COM CLAIMING STKS 2m (P)
12:30 (12:30) (Class 6) 4-Y-0+ **£2,045** (£603; £302) **Stalls** Low

Form RPR

002- **1** **Right Stuff (FR)**[29] 8153 10-9-9 87.......... GeorgeBaker 1 89
(Gary Moore) *t.k.h: hld up wl in tch: trckd ldng pair 5f out: upsides ldr on bit ent fnl f: rdn and asked for effrt ins fnl f: fnd enough and led towards fin* **2/1**[2]

11-1 **2** nk **La Estrella (USA)**[15] 1 10-9-12 89.......... AdamKirby 6 92
(Don Cantillon) *hld up wl in tch: trckd ldrs 5f out: rdn to ld ent fnl 2f: jnd and drvn ent fnl f: r.o wl u.p tl hdd and no ex towards fin* **1/2**[1]

5-13 **3** 25 **Activate**[4] 183 6-9-7 70..........(be) LukeMorris 5 57
(Phil McEntee) *chsd ldrs: wnt 2nd 7f out: led over 3f out: rdn and hdd ent fnl 2f: sn wknd: wl btn 1f out* **12/1**[3]

0/4- **4** 11 **Watch The Birdie (IRE)**[32] 8135 5-8-11 60.......... WilliamCarson 2 34
(Ronald Harris) *led tl over 3f out: 4th and wknd over 2f out: wl bhd fnl f: t.o over 1f out* **33/1**

00/ **5** 6 **Cinematique (IRE)**[529] 4800 5-9-9 0.......... IanMongan 3 39
(Laura Mongan) *a in rr: rdn after 4f: lost tch 4f out: t.o over 2f out* **66/1**

/0-0 **6** 50 **Sonara (IRE)**[14] 22 9-8-8 57..........(v[1]) PhilipPrince[(7)] 4
(David Evans) *chsd ldr tl 7f out: lost pl u.p 5f out: wl t.o over 2f out* **50/1**

3m 20.35s (-5.35) **Going Correction** -0.05s/f (Stan) **6** Ran SP% **114.1**
Speed ratings (Par 101): **111,110,98,92,89 64**
toteswingers 1&2 £1.50, 1&3 £1.10, 2&3 £1.40 CSF £3.41 TOTE £3.20: £1.40, £1.10; EX 3.70 Trifecta £8.30 Pool: £2463.37 - 221.87 winning units..
Owner The Ashden Partnership & Partners **Bred** N P Bloodstock Ltd **Trained** Lower Beeding, W Sussex

FOCUS
Visibility was down to 1f. A bitterly cold day with snow lying in the centre of the course but the track unaffected. A typical claimer with a wide spread of ability amongst the runners, judged on official ratings, but this was all about La Estrella. He's rated to form, while the winner was entitled to beat the favourite on his best form.

228 CROWHURST MEDIAN AUCTION MAIDEN STKS 7f (P)
1:00 (1:02) (Class 6) 3-Y-0 **£2,045** (£603; £302) **Stalls** Low

Form RPR

304- **1** **Black Dave (IRE)**[63] 7708 3-9-5 56.......... AdamKirby 3 69
(David Evans) *t.k.h: hld up in midfield: rdn and effrt 2f out: hung lft over 1f out: stened and hdwy to chse ldr ins fnl f: r.o wl to ld towards fin* **5/1**

5- **2** 1 **Jimmy The Snooze (IRE)**[85] 7304 3-9-5 0..........(t) AndreaAtzeni 8 66
(Stuart Williams) *led: rdn 2f out: kpt on wl u.p tl hdd and no ex towards fin* **9/2**[3]

0- **3** 1 1/4 **Shaolin (IRE)**[216] 3067 3-9-5 0.......... JohnFahy 6 63
(Seamus Durack) *t.k.h: hld up in tch in midfield: hdwy to chse ldrs 2f out: rdn and styd on to chse ldng pair ins fnl f: one pce fnl 100yds* **6/4**[1]

4 nk **Wotabooty** 3-9-0 0.......... MartinLane 5 57+
(Hugo Palmer) *dwlt: hld up in tch in rr: rdn and hdwy ent fnl f: styd on wl: nt rch ldrs* **25/1**

04- **5** 1 1/2 **Spreading**[117] 6437 3-9-0 0.......... LiamKeniry 7 53
(Michael Blanshard) *chsd ldng pair: rdn and chsd ldr wl over 1f out tl ins fnl f: wknd fnl 100yds* **33/1**

- **6** hd **Excellent Puck (IRE)** 3-9-5 0.......... FergusSweeney 2 57
(Jamie Osborne) *s.i.s: hld up in tch in rr: rdn and hdwy 1f out: styd on wl ins fnl f: nt rch ldrs* **10/1**

5- **7** 1/2 **Two No Bids (IRE)**[48] 7926 3-9-5 0.......... SebSanders 1 56
(J W Hills) *in tch in midfield: rdn and effrt on inner to chse ldrs over 1f out: no imp 1f out: wknd ins fnl f* **5/1**

22-3 **8** 3 1/2 **Liliana (IRE)**[9] 90 3-9-0 66.......... LukeMorris 9 41
(Peter Chapple-Hyam) *chsd ldr tl wl over 1f out: sn wknd u.p* **4/1**[2]

5- **9** 1/2 **Hammer Shaft (IRE)**[16] 8303 3-9-5 0.......... StevieDonohoe 4 45
(Amy Weaver) *hld up in rr: pushed along 4f out: wknd over 1f out* **25/1**

1m 26.85s (2.05) **Going Correction** -0.05s/f (Stan) **9** Ran SP% **131.2**
Speed ratings (Par 95): **86,84,83,83,81 81,80,76,76**
toteswingers 1&2 £5.30, 1&3 £3.90, 2&3 £3.00 CSF £31.34 TOTE £7.90: £2.90, £2.50, £1.10; EX 38.90 Trifecta £122.30 Pool: £1485.05 - 9.10 winning units..
Owner Mrs E Evans **Bred** Richard Frayne **Trained** Pandy, Monmouths

FOCUS
A moderate maiden with only a couple having significant experience. The winner posted a clear personal best but the time was slow.

229 DORMANSLAND CLASSIFIED CLAIMING STKS 7f (P)
1:30 (1:32) (Class 6) 4-Y-0+ **£2,726** (£805; £402) **Stalls** Low

Form RPR

0-21 **1** **Paphos**[2] 199 6-8-2 64..........(v) DavidProbert 4 71
(Stuart Williams) *rdn along leaving stalls: chsd ldr tl led over 2f out: rdn ent fnl 2f: hrd pressed ins fnl f: hld on wl* **4/5**[1]

23-1 **2** shd **Restless Bay (IRE)**[4] 186 5-8-7 68..........(v) LukeMorris 1 76
(Mrs K Burke) *reluctant to go to post and led to post: t.k.h: trckd ldrs: rdn to chse wnr 2f out: drvn to chal jst ins fnl f: a jst hld* **6/4**[2]

30-3 **3** 13 **Abhaath (USA)**[9] 97 4-8-4 66..........(p) WilliamCarson 6 38
(Ronald Harris) *chsd ldrs: rdn over 3f out: struggling over 2f out: 3rd and wl btn over 1f out* **8/1**[3]

54-1 **4** 3 **Gaelic Wizard (IRE)**[13] 37 5-8-8 68.......... JoshBaudains[(7)] 2 41
(Dominic Ffrench Davis) *led tl over 2f out: sn rdn and struggling: bhd over 1f out* **20/1**

1m 22.73s (-2.07) **Going Correction** -0.05s/f (Stan) **4** Ran SP% **111.4**
Speed ratings (Par 101): **109,108,94,90**
CSF £2.38 TOTE £1.60; EX 2.50 Trifecta £3.80 Pool: £868.34 - 168.64 winning units..Restless Bay was claimed by Mr C R Dore for £8,500.
Owner Stuart C Williams **Bred** L Ellinas And Old Mill Stud Ltd **Trained** Newmarket, Suffolk

FOCUS
Two non-runners but this looked a pretty competitive claimer and all the runners came here race-fit. However, the market leaders came clear. The form is rated through the runner-up.

230 BLUE SQUARE BET MAIDEN FILLIES' STKS 1m (P)
2:05 (2:05) (Class 5) 3-Y-0+ **£2,726** (£805; £402) **Stalls** High

Form RPR

0- **1** **Maxi Dress (IRE)**[27] 8185 3-8-7 0.......... RobertHavlin 3 69+
(John Gosden) *t.k.h: led for 1f: chsd ldr after tl led again jst over 2f out: clr and edgd lft over 1f out: styd on wl: eased nr fin* **3/1**[3]

2 2 **Lily Edge** 4-9-13 0.......... KieranO'Neill 1 66
(John Bridger) *wnt lft s and v.s.a: racd in last pair: rdn and struggling 3f out: stl modest 6th over 1f out: str run ins fnl f to snatch 2nd last stride: no threat to wnr* **66/1**

33-2 **3** shd **Lady Lunchalot (USA)**[14] 16 3-8-7 64.......... LukeMorris 5 61
(J S Moore) *chsd ldrs: rdn over 2f out: chsd clr wnr and drvn over 1f out: no real imp and styd on same pce fnl f: lost 2nd last stride* **5/2**[2]

4- **4** hd **Mistral Wind (IRE)**[26] 8201 3-8-7 0.......... ChrisCatlin 7 61
(Ed Dunlop) *hld up in last pair: hdwy to chse ldrs 2f out: chsd ldng pair over 1f out: kpt on but no threat to wnr: lost 3rd last strides* **5/1**

5- **5** 3 1/4 **Wakeup Little Suzy (IRE)**[91] 7159 3-8-7 0.......... AndreaAtzeni 6 53
(Marco Botti) *in tch in midfield: rdn and effrt to chse ldrs 2f out: unable qck over 1f out: wknd 1f out* **6/4**[1]

03- **6** 5 **Star Sequence (IRE)**[16] 8303 3-8-7 0.......... MartinDwyer 2 41
(Hugo Palmer) *sn bustled along to chse ldr: led after 1f: rdn and hdd jst over 2f out: wknd over 1f out: fdd fnl f* **16/1**

00 **7** 9 **Elusive**[3] 197 7-9-8 0.......... AnnStokell[(5)] 4 24
(Ann Stokell) *stdd s: t.k.h: hld up in tch in midfield: rdn and struggling over 2f out: bhd over 1f out* **100/1**

1m 38.5s (0.30) **Going Correction** -0.05s/f (Stan)
WFA 3 from 4yo+ 20lb **7** Ran SP% **118.6**
Speed ratings (Par 100): **96,94,93,93,90 85,76**
toteswingers 1&2 £13.10, 1&3 £2.60, 2&3 £7.70 CSF £131.87 TOTE £5.80: £2.80, £13.60; EX 149.60 Trifecta £470.90 Pool: £2036.82 - 3.24 winning units..
Owner HRH Princess Haya Of Jordan **Bred** Denis McDonnell **Trained** Newmarket, Suffolk

FOCUS
Lady Lunchalot set a modest standard in this fillies' maiden but there were several others that were unexposed and representing major yards. The time was slow and the third is perhaps the key.

231 HOLTYE H'CAP — 1m 2f (P)
2:35 (2:35) (Class 5) (0-75,74) 3-Y-O — £2,726 (£805; £402) Stalls Low

Form — RPR
11-1 1 **Gabrial The Boss (USA)**[2] 209 3-9-13 74 6ex..........(t) AndreaAtzeni 2 78+
(David Simcock) *mde all: set stdy gallop tl shkn up and qcknd 2f out: clr and in command 1f out: eased towards fin* 4/6[1]
55-4 2 2 **Inessa Armand (IRE)**[6] 141 3-8-13 60..........(p) LiamKeniry 1 57
(J S Moore) *chsd wnr tl 7f out: rdn over 2f out: drvn to chse clr wnr over 1f out: no imp and wl hld tl clsd on eased wnr towards fin* 4/1[3]
3 5 **Rose Ransom (IRE)**[81] 7420 3-9-2 63.......... JoeFanning 3 53
(Mark Johnston) *hld up in 3rd tl chsd wnr 7f out: rdn and outpcd 2f out: 3rd and wl btn 1f out: eased wl ins fnl f* 5/2[2]
2m 8.33s (1.73) **Going Correction** -0.05s/f (Stan) 3 Ran SP% **108.6**
Speed ratings (Par 97): **91,89,85**
CSF £3.53 TOTE £2.10; EX 3.60 Trifecta £4.70 Pool: £738.65 - 115.44 winning units..
Owner Dr Marwan Koukash **Bred** Hunter Valley Farm Et Al **Trained** Newmarket, Suffolk
FOCUS
A very modest handicap in which the pace was steady and this was straightforward for the favourite, who continues on the up.

232 BREATHE SPA AT LINGFIELD MARRIOTT H'CAP — 5f (P)
3:10 (3:10) (Class 5) (0-75,74) 4-Y-O+ — £2,726 (£805; £402) Stalls High

Form — RPR
43-2 1 **Picansort**[4] 186 6-8-13 66..........(b[1]) ShaneKelly 6 81
(Peter Crate) *in tch in midfield: 3rd 2f out: in clr ld towards fin* 11/4[2]
461- 2 3 **The Strig**[49] 7902 6-9-7 74..........(v) DavidProbert 2 78
(Stuart Williams) *chsd ldrs: 4th 2f out: 2nd and no threat to wnr towards fin* 4/1[3]
0-13 3 1 ¾ **Roy's Legacy**[7] 113 4-9-7 74..........(t) AdamKirby 7 72
(Shaun Harris) *led: rdn 2f out: hoilding on to 3rd but wl hld towards fin* 5/2[1]
30-2 4 shd **Billy Red**[13] 29 9-9-2 69..........(b) JoeFanning 8 67
(J R Jenkins) *chsd ldr: led and rdn 2f out: battling for 3rd and wl hld towards fin* 7/1
100- 5 ½ **Peter Island (FR)**[121] 6303 10-8-6 66..........(v) RyanTate(7) 1 62
(John Gallagher) *in tch in midfield: 5th and rdn 2f out: pressing for 3rd but wl hld towards fin* 12/1
000- 6 2 **Foxtrot India (IRE)**[158] 5097 4-9-3 70..........[1] RenatoSouza 4 59
(Jeremy Gask) *hld up in detached last: 6th and wl btn towards fin* 5/1
33-6 7 4 **Amenable (IRE)**[12] 56 6-8-10 68.......... CharlesBishop(5) 5 42
(Violet M Jordan) *in tch in midfield: 6th and effrt u.p 2f out: bhd towards fin* 14/1
57.88s (-0.92) **Going Correction** -0.05s/f (Stan) 7 Ran SP% **118.8**
Speed ratings (Par 103): **105,100,97,97,96 93,86**
toteswingers 1&2 £2.20, 1&3 £3.10, 2&3 £2.40 CSF £15.08 CT £30.89 TOTE £3.80: £1.80, £2.90; EX 17.00 Trifecta £47.40 Pool: £2707.58 - 42.76 winning units..
Owner Peter Crate **Bred** Miss Brooke Sanders **Trained** Newdigate, Surrey
FOCUS
An ordinary sprint handicap that was mostly hidden in a blanket of fog. The winner is rated back to his best.

233 ENOUGH SAID, JUST BET AT BLUESQ.COM APPRENTICE H'CAP — 6f (P)
3:40 (3:43) (Class 6) (0-60,57) 4-Y-O+ — £2,196 (£754) Stalls Low

Form — RPR
23-2 1 **Baby Dottie**[5] 156 6-9-0 57..........(tp) SophieRalston(7) 5 66
(Pat Phelan) *dwlt: sn rcvrd to chse ldrs: led 2f out: wl clr nr fin* 4/1[3]
3-33 2 6 **Spartic**[6] 139 5-9-7 57..........(p) ShirleyTeasdale 7 47
(Alan McCabe) *in tch in last trio: 4th and effrt 2f out: modest 2nd nr fin* 2/1[1]
44-5 0 **Brandywell Boy (IRE)**[7] 124 10-9-2 52.......... JoshBaudains 6
(Dominic Ffrench Davis) *sn bustled along: in tch in rr: 7th and effrt 2f out* 16/1
0-60 0 **Steel City Boy (IRE)**[7] 124 10-9-2 52.......... GeorgeChaloner 2
(Ann Stokell) *chsd ldr: 3rd and rdn 2f out* 25/1
536- 0 **Chjimes (IRE)**[16] 8307 9-9-2 55..........(b) RyanWhile(3) 3
(Conor Dore) *dwlt: in tch in last trio: 6th and rdn 2f out* 12/1
36-2 0 **Dixie Gwalia**[9] 92 5-9-0 50.......... PhilipPrince 4
(David Evans) *chsd ldrs: 5th and rdn 2f out* 11/4[2]
6-30 0 **Russian Bullet**[5] 163 4-9-4 57.......... RyanTate(3) 1
(Jamie Osborne) *led: 2nd and rdn 2f out* 9/2
1m 11.2s (-0.70) **Going Correction** -0.05s/f (Stan) 7 Ran SP% **115.6**
Speed ratings (Par 101): **102,94,94,94,94 94,94**
CSF £12.75 TOTE £5.20: £2.10, £1.30; EX 14.40 Trifecta £13.80 Trifecta paid on 1st, 2nd and any other. Pool: £3886.99 - 210.35 winning units..
Owner Tony Smith **Bred** Tony J Smith **Trained** Epsom, Surrey
■ Sophie Ralston's first winner, on her second ride.
FOCUS
A moderate apprentice handicap but all the runners had had a recent start. The weather had closed in so much that virtually nothing could be seen of the race. Controversially, only the first two placings were made official, and that after the judge had deliberated for 40 minutes. Brandywell Boy's rider claimed he was third. Unconvincing form.
T/Plt: £86.80 to a £1 stake. Pool of £52,749.63 - 443.40 winning tickets. T/Qpdt: £53.80 to a £1 stake. Pool of £5,196.44 - 71.40 winning tickets. SP

213 WOLVERHAMPTON (A.W) (L-H)
Thursday, January 17

OFFICIAL GOING: Standard
Wind: Light across Weather: Snow showers

234 CORAL.CO.UK FILLIES' H'CAP — 5f 216y(P)
4:30 (4:30) (Class 5) (0-70,74) 4-Y-O+ — £2,587 (£770; £384; £192) Stalls Low

Form — RPR
6-12 1 **Aubrietia**[4] 196 4-9-11 74 6ex..........(b) LukeMorris 2 82
(Alan McCabe) *s.i.s: hdwy to ld 5f out: rdn over 1f out: all out* 8/13[1]
40-3 2 nk **Avonrose**[8] 116 6-8-13 69..........(v) AdamMcLean(7) 7 76
(Derek Shaw) *broke wl: sn stdd and lost pl: hdwy and n.m.r over 1f out: rdn to chse wnr ins fnl f: r.o* 11/1
2-11 3 3 ½ **Miss Bunter**[13] 54 4-9-7 70.......... DanielTudhope 4 66
(David O'Meara) *chsd ldrs: rdn over 1f out: no ex ins fnl f* 5/2[2]
5-43 4 8 **Mother Jones**[13] 56 5-9-0 70.......... PhilipPrince(7) 1 40
(David Evans) *sn led: hdd 5f out: chsd ldr: rdn over 1f out: wknd fnl f* 8/1[3]
1m 13.6s (-1.40) **Going Correction** -0.05s/f (Stan) 4 Ran SP% **109.9**
Speed ratings (Par 100): **107,106,101,91**
CSF £7.91 TOTE £1.40; EX 5.80 Trifecta £21.90 Pool: £1631.24 - 55.65 winning units..
Owner Shropshire Wolves 4 **Bred** C J Murfitt **Trained** Averham Park, Notts
FOCUS
A snowfall arrived shortly before racing commenced and Luke Morris claimed after winning the opener that the surface felt a little slower than standard. Not a bad little fillies' handicap for the class and it was a proper test. The winner is rated close to her penultimate form over C&D.

235 HORSE RACING BEST BETS AT BOOKMAKERS.CO.UK CLAIMING STKS — 1m 5f 194y(P)
5:00 (5:01) (Class 6) 4-Y-O+ — £1,940 (£577; £288; £144) Stalls Low

Form — RPR
15-1 1 **Stand Guard**[6] 166 9-9-8 87.......... AdamKirby 4 88+
(John Butler) *chsd ldr over 2f: remained handy: wnt 2nd again 3f out: led over 1f out: pushed clr: eased towards fin* 2/9[1]
221- 2 14 **Priestley's Reward (IRE)**[17] 8301 4-9-0 67..........(p) LukeMorris 3 64
(Mrs K Burke) *sn drvn along to ld: reminders 7f out: hdd over 1f out: sn outpcd* 5/1[2]
000/ 3 hd **Esteem**[43] 504 10-8-13 55..........(t) WilliamCarson 2 57?
(David Evans) *hld up: hdwy over 1f out: sn rdn and outpcd* 20/1[3]
-654 4 21 **Dubai Story**[3] 201 4-7-9 39..........(p) ShelleyBirkett(7) 1 18
(Alastair Lidderdale) *prom: chsd ldr over 11f out tl pushed along 3f out: wknd over 1f out* 20/1[3]
3m 3.68s (-2.32) **Going Correction** -0.05s/f (Stan)
WFA 4 from 5yo+ 6lb 4 Ran SP% **108.0**
Speed ratings (Par 101): **104,96,95,83**
CSF £1.71 TOTE £1.10; EX 1.70 Trifecta £4.40 Pool: £1894.47 - 316.66 winning units..
Owner J Butler **Bred** Juddmonte Farms Ltd **Trained** Newmarket, Suffolk
FOCUS
A very weak affair and a walk in the park for long odds-on favourite. The second did not look straightforward and there are doubts over the form.

236 CORAL.CO.UK MOBILE CASINO MEDIAN AUCTION MAIDEN STKS — 5f 216y(P)
5:30 (5:35) (Class 5) 3-5-Y-O — £2,587 (£770; £384; £192) Stalls Low

Form — RPR
2 1 **Iggy**[13] 59 3-8-10 0.......... JamesSullivan 4 62
(Michael Easterby) *led 5f out: rdn over 1f out: r.o* 3/1[3]
05-3 2 1 ½ **Sewn Up**[9] 106 3-8-10 67..........(t) BarryMcHugh 2 58
(Reg Hollinshead) *chsd ldrs: lost pl over 4f out: hdwy over 2f out: rdn over 1f out: styd on* 15/8[1]
2- 3 shd **Black Rider (IRE)**[26] 8230 3-8-10 0.......... AmyRyan 1 57+
(Kevin Ryan) *dwlt: outpcd: hdwy on outer over 2f out: rdn over 1f out: edgd lft: styd on* 9/4[2]
4 ½ **Secret Advice** 3-8-5 0.......... JoeFanning 3 51
(Keith Dalgleish) *sn prom: rdn and ev ch over 1f out: edgd lft: styd on same pce fnl f* 9/2
606- 5 ½ **Stoneacre Hull (IRE)**[34] 8109 4-9-7 43.......... AdamKirby 8 53?
(Peter Grayson) *led 1f: chsd ldrs: rdn over 1f out: styd on same pce ins fnl f* 80/1
5-3 6 8 **Ches Jicaro (IRE)**[13] 51 5-9-12 0.......... AdamBeschizza 5 32
(James Unett) *s.i.s: sn pushed along to chse ldrs: rdn and ev ch 2f out: wknd fnl f* 40/1
7 3 ¾ **Twist And Twirl** 3-7-12 0.......... AdamMcLean(7) 9
(Derek Shaw) *prom: lost pl 4f out: wknd over 2f out* 100/1
1m 15.52s (0.52) **Going Correction** -0.05s/f (Stan)
WFA 3 from 4yo+ 16lb 7 Ran SP% **113.4**
Speed ratings (Par 103): **94,92,91,91,90 79,74**
toteswingers 1&2 £1.40, 1&3 £1.90, 2&3 £1.70 CSF £8.91 TOTE £4.00: £1.80, £2.00; EX 10.70 Trifecta £22.40 Pool: £2144.87 - 71.80 winning units..
Owner T Dewhirst & R Moore **Bred** M W Easterby **Trained** Sheriff Hutton, N Yorks
FOCUS
There was a tight finish to this sprint maiden and it's ordinary form, with the proximity of the fifth a big doubt. The winner is rated up a length on his debut effort.

237 FREE SPORTS BETTING AT BOOKMAKERS.CO.UK H'CAP — 1m 4f 50y(P)
6:00 (6:00) (Class 6) (0-65,63) 3-Y-O — £1,940 (£577; £288; £144) Stalls Low

Form — RPR
2-02 1 **Great Ormond (IRE)**[3] 212 3-8-11 53.......... AndreaAtzeni 7 61+
(David Simcock) *hld up: hdwy over 2f out: led over 1f out: sn rdn and edgd lft: styd on wl* 2/1[2]
25-2 2 2 **Rakticate (IRE)**[7] 141 3-8-11 60.......... CharlotteJenner(7) 9 65
(J S Moore) *hld up: hdwy over 2f out: rdn over 1f out: styd on same pce ins fnl f* 17/2
05-5 3 7 **Rosie Future (IRE)**[10] 103 3-8-12 54.......... DavidProbert 8 48
(Rae Guest) *chsd ldrs tl led 9f out: rdn over 2f out: hdd over 1f out: wknd ins fnl f* 9/2[3]
054- 4 ¾ **Honey Haven (IRE)**[33] 8140 3-8-3 45.......... JamesSullivan 2 38
(Mark Brisbourne) *prom: pushed along and lost pl over 6f out: hmpd 5f out: styd on ins fnl f* 50/1
006- 5 4 **Pacquiao (IRE)**[34] 8112 3-8-10 52 ow1.......... MichaelO'Connell 5 38
(John Quinn) *prom: rdn over 5f out: wknd over 2f out* 10/1
060- 6 nse **By A Wiska**[45] 7973 3-8-13 55.......... TomEaves 1 41
(Ann Duffield) *led: hdd 9f out: chsd ldr: rdn over 2f out: wknd fnl f* 33/1
032- 7 25 **Misleading Promise (IRE)**[19] 8289 3-9-7 63.......... AdamKirby 6
(John Butler) *hld up: plld hrd: hdwy over 4f out: rdn over 2f out: wknd over 1f out: t.o* 15/8[1]
50-0 8 39 **Crafty Wonder (IRE)**[10] 103 3-8-9 51.......... WilliamCarson 3
(David Evans) *w ldr 4f: remained handy tl rdn over 3f out: sn wknd: t.o* 33/1
00-0 9 8 **Upper Echelon**[12] 74 3-8-8 50.......... JoeFanning 4
(Mark Johnston) *s.i.s: hld up: bhd fnl 4f: t.o* 20/1
2m 41.67s (0.57) **Going Correction** -0.05s/f (Stan) 9 Ran SP% **118.5**
Speed ratings (Par 95): **96,94,90,89,86 86,70,44,38**
toteswingers 1&2 £2.60, 1&3 £2.80, 2&3 £5.40 CSF £19.10 CT £70.96 TOTE £2.80: £1.10, £1.70, £1.50; EX 13.80 Trifecta £33.60 Pool: £1583.90 - 35.26 winning units..
Owner Dr Marwan Koukash **Bred** David Eiffe **Trained** Newmarket, Suffolk
■ Stewards' Enquiry : Charlotte Jenner one-day ban: careless riding (Jan 31)

The Form Book Flat, Raceform Ltd, Compton, RG20 6NL.

FOCUS
A moderate 3yo handicap, run at an average pace and two pulled clear. They both rate personal bests.

238 ONLINE BETTING OFFERS AT BOOKMAKERS.CO.UK (S) STKS 1m 1f 103y(P)
6:30 (6:30) (Class 6) 4-Y-O+ £1,940 (£577; £288; £144) Stalls Low

Form RPR
40-0 1 **West End Lad**11 82 10-9-1 68 ow1 (b) AdamKirby 2 71
(Roy Bowring) *sn pushed along to ld: clr over 7f out: rdn over 1f out: styd on u.p* 4/1[2]
00-3 2 2 1/2 **Yourinthewill (USA)**11 84 5-9-0 61 JoeFanning 1 65
(Daniel Mark Loughnane) *hld up: hdwy over 2f out: rdn over 1f out: styd on to go 2nd wl ins fnl f: nt rch wnr* 12/1
50-0 3 1/2 **Chosen Forever**7 146 8-9-0 77 TomEaves 4 64
(Geoffrey Oldroyd) *sn pushed along and prom: chsd wnr over 7f out: rdn over 1f out: styd on same pce ins fnl f* 11/2[3]
/6-4 4 3 **Syrian**3 206 6-9-0 73 LukeMorris 6 58
(Thomas McLaughlin, Ire) *hld up: hdwy over 3f out: rdn over 1f out: no ex fnl f* 10/11[1]
40-0 5 7 **Time Square (FR)**15 9 6-9-0 52 (t) DavidProbert 3 43
(Tony Carroll) *chsd ldrs: rdn over 3f out: wknd over 2f out* 20/1
025- 6 nk **Guava**19 8288 4-8-6 48 ow1 MarkCoumbe(3) 5 38
(Shaun Harris) *hld up: rdn over 3f out: hdwy over 2f out: wknd over 1f out* 16/1
04-6 7 3/4 **Gangsterbanksters (FR)**10 100 4-8-10 49 (p) DeclanCannon(3) 7 41
(Mrs K Burke) *prom: pushed along and lost pl 4f out: wknd over 2f out* 12/1

2m 0.27s (-1.43) **Going Correction** -0.05s/f (Stan)
WFA 4 from 5yo+ 1lb 7 Ran SP% 113.8
Speed ratings (Par 101): **104,101,101,98,92 92,91**
toteswingers 1&2 £7.00, 1&3 £3.70, 2&3 £5.50 CSF £47.99 TOTE £4.50: £2.60, £3.90; EX 38.30 Trifecta £156.40 Pool: £1490.20 - 7.14 winning units..There was no bid for the winner.
Owner K Nicholls **Bred** Keith Nicholls **Trained** Edwinstowe, Notts

FOCUS
There was certainly no hanging about in this seller. It wasn't a bad race for the grade on paper, but there are doubts over the form as the first three all arrived on the back of poor runs.

239 COMPARE BOOKIES WITH BOOKMAKERS.CO.UK H'CAP 1m 1f 103y(P)
7:00 (7:00) (Class 4) (0-85,85) 4-Y-O+ £4,690 (£1,395; £697; £348) Stalls Low

Form RPR
33-2 1 **Desert Vision**15 23 9-9-4 82 (vt) GrahamGibbons 6 91
(Michael Easterby) *a.p: chsd ldr 2f out: rdn to ld over 1f out: hdd wl ins fnl f: rallied to ld post* 4/1[3]
21-2 2 shd **Knowe Head (NZ)**7 146 6-8-8 72 (v) DavidProbert 3 81
(James Unett) *hld up: hdwy over 3f out: rdn to ld wl ins fnl f: hdd post* 6/4[1]
324- 3 2 1/4 **Dubawi Island (FR)**43 7986 4-9-6 85 (b) LukeMorris 8 89
(James Tate) *led: hdd 8f out: chsd ldr tl led again over 2f out: rdn and hdd over 1f out: no ex ins fnl f* 9/4[2]
0/ 4 2 1/4 **Boom To Bust (IRE)**29 3895 5-9-6 84 (b) JohnFahy 4 84
(Paul Rich) *hld up: hdwy 5f out: rdn over 2f out: styd on same pce fr over 1f out* 25/1
206- 5 1 1/4 **Change The Subject (USA)**20 8275 5-9-0 78 ow1..(bt) SebSanders 11 75
(Peter Salmon) *led 8f out: clr 7f out: rdn and hdd over 2f out: wknd fnl f* 14/1
522- 6 1/2 **Red Inca**180 3628 5-8-12 79 ow2 PaulPickard(3) 9 75
(Brian Ellison) *mid-div: sn drvn along: styd on fr over 1f out: nvr trbld ldrs* 28/1
114- 7 1/2 **Calaf**52 7069 5-8-11 75 DaleSwift 7 70
(Brian Ellison) *hld up: rdn over 3f out: nvr on terms* 11/2
0-45 8 24 **Copperwood**12 79 8-8-12 76 JoeFanning 1 20
(Mark Johnston) *mid-div: hmpd and lost pl after 1f: bhd fnl 3f: t.o* 25/1
9 5 **Cawett Cove (IRE)**210 5-9-0 85 IanBurns(7) 10 19
(Jane Chapple-Hyam) *chsd ldrs: rdn over 3f out: wknd over 2f out: t.o* 50/1

2m 0.2s (-1.50) **Going Correction** -0.05s/f (Stan)
WFA 4 from 5yo+ 1lb 9 Ran SP% 125.9
Speed ratings (Par 105): **104,103,101,99,98 98,97,76,72**
toteswingers 1&2 £4.10, 1&3 £2.90, 2&3 £2.40 CSF £11.16 CT £17.89 TOTE £3.80: £2.00, £1.80, £1.20; EX 20.70 Trifecta £58.30 Pool: £1751.12 - 22.50 winning units..
Owner A Black,R Edmonds,J Holdroyd,J Quickfall **Bred** Gainsborough Stud Management Ltd **Trained** Sheriff Hutton, N Yorks
■ Stewards' Enquiry : Luke Morris three-day ban: careless riding (Jan 31-Feb 2)

FOCUS
It paid to race handily in this modest handicap. The winner is rated to his old best.

240 £50 FREE BET AT CORAL.CO.UK H'CAP 7f 32y(P)
7:30 (7:34) (Class 7) (0-50,56) 4-Y-O+ £1,940 (£577; £288; £144) Stalls High

Form RPR
05-6 1 **Media Jury**11 87 6-9-3 48 (p) BarryMcHugh 10 56
(John Wainwright) *hld up: hdwy over 2f out: rdn to ld wl ins fnl f* 33/1
0-20 2 hd **Under Par**6 163 5-9-4 49 (t) GrahamGibbons 6 56
(Michael Easterby) *led 6f out: rdn over 1f out: hdd wl ins fnl f* 11/2
00-6 3 1 **Hold The Star**11 88 7-8-11 47 AnnStokell(5) 2 51
(Ann Stokell) *led 1f: chsd ldrs: rdn over 1f out: styd on* 20/1
2-55 4 1/2 **Lord Paget**9 110 4-9-0 50 (p) ShirleyTeasdale(5) 8 53+
(Reg Hollinshead) *hld up: hdwy over 1f out: r.o: nt rch ldrs* 6/1
6-20 5 nse **Dixie Gwalia**1 233 5-9-5 50 LukeMorris 1 53+
(David Evans) *mid-div: hdwy over 1f out: r.o: nt rch ldrs* 3/1[2]
0/6- 6 nse **Aljosan**276 1413 4-9-1 49 (bt[1]) MarkCoumbe(3) 5 52
(Frank Sheridan) *hld up: rdn over 1f out: r.o ins fnl f: nvr nrr* 50/1
60-0 7 nk **Very First Blade**14 42 4-9-2 47 FrannyNorton 4 49
(Mark Brisbourne) *prom: chsd ldr over 5f out: rdn over 1f out: styd on same pce ins fnl f* 33/1
346- 8 1 3/4 **Huzzah (IRE)**28 8180 8-9-4 49 (t[1]) MichaelStainton 9 46
(Paul Howling) *dwlt: hld up: rdn over 2f out: nvr trbld ldrs* 17/2
00-6 9 1 1/4 **Rise To Glory (IRE)**14 35 5-9-5 50 (t) JoeFanning 3 44
(Shaun Harris) *prom: rdn over 1f out: no ex ins fnl f* 4/1[3]
02-1 10 1 **Coastal Passage**9 105 5-9-11 56 6ex AdamKirby 11 47
(Charles Smith) *chsd ldrs: rdn over 2f out: wkng whn hmpd ins fnl f* 9/4[1]
242- 11 1/2 **Flow Chart (IRE)**244 2225 6-8-11 47 (b) SladeO'Hara(5) 7 37
(Peter Grayson) *hld up: rdn over 1f out: n.d* 16/1

1m 30.73s (1.13) **Going Correction** -0.05s/f (Stan) 11 Ran SP% 134.5
Speed ratings (Par 97): **91,90,89,89,89 88,88,86,85,84 83**
toteswingers 1&2 £4.10, 1&3 £2.90, 2&3 £2.40 CSF £227.62 CT £3880.39 TOTE £36.80: £5.60, £2.70, £5.00; EX 151.90 Trifecta £1383.80 Part won. Pool: £1845.15 - 0.03 winning units..
Owner S Enwright **Bred** J S Wainwright **Trained** Kennythorpe, N Yorks

FOCUS
A bottom-drawer handicap. The pace held up well in worsening conditions as the snow carried on falling. The surprise winner was close to last year's best.
T/Plt: £23.70 to a £1 stake. Pool of £73,597.12 - 2,261.91 winning tickets. T/Qpdt: £9.50 to a £1 stake. Pool of £8,625.86 - 668.68 winning tickets. CR

149 MEYDAN (L-H)
Thursday, January 17

OFFICIAL GOING: Tapeta: standard; turf: good

241a DUBAI DUTY FREE FINEST SURPRISE (H'CAP) (TAPETA) 1m
2:30 (2:30) (95-105,105) 3-Y-O+
£40,490 (£13,496; £6,748; £3,374; £2,024; £1,349)

RPR
1 **Capital Attraction (USA)**6 180 6-9-0 104 TadhgO'Shea 13 110
(Ernst Oertel, UAE) *trckd ldrs: led after 1 1/2f: kicked clr 3f out: r.o wl: comf* 12/1
2 1 3/4 **Elderly Paradise (AUS)**40 6-9-1 105 (e) ODoleuze 7 107+
(M C Tam, Macau) *sn led: hdd after 1 1/2f: trckd wnr: ev ch 2f out: one pce fnl 1 1/2f* 8/1[3]
3 1 1/4 **Sandagiyr (FR)**126 6166 5-8-11 101 PatDobbs 14 100+
(Saeed bin Suroor) *settled in rr: nvr nr to chal but r.o fnl 1 1/2f: nrst fin* 14/1
4 1/4 **Banna Boirche (IRE)**62 7759 7-8-13 102 ShaneFoley 2 102+
(M Halford, Ire) *rr of mid-div: r.o fnl 2f: nrst fin* 10/1
5 1 1/4 **Not A Given (USA)**166 4-8-13 102 KierenFallon 3 98+
(Mahmood Al Zarooni) *mid-div: kpt on same pce fnl 1 1/2f* 7/1[2]
6 hd **Con Artist (IRE)**194 3878 6-8-13 102 SilvestreDeSousa 11 99+
(Saeed bin Suroor) *a mid-div: kpt on: nrst fin* 12/1
7 1/4 **Finjaan**28 8198 7-9-0 104 (bt) PaulHanagan 6 99+
(Doug Watson, UAE) *mid-div on rail: chsd ldrs 2 1/2f out: kpt on same pce fnl 1 1/2f* 20/1
8 1/2 **Spirit Of Battle (USA)**7 149 5-8-13 102 (b) PatCosgrave 15 96+
(A bin Huzaim, UAE) *trckd ldrs: ev ch 3f out: one pce fnl 1 1/2f* 14/1
9 1 1/2 **Iver Bridge Lad**7 149 6-8-13 102 DaraghO'Donohoe 16 93
(John Ryan) *trckd ldrs tl outpcd 1 1/2f out* 14/1
10 3/4 **Jardim (BRZ)**313 876 7-9-0 104 JGeroudis 1 92+
(M F De Kock, South Africa) *rr of mid-div: nvr nr to chal* 16/1
11 hd **Belgian Bill**7 149 5-9-0 104 (t) RyanMoore 8 92+
(George Baker) *a mid-div* 14/1
12 1/2 **Mariner's Cross (IRE)**257 1859 4-9-1 105 MickaelBarzalona 5 92+
(Mahmood Al Zarooni) *nvr bttr than mid-div* 7/2[1]
13 1 1/4 **Nordic Truce (USA)**123 6291 6-9-1 105 JamieSpencer 12 89+
(P Schiergen, Germany) *settled in rr: nvr nr to chal* 16/1
14 7 1/2 **Akeed Wafi (IRE)**7 149 4-8-13 102 RoystonFfrench 4 70+
(A Al Raihe, UAE) *slowly away: nvr nr to chal* 16/1
15 8 1/2 **Storm Ultralight (ARG)**20 8281 7-9-0 104 RichardMullen 9 51+
(S Seemar, UAE) *nvr bttr than mid-div* 33/1
16 2 1/2 **Modern History (IRE)**378 47 5-9-1 105 AhmedAjtebi 10 46+
(Mahmood Al Zarooni) *nvr bttr than mid-div* 16/1

1m 36.9s (-0.60) 16 Ran SP% 128.2
WIN: 12.00. CSF: 110.00. TRICAST: 1,397.64.
Owner H E Sheikh Sultan Bin Khalifa Al Nahyan **Bred** WinStar Farm LLC **Trained** United Arab Emirates

FOCUS
The story of this race was an excellent bit of pace judgement from Tadhg O'Shea aboard the winner. The others had little hope of landing a blow. The winner is progressive.

242a DUBAI DUTY FREE TENNIS CHAMPIONSHIP (H'CAP) (TURF) 1m 2f
3:05 (3:05) (100-110,108) 3-Y-O+
£44,171 (£14,723; £7,361; £3,680; £2,208; £1,472)

RPR
1 **Laajooj (IRE)**152 5364 5-9-2 107 MickaelBarzalona 8 110+
(Mahmood Al Zarooni) *settled in rr: smooth prog to chse ldrs 2f out: r.o wl: led fnl strides* 7/2[1]
2 hd **Naqshabban (USA)**371 143 5-9-3 108 KierenFallon 4 111
(Mahmood Al Zarooni) *trckd ldng trio: led 1f out: hdd fnl strides* 5/1[3]
3 1 1/4 **Tanfeeth**7 151 5-8-9 100 (t) DaneO'Neill 1 100
(M Al Muhairi, UAE) *s.i.s: settled in rr: r.o fnl 1 1/2f nrst fin* 10/1
4 1 **Al Shemali**7 152 9-8-13 104 (t) RyanMoore 3 102
(A Al Raihe, UAE) *rr of mid-div: rdn 3f out: kpt on same pce fnl 1 1/2f* 11/1
5 hd **Anaerobio (ARG)**7 154 6-8-10 101 (t) PatCosgrave 2 99
(M F De Kock, South Africa) *trckd ldng pair: smooth prog 2f out: ev ch 1f out: one pce fnl 1/2f* 4/1[2]
6 hd **Lindenthaler (GER)**198 3746 5-9-1 106 JamieSpencer 5 103
(P Schiergen, Germany) *rr of mid-div: chsd ldrs 2f out: one pce ins fnl f* 14/1
7 4 1/2 **Blue Corner (IRE)**161 5027 4-8-10 102 (t) SilvestreDeSousa 6 91
(Saeed bin Suroor) *slowly away: nvr bttr than mid-div* 5/1[3]
8 hd **Red Dubawi (IRE)**103 6898 5-9-0 105 FergalLynch 11 93
(David Marnane, Ire) *settled in rr: t.k.h: nvr able to chal but: kpt on fnl 1 1/2f* 12/1
9 3 1/2 **War Monger (USA)**39 9-8-10 101 PaulHanagan 7 82
(Doug Watson, UAE) *Soon led: kicked clr 3f out: hdd & wknd 1 1/2f out* 33/1
10 dist **Florentino (JPN)**39 7-8-9 100 (t) RichardMullen 9
(S Seemar, UAE) *trckd ldrs: outpcd and wknd 4f out* 33/1
P **Wealthy (IRE)**320 793 6-8-13 104 (t) TedDurcan 10
(Saeed bin Suroor) *p.u after 4f* 12/1

2m 1.75s (121.75)
WFA 4 from 5yo+ 2lb 11 Ran SP% 120.9
WIN: 4.80. PLACES: 1.40, 3.00, 2.50. CSF: 21.65, TRICAST: 161.50..
Owner Sheikh Ahmed Al Maktoum **Bred** Kildaragh Stud **Trained** Newmarket, Suffolk

FOCUS
There was a slow-fast-slow pace thanks to War Monger, who took them along in splits of 26.34 (standing start), 23.11, 23.32 and 24.18, before being passed, and Laajooj stayed on from last to get up on the line.

243a UAE 1000 GUINEAS TRIAL SPONSORED BY DUBAI DUTY FREE GOLF WORLD CUP (CONDITIONS) (FILLIES) (TAPETA) 7f
3:40 (3:40) 3-Y-O

£18,404 (£6,134; £3,067; £1,533; £920; £613)

RPR

1 **Music Chart (USA)**[131] 6021 3-8-8 94 MickaelBarzalona 1 102+
(Mahmood Al Zarooni) *settled in rr: smooth prog: trck ldrs 2f out: rdn 1 1/2f out: led ins fnl f* **3/1**[1]

2 ¾ **Shuruq (USA)**[92] 7159 3-8-8 85 SilvestreDeSousa 6 100
(Saeed bin Suroor) *settled in rr: smooth prog to ld 1 1/2f out: r.o but hdd ins fnl f* **3/1**[1]

3 5½ **More Than Sotka (FR)**[125] 6225 3-8-8 99 FergalLynch 10 85
(David Marnane, Ire) *mid-div: chsd ldrs 1 1/2f out: nt qckn ins fnl f* **6/1**[2]

4 shd **Mar Mar (IRE)**[68] 7686 3-8-8 86 (v) TedDurcan 4 85
(Saeed bin Suroor) *mid-div: r.o same pce fnl 1 1/2f* **11/1**

5 3½ **My Special J'S (USA)**[102] 6909 3-8-13 105 TadhgO'Shea 9 80
(John Patrick Shanahan, Ire) *trckd ldng pair: rdn to ld 2f out: hdd & wknd 1f out* **3/1**[1]

6 ¼ **Ana Emaratiya**[28] 8196 3-8-8 78 (t) HarryBentley 3 75
(A Al Raihe, UAE) *mid-div on rail: chsd ldrs 2 1/2f out: rdn and one pce fnl 1 1/2f out* **33/1**

7 1½ **Daar Zayed (USA)**[96] 3-8-8 85 (t) WayneSmith 5 71
(M Al Muhairi, UAE) *trckd ldng trio tl outpcd 1 1/2f out* **14/1**

8 5½ **Kosika (USA)**[237] 2450 3-8-8 75 AhmedAjtebi 7 56
(Mahmood Al Zarooni) *trckd ldrs tl outpcd 1 1/2f out* **9/1**[3]

9 12 **Ghibli** 3-8-8 JuanPaulV'DMerwe 8 23
(R Bouresly, Kuwait) *slowly away: sn rdn in rr: nvr involved* **100/1**

10 21 **Bint Youmzain (IRE)**[120] 6355 3-8-8 53 (b) RoystonFfrench 2
(M Ramadan, UAE) *sn led: hdd & wknd 2f out* **100/1**

1m 24.59s (-0.61) **10** Ran SP% **119.2**
WIN: 4.80, PLACES: 1.30, 2.10, 2.40. CSF: 11.84..
Owner Godolphin **Bred** Bedford Bloodstock Llc **Trained** Newmarket, Suffolk

FOCUS
The runner-up from this trial in 2011, Mahbooba, went one better in the UAE 1000 Guineas, and last year Gamilati won both races. A look at the sectionals, with the splits for the later 2000 Guineas Trial in brackets, shows the pace was quick enough early on before slowing: 25.31 (25.74), 23.35 (23.55), 23.95 (22.71), 11.94 (11.68). That set things up nicely for the winner and runner-up, who were able to save plenty in the opening stages and raced more evenly than those on the speed. They pulled clear and seemed to run to a decent level. The fourth and sixth help with the standard.

244a DUBAI DUTY FREE MILLENNIUM MILLIONAIRE (H'CAP) (TURF) 6f
4:15 (4:15) (100-110,110) 3-Y-O+

£44,171 (£14,723; £7,361; £3,680; £2,208; £1,472)

RPR

1 **Tamaathul**[7] 154 6-9-5 110 (t) PaulHanagan 15 117
(A Al Raihe, UAE) *rr of mid-div: smooth prog 3f out: led 1f out: comf* **6/1**[1]

2 1¼ **Russian Soul (IRE)**[48] 7941 5-8-9 100 (p) ShaneFoley 3 103
(M Halford, Ire) *trckd ldrs: ev ch 1 1/2f out: one pce ins fnl f* **12/1**

3 2¾ **Inxile (IRE)**[7] 150 8-9-3 108 (p) AdrianNicholls 1 102
(David Nicholls) *trckd ldrs: ev ch 1f out: nt qckn ins fnl f* **14/1**

4 1¼ **Russian Rock (IRE)**[6] 182 6-8-13 104 WayneSmith 12 94
(M Al Muhairi, UAE) *Chased ldrs: led 2f out: hdd 1f out but kpt on* **12/1**

5 ¼ **Invincible Ash (IRE)**[7] 150 8-9-3 108 (p) JamieSpencer 16 97
(M Halford, Ire) *slowly away: racd in rr: kpt on fnl 1 1/2f: nrst fin* **10/1**

6 hd **Lui Rei (ITY)**[7] 150 7-8-11 102 TadhgO'Shea 5 91
(Fawzi Abdulla Nass, Bahrain) *settled in rr: r.o fnl 2f: nrst fin* **9/1**

7 ¾ **Cheviot (USA)**[7] 150 7-8-13 104 (p) FergalLynch 2 90
(Kevin Ryan) *mid-div: kpt on one pce fnl 1 1/2f* **20/1**

8 ½ **Final Button (SAF)**[7] 149 5-8-11 102 PatCosgrave 7 87
(M F De Kock, South Africa) *mid-div: kpt on same pce fnl f* **8/1**[3]

9 1 **Rosendhal (IRE)**[67] 7697 6-9-3 108 (bt) MickaelBarzalona 10 90
(G Botti, France) *nvr bttr than mid-div* **16/1**

10 hd **Devil's Cut (AUS)**[32] 5-8-9 100 (t) TedDurcan 13 81
(S Burridge, Singapore) *nvr bttr than mid-div* **7/1**[2]

11 ½ **Happy Dubai (IRE)**[7] 150 6-9-5 110 (t) RyanMoore 6 89
(A Al Raihe, UAE) *nvr nr to chal* **12/1**

12 3¾ **Alo Pura**[28] 8197 9-8-9 100 (e) JamesDoyle 4 67
(D Selvaratnam, UAE) *nvr bttr than mid-div* **25/1**

13 hd **Confessional**[7] 150 6-9-1 106 RichardMullen 8 73
(Tim Easterby) *s.i.s: nvr nr to chal* **16/1**

14 1¼ **Stonefield Flyer**[256] 1877 4-8-10 101 RoystonFfrench 14 64
(Keith Dalgleish) *sn led: hdd & wknd 1 1/2f out* **20/1**

15 ¾ **The Reaper (IRE)**[151] 5392 5-9-5 110 (b) GaryCarroll 9 70
(G M Lyons, Ire) *nvr able to chal* **9/1**

16 6 **Es Que Love (IRE)**[114] 6557 4-8-13 104 KierenFallon 11 45
(Mark Johnston) *trckd ldrs tl wknd 2f out* **14/1**

1m 9.04s (69.04) **16** Ran SP% **128.5**
WIN: 3.20. CSF: 78.87. TRICAST: 1,000.80..
Owner Hamdan Al Maktoum **Bred** Shadwell Estate Co Ltd **Trained** UAE

FOCUS
The pace setup seemed fair enough. The progressive winner ran a personal best, with the second to his mark.

245a UAE 2000 GUINEAS TRIAL SPONSORED BY DUBAI DUTY FREE JUMEIRAH CREEKSIDE (CONDITIONS RACE) (TAPETA) 7f
4:50 (4:50) 3-Y-O

£18,404 (£6,134; £3,067; £1,533; £920; £613)

RPR

1 **Soft Falling Rain (SAF)**[264] 4-9-11 113 PaulHanagan 6 112+
(M F De Kock, South Africa) *sn led: kicked clr 2 1/2f out: r.o wl: easily* **7/4**[1]

2 2½ **I'm Back (IRE)**[106] 6775 3-8-8 89 (t) SilvestreDeSousa 14 95
(Saeed bin Suroor) *trckd ldrs: ev ch 3f out: otpced 1 1/2f out but kpt on wl* **12/1**

3 2¼ **Snowboarder (USA)**[98] 7009 3-8-8 91 KierenFallon 3 89+
(Mahmood Al Zarooni) *mid-div: rdn 3f out: kpt on same pce fnl 1 1/2f* **12/1**

4 ½ **Zahee (NZ)**[127] 4-9-4 98 JGeroudis 8 90+
(M F De Kock, South Africa) *settled in rr: r.o fnl 2f but nvr nr to chal* **14/1**

5 1 **Glass Office**[131] 6038 3-8-10 108 JamieSpencer 5 87+
(David Simcock) *rr of mid-div: n.m.r 2 1/2f out: kpt on one pce fnl f* **4/1**[2]

6 ½ **Filfil (USA)**[72] 7614 3-8-8 87 MickaelBarzalona 10 84+
(Mahmood Al Zarooni) *mid-div: chsd ldrs 3f out: nt qckn fnl 1 1/2f* **14/1**

7 ¾ **El Estruendoso (ARG)**[261] 4-9-4 90 ChristopheSoumillon 11 84+
(M F De Kock, South Africa) *settled in rr: nvr nr to chal* **6/1**[3]

8 1¼ **Bravo Youmzain (IRE)**[90] 7207 3-8-8 88 HarryBentley 2 78
(A Al Raihe, UAE) *trckd ldng pair tl outpcd 3f out* **33/1**

9 1¾ **Tarbawi (IRE)**[63] 7723 3-8-8 75 TedDurcan 12 73+
(M bin Shafya, UAE) *nvr nr to chal* **50/1**

10 ¼ **Luhaif**[88] 7283 3-8-8 100 MartinHarley 9 73+
(Mick Channon) *rr of mid-div: n.d* **14/1**

11 nse **Related**[14] 46 3-8-8 84 TadhgO'Shea 1 73+
(Ernst Oertel, UAE) *v.s.a: nvr bttr than mid-div* **20/1**

12 ¼ **Desert Of Dreams**[14] 46 3-8-8 83 RoystonFfrench 7 72+
(A Al Raihe, UAE) *nvr bttr than mid-div* **28/1**

13 ¼ **Timoneer (USA)**[139] 5787 3-8-8 98 AhmedAjtebi 13 71+
(Mahmood Al Zarooni) *sn struggling in rr* **12/1**

14 1¾ **Bircham (IRE)**[97] 7028 3-8-8 79 AntiocoMurgia 4 67+
(Ismail Mohammed) *nvr bttr than mid-div* **100/1**

1m 23.68s (-1.52)
WFA 3 from 4yo 18lb **14** Ran SP% **127.8**
WIN: 2.60. PLACES: 1.00, 3.30, 3.80. CSF: 25.98..
Owner Hamdan Al Maktoum **Bred** Highlands Farm Stud (pty) Ltd **Trained** South Africa

FOCUS
This race has produced the Guineas winner in each of the three years that it's officially been named as a trial. Musir won both races in 2010, while Zanzamar in 2011 and Kinglet in 2012 ran second before taking the main event. There are a couple of ways of looking at this year's race. The winner breaks the race averages but had the run of the race up front.

246a DUBAI DUTY FREE FULL OF SURPRISES (H'CAP) (TURF) 1m 4f 11y
5:25 (5:25) (95-105,102) 3-Y-O+

£40,490 (£13,496; £6,748; £3,374; £2,024; £1,349)

RPR

1 **Anatolian**[208] 3372 5-9-3 102 MickaelBarzalona 2 100+
(Mahmood Al Zarooni) *trckd ldrs: led ins fnl f: jst hld on* **8/1**[3]

2 hd **Ahzeemah (IRE)**[131] 6025 4-9-0 102 (p) SilvestreDeSousa 4 101+
(Saeed bin Suroor) *mid-div: rdn 3f out: r.o fnl 1 1/2f: jst failed* **3/1**[2]

3 ¼ **Star Empire (SAF)**[693] 677 7-9-3 102 ChristopheSoumillon 15 100+
(M F De Kock, South Africa) *mid-div: chsd ldrs 2f out: one pce fnl f* **10/1**

4 ¼ **In The Spotlight (IND)**[109] 5-9-3 102 RyanMoore 5 99
(S Padmanabhan, India) *trckd ldrs: rdn 3f out: led 1 1/2f out: hdd ins fnl f: kpt on one pce* **9/4**[1]

5 ¼ **Certerach (IRE)**[90] 7233 5-9-3 102 ShaneFoley 7 99
(M Halford, Ire) *settled in rr: r.o fnl 2f: nrst fin* **16/1**

6 ¾ **Art Scholar (IRE)**[50] 7895 6-9-0 99 MartinHarley 8 95
(Michael Appleby) *settled in rr: r.o fnl 1 1/2f: nrst fin* **14/1**

7 1½ **Eddie Jock (IRE)**[20] 8282 9-8-9 95 (t) HarryBentley 1 87
(S Seemar, UAE) *mid-div: kpt on same pce fnl 1 1/2f* **25/1**

8 1¼ **Ithoughtitwasover (IRE)**[208] 3372 5-9-1 100 KierenFallon 10 91
(Mark Johnston) *in rr of mid-div: kpt on one pce fnl 1 1/2f* **16/1**

9 ½ **Sadeek's Song (USA)**[244] 2253 5-9-0 99 AhmedAjtebi 3 89
(Mahmood Al Zarooni) *in rr of mid-div: kpt on same pce fnl 1 1/2f* **25/1**

10 ½ **Royaaty (IRE)**[14] 45 7-8-9 95 TedDurcan 11 84
(M bin Shafya, UAE) *trckd ldng pair tl wknd 2 1/2f* **12/1**

11 ¾ **Bob Le Beau (IRE)**[145] 5600 6-9-1 100 GaryCarroll 13 88
(Mrs John Harrington, Ire) *nvr bttr than mid-div* **16/1**

12 1¾ **Concordat**[62] 7764 5-8-13 98 (bt) RichardMullen 16 84
(S Seemar, UAE) *settled in rr: n.d* **40/1**

13 ¾ **Chicago (IRE)**[149] 5462 4-8-10 99 TadhgO'Shea 6 83
(John Patrick Shanahan, Ire) *slowly away: settled in rr: n.d* **14/1**

14 ¼ **Sham Sheer**[7] 152 7-9-1 100 WayneSmith 14 84
(Fawzi Abdulla Nass, Bahrain) *sn led: kicked clr 4f out: hdd & wknd 1 1/1f out* **12/1**

15 hd **Submariner (USA)**[6] 179 7-9-2 101 PatCosgrave 9 85
(A bin Huzaim, UAE) *in rr of mid-div: nvr able to chal* **33/1**

16 ¼ **Kidnapped (AUS)**[329] 678 7-8-13 98 (vt) RoystonFfrench 12 81
(S Seemar, UAE) *settled in rr: nvr nr to chal* **40/1**

2m 31.59s (151.59)
WFA 4 from 5yo+ 4lb **16** Ran SP% **137.8**
WIN: 11.70. CSF: 34.86. TRICAST: 266.25. PLACEPOT: £29.30. Pool £8,239.25 - 204.95 winning units. QUADPOT: £10.20. Pool £447.80 - 32.10 winning units..
Owner Godolphin **Bred** Darley **Trained** Newmarket, Suffolk

FOCUS
Ignoring the clear leader (and ultimately well-beaten) Sham Sheer, the main pack were taken along by In The Spotlight and her sectionals showed she gradually upped the ante, going 27.18, 26.06, 25.86, 25.11, 23.46, 24.05 (last split ten metres longer than the others). There was a bunch finish but the form makes sense.

227 LINGFIELD (L-H)
Friday, January 18
247 Meeting Abandoned - snow

234 WOLVERHAMPTON (A.W) (L-H)
Friday, January 18
254 Meeting Abandoned - snow

262 - 269a (Foreign Racing) - See Raceform Interactive

CAGNES-SUR-MER

Friday, January 18

OFFICIAL GOING: Fibresand: standard

270a PRIX CHERET (MAIDEN) (3YO) (FIBRESAND) 1m (F)

1:20 (12:00) 3-Y-O £9,756 (£3,902; £2,926; £1,951; £975)

RPR

1 **Julius Quercus (IRE)**[105] 3-8-10 0.......................... AntoineCoutier(6) 9 78
(F Chappet, France) 49/10

2 3 1/2 **Carletti (IRE)**[29] 8192 3-9-2 0.......................... MircoDemuro 3 70
(G Botti, France) 48/10[3]

3 nk **Serenissime (USA)**[34] 3-8-13 0.......................... StephanePasquier 5 66
(C Ferland, France) 23/10[1]

4 1/2 **Snowy Dawn**[77] 7517 3-9-2 0.......................... Francois-XavierBertras 8 68
(Reg Hollinshead) *racd in midfield on outside: swung wd into st: r.o u.p fnl f: wnt 4th 50yds out* 14/1

5 1/2 **Chrysos (GER)**[161] 3-9-2 0.......................... GregoryBenoist 6 67
(J-C Rouget, France) 7/2[2]

6 3/4 **Elabela (IRE)**[67] 3-8-13 0.......................... FabienLefebvre 10 62
(J E Hammond, France) 20/1

7 2 **Moorway (IRE)**[88] 7289 3-9-2 0.......................... JackDuern 4 60
(Reg Hollinshead) *racd in midfield on ins: rdn early in st: chsd ldrs: no ex fnl f* 40/1

8 6 **Saluberlin (FR)** 3-8-8 0.......................... SoufianeSaadi(8) 2 47
(J-C Rouget, France) 9/1

9 1 1/2 **Mesharc (FR)**[35] 3-9-2 0.......................... TonyPiccone 1 43
(Mme C Barande-Barbe, France) 31/1

10 3 **Primadonna Girl (IRE)**[9] 126 3-8-13 0.......................... MickaelForest 7 33
(C Boutin, France) 34/1

1m 38.17s (98.17) 10 Ran SP% 116.6
WIN (incl. 1 euro stake): 5.90. PLACES: 1.80, 1.50, 1.40. DF: 11.20. SF: 21.90.
Owner Ecurie Loic Appere **Bred** D Chassagneux **Trained** France

220 KEMPTON (A.W) (R-H)

Saturday, January 19

OFFICIAL GOING: Standard changing to standard to slow after race 3 (2:55)

Wind: Moderate, across towards stands Weather: Lying snow, overcast

271 WILLIAM HILL - DOWNLOAD THE APP FILLIES' H'CAP 7f (P)

1:45 (1:47) (Class 5) (0-70,70) 4-Y-O+ £2,911 (£866; £432; £216) Stalls Low

Form RPR

41-2 1 **Big Sylv (IRE)**[15] 61 4-8-8 57.......................... (p) DavidProbert 1 70
(James Unett) *t.k.h: prom: led over 1f out: rdn clr: readily* 11/4[2]

425- 2 3 **Amosite**[19] 8305 7-9-0 66 ow2.......................... (p) PatrickHills(3) 2 71
(J R Jenkins) *led: rdn over 2f out: hdd over 1f out: unable qck* 12/1

3-22 3 3/4 **Climaxfortackle (IRE)**[4] 214 5-8-13 62.......................... FrannyNorton 4 65
(Derek Shaw) *s.s: hld up in rr: hdwy over 2f out: one pce appr fnl f* 7/2[3]

63-5 4 1 1/4 **Chambles**[10] 116 4-9-0 63.......................... SeanLevey 3 63
(Alan McCabe) *dwlt: sn in tch: rdn over 2f out: one pce* 8/1

21-2 5 3/4 **Glastonberry**[10] 116 5-9-6 69.......................... GeorgeBaker 7 67
(Geoffrey Deacon) *hld up in rr: sme hdwy in 5th whn n.m.r ent fnl f: nvr able to chal* 15/8[1]

60-6 6 1 1/4 **Dancing Welcome**[13] 86 7-8-13 69.......................... (b) RyanTate(7) 8 63
(Milton Bradley) *chsd ldrs: rdn 3f out: sn outpcd* 20/1

40-0 7 8 **Ishiamiracle**[8] 159 4-8-4 58.......................... (v[1]) LeonnaMayor(5) 5 31
(Phil McEntee) *plld hrd: pressed ldr: rdn 3f out: wknd qckly 2f out* 50/1

1m 26.63s (0.63) **Going Correction** +0.175s/f (Slow) 7 Ran SP% 109.2
Speed ratings (Par 100): **103,99,98,97,96 95,85**
toteswingers 1&2 £5.20, 1&3 £2.20, 2&3 £3.90 CSF £30.99 CT £105.28 TOTE £4.10: £2.30, £5.30; EX 34.10 Trifecta £100.70 Pool: £6,969.74 - 51.89 winning units..
Owner Miss Ciara Doyle **Bred** John Doyle **Trained** Tedsmore Hall, Shropshire

FOCUS

Little got into this modest handicap.

272 WILLIAM HILL - IPAD APP NOW AVAILABLE H'CAP 1m (P)

2:20 (2:20) (Class 4) (0-80,77) 4-Y-O+ £5,175 (£1,540; £769; £384) Stalls Low

Form RPR

15-1 1 **Toga Tiger (IRE)**[11] 104 6-8-13 72.......................... RaulDaSilva(3) 9 79
(Jeremy Gask) *trckd ldr: rdn to ld briefly over 2f out: edgd lft: rallied fnl f: led again on line* 4/1[3]

5-00 2 nse **Diplomatic (IRE)**[3] 222 8-8-5 68.......................... (p) RobertTart(7) 4 75
(Michael Squance) *hld up in rr: rdn over 2f out: gd hdwy fr over 1f out: fin wl* 25/1

41-2 3 shd **Light From Mars**[4] 217 8-9-7 77.......................... LukeMorris 5 84
(Ronald Harris) *prom: led 2f out: hrd rdn fnl f: jst ct* 3/1[2]

12-3 4 hd **Haftohaf**[9] 133 4-9-5 75.......................... AndreaAtzeni 6 81
(Marco Botti) *hld up in tch: effrt 2f out: styd on fnl f* 2/1[1]

53-5 5 3/4 **Angelic Upstart (IRE)**[18] 6 5-9-0 77.......................... (v[1]) ThomasBrown(7) 7 82
(Andrew Balding) *hld up in rr: rdn 3f out: styd on wl fnl f* 4/1[3]

11-3 6 2 **Storm Runner (IRE)**[9] 138 5-8-4 67.......................... JordanVaughan(7) 8 67
(George Margarson) *chsd ldrs: rdn over 2f out: btn over 1f out* 16/1

21-1 7 2 1/2 **Avertis**[9] 138 8-8-13 74.......................... AmyScott(5) 3 68
(Alastair Lidderdale) *led tl over 2f out: wknd over 1f out* 12/1

1m 40.53s (0.73) **Going Correction** +0.175s/f (Slow) 7 Ran SP% 115.8
Speed ratings (Par 105): **103,102,102,102,101 99,97**
toteswingers 1&2 £18.20, 1&3 £3.70, 2&3 £8.80 CSF £87.60 CT £341.15 TOTE £5.70: £2.80, £7.20; EX 157.10 Trifecta £503.00 Pool: £5,695.21 - 8.49 winning units..
Owner For Sale **Bred** Daniel Spaight **Trained** Sutton Veny, Wilts

FOCUS

The early pace was steady in what looked a fair race for the grade and the race produced a predictably tight finish, with the first four being split by a whisker.

273 WILLIAM HILL - IPHONE, IPAD, IPAD MINI H'CAP (LONDON MIDDLE DISTANCE QUALIFIER) 1m 3f (P)

2:55 (2:55) (Class 3) (0-95,88) 4-Y-O+ £7,762 (£2,310; £1,154; £577) Stalls Low

Form RPR

063- 1 **Spifer (IRE)**[23] 8259 5-9-4 85.......................... (p) AndreaAtzeni 5 93
(Marco Botti) *hld up in 5th: effrt 2f out: styd on to ld fnl 75yds* 9/2[3]

566- 2 shd **Greylami (IRE)**[58] 7825 8-8-11 85.......................... RyanTate(7) 6 93
(Clive Cox) *chsd ldrs: rdn to ld 1f out: hdd fnl 75yds: kpt on wl* 8/1

22-1 3 1/2 **Noble Silk**[12] 93 4-8-13 83.......................... (p) LukeMorris 1 90
(Lucy Wadham) *prom: rdn to ld briefly over 1f out: kpt on* 11/4[2]

153- 4 nk **Fluctuate (USA)**[156] 5273 4-9-4 88.......................... (b[1]) RobertHavlin 4 94
(John Gosden) *t.k.h: trckd ldr: led 2f out tl over 1f out: kpt on* 7/4[1]

-121 5 9 **Kames Park (IRE)**[6] 198 11-9-0 81 6ex.......................... RobbieFitzpatrick 3 71
(Richard Guest) *stdd s: t.k.h: hld up and bhd: rdn and sme hdwy over 1f out: sn wknd* 20/1

0/ 6 1 1/2 **Gaelic Silver (FR)**[24] 7-9-4 85.......................... GeorgeBaker 7 73
(Gary Moore) *stdd s: hld up and bhd: effrt 2f out: no imp* 33/1

11-2 7 2 1/2 **Aquilonius (IRE)**[18] 6 4-9-1 85.......................... (t) SeanLevey 2 68
(Stuart Williams) *led: lugged lft on home turn: hdd & wknd 2f out* 7/1

2m 22.08s (0.18) **Going Correction** +0.175s/f (Slow)
WFA 4 from 5yo+ 3lb 7 Ran SP% **112.5**
Speed ratings (Par 107): **106,105,105,105,98 97,95**
toteswingers 1&2 £5.10, 1&3 £5.10, 2&3 £4.80 CSF £37.84 TOTE £4.70: £1.60, £4.60; EX 33.90 Trifecta £125.80 Pool: £7,538.72 - 44.94 winning units..
Owner Op Center One **Bred** Tullamaine Castle Stud **Trained** Newmarket, Suffolk

FOCUS

A decent handicap that should produce winners. It developed into something of a dash down the straight.

274 WILLIAM HILL - NO.1 DOWNLOADED BETTING APP H'CAP 7f (P)

3:30 (3:30) (Class 6) (0-57,57) 4-Y-O+ £2,264 (£673; £336; £168) Stalls Low

Form RPR

12-5 1 **Welsh Inlet (IRE)**[16] 35 5-9-2 57.......................... WilliamTwiston-Davies(5) 1 67
(John Bridger) *mid-div on rail: hdwy 2f out: styd on to ld ins fnl f: rdn out* 5/1[2]

00-6 2 3/4 **Katmai River (IRE)**[15] 50 6-8-13 56.......................... EmilyMelbourn(7) 3 64
(Mark Usher) *prom: led 2f out tl ins fnl f: kpt on* 12/1

5-04 3 1/2 **Spinning Ridge (IRE)**[10] 118 8-9-7 57.......................... (v) LukeMorris 9 64
(Ronald Harris) *dwlt: hld up towards rr: hdwy over 2f out: pressed ldrs 1f out: unable qck* 5/1[2]

0-05 4 1 3/4 **Dvinsky (USA)**[9] 130 12-9-5 55.......................... (b) FrannyNorton 4 57
(Paul Howling) *drvn to ld: hdd 2f out: one pce fnl f* 14/1

433- 5 1 1/4 **Michael's Nook**[23] 8257 6-8-7 48.......................... (p) LeonnaMayor(5) 11 47
(Alastair Lidderdale) *s.s: t.k.h in rr: sltly wd on home turn: shkn up and styd on fr over 1f out: nvr nrr* 5/1[2]

60-0 6 1 **Mambo Spirit (IRE)**[16] 30 9-9-7 57.......................... WilliamCarson 6 53
(Tony Newcombe) *s.i.s: bhd: rdn 3f out: sme late hdwy* 16/1

0-6 7 1 1/4 **Back For Tea (IRE)**[10] 114 5-8-3 46 oh1.......................... (v) RyanTate(7) 2 38
(Phil McEntee) *chsd ldrs: rdn over 2f out: sn outpcd* 25/1

21-0 8 1 3/4 **Jackie Love (IRE)**[10] 117 5-9-1 51.......................... (v) KirstyMilczarek 7 39
(Olivia Maylam) *in rr of midfield: rdn 3f out: sn struggling* 6/1[3]

03-0 9 1/2 **Rogue Reporter (IRE)**[15] 61 4-9-6 56.......................... (v) AndreaAtzeni 8 42
(Stuart Williams) *in tch: hrd rdn over 2f out: sn wknd* 7/2[1]

00-0 10 10 **Justbookies Dotnet**[10] 115 4-9-5 55.......................... (v) IanMongan 10 14
(Louise Best) *chsd ldr tl wknd over 2f out* 20/1

1m 27.18s (1.18) **Going Correction** +0.175s/f (Slow) 10 Ran SP% **115.4**
Speed ratings (Par 101): **100,99,98,96,95 94,92,90,90,78**
toteswingers 1&2 £8.50, 1&3 £5.90, 2&3 £10.90 CSF £62.61 CT £322.37 TOTE £4.20: £1.50, £3.50, £2.60; EX 74.40 Trifecta £428.90 Pool: £81,901.33 - 143.19 winning units..
Owner Kevin J Walls **Bred** Patrick Gleeson **Trained** Liphook, Hants

FOCUS

A moderate handicap.

275 WILLIAM HILL - IPAD APP NOW AVAILABLE MAIDEN FILLIES' STKS 1m 3f (P)

4:05 (4:07) (Class 5) 3-Y-O+ £3,067 (£905; £453) Stalls Low

Form RPR

53-2 1 **Gertrude Versed**[14] 74 3-8-4 66.......................... FrannyNorton 1 79+
(John Gosden) *mde all: shkn up and qcknd clr 1f out: easily* 4/5[1]

42-2 2 7 **Easy Life**[12] 90 3-8-4 63.......................... KieranO'Neill 3 64
(Marcus Tregoning) *prom: rdn over 3f out: wnt 2nd over 1f out: no ch w wnr* 7/1[3]

22- 3 1 3/4 **Lascaux**[256] 1957 4-9-11 0.......................... IanMongan 5 64
(Luke Dace) *s.i.s: bhd: hdwy 6f out: rdn to chal for 2nd over 1f out: no ex* 10/1

2-4 4 4 1/2 **Too Difficult (IRE)**[14] 74 3-8-4 0.......................... DavidProbert 6 53
(Andrew Balding) *pressed wnr: rdn over 2f out: wknd over 1f out* 4/1[2]

3- 5 8 **Taming The Tweet**[22] 8270 3-8-4 0.......................... AndreaAtzeni 7 38
(Alan McCabe) *hld up in 5th: pushed along fr 1m out: lost pl over 4f out: n.d after* 8/1

0/ 6 12 **Narla**[436] 7343 4-9-11 0.......................... GeorgeBaker 9 20
(Clive Cox) *chsd ldrs tl wknd over 2f out* 14/1

00-4 7 3 1/4 **Lea Valley**[17] 14 4-9-4 42.......................... ShelleyBirkett(7) 4 14
(Julia Feilden) *hld up in 6th: rdn 4f out: sn bhd* 100/1

8 10 **Santorini Sunset** 4-9-8 0.......................... PatrickHills(3) 2
(J R Jenkins) *rn green: sn bhd: reminder 5f out: no ch fnl 3f* 50/1

2m 22.24s (0.34) **Going Correction** +0.175s/f (Slow)
WFA 3 from 4yo 24lb 4 from 5yo 3lb 8 Ran SP% **117.9**
Speed ratings (Par 100): **105,99,98,95,89 80,78,71**
toteswingers 1&2 £2.30, 1&3 £2.90, 2&3 £5.00 CSF £7.65 TOTE £1.80: £1.10, £1.40, £1.10; EX 6.10 Trifecta £27.70 Pool: £5,415.03 - 146.24 winning units..
Owner Ms Rachel D S Hood **Bred** Ms Rachel Hood **Trained** Newmarket, Suffolk

FOCUS

No great depth to this moderate maiden and a straightforward success for the odds-on favourite.

276 WILLIAM HILL - DOWNLOAD APP H'CAP (DIV I) 6f (P)

4:35 (4:36) (Class 6) (0-55,55) 4-Y-O+ £2,264 (£673; £336; £168) Stalls Low

Form RPR

32- 1 **Valdaw**[21] 8287 5-9-7 55.......................... EddieAhern 1 70+
(Mike Murphy) *hld up in 5th: effrt over 2f out: led over 1f out: drvn out* 10/11[1]

10-0 2 2 1/4 **Lord Buffhead**[14] 76 4-9-6 54.......................... (v) RobbieFitzpatrick 3 62
(Richard Guest) *w ldrs on rail: led 4f out tl over 1f out: unable qck fnl f* 8/1

00-0 3 2 3/4 **Venetias Dream (IRE)**[15] 62 4-9-0 48.......................... (vt[1]) SeanLevey 4 47
(Stuart Williams) *dwlt and rdn s: sn in midfield: hdwy over 1f out: styd on same pce fnl f* 14/1

4-56 4 1 1/4 **Brandywell Boy (IRE)**[3] 233 10-8-10 51.......................... JoshBaudains(7) 6 46
(Dominic Ffrench Davis) *w ldrs: rdn over 2f out: sn outpcd* 12/1

600- 5 1 **The Bendy Fella (IRE)**[304] 981 5-9-7 55.......................... GeorgeBaker 7 47
(Mark Usher) *stdd s: hld up and bhd: shkn up and styd on fnl 2f: nvr nrr* 11/2[2]

65-1 6 3 3/4 **Glennten**13 87 4-9-2 55 LeeNewnes(5) 11 35
(Sylvester Kirk) *w ldrs on outer tl rdn and btn over 2f out* 6/1³
2-24 7 15 **Summer Sun**10 114 4-9-4 52 DavidProbert 10
(Phil McEntee) *slt ld 2f: rdn over 2f out: sn hanging and wknd* 12/1
00-0 8 2 1/2 **Takajan (IRE)**13 87 6-8-12 46 oh1 FrannyNorton 8
(Mark Brisbourne) *in rr of midfield: rdn over 2f out: n.d after* 50/1
1m 13.28s (0.18) **Going Correction** +0.175s/f (Slow) 8 Ran SP% **117.2**
Speed ratings (Par 101): **105,102,98,96,95 90,70,67**
toteswingers 1&2 £3.10, 1&3 £4.60, 2&3 £16.20 CSF £9.47 CT £65.28 TOTE £1.50: £1.02, £3.20, £3.80; EX 11.90 Trifecta £121.60 Pool: £3,593.57 - 22.16 winning units..
Owner D Spratt **Bred** Mayden Stud, J A And D S Dewhurst **Trained** Westoning, Beds
FOCUS
A moderate sprint handicap.

277 WILLIAM HILL - DOWNLOAD APP H'CAP (DIV II) 6f (P)
5:05 (5:05) (Class 6) (0-55,55) 4-Y-O+ £2,264 (£673; £336; £168) **Stalls** Low

Form RPR
05-3 1 **Whipphound**9 143 5-9-7 55 GeorgeBaker 9 62+
(Mark Brisbourne) *prom: led wl over 1f out: hrd rdn ent fnl f: hld on under hands and heels fnl 100yds* 7/2²
100- 2 nk **Artful Lady (IRE)**29 8205 4-9-2 50 IanMongan 4 56
(George Margarson) *in tch: rdn over 2f out: styd on fnl f: wnt 2nd nr fin* 11/2³
5-24 3 nk **Sherjawy (IRE)**8 156 9-9-4 52 KirstyMilczarek 2 57
(Zoe Davison) *cl up: rdn to press wnr over 1f out: r.o* 10/1
-244 4 nse **Ryedale Dancer (IRE)**4 213 5-9-7 55 RobbieFitzpatrick 6 60
(Richard Guest) *hld up in rr: hdwy 2f out: drvn to press wnr ins fnl f: r.o* 3/1¹
-603 5 1/2 **Jonnie Skull (IRE)**8 156 7-9-6 54 (vt) DavidProbert 3 57
(Phil McEntee) *led tl wl over 1f out: kpt on wl u.p* 7/2²
00-0 6 3 1/4 **Flying Kitty**10 120 4-8-12 46 oh1 (v¹) KieranO'Neill 1 39
(John Bridger) *in tch: effrt 2f out: wknd over 1f out* 14/1
4-00 7 3 **Fantasy Fighter (IRE)**9 128 8-8-13 47 (be¹) LukeMorris 8 30
(Ronald Harris) *towards rr: mod effrt over 2f out: wknd over 1f out* 8/1
-653 8 2 1/4 **Slatey Hen (IRE)**10 111 5-9-1 49 (p) WilliamCarson 10 25
(Violet M Jordan) *chsd ldr tl wknd 2f out* 10/1
1m 13.95s (0.85) **Going Correction** +0.175s/f (Slow) 8 Ran SP% **120.8**
Speed ratings (Par 101): **101,100,100,100,99 95,91,88**
toteswingers 1&2 £4.20, 1&3 £8.40, 2&3 £11.60 CSF £24.59 CT £182.23 TOTE £2.70: £1.50, £1.50, £3.70; EX 28.50 Trifecta £242.80 Pool: £3,096.42 - 9.56 winning units..
Owner W M Clare **Bred** Mrs B Skinner **Trained** Great Ness, Shropshire
FOCUS
More competitive than the first division.
T/Plt: £256.40 to a £1 stake. Pool: £167,780.78 - 477.60 winning tickets T/Qpdt: £18.70 to a £1 stake. Pool: £13,882.00 - 547.98 winning tickets LM

227 LINGFIELD (L-H)
Saturday, January 19
278 Meeting Abandoned - snow

270 CAGNES-SUR-MER
Saturday, January 19
OFFICIAL GOING: Fibresand: standard

286a PRIX JOSEPH COLLIGNON (CONDITIONS) (3YO) (FIBRESAND) 1m (F)
1:15 (12:00) 3-Y-O £15,040 (£6,016; £4,512; £3,008; £1,504)

RPR
1 **Calvin Williams (FR)**53 3-8-11 0 AnthonyCrastus 9 90
(E Lellouche, France) 58/10
2 2 **Courcy (FR)**151 5471 3-9-1 0 GregoryBenoist 6 89
(J-C Rouget, France) 43/10³
3 snk **Aldo Bere (FR)**20 3-8-11 0 (b) JohanVictoire 4 85
(C Boutin, France) 21/1
4 1 **Le Ring (FR)**70 7692 3-9-1 0 FranckBlondel 8 86
(F Rossi, France) 5/1
5 3 **San Juan (FR)**46 7984 3-9-1 0 (b) MarcLerner 1 79
(C Lerner, France) 32/1
6 1 **Dha Chara (IRE)**57 7840 3-8-11 0 JackDuern 2 73?
(Reg Hollinshead) *broke slowly: rdn to r in midfield on ins: proged to 4th ent st: r.o u.p: no ex fr 1 1/2f out: styd on one pce* 59/1
7 1 1/2 **Number Winner (FR)** 3-8-11 0 MircoDemuro 7 70
(M Gentile, France) 7/1
8 1 1/2 **Linngaro (FR)**26 3-9-1 0 ThierryThulliez 5 70
(Mario Hofer, Germany) 4/1²
9 4 1/2 **Victory De Rebecq (USA)**120 3-8-11 0 PaulineProd'homme 3 56
(D Prod'Homme, France) 3/1¹
1m 37.33s (97.33) 9 Ran SP% **117.0**
WIN (incl. 1 euro stake): 6.80. PLACES: 2.30, 2.20, 4.10. DF: 12.00. SF: 26.80.
Owner Jean-Andre Zay **Bred** M Chartier **Trained** Lamorlaye, France

287 - 289a (Foreign Racing) - See Raceform Interactive

241 MEYDAN (L-H)
Saturday, January 19
OFFICIAL GOING: Tapeta: standard; turf: good

290a AL NABOODAH CONSTRUCTION GROUP TROPHY (H'CAP) (TURF) 6f
4:15 (4:15) (85-100,99) 3-Y-O+ £9,045 (£3,015; £1,658; £904; £452)

RPR
1 **Take Ten**44 8012 6-8-11 91 PatCosgrave 9 95
(S Seemar, UAE) *trckd ldrs: led 1f out: r.o wl* 20/1
2 3/4 **Les Troyens**308 948 5-9-0 94 TedDurcan 7 96
(Saeed bin Suroor) *nvr bttr than mid-div* 15/2³
3 1/4 **Golden Shaheen (IRE)**8 181 6-8-3 93 ow5 AAlSubosi(10) 16 89
(M bin Shafya, UAE) *mid-div: r.o fnl 2f: nrst fin* 50/1
4 hd **Silaah**8 182 9-8-10 90 (p) PatDobbs 15 90
(M Ramadan, UAE) *chsd ldrs: ev ch 1 1/2f out: nt qckn fnl 110yds* 20/1
5 1/2 **Royal Ridge (SAF)**294 5-9-5 99 PaulHanagan 3 98
(M F De Kock, South Africa) *trckd ldrs: led 2 1/2f out: hdd 1f out: kpt on same pce* 6/1²
6 1/4 **Ahtoug**161 5077 5-9-5 99 KierenFallon 4 97
(Mahmood Al Zarooni) *chsd ldrs: ev ch 1f out: nt qckn fnl 110yds* 5/2¹
7 1/4 **Mutheeb (USA)**22 8283 8-9-3 97 DaneO'Neill 1 94
(M Al Muhairi, UAE) *mid-div: smooth prog 2f out: nt qckn fnl f* 16/1
8 1/2 **Santefisio**66 7709 7-9-4 98 (b) GaryCarroll 14 93
(Keith Dalgleish) *nvr bttr than mid-div* 9/1
9 hd **Hajoum (IRE)**36 8128 7-9-2 96 (bt) HarryBentley 8 91
(A Al Raihe, UAE) *chsd ldrs: ev ch 1f out: nt qckn fnl 110yds* 11/1
10 2 1/4 **Firestreak**22 8280 8-9-3 97 WayneSmith 2 85
(M Al Muhairi, UAE) *nvr able to chal* 14/1
11 2 1/2 **Kaiss (USA)**22 8280 6-8-13 93 (t) RichardMullen 11 73
(S Seemar, UAE) *nvr nr to chal* 12/1
12 3 **Noor Zabeel (USA)**30 8196 4-9-3 97 RoystonFfrench 10 67
(A Al Raihe, UAE) *trckd ldrs tl outpcd 1 1/2f out* 16/1
13 2 1/4 **Mon Cadeaux**8 181 6-9-4 98 DaraghO'Donohoe 6 61
(A bin Huzaim, UAE) *slowly away: nvr able to chal* 33/1
14 3/4 **Mysticism (USA)**155 5-9-4 98 (v) SilvestreDeSousa 5 58
(Saeed bin Suroor) *sn led: hdd 2 1/2f out: kpt on same pce fnl f* 8/1
15 1 **Hazaz (IRE)**16 43 4-8-8 95 (t) SaeedAlMazrooei(7) 13 52
(A Al Raihe, UAE) *a in rr* 16/1
16 2 1/4 **League Champion (USA)**330 705 10-8-7 87 ow2 AhmedAjtebi 12 35
(M Ramadan, UAE) *nvr able to chal* 50/1
1m 10.88s (70.88) 16 Ran SP% **132.5**
WIN: 77.60 CSF: 169.65 EX: 2710.00 TRICAST: 7345.35 TRIFECTA: 15311.70.
Owner Sheikh Hamdan Bin Mohammed Al Maktoum **Bred** Whitsbury Manor Stud & Mrs M E Slade **Trained** United Arab Emirates

291 - 292a (Foreign Racing) - See Raceform Interactive

271 KEMPTON (A.W) (R-H)
Sunday, January 20
293 Meeting Abandoned - snow

271 KEMPTON (A.W) (R-H)
Monday, January 21
300 Meeting Abandoned - snow

234 WOLVERHAMPTON (A.W) (L-H)
Monday, January 21
OFFICIAL GOING: Slow changing to standard to slow after race 1 (2.35)
Wind: Light across Weather: Overcast

308 EXCLUSIVE FREE BETS AT BOOKMAKERS.CO.UK H'CAP 5f 20y(P)
2:35 (2:35) (Class 5) (0-70,70) 4-Y-O+ £2,587 (£770; £384; £192) **Stalls** Low

Form RPR
00-3 1 **Cardinal**19 27 8-9-6 69 TomEaves 3 79
(Robert Cowell) *hld up: hdwy over 1f out: rdn to ld and edgd rt ins fnl f: r.o* 6/1³
4-10 2 1 1/2 **Desert Strike**9 187 7-9-2 70 (p) WilliamTwiston-Davies(5) 1 75
(Conor Dore) *led 1f: chsd ldrs: pushed along 1/2-way: edgd rt and ev ch ins fnl f: styd on same pce* 14/1
01-2 3 nk **Strong Man**15 86 5-9-5 68 (b) GrahamGibbons 9 72
(Michael Easterby) *chsd ldrs: rdn over 1f out: edgd lft ins fnl f: styd on same pce* 9/4²
30-0 4 3/4 **Shawkantango**15 86 6-8-9 65 (v) AdamMcLean(7) 8 67
(Derek Shaw) *s.i.s: bhd: rdn and r.o ins fnl f: nt rch ldrs* 25/1
021- 5 shd **Passionada**49 7969 4-9-5 68 RobertWinston 7 70+
(Ed McMahon) *prom: hmpd and lost pl wl over 3f out: hdwy over 1f out: r.o* 15/8¹
000- 6 1 **No Mean Trick (USA)**23 8285 7-8-12 61 MickyFenton 2 60
(Paul Midgley) *w ldrs tl rdn to ld over 1f out: hdd ins fnl f: hmpd and no ex sn after* 8/1
2-64 7 3/4 **Master Of Disguise**6 214 7-9-2 65 (vt¹) DuranFentiman 6 61
(Brian Baugh) *led 4f out: rdn and hdd over 1f out: hmpd and no ex ins fnl f* 13/2
000- 8 1/2 **Crimson Queen**23 8285 6-9-4 70 (b) MarkCoumbe(3) 4 64
(Roy Brotherton) *prom: rdn over 1f out: hmpd ins fnl f: wknd towards fin* 40/1
646- 9 2 **You'relikemefrank**221 3065 7-8-5 61 (p) VictorSantos(7) 5 49
(Richard Ford) *sn pushed along in rr: rdn over 1f out: wknd fnl f* 40/1
1m 2.6s (0.30) **Going Correction** +0.225s/f (Slow) 9 Ran SP% **119.7**
Speed ratings (Par 103): **106,103,103,101,101 100,98,98,94**
Tote Swingers: 1&2 £10.10, 1&3 £2.70, 2&3 £6.80 CSF £85.21 CT £246.84 TOTE £6.00: £1.50, £3.70, £1.40; EX 41.90 Trifecta £201.30 Pool: £4,477.52 - 16.67 winning units..
Owner Mrs J May **Bred** The Queen **Trained** Six Mile Bottom, Cambs
FOCUS
The surface was described as 'slow'. A modest sprint handicap but some in-form horses in opposition. The pace was good and the winner is rated to last year's turf form.

309 CORAL.CO.UK H'CAP 1m 5f 194y(P)
3:05 (3:05) (Class 5) (0-75,75) 4-Y-O+ £2,587 (£770; £384; £192) **Stalls** Low

Form RPR
640- 1 **Rapid Heat Lad (IRE)**84 3345 4-9-3 72 (p) DanielTudhope 6 81
(Reg Hollinshead) *a.p: chsd ldr 8f out: led over 2f out: rdn over 1f out: styd on wl* 13/2³
213- 2 1 1/2 **Alborz (IRE)**35 5528 4-9-2 71 ShaneKelly 4 78+
(Tim Vaughan) *led 1f: chsd ldr tl 8f out: hmpd over 3f out: rdn to go 2nd again over 1f out: unable qck wl ins fnl f* 9/2²
323- 3 2 **Thundering Home**26 6232 6-9-4 67 RobertWinston 7 71
(Richard Mitchell) *hld up: hdwy over 1f out: sn rdn: styd on same pce ins fnl f* 13/2³
66-1 4 shd **Sohcahtoa (IRE)**17 57 7-9-4 72 LMcNiff(5) 1 76
(David Barron) *chsd ldrs: rdn over 1f out: styd on same pce ins fnl f* 11/4¹

/3-2 5 3 ½ **Priors Gold**[10] 166 6-9-5 75 JacobButterfield(7) 2 74
(Ollie Pears) *prom: hmpd over 3f out: nt clr run wl over 1f out: styd on same pce* 11/4[1]

40-0 6 13 **Volcanic Jack (IRE)**[8] 198 5-8-13 62 BarryMcHugh 3 43
(Tony Coyle) *led after 1f at stdy pce: qcknd 3f out: hdd over 2f out: wkng whn hung rt fnl f* 12/1

00-6 P **All The Winds (GER)**[17] 52 8-9-7 75 (t) WilliamTwiston-Davies(5) 8
(Shaun Lycett) *hld up: hdwy over 7f out: rdn and wknd over 2f out: sn p.u* 14/1

3m 8.23s (2.23) **Going Correction** +0.225s/f (Slow)
WFA 4 from 5yo+ 6lb 7 Ran SP% **112.5**
Speed ratings (Par 103): **102,101,100,99,97 90,**
Tote Swingers: 1&2 £6.20, 1&3 £6.00, 2&3 £2.10 CSF £34.32 CT £196.22 TOTE £9.90: £4.00, £2.70; EX 38.50 Trifecta £175.40 Pool: £3,963.95 - 16.94 winning units..
Owner Graham Brothers Racing Partnership **Bred** Roundhill Stud & Gleadhill House Stud Ltd **Trained** Upper Longdon, Staffs

FOCUS
The going was changed from slow to standard to slow after the first race. A fair staying handicap, but the pace was ordinary and the form isn't entirely convincing. It's been taken at face value.

310 GET THE INSIDE TRACK AT BOOKMAKERS.CO.UK H'CAP 7f 32y(P)
3:35 (3:35) (Class 6) (0-55,55) 3-Y-O **£1,940** (£577; £288; £144) **Stalls** High

Form RPR

336- 1 **Maypole Joe (IRE)**[32] 8186 3-9-7 55 (v) GrahamGibbons 2 60
(David Evans) *mde all: rdn clr fr over 1f out: styd on* 4/1[2]

50-3 2 2 ¼ **Armada Bay (IRE)**[14] 102 3-9-6 54 TomEaves 8 53
(Bryan Smart) *hld up: hdwy over 2f out: rdn over 1f out: swtchd rt ins fnl f: styd on to go 2nd towards fin: no ch w wnr* 10/1

260- 3 ¾ **Frans Hals**[24] 8274 3-8-11 52 (p) JoshBaudains(7) 4 49
(Dominic Ffrench Davis) *chsd ldrs: rdn over 1f out: styd on same pce* 7/1[3]

24-3 4 hd **Devout (IRE)**[18] 31 3-9-3 51 FergusSweeney 1 48
(Jamie Osborne) *prom: rdn over 1f out: styd on same pce* 13/8[1]

00-0 5 ½ **Chelsea Grey (IRE)**[17] 55 3-8-12 46 (p) RobertWinston 5 41
(Ronald Harris) *chsd wnr: rdn over 2f out: no ex ins fnl f* 15/2

00-0 6 nk **Jonny Wombat**[7] 207 3-8-5 46 oh1 VictorSantos(7) 9 40
(Richard Ford) *s.i.s: hld up: hdwy over 1f out: nt trbld ldrs* 33/1

450- 7 3 **Annalova**[125] 6335 3-8-13 47 TonyHamilton 6 33
(Richard Fahey) *hld up: rdn 1/2-way: nvr on terms* 4/1[2]

52-0 8 1 ¼ **Fat Bottom Girl**[8] 195 3-8-5 46 MatthewHopkins(7) 7 29
(Michael Easterby) *s.i.s: sn pushed along in rr: rdn over 2f out: wknd over 1f out* 25/1

06- 9 11 **Firey Sally (IRE)**[25] 8254 3-8-13 50 (bt[1]) MarkCoumbe(3) 10
(Frank Sheridan) *prom: rdn over 2f out: wknd wl over 1f out* 50/1

1m 32.29s (2.69) **Going Correction** +0.225s/f (Slow) 9 Ran SP% **120.2**
Speed ratings (Par 95): **93,90,89,89,88 88,85,83,71**
Tote Swingers: 1&2 £4.80, 1&3 £5.00, 2&3 £8.30 CSF £44.17 CT £279.44 TOTE £4.80: £1.70, £3.30, £2.70; EX 33.30 Trifecta £156.00 Pool: £4,246.46 - 20.41 winning units..
Owner Dukes Head Racing **Bred** T M Jennings **Trained** Pandy, Monmouths

FOCUS
A poor handicap, run at a steady pace. The time was fair and the winner confirmed his selling/claiming form.

311 WINNERS LOVE BOOKMAKERS.CO.UK (S) STKS 1m 141y(P)
4:05 (4:05) (Class 6) 4-Y-O+ **£1,940** (£577; £288; £144) **Stalls** Low

Form RPR

22-6 1 **Red Somerset (USA)**[11] 133 10-9-0 77 KieranO'Neill 4 83
(Mike Murphy) *hld up in tch: plld hrd: shkn up to ld 2f out: sn clr: easily* 1/1[1]

53-0 2 7 **Jack Who's He (IRE)**[11] 133 4-8-13 77 (v) GrahamGibbons 3 66
(David Evans) *trckd ldrs: rdn over 1f out: sn outpcd* 11/10[2]

035- 3 1 ½ **Faithful Ruler (USA)**[26] 8238 9-9-0 67 (p) RobertWinston 1 62
(Ronald Harris) *chsd ldr: rdn and ev ch 2f out: wknd ins fnl f* 16/1

23-3 4 7 **Imprimis Tagula (IRE)**[10] 155 9-8-9 68 (v) NatashaEaton(5) 5 46
(Alan Bailey) *led: pushed along and hdd 2f out: wknd fnl f* 12/1[3]

1m 53.08s (2.58) **Going Correction** +0.225s/f (Slow)
WFA 4 from 8yo+ 1lb 4 Ran SP% **111.2**
Speed ratings (Par 101): **97,90,89,83**
CSF £2.50 TOTE £1.40; EX 3.00 Trifecta £9.70 Pool: £2,763.84 - 212.28 winning units..The winner was bought in for 4,750gns.
Owner M Murphy **Bred** Haras D'Etreham **Trained** Westoning, Beds

FOCUS
A fair seller, despite the small field, but the time was slow and the form is shaky.

312 CASINO AT CORAL.CO.UK H'CAP 1m 141y(P)
4:35 (4:35) (Class 6) (0-55,55) 4-Y-O+ **£1,940** (£577; £288; £144) **Stalls** Low

Form RPR

050- 1 **Monzino (USA)**[56] 7731 5-9-0 55 GerardGalligan(7) 4 73
(Michael Chapman) *s.i.s: sn prom: rdn to ld wl over 1f out: clr fnl f* 12/1

50-3 2 7 **This Ones For Eddy**[8] 193 8-9-5 53 (b) DanielTudhope 9 55
(John Balding) *hld up: pushed along over 5f out: hdwy over 2f out: sn rdn: styd on to go 2nd ins fnl f: no ch w wnr* 13/2

00-2 3 3 **Meglio Ancora**[8] 193 6-9-2 55 RachealKneller(5) 7 50
(Richard Ford) *s.i.s: hld up: hdwy and swtchd lft over 1f out: nvr trbld ldrs* 3/1[2]

54-3 4 1 **Harvest Mist (IRE)**[13] 108 5-8-10 49 WilliamTwiston-Davies(5) 5 42
(Shaun Lycett) *chsd ldrs: led wl over 2f out: rdn and hdd wl over 1f out: wknd fnl f* 5/1[3]

0-20 5 1 **Justcallmehandsome**[18] 41 11-8-7 48 (be) JoshBaudains(7) 1 38
(Dominic Ffrench Davis) *sn led: hdd over 6f out: remained handy: nt clr run over 2f out: sn rdn: wknd over 1f out* 9/1

036- 6 2 ½ **Athletic**[43] 8051 4-9-6 55 (p) RobertWinston 6 40
(Alan McCabe) *prom: hung rt over 4f out: rdn over 2f out: nt run on* 5/4[1]

00-0 7 7 **Johnson's Cat (IRE)**[15] 88 4-8-6 46 oh1 ShirleyTeasdale(5) 2 15
(Mandy Rowland) *chsd ldr tl led over 6f out: hdd wl over 2f out: wknd over 1f out* 80/1

1m 51.42s (0.92) **Going Correction** +0.225s/f (Slow)
WFA 4 from 5yo+ 1lb 7 Ran SP% **118.4**
Speed ratings (Par 101): **104,97,95,94,93 91,84**
Tote Swingers: 1&2 £7.40, 1&3 £6.40, 2&3 £3.50 CSF £89.38 CT £299.56 TOTE £23.00: £10.40, £1.10; EX 83.00 Trifecta £385.20 Pool: £2,942.20 - 5.72 winning units..
Owner Mrs M Chapman **Bred** Pillar Property Services Inc **Trained** Market Rasen, Lincs
■ Gerard Galligan's first Flat winner.

FOCUS
A desperately weak handicap. The winner is rated back to form.

313 FREE BETS GALORE AT BOOKMAKERS.CO.UK MAIDEN STKS 1m 1f 103y(P)
5:05 (5:05) (Class 5) 4-Y-O+ **£2,587** (£770; £384; £192) **Stalls** Low

Form RPR

224- 1 **Exning Halt**[97] 7131 4-9-5 74 TomEaves 4 74+
(John Quinn) *chsd ldrs: led on bit over 2f out: shkn up and clr fr over 1f out* 2/7[1]

450- 2 7 **Yojojo (IRE)**[83] 7470 4-9-0 55 StevieDonohoe 7 54
(Gay Kelleway) *trckd ldr: racd keenly: led over 6f out: hdd 4f out: rdn over 1f out: styd on same pce* 12/1[3]

3 10 **Pullmen**[346] 5-9-6 0 RobertWinston 3 38
(Alan McCabe) *hld up: rdn over 2f out: hung lft and wknd over 1f out* 4/1[2]

4 3 ½ **Miss Chardonay**[208] 6-9-1 0 TomMcLaughlin 1 26
(Mandy Rowland) *s.i.s: hdwy to ld 4f out: rdn and hdd over 2f out: wknd fnl f* 125/1

00-4 5 3 ¼ **Kuraanda**[19] 28 4-9-0 45 (p) PaddyAspell 6 19
(John Wainwright) *led: hdd over 6f out: chsd ldrs: rdn over 2f out: wknd over 1f out* 40/1

6 11 **Gallant Leader (USA)**[11] 4-9-5 0 BarryMcHugh 5
(Tony Coyle) *prom: pushed along 1/2-way: wknd over 3f out: t.o* 16/1

2m 5.83s (4.13) **Going Correction** +0.225s/f (Slow)
WFA 4 from 5yo+ 1lb 6 Ran SP% **114.6**
Speed ratings (Par 103): **90,83,74,71,68 59**
Tote Swingers: 1&2 £1.60, 1&3 £1.20, 2&3 £2.10 CSF £5.66 TOTE £1.20: £1.02, £3.80; EX 5.10 Trifecta £10.30 Pool: £3,534.26 - 254.91 winning units..
Owner Highfield Racing 4 **Bred** Bolton Grange **Trained** Settrington, N Yorks

FOCUS
A one-horse race according to the market and that was played out in the race itself. It was slowly run and the winner is rated 7lb off his best.

314 DOWNLOAD CORAL.CO.UK MOBILE APP H'CAP 1m 1f 103y(P)
5:35 (5:36) (Class 5) (0-75,75) 4-Y-O+ **£2,587** (£770; £384; £192) **Stalls** Low

Form RPR

36-1 1 **Noble Jack (IRE)**[19] 23 7-9-5 73 (b) J-PGuillambert 2 84
(Jo Hughes) *s.s: hld up: hdwy over 2f out: rdn to ld and edgd lft wl ins fnl f: r.o* 11/4[2]

1-46 2 1 ¼ **On The Hoof**[6] 217 4-8-13 75 MatthewHopkins(7) 9 83
(Michael Easterby) *chsd ldr tl led 7f out: rdn and hdd ins fnl f: styd on same pce* 15/2

02-5 3 ¾ **Dakota Canyon (IRE)**[15] 82 4-9-3 72 (v[1]) TonyHamilton 8 79
(Richard Fahey) *chsd ldrs: rdn over 1f out: led ins fnl f: sn hdd and unable qck* 7/1[3]

15-1 4 1 ½ **Lean On Pete (IRE)**[15] 82 4-9-6 75 ShaneKelly 6 79
(Ollie Pears) *hld up: hdwy over 2f out: rdn over 1f out: edgd lft and styd on same pce ins fnl f* 2/1[1]

04-2 5 3 ¾ **Follow The Flag (IRE)**[15] 82 9-9-4 72 (v) RobertWinston 4 68
(Alan McCabe) *hld up: rdn 3f out: styd on fr over 1f out: nvr nrr* 10/1

60-2 6 1 ¼ **Scamperdale**[15] 83 11-8-9 63 (p) KellyHarrison 10 58
(Brian Baugh) *hld up and bhd: nt clr run over 2f out: styd on ins fnl f: nvr nrr* 14/1

0-53 7 2 **Aviso (GER)**[9] 190 9-8-7 61 oh1 FrannyNorton 7 50
(David Evans) *hld up: rdn over 2f out: nvr on terms* 28/1

00-6 8 4 ½ **Spanish Plume**[11] 146 5-9-2 70 GrahamGibbons 5 50
(Reg Hollinshead) *prom: rdn over 2f out: wknd fnl f* 14/1

6-30 9 2 ½ **Standpoint**[9] 190 7-9-0 73 WilliamTwiston-Davies(5) 3 47
(Conor Dore) *prom: rdn over 2f out: wknd over 1f out* 18/1

42-1 10 1 **Honey Of A Kitten (USA)**[9] 183 5-9-1 69 (v) TomMcLaughlin 1 41
(David Evans) *led: hdd 7f out: chsd ldr: rdn and ev ch over 2f out: wknd fnl f* 20/1

2m 1.19s (-0.51) **Going Correction** +0.225s/f (Slow)
WFA 4 from 5yo+ 1lb 10 Ran SP% **120.2**
Speed ratings (Par 103): **111,109,109,107,104 103,101,97,95,94**
Tote Swingers: 1&2 £5.40, 1&3 £4.80, 2&3 £11.00 CSF £24.85 CT £134.89 TOTE £3.70: £1.10, £3.30, £2.20; EX 27.40 Trifecta £174.60 Pool: £3,042.74 - 13.06 winning units..
Owner Darren & Annaley Yates **Bred** Team Hogdala Ab **Trained** Lambourn, Berks

FOCUS
A competitive handicap, run at a brisk pace. The form is rated on the positive side, with the winner back to his old best.
T/Plt: £158.90 to a £1 stake. Pool: £146,825.00 - 674.52 winning tickets. T/Qpdt: £24.50 to a £1 stake. Pool: £11,068.00 - 333.17 winning tickets. CR

286 CAGNES-SUR-MER
Monday, January 21

OFFICIAL GOING: Turf: heavy

315a PRIX ROBERT VILLENEUVE-BARGEMON (CONDITIONS) (5YO+) (TURF) 1m 4f
1:20 (12:00) 5-Y-O+ **£11,382** (£4,552; £3,414; £2,276; £1,138)

RPR

1 **Griraz (FR)**[43] 8-9-7 0 Francois-XavierBertras 6 102
(P Sogorb, France) 2/5[1]

2 3 **Le Roi Mage (IRE)**[94] 8-8-11 0 MathieuAndrouin 5 88
(P Monfort, France) 11/1

3 1 **Galeo Des Flandres (FR)**[17] 7-8-11 0 ThierryThulliez 3 86
(P Demercastel, France) 14/1

4 5 ½ **Validor (FR)**[66] 7766 7-9-1 0 (b) StephanePasquier 1 81
(S Labate, France) 63/10[2]

5 3 **Lord Emery (GER)**[105] 5-8-11 0 AlexisBadel 2 72
(M Figge, Germany) 13/1

6 8 **Uphold**[30] 8228 6-8-11 0 (e) MickaelForest 7 60
(Gay Kelleway) *sn led: clr ld ent bk st: margin reduced 4f out: rdn and hdd bef st 3f out: no ex u.p in st: dropped away: nt hrd rdn fnl f* 68/10[3]

2m 47.55s (167.55) 6 Ran SP% **120.1**
WIN (incl. 1 euro stake): 1.40. PLACES: 1.20, 2.10. SF: 8.10.
Owner Serge Kinast **Bred** M Berlato **Trained** France

[227]LINGFIELD (L-H)
Tuesday, January 22

OFFICIAL GOING: Standard

Wind: Virtually nil Weather: grey cloud and cold

316 STAY AT THE MARRIOTT HOTEL (S) STKS 5f (P)
12:20 (12:20) (Class 6) 4-Y-0+ £2,045 (£603; £302) Stalls High

Form RPR

04-4 1 **Where's Reiley (USA)**[15] 92 7-9-5 70 (b) LukeMorris 1 69
(Alastair Lidderdale) *trckd ldng pair: pushed along 1/2-way: hdwy to chse ldr over 1f out: rdn to ld ins fnl f: styd on strly* 9/4[2]

0-12 2 2 ¼ **Johnny Splash (IRE)**[12] 135 4-9-0 57 (b) NathanAlison(5) 4 61
(Roger Teal) *sn led: rdn along wl over 1f out: hdd and drvn ins fnl f: kpt on same pce* 7/1[3]

050- 3 ¾ **Wicked Wench**[102] 7019 4-8-9 76 J-PGuillambert 5 48
(Jo Hughes) *sn cl up: effrt to chal 2f out: sn rdn along: drvn and one pce appr fnl f* 4/7[1]

600- 4 6 **Pytheas (USA)**[34] 8167 6-9-0 49 (b) WilliamCarson 2 32
(Alastair Lidderdale) *dwlt and awkward s: sn rdn along on outer and a in rr* 16/1

59.1s (0.30) **Going Correction** +0.05s/f (Slow) 4 Ran SP% **112.8**
Speed ratings (Par 101): **99,95,94,84**
CSF £15.64 TOTE £2.80; EX 10.80 Trifecta £14.50 Pool: £848.87 - 43.77 winning units..There was no bid for winner. Wicked Wench was claimed by Horses First Racing Limited £6,000.
Owner Chris Beek & Steve Jakes **Bred** Overbrook Farm **Trained** Lambourn, Berks

FOCUS
An uncompetitive seller, run at a fair pace. Shaky form, with the favourite disappointing.

317 BOOK HOSPITALITY AT LINGFIELD PARK (S) STKS 7f (P)
12:50 (12:50) (Class 6) 4-Y-0+ £2,045 (£603; £302) Stalls Low

Form RPR

035- 1 **Homeboy (IRE)**[66] 7770 5-9-0 63 EddieAhern 5 65
(Marcus Tregoning) *t.k.h: trckd ldrs: hdwy over 1f out: shkn up to chse ldr ent fnl f: sn edgd lft: styd on wl under hand riding to ld nr line* 6/1[2]

0-33 2 hd **Abhaath (USA)**[6] 229 4-9-0 64 (v[1]) LukeMorris 6 65
(Ronald Harris) *cl up: chal 2f out: rdn to ld over 1f out: drvn ins fnl f: hdd and no ex nr line* 6/1[2]

000- 3 4 **Not My Choice (IRE)**[23] 8298 8-9-0 43 (t) AmirQuinn 3 54?
(Paul Howling) *sn led: rdn along wl over 1f out: sn hdd & wknd fnl f* 33/1

060- 4 shd **Katy's Secret**[63] 7794 6-8-9 60 DavidProbert 7 49
(William Jarvis) *dwlt and in rr: rdn along 2f out: kpt on u.p fnl f: n.d* 10/1[3]

6-65 5 nk **Irish Heartbeat (IRE)**[7] 217 8-9-0 76 (p) FergusSweeney 1 53
(Jamie Osborne) *t.k.h early: trckd ldrs on inner: effrt 2f out: sn rdn: drvn ent fnl f and fnd nil* 2/5[1]

1m 24.84s (0.04) **Going Correction** +0.05s/f (Slow) 5 Ran SP% **112.0**
Speed ratings (Par 101): **101,100,96,96,95**
CSF £38.59 TOTE £7.10: £2.60, £1.90; EX 33.20 Trifecta £110.40 Pool: £2,073.37 - 14.07 winning units..There was no bid for winner. Irish Heartbeat was claimed by Mr Barry Leavy for £5,000.
Owner Home Marketing Limited **Bred** J Costello **Trained** Whitsbury, Hants

FOCUS
A moderate seller, run at a steady pace with the front two pulling clear inside the final furlong. Shaky and unconvincing form.

318 LINGFIELD PARK MARRIOTT HOTEL H'CAP 1m 4f (P)
1:20 (1:20) (Class 4) (0-85,84) 4-Y-0+ £4,690 (£1,395; £697; £348) Stalls Low

Form RPR

21-1 1 **Harry Buckle**[19] 32 4-8-12 76 WilliamCarson 5 88+
(Philip McBride) *trckd ldr: hdwy and cl up over 4f out: effrt to ld 2f out: rdn clr wl over 1f out: kpt on wl u.p fnl f* 2/1[1]

12-2 2 2 **Focail Maith**[18] 52 5-9-9 83 (p) FergusSweeney 2 90
(John Ryan) *hld up and bhd: hdwy 3f out: rdn to chse wnr over 1f out: edgd lft ins fnl f: sn no imp* 4/1[2]

50-5 3 5 **Solfilia**[15] 93 4-8-13 82 WilliamTwiston-Davies(5) 8 81
(Hughie Morrison) *in tch: effrt 3f out: sn rdn along and one pce fr wl over 1f out* 5/1[3]

621- 4 nse **Scottish Boogie (IRE)**[15] 6933 6-9-3 77 SebSanders 4 76
(Brendan Powell) *dwlt and hld up towards rr: hdwy over 4f out: pushed along to chse ldng pair over 2f out: rdn wl over 1f out: sn one pce* 12/1

412- 5 nk **Cayuga**[34] 8174 4-9-6 84 IanMongan 3 82
(Brett Johnson) *hld up: hdwy 1/2-way: rdn along 3f out and sn outpcd: styd on fnl f* 2/1[1]

-133 6 3 ¾ **Activate**[6] 227 6-8-5 70 (b) LeonnaMayor(5) 1 62
(Phil McEntee) *led: rdn along 3f out: hdd over 2f out: sn wknd* 20/1

0/0- 7 11 **While You Wait (IRE)**[24] 3600 4-9-0 78 ChrisCatlin 6 53
(Gary Moore) *chsd ldng pair: rdn along on inner 4f out: drvn 3f out: sn wknd* 25/1

2m 29.73s (-3.27) **Going Correction** +0.05s/f (Slow)
WFA 4 from 5yo+ 4lb 7 Ran SP% **119.6**
Speed ratings (Par 105): **112,110,107,107,107 104,97**
toteswingers 1&2 £2.60, 1&3 £3.10, 2&3 £4.20 CSF £11.27 CT £35.98 TOTE £3.40: £1.40, £3.10; EX 10.20 Trifecta £27.60 Pool: £2,682.75 - 72.64 winning units..
Owner Four Winds Racing Partnership **Bred** Wood Farm Stud (Waresley) **Trained** Newmarket, Suffolk

FOCUS
This was competitive enough, the pace was honest with the winner scoring well.The winner more than confirmed his recent form, and the first two were clear.

319 LINGFIELD PARK OWNERS GROUP H'CAP 5f (P)
1:50 (1:50) (Class 2) (0-100,101) 4-Y-0+ £12,291 (£3,657; £1,827; £913) Stalls High

Form RPR

12-1 1 **Woolfall Sovereign (IRE)**[21] 3 7-9-3 96 IanMongan 8 105+
(George Margarson) *hld up in tch: hdwy on outer 2f out: rdn and str run ins fnl f to ld last 50yds* 2/1[1]

000- 2 ½ **Even Stevens**[42] 8066 5-8-13 92 (p) TomMcLaughlin 5 99
(Scott Dixon) *awkward s: trckd ldrs on inner: hdwy wl over 1f out: rdn to take slt ld jst ins fnl f: sn hung rt: hdd and no ex last 50yds* 25/1

36-0 3 ½ **Alaskan Bullet (IRE)**[9] 196 4-8-2 86 oh7 NathanAlison(5) 4 91
(Brian Ellison) *dwlt and towards rr: hdwy wl over 1f out: trckd ldrs and effrt whn nt clr run and swtchd lft ins fnl f: kpt on* 10/1

00-5 4 ¾ **Fratellino**[17] 78 6-9-2 100 (t) WilliamTwiston-Davies(5) 7 103
(Alan McCabe) *trckd ldrs: hdwy 2f out: rdn and ch whn n.m.r jst ins fnl f: sn one pce* 3/1[2]

460- 5 ½ **Bajan Tryst (USA)**[40] 8098 7-8-11 93 (p) JulieBurke(3) 1 94
(Kevin Ryan) *sn rdn along and outpcd in rr: hdwy on outer over 1f out: styd on fnl f: nrst fin* 6/1

22-3 6 ¾ **Moorhouse Lad**[21] 3 10-8-7 86 oh1 LukeMorris 6 84
(Garry Moss) *cl up: rdn along wl over 1f out: ev ch tl drvn and wknd ent fnl f* 8/1

24-6 7 1 **Swiss Cross**[17] 78 6-9-8 101 (t) DavidProbert 3 96
(Phil McEntee) *cl up: rdn and ev ch over 1f out: sn drvn and wknd fnl f* 9/2[3]

256- 8 4 ½ **Six Wives**[42] 8066 6-8-4 86 oh6 (p) RaulDaSilva(3) 2 64
(Scott Dixon) *set str pce: rdn along 2f out: hdd ent fnl f: sn drvn and wknd* 25/1

57.98s (-0.82) **Going Correction** +0.05s/f (Slow) 8 Ran SP% **118.7**
Speed ratings (Par 109): **108,107,106,105,104 103,101,94**
toteswingers 1&2 £22.90, 1&3 £4.00, 2&3 £9.20 CSF £57.04 CT £413.35 TOTE £1.70: £1.10, £6.30, £5.40; EX 68.80 Trifecta £347.60 Pool: £3,135.59 - 6.76 winning units..
Owner Wildcard Racing Syndicate **Bred** Saud Bin Saad **Trained** Newmarket, Suffolk

FOCUS
A nice prize for this decent handicap, run at a fair pace with the hold-up performers dominating. The winner continues to improve and looked a bit better than the bare form.

320 BOOK TICKETS ONLINE @ LINGFIELDPARK.CO.UK H'CAP 1m (P)
2:25 (2:26) (Class 6) (0-60,60) 4-Y-0+ £2,045 (£603; £302) Stalls High

Form RPR

66-1 1 **Mubtadi**[8] 205 5-8-11 57 ThomasBrown(7) 9 65
(Ismail Mohammed) *cl up: led over 2f out: rdn ent fnl f: kpt on wl towards fin* 5/4[1]

060- 2 nk **Spirit Of Xaar (IRE)**[32] 8199 7-9-5 58 (p) RobertHavlin 11 65
(Linda Jewell) *in tch: smooth hdwy to trck ldrs over 2f out: rdn to chse wnr ent fnl f: sn drvn and kpt on* 20/1

-043 3 ½ **Spinning Ridge (IRE)**[3] 274 8-9-4 57 (v) LukeMorris 7 63
(Ronald Harris) *hld up in tch: hdwy 3f out: chsd ldrs 2f out: sn rdn: drvn ins fnl f: kpt on same pce* 6/1[2]

40-4 4 hd **Litmus (USA)**[13] 120 4-8-2 46 oh1 (b) NathanAlison(5) 4 52
(Simon Dow) *hld up in tch: hdwy on inner over 3f out: rdn to chse ldrs wl over 1f out: kpt on u.p fnl f: nrst fin* 14/1

33-0 5 1 ¾ **Sudden Wish (IRE)**[15] 89 4-9-2 55 (v[1]) TomMcLaughlin 8 57
(David Evans) *led: rdn along 3f out: hdd over 2f out: cl up tl drvn and wknd ins fnl f* 14/1

60-2 6 nk **Mafi (IRE)**[8] 205 5-8-13 59 (t) PhilipPrince(7) 3 60
(Mark Hoad) *trckd ldrs on inner: hdwy 2f out: rdn to chse ldrs whn n.m.r and hmpd jst ins fnl f: swtchd rt and kpt on towards fin* 6/1[2]

1-03 7 1 ½ **Daniel Thomas (IRE)**[8] 200 11-9-7 60 (tp) WilliamCarson 2 57
(Violet M Jordan) *dwlt and in rr: hdwy wl over 2f out: sn rdn and kpt on: nrst fin* 10/1

035- 8 ½ **Finlodex**[26] 8248 6-9-3 56 FrankieMcDonald 5 52
(Murty McGrath) *hld up: a towards rr* 8/1[3]

00-0 9 1 ¼ **Salient**[8] 205 9-8-12 51 (b) SebSanders 10 44
(Michael Attwater) *sn prom on outer: hdwy and cl up 1/2-way: rdn along over 2f out and sn wknd* 16/1

120- 10 nse **Ensnare**[33] 8179 8-9-3 56 StevieDonohoe 1 49
(Willie Musson) *midfield whn n.m.r and lost pl after 1f: a towards rr after* 25/1

1m 39.87s (1.67) **Going Correction** +0.05s/f (Slow) 10 Ran SP% **121.0**
Speed ratings (Par 101): **93,92,92,92,90 89,88,87,86,86**
toteswingers 1&2 £9.70, 1&3 £3.10, 2&3 £26.60 CSF £33.42 CT £124.17 TOTE £2.20: £1.40, £7.50, £1.90; EX 43.80 Trifecta £366.70 Pool: £4,092.38 - 8.36 winning units..
Owner Abdulla Al Mansoori **Bred** Whitsbury Manor Stud **Trained** Newmarket, Suffolk

FOCUS
This weak handicap was run at an ordinary pace and it proved an advantage to race handily. The first three were all on good marks and the winner is rated similarly to last week's win.

321 FOLLOW US ON TWITTER @LINGFIELDPARK H'CAP 1m (P)
3:00 (3:03) (Class 6) (0-60,61) 3-Y-O £2,045 (£603; £302) Stalls High

Form RPR

36-3 1 **Darkest Night (IRE)**[18] 55 3-9-2 55 FergusSweeney 7 63
(Jamie Osborne) *trckd ldrs: hdwy 2f out: swtchd lft and rdn to chal ent fnl f: kpt on u.p to ld nr fin* 5/1[3]

6-22 2 hd **Derwentwater (IRE)**[13] 122 3-9-7 60 (b) RobertHavlin 2 68
(John Gosden) *cl up: led 2f out: rdn and edgd rt ent fnl f: drvn: hdd and no ex towards fin* 2/1[1]

24-1 3 2 ¼ **Flying Tempo**[18] 55 3-9-4 57 (b) StevieDonohoe 8 59
(Ed Dunlop) *t.k.h early: hld up towards rr: hdwy on outer 2f out: rdn to chse ldrs and edgd lft ent fnl f: sn drvn and kpt on same pce* 2/1[1]

350- 4 2 ¾ **Napinda**[101] 7056 3-8-13 52 WilliamCarson 5 48
(Philip McBride) *trckd ldrs: effrt over 2f out: sn rdn and kpt on same pce appr fnl f* 20/1

32-4 5 1 **Dream About You (IRE)**[15] 103 3-8-11 57 (p) RobertTart(7) 9 51
(Robert Mills) *in tch on outer: hdwy 3f out: rdn along 2f out: drvn and no imp fnl f* 7/2[2]

36-1 6 6 **Maypole Joe (IRE)**[1] 310 3-9-8 61 6ex (v) TomMcLaughlin 1 41
(David Evans) *set stdy pce: rdn along and hdd 2f out: sn drvn and wknd* 12/1

04-0 7 ½ **Vergality Ridge (IRE)**[13] 122 3-9-3 56 (b) LukeMorris 3 35
(Ronald Harris) *trckd ldrs on inner: pushed along 3f out: rdn over 2f out: sn wknd* 16/1

036- 8 13 **Paige Flyer**[97] 7165 3-9-7 60 AndreaAtzeni 6
(Mick Quinn) *stmbld and dwlt s: in rr and rdn along 1/2-way: sn bhd* 33/1

1m 38.51s (0.31) **Going Correction** +0.05s/f (Slow) 8 Ran SP% **126.8**
Speed ratings (Par 95): **100,99,97,94,93 87,87,74**
toteswingers 1&2 £3.80, 1&3 £3.20, 2&3 £1.90 CSF £17.35 CT £28.49 TOTE £5.00: £2.00, £1.40, £2.20; EX 21.20 Trifecta £86.40 Pool: £3,669.65 - 31.84 winning units..
Owner Miss E Asprey **Bred** M McGinn **Trained** Upper Lambourn, Berks

FOCUS
A moderate contest run at a fair pace, with the front two fighting out an exciting finish. A personal best from the winner.

322 PLAY GOLF AT LINGFIELD PARK RACECOURSE H'CAP (DIV I) 6f (P)
3:35 (3:35) (Class 6) (0-60,58) 4-Y-0+ £2,045 (£603; £302) Stalls Low

Form RPR

000- 1 **Dorothy's Dancing (IRE)**[35] 8159 5-9-7 58 GeorgeBaker 5 64
(Gary Moore) *trckd ldrs: hdwy on inner 2f out: rdn over 1f out: chal ins fnl f: drvn and kpt on to ld nr fin* 10/11[1]

50-0 2 nk **Waterloo Dock**[17] 76 8-9-4 55 (v) AndreaAtzeni 3 60
(Mick Quinn) *led: pushed along 2f out: rdn over 1f out: drvn ent fnl f: hdd and no ex nr fin* 12/1

-60 **3** 3/4 **Back For Tea (IRE)**[3] [274] 5-8-8 **45**............................(b) DavidProbert 8 48
(Phil McEntee) *chsd ldng pair: rdn along and sltly outpcd 2f out: kpt on u.p fnl f* **5/1**[3]
0-40 **4** 1 1/2 **Imaginary Diva**[12] [139] 7-9-6 **57**.. IanMongan 6 55
(George Margarson) *trckd ldrs: hdwy on outer 2f out: rdn over 1f out: sn drvn and one pce* **6/1**
36-4 **5** 1 **Chjimes (IRE)**[6] [233] 9-8-13 **55**.................(b) WilliamTwiston-Davies(5) 9 50
(Conor Dore) *cl up: rdn along 2f out: drvn over 1f out: wknd ent fnl f* **3/1**[2]
1m 12.38s (0.48) **Going Correction** +0.05s/f (Slow) **5** Ran SP% **116.0**
Speed ratings (Par 101): **98,97,96,94,93**
CSF £13.65 TOTE £1.80: £1.20, £6.70; EX 13.70 Trifecta £45.90 Pool: £2,773.22 - 45.24 winning units..
Owner Tom Glynn **Bred** Patrick Carroll **Trained** Lower Beeding, W Sussex
FOCUS
A modest handicap, run at a fair pace and slightly faster than division II. The poor third offers perspective.

323 PLAY GOLF AT LINGFIELD PARK RACECOURSE H'CAP (DIV II) 6f (P)
4:05 (4:05) (Class 6) (0-60,58) 4-Y-0+ **£2,045** (£603; £302) **Stalls** Low

Form RPR
-205 **1** **Dixie Gwalia**[5] [240] 5-9-3 **54**....................................(v1) TomMcLaughlin 1 62
(David Evans) *mde all: rdn along wl over 1f out: kpt on wl towards fin* **6/1**[3]
3-21 **2** 3/4 **Baby Dottie**[6] [233] 6-9-1 **57**..................................(tp) JemmaMarshall(5) 6 63
(Pat Phelan) *trckd ldrs: hdwy wl over 1f out: rdn to chse wnr ins fnl f: sn no imp* **4/7**[1]
0-00 **3** nk **Cut The Cackle (IRE)**[13] [117] 7-8-11 **48**.................(bt) WilliamCarson 2 53
(Violet M Jordan) *dwlt and in rr: hdwy on wd outside wl over 1f out: sn rdn and styd on strly fnl f* **8/1**
5-05 **4** 1 1/2 **Lady Mango (IRE)**[12] [139] 5-9-7 **58**............................(p) LukeMorris 7 58
(Ronald Harris) *cl up on outer: rdn along 2f out: drvn and wknd fnl f* **9/2**[2]
05-4 **5** 2 **Desert Red (IRE)**[12] [136] 4-8-9 **46**..............................(vt) DavidProbert 3 39
(Phil McEntee) *trckd ldrs on inner: effrt 2f out: sn rdn and one pce appr fnl f* **25/1**
000- **6** 1/2 **Punching**[83] [7482] 9-8-12 **56**.. PhilipPrince(7) 5 48
(Conor Dore) *in tch: rdn along over 2f out: n.d* **25/1**
00-0 **7** 1 **Ace Of Spies (IRE)**[17] [77] 8-9-1 **55**.......................... SimonPearce(3) 4 44
(Conor Dore) *cl up: rdn 2f out: sn wknd* **33/1**
1m 12.47s (0.57) **Going Correction** +0.05s/f (Slow) **7** Ran SP% **117.9**
Speed ratings (Par 101): **98,97,96,94,91 91,90**
toteswingers 1&2 £2.00, 1&3 £4.80, 2&3 £2.60 CSF £10.24 CT £29.47 TOTE £7.50: £3.30, £1.10; EX 14.80 Trifecta £49.80 Pool: £3,222.89 - 48.45 winning units..
Owner Mrs I M Folkes **Bred** Charlie Wyatt **Trained** Pandy, Monmouths
FOCUS
An uncompetitive handicap run at a sound pace with the winner making all under a strong ride. Slightly the slower division. The winner seemed to confirm her Kempton claiming form.
T/Plt: £49.10 to a £1 stake. Pool: £54,932.39 - 815.45 winning tickets T/Qpdt: £4.50 to a £1 stake. Pool: £8,149.04 - 1,321.63 winning tickets JR

308 WOLVERHAMPTON (A.W) (L-H)
Tuesday, January 22
OFFICIAL GOING: Standard to slow
Wind: Light against becoming fresher as the afternoon went on Weather: Cloudy

324 GET FREE BETS WITH BOOKMAKERS.CO.UK MAIDEN STKS 7f 32y(P)
2:00 (2:06) (Class 5) 3-Y-0+ **£3,234** (£962; £481; £240) **Stalls** High

Form RPR
1 **Street Battle (USA)** 3-8-9 0.. BarryMcHugh 5 74
(Tony Coyle) *a.p: led over 2f out: rdn clr fr over 1f out* **17/2**
56- **2** 7 **Village Green**[36] [8151] 4-9-6 0..................................(b1) JacobButterfield(7) 3 60
(Ollie Pears) *a.p: rdn to chse wnr over 1f out: sn hung lft: styd on same pce* **33/1**
33-4 **3** nk **Peak Storm**[18] [59] 4-9-8 58..................................(v1) CharlesBishop(5) 6 59
(John O'Shea) *hld up: hdwy over 2f out: rdn over 1f out: sn hung lft: styd on same pce* **11/4**[2]
222- **4** 1/2 **Lady Malet**[26] [8254] 3-8-5 70 ow1.......................................[1] AdamBeschizza 2 49
(William Haggas) *hld up: hdwy over 1f out: sn rdn no imp fnl f* **1/1**[1]
6 **5** 1 1/4 **Always Fabulous**[15] [102] 3-8-4 0.. JoeFanning 4 44
(Mark Johnston) *led over 4f: wknd fnl f* **7/1**[3]
64- **6** nk **Polar Forest**[26] [8254] 3-8-9 0...................................... RobbieFitzpatrick 7 48
(Richard Guest) *hld up: rdn over 1f out: nvr on terms* **10/1**
000 **7** 11 **Elusive**[6] [230] 7-9-3 0.. AnnStokell(5) 1 19
(Ann Stokell) *chsd ldrs tl wknd wl over 1f out* **150/1**
1m 31.33s (1.73) **Going Correction** +0.275s/f (Slow)
WFA 3 from 4yo+ 18lb **7** Ran SP% **112.4**
Speed ratings (Par 103): **101,93,92,92,90 90,77**
toteswingers 1&2 £22.90, 1&3 £4.00, 2&3 £9.20 CSF £200.09 TOTE £16.50: £6.20, £26.50; EX 243.60 Trifecta £633.80 Pool: £2,795.68 - 3.30 winning units..
Owner B Dunn **Bred** David Garvin **Trained** Norton, N Yorks
FOCUS
Little depth to this maiden.

325 CORAL.CO.UK H'CAP 7f 32y(P)
2:35 (2:40) (Class 4) (0-85,79) 3-Y-0 **£5,175** (£1,540; £769) **Stalls** High

Form RPR
51-2 **1** **Ashamaly**[12] [129] 3-9-7 79.. JoeFanning 2 90+
(James Tate) *trckd ldr tl led over 1f out: shkn up and r.o wl* **4/9**[1]
54-0 **2** 3 **Red Gift (IRE)**[8] [202] 3-8-11 69.. TomEaves 1 66
(Brian Ellison) *hung rt almost thrght: led at stdy pce tl qcknd over 2f out: hdd over 1f out: styd on same pce* **20/1**[3]
01-1 **3** 1 1/2 **Hazza The Jazza**[20] [8] 3-8-6 64...............................(b) FrannyNorton 3 57
(Richard Guest) *s.s: hld up: effrt over 1f out: no imp* **5/2**[2]
1m 33.53s (3.93) **Going Correction** +0.275s/f (Slow) **3** Ran SP% **102.6**
Speed ratings (Par 99): **88,84,82**
CSF £6.36 TOTE £1.30; EX 5.50 Trifecta £3.40 Pool: £1,190.99 - 255.83 winning units..
Owner Saif Ali **Bred** Hascombe And Valiant Studs **Trained** Newmarket, Suffolk
FOCUS
Straightforward enough form.

326 BOOKMAKER REVIEWS AT BOOKMAKERS.CO.UK H'CAP 5f 20y(P)
3:10 (3:15) (Class 6) (0-55,54) 4-Y-0+ **£1,940** (£577; £288; £144) **Stalls** Low

Form RPR
-162 **1** **Hab Reeh**[7] [213] 5-9-0 54..(t) GemmaTutty(7) 1 64
(Ruth Carr) *a.p: chsd ldr over 3f out: rdn to ld 1f out: r.o* **2/1**[1]
160- **2** 3 **Yungaburra (IRE)**[22] [8304] 9-9-3 50..............................(tp) FrannyNorton 9 51
(David C Griffiths) *mid-div: hdwy u.p over 1f out: r.o to go 2nd post: no ch w wnr* **8/1**
6-23 **3** hd **Miserere Mei (IRE)**[7] [213] 4-9-0 47.......................... RobbieFitzpatrick 6 47
(Richard Guest) *chsd ldrs: rdn over 1f out: styd on same pce ins fnl f* **9/2**[2]
653- **4** 1 **Love Club**[39] [8109] 5-9-2 49.. GrahamGibbons 7 46
(Brian Baugh) *led early: chsd ldrs: rdn 1/2-way: styd on same pce ins fnl f* **13/2**[3]
05-5 **5** 1/2 **Rightcar**[12] [128] 6-8-13 46.. LiamKeniry 4 41
(Peter Grayson) *sn pushed along in rr: r.o ins fnl f: nvr nrr* **8/1**
3-40 **6** 4 1/2 **Nafa (IRE)**[12] [142] 5-9-4 51.. ShaneKelly 8 32
(Daniel Mark Loughnane) *sn led: clr 1/2-way: rdn and hdd 1f out: wknd wl ins fnl f* **14/1**
00-0 **7** 1 1/2 **Dancing Ellie Mae**[13] [114] 4-8-13 46 ow1........................... DaleSwift 3 22
(Derek Shaw) *in rr whn hmpd sn after s: nvr on terms* **28/1**
000- **8** 1 1/2 **Lowtherwood**[140] [5918] 4-8-12 45...................................... JoeFanning 11 16
(William Muir) *s.s: a in rr* **9/1**
000- **9** 2 1/4 **Duke Of Rainford**[69] [7703] 6-8-12 45.................................... TomEaves 2
(Michael Herrington) *in rr whn hmpd sn after s: drvn along 1/2-way: sn lost tch* **14/1**
604- **10** hd **Busy Bimbo (IRE)**[39] [8109] 4-8-12 45.....................(b) BarryMcHugh 10
(Alan Berry) *chsd ldrs: rdn 1/2-way: wknd over 1f out* **40/1**
1m 3.0s (0.70) **Going Correction** +0.275s/f (Slow) **10** Ran SP% **116.3**
Speed ratings (Par 101): **105,100,99,98,97 90,87,85,81,81**
toteswingers 1&2 £5.50, 1&3 £1.90, 2&3 £7.80 CSF £18.62 CT £67.10 TOTE £2.30: £1.20, £2.40, £1.50; EX 18.90 Trifecta £62.60 Pool: £1,396.25 - 16.75 winning units..
Owner Mrs B Taylor, A Dickman, Mrs R Carr **Bred** The Anglo Irish Choral Society **Trained** Huby, N Yorks
FOCUS
A weak sprint handicap, run at a strong pace.

327 CORAL.CO.UK MOBILE BETTING H'CAP 5f 216y(P)
3:40 (3:50) (Class 6) (0-53,52) 4-Y-0+ **£1,940** (£577; £288; £144) **Stalls** Low

Form RPR
-605 **1** **Steel City Boy (IRE)**[6] [233] 10-9-2 52............................ AnnStokell(5) 1 59
(Ann Stokell) *mde all: rdn and edgd rt fnl f: jst hld on* **14/1**
00-4 **2** nk **Exkaliber**[12] [139] 4-9-2 47...(t) JoeFanning 4 53
(Jeremy Gask) *a.p: rdn over 1f out: edgd rt ins fnl f: r.o* **3/1**[1]
00-4 **3** nk **Blue Noodles**[16] [88] 7-9-0 45.......................................(p) BarryMcHugh 9 50
(John Wainwright) *hld up: rdn over 1f out: edgd lft and r.o wl ins fnl f: nt rch ldrs* **11/2**[3]
00-5 **4** 1 3/4 **Chester Deelyte (IRE)**[11] [163] 5-9-2 52.............(v) ShirleyTeasdale(5) 8 51
(Lisa Williamson) *hld up: hdwy over 1f out: r.o* **11/2**[3]
56-5 **5** 1 **Script**[19] [37] 4-8-9 47.. JordanHibberd(7) 2 43
(Alan Berry) *chsd ldrs: rdn over 1f out: n.m.r and no ex ins fnl f* **33/1**
0-46 **6** 1 1/2 **Vhujon (IRE)**[13] [111] 8-9-0 45.. LiamKeniry 5 36
(Peter Grayson) *s.i.s: hld up: hdwy over 2f out: rdn over 1f out: wkng whn hung rt ins fnl f* **13/2**
05-0 **7** 2 3/4 **Dingaan (IRE)**[13] [117] 10-8-10 46 ow1........................ SladeO'Hara(5) 7 29
(Peter Grayson) *s.i.s: hld up: nt clr run over 2f out: n.m.r over 1f out: wkd fnl f* **12/1**
06-0 **8** 1 1/2 **Replicator**[12] [143] 8-9-0 45...(e) MickyFenton 10 23
(Patrick Gilligan) *chsd ldrs: lost pl 5f out: rdn and wknd over 2f out* **40/1**
000- **9** 2 3/4 **Lady By Red (IRE)**[77] [7611] 5-9-0 45.............................. JamesSullivan 3 14
(Ann Duffield) *chsd ldrs: rdn over 2f out: wknd over 1f out* **10/1**
05-6 **10** nse **Cheyenne Red (IRE)**[12] [128] 7-9-0 45...........................(b) TomEaves 6 14
(Michael Herrington) *prom tl rdn and wknd over 2f out* **5/1**[2]
1m 16.57s (1.57) **Going Correction** +0.275s/f (Slow) **10** Ran SP% **114.6**
Speed ratings (Par 101): **100,99,99,96,95 93,89,87,84,84**
toteswingers 1&2 £9.10, 1&3 £16.90, 2&3 £4.90 CSF £54.95 CT £272.33 TOTE £8.80: £5.00, £1.10, £2.70; EX 70.20 Trifecta £1105.60 Part won. Pool: £1,474.20 - 0.81 winning units..
Owner Ms Caron Stokell **Bred** Mrs A B McDonnell **Trained** Southwell, Notts
FOCUS
An ordinary handicap.

328 BOOKMAKERS.CO.UK GIVES YOU FREE BETS H'CAP 5f 216y(P)
4:10 (4:20) (Class 5) (0-70,67) 3-Y-0 **£2,911** (£866; £432; £216) **Stalls** Low

Form RPR
45-5 **1** **Roland**[21] [5] 3-9-0 60..(b) FrannyNorton 1 63
(Kevin Ryan) *led: hdd over 4f out: chsd ldrs: reminders over 3f out: led ins fnl f: styd on* **5/2**[2]
5-32 **2** 1 1/4 **Sewn Up**[5] [236] 3-9-7 67...(tp) BarryMcHugh 3 66
(Reg Hollinshead) *a.p: chsd ldr over 4f out: rdn to ld over 1f out: hdd and nt qckn ins fnl f* **1/1**[1]
021- **3** 1 **Faffa**[24] [8286] 3-8-7 58.. AdamCarter(5) 4 54
(Tim Easterby) *stdd s: racd in last pl: shkn up ins fnl f: nvr nr to chal* **7/2**[3]
3-50 **4** 3/4 **Duchess Of Dreams**[9] [195] 3-8-11 57.................................. JohnFahy 2 50
(Richard Guest) *chsd ldr tl led over 4f out: rdn and hdd over 1f out: no ex ins fnl f* **12/1**
1m 17.05s (2.05) **Going Correction** +0.275s/f (Slow) **4** Ran SP% **108.5**
Speed ratings (Par 97): **97,95,94,93**
CSF £5.47 TOTE £1.90; EX 5.80 Trifecta £11.20 Pool: £1,946.65 - 129.56 winning units..
Owner Mrs Angie Bailey **Bred** Minster Stud And Bickerton Racing **Trained** Hambleton, N Yorks
■ Stewards' Enquiry : Adam Carter ten-day ban: failed to take all reasonable and permissable measures to obtain the best possible placing (Feb 5-14)
FOCUS
A moderate little handicap, run at a solid pace.

329 COMPARE ONLINE BOOKIES AT BOOKMAKERS.CO.UK H'CAP1m 1f 103y(P)
4:40 (4:50) (Class 4) (0-85,77) 4-Y-0+ **£5,175** (£1,540; £769; £384) **Stalls** Low

Form RPR
3-33 **1** **Strike Force**[7] [219] 9-8-8 69.......................................(t) NatashaEaton(5) 2 77
(Alison Hutchinson) *a.p: led over 1f out: rdn out* **8/1**
0-32 **2** nk **One Scoop Or Two**[7] [219] 7-8-10 71..................(p) ShirleyTeasdale(5) 4 78
(Reg Hollinshead) *hld up: hdwy over 1f out: rdn to chse wnr and edgd lft ins fnl f: styd on* **10/3**[2]
14-0 **3** 2 1/2 **Calaf**[5] [239] 5-9-5 75.. DaleSwift 3 77
(Brian Ellison) *chsd ldrs: shkn up and nt clr run over 2f out: rdn over 1f out: edgd lft and styd on same pce ins fnl f* **4/1**[3]
46-2 **4** 1 **Presburg (IRE)**[13] [112] 4-9-6 77.. LiamKeniry 1 77
(Joseph Tuite) *led 1f: chsd ldr tl led 2f out: rdn and hdd over 1f out:* **2/1**[1]
450- **5** 4 1/2 **Musnad (USA)**[25] [8275] 5-8-12 68...................................(b) TomEaves 5 59
(Brian Ellison) *sn pushed along: led over 8f out: rdn and hdd 2f out: wknd fnl f* **7/1**

4-25 **6** *4* **Follow The Flag (IRE)**[1] 314 9-9-2 72..........................(v) SeanLevey 7 54
(Alan McCabe) *hld up: pushed along over 4f out: rdn and wknd over 2f out* **8/1**

2m 2.78s (1.08) **Going Correction** +0.275s/f (Slow)
WFA 4 from 5yo+ 1lb **6** Ran SP% **111.1**
Speed ratings (Par 105): **106,105,103,102,98 95**
toteswingers 1&2 £3.40, 1&3 £4.70, 2&3 £3.00 CSF £33.71 TOTE £9.50: £3.90, £2.30; EX 24.90 Trifecta £130.10 Pool: £3,421.53 - 19.71 winning units..
Owner Miss A L Hutchinson **Bred** Cheveley Park Stud Ltd **Trained** Exning, Suffolk
FOCUS
Sound form for the grade.

330 POKER AT CORAL.CO.UK H'CAP 1m 1f 103y(P)
5:10 (5:20) (Class 6) (0-60,60) 4-Y-O+ **£1,940** (£577; £288; £144) **Stalls** Low

Form RPR
0-32 **1** **Yourinthewill (USA)**[5] 238 5-9-4 57................................ ShaneKelly 7 68+
(Daniel Mark Loughnane) *hld up: hdwy and n.m.r over 1f out: shkn up ins fnl f: r.o to ld post: comf* **6/1**[3]
00-0 **2** *nk* **Edgware Road**[18] 61 5-9-4 57................................ AdamBeschizza 9 65
(Sean Curran) *chsd ldr after 1f tl led over 1f out: rdn ins fnl f: hdd post* **20/1**
50-6 **3** *2 ¼* **Imaginary World (IRE)**[7] 218 5-9-7 60..................(p) GrahamGibbons 6 63
(John Balding) *hld up: hdwy and nt clr run over 1f out: rdn ins fnl f: styd on* **9/2**[2]
34-1 **4** *hd* **Precision Five**[11] 158 4-9-1 55....................................(p) JoeFanning 1 58
(Jeremy Gask) *trckd ldrs: rdn and edgd lft over 1f out: styd on same pce ins fnl f* **2/1**[1]
306- **5** *2* **Shaker Style (USA)**[25] 7454 7-9-3 56........................ JamesSullivan 4 55
(Barry Murtagh) *prom: rdn over 3f out: styd on same pce fnl f* **20/1**
6-16 **6** *½* **Sinchiroka (FR)**[8] 201 7-9-4 57................................(t) JamieGoldstein 3 55
(Ralph Smith) *led: rdn and hdd over 1f out: no ex ins fnl f* **9/2**[2]
110/ **7** *1* **True Pleasure (IRE)**[939] 3521 6-8-10 52................ DeclanCannon(3) 11 48
(James Bethell) *s.s: hld up: hdwy over 1f out: sn rdn: nt trble ldrs* **33/1**
00-4 **8** *1* **Shelovestobouggie**[12] 145 5-9-2 55..........................(t) FrannyNorton 2 48
(Mark Brisbourne) *prom: rdn and nt clr run over 1f out: wknd ins fnl f* **16/1**
00-6 **9** *7* **John Potts**[16] 82 8-9-4 57....................................... KellyHarrison 10 36
(Brian Baugh) *prom: rdn over 2f out: wknd fnl f* **7/1**
00/0 **10** *1* **Catawollow**[6] 220 6-8-7 46 oh1..................................(e) JohnFahy 5 23
(Richard Guest) *hld up: plld hrd: hdwy over 2f out: wknd over 1f out* **100/1**

2m 4.22s (2.52) **Going Correction** +0.275s/f (Slow)
WFA 4 from 5yo+ 1lb **10** Ran SP% **115.8**
Speed ratings (Par 101): **99,98,96,96,94 94,93,92,86,85**
toteswingers 1&2 £16.30, 1&3 £5.90, 2&3 £14.30 CSF £118.82 CT £590.84 TOTE £4.40: £2.00, £7.00, £2.00; EX 80.80 Trifecta £880.80 Pool: £3,608.40 - 3.07 winning units..
Owner Mrs C Loughnane **Bred** Branch Equine Llc **Trained** Baldwin's Gate, Staffs
FOCUS
This was run at a steady pace and the field bunched rounding the final bend.
T/Jkpt: Not won. T/Plt: £8,672.40 to a £1 stake. Pool: £81,972.2 - 6.90 winning tickets T/Qpdt: £21.70 to a £1 stake. Pool: £11,482.00 - 390.21 winning tickets CR

315 CAGNES-SUR-MER
Tuesday, January 22
OFFICIAL GOING: Fibresand: standard

331a PRIX DES CITRONNIERS (CLAIMER) (3YO COLTS & GELDINGS) (FIBRESAND) 1m 2f (D)
1:50 (12:00) 3-Y-O **£6,504** (£2,601; £1,951; £1,300; £650)

RPR
1 **Mahyar Glaz (FR)**[10] 3-9-0 0....................................(b) JohanVictoire 12 76
(C Boutin, France) **15/2**[2]
2 *shd* **Varing (FR)**[126] 3-9-0 0...(b) FabriceVeron 16 76
(H-A Pantall, France) **19/5**[1]
3 *1* **Ciel D'Automne (FR)**[17] 3-8-9 0........................ Pierre-CharlesBoudot 8 69
(J-P Gauvin, France) **11/1**
4 *5* **Houghton Hill (FR)**[39] 3-8-9 0.......................................(p) GeraldPardon 5 59
(J Rossi, France) **78/10**[3]
5 *shd* **Kawa Blanc (FR)** 3-9-0 0.. FranckBlondel 3 64
(P Khozian, France) **20/1**
6 *hd* **Mister Black (FR)**[17] 3-8-4 0........................... ChristopherGrosbois(5) 7 58
(F-X De Chevigny, France) **16/1**
7 *shd* **Peintre Francais (FR)**[28] 3-8-8 0.............................. CesarPasserat(6) 4 63
(F-X De Chevigny, France) **78/10**[3]
8 *shd* **Stenka Razine (FR)**[34] 3-8-9 0...................................(b) MickaelForest 13 58
(C Boutin, France) **35/1**
9 *1* **Jean De Medicis (FR)**[25] 3-8-6 0.............................. RomainAuray(3) 15 56
(J Heloury, France) **42/1**
10 *nse* **Zapata Rebel (FR)**[34] 3-8-4 0.............................. NicolasLarenaudie(5) 9 56
(J-M Lefebvre, France) **85/1**
0 **Ascha (FR)**[127] 3-9-0 0..(b) ThomasMessina 2
(Mme Pia Brandt, France) **19/5**[1]
0 **Woza Moya (USA)**[24] 8289 3-9-0 0.................................(b) LouisBeuzelin 6
(Gay Kelleway) *broke wl: racd in midfield under restraint: mde gd prog at end of bk st to go 4th: swtchd to outside: rdn early in st: no ex: styd on fnl 2f* **37/1**
0 **Beau Slam (FR)**[28] 3-8-2 0..............................(p) SebastienMartino(7) 10
(H-A Pantall, France) **14/1**
0 **Ginger Beer (FR)**[38] 3-8-9 0.. TheoBachelot 14
(J Heloury, France) **39/1**
0 **Poco De Oro (FR)** 3-9-0 0.. TonyPiccone 1
(M Gentile, France) **66/1**
P **Raineon (FR)**[10] 3-8-2 0..................................... JulienMagniez(7) 11
(Mme C Barande-Barbe, France) **39/1**

2m 6.54s (126.54) **16** Ran SP% **117.2**
WIN (incl. 1 euro stake): 8.50. PLACES: 2.70, 2.10, 4.00. DF: 12.60. SF: 29.10.
Owner Stephan Hoffmeister **Bred** Thierry Grandsir **Trained** France

271 KEMPTON (A.W) (R-H)
Wednesday, January 23
OFFICIAL GOING: Standard to slow
Wind: Brisk; behind Weather: Chilly

332 WIN BIG WITH BETDAQ MULTIPLES MAIDEN FILLIES' STKS 7f (P)
4:30 (4:31) (Class 5) 3-Y-O+ **£2,587** (£770; £384; £192) **Stalls** Low

Form RPR
4 **1** **Poet's Prospect (IRE)**[13] 148 3-8-10 0........................ AndreaAtzeni 4 68+
(Marco Botti) *trckd ldrs: led wl over 1f out: shkn up clsng stages and edgd lft: comf* **7/4**[1]
2 *hd* **Movementneverlies** 3-8-10 0.................................... RobertWinston 8 65+
(Charles Hills) *in tch: hdwy and drvn appr fnl f: wnt 2nd ins fnl f: kpt on clsng stages but a readily hld by wnr* **7/2**[3]
05- **3** *3 ¼* **Prom Dress**[40] 8102 3-8-10 0.. ShaneKelly 2 56
(Robert Cowell) *chsd ldrs: drvn to chal ins fnl 2f and stl ev ch over 1f out: outpcd into 3rd fnl f* **20/1**
40- **4** *3 ¼* **Bubblina**[49] 7996 6-10-0 0... GeorgeBaker 5 52
(Alastair Lidderdale) *in rr: hdwy fr 2f out: hung lft but styd on fnl f: nvr a threat* **14/1**
5 *¾* **Hawaiian Dream (IRE)** 3-8-10 0.................................. MartinLane 3 45
(Roger Teal) *in tch: drvn and hdwy 2f out: nvr gng pce to press ldrs* **8/1**
36- **6** *1 ½* **Special Meaning**[33] 8201 3-8-10 0............................... JoeFanning 1 41
(Mark Johnston) *led tl hdd over 4f out: led again appr fnl 2f: hdd & wknd* **11/4**[2]
4 **7** *3 ½* **Petra**[16] 102 3-8-10 0.. LiamKeniry 6 32
(Michael Appleby) *trckd ldr: led over 4f out: hdd & wknd wl over 1f out* **25/1**
0- **8** *1 ¼* **Quelle Affaire**[35] 8165 3-8-8 0 ow1.......................... BrendanPowell(3) 7 30
(Brendan Powell) *s.i.s: t.k.h: rdn over 2f out: a outpcd* **50/1**
000- **9** *1 ¾* **Twilight Legend (IRE)**[26] 8265 4-10-0 34...................... FrannyNorton 9 29
(Seamus Mullins) *chsd ldrs: drvn 3f out: sn btn* **100/1**

1m 26.95s (0.95) **Going Correction** +0.05s/f (Slow)
WFA 3 from 4yo+ 18lb **9** Ran SP% **114.6**
Speed ratings (Par 100): **96,95,92,88,87 85,81,80,78**
toteswingers 1&2 £1.90, 1&3 £12.20, 2&3 £13.50 CSF £7.73 TOTE £2.60: £1.10, £2.20, £7.70; EX 8.60 Trifecta £105.20 Pool: £2,678.02 - 19.09 winning units..
Owner Ahmed Ali **Bred** Rabbah Bloodstock Limited **Trained** Newmarket, Suffolk
FOCUS
Quite a weak maiden with the favourite disappointing, and it was slowly run. The first two may rate higher.

333 BACK AND LAY AT BETDAQ.COM MAIDEN STKS 1m 3f (P)
5:00 (5:00) (Class 5) 3-Y-O+ **£2,587** (£770; £288; £288) **Stalls** Low

Form RPR
1 **Magical Kingdom (IRE)** 3-8-4 0.................................. AndreaAtzeni 7 75+
(Marco Botti) *trckd ldrs: led over 1f out: drvn and styd on strly fnl f* **4/1**[3]
5 **2** *2 ¾* **El Massivo (IRE)**[18] 74 3-8-4 0.................................. JimmyQuinn 10 68
(William Jarvis) *sn chsng ldr: dropped to cl 4th 6f out: drvn and styd on wl fnl f to re-take 2nd clsng stages: no imp on wnr* **5/1**
225- **3** *½* **Luggers Hall (IRE)**[26] 3564 5-10-0 77............................ JimCrowley 5 70
(Tony Carroll) *hld up in rr: hdwy over 2f out: styd on u.p fnl f to share 3rd cl home but no imp on wnr* **9/4**[1]
5- **3** *dht* **Bin Manduro**[51] 7963 3-8-4 0.................................... LukeMorris 8 67
(James Tate) *sn led: drvn over 2f out: hdd over 1f out: one pce fnl f and dropped to share of 3rd cl home* **7/2**[2]
5 *9* **Rayadour (IRE)**[74] 4-9-11 75...................................... FergusSweeney 3 54
(Alan King) *hld up in tch: hdwy over 3f out: rdn over 2f out and sn btn* **8/1**
6 *3* **Federal Blue (USA)** 3-8-4 0... JoeFanning 6 46
(Mark Johnston) *in rr and green in rr: mod prog fr 2f out* **8/1**
00- **7** *3* **Sassi Sioux**[100] 7112 4-9-3 0..................................... RyanClark(3) 2 38
(Tom Keddy) *in tch: rdn and hung rt ins fnl 3f: sn btn* **100/1**
0- **8** *nk* **Sings Poet**[67] 7780 3-8-4 0.. MartinLane 4 40
(James Tate) *chsd ldrs: rdn 4f out: wknd 3f out* **66/1**
000- **9** *19* **Fleeting Indian (IRE)**[138] 5989 4-9-11 40...............(p) FrankieMcDonald 9
(Linda Jewell) *in rr but in tch: rdn 3f out: sn btn* **100/1**

2m 24.56s (2.66) **Going Correction** +0.05s/f (Slow)
WFA 3 from 4yo 24lb 4 from 5yo 3lb **9** Ran SP% **115.4**
Speed ratings (Par 103): **92,90,89,89,83 80,78,78,64**
CSF £24.30 TOTE £3.70: £1.30, £3.00; EX 30.80 TRIFECTA Pool: £2,445.77 - 11.16 & 12.79 winning units..
Owner Michael Tabor, John Magnier & Derrick Smith **Bred** Lynch Bages Ltd **Trained** Newmarket, Suffolk
FOCUS
An ordinary maiden run at a steady gallop. Still, the right horses came clear. The form has a fluid feel.

334 BETDAQ MOBILE APPS H'CAP (DIV I) 1m (P)
5:30 (5:33) (Class 6) (0-55,61) 4-Y-O+ **£1,940** (£577; £288; £144) **Stalls** Low

Form RPR
014- **1** **Ermyntrude**[83] 7500 6-9-5 53.......................................(v) IanMongan 10 61
(Pat Phelan) *trckd ldr: led over 2f out: strly chal fr over 1f out: stl hrd pressed fnl f: hld on all out* **9/2**[3]
2-36 **2** *shd* **Divine Rule (IRE)**[7] 223 5-9-0 55..........................(v) ThomasBrown(7) 5 63
(Laura Mongan) *chsd ldrs: wnt 2nd 2f out: str chal fr over 1f out and stl upsides ins fnl f: no ex last strides* **6/1**
02-0 **3** *½* **Flamborough Breeze**[14] 116 4-9-7 55..........................(t) LukeMorris 4 62
(Ed Vaughan) *in rr: hdwy wl over 1f out: styd on wl u.p fnl f: clsng in 3rd nr fin but nt rch ldng duo* **14/1**
63-1 **4** *1 ¾* **Vitznau (IRE)**[7] 223 9-9-13 61 6ex.................................. ChrisCatlin 1 64
(John Butler) *hld up in tch: hdwy travelling smoothly wl over 1f out: sn rdn: fnd no ex and one pce fnl f* **2/1**[1]
01-6 **5** *nk* **Aegean King**[15] 110 7-9-4 52.......................................(p) JimCrowley 2 54
(Michael Wigham) *s.i.s: in rr: hdwy over 1f out: styd on ins fnl f: nt rch ldrs* **4/1**[2]
00-6 **6** *1 ¾* **Shared Moment (IRE)**[13] 138 7-9-7 55.................(b) FergusSweeney 3 53
(Luke Dace) *chsd ldrs: rdn 2f out: wknd ins fnl f* **10/1**
54-2 **7** *3* **Fairy Mist (IRE)**[14] 120 6-8-12 46................................ KieranO'Neill 8 37
(John Bridger) *led tl hdd over 2f out: wknd over 1f out* **7/1**
0-40 **8** *8* **Georgebernardshaw (IRE)**[15] 110 8-9-3 51...(tp) RobbieFitzpatrick 12 24
(Richard Guest) *s.i.s: sn t.k.h: and in tch: rdn and btn 2f out* **25/1**

000/ **9** 3/4 **Valkov**[550] 4317 6-8-12 **46** oh1 .... MartinLane 11 17
(Tony Carroll) *s.i.s: rdn 4f out: a bhd* **66/1**
1m 40.89s (1.09) **Going Correction** +0.05s/f (Slow) **9** Ran SP% **119.4**
Speed ratings (Par 101): **96,95,95,93,93 91,88,80,79**
toteswingers 1&2 £5.70, 1&3 £7.50, 2&3 £12.60 CSF £32.85 CT £355.92 TOTE £6.60: £1.70, £2.70, £3.40; EX 32.50 Trifecta £313.60 Pool: £2,065.85 - 4.94 winning units..

Owner Epsom Racegoers No. 2 **Bred** Ermyn Lodge Stud Limited **Trained** Epsom, Surrey

■ Stewards' Enquiry : Ian Mongan two-day ban: ise of whip (7-8 Feb)

FOCUS
The complexion of the race changed when likely front-runner Georgebernardshaw missed the break, and the pace ended up being steady. Ordinary form.

335 BETDAQ MOBILE APPS H'CAP (DIV II) 1m (P)
6:00 (6:00) (Class 6) (0-55,55) 4-Y-0+ **£1,940** (£577; £288; £144) **Stalls** Low

Form RPR
40-4 **1** **Strategic Action (IRE)**[12] 158 4-9-6 **54** .... RobertHavlin 3 63
(Linda Jewell) *chsd ldrs: wnt 2nd 2f out: sn drvn: styd on to ld fnl 75yds: hld on wl* **9/2**[3]

240- **2** 3/4 **Exopuntia**[34] 8179 7-9-3 **51** .... AdamBeschizza 11 58
(Julia Feilden) *s.i.s: sn rcvrd and led after 1f: drvn 2f out: jnd ins fnl f: hdd and nt qckn fnl 75yds* **12/1**

-040 **3** 2 3/4 **Sleepy Lucy**[10] 193 4-8-12 **46** oh1 .... (e) RobbieFitzpatrick 6 46
(Richard Guest) *s.i.s: in rr: drvn and hdwy over 1f out: styd on to take 3rd ins fnl f: no imp on ldng duo* **33/1**

43-3 **4** 1 1/2 **Tijuca (IRE)**[21] 28 4-9-7 **55** .... LiamKeniry 8 52
(Ed de Giles) *sn led: hdd after 1f: styd chsng ldr to 2f out: styd on same pce fnl f* **16/1**

540- **5** *nk* **Leitrim King (IRE)**[69] 7731 4-9-7 **55** .... ShaneKelly 7 51+
(Gary Moore) *s.i.s: in rr: drvn and hdwy over 1f out: kpt on clsng stages* **9/4**[1]

50-5 **6** 3/4 **Olney Lass**[13] 145 6-9-2 **53** .... SimonPearce(3) 2 48
(Lydia Pearce) *towards rr: drvn over 2f out: kpt on same pce ins fnl f* **20/1**

00-6 **7** 3/4 **Rapid Water**[13] 147 7-9-7 **55** .... (p) LukeMorris 1 48
(Pat Eddery) *in rr but in tch: drvn and styd on to chse ldrs wl over 1f out: wknd ins fnl f* **8/1**

00-3 **8** 6 **Boris The Bold**[7] 220 4-8-12 **46** .... RobertWinston 4 25
(John Best) *outpcd most of way* **11/4**[2]

000- **9** 1 1/4 **Just Breathe (IRE)**[23] 8304 4-9-7 **55** .... KirstyMilczarek 9 31
(Olivia Maylam) *in tch: racd wd: hung lft and wknd fnl 2f* **25/1**

000- **10** 10 **Kiss My Heart**[24] 8295 4-8-12 **46** oh1 .... JimmyQuinn 10
(Eric Wheeler) *chsd ldrs: rdn 3f out: sn btn* **100/1**

1m 39.99s (0.19) **Going Correction** +0.05s/f (Slow) **10** Ran SP% **112.8**
Speed ratings (Par 101): **101,100,97,96,95 94,94,88,86,76**
toteswingers 1&2 £11.00, 1&3 £13.20, 2&3 £23.00 CSF £51.93 CT £1604.01 TOTE £6.50: £2.30, £2.30, £7.10; EX 61.50 Trifecta £812.20 Pool: £1,789.26 - 1.65 winning units..

Owner M J Boutcher **Bred** Martin O'Hanlon **Trained** Sutton Valence, Kent

FOCUS
Another race that went the way of the prominent racers. The pick of the three C&D times, but ordinary form.

336 BETDAQ CASINO GAMES H'CAP 1m (P)
6:30 (6:30) (Class 6) (0-55,55) 3-Y-0 **£1,940** (£577; £288; £144) **Stalls** Low

Form RPR
05-1 **1** **Taxiformissbyron**[13] 134 3-9-4 **52** .... TomEaves 4 58+
(Michael Herrington) *trckd ldrs: led 2f out: drvn and styd on strly fnl f* **9/4**[1]

0-56 **2** 1 1/4 **Icanboogie**[9] 212 3-8-5 **46** .... RobertTart(7) 3 49
(Karen George) *s.i.s: sn in tch: hdwy over 2f out: chsd ldr: over 1f out: no imp fnl f: hld on wl for 2nd clsng stages* **20/1**

03-4 **3** *nk* **Mystery Woman (IRE)**[11] 184 3-9-6 **54** .... LukeMorris 6 56
(Peter Chapple-Hyam) *chsd ldrs: drvn 3f out: styd on fnl f to cl on 2nd nr fin but no imp on wnr* **3/1**[2]

04-6 **4** 1 1/4 **Poetic Verse**[16] 103 3-9-0 **55** .... PatMillman(7) 7 54
(Rod Millman) *in rr: drvn and hdwy fr 2f out: styd on fnl f: no imp on ldrs* **8/1**

-634 **5** 2 **Precision Strike**[9] 212 3-8-9 **50** .... (v[1]) PhilipPrince(7) 10 45
(Richard Guest) *chsd ldrs: drvn and one pce over 2f out: styd on again fnl f* **7/1**

000- **6** 4 **World Freight Girl**[33] 8203 3-8-13 **47** .... JimmyQuinn 9 33
(Dean Ivory) *chsd ldrs: rdn over 2f out: wknd fnl f* **20/1**

065- **7** 3/4 **Ely Valley**[35] 8164 3-8-12 **46** oh1 .... WilliamCarson 2 30
(William Muir) *sn led: hdd 2f out: wknd over 1f out* **25/1**

005- **8** 3/4 **Multi Fours**[76] 7653 3-9-7 **55** .... MartinDwyer 5 37
(Daniel Kubler) *s.i.s: in rr: rdn over 2f out: no prog whn hung lft over 1f out* **5/1**[3]

53-3 **9** *nse* **Alfaisaliah (IRE)**[8] 216 3-9-4 **52** .... (b) LiamKeniry 8 34
(J S Moore) *rdn 3f out: outpcd most of way* **20/1**

1m 41.12s (1.32) **Going Correction** +0.05s/f (Slow) **9** Ran SP% **114.2**
Speed ratings (Par 95): **95,93,93,92,90 86,85,84,84**
toteswingers 1&2 £6.50, 1&3 £2.50, 2&3 £7.10 CSF £52.36 CT £137.32 TOTE £3.00: £2.10, £4.50, £1.50; EX 65.90 Trifecta £196.50 Pool: £1,320.14 - 5.03 winning units..

Owner H Hurst **Bred** Hugh M Hurst **Trained** Cold Kirby, N Yorks

FOCUS
Continuing the theme, the winner of this low-grade 3yo handicap was again well placed. The winner built on her C&D latest.

337 TIME ORDERED CARDS IN RACING PLUS H'CAP 6f (P)
7:00 (7:00) (Class 4) (0-85,94) 3-Y-0 **£4,690** (£1,395) **Stalls** Low

Form RPR
11- **1** **Foxtrot Jubilee (IRE)**[24] 8293 3-9-5 **83** .... JimCrowley 3 86+
(Ralph Beckett) *racd in cl 2nd: shkn up 2f out: qcknd to ld fnl 110yds: readily* **2/11**[1]

1-41 **2** 1 1/2 **Equitania**[9] 203 3-9-9 **94** 6ex .... PhilipPrince(7) 1 92
(Alan Bailey) *led: drvn over 2f out: hdd fnl 110yds: sn one pce* **4/1**[2]

1m 13.08s (-0.02) **Going Correction** +0.05s/f (Slow) **2** Ran SP% **104.6**
Speed ratings (Par 99): **102,100**
TOTE £1.10.

Owner Foxtrot Racing Partnership IV **Bred** Patrick Roche **Trained** Kimpton, Hants

FOCUS
Straightforward form. The winner did not need to improve on his Lingfield win, but is likely to do so.

338 KEMPTON FOR WEDDINGS H'CAP 1m 4f (P)
7:30 (7:30) (Class 6) (0-65,65) 4-Y-0+ **£1,940** (£577; £288; £144) **Stalls** Centre

Form RPR
23-0 **1** **Mcbirney (USA)**[21] 22 6-9-3 **65** .... PhilipPrince(7) 8 75
(Paul D'Arcy) *in rr: hdwy 2f out: swtchd rt and qcknd to ld ins fnl f: drvn out* **20/1**

464- **2** 2 **Wordiness**[33] 8214 5-9-3 **63** .... (t) WilliamTwiston-Davies(5) 7 70
(Seamus Durack) *in tch: chsd ldrs 3f out: swtchd lft over 2f out: styd on fnl f to take 2nd last strides: nt rch wnr* **10/1**[3]

3-11 **3** *nk* **Sweet Liberta (IRE)**[9] 201 4-8-13 **65** 6ex .... DanielMuscutt(7) 3 72+
(Andrew Balding) *chsd ldrs: led ins fnl 2f: hdd ins fnl f: styd on same pce: lost 2nd last strides* **5/2**[1]

000- **4** 3/4 **Simayill**[35] 8162 5-9-9 **64** .... (b) TomMcLaughlin 4 69
(John Berry) *chsd ldrs: drvn to chal ins fnl 2f: one pce fnl f* **25/1**

056- **5** 1 1/2 **Soweto Star (IRE)**[34] 8189 5-9-3 **58** .... RobertWinston 12 61
(John Best) *hld up in rr: drvn and hdwy over 1f out: styd on fnl f: nt rch ldrs* **25/1**

/06- **6** *hd* **Al Amaan**[35] 8162 8-9-9 **64** .... GeorgeBaker 9 67
(Gary Moore) *in rr: hdwy over 2f out: styd on u.p over 1f out: nvr gng pce to rch ldrs* **14/1**

06-4 **7** 1/2 **Shalambar (IRE)**[21] 20 7-9-9 **64** .... JimCrowley 5 66
(Tony Carroll) *trckd ldr: led ins fnl 4f: drvn 3f out: hdd ins fnl 2f: wknd ins fnl f* **7/1**[2]

221- **8** 2 **Langham Lily (USA)**[56] 7921 4-9-4 **63** .... SebSanders 14 62
(Chris Wall) *chsd ldrs: rdn 2f out: wknd fnl f* **7/1**[2]

10-1 **9** *nk* **Refreshestheparts (USA)**[10] 192 4-8-13 **65** .... (t) AaronJones(7) 11 63
(George Baker) *in rr: racd wd into st: sme hdwy on outside fr 2f out: nvr rchd ldrs* **14/1**

0441 **10** 9 **Nolecce**[7] 226 6-9-1 **56** 6ex .... (p) JimmyQuinn 10 40
(Richard Guest) *in rr: rdn and sme hdwy 3f out: wknd ins fnl 2f* **12/1**

300- **11** 3 3/4 **The Blue Dog (IRE)**[170] 4875 6-9-8 **63** .... AndreaAtzeni 6 41
(Michael Wigham) *in rr: rdn and sme prog over 2f out: sn btn* **33/1**

00-0 **12** 19 **Trip Switch**[15] 107 7-9-8 **63** .... [1] LiamKeniry 1
(John Butler) *in tch: rdn: n.m.r and btn 3f out* **50/1**

15-4 **13** 6 **Honoured (IRE)**[15] 107 6-9-8 **63** .... (t) LukeMorris 13
(Michael Appleby) *chsd ldrs: rdn 3f out and sn wknd: eased whn no ch 2f out* **10/1**[3]

650- **14** 8 **Port Charlotte**[26] 8273 4-9-4 **63** .... (b) RobertHavlin 2
(Hughie Morrison) *led: hdd ins fnl 4f: n.m.r: hmpd and wknd 3f out* **12/1**

2m 33.54s (-0.96) **Going Correction** +0.05s/f (Slow)
WFA 4 from 5yo+ 4lb **14** Ran SP% **117.8**
Speed ratings (Par 101): **105,103,103,102,101 101,101,100,99,93 91,78,74,69**
toteswingers 1&2 £49.70, 1&3 £13.70, 2&3 £7.70 CSF £194.40 CT £682.85 TOTE £27.20: £5.00, £3.20, £1.60; EX 262.10 Trifecta £864.50 Pool: £1,152.72 - 0.13 winning units..
Owner Mrs Sue D'Arcy **Bred** Charles H Wacker **Trained** Newmarket, Suffolk

FOCUS
Not much pace early but still reasonable form for the grade. The second helps set the standard.

339 BOOK FOR RACING PLUS CHASE DAY H'CAP 6f (P)
8:00 (8:01) (Class 7) (0-50,53) 4-Y-0+ **£1,455** (£433; £216; £108) **Stalls** Low

Form RPR
00-5 **1** **Mr Optimistic**[14] 111 5-9-4 **48** .... KieranO'Neill 12 61
(Paul Howling) *hld up in rr: drvn and hdwy fr 2f out to ld over 1f out: r.o wl* **9/2**

0-50 **2** 2 1/4 **Ishetoo**[12] 163 9-9-1 **50** .... SladeO'Hara(5) 3 56
(Peter Grayson) *in tch: rdn and outpcd over 2f out: hdwy over 1f out to chse wnr fnl f: no imp* **16/1**

5-55 **3** 3 1/2 **Rightcar**[1] 326 6-9-2 **46** .... LukeMorris 4 41
(Peter Grayson) *in rr: hdwy and hmpd over 2f out: styd on fr over 1f out to take one pce 3rd fnl f* **4/1**[3]

000- **4** 1 1/4 **Smoky Cloud (IRE)**[34] 8184 6-9-2 **46** .... (p) RobertWinston 10 37
(Terry Clement) *led after 1f: rdn over 2f out: hdd over 1f out: sn btn* **14/1**

54-2 **5** 1 1/4 **Adaeze (IRE)**[13] 143 5-9-4 **48** .... (v) JohnFahy 1 35
(Jonathan Portman) *led 1f: chsd ldrs: rdn 2f out: wknd over 1f out* **6/1**

35-2 **6** 2 3/4 **First Rebellion**[13] 128 4-9-0 **47** .... RaulDaSilva(3) 11 25
(Tony Carroll) *s.i.s: sn in tch: rdn and effrt over 2f out: edgd rt and sn btn* **5/2**[1]

03-0 **7** 5 **Greek Islands (IRE)**[14] 117 5-9-4 **48** .... (b) LiamKeniry 7
(Ed de Giles) *t.k.h: chsd ldrs: rdn 2f out: sn btn* **7/2**[2]

1m 12.34s (-0.76) **Going Correction** +0.05s/f (Slow) **7** Ran SP% **115.8**
Speed ratings (Par 97): **107,104,99,97,96 92,85**
toteswingers 1&2 £2.90, 1&3 £5.50, 2&3 £7.20 CSF £69.64 CT £311.86 TOTE £5.00: £1.90, £4.30; EX 83.20 Trifecta £308.50 Pool: £1,017.45 - 2.47 winning units..
Owner Eclipse Horse Racing **Bred** C J Murfitt **Trained** Lee-On-The-Solent, Hants

FOCUS
The only race of the night to be run at a good clip. The first two had both come down a long way in the weights.
T/Plt: £59.10 to a £1 stake. Pool: £68,248.32 - 841.61 winning units T/Qpdt: £27.30 to a £1 stake. Pool: £7,017.82 - 189.80 winning units ST

[316]LINGFIELD (L-H)
Wednesday, January 23

OFFICIAL GOING: Standard
Wind: Light; across Weather: Heavy grey cloud

340 BET ON YOUR MOBILE @BLUESQ.COM CLAIMING STKS 1m (P)
1:00 (1:00) (Class 6) 4-Y-0+ **£2,045** (£603; £302) **Stalls** High

Form RPR
-211 **1** **Paphos**[7] 229 6-8-7 64 .... (v) AndreaAtzeni 5 79
(Stuart Williams) *led 2f: trckd ldr tl cl up over 2f out: led wl over 1f out: rdn clr ent fnl f: kpt on strly* **6/4**[1]

2-61 **2** 3 3/4 **Red Somerset (USA)**[2] 311 10-9-1 77 .... KieranO'Neill 2 78
(Mike Murphy) *hld up in tch: smooth hdwy over 3f out: trckd ldrs 2f out: rdn over 1f out: chsd wnr ins fnl f: no imp* **7/4**[2]

15-4 **3** 2 1/2 **The Mongoose**[13] 130 5-8-11 65 .... (t) LukeMorris 1 69
(David Evans) *chsd ldng pair: hdwy over 2f out: rdn wl over 1f out: drvn and one pce fnl f* **16/1**

036- **4** *nk* **Tornado Force (IRE)**[32] 8228 5-9-5 77 .... GeorgeBaker 3 76
(Chris Dwyer) *hld up in rr: stdy hdwy over 3f out: chsd ldrs wl over 1f out: sn rdn and no imp* **8/1**

15-0 **5** 2 1/4 **Ertikaan**[14] 127 6-8-8 81 ....(tp) ConnorKing(7) 6 67
(Brendan Powell) *chsd ldr tl led after 2f: jnd and rdn along over 2f out: hdd wl over 1f out: sn drvn and wknd ent fnl f* **9/2**[3]

05-0 **6** 24 **Mcconnell (USA)**[19] 49 8-8-7 63 ....(b) WilliamCarson 4
(Violet M Jordan) *stdd s: hld up in rr: rdn along over 3f out: sn outpcd and bhd* **66/1**

1m 36.04s (-2.16) **Going Correction** +0.05s/f (Slow) **6** Ran SP% **113.0**
Speed ratings (Par 101): **112,108,105,105,103 79**
toteswingers 1&2 £1.10, 1&3 £2.40, 2&3 £5.40 CSF £4.48 TOTE £2.50: £1.20, £1.40; EX 5.10 Trifecta £21.00 Pool: £1,226.58 - 43.73 winning units..Paphos was claimed by Mr C. B. Hills for £6,000
Owner Stuart C Williams **Bred** L Ellinas And Old Mill Stud Ltd **Trained** Newmarket, Suffolk

FOCUS
Not a bad claimer in which they went a decent gallop. The winning time was under a second outside the par.

341 PLAY GOLF AT LINGFIELD MARRIOTT MAIDEN STKS 6f (P)
1:30 (1:30) (Class 5) 3-Y-O **£2,726** (£805; £402) **Stalls** Low

Form RPR

026- **1** **Keene's Pointe**[132] 6167 3-9-5 78 .... SebSanders 2 72
(J W Hills) *trckd ldng pair: effrt on inner 2f out: rdn ent fnl f: styd on to ld last 75yds* **7/4**[1]

6 **2** 1 **Irish Dream (IRE)**[11] 185 3-9-0 0 .... JoeFanning 6 64
(Mark Johnston) *sn led: pushed along 2f out: rdn over 1f out: hdd and no ex last 75yds* **10/1**

443- **3** 1 **Not Rigg (USA)**[41] 8092 3-9-5 72 ....(t) LiamKeniry 3 66
(Andrew Balding) *trckd ldr: effrt 2f out: sn rdn: drvn and one pce fnl f* **2/1**[2]

4 **4** nk **Laudation**[11] 185 3-9-5 0 .... JimmyQuinn 4 65
(William Jarvis) *trckd ldrs: niggled along wl over 2f out: rdn wl over 1f out: kpt on towards fin* **5/1**[3]

0- **5** 3 1/2 **Limoges**[101] 7078 3-9-0 0 .... IanMongan 1 48
(Luke Dace) *dwlt: in tch on inner: rdn along over 2f out and n.d* **8/1**

6 nk **Mighty Mata** 3-9-5 0 .... RobertHavlin 5 52
(Mark Usher) *dwlt: a in rr* **16/1**

1m 13.02s (1.12) **Going Correction** +0.05s/f (Slow) **6** Ran SP% **112.4**
Speed ratings (Par 97): **94,92,91,90,86 85**
toteswingers 1&2 £2.70, 1&3 £1.40, 2&3 £2.70 CSF £19.40 TOTE £2.50: £1.60, £7.50; EX 16.50 Trifecta £46.70 Pool: £1,732.14 - 27.76 winning units..
Owner Mrs Paul Abberley **Bred** Christopher & Annabelle Mason **Trained** Upper Lambourn, Berks

FOCUS
A modest 3yo maiden in which they went a fair pace.

342 LINGFIELD PARK MEDIAN AUCTION MAIDEN STKS 1m 4f (P)
2:00 (2:00) (Class 6) 4-6-Y-O **£2,045** (£603; £302) **Stalls** Low

Form RPR

05- **1** **Waving**[54] 7933 4-9-3 68 ....(t) LukeMorris 2 74
(Tony Carroll) *hld up: stdy hdwy over 3f out: trckd ldrs over 2f out: rdn to ld jst ins fnl f: sn clr* **9/2**[3]

2 **2** 2 3/4 **Story Writer**[19] 63 4-9-3 0 .... GeorgeBaker 6 70
(William Knight) *hld up and bhd: stdy hdwy 5f out: trckd ldrs 3f out: rdn to ld 2f out: drvn ent fnl f: sn edgd lft and hdd: kpt on same pce* **5/2**[1]

00-2 **3** 1 1/2 **Linkable**[12] 161 4-9-0 63 ....(t) BrendanPowell(3) 3 67
(Brendan Powell) *trckd ldrs: hdwy over 2f out: effrt and rdn over 1f out: n.m.r and swtchd rt ins fnl f: kpt on* **4/1**[2]

35-3 **4** nk **Viola Da Gamba (IRE)**[19] 53 4-8-12 60 .... JimCrowley 8 62
(William Knight) *trckd ldr: cl up 4f out: led 3f out: rdn and hdd 2f out: cl up and ev ch ent fnl f: sn drvn and one pce* **5/2**[1]

05-3 **5** 5 **Frosty Friday**[20] 33 5-9-2 57 ....(p) JoeFanning 1 54
(J R Jenkins) *trckd ldng pair on inner: effrt over 2f out and sn rdn along: drvn and wknd appr fnl f* **10/1**

-6 **6** 3 **Shirazz**[8] 215 4-8-12 0 .... FrannyNorton 4 49
(Jeremy Noseda) *dwlt: a towards rr* **10/1**

0-0 **7** 2 **Nadia Naes (IRE)**[21] 12 4-8-12 43 ....(b) RobertHavlin 7 46
(Roger Ingram) *led and sn clr: pushed along 4f out: hdd 3f out and sn wknd* **33/1**

000/ **8** 46 **Drumadoon (IRE)**[16] 7639 5-9-0 47 ....(tp) PhilipPrince(7) 9
(Liam Corcoran) *trckd ldrs: pushed along over 5f out: rdn over 4f out: sn lost pl and bhd* **50/1**

2m 32.61s (-0.39) **Going Correction** +0.05s/f (Slow)
WFA 4 from 5yo 4lb **8** Ran SP% **118.4**
Speed ratings: **103,101,100,99,96 94,93,62**
toteswingers 1&2 £3.30, 1&3 £3.98, 2&3 £3.00 CSF £16.85 TOTE £7.90: £2.70, £1.10, £2.80; EX 20.00 Trifecta £80.50 Pool: £2,454.38 - 22.86 winning units..
Owner Carl Hodgson **Bred** Theakston Stud **Trained** Cropthorne, Worcs
■ Stewards' Enquiry : Jim Crowley one-day ban: did not keep straight out of the stalls

FOCUS
A moderate middle-distance maiden.

343 DEAN WILSON FAMILY FUNERAL DIRECTORS H'CAP 1m 5f (P)
2:30 (2:30) (Class 6) (0-60,60) 4-Y-O+ **£2,045** (£603; £302) **Stalls** Low

Form RPR

0-64 **1** **Broxbourne (IRE)**[10] 198 4-8-12 53 .... JoeFanning 11 65
(Mark Johnston) *trckd ldrs: hdwy over 2f out: effrt and n.m.r whn swtchd rt ent fnl f: sn led and rdn clr: styd on* **6/1**[3]

052- **2** 2 1/2 **Comedy House**[49] 7991 5-9-9 59 .... GeorgeBaker 14 67+
(Michael Madgwick) *hld up towards rr: hdwy 4f out: chsd ldrs whn n.m.r and swtchd rt 2f out: wd st and rdn: styd on fnl f* **5/2**[1]

54-4 **3** 3 1/4 **Handsome Molly**[13] 140 4-8-11 52 .... LiamKeniry 6 55
(David Elsworth) *hld up in rr: hdwy 3f out: rdn wl over 1f out: styd on fnl f: nrst fin* **8/1**

236- **4** 1/2 **Celtic Charlie (FR)**[55] 7927 8-9-5 55 .... IanMongan 13 57
(Pat Phelan) *hld up: hdwy on outer 4f out: chal 2f out: rdn and slt ld over 1f out: drvn and hdd ins fnl f: sn wknd* **11/4**[2]

4U- **5** 1 3/4 **Sing Alana Sing**[70] 7717 5-8-3 46 oh1 ....(t) JakePayne(7) 8 46
(Bill Turner) *chsd ldr: hdwy 3f out: cl up 2f out: sn rdn and ev ch tl wknd appr fnl f* **50/1**

0-44 **6** nk **Formidable Guest**[12] 161 9-9-1 51 .... RobertHavlin 3 50
(Jamie Poulton) *trckd ldrs on inner: hdwy whn nt clr run and hmpd wl over 1f out: one pce after* **25/1**

5-05 **7** 1 1/4 **Sommersturm (GER)**[10] 193 9-9-1 51 .... WilliamCarson 10 48
(David Evans) *led: rdn along 3f out: drvn and hdd over 1f out: wknd fnl f* **14/1**

56-6 **8** nk **Midnight Sequel**[12] 169 4-8-6 47 ....(b1) MartinLane 1 44
(Michael Blake) *midfield: effrt on inner wl over 2f out: sn rdn along and n.d* **14/1**

000- **9** 1 1/2 **Broughton Place**[43] 8067 5-8-10 46 oh1 .... EddieAhern 7 41
(Willie Musson) *hld up: a towards rr* **10/1**

006- **10** 2 1/2 **Cozy Tiger (USA)**[197] 3942 8-9-7 57 .... JamieMackay 12 48
(Willie Musson) *prom: effrt on outer 3f out: rdn along 2f out: wknd over 1f out* **16/1**

34/5 **11** 7 **Corres (IRE)**[22] 2 6-9-3 58 ....(tp) WilliamTwiston-Davies(5) 2 38
(Paul Fitzsimons) *nvr bttr than midfield* **25/1**

460- **12** 10 **Total Obsession**[230] 2851 6-8-3 46 oh1 .... PhilipPrince(7) 5 11
(Mark Hoad) *in tch: rdn along over 5f out: sn lost pl and bhd* **66/1**

/00- **13** 11 **Benozzo Gozzoli**[36] 632 7-9-0 50 .... FergusSweeney 9
(Simon Earle) *a in rr: bhd fnl 4f* **25/1**

2m 45.19s (-0.81) **Going Correction** +0.05s/f (Slow)
WFA 4 from 5yo+ 5lb **13** Ran SP% **123.9**
Speed ratings (Par 101): **104,102,100,100,99 98,98,97,97,95 91,85,78**
toteswingers 1&2 £5.30, 1&3 £6.40, 2&3 £4.50 CSF £21.13 CT £127.56 TOTE £6.80: £2.50, £1.10, £3.60; EX 21.40 Trifecta £139.90 Pool: £1,719.07 - 9.21 winning units..
Owner Ready To Run Partnership **Bred** Mount Coote Stud And M Johnston **Trained** Middleham Moor, N Yorks

FOCUS
A moderate middle-distance handicap.

344 LINGFIELDPARK.CO.UK H'CAP 1m (P)
3:00 (3:02) (Class 5) (0-75,73) 4-Y-O+ **£2,726** (£805; £402) **Stalls** High

Form RPR

1-36 **1** **Storm Runner (IRE)**[4] 272 5-9-1 67 .... IanMongan 6 74+
(George Margarson) *trckd ldrs: pushed along and sltly outpcd over 2f out: rdn wl over 1f out: styd on u.p fnl f to ld last 75yds* **5/2**[1]

630- **2** 1/2 **Super Duplex**[67] 4983 6-8-8 65 .... JemmaMarshall(5) 5 71
(Pat Phelan) *led: pushed along over 2f out: rdn wl over 1f out: drvn ins fnl f: hdd and no ex last 75yds* **16/1**

1-22 **3** 1 **Muhandis (IRE)**[9] 199 5-9-4 70 ....(b) SebSanders 7 75
(Nick Littmoden) *dwlt and hld up towards rr: hdwy 1/2-way: chsd ldrs over 1f out: rdn and ev ch ins fnl f: hld whn n.m.r towards fin* **11/4**[2]

52-3 **4** 3/4 **Only Ten Per Cent (IRE)**[20] 34 5-9-7 73 .... ShaneKelly 3 75
(J R Jenkins) *hld up towards rr: hdwy on outer 2f out: rdn to chse ldrs ent fnl f: kpt on same pce towards fin* **6/1**

10-6 **5** nk **The Happy Hammer (IRE)**[18] 79 7-8-11 68 WilliamTwiston-Davies(5) 2 69
(Eugene Stanford) *trckd ldng pair: hdwy to chse ldr over 2f out: sn chal and ev ch tl drvn and one pce fnl f* **10/1**

100- **6** nk **Perfect Mission**[37] 8152 5-9-0 73 ....(v) ThomasBrown(7) 4 74
(Andrew Balding) *cl up on inner: effrt 2f out: sn rdn: one pce fnl f* **7/2**[3]

000- **7** 1 1/4 **Titan Triumph**[40] 8105 9-9-5 71 ....(t) JimCrowley 1 69
(William Knight) *hld up in rr: hdwy on outer over 2f out: rdn to chse ldng pair over 1f out: sn drvn and wknd ins fnl f* **10/1**

1m 38.07s (-0.13) **Going Correction** +0.05s/f (Slow) **7** Ran SP% **115.8**
Speed ratings (Par 103): **102,101,100,99,99 99,97**
toteswingers 1&2 £8.50, 1&3 £1.60, 2&3 £9.80 CSF £42.21 TOTE £3.30: £1.60, £7.70; EX 38.30 Trifecta £252.80 Pool: £2,141.95 - 6.35 winning units..
Owner Pitfield Partnership **Bred** Kevin Foley **Trained** Newmarket, Suffolk
■ Stewards' Enquiry : Seb Sanders one-day ban: careless riding (Feb 6)

FOCUS
A fair handicap in which they went a steady gallop. The winning time was two seconds slower than the earlier 1m claimer.

345 BLUE SQUARE BET H'CAP 7f (P)
3:30 (3:31) (Class 4) (0-85,84) 4-Y-O+ **£4,690** (£1,395; £697; £348) **Stalls** Low

Form RPR

2-11 **1** **Al's Memory (IRE)**[18] 80 4-9-0 77 .... LukeMorris 3 87
(David Evans) *trckd ldrs: effrt and n.m.r wl over 1f out: sn swtchd rt and rdn: styd on to ld ins fnl f* **3/1**[2]

000- **2** 1 1/4 **Docofthebay (IRE)**[41] 8095 9-9-7 84 ....(b) IanMongan 5 91
(Scott Dixon) *rdn along early: hld up in tch: hdwy on outer over 2f out: chal wl over 1f out: sn rdn and led jst over 1f out: hdd ins fnl f: drvn and kpt on same pce* **7/1**

36-0 **3** 3/4 **Key Ambition**[17] 86 4-8-7 70 ....(tp) JimmyQuinn 7 75
(Garry Moss) *hld up towards rr: hdwy on inner wl over 1f out: rdn and ev ch ent fnl f: kpt on same pce* **20/1**

014- **4** 3/4 **Scottish Lake**[70] 7716 5-9-1 78 ....(v1) KirstyMilczarek 6 81
(Olivia Maylam) *led: rdn along 2f: hdd over 1f out: drvn and one pce fnl f* **6/1**[3]

00-6 **5** shd **Prince Of Burma (IRE)**[12] 164 5-9-1 78 ....(b) HayleyTurner 1 81
(Jeremy Gask) *trckd ldrs: effrt and nt clr run over 1f out and again whn hmpd ins fnl f: nt rcvr* **11/4**[1]

5-0U **6** 1 **Decent Fella (IRE)**[18] 78 7-9-6 83 ....(t) WilliamCarson 2 83
(Violet M Jordan) *dwlt and in rr: hdwy 2f out: rdn over 1f out: no imp fnl f* **20/1**

320- **7** nse **Delft**[51] 7966 4-9-6 83 .... JimCrowley 8 83
(Jeremy Noseda) *cl up: rdn along and ev ch wl over 1f out: drvn and wknd ent fnl f* **11/4**[1]

1m 24.7s (-0.10) **Going Correction** +0.05s/f (Slow) **7** Ran SP% **114.6**
Speed ratings (Par 105): **102,100,99,98,98 97,97**
toteswingers 1&2 £4.60, 1&3 £5.70, 2&3 £10.20 CSF £24.08 CT £346.80 TOTE £3.10: £1.50, £4.00; EX 28.20 Trifecta £233.50 Pool: £2,913.66 - 9.35 winning units..
Owner Will Dawson **Bred** Brian Miller **Trained** Pandy, Monmouths

346 GET STRAIGHT TO THE BET AT BLUESQ.COM APPRENTICE H'CAP 7f (P)
4:00 (4:00) (Class 6) (0-60,60) 4-Y-O+ **£2,045** (£603; £302) **Stalls** Low

Form RPR

36-4 **1** **Amis Reunis**[12] 162 4-9-5 58 ....(p) RobertTart 7 66
(Anthony Carson) *hld up in rr: pushed along 2f out: gd hdwy on inner over 1f out: rdn to ld ins fnl f: styd on* **9/4**[1]

60-2 **2** 1 **Cuthbert (IRE)**[20] 35 6-8-2 48 ow1 ....(b) PaigeBolton(7) 2 53
(Michael Attwater) *trckd ldrs: hdwy 2f out: chal and ev ch ent fnl f: sn rdn and edgd rt: one pce towards fin* **5/1**

504- **3** 2 1/4 **Miakora**[27] 8251 5-8-6 50 .... ShelleyBirkett(5) 1 51
(Mick Quinn) *trckd ldng pair: effrt 2f out: ch whn nt clr run and hmpd ent fnl f: kpt on same pce* **16/1**

61-1 **4** 1 **Basle**[19] 50 6-9-2 60 ....(t) AaronJones(5) 5 56
(Michael Blake) *trckd ldrs: effrt 2f out: sn rdn and one pce fnl f* **7/2**[3]

-332 **5** 1 1/4 **Spartic**[7] 233 5-9-5 58 ....(p) PatMillman 3 51
(Alan McCabe) *led: rdn along 2f out: rdr dropped whip over 1f out: sn edgd rt and hdd ins fnl f: grad wknd* **5/2**[2]

 The Form Book Flat, Raceform Ltd, Compton, RG20 6NL.

-603 6 1/2 **Back For Tea (IRE)**[1] 322 5-8-7 **46** oh1....(b) RyanTate 6 38
(Phil McEntee) *cl up: rdn and ev ch wl over 1f out: wknd appr fnl f* **8/1**
1m 25.27s (0.47) **Going Correction** +0.05s/f (Slow) **6** Ran SP% **115.2**
Speed ratings (Par 101): **99,97,95,94,92 92**
toteswingers 1&2 £3.00, 1&3 £5.40, 2&3 £4.60 CSF £14.39 TOTE £2.90: £1.40, £3.60; EX 14.90 Trifecta £113.90 Pool: £2,499.02 - 16.44 winning units..
Owner W Carson P Huntbach & D Rutter **Bred** Paddock Space **Trained** Newmarket, Suffolk
■ Stewards' Enquiry : Paige Bolton two-day ban: careless riding (7-7 Feb)
FOCUS
A moderate handicap for apprentice riders.
T/Plt: £71.50 to a £1 stake. Pool: £62,648.20 - 639.23 winning units T/Qpdt: £22.40 to a £1 stake. Pool: £6,180.69 - 203.80 winning units JR

332 KEMPTON (A.W) (R-H)
Thursday, January 24

OFFICIAL GOING: Standard to slow
Wind: Moderate; across Weather: Chilly

347 BOOK TICKETS FOR RACING PLUS CHASE DAY H'CAP (DIV I) 1m (P)
4:00 (4:01) (Class 6) (0-60,60) 4-Y-0+ **£1,940** (£577; £288; £144) **Stalls** Low

Form RPR
523- 1 **Bowstar**[27] 8267 4-9-7 **60**....(p) RobertHavlin 10 69
(Michael Attwater) *trckd ldr over 4f out: led appr fnl 2f: sn drvn along: hld on wl clsng stages: all out* **6/1**[3]
35-2 2 nk **West Leake (IRE)**[14] 130 7-9-4 **57**.... JohnFahy 9 65
(Paul Burgoyne) *in tch: drvn and hdwy 2f out: chal thrght fnl f: nt quite get up* **9/2**[1]
53-2 3 nk **Arabian Flight**[17] 98 4-9-6 **59**.... FrannyNorton 6 66
(Michael Appleby) *chsd ldrs: drvn over 2f out: styd on thrght fnl f: nt quite pce of ldng duo cl home* **5/1**[2]
201- 4 2 1/2 **Bahri Sheen (IRE)**[35] 8179 5-9-6 **59**.... GeorgeBaker 2 61
(John Best) *in rr: pushed along over 2f out: styd on fnl f: nt rch ldrs* **9/2**[1]
0-40 5 1 3/4 **Gallantry**[10] 205 11-9-3 **56**.... MichaelStainton 5 53
(Paul Howling) *led after 2f: hdd appr fnl 2f: wknd fnl f* **20/1**
0-43 6 1 **Moheebb (IRE)**[17] 98 9-9-4 **57**....(b) RobbieFitzpatrick 7 52
(Robert Johnson) *in rr: drvn along 3f out: mod prog fnl f* **9/2**[1]
/4-2 7 shd **Cape Crossing**[16] 108 4-9-1 **54**.... LiamKeniry 3 49
(Andrew Balding) *sn led: hdd after 2f: rdn over 2f out: wknd over 1f out* **7/1**
52-5 8 2 1/2 **Community (USA)**[10] 205 5-9-0 **58**.... LeonnaMayor(5) 1 47
(Jamie Osborne) *in tch: rdn 3f out: wknd 2f out* **10/1**
1m 39.02s (-0.78) **Going Correction** -0.05s/f (Stan) **8** Ran SP% **111.9**
Speed ratings (Par 101): **101,100,100,97,96 95,95,92**
toteswingers 1&2 £5.00, 1&3 £5.30, 2&3 £3.90 CSF £31.57 CT £142.37 TOTE £6.00: £2.20, £2.00, £2.10; EX 30.80 Trifecta £127.50 Pool: £1,731.33 - 10.18 winning units..
Owner Canisbay Bloodstock **Bred** Juddmonte Farms Ltd **Trained** Epsom, Surrey
FOCUS
Few got involved from off what was a steady pace. The winner was back to her C&D best from November.

348 BOOK TICKETS FOR RACING PLUS CHASE DAY H'CAP (DIV II) 1m (P)
4:35 (4:35) (Class 6) (0-60,60) 4-Y-0+ **£1,940** (£577; £288; £144) **Stalls** Low

Form RPR
305- 1 **South Cape**[85] 7496 10-8-12 **58**.... NedCurtis(7) 5 69
(Gary Moore) *stdd s: hld up in rr: gd hdwy appr fnl f: edgd rt and qcknd fnl 100yds: led last strides* **7/1**
413- 2 nk **Pastoral Jet**[36] 8167 5-8-10 **56**.... ThomasBrown(7) 1 66
(Richard Rowe) *in tch: hdwy 2f out: drvn to ld jst ins fnl f: edgd lft fnl 100yds: hd last strides* **7/4**[1]
00-6 3 2 **Hip Hip Hooray**[22] 13 7-9-7 **60**.... GeorgeBaker 7 67
(Luke Dace) *stdd s: in rr: hdwy over 1f out: styng on to chal whn hmpd and nt rcvr fnl 100yds* **11/2**
0-66 4 1 1/2 **Meydan Style (USA)**[8] 220 7-8-0 **46** oh1.... VictorSantos(7) 3 48
(Richard Ford) *chsd ldrs: led over 1f out: hdd jst ins fnl f: sn outpcd* **33/1**
42-3 5 1/2 **Silly Billy (IRE)**[10] 205 5-9-1 **54**....(v) IanMongan 6 56
(Pat Phelan) *chsd ldrs: led ins fnl 2f: hdd over 1f out: styng on whn hmpd fnl 100yds: nt rcvr* **5/1**[3]
54-0 6 1 3/4 **Menadati (USA)**[17] 94 5-9-6 **59**.... KirstyMilczarek 4 59
(Peter Hiatt) *chsd ldrs: drvn to press ldrs whn hmpd and nt rcvr fnl 100yds* **7/2**[2]
04-6 7 3 **Songbird Blues**[11] 192 4-8-13 **57**.... RachealKneller(5) 8 47
(Mark Usher) *stdd s: in rr: hdwy over 2f out: chsd ldrs sn after: wknd fnl f* **16/1**
00-0 8 9 **Pipers Piping (IRE)**[17] 98 7-9-4 **57**.... LiamKeniry 2 26
(John Butler) *led tl hdd jst ins fnl 2f: sn wknd* **20/1**
1m 39.82s (0.02) **Going Correction** -0.05s/f (Stan) **8** Ran SP% **116.7**
Speed ratings (Par 101): **97,96,94,93,92 90,87,78**
toteswingers 1&2 £3.60, 1&3 £8.00, 2&3 £3.60 CSF £20.15 CT £74.82 TOTE £8.60: £2.80, £1.20, £2.60; EX 27.30 Trifecta £158.00 Pool: £2,569.98 - 12.19 winning units..
Owner Heart Of The South Racing & Friends **Bred** John And Mrs Caroline Penny **Trained** Lower Beeding, W Sussex
■ Stewards' Enquiry : Ned Curtis two-day ban: careless riding (Feb 7-8)
Thomas Brown two-day ban: careless riding (Feb 7-8)
FOCUS
A few of these took each other on early and the race set up for the closers. Certainly the stronger of the two divisions, although it was slower.

349 TRY OUR HOSPITALITY H'CAP 7f (P)
5:05 (5:05) (Class 7) (0-50,53) 4-Y-0+ **£1,455** (£433; £216; £108) **Stalls** Low

Form RPR
33-5 1 **Michael's Nook**[5] 274 6-9-5 **48**....(p) LukeMorris 13 58
(Alastair Lidderdale) *stdd s: hld up in rr: drvn and hdwy over 1f out: str run u.p fnl f to ld fnl 50yds* **5/1**[3]
42-0 2 1 1/4 **Flow Chart (IRE)**[7] 240 6-8-13 **47**.... SladeO'Hara(5) 2 54
(Peter Grayson) *chsd ldrs: drvn to ld appr fnl 2f: kpt on fnl f: hdd and outpcd fnl 50yds* **25/1**
64-1 3 1 1/4 **Teen Ager (FR)**[15] 117 9-9-7 **50**.... TomMcLaughlin 3 54
(Paul Burgoyne) *chsd ldrs: drvn and styd on to go 2nd over 1f out: styd on same pce into 3rd ins fnl f* **6/1**
35-6 4 nk **Vale Of Lingfield (IRE)**[15] 117 4-9-2 **45**....(t[1]) FergusSweeney 5 48
(John Best) *stdd s: in rr: drvn and hdwy over 1f out: styd on wl clsng stages: nt rch ldrs* **11/2**
00-2 5 1 1/4 **Invincible Beauty (IRE)**[15] 117 4-9-5 **48**....(t) MickyFenton 12 47
(Seamus Durack) *in tch: pushed along over 2f out: styd on fnl f: nt rch ldrs* **10/1**
-466 6 3/4 **Vhujon (IRE)**[2] 327 8-9-2 **45**.... LiamKeniry 1 42
(Peter Grayson) *in rr drvn over 2f out: styd on fnl f: nvr a threat* **14/1**
00-0 7 nse **Vermeyen**[15] 117 4-9-7 **50**.... GeorgeBaker 11 47
(Geoffrey Deacon) *stdd s: in rr: drvn and hdwy to chse ldrs 2f out: sn one pce u.p* **3/1**[1]
0-23 8 nk **Compton Target (IRE)**[15] 117 4-9-4 **47**....(t) RobertWinston 10 43
(Milton Bradley) *chsd ldr: drvn to chal appr fnl 2f: wknd ins fnl f* **9/2**[2]
0-60 9 2 **Rise To Glory (IRE)**[7] 240 5-9-0 **50**....(t) JordanNason(7) 7 41
(Shaun Harris) *chsd ldrs: rdn over 2f out: wknd over 1f out* **16/1**
0-40 10 hd **Bygones For Coins (IRE)**[17] 99 5-9-0 **48**(p) WilliamTwiston-Davies(5) 4 39
(Robert Johnson) *led tl hdd appr fnl 2f: wknd appr fnl f* **14/1**
5-45 11 2 3/4 **Desert Red (IRE)**[2] 323 4-9-3 **46**....(vt) KirstyMilczarek 8 29
(Phil McEntee) *s.i.s: outpcd most of way* **33/1**
1m 26.06s (0.06) **Going Correction** -0.05s/f (Stan) **11** Ran SP% **124.6**
Speed ratings (Par 97): **97,95,94,93,92 91,91,91,88,88 85**
toteswingers 1&2 £14.80, 1&3 £4.40, 2&3 £18.10 CSF £128.60 CT £798.32 TOTE £5.40: £2.30, £8.90, £2.70; EX 161.80 Trifecta £1111.70 Pool: £3,112.70 - 2.09 winning units..
Owner C S J Beek **Bred** D R Tucker **Trained** Lambourn, Berks
FOCUS
Weak handicap form. The winner is rated up a length.

350 GET THE BETVICTOR APP MEDIAN AUCTION MAIDEN STKS 7f (P)
5:35 (5:35) (Class 6) 3-5-Y-0 **£1,940** (£577; £288; £144) **Stalls** Low

Form RPR
1 **Holy Warrior (IRE)** 3-8-10 0.... AndreaAtzeni 6 87+
(Marco Botti) *s.i.s: sn drvn to chse ldrs: pushed along and qcknd fr 2f out to ld 1f out: comf* **9/4**[1]
026- 2 3 1/4 **Great Demeanor (USA)**[47] 8033 3-8-10 75....(v[1]) LiamKeniry 9 78
(David Elsworth) *trckd ldr: drvn to ld 2f out: hdd 1f out: sn outpcd by wnr but kpt on wl for 2nd* **9/4**[1]
3 5 **Continental Divide (IRE)** 3-8-10 0.... FergusSweeney 7 65+
(Jamie Osborne) *chsd ldrs: pushed along and green fr over 2f out: styd on for wl hld 3rd fr over 1f out* **10/1**[2]
5-6 4 7 **Mastered (IRE)**[12] 184 3-8-10 0.... LukeMorris 1 46
(John Best) *in rr: pushed along over 2f out: mod prog fnl f* **20/1**[3]
5- 5 nk **Shenval**[36] 8165 3-8-10 0.... RobertWinston 8 45
(Noel Quinlan) *led tl hdd 2f out: wknd appr f* **9/4**[1]
0/ 6 1/2 **South Kenter (USA)**[504] 5863 4-9-9 0....(t) WilliamTwiston-Davies(5) 2 48
(Heather Main) *in rr: pushed along and mod prog fnl f* **33/1**
60-3 7 4 **Hanga Roa (IRE)**[15] 114 3-8-10 59.... ChrisCatlin 4 33
(Gary Moore) *chsd ldrs: rdn 3f out: wknd wl over 2f out* **20/1**[3]
30-0 8 1 3/4 **Kalahari Breeze (IRE)**[21] 31 3-8-5 48.... WilliamCarson 5 23
(William Muir) *towards rr most of way* **33/1**
60 9 9 **It Ain't To Grand**[15] 123 4-10-0 0.... RobertHavlin 3
(Roger Ingram) *bhd most of way* **66/1**
1m 25.28s (-0.72) **Going Correction** -0.05s/f (Stan)
WFA 3 from 4yo 18lb **9** Ran SP% **118.3**
Speed ratings (Par 101): **102,98,92,84,84 83,79,77,66**
toteswingers 1&2 £1.70, 1&3 £3.90, 2&3 £6.10 CSF £7.09 TOTE £3.00: £2.30, £1.10, £2.90; EX 9.50 Trifecta £71.60 Pool: £1,483.94 - 15.54 winning units..
Owner Clive Washbourn & Chris McHale **Bred** Chris McHale And Oghill House Stud **Trained** Newmarket, Suffolk
FOCUS
A moderate maiden that lacked depth. The runner-up isn't worth his rating of 75 but the winner did it well.

351 BETVICTOR CHELTENHAM FESTIVAL ANTEPOST PIONEERS H'CAP 2m (P)
6:05 (6:05) (Class 5) (0-70,70) 4-Y-0+ **£2,587** (£770; £384; £192) **Stalls** Low

Form RPR
01-3 1 **Llamadas**[14] 131 11-9-2 **58**.... IanMongan 10 66
(Olivia Maylam) *in rr: hdwy 3f out: drvn to ld wl over 1f out: fading clsng stages: jst hld on* **10/1**
0-21 2 shd **Bold Adventure**[16] 109 9-9-0 **56**.... JamieMackay 5 64
(Willie Musson) *in rr: hdwy and nt clr run over 2f out: edgd rt over 1f out: styd on wl fnl f: fin strly: jst failed* **10/1**
044- 3 hd **The Absent Mare**[26] 8290 5-9-10 **66**.... LukeMorris 8 74
(Robin Dickin) *in tch: hdwy 2f out: styd on wl fnl f: fin strly: nt quite get up* **7/1**
100- 4 1 **Dr Finley (IRE)**[81] 6407 6-9-6 **65**.... SimonPearce(3) 3 71
(Lydia Pearce) *in tch: rdn and outpcd 3f out: styd on again over 1f out: kpt on wl clsng stages* **33/1**
643- 5 3 1/2 **Ginger Fizz**[36] 8170 6-9-13 **69**.... JimCrowley 6 71
(Ben Case) *chsd ldrs: led 9f out: drvn 3 l clr ins fnl 3f: hdd wl over 1f out: wknd fnl f* **4/1**[2]
00-6 6 nk **Rocky Rebel**[14] 131 5-9-8 **64**....(b) LiamKeniry 4 66
(Chris Bealby) *chsd ldrs: rdn wl over 2f out: styd on same pce* **14/1**
053- 7 1 1/2 **Native Colony**[23] 4831 5-9-10 **66**.... HayleyTurner 7 66
(Neil King) *in rr: rdn 3f out: mod prog u.p fr over 1f out* **20/1**
656/ 8 3 1/4 **Buckie Boy (IRE)**[17] 4656 7-10-0 **70**.... EddieAhern 9 66
(Nicky Henderson) *in rr: hdwy 4f out: chsd ldr over 2f out: wknd fnl f* **12/1**
66-2 9 13 **Sherman McCoy**[20] 57 7-9-9 **70**.... WilliamTwiston-Davies(5) 2 51
(Daniel Kubler) *sn led: hdd after 2f: styd chsng ldrs: rdn over 3f out: sn wknd* **6/1**[3]
20-1 10 99 **Honourable Knight (IRE)**[15] 119 5-9-13 **69**.... GeorgeBaker 11
(Mark Usher) *in tch: chsd ldrs 1/2-way: dropped to rr 7f out: sn rdn and no ch: t.o wl over 2f out* **7/2**[1]
62-3 F **Reaction**[20] 57 7-9-5 **61**....(v) WilliamCarson 1
(Michael Appleby) *led after 2f: hdd 9f out: rdn fr 6f out: wknd 2f out: no ch whn fell wl over 1f out* **8/1**
3m 29.13s (-0.97) **Going Correction** -0.05s/f (Stan)
WFA 4 from 5yo+ 7lb **11** Ran SP% **120.4**
Speed ratings (Par 103): **100,99,99,99,97 97,96,95,88,39**
toteswingers 1&2 £9.80, 1&3 £14.30, 2&3 £11.60 CSF £108.45 CT £757.13 TOTE £13.40: £3.40, £2.20, £2.70; EX 68.40 Trifecta £467.00 Pool: £1,249.53 - 2.00 winning units..
Owner K Tyre **Bred** Burton Agnes Stud Co Ltd **Trained** Epsom, Surrey

FOCUS
They got racing a fair way out in this. The first three are all possibly better than the bare form.

352 BETVICTOR NON RUNNER FREE BET AT CHELTENHAM H'CAP 1m 4f (P)
6:35 (6:36) (Class 5) (0-75,79) 4-Y-0+ **£2,587** (£770; £384; £192) **Stalls** Centre

Form RPR

1-21 **1** **English Summer**[10] 208 6-10-1 **79** 6ex..........(t) AndreaAtzeni 6 86+
(David Simcock) *trckd ldrs in 3rd: drvn over 2f out: chsd ldr ins fnl f: led fnl 100yds: readily* **6/4**[1]

01-4 **2** *1* **Tingo In The Tale (IRE)**[14] 144 4-9-3 **71**.......... HayleyTurner 7 76
(David Arbuthnot) *chsd ldr: rdn over 2f out: led jst ins fnl f: hdd and outpcd fnl 100yds* **8/1**

13-1 **3** *4* **Purple 'n Gold (IRE)**[15] 112 4-9-1 **74**......(v) WilliamTwiston-Davies(5) 3 73
(David Pipe) *led: rdn over 2f out: hdd jst ins fnl f: sn btn* **2/1**[2]

50-4 **4** *1 ¾* **Parigino (FR)**[12] 190 5-9-10 **74**..........(p) JimCrowley 4 70
(Nick Gifford) *a in last pl: rdn and no prog fr over 2f out* **7/2**[3]

2m 36.56s (2.06) **Going Correction** -0.05s/f (Stan)
WFA 4 from 5yo+ 4lb **4** Ran SP% **106.7**
Speed ratings (Par 103): **91,90,87,86**
CSF £11.70 TOTE £2.00; EX 6.60 Trifecta £22.60 Pool: £718.41 - 23.76 winning units..

Owner Dr Marwan Koukash **Bred** Juddmonte Farms Ltd **Trained** Newmarket, Suffolk

FOCUS
This developed into something of a dash late on. Muddling form, rated around the runner-up.

353 BETVICTOR EXCLUSIVE ANTEPOST OFFER CHELTENHAM 2013 H'CAP 6f (P)
7:05 (7:05) (Class 4) (0-85,85) 4-Y-0+ **£4,690** (£1,395; £697; £348) **Stalls** Low

Form RPR

600- **1** **Burnhope**[89] 7411 4-8-7 **71** oh1..........(p) LukeMorris 4 82
(Scott Dixon) *trckd ldr: drvn over 2f out: chal over 1f out: slt ld jst ins fnl f but remained hrd pressed: hld on all out* **10/1**

00-1 **2** *nk* **Profile Star (IRE)**[20] 58 4-9-5 **83**.......... GrahamGibbons 8 93
(David Barron) *led: drvn 2f out: jnd over 1f out: narrowly hdd jst ins fnl f: styd chalng and upsides tl no ex last strides* **9/2**

-244 **3** *2* **Dorback**[11] 196 6-9-4 **82**.......... FrannyNorton 3 86
(David Nicholls) *t.k.h: chsd ldrs in 3rd: rdn ins fnl 2f: styd on same pce fnl f* **7/2**[3]

221- **4** *¾* **Lujeanie**[34] 8202 7-8-10 **79**..........(p) WilliamTwiston-Davies(5) 7 80
(Dean Ivory) *hld up in rr: hdwy ins fnl 2f: hung rt fnl f: styd on one pce* **8/1**

01-0 **5** *shd* **Kakatosi**[13] 164 6-9-7 **85**.......... EddieAhern 1 86
(Mike Murphy) *in rr: pushed along over 2f out: drvn and styd on fnl f: nt rch ldrs* **11/4**[1]

2-42 **6** *½* **Majuro (IRE)**[13] 155 9-8-13 **77**..........(t) WilliamCarson 2 76
(Violet M Jordan) *in tch: rdn over 2f out: styd on same pce* **12/1**

1-21 **7** *1* **Lastkingofscotland (IRE)**[17] 95 7-9-3 **81**..........(b) HayleyTurner 5 77
(Conor Dore) *in tch: rdn over 2f out: wknd ins fnl f* **3/1**[2]

001- **8** *nk* **Gorgeous Goblin (IRE)**[164] 5165 6-9-2 **80**..........(t) KirstyMilczarek 6 75
(David C Griffiths) *s.i.s: hld up in rr: rdn and no prog fnl 2f* **33/1**

1m 11.61s (-1.49) **Going Correction** -0.05s/f (Stan) **8** Ran SP% **122.9**
Speed ratings (Par 105): **107,106,103,102,102 102,100,100**
toteswingers 1&2 £10.20, 1&3 £5.00, 2&3 £6.30 CSF £58.56 CT £197.34 TOTE £10.10: £3.70, £1.80, £1.50; EX 111.20 Trifecta £682.00 Part won. Pool: £909.36 - 0.28 winning units..

Owner Paul J Dixon **Bred** Mrs S M Roy **Trained** Babworth, Notts

FOCUS
They appeared to go a decent gallop, but still little got into it from off the pace. A clear best from the winner.

354 FOLLOW US ON TWITTER@BETVICTORRACING H'CAP 6f (P)
7:35 (7:35) (Class 6) (0-65,65) 4-Y-0+ **£1,940** (£577; £288; £144) **Stalls** Low

Form RPR

6-65 **1** **Lucky Mark (IRE)**[13] 162 4-9-1 **59**.......... GrahamGibbons 9 70
(Garry Moss) *mde all: drvn and styd on strly fnl f* **7/2**[2]

-212 **2** *1 ¼* **Baby Dottie**[2] 323 6-8-8 **57**..........(tp) JemmaMarshall(5) 1 64
(Pat Phelan) *disp 2nd tl chsd wnr fr 2f out: rdn and no imp fnl f* **5/2**[1]

536- **3** *½* **Foot Tapper**[24] 8304 4-9-2 **60**.......... GeorgeBaker 8 65+
(Chris Wall) *s.i.s: in rr: hdwy over 2f out: sn rdn: styd on to take 3rd clsng stages but no imp on ldng duo* **5/1**[3]

210- **4** *½* **Mack's Sister**[27] 8268 6-9-1 **59**..........(p) JimCrowley 6 63
(Dean Ivory) *s.i.s: sn in tch: drvn and hdwy over 1f out: styd on fnl f: nt rch ldrs* **5/1**[3]

/0-0 **5** *½* **Lady Prodee**[15] 124 5-9-5 **63**.......... SebSanders 2 65
(Bill Turner) *chsd ldrs: rdn over 2f out: styd on same pce fnl f* **33/1**

00-4 **6** *1 ¼* **Swendab (IRE)**[17] 95 5-9-4 **62**..........(v) LukeMorris 5 60
(John O'Shea) *in rr: drvn and hdwy to chse ldrs over 1f out: wknd ins fnl f* **8/1**

16-6 **7** *2* **Efistorm**[15] 115 12-9-5 **63**.......... HayleyTurner 3 55
(Conor Dore) *in tch: rdn over 2f out: sn btn* **14/1**

200- **8** *nse* **Batgirl**[93] 7314 6-9-7 **65**.......... RobertWinston 10 57
(Terry Clement) *a towards rr* **10/1**

24-0 **9** *11* **Illustrious Lad (IRE)**[13] 156 4-8-11 **55**..........(p) WilliamCarson 7 11
(Roger Ingram) *disp 2nd tl over 2f out: sn wknd* **33/1**

1-35 **10** *3 ¼* **Pharoh Jake**[13] 156 5-8-9 **58**.......... WilliamTwiston-Davies(5) 11
(John Bridger) *outpcd most of way* **14/1**

1m 12.0s (-1.10) **Going Correction** -0.05s/f (Stan) **10** Ran SP% **123.5**
Speed ratings (Par 101): **105,103,102,102,101 99,97,96,82,77**
toteswingers 1&2 £3.90, 1&3 £4.00, 2&3 £5.00 CSF £13.57 CT £45.46 TOTE £3.70: £1.50, £1.70, £2.40; EX 18.30 Trifecta £106.30 Pool: £1,380.82 - 9.73 winning units..

Owner Ron Hull **Bred** Mrs Lisa Kelly **Trained** Tickhill, S Yorks

FOCUS
The time was reasonable and the field were soon quite well strung out. A length best from the winner.

T/Jkpt: Not won. T/Plt: £47.10 to a £1 stake. Pool of £76,948.54 - 1,192.44 winning units T/Qpdt: £15.70 to a £1 stake. Pool of £9,289.40 - 436.95 winning units ST

340 LINGFIELD (L-H)
Thursday, January 24

OFFICIAL GOING: Standard
Wind: Virtually nil Weather: Cloudy

355 LINGFIELD (S) STKS 6f (P)
1:15 (1:15) (Class 6) 4-Y-0+ **£2,045** (£603; £302) **Stalls** Low

Form RPR

35-1 **1** **Homeboy (IRE)**[2] 317 5-9-6 63.......... HayleyTurner 5 71
(Marcus Tregoning) *trckd ldr: cl up after 2f: led 1/2-way: rdn and qcknd clr 1 1/2f out: styd on strly* **6/4**[2]

1-51 **2** *3* **Dark Lane**[17] 92 7-9-6 70.......... GrahamGibbons 1 61
(David Evans) *trckd ldng pair: hdwy to trck wnr over 2f out: rdn wl over 1f out: sn no imp* **4/7**[1]

4-01 **3** *3* **Athaakeel (IRE)**[18] 88 7-9-1 49..........(b) LukeMorris 4 46
(Ronald Harris) *set stdy pce: jnd after 2f: hdd 1/2-way: rdn along 2f out: drvn wl over 1f out and sn one pce* **16/1**[3]

00-0 **4** *2* **Prophet In A Dream**[8] 220 5-9-0 42..........(p) RobertWinston 3 39
(Paddy Butler) *hld up: a in rr* **66/1**

1m 12.45s (0.55) **Going Correction** -0.025s/f (Stan) **4** Ran SP% **111.0**
Speed ratings (Par 101): **95,91,87,84**
CSF £2.79 TOTE £2.70; EX 4.20 Trifecta £4.80 Pool: £1,421.31 - 218.98 winning units..The winner was bought in for 6,500gns.

Owner Home Marketing Limited **Bred** J Costello **Trained** Whitsbury, Hants

FOCUS
Despite three of the four runners winning last time, this was uncompetitive. The winner looks the best guide.

356 LINGFIELDPARK.CO.UK MAIDEN STKS 5f (P)
1:45 (1:45) (Class 5) 3-Y-0+ **£2,726** (£805; £402) **Stalls** High

Form RPR

3 **1** **Dangerous Age**[22] 19 3-8-6 0.......... JoeFanning 10 53+
(J W Hills) *trckd ldrs on outer: hdwy 2f out: rdn over 1f out: styd on to ld ins fnl f* **7/2**[3]

0 **2** *nk* **Twist And Twirl**[7] 236 3-7-13 0.......... AdamMcLean(7) 7 52
(Derek Shaw) *cl up: led over 2f out: rdn wl over 1f out: hdd ins fnl f: no ex towards fin* **66/1**

52- **3** *¾* **Magic Ice**[26] 8286 3-8-6 0.......... FrannyNorton 2 50
(John Berry) *trckd ldrs on inner: hdwy wl over 1f out: rdn and ev ch ent fnl f: kpt on same pce* **5/1**

3-33 **4** *¾* **Island Express (IRE)**[14] 136 6-9-7 53..........(tp) AnnStokell(5) 6 58?
(Ann Stokell) *towards rr: rdn and hdwy on outer wl over 1f out: kpt on fnl f: nrst fin* **16/1**

2-42 **5** *½* **Jermatt**[14] 136 4-9-12 59.......... IanMongan 3 56
(J R Jenkins) *led: pushed along 1/2-way and sn: hdd: rdn wl over 1f out and sn one pce* **11/4**[2]

04- **6** *nk* **Copper Leyf**[33] 8230 3-8-11 0.......... LiamKeniry 4 49
(Jeremy Gask) *dwlt and in rr: hdwy on inner wl over 1f out: chsd ldrs whn n.m.r ins fnl f: one pce after* **33/1**

7 *2* **Green Millionaire** 3-8-11 0.......... FergusSweeney 9 42+
(Jeremy Gask) *sn outpcd and in rr: hdwy over 1f out: swtchd rt ins fnl f and kpt on towards fin* **8/1**

65-3 **8** *7* **First Serve (IRE)**[11] 197 3-8-6 0.......... LukeMorris 5 12
(David Barron) *dwlt: sn chsng ldrs: rdn along over 2f out: sn wknd and eased fnl f* **5/2**[1]

59.34s (0.54) **Going Correction** -0.025s/f (Stan)
WFA 3 from 4yo+ 15lb **8** Ran SP% **115.6**
Speed ratings (Par 103): **94,93,92,91,90 89,86,75**
toteswingers 1&2 £32.30, 1&3 £4.10, 2&3 £44.00 CSF £166.16 TOTE £2.80: £1.10, £20.20, £3.00; EX 264.80 Trifecta £740.70 Pool: £3,068.89 - 3.10 winning units..

Owner Ross Hunter & David Klein **Bred** Mrs T Brudenell **Trained** Upper Lambourn, Berks

FOCUS
A poor sprint maiden, limited by the fourth.

357 PLAY GOLF AT LINGFIELD PARK RACECOURSE H'CAP 6f (P)
2:15 (2:15) (Class 6) (0-60,62) 3-Y-0 **£2,045** (£603; £302) **Stalls** Low

Form RPR

04-1 **1** **Black Dave (IRE)**[8] 228 3-9-9 **62** 6ex.......... GrahamGibbons 5 69
(David Evans) *cl up: led after 1f: rdn over 1f out: drvn ins fnl f: hld on wl* **7/4**[1]

5-22 **2** *½* **Holding Fast (IRE)**[10] 207 3-8-12 **51**.......... MartinLane 4 56
(Tobias B P Coles) *dwlt: sn trcking ldrs: hdwy to chse ldng pair over 1f out and sn rdn: styd on wl u.p ins fnl f: jst hld* **7/2**[3]

31-2 **3** *hd* **Katy Spirit (IRE)**[21] 31 3-9-6 **59**.......... LiamKeniry 1 63
(Michael Blanshard) *led 1f: trckd ldng pair: hdwy on inner wl over 1f out: rdn to chal ent fnl f: ev ch tl drvn and no ex last 50yds* **7/1**

505- **4** *2 ½* **Jordanstown**[209] 3576 3-9-3 **56**.......... RobertWinston 2 52
(Kevin Ryan) *trckd ldrs: hdwy on outer over 2f out: rdn wl over 1f out: sn no imp* **5/2**[2]

54-0 **5** *3* **We Are City**[16] 106 3-9-0 **60**.......... RobertTart(7) 3 47
(Michael Bell) *in rr: sme hdwy whn n.m.r on inner wl over 1f out: sn rdn and n.d* **10/1**

4-00 **6** *13* **Vergality Ridge (IRE)**[2] 321 3-9-3 **56**..........(b) LukeMorris 6
(Ronald Harris) *cl up: rdn along over 2f out: wknd wl over 1f out* **12/1**

1m 11.96s (0.06) **Going Correction** -0.025s/f (Stan) **6** Ran SP% **116.4**
Speed ratings (Par 95): **98,97,97,93,89 72**
toteswingers 1&2 £1.60, 1&3 £2.80, 2&3 £2.30 CSF £8.71 TOTE £2.70: £1.20, £2.90; EX 10.80 Trifecta £22.00 Pool: £2,916.05 - 99.04 winning units..

Owner Mrs E Evans **Bred** Richard Frayne **Trained** Pandy, Monmouths

FOCUS
A modest sprint handicap for 3yos. The first two were well in and are rated to form.

358 BOOK TICKETS ONLINE @ LINGFIELDPARK.CO.UK H'CAP 7f (P)
2:45 (2:45) (Class 5) (0-75,75) 4-Y-0+ **£2,726** (£805; £402) **Stalls** Low

Form RPR

11-5 **1** **Balti's Sister (IRE)**[22] 25 4-9-6 **74**.......... RobertWinston 8 83
(Terry Clement) *hld up in rr: gd hdwy on inner 1 1/2f out: rdn to chse ldrs ent fnl f: styd on to ld last 100yds* **8/1**

/34- **2** *1 ½* **Chokidar (IRE)**[108] 6934 5-9-7 **75**..........(v) IanMongan 10 80
(Scott Dixon) *hld up in tch: hdwy 2f out: rdn to chse ldrs over 1f out: drvn and ch ins fnl f: kpt on same pce* **8/1**

The Form Book Flat, Raceform Ltd, Compton, RG20 6NL.

-223 **3** *nse* **Muhandis (IRE)**[1] 344 5-9-2 **70**....(b) SebSanders 9 75
(Nick Littmoden) *dwlt: hld up in rr: hdwy on inner over 1f out: sn rdn and styd on wl towards fin* **5/1**[3]

01-1 **4** *½* **Captain Kendall (IRE)**[15] 115 4-9-0 **68**.... LukeMorris 1 72+
(David Evans) *chsd ldr: hdwy 2f out: rdn over 1f out: led ent fnl f: drvn and hdd last 100yds: wknd* **7/2**[2]

660- **5** *2 ¾* **Blue Jack**[35] 8188 8-9-5 **73**....(t) AndreaAtzeni 3 69
(Stuart Williams) *led: rdn along wl over 1f out: hdd ent fnl f: grad wknd* **25/1**

00-0 **6** *¾* **The Guru Of Gloom (IRE)**[21] 34 5-9-4 **72**.... JimCrowley 4 66
(William Muir) *t.k.h early: in tch: rdn over 1f out: no imp* **10/1**

003- **7** *hd* **Avonmore Star**[116] 6705 5-9-1 **74**.... WilliamTwiston-Davies(5) 2 68
(Mike Murphy) *chsd ldrs: rdn 2f out: wknd appr fnl f* **6/1**

0-32 **8** *1 ¼* **Avonrose**[7] 234 6-8-7 **68**....(v) AdamMcLean(7) 7 58
(Derek Shaw) *a towards rr* **7/1**

42-2 **9** *2* **Paperetto**[19] 80 5-8-4 **65**.... RyanTate(7) 6 50
(Robert Mills) *chsd ldrs on outer: rdn along 2f out: sn wknd* **3/1**[1]

1m 23.33s (-1.47) **Going Correction** -0.025s/f (Stan) **9** Ran SP% **125.8**
Speed ratings (Par 103): **107,105,105,104,101 100,100,99,96**
toteswingers 1&2 £11.40, 1&3 £7.30, 2&3 £8.30 CSF £76.40 CT £296.59 TOTE £10.70: £3.10, £3.60, £1.90; EX 106.00 Trifecta £601.60 Pool: £2,022.47 - 2.52 winning units..
Owner Mrs Michelle Smith **Bred** P Monaghan, J Collins & G Dillon **Trained** Newmarket, Suffolk

FOCUS
A modest handicap, though a competitive one. It was well run, which suited the winner.

359 CROWHURST H'CAP 1m (P)
3:15 (3:15) (Class 4) (0-85,83) 3-Y-O £4,690 (£1,395; £697; £348) **Stalls High**

Form RPR

013- **1** **Hipster**[34] 8211 3-9-7 **83**....(b) JimCrowley 6 88
(Ralph Beckett) *mde all: rdn wl over 1f out: drvn and edgd lft ins fnl f: kpt on* **5/1**[3]

3- **2** *1 ¼* **King George River (IRE)**[33] 8223 3-8-13 **82**.... PhilipPrince(7) 2 84
(Alan Bailey) *trckd wnr: effrt 2f out: rdn wl over 1f out: drvn and kpt on same pce ins fnl f* **7/4**[1]

14-2 **3** *1* **Tight Knit (USA)**[10] 209 3-8-13 **75**....(b[1]) LukeMorris 3 75
(James Tate) *trckd ldrs: hdwy 2f out: rdn over 1f out: ch whn n.m.r jst ins fnl f: one pce after* **11/4**[2]

4-11 **4** *1* **Club House (IRE)**[12] 188 3-8-5 **74**.... RobertTart(7) 4 72
(Robert Mills) *hld up in rr: hdwy wl over 1f out: rdn to chse ldrs and styng on whn n.m.r and hmpd jst ins fnl f: one pce after* **6/1**

021- **5** *nk* **Sherinn**[24] 8303 3-8-10 **72**.... AndreaAtzeni 5 69
(Roger Varian) *hld up in rr: hdwy wl over 1f out: sn rdn and no imp fnl f* **7/1**

214- **6** *hd* **Blue Wave (IRE)**[143] 5890 3-9-3 **79**.... JoeFanning 1 75
(Mark Johnston) *dwlt: sn cl up: rdn along 3f out: wknd over 2f out* **14/1**

1m 37.09s (-1.11) **Going Correction** -0.025s/f (Stan) **6** Ran SP% **113.1**
Speed ratings (Par 99): **104,102,101,100,100 100**
toteswingers 1&2 £2.40, 1&3 £3.20, 2&3 £2.00 CSF £14.47 TOTE £5.30: £2.80, £1.40; EX 16.10 Trifecta £63.50 Pool: £2,460.59 - 29.01 winning units..
Owner R Roberts **Bred** Cheveley Park Stud Ltd **Trained** Kimpton, Hants

FOCUS
A field of in-form and progressive 3yos lined up for this, but it was spoilt by a lack of pace and the winner had the run of the race. The form is taken at something like face value.

360 ANNUAL MEMBERSHIP AT LINGFIELD PARK GOLF CLUB H'CAP 5f (P)
3:45 (3:45) (Class 5) (0-75,74) 4-Y-O+ £2,587 (£770; £384; £192) **Stalls High**

Form RPR

3-21 **1** **Picansort**[8] 232 6-9-5 **72** 6ex....(b) ShaneKelly 1 83
(Peter Crate) *trckd ldng pair: cl up 1/2-way: led 2f out: rdn over 1f out: kpt on fnl f* **5/4**[1]

61-5 **2** *1 ¼* **Danzoe (IRE)**[12] 186 6-9-3 **70**.... TomMcLaughlin 2 76
(Christine Dunnett) *prom: rdn to chse wnr ent fnl f: kpt on* **6/1**

61-2 **3** *3 ¼* **The Strig**[8] 232 6-9-7 **74**....(v) AndreaAtzeni 3 68
(Stuart Williams) *s.i.s and bhd: hdwy 2f out: sn rdn: kpt on fnl f* **7/4**[2]

000- **4** *1* **Berberana (IRE)**[85] 7489 5-8-13 **66**....(p) JimCrowley 5 57
(Jeremy Gask) *led: pushed along and hdd 2f out: wknd fnl f* **5/1**[3]

58.34s (-0.46) **Going Correction** -0.025s/f (Stan) **4** Ran SP% **111.8**
Speed ratings (Par 103): **102,100,94,93**
CSF £8.83 TOTE £1.70; EX 5.00 Trifecta £11.00 Pool: £1,423.27 - 96.70 winning units..
Owner Peter Crate **Bred** Miss Brooke Sanders **Trained** Newdigate, Surrey

FOCUS
A modest sprint handicap. The winner confirmed that he's better than ever.

361 FOLLOW US ON TWITTER @LINGFIELDPARK H'CAP 1m 4f (P)
4:15 (4:17) (Class 6) (0-60,60) 4-Y-O+ £2,045 (£603; £302) **Stalls Low**

Form RPR

2/0- **1** **Wom**[45] 4683 5-9-7 **57**....(v[1]) HayleyTurner 4 66
(Neil King) *hld up in rr: hdwy 2f out: rdn ins fnl f: styd on wl to ld nr fin* **12/1**

240- **2** *hd* **Broughtons Bandit**[247] 2371 6-9-3 **53**.... J-PGuillambert 3 61
(Willie Musson) *hld up towards rr: hdwy 2f out: rdn over 1f out: styd on wl fnl f: jst hld* **5/1**[3]

15-2 **3** *hd* **Liberty Love (IRE)**[17] 100 8-9-2 **52**....(bt) WilliamCarson 5 60
(Shaun Harley, Ire) *hld up towards rr: stdy hdwy over 4f out: trckd ldrs over 2f out: rdn to chal over 1f out: led wl ins fnl f: hdd and no ex nr fin* **2/1**[1]

006- **4** *½* **Extremely Alert**[33] 8229 4-7-13 **46** oh1.... RyanTate(7) 10 53
(Michael Bell) *trckd ldng pair: hdwy and cl up over 2f out: rdn to ld over 1f out: drvn and hdd wl ins fnl f: one pce towards fin* **3/1**[2]

/0-0 **5** *2* **State Senator (USA)**[20] 53 5-9-5 **55**.... JimCrowley 2 59
(Richard Ford) *chsd ldrs: rdn along 2f out: drvn and one pce fnl f* **20/1**

01-3 **6** *nse* **El Bravo**[22] 9 7-9-3 **58**.... ShirleyTeasdale(5) 9 62
(Shaun Harris) *trckd ldr: cl up 3f out: rdn to ld wl over 1f out: hdd and drvn appr fnl f: one pce* **5/1**[3]

060- **7** *1 ¼* **Scary Movie (IRE)**[48] 8030 8-9-10 **60**.... ShaneKelly 7 62
(Thomas McLaughlin, Ire) *hld up in rr: hdwy on outer over 3f out: rdn along over 2f out: kpt on same pce fnl f* **12/1**

40-0 **8** *2 ¼* **Bennelong**[14] 132 7-9-5 **55**....(p) AmirQuinn 11 53
(Richard Rowe) *hld up: a towards rr* **25/1**

0-06 **9** *9* **Penbryn (USA)**[10] 205 6-9-9 **59**.... SebSanders 6 43
(Nick Littmoden) *led: rdn along 3f out: hdd and drvn wl over 1f out: sn wknd* **12/1**

540- **10** *1 ¼* **Persian Herald**[23] 5012 5-9-10 **60**....(p) EddieAhern 8 42
(Neil King) *in tch: effrt on outer over 3f out: rdn along over 2f out: sn wknd* **20/1**

2m 32.25s (-0.75) **Going Correction** -0.025s/f (Stan)
WFA 4 from 5yo+ 4lb **10** Ran SP% **128.1**
Speed ratings (Par 101): **101,100,100,100,99 99,98,96,90,89**
toteswingers 1&2 £14.30, 1&3 £7.60, 2&3 £4.50 CSF £76.09 CT £178.02 TOTE £17.30: £5.60, £3.00, £1.10; EX 123.60 Trifecta £1873.10 Pool: £2,790.90 - 1.11 winning units..
Owner Mark Harrod & John Hitchin **Bred** Genesis Green Stud **Trained** Newmarket, Suffolk

FOCUS
A moderate middle-distance handicap run at a fair pace. A Flat best from the winner.
T/Plt: £427.30 to a £1 stake. Pool: £70,333.53 - 120.14 winning tickets T/Qpdt: £24.90 to a £1 stake. Pool: £8,325.18 - 247.05 winning tickets JR

287 MEYDAN (L-H)
Thursday, January 24

OFFICIAL GOING: Tapeta: standard; turf: good

362a ZABEEL FEEDMILL TROPHY (H'CAP) (TAPETA) 1m 3f
2:30 (2:31) (95-105,104) 3-Y-O+
£40,490 (£13,496; £6,748; £3,374; £2,024; £1,349)

RPR

1 **Bay Willow (IRE)**[21] 45 6-9-3 **102**....(tp) RichardMullen 5 102
(S Seemar, UAE) *sn led: rdn 3f out: r.o wl: hld on gamely* **6/1**[3]

2 *½* **Layali Al Andalus**[5] 292 6-8-5 **97** ow2.... MarcMonaghan(6) 4 93+
(S Seemar, UAE) *mid-div: rdn 3f out: r.o fnl 2f: nrst fin* **13/2**

3 *1 ½* **Pisco Sour (USA)**[120] 6575 5-9-3 **102**.... SilvestreDeSousa 1 98
(Saeed bin Suroor) *trckd ldng pair: nvr nr to chal* **7/1**

4 *2* **Art Scholar (IRE)**[7] 246 6-9-0 **99**.... KierenFallon 3 92
(Michael Appleby) *mid-div: chsd ldrs 2 1/2f out: one pce fnl 1 1/2f* **10/3**[2]

5 *hd* **Ottoman Empire (FR)**[14] 151 7-8-13 **98**.... HarryBentley 10 90+
(David Simcock) *settled in rr: kpt on fnl 2f but nvr nr to chal* **6/1**[3]

6 *¼* **Arthur's Tale (USA)**[14] 151 5-8-13 **98**....(b) MickaelBarzalona 2 90
(Mahmood Al Zarooni) *trckd ldrs: t.k.h: rdn 4f out: one pce fnl 1 1/2f* **3/1**[1]

7 *3 ¼* **Eddie Jock (IRE)**[7] 246 9-8-9 **95**....(t) TadhgO'Shea 8 80+
(S Seemar, UAE) *settled in rr: nvr able to chal* **25/1**

8 *3 ¾* **Topclas (FR)**[14] 151 7-9-3 **102**....(vt) ADeVries 6 81
(M bin Shafya, UAE) *slowly away: nvr bttr than mid-div* **25/1**

9 *3 ¼* **Rochdale**[14] 151 10-9-3 **102**....(t) RoystonFfrench 9 75
(A Al Raihe, UAE) *in rr of mid-div: nvr nr to chal* **33/1**

10 *9 ¾* **Jardim (BRZ)**[7] 241 7-9-4 **104**.... PatCosgrave 7 59
(M F De Kock, South Africa) *in rr of mid-div: nvr able to chal* **14/1**

2m 20.85s (2.45) **10** Ran SP% **119.8**
WIN: 4.60. PL: 1.60, 2.30, 2.90. EX: 46.60. CSF: 45.01; TRICAST: 284.29.
Owner Sheikh Majid Bin Mohammed al Maktoum **Bred** Philip Brady **Trained** United Arab Emirates

FOCUS
There was a distinct lack of initiative from most of the beaten riders in this weak handicap, with Bay Willow allowed a totally uncontested lead. He was able to crawl through the early stages before gradually upping the tempo, recording the following splits: 28.20, 26.87, 26.49, 24.16, 23.11 and 12.02.

363a MEYDAN HOTEL TROPHY (H'CAP) (TURF) 1m 1f
3:05 (3:05) (95-110,110) 3-Y-O+
£55,214 (£18,404; £9,202; £4,601; £2,760; £1,840)

RPR

1 **Masteroftherolls (IRE)**[110] 6879 5-8-10 **100**.... SilvestreDeSousa 8 103
(Saeed bin Suroor) *mid-div: smooth prog 3f out: led over 1f out: r.o wl* **2/1**[1]

2 *¾* **Burano (IRE)**[82] 7557 4-8-8 **99**.... KierenFallon 3 100
(Brian Meehan) *in rr of mid-div: rdn over 2f out: r.o fnl 1 1/2f: nrst fin* **12/1**

3 *¾* **Counterglow (IRE)**[126] 6400 4-8-9 **100**.... AntiocoMurgia 2 99+
(Mahmood Al Zarooni) *in rr of mid-div: r.o fnl 2f: nrst fin* **16/1**

4 *1* **Mushreq (AUS)**[14] 151 5-9-0 **104**.... PaulHanagan 7 101+
(M F De Kock, South Africa) *mid-div: n.m.r 2f out: r.o wl fnl f: nrst fin* **8/1**

5 *2 ¼* **Tajaaweed (USA)**[14] 153 8-9-6 **110**.... DaneO'Neill 9 103
(Doug Watson, UAE) *trckd ldng pair: ev ch over a f out: one pce* **25/1**

6 *hd* **Famous Warrior (IRE)**[13] 180 6-8-9 **99**....(t) PatDobbs 5 91
(Doug Watson, UAE) *sn led: rdn 2f out: hdd over 1f out: kpt on same pce* **20/1**

7 *12* **Samurai Sword**[453] 7166 5-8-8 **98**.... AhmedAjtebi 1 65
(Mahmood Al Zarooni) *slowly away: settled in last: nvr nr to chal* **6/1**[3]

8 *3* **Paene Magnus (IRE)**[69] 7759 4-8-8 **99**....(t) KevinManning 4 60
(J S Bolger, Ire) *s.i.s: trckd ldrs: rdn 4f out: outpcd fnl 1 1/2f* **7/2**[2]

9 *1 ¾* **Theo Danon (GER)**[14] 152 5-9-1 **105**.... ADeVries 6 62
(Mario Hofer, Germany) *settled in rr: nvr able to chal* **16/1**

10 *4 ¾* **Rostrum (FR)**[329] 759 6-9-1 **105**.... MickaelBarzalona 10 52
(Mahmood Al Zarooni) *trckd ldng pair tl outpcd 2f out* **7/1**

1m 49.36s (109.36)
WFA 4 from 5yo+ 1lb **10** Ran SP% **121.5**
WIN: 2.40. PL: 1.00, 5.80, 6.70. EX: 48.00. CSF: 29.90; TRICAST: 318.32 TRIFECTA: 450.40.
Owner Godolphin **Bred** Helen Smith & Sally Mullen **Trained** Newmarket, Suffolk

FOCUS
Famous Warrior had to work hard for the lead, being pressed by Paene Magnus, and the sectionals showed he set an unsustainable pace, going 24.98 (from standing start) and 23.14, before the tempo inevitably slowed. The first two set the standard.

364a BAB AL SHAMS TROPHY (H'CAP) (TAPETA) 1m 2f
3:40 (3:40) (95-112,112) 3-Y-O+
£55,214 (£18,404; £9,202; £4,601; £2,760; £1,840)

RPR

1 **Elderly Paradise (AUS)**[7] 241 6-9-0 **106**....(e) ChristopheSoumillon 2 106
(M C Tam, Macau) *sn led: kicked clr over 2f out: r.o wl* **5/2**[2]

2 *1 ¼* **Jamr**[14] 153 5-9-1 **107**....(v) ADeVries 4 104+
(M bin Shafya, UAE) *mid-div: r.o fnl 2f: nrst fin but nvr able to chal* **5/2**[2]

3 *hd* **High Twelve (IRE)**[27] 8281 6-8-5 **95**....(v) RichardMullen 1 94
(S Seemar, UAE) *trckd ldrs: ev ch 2f out: one pce fnl f* **20/1**

4 *1* **Novelty Seeker (USA)**[100] 4-8-5 **98**.... MickaelBarzalona 3 94
(Mahmood Al Zarooni) *in rr of mid-div: n.m.r sn after s: r.o fnl 2f: nrst fin* **9/4**[1]

5 *2 ½* **Muck 'N' Brass (IRE)**[14] 151 4-8-5 **97**....(t) TadhgO'Shea 6 89
(Edward Lynam, Ire) *slowly away: settled in rr: nvr able to chal but kpt on fnl f* **16/1**

6 1 ¼ **Ostinato (GER)**[81] 7586 5-9-5 **111**.....(bt) KierenFallon 8 98
(Sandor Kovacs, Hungary) *slowly away: trckd ldrs: led 4f out: hdd 2f out: wknd fnl f* **8/1**[3]
7 2 **Marching Time**[14] 151 7-8-8 **100**.....(v) PaulHanagan 7 83
(Doug Watson, UAE) *trckd ldng pair: ev ch 3f out: outpcd fnl f* **20/1**
2m 7.64s (2.94)
WFA 4 from 5yo+ 2lb 7 Ran SP% **114.4**
WIN: 3.00. EX: 10.50. CSF: 9.23; TRICAST: 93.84 TRIFECTA: 102.00.
Owner Wong Yun Sang, Choi Yuet Wing & Ng Kang So **Bred** Fowlston Bloodstock, Classic Park Bloodstock Pty L **Trained** Macau

FOCUS
Elderly Paradise was allowed to set a slow early pace. Here are his sectionals in full: 28.65, 26.70, 24.44, 24.76, 23.09.

365a MEYDAN GOLF TROPHY (CONDITIONS RACE) (TAPETA) 6f
4:15 (4:15) 3-Y-O+
£36,809 (£12,269; £6,134; £3,067; £1,840; £1,226)

RPR
1 **Reynaldothewizard (USA)**[35] 8198 7-9-0 107.....(bt) RichardMullen 6 111
(S Seemar, UAE) *trckd ldng pair: rdn over 2f out: r.o to ld fnl 55yds* **20/1**
2 ½ **Balmont Mast (IRE)**[14] 150 5-9-0 108..... GaryCarroll 7 109+
(Edward Lynam, Ire) *trckd ldrs: rdn over 2f out: r.o wl fnl 1 1/2f: nrst fin* **6/1**[3]
3 ¾ **Ganas (IRE)**[35] 8197 5-9-0 102..... TadhgO'Shea 10 107
(Ernst Oertel, UAE) *sn led: kicked clr 3f out: wknd 110yds out: hdd fnl 55yds* **9/1**
4 2 ¼ **Smooth Operator (GER)**[14] 150 7-9-0 107.....(v) ADeVries 12 100
(Mario Hofer, Germany) *mid-div: kpt on fnl 2f: nrst fin* **16/1**
5 ¼ **Kavanagh (SAF)**[264] 6-9-0 112..... JGeroudis 1 99
(M F De Kock, South Africa) *chsd ldrs: kpt on same pce fnl 1 1/2f* **10/1**
6 ¾ **Govinda (USA)**[14] 150 6-9-0 107..... TedDurcan 14 96
(Vanja Sandrup, Sweden) *a in rr* **33/1**
7 3 ½ **Ballista (IRE)**[68] 7772 5-9-0 109..... RichardKingscote 2 85
(Tom Dascombe) *mid-div: chsd ldrs 2f out: one pce fnl 55yds* **4/1**[2]
8 2 ¼ **Hitchens (IRE)**[138] 6030 8-9-0 113..... SilvestreDeSousa 9 78
(David Barron) *mid-div: kpt on same pce fnl 2f* **3/1**[1]
9 ½ **Garbah (IRE)**[32] 5-8-9 105..... RoystonFfrench 5 71
(A Al Raihe, UAE) *trckd ldng pair: ev ch 3f out: one pce fnl f* **10/1**
10 1 ¼ **Waffle (IRE)**[110] 6867 7-9-0 102..... HarryBentley 13 72
(David Barron) *nvr able to chal* **16/1**
11 ¼ **Oasis Dancer**[14] 149 6-9-0 102..... KierenFallon 3 71
(Kevin Ryan) *chsd ldrs: nt qckn fnl f* **14/1**
12 5 ¼ **Dohasa (IRE)**[321] 861 8-9-0 107..... AntiocoMurgia 11 55
(Ismail Mohammed) *nvr nr to chal* **33/1**
13 13 **Addictive Dream (IRE)**[14] 150 6-9-0 107..... AdrianNicholls 4 13
(David Nicholls) *trckd ldrs tl outpcd over 3f out* **25/1**
U **Whaileyy (IRE)**[19] 78 5-9-0 105.....(b) MartinHarley 8
(Marco Botti) *uns rdr at s* **7/1**
1m 11.21s (-0.39) 14 Ran SP% **132.9**
WIN: 25.00. PL: 6.60, 3.50, 2.20. EX: 261.20. CSF: 144.73; TRIFECTA: 1,664.60.
Owner Zabeel Racing International, Corp **Bred** Gibraltar Group Lp **Trained** United Arab Emirates

FOCUS
There wasn't the anticipated battle for the lead as one of the expected pacesetters Ballista ruined his chance with a sluggish start and Ganas just blasted away from the others. The leader's 800m split of 46.66 was just 0.08 off the record set by Rocket Man in last year's Golden Shaheen. The winner is rated to his mark.

366a CAPE VERDI SPONSORED BY MEYDAN HOTELS (F&M) (GROUP 2) (TURF) 1m
4:50 (4:50) 3-Y-O+
£73,619 (£24,539; £12,269; £6,134; £3,680; £2,453)

RPR
1 **Sajjhaa**[75] 7688 6-9-0 110..... SilvestreDeSousa 8 109+
(Saeed bin Suroor) *trckd ldrs: rdn over 2 1/2f out: led 2f out: r.o wl: comf* **4/6**[1]
2 1 ¼ **First City**[32] 7-9-0 110..... RoystonFfrench 7 97
(A Al Raihe, UAE) *settled in rr: smooth prog over 2f out: chsd wnr fr 1f out: wknd fnl 110yds* **10/1**
3 2 ½ **Falls Of Lora (IRE)**[118] 6633 4-9-0 107..... MickaelBarzalona 4 91
(Mahmood Al Zarooni) *mid-div: kpt on same pce fnl f* **6/1**[2]
4 4 ¾ **Dark Orchid (USA)**[156] 5472 4-9-0 108..... TedDurcan 1 80
(Saeed bin Suroor) *sn led: clr 4f out: hdd & wknd 2f out* **9/1**
5 3 ¾ **Naseem Alyasmeen (IRE)**[5] 292 4-9-0 95..... PaulHanagan 3 72
(A Al Raihe, UAE) *trckd ldrs tl outpcd 3f out* **40/1**
6 12 **Spellwork (USA)**[144] 5870 4-9-0 102..... KierenFallon 5 44
(Saeed bin Suroor) *settled in rr: nvr nr to chal* **8/1**[3]
7 2 ½ **Forever Snow (USA)**[141] 4-9-0 95.....(v) HarryBentley 6 38
(Fabricio Borges, Sweden) *settled in rr: n.d* **33/1**
D 3 ¾ **Amanee (AUS)**[14] 154 5-9-0 102..... ChristopheSoumillon 2 102+
(M F De Kock, South Africa) *trckd ldrs: ev ch over 2f out: outpcd last f but kpt on wl* **12/1**
1m 36.68s (96.68) 8 Ran SP% **117.5**
WIN: 1.70. PL: 1.00, 2.10, 3.00. EX: 9.50. CSF: 10.96; TRIFECTA: 37.60.
Owner Godolphin **Bred** Darley **Trained** Newmarket, Suffolk

FOCUS
Whilst this wasn't a competitive race, and the winner and runner-up both had tough trips, the form actually makes sense and looks solid enough. They went a fast-slow pace thanks to Dark Orchid, who took them along in splits of 25.88, 22.80, 23.46, before Sajjhaa came home in 24.45.

367a MEYDAN BEACH TROPHY (H'CAP) (TURF) 1m
5:25 (5:25) (100-110,109) 3-Y-O+
£44,171 (£14,723; £7,361; £3,680; £2,208; £1,472)

RPR
1 **Mandaean**[103] 7054 4-9-0 **105**..... MickaelBarzalona 3 111
(Mahmood Al Zarooni) *mid-div on rail: smooth prog to ld 1 1/2f out: r.o wl* **6/1**[3]
2 1 ½ **Don't Call Me (IRE)**[14] 154 6-9-0 **105**.....(t) RichardMullen 7 108+
(David Nicholls) *settled in rr: r.o fnl 2f: nrst fin* **7/2**[1]
3 3 ¼ **Iguazu Falls (USA)**[21] 46 8-8-11 **102**.....(t) ADeVries 5 97
(M bin Shafya, UAE) *trckd ldrs: ev ch 2 1/2f out: one pce fnl 1 1/2f* **33/1**
4 hd **Disa Leader (SAF)**[14] 154 8-9-2 **107**..... JGeroudis 2 102
(M F De Kock, South Africa) *settled in rr: smooth prog 3f out: led 2 1/2f out: hdd 1 1/2f out: wknd fnl 110yds* **6/1**[3]
5 1 ¾ **Malossol (USA)**[51] 7985 4-9-4 **109**.....(bt) CO'Donoghue 1 100
(G Botti, France) *trckd ldrs: ev ch 1 1/2f out: wknd fnl 110yds* **33/1**
6 ¼ **Quick Wit**[82] 7558 6-9-2 **107**..... TedDurcan 6 97
(Saeed bin Suroor) *trckd ldng duo: ev ch 3f out: wknd fnl f* **14/1**
7 ¼ **Finjaan**[7] 241 7-8-13 **104**.....(bt) DaneO'Neill 10 93
(Doug Watson, UAE) *slowly away: settled in rr: nvr nr to chal* **25/1**
8 4 **Jet Legend (SAF)**[310] 6-8-9 **100**..... PaulHanagan 9 80
(M F De Kock, South Africa) *in rr of mid-div: nvr nr to chal* **7/2**[1]
9 4 ¾ **Canwinn (IRE)**[14] 149 7-8-10 **101**..... KierenFallon 4 70
(D Selvaratnam, UAE) *trckd ldrs tl outpcd 2 1/2f out* **25/1**
10 2 ½ **Energia Dust (BRZ)**[14] 152 5-8-11 **102**.....(t) GaryCarroll 11 65
(Fabricio Borges, Sweden) *settled in rr: n.d* **25/1**
11 1 **Trade Storm**[133] 6166 5-8-13 **104**..... ChristopheSoumillon 8 65
(David Simcock) *settled in rr: nvr able to chal* **9/2**[2]
12 4 ¼ **Rex Imperator**[131] 6244 4-8-11 **102**..... AdrianNicholls 13 53
(David Nicholls) *sn led: hdd & wknd 2 1/2f out* **16/1**
13 2 ¾ **Rassam (IRE)**[132] 6201 4-8-9 **100**..... SilvestreDeSousa 12 45
(Saeed bin Suroor) *settled in last: n.d* **9/1**
14 ¾ **Il Grande Maurizio (IRE)**[14] 149 9-8-9 **100**..... RoystonFfrench 14 43
(A Al Raihe, UAE) *trckd ldrs tl wknd 2 1/2f out* **33/1**
1m 36.65s (96.65) 14 Ran SP% **134.1**
WIN: 6.60. PL: 2.70, 1.80, 10.50. EX: 45.40. CSF: 28.52; TRICAST: 678.60; TRIFECTA: £1,692.20. PLACEPOT: £136.60. Pool £11,643.37 - 62.20 winning units. QUADPOT: £11.90. Pool £731.70 - 45.40 winning units..
Owner Godolphin **Bred** Darley **Trained** Newmarket, Suffolk

FOCUS
The pace wasn't overly strong (splits for the first three quarters were 25.09, 23.84, 24.02), but a couple of nicely handicapped types were well on top at the line.

355 LINGFIELD (L-H)
Friday, January 25

OFFICIAL GOING: Standard
Wind: Light; half behind Weather: Dry; cold

368 BET AT BLUESQ.COM CLAIMING STKS 5f (P)
1:00 (1:00) (Class 6) 3-Y-O **£2,045** (£603; £302) **Stalls** High

Form RPR
1-22 1 **Windforpower (IRE)**[17] 106 3-8-6 68.....(be) LukeMorris 2 58
(Ronald Harris) *trckd ldrs: wnt 2nd wl over 1f out: cajoled along to go upsides ldr ins fnl f: asked for effrt fnl 100yds: drvn and fnd jst enough to ld last strides* **1/1**[1]
444- 2 hd **Marmot Bay (IRE)**[29] 8258 3-7-12 57 ow1.....(p) RaulDaSilva(3) 1 52
(Alastair Lidderdale) *led: rdn over 1f out: kpt on u.p tl hdd and no ex last strides* **8/1**
62-2 3 ½ **Princess Cammie (IRE)**[11] 202 3-8-5 0..... KieranO'Neill 3 54
(Mike Murphy) *stdd s: hld up in last: rdn and effrt whn swtchd rt over 1f out: styd on wl ins fnl f: nt quite rch ldrs* **4/1**[3]
356- 4 7 **Just Past Andover (IRE)**[184] 4462 3-8-8 74..... JoeFanning 4 32
(Bill Turner) *dwlt: sn chsng ldr: rdn and unable qck wl over 1f out: 4th and btn 1f out: wknd fnl f* **9/4**[2]
59.58s (0.78) **Going Correction** +0.05s/f (Slow) 4 Ran SP% **111.9**
Speed ratings (Par 95): **95,94,93,82**
CSF £9.16 TOTE £1.60; EX 9.50 Trifecta £12.10 Pool: £909.85 - 56.16 winning units.
Owner Anthony Cooke **Bred** Tally-Ho Stud **Trained** Earlswood, Monmouths

FOCUS
A modest claimer.

369 LINGFIELDPARK.CO.UK H'CAP 5f (P)
1:30 (1:30) (Class 6) (0-60,60) 4-Y-O+ **£2,045** (£603; £302) **Stalls** High

Form RPR
006- 1 **Secret Millionaire (IRE)**[56] 7936 6-9-5 **58**..... JimCrowley 2 69+
(Tony Carroll) *hld up in tch in midfield: rdn and hdwy over 1f out: led ins fnl f: r.o wl and gng away at fin* **6/4**[1]
-303 2 1 ½ **Russian Bullet**[9] 233 4-9-4 **57**..... MartinLane 7 62
(Jamie Osborne) *chsd ldrs: rdn and ev ch over 1f out: led 1f out: hdd ins fnl f: styd on same pce after* **14/1**
-122 3 nk **Johnny Splash (IRE)**[3] 316 4-8-13 **57**.....(b) NathanAlison(5) 4 61
(Roger Teal) *wnt lft s: chsd ldr: ev ch over 1f out: styd on same pce ins fnl f* **9/2**[2]
243 4 1 ¼ **Sherjawy (IRE)**[6] 277 9-8-13 **52**..... KirstyMilczarek 1 51
(Zoe Davison) *in tch in midfield: effrt on inner over 1f out: pressing ldrs whn nt clr run and eased briefly ins fnl f: nt rcvr and styd on same pce towards fin* **14/1**
353- 5 shd **Speedyfix**[58] 7915 6-9-3 **56**.....(t) TomMcLaughlin 6 55
(Christine Dunnett) *in tch in midfield: rdn and effrt 2f out: hdwy u.p 1f out: kpt on but no threat to wnr* **8/1**
00-4 6 ½ **Atlantic Beach**[15] 135 8-9-7 **60**.....(p) RobertWinston 5 57
(Milton Bradley) *s.i.s: hld up in rr: rdn and hdwy over 1f out: styd on fnl f: nvr trbld ldrs* **10/1**
20-0 7 1 **Volcanic Dust (IRE)**[20] 77 5-9-5 **58**.....(be) SebSanders 8 51
(Milton Bradley) *s.i.s: in tch in midfield: rdn and unable qck wl over 1f out: no imp after* **16/1**
42-0 8 1 ½ **Red Ramesses (IRE)**[14] 163 4-8-13 **52**.....(b[1]) LukeMorris 9 40
(John Best) *led: rdn wl over 1f out: hdd 1f out: wknd fnl f* **5/1**[3]
0-11 9 6 **Beach Candy (IRE)**[15] 128 4-9-5 **58**.....(vt) MickyFenton 3 24
(Phil McEntee) *short of room: hmpd and dropped to rr after s: rdn and struggling over 2f out: wknd over 1f out* **10/1**
59.0s (0.20) **Going Correction** +0.05s/f (Slow) 9 Ran SP% **123.4**
Speed ratings (Par 101): **100,97,97,95,94 94,92,90,80**
toteswingers 1&2 £7.90, 1&3 £3.40, 2&3 £18.80 CSF £28.24 CT £87.04 TOTE £3.20: £1.20, £6.00, £1.80; EX 34.50 Trifecta £624.30 Pool: £1,970.40 - 2.36 winning units.
Owner T P Ramsden **Bred** James Delaney **Trained** Cropthorne, Worcs

370 LINGFIELDPARK.CO.UK CLASSIFIED CLAIMING STKS 7f (P)
2:00 (2:00) (Class 5) 4-Y-O+ **£2,726** (£805; £402) **Stalls** Low

Form RPR
1-61 1 **Polar Kite (IRE)**[11] 206 5-8-12 73..... RobertWinston 9 86
(Sean Curran) *stdd s: hld up in last pair: hdwy and swtchd lft jst over 1f out: led ins fnl f: sn in command: eased cl home* **7/4**[1]
3-50 2 2 ¾ **Cyflymder (IRE)**[10] 217 7-7-12 69..... IanBurns(7) 10 71
(David C Griffiths) *in tch in midfield: lost pl and pushed along 4f out: hdwy to chse ldr whn wd bnd 2f out: sn rdn: led ins fnl f: sn hdd and outpcd by wnr: kpt on* **7/1**

52-3 **3** ½ **Azrael**[17] 104 5-8-10 72 (p) SeanLevey 2 75
(Alan McCabe) *led: rdn 2f out: hdd jst ins fnl f: kpt on but no ch w wnr fnl 100yds* **9/4**[2]

11-0 **4** 2½ **Mr Knightley (IRE)**[17] 104 4-9-2 75 (b) JimCrowley 6 74
(Roger Ingram) *in tch in midfield: rdn and effrt to chal over 1f out: led jst ins fnl f: sn hdd: wknd fnl 100yds* **7/1**

003- **5** 1½ **Khajaaly (IRE)**[56] 7935 6-7-13 70 RaulDaSilva(3) 5 56
(Julia Feilden) *chsd ldrs: rdn and unable qck over 1f out: wknd ins fnl f* **5/1**[3]

066- **6** shd **Aquilifer (IRE)**[44] 8083 5-7-9 63 (t) NatashaEaton(5) 8 54
(Mrs K Burke) *stdd s: hld up in last pair: clsd on ldrs over 2f out: rdn and keeping on same pce whn pushed lft and hmpd jst over 1f out: sn rdn: wknd ins fnl f* **12/1**

6-50 **7** 9 **Lindoro**[9] 223 8-8-1 55 ow1 MartinLane 4 31
(Sean Curran) *t.k.h: chsd ldr tl rdn and lost pl over 2f out: bhd fnl f* **50/1**

1m 23.58s (-1.22) **Going Correction** +0.05s/f (Slow) 7 Ran SP% 118.5
Speed ratings (Par 103): **108,104,104,101,99 99,89**
toteswingers 1&2 £3.90, 1&3 £2.00, 2&3 £4.30 CSF £15.75 TOTE £2.80: £1.70, £4.20; EX 17.80 Trifecta £69.10 Pool: £2,944.57 - 31.92 winning units.
Owner Power Bloodstock Ltd **Bred** Holborn Trust Co **Trained** Hatford, Oxon

FOCUS
A fair race of its type.

371 BLACKBERRY LANE H'CAP 7f (P)

2:30 (2:30) (Class 6) (0-65,68) 3-Y-O £2,045 (£603; £302) Stalls Low

Form RPR

01-4 **1** **It's Only Business**[12] 195 3-9-2 60 (p) JoeFanning 6 63
(Bill Turner) *stdd s: chsd ldr: rdn and chal wl over 1f out: led 1f out: r.o wl and clr fnl 75yds: eased cl home* **5/1**[2]

00-2 **2** 2 **Rhyolite (IRE)**[12] 195 3-9-3 61 (tp) AndreaAtzeni 2 59
(Marco Botti) *chsd ldng pair: rdn and outpcd wl over 1f out: rallied ins fnl f and r.o to go 2nd last strides* **4/9**[1]

50-4 **3** nk **Napinda**[3] 321 3-8-5 52 RaulDaSilva(3) 1 49
(Philip McBride) *led: set stdy gallop: rdn and qcknd 2f out: hdd 1f out: one pce after: lost 2nd last strides* **12/1**[3]

01- **4** ¾ **Byroness**[37] 8166 3-9-0 65 RyanTate(7) 3 60
(Heather Main) *t.k.h: hld up in tch in last: outpcd over 2f out: rdn and rallied 1f out: styd on but no threat to wnr* **5/1**[2]

1m 28.38s (3.58) **Going Correction** +0.05s/f (Slow) 4 Ran SP% 110.3
Speed ratings (Par 95): **81,78,78,77**
CSF £8.10 TOTE £4.30; EX 8.50 Trifecta £29.40 Pool: £2,015.93 - 51.28 winning units.
Owner Ansells Of Watford **Bred** South Wind Bloodstock **Trained** Sigwells, Somerset

FOCUS
There wasn't much pace on here and there was a bit of a shock result.

372 BLUE SQUARE BET H'CAP 6f (P)

3:05 (3:05) (Class 5) (0-75,75) 4-Y-O+ £3,234 (£962; £481; £240) Stalls Low

Form RPR

15-1 **1** **Polar Venture**[13] 187 4-9-1 69 AdamBeschizza 4 77+
(William Haggas) *hld up in detached last: stl plenty to do and effrt on inner over 1f out: str run fnl f to ld fnl 50yds: r.o wl* **2/1**[2]

00-1 **2** ½ **Khawatim**[19] 86 5-9-7 75 StevieDonohoe 3 81+
(Noel Quinlan) *hld up in tch in last quartet: rdn and effrt over 1f out: hdwy ins fnl f: swtchd lft wl ins fnl f: r.o wl to snatch 2nd last stride* **7/4**[1]

66-1 **3** shd **Alnoomaas (IRE)**[23] 11 4-9-5 73 TomMcLaughlin 9 79
(Luke Dace) *led: rdn and qcknd over 1f out: drvn ins fnl f: hdd fnl 50yds: no ex and lost 2nd last stride* **6/1**[3]

5-03 **4** nk **Gung Ho Jack**[13] 187 4-9-2 70 AndreaAtzeni 2 75
(John Best) *sn chsng ldr: rdn over 1f out: drvn and kpt on same pce ins fnl f* **8/1**

46-6 **5** nk **Gabbiano**[23] 11 4-9-6 74 (p) IanMongan 8 78
(Jeremy Gask) *t.k.h: hld up in midfield on outer: rdn and effrt wl over 1f out: kpt on u.p ins fnl f* **8/1**

32-4 **6** nk **Catalinas Diamond (IRE)**[20] 77 5-8-12 65 ow1 (t) SebSanders 5 69
(Pat Murphy) *hld up in tch in midfield: rdn and n.m.r over 1f out: drvn and kpt on ins fnl f* **16/1**

400- **7** ½ **Proper Charlie**[28] 8266 5-9-4 72 JimCrowley 7 74
(William Knight) *chsd ldrs: rdn and effrt 2f out: unable qck u.p over 1f out: one pce fnl f* **14/1**

00-0 **8** nk **Black Cadillac (IRE)**[18] 95 5-8-8 69 DanielMuscutt(7) 6 70
(Andrew Balding) *hld up in tch in last trio: rdn and effrt over 1f out: kpt on ins fnl f: no threat to ldrs* **33/1**

430- **9** 2½ **Courageous (IRE)**[112] 6837 7-9-6 74 (t) RobertWinston 1 67
(Milton Bradley) *chsd ldrs: rdn and unable qck wl over 1f out: wknd ins fnl f:* **20/1**

1m 12.29s (0.39) **Going Correction** +0.05s/f (Slow) 9 Ran SP% 126.5
Speed ratings (Par 103): **99,98,98,97,97 97,96,95,92**
toteswingers 1&2 £2.40, 1&3 £3.70, 2&3 £4.40 CSF £6.64 CT £19.18 TOTE £3.30: £1.20, £2.10, £2.40; EX 9.60 Trifecta £46.40 Pool: £5,818.48 - 94.03 winning units.
Owner Cheveley Park Stud **Bred** F C T Wilson **Trained** Newmarket, Suffolk

FOCUS
The right horses came to the fore here.

373 LINGFIELDPARK.CO.UK MAIDEN STKS 1m 2f (P)

3:40 (3:41) (Class 5) 3-Y-O £2,726 (£805; £402) Stalls Low

Form RPR

0- **1** **Ray Ward (IRE)**[44] 8071 3-9-5 0 MartinLane 3 74+
(David Simcock) *chsd ldrs: rdn and chal over 1f out: led jst ins fnl f: rn green and drifted rt fnl 100yds: styd on: rdn out* **8/1**

0- **2** 1¼ **Countess Lovelace**[35] 8200 3-9-0 0 IanMongan 9 66
(Pat Phelan) *chsd ldrs: rdn and pressed ldrs over 1f out: chsd wnr fnl 100yds: styng on same pce and hld whn carried rt wl ins fnl f* **25/1**

5 **3** nk **Edwyn Ralph**[13] 184 3-9-5 0 LiamKeniry 1 71+
(David Simcock) *racd off the pce in last trio: sme hdwy 3f out: chsd clr ldng quartet and clsng wl over 1f out: styd on to chse ldrs ins fnl f: one pce towards fin* **10/1**

52-2 **4** ¾ **Solace (USA)**[14] 168 3-9-0 66 (p) RobertHavlin 8 64
(John Gosden) *led: rdn ent fnl 2f: hdd and unable qck jst ins fnl f: styd on same pce fnl 100yds* **11/4**[2]

0 **5** 4½ **Moscow Circus (IRE)**[11] 211 3-9-5 0 JoeFanning 7 60
(Mark Johnston) *chsd ldr: rdn and unable qck whn hung lft over 1f out: wknd fnl f* **7/2**[3]

0- **6** 2¼ **Royal Barge (IRE)**[90] 7403 3-9-0 0 JimCrowley 4 51
(Eve Johnson Houghton) *in tch in midfield: outpcd and rdn over 2f out: no imp over 1f out: wknd ins fnl f* **20/1**

7 4 **Mighty Thor** 3-9-5 0 AdamBeschizza 2 48
(Simon Dow) *rrd as stalls opened and v.s.a: bhd: clsd on to bk of field 8f out: rdn and struggling 3f out: bhd fnl 2f* **33/1**

8 2¾ **Nadmah** 3-9-0 0 AndreaAtzeni 6 37
(Roger Varian) *in tch towards rr: rdn and struggling 3f out: bhd fnl 2f* **14/1**

042- **9** 117 **Dali's Lover (IRE)**[120] 6607 3-9-0 66 RobertWinston 5
(Charles Hills) *in tch in midfield: pushed along briefly and lost pl 4f out: sn eased and t.o* **9/4**[1]

2m 7.08s (0.48) **Going Correction** +0.05s/f (Slow) 9 Ran SP% 118.1
Speed ratings (Par 97): **100,99,98,98,94 92,89,87,**
toteswingers 1&2 £23.30, 1&3 £9.30, 2&3 £12.70 CSF £187.18 TOTE £9.30: £2.70, £5.30, £3.40; EX 235.20 Trifecta £2691.80 Pool: £4,631.99 - 1.29 winning units.
Owner Mrs Fitri Hay **Bred** Churchtown House Stud **Trained** Newmarket, Suffolk

FOCUS
A modest maiden.

374 ENOUGH SAID, JUST BET AT BLUESQ.COM H'CAP 5f (P)

4:10 (4:12) (Class 6) (0-65,63) 3-Y-O £2,045 (£603; £302) Stalls High

Form RPR

423- **1** **Ada Lovelace**[47] 8044 3-9-6 62 JimCrowley 2 71
(Dean Ivory) *chsd ldrs: wnt 2nd 2f out: rdn and qcknd to ld ent fnl f: clr and in command fnl f: r.o wl* **3/1**[2]

23-3 **2** 2½ **Modern Lady**[20] 75 3-9-2 63 WilliamTwiston-Davies(5) 3 63
(Richard Guest) *led: rdn wl over 1f out: hdd and nt pce of wnr ent fnl f: no ch w wnr but hld on gamely for 2nd fnl f* **6/1**[3]

202- **3** nk **Tregereth (IRE)**[95] 7296 3-9-5 61 JohnFahy 10 60
(Jonathan Portman) *chsd ldrs: rdn and hung lft over 1f out: kpt on u.p ins fnl f: no ch w wnr* **10/1**

500- **4** ½ **Southern Sapphire**[80] 7613 3-8-5 52 RachealKneller(5) 5 49
(Linda Stubbs) *s.i.s: hld up in tch towards rr: rdn and hdwy on inner over 1f out: no ch w wnr and kpt on same pce fnl f* **12/1**

03-1 **5** 1½ **Outbid**[23] 19 3-8-13 60 LeonnaMayor(5) 7 52
(Jamie Osborne) *t.k.h: hld up in midfield: wnt wd bnd 4f out: rdn and no prog wl over 1f out:* **7/1**

24-1 **6** shd **Prince Of Prophets (IRE)**[22] 36 3-9-0 56 (t) AndreaAtzeni 4 47+
(Stuart Williams) *rrd jst bef stalls opened and lost many l s: clsd over 3f out: rdn and hdwy over 1f out: swtchd rt and styd on fnl f: n.d* **7/4**[1]

216- **7** 1½ **Iwilsayzisonlyonce**[86] 7476 3-9-0 63 NoraLooby(7) 6 49
(Joseph Tuite) *chsd ldr tl 2f out: rdn and no ex over 1f out: wknd ins fnl f* **12/1**

630- **8** 4½ **Fiance Fiasco**[38] 8155 3-8-0 45 (v[1]) SimonPearce(3) 1 15
(Luke Dace) *awkward and wnt lft s: slowly away: hld up in tch towards rr: rdn and effrt wl over 1f out: sn wknd* **33/1**

59.47s (0.67) **Going Correction** +0.05s/f (Slow) 8 Ran SP% 115.6
Speed ratings (Par 95): **96,92,91,90,88 88,85,78**
toteswingers 1&2 £3.30, 1&3 £7.10, 2&3 £5.50 CSF £21.65 CT £160.89 TOTE £4.10: £1.40, £2.20, £2.90; EX 23.20 Trifecta £141.60 Pool: £5,002.50 - 26.48 winning units.
Owner D A Clark **Bred** D A Clark **Trained** Radlett, Herts

FOCUS
This proved pretty straightforward for the winner.
T/Plt: £1,600.00 to a £1 stake. Pool of £63,345.82 - 28.90 winning units T/Qpdt: £195.60 to a £1 stake. Pool of £7,211.79 - 27.28 winning units SP

324 WOLVERHAMPTON (A.W) (L-H)

Friday, January 25

OFFICIAL GOING: Standard to slow
Wind: strong, behind Weather: Light, snow

375 WIN MORE ON BETTING AT BOOKMAKERS.CO.UK APPRENTICE H'CAP 1m 1f 103y(P)

4:30 (4:31) (Class 6) (0-55,55) 4-Y-O+ £1,940 (£577; £288; £144) Stalls Low

Form RPR

00-3 **1** **Young Jackie**[16] 120 5-8-7 46 (b) JordanVaughan(5) 6 56
(George Margarson) *hld up in midfield: hdwy over 2f out: styd on to ld narrowly ins fnl f: rdn out* **3/1**[1]

/50- **2** nk **Tyrur Ted**[51] 7991 8-9-3 54 (t) PhilipPrince(3) 10 63
(Frank Sheridan) *hld up: rdn and hdwy 3f out: led over 2f out: hdd narrowly ins fnl f: kpt on u.p: hld cl home* **8/1**

3-05 **3** 3 **Sudden Wish (IRE)**[3] 320 4-9-3 55 JoshBaudains(3) 2 58
(David Evans) *hld up in midfield: hdwy 2f out: styd on to chse ldrs fnl f: nt trble front pair* **6/1**

44-3 **4** nk **Landown Littlerock**[18] 99 4-8-13 51 (p) ShirleyTeasdale(3) 5 53
(Reg Hollinshead) *in tch: effrt to chse ldrs over 1f out: styd on same pce and no imp ins fnl f* **7/2**[2]

06-5 **5** 3¾ **Justine Time (IRE)**[18] 98 4-8-11 46 oh1 CharlesBishop 11 41
(Julie Camacho) *in tch on outer: effrt 3f out: led wl over 2f out: sn hdd: stl in contention wl over 1f out: wknd ins fnl f* **33/1**

0-40 **6** 1¼ **Shelovestobouggie**[3] 330 5-9-2 55 (t) MatthewHopkins(5) 9 47
(Mark Brisbourne) *hld up: hdwy on outer over 2f out: one pce u.p fr over 1f out: nvr able to chal* **12/1**

4-34 **7** 5 **American Lover (FR)**[12] 192 6-8-11 50 KevinStott(5) 4 31
(John Wainwright) *hld up in rr: detached early: kpt on modly fr over 1f out: nvr a threat* **14/1**

00-6 **8** 3½ **I'm Harry**[24] 7 4-8-13 53 (tp) AaronJones(5) 1 27
(George Baker) *prom tl rdn and wknd over 2f out* **5/1**[3]

0-45 **9** 8 **Kuraanda**[4] 313 4-8-11 46 oh1 (p) AdamCarter 8
(John Wainwright) *prom: led under 3f out: sn hdd and btn: dropped away wl over 1f out* **66/1**

004- **10** 4½ **Nurse Dominatrix (IRE)**[16] 8111 4-8-5 47 LisaTodd(7) 3
(Richard Guest) *led: hdd under 3f out: n.m.r sn after whn wkng* **14/1**

2m 4.18s (2.48) **Going Correction** +0.20s/f (Slow)
WFA 4 from 5yo+ 1lb 10 Ran SP% 114.7
Speed ratings (Par 101): **96,95,93,92,89 88,83,80,73,69**
toteswingers 1&2 £6.60, 1&3 £4.20, 2&3 £10.10 CSF £27.14 CT £135.01 TOTE £2.90: £1.20, £3.40, £2.30; EX 40.30 Trifecta £183.40 Pool: £1,996.36 - 8.16 winning units.
Owner Exors of the Late M Kentish **Bred** M F Kentish **Trained** Newmarket, Suffolk
■ Stewards' Enquiry : Matthew Hopkins two-day ban; used whip above permitted level (8th&9th Feb).

FOCUS
A low-grade apprentice handicap, and weak, muddling form.

376 CORAL.CO.UK CLASSIFIED CLAIMING STKS 1m 141y(P)
5:00 (5:01) (Class 5) 4-Y-0+ **£2,587** (£770; £384; £192) **Stalls** Low

Form RPR
000- **1** **Toymaker**[72] 7715 6-8-12 69 JamesSullivan 6 81
(James Given) *hld up in tch: clsd 3f out: led over 1f out: sn rdn: r.o and a in command ins fnl f* **20/1**
-311 **2** *1 ¼* **One Way Or Another (AUS)**[16] 118 10-8-7 69 (t) LukeMorris 7 73
(David Evans) *hld up: hdwy 2f out: forced wd ent st wl over 1f out: chsd wnr fr 1f out: styd on but hld ins fnl f* **4/1**[2]
42- **3** *1 ¾* **Ferryview Place**[35] 8213 4-8-7 65 (v) TomEaves 3 70
(Ian Williams) *in tch: effrt over 1f out: chsd ldrs ins fnl f: kpt on* **4/1**[2]
052- **4** *1 ¾* **Hail Promenader (IRE)**[126] 6452 7-8-9 68 (p) WilliamCarson 8 67
(Anthony Carson) *chsd ldr tl rdn over 1f out: sn one pce* **17/2**[3]
-420 **5** *nse* **Resplendent Alpha**[12] 192 9-8-4 63 ow1 ChrisCatlin 5 62
(Jamie Osborne) *dwlt: in rr: rdn over 2f out: kpt on ins fnl f: no imp on ldrs* **25/1**
4 **6** *hd* **Creek Falcon (IRE)**[10] 217 4-8-11 69 GrahamGibbons 2 70
(David O'Meara) *led after 1f: rdn over 2f out: hdd over 1f out: no ex fnl 100yds* **6/5**[1]
00-2 **7** *5* **Violent Velocity (IRE)**[18] 97 10-7-13 68 KevinLundie(7) 1 52
(John Quinn) *led for 1f: chsd ldrs after: rdn 2f out: wknd fnl f* **14/1**

1m 51.21s (0.71) **Going Correction** +0.20s/f (Slow)
WFA 4 from 5yo+ 1lb 7 Ran SP% **111.3**
Speed ratings (Par 103): **104,102,101,99,99 99,95**
toteswingers 1&2 £10.80, 1&3 £9.50, 2&3 £2.90 CSF £92.21 TOTE £24.20: £11.60, £1.30; EX 147.70 Trifecta £377.60 Pool: £2,813.60 - 5.58 winning units.Resplendent Alpha was claimed by Mr A. J. D. Lidderdale for £3,000
Owner Antoniades Family **Bred** A G Antoniades **Trained** Willoughton, Lincs

FOCUS
The market favoured the two 4yos in this classified claimer, but it was the older brigade who came to the fore. The winner is rated back to last year's winning Pontefract form.

377 CHOOSE THE RIGHT BOOKIE AT BOOKMAKERS.CO.UK MAIDEN FILLIES' STKS 1m 141y(P)
5:30 (5:30) (Class 5) 3-Y-0+ **£2,587** (£770; £384; £192) **Stalls** Low

Form RPR
22- **1** **Iridescence**[37] 8171 3-8-5 0 ChrisCatlin 4 77+
(Jeremy Noseda) *a.p: led 3f out: rdn whn strly pressed fr 2f out: styd on and plld out more towards fin* **11/8**[1]
0-3 **2** *1 ¼* **Passionate Diva (USA)**[11] 211 3-8-5 0 LukeMorris 2 74
(Ed Vaughan) *led for 1f: remained handy: str chal fr 2f out: no ex towards fin* **4/1**[3]
3-2 **3** *4 ½* **Empowermentofwomen (IRE)**[13] 184 3-8-5 0 HayleyTurner 8 64
(Michael Bell) *in tch: effrt to chse ldrs 2f out: lugged lft u.p over 1f out: one pce ins fnl f* **13/8**[2]
4 *4* **Short Shrift (IRE)** 3-8-5 0 KirstyMilczarek 3 54
(James Toller) *in tch: effrt to chse ldrs 2f out: wl btn ins fnl f* **33/1**
5 *21* **Au Renoir** 3-8-5 0 FrannyNorton 7
(Kevin Ryan) *missed break: a bhd: pushed along over 2f out: nvr a threat* **14/1**
/0-0 **6** *¾* **Supastarqueen (USA)**[23] 28 5-9-13 30 GrahamGibbons 6
(Brian Baugh) *led after 1f: rdn and hdd 3f out: sn wknd* **200/1**
0-0 **7** *¾* **Sarahs Pal**[18] 102 3-8-5 0 JamieMackay 5
(Mandy Rowland) *missed break: a bhd: pushed along 4f out: nvr a threat* **200/1**

1m 52.28s (1.78) **Going Correction** +0.20s/f (Slow)
WFA 3 from 4yo 22lb 4 from 5yo 1lb 7 Ran SP% **110.8**
Speed ratings (Par 100): **100,98,94,91,72 72,71**
toteswingers 1&2 £1.60, 1&3 £1.20, 2&3 £1.60 CSF £6.89 TOTE £2.10: £1.50, £1.90; EX 7.30 Trifecta £11.30 Pool: £3,547.94 - 234.36 winning units.
Owner Cheveley Park Stud **Bred** Cheveley Park Stud Ltd **Trained** Newmarket, Suffolk

FOCUS
A modest fillies' maiden with the first three in the market having been placed on their most recent starts. The winner was back to her debut level.

378 FIND THE BEST ODDS AT BOOKMAKERS.CO.UK H'CAP 2m 119y(P)
6:00 (6:02) (Class 4) (0-85,84) 4-Y-0+ **£4,690** (£1,395; £697; £348) **Stalls** Low

Form RPR
26-5 **1** **Bradbury (IRE)**[17] 107 5-8-13 **69** (p) TomEaves 4 76
(Donald McCain) *s.i.s: hld up: hdwy over 3f out: sn rdn to chse ldr: abt 4 l down 2f out: styd on for press ins fnl f: got up fnl stride* **6/1**[3]
41/1 **2** *hd* **Murcar**[22] 40 8-9-1 **78** (b) PhilipPrince(7) 6 85+
(Liam Corcoran) *hld up: hdwy 5f out: led 4f out: rdn 4 l clr 2f out: reduced advantage ins fnl f: worn down fnl stride* **9/2**[1]
00-0 **3** *¾* **Art History (IRE)**[14] 167 5-10-0 **84** (b) DanielTudhope 5 90
(David O'Meara) *prom: lost pl over 4f out: rallied u.p over 2f out: styd on to cl ins fnl f: jst hld nr fin* **7/1**
55-4 **4** *9* **Odin (IRE)**[18] 93 5-9-9 **79** EddieAhern 2 74
(Don Cantillon) *in tch: lost pl over 3f out: rdn over 2f out: plugged on at one pce fnl f: nvr able to chal* **9/2**[1]
45/2 **5** *5* **Experimentalist**[15] 131 5-8-9 **65** (t) FergusSweeney 7 54
(Tim Vaughan) *hld up: hdwy to go prom after 3f: wknd over 2f out* **9/2**[1]
563- **6** *6* **Valid Reason**[30] 7068 6-9-10 **80** LukeMorris 3 62
(Dean Ivory) *led: hdd after 5f: remained prom: rdn over 4f out: wknd over 3f out* **5/1**[2]
00-3 **7** *82* **Wild Desert (FR)**[14] 166 8-9-0 **77** AliceWhite(7) 8
(John Gallagher) *prom: led after 5f: hdd 4f out: wknd over 3f out: t.o* **16/1**

3m 44.47s (2.67) **Going Correction** +0.20s/f (Slow)
WFA 4 from 5yo+ 7lb 7 Ran SP% **103.9**
Speed ratings (Par 105): **101,100,100,96,93 91,52**
toteswingers 1&2 £3.30, 1&3 £3.10, 2&3 £3.40 CSF £26.21 CT £121.22 TOTE £6.40: £3.40, £1.40; EX 24.00 Trifecta £319.00 Pool: £1,185.12 - 2.78 winning units.
Owner D Charlesworth **Bred** Pat Harnett **Trained** Cholmondeley, Cheshire

FOCUS
A wide-open contest in which Murcar was wron down late. The winner is rated to form.

379 PICK TODAY'S WINNERS AT BOOKMAKERS.CO.UK CLAIMING STKS 5f 20y(P)
6:30 (6:30) (Class 6) 4-Y-0+ **£1,940** (£577; £288; £144) **Stalls** Low

Form RPR
231- **1** **Hamoody (USA)**[27] 8285 9-9-1 79 SebSanders 5 91
(David Nicholls) *s.i.s: hld up: hdwy over 1f out: led 1f out: edgd lft ins fnl f: r.o* **2/1**[1]
014- **2** *1 ¾* **Noverre To Go (IRE)**[35] 8202 7-9-5 88 LukeMorris 3 89
(Ronald Harris) *chsd ldrs: rdn and ev ch ent fnl f: nt qckn towards fin* **11/4**[2]
3-32 **3** *1 ¾* **Above The Stars**[15] 135 5-8-3 62 PatrickMathers 1 66
(Richard Fahey) *hld up: rdn over 1f out: styd on ins fnl f: unable to rch ldrs* **16/1**
0-52 **4** *1 ¼* **Le Toreador**[21] 56 8-8-13 85 (tp) KevinStott(7) 6 79
(Kevin Ryan) *led: rdn and hdd 1f out: no ex fnl 100yds* **8/1**[3]
00-0 **5** *6* **Lesley's Choice**[21] 56 7-9-0 64 WilliamCarson 2 51
(Sean Curran) *w ldr: pushed along over 2f out: wknd over 1f out* **50/1**
11-1 **6** *nk* **Drawnfromthepast (IRE)**[21] 56 8-9-0 83 FergusSweeney 7 50
(Jamie Osborne) *chsd ldrs: rdn over 1f out: sn wknd* **2/1**[1]

1m 2.41s (0.11) **Going Correction** +0.20s/f (Slow) 6 Ran SP% **112.3**
Speed ratings (Par 101): **107,104,101,99,89 89**
toteswingers 1&2 £1.80, 1&3 £4.10, 2&3 £3.30 CSF £7.85 TOTE £3.60: £1.80, £1.60; EX 8.50 Trifecta £54.30 Pool: £2,518.16 - 34.76 winning units.Above The Stars was claimed by Mr J. A. Osborne for £3,000.
Owner Hart Inn I **Bred** Ragged Mountain Farm **Trained** Sessay, N Yorks

FOCUS
A competitive claimer over the minimum trip. The winner rates close to his best since he was a 2yo at face value.

380 CORAL.CO.UK MOBILE CASINO H'CAP 7f 32y(P)
7:00 (7:01) (Class 6) (0-65,71) 4-Y-0+ **£1,940** (£577; £288; £144) **Stalls** High

Form RPR
14-4 **1** **Nant Saeson (IRE)**[15] 147 4-8-13 **57** (p) MichaelO'Connell 5 66
(John Quinn) *led: hdd narrowly jst over 2f out: rdn and continued to chal: regained ld towards fin* **8/1**
1-12 **2** *hd* **Bussa**[15] 139 5-9-4 **62** (t) WilliamCarson 10 70
(David Evans) *chsd ldr: narrow ld jst over 2f out: a hrd pressed: kpt on u.p: hdd towards fin* **5/1**[3]
332 **3** *1 ¼* **Abhaath (USA)**[3] 317 4-8-13 **64** (b[1]) GaryPhillips(7) 9 69
(Ronald Harris) *s.i.s: hld up in rr: hdwy over 2f out: styd on to take 3rd fnl 150yds: nt quite able to rch ldrs* **10/1**
000- **4** *1 ¼* **Fighter Boy (IRE)**[42] 8114 6-9-2 **60** (t) GrahamGibbons 1 62
(Michael Easterby) *chsd ldrs: rdn over 2f out: unable to go w front pair: styd on ins fnl f tl no ex towards fin* **4/1**[2]
00-1 **5** *nse* **Boy The Bell**[23] 24 6-8-5 **56** (b) JacobButterfield(7) 4 58
(Ollie Pears) *slowly into strde: in rr: rdn over 3f out: edgd rt over 1f out: styd on ins fnl f: nt pce to chal* **10/1**
5-21 **6** *6* **Kai**[14] 162 4-9-0 **58** (b) SeanLevey 7 43
(Alan McCabe) *in tch: rdn and outpcd over 2f out: wl btn ins fnl f* **13/2**
00-0 **7** *16* **Green Mitas (ITY)**[23] 27 4-9-1 **62** MarkCoumbe(3) 8 4
(Frank Sheridan) *racd keenly: in tch wout cover: rdn and wknd over 2f out* **9/1**
13-1 **8** *1* **Bassett Road (IRE)**[12] 194 5-9-13 **71** 6ex (p) TomEaves 2 10
(Keith Dalgleish) *hld up: niggled along 4f out: lft bhd over 2f out: nvr a threat* **3/1**[1]

1m 30.39s (0.79) **Going Correction** +0.20s/f (Slow) 8 Ran SP% **114.3**
Speed ratings (Par 101): **103,102,101,99,99 93,74,73**
toteswingers 1&2 £7.70, 1&3 £12.20, 2&3 £9.20 CSF £47.45 CT £407.91 TOTE £8.20: £2.80, £1.10, £3.40; EX 50.90 Trifecta £582.50 Pool: £1,817.41 - 2.33 winning units.
Owner R A Kaye **Bred** Dr Myles Sweeney **Trained** Settrington, N Yorks

FOCUS
On paper this shaped up to be a decent handicap. However, with favourite Bassett Road disappointing it proved a modest affair, with only first two ever able to land a blow. It was the best relative time on the card.

381 £50 FREE BET AT CORAL.CO.UK H'CAP 1m 141y(P)
7:30 (7:30) (Class 7) (0-50,54) 4-Y-0+ **£1,940** (£577; £288; £144) **Stalls** Low

Form RPR
0-42 **1** **Delightful Sleep**[9] 220 5-9-5 **50** WilliamCarson 10 62
(David Evans) *chsd ldrs: wnt 2nd over 2f out: rdn to ld 1f out: styd on wl and in command towards fin* **6/1**[2]
-202 **2** *2* **Under Par**[8] 240 5-9-4 **49** (t) GrahamGibbons 12 56
(Michael Easterby) *a.p: led over 2f out: rdn whn hdd 1f out: no ex fnl 50yds* **9/1**
25-3 **3** *2* **Monsieur Pontaven**[22] 42 6-9-2 **47** (b) DanielTudhope 3 49+
(Robin Bastiman) *hld up in midfield: lost pl over 2f out: nt clr run briefly under 2f out: hdwy sn after: styd on ins fnl f to take 3rd fnl stride: nt trble front two* **11/4**[1]
00-4 **4** *nk* **Pytheas (USA)**[3] 316 6-9-4 **49** (b) LukeMorris 4 51
(Alastair Lidderdale) *hld up: hdwy over 2f out: rdn to chse ldrs over 1f out: kpt on ins fnl f* **17/2**[3]
02-0 **5** *1 ¼* **Stamp Duty (IRE)**[22] 41 5-9-2 **47** TomEaves 8 46
(Suzzanne France) *hld up: rdn over 1f out: hdwy ent fnl f: styd on ins fnl f: nt trble ldrs* **18/1**
632- **6** *4* **Avon Supreme**[35] 8212 5-9-2 **47** StevieDonohoe 2 37
(Gay Kelleway) *chsd ldrs: rdn over 2f out: wknd fnl f* **17/2**[3]
-554 **7** *1 ¼* **Lord Paget**[8] 240 4-8-11 **48** (p) ShirleyTeasdale(5) 7 35
(Reg Hollinshead) *hld up: rdn over 1f out: nvr a threat* **9/1**
006- **8** *1 ¼* **Autumnus (IRE)**[29] 8257 4-9-4 **50** (t) ShaneKelly 1 34
(Ismail Mohammed) *led: rdn and hdd over 2f out: wknd over 1f out* **11/4**[1]
/6-6 **9** *6* **Aljosan**[8] 240 4-9-0 **49** (tp) MarkCoumbe(3) 11 19
(Frank Sheridan) *chsd ldrs: rdn over 2f out: wknd over 1f out* **40/1**

1m 52.54s (2.04) **Going Correction** +0.20s/f (Slow)
WFA 4 from 5yo+ 1lb 9 Ran SP% **116.4**
Speed ratings (Par 97): **98,96,94,94,93 89,88,87,81**
toteswingers 1&2 £3.70, 1&3 £3.70, 2&3 £5.00 CSF £59.00 CT £182.93 TOTE £6.00: £1.60, £3.00, £1.50; EX 24.90 Trifecta £129.90 Pool: £1,619.55 - 9.34 winning units.
Owner Mrs E Evans **Bred** Theresa Fitsall **Trained** Pandy, Monmouths

FOCUS
A low-grade contest, but not without interest. The winner was unexposed and the second sets the standard.

T/Plt: £107.30 to a £1 stake. Pool: £8,4617.55 - 575.45 winning tickets T/Qpdt: £23.70 to a £1 stake. Pool: £9,346.27 - 291.60 winning tickets DO

382 - 393a (Foreign Racing) - See Raceform Interactive

[178] JEBEL ALI (L-H)

Friday, January 25

OFFICIAL GOING: Dirt: fast

394a MARSH INSCO (H'CAP) (DIRT) 7f

12:25 (12:25) (55-70,70) 3-Y-0+ **£6,030** (£2,010; £1,105; £603; £301)

RPR

1 **Suited And Booted (IRE)**[22] 46 6-9-6 **70**...............(b) WayneSmith 13 74
(M Al Muhairi, UAE) *led nr side: kicked clr 2 1/2f out: r.o gamely* **16/1**

2 3/4 **Momaris**[56] 7951 5-9-5 **69**...............(v) KierenFallon 9 71
(D Selvaratnam, UAE) *s.i.s: trckd ldrs: ev ch 1f out: nt qckn fnl 50yds* **2/1**[1]

3 2 1/4 **I Got You Babe (IRE)**[22] 43 5-9-1 **65**............... PatDobbs 5 61
(Doug Watson, UAE) *mid-div: kpt on same pce fnl 1 1/2f but no ch w first two* **14/1**

4 1 1/2 **Extroverted**[56] 7951 5-8-9 **60**............... DaneO'Neill 7 51
(Doug Watson, UAE) *mid-div: kpt on same pce fnl 1 1/2f* **25/1**

5 1 **Hannibal Hayes (USA)**[126] 6439 4-8-11 **62**............... PaulHanagan 6 50
(M Al Muhairi, UAE) *prom in centre: kpt on same pce fnl 1 1/2f* **10/1**[3]

6 3 1/4 **Broughtons Day**[14] 178 6-8-5 **62**...............(bt) SaeedAlMazrooei(6) 3 41
(M Ramadan, UAE) *nvr nr to chal* **25/1**

7 1/2 **Pulpit Point (USA)**[64] 7836 7-9-6 **70**...............(bt) RichardMullen 10 49
(S Seemar, UAE) *a mid-div* **25/1**

8 1 3/4 **Liberation (IRE)**[22] 47 7-9-6 **70**...............(bt) TadhgO'Shea 14 44
(Ismail Mohammed) *trckd ldrs tl outpcd 3f out* **16/1**

9 1/2 **Divine Force**[27] 7-9-1 **65**............... DSmith 1 38
(M Ibrahim, UAE) *nvr able to chal* **33/1**

10 5 **Masaalek**[41] 8-8-8 **68**...............(v) OAhmad(10) 4 27
(Doug Watson, UAE) *nvr able to chal* **7/1**[2]

11 1 **Fa'Iz (IRE)**[5] 4-9-1 **65**...............(b) SamHitchcott 11 22
(E Charpy, UAE) *nvr nr to chal* **16/1**

12 10 **Spice Souk**[70] 7763 6-9-1 **65**...............(t) DaraghO'Donohoe 12
(A bin Huzaim, UAE) *nvr nr to chal* **25/1**

1m 26.0s (86.00) 12 Ran SP% **97.6**
CSF: 31.84; TRICAST: 286.95; EXACTA: 52.10; TRIFECTA: 434.20.
Owner Fahad Al Mutairi **Bred** Carpet Lady Partnership **Trained** UAE

395 - (Foreign Racing) - See Raceform Interactive

[368] LINGFIELD (L-H)

Saturday, January 26

OFFICIAL GOING: Standard

Wind: light, half behind Weather: dry, bright

396 BET ON TODAY'S FOOTBALL AT BLUESQ.COM MAIDEN STKS 1m (P)

12:20 (12:21) (Class 5) 3-Y-0+ **£2,726** (£805; £402) **Stalls** High

Form RPR

60- 1 **Tribal Path (IRE)**[136] 6133 3-8-7 0............... JoeFanning 10 79+
(Mark Johnston) *mde all: rdn and qckmd clr over 1f out: in command and r.o wl fnl f: readily* **7/2**[2]

54- 2 3 3/4 **Silver Dixie (USA)**[54] 7962 3-8-7 0............... FrannyNorton 2 70+
(Jeremy Noseda) *hld up in tch in midfield: rdn and sltly outpcd wl over 1f out: rallied and n.m.r ent fnl f: hdwy 1f out: r.o wl to go 2nd wl ins fnl f: no ch w wnr* **7/2**[2]

3 3/4 **St Georges Hill (IRE)** 3-8-7 0............... ShaneFoley 1 69+
(Michael Wigham) *dwlt: sn rcvrd and in tch in midfield: nt clr run wl over 1f out: rdn and hdwy over 1f out: chsd wnr ins fnl f: no imp: lost 2nd wl ins fnl f* **5/4**[1]

00- 4 1 1/2 **Tenure**[184] 4516 4-9-13 0............... RyanMoore 3 70+
(Gary Moore) *in tch in midfield: effrt to chse ldrs and rdn wl over 1f out: styd on same pce and no threat to wnr fnl f* **7/1**[3]

0-6 5 nk **True Spirit**[21] 74 3-8-0 0............... PhilipPrince(7) 9 64
(Paul D'Arcy) *chsd ldr: rdn and unable qck over 1f out: lost 2nd 1f out and wknd ins fnl f* **10/1**

0- 6 2 3/4 **Alshan Fajer**[29] 8262 3-8-7 0............... AndreaAtzeni 8 58
(Paul Howling) *stdd after s: hld up in tch in last trio: rdn and no prog over 2f out: nvr trbld ldrs* **66/1**

5- 7 1 **Desert Donkey**[38] 8172 3-8-8 0 ow1............... LiamKeniry 6 56
(Andrew Balding) *t.k.h: chsd ldrs: rdn and unable qck over 1f out: wknd ins fnl f* **33/1**

8 10 **Culture Trip** 3-8-7 0............... FrankieMcDonald 7 31
(Murty McGrath) *bhd: pushed along over 4f out: rdn over 3f out: wknd wl over 1f out: bhd and eased wl ins fnl f* **50/1**

1m 37.43s (-0.77) **Going Correction** -0.075s/f (Stan)
WFA 3 from 4yo 20lb 8 Ran SP% **116.9**
Speed ratings (Par 103): **100,96,95,94,93 90,89,79**
Tote Swingers 1&2 £1.70, 2&3 £2.20, 1&3 £3.00 CSF £16.47 TOTE £4.20: £2.00, £1.40, £1.10; EX 14.90 Trifecta £36.30 Pool: £3700.57 - 76.32 winning tickets..
Owner Racegoers Club Owners Group **Bred** S F Bloodstock LLC **Trained** Middleham Moor, N Yorks

FOCUS
An interesting maiden for the time of year.

397 LINGFIELD PARK OWNERS GROUP MAIDEN STKS 1m 4f (P)

12:50 (12:50) (Class 5) 4-Y-0+ **£2,726** (£805; £402) **Stalls** Low

Form RPR

232- 1 **Elysian**[36] 8206 4-9-0 66............... RyanMoore 8 73
(Sir Michael Stoute) *hld up in tch in midfield: effrt to chse ldr over 2f out: rdn to ld wl over 1f out: sn clr and styd on wl: rdn out* **3/1**[2]

2 4 **Full Swing** 4-9-5 0............... AndreaAtzeni 1 72
(Roger Varian) *chsd ldrs: rdn and outpcd by wnr wl over 1f out: styd on ins fnl f to go 2nd fnl 75yds: no threat to wnr* **14/1**

42-2 3 1 1/4 **Harlestone Wood**[15] 157 4-9-5 80............... JimCrowley 9 70
(Peter Hedger) *t.k.h: jnd ldr 10f out tl led over 2f out: rdn and hdd wl over 1f out: sn outpcd and btn: lost 2nd fnl 75yds* **4/6**[1]

0/ 4 4 1/2 **Mister Bob (GER)**[546] 4525 4-9-5 0............... GeorgeBaker 3 62
(James Bethell) *stdd s: t.k.h: hld up in rr: hdwy on outer over 2f out: rn green and wnt v wd bnd 2f out: lost pl and bhd after: rallied and styd on again ins fnl f* **25/1**

4 5 1/2 **Ice Tres**[11] 215 4-9-0 0............... ChrisCatlin 6 57
(Rod Millman) *stdd s: hld up in last quartet: pushed along and hdwy over 2f out: outpcd 2f out: wl btn and one pce after* **33/1**

52-5 6 2 1/2 **Minority Interest**[16] 140 4-9-5 73............... JoeFanning 2 58
(Brett Johnson) *t.k.h: led tl over 2f out: sn rdn and outpcd 2f out: wknd over 1f out* **20/1**

503- 7 2 1/4 **Torero**[219] 3305 4-9-5 66............... TomEaves 4 54
(Kevin Ryan) *chsd ldrs: rdn and no ex over 2f out: fdd over 1f out* **10/1**[3]

8 1/2 **Zafaraban (IRE)**[70] 6-9-4 0............... GeorgeDowning(5) 5 53
(Tony Carroll) *hld up in rr: rdn 4f out: wknd over 2f out: bhd fnl f* **33/1**

0- 9 1 1/4 **Rahy's Promise (USA)**[27] 8295 4-8-12 0............... ThomasBrown(7) 7 51
(Andrew Balding) *in tch in midfield: rdn over 4f out: no prog 2f out: sn wknd* **50/1**

2m 30.81s (-2.19) **Going Correction** -0.075s/f (Stan)
WFA 4 from 6yo 4lb 9 Ran SP% **117.2**
Speed ratings (Par 103): **104,101,100,97,97 95,94,93,92**
Tote Swingers 1&2 £3.50, 2&3 £3.30, 1&3 £1.30 CSF £38.25 TOTE £2.70: £1.40, £3.70, £1.02; EX 35.30 Trifecta £70.70 Pool: £3,393.44 - 35.99 winning tickets..
Owner Cheveley Park Stud **Bred** Cheveley Park Stud Ltd **Trained** Newmarket, Suffolk

FOCUS
This didn't take much winning.

398 BLUE SQUARE BET SPRINT SERIES ROUND 4 H'CAP (QUALIFIER) (DIV I) 6f (P)

1:25 (1:25) (Class 6) (0-65,68) 4-Y-0+ **£3,067** (£905; £453) **Stalls** Low

Form RPR

220/ 1 **Sister Guru**[481] 6590 4-9-6 **64**............... JohnFahy 4 74
(Peter Hedger) *stdd s: wl off the pce in last: clsng but stl last over 1f out: str run on inner ins fnl f to ld cl home* **33/1**

30-2 2 nk **Jack My Boy (IRE)**[13] 194 6-9-10 **68**...............(v) TomMcLaughlin 9 77
(David Evans) *racd off the pce in midfield: rdn and clsd over 1f out: ev ch wl ins fnl f: kpt on* **4/1**[2]

3-06 3 1/2 **Speak The Truth (IRE)**[14] 187 7-9-5 **63**...............(p) JimCrowley 2 70
(Roger Ingram) *hld up in midfield: rdn and clsd over 1f out: drvn to ld fnl 100yds: hdd and lost 2 pls cl home* **7/2**[1]

5-20 4 3/4 **Waabel**[14] 186 6-9-7 **65**...............(t) WilliamCarson 5 70
(Violet M Jordan) *hld up wl off the pce in last pair: rdn and hdwy whn nt clr run 1f out: swtchd rt ins fnl f: r.o strly: nt rch ldrs* **8/1**

4-24 5 1 3/4 **My Own Way Home**[14] 186 5-9-4 **62**............... RyanMoore 7 61
(David Evans) *racd off the pce in midfield: rdn and clsd over 1f out: styd on same pce and no imp fnl 100yds* **4/1**[2]

4-30 6 nse **Dancing Freddy (IRE)**[14] 187 6-9-1 **64**...............(tp) CharlesBishop(5) 3 63
(Violet M Jordan) *chsd ldr tl led over 4f out: sn dashed clr: rdn over 1f out: hdd fnl 100yds: wknd towards fin* **16/1**

60-2 7 3/4 **Yungaburra (IRE)**[4] 326 9-8-7 **51** oh1...............(tp) FrannyNorton 12 47+
(David C Griffiths) *hld up wl off the pce towards rr: styng on whn nt clr run 1f out tl wl ins fnl f: kpt on towards fin: nvr trbld ldrs* **20/1**

53-5 8 hd **Speedyfix**[1] 369 6-8-12 **56**...............(t) SebSanders 10 52
(Christine Dunnett) *racd off the pce in midfield on outer: rdn and clsd to press ldrs jst over 1f out: styd on same pce ins fnl f* **16/1**

6035 9 1/2 **Jonnie Skull (IRE)**[7] 277 7-8-10 **54**...............(vt) AndreaAtzeni 8 48
(Phil McEntee) *prom in main gp: rdn and effrt wl over 1f out: no imp ins fnl f* **20/1**

406- 10 1/2 **Diamond Vine (IRE)**[26] 8305 5-9-5 **63**...............(b[1]) JoeFanning 11 56
(Ronald Harris) *hld up wl off the pce in rr of main gp: rdn and hdwy over 1f out: styd on same pce ins fnl f* **7/1**[3]

006- 11 1 1/2 **Ice Trooper**[82] 7591 5-9-7 **65**...............(p) TomEaves 1 53
(Linda Stubbs) *led tl over 4f out: chsd clr ldr after tl jst over 1f out: wknd fnl f* **16/1**

110 12 1 **Beach Candy (IRE)**[1] 369 4-9-0 **58**...............(vt) MickyFenton 6 43
(Phil McEntee) *chsd ldrs tl over 1f out: wknd u.p 1f out* **20/1**

1m 10.8s (-1.10) **Going Correction** -0.075s/f (Stan) 12 Ran SP% **120.7**
Speed ratings (Par 101): **104,103,102,101,99 99,98,98,97,96 94,93**
Tote Swingers 1&2 £26.30, 2&3 £4.20, 1&3 £35.10 CSF £157.26 CT £611.22 TOTE £39.70: £11.00, £1.30, £1.50; EX 263.20 Trifecta £1933.90 Pool: £3,273.18 - 1.26 winning tickets..
Owner John McHale **Bred** Geoffrey J Hamer **Trained** Dogmersfield, Hampshire

FOCUS
There was a good pace on here.

399 BLUE SQUARE BET SPRINT SERIES ROUND 4 H'CAP (QUALIFIER) (DIV II) 6f (P)

2:00 (2:00) (Class 6) (0-65,65) 4-Y-0+ **£3,067** (£905; £453) **Stalls** Low

Form RPR

63-3 1 **Frognal (IRE)**[21] 76 7-9-6 **64**...............(bt) WilliamCarson 8 76
(Violet M Jordan) *hmpd and swtchd lft after s: hld up in rr: rdn and str run over 1f out: led fnl 100yds: sn clr and r.o strly* **8/1**

451- 2 2 **Rich Again (IRE)**[46] 8064 4-9-5 **63**............... RobertWinston 4 73+
(James Bethell) *t.k.h: hld up towards rr: hdwy over 1f out: styng on whn nt clr run 1f out: swtchd rt and r.o ins fnl f to go 2nd fnl 75yds: no threat to wnr* **11/4**[1]

2051 3 1 1/4 **Dixie Gwalia**[4] 323 5-8-11 **55** 6ex...............(v) TomMcLaughlin 5 57
(David Evans) *led tl 5f out: chsd ldrs after: rdn 2f out: led ins fnl f: hdd and outpcd fnl 100yds* **8/1**

1200 4 1/2 **Putin (IRE)**[14] 187 5-8-5 **54**...............(bt) LeonnaMayor(5) 6 54
(Phil McEntee) *chsd ldr: rdn and effrt over 1f out: led 1f out: sn hdd and styd on same pce after* **25/1**

46-2 5 shd **Loyal Royal (IRE)**[16] 142 10-9-0 **58**...............(bt) SebSanders 9 58
(Milton Bradley) *stdd and wnt lft after s: t.k.h: hld up in rr: rdn and effrt over 1f out: styd on ins fnl f: nt rch ldrs* **20/1**

01-1 6 1/2 **Reginald Claude**[16] 139 5-9-0 **63**............... RachealKneller(5) 11 61
(Mark Usher) *hld up in midfield: clsd over 1f out: rdn 1f out: styd on same pce and no imp after* **6/1**[3]

04-5 7 1 **Haadeeth**[14] 187 6-9-2 **60**............... RyanMoore 1 55
(David Evans) *in tch in midfield: effrt u.p over 1f out: styd on same pce ins fnl f* **3/1**[2]

36-1 8 3/4 **Ivestar (IRE)**[16] 143 8-9-6 **64**...............(vt) JimCrowley 7 56+
(Michael Easterby) *hmpd sn after s: in tch in midfield: effrt and chsng ldrs whn nt clr run over 1f out tl ins fnl f: nt rcvr and one pce fnl 100yds* **6/1**[3]

110- 9 2 1/4 **Festival Dance**[183] 4535 5-9-0 **65**............... PhilipPrince(7) 3 50
(Ron Hodges) *chsd ldrs tl led after 1f: rdn over 1f out: hdd 1f out: wknd ins fnl f* **25/1**

65-5 10 1/2 **Fairy Wing (IRE)**[19] 92 6-9-2 **65**...............(b[1]) CharlesBishop(5) 12 49
(Violet M Jordan) *t.k.h: in tch in midfield: rdn and no prog over 1f out: wknd ins fnl f* **33/1**

1-26 **11** 2 1/4 **Liberal Lady**[15] 156 5-9-4 **62** .... JoeFanning 2 38+
(Ralph Smith) *hld up towards rr: clsng on ldrs whn nt clr run 1f out tl wl ins fnl f: nt rcvr and eased towards fin* **20/1**

1m 11.21s (-0.69) **Going Correction** -0.075s/f (Stan) **11** Ran SP% **122.6**
Speed ratings (Par 101): **101,98,96,96,95 95,93,92,89,89 86**
Tote Swingers 1&2 £4.30, 2&3 £5.00, 1&3 £12.40 CSF £29.44 CT £190.99 TOTE £11.30: £3.40, £1.60, £3.90; EX 41.10 Trifecta £312.30 Pool: £2,295.03 - 5.51 winning tickets..
Owner Rakebackmypoker.com **Bred** Bryan Ryan **Trained** Moreton Morrell, Warwicks

FOCUS
Nowhere near as strong a pace as in the first division, but the winner and runner-up still came from well back.

400 FOLLOW US ON TWITTER @LINGFIELDPARK H'CAP 1m (P)
2:35 (2:37) (Class 4) (0-85,85) 4-Y-0+ **£4,690** (£1,395; £697; £348) **Stalls** High

Form RPR

534- **1** **Mister Musicmaster**[52] 7997 4-8-9 **73** .... WilliamCarson 6 82
(Ron Hodges) *chsd ldrs: rdn to chal over 1f out: led ins fnl f: kpt on wl: drvn out* **12/1**

100- **2** *shd* **Maverik**[104] 7083 5-9-6 **84** .... JimCrowley 9 93
(Ralph Beckett) *chsd ldrs: wnt 2nd 5f out: rdn and ev ch over 1f out: led briefly jst ins fnl f: sn hdd: kpt on u.p but a jst hld* **3/1**[1]

21-0 **3** 1 1/4 **Silverware (USA)**[11] 217 5-9-0 **78** .... TomEaves 10 84
(Linda Stubbs) *led and grad crossed to inner: rdn wl over 1f out: hdd jst ins fnl f: styd on same pce fnl 100yds* **25/1**

44-3 **4** *hd* **Patriotic (IRE)**[17] 121 5-8-10 **77** ....(p) RaulDaSilva(3) 4 82
(Chris Dwyer) *hld up in tch in last quartet: rdn and effrt wl over 1f out: styd on wl ins fnl f: nt rch ldrs* **7/1**

-111 **5** 1/2 **Al's Memory (IRE)**[3] 345 4-9-5 **83** 6ex........ TomMcLaughlin 3 87
(David Evans) *t.k.h: hld up wl in tch in midfield: rdn and effrt to press ldrs on inner 1f out: styd on same pce ins fnl f* **6/1**[3]

22-2 **6** *shd* **Fast Finian (IRE)**[17] 121 4-9-0 **85** .... PhilipPrince(7) 5 89
(Paul D'Arcy) *taken down early: t.k.h: hld up wl in tch: effrt u.p wl over 1f out: n.m.r briefly 1f out: styd on same pce ins fnl f* **4/1**[2]

03-1 **7** 1 3/4 **Beautiful Day**[22] 49 5-9-0 **78** .... RyanMoore 8 78
(Kevin Ryan) *chsd ldr tl 5f out: styd chsng ldrs: rdn and unable qck over 1f out: wknd ins fnl f* **10/1**

44-4 **8** 1 1/4 **Crew Cut (IRE)**[17] 121 5-9-0 **78** ....(p) RobertWinston 1 75
(Jeremy Gask) *hld up in tch in rr: rdn and effrt over 1f out: no imp ins fnl f* **16/1**

/00- **9** *nse* **Tadabeer**[74] 7083 5-8-12 **76** ....(t) StevieDonohoe 7 73
(Ian Williams) *stdd s: hld up in tch in rr: wd bnd 2f out: one pce and no imp after* **16/1**

0-11 **10** 3 3/4 **Loyalty**[14] 189 6-9-7 **85** ....(v) JoeFanning 2 73
(Derek Shaw) *dwlt: in tch in last trio: rdn and no hdwy over 1f out: wknd ins fnl f* **4/1**[2]

1m 37.18s (-1.02) **Going Correction** -0.075s/f (Stan) **10** Ran SP% **124.2**
Speed ratings (Par 105): **102,101,100,100,99 99,98,96,96,93**
Tote Swingers 1&2 £9.20, 2&3 £14.90, 1&3 £31.50 CSF £51.25 CT £930.55 TOTE £17.60: £5.00, £1.90, £8.50; EX 90.10 Trifecta £3104.60 Part won..
Owner Mrs L Sharpe & Mrs S G Clapp **Bred** Mrs J Fuller And S Dutfield **Trained** Charlton Mackrell, Somerset

FOCUS
There wasn't much pace on and it paid to be handy.

401 LINGFIELDPARK.CO.UK H'CAP 1m 2f (P)
3:10 (3:10) (Class 2) (0-100,96) 4-Y-0+ **£12,291** (£3,657; £1,827; £913) **Stalls** Low

Form RPR

24-3 **1** **Robin Hoods Bay**[14] 189 5-9-3 **92** .... RyanMoore 8 103
(Ed Vaughan) *stdd after s: hld up in last trio: rdn and hdwy over 2f out: chsd ldr over 1f out: led fnl 100yds: r.o wl* **9/2**[2]

263- **2** 1 1/4 **Strictly Silver (IRE)**[35] 8226 4-8-8 **92** .... PhilipPrince(7) 9 100
(Alan Bailey) *in tch in midfield: rdn and effrt on inner over 1f out: kpt on u.p ins fnl f: snatched 2nd on post* **9/2**[2]

22-5 **3** *nse* **Emerald Wilderness (IRE)**[14] 189 9-9-6 **95** .... SebSanders 6 103
(Mark Rimmer) *chsd ldrs tl led 9f out: sn clr: rdn and fnd ex wl over 1f out: hdd and styd on same pce fnl 100yds: lost 2nd on post* **10/1**

424- **4** 3/4 **Mia's Boy**[35] 8226 9-9-5 **94** .... GeorgeBaker 3 100
(Chris Dwyer) *short of room leaving stalls: hld up in rr: clsd 2f out: rdn over 1f out: styd on wl ins fnl f: nt rch ldrs* **12/1**

15-4 **5** 1/2 **Mawaakef (IRE)**[14] 189 5-9-1 **90** .... JimCrowley 7 95
(J R Jenkins) *hld up in midfield: rdn and unable qck over 1f out: styd on again ins fnl f: nt rch ldrs* **14/1**

414- **6** 1/2 **Tinshu (IRE)**[35] 8227 7-9-6 **95** ....(p) WilliamCarson 5 99
(Derek Haydn Jones) *chsd ldrs: rdn and unable qck over 1f out: no ex and wknd fnl 100yds* **8/1**[3]

623- **7** 3 **Be Perfect (USA)**[35] 8227 4-9-4 **95** ....(tp) AndreaAtzeni 2 93
(Marco Botti) *chsd ldrs: rdn and unable qck over 1f out: wknd fnl f* **6/4**[1]

040- **8** 4 1/2 **Nazreef**[44] 8095 6-9-7 **96** ....(vt) RobertWinston 1 85
(Hughie Morrison) *led tl 9f out: rdn and effrt to press ldr over 2f out tl wl over 1f out: wknd over 1f out* **16/1**

9 6 **Teshali (IRE)**[21] 7-8-5 **85** ....(vt[1]) LeonnaMayor(5) 4 62
(Anthony Middleton) *awkward and wnt lft leaving stalls: hld up in rr: rdn 4f out: wknd over 2f out* **33/1**

2m 2.41s (-4.19) **Going Correction** -0.075s/f (Stan)
WFA 4 from 5yo+ 2lb **9** Ran SP% **119.7**
Speed ratings (Par 109): **113,112,111,111,110 110,108,104,99**
Tote Swingers 1&2 £5.00, 2&3 £11.50, 1&3 £8.30 CSF £26.14 CT £196.38 TOTE £5.70: £1.30, £2.20, £3.40; EX 34.80 Trifecta £261.70 Pool: £3,438.12 - 9.84 winning tickets..
Owner A M Pickering **Bred** Palm Tree Thoroughbreds **Trained** Newmarket, Suffolk

FOCUS
Not that strong a race for the class, but they seemed to go a fair enough pace.

402 6TH SHAREN BLAQUIERE "CELEBRATE A LIFE" H'CAP 6f (P)
3:45 (3:46) (Class 5) (0-70,74) 3-Y-O **£2,726** (£805; £402) **Stalls** Low

Form RPR

4-44 **1** **The Black Jacobin**[12] 204 3-9-1 **64** ....(b) RyanMoore 4 67
(J S Moore) *hld up in last: effrt and rdn 2f out: chsd clr ldr jst ins fnl f: str run fnl 100yds to ld last strides* **9/2**[3]

-113 **2** *hd* **Lager Time (IRE)**[13] 195 3-9-1 **64** .... WilliamCarson 2 66+
(David Evans) *led tl over 4f out: chsd ldr after tl led again over 2f out: drvn clr over 1f out: kpt on u.p tl hdd and no ex last strides* **4/5**[1]

36-6 **3** 7 **Betzyoucan**[12] 209 3-8-11 **60** .... JoeFanning 1 40
(Mark Johnston) *chsd ldng pair: rdn and effrt ent fnl 2f: chsd clr ldr wl over 1f out tl jst ins fnl f: wknd* **8/1**

61- **4** 5 **Buy Art**[221] 3244 3-9-7 **70** .... GeorgeBaker 3 34
(Gary Moore) *chsd ldr tl led over 4f out: hdd over 2f out: wknd over 1f out: bhd fnl f* **5/2**[2]

1m 11.59s (-0.31) **Going Correction** -0.075s/f (Stan) **4** Ran SP% **113.4**
Speed ratings (Par 97): **99,98,89,82**
CSF £9.17 TOTE £4.60; EX 8.00 Trifecta £33.10 Pool: £1,768.11 - 39.99 wining tickets..
Owner Norton Common Farm Racing **Bred** T R Watson & Miss D S Peasley **Trained** Upper Lambourn, Berks

FOCUS
Only four runners, but the front two finished well clear of the other pair and look to have run to a fair enough level.

403 GET STRAIGHT TOTHE BET AT BLUESQ.COM H'CAP 1m 2f (P)
4:15 (4:16) (Class 5) (0-70,70) 4-Y-0+ **£2,726** (£805; £402) **Stalls** Low

Form RPR

26-1 **1** **Conducting**[21] 73 5-9-3 **66** .... RobertWinston 13 74
(Gay Kelleway) *mde virtually all: dictated stdy gallop tl qcknd 3f out: rdn and fnd ex whn drifted rt wl over 1f out: styd on wl fnl f* **8/1**

021- **2** 1 1/4 **Bert The Alert**[27] 8292 5-9-7 **70** .... GeorgeBaker 6 76
(Gary Moore) *hld up in midfield: effrt and swtchd lft jst over 1f out: chsd wnr fnl 100yds: kpt on but no real imp* **5/2**[1]

150- **3** 1 **Fire King**[132] 6275 7-9-3 **66** .... TomEaves 4 70
(Philip Hide) *t.k.h: chsd ldrs: rdn and effrt over 1f out: drvn and chsd wnr 1f out: no imp and lost 2nd fnl 100yds* **16/1**

000- **4** *nk* **Rezwaan**[36] 8199 6-8-13 **62** ....(be) JoeFanning 7 65
(Murty McGrath) *t.k.h: hld up in tch in midfield: rdn and effrt over 1f out: styd on wl ins fnl f: nt rch ldrs* **16/1**

060- **5** 3/4 **Attwaal (IRE)**[38] 3345 4-9-0 **65** .... SebSanders 12 66
(Neil King) *hld up in tch towards rr: rdn and wd bnd 2f out: rallied and styd on wl ins fnl f: nt rch ldrs* **7/1**

30-6 **6** *shd* **Officer In Command (USA)**[21] 73 7-9-2 **65** ....(p) JohnFahy 1 66
(Sean Curran) *rdn along leaving stalls: hld up in tch in midfield: rdn and effrt to chse ldrs on inner over 1f out: drvn and styd on same pce fnl f* **14/1**

2-10 **7** 1/2 **Honey Of A Kitten (USA)**[5] 314 5-9-6 **69** ....(v) RyanMoore 11 69
(David Evans) *t.k.h: hld up in tch in midfield: drvn and styd on same pce fr over 1f out* **5/1**[2]

00-0 **8** 1 1/4 **Legal Legacy**[21] 73 7-8-12 **61** .... WilliamCarson 5 59
(Richard Rowe) *hld up in tch in rr: effrt 2f out: hdwy u.p 1f out: styd on: nvr trbld ldrs* **20/1**

400- **9** *nk* **Confirmed**[26] 8308 4-8-12 **63** .... RenatoSouza 10 60
(Alison Batchelor) *t.k.h: hld up in tch in rr: rdn and effrt whn n.m.r over 1f out: styd on ins fnl f: nt rch ldrs* **50/1**

35-6 **10** 3/4 **Hurricane Hymnbook (USA)**[17] 112 8-9-3 **66** .... TomMcLaughlin 9 62
(Willie Musson) *stdd s: hld up in rr: rdn and effrt over 1f out: kpt on ins fnl f: nvr trbld ldrs* **6/1**[3]

10-5 **11** *nk* **Zafranagar (IRE)**[22] 52 8-9-2 **70** .... GeorgeDowning(5) 8 65
(Tony Carroll) *t.k.h: chsd ldrs: ev ch 3f out: rdn and unable qck wl over 1f out: wknd ins fnl f* **14/1**

304- **12** 1 3/4 **Palmyra (IRE)**[242] 2577 4-8-10 **61** .... ChrisCatlin 14 53
(Martin Hill) *pressed wnr tl unable qck over 1f out: btn 1f out: wknd ins fnl f* **25/1**

06-0 **13** 3 1/4 **L'Hirondelle (IRE)**[17] 112 9-9-4 **67** .... JimCrowley 2 52
(Michael Attwater) *chsd ldrs: rdn and no ex wl over 1f out: wknd ent fnl f* **20/1**

2m 8.94s (2.34) **Going Correction** -0.075s/f (Stan)
WFA 4 from 5yo+ 2lb **13** Ran SP% **123.6**
Speed ratings (Par 103): **87,86,85,84,84 84,83,82,82,82 81,80,77**
Tote Swingers 1&2 £4.40, 2&3 £11.00, 1&3 £25.60 CSF £27.89 CT £330.41 TOTE £8.10: £3.10, £1.60, £5.90; EX 26.40 Trifecta £309.90 Pool: £2,805.41 - 6.78 winning tickets..
Owner J Farley, M Brunner & M Whatley **Bred** David J Brown **Trained** Exning, Suffolk

FOCUS
The pace was slow.
T/Plt: £46.50 to a £1 stake. Pool: £69,805.41 - 1095.41 winning tickets. T/Qpdt: £51.00 to a £1 stake. Pool: £4,872.29 - 70.68 winning tickets. SP

375 WOLVERHAMPTON (A.W) (L-H)
Saturday, January 26

OFFICIAL GOING: Standard to slow
Wind: Light to Moderate, half behind Weather: Cloudy

404 BEST RACING ODDS GUARANTEED AT BOOKMAKERS.CO.UK MAIDEN STKS 5f 216y(P)
1:40 (1:41) (Class 5) 3-Y-0+ **£2,587** (£770; £384; £192) **Stalls** Low

Form RPR

-322 **1** **Sewn Up**[4] 328 3-8-11 66 ....(tp) ShaneKelly 7 69
(Reg Hollinshead) *hld up: hdwy 2f out: swtchd rt and shkn up to go through gap over 1f out: kidded to move upsides wl ins fnl f: sn led: cheekily: gd ride* **10/3**[2]

2/ **2** 1 **Danziger (IRE)**[124] 6548 4-9-8 0 .... GrahamGibbons 4 65
(David Evans) *led: rdn over 1f out: jnd wl ins fnl f: sn hdd and hld* **9/1**

43- **3** 1/2 **Next Door (IRE)**[140] 6042 3-8-6 0 .... HayleyTurner 1 59
(David Barron) *chsd ldr: chalng 2f out: rdn and nt qckn over 1f out: kpt on u.p towards fin* **15/8**[1]

2-3 **4** 2 1/4 **Black Rider (IRE)**[9] 236 3-8-11 0 .... AmyRyan 3 57
(Kevin Ryan) *racd keenly: a.p: chalng 2f out: rdn over 1f out: styd on same pce fnl 100yds* **7/2**[3]

5 1 **Jofranka** 3-8-6 0 .... MartinLane 2 49
(David Barron) *s.i.s: racd keenly: sn in tch: pushed along 2f out: rdn whn chsng ldrs over 1f out: kpt on same pce ins fnl f* **16/1**

6 **6** 1 1/2 **Dutch Delight**[13] 197 3-8-6 0 .... BarryMcHugh 6 44
(Tony Coyle) *hld up in midfield: pushed along 3f out: rdn and wknd wl over 1f out* **11/1**

-334 **7** 9 **Island Express (IRE)**[2] 356 6-9-8 53 ....(tp) AnnStokell(5) 5 24
(Ann Stokell) *racd keenly on outer: in tch: rdn and wknd over 2f out* **25/1**

06-5 **8** 2 1/4 **Proventi**[16] 136 3-8-11 50 ....(be) SeanLevey 8 13
(Alan McCabe) *s.i.s: in rr: pushed along over 2f out: toiling after* **66/1**

1m 15.89s (0.89) **Going Correction** +0.125s/f (Slow)
WFA 3 from 4yo+ 16lb **8** Ran SP% **109.6**
Speed ratings (Par 103): **99,97,97,94,92 90,78,75**
Tote Swingers: 1&2 £6.90, 1&3 £1.40, 2&3 £4.00 CSF £30.14 TOTE £2.80: £1.10, £3.20, £1.30; EX 33.20 Trifecta £94.20 Pool: £1,859.87 - 14.80 winning units..
Owner John L Marriott **Bred** M E Broughton **Trained** Upper Longdon, Staffs

FOCUS
An ordinary maiden.

405 FREE BET BONANZA NOW AT BOOKMAKERS.CO.UK H'CAP 5f 216y(P)
2:15 (2:15) (Class 3) (0-95,88) 4-Y-0+ £7,439 (£2,213; £1,106; £553) Stalls Low

Form RPR

P1-1 1 **Tarooq (USA)**[15] 155 7-9-7 88 (t) SeanLevey 2 98
(Stuart Williams) *chsd ldrs: wnt 2nd 2f out: rdn over 1f out: led jst ins fnl f: r.o* 9/2[2]

660- 2 1 **Thunderball**[44] 8098 7-9-4 85 (p) AdamBeschizza 4 92
(Scott Dixon) *sn led: rdn over 1f out: hdd jst ins fnl f: kpt on but u.p hld* 8/1

0-12 3 3/4 **Profile Star (IRE)**[2] 353 4-9-2 83 GrahamGibbons 5 87
(David Barron) *midfield: pushed along 3f out: hdwy over 1f out: styd on ins fnl f: nt quite pce to chal ldrs* 15/8[1]

00-1 4 1 3/4 **Seek The Fair Land**[15] 164 7-9-2 88 (b) WilliamTwiston-Davies(5) 10 87
(Jamie Osborne) *chsd ldrs: rdn over 2f out: kpt on same pce ins fnl f* 8/1

43-4 5 nk **Sulis Minerva (IRE)**[21] 78 6-8-12 86 RyanTate(7) 9 84
(Jeremy Gask) *s.i.s: hld up: rdn over 1f out: styd on ins fnl f: nvr able to get to ldrs* 8/1

42-0 6 3/4 **Speightowns Kid (USA)**[15] 164 5-8-2 74 oh3 JemmaMarshall(5) 8 69
(Jo Hughes) *chsd ldr tl pushed along 2f out: rdn over 1f out: no ex fnl 100yds* 33/1

3-51 7 hd **Waking Warrior**[13] 196 5-8-12 82 (tp) JulieBurke(3) 1 77
(Kevin Ryan) *hld up: pushed along 2f out: kpt on ins fnl f: nvr able to chal* 6/1[3]

10-0 8 3 **Forest Edge (IRE)**[21] 78 4-9-5 86 (b) ShaneKelly 7 71
(David Evans) *towards rr: niggled along 4f out: u.p over 2f out: nvr a threat* 12/1

0-60 9 12 **Royal Bajan (USA)**[17] 113 5-8-12 79 JamesSullivan 6 26
(James Given) *plld hrd: prom tl pushed along and wknd over 2f out* 40/1

1m 14.63s (-0.37) **Going Correction** +0.125s/f (Slow) 9 Ran SP% 113.7
Speed ratings (Par 107): **107,105,104,102,101 100,100,96,80**
Tote Swingers: 1&2 £7.10, 1&3 £2.90, 2&3 £6.30 CSF £39.49 CT £88.72 TOTE £4.80: £1.40, £2.20, £1.10; EX 37.80 Trifecta £103.90 Pool: £1,642.70 - 11.85 winning units..
Owner H Chamberlain, I Pearce **Bred** Kirsten Rausing **Trained** Newmarket, Suffolk

FOCUS
A burn-up looked possible here, but in the event very few got into it, with Thunderball leading most of the way.

406 CORAL.CO.UK MOBILE BETTING H'CAP 1m 5f 194y(P)
2:50 (2:55) (Class 6) (0-60,59) 4-Y-0+ £1,940 (£577; £288; £144) Stalls Low

Form RPR

1 **Speed Steed (IRE)**[247] 1350 6-8-9 51 DanielMuscutt(7) 2 59
(Tim Vaughan) *hld up: hdwy over 3f out: wnt 2nd over 1f out: rdn over 1f out: r.o to ld ins fnl f: a doing enough nr fin* 16/1

5-23 2 3/4 **Liberty Love (IRE)**[2] 361 8-9-3 52 (bt) SeanLevey 7 59
(Shaun Harley, Ire) *hld up: hdwy over 1f out: r.o ins fnl f: tk 2nd fnl 75yds: clsd on wnr nr fin* 9/4[1]

0U-5 3 1 3/4 **Crimson Monarch (USA)**[19] 100 9-8-10 45 (b) KirstyMilczarek 6 50
(Peter Hiatt) *midfield: hdwy over 3f out: led 2f out: hung lft 1f out: sn hdd: no ex fnl 75yds* 11/1

2-32 4 3/4 **Peace In Our Time**[10] 226 4-8-3 51 ow1 RobertTart(7) 10 55
(Anthony Carson) *a.p: rdn over 1f out: sn edgd lft: styd on same pce fnl 100yds* 11/4[2]

0/0- 5 shd **Richo**[29] 8265 7-8-7 45 MarkCoumbe(3) 3 48
(Shaun Harris) *s.v.s: in rr: pushed along and hdwy 2f out: styd on ins fnl f: unable to chal* 100/1

060- 6 16 **Grey Command (USA)**[25] 3437 8-9-9 58 HayleyTurner 1 39
(Philip Kirby) *midfield tl rdn and wknd over 2f out* 9/1

0-05 7 hd **Dubai Emerald (USA)**[15] 169 4-8-7 48 BarryMcHugh 4 29
(Chris Dwyer) *led: hdd 2f out: rdn and wknd over 1f out* 20/1

006- 8 2 1/4 **Merevale**[87] 7494 4-8-4 45 JamesSullivan 11 23
(Michael Appleby) *in tch: pushed along over 3f out: wknd 2f out* 9/2[3]

06-6 9 23 **Rasteau (IRE)**[12] 200 5-8-3 45 (p) DanielleMooney(7) 5
(Tom Keddy) *hld up in midfield: rdn and wknd 3f out* 50/1

00-5 10 6 **Asterales**[12] 201 6-9-4 53 J-PGuillambert 8
(Jo Hughes) *rdn along s: hdwy to chse ldr after over 2f: pushed along over 3f out: lost 2nd over 2f out: sn wknd* 14/1

3m 7.59s (1.59) **Going Correction** +0.125s/f (Slow)
WFA 4 from 5yo+ 6lb 10 Ran SP% 114.2
Speed ratings (Par 101): **100,99,98,98,98 88,88,87,74,70**
Tote Swingers: 1&2 £10.10, 1&3 £17.40, 2&3 £4.80 CSF £50.65 CT £426.42 TOTE £8.80: £2.10, £1.30, £3.10; EX 62.10 Trifecta £371.80 Pool: £1,088.13 - 2.19 winning units..
Owner J H Frost **Bred** Michael Thornton **Trained** Aberthin, Vale of Glamorgan
■ Stewards' Enquiry : Kirsty Milczarek two-day ban; careless riding (9th&10th Feb).

FOCUS
Just a moderate staying handicap.

407 CLAIM FREE BETS TODAY AT BOOKMAKERS.CO.UK CONDITIONS STKS 7f 32y(P)
3:25 (3:27) (Class 4) 4-Y-0+ £4,851 (£1,443; £721; £360) Stalls High

Form RPR

/12- 1 **Anaconda (FR)**[35] 8226 4-9-5 97 StephenCraine 2 99
(Tom Dascombe) *mde all: rdn over 1f out: kpt on wl towards fin* 7/4[1]

01-3 2 1 1/4 **Piscean (USA)**[21] 78 8-8-13 98 RyanClark(3) 3 93
(Tom Keddy) *hld up in rr: effrt on outer over 1f out: sn wnt 2nd: styd on ins fnl f: hld towards fin* 3/1[2]

1-22 3 3/4 **Chapter And Verse (IRE)**[22] 60 7-9-2 90 EddieAhern 1 91
(Mike Murphy) *hld up: rdn over 1f out: prog ins fnl f: styd on towards fin: nt pce to chal* 5/1[3]

16-1 4 3/4 **Kung Hei Fat Choy (USA)**[24] 25 4-9-2 82 (b) DaleSwift 5 89
(James Given) *chsd ldr: ev ch 2f out: lost 2nd whn rdn 1f out: one pce fnl 75yds* 10/1

60-1 5 1 3/4 **Verse Of Love**[22] 60 4-9-5 89 GrahamGibbons 4 87
(David Evans) *awkward s: chsd ldrs: pushed along 3f out: rdn over 1f out: eased whn no ex fnl 100yds* 3/1[2]

1m 29.01s (-0.59) **Going Correction** +0.125s/f (Slow) 5 Ran SP% 112.1
Speed ratings (Par 105): **108,106,105,104,102**
CSF £7.44 TOTE £2.40: £1.20, £2.90; EX 6.70 Trifecta £18.10 Pool: £1,184.47 - 49.06 winning units..
Owner The MHS 8X8 Partnership **Bred** Haras Du Quesnay **Trained** Malpas, Cheshire

FOCUS
Quite a competitive little conditions race on paper but the winner made all.

408 HORSE RACING FREE BETS AT BOOKMAKERS.CO.UK H'CAP (DIV I) 7f 32y(P)
4:00 (4:00) (Class 6) (0-55,55) 4-Y-0+ £1,940 (£577; £288; £144) Stalls High

Form RPR

3-43 1 **Lieutenant Dan (IRE)**[10] 223 6-9-5 53 (v) DanielTudhope 6 62
(Michael Appleby) *midfield: effrt over 2f out: rdn and chalng over 1f out: styd on to ld towards fin* 5/2[1]

6-32 2 3/4 **Kielty's Folly**[18] 105 9-9-6 54 GrahamGibbons 5 61
(Brian Baugh) *hld up: smooth hdwy 3f out: on bit coming to chal over 1f out: shkn up and led ins fnl f: sn rdn: hdd and outbattled towards fin* 11/4[2]

-400 3 1 1/2 **Georgebernardshaw (IRE)**[3] 334 8-9-3 51 (vt[1]) KellyHarrison 8 54
(Richard Guest) *chsd ldrs: led over 2f out: rdn and carried hd awkwardly over 1f out: hdd ins fnl f: kpt on same pce towards fin* 14/1

5-61 4 1 1/2 **Media Jury**[9] 240 6-9-3 51 (p) BarryMcHugh 9 50
(John Wainwright) *bhd: hdwy 2f out: chsd ldrs over 1f out: lugged lft ins fnl f: styd on same pce fnl 100yds* 9/1

0-63 5 hd **Hold The Star**[9] 240 7-8-8 47 AnnStokell(5) 4 45
(Ann Stokell) *chsd ldrs: rdn over 1f out: one pce ins fnl f* 16/1

0-06 6 hd **Mambo Spirit (IRE)**[7] 274 9-9-6 54 SeanLevey 10 52
(Tony Newcombe) *s.v.s: bhd: rdn over 1f out: kpt on ins fnl f: nvr able to chal* 9/1

3-00 7 1/2 **Rogue Reporter (IRE)**[7] 274 4-9-7 55 (p) KirstyMilczarek 3 51
(Stuart Williams) *led: hdd narrowly over 4f out: regained ld 3f out: hdd over 2f out: stl in contention over 1f out: fdd ins fnl f* 4/1[3]

6-60 8 2 1/2 **Aljosan**[1] 381 4-8-11 48 (tp) MarkCoumbe(3) 1 38
(Frank Sheridan) *chsd ldrs: rdn over 3f out: wknd 2f out* 33/1

006- 9 2 3/4 **Schoolboy Champ**[27] 8299 6-8-9 46 oh1 (bt) RyanClark(3) 2 28
(Lisa Williamson) *dwlt: a towards rr: sn rdn along: eased whn bhd and wl btn ins fnl f* 20/1

0-06 10 7 **The Jailer**[19] 92 10-8-5 46 oh1 (v) AaronJones(7) 7 9
(John O'Shea) *pushed along early to go prom: led over 4f out: hdd 3f out: rdn and wknd over 2f out* 66/1

1m 30.78s (1.18) **Going Correction** +0.125s/f (Slow) 10 Ran SP% 117.0
Speed ratings (Par 101): **98,97,95,93,93 93,92,89,86,78**
Tote Swingers: 1&2 £2.70, 1&3 £6.70, 2&3 £5.90 CSF £9.36 CT £78.52 TOTE £3.30: £1.40, £1.20, £4.00; EX 10.70 Trifecta £119.10 Pool: £1,853.92 - 11.67 winning units..
Owner Dallas Racing **Bred** Hong Kong Breeders Club **Trained** Danethorpe, Notts

FOCUS
There was a good gallop on here and it was set up for the closers.

409 HORSE RACING FREE BETS AT BOOKMAKERS.CO.UK H'CAP (DIV II) 7f 32y(P)
4:30 (4:31) (Class 6) (0-55,55) 4-Y-0+ £1,940 (£577; £288; £144) Stalls High

Form RPR

4-34 1 **Harvest Mist (IRE)**[5] 312 5-8-10 49 WilliamTwiston-Davies(5) 7 58
(Shaun Lycett) *chsd ldrs: rdn to ld over 1f out: r.o ins fnl f: hld on wl cl home* 11/1

02- 2 nk **Phils Wish (IRE)**[81] 7616 4-9-3 51 AmyRyan 2 59
(John C McConnell, Ire) *chsd ldrs: rdn to take 2nd jst over 1f out: styd on ins fnl f: clsd on wnr cl home* 13/8[1]

40-5 3 4 **Brown Volcano (IRE)**[22] 54 4-9-4 55 MarkCoumbe(3) 6 52
(John O'Shea) *hld up: pushed aong over 2f out: rdn and swtchd rt whn hdwy jst over 1f out: styd on to take 3rd ins fnl f: no imp on front two* 12/1

44-0 4 2 1/2 **Littlecote Lady**[10] 223 4-9-0 53 LeeNewnes(5) 9 44
(Mark Usher) *racd keenly in midfield: pushed along 3f out: rdn over 1f out: kpt on ins fnl f: nvr able to chal* 14/1

-600 5 2 1/2 **Rise To Glory (IRE)**[2] 349 5-8-13 47 (t) DuranFentiman 1 31
(Shaun Harris) *chsd ldr: rdn 2f out: sn lost 2nd: stl chsng ldrs but no imp over 1f out: no ex fnl 100yds* 10/1

0-30 6 1/2 **Onceaponatime (IRE)**[15] 163 8-9-4 52 KirstyMilczarek 5 35
(Michael Squance) *hld up: pushed along 2f out: rdn over 1f out: nvr a threat* 12/1

3-15 7 shd **Dhhamaan (IRE)**[18] 105 8-9-6 54 (b) JamesSullivan 4 36
(Ruth Carr) *led: rdn and hdd over 1f out: wknd ins fnl f* 4/1[2]

0403 8 hd **Sleepy Lucy**[3] 335 4-8-12 46 oh1 (e) RobbieFitzpatrick 3 28
(Richard Guest) *dwlt: midfield: rdn over 1f out: one pce u.p over 1f out: nvr able to chal* 15/2[3]

0-0 9 30 **Minty Jones**[23] 42 4-8-13 47 GrahamGibbons 8
(Michael Mullineaux) *s.i.s: a bhd: lost tch 3f out: virtually p.u wl over 1f out* 25/1

1m 30.39s (0.79) **Going Correction** +0.125s/f (Slow) 9 Ran SP% 113.2
Speed ratings (Par 101): **100,99,95,92,89 88,88,88,54**
Tote Swingers: 1&2 £5.20, 1&3 £17.80, 2&3 £6.70 CSF £28.68 CT £224.87 TOTE £9.70: £3.70, £1.02, £4.40; EX 32.10 Trifecta £602.70 Pool: £2,535.07 - 3.15 winning units..
Owner Chris Buckingham **Bred** Mrs Amanda Brudenell **Trained** Clapton-on-the-Hill, Gloucs
■ Stewards' Enquiry : William Twiston-Davies two-day ban; used whip above permitted level (9th Feb, other day tbd).

FOCUS
The quicker of the two divisions by 0.39sec.

410 CORAL.CO.UK H'CAP 1m 141y(P)
5:00 (5:00) (Class 6) (0-65,65) 4-Y-0+ £1,940 (£577; £288; £144) Stalls Low

Form RPR

50-1 1 **Monzino (USA)**[5] 312 5-8-10 61 6ex GerardGalligan(7) 6 71
(Michael Chapman) *racd keenly in tch: rdn over 2f out: led ins fnl f: r.o and in command fnl 75yds* 7/2[2]

6-1 2 1 3/4 **Jumbo Prado (USA)**[16] 147 4-9-4 63 ShaneKelly 2 69
(Daniel Mark Loughnane) *hld up: hdwy 2f out: rdn and ev ch ins fnl f: outpcd by wnr fnl 75yds* 11/10[1]

003- 3 1 3/4 **Stylistickhill (IRE)**[48] 8051 5-9-5 63 (tp) GrahamGibbons 5 65
(Scott Dixon) *hld up: hdwy 2f out: styd on ins fnl f: nvr able to get to ldrs* 12/1

40-0 4 nk **Haywain**[11] 219 4-9-5 64 (b[1]) FrannyNorton 1 65
(Kevin Ryan) *chsd ldrs: rdn over 1f out: styd on u.p ins fnl f: nt pce of ldrs* 12/1

30-2 5 hd **Dundrum Dancer (IRE)**[11] 218 6-9-2 65 WilliamTwiston-Davies(5) 7 66
(Alex Hales) *hld up: rdn over 1f out: styd on ins fnl f: nvr nrr* 20/1

0-50 6 1 1/4 **Lord Of The Dance (IRE)**[11] 218 7-9-5 63 DanielTudhope 9 61
(Michael Mullineaux) *chsd ldr: led 2f out: rdn and hdd ins fnl f: no ex fnl 100yds* 25/1

4-60 7 2 3/4 **Elijah Pepper (USA)**[11] 219 8-9-6 64 HayleyTurner 4 56
(Conor Dore) *in tch: outpcd 2f out: no imp fnl f* 20/1

11-5 **8** 1 1/4 **Outlaw Torn (IRE)**[22] 61 4-9-5 64......................(e) RobbieFitzpatrick 3 53
(Richard Guest) *racd keenly: led: hdd 2f out: rdn over 1f out: wknd ins fnl f* **11/2**[3]
00-0 **9** 7 **King Of Windsor (IRE)**[13] 192 6-9-4 62......................(p) DaleSwift 10 35
(John Wainwright) *s.s: a bhd* **25/1**
00-0 **10** 18 **Qeethaara (USA)**[19] 89 9-8-13 57............................(p) EddieAhern 11
(Mark Brisbourne) *chsd ldrs tl rdn and wknd 2f out* **66/1**

1m 50.79s (0.29) **Going Correction** +0.125s/f (Slow)
WFA 4 from 5yo+ 1lb **10** Ran SP% **119.3**
Speed ratings (Par 101): **103,101,99,99,99 98,95,94,88,72**
Tote Swingers: 1&2 £2.70, 1&3 £2.20, 2&3 £8.50 CSF £7.36 CT £41.45 TOTE £5.60: £1.40, £1.30, £3.40; EX 13.00 Trifecta £73.30 Pool: £3,092.83 - 31.62 winning units..
Owner Mrs M Chapman **Bred** Pillar Property Services Inc **Trained** Market Rasen, Lincs
FOCUS
The market principals came to the fore here.

411 POKER AT CORAL.CO.UK H'CAP 1m 1f 103y(P)
5:30 (5:30) (Class 6) (0-60,60) 3-Y-O **£1,940** (£577; £288; £144) **Stalls** Low

Form RPR
6345 **1** **Precision Strike**[3] 336 3-8-11 50......................(v) KellyHarrison 5 52
(Richard Guest) *hld up: hdwy 3f out: led 2f out: a hrd pressed after: all out in driving fin* **8/1**[3]
5-22 **2** *nse* **Subtle Difference**[16] 134 3-9-6 59............................ KirstyMilczarek 4 61
(Andrew Balding) *led tl 8f out: remained handy: rdn and nt qckn whn carried hd high over 1f out: styd on ins fnl f: clsd nr fin: jst failed* **11/4**[1]
06-1 **3** *nk* **Salute To Seville (IRE)**[19] 103 3-9-7 60......................(b) LiamKeniry 6 61
(J S Moore) *a.p: led wl over 2f out: sn hdd: continued to chal strly: styd on in driving fin: jst hld* **3/1**[2]
003- **4** 5 **Sand Grouse**[68] 7785 3-8-10 56......................(b) RyanTate(7) 2 47
(Marco Botti) *in tch: outpcd 2f out: n.d after* **11/4**[1]
03-4 **5** 24 **Rainford Glory (IRE)**[12] 209 3-8-13 57...(p) WilliamTwiston-Davies(5) 7
(Patrick Morris) *prom: led 8f out: hdd wl over 2f out: sn wknd* **10/1**
06-P **6** 10 **Charm Cry (USA)**[12] 212 3-9-6 59............................ FrannyNorton 8
(Mark Johnston) *hld up: outpcd over 2f out: sn lft wl bhd* **8/1**[3]

2m 3.84s (2.14) **Going Correction** +0.125s/f (Slow) **6** Ran SP% **109.6**
Speed ratings (Par 95): **95,94,94,90,68 60**
Tote Swingers: 1&2 £4.00, 1&3 £5.20, 2&3 £1.60 CSF £28.72 CT £74.60 TOTE £8.80: £6.10, £1.10; EX 33.00 Trifecta £119.40 Pool: £2,058.34 - 12.92 winning units..
Owner Future Racing (Notts) Limited **Bred** Mickley Stud **Trained** Wetherby, W Yorks
FOCUS
No-one really wanted to go, but eventually Rainford Glory was taken to the front, and he set an ordinary gallop.
T/Plt: £12.50 to a £1 stake. Pool: £64,947.20 - 3,783.55 winning tickets. T/Qpdt: £6.30 to a £1 stake. Pool: £5,757.01 - 667.54 winning tickets. DO

ABU DHABI
Sunday, January 27
OFFICIAL GOING: Turf: good to firm

412a RAJAI H'CAP (TURF) 1m (T)
2:00 (2:00) (75-95,95) 3-Y-O+ **£7,537** (£2,512; £1,381; £753; £376)

RPR
1 **El Wasmi**[58] 7950 5-8-5 82......................(bt) SaeedAlMazrooei(6) 3 83
(A Al Raihe, UAE) *well away, sn led, rdn 2f out, ran on well*
2 1/4 **Entifaadha**[38] 8196 4-9-11 95............................ PaulHanagan 11 95
(M Al Muhairi, UAE) *mid-division, ran on wl fnl 1 1/2f, jst failed*
3 1/2 **Musaafer (IRE)**[8] 291 6-9-3 87............................ DaneO'Neill 6 86
(M Al Muhairi, UAE) *mid-division ran on wl fnl 1 1/2f, nrst finish*
4 3/4 **Among Equals**[8] 289 4-9-1 85......................(t) PatCosgrave 4 83
(Doug Watson, UAE) *mid-division, kpt on wl fnl 1 1/2f*
5 3/4 **Furnace (IRE)**[8] 288 9-8-13 83......................(tp) SamHitchcott 10 79
(E Charpy, UAE) *tracked ldg pair, one pace fnl 1 1/2f*
6 1/4 **Black Snowflake (USA)**[30] 8282 6-9-0 84......................(t) RichardMullen 2 79
(S Seemar, UAE) *always mid-division*
7 3/4 **Sailorman (IRE)**[345] 615 6-9-1 85............................ AntiocoMurgia 13 79
(Ismail Mohammed) *tracked leaders, ev ch 3f out, one pace fnl 2f*
8 *nse* **Classic Blade (IRE)**[30] 8280 7-9-6 90............................ PatDobbs 7 83
(Doug Watson, UAE) *always mid-division*
9 1/4 **Kingship Spirit (IRE)**[29] 7-8-11 82............................ CSanchez 14 74
(M Ramadan, UAE) *settled rear, nvr able to chal, but kpt on fnl 1 1/2f*
10 1/2 **Ukrainian (IRE)**[8] 291 4-9-0 84......................(v) RoystonFfrench 8 76
(A Al Raihe, UAE) *never better than mid-division*
11 1/4 **Izaaj (USA)**[8] 291 6-9-3 87............................ ADeVries 5 78
(M bin Shafya, UAE) *never nr to challenge*
12 3 **Mazeydd**[143] 5973 4-9-4 88............................ KierenFallon 1 72
(D Selvaratnam, UAE) *tracked ldg pair til outpcd 3f out*
13 4 1/4 **Maath Gool**[8] 289 6-9-0 84............................ WayneSmith 9 58
(M Al Muhairi, UAE) *always in rear*
14 12 **Nabah**[7] 5-9-4 88............................ SilvestreDeSousa 12 35
(A Al Raihe, UAE) *always in rear*

1m 34.78s (-1.19) **14** Ran

Owner Saeed Manana **Bred** Glebe Stud & Partners **Trained** UAE

TURFWAY PARK (L-H)
Sunday, January 27
OFFICIAL GOING: Polytrack: fast

413a CLAIMING RACE (CLAIMER) (4YO+) (POLYTRACK) 1m
8:40 (12:00) 4-Y-O+
£5,153 (£1,717; £858; £429; £257; £85)

RPR
1 **Gold Trader (USA)**[840] 5-8-9 0............................ PWOuzts 4
(Joe Woodard, U.S.A) **29/10**[2]
2 1 1/2 **Slick Pardoned Me (USA)**[484] 7-8-9 0......................(b) TPompell 1
(Vernon Obermeier, U.S.A) **9/5**[1]
3 *hd* **Master Rocket (USA)** 5-8-9 0............................ ATTamburello 5
(Kris Nemann, U.S.A) **19/2**
4 8 1/4 **Jo Bob (USA)** 5-8-9 0............................ SSellers 2
(Colleen Patterson, U.S.A) **166/10**
5 5 1/2 **Gambling Don (USA)** 4-8-9 0......................(b) RHernandez 3
(Daniel E Sanner, U.S.A) **47/10**[3]
6 4 1/4 **Pure Sovereignty (USA)** 5-8-9 0......................(b) NArroyoJr 7
(Tanya Boulmetis, U.S.A) **31/5**
7 23 **Marford Missile (IRE)**[30] 8279 4-8-9 0............................ BFayosMartin 6
(Amy Weaver) *trckd ldr in 2nd on outer: rdn and lost pl rapidly 3f out: last and btn on turn into st: eased and t.o* **56/10**

1m 41.65s (101.65) **7** Ran SP% **123.1**
PARI-MUTUEL (all including $2 stakes): WIN 7.80; PLACE (1-2) 3.60, 3.20; SHOW (1-2-3) 3.40, 2.80, 5.00; SF 23.20.
Owner Billy, Donna & Justin Hays **Bred** Phipps Stable **Trained** North America

347 KEMPTON (A.W) (R-H)
Monday, January 28
OFFICIAL GOING: Standard
Wind: light, half behind Weather: light rain

414 BOOK TICKETS FOR RACING PLUS CHASE DAY H'CAP 1m (P)
1:20 (1:21) (Class 6) (0-65,65) 3-Y-O **£1,940** (£577; £288; £144) **Stalls** Low

Form RPR
64-4 **1** **Camachoice (IRE)**[17] 168 3-9-7 65......................(tp) AdamKirby 5 73
(Marco Botti) *chsd ldrs: effrt to ld wl over 1f out: pricking ears in front but sn rdn clr: in n.d fnl f: eased cl home* **7/4**[2]
-222 **2** 3 3/4 **Derwentwater (IRE)**[6] 321 3-9-2 60......................(b) NickyMackay 4 59
(John Gosden) *chsd ldr tl led after 1f: rdn and hdd wl over 1f out: nt qckn and sn outpcd by wnr: plugged on same pce fnl f* **5/4**[1]
66-4 **3** 1 **Entrapping**[18] 134 3-9-0 58............................ SeanLevey 3 55
(Richard Hannon) *stdd s: t.k.h: hld up in last pair: rdn and no prog over 2f out: styd on past btn horses and edgd rt ins fnl f* **10/1**
650- **4** 1/2 **Mudaawem (USA)**[118] 6753 3-9-7 65............................ FrannyNorton 6 61
(Mark Johnston) *t.k.h: chsd ldr tl wnt 2nd after 2f: rdn over 3f out: drvn and unable qck over 2f out: outpcd and wl btn wl over 1f out: plugged on* **8/1**[3]
2-42 **5** *nse* **Ishigunnaeatit**[13] 216 3-8-13 64......................(p) RobertTart(7) 1 60
(Mrs K Burke) *broke wl: t.k.h: led for 1f: chsd ldrs after: rdn and unable qck 2f out: wl hld and plugged on same pce after* **14/1**
05-4 **6** 3 3/4 **Man In The Arena**[26] 17 3-8-13 57............................ WilliamCarson 2 44
(Dr Jon Scargill) *hld up in last pair: rdn and effrt whn swtchd lft ent fnl 2f: styng on same pce and wl hld whn short of room and hmpd ins fnl f: eased towards fin* **20/1**

1m 41.31s (1.51) **Going Correction** +0.10s/f (Slow) **6** Ran SP% **112.4**
Speed ratings (Par 95): **96,92,91,90,90 86**
Tote Swingers: 1&2 £1.10, 1&3 £1.90, 2&3 £2.60 CSF £4.31 TOTE £2.30: £1.80, £1.10; EX 4.60 Trifecta £22.40 Pool: £2,581.78 - 86.11 winning units..
Owner Giuliano Manfredini **Bred** Doc Bloodstock **Trained** Newmarket, Suffolk
FOCUS
A weak 3-y-o handicap best rated around the third and fourth.

415 GET THE BETVICTOR APP H'CAP 1m (P)
1:50 (1:50) (Class 5) (0-75,75) 4-Y-O+ **£2,587** (£770; £384; £192) **Stalls** Low

Form RPR
-002 **1** **Diplomatic (IRE)**[9] 272 8-8-7 68......................(p) RobertTart(7) 5 75
(Michael Squance) *hld up in last quartet: rdn and gd hdwy wl over 1f out: chal 1f out: led ins fnl f: hld on wl u.p: all out* **9/2**[2]
00- **2** *nk* **Kindia (IRE)**[54] 7986 5-9-4 72............................ SebSanders 6 78
(Michael Attwater) *stdd s: hld up in rr: rdn and effrt 2f out: gd hdwy 1f out: nt clr run and swtchd lft ins fnl f: r.o strly fnl 100yds to snatch 2nd fnl strides* **50/1**
01-1 **3** *hd* **Hurricane Spirit (IRE)**[12] 221 9-8-12 71............... NicoleNordblad(5) 4 76
(Hans Adielsson) *hld up in last quartet: swtchd rt and gd hdwy ent fnl 2f: led ent fnl f: hdd ins fnl f: ev ch after but a jst hld: lost 2nd last strides* **7/2**[1]
-145 **4** *hd* **Breakheart (IRE)**[12] 222 6-8-1 62......................(p) JoeyHaynes(7) 3 67
(Andrew Balding) *hld up in midfield: rdn and hdwy 2f out: chsd ldrs: stdy on u.p to press ldrs fnl 75yds: kpt on* **8/1**
32-6 **5** 1 1/4 **Masai Moon**[25] 34 9-8-13 74............................ PatMillman(7) 8 76
(Rod Millman) *chsd ldrs: rdn and effrt over 2f out: styd on same pce ins fnl f* **12/1**
01-0 **6** 1 1/4 **Greyfriarschorista**[13] 217 6-9-4 75............................ RyanClark(3) 10 74
(Tom Keddy) *hld up in midfield: rdn and effrt 2f out: nt clr run over 1f out: hdwy 1f out: styd on same pce fnl 100yds* **20/1**
030- **7** 2 **Master Mylo (IRE)**[86] 7559 6-9-6 74............................[1] GeorgeBaker 7 69
(Martin Bosley) *hld up in tch: swtchd lft and effrt jst over 2f out: no imp: styd on same pce and no threat fnl f* **6/1**[3]
03-1 **8** 3 **Shaunas Spirit (IRE)**[19] 116 5-9-4 72......................(p) AdamKirby 11 60
(Dean Ivory) *racd keenly: led and sn clr: rdn over 2f out: hdd ent fnl f: wknd ins fnl f* **9/2**[2]
-450 **9** 1 1/2 **Copperwood**[11] 239 8-9-7 75............................ FrannyNorton 1 59
(Mark Johnston) *chsd ldrs: rdn and unable qck over 1f out: wknd u.p over 1f out* **16/1**
605- **10** 8 **Take Two**[19] 7376 4-9-6 74............................ WilliamCarson 2 40
(John O'Shea) *chsd clr ldr: clsd 3f out: lost 2nd and struggling over 2f out: sn wknd* **8/1**
00-0 **11** 1 3/4 **Dream Prospector**[26] 13 4-8-13 67............................ ChrisCatlin 9 29
(James Evans) *hld up in last quartet: rdn and no hdwy over 2f out: bhd over 1f out* **20/1**

1m 39.92s (0.12) **Going Correction** +0.10s/f (Slow) **11** Ran SP% **120.2**
Speed ratings (Par 103): **103,102,102,102,101 99,97,94,93,85 83**
Tote Swingers: 1&2 £45.90, 1&3 £3.00, 2&3 £19.80 CSF £221.96 CT £888.58 TOTE £6.00: £2.20, £11.50, £1.20; EX 217.50 Trifecta £1960.90 Part won. Pool: £2,614.65 - 0.99 winning units..
Owner Miss K Squance **Bred** Darley **Trained** Newmarket, Suffolk
■ Stewards' Enquiry : Robert Tart two-day ban: used whip above permitted level (Feb 11-12)

The Form Book Flat, Raceform Ltd, Compton, RG20 6NL.

FOCUS
This was wide open and, after a quick early pace, it saw a bunched finish. The winner backed up a recent good effort and the third and fourth set the level in line with recent efforts.

416 BETVICTOR CHELTENHAM FESTIVAL ANTEPOST PIONEERS MEDIAN AUCTION MAIDEN STKS 6f (P)
2:20 (2:20) (Class 5) 3-5-Y-O **£2,587** (£770; £384; £192) **Stalls** Low

Form RPR
0-3 **1** **Sand Boy (IRE)**[16] [185] 3-8-12 0 RobertWinston 3 76
(Charles Hills) *chsd ldr tl led over 2f out: rdn clr over 1f out: in command whn rn green and veered rt ins fnl f: comf* **8/13**[1]

63-2 **2** 4 ½ **Clock Opera (IRE)**[25] [37] 3-8-7 67 FrannyNorton 1 57
(Mrs K Burke) *led tl rdn and hdd over 2f out: outpcd and btn over 1f out: hld on for 2nd fnl f* **3/1**[2]

0-2 **3** 1 ¼ **Batchworth Lady**[19] [114] 3-8-7 0 WilliamCarson 5 53
(Dean Ivory) *hld up in tch: rdn and outpcd 2f out: kpt on to press for 2nd ins fnl f: no ch w wnr* **4/1**[3]

0-0 **4** 4 ½ **Quelle Affaire**[5] [332] 3-8-7 0 ChrisCatlin 2 38
(Brendan Powell) *s.i.s: in tch in rr: rdn and outpcd over 2f out: tried to rally in centre over 1f out: sn wknd* **50/1**

00-4 **5** 1 ½ **Bonbon Bonnie**[14] [202] 5-9-2 40 (v) RyanTate(7) 4 37
(Phil McEntee) *chsd ldng pair tl over 2f out: sn wknd u.p* **66/1**

1m 13.53s (0.43) **Going Correction** +0.10s/f (Slow)
WFA 3 from 5yo 16lb **5** Ran SP% **110.4**
Speed ratings (Par 103): **101,95,93,87,85**
CSF £2.81 TOTE £2.30: £1.30, £1.20; EX 2.40 Trifecta £4.30 Pool: £2,696.69 - 469.89 winning units..
Owner Sir A Ferguson,Mr,Mrs J Cotton,J Hanson **Bred** P Kelly **Trained** Lambourn, Berks

FOCUS
A weak maiden and another plunge horse completed the task. The form is fluid but is taken at face value for now.

417 COME DINE IN THE PANORAMIC RESTAURANT H'CAP (DIV I) 1m 4f (P)
2:50 (2:51) (Class 6) (0-60,60) 4-Y-0+ **£1,940** (£577; £288; £144) **Stalls** Centre

Form RPR
03-1 **1** **Irene Kennet**[26] [9] 6-9-0 53 [1] TomMcLaughlin 5 62
(Paul Burgoyne) *t.k.h: chsd ldrs: rdn to ld ent fnl f: kpt on wl u.p: rdn out* **11/2**[2]

03-0 **2** 1 **Youm Jamil (USA)**[15] [193] 6-8-8 54 RyanTate(7) 1 61
(Tony Carroll) *hld up in tch towards rr: hdwy into midfield over 3f out: clsng on ldrs whn nt clr run over 1f out: drvn to chse ldrs ins fnl f: styd on wl to go 2nd fnl 50yds* **12/1**

00-6 **3** ½ **Shirataki (IRE)**[26] [9] 5-9-5 58 ChrisCatlin 2 64
(Peter Hiatt) *t.k.h: hld up in tch: rdn and effrt wl over 1f out: drvn and chsd wnr ins fnl f: kpt on same pce fnl 100yds: lost 2nd fnl 50yds* **6/1**[3]

553- **4** 1 ¾ **If You Whisper (IRE)**[41] [8153] 5-9-2 55 EddieAhern 14 58
(Mike Murphy) *chsd ldr tl 9f out: hdd but styd upsides ldr 4f out: rdn wl over 1f out: no ex 1f out: wknd u.p ins fnl f* **6/1**[3]

404- **5** ½ **Lady of Burgundy**[135] [6255] 7-9-2 60 LeeNewnes(5) 4 63
(Mark Usher) *stdd s: t.k.h: hld up in rr: hdwy over 2f out: swtchd rt and drvn to chse ldrs jst over 1f out: styd on same pce ins fnl f* **7/1**

54/3 **6** 2 ½ **Polarity**[17] [157] 7-9-0 60 NedCurtis(7) 8 59
(Gerry Enright) *in tch in midfield: rdn and unable qck over 2f out: no imp tl kpt on ins fnl f: no threat to ldrs* **25/1**

00-5 **7** ¾ **Bubbly Braveheart (IRE)**[14] [200] 6-8-7 51 (p) JemmaMarshall(5) 7 48
(Pat Phelan) *chsd ldrs tl led 4f out: rdn and hdd ent fnl f: wknd ins fnl f* **16/1**

5-20 **8** 3 **Turjuman (USA)**[15] [198] 8-9-0 53 (p) NickyMackay 9 46
(Alan Bailey) *dwlt and rdn along leaving stalls: hdwy to chse ldrs 8f out: rdn and unable qck 2f out: btn 1f out: wknd* **14/1**

200- **9** 3 ¾ **Novel Dancer**[39] [8189] 5-8-12 51 (e) FrannyNorton 11 38
(Lydia Richards) *in tch in midfield: rdn and unable qck over 2f out: wknd over 1f out* **8/1**

400- **10** hd **Imperial Elegance**[11] [6280] 4-7-12 46 oh1 NathanAlison(5) 3 32
(Sheena West) *in tch towards rr: reminders 5f out: wknd u.p over 1f out* **16/1**

20-4 **11** 2 ¾ **Roman Senate (IRE)**[21] [94] 4-8-10 53 (tp) MartinLane 10 35
(Martin Bosley) *led tl 9f out: styd chsng ldrs: rdn and struggling 2f out: wknd over 1f out* **5/1**[1]

400- **12** 12 **Avison (IRE)**[14] [7490] 5-8-9 48 KirstyMilczarek 6 11
(Lawney Hill) *stdd s: t.k.h: hld up in tch towards rr: lost tch 2f out* **20/1**

0/00 **13** hd **Catawollow**[6] [330] 6-8-0 46 oh1 (e) PhilipPrince(7) 12 8
(Richard Guest) *t.k.h: hld up in tch in rr: lost tch 2f out* **66/1**

555- **14** ½ **Superstiction**[75] [7710] 4-8-2 48 SimonPearce(3) 13 10
(Michael Madgwick) *in tch in midfield on outer: rdn over 4f out: lost tch 2f out* **33/1**

2m 35.13s (0.63) **Going Correction** +0.10s/f (Slow)
WFA 4 from 5yo+ 4lb **14** Ran SP% **123.4**
Speed ratings (Par 101): **101,100,100,98,98 96,96,94,91,91 89,81,81,81**
Tote Swingers: 1&2 £17.10, 1&3 £5.90, 2&3 £23.10 CSF £69.21 CT £420.17 TOTE £5.40: £2.10, £6.20, £2.70; EX 92.20 Trifecta £485.60 Pool: £2,572.38 - 3.97 winning units..
Owner R W Floyd **Bred** Jim Duncan And Richard William Floyd **Trained** Shepton Montague, Somerset

■ Stewards' Enquiry : Tom McLaughlin two-day ban: used whip above permitted level (Feb 11-12)
Nathan Alison 12-day ban: used whip above permitted level when out of contention (Feb 11-16,18-23)

FOCUS
Another wide-open handicap. It was run at a sound pace and the form looks straightforward rated through the runner-up.

418 COME DINE IN THE PANORAMIC RESTAURANT H'CAP (DIV II) 1m 4f (P)
3:20 (3:22) (Class 6) (0-60,60) 4-Y-0+ **£1,940** (£577; £288; £144) **Stalls** Centre

Form RPR
003- **1** **Asia Minor (IRE)**[31] [8265] 4-8-9 52 MartinLane 2 65
(Dr Jon Scargill) *hld up off the pce in rr: rdn and effrt over 2f out: drvn and str run over 1f out: led jst ins fnl f: edgd rt but r.o strly* **8/1**

000- **2** 2 ¾ **Evergreen Forest (IRE)**[61] [7905] 5-9-3 59 (b) RyanClark(3) 3 67
(Tom Keddy) *chsd ldr: rdn and clsd over 1f out: led 1f out: sn hdd and kpt on same pce after* **2/1**[1]

4410 **3** 5 **Nolecce**[5] [338] 6-8-9 55 (p) PhilipPrince(7) 4 55
(Richard Guest) *taken down early: chsd ldrs: chsd clr ldng pair and drvn over 1f out: plugged on to go 3rd nr fin: no threat to ldrs* **6/1**[3]

000- **4** hd **Sovento (GER)**[51] [8039] 9-8-10 54 CharlesBishop(5) 12 54
(Alan McCabe) *led: clr after 2f: stl clr and rdn over 1f out: hdd jst ins fnl f: sn wknd* **14/1**

400/ **5** ¾ **Zelos Diktator**[13] [7206] 7-8-11 50 RobertWinston 14 49
(Sean Curran) *racd off the pce in midfield: rdn and effrt over 2f out: plugged on u.p fnl f: no threat to ldrs* **25/1**

4-00 **6** 2 **Sir Dylan**[18] [132] 4-8-12 55 WilliamCarson 10 51
(Ronald Harris) *stdd s: hld up wl off the pce in rr: styd on past btn horses fnl f: n.d* **20/1**

422- **7** 1 ¼ **Clapped**[47] [8075] 4-9-0 57 LiamKeniry 7 51
(Ed Vaughan) *stdd s: hld up off the pce in midfield: rdn and sme hdwy 2f out: no imp and wl hld whn hung lft ins fnl f* **9/2**[2]

00-0 **8** 1 ½ **Burnbrake**[18] [131] 8-8-4 46 oh1 SimonPearce(3) 13 37
(Richard Rowe) *hld up off the pce towards rr: rdn and effrt over 2f out: plugged on fnl f: nvr trbld ldrs* **50/1**

0-40 **9** 1 ½ **Lea Valley**[9] [275] 4-8-3 46 oh1 NickyMackay 11 35
(Julia Feilden) *hmpd and slowly away: grad rcvrd and chsd ldrs after 2f: rdn 4f out: wknd over 2f out* **66/1**

60-0 **10** ½ **Before Bruce**[26] [12] 6-8-8 47 KirstyMilczarek 1 35
(Brendan Powell) *racd off the pce in midfield: rdn over 4f out: no imp and n.d* **25/1**

000- **11** 3 **Saffron Park**[31] [8265] 4-8-5 48 ow2 ChrisCatlin 8 31
(John Best) *hld up off the pce in rr: rdn and no prog 4f out: no ch fnl 2f* **16/1**

0-06 **12** nk **Boston Blue**[14] [208] 6-9-2 60 GeorgeDowning(5) 5 43
(Tony Carroll) *s.i.s and pushed along early: a bhd: no ch fnl 2f* **33/1**

420- **13** 2 ¾ **Hill Of Dreams (IRE)**[50] [8050] 4-8-12 55 EddieAhern 6 33
(Dean Ivory) *racd off the pce in midfield: rdn and no prog over 2f out: wknd 2f out* **10/1**

400/ **14** 10 **Our Play (IRE)**[432] [7515] 5-9-5 58 FrannyNorton 9 20
(Lydia Richards) *prom in main gp but off the pce: rdn and wknd wl over 2f out: bhd and eased wl ins fnl f* **8/1**

2m 34.79s (0.29) **Going Correction** +0.10s/f (Slow)
WFA 4 from 5yo+ 4lb **14** Ran SP% **128.5**
Speed ratings (Par 101): **103,101,97,97,97 95,95,94,93,92 90,90,88,82**
Tote Swingers: 1&2 £4.90, 1&3 £4.20, 2&3 £5.40 CSF £24.38 CT £112.90 TOTE £6.30: £2.40, £1.60, £2.20; EX 27.00 Trifecta £99.80 Pool: £3,276.12 - 24.60 winning units..
Owner Strawberry Fields Stud **Bred** Darley **Trained** Newmarket, Suffolk

FOCUS
The second division of the 1m4f handicap and it was run at a strong pace. The winner built on a recent effort and the placed horses help set the level.

419 BETVICTOR NON RUNNER FREE BET AT CHELTENHAM H'CAP 1m 3f (P)
3:50 (3:51) (Class 6) (0-65,65) 3-Y-0 **£1,940** (£577; £216; £216) **Stalls** Low

Form RPR
3 **1** **Rose Ransom (IRE)**[12] [231] 3-9-4 62 (b) FrannyNorton 7 76
(Mark Johnston) *racd off the pce in 4th: clsd on ldr over 3f out: rdn to ld over 1f out: sn clr and in n.d fnl f: eased towards fin* **14/1**

0-41 **2** 10 **Hidden Link**[14] [212] 3-9-5 63 WilliamCarson 2 59
(Ronald Harris) *racd off the pce in 3rd: clsd qckly on ldr to ld 3f out: hdd and wandered u.p over 1f out: sn wl btn but plugged on to hold 2nd* **5/2**[2]

-021 **3** 3 ¾ **Great Ormond (IRE)**[11] [237] 3-9-4 62 AdamKirby 5 51
(David Simcock) *slowly away: hld up wl off the pce in last trio: clsd on ldr over 3f out: drvn and no ex 2f out: no ch and battling for 3rd fnl f* **2/1**[1]

5-42 **3** dht **Inessa Armand (IRE)**[12] [231] 3-9-1 59 (p) LiamKeniry 4 48
(J S Moore) *chsd clr ldr: clsd on ldr and ev ch whn rdn 3f out: wknd over 1f out: battling for modest 3rd fnl f* **16/1**

600- **5** 5 **Spirit Of Success**[51] [8033] 3-8-13 62 WilliamTwiston-Davies(5) 1 42
(Michael Bell) *v.s.a: hld up wl off pce in last trio: clsd on ldr over 3f out: drvn and wknd 2f out* **6/1**

32-0 **6** 10 **Misleading Promise (IRE)**[11] [237] 3-9-7 65 GeorgeBaker 3 27
(John Butler) *v.s.a: alway bhd: clsd on ldr over 3f out: wknd qckly jst over 2f out: wl bhd fnl f* **10/1**

2-22 **7** 26 **Easy Life**[9] [275] 3-9-0 65 (v[1]) CharlieBennett(7) 6
(Marcus Tregoning) *led and wnt wl clr after 1f: hdd 3f out: sn dropped out and bhd: t.o and eased over 1f out* **11/2**[3]

2m 23.83s (1.93) **Going Correction** +0.10s/f (Slow) **7** Ran SP% **113.2**
Speed ratings (Par 95): **96,88,86,86,82 75,56**
Trifecta: 6-3-5 £143.40 (8.81 winning units), 6-3-7 £111.90 (11.29 winning units). Pool: £3,371.49. Tote Swingers: 3&5 £0.90, 3&6 £7.40, 3&7 £2.90, 5&6 £2.60, 6&7 £4.40. CSF £48.16 TOTE £20.50: £5.70, £1.20; EX 66.60.
Owner Lady O'Reilly **Bred** Castlemartin Sky & Skymarc Farm **Trained** Middleham Moor, N Yorks

FOCUS
This was run at a scorching pace courtesy of Easy Life, who ran away with her apprentice rider in a first-time visor and unsurprisingly capitulated off the home turn. The form is hard to assess but could be worth more than rated.

420 BETVICTOR EXCLUSIVE ANTEPOST OFFERS CHELTENHAM 2013 H'CAP 1m 3f (P)
4:20 (4:20) (Class 4) (0-85,86) 4-Y-0+ **£4,690** (£1,395; £697; £348) **Stalls** Low

Form RPR
4-25 **1** **Reflect (IRE)**[18] [144] 5-8-13 73 (t) FrannyNorton 7 80
(Derek Shaw) *hld up in last trio: rdn and hdwy to chse ldrs and hung rt over 1f out: drvn and str run ins fnl f to ld on post* **7/1**

26-3 **2** nse **Noguchi (IRE)**[21] [93] 8-9-3 77 TomMcLaughlin 5 84
(Michael Murphy) *chsd ldrs: rdn and effrt to ld 2f out: edgd rt ins fnl f: hdd on post* **6/1**[3]

324- **3** nse **Brimstone Hill (IRE)**[31] [8275] 4-9-0 77 WilliamCarson 9 84
(Anthony Carson) *stdd s: hld up in last pair: rdn and gd hdwy over 1f out: drvn and styd on wl ins fnl f: jst hld* **11/4**[2]

1-22 **4** 2 **Wildomar**[12] [224] 4-9-4 81 AdamKirby 2 84
(John Ryan) *hld up in midfield: effrt on inner 2f out: ev ch ins fnl f: styng on same pce and hld whn squeezed for room and snatched up wl ins fnl f* **9/4**[1]

03-3 **5** 4 **Nave (USA)**[17] [161] 6-8-9 69 MartinLane 1 65
(David Simcock) *mde most: rdn over 2f out: drvn and hdd 2f out: wknd u.p 2f out* **6/1**[3]

1215 **6** 1 ¼ **Kames Park (IRE)**[9] [273] 11-8-8 75 PhilipPrince(7) 6 69
(Richard Guest) *stdd s: hld up in rr: effrt on inner 2f out: drvn and no prog over 1f out: wknd ins fnl f* **16/1**

0/6 **7** 4 **Gaelic Silver (FR)**[9] [273] 7-9-4 78 GeorgeBaker 3 65
(Gary Moore) *chsd ldrs: wnt 2nd and stl travelling wl over 2f out: rdn and unable qck over 1f out: wknd fnl f* **25/1**

50-5 **8** 8 **St Ignatius**[19] [112] 6-8-5 72 (p) RobertTart(7) 4 44
(Alan Bailey) *pressed ldr tl wl over 2f out: sn lost pl: bhd fnl f* **16/1**

00/0 9 1 **King Olav (UAE)**[21] [93] 8-9-3 **77**.............................. KirstyMilczarek 10 47
(Tony Carroll) *hld up in tch: lost pl over 2f out: rdn and lost tch 2f out* **33/1**

2m 21.82s (-0.08) **Going Correction** +0.10s/f (Slow)
WFA 4 from 5yo+ 3lb **9** Ran SP% **117.1**
Speed ratings (Par 105): **104,103,103,102,99 98,95,89,89**
Tote Swingers: 1&2 £8.80, 1&3 £6.00, 2&3 £4.30 CSF £49.21 CT £144.59 TOTE £9.90: £2.30, £1.50, £1.60; EX 50.60 Trifecta £176.80 Pool: £2,440.07 - 10.34 winning units..
Owner Chris Hamilton **Bred** D Harron & J G Davis **Trained** Sproxton, Leics
■ Stewards' Enquiry : Tom McLaughlin two-day ban: used whip in incorrect place (Feb 13-14)
William Carson two-day ban: used whip above permitted level (Feb 11-12)

FOCUS
A modest handicap, run at a fair pace and there was a desperate three-way finish. The first two built slightly on recent form.

421 FOLLOW US ON TWITTER @BETVICTORRACING FILLIES' H'CAP 7f (P)
4:50 (4:50) (Class 5) (0-75,74) 4-Y-0+ **£2,587** (£770; £384; £192) **Stalls** Low

Form RPR
03-1 1 **Compton Rainbow**[21] [90] 4-8-9 **69**..............................(t) RyanTate[(7)] 3 78
(Hans Adielsson) *hld up off the pce in midfield: hdwy to chse clr ldr 2f out: rdn and clsd to ld ins fnl f: fnd ex and asserted fnl 50yds* **5/2**[2]

02-5 2 1 1/4 **Russian Ice**[25] [34] 5-9-5 **72**..............................(b) GeorgeBaker 2 78
(Dean Ivory) *stdd s: hld up in rr: hdwy to go 3rd but stl plenty to do 2f out: clsd and rdn to chal ins fnl f: no ex and btn fnl 50yds* **3/1**[3]

1-42 3 3 1/4 **Fairyinthewind (IRE)**[12] [222] 4-9-7 **74**..............................(b[1]) SebSanders 1 71
(Paul D'Arcy) *led: clr 1/2-way: rdn over 1f out: hdd ins fnl f: sn btn: wknd fnl 100yds* **9/4**[1]

235- 4 4 **Sugarformyhoney (IRE)**[67] [7827] 4-8-13 **71**.............. CharlesBishop[(5)] 4 57
(Seamus Durack) *hld up off the pce on last pair: rdn and effrt in modest 4th 2f out: no prog and wl hld after* **4/1**

100- 5 13 **Demoiselle Bond**[28] [8305] 5-8-7 **60**.............................. FrannyNorton 6 11
(Lydia Richards) *chsd ldng pair on outer: rdn and wknd over 2f out: t.o fnl f* **14/1**

4030 6 11 **Sleepy Lucy**[2] [409] 4-7-10 **55** oh10 ow1..............................(e) PhilipPrince[(7)] 5
(Richard Guest) *chsd ldr tl 2f out: sn dropped out: t.o fnl f* **33/1**

1m 26.41s (0.41) **Going Correction** +0.10s/f (Slow) **6** Ran SP% **113.9**
Speed ratings (Par 100): **101,99,95,91,76 63**
Tote Swingers: 1&2 £2.40, 1&3 £1.80, 2&3 £2.00 CSF £10.70 TOTE £3.70: £2.10, £2.50; EX 13.90 Trifecta £37.40 Pool: £2,082.08 - 41.66 winning units..
Owner Erik Penser **Bred** Pegasus Racing Ltd **Trained** Kingston Lisle, Oxon

FOCUS
A tight fillies' handicap and there was plenty of pace on. The runner-up sets the standard.
T/Jkpt: £7,311.40 to a £1 stake. Pool: £10,298.00 - 1.00 winning ticket. T/Plt: £24.10 to a £1 stake. Pool: £70,801.00 - 2,136.79 winning tickets. T/Qpdt: £11.30 to a £1 stake. Pool: £5,772.00 - 374.85 winning tickets. SP

404 WOLVERHAMPTON (A.W) (L-H)
Monday, January 28

OFFICIAL GOING: Standard
Wind: Strong, half behind Weather: Overcast

422 CLAIM FREE BETS TODAY AT BOOKMAKERS.CO.UK AMATEUR RIDERS' H'CAP (DIV I) 5f 216y(P)
1:40 (1:40) (Class 6) (0-55,58) 4-Y-0+ **£1,871** (£580; £290; £145) **Stalls** Low

Form RPR
1621 1 **Hab Reeh**[6] [326] 5-11-3 **58** 6ex..............................(t) MissSBrotherton 6 71
(Ruth Carr) *racd keenly: led for 1f: remained prom: regained ld over 2f out: drew clr wl over 1f out: in command after: pushed out* **7/4**[1]

5-16 2 2 1/4 **Glennten**[9] [276] 4-10-11 **55**.............................. MissCBoxall[(3)] 8 60
(Sylvester Kirk) *chsd ldrs: rdn and lugged lft and wnt 2nd wl over 1f out: kpt on ins fnl f: no real imp on wnr* **6/1**[3]

40-0 3 3 **Bachelor Knight (IRE)**[25] [42] 5-9-12 **46** oh1.............. MrJPearce[(7)] 10 41
(Suzzanne France) *uns on way to post but sn stopped running: s.i.s: in rr: hdwy on outer over 1f out: chsd ldrs ins fnl f: styd on: nvr able to chal* **14/1**

3-51 4 nk **Michael's Nook**[4] [349] 6-10-6 **54** 6ex..............................(p) MissJGordon[(7)] 3 48
(Alastair Lidderdale) *hd over side of stall s and s.i.s: hld up: hmpd after 1f: hdwy wl over 1f out: styd on ins fnl f: nvr able to chal* **3/1**[2]

-233 5 1 1/4 **Miserere Mei (IRE)**[6] [326] 4-10-7 **48**.............................. MrSWalker 12 38+
(Richard Guest) *hld up in midfield: swtchd lft after 1f: effrt whn n.m.r and bdly hmpd over 1f out: styd on u.p to chse ldrs after: one pce fnl 75yds* **7/1**

00-3 6 4 **Prigsnov Dancer (IRE)**[22] [81] 8-10-0 **46** oh1.....(t) MissCHJones[(5)] 11 23
(Frank Sheridan) *hmpd after 1f: racd keenly on outer in midfield: hdwy 2f out: chsd ldrs but no imp over 1f out: rdn and wknd ins fnl f* **40/1**

065- 7 1/2 **Spread Boy (IRE)**[82] [7638] 6-9-12 **46** oh1.............................. MrAFrench[(7)] 4 22
(Alan Berry) *prom: pushed along and lost pl 3f out: struggling after* **25/1**

00-5 8 2 3/4 **Charmel's Delight**[18] [148] 4-10-4 **50**..............................(p) MrAaronJames[(5)] 9 17
(Geoffrey Oldroyd) *missed break: racd keenly: hld up: rdn over 3f out: nvr on terms: b.b.v* **16/1**

00-0 9 nse **Cape Of Storms**[22] [88] 10-10-8 **52**..............................(b) MrChrisMartin[(3)] 2 19
(Roy Brotherton) *s.i.s: sn pushed along and rcvrd to ld after 1f: hdd over 2f out: u.p after: wknd 1f out* **16/1**

1m 16.94s (1.94) **Going Correction** +0.20s/f (Slow) **9** Ran SP% **112.9**
Speed ratings (Par 101): **95,92,88,87,85 80,79,76,76**
Tote Swingers: 1&2 £2.80, 1&3 £6.30, 2&3 £15.60 CSF £12.33 CT £107.86 TOTE £2.00: £1.10, £1.60, £5.20; EX 11.30 Trifecta £137.80 Pool: £2,303.81 - 12.53 winning units..
Owner Mrs B Taylor, A Dickman, Mrs R Carr **Bred** The Anglo Irish Choral Society **Trained** Huby, N Yorks
■ Stewards' Enquiry : Mr S Walker three-day ban: careless riding (Feb 18, Mar 27,Apr 20)

FOCUS
A low-grade sprint but sound enough form rated around the first two.

423 CLAIM FREE BETS TODAY AT BOOKMAKERS.CO.UK AMATEUR RIDERS' H'CAP (DIV II) 5f 216y(P)
2:10 (2:11) (Class 6) (0-55,55) 4-Y-0+ **£1,871** (£580; £290; £145) **Stalls** Low

Form RPR
0-02 1 **Lord Buffhead**[9] [276] 4-10-13 **54**..............................(v) MrSWalker 8 62
(Richard Guest) *chsd ldrs: led over 1f out: sn asserted: drvn out and styd on ins fnl f* **3/1**[1]

6-55 2 1 1/4 **Script**[6] [327] 4-10-1 **47**.............................. MrsVDavies[(5)] 5 51
(Alan Berry) *midfield: hdwy 2f out: wnt 2nd ins fnl f: styd on: unable to chal wnr* **28/1**

0-43 3 1 1/2 **Blue Noodles**[6] [327] 7-9-12 **46** oh1..............................(p) MrAFrench[(7)] 1 45
(John Wainwright) *in tch: clsd to chal over 1f out: nt qckn ent fnl f: styd on same pce fnl 100yds* **7/2**[2]

00-2 4 3 **Artful Lady (IRE)**[9] [277] 4-10-5 **51**.............................. MissKMargarson[(5)] 3 41
(George Margarson) *dwlt: bhd: hdwy over 1f out: styd on ins fnl f: nt rch ldrs* **5/1**[3]

030- 5 1 1/2 **Mango Music**[61] [7906] 10-10-9 **55**..............................(p) MrGRSmith[(5)] 2 40
(David Thompson) *prom: led 3f out: rdn and hdd over 1f out: wknd fnl 100yds* **8/1**

60-0 6 1 1/4 **Olynard (IRE)**[19] [117] 7-10-2 **46** oh1..............................(p) MissMMullineaux[(3)] 9 27
(Michael Mullineaux) *midfield: rdn 3f out: sn outpcd: no imp on ldrs* **12/1**

0-04 7 2 1/2 **Prophet In A Dream**[4] [355] 5-10-0 **46** oh1..............(p) MissMBryant[(5)] 11 19
(Paddy Butler) *slowly int stride: hld up: hdwy 2f out: rdn and no imp on ldrs over 1f out: one pce ins fnl f* **66/1**

26-3 8 1 **Whiskey Junction**[17] [163] 9-10-7 **55**.............. MrGrahamCarson[(7)] 12 25
(Mick Quinn) *led narrowly racing 4 wd: hdd 3f out: rdn over 1f out: sn btn: dropped away fnl f* **12/1**

030- 9 2 3/4 **Lady Platinum Club**[73] [7747] 5-10-5 **53**.............. MissMKeegan[(7)] 10 14
(Linda Stubbs) *prom tl rdn and wknd over 2f out* **20/1**

06-0 10 1 **Cadmium Loch**[26] [24] 5-10-4 **50**..............................(p) MrFMitchell[(5)] 4 8
(Reg Hollinshead) *prom: rdn and ev ch 2f out: wknd over 1f out* **13/2**

005- 11 hd **Bond Blade**[38] [8210] 5-10-0 **46** oh1.............................. MrAaronJames[(5)] 6 3
(Suzzanne France) *s.i.s: u.p over 2f out: a bhd* **20/1**

1m 17.76s (2.76) **Going Correction** +0.20s/f (Slow) **11** Ran SP% **118.2**
Speed ratings (Par 101): **89,87,85,81,79 77,74,73,69,68 67**
Tote Swingers: 1&2 £14.70, 1&3 £4.20, 2&3 £19.70 CSF £97.17 CT £317.61 TOTE £4.80: £1.80, £7.60, £1.20; EX 70.20 Trifecta £413.80 Pool: £2,575.41 - 4.66 winning units..
Owner Miss Alex Ingram **Bred** T K & Mrs P A Knox **Trained** Wetherby, W Yorks

FOCUS
The four who raced upsides took each other on and the pace was strong. The winner is rated close to his previous Kempton form.

424 FREE BET BONANZA NOW AT BOOKMAKERS.CO.UK CLAIMING STKS 5f 216y(P)
2:40 (2:40) (Class 6) 3-Y-O **£1,940** (£577; £288; £144) **Stalls** Low

Form RPR
36-1 1 **Hiddon Coin (IRE)**[25] [38] 3-9-3 75.............................. DanielTudhope 8 75
(David O'Meara) *mde all: rdn 1f out: pressed ins fnl f: plld out more towards fin* **11/8**[1]

-221 2 1/2 **Windforpower (IRE)**[3] [368] 3-8-7 68..............................(be) JoeFanning 7 64
(Ronald Harris) *trckd ldrs: wnt 2nd 1f out: chalng wnr ins fnl f: hld towards fin* **10/3**[2]

250- 3 1 1/2 **Elusive Thought (IRE)**[45] [8112] 3-8-7 58.............................. JohnFahy 1 59
(J S Moore) *in tch: outpcd over 2f out: styd on ins fnl 75yds: nt gng pce to rch front two* **14/1**

20-5 4 nk **Hillbilly Boy (IRE)**[16] [188] 3-8-8 78.............................. RyanWhile[(7)] 5 66
(Bill Turner) *hld up in rr: hdwy 2f out: chsd ldrs over 1f out: styd on same pce ins fnl f* **7/2**[3]

44-2 5 3/4 **Marmot Bay (IRE)**[3] [368] 3-7-11 57..............................(p) RaulDaSilva[(3)] 3 49
(Alastair Lidderdale) *rrd jst bef s and anticipated s: chsd ldr and ref to settle: rdn and lost 2nd 1f out: no ex fnl 100yds* **11/2**

5-40 6 16 **Scoobys Girl (IRE)**[14] [207] 3-8-1 44 ow1.............. FrankieMcDonald 2
(Daniel Mark Loughnane) *hdwy to chse ldrs over 4f out: rdn over 2f out: sn wknd* **125/1**

0 7 9 **Hester Street**[16] [185] 3-7-9 0 ow2.............................. IanBurns[(7)] 6
(Rae Guest) *slowly int stride: a outpcd and wl bhd* **125/1**

1m 16.78s (1.78) **Going Correction** +0.20s/f (Slow) **7** Ran SP% **111.0**
Speed ratings (Par 95): **96,95,93,92,91 70,58**
Tote Swingers: 1&2 £1.60, 1&3 £4.20, 2&3 £5.00 CSF £5.80 TOTE £1.60: £1.20, £2.30; EX 5.30 Trifecta £40.60 Pool: £1,991.51 - 36.71 winning units..
Owner Hambleton Racing Ltd - Three In One **Bred** Noel & Anthony O'Callaghan **Trained** Nawton, N Yorks

FOCUS
A fair claimer with the winner rated to recent C&D form.

425 BEST RACING ODDS GUARANTEED AT BOOKMAKERS.CO.UK MAIDEN STKS 7f 32y(P)
3:10 (3:10) (Class 5) 3-Y-O **£2,587** (£770; £384; £192) **Stalls** High

Form RPR
1 **Henry The Aviator (USA)** 3-9-5 0.............................. JoeFanning 6 76+
(Mark Johnston) *in tch: rdn whn lugged lft and rn green fr over 1f out: styd on to ld wl ins fnl f: wl on top at fin* **9/4**[1]

33-2 2 1 1/4 **Bouyrin (IRE)**[15] [197] 3-9-0 66.............................. HayleyTurner 5 68
(Michael Bell) *chsd ldr: rdn to ld narrowly over 1f out: leant lft on to rival wl ins fnl f: sn hdd and hld* **4/1**[3]

23-3 3 2 **Go Far**[18] [129] 3-9-5 68..............................(p) GrahamGibbons 1 71+
(Alan Bailey) *led: rdn 2f out: hdd narrowly over 1f out: stl chalng for press whn hmpd wl ins fnl f: unable to rcvr after* **3/1**[2]

0 4 1 1/2 **Triple Aitch (USA)**[14] [211] 3-9-5 0.............................. ShaneKelly 3 67+
(Peter Chapple-Hyam) *trckd ldrs: effrt on inner and trying to chal over 1f out: keeping on for press but looking hld in cl 4th whn n.m.r and hmpd wl ins fnl f: nt rcvr* **50/1**

5 11 **Botteen (IRE)** 3-9-5 0.............................. AdamBeschizza 7 34
(William Haggas) *s.i.s: in rr: niggled along 3f out: sn outpcd: lft bhd wl over 1f out* **8/1**

6 6 **King Wood (TUR)** 3-9-5 0.............................. JimmyFortune 4 18
(Charles Hills) *s.i.s: racd keenly: hld up: pushed along 3f out: sn outpcd: lft bhd wl over 1f out* **4/1**[3]

1m 31.67s (2.07) **Going Correction** +0.20s/f (Slow) **6** Ran SP% **108.8**
Speed ratings (Par 97): **96,94,92,90,78 71**
Tote Swingers: 1&2 £1.90, 1&3 £2.00, 2&3 £1.80 CSF £10.79 TOTE £2.80: £2.60, £1.20; EX 9.30 Trifecta £23.20 Pool: £3,107.32 - 100.29 winning units..
Owner Crone Stud Farms Ltd **Bred** Summer Wind Farm **Trained** Middleham Moor, N Yorks

FOCUS
A modest 3-y-o maiden but an unraced winner of some potential. The placed horses set the level.

426 CORAL.CO.UK H'CAP 7f 32y(P)
3:40 (3:40) (Class 5) (0-70,70) 4-Y-0+ **£2,587** (£770; £384; £192) **Stalls** High

Form RPR
-506 1 **Lord Of The Dance (IRE)**[2] [410] 7-9-0 **63**.............................. TomEaves 1 73
(Michael Mullineaux) *chsd ldrs: wnt 2nd wl over 1f out: led jst over 1f out: r.o wl to draw away fnl 100yds* **16/1**

-122 2 2 **Bussa**[3] [380] 5-8-6 **62**..............................(t) JoshBaudains[(7)] 2 67
(David Evans) *w ldr: led over 4f out: rdn and hdd jst over 1f out: outpcd fnl 100yds* **7/4**[1]

3-12 **3** 2 **Restless Bay (IRE)**[12] 229 5-9-7 **70**........................(v) HayleyTurner 11 69
(Conor Dore) *midfield: hdwy 3f out: rdn to chse ldrs over 1f out: styd on ins fnl f: nt pce to chal* **5/1**[2]

6-03 **4** hd **Key Ambition**[5] 345 4-9-7 **70**..................................(tp) DanielTudhope 5 69
(Garry Moss) *in tch: lost pl over 2f out: rdn over 1f out: styd on ins fnl f: nt trble ldrs* **6/1**[3]

445- **5** 2 **For Shia And Lula (IRE)**[31] 8269 4-9-4 **67**........................ ShaneKelly 6 60
(Daniel Mark Loughnane) *hld up: shkn up over 1f out: rdn ins fnl f: kpt on but nt trble ldrs* **9/1**

000- **6** ½ **Masked Dance (IRE)**[86] 7559 6-9-1 **64**..........................(p) IanMongan 4 56
(Scott Dixon) *led: hdd over 4f out: rdn and stl ev ch 2f out: lost 2nd wl over 1f out: sn edgd rt and outpcd by front two: wknd fnl 100yds* **7/1**

4-05 **7** 2¾ **George Fenton**[19] 115 4-8-9 **58**..................................(p) J-PGuillambert 8 42
(Richard Guest) *racd keenly in midfield: pushed along over 2f out: hdwy to chse ldrs over 1f out: sn no further imp: wl btn fnl 100yds* **20/1**

50-0 **8** 3 **Unlimited**[21] 96 11-8-6 **62**.................................... AidenBlakemore(7) 3 38
(Tony Carroll) *s.i.s: bhd: sme hdwy over 3f out: rdn and btn wl over 1f out* **66/1**

210- **9** ¾ **July Days (IRE)**[136] 6217 7-8-12 **61**............................ GrahamGibbons 7 35
(Brian Baugh) *chsd ldrs tl rdn and wknd over 1f out* **8/1**

60-6 **10** 3 **Needwood Ridge**[14] 206 6-8-13 **65**......................(bt) MarkCoumbe(3) 9 31
(Frank Sheridan) *missed break: bhd: hrd at work over 3f out: nvr on terms* **40/1**

1m 30.78s (1.18) **Going Correction** +0.20s/f (Slow) **10** Ran SP% **115.5**
Speed ratings (Par 103): **101,98,96,96,93 93,90,86,85,82**
Tote Swingers: 1&2 £5.80, 1&3 £10.50, 2&3 £2.80 CSF £43.44 CT £172.68 TOTE £19.20: £3.80, £1.30, £1.70; EX 36.20 Trifecta £97.90 Pool: £3,888.23 - 29.76 winning units..
Owner H Clewlow **Bred** Bridgewater Equine Ltd **Trained** Alpraham, Cheshire

FOCUS
A modest handicap in which the first two home were in the firing line throughout. The winner is rated as having run his best race for nearly two years.

427 POKER AT CORAL.CO.UK (S) STKS 1m 141y(P)
4:10 (4:10) (Class 6) 3-Y-0 **£1,940** (£577; £288; £144) **Stalls** Low

Form RPR

34-2 **1** **Mick Dundee (IRE)**[14] 210 3-8-12 **62**......................(vt[1]) HayleyTurner 5 61
(J W Hills) *mde all: pushed clr fnl f and a in command: comf* **1/1**[1]

64-1 **2** 2¾ **Amelia Hull**[21] 103 3-8-13 **58**....................................(p) ShaneKelly 1 55
(J S Moore) *chsd ldrs: disp 2nd over 6f out: rdn to go def 2nd over 2f out: no imp over 1f out: no ch w wnr fnl f* **5/2**[2]

00-6 **3** ½ **Silk Scarf (IRE)**[18] 134 3-8-7 **50**..................................(b[1]) JoeFanning 6 48?
(Mark H Tompkins) *s.s: in rr: pushed along 3f out: rdn to go 3rd over 1f out and wanted to lugg lft: kpt on towards fin: nvr able to chal* **20/1**

4-65 **4** 4½ **Handsome Stranger (IRE)**[18] 134 3-8-12 **58**.....(v[1]) GrahamGibbons 4 46
(David Evans) *chsd wnr: jnd for 2nd over 6f out: lost 2nd over 2f out: rdn over 1f out: sn btn: eased fnl f* **3/1**[3]

1m 52.94s (2.44) **Going Correction** +0.20s/f (Slow) **4** Ran SP% **108.3**
Speed ratings (Par 95): **97,94,94,90**
CSF £3.78 TOTE £1.80; EX 3.10 Trifecta £12.80 Pool: £2,068.94 - 120.55 winning units..Winner bought in 3,750gns.
Owner R J Tufft **Bred** Kildare Racing Syndicate **Trained** Upper Lambourn, Berks

FOCUS
An uncompetitive 3-y-o seller and all of the runners had some sort of headgear. The form makes sense at face value.

428 CORAL.CO.UK MOBILE BETTING H'CAP 1m 1f 103y(P)
4:40 (4:40) (Class 5) (0-75,70) 3-Y-0 **£2,587** (£770; £384; £192) **Stalls** Low

Form RPR

0-1 **1** **Naru (IRE)**[14] 211 3-9-7 **70**.................................... JoeFanning 5 76+
(James Tate) *led: hdd over 6f out: racd in 2nd pl: chalng 2f out: regained ld wl over 1f out: rdn and r.o ins fnl f: eased whn in command fnl 50yds: shkn up fnl strides* **9/4**[1]

001- **2** ½ **Good Speech (IRE)**[45] 8112 3-9-0 **63**............................ JohnFahy 3 66+
(Tom Tate) *chsd ldrs: pushed along over 3f out: n.m.r and hmpd sn after: sn shuffled bk to last pl and outpcd: rallied over 1f out: styd on to take 2nd ins fnl f: clsd on wnr nr fin: sltly flattered* **5/1**[3]

404- **3** 2½ **Lucky Mountain**[51] 8032 3-9-3 **66**.............................. IanMongan 6 64
(Scott Dixon) *hld up: pushed along over 2f out: rdn and hdwy to chse ldrs over 1f out: kpt on ins fnl f: nvr able to chal* **4/1**[2]

4-12 **4** ¾ **Walter White (IRE)**[14] 204 3-8-11 **67**....................(v) ThomasBrown(7) 2 63
(Andrew Balding) *chsd ldr: led over 6f out: pressed 2f out: hdd wl over 1f out: lost 2nd and edgd rt ins fnl f: no ex* **11/2**

6-13 **5** 4½ **Salute To Seville (IRE)**[2] 411 3-8-4 **60**..............(b) CharlotteJenner(7) 1 47
(J S Moore) *chsd ldrs: rdn and c wd off fnl bnd wl over 1f out: sn wknd* **5/1**[3]

46-5 **6** 6 **Abraq**[18] 141 3-9-4 **67**.. ShaneKelly 4 41
(Ed Dunlop) *in rr: hdwy and effrt on outer over 3f out: rdn over 2f out: wknd wl over 1f out* **8/1**

2m 2.68s (0.98) **Going Correction** +0.20s/f (Slow) **6** Ran SP% **110.6**
Speed ratings (Par 97): **103,102,100,99,95 90**
Tote Swingers: 1&2 £2.40, 1&3 £2.90, 2&3 £4.80 CSF £13.28 TOTE £2.70: £2.00, £3.20; EX 8.10 Trifecta £45.90 Pool: £2,681.51 - 43.71 winning units..
Owner Saeed Manana **Bred** Rabbah Bloodstock Limited **Trained** Newmarket, Suffolk

FOCUS
The two with a progressive profile filled the first two places in this 3-y-o handicap. The third sets the standard initially.

429 HORSE RACING FREE BETS AT BOOKMAKERS.CO.UK FILLIES' H'CAP 1m 4f 50y(P)
5:10 (5:10) (Class 5) (0-75,73) 4-Y-0+ **£2,587** (£770; £384; £192) **Stalls** Low

Form RPR

/2-2 **1** **Hepworth**[13] 215 4-9-3 **70**...(b[1]) JoeFanning 2 81
(John Gosden) *in tch: led over 1f out: hrd pressed ins fnl f: kpt on wl fnl strides* **13/8**[1]

36-0 **2** ½ **Dazzling Valentine**[22] 82 5-8-13 **67**...................... NatashaEaton(5) 12 77
(Alan Bailey) *midfield: hdwy over 1f out: rdr dropped whip 1f out: chalng and upsides wl ins fnl f: hld fnl strides* **11/1**

-110 **3** 5 **Rosie's Lady (IRE)**[20] 110 4-8-13 **66**......................... DanielTudhope 1 68
(David O'Meara) *chsd ldrs: rdn over 1f out: styd on same pce fnl 100yds* **9/2**[2]

34-3 **4** nk **Sail Home**[26] 21 6-8-7 **63**.. ShelleyBirkett(7) 4 65
(Julia Feilden) *chsd ldr: led 2f out: rdn and hdd over 1f out: no ex fnl 100yds* **8/1**

155- **5** 1 **Candelita**[56] 7968 6-8-13 **62**.. J-PGuillambert 5 62
(Jo Hughes) *midfield: outpcd over 3f out: hdwy over 1f out: styd on ins fnl f: nvr able to rch ldrs* **6/1**[3]

130- **6** 4½ **Bernisdale**[60] 7301 5-9-0 **63**.. JohnFahy 9 56
(John Flint) *racd keenly in midfield: lost pl 4f out: kpt on modly ins fnl f: nvr able to trble ldrs* **16/1**

00-6 **7** 5 **Mazij**[25] 39 5-9-2 **65**.. HayleyTurner 7 50
(Peter Hiatt) *led: hdd 2f out: rdn and stl in contention over 1f out: wknd ins fnl f* **20/1**

10-3 **8** 1¼ **Cheers For Thea (IRE)**[14] 208 8-9-6 **69**.............(bt) DuranFentiman 11 52
(Tim Easterby) *s.i.s: hld up: hdwy over 6f out: chsd ldrs over 3f out: effrt over 2f out: wknd over 1f out* **25/1**

433- **9** ¾ **Queen Of Skies (IRE)**[72] 7782 4-8-13 **66**........................ ShaneKelly 8 48
(Tim Pitt) *midfield: pushed along 3f out: wknd over 2f out* **16/1**

32-4 **10** nk **Mediterranean Sea (IRE)**[24] 57 7-9-7 **73**................ PatrickHills(3) 10 54
(J R Jenkins) *hld up: pushed along over 3f out: nvr able to get on terms* **12/1**

03-0 **11** 21 **Elizabeth Coffee (IRE)**[22] 82 5-9-3 **66**......................... TomEaves 3 13
(John Weymes) *racd keenly: trckd ldrs: rdn 3f out: sn wknd* **33/1**

02-0 **12** 8 **Amana (USA)**[13] 219 9-9-2 **65**.................................... RobbieFitzpatrick 6
(Mark Brisbourne) *s.i.s: rdn over 3f out: a in rr* **66/1**

2m 41.34s (0.24) **Going Correction** +0.20s/f (Slow)
WFA 4 from 5yo+ 4lb **12** Ran SP% **122.5**
Speed ratings (Par 100): **107,106,103,103,102 99,96,95,94,94 80,75**
Tote Swingers: 1&2 £6.20, 1&3 £3.20, 2&3 £11.60 CSF £21.45 CT £74.12 TOTE £2.40: £1.10, £4.30, £1.60; EX 29.20 Trifecta £117.70 Pool: £3,216.47 - 20.49 winning units..
Owner Denford Stud **Bred** Denford Stud Ltd **Trained** Newmarket, Suffolk

FOCUS
A tactical affair with just a steady pace until the final 4f in this fillies' handicap. The runner-up sets the standard running close to last year's best.
T/Plt: £9.00 to a £1 stake. Pool: £83,676.00 - 6,780.48 winning tickets. T/Qpdt: £3.70 to a £1 stake. Pool: £7,637.00 - 1,521.68 winning tickets. DO

422 WOLVERHAMPTON (A.W) (L-H)
Tuesday, January 29

OFFICIAL GOING: Standard
Wind: Fresh, behind Weather: Overcast

430 CORAL.CO.UK AMATEUR RIDERS' H'CAP 1m 5f 194y(P)
2:00 (2:00) (Class 5) (0-70,68) 4-Y-0+ **£2,495** (£774; £386; £193) **Stalls** Low

Form RPR

40/4 **1** **Blazing Desert**[2] 22 9-10-10 **64**....................................... MrSWalker 3 72
(William Kinsey) *trckd ldrs: effrt over 2f out: led 1 1/2f out: sn rdn clr: styd on* **11/2**

32-1 **2** 2 **Stormy Morning**[27] 22 7-10-5 **62**..........................(p) MissHBethell(3) 5 67
(Philip Kirby) *hld up in tch: hdwy 3f out: rdn to chse ldng pair wl over 1f out: kpt on ins fnl f* **5/2**[1]

6-43 **3** 1 **Daring Damsel (IRE)**[16] 198 4-10-0 **60**.................... MissSBrotherton 1 64
(Brian Baugh) *set stdy pce: hdd after 4f: cl up: led again over 4f out: rdn along over 2f out: hdd 1 1/2f out: one pce* **7/2**[3]

0-34 **4** 1¾ **Blizzard Blues (USA)**[18] 166 7-10-9 **68**........(b) MrJamieJenkinson(5) 2 69
(Aytach Sadik) *hld up on inner to trck ldrs after 4f: effrt and pushed along over 2f out: rdn wl over 1f out: kpt on same pce* **25/1**

23-2 **5** 1¼ **Baan (USA)**[27] 22 10-9-8 **55**.................................. StevieSanders(7) 7 54
(James Eustace) *hld up in rr: hdwy over 4f out: rdn over 2f out: sn no imp* **3/1**[2]

000/ **6** 3¼ **Worth A King'S**[86] 4601 7-10-6 **67**...................... MissEmmaBedford(7) 8 62
(Philip Kirby) *in rr: sme hdwy on outer 6f out: rdn along wl over 2f out: n.d* **16/1**

460- **7** 6 **Overrule (USA)**[211] 3693 9-10-4 **65**..............(p) MissFrancesHarper(7) 6 51
(Chris Bealby) *trckd ldrs: hdwy to ld after 4f: hdd and pushed along 4f out: rdn wl over 2f out and sn wknd* **33/1**

205- **8** 28 **Frosty Berry**[153] 5731 4-10-0 **67**.................................... MrAFrench(7) 4 14
(John Wainwright) *t.k.h: cl up: pushed along over 4f out: sn rdn and wknd* **8/1**

3m 14.38s (8.38) **Going Correction** +0.15s/f (Slow)
WFA 4 from 7yo+ 6lb **8** Ran SP% **115.0**
Speed ratings (Par 103): **82,80,80,79,78 76,73,57**
toteswingers 1&2 £4.10, 2&3 £2.10, 1&3 £4.70 CSF £19.79 CT £54.76 TOTE £6.90: £1.30, £1.70, £2.00; EX 13.80 Trifecta £69.20 Pool: £2555.85 - 27.66 winning units..
Owner The Deeside Partnership **Bred** Mrs Brenda Howlett-Nye **Trained** Ashton, Cheshire

FOCUS
This handicap for amateur riders was run at a steady early pace and the two most experience riders were best placed turning for home. Muddling form, the winner reversing latest with the runner-up.

431 BOOKMAKERS.CO.UK FILLIES' H'CAP 5f 216y(P)
2:30 (2:30) (Class 5) (0-75,75) 4-Y-0+ **£2,911** (£866; £432; £216) **Stalls** Low

Form RPR

-223 **1** **Climaxfortackle (IRE)**[10] 271 5-8-9 **63**......................... JoeFanning 8 65
(Derek Shaw) *dwlt and in rr: hdwy 1/2-way: chsd ldrs on outer over 1f out: sn rdn and styd on wl to ld nr fin* **9/4**[1]

055- **2** ½ **Night Trade (IRE)**[117] 6825 6-9-2 **73**........................(p) RaulDaSilva(3) 5 73
(Ronald Harris) *t.k.h early: trckd ldrs: hdwy 1/2-way: rdn to chal over 1f out: styd on to ld last 100yds: hdd and no ex nr fin* **9/2**[3]

40-0 **3** hd **Little China**[22] 101 4-8-13 **67**.................................... WilliamCarson 1 67
(William Muir) *set stdy pce: qcknd 2f out: jnd and rdn over 1f out: drvn ins fnl f: hdd last 100yds: kpt on* **8/1**

100- **4** ¾ **Zing Wing**[104] 7171 5-9-2 **70**.. AdamKirby 3 67
(David Evans) *trckd ldrs: hdwy 2f out: rdn to chse ldrs ent fnl f: n.m.r and sn swtchd rt: kpt on wl towards fin* **11/4**[2]

00-0 **5** 2 **Song Of Parkes**[25] 58 6-9-2 **75**.............................. SladeO'Hara(5) 4 66
(Peter Grayson) *t.k.h early: trckd ldrs on inner: effrt 2f out: sn rdn along and wknd ins fnl f* **8/1**

00-0 **6** 3¼ **Lady Royale**[25] 58 5-9-7 **75**..(p) TomEaves 2 56
(Geoffrey Oldroyd) *dwlt: a in rr* **16/1**

0R-6 **7** 5 **Blodwen Abbey**[22] 101 4-8-4 **65**................................... RobertTart(7) 9 30
(Michael Mullineaux) *s.i.s: t.k.h and rapid hdwy to chse ldrs on outer after 1 1/2f: pushed along over 2f out: sn rdn and wknd* **10/1**

1m 16.71s (1.71) **Going Correction** +0.15s/f (Slow) **7** Ran SP% **112.8**
Speed ratings (Par 100): **94,93,93,92,89 85,78**
toteswingers 1&2 £2.10, 2&3 £5.70, 1&3 £3.40 CSF £12.36 CT £66.22 TOTE £2.00: £1.10, £2.90; EX 10.50 Trifecta £41.50 Pool: £2938.88 - 53.03 winning units..
Owner Shakespeare Racing **Bred** Pat Fullam **Trained** Sproxton, Leics

FOCUS
This moderate fillies' handicap was run at a slow early pace and there was a tight finish as a result. The form is rated around the cosy winner.

432 HORSE RACING FREE BETS WITH BOOKMAKERS.CO.UK (S) STKS 1m 4f 50y(P)
3:00 (3:01) (Class 6) 4-Y-O+ **£1,940** (£577; £288; £144) **Stalls** Low

Form RPR
5-11 **1** **Stand Guard**[12] 235 9-9-5 87 AdamKirby 1 68+
(John Butler) *hld up in rr: hdwy on inner over 3f out: sn chsng ldr: shkn up and hdwy to chal ent fnl f: led on bit last 100yds: sn clr* **1/8**[1]
1336 **2** 2 1/4 **Activate**[7] 318 6-9-5 68 (b) GrahamGibbons 4 64
(Phil McEntee) *led: rdn pushed clr 3f out: rdn wl over 1f out: jnd and drvn ins fnl f: hdd and one pce last 100yds* **8/1**[2]
0-06 **3** 10 **Volcanic Jack (IRE)**[8] 309 5-9-0 61 BarryMcHugh 2 43
(Tony Coyle) *trckd ldng pair: pushed along over 3f out: sn rdn and outpcd* **25/1**[3]
U-5 **4** 7 **Sing Alana Sing**[6] 343 5-8-2 44 (t) JakePayne(7) 3 27
(Bill Turner) *chsd ldr: rdn along over 4f out: sn wknd* **100/1**
2m 41.2s (0.10) **Going Correction** +0.15s/f (Slow) **4** Ran SP% **104.8**
Speed ratings (Par 101): **105,103,96,92**
CSF £1.40 TOTE £1.10; EX 1.90 Trifecta £1.90 Pool: £2419.69 - 927.71 winning units..There was no bid for the winner.
Owner J Butler **Bred** Juddmonte Farms Ltd **Trained** Newmarket, Suffolk

FOCUS
The second sets the standard with the winner rated way off his best.

433 CASINO AT CORAL.CO.UK (S) STKS 1m 1f 103y(P)
3:30 (3:30) (Class 6) 4-Y-O+ **£1,940** (£577; £288; £144) **Stalls** Low

Form RPR
35-3 **1** **Faithful Ruler (USA)**[8] 311 9-8-6 67 (p) GaryPhillips(7) 1 67
(Ronald Harris) *trckd ldrs: hdwy over 2f out: rdn to chse ldng pair over 1f out: styd on ins fnl f to ld last 75yds* **16/1**
0-01 **2** 1 **West End Lad**[12] 238 10-9-5 65 (b) AdamKirby 4 71
(Roy Bowring) *reminders s and rdn along to ld: pushed along 3f out: jnd and rdn 2f out: drvn ent fnl f: hdd and no ex last 75yds* **5/2**[2]
30-4 **3** nk **Five Hearts**[19] 132 5-8-8 49 (b) MartinLane 7 59?
(Mark H Tompkins) *hld up in rr: hdwy over 2f out: rdn over 1f out: kpt on u.p fnl f* **33/1**
051/ **4** 3 1/2 **Asterism**[503] 6054 5-8-8 75 JamieSpencer 2 52
(Ian Williams) *trckd ldng pair: hdwy over 3f out: cl up 2f out: sn chal and rdn: drvn appr fnl f and sn wknd* **6/4**[1]
0-03 **5** 5 **Chosen Forever**[12] 238 8-8-13 64 TomEaves 6 46
(Geoffrey Oldroyd) *trckd ldrs: effrt and hdwy on outer over 2f out: rdn along wl over 1f out and sn wknd* **6/1**
00-1 **6** 2 1/2 **Temuco (IRE)**[20] 120 4-9-4 59 (v) GrahamGibbons 5 47
(David Evans) *chsd ldr: rdn along over 3f out: sn wknd* **9/2**[3]
2m 2.2s (0.50) **Going Correction** +0.15s/f (Slow)
WFA 4 from 5yo+ 1lb **6** Ran SP% **109.9**
Speed ratings (Par 101): **103,102,101,98,94 92**
totewingers 1&2 £2.90, 2&3 £6.30, 1&3 £6.40 CSF £53.48 TOTE £12.20: £3.70, £1.10; EX 75.00 Trifecta £472.60 Pool: £3047.38 - 4.83 winning units..There was no bid for the winner.
Owner Ridge House Stables Ltd **Bred** WinStar Farm LLC **Trained** Earlswood, Monmouths

FOCUS
A weak affair and shaky form, with the moderate third the key.

434 BEST HORSE RACING ODDS WITH BOOKMAKERS.CO.UK MAIDEN STKS 1m 141y(P)
4:00 (4:01) (Class 5) 4-5-Y-O **£2,911** (£866; £432; £216) **Stalls** Low

Form RPR
34-2 **1** **Stormbound (IRE)**[19] 138 4-9-2 72 RaulDaSilva(3) 4 76
(Paul Cole) *trckd ldrs: hdwy 2f out: swtchd to inner ent fnl f: sn ev ch and n.m.r: styd on wl to ld fnl 100yds* **2/1**[2]
4-2 **2** 1 **Pategonia**[18] 160 4-9-5 NickyMackay 7 74
(John Gosden) *trckd ldrs: hdwy over 2f out: rdn to ld over 1f out: drvn ins fnl f: hdd and one pce last 100yds* **1/1**[1]
3 2 **Pacific Ridge (USA)**[173] 5028 4-9-5 73 (t) GeorgeBaker 3 69
(Amy Weaver) *stdd s and hld up in rr: hdwy over 2f out: chal over 1f out: rdn and ev ch whn edgd lft ins fnl f: sn btn* **11/4**[3]
6-3 **4** 7 **Exclusive Predator**[25] 59 4-9-5 TomEaves 1 53
(Geoffrey Oldroyd) *led: rdn along over 2f out: hdd over 1f out: grad wknd* **33/1**
54-2 **5** 1 1/4 **Merrjanah**[27] 28 5-9-1 54 PaddyAspell 2 45
(John Wainwright) *trckd ldrs: rdn along over 2f out: sn one pce* **50/1**
5-0 **6** 10 **Golden Share (USA)**[14] 215 4-9-5 (t) AdamKirby 6 27
(Marco Botti) *dwlt: sn cl up: rdn along over 2f out: sn wknd* **12/1**
6 **7** 17 **Gallant Leader (USA)**[8] 313 4-9-5 (b[1]) BarryMcHugh 5
(Tony Coyle) *towards rr: rdn along over 4f out: sn bhd* **100/1**
1m 51.1s (0.60) **Going Correction** +0.15s/f (Slow)
WFA 4 from 5yo 1lb **7** Ran SP% **123.6**
Speed ratings: **103,102,100,94,93 84,69**
totewingers 1&2 £1.30, 2&3 £2.10, 1&3 £1.70 CSF £4.88 TOTE £3.20: £1.30, £1.60; EX 6.70 Trifecta £14.90 Pool: £3070.94 - 153.59 winning units..
Owner P F I Cole Ltd **Bred** A Footstep Away Syndicate **Trained** Whatcombe, Oxon

FOCUS
An ordinary maiden, run at a fair pace. The first two recorded slight personal bests.

435 DOWNLOAD CORAL.CO.UK MOBILE APP H'CAP 1m 141y(P)
4:30 (4:30) (Class 6) (0-60,60) 4-Y-O+ **£1,940** (£577; £288; £144) **Stalls** Low

Form RPR
00-4 **1** **Fighter Boy (IRE)**[4] 380 6-9-7 60 (bt) GrahamGibbons 7 73
(Michael Easterby) *hld up in rr: hdwy 1/2-way: rdn to chse ldrs on outer over 1f out: styd on strly fnl f to ld fnl 75yds* **11/2**[2]
3-23 **2** 1 1/4 **Arabian Flight**[5] 347 4-9-5 59 JoeFanning 11 69
(Michael Appleby) *trckd ldrs: hdwy to ld wl over 1f out: rdn clr ent fnl f: hdd and no ex fnl 75yds* **9/1**
40-2 **3** 1 1/2 **Dubai Celebration**[19] 147 5-9-6 59 PaddyAspell 5 66
(Julie Camacho) *trckd ldng pair: effrt 2f out: sn rdn and kpt on same pce fnl f* **11/2**[2]
664/ **4** hd **William Van Gogh**[582] 3475 6-9-1 54 JamesSullivan 8 60
(Michael Easterby) *s.i.s: in rr: hdwy 3f out: chsd ldrs and n.m.r over 1f out: sn rdn and kpt on: nrst fin* **20/1**
0-31 **5** 2 1/4 **Spirit Of Gondree (IRE)**[16] 193 5-9-7 60 (b) RobertWinston 4 61
(Milton Bradley) *hld up towards rr: hdwy over 2f out: chsd ldrs and n.m.r over 1f out: sn rdn and kpt on: nrst fin* **9/1**
03-6 **6** 6 **Flying Applause**[23] 83 8-9-1 57 (b) MarkCoumbe(3) 9 44
(Roy Bowring) *in tch: effrt over 2f out: sn rdn and no imp* **40/1**
1/0- **7** 3/4 **Belle Noverre (IRE)**[293] 1310 9-8-13 52 ow1 AdamKirby 10 37
(John Butler) *led: rdn along over 2f out: sn hdd & wknd* **8/1**
-421 **8** shd **Delightful Sleep**[4] 381 5-9-5 58 6ex WilliamCarson 2 43
(David Evans) *hld up towards rr: hdwy over 3f out: rdn to chse ldrs over 1f out: sn drvn and wknd* **6/1**[3]
13-2 **9** 1 1/2 **Bertie Blu Boy**[21] 110 5-9-3 56 (b) GeorgeBaker 12 38
(Lisa Williamson) *cl up: led 2f out and sn rdn: hdd & wknd wl over 1f out* **9/1**
0-32 **10** 1 **This Ones For Eddy**[8] 312 8-8-13 52 (b) MartinLane 1 31
(John Balding) *chsd ldrs: rdn along over 2f out: sn wknd* **16/1**
00-6 **11** 9 **Bartley**[18] 162 4-9-3 57 TomEaves 3 16
(Bryan Smart) *a towards rr* **20/1**
006- **12** 2 1/4 **Aureolin Gulf**[73] 7782 4-9-3 57 LiamKeniry 13 11
(Reg Hollinshead) *a towards rr* **100/1**
0-11 **13** 3 1/4 **Kyllachykov (IRE)**[21] 110 5-9-3 56 DanielTudhope 6
(Robin Bastiman) *a towards rr* **9/2**[1]
1m 50.15s (-0.35) **Going Correction** +0.15s/f (Slow)
WFA 4 from 5yo+ 1lb **13** Ran SP% **123.2**
Speed ratings (Par 101): **107,105,104,104,102 97,96,96,94,94 86,84,81**
toteswingers 1&2 £12.50, 2&3 £12.20, 1&3 £8.50 CSF £54.12 CT £303.11 TOTE £6.80: £2.00, £3.30, £2.40; EX 77.60 Trifecta £564.70 Pool: £3260.15 - 4.32 winning units..
Owner A G Greenwood **Bred** Rockhart Trading Ltd **Trained** Sheriff Hutton, N Yorks

FOCUS
A competitive handicap. There was a fair enough pace set and it proved a little rough around 2f from home, but they got sorted out in the straight. Fair form.

436 NO DEPOSIT FREE BETS WITH BOOKMAKERS.CO.UK H'CAP (DIV I) 7f 32y(P)
5:00 (5:00) (Class 6) (0-60,60) 4-Y-O+ **£1,940** (£577; £288; £144) **Stalls** High

Form RPR
00-0 **1** **Prince James**[27] 27 6-9-7 60 GrahamGibbons 7 68
(Michael Easterby) *sn led: rdn along 2f out: drvn ent fnl f: hdd fnl 100yds: rallied gamely to ld again towards fin* **11/2**
0433 **2** nk **Spinning Ridge (IRE)**[7] 320 8-9-4 57 (b) WilliamCarson 3 64
(Ronald Harris) *dwlt and towards rr: hdwy 3f out: swtchd rt and rdn to chse ldrs over 1f out: styd on to take slt ld fnl 100yds: hdd and no ex towards fin* **5/1**[3]
3-62 **3** 1 **Bitaphon (IRE)**[18] 162 4-9-5 58 DanielTudhope 4 63
(Michael Appleby) *dwlt: trckd ldrs on inner: hdwy 2f out: rdn to chal ent fnl f: ev ch tl drvn: n.m.r and one pce fnl 100yds* **9/4**[1]
000- **4** 3/4 **Daunt (IRE)**[136] 6261 4-9-4 57 [1] MichaelO'Connell 8 59
(John Quinn) *hld up towards rr: hdwy 2f out: sn rdn and kpt on fnl f: nrst fin* **10/3**[2]
06-0 **5** 1 3/4 **Schoolboy Champ**[3] 408 6-8-2 48 oh1 ow2 (vt) RobertTart(7) 9 45
(Lisa Williamson) *in tch: effrt on outer over 2f out: sn rdn and one pce* **50/1**
04-6 **6** 1/2 **Cornus**[24] 77 11-9-1 59 (be) WilliamTwiston-Davies(5) 6 55
(Alan McCabe) *trckd ldrs: effrt 2f out: sn rdn and one pce* **16/1**
3-43 **7** 1 **Peak Storm**[7] 324 4-9-0 58 (v) CharlesBishop(5) 1 51
(John O'Shea) *chsd ldr: hdwy and cl up 2f out: sn rdn and wknd over 1f out* **7/1**
00-4 **8** 26 **Code Six (IRE)**[22] 101 4-9-7 60 [1] TomEaves 2
(Bryan Smart) *t.k.h: chsd ldng pair: rdn along over 3f out: sn wknd* **14/1**
1m 30.34s (0.74) **Going Correction** +0.15s/f (Slow) **8** Ran SP% **112.9**
Speed ratings (Par 101): **101,100,99,98,96 96,94,65**
toteswingers 1&2 £4.40, 2&3 £2.00, 1&3 £3.70 CSF £32.14 CT £78.39 TOTE £6.90: £2.00, £1.70, £1.10; EX 36.90 Trifecta £124.90 Pool: £3665.00 - 22.00 winning units..
Owner A Saha **Bred** A C M Spalding **Trained** Sheriff Hutton, N Yorks

FOCUS
A slightly faster time than division II and the winner's best form since his 2011 peak.

437 NO DEPOSIT FREE BETS WITH BOOKMAKERS.CO.UK H'CAP (DIV II) 7f 32y(P)
5:30 (5:30) (Class 6) (0-60,60) 4-Y-O+ **£1,940** (£577; £288; £144) **Stalls** High

Form RPR
00-4 **1** **Prince Of Passion (CAN)**[20] 115 5-9-7 60 (v) JoeFanning 7 67
(Derek Shaw) *trckd ldrs: hdwy over 2f out: rdn to chse ldr ent fnl f: drvn and styd on to ld fnl 50yds* **4/1**[2]
04-3 **2** 1/2 **Ace Master**[25] 54 5-9-1 57 (b) MarkCoumbe(3) 6 63
(Roy Bowring) *sn led and clr: rdn over 2f out: drvn over 1f out: kpt on gamely tl hdd and no ex fnl 50yds* **4/1**[2]
0-53 **3** hd **Brown Volcano (IRE)**[3] 409 4-8-9 55 ThomasBrown(7) 9 60
(John O'Shea) *dwlt and towards rr: hdwy 2f out: rdn over 1f out: styd on wl ins fnl f: nrst fin* **12/1**
63-4 **4** nk **Piccolo Express**[22] 96 7-9-5 58 WilliamCarson 1 63
(Brian Baugh) *hld up in tch: hdwy 2f out: rdn over 1f out: drvn and styd on ins fnl f* **9/2**[3]
101- **5** shd **Maggie Pink**[62] 7917 4-9-6 59 DanielTudhope 2 63
(Michael Appleby) *chsd clr ldr: hdwy over 2f out: tk clsr order over 1f out: sn rdn and ev ch tl drvn and one pce fnl 100yds* **15/8**[1]
34-0 **6** 9 **Silver Wind**[19] 143 8-8-13 57 (v) WilliamTwiston-Davies(5) 3 37
(Alan McCabe) *a in rr: outpcd fnl 2f* **8/1**
1m 30.76s (1.16) **Going Correction** +0.15s/f (Slow) **6** Ran SP% **111.8**
Speed ratings (Par 101): **99,98,98,97,97 87**
toteswingers 1&2 £1.70, 2&3 £5.90, 1&3 £5.50 CSF £19.88 CT £170.19 TOTE £4.50: £1.70, £1.70; EX 18.20 Trifecta £157.80 Pool: £2439.45 - 11.58 winning units..
Owner Chris Hamilton **Bred** Majestic Thoroughbred Investments Inc **Trained** Sproxton, Leics

■ Stewards' Enquiry : Mark Coumbe four-day ban: used whip above permitted level (Feb 12-15)

FOCUS
The second division of the 7f handicap and another tight race, which resulted in a blanket finish. The slightly slower division, and ordinary form.

T/Plt: £23.20 to a £1 stake. Pool of £82902.89 - 2606.44 winning tickets. T/Qpdt: £9.70 to a £1 stake. Pool of £5895.73 - 449.18 winning tickets. JR

[414]KEMPTON (A.W) (R-H)

Wednesday, January 30

OFFICIAL GOING: Standard

Wind: Strong, across (away from stands) Weather: Fine

438 BETDAQ MEMBERS FREE ENTRY EVERY WEDNESDAY MEDIAN AUCTION MAIDEN STKS 5f (P)

4:50 (4:50) (Class 5) 3-5-Y-O **£2,587** (£770; £384; £192) **Stalls** Low

Form RPR

0-3 **1** **Panther Patrol (IRE)**[16] 202 3-8-13 0 JohnFahy 4 71+
(Eve Johnson Houghton) *hld up: prog arnd rivals to go 2nd 2f out but inclined to hang: led over 1f out: sn pushed clr: eased fnl 100yds* **4/9**[1]

306- **2** *4 ½* **Con Leche**[50] 8065 3-8-13 57 (p) LukeMorris 5 49
(Scott Dixon) *awkward s but led: shkn up and hdd over 1f out: sn btn* **9/4**[2]

0-45 **3** *3 ½* **Bonbon Bonnie**[2] 416 5-9-2 40 (v) RyanTate(7) 2 37
(Phil McEntee) *chsd ldr to 2f out: wknd qckly over 1f out* **50/1**

0 **4** *4* **Don't Be Scilly**[16] 202 5-9-2 0 JoeyHaynes(7) 1 17
(Eric Wheeler) *dwlt: t.k.h: hld up in last: effrt to dispute 2nd 1/2-way: wknd rapidly over 1f out* **20/1**[3]

1m 1.46s (0.96) **Going Correction** +0.125s/f (Slow)
WFA 3 from 5yo 15lb **4** Ran SP% **106.7**
Speed ratings (Par 103): **97,89,84,77**
CSF £1.63 TOTE £1.20; EX 2.00 Trifecta £5.00 Pool: £1756.16 - 260.80 winning units..
Owner G C Stevens **Bred** Kilfrush Stud **Trained** Blewbury, Oxon

FOCUS
A weak maiden, and a straightforward success for the favourite. The form is rated a bit cautiously.

439 WIN BIG WITH BETDAQ MULTIPLES H'CAP 1m 2f (P)

5:20 (5:21) (Class 5) (0-75,74) 4-Y-O+ **£2,587** (£770; £384; £192) **Stalls** Low

Form RPR

00-4 **1** **Canary Wharf (IRE)**[20] 146 4-9-4 **73** (b) AdamKirby 6 82
(Marco Botti) *s.i.s and rousted along early to take 5th: quick prog 1/2-way to ld 4f out: drvn 2f out: narrowly hdd jst ins fnl f: rallied to ld post* **7/2**[3]

3-13 **2** *shd* **Purple 'n Gold (IRE)**[6] 352 4-9-0 **74** (v) WilliamTwiston-Davies(5) 8 83
(David Pipe) *hld up in last trio: prog on outer over 2f out: clsd to ld narrowly jst ins fnl f: kpt on but hdd post* **3/1**[2]

-462 **3** *2 ¾* **On The Hoof**[9] 314 4-8-12 **74** MatthewHopkins(7) 1 77
(Michael Easterby) *led to 4f out: rdn 3f out: disp 2nd to over 1f out: one pce after* **9/4**[1]

00-4 **4** *nse* **White Diamond**[26] 52 6-8-10 **63** LukeMorris 9 66
(Michael Appleby) *trckd ldrs: rdn to dispute 2nd 3f out to over 1f out: one pce* **14/1**

51-3 **5** *1* **Whitby Jet (IRE)**[21] 112 5-9-7 **74** WilliamCarson 5 75
(Ed Vaughan) *hld up in last trio: prog on outer over 2f out: rdn and nt qckn wl over 1f out: one pce after* **9/2**

0-05 **6** *5* **Final Drive (IRE)**[15] 219 7-9-0 **67** (tp) LiamKeniry 2 58
(John Butler) *chsd ldrs: rdn wl over 2f out: wknd qckly over 1f out* **20/1**

00/ **7** *1* **Gracchus (USA)**[242] 2039 7-8-10 **63** JimmyQuinn 3 52
(Tony Carroll) *dwlt: hld up in last trio: pushed along and no prog 3f out: n.d over 1f out* **50/1**

604- **8** *8* **On The Cusp (IRE)**[252] 2405 6-8-9 **67** (p) CharlesBishop(5) 4 40
(Violet M Jordan) *rn wout declared tongue-strap: chsd ldr to over 4f out: wknd qckly over 2f out* **50/1**

54-1 **9** *8* **Malindi**[28] 28 4-9-0 **69** JamesSullivan 10 26
(James Given) *racd wd and sn in rr: rdn over 4f out: sn wknd: t.o* **25/1**

2m 7.8s (-0.20) **Going Correction** +0.125s/f (Slow)
WFA 4 from 5yo+ 2lb **9** Ran SP% **115.4**
Speed ratings (Par 103): **105,104,102,102,101 97,97,90,84**
toteswingers 1&2 £3.00, 1&3 £3.50, 2&3 £2.20 CSF £13.89 CT £27.45 TOTE £2.80: £1.60, £1.60, £1.10; EX 15.70 Trifecta £49.30 Pool: £2378.80 - 36.17 winning units..
Owner G Manfredini & J Allison **Bred** Michael Lowry **Trained** Newmarket, Suffolk

FOCUS
There was a slackening of the pace down the far side and the field bunched up. The winner is rated back to his best.

440 BACK AND LAY AT BETDAQ.COM H'CAP 7f (P)

5:50 (5:53) (Class 7) (0-50,54) 4-Y-O+ **£1,455** (£433; £216; £108) **Stalls** Low

Form RPR

5-44 **1** **Fleetwoodsands (IRE)**[22] 110 6-9-7 **50** (bt[1]) RobertWinston 13 59
(Milton Bradley) *dwlt: hld up in last pair fr wdst draw: gd prog on outer fr 2f out: drvn to ld last 75yds: kpt on* **7/1**[3]

4-13 **2** *½* **Teen Ager (FR)**[6] 349 9-9-7 **50** (p) JimmyQuinn 10 57
(Paul Burgoyne) *t.k.h: hld up in midfield: swtchd lft over 2f out: smooth prog to ld over 1f out: shkn up and fnd little fnl f: hdd last 75yds* **8/1**

-003 **3** *hd* **Cut The Cackle (IRE)**[8] 323 7-9-5 **48** (bt) WilliamCarson 11 55
(Violet M Jordan) *chsd ldr: hrd rdn over 2f out: led v briefly over 1f out: pressed new ldr tl no ex last 100yds* **12/1**

5-64 **4** *nk* **Vale Of Lingfield (IRE)**[6] 349 4-9-2 **45** (t) GeorgeBaker 2 54+
(John Best) *hld up in midfield: gng strly whn nowhere to go over 1f out and dropped to last trio: plld out wd and r.o wl fnl f: gaining at fin* **3/1**[2]

-514 **5** *1 ¾* **Michael's Nook**[2] 422 6-9-11 **54** 6ex (p) LukeMorris 6 55
(Alastair Lidderdale) *hld up wl in rr: rdn and prog over 2f out: cl up bhd ldrs jst over 1f out: nt qckn after* **5/2**[1]

0-03 **6** *1 ¼* **Venetias Dream (IRE)**[11] 276 4-9-4 **47** (vt) SeanLevey 4 45
(Stuart Williams) *chsd ldng pair: hrd rdn over 2f out: tried to chal over 1f out: fdd fnl f* **16/1**

1-00 **7** *½* **Ishi**[20] 128 4-8-11 **47** (b) PatMillman(7) 1 44
(Rod Millman) *hld up in last trio: prog on inner 2f out: tried to cl 1f out: fdd fnl f* **20/1**

60-0 **8** *1* **Doctor Hilary**[14] 223 11-8-10 **46** (v) PhilipPrince(7) 8 40
(Mark Hoad) *nvr beyond midfield on outer: dropped to rr over 2f out: n.d after* **33/1**

-664 **9** *¾* **Meydan Style (USA)**[6] 348 7-8-9 **45** (b) VictorSantos(7) 5 37
(Richard Ford) *s.s: bmpd along in last: effrt on inner 2f out: no imp on ldrs 1f out: fdd* **16/1**

00-3 **10** *½* **Not My Choice (IRE)**[8] 317 8-9-2 **45** (t) AmirQuinn 3 35
(Paul Howling) *reluctant to enter stalls: led to over 1f out: wknd* **20/1**

0-00 **11** *¾* **Very First Blade**[13] 240 4-9-3 **46** (b[1]) FrannyNorton 9 34
(Mark Brisbourne) *chsd ldrs: rdn over 2f out: trying to cl whn short of room then hmpd over 1f out: no ch after* **33/1**

600/ **12** *2 ¼* **Poyle Todream**[503] 6084 5-9-5 **48** TomEaves 12 30
(Roy Brotherton) *chsd ldrs: rdn over 2f out: losing pl whn n.m.r over 1f out: wknd* **50/1**

04-3 **13** *3 ¾* **Miakora**[7] 346 5-9-7 **50** AdamKirby 7 22
(Mick Quinn) *hld up in last trio: pushed along and no prog over 2f out: no ch after* **14/1**

1m 27.56s (1.56) **Going Correction** +0.125s/f (Slow) **13** Ran SP% **120.7**
Speed ratings (Par 97): **96,95,95,94,92 91,90,89,88,88 87,84,80**
toteswingers 1&2 £11.30, 1&3 £14.00, 2&3 £6.90 CSF £58.65 CT £487.49 TOTE £6.90: £3.00, £1.60, £4.30; EX 72.50 Trifecta £1267.60 Pool: £2357.01 - 1.39 winning units..
Owner E R Griffiths **Bred** Gary O'Reilly **Trained** Sedbury, Gloucs

FOCUS
A poor race but a good pace and a close finish. Typical bottom-grade form.

441 BETDAQ GAMES £50 CASH BONUS H'CAP 1m (P)

6:20 (6:25) (Class 7) (0-50,50) 4-Y-O+ **£1,455** (£433; £216; £108) **Stalls** Low

Form RPR

0-44 **1** **Litmus (USA)**[8] 320 4-9-2 **45** (b) HayleyTurner 11 58+
(Simon Dow) *pressed ldr: led over 2f out: pushed clr over 1f out and in n.d after: 5 l clr fnl f: unchal* **5/1**[1]

40-0 **2** *2 ½* **Compton Crofter**[14] 226 4-8-11 **45** (t) NicoleNordblad(5) 10 52
(Hans Adielsson) *hld up in midfield disputing 7th: shkn up on outer 2f out: styd on fr over 1f out to take 2nd last 100yds: no ch w wnr* **10/1**

0-30 **3** *1 ¼* **Boris The Bold**[7] 335 4-9-5 **48** GeorgeBaker 14 52+
(John Best) *hld up wl in rr: nt clr run on inner over 2f out: sme prog over 1f out but already no ch: drvn and r.o fnl f to take 3rd last strides* **7/1**[2]

000- **4** *nk* **Byrd In Hand (IRE)**[49] 8078 6-9-5 **48** SeanLevey 2 51
(John Bridger) *chsd ldrs disputing 5th: drvn to take 2nd 1f out but no ch w wnr: lost 2 pls last 100yds* **20/1**

-230 **5** *2 ½* **Compton Target (IRE)**[6] 349 4-9-4 **47** (t) RobertWinston 6 45
(Milton Bradley) *hld up in midfield disputing 5th: effrt towards inner 2f out: outpcd over 1f out: kpt on* **7/1**[2]

635- **6** *2* **Give Us A Belle (IRE)**[34] 8257 4-9-4 **47** (t) TomMcLaughlin 8 40
(Christine Dunnett) *chsd ldng pair: rdn over 2f out: tried to chal for 2nd over 1f out: fdd and eased* **25/1**

32-6 **7** *hd* **Avon Supreme**[5] 381 5-8-13 **47** NatashaEaton(5) 5 40
(Gay Kelleway) *led to over 2f out: sn no ch w wnr: lost 2nd and wknd 1f out* **8/1**[3]

40-0 **8** *1* **Rigid**[22] 110 6-9-1 **49** GeorgeDowning(5) 4 39
(Tony Carroll) *chsd ldrs disputing 5th: rdn over 2f out: nt qckn wl over 1f out: wknd fnl f* **10/1**

4-64 **9** *½* **Crucis Abbey (IRE)**[14] 220 5-9-2 **45** (p) EddieAhern 3 34
(Mark Brisbourne) *slowly away: wl in rr: sme prog on inner 2f out: no hdwy over 1f out: wknd* **8/1**[3]

560- **10** *1* **The Which Doctor**[32] 8288 8-9-7 **50** (p) WilliamCarson 1 37
(Violet M Jordan) *slowly away: a in rr: shkn up over 2f out: hanging and no prog* **16/1**

16-5 **11** *nk* **Gay Gallivanter**[28] 15 5-9-6 **49** (p) FrannyNorton 12 35
(Mick Quinn) *chsd ldng pair: rdn over 2f out: wknd wl over 1f out* **25/1**

600- **12** *1* **Surrey Dream (IRE)**[21] 8001 4-9-2 **50** WilliamTwiston-Davies(5) 7 34
(John Bridger) *slowly away: a in rr: rdn and hanging over 2f out: no prog* **9/1**

0-44 **13** *37* **Pytheas (USA)**[5] 381 6-9-6 **49** (tp) LukeMorris 13
(Alastair Lidderdale) *restless in stalls: c out of them w blindfold stl on: a in rr: wknd 3f out: t.o and eased: b.b.v* **14/1**

1m 40.91s (1.11) **Going Correction** +0.125s/f (Slow) **13** Ran SP% **117.1**
Speed ratings (Par 97): **99,96,95,94,92 90,90,89,88,87 87,86,49**
toteswingers 1&2 £15.90, 1&3 £9.10, 2&3 £17.90 CSF £51.89 CT £274.88 TOTE £5.00: £1.90, £4.20, £2.70; EX 60.00 Trifecta £682.70 Pool: £1413.72 - 1.55 winning units..
Owner T G Parker **Bred** Millsec Ltd **Trained** Epsom, Surrey

FOCUS
This looked an open handicap on paper. The second sets the standard and the winner is probably better than the bare form.

442 TIME ORDERED CARDS IN RACING PLUS H'CAP 6f (P)

6:50 (6:54) (Class 6) (0-55,55) 3-Y-O **£1,940** (£577; £288; £144) **Stalls** Low

Form RPR

0-05 **1** **Chelsea Grey (IRE)**[9] 310 3-8-12 **46** (b[1]) LukeMorris 2 49
(Ronald Harris) *chsd ldr: chal 3f out: rdn and lost 2nd wl over 1f out: pressed new ldr fnl f: drvn to ld nr fin* **12/1**

054- **2** *nk* **Sally Bruce**[42] 8166 3-8-6 **47** JenniferFerguson(7) 5 49
(Louise Best) *hld up in 5th: prog on inner over 2f out: pushed into ld over 1f out: edgd lft fnl f: hdd and nt qckn nr fin* **33/1**

36-3 **3** *¾* **Black Truffle (FR)**[21] 122 3-8-10 **49** RachealKneller(5) 1 49
(Mark Usher) *trckd ldng pair: rdn over 2f out: shkn up and tried to cl over 1f out: urged along and kpt on to take 3rd nr fin* **3/1**[2]

60-3 **4** *nk* **Frans Hals**[9] 310 3-8-11 **52** (p) JoshBaudains(7) 6 51
(Dominic Ffrench Davis) *dwlt: hld up in last trio: prog over 2f out: pressed ldrs over 1f out: one pce after* **7/1**[3]

00-6 **5** *1* **Actonetaketwo**[20] 136 3-8-12 **46** oh1 WilliamCarson 10 41
(Ron Hodges) *stdd s: hld up in detached last: rdn over 2f out: stl last over 1f out: styd on fnl f: nrst fin* **50/1**

-222 **6** *¾* **Holding Fast (IRE)**[6] 357 3-9-7 **55** MartinLane 8 48
(Tobias B P Coles) *plld hrd: hld up in last trio: rdn and nt qckn 2f out: kpt on one pce fr over 1f out: no imp* **7/4**[1]

24-6 **7** *½* **Cromwell Rose (IRE)**[16] 207 3-9-1 **49** (b) TomEaves 4 40
(John Weymes) *led to over 1f out: wknd fnl f* **25/1**

503- **8** *2 ¼* **Otto The First**[67] 7865 3-9-7 **55** GeorgeBaker 9 39
(John Best) *chsd ldng pair to over 2f out: drvn and sn lost pl: no ch over 1f out* **10/1**

0-50 **9** *3 ¾* **Woodland Fleur**[16] 207 3-9-4 **52** JimmyQuinn 7 24
(Tony Carroll) *in tch: dropped to rr and drvn 2f out: sn wknd* **25/1**

1m 15.62s (2.52) **Going Correction** +0.125s/f (Slow) **9** Ran SP% **103.2**
Speed ratings (Par 95): **88,87,86,86,84 83,83,80,75**
toteswingers 1&2 £46.90, 1&3 £8.40, 2&3 £14.90 CSF £253.95 CT £950.52 TOTE £10.00: £4.70, £9.20, £1.10; EX 474.90 Trifecta £878.50 Part won. Pool: £1171.46 - 0.65 winning units..
Owner Leslie Scadding **Bred** Jaykayeen **Trained** Earlswood, Monmouths

FOCUS
There was a modest pace here and a slow time. The form looks weak but has been rated at face value.

443 YEONGCHEON CITY RACING H'CAP — 7f (P)
7:20 (7:22) (Class 4) (0-85,85) 4-Y-0+ £4,690 (£1,395; £697; £348) Stalls Low

Form RPR
1-23 **1** **Light From Mars**[11] 272 8-9-2 80 LukeMorris 9 91
(Ronald Harris) *trckd ldrs in 6th: followed runner-up through fr over 1f out: drvn and r.o fnl f to ld last 100yds* 9/1
3- **2** ¾ **Free Spin (IRE)**[103] 7229 4-9-3 81 GrahamGibbons 7 90
(David Barron) *t.k.h early: trckd ldng pair: c between rivals to ld over 1f out: drvn and styd on but hdd last 100yds* 4/1[3]
1-21 **3** nk **Atlantis Crossing (IRE)**[15] 217 4-9-7 85 AdamKirby 10 93+
(Roger Ingram) *hld up in last trio: gng wl enough over 2f out: shkn up and prog over 1f out: rdn and r.o to take 3rd nr fin: too much to do* 3/1[2]
U3-1 **4** 1 **Haaf A Sixpence**[21] 121 4-9-5 83 SebSanders 1 88
(Ralph Beckett) *trckd ldng pair on inner: drvn to chal wl over 1f out: nt qckn and hld fnl f* 5/2[1]
13-3 **5** 2¾ **Fame Again**[20] 146 5-8-8 72 JamesSullivan 8 70
(Michael Easterby) *led to over 1f out: wknd fnl f* 14/1
00-2 **6** nse **Docofthebay (IRE)**[7] 345 9-9-6 84 (b) TomMcLaughlin 2 82
(Scott Dixon) *dwlt: hld up in last: effrt over 2f out: no imp on ldrs fr over 1f out* 16/1
21-4 **7** nk **Lujeanie**[6] 353 7-8-8 79 (p) PaulBooth(7) 3 76
(Dean Ivory) *dwlt: hld up in last trio: effrt over 2f out: no real hdwy over 1f out* 33/1
14-4 **8** 1¼ **Scottish Lake**[7] 345 5-9-0 78 (v) KirstyMilczarek 11 72
(Olivia Maylam) *t.k.h: racd on outer: chsd ldng pair to over 2f out: steadily wknd* 25/1
-426 **9** 3 **Majuro (IRE)**[6] 353 9-8-13 77 (t) WilliamCarson 4 63
(Violet M Jordan) *in tch in midfield: rdn over 2f out: sn btn* 33/1
6-14 **10** nk **Kung Hei Fat Choy (USA)**[4] 407 4-9-4 82 (b) DaleSwift 6 67
(James Given) *rousted along to press ldr: drvn to chal and upsides 2f out: wknd qckly over 1f out* 6/1

1m 25.07s (-0.93) **Going Correction** +0.125s/f (Slow) **10** Ran SP% **120.1**
Speed ratings (Par 105): **110,109,108,107,104 104,104,102,99,98**
toteswingers 1&2 £4.30, 1&3 £6.10, 2&3 £4.30 CSF £45.60 CT £136.05 TOTE £7.30: £2.40, £1.70, £1.80; EX 57.40 Trifecta £141.60 Pool: £1829.24 - 9.68 winning units..
Owner Mrs N Macauley **Bred** Harts Farm And Stud **Trained** Earlswood, Monmouths
FOCUS
A decent race for the grade. Plenty of these came here in good heart, there was a sound gallop and the form should prove pretty reliable.

444 KEMPTON FOR WEDDINGS H'CAP — 7f (P)
7:50 (7:50) (Class 5) (0-75,74) 3-Y-0 £2,587 (£770; £384) Stalls Low

Form RPR
21- **1** **Prophets Pride**[57] 7979 3-9-6 73 SebSanders 3 84+
(Jeremy Noseda) *pressed ldr: shkn up to ld 2f out: rdn to assert fnl f* 8/11[1]
61-1 **2** 1¾ **Red Dragon (IRE)**[17] 195 3-9-1 68 RobertWinston 2 71
(Charles Hills) *pushed up to ld: rdn over 2f out: sn hdd: pressed wnr to 1f out: one pce after* 9/4[2]
-114 **3** ¾ **Club House (IRE)**[6] 359 3-9-0 74 RyanTate(7) 4 75
(Robert Mills) *hld up in last: cl enough whn asked for effrt 2f out: hanging and fnd little fr over 1f out* 9/2[3]

1m 26.8s (0.80) **Going Correction** +0.125s/f (Slow) **3** Ran SP% **106.9**
Speed ratings (Par 97): **100,98,97**
CSF £2.59 TOTE £1.60; EX 2.20 Trifecta £2.60 Pool: £700.43 - 195.80 winning units..
Owner Saeed Suhail **Bred** Rabbah Bloodstock Limited **Trained** Newmarket, Suffolk
FOCUS
A fair pace given the small field. The winner improved past the second and both look ahead of their marks.
T/Plt: £85.60 to a £1 stake. Pool of £66,240.15 - 564.39 winning tickets. T/Qpdt: £36.70 to a £1 stake. Pool of £7,848.48 - 158.00 winning tickets. JN

331 CAGNES-SUR-MER
Monday, January 28
OFFICIAL GOING: Fibresand: standard

445a PRIX DE GRIMAUD (MAIDEN) (3YO COLTS & GELDINGS) (FIBRESAND) — 1m 2f (D)
12:30 (12:00) 3-Y-0 £9,756 (£3,902; £2,926; £1,951; £975)

RPR
1 **Face Surface (GER)** 3-9-2 0 Francois-XavierBertras 8 78
(F Rohaut, France) 19/10[1]
2 ½ **Baileys Auteur (FR)** 3-9-2 0 (p) MickaelForest 10 77
(W Walton, France) 26/1
3 1 **Lucio Silla**[31] 3-9-2 0 (b) FabriceVeron 13 75
(H-A Pantall, France) 68/10[2]
4 ¾ **Yeoman (USA)**[45] 3-9-2 0 (b[1]) JulienAuge 3 74
(C Ferland, France) 9/1
5 1½ **Sango (IRE)**[171] 3-9-2 0 IoritzMendizabal 12 71
(J-C Rouget, France) 10/1
6 ½ **Kenasie (FR)** 3-9-2 0 Pierre-CharlesBoudot 15 70
(J-M Capitte, France) 7/1[3]
7 nse **Kareman (FR)** 3-9-2 0 ThierryThulliez 16 69
(T Lemer, France) 65/1
8 nse **Snowy Dawn**[10] 270 3-9-2 0 JackDuern 6 69
(Reg Hollinshead) *hld up towards rr: gd prog towards end of bk st: swung wd: short of room 2f out: r.o u.p fnl f: nrest at fin* 18/1
9 ½ **King Lollipop (FR)**[31] 3-9-2 0 FranckBlondel 4 68
(T Lemer, France) 18/1
10 nk **Shabaka (FR)** 3-9-2 0 (p) FranckForesi 5 68
(F Foresi, France) 22/1
0 **Welcome Sir (FR)**[185] 3-9-2 0 AnthonyCrastus 1
(E Lellouche, France) 57/1
0 **Moorway (IRE)**[10] 270 3-9-2 0 FilipMinarik 7
(Reg Hollinshead) *settled in midfield on ins: rdn but no ex 2f out: styd on one pce fnl f* 63/1
0 **Gorki Park (FR)**[24] 72 3-9-2 0 FabienLefebvre 11
(Mme G Rarick, France) 82/1
0 **Toni Fortebracci (FR)**[44] 3-9-2 0 StephanePasquier 9
(G Botti, France) 15/2
0 **Gimli (FR)** 3-8-8 0 NicolasLarenaudie(8) 2
(G Collet, France) 35/1

2m 3.02s (123.02) **15** Ran SP% **118.0**
WIN (incl. 1 euro stake): 2.90. PLACES: 1.50, 5.10, 2.30. DF: 36.60. SF: 44.90.
Owner Berend Van Dalfsen **Bred** B Van Dalfsen **Trained** Sauvagnon, France

396 LINGFIELD (L-H)
Thursday, January 31
OFFICIAL GOING: Standard
Wind: Strong across Weather: Dry and blustery

446 LINGFIELD (S) STKS — 7f (P)
1:30 (1:30) (Class 6) 4-Y-0+ £2,045 (£603; £302) Stalls Low

Form RPR
3-54 **1** **Chambles**[12] 271 4-8-5 61 DavidProbert 4 63
(J R Jenkins) *trckd ldng pair: pushed along and cl up on outer 2f out: rdn to chal over 1f out: styd on to ld last 100yds* 5/2[3]
4260 **2** nk **Majuro (IRE)**[1] 443 9-9-1 77 (t) WilliamCarson 2 72
(Violet M Jordan) *hld up in rr: hdwy on outer wl over 1f out: rdn and styd on to chal ins fnl f: ev ch tl drvn and no ex towards fin* 6/4[1]
5-43 **3** 1¼ **The Mongoose**[8] 340 5-9-1 65 (t) TomMcLaughlin 1 69
(David Evans) *trckd ldr: hdwy 2f out: rdn to chal wl over 1f out: sn ev ch: drvn and one pce last 100yds* 9/4[2]
00-0 **4** nk **Leelu**[22] 116 7-8-5 54 KirstyMilczarek 3 58
(David Arbuthnot) *led: rdn along and jnd 2f out: drvn over 1f out: hdd & wknd last 100yds* 12/1

1m 24.34s (-0.46) **Going Correction** +0.025s/f (Slow) **4** Ran SP% **107.0**
Speed ratings (Par 101): **103,102,101,100**
CSF £6.54 TOTE £4.50; EX 6.30 Trifecta £6.70 Pool: £1096.74 - 121.55 winning units..There was no bid for the winner.
Owner A S Reid **Bred** A S Reid **Trained** Royston, Herts
FOCUS
An uncompetitive seller and the four runners were in a line across the track entering the last furlong. Muddling form, rated tentatively.

447 GOLF & RACING AT LINGFIELD PARK RESORT (S) STKS — 1m (P)
2:00 (2:00) (Class 6) 3-Y-0 £2,045 (£603; £302) Stalls High

Form RPR
4-21 **1** **Mick Dundee (IRE)**[3] 427 3-9-3 62 (vt) SebSanders 2 67
(J W Hills) *mde all: pushed clr over 3f out: rdn wl over 1f out: kpt on strly* 1/1[1]
50-3 **2** 3 **Elusive Thought (IRE)**[3] 424 3-8-11 58 DavidProbert 1 54
(J S Moore) *trckd ldng pair: hdwy over 3f out: rdn to chse wnr over 1f out: drvn and no imp fnl f* 6/4[2]
6-63 **3** 6 **Betzyoucan**[5] 402 3-8-6 60 FrannyNorton 4 35
(Mark Johnston) *trckd wnr: pushed along over 2f out: rdn wl over 1f out: wknd appr fnl f* 9/2[3]
36-0 **4** 21 **Paige Flyer**[9] 321 3-8-6 58 (v[1]) AndreaAtzeni 3
(Mick Quinn) *dwlt: trckd ldrs: pushed along 4f out: rdn over 3f out: sn outpcd* 33/1

1m 37.86s (-0.34) **Going Correction** +0.025s/f (Slow) **4** Ran SP% **111.1**
Speed ratings (Par 95): **102,99,93,72**
CSF £2.91 TOTE £1.60; EX 2.70 Trifecta £3.40 Pool: £989.47 - 216.27 winning units..There was no bid for the winner.
Owner R J Tufft **Bred** Kildare Racing Syndicate **Trained** Upper Lambourn, Berks
FOCUS
Another modest seller. The winner had an easy lead and is rated up 4lb.

448 BOOK HOSPITALITY AT LINGFIELD PARK H'CAP — 5f (P)
2:30 (2:30) (Class 6) (0-65,65) 4-Y-0+ £2,385 (£704; £352) Stalls High

Form RPR
2-10 **1** **Charming (IRE)**[20] 156 4-9-7 65 (e) SebSanders 2 72
(Olivia Maylam) *a.p: rdn to chal over 1f out: r.o to ld narrowly wl ins fnl f: jst hld on in driving fin* 7/1[3]
06-1 **2** nse **Secret Millionaire (IRE)**[6] 369 6-9-6 64 6ex JimCrowley 7 71+
(Tony Carroll) *hld up: effrt over 1f out: clsd ins fnl f: r.o and str chal cl home: jst failed* 4/5[1]
2004 **3** hd **Putin (IRE)**[5] 399 5-8-10 54 (bt) DavidProbert 1 60
(Phil McEntee) *led: rdn over 1f out: hdd narrowly wl ins fnl f: hld fnl stride in driving fin* 12/1
5-40 **4** 1½ **Greenhead High**[16] 214 5-8-13 62 ShirleyTeasdale(5) 6 63
(David Nicholls) *chsd ldrs: rdn and nt qckn over 1f out: styd on ins fnl f but nt pace to chal front trio* 9/2[2]
434 **5** 1¼ **Sherjawy (IRE)**[6] 369 9-8-8 52 KirstyMilczarek 3 48
(Zoe Davison) *hld up: pushed along 2f out: rdn and kpt on ins fnl f: nvr able to chal* 14/1
00-6 **6** 2½ **Foxtrot India (IRE)**[15] 232 4-9-7 65 RenatoSouza 4 52
(Jeremy Gask) *dwlt: sn chsd ldrs: rdn over 1f out: wknd fnl 100yds* 16/1
-260 **7** ½ **Liberal Lady**[5] 399 5-9-4 62 GeorgeBaker 5 47
(Ralph Smith) *a bhd: wl outpcd over 1f out: nvr on terms* 10/1

58.43s (-0.37) **Going Correction** +0.025s/f (Slow) **7** Ran SP% **115.6**
Speed ratings (Par 101): **103,102,102,100,98 94,93**
toteswingers 1&2 £2.50, 1&3 £5.80, 2&3 £3.40 CSF £13.38 TOTE £8.90: £4.10, £1.20; EX 15.20 Trifecta £125.50 Pool: £1823.37 - 10.89 winning units..
Owner Mrs V A Ward **Bred** Rabbah Bloodstock Limited **Trained** Epsom, Surrey
■ Stewards' Enquiry : David Probert two-day ban: use of whip (14-15 Feb)
FOCUS
A moderate sprint handicap. The winner and third were always to the fore and are rated close to their best, with the second matching his C&D win latest.

449 LINGFIELD PARK MARRIOTT HOTEL H'CAP — 6f (P)
3:00 (3:00) (Class 6) (0-60,60) 4-Y-0+ £2,385 (£704; £352) Stalls Low

Form RPR
32-1 **1** **Valdaw**[12] 276 5-9-2 60 WilliamTwiston-Davies(5) 7 71+
(Mike Murphy) *trckd ldng pair: hdwy to chal over 1f out: sn rdn and led ins fnl f: pushed out* 5/4[1]
0-02 **2** ½ **Waterloo Dock**[9] 322 8-9-2 55 (v) AndreaAtzeni 8 64
(Mick Quinn) *sn led: rdn along 2f out: drvn over 1f out: hdd ins fnl f: kpt on* 16/1

-162 **3** 1 ½ **Glennten**[3] 422 4-9-2 **55** GeorgeBaker 3 60
(Sylvester Kirk) *chsd ldr: effrt 2f out: rdn over 1f out: kpt on same pce* **11/4**[2]
0-36 **4** 1 ½ **John Coffey (IRE)**[16] 213 4-8-13 **52** (b[1]) SebSanders 5 52
(David Nicholls) *awkward and hmpd s: t.k.h and hld up in rr: hdwy and wd st: rdn and wandered over 1f out: styd on and hung lft ins fnl f: nrst fin* **9/2**[3]
6036 **5** ½ **Back For Tea (IRE)**[8] 346 5-8-7 **46** oh1 (b) DavidProbert 2 44
(Phil McEntee) *chsd ldrs: rdn along wl over 1f out: drvn and one pce appr fnl f* **33/1**
000- **6** ½ **Johnstown Lad (IRE)**[31] 8305 9-9-7 **60** (bt) ShaneKelly 4 57
(Daniel Mark Loughnane) *hld up towards rr: hdwy wl over 1f out: sn rdn and no imp fnl f* **12/1**
-054 **7** 1 **Lady Mango (IRE)**[9] 323 5-9-5 **58** (b[1]) WilliamCarson 9 51
(Ronald Harris) *dwlt and towards rr: hdwy on outer 1/2-way: rdn wl over 1f out: hld whn sltly hmpd ins fnl f* **14/1**
6-45 **8** ½ **Chjimes (IRE)**[9] 322 9-9-1 **54** (b) LiamKeniry 6 46
(Conor Dore) *t.k.h early: hld up: hdwy wl over 1f out: sn rdn and no imp* **25/1**
050- **9** 14 **Cliffords Reprieve**[119] 6823 5-8-9 **55** (b) JoeyHaynes[(7)] 1
(Eric Wheeler) *a towards rr* **50/1**

1m 12.48s (0.58) **Going Correction** +0.025s/f (Slow) **9** Ran SP% **118.3**
Speed ratings (Par 101): **97,96,94,92,91 91,89,89,70**
toteswingers 1&2 £4.10, 1&3 £1.50, 2&3 £8.40 CSF £25.29 CT £51.66 TOTE £1.70: £1.10, £3.40, £2.90; EX 23.50 Trifecta £77.20 Pool: £3424.62 - 33.22 winning units..
Owner D Spratt **Bred** Mayden Stud, J A And D S Dewhurst **Trained** Westoning, Beds

FOCUS
Another modest sprint handicap where few got involved. The winner is starting to fulfil his earlier promise.

450 PLAY GOLF AT LINGFIELD PARK RACECOURSE H'CAP 1m 2f (P)
3:30 (3:30) (Class 5) (0-70,75) 4-Y-0+ £2,587 (£770; £384; £192) Stalls Low

Form RPR
514- **1** **Norfolk Sky**[40] 8229 4-9-2 **66** JimCrowley 2 76
(Laura Mongan) *trckd ldrs: hdwy over 3f out: led 1 1/2f out: sn rdn and kpt on strly* **4/1**
0/0- **2** 1 ¾ **Ze King**[247] 2584 4-9-2 **66** GeorgeBaker 1 73
(Chris Wall) *trckd ldng pair: hdwy to chse wnr over 1f out: drvn and kpt on fnl f* **5/2**[2]
1-04 **3** ¾ **Brown Pete (IRE)**[21] 138 5-9-5 **67** WilliamCarson 7 72
(Violet M Jordan) *hld up in rr: hdwy over 3f out: rdn to chse ldrs over 1f out: kpt on fnl f* **10/1**
234- **4** nk **Whinging Willie (IRE)**[34] 8263 4-8-12 **62** FergusSweeney 5 66
(Gary Moore) *in tch on inner: effrt over 2f out: sn rdn and kpt on fnl f: nrst fin* **7/2**[3]
5-25 **5** 2 ¼ **Understory (USA)**[19] 190 6-9-6 **68** SebSanders 6 68
(Tim McCarthy) *led: rdn along over 2f out: hdd 1 1/2f: out: grad wknd* **10/1**
21-2 **6** 3 ¼ **Neige D'Antan**[21] 145 4-9-2 **66** ChrisCatlin 3 59
(Sir Mark Prescott Bt) *towards rr: pushed along on outer 1/2-way: rdn along over 4f out and sn btn* **9/4**[1]
6-00 **7** 9 **L'Hirondelle (IRE)**[5] 403 9-9-5 **67** (b[1]) JohnFahy 4 42
(Michael Attwater) *dwlt: sn cl up: rdn along over 2f out: sn wknd* **50/1**

2m 5.6s (-1.00) **Going Correction** +0.025s/f (Slow)
WFA 4 from 5yo+ 2lb **7** Ran SP% **121.7**
Speed ratings (Par 103): **105,103,103,102,100 98,91**
toteswingers 1&2 £3.20, 1&3 £4.50, 2&3 £5.20 CSF £15.73 CT £96.64 TOTE £4.50: £3.20, £5.60; EX 17.20 Trifecta £159.20 Pool: £3314.54 - 15.61 winning units..
Owner Condover Racing **Bred** Farmers Hill Stud **Trained** Epsom, Surrey

FOCUS
An ordinary handicap, but the pace was solid which helped the winner, who improved on his recent form. The second improved.

451 MORE THAN JUST A RACECOURSE H'CAP 1m (P)
4:00 (4:00) (Class 5) (0-70,72) 4-Y-0+ £2,587 (£770; £384; £192) Stalls High

Form RPR
61-1 **1** **Whispering Warrior (IRE)**[15] 222 4-9-7 **70** JimCrowley 4 85+
(David Simcock) *trckd ldng pair: smooth hdwy on inner to ld appr fnl f: sn pushed clr: readily* **2/5**[1]
-361 **2** 2 **Storm Runner (IRE)**[8] 344 5-9-9 **72** 6ex GeorgeBaker 2 77
(George Margarson) *slt ld: rdn along wl over 1f out: hdd and drvn appr fnl f: kpt on same pce* **6/1**[2]
24-4 **3** hd **Warbond**[15] 222 5-8-11 **60** FergusSweeney 3 65
(Michael Madgwick) *in tch: hdwy wl over 1f out: sn rdn and kpt on fnl f: nrst fin* **12/1**
040- **4** ¾ **Hereford Boy**[34] 8268 9-8-13 **62** (p) AndreaAtzeni 5 65
(Dean Ivory) *cl up: rdn along wl over 1f out: drvn and one pce fnl f* **20/1**
42-3 **5** 1 **Chrissycross (IRE)**[20] 159 4-8-9 **65** (v) ThomasBrown[(7)] 1 66
(Roger Teal) *hld up in rr: hdwy 2f out: rdn over 1f out: no imp fnl f* **8/1**[3]

1m 38.8s (0.60) **Going Correction** +0.025s/f (Slow) **5** Ran SP% **109.3**
Speed ratings (Par 103): **98,96,95,95,94**
CSF £3.20 TOTE £1.60: £1.30, £1.70; EX 4.10 Trifecta £10.00 Pool: £1043.76 - 78.00 winning units..
Owner Daniel Pittack **Bred** Epona Bloodstock Ltd **Trained** Newmarket, Suffolk

FOCUS
A very one-sided betting market, but it proved totally accurate. The form is rated around the third and fourth, and there could be more to come from the winner.

452 FOLLOW US ON TWITTER @LINGFIELDPARK APPRENTICE H'CAP 7f (P)
4:30 (4:30) (Class 5) (0-70,70) 4-Y-0+ £2,587 (£770; £384; £192) Stalls Low

Form RPR
0-22 **1** **Jack My Boy (IRE)**[5] 398 6-9-0 **68** (v) ThomasBrown[(5)] 2 76
(David Evans) *trckd ldng pair: effrt over 1f out: hdwy to ld jst ins fnl f: sn rdn and kpt on* **7/4**[1]
62-2 **2** nk **Hierarch (IRE)**[24] 89 6-8-9 **65** (p) SiobhanMiller[(7)] 3 72
(David Simcock) *prom: cl up 1/2-way: rdn to ld jst over 1f out: hdd jst ins fnl f: kpt on wl u.p towards fin* **6/1**
2-51 **3** 1 **Welsh Inlet (IRE)**[12] 274 5-8-9 **61** ow1 WilliamTwiston-Davies[(3)] 4 65
(John Bridger) *hld up in tch: hdwy 2f out: rdn to chse ldng pair ins fnl f: kpt on same pce* **8/1**
45-5 **4** ½ **For Shia And Lula (IRE)**[3] 426 4-9-4 **67** RyanClark 5 70
(Daniel Mark Loughnane) *in tch: hdwy 2f out: rdn over 1f out: kpt on same pce fnl f* **6/1**

0-03 **5** ¾ **Dunn'o (IRE)**[17] 206 8-8-10 **64** (t) ShirleyTeasdale[(5)] 1 65
(David Nicholls) *led: rdn along 2f out: hdd jst over 1f out: wknd ins fnl f* **9/2**[3]
-123 **6** 1 ½ **Restless Bay (IRE)**[3] 426 5-9-7 **70** (v) AshleyMorgan 6 67
(Conor Dore) *hld up in rr: effrt 2f out: sn rdn and no imp* **7/2**[2]

1m 25.17s (0.37) **Going Correction** +0.025s/f (Slow) **6** Ran SP% **116.5**
Speed ratings (Par 103): **98,97,96,95,95 93**
toteswingers 1&2 £3.40, 1&3 £1.80, 2&3 £6.10 CSF £13.49 TOTE £2.60: £1.60, £2.40; EX 12.60 Trifecta £32.90 Pool: £2194.47 - 49.98 winning units..
Owner T Earle & G Evans **Bred** Mrs Sheila Walker **Trained** Pandy, Monmouths

FOCUS
An ordinary apprentice handicap, rated around the runner-up and the fifth.
T/Plt: £44.50 to a £1 stake. Pool of £48647.61 - 796.92 winning tickets. T/Qpdt: £7.80 to a £1 stake. Pool of £4550.04 - 428.42 winning tickets. JR

430 WOLVERHAMPTON (A.W) (L-H)
Thursday, January 31

OFFICIAL GOING: Standard
Wind: Strong, behind Weather: Overcast, dry

453 BOOKIE FREE BETS AT BOOKMAKERS.CO.UK APPRENTICE H'CAP 5f 216y(P)
4:50 (4:50) (Class 5) (0-75,71) 4-Y-0+ £2,587 (£770; £384; £192) Stalls Low

Form RPR
2-26 **1** **Holy Angel (IRE)**[16] 214 4-8-8 **63** (e) RachelRichardson[(5)] 4 78
(Tim Easterby) *t.k.h: mde all at decent gallop: clr 2f out: pushed out fnl f* **5/1**[3]
61-0 **2** 3 ¼ **Dickie Le Davoir**[29] 27 9-9-2 **66** (b) PhilipPrince 1 71
(Richard Guest) *dwlt: bhd: rdn and hdwy over 1f out: chsd (clr) wnr ins fnl f: no imp* **8/1**
035- **3** 1 ½ **Mazovian (USA)**[40] 8236 5-9-0 **69** GerardGalligan[(5)] 6 69
(Michael Chapman) *prom: effrt and rdr dropped whip over 1f out: kpt on same pce fnl f* **20/1**
01-6 **4** nk **Hot Sugar (USA)**[28] 29 4-9-2 **66** JoshBaudains 3 65
(Michael Appleby) *hld up in tch: rdn over 2f out: effrt and edgd lft over 1f out: sn no imp* **7/1**
02-1 **5** 3 ½ **Colbyor**[29] 27 4-8-11 **68** (v) EireannCagney[(7)] 7 56
(Richard Fahey) *chsd clr ldng pair: effrt over 2f out: wknd fnl f* **9/4**[2]
00-5 **6** 1 ¾ **Perlachy**[24] 95 9-8-11 **64** (v) GaryPhillips[(3)] 2 46
(Ronald Harris) *sn towards rr: rdn and effrt over 2f out: sn no imp: btn fnl f* **10/1**
1-23 **7** 2 ¼ **Strong Man**[10] 308 5-8-13 **68** (b) MatthewHopkins[(5)] 5 43
(Michael Easterby) *w wnr: rdn and outpcd 2f out: wknd appr fnl f* **2/1**[1]

1m 15.44s (0.44) **Going Correction** +0.175s/f (Slow) **7** Ran SP% **118.2**
Speed ratings (Par 103): **104,99,97,97,92 90,87**
toteswingers 1&2 £9.00, 2&3 £12.00, 1&3 £8.50 CSF £45.37 CT £742.91 TOTE £5.20: £3.90, £4.40; EX 54.00 Trifecta £383.50 Pool: £1620.30 - 3.16 winning units..
Owner Three Jolly Farmers **Bred** Yeomanstown Stud **Trained** Great Habton, N Yorks

FOCUS
A weak sprint and suspect form, but the winner's improvement seems no fluke.

454 CORALCHAMPIONSCLUB.CO.UK CLASSIFIED CLAIMING STKS 5f 216y(P)
5:20 (5:20) (Class 5) 3-Y-0+ £2,587 (£770; £384; £192) Stalls Low

Form RPR
105- **1** **Clubland (IRE)**[103] 7254 4-9-5 68 MarkCoumbe[(3)] 2 70
(Roy Bowring) *trckd ldrs: rdn to ld over 1f out: kpt on wl fnl f* **8/1**
00-0 **2** ¾ **Proper Charlie**[6] 372 5-9-12 72 AdamKirby 8 72
(William Knight) *hld up in tch: hdwy on outside over 2f out: edgd lft and chsd wnr ins fnl f: r.o* **13/8**[1]
00-0 **3** hd **Point North (IRE)**[17] 206 6-9-10 67 DanielTudhope 1 69
(John Balding) *t.k.h: chsd ldrs: hmpd after 1f: smooth hdwy 2f out: sn rdn: one pce fnl f* **16/1**
3-50 **4** 1 ¾ **Frequency**[16] 217 6-9-11 72 (b) RobertWinston 5 65
(Keith Dalgleish) *rrd and uns rdr in stalls: s.i.s: t.k.h in rr: hdwy on outside over 1f out: r.o fnl f: nrst fin* **7/1**
-512 **5** nse **Dark Lane**[7] 355 7-9-8 70 GrahamGibbons 7 62
(David Evans) *w ldr: led 1/2-way to over 1f out: n.m.r briefly and outpcd ins fnl f* **11/4**[2]
040- **6** 6 **Takealookatmenow (IRE)**[93] 7451 4-9-10 70 FrannyNorton 3 44
(David Nicholls) *t.k.h: led to 1/2-way: rdn: edgd lft and wknd over 1f out* **4/1**[3]

1m 15.45s (0.45) **Going Correction** +0.175s/f (Slow)
WFA 3 from 4yo+ 16lb **6** Ran SP% **114.3**
Speed ratings (Par 103): **104,103,102,100,100 92**
toteswingers 1&2 £3.40, 2&3 £5.40, 1&3 £4.80 CSF £22.13 TOTE £9.70: £4.30, £2.30; EX 31.40 Trifecta £292.10 Pool: £2538.33 - 6.51 winning units..
Owner S R Bowring **Bred** Mrs Sharon Slattery **Trained** Edwinstowe, Notts

FOCUS
Not a bad claimer. The winner matched his 5f best.

455 CORAL CHAMPIONS CLUB FREE TO JOIN H'CAP 1m 4f 50y(P)
5:50 (5:50) (Class 6) (0-55,67) 4-Y-0+ £1,259 (£1,259; £288; £144) Stalls Low

Form RPR
63-2 **1** **Midnight Bahia (IRE)**[20] 169 4-8-10 **48** FrannyNorton 11 57
(Dean Ivory) *t.k.h: led 2f: chsd ldr: led over 3f out: clr 2f out: kpt on ins fnl f: jnd on line* **11/2**[3]
-006 **1** dht **Sir Dylan**[3] 418 4-9-3 **55** RobertWinston 1 64
(Ronald Harris) *s.i.s: bhd: gd hdwy on outside to chse (clr) wnr over 1f out: hung lft: styd on wl ins fnl f to dead-heat on line* **12/1**
40-5 **3** 2 ¼ **Leitrim King (IRE)**[8] 335 4-9-3 **55** AdamKirby 7 60+
(Gary Moore) *in tch: effrt whn n.m.r and outpcd wl over 2f out: rallied over 1f out: edgd lft and styd on wl ins fnl f* **11/4**[1]
50-2 **4** 1 **Tyrur Ted**[6] 375 8-8-13 **54** (t) PhilipPrince[(7)] 4 58+
(Frank Sheridan) *hld up on ins: stdy hdwy over 3f out: rdn and kpt on same pce fr 2f out* **6/1**
0-11 **5** 3 **Monzino (USA)**[5] 410 5-9-12 **67** 12ex GerardGalligan[(7)] 2 66
(Michael Chapman) *in tch: effrt and hdwy on outside over 2f out: outpcd over 1f out* **4/1**[2]
05-0 **6** 1 **Newington**[30] 7 4-8-11 **52** SimonPearce[(3)] 3 49
(Lydia Pearce) *bhd: drvn along over 3f out: kpt on fnl f: nvr able to chal* **33/1**
00-2 **7** 1 ¼ **Seawood**[24] 99 7-8-10 **47** MarkCoumbe[(3)] 9 42
(Roy Bowring) *chsd ldrs: wnt 2nd over 2f out to over 1f out: wknd fnl f* **14/1**

0-65 **8** ½ **Pirate Chest (IRE)**[20] 166 5-9-5 **53**.......................(bt) DuranFentiman 10 48
(Patrick Holmes) *bhd: drvn along 4f out: kpt on fnl f: nvr able to chal* **50/1**

0-30 **9** 10 **Pobs Trophy**[15] 226 6-8-13 **47**..............................(b) RobbieFitzpatrick 5 26
(Richard Guest) *chsd ldrs: rdn over 3f out: wknd 2f out* **33/1**

10 1 ¾ **Houdini Bright (USA)**[13] 269 5-8-13 **47**.............. GrahamGibbons 8 23
(Dermot Anthony McLoughlin, Ire) *hld up in tch: sn pushed along: drvn 1/2-way: wknd 3f out* **7/1**

510- **11** ¾ **Hyde Lea Flyer**[125] 6626 8-9-7 **55**.................... KirstyMilczarek 6 30
(Barry Leavy) *t.k.h: led after 2f and sn clr: hdd over 3f out: wknd 2f out* **25/1**

636- **12** 6 **No Diamond**[35] 8260 6-9-4 **52**...........................(p) AndrewMullen 12 17
(Michael Appleby) *missed break: bhd: stdy hdwy on outside over 5f out: wknd fr 3f out* **8/1**

2m 43.93s (2.83) **Going Correction** +0.175s/f (Slow)
WFA 4 from 5yo+ 4lb 12 Ran SP% **126.0**
Speed ratings (Par 101): **97,97,95,94,92 92,91,91,84,83 82,78**WIN: Sir Dylan £7.20 Midnight Bahia £2.60 PL: SD £3.30 MB £2.00 LK £1.70. EX: SD/MB £52.90 MB/SD £28.20 CSF: SD/MB £39.72 MB/SD £35.96 TRI: SD/MB/Leitrim King £121.41 MB/SD/LK £113.52 toteswingers: SD&MB £1.30, SD&3 £11.30, 3&MB £3.00, £1.70 27 Trifecta £Owner K B Taylor Bred.
Owner Ridge House Stables Ltd **Bred** Cavendish Bloodstock **Trained** Earlswood, Monmouths

FOCUS
A dead-heat after a muddling race. The third and fourth are perhaps a bit better than the bare form.

456 MONEY BACK RACING SPECIALS AT BOOKMAKERS.CO.UK H'CAP 1m 1f 103y(P)
6:20 (6:22) (Class 7) (0-50,50) 4-Y-0+ **£1,940** (£577; £288; £144) **Stalls** Low

Form RPR

0-31 **1** **Young Jackie**[6] 375 5-8-10 **46**..............................(b) JordanVaughan(7) 6 58
(George Margarson) *t.k.h: hld up in tch: gd hdwy on outside to ld over 1f out: sn kicked clr: hld on wl fnl f* **7/4**[1]

060- **2** 1 **Angelena Ballerina (IRE)**[255] 2348 6-9-2 **45**..................(v) AdamKirby 4 55+
(Sean Curran) *t.k.h: trckd ldrs: effrt over 2f out: hdwy and edgd lft over 1f out: chsd wnr ins fnl f: r.o* **9/1**

06-4 **3** 1 ¾ **Extremely Alert**[7] 361 4-8-8 **45**.. RyanTate(7) 9 51
(Michael Bell) *led: rdn and hdd over 1f out: one pce and lost 2nd ins fnl f* **2/1**[2]

0-03 **4** 4 **Titan Diamond (IRE)**[23] 110 5-8-11 **45**................. RachealKneller(5) 2 43
(Mark Usher) *t.k.h: chsd ldrs: rdn 2f out: outpcd fnl f* **14/1**

0-05 **5** ¾ **Sun Dream**[15] 220 6-9-2 **45**.. JimmyQuinn 7 41
(Tony Carroll) *sn cl up: rdn over 2f out: no ex over 1f out* **25/1**

600/ **6** 1 **Atacama Sunrise**[663] 1233 7-9-6 **49**.................................. JoeFanning 11 43
(John Butler) *t.k.h: in tch: effrt and rdn 2f out: wknd appr fnl f* **7/1**[3]

404- **7** hd **Supa Seeker (USA)**[41] 8212 7-8-12 **46**.................. GeorgeDowning(5) 8 40
(Tony Carroll) *missed break: hld up: rdn along 3f out: nvr able to chal* **14/1**

04-0 **8** hd **Nurse Dominatrix (IRE)**[6] 375 4-9-3 **47**.............. RobbieFitzpatrick 13 40
(Richard Guest) *hld up: rdn along over 3f out: nvr rchd ldrs* **40/1**

423- **9** hd **Kheskianto (IRE)**[128] 6561 7-8-9 **45**............................(t) AaronJones(7) 5 38
(Michael Chapman) *dwlt: bhd: drvn over 2f out: nvr on terms* **20/1**

0-00 **10** 2 ¼ **Vermeyen**[7] 349 4-9-6 **50**... KirstyMilczarek 12 38
(Geoffrey Deacon) *stdd s: t.k.h in rr: rdn over 2f out: nvr on terms* **12/1**

300- **11** 6 **Tous Les Deux**[54] 8038 10-9-2 **45**................................ RichardThomas 3 20
(Dr Jeremy Naylor) *hld up on ins: rdn along 3f out: struggling fnl 2f* **50/1**

2m 4.17s (2.47) **Going Correction** +0.175s/f (Slow)
WFA 4 from 5yo+ 1lb 11 Ran SP% **126.2**
Speed ratings (Par 97): **96,95,93,90,89 88,88,88,87,85 80**
toteswingers 1&2 £5.90, 2&3 £7.80, 1&3 £1.90 CSF £19.73 CT £37.16 TOTE £3.00: £1.40, £2.50, £1.50; EX 23.60 Trifecta £102.60 Pool: £2410.35 - 17.61 winning units..
Owner Exors of the Late M Kentish **Bred** M F Kentish **Trained** Newmarket, Suffolk

FOCUS
A weak handicap, and rather muddling, but not bad form for the class. The winner was well in and confirmed the form of her previous C&D win.

457 FREE BETS CORAL CHAMPIONS CLUB MEMBERS H'CAP 5f 20y(P)
6:50 (6:50) (Class 4) (0-85,81) 4-Y-0+ **£4,690** (£1,395; £697; £348) **Stalls** Low

Form RPR

-600 **1** **Royal Bajan (USA)**[5] 405 5-9-5 **79**............................(b) JamesSullivan 1 87
(James Given) *mde all at decent gallop: rdn 2f out: edgd lft ins fnl f: hld on wl* **20/1**

4-23 **2** nk **Triple Dream**[18] 196 8-9-3 **77**...............................(tp) RobertWinston 8 84
(Milton Bradley) *towards rr: rdn over 2f out: angled to outside over 1f out: chsd wnr ins fnl f: r.o* **6/1**[3]

050- **3** ½ **Tyfos**[179] 4849 8-9-5 **79**.. DuranFentiman 2 84
(Brian Baugh) *cl up: effrt and rdn 2f out: ch ins fnl f: hld nr fin* **22/1**

2443 **4** 1 ¼ **Dorback**[7] 353 6-9-7 **81**.. FrannyNorton 4 82
(David Nicholls) *prom: hung rt appr st: effrt wl over 1f out: kpt on same pce fnl f* **11/4**[2]

10-6 **5** nk **Rocket Rob (IRE)**[22] 113 7-9-0 **74**........................... J-PGuillambert 10 74
(Willie Musson) *s.i.s: bhd tl hdwy over 1f out: kpt on: nvr able to chal* **12/1**

6-03 **6** ½ **Alaskan Bullet (IRE)**[9] 319 4-9-3 **77**........................ GrahamGibbons 6 75
(Brian Ellison) *dwlt: bhd: hdwy on ins and in tch over 2f out: sn rdn: outpcd fr 2f out* **2/1**[1]

610- **7** 3 ½ **Rylee Mooch**[64] 7918 5-9-3 **77**...........................(e) RobbieFitzpatrick 3 62
(Richard Guest) *cl up tl rdn and wknd 2f out* **16/1**

56-0 **8** 2 ¼ **Six Wives**[9] 319 6-9-6 **80**..(p) AdamKirby 5 57
(Scott Dixon) *cl up: drvn over 2f out: wknd wl over 1f out* **9/1**

01-0 **9** 1 ½ **Island Legend (IRE)**[22] 113 7-9-7 **81**..........................(p) SebSanders 9 53
(Milton Bradley) *towards rr: drvn along 1/2-way: btn fnl 2f* **20/1**

06-0 **10** 5 **Verinco**[18] 196 7-9-4 **78**..(v) TomEaves 7 32
(Bryan Smart) *midfield: struggling over 2f out: sn btn* **14/1**

1m 2.25s (-0.05) **Going Correction** +0.175s/f (Slow) 10 Ran SP% **118.4**
Speed ratings (Par 105): **107,106,105,103,103 102,96,93,90,82**
toteswingers 1&2 £30.50, 2&3 £22.60, 1&3 £45.50 CSF £134.08 CT £2765.26 TOTE £18.90: £4.80, £2.00, £6.70; EX 171.70 Trifecta £1483.50 Part won. Pool: £1978.13 - 0.19 winning units..
Owner Danethorpe Racing Partnership **Bred** West Wind Farm **Trained** Willoughton, Lincs

FOCUS
This modest sprint handicap was run at a sound pace, but it proved another race where it paid to race handily. The winner is rated back to his best.

458 HORSE RACING BEST BETS AT BOOKMAKERS.CO.UK H'CAP 2m 119y(P)
7:20 (7:21) (Class 6) (0-60,60) 4-Y-0+ **£1,940** (£577; £288; £144) **Stalls** Low

Form RPR

12-3 **1** **Goldan Jess (IRE)**[29] 22 9-9-4 **52**.................................... AdamKirby 9 60
(Philip Kirby) *led at ordinary gallop: rdn and qcknd 2f out: kpt on fnl f: unchal* **1/1**[1]

040- **2** 1 ½ **Life Of Laughter (USA)**[41] 8214 5-9-0 **48**................... StevieDonohoe 7 54
(Willie Musson) *t.k.h in midfield: effrt over 2f out: hung lft and chsd wnr ins fnl f: r.o* **7/1**[3]

00/3 **3** 1 ¼ **Esteem**[14] 235 10-9-7 **55**......................................(t) TomMcLaughlin 13 59
(David Evans) *hld up in tch: effrt over 2f out: kpt on u.p ins fnl f* **25/1**

06-5 **4** nk **Jezza**[17] 208 7-9-5 **60**.. RyanTate(7) 5 64
(Karen George) *s.i.s: bhd: hdwy to chse wnr 2f out: sn rdn: hung lft ins fnl f: sn no ex* **12/1**

060/ **5** ¾ **Kijivu**[36] 6753 8-8-5 **46** oh1.......................................(bt) SemiraPashai(7) 2 49
(Alastair Lidderdale) *prom: outpcd over 2f out: rallied fnl f: kpt on: no imp* **40/1**

1-36 **6** ½ **El Bravo**[7] 361 7-9-10 **58**... RobertWinston 4 61
(Shaun Harris) *prom: effrt whn n.m.r on ins over 2f out: no imp over 1f out* **4/1**[2]

63-3 **7** 2 **Party Palace**[20] 165 9-8-13 **47**....................................... JimmyQuinn 1 47
(Stuart Howe) *t.k.h: chsd wnr to 2f out: sn drvn and outpcd* **14/1**

/0-6 **8** 7 **Dane Cottage**[29] 22 6-8-11 **50**.............................. RachealKneller(5) 3 42
(Richard Ford) *hld up: drvn and struggling over 3f out: btn fnl 2f* **20/1**

50/6 **9** 6 **Poppy Gregg**[29] 12 8-8-12 **46** oh1..........................(v) RichardThomas 10 31
(Dr Jeremy Naylor) *hld up: struggling 4f out: sn btn* **33/1**

350/ **10** 1 **Postmaster**[194] 5020 11-9-1 **49**...................................(t) DavidProbert 12 32
(Tim Vaughan) *hld up: rdn over 3f out: sn n.d* **12/1**

00/0 **11** 1 ½ **Share Option**[21] 132 11-8-12 **46** oh1..................... MichaelO'Connell 11 28
(Tony Carroll) *hld up: rdn over 3f out: nvr on terms* **50/1**

60-6 **12** 3 **Arbeejay**[28] 33 4-8-5 **46** oh1......................................(t) JoeFanning 8 24
(Simon Hodgson) *cl up tl rdn and wknd over 2f out* **50/1**

06-0 **13** 74 **Merevale**[5] 406 4-8-5 **46** oh1.......................................[1] AndrewMullen 6
(Michael Appleby) *hld up in midfield: hung lft and lost pl 4f out: sn struggling and eased: t.o* **10/1**

3m 45.33s (3.53) **Going Correction** +0.175s/f (Slow)
WFA 4 from 5yo+ 7lb 13 Ran SP% **131.6**
Speed ratings (Par 101): **98,97,96,96,96 95,95,91,88,88 87,86,51**
toteswingers 1&2 £3.30, 2&3 £65.40, 1&3 £10.30 CSF £9.18 CT £132.22 TOTE £2.10: £1.10, £3.50, £8.70; EX 11.70 Trifecta £239.20 Pool: £1484.78 - 4.65 winning units..
Owner The Jessies,Colin Fletcher,Philip Kirby **Bred** Bendis Partnership **Trained** Middleham, N Yorks

FOCUS
An ordinary staying handicap and another winner from the front. Pretty straightforward form.

459 FREE SPORTS BETTING AT BOOKMAKERS.CO.UK H'CAP 1m 141y(P)
7:50 (7:50) (Class 6) (0-60,58) 3-Y-O **£1,940** (£577; £288; £144) **Stalls** Low

Form RPR

5-11 **1** **Taxiformissbyron**[8] 336 3-9-7 **58** 6ex........................... DanielTudhope 4 69
(Michael Herrington) *trckd ldrs: led on bit ent fnl f: qcknd clr: readily* **8/11**[1]

0-32 **2** 6 **Armada Bay (IRE)**[10] 310 3-9-3 **54**................................... TomEaves 5 51
(Bryan Smart) *led: rdn wl over 2f out: hdd appr fnl f: no ch w wnr* **9/2**[3]

000- **3** 3 ¼ **Silver Fawn (IRE)**[142] 6121 3-8-9 **46**............................ DuranFentiman 2 36
(John Weymes) *in tch: drvn and outpcd 3f out: styd on fnl f: nvr able to chal* **22/1**

000- **4** ¾ **Faither**[64] 7900 3-9-6 **57**... JoeFanning 7 45
(Keith Dalgleish) *trckd ldrs: rdn over 2f out: wknd over 1f out* **5/2**[2]

0-06 **5** 9 **Jonny Wombat**[10] 310 3-8-1 **45**..................................(b[1]) VictorSantos(7) 3 12
(Richard Ford) *hld up in tch: struggling 3f out: btn fnl 2f* **28/1**

1m 53.41s (2.91) **Going Correction** +0.175s/f (Slow) 5 Ran SP% **112.5**
Speed ratings (Par 95): **94,88,85,85,77**
CSF £4.70 TOTE £1.80: £1.10, £2.10; EX 3.60 Trifecta £17.50 Pool: £1309.49 - 55.99 winning units..
Owner H Hurst **Bred** Hugh M Hurst **Trained** Cold Kirby, N Yorks

FOCUS
This was run at an uneven pace and the in-form winner hosed up. It was a weak race though.
T/Jkpt: Not won. T/Plt: £223.80 to a £1 stake. Pool of £87823.44 - 286.34 winning tickets.
T/Qpdt: £18.50 to a £1 stake. Pool of £12247.74 - 488.24 winning tickets. RY

[445]CAGNES-SUR-MER
Thursday, January 31
OFFICIAL GOING: Fibresand: standard

460a PRIX DE L'ILE SAINT-HONORAT (MAIDEN) (3YO COLTS & GELDINGS) (FIBRESAND) 1m (F)
12:30 (12:00) 3-Y-O **£9,756** (£3,902; £2,926; £1,951; £975)

RPR

1 **Villequier (FR)** 3-8-13 0.. IoritzMendizabal 11 78
(J-C Rouget, France) **7/2**[2]

2 2 **Dha Chara (IRE)**[12] 286 3-8-13 0............................ ThomasMessina 4 73
(Reg Hollinshead) *racd in midfield: prog bhd ldng gp end of bk st: swtchd to outside: rdn 2f out: tk ld u.p 1 1/2f out: wnt 3 l clr: chal and hdd 100yds out: styd on wl* **16/1**

3 3 **Dark Flinch (FR)** 3-8-13 0..................................... FabienLefebvre 12 66
(G Martin, Austria) **43/1**

4 2 ½ **Janaab (IRE)** 3-8-13 0.......................................(p) LouisBeuzelin 9 60
(J E Hammond, France) **14/1**

5 1 **Iftikaar (IRE)** 3-9-2 0........................... Francois-XavierBertras 10 61
(F Rohaut, France) **6/1**

6 2 ½ **Indian Walk (FR)** 3-9-2 0.. GuillaumeMillet 8 55
(M Gentile, France) **43/10**[3]

7 1 ½ **Microtheos (FR)** 3-8-13 0................................... SebastienMaillot 3 49
(M Boutin, France) **59/1**

8 ½ **Le Meltem (FR)** 3-8-13 0.. DarioVargiu 7 48
(Laura Grizzetti, Italy) **126/1**

9 ½ **Everest Hill** 3-8-9 0... VJanacek 2 43
(V Luka Jr, Czech Republic) **55/1**

10 nk **I'Ll Be Your Man** 3-8-13 0.. FilipMinarik 6 46
(M Figge, Germany) **37/1**

0 **Tiberio (SPA)**[27] 72 3-8-13 0..............................(b[1]) StephanePasquier 1
(M Delzangles, France) **15/2**

0 **Carletti (IRE)**[13] 270 3-9-2 0.. ThierryThulliez 5
(G Botti, France) **5/2**[1]

1m 37.28s (97.28) 12 Ran SP% **117.4**
WIN (incl. 1 euro stake): 4.50. PLACES: 2.30, 3.90, 8.40. DF: 40.10. 58.70.
Owner Gerard Augustin-Normand **Bred** Mat Daguzan-Garros & Rolling Hills Farm **Trained** Pau, France

The Form Book Flat, Raceform Ltd, Compton, RG20 6NL.

461a PRIX DE THEOULE-SUR-MER (CLAIMER) (3YO) (FIBRESAND) 1m (F)
1:35 (12:00) 3-Y-O £6,910 (£2,764; £2,073; £1,382; £691)

RPR

1 **Lily Merrill**[26] 3-8-8 0 IoritzMendizabal 3 69
(J-M Lefebvre, France) **138/10**

2 1 **Bijou Bijou (FR)**[89] 3-9-6 0 DarioVargiu 6 79
(Laura Grizzetti, Italy) **63/10**[3]

3 ¾ **Got Bird (FR)**[47] 3-8-13 0 (p) JulienAuge 13 70
(C Ferland, France) **19/1**

4 1 ½ **Shareel (FR)**[22] 3-8-8 0 (p) ThierryThulliez 10 62
(N Clement, France) **12/1**

5 ½ **Tempete En Mer (FR)**[83] 3-8-3 0 (p) AntoineCoutier(5) 4 60
(F Chappet, France) **27/1**

6 1 **Green Medi (FR)**[82] 7692 3-9-3 0 (p) MarcLerner(3) 8 70
(Y Durepaire, France) **19/5**[2]

7 shd **Maderienne (FR)**[22] 3-8-8 0 ThomasMessina 12 58
(L Baudron, France) **35/1**

8 snk **Woza Moya (USA)**[9] 331 3-9-2 0 (b) LouisBeuzelin 1 66
(Gay Kelleway) *broke wl on ins: stdd to r in 3rd: r.o u.p in st to go 2nd 1 1/2f out: no ex ent fnl f: fdd* **46/1**

9 2 ½ **Daloisi (FR)** 3-8-13 0 (p) FabriceVeron 11 57
(C Scandella, France) **8/1**

10 2 ½ **Nulera (FR)** 3-8-8 0 JohanVictoire 5 46
(C Ferland, France) **12/1**

0 **Safrana (FR)**[104] 3-8-8 0 StephanePasquier 7
(D Prod'Homme, France) **5/2**[1]

0 **La Best (FR)** 3-8-8 0 (b[1]) FilipMinarik 9
(M Figge, Germany) **12/1**

1m 38.96s (98.96) **12** Ran SP% **117.5**
WIN (incl. 1 euro stake): 14.80. PLACES: 4.30, 2.60, 6.00. DF: 52.50. SF: 132.10.
Owner Mme Isabelle Garcon **Bred** E Ciampi & P Nataf **Trained** France

362 MEYDAN (L-H)
Thursday, January 31
OFFICIAL GOING: Tapeta: standard; turf: good

462a DUBAL BILLET TROPHY (H'CAP) (TURF) 1m 2f
2:30 (2:30) (95-108,108) 3-Y-O+
£55,214 (£18,404; £9,202; £4,601; £2,760; £1,840)

RPR

1 **Mushreq (AUS)**[7] 363 5-9-1 104 PaulHanagan 1 111
(M F De Kock, South Africa) *mid-div: smooth prog 2f out: led 1f out: r.o wl: comf* **13/8**[1]

2 1 ½ **Royal Empire (IRE)**[21] 151 4-9-2 106 SilvestreDeSousa 11 111
(Saeed bin Suroor) *mid-div: led 2f out: hdd 1f out: kpt on same pce* **4/1**[2]

3 5 ¾ **Start Right**[21] 151 6-8-8 97 (p) TedDurcan 13 90
(Saeed bin Suroor) *settled in rr: r.o fnl 2f but no ch w fnl two* **14/1**

4 1 ½ **Tanfeeth**[14] 242 5-8-11 100 (t) DaneO'Neill 14 90
(M Al Muhairi, UAE) *settled in rr: kpt on same pce fnl 1 1/2f but no ch w fnl two* **16/1**

5 1 ½ **Adroitly (AUS)**[229] 6-9-1 104 MickaelBarzalona 4 91
(Saeed bin Suroor) *settled in rr: chsd ldrs 2 1/2f out: kpt on same pce fnl 1 1/2f* **12/1**

6 hd **Anaerobio (ARG)**[14] 242 6-8-13 101 (t) PatCosgrave 12 88
(M F De Kock, South Africa) *in rr of mid-div: chsd ldrs 2f out: one pce fnl f* **14/1**

7 ¼ **Energia Davos (BRZ)**[102] 7282 5-9-2 105 (b) TadhgO'Shea 6 91
(Fabricio Borges, Sweden) *settled in rr: nvr able to chal but r.o fnl 1 1/2f* **33/1**

8 1 **Bank Of Burden (USA)**[126] 6-9-5 108 (t) Per-AndersGraberg 10 92
(Niels Petersen, Norway) *settled in rr: nr nrr to chal* **25/1**

9 9 **Universal (IRE)**[21] 151 4-8-9 99 AdrianNicholls 9 66
(Mark Johnston) *trckd ldrs tl wknd 2f out* **20/1**

10 hd **Malthouse (GER)**[67] 5-8-8 97 RichardMullen 15 62
(S Seemar, UAE) *trckd ldrs: ev ch 2f out: wknd fnl f* **25/1**

11 ½ **Court Circle**[144] 6091 6-9-0 102 PatDobbs 7 67
(Rune Haugen, Norway) *trckd ldrs tl outpcd 2f out* **25/1**

12 ¼ **Akeed Wafi (IRE)**[6] 393 4-8-10 100 RoystonFfrench 2 65
(A Al Raihe, UAE) *in rr of mid-div: n.d* **33/1**

13 ¾ **Alkimos (IRE)**[12] 292 5-8-13 101 (p) KierenFallon 8 64
(Saeed bin Suroor) *s.i.s: nvr nr to chal* **5/1**[3]

14 ¾ **Salon Soldier (GER)**[165] 5402 4-9-3 107 AStarke 3 69
(P Schiergen, Germany) *trckd ldrs tl wknd 2f out* **14/1**

15 ¼ **Paene Magnus (IRE)**[7] 363 4-8-9 99 (tp) KevinManning 5 60
(J S Bolger, Ire) *sn led: hdd & wknd 2f out* **20/1**

2m 1.93s (121.93)
WFA 4 from 5yo+ 2lb **15** Ran SP% **135.3**
CSF: 7.72 TRICAST: 78.64 WIN: 2.30 PLACES: 2.60, 1.40, 5.30 EXACTA: 12.00 TRIFECTA 171.00.
Owner Hamdan Al Maktoum **Bred** Shadwell Stud Australasia Ltd **Trained** South Africa

FOCUS
The sectionals show they went a nice even gallop (25.73, 24.16, 24.55, 24.51) before the winner came home in a rapid 22.92. The front two pulled a long way clear of a couple of proven handicappers in Start Right and Tanfeeth, and this is really strong form.

463a DUBAL POTLINES TROPHY (H'CAP) (TAPETA) 1m 1f 110y
3:05 (3:05) (95-105,105) 3-Y-O+
£40,490 (£13,496; £6,748; £3,374; £2,024; £1,349)

RPR

1 **Kassiano (GER)**[21] 151 4-8-11 98 TedDurcan 9 105+
(Saeed bin Suroor) *mid-div: smooth prog 2 1/2f out: led 1f out: comf* **5/2**[1]

2 ¼ **Con Artist (IRE)**[14] 241 6-9-3 102 SilvestreDeSousa 7 108
(Saeed bin Suroor) *trckd ldrs: led 2f out: hdd 1f out: kpt on same pce* **7/2**[2]

3 3 ¼ **Farrier (USA)**[21] 151 5-8-10 96 RichardMullen 11 94+
(S Seemar, UAE) *settled in rr: r.o fnl 2f: nrst fin* **14/1**

4 ½ **Banna Boirche (IRE)**[14] 241 7-9-3 102 ShaneFoley 4 100
(M Halford, Ire) *in rr of mid-div: r.o same pce fnl 2f* **11/1**

5 shd **Not A Given (USA)**[14] 241 4-9-2 102 MickaelBarzalona 1 101
(Mahmood Al Zarooni) *trckd ldrs: ev ch 2f out: one pce fnl 110yds* **10/1**

6 1 ¼ **Maritimer (CAN)**[82] 4-9-3 104 (t) ChristopheSoumillon 5 100
(Seth Benzel, U.S.A) *sn led: hdd 2 out: wknd fnl 1f* **20/1**

7 1 ¼ **Sandagiyr (FR)**[14] 241 5-9-2 101 PatDobbs 3 94
(Saeed bin Suroor) *in rr of mid-div: nvr able to chal* **7/1**[3]

8 ½ **Plantagenet (SPA)**[21] 151 6-9-3 102 CO'Donoghue 8 94
(G Arizkorreta Elosegui, Spain) *settled in rr: nvr nr to chal* **10/1**

9 2 **Mustaheel (IRE)**[177] 4935 4-9-4 105 PaulHanagan 13 93
(A Al Raihe, UAE) *s.i.s: settled ld: nvr nr to chal* **12/1**

10 3 ¾ **Royal Destination (IRE)**[12] 292 8-8-9 95 (vt) WayneSmith 10 74
(Fawzi Abdulla Nass, Bahrain) *mid-div: chsd ldrs 3f out: wknd fnl 1 1/2f* **33/1**

11 17 **Without Fear (FR)**[126] 5-9-1 100 Per-AndersGraberg 12 45
(Niels Petersen, Norway) *settled in rr: nvr in tch* **33/1**

12 1 ½ **Burj Alzain (IRE)**[75] 7772 5-9-1 100 KierenFallon 2 42
(Fawzi Abdulla Nass, Bahrain) *s.i.s: a in rr* **20/1**

13 1 ¾ **Kingsdesire (IRE)**[145] 6029 4-8-13 99 (t) MartinHarley 6 39
(Marco Botti) *trckd ldrs: ev ch 3f out: wknd fnl 1 1/2f* **9/1**

1m 58.64s (-0.36)
WFA 4 from 5yo+ 1lb **13** Ran SP% **129.6**
CSF: 11.24 TRICAST 109.52 EXACTA 16.60 TRIFECTA 127.90 WIN 2.60 PLACES: 1.00, 1.80, 4.40.
Owner Godolphin **Bred** Gestut Rottgen **Trained** Newmarket, Suffolk

FOCUS
Maritimer took the field along at steady early pace, going 26.64, 25.13, 25.34, 23.75 to the 1600m point. It paid to be handy, but the first two finishers were probably just the best two horses on the day and they had the race to themselves in the closing stages.

464a DUBAL EXCELLENCE TROPHY (H'CAP) (TURF) 5f
3:40 (3:40) (100-119,119) 3-Y-O+
£64,417 (£21,472; £10,736; £5,368; £3,220; £2,147)

RPR

1 **Medicean Man**[103] 7236 7-8-8 107 (p) HarryBentley 1 109
(Jeremy Gask) *s.i.s: chsd ldrs: led 1 1/2f out: jst hld on* **14/1**

2 ¾ **Russian Soul (IRE)**[14] 244 5-8-5 101 (p) ShaneFoley 11 103
(M Halford, Ire) *broke awkwardly: mid-div: r.o wl 1 1/2f: nrst fin* **9/2**[2]

3 ½ **Bear Behind (IRE)**[21] 150 4-8-5 104 RichardKingscote 4 102
(Tom Dascombe) *sn led: hdd 1 1/2f out: kpt on same pce fnl f* **8/1**[3]

4 ½ **Inxile (IRE)**[14] 244 8-8-8 107 (p) AdrianNicholls 15 103
(David Nicholls) *mid-div: r.o fnl 2f: nrst fin* **8/1**[3]

5 ¼ **Sholaan (IRE)**[124] 6666 4-8-5 102 (v) TadhgO'Shea 13 99
(D Selvaratnam, UAE) *mid-div: r.o fnl 1 1/2f* **14/1**

6 3 **Humidor (IRE)**[116] 6908 6-8-10 109 (t) JamesDoyle 6 93
(George Baker) *mid-div: kpt on same pce fnl 1 1/2f* **14/1**

7 shd **Shea Shea (SAF)**[278] 6-9-6 119 ChristopheSoumillon 3 103
(M F De Kock, South Africa) *trckd ldrs: ev ch 1 1/2f out: nt qckn fnl f* **15/8**[1]

8 hd **Beat Baby (IRE)**[126] 6-8-5 104 (t) Per-AndersGraberg 2 87
(Niels Petersen, Norway) *trckd ldrs tl outpcd fnl 2f* **25/1**

9 2 ½ **Desert Law (IRE)**[21] 150 5-8-5 104 SilvestreDeSousa 10 78
(Saeed bin Suroor) *nvr bttr than mid-div* **16/1**

10 1 ¼ **Pabusar**[21] 150 5-8-5 102 (b) HayleyTurner 5 73
(Jamie Osborne) *nvr bttr than mid-div* **25/1**

11 shd **Stonefield Flyer**[14] 244 4-8-5 101 RoystonFfrench 14 73
(Keith Dalgleish) *nvr able to chal* **33/1**

12 1 **Temple Meads**[21] 150 5-8-6 105 (v) RichardMullen 9 70
(David Brown) *trckd ldrs: hung lft 3f out: sn btn* **9/2**[2]

57.13s (57.13) **12** Ran SP% **129.9**
CSF: 81.90 TRICAST 568.11 EXACTA: 159.80 TRIFECTA 1022.90 WIN: 32.40, PLACES: 6.30, 1.90, 2.30.
Owner Stuart Dobb & Miss Kate Dobb **Bred** Barry Taylor **Trained** Sutton Veny, Wilts

FOCUS
Most of the runners were held in the stalls for longer than ideal after Beat Baby burst out of his gate just before the off. He didn't go far and was re-loaded, and the only other runner not in the stalls during the delay was Inxile. The field were spread across the track in the closing stages

465a DUBAL CASTHOUSE TROPHY (H'CAP) (TAPETA) 7f
4:15 (4:15) (100-110,110) 3-Y-O+
£44,171 (£14,723; £7,361; £3,680; £2,208; £1,472)

RPR

1 **Rerouted (USA)**[21] 152 5-9-3 108 ChristopheSoumillon 3 111
(M F De Kock, South Africa) *mid-div: smooth prog 3f out: rdn to ld fnl 55yds* **6/1**[2]

2 1 **Van Ellis**[103] 7236 4-9-1 106 MickaelBarzalona 8 106
(Mahmood Al Zarooni) *sn led: kicked clr 3f out: wknd fnl f: hdd cl home* **5/1**[1]

3 1 ¼ **Free Wheeling (AUS)**[82] 5-9-3 108 (tp) PatDobbs 10 105
(Saeed bin Suroor) *settled in rr: r.o fnl 2f: nrst fin* **16/1**

4 2 **Iver Bridge Lad**[14] 241 6-8-11 102 DaneO'Neill 5 93
(John Ryan) *mid-div: kpt on same pce fnl 2f* **8/1**[3]

5 3 **Smooth Operator (GER)**[7] 365 7-9-1 106 (b) TedDurcan 13 89
(Mario Hofer, Germany) *s.i.s: settled in rr: r.o fnl 1 1/2f: nrst fin* **14/1**

6 ¼ **Arnold Lane (IRE)**[21] 154 4-9-0 105 MartinHarley 7 87
(Mick Channon) *mid-div: kpt on same pce fnl 1 1/2f* **16/1**

7 1 ¼ **Pied A Terre (AUS)**[138] 5-9-0 105 KierenFallon 1 84
(Saeed bin Suroor) *trckd ldrs tl outpcd 3f out* **6/1**[2]

8 ½ **Ariete Arrollador**[21] 149 6-8-11 102 (e) CO'Donoghue 2 80
(G Arizkorreta Elosegui, Spain) *slowly away: nvr bttr than mid-div* **5/1**[1]

9 1 ½ **Nordic Truce (USA)**[14] 241 6-9-0 105 AStarke 9 79
(P Schiergen, Germany) *nvr rr to chal* **25/1**

10 3 **Lockwood**[21] 154 4-9-4 109 SilvestreDeSousa 14 75
(Saeed bin Suroor) *trckd ldrs: ev ch 3f out: wknd fnl 2f* **6/1**[2]

11 ¾ **Saint Bernard**[88] 7587 4-9-2 107 JamesDoyle 6 71
(Robert Cowell) *in rr of mid-div: nvr nr to chal* **20/1**

12 1 ¾ **Silver Ocean (USA)**[144] 5-9-5 110 Per-AndersGraberg 12 69
(Niels Petersen, Norway) *trckd ldrs: ev ch tl outpcd 3f out* **20/1**

13 ¾ **Alazeyab (USA)**[20] 180 7-9-2 107 (vt) PaulHanagan 4 64
(A Al Raihe, UAE) *trckd ldrs tl outpcd 3f out* **14/1**

14 1 ¾ **First City**[7] 366 7-9-3 108 RoystonFfrench 11 60
(A Al Raihe, UAE) *nvr bttr than mid-div* **16/1**

1m 24.2s (-1.00) **14** Ran SP% **131.7**
CSF: 38.64 TRICAST 485.75 WIN: 4.40 PLACES: 1.30, 1.90, 4.70 EXACTA: 36.50, TRIFECTA 695.50.
Owner Mssrs Chandler, Westwood Et Al **Bred** Juddmonte Farms Inc **Trained** South Africa

FOCUS
The front-running Van Ellis opened up a significant advantage rounding the bend, but the sectionals show he did so at great cost to his chance. He went 24.94 (400m), 22.83 (800m), 23.46 (1200m) before crawling through the final 200m in 13.15 (compared to 12.26 for the winner). It must be noted, while the winner was sat sixth at the 800m point, the third, fourth and fifth home filled the bottom three places, and clearly the closers are flattered. The winner is rated back to his best.

466a AL RASHIDIYA SPONSORED BY DUBAL (GROUP 2) (TURF) 1m 1f
4:50 (4:50) 3-Y-0+

£73,619 (£24,539; £12,269; £6,134; £3,680; £2,453)

RPR

1 **The Apache (SAF)**369 6-9-0 115.......... ChristopheSoumillon 6 116
(M F De Kock, South Africa) *trckd ldrs: led 1 1/2f out: r.o wl* **12/1**

2 3/4 **City Style (USA)**208 [3880] 7-9-0 115.......... MickaelBarzalona 5 114
(Mahmood Al Zarooni) *settled in rr: r.o fnl 2f: nrst fin* **6/1**2

3 2 1/4 **Sharestan (IRE)**21 [152] 5-9-0 113.......... SilvestreDeSousa 1 112+
(Saeed bin Suroor) *trckd: n.m.r 2 1/2f out: r.o fnl 1 1/2f: nrst fin* **8/13**1

4 1/2 **Aesop's Fables (USA)**169 [5250] 4-9-4 117.......... KierenFallon 3 114
(Saeed bin Suroor) *mid-div: chsd ldrs 2 1/2f out: could nt qckn fnl f* **8/1**3

5 hd **Albaasil (IRE)**327 [879] 5-9-0 115.......... PatDobbs 2 108
(Doug Watson, UAE) *mid-div: kpt on same pce fnl 1 1/2f* **20/1**

6 1 1/4 **So Beautiful (FR)**21 [152] 4-8-13 113.......... PaulHanagan 9 106
(Doug Watson, UAE) *mid-div: chsd ldrs 2f out: one pce fnl f* **8/1**3

7 1/2 **Light Heavy (IRE)**118 [6855] 4-8-13 113..........(tp) KevinManning 10 105
(J S Bolger, Ire) *settled in rr: nvr nr to chal* **16/1**

8 3/4 **Derbaas (USA)**53 7-9-0 113..........(t) DaneO'Neill 8 103
(A Al Raihe, UAE) *trckd ldng pair: led 3f out: hdd 1 1/2f out: wknd fnl f* **16/1**

9 22 **Fanunalter**21 [153] 7-9-3 113.......... CO'Donoghue 4 60
(Marco Botti) *in rr of mid-div: nvr able to chal* **33/1**

10 18 **Do It All (USA)**306 [1143] 6-9-0 113..........(t) TedDurcan 7 19
(Saeed bin Suroor) *sn led: hdd & wknd 3f out* **25/1**

1m 49.68s (109.68)
WFA 4 from 5yo+ 1lb **10** Ran SP% **129.4**
CSF: 89.33 EXACTA: 61.50, TRIFECTA: 195.30 WIN: 6.30, PLACES: 1.40, 2.90, 1.00.
Owner Sh Mohd Bin Khalifa Al Maktoum & Winston Chow **Bred** Scott Bros **Trained** South Africa

FOCUS
The third straight year this race has held Group 2 status. It didn't look a strong contest beforehand, and the favourite got no sort of run, but the winner is open to considerable improvement. Do It All gradually upped the tempo, going 26.42 (400m), 24.42 (800m), 24.06 (1200m).

467a DUBAL TROPHY (H'CAP) (TURF) 7f
5:25 (5:25) (100-113,113) 3-Y-0+

£64,417 (£21,472; £10,736; £5,368; £3,220; £2,147)

RPR

1 **Time Prisoner (USA)**350 [590] 6-9-4 **112**.......... MickaelBarzalona 9 114+
(Mahmood Al Zarooni) *mid-div: smooth prog 2f out: led 55yds out: r.o wl* **4/1**2

2 3/4 **Dux Scholar**91 [7515] 5-9-4 **112**..........(bt) KierenFallon 13 112
(Seth Benzel, U.S.A) *trckd ldrs: led 1 1/2f out: hdd fnl 55yds* **14/1**

3 2 1/2 **Dubawi Sound**159 [5597] 5-8-7 **101**..........(t) HarryBentley 8 94
(David Brown) *mid-div: chsd ldrs 3f out: kpt on same pce fnl f* **11/2**3

4 shd **Kenny Powers**21 [154] 4-8-11 **106**..........(vt) DaneO'Neill 5 98
(Tom Dascombe) *slowly away: mid-div: kpt on same pce fnl 1 1/2f* **7/1**

5 shd **Justineo**21 [154] 4-8-6 **100**.......... ShaneFoley 16 93
(Roger Varian) *trckd ldrs: led 2f out: hdd 1 1/2f out: kpt on same pce* **20/1**

6 1 **Final Button (SAF)**14 [244] 5-8-9 **103** ow1..........(b) PatCosgrave 7 93+
(M F De Kock, South Africa) *mid-div: n.d but kpt on fnl 1 1/2f* **16/1**

7 nse **Field Of Dream**117 [6868] 6-8-8 **102**..........(b) HayleyTurner 11 90+
(Jamie Osborne) *s.i.s: n.d but kpt on fnl 1 1/2f* **14/1**

8 3/4 **Jaasoos (IRE)**21 [154] 9-8-10 **105**.......... JamesDoyle 6 96+
(D Selvaratnam, UAE) *nvr bttr than mid-div* **33/1**

9 shd **Red Dubawi (IRE)**14 [242] 5-8-10 **105**.......... FergalLynch 10 92
(David Marnane, Ire) *in rr of mid-div: nvr nr to chal but kpt on fnl 1 1/2f* **18/1**

10 1 1/4 **Saamidd**250 [2505] 5-9-5 **113**..........(t) SilvestreDeSousa 14 97
(Saeed bin Suroor) *slowly away: nvr nr to chal* **3/1**1

11 1/4 **Captain Ramius (IRE)**21 [154] 7-9-0 **108**.......... PaulHanagan 2 92
(Kevin Ryan) *a in mid-div* **20/1**

12 1 1/2 **Rosendhal (IRE)**14 [244] 6-9-0 **108**..........(bt) CO'Donoghue 3 87
(G Botti, France) *trckd ldrs tl outpcd 2 1/2f out* **33/1**

13 3/4 **Kavanagh (SAF)**7 [365] 6-9-4 **112**.......... JGeroudis 1 89
(M F De Kock, South Africa) *trckd ldrs tl outpcd 3f out* **6/1**

14 2 1/2 **Benji's Empire (AUS)**21 [150] 7-8-7 **101**..........(e) TedDurcan 4 72
(S Burridge, Singapore) *sn led: hdd 3f out: sn btn* **16/1**

15 5 1/4 **Tertio Bloom (SWE)**21 [149] 8-8-8 **102**..........(t) TadhgO'Shea 15 59
(Fabricio Borges, Sweden) *nvr able to chal* **33/1**

16 12 **Montmorency (IRE)**21 [149] 7-8-6 **100**..........(vt) RichardMullen 12 24
(S Seemar, UAE) *nvr able to chal* **16/1**

1m 24.27s (84.27) **16** Ran SP% **141.8**
CSF: 66.10 TRICAST 333.63 EXACTA 40.20 WIN: 4.50 TRIFECTA: 637.80 PLACEPOT: £36.80 to a £1 stake. Pool: £10004.17 - 198.24 winning tickets; QUADPOT: £16.00 to a £1 stake. Pool: £448.30 - 20.70 winning tickets..
Owner Godolphin **Bred** Darley **Trained** Newmarket, Suffolk

FOCUS
Just an ordinary gallop (25.27, 23.23, 23.11 to 1200m) in this good-quality handicap.

446 LINGFIELD (L-H)
Friday, February 1

OFFICIAL GOING: Standard
Wind: Light, against Weather: Rain before racing, becoming fine

468 BET ON YOUR MOBILE AT BLUESQ.COM CLAIMING STKS 7f (P)
12:30 (12:30) (Class 6) 3-Y-0 **£2,045** (£603; £302) **Stalls** Low

Form RPR

1-41 1 **It's Only Business**7 [371] 3-9-2 58..........(p) JimmyQuinn 3 67
(Bill Turner) *t.k.h: trckd ldng pair: wnt 2nd wl over 1f out: drvn and styd on fnl f to ld last 75yds* **7/2**3

3-33 2 1/2 **Go Far**4 [425] 3-9-2 68..........(p) NatashaEaton(5) 1 71
(Alan Bailey) *led and set gd pce: pushed 2 l clr over 1f out: rdn fnl f: hdd and nt qckn last 75yds* **7/4**2

-441 3 8 **The Black Jacobin**6 [402] 3-9-1 64..........(b) RyanMoore 4 43
(J S Moore) *trckd ldr: rdn 2f out: fnd nil and sn lost 2nd: wknd qckly over 1f out* **6/4**1

2-44 4 2 3/4 **Hardy Red (IRE)**17 [216] 3-8-13 68.......... FergusSweeney 6 34
(Jamie Osborne) *t.k.h: trckd ldng pair on outer: rdn 1/2-way: wknd over 2f out* **8/1**

0-0 5 1 1/4 **How You Fixed (IRE)**18 [211] 3-9-7 0.......... AndreaAtzeni 5 39
(Denis Quinn) *sn pushed along: a in last: struggling fr 1/2-way* **100/1**

1m 24.18s (-0.62) **Going Correction** -0.05s/f (Stan) **5** Ran SP% **110.7**
Speed ratings (Par 95): **101,100,91,88,86**
CSF £10.14 TOTE £4.30: £2.50, £1.10; EX 11.60 Trifecta £26.70 Pool: £1,765.95 - 49.65 winning units..
Owner Ansells Of Watford **Bred** South Wind Bloodstock **Trained** Sigwells, Somerset

FOCUS
A modest claimer, but featuring a couple of recent winners and one of those proved strongest in the latter stages.

469 ASHDOWN FOREST (S) H'CAP 2m (P)
1:00 (1:00) (Class 6) (0-60,60) 4-Y-0+ **£2,045** (£603; £302) **Stalls** Low

Form RPR

040- 1 **Hoonose**41 [8229] 4-8-4 **46** oh1..........(v1) JoeFanning 8 59
(Pat Eddery) *hld up in midfield: smooth prog fr 4f out to trck ldr wl over 2f out: rdn to ld over 1f out: drew away* **6/1**

635- 2 6 **On The Feather**18 [8060] 7-9-5 **60**..........(b) WilliamTwiston-Davies(5) 10 66
(Jim Best) *hld up in last quartet: gng easily 4f out: nt clr passage over 3f out: gd prog wl over 2f out to go 4th: sn rdn: styd on to take 2nd fnl f: no ch w wnr* **12/1**

505- 3 nk **Galiotto (IRE)**49 [8104] 7-9-9 **59**..........(v) RyanMoore 12 65
(Gary Moore) *hld up in last quartet: prog on outer over 3f out: rdn to dispute 2nd fnl f: no ch w wnr* **5/2**1

24-0 4 3 1/4 **Red Mystique (IRE)**30 [12] 4-8-8 **50**..........(b) FergusSweeney 4 52
(Philip Hide) *trckd ldrs: prog gng easily to ld over 4f out: drvn and hdd over 1f out: wknd* **3/1**2

02-4 5 9 **Perfect Shot (IRE)**30 [12] 7-8-12 **51**.......... MarkCoumbe(3) 1 42
(Michael Attwater) *cl up on inner: lost pl 4f out: nt clr run over 3f out and only 8th over 2f out: drvn and kpt on to take 5th wl over 1f out: no ch* **9/2**3

00-0 6 14 **Imperial Elegance**4 [417] 4-8-1 **46** oh1.......... SimonPearce(3) 5 20
(Sheena West) *trckd ldr 5f: styd prom: rdn to go 2nd again over 3f out to wl over 2f out: wknd qckly* **50/1**

00-0 7 2 1/4 **Za'Lan (USA)**22 [131] 4-8-10 **52**..........(v) LiamKeniry 13 23
(Chris Gordon) *dwlt: mostly in last pair: pushed along and no prog 4f out: bhd after* **20/1**

000/ 8 nk **Ede's**17 [7490] 13-8-3 **46** oh1.......... SophieRalston(7) 6 17
(Pat Phelan) *s.s: hld up in last: pushed along over 4f out: nvr a factor* **33/1**

/4-4 9 1/2 **Watch The Birdie (IRE)**16 [227] 5-9-7 **57**.......... WilliamCarson 2 27
(Ronald Harris) *t.k.h: led to over 10f out: rdn over 4f out: wknd wl over 2f out* **25/1**

-446 10 9 **Formidable Guest**9 [343] 9-9-1 **51**.......... RobertHavlin 7 11
(Jamie Poulton) *hld up bhd ldrs: quick move to ld over 10f out: hdd 7f out: short of room 6f out: rdn over 3f out: sn wknd* **16/1**

/0-0 11 3 3/4 **Bet Noir (IRE)**22 [132] 8-8-10 **46** oh1.......... DavidProbert 11
(Tony Carroll) *hld up in midfield: rdn over 4f out: wknd 3f out: eased fnl 2f* **50/1**

30-5 12 34 **Faraway Land (USA)**21 [157] 5-8-9 **52**..........(b1) ShelleyBirkett(7) 9
(Julia Feilden) *dwlt: t.k.h: rapid prog on outer to go prom after 4f: led 7f out to over 4f out: wknd rapidly: t.o* **14/1**

3m 22.1s (-3.60) **Going Correction** -0.05s/f (Stan)
WFA 4 from 5yo+ 6lb **12** Ran SP% **121.8**
Speed ratings (Par 101): **107,104,103,102,97 90,89,89,89,84 82,65**
toteswingers 1&2 £13.40, 1&3 £4.00, 2&3 £6.20 CSF £73.03 CT £228.87 TOTE £6.00: £2.50, £3.50, £1.10; EX 151.40 Trifecta £938.50 Pool: £2,259.42 - 1.80 winning units..The winner was bought in for 5,200gns.
Owner Miss Emma L Owen **Bred** Mrs R F Johnson Houghton **Trained** Nether Winchendon, Bucks
■ Stewards' Enquiry : Shelley Birkett one-day ban; careless riding (15th Feb).

FOCUS
A big field for this long-distance seller.

470 DORMANSLAND H'CAP 6f (P)
1:30 (1:31) (Class 6) (0-65,63) 3-Y-0 **£2,045** (£603; £302) **Stalls** Low

Form RPR

646- 1 **Malaysian Boleh**32 [8302] 3-9-7 **63**.......... HayleyTurner 4 69
(Simon Dow) *sn hld up bhd ldrs gng wl: shkn up to chal over 1f out: led ins fnl f: drvn and edgd lft: styd on* **2/1**1

4-34 2 3/4 **Devout (IRE)**11 [310] 3-8-9 **51**.......... FergusSweeney 1 55
(Jamie Osborne) *trckd ldrs: effrt 2f out: led jst over 1f out to ins fnl f: styd on but hld after* **8/1**

45-3 3 1 1/2 **Gebayl**22 [148] 3-9-5 **61**.......... AdamKirby 6 60
(James Tate) *led: rdn and hung rt bnd 2f out: continued to edge rt and hdd jst over 1f out: one pce* **2/1**1

2-23 4 1 **Princess Cammie (IRE)**7 [368] 3-8-12 **59**.. WilliamTwiston-Davies(5) 5 55
(Mike Murphy) *s.i.s: sn in 6th: taken wd bnd 4f out and keen: rdn and effrt on inner over 1f out: no imp fnl f* **7/1**3

04-5 5 2 3/4 **Spreading**16 [228] 3-9-0 **56**.......... LiamKeniry 7 43
(Michael Blanshard) *sn chsd ldr: rdn and wd bnd 2f out: fdd over 1f out* **20/1**

4-25 6 nk **Marmot Bay (IRE)**4 [424] 3-9-1 **57**.......... RyanMoore 2 43
(Alastair Lidderdale) *t.k.h on outer of ldrs: wd bnd 2f out: sn rdn and nt qckn: wknd* **5/1**2

060- 7 2 3/4 **Exit Clause**35 [8274] 3-8-13 **60**..........(t) GeorgeDowning(5) 3 37
(Tony Carroll) *slowly away: a last: urged along and no prog 3f out* **25/1**

1m 12.33s (0.43) **Going Correction** -0.05s/f (Stan) **7** Ran SP% **115.6**
Speed ratings (Par 95): **95,94,92,90,87 86,82**
CSF £20.09 TOTE £3.20: £2.60, £4.50; EX 24.30 Trifecta £83.80 Pool: £2,843.24 - 25.42 winning units..
Owner JCG Chua & CK Ong **Bred** John & Sue Davis **Trained** Epsom, Surrey

FOCUS
A modest 3-y-o sprint and a well-supported winner.

471 MARRIOTT HOTEL AT LINGFIELD PARK H'CAP (DIV I) 6f (P)
2:00 (2:01) (Class 6) (0-52,52) 4-Y-0+ **£2,045** (£603; £302) **Stalls** Low

Form RPR

0-24 1 **Artful Lady (IRE)**4 [423] 4-9-6 **51**.......... RyanMoore 1 59
(George Margarson) *disp ld on inner to 1/2-way: lost pl and rdn over 2f out: rallied over 1f out: drvn to ld ins fnl f: hld on wl* **6/4**1

22-4 **2** *nk* **My Scat Daddy (USA)**[18] 205 4-9-4 **49**......................... DavidProbert 9 56
(Brett Johnson) *fractious preliminaries: hld up in 9th: prog 2f out: drvn to take 2nd ins fnl f: styd on but hld nr fin* **2/1**[2]

03-0 **3** *¾* **Christopher Chua (IRE)**[22] 139 4-9-7 **52**.................... HayleyTurner 7 57
(Simon Dow) *hld up bhd ldrs: cl up 2f out: drvn over 1f out: styd on but nvr quite pce to chal* **9/2**[3]

446- **4** *½* **Metropolitan Chief**[270] 1910 9-9-1 **46**......................... TomMcLaughlin 5 49
(Paul Burgoyne) *racd freely: disp ld tl def advantage over 2f out: urged along over 1f out: hdd and fdd ins fnl f* **20/1**

5-00 **5** *nse* **Dingaan (IRE)**[10] 327 10-9-1 **46** oh1.................................. LiamKeniry 2 49
(Peter Grayson) *hld up bhd ldrs: effrt on inner over 1f out: rdn and kpt on but nvr able to chal* **33/1**

-013 **6** *½* **Athaakeel (IRE)**[8] 355 7-9-4 **49**...............................(b) KirstyMilczarek 4 50
(Ronald Harris) *pushed along in last after 2f: brought wdst of all bnd 2f out: nrly agains nr side rail fnl f: r.o: nrst fin* **14/1**

240 **7** *1¾* **Summer Sun**[13] 276 4-9-5 **50**..(p) AdamKirby 6 46
(Phil McEntee) *stdd s: hld up bhd ldrs: shkn up and nt qckn wl over 1f out: n.d after* **14/1**

5-26 **8** *1¼* **First Rebellion**[9] 339 4-8-13 **47**.................................[1] RaulDaSilva(3) 8 39
(Tony Carroll) *disp ld to 1/2-way: rdn in 2nd over 2f out: wknd over 1f out* **14/1**

-054 **9** *½* **Dvinsky (USA)**[13] 274 12-9-7 **52**..................................(b) JimmyQuinn 3 42
(Paul Howling) *drvn to dispute ld and nvr able to dominate: lost pl over 2f out: fdd over 1f out* **12/1**

5-00 **10** *2¾* **Spoof Master (IRE)**[22] 143 9-8-12 **46** oh1............(t) SimonPearce(3) 10 27
(Lydia Pearce) *racd wd bhd ldrs: lost grnd bnd 2f out: wknd* **50/1**

1m 12.19s (0.29) **Going Correction** -0.05s/f (Stan) **10** Ran SP% **128.9**
Speed ratings (Par 101): **96,95,94,93,93 93,90,89,88,84**
toteswingers 1&2 £1.80, 1&3 £3.20, 2&3 £2.50 CSF £5.19 CT £12.44 TOTE £2.80: £1.10, £1.10, £1.50; EX 7.90 Trifecta £27.30 Pool: £4,518.85 - 123.92 winning units..
Owner Graham Lodge Partnership **Bred** Michael Begley **Trained** Newmarket, Suffolk

FOCUS
This moderate older-horse handicap was run only slightly faster than the preceding race for 3-y-os.

472 MARRIOTT HOTEL AT LINGFIELD PARK H'CAP (DIV II) 6f (P)
2:35 (2:35) (Class 6) (0-52,52) 4-Y-0+ **£2,045** (£603; £302) **Stalls** Low

Form RPR

03- **1** **Spellmaker**[192] 4424 4-9-1 **46**... WilliamCarson 3 55
(Tony Newcombe) *dwlt: t.k.h and sn in midfield: prog to chse clr ldr 2f out: clsd to ld last 100yds: edgd lft after: hld on* **2/1**[1]

-535 **2** *nk* **Do More Business (IRE)**[16] 223 6-8-11 **49**...............(v) NedCurtis(7) 8 57
(Alison Batchelor) *stdd s: hld up wl off the pce and last to 1/2-way: prog over 2f out: rdn to chal ins fnl f: carried lft then bmpd last stride* **5/2**[2]

00-0 **3** *1¼* **Mary's Pet**[23] 115 6-9-7 **52**...(p) AdamKirby 1 56
(Lee Carter) *pushed up to ld and set str pce: 3 l clr 2f out: hdd and no ex last 100yds* **9/2**[3]

-000 **4** *1¼* **Fantasy Fighter (IRE)**[13] 277 8-9-1 **46** oh1...............(p) JimmyQuinn 9 46
(Ronald Harris) *hld up: last fr 1/2-way: pushed along and prog over 1f out: reminders to take 4th fnl f: no imp after* **14/1**

006- **5** *2¼* **Rooknrasbryripple**[132] 6496 4-9-2 **47**.............................. JoeFanning 2 40
(Ralph Smith) *chsd ldng pair to 1/2-way: sn lost pl: brief effrt over 1f out: no hdwy fnl f* **25/1**

05-0 **6** *1¼* **Le King Beau (USA)**[22] 139 4-9-7 **52**...........................(v) SeanLevey 7 41
(John Bridger) *a towards rr: rdn and no prog 2f out: wknd* **12/1**

06-5 **7** *2¼* **Stoneacre Hull (IRE)**[15] 236 4-9-5 **50**............................... LiamKeniry 5 32
(Peter Grayson) *chsd ldrs on outer: wd bnd 2f out: sn wknd* **16/1**

00-0 **8** *2½* **Fast Samurai (USA)**[23] 111 5-8-12 **46**...................(v[1]) RaulDaSilva(3) 4 20
(Tony Carroll) *chsd clr ldr to 2f out: wknd* **7/1**

1m 11.57s (-0.33) **Going Correction** -0.05s/f (Stan) **8** Ran SP% **116.7**
Speed ratings (Par 101): **100,99,97,96,93 91,88,85**
toteswingers 1&2 £2.00, 1&3 £3.40, 2&3 £3.50 CSF £7.33 CT £19.45 TOTE £2.70: £1.30, £1.20, £1.40; EX 8.40 Trifecta £26.10 Pool: £4,815.46 - 138.23 winning units..
Owner Joli Racing **Bred** Dxb Bloodstock Ltd **Trained** Yarnscombe, Devon
■ Stewards' Enquiry : William Carson three-day ban; careless riding (15th,16th&18th Feb).

FOCUS
The second leg of this sprint handicap was run 0.62 secs faster than the first division and produced a desperate finish.

473 SHARPTHORNE MAIDEN STKS 1m 2f (P)
3:10 (3:10) (Class 5) 3-Y-O+ **£2,726** (£805; £402) **Stalls** Low

Form RPR

42-0 **1** **Dali's Lover (IRE)**[7] 373 3-8-0 66.................................... JimmyQuinn 4 66
(Charles Hills) *shoved along early in 4th: rdn over 2f out: mounted chal on outer fnl f: drvn and styd on to ld post* **16/1**

2 *hd* **Cousin Khee**[15] 6-9-13 0... GeorgeBaker 1 74
(Hughie Morrison) *trckd ldr 2f: mostly in 3rd after: looking for room over 1f out: clsd to ld 150yds out: rdn and kpt on same pce after: hdd post* **5/2**[2]

5-5 **3** *1* **Ofcoursewecan (USA)**[18] 211 3-8-5 0............................... JoeFanning 6 68
(Mark Johnston) *trckd ldr after 2f: shkn up to ld wl over 1f out: hdd and one pce last 150yds* **9/2**[3]

6-2 **4** *hd* **Good Evans**[18] 211 3-8-5 0.. HayleyTurner 5 68
(Tom Dascombe) *sn led and set mod pce: hdd and nt qckn wl over 1f out: kpt on one pce after* **5/4**[1]

0-0 **5** *hd* **Pencombe (FR)**[18] 211 3-8-5 0...................................... DavidProbert 2 68
(David Simcock) *hld up in last pair: nt clr run briefly 2f out: swtiched ins over 1f out: kpt on fnl f but nvr able to chal* **5/1**

6 *6* **Revert (USA)**[66] 4-9-0 0... NedCurtis(7) 3 55?
(Gerry Enright) *dwlt: hld up in last: effrt on outer 3f out: rdn and wknd wl over 1f out* **50/1**

2m 9.15s (2.55) **Going Correction** -0.05s/f (Stan)
WFA 3 from 4yo 22lb 4 from 6yo 1lb **6** Ran SP% **115.7**
Speed ratings (Par 103): **87,86,86,85,85 80**
toteswingers 1&2 £3.90, 1&3 £3.50, 2&3 £2.20 CSF £57.85 TOTE £13.20: £5.10, £1.90; EX 39.00 Trifecta £139.40 Pool: £5,929.16 - 31.89 winning units..
Owner Triermore Stud **Bred** W Maxwell Ervine **Trained** Lambourn, Berks

FOCUS
A fairly interesting maiden with several major yards represented.

474 BLUE SQUARE BET H'CAP 1m 2f (P)
3:45 (3:45) (Class 4) (0-85,83) 3-Y-0 **£4,942** (£1,459; £730) **Stalls** Low

Form RPR

142- **1** **Infinite Magic (USA)**[37] 8240 3-9-7 **83**..........................(p) RyanMoore 1 91+
(Jeremy Noseda) *trckd ldng pair to 3f out: sn shkn up: effrt to chse ldr over 1f out: hrd drvn and styd on to ld post* **9/4**[2]

3-2 **2** *nse* **King George River (IRE)**[8] 359 3-9-6 **82**......................... AdamKirby 3 90+
(Alan Bailey) *hld up in 4th: quick move to ld 3f out and wnt for home: hrd rdn over 1f out: styd on but hdd post* **5/4**[1]

14-6 **3** *6* **Blue Wave (IRE)**[8] 359 3-9-3 **79**.................................... JoeFanning 6 75
(Mark Johnston) *sltly impeded after 1f: trckd ldr to 3f out: sn dropped to last and outpcd: kpt on fnl f to take 3rd last strides* **10/1**

1-11 **4** *nk* **Gabrial The Boss (USA)**[16] 231 3-9-1 **77**...................(t) AndreaAtzeni 2 72
(David Simcock) *hld up in last: outpcd over 2f out: drvn and no imp wl over 1f out: chal for 3rd fnl f* **5/1**

22-1 **5** *1¼* **Rangi**[30] 16 3-9-0 **76**.. RobertHavlin 5 69
(John Gosden) *led: jinked rt after 1f: hdd 3f out: lost 2nd and wknd over 1f out* **4/1**[3]

2m 4.72s (-1.88) **Going Correction** -0.05s/f (Stan) **5** Ran SP% **121.0**
Speed ratings (Par 99): **105,104,100,99,98**
CSF £6.18 TOTE £3.30: £1.90, £1.90; EX 6.50 Trifecta £28.60 Pool: £4,676.67 - 122.30 winning units..
Owner Tom Ludt **Bred** Grapestock Llc **Trained** Newmarket, Suffolk
■ Stewards' Enquiry : Ryan Moore two-day ban; used whip above permitted level (15th-16th Feb).

FOCUS
A decent handicap despite the small field and another very close finish.

475 ENOUGH SAID, JUST BET AT BLUESQ.COM AMATEUR RIDERS' H'CAP 1m 4f (P)
4:20 (4:20) (Class 5) (0-70,68) 4-Y-0+ **£2,634** (£810; £405) **Stalls** Low

Form RPR

00-1 **1** **Stentorian (IRE)**[30] 20 5-10-7 **66**...............................(v) MrFMitchell(5) 7 76
(Gary Moore) *hld up in rr: stdy prog fr 4f out: trckd ldrs 2f out: clsd to ld ins fnl f: rdn out* **5/2**[1]

05-0 **2** *2* **Maslak (IRE)**[19] 198 9-9-8 **55**... MissMEdden(7) 1 62
(Peter Hiatt) *prom in chsng gp: clsd 4f out: led 3f out: pushed along and hdd ins fnl f: one pce* **14/1**

051- **3** *1* **Teide Peak (IRE)**[46] 8145 4-9-13 **61**............................... MrsRWilson(5) 5 66
(Paul D'Arcy) *trckd ldrs in chsng gp: effrt 3f out: pushed along and styd on to take 3rd fnl f: unable to threaten* **4/1**[2]

006- **4** *3* **Manshoor (IRE)**[66] 7793 8-9-7 **54** oh2........................... MrSamDavis(7) 6 54
(Lucy Wadham) *hld up towards rr: taken to outer and sme prog over 3f out: outpcd over 2f out: styd on to take 4th nr fin* **12/1**

0-23 **5** *½* **Linkable**[9] 342 4-9-13 **63**.. MissJenniferPowell(7) 9 62
(Brendan Powell) *prom in chsng gp: lost pl 5f out and sn in rr: effrt over 2f out: styd on fnl f* **5/1**[3]

0- **6** *hd* **Capellini**[3] 8162 6-10-0 **61**.. AnnaHesketh(7) 11 60
(Charles Egerton) *led after 2f and sn clr w one rival: c bk to field fr 4f out: hdd 3f out: wknd qckly fnl f* **20/1**

053- **7** *2¼* **Foxhaven**[44] 8175 11-11-0 **68**.....................................(v) NicodeBoinville 8 63
(Patrick Chamings) *t.k.h: prom in chsng gp: clsd 4f out: rdn to dispute 2nd over 2f out: wknd jst over 1f out* **5/1**[3]

36-0 **8** *½* **Love Pegasus (USA)**[21] 158 7-9-9 **54** oh2.............(p) MissMBryant(5) 2 49
(Paddy Butler) *hld up in last pair: rdn 3f out: kpt on one pce fnl 2f: nvr on terms* **33/1**

60/0 **9** *14* **Jakeys Girl**[16] 226 6-9-7 **54** oh9.................................. MissLWilliams(7) 3 26
(Pat Phelan) *a in rr: lost tch over 3f out: t.o* **50/1**

0-02 **10** *1* **Edgware Road**[10] 330 5-9-10 **57**.................................. MissBHampson(7) 4 28
(Sean Curran) *hld up in detached last: nvr any prog: t.o* **8/1**

/00- **11** *14* **Murfreesboro**[44] 7819 10-9-12 **59**................................ MissRDorrell(7) 10
(Raymond York) *led 2f: chsd ldr and clr of rest tl wknd rapidly over 3f out: wl t.o* **33/1**

2m 34.59s (1.59) **Going Correction** -0.05s/f (Stan)
WFA 4 from 5yo+ 3lb **11** Ran SP% **120.0**
Speed ratings (Par 103): **92,90,90,88,87 87,86,85,76,75 66**
toteswingers 1&2 £9.30, 1&3 £2.60, 2&3 £12.20 CSF £40.04 CT £141.19 TOTE £3.10: £2.40, £3.40, £1.60; EX 42.60 Trifecta £317.60 Pool: £5,670.69 - 13.39 winning units..
Owner B Homewood **Bred** Ceka Ireland Limited **Trained** Lower Beeding, W Sussex
■ Stewards' Enquiry : Miss B Hampson ten-day ban; failed to take all reasonable and permissible measures to obtain best possible placing (dates tba).

FOCUS
A modest amateur riders' handicap.
T/Jkpt: Part won. £39,110.50 to a £1 stake. Pool: £55,085.35 - 0.50 winning tickets. T/Plt: £66.60 to a £1 stake. Pool: £59,029.37 - 646.83 winning tickets T/Qpdt: £9.90 to a £1 stake. Pool: £7,957.78 - 593.32 winning tickets JN

453 WOLVERHAMPTON (A.W) (L-H)
Friday, February 1

OFFICIAL GOING: Standard
Wind: Light; behind Weather: Overcast, turning to rain after race 1

476 CORAL.CO.UK CLAIMING STKS 1m 1f 103y(P)
4:50 (4:50) (Class 5) 4-Y-0+ **£2,587** (£770; £384; £192) **Stalls** Low

Form RPR

1-13 **1** **Hurricane Spirit (IRE)**[4] 415 9-8-7 71.................... NicoleNordblad(5) 4 57
(Hans Adielsson) *hld up: racd keenly: hdwy over 2f out: rdn to ld and edgd lft wl ins fnl f* **8/11**[1]

-321 **2** *shd* **Yourinthewill (USA)**[10] 330 5-9-0 59................................ ShaneKelly 7 59
(Daniel Mark Loughnane) *dwlt: hld up: shkn up over 1f out: hung lft ins fnl f: sn rdn: r.o wl* **6/1**[2]

400- **3** *nk* **Elspeth's Boy (USA)**[87] 7607 6-8-12 73...................... GarryWhillans(5) 5 61
(Philip Kirby) *trckd ldrs: plld hrd: wnt 2nd over 3f out: rdn to ld and edgd lft 1f out: hdd wl ins fnl f* **15/2**

-100 **4** *½* **Honey Of A Kitten (USA)**[6] 403 5-8-10 69..........(v) ThomasBrown(7) 1 60
(David Evans) *hld up: hdwy over 2f out: rdn over 1f out: r.o: n.m.r towards fin* **7/1**[3]

000- **5** *shd* **Bashama**[74] 7612 5-8-5 43.......................................(b[1]) FrankieMcDonald 3 48
(Nikki Evans) *sn pushed along to ld: rdn and hdd 1f out: styd on* **250/1**

4-10 **6** *3¼* **Malindi**[2] 439 4-8-9 69.. JamesSullivan 2 45
(James Given) *prom: rdn over 2f out: styd on same pce fnl f* **12/1**

0/ **7** *17* **Platinum (IRE)**[438] 5963 6-9-5 85..................................... ChrisCatlin 6 19
(Philip Kirby) *chsd ldr tl pushed along over 3f out: wknd over 2f out* **12/1**

2m 3.28s (1.58) **Going Correction** +0.125s/f (Slow) **7** Ran SP% **112.2**
Speed ratings (Par 103): **97,96,96,96,96 93,78**
toteswingers 1&2 £1.90, 1&3 £3.00, 2&3 £5.00 CSF £5.36 TOTE £1.80: £1.10, £1.80; EX 4.10 Trifecta £27.30 Pool: £11,550.66 - 316.23 winning units..
Owner Hans Adielsson A B **Bred** Knocktoran Stud **Trained** Kingston Lisle, Oxon

FOCUS
Quite a competitive claimer.

477 ONLINE BETTING OFFERS AT BOOKMAKERS.CO.UK APPRENTICE H'CAP 1m 1f 103y(P)
5:25 (5:25) (Class 6) (0-65,65) 4-Y-0+ £1,940 (£577; £288; £144) Stalls Low

Form RPR
642- 1 **Silver Alliance**^{46} [8145] 5-9-2 65 ShelleyBirkett$^{(5)}$ 1 74
(Julia Feilden) *chsd ldrs: led over 1f out: sn rdn: edgd rt ins fnl f: styd on* 5/1
1454 2 ¾ **Breakheart (IRE)**^{4} [415] 6-8-13 62 (p) JoeyHaynes$^{(5)}$ 3 69
(Andrew Balding) *prom: lost pl 5f out: rdn over 2f out: wnt 2nd ins fnl f: r.o: nt rch wnr* 4/1^{2}
0-24 3 1¾ **Tyrur Ted**^{1} [455] 8-8-3 54 (t) DanaZamecnikova$^{(7)}$ 5 58
(Frank Sheridan) *s.i.s: hld up: hdwy over 3f out: styd on same pce ins fnl f* 9/2^{3}
0-44 4 3½ **White Diamond**^{2} [439] 6-9-5 63 PatMillman 7 59
(Michael Appleby) *w ldr tl led over 6f out: rdn over 2f out: hdd over 1f out: no ex ins fnl f* 4/1^{2}
4205 5 6 **Resplendent Alpha**^{7} [376] 9-8-12 63 (p) SemiraPashai$^{(7)}$ 2 47
(Alastair Lidderdale) *dwlt: hld up: hdwy over 3f out: wknd over 1f out* 22/1
2-01 6 1 **Royal Sea (IRE)**^{22} [145] 4-9-4 62 RyanWhile 4 44
(Michael Mullineaux) *chsd ldrs: rdn over 3f out: wknd over 2f out* 3/1^{1}
03-3 7 3¼ **Apache Glory (USA)**^{22} [147] 5-9-3 61 GaryPhillips 6 36
(John Stimpson) *led: hdd over 6f out: chsd ldr: rdn over 2f out: wknd and eased fnl f* 5/1

2m 2.62s (0.92) **Going Correction** +0.125s/f (Slow) 7 Ran SP% **120.9**
Speed ratings (Par 101): **100,99,97,94,89 88,85**
toteswingers 1&2 £4.70, 1&3 £4.40, 2&3 £4.50 CSF £27.08 TOTE £3.90: £1.70, £3.40; EX 27.10 Trifecta £129.00 Pool: £18,161.89 - 105.51 winning units..
Owner In It To Win Partnership **Bred** Peter Harris **Trained** Exning, Suffolk
■ Shelley Birkett's first winner as an apprentice.
■ Stewards' Enquiry : Gary Phillips caustion; failing to ride out.

FOCUS
Several of the runners came into this apprentice handicap in good form.

478 COMPARE BOOKIES WITH BOOKMAKERS.CO.UK H'CAP 1m 141y(P)
6:00 (6:00) (Class 5) (0-70,70) 4-Y-0+ £2,587 (£770; £384; £192) Stalls Low

Form RPR
1-41 1 **Idol Deputy (FR)**^{17} [219] 7-9-2 70 (p) RachealKneller$^{(5)}$ 4 78
(Mark Usher) *a.p: shkn up to ld wl ins fnl f: r.o* 11/2^{3}
23-4 2 nk **Exceedexpectations (IRE)**^{20} [187] 4-8-13 67 WilliamTwiston-Davies$^{(5)}$ 9 74
(Michael Bell) *hld up in tch: rdn and ev ch wl ins fnl f: r.o* 7/2^{2}
0-2 3 ½ **Miami Gator (IRE)**^{23} [118] 6-8-6 62 (v) RyanTate$^{(7)}$ 3 68
(Mrs K Burke) *chsd ldr: rdn over 2f out: led 1f out: hdd wl ins fnl f* 8/1
22-1 4 ½ **Goldstorm**^{17} [218] 5-9-3 66 (p) WilliamCarson 5 71+
(Brian Baugh) *hld up: stmbld over 7f out: rdn over 2f out: swtchd rt and bmpd 1f out: r.o wl: nt rch ldrs* 3/1^{1}
34-5 5 ¾ **Thereabouts (USA)**^{24} [104] 4-9-3 66 AndrewMullen 7 69
(Michael Appleby) *s.i.s: hld up: rdn over 1f out: r.o ins fnl f: nt rch ldrs* 10/1
1-50 6 ¾ **Outlaw Torn (IRE)**^{6} [410] 4-8-8 64 (e) PhilipPrince$^{(7)}$ 2 65
(Richard Guest) *led: clr 5f out: rdn and hdd 1f out: styd on same pce* 10/1
6-12 7 1¼ **Jumbo Prado (USA)**^{6} [410] 4-9-0 63 ShaneKelly 8 61
(Daniel Mark Loughnane) *hld up: effrt and hmpd 1f out: nvr trbld ldrs* 7/2^{2}
3-50 8 1 **Crowning Star (IRE)**^{22} [138] 4-9-5 68 (t) StevieDonohoe 1 64
(Gay Kelleway) *chsd ldrs: rdn over 1f out: no ex ins fnl f* 25/1
00-0 9 2¼ **Beauchamp Xerxes**^{30} [13] 7-9-1 64 (t) FrannyNorton 10 55
(Hans Adielsson) *stdd s: sn swtchd lft: hld up: shkn up over 1f out: eased whn btn ins fnl f* 33/1

1m 52.37s (1.87) **Going Correction** +0.125s/f (Slow) 9 Ran SP% **120.9**
Speed ratings (Par 103): **96,95,95,94,94 93,92,91,89**
toteswingers 1&2 £3.30, 1&3 £4.60, 2&3 £5.80 CSF £26.40 CT £159.24 TOTE £7.00: £2.50, £2.30, £3.10; EX 32.80 Trifecta £278.00 Pool: £8,028.38 - 21.65 winning units..
Owner Miss J C Blackwell **Bred** Sheikh Sultan Bin Khalifa Al Nayan **Trained** Upper Lambourn, Berks
■ Stewards' Enquiry : William Carson three-day ban; careless riding (19th-21st Feb).

FOCUS
The most competitive race on the cards in terms of numbers and it included a few progressive horses. This rates strong form for the grade.

479 GET FREE BETS WITH BOOKMAKERS.CO.UK MEDIAN AUCTION MAIDEN STKS 1m 141y(P)
6:30 (6:31) (Class 5) 3-5-Y-0 £2,587 (£770; £384; £192) Stalls Low

Form RPR
3- 1 **Rouge Nuage (IRE)**^{43} [8178] 3-8-0 0 RyanTate$^{(7)}$ 2 73
(Conrad Allen) *chsd ldrs: shkn up to ld ins fnl f: r.o* 3/1^{2}
3 2 ¾ **Aryal**^{27} [74] 3-8-7 0 FrannyNorton 3 71
(Mark Johnston) *led 2f: chsd ldr tl led again over 3f out: rdn over 1f out: hdd ins fnl f: styd on* 2/9^{1}
3 6 **Scarlette D'Or** 4-9-4 0 AmyScott$^{(5)}$ 1 57?
(Alastair Lidderdale) *s.i.s: hld up: pushed along over 2f out: styd on same pce fr over 1f out* 33/1^{3}
0 4 ½ **Ivy Port**^{19} [197] 3-8-2 0 AndrewMullen 4 51?
(Michael Appleby) *plld hrd: trckd ldrs: wnt 2nd over 2f out: rdn and hung lft over 1f out: wknd ins fnl f* 66/1
5-0 5 37 **Arabougg**^{25} [102] 3-8-7 0 FrankieMcDonald 5
(Nikki Evans) *hld up: plld hrd: hdwy to ld over 6f out: hdd over 3f out: rdn and wknd over 2f out: t.o* 100/1

1m 54.69s (4.19) **Going Correction** +0.125s/f (Slow)
WFA 3 from 4yo 21lb 5 Ran SP% **112.3**
Speed ratings (Par 103): **86,85,80,79,46**
CSF £4.26 TOTE £4.00: £1.30, £1.10; EX 7.30 Trifecta £16.90 Pool: £25,556.39 - 1,129.08 winning units..
Owner sportsdays.co.uk **Bred** Dermot Farrington **Trained** Newmarket, Suffolk

FOCUS
The market for this median auction maiden concerned only two runners. Despite finishing first and second, the long odds-on favourite was beaten.

480 POKER AT CORAL.CO.UK CONDITIONS STKS 5f 216y(P)
7:00 (7:00) (Class 4) 4-Y-0+ £4,690 (£1,395; £697; £348) Stalls Low

Form RPR
1-32 1 **Piscean (USA)**^{6} [407] 8-9-2 98 GeorgeBaker 2 107
(Tom Keddy) *s.i.s and hld up: hdwy over 1f out: r.o u.p to ld nr fin* 7/2^{2}
011- 2 ¾ **York Glory (USA)**^{65} [7918] 5-9-2 103 (b) FrannyNorton 3 105
(Kevin Ryan) *chsd ldrs: led 2f out: sn pushed clr: wknd and hdd nr fin* 4/5^{1}
410- 3 4½ **Capone (IRE)**^{76} [7772] 8-9-5 102 ShaneKelly 6 93
(Garry Moss) *s.i.s: hld up: rdn over 1f out: styd on same pce: wnt 3rd wl ins fnl f* 6/1^{3}
0-00 4 ¾ **Forest Edge (IRE)**^{6} [405] 4-9-2 86 (b) GrahamGibbons 1 88
(David Evans) *led: rdn and hdd over 2f out: wknd ins fnl f* 16/1
4-60 5 1¾ **Swiss Cross**^{10} [319] 6-9-2 101 (t) WilliamCarson 4 82
(Phil McEntee) *chsd ldr tl rdn to ld over 2f out: sn hdd: wknd fnl f* 15/2

1m 13.49s (-1.51) **Going Correction** +0.125s/f (Slow) 5 Ran SP% **109.7**
Speed ratings (Par 105): **115,114,108,107,104**
CSF £6.73 TOTE £4.00: £1.70, £1.10; EX 8.10 Trifecta £18.90 Pool: £14,258.39 - 562.90 winning units..
Owner Andrew Duffield **Bred** Connie And John Iacoune **Trained** Newmarket, Suffolk

FOCUS
The feature on the card was a conditions sprint over 6f and, with the first four in the market rated between 98-103, this was a strong contest.

481 CORAL.CO.UK MOBILE BETTING H'CAP 5f 20y(P)
7:30 (7:30) (Class 5) (0-75,75) 4-Y-0+ £2,587 (£770; £384; £192) Stalls Low

Form RPR
1-41 1 **M J Woodward**^{17} [213] 4-8-10 64 JamesSullivan 6 72
(Paul Green) *chsd ldr: rdn to ld ins fnl f: jst hld on* 7/1
0-31 2 nk **Cardinal**^{11} [308] 8-9-7 75 6ex TomEaves 8 82+
(Robert Cowell) *hld up: nt clr run over 1f out: rdn and r.o wl ins fnl f* 5/1^{3}
20-2 3 shd **Sole Danser (IRE)**^{21} [164] 5-9-7 75 SebSanders 5 82
(Milton Bradley) *hld up: hdwy over 1f out: sn rdn: r.o* 9/4^{1}
00-0 4 ½ **Crimson Queen**^{11} [308] 6-8-13 70 (b) MarkCoumbe$^{(3)}$ 2 75
(Roy Brotherton) *led: rdn and hdd ins fnl f: styd on* 40/1
6-35 5 ¾ **Lucky Dan (IRE)**^{19} [196] 7-9-6 74 (b^{1}) FrannyNorton 3 77
(Paul Green) *hld up: hdwy over 1f out: sn rdn r.o* 3/1^{2}
0-04 6 nk **Shawkantango**^{11} [308] 6-8-4 65 (v) AdamMcLean$^{(7)}$ 1 66
(Derek Shaw) *sn pushed along and prom: losing pl whn brushed rails wl over 2f out: hdwy over 1f out: r.o* 16/1
-102 7 3¾ **Desert Strike**^{11} [308] 7-8-11 70 (p) WilliamTwiston-Davies$^{(5)}$ 7 58
(Conor Dore) *chsd ldrs: rdn 1/2-way: wknd ins fnl f* 10/1
000- 8 2¾ **Sir Geoffrey (IRE)**^{63} [7937] 7-8-11 65 (p) NickyMackay 4 43
(Scott Dixon) *chsd ldrs: rdn 1/2-way: wknd fnl f* 11/2

1m 1.93s (-0.37) **Going Correction** +0.125s/f (Slow) 8 Ran SP% **117.7**
Speed ratings (Par 103): **107,106,106,105,104 103,97,93**
toteswingers 1&2 £5.80, 1&3 £3.50, 2&3 £3.90 CSF £43.03 CT £104.86 TOTE £6.80: £1.90, £1.50, £1.10; EX 33.80 Trifecta £99.80 Pool: £6,997.01 - 52.57 winning units..
Owner E Sciarrillo **Bred** Paul Green **Trained** Lydiate, Merseyside

FOCUS
A competitive 61-75 handicap over the minimum trip.

482 COMPARE ONLINE BOOKIES AT BOOKMAKERS.CO.UK H'CAP 7f 32y(P)
8:00 (8:00) (Class 6) (0-60,61) 3-Y-0 £1,940 (£577; £288; £144) Stalls High

Form RPR
2222 1 **Derwentwater (IRE)**^{4} [414] 3-9-7 60 (b) NickyMackay 3 69
(John Gosden) *n.m.r sn after s: hld up: hdwy over 1f out: led wl ins fnl f: edgd lft: r.o* 5/4^{1}
00-4 2 2¼ **Shearian**^{28} [55] 3-8-9 53 ow1 WilliamTwiston-Davies$^{(5)}$ 2 56
(Tony Carroll) *a.p: chsd ldr over 1f out: rdn to ld ins fnl f: sn hdd and unable qck* 3/1^{2}
33-5 3 3 **Petite Georgia (IRE)**^{29} [31] 3-9-4 57 GeorgeBaker 9 52
(George Baker) *sn led: rdn: hdd and no ex ins fnl f* 7/1^{3}
3-51 4 ¾ **Schottische**^{17} [216] 3-9-7 60 (p) WilliamCarson 7 53
(Derek Haydn Jones) *hld up: rdn 1/2-way: hdwy u.p over 1f out: styd on same pce fnl f* 10/1
6-16 5 nk **Maypole Joe (IRE)**^{10} [321] 3-9-1 61 6ex (v) ThomasBrown$^{(7)}$ 4 53
(David Evans) *hld up: hdwy over 1f out: styd on same pce ins fnl f* 10/1
-504 6 5 **Duchess Of Dreams**^{10} [328] 3-8-8 54 PhilipPrince$^{(7)}$ 6 33
(Richard Guest) *hld up: rdn over 1f out: wknd fnl f* 33/1
33-4 7 nk **Lincolnrose (IRE)**^{23} [122] 3-8-12 51 (p) GrahamGibbons 5 29
(Alan McCabe) *prom: rdn over 1f out: wknd ins fnl f* 8/1
06-0 8 8 **Firey Sally (IRE)**^{11} [310] 3-8-8 50 (t) MarkCoumbe$^{(3)}$ 1
(Frank Sheridan) *chsd ldr: rdn over 2f out: wknd over 1f out* 66/1
000- 9 1½ **Cash Rich**^{94} [7459] 3-8-7 46 oh1 ChrisCatlin 8
(Jamie Osborne) *chsd ldrs: rdn 1/2-way: wkng whn n.m.r over 1f out* 33/1

1m 30.06s (0.46) **Going Correction** +0.125s/f (Slow) 9 Ran SP% **118.6**
Speed ratings (Par 95): **102,99,96,95,94 89,88,79,77**
toteswingers 1&2 £2.20, 1&3 £2.60, 2&3 £4.60 CSF £5.11 CT £18.75 TOTE £2.00: £1.10, £1.50, £2.60; EX 6.70 Trifecta £43.40 Pool: £1,320.94 - 22.80 winning units..
Owner HRH Princess Haya Of Jordan **Bred** D Farrington, P Gately, T Killarney **Trained** Newmarket, Suffolk

FOCUS
Not the most competitive.
T/Plt: £17.20 to a £1 stake. Pool: £93,730.14 - 3,967.29 winning units T/Qpdt: £6.10 to a £1 stake. Pool: £9,033.82 - 1,082.99 winning units CR

468 LINGFIELD (L-H)
Saturday, February 2

OFFICIAL GOING: Standard
Wind: Fresh, half against Weather: Fine, becoming cloudy by race 2

490 BET ON TODAY'S FOOTBALL AT BLUESQ.COM (S) STKS 1m (P)
12:40 (12:42) (Class 6) 4-Y-0+ £2,215 (£490; £490) Stalls High

Form RPR
-433 1 **The Mongoose**^{2} [446] 5-9-5 64 (t) AdamKirby 5 69
(David Evans) *mde all: set stdy pce: qcknd over 2f out: tired fnl f: jst hld on* 11/4^{2}
55F- 2 ½ **Spin Again (IRE)**^{36} [8261] 8-8-13 63 MichaelO'Connell 3 62
(John Ryan) *t.k.h in 4th: rdn over 2f out: r.o to dead-heat for 2nd on line* 14/1
5-10 2 dht **Electrician**^{21} [190] 4-9-5 63 (p) ShaneKelly 6 68
(Tim Pitt) *chsd wnr tl over 1f out: kpt on again ins fnl f* 8/1
3323 4 nse **Abhaath (USA)**^{8} [380] 4-8-6 64 (b) GaryPhillips$^{(7)}$ 4 62
(Ronald Harris) *t.k.h: trckd ldrs: rdn to chse wnr over 1f out: kpt on u.p: lost 2nd fnl strides* 4/1^{3}
0-66 5 nk **Officer In Command (USA)**^{7} [403] 7-8-13 64 (b) WilliamCarson 2 61
(Sean Curran) *s.s: bhd: rdn over 3f out: styd on wl fnl f: clsng fast at fin* 6/1

The Form Book Flat, Raceform Ltd, Compton, RG20 6NL.

3112 **6** 1 ¼ **One Way Or Another (AUS)**[8] [376] 10-9-5 69......(t) GrahamGibbons 1 64
(David Evans) *t.k.h in 5th: rdn over 2f out: kpt on same pce* **9/4[1]**
1m 38.04s (-0.16) **Going Correction** +0.05s/f (Slow) **6** Ran SP% **109.5**
Speed ratings (Par 101): **102,101,101,101,101 99**
PL: E £1.70, SA £3.80 EX: TM/E £11.40, TM/SA £22.50 CSF: TM/E £11.30, TM/SA £17.40 TRIFECTA TM/E/SA £83.20, TM/SA/E £105.80 toteswingers TM&E £3.00, TM&SA £7.50, E&SA £7.10 TOTE £3.30: £1.40.There was no bid for the winner.
Owner G Evans & P D Evans **Bred** Kincorth Investments Inc **Trained** Pandy, Monmouths

FOCUS
An open-looking seller.

491 FOLLOW US ON TWITTER @LINGFIELDPARK MEDIAN AUCTION MAIDEN STKS 1m (P)
1:10 (1:10) (Class 6) 3-5-Y-O **£2,385** (£704; £352) **Stalls** High

Form RPR
0-3 **1** **Shaolin (IRE)**[17] [228] 3-8-9 .... JohnFahy 3 60
(Seamus Durack) *led 1f: sttd bk to 3rd and t.k.h: qcknd bk into ld over 1f out: hrd rdn fnl f: jst hld on* **7/4[1]**
2 *hd* **King Bertie (IRE)** 3-8-9 .... DavidProbert 6 59+
(Peter Chapple-Hyam) *chsd ldrs: carried wd and lost pl bnd into st: rallied and r.o wl fnl f: jst hld* **2/1[2]**
5-0 **3** 2 ¼ **Two No Bids (IRE)**[17] [228] 3-8-9 .... FrannyNorton 5 54
(J W Hills) *t.k.h: sn chsng ldr: rdn and carried sltly wd bnd into st: one pce appr fnl f* **8/1**
0- **4** 1 ¾ **Al Sulaimi (IRE)**[107] [7199] 3-8-9 .... WilliamCarson 8 50
(Ronald Harris) *led after 1f: rdn and increased tempo over 2f out: sltly wd bnd into st: hdd over 1f out: no ex fnl f* **16/1**
5 1 ½ **Gambolling Den (IRE)** 3-8-9 .... AndreaAtzeni 2 47+
(David Simcock) *s.i.s: bhd: rdn 3f out: nvr rchd ldrs* **4/1[3]**
00-0 **6** ¾ **Fleeting Indian (IRE)**[10] [333] 4-10-0 34..............(p) FrankieMcDonald 4 49?
(Linda Jewell) *towards rr: rdn over 2f out: nvr able to chal* **100/1**
5-0 **7** ½ **Hammer Shaft (IRE)**[17] [228] 3-8-9 .... HayleyTurner 1 44
(Amy Weaver) *in tch tl outpcd fnl 2f* **33/1**
1m 40.1s (1.90) **Going Correction** +0.05s/f (Slow)
WFA 3 from 4yo 19lb **7** Ran SP% **110.6**
Speed ratings (Par 101): **92,91,89,87,86 85,85**
toteswingers 1&2 £1.60, 1&3 £2.70, 2&3 £3.30 CSF £5.10 TOTE £2.40: £2.00, £1.10; EX 6.70 Trifecta £16.80 Pool: £4062.40 - 181.28 winning units..
Owner P A Deal **Bred** Joe Fogarty **Trained** Baydon, Wilts

FOCUS
Just an ordinary winter all-weather maiden.

492 MICHAEL HUGHES 30TH BIRTHDAY MAIDEN STKS 7f (P)
1:45 (1:45) (Class 5) 3-Y-0+ **£2,726** (£805; £402) **Stalls** Low

Form RPR
26-2 **1** **Great Demeanor (USA)**[9] [350] 3-8-10 75.................. LiamKeniry 1 78
(David Elsworth) *mde all: rdn 2f out: hld on wl fnl f* **7/4[2]**
2 ¾ **Kabbaas (IRE)** 3-8-10 0.................. AndreaAtzeni 3 76
(Roger Varian) *chsd wnr: rdn 2f out: kpt on fnl f: a hld* **6/4[1]**
3 4 ½ **Jolaine** 4-9-8 0.................. JimCrowley 4 64
(Ralph Beckett) *in tch: rdn over 2f out: styd on same pce* **9/2[3]**
4 ½ **Fearless Lad (IRE)** 3-8-10 0..................(t) HayleyTurner 6 62
(John Best) *dwlt: hld up in rr: rdn 2f out: styd on fnl f: nvr nrr* **16/1**
0- **5** *nk* **Lively Little Lady**[308] [1136] 3-8-5 0.................. DavidProbert 2 57?
(Tim Pitt) *prom: hrd rdn over 1f out: sn wknd* **100/1**
0-4 **6** 2 ¾ **Fire Fairy (USA)**[20] [197] 3-8-5 0.................. WilliamCarson 7 49
(Charles Hills) *chsd ldrs tl outpcd fnl 2f* **12/1**
7 3 ¾ **One Dark Night** 3-8-10 0.................. FergusSweeney 5 44
(Gary Moore) *sttd s and awkward leaving stalls: plld hrd in 6th: rdn and n.d fnl 2f* **33/1**
1m 27.55s (2.75) **Going Correction** +0.05s/f (Slow)
WFA 3 from 4yo 17lb **7** Ran SP% **112.1**
Speed ratings (Par 103): **86,85,80,79,79 75,71**
toteswingers 1&2 £1.80, 1&3 £1.70, 2&3 £2.30 CSF £4.52 TOTE £3.30: £1.10, £3.70; EX 5.30 Trifecta £14.40 Pool: £2843.21 - 148.02 winning units..
Owner Vinci Wong **Bred** Brick Kiln Stud **Trained** Newmarket, Suffolk

FOCUS
Probably a fair maiden.

493 BLUE SQUARE BET SPRINT SERIES ROUND 5 H'CAP (QUALIFIER) (DIV I) 6f (P)
2:20 (2:22) (Class 6) (0-65,70) 4-Y-0+ **£3,067** (£905; £453) **Stalls** Low

Form RPR
3-31 **1** **Frognal (IRE)**[7] [399] 7-9-12 70..................(bt) WilliamCarson 7 79
(Violet M Jordan) *sttd s: hld up in rr: gd hdwy over 1f out: edgd lft: r.o to ld fnl 75yds: drvn out* **9/2[2]**
4-50 **2** *nk* **Haadeeth**[7] [399] 6-9-2 60.................. TomMcLaughlin 4 68
(David Evans) *prom in chsng gp: clsd and led ins fnl f: hdd fnl 75yds: r.o* **7/1**
500- **3** ½ **Aqua Ardens (GER)**[129] [6577] 5-9-7 65.................. KirstyMilczarek 2 71
(George Baker) *hld up in rr: rdn and gd hdwy over 1f out: hmpd ins fnl f: r.o wl fnl 100yds* **6/1[3]**
51-2 **4** 1 **Rich Again (IRE)**[7] [399] 4-9-7 65.................. GrahamGibbons 12 68
(James Bethell) *mid-div on outer: drvn along and styd on fr over 1f out: nvr nrr* **2/1[1]**
3-50 **5** *shd* **Speedyfix**[7] [398] 6-8-11 55..................(t) FrannyNorton 11 58
(Christine Dunnett) *mid-div: drvn to chse ldrs over 1f out: kpt on same pce fnl f* **20/1**
2122 **6** 1 ¼ **Baby Dottie**[9] [354] 6-8-11 62..................(tp) SophieRalston[(7)] 10 61
(Pat Phelan) *led after 1f: wnt 6 l clr over 3f out: hdd and fdd ins fnl f* **10/1**
5-50 **7** ¾ **Fairy Wing (IRE)**[7] [399] 6-9-2 60.................. SeanLevey 5 56
(Violet M Jordan) *hld up in 5th: rdn and no imp fnl 2f* **33/1**
2-41 **8** ½ **Colourbearer (IRE)**[18] [214] 6-9-7 65..................(t) SebSanders 3 60
(Milton Bradley) *sn towards rr: rdn over 2f out: nvr rchd ldrs* **7/1**
430- **9** *nk* **Excellent Aim**[166] [5416] 6-8-11 62.................. PaulHainey[(7)] 1 56
(George Margarson) *hld up towards rr: nvr rchd chalng position* **20/1**
3-60 **10** 2 ¾ **Amenable (IRE)**[17] [232] 6-9-2 65.................. CharlesBishop[(5)] 8 50
(Violet M Jordan) *led 1f: prom: rdn over 2f out: wknd over 1f out* **33/1**
2600 **11** 12 **Liberal Lady**[2] [448] 5-9-3 61.................. JoeFanning 9
(Ralph Smith) *prom in chsng gp tl wknd 2f out* **33/1**
1m 11.84s (-0.06) **Going Correction** +0.05s/f (Slow) **11** Ran SP% **118.2**
Speed ratings (Par 101): **102,101,100,99,99 97,96,96,95,92 76**
toteswingers 1&2 £5.60, 1&3 £6.60, 2&3 £9.20 CSF £33.40 CT £187.54 TOTE £4.00: £1.20, £3.20, £2.50; EX 36.40 Trifecta £248.40 Pool: £3600.05 - 10.86 winning units..
Owner Rakebackmypoker.com **Bred** Bryan Ryan **Trained** Moreton Morrell, Warwicks
■ Stewards' Enquiry : William Carson caution; careless riding.

FOCUS
A race run at a very strong pace.

494 BLUE SQUARE BET SPRINT SERIES ROUND 5 H'CAP (QUALIFIER) (DIV II) 6f (P)
2:55 (2:56) (Class 6) (0-65,71) 4-Y-0+ **£3,067** (£905; £453) **Stalls** Low

Form RPR
-063 **1** **Speak The Truth (IRE)**[7] [398] 7-9-6 64..................(p) JimCrowley 7 75
(Roger Ingram) *towards rr: drvn along and hdwy over 1f out: led ins fnl f: all out* **9/2[1]**
14-5 **2** *shd* **Tidal's Baby**[26] [96] 4-9-1 64.................. GeorgeDowning[(5)] 6 75
(Tony Carroll) *s.i.s: bhd: rapid hdwy in centre to join wnr ins fnl f: r.o* **5/1[2]**
-306 **3** 1 ¾ **Dancing Freddy (IRE)**[7] [398] 6-8-13 62..............(tp) CharlesBishop[(5)] 3 67
(Violet M Jordan) *led: drvn along over 2f out: hdd and one pce ins fnl f* **16/1**
0043 **4** ½ **Putin (IRE)**[2] [448] 5-8-10 54..................(bt) JoeFanning 12 57
(Phil McEntee) *prom: rdn 2f out: wnt 2nd jst over 1f out: one pce fnl f* **20/1**
6-25 **5** ½ **Loyal Royal (IRE)**[7] [399] 10-9-0 58..................(bt) RichardKingscote 10 60
(Milton Bradley) *hld up in midfield on outer: effrt 2f out: styd on same pce* **20/1**
-204 **6** *hd* **Waabel**[7] [398] 6-9-7 65..................(t) WilliamCarson 5 66
(Violet M Jordan) *bhd tl rdn and r.o fr over 1f out: nrst fin* **6/1[3]**
06-0 **7** *nse* **Diamond Vine (IRE)**[7] [398] 5-9-2 60..................(b) SeanLevey 1 61
(Ronald Harris) *nvr gng wl: chsd ldrs: one pce appr fnl f* **10/1**
-245 **8** ½ **My Own Way Home**[7] [398] 5-9-3 61.................. TomMcLaughlin 11 60
(David Evans) *in tch tl outpcd fnl 2f* **16/1**
31-6 **9** *nk* **Stepturn**[28] [80] 4-9-7 65..................(b[1]) ChrisCatlin 9 63
(Michael Wigham) *chsd ldr tl wknd over 1f out* **5/1[2]**
-323 **10** 1 ¼ **Above The Stars**[8] [379] 5-9-4 62.................. FergusSweeney 2 59
(Jamie Osborne) *hld up in midfield: n.m.r ent fnl f: nvr able to chal* **10/1**
0-00 **11** 1 **Time Medicean**[20] [196] 7-9-7 65.................. DavidProbert 4 63
(Tony Carroll) *mid-div: pushed along 3f out: hld whn n.m.r ent fnl f* **8/1**
1m 11.73s (-0.17) **Going Correction** +0.05s/f (Slow) **11** Ran SP% **116.4**
Speed ratings (Par 101): **103,102,100,99,99 98,98,98,97,96 94**
toteswingers 1&2 £5.10, 1&3 £8.40, 2&3 £15.80 CSF £26.29 CT £323.34 TOTE £3.90: £1.10, £4.00, £5.30; EX 32.70 Trifecta £95.90 Pool: £1327.32 - 10.37 winning units..
Owner Inside Track Racing Club **Bred** Gerard Mulligan **Trained** Epsom, Surrey
■ Stewards' Enquiry : Charles Bishop two-day ban; used whip above permitted level (16th&18th Feb)

FOCUS
Similarly run to the first division and once again the finish was dominated by horses who flashed home from well off the pace.

495 LINGFIELDPARK.CO.UK H'CAP 1m (P)
3:30 (3:31) (Class 3) (0-95,95) 4-Y-0+ **£7,439** (£2,213; £1,106; £553) **Stalls** High

Form RPR
2-53 **1** **Emerald Wilderness (IRE)**[7] [401] 9-9-7 95.................. SebSanders 7 104
(Mark Rimmer) *hld up in midfield: hdwy over 1f out: r.o to ld ins fnl f: drvn out* **12/1**
361- **2** ½ **Grey Mirage**[34] [8296] 4-8-12 86..................(p) AndreaAtzeni 10 94
(Marco Botti) *led after 1f: rdn and hdd ins fnl f: kpt on* **3/1[1]**
-110 **3** 1 **Loyalty**[7] [400] 6-8-4 85..................(v) AdamMcLean[(7)] 4 91
(Derek Shaw) *mid-div: hdwy to press ldrs over 1f out: kpt on same pce* **20/1**
415- **4** ½ **George Guru**[34] [8296] 6-9-3 94.................. MarkCoumbe[(3)] 5 99
(Michael Attwater) *t.k.h in midfield: smooth hdwy to press ldrs 1f out: unable qck ins fnl f* **8/1[3]**
1-21 **5** *nk* **Lowther**[23] [133] 8-8-8 82..................(b) FrannyNorton 8 86
(Lee Carter) *towards rr: rdn 3f out: hdwy over 1f out: no imp fnl f* **4/1[2]**
4-42 **6** ½ **Rakaan (IRE)**[19] [206] 6-8-12 86..................(p) FergusSweeney 6 89
(Jamie Osborne) *hld up in rr: styd on fnl f: nrest at fin* **16/1**
222- **7** *shd* **Webbow (IRE)**[34] [8296] 11-9-7 95.................. JimCrowley 3 98
(Julie Camacho) *led 1f: chsd ldrs: outpcd and n.m.r over 1f out: kpt on again fnl f* **8/1[3]**
1-20 **8** ¾ **Aquilonius (IRE)**[14] [273] 4-8-11 85..................(t) DavidProbert 12 86
(Stuart Williams) *chsd ldrs tl hrd rdn and btn jst over 1f out* **14/1**
05-1 **9** *shd* **Spirit Of Sharjah (IRE)**[31] [10] 8-9-4 92.................. JoeFanning 11 93
(Julia Feilden) *towards rr: rdn 2f out: nvr able to chal* **20/1**
550- **10** *shd* **Mr Red Clubs (IRE)**[149] [5363] 4-9-4 92.................. ShaneKelly 9 93
(Tim Pitt) *towards rr: rdn 2f out: n.d* **8/1[3]**
000- **11** 2 ¼ **Askaud (IRE)**[127] [6638] 5-8-8 82..................(p) NickyMackay 2 77
(Scott Dixon) *prom tl wknd over 1f out* **20/1**
0-15 **12** ¾ **Verse Of Love**[7] [407] 4-9-1 89.................. GrahamGibbons 1 83
(David Evans) *chsd ldr tl 2f out: sn wknd* **14/1**
1m 35.39s (-2.81) **Going Correction** +0.05s/f (Slow) **12** Ran SP% **119.5**
Speed ratings (Par 107): **116,115,114,114,113 113,113,112,112,112 109,109**
toteswingers 1&2 £7.40, 1&3 £35.60, 2&3 £17.80 CSF £46.85 CT £728.48 TOTE £16.50: £4.40, £1.10, £8.70; EX 61.10 Trifecta £210.70 Pool: £40218.91 - 24.88 winning units..
Owner F J Perry **Bred** Mrs Joan Murphy **Trained** Newmarket, Suffolk
■ Stewards' Enquiry : Mark Coumbe two-day ban; used whip above permitted level (16th&18th Feb)

FOCUS
A competitive handicap in which the pace was strong.

496 LINGFIELD PARK OWNERS GROUP H'CAP 1m 4f (P)
4:05 (4:05) (Class 3) (0-95,88) 4-Y-0+ **£7,439** (£2,213; £1,106; £553) **Stalls** Low

Form RPR
2-13 **1** **Noble Silk**[14] [273] 4-8-13 83..................(p) DavidProbert 2 94
(Lucy Wadham) *towards rr: hdwy over 1f out: led jst ins fnl f: rdn out* **6/1[3]**
-211 **2** 1 ¼ **English Summer**[9] [352] 6-9-1 82..................(t) AndreaAtzeni 1 91
(David Simcock) *in tch: effrt 2f out: styd on to take 2nd ins fnl f* **10/1**
-224 **3** 1 ¼ **Wildomar**[5] [420] 4-8-11 81.................. MichaelO'Connell 7 88
(John Ryan) *towards rr: rdn and r.o fr over 1f out: nrest at fin* **16/1**
1-11 **4** ½ **Harry Buckle**[11] [318] 4-8-13 83.................. WilliamCarson 6 89
(Philip McBride) *sn led: hdd 7f out: one pce appr fnl f* **3/1[2]**
3-22 **5** 1 ¼ **Ajeeb (USA)**[21] [183] 5-8-13 80.................. JimCrowley 5 84
(Michael Scudamore) *mid-div: effrt 3f out: one pce appr fnl f* **25/1**
61-1 **6** *shd* **Mica Mika (IRE)**[22] [167] 5-9-2 83.................. BarryMcHugh 10 87
(Richard Fahey) *prom: led 7f out tl 5f out: wknd 1f out* **16/1**
124- **7** ½ **Thecornishcockney**[42] [8228] 4-9-4 88..................(tp) GeorgeBaker 8 91
(John Ryan) *hld up in rr: hdwy on outer 2f out: rdn and btn over 1f out* **16/1**
51-1 **8** *nk* **De Rigueur**[29] [52] 5-9-1 82..................(t) AdamKirby 9 85
(Marco Botti) *chsd ldrs: rdn to ld 2f out: hdd & wknd jst ins fnl f* **2/1[1]**
015- **9** *nk* **Incendo**[38] [8242] 7-9-5 86..................(t) StevieDonohoe 3 88
(Ian Williams) *bhd: shkn up over 1f out: nvr rchd ldrs* **20/1**

2-22 **10** 2 **Focail Maith**[11] 318 5-9-4 85........(p) JoeFanning 11 84
(John Ryan) *prom: led 5f out tl 2f out: n.m.r and wknd ent fnl f* **9/1**
000/ **11** 6 **Dubawi Phantom**[156] 784 6-9-4 85........ FrannyNorton 12 74
(David C Griffiths) *a bhd* **50/1**
100/ **12** 2 3/4 **Topolski (IRE)**[21] 6528 7-9-4 85........(t) LiamKeniry 4 70
(David Arbuthnot) *chsd ldrs: hrd rdn over 3f out: wknd over 2f out* **66/1**

2m 30.63s (-2.37) **Going Correction** +0.05s/f (Slow)
WFA 4 from 5yo+ 3lb **12** Ran SP% **121.4**
Speed ratings (Par 107): **109,108,107,107,106 106,105,105,105,104 100,98**
toteswinger: 1&2 £11.10, 1&3 £21.20, 2&3 £44.80 CSF £64.01 CT £928.63 TOTE £4.60: £1.20, £4.30, £7.00; EX 44.40 Trifecta £818.70 Pool: £2621.50 - 2.40 winning units..
Owner The FOPS **Bred** Mr & Mrs A E Pakenham **Trained** Newmarket, Suffolk

FOCUS
An extremely competitive handicap featuring the a whole raft of in-form performers and the pace was solid so this is strong form.

497 GET STRAIGHT TO THE BET AT BLUESQ.COM APPRENTICE H'CAP 7f (P)
4:35 (4:36) (Class 6) (0-60,60) 4-Y-0+ £2,045 (£603; £302) Stalls Low

Form RPR
4332 **1** **Spinning Ridge (IRE)**[4] 436 8-8-13 57........(b) GaryPhillips(5) 9 68
(Ronald Harris) *dwlt: hld up in 5th: hdwy 2f out: led over 1f out: rdn out* **5/2**[1]
22-3 **2** 1 1/2 **Rose Garnet (IRE)**[23] 142 5-9-2 58........ GeorgeDowning(3) 7 65
(Tony Carroll) *prom: rdn to chal 1f out: unable qck fnl 100yds* **7/2**[3]
0-22 **3** 1 1/2 **Cuthbert (IRE)**[10] 346 6-8-2 48........(b) PaigeBolton(7) 4 51
(Michael Attwater) *mid-div to rr: effrt 2f out: styd on same pce appr fnl f* **15/2**
1-00 **4** nse **Jackie Love (IRE)**[14] 274 5-8-6 50........(v) CharlotteJenner(5) 1 53
(Olivia Maylam) *towards rr: rdn and styd on fr over 1f out: nvr nrr* **14/1**
6-41 **5** 3/4 **Amis Reunis**[10] 346 4-9-4 60........(p) RyanTate(3) 6 61
(Anthony Carson) *rrd s: bhd: hdwy over 1f out: no imp* **3/1**[2]
-203 **6** 1/2 **Marshall Art**[22] 162 4-9-2 58........(v[1]) ThomasBrown(3) 3 57
(David Evans) *disp ld: led 3f out tl wknd over 1f out* **7/1**
5-00 **7** 1 1/2 **Rainbow Riches (IRE)**[17] 220 4-8-4 46 oh1........(p) NedCurtis(3) 5 41
(Roger Curtis) *chsd clr ldrs tl wknd wl over 1f out* **33/1**
65-5 **8** 14 **King's Future**[22] 160 4-8-10 49........[1] NathanAlison 2
(Lee Carter) *disp ld 3f: wknd wl over 1f out* **16/1**

1m 24.68s (-0.12) **Going Correction** +0.05s/f (Slow) **8** Ran SP% **115.5**
Speed ratings (Par 101): **102,100,98,98,97 97,95,79**
toteswingers: 1&2 £1.70, 1&3 £4.40, 2&3 £5.20 CSF £11.64 CT £56.89 TOTE £3.70: £1.20, £1.40, £4.30; EX 12.00 Trifecta £71.50 Pool: £1543.66 - 16.16 winning units..
Owner Ridge House Stables Ltd **Bred** Eddie O'Leary **Trained** Earlswood, Monmouths
■ Stewards' Enquiry : Gary Phillips two-day ban; careless riding (16th&18th Feb)

FOCUS
The leaders went off way too fast here and this race fell into the lap of the perfectly placed winner.
T/Plt: £111.30 to a £1 stake. Pool: £67313.58 - 441.31 winning tickets T/Qpdt: £24.50 to a £1 stake. Pool: £5776.29 - 174.39 winning tickets LM

[460] CAGNES-SUR-MER
Saturday, February 2

OFFICIAL GOING: Fibresand: standard

498a PRIX DU HAUT DE CAGNES (CLAIMER) (4YO+) (FIBRESAND) 1m 4f
11:45 (12:00) 4-Y-0+ £6,910 (£2,764; £2,073; £1,382; £691)

RPR
1 **Renaione (IRE)**[29] 7-9-0 0........(b) AntoineCoutier(5) 1 85
(F Chappet, France) **21/10**[2]
2 nse **Rento (FR)**[137] 10-9-1 0........(p) StephanePasquier 5 81
(D Prod'Homme, France) **11/2**[3]
3 1 1/2 **Doctor Sim (IRE)**[49] 4-9-6 0........ JohanVictoire 4 87
(C Ferland, France) **2/1**[1]
4 3/4 **Thomaraz (FR)**[93] 6-8-11 0........(b) MarcLerner(4) 3 77
(P Sogorb, France) **63/10**
5 3/4 **Benjamin (FR)**[165] 8-8-9 0........(b) ChristopherGrosbois(6) 9 76
(L A Urbano-Grajales, France) **23/1**
6 3/4 **Uphold**[12] 315 6-9-1 0........(b) IoritzMendizabal 2 75
(Gay Kelleway) *broke wl: sn led: 2 l clr down bk st: set gd pce: chal early in st: hdd 350yds out: rdn but no ex fr 1 1/2f: styd on fnl f* **14/1**
7 1 1/2 **Babel Ouest (FR)**[60] 5-9-1 0........(p) ThierryThulliez 10 73
(J Van Handenhove, France) **14/1**
8 11 **Camacarin** 5-8-11 0........ FabienLefebvre 6 51
(G Collet, France) **23/1**
9 20 **Abrasivo (ITY)**[346] 661 4-8-11 0........ SUrru 7 22
(P Caravati, Italy) **91/1**
10 2 **Okhtay (FR)** 5-9-1 0........ MircoDemuro 8 20
(P Olsanik, Germany) **79/1**

2m 31.83s (151.83)
WFA 4 from 5yo+ 3lb **10** Ran SP% **118.7**
WIN (incl. 1 euro stake): 3.10. PLACES: 1.20, 1.50, 1.30. DF: 7.10. SF: 11.00.
Owner Gerard Augustin-Normand **Bred** Giuseppe Rossi **Trained** France

499 - 502a (Foreign Racing) - See Raceform Interactive

[462] MEYDAN (L-H)
Saturday, February 2

OFFICIAL GOING: Tapeta: round course - standard; sprint course - fast; turf: good

503a LONGINES SAINT IMIER (H'CAP) (TURF) 1m
5:10 (5:10) (85-99,98) 3-Y-0+ £9,045 (£3,015; £1,658; £904; £452)

RPR
1 **Nawwaar (USA)**[14] 289 4-8-10 90........ PaulHanagan 1 94
(A Al Raihe, UAE) *sn led: t.k.h: kicked clr 1 1/2f out: comf* **5/1**[2]
2 1 3/4 **Les Troyens**[14] 290 5-9-2 96........ MickaelBarzalona 7 96
(Saeed bin Suroor) *trckd ldrs: ev ch 1 1/2f out: kpt on same pce fnl f but no ch w wnr* **7/1**[3]
3 1/4 **Specific Gravity (FR)**[133] 6484 5-9-4 98........ ChristopheSoumillon 12 97+
(M F De Kock, South Africa) *mid-div: kpt on same pce fnl 1 1/2f* **8/1**
4 1/4 **My Freedom (IRE)**[84] 7691 5-8-11 91........ TedDurcan 14 90+
(Saeed bin Suroor) *settled in rr: nvr nr to chal but kpt on fnl 1 1/2f* **16/1**
5 1/4 **Redemptor**[22] 180 5-9-4 98........(t) DaneO'Neill 9 96+
(E Charpy, UAE) *settled in rr: nvr nr to chal but r.o fnl 1 1/2f* **25/1**
6 1/4 **Santefisio**[14] 290 7-9-4 98........(b) KierenFallon 10 95
(Keith Dalgleish) *mid-div: chsd ldrs 2f out: one pce fnl f* **11/1**
7 3/4 **Flag Officer**[14] 292 5-9-1 95........(t) SilvestreDeSousa 2 90
(Saeed bin Suroor) *trckd ldrs: ev ch 3f out: outpcd fr 2f out* **6/5**[1]
8 1/4 **Trojan Nights (USA)**[22] 178 5-9-1 95........ WayneSmith 8 90
(M Al Muhairi, UAE) *trckd ldrs tl outpcd 2 1/2f out* **16/1**
9 3/4 **Mutajare (IRE)**[8] 393 5-8-0 87........(t) SaeedAlMazrooei(7) 5 80
(A Al Raihe, UAE) *s.i.s: nvr bttr than mid-div* **33/1**
10 shd **Among Equals**[6] 412 4-8-5 85........(t) HarryBentley 3 78
(Doug Watson, UAE) *a mid-div* **25/1**
11 1/2 **Maqaraat (IRE)**[44] 8195 5-8-10 90........(t) PatDobbs 11 82
(Doug Watson, UAE) *settled in rr: nvr able to chal* **25/1**
12 1/2 **Mon Cadeaux**[14] 290 6-9-1 95........(b) TadhgO'Shea 6 86
(A bin Huzaim, UAE) *nvr nr to chal* **33/1**
13 shd **Noor Zabeel (USA)**[14] 290 4-9-3 97........ RoystonFfrench 4 87
(A Al Raihe, UAE) *nvr nr to chal* **28/1**
14 78 **Terdaad (IRE)**[87] 7631 5-8-11 91........(tp) DaraghO'Donohoe 13 40
(Saeed bin Suroor) *trckd ldrs tl wknd 2 1/2f out* **12/1**

1m 40.71s (100.71) **14** Ran SP% **134.4**
CSF: £41.71; TRICAST: £293.13; WIN: £8.30; EXACTA: £39.30; TRIFECTA £149.50.
Owner Hamdan Al Maktoum **Bred** Shadwell Farm LLC **Trained** UAE

504 - 505a (Foreign Racing) - See Raceform Interactive

[490] LINGFIELD (L-H)
Sunday, February 3

OFFICIAL GOING: Standard
Wind: Fresh, half behind Weather: Overcast

506 BET ON YOUR TABLET AT BLUESQ.COM H'CAP 1m (P)
1:40 (1:40) (Class 6) (0-65,65) 3-Y-O £2,215 (£654; £327) Stalls High

Form RPR
6-31 **1** **Darkest Night (IRE)**[12] 321 3-9-1 59........ FergusSweeney 1 62
(Jamie Osborne) *sn led: mde virtually all: set modest pce tl qcknd 3f out: hrd rdn and jnd ins fnl f: all out* **5/2**[2]
-111 **2** nse **Taxiformissbyron**[3] 459 3-9-1 64 6ex........ WilliamTwiston-Davies(5) 2 67
(Michael Herrington) *broke best: stdd and t.k.h in 3rd: drvn to chse wnr over 1f out: drew level ins fnl f: r.o wl* **4/7**[1]
01-4 **3** 3/4 **Byroness**[9] 371 3-9-0 65........ RyanTate(7) 4 66
(Heather Main) *plld hrd in cl 4th: chsd wnr 3f out tl over 1f out: kpt on wl fnl 100yds* **14/1**
-562 **4** 8 **Icanboogie**[11] 336 3-8-4 48........ LukeMorris 3 31
(Karen George) *t.k.h: chsd wnr tl 3f out: sn outpcd and btn* **10/1**[3]

1m 39.52s (1.32) **Going Correction** 0.0s/f (Stan) **4** Ran SP% **108.0**
Speed ratings (Par 95): **93,92,92,84**
CSF £4.37 TOTE £4.00; EX 4.00 Trifecta £9.00 Pool: £1,525.28 - 126.99 winning units..
Owner Miss E Asprey **Bred** M McGinn **Trained** Upper Lambourn, Berks

FOCUS
There was a tight finish in this tactical handicap. The hot favourite didn't have the run of things and was just denied.

507 LINGFIELDPARK.CO.UK H'CAP 1m 2f (P)
2:10 (2:10) (Class 6) (0-60,60) 3-Y-O £2,385 (£704; £352) Stalls Low

Form RPR
3451 **1** **Precision Strike**[8] 411 3-8-6 52........(v) PhilipPrince(7) 6 57
(Richard Guest) *hld up in rr: qcknd past all rivals to ld over 2f out: sn clr: drvn along and kpt gng ins fnl f* **6/1**
041- **2** 1 1/4 **Close Together (IRE)**[109] 7165 3-9-1 59........ WilliamTwiston-Davies(5) 3 61
(Robert Mills) *plld hrd: cl up: outpcd over 2f out: hrd rdn and styd on fr over 1f out: tk 2nd on line* **3/1**[2]
3-43 **3** shd **Mystery Woman (IRE)**[11] 336 3-9-2 55........ LukeMorris 2 57
(Peter Chapple-Hyam) *led: set slow pce: hdd and outpcd by wnr over 2f out: kpt on u.p fr over 1f out: lost 2nd on line* **4/1**[3]
000- **4** 3 1/4 **Jd Rockefeller**[45] 8178 3-9-4 57........ SebSanders 5 52
(Paul D'Arcy) *cl up on outer: outpcd and hrd rdn 2f out: sn btn* **6/4**[1]
664- **5** 3/4 **She's Some Girl (IRE)**[36] 8289 3-8-7 46 oh1........ BarryMcHugh 7 40
(Richard Fahey) *in tch: jnd ldr 7f out tl 3f out: sn outpcd* **8/1**
50-0 **6** 3/4 **Annalova**[13] 310 3-8-7 46 oh1........ TomEaves 1 38
(Richard Fahey) *cl up tl outpcd and struggling to stay in tch over 2f out* **25/1**

2m 9.31s (2.71) **Going Correction** 0.0s/f (Stan) **6** Ran SP% **114.2**
Speed ratings (Par 95): **89,88,87,85,84 84**
Tote Swingers: 1&2 £3.10, 1&3 £3.00, 2&3 £1.70 CSF £24.78 TOTE £8.20: £4.50, £2.00; EX 26.60 Trifecta £85.10 Pool: £2,560.59 - 22.56 winning units..
Owner Future Racing (Notts) Limited **Bred** Mickley Stud **Trained** Wetherby, W Yorks

FOCUS
The pace was steady. They were tightly bunched for a long way in this minor handicap and the winner completed a double under a good ride.

508 LINGFIELD PARK OWNERS GROUP H'CAP 1m 2f (P)
2:40 (2:40) (Class 6) (0-60,60) 4-Y-0+ £2,385 (£704; £352) Stalls Low

Form RPR
12-6 **1** **Bridge That Gap**[27] 94 5-9-2 55........(p) AdamKirby 4 64
(Roger Ingram) *hld up in midfield: rdn and hdwy over 1f out: led ins fnl f: drvn out* **9/4**[2]
51-2 **2** 1/2 **Safwaan**[23] 158 6-9-5 58........ StevieDonohoe 9 66
(Willie Musson) *dwlt: hld up towards rr: pushed along over 2f out: hdwy over 1f out: r.o u.p to take 2nd fnl 100yds: nt rch wnr* **2/1**[1]
20-3 **3** 1 1/4 **Barachiel**[25] 118 5-9-6 59........ LukeMorris 10 64
(Luke Dace) *prom: drvn to chse ldr over 1f out: kpt on same pce* **6/1**[3]
40-2 **4** 1 1/4 **Gunner Will (IRE)**[30] 51 4-9-6 60........ FergusSweeney 3 63
(Jamie Osborne) *trckd ldrs: effrt 2f out: one pce appr fnl f* **14/1**
-060 **5** 1/2 **Penbryn (USA)**[10] 361 6-9-3 56........ SebSanders 5 58
(Nick Littmoden) *t.k.h: pressed ldr: led 2f out: hdd & wknd ins fnl f* **25/1**
4-46 **6** shd **Silkee Supreme**[24] 132 4-8-11 56........(b) WilliamTwiston-Davies(5) 7 57
(Richard Hannon) *mid-div: rdn and rn wd bnd into st: styd on fnl f* **10/1**
-030 **7** hd **Daniel Thomas (IRE)**[12] 320 11-9-6 59........(tp) WilliamCarson 1 60
(Violet M Jordan) *dwlt: bhd: rdn 3f out: styd on fr over 1f out: nvr nrr* **12/1**
00-2 **8** 4 **Dolly Colman (IRE)**[20] 200 5-8-8 47........ ChrisCatlin 2 40
(Zoe Davison) *in rr of midfield: rdn 3f out: n.d* **25/1**

The Form Book Flat, Raceform Ltd, Compton, RG20 6NL.

00-0 **9** *2 ¼* **Archelao (IRE)**[27] 94 5-9-3 **56**.......................................(t) AmirQuinn 8 44
(Richard Rowe) *sn led: rdn and hdd 2f out: wknd over 1f out* **25/1**

56-0 **10** *14* **Arte Del Calcio**[22] 53 4-9-5 **59**....................................... DavidProbert 6 19
(Tony Carroll) *towards rr: rdn over 3f out: sn trailing: virtually p.u over 1f out* **33/1**

2m 4.85s (-1.75) **Going Correction** 0.0s/f (Stan)
WFA 4 from 5yo+ 1lb **10** Ran SP% **116.3**
Speed ratings (Par 101): **107,106,105,104,104 104,103,100,98,87**
Tote Swingers: 1&2 £2.00, 1&3 £3.00, 2&3 £3.20 CSF £6.74 CT £22.53 TOTE £2.10: £1.10, £1.20, £2.50; EX 9.00 Trifecta £29.50 Pool: £3,777.38 - 95.81 winning units..
Owner The Stargazers **Bred** Michael Joy **Trained** Epsom, Surrey

FOCUS
The two market leaders came from off the pace to fill the first two positions in this strongly run handicap.

509 MARSH GREEN MAIDEN FILLIES' STKS (SUNDAY £5K BONUS RACE) 6f (P)
3:10 (3:12) (Class 5) 3-Y-0+ **£2,587** (£770; £384; £192) **Stalls** Low

Form RPR

2 **1** **Hard Walnut (IRE)**[22] 185 3-8-9 71.............................. WilliamCarson 1 69
(Olly Stevens) *mde all: pushed clr over 1f out: unchal* **1/3**[1]

0-0 **2** *4 ½* **Club Electra (IRE)**[21] 197 3-8-9 0.................................... LukeMorris 4 55
(Tobias B P Coles) *sn drvn along in 4th: styd on to take 2nd fnl strides: nt trble wnr* **33/1**

0-4 **3** *nk* **Dubai Applause**[25] 123 3-8-9 0....................................... DavidProbert 5 54
(Charles Hills) *chsd wnr: rdn 2f out: no ch w wnr: lost 2nd fnl strides* **8/1**[2]

0 **4** *½* **Lady Farah**[21] 197 3-8-9 0.. HayleyTurner 2 52
(Robert Cowell) *prom: rdn 2f out: one pce* **12/1**[3]

0-5 **5** *2 ½* **Limoges**[11] 341 3-8-9 0.. EddieAhern 8 44
(Luke Dace) *sn rdn along towards rr: n.d* **25/1**

0- **6** *hd* **Made It (IRE)**[117] 6966 3-8-2 0.. RobertTart(7) 6 43
(Anthony Carson) *s.i.s: outpcd in rr: nvr nr ldrs* **12/1**[3]

6 **7** *shd* **Lasaraleen (IRE)**[20] 202 3-8-9 0.................................. BarryMcHugh 7 43
(Richard Fahey) *modest 5th most of way: rdn and n.d fnl 2f* **20/1**

1m 11.51s (-0.39) **Going Correction** 0.0s/f (Stan) **7** Ran SP% **113.1**
Speed ratings (Par 100): **102,96,95,94,91 91,91**
Tote Swingers: 1&2 £5.20, 1&3 £2.00, 2&3 £9.60 CSF £19.25 TOTE £1.40: £1.10, £10.30; EX 12.80 Trifecta £42.50 Pool: £3,325.86 - 58.68 winning units..
Owner Qatar Racing Limited **Bred** Barbara Prendergast **Trained** Chiddingfold, Surrey

FOCUS
The hot favourite had no trouble taking advantage of a golden opportunity in this maiden.

510 FOLLOW LINGFIELD PARK ON FACEBOOK H'CAP 1m (P)
3:40 (3:41) (Class 6) (0-55,56) 4-Y-0+ **£2,385** (£704; £352) **Stalls** High

Form RPR

05-5 **1** **Fonterutoli (IRE)**[23] 158 6-9-6 **54**................................(e) AdamKirby 11 62
(Roger Ingram) *sn prom: rdn to ld over 2f out: drvn out* **7/1**[2]

03-0 **2** *¾* **Teth**[33] 7 4-9-5 **53**.. WilliamCarson 1 59
(Anthony Carson) *chsd ldrs: rdn over 2f out: wnt 2nd ins fnl f: r.o* **20/1**

-362 **3** *nk* **Divine Rule (IRE)**[11] 334 5-9-1 **56**.........................(v) ThomasBrown(7) 7 62+
(Laura Mongan) *towards rr: rdn and hdwy over 1f out: styd on wl fnl f* **8/1**[3]

00-3 **4** *¾* **Automotive**[32] 14 5-9-6 **54**... LukeMorris 5 58
(Julia Feilden) *sn chsng ldr: jnd wnr over 2f out: unable qck fnl f* **25/1**

36-6 **5** *hd* **Athletic**[13] 312 4-9-5 **53**..(v[1]) EddieAhern 3 56
(J R Jenkins) *t.k.h in midfield: hdwy on inner to chse ldrs over 1f out: one pce fnl f* **16/1**

441 **6** *nk* **Litmus (USA)**[4] 441 4-9-4 **52** 6ex...................................(b) HayleyTurner 6 55+
(Simon Dow) *bhd: rdn and hdwy over 1f out: nrest at fin* **3/1**[1]

2-42 **7** *1 ¾* **My Scat Daddy (USA)**[2] 471 4-9-1 **49**............................ DavidProbert 4 48
(Brett Johnson) *bhd: rdn 3f out: styd on fr over 1f out: nvr nrr* **3/1**[1]

1-65 **8** *1* **Aegean King**[11] 334 7-9-4 **52**....................................... GeorgeBaker 10 48
(Michael Wigham) *t.k.h: in tch: rdn over 2f out: sn outpcd* **3/1**[1]

4-20 **9** *2 ¼* **Fairy Mist (IRE)**[11] 334 6-8-12 **46**................................ SeanLevey 12 37
(John Bridger) *wnt lft s: in tch tl wkng and hung lft over 1f out* **25/1**

00-3 **10** *1* **Missionaire (USA)**[27] 94 6-9-0 **55**..............................(p) RyanTate(7) 8 44
(Tony Carroll) *mid-div on outer: rdn over 2f out: sn btn* **16/1**

460- **11** *2 ½* **Indian Violet (IRE)**[38] 8248 7-9-6 **54**.............................(p) LiamKeniry 2 37
(Zoe Davison) *led tl over 2f out: sn wknd* **33/1**

00-0 **12** *1 ¼* **Sangrail**[23] 158 4-9-2 **50**...(b[1]) TomEaves 9 30
(William Muir) *towards rr: rdn and n.d fnl 3f* **33/1**

1m 37.83s (-0.37) **Going Correction** 0.0s/f (Stan) **12** Ran SP% **128.7**
Speed ratings (Par 101): **101,100,99,99,99 98,96,95,93,92 90,88**
Tote Swingers: 1&2 £28.30, 1&3 £7.20, 2&3 £26.20 CSF £149.30 CT £1183.27 TOTE £6.20: £2.00, £6.50, £2.10; EX 149.80 Trifecta £2497.30 Pool: £3,518.04 - 1.05 winning units..
Owner Mrs Cathy Hallam & Martyn Cruse **Bred** Massimo Parri **Trained** Epsom, Surrey
■ Stewards' Enquiry : Sean Levey one-day ban; failed to ride to draw (Feb 18)

FOCUS
Another tactical handicap. The leaders quickened up around the final turn and not many got involved.

511 BLUE SQUARE BET H'CAP 1m (P)
4:10 (4:12) (Class 5) (0-75,77) 4-Y-0+ **£3,408** (£1,006; £251; £251) **Stalls** High

Form RPR

34-1 **1** **Mister Musicmaster**[8] 400 4-9-9 **77**............................ WilliamCarson 1 85
(Ron Hodges) *chsd ldr most of way: led ins fnl f: drvn out* **4/1**[1]

324- **2** *1 ¾* **Piceno (IRE)**[65] 7935 5-9-7 **75**.....................................(p) LukeMorris 9 79
(Scott Dixon) *led: hrd rdn and hdd ins fnl f: unable qck* **5/1**[2]

60-5 **3** *shd* **Push Me (IRE)**[23] 159 6-8-10 **71**.............................. RobertTart(7) 6 75
(Jamie Poulton) *towards rr: rdn and r.o fr over 1f out: clsng at fin* **7/1**[3]

625- **3** *dht* **Lady Sylvia**[135] 6434 4-8-13 **67**.................................... LiamKeniry 2 71
(Joseph Tuite) *t.k.h: chsd ldrs: rdn over 2f out: kpt on fnl f* **33/1**

20-1 **5** *nk* **Travelling**[27] 89 4-8-7 **68**....................................... RyanTate(7) 11 71
(Tony Carroll) *hld up in rr: rdn and r.o fnl 2f: nrst fin* **8/1**

3612 **6** *hd* **Storm Runner (IRE)**[3] 451 5-8-10 **71**.................. JordanVaughan(7) 10 74
(George Margarson) *mid-div on outer: rdn over 2f out: styd on fnl f* **5/1**[2]

2233 **7** *nse* **Muhandis (IRE)**[10] 358 5-9-2 **70**................................(b) SebSanders 7 73
(Nick Littmoden) *plld hrd towards rr: rdn and hdwy over 1f out: styd on* **5/1**[2]

2-34 **8** *nk* **Only Ten Per Cent (IRE)**[11] 344 5-9-5 **73**.................. HayleyTurner 4 75
(J R Jenkins) *prom: rdn over 2f out: one pce fnl f* **20/1**

04-5 **9** *¾* **Availed Speaker (IRE)**[24] 146 4-8-13 **67**..................... BarryMcHugh 3 67
(Richard Fahey) *trckd ldrs: rdn over 2f out: one pce appr fnl f* **14/1**

5-06 **10** *5* **Mcconnell (USA)**[11] 340 8-8-2 **61** oh1...................(b) NatashaEaton(5) 5 50
(Violet M Jordan) *mid-div: rdn over 2f out: sn outpcd* **100/1**

360- **11** *6* **Cathedral**[60] 7997 4-9-3 **71**.. GeorgeBaker 8 46
(Michael Wigham) *stdd in rr s: rdn and n.d fnl 2f* **8/1**

1m 38.75s (0.55) **Going Correction** 0.0s/f (Stan) **11** Ran SP% **120.1**
Speed ratings (Par 103): **97,95,95,95,94 94,94,94,93,88 82**PL: Push Me £1.60 Lady Sylvia £3.50. Tricast: Mister Musicmaster, Piceno, Push Me £70.57, Mister Musicmaster, Piceno, Lady Sylvia £299.36. Trifecta: 1-2-5 £109.00 1-2-9 £331.30. Tote Swingers: 1&2 £4.60, 1&P £2.60, 1&L £6.80, 2&P £4.20, 2&L £11.30. CSF £23.95 CT £27 TOTE £Owner: £Mrs L Sharpe & Mrs S G Clapp, £Bred, £Mrs J Fuller And S Dutfield, £TrainedCharlton Mackrell, Somerset.

FOCUS
A competitive handicap. The pace was steady but the favourite scored in good style.

512 ENOUGH SAID, JUST BET AT BLUESQ.COM H'CAP 1m 4f (P)
4:40 (4:40) (Class 6) (0-60,60) 4-Y-0+ **£2,385** (£704; £352) **Stalls** Low

Form RPR

40-0 **1** **Maison Brillet (IRE)**[30] 53 6-9-7 **60**............................(p) SebSanders 6 69
(Clive Drew) *dwlt: towards rr: hdwy 3f out: led wl over 1f out: sn in command: rdn out* **6/1**[3]

2-03 **2** *1 ½* **El Libertador (USA)**[20] 201 7-8-9 **55**.......................(b) JoeyHaynes(7) 3 62
(Eric Wheeler) *towards rr: hdwy over 2f out: styd on to take 2nd ent fnl f* **5/1**[2]

413- **3** *1 ½* **Uncle Roger (IRE)**[29] 7718 4-9-4 **60**................................(v) LukeMorris 2 65
(Eve Johnson Houghton) *prom: rdn over 2f out: one pce* **6/4**[1]

03-4 **4** *½* **Petersboden**[27] 98 4-8-4 **49** oh1................................ NickyMackay 8 50
(Michael Blanshard) *bhd: nt clr run 3f out: hdwy 2f out: styd on same pce* **5/1**[2]

0-05 **5** *5* **Gower Rules (IRE)**[24] 132 5-8-10 **49**................................ SeanLevey 7 45
(John Bridger) *led: qcknd over 2f out: hdd & wknd wl over 1f out* **14/1**

606- **6** *3 ¾* **Rulbin Realta**[28] 7077 6-8-5 **49**..............................(p) JemmaMarshall(5) 9 39
(Pat Phelan) *chsd ldrs on outer: rdn 4f out: outpcd fnl 3f* **20/1**

00-0 **7** *½* **Broughton Place**[11] 343 5-8-7 **46** oh1.............................. JamieMackay 1 35
(Willie Musson) *plld hrd: hld up in 5th: squeezed out 3f out: sn hrd rdn and btn* **20/1**

450- **8** *16* **Murphy (IRE)**[46] 8170 11-9-1 **54**................................... HayleyTurner 4 17
(Nick Gifford) *sn chsng ldr: rdn and wknd 3f out: sn bhd* **6/1**[3]

2m 30.81s (-2.19) **Going Correction** 0.0s/f (Stan)
WFA 4 from 5yo+ 3lb **8** Ran SP% **118.1**
Speed ratings (Par 101): **107,106,105,104,101 98,98,87**
Tote Swingers: 1&2 £6.70, 1&3 £3.20, 2&3 £1.90 CSF £37.19 CT £66.69 TOTE £8.50: £1.60, £1.70, £1.60; EX 47.70 Trifecta £131.40 Pool: £2,518.80 - 14.37 winning units..
Owner C Drew **Bred** Liam Webb **Trained** Rampton, Cambs

FOCUS
The winner bounced back and scored in good style in this low-grade handicap.
T/Jkpt: Part won. £4,390.00 to a £1 stake. Pool: £6,184.18 - 0.50 winning tickets. T/Plt: £123.70 to a £1 stake. Pool: £71,706.76 - 423.15 winning tickets. T/Qpdt: £33.40 to a £1 stake. Pool: £5,066.50 - 112.24 winning tickets. LM

ST MORITZ (R-H)
Sunday, February 3

OFFICIAL GOING: Snow: frozen

513a GRAND PRIX AMERICAN AIRLINES (CONDITIONS) (4YO+) (GENTLEMEN RIDERS) (SNOW) 1m
1:15 (12:00) 4-Y-0+
£4,228 (£2,114; £1,510; £1,006; £503; £302)

RPR

1 **Ancient Greece**[29] 79 6-10-7 0.. MrFMitchell 7
(George Baker) *midfield on outside: hdwy to join ldng gp 3f out: tk narrow ld over 1 1/2f out: drvn out fnl f* **9/2**

2 *3* **Song Of Victory (GER)**[153] 9-10-1 0................................ MrJEFlynn 2
(M Weiss, Switzerland) **23/10**[2]

3 *4 ½* **Niya (FR)**[350] 631 6-9-13 0 ow1.................................. MrPatrickDeno 5
(P Schaerer, Switzerland) **32/5**

4 *¾* **Mont Pelato (USA)**[424] 7668 5-10-6 0.................... MrEdouardMonfort 4
(M Weiss, Switzerland) **1/1**[1]

5 *4* **Pasalsa (FR)**[158] 5-10-4 0....................................... MrFabrizioPerego 1
(Carmen Bocskai, Switzerland) **4/1**[3]

6 *1* **Oasis Knight (IRE)**[258] 2316 7-10-0 0.................. MrDennisSchiergen 3
(C Von Der Recke, Germany) **111/10**

7 **Akarali (IRE)** 4-10-7 0.. MrAlexandreLemarie 6
(Th Von Ballmoos, Switzerland) **156/10**

7 Ran SP% **146.3**
PARI-MUTUEL (all including 1 chf stakes): WIN 5.50; PLACE 1.50, 1.30; SF 10.30.
Owner Inkin, Inkin, Byng, Baker & Partners **Bred** Darley **Trained** Manton, Wilts

514a GRAND PRIX GUARDAVAL IMMOBILIEN (CONDITIONS) (4YO+) (SNOW) 1m 1f
2:15 (12:00) 4-Y-0+
£5,919 (£2,959; £2,114; £1,409; £704; £422)

RPR

1 **Amazing Beauty (GER)**[94] 6-9-1 0.............................. MircoDemuro 4
(M Figge, Germany) **8/5**[1]

2 *4* **Nightdance Paolo (GER)**[105] 7282 6-9-2 0.............. FredericSpanu 12
(A Schaerer, Switzerland) **13/2**

3 *10* **Tepmokea (IRE)**[25] 125 7-9-2 0.. ShaneKelly 8
(Mrs K Burke) *pressed ldr on ins: pushed along to hold pl 3f out: rdn and outpcd by front two fr ins fnl 2f: kpt on at one pce fnl f* **237/10**

4 *½* **Earl Of Winds (GER)**[350] 630 8-9-0 0............................(b) AndreBest 3
(P Schaerer, Switzerland) **43/5**

5 *6* **Flash Dance (GER)**[134] 6-9-2 0.. TimBurgin 6
(A Schennach, Switzerland) **4/1**[2]

6 *2 ½* **Halling River (IRE)**[350] 630 6-9-0 0..........................(b) RobertHavlin 2
(M Weiss, Switzerland) **11/2**[3]

7 **African Art (USA)**[350] 630 7-9-6 0.. DPorcu 7
(P Schaerer, Switzerland) **63/10**

8 **Exchange**[350] 629 5-9-0 0... AndreaAtzeni 13
(Frau M Muller, Switzerland) **118/10**

9 **Primatist (GER)**[77] 4-9-1 0...................................... LennartHammer-Hansen 10
(M Weber, Germany) **208/10**

10 **My Mary (GER)**[959] 6-8-10 0....................................... OlivierPlacais 5
(M Weiss, Switzerland) **156/10**

11	**Leiloken (FR)**[37] 6-9-0 0 ... AurelienLemaitre 1 (Christina Bucher, Switzerland) **26/1**		
12	**Sumatra Tiger (GER)**[264] 8-9-2 0 ... MrDennisSchiergen 11 (P Vovcenko, Germany) **206/10**		
13	**Letty**[344] 717 6-8-8 0 ... ZsuzsaTimar 9 (A Klimscha Jr, Hungary) **64/1**		

13 Ran SP% **143.6**

PARI-MUTUEL (all including 1 chf stakes): WIN 2.60; PLACE 2.80, 3.60, 3.70; SF 48.50.
Owner Stall Eivissa **Bred** Gestut Hachtsee **Trained** Germany

[476]WOLVERHAMPTON (A.W) (L-H)
Monday, February 4

OFFICIAL GOING: Standard
Wind: Fresh behind Weather: Cloudy

515 COMPARE ONLINE BOOKIES AT BOOKMAKERS.CO.UK ALL WEATHER "HANDS AND HEELS" APPRENTICE SERIES H'CAP 1m 5f 194y(P)
2:45 (2:45) (Class 6) (0-60,60) 4-Y-O+ **£1,940** (£577; £288; £144; £15) **Stalls** Low

Form	Pos	Btn	Horse / Comment	RPR
3-30	1		**Party Palace**[4] 458 9-8-10 **47** ... JordanVaughan(3) 10 (Stuart Howe) *chsd ldrs: led over 3f out: pushed clr over 1f out: styd on* **8/1**	55
2-11	2	¾	**Easydoesit (IRE)**[24] 169 5-9-12 **60** ... RyanTate 2 (Tony Carroll) *prom: pushed along over 3f out: styd on wl: nt rch wnr* **6/4**[1]	66+
506-	3	1 ¾	**Royal Defence (IRE)**[34] 7472 7-9-0 **48** ... RobertTart 3 (Mick Quinn) *led after 1f: hdd over 3f out: sn pushed along: styd on same pce ins fnl f* **28/1**	52
1-02	4	¾	**Scribe (IRE)**[24] 165 5-9-6 **54** ... (t) DanielMuscutt 6 (David Evans) *broke wl: lost pl after 2f: hdwy over 2f out: styd on: nt rch ldrs* **3/1**[2]	57+
/0-5	5	nk	**Richo**[5] 406 7-8-9 **46** oh1 ... JordanNason(3) 7 (Shaun Harris) *s.i.s: hld up: pushed along over 3f out: hdwy over 2f out: styd on: nrst fin* **20/1**	49
0/	6	8	**Table Forty Six (IRE)**[127] 6719 7-9-2 **50** ... (t) RossCoakley 8 (Jarlath P Fahey, Ire) *hld up: hdwy over 3f out: sn pushed along: wknd over 1f out* **10/1**	41
2-45	7	1 ½	**Perfect Shot (IRE)**[3] 469 7-8-12 **51** ... PaigeBolton(5) 1 (Michael Attwater) *led 1f: chsd ldrs: pushed along over 2f out: wknd over 1f out* **7/2**[3]	40
4-40	8	7	**Watch The Birdie (IRE)**[3] 469 5-9-9 **57** ... (p) GaryPhillips 5 (Ronald Harris) *s.i.s: sn prom: pushed along over 3f out: wknd over 2f out* **25/1**	36
/00-	9	9	**Artful Dodger**[38] 8267 6-8-9 **46** oh1 ... CharlotteJenner(3) 4 (Olivia Maylam) *prom over 9f* **33/1**	13
06-5	10	2 ½	**Shaker Style (USA)**[13] 330 7-9-6 **54** ... GemmaTutty 12 (Barry Murtagh) *hld up: wknd over 3f out* **20/1**	17
000-	11	22	**Royal Gig**[25] 7384 4-8-2 **46** oh1 ... RichardOliver(5) 11 (Tim Etherington) *hld up: bhd fnl 5f: t.o* **66/1**	

3m 6.39s (0.39) **Going Correction** +0.05s/f (Slow)
WFA 4 from 5yo+ 5lb 11 Ran SP% **128.7**
Speed ratings (Par 101): **100,99,98,98,97 93,92,88,83,81 69**
Tote Swingers: 1&2 £4.60, 1&3 £36.50, 2&3 £11.20 CSF £21.00 CT £358.88 TOTE £11.20: £2.60, £1.40, £6.00; EX 31.00 Trifecta £962.10 Pool: £5,806.18 - 4.52 winning units..
Owner B P Jones **Bred** Llety Stud **Trained** Oakford, Devon

FOCUS
A weak handicap, won in good style by the enterprisingly ridden winner.

516 BOOKMAKER REVIEWS AT BOOKMAKERS.CO.UK H'CAP 5f 20y(P)
3:20 (3:20) (Class 6) (0-60,60) 4-Y-O+ **£2,264** (£673; £336; £168) **Stalls** Low

Form	Pos	Btn	Horse / Comment	RPR
060-	1		**Bailadeira**[52] 8107 5-9-0 **53** ... JamesSullivan 1 (Tim Etherington) *hld up: hdwy over 1f out: rdn to ld wl ins fnl f: r.o* **16/1**	62
05-5	2	nk	**Imjin River (IRE)**[25] 143 6-8-10 **54** ... (t) NatashaEaton(5) 10 (William Stone) *s.i.s: hld up: hdwy over 1f out: rdn and ev ch wl ins fnl f: r.o* **12/1**	62
0004	3	½	**Fantasy Fighter (IRE)**[3] 472 8-8-7 **46** oh1 ... (b) LukeMorris 2 (Ronald Harris) *trckd ldrs: led ins fnl f: sn rdn and hdd: styd on* **7/1**[2]	52
1-40	4	½	**Methaaly (IRE)**[20] 214 10-9-0 **60** ... (be) RobertTart(7) 9 (Michael Mullineaux) *hld up: hdwy over 1f out: r.o* **9/1**	64
00-6	5	1 ¼	**No Mean Trick (USA)**[14] 308 7-9-6 **59** ... MickyFenton 7 (Paul Midgley) *led: rdn over 1f out: hdd and unable qck ins fnl f* **7/2**[1]	59
6051	6	1 ¼	**Steel City Boy (IRE)**[13] 327 10-8-11 **55** ... AnnStokell(5) 5 (Ann Stokell) *chsd ldrs: rdn 1/2-way: styd on same pce fnl f* **20/1**	50
3032	7	hd	**Russian Bullet**[10] 369 4-9-5 **58** ... FergusSweeney 3 (Jamie Osborne) *hld up: hdwy over 1f out: sn rdn: no imp ins fnl f* **7/2**[1]	53
6-30	8	hd	**Whiskey Junction**[7] 423 9-9-2 **55** ... WilliamCarson 6 (Mick Quinn) *sn pushed along and prom: rdn 1/2-way: styd on same pce fr over 1f out* **12/1**	49
0-20	9	1	**Yungaburra (IRE)**[9] 398 9-8-11 **50** ... (tp) FrannyNorton 11 (David C Griffiths) *hld up: nvr trbld ldrs* **15/2**[3]	40
5-36	10	1	**Ches Jicaro (IRE)**[18] 236 5-8-7 **46** oh1 ... (v[1]) DavidProbert 8 (James Unett) *s.i.s: sn prom: rdn over 1f out: no ex* **8/1**	33
050-	11	¾	**Jolly Ranch**[87] 7673 7-9-2 **55** ... SeanLevey 4 (Tony Newcombe) *w ldr tl rdn over 1f out: wknd ins fnl f* **8/1**	39

1m 2.3s **Going Correction** +0.05s/f (Slow) 11 Ran SP% **127.0**
Speed ratings (Par 101): **102,101,100,99,97 95,95,95,93,92 90**
Tote Swingers: 1&2 £46.50, 1&3 £27.20, 2&3 £13.30 CSF £208.93 CT £1517.93 TOTE £39.60: £8.40, £4.60, £2.60; EX 390.50 Trifecta £2456.30 Pool: £5,242.07 - 1.60 winning units..
Owner World Wide Racing Partners **Bred** Summerville Bloodstock Associates Llp **Trained** Norton, N Yorks

FOCUS
A low-grade handicap, run at a fierce pace.

517 BOOKMAKERS.CO.UK GIVES YOU FREE BETS (S) STKS 7f 32y(P)
3:50 (3:51) (Class 6) 3-Y-O+ **£1,940** (£577; £288; £144) **Stalls** High

Form	Pos	Btn	Horse / Comment	RPR
46-3	1		**Classic Colori (IRE)**[33] 23 6-9-10 **78** ... (b[1]) DanielTudhope 4 (David O'Meara) *trckd ldrs: rdn to ld and hung lft ins fnl f: styd on* **7/4**[1]	83
2-33	2	1	**Azrael**[10] 370 5-9-5 **72** ... (p) WilliamTwiston-Davies(5) 3 (Alan McCabe) *led: rdn and hdd ins fnl f: styd on same pce* **7/2**[3]	80
64-2	3	¾	**Saharia (IRE)**[19] 221 6-9-10 **77** ... (v) ShaneKelly 1 (Daniel Mark Loughnane) *hld up: hdwy over 1f out: sn rdn: styd on* **5/2**[2]	78
00-4	4	hd	**Zing Wing**[6] 431 5-9-5 **70** ... AdamKirby 9 (David Evans) *prom: rdn over 2f out: styd on* **7/2**[3]	72
03-5	5	5	**Khajaaly (IRE)**[10] 370 6-9-7 **70** ... RaulDaSilva(3) 5 (Julia Feilden) *trckd ldr: rdn over 2f out: hung lft and no ex fnl f* **16/1**	64
3-14	6	2 ¼	**Vitznau (IRE)**[12] 334 9-10-0 **61** ... ChrisCatlin 8 (John Butler) *s.i.s: hld up: nvr on terms* **25/1**	62
000-	7	4	**The Kernigal (IRE)**[52] 8111 4-9-10 **46** ... (bt) DavidProbert 7 (Paul Howling) *hld up: pushed along 1/2-way: rdn and wknd 2f out* **80/1**	47
0-50	8	2 ¾	**Amber Moon**[22] 193 8-9-0 **39** ... (b) AnnStokell(5) 10 (Ann Stokell) *prom: racd keenly: hung rt and wknd over 2f out* **150/1**	35

1m 29.48s (-0.12) **Going Correction** +0.05s/f (Slow)
WFA 3 from 4yo+ 17lb 8 Ran SP% **121.0**
Speed ratings (Par 101): **102,100,100,99,94 91,86,83**
Tote Swingers: 1&2 £1.90, 1&3 £1.70, 2&3 £2.30 CSF £8.96 TOTE £2.40: £1.20, £1.70, £1.10; EX 9.30 Trifecta £25.10 Pool: £4,717.95 - 140.51 winning units..No bid for the winner.
Owner The Classic Strollers Partnership **Bred** Frank Dunne **Trained** Nawton, N Yorks

FOCUS
A modest seller.

518 CORAL.CO.UK H'CAP 7f 32y(P)
4:25 (4:26) (Class 5) (0-75,75) 4-Y-O+ **£3,234** (£962; £481; £240) **Stalls** High

Form	Pos	Btn	Horse / Comment	RPR
0-06	1		**The Guru Of Gloom (IRE)**[11] 358 5-9-1 **69** ... LukeMorris 2 (William Muir) *hld up: hdwy over 1f out: sn rdn: r.o u.p to ld post* **16/1**	78
2-34	2	shd	**Haftohaf**[16] 272 4-9-7 **75** ... (p) AdamKirby 4 (Marco Botti) *chsd ldrs: led over 1f out: sn rdn: r.o: hdd post* **10/11**[1]	83
2-1	3	2	**Frontier Fighter**[27] 108 5-9-1 **69** ... DanielTudhope 6 (David O'Meara) *chsd ldrs tl led 2f out: rdn and hdd over 1f out: styd on same pce ins fnl f* **4/1**[2]	72
34-5	4	5	**Showboating (IRE)**[24] 164 5-9-7 **75** ... (p) SeanLevey 7 (Alan McCabe) *s.i.s: hld up: hung rt 1/2-way: rdn over 1f out: nvr trbld ldrs* **7/1**[3]	65
5061	5	hd	**Lord Of The Dance (IRE)**[7] 426 7-9-0 **68** 6ex ... TomEaves 1 (Michael Mullineaux) *prom: rdn over 1f out: wknd fnl f* **9/1**	57
0-40	6	3 ¼	**Smalljohn**[20] 217 7-9-1 **74** ... (v) WilliamTwiston-Davies(5) 5 (Bryan Smart) *led 1f: chsd ldrs: rdn over 2f out: wknd over 1f out* **9/1**	53
2-00	7	6	**Beauty Pageant (IRE)**[22] 196 6-9-4 **72** ... WilliamCarson 3 (David Evans) *sn pushed along: led 6f out: rdn and hdd 2f out: wknd over 1f out* **50/1**	35

1m 29.09s (-0.51) **Going Correction** +0.05s/f (Slow) 7 Ran SP% **112.7**
Speed ratings (Par 103): **104,103,101,95,95 91,84**
Tote Swingers: 1&2 £1.70, 1&3 £3.70, 2&3 £7.40 CSF £30.48 TOTE £23.40: £7.00, £1.30; EX 35.30 Trifecta £182.50 Pool: £4,691.05 - 19.27 winning units..
Owner R Haim **Bred** Oak Lodge Bloodstock **Trained** Lambourn, Berks
■ Stewards' Enquiry : William Twiston-Davies one-day ban: careless riding (Feb 18)

FOCUS
A fair handicap, run at a strong pace and it served up a thrilling finish.

519 CASINO AT CORAL.CO.UK CLAIMING STKS 1m 141y(P)
4:55 (4:55) (Class 6) 4-Y-O+ **£1,988** (£625; £336) **Stalls** Low

Form	Pos	Btn	Horse / Comment	RPR
5-31	1		**Faithful Ruler (USA)**[6] 433 9-8-5 **65** ... (p) GaryPhillips(7) 1 (Ronald Harris) *chsd ldr to over 5f out: lft in ld wl over 3f out: rdn and hdd over 1f out: rallied to ld wl ins fnl f* **10/1**[3]	67
5-54	2	½	**For Shia And Lula (IRE)**[4] 452 4-9-0 **67** ... ShaneKelly 3 (Daniel Mark Loughnane) *hld up: hmpd wl over 3f out: rdn: edgd lft and r.o wl ins fnl f: wnt 2nd post: nt rch wnr* **16/1**	68
4331	3	hd	**The Mongoose**[2] 490 5-9-0 **64** ... (bt[1]) AdamKirby 4 (David Evans) *trckd ldrs: wnt 2nd over 5f out: hmpd wl over 3f out: shkn up to ld over 1f out: hrd rdn and hdd wl ins fnl f* **7/1**[2]	68
3-21	U		**Desert Vision**[18] 239 9-9-3 **86** ... (vt) GrahamGibbons 2 (Michael Easterby) *led at stdy pce tl broke leg and uns rdr wl over 3f out: fatally injured* **1/4**[1]	

1m 53.72s (3.22) **Going Correction** +0.05s/f (Slow) 4 Ran SP% **107.5**
Speed ratings (Par 101): **87,86,86,**
CSF £85.62 TOTE £10.10; EX 34.70 Trifecta £62.80 Pool: £2,315.98 - 27.62 winning units..
Owner Ridge House Stables Ltd **Bred** WinStar Farm LLC **Trained** Earlswood, Monmouths
■ Stewards' Enquiry : Gary Phillips two-day ban: used whip above permitted level (Feb 19-20)

FOCUS
A fair claimer, marred by the fatal injury of Desert Vision which impacted heavily on the result. The form clearly amounts to very little.

520 DOWNLOAD CORAL.CO.UK MOBILE APP H'CAP 1m 4f 50y(P)
5:25 (5:25) (Class 6) (0-65,65) 4-Y-O+ **£2,264** (£673; £336; £168) **Stalls** Low

Form	Pos	Btn	Horse / Comment	RPR
64-2	1		**Wordiness**[12] 338 5-9-1 **64** ... WilliamTwiston-Davies(5) 5 (Seamus Durack) *a.p: hit over hd by rivals whip over 2f out: led over 1f out: sn rdn: styd on wl: eased nr fin* **5/2**[1]	75
33-6	2	2 ¾	**Day Of Destiny (IRE)**[24] 165 8-9-4 **62** ... JamesSullivan 1 (James Given) *a.p: rdn to chse wnr over 1f out: hung lft and styd on same pce ins fnl f* **5/1**[2]	69
0/	3	8	**Walter De La Mare (IRE)**[27] 6269 6-8-9 **53** ... LukeMorris 4 (Anabel K Murphy) *led 1f: chsd ldr tl led over 2f out: rdn and hdd over 1f out: wknd ins fnl f* **10/1**	47
63-2	4	8	**Annelko**[31] 53 6-9-4 **62** ... RichardKingscote 6 (Michael Blake) *s.i.s: rcvrd to ld after 1f: rdn and hdd over 2f out: wknd over 1f out* **5/2**[1]	43
03-0	5	1	**Torero**[9] 397 4-9-4 **65** ... TomEaves 2 (Kevin Ryan) *chsd ldrs: rdn over 4f out: wknd over 2f out* **8/1**[3]	44
2-00	6	13	**Amana (USA)**[7] 429 9-9-7 **65** ... ShaneKelly 7 (Mark Brisbourne) *s.i.s: hld up: rdn over 3f out: sn wknd: t.o* **33/1**	24
303-	7	12	**Ashkalara**[96] 7473 6-9-2 **60** ... AdamKirby 3 (Stuart Howe) *hld up: rdn over 3f out: sn wknd: t.o* **5/1**[2]	

2m 39.02s (-2.08) **Going Correction** +0.05s/f (Slow)
WFA 4 from 5yo+ 3lb 7 Ran SP% **113.6**
Speed ratings (Par 101): **108,106,100,95,94 86,78**
Tote Swingers: 1&2 £3.10, 1&3 £5.30, 2&3 £7350.00 CSF £15.24 TOTE £3.20: £1.70, £2.10; EX 14.50 Trifecta £100.80 Pool: £2,730.56 - 20.30 winning units..
Owner W A Harrison-Allan **Bred** Juddmonte Farms Ltd **Trained** Baydon, Wilts

FOCUS
A modest handicap, run only at a steady pace but a lot to like about the performance of the winner.

521 EXCLUSIVE FREE BETS AT BOOKMAKERS.CO.UK MAIDEN STK$m 4f 50y(P)
5:55 (5:55) (Class 5) 4-Y-O+ **£2,587** (£770; £384; £192) **Stalls** Low

Form	Pos	Btn	Horse / Comment	RPR
	1		**Wyborne**[157] 4-9-5 0 ... DaleSwift 6 (Brian Ellison) *chsd ldr tl led over 2f out: pushed clr over 1f out: eased nr fin* **1/1**[1]	66+

3 **2** 3 ¼ **Pullmen**[14] 313 5-9-8 0 DavidProbert 9 57
(J R Jenkins) *chsd ldrs: pushed along 7f out: rdn over 2f out: styd on same pce fr over 1f out* **20/1**

5 **3** shd **Lacey**[20] 215 4-9-5 0 AdamKirby 4 56
(Reg Hollinshead) *hld up: pushed along over 5f out: rdn over 2f out: styd on same pce fr over 1f out* **9/1**

4 4 **The Great Gabrial** 4-9-5 0 TomEaves 1 50
(Ian Williams) *trckd ldrs: wnt 2nd 2f out: sn rdn: wknd fnl f* **11/4**[2]

/ **5** 9 **Bathcounty (IRE)**[45] 6-9-8 0 SebSanders 2 41
(Barry Brennan) *led: rdn and hdd over 2f out: wknd over 1f out* **13/2**[3]

4 **6** 47 **Chain Reactor**[24] 157 7-9-8 0 (b) RobertHavlin 8
(Amy Weaver) *s.i.s: hld up: pushed along 7f out: rdn and wknd over 5f out* **14/1**

2m 41.37s (0.27) **Going Correction** +0.05s/f (Slow)
WFA 4 from 5yo+ 3lb **6** Ran SP% **111.4**
Speed ratings (Par 103): **101,98,98,96,90 58**
Tote Swingers: 1&2 £5.00, 1&3 £2.20, 2&3 £7.00 CSF £22.53 TOTE £1.80: £1.60, £6.50; EX 20.30 Trifecta £103.40 Pool: £2,228.65 - 16.15 winning units..
Owner D Gilbert, M Lawrence, A Bruce **Bred** Juddmonte Farms Ltd **Trained** Norton, N Yorks

FOCUS
A weak maiden, run at a sound pace.
T/Plt: £464.50 to a £1 stake. Pool: £83,582.00 - 131.55 winning tickets. T/Qpdt: £36.10 to a £1 stake. Pool: £8,837.00 - 180.70 winning tickets. CR

SOUTHWELL (L-H)
Tuesday, February 5

OFFICIAL GOING: Standard to slow
Wind: Fresh half behind Weather: Bright, dry and cold

522 BOOKIE FREE BETS WITH BOOKMAKERS.CO.UK AMATEUR RIDERS' H'CAP 1m 3f (F)
1:40 (1:45) (Class 6) (0-52,52) 4-Y-O+ **£1,975** (£607; £303) **Stalls** Low

Form RPR

-324 **1** **Peace In Our Time**[10] 406 4-10-4 **50** (p) MrGrahamCarson(7) 1 59
(Anthony Carson) *trckd ldrs on inner: hdwy over 2f out: swtchd rt wl over 1f out: rdn to ld appr fnl f: styd on* **5/1**[1]

00-0 **2** 2 ¾ **Silver Marizah (IRE)**[28] 110 4-10-3 **49** (e) MissRBIngram(7) 3 53
(Roger Ingram) *a.p: cl up over 3f out: rdn 2f out: kpt on u.p fnl f* **40/1**

04-0 **3** ½ **Supa Seeker (USA)**[5] 456 7-10-4 **46** MrCCarroll(5) 12 49
(Tony Carroll) *trckd ldrs: hdwy 3f out: rdn wl over 1f out: drvn and kpt on fnl f* **15/2**[3]

6-0 **4** nse **Revolving World (IRE)**[25] 169 10-10-3 **45** (t) MrAaronJames(5) 9 48
(Lee James) *towards rr: rapid hdwy on outer to join ldrs after 3f: cl up 1/2-way: led 3f out: rdn 2f out: drvn and hdd appr fnl f: one pce* **12/1**

4-40 **5** 1 **May Boy**[20] 226 7-10-1 **45** MissMorganKerr(7) 13 46
(Ron Hodges) *hld up towards rr: hdwy 3f out: swtchd wd and rdn wl over 1f out: kpt on wl fnl f: nrst fin* **14/1**

60-2 **6** 1 ¾ **Angelena Ballerina (IRE)**[5] 456 6-10-1 **45** (v) MissBHampson(7) 4 43
(Sean Curran) *cl up: rdn along 3f out: wknd over 1f out* **7/1**[2]

66-6 **7** 3 ¾ **Skyblue**[27] 120 4-10-3 **45** (bt) MrChrisMartin(3) 6 36
(Tobias B P Coles) *in tch: effrt over 3f out: rdn along wl over 2f out: no hdwy* **14/1**

506- **8** hd **General Tufto**[46] 8212 8-10-11 **48** (b) MissSBrotherton 2 39
(Charles Smith) *hld up in rr: sme hdwy fnl 2f: nvr a factor* **15/2**[3]

0-0 **9** 1 ¾ **Son Of May**[28] 105 4-10-4 **50** (p[1]) MissJGordon(7) 10 38
(Jo Hughes) *led: rdn along and hdd 3f out: grad wknd fnl 2f* **16/1**

0/00 **10** 1 **Jakeys Girl**[4] 475 6-10-1 **45** MissLWilliams(7) 8 31
(Pat Phelan) *in tch: hdwy over 2f out: sn rdn and n.d* **66/1**

440- **11** 3 ½ **Heading To First**[91] 7605 6-10-3 **45** (p) MissMBryant(5) 11 25
(Paddy Butler) *a in rr* **28/1**

6/ **12** 22 **Lady Lyrath (IRE)**[18] 268 6-10-7 **51** (be) MissEMcCutcheon(7) 5 44
(S M Duffy, Ire) *hld up: hdwy on inner and in tch 4f out: rdn along 2f out: sn wknd and eased fnl f* **5/1**[1]

0-00 **13** 51 **Za'Lan (USA)**[4] 469 4-10-6 **52** (b) MissMTrainor(7) 7
(Chris Gordon) *s.i.s: reminders and outpcd after 3f: sn bhd: t.o fr 1/2-way* **8/1**

2m 31.31s (3.31) **Going Correction** +0.20s/f (Slow)
WFA 4 from 6yo+ 2lb **13** Ran SP% **114.8**
Speed ratings (Par 101): **95,93,92,92,91 90,87,87,86,85 83,67,30**
toteswingers 1&2 £34.10, 1&3 £7.30, 2&3 £56.40 CSF £216.89 CT £1480.52 TOTE £5.20: £1.50, £8.20, £2.80; EX 237.10 Trifecta £977.80 Pool: £4092.45 - 3.13 winning units..
Owner Neville Chamberlain Syndicate 1 **Bred** Darley **Trained** Newmarket, Suffolk
■ The first winner for Graham Carson, son of trainer Anthony and brother of jockey William.

FOCUS
The moment AW aficionados had been waiting for, this being the first meeting at Southwell since floods hit the course in November and both the back and home straight had been relaid. Officials expected it to ride on the slow side while still bedding in. The 5f chute is still out of action so all races were on the round course. An amateur riders' handicap kicked off proceeding and it was wide open. The went a solid early pace, but slowed up around 5f out and it did pay to be up there.

523 MONEY BACK RACING SPECIALS AT BOOKMAKERS.CO.UK H'CAP 7f (F)
2:10 (2:15) (Class 6) (0-60,60) 4-Y-O+ **£2,045** (£603; £302) **Stalls** Low

Form RPR

00-0 **1** **Hellbender (IRE)**[29] 96 7-9-7 60 (t) DavidProbert 10 71
(Shaun Harris) *in tch: hdwy on outer wl over 2f out: rdn to chse ldr wl over 1f out: led ent fnl f: drvn out* **12/1**

044- **2** ¾ **Kashmiri Star**[80] 7769 4-9-6 59 (v) AndreaAtzeni 7 68
(Mick Quinn) *trckd ldrs: hdwy and cl up 1/2-way: led wl over 2f out and sn rdn clr: hdd and drvn ent fnl f: kpt on* **6/1**[2]

0-60 **3** 2 ¾ **Bartley**[7] 435 4-9-4 57 (e[1]) TomEaves 11 59
(Bryan Smart) *dwlt and towards rr on wd outside: hdwy wl over 2f out: rdn over 1f out: kpt on wl fnl f: nrst fin* **11/1**

0-00 **4** 1 ¾ **Ace Of Spies (IRE)**[14] 323 8-9-0 53 HayleyTurner 1 50
(Conor Dore) *chsd ldrs: rdn along 2f out: sn one pce* **6/1**[2]

6640 **5** ¾ **Meydan Style (USA)**[6] 440 7-8-7 46 oh1 JoeFanning 3 41
(Richard Ford) *midfield: n.m.r towards inner 3f out: effrt and nt clr run wl over 1f out: sn swtchd rt to outer and rdn: kpt on fnl f: nrst fin* **10/1**

0-15 **6** nk **Boy The Bell**[11] 380 6-8-10 56 (b) JacobButterfield(7) 2 50
(Ollie Pears) *dwlt and sn pushed along in rr: hdwy on inner whn n.m.r 3f out: rdn and in tch 2f out: sn drvn and no imp* **7/2**[1]

00-0 **7** ¾ **Upper Lambourn (IRE)**[29] 96 5-8-11 55 (t) JemmaMarshall(5) 6 47
(Christopher Kellett) *nvr bttr then midfield* **7/1**[3]

3-00 **8** 5 **Greek Islands (IRE)**[13] 339 5-8-7 46 (v) LiamKeniry 5 24
(Ed de Giles) *disp ld to 1/2-way: cl up and rdn along 3f out: sn wknd* **16/1**

65-0 **9** 2 ¾ **Spread Boy (IRE)**[8] 422 6-8-0 46 oh1 JordanHibberd(7) 8 17
(Alan Berry) *a towards rr* **50/1**

0-00 **10** 4 ½ **Pipers Piping (IRE)**[12] 348 7-9-2 55 (p[1]) AdamKirby 9 14
(John Butler) *disp ld tl led 1/2-way: rdn along and hdd wl over 2f out: sn drvn and wknd wl over 1f out* **7/1**[3]

0-00 **11** 10 **Ishiamiracle**[17] 271 4-9-1 54 (p) LukeMorris 4
(Phil McEntee) *chsd ldrs: rdn along 1/2-way: sn lost pl and bhd fnl 2f* **12/1**

1m 31.34s (1.04) **Going Correction** +0.20s/f (Slow) **11** Ran SP% **116.4**
Speed ratings (Par 101): **102,101,98,96,95 94,93,88,85,79 68**
toteswingers 1&2 £13.80, 2&3 £13.90, 1&3 £24.40 CSF £81.55 CT £824.44 TOTE £18.30: £4.90, £2.00, £3.90; EX 101.60 Trifecta £851.40 Pool: £4327.45 - 3.81 winning units..Activate was claimed by Keith Dalgleish for £5,000.
Owner Wilf Hobson **Bred** James Lombard **Trained** Carburton, Notts

FOCUS
This moderate handicap was another open affair.

524 CORAL.CO.UK CLAIMING STKS 1m 4f (F)
2:40 (2:45) (Class 6) 4-Y-O+ **£2,045** (£603; £302) **Stalls** Low

Form RPR

-111 **1** **Stand Guard**[7] 432 9-9-8 87 AdamKirby 4 89+
(John Butler) *trckd ldng pair: hdwy and cl up after 4f: led on bit over 2f out: sn clr: unchal* **8/15**[1]

3362 **2** 10 **Activate**[7] 432 6-9-1 65 (b) DavidProbert 6 63
(Phil McEntee) *led: rdn along over 3f out: hdd over 2f out: sn drvn and kpt on same pce: no ch w wnr* **5/1**[3]

060- **3** 41 **Jack Dawkins (USA)**[52] 8136 8-9-4 61 SebSanders 3 24
(David Nicholls) *trckd ldr: cl up 1/2-way: rdn along over 3f out: sn wknd and eased fnl 2f* **10/3**[2]

00-0 **4** 26 **Avison (IRE)**[8] 417 5-8-5 48 (tp) RyanTate(7) 1
(Lawney Hill) *a in rr: rdn along and outpcd bef 1/2-way: sn wl bhd* **66/1**

2m 39.31s (-1.69) **Going Correction** +0.20s/f (Slow) **4** Ran SP% **106.5**
Speed ratings (Par 101): **113,106,79,61**
CSF £3.48 TOTE £1.50; EX 2.60 Trifecta £3.40 Pool: £3075.84 - 674.86 winning units..
Owner J Butler **Bred** Juddmonte Farms Ltd **Trained** Newmarket, Suffolk

FOCUS
An easy success for the highest-rated runner.

525 HORSE RACING BEST BETS AT BOOKMAKERS.CO.UK MAIDEN STKS 6f (F)
3:10 (3:15) (Class 5) 3-Y-O+ **£2,726** (£805; £402) **Stalls** Low

Form RPR

1 **Repetition** 3-8-12 0 TomEaves 8 75+
(Kevin Ryan) *dwlt: sn chsng ldrs: pushed along and n.m.r wl over 1f out: swtchd lft to inner and rdn ent fnl f: styd on strly to ld last 75yds* **5/2**[1]

0- **2** 1 ¾ **Moe's Place (IRE)**[99] 7434 3-8-9 0 JulieBurke(3) 10 66
(Kevin Ryan) *disp ld tl led 1/2-way: rdn over 1f out: drvn ins fnl f: hdd and no ex last 75yds* **7/1**

000- **3** 1 **Shining Cross (IRE)**[95] 7517 3-8-7 30 JemmaMarshall(5) 11 63
(Jo Hughes) *chsd ldrs: hdwy over 2f out: rdn to chse ldr over 1f out: drvn and kpt on same pce fnl f* **100/1**

2-34 **4** 2 ¾ **Black Rider (IRE)**[10] 404 3-8-12 65 AmyRyan 3 54
(Kevin Ryan) *in rr: hdwy on wd outside wl over 1f out: sn rdn and kpt on fnl f: nrst fin* **7/2**[2]

0-5 **5** 2 **Big Storm Coming**[22] 202 3-8-12 0 DaleSwift 4 48
(Brian Ellison) *chsd ldrs on inner: rdn along over 2f out: kpt on same pce* **33/1**

6 1 ¼ **Derby To Dubai** 3-8-5 0 KevinStott(7) 1 44
(Kevin Ryan) *in rr tl sme late hdwy* **20/1**

-552 **7** ½ **Script**[8] 423 4-9-3 45 SladeO'Hara(5) 5 41
(Alan Berry) *trckd ldrs: hdwy and cl up wl over 2f out: sn rdn and wknd over 1f out* **22/1**

66 **8** ¾ **Dutch Delight**[10] 404 3-8-7 0 JamesSullivan 9 35
(Tony Coyle) *hld up: a towards rr* **16/1**

22-4 **9** 1 ¾ **Lady Malet**[14] 324 3-8-7 67 AdamBeschizza 2 29
(William Haggas) *hld up towards rr: effrt and sme hdwy on inner over 2f out: sn rdn along and nvr a factor* **4/1**[3]

56-2 **10** 2 **Village Green**[14] 324 4-9-6 60 (b) JacobButterfield(7) 7 32
(Ollie Pears) *disp ld: rdn along wl over 2f out: drvn and wknd wl over 1f out* **15/2**

06- **11** 7 **Eliya**[210] 3948 3-8-0 0 KirstenSmith(7) 6
(Jo Hughes) *a towards rr* **66/1**

1m 18.06s (1.56) **Going Correction** +0.20s/f (Slow)
WFA 3 from 4yo 15lb **11** Ran SP% **115.5**
Speed ratings (Par 103): **97,94,93,89,87 85,84,83,81,78 69**
toteswingers 1&2 £5.90, 1&3 £27.00, 2&3 £75.90 CSF £19.10 TOTE £2.80: £1.20, £3.20, £16.80; EX 26.10 Trifecta £2798.10 Part won. Pool: £3730.86 - 0.91 winning units..
Owner Exors of The Late Guy Reed **Bred** G Reed **Trained** Hambleton, N Yorks

FOCUS
An ordinary sprint maiden, run at a sound pace and unsurprisingly trainer Kevin Ryan held the key as he saddled a one-two from his four runners.

526 POKER AT CORAL.CO.UK H'CAP 6f (F)
3:40 (3:45) (Class 4) (0-85,85) 4-Y-O+ **£4,690** (£1,395; £697; £348) **Stalls** Low

Form RPR

-121 **1** **Aubrietia**[19] 234 4-8-13 **77** (b) HayleyTurner 4 91
(Alan McCabe) *mde all: rdn 2f out: drvn over 1f out: kpt on wl u.p fnl f* **9/2**[1]

00-1 **2** 2 ½ **Burnhope**[12] 353 4-8-11 **75** (p) LukeMorris 5 81
(Scott Dixon) *chsd wnr: rdn 2f out: drvn and ch ent fnl f: kpt on* **8/1**

1-02 **3** 2 **Dickie Le Davoir**[5] 453 9-8-2 **66** (be) KellyHarrison 7 66
(Richard Guest) *in rr: hdwy on wd outside wl over 1f out: sn rdn and styd on wl fnl f: nrst fin* **16/1**

000- **4** ½ **Sans Loi (IRE)**[185] 4819 4-9-1 **79** ShaneKelly 8 77
(Brian Ellison) *chsd ldrs: hdwy to chse ldng pair 2f out: rdn and ch over 1f out tl edgd lft and one pce fnl f* **5/1**[2]

20-0 **5** shd **Bandstand**[32] 58 7-8-12 **76** TomEaves 6 74
(Bryan Smart) *dwlt and towards rr: hdwy and in tch 1/2-way: rdn 2f out and sn no imp* **11/2**[3]

-510 **6** 5 **Waking Warrior**[10] 405 5-9-1 **82** (tp) JulieBurke(3) 3 64
(Kevin Ryan) *dwlt and in rr tl sme late hdwy* **11/2**[3]

35-3 **7** nse **Mazovian (USA)**[5] 453 5-7-12 **69** NoelGarbutt(7) 9 51
(Michael Chapman) *chsd ldrs on outer: rdn along wl over 2f out: grad wknd* **7/1**

00-6 **8** *3 ¼* **Masked Dance (IRE)**[8] 426 6-8-2 **66** oh2..................(p) NickyMackay 1 38
(Scott Dixon) *midfield on inner: rdn along over 2f out: sn wknd* **28/1**
223- **9** *2 ½* **Sound Amigo (IRE)**[151] 6008 5-9-7 **85**.............................. GrahamLee 2 49
(Ollie Pears) *chsd ldrs: rdn along wl over 2f out: sn wknd* **11/2**[3]
1m 16.06s (-0.44) **Going Correction** +0.20s/f (Slow) **9** Ran SP% **113.9**
Speed ratings (Par 105): **110,106,104,103,103 96,96,92,88**
toteswingers 1&2 £6.30, 1&3 £5.10, 2&3 £13.60 CSF £39.95 CT £524.32 TOTE £3.70: £2.90, £2.50, £4.40; EX 18.50 Trifecta £105.20 Pool: £4524.20 - 32.24 winning units..
Owner Shropshire Wolves 4 **Bred** C J Murfitt **Trained** Averham Park, Notts

FOCUS
A lively betting heat. There was a decent pace on, but again it was a race where it paid to race handily.

527 CORAL.CO.UK MOBILE BETTING MAIDEN H'CAP 1m (F)
4:10 (4:15) (Class 6) (0-55,55) 3-Y-O **£2,045** (£603; £302) **Stalls** Low

Form RPR
4-64 **1** **Poetic Verse**[13] 336 3-9-7 **55**.............................. AndreaAtzeni 9 61
(Rod Millman) *trckd ldrs: hdwy wl over 2f out: rdn to chal over 1f out: drvn to ld ins fnl f: kpt on wl* **7/1**
0-43 **2** *½* **Napinda**[11] 371 3-9-3 **51**.............................. WilliamCarson 6 56
(Philip McBride) *prom: cl up 3f out: rdn to ld over 2f out: drvn and hdd ins fnl f: no ex last 50yds* **25/1**
604- **3** *3 ¼* **Naughtybychoice**[204] 4140 3-9-7 **55**.............................. TomEaves 8 52
(Ollie Pears) *dwlt: hld up towards rr: smooth hdwy on outer over 3f out: chal wl over 1f out and sn ev ch: rdn ent fnl f and kpt on same pce* **14/1**
0-42 **4** *shd* **Shearian**[4] 482 3-8-11 **52**.............................. RyanTate(7) 2 49+
(Tony Carroll) *in tch: rdn along over 2f out: styd on fnl f: nrst fin* **9/2**[3]
000- **5** *3 ¼* **Aphrodite Spirit (IRE)**[54] 8094 3-8-13 **47**.............................. LukeMorris 7 37
(Pat Eddery) *chsd ldrs: rdn along wl over 2f out: grad wknd* **12/1**
040- **6** *nse* **Birdy Boy (USA)**[89] 7650 3-8-12 **46** oh1.............................. JoeFanning 4 36
(Mark Johnston) *slt ld: rdn along wl over 2f out: sn hdd and drvn: wknd over 1f out* **4/1**[2]
2226 **7** *¾* **Holding Fast (IRE)**[6] 442 3-9-7 **55**.............................. AdamKirby 1 43
(Tobias B P Coles) *chsd ldrs: rdn along wl over 2f out: sn wknd* **15/2**
0-30 **8** *17* **Hanga Roa (IRE)**[12] 350 3-9-7 **55**.............................. GeorgeBaker 5
(Gary Moore) *a in rr: bhd fnl 2f* **10/1**
4-23 **9** *13* **Una Bella Cosa**[22] 212 3-9-5 **53**..............................(p) SebSanders 3
(Alan McCabe) *cl up on inner: rdn along 3f out: sn wknd and bhd whn eased wl over 1f out* **7/2**[1]
1m 45.59s (1.89) **Going Correction** +0.20s/f (Slow) **9** Ran SP% **112.0**
Speed ratings (Par 95): **98,97,94,94,90 90,90,73,60**
toteswingers 1&2 £19.00, 1&3 £18.00, 2&3 £17.90 CSF £153.26 CT £2340.18 TOTE £6.10: £2.40, £4.10, £4.60; EX 125.50 Trifecta £2811.30 Part won. Pool: £3748.50 - 0.83 winning units..
Owner The Links Partnership **Bred** The Links Partnership **Trained** Kentisbeare, Devon

FOCUS
A typically weak 3yo maiden handicap.

528 ONLINE BETTING OFFERS AT BOOKMAKERS.CO.UK H'CAP 1m 4f (F)
4:40 (4:45) (Class 5) (0-70,70) 4-Y-O+ **£2,587** (£770; £384; £192) **Stalls** Low

Form RPR
030- **1** **Discay**[120] 6924 4-8-13 **65**.............................. JoeFanning 3 74
(Mark Johnston) *trckd ldr: cl up over 3f out: led over 2f out: rdn and hung lft 1f out: drvn and edgd lft ins fnl f: kpt on* **8/1**
01-6 **2** *nk* **Goldmadchen (GER)**[23] 198 5-8-13 **62**.............................. TomEaves 4 70
(Keith Dalgleish) *t.k.h: trckd ldng pair on inner: hdwy over 2f out: chal wl over 1f out: rdn whn sltly hmpd 1f out: sn drvn and ev ch tl n.m.r on inner and no ex nr fin* **4/1**[3]
3-20 **3** *¾* **Stanley Rigby**[26] 144 7-8-9 **65**.............................. LauraBarry(7) 7 72
(Richard Fahey) *trckd ldng pair on outer: hdwy over 2f out: rdn to chal over 1f out and ev ch tl hung lft and one pce last 100yds* **7/2**[2]
-113 **4** *3* **Sweet Liberta (IRE)**[13] 338 4-9-1 **67**.............................. DavidProbert 6 69
(Andrew Balding) *hld up in tch: hdwy on outer over 2f out: sn rdn and no imp appr fnl f* **11/4**[1]
-256 **5** *3 ½* **Follow The Flag (IRE)**[14] 329 9-9-7 **70**..............................(be) ShaneKelly 1 67
(Alan McCabe) *trckd ldrs: effrt 3f out: rdn along over 2f out and sn btn* **16/1**
3-01 **6** *15* **Mcbirney (USA)**[13] 338 6-9-0 **70**.............................. PhilipPrince(7) 5 43
(Paul D'Arcy) *hld up: effrt on inner over 3f out: rdn along wl over 2f out and sn wknd* **5/1**
0-60 **7** *8* **Mazij**[8] 429 5-9-2 **65**.............................. WilliamCarson 2 25
(Peter Hiatt) *led: rdn along 3f out: hdd over 2f out and sn wknd* **9/1**
2m 44.64s (3.64) **Going Correction** +0.20s/f (Slow)
WFA 4 from 5yo+ 3lb **7** Ran SP% **112.5**
Speed ratings (Par 103): **95,94,94,92,89 79,74**
toteswingers 1&2 £8.60, 1&3 £6.20, 2&3 £3.50 CSF £38.44 TOTE £8.80: £5.50, £4.00; EX 63.30 Trifecta £460.00 Pool: £2669.31 - 4.35 winning units..
Owner C H Greensit & W A Greensit **Bred** C H And W A Greensit **Trained** Middleham Moor, N Yorks

FOCUS
A tight handicap. It was run at an average pace and the first four had it to themselves from 2f out.
T/Plt: £4,162.50 to a £1 stake. Pool: £72,416.16 - 12.70 winning tickets. T/Qpdt: £233.30 to a £1 stake. Pool: £9,303.84 - 29.50 winning tickets. JR

438 KEMPTON (A.W) (R-H)
Wednesday, February 6

OFFICIAL GOING: Standard
Wind: Very strong, against Weather: Fine but cloudy, cold

529 WIN BIG WITH BETDAQ MULTIPLES H'CAP 5f (P)
5:05 (5:05) (Class 7) (0-50,50) 4-Y-O+ **£1,455** (£433; £216; £108) **Stalls** Low

Form RPR
05-4 **1** **Burnt Cream**[28] 111 6-9-2 **45**..............................(t) JimCrowley 7 54
(Martin Bosley) *settled in last trio: pushed along and prog over 1f out: rdn and styd on wl fnl f to ld last 75yds* **11/2**
2335 **2** *1* **Miserere Mei (IRE)**[9] 422 4-9-5 **48**.............................. KellyHarrison 2 53
(Richard Guest) *wl away fr gd draw: led: more than a l clr 1f out: drvn and hdd last 75yds* **9/2**[3]
4-20 **3** *1* **Deveze (IRE)**[28] 111 5-9-2 **45**..............................(b) LukeMorris 9 46
(Milton Bradley) *slowest away and swtchd to inner: t.k.h and sn in tch: prog fr 1/2-way: rdn to chse ldr over 1f out to 1f out: kpt on same pce* **10/1**
055- **4** *½* **Cincinnati Kit**[144] 6249 4-9-7 **50**..............................(t) DavidProbert 5 50
(Stuart Williams) *s.i.s: racd wd in midfield: lost grnd bnd 2f out: drvn and kpt on fnl f: unable to chal* **7/2**[2]
2-00 **5** *¾* **Red Ramesses (IRE)**[12] 369 4-9-7 **50**.............................. AdamKirby 8 47+
(John Best) *hung lft bnd after 1f and dropped to last pair: swtchd lft and shkn up over 1f out: styd on fnl f: nvr nrr* **11/4**[1]
06-5 **6** *nse* **Rooknrasbryripple**[5] 472 4-9-4 **47**.............................. WilliamCarson 1 44
(Ralph Smith) *chsd ldng pair: shoved along bef 1/2-way: chsd ldr 2f out to over 1f out: wknd* **14/1**
4-65 **7** *1 ½* **Chateau Lola**[27] 142 4-9-7 **50**.............................. FrannyNorton 3 41
(Derek Shaw) *chsd ldrs: lost pl and shkn up wl over 1f out: n.d after: eased nr fin* **7/1**
056/ **8** *3* **Old Peg**[835] 7129 8-9-7 **50**.............................. RobbieFitzpatrick 4 31
(Dai Burchell) *s.i.s: a in rr: shkn up and no prog over 1f out* **33/1**
00-0 **9** *¾* **Lowtherwood**[15] 326 4-9-2 **45**..............................(bt[1]) FergusSweeney 6 23
(William Muir) *chsd ldr to 2f out: wknd* **16/1**
1m 0.39s (-0.11) **Going Correction** 0.0s/f (Stan) **9** Ran SP% **119.5**
Speed ratings (Par 97): **100,98,96,96,94 94,92,87,86**
toteswingers 1&2 £4.50, 1&3 £7.60, 2&3 £5.50 CSF £31.64 CT £247.24 TOTE £7.50: £2.60, £1.30, £2.20; EX 24.30 Trifecta £178.20 Pool: £1,607.31 - 6.76 winning units..
Owner Mrs Patricia Brown **Bred** C Eddington And Partners **Trained** Chalfont St Giles, Bucks

FOCUS
A modest handicap run at a decent pace. The winner came from some way back and there was a strong headwind in the straight.

530 BACK OR LAY AT BETDAQ.COM H'CAP 1m 2f (P)
5:35 (5:36) (Class 7) (0-50,50) 4-Y-O+ **£1,455** (£433; £216; £108) **Stalls** Low

Form RPR
450- **1** **Lytham (IRE)**[39] 8288 12-9-2 **45**.............................. FergusSweeney 4 54
(Tony Carroll) *t.k.h early: hld up in last quartet: taken to outer and prog wl over 1f out: styd on wl to ld last 75yds* **5/1**[2]
15-0 **2** *1 ¼* **Brave Decision**[26] 158 6-9-4 **47**.............................. LukeMorris 7 53
(Suzy Smith) *sn trckd ldr: led 2f out: drvn over 1f out: hdd and outpcd last 75yds* **10/1**
-050 **3** *¾* **Sommersturm (GER)**[14] 343 9-9-6 **49**.............................. WilliamCarson 1 54+
(David Evans) *t.k.h: hld up in last quartet: pushed along 3f out and trapped on inner: plld out over 1f out but only 7th: fin wl to take 3rd post* **7/2**[1]
00-4 **4** *hd* **Byrd In Hand (IRE)**[7] 441 6-9-5 **48**..............................(v) SeanLevey 12 52
(John Bridger) *t.k.h on outer: sn prom: trckd ldng pair 3f out: rdn to chse ldr wl over 1f out: chal fnl f: nt qckn and lost pls nr fin* **8/1**[3]
0-43 **5** *1 ¼* **Five Hearts**[8] 433 5-9-6 **49**..............................(b) JimCrowley 9 54+
(Mark H Tompkins) *t.k.h: hld up in midfield: prog over 2f out: disp 2nd on inner and tried to chal over 1f out: making heavy weather of it whn squeezed out jst ins fnl f: no ch after* **7/2**[1]
00-6 **6** *hd* **Brandy Snapping**[21] 226 4-9-3 **47**..............................(t) TomMcLaughlin 5 48
(Mark Brisbourne) *chsd ldng pair to 3f out: sn rdn: plugged on same pce fr over 1f out* **14/1**
35/4 **7** *1* **Seaquel**[30] 99 7-9-2 **45**.............................. JimmyQuinn 13 44
(Tony Carroll) *hld up in midfield: rdn and no prog 3f out: sme hdwy over 1f out: fdd fnl f* **12/1**
00-0 **8** *1* **Saffron Park**[9] 418 4-9-2 **46**.............................. DavidProbert 10 43
(John Best) *settled in last pair: pushed along fr 1/2-way: struggling over 2f out: kpt on fnl f* **25/1**
605- **9** *6* **Willow Beauty**[40] 8267 4-9-1 **45**.............................. EddieAhern 3 30
(J R Jenkins) *chsd ldrs tl wknd qckly over 1f out* **33/1**
000- **10** *9* **King Of The Moors (USA)**[144] 6259 10-9-2 **45**....(p) RobbieFitzpatrick 6 12
(Dai Burchell) *trckd ldrs: rdn 3f out: sn wknd qckly: t.o* **25/1**
45-0 **11** *2 ¾* **Rosa Lockwood**[21] 223 4-9-1 **45**.............................. FrannyNorton 8 7
(Tony Carroll) *a in last pair: struggling bef 1/2-way: t.o* **33/1**
00-0 **12** *2* **Surrey Dream (IRE)**[7] 441 4-9-6 **50**.............................. AdamKirby 2 8
(John Bridger) *rousted along to ld: hrd rdn and hdd 2f out: wknd rapidly: t.o* **12/1**
2m 9.04s (1.04) **Going Correction** 0.0s/f (Stan)
WFA 4 from 5yo+ 1lb **12** Ran SP% **116.9**
Speed ratings (Par 97): **95,94,93,93,92 92,91,90,85,78 76,74**
toteswingers 1&2 £7.10, 1&3 £5.80, 2&3 £6.90 CSF £51.02 CT £196.16 TOTE £6.00: £2.00, £3.80, £1.80; EX 99.10 Trifecta £203.80 Pool: £1,938.75 - 7.13 winning units..
Owner Morgan, Clarke & Parris **Bred** Mrs A S O'Brien And Lars Pearson **Trained** Cropthorne, Worcs
■ Stewards' Enquiry : Luke Morris two-day ban: careless riding (Feb 20-21)

FOCUS
An ordinary handicap in which a veteran finished well to record his 11th win and his first success since May 2011.

531 BETDAQ MOBILE APPS H'CAP 5f (P)
6:05 (6:06) (Class 5) (0-75,75) 3-Y-O **£2,587** (£770; £384; £192) **Stalls** Low

Form RPR
2212 **1** **Windforpower (IRE)**[9] 424 3-9-0 **68**..............................(be) LukeMorris 2 70
(Ronald Harris) *in tch: prog over 1f out: brought between rivals fnl f: urged into ld last 50yds: immediately hung lft: hld on* **6/1**[3]
3-32 **2** *hd* **Modern Lady**[12] 374 3-8-3 **64**.............................. PhilipPrince(7) 7 65
(Richard Guest) *chsd ldr: drvn 2f out: clsd u.p to ld 150yds out: one pce and hdd last 50yds* **8/1**
5-41 **3** *nk* **Marvelino**[23] 202 3-8-13 **67**..............................(p) LiamKeniry 3 67
(Pat Eddery) *led at brisk pce: gng strly over 1f out: hdd and nt qckn 150yds out: kpt on* **7/2**[2]
23-1 **4** *1 ½* **Ada Lovelace**[12] 374 3-9-3 **71**.............................. JimCrowley 5 66+
(Dean Ivory) *w.w in 6th: taken wd and shkn up over 1f out: styd on u.p fnl f but nt pce to reel in ldrs* **7/4**[1]
015- **5** *2 ¾* **Mossgo (IRE)**[41] 8245 3-9-0 **68**.............................. AdamKirby 6 53
(John Best) *in tch: rdn on outer 1/2-way: nt qckn over 1f out: wl hld after* **9/1**
610- **6** *3* **La Sylphe**[110] 7220 3-9-0 **75**.............................. AdamMcLean(7) 1 49
(Derek Shaw) *chsd ldng pair to wl over 1f out: unbalanced u.p and wknd sn after* **6/1**[3]
16-0 **7** *1* **Iwilsayzisonlyonce**[12] 374 3-7-13 **60**.............................. NoraLooby(7) 4 31
(Joseph Tuite) *dwlt: outpcd* **16/1**
1m 0.32s (-0.18) **Going Correction** 0.0s/f (Stan) **7** Ran SP% **114.2**
Speed ratings (Par 97): **101,100,100,97,93 88,87**
toteswingers 1&2 £3.60, 1&3 £3.60, 2&3 £2.10 CSF £51.30 CT £192.72 TOTE £6.10: £2.30, £5.90; EX 22.40 Trifecta £114.60 Pool: £1,743.58 - 11.40 winning units..
Owner Anthony Cooke **Bred** Tally-Ho Stud **Trained** Earlswood, Monmouths

The Form Book Flat, Raceform Ltd, Compton, RG20 6NL.

FOCUS
There was a tight three-way finish in this competitive handicap and the favourite couldn't land a blow from off the pace.

532 BETDAQ CASINO GAMES MAIDEN FILLIES' STKS 7f (P)
6:35 (6:35) (Class 5) 3-Y-0+ £2,587 (£770; £384; £192) Stalls Low

Form RPR
000- **1** **Golden Causeway**[153] 5977 3-8-11 67 .... WilliamCarson 7 67+
(Charles Hills) *hld up in 4th: prog to trck ldr over 2f out: shkn up to ld jst over 1f out: hrd pressed and drvn last 100yds: hld on wl* **4/6**[1]
5-5 **2** *hd* **Wakeup Little Suzy (IRE)**[21] 230 3-8-11 0 ....(t) LukeMorris 3 66+
(Marco Botti) *chsd ldr 2f: rdn in 3rd 3f out w rest all gng much bttr: rallied over 1f out: wnt 2nd ins fnl f and pressed wnr hrd last 100yds: jst hld* **7/2**[2]
4 **3** *2* **Wotabooty**[21] 228 3-8-4 0 .... NoelGarbutt(7) 4 61
(Hugo Palmer) *t.k.h: trckd ldr after 2f: led wl over 2f out but stl green once in front: hdd jst over 1f out: fdd* **5/1**[3]
4 *2 ¾* **Viva L'Inghilterra (IRE)** 3-8-13 0 ow2 .... EddieAhern 1 56
(Robert Cowell) *hld up in 5th: pushed along and effrt 2f out: one pce and no imp on ldrs* **20/1**
5 *2* **Shaken Not Stirred** 3-8-11 0 .... LiamKeniry 6 48
(Milton Bradley) *dwlt: hld up in last: pushed along and effrt 2f out: no hdwy fnl f* **66/1**
65 **6** *2* **Always Fabulous**[15] 324 3-8-11 0 .... FrannyNorton 2 43
(Mark Johnston) *led to wl over 2f out: sn wknd qckly* **14/1**
1m 28.6s (2.60) **Going Correction** 0.0s/f (Stan) 6 Ran SP% **111.8**
Speed ratings (Par 100): **85,84,82,79,77 74**
toteswingers 1&2 £1.10, 1&3 £1.80, 2&3 £2.20 CSF £3.27 TOTE £1.40: £1.10, £2.70; EX 4.20 Trifecta £9.20 Pool: £1,592.77 - 128.95 winning units..
Owner Swettenham Stud & Marston Stud **Bred** Swettenham Stud **Trained** Lambourn, Berks
FOCUS
The odds-on favourite just held off her main market rival in this ordinary fillies' maiden.

533 TIME ORDERED CARDS IN RACING PLUS H'CAP 7f (P)
7:05 (7:05) (Class 4) (0-85,85) 3-Y-0 £4,690 (£1,395; £697; £348) Stalls Low

Form RPR
1-21 **1** **Ashamaly**[15] 325 3-9-7 85 .... ShaneKelly 4 89
(James Tate) *hld up in 4th: smooth prog 2f out to ld over 1f out: sn shkn up: pressed and hrd rdn ins fnl f: jst hld on* **7/2**[2]
4-11 **2** *shd* **Black Dave (IRE)**[13] 357 3-8-4 68 .... LukeMorris 1 71
(David Evans) *t.k.h early: trckd ldng pair: rdn over 2f out: tried to chal over 1f out: chsd wnr after: rallied and nrly upsides last 50yds: jst failed* **6/1**[3]
-1 **3** *2 ½* **Al Raqeeb (IRE)**[26] 160 3-9-0 78 .... AdamKirby 5 74
(Marco Botti) *dwlt: mostly in last and nvr gng that wl: rdn and no prog over 2f out: kpt on u.p to take 3rd ins fnl f* **1/1**[1]
641- **4** *¾* **Overrider**[47] 8207 3-8-12 76 .... WilliamCarson 6 70
(Charles Hills) *led: rdn over 2f out: hdd over 1f out: steadily wknd* **6/1**[3]
21-5 **5** *½* **Sherinn**[13] 359 3-8-7 71 .... ChrisCatlin 3 64
(Roger Varian) *t.k.h early: trckd ldr: rdn to chal 2f out: nt qckn over 1f out: fdd* **12/1**
1m 26.4s (0.40) **Going Correction** 0.0s/f (Stan) 5 Ran SP% **108.5**
Speed ratings (Par 99): **97,96,94,93,92**
CSF £22.18 TOTE £5.20: £3.00, £5.70; EX 10.80 Trifecta £19.80 Pool: £1,638.79 - 61.94 winning units..
Owner Saif Ali **Bred** Hascombe And Valiant Studs **Trained** Newmarket, Suffolk
FOCUS
A fair handicap, involving four last-time-out winners.

534 KEMPTON FOR WEDDINGS H'CAP 1m 4f (P)
7:35 (7:36) (Class 6) (0-65,68) 3-Y-0 £1,940 (£577; £288; £144) Stalls Centre

Form RPR
53-3 **1** **Crystal Peaks**[27] 134 3-9-5 62 .... DaleSwift 1 69
(James Given) *trckd ldr: led over 2f out: drvn wl over 1f out: kpt on fnl f: jst hld on* **6/1**[3]
04-4 **2** *hd* **Masaadr**[23] 211 3-9-7 64 .... AdamKirby 4 71
(James Tate) *hld up in last: prog to trck wnr 2f out: edgd lft and rdn over 1f out: clsd grad fnl f: jst failed* **11/8**[2]
31 **3** *9* **Rose Ransom (IRE)**[9] 419 3-9-11 68 6ex ....(b) FrannyNorton 2 61
(Mark Johnston) *led at fair pce: hdd over 2f out: hrd rdn and no rspnse: wl btn 3rd over 1f out* **11/10**[1]
0-63 **4** *40* **Silk Scarf (IRE)**[9] 427 3-8-7 50 ....(b) JimmyQuinn 3
(Mark H Tompkins) *disp 2nd pl to over 3f out: wknd rapidly: eased and t.o* **33/1**
2m 35.98s (1.48) **Going Correction** 0.0s/f (Stan) 4 Ran SP% **107.0**
Speed ratings (Par 95): **95,94,88,62**
CSF £14.47 TOTE £5.80; EX 12.40 Trifecta £14.90 Pool: £992.50 - 49.79 winning units..
Owner Danethorpe Racing Partnership **Bred** Mrs Hugh Maitland-Jones **Trained** Willoughton, Lincs
FOCUS
There was a tight finish in this handicap and the favourite was disappointing.

535 RACING PLUS CHASE 23.02.13 H'CAP 6f (P)
8:05 (8:07) (Class 5) (0-70,70) 4-Y-0+ £2,587 (£770; £384; £192) Stalls Low

Form RPR
1-14 **1** **Captain Kendall (IRE)**[13] 358 4-9-5 68 .... AdamKirby 2 81+
(David Evans) *hld up in midfield on inner: prog jst over 2f out to ld over 1f out: drvn and hrd pressed ins fnl f: hld on wl* **11/8**[1]
60-0 **2** *nk* **Jake The Snake (IRE)**[35] 11 12-9-4 70 .... AmyBaker(3) 6 82
(Tony Carroll) *hld up in last trio: prog on outer 2f out: chsd wnr 1f out: urged along and chal fnl f: jst hld* **20/1**
14-3 **3** *3* **Fortrose Academy (IRE)**[35] 11 4-9-4 67 .... DavidProbert 11 69
(Andrew Balding) *hld up in midfield: prog 2f out: rdn to chal over 1f out: one pce and wl hld in 3rd ins fnl f* **7/2**[2]
600- **4** *1 ¾* **Dressed In Lace**[65] 7967 4-9-4 67 .... LiamKeniry 4 64
(Jo Crowley) *hld up in last trio: nt clr run jst over 2f out: outpcd whn sme prog over 1f out: kpt on to take 4th last strides* **20/1**
40-0 **5** *nk* **Rambo Will**[35] 11 5-9-4 67 .... KirstyMilczarek 3 63
(J R Jenkins) *led at str pce: hdd over 1f out: wknd fnl f* **14/1**
0-05 **6** *½* **Lady Prodee**[13] 354 5-8-12 61 .... FergusSweeney 7 55
(Bill Turner) *hld up in last trio: effrt 2f out: outpcd over 1f out: nvr on terms after* **20/1**
1-45 **7** *1 ¼* **Belle Bayardo (IRE)**[31] 86 5-9-5 68 .... LukeMorris 12 58
(Ronald Harris) *t.k.h: hld up in midfield: effrt 2f out: outpcd over 1f out: nt on terms after* **8/1**
-651 **8** *2 ¾* **Lucky Mark (IRE)**[13] 354 4-9-1 64 .... JimmyQuinn 5 45
(Garry Moss) *racd freely: chsd ldng pair to 2f out: wknd over 1f out* **6/1**[3]
0-03 **9** *1* **Little China**[8] 431 4-9-4 67 .... WilliamCarson 1 45
(William Muir) *prom: disp 2nd and rdn 2f out: wknd over 1f out* **25/1**
00-5 **10** *nk* **Peter Island (FR)**[21] 232 10-9-1 64 ....(v) ChrisCatlin 10 41
(John Gallagher) *dwlt: rcvrd on wd outside to chse ldng trio after 2f: wknd qckly over 1f out* **50/1**
0-00 **11** *1 ¼* **Ziefhd**[27] 130 4-8-7 63 ....(p) RyanTate(7) 9 36
(Tim McCarthy) *tried to match strides w ldr: btn off over 2f out: wknd qckly over 1f out* **50/1**
1m 12.76s (-0.34) **Going Correction** 0.0s/f (Stan) 11 Ran SP% **118.4**
Speed ratings (Par 103): **102,101,97,95,94 94,92,88,87,87 85**
toteswingers 1&2 £7.20, 1&3 £2.50, 2&3 £27.30 CSF £39.05 CT £86.93 TOTE £2.40: £1.50, £5.10, £1.90; EX 45.20 Trifecta £186.70 Pool: £2,201.19 - 8.84 winning units..
Owner J G White **Bred** Pier House Stud **Trained** Pandy, Monmouths
FOCUS
A big gamble was landed in this strongly run handicap and the first two pulled clear.
T/Jkpt: Not won. T/Plt: £263.90 to a £1 stake. Pool of £66,058.29 - 182.72 winning units T/Qpdt: £40.40 to a £1 stake. Pool of £6,757.40 - 123.75 winning units JN

522 SOUTHWELL (L-H)
Wednesday, February 6

OFFICIAL GOING: Standard to slow
Wind: Fresh; behind Weather: Cloudy

536 GET FREE BETS WITH BOOKMAKERS.CO.UK H'CAP 1m (F)
1:30 (1:30) (Class 6) (0-65,64) 4-Y-0+ £1,940 (£577; £288; £144) Stalls Low

Form RPR
000- **1** **Our Ivor**[42] 8241 4-8-7 50 oh5 .... AndrewMullen 7 61
(Michael Appleby) *slt ld 2f: cl up tl led narrowly wl over 2f out: sn rdn: drvn and edgd lft ent fnl f: kpt on* **8/1**[3]
-23 **2** *1* **Miami Gator (IRE)**[5] 478 6-8-13 63 ow1 ....(v) ConorHarrison(7) 2 72
(Mrs K Burke) *cl up: slt ld after 2f: pushed along and hdd wl over 2f out: sn rdn and ev ch tl drvn and no ex wl ins fnl f* **5/2**[1]
0-05 **3** *4 ½* **Minortransgression (USA)**[21] 221 6-8-12 62 .... RobertTart(7) 6 61
(Sean Curran) *hld up in rr: pushed along bef 1/2-way: hdwy over 2f out: sn rdn and chsd ldng pair over 1f out: no imp* **5/2**[1]
6-50 **4** *7* **Gay Gallivanter**[7] 441 5-8-7 50 oh1 ....(p) AndreaAtzeni 1 33
(Mick Quinn) *towards rr and reminders after 2f: rdn along 3f out and sme hdwy: n.d* **10/1**
140- **5** *4* **Bladewood Girl**[47] 8199 5-9-7 64 .... GrahamLee 4 37
(J R Jenkins) *chsd ldrs: rdn along 3f out: sn btn* **4/1**[2]
660- **6** *16* **Mystical Witch**[40] 8263 4-8-7 50 oh5 ....(v) JoeFanning 3
(Christine Dunnett) *chsd ldng pair on inner: rdn along 3f out: wknd fnl 2f* **16/1**
6-60 **7** *28* **Efistorm**[13] 354 12-9-4 61 .... HayleyTurner 5
(Conor Dore) *chsd ldrs: rdn along over 3f out: sn wknd* **9/1**
1m 43.94s (0.24) **Going Correction** +0.025s/f (Slow) 7 Ran SP% **113.2**
Speed ratings (Par 101): **99,98,93,86,82 66,38**
toteswingers 1&2 £4.40, 1&3 £9.70, 2&3 £2.10 CSF £27.78 TOTE £15.30: £5.20, £1.30; EX 45.50 Trifecta £309.40 Pool: £1,990.55 - 4.82 winning units..
Owner J&G Bacciochi, A Taylor, Bruce W Wyatt **Bred** B W Wyatt **Trained** Danethorpe, Notts
FOCUS
Very few ever got into this moderate handicap. The front pair disputed the lead from the start and there was never much between them.

537 COMPARE ONLINE BOOKIES AT BOOKMAKERS.CO.UK (S) H'CAP 6f (F)
2:00 (2:01) (Class 6) (0-60,58) 4-Y-0+ £2,102 (£625; £312; £156) Stalls Low

Form RPR
2036 **1** **Marshall Art**[4] 497 4-9-2 58 .... ThomasBrown(5) 12 67
(David Evans) *trckd ldrs: chsd ldr 1/2-way: rdn to ld over 1f out: edgd lft ent fnl f: drvn out* **7/1**[2]
05-0 **2** *2* **Red Shadow**[26] 162 4-9-4 55 ....(p) TomEaves 11 58
(Alan Brown) *dwlt: gd hdwy on wd outside after 2f: chsd ldrs over 2f out: rdn wl over 1f out: styd on fnl f* **14/1**
-000 **3** *1* **Ishi**[7] 440 4-8-10 47 ....(b) AndreaAtzeni 5 47
(Rod Millman) *towards rr: hdwy on outer wl over 2f out: sn rdn and kpt on fnl f: nrst fin* **7/1**[2]
1-4 **4** *nk* **Hittin'The Skids (IRE)**[34] 42 5-9-4 55 ....(p) PaddyAspell 10 54
(Kevin Ryan) *led: rdn along and jnd 2f out: hdd over 1f out: wknd ins fnl f* **5/1**[1]
-004 **5** *2 ¼* **Ace Of Spies (IRE)**[1] 523 8-9-2 53 .... HayleyTurner 8 45
(Conor Dore) *chsd ldrs: rdn along over 2f out: sn one pce* **5/1**[1]
2305 **6** *4* **Compton Target (IRE)**[7] 441 4-8-10 47 ....(bt[1]) RichardKingscote 4 26
(Milton Bradley) *trckd ldrs on inner: effrt over 2f out: sn rdn and wknd over 1f out* **5/1**[1]
0-46 **7** *¾* **Atlantic Beach**[12] 369 8-9-7 58 ....(v) GrahamLee 3 34
(Milton Bradley) *midfield: rdn along 2f out: no imp* **20/1**
402- **8** *hd* **Elusive Warrior (USA)**[83] 7733 10-8-13 57 ....(p) NoraLooby(7) 7 33
(Alan McCabe) *dwlt: keen and sn chsng ldrs: n.m.r over 3f out: sn lost pl and rr* **8/1**[3]
02-0 **9** *1 ¼* **Mucky Molly**[27] 128 5-8-13 50 ....(bt[1]) SebSanders 2 22
(Alison Hutchinson) *a towards rr* **16/1**
045- **10** *4 ½* **Catalyze**[92] 7612 5-8-10 47 ....(t) RobbieFitzpatrick 6
(Charles Smith) *a in rr* **8/1**[3]
006- **11** *6* **Bird Dog**[41] 8246 7-8-8 45 ....(v) JoeFanning 9
(Phil McEntee) *chsd ldrs: rdn along wl over 2f out: sn wknd* **33/1**
000- **12** *25* **Skiddaw View**[141] 6341 5-8-8 45 .... DuranFentiman 1
(John Weymes) *cl up on inner: sn rdn along: lost pl after 2f and bhd fr 1/2-way* **66/1**
1m 16.8s (0.30) **Going Correction** +0.025s/f (Slow) 12 Ran SP% **120.9**
Speed ratings (Par 101): **99,96,95,94,91 86,85,85,83,77 69,36**
toteswingers 1&2 £22.40, 1&3 £12.40, 2&3 £14.80 CSF £103.04 CT £732.87 TOTE £10.00: £3.20, £4.70, £3.90; EX 130.80 Trifecta £886.70 Pool: £2,375.54 - 2.00 winning units..There was no bid for the winner. Catalyze was claimed by Mr S Arnold for £4000.
Owner Mrs E Evans **Bred** Plantation Stud **Trained** Pandy, Monmouths
■ Stewards' Enquiry : Andrea Atzeni two-day ban: used whip above permitted level (Feb 20-21)
FOCUS
A moderate selling handicap, but quite a competitive race.

538 CORAL.CO.UK H'CAP 1m (F)
2:30 (2:31) (Class 5) (0-75,75) 3-Y-0 £3,105 (£924; £461; £230) Stalls Low

Form RPR
2-06 **1** **Misleading Promise (IRE)**[9] 419 3-8-11 65 ....(t) LiamKeniry 4 69
(John Butler) *trckd ldrs: smooth hdwy 3f out: chal jst over 2f out: sn led: rdn ent fnl f and kpt on wl* **7/1**[2]

4-02 **2** 1 1/2 **Red Gift (IRE)**[15] 325 3-8-11 65 .... TomEaves 5 66
(Brian Ellison) *chsd ldr: hdwy to chal wl over 2f out: sn rdn and ev ch tl drvn and kpt on one pce fnl f* **8/1**[3]

4-23 **3** *nk* **Tight Knit (USA)**[13] 359 3-9-7 75 ....(b) JoeFanning 2 75
(James Tate) *led: jnd and rdn over 2f out: sn hdd: drvn and one pce fnl f* **4/9**[1]

-1 **4** *14* **Little Dolly**[30] 102 3-8-13 67 .... SebSanders 1 41
(Alan McCabe) *trckd ldng pair on inner: rdn along over 2f out: sn drvn and wknd* **10/1**

64-6 **5** *29* **Polar Forest**[15] 324 3-8-1 62 .... PhilipPrince(7) 3
(Richard Guest) *a in rr: outpcd and bhd fr 1/2-way* **14/1**

1m 44.66s (0.96) **Going Correction** +0.025s/f (Slow) 5 Ran SP% **108.6**
Speed ratings (Par 97): **96,94,94,80,51**
CSF £52.09 TOTE £8.20: £1.90, £1.70; EX 47.30 Trifecta £93.50 Pool: £2,341.72 - 18.76 winning units..
Owner J Butler **Bred** James Waldron **Trained** Newmarket, Suffolk
FOCUS
A fair 3yo handicap.

539 CASINO AT CORAL.CO.UK H'CAP — 1m 4f (F)
3:05 (3:05) (Class 6) (0-60,60) 4-Y-O+ — **£1,940** (£577; £288; £144) **Stalls** Low

Form — RPR

/23- **1** **Lakota Ghost (USA)**[123] 6399 5-9-6 59 ....(t) JohnFahy 8 72+
(Seamus Durack) *hld up: tk clsr order 1/2-way: gd hdwy on outer over 3f out: led wl over 2f out: sn rdn clr: styd on* **11/4**[2]

46-0 **2** 3 1/4 **Corn Maiden**[26] 169 4-8-4 46 oh1 .... JoeFanning 4 52
(Mark Rimmer) *trckd ldrs: hdwy 4f out: rdn to chse wnr 2f out: drvn and no imp fnl f* **16/1**

32/ **3** *11* **Waterloo Sunrise (IRE)**[26] 175 8-9-2 60 ......(be) DerekMcCormack(5) 3 48
(S M Duffy, Ire) *awkward s and sn pushed along in rr: bhd after 3f: hdwy 5f out: effrt on inner and n.m.r 3f out: sn rdn to chse ldng pair over 2f out: drvn and one pce fr wl over 1f out* **7/1**

301- **4** 3/4 **Bocamix (FR)**[63] 7793 7-9-0 53 ....(v) TomEaves 7 40
(Andrew Crook) *trckd ldrs: pushed along and outpcd 4f out: sn rdn: drvn over 2f out: kpt on fnl f* **9/2**[3]

31-5 **5** *2* **Honest Strike (USA)**[35] 20 6-8-13 52 ....(b) ShaneKelly 6 36
(Daniel Mark Loughnane) *prom: hdwy and cl up 5f out: led 4f out and rdn clr: hdd and sltly hmpd wl over 2f out: sn wknd* **2/1**[1]

320- **6** *11* **Lakeman (IRE)**[32] 8139 7-9-2 55 ....(p) DaleSwift 2 21
(Brian Ellison) *chsd clr ldr: led over 5f out: rdn along and hdd 4f out: drvn over 3f out and sn wknd* **10/1**

-200 **7** *14* **Turjuman (USA)**[9] 417 8-8-9 53 ....(p) ShirleyTeasdale(5) 5
(Simon West) *a in rr: outpcd and bhd fr 1/2-way* **20/1**

0-05 **8** *38* **State Senator (USA)**[13] 361 5-9-1 54 ....(b[1]) MickyFenton 1
(Richard Ford) *led at str pce and sn clr: pushed along after 5f: rdn and hdd over 5f out: sn wknd and bhd* **20/1**

2m 40.57s (-0.43) **Going Correction** +0.025s/f (Slow)
WFA 4 from 5yo+ 3lb 8 Ran SP% **115.2**
Speed ratings (Par 101): **102,99,92,92,90 83,74,48**
toteswingers 1&2 £6.50, 1&3 £4.60, 2&3 £11.90 CSF £45.18 CT £275.39 TOTE £3.60: £1.40, £2.90, £1.60; EX 44.80 Trifecta £441.10 Pool: £2,928.63 - 4.97 winning units..
Owner Grandpa's **Bred** Extern Developments **Trained** Baydon, Wilts
FOCUS
A modest handicap and a war of attrition in the conditions.

540 DOWNLOAD CORAL.CO.UK MOBILE APP CLASSIFIED CLAIMING STKS — 1m (F)
3:40 (3:40) (Class 6) 4-Y-O+ — **£2,045** (£603; £302) **Stalls** Low

Form — RPR

62-3 **1** **Caledonia Prince**[33] 49 5-8-12 67 ....(b) JoeFanning 2 77
(Jo Hughes) *hld up in tch: smooth hdwy 3f out: chal 2f out: rdn to ld and edgd rt over 1f out: kpt on wl fnl f* **9/4**[1]

150- **2** *1* **Flying Pickets (IRE)**[58] 8055 4-8-10 69 ....(be) JohnFahy 5 73
(Alan McCabe) *in rr: hdwy on inner 3f out: rdn to ld 2f out: hdd over 1f out: ev ch tl drvn and one pce ins fnl f* **9/1**

50-0 **3** 2 1/2 **Fluctuation (IRE)**[35] 13 5-8-9 65 ow1 ....(v) TomEaves 6 66
(Ian Williams) *hld up in tch: smooth hdwy 3f out: cl up 2f out: sn rdn and ev ch tl drvn and one pce fnl f* **6/1**[3]

43-4 **4** 2 1/4 **Bold Marc (IRE)**[30] 97 11-8-4 64 .... HayleyTurner 4 56
(Mrs K Burke) *cl up: led 3f out: sn rdn and hdd 2f out: grad wknd* **7/1**

3-34 **5** *3* **Imprimis Tagula (IRE)**[16] 311 9-8-4 67 ....(v) NatashaEaton(5) 8 54
(Alan Bailey) *trckd ldng pair: effrt wl over 2f out: sn rdn and grad wknd* **12/1**

-102 **6** *nse* **Electrician**[4] 490 4-8-4 63 ....(p) AndreaAtzeni 3 49
(Tim Pitt) *trckd ldrs: effrt 3f out: rdn along over 2f out: sn wknd* **5/1**[2]

50-5 **7** 1 1/4 **Musnad (USA)**[15] 329 5-8-11 66 ....(v[1]) DaleSwift 7 53
(Brian Ellison) *in tch on outer: hdwy over 3f out: rdn along over 2f out: sn btn* **5/1**[2]

46 **8** *23* **Creek Falcon (IRE)**[12] 376 4-8-8 67 .... RaulDaSilva(3) 1
(David O'Meara) *slt ld: rdn along and hdd 3f out: sn wknd* **12/1**

1m 42.91s (-0.79) **Going Correction** +0.025s/f (Slow) 8 Ran SP% **116.3**
Speed ratings (Par 101): **104,103,100,98,95 95,93,70**
toteswingers 1&2 £7.10, 1&3 £3.70, 2&3 £7.60 CSF £24.22 TOTE £3.00: £1.30, £2.20, £2.40; EX 28.80 Trifecta £143.60 Pool: £2,355.13 - 12.29 winning units..
Owner Isla & Colin Cage **Bred** Mrs I M Cage And C J Cage **Trained** Lambourn, Berks
FOCUS
A tight classified claimer with 5lb covering the eight runners on adjusted official ratings.

541 BOOKMAKER REVIEWS AT BOOKMAKERS.CO.UK MAIDEN FILLIES' STKS — 1m (F)
4:15 (4:15) (Class 5) 3-Y-O+ — **£3,135** (£925; £463) **Stalls** Low

Form — RPR

323- **1** **Naalatt (IRE)**[140] 6366 3-8-9 77 ....[1] AndreaAtzeni 5 79+
(Roger Varian) *cl up: led over 3f out: shkn up and pushed clr wl over 1f out: readily* **1/2**[1]

2 *8* **Mirth** 3-8-9 0 .... JoeFanning 4 58+
(Mark Johnston) *prom: pushed along 3f out: chsd wnr 2f out: sn no imp* **9/4**[2]

3-5 **3** 3 1/4 **Taming The Tweet**[18] 275 3-8-6 0 .... RaulDaSilva(3) 6 48
(J R Jenkins) *hld up in rr: hdwy over 2f out: sn rdn and kpt on appr fnl f* **9/1**[3]

0- **4** *14* **Dolly Bantry**[231] 3282 3-8-9 0 .... JohnFahy 2 16
(Alan McCabe) *trckd ldrs: rdn along 3f out: sn outpcd* **40/1**

4 **5** *3* **Miss Chardonay**[16] 313 6-10-0 0 .... JamieMackay 3 14
(Mandy Rowland) *dwlt: keen and sn chsng ldrs on outer: rdn along 3f out: sn wknd* **100/1**

0000 **6** 1 3/4 **Elusive**[15] 324 7-9-9 29 .... AnnStokell(5) 1 10
(Ann Stokell) *cl up: slt ld after 2f: rdn along and hdd over 3f out: sn wknd* **100/1**

1m 43.96s (0.26) **Going Correction** +0.025s/f (Slow)
WFA 3 from 6yo+ 19lb 6 Ran SP% **111.9**
Speed ratings (Par 100): **99,91,87,73,70 69**
toteswingers 1&2 £1.10, 1&3 £1.40, 2&3 £1.80 CSF £1.86 TOTE £1.50: £1.10, £2.30; EX 2.40 Trifecta £3.60 Pool: £2,220.83 - 458.99 winning units..
Owner Sheikh Ahmed Al Maktoum **Bred** Darley **Trained** Newmarket, Suffolk
FOCUS
An uncompetitive fillies' maiden and ultimately a one-horse race.

542 BOOKMAKERS.CO.UK GIVES YOU FREE BETS H'CAP — 2m (F)
4:45 (4:45) (Class 5) (0-70,67) 4-Y-O+ — **£2,975** (£885; £442; £221) **Stalls** Low

Form — RPR

-024 **1** **Scribe (IRE)**[2] 515 5-8-8 54 ....(t) ThomasBrown(5) 2 62
(David Evans) *in tch: hdwy 4f out: cl up 3f out: rdn to ld over 2f out: hdd over 1f out: sn drvn and rallied gamely ins fnl f to ld last 40yds* **5/1**[2]

06-2 **2** 1/2 **Neil's Pride**[23] 201 4-8-4 51 ....(v) PatrickMathers 1 58
(Richard Fahey) *t.k.h: trckd ldrs on inner: effrt 3f out: chal over 2f out: rdn to ld over 1f out: drvn ent fnl f: hdd and no ex last 40yds* **8/1**[3]

/0-3 **3** *10* **White Fusion**[22] 215 5-9-12 67 .... DanielTudhope 5 64
(David O'Meara) *set stdy pce: pushed along 4f out: rdn 3f out: hdd over 2f out: drvn and wknd over 1f out* **9/4**[1]

60-0 **4** *11* **Lyric Poet (USA)**[27] 145 6-9-5 60 ....(bt[1]) JohnFahy 8 42
(Charlie Longsdon) *cl up: pushed along over 4f out: rdn over 3f out: sn wknd* **10/1**

010- **5** 1/2 **Zefooha (FR)**[39] 7603 9-9-9 64 ....(p) PaddyAspell 6 45
(Tim Walford) *trckd ldrs: niggled along 7f out: rdn over 5f out: sn wknd* **11/1**

43-1 **6** *20* **Entitlement**[27] 131 4-9-1 62 .... HayleyTurner 4
(James Fanshawe) *hld up in rr: pushed along 6f out: rdn over 4f out: sn wknd* **9/4**[1]

54-0 **7** *48* **Low Key (IRE)**[28] 119 6-9-12 67 ....(p[1]) MickyFenton 7
(John Butler) *trckd ldng pair: rdn along 6f out: sn wknd and wl bhd fnl 3f* **20/1**

3m 44.41s (-1.09) **Going Correction** +0.025s/f (Slow)
WFA 4 from 5yo+ 6lb 7 Ran SP% **111.5**
Speed ratings (Par 103): **103,102,97,92,92 82,58**
toteswingers 1&2 £3.60, 1&3 £2.30, 2&3 £5.30 CSF £41.07 CT £110.56 TOTE £3.70: £1.70, £2.80; EX 20.30 Trifecta £102.20 Pool: £2,272.33 - 16.66 winning units..
Owner Shropshire Wolves/John Wilcox **Bred** Lynch Bages Ltd & Samac Ltd **Trained** Pandy, Monmouths
■ Stewards' Enquiry : Thomas Brown two-day ban: used whip above permitted level (Feb 20-21)
FOCUS
Despite the pace being ordinary, 2m on this slow Fibresand surface was still a demanding test.
T/Plt: £485.30 to a £1 stake. Pool of £58,573.35 - 88.09 winning units T/Qpdt: £32.60 to a £1 stake. Pool of £5,294.46 - 120.15 winning units JR

498 CAGNES-SUR-MER
Wednesday, February 6

OFFICIAL GOING: Fibresand: standard

543a PRIX DU BORD DE MER (MAIDEN) (3YO) (FIBRESAND) — 1m 2f (D)
12:00 (12:00) 3-Y-O — **£9,756** (£3,902; £2,926; £1,951; £975)

RPR

1 **Lucio Silla**[9] 445 3-9-2 0 ....(b) FabriceVeron 3 82
(H-A Pantall, France) **11/10**[1]

2 *3* **Kenasie (FR)**[9] 445 3-9-2 0 ....(p) Pierre-CharlesBoudot 1 76
(J-M Capitte, France) **48/10**[2]

3 *3* **Shabaka (FR)**[9] 445 3-9-2 0 ....(b) FranckForesi 11 70
(F Foresi, France) **19/1**

4 2 1/2 **Si Violente (FR)** 3-8-13 0 .... WilliamsSaraiva 7 62
(J Parize, France) **7/1**[3]

5 1 1/2 **Performance (IRE)**[110] 7228 3-9-2 0 .... ThierryThulliez 6 62
(D Grilli, Italy) **78/10**

6 *1* **Taboule** 3-8-6 0 .... NicolasLarenaudie(5) 2 55
(G Martin, Austria) **65/1**

7 *nk* **Moorway (IRE)**[9] 445 3-9-2 0 .... IoritzMendizabal 8 59
(Reg Hollinshead) *broke wl: trckd ldrs: 2nd and ev ch 3f out: rdn and nt qckn over 2f out: wknd fnl 1 1/2f* **16/1**

8 1/2 **Sharp Anna (FR)**[162] 3-8-13 0 .... MickaelForest 4 55
(P Vidotto, France) **81/1**

9 1 1/2 **Stenka Razine (FR)**[15] 331 3-8-10 0 .... SoufyaneMoulin(6) 9 55
(C Boutin, France) **34/1**

10 *1* **Lagonda Blue (FR)** 3-8-13 0 ....(b[1]) Roberto-CarlosMontenegro 10 50
(C Baillet, France) **13/1**

11 **Pegasus Bridge (FR)**[83] 3-9-2 0 .... NicolasPerret 5 53
(K Borgel, France) **21/1**

2m 4.65s (124.65) 11 Ran SP% **116.9**
PARI-MUTUEL (all including 1 euro stakes): WIN 2.10; PLACE (1-2) 1.20, 1.60, 2.70; DF 3.70; SF 4.80.
Owner Alexandre Pereira **Bred** Newsells Park Stud **Trained** France

544a PRIX DES MIMOSAS (CLAIMER) (3YO) (FIBRESAND) — 1m 2f (D)
1:05 (12:00) 3-Y-O — **£6,910** (£2,764; £2,073; £1,382; £691)

RPR

1 **Russian Reel (FR)**[38] 3-8-13 0 .... RomainAuray(3) 2 80
(J Heloury, France) **5/1**[3]

2 *1* **Royalitta (FR)**[25] 3-8-8 0 .... StephanePasquier 7 70
(M Boutin, France) **14/5**[1]

3 1/2 **Mahyar Glaz (FR)**[15] 331 3-9-6 0 ....(b) JohanVictoire 5 81
(C Boutin, France) **3/1**[2]

4 *nk* **Zapata Rebel (FR)**[15] 331 3-8-6 0 ....(p) NicolasLarenaudie(5) 8 71
(J-M Lefebvre, France) **71/1**

5 *1* **Litian Rocket (FR)**[25] 3-8-10 0 .... AlexandreChampenois(6) 4 74
(M Boutin, France) **6/1**

6 *3* **Symphony Break (IRE)**[40] 3-8-5 0 .... AntoineCoutier(3) 3 60
(N Caullery, France) **14/1**

7 1 1/2 **Mister Black (FR)**[15] 331 3-8-6 0 .... ChristopherGrosbois(5) 10 60
(F-X De Chevigny, France) **16/1**

The Form Book Flat, Raceform Ltd, Compton, RG20 6NL.

8 1/2 **Woza Moya (USA)**6 461 3-9-2 0 JackDuern 9 64
(Gay Kelleway) *towards rr on outside: prog to trck ldrs 1/2-way: 3rd on outside and shkn up over 2 1/2f out: hrd rdn and nt qckn over 2f out: sn lost pl and wl hld fnl 1 1/2f* **38/1**
9 1 1/2 **Fleur De Guerre (FR)**25 3-8-8 0 MircoDemuro 6 53
(W Mongil, Germany) **14/1**
10 3 **Waris Magic (FR)** 3-8-13 0 WilliamsSaraiva 1 52
(J Parize, France) **15/2**
2m 4.95s (124.95) **10** Ran SP% **117.2**
PARI-MUTUEL (all including 1 euro stakes): WIN 6.00; PLACE (1-2) 1.60, 1.50, 1.50; DF 11.50; SF 24.80.
Owner Vincent Moreau **Bred** Mme M Reynolds **Trained** France

515 WOLVERHAMPTON (A.W) (L-H)
Thursday, February 7

OFFICIAL GOING: Standard
Wind: Fresh behind Weather: Raining

545 CORAL.CO.UK APPRENTICE H'CAP 1m 1f 103y(P)
5:05 (5:05) (Class 6) (0-58,65) 4-Y-0+ **£1,940** (£577; £288; £144) **Stalls** Low

Form RPR
-243 1 **Tyrur Ted**6 477 8-8-13 **57** (t) DanaZamecnikova(7) 4 69
(Frank Sheridan) *chsd ldrs: led 1f out: rdn out* **13/2**
21-0 2 3 1/4 **Norwegian Reward (IRE)**24 200 5-9-1 **57** RobertTart(5) 3 62
(Michael Wigham) *chsd ldrs: pushed along over 3f out: led over 1f out: sn rdn: hung lft and hdd: no ex ins fnl f* **3/1**2
550- 3 4 **Rockgoat (IRE)**48 8213 4-9-4 **58** JacobButterfield(3) 5 55
(Ian McInnes) *led: hdd over 6f out: led again 3f out: rdn and hdd over 1f out: wknd ins fnl f* **16/1**
4-00 4 7 **Nurse Dominatrix (IRE)**7 456 4-8-3 **47** LisaTodd(7) 2 29
(Richard Guest) *hld up: racd keenly: hdwy over 5f out: rdn and wknd 2f out* **33/1**
4-34 5 3 1/2 **Landown Littlerock**13 375 4-8-10 **50** (p) ShirleyTeasdale(3) 7 25
(Reg Hollinshead) *prom: lost pl over 5f out: rdn and wknd over 2f out* **5/1**3
/0-0 6 5 **Chorister Girl**30 105 4-8-9 **46** oh1 RachealKneller 1 10
(Richard Ford) *hld up: a in rr: lost tch fnl 3f* **50/1**
0-41 7 24 **Fighter Boy (IRE)**9 435 6-9-9 **65** 7ex (bt) MatthewHopkins(5) 8
(Michael Easterby) *s.i.s: hld up: plld hrd: hdwy to ld over 6f out: hdd & wknd 3f out: t.o* **11/10**1
2m 3.73s (2.03) **Going Correction** +0.20s/f (Slow) **7** Ran SP% **113.4**
Speed ratings (Par 101): **98,95,91,85,82 77,56**
toteswingers 1&2 £2.10, 1&3 £7.60, 2&3 £8.10 CSF £25.83 CT £297.61 TOTE £8.40: £1.90, £2.10; EX 29.10 Trifecta £168.10 Pool: £1546.82 - 6.89 winning units..
Owner Frank Sheridan **Bred** A G Greenwood **Trained** Wolverhampton, W Midlands
■ Dana Zamecnikova's first winner.

FOCUS
Fighter Boy pulled his way to the front and was soon setting a serious gallop, but the others largely ignored him. The winner is rated in line with last month's C&D second.

546 GET THE INSIDE TRACK AT BOOKMAKERS.CO.UK H'CAP 7f 32y(P)
5:35 (5:36) (Class 6) (0-65,65) 4-Y-0+ **£1,940** (£577; £288; £144) **Stalls** High

Form RPR
1222 1 **Bussa**10 426 5-9-6 **64** (t) WilliamCarson 7 76
(David Evans) *a.p: chsd ldr 2f out: sn rdn: styd on u.p to ld nr fin* **3/1**1
0-04 2 hd **Haywain**12 410 4-9-6 **64** (b) GrahamLee 2 75
(Kevin Ryan) *chsd ldrs tl led over 2f out: rdn over 1f out: hdd nr fin* **5/1**3
2-22 3 4 1/2 **Hierarch (IRE)**7 452 6-9-0 **65** (p) SiobhanMiller(7) 8 64
(David Simcock) *hld up: hdwy over 1f out: styd on to go 3rd nr fin: nt trble ldrs* **9/2**2
25-2 4 3/4 **Amosite**19 271 7-9-3 **64** (p) PatrickHills(3) 11 61
(J R Jenkins) *chsd ldrs: rdn over 1f out: no ex ins fnl f* **14/1**
-323 5 nse **Aragorn Rouge**23 218 5-9-3 **61** (b1) JoeFanning 12 58
(Keith Dalgleish) *hld up: hdwy over 2f out: rdn over 1f out: no ex ins fnl f* **5/1**3
-431 6 7 **Lieutenant Dan (IRE)**12 408 6-8-13 **57** (v) AndrewMullen 9 35
(Michael Appleby) *hld up: pushed along 4f out: hdwy u.p over 1f out: wknd fnl f* **14/1**
0-60 7 4 **Needwood Ridge**10 426 6-9-7 **65** (bt) AdamKirby 3 32
(Frank Sheridan) *s.i.s: pushed along early in rr: hdwy u.p over 1f out: wknd and eased fnl f* **10/1**
240/ 8 2 **Fantastic Smartie**497 6492 4-9-2 **60** FergusSweeney 6 22
(Richard Phillips) *hld up: nvr on terms* **66/1**
0-66 9 10 **Foxtrot India (IRE)**7 448 4-9-0 **65** RyanTate(7) 4
(Jeremy Gask) *led: hung rt almost thrght: hdd over 2f out: wknd over 1f out* **40/1**
-150 10 10 **Dhhamaan (IRE)**12 409 8-8-9 **53** (b) JamesSullivan 5
(Ruth Carr) *chsd ldr tl rdn and wknd over 2f out: t.o* **20/1**
1m 29.92s (0.32) **Going Correction** +0.20s/f (Slow) **10** Ran SP% **107.6**
Speed ratings (Par 101): **106,105,100,99,99 91,87,84,73,62**
toteswingers 1&2 £3.60, 1&3 £3.30, 2&3 £5.60 CSF £14.11 CT £43.73 TOTE £3.00: £1.10, £1.80, £1.80; EX 18.20 Trifecta £88.20 Pool: £750.86 - 6.38 winning units..
Owner Nick Shutts **Bred** Natton House Thoroughbreds & Mark Woodall **Trained** Pandy, Monmouths
■ Hawk Moth was withdrawn (9/2, unruly in stalls). R4 applies; deduct 15p in the £.

FOCUS
The pace was good in this middling handicap, but the two who contested the finish were both always prominent. The winner is rated closer to his old form.

547 WINNERS LOVE BOOKMAKERS.CO.UK CLAIMING STKS 1m 141y(P)
6:05 (6:05) (Class 6) 3-Y-0 **£1,940** (£577; £288; £144) **Stalls** Low

Form RPR
-411 1 **It's Only Business**6 468 3-9-3 64 (p) JimmyQuinn 2 72
(Bill Turner) *racd keenly: led 1f: chsd ldrs: led again over 3f out: rdn over 1f out: styd on gamely* **7/4**2
-361 2 shd **Run It Twice (IRE)**24 210 3-9-4 69 (b) LukeMorris 1 73
(David Evans) *hld up: hdwy to ld over 4f out: hdd over 3f out: rdn and ev ch fr over 1f out: styd on* **1/1**1
4-12 3 4 **Amelia Hull**10 427 3-8-6 58 (b1) JohnFahy 5 52
(J S Moore) *led at stdy pce after 1f: hdd over 4f out: rdn over 2f out: hung lft over 1f out: styd on same pce* **5/1**3
556- 4 26 **Bix (IRE)**42 8258 3-8-9 63 SladeO'Hara(5) 4
(Alan Berry) *prom: chsd ldr over 6f out tl over 4f out: rdn and wknd over 2f out* **25/1**
1m 54.59s (4.09) **Going Correction** +0.20s/f (Slow) **4** Ran SP% **106.9**
Speed ratings (Par 95): **89,88,85,62**
CSF £3.81 TOTE £3.30; EX 4.10 Trifecta £5.80 Pool: £1012.61 - 129.23 winning units..
Owner Ansells Of Watford **Bred** South Wind Bloodstock **Trained** Sigwells, Somerset

FOCUS
The first two set a decent standard in this grade, but the tempo was weak until between them they suddenly quickened at halfway. The runner-up sets the standard.

548 FREE BETS GALORE AT BOOKMAKERS.CO.UK H'CAP 1m 1f 103y(P)
6:35 (6:35) (Class 5) (0-75,71) 4-Y-0+ **£2,587** (£770; £384; £192) **Stalls** Low

Form RPR
-331 1 **Strike Force**16 329 9-9-2 **71** (t) NatashaEaton(5) 7 82
(Alison Hutchinson) *hld up: hdwy on outer to chse ldr over 2f out: led over 1f out: styd on wl* **6/1**3
-115 2 4 1/2 **Monzino (USA)**7 455 5-8-11 **68** GerardGalligan(7) 2 70
(Michael Chapman) *a.p: chsd ldr 7f out tl rdn over 2f out: styd on same pce fr over 1f out* **4/1**2
03-3 3 2 3/4 **Stylistickhill (IRE)**12 410 5-8-13 **63** (tp) LukeMorris 6 59
(Scott Dixon) *s.i.s: hld up: drvn along over 3f out: styd on u.p to go 3rd wl ins fnl f: nt trble ldrs* **7/1**
00-3 4 hd **Going Grey (IRE)**28 145 4-8-9 **59** PatrickMathers 3 54
(Richard Fahey) *chsd ldrs: rdn over 2f out: sn outpcd* **13/2**
00/4 5 nk **Ortea**23 219 4-9-6 **70** StevieDonohoe 8 65
(Ian Williams) *hld up: rdn over 2f out: nvr on terms* **10/1**
035- 6 1 **Basingstoke (IRE)**99 7494 4-9-5 **69** JoeFanning 1 62
(Keith Dalgleish) *racd keenly: trckd ldr over 2f: remained handy: rdn over 2f out: wknd over 1f out* **2/1**1
120- 7 1 1/2 **Elusive Hawk (IRE)**101 7436 9-9-3 **67** WilliamCarson 4 56
(David Evans) *led at str pce: rdn and hdd over 1f out: wknd fnl f* **7/1**
2m 3.29s (1.59) **Going Correction** +0.20s/f (Slow) **7** Ran SP% **115.0**
Speed ratings (Par 103): **100,96,93,93,93 92,90**
toteswingers 1&2 £2.90, 1&3 £3.30, 2&3 £2.20 CSF £30.39 CT £172.04 TOTE £8.40: £2.40, £2.50; EX 33.80 Trifecta £70.40 Pool: £1126.15 - 11.98 winning units..
Owner Miss A L Hutchinson **Bred** Cheveley Park Stud Ltd **Trained** Exning, Suffolk

FOCUS
This turned out be be surprisingly uncompetitive, with the winner proving to be far too good.

549 CORAL.CO.UK MOBILE CASINO MAIDEN STKS 5f 20y(P)
7:05 (7:05) (Class 5) 3-Y-0 **£2,587** (£770; £384; £192) **Stalls** Low

Form RPR
2- 1 **Hand In Glove**54 8138 3-9-0 0 ShaneKelly 1 66+
(Robert Cowell) *trckd ldr tl shkn up to ld and edgd lft ins fnl f: r.o: comf* **2/7**1
0 2 1 1/2 **Green Millionaire**14 356 3-9-5 0 FergusSweeney 2 63+
(Jeremy Gask) *chsd ldrs: rdn and ev ch ins fnl f: unable qck towards fin* **7/1**3
2-6 3 3 3/4 **Lady Calantha**35 36 3-9-0 48 TomEaves 3 44
(Alan Berry) *sn led: rdn over 1f out: hdd and no ex ins fnl f* **66/1**
4 1/2 **Belle Isle** 3-9-0 0 ChrisCatlin 4 42+
(Jeremy Noseda) *s.i.s: shkn up over 1f out: nvr on terms* **11/2**2
1m 4.06s (1.76) **Going Correction** +0.20s/f (Slow) **4** Ran SP% **107.1**
Speed ratings (Par 97): **93,90,84,83**
CSF £2.76 TOTE £1.10; EX 2.70 Trifecta £13.70 Pool: £1019.04 - 55.43 winning units..
Owner Joseph Barton **Bred** Highfield Farm Llp **Trained** Six Mile Bottom, Cambs

FOCUS
An uncompetitive maiden, the form limited by the third. The odds-on favourite had to work harder than expected to win, the next two came into the race with little form in the bank, and the debutante finished a never-dangerous last.

550 £50 FREE BET AT CORAL.CO.UK H'CAP 5f 216y(P)
7:35 (7:36) (Class 4) (0-85,80) 3-Y-0 **£4,690** (£1,395; £697; £348) **Stalls** Low

Form RPR
3221 1 **Sewn Up**12 404 3-8-9 **68** (tp) ShaneKelly 1 71
(Reg Hollinshead) *hld up: hdwy over 1f out: shkn up and edgd lft ins fnl f: r.o to ld post* **9/1**
15-2 2 nse **Midnight Dream (FR)**32 85 3-9-4 **77** GrahamLee 7 80
(Kristin Stubbs) *a.p: chsd ldr over 3f out: hmpd over 1f out: rdn to ld wl ins fnl f: hdd post* **7/2**3
063- 3 1 1/4 **Blackdown Spirit**124 6871 3-9-7 **80** (b1) AdamKirby 2 79
(Paul D'Arcy) *trckd ldrs: racd keenly: shkn up to ld over 1f out: sn rdn and hung lft: hdd and unable qck wl ins fnl f* **11/4**2
26-1 4 3/4 **Keene's Pointe**15 341 3-9-5 **78** FrannyNorton 6 75
(J W Hills) *led: rdn and hdd over 1f out: nt clr run wl ins fnl f: styd on* **12/1**
1-13 5 3 **Hazza The Jazza**16 325 3-8-5 **64** (b) LukeMorris 4 51
(Richard Guest) *s.i.s: hld up: hdwy over 1f out: r.o: nt rch ldrs* **11/1**
04-1 6 1 **Blazing Knight (IRE)**22 225 3-9-4 **77** JimCrowley 9 61
(Ralph Beckett) *broke wl: sn stdd and lost pl: racd wd: shkn up over 1f out: nvr nr to chal* **2/1**1
455- 7 1 3/4 **Sylvia Pankhurst (IRE)**121 6955 3-8-12 **71** GrahamGibbons 5 49
(David C Griffiths) *mid-div: effrt over 2f out: wknd over 1f out* **16/1**
23-1 8 7 **Tanghan (IRE)**28 136 3-9-4 **77** DavidNolan 8 33
(Richard Fahey) *prom: pushed along and hung rt over 2f out: sn wknd* **12/1**
0-00 9 4 **Sylvia's Diamond**25 195 3-7-10 **62** oh16 ow1 (p) PhilipPrince(7) 3
(Richard Guest) *chsd ldr tl rdn over 3f out: wknd 2f out* **100/1**
1m 16.08s (1.08) **Going Correction** +0.20s/f (Slow) **9** Ran SP% **122.8**
Speed ratings (Par 99): **100,99,98,97,93 91,89,80,74**
toteswingers 1&2 £6.20, 1&3 £6.10, 2&3 £2.70 CSF £43.29 CT £114.64 TOTE £4.40: £2.70, £1.70, £1.50; EX 37.90 Trifecta £248.00 Pool: £1524.61 - 4.60 winning units..
Owner John L Marriott **Bred** M E Broughton **Trained** Upper Longdon, Staffs

FOCUS
They went just an ordinary gallop, which probably wasn't ideal for the winner in this decent Polytrack handicap. Ordinary form for the grade.

551 WIN MORE ON BETTING AT BOOKMAKERS.CO.UK H'CAP 5f 216y(P)
8:05 (8:08) (Class 7) (0-50,50) 4-Y-0+ **£1,940** (£577; £288; £144) **Stalls** Low

Form RPR
2-02 1 **Flow Chart (IRE)**14 349 6-8-12 **48** SladeO'Hara(5) 6 58
(Peter Grayson) *hld up: hdwy over 1f out: rdn to ld ins fnl f: jst hld on* **12/1**
6-00 2 nk **Cadmium Loch**10 423 5-9-5 **50** (p) AdamKirby 11 59
(Reg Hollinshead) *hld up: hdwy over 1f out: rdn and ev ch ins fnl f: r.o* **10/1**

-260 **3** *1 ¼* **First Rebellion**[6] 471 4-9-1 **46**.. DavidProbert 3 51
(Tony Carroll) *led: rdn and hung rt over 1f out: hdd and unable qck ins fnl f* **12/1**

0-42 **4** *¾* **Exkaliber**[16] 327 4-9-4 **49**...(t) JoeFanning 1 52
(Jeremy Gask) *trckd ldrs: racd keenly: shkn up over 1f out: styd on same pce ins fnl f* **3/1**[1]

0136 **5** *nk* **Athaakeel (IRE)**[6] 471 7-9-4 **49**.............................(b) LukeMorris 2 51
(Ronald Harris) *hld up in tch: shkn up over 1f out: styd on same pce ins fnl f* **5/1**[2]

-433 **6** *¾* **Blue Noodles**[10] 423 7-9-1 **46**...................................(p) PaddyAspell 4 45
(John Wainwright) *hld up: nt clr run over 1f out: edgd lft and r.o ins fnl f: nrst fin* **8/1**

0-03 **7** *1* **Bachelor Knight (IRE)**[10] 422 5-8-7 **45**.............. JacobButterfield(7) 7 41
(Suzzanne France) *hld up: hdwy over 1f out: no ex ins fnl f* **22/1**

0-54 **8** *½* **Chester Deelyte (IRE)**[16] 327 5-9-0 **50**.............(v) ShirleyTeasdale(5) 8 44
(Lisa Williamson) *mid-div: hdwy over 1f out: rdn and edgd lft ins fnl f: styd on same pce* **14/1**

-000 **9** *1 ¼* **Very First Blade**[8] 440 4-9-1 **46**..............................(b) FrannyNorton 5 36
(Mark Brisbourne) *trckd ldrs: plld hrd: n.m.r over 1f out: wknd ins fnl f* **25/1**

0-00 **10** *3 ¼* **Fast Samurai (USA)**[6] 472 5-9-1 **46**............................. JimmyQuinn 13 26
(Tony Carroll) *hld up: rdn over 1f out: edgd lft ins fnl f: nvr on terms* **50/1**

4-25 **11** *2* **Adaeze (IRE)**[15] 339 5-9-3 **48**..(b) JohnFahy 12 22
(Jonathan Portman) *chsd ldrs: rdn over 1f out: wknd ins fnl f* **25/1**

-306 **12** *shd* **Onceaponatime (IRE)**[12] 409 8-8-12 **50**....................... RobertTart(7) 10 23
(Michael Squance) *prom: rdn over 2f out: wknd over 1f out* **7/1**[3]

206- **13** *8* **Dear Ben**[182] 5000 4-9-5 **50**..[1] WilliamCarson 9
(Brian Baugh) *chsd ldr: rdn over 2f out: wknd over 1f out* **5/1**[2]

1m 15.79s (0.79) **Going Correction** +0.20s/f (Slow) **13** Ran SP% **127.1**
Speed ratings (Par 97): **102,101,99,98,98 97,96,95,93,89 86,86,76**
toteswingers 1&2 £36.90, 1&3 £9.00, 2&3 £33.70 CSF £129.59 CT £1544.64 TOTE £14.30: £4.10, £4.10, £4.40; EX 151.70 Trifecta £1261.20 Part won. Pool: £1681.72 - 0.42 winning units..
Owner E Grayson **Bred** John Starbuck **Trained** Formby, Lancs
■ Stewards' Enquiry : David Probert two-day ban: used whip above permitted level (Feb 21-22)

FOCUS
This was a low-grade race, and the first 2f didn't look that strongly run, with many hard pullers. However, the first two were held up and the third made the running, so the pace looks to have been fair to all. The winner's best form since he was a 3yo.
T/Plt: £61.50 to a £1 stake. Pool of £72184.68 - 856.11 winning units T/Qpdt: £18.60 to a £1 stake. Pool of £9058.76 - 359 winning units CR

499 MEYDAN (L-H)

Thursday, February 7

OFFICIAL GOING: Tapeta: standard; turf: good

552a GN FOCUS (H'CAP) (TAPETA) 1m 2f

3:15 (3:15) (95-105,105) 3-Y-O+

£40,490 (£13,496; £6,748; £3,374; £2,024; £1,349)

RPR

1 **Ottoman Empire (FR)**[14] 362 7-9-0 **98**......................... HarryBentley 1 105
(David Simcock) *trckd ldrs: smooth prog 2 1/f out: led 1 1/2f out* **9/2**[2]

2 *1 ½* **Arthur's Tale (USA)**[14] 362 5-8-13 **97**......................... AhmedAjtebi 3 101+
(Mahmood Al Zarooni) *settled in rr: r.o wl fnl 2f: nrst fin* **9/1**

3 *¼* **Universal (IRE)**[7] 462 4-8-11 **97**.............................. KierenFallon 10 100
(Mark Johnston) *in rr of mid-div: rdn 4f out: chsd ldrs 2f out: kpt on one pce fnl f* **16/1**

4 *1 ¾* **Jardim (BRZ)**[14] 362 7-9-4 **102**........................... ChristopheSoumillon 9 102+
(M F De Kock, South Africa) *settled in rr: r.o fnl 2f but nvr nr to chal* **9/1**

5 *1 ¾* **Modern History (IRE)**[21] 241 5-9-6 **105**.................. MickaelBarzalona 5 101
(Mahmood Al Zarooni) *sn led: hdd 1 1/2f out: kpt on same pce fnl f* **10/1**

6 *½* **Mustaheel (IRE)**[7] 463 4-9-5 **105**................................. PaulHanagan 11 100
(A Al Raihe, UAE) *s.i.s: in rr of mid-div: kpt on same pce fnl 1 1/2f* **10/1**

7 *¼* **Layali Al Andalus**[14] 362 6-8-13 **97**.......................... RichardMullen 8 92
(S Seemar, UAE) *settled in rr: nvr able to chal* **11/4**[1]

8 *9 ½* **Dorian Crown**[118] 7-9-2 **100**..(t) KUlubaev 6 76
(Seth Benzel, U.S.A) *nvr bttr than mid-div* **14/1**

9 *6* **Muck 'N' Brass (IRE)**[14] 364 4-8-11 **97**.....................(bt) GaryCarroll 4 60
(Edward Lynam, Ire) *trckd ldrs tl outpcd 3 1/2f out* **12/1**

10 *29* **Theo Danon (GER)**[14] 363 5-9-4 **102**..........................(p) TedDurcan 7 8
(Mario Hofer, Germany) *trckd ldrs tl outpcd 2 1/2f out* **20/1**

11 *½* **Blue Corner (IRE)**[21] 242 4-9-3 **102**..................(t) SilvestreDeSousa 2 7
(Saeed bin Suroor) *nvr bttr than mid-div* **5/1**[3]

2m 4.3s (-0.40)
WFA 4 from 5yo+ 1lb **11** Ran SP% **124.7**
CSF: 46.89 TRICAST: 611.14 EXACTA: 34.90 TRIFECTA: 335.90 WIN: 5.50 PL: 3.10, 1.70, 4.10.
Owner Ahmad Abdulla Al Shaikh **Bred** S C E A Haras De La Perelle **Trained** Newmarket, Suffolk

FOCUS
A weak handicap for the grade run at a fair gallop, with Modern History taking the field to the 1600m point in splits of 25.83, 24.04, 24.53, 25.20, before \the winner came home in 24.64.

553a MEYDAN CLASSIC TRIAL SPONSORED BY WEEKEND REVIEW (CONDITIONS RACE) (TURF) 7f

3:50 (3:50) 3-Y-O

£36,809 (£12,269; £6,134; £3,067; £1,840; £1,226)

RPR

1 **Elleval (IRE)**[48] 8219 3-8-9 **88**.................................... FergalLynch 7 106+
(David Marnane, Ire) *mid-div: rdn 2 1/2f out: r.o wl fnl f: led fnl 55yds* **12/1**

2 *½* **El Estruendoso (ARG)**[21] 245 4-9-4 **90**......... ChristopheSoumillon 11 106
(M F De Kock, South Africa) *trckd ldrs: rdn 2 1/2f out: led 1 1/2f out: hdd cl home* **5/1**[2]

3 *2 ½* **Luhaif**[21] 245 3-8-9 **100**...(v) MartinHarley 10 97
(Mick Channon) *sn led: kicked clr 2 1/2f out: hdd 1/2f out: kpt on* **10/1**

4 *2* **Tarbawi (IRE)**[21] 245 3-8-9 **80**....................................... TedDurcan 9 92
(M bin Shafya, UAE) *mid-div: rdn 3f out: kpt on same pce fnl 1 1/2f* **33/1**

5 *2 ¼* **Filfil (USA)**[21] 245 3-8-9 **87**................................ MickaelBarzalona 16 85+
(Mahmood Al Zarooni) *nvr nr to chal but r.o fnl 1 1/2f* **11/1**

6 *¾* **I'm Back (IRE)**[21] 245 3-8-9 **96**.........................(t) SilvestreDeSousa 5 83
(Saeed bin Suroor) *trckd ldrs: ev ch 1 1/2f out: wknd fnl 1/2f* **9/4**[1]

7 *¾* **Stasio (USA)**[82] 7773 3-8-9 **90**.. WilliamBuick 15 81
(David Simcock) *nvr bttr than mid-div* **8/1**[3]

8 *hd* **Energia El Gigante (BRZ)**[19] 288 4-9-4 **80**........................ GaryCarroll 6 83
(Fabricio Borges, Sweden) *nvr nr to chal but kpt on same pce fnl 1 1/2f* **33/1**

9 *1 ¼* **Mister Big Shuffle (GER)**[96] 7565 3-8-9 **97**...................... RyanMoore 12 77
(Niels Petersen, Norway) *nvr nr to chal* **12/1**

10 *1 ½* **Bravo Youmzain (IRE)**[21] 245 3-8-9 **88**................. RoystonFfrench 13 73
(A Al Raihe, UAE) *chsd ldrs tl wknd 2f* **20/1**

11 *½* **Ouzinkie (IRE)**[99] 7476 3-8-9 **70**.. DaneO'Neill 3 72
(A Al Raihe, UAE) *nvr nr to chal* **33/1**

12 *4* **Bircham (IRE)**[21] 245 3-8-9 **79**.. AhmedAjtebi 8 61
(Ismail Mohammed) *trckd ldrs tl outpcd fnl 1 1/2f* **50/1**

13 *¾* **Hototo**[117] 7049 3-8-9 **104**.. KierenFallon 1 59
(Fawzi Abdulla Nass, Bahrain) *wl away: chsd ldrs: t.k.h: wknd fnl 2f* **5/1**[2]

14 *¼* **Related**[21] 245 3-8-9 **84**.. TadhgO'Shea 14 59
(Ernst Oertel, UAE) *s.i.s: settled in rr: n.d* **20/1**

15 *7 ¼* **Ana Emaratiya**[21] 243 3-8-5 **78**....................................(t) HarryBentley 4 35
(A Al Raihe, UAE) *trckd ldrs tl wknd room 1 1/2f out* **40/1**

16 *4* **Bint Youmzain (IRE)**[21] 243 3-7-12 **53**................. SaeedAlMazrooei(7) 2 24
(M Ramadan, UAE) *nvr nr to chal* **150/1**

1m 24.65s (0.35)
WFA 3 from 4yo 17lb **16** Ran SP% **131.4**
CSF: 71.44 EXACTA: 164.30 TRIFECTA: 2300.10 WIN 25.10 PL: 6.10, 2.90, 5.60.
Owner Damian Lavelle **Bred** P G Lyons **Trained** Bansha, Co Tipperary

FOCUS
This trial for the Meydan Classic wasn't much of a race - nothing appealed beforehand and Tarbawi holds the form down - but the speed shown by the winner up the straight suggests he's pretty smart.

554a UAE 1000 GUINEAS SPONSORED BY GULF NEWS (LISTED RACE) (FILLIES) (TAPETA) 1m

4:25 (4:25) 3-Y-O

£92,024 (£30,674; £15,337; £7,668; £4,601; £3,067)

RPR

1 **Lovely Pass (IRE)**[152] 6021 3-8-9 **99**............................(p) AhmedAjtebi 8 102
(Mahmood Al Zarooni) *trckd ldng pair: rdn 2 1/2f uut: led 1f out: r.o wl* **7/1**

2 *½* **Shuruq (USA)**[21] 243 3-8-9 **99**.............................. SilvestreDeSousa 6 101+
(Saeed bin Suroor) *mid-div: smooth prog 2 1/2 out: kpt on fnl f: nrst fin* **6/1**[3]

3 *1 ¼* **Music Chart (USA)**[21] 243 3-8-9 **102**.................... MickaelBarzalona 10 98+
(Mahmood Al Zarooni) *settled it rr: smooth prog 1 1/2f out: kpt on fnl f* **5/2**[2]

4 *¼* **Mar Mar (IRE)**[21] 243 3-8-9 **86**....................................(b) WilliamBuick 7 98
(Saeed bin Suroor) *sn led: hdd 1f out: wknd fnl 55yds* **25/1**

5 *¾* **Emotif (ARG)**[261] 4-9-5 **98**.......................... ChristopheSoumillon 2 99+
(M F De Kock, South Africa) *slowly away: r of mid-div: hung 3f out: kpt on same pce fnl 1 1/2f* **6/4**[1]

6 *4 ½* **More Than Sotka (FR)**[21] 243 3-8-9 **99**.............................. FergalLynch 4 85
(David Marnane, Ire) *trckd ldng trio tl one pce fnl 1 1/2f* **16/1**

7 *2 ½* **My Special J'S (USA)**[21] 243 3-8-9 **105**...................(bt) TadhgO'Shea 1 80
(John Patrick Shanahan, Ire) *settled in rr: nvr nr to chal* **20/1**

8 *2* **Daar Zayed (USA)**[21] 243 3-8-9 **85**..................................(t) JamesDoyle 3 75
(M Al Muhairi, UAE) *nvr bttr than mid-div* **66/1**

9 *3 ¼* **Pure Excellence**[96] 7555 3-8-9 **101**................................... KierenFallon 9 68
(Mark Johnston) *trckd ldrs tl outpcd 2 1/2f out* **10/1**

10 *5 ½* **Go Angellica (IRE)**[117] 7052 3-8-9 **98**............................ RichardMullen 5 55
(David Simcock) *settled in rr: n.d* **16/1**

1m 38.99s (1.49)
WFA 3 from 4yo 19lb **10** Ran SP% **126.3**
CSF: 51.92 WIN: 10.90 PL: 2.30, 1.70, 1.00 EXACTA: 43.30 TRIFECTA: 237.90.
Owner Godolphin **Bred** Stowell Park Stud **Trained** Newmarket, Suffolk

FOCUS
The first classic of the UAE season, but the form is worth little. A really slow early pace turned this into a sprint, and it paid to be handy.

555a CLASSIFIEDS (H'CAP) (TURF) 1m 6f 11y

5:00 (5:00) (95-104,104) 3-Y-O+

£55,214 (£18,404; £9,202; £4,601; £2,760; £1,840)

RPR

1 **Star Empire (SAF)**[21] 246 7-9-5 **102**.............. ChristopheSoumillon 14 103+
(M F De Kock, South Africa) *s.i.s: settled in rr: smooth prog 2f out: led fnl 55yds* **11/2**[3]

2 *¼* **Ahzeemah (IRE)**[21] 246 4-9-2 **104**.......................(p) SilvestreDeSousa 4 105+
(Saeed bin Suroor) *mid-div: n.m.r 2 1/2f out: r.o to ld briefly 1f out: hdd fnl 55yds* **5/2**[1]

3 *hd* **Certerach (IRE)**[21] 246 5-9-5 **102**.................................... ShaneFoley 7 102+
(M Halford, Ire) *in rr of mid-div: r.o wl fnl 1 1/2f: nrst fin* **9/1**

4 *¼* **Bob Le Beau (IRE)**[21] 246 6-9-3 **100**............................(p) GaryCarroll 10 100
(Mrs John Harrington, Ire) *sn led: rdn 3f out: hdd 1f out: kpt on same pce* **33/1**

5 *3 ½* **Chicago (IRE)**[21] 246 4-8-11 **99**..................................... TadhgO'Shea 6 94+
(John Patrick Shanahan, Ire) *settled in rr: r.o fnl 2f: nrst fin but n.d* **33/1**

6 *½* **In The Spotlight (IND)**[21] 246 5-9-5 **102**........................ RyanMoore 15 96
(S Padmanabhan, India) *trckd ldrs: wd: ev ch 1 1/2f out: wknd fnl 110yds* **9/2**[2]

7 *3 ¼* **Novelty Seeker (USA)**[14] 364 4-8-10 **98**................... MickaelBarzalona 11 88
(Mahmood Al Zarooni) *mid-div: kpt on same pce fnl 3 1/2f* **8/1**

8 *shd* **Bay Willow (IRE)**[14] 362 6-8-11 **95**...........................(tp) RichardMullen 12 84
(S Seemar, UAE) *trckd ldrs tl outpcd 1 1/2f out* **9/1**

9 *1 ¼* **Kidnapped (AUS)**[21] 246 7-8-8 **98**......................(bt) MarcMonaghan(7) 5 86
(S Seemar, UAE) *nvr bttr than mid div* **66/1**

10 *½* **Ithoughtitwasover (IRE)**[21] 246 5-9-3 **100**........................ KierenFallon 1 87
(Mark Johnston) *trckd ldrs tl outpcd 2f out* **14/1**

11 *½* **Trois Rois (FR)**[28] 151 8-9-4 **101**.................................(b) AnticoMurgia 9 88
(Ismail Mohammed) *a in rr* **33/1**

12 *shd* **Pisco Sour (USA)**[14] 362 5-9-5 **102**............................... WilliamBuick 3 88
(Saeed bin Suroor) *settled in rr: nvr nr to chal* **14/1**

13 *¼* **Art Scholar (IRE)**[14] 362 6-9-2 **99**................................... JamesDoyle 8 85
(Michael Appleby) *settled in rr: nvr nr to chal* **12/1**

14 *3 ½* **Royaaty (IRE)**[21] 246 7-8-11 **95**.. XZiani 13 75
(M bin Shafya, UAE) *in rr of mid-div: wd: wknd fnl 2 1/2f* **33/1**

2m 59.88s (179.88)
WFA 4 from 5yo+ 5lb **14** Ran SP% **127.5**
CSF: 20.05 TRICAST: 131.04 EXACTA: 21.00 TRIFECTA: 158.30 WIN: 7.90 PL: 2.50, 1.80, 4.20.
Owner Mohd Khaleel Ahmed **Bred** Sydney A Muller, F M Ratner & L M Salzman **Trained** South Africa

FOCUS
Ten of these had contested a 1m4f handicap here last month. The pace was slow and there was a bunch finish.

556a AL MAKTOUM CHALLENGE R2 SPONSORED BY TABLOID (GROUP 2) (TAPETA) 1m 1f 110y
5:35 (5:35) 3-Y-0+
£92,024 (£30,674; £15,337; £7,668; £4,601; £3,067)

RPR
1 **Hunter's Light (IRE)**[95] 7586 5-9-0 117 SilvestreDeSousa 6 116
(Saeed bin Suroor) *trckd ldrs: rdn 2 1/2f out: led 1f out: comf* 7/2[2]
2 3 1/4 **Surfer (USA)**[49] 8196 4-8-13 106 RichardMullen 11 109
(S Seemar, UAE) *trckd ldrs: led 3f out: hdd 1f out: r.o gamely* 20/1
3 1/2 **Prince Bishop (IRE)**[313] 1150 6-9-0 115 RyanMoore 1 108
(Saeed bin Suroor) *sn led: hdd 3f out: kpt on same pce* 12/1
4 1 3/4 **Saint Baudolino (IRE)**[176] 5250 4-8-13 115 (t) MickaelBarzalona 4 105+
(Mahmood Al Zarooni) *in rr of mid-div: r.o fnl 1 1/2f: nrst fin* 2/1[1]
5 1 1/2 **Mendip (USA)**[313] 1150 6-9-0 113 KierenFallon 8 102+
(Saeed bin Suroor) *mid-div: r.o fnl 1 1/2f but nvr nr to chal* 12/1
6 shd **Mushreq (AUS)**[7] 462 5-9-0 112 PaulHanagan 12 101+
(M F De Kock, South Africa) *settled in rr: nvr able to chal but r.o fnl 1 1/2f* 11/2[3]
7 1/4 **Jamr**[14] 364 5-9-0 107 (v) TedDurcan 10 101+
(M bin Shafya, UAE) *in rr of mid-div: kpt on same pce fnl 2f* 20/1
8 hd **Mufarrh (IRE)**[28] 153 6-9-0 112 DaneO'Neill 5 101
(A Al Raihe, UAE) *trckd ldrs: ev ch 1 1/2f out: one pce fnl 110yds* 10/1
9 hd **Await The Dawn (USA)**[313] 1148 6-9-0 118 PatCosgrave 2 100+
(M F De Kock, South Africa) *break awkwardly: settled in rr: nvr nr to chal* 9/1
10 3/4 **Zain Shamardal (IRE)**[37] 5-9-0 105 (t) RoystonFfrench 7 99+
(A Al Raihe, UAE) *nvr bttr than mid-div* 33/1
11 1 1/2 **So Beautiful (FR)**[7] 466 4-8-13 112 PatDobbs 9 96+
(Doug Watson, UAE) *settled in last: nvr nr to chal* 16/1
12 2 **Alpha (USA)**[95] 7576 4-8-13 116 WilliamBuick 3 91+
(Saeed bin Suroor) *nvr bttr than mid-div* 16/1
1m 58.19s (-0.81) 12 Ran SP% 129.6
CSF: 81.29 EXACTA: 106.70 WIN: 6.10 PL: 1.90 4.10 3.60 TRIFECTA: 860.80.
Owner Godolphin **Bred** Darley **Trained** Newmarket, Suffolk

FOCUS
Moon Ballad remains the only horse to take this en-route to winning the Dubai World Cup (did so back in 2003). It paid to be handy. It's true this was run at a desperately slow early pace, as the sectionals show: 27.21 (440m) 26.23 (800m), 25.28 (1200m), 22.66 (1600m), so the obvious conclusion is this is misleading form, but Hunter's Light impressed.

557a FREEHOLD (H'CAP) (TAPETA) 1m
6:10 (6:10) (100-110,109) 3-Y-0+
£44,171 (£14,723; £7,361; £3,680; £2,208; £1,472)

RPR
1 **Royal Ridge (SAF)**[13] 393 5-9-2 105 PaulHanagan 12 109
(M F De Kock, South Africa) *trckd ldng pair: led 2 1/2f out* 5/1[2]
2 hd **Producer**[78] 7809 4-9-5 108 RichardHughes 1 112
(Richard Hannon) *mid-div: chsd ldrs 2f out: ev ch 110yds out: nt qckn fnl 55yds* 10/1
3 hd **Mariner's Cross (IRE)**[21] 241 4-9-2 105 AhmedAjtebi 9 109
(Mahmood Al Zarooni) *mid-div: chsd ldrs 2 1/2f out: kpt on fnl 1 1/2f* 12/1
4 1 **Don't Call Me (IRE)**[14] 367 6-9-4 107 (t) RichardMullen 7 108
(David Nicholls) *in rr of mid-div: r.o fnl 1 1/2f: nrst fin* 9/2[1]
5 1/4 **Ariete Arrollador**[7] 465 6-9-0 102 CO'Donoghue 4 104
(G Arizkorreta Elosegui, Spain) *in rr of mid-div: smooth prog 2 1/2f out: could nt qckn fnl 110yds* 12/1
6 1/2 **Red Duke (USA)**[28] 152 4-9-4 107 WilliamBuick 6 107
(David Simcock) *settled in rr: nvr nr to chal* 14/1
7 nse **Kinglet (USA)**[313] 1145 4-9-3 106 MickaelBarzalona 14 105
(Mahmood Al Zarooni) *settled in last: nvr nr to chal* 7/1[3]
8 3/4 **Yaa Wayl (IRE)**[28] 149 6-9-0 102 (vt) SilvestreDeSousa 8 101
(Saeed bin Suroor) *mid-div: kpt on same pce fnl 1 1/2f* 7/1[3]
9 1 1/2 **Banna Boirche (IRE)**[7] 463 7-8-13 101 ShaneFoley 2 96
(M Halford, Ire) *nvr bttr than mid-div* 10/1
10 hd **Red Dubawi (IRE)**[7] 467 5-9-1 104 FergalLynch 3 98
(David Marnane, Ire) *slowly away: nvr nr to chal* 25/1
11 4 1/4 **Rutland Boy**[28] 153 5-9-6 109 HarryBentley 13 93
(A Al Raihe, UAE) *trckd ldrs tl outpcd 2f out* 16/1
12 4 1/2 **Famous Warrior (IRE)**[14] 363 6-8-13 101 (t) PatDobbs 11 76
(Doug Watson, UAE) *sn led: hdd & wknd 2 1/2f out* 16/1
13 5 3/4 **Freezemaster (AUS)**[28] 154 6-8-11 100 (t) TedDurcan 10 60
(S Burridge, Singapore) *trckd ldng pair tl outpcd 2 1/2f out* 20/1
P **Jet Legend (SAF)**[14] 367 6-8-11 100 DaneO'Neill 5
(M F De Kock, South Africa) *p.u after 2 1/2f* 10/1
1m 36.17s (-1.33) 14 Ran SP% 131.4
CSF: 60.04 TRICAST: 600.47 EXACTA 78.90 WIN: 5.50 PL: 2.20, 4.00, 5.30, TRIFECTA: 1492.10. Placepot: £256.00 to a £1 stake. Pool of £5856.75 - 16.70 winning units. Quadpot: £36.30 to a £1 stake. Pool of £501.60 - 10.20 winning units..
Owner Hamdan Al Maktoum **Bred** F W Sharp **Trained** South Africa

FOCUS
Famous Warrior, pressed for the lead by Rutland Boy, went a fair pace, clocking 25.35, 23.09, 23.92, and the winner went 23.75 over the last quarter.

545 WOLVERHAMPTON (A.W) (L-H)
Friday, February 8

OFFICIAL GOING: Standard
Wind: Fresh across Weather: Overcast

558 CORAL.CO.UK H'CAP 5f 20y(P)
5:00 (5:00) (Class 6) (0-65,65) 4-Y-0+ £1,940 (£577; £288; £144) Stalls Low

Form RPR
-261 1 **Holy Angel (IRE)**[8] 453 4-8-12 63 (e) RachelRichardson(7) 9 75+
(Tim Easterby) *hld up: hdwy over 1f out: r.o to ld wl ins fnl f: comf* 9/4[1]
01-3 2 1 1/2 **Sunrise Dance**[24] 214 4-9-6 64 AndrewMullen 10 71
(Robert Johnson) *chsd ldr tl rdn to ld and edgd lft over 1f out: hdd and unable qck wl ins fnl f* 9/1
0320 3 1 1/4 **Russian Bullet**[4] 516 4-9-0 58 DavidProbert 5 61
(Jamie Osborne) *chsd ldrs: rdn over 1f out: styd on same pce ins fnl f* 12/1
0-04 4 1 1/2 **Crimson Queen**[7] 481 6-9-4 65 (b) MarkCoumbe(3) 2 62
(Roy Brotherton) *led: rdn and hdd over 1f out: no ex ins fnl f* 7/1[3]
6-10 5 1/2 **Ivestar (IRE)**[13] 399 8-9-6 64 (vt) JamesSullivan 4 59
(Michael Easterby) *hld up: rdn over 1f out: r.o ins fnl f: nt rch ldrs* 17/2
0-56 6 hd **Perlachy**[8] 453 9-9-6 64 (v) LukeMorris 6 59
(Ronald Harris) *mid-div: rdn over 1f out: styd on: nt trble ldrs* 12/1
-046 7 nk **Shawkantango**[7] 481 6-9-6 64 (v) JoeFanning 1 58
(Derek Shaw) *s.i.s: outpcd: r.o ins fnl f: nvr nrr* 4/1[2]
10-0 8 2 **Festival Dance**[13] 399 5-9-0 65 PhilipPrince(7) 8 51
(Ron Hodges) *hld up in tch: racd keenly: rdn over 1f out: wknd ins fnl f* 20/1
06-0 9 1/2 **Ice Trooper**[13] 398 5-9-4 62 (p) TomEaves 11 47
(Kristin Stubbs) *chsd ldrs: pushed along 1/2-way: wknd fnl f* 33/1
100- 10 1/2 **Ingleby Star (IRE)**[116] 7101 8-9-4 62 (p) DaleSwift 7 45
(Ian McInnes) *mid-div: rdn and wknd over 1f out* 50/1
-021 11 14 **Lord Buffhead**[11] 423 4-9-2 60 6ex (v) RobbieFitzpatrick 3
(Richard Guest) *s.i.s: outpcd* 7/1[3]
1m 1.73s (-0.57) **Going Correction** 0.0s/f (Stan) 11 Ran SP% 121.3
Speed ratings (Par 101): **104,101,99,97,96 96,95,92,91,90 68**
toteswingers 1&2 £5.10, 1&3 £8.20, 2&3 £13.80 CSF £24.09 CT £211.97 TOTE £3.30: £1.60, £1.90, £5.90; EX 16.00 Trifecta £253.00 Pool: £5,385.77 - 15.96 winning units..
Owner Three Jolly Farmers **Bred** Yeomanstown Stud **Trained** Great Habton, N Yorks

FOCUS
Track Gallop Mastered after race four. A sprint handicap that revolved around the well-in winner. The form is sound, set around the second and third.

559 PICK THE BEST BOOKIES AT BOOKMAKERS.CO.UK H'CAP (DIV I) 5f 216y(P)
5:30 (5:30) (Class 6) (0-60,60) 4-Y-0+ £1,940 (£577; £288; £144) Stalls Low

Form RPR
-050 1 **George Fenton**[11] 426 4-8-12 58 (v[1]) PhilipPrince(7) 10 70
(Richard Guest) *a.p: rdn to ld wl ins fnl f: styd on* 7/1
00-1 2 1/2 **Dorothy's Dancing (IRE)**[17] 322 5-9-7 60 GeorgeBaker 8 70
(Gary Moore) *hld up: nt clr run over 1f out: swtchd rt and r.o wl ins fnl f: nt rch wnr* 3/1[1]
10-4 3 1 3/4 **Mack's Sister**[15] 354 6-9-6 59 (p) AdamKirby 3 63
(Dean Ivory) *a.p: pushed along 1/2-way: rdn and ev ch ins fnl f: styd on same pce* 9/2[2]
5-31 4 shd **Whipphound**[20] 277 5-9-4 57 RobbieFitzpatrick 5 62
(Mark Brisbourne) *chsd ldrs: wnt 2nd over 2f out: rdn and ev ch whn hmpd ins fnl f: styd on same pce* 8/1
000- 5 shd **Almaty Express**[126] 6836 11-9-2 55 (b) LukeMorris 7 59
(John Weymes) *led: rdn over 1f out: edgd rt and hdd wl ins fnl f: styd on same pce* 25/1
-216 6 1 3/4 **Kai**[14] 380 4-9-5 58 (b) SeanLevey 2 56
(Alan McCabe) *chsd ldrs: rdn over 1f out: no ex ins fnl f* 5/1[3]
4-5 7 1 1/2 **Scommettitrice (IRE)**[36] 30 5-9-3 56 (p) AndreaAtzeni 4 49
(Mark Gillard) *s.i.s: hld up: rdn over 2f out: nvr trbld ldrs* 20/1
45-0 8 shd **Powerful Pierre**[24] 214 6-9-7 60 (b) GrahamGibbons 1 62+
(Ian McInnes) *hld up: hdwy over 1f out: running on whn bdly hmpd ins fnl f: nt rcvr* 9/2[2]
430- 9 7 **Petrarchan**[156] 5935 5-8-7 46 oh1 (bt) ChrisCatlin 9 17
(Milton Bradley) *chsd ldr tl pushed along over 2f out: wknd over 1f out* 66/1
103- 10 1 3/4 **True Prince (USA)**[107] 7326 4-9-0 53 TomEaves 6 18
(Brian Ellison) *a in rr: rdn and lost tch over 2f out* 7/1
1m 15.07s (0.07) **Going Correction** 0.0s/f (Stan) 10 Ran SP% 124.2
Speed ratings (Par 101): **99,98,96,95,95 93,91,91,81,79**
toteswingers 1&2 £7.40, 1&3 £7.40, 2&3 £3.10 CSF £29.80 CT £112.69 TOTE £9.10: £3.30, £1.50, £1.60; EX 46.90 Trifecta £246.50 Pool: £6,164.64 - 18.75 winning units..
Owner Maze Rattan Limited **Bred** R P Williams **Trained** Wetherby, W Yorks
■ Stewards' Enquiry : Luke Morris three-day ban; careless riding (22nd,23rd&25th Feb)

FOCUS
The first division of the 6f handicap rated a strong affair for the grade, with several in-form participants. However, the two last-time-out winners were weak in the market. It was slightly the slower division and the form is rated around the third.

560 PICK THE BEST BOOKIES AT BOOKMAKERS.CO.UK H'CAP (DIV II)5f 216y(P)
6:00 (6:02) (Class 6) (0-60,60) 4-Y-0+ £1,940 (£577; £288; £144) Stalls Low

Form RPR
-404 1 **Methaaly (IRE)**[4] 516 10-9-0 60 (be) RobertTart(7) 7 69
(Michael Mullineaux) *hld up: hdwy over 1f out: rdn to ld wl ins fnl f: r.o* 4/1[2]
1623 2 2 3/4 **Glennten**[8] 449 4-9-2 55 (b[1]) LiamKeniry 1 55
(Sylvester Kirk) *sn pushed along and prom: chsd ldr over 2f out: led over 1f out: rdn and hdd wl ins fnl f* 11/4[1]
06-1 3 1 3/4 **Romanticize**[28] 163 7-9-4 57 DaleSwift 8 52
(Jason Ward) *hld up: pushed along 1/2-way: hdwy over 2f out: rdn over 1f out: styd on same pce fnl f* 5/1[3]
000- 4 1 1/2 **Sweet Ovation**[39] 8304 4-9-7 60 HayleyTurner 4 50
(Mark Usher) *hld up: hdwy over 2f out: rdn over 1f out: wknd ins fnl f* 11/1
04-6 5 2 1/4 **Sannibel**[29] 139 5-9-4 57 DavidProbert 6 40
(Graeme McPherson) *sn pushed along in rr: rdn over 2f out: styd on same pce* 6/1
0350 6 nk **Jonnie Skull (IRE)**[13] 398 7-9-0 53 (vt) LukeMorris 5 35
(Phil McEntee) *prom: rdn and lost pl over 2f out: n.d after* 10/1
2444 7 2 3/4 **Ryedale Dancer (IRE)**[20] 277 5-9-2 55 RobbieFitzpatrick 3 28
(Richard Guest) *chsd ldr tl rdn and hung rt over 2f out: wknd fnl f* 13/2
044- 8 1 1/2 **Jawking**[357] 605 4-9-6 59 (bt[1]) AdamKirby 9 27
(Frank Sheridan) *led: rdn and hdd over 1f out: wknd fnl f* 12/1
46-0 9 nk **You'relikemefrank**[18] 308 7-8-12 58 VictorSantos(7) 2 25
(Richard Ford) *chsd ldrs: rdn over 2f out: wknd over 1f out* 40/1
1m 15.0s **Going Correction** 0.0s/f (Stan) 9 Ran SP% 118.5
Speed ratings (Par 101): **100,96,94,92,89 88,84,82,82**
toteswingers 1&2 £3.90, 1&3 £4.60, 2&3 £2.90 CSF £15.90 CT £56.94 TOTE £7.40: £2.30, £1.30, £2.40; EX 21.60 Trifecta £120.60 Pool: £8,183.76 - 50.86 winning units..
Owner S A Pritchard **Bred** Scuderia Golden Horse S R L **Trained** Alpraham, Cheshire

FOCUS
The weaker if slightly faster of the two divisions of the 6f handicap and plenty who hadn't been at the top of their game recently. The form is rated a bit cautiously.

561 POKER AT CORAL.CO.UK MEDIAN AUCTION MAIDEN STKS 5f 216y(P)
6:30 (6:30) (Class 6) 3-5-Y-0 £1,940 (£577; £288; £144) Stalls Low

Form RPR
454- 1 **Newstead Abbey**[123] 6920 3-8-12 76 GrahamGibbons 1 71+
(David Barron) *s.v.s: bhd: smooth hdwy over 1f out: led on bit ins fnl f: easily* 2/9[1]

43-6 **2** 1 ½ **Loulou Vuitton**[31] 106 3-8-7 60....(p[1]) WilliamCarson 2 61
(Brian Baugh) *led 1f: chsd ldrs: rdn to ld over 1f out: hung lft and hdd ins fnl f: no ex* **8/1**[2]
3 3 ½ **Green Special (ITY)** 3-8-12 0.... LukeMorris 3 55
(Frank Sheridan) *s.s: sn pushed along in rr: in tch 1/2-way: rdn over 1f out: sn hung lft and styd on same pce* **14/1**[3]
0-23 **4** 4 ½ **Batchworth Lady**[11] 416 3-8-7 0.... JimmyQuinn 6 35
(Dean Ivory) *chsd ldr: led over 2f out: rdn and hdd over 1f out: wknd fnl f* **8/1**[2]
50-3 **5** 10 **Eyeline**[25] 207 3-8-12 54....(p) ChrisCatlin 5
(Reg Hollinshead) *sn pushed along: led after 1f: rdn and hdd over 2f out: wknd over 1f out* **16/1**

1m 15.64s (0.64) **Going Correction** 0.0s/f (Stan)
WFA 3 from 4yo 15lb **5** Ran SP% **116.6**
Speed ratings (Par 101): **95,93,88,82,69**
CSF £3.34 TOTE £1.70: £1.10, £2.50; EX 4.70 Trifecta £22.00 Pool: £26,577.37 - 905.13 winning units..
Owner Let's Be Lucky Partnership **Bred** Grasshopper 2000 Ltd **Trained** Maunby, N Yorks

FOCUS
A weak median auction maiden in which the winner cruised home. The form is rated around the runner-up.

562 CORAL.CO.UK MOBILE BETTING H'CAP 1m 5f 194y(P)
7:00 (7:00) (Class 5) (0-75,75) 4-Y-0+ **£2,587** (£770; £384; £192) **Stalls** Low

Form RPR
-641 **1** **Broxbourne (IRE)**[16] 343 4-8-7 **61**.... JoeFanning 1 73+
(Mark Johnston) *chsd ldrs: wnt 2nd over 2f out: edgd rt and led over 1f out: styd on wl: readily* **13/8**[1]
1-42 **2** 4 **Tingo In The Tale (IRE)**[15] 352 4-9-3 **71**.... HayleyTurner 3 77
(David Arbuthnot) *led: rdn: edgd rt and hdd over 1f out: styd on same pce ins fnl f* **5/2**[2]
0-40 **3** 10 **Epic Storm (IRE)**[23] 224 5-9-10 **73**.... AdamKirby 5 65
(Sean Curran) *chsd ldr after 2f tl rdn over 2f out: wknd over 1f out* **13/8**[1]
000- **4** 3 **Oneofapear (IRE)**[43] 8259 7-9-12 **75**.... DaleSwift 6 63
(Ian McInnes) *hld up: pushed along over 4f out: wknd over 2f out* **28/1**
0-30 **5** 17 **Wild Desert (FR)**[14] 378 8-9-12 **75**.... GeorgeBaker 4 39
(John Gallagher) *chsd ldr 2f: remained handy: rdn over 2f out: sn wknd: t.o* **8/1**[3]

3m 3.24s (-2.76) **Going Correction** 0.0s/f (Stan)
WFA 4 from 5yo+ 5lb **5** Ran SP% **119.3**
Speed ratings (Par 103): **107,104,99,97,87**
CSF £6.77 TOTE £2.20: £1.20, £1.80; EX 4.20 Trifecta £6.80 Pool: £15,868.78 - 1,726.29 winning units..
Owner Ready To Run Partnership **Bred** Mount Coote Stud And M Johnston **Trained** Middleham Moor, N Yorks

FOCUS
Only five runners lined up but this was still a decent staying handicap. The winner is progressing now.

563 CHOOSE THE RIGHT BOOKIE AT BOOKMAKERS.CO.UK H'CAP 1m 4f 50y(P)
7:30 (7:30) (Class 4) (0-85,84) 4-Y-0+ **£4,690** (£1,395; £697; £348) **Stalls** Low

Form RPR
11-3 **1** **Flying Power**[28] 167 5-9-7 **84**.... PaddyAspell 9 92
(John Norton) *trckd ldr: plld hrd: shkn up ins fnl f: styd on to ld post* **4/1**[1]
02-1 **2** hd **Illustrious Forest**[36] 39 5-8-13 **76**.... GrahamGibbons 1 83
(John Mackie) *led at stdy pce tl qcknd over 3f out: rdn over 1f out: hdd post* **11/2**[2]
3 1 ½ **Roman Flight (IRE)**[70] 1080 5-9-0 **77**.... DanielTudhope 7 82
(David O'Meara) *chsd ldrs: rdn and hung lft over 1f out: styd on u.p* **8/1**
-132 **4** 1 ¾ **Sir Boss (IRE)**[29] 144 8-9-3 **80**.... TomEaves 12 82
(Michael Mullineaux) *mid-div: hdwy over 2f out: rdn over 1f out: styd on: nt rch ldrs* **9/1**
4623 **5** ½ **On The Hoof**[9] 439 4-8-10 **76**.... JamesSullivan 5 77
(Michael Easterby) *a.p: nt clr run over 2f out: rdn over 1f out: styd on same pce ins fnl f* **7/1**[3]
-344 **6** nk **Blizzard Blues (USA)**[10] 430 7-8-4 **70** oh2....(b) RaulDaSilva[(3)] 8 71
(Aytach Sadik) *s.i.s: hld up: rdn and r.o ins fnl f: nvr nrr* **66/1**
0/4 **7** 2 ¾ **Boom To Bust (IRE)**[22] 239 5-9-6 **83**....(p) WilliamCarson 4 80
(Sean Curran) *chsd ldrs: rdn over 2f out: hung lft and wknd ins fnl f* **20/1**
/24- **8** 1 **Monte Cavallo (SAF)**[62] 7300 8-9-3 **80**.... AdamKirby 2 75
(Rebecca Curtis) *s.i.s: hld up: rdn over 2f out: edgd lft over 1f out: nt trble ldrs* **4/1**[1]
2156 **9** 1 ¾ **Kames Park (IRE)**[11] 420 11-8-5 **75**.... PhilipPrince[(7)] 3 67
(Richard Guest) *hld up: rdn over 2f out: nvr on terms* **25/1**
0/ **10** hd **Capellanus (IRE)**[12] 2902 7-8-11 **74**.... DaleSwift 10 66
(Brian Ellison) *hld up: rdn over 3f out: hdwy over 2f out: wknd over 1f out* **8/1**
40-1 **11** 33 **Rapid Heat Lad (IRE)**[18] 309 4-8-10 **76**....(p) JoeFanning 11 15
(Reg Hollinshead) *hld up: hdwy over 5f out: rdn and wknd over 2f out* **11/1**

2m 38.27s (-2.83) **Going Correction** 0.0s/f (Stan)
WFA 4 from 5yo+ 3lb **11** Ran SP% **118.5**
Speed ratings (Par 105): **109,108,107,106,106 106,104,103,102,102 80**
toteswingers 1&2 £5.90, 1&3 £9.90, 2&3 £11.80 CSF £25.34 CT £170.46 TOTE £5.40: £2.10, £1.60, £4.80; EX 31.10 Trifecta £241.60 Pool: £3,309.95 - 10.27 winning units..
Owner Jaffa Racing Syndicate **Bred** Rabbah Bloodstock Limited **Trained** High Hoyland, S Yorks

FOCUS
A competitive 0-85 1m4f handicap, in which it paid to race handy. Ordinary form, but the winner continues to improve.

564 FIND THE BEST ODDS AT BOOKMAKERS.CO.UK MEDIAN AUCTION MAIDEN STKS 1m 1f 103y(P)
8:00 (8:01) (Class 6) 3-5-Y-0 **£1,940** (£577; £288; £144) **Stalls** Low

Form RPR
1 **Welsh Sunrise** 3-8-2 0.... LukeMorris 2 54+
(Gerard Butler) *a.p: chsd ldr over 2f out: led over 1f out: styd on wl* **4/1**
2 3 ½ **Lignum Vitae** 3-8-7 0.... PatrickMathers 3 51+
(Richard Fahey) *s.i.s: hld up: rn green in rr: hdwy over 1f out: r.o ins fnl f: no ch w wnr* **5/2**[2]
564/ **3** 2 **Big City Boy (IRE)**[710] 720 5-10-0 35.... DavidProbert 4 52?
(Phil McEntee) *led: rdn and hdd over 1f out: wknd ins fnl f* **50/1**
4 shd **Pereira** 3-8-2 0.... NickyMackay 1 42
(David Simcock) *unruly in stalls: chsd ldrs: pushed along and edgd lft wl over 2f out: wknd ins fnl f* **6/4**[1]
50- **5** 20 **Mayforde Jack**[314] 1138 4-10-0 0.... J-PGuillambert 5
(Jo Hughes) *s.i.s: hld up: rdn over 3f out: wknd over 2f out* **7/2**[3]
6 **6** 1 ¼ **Reggie Rabbit**[35] 63 4-9-9 0....(v[1]) HarryChalloner[(5)] 6
(Richard Ford) *chsd ldr tl rdn: hmpd and wknd wl over 2f out* **16/1**

2m 3.55s (1.85) **Going Correction** 0.0s/f (Stan)
WFA 3 from 4yo+ 21lb **6** Ran SP% **118.6**
Speed ratings (Par 101): **91,87,86,86,68 67**
toteswingers 1&2 £1.50, 1&3 £3.70, 2&3 £6.40 CSF £15.44 TOTE £5.50: £2.70, £1.20; EX 12.20 Trifecta £112.60 Pool: £1,114.50 - 7.41 winning units..
Owner Seize The Day Racing Partnership **Bred** Mr & Mrs Sells **Trained** Newmarket, Suffolk

FOCUS
The only runner to have achieved a mark came into this rated 35 and he wasn't beaten far, so this has to be considered a very modest maiden. The time was slow and the form is rated negatively.

565 PICK TODAY'S WINNERS AT BOOKMAKERS.CO.UK H'CAP 7f 32y(P)
8:30 (8:32) (Class 7) (0-50,50) 4-Y-0+ **£1,940** (£577; £288; £144) **Stalls** High

Form RPR
6005 **1** **Rise To Glory (IRE)**[13] 409 5-9-0 **45**....(p) DuranFentiman 3 55
(Shaun Harris) *mde all: pushed clr over 2f out: drvn out* **14/1**
-034 **2** 1 ¾ **Titan Diamond (IRE)**[8] 456 5-8-9 **45**.... RachealKneller[(5)] 9 50
(Mark Usher) *prom: rdn over 2f out: styd on to go 2nd nr fin: nt rch wnr* **7/1**[3]
614 **3** nk **Media Jury**[13] 408 6-9-5 **50**....(p) DavidNolan 2 54
(John Wainwright) *chsd wnr: rdn over 2f out: edgd lft and styd on same pce ins fnl f: lost 2nd nr fin* **9/1**
2-60 **4** ½ **Avon Supreme**[9] 441 5-9-2 **47**....(v[1]) LukeMorris 1 50
(Gay Kelleway) *chsd ldrs: rdn over 2f out: styd on same pce ins fnl f* **12/1**
0365 **5** shd **Back For Tea (IRE)**[8] 449 5-9-0 **45**....(b) DavidProbert 8 48
(Phil McEntee) *hld up: hdwy over 1f out: r.o: nt rch ldrs* **20/1**
0-30 **6** ¾ **Not My Choice (IRE)**[9] 440 8-9-3 **48**....(t) TomMcLaughlin 7 49
(Paul Howling) *chsd ldrs: rdn over 1f out: styd on same pce fnl f* **20/1**
0-06 **7** hd **Olynard (IRE)**[11] 423 7-9-0 **45**.... TomEaves 5 45
(Michael Mullineaux) *prom: rdn over 2f out: styd on same pce fr over 1f out* **14/1**
5-33 **8** 1 ¼ **Monsieur Pontaven**[14] 381 6-9-2 **47**....(b) DanielTudhope 11 44
(Robin Bastiman) *s.i.s: hld up: rdn over 1f out: nt rch ldrs* **9/4**[1]
-635 **9** ¾ **Hold The Star**[13] 408 7-8-10 **46**.... AnnStokell[(5)] 6 41
(Ann Stokell) *s.i.s: hld up: rdn over 1f out: nvr on terms* **18/1**
0033 **10** 1 **Cut The Cackle (IRE)**[9] 440 7-9-3 **48**....(bt) WilliamCarson 4 40
(Violet M Jordan) *hld up: pushed along 1/2-way: rdn over 1f out: n.d* **5/2**[2]
-600 **11** 8 **Aljosan**[13] 408 4-8-8 **46**....(bt) RobertTart[(7)] 10 16
(Frank Sheridan) *hld up: rdn and wknd over 1f out* **25/1**

1m 30.54s (0.94) **Going Correction** 0.0s/f (Stan) **11** Ran SP% **121.5**
Speed ratings (Par 97): **94,92,91,91,90 90,89,88,87,86 77**
toteswingers 1&2 £15.80, 1&3 £15.60, 2&3 £4.90 CSF £109.15 CT £963.22 TOTE £13.80: £1.90, £3.10, £3.00; EX 149.80 Trifecta £615.50 Pool: £1,563.83 - 1.90 winning units..
Owner The Moorhouse Partnership **Bred** Bryan Ryan **Trained** Carburton, Notts

FOCUS
A desperate finale.
T/Plt: £16.10 to a £1 stake. Pool: £84,879.12 - 3,835.52 winning tickets T/Qpdt: £3.70 to a £1 stake. Pool: £9,092.95 - 1,791.30 winning tickets CR

566 - 574a (Foreign Racing) - See Raceform Interactive

390 JEBEL ALI (L-H)
Friday, February 8

OFFICIAL GOING: Dirt: fast

575a SHADWELL (H'CAP) (DIRT) 6f (D)
11:15 (11:15) (95-110,108) 3-Y-O£11,557 (£3,852; £2,118; £1,155; £577)

RPR
1 **Kilt Rock (IRE)**[28] 182 6-9-0 **101**.... PatDobbs 5 106
(Doug Watson, UAE) *sn led: kicked clr 1 1/2f out: r.o wl: comf* **5/1**[3]
2 4 **Murbeh (IRE)**[322] 1029 5-8-8 **96**....(t) PaulHanagan 7 87
(A Al Raihe, UAE) *trckd ldrs tl wknd fnl f* **16/1**
3 2 ½ **United Color (USA)**[14] 393 4-9-6 **108**....(e) JamesDoyle 2 91
(D Selvaratnam, UAE) *mid-div: kpt on same pce fnl 2f but nvr able to chal* **2/1**[1]
4 1 ¼ **Alazeyab (USA)**[8] 465 7-9-0 **101**....(vt) DaneO'Neill 3 81
(A Al Raihe, UAE) *mid-div: rdn 3f out: kpt on same pce fnl f* **20/1**
5 ½ **Dohasa (IRE)**[15] 365 8-9-1 **102**....(b) AntiocoMurgia 1 81
(Ismail Mohammed) *nvr bttr than mid-div* **16/1**
6 1 ¼ **Take Ten**[20] 290 6-8-8 **96**.... RichardMullen 9 70
(S Seemar, UAE) *trckd ldrs tl outpcd 1 1/2f out* **7/1**
7 1 ¼ **Youm Mutamiez (USA)**[14] 393 6-9-4 **106**....(vt) WayneSmith 8 76
(M Al Muhairi, UAE) *trckd ldrs tl outpcd 2f out* **11/4**[2]
8 shd **Spirit Of Battle (USA)**[22] 241 5-9-0 **101**....(b) TadhgO'Shea 4 71
(A bin Huzaim, UAE) *slowly away: nvr nr to chal* **12/1**
9 7 ¼ **Silaah**[20] 290 9-8-6 **100**....(p) SaeedAlMazrooei[(7)] 6 47
(M Ramadan, UAE) *s.i.s: a in rr* **12/1**

1m 10.94s (-2.47) **9** Ran SP% **121.1**
CSF: 84.12; EX: 43.00; TRICAST: 214.58; TRIFECTA: 334.70; WIN: 8.00; PL: 1.20, 2.00, 1.30.
Owner EERC (Mngr: Mrs Rebecca Byrne) **Bred** Strategy Bloodstock **Trained** United Arab Emirates

576 - 578a (Foreign Racing) - See Raceform Interactive

506 LINGFIELD (L-H)
Saturday, February 9

OFFICIAL GOING: Standard
Wind: Light, half behind Weather: Dull and damp

579 BET ON TODAY'S FOOTBALL AT BLUESQ.COM H'CAP 1m 4f (P)
12:50 (12:51) (Class 6) (0-52,52) 4-Y-0+ **£2,045** (£603; £302) **Stalls** Low

Form RPR
0503 **1** **Sommersturm (GER)**[3] 530 9-9-4 **49**....(t) AdamKirby 15 59
(David Evans) *hld up in midfield: plld wd and effrt 3f out: rdn to chse ldrs over 1f out: styd on to ld nr fin* **9/2**[1]
4-04 **2** ¾ **Red Mystique (IRE)**[8] 469 4-9-1 **49**....(b) FergusSweeney 14 58
(Philip Hide) *hld up in midfield: hdwy over 2f out: led wl over 1f out: hung lft and idled ins fnl f: ct nr fin* **9/2**[1]
-311 **3** 1 ¾ **Young Jackie**[9] 456 5-9-0 **52**....(b) JordanVaughan[(7)] 1 58+
(George Margarson) *hld up in tch: effrt over 1f out: styd on to take 3rd ins fnl f* **6/1**[3]
02-0 **4** ½ **High 'n Dry (IRE)**[29] 158 9-9-0 **52**.... NedCurtis[(7)] 9 57
(Roger Curtis) *hld up towards rr: rdn and hdwy over 1f out: styd on same pce* **33/1**

40-4 **5** *hd* **Hollywood All Star (IRE)**[24] 226 4-9-1 **49** LukeMorris 11 54
(William Muir) *hld up in midfield: hdwy 3f out: one pce appr fnl f* **14/1**

40-4 **6** *nk* **Here Comes Jeanie**[38] 9 4-8-12 **46** oh1 AndreaAtzeni 13 51
(Michael Madgwick) *s.s: hld up towards rr: rdn 3f out: r.o fr over 1f out: nrest at fin* **16/1**

050- **7** *1* **Rajeh (IRE)**[194] 4652 10-9-2 **52** SladeO'Hara(5) 2 55
(Peter Grayson) *s.s: bhd tl rdn and styd on fnl 2f: nvr nrr* **66/1**

60/5 **8** *4* **Kijivu**[9] 458 8-9-1 **46** oh1 (bt) RichardKingscote 7 43
(Alastair Lidderdale) *led tl over 2f out: wknd over 1f out* **16/1**

000- **9** *3/4* **Lady Barastar (IRE)**[66] 7991 5-9-7 **52** (b1) JimCrowley 6 47
(Amanda Perrett) *prom: led over 2f out tl wl over 1f out: sn wknd* **10/1**

4-43 **10** *9* **Handsome Molly**[17] 343 4-9-4 **52** LiamKeniry 10 33
(David Elsworth) *towards rr: rdn over 4f out: sn bhd* **5/1**[2]

6-00 **11** *3* **Love Pegasus (USA)**[8] 475 7-9-5 **50** WilliamCarson 8 26
(Paddy Butler) *prom: rdn 5f out: wknd over 3f out* **33/1**

5-06 **12** *3 1/2* **Newington**[9] 455 4-8-13 **50** SimonPearce(3) 16 21
(Lydia Pearce) *chsd ldrs on outer: rdn over 3f out: sn wknd* **50/1**

664- **13** *2 1/4* **If What And Maybe**[262] 2391 5-9-5 **50** JohnFahy 12 17
(John Ryan) *prom: rdn 4f out: wknd 3f out* **20/1**

55-0 **14** *1 1/2* **Superstician**[12] 417 4-8-5 **46** oh1 (v1) PhilipPrince(7) 3 11
(Michael Madgwick) *in tch: drvn along 7f out: bhd fnl 4f* **66/1**

2m 31.96s (-1.04) **Going Correction** 0.0s/f (Stan)
WFA 4 from 5yo+ 3lb **14** Ran SP% **110.4**
Speed ratings (Par 101): **103,102,101,101,100 100,100,97,96,90 88,86,85,84**
Tote Swingers: 1&2 £3.70, 1&3 £4.40, 2&3 £4.40 CSF £18.86 CT £90.94 TOTE £5.00: £1.90, £1.50, £1.80; EX 24.30 Trifecta £93.70 Pool: £2,760.70 - 22.08 winning units..
Owner Ms S Howell **Bred** Gestut Schlenderhan **Trained** Pandy, Monmouths
■ Stewards' Enquiry : Richard Kingscote one-day ban; did not keep straight leaving stalls (23rd Feb)

FOCUS
An open if moderate handicap, but the market got it right. The form seems sound enough.

580 BREATHE SPA AT LINGFIELD MARRIOTT MAIDEN STKS 1m (P)
1:25 (1:27) (Class 5) 3-Y-O **£2,726** (£805; £402) **Stalls** High

Form RPR

0- **1** **Al Enbess (IRE)**[116] 7127 3-9-5 0 JamieSpencer 1 72+
(David Simcock) *trckd ldrs gng wl: rdn to ld wl over 1f out: r.o wl* **3/1**[2]

2 *1 1/4* **Huffoof (IRE)** 3-9-0 0 AndreaAtzeni 9 64+
(Roger Varian) *s.i.s: sn chsng ldrs: rdn 3f out: kpt on to take 2nd ins fnl f* **9/2**[3]

3 *1 3/4* **Awattan** 3-9-0 0 LukeMorris 8 60+
(Ed Vaughan) *bhd: pushed along 4f out: hdwy over 1f out: r.o ins fnl f* **12/1**

3 **4** *1 3/4* **Lady Who**[28] 184 3-9-0 0 JimCrowley 7 56
(Ralph Beckett) *chsd ldrs: rdn over 2f out: one pce appr fnl f* **9/2**[3]

5 *hd* **Landau (IRE)** 3-9-5 0 LiamKeniry 5 60
(Sylvester Kirk) *rn green in rr: rdn over 4f out: hdwy fnl f: r.o* **33/1**

0-05 **6** *1/2* **Bubbly Bailey**[27] 195 3-9-5 59 (v1) AdamKirby 3 59
(Alan Bailey) *led: rdn over 3f out: hdd wl over 1f out: no ex ent fnl f* **7/1**

7 *3/4* **Tranquility Cove (USA)** 3-9-0 0 GrahamGibbons 4 52
(David Barron) *dwlt: sn in midfield: rdn 4f out: short-lived effrt over 1f out* **11/4**[1]

0-6 **8** *1* **Alshan Fajer**[14] 396 3-9-5 0 JimmyQuinn 2 55
(Paul Howling) *in tch: rdn 3f out: sn outpcd* **66/1**

0 **9** *11* **Culture Trip**[14] 396 3-9-5 0 ShaneKelly 6 28
(Murty McGrath) *broke wl: t.k.h and sn stdd into midfield: rdn 3f out: sn wknd* **66/1**

1m 39.02s (0.82) **Going Correction** 0.0s/f (Stan) **9** Ran SP% **114.1**
Speed ratings (Par 97): **95,93,92,90,90 89,88,87,76**
Tote Swingers: 1&2 £3.80, 1&3 £5.30, 2&3 £10.30 CSF £16.60 TOTE £3.10: £1.10, £2.00, £3.30; EX 18.90 Trifecta £154.10 Pool: £4,254.07 - 20.69 winning tickets..
Owner Ziad A Galadari **Bred** Galadari Sons Stud Company Limited **Trained** Newmarket, Suffolk

FOCUS
A modest maiden, run at a steady pace, but some of these gave the impression they would come on for the experience and the form is a bit fluid.

581 CYPRIUM BAR & GRILL AT LINGFIELD MARRIOTT MAIDEN STKS 5f (P)
2:00 (2:00) (Class 5) 3-Y-O+ **£2,726** (£805; £402) **Stalls** High

Form RPR

2/2 **1** **Danziger (IRE)**[14] 404 4-9-8 60 AdamKirby 1 72+
(David Evans) *mde all: rdn clr over 1f out: pushed out nr fin: readily* **11/10**[1]

00- **2** *1 3/4* **Firmdecisions (IRE)**[208] 4149 3-8-13 0 (v1) DavidProbert 2 65
(Brett Johnson) *in tch: chsd wnr 2f out: kpt on u.p fnl f: a hld* **5/1**

3340 **3** *5* **Island Express (IRE)**[14] 404 6-9-8 53 (tp) AnnStokell(5) 7 53
(Ann Stokell) *outpcd in rr: wnt mod 4th ent st: kpt on u.p to take 3rd fnl 50yds* **20/1**

5 **4** *nk* **Jofranka**[14] 404 3-8-8 0 GrahamGibbons 4 41
(David Barron) *plld hrd: pressed wnr tl 2f out: wknd over 1f out* **9/2**[3]

04 **5** *2 3/4* **Don't Be Scilly**[10] 438 5-9-1 0 JoeyHaynes(7) 3 37
(Eric Wheeler) *in tch: rdn over 2f out: sn outpcd* **66/1**

-453 **6** *6* **Bonbon Bonnie**[10] 438 5-9-8 40 (v) LukeMorris 6 15
(Phil McEntee) *chsd ldrs tl wknd over 2f out* **66/1**

U **Holley Shiftwell** 3-8-8 0 AndreaAtzeni 5
(Stuart Williams) *fly-jmpd and uns rdr leaving stalls* **3/1**[2]

58.95s (0.15) **Going Correction** 0.0s/f (Stan)
WFA 3 from 4yo+ 14lb **7** Ran SP% **115.2**
Speed ratings (Par 103): **98,95,87,86,82 72,**
Tote Swingers: 1&2 £2.20, 1&3 £3.20, 2&3 £7.90 CSF £7.33 TOTE £2.10: £1.40, £2.70; EX 9.20 Trifecta £94.00 Pool: £4,155.03 - 33.13 winning tickets..
Owner Mrs E Evans **Bred** Castleton Lyons & Kilboy Estate **Trained** Pandy, Monmouths

FOCUS
A weak sprint maiden but the time wasn't bad. The winner gave the fourth a bigger beating than at Wolverhampton.

582 BLUE SQUARE BET SPRINT SERIES ROUND 6 H'CAP (QUALIFIER) (DIV I) 6f (P)
2:35 (2:36) (Class 5) (0-75,75) 4-Y-O+ **£3,067** (£905; £453) **Stalls** Low

Form RPR

60-5 **1** **Blue Jack**[16] 358 8-9-3 **71** (t) AndreaAtzeni 5 80
(Stuart Williams) *broke wl: trckd ldr: led ins fnl f: rdn out* **5/1**[3]

4-54 **2** *3/4* **Showboating (IRE)**[5] 518 5-9-7 **75** (vt1) SeanLevey 1 82
(Alan McCabe) *hld up in midfield: hdwy 2f out: rdn and r.o wl fnl f: wnt 2nd nr fin* **6/1**

0-00 **3** *1/2* **Black Cadillac (IRE)**[15] 372 5-8-6 **67** DanielMuscutt(7) 4 72
(Andrew Balding) *hld up in tch: n.m.r ent st: effrt over 1f out: r.o to take 3rd on line* **8/1**

-034 **4** *nse* **Key Ambition**[12] 426 4-9-1 **69** (vt) AdamKirby 11 74
(Garry Moss) *sn led: rdn and hdd ins fnl f: one pce* **10/1**

0-23 **5** *3/4* **Sole Danser (IRE)**[8] 481 5-9-7 **75** RichardKingscote 7 77
(Milton Bradley) *chsd ldrs and sltly outpcd 2f out: kpt on fnl f* **3/1**[1]

000- **6** *3/4* **Dishy Guru**[61] 8059 4-9-0 **68** LiamKeniry 2 68
(Michael Blanshard) *chsd ldrs tl no ex ent fnl f* **12/1**

20-5 **7** *nk* **Avonvalley**[33] 101 6-8-8 **67** SladeO'Hara(5) 6 66
(Peter Grayson) *hld up towards rr: rdn and sme hdwy over 1f out: no imp fnl f* **33/1**

-311 **8** *nse* **Frognal (IRE)**[7] 493 7-9-5 **73** (bt) WilliamCarson 3 72
(Violet M Jordan) *s.s: hld up in rr: rdn and sme hdwy fr over 1f out: nt rch ldrs* **4/1**[2]

505- **9** *2* **Hatta Stream (IRE)**[73] 7902 7-9-0 **71** SimonPearce(3) 12 64
(Lydia Pearce) *in tch on outer: rdn over 2f out: sn outpcd* **20/1**

4-41 **10** *1/2* **Where's Reiley (USA)**[18] 316 7-8-13 **70** (v1) MarkCoumbe(3) 10 61
(Michael Attwater) *towards rr: rdn over 2f out: n.d* **25/1**

55-2 **11** *4 1/2* **Night Trade (IRE)**[11] 431 6-9-5 **73** (p) LukeMorris 9 50
(Ronald Harris) *towards rr: rdn whn n.m.r on rail over 2f out: bhd whn eased over 1f out: fin lame* **14/1**

1m 11.43s (-0.47) **Going Correction** 0.0s/f (Stan) **11** Ran SP% **122.1**
Speed ratings (Par 103): **103,102,101,101,100 99,98,98,96,95 89**
Tote Swingers: 1&2 £8.20, 1&3 £9.70, 2&3 £11.40 CSF £35.73 CT £243.39 TOTE £6.50: £2.50, £2.70, £3.40; EX 44.60 Trifecta £337.00 Pool: £3,581.37 - 7.96 winning units..
Owner Darren Hudson-Wood **Bred** Miss S N Ralphs **Trained** Newmarket, Suffolk
■ Stewards' Enquiry : Slade O'Hara two-day ban; careless riding (23rd-25th Feb)

FOCUS
The latest qualifier in this series and a competitive race. It was slightly the faster division. The level is set around the fourth and there's a chance the winner can do better.

583 BLUE SQUARE BET SPRINT SERIES ROUND 6 H'CAP (QUALIFIER) (DIV II) 6f (P)
3:10 (3:15) (Class 5) (0-75,75) 4-Y-O+ **£3,067** (£905; £453) **Stalls** Low

Form RPR

11-3 **1** **Temple Road (IRE)**[28] 186 5-8-13 **67** RichardKingscote 5 81+
(Milton Bradley) *hld up in tch and patiently rdn: stdy hdwy gng wl over 1f out: qcknd to ld 100yds out* **7/2**[1]

-221 **2** *3/4* **Jack My Boy (IRE)**[9] 452 6-9-2 **70** (b) AdamKirby 1 78
(David Evans) *prom: rdn to join ldr ent fnl f: unable qck fnl 100yds* **4/1**[2]

0-05 **3** *1* **Song Of Parkes**[11] 431 6-9-5 **73** LiamKeniry 4 78
(Peter Grayson) *chsd ldr: led and kicked on over 2f out: hdd and one pce 100yds out* **50/1**

-450 **4** *3/4* **Belle Bayardo (IRE)**[3] 535 5-9-0 **68** LukeMorris 7 70
(Ronald Harris) *chsd ldrs: hrd rdn over 1f out: kpt on fnl f* **6/1**

-211 **5** *shd* **Picansort**[16] 360 6-9-7 **75** (b) ShaneKelly 3 77
(Peter Crate) *dwlt: hld up towards rr: shkn up and hdwy over 1f out: styd on same pce ins fnl f* **8/1**

5-52 **6** *nk* **Welease Bwian (IRE)**[28] 187 4-8-13 **67** AndreaAtzeni 10 68+
(Stuart Williams) *towards rr: rdn 2f out: styd on fnl f* **8/1**

1236 **7** *shd* **Restless Bay (IRE)**[9] 452 5-9-1 **69** (v) HayleyTurner 8 70
(Conor Dore) *hld up in midfield: effrt 2f out: no imp* **14/1**

6-65 **8** *3/4* **Gabbiano**[15] 372 4-9-5 **73** JamieSpencer 9 71
(Jeremy Gask) *stdd s: hld up towards rr: hung lft fnl 2f: nt clr run over 1f out: nt trble ldrs* **9/2**[3]

2046 **9** *2* **Waabel**[7] 494 6-8-10 **64** (t) WilliamCarson 2 56
(Violet M Jordan) *led tl over 2f out: wknd over 1f out* **16/1**

30-0 **10** *1* **Courageous (IRE)**[15] 372 7-9-4 **72** (t) ChrisCatlin 12 61
(Milton Bradley) *a in rr* **66/1**

2-06 **11** *5* **Speightowns Kid (USA)**[14] 405 5-9-3 **71** J-PGuillambert 11 44
(Jo Hughes) *prom tl wknd over 2f out* **33/1**

1m 11.5s (-0.40) **Going Correction** 0.0s/f (Stan) **11** Ran SP% **115.9**
Speed ratings (Par 103): **102,101,99,98,98 98,98,97,94,93 86**
Tote Swingers: 1&2 £3.00, 1&3 £37.80, 2&3 £34.90 CSF £16.30 CT £517.53 TOTE £3.70: £1.70, £1.90, £13.70; EX 15.10 Trifecta £451.90 Pool: £3,582.43 - 5.94 winning units..
Owner Darren Hudson-Wood **Bred** Paul Monaghan **Trained** Sedbury, Gloucs

FOCUS
The winning time was 7/100ths of a second slower than division one. The third is a doubt but the winner is progressing nicely.

584 LINGFIELD PARK OWNERS GROUP H'CAP 6f (P)
3:45 (3:48) (Class 2) (0-100,100) 4-Y-O+ **£12,291** (£3,657; £1,827; £913) **Stalls** Low

Form RPR

1-11 **1** **Tarooq (USA)**[14] 405 7-9-0 **93** (t) SeanLevey 3 101+
(Stuart Williams) *hld up in tch: effrt over 1f out: qcknd through on rail to ld 100yds out: jst hld on* **7/2**[1]

-321 **2** *hd* **Piscean (USA)**[8] 480 8-9-7 **100** GeorgeBaker 7 107+
(Tom Keddy) *stdd s: hld up in rr: effrt and wd ent st: str run fnl f: nt quite able to catch wnr* **5/1**[2]

-123 **3** *nk* **Profile Star (IRE)**[14] 405 4-8-7 **86** oh1 GrahamGibbons 10 92
(David Barron) *led: hrd rdn over 1f out: hdd 100yds out: kpt on* **7/1**[3]

00-2 **4** *nk* **Even Stevens**[18] 319 5-9-0 **93** (p) TomMcLaughlin 1 98
(Scott Dixon) *chsd ldrs: rdn to chse ldr 1f out: kpt on* **16/1**

0-54 **5** *nk* **Fratellino**[18] 319 6-9-6 **99** (t) SebSanders 8 103
(Alan McCabe) *mid-div: rdn over 2f out: styd on fnl f* **12/1**

14-2 **6** *1/2* **Noverre To Go (IRE)**[15] 379 7-8-8 **87** LukeMorris 6 89
(Ronald Harris) *t.k.h: chsd ldrs: rdn 2f out: kpt on fnl f* **8/1**

2-11 **7** *1 1/4* **Woolfall Sovereign (IRE)**[18] 319 7-9-6 **99** IanMongan 5 97
(George Margarson) *towards rr: rdn over 2f out: nvr rchd ldrs* **7/2**[1]

60-2 **8** *hd* **Thunderball**[14] 405 7-8-8 **87** (p) NickyMackay 2 85
(Scott Dixon) *dwlt: hld up in rr: rdn 2f out: styng on at fin: n.d* **10/1**

002- **9** *3/4* **Elna Bright**[65] 8008 8-8-7 **86** oh1 JimmyQuinn 4 81
(Peter Crate) *t.k.h: chsd ldr tl wknd 1f out* **25/1**

-605 **10** *shd* **Swiss Cross**[8] 480 6-9-4 **97** (t) DavidProbert 11 92
(Phil McEntee) *prom: rdn over 2f out: wknd over 1f out* **20/1**

1m 11.33s (-0.57) **Going Correction** 0.0s/f (Stan) **10** Ran SP% **116.0**
Speed ratings (Par 109): **103,102,102,101,101 100,99,98,97,97**
Tote Swingers: 1&2 £4.10, 1&3 £4.50, 2&3 £6.30 CSF £20.59 CT £119.06 TOTE £4.20: £1.90, £1.60, £2.30; EX 15.60 Trifecta £86.40 Pool: £4,090.05 - 35.94 winning units..
Owner H Chamberlain, I Pearce **Bred** Kirsten Rausing **Trained** Newmarket, Suffolk

FOCUS
A cracking 86-100 sprint handicap and a field worthy of the decent prize on offer, though the pace wasn't breakneck by any means. There was a bunch finish but the form still makes sense at face value.

585 LINGFIELD PARK RESORT H'CAP — 1m 2f (P)
4:15 (4:17) (Class 3) (0-95,99) 4-Y-O+ £7,439 (£2,213; £1,106; £553) Stalls Low

Form RPR
-200 1 **Aquilonius (IRE)**[7] 495 4-8-9 84 (t) JamieSpencer 5 92
(Stuart Williams) *mde all: strly pressed 1f out: hld on gamely* 6/1[3]
24-4 2 ½ **Mia's Boy**[14] 401 9-9-5 93 GeorgeBaker 11 100
(Chris Dwyer) *stdd s: hld up in rr: hdwy to chse ldrs whn n.m.r ent fnl f: r.o wl fnl 100yds: jst hld* 9/2[2]
5-45 3 ¾ **Mawaakef (IRE)**[14] 401 5-9-0 88 JimCrowley 6 93
(J R Jenkins) *chsd ldrs: rdn and lost pl 2f out: rallied and r.o again ins fnl f* 6/1[3]
-531 4 ½ **Emerald Wilderness (IRE)**[7] 495 9-9-6 99 TobyAtkinson(5) 1 103
(Mark Rimmer) *t.k.h: chsd wnr tl one pce ent fnl f: kpt on nr fin* 6/1[3]
00/0 5 ½ **Dubawi Phantom**[7] 496 6-8-7 81 oh2 (b) WilliamCarson 10 84?
(David C Griffiths) *mid-div: rdn whn forced wd bnd into st: carried even wdr over 1f out: styd on fnl f* 50/1
50-0 6 nk **Mr Red Clubs (IRE)**[7] 495 4-9-1 90 ShaneKelly 3 92
(Tim Pitt) *chsd ldrs: rdn to chal over 1f out: one pce fnl f* 8/1
600- 7 nk **Starluck (IRE)**[15] 6018 8-8-12 86 HayleyTurner 4 88
(David Arbuthnot) *hld up towards rr: rdn over 2f out: styng on wl at fin* 14/1
-225 8 ¾ **Ajeeb (USA)**[7] 496 5-8-7 81 oh2 NickyMackay 8 81
(Michael Scudamore) *in tch: rdn to chse ldrs on inner over 1f out: no ex fnl f* 20/1
6-24 9 3¼ **Presburg (IRE)**[18] 329 4-7-13 81 oh6 NoraLooby(7) 7 75
(Joseph Tuite) *a towards rr: rdn and n.d fnl 2f* 25/1
23-0 10 ½ **Be Perfect (USA)**[14] 401 4-9-5 94 (t) AdamKirby 2 87
(Marco Botti) *prom: hrd rdn 2f out: edgd rt and wknd over 1f out* 11/4[1]
2m 3.44s (-3.16) **Going Correction** 0.0s/f (Stan)
WFA 4 from 5yo+ 1lb 10 Ran SP% 116.1
Speed ratings (Par 107): **112,111,111,110,110 109,109,109,106,106**
Tote Swingers: 1&2 £5.80, 1&3 £7.60, 2&3 £7.10 CSF £32.28 CT £170.11 TOTE £8.40: £2.30, £1.80, £2.50; EX 44.40 Trifecta £356.20 Pool: £2,824.53 - 5.94 winning units..
Owner T W Morley & Mrs J Morley **Bred** Redmondstown Stud **Trained** Newmarket, Suffolk
FOCUS
Another decent handicap, but the pace didn't look that strong and it saw a fine front-running ride from Jamie Spencer. The form is taken at face value though it's not hard to have doubts.

586 GET STRAIGHT TO THE BET AT BLUESQ.COM H'CAP — 5f (P)
4:45 (4:47) (Class 4) (0-85,85) 4-Y-O+ £4,690 (£1,395; £697; £348) Stalls High

Form RPR
-232 1 **Triple Dream**[9] 457 8-9-1 79 (tp) RichardKingscote 8 86
(Milton Bradley) *prom: led ins fnl f: drvn out* 7/1
31-1 2 shd **Hamoody (USA)**[15] 379 9-9-4 82 SebSanders 10 89
(David Nicholls) *in tch: hrd rdn over 1f out: str chal ins fnl f: kpt on wl nr fin* 4/1[1]
-004 3 nk **Forest Edge (IRE)**[8] 480 4-9-7 85 (b) AdamKirby 3 91
(David Evans) *pressed ldr: rdn over 2f out: str chal ins fnl f: r.o* 6/1
203- 4 ¾ **Sandfrankskipsgo**[147] 6226 4-9-1 79 ShaneKelly 6 82+
(Peter Crate) *stdd s: hld up in rr: effrt over 1f out: r.o wl fnl f* 8/1
01-0 5 hd **Gorgeous Goblin (IRE)**[16] 353 6-9-0 78 (t) DavidProbert 5 80
(David C Griffiths) *cl up: drvn to press ldrs ins fnl f: r.o* 16/1
020- 6 ¾ **Rowe Park**[77] 7859 10-9-7 85 (p) LiamKeniry 9 84
(Linda Jewell) *bhd: effrt and hrd rdn over 1f out: r.o fnl f* 25/1
3-45 7 nse **Sulis Minerva (IRE)**[14] 405 6-8-13 84 (b) RyanTate(7) 7 83+
(Jeremy Gask) *towards rr: effrt over 1f out: r.o fnl f* 5/1[3]
2-36 8 nse **Moorhouse Lad**[18] 319 10-9-6 84 JimCrowley 4 83
(Garry Moss) *led: hrd rdn over 1f out: hdd & wknd ins fnl f* 9/2[2]
6/3- 9 1 **Lenny Bee**[280] 1868 7-9-2 80 (t) GrahamGibbons 1 75
(Garry Moss) *in tch: effrt over 1f out: no imp* 7/1
-0U6 10 nse **Decent Fella (IRE)**[17] 345 7-9-3 81 (bt) WilliamCarson 2 76
(Violet M Jordan) *stdd s: bhd: rdn over 1f out: nvr able to chal* 16/1
58.53s (-0.27) **Going Correction** 0.0s/f (Stan) 10 Ran SP% 120.9
Speed ratings (Par 105): **102,101,101,100,99 98,98,98,96,96**
Tote Swingers: 1&2 £3.60, 1&3 £7.60, 2&3 £4.80 CSF £36.53 CT £186.88 TOTE £6.30: £2.20, £1.30, £2.60; EX 22.40 Trifecta £119.80 Pool: £2,153.25 - 13.47 winning units..
Owner J M Bradley **Bred** Hesmonds Stud Ltd **Trained** Sedbury, Gloucs
FOCUS
A fair sprint handicap and they finished in a heap off an ordinary pace. There are slight doubts but the winner has been rated to his old best.
T/Plt: £97.40 to a £1 stake. Pool: £60,261.14 - 451.21 winning tickets. T/Qpdt: £17.70 to a £1 stake. Pool: £4,313.28 - 179.69 winning tickets. LM

558 WOLVERHAMPTON (A.W) (L-H)
Saturday, February 9

OFFICIAL GOING: Standard
Track Gallop Mastered after race 4.
Wind: Light across Weather: Overcast

587 CORAL.CO.UK AMATEUR RIDERS' H'CAP — 1m 141y(P)
6:20 (6:20) (Class 6) (0-60,61) 4-Y-O+ £1,871 (£580; £290; £145) Stalls Low

Form RPR
4-10 1 **Flag Of Glory**[27] 193 6-10-7 60 MissMEdden(7) 2 68
(Peter Hiatt) *chsd ldr tl led over 3f out: rdn over 1f out: edgd lft: jst hld on* 7/1[2]
0-60 2 nk **John Potts**[18] 330 8-10-4 53 (p) MissCBoxall(3) 12 60
(Brian Baugh) *a.p: shkn up over 1f out: chsd wnr ins fnl f: styd on* 14/1
-205 3 hd **Justcallmehandsome**[19] 312 11-9-8 47 (be) MrBenFfrenchDavis(7) 7 54
(Dominic Ffrench Davis) *s.i.s: hld up: hdwy over 1f out: rdn and r.o wl: nt quite rch ldrs* 18/1
-232 4 2¼ **Arabian Flight**[11] 435 4-11-1 61 MrSWalker 3 63
(Michael Appleby) *a.p: rdn and bmpd over 1f out: no ex ins fnl f* 6/5[1]
4-25 5 ½ **Merrjanah**[11] 434 5-10-0 53 MrAFrench(7) 13 54
(John Wainwright) *s.i.s: in rr tl r.o ins fnl f: nvr nrr* 40/1
3-20 6 2 **Bertie Blu Boy**[11] 435 5-10-2 55 (b) MrCEllingham(7) 11 51
(Lisa Williamson) *led 5f: rdn and hung lft over 1f out: styd on same pce* 7/1[2]
66-0 7 nk **Querido (GER)**[24] 220 9-9-10 47 (tp) MissMBryant(5) 1 42
(Paddy Butler) *prom: rdn over 2f out: styd on same pce fr over 1f out* 25/1
00-6 8 1¼ **Kyle Of Bute**[25] 219 7-10-9 55 (p) MissSBrotherton 4 47
(Brian Baugh) *hld up: hdwy 1/2-way: wknd fnl f* 7/1[2]
44-4 9 1 **Sir George (IRE)**[38] 23 8-10-8 59 MrAaronJames(5) 10 49
(Suzzanne France) *prom: rdn over 2f out: wknd over 1f out* 9/1[3]
06-0 10 8 **Aureolin Gulf**[11] 435 4-10-4 53 (p) MrFMitchell(3) 5 25
(Reg Hollinshead) *hld up: racd keenly: hdwy over 5f out: rdn and wknd over 3f out* 28/1
1m 51.93s (1.43) **Going Correction** +0.05s/f (Slow) 10 Ran SP% 114.6
Speed ratings (Par 101): **95,94,94,92,92 90,90,88,88,80**
Tote Swingers: 1&2 £15.50, 1&3 £30.30, 2&3 £22.80 CSF £95.14 CT £1712.16 TOTE £6.50: £2.20, £4.80, £5.10; EX 104.50 Trifecta £1419.00 Part won. Pool: £1,892.10 - 0.65 winning units..
Owner N D Edden **Bred** Follow The Flag Partnership **Trained** Hook Norton, Oxon
FOCUS
Exposed performers in a modest amateur riders' handicap. The gallop was no more than fair and the winner raced towards the inside rail in the straight.

588 CLAIM FREE BETS TODAY AT BOOKMAKERS.CO.UK (S) STKS — 7f 32y(P)
6:50 (6:50) (Class 6) 3-Y-O £1,940 (£577; £288; £144) Stalls High

Form RPR
0-54 1 **Hillbilly Boy (IRE)**[12] 424 3-9-4 73 LukeMorris 5 68
(Bill Turner) *a.p: chsd ldr 3f out: shkn up to ld over 1f out: pushed out* 4/6[1]
266- 2 2¾ **Finaz**[71] 7931 3-8-12 68 (b[1]) TomEaves 1 55
(Noel Quinlan) *chsd ldrs: rdn over 1f out: styd on same pce fnl f: wnt 2nd towards fin* 9/2[3]
-165 3 ¾ **Maypole Joe (IRE)**[8] 482 3-8-11 60 (v) EoinWalsh(7) 6 59
(David Evans) *sn pushed along to chse ldr: led over 4f out: rdn and hdd over 1f out: no ex ins fnl f* 7/2[2]
0-00 4 8 **Kalahari Breeze (IRE)**[16] 350 3-8-7 45 (b[1]) JoeFanning 4 26
(William Muir) *led: hdd over 4f out: rdn 1/2-way: wknd 2f out* 16/1
605- 5 4½ **Lady Jean**[67] 7977 3-8-2 43 ShirleyTeasdale(5) 3 14
(Reg Hollinshead) *s.i.s: a in rr: rdn and wknd over 2f out* 33/1
1m 30.02s (0.42) **Going Correction** +0.05s/f (Slow) 5 Ran SP% 109.2
Speed ratings (Par 95): **99,95,95,85,80**
CSF £4.00 TOTE £1.60: £1.40, £1.70; EX 5.00 Trifecta £9.10 Pool: £1,563.52 - 127.67 winning units..There was no bid for the winner.
Owner E A Brook **Bred** Tipper House Stud **Trained** Sigwells, Somerset
FOCUS
An uncompetitive seller in which the gallop was just an ordinary one. The winner came down the centre in the straight.

589 FREE BET BONANZA NOW AT BOOKMAKERS.CO.UK FILLIES' H'CAP — 7f 32y(P)
7:20 (7:21) (Class 5) (0-75,74) 4-Y-O+ £2,587 (£770; £384; £192) Stalls High

Form RPR
0-44 1 **Zing Wing**[5] 517 5-8-9 70 (v[1]) EoinWalsh(7) 3 77
(David Evans) *s.i.s: hld up: pushed along 1/2-way: hdwy over 1f out: rdn to ld ins fnl f: r.o wl* 8/1
40-1 2 3 **Al Freej (IRE)**[29] 159 4-9-3 74 RyanClark(3) 1 73
(Brian Ellison) *led: rdn and edgd lft over 1f out: hdd and unable qck ins fnl f* 2/1[2]
1-13 3 hd **Spark Of Genius**[27] 194 4-9-2 70 LukeMorris 2 68
(Alan McCabe) *chsd ldr 6f out: rdn and ev ch over 1f out: styd on same pce ins fnl f* 5/4[1]
3-10 4 3½ **Shaunas Spirit (IRE)**[12] 415 5-9-4 72 (p) FrannyNorton 4 61
(Dean Ivory) *plld hrd: trckd ldr 1f: remained handy: rdn over 1f out: no ex fnl f* 7/2[3]
1m 28.91s (-0.69) **Going Correction** +0.05s/f (Slow) 4 Ran SP% 111.1
Speed ratings (Par 100): **105,101,101,97**
CSF £24.06 TOTE £6.20; EX 26.90 Trifecta £37.80 Pool: £1,094.46 - 21.70 winning units..
Owner Exors of the late Mrs Sally Edwards **Bred** Deepwood Farm Stud **Trained** Pandy, Monmouths
FOCUS
Only four runners but three recent winners in a fair fillies' handicap. The gallop was an ordinary one and the winner raced in the centre in the straight.

590 CASINO AT CORAL.CO.UK MAIDEN FILLIES' STKS — 1m 141y(P)
7:50 (7:51) (Class 5) 3-Y-O+ £2,587 (£770; £384; £192) Stalls Low

Form RPR
3-23 1 **Empowermentofwomen (IRE)**[15] 377 3-8-5 67 HayleyTurner 1 62+
(Michael Bell) *mde all: set stdy pce tl qcknd 3f out: shkn up ins fnl f: comf* 7/4[1]
0- 2 1½ **Hamla**[115] 7160 3-8-5 0 JoeFanning 6 59+
(Mark Johnston) *chsd wnr: rdn over 2f out: styd on same pce fnl f* 85/40[2]
3 6 **Impeccability** 3-8-5 0 FrannyNorton 5 45
(John Mackie) *chsd ldrs: rdn over 2f out: wknd fnl f* 16/1
4 ½ **Conas Ata Tu**[28] 4-9-5 0 AdamMcLean(7) 4 49
(Derek Shaw) *plld hrd and sn prom: rdn over 2f out: sn outpcd: edgd lft over 1f out: styd on ins fnl f* 66/1
45 5 2½ **Miss Chardonay**[3] 541 6-9-12 0 JimmyQuinn 2 43
(Mandy Rowland) *hld up: hdwy over 2f out: sn rdn: wknd fnl f* 100/1
6 6 **Half To You** 3-8-5 0 LukeMorris 7 24
(Kevin Ryan) *dwlt: hld up: rdn over 2f out: sn wknd* 4/1[3]
7 3½ **Keladiva** 3-8-5 0 NickyMackay 8 16
(David Simcock) *chsd ldrs: lost pl 7f out: hdwy over 3f out: rdn and wknd over 2f out* 6/1
8 3¾ **Just Gwen** 4-9-12 0 (p) DanielTudhope 3 12
(Brian Baugh) *s.s: a in rr* 33/1
1m 51.92s (1.42) **Going Correction** +0.05s/f (Slow)
WFA 3 from 4yo+ 21lb 8 Ran SP% 114.0
Speed ratings (Par 100): **95,93,88,87,85 80,77,73**
Tote Swingers: 1&2 £1.30, 1&3 £4.10, 2&3 £8.60 CSF £5.64 TOTE £2.50: £1.10, £1.20, £4.10; EX 5.70 Trifecta £40.80 Pool: £1,723.94 - 31.65 winning units..
Owner W J Gredley **Bred** Stetchworth & Middle Park Studs **Trained** Newmarket, Suffolk
FOCUS
An uncompetitive maiden in which the gallop was a modest one. The first two pulled clear and the winner raced towards the inside rail in the straight.

591 BEST RACING ODDS GUARANTEED AT BOOKMAKERS.CO.UK (S) STKS — 1m 1f 103y(P)
8:20 (8:20) (Class 6) 3-Y-O £1,940 (£577; £288; £144) Stalls Low

Form RPR
6-24 1 **Good Evans**[8] 473 3-8-12 68 RichardKingscote 3 70
(Tom Dascombe) *led: hdd over 7f out: chsd ldr: pushed along 4f out: swtchd rt over 2f out: led over 1f out: r.o wl* 2/13[1]

The Form Book Flat, Raceform Ltd, Compton, RG20 6NL.

660 **2** 12 **Dutch Delight**[4] 525 3-8-7 0.. JamesSullivan 2 40
(Tony Coyle) *prom: pushed along 1/2-way: rdn over 2f out: wknd over 1f out: wnt 2nd ins fnl f* **9/1**[2]
05-0 **3** 2 **Multi Fours**[17] 336 3-8-7 53..(p) LukeMorris 5 36
(Daniel Kubler) *w wnr tl led over 7f out: rdn over 2f out: hdd over 1f out: wknd fnl f* **14/1**[3]
6-00 **4** 19 **Firey Sally (IRE)**[8] 482 3-8-7 40..............................(t) AndrewMullen 4
(Frank Sheridan) *chsd ldrs tl rdn and wknd over 2f out: t.o* **50/1**

2m 1.41s (-0.29) **Going Correction** +0.05s/f (Slow) **4** Ran SP% **105.3**
Speed ratings (Par 95): **103,92,90,73**
CSF £1.87 TOTE £1.10; EX 1.50 Trifecta £2.40 Pool: £946.09 - 294.22 winning units..Winner was bought in for 11,500gns.
Owner Manor House Stables LLP **Bred** Newsells Park Stud **Trained** Malpas, Cheshire

FOCUS
A most uncompetitive seller. The gallop was a steady one and the winner came down the centre in the straight.

592 DOWNLOAD CORAL.CO.UK MOBILE APP H'CAP 1m 4f 50y(P)
8:50 (8:50) (Class 5) (0-75,72) 4-Y-0+ **£2,587** (£770; £384; £192) **Stalls** Low

Form RPR
05-1 **1** **Waving**[17] 342 4-9-2 **70**..(t) DavidProbert 1 77
(Tony Carroll) *a.p: shkn up over 1f out: rdn to ld nr fin* **2/1**[1]
0/41 **2** *nk* **Blazing Desert**[11] 430 9-9-3 **68**.. LukeMorris 3 74
(William Kinsey) *chsd ldr tl over 5f out: wnt 2nd again over 3f out: rdn to ld over 1f out: hdd nr fin* **11/4**[2]
06-6 **3** 1 ¾ **Brunston**[30] 144 7-9-7 **72**..(t) RobbieFitzpatrick 4 75
(Anthony Middleton) *s.i.s: hld up: hdwy over 2f out: sn rdn: r.o: nt rch ldrs* **9/2**
035- **4** 1 ¼ **Toughness Danon**[56] 8136 7-9-2 **67**..............................(tp) ChrisCatlin 2 68
(Anthony Middleton) *led: pushed along over 3f out: rdn and hdd over 1f out: no ex ins fnl f* **7/2**[3]
226- **5** 13 **Arashi**[166] 5665 7-8-6 **64**.. AdamMcLean(7) 5 44
(Derek Shaw) *chsd ldrs: wnt 2nd over 5f out tl over 3f out: wknd over 2f out* **10/1**

2m 43.37s (2.27) **Going Correction** +0.05s/f (Slow)
WFA 4 from 5yo+ 3lb **5** Ran SP% **109.5**
Speed ratings (Par 103): **94,93,92,91,83**
CSF £7.65 TOTE £3.00: £1.70, £1.80; EX 6.60 Trifecta £14.10 Pool: £641.23 - 33.88 winning units..
Owner Carl Hodgson **Bred** Theakston Stud **Trained** Cropthorne, Worcs

FOCUS
Just a fair handicap. The gallop was on the steady side to the home turn and the winner came down the centre in the straight.

593 HORSERACING FREE BETS AT BOOKMAKERS.CO.UK H'CAP 1m 141y(P)
9:20 (9:20) (Class 5) (0-75,74) 4-Y-0+ **£2,587** (£770; £384; £192) **Stalls** Low

Form RPR
-322 **1** **One Scoop Or Two**[18] 329 7-8-12 **72**..............................(p) RobertTart(7) 3 81
(Reg Hollinshead) *hld up: hdwy over 1f out: rdn to ld wl ins fnl f* **11/4**[2]
0-11 **2** *hd* **Berlusca (IRE)**[34] 83 4-9-4 **71**.. DanielTudhope 6 79
(David O'Meara) *trckd ldrs: led over 1f out: rdn and hdd wl ins fnl f: r.o* **2/1**[1]
4-55 **3** ¾ **Thereabouts (USA)**[8] 478 4-8-12 **65**.............................. AndrewMullen 4 71
(Michael Appleby) *hld up: hdwy over 2f out: sn rdn: r.o* **13/2**
4500 **4** 2 ¾ **Copperwood**[12] 415 8-9-6 **73**.. JoeFanning 1 73
(Mark Johnston) *a.p: chsd ldr 3f out: rdn and ev ch over 1f out: styd on same pce ins fnl f* **12/1**
0-26 **5** ¾ **California English (IRE)**[24] 222 4-9-7 **74**..................(p) JimmyQuinn 7 72
(Marco Botti) *hld up: rdn over 3f out: styd on u.p: nt trble ldrs* **6/1**[3]
-506 **6** 1 **Outlaw Torn (IRE)**[8] 478 4-8-10 **63**..............................(e) RobbieFitzpatrick 9 59
(Richard Guest) *led: rdn and hdd over 1f out: wknd ins fnl f* **16/1**
060/ **7** 1 ½ **Matraash (USA)**[820] 7436 7-9-2 **69**.. LukeMorris 5 62
(Daniel Mark Loughnane) *hld up: rdn over 1f out: wknd fnl f* **28/1**
-355 **8** ½ **Lucky Dan (IRE)**[8] 481 7-9-6 **73**.. FrannyNorton 2 64
(Paul Green) *plld hrd and prom: hmpd over 7f out: rdn over 1f out: wknd ins fnl f* **9/1**
0-63 **9** 34 **Dream Win**[27] 192 7-8-8 **61**..(bt[1]) TomEaves 8
(Brian Ellison) *dwlt: hdwy over 7f out: chsd ldr over 6f out tl rdn 3f out: sn wknd: t.o* **14/1**

1m 49.25s (-1.25) **Going Correction** +0.05s/f (Slow) **9** Ran SP% **121.3**
Speed ratings (Par 103): **107,106,106,103,103 102,100,100,70**
Tote Swingers: 1&2 £1.40, 1&3 £5.10, 2&3 £7.70 CSF £9.20 CT £33.27 TOTE £3.40: £1.30, £1.50, £1.50; EX 11.00 Trifecta £70.60 Pool: £1,256.25 - 13.33 winning units..
Owner Showtime Ice Cream Concessionaire **Bred** S And R Ewart **Trained** Upper Longdon, Staffs

FOCUS
Mainly exposed sorts in a fair handicap in which the gallop was just an ordinary one. The first three pulled a few lengths clear and the winner edged towards the inside rail late on.
T/Plt: £188.60 to a £1 stake. Pool: £75,878.00 - 293.58 winning tickets. T/Qpdt: £18.10 to a £1 stake. Pool: £6,961.00 - 284.40 winning tickets. CR

594 - 596a (Foreign Racing) - See Raceform Interactive

536 SOUTHWELL (L-H)
Sunday, February 10

OFFICIAL GOING: Standard to slow
Wind: light 1/2 against Weather: overcast, rain

597 WINNERS LOVE BOOKMAKERS.CO.UK (S) H'CAP 1m 4f (F)
1:50 (1:50) (Class 6) (0-60,59) 4-Y-0+ **£1,940** (£577; £288; £144) **Stalls** Low

Form RPR
5-02 **1** **Maslak (IRE)**[9] 475 9-9-5 **57**.. ChrisCatlin 5 63
(Peter Hiatt) *led 1f: chsd ldr: led over 3f out: narrowly hdd appr fnl f: kpt on to ld nr fin* **11/4**[2]
4-65 **2** ½ **Layla's Boy**[28] 198 6-9-2 **59**..(bt) ShirleyTeasdale(5) 3 64
(Simon West) *trckd ldrs: effrt over 2f out: narrow ld appr fnl f: hdd and no ex nr fin* **15/8**[1]
660- **3** 2 ¼ **Isola Bella**[53] 7108 4-8-4 **45**.. WilliamCarson 7 47
(Jonathan Portman) *trckd ldrs: chal 3f out: one pce over 1f out* **14/1**
06-0 **4** 3 ¾ **General Tufto**[5] 522 8-8-10 **48**..............................(b) RobbieFitzpatrick 2 44
(Charles Smith) *hld up in rr: drvn over 3f out: modest 4th over 2f out: one pce: eased nr fin* **7/1**
40/- **5** 10 **Mighty Whitey (IRE)**[23] 269 7-9-1 **58**..............................(t) LMcNiff(5) 4 38
(Noel C Kelly, Ire) *hld up in rr: effrt over 3f out: sn lost pl and bhd* **9/2**[3]
500/ **6** ½ **Florimund**[295] 1537 10-8-7 **45**..(t) JimmyQuinn 1 24
(Michael Butler, Ire) *hld up in rr: drvn over 4f out: lost pl over 3f out: sn bhd* **6/1**
004- **7** 2 ½ **Penderyn**[103] 7472 6-8-0 **45**.. IanBurns(7) 6 20
(Charles Smith) *stmbld s: led after 1f: hdd over 3f out: sn lost pl and bhd* **40/1**

2m 43.56s (2.56) **Going Correction** +0.05s/f (Slow)
WFA 4 from 6yo+ 3lb **7** Ran SP% **115.5**
Speed ratings (Par 101): **93,92,91,88,82 81,80**
toteswingers 1&2 £1.70, 1&3 £3.60, 2&3 £5.90 CSF £8.54 CT £58.22 TOTE £3.20: £2.10, £2.10; EX 5.10 Trifecta £58.50 Pool: £2865.03 - 36.68 winning units..No bids for the winner.
Owner P W Hiatt **Bred** Shadwell Estate Company Limited **Trained** Hook Norton, Oxon
■ Stewards' Enquiry : Shirley Teasdale four-day ban: used whip above permitted level (Feb 25-28)

FOCUS
The ground was still riding on the slow side of standard for this meeting. A moderate seller featuring a couple of course specialists nearing the veteran stage and one of them ran out a game winner.

598 GET THE INSIDE TRACK AT BOOKMAKERS.CO.UK H'CAP 6f (F)
2:20 (2:20) (Class 6) (0-60,55) 3-Y-0 **£1,940** (£577; £288; £144) **Stalls** Low

Form RPR
000- **1** **Hannahs Turn**[52] 8185 3-8-11 **45**.. HayleyTurner 1 58
(Chris Dwyer) *sn led: rdn over 1f out: kpt on wl* **8/1**
-342 **2** 2 **Devout (IRE)**[9] 470 3-9-5 **53**.. FergusSweeney 4 59
(Jamie Osborne) *broke smartly: led early: trckd wnr: rdn 2f out: kpt on same pce fnl f* **4/1**[3]
02-1 **3** 8 **Hazard Warning (IRE)**[27] 207 3-9-6 **54**..................(b) DuranFentiman 5 34
(Tim Easterby) *t.k.h: trckd ldrs: drvn 3f out: hung lft 2f out: fdd fnl f* **7/4**[2]
05-4 **4** 7 **Jordanstown**[17] 357 3-9-7 **55**..(b[1]) AmyRyan 3 13
(Kevin Ryan) *s.s: t.k.h in last: effrt over 3f out: sn rdn and outpcd: edgd lft and wknd over 1f out* **5/4**[1]
-065 **5** 17 **Jonny Wombat**[10] 459 3-8-11 **45**..(b) JoeFanning 2
(Richard Ford) *s.i.s: sn chsng ldrs: outpcd and lost pl 3f out: sn bhd: t.o* **25/1**

1m 17.19s (0.69) **Going Correction** +0.05s/f (Slow) **5** Ran SP% **115.8**
Speed ratings (Par 95): **97,94,83,74,51**
CSF £39.78 TOTE £10.80: £3.40, £1.50; EX 40.70 Trifecta £104.40 Pool: £2788.75 - 20.01 winning units..
Owner Mrs K W Sneath **Bred** Wayland Stud **Trained** Newmarket, Suffolk

FOCUS
A moderate 3-y-o sprint with the top weight rated 5lb below the race ceiling.

599 CORAL.CO.UK H'CAP 1m (F)
2:50 (2:50) (Class 6) (0-60,67) 3-Y-0 **£1,940** (£577; £288) **Stalls** Low

Form RPR
-432 **1** **Napinda**[5] 527 3-8-12 **51**.. WilliamCarson 1 55
(Philip McBride) *chsd wnr: chal over 3f out: drvn over 2f out: styd on ins fnl f: led last 50yds* **6/4**[1]
-424 **2** 1 ½ **Shearian**[5] 527 3-8-10 **56**.. RyanTate(7) 2 57
(Tony Carroll) *led: edgd lft over 1f out: hdd and no ex clsng stages* **7/4**[2]
-311 **3** 7 **Darkest Night (IRE)**[7] 506 3-10-0 **67** 6ex.................. FergusSweeney 3 53
(Jamie Osborne) *hld up in last: hdwy to trck other pair over 3f out: drvn over 2f out: nvr able to land blow: wknd fnl f* **2/1**[3]

1m 45.73s (2.03) **Going Correction** +0.05s/f (Slow) **3** Ran SP% **109.7**
Speed ratings (Par 95): **91,89,82**
CSF £4.39 TOTE £2.20; EX 3.40 Trifecta £2.50 Pool: £1498.59 - 448.04 winning units..
Owner Peter Wagstaffe **Bred** Stuart McPhee Bloodstock Ltd **Trained** Newmarket, Suffolk

FOCUS
Only three runners in this mile handicap.

600 EXCLUSIVE FREE BETS AT BOOKMAKERS.CO.UK H'CAP 1m (F)
3:20 (3:20) (Class 6) (0-60,60) 4-Y-0+ **£1,940** (£577; £288; £144) **Stalls** Low

Form RPR
00-1 **1** **Our Ivor**[4] 536 4-8-12 **51** 6ex.. AndrewMullen 8 67
(Michael Appleby) *mde all: drvn over 2f out: forged clr over 1f out: styd on wl* **4/5**[1]
204- **2** 6 **Bentley**[365] 532 9-8-5 **51**.. RobertTart(7) 10 53
(Brian Baugh) *chsd wnr: kpt on same pce fnl 2f: no imp* **16/1**
/00- **3** 6 **Doyouknowwhoiam**[79] 7837 4-8-9 **48**.. TomEaves 9 36
(John Quinn) *s.s: hdwy on outside to chse ldrs after 2f: one pce fnl 2f* **16/1**
-320 **4** 2 ¼ **This Ones For Eddy**[12] 435 8-8-13 **52**..................(b) GrahamGibbons 11 35
(John Balding) *chsd ldrs: drvn 3f out: wknd over 1f out* **4/1**[2]
60-0 **5** 1 ¼ **Bonnie Prince Blue**[34] 98 10-9-0 **53**..............................(b) DaleSwift 7 33
(Ian McInnes) *sn bhd: kpt on fnl 2f: nvr on terms* **16/1**
6-55 **6** *nk* **Justine Time (IRE)**[16] 375 4-8-7 **46** oh1..................(e[1]) JamesSullivan 2 26
(Julie Camacho) *chsd ldrs: rdn and lost pl over 4f out: no ch after* **25/1**
002- **7** 11 **Balmoral Castle**[52] 8177 4-9-4 **57**.. JohnFahy 3 11
(Jonathan Portman) *chsd ldrs: rdn and lost pl over 4f out* **8/1**[3]
60-6 **8** 29 **Mystical Witch**[4] 536 4-8-7 **46** oh1..............................(b[1]) JimmyQuinn 4
(Christine Dunnett) *chsd ldrs: rdn over 3f out: sn lost pl and bhd: t.o* **25/1**
00-0 **9** 2 **Confirmed**[15] 403 4-9-7 **60**.. RenatoSouza 6
(Alison Batchelor) *s.i.s: in rr: outpcd over 3f out: sn bhd: t.o 2f out* **9/1**
0-00 **10** 21 **Trip Switch**[18] 338 7-9-7 **60**.. LiamKeniry 5
(John Butler) *sn bhd: t.o 3f out: virtually p.u over 1f out* **25/1**

1m 42.89s (-0.81) **Going Correction** +0.05s/f (Slow) **10** Ran SP% **125.9**
Speed ratings (Par 101): **106,100,94,91,90 90,79,50,48,27**
toteswingers 1&2 £4.40, 1&3 £6.10, 2&3 £19.70 CSF £18.71 CT £132.26 TOTE £1.70: £1.10, £3.00, £5.20; EX 15.20 Trifecta £176.60 Pool: £3328.27 - 14.12 winning units..
Owner J&G Bacciochi, A Taylor, Bruce W Wyatt **Bred** B W Wyatt **Trained** Danethorpe, Notts

FOCUS
This race was run 2.84secs faster than the preceding 3-y-o contest.

601 CORAL.CO.UK MOBILE CASINO FILLIES' H'CAP (THE SUNDAY £5K BONUS RACE) 1m (F)
3:50 (3:50) (Class 5) (0-75,72) 4-Y-0+ **£2,587** (£770; £384; £192) **Stalls** Low

Form RPR
225- **1** **Dewala**[63] 8048 4-8-7 **58** oh3.. AndrewMullen 1 79
(Michael Appleby) *mde all: qcknd over 3f out: sn clr: unchal* **11/4**[3]
3-11 **2** 8 **Compton Rainbow**[13] 421 4-9-0 **72**..............................(t) RyanTate(7) 5 75
(Hans Adielsson) *chsd wnr: effrt over 2f out: kpt on: no imp* **15/8**[1]
0-25 **3** 7 **Dundrum Dancer (IRE)**[15] 410 6-9-0 **65**.. HayleyTurner 3 52
(Alex Hales) *dwlt: sn chsng ldrs: drvn over 2f out: one pce* **9/2**
-504 **4** 1 ¼ **Gay Gallivanter**[4] 536 5-8-0 **58** oh11.. ShelleyBirkett(7) 4 42
(Mick Quinn) *chsd ldrs: outpcd and lost pl after 3f: kpt on fnl 2f* **20/1**

40-4 **5** *5* **Roedean (IRE)**[32] 116 4-9-4 **69**....................(tp) GrahamLee 2 41
(William Stone) *chsd ldrs: drvn over 3f out: wknd over 2f out* **9/4**[2]
1m 42.77s (-0.93) **Going Correction** +0.05s/f (Slow) **5** Ran SP% **115.2**
Speed ratings (Par 100): **106,98,91,89,84**
CSF £8.80 TOTE £4.10: £3.60, £1.20; EX 8.00 Trifecta £29.90 Pool: £2524.54 - 63.12 winning units..
Owner Goldform Racing **Bred** A M Wragg **Trained** Danethorpe, Notts
FOCUS
Not the most competitive fillies' handicap with two of the five racing from out of the weights, but one of those was a runaway winner.

602 WIN MORE ON BETTING AT BOOKMAKERS.CO.UK MAIDEN STKS 7f (F)
4:20 (4:20) (Class 5) 3-Y-0+ **£3,234** (£962; £481; £240) **Stalls** Low

Form RPR
2 **1** **Kabbaas (IRE)**[8] 492 3-8-10 0.................... ChrisCatlin 4 79
(Roger Varian) *trckd ldr: led over 2f out: sn nudged clr: edgd lft over 1f out: v easily* **1/12**[1]
2 *20* **Quintain (IRE)**[31] 5-9-13 0.................... DuranFentiman 5 30
(Tim Easterby) *s.s: drvn along on outer: outpcd over 3f out: wnt remote 4th over 1f out: kpt on to take distant 2nd clsng stages* **7/1**[3]
005- **3** *nk* **Dr Victoria**[55] 8151 4-9-8 36....................(t) PaddyAspell 1 24
(John Norton) *trckd ldrs: outpcd over 3f out: remote 3rd over 2f out: distant 2nd last 100yds: lost 2nd nr fin* **20/1**
64/3 **4** *4 1/2* **Big City Boy (IRE)**[2] 564 5-9-13 35.................... WilliamCarson 3 17
(Phil McEntee) *led: hdd over 2f out: wknd and lost 2 pls fnl 150yds* **5/1**[2]
0006 **5** *11* **Elusive**[4] 541 7-9-3 29....................(p) AnnStokell[(5)] 2
(Ann Stokell) *chsd ldng pair: drvn over 4f out: wknd over 2f out: sn bhd* **33/1**
1m 29.87s (-0.43) **Going Correction** +0.05s/f (Slow)
WFA 3 from 4yo+ 17lb **5** Ran SP% **129.2**
Speed ratings (Par 103): **104,81,80,75,63**
CSF £2.82 TOTE £1.10: £1.02, £3.00; EX 2.60 Trifecta £9.70 Pool: £3086.63 - 238.21 winning units..
Owner Sheikh Ahmed Al Maktoum **Bred** Darley **Trained** Newmarket, Suffolk
FOCUS
A totally uncompetitive maiden.

603 £50 FREE BET AT CORAL.CO.UK H'CAP 7f (F)
4:50 (4:50) (Class 5) (0-70,70) 4-Y-0+ **£2,587** (£770; £384; £192) **Stalls** Low

Form RPR
-623 **1** **Bitaphon (IRE)**[12] 436 4-8-9 **58**.................... AndrewMullen 8 67
(Michael Appleby) *mde all: drvn over 2f out: hld on nr fin* **4/1**[2]
50-2 **2** *3/4* **Flying Pickets (IRE)**[4] 540 4-9-6 **69**....................(be) JohnFahy 6 76
(Alan McCabe) *in rr: hdwy over 2f out: styd on wl fnl f: fin strly to snatch 2nd line* **3/1**[1]
2-13 **3** *hd* **Frontier Fighter**[6] 518 5-9-6 **69**.................... DanielTudhope 1 76
(David O'Meara) *chsd ldrs: nt clr run and swtchd lft wl over 1f out: chsd wnr jst ins fnl f: styd on same pce* **4/1**[2]
5-30 **4** *2 1/2* **Mazovian (USA)**[5] 526 5-8-12 **68**.................... GerardGalligan[(7)] 4 68
(Michael Chapman) *chsd ldrs: drvn over 3f out: outpcd over 2f out: kpt on appr fnl f* **12/1**
3-10 **5** *2 1/4* **Bassett Road (IRE)**[16] 380 5-9-6 **69**....................(p) JoeFanning 9 63
(Keith Dalgleish) *s.i.s: in rr: hdwy over 3f out: kpt on same pce over 1f out* **7/1**
12-4 **6** *1 3/4* **Royal Holiday (IRE)**[28] 194 6-9-2 **65**....................(p) JamesSullivan 3 54
(Marjorie Fife) *chsd ldrs: drvn over 4f out: one pce fnl 2f* **5/1**[3]
65-6 **7** *1 1/2* **Caramelita**[30] 159 6-9-5 **68**....................(v) GrahamLee 7 53
(J R Jenkins) *in rr: hdwy on outside over 3f out: outpcd over 2f out: kpt on ins fnl f* **10/1**
-056 **8** *nse* **Final Drive (IRE)**[11] 439 7-9-2 **65**....................(tp) LiamKeniry 2 50
(John Butler) *s.i.s: bhd tl kpt on ins fnl f* **33/1**
1020 **9** *2 1/2* **Desert Strike**[9] 481 7-9-7 **70**....................(p) HayleyTurner 10 48
(Conor Dore) *w ldrs: t.k.h: wnt 2nd over 2f out: wknd over 1f out* **33/1**
50-6 **10** *nk* **Victorian Bounty**[29] 186 8-9-2 **65**.................... WilliamCarson 5 42
(Tony Newcombe) *mid-div: rdn and outpcd over 3f out: hdwy over 2f out: wknd appr fnl f* **20/1**
1m 30.56s (0.26) **Going Correction** +0.05s/f (Slow) **10** Ran SP% **121.6**
Speed ratings (Par 103): **100,99,98,96,93 91,89,89,86,86**
toteswingers 1&2 £3.50, 1&3 £4.30, 2&3 £3.60 CSF £16.89 CT £52.79 TOTE £6.10: £1.70, £1.50, £2.10; EX 17.00 Trifecta £84.20 Pool: £3110.37 - 27.67 winning units..
Owner Dallas Racing **Bred** Pitrizzia Partnership **Trained** Danethorpe, Notts
FOCUS
A modest but pretty competitive handicap and a game winner.
T/Plt: £26.60 to a £1 stake. Pool: £72,915.99 - 1,999.00 winning tickets. T/Qpdt: £4.00 to a £1 stake. Pool: £4,505.68 - 813.83 winning tickets. WG

[543] CAGNES-SUR-MER
Sunday, February 10
OFFICIAL GOING: Fibresand: standard

604a PRIX DE MOSCOU (MAIDEN) (3YO) (FIBRESAND) 6f 110y
12:45 (12:00) 3-Y-0 **£9,756** (£3,902; £2,926; £1,951; £975)

RPR
1 **African Waters (USA)** 3-9-2 0.................... IoritzMendizabal 7 73
(J-C Rouget, France) **5/2**[2]
2 *snk* **Dha Chara (IRE)**[10] 460 3-9-2 0.................... ThomasMessina 3 73
(Reg Hollinshead) *racd in 4th on rail: gd prog ent st: rdn 1 1/2f out to go 3rd: r.o wl u.p ins fnl f to go 2nd 100yds out: fin strly: narrowly failed* **19/5**[3]
3 *1 1/2* **Wunderbar (GER)** 3-9-2 0.................... Christophe-PatriceLemaire 6 69
(J-C Rouget, France) **1/1**[1]
4 *1/2* **Indian Walk (FR)**[10] 460 3-9-2 0.................... FranckBlondel 5 67
(M Gentile, France) **5/1**
5 *20* **Kiss And Kill (FR)** 3-8-9 0....................(p) TonyPiccone 2 2
(J-M Capitte, France) **20/1**
1m 19.24s (79.24) **5** Ran SP% **120.8**
WIN (incl. 1 euro stake): 3.50. PLACES: 2.30, 2.20. SF: 14.50.
Owner Joseph Allen **Bred** Joe Allen Stables **Trained** Pau, France

605a PRIX DES CHEVREFEUILLES (MAIDEN) (3YO COLTS & GELDINGS) (FIBRESAND) 1m 2f (D)
1:15 (12:00) 3-Y-0 **£9,756** (£3,902; £2,926; £1,951; £975)

RPR
1 **Snap Call** 3-9-2 0.................... IoritzMendizabal 3 81
(J-C Rouget, France) **1/2**[1]
2 *2* **Baileys Auteur (FR)**[13] 445 3-9-2 0....................(p) MickaelForest 2 77
(W Walton, France) **19/5**[2]
3 *1* **Destiny Highway (FR)**[109] 7332 3-8-13 0.................... JohanVictoire 9 72
(Gay Kelleway) *hld up towards rr: gd prog on wd outside 2f out: r.o wl u.p fnl f to go 3rd: clst at fin* **27/1**
4 *3 1/2* **Snowy Dawn**[13] 445 3-9-2 0.................... ThomasMessina 5 68
(Reg Hollinshead) *racd in 4th: chsd along down bk st to keep position: relegated to 6th 2f out: r.o u.p fnl f to get up for 3rd on line* **12/1**[3]
5 *snk* **Hello Pump Pump (FR)** 3-9-2 0....................(b) FranckBlondel 7 68
(M Pimbonnet, France) **15/1**
6 *1* **Le Tholoney (FR)** 3-8-13 0....................(p) Francois-XavierBertras 8 63
(F Rohaut, France) **12/1**[3]
7 *shd* **Taboule**[4] 543 3-8-7 0.................... NicolasLarenaudie[(6)] 1 63
(G Martin, Austria) **61/1**
8 *4* **Super Blue Cat (USA)** 3-8-9 0....................(b[1]) RomainAuray[(4)] 6 55
(J Heloury, France) **29/1**
9 *snk* **Stenka Razine (FR)**[4] 543 3-8-10 0.................... SoufyaneMoulin[(6)] 4 57
(C Boutin, France) **40/1**
2m 3.02s (123.02) **9** Ran SP% **120.1**
WIN (incl. 1 euro stake): 1.50. PLACES: 1.10, 1.20, 2.20. DF: 2.00. SF: 2.50.
Owner Daniel-Yves Treves **Bred** Canary Thoroughbreds **Trained** Pau, France

606 - 607a (Foreign Racing) - See Raceform Interactive

[595] GULFSTREAM PARK (L-H)
Sunday, February 10
OFFICIAL GOING: Turf: firm; dirt: fast

608a CLAIMING RACE (CLAIMER) (4YO+) (TURF) 1m 1f
7:37 (7:39) 4-Y-0+
£12,515 (£5,423; £2,607; £1,042; £208; £208)

RPR
1 **Dark Cove (USA)**[526] 6-8-7 0.................... JRosario 8 104
(Michael J Maker, U.S.A) **23/10**[1]
2 *3/4* **Nineinthenine (USA)** 7-8-7 0....................(b) LSaez 4 102
(Humberto Toledo, U.S.A) **49/10**
3 *nk* **Clement Rock (USA)**[168] 5-8-7 0....................(b) JLezcano 5 102
(Mark Casse, Canada) **23/10**[2]
4 *nk* **Political Courage (USA)** 4-8-7 0.................... JRoccoJr 3 101
(Michael Matz, U.S.A) **61/10**
5 *5 3/4* **Julius Geezer (IRE)**[44] 8278 5-8-7 0.................... CLanerie 1 89
(Amy Weaver) *broke wl: led: hdd 3f out: sn no ex and btn: fdd* **29/1**
6 *3/4* **Minnie Punt (USA)**[154] 7-8-7 0....................(b) JJCastellano 7 88
(J David Braddy, U.S.A) **19/5**[3]
7 *4 1/4* **Decaf Again (USA)**[22] 7-8-7 0....................(b) JDelgado 6 79
(Barry Rose, U.S.A) **76/1**
8 *1/2* **Ojibway Signal (CAN)**[147] 6299 5-8-7 0....................(b[1]) LContreras 2 78
(David R Bell, Canada) **191/10**
1m 46.98s (106.98) **8** Ran SP% **122.1**
PARI-MUTUEL (all including $2 stakes): WIN 6.60; PLACE (1-2) 3.80, 4.60; SHOW (1-2-3) 2.60, 2.80, 2.60; SF 29.00.
Owner Kenneth L & Sarah K Ramsey **Bred** Stonewall Farm Stallions **Trained** USA

[513] ST MORITZ (R-H)
Sunday, February 10
OFFICIAL GOING: Snow: frozen

609a PREIS TOP EVENTS OF SWITZERLAND UND GALOPPRENNFREUNDE SCHWEIZ (CONDITIONS) (4YO+) (SNOW) 1m 1f 110y
2:45 (12:00) 4-Y-0+
£2,818 (£1,409; £1,006; £671; £335; £201)

RPR
1 **Ancient Greece**[7] 513 6-9-6 0.................... JBojko 7 82
(George Baker) *trckd ldrs on outside: hdwy 3f out: sn pressing ldr on outside: led under 2f out: hrd rdn appr fnl f: kpt on wl u.p* **13/10**[1]
2 *1 1/4* **Run The Show (FR)**[602] 3210 5-9-4 0....................(p) DPorcu 4 77
(P Schaerer, Switzerland) **19/5**[2]
3 *hd* **Ziking (FR)**[357] 630 8-9-4 0.................... FredericSpanu 2 77
(A Schaerer, Switzerland) **126/10**
4 *6* **Cappuccino (SWI)**[162] 5-9-6 0....................(b) AndreBest 5 67
(P Schaerer, Switzerland) **76/10**
5 *dist* **Flash Dance (GER)**[7] 514 6-8-9 0.................... TimBurgin[(7)] 1
(A Schennach, Switzerland) **13/10**[1]
6 *2 1/2* **Harvest (GER)** 6-8-8 0.................... MiguelLopez 3
(K Klein, Switzerland) **32/5**[3]
7 *dist* **Hashanar (IRE)** 5-9-6 0.................... OlivierPlacais 6
(M Weiss, Switzerland) **176/10**
2m 2.5s (122.50) **7** Ran SP% **145.7**
PARI-MUTUEL (all including 1 chf stakes): WIN 2.30; PLACE 2.30, 2.00; SF 6.30.
Owner Inkin, Inkin, Byng, Baker & Partners **Bred** Darley **Trained** Manton, Wilts

The Form Book Flat, Raceform Ltd, Compton, RG20 6NL.

[587]WOLVERHAMPTON (A.W) (L-H)

Monday, February 11

OFFICIAL GOING: Standard to slow

Wind: Fresh against Weather: Overcast

610 BOOKMAKERS.CO.UK H'CAP 5f 20y(P)

2:30 (2:30) (Class 6) (0-52,52) 4-Y-0+ **£1,940** (£577; £288; £144) **Stalls** Low

Form RPR

03-0 **1** **Divertimenti (IRE)**[36] 88 9-8-12 **46** oh1................(b) MarkCoumbe(3) 6 56
(Roy Bowring) *a.p: shkn up over 1f out: rdn to ld and hung lft wl ins fnl f: r.o wl* **11/1**

3352 **2** *1 3/4* **Miserere Mei (IRE)**[5] 529 4-8-10 **48**............................ PhilipPrince(7) 1 52
(Richard Guest) *s.i.s: hdwy over 3f out: rdn and ev ch ins fnl f: styd on same pce* **11/4**[1]

-406 **3** *3/4* **Nafa (IRE)**[20] 326 5-9-4 **49**.. StephenCraine 8 50
(Daniel Mark Loughnane) *chsd ldr tl led over 1f out: rdn: edgd lft and hdd wl ins fnl f* **16/1**

-360 **4** *nse* **Ches Jicaro (IRE)**[7] 516 5-9-1 **46** oh1........................(v) DavidProbert 2 47
(James Unett) *chsd ldrs: rdn over 1f out: hmpd ins fnl f: styd on* **12/1**

4-00 **5** *1* **Illustrious Lad (IRE)**[18] 354 4-9-7 **52**.......................(bt[1]) AdamKirby 10 49
(Roger Ingram) *chsd ldrs: pushed along 1/2-way: rdn and ev ch over 1f out: styd on same pce ins fnl f* **15/2**

-650 **6** *nk* **Chateau Lola**[5] 529 4-9-5 **50**...(v) JoeFanning 4 46
(Derek Shaw) *s.i.s: pushed along early in rr: hdwy over 1f out: r.o: nt trble ldrs* **7/1**

53-4 **7** *nk* **Love Club**[20] 326 5-9-3 **48**.. GrahamGibbons 3 45
(Brian Baugh) *led: rdn and hdd over 1f out: styng on same pce whn hmpd wl ins fnl f* **4/1**[3]

0043 **8** *hd* **Fantasy Fighter (IRE)**[7] 516 8-9-1 **46** oh1....................(b) LukeMorris 7 40
(Ronald Harris) *hld up: plld hrd: hdwy over 1f out: sn rdn: styd on same pce* **7/2**[2]

0-36 **9** *3 1/4* **Prigsnov Dancer (IRE)**[14] 422 8-9-1 **46** oh1............(t) AndrewMullen 5 29
(Frank Sheridan) *hld up: effrt over 1f out: wknd fnl f* **25/1**

04-0 **10** *6* **Busy Bimbo (IRE)**[20] 326 4-9-1 **46** oh1...................(b) RobertWinston 9
(Alan Berry) *sn outpcd* **66/1**

1m 3.07s (0.77) **Going Correction** +0.15s/f (Slow) **10** Ran SP% **120.4**

Speed ratings (Par 101): **99,96,95,94,93 92,92,92,86,77**

Tote Swingers: 1&2 £7.80, 1&3 £22.60, 2&3 £8.80 CSF £42.81 CT £512.86 TOTE £12.40: £2.90, £1.30, £4.70; EX 78.00 Trifecta £1302.60 Pool: £3,496.85 - 2.01 winning units..

Owner K Nicholls **Bred** Airlie Stud **Trained** Edwinstowe, Notts

FOCUS

A competitive albeit low-grade handicap over the minimum trip. There was a bunch finish and the runner-up is the best guide.

611 CORAL.CO.UK (S) STKS 5f 216y(P)

3:00 (3:00) (Class 6) 3-Y-0+ **£1,940** (£577; £288; £144) **Stalls** Low

Form RPR

1365 **1** **Athaakeel (IRE)**[4] 551 7-9-1 49...............................(b) GaryPhillips(7) 3 61
(Ronald Harris) *hld up: pushed along over 2f out: hdwy over 1f out: rdn to ld and edgd lft ins fnl f: r.o* **25/1**

125 **2** *1 1/4* **Dark Lane**[11] 454 7-9-13 66..(p) AdamKirby 4 62
(David Evans) *chsd ldrs: rdn and ev ch ins fnl f: styd on same pce* **7/2**[2]

3230 **3** *2* **Above The Stars**[9] 494 5-9-3 62............................... FergusSweeney 7 46
(Jamie Osborne) *chsd ldr tl led over 2f out: rdn over 1f out: hdd and unable qck ins fnl f* **7/2**[2]

-434 **4** *1/2* **Mother Jones**[25] 234 5-9-1 68... EoinWalsh(7) 8 49
(David Evans) *plld hrd and prom: chsd ldr 2f out: sn rdn: no ex ins fnl f* **6/1**

-504 **5** *1 3/4* **Frequency**[11] 454 6-9-8 69...(b) JoeFanning 6 43
(Keith Dalgleish) *broke wl and led early: sn stdd to trck ldrs: effrt and nt clr run over 1f out: swtchd lft: no ex* **9/4**[1]

-430 **6** *2 1/4* **Peak Storm**[13] 436 4-9-8 58..(v) LukeMorris 1 36
(John O'Shea) *hld up: rdn over 2f out: wknd fnl f* **12/1**

-056 **7** *5* **Lady Prodee**[5] 535 5-9-3 61.. JimmyQuinn 5 15
(Bill Turner) *s.i.s: sn rcvrd to ld: rdn and hdd over 2f out: wknd over 1f out* **11/2**[3]

1m 15.74s (0.74) **Going Correction** +0.15s/f (Slow) **7** Ran SP% **116.4**

Speed ratings (Par 101): **101,99,96,96,93 90,84**

Tote Swingers: 1&2 £4.80, 1&3 £7.30, 2&3 £3.30 CSF £113.25 TOTE £18.90: £5.00, £1.90; EX 49.00 Trifecta £296.60 Pool: £3,372.45 - 8.52 winning units..No bid for the winner.

Owner Drag Star On Swan **Bred** Shadwell Estate Company Limited **Trained** Earlswood, Monmouths

FOCUS

A very ordinary seller with the usual doubts over the form, not least the winner who had the worst chance at the weights.

612 HORSE RACING FREE BETS WITH BOOKMAKERS.CO.UK MAIDEN STKS 1m 4f 50y(P)

3:30 (3:30) (Class 5) 4-Y-0+ **£2,587** (£770; £384; £192) **Stalls** Low

Form RPR

32-2 **1** **Suffice (IRE)**[32] 140 4-9-5 71... DavidNolan 4 79
(Richard Fahey) *chsd ldrs: led over 1f out: shkn up and styd on wl* **3/1**[2]

2 **2** *3* **Full Swing**[16] 397 4-9-5 0... AndreaAtzeni 1 74
(Roger Varian) *sn led: hdd over 10f out: chsd ldrs: shkn up to go 2nd over 3f out: led 2f out: rdn and hdd over 1f out: styd on same pce* **4/11**[1]

5 **3** *12* **Rayadour (IRE)**[19] 333 4-9-5 68...........................(b[1]) FergusSweeney 6 57
(Alan King) *chsd ldr tl led 5f out: rdn and hdd 2f out: wknd fnl f* **14/1**[3]

0 **4** *1 1/4* **Zafaraban (IRE)**[16] 397 6-9-3 0.............................. GeorgeDowning(5) 3 53
(Tony Carroll) *hld up: rdn and wknd over 2f out* **66/1**

5 *31* **Knight In Purple**[254] 9-9-8 0..................................(vt) MichaelO'Connell 2
(John Mackie) *s.i.s: sn pushed along: hdwy to ld over 10f out: hdd 5f out: rdn over 3f out: wknd over 2f out: t.o* **16/1**

2m 41.7s (0.60) **Going Correction** +0.15s/f (Slow)

WFA 4 from 6yo+ 3lb **5** Ran SP% **112.4**

Speed ratings (Par 103): **104,102,94,93,72**

CSF £4.60 TOTE £2.60: £1.10, £1.10; EX 4.30 Trifecta £13.30 Pool: £3,634.34 - 204.86 winning units..

Owner R A Fahey **Bred** Roalso Ltd **Trained** Musley Bank, N Yorks

FOCUS

The front two pulled a long way clear in this 1m4f maiden for older horses and there was a minor upset. The winner is rated back to his debut level.

613 BEST HORSE RACING ODDS WITH BOOKMAKERS.CO.UK H'CAP 1m 1f 103y(P)

4:00 (4:00) (Class 5) (0-75,75) 3-Y-O **£2,587** (£770; £384) **Stalls** Low

Form RPR

51-5 **1** **Diletta Tommasa (IRE)**[28] 209 3-8-12 **66**.................... AndreaAtzeni 4 66
(John Stimpson) *hld up in tch: qcknd on outer to ld over 2f out: sn rdn: edgd lft ins fnl f: styd on* **25/1**[3]

0-11 **2** *nk* **Naru (IRE)**[14] 428 3-9-7 **75**.. AdamKirby 1 74
(James Tate) *racd keenly: led 1f: chsd ldr: hung rt over 7f out: jnd wnr over 2f out: rdn and hung lft ins fnl f: styd on* **2/9**[1]

50-4 **3** *15* **Mudaawem (USA)**[14] 414 3-8-8 **62**.................................. JoeFanning 2 45
(Mark Johnston) *led over 8f out: rdn and hdd over 2f out: wknd sn after* **4/1**[2]

2m 5.93s (4.23) **Going Correction** +0.15s/f (Slow) **3** Ran SP% **105.7**

Speed ratings (Par 97): **87,86,73**

CSF £33.43 TOTE £7.10; EX 14.80 Trifecta £11.30.

Owner J T Stimpson **Bred** Ms Sheila Lavery **Trained** Butterton, Staffs

■ John Stimpson's first Flat winner since June 2008.

FOCUS

The extended 1m1f handicap for 3yos provided a massive upset. It was slowly run and the form is shaky.

614 CORAL.CO.UK MOBILE CASINO H'CAP 1m 1f 103y(P)

4:30 (4:32) (Class 4) (0-80,79) 4-Y-0+ **£4,690** (£1,395; £697; £348) **Stalls** Low

Form RPR

4-34 **1** **Patriotic (IRE)**[16] 400 5-9-5 **77**..(p) AdamKirby 2 86
(Chris Dwyer) *trckd ldrs tl led over 5f out: rdn clr over 1f out: all out* **4/1**[1]

1-22 **2** *shd* **Knowe Head (NZ)**[25] 239 6-9-3 **75**...........................(v) DavidProbert 8 84
(James Unett) *hld up in tch: chsd wnr fnl f: sn rdn: r.o: jst failed* **8/1**

24-3 **3** *1 3/4* **Brimstone Hill (IRE)**[14] 420 4-9-7 **79**............................. GrahamLee 9 84
(Anthony Carson) *a.p: rdn over 1f out: styd on* **15/2**[3]

6-02 **4** *2 1/4* **Dazzling Valentine**[14] 429 5-8-7 **70**.......................... NatashaEaton(5) 6 70
(Alan Bailey) *hld up: pushed along over 2f out: r.o ins fnl f: nt rch ldrs* **16/1**

2-53 **5** *nk* **Dakota Canyon (IRE)**[21] 314 4-9-0 **72**.....................(p) FrederikTylicki 5 72
(Richard Fahey) *mid-div: pushed along over 5f out: rdn and outpcd over 2f out: r.o ins fnl f* **11/2**[2]

1004 **6** *hd* **Honey Of A Kitten (USA)**[10] 476 5-8-8 **66**...................(v) LukeMorris 4 65
(David Evans) *led 1f: chsd ldr: tl over 5f out: chsd wnr over 4f out: rdn over 2f out: no ex fnl f* **33/1**

24-1 **7** *nk* **Exning Halt**[21] 313 4-9-2 **74**...................................... MichaelO'Connell 10 73
(John Quinn) *led over 8f out: hdd over 5f out: rdn over 2f out: styd on same pce fr over 1f out* **8/1**

000- **8** *3 1/4* **Mountain Range (IRE)**[124] 6987 5-9-2 **74**................... JamieMackay 11 66
(Willie Musson) *hld up: pushed along over 2f out: nvr nr to chal* **16/1**

-411 **9** *1* **Idol Deputy (FR)**[10] 478 7-8-10 **73**.......................(p) RachealKneller(5) 1 63
(Mark Usher) *hld up: lost pl over 2f out: n.d after* **8/1**

2m 3.12s (1.42) **Going Correction** +0.15s/f (Slow) **9** Ran SP% **95.2**

Speed ratings (Par 105): **99,98,97,95,95 94,94,91,90**

Tote Swingers: 1&2 £5.20, 1&3 £5.90, 2&3 £4.80 CSF £22.74 CT £99.80 TOTE £3.80: £1.90, £1.40, £2.00; EX 18.40 Trifecta £48.50 Pool: £1,334.12 - 20.59 winning units..

Owner M M Foulger **Bred** Darley **Trained** Newmarket, Suffolk

FOCUS

There was no pace until the winner went on at halfway. He is rated back to his best.

615 £50 FREE BET AT CORAL.CO.UK H'CAP 1m 141y(P)

5:00 (5:00) (Class 5) (0-70,69) 3-Y-O **£2,587** (£770; £384; £192) **Stalls** Low

Form RPR

3612 **1** **Run It Twice (IRE)**[4] 547 3-9-4 **69**................................(b) LukeMorris 3 75
(David Evans) *hld up: hdwy over 3f out: led over 1f out: rdn and edgd lft ins fnl f: styd on* **10/3**[2]

5-33 **2** *nk* **Tanawar (IRE)**[31] 160 3-9-2 **67**................................(b[1]) AdamBeschizza 4 72
(William Haggas) *trckd ldr: racd keenly: rdn over 2f out: ev ch fr over 1f out: styd on* **15/8**[1]

-211 **3** *3 1/4* **Mick Dundee (IRE)**[11] 447 3-9-3 **68**............................(vt) AdamKirby 2 66
(J W Hills) *led: rdn and hdd over 1f out: styd on same pce ins fnl f* **7/2**[3]

1112 **4** *3 1/4* **Taxiformissbyron**[8] 506 3-9-3 **68**...................................... TomEaves 5 58
(Michael Herrington) *s.i.s: hld up: rdn over 2f out: nvr on terms* **15/2**

5-53 **5** *26* **Ofcoursewecan (USA)**[10] 473 3-9-3 **68**.......................... JoeFanning 1
(Mark Johnston) *chsd ldrs: pushed along and lost pl over 3f out: wknd over 2f out: t.o* **7/2**[3]

1m 51.23s (0.73) **Going Correction** +0.15s/f (Slow) **5** Ran SP% **114.1**

Speed ratings (Par 97): **102,101,98,95,72**

CSF £10.44 TOTE £3.30: £1.20, £2.20; EX 9.10 Trifecta £31.00 Pool: £2,379.43 - 57.43 winning units..

Owner Shropshire Wolves 4 **Bred** Yeomanstown Stud **Trained** Pandy, Monmouths

FOCUS

A small field but several in-form or unexposed participants in this extended 1m handicap for 3yos. It wasn't strong run but the form is taken at face value.

616 NO DEPOSIT FREE BETS WITH BOOKMAKERS.CO.UK H'CAP (DIV I) 7f 32y(P)

5:30 (5:30) (Class 6) (0-60,60) 4-Y-O+ **£1,940** (£577; £288; £144) **Stalls** High

Form RPR

4-32 **1** **Ace Master**[13] 437 5-9-2 **58**......................................(b) MarkCoumbe(3) 10 69
(Roy Bowring) *mde all: clr 5f out: rdn over 1f out: styd on* **5/1**[3]

0-00 **2** *2 1/4* **Unlimited**[14] 426 11-9-1 **59**................................ GeorgeDowning(5) 3 64
(Tony Carroll) *dwlt: hld up: hdwy over 1f out: styd on to go 2nd nr fin: nt rch wnr* **20/1**

1-14 **3** *hd* **Basle**[19] 346 6-9-6 **59**..(t) AdamKirby 8 63
(Michael Blake) *hld up: hdwy over 1f out: styd on: wnt 3rd nr fin: nt trble ldrs* **10/1**

3321 **4** *1/2* **Spinning Ridge (IRE)**[9] 497 8-9-0 **60**......................(b) GaryPhillips(7) 6 63
(Ronald Harris) *s.i.s: hld up: hdwy on outer over 2f out: chsd wnr over 1f out: hung lft ins fnl f: no ex towards fin* **9/4**[1]

00-4 **5** *1 1/2* **Daunt (IRE)**[13] 436 4-9-3 **56**.. MichaelO'Connell 1 55
(John Quinn) *prom: chsd wnr 4f out tl rdn over 1f out: no ex ins fnl f* **6/1**

0-46 **6** *1/2* **Swendab (IRE)**[18] 354 5-9-2 **60**............................(p) ThomasBrown(5) 11 58
(John O'Shea) *mid-div: drvn along 1/2-way: hdwy over 2f out: styd on: nt trble ldrs* **14/1**

0-62 **7** *1 3/4* **Katmai River (IRE)**[23] 274 6-8-13 **57**.....................(v) RachealKneller(5) 2 50
(Mark Usher) *sn pushed along in rr: nvr on terms* **7/1**

2166 **8** *2* **Kai**[3] 559 4-8-12 **58**..........(b) PhilipPrince(7) 4 46
(Alan McCabe) *chsd ldrs: rdn over 2f out: wknd wl over 1f out* **4/1**[2]
10-0 **9** *15* **July Days (IRE)**[14] 426 7-9-7 **60**.......... GrahamGibbons 7
(Brian Baugh) *chsd wnr 3f: remained handy: rdn and wkng whn hmpd over 2f out* **16/1**
1m 30.34s (0.74) **Going Correction** +0.15s/f (Slow) **9** Ran SP% **120.6**
Speed ratings (Par 101): **101,98,98,97,95 95,93,91,73**
Tote Swingers: 1&2 £18.10, 1&3 £5.40, 2&3 £37.10 CSF £101.05 CT £985.39 TOTE £6.00: £2.50, £10.50, £4.20; EX 134.00 Trifecta £1912.30 Part won. Pool: £2,549.85 - 0.67 winning units..
Owner S R Bowring **Bred** S R Bowring **Trained** Edwinstowe, Notts
FOCUS
The way the surface was riding clearly affected this low-grade 7f handicap as most of the field were off the bridle 4f out. The winner is rated in line with his Wolverhampton best.

617 NO DEPOSIT FREE BETS WITH BOOKMAKERS.CO.UK H'CAP (DIV II) 7f 32y(P)
6:00 (6:01) (Class 6) (0-60,60) 4-Y-0+ **£1,940** (£577; £288; £144) **Stalls** High

Form RPR
000- **1** **Dashwood**[98] 7589 6-9-7 **60**..........(t) GrahamLee 5 74+
(Anthony Carson) *chsd ldrs: led ins fnl f: r.o: comf* **6/4**[1]
-322 **2** *2 1/4* **Kielty's Folly**[16] 408 9-9-3 **56**..........(v[1]) GrahamGibbons 11 61
(Brian Baugh) *hld up: hdwy over 1f out: rdn and hung lft ins fnl f: styd on same pce* **8/1**
60-6 **3** *1 1/2* **Purley Queen (IRE)**[33] 116 4-9-6 **59**.......... JDSmith 8 60
(Sylvester Kirk) *s.i.s: hld up: hdwy over 1f out: r.o: nt rch ldrs* **33/1**
01-5 **4** *1* **Maggie Pink**[13] 437 4-9-6 **59**.......... AndrewMullen 6 57
(Michael Appleby) *led: rdn and hdd ins fnl f: no ex* **5/2**[2]
-533 **5** *3/4* **Brown Volcano (IRE)**[13] 437 4-8-11 **55**.......... ThomasBrown(5) 3 51
(John O'Shea) *sn chsng ldr: rdn over 1f out: no ex ins fnl f* **6/1**
3-44 **6** *3 1/4* **Piccolo Express**[13] 437 7-9-5 **58**..........(p) AdamKirby 1 45
(Brian Baugh) *trckd ldrs: plld hrd: rdn over 1f out: wknd ins fnl f* **9/2**[3]
40-0 **7** *4 1/2* **Jericho (IRE)**[27] 218 4-9-5 **58**..........(b[1]) FergusSweeney 9 33
(Jamie Osborne) *s.i.s: rdn 1/2-way: nvr on terms* **25/1**
30-0 **8** *8* **Petrarchan**[3] 559 5-8-7 **46** oh1..........(bt) LukeMorris 4
(Milton Bradley) *prom: rdn and hung lft over 4f out: wknd over 2f out* **40/1**
1m 29.62s (0.02) **Going Correction** +0.15s/f (Slow) **8** Ran SP% **121.4**
Speed ratings (Par 101): **105,102,100,99,98 95,89,80**
Tote Swingers: 1&2 £1.60, 1&3 £13.50, 2&3 £13.80 CSF £15.67 CT £300.90 TOTE £3.40: £1.10, £2.10, £7.50; EX 12.70 Trifecta £237.50 Pool: £3,275.54 - 10.34 winning units..
Owner Macattack, William Lea Screed & Form IT **Bred** Darley **Trained** Newmarket, Suffolk
FOCUS
The closing contest was the scene of a successful gamble. It was sound run and the runner-up sets a sound standard.
T/Plt: £935.80 to a £1 stake. Pool: £85,314.00 - 66.55 winning tickets. T/Qpdt: £76.10 to a £1 stake. Pool: £8,066.00 - 78.40 winning tickets. CR

597 SOUTHWELL (L-H)
Tuesday, February 12
OFFICIAL GOING: Standard to slow
Wind: Light across Weather: Overcast

618 BEST RACING ODDS GUARANTEED AT BOOKMAKERS.CO.UK H'CAP 6f (F)
1:40 (1:43) (Class 6) (0-55,55) 4-Y-0+ **£1,940** (£577; £288; £144) **Stalls** Low

Form RPR
610/ **1** **Seamster**[407] 14 6-9-4 **52**..........(vt) GrahamLee 10 65
(Richard Ford) *qckly away: made all: rdn clr 2f out: kpt on strly* **4/1**[2]
46-0 **2** *2 1/4* **Ridgeway Hawk**[32] 162 5-9-5 **53**..........(v) RobertHavlin 14 58
(Mark Usher) *sn chsng wnr: rdn 2f out: kpt on u.p fnl f* **8/1**
0516 **3** *3/4* **Steel City Boy (IRE)**[8] 516 10-9-2 **55**.......... AnnStokell(5) 5 58
(Ann Stokell) *prom: rdn along over 2f out: kpt on fnl f* **20/1**
30-5 **4** *1* **Mango Music**[15] 423 10-9-4 **52**.......... BarryMcHugh 11 52
(David Thompson) *dwlt and in rr: wd st and hdwy over 2f out: sn rdn and edgd lft wl over 1f out: kpt on u.p fnl f: nrst fin* **20/1**
0-00 **5** *1* **Upper Lambourn (IRE)**[7] 523 5-9-7 **55**..........(t) GrahamGibbons 13 52
(Christopher Kellett) *dwlt: in tch and wd st: hdwy on outer over 2f out: sn rdn and kpt on fnl f* **4/1**[2]
-320 **6** *1 3/4* **Mataajir (USA)**[27] 223 5-9-0 **55**.......... AdamMcLean(7) 2 46+
(Derek Shaw) *midfield on inner: rdn along and outpcd bef 1/2-way: styd on u.p appr fnl f* **7/2**[1]
-505 **7** *1 1/2* **Speedyfix**[10] 493 6-9-7 **55**..........(t) IanMongan 7 41
(Christine Dunnett) *in tch: hdwy 3f out: rdn to chse ldrs over 2f out: drvn and wknd over 1f out* **11/1**
5-02 **8** *1/2* **Red Shadow**[6] 537 4-9-7 **55**..........(p) TomEaves 6 40
(Alan Brown) *sn rdn along in rr: drvn over 2f out: sme late hdwy* **9/2**[3]
000- **9** *2 1/2* **Fathey (IRE)**[187] 5013 7-8-12 **46** oh1.......... RobbieFitzpatrick 12 23
(Charles Smith) *chsd ldrs: rdn along wl over 2f out: sn wknd* **66/1**
06-0 **10** *7* **Bird Dog**[6] 537 7-8-12 **46** oh1..........(v) DavidProbert 9
(Phil McEntee) *a towards rr* **40/1**
0-00 **11** *1 1/2* **Johnson's Cat (IRE)**[22] 312 4-8-12 **46** oh1..........(b[1]) JimmyQuinn 4
(Mandy Rowland) *a towards rr* **50/1**
220- **12** *8* **Tenancy (IRE)**[89] 7733 9-9-2 **50**.......... LiamKeniry 1
(Shaun Harris) *chsd ldrs on inner: rdn along 1/2-way: sn wknd* **14/1**
1m 16.59s (0.09) **Going Correction** -0.025s/f (Stan) **12** Ran SP% **121.9**
Speed ratings (Par 101): **98,95,94,92,91 89,87,86,83,73 71,61**
toteswingers 1&2 £8.30, 2&3 £21.10, 1&3 £16.90 CSF £35.12 CT £595.51 TOTE £4.60: £1.60, £2.80, £3.90; EX 53.90 Trifecta £686.30 Pool: £3059.37 - 3.34 winning units..
Owner The Haydock Club **Bred** D G Hardisty Bloodstock **Trained** Garstang, Lancs
FOCUS
A moderate handicap and those that raced prominently dominated.

619 HORSE RACING FREE BETS AT BOOKMAKERS.CO.UK MAIDEN STKS 1m (F)
2:10 (2:10) (Class 5) 3-Y-0+ **£2,726** (£805; £402) **Stalls** Low

Form RPR
54-4 **1** **Makinson Lane (IRE)**[33] 129 3-8-8 **66**.......... BarryMcHugh 3 68
(Richard Fahey) *cl up: rdn along and sltly outpcd 3f out: hdwy u.p to chal over 1f out: led ent fnl f: drvn out* **1/1**[1]
332- **2** *2* **Ifan (IRE)**[60] 8115 5-9-13 **64**.......... DavidProbert 1 69
(Tim Vaughan) *t.k.h: set stdy pce: qcknd 3f out: rdn and edgd lft wl over 1f out: hdd ent fnl f: sn drvn and hung rt: one pce* **5/4**[2]
5-35 **3** *6* **Frosty Friday**[20] 342 5-9-8 **57**..........(p) IanMongan 4 50
(J R Jenkins) *trckd ldng pair: effrt 3f out: sn rdn along and outpcd fr wl over 1f out* **7/1**[3]
4 *15* **Chancealot**[34] 5-9-13 **0**..........[1] LiamKeniry 2 21
(Neil Mulholland) *s.i.s: t.k.h and sn trcking ldng pair: rdn along 3f out: sn outpcd and bhd fnl 2f* **40/1**
1m 44.79s (1.09) **Going Correction** -0.025s/f (Stan)
WFA 3 from 5yo 19lb **4** Ran SP% **109.4**
Speed ratings (Par 103): **93,91,85,70**
CSF £2.58 TOTE £2.00; EX 2.70 Trifecta £3.30 Pool: £1372.64 - 304.80 winning units..
Owner David W Armstrong **Bred** M Fahy & Rathbarry Stud **Trained** Musley Bank, N Yorks
■ Stewards' Enquiry : Barry McHugh two-day ban: use of whip (26-27 Feb)
FOCUS
A weak and uncompetitive maiden.

620 PICK THE BEST BOOKIES AT BOOKMAKERS.CO.UK (S) STKS 7f (F)
2:45 (2:45) (Class 6) 4-Y-0+ **£1,940** (£577; £288) **Stalls** Low

Form RPR
0-22 **1** **Flying Pickets (IRE)**[2] 603 4-9-4 **69**..........(be) JohnFahy 4 74
(Alan McCabe) *trckd ldr on outer: cl up 1/2-way: led wl over 2f out: rdn over 1f out: edgd rt and kpt on fnl f* **4/5**[1]
0-03 **2** *1* **Fluctuation (IRE)**[6] 540 5-8-13 **65** ow1..........(v) StevieDonohoe 1 66
(Ian Williams) *trckd ldr on inner: effrt 3f out: sn swtchd to outer and rdn to chse wnr wl 2f out: drvn and kpt on fnl f* **5/4**[2]
02-0 **3** *9* **Elusive Warrior (USA)**[6] 537 10-8-5 **57**..........(p) NoraLooby(7) 2 42
(Alan McCabe) *led: pushed along 1/2-way: sn hdd and rdn: wknd wl over 1f out* **9/1**[3]
1m 29.86s (-0.44) **Going Correction** -0.025s/f (Stan) **3** Ran SP% **110.0**
Speed ratings (Par 101): **101,99,89**
CSF £2.20 TOTE £1.40; EX 2.40 Trifecta £1.90 Pool: £2053.26 - 772.38 winning units..There was no bid for the winner.
Owner Tariq Al Nisf **Bred** Richard Frayne **Trained** Averham Park, Notts
FOCUS
A moderate seller and the market suggested it was a match.

621 WIN MORE ON BETTING AT BOOKMAKERS.CO.UK H'CAP 7f (F)
3:15 (3:18) (Class 3) (0-95,94) 4-Y-0+ **£7,439** (£2,213; £1,106; £553) **Stalls** Low

Form RPR
0-26 **1** **Docofthebay (IRE)**[13] 443 9-8-10 **83**..........(b) LukeMorris 2 95
(Scott Dixon) *trckd ldrs: hdwy to chse ldr 2f out: sn swtchd rt and rdn to chal: led 1f out: one l up and drvn whn hung bdly rt ins fnl f: kpt on nr fin* **7/1**
40-0 **2** *nk* **Nazreef**[17] 401 6-9-7 **94**..........(vt) RobertWinston 8 105
(Hughie Morrison) *cl up: led 1/2-way: rdn wl over 1f out: hdd appr 1f out: drvn and rallied wl ins fnl f: no ex nr fin* **3/1**[2]
311- **3** *5* **Chookie Royale**[76] 7920 5-8-9 **82**..........(p) JoeFanning 6 80
(Keith Dalgleish) *dwlt and towards rr: hdwy on outer 3f out: rdn and edgd lft wl over 1f out: kpt on u.p fnl f: nrst fin* **11/4**[1]
330- **4** *2* **Shahzan (IRE)**[54] 8188 5-8-10 **83**.......... AndreaAtzeni 7 76
(Roger Varian) *prom: rdn along over 2f out: drvn and one pce fr over 1f out* **6/1**[3]
-140 **5** *3 1/4* **Kung Hei Fat Choy (USA)**[13] 443 4-8-9 **82**..........(b) DaleSwift 1 66
(James Given) *in tch on inner: rdn along 3f out: n.d* **8/1**
01-3 **6** *3 1/4* **Kickingthelilly**[38] 79 4-8-10 **83**.......... ChrisCatlin 9 59
(Rae Guest) *dwlt and in rr: rdn and sme hdwy on wd outside 2f out: nr a factor* **7/1**
400- **7** *1 1/2* **Gouray Girl (IRE)**[82] 7826 6-8-7 **80**..........[1] TomEaves 4 52
(Brian Ellison) *dwlt: a towards rr* **25/1**
0-20 **8** *7* **Thunderball**[3] 584 7-9-0 **87**..........(p) IanMongan 3 41
(Scott Dixon) *slt ld: hdd 1/2-way: rdn along wl over 2f out: sn wknd* **10/1**
/50- **9** *8* **Red Aggressor (IRE)**[153] 6143 4-9-3 **90**.......... FrederikTylicki 5 23
(Clive Brittain) *chsd ldrs: rdn wl over 2f out: sn wknd* **20/1**
1m 27.97s (-2.33) **Going Correction** -0.025s/f (Stan) **9** Ran SP% **119.8**
Speed ratings (Par 107): **112,111,105,103,99 96,94,86,77**
toteswingers 1&2 £5.70, 2&3 £2.90, 1&3 £4.60 CSF £29.44 CT £74.16 TOTE £11.60: £2.40, £1.70, £1.20; EX 34.20 Trifecta £123.30 Pool: £3433.50 - 20.87 winning units..
Owner Paul J Dixon **Bred** G And Mrs Middlebrook **Trained** Babworth, Notts
FOCUS
A decent Fibresand handicap, run at a good pace, and the front pair pulled clear.

622 CORAL.CO.UK H'CAP 2m (F)
3:50 (3:50) (Class 5) (0-75,74) 4-Y-0+ **£2,587** (£770; £384; £192) **Stalls** Low

Form RPR
406- **1** **Kazbow (IRE)**[71] 7972 7-9-10 **72**..........(t) GrahamLee 5 80
(Richard Ford) *trckd ldr: cl up 1/2-way: led over 4f out: rdn 2f out: pushed out and styd on wl ins fnl f* **4/1**[2]
234- **2** *1 3/4* **Tartan Jura**[54] 8191 5-9-12 **74**..........(b) JoeFanning 1 80
(Mark Johnston) *trckd ldng pair: pushed along and outpcd 6f out: rdn and hdwy to chse wnr over 3f out: drvn wl over 1f out: kpt on ins fnl f* **4/5**[1]
302- **3** *30* **Inside Knowledge (USA)**[47] 7710 7-8-7 **55** oh4..........(b) LukeMorris 4 25
(Garry Woodward) *led: jnd 1/2-way: rdn along and hdd over 4f out: drvn over 3f out: outpcd fr over 2f out* **7/1**
4 *5* **Almadan (IRE)**[92] 5-9-7 **69**..........(t) PaddyAspell 3 33
(Ferdy Murphy, France) *s.i.s: sn in tch: rdn along 6f out: outpcd fnl 4f* **20/1**
00-4 **5** *5* **Lifetime (IRE)**[9] 40 5-9-11 **73**.......... DaleSwift 2 31
(Brian Ellison) *in rr: pushed along over 6f out: rdn 4f out: sn outpcd and bhd* **9/2**[3]
3m 41.33s (-4.17) **Going Correction** -0.025s/f (Stan) **5** Ran SP% **111.0**
Speed ratings (Par 103): **109,108,93,90,88**
CSF £7.79 TOTE £3.10: £2.40, £1.10; EX 9.40 Trifecta £23.50 Pool: £2908.94 - 92.83 winning units..
Owner The Most Wanted Partnership **Bred** Airlie Stud **Trained** Garstang, Lancs
FOCUS
This staying handicap was exhausting to watch.

623 POKER AT CORAL.CO.UK H'CAP 7f (F)
4:20 (4:20) (Class 6) (0-65,64) 3-Y-O **£1,940** (£577; £288; £144) **Stalls** Low

Form RPR
601- **1** **Apache Rising**[98] 7606 3-9-1 **58**.......... TomEaves 4 61
(Bryan Smart) *sn led: jnd and rdn 2f out: drvn and hdd ins fnl f: sn edgd rt: rallied gamely to ld again nr fin* **5/4**[1]
5-33 **2** *nse* **Gebayl**[11] 470 3-9-3 **60**..........(p) JoeFanning 5 63
(James Tate) *cl up: chal 2f out: sn rdn: styd on to take slt ld ins fnl f: drvn: hdd and no ex nr fin* **7/2**[2]

00-4 **3** *11* **Faither**[12] 459 3-8-11 **54**....(p) ShaneKelly 6 28
(Keith Dalgleish) *dwlt: sn trcking ldrs on outer: effrt over 2f out: rdn wl over 1f out: sn one pce* **12/1**

40-5 **4** *3 ¾* **Whitford (IRE)**[29] 204 3-9-3 **60**.... AndreaAtzeni 1 25
(Chris Dwyer) *dwlt: sn trcking ldrs: pushed along on inner and sltly outpcd 3f out: rdn and hdwy 2f out: sn drvn and btn* **5/1**[3]

5-51 **5** *3* **Roland**[21] 328 3-9-7 **64**....(b) GrahamLee 2 21
(Kevin Ryan) *cl up: rdn 2f out and ev ch tl drvn over 1f out and sn wknd* **5/1**[3]

1m 30.43s (0.13) **Going Correction** -0.025s/f (Stan) 5 Ran SP% **107.7**
Speed ratings (Par 95): **98,97,85,81,77**
CSF £5.52 TOTE £2.10: £1.40, £2.00; EX 5.90 Trifecta £26.80 Pool: £1429.27 - 39.87 winning units..
Owner The Smart Distant Music Partnership **Bred** Southill Stud **Trained** Hambleton, N Yorks

FOCUS
A moderate handicap and the front pair pulled a long way clear of the other trio.

624 CORAL.CO.UK MOBILE BETTING H'CAP 1m 4f (F)
4:50 (4:52) (Class 6) (0-65,65) 4-Y-0+ **£1,940** (£577; £288; £144) **Stalls** Low

Form RPR

1-62 **1** **Goldmadchen (GER)**[7] 528 5-9-4 **62**.... JoeFanning 5 73+
(Keith Dalgleish) *trckd ldrs: smooth hdwy 3f out: chal over 2f out: led wl over 1f out: sn rdn clr: styd on* **7/4**[1]

3-62 **2** *3 ¾* **Day Of Destiny (IRE)**[8] 520 8-9-4 **62**.... JamesSullivan 3 66
(James Given) *cl up on inner: led over 4f out: rdn over 2f out: hdd wl over 1f out: sn drvn and one pce* **2/1**[2]

066- **3** *2 ¾* **Kingaroo (IRE)**[43] 7731 7-9-0 **58**.... LukeMorris 7 58
(Garry Woodward) *slt ld: rdn along over 5f out: hdd over 4f out: cl up and drvn 3f out: kpt on same pce fnl 2f* **7/1**

3-05 **4** *11* **Torero**[8] 520 4-9-4 **65**....(b[1]) GrahamLee 8 47
(Kevin Ryan) *trckd ldng pair: cl up on outer 5f out: rdn along 3f out: wknd 2f out* **6/1**[3]

606/ **5** *3 ¾* **Calculating (IRE)**[411] 7914 9-8-13 **62**.... LeeNewnes(5) 6 38
(Mark Usher) *a in rr: pushed along and outpcd fr 1/2-way* **25/1**

2m 42.43s (1.43) **Going Correction** -0.025s/f (Stan)
WFA 4 from 5yo+ 3lb 5 Ran SP% **100.3**
Speed ratings (Par 101): **94,91,89,82,79**
CSF £4.47 TOTE £2.10: £1.20, £1.30; EX 3.50 Trifecta £975.00 Part won. Pool: £1300.11 - 0.07 winning units..
Owner Keith Dalgleish **Bred** Gestut Gorlsdorf **Trained** Carluke, S Lanarks
■ Rano Pano was withdrawn (14/1, ref to ent stalls). Deduct 5p in the £ under R4.

FOCUS
A moderate middle-distance handicap, run at a fair pace.
T/Jkpt: Not won. T/Plt: £83.10 to £1 stake. Pool of £61955.21 - 543.94 winning tickets. T/Qpdt: £5.10 to a £1 stake. Pool of £5374.38 - 770.76 winning tickets. JR

529 KEMPTON (A.W) (R-H)
Wednesday, February 13

OFFICIAL GOING: Standard
Wind: Brisk, across (away from stands) Weather: Overcast, cold; first race run in a blizzard

625 WIN BIG WITH BETDAQ MULTIPLES APPRENTICE H'CAP 1m 2f (P)
5:00 (5:01) (Class 7) (0-50,55) 4-Y-0+ **£1,455** (£433; £216; £108) **Stalls** Low

Form RPR

0-05 **1** **Time Square (FR)**[27] 238 6-9-2 **50**.... JoeyHaynes(5) 7 59
(Tony Carroll) *t.k.h: w ldrs: led after 4f: clr over 3f out: urged along and looked vulnerable fnl f: hld on* **14/1**

0-26 **2** *½* **Angelena Ballerina (IRE)**[8] 522 6-9-0 **48**....(v) JordanVaughan(5) 12 56
(Sean Curran) *hld up in rr: prog to go 3rd 2f out: bmpd along to chse wnr 1f out: clsd 100yds out: effrt flattened out nr fin* **11/2**

-405 **3** *½* **May Boy**[8] 522 7-8-13 **45**.... PhilipPrince(3) 2 52
(Ron Hodges) *hld up in midfield: prog to chse wnr jst over 2f out to 1f out: kpt on same pce fnl f* **5/1**[3]

50-1 **4** *1 ½* **Lytham (IRE)**[7] 530 12-9-5 **51** 6ex.... RyanTate(3) 13 55
(Tony Carroll) *hld up in rr: effrt and v wd bnd 2f out: styd on to take 4th ins fnl f: no ch but nrst fin* **7/2**[1]

0-50 **5** *5* **Bubbly Braveheart (IRE)**[16] 417 6-9-3 **49**....(p) GaryPhillips(3) 3 43
(Pat Phelan) *led 4f: chsd wnr tl wknd jst over 2f out* **9/2**[2]

00-0 **6** *1* **Smirfy's Silver**[36] 110 9-9-0 **46**.... RobertTart(3) 8 38
(Michael Mullineaux) *racd wd in midfield: effrt and wdst of all bnd 2f out: lost grnd and no ch after* **50/1**

6-00 **7** *1 ¾* **Querido (GER)**[4] 587 9-9-1 **47**....(vt) NicoleNordblad(3) 11 36
(Paddy Butler) *s.s: hld up in last: pushed along over 2f out: nvr on terms* **10/1**

-004 **8** *2* **Nurse Dominatrix (IRE)**[6] 545 4-8-9 **46**.... LisaTodd(7) 1 31
(Richard Guest) *trckd ldrs: cl up over 2f out: sn pushed along and wknd* **33/1**

650- **9** *½* **Firefly**[162] 5917 4-8-12 **45**.... IanBurns(3) 9 29
(John Weymes) *broke out of front of stalls bef s: wl in rr: prog on outer fr 1/2-way to chse ldrs 3f out: wknd 2f out* **16/1**

30-0 **10** *12* **Mayan Flight (IRE)**[42] 9 5-8-12 **48**.... AidenBlakemore(7) 4 8
(Tony Carroll) *chsd ldrs tl wknd rapidly 3f out: t.o* **20/1**

5-02 **11** *4* **Brave Decision**[7] 530 6-9-1 **47**.... JakePayne(3) 5
(Suzy Smith) *plld hrd: prom to over 3f out: wknd rapidly: t.o* **6/1**

2m 7.14s (-0.86) **Going Correction** -0.05s/f (Stan)
WFA 4 from 5yo+ 1lb 11 Ran SP% **118.0**
Speed ratings (Par 97): **101,100,100,99,95 94,92,91,90,81 78**
toteswingers 1&2 £13.50, 1&3 £14.50, 2&3 £5.00 CSF £88.03 CT £448.06 TOTE £23.50: £4.30, £2.20, £1.70; EX 162.50 Trifecta £801.30 Pool: £2,075.13 - 1.94 winning units..
Owner M S Cooke **Bred** Mme Therese Bouche & Isabelle Roussel **Trained** Cropthorne, Worcs

FOCUS
There was a steady early pace here.

626 BACK OR LAY AT BETDAQ.COM H'CAP 1m 2f (P)
5:30 (5:30) (Class 6) (0-60,60) 4-Y-0+ **£1,940** (£577; £216; £216) **Stalls** Low

Form RPR

-466 **1** **Silkee Supreme**[10] 508 4-9-2 **56**....(b) SeanLevey 9 64
(Richard Hannon) *s.s: hld up in rr: smooth prog 3f out: rdn to cl on ldrs 1f out: r.o to ld last 75yds* **14/1**

0605 **2** *½* **Penbryn (USA)**[10] 508 6-9-3 **56**.... SebSanders 12 63
(Nick Littmoden) *trckd ldrs: prog over 2f out: drvn and clsd to ld ins fnl f: hdd and outpcd last 75yds* **12/1**

-315 **3** *1 ¼* **Spirit Of Gondree (IRE)**[15] 435 5-9-7 **60**....(b) RobertWinston 2 68+
(Milton Bradley) *stdd s: hld up in 11th and wl off the pce: prog over 2f out: clsng on ldrs whn nowhere to go on inner and stopped in trcks jst over 1f out: plld out and only 7th ins fnl f: r.o wl nr fin* **8/1**

50-5 **3** *dht* **Landesherr (GER)**[42] 9 6-9-4 **57**....(p) AdamKirby 6 62
(Steve Gollings) *stdd s: hld up towards rr: prog over 2f out: rdn and cl up bhd ldrs over 1f out: styd on same pce* **4/1**[2]

00/0 **5** *1* **Gracchus (USA)**[14] 439 7-9-7 **60**....(t) DavidProbert 4 63
(Tony Carroll) *trckd ldrs: wnt 2nd jst over 2f out: drvn ahd over 1f out: hdd & wknd ins fnl f* **20/1**

030- **6** *¾* **Tallevu (IRE)**[53] 8229 4-9-1 **55**.... EddieAhern 5 56
(Noel Chance) *prom: rdn and nt qckn wl over 1f out: kpt on same pce after* **8/1**

4-06 **7** *1 ¾* **Menadati (USA)**[20] 348 5-9-5 **58**.... WilliamCarson 11 56
(Peter Hiatt) *led: drvn over 2f out: hdd & wknd over 1f out* **7/1**[3]

0-00 **8** *½* **Legal Legacy**[18] 403 7-9-6 **59**.... AmirQuinn 1 56
(Richard Rowe) *s.s: hld up in detached last and wl off the pce: no prog 2f out: pushed along and kpt on fr over 1f out: no ch* **33/1**

1-02 **9** *4 ½* **Norwegian Reward (IRE)**[6] 545 5-9-4 **57**.... JimCrowley 3 45
(Michael Wigham) *t.k.h: prom: chsd ldr 3f out tl hung lft and wd bnd jst over 2f out: wknd* **5/2**[1]

660- **10** *½* **Flying Phoenix**[69] 8010 5-8-11 **50**.... KellyHarrison 10 37
(Dai Burchell) *chsd ldr to 3f out: wknd qckly* **50/1**

-406 **11** *1 ¼* **Shelovestobouggie**[19] 375 5-8-13 **52**....(t) ShaneKelly 8 36
(Mark Brisbourne) *a towards rr: no prog over 2f out: no ch after* **33/1**

0061 **12** *5* **Sir Dylan**[13] 455 4-9-4 **58**.... LukeMorris 7 32
(Ronald Harris) *chsd ldrs: hanging lft and reminder 4f out: wknd 3f out* **12/1**

2m 6.92s (-1.08) **Going Correction** -0.05s/f (Stan)
WFA 4 from 5yo+ 1lb 12 Ran SP% **117.9**
Speed ratings (Par 101): **102,101,100,100,99 99,97,97,93,93 92,88**PL: Landesherr: £0.70, Spirit Of Gondree: £1.20. T/C: SS&P&SOG£722.26, SS&P&L £402.59. toteswingers 1&2 £12.80, 1&SOG £6.90, 1&L £5.70 2&SOG £8.50, 2&L £4.50 CSF £163.88 TOTE £20.10: £5.80, £2.40; EX 127.70 TRIFECTA Pool: £2,034.64 - SS/P/SOG £693.1027 Owner.

FOCUS
It paid to be ridden with a bit of patience here.

627 BETDAQ MOBILE APPS H'CAP 5f (P)
6:00 (6:00) (Class 5) (0-75,75) 4-Y-0+ **£2,587** (£770; £384; £192) **Stalls** Low

Form RPR

2115 **1** **Picansort**[4] 583 6-9-7 **75**....(b) ShaneKelly 6 86
(Peter Crate) *trckd ldrs: wnt 2nd wl over 1f out: drvn to ld 150yds out: steadily drew clr* **4/1**[2]

41-4 **2** *2* **Novabridge**[35] 124 5-9-1 **69**....(b) AdamKirby 1 73
(Neil Mulholland) *drvn furiously to ld on inner after 100yds: hdd and outpcd last 150yds* **10/1**

6-00 **3** *1* **Bubbly Ballerina**[31] 196 4-9-0 **75**.... RobertTart(7) 2 75
(Alan Bailey) *s.s: hld up in last: prog on inner over 1f out: drvn and styd on to take 3rd ins fnl f: no threat to wnr* **9/2**[3]

1-64 **4** *nk* **Hot Sugar (USA)**[13] 453 4-8-11 **65**.... AndrewMullen 4 64
(Michael Appleby) *trckd ldng pair on outer: quite wd bnd 2f out and nt qckn sn after: styd on again fnl f* **16/1**

00-5 **5** *1 ¼* **Quality Art (USA)**[35] 113 5-9-2 **70**.... EddieAhern 9 65
(Richard Guest) *trckd ldrs: rdn and nt qckn wl over 1f out: fdd fnl f* **10/1**

6-13 **6** *2* **Alnoomaas (IRE)**[19] 372 4-8-13 **74**.... PhilipPrince(7) 5 61
(Luke Dace) *racd wd: trckd ldrs: lost grnd bnd 2f out: nt qckn after and sn btn* **2/1**[1]

-133 **7** *shd* **Roy's Legacy**[28] 232 4-9-5 **73**....(t) DavidProbert 3 60
(Shaun Harris) *led 100yds: chsd ldr to wl over 1f out: wknd* **7/1**

-101 **8** *4 ½* **Charming (IRE)**[13] 448 4-8-13 **67**....(e) SebSanders 8 38
(Olivia Maylam) *racd wdst of all: in tch tl lost grnd bnd 2f out: wknd* **16/1**

59.48s (-1.02) **Going Correction** -0.05s/f (Stan) 8 Ran SP% **114.0**
Speed ratings (Par 103): **106,102,101,100,98 95,95,88**
toteswingers 1&2 £6.10, 1&3 £4.60, 2&3 £10.10 CSF £42.55 CT £187.44 TOTE £4.40: £1.70, £2.50, £2.30; EX 26.20 Trifecta £61.30 Pool: £1,627.67 - 19.90 winning units..
Owner Peter Crate **Bred** Miss Brooke Sanders **Trained** Newdigate, Surrey

FOCUS
The first three all saved ground by hugging the rail into the straight.

628 BETDAQ CASINO GAMES H'CAP 6f (P)
6:30 (6:32) (Class 5) (0-75,75) 3-Y-O **£1,678** (£1,678; £384; £192) **Stalls** Low

Form RPR

253- **1** **Indian Affair**[81] 7866 3-8-5 **66**.... PhilipPrince(7) 2 68
(Milton Bradley) *racd freely: disp thrght: stdy pce tl over 2f out: kpt on wl fnl f* **5/1**[2]

1-23 **1** *dht* **Katy Spirit (IRE)**[20] 357 3-8-8 **62**.... LiamKeniry 9 64
(Michael Blanshard) *racd freely: disp thrght: stdy pce tl over 2f out: kpt on wl fnl f* **20/1**

1- **3** *½* **Studfarmer**[282] 1904 3-9-0 **68**.... AdamKirby 1 68
(David Evans) *dwlt: sn in 6th: drvn and styd on fr 2f out: wnt 3rd ins fnl f: nvr quite able to chal* **14/1**

2121 **4** *¾* **Windforpower (IRE)**[7] 531 3-9-3 **71** 6ex....(be) LukeMorris 5 69
(Ronald Harris) *t.k.h: trckd ldng pair: rdn and kpt trying for run between them fr over 1f out but no gap: one pce ins fnl f* **6/1**[3]

0-31 **5** *1* **Sand Boy (IRE)**[16] 416 3-9-7 **75**.... RobertWinston 8 73
(Charles Hills) *t.k.h: trckd ldng pair on outer: rdn 2f out: trying to cl whn edgd rt then sltly impeded jst ins fnl f: wl hld after* **10/11**[1]

630- **6** *1* **Forceful Flame**[61] 8103 3-9-0 **68**.... AndreaAtzeni 7 60
(Robert Eddery) *dwlt: hld up in last in steadily run event: nt qckn whn pce lifted over 2f out: kpt on fnl f: no ch* **33/1**

355- **7** *hd* **Miako (USA)**[47] 8274 3-8-8 **62**.... AndrewMullen 6 53
(Michael Appleby) *t.k.h: hld up in 5th: nt qckn whn pce lifted over 2f out: no imp after* **12/1**

055- **8** *1 ¾* **Claude Greenwood**[75] 7932 3-8-12 **66**.... HayleyTurner 3 51
(David Simcock) *t.k.h: hld up in rr in steadily run event: nt qckn whn pce lifted over 2f out: nvr on terms after* **12/1**

040- **9** *1 ¼* **Echo Brava**[155] 6114 3-9-2 **70**.... IanMongan 10 51
(Luke Dace) *hld up in last trio in steadily run event: nt qckn whn pce lifted over 2f out: wknd fnl f* **20/1**

1m 14.17s (1.07) **Going Correction** -0.05s/f (Stan) 9 Ran SP% **117.9**
Speed ratings (Par 97): **90,90,89,88,87 85,85,83,81**WIN: Indian Affair £3.40, Katy Spirit £6.30; PLACE: IA £2.50, KS £3.30, S £4.60; EXACTA: IA&KS £50.70, KS&IA £40.70; CSF IA&KS £50.12, KS&IA £58.31. T/C: IA&KS&S £662.48, KS&IA&S £739.91. totewingers IA&KS £18.00, KS&S £18.40, IA&S £7.10.: £027, £Owner, £A D Jones, £BredAllevamento Pian Di Neve Srl Trained Trifecta £Upper Lambourn, Berks.
Owner J M Bradley **Bred** Mette Campbell-Andenaes **Trained** Sedbury, Gloucs

FOCUS
There wasn't a hectic early pace here and it was an advantage to race prominently. The dead-heaters duelled all the way up the straight.

629 KEMPTON.CO.UK H'CAP — 7f (P)
7:00 (7:00) (Class 4) (0-85,84) 4-Y-0+ — **£4,690** (£1,395; £697; £348) **Stalls** Low

Form — RPR

-231 **1** **Light From Mars**[14] 443 8-9-7 **84** .... LukeMorris 2 — 91
(Ronald Harris) *trckd ldng pair: wnt 2nd on inner 2f out: drvn ahd over 1f out: hrd pressed after: hld on wl* **13/8**[1]

-611 **2** *hd* **Polar Kite (IRE)**[19] 370 5-9-3 **80** .... RobertWinston 5 — 86
(Sean Curran) *hld up in last pair: prog over 2f out: rdn to chal jst over 1f out: upsides and looked likeliest wnr ins fnl f: nt qckn last 75yds* **9/4**[2]

1-03 **3** *hd* **Silverware (USA)**[18] 400 5-9-1 **78** .... TomEaves 1 — 84
(Kristin Stubbs) *led at gd pce: drvn and hdd over 1f out: rallied and nrly upsides ins fnl f: kpt on wl but lost 2nd* **10/1**

204- **4** *2 ¾* **Afkar (IRE)**[121] 7113 5-9-0 **77** .... ChrisCatlin 6 — 75
(Clive Brittain) *chsd ldr to 2f out: sn one pce u.p* **8/1**

1115 **5** *½* **Al's Memory (IRE)**[18] 400 4-9-6 **83** .... AdamKirby 4 — 80
(David Evans) *chsd ldrs in 4th: rdn over 2f out: outpcd wl over 1f out: no imp after* **6/1**[3]

520- **6** *¾* **Ocean Legend (IRE)**[158] 6040 8-8-12 **75** .... MichaelO'Connell 3 — 70
(Tony Carroll) *hld up in last pair: rdn 2f out: no prog and wl hld over 1f out* **14/1**

310- **7** *9* **Brocklebank (IRE)**[44] 8306 4-9-2 **79** .... (v[1]) JimCrowley 7 — 50
(Simon Dow) *racd on outer in last trio: pushed along 1/2-way: wknd over 2f out* **12/1**

1m 24.96s (-1.04) **Going Correction** -0.05s/f (Stan) **7** Ran SP% **117.7**
Speed ratings (Par 105): **103,102,102,99,98 97,87**
toteswingers 1&2 £1.10, 1&3 £2.90, 2&3 £4.10 CSF £5.76 CT £26.34 TOTE £2.90: £2.20, £2.10; EX 6.90 Trifecta £27.50 Pool: £1,557.80 - 42.61 winning units..
Owner Mrs N Macauley **Bred** Harts Farm And Stud **Trained** Earlswood, Monmouths

FOCUS
Once again the first three raced on the inside rail throughout.

630 KEMPTON FOR WEDDINGS H'CAP (DIV I) — 1m (P)
7:30 (7:30) (Class 6) (0-55,55) 4-Y-0+ — **£1,940** (£577; £288; £144) **Stalls** Low

Form — RPR

1-32 **1** **Reasons Unknown (IRE)**[31] 198 5-9-6 **54** .... ShaneKelly 4 — 63+
(Thomas McLaughlin, Ire) *hld up in last trio: stdy prog gng strly fr 2f out: wnt 2nd 1f out: drvn to ld last 100yds: hld on wl* **3/1**[1]

00/1 **2** *shd* **Commercial (IRE)**[28] 220 5-9-5 **53** .... FergusSweeney 6 — 62
(Jamie Osborne) *led: untrbld in front and travelled wl: shkn up 2f out: hdd last 100yds: fought bk wl but jst hld* **9/2**[3]

416 **3** *1 ½* **Litmus (USA)**[10] 510 4-9-3 **51** .... (b) HayleyTurner 2 — 57
(Simon Dow) *chsd ldr: rdn over 2f out: lost 2nd 1f out: one pce after* **7/2**[2]

0-44 **4** *½* **Byrd In Hand (IRE)**[7] 530 6-8-12 **46** .... SeanLevey 5 — 50
(John Bridger) *trckd ldng pair: drvn to dispute 2nd fr wl over 1f out tl one pce fnl f* **5/1**

-405 **5** *hd* **Gallantry**[20] 347 11-9-4 **52** .... JimmyQuinn 3 — 56
(Paul Howling) *trckd ldrs: rdn and effrt on inner over 2f out: one pce fr over 1f out* **16/1**

0-00 **6** *2 ¾* **Rigid**[14] 441 6-8-12 **46** .... DavidProbert 8 — 44
(Tony Carroll) *stdd after s and hld up towards rr: clsd on ldrs 2f out: jst pushed along fr over 1f out: fdd fnl f* **16/1**

14-1 **7** *1* **Ermyntrude**[21] 334 6-9-7 **55** .... (v) IanMongan 10 — 50
(Pat Phelan) *prom on outer: drvn over 2f out: sn lost pl and steadily wknd* **5/1**

340/ **8** *1 ¼* **Anrheg**[469] 7229 5-9-3 **51** .... KellyHarrison 1 — 43
(Dai Burchell) *hld up in rr: plld out over 2f out: reminder over 1f out: nvr involved* **66/1**

0-00 **9** *¾* **Doctor Hilary**[14] 440 11-8-5 **46** oh1 .... (v) PhilipPrince[(7)] 9 — 37
(Mark Hoad) *chsd ldrs: rdn over 2f out: fdd wl over 1f out* **50/1**

130- **10** *14* **High Five Prince (IRE)**[132] 6814 4-9-5 **53** .... RobertWinston 11 — 12
(Milton Bradley) *t.k.h: hld up and r wd: wknd over 2f out: t.o* **20/1**

00-0 **11** *9* **Murfreesboro**[12] 475 10-9-7 **55** .... AdamKirby 7
(Raymond York) *hld up but reminders after 1f: nvr gng wl and sn bhd: t.o* **25/1**

1m 40.24s (0.44) **Going Correction** -0.05s/f (Stan) **11** Ran SP% **122.6**
Speed ratings (Par 101): **95,94,93,92,92 89,88,87,86,72 63**
toteswingers 1&2 £5.00, 1&3 £3.30, 2&3 £6.90 CSF £16.97 CT £51.03 TOTE £4.40: £1.10, £3.30, £1.40; EX 21.00 Trifecta £88.80 Pool: £1,321.62 - 11.15 winning units..
Owner Andrew Stinchon **Bred** Martyn J McEnery **Trained** Rathmullan, Co Donegal

FOCUS
They seemed to go a fair gallop here and, while the second and third were in the first two places for much of the race, the winner came from well off the gallop.

631 KEMPTON FOR WEDDINGS H'CAP (DIV II) — 1m (P)
8:00 (8:00) (Class 6) (0-55,55) 4-Y-0+ — **£1,940** (£577; £288; £144) **Stalls** Low

Form — RPR

2-03 **1** **Flamborough Breeze**[21] 334 4-9-7 **55** .... (t) GeorgeBaker 4 — 68
(Ed Vaughan) *hld up in 9th: smooth prog on inner 2f out: swept into the ld over 1f out: reminders fnl f but wl on top nr fin: quite impressive* **13/2**[3]

6-65 **2** *2* **Athletic**[10] 510 4-9-5 **53** .... (v) EddieAhern 8 — 60
(J R Jenkins) *t.k.h: hld up in midfield: prog 2f out: drvn to go 2nd jst ins fnl f: no ch w wnr* **10/1**

525- **3** *hd* **Thane Of Cawdor (IRE)**[110] 7385 4-9-5 **53** .... LiamKeniry 5 — 60
(Joseph Tuite) *chsd ldrs: rdn over 2f out: styd on fr over 1f out: pressed runner-up nr fin* **9/4**[1]

35-0 **4** *hd* **Finlodex**[22] 320 6-9-7 **55** .... ShaneKelly 6 — 61
(Murty McGrath) *hld up in midfield: rdn 2f out: styd on to press for a pl fnl f* **7/2**[2]

0-60 **5** *½* **Rapid Water**[21] 335 7-9-5 **53** .... (b) LukeMorris 9 — 58
(Pat Eddery) *hld up in last trio: tried to creep clsr fr 2f out jst as wnr was cruising to the front: ch of a pl 1f out: limited rspnse whn rdn* **16/1**

0-02 **6** *shd* **Compton Crofter**[14] 441 4-8-7 **46** .... (t) NicoleNordblad[(5)] 10 — 51
(Hans Adielsson) *s.s: hld up in detached last: plld out wd over 2f out: prog over 1f out: pushed along and styd on fnl f: nrst fin* **9/1**

0-00 **7** *2* **Salient**[22] 320 9-8-12 **46** .... (b) SebSanders 1 — 47
(Michael Attwater) *led: stretched on fr 1/2-way: hdd over 1f out and no ch w wnr: wknd ins fnl f* **16/1**

40-2 **8** *¾* **Exopuntia**[21] 335 7-9-4 **52** .... AdamBeschizza 2 — 51
(Julia Feilden) *pressed ldr: hd to one side over 2f out: lost 2nd and fdd wl over 1f out* **8/1**

-132 **9** *1 ¾* **Teen Ager (FR)**[14] 440 9-9-3 **51** .... (p) JimmyQuinn 3 — 46+
(Paul Burgoyne) *trckd ldng pair: gng strly over 2f out: nt qckn wl over 1f out: wknd fnl f* **7/1**

-055 **10** *18* **Sun Dream**[13] 456 6-8-12 **46** oh1 .... MichaelO'Connell 7
(Tony Carroll) *prom on outer: rdn over 3f out: sn wknd: t.o* **50/1**

1m 39.31s (-0.49) **Going Correction** -0.05s/f (Stan) **10** Ran SP% **122.8**
Speed ratings (Par 101): **100,98,97,97,97 97,95,94,92,74**
toteswingers 1&2 £10.20, 1&3 £4.60, 2&3 £8.30 CSF £73.48 CT £195.21 TOTE £3.80: £2.50, £4.40, £1.70; EX 83.30 Trifecta £428.70 Pool: £1,246.12 - 2.17 winning units..
Owner A M Pickering **Bred** Windymains Farm Ltd **Trained** Newmarket, Suffolk

FOCUS
A good pace wasn't guaranteed on paper but as it turned out Salient was taken on by Exopuntia up front and the race was set up for a closer. The time was 0.93sec faster than the first division.

632 RACING PLUS CHASE DAY 23.02.13 H'CAP — 1m (P)
8:30 (8:30) (Class 6) (0-65,65) 3-Y-O — **£1,940** (£577; £288; £144) **Stalls** Low

Form — RPR

1-43 **1** **Byroness**[10] 506 3-9-0 **65** .... RyanTate[(7)] 2 — 68
(Heather Main) *t.k.h: trckd ldng pair: wnt 2nd 2f out: shkn up to cl and ld jst ins fnl f: edgd lft after but a holding on* **8/1**

253- **2** *½* **Beau Select (IRE)**[63] 8072 3-9-7 **65** .... AndreaAtzeni 5 — 67
(Robert Eddery) *hld up in 4th: rdn and no prog over 2f out: styd on fr over 1f out: tk 2nd last 75yds and clsd on wnr fin* **4/1**[3]

00-6 **3** *1* **World Freight Girl**[21] 336 3-8-7 **51** oh6 .... (b[1]) JimmyQuinn 6 — 51
(Dean Ivory) *hld up in last: rdn over 2f out: styd on fr over 1f out to take 3rd nr fin: no threat to wnr* **66/1**

3-45 **4** *shd* **Rainford Glory (IRE)**[18] 411 3-8-9 **53** .... DavidProbert 3 — 52
(David Simcock) *hld up in 5th: pushed along over 2f out: rdn and styd on fnl f to press for 3rd nr fin: nvr cl enough to chal* **10/1**

-412 **5** *nk* **Hidden Link**[16] 419 3-9-6 **64** .... LukeMorris 4 — 63
(Ronald Harris) *led: rdn 2f out: hdd jst ins fnl f: wknd last 100yds* **3/1**[2]

333- **6** *2 ½* **Scepticism (USA)**[114] 7289 3-9-2 **60** .... FrannyNorton 7 — 53
(Mark Johnston) *trckd ldr: rdn over 2f out: sn lost 2nd and grad wknd* **5/4**[1]

1m 40.03s (0.23) **Going Correction** -0.05s/f (Stan) **6** Ran SP% **111.1**
Speed ratings (Par 95): **96,95,94,94,94 91**
toteswingers 1&2 £11.60, 1&3 £11.60, 2&3 £48.40 CSF £38.40 TOTE £9.40: £3.20, £3.50; EX 42.10 Trifecta £598.60 Pool: £1,806.54 - 2.26 winning units..
Owner Les Chevaliers **Bred** J P M Main **Trained** Kingston Lisle, Oxon
■ Stewards' Enquiry : Andrea Atzeni two-day ban: used whip above permitted level (Feb 27-28)

FOCUS
Not for the first time on the night those that stuck to the inside rail proved to be at an advantage.
T/Jkpt: Not won. T/Plt: £380.90 to a £1 stake. Pool: £72,903.36 - 139.69 winning tickets T/Qpdt: £46.10 to a £1 stake. Pool: £8,855.46 - 142.10 winning tickets JN

579 LINGFIELD (L-H)
Wednesday, February 13

OFFICIAL GOING: Standard
Wind: fresh, behind Weather: overcast, dry

633 BET ON YOUR MOBILE AT BLUESQ.COM (S) STKS — 1m 2f (P)
1:30 (1:31) (Class 6) 4-6-Y-0 — **£2,045** (£603; £302) **Stalls** Low

Form — RPR

0-24 **1** **Gunner Will (IRE)**[10] 508 4-8-12 60 .... FergusSweeney 5 — 64
(Jamie Osborne) *t.k.h: chsd ldrs: jnd ldrs 3f out: drvn to ld over 1f out: clr ins fnl f: r.o wl* **4/1**[1]

100- **2** *1 ¾* **Royal Etiquette (IRE)**[19] 8162 6-9-5 64 .... (v) LukeMorris 2 — 66
(Lawney Hill) *bmpd s: t.k.h: hld up in tch in last trio: effrt and carried rt over 1f out: hdwy 1f out: chsd wnr fnl 100yds: kpt on wl but unable to chal* **8/1**

3623 **3** *½* **Divine Rule (IRE)**[10] 510 5-8-13 56 .... (v) JimCrowley 1 — 59
(Laura Mongan) *t.k.h: wnt rt s: hld up in midfield: shuffled bk over 4f out: nt clr run ent fnl 2f: swtchd rt and hdwy 1f out: kpt on u.p: no threat to wnr* **9/2**[2]

6-44 **4** *½* **Syrian**[27] 238 6-8-13 71 .... ShaneKelly 4 — 58
(Thomas McLaughlin, Ire) *t.k.h: hld up wl in tch: effrt and swtchd rt over 1f out: kpt on u.p fnl f: nvr threatened wnr* **4/1**[1]

1026 **5** *1 ½* **Electrician**[7] 540 4-9-4 63 .... (p) DavidProbert 7 — 61
(Tim Pitt) *led tl over 6f out: chsd ldr: ev ch over 2f out: rdn and unable qck w wnr ent fnl f: lost 2nd and wknd fnl 100yds* **4/1**[1]

0-16 **6** *½* **Temuco (IRE)**[15] 433 4-9-4 59 .... (v) AdamKirby 8 — 60
(David Evans) *v.s.a: hld up in rr: swtchd rt and rapid hdwy to ld over 6f out: jnd and rdn over 2f out: hdd over 1f out: wknd ins fnl f* **5/1**[3]

44-3 **7** *2 ½* **Maz**[38] 83 5-8-3 58 .... (p) NatashaEaton[(5)] 3 — 44
(Alan Bailey) *chsd ldr tl over 6f out: chsd ldrs after tl outpcd and rdn 2f out: wknd 1f out: wl hld and edgd rt ins fnl f* **8/1**

000- **8** *7* **Darwinian**[88] 7769 4-8-7 39 .... JimmyQuinn 6 — 30
(Dave Morris) *t.k.h: hld up in tch towards rr: rdn and struggling over 2f out: bhd fnl f* **100/1**

2m 9.06s (2.46) **Going Correction** +0.20s/f (Slow) **8** Ran SP% **118.1**
WFA 4 from 5yo+ 1lb
Speed ratings: **98,96,96,95,94 94,92,86**
toteswingers 1&2 £6.10, 1&3 £3.30, 2&3 £7.00 CSF £37.61 TOTE £5.40: £1.80, £2.50, £1.50; EX 50.40 Trifecta £194.50 Pool: £2637.50 - 10.16 winning units..There was no bid for the winner.
Owner J A Osborne **Bred** Lord Harrington **Trained** Upper Lambourn, Berks

FOCUS
A competitive if only modest seller, run at a steady pace.

634 YOUR GUIDE TO LINGFIELD AT LINGFIELDRACECOURSETIPS.CO.UK H'CAP — 1m 2f (P)
2:00 (2:00) (Class 6) (0-60,61) 3-Y-O — **£2,045** (£603; £302) **Stalls** Low

Form — RPR

0-05 **1** **Gabrial The Duke (IRE)**[30] 212 3-9-1 53 .... JimCrowley 4 — 61+
(David Simcock) *hld up in tch in last pair: effrt and nt clr run over 1f out: swtchd lft and hdwy 1f out: led fnl 75yds: sn in command: r.o wl* **9/4**[1]

-641 **2** *1* **Poetic Verse**[8] 527 3-9-9 61 6ex .... AndreaAtzeni 2 — 65
(Rod Millman) *chsd ldr for 2f: styd chsng ldrs: rdn 3f out: ev ch wl over 1f out: led jst over 1f out: hdd and styd on same pce fnl 75yds* **6/1**

6-43 **3** *hd* **Entrapping**[16] 414 3-9-4 56 .... SeanLevey 5 — 60
(Richard Hannon) *hld up in midfield: sltly hmpd after 1f out: rdn and effrt 2f out: ev ch but racing awkwardly ins fnl f: nt qckn and one pce fnl 100yds* **7/2**[2]

The Form Book Flat, Raceform Ltd, Compton, RG20 6NL.

41-2 **4** *1 ¾* **Close Together (IRE)**[10] 507 3-9-0 59 .... RobertTart(7) 3 59
(Robert Mills) *led but looking arnd in front: wnt rt after 1f out: hdd and rdn over 2f out: led again over 1f out: sn hdd and unable qck: wknd ins fnl f* **9/4**[1]

03-4 **5** *3 ¼* **Sand Grouse**[18] 411 3-9-4 56 .... (b) AdamKirby 7 50
(Marco Botti) *hld up in midfield: sltly hmpd after 1f: hdwy to chse ldr 8f out: led over 2f out: rdn 2f out: hdd and no ex over 1f out: wkng whn short of room ins fnl f* **4/1**[3]

00-3 **6** *10* **Silver Fawn (IRE)**[13] 459 3-8-7 45 .... (p) DuranFentiman 1 19
(John Weymes) *stdd s: t.k.h: hld up in tch in rr: rdn and no hdwy whn racd awkwardly bnd 2f out: wknd over 1f out* **33/1**

2m 9.13s (2.53) **Going Correction** +0.20s/f (Slow) **6** Ran SP% **121.0**
Speed ratings (Par 95): **97,96,96,94,92 84**
toteswingers 1&2 £3.70, 1&3 £2.60, 2&3 £3.30 CSF £18.03 TOTE £3.60: £1.80, £3.60; EX 19.50 Trifecta £93.60 Pool: £1846.08 - 14.78 winning units..
Owner Dr Marwan Koukash **Bred** Old Carhue & Graeng Bloodstock **Trained** Newmarket, Suffolk

FOCUS
There was very little in the way of early pace in this 3yo handicap and it resulted in a messy finish.

635 CROWHURST H'CAP — 2m (P)
2:30 (2:30) (Class 6) (0-60,60) 4-Y-0+ **£2,045** (£603; £302) **Stalls** Low

Form RPR

50-5 **1** **Rollin 'n Tumblin**[42] 12 9-8-10 **46** oh1 .... JimmyQuinn 12 56
(Michael Attwater) *hld up in midfield: hdwy to chse ldr and travelling wl over 2f out: rdn and led over 1f out: clr ins fnl f: pressed and rdn towards fin: a holding on* **9/2**[3]

40-2 **2** *nk* **Broughtons Bandit**[20] 361 6-9-5 **55** .... J-PGuillambert 1 64
(Willie Musson) *hld up in tch in midfield: rdn and effrt to chse ldrs over 2f out: wnt 3rd and swtchd rt over 1f out: chsd wnr ins fnl f: styd on wl and pressing wnr towards fin: nvr quite gng to rch wnr* **7/4**[1]

060/ **3** *2 ¾* **Cecily Parsley**[264] 6445 7-9-5 **55** .... (t) RobertHavlin 11 61
(Hughie Morrison) *in tch in midfield: hdwy to chse ldrs 8f out: pushed along to ld over 3f out: drvn over 2f out: hdd over 1f out: no ex and one pce fnl f* **14/1**

35-2 **4** *6* **On The Feather**[12] 469 7-9-10 **60** .... (b) FergusSweeney 9 59
(Jim Best) *hld up in tch in last trio: rdn and hdwy on outer to chse ldrs wl over 2f out: 4th and no ex over 1f out: wknd fnl f* **5/1**

-060 **5** *2 ¾* **Boston Blue**[16] 418 6-9-5 **55** .... JimCrowley 7 51
(Tony Carroll) *dwlt and rdn along leaving stalls: hld up in tch in last trio: rdn and effrt over 3f out: sme hdwy into modest 5th 2f out: no imp after* **4/1**[2]

-54 **6** *1 ½* **Sing Alana Sing**[15] 432 5-8-3 **46** oh1 .... (t) JakePayne(7) 5 40
(Bill Turner) *chsd ldrs: nt clr run and shuffled bk fr 3f out: modest 7th whn eventually swtchd rt wl over 1f out: no imp* **25/1**

0-00 **7** *20* **Burnbrake**[16] 418 8-8-10 **46** oh1 .... ChrisCatlin 4 16
(Richard Rowe) *in tch in last trio: niggled along 9f out: rdn and lost tch over 2f out: wl bhd fnl f: t.o* **66/1**

64-0 **8** *1 ¼* **If What And Maybe**[4] 579 5-9-1 **51** ow1 .... (p) AdamKirby 8 19
(John Ryan) *led but immediately rdn along: drvn and hdd over 3f out: 6th and wkng 2f out: wl bhd fnl f: t.o* **7/1**

0-00 **9** *5* **Nadia Naes (IRE)**[21] 342 4-8-4 **46** oh1 .... (e) LukeMorris 10
(Roger Ingram) *chsd ldr tl over 3f out: sn rdn and dropped out: wl bhd over 1f out: t.o* **16/1**

4/36 **10** *36* **Polarity**[16] 417 7-9-0 **57** .... NedCurtis(7) 6
(Gerry Enright) *t.k.h: wl in tch in midfield tl dropped to rr 4f out: lost tch 3f out: wl t.o over 1f out: b.b.v* **12/1**

3m 23.17s (-2.53) **Going Correction** +0.20s/f (Slow)
WFA 4 from 5yo+ 6lb **10** Ran SP% **129.3**
Speed ratings (Par 101): **114,113,112,109,108 107,97,96,94,76**
toteswingers 1&2 £3.00, 1&3 £7.80, 2&3 £9.30 CSF £14.33 CT £112.67 TOTE £4.70: £1.60, £1.40, £3.40; EX 21.70 Trifecta £358.10 Pool: £2205.98 - 4.61 winning units..
Owner Canisbay Bloodstock **Bred** Canisbay Bloodstock Ltd **Trained** Epsom, Surrey

FOCUS
A poor staying handicap, run at an honest pace.

636 BLUE SQUARE BET MAIDEN STKS — 7f (P)
3:00 (3:00) (Class 5) 3-Y-0 **£2,726** (£805; £402) **Stalls** Low

Form RPR

5-2 **1** **Jimmy The Snooze (IRE)**[28] 228 3-9-5 0 .... (t) AndreaAtzeni 2 72+
(Stuart Williams) *mde all: rdn and qcknd clr over 1f out: in command and pushed out fnl f: eased cl home* **5/4**[1]

4 **2** *1* **Fearless Lad (IRE)**[11] 492 3-9-5 0 .... (t) HayleyTurner 6 67
(John Best) *pushed along leaving stalls: sn chsng ldrs and t.k.h: chsd wnr over 4f out: rdn and outpcd by wnr over 1f out: styd on but a hld ins fnl f* **4/1**[3]

5 **3** *½* **Botteen (IRE)**[16] 425 3-9-5 0 .... AdamBeschizza 3 66
(William Haggas) *in tch in last pair: swtchd rt and hdwy over 1f out: disputing 2nd and kpt on u.p fnl f* **8/1**

4 *1* **Sharaar (IRE)** 3-9-5 0 .... LukeMorris 5 63+
(Gerard Butler) *rn green and rdn along at times: in tch in last pair: rdn and outpcd over 1f out: rallied and kpt on again ins fnl f: no threat to wnr* **3/1**[2]

0- **5** *6* **Douglas Pasha (IRE)**[123] 7057 3-9-5 0 .... SeanLevey 4 47
(Richard Hannon) *chsd ldr tl over 4f out: rdn and unable qck over 2f out: wknd over 1f out* **8/1**

1m 25.59s (0.79) **Going Correction** +0.20s/f (Slow) **5** Ran SP% **111.7**
Speed ratings (Par 97): **103,101,101,100,93**
CSF £6.72 TOTE £2.20: £1.10, £1.80; EX 3.60 Trifecta £9.70 Pool: £1937.80 - 149.07 winning units..
Owner Eclipse Horse Racing **Bred** L Queally **Trained** Newmarket, Suffolk

FOCUS
A weak maiden.

637 BREATHE SPA AT MARRIOTT LINGFIELD MAIDEN STKS — 1m 5f (P)
3:30 (3:30) (Class 5) 4-Y-0+ **£2,726** (£805; £201; £201) **Stalls** Low

Form RPR

2 **1** **Cousin Khee**[12] 473 6-9-9 0 .... GeorgeBaker 7 77+
(Hughie Morrison) *hld up in tch in midfield: hdwy to join ldrs and wnt clr over 2f out: led over 1f out: in command and edgd lft ins fnl f: comf* **5/4**[1]

/ **2** *1 ¾* **Fulgora**[19] 5-9-4 0 .... SebSanders 6 63
(Brendan Powell) *chsd ldrs: rdn and ev ch over 2f out: unable qck and outpcd over 1f out: no threat to wnr but kpt on to go 2nd again towards fin* **20/1**

25-3 **3** *½* **Luggers Hall (IRE)**[21] 333 5-9-9 70 .... LukeMorris 2 67
(Tony Carroll) *chsd ldrs: clsd on ldrs wl over 3f out: rdn to ld 3f out: hdd and unable qck over 1f out: no threat to wnr and styd on same pce ins fnl f* **6/1**

2-23 **3** *dht* **Harlestone Wood**[18] 397 4-9-5 77 .... (p) IanMongan 8 67+
(Peter Hedger) *stdd and swtchd lft after s: t.k.h: hld up in last trio: clsd over 2f out: rdn and effrt in modest 5th over 1f out: styd on wl ins fnl f: no ch w wnr* **9/4**[2]

22 **5** *2 ¾* **Story Writer**[21] 342 4-9-5 0 .... JimCrowley 5 63
(William Knight) *stdd and swtchd lft after s: hld up in last trio: rdn and hdwy over 2f out: no imp and hung lft over 1f out: stl hanging and no imp ins fnl f* **9/2**[3]

2-56 **6** *3* **Minority Interest**[18] 397 4-9-5 70 .... WilliamCarson 4 58
(Brett Johnson) *stdd s: t.k.h: hld up in last trio: nt clr run over 2f out: hmpd on inner wl over 1f out: no ch after: swtchd rt jst over 1f out: edgd rt and kpt on ins fnl f* **20/1**

0-0 **7** *1 ¼* **Rahy's Promise (USA)**[18] 397 4-9-5 0 .... (t) DavidProbert 1 57?
(Andrew Balding) *hld up in midfield: rdn and struggling over 3f out: wknd 2f out* **50/1**

0/ **8** *¾* **King Of Forces**[586] 3823 4-9-5 0 .... AndreaAtzeni 3 55?
(Denis Quinn) *led tl 3f out: sn struggling u.p: wknd 2f out* **50/1**

2m 53.38s (7.38) **Going Correction** +0.20s/f (Slow)
WFA 4 from 5yo+ 4lb **8** Ran SP% **121.1**
Speed ratings (Par 103): **85,83,83,83,81 80,79,78**PL: LH £0.90, HW £0.50, TRIFECTA: CK/F/LH £81.50, CK/F/HW £69.40, toteswingers CK&F £5.30, CK&LH £1.40, CK&HW £0.80, F&LH £2.90, F&HW £3.00 CSF £33.04 TOTE £2.50: £1.10, £3.80; EX 28.70 TRIFECTA Pool: £4144.06 - CK/F/LH 19.06 winning units, CK/F/HW 22.36 w27 Owner.

FOCUS
An informative, if only low-grade maiden.

638 FALKO REGIONAL AIRCRAFT H'CAP — 1m (P)
4:00 (4:00) (Class 5) (0-70,69) 4-Y-0+ **£2,726** (£805; £402) **Stalls** High

Form RPR

0-26 **1** **Mafi (IRE)**[22] 320 5-8-10 **58** .... (t) RobertHavlin 1 65
(Mark Hoad) *trckd ldrs: swtchd rt and effrt over 1f out: rdn and ev ch 1f out: led ins fnl f: hrd pressed and hld on fnl 100yds* **8/1**

04-3 **2** *hd* **Ellie In The Pink (IRE)**[42] 13 5-9-3 **65** .... IanMongan 3 71
(Pat Phelan) *t.k.h: hld up wl in tch: effrt u.p over 1f out: drvn and ev ch ins fnl f: kpt on but a jst hld* **7/2**[2]

0046 **3** *nk* **Honey Of A Kitten (USA)**[2] 614 5-8-11 **66** .... (v) EoinWalsh(7) 2 71
(David Evans) *hld up in tch in rr: swtchd rt and effrt over 1f out: pressed ldrs ins fnl f: kpt on but hld towards fin* **7/2**[2]

240- **4** *2 ¼* **Manomine**[88] 7768 4-9-1 **63** .... ChrisCatlin 5 63
(Clive Brittain) *chsd ldrs: rdn and pressed ldr 2f out: unable qck u.p 1f out: wknd ins fnl f* **4/1**[3]

-500 **5** *½* **Crowning Star (IRE)**[12] 478 4-9-4 **66** .... JimmyQuinn 6 65
(Gay Kelleway) *led after 1f: rdn wl over 1f out: hdd ins fnl f: no ex and wknd ins fnl f* **8/1**

2-03 **6** *1 ¾* **Zaheeb**[34] 130 5-8-13 **61** .... WilliamCarson 4 56
(Dave Morris) *led for 1f: chsd ldr after: drvn an unable qck ent fnl 2f: wknd fnl f* **11/4**[1]

1m 38.75s (0.55) **Going Correction** +0.20s/f (Slow) **6** Ran SP% **113.3**
Speed ratings (Par 103): **105,104,104,102,101 100**
toteswingers 1&2 £3.40, 1&3 £3.20, 2&3 £2.80 CSF £36.20 TOTE £10.70: £3.30, £2.10; EX 33.60 Trifecta £132.20 Pool: £2250.46 - 12.76 winning units..
Owner Mrs J E Taylor **Bred** Kilboy Estate **Trained** Lewes, E Sussex

FOCUS
A fair handicap, despite the small field, and it served up a thrilling finish.

639 ENOUGH SAID, JUST BET AT BLUESQ.COM H'CAP — 1m 2f (P)
4:30 (4:30) (Class 5) (0-70,70) 4-Y-0+ **£2,726** (£805; £402) **Stalls** Low

Form RPR

-255 **1** **Understory (USA)**[13] 450 6-9-4 **67** .... HayleyTurner 3 73
(Tim McCarthy) *mde all: rdn and clr w rival 2 out: forged ahd u.p 1f out: styd on wl: all out* **12/1**

0/60 **2** *½* **Gaelic Silver (FR)**[16] 420 7-9-7 **70** .... GeorgeBaker 10 75+
(Gary Moore) *stdd and swtchd lft after s: hld up in last trio: rdn and effrt over 1f out: styd on strly ins fnl f: wnt 2nd cl home* **8/1**[3]

6-11 **3** *nk* **Conducting**[18] 403 5-9-7 **70** .... JimmyQuinn 8 74
(Gay Kelleway) *t.k.h: chsd wnr tl 3f out: short of room and sltly outpcd over 2f out: hrd drvn and rallied to chse wnr again wl ins fnl f: kpt on but lost 2nd cl home* **8/1**[3]

30-2 **4** *nk* **Super Duplex**[21] 344 6-9-4 **67** .... IanMongan 9 70
(Pat Phelan) *t.k.h: hld up wl in tch in midfield: hdwy to press ldr and wnt clr over 2f out: rdn wl over 1f out: no ex 1f out: styd on same pce and lost 2 pls wl ins fnl f* **8/1**[3]

-024 **5** *shd* **Dazzling Valentine**[2] 614 5-9-2 **70** .... NatashaEaton(5) 5 73
(Alan Bailey) *chsd ldrs: pushed along and sltly outpcd over 2f out: rallied ent fnl f: kpt on* **5/1**[2]

215- **6** *¾* **Mcvicar**[48] 4578 4-9-3 **67** .... FergusSweeney 2 69
(Alan King) *chsd ldrs: rdn and outpcd over 2f out: rallied u.p ent fnl f: kpt on same pce fnl 100yds* **3/1**[1]

000- **7** *1 ¼* **Smokey Oakey (IRE)**[131] 6639 9-9-4 **70** .... SimonPearce(3) 4 69
(Mark H Tompkins) *hld up in tch in midfield: rdn and effrt over 1f out: kpt on same pce ins fnl f* **33/1**

640- **8** *1* **Whipcrackaway (IRE)**[57] 6146 4-9-5 **69** .... (p) JohnFahy 7 66
(Peter Hedger) *hld up in tch in last trio: rdn and hdwy into midfield 3f out: no imp 2f out: kpt on but no threat to ldrs fnl f* **12/1**

-530 **9** *nk* **Aviso (GER)**[23] 314 9-8-11 **60** .... AndreaAtzeni 6 57
(David Evans) *hld up in tch in midfield: dropped towards rr but stl in tch 4f out: rdn and styd on same pce fr over 1f out* **20/1**

1-22 **10** *1 ¾* **Safwaan**[10] 508 6-8-9 **58** .... JamieMackay 1 51
(Willie Musson) *s.i.s: a in rr: rdn and no imp over 2f out: n.d but plugged on fnl f* **3/1**[1]

2m 9.53s (2.93) **Going Correction** +0.20s/f (Slow)
WFA 4 from 5yo+ 1lb **10** Ran SP% **123.1**
Speed ratings (Par 103): **96,95,95,95,95 94,93,92,92,91**
toteswingers 1&2 £16.80, 1&3 £6.80, 2&3 £12.00 CSF £110.07 CT £833.14 TOTE £18.90: £3.80, £3.20, £2.90; EX 186.30 Trifecta £1504.00 Pool: £2005.44 - 0.63 winning units..
Owner Homecroft Wealth Racing **Bred** Darley **Trained** Godstone, Surrey

FOCUS
Another steadily run affair.

T/Plt: £61.80 to a £1 stake. Pool of £58327.72 - 688.77 winning tickets. T/Qpdt: £4.50 to a £1 stake. Pool of £5350.77 - 867.85 winning tickets. SP

[618]SOUTHWELL (L-H)

Wednesday, February 13

OFFICIAL GOING: Standard

Wind: Moderate across Weather: Sleet and snow showers

640 CASINO AT CORAL.CO.UK H'CAP 6f (F)

1:50 (1:51) (Class 6) (0-65,65) 4-Y-O+ **£1,940** (£577; £288; £144) **Stalls** Low

Form RPR

-411 **1** **M J Woodward**[12] 481 4-9-7 65 JoeFanning 7 74
(Paul Green) *cl up: led wl over 2f out: rdn to chse ldrs over 1f out: kpt on wl towards fin* **3/1**[1]

0501 **2** *½* **George Fenton**[5] 559 4-8-12 63 6ex (v) JoshBaudains(7) 8 70
(Richard Guest) *in rr: hdwy 2f out: rdn over 1f out: styd on wl fnl f* **9/2**[3]

6-13 **3** *1¼* **Romanticize**[5] 560 7-8-13 57 DaleSwift 2 60
(Jason Ward) *chsd ldrs on inner: effrt 2f out and sn rdn: kpt on same pce fnl f* **16/1**

0434 **4** *nse* **Putin (IRE)**[11] 494 5-8-10 54 (bt) MickyFenton 3 57
(Phil McEntee) *slt ld: pushed along 1/2-way and sn hdd: styd cl up: rdn and ev ch over 1f out: drvn and wknd fnl f* **14/1**

-404 **5** *1½* **Greenhead High**[13] 448 5-9-3 61 FrannyNorton 1 59
(David Nicholls) *cl up on inner: effrt over 2f out and sn rdn: swtchd rt and drvn over 1f out: sn one pce* **9/2**[3]

2-32 **6** *1¾* **Rose Garnet (IRE)**[11] 497 5-9-0 58 GrahamLee 4 50
(Tony Carroll) *in tch: hdwy over 2f out: sn rdn and no imp fr over 1f out* **7/2**[2]

0210 **7** *8* **Lord Buffhead**[5] 558 4-9-1 59 (ve) RobbieFitzpatrick 9 26
(Richard Guest) *dwlt: sn swtchd lft to inner: a in rr* **20/1**

200- **8** *3¼* **Orwellian**[60] 8142 4-9-7 65 (e[1]) TomEaves 6 21
(Bryan Smart) *a towards rr: outpcd and bhd fnl 2f* **6/1**

1m 16.8s (0.30) **Going Correction** +0.15s/f (Slow) **8** Ran SP% **115.2**
Speed ratings (Par 101): **104,103,101,101,99 97,86,82**
toteswingers 1&2 £4.20, 1&3 £7.20, 2&3 £13.10 CSF £16.92 CT £184.56 TOTE £3.70: £1.10, £1.90, £4.00; EX 24.50 Trifecta £98.60 Pool: £2637.51 - 20.05 winning units..
Owner E Sciarrillo **Bred** Paul Green **Trained** Lydiate, Merseyside
■ Stewards' Enquiry : Joe Fanning Caution: careless riding.

FOCUS
It was snowing throughout the afternoon and there was a covering on the track. A modest but competitive event.

641 FIND THE BEST ODDS AT BOOKMAKERS.CO.UK MEDIAN AUCTION MAIDEN STKS 1m 4f (F)

2:20 (2:21) (Class 5) 4-6-Y-O **£2,587** (£770; £384; £192) **Stalls** Low

Form RPR

0/4 **1** **Mister Bob (GER)**[18] 397 4-9-5 0 GrahamLee 1 60+
(James Bethell) *trckd ldr: led over 4f out: pushed clr whn rn green and jinked 1 1/2f out: kpt on: readily* **4/7**[1]

-400 **2** *4* **Lea Valley**[16] 418 4-9-0 40 (b[1]) NickyMackay 6 46
(Julia Feilden) *a.p: cl up 4f out: rdn to chal 3f out: drvn 2f out and kpt on same pce* **16/1**

0 **3** *27* **Santorini Sunset**[25] 275 4-9-0 0 FrannyNorton 2
(J R Jenkins) *led: rdn along and hdd over 4f out: drvn wl over 2f out and sn wknd* **14/1**

0 **4** *5* **Princess Kheleyf**[42] 28 4-9-0 0 FrederikTylicki 4
(Geoffrey Oldroyd) *in tch: pushed along 5f out: sn rdn and outpcd fnl 4f* **25/1**

5 *hd* **Sweetie Royale (IRE)**[8] 4-9-0 0 TomEaves 3
(John Wainwright) *trckd ldrs: effrt over 3f out: sn rdn along and wknd* **5/1**[3]

6 *21* **Terntheothercheek**[29] 4-9-0 0 JoeFanning 5
(Jennie Candlish) *s.i.s: rdn along bef 1/2-way: sn outpcd and wl bhd* **9/2**[2]

2m 46.45s (5.45) **Going Correction** +0.15s/f (Slow) **6** Ran SP% **114.9**
Speed ratings: **87,84,66,63,62 48**
toteswingers 1&2 £3.10, 1&3 £3.00, 2&3 £4.80 CSF £12.53 TOTE £1.60: £1.10, £6.10; EX 9.60 Trifecta £61.50 Pool: £2111.71 - 25.72 winning units..
Owner Robert Gibbons **Bred** Newsells Park Stud Ltd **Trained** Middleham Moor, N Yorks

FOCUS
A shocker of a contest.

642 PICK TODAY'S WINNERS AT BOOKMAKERS.CO.UK H'CAP 1m 4f (F)

2:50 (2:50) (Class 5) (0-75,72) 4-Y-O+ **£2,587** (£770; £384; £192) **Stalls** Low

Form RPR

2-40 **1** **Mediterranean Sea (IRE)**[16] 429 7-9-7 72 FrederikTylicki 4 81
(J R Jenkins) *hld up in tch: gd hdwy on outer over 3f out: chal wl over 2f out: sn rdn: led over 1f out: drvn and kpt on wl fnl f* **7/1**

20-3 **2** *nk* **Honest Deal**[34] 144 5-9-5 70 RussKennemore 5 78
(Alan Swinbank) *t.k.h: trckd ldng pair: hdwy and cl up 1/2-way: led over 4f out: rdn along wl over 2f out: drvn and hdd over 1f out: kpt on u.p fnl f* **11/4**[2]

001/ **3** *6* **Masterful Act (USA)**[65] 7579 6-9-2 67 (t) GrahamLee 2 66
(Alan McCabe) *cl up on inner: slt ld after 2f: pushed along and hdd over 4f out: rdn over 3f out: kpt on same pce fnl 2f* **7/1**

00-4 **4** *4* **Admirable Duque (IRE)**[30] 208 7-8-12 70 (be) JoshBaudains(7) 3 62
(Dominic Ffrench Davis) *hld up in tch: hdwy 5f out and sn cl up: chal over 3f out: rdn wl over 2f out and grad wknd* **4/1**[3]

13-2 **5** *32* **Alborz (IRE)**[23] 309 4-9-4 72 DanielTudhope 6 13
(Tim Vaughan) *slt ld 2f: cl up: rdn along 4f out: wknd over 3f out: sn bhd and eased fnl 2f* **6/4**[1]

2m 42.57s (1.57) **Going Correction** +0.15s/f (Slow)
WFA 4 from 5yo+ 3lb **5** Ran SP% **111.7**
Speed ratings (Par 103): **100,99,95,93,71**
CSF £26.41 TOTE £6.70: £1.50, £2.50; EX 23.80 Trifecta £126.30 Pool: £1116.36 - 6.62 winning units..
Owner Mrs Wendy Jenkins **Bred** D H W Dobson **Trained** Royston, Herts

FOCUS
A decent middle-distance event for the surface, won by a course specialist.

643 DOWNLOAD CORAL.CO.UK MOBILE APP CLAIMING STKS 6f (F)

3:20 (3:20) (Class 6) 3-Y-O **£1,940** (£577; £288) **Stalls** Low

Form RPR

04-5 **1** **Girl At The Sands (IRE)**[28] 225 3-8-9 67 JamesSullivan 2 69
(James Given) *outpcd early: hdwy to chse ldr after 1 1/2f: rdn 2f out: styd on to ld ent fnl f: drvn out* **11/4**[3]

10-6 **2** *½* **La Sylphe**[7] 531 3-7-13 75 AdamMcLean(7) 4 64
(Derek Shaw) *led: rdn over 2f out: drvn and hdd ent fnl f: kpt on u.p towards fin* **5/2**[2]

6-11 **3** *2* **Hiddon Coin (IRE)**[16] 424 3-8-12 75 DavidBergin(7) 1 71
(David O'Meara) *chsd ldr 1f: pushed along 1/2-way: rdn 2f out: no imp fnl f* **4/5**[1]

1m 18.87s (2.37) **Going Correction** +0.15s/f (Slow) **3** Ran SP% **110.8**
Speed ratings (Par 95): **90,89,86**
CSF £8.68 TOTE £4.80; EX 8.50 Trifecta £8.80 Pool: £956.57 - 81.48 winning units..Girl At The Sands was claimed by Mr E J Creighton for £8,000.
Owner Peter Swann **Bred** Rossenarra Bloodstock Limited **Trained** Willoughton, Lincs

FOCUS
Not a result to take that seriously considering conditions and the size of the field.

644 CLAIM FREE BETS TODAY AT BOOKMAKERS H'CAP 1m (F)

3:50 (3:50) (Class 4) (0-85,85) 4-Y-O+ **£4,690** (£1,395; £697; £348) **Stalls** Low

Form RPR

40-6 **1** **The Lock Master (IRE)**[33] 167 6-8-10 79 ShirleyTeasdale(5) 1 89
(Michael Appleby) *broke wl: sn pushed along and outpcd after 1f: in tch 1/2-way: rdn along on outer over 2f out: gd hdwy over 1f out: chal ent fnl f: styd on to ld last 100yds: rdr dropped reins: kpt on* **9/1**

24-3 **2** *½* **Dubawi Island (FR)**[27] 239 4-9-7 85 (b) GrahamLee 7 94
(James Tate) *cl up: led after 2f: qcknd clr over 2f out: rdn over 1f out: jnd and drvn ent fnl f: hdd and one pce last 100yds* **11/10**[1]

1103 **3** *6* **Loyalty**[11] 495 6-9-0 85 (v) AdamMcLean(7) 8 80
(Derek Shaw) *dwlt and in rr: hdwy over 2f out: sn rdn and styd on fnl f: nrst fin* **8/1**[3]

00-0 **4** *1* **Askaud (IRE)**[11] 495 5-9-0 78 (b) FrederikTylicki 4 71
(Scott Dixon) *broke wl: chsd ldrs on inner: rdn along wl over 2f out: sn one pce* **9/1**

5004 **5** *2¾* **Copperwood**[4] 593 8-8-9 73 JoeFanning 5 59
(Mark Johnston) *chsd ldrs: rdn along wl over 2f out: grad wknd* **9/1**

24-3 **6** *½* **Chookie Avon**[29] 217 6-8-8 77 ow1 (p) GarryWhillans(5) 3 62
(Keith Dalgleish) *broke wl: sn pushed along and outpcd early: a towards rr after* **20/1**

24-2 **7** *¾* **Piceno (IRE)**[10] 511 5-8-11 75 (p) NickyMackay 6 59
(Scott Dixon) *sn led: hdd after 2f: cl up on inner: rdn along wl over 2f out: sn wknd* **5/1**[2]

000- **8** *3¼* **Dubaianswer**[9] 7715 5-8-11 82 JacobButterfield(7) 2 58
(Tony Coyle) *a in rr* **11/1**

1m 42.93s (-0.77) **Going Correction** +0.15s/f (Slow) **8** Ran SP% **118.5**
Speed ratings (Par 105): **109,108,102,101,98 98,97,94**
toteswingers 1&2 £3.10, 1&3 £6.90, 2&3 £3.30 CSF £20.15 CT £89.59 TOTE £10.70: £2.30, £1.50, £1.90; EX 27.70 Trifecta £197.70 Pool: £2955.02 - 11.20 winning units..
Owner K G Kitchen **Bred** Patrick F Kelly **Trained** Danethorpe, Notts

FOCUS
Another good result for those who follow course form.

645 FREE BET BONANZA NOW AT BOOKMAKERS.CO.UK H'CAP 6f (F)

4:20 (4:25) (Class 5) (0-75,75) 4-Y-O+ **£2,587** (£770; £384; £192) **Stalls** Low

Form RPR

-023 **1** **Dickie Le Davoir**[8] 526 9-8-12 66 (be) RobbieFitzpatrick 2 73
(Richard Guest) *sn outpcd and bhd: hdwy over 2f out: rdn over 1f out: styd on strly ent fnl f to ld last 100yds* **8/1**[3]

2-65 **2** *nk* **Masai Moon**[16] 415 9-8-12 73 (b) PatMillman(7) 8 79
(Rod Millman) *dwlt and bhd: hdwy over 3f out: rdn 2f out: sn chsng pcemaking duo: styd on to ld jst ins fnl f: sn edgd lft: hdd and no ex last 100yds* **5/2**[1]

000- **3** *6* **Alpha Tauri (USA)**[90] 7732 7-9-7 75 GrahamLee 7 62
(Scott Dixon) *slt ld and set str pce: rdn over 2f out: drvn over 1f out: hdd jst ins fnl f: sn wknd* **5/2**[1]

0-03 **4** *2* **Point North (IRE)**[13] 454 6-8-13 67 JamesSullivan 5 47
(John Balding) *disp ld at str pce: rdn wl over 2f out: drvn over 1f out: wknd fnl f* **14/1**

6211 **5** *3* **Hab Reeh**[16] 422 5-8-3 64 (t) GemmaTutty(7) 4 35
(Ruth Carr) *chsd ldng pair: rdn along wl over 2f out: sn wknd* **6/1**[2]

4-14 **6** *2* **Gaelic Wizard (IRE)**[28] 229 5-8-6 67 JoshBaudains(7) 3 31
(Dominic Ffrench Davis) *a towards rr* **14/1**

1m 17.34s (0.84) **Going Correction** +0.15s/f (Slow) **6** Ran SP% **95.9**
Speed ratings (Par 103): **100,99,91,88,84 82**
toteswingers 1&2 £2.40, 1&3 £2.90, 2&3 £2.10 CSF £20.30 CT £36.12 TOTE £8.20: £2.80, £1.60; EX 19.00 Trifecta £63.70 Pool: £1486.46 - 17.49 winning units..
Owner Glen Wilton **Bred** P And Mrs A G Venner **Trained** Wetherby, W Yorks

FOCUS
Admiralty (9/2) unseated his rider going down to the start and Caldercruix (9/2) broke out of the stalls. Both were withdrawn, which weakened the race somewhat considering their position in the betting. Deduct 30p in the £ under R4, new market formed. The two leaders went off much too fast.

646 CORAL.CO.UK APPRENTICE H'CAP 1m 3f (F)

4:50 (4:50) (Class 6) (0-60,61) 4-Y-O+ **£1,940** (£577; £288; £144) **Stalls** Low

Form RPR

25-1 **1** **Dewala**[3] 601 4-9-5 61 6ex CharlesBishop(3) 9 81
(Michael Appleby) *mde all: pushed clr 3f out: rdn out fnl f: unchal* **10/11**[1]

-112 **2** *12* **Easydoesit (IRE)**[9] 515 5-9-4 60 GeorgeDowning(5) 8 58
(Tony Carroll) *towards rr and pushed along early: swtchd to wd outside and hdwy over 6f out: sn chsng ldrs: rdn along over 3f out: kpt on to take 2nd ins fnl f: no ch w wnr* **4/1**[2]

5-30 **3** *9* **Icy Quiet**[33] 169 5-8-7 49 DavidBergin(5) 3 31
(David O'Meara) *trckd wnr: rdn along over 3f out: drvn and outpcd over 2f out: lost 2nd ins fnl f* **12/1**

-652 **4** *2¾* **Layla's Boy**[3] 597 6-9-3 59 (vt) ShirleyTeasdale(5) 4 36
(Simon West) *trckd ldrs: effrt 4f out: rdn along over 3f out: plugged on one pce* **9/2**[3]

646- **5** *2¼* **My New Angel (IRE)**[49] 8241 4-8-7 46 oh1 (e[1]) JulieBurke 10 19
(Paul Green) *chsd ldrs: rdn along 4f out: sn outpcd* **25/1**

30-6 **6** *2* **Sygnature**[34] 145 4-9-4 57 PatrickHills 5 26
(Alan Swinbank) *in tch: rdn along over 4f out: sn outpcd* **16/1**

0-6 **7** *9* **Capellini**[12] 475 6-9-6 60 (b) RachealKneller(3) 1 13
(Charles Egerton) *a in rr: bhd fnl 4f* **25/1**

050- **8** *3¼* **Kingarrick**[49] 8241 5-9-2 58 (t) ConorHarrison(5) 7
(Noel Wilson) *a in rr: wl bhd fnl 4f* **20/1**

23-0 **9** *27* **Kheskianto (IRE)**[13] 456 7-8-2 **46** oh1........................(t) AaronJones(7) 2
(Michael Chapman) *chsd ldrs on inner: lost pl bef 1/2-way: sn bhd* **50/1**
2m 26.64s (-1.36) **Going Correction** +0.15s/f (Slow)
WFA 4 from 5yo+ 2lb 9 Ran SP% **118.6**
Speed ratings (Par 101): **110,101,94,92,91 89,83,80,61**
toteswingers 1&2 £2.00, 1&3 £3.20, 2&3 £4.30 CSF £4.61 CT £26.97 TOTE £1.90: £1.10, £1.50, £2.70; EX 5.40 Trifecta £19.20 Pool: £2469.26 - 95.05 winning units..
Owner Goldform Racing **Bred** A M Wragg **Trained** Danethorpe, Notts

FOCUS
A modest event won easily by an in-form filly.
T/Plt: £230.10 to a £1 stake. Pool of £53226.85 - 168.85 winning tickets. T/Qpdt: £47.20 to a £1 stake. Pool of £3385.92 - 53.00 winning tickets. JR

604 CAGNES-SUR-MER
Wednesday, February 13
OFFICIAL GOING: Turf: soft; fibresand: standard

647a PRIX DES SPIREES (CLAIMER) (3YO) (TURF) 7f 110y
2:20 (12:00) 3-Y-0 **£6,910** (£2,764; £2,073; £1,382; £691)

RPR
1 **Celtic Filly (IRE)**[40] 3-8-13 0.. MircoDemuro 3 77
(S Botti, Italy) **21/10**[1]
2 *1* **Halloween Chope (FR)**[47] 8276 3-9-3 0.................. IoritzMendizabal 7 78
(D Prod'Homme, France) **3/1**[2]
3 *2* **Litian Rocket (FR)**[7] 544 3-8-10 0.............. AlexandreChampenois(6) 5 72
(M Boutin, France) **9/1**
4 *1* **Medipearl (FR)**[96] 3-8-11 0... AnthonyCrastus 8 65
(F Chappet, France) **12/1**
5 *1* **Mesharc (FR)**[26] 270 3-8-4 0.................................(p) JulienMagniez(7) 2 62
(Mme C Barande-Barbe, France) **37/1**
6 *hd* **City Chope (FR)**[32] 3-8-9 0 ow1.................................... JohanVictoire 1 60
(C Boutin, France) **26/1**
7 *1* **Gorki Park (FR)**[16] 445 3-9-2 0.................................... FabienLefebvre 9 64
(Mme G Rarick, France) **33/1**
8 *2* **Safrana (FR)**[13] 461 3-8-8 0.. MaximeGuyon 10 51
(D Prod'Homme, France) **43/10**[3]
9 *¾* **Freestyler (FR)**[78] 3-9-5 0... JimmyTastayre(6) 4 66
(C Boutin, France) **83/10**
10 *4* **Moorway (IRE)**[7] 543 3-9-2 0..(p) JackDuern 11 47
(Reg Hollinshead) *racd in midfield on wd outside: proged to 4th ent st: shkn up 2f out: no ex: styd on one pce* **44/1**
11 **Gimli (FR)**[16] 445 3-8-4 0...................................... NicolasLarenaudie(7) 6 42
(G Collet, France) **58/1**
1m 39.07s (99.07) 11 Ran SP% **117.8**
WIN (incl. 1 euro stake): 3.10. PLACES: 1.70, 1.50, 2.20. DF: 7.00. SF: 12.10.
Owner Dioscuri Srl **Bred** Jim McDonald **Trained** Italy

648a PRIX DE JUAN-LES-PINS (H'CAP) (5YO+) (FIBRESAND) 1m 4f
4:25 (12:00) 5-Y-0+ **£10,569** (£4,227; £3,170; £2,113; £1,056)

RPR
1 **Kourdo (FR)**[270] 5-9-5 **0**.. ThomasMessina 1 78
(J Parize, France) **9/2**[2]
2 *1½* **Rainbow Knight**[479] 5-9-5 **0**.............................. Pierre-CharlesBoudot 2 76
(J-M Capitte, France) **48/10**[3]
3 *1½* **Eskadi (FR)**[182] 5-9-1 **0**..(b) RomainAuray 11 69
(J Helouny, France) **44/1**
4 *2* **Uphold**[11] 498 6-9-6 **0**...(b) MaximeGuyon 7 71
(Gay Kelleway) *broke wl: racd in 2nd: first two wnt wl clr down bk st: led 3 1/2f out: rdn 2f out: hdd 1 1/2f out: no ex u.p: styd on fnl frlong* **10/1**
5 *1½* **Topaze Du Paon (FR)** 6-8-8 **0**....................(b) Francois-XavierBertras 8 57
(J-L Dubord, France) **44/5**
6 *nse* **Gonetrio (USA)**[71] 6-8-3 **0**... EddyHardouin 5 52
(N Caullery, France) **19/1**
7 *1* **Rousseau (FR)**[71] 7-8-13 **0**......................................(b) RonanThomas 9 60
(Carmen Bocskai, Switzerland) **18/1**
8 *1* **Commando Cat (FR)**[40] 6-9-2 **0**...................................... JulienAuge 4 61
(P Nicot, France) **20/1**
9 *hd* **Romeo Saint Cyr (FR)**[45] 7-9-0 **0**..............................(b) FabriceVeron 6 59
(C Martinon, France) **28/1**
10 *1* **Notion (IRE)**[411] 5-9-4 **0**.. IoritzMendizabal 12 61
(F Chappet, France) **2/1**[1]
0 **Kel Away (FR)**[45] 6-8-8 **0**...(p) TheoBachelot 3
(Mlle M Henry, France) **19/1**
0 **Golden Beau (FR)**[40] 5-9-4 **0**...................................(p) BriceRaballand 10
(J-P Delaporte, France) **25/1**
2m 31.65s (151.65) 12 Ran SP% **117.6**
WIN (incl. 1 euro stake): 5.50. PLACES: 2.20, 2.30, 8.00. DF: 13.40. SF: 33.50.
Owner Philippe Walter **Bred** Sarl Euro Normandy **Trained** France

625 KEMPTON (A.W) (R-H)
Thursday, February 14
OFFICIAL GOING: Standard
Wind: Light, across Weather: Fine but cloudy, mild

649 RACING PLUS CHASE 23.02.13 H'CAP 6f (P)
5:00 (5:01) (Class 7) (0-50,50) 4-Y-0+ **£1,455** (£433; £216; £108) **Stalls** Low

Form RPR
-005 **1** **Red Ramesses (IRE)**[8] 529 4-9-6 **50**................................ LukeMorris 7 58
(John Best) *hld up in 7th: prog jst over 2f out: rdn to ld over 1f out: drvn out fnl f: hld on* **6/1**[3]
3-1 **2** *nk* **Spellmaker**[13] 472 4-9-6 **50**.................................. WilliamCarson 10 57+
(Tony Newcombe) *stdd s: t.k.h and hld up in last pair: taken out wd and prog 2f out: drvn and styd on fnl f to take 2nd last 75yds: nt rch wnr* **11/4**[1]
4336 **3** *nk* **Blue Noodles**[7] 551 7-9-2 **46**...................................(p) PaddyAspell 1 52
(John Wainwright) *led: drvn and hdd over 1f out: kpt on same pce: lost 2nd last 75yds* **8/1**
300- **4** *nk* **Flaxen Lake**[150] 6322 6-9-6 **50**............................(p) RobertWinston 4 55
(Milton Bradley) *t.k.h: trckd ldrs: lost pl sltly over 2f out: rallied over 1f out: kpt on u.p fnl f* **16/1**
334- **5** *2¾* **Kerfuffle (IRE)**[56] 8184 4-9-2 **46**....................................(b[1]) SebSanders 2 42
(Simon Dow) *s.i.s: sn prom on inner: rdn to try to chal 2f out: could nt qckn over 1f out: wknd fnl f* **11/2**[2]
4-50 **6** *nk* **Lisselton Cross**[36] 111 5-9-4 **48**...................................(p) JimCrowley 8 43
(Martin Bosley) *slowest away: hld up in last pair: prog on inner over 2f out: pressed ldrs over 1f out: wknd fnl f* **7/1**
-564 **7** *4* **Brandywell Boy (IRE)**[26] 276 10-8-13 **50**............... JoshBaudains(7) 9 33
(Dominic Ffrench Davis) *a in rr and nvr gng wl: struggling sn after 1/2-way: modest late prog* **25/1**
5-06 **8** *nk* **Le King Beau (USA)**[13] 472 4-9-5 **49**............................(v) AdamKirby 3 31
(John Bridger) *drvn fr s but unable to ld: pressed ldr to over 2f out: steadily lost pl* **10/1**
46-4 **9** *½* **Metropolitan Chief**[13] 471 9-8-11 **46**....................... NatashaEaton(5) 5 26
(Paul Burgoyne) *cl up tl steadily wknd fr jst over 2f out* **20/1**
006- **10** *1¾* **Royal Envoy (IRE)**[65] 8061 10-9-2 **46**...................(p) MichaelStainton 12 20
(Paul Howling) *racd wd: a in rr: no prog and btn 2f out* **33/1**
56/0 **11** *½* **Old Peg**[8] 529 8-9-6 **50**... RobbieFitzpatrick 6 23
(Dai Burchell) *dwlt: a towards rr: brief effrt over 2f out: sn wknd* **66/1**
20-4 **12** *2½* **Kaylee**[35] 128 4-9-5 **49**... GeorgeBaker 11 14
(Gary Moore) *racd wdst of all: prom: wknd fr over 2f out* **6/1**[3]
1m 12.92s (-0.18) **Going Correction** 0.0s/f (Stan) 12 Ran SP% **122.2**
Speed ratings (Par 97): **101,100,100,99,96 95,90,90,89,87 86,83**
toteswingers 1&2 £5.60, 2&3 £5.80, 1&3 £8.60 CSF £22.74 CT £140.33 TOTE £6.20: £2.10, £1.50, £3.30; EX 26.30 Trifecta £450.00 Pool: £2279.40 - 3.79 winning units..
Owner John Best **Bred** Wardstown Stud Ltd **Trained** Hucking, Kent

FOCUS
A bottom-drawer sprint handicap, run at a sound enough pace that saw a bunched four-way finish.

650 BETVICTOR NON RUNNER CHELTENHAM FREE BET H'CAP 7f (P)
5:30 (5:30) (Class 5) (0-75,75) 4-Y-0+ **£2,587** (£770; £384; £192) **Stalls** Low

Form RPR
2-52 **1** **Russian Ice**[17] 421 5-9-4 **72**..(b) JimCrowley 13 79
(Dean Ivory) *stdd s and swtchd sharply to inner fr wdst draw: hld up in last: prog whn nt clr run over 1f out and swtchd out wd: 10th ent fnl f: styd on strly to ld post* **10/1**
2221 **2** *hd* **Bussa**[7] 546 5-8-11 **70** 6ex.......................................(t) ThomasBrown(5) 10 76
(David Evans) *hld up in midfield: prog over 2f out: drvn over 1f out: chsd ldr ins fnl f: clsd to ld last strides: hdd post* **3/1**[1]
0-02 **3** *nk* **Jake The Snake (IRE)**[8] 535 12-8-13 **70**...................... AmyBaker(3) 9 75
(Tony Carroll) *hld up in rr: prog over 2f out: drvn over 1f out: kpt on wl fr over 1f out but jst lacked pce of wnr* **7/1**
03-0 **4** *shd* **Avonmore Star**[21] 358 5-9-4 **72**.. EddieAhern 6 77
(Mike Murphy) *pressed ldrs: rdn to ld over 2f out: hrd drvn fnl f: hdd and lost pls last strides* **8/1**
1-23 **5** *nk* **The Strig**[21] 360 6-9-5 **73**... SeanLevey 1 77
(Stuart Williams) *hld up in midfield: prog over 2f out: drvn to chse ldr jst over 1f out: kpt on but a hld: lost pls last 50yds* **16/1**
505- **6** *nk* **Ted's Brother (IRE)**[108] 7436 5-8-2 **63**.................... PhilipPrince(7) 4 66
(Richard Guest) *t.k.h: hld up in last pair: prog 2f out: styd on fr over 1f out: clsd on ldrs fnl f: jst outpcd* **16/1**
0021 **7** *hd* **Diplomatic (IRE)**[17] 415 8-8-8 **69**.............................(p) RobertTart(7) 3 72
(Michael Squance) *hld up in rr: prog on inner over 2f out: drvn wl over 1f out: pressed ldrs fnl f: one pce last 100yds* **11/2**[2]
03-1 **8** *1½* **Golden Desert (IRE)**[35] 130 9-9-0 **68**.............................. GrahamLee 7 67
(Simon Dow) *stdd s: hld up in rr: effrt over 2f out: kpt on fr over 1f out: nvr rchd ldrs* **6/1**[3]
-035 **9** *2½* **Dunn'o (IRE)**[14] 452 8-8-8 **62**.......................................(t) FrannyNorton 5 54
(David Nicholls) *led 3f: lost 2nd wl over 2f out: kpt on and stl prom tl wknd fnl f* **8/1**
4-40 **10** *1¾* **Scottish Lake**[15] 443 5-9-7 **75**................................(b) KirstyMilczarek 11 62
(Olivia Maylam) *t.k.h: hld up bhd ldrs and racd wd: lost grnd fr 1/2-way: last whn sltly impeded over 1f out: plugged on late* **12/1**
030- **11** *3½* **Chevise (IRE)**[58] 8158 5-8-11 **65**.................................. WilliamCarson 2 43
(Steve Woodman) *chsd ldrs: u.p by 1/2-way: wknd over 2f out* **50/1**
20-0 **12** *hd* **Elusive Hawk (IRE)**[7] 548 9-8-13 **67**.............................. ShaneKelly 8 44
(David Evans) *pressed ldr: led after 3f: hdd & wknd over 2f out* **25/1**
000- **13** *8* **Quasi Congaree (GER)**[45] 8306 7-9-7 **75**...............(bt[1]) GeorgeBaker 12 31
(Paul Fitzsimons) *t.k.h: pressed ldrs on outer: wknd wl over 2f out: eased: t.o* **50/1**
1m 24.77s (-1.23) **Going Correction** 0.0s/f (Stan) 13 Ran SP% **125.7**
Speed ratings (Par 103): **107,106,106,106,105 105,105,103,100,98 94,94,85**
toteswingers 1&2 £8.10, 2&3 £10.70, 1&3 £8.60 CSF £41.70 CT £205.69 TOTE £10.80: £3.50, £2.20, £3.20; EX 50.80 Trifecta £408.20 Pool: £1664.77 - 3.05 winning units..
Owner Roger S Beadle **Bred** Kingwood Bloodstock & Mrs M Gutkin **Trained** Radlett, Herts

FOCUS
This moderate handicap appeared wide open and, despite a fair pace set, the first six were closely covered at the death.

651 BET EUROPA LEAGUE NOW WITH BETVICTOR MEDIAN AUCTION MAIDEN FILLIES' STKS 1m (P)
6:00 (6:01) (Class 5) 3-5-Y-0 **£2,587** (£770; £384; £192) **Stalls** Low

Form RPR
2 **1** **Lily Edge**[29] 230 4-10-0 0.. SeanLevey 3 67
(John Bridger) *hld up in midfield: plenty to do whn plld out over 2f out: prog to take 2nd 1f out: clsd qckly to ld last 100yds: sn clr* **9/4**[2]
2 *2* **Oratorio's Joy (IRE)** 3-8-9 0..................................... FergusSweeney 1 58
(Jamie Osborne) *dwlt: t.k.h in last pair: bmpd over 5f out: pushed along and prog on inner 2f out: styd on quite wl to take 2nd nr fin* **12/1**
5 **3** *hd* **Hawaiian Dream (IRE)**[22] 332 3-8-9 0........................ RobertWinston 6 57
(Roger Teal) *t.k.h: trckd ldrs: rdn to chse clr ldr wl over 1f out: no imp and lost 2nd 1f out: kpt on* **8/1**
4 *1¼* **Floralys (USA)**[487] 6897 4-10-0 73................................(b) AdamKirby 8 59
(John Butler) *led: rdn and drew 3 l clr wl over 1f out: wknd qckly and hdd last 100yds* **13/8**[1]
6- **5** *1½* **Bullseye Babe**[57] 8166 3-8-9 0... LiamKeniry 5 51
(Mark Usher) *t.k.h: hld up in rr: tried to cl fr 2f out: one pce* **66/1**
-004 **6** *1½* **Kalahari Breeze (IRE)**[5] 588 3-8-9 45............................ LukeMorris 7 47?
(William Muir) *mostly chsd ldr to over 2f out: steadily lost pl* **25/1**
7 *2¼* **Early One Morning** 3-8-9 0.. HayleyTurner 9 42
(Hugo Palmer) *dwlt: prog on outer fr rr into midfield 1/2-way: dropped to rr again over 2f out: no ch after* **6/1**[3]
05-0 **8** *1¾* **Willow Beauty**[8] 530 4-10-0 42... EddieAhern 2 42
(J R Jenkins) *t.k.h: prom: rdn to chse ldr over 2f out to wl over 1f out: wknd qckly fnl f* **66/1**

45 **9** *nse* **Ice Tres**[19] 397 4-9-7 0 .... PatMillman(7) 4 42
(Rod Millman) *dwlt: t.k.h and racd awkwardly in last pair: lost tch over 2f out* **6/1**[3]

1m 40.69s (0.89) **Going Correction** 0.0s/f (Stan)
WFA 3 from 4yo 19lb **9** Ran SP% **123.1**
Speed ratings (Par 100): **95,93,92,91,90 88,86,84,84**
toteswingers 1&2 £10.00, 2&3 £17.00, 1&3 £5.00 CSF £31.29 TOTE £4.30: £1.50, £4.20, £2.40; EX 59.40 Trifecta £335.40 Pool: £1528.47 - 3.41 winning units..
Owner Allsorts **Bred** W J Wyatt **Trained** Liphook, Hants

FOCUS
This weak maiden saw changing fortunes inside the final furlong.

652 BETVICTOR NON RUNNER AINTREE FREE BET H'CAP 1m (P)
6:30 (6:31) (Class 6) (0-65,65) 4-Y-0+ **£1,940** (£577; £288; £144) **Stalls** Low

Form RPR

-665 **1** **Officer In Command (USA)**[12] 490 7-9-5 **63** ......(v[1]) RobertWinston 6 73
(Sean Curran) *dwlt: hld up and sn in last: pushed along 3f out: prog on inner over 2f out: swtchd lft over 1f out: drvn and r.o to ld last 50yds: won gng away* **8/1**

23-1 **2** 1¼ **Bowstar**[21] 347 4-9-4 **62** ....(p) RobertHavlin 4 69
(Michael Attwater) *trckd ldr: led over 2f out gng strly: drvn over 1f out and idled: hrd pressed fnl f: hdd and outpcd last 50yds* **11/4**[1]

4-43 **3** *nse* **Warbond**[14] 451 5-9-2 **60** .... LukeMorris 5 67
(Michael Madgwick) *trckd ldrs: rdn to go 2nd jst over 2f out: grad clsd fr over 1f out: upsides jst as wnr flashed by 50yds out* **11/2**[2]

5F-2 **4** 1½ **Spin Again (IRE)**[12] 490 8-9-4 **62** .... MichaelO'Connell 8 66
(John Ryan) *trckd ldrs in 6th: rdn over 2f out: kpt on same pce fr over 1f out: nvr able to chal* **16/1**

0-63 **5** 3 **Hip Hip Hooray**[21] 348 7-9-2 **60** .... IanMongan 3 57
(Luke Dace) *hld up towards rr: outpcd whn effrt over 2f out: one pce and nvr on terms after* **6/1**[3]

00-6 **6** 3 **Standing Strong (IRE)**[35] 130 5-9-7 **65** ....(p) JamieGoldstein 10 55
(Zoe Davison) *reluctant to enter stalls: hld up in last pair: coaxed along and no prog over 2f out: kpt on whn r was over* **33/1**

-500 **7** *nse* **Fairy Wing (IRE)**[12] 493 6-9-0 **58** .... WilliamCarson 1 48
(Violet M Jordan) *dwlt but rushed up to ld on inner and set gd pce: hdd over 2f out: sn wknd* **20/1**

0-41 **8** 2½ **Prince Of Passion (CAN)**[16] 437 5-9-4 **62** ....(v) JoeFanning 11 46
(Derek Shaw) *hld up in rr: shkn up over 2f out: sn lost tch w ldrs* **14/1**

00-4 **9** 5 **Rezwaan**[19] 403 6-9-4 **62** ....(be) ShaneKelly 12 34
(Murty McGrath) *chsd ldrs: lost pl and wknd over 2f out* **20/1**

3313 **10** 2¼ **The Mongoose**[10] 519 5-9-6 **64** ....(vt) AdamKirby 7 31
(David Evans) *chsd ldng pair to over 2f out: wknd qckly* **6/1**[3]

-146 **U** **Vitznau (IRE)**[10] 517 9-9-3 **61** ....(t) JamieMackay 2
(K F Clutterbuck) *virtually ref to r: c out of stalls 20 l bhd and promptly uns the rdr* **20/1**

1m 38.88s (-0.92) **Going Correction** 0.0s/f (Stan) **11** Ran SP% **117.9**
Speed ratings (Par 101): **104,102,102,101,98 95,95,92,87,85**
toteswingers 1&2 £6.70, 2&3 £3.80, 1&3 £6.70 CSF £29.52 CT £134.95 TOTE £11.40: £2.10, £1.90, £1.90; EX 49.10 Trifecta £298.20 Pool: £1691.37 - 4.25 winning units..
Owner P M Rich **Bred** Blooming Hills Inc **Trained** Hatford, Oxon
■ Stewards' Enquiry : Ian Mongan one-day ban: careless riding (Feb 28)

FOCUS
An ordinary handicap which looked another open affair, but few landed a serious blow.

653 BETVICTOR AINTREE GRAND NATIONAL NON RUNNER FREE BET H'CAP 1m 4f (P)
7:00 (7:02) (Class 6) (0-60,60) 4-Y-0+ **£1,940** (£577; £288; £144) **Stalls** Centre

Form RPR

00-2 **1** **Evergreen Forest (IRE)**[17] 418 5-9-7 **60** ....(b) GeorgeBaker 7 71
(Tom Keddy) *hld up in 7th: prog over 2f out to trck ldr over 1f out: hanging rt but coaxed along to ld 150yds out: drvn out* **4/1**[2]

3-11 **2** ½ **Irene Kennet**[17] 417 6-9-3 **56** .... HayleyTurner 11 66
(Paul Burgoyne) *t.k.h: hld up in 10th: prog on outer over 2f out: drvn over 1f out: styd on to take 2nd nr fin: nt rch wnr* **11/2**[3]

03-1 **3** *shd* **Asia Minor (IRE)**[17] 418 4-9-2 **58** .... LukeMorris 12 68
(Dr Jon Scargill) *s.i.s: hld up in last trio: prog on wd outside over 2f out: drvn over 1f out: styd on to press for 2nd nr fin: nt rch wnr* **5/2**[1]

0-63 **4** 1½ **Shirataki (IRE)**[17] 417 5-9-5 **58** .... ChrisCatlin 14 65
(Peter Hiatt) *t.k.h: hld up in 5th: prog to ld over 2f out and kicked on: hdd and one pce last 150yds* **12/1**

3-21 **5** ¾ **Midnight Bahia (IRE)**[14] 455 4-8-9 **51** .... FrannyNorton 9 58
(Dean Ivory) *t.k.h: trckd ldng pair: chsd ldr over 2f out to over 1f out: fdd* **14/1**

00-0 **6** ½ **The Blue Dog (IRE)**[22] 338 6-9-0 **60** .... RobertTart(7) 5 65
(Michael Wigham) *trckd ldng pair: bmpd on inner over 2f out: drvn and kpt on one pce fnl 2f: hld whn short of room briefly ins fnl f* **33/1**

04-5 **7** 1¼ **Lady of Burgundy**[17] 417 7-9-1 **59** .... LeeNewnes(5) 3 62
(Mark Usher) *hld up in last trio: rdn over 2f out: kpt on one pce fr over 1f out: n.d* **20/1**

53-4 **8** 1½ **If You Whisper (IRE)**[17] 417 5-9-1 **54** .... EddieAhern 8 55
(Mike Murphy) *stdd s: hld up in last: prog on inner over 2f out: no hdwy over 1f out* **14/1**

3-02 **9** *shd* **Youm Jamil (USA)**[17] 417 6-8-9 **55** .... RyanTate(7) 2 56
(Tony Carroll) *trckd ldrs in 6th: rdn over 2f out: no imp on ldrs over 1f out* **20/1**

01-0 **10** 1½ **Rodrigo De Freitas (IRE)**[43] 9 6-9-7 **60** ....(v) AdamKirby 4 58
(Roger Ingram) *slowly away and rousted along to rch midfield: drvn and no prog over 2f out: btn after* **10/1**

65-3 **11** 4½ **Ice Apple**[35] 132 5-8-4 **46** oh1 .... NataliaGemelova(3) 6 37
(John E Long) *pushed up to join ldr: losing pl qckly whn crowded over 2f out: sn bhd* **66/1**

0-53 **12** 4½ **Leitrim King (IRE)**[14] 455 4-8-13 **55** ....(p) FergusSweeney 10 39
(Gary Moore) *racd on outer: nvr bttr than midfield: wknd over 2f out* **12/1**

02-2 **13** 14 **Highly Likely (IRE)**[35] 132 4-9-1 **57** .... WilliamCarson 1 19+
(Steve Woodman) *mde most: hdd over 2f out: wkng whn crowded sn after: eased and t.o* **33/1**

2m 33.62s (-0.88) **Going Correction** 0.0s/f (Stan)
WFA 4 from 5yo+ 3lb **13** Ran SP% **118.7**
Speed ratings (Par 101): **102,101,101,100,100 99,98,97,97,96 93,90,81**
toteswingers 1&2 £6.70, 2&3 £3.50, 1&3 £4.60 CSF £24.37 CT £66.36 TOTE £5.30: £2.00, £1.80, £1.60; EX 28.10 Trifecta £43.50 Pool: £1141.32 - 19.66 winning units..
Owner Evergreen Racing Newmarket **Bred** Shadwell Estate Company Limited **Trained** Newmarket, Suffolk

FOCUS
Not a bad handicap for the class and there was a fair pace on. Solid form.

654 BETVICTOR EXCLUSIVE NON RUNNER FREE BET H'CAP 2m (P)
7:30 (7:31) (Class 4) (0-85,87) 4-Y-0+ **£4,690** (£1,395; £697; £348) **Stalls** Low

Form RPR

24-0 **1** **Thecornishcockney**[12] 496 4-9-8 **87** ....(t) AdamKirby 5 99+
(John Ryan) *s.v.s: hld up in last trio: smooth prog on inner over 2f out: led over 1f out: pushed along and sn clr: eased last 50yds* **4/1**[2]

1/12 **2** 2½ **Murcar**[20] 378 8-9-0 **80** ....(b) PhilipPrince(7) 3 87
(Liam Corcoran) *trckd ldrs: drvn over 2f out: styd on fr over 1f out to take 2nd last 100yds: no ch w wnr* **6/1**[3]

2/0- **3** 2½ **Desert Recluse (IRE)**[84] 7825 6-9-11 **84** .... JoeFanning 4 88
(Pat Eddery) *led at stdy pce: kicked on fr 3f out: hdd and easily outpcd fr over 1f out* **10/1**

50-6 **4** *nk* **Phoenix Flight (IRE)**[29] 224 8-9-0 **80** .... RyanTate(7) 10 84
(James Evans) *t.k.h: trckd ldrs: prog over 3f out: rdn to chal 2f out: upsides whn wnr cruised by over 1f out: fdd fnl f* **9/1**

56/0 **5** 2¼ **Buckie Boy (IRE)**[21] 351 7-8-9 **68** .... EddieAhern 6 69
(Nicky Henderson) *hld up in last trio: hanging bdly rt and wouldn't make prog fr 3f out: passed wkng rivals fnl f* **20/1**

523- **6** *hd* **Rysbrack (USA)**[18] 5430 7-9-2 **75** .... GrahamLee 8 76
(Paul Webber) *hld up in midfield: effrt wl over 2f out: drvn and wl outpcd fnl 2f* **11/4**[1]

0/0- **7** 3½ **Bahrain Storm (IRE)**[90] 7367 10-9-3 **76** ....(b) StevieDonohoe 7 73
(Noel Quinlan) *mostly trckd ldr: hd to one side whn rdn wl over 2f out: sn wknd* **66/1**

44-3 **8** 1½ **The Absent Mare**[21] 351 5-8-9 **68** .... LukeMorris 11 63
(Robin Dickin) *hld up tl prog to trck ldrs after 6f: wknd over 2f out* **8/1**

203- **9** *nk* **Dunhoy (IRE)**[122] 7109 5-9-7 **80** .... WilliamCarson 1 74
(Tony Newcombe) *dwlt: hld up in rr: pushed along 6f out: struggling fr 3f out* **7/1**

00-4 **10** 2 **Dr Finley (IRE)**[21] 351 6-8-4 **66** .... SimonPearce(3) 2 58
(Lydia Pearce) *trckd ldng pair: pushed along 5f out: wknd over 2f out* **33/1**

3m 32.18s (2.08) **Going Correction** 0.0s/f (Stan)
WFA 4 from 5yo+ 6lb **10** Ran SP% **112.9**
Speed ratings (Par 105): **94,92,91,91,90 90,88,87,87,86**
toteswingers 1&2 £2.10, 2&3 £12.50, 1&3 £11.30 CSF £26.69 CT £220.36 TOTE £4.90: £2.00, £1.70, £3.80; EX 21.90 Trifecta £172.00 Pool: £1238.95 - 5.40 winning units..
Owner C Letcher & J Ryan **Bred** D Robb **Trained** Newmarket, Suffolk

FOCUS
A modest staying handicap.

655 COME DINE IN THE PANORAMIC RESTAURANT H'CAP 7f (P)
8:00 (8:01) (Class 6) (0-55,55) 4-Y-0+ **£1,940** (£577; £288; £144) **Stalls** Low

Form RPR

560- **1** **Chandrayaan**[46] 8299 6-8-12 **46** oh1 ....(v) KirstyMilczarek 1 55
(John E Long) *mde all: drvn over 1f out: hrd pressed last 100yds: hld on wl* **33/1**

4-04 **2** ¾ **Littlecote Lady**[19] 409 4-9-3 **51** ....(v) RobertHavlin 5 58
(Mark Usher) *hld up in midfield: rdn and prog 2f out: chsd wnr jst ins fnl f: clsd 100yds out: no imp nr fin* **16/1**

34-0 **3** 1¾ **Renoir's Lady**[34] 162 5-9-7 **55** .... HayleyTurner 6 57
(Simon Dow) *trckd ldrs: rdn over 2f out: prog to chse wnr briefly 1f out: one pce after* **5/1**[3]

143 **4** 1¼ **Media Jury**[6] 565 6-9-2 **50** ....(p) PaddyAspell 10 49
(John Wainwright) *racd wd in midfield: rdn over 2f out: kpt on fr over 1f out: nvr able to chal* **20/1**

-341 **5** ¾ **Harvest Mist (IRE)**[19] 409 5-9-5 **53** .... AdamKirby 3 50
(Shaun Lycett) *prom: chsd wnr over 2f out to 1f out: fdd* **3/1**[1]

6232 **6** ¾ **Glennten**[6] 560 4-9-7 **55** ....(b) LiamKeniry 11 50
(Sylvester Kirk) *mostly chsd wnr to over 2f out: styd prom but steadily fdd fr over 1f out* **11/2**

060- **7** ¾ **Yalding Dancer**[331] 970 4-9-7 **55** .... LukeMorris 2 48
(John Best) *sn in last quartet: rdn and no prog over 2f out: late hdwy but n.d* **66/1**

0-00 **8** *hd* **Surrey Dream (IRE)**[8] 530 4-8-12 **46** ....(p) EddieAhern 9 38
(John Bridger) *settled in midfield: effrt on inner jst over 2f out: no imp on ldrs over 1f out: fdd* **33/1**

02-0 **9** ½ **Signora Frasi (IRE)**[34] 158 8-9-7 **55** .... WilliamCarson 8 46
(Tony Newcombe) *dwlt: sn rdn in last trio: no prog tl kpt on fnl f: no ch* **13/2**

00-5 **10** *hd* **The Bendy Fella (IRE)**[26] 276 5-9-5 **53** .... GrahamLee 7 43+
(Mark Usher) *dwlt: detached in last and pushed along after 3f: trying to make prog but no ch whn short of room 1f out: eased* **4/1**[2]

-005 **11** ¾ **Dingaan (IRE)**[13] 471 10-8-9 **48** oh1 ow2 .... SladeO'Hara(5) 4 36
(Peter Grayson) *a towards rr: rdn and no prog over 2f out* **25/1**

0540 **12** 1¼ **Dvinsky (USA)**[13] 471 12-9-3 **51** ....(b) IanMongan 14 36
(Paul Howling) *spd fr wdst draw to press ldrs: drvn wl over 2f out: losing pl whn hmpd jst over 1f out: eased* **16/1**

0003 **13** 3¼ **Ishi**[8] 537 4-8-12 **46** oh1 ....(b) ChrisCatlin 12 22
(Rod Millman) *dwlt: racd wd: nvr beyond midfield: wknd over 2f out* **16/1**

1m 26.32s (0.32) **Going Correction** 0.0s/f (Stan) **13** Ran SP% **124.0**
Speed ratings (Par 101): **98,97,95,93,92 92,91,90,90,90 89,87,84**
toteswingers 1&2 £74.20, 2&3 £16.70, 1&3 £25.30 CSF £483.45 CT £3096.88 TOTE £35.60: £11.40, £4.00, £2.10; EX 905.50 Trifecta £1205.10 Part won. Pool: £1606.86 - 0.52 winning units..
Owner R D John **Bred** Whatton Manor Stud **Trained** Caterham, Surrey

FOCUS
A weak handicap.

T/Jkpt: Not won. T/Plt: £15.40 to a £1 stake. Pool of £83433.85 - 3951.77 winning tickets. T/Qpdt: £6.60 to a £1 stake. Pool of £8514.0 - 951.40 winning tickets. JN

[552]MEYDAN (L-H)

Thursday, February 14

OFFICIAL GOING: Tapeta: standard; turf: good

656a RANGE ROVER EVOQUE TROPHY (H'CAP) (TAPETA) 1m 3f

2:45 (2:45) (100-110,110) 3-Y-0+

£44,171 (£14,723; £7,361; £3,680; £2,208; £1,472)

RPR

1 **Kassiano (GER)**[14] 463 4-8-10 **102** SilvestreDeSousa 4 104+
(Saeed bin Suroor) *mid-div: smooth prog 2 1/2f out: led 1 1/2f out: r.o wl* **13/8**[1]

2 ¼ **Royal Empire (IRE)**[14] 462 4-9-4 **110** MickaelBarzalona 3 111+
(Saeed bin Suroor) *settled in rr: chsd ldrs 2f out: r.o fnl f: nrst fin* **5/2**[2]

3 3 **Modun (IRE)**[99] 7630 6-9-3 **107** KierenFallon 6 103
(Saeed bin Suroor) *sn led: kicked clr 3f out: hdd 1 1/2f out: kpt on same pce* **6/1**

4 ½ **Ostinato (GER)**[21] 364 5-9-6 **110** (bt) TedDurcan 5 105+
(Sandor Kovacs, Hungary) *slowly away: settled in rr: r.o fnl 2f but nvr able to chal* **28/1**

5 shd **Jardim (BRZ)**[7] 552 7-8-13 **102** ChristopheSoumillon 1 98+
(M F De Kock, South Africa) *trckd ldng tl outpcd 2f out* **10/1**

6 nk **Jamr**[7] 556 5-9-3 **107** (v) ADeVries 2 101
(M bin Shafya, UAE) *s.i.s: trckd ldrs rdn 4 1/2f out: ev ch 2f out: wknd fnl f* **11/2**[3]

7 8 ¼ **Tajaaweed (USA)**[21] 363 8-9-4 **108** PaulHanagan 7 87
(Doug Watson, UAE) *mid-div tl wknd fnl 2f* **20/1**

2m 18.04s (-0.36)
WFA 4 from 5yo+ 2lb 7 Ran SP% **113.6**
CSF 5.76 WIN 2.20 EX 6.00 TRIFECTA 23.50.
Owner Godolphin **Bred** Gestut Rottgen **Trained** Newmarket, Suffolk

FOCUS
The sectionals tell the story of a slow-fast-slow pace, set by Modun: 26.92 (400m), 24.41 (800m), 23.73 (1200m), 24.38 (1600m), 25.25 (2000m), before the winner clocked 13.30 (finish). Consequently, there was something of a bunch finish and this is muddling form.

657a JAGUAR XF TROPHY (H'CAP) (TURF) 1m 1f

3:20 (3:20) (100-115,115) 3-Y-0+

£64,417 (£21,472; £10,736; £5,368; £3,220; £2,147)

RPR

1 **Trade Storm**[21] 367 5-8-9 **104** JamieSpencer 7 114+
(David Simcock) *slowly away: settled in rr: smooth prog 2f out: led 1f out: comf* **9/1**

2 3 ¾ **Anaerobio (ARG)**[14] 462 6-8-6 **100** (t) WayneSmith 3 102
(M F De Kock, South Africa) *Soon led: rdn 2f out: hdd fnl 110yds* **14/1**

3 2 **Mikhail Glinka (IRE)**[130] 6912 6-9-6 **115** (bt) TedDurcan 12 112
(Seth Benzel, U.S.A) *trckd ldrs: rdn 3 1/2f out: kpt on same pce fnl 1 1/2f* **16/1**

4 shd **Rerouted (USA)**[14] 465 5-9-3 **111** ChristopheSoumillon 9 109
(M F De Kock, South Africa) *in rr of mid-div: r.o fnl 2f: nrst fin* **4/1**[2]

5 ½ **Masteroftherolls (IRE)**[21] 363 5-8-9 **104** SilvestreDeSousa 5 100
(Saeed bin Suroor) *settled in rr: nvr nr to chal but r.o fnl 1 1/2f* **11/4**[1]

6 ½ **Mustaheel (IRE)**[7] 552 4-8-9 **104** DaneO'Neill 1 95
(A Al Raihe, UAE) *trckd ldrs: ev ch 1 1/2 out: one pce fnl f* **16/1**

7 hd **Quick Wit**[21] 367 6-8-13 **107** (p) MickaelBarzalona 4 102
(Saeed bin Suroor) *settled in rr: nvr able to chal* **9/1**

8 1 ½ **Final Button (SAF)**[14] 467 5-8-8 **102** (b) PatDobbs 10 97
(M F De Kock, South Africa) *nvr bttr tham mid-div* **11/1**

9 ½ **Finjaan**[21] 367 7-8-9 **104** (bt) PaulHanagan 8 94
(Doug Watson, UAE) *slowly away: nvr nr to chal* **20/1**

10 2 ¾ **Burano (IRE)**[21] 363 4-8-6 **100** KierenFallon 2 85
(Brian Meehan) *nvr bttr than mid-div* **9/2**[3]

11 nse **Rochdale**[21] 362 10-8-7 **101** (t) RoystonFfrench 11 86
(A Al Raihe, UAE) *nvr bttr than mid-div* **33/1**

12 1 ½ **Energia Dust (BRZ)**[21] 367 5-8-8 **102** (t) TadhgO'Shea 6 84
(Fabricio Borges, Sweden) *trckd ldrs tl outpcd 2 1/2f out* **33/1**

1m 49.06s (109.06) 12 Ran SP% **122.3**
CSF: 129.31 TRICAST 1990.58 EX 73.00 TRIFECTA 922.20 WIN 10.10 PL 3.10, 4.10, 2.90.
Owner Universal Racing **Bred** Gt Lucas **Trained** Newmarket, Suffolk

FOCUS
This was visually really impressive from the winner. Here's a look at the sectionals posted by long-time leader Anaerobio, with the winner's splits in brackets: 25.74 (26.89), 23.37 (23.46), 23.78 (23.84), 23.84 (22.86), 12.93 (12.01). The first two are both rated to their marks.

658a UAE 2000 GUINEAS SPONSORED BY AL TAYER MOTORS (GROUP 3) (TAPETA) 1m

3:55 (3:56) 3-Y-0

£92,024 (£30,674; £15,337; £7,668; £4,601; £3,067)

RPR

1 **Soft Falling Rain (SAF)**[28] 245 4-9-5 113 PaulHanagan 8 106+
(M F De Kock, South Africa) *trckd ldrs: t.k.h: rdn to ld 2 1/2f out: r.o wl: comf* **8/11**[1]

2 2 ¼ **Snowboarder (USA)**[28] 245 3-8-9 91 SilvestreDeSousa 3 98+
(Mahmood Al Zarooni) *settled in rr: r.o fnl 2f: nrst fin but no ch w wnr* **16/1**

3 ¾ **Zahee (NZ)**[28] 245 4-9-5 98 ChristopheSoumillon 5 99
(M F De Kock, South Africa) *mid-div: chsd ldrs 2f out: kpt on same pce fnl f* **12/1**

4 nse **Deauville Prince (FR)**[124] 7076 3-8-9 105 RichardKingscote 2 96
(Tom Dascombe) *sn led: hdd 2f out: r.o gamely tl wknd 1f out* **20/1**

5 2 ½ **Filfil (USA)**[7] 553 3-8-9 87 AhmedAjtebi 1 90
(Mahmood Al Zarooni) *trckd ldrs: ev ch 2f out: one pce fnl f* **50/1**

6 ¾ **Fortify (USA)**[103] 7572 3-8-9 109 (t) MickaelBarzalona 4 89
(Mahmood Al Zarooni) *mid-div: smooth prog 2 1/2f out: wknd fnl f* **7/2**[2]

7 3 ½ **Glass Office**[28] 245 3-8-9 108 JamieSpencer 7 81
(David Simcock) *settled in rr: nvr nr to chal* **5/1**[3]

8 8 ¼ **Pure Excellence**[7] 554 3-8-5 101 AdrianNicholls 6 58
(Mark Johnston) *trckd ldrs tl wknd 2f out* **50/1**

1m 36.7s (-0.80)
WFA 3 from 4yo 19lb 8 Ran SP% **119.1**
CSF 16.21 EX 12.10 TRIFECTA 41.50 WIN 1.50 PL 1.00, 2.30, 4.30.
Owner Hamdan Al Maktoum **Bred** Highlands Farm Stud (pty) Ltd **Trained** South Africa

FOCUS
Hard to be positive about the form. While the pace was good early, it slowed on the bend (25.87, 23.14, 24.10). The overall time was 0.31 seconds slower than the Firebreak Stakes, which unfolded in similar fashion. The winner did not need to run to his best.

659a FIREBREAK STKS SPONSORED BY RANGE ROVER (GROUP 3) (TAPETA) 1m

4:30 (4:30) 3-Y-0+

£73,619 (£24,539; £12,269; £6,134; £3,680; £2,453)

RPR

1 **Moonwalk In Paris (FR)**[172] 5649 5-9-0 113 AhmedAjtebi 1 115
(Mahmood Al Zarooni) *mid-div: smooth prog 2 1/2f out: led 1 1/2f out: comf* **9/1**

2 2 **Fulbright**[35] 153 4-9-3 113 (t) MickaelBarzalona 5 113
(Mahmood Al Zarooni) *mid-div: chsd ldrs 2f out: ev ch 110yds out: one pce fnl 55yds* **5/1**[3]

3 ¼ **Barbecue Eddie (USA)**[35] 153 9-9-3 113 (b) PaulHanagan 4 112
(Doug Watson, UAE) *mid-div: chsd ldrs 2 1/2f out: r.o fnl 1 1/2f: nrst fin* **4/1**[2]

4 1 ¾ **Haatheq (USA)**[20] 392 6-9-0 112 RoystonFfrench 14 105
(A Al Raihe, UAE) *trckd ldng trio: ev ch 1 1/2f out: could nt qckn fnl f* **16/1**

5 ¾ **Saamidd**[14] 467 5-9-0 113 (tp) KierenFallon 6 104
(Saeed bin Suroor) *slowly away: settled in rr: nvr nr to chal but r.o fnl 110yds* **16/1**

6 nse **Santefisio**[12] 503 7-9-0 97 (b) GaryCarroll 12 104
(Keith Dalgleish) *slowly away: settled in rr: nvr able to chal but r.o fnl 2f* **66/1**

7 hd **Elderly Paradise (AUS)**[21] 364 6-9-0 111 (e) ODoleuze 10 103
(M C Tam, Macau) *trckd ldrs: led 1 1/2f out: wknd fnl 55yds* **16/1**

8 1 **Capital Attraction (USA)**[20] 392 6-9-0 110 TadhgO'Shea 2 101
(Ernst Oertel, UAE) *trckd ldrs: ev ch 1 1/2f out: could nt qckn fnl 110yds* **25/1**

9 ¾ **Derbaas (USA)**[14] 466 7-9-0 113 (t) DaneO'Neill 11 99
(A Al Raihe, UAE) *nvr bttr than mid-div* **25/1**

10 ¾ **Out Of Bounds (USA)**[35] 153 4-9-0 110 SilvestreDeSousa 3 97
(Saeed bin Suroor) *mid-div: chsd ldrs 2f out: could nt qckn fnl f* **7/2**[1]

11 2 **Treble Jig (USA)**[20] 392 6-9-2 105 WayneSmith 8 95
(M Al Muhairi, UAE) *sn led: hdd & wknd 1 1/2f out* **18/1**

12 2 ½ **Malossol (USA)**[21] 367 4-9-0 109 (bt) CO'Donoghue 9 87
(G Botti, France) *nvr bttr than mid-div* **33/1**

13 ¼ **Daddy Long Legs (USA)**[159] 6063 4-9-0 113 ChristopheSoumillon 7 86
(M F De Kock, South Africa) *nvr bttr than mid-div* **4/1**[2]

14 2 ¾ **Silver Ocean (USA)**[14] 465 5-9-2 110 Per-AndersGraberg 13 82
(Niels Petersen, Norway) *nvr nr to chal* **40/1**

1m 36.39s (-1.11) 14 Ran SP% **126.4**
CSF 53.98 WIN 8.90 PL 2.70, 2.10, 1.50 EX 49.80 TRIFECTA 293.80.
Owner Godolphin **Bred** S A R L Neustrian Associates Et Al **Trained** Newmarket, Suffolk

FOCUS
The pace, which was good early, slowed around the bend and they then quickened up the straight: 25.04 (400m), 23.08 (800m), 24.19 (1200m), before the winner clocked 23.49 to the finish. The form is a bit muddling but the third is a decent guide.

660a AL SHINDAGHA SPRINT SPONSORED BY JAGUAR XJ (GROUP 3) (TAPETA) 6f

5:05 (5:05) 3-Y-0+

£73,619 (£24,539; £12,269; £6,134; £3,680; £2,453)

RPR

1 **Mental (AUS)**[96] 7695 5-9-5 121 MickaelBarzalona 6 121+
(Mahmood Al Zarooni) *slowly away: smooth prog 2f out: led fnl 110yds comf* **7/2**[2]

2 1 **Kavanagh (SAF)**[14] 467 6-9-0 110 ChristopheSoumillon 1 113
(M F De Kock, South Africa) *trckd ldng: led 1 1/2f out: hdd fnl 110yds* **22/1**

3 ¾ **Krypton Factor**[236] 3370 5-9-0 123 (b) KierenFallon 3 111+
(Fawzi Abdulla Nass, Bahrain) *mid-div: chsd ldrs 2f out: nt qckn fnl 110yds* **5/2**[1]

4 ¼ **Balmont Mast (IRE)**[21] 365 5-9-0 110 CO'Donoghue 7 110
(Edward Lynam, Ire) *in rr of mid-div: r.o fnl 1 1/2f: nrst fin* **10/1**

5 hd **Iver Bridge Lad**[14] 465 6-9-0 101 DaraghO'Donohoe 13 109
(John Ryan) *settled in rr: kpt on fnl 2f but nvr able to chal* **25/1**

6 ¾ **Tamaathul**[28] 244 6-9-0 115 (t) PaulHanagan 12 107+
(A Al Raihe, UAE) *settled in rr: r.o fnl 2f: nrst fin* **9/2**[3]

7 2 ¼ **Dubawi Sound**[14] 467 5-9-0 101 (t) JamesDoyle 8 100
(David Brown) *in rr of mid-div: kpt on same pce fnl 1 1/2f* **20/1**

8 ½ **Hitchens (IRE)**[21] 365 8-9-0 113 JamieSpencer 9 98
(David Barron) *nvr nr to chal* **10/1**

9 1 ¼ **Govinda (USA)**[21] 365 6-9-0 105 TedDurcan 14 94
(Vanja Sandrup, Sweden) *nvr bttr than mid-div* **33/1**

10 ¼ **Es Que Love (IRE)**[28] 244 4-9-0 104 AdrianNicholls 11 93
(Mark Johnston) *trckd ldrs tl outpcd 1 1/2f out* **33/1**

11 2 ½ **Ganas (IRE)**[21] 365 5-9-0 108 TadhgO'Shea 10 85
(Ernst Oertel, UAE) *sn led: hdd & wknd 1 1/2f out* **8/1**

12 5 ¾ **Alazeyab (USA)**[6] 575 7-9-0 105 (vt) DaneO'Neill 4 67
(A Al Raihe, UAE) *slowly away: sn rdn in rr: nvr nr to chal* **40/1**

13 ¼ **Ballista (IRE)**[21] 365 5-9-0 109 RichardKingscote 2 66
(Tom Dascombe) *trckd ldng tl outpcd 1 1/2f out* **16/1**

14 2 ¾ **Global City (IRE)**[92] 7709 7-9-0 102 (t) SilvestreDeSousa 5 57
(Saeed bin Suroor) *slowly away: nvr bttr than mid-div* **25/1**

1m 10.59s (-1.01) 14 Ran SP% **129.3**
CSF: 88.51 EXACTA 43.50 TRIFECTA 124.70 WIN 3.50 PL 1.60, 3.00, 1.40.
Owner Godolphin **Bred** Darley **Trained** Newmarket, Suffolk

FOCUS
A quality Group 3 sprint and Ganas set the quickest-ever 800m split on this surface, clocking 46.47. He was hassled up front by Ballista and neither of them had a chance of seeing it out. The pace scenario set things up nicely for the winner, who is rated a bit below his Australian best.

661a RANGE ROVER SPORT TROPHY (H'CAP) (TURF) 1m 4f 38y

5:40 (5:40) (100-115,115) 3-Y-0+

£64,417 (£21,472; £10,736; £5,368; £3,220; £2,147)

RPR

1 **Anatolian**[28] 246 5-8-10 **105** MickaelBarzalona 2 108+
(Mahmood Al Zarooni) *mid-div: smooth prog 2 1/2f out: led 1 1/2f out: comf* **13/8**[1]

2 1¼ **Topclas (FR)**[21] 362 7-8-7 **101**.................................(tp) WayneSmith 12 103+
(M bin Shafya, UAE) *settled in rr: smooth prog 2 1/2f out: r.o wl fnl 1 1/2f but no ch w wnr* **33/1**

3 1¾ **Dormello (IRE)**[20] 392 5-8-9 **104**.................................... JamesDoyle 6 102
(D Selvaratnam, UAE) *slowly away: settled in rr: smooth prog 3f out: r.o fnl 1 1/2f* **16/1**

4 2½ **Jutland**[34] 179 6-8-13 **107**.. PatDobbs 1 102
(Doug Watson, UAE) *trckd ldrs: led after 2 1/2f: rdn 3f out: hdd 1 1/2f out: kpt on same pce* **14/1**

5 ¼ **Bob Le Beau (IRE)**[7] 555 6-8-7 **101**.........................(p) TadhgO'Shea 11 96
(Mrs John Harrington, Ire) *sn led: hdd after 2 1/2f: rdn 3 1/2f out: kpt on same pce fnl 2f* **10/1**

6 1½ **Shimraan (FR)**[320] 1149 6-9-6 **115**.................................. AhmedAjtebi 10 106
(Mahmood Al Zarooni) *settled in rr: nvr nr to chal but kpt on fnl 1 1/2f* **10/1**

7 ¼ **Fattsota**[110] 7405 5-8-13 **107**.. CO'Donoghue 5 99
(Marco Botti) *trckd ldng pair tl 4 1/2f out* **7/1**[3]

8 2 **Silvaner (GER)**[165] 5-9-2 **110**... TedDurcan 3 99
(P Schiergen, Germany) *settled in rr: kpt on same pce fnl 2f* **20/1**

9 nse **Bank Of Burden (USA)**[14] 462 6-9-0 **108**........(t) Per-AndersGraberg 7 97
(Niels Petersen, Norway) *settled in rr: nvr nr to chal but r.o fnl 1 1/2f* **25/1**

10 1 **Lindenthaler (GER)**[26] 242 5-8-11 **106**................................ AStarke 8 92
(P Schiergen, Germany) *trckd ldng pair tl 4f out* **11/1**

11 4 **Adroitly (AUS)**[14] 462 6-8-9 **104**.............................. SilvestreDeSousa 4 84
(Saeed bin Suroor) *settled in rr: nvr nr to chal* **5/1**[2]

12 9½ **Induna (AUS)**[137] 5-8-9 **104**..................................(t) PaulHanagan 13 69
(Saeed bin Suroor) *in rr of mid-div: nvr able to chal* **14/1**

13 22 **Court Circle**[14] 462 6-8-8 **102**..(b) KierenFallon 9 32
(Rune Haugen, Norway) *nvr bttr than mid-div* **25/1**

2m 32.14s (152.14) **13 Ran SP% 128.4**
CSF: 84.49 TRICAST 723.85 EX 100.00 WIN 2.00 PL: 1.00, 14.10, 5.00 TRIFECTA 3349.70.
Placepot: £282.40 to a £1 stake. Pool: £13482.61 - 34.85 winning tickets. Quadpot: £8.80 to a £1 stake. Pool: £648.50 - 54.10 winning tickets.
Owner Godolphin **Bred** Darley **Trained** Newmarket, Suffolk

FOCUS
They went a nice, even gallop thanks to Jutland. The sectionals were 26.50 (400m), 24.25 (800m), 24.38 (1200m), 24.70 (1600m), 24.74 (2000m).

633 LINGFIELD (L-H)
Friday, February 15

OFFICIAL GOING: Standard
Wind: light, across Weather: dry

662 BET AT BLUESQ.COM APPRENTICE (S) STKS 1m 4f (P)
1:30 (1:30) (Class 6) 4-Y-0+ **£2,045** (£603; £302) **Stalls** Low

Form RPR

2/6- 1 **Discovery Bay**[21] 389 5-9-0 78.................................. RobertTart(5) 2 76
(C F Swan, Ire) *stdd s: hld up off the pce in last trio: hdwy and clsd on ldr 4f out: rdn to ld 2f out: drvn clr and in command 1f out: comf* **4/6**[1]

053- 2 7 **Mount Abora (IRE)**[46] 8301 6-8-9 61.............................. ThomasBrown(5) 8 60
(Laura Mongan) *racd off the pce in midfield: chsd ldng pair 7f out: clsd over 4f out: rdn and effrt 2f out: chsd clr wnr ent fnl f: no imp* **6/1**[3]

-321 3 1½ **Reasons Unknown (IRE)**[2] 630 5-9-7 54.................... CharlesBishop(3) 3 67
(Thomas McLaughlin, Ire) *stdd s: t.k.h: hld up off the pce in rr: clsd on ldrs over 4f out: rdn and chsd ldng trio over 2f out: 3rd and no ch w wnr fnl f* **7/2**[2]

0265 4 4½ **Electrician**[2] 633 4-9-2 63..(p) NoelGarbutt(5) 7 60
(Tim Pitt) *led: clr 8f out: rdn and hdd 2f out: btn and lost 2nd ent fnl f: wknd* **14/1**

214- 5 13 **Locum**[151] 6305 8-8-12 59.................................. JordonMcMurray(7) 4 34
(Mark H Tompkins) *t.k.h: hld up off the pce in midfield: clsd on ldrs over 4f out: 5th and struggling u.p over 2f out: wl btn fnl 2f* **16/1**

0-00 6 14 **Sangrail**[12] 510 4-8-6 50.. RyanTate(5) 1 7
(William Muir) *broke wl: chsd ldrs but allowed ldng pair to go clr after 1f: rdn and dropped to rr 3f out: t.o fnl f* **66/1**

60-0 7 1 **Total Obsession**[23] 343 6-8-9 43...........................(v[1]) PhilipPrince(5) 5 5
(Mark Hoad) *chsd ldr and wnt clr of field after 1f: lost pl u.p wl over 2f out: t.o fnl f* **100/1**

2m 30.43s (-2.57) **Going Correction** +0.05s/f (Slow)
WFA 4 from 5yo+ 3lb **7 Ran SP% 111.5**
Speed ratings (Par 101): **110,105,104,101,92 83,82**
Tote Swingers: 1&2 £1.80, 1&3 £1.10, 2&3 £1.60 CSF £5.01 TOTE £1.80: £1.30, £2.20; EX 4.20 Trifecta £7.70 Pool: £2,594.17 - 250.90 winning units..Winner was bought in for 10,400gns.
Owner Keoghan Carthy Partnership **Bred** The Queen **Trained** Cloughjordan, Co Tipperary

FOCUS
A strongly run seller and a winner far too good for this level. He did not need to match his Irish form.

663 MORE THAN JUST A RACECOURSE MEDIAN AUCTION MAIDEN STKS 1m 2f (P)
2:00 (2:00) (Class 6) 3-Y-0 **£2,045** (£603; £302) **Stalls** Low

Form RPR

53 1 **Edwyn Ralph**[21] 373 3-9-5 0... JimCrowley 3 74
(David Simcock) *broke wl but sn stdd: chsd ldr 7f out: rdn and ev ch 2f out: drvn over 1f out: kpt on u.p to ld last strides* **5/4**[1]

32 2 hd **Aryal**[14] 479 3-9-5 0.. JoeFanning 6 74
(Mark Johnston) *sn led: rdn ent fnl 2f: sustained duel w wnr after: kpt on u.p tl hdd and no ex last strides* **6/4**[2]

3 ¾ **Incorporate** 3-9-5 0... LukeMorris 4 73
(Pat Eddery) *t.k.h early: chsd ldr tl 7f out: chsd ldng pair after: rdn over 3f out: sltly outpcd 2f out: rallied u.p fnl f: kpt on wl: no imp cl home* **8/1**

32- 4 10 **Minimee**[73] 7979 3-9-5 0.. AdamKirby 2 53
(Alan Bailey) *in tch in midfield: 4th and struggling u.p over 2f out: wl btn over 1f out* **6/1**[3]

00- 5 5 **Frederick Alfred**[114] 7323 3-9-5 0.................................. J-PGuillambert 5 43
(Mark H Tompkins) *in tch in rr: rdn and struggling 3f out: sn bhd* **66/1**

6 20 **Tavistock Fair** 3-9-0 0... HarryPoulton(5) 1
(Michael Squance) *t.k.h: hld up in tch: rdn and dropped to rr over 3f out: lost tch over 2f out: t.o* **66/1**

2m 6.86s (0.26) **Going Correction** +0.05s/f (Slow) **6 Ran SP% 112.8**
Speed ratings (Par 95): **100,99,99,91,87 71**
Tote Swingers: 1&2 £1.10, 1&3 £1.80, 2&3 £2.10 CSF £3.43 TOTE £2.50: £1.60, £1.10; EX 3.80 Trifecta £11.20 Pool: £2,351.27 - 157.01 winning units..
Owner Gee Ceffyl Bach Club **Bred** Azienda Agricola Rosati Colarieti **Trained** Newmarket, Suffolk

FOCUS
A modest maiden. The form is a little muddling, rated around the runner-up.

664 CYPRIUM BAR AT MARRIOTT LINGFIELD (S) STKS 7f (P)
2:30 (2:30) (Class 6) 3-Y-0+ **£2,045** (£603; £302) **Stalls** Low

Form RPR

-200 1 **Fairy Mist (IRE)**[12] 510 6-9-8 46... AdamKirby 2 48
(John Bridger) *chsd ldrs: rdn 3f out: drvn ent fnl 2f: hdwy to ld 1f out: clr but stl drvn ins fnl f: a jst lasting home* **4/6**[1]

-500 2 nk **Amber Moon**[11] 517 8-8-12 39.................................... AnnStokell(5) 4 42
(Ann Stokell) *in tch in last pair: niggled along 5f out: rdn and no imp over 1f out: hdwy and styd on strly ins fnl f: chsd wnr and clsng qckly towards fin* **25/1**

0-06 3 2¼ **Flying Kitty**[27] 277 4-9-3 39..(v) SeanLevey 1 36
(John Bridger) *t.k.h: led tl over 5f out: chsd ldr after: rdn and ev ch ent fnl 2f: carried rt wl over 1f out: rdr dropped whip and no ex 1f out: wknd towards fin* **6/1**[3]

-306 4 ¾ **Not My Choice (IRE)**[7] 565 8-9-8 45..............................(b) AmirQuinn 5 39
(Paul Howling) *dwlt: rcvrd to ld over 5f out: pressed and rdn 2f out: edgd rt wl over 1f out: hdd 1f out: wknd wl ins fnl f* **5/2**[2]

00 5 9 **Hester Street**[18] 424 3-7-7 0.....................................(bt[1]) NoelGarbutt(7) 3 10
(Rae Guest) *s.i.s: rdn along in rr thrght: lost tch over 1f out* **20/1**

1m 26.04s (1.24) **Going Correction** +0.05s/f (Slow)
WFA 3 from 4yo+ 17lb **5 Ran SP% 111.5**
Speed ratings (Par 101): **94,93,91,90,79**
CSF £18.68 TOTE £1.60: £1.10, £4.00; EX 15.40 Trifecta £44.40 Pool: £1,307.87 - 22.07 winning units..No bid for the winner.
Owner J J Bridger **Bred** Sandro Garavelli **Trained** Liphook, Hants

FOCUS
A desperately weak seller, rated around the runner-up.

665 FOLLOW US ON TWITTER @LINGFIELDPARK H'CAP 7f (P)
3:05 (3:05) (Class 6) (0-60,60) 4-Y-0+ **£2,045** (£603; £302) **Stalls** Low

Form RPR

40-4 1 **Hereford Boy**[15] 451 9-9-7 60...(p) AdamKirby 1 68
(Dean Ivory) *trckd ldng pair: swtchd out rt and effrt u.p wl over 1f out: styd on to ld wl ins fnl f: r.o wl* **5/1**[2]

4-65 2 nk **Sannibel**[7] 560 5-8-11 57..................................... RobertTart(7) 3 64
(Graeme McPherson) *hld up in tch in midfield: rdn and effrt to chse ldrs over 1f out: styd on wl u.p to chse wnr wl ins fnl f: r.o* **25/1**

60-2 3 ½ **Spirit Of Xaar (IRE)**[24] 320 7-9-6 59.......................(p) RobertHavlin 11 65
(Linda Jewell) *chsd ldr: rdn and ev ch over 1f out: unable qck u.p fnl 100yds* **7/1**[3]

06-2 4 nk **Arachnophobia (IRE)**[30] 223 7-9-4 57........................(b) GeorgeBaker 2 62
(Martin Bosley) *led: rdn and hrd pressed over 1f out: hdd and no ex wl ins fnl f* **5/1**[2]

641- 5 ¾ **Patavium Prince (IRE)**[59] 8156 10-9-7 60.......................... IanMongan 9 63
(Jo Crowley) *hld up in tch in midfield: effrt u.p over 1f out: styng on whn swtchd rt ins fnl f: kpt on fnl 100yds but nvr able to chal* **7/2**[1]

-513 6 ½ **Welsh Inlet (IRE)**[15] 452 5-9-7 60.................................... SeanLevey 5 62
(John Bridger) *chsd ldrs: effrt u.p over 1f out: styd on same pce ins fnl f* **8/1**

0-63 7 ½ **Purley Queen (IRE)**[4] 617 4-9-6 59...................................... JDSmith 6 59
(Sylvester Kirk) *s.i.s: hld up in tch in rr: rdn and effrt wl over 1f out: kpt on ins fnl f: nvr trbld ldrs* **8/1**

1226 8 1¼ **Baby Dottie**[13] 493 6-9-2 60.............................(tp) JemmaMarshall(5) 8 57
(Pat Phelan) *t.k.h: hld up in tch in midfield: rdn and no imp over 1f out: one pce and no threat to ldrs fnl f* **12/1**

-004 9 hd **Jackie Love (IRE)**[13] 497 5-8-10 49.......................(v) KirstyMilczarek 10 45
(Olivia Maylam) *hld up in tch in last trio: rdn and effrt over 1f out: no imp: nvr trbld ldrs* **12/1**

20-0 10 ½ **Ensnare**[24] 320 8-9-2 55...(b) J-PGuillambert 4 50
(Willie Musson) *hld up in last pair: rdn and no hdwy over 1f out: nvr trbld ldrs* **16/1**

1m 24.72s (-0.08) **Going Correction** +0.05s/f (Slow) **10 Ran SP% 115.4**
Speed ratings (Par 101): **102,101,101,100,99 99,98,97,97,96**
Tote Swingers: 1&2 £23.30, 1&3 £3.10, 2&3 £31.50 CSF £118.01 CT £894.50 TOTE £5.60: £2.80, £5.20, £2.10; EX 154.40 Trifecta £1403.20 Part won. Pool: £1,871.01 - 0.79 winning units..
Owner Recycled Products Limited **Bred** Mrs L R Burrage **Trained** Radlett, Herts

FOCUS
A moderate handicap. The pace was ordinary and the first four were never far away. The winner is rated to his best form of last summer.

666 BLUE SQUARE BET H'CAP 1m (P)
3:40 (3:40) (Class 4) (0-85,86) 3-Y-0 **£4,690** (£1,395; £697; £348) **Stalls** High

Form RPR

3-22 1 **King George River (IRE)**[14] 474 3-9-1 86.................. RobertTart(7) 3 93+
(Alan Bailey) *hld up wl in tch in last pair: nt clr run and waiting for gap ent fnl f: drvn and qcknd between horses ins fnl f: led wl ins fnl f: edgd rt nr fin* **6/4**[1]

1 2 hd **Henry The Aviator (USA)**[18] 425 3-8-11 75.................. JoeFanning 5 80
(Mark Johnston) *chsd ldr: drvn and ev ch over 1f out: led fnl 100yds: hdd and kpt on same pce wl ins fnl f* **2/1**[2]

6-21 3 ½ **Great Demeanor (USA)**[13] 492 3-8-11 75..................... AndreaAtzeni 6 79
(David Elsworth) *led and grad crossed to inner: rdn and hrd pressed over 1f out: drvn and hdd fnl 100yds: styd on same pce after* **8/1**

3-1 4 ½ **Rouge Nuage (IRE)**[14] 479 3-8-3 74.............................. RyanTate(7) 4 77
(Conrad Allen) *t.k.h: chsd ldrs: rdn and chal ent fnl f: no ex wl ins fnl f* **12/1**

51-2 5 ¾ **Ningara**[39] 91 3-8-10 74.. HayleyTurner 2 76+
(Andrew Balding) *stdd s: hld up in tch in rr: rdn and effrt over 1f out: styng on and chsng ldrs whn short of room and eased cl home* **6/1**[3]

-114 6 2½ **Gabrial The Boss (USA)**[14] 474 3-8-12 76......................(t) JimCrowley 1 71
(David Simcock) *chsd ldrs: effrt u.p to chal on inner over 1f out: no ex and wknd ins fnl f* **12/1**

1m 38.72s (0.52) **Going Correction** +0.05s/f (Slow) **6 Ran SP% 114.1**
Speed ratings (Par 99): **99,98,98,97,97 94**
Tote Swingers: 1&2 £2.90, 1&3 £3.20, 2&3 £1.80 CSF £4.88 TOTE £2.30: £1.90, £2.20; EX 6.80 Trifecta £30.10 Pool: £3,549.33 - 15.27 winning units..
Owner John Stocker **Bred** Barronstown Stud **Trained** Newmarket, Suffolk
■ Stewards' Enquiry : Robert Tart two-day ban: careless riding (Mar 1-2)

FOCUS
A fascinating, not to mention competitive 3yo handicap, run at a steady pace. Because of the bunch finish it's hard to be too positive about the form.

667 GOLF MEMBERSHIP AT MARRIOTT LINGFIELD MAIDEN STKS 6f (P)
4:15 (4:15) (Class 5) 3-Y-O+ **£2,726** (£805; £402) **Stalls** Low

Form RPR
1 **Secret Of Success** 3-8-6 0 ChrisCatlin 3 57
(Rae Guest) *mde all: rdn over 1f out: drew clr and sustained duel w rival fnl f: hld on wl* **5/1**[3]
5-0 2 *shd* **Desert Donkey**[20] [396] 3-8-4 0 JoeyHaynes[(7)] 5 62
(Andrew Balding) *upsides wnr thrght: rdn over 1f out: sustained duel w wnr fnl f: r.o but jst hld* **7/4**[1]
3403 3 *5* **Island Express (IRE)**[6] [581] 6-9-7 53 (tp) AnnStokell[(5)] 10 50
(Ann Stokell) *dwlt: in tch in last trio: wd bnd 2f out: sn rdn: styd on fnl f to go 3rd fnl 50yds: no threat to ldng pair* **20/1**
5-50 4 *¾* **King's Future**[13] [497] 4-9-12 46 KierenFox 8 48
(Lee Carter) *in tch in midfield on outer: 3rd and unable qck u.p over 1f out: wknd ins fnl f: lost 3rd fnl 50yds* **20/1**
3655 5 *1* **Back For Tea (IRE)**[7] [565] 5-9-12 44 (be) GeorgeBaker 6 44
(Phil McEntee) *hld up in tch in last trio: rdn and effrt wl over 1f out: wknd ins fnl f* **10/1**
6 *2* **Purford Green** 4-9-7 0 JoeFanning 2 33
(Michael Attwater) *chsd ldrs: rdn and unable qck over 1f out: wknd ins fnl f* **20/1**
442- 7 *nk* **Jimmy Elder**[189] [5061] 3-8-11 65 SeanLevey 7 33
(Richard Hannon) *v free to post: plld hrd: chsd ldrs: lost pl and rdn whn hmpd wl over 1f out: sn drvn and foung nil: bhd fnl f* **2/1**[2]
0-5 8 *½* **Lively Little Lady**[13] [492] 3-7-13 0 NoelGarbutt[(7)] 9 26
(Tim Pitt) *hld up in tch in rr: rdn and hdwy on inner over 1f out: wknd fnl f* **14/1**

1m 12.13s (0.23) **Going Correction** +0.05s/f (Slow)
WFA 3 from 4yo+ 15lb 8 Ran SP% **116.4**
Speed ratings (Par 103): **100,99,93,92,90 88,87,87**
Tote Swingers: 1&2 £3.30, 1&3 £10.20, 2&3 £8.40 CSF £14.04 TOTE £4.90: £2.20, £1.10, £3.20; EX 18.40 Trifecta £174.30 Pool: £3,155.60 - 6.08 winning units..
Owner J H Metzger **Bred** J H Metzger **Trained** Newmarket, Suffolk
■ Stewards' Enquiry : Sean Levey five-day ban: used whip when out of contention (Mar 1-2,4-6)

FOCUS
A weak maiden. The first pair finished clear but this is very limted form.

668 GET STRAIGHT TO THE BET AT BLUESQ.COM H'CAP 1m 5f (P)
4:50 (4:50) (Class 6) (0-65,66) 4-Y-O+ **£2,045** (£603; £302) **Stalls** Low

Form RPR
-235 1 **Linkable**[14] [475] 4-9-5 62 (t) SebSanders 8 69
(Brendan Powell) *dwlt: hld up in tch in rr: hdwy on outer 3f out: drvn and no prog over 1f out: rallied and str run ins fnl f to ld last strides* **10/1**
060- 2 *hd* **Bramshill Lass**[55] [8229] 4-9-5 62 (b) JimCrowley 4 69
(Amanda Perrett) *chsd ldr tl 3f: styd chsng ldrs: swtchd rt and rdn over 1f out: rallied u.p to ld wl ins fnl f: hdd last strides* **7/1**[3]
-032 3 *¾* **El Libertador (USA)**[12] [512] 7-8-9 55 (b) JoeyHaynes[(7)] 3 61
(Eric Wheeler) *in tch in midfield: shuffled bk on inner over 2f out: rdn and hdwy over 1f out: led ins fnl f: hdd and no ex wl ins fnl f* **10/1**
52-2 4 *1* **Comedy House**[23] [343] 5-9-3 63 RyanTate[(7)] 7 67
(Michael Madgwick) *in tch in midfield: effrt u.p over 1f out: kpt on ins fnl f: nvr quite gng pce to chal* **5/2**[2]
36-4 5 *¾* **Celtic Charlie (FR)**[23] [343] 8-8-10 54 JemmaMarshall[(5)] 10 57
(Pat Phelan) *taken down early: t.k.h: hld up in tch in midfield on outer: hdwy to chse ldrs 3f out: styd on same pce u.p fr over 1f out* **7/1**[3]
330- 6 *hd* **Masters Blazing**[55] [8229] 4-9-5 62 (p) KirstyMilczarek 1 65
(John Ryan) *hld up in tch in last pair: hdwy u.p on inner jst over 1f out: no ex and styd on same pce ins fnl f* **25/1**
21-0 7 *shd* **Langham Lily (USA)**[23] [338] 4-9-5 62 GeorgeBaker 9 66
(Chris Wall) *chsd ldrs: wnt 2nd 3f out: rdn and ev ch 2f out: drvn to ld over 1f out: hdd ins fnl f: no ex and btn whn short room and hmpd wl ins fnl f* **2/1**[1]
-021 8 *2* **Maslak (IRE)**[5] [597] 9-9-10 63 6ex ChrisCatlin 6 63
(Peter Hiatt) *led: rdn ent fnl 2f: hdd and no ex over 1f out: wknd ins fnl f* **16/1**

2m 48.7s (2.70) **Going Correction** +0.05s/f (Slow)
WFA 4 from 5yo+ 4lb 8 Ran SP% **114.8**
Speed ratings (Par 101): **93,92,92,91,91 91,91,89**
Tote Swingers: 1&2 £7.90, 1&3 £7.50, 2&3 £10.40 CSF £77.52 CT £721.54 TOTE £10.10: £2.20, £2.70, £2.10; EX 52.90 Trifecta £388.60.
Owner Jonathan H Ross **Bred** Juddmonte Farms Ltd **Trained** Upper Lambourn, Berks
■ Stewards' Enquiry : Joey Haynes one-day ban: careless riding (Mar 1)
Jim Crowley two-day ban: careless riding Mar 1-2)

FOCUS
An ordinary staying handicap, and another muddling race. The winner is a still a few pounds off his 3yo best.
T/Plt: £14.90 to a £1 stake. Pool: £52,951.67 - 2,580.67 winning tickets. T/Qpdt: £11.70 to a £1 stake. Pool: £3,263.85 - 206.08 winning tickets. SP

610 WOLVERHAMPTON (A.W) (L-H)
Friday, February 15

OFFICIAL GOING: Standard
Wind: Light across Weather: Overcast

669 MONEY BACK RACING SPECIALS AT BOOKMAKERS.CO.UK H'CAP 5f 20y(P)
5:00 (5:01) (Class 6) (0-60,60) 3-Y-O **£1,940** (£577; £288; £144) **Stalls** Low

Form RPR
31 1 **Dangerous Age**[22] [356] 3-9-3 56 JamieSpencer 4 62+
(J W Hills) *broke wl: sn stdd and lost pl: hdwy over 1f out: shkn up to ld and hung lft ins fnl f: pushed out* **10/11**[1]
64-3 2 *1¼* **Lexi's Beauty (IRE)**[43] [36] 3-8-7 46 oh1 FrannyNorton 7 47
(Patrick Morris) *s.i.s: hld up: swtchd lft and hdwy over 1f out: chsd wnr ins fnl f: styd on* **25/1**
5-65 3 *2¾* **Whiteflats**[34] [185] 3-8-7 46 oh1 (v) JimmyQuinn 1 37
(Derek Shaw) *dwlt: hld up: rdn and r.o ins fnl f: nt rch ldrs* **16/1**
4 *1* **Samara Jazz (IRE)**[126] [7036] 3-8-11 50 GrahamGibbons 3 38
(Patrick Carey, Ire) *chsd ldrs: led over 3f out: rdn and hdd ins fnl f: no ex* **7/1**

6-30 5 *¾* **Scarlet Strand**[33] [197] 3-9-4 57 RobertWinston 2 42
(Reg Hollinshead) *chsd ldrs: rdn over 1f out: no ex ins fnl f* **11/1**
52-3 6 *½* **Magic Ice**[22] [356] 3-9-0 53 TomMcLaughlin 5 36
(John Berry) *chsd ldrs: shkn up over 1f out: no ex fnl f* **13/2**[3]
-63 7 *2½* **Lady Calantha**[8] [549] 3-8-9 48 TomEaves 8 22
(Alan Berry) *sn led: hdd over 3f out: ev ch 2f out: wknd over 1f out* **40/1**
3-15 8 *hd* **Outbid**[21] [374] 3-9-7 60 FergusSweeney 6 33
(Jamie Osborne) *chsd ldrs: rdn over 1f out: wknd fnl f* **6/1**[2]

1m 3.14s (0.84) **Going Correction** +0.025s/f (Slow) 8 Ran SP% **113.0**
Speed ratings (Par 95): **94,92,87,86,84 84,80,79**
toteswingers: 1&2 £5.60, 1&3 £5.20, 2&3 £28.40. CSF £27.92 CT £230.85 TOTE £2.00: £1.10, £3.20, £3.40; EX 18.60 Trifecta £206.50 Pool: £3,067.15 - 11.13 winning units..
Owner Ross Hunter & David Klein **Bred** Mrs T Brudenell **Trained** Upper Lambourn, Berks

FOCUS
A weak handicap, but it was strongly run. The winner has more to offer.

670 HORSE RACING BEST BETS AT BOOKMAKERS.CO.UK H'CAP 5f 20y(P)
5:30 (5:30) (Class 7) (0-50,50) 4-Y-O+ **£1,940** (£577; £288; £144) **Stalls** Low

Form RPR
55-4 1 **Cincinnati Kit**[9] [529] 4-9-7 50 (t) JamieSpencer 7 65+
(Stuart Williams) *s.i.s: hld up: hdwy over 1f out: led wl ins fnl f: comf* **4/1**[2]
2 *1½* **Majestic Timeline (IRE)**[42] [66] 4-9-3 46 (t) StevieDonohoe 11 53
(Adrian Brendan Joyce, Ire) *chsd ldrs: led over 1f out: rdn and hdd wl ins fnl f* **14/1**
6530 3 *¾* **Slatey Hen (IRE)**[27] [277] 5-9-0 48 (p) CharlesBishop[(5)] 2 52
(Violet M Jordan) *chsd ldrs: pushed along 1/2-way: rdn and ev ch over 1f out: styd on same pce ins fnl f* **12/1**
-002 4 *hd* **Cadmium Loch**[8] [551] 5-9-5 48 (p) ShaneKelly 1 51
(Reg Hollinshead) *hld up: hdwy over 1f out: sn rdn: styd on same pce ins fnl f* **11/4**[1]
-553 5 *nse* **Rightcar**[23] [339] 6-8-11 45 SladeO'Hara[(5)] 8 48+
(Peter Grayson) *hld up: nt clr run and swtchd rt ins fnl f: r.o: nt rch ldrs* **9/1**
-203 6 *3½* **Deveze (IRE)**[9] [529] 5-9-2 45 (b) RobertWinston 4 36
(Milton Bradley) *chsd ldrs: rdn over 1f out: wknd ins fnl f* **13/2**[3]
06-0 7 *¾* **Dear Ben**[8] [551] 4-9-7 50 (t[1]) GrahamGibbons 6 38
(Brian Baugh) *sn led: rdn and hdd over 1f out: wknd ins fnl f* **7/1**
6-50 8 *1¼* **Stoneacre Hull (IRE)**[14] [472] 4-9-3 46 TomEaves 5 29
(Peter Grayson) *mid-div: pushed along and lost pl 1/2-way: wknd over 1f out* **33/1**
6506 9 *1* **Chateau Lola**[4] [610] 4-9-7 50 (v) FrannyNorton 3 30
(Derek Shaw) *mid-div: rdn over 1f out: wknd fnl f* **7/1**

1m 2.59s (0.29) **Going Correction** +0.025s/f (Slow) 9 Ran SP% **112.3**
Speed ratings (Par 97): **98,95,94,94,94 88,87,85,83**
toteswingers: 1&2 £12.40, 1&3 £9.10, 2&3 £22.60. CSF £55.80 CT £612.63 TOTE £5.40: £1.40, £5.20, £3.60; EX 77.20 Trifecta £827.30 Pool: £2,139.21 - 1.93 winning units..
Owner J W Parry **Bred** Old Mill Stud & S Williams & J Parry **Trained** Newmarket, Suffolk

FOCUS
A competitive, low-grade handicap, run at a sound pace. There's every chance the winner can do better.

671 CORAL.CO.UK H'CAP 1m 5f 194y(P)
6:00 (6:01) (Class 6) (0-65,60) 4-Y-O+ **£1,940** (£577; £288; £144) **Stalls** Low

Form RPR
6-54 1 **Jezza**[15] [458] 7-9-12 60 LukeMorris 3 68
(Karen George) *s.s: hld up: hdwy over 1f out: sn rdn: styd on u.p to ld nr fin* **9/2**[3]
-301 2 *¾* **Party Palace**[11] [515] 9-8-13 47 JimmyQuinn 4 54
(Stuart Howe) *chsd ldrs: rdn over 3f out: styd on to ld wl ins fnl f: hdd nr fin* **16/1**
-433 3 *½* **Daring Damsel (IRE)**[17] [430] 4-9-7 60 GrahamGibbons 1 66
(Brian Baugh) *led: pushed clr over 7f out: drvn along 5f out: hdd and no ex wl ins fnl f* **12/1**
61-6 4 *1¼* **Tram Express (FR)**[42] [57] 9-9-8 56 (t) JamieGoldstein 6 61
(Shaun Lycett) *hld up: hdwy over 1f out: sn rdn: styd on same pce ins fnl f* **20/1**
1 5 *1* **Speed Steed (IRE)**[20] [406] 6-8-13 54 DanielMuscutt[(7)] 2 57
(Tim Vaughan) *chsd ldrs: rdn over 1f out: styd on same pce fnl f* **3/1**[2]
-366 6 *4* **El Bravo**[15] [458] 7-9-10 58 RobertWinston 5 58
(Shaun Harris) *chsd ldr: rdn over 2f out: wknd ins fnl f* **11/2**
23-0 7 *10* **Gabrial's Hope (FR)**[33] [198] 4-9-6 59 (t) JamieSpencer 8 43
(Ian Williams) *s.i.s: hld up: racd keenly: rdn over 2f out: wknd over 1f out* **11/4**[1]
253- 8 *5* **White Deer (USA)**[50] [8260] 9-9-9 57 (v) PaddyAspell 7 42
(Geoffrey Harker) *hld up in tch: disputing cl 3rd and pushed along whn wnt wrong over 1f out: eased* **12/1**

3m 7.07s (1.07) **Going Correction** +0.025s/f (Slow)
WFA 4 from 6yo+ 5lb 8 Ran SP% **111.3**
Speed ratings (Par 101): **97,96,96,95,95 92,87,84**
toteswingers: 1&2 £6.50, 1&3 £3.80, 2&3 £7.30. CSF £66.99 CT £778.85 TOTE £6.00: £1.40, £2.90, £3.10; EX 42.70 Trifecta £152.40 Pool: £1,824.99 - 8.97 winning units..
Owner Kilcash Bloodstock Limited **Bred** C P Ranson **Trained** Higher Eastington, Devon

FOCUS
A few in-form contenders, however in the absence of anything unexposed this was just a modest staying contest. The form is rated around the third.

672 POKER AT CORAL.CO.UK CLASSIFIED CLAIMING STKS 1m 1f 103y(P)
6:30 (6:30) (Class 5) 4-Y-O+ **£2,587** (£770; £384; £192) **Stalls** Low

Form RPR
0-10 1 **Refreshestheparts (USA)**[23] [338] 4-8-10 69 (t) AaronJones[(7)] 1 80
(George Baker) *chsd ldrs: wnt 2nd over 3f out: rdn to ld over 1f out: styd on* **5/2**[1]
3212 2 *1¼* **Yourinthewill (USA)**[14] [476] 5-8-11 64 ShaneKelly 3 71
(Daniel Mark Loughnane) *hld up: hdwy over 1f out: rdn to chse wnr fnl f: r.o* **3/1**[2]
0463 3 *1¼* **Honey Of A Kitten (USA)**[2] [638] 5-8-8 66 (v) EoinWalsh[(7)] 5 73
(David Evans) *chsd ldrs: rdn over 2f out: styd on* **4/1**[3]
-311 4 *1¾* **Faithful Ruler (USA)**[11] [519] 9-8-2 65 (p) GaryPhillips[(7)] 7 63
(Ronald Harris) *hld up: rdn over 1f out: styd on ins fnl f: nvr nrr* **11/2**
0/0 5 *1¼* **Platinum (IRE)**[14] [476] 6-9-3 75 MichaelO'Connell 8 68
(Philip Kirby) *hld up: hdwy over 2f out: sn rdn: styd on same pce fnl f* **66/1**
0-54 6 *7* **Jordaura**[40] [84] 7-8-13 60 RobertWinston 4 50
(Alan Berry) *hld up: rdn over 3f out: wknd over 2f out* **16/1**

1126 7 1 **One Way Or Another (AUS)**[13] 490 10-8-11 68..(t) TomMcLaughlin 6 46
(David Evans) *sn pushed along to ld: clr 7f out: rdn over 2f out: hdd over 1f out: wknd and eased ins fnl f* **6/1**

8 31 **Strove For Gold (IRE)**[56] 8218 8-9-1 47.................... FergusSweeney 2
(Thomas McLaughlin, Ire) *chsd clr ldr tl rdn over 3f out: wknd and eased over 2f out: t.o* **100/1**

2m 1.09s (-0.61) **Going Correction** +0.025s/f (Slow) **8** Ran SP% **111.6**
Speed ratings (Par 103): **103,101,100,99,98 91,91,63**
toteswingers: 1&2 £2.70, 1&3 £4.10, 2&3 £2.00. CSF £9.65 TOTE £3.00: £1.40, £1.30, £1.50; EX 14.60 Trifecta £33.10 Pool: £1,759.22 - 39.74 winning units..Refreshestheparts was the subject of a friendly claim.
Owner Keith Jones & Family **Bred** Lazy Lane Farms Inc **Trained** Manton, Wilts

FOCUS
The usual standing dishes lined up for this classified claimer. The pace was decent and the winer recorded a small personal best.

673 FREE SPORTS BETTING AT BOOKMAKERS.CO.UK MAIDEN STKS 7f 32y(P)
7:00 (7:02) (Class 5) 3-Y-O+ **£2,587** (£770; £384; £192) **Stalls** High

Form RPR
05- 1 **Striking Echo**[49] 8270 3-8-9 0....................................... FergusSweeney 3 69
(Reg Hollinshead) *mde virtually all: rdn over 1f out: edgd lft ins fnl f: styd on* **40/1**

423- 2 1 ½ **He's A Striker (IRE)**[132] 6880 3-8-9 78.......................... BarryMcHugh 5 65
(Tony Coyle) *trckd wnr: pushed along over 2f out: rdn and hung lft over 1f out: no imp ins fnl f* **1/4**[1]

0-4 3 4 ½ **Al Sulaimi (IRE)**[13] 491 3-8-9 0.. LukeMorris 7 53
(Ronald Harris) *hld up: drvn along 1/2-way: styd on u.p ins fnl f: nt trble ldrs* **10/1**[3]

4 1 ¼ **Deal Me In (IRE)** 4-9-12 0.. MichaelO'Connell 2 56
(Ian Williams) *s.i.s: hld up: drvn along 1/2-way: styd on ins fnl f: nvr nrr* **33/1**

4 5 2 ½ **Secret Advice**[29] 236 3-8-4 0.. FrannyNorton 6 38
(Keith Dalgleish) *trckd ldrs: plld hrd: rdn over 2f out: wknd fnl f* **6/1**[2]

5 6 4 ½ **Shaken Not Stirred**[9] 532 3-8-4 0.................................... JimmyQuinn 1 26
(Milton Bradley) *s.i.s: sn prom: rdn over 2f out: wknd over 1f out* **25/1**

7 3 ½ **Logans Lad (IRE)** 3-8-9 0.......................................(t) FrankieMcDonald 4 21
(Daniel Mark Loughnane) *hld up: rdn and hung rt 1/2-way: sn lost tch* **40/1**

1m 31.0s (1.40) **Going Correction** +0.025s/f (Slow)
WFA 3 from 4yo 17lb **7** Ran SP% **115.0**
Speed ratings (Par 103): **93,91,86,84,81 76,72**
toteswingers: 1&2 £6.00, 1&3 £9.50, 2&3 £1.60. CSF £52.43 TOTE £37.30: £17.30, £1.10; EX 103.40 Trifecta £554.20 Pool: £2,481.85 - 3.35 winning units..
Owner Geoff Lloyd **Bred** Peter Webb **Trained** Upper Longdon, Staffs

FOCUS
A very modest maiden which saw a big upset with the 78-rated long odds on favourite getting turned over by a gelding who had showed little in two starts to date. The time was slow and the form is shaky.

674 ONLINE BETTING OFFERS AT BOOKMAKERS.CO.UK H'CAP 7f 32y(P)
7:30 (7:30) (Class 4) (0-85,83) 3-Y-O **£4,690** (£1,395; £697; £348) **Stalls** High

Form RPR
014- 1 **Teophilip (IRE)**[90] 7773 3-9-7 83......................................(t) AdamKirby 4 97
(Marco Botti) *hld up: hdwy 1/2-way: rdn to ld ins fnl f: r.o* **7/2**[2]

631- 2 ¾ **Grilletto (USA)**[125] 7059 3-8-9 71.................................(b) AndreaAtzeni 6 83
(James Tate) *led: rdn and hung lft over 1f out: hdd ins fnl f: styd on* **2/1**[1]

112 3 3 **Black Dave (IRE)**[9] 533 3-8-6 68.. LukeMorris 1 72
(David Evans) *prom: drvn along 4f out: outpcd 1/2-way: styd on u.p ins fnl f* **9/2**[3]

2-23 4 ½ **Staffhoss**[34] 188 3-9-4 80.. FrannyNorton 2 83
(Mark Johnston) *chsd ldrs: rdn over 2f out: styd on same pce fr over 1f out* **11/2**

1 5 1 **Street Battle (USA)**[24] 324 3-9-1 77.................................. BarryMcHugh 3 77
(Tony Coyle) *prom: chsd ldr over 5f out tl rdn over 1f out: no ex ins fnl f* **7/2**[2]

12-2 6 2 ¼ **Lucky Di**[30] 225 3-9-2 78.. RobertWinston 5 72
(Peter Hedger) *s.i.s: hld up: rdn over 2f out: nvr on terms* **10/1**

1m 29.02s (-0.58) **Going Correction** +0.025s/f (Slow) **6** Ran SP% **120.4**
Speed ratings (Par 99): **104,103,99,99,98 95**
toteswingers: 1&2 £2.50, 1&3 £4.20, 2&3 £2.80. CSF £11.97 TOTE £5.20: £2.80, £1.50; EX 16.10 Trifecta £66.70 Pool: £1,674.39 - 18.82 winning units..
Owner Giuliano Manfredini **Bred** Mount Coote Stud, Richard Pegum & M Bell Racing **Trained** Newmarket, Suffolk

FOCUS
An interesting 7f handicap for 3yos featuring either in-form or unexposed participants. The pace was decent and the first two took biggish steps forward.

675 CORAL.CO.UK MOBILE BETTING FILLIES' H'CAP 1m 4f 50y(P)
8:00 (8:00) (Class 5) (0-70,68) 4-Y-O+ **£2,587** (£770; £384; £192) **Stalls** Low

Form RPR
6411 1 **Broxbourne (IRE)**[7] 562 4-9-3 67 6ex............................ FrannyNorton 3 79
(Mark Johnston) *hld up: hdwy over 4f out: chsd ldr over 2f out: rdn to ld over 1f out: styd on wl* **11/10**[1]

1103 2 3 ¾ **Rosie's Lady (IRE)**[18] 429 4-9-1 65............................ DanielTudhope 4 71
(David O'Meara) *a.p: rdn over 1f out: styd on same pce: wnt 2nd wl ins fnl f* **3/1**[2]

30-6 3 ¾ **Bernisdale**[18] 429 5-8-13 60.. JohnFahy 7 65
(John Flint) *led: rdn and hdd over 1f out: no ex ins fnl f* **12/1**

51/4 4 8 **Asterism**[17] 433 5-9-7 68.. JamieSpencer 6 60
(Ian Williams) *hld up rdn over 2f out: nvr on terms* **11/1**

00-4 5 3 **Simayill**[23] 338 5-9-3 64....................................(p) TomMcLaughlin 1 51
(John Berry) *prom: chsd ldr over 6f out tl rdn over 2f out: wknd fnl f* **5/1**[3]

630- 6 8 **Adorable Choice (IRE)**[50] 8252 5-9-4 65..................(v) StephenCraine 5 39
(Tom Dascombe) *chsd ldr over 5f: remained handy tl rdn over 2f out: wknd wl over 1f out* **25/1**

2m 39.75s (-1.35) **Going Correction** +0.025s/f (Slow)
WFA 4 from 5yo 3lb **6** Ran SP% **109.2**
Speed ratings (Par 100): **105,102,102,96,94 89**
toteswingers: 1&2 £1.10, 1&3 £4.10, 2&3 £6.60. CSF £4.23 TOTE £2.00: £1.10, £1.50; EX 4.10 Trifecta £44.10 Pool: £1,728.36 - 29.33 winning units..
Owner Ready To Run Partnership **Bred** Mount Coote Stud And M Johnston **Trained** Middleham Moor, N Yorks

FOCUS
A fair fillies' handicap, which saw a winner who should be able to acquit herself well in far higher company. The second ran as well as ever.
T/Jkpt: Not won. T/Plt: £78.70 to a £1 stake. Pool: £79,591.89 - 737.75 winning tickets. T/Qpdt: £13.80 to a £1 stake. Pool: £8,797.41 - 468.64 winning tickets. CR

676 - 678a (Foreign Racing) - See Raceform Interactive

566 DUNDALK (A.W) (L-H)
Friday, February 15

OFFICIAL GOING: Standard

679a WWW.DUNDALKSTADIUM.COM H'CAP 6f (P)
7:20 (7:22) 4-Y-O+ **£5,609** (£1,300; £569; £325)

RPR
1 **Khawatim**[21] 372 5-9-5 76.. BenCurtis 5 87+
(Noel Quinlan) *hld up in mid-div: 6th 1/2-way: hdwy 2f out to cl between horses and ld jst ins fnl f: pushed out towards fin: comf* **4/6**[1]

2 3 **Almadaa**[28] 262 6-9-9 80... FergalLynch 2 80
(David Marnane, Ire) *chsd ldrs: pushed along in 5th 1/2-way: prog into st to ld narrowly under 2f out: strly pressed and hdd jst ins fnl f: no ex cl home* **9/2**[2]

3 1 **Fastidious**[21] 384 4-9-2 80... LukeDempsey(7) 9 77
(M D O'Callaghan, Ire) *chsd ldrs: 5th 1/2-way: rdn 2f out and no imp in 5th ins fnl f: kpt on u.p into nvr threatening 3rd fnl 50yds* **14/1**

4 nk **Harry Trotter (IRE)**[28] 262 4-9-9 80.................................. ShaneFoley 4 76
(David Marnane, Ire) *racd in mid-div: 8th 1/2-way: pushed along into st and hdwy into 5th ent fnl f: sn no ex: kpt on same pce* **20/1**

5 ½ **Big Typhoon (IRE)**[84] 7850 6-8-1 61 oh7......................... IJBrennan(3) 1 55
(T G McCourt, Ire) *sn led: strly pressed over 2f out: sn hdd and no ex in 3rd ent fnl f: dropped to 5th cl home* **33/1**

6 ¾ **Copper Dock (IRE)**[14] 483 9-9-0 78............................... KarenKenny(7) 11 70
(T G McCourt, Ire) *w.w towards rr: 11th 1/2-way: rdn and hdwy under 2f out: nrst fin* **16/1**

7 nk **Elusive Prince**[181] 5370 5-10-1 91................................ ConorHoban(5) 7 82
(T Hogan, Ire) *awkward s: settled in rr of mid-div: rdn under 2f out and sme hdwy: no imp ent fnl f* **14/1**

8 nk **Fol Hollow (IRE)**[21] 383 8-8-3 67............................ KatherineSO'Brien(7) 12 57
(T Hogan, Ire) *trckd ldr: 2nd 1/2-way: effrt on outer 2f out: sn rdn and wknd ent fnl f* **12/1**

9 2 ½ **Jembatt (IRE)**[133] 6854 6-9-8 79.................................(p) PatSmullen 10 61
(Michael Mulvany, Ire) *w.w in rr: swtchd rt 2f out and sme modest hdwy on outer ent fnl f: kpt on same pce towards fin* **20/1**

10 ¾ **Thats A Fret (IRE)**[14] 483 7-8-3 70..........................(b) ConnorKing(10) 13 50
(Liam McAteer, Ire) *trckd ldr: 4th 1/2-way: pushed along over 2f out and sn wknd* **16/1**

11 1 ¾ **Pencil Hill (IRE)**[14] 483 8-9-6 84............................... MeganCarberry(7) 3 58
(Tracey Collins, Ire) *in rr of mid-div: 8th 1/2-way: pushed along over 2f out and no ex u.p ent fnl f* **10/1**[3]

12 3 **Right Divine (IRE)**[91] 7757 4-9-2 73............................. MichaelHussey 8 37
(Peter Fahey, Ire) *towards rr thrght: nvr a factor* **33/1**

13 1 ¼ **Sweet Annathea (IRE)**[35] 171 4-8-4 61 oh3................(b) RoryCleary 6 21
(Thomas Cleary, Ire) *racd in mid-div: 7th 1/2-way: rdn over 2f out and sn no imp: wknd: lame* **20/1**

1m 11.33s (71.33) **13** Ran SP% **140.2**
CSF £4.45 CT £34.22 TOTE £1.90: £1.40, £1.40, £4.20; DF 3.50.
Owner The Unique Partnership **Bred** Baroness Bloodstock **Trained** Newmarket, Suffolk

FOCUS
His status as an odds-on chance in this race was there to be questioned but Khawatim made absolutely no mistake. The runner-up sets the standard.

680 - 683a (Foreign Racing) - See Raceform Interactive

662 LINGFIELD (L-H)
Saturday, February 16

OFFICIAL GOING: Standard
Wind: Virtually nil Weather: Dry

684 BET ON TODAY'S FOOTBALL AT BLUESQ.COM CLAIMING STKS 1m (P)
12:40 (12:40) (Class 6) 3-Y-O **£2,045** (£603; £302) **Stalls** High

Form RPR
-541 1 **Hillbilly Boy (IRE)**[7] 588 3-8-10 73................................ RyanWhile(7) 4 70
(Bill Turner) *trckd ldrs: swtchd rt and effrt wl over 1f out: led fnl 100yds: r.o wl: rdn out* **1/1**[1]

3-23 2 2 ¼ **Lady Lunchalot (USA)**[31] 230 3-8-3 64................ CharlotteJenner(7) 3 58
(J S Moore) *t.k.h: trckd ldrs tl hdwy to chal and edgd lft over 2f out: rdn to ld wl over 1f out: hdd and one pce fnl 100yds* **5/2**[2]

4321 3 hd **Napinda**[6] 599 3-8-6 54...(v[1]) AndreaAtzeni 2 54
(Philip McBride) *t.k.h: chsd ldr tl led after 1f: rdn and hdd over 1f out: drvn and styd on same pce fnl f* **4/1**[3]

1653 4 1 ¼ **Maypole Joe (IRE)**[7] 588 3-8-10 62...............................(v) LukeMorris 1 55
(David Evans) *t.k.h: led for 1f: chsd ldr tl unable qck and sltly short of room over 2f out: drvn and one pce fnl 2f* **12/1**

1m 40.47s (2.27) **Going Correction** +0.05s/f (Slow) **4** Ran SP% **106.3**
Speed ratings (Par 95): **90,87,87,86**
CSF £3.60 TOTE £1.70; EX 3.90 Trifecta £5.50 Pool: £772.60 - 104.43 winning units..
Owner E A Brook **Bred** Tipper House Stud **Trained** Sigwells, Somerset

FOCUS
Modest form to this muddling claimer. The winner only needed to run to his more recent form.

685 MATT GROUT 21ST BIRTHDAY MAIDEN STKS 1m (P)
1:10 (1:10) (Class 5) 3-Y-O **£2,726** (£805; £402) **Stalls** High

Form RPR
5 1 **Gambolling Den (IRE)**[14] 491 3-9-5 0.......................... AndreaAtzeni 2 67
(David Simcock) *t.k.h: hld up wl in tch in midfield: rdn and hdwy to chal on inner ent fnl f: r.o wl to ld wl ins fnl f: hld on last strides* **16/1**

2 hd **Lady Guinevere** 3-9-0 0.. DavidProbert 7 62
(Stuart Williams) *stdd s: hld up wl in tch towards rr: hdwy u.p ent fnl f: r.o wl to go 2nd cl home: jst hld* **8/1**

0- 3 nk **India's Song**[93] 7720 3-9-0 0.. JamieSpencer 3 61
(David Simcock) *led and set stdy gallop: edgd out rt and rdn wl over 1f out: drvn and kpt on fnl f tl hdd and lost 2 pls wl ins fnl f* **5/4**[1]

00- 4 1 **Zhuba (IRE)**[64] 8102 3-9-5 0.. GeorgeBaker 8 64
(John Best) *t.k.h early: hld up in tch in midfield on outer: effrt and wdst bnd 2f out: kpt on ins fnl f: nt pce to chal* **20/1**

5 ¾ **Mad About Harry (IRE)** 3-9-5 0.. LukeMorris 6 62
(John Best) *dwlt: rn green: sn rdn along: in tch in rr: styd on u.p ins fnl f: nt threaten ldrs* **20/1**

6- **6** 1 ¼ **Gunning For Glory**[58] 8178 3-9-5 0 .... StevieDonohoe 1 59
(Martin Bosley) *chsd ldrs: reminder over 4f out: rdn and unable qck over 1f out: styd on same pce ins fnl f* **50/1**

7 1 ½ **Red To Amber (IRE)** 3-9-5 0 .... AdamKirby 4 55
(Clive Cox) *dwlt: rn green: rdn along and in tch in rr: styd on same pce and no imp fr over 1f out* **7/2**[2]

0-2 **8** 1 ½ **Hamla**[7] 590 3-9-0 0 .... JoeFanning 9 47
(Mark Johnston) *dwlt: rcvrd to chse ldr over 6f out: rdn and unable qck over 1f out: fdd ins fnl f* **4/1**[3]

00-0 **9** 7 **Positive Parenting (IRE)**[40] 103 3-9-0 38 .... SeanLevey 5 30
(Stuart Williams) *chsd ldr tl over 6f out: 4th and drvn 5f out: lost pl over 2f out: bhd fnl f* **100/1**

1m 38.64s (0.44) **Going Correction** +0.05s/f (Slow) 9 Ran SP% **116.1**
Speed ratings (Par 97): **99,98,98,97,96 95,94,92,85**
toteswingers 1&2 £13.60, 1&3 £3.20, 2&3 £3.30 CSF £130.05 TOTE £20.10: £2.60, £2.40, £1.10; EX 197.20 Trifecta £620.10 Pool: £3,772.97 - 4.56 winning units..
Owner Whitfield Associates **Bred** Moyglare Stud Farm Ltd **Trained** Newmarket, Suffolk

FOCUS
A modest maiden run at a nuddling pace. Shaky form, although the winner was certainly much improved.

686 MARSH GREEN MEDIAN AUCTION MAIDEN STKS 5f (P)
1:40 (1:40) (Class 6) 3-Y-O **£2,045** (£603; £302) **Stalls** High

Form RPR

U **1** **Holley Shiftwell**[7] 581 3-9-0 0 .... AndreaAtzeni 2 70+
(Stuart Williams) *mde all: rdn and qcknd wl over 1f out: in command kpt on wl ins fnl f: rdn out* **3/1**[2]

00-2 **2** 1 ¼ **Firmdecisions (IRE)**[7] 581 3-9-5 60 .... DavidProbert 6 70
(Brett Johnson) *sn chsng wnr: rdn and unable qckn over 1f out: rallied u.p: kpt on but a comf hld* **1/1**[1]

-234 **3** 4 **Princess Cammie (IRE)**[15] 470 3-9-0 59 .... EddieAhern 5 51
(Mike Murphy) *s.i.s: in tch in last pair: hdwy 1/2-way: rdn and unable qck wl over 1f out: no threat to wnr but plugged on to go 3rd ins fnl f* **3/1**[2]

06-2 **4** 1 ½ **Con Leche**[17] 438 3-9-5 55 .... LukeMorris 3 50
(Scott Dixon) *t.k.h: chsd ldrs: rdn and unable qck over 1f out: drvn 1f out: wknd ins fnl f* **8/1**[3]

50-2 **5** 3 **Twinwood Star (IRE)**[44] 36 3-9-0 49 .... ChrisCatlin 4 34
(John Weymes) *s.i.s: in tch in last pair: rdn and struggling 2f out: wknd over 1f out* **25/1**

000- **6** 3 ½ **Highway United (IRE)**[130] 6954 3-8-7 30 .... IanBurns[(7)] 1 22
(John Weymes) *chsd ldrs: lost pl and rdn over 2f out: bhd over 1f out* **66/1**

59.31s (0.51) **Going Correction** +0.05s/f (Slow) 6 Ran SP% **116.4**
Speed ratings (Par 95): **97,95,88,86,81 75**
toteswingers 1&2 £1.80, 1&3 £1.90, 2&3 £1.30 CSF £6.74 TOTE £4.20: £1.50, £2.00; EX 9.20 Trifecta £27.20 Pool: £3,697.92 - 101.85 winning units..
Owner J W Parry **Bred** Mr & Mrs K W Grundy, Mr & Mrs P Hopper **Trained** Newmarket, Suffolk

FOCUS
This didn't take much winning, but the pace was fair. The winner should start in handicaps on a modest mark.

687 BLUE SQUARE BET SPRINT SERIES ROUND 7 H'CAP (QUALIFIER) (DIV I) 6f (P)
2:15 (2:17) (Class 5) (0-70,73) 4-Y-0+ **£3,067** (£905; £453) **Stalls** Low

Form RPR

0-24 **1** **Billy Red**[31] 232 9-9-5 68 ....(b) JoeFanning 4 76
(J R Jenkins) *mde all and dictated uncontested ld: rdn 1f out: kpt on wl and a hoding rivals: rdn out* **16/1**

-526 **2** 1 ¼ **Welease Bwian (IRE)**[7] 583 4-9-3 66 .... AndreaAtzeni 6 70+
(Stuart Williams) *in tch in midfield: rdn and hdwy towards inner over 1f out: chsd wnr fnl 100yds: kpt on but no imp* **9/2**[3]

2212 **3** hd **Jack My Boy (IRE)**[7] 583 6-9-10 73 ....(v) AdamKirby 5 76+
(David Evans) *chsd ldrs: rdn over 2f out: drvn and chsd ldng pair jst ins fnl f: kpt on but no imp* **2/1**[1]

0200 **4** 1 **Desert Strike**[6] 603 7-9-7 70 ....(p) HayleyTurner 1 70
(Conor Dore) *chsd wnr: rdn over 1f out: drvn and lost 2nd 1f out: styd on same pce ins fnl f* **20/1**

4-52 **5** nk **Tidal's Baby**[14] 494 4-8-13 67 .... GeorgeDowning[(5)] 7 66+
(Tony Carroll) *s.i.s: hld up in tch towards rr: hdwy u.p jst over 1f out: swtchd lft ins fnl f: keeping on but hld whn nt clr run towards fin* **5/2**[2]

2303 **6** nse **Above The Stars**[5] 611 5-8-13 62 .... FergusSweeney 2 61
(Jamie Osborne) *chsd ldrs: effrt u.p over 1f out: chsd wnr 1f out tl fnl 100yds: no ex* **14/1**

2450 **7** ¾ **My Own Way Home**[14] 494 5-8-10 59 .... LukeMorris 8 56
(David Evans) *in tch in midfield: effrt u.p and no imp over 1f out: kpt on same pce ins fnl f* **10/1**

0361 **8** 2 ¼ **Marshall Art**[10] 537 4-8-9 63 .... ThomasBrown[(5)] 10 52
(David Evans) *s.i.s: hld up in tch towards rr: rdn and no imp fr over 1f out: n.d* **14/1**

030- **9** 3 ¾ **Duke Of Aricabeau (IRE)**[60] 8159 4-9-0 66 .... SimonPearce[(3)] 11 43
(Lydia Pearce) *a towards rr: rdn and no prog jst over 2f out: n.d* **50/1**

-600 **10** 2 **Amenable (IRE)**[14] 493 6-8-13 62 ....(b) SeanLevey 3 33
(Violet M Jordan) *taken down early: in tch in midfield: rdn and struggling over 2f out: wknd over 1f out* **33/1**

1m 11.28s (-0.62) **Going Correction** +0.05s/f (Slow) 10 Ran SP% **118.1**
Speed ratings (Par 103): **106,104,104,102,102 102,101,98,93,90**
toteswingers 1&2 £10.90, 1&3 £5.00, 2&3 £2.40 CSF £86.29 CT £212.06 TOTE £10.80: £3.10, £1.90, £1.30; EX 73.80 Trifecta £290.20 Pool: £4,562.59 - 11.79 winning units..
Owner Mrs Irene Hampson **Bred** D R Tucker **Trained** Royston, Herts

FOCUS
They didn't go that fast early and few got into the race. The winner had the run of things and is rated to his best form since the summer.

688 BLUE SQUARE BET SPRINT SERIES ROUND 7 H'CAP (QUALIFIER) (DIV II) 6f (P)
2:50 (2:50) (Class 5) (0-70,70) 4-Y-0+ **£3,067** (£905; £453) **Stalls** Low

Form RPR

-003 **1** **Black Cadillac (IRE)**[7] 582 5-8-11 67 .... DanielMuscutt[(7)] 6 76+
(Andrew Balding) *dwlt: hld up in tch in last trio: rdn and effrt on outer over 1f out: qcknd wl and str run to ld wl ins fnl f: sn in command* **6/1**[3]

4504 **2** 1 ¼ **Belle Bayardo (IRE)**[7] 583 5-9-4 67 .... LukeMorris 4 72
(Ronald Harris) *in tch in midfield: rdn and effrt over 2f out: drvn and hdwy to chal 1f out: led ins fnl f: hedaed and outpcd wl ins fnl f: kpt on* **4/1**[1]

4041 **3** shd **Methaaly (IRE)**[8] 560 10-8-8 64 ....(be) RobertTart[(7)] 5 69
(Michael Mullineaux) *hld up in tch in last pair: rdn and hdwy on inner over 1f out: drvn and ev ch ins fnl f: no ex and one pce fnl 100yds* **10/1**

252 **4** 1 ½ **Dark Lane**[5] 611 7-9-3 66 .... AdamKirby 2 66
(David Evans) *led: rdn wl over 1f out: hdd ins fnl f: wknd fnl 75yds* **5/1**[2]

0-02 **5** ¾ **Proper Charlie**[16] 454 5-9-7 70 .... GeorgeBaker 9 67
(William Knight) *stdd s: hld up in tch in last pair: hdwy on inner over 1f out: drvn and chsd ldrs 1f out: no ex and wknd fnl 75yds* **4/1**[1]

2360 **6** ½ **Restless Bay (IRE)**[7] 583 5-9-5 68 ....(b) HayleyTurner 8 64
(Conor Dore) *taken down early and led to s: in tch in midfield: hdwy on outer to chse ldrs over 3f out: drvn: unable qck and edgd rt over 1f out: wknd ins fnl f* **7/1**

-502 **7** nse **Haadeeth**[14] 493 6-8-13 62 .... TomMcLaughlin 3 58
(David Evans) *taken down early: chsd ldrs: lost pl 2f out: rdn and hmpd over 1f out: swtchd lft 1f out and no imp after: eased towards fin* **5/1**[2]

5000 **8** 3 ½ **Fairy Wing (IRE)**[2] 652 6-8-9 58 .... SeanLevey 1 43
(Violet M Jordan) *t.k.h: chsd ldr tl over 3f out: rdn and struggling over 2f out: wknd over 1f out* **16/1**

1m 10.94s (-0.96) **Going Correction** +0.05s/f (Slow) 8 Ran SP% **115.1**
Speed ratings (Par 103): **108,106,106,104,103 102,102,97**
toteswingers 1&2 £7.30, 1&3 £8.80, 2&3 £11.00 CSF £30.41 CT £236.56 TOTE £7.00: £2.00, £2.70, £2.30; EX 30.80 Trifecta £168.90 Pool: £2,409.39 - 10.69 winning units..
Owner N Botica **Bred** John Foley & Miss Ann Aungier **Trained** Kingsclere, Hants

FOCUS
In contrast to the first division there was a good early gallop on here and the winner came from off the pace. The winning time was 0.34sec faster than the first division. The second and third set the standard.

689 WEDDINGS AT LINGFIELD MARRIOTT HOTEL H'CAP 1m (P)
3:30 (3:31) (Class 5) (0-75,75) 4-Y-0+ **£2,726** (£805; £402) **Stalls** High

Form RPR

5-11 **1** **Toga Tiger (IRE)**[28] 272 6-9-6 74 .... RobertWinston 1 84
(Jeremy Gask) *broke wl: sn stdd and chsd ldrs: gng wl but nt clr run 2f out: swtchd out rt wl over 1f out: rdn and hdwy over 1f out: led ins fnl f: sn in command: comf* **9/4**[1]

0-53 **2** 1 ¾ **Push Me (IRE)**[13] 511 6-8-10 71 .... RobertTart[(7)] 5 78
(Jamie Poulton) *hld up in tch in last pair: effrt and clsng whn nt clr run and hmpd over 1f out: rallied u.p ins fnl f: wnt 2nd towards fin: no threat to wnr* **7/2**[2]

1-10 **3** nk **Avertis**[28] 272 8-9-0 73 .... AmyScott[(5)] 8 78
(Alastair Lidderdale) *v awkward leaving stalls: rcvrd to chse ldr after 2f: rdn to ld over 1f out: drvn and hdd ins fnl f: sn outpcd and no ch w wnr: lost 2nd towards fin* **10/1**

-441 **4** 1 **Zing Wing**[7] 589 5-8-13 74 ....(v) EoinWalsh[(7)] 7 77
(David Evans) *stdd and dropped in bhd after s: swtchd lft and hdwy on inner over 1f out: drvn and styd on same pce ins fnl f* **20/1**

54-2 **5** 4 **Blue Deer (IRE)**[38] 115 5-8-8 62 .... KierenFox 2 56
(Lee Carter) *sn led: rdn and hdd over 1f out: wknd ins fnl f* **16/1**

36-4 **6** 2 **Tornado Force (IRE)**[24] 340 5-9-7 75 .... AdamKirby 3 64
(Chris Dwyer) *chsd ldr for 2f: rdn and unable qck 2f out: wknd ent fnl f* **6/1**[3]

4-32 **7** ¾ **Ellie In The Pink (IRE)**[3] 638 5-8-6 65 .... JemmaMarshall[(5)] 6 52
(Pat Phelan) *in tch in midfield on outer: rdn and unable qck 2f out: wknd ent fnl f* **8/1**

1m 37.36s (-0.84) **Going Correction** +0.05s/f (Slow) 7 Ran SP% **98.1**
Speed ratings (Par 103): **106,104,103,102,98 96,96**
toteswingers 1&2 £1.50, 1&3 £3.60, 2&3 £4.50 CSF £7.29 CT £35.23 TOTE £2.60: £1.40, £2.40; EX 8.40 Trifecta £43.70 Pool: £831.19 - 14.23 winning units..
Owner For Sale **Bred** Daniel Spaight **Trained** Sutton Veny, Wilts

FOCUS
They didn't got a great pace early, but the most interesting pair were 1-2 and the form seems sound enough rated around the third.

690 DOUG GROUT 65TH BIRTHDAY H'CAP 1m (P)
4:00 (4:02) (Class 2) (0-100,98) 4-Y-0+ **£12,291** (£3,657; £1,827; £913) **Stalls** High

Form RPR

11-3 **1** **Solar Deity (IRE)**[43] 60 4-9-1 92 .... MartinHarley 5 102+
(Marco Botti) *trckd ldrs: nt clr run and wating for gap over 1f out: rdn and qcknd between horses to ld wl ins fnl f: r.o wl* **5/2**[1]

15-4 **2** ¾ **George Guru**[14] 495 6-9-3 94 .... JoeFanning 9 101
(Michael Attwater) *t.k.h: hld up in tch in midfield: hdwy to press ldrs and rdn 2f out: ev ch fnl f: kpt on but outpcd by wnr towards fin: wnt 2nd last strides* **5/1**[2]

01-1 **3** nk **Alfred Hutchinson**[46] 6 5-8-10 92 .... WilliamTwiston-Davies[(5)] 6 98
(Geoffrey Oldroyd) *chsd ldrs tl hdwy to join ldr over 2f out: rdn wl over 1f out: led 1f out: kpt on u.p tl hdd and outpcd by wnr wl ins fnl f: lost 2nd last strides* **7/1**[3]

4-42 **4** ½ **Mia's Boy**[7] 585 9-9-3 94 .... GeorgeBaker 7 99
(Chris Dwyer) *stdd after s: hld up in last trio: clsng and nt clr run 2f out: rdn and hdwy over 1f out: kpt on ins fnl f* **7/1**[3]

-213 **5** ¾ **Atlantis Crossing (IRE)**[17] 443 4-8-10 87 .... JamieSpencer 8 90+
(Roger Ingram) *awkward leaving stalls: hld up in tch towards rr: pushed along and hdwy 3f out: hung lft and styd on same pce ins fnl f* **5/1**[2]

-426 **6** ½ **Rakaan (IRE)**[14] 495 6-8-9 86 ....(p) FergusSweeney 2 88
(Jamie Osborne) *t.k.h: hld up wl in tch in midfield: rdn and effrt over 1f out: styd on same pce ins fnl f* **16/1**

22-0 **7** nk **Webbow (IRE)**[14] 495 11-9-4 95 .... AdamKirby 1 97
(Julie Camacho) *led: rdn ent fnl 2f: hdd 1f out: wknd ins fnl f* **8/1**

-150 **8** 1 ¼ **Verse Of Love**[14] 495 4-8-11 88 .... LukeMorris 10 87
(David Evans) *chsd ldr tl over 2f out: sn rdn and unable qck: btn and styd on same pce fnl f* **25/1**

000- **9** nse **Monsieur Chevalier (IRE)**[91] 7774 6-9-7 98 .... TomMcLaughlin 4 97
(P J O'Gorman) *v.s.a: hld up in rr: rdn but stl plenty to do over 1f out: kpt on ins fnl f: nvr trbld ldrs* **20/1**

063- **10** ¾ **Lord Ofthe Shadows (IRE)**[86] 7824 4-8-8 85 .... SeanLevey 3 82
(Richard Hannon) *in tch in midfield: lost pl and rdn over 2f out: bhd and styd on same pce fr over 1f out* **14/1**

1m 37.96s (-0.24) **Going Correction** +0.05s/f (Slow) 10 Ran SP% **119.2**
Speed ratings (Par 109): **103,102,101,101,100 100,99,98,98,97**
toteswingers 1&2 £4.30, 1&3 £4.70, 2&3 £7.60 CSF £15.07 CT £79.22 TOTE £2.80: £2.20, £2.10, £1.40; EX 9.30 Trifecta £69.80 Pool: £2,891.55 - 31.04 winning units..
Owner G Manfredini & A Tinkler **Bred** Castlemartin Stud And Skymarc Farm **Trained** Newmarket, Suffolk

FOCUS
A decent handicap, but the early gallop wasn't strong. There's every chance the winner can do a bit better.

691 ENOUGH SAID, JUST BET AT BLUESQ.COM H'CAP 1m 4f (P)
4:35 (4:35) (Class 4) (0-85,85) 4-Y-0+ £4,690 (£1,395; £697; £348) Stalls Low

Form RPR
-114 1 **Harry Buckle**[14] 496 4-9-2 83 LukeMorris 5 92+
(Philip McBride) *mde all: rdn and qcknd wl over 2f out: kpt on u.p: a jst holding runner-up* 9/4[1]
31-1 2 hd **Saoi (USA)**[37] 146 6-9-5 83 GeorgeBaker 3 91+
(William Knight) *t.k.h early: hld up in tch in midfield: rdn and effrt on inner to chse ldng pair wl over 1f out: chsd wnr ins fnl f: kpt on wl: nt quite rch wnr* 3/1[3]
/6-1 3 2 1/2 **Discovery Bay**[1] 662 5-9-0 78 JamieSpencer 7 82
(C F Swan, Ire) *stdd s and dropped in bhd after s: hld up in rr: swtchd to outer and gd hdwy over 3f out: chsd wnr and clr of field over 2f out: no ex 1f out: lost 2nd and onepced ins fnl f* 11/4[2]
1324 4 1/2 **Sir Boss (IRE)**[8] 563 8-8-8 79 RobertTart(7) 2 83
(Michael Mullineaux) *hld up in last quartet: rdn and effrt wl over 1f out: styd on ins fnl f: nvr threatened ldrs* 8/1
21-4 5 1 **Scottish Boogie (IRE)**[25] 318 6-8-12 76 ow1 SebSanders 9 78
(Brendan Powell) *stdd and dropped in bhd after s: t.k.h: hld up in last quartet: rdn and effrt on outer over 2f out: plugged on but no real impressn fnl f* 25/1
1- 6 1/2 **Solaras Exhibition (IRE)**[210] 3610 5-9-7 85 DavidProbert 8 86
(Tim Vaughan) *hld up in tch in last quartet: rdn and outpcd over 2f out: styd on same pce and no imp over 1f out* 20/1
3311 7 2 3/4 **Strike Force**[9] 548 9-8-9 78 (t) NatashaEaton(5) 6 75
(Alison Hutchinson) *chsd ldrs: wnt 2nd 10f out tl over 2f out: sn outpcd and struggling: onepced and wl hld fr over 1f out* 20/1
105/ 8 shd **Palio Square (USA)**[93] 1030 6-8-13 84 (b) NedCurtis(7) 1 81
(John Flint) *chsd ldrs: rdn and outpcd over 2f out: wknd over 1f out* 50/1
100- 9 6 **Grandiloquent**[17] 6045 4-9-2 83 (b[1]) EddieAhern 4 70
(Donald McCain) *hld up wl in tch in midfield: struggling and rdn over 2f out: wknd over 1f out: bhd fnl f* 7/1

2m 34.53s (1.53) **Going Correction** +0.05s/f (Slow)
WFA 4 from 5yo+ 3lb 9 Ran SP% 121.4
Speed ratings (Par 105): **96,95,94,93,93 92,91,90,86**
toteswingers 1&2 £1.90, 1&3 £2.50, 2&3 £3.30 CSF £9.35 CT £19.67 TOTE £2.10: £1.30, £2.10, £1.30; EX 7.20 Trifecta £32.20 Pool: £2,665.90 - 62.03 winning units..
Owner Four Winds Racing Partnership **Bred** Wood Farm Stud (Waresley) **Trained** Newmarket, Suffolk

FOCUS
A fair handicap in which the right horses came to the fore. The winner set just a modest pace.
T/Plt: £20.80 to a £1 stake. Pool: £50,040.80 - 1,750.84 winning units T/Qpdt: £7.10 to a £1 stake. Pool: £4,187.67 - 433.00 winning units SP

647 CAGNES-SUR-MER
Saturday, February 16
OFFICIAL GOING: Fibresand: standard

692a PRIX DES SEMBOULES (CONDITIONS) (3YO) (FIBRESAND) 1m (F)
12:00 (12:00) 3-Y-0 £11,788 (£4,715; £3,536; £2,357; £1,178)

RPR
1 **Gotham News (USA)** 3-8-13 0 MircoDemuro 5 94
(J-C Rouget, France) 1/2[1]
2 hd **Carlton Blue (IRE)**[81] 3-8-13 0 (p) MaximeGuyon 6 94
(Y Durepaire, France) 43/10[2]
3 6 **Dha Chara (IRE)**[6] 604 3-8-13 0 ThomasMessina 3 80
(Reg Hollinshead) *racd in 4th: dropped to 5th ent st: shkn up and r.o wl ent fnl 2f: wnt 3rd 350yds out: styd on wl but no ch w first two* 13/2[3]
4 3 **Deodora (FR)**[42] 3-8-9 0 JohanVictoire 2 69
(C Boutin, France) 8/1
5 nk **Silvy Du Normandy (IRE)**[58] 3-8-9 0 (p) IoritzMendizabal 4 68
(J Heloury, France) 29/1
6 3 **Destiny Highway (FR)**[6] 605 3-8-7 0 CesarPasserat(6) 1 65
(Gay Kelleway) *racd in 3rd on ins: rdn ent st: no ex u.p: styd on one pce fnl 2f* 23/1

1m 38.64s (98.64) 6 Ran SP% 117.5
WIN (incl. 1 euro stake):1.50. PLACES: 1.10, 1.60. SF: 3.90.
Owner Joseph Allen **Bred** J Allen **Trained** Pau, France

609 ST MORITZ (R-H)
Sunday, February 17
OFFICIAL GOING: Snow: frozen

700a GRAND PRIX MOYGLARE STUD (CONDITIONS) (4YO+) (SNOW) 6f 110y
11:40 (12:00) 4-Y-0+

£8,456 (£4,228; £3,020; £2,013; £1,006; £604)

RPR
1 **Lipocco**[103] 9-8-11 0 MircoDemuro 10 68
(J D Hillis, Germany) 107/10
2 3/4 **Le Big (GER)**[348] 814 9-9-4 0 AndreBest 4 73
(P Schaerer, Switzerland) 8/5[1]
3 nk **Exchange**[14] 514 5-9-2 0 FredericSpanu 7 70
(Frau M Muller, Switzerland) 114/10
4 nk **Zack Tiger (IRE)**[106] 7565 4-9-2 0 DPorcu 2 69
(P Schaerer, Switzerland) 68/10
5 3 **Just In Time (SLO)** 5-8-11 0 OlivierPlacais 1 55
(M Weiss, Switzerland) 7/2[3]
6 8 **Boccalino (GER)**[364] 629 5-9-2 0 (b) EPedroza 6 37
(P Schaerer, Switzerland) 56/10
7 1/2 **Chapman (GER)**[252] 4-9-6 0 FilipMinarik 3 40
(P Schiergen, Germany) 54/10
8 dist **Paphos**[25] 340 6-9-0 0 (v) JimCrowley 8
(Charles Hills) *in rr on outside: scrubbed along: lost grnd and wl bhd fr 1/2-way: t.o* 33/10[2]

1m 21.34s (81.34) 8 Ran SP% 144.1
PARI-MUTUEL (all including 1 chf stakes): WIN 11.70; PLACE 2.00, 1.40, 2.50; SF 20.30.
Owner Plersch Breeding Sarl **Bred** C Scott & T Leigh **Trained** Germany

701a GUBELIN 74 GROSSER PREIS VON ST MORITZ (LOCAL GROUP 2) (4YO+) (SNOW) 1m 2f
1:10 (12:00) 4-Y-0+

£38,093 (£19,046; £13,604; £9,067; £4,530; £2,718)

RPR
1 **Russian Tango (GER)**[88] 6-8-11 0 JBojko 3
(A Wohler, Germany) 9/5[1]
2 1/2 **Winterwind (IRE)**[287] 8-8-11 0 (b) FilipMinarik 9
(Carmen Bocskai, Switzerland) 124/10
3 6 **Nightdance Paolo (GER)**[14] 514 6-9-4 0 FredericSpanu 11
(A Schaerer, Switzerland) 76/10
4 1 1/4 **Saltas (GER)**[39] 125 5-8-13 0 ow2 (b) EPedroza 8
(P Schaerer, Switzerland) 234/10
5 1 **Amazing Beauty (GER)**[14] 514 6-9-3 0 MircoDemuro 2
(M Figge, Germany) 11/5[2]
6 1 1/4 **Tepmokea (IRE)**[14] 514 7-9-0 0 ShaneKelly 5
(Mrs K Burke) *pressed ldr: led over 4f out: hdd 3f out: styd prom tl rdn and wknd fr 1 1/2f out* 39/1
7 4 **Earl Of Winds (GER)**[14] 514 8-8-11 0 (p) AndreBest 14
(P Schaerer, Switzerland) 195/10
8 9 **Halling River (IRE)**[14] 514 6-8-11 0 (p) RobertHavlin 13
(M Weiss, Switzerland) 154/10
9 6 **African Art (USA)**[14] 514 7-9-8 0 DPorcu 10
(P Schaerer, Switzerland) 122/10
10 10 **Maverik**[22] 400 5-8-11 0 JimCrowley 12
(Ralph Beckett) *sn prom fr wd draw: cl 3rd whn rdn and lost pl over 4f out: sn bhd* 131/10
11 2 1/2 **Dreamspeed (IRE)**[142] 6637 6-8-11 0 SabrinaWandt 1
(C Von Der Recke, Germany) 66/10[3]
12 dist **Song Of Victory (GER)**[14] 513 9-8-11 0 (p) OlivierPlacais 6
(M Weiss, Switzerland) 40/1
13 7 **Quinindo (GER)**[91] 7784 5-9-2 0 SHellyn 4
(Elfie Schnakenberg, Germany) 16/1
P **Sumatra Tiger (GER)**[14] 514 8-9-0 0 MiguelLopez 7
(P Vovcenko, Germany) 228/10

2m 13.74s (133.74) 14 Ran SP% 144.0
PARI-MUTUEL (all including 1 chf stakes): WIN 2.80; PLACE 1.90, 2.90, 2.30; SF 10.40.
Owner Rennstall Darboven **Bred** Gestut Idee **Trained** Germany

702a GRAND PRIX THE ST LEGER CLUB OF LUCERNE (CONDITIONS) (4YO+) (SNOW) 1m 1f
2:45 (12:00) 4-Y-0+

£4,228 (£2,114; £1,510; £1,006; £503; £302)

RPR
1 **Ancient Greece**[7] 609 6-9-8 0 JimCrowley 11
(George Baker) *broke wl fr wd draw: trckd ldrs on outside: outpcd briefly 5f out: sn rcvrd to press ldr fr 4f out: rdn over 2f out: styd on wl u.p fnl f to ld cl home* 1/2[1]
2 nk **Mont Pelato (USA)**[14] 513 5-9-4 0 OlivierPlacais 9
(M Weiss, Switzerland) 178/10
3 1/2 **Alberto Hawaii (GER)**[119] 4-8-9 0 JBojko 3
(Elfie Schnakenberg, Germany) 29/1
4 1 1/4 **Prince Caracallo (FR)**[609] 3210 5-8-5 0 SibylleVogt(9) 4
(Carmen Bocskai, Switzerland) 5/1[3]
5 3 1/2 **Story Of Dubai**[364] 631 6-9-3 0 RobertHavlin 10
(M Weiss, Switzerland) 212/10
6 nk **Ziking (FR)**[7] 609 8-9-8 0 FredericSpanu 8
(A Schaerer, Switzerland) 22/5[2]
7 dist **Niya (FR)**[14] 513 6-8-6 0 AndreBest 7
(P Schaerer, Switzerland) 65/1
8 dist **Flash Dance (GER)**[7] 609 6-9-4 0 TimBurgin(7) 2
(A Schennach, Switzerland) 78/10
8 dht **Ciocco Sam (GER)**[154] 5-8-11 0 SabrinaWandt 1
(C Von Der Recke, Germany) 242/10
10 nse **Pasalsa (FR)**[14] 513 5-9-3 0 (p) FilipMinarik 5
(Carmen Bocskai, Switzerland) 193/10
11 nk **Cappuccino (SWI)**[7] 609 5-9-11 0 (b) DPorcu 6
(P Schaerer, Switzerland) 134/10

1m 59.1s (119.10) 11 Ran SP% 143.7
PARI-MUTUEL (all including 1 chf stakes): WIN 1.50; PLACE 1.50, 2.10, 4.90; SF 8.30.
Owner Inkin, Inkin, Byng, Baker & Partners **Bred** Darley **Trained** Manton, Wilts

669 WOLVERHAMPTON (A.W) (L-H)
Monday, February 18
OFFICIAL GOING: Standard
Wind: Light across Weather: Fine

703 BOOKMAKER REVIEWS AT BOOKMAKERS.CO.UK AMATEUR RIDERS' H'CAP (DIV I) 1m 4f 50y(P)
2:10 (2:11) (Class 6) (0-52,52) 4-Y-0+ £1,871 (£580; £290; £145) Stalls Low

Form RPR
2000 1 **Turjuman (USA)**[12] 539 8-10-11 49 NicodeBoinville 7 59
(Simon West) *hld up: hdwy over 2f out: chsd ldr over 1f out: styd on u.p to ld nr fin* 14/1
-042 2 nk **Red Mystique (IRE)**[9] 579 4-10-4 52 (b) MissChelseyBanks(7) 2 61
(Philip Hide) *led: rdn over 1f out: hdd nr fin* 3/1[1]
5/ 3 5 **Faranadooney (USA)**[17] 484 6-10-5 48 (b) MrJCBarry(5) 12 49
(S M Duffy, Ire) *hld up: hdwy over 3f out: rdn over 1f out: styd on same pce: wnt 3rd wl ins fnl f* 4/1[2]
66-6 4 3/4 **Waldsee (GER)**[42] 99 8-10-6 47 MrFMitchell(3) 4 47
(Sean Curran) *a.p: chsd ldr over 5f out: rdn over 1f out: no ex ins fnl f* 7/1
-255 5 1 **Merrjanah**[9] 587 5-10-7 52 MrAFrench(7) 3 50
(John Wainwright) *prom: lost pl over 4f out: styd on ins fnl f* 22/1

The Form Book Flat, Raceform Ltd, Compton, RG20 6NL.

4-03 **6** ¾ **Supa Seeker (USA)**[13] 522 7-10-3 **46** .... MrCCarroll(5) 1 43
(Tony Carroll) *chsd ldr over 6f: remained handy: rdn over 2f out: wknd fnl f* **10/1**

-000 **7** ½ **Love Pegasus (USA)**[9] 579 7-10-4 **47** .... MissMBryant(5) 8 43
(Paddy Butler) *hld up: nvr nrr* **33/1**

0-55 **8** *hd* **Richo**[6] 515 7-10-5 **46** oh1 .... MissBeckyBrisbourne(3) 6 42
(Shaun Harris) *s.i.s: hld up: effrt over 2f out: n.d* **12/1**

-050 **9** ½ **State Senator (USA)**[12] 539 5-10-7 **52** .... MrTGreenwood(7) 11 47
(Richard Ford) *prom: rdn over 2f out: wknd over 1f out* **16/1**

614- **10** 3 **Shamo Hill Theatre**[65] 8139 6-10-7 **50** ....(p) MissVickiWood(5) 9 40
(Lawrence Mullaney) *hld up: effrt over 2f out: wknd over 1f out* **9/2**[3]

060- **11** 7 **Blue Pencil**[179] 5508 4-10-0 **46** oh1 .... MrFTett(5) 5 25
(Roger Curtis) *chsd ldrs: pushed along over 3f out: wknd over 2f out* **11/1**

6-60 **12** 2 **Rasteau (IRE)**[23] 406 5-10-3 **46** oh1 .... MrGrahamCarson(5) 10 22
(Tom Keddy) *hld up: a in rr: wknd over 2f out* **66/1**

2m 43.69s (2.59) **Going Correction** +0.10s/f (Slow)
WFA 4 from 5yo+ 3lb **12** Ran SP% **122.1**
Speed ratings (Par 101): **95,94,91,90,90 89,89,89,89,87 82,81**
toteswingers 1&2 £8.60, 1&3 £15.90, 2&3 £3.50 CSF £56.77 CT £209.93 TOTE £18.30: £3.60, £2.40, £2.10; EX 60.30 Trifecta £335.60 Pool: £1,931.30 - 4.31 winning units..
Owner S G West **Bred** Shadwell Farm LLC **Trained** Middleham Moor, N Yorks
■ Stewards' Enquiry : Mr J C Barry 11-day ban: used whip above permitted level (tbn)
Miss Chelsey Banks 11-day ban: used whip above permitted level without giving gelding time to respond (tbn)

FOCUS
The first division of a low-grade amateur riders' handicap.

704 BOOKMAKER REVIEWS AT BOOKMAKERS.CO.UK AMATEUR RIDERS' H'CAP (DIV II) 1m 4f 50y(P)
2:40 (2:40) (Class 6) (0-52,52) 4-Y-0+ **£1,871** (£580; £290; £145) **Stalls** Low

Form RPR

000- **1** **Tidy Affair (IRE)**[52] 8264 4-10-4 **52** .... MrGeorgeCrate(7) 9 64
(Gary Moore) *hld up: hdwy over 2f out: rdn to ld over 1f out: r.o wl* **7/2**[1]

0-66 **2** 4 **Brandy Snapping**[12] 530 4-10-2 **46** ....(t) MissBeckyBrisbourne(3) 3 52
(Mark Brisbourne) *hld up: hdwy over 2f out: rdn over 1f out: hung lft ins fnl f: styd on same pce* **10/1**

-650 **3** 2 ¼ **Pirate Chest (IRE)**[18] 455 5-10-7 **50** ....(bt) MrsFreyaBrewer(5) 8 52
(Patrick Holmes) *mid-div: hdwy over 3f out: ev ch over 1f out: no ex ins fnl f* **11/1**

400- **4** 6 **Needwood Park**[202] 4682 5-10-9 **52** ....(p) MrGRSmith(5) 6 45
(Ray Craggs) *prom: rdn over 1f out: wknd fnl f* **11/1**

0/0- **5** *nse* **Commerce**[262] 2137 6-10-5 **50** ....(p) MissSLewis(7) 2 43
(Dai Burchell) *trckd ldrs: racd keenly: led over 3f out: hdd over 1f out: wknd ins fnl f* **50/1**

00/5 **6** *shd* **Zelos Diktator**[21] 418 7-10-7 **48** .... MissSallyRandell(3) 5 41
(Sean Curran) *hld up: racd wd fr over 3f out tl over 1f out: hung lft and styd on ins fnl f: nvr nrr* **11/2**[2]

60-3 **7** 7 **Isola Bella**[8] 597 4-10-0 **46** oh1 .... MrJHarding(5) 10 27
(Jonathan Portman) *chsd ldrs tl rdn and wknd over 2f out* **8/1**

56/ **8** 5 **Peintre Du Roi (USA)**[77] 407 9-10-1 **46** oh1 ...... MrEdwardSibbick(7) 4 19
(Natalie Lloyd-Beavis) *led: hdd over 9f out: led again 6f out: hdd over 3f out: wknd 2f out* **66/1**

000- **9** 2 **Maccabees**[41] 7793 4-10-3 **49** .... MrFTett(5) 11 19
(Roger Curtis) *s.i.s: hld up: hdwy over 2f out: rdn and wknd wl over 1f out* **15/2**

0-04 **10** 1 ¼ **Fromthestables Com (IRE)**[39] 131 4-10-3 **51** MissJenniferPowell(7) 7 19
(Brendan Powell) *chsd ldrs: led over 9f out tl 6f out: wknd over 2f out* **7/1**[3]

0-02 **11** 5 **Silver Marizah (IRE)**[13] 522 4-10-2 **50** ....(e) MissRBIngram(7) 1 10
(Roger Ingram) *prom: lost pl over 6f out: bhd fnl 5f: t.o* **7/1**[3]

604- **12** 23 **Carlton Scroop (FR)**[61] 8173 10-10-3 **46** oh1 ....(b) MissMBryant(5) 12
(Paddy Butler) *prom over 7f: t.o* **40/1**

2m 43.8s (2.70) **Going Correction** +0.10s/f (Slow)
WFA 4 from 5yo+ 3lb **12** Ran SP% **117.1**
Speed ratings (Par 101): **95,92,90,86,86 86,82,78,77,76 73,57**
toteswingers 1&2 £10.90, 1&3 £12.80, 2&3 £29.70 CSF £38.73 CT £352.16 TOTE £3.70: £2.10, £3.80, £3.70; EX 59.50 Trifecta £998.70 Pool: £1,948.69 - 1.46 winning units..
Owner Gallagher, O'Rourke **Bred** Jim McCormack **Trained** Lower Beeding, W Sussex
■ A winner on his first ride under rules for George Crate.

FOCUS
The second division of the amateur riders' handicap was notable for gamble on the winner.

705 GET FREE BETS WITH BOOKMAKERS.CO.UK H'CAP 7f 32y(P)
3:15 (3:15) (Class 5) (0-70,70) 4-Y-0+ **£2,587** (£770; £384; £192) **Stalls** High

Form RPR

44-5 **1** **Yankee Storm**[35] 199 8-9-3 **66** ....(v) GeorgeBaker 6 74
(Michael Wigham) *dwlt: hld up: hdwy over 1f out: shkn up to ld ins fnl f: rdn out* **20/1**

-002 **2** ½ **Unlimited**[7] 616 11-8-10 **59** .... JimmyQuinn 3 66
(Tony Carroll) *hld up: hdwy over 2f out: rdn and ev ch ins fnl f: unable qck nr fin* **20/1**

2324 **3** ¾ **Arabian Flight**[9] 587 4-8-11 **60** .... AndrewMullen 7 65
(Michael Appleby) *mid-div: drvn along 1/2-way: outpcd over 2f out: rallied over 1f out: r.o* **15/2**

4-41 **4** ½ **Nant Saeson (IRE)**[24] 380 4-8-11 **60** ....(p) MichaelO'Connell 2 63
(John Quinn) *led: hdd over 5f out: chsd ldr tl led again over 2f out: rdn and edgd rt 1f out: hdd and unable qck ins fnl f* **5/1**[2]

3234 **5** ½ **Abhaath (USA)**[16] 490 4-9-0 **63** ....(b) LukeMorris 1 65
(Ronald Harris) *a.p: chsd ldr over 1f out: rdn and ev ch whn bmpd sn after: no ex ins fnl f* **15/2**

3-43 **6** 1 **Buckland (IRE)**[33] 222 5-9-2 **70** .... NicoleNordblad(5) 11 69
(Hans Adielsson) *s.i.s: hld up: hdwy over 1f out: sn rdn and edgd lft: nt trble ldrs* **7/1**[3]

2212 **7** 1 ¼ **Bussa**[4] 650 5-9-6 **69** ....(t) AdamKirby 5 65
(David Evans) *hld up: rdn over 1f out: nvr on terms* **13/8**[1]

300/ **8** 1 ½ **Youhavecontrol (IRE)**[485] 7024 5-9-6 **69** ....(t) ShaneKelly 12 61
(Nicky Vaughan) *chsd ldr tl led over 5f out: rdn and hdd over 2f out: wknd ins fnl f* **50/1**

0615 **9** *nse* **Lord Of The Dance (IRE)**[14] 518 7-9-6 **69** .... TomEaves 4 61
(Michael Mullineaux) *hld up: rdn over 2f out: hung lft ins fnl f: n.d* **16/1**

5066 **10** 4 ½ **Outlaw Torn (IRE)**[9] 593 4-8-13 **62** ....(e) RobbieFitzpatrick 9 42
(Richard Guest) *chsd ldrs: rdn over 2f out: wknd and eased fnl f* **20/1**

020- **11** 3 ¼ **Consistant**[151] 6403 5-8-13 **62** .... DuranFentiman 10 33
(Brian Baugh) *chsd ldrs tl rdn over 1f out: sn wknd* **40/1**

1m 29.39s (-0.21) **Going Correction** +0.10s/f (Slow) **11** Ran SP% **115.4**
Speed ratings (Par 103): **105,104,103,103,102 101,99,98,98,92 89**
toteswingers 1&2 £20.50, 1&3 £13.70, 2&3 £13.50 CSF £336.77 CT £3246.72 TOTE £18.00: £4.20, £3.80, £2.40; EX 247.10 Trifecta £1304.00 Pool: £3,280.80 - 1.88 winning units..
Owner R L Maynard **Bred** Mark Johnston Racing Ltd **Trained** Newmarket, Suffolk

FOCUS
It paid to be drawn low in this modest 7f handicap.

706 CASINO AT CORAL.CO.UK MAIDEN FILLIES' STKS 7f 32y(P)
3:50 (3:50) (Class 5) 3-Y-0+ **£2,587** (£770; £384; £192) **Stalls** High

Form RPR

2 **1** **Movementneverlies**[26] 332 3-8-7 0 .... RobertWinston 3 76
(Charles Hills) *chsd ldr tl rdn to ld ins fnl f: r.o* **5/6**[1]

2 ½ **Fizzy Pink** 3-8-7 0 .... LukeMorris 6 75
(Mrs K Burke) *a.p: shkn up over 2f out: rdn to chse wnr ins fnl f: hung rt: r.o* **12/1**

6- **3** 5 **Scent Of Roses (IRE)**[232] 3674 3-8-0 0 .... RyanTate(7) 1 61
(Clive Cox) *led: rdn over 1f out: hdd and no ex ins fnl f* **11/4**[2]

4 3 ¼ **Nellie Bly** 3-8-7 0 .... JoeFanning 2 52
(Mark Johnston) *chsd ldrs: rdn over 2f out: wknd fnl f* **6/1**[3]

4 **5** 1 ½ **Conas Ata Tu**[9] 590 4-9-3 0 .... AdamMcLean(7) 8 54
(Derek Shaw) *hld up: r.o ins fnl f: nvr nrr* **40/1**

04 **6** 3 ½ **Ivy Port**[17] 479 3-8-7 0 .... AndrewMullen 9 39
(Michael Appleby) *hld up: pushed along 1/2-way: wknd over 2f out* **33/1**

7 3 ¾ **Madam Fifi** 3-8-7 0 .... JohnFahy 7 29
(Alan McCabe) *s.i.s: hld up: a in rr: wknd over 2f out* **66/1**

3- **8** ½ **Fleurtille**[286] 1953 4-9-10 0 .... PaddyAspell 10 33
(Ray Craggs) *hld up: effrt over 2f out: sn wknd* **25/1**

9 ½ **Auntie Mildred (IRE)** 3-8-4 0 .... RaulDaSilva(3) 4 26
(David O'Meara) *prom: rdn over 2f out: wknd over 1f out* **14/1**

0 **10** 9 **Bella Cinderella**[39] 148 3-8-7 0 .... DuranFentiman 5
(George Moore) *s.i.s: a in rr: bhd fr 1/2-way* **66/1**

1m 29.67s (0.07) **Going Correction** +0.10s/f (Slow)
WFA 3 from 4yo 17lb **10** Ran SP% **122.1**
Speed ratings (Par 100): **103,102,96,93,91 87,83,82,81,71**
toteswingers 1&2 £4.10, 1&3 £1.30, 2&3 £4.50 CSF £13.76 TOTE £1.90: £1.10, £3.20, £1.40; EX 15.30 Trifecta £43.80 Pool: £2,838.91 - 48.55 winning units..
Owner Nicholas Roberts & Mrs E Roberts **Bred** Maywood Stud **Trained** Lambourn, Berks

FOCUS
The first two home in this fillies' maiden could turn out to be useful types.

707 BOOKMAKERS.CO.UK GIVES YOU FREE BETS (S) STKS 1m 141y(P)
4:20 (4:20) (Class 6) 4-Y-0+ **£1,940** (£577; £288; £144) **Stalls** Low

Form RPR

4-23 **1** **Saharia (IRE)**[14] 517 6-9-0 77 ....(be[1]) ShaneKelly 5 67+
(Daniel Mark Loughnane) *hld up: hdwy to chse ldr 2f out: led on bit over 1f out: canter* **4/11**[1]

204- **2** 2 ½ **Xpres Maite**[104] 7608 10-9-0 69 ....(b) AdamKirby 1 61
(Roy Bowring) *s.i.s: sn pushed along and rcvrd to ld after 1f: rdn over 2f out: hdd over 1f out: styd on same pce* **11/4**[2]

00-5 **3** 3 ½ **Bashama**[17] 476 5-8-9 49 ....(vt[1]) FrankieMcDonald 2 48
(Nikki Evans) *led 1f: chsd ldrs: rdn over 3f out: ev ch over 1f out: no ex ins fnl f* **33/1**

003- **4** 14 **Captain Cavallo**[76] 7978 6-9-0 44 ....(vt) LukeMorris 4 21
(Nicky Vaughan) *prom: chsd ldr 7f out: rdn over 3f out: wknd over 1f out* **25/1**[3]

1m 51.71s (1.21) **Going Correction** +0.10s/f (Slow) **4** Ran SP% **106.8**
Speed ratings (Par 101): **98,95,92,80**
CSF £1.56 TOTE £1.20; EX 2.00 Trifecta £4.00 Pool: £1,369.88 - 250.94 winning units..The winner was bought in for 5,500gns.
Owner Brooklands Racing **Bred** Woodcote Stud Ltd **Trained** Baldwin's Gate, Staffs

FOCUS
An uncompetitive seller.

708 COMPARE ONLINE BOOKIES WITH BOOKMAKERS.CO.UK MAIDEN STKS 1m 1f 103y(P)
4:50 (4:50) (Class 5) 3-Y-0+ **£2,587** (£770; £384; £192) **Stalls** Low

Form RPR

5 **1** **He's No Angel (IRE)**[41] 108 4-9-12 0 .... AdamKirby 10 78+
(Clive Cox) *chsd ldr tl led over 2f out: rdn clr fr over 1f out: eased nr fin* **8/1**

0 **2** 7 **Shockingdancer (IRE)**[35] 211 3-8-5 0 .... AndreaAtzeni 3 58+
(Marco Botti) *a.p: shkn up over 2f out: rdn to chse wnr over 1f out: no imp* **7/4**[1]

2 **3** 1 ¼ **Quintain (IRE)**[8] 602 5-9-12 0 .... DuranFentiman 8 61
(Tim Easterby) *led: rdn and hdd over 2f out: styd on same pce appr fnl f* **25/1**

4 **4** ¾ **The Great Gabrial**[14] 521 4-9-12 0 .... TomEaves 4 59
(Ian Williams) *trckd ldrs: plld hrd: stdd and lost pl 7f out: hdwy over 2f out: rdn over 1f out: styd on* **11/2**[3]

0- **5** 2 ½ **Autrisk (IRE)**[68] 8071 3-8-5 0 .... JimmyQuinn 9 48+
(Marco Botti) *prom: pushed along and nt clr run over 2f out: sn outpcd* **7/2**[2]

04 **6** 6 **Zafaraban (IRE)**[7] 612 6-9-7 0 .... GeorgeDowning(5) 5 42
(Tony Carroll) *hld up: wknd over 2f out* **33/1**

7 ½ **Omotesando** 3-8-5 0 .... JoeFanning 6 35
(Mark Johnston) *prom: pushed along over 2f out: sn wknd* **7/2**[2]

8 ¾ **Dorlesh Way (IRE)**[255] 6-9-12 0 .... PaddyAspell 1 39
(Patrick Holmes) *s.s: hld up and a in rr: wknd over 2f out* **100/1**

0-4 **9** 6 **Dolly Bantry**[12] 541 3-7-9 0 .... ShirleyTeasdale(5) 2
(Alan McCabe) *hld up: a in rr: wknd over 2f out* **100/1**

2m 2.57s (0.87) **Going Correction** +0.10s/f (Slow)
WFA 3 from 4yo+ 21lb **9** Ran SP% **116.1**
Speed ratings (Par 103): **100,93,92,92,89 84,84,83,78**
toteswingers 1&2 £4.30, 1&3 £7.00, 2&3 £7.20 CSF £22.34 TOTE £8.10: £1.90, £1.10, £3.80; EX 28.50 Trifecta £180.60 Pool: £2,536.11 - 10.52 winning units..
Owner B Ecclestone & J Humphreys **Bred** Lynch Bages Ltd & Samac Ltd **Trained** Lambourn, Berks

FOCUS
All four previous runnings of this maiden have been won by 3-y-os, but it was a 4-y-o colt who prevailed here.

709 DOWNLOAD CORAL.CO.UK MOBILE APP H'CAP 1m 1f 103y(P)
5:25 (5:25) (Class 6) (0-65,65) 4-Y-0+ £1,940 (£577; £288; £144) Stalls Low

Form RPR
6-11 **1** **Mubtadi**[27] 320 5-8-13 62 ThomasBrown(5) 4 71
(Ismail Mohammed) *trckd ldrs: led over 1f out: pushed out* **4/1**[2]
02-4 **2** 1 **Fly Haaf (IRE)**[41] 108 4-9-5 63 [1] GeorgeBaker 11 70
(William Knight) *hld up: hdwy on outer over 2f out: chsd wnr over 1f out: rdn and edgd lft ins fnl f: styd on* **5/1**[3]
60-5 **3** 3/4 **Attwaal (IRE)**[23] 403 4-9-7 65 SebSanders 9 70
(Neil King) *hld up: hdwy over 2f out: nt clr run wl over 1f out: sn rdn: styd on* **10/1**
-553 **4** 1 1/4 **Thereabouts (USA)**[9] 593 4-9-7 65 AndrewMullen 2 68
(Michael Appleby) *a.p: rdn over 2f out: styd on* **5/2**[1]
3-30 **5** hd **Apache Glory (USA)**[17] 477 5-9-2 60 AndreaAtzeni 10 62
(John Stimpson) *hld up: hdwy over 1f out: nt clr run ins fnl f: swtchd lft: r.o: nt rch ldrs* **20/1**
0-55 **6** 3 1/2 **Yeomanoftheguard**[34] 218 4-9-4 62 TonyHamilton 8 57
(Richard Fahey) *mid-div: effrt and hmpd over 2f out: rdn over 1f out: r.o: nt trble ldrs* **12/1**
0-26 **7** 3/4 **Scamperdale**[28] 314 11-9-4 62 (p) GrahamGibbons 1 55
(Brian Baugh) *hld up: hdwy over 3f out: rdn over 1f out: wknd wl ins fnl f* **8/1**
5-05 **8** 2 1/4 **Count Ceprano (IRE)**[39] 147 9-8-4 51 SimonPearce(3) 7 40
(Lydia Pearce) *hld up: hdwy over 1f out: wknd ins fnl f* **20/1**
-020 **9** 1/2 **Edgware Road**[17] 475 5-9-2 60 RobertWinston 3 48
(Sean Curran) *led: rdn over 2f out: hdd over 1f out: wknd ins fnl f* **16/1**
26-5 **10** 2 1/4 **Arashi**[9] 592 7-8-11 62 AdamMcLean(7) 5 45
(Derek Shaw) *hld up: swtchd lft over 1f out: nvr on terms* **50/1**
-012 **11** 15 **West End Lad**[20] 433 10-9-7 65 (b) AdamKirby 13 16
(Roy Bowring) *sn drvn along to chse ldrs: rdn over 3f out: hmpd and wknd 2f out* **8/1**
666- **12** 2 1/4 **Forster Street (IRE)**[37] 5680 4-9-5 63 DuranFentiman 12 10
(Tim Easterby) *chsd ldr tl drvn along over 2f out: sn wknd* **25/1**
2m 1.11s (-0.59) **Going Correction** +0.10s/f (Slow) **12 Ran SP% 125.5**
Speed ratings (Par 101): **106,105,104,103,103 100,99,97,96,94 81,79**
toteswingers 1&2 £6.60, 1&3 £12.00, 2&3 £11.40 CSF £24.77 CT £196.17 TOTE £5.20: £1.60, £2.30, £4.10; EX 28.70 Trifecta £260.80 Pool: £2,649.96 - 7.61 winning units..
Owner Abdulla Al Mansoori **Bred** Whitsbury Manor Stud **Trained** Newmarket, Suffolk
FOCUS
A very moderate handicap.

710 CORAL.CO.UK H'CAP 5f 20y(P)
5:55 (5:58) (Class 5) (0-75,72) 3-Y-0 £2,587 (£770; £384; £192) Stalls Low

Form RPR
1-62 **1** **Boxing Shadows**[35] 203 3-9-2 72 WilliamTwiston-Davies(5) 7 75
(Bryan Smart) *hld up in tch: rdn to ld wl ins fnl f: jst hld on* **7/2**[1]
1132 **2** shd **Lager Time (IRE)**[23] 402 3-9-1 66 AdamKirby 8 68
(David Evans) *hld up: hung rt over 3f out: rdn over 1f out: edgd lft and r.o wl ins fnl f: jst failed* **7/2**[1]
1214 **3** 3/4 **Windforpower (IRE)**[5] 628 3-9-6 71 (be) LukeMorris 4 70
(Ronald Harris) *a.p: rdn ins fnl f: r.o* **8/1**
-322 **4** nk **Modern Lady**[12] 531 3-8-8 66 PhilipPrince(7) 3 64
(Richard Guest) *led: rdn over 1f out: hdd ins fnl f: styd on* **14/1**
2211 **5** hd **Sewn Up**[11] 550 3-9-6 71 (tp) ChrisCatlin 1 68
(Reg Hollinshead) *hld up: pushed along 1/2-way: rdn and r.o ins fnl f* **10/1**
55-0 **6** shd **Miako (USA)**[5] 628 3-8-11 62 AndrewMullen 2 59
(Michael Appleby) *chsd ldrs: rdn to ld ins fnl f: sn hdd and unable qck* **10/1**
61-4 **7** 3 1/2 **Buy Art**[23] 402 3-9-2 67 FergusSweeney 6 51
(Gary Moore) *hld up: effrt over 1f out: styd on same pce fnl f* **25/1**
3-1 **8** 1 **Lead Role**[36] 197 3-9-4 69 AndreaAtzeni 5 50
(James Tate) *chsd ldr: rdn over 1f out: wknd ins fnl f* **9/2**[2]
2-1 **9** 2 3/4 **Hand In Glove**[11] 549 3-9-2 67 ShaneKelly 9 38
(Robert Cowell) *chsd ldrs: pushed along over 1f out: wknd fnl f* **5/1**[3]
1m 2.52s (0.22) **Going Correction** +0.10s/f (Slow) **9 Ran SP% 119.1**
Speed ratings (Par 97): **102,101,100,100,99 99,94,92,88**
toteswingers 1&2 £3.70, 1&3 £8.50, 2&3 £4.50 CSF £16.15 CT £93.34 TOTE £4.70: £1.80, £1.60, £3.20; EX 18.50 Trifecta £85.10 Pool: £2,271.24 - 20.01 winning units..
Owner Fromthestables.com Racing **Bred** Catridge Farm Stud Ltd **Trained** Hambleton, N Yorks
FOCUS
An interesting closer that pitted in-form sprint handicappers against unexposed maiden winners. There was a bunched finish.
T/Plt: £102.00 to a £1 stake. Pool: £67,938.77 - 485.91 winning tickets T/Qpdt: £18.00 to a £1 stake. Pool: £5,581.98 - 229.05 winning tickets CR

692 CAGNES-SUR-MER
Monday, February 18

OFFICIAL GOING: Turf: soft

711a PRIX DE LONGCHAMP (H'CAP) (3YO) (TURF) 1m 2f 165y
1:05 (12:00) 3-Y-0 £8,943 (£3,577; £2,682; £1,788; £894)

RPR
1 **Kingzar (FR)**[52] 3-9-4 0 FredericSpanu 6 90
(Mme C Barande-Barbe, France) **10/1**
2 snk **Russian Reel (FR)**[12] 544 3-9-1 0 RomainAuray 1 87
(J Heloury, France) **15/1**
3 2 **Saphir Nonantais (FR)**[55] 3-8-0 0 (b) AlexisBadel 12 68
(W Walton, France) **18/1**
4 1 1/2 **Lucio Silla**[12] 543 3-9-3 0 (b) MaximeGuyon 11 82
(H-A Pantall, France) **5/2**[1]
5 3/4 **Bien Determinee (FR)**[206] 3-8-0 0 AnthonyCrastus 3 63
(T Doumen, France) **72/1**
6 3/4 **Shabaka (FR)**[12] 543 3-8-9 0 (p) IoritzMendizabal 10 71
(F Foresi, France) **10/1**
7 1 1/2 **Snowy Dawn**[8] 605 3-8-13 0 (p) ThomasMessina 2 70
(Reg Hollinshead) *chsd clr ldr: clsd fr 3f out: rdn to chal over 2f out: outpcd and lost pl over 1f out: plugged on: fin 8th: plcd 7th* **10/1**
8 nse **Sara Francesca (FR)** 3-8-4 0 LouisBeuzelin 9 61
(S-R Simon, France) *fin 9th: plcd 8th* **25/1**
9 2 1/2 **Broken Spirit (FR)** 3-9-0 0 RemiCampos 4 66
(T Larriviere, France) *fin 10th: plcd 9th* **34/1**
10 **Kitten Rock (FR)** 3-9-2 0 NicolasPerret 8 68
(K Borgel, France) *fin 11th: plcd 10th* **17/1**
11 **Moorway (IRE)**[5] 647 3-8-0 0 DavidBreux 13 52
(Reg Hollinshead) *dwlt: qckly rcvrd and sent forward fr wdst draw to ld: over 6 l clr 4f out: diminishing advantage fr 3f out: rdn and hdd over 2f out: wknd and eased: fin 12th: plcd 11th* **66/1**
12 **Smart Casual (FR)**[100] 3-8-7 0 (p) JeromeClaudic 7 59
(R Laplanche, France) *fin 13th: plcd 12th* **9/1**[3]
D 1 **Varing (FR)**[27] 331 3-8-11 0 (b) FabriceVeron 5 71
(H-A Pantall, France) *fin 7th: disqualified: jockey failed to weigh in* **3/1**[2]
2m 22.96s (142.96) **13 Ran SP% 117.5**
PARI-MUTUEL (all including 1 euro stakes): WIN 11.00; PLACE 3.90, 4.60, 5.50; DF 74.50; SF 152.60.
Owner Jean-Claude-Alain Dupouy **Bred** I Shenkin **Trained** France

640 SOUTHWELL (L-H)
Tuesday, February 19

OFFICIAL GOING: Standard
Wind: Virtually nil Weather: Fine and dry

712 FREE SPORTS BETTING AT BOOKMAKERS.CO.UK MAIDEN STKS 1m 3f (F)
1:50 (1:50) (Class 5) 3-Y-0+ £2,726 (£805; £402) Stalls Low

Form RPR
1 **Dorfman** 3-8-5 0 JoeFanning 6 77+
(Mark Johnston) *in tch: hdwy to trck ldrs 1/2-way: effrt on bit to chse ldr 3f out: slt ld 2f out: rn green: edgd lft and shkn up ent fnl f: kpt on* **5/1**[3]
33- **2** 1 1/4 **Gods Gift (IRE)**[112] 7468 3-8-5 0 ChrisCatlin 5 68
(Rae Guest) *trckd ldr: hdwy and cl up over 5f out: led over 4f out: rdn wl over 2f out: sn jnd and hdd wl over 1f out: rallied and ev ch ent fnl f: sn drvn and one pce* **6/4**[2]
020- **3** 14 **Roc De Prince**[131] 7011 4-9-12 73 DanielTudhope 3 47
(David O'Meara) *trckd ldrs: hdwy to chse ldng pair over 3f out: rdn over 2f out and sn one pce* **5/4**[1]
4 18 **Nevermindapete**[7] 5-10-0 0 (t) AdamKirby 8 14
(David Evans) *s.i.s and bhd: sme hdwy on wd outside 1/2-way: sn pushed along: rdn wl over 3f out: n.d* **14/1**
0065 **5** 1 3/4 **Elusive**[9] 602 7-9-4 29 AnnStokell(5) 1 6
(Ann Stokell) *hld up in tch: sme hdwy 4f out: sn rdn along and n.d* **100/1**
0/0 **6** 2 1/4 **King Of Forces**[6] 637 4-9-12 0 AndreaAtzeni 2 7
(Denis Quinn) *chsd ldrs on inner: pushed along 1/2-way: sn rdn and outpcd: bhd fnl 4f* **25/1**
46 **7** 15 **Chain Reactor**[15] 521 7-10-0 0 RobertHavlin 7
(Amy Weaver) *reminders s: in tch: rdn along after 4f: sn lost pl and bhd fnl 4f* **33/1**
0-05 **8** 21 **How You Fixed (IRE)**[18] 468 3-7-13 0 ow1 (b[1]) TimClark(7) 4
(Denis Quinn) *led and sn clr: rdn along 1/2-way: hdd over 4f out and wknd qckly: sn wl bhd* **66/1**
2m 26.74s (-1.26) **Going Correction** -0.075s/f (Stan)
WFA 3 from 4yo 23lb 4 from 5yo+ 2lb **8 Ran SP% 117.0**
Speed ratings (Par 103): **101,100,89,76,75 73,63,47**
toteswingers 1&2 £2.30, 1&3 £1.70, 2&3 £1.10 CSF £13.17 TOTE £5.10: £2.30, £1.10, £1.10; EX 14.10 Trifecta £26.50 Pool: £2147.83 - 60.58 winning units..
Owner Sheikh Hamdan Bin Mohammed Al Maktoum **Bred** Darley **Trained** Middleham Moor, N Yorks
FOCUS
An uncompetitive maiden which only concerned the front three from some way out. The form is fluid.

713 ONLINE BETTING OFFERS AT BOOKMAKERS.CO.UK CLAIMING STKS 2m (F)
2:20 (2:24) (Class 6) 4-Y-0+ £2,045 (£603; £302) Stalls Low

Form RPR
06-1 **1** **Kazbow (IRE)**[7] 622 7-9-1 72 (t) GrahamLee 1 81
(Richard Ford) *prom on inner: cl up 6f out: led 4f out: rdn along and hdd wl over 1f out: rallied u.p ins fnl f to ld again nr fin* **2/1**[2]
1111 **2** nk **Stand Guard**[14] 524 9-9-10 87 AdamKirby 4 90
(John Butler) *hld up: smooth hdwy to trck ldrs 5f out: effrt 3f out: rdn to ld wl over 1f out: hung rt to stands' rail and drvn ent fnl f: hdd and no ex towards fin* **1/1**[1]
050- **3** 17 **Omid**[67] 8104 5-9-6 58 (vt) LukeMorris 5 65
(Nicky Vaughan) *trckd ldrs: cl up 6f out: rdn along over 3f out: grad wknd fr over 2f out* **33/1**
0/33 **4** 4 1/2 **Esteem**[19] 458 10-8-13 55 (t) ShaneKelly 7 53
(David Evans) *hld up in rr: hdwy on outer 1/2-way: rdn along to chse ldrs over 3f out: drvn to chse ldng pair over 2f out: sn one pce: lost poor 3rd ins fnl f* **40/1**
50-0 **5** 37 **One For The Girls**[35] 215 4-8-2 45 (p) RachealKneller(5) 6 8
(Nicky Vaughan) *led: rdn along and hdd 4f out: sn wknd and bhd fnl 2f* **100/1**
6 36 **Vin Chaud**[173] 5-8-1 0 PhilipPrince(7) 2
(Bill Turner) *t.k.h: chsd ldrs on inner: rdn along over 6f out: sn wknd* **66/1**
360- **P** **Captain Bellamy (USA)**[70] 7377 5-9-4 78 GeorgeBaker 3
(Hughie Morrison) *prom on outer: pushed along wl over 4f out: sn lost pl and p.u over 3f out: b.b.v* **4/1**[3]
3m 42.45s (-3.05) **Going Correction** -0.075s/f (Stan)
WFA 4 from 5yo+ 6lb **7 Ran SP% 111.2**
Speed ratings (Par 101): **104,103,95,93,74 56,**
toteswingers 1&2 £1.20, 1&3 £6.70, 2&3 £5.60 CSF £4.10 TOTE £3.10: £1.20, £1.10; EX 4.70 Trifecta £24.10 Pool: £2200.15 - 68.40 winning units..
Owner The Most Wanted Partnership **Bred** Airlie Stud **Trained** Garstang, Lancs
FOCUS
A fascinating claimer in which the third sets the level.

714 COMPARE BOOKIES WITH BOOKMAKERS.CO.UK H'CAP 1m 4f (F)
2:50 (2:50) (Class 6) (0-60,60) 4-Y-0+ £2,045 (£603; £302) Stalls Low

Form RPR
6-02 **1** **Corn Maiden**[13] 539 4-8-5 47 JoeFanning 1 58
(Mark Rimmer) *trckd ldr on inner: hdwy over 2f out: rdn to ld over 1f out: edgd rt ins fnl f: sn drvn and kpt on* **3/1**[2]

The Form Book Flat, Raceform Ltd, Compton, RG20 6NL.

1-55 **2** *2* **Honest Strike (USA)**[13] 539 6-8-12 **51**..........................(b) ShaneKelly 6 59
(Daniel Mark Loughnane) *hld up: hdwy on outer 3f out: chsd ldrs 2f out: rdn to chal over 1f out and ev ch tl drvn and one pce ins fnl f: b.b.v* **7/2**[3]
55-5 **3** *2* **Candelita**[22] 429 6-9-7 **60**.. J-PGuillambert 3 65
(Jo Hughes) *hld up in tch: hdwy to trck ldrs over 4f out: effrt over 2f out: rdn wl over 1f out and ev ch tl drvn and one pce ins fnl f* **9/4**[1]
66-3 **4** *4* **Kingaroo (IRE)**[7] 624 7-9-5 **58**.......................... LukeMorris 2 56
(Garry Woodward) *led: pushed along 3f out: rdn over 2f out: drvn and hdd over 1f out: grad wknd* **8/1**
-04 **5** *1 3/4* **Revolving World (IRE)**[14] 522 10-8-7 **46** oh1..........(t) AndrewMullen 8 42
(Lee James) *hld up towards rr: hdwy on outer over 2f out: rdn wl over 1f out: sn no imp* **16/1**
0 **6** *1/2* **Houdini Bright (USA)**[19] 455 5-8-7 **46**.................... JamesSullivan 4 41
(James Given) *chsd ldrs: rdn along over 4f out: wknd wl over 2f out* **8/1**
50-0 **7** *3* **Rajeh (IRE)**[10] 579 10-8-7 **51**.............................. SladeO'Hara(5) 5 41
(Peter Grayson) *a towards rr* **20/1**
000- **8** *45* **La Giaconda**[111] 7477 4-8-9 **51** ow1............................(t) RobertWinston 7
(Olivia Maylam) *racd wd: cl up: rdn along over 4f out: sn wknd and bhd fnl 2f* **33/1**

2m 42.17s (1.17) **Going Correction** -0.075s/f (Stan)
WFA 4 from 5yo+ 3lb **8** Ran SP% **113.8**
Speed ratings (Par 101): **93,91,90,87,86 86,84,54**
toteswingers 1&2 £2.60, 1&3 £2.60, 2&3 £1.60 CSF £13.82 CT £26.70 TOTE £4.80: £1.50, £1.40, £1.10; EX 15.80 Trifecta £47.60 Pool: £1495.84 - 23.52 winning units..
Owner Ms Johanna McHugh **Bred** G B Turnbull Ltd **Trained** Newmarket, Suffolk

FOCUS
A modest middle-distance handicap but the form seems sound rated around the first three.

715 GET FREE BETS WITH BOOKMAKERS.CO.UK H'CAP 7f (F)
3:25 (3:25) (Class 4) (0-80,80) 4-Y-0+ **£4,690** (£1,395; £697; £348) **Stalls** Low

Form RPR
135- **1** **Light Burst (USA)**[89] 7824 4-9-2 **80**.......................... ThomasBrown(5) 9 90+
(Ismail Mohammed) *trckd ldrs on outer: hdwy 2f out: rdn to ld jst over 1f out: drvn ins fnl f and kpt on wl* **2/1**[1]
0-01 **2** *3/4* **Hellbender (IRE)**[14] 523 7-8-7 **66** oh3..........................(t) DavidProbert 5 74
(Shaun Harris) *cl up: led over 2f out and sn rdn: hdd and drvn over 1f out: kpt on wl u.p fnl f* **16/1**
4-20 **3** *1* **Piceno (IRE)**[6] 644 5-9-2 **75**..(p) LukeMorris 4 80
(Scott Dixon) *dwlt: sn prom: slt ld after 2f: rdn along and hdd over 2f out: cl up and drvn over 1f out: kpt on same pce fnl f* **9/2**[2]
-221 **4** *2 3/4* **Flying Pickets (IRE)**[7] 620 4-9-1 **74** 6ex.......................(be) JohnFahy 6 72
(Alan McCabe) *in tch: hdwy to chse ldrs 2f out: sn rdn and no imp fnl f* **7/1**[3]
0344 **5** *1* **Key Ambition**[10] 582 4-8-9 **68**.................................(tp) RobertWinston 8 63
(Garry Moss) *squeezed out s and towards rr: hdwy 3f out: rdn wl over 1f out: kpt on: nrst fin* **9/1**
23-0 **6** *3 3/4* **Sound Amigo (IRE)**[14] 526 5-9-7 **80**.............................. GrahamLee 7 65
(Ollie Pears) *trckd ldrs: effrt 2f out: sn rdn and wknd appr fnl f* **10/1**
0U60 **7** *2 3/4* **Decent Fella (IRE)**[10] 586 7-9-6 **79**..........................(tp) MartinHarley 1 57
(Violet M Jordan) *a towards rr* **16/1**
-304 **8** *nk* **Mazovian (USA)**[9] 603 5-8-1 **67**.................................. NoelGarbutt(7) 2 44
(Michael Chapman) *broke wl and prom 2f: sn lost pl and bhd* **16/1**
-345 **9** *shd* **Imprimis Tagula (IRE)**[13] 540 9-8-2 **66** oh1..........(v) NatashaEaton(5) 10 43
(Alan Bailey) *sn led: hdd after 2f and cl up tl rdn along wl over 2f out and sn wknd* **10/1**
000- **10** *10* **Abi Scarlet (IRE)**[153] 6367 4-9-7 **80**............................... HayleyTurner 3 30
(Hughie Morrison) *prom on inner: rdn along wl over 2f out: sn wknd and towards rr whn lost action and eased over 1f out* **8/1**

1m 28.79s (-1.51) **Going Correction** -0.075s/f (Stan) **10** Ran SP% **121.0**
Speed ratings (Par 105): **105,104,103,99,98 94,91,90,90,79**
toteswingers 1&2 £12.80, 1&3 £2.50, 2&3 £10.70 CSF £40.11 CT £139.92 TOTE £2.30: £1.70, £5.00, £1.40; EX 53.70 Trifecta £366.50 Pool: £2499.01 - 5.11 winning units..
Owner Saeed H Altayer **Bred** C Kidder, N Cole & B Kidder **Trained** Newmarket, Suffolk

FOCUS
A decent handicap and truly run, with the third setting the standard.

716 CORAL.CO.UK (S) STKS 6f (F)
4:00 (4:00) (Class 6) 3-Y-0+ **£2,045** (£603; £302) **Stalls** Low

Form RPR
0-60 **1** **Masked Dance (IRE)**[14] 526 6-9-8 60..............................(bt) LukeMorris 3 63
(Scott Dixon) *cl up: rdn to chal over 2f out: led over 1f out: drvn and edgd rt ent fnl f: hld on wl towards fin* **6/4**[2]
0000 **2** *3/4* **Very First Blade**[12] 551 4-9-8 43.................................(p) FrannyNorton 6 61?
(Mark Brisbourne) *led: rdn along 2f out: hdd over 1f out: drvn and rallied gamely ins fnl f: ev ch tl no ex towards fin* **4/1**[3]
4344 **3** *4* **Mother Jones**[8] 611 5-9-8 68.. AdamKirby 5 48
(David Evans) *trckd ldrs: hdwy over 2f out: swtchd rt and rdn wl over 1f out: sn ev ch: drvn and one pce appr fnl f* **5/4**[1]
600- **4** *7* **Munaawib**[222] 3988 5-9-8 40....................................(t) RobbieFitzpatrick 2 26
(Charles Smith) *in rr: sme hdwy over 2f out: sn rdn and n.d* **25/1**
6-00 **5** *28* **Bird Dog**[7] 618 7-9-1 41...(v) RyanTate(7) 1
(Phil McEntee) *broke wl: prom: rdn along bef 1/2-way: sn outpcd and bhd whn eased fnl f* **25/1**

1m 16.72s (0.22) **Going Correction** -0.075s/f (Stan)
WFA 3 from 4yo+ 15lb **5** Ran SP% **112.1**
Speed ratings (Par 101): **95,94,88,79,42**
CSF £8.04 TOTE £2.70: £1.10, £1.30; EX 8.20 Trifecta £12.70 Pool: £2104.83 - 140.97 winning units..There were no bids for the winner.
Owner Ontoawinner 4 **Bred** Canice Farrell Jnr **Trained** Babworth, Notts

FOCUS
A poor seller dominated by the pair that raced on the pace. the runner-up is rated to his previous course form.

717 POKER AT CORAL.CO.UK H'CAP 1m (F)
4:35 (4:35) (Class 6) (0-55,55) 3-Y-0 **£2,045** (£603; £302) **Stalls** Low

Form RPR
656- **1** **Luv U Whatever**[141] 6733 3-9-2 **50**.................................. J-PGuillambert 4 60
(Jo Hughes) *prom: cl up 1/2-way: slt ld wl over 2f out: drvn ent fnl f: kpt on wl towards fin* **7/1**
000- **2** *nk* **Suspension**[69] 8068 3-8-13 **52**........................ WilliamTwiston-Davies(5) 1 61
(Hughie Morrison) *trckd ldrs on inner: smooth hdwy over 2f out: rdn to chal over 1f out: disp ld and drvn ent fnl f: ev ch tl no ex towards fin* **9/1**
04-3 **3** *5* **Naughtybychoice**[14] 527 3-9-6 **54**.................................... GrahamLee 6 52
(Ollie Pears) *trckd ldrs: hdwy over 2f out: swtchd rt and rdn to chal wl over 1f out: ev ch tl drvn and hung rt ent fnl f: sn one pce* **7/4**[1]
0-43 **4** *4 1/2* **Faither**[7] 623 3-9-6 **54**..(b[1]) JoeFanning 5 41
(Keith Dalgleish) *t.k.h: cl up: disp ld 3f out: rdn and ev ch 2f out: drvn and wknd appr fnl f* **7/1**
5-53 **5** *2* **Rosie Future (IRE)**[33] 237 3-9-5 **53**..................................[1] DavidProbert 7 36
(Rae Guest) *sn rdn along and bhd tl sme hdwy fnl 2f: n.d* **3/1**[2]
-322 **6** *6* **Armada Bay (IRE)**[19] 459 3-9-7 **55**.................................. TomEaves 8 24
(Bryan Smart) *prom on outer: rdn along 3f out: wknd over 2f out* **6/1**[3]
5-03 **7** *9* **Multi Fours**[10] 591 3-9-1 **49**...(p) LukeMorris 2
(Daniel Kubler) *led: rdn along over 3f out: hdd wl over 2f out and sn wknd* **14/1**
-000 **8** *23* **Sylvia's Diamond**[12] 550 3-8-5 **46** oh1......................(v[1]) PhilipPrince(7) 3
(Richard Guest) *a in rr: outpcd and bhd fnl 3f* **80/1**

1m 43.82s (0.12) **Going Correction** -0.075s/f (Stan) **8** Ran SP% **118.6**
Speed ratings (Par 95): **96,95,90,86,84 78,69,46**
toteswingers 1&2 £12.90, 1&3 £4.90, 2&3 £4.10 CSF £69.60 CT £160.82 TOTE £10.20: £2.30, £3.00, £1.20; EX 118.30 Trifecta £225.20 Pool: £2896.38 - 9.64 winning units..
Owner 21C Telecom.co.uk **Bred** Richard Hunt **Trained** Lambourn, Berks

FOCUS
A moderate 3-y-o handicap rated at face value with the third to his latest C&D mark..

718 CORAL.CO.UK MOBILE BETTING H'CAP 1m (F)
5:10 (5:10) (Class 5) (0-70,69) 4-Y-0+ **£2,587** (£770; £384; £192) **Stalls** Low

Form RPR
0-11 **1** **Our Ivor**[9] 600 4-8-10 **58** 6ex... AndrewMullen 9 79
(Michael Appleby) *trckd ldrs: cl up over 3f out: rdn to ld 2f out: clr whn wandered bdly and drvn along ent fnl f: styd on strly* **5/4**[1]
2565 **2** *8* **Follow The Flag (IRE)**[14] 528 9-9-5 **67**..........................(be) JohnFahy 5 69
(Alan McCabe) *sn rdn along and outpcd in rr: wd st: hdwy wl over 2f out: styd on u.p appr fnl f: no ch w wnr* **9/1**
232 **3** *1/2* **Miami Gator (IRE)**[13] 536 6-9-1 **63**................................(v) LukeMorris 10 64
(Mrs K Burke) *cl up: led wl 3f out: hdd 2f out: sn drvn and one pce* **5/1**[2]
422- **4** *shd* **River Ardeche**[91] 7798 8-9-1 **63**....................................... BarryMcHugh 7 64
(Tracy Waggott) *led 1f: prom on inner: rdn along 3f out: drvn and one pce fr over 2f out* **7/1**[3]
4-50 **5** *2 1/4* **Availed Speaker (IRE)**[16] 511 4-8-10 **65**................. SamanthaBell(7) 4 61
(Richard Fahey) *chsd ldrs: rdn along 3f out: sn one pce* **16/1**
-060 **6** *1 1/2* **Mcconnell (USA)**[16] 511 8-8-4 **57**.........................(b) NatashaEaton(5) 6 49
(Violet M Jordan) *chsd ldrs: effrt 3f out: rdn along over 2f out: sn wknd* **33/1**
04-0 **7** *14* **On The Cusp (IRE)**[20] 439 6-8-10 **63**..................(p) CharlesBishop(5) 8 23
(Violet M Jordan) *cl up: led after 1f: rdn along and hdd wl over 3f out: sn wknd* **20/1**
0-50 **8** *3 1/4* **St Ignatius**[22] 420 6-9-7 **69**.. AdamKirby 3 21
(Alan Bailey) *sn outpcd in rr: bhd fr 1/2-way* **5/1**[2]

1m 41.83s (-1.87) **Going Correction** -0.075s/f (Stan) **8** Ran SP% **113.9**
Speed ratings (Par 103): **106,98,97,97,95 93,79,76**
toteswingers 1&2 £2.50, 1&3 £2.40, 2&3 £5.40 CSF £13.57 CT £43.20 TOTE £2.20: £1.20, £2.30, £1.30; EX 11.80 Trifecta £38.40 Pool: £3101.47 - 60.42 winning units..
Owner J&G Bacciochi, A Taylor, Bruce W Wyatt **Bred** B W Wyatt **Trained** Danethorpe, Notts

FOCUS
An ordinary handicap, but a few of these like to force it so the pace was solid enough. The form is a bit fluid but the runner-up is the best guide rated to his November C&D mark.
T/Plt: £16.30 to a £1 stake. Pool of £54428.18 - 2433.05 winning units. T/Qpdt: £15.30 to a £1 stake. Pool: £3334.77 - 160.80 winning tickets JR

649 KEMPTON (A.W) (R-H)
Wednesday, February 20

OFFICIAL GOING: Standard
Wind: Fresh, across (towards stands) Weather: Fine, cold

719 FREE ENTRY EVERY WEDNESDAY FOR BETDAQ MEMBERS H'CAP 5f (P)
5:30 (5:31) (Class 5) (0-70,70) 4-Y-0+ **£2,587** (£770; £384; £192) **Stalls** Low

Form RPR
2/21 **1** **Danziger (IRE)**[11] 581 4-9-0 **63**... AdamKirby 1 72
(David Evans) *s.i.s and rousted along early: prog fr rr 2f out: chsd ldr jst over 1f out: drvn ahd last 100yds: styd on* **5/4**[1]
0-00 **2** *1/2* **Courageous (IRE)**[11] 583 7-9-6 **69**................................(t) JimmyQuinn 6 76
(Milton Bradley) *led: drvn over 1f out: kpt on but hdd and hld last 100yds* **12/1**
3203 **3** *2 1/4* **Russian Bullet**[12] 558 4-8-8 **57**.. DavidProbert 3 56
(Jamie Osborne) *cl up on inner: drvn to dispute 2nd over 1f out: outpcd fnl f* **8/1**
1010 **4** *1* **Charming (IRE)**[7] 627 4-9-4 **67**...(e) IanMongan 4 62
(Olivia Maylam) *lost pl after 1f: rdn in 5th 2f out: no imp over 1f out: kpt on nr fin* **14/1**
0-55 **5** *hd* **Quality Art (USA)**[7] 627 5-9-7 **70**............................ RobbieFitzpatrick 7 65
(Richard Guest) *mostly chsd ldr to jst over 1f out: fdd fnl f* **7/1**[3]
0-05 **6** *1/2* **Rambo Will**[14] 535 5-9-2 **65**... AmyRyan 5 58
(J R Jenkins) *racd v wd thrght: hld up: lost grnd bnd 2f out: no ch after: kpt on last 100yds* **3/1**[2]
204- **7** *1/2* **Even Bolder**[60] 8225 10-8-4 **60**....................................(b) JoeyHaynes(7) 2 51
(Eric Wheeler) *t.k.h: racd wd: in tch in rr: lost grnd bnd 2f out: nvr on terms after* **12/1**

59.29s (-1.21) **Going Correction** -0.05s/f (Stan) **7** Ran SP% **115.1**
Speed ratings (Par 103): **107,106,102,101,100 99,99**
Tote Swingers: 1&2 £5.70, 1&3 £1.60, 2&3 £15.50 CSF £18.40 TOTE £1.90: £1.10, £6.90; EX 25.30 Trifecta £131.60 Pool: £1,718.71 - 9.79 winning units..
Owner Mrs E Evans **Bred** Castleton Lyons & Kilboy Estate **Trained** Pandy, Monmouths
■ Stewards' Enquiry : Adam Kirby four-day ban: used whip in incorrect place (Mar 6-9)

FOCUS
A modest handicap in which the gallop was an ordinary one for a sprint. The winner raced towards the far side in the straight.

720 BACK AND LAY AT BETDAQ.COM H'CAP 1m 2f (P)
6:00 (6:02) (Class 5) (0-75,73) 4-Y-0+ **£2,587** (£770; £384; £192) **Stalls** Low

Form RPR
-436 **1** **Buckland (IRE)**[2] 705 5-8-13 **70**.............................. NicoleNordblad(5) 6 85
(Hans Adielsson) *hld up in 5th: clsd over 2f out: prog on outer and pushed into ld over 1f out: sn clr: readily* **4/1**[2]
0-15 **2** *2 3/4* **Travelling**[17] 511 4-8-8 **68**... RyanTate(7) 3 77
(Tony Carroll) *reluctant to enter stalls: hld up in last: prog on inner wl over 1f out: drvn to chse wnr fnl f: styd on but no imp* **5/1**[3]

1-35 **3** 2 1/2 **Whitby Jet (IRE)**[21] 439 5-9-7 **73** GeorgeBaker 2 77
(Ed Vaughan) *led at decent pce: shkn up and hrd pressed over 2f out: hdd over 1f out: fdd* **6/4**[1]

-113 **4** 1 **Conducting**[7] 639 5-9-4 **70** JimmyQuinn 4 72
(Gay Kelleway) *awkward s: chsd ldrs: drvn over 2f out: no rspnse and wl btn over 1f out* **11/2**

03-2 **5** 1 3/4 **Abigails Angel**[40] 159 6-9-7 **73** DavidProbert 5 72
(Brett Johnson) *trckd ldr: rdn to chal over 2f out: wknd over 1f out* **8/1**

0/00 **6** 99 **King Olav (UAE)**[23] 420 8-9-3 **69** AdamKirby 8
(Tony Carroll) *trckd ldrs on outer: hanging bdly and dropped to last 3f out: sn t.o and eased* **10/1**

2m 5.72s (-2.28) **Going Correction** -0.05s/f (Stan)
WFA 4 from 5yo+ 1lb **6** Ran SP% **112.3**
Speed ratings (Par 103): **107,104,102,102,100 21**
Tote Swingers: 1&2 £3.80, 2&3 £2.70 CSF £23.67 CT £41.50 TOTE £4.90: £2.60, £4.40; EX 24.00 Trifecta £88.30 Pool: £1,770.28 - 15.02 winning units..
Owner P S McNally **Bred** Airlie Stud And Sir Thomas Pilkington **Trained** Kingston Lisle, Oxon

FOCUS
A fair handicap. The gallop was an ordinary one to the home turn and the winner came down the centre.

721 WIN BIG WITH BETDAQ MULTIPLES CLAIMING STKS 7f (P)
6:30 (6:30) (Class 6) 4-Y-0+ **£1,940** (£577; £288; £144) **Stalls** Low

Form RPR

-131 **1** **Hurricane Spirit (IRE)**[19] 476 9-8-8 71 NicoleNordblad(5) 1 72+
(Hans Adielsson) *t.k.h: hld up: trckd ldr 3f out: led on inner 2f out and sn dashed clr: rdn out* **1/2**[1]

-340 **2** 5 **Only Ten Per Cent (IRE)**[17] 511 5-9-9 73 IanMongan 3 68
(J R Jenkins) *awkward s: t.k.h: hld up: effrt over 2f out: rdn to chse clr wnr over 1f out: no imp* **5/1**[3]

-652 **3** 3/4 **Masai Moon**[7] 645 9-9-0 73 PatMillman(7) 6 64
(Rod Millman) *t.k.h: racd wd thrght: in tch: lost grnd bnd 3f out: no ch 2f out: pushed along and kpt on fnl f* **9/2**[2]

-605 **4** 1/2 **Rapid Water**[7] 631 7-8-13 53 (b) RobertWinston 4 55
(Pat Eddery) *t.k.h: chsd ldr to 3f out: outpcd fr 2f out: fdd* **16/1**

-063 **5** 3/4 **Flying Kitty**[5] 664 4-7-11 39 (v) PhilipPrince(7) 2 44
(John Bridger) *t.k.h: led to 2f out: no ch w wnr after: fdd fnl f* **66/1**

1m 24.9s (-1.10) **Going Correction** -0.05s/f (Stan) **5** Ran SP% **108.9**
Speed ratings (Par 101): **104,98,97,96,96**
CSF £3.35 TOTE £1.30: £1.10, £2.50; EX 3.70 Trifecta £7.00 Pool: £1,739.15 - 185.46 winning units..
Owner Hans Adielsson A B **Bred** Knocktoran Stud **Trained** Kingston Lisle, Oxon

FOCUS
An uncompetitive claimer in which the gallop was an ordinary one to the intersection. The winner raced against the inside rail throughout.

722 BETDAQ GAMES £50 HARD CASH BONUS H'CAP 1m 3f (P)
7:00 (7:00) (Class 6) (0-60,60) 4-Y-0+ **£1,940** (£577; £288; £72; £72) **Stalls** Low

Form RPR

-051 **1** **Time Square (FR)**[7] 625 6-8-4 **50** JoeyHaynes(7) 10 59
(Tony Carroll) *t.k.h: trckd ldr: led jst over 3f out and sn 3 l clr gng strly: rdn over 1f out: kpt on wl: unchal* **8/1**

-006 **2** 1 1/2 **Amana (USA)**[16] 520 9-9-6 **59** ShaneKelly 9 65+
(Mark Brisbourne) *hld up in 9th: nt clr run on inner wl over 2f out: gd prog wl over 1f out: drvn to take 2nd ins fnl f: styd on but unable to chal* **33/1**

0-20 **3** 1 3/4 **Dolly Colman (IRE)**[17] 508 5-8-7 **46** ChrisCatlin 3 49
(Zoe Davison) *hld up in 7th: prog on inner over 2f out: drvn to chal for a pl fr over 1f out: kpt on same pce* **33/1**

3153 **4** hd **Spirit Of Gondree (IRE)**[7] 626 5-9-7 **60** (b) RobertWinston 11 63
(Milton Bradley) *s.s: hld up in 10th: gd prog over 2f out to chse wnr wl over 1f out: no imp after: lost 2nd ins fnl f* **3/1**[2]

04-0 **4** dht **Beggers Belief**[44] 94 5-9-1 **54** (b) JimmyQuinn 5 57
(Eric Wheeler) *trckd ldrs in 5th: drvn over 2f out: kpt on same pce to chal for pls fnl f* **11/1**

5031 **6** nk **Sommersturm (GER)**[11] 579 9-9-1 **54** (t) AdamKirby 1 56
(David Evans) *trckd ldng pair: hrd rdn to chse wnr wl over 2f out to wl over 1f out: one pce after* **5/2**[1]

00-2 **7** 2 **Tinkerbell Will**[44] 94 6-8-9 **51** NataliaGemelova(3) 7 50
(John E Long) *hld up in 6th: rdn on outer over 2f out: tried to cl on ldrs over 1f out: wknd fnl f* **8/1**

0-00 **8** 6 **Confirmed**[10] 600 4-9-5 **60** (t) GeorgeBaker 4 48
(Alison Batchelor) *stdd s: t.k.h: hld up in last: v modest prog 2f out: nvr in it* **33/1**

-430 **9** 8 **Handsome Molly**[11] 579 4-8-10 **51** (v[1]) LiamKeniry 13 24
(David Elsworth) *hld up in 8th: rdn over 3f out: sn struggling: t.o* **14/1**

050- **10** 1 **Navajo Charm**[75] 8020 4-8-12 **60** DavidParkes(7) 2 32
(Alan Jarvis) *led to jst over 3f out: wknd qckly: t.o* **7/1**[3]

0300 **11** 1/2 **Daniel Thomas (IRE)**[17] 508 11-9-4 **57** (tp) MartinHarley 14 28
(Violet M Jordan) *trckd ldng trio: drvn to dispute 2nd briefly over 2f out: sn wknd qckly: t.o* **20/1**

2m 22.21s (0.31) **Going Correction** -0.05s/f (Stan)
WFA 4 from 5yo+ 2lb **11** Ran SP% **116.9**
Speed ratings (Par 101): **96,94,93,93,93 93,91,87,81,80 80**
Tote Swingers: 1&2 £17.00, 1&3 £24.00, 2&3 £68.90 CSF £249.08 CT £7915.56 TOTE £16.60: £4.20, £13.90, £11.20; EX 401.50 Trifecta £1190.00 Part won. Pool: £1,586.67 - 0.02 winning units..
Owner M S Cooke **Bred** Mme Therese Bouche & Isabelle Roussel **Trained** Cropthorne, Worcs

FOCUS
A moderate handicap run at an ordinary gallop to early in the home straight. The winner raced towards the centre.

723 TIME ORDERED CARDS IN RACING PLUS H'CAP 6f (P)
7:30 (7:30) (Class 4) (0-85,85) 4-Y-0+ **£4,690** (£1,395; £697; £348) **Stalls** Low

Form RPR

4-40 **1** **Crew Cut (IRE)**[25] 400 5-8-12 **76** (b[1]) RobertWinston 1 85
(Jeremy Gask) *trckd ldrs on inner: prog to go 2nd 2f out: urged along to ld jst over 1f out: kpt on wl* **8/1**[3]

3-2 **2** 1 **Free Spin (IRE)**[21] 443 4-9-5 **83** GrahamGibbons 3 89+
(David Barron) *hld up in midfield: pushed along to chse ldrs 2f out: drvn over 1f out: styd on fnl f to take 2nd post: nvr cl enough to chal* **11/10**[1]

-450 **3** nse **Sulis Minerva (IRE)**[11] 586 6-9-2 **83** RyanClark(3) 7 89+
(Jeremy Gask) *hld up in last: gd prog over 1f out: drvn to chse wnr ins fnl f: nt qckn and hld last 100yds: lost 2nd post* **10/1**

0043 **4** 1 3/4 **Forest Edge (IRE)**[11] 586 4-9-7 **85** (b) AdamKirby 11 85
(David Evans) *led and crossed fr wdst draw to inner: hdd jst over 1f out: fdd* **16/1**

23-3 **5** 1 1/2 **Roy The Boy (USA)**[49] 25 5-8-12 **76** (v) NickyMackay 5 71
(Alan Bailey) *chsd ldng pair: rdn on outer 2f out: nt qckn wl over 1f out: one pce after* **12/1**

6- **6** 1/2 **Albaqaa**[75] 8022 8-9-3 **81** J-PGuillambert 9 75
(P J O'Gorman) *racd wd: towards rr: dropped to last 2f out: jst pushed along and kpt on one pce after: nvr involved* **33/1**

22-3 **7** 1 1/2 **Clear Praise (USA)**[40] 164 6-9-4 **82** HayleyTurner 2 71
(Simon Dow) *plld hrd early: hld up in last pair: pushed along and effrt on inner 2f out: no hdwy over 1f out: fdd* **7/1**[2]

02-0 **8** nse **Elna Bright**[11] 584 8-9-6 **84** JimmyQuinn 8 73
(Peter Crate) *hld up towards rr: pushed along and effrt on inner 2f out: shkn up and no prog over 1f out: fdd* **20/1**

106- **9** 8 **Tioman Pearl**[228] 3861 4-9-4 **82** JamieSpencer 10 45
(Roger Varian) *racd freely: chsd ldr to 2f out: wknd qckly: t.o* **8/1**[3]

1m 12.44s (-0.66) **Going Correction** -0.05s/f (Stan) **9** Ran SP% **112.7**
Speed ratings (Par 105): **102,100,100,98,96 95,93,93,82**
Tote Swingers: 1&2 £2.50, 1&3 £13.40, 2&3 £5.10 CSF £16.70 CT £90.22 TOTE £12.60: £2.50, £1.02, £3.70; EX 24.80 Trifecta £127.30 Pool: £1,501.94 - 8.84 winning units..
Owner Coral Champions Club **Bred** Rathbarry Stud **Trained** Sutton Veny, Wilts
■ Stewards' Enquiry : Robert Winston six-day ban: used whip in incorrect place (Mar 6-9, 12-13)

FOCUS
A useful handicap in which the pace seemed reasonable. The winner came down the centre.

724 RACING PLUS CHASE DAY 23.02.13 H'CAP 2m (P)
8:00 (8:01) (Class 6) (0-60,60) 4-Y-0+ **£1,940** (£577; £288; £144) **Stalls** Low

Form RPR

/41- **1** **Guards Chapel**[356] 221 5-9-7 **60** (v) GeorgeBaker 13 71+
(Gary Moore) *trckd ldng trio: smooth prog to ld over 1f out: sn clr: easily* **7/1**[3]

0241 **2** 2 **Scribe (IRE)**[14] 542 5-9-5 **58** (t) AdamKirby 2 63
(David Evans) *trckd ldng pair: drvn jst over 2f out: kpt on u.p to take 2nd nr fin: no ch w wnr* **2/1**[1]

-055 **3** 1/2 **Gower Rules (IRE)**[17] 512 5-8-8 **47** (v[1]) HayleyTurner 7 51
(John Bridger) *trckd ldr: chal over 3f out: stl pressing as wnr breezed past over 1f out: kpt on* **20/1**

56-5 **4** shd **Soweto Star (IRE)**[28] 338 5-9-4 **57** RobertWinston 10 61+
(John Best) *hld up in last pair in steadily run event: prog 2f out: rdn and styd on fnl f: nrst fin* **6/1**[2]

4-00 **5** nk **If What And Maybe**[7] 635 5-8-8 **47** (p) JohnFahy 14 51
(John Ryan) *led: set mod pce to 1/2-way: tried to up the tempo after but mde heavy weather of it: kpt on whn pressed over 3f out: hdd over 1f out: lost 3 pls nr fin* **33/1**

6 1 1/4 **Numen (IRE)**[34] 3965 9-9-2 **55** LiamKeniry 11 57
(Barry Brennan) *trckd ldrs: rdn over 2f out: one pce and no imp* **50/1**

40-2 **7** 1 **Life Of Laughter (USA)**[20] 458 5-8-11 **50** StevieDonohoe 4 51
(Willie Musson) *hld up in 8th: pushed along and sme prog over 2f out: no hdwy over 1f out* **6/1**[2]

5/40 **8** nk **Seaquel**[14] 530 7-8-7 **46** oh1 JimmyQuinn 12 46
(Tony Carroll) *hld up in rr: rdn and effrt over 2f out: no prog over 1f out* **33/1**

4-50 **9** 2 **Lady of Burgundy**[6] 653 7-9-1 **59** LeeNewnes(5) 1 57+
(Mark Usher) *hld up in detached last in steadily run event: taken wd and shkn up wl over 2f out: no ch to be involved* **9/1**

224- **10** 1 **Silver Six**[188] 4510 4-8-10 **55** (t) EddieAhern 8 52
(Sheena West) *prog to trck ldrs on outer after 5f: wknd 2f out* **10/1**

0-46 **11** nse **Here Comes Jeanie**[11] 579 4-7-12 **46** SimonPearce(3) 6 43
(Michael Madgwick) *hld up in last trio in steadily run event: rdn and no prog 3f out* **9/1**

4/50 **12** 1/2 **Corres (IRE)**[13] 343 6-9-2 **55** (tp) ShaneKelly 9 51
(Paul Fitzsimons) *trckd ldrs: urged along and no rspnse over 2f out: sn wknd* **66/1**

3m 34.76s (4.66) **Going Correction** -0.05s/f (Stan)
WFA 4 from 5yo+ 6lb **12** Ran SP% **117.6**
Speed ratings (Par 101): **86,85,84,84,84 83,83,83,82,81 81,81**
Tote Swingers: 1&2 £2.40, 1&3 £36.70, 2&3 £14.10 CSF £20.23 CT £274.61 TOTE £11.40: £2.70, £1.10, £6.50; EX 24.30 Trifecta £590.60 Pool: £1,301.57 - 1.65 winning units..
Owner Andrew Bradmore **Bred** Mrs J Chandris **Trained** Lower Beeding, W Sussex

FOCUS
A moderate handicap run at a modest gallop. The winner came down the centre in the straight.

725 ALL-WEATHER "HANDS AND HEELS" APPRENTICE SERIES H'CAP (PART OF THE RACING EXCELLENCE INITIATIVE) 1m (P)
8:30 (8:30) (Class 7) (0-50,51) 4-Y-0+ **£1,455** (£433; £216; £108) **Stalls** Low

Form RPR

0-14 **1** **Lytham (IRE)**[7] 625 12-9-6 **49** RyanTate 7 58
(Tony Carroll) *hld up in tch: pushed along and prog over 2f out: chsd ldr over 1f out: clsd to ld ins fnl f: styd on wl* **4/1**[2]

-604 **2** 1 3/4 **Avon Supreme**[12] 565 5-8-11 **45** LaurenHunter(5) 9 50
(Gay Kelleway) *led and sn clr: hld together fr over 2f out: hdd and nt qckn ins fnl f* **20/1**

000- **3** 4 **Hawaiian Freeze**[202] 4734 4-8-13 **45** JordanVaughan(3) 2 41
(John Stimpson) *chsd ldrs: prog 2f out: urged along to take 3rd fnl f: no imp ldng pair* **66/1**

2001 **4** 2 **Fairy Mist (IRE)**[5] 664 6-9-8 **51** 6ex RyanWhile 5 42
(John Bridger) *prom: chsd clr ldr 1/2-way to over 1f out: wknd* **14/1**

-026 **5** 1 **Compton Crofter**[7] 631 4-9-3 **46** (t) PhilipPrince 4 35
(Hans Adielsson) *v awkward sn after s and dropped to detached last: urged along and struggling 3f out: sme prog over 1f out: no threat* **11/8**[1]

6-05 **6** 1 **Schoolboy Champ**[22] 436 6-8-13 **45** (tp) CharlotteJenner(3) 1 32
(Lisa Williamson) *racd wd in rr: struggling in last pair 3f out: sme prog over 1f out: n.d* **25/1**

-006 **7** 8 **Rigid**[7] 630 6-9-0 **46** JoeyHaynes(3) 6 14
(Tony Carroll) *racd wd: chsd ldrs tl wknd over 2f out: t.o* **9/2**[3]

0-00 **8** 3 1/4 **Son Of May**[15] 522 4-9-4 **47** (p) PatMillman 3
(Jo Hughes) *chsd clr ldr to 1/2-way: wknd qckly: t.o* **14/1**

-223 **9** 10 **Cuthbert (IRE)**[18] 497 6-9-0 **48** (b) PaigeBolton(5) 8
(Michael Attwater) *racd wd: in tch tl wknd rapidly 3f out: wl t.o* **8/1**

1m 40.2s (0.40) **Going Correction** -0.05s/f (Stan) **9** Ran SP% **114.8**
Speed ratings (Par 97): **96,94,90,88,87 86,78,75,65**
Tote Swingers: 1&2 £11.80, 1&3 £65.40, 2&3 £65.40 CSF £79.10 CT £4510.41 TOTE £4.70: £2.50, £4.20, £13.50; EX 49.10 Trifecta £1000.60 Part won. Pool: £1,334.21 - 0.85 winning units..
Owner Morgan, Clarke & Parris **Bred** Mrs A S O'Brien And Lars Pearson **Trained** Cropthorne, Worcs

FOCUS
A very moderate handicap run at a reasonable gallop. The winner came down the centre.

T/Plt: £255.50 to a £1 stake. Pool: £64292.30 - 183.67 winning tickets. T/Qpdt: £15.30 to a £1 stake. Pool: £6,963.72 - 335.90 winning tickets. JN

[684] LINGFIELD (L-H)

Wednesday, February 20

OFFICIAL GOING: Standard

Wind: Fresh; across Weather: Dry

726 BET ON YOUR TABLET AT BLUESQ.COM CLAIMING STKS — 1m 2f (P)

1:30 (1:30) (Class 6) 3-Y-O — **£2,045** (£603; £302) **Stalls** Low

Form — RPR

4111 **1** **It's Only Business**[13] [547] 3-9-3 69 (p) JimmyQuinn 3 — 72
(Bill Turner) *handed clr ld s and mde all: set stdy gallop: rdn and qcknd ent fnl 2f: in command 1f out: rdn out hands and heels* — **4/5**[1]

-061 **2** 3 ¾ **Misleading Promise (IRE)**[14] [538] 3-9-5 69 (t) AdamKirby 4 — 67
(John Butler) *v.s.a: hld up in last: rdn to chse wnr ent fnl 2f: drvn and btn 1f out* — **5/2**[2]

040- **3** 2 ¼ **Tebbit (USA)**[84] [7900] 3-9-0 68 FergusSweeney 2 — 57
(Philip Hide) *s.i.s: chsd wnr tl jst over 2f out: sn drvn and struggling: wl hld 1f out* — **3/1**[3]

2m 15.52s (8.92) **Going Correction** +0.075s/f (Slow) **3** Ran SP% **109.1**
Speed ratings (Par 95): **67,64,62**
CSF £3.09 TOTE £2.00; EX 2.60 Trifecta £2.00 Pool: £841.32 - 317.74 winning units..It's Only Business was claimed by Mr Jack Callaghan for £10,000.
Owner Ansells Of Watford **Bred** South Wind Bloodstock **Trained** Sigwells, Somerset

FOCUS
The opening claimer was also the first of five races confined to 3yos.

727 BREATHE SPA @ LINGFIELD MARRIOTT CLAIMING STKS — 5f (P)

2:00 (2:00) (Class 6) 4-Y-0+ — **£2,045** (£603; £302) **Stalls** High

Form — RPR

-410 **1** **Where's Reiley (USA)**[11] [582] 7-8-12 67 ow1 (v) SebSanders 4 — 75
(Michael Attwater) *mde all: rdn ent fnl 2f: hrd pressed ins fnl f: hld on gamely: all out* — **14/1**

1-12 **2** hd **Hamoody (USA)**[11] [586] 9-9-2 83 ShirleyTeasdale(5) 3 — 84
(David Nicholls) *taken down early: hld up in tch in 4th: effrt and wdst bnd wl over 1f out: styd on to press wnr wl ins fnl f: kpt on cl home: jst hld* — **5/4**[1]

113- **3** ¾ **Angelo Poliziano**[67] [8144] 7-8-7 66 JoeFanning 5 — 67
(Jo Hughes) *stdd and dropped in bhd after s: hld up in tch in rr: rdn and hdwy on inner over 1f out: chsd ldrs ins fnl f: no ex towards fin* — **7/1**

1-16 **4** ½ **Drawnfromthepast (IRE)**[26] [379] 8-9-1 81 FergusSweeney 1 — 73
(Jamie Osborne) *chsd wnr: rdn and pressed wnr over 1f out: unable qck ins fnl f: wknd towards fin* — **9/4**[2]

2524 **5** ½ **Dark Lane**[4] [688] 7-8-5 66 DavidProbert 2 — 61
(David Evans) *chsd ldrs: rdn ent fnl 2f: outpcd u.p over 1f out: styd on same pce ins fnl f* — **5/1**[3]

59.42s (0.62) **Going Correction** +0.075s/f (Slow) **5** Ran SP% **111.0**
Speed ratings (Par 101): **98,97,96,95,94**
CSF £32.75 TOTE £19.20: £5.60, £1.10; EX 40.30 Trifecta £152.40 Pool: £1,662.11 - 8.17 winning units..
Owner J M Duggan & T P Duggan **Bred** Overbrook Farm **Trained** Epsom, Surrey
■ Stewards' Enquiry : Seb Sanders two-day ban: used whip above permitted level (Mar 6-7)

FOCUS
A run-of-the-mill claimer.

728 CYPRIUM BAR AT MARRIOTT LINGFIELD H'CAP — 6f (P)

2:30 (2:30) (Class 6) (0-65,65) 4-Y-O+ — **£2,045** (£603; £302) **Stalls** Low

Form — RPR

2-46 **1** **Catalinas Diamond (IRE)**[26] [372] 5-9-7 **65** (t) SebSanders 5 — 73
(Pat Murphy) *hld up in tch in midfield: rdn and effrt over 1f out: drvn ins fnl f: r.o u.p to ld last strides* — **7/1**[3]

0-12 **2** hd **Dorothy's Dancing (IRE)**[12] [559] 5-9-5 **63** (p) GeorgeBaker 7 — 70
(Gary Moore) *hld up in tch: hdwy and nt clr run wl over 1f out: sn swtchd rt and effrt: rdn to ld ins fnl f: r.o tl hdd and no ex last strides* — **3/1**[1]

1-16 **3** ¾ **Reginald Claude**[25] [399] 5-9-0 **63** RachealKneller(5) 3 — 68
(Mark Usher) *hld up in last pair: asked for effrt and gd hdwy on inner 1f out: chsd ldrs fnl 100yds: no imp after* — **7/1**[3]

221- **4** ½ **Amethyst Dawn (IRE)**[130] [7055] 7-9-5 **63** (t) JoeFanning 1 — 66
(J R Jenkins) *hld up in tch towards rr: rdn and hdwy over 1f out: swtchd rt and styd on to chse ldrs ins fnl f: no imp fnl 100yds* — **6/1**[2]

2-11 **5** nk **Valdaw**[20] [449] 5-9-7 **65** EddieAhern 10 — 67
(Mike Murphy) *dwlt: sn rcvrd to chse ldrs: rdn and pressed ldrs 2f out: styd on same pce fnl f* — **3/1**[1]

3506 **6** 2 ¼ **Jonnie Skull (IRE)**[12] [560] 7-8-7 **51** (vt) DavidProbert 9 — 46
(Phil McEntee) *led: rdn and hdd ent fnl 2f: unable qck and nudged by rival over 1f out: wknd ins fnl f* — **20/1**

5-30 **7** hd **Molly Jones**[36] [213] 4-8-8 **52** JohnFahy 4 — 47
(Derek Haydn Jones) *in tch in midfield: rdn and effrt on inner to chal over 1f out: wknd ins fnl f* — **33/1**

005- **8** 1 ½ **Athwaab**[60] [8231] 6-9-1 **59** GrahamLee 8 — 49
(Noel Chance) *taken down early: chsd ldr tl led ent fnl 2f: hdd ins fnl f: sn wknd* — **16/1**

-000 **9** 2 ¾ **Time Medicean**[18] [494] 7-9-5 **63** RobertWinston 6 — 44
(Tony Carroll) *chsd ldrs early: pushed along and lost pl 4f out: rdn and hdwy over 1f out: wknd ins fnl f* — **6/1**[2]

24-0 **10** ½ **Running Mate (IRE)**[42] [115] 6-9-2 **60** (t) IanMongan 2 — 39
(Jo Crowley) *taken down early and led rdrless to post: sn rdn in rr: sme hdwy over 2f out: wknd ent fnl f* — **7/1**[3]

1m 12.08s (0.18) **Going Correction** +0.075s/f (Slow) **10** Ran SP% **129.7**
Speed ratings (Par 101): **101,100,99,99,98 95,95,93,89,89**
toteswingers 1&2 £4.40, 1&3 £9.30, 2&3 £4.90 CSF £31.71 CT £164.31 TOTE £10.10: £2.50, £1.90, £2.40; EX 28.90 Trifecta £178.50 Pool: £2,179.18 - 9.15 winning units..
Owner Briton International **Bred** Sean Gorman **Trained** East Garston, Berks

FOCUS
A competitive sprint handicap.

729 BLUE SQUARE BET MEDIAN AUCTION MAIDEN STKS — 6f (P)

3:05 (3:05) (Class 6) 3-5-Y-O — **£2,045** (£603; £302) **Stalls** Low

Form — RPR

1 **Riskit Fora Biskit (IRE)** 3-8-6 0 HayleyTurner 2 — 72
(Michael Bell) *led for 1f: chsd ldr after tl led again wl over 2f out: clr and rdn wl over 1f out: drvn and edgd sltly rt ins fnl f: a gng to hold on* — **5/4**[1]

2 nk **Can You Conga** 3-8-11 0 JamieSpencer 1 — 76
(Kevin Ryan) *dwlt: sn chsd ldng pair: wnt 2nd and rn green ent fnl 2f: rdn over 1f out: styd on ins fnl f: clsng on wnr towards fin but nvr quite getting up* — **4/1**[3]

5-03 **3** 7 **Two No Bids (IRE)**[18] [491] 3-8-11 64 (v[1]) DavidProbert 4 — 54
(Phil McEntee) *chsd wnr tl led after 1f: hdd and rdn wl over 2f out: 3rd and btn over 1f out: wknd* — **6/1**

6 **4** 2 **Mighty Mata**[28] [341] 3-8-11 0 LiamKeniry 3 — 48
(Mark Usher) *sn pushed along and outpcd in 4th: no threat to ldrs fr over 2f out* — **25/1**

5 9 **Tornado Battle** 3-8-11 0 JoeFanning 6 — 19+
(Mark Johnston) *rn green: sn outpcd in last pair: wl bhd fnl 2f* — **5/2**[2]

00- **6** 8 **Eton Miss (IRE)**[104] [7653] 3-8-6 0 JimmyQuinn 5
(Mike Murphy) *s.i.s: a bhd: lost tch over 2f out* — **33/1**

1m 12.55s (0.65) **Going Correction** +0.075s/f (Slow) **6** Ran SP% **114.1**
Speed ratings (Par 101): **98,97,88,85,73 62**
toteswingers 1&2 £2.00, 1&3 £2.30, 2&3 £1.60 CSF £6.93 TOTE £2.20: £1.80, £1.60; EX 6.70 Trifecta £9.50 Pool: £3,230.83 - 254.01 winning units..
Owner Chris Wright & The Hon Mrs J M Corbett **Bred** Edmond Kent **Trained** Newmarket, Suffolk

FOCUS
Three newcomers headed the market for this 6f median auction maiden in which all of the six participants were 3yos.

730 LINGFIELD PARK OWNERS GROUP H'CAP — 6f (P)

3:35 (3:40) (Class 4) (0-85,80) 3-Y-O — **£4,690** (£1,395; £697; £348) **Stalls** Low

Form — RPR

0-31 **1** **Panther Patrol (IRE)**[21] [438] 3-8-13 **72** JohnFahy 6 — 81
(Eve Johnson Houghton) *in tch: rdn and effrt towards inner over 1f out: hdwy to ld 1f out: drvn and hld on wl fnl 50yds* — **10/1**

3-1 **2** nk **Upavon**[39] [185] 3-9-7 **80** LiamKeniry 3 — 88
(David Elsworth) *hld up in tch: rdn and effrt towards inner over 1f out: drvn and ev ch ins fnl f: styd on wl but a jst hld* — **4/1**[3]

1322 **3** 1 ¾ **Lager Time (IRE)**[2] [710] 3-8-0 **66** NoelGarbutt(7) 5 — 68
(David Evans) *sn detached in last: pushed along and clsd over 2f out: rdn and hdwy over 1f out: pressed ldrs jst ins fnl f: no ex and btn fnl 75yds* — **4/1**[3]

21 **4** ¾ **Hard Walnut (IRE)**[17] [509] 3-9-1 **74** JamieSpencer 4 — 74
(Olly Stevens) *led: rdn and edgd rt over 1f out: hdd over 1f out: no ex and one pce ins fnl f* — **11/4**[1]

34-1 **5** 1 ¾ **Groove On (IRE)**[43] [106] 3-9-0 **73** (t) AdamKirby 1 — 67
(Marco Botti) *chsd ldrs: rdn and sltly hmpd over 1f out: sn drvn and unable qck: wknd ins fnl f* — **7/2**[2]

5-22 **6** nk **Midnight Dream (FR)**[13] [550] 3-9-6 **79** GrahamLee 2 — 72
(Kristin Stubbs) *chsd ldrs: rdn and unable qck over 1f out: wknd ins fnl f* — **5/1**

1m 11.71s (-0.19) **Going Correction** +0.075s/f (Slow) **6** Ran SP% **114.6**
Speed ratings (Par 99): **104,103,101,100,97 97**
toteswingers 1&2 £5.70, 1&3 £5.60, 2&3 £3.00 CSF £50.04 TOTE £15.70: £6.30, £2.30; EX 65.40 Trifecta £146.50 Pool: £2,859.23 - 14.81 winning units..
Owner G C Stevens **Bred** Kilfrush Stud **Trained** Blewbury, Oxon

FOCUS
All six runners came into this handicap on the back of winning or finishing runner-up, therefore this can be considered strong form.

731 LINGFIELDPARK.CO.UK H'CAP — 1m 2f (P)

4:05 (4:07) (Class 5) (0-75,72) 3-Y-O — **£2,726** (£805; £402) **Stalls** Low

Form — RPR

54-2 **1** **Silver Dixie (USA)**[25] [396] 3-9-2 **67** GrahamLee 5 — 74+
(Jeremy Noseda) *chsd ldrs: jnd ldr and gng wl over 2f out: shkn up to ld and rn green over 1f out: rdn and asserted ins fnl f: r.o wl* — **4/5**[1]

0-05 **2** 1 ½ **Pencombe (FR)**[19] [473] 3-9-3 **68** JamieSpencer 3 — 72
(David Simcock) *hld up wl in tch: rdn and effrt ent fnl 2f: chsd wnr ins fnl f: kpt on same pce fnl 100yds* — **9/2**[2]

0-31 **3** ¾ **Shaolin (IRE)**[18] [491] 3-9-4 **69** JohnFahy 2 — 71
(Seamus Durack) *hld up in tch in rr: rdn and effrt on inner over 1f out: chsd ldrs and styd on same pce ins fnl f* — **8/1**

1-4 **4** 1 **Azma (USA)**[39] [188] 3-9-0 **72** RyanTate(7) 1 — 72
(Conrad Allen) *chsd ldr: rdn and unable qck over 1f out: edgd rt and styd on same pce ins fnl f* — **7/1**

062- **5** 3 **Raven's Tower (USA)**[149] [6532] 3-9-6 **71** JoeFanning 4 — 65
(Mark Johnston) *led: jnd and rdn over 2f out: hdd and unable qck over 1f out: wknd ins fnl f* — **5/1**[3]

2m 7.53s (0.93) **Going Correction** +0.075s/f (Slow) **5** Ran SP% **114.0**
Speed ratings (Par 97): **99,97,97,96,94**
CSF £5.09 TOTE £1.50: £1.10, £1.50; EX 5.30 Trifecta £28.10 Pool: £1,021.54 - 27.23 winning units..
Owner Mrs Susan Roy **Bred** Lantern Hill Farm Llc **Trained** Newmarket, Suffolk

FOCUS
Only the five runners, but with some big stables represented this was an interesting contest.

732 GET STRAIGHT TO BET AT BLUESQ.COM H'CAP — 7f (P)

4:40 (4:40) (Class 6) (0-60,57) 3-Y-O — **£2,045** (£603; £302) **Stalls** Low

Form — RPR

3422 **1** **Devout (IRE)**[10] [598] 3-9-3 **53** FergusSweeney 1 — 60
(Jamie Osborne) *chsd ldr for 1f: chsd ldrs after: rdn and edgd out rt to chse ldr over 1f out: r.o wl to ld wl ins fnl f: rdn out* — **9/2**[3]

0-65 **2** ½ **Actonetaketwo**[21] [442] 3-8-9 **45** HayleyTurner 3 — 51
(Ron Hodges) *led: rdn and fnd ex over 1f out: drvn ins fnl f: hdd wl ins fnl f: kpt on but a hld* — **5/1**

6-33 **3** 1 ¾ **Black Truffle (FR)**[21] [442] 3-8-13 **49** RobertHavlin 7 — 50
(Mark Usher) *hld up in tch in midfield: rdn and effrt on inner to chse ldrs over 1f out: no imp fnl f* — **4/1**[2]

4-55 **4** ¾ **Spreading**[19] [470] 3-9-5 **55** LiamKeniry 2 — 54
(Michael Blanshard) *hld up in tch towards rr: rdn and outpcd over 1f out: rallied and kpt on ins fnl f: no threat to ldrs* — **16/1**

0-34 **5** ¾ **Frans Hals**[21] [442] 3-9-1 **51** (p) EddieAhern 5 — 48
(Dominic Ffrench Davis) *s.i.s: bhd and sn pushed along: hdwy u.p 1f out: kpt on but nvr trbld ldrs* — **7/1**

60-0 **6** ½ **Exit Clause**[19] [470] 3-9-7 **57** (t) GrahamLee 6 — 53
(Tony Carroll) *hld up in tch in midfield: effrt u.p over 1f out: no prog and btn 1f out: plugged on same pce fnl f* — **10/1**

-514 **7** ¾ **Schottische**[19] [482] 3-9-7 **57** (p) JohnFahy 8 — 51
(Derek Haydn Jones) *chsd ldrs: wnt 2nd 5f out tl over 1f out: sn no ex u.p: wknd ins fnl f* — **6/1**

0-43 **8** 2¼ **Dubai Applause**[17] 509 3-9-5 **55**.................................. RobertWinston 4 43
(Charles Hills) *in tch towards rr: hdwy on outer into midfield over 2f out: no hdwy bnd 2f out: wknd over 1f out* **7/2**[1]

1m 26.04s (1.24) **Going Correction** +0.075s/f (Slow) **8** Ran SP% **118.8**
Speed ratings (Par 95): **95,94,92,91,90 90,89,86**
toteswingers 1&2 £7.90, 1&3 £2.80, 2&3 £5.80 CSF £28.40 CT £99.50 TOTE £3.10: £2.50, £2.20, £1.70; EX 39.20 Trifecta £261.30 Pool: £1,285.24 - 3.68 winning units..
Owner Dean Margolis, Paul Hearn & Partners **Bred** Edgeridge Ltd **Trained** Upper Lambourn, Berks

FOCUS
A modest handicap for 3yos to close the card.
T/Plt: £43.70 to a £1 stake. Pool: £44,335.40 - 739.06 winning units T/Qpdt: £11.50 to a £1 stake. Pool: £3,561.04 - 228.50 winning units SP

719 KEMPTON (A.W) (R-H)
Thursday, February 21

OFFICIAL GOING: Standard
Wind: Moderate; across Weather: Chilly

733 RACING PLUS CHASE 23.02.2013 H'CAP 7f (P)
5:30 (5:33) (Class 7) (0-50,50) 4-Y-O+ **£1,455** (£433; £216; £108) **Stalls** Low

Form RPR

-000 **1** **Greek Islands (IRE)**[16] 523 5-9-2 **45**.................................. LiamKeniry 3 59
(Ed de Giles) *hld up towards rr: hdwy 2f out: drvn: edgd rt and qcknd to ld jst ins fnl f: styd on strly* **16/1**

434 **2** 2¾ **Media Jury**[7] 655 6-9-6 **49**...(p) DaleSwift 4 56
(John Wainwright) *in tch: hdwy 2f out: styd on wl fnl f to take 2nd fnl 75yds: no imp on wnr* **10/1**

0051 **3** 1 **Rise To Glory (IRE)**[13] 565 5-9-5 **48**......................(p) DuranFentiman 7 52
(Shaun Harris) *sn led: rdn 2f out: hdd and outpcd jst ins fnl f: lost 2nd fnl 75yds* **11/2**[2]

3363 **4** nk **Blue Noodles**[7] 649 7-9-2 **45**..(p) PaddyAspell 2 48
(John Wainwright) *in rr: hdwy 2f out: styd on ins fnl f: nt rch ldrs* **13/2**[3]

0-40 **5** 2 **Kaylee**[7] 649 4-9-6 **49**.. GeorgeBaker 5 47
(Gary Moore) *stdd s: in rr: hdwy towards ins appr fnl 2f: drvn and one pce fnl f* **11/2**[2]

0-25 **6** shd **Invincible Beauty (IRE)**[28] 349 4-9-5 **48**.....................(t) MickyFenton 6 46
(Seamus Durack) *chsd ldrs: drvn 2f out: wknd ins fnl f* **4/1**[1]

2-05 **7** ¾ **Stamp Duty (IRE)**[27] 381 5-9-2 **45**................................... RussKennemore 12 41
(Suzzanne France) *s.i.s: in rr: hdwy ins fnl 2f: kpt on clsng stages* **8/1**

6350 **8** 1¼ **Hold The Star**[13] 565 7-8-11 **45**................................... AnnStokell(5) 10 37
(Ann Stokell) *chsd ldrs: rdn 2f out: wknd fnl f* **33/1**

00/0 **9** 1 **Poyle Todream**[22] 440 5-9-0 **46**................................ MarkCoumbe(3) 8 36
(Roy Brotherton) *chsd ldrs: wknd appr fnl f* **33/1**

000- **10** 3 **Rose Madder**[108] 7591 4-9-0 **50**...................................... NedCurtis(7) 1 32
(Roger Curtis) *hmpd ins fnl 3f: a towards rr* **9/1**

200/ **11** 16 **Concordia Notte (IRE)**[542] 5535 4-9-5 **48**......................(t) MartinHarley 9
(Violet M Jordan) *chsd ldrs to 1/2-way* **14/1**

1m 25.39s (-0.61) **Going Correction** 0.0s/f (Stan) **11** Ran SP% **112.7**
Speed ratings (Par 97): **103,99,98,98,96 95,95,93,92,89 70**
toteswingers 1&2 £28.10, 1&3 £22.00, 2&3 £7.90 CSF £152.34 CT £861.81 TOTE £18.70: £5.70, £2.10, £2.30; EX 131.40 Trifecta £503.30 Part won. Pool: £671.10 - 0.43 winning units..
Owner E B De Giles **Bred** Petra Bloodstock Agency Ltd **Trained** Ledbury, H'fords
■ Stewards' Enquiry : Dale Swift two-day ban: careless riding (Mar 7-8)

FOCUS
A poor-quality handicap run at a fair gallop. The runner-up reversed placings with the third off this better gallop and helps set the level.

734 EASTER FAMILY FUN 30.03.13 MEDIAN AUCTION MAIDEN STKS 7f (P)
6:00 (6:01) (Class 6) 3-5-Y-O **£1,940** (£577; £288; £144) **Stalls** Low

Form RPR

42- **1** **Emperor Julius (IRE)**[99] 7707 3-8-11 0...................... FergusSweeney 1 72+
(Jo Crowley) *disp 2nd tl trckd ldr over 3f out: led jst ins fnl 2f: shkn up fnl f: comf* **1/3**[1]

2 3 **Back On The Trail** 3-8-11 0.................................. StevieDonohoe 2 64+
(Rae Guest) *s.i.s: in rr and green: pushed along and hdwy over 2f out: styd on to take 2nd ins fnl f but no ch w wnr* **7/1**[3]

4 **3** 4 **Viva L'Inghilterra (IRE)**[15] 532 3-8-6 0.......................... HayleyTurner 4 48
(Robert Cowell) *led: pushed along and hdd jst ins fnl 2f: sn no ch w wnr: lost 2nd ins fnl f* **6/1**[2]

003- **4** 4½ **Guru Baby**[64] 8166 3-8-6 55.................................. RichardThomas 5 36
(John E Long) *disp 2nd tl over 3f out: sn rdn: no ch fnl 2f* **20/1**

0/0- **5** 2¼ **Sid**[386] 379 5-10-0 30... JamieGoldstein 3 41?
(Zoe Davison) *a towards rr: no ch fnl 3f* **100/1**

1m 26.96s (0.96) **Going Correction** 0.0s/f (Stan)
WFA 3 from 5yo 17lb **5** Ran SP% **107.6**
Speed ratings (Par 101): **94,90,86,80,78**
CSF £3.01 TOTE £1.40: £1.10, £2.50; EX 2.80 Trifecta £5.30 Pool: £1,270.57 - 178.67 winning units..
Owner Kilstone Limited **Bred** Noel Brosnan **Trained** Whitcombe, Dorset

FOCUS
A weak maiden, run in a slow time, but an easy winner who set the level.

735 GET THE BETVICTOR APP H'CAP (DIV I) 6f (P)
6:30 (6:30) (Class 6) (0-55,55) 4-Y-O+ **£1,940** (£577; £288; £144) **Stalls** Low

Form RPR

-042 **1** **Littlecote Lady**[7] 655 4-9-3 **51**.......................................(v) RobertHavlin 9 57
(Mark Usher) *trckd ldrs: drvn to ld fnl 120yds: rdn out* **7/2**[1]

5163 **2** ½ **Steel City Boy (IRE)**[9] 618 10-9-1 **54**.............................. AnnStokell(5) 2 58
(Ann Stokell) *chsd ldrs: drvn to chal 1f out: sn slt ld: hdd and nt qckn fnl 120yds* **9/1**

-000 **3** ½ **Spoof Master (IRE)**[20] 471 9-8-9 **46** oh1...............(t) SimonPearce(3) 3 48
(Lydia Pearce) *led: jnd over 1f out: hdd jst ins fnl f: one pce fnl 120yds* **50/1**

3060 **4** 1 **Onceaponatime (IRE)**[14] 551 8-8-13 **47**........................... ShaneKelly 6 46
(Michael Squance) *mid-div: drvn swtchd lft and hdwy fnl f: kpt on clsng stages* **8/1**

4345 **5** ½ **Sherjawy (IRE)**[21] 448 9-9-3 **51**... LiamKeniry 5 49
(Zoe Davison) *chsd ldrs: drvn over 3f out: stl wl there over 1f out: no ex fnl f* **7/1**[3]

5050 **6** 2 **Speedyfix**[9] 618 6-9-7 **55**..(t) TomMcLaughlin 7 46
(Christine Dunnett) *in tch: rdn and effrt over 1f out: kpt on same pce* **5/1**[2]

4440 **7** 1¾ **Ryedale Dancer (IRE)**[13] 560 5-9-6 **54**.................... RobbieFitzpatrick 10 40
(Richard Guest) *in rr: drvn over 2f out: sme hdwy fnl f* **8/1**

-500 **8** 4 **Lindoro**[27] 370 8-9-4 **52**.. AdamKirby 4 25
(Sean Curran) *chsd ldrs: rdn 2f out: sn btn* **7/2**[1]

40/0 **9** 5 **Fantastic Smartie**[14] 546 4-9-7 **55**................................ FergusSweeney 1 12
(Richard Phillips) *sn bhd* **10/1**

1m 12.89s (-0.21) **Going Correction** 0.0s/f (Stan) **9** Ran SP% **116.9**
Speed ratings (Par 101): **101,100,99,98,97 95,92,87,80**
toteswingers 1&2 £3.00, 1&3 £15.20, 2&3 £32.20 CSF £36.53 CT £1347.70 TOTE £3.80: £1.10, £1.60, £20.30; EX 19.50 Trifecta £913.50 Part won. Pool: £1,218.12 - 0.58 winning units..
Owner Littlecote House Racing **Bred** Ridgeway Bloodstock **Trained** Upper Lambourn, Berks

FOCUS
Little got into division one of what was a weak sprint handicap. The third sets the level and limits the form.

736 GET THE BETVICTOR APP H'CAP (DIV II) 6f (P)
7:00 (7:00) (Class 6) (0-55,55) 4-Y-O+ **£1,940** (£577; £288; £144) **Stalls** Low

Form RPR

0-51 **1** **Mr Optimistic**[29] 339 5-9-6 **54**.. SeanLevey 1 62+
(Paul Howling) *in rr: hdwy over 1f out: str chal jst ins fnl f: led fnl 120yds: drvn out* **6/4**[1]

50 **2** ¾ **Scommettitrice (IRE)**[13] 559 5-9-7 **55**.........................(b) GeorgeBaker 7 61
(Mark Gillard) *chsd ldrs: drvn to chal 1f out: nt qckn w wnr fnl 120yds* **16/1**

-005 **3** ½ **Illustrious Lad (IRE)**[10] 610 4-8-13 **52**.(vt[1]) WilliamTwiston-Davies(5) 4 56
(Roger Ingram) *chsd ldrs: drvn to chal 1f out: nt qckn fnl 120yds* **14/1**

000- **4** hd **Microlight**[64] 8168 5-8-12 **46** oh1.................................(b) RichardThomas 2 49
(John E Long) *chsd ldrs: drvn to ld over 1f out: sn jnd: one pce fnl 120yds* **25/1**

5303 **5** ½ **Slatey Hen (IRE)**[6] 670 5-8-9 **48**..............................(p) CharlesBishop(5) 3 50
(Violet M Jordan) *in rr: hdwy over 1f out: styd on fnl f: nt pce to rch ldrs* **10/1**

0-4 **6** 4 **Sextons House (IRE)**[36] 223 5-9-3 **51**.............................. MartinHarley 8 40
(Alan McCabe) *stdd s: in rr: pushed along and carried hd awkwardly over 2f out: edgd lft and rdn sn after: styd on fnl f: nvr a threat* **11/4**[2]

0-50 **7** hd **The Bendy Fella (IRE)**[7] 655 5-9-5 **53**.......................(v[1]) RobertHavlin 5 41
(Mark Usher) *s.i.s: sn drvn and in tch: wknd wl over 1f out* **6/1**[3]

00-5 **8** 1 **Almaty Express**[13] 559 11-9-6 **54**................................(b) DuranFentiman 9 39
(John Weymes) *sn led: rdn over 2f out: hdd over 1f out: sn btn* **16/1**

-000 **9** 3 **Rainbow Riches (IRE)**[19] 497 4-8-7 **48** oh1 ow2......(p) NedCurtis(7) 10 24
(Roger Curtis) *chsd ldrs: wknd wl over 1f out* **50/1**

1m 12.62s (-0.48) **Going Correction** 0.0s/f (Stan) **9** Ran SP% **114.3**
Speed ratings (Par 101): **103,102,101,101,100 95,94,93,89**
toteswingers 1&2 £7.90, 1&3 £4.00, 2&3 £9.80 CSF £28.49 CT £248.91 TOTE £2.40: £1.10, £3.20, £3.00; EX 23.60 Trifecta £151.30 Pool: £1,475.63 - 7.31 winning units..
Owner Eclipse Horse Racing **Bred** C J Murfitt **Trained** Lee-On-The-Solent, Hants

FOCUS
This had looked less open than the first division and the short-priced favourite duly obliged. The runner-up sets the level.

737 BETVICTOR CHELTENHAM FESTIVAL ANTEPOST PIONEERS H'CAP 1m (P)
7:30 (7:30) (Class 6) (0-55,61) 4-Y-O+ **£1,940** (£577; £288; £144) **Stalls** Low

Form RPR

-031 **1** **Flamborough Breeze**[8] 631 4-9-13 **61** 6ex..................(t) GeorgeBaker 6 77+
(Ed Vaughan) *hld up in rr: stdy hdwy on bit 2f out: led wl over 1f out: pushed clr fnl f: easily* **3/1**[1]

-652 **2** 5 **Athletic**[8] 631 4-9-4 **52**...(v) EddieAhern 5 57
(J R Jenkins) *chsd ldrs: led 2f out: hdd wl over 1f out: kpt on but no ch w easy wnr* **13/2**

0-00 **3** 2¼ **Qeethaara (USA)**[26] 410 9-9-4 **52**...............................(p) ShaneKelly 12 51
(Mark Brisbourne) *mid-div: hdwy 2f out: styd on to take 3rd ins fnl f: no imp on ldng duo* **16/1**

441 **4** 1 **Fleetwoodsands (IRE)**[22] 440 6-9-4 **52**................(bt) RobertWinston 7 49
(Milton Bradley) *in rr: hdwy and rdn over 2f out: kpt on fnl f: nt trble ldrs* **7/1**

6-00 **5** 1¾ **Arte Del Calcio**[18] 508 4-9-0 **55**.......................................[1] JoeyHaynes(7) 2 48
(Tony Carroll) *s.i.s: in rr: hdwy 2f out: styd on fnl f: nt rch ldrs* **33/1**

4055 **6** 1¾ **Gallantry**[8] 630 11-9-4 **52**... JimmyQuinn 10 41
(Paul Howling) *chsd ldrs: rdn over 2f out: wknd over 1f out* **14/1**

4210 **7** 1¾ **Delightful Sleep**[23] 435 5-9-7 **55**....................................... AdamKirby 1 40+
(David Evans) *sn led: hdd 6f out: styd chsng ldr and ev ch 2f out: sn wknd* **5/1**[3]

0/12 **8** ½ **Commercial (IRE)**[8] 630 5-9-5 **53**................................ FergusSweeney 11 37+
(Jamie Osborne) *trckd ldr: led 6f out: hdd 2f out: sn btn* **4/1**[2]

2053 **9** ½ **Justcallmehandsome**[12] 587 11-8-7 **48**...........(be) JoshBaudains(7) 4 31
(Dominic Ffrench Davis) *s.i.s: in rr: rdn over 2f out: hd high and hanging rt sn after: sme late prog* **25/1**

660- **10** ¾ **Snowy Valley**[63] 8179 4-8-10 **51**... RyanTate(7) 3 32
(Simon Earle) *s.i.s: sme hdwy over 2f out: wknd over 1f out* **20/1**

-444 **11** 1½ **Byrd In Hand (IRE)**[8] 630 6-8-9 **48**.......... WilliamTwiston-Davies(5) 14 25
(John Bridger) *chsd ldrs: rdn 2f out: sn btn* **16/1**

500- **12** ¾ **Doc Hill**[92] 7811 4-8-12 **46** oh1...(b[1]) LiamKeniry 8 22
(Michael Blanshard) *chsd ldrs: rdn over 3f out: wknd over 2f out* **33/1**

30-0 **13** 3 **High Five Prince (IRE)**[8] 630 4-8-12 **53**........................ PhilipPrince(7) 13 22
(Milton Bradley) *bhd most of way* **66/1**

1m 38.71s (-1.09) **Going Correction** 0.0s/f (Stan) **13** Ran SP% **121.9**
Speed ratings (Par 101): **105,100,97,96,95 93,91,91,90,89 88,87,84**
toteswingers 1&2 £3.30, 1&3 £7.60, 2&3 £12.90 CSF £21.80 CT £287.31 TOTE £2.50: £1.80, £2.50, £4.10; EX 17.90 Trifecta £147.70 Pool: £1,638.08 - 8.31 winning units..
Owner A M Pickering **Bred** Windymains Farm Ltd **Trained** Newmarket, Suffolk

FOCUS
What had looked quite an open and competitive handicap was turned into a rout by in-form filly. The winner has more to offer and the third sets the standard.

738 BETVICTOR NON RUNNER FREE BET AT CHELTENHAM H'CAP (LONDON MILE QUALIFIER) 1m (P)
8:00 (8:00) (Class 5) (0-75,75) 3-Y-O **£2,587** (£770; £384; £192) **Stalls** Low

Form RPR

1-12 **1** **Red Dragon (IRE)**[22] 444 3-9-0 **68**................................... RobertWinston 3 76
(Charles Hills) *trckd ldr: led over 2f out: sn drvn clr: kpt on wl fnl f* **11/2**[3]

123 **2** 3¼ **Black Dave (IRE)**[6] 674 3-9-3 **71**... AdamKirby 5 72
(David Evans) *chsd ldrs: drvn and one pce 3f out: hdwy to chse wnr wl over 1f out: styd on but no imp fnl f* **8/1**

-213 **3** 6 **Great Demeanor (USA)**[6] 666 3-9-7 **75**............................ LiamKeniry 2 62
(David Elsworth) *led: hdd over 2f out: wknd into 3rd over 1f out* **3/1**[2]

-022 **4** ¾ **Red Gift (IRE)**[15] 538 3-8-12 **66**...................................(b[1]) DaleSwift 1 51
(Brian Ellison) *s.i.s: sn chsng ldrs: rdn 3f out: wknd 2f out* **16/1**

The Form Book Flat, Raceform Ltd, Compton, RG20 6NL.

0-1 **5** 23 **Al Enbess (IRE)**[12] 580 3-9-1 **69** .... JamieSpencer 4
(David Simcock) *in rr but in tch: rdn 3f out: sn btn* **4/5**[1]

1m 38.68s (-1.12) **Going Correction** 0.0s/f (Stan) 5 Ran SP% **112.9**
Speed ratings (Par 97): **105,101,95,95,72**
CSF £43.52 TOTE £10.30: £2.10, £2.60; EX 17.30 Trifecta £35.60 Pool: £719.49 - 15.12 winning units..
Owner The Hon R J Arculli & Des Anderson **Bred** N Hartery **Trained** Lambourn, Berks

FOCUS
An unsatisfactory race, with red-hot favourite Al Enbess running as though something was amiss and Great Demeanour failing to run up to his best. The runner-up is rated close to previous course form.

739 BETVICTOR EXCLUSIVE ANTEPOST OFFER CHELTENHAM 2013 CONDITIONS STKS 1m 4f (P)
8:30 (8:30) (Class 4) 4-Y-0+ **£4,690** (£1,395; £697; £348) **Stalls** Centre

Form				RPR
2243	**1**		**Wildomar**[19] 496 4-8-13 82 .... MichaelO'Connell 3 (John Ryan) *trckd ldrs in 3rd: drvn and styd on to take slt ld appr fnl f: hld on wl clsng stages* **11/4**[3]	91
-453	**2**	½	**Mawaakef (IRE)**[12] 585 5-9-2 88 .... JimCrowley 5 (J R Jenkins) *trckd ldr: chal over 6f out tl led wl over 2f out: sn rdn: hdd appr fnl f: kpt on but a hld clsng stages* **9/4**[2]	90
305-	**3**	1¼	**Tappanappa (IRE)**[106] 7630 6-9-2 93 ....(b) DaleSwift 4 (Brian Ellison) *led: jnd over 6f out: rdn 3f out: hdd wl over 2f out: styd pressing wnr tl jst ins fnl f: no ex fnl 110yds* **7/4**[1]	88
03-0	**4**	4½	**First Avenue**[36] 224 8-9-2 83 .... IanMongan 1 (Laura Mongan) *a in last pl: rdn and no imp wl over 2f out* **7/1**	82

2m 38.42s (3.92) **Going Correction** 0.0s/f (Stan)
WFA 4 from 5yo+ 3lb 4 Ran SP% **106.3**
Speed ratings (Par 105): **86,85,84,81**
CSF £8.82 TOTE £3.60; EX 5.60 Trifecta £13.80 Pool: £423.64 - 22.97 winning units..
Owner W McLuskey **Bred** Wood Hall Stud Limited **Trained** Newmarket, Suffolk

FOCUS
The early pace was quite steady in this competitive small-field conditions contest, but the form is muddling and probably best not to take literally.

740 FOLLOW US ON TWITTER @BETVICTORRACING H'CAP 7f (P)
9:00 (9:00) (Class 5) (0-75,74) 4-Y-0+ **£2,587** (£770; £384; £192) **Stalls** Low

Form				RPR
021-	**1**		**Admiralty**[132] 7022 4-9-3 70 .... JoeFanning 7 (Ismail Mohammed) *wnt lft s: sn led: drvn and styd on wl fnl f* **6/4**[1]	80+
05-0	**2**	1¾	**Hatta Stream (IRE)**[12] 582 7-8-13 69 .... SimonPearce(3) 3 (Lydia Pearce) *chsd ldrs: rdn to go 2nd fr 2f out: kpt on fnl f but a hld* **25/1**	73
/55-	**3**	¾	**Macdonald Mor (IRE)**[330] 1063 4-9-7 74 .... ChrisCatlin 5 (Michael Wigham) *in tch: rdn 2f out: hdwy over 1f out: styd on to take 3rd fnl 100yds: no imp on ldng duo* **16/1**	76
-023	**4**	nk	**Jake The Snake (IRE)**[7] 650 12-9-3 73 .... AmyBaker(3) 6 (Tony Carroll) *in rr but in tch: drvn and hdwy fr 2f out: styd on fnl f to cl on 3rd but no imp on ldng duo* **5/1**[3]	74
05-6	**5**	¾	**Ted's Brother (IRE)**[7] 650 5-8-3 63 .... PhilipPrince(7) 4 (Richard Guest) *t.k.h towards rr: rdn over 2f out: styd on fnl f but nvr gng pce to rch ldrs* **5/1**[3]	62
30-0	**6**	1½	**Master Mylo (IRE)**[24] 415 6-9-5 72 .... GeorgeBaker 1 (Martin Bosley) *t.k.h: chsd ldrs: drvn over 1f out and sn btn* **8/1**	67
-061	**7**	shd	**The Guru Of Gloom (IRE)**[17] 518 5-9-5 72 .... JackMitchell 2 (William Muir) *t.k.h: chsd ldrs: rdn 2f out: sn btn* **9/2**[2]	67

1m 26.37s (0.37) **Going Correction** 0.0s/f (Stan) 7 Ran SP% **112.4**
Speed ratings (Par 103): **97,95,94,93,92 91,91**
toteswingers 1&2 £12.00, 1&3 £9.60, 2&3 £9.70 CSF £40.95 TOTE £2.70: £1.60, £10.00; EX 42.80 Trifecta £481.30 Pool: £1,138.76 - 1.77 winning units..
Owner Ahmad Abdulla Al Shaikh **Bred** Mrs Fiona Denniff **Trained** Newmarket, Suffolk

FOCUS
Modest handicap form best rated through the runner-up.
T/Jkpt: Part won. £14,524.80 to a £1 stake. Pool: £20,457.51 - 0.50 winning units. T/Plt: £63.00 to a £1 stake. Pool: £62,931.45 - 728.14 winning units T/Qpdt: £22.70 to a £1 stake. Pool: £6,660.99 - 216.55 winning units ST

694 MEYDAN (L-H)
Thursday, February 21
OFFICIAL GOING: Tapeta - standard; turf - good

741a AL NABOODAH COMMERCIAL GROUP TROPHY (H'CAP) (TURF) 1m 2f
3:15 (3:15) (100-118,118) 3-Y-0+
£64,417 (£21,472; £10,736; £5,368; £3,220; £2,147)

			RPR
1		**Await The Dawn (USA)**[14] 556 6-9-6 **118** .... PatCosgrave 4 (M F De Kock, South Africa) *in rr of mid-div: smooth prog 2 1/2f out: led 1 1/2f out: comf* **5/2**[1]	122+
2	2¾	**So Beautiful (FR)**[14] 556 4-8-10 **109** .... PaulHanagan 3 (Doug Watson, UAE) *mid-div: smooth prog 3f out: ev ch 1 1/2f out: nt qckn fnl 110yds* **6/1**	108
3	4	**Salon Soldier (GER)**[21] 462 4-8-9 **107** ow1 .... ADeVries 7 (P Schiergen, Germany) *settled rr: kpt on same pce fnl 1 1/2f but nvr nr to chal* **33/1**	99
4	shd	**Without Fear (FR)**[21] 463 5-8-5 **100** .... Per-AndersGraberg 6 (Niels Petersen, Norway) *trckd ldng pair tl outpcd 2f out* **40/1**	93
5	1	**Mikhail Glinka (IRE)**[7] 657 6-9-3 **115** ....(bt) KUlubaev 1 (Seth Benzel, U.S.A) *sn led: hdd 6 1/2f out: rdn 4f out: wknd fnl 2f* **3/1**[2]	103
6	1¼	**Starboard**[152] 6508 4-9-0 **112** .... KierenFallon 2 (E Charpy, UAE) *trckd ldrs: keen: led 6 1/2f out: hdd & wknd 1 1/2f out* **9/2**	96
7	1½	**Light Heavy (IRE)**[21] 466 4-9-1 **113** ....(tp) KevinManning 5 (J S Bolger, Ire) *a in rr* **10/3**[3]	100

2m 1.54s (-1.96)
WFA 4 from 5yo+ 1lb 7 Ran SP% **114.5**
WIN: 2.70; CSF: 18.13; EXACTA:14.10; TRIFECTA: 133.30.
Owner Ms Partridge, M De Kock, C Haynes Et Al **Bred** Juddmonte Farms Inc **Trained** South Africa

FOCUS
All of these had something prove, and the early pace was too quick, so not obviously strong form. Mikhail Glinka tried to dominate, but was soon taken on past by Starboard, who went clear. Here are the sectionals: 26.13 (400m), 23.01 (800m), 23.81 (1200m), 24.24 (1600m), and the winner's closing split was 23.88. Await The Dawn is rated back to form, with the second to his recent course best.

742a AL NABOODAH TRAVEL & TOURISM AGENCIES TROPHY (H'CAP) (TAPETA) 1m 1f 110y
3:50 (3:50) (95-105,105) 3-Y-0+
£40,490 (£13,496; £6,748; £3,374; £2,024; £1,349)

			RPR
1		**Con Artist (IRE)**[21] 463 6-9-6 **105** .... SilvestreDeSousa 1 (Saeed bin Suroor) *sn led: rdn clr 2 1/2f out: r.o wl: comf* **11/8**[1]	108+
2	3¾	**Plantagenet (SPA)**[21] 463 6-9-3 **101** .... J-LMartinez 6 (G Arizkorreta Elosegui, Spain) *mid-div: smooth prog 3f out: outpcd 2f out: kpt on fnl 1 1/2f but no ch w wnr* **11/1**	97+
3	2¼	**Specific Gravity (FR)**[5] 698 5-9-1 **99** .... ChristopheSoumillon 4 (M F De Kock, South Africa) *settled in rr: smooth prog 2 1/2f out: kpt on same pce fnl 1 1/2f* **3/1**[2]	91+
4	¾	**Zain Shamardal (IRE)**[14] 556 5-9-6 **105** ....(t) RoystonFfrench 7 (A Al Raihe, UAE) *settled in rr: kpt on same pce fnl 1 1/2f: nrst fin* **12/1**	94+
5	3¼	**Treble Jig (USA)**[7] 659 6-9-6 **105** .... JamesDoyle 3 (M Al Muhairi, UAE) *trckd ldrs: ev ch 2f out: wknd fnl f* **9/1**	88+
6	2¼	**Not A Given (USA)**[21] 463 4-9-2 **101** .... MickaelBarzalona 2 (Mahmood Al Zarooni) *trckd ldng duo: ev ch 2f out: wknd fnl f* **7/1**[3]	80+
7	1¼	**Muck 'N' Brass (IRE)**[14] 552 4-8-9 **95** ....(t) GaryCarroll 8 (Edward Lynam, Ire) *settled in rr: rdn 4f out: nvr nr to chal* **28/1**	70+
8	hd	**Yaa Wayl (IRE)**[14] 557 6-9-3 **101** ....(vt) PaulHanagan 5 (Saeed bin Suroor) *mid-div: rdn 5f out: sn btn* **10/1**	77+

1m 57.87s (-1.13) 8 Ran SP% **118.2**
WIN: 1.70; PL: 1.00, 2.60, 2.10 CSF: 19.25; EXACTA: 24.60; TRIFECTA: 118.40.
Owner Godolphin **Bred** Airlie Stud **Trained** Newmarket, Suffolk

FOCUS
Con Artist was the best horse in the field and his task was made easier by dominating from the inside stall and saving plenty through the early stages, going 27.64 (400m), 24.10 (800m), 23.49 (1200m), 23.89 (1600m). He only needed to match his C&D form on his previous run.

743a BALANCHINE (GROUP 2) (F&M) (TURF) (SPONSORED BY AL NABOODAH CONSTRUCTION GROUP) 1m 1f (T)
4:25 (4:25) 3-Y-0+
£73,619 (£24,539; £12,269; £6,134; £3,680; £2,453)

			RPR
1		**Sajjhaa**[28] 366 6-9-3 112 .... SilvestreDeSousa 4 (Saeed bin Suroor) *mid-div: smooth prog to ld 2f out: r.o wl: comf* **5/2**[2]	112
2	1	**Prussian**[138] 6875 4-9-0 100 .... MickaelBarzalona 2 (Mahmood Al Zarooni) *settled in rr: r.o wl fnl 2f: nrst fin* **20/1**	107
3	3¼	**Igugu (AUS)**[390] 6-9-0 118 .... ChristopheSoumillon 6 (M F De Kock, South Africa) *trckd ldrs: led over 8f out: hdd 2f out: kpt on same pce* **4/7**[1]	100+
4	7	**Lily's Angel (IRE)**[42] 149 4-9-0 108 .... GaryCarroll 1 (G M Lyons, Ire) *mid-div: chsd ldrs 3f out: one pce fnl f* **7/1**[3]	85
5	4½	**Spellwork (USA)**[28] 366 4-9-0 102 .... PaulHanagan 7 (Saeed bin Suroor) *settled in rr: nvr nr to chal* **40/1**	76
6	3½	**Dark Orchid (USA)**[28] 366 4-9-0 108 .... KierenFallon 3 (Saeed bin Suroor) *sn led: hdd over 8f out: chsd ldr tl outpcd 3f out* **25/1**	69+
7	dist	**Colliding Worlds (IRE)**[42] 153 4-9-0 100 .... TadhgO'Shea 5 (John Patrick Shanahan, Ire) *s.i.s: sn struggling in rr* **50/1**	

1m 48.58s (-2.12) 7 Ran SP% **117.7**
WIN: 3.80; CSF: 45.07; EXACTA: 28.40; TRIFECTA: 59.40.
Owner Godolphin **Bred** Darley **Trained** Newmarket, Suffolk

FOCUS
To put into some sort of perspective just how fast Igugu was asked to go, it's worth comparing the sectionals with the earlier strongly 1m2f handicap, for although that was run over a furlong further, the first 800m of both are down the back of the track. Here are the splits to the 1200m point with the times for the handicap in brackets: 25.45 (26.13), 22.42 (23.01), 23.81 (23.79). The form is rated around the first two.

744a SMKA TROPHY (H'CAP) (TAPETA) 1m
5:00 (5:00) (95-105,105) 3-Y-0+
£40,490 (£13,496; £6,748; £3,374; £2,024; £1,349)

			RPR
1		**Unbridled Ocean (USA)**[127] 5-9-0 **98** .... RichardMullen 15 (S Seemar, UAE) *trckd ldrs: led over 1f out: r.o wl* **16/1**	103
2	¾	**Sandagiyr (FR)**[21] 463 5-9-3 **101** .... SilvestreDeSousa 1 (Saeed bin Suroor) *trckd ldng trio: rdn over 2f out: r.o fnl f: jst failed* **7/2**[1]	104
3	¼	**Rostrum (FR)**[28] 363 6-9-6 **105** .... MickaelBarzalona 4 (Mahmood Al Zarooni) *in rr of mid-div: r.o fnl 2f: nrst fin* **10/1**	107
4	¾	**Ariete Arrollador**[14] 557 6-9-3 **101** .... ShaneFoley 9 (G Arizkorreta Elosegui, Spain) *settled last: r.o fnl 2f but nvr able to chal* **9/1**	102
5	2¼	**Field Of Dream**[21] 467 6-9-4 **102** ....(b) JamesDoyle 12 (Jamie Osborne) *in rr of mid-div: kpt on same pce fnl 2f* **7/1**[3]	98
6	¼	**Famous Warrior (IRE)**[14] 557 6-9-2 **100** ....(t) TadhgO'Shea 10 (Doug Watson, UAE) *sn led: rdn over 2f out: hdd bef fnl f: kpt on same pce* **25/1**	95
7	¼	**Canwinn (IRE)**[28] 367 7-8-7 **98** .... MarcMonaghan(7) 6 (D Selvaratnam, UAE) *mid-div: kpt on same pce* **25/1**	93
8	3¼	**Santefisio**[7] 659 7-9-5 **104** ....(b) GaryCarroll 11 (Keith Dalgleish) *slowly away: nvr able to chal* **12/1**	90
9	1	**Muraweg (IRE)**[5] 696 7-8-13 **97** ....(v) GeraldAvranche 8 (Fawzi Abdulla Nass, Bahrain) *nvr bttr than mid-div* **8/1**	81
10	¼	**My Freedom (IRE)**[19] 503 5-9-1 **99** .... TedDurcan 14 (Saeed bin Suroor) *s.i.s: nvr bttr than mid-div* **13/2**[2]	83
11	11	**Saint Bernard**[21] 465 4-9-6 **105** ....(p) KierenFallon 2 (Robert Cowell) *chsd ldrs tl outpcd 2f out* **16/1**	63
12	1	**Smooth Operator (GER)**[21] 465 7-9-5 **104** ....(b) ADeVries 3 (Mario Hofer, Germany) *nvr bttr than mid-div* **14/1**	60
13	11	**Finjaan**[7] 657 7-9-4 **102** .... PaulHanagan 13 (Doug Watson, UAE) *trckd ldrs: rdn 3f out: sn btn* **16/1**	33
14	5½	**Maritimer (CAN)**[21] 463 4-9-5 **104** ....(bt[1]) ChristopheSoumillon 5 (Seth Benzel, U.S.A) *trckd ldrs tl wknd 3f out* **9/1**	22

15 *dist* **Mysticism (USA)**[33] 290 5-9-0 **98**........................ DaraghO'Donohoe 16
(Saeed bin Suroor) *nvr able to chal: virtually p.u fr over 2f out* **33/1**
1m 36.81s (-0.69) **15** Ran SP% **130.9**
WIN: 16.80; PL: 5.00, 1.00, 5.90 CSF: 75.50; EXACTA: 66.30; TRIFECTA: 965.70.
Owner Besilu Stables Llc - Benjamin Leon Jr **Bred** Sybon Racing Stable Llc & Racehorse Management Llc **Trained** United Arab Emirates

FOCUS
There was a fast-slow gallop thanks to Famous Warrior (went 25.14, 22.95, 23.72, before the winner came home in 24.94), yet not much got involved from off the pace.

745a AL FAHIDI FORT (GROUP 2) (TURF) (SPONSORED BY SAEED & MOHAMMED AL NABOODAH GROUP) 1m
5:35 (5:35) 3-Y-O+

£92,024 (£30,674; £15,337; £7,668; £4,601; £3,067)

RPR

1 **Mushreq (AUS)**[14] 556 5-9-0 112.................................... PaulHanagan 2 116+
(M F De Kock, South Africa) *mid-div: rdn 2 1/2f out: chsd ldrs 2f out: led ins fnl f: comf* **4/1**[3]

2 *3 ¼* **Master Of Hounds (USA)**[74] 8042 5-9-3 115...............(t) PatCosgrave 4 112
(M F De Kock, South Africa) *trckd ldrs: ev ch over a f out: one pce* **9/1**

3 *shd* **Iguazu Falls (USA)**[5] 697 8-9-0 102...............(t) ADeVries 8 108
(M bin Shafya, UAE) *in rr of mid-div: r.o over a f out: nrst fin* **25/1**

4 *¾* **Musir (AUS)**[291] 1902 7-9-0 117......................... ChristopheSoumillon 10 107
(M F De Kock, South Africa) *mid-div: smooth prog to ld over a f out: hdd fnl f* **11/4**[2]

5 *1* **Don't Call Me (IRE)**[14] 557 6-9-0 107........................(t) AdrianNicholls 1 104
(David Nicholls) *s.i.s: settled in rr: r.o fnl 2f: nrst fin* **11/1**

6 *¼* **Mandaean**[28] 367 4-9-0 111.................................. MickaelBarzalona 6 104+
(Mahmood Al Zarooni) *settled in rr: nvr nr to chal* **13/8**[1]

7 *1 ½* **Le Drakkar (AUS)**[42] 154 8-9-0 109...............................(t) DaneO'Neill 5 100
(A bin Huzaim, UAE) *slowly away: settled in rr: nvr able to chal* **14/1**

8 *2 ¾* **Across The Rhine (USA)**[431] 7815 7-9-0 107............... TadhgO'Shea 7 94
(S Seemar, UAE) *sn led: kicked clr 3f out: hdd & wknd fnl f* **40/1**

9 *2 ½* **Fiscal**[42] 154 4-9-0 104.. RoystonFfrench 9 88
(M Al Jahouri, UAE) *nvr bttr than mid-div* **66/1**

10 *5 ¾* **Do It All (USA)**[21] 466 6-9-0 113.......................... SilvestreDeSousa 3 75
(Saeed bin Suroor) *trckd ldrs tl outpcd 3f out* **14/1**

1m 36.6s (-1.20) **10** Ran SP% **124.2**
WIN: 4.70; PL: 1.90, 2.00, 6.20 CSF: 42.14; EXACTA: 38.50; TRIFECTA: 337.10.
Owner Hamdan Al Maktoum **Bred** Shadwell Stud Australasia Ltd **Trained** South Africa

FOCUS
The bare form probably isn't anything special - the runner-up and fourth were expected to need the run - but there was a good, even gallop and Mushreq came clear. The sectionals were 26.00 (400m), 23.21 (800m), 23.55 (1200m), before the winner clocked 23.20 to the finish. The third offers some limit to the form.

746a AL NABOODAH CONSTRUCTION GROUP TROPHY (H'CAP) (TURF) 5f (T)
6:10 (6:10) (100-112,112) 3-Y-O+

£64,417 (£21,472; £10,736; £5,368; £3,220; £2,147)

RPR

1 **Dux Scholar**[21] 467 5-9-6 **112**..(bt) KUlubaev 14 115
(Seth Benzel, U.S.A) *mid-div: smooth prog over 2f out: led 55yds out: comf* **7/1**

2 *1 ¼* **Russian Soul (IRE)**[21] 464 5-8-13 **105**.......................(p) ShaneFoley 10 103
(M Halford, Ire) *mid-div: smooth prog over 2f out: ev ch fnl f: one pce* **9/4**[1]

3 *¼* **Medicean Man**[21] 464 7-9-4 **110**.......................(p) PatCosgrave 5 108
(Jeremy Gask) *mid-div: chsd ldrs 2f out: ev ch fnl f: nt qckn fnl 55yds* **9/2**[2]

4 *¾* **Bear Behind (IRE)**[21] 464 4-8-11 **104**............. RichardKingscote 8 98
(Tom Dascombe) *sn led: hdd 2f out but r.o gamely* **13/2**[3]

5 *¼* **Lui Rei (ITY)**[35] 244 7-8-10 **102**...........................(v) KierenFallon 11 96
(Fawzi Abdulla Nass, Bahrain) *nvr bttr than mid-div* **12/1**

6 *¼* **Inxile (IRE)**[21] 464 8-9-0 **106**...................................(p) AdrianNicholls 6 99
(David Nicholls) *trckd ldrs: led 2f out: hdd 55yds out: kpt on same pce* **8/1**

7 *2* **Invincible Ash (IRE)**[35] 244 8-8-7 **106**...............(b) MarcMonaghan[(7)] 2 92
(M Halford, Ire) *slowly away: racd in rr: nvr able to chal* **8/1**

8 *1 ¼* **Beat Baby (IRE)**[21] 464 6-8-11 **104**.................(t) Per-AndersGraberg 13 84
(Niels Petersen, Norway) *nvr bttr than mid-div* **33/1**

9 *1 ¾* **Kanaf (IRE)**[83] 7948 6-8-11 **104**....................................... PaulHanagan 3 78
(M Al Muhairi, UAE) *settled in rr: nvr nr to chal* **20/1**

10 *1* **Factory Time (IRE)**[335] 1026 4-8-8 **100**................. RoystonFfrench 7 72
(M Ibrahim, UAE) *trckd ldrs tl outpcd over 2f out* **28/1**

11 *2* **Pabusar**[21] 464 5-8-9 **101**... JamesDoyle 4 65
(Jamie Osborne) *nvr bttr than mid-div* **33/1**

12 *2 ¼* **Stonefield Flyer**[21] 464 4-8-8 **100**.................................(b[1]) GaryCarroll 12 56
(Keith Dalgleish) *nvr able to chal* **33/1**

13 *¼* **Temple Meads**[21] 464 5-8-13 **105**............................. RichardMullen 1 59
(David Brown) *broke awkwardly: nvr bttr than mid-div* **14/1**

57.75s (-0.75) **13** Ran SP% **128.4**

Owner Ramzan Kadyrov **Bred** Juddmonte Farms Ltd **Trained** North America

FOCUS
A typical Meydan sprint. Solid form.

[726] LINGFIELD (L-H)
Friday, February 22

OFFICIAL GOING: Standard
Wind: fresh, across Weather: mainly dry, light snow flurries

747 BET ON YOUR MOBILE AT BLUESQ.COM (S) STKS 1m 2f (P)
1:30 (1:30) (Class 6) 4-Y-O+ **£2,045** (£603; £302) **Stalls** Low

Form RPR

4633 **1** **Honey Of A Kitten (USA)**[7] 672 5-9-6 66...................(v) MartinHarley 2 73
(David Evans) *chsd clr and clr of field: rdn and clsd 2f out: styd on to ld 1f out: sn clr and in command: eased cl home* **6/1**

2654 **2** *3 ¼* **Electrician**[7] 662 4-9-5 63.....................................(b[1]) AndreaAtzeni 8 66
(Tim Pitt) *led to post: sn led and clr 8f out: stl clr and rdn 2f out: hdd 1f out: sn no threat to wnr but kpt on to hold 2nd* **10/1**

060- **3** *½* **Alhaban (IRE)**[163] 6141 7-9-1 68.................................. JamieSpencer 6 60
(Ronald Harris) *hld up off the pce in midfield: nt clr run and shuffled bk towards rr over 2f out: rdn and rallied over 1f out: r.o strly fnl f: no threat to wnr* **9/2**[2]

00-2 **4** *1* **Royal Etiquette (IRE)**[9] 633 6-9-6 64.........................(v) GeorgeBaker 7 63
(Lawney Hill) *hld up off the pce in midfield: hdwy to chse ldng pair 3f out: drvn 2f out: no imp and plugged on same pce fnl f* **8/1**

5300 **5** *1 ½* **Aviso (GER)**[9] 639 9-8-10 60.................................. ThomasBrown[(5)] 5 55
(David Evans) *hld up off the pce towards rr: hdwy 3f out: rdn and kpt on fr over 1f out: nvr trbld ldrs* **20/1**

2122 **6** *1 ½* **Yourinthewill (USA)**[7] 672 5-9-6 64................................ ShaneKelly 4 57
(Daniel Mark Loughnane) *hld up off the pce in midfield: nt clr run and shuffled bk over 2f out: swtchd arnd wkng rival over 1f out: no imp: nvr trbld ldrs* **5/1**[3]

3-40 **7** *1 ¼* **If You Whisper (IRE)**[8] 653 5-9-1 54.............................. EddieAhern 9 50
(Mike Murphy) *stdd s: hld up off the pce in rr: hdwy into midfield 4f out: rdn over 2f out: no hdwy wl over 1f out: wknd fnl f* **7/1**

-060 **8** *10* **Le King Beau (USA)**[8] 649 4-8-9 49......(v) WilliamTwiston-Davies[(5)] 10 30
(John Bridger) *hld up off the pce in rr: strugging u.p 4f out: n.d* **50/1**

4-30 **9** *1 ½* **Maz**[9] 633 5-8-5 58.. NatashaEaton[(5)] 1 22
(Alan Bailey) *chsd clr ldng pair tl 3f out: wknd wl over 1f out: bhd fnl f* **25/1**

640/ **10** *nk* **Emerging Artist (FR)**[68] 1381 7-9-1 87........................(tp) JimCrowley 3 26
(Evan Williams) *chsd clr ldng trio: rdn and struggling over 2f out: wknd 2f out: bhd fnl f* **5/2**[1]

2m 4.08s (-2.52) **Going Correction** +0.10s/f (Slow)
WFA 4 from 5yo+ 1lb **10** Ran SP% **121.0**
Speed ratings (Par 101): **114,111,111,110,109 107,106,98,97,97**
.There was no bid for the winner.\n\x\x

Owner Mrs E Evans **Bred** Kenneth L Ramsey And Sarah K Ramsey **Trained** Pandy, Monmouths

FOCUS
A fair selling stakes in which they went a decent gallop. The form is rated around the first two.

748 BREATHE SPA AT MARRIOTT LINGFIELD MEDIAN AUCTION MAIDEN STKS 1m (P)
2:00 (2:02) (Class 6) 3-4-Y-O **£2,045** (£603; £302) **Stalls** High

Form RPR

2 **1** **King Bertie (IRE)**[20] 491 3-8-8 0................................... JamieSpencer 5 72+
(Peter Chapple-Hyam) *t.k.h: hld up in midfield: effrt and qckn to ld 3f out: rdn hands and heels fnl f: kpt on and a doing enough* **4/5**[1]

-6 **2** *½* **Excellent Puck (IRE)**[37] 228 3-8-8 0......................... FergusSweeney 4 70
(Jamie Osborne) *chsd ldr: short of room 3f out: rdn to chse wnr 2f out: keeping on whn rn green and hung lft ent fnl f: kpt on towards fin but a hld* **7/1**[3]

42 **3** *hd* **Fearless Lad (IRE)**[9] 636 3-8-8 0.................................(t) HayleyTurner 1 70+
(John Best) *chsd ldrs: rdn and sltly outpcd over 2f out: rallied 1f out: kpt on wl ins fnl f: nvr quite getting to wnr* **11/4**[2]

5 **4** *1 ½* **Landau (IRE)**[13] 580 3-8-8 0... LiamKeniry 6 66
(Sylvester Kirk) *led tl hdd 3f out: sn rdn: kpt on same pce fr over 1f out* **7/1**[3]

5 *6* **Kingston Eucalypt** 3-8-3 0.. AndreaAtzeni 2 47
(Ed Vaughan) *hld up in tch in last trio: rdn and outpcd over 2f out: wl hld and plugged on same pce fr over 1f out* **25/1**

6 *¾* **Flamingo Beat** 3-8-8 0.. ChrisCatlin 3 50
(Rae Guest) *s.i.s: rn green and pushed along in last pair: rdn and outpcd over 2f out: wl btn over 1f out: no ch but styd on again ins fnl f* **25/1**

7 *5* **Baytown Bertie** 4-9-13 0.. RobertHavlin 7 38
(Lydia Richards) *s.i.s: rn green and pushed along in last pair: rdn and struggling wl over 2f out: bhd over 1f out* **100/1**

1m 40.59s (2.39) **Going Correction** +0.10s/f (Slow)
WFA 3 from 4yo 19lb **7** Ran SP% **115.9**
Speed ratings (Par 101): **92,91,91,89,83 83,78**
toteswingers 1&2 £1.90, 2&3 £2.50, 1&3 £1.50 CSF £7.52 TOTE £1.60: £1.30, £2.30; EX 7.40 Trifecta £21.90 Pool: £3964.50 - 135.58 winning units..

Owner Paul Hancock **Bred** P J Fahey **Trained** Newmarket, Suffolk

FOCUS
A modest median auction maiden in which they went a steady gallop. The form is rated loosely around the third, with the winner capable of better.

749 HOLLOW LANE H'CAP 1m (P)
2:30 (2:30) (Class 5) (0-70,69) 4-Y-O+ **£2,726** (£805; £402) **Stalls** High

Form RPR

-261 **1** **Mafi (IRE)**[9] 638 5-8-11 **64** 6ex.............................(t) ThomasBrown[(5)] 1 70
(Mark Hoad) *chsd ldr for 2f: chsd ldrs after: rdn and ev ch ins fnl f: kpt on wl u.p to ld towards fin* **6/1**[3]

-502 **2** *hd* **Cyflymder (IRE)**[28] 370 7-8-13 **68**.................................... IanBurns[(7)] 5 74
(David C Griffiths) *led for 2f: chsd ldr after: rdn and chal 2f out: led over 1f out: kpt on wl u.p tl hdd and no ex towards fin* **9/2**[2]

F-24 **3** *nk* **Spin Again (IRE)**[8] 652 8-9-0 **62**............................... HayleyTurner 7 67
(John Ryan) *t.k.h: hld up in tch in last trio: rdn and clsng whn nt clr run and switching rt ins fnl f: squeezed between horses and kpt on wl towards fin* **7/1**

-542 **4** *shd* **For Shia And Lula (IRE)**[18] 519 4-9-4 **66**........................ ShaneKelly 4 71
(Daniel Mark Loughnane) *hld up in tch in last trio: rdn and effrt ent fnl f: hanging lft and styd on same pce fnl 100yds* **8/1**

00-0 **5** *1* **Titan Triumph**[30] 344 9-9-7 **69**................................(t) JimCrowley 3 71
(William Knight) *stdd after s: hld up in tch in rr: nt clr run 2f out: swtchd lft and hdwy on inner over 1f out: chal ins fnl f: no ex and wknd towards fin* **6/1**[3]

51-4 **6** *1 ¼* **Flavius Victor (IRE)**[48] 80 4-9-6 **68**............................. GeorgeBaker 6 67
(Patrick Chamings) *t.k.h: hld up in midfield tl hdwy to ld after 2f: rdn and pressed 2f out: hdd over 1f out: no ex 1f out: wknd wl ins fnl f* **7/4**[1]

25-3 **7** *nk* **Lady Sylvia**[19] 511 4-9-5 **67**.. LiamKeniry 2 65
(Joseph Tuite) *chsd ldrs: rdn and unable qck over 1f out: one pce and btn fnl f* **8/1**

1m 38.03s (-0.17) **Going Correction** +0.10s/f (Slow) **7** Ran SP% **117.8**
Speed ratings (Par 103): **104,103,103,103,102 101,100**
toteswingers 1&2 £4.40, 2&3 £5.90, 1&3 £5.70 CSF £34.32 TOTE £8.00: £3.80, £1.10; EX 31.20 Trifecta £148.80 Pool: £2957.01 - 14.89 winning units..
Owner Mrs J E Taylor **Bred** Kilboy Estate **Trained** Lewes, E Sussex

The Form Book Flat, Raceform Ltd, Compton, RG20 6NL.

FOCUS
A modest handicap and muddling form. The winner is rated in line with his winter form.

750 BLUE SQUARE BET H'CAP 6f (P)
3:05 (3:06) (Class 6) (0-60,60) 4-Y-0+ **£2,045** (£603; £302) **Stalls** Low

Form RPR

1223 **1** **Johnny Splash (IRE)**[28] [369] 4-9-4 **57**........................(b) JimCrowley 11 67
(Roger Teal) *t.k.h: hld up in tch in midfield: rdn and effrt over 1f out: styd on wl to ld towards fin* **6/1**

6-00 **2** *nk* **Diamond Vine (IRE)**[20] [494] 5-9-5 **58**..........................(p) MartinHarley 9 67
(Ronald Harris) *chsd ldrs: rdn and effrt over 1f out: led ins fnl f: kpt on wl tl hdd and no ex towards fin* **9/2**[2]

-350 **3** *1 ¼* **Pharoh Jake**[29] [354] 5-8-13 **57**..................... WilliamTwiston-Davies(5) 4 62
(John Bridger) *chsd ldrs: gng wl 2f out: rdn and chal ins fnl f: drvn and no ex fnl 100yds: wknd towards fin* **14/1**

5-00 **4** *½* **Powerful Pierre**[14] [559] 6-9-7 **60**....................................(b) ShaneKelly 6 63
(Ian McInnes) *hld up in midfield: nt clr run and swtchd lft over 1f out: hdwy 1f out: styng on whn nt clr run and swtchd rt wl ins fnl f: nt rch ldrs* **7/1**

-200 **5** *1* **Yungaburra (IRE)**[18] [516] 9-8-5 **49**......................(tp) RachealKneller(5) 1 49
(David C Griffiths) *taken down early and led to post: hld up in midfield: pushed along and effrt over 1f out: rdn and kpt on ins fnl f: nvr trbld ldrs* **20/1**

303- **6** *¾* **Comadoir (IRE)**[56] [8268] 7-9-0 **58**.........................(p) NathanSweeney(5) 5 56
(Jo Crowley) *dwlt and bustled along leaving stalls: in tch in midfield: rdn and no imp 2f out: kpt on fnl f but nvr gng pce to threaten ldrs* **4/1**[1]

00-4 **7** *½* **Sweet Ovation**[14] [560] 4-9-4 **57**................................... HayleyTurner 3 53
(Mark Usher) *hld up off the pce in last trio: rdn and effrt wl over 1f out: kpt on ins fnl f: nvr trbld ldrs* **7/1**

5-52 **8** *½* **Imjin River (IRE)**[18] [516] 6-8-12 **56**........................(t) NatashaEaton(5) 10 51
(William Stone) *hld up off the pce in last trio: swtchd lft and hdwy over 1f out: nvr clr enough run despite switching rt ins fnl f: nvr trbld ldrs* **7/1**

-022 **9** *nk* **Waterloo Dock**[22] [449] 8-9-5 **58**....................................(v) AndreaAtzeni 2 52
(Mick Quinn) *pressed ldrs: rdn and no ex wl over 1f out: wknd ins fnl f* **5/1**[3]

6-00 **10** *hd* **Ice Trooper**[14] [558] 5-9-5 **58**.. PatrickMathers 8 51
(Kristin Stubbs) *led: rdn over 1f out: hdd ins fnl f: wknd* **20/1**

11 *28* **Gemara (USA)**[441] [7705] 5-9-4 **57**....................................... LiamKeniry 7
(Gary Brown) *a bhd: lost tch 3f out: t.o* **25/1**

1m 11.88s (-0.02) **Going Correction** +0.10s/f (Slow) **11** Ran SP% **126.7**
Speed ratings (Par 101): **104,103,101,101,99 98,98,97,97,96 59**
toteswingers 1&2 £6.20, 2&3 £19.10, 1&3 £14.70 CSF £34.99 CT £386.56 TOTE £8.30: £2.80, £2.00, £6.10; EX 53.50 Trifecta £854.90 Pool: £4143.44 - 3.63winning units..
Owner Epping Racing **Bred** J Connolly **Trained** Ashtead, Surrey

FOCUS
A moderate sprint handicap in which they went a strong, contested gallop. The winner rates better than ever.

751 LINGFIELDPARK.CO.UK H'CAP 7f (P)
3:40 (3:40) (Class 4) (0-85,85) 4-Y-0+ **£4,690** (£1,395; £697; £348) **Stalls** Low

Form RPR

-542 **1** **Showboating (IRE)**[13] [582] 5-8-11 **75**........................(vt) MartinHarley 4 84
(Alan McCabe) *taken down early: hld up in tch: rdn and effrt over 1f out: drvn to ld ins fnl f: r.o wl* **5/1**[3]

1155 **2** *1* **Al's Memory (IRE)**[9] [629] 4-9-0 **83**........................... ThomasBrown(5) 1 89
(David Evans) *chsd ldr: rdn and ev ch 2f out: led ins fnl f: sn hdd and styd on same pce after* **4/1**[2]

243- **3** *1* **Dr Red Eye**[115] [7453] 5-9-4 **82**...................................(p) TomMcLaughlin 6 86
(Scott Dixon) *led and set stdy gallop: rdn 2f out: drvn and hdd ins fnl f: no ex and one pce after* **7/1**

0610 **4** *1* **The Guru Of Gloom (IRE)**[1] [740] 5-8-8 **72**.................... JackMitchell 2 73
(William Muir) *stdd s: hld up in tch in rr: rdn and effrt over 1f out: edgd lft u.p jst ins fnl f: nvr gng pce to chal* **8/1**

-033 **5** *hd* **Silverware (USA)**[9] [629] 5-9-0 **78**............................... PatrickMathers 3 78
(Kristin Stubbs) *t.k.h: hld up wl in tch in midfield: rdn and effrt on inner over 1f out: pressd ldrs 1f out: wknd fnl 100yds* **7/1**

4-32 **6** *½* **Dubawi Island (FR)**[9] [644] 4-9-7 **85**...............................(b) ShaneKelly 5 84
(James Tate) *chsd ldrs: hdwy to join ldrs 3f out: rdn and unable qck 2f out: drvn and styd on same pce fr over 1f out* **5/4**[1]

1m 25.67s (0.87) **Going Correction** +0.10s/f (Slow) **6** Ran SP% **117.2**
Speed ratings (Par 105): **99,97,96,95,95 94**
toteswingers 1&2 £2.40, 2&3 £4.30, 1&3 £4.20 CSF £26.21 TOTE £6.80: £2.10, £2.60; EX 29.60 Trifecta £87.50 Pool: £4156.48 - 35.59 winning units..
Owner Mr & Mrs L Cooke A Pierce A McCabe **Bred** Crone Stud Farms Ltd **Trained** Averham Park, Notts

FOCUS
A decent handicap in which they went steady until the tempo increased about 3f out. A muddling race, with the winner rated to last year's best.

752 LINGFIELD PARK OWNERS GROUP MAIDEN STKS 1m 4f (P)
4:10 (4:10) (Class 5) 4-Y-0+ **£2,726** (£805; £402) **Stalls** Low

Form RPR

1 **Kent Ragstone (USA)** 4-9-5 0... ShaneKelly 8 76+
(William Haggas) *chsd ldrs: led over 3f out: clr and rn green over 1f out: styd on strly: readily* **6/4**[2]

2 *6* **Keep Kicking (IRE)**[24] 6-9-8 0... GeorgeBaker 9 64
(Jonjo O'Neill) *stdd s: hld up in last pair: hdwy 4f out: chsd clr ldr over 2f out: rdn and no imp over 1f out: wl hld and eased towards fin* **7/1**[3]

/50- **3** *2 ¼* **Lord Golan**[86] [7896] 5-9-8 59.. MartinHarley 2 60
(Violet M Jordan) *in tch in midfield: 4th and unable qck over 2f out: no ch w wnr but kpt on to go 3rd ins fnl f* **33/1**

32 **4** *½* **Pullmen**[18] [521] 5-9-8 0.. EddieAhern 6 59
(J R Jenkins) *t.k.h: chsd ldrs: lft in ld 9f out tl 8f out: chsd ldrs after: rdn and outpcd 2f out: wl btn fnl f* **14/1**

5 *5* **Clover Nova**[147] 6-9-0 0...(t) MarkCoumbe(3) 5 46
(Jo Davis) *s.i.s: hld up in rr: hdwy into midfield: 5th and no prog over 2f out: wknd over 1f out* **50/1**

4 **6** *5* **Nevermindapete**[3] [712] 5-9-3 0..................................(t) ThomasBrown(5) 1 43
(David Evans) *hld up in tch in midfield: rdn and struggling whn sltly hmpd and swtchd rt over 2f out: sn wl btn* **33/1**

6 **7** *7* **Revert (USA)**[21] [473] 4-9-0 0...................................... TomMcLaughlin 7 27
(Gerry Enright) *chsd ldr: hmpd and carried rt bnd 9f out: hdwy to ld over 7f out tl over 3f out: sn wknd* **33/1**

8 *11* **Miss Glorioso** 4-9-0 0... LiamKeniry 10 9
(Stuart Kittow) *in tch in midfield: hung rt bnd 4f out: sn bhd: t.o* **33/1**

22 **P** **Full Swing**[11] [612] 4-9-5 0... AndreaAtzeni 4
(Roger Varian) *t.k.h: refused tl hung rt to paddock exit and hdd bnd 9f out: rcvrd to ld 8f out: sn hdd and chsd ldr after: ev ch over 3f out: lost action and eased wl over 2f out: p.u and dismntd 2f out: fatally injured* **4/5**[1]

2m 34.4s (1.40) **Going Correction** +0.10s/f (Slow)
WFA 4 from 5yo+ 3lb **9** Ran SP% **128.4**
Speed ratings (Par 103): **99,95,93,93,89 86,81,74,**
toteswingers 1&2 £2.00, 2&3 £19.30, 1&3 £18.00 CSF £13.71 TOTE £2.30: £1.40, £2.00, £11.60; EX 15.20 Trifecta £201.00 Pool: £4004.95 - 14.93 winning units..
Owner Gallagher Equine Ltd **Bred** Gsb Racing & Breeding Stock Inc **Trained** Newmarket, Suffolk

FOCUS
A fair middle-distance maiden in which there was a muddling early gallop. There is some doubt as to what the winner beat.

753 ENOUGH SAID, JUST BET AT BLUESQ.COM FILLIES' H'CAP 1m 2f (P)
4:40 (4:41) (Class 5) (0-70,70) 4-Y-0+ **£2,726** (£805; £402) **Stalls** Low

Form RPR

4-34 **1** **Sail Home**[25] [429] 6-8-6 **62**... ShelleyBirkett(7) 4 70
(Julia Feilden) *hld up in tch: rdn and effrt to press ldr 1f out: led ins fnl f: r.o wl* **5/2**[1]

00-6 **2** *2 ¼* **Ogaritmo**[41] [190] 4-9-5 **69**.. GeorgeBaker 1 72
(Alastair Lidderdale) *hld up wl in tch in midfield: rdn and hdwy 1f out: styd on wl ins fnl f to go 2nd fnl 50yds: no threat to wnr* **8/1**

205- **3** *½* **Elsie Bay**[64] [8182] 4-8-2 **57**....................................... RachealKneller(5) 8 59
(Mark Usher) *rdn along leaving stalls: w ldr tl led 8f out: rdn and edgd rt over 1f out: hdd and no ex ins fnl f* **4/1**[3]

0245 **4** *½* **Dazzling Valentine**[9] [639] 5-9-2 **70**........................ NatashaEaton(5) 6 71
(Alan Bailey) *hld up wl in tch: hdwy to chse ldr jst over 2f out: short of room and swtchd rt 1f out: edgd lft and one pce fnl f* **3/1**[2]

3-33 **5** *1 ¼* **Stylistickhill (IRE)**[15] [548] 5-8-13 **62**.....................(tp) TomMcLaughlin 2 62
(Scott Dixon) *hld up wl in tch in last pair: rdn and hdwy on inner over 1f out: styng on but hld whn nt clr run and eased wl ins fnl f* **10/1**

1-26 **6** *1 ½* **Neige D'Antan**[22] [450] 4-9-1 **65**.. ChrisCatlin 7 61
(Sir Mark Prescott Bt) *rdn along leaving stalls: chsd ldrs: wnt 2nd 6f out tl over 2f out: rdn and unable qck 2f out: wknd ins fnl f* **9/2**

264/ **7** *3 ¼* **Tartaria**[987] [2921] 7-8-9 **58** ow1.. LiamKeniry 3 47
(Edward Creighton) *hld up in last pair: rdn and outpcd 2f out: wknd over 1f out* **20/1**

313- **8** *2 ¾* **Bondi Mist (IRE)**[179] [5653] 4-9-0 **64**.............................. RobertHavlin 5 48
(Jonathan Geake) *wl in tch in midfield: rdn and unable qck wl over 1f out: wknd 1f out* **14/1**

2m 5.61s (-0.99) **Going Correction** +0.10s/f (Slow)
WFA 4 from 5yo+ 1lb **8** Ran SP% **123.4**
Speed ratings (Par 100): **107,105,104,104,103 102,99,97**
toteswingers 1&2 £5.10, 2&3 £5.90, 1&3 £3.50 CSF £25.60 CT £82.08 TOTE £3.70: £1.50, £2.70, £2.30; EX 23.30 Trifecta £179.10 Pool: £3158.01 - 13.22 winning units..
Owner Peter Foster **Bred** Juddmonte Farms Ltd **Trained** Exning, Suffolk
■ Stewards' Enquiry : Natasha Eaton two-day ban: careless riding (Mar 8-9)

FOCUS
A fair fillies' handicap, but only fillies' form and it's not rated too positively.
T/Plt: £1,018.80 to a £1 stake. Pool: £59230.61 - 42.44 winning tickets. T/Qpdt: £98.80 to a £1 stake. Poo: £5165.98 - 38.67 winning tickets. SP

703 WOLVERHAMPTON (A.W) (L-H)
Friday, February 22

OFFICIAL GOING: Standard
Wind: Moderate, across Weather: Cloudy

754 FREE BETS GALORE AT BOOKMAKERS.CO.UK APPRENTICE H'CAP 5f 216y(P)
5:30 (5:30) (Class 7) (0-50,54) 4-Y-0+ **£1,940** (£577; £288; £144) **Stalls** Low

Form RPR

0002 **1** **Very First Blade**[3] [716] 4-8-13 **45**.......................(p) MatthewHopkins(3) 3 56+
(Mark Brisbourne) *racd keenly: trckd ldrs: gng wl 2f out: led wl over 1f out: pushed out ins fnl f* **9/2**[2]

651 **2** *1 ¾* **Athaakeel (IRE)**[11] [611] 7-9-11 **54** 6ex.......................(b) GemmaTutty 11 59+
(Ronald Harris) *racd keenly towards rr: impr into midfield after 2f: clsd over 2f out: effrt whn hmpd on inner over 1f out: styd on to take 2nd wl ins fnl f: no imp on wnr* **4/1**[1]

060/ **3** *1 ¼* **Spirit Of Dixie**[445] [7351] 6-9-2 **45**... PatMillman 6 46
(Alan McCabe) *w ldr: rdn to ld narrowly 2f out: hdd wl over 1f out: styd on same pce fnl 100yds* **16/1**

00-4 **4** *¾* **Flaxen Lake**[8] [649] 6-9-7 **50**...(p) SamanthaBell 2 49
(Milton Bradley) *dwlt: rcvrd to chse ldrs after 1f: effrt and swtchd lft over 1f out: nvr able to mount serious chal: one pce wl ins fnl f* **9/2**[2]

3-40 **5** *½* **Love Club**[11] [610] 5-9-0 **48**... AaronJones(5) 1 45
(Brian Baugh) *led: hdd narrowly 2f out: rdn and stl ev ch wl over 1f out: no ex fnl 75yds* **12/1**

00-0 **6** *nk* **Fathey (IRE)**[10] [618] 7-9-2 **45**.. RyanWhile 8 41
(Charles Smith) *trckd ldrs: rdn over 2f out: edgd lft whn outpcd over 1f out: n.d after* **33/1**

-030 **7** *½* **Bachelor Knight (IRE)**[15] [551] 5-8-13 **45**............ JordanVaughan(3) 10 39
(Suzzanne France) *s.i.s: hld up: nt clr run on inner over 1f out: kpt on ins fnl f: no imp* **8/1**

2603 **8** *1 ¼* **First Rebellion**[15] [551] 4-8-11 **45**................................... JoeyHaynes(5) 4 35
(Tony Carroll) *midfield: rdn 2f out: no imp over 1f out: one pce fnl f* **4/1**[1]

365/ **9** *1 ¼* **Mousie**[487] [7067] 4-9-2 **50**.. KevinLundie(5) 9 36
(Alan McCabe) *hld up in rr: niggled along over 3f out: nvr able to get on terms* **25/1**

060 **10** *1 ¼* **Olynard (IRE)**[14] [565] 7-8-13 **45**..............................(be) JordanNason(3) 7 27
(Michael Mullineaux) *a bhd: toiling fnl 2f* **7/1**[3]

1m 16.12s (1.12) **Going Correction** +0.05s/f (Slow) **10** Ran SP% **120.3**
Speed ratings (Par 97): **94,91,90,89,88 87,87,85,83,82**
toteswingers 1&2 £4.10, 1&3 £28.90, 2&3 £18.70 CSF £23.72 CT £275.97 TOTE £4.60: £2.60, £1.10, £4.80; EX 20.20 Trifecta £259.10 Pool: £1477.12 - 5.30 winning units..
Owner L R Owen **Bred** L R Owen **Trained** Great Ness, Shropshire
■ Stewards' Enquiry : Samantha Bell one-day ban: careless riding (Mar 8)

FOCUS
A low-grade apprentice handicap and weak form, but it makes sense. The winner was well in if her latest Southwell form can be believed.

755 WINNERS LOVE BOOKMAKERS.CO.UK H'CAP 1m 5f 194y(P)
6:00 (6:00) (Class 6) (0-60,60) 4-Y-0+ £1,940 (£577; £288; £144) Stalls Low

Form RPR
0316 1 **Sommersturm (GER)**[2] 722 9-8-11 54........................(t) EoinWalsh(7) 8 64
(David Evans) *hld up: hdwy under 2f out: led jst over 1f out: r.o and in command ins fnl f* 7/2[1]
0-06 2 2 ¾ **The Blue Dog (IRE)**[8] 653 6-9-3 60................................ RobertTart(7) 1 66
(Michael Wigham) *midfield: hdwy whn nt clr run and swtchd rt over 1f out: styd on ins fnl f: tk 2nd towards fin: nt rch wnr* 6/1
/00- 3 ½ **Mr Plod**[352] 825 8-9-4 54.. FrederikTylicki 2 59
(J R Jenkins) *chsd ldrs: effrt and ch over 1f out: styd on same pce ins fnl f* 9/1
4333 4 ½ **Daring Damsel (IRE)**[7] 671 4-9-5 60.................(v[1]) GrahamGibbons 10 65
(Brian Baugh) *chsd ldr: led after 4f: rdn 2f out: hdd jst over 1f out: no ex ins fnl 75yds* 5/1[3]
000- 5 2 ¼ **Uncut Stone (IRE)**[49] 6407 5-9-6 56....................................(b) DaleSwift 5 57
(Peter Niven) *midfield: pushed along 3f out: outpcd whn hung lft over 1f out: kpt on ins fnl f: nt trble ldrs* 9/2[2]
263- 6 ¾ **Aegean Destiny**[58] 7018 6-9-1 51.................................... FrannyNorton 7 51
(John Mackie) *s.i.s: hld up: effrt on outer whn hmpd over 1f out: kpt on ins fnl f: nvr a danger* 10/1
3012 7 ¾ **Party Palace**[7] 671 9-9-0 50.. JimmyQuinn 4 49
(Stuart Howe) *in tch: u.p whn forced wd over 1f out: wknd* 11/2
0/0- 8 1 **I'Lldoit**[100] 7710 6-8-10 49 ow2.. RyanClark(3) 6 47
(Michael Scudamore) *sn rdn and nvr gng wl in rr: nvr on terms* 7/1
060- 9 1 ¾ **Trumpet Voluntary (IRE)**[76] 6647 4-9-5 60.............(t) WilliamCarson 11 56
(Nicky Vaughan) *led: hdd after 4f: remained prom: rdn over 2f out: wknd ins fnl f* 25/1
0-00 10 33 **Bet Noir (IRE)**[21] 469 8-8-3 46 oh1.............................[1] JoeyHaynes(7) 9
(Tony Carroll) *racd keenly in midfield: lost pl 4f out: bhd after* 66/1

3m 5.27s (-0.73) **Going Correction** +0.05s/f (Slow)
WFA 4 from 5yo+ 5lb 10 Ran SP% **123.7**
Speed ratings (Par 101): **104,102,102,101,100 100,99,99,98,79**
toteswingers 1&2 £5.80, 1&3 £10.80, 2&3 £8.20 CSF £26.52 CT £181.99 TOTE £2.60: £1.80, £1.80, £3.00; EX 34.40 Trifecta £361.40 Pool: £1683.59 - 3.49 winning units..
Owner Ms S Howell **Bred** Gestut Schlenderhan **Trained** Pandy, Monmouths

FOCUS
A modest staying handicap run at a reasonable pace, and the form looks sound enough. The winner built on his recent form over shorter.

756 £50 FREE BET AT CORAL.CO.UK H'CAP 5f 20y(P)
6:30 (6:30) (Class 7) (0-50,50) 4-Y-0+ £1,940 (£577; £288; £144) Stalls Low

Form RPR
5060 1 **Chateau Lola**[7] 670 4-9-5 48..(v) JoeFanning 2 54
(Derek Shaw) *chsd ldrs: wnt 2nd over 1f out: rdn to ld ins fnl f: r.o: in command towards fin* 13/2
5535 2 1 **Rightcar**[7] 670 6-8-11 45... SladeO'Hara(5) 9 48
(Peter Grayson) *in rr: rdn and hdwy over 1f out: wnt 2nd ins fnl f: tried to chal fnl 100yds: hld towards fin* 11/4[2]
00-5 3 1 ½ **Sophie's Beau (USA)**[47] 81 6-8-9 45.............(bt) DanielleMooney(7) 1 43
(Michael Chapman) *led: rdn over 1f out: hdd ins fnl f: styd on same pce towards fin* 20/1
3604 4 ¾ **Ches Jicaro (IRE)**[11] 610 5-9-2 45........................(v) AdamBeschizza 3 41
(James Unett) *hld up: pushed along 3f out: rdn and hdwy over 1f out: kpt on ins fnl f: nt pce to chal* 5/1[3]
0430 5 1 ½ **Fantasy Fighter (IRE)**[11] 610 8-9-3 46........................(b) JimmyQuinn 7 37
(Ronald Harris) *chsd ldrs tl rdn and outpcd over 1f out: n.d after* 7/1
2036 6 nk **Deveze (IRE)**[7] 670 5-9-2 45.................................(b) RobertWinston 8 35
(Milton Bradley) *plld hrd: hld up: rdn over 1f out: no imp* 8/1
3522 7 2 ¾ **Miserere Mei (IRE)**[11] 610 4-9-0 50..........................(e) PhilipPrince(7) 5 31
(Richard Guest) *chsd ldr: rdn and lost 2nd over 1f out: wknd fnl 100yds* 9/4[1]

1m 2.88s (0.58) **Going Correction** +0.05s/f (Slow) 7 Ran SP% **115.8**
Speed ratings (Par 97): **97,95,93,91,89 88,84**
toteswingers 1&2 £4.30, 1&3 £10.30, 2&3 £5.10 CSF £25.38 CT £341.70 TOTE £10.30: £3.60, £2.10; EX 24.60 Trifecta £482.60 Pool: £1615.98 - 2.51 winning units..
Owner Basingstoke Commercials & Ownaracehorse **Bred** Basingstoke Commercials **Trained** Sproxton, Leics

FOCUS
Another low-grade handicap. The winner is rated to his earlier C&D form.

757 GET THE INSIDE TRACK AT BOOKMAKERS.CO.UK MAIDEN STKS 1m 141y(P)
7:00 (7:02) (Class 5) 3-Y-0 £2,587 (£770; £384; £192) Stalls Low

Form RPR
30- 1 **Yellow Mountain (IRE)**[216] 4330 3-9-5 0........................... AdamKirby 1 65+
(Marco Botti) *a.p: swtchd lft over 1f out: rdn to ld ins fnl f: sn edgd rt: pushed out after: readily* 4/6[1]
2 3 ½ **Off The Pulse** 3-9-5 0... GrahamGibbons 3 57
(John Mackie) *hld up: impr to chse ldrs after 2f: rdn and hung lft whn led jst over 1f out: hdd ins fnl f: sn no ch w wnr: eased towards fin* 16/1
0-36 3 1 ¼ **Silver Fawn (IRE)**[9] 634 3-9-5 43...........................(be[1]) JimmyQuinn 2 54?
(John Weymes) *racd keenly: hld up: effrt over 1f out: kpt on ins fnl f: nvr able to trble ldrs* 50/1
3 4 hd **Impeccability**[13] 590 3-9-0 0.. FrannyNorton 4 49
(John Mackie) *led: rdn and hdd jst over 1f out: no ex fnl 75yds* 12/1
5 1 ½ **Spider House** 3-9-5 0... DanielTudhope 7 50
(David O'Meara) *hld up in rr: swtchd lft over 1f out: nvr able to chal* 8/1[3]
00- 6 1 ¼ **Conversing (USA)**[142] 6795 3-9-5 0.................................... JoeFanning 5 47
(Mark Johnston) *prom: lost pl and intimidated over 1f out: wl btn fnl f* 11/4[2]

1m 54.08s (3.58) **Going Correction** +0.05s/f (Slow) 6 Ran SP% **113.3**
Speed ratings (Par 97): **86,82,81,81,80 79**
toteswingers 1&2 £3.30, 1&3 £7.50, 2&3 £12.20 CSF £14.03 TOTE £1.40: £1.10, £6.60; EX 11.10 Trifecta £114.70 Pool: £2004.05 - 13.09 winning units..
Owner Mrs John Magnier, D Smith & M Tabor **Bred** Lynch Bages Ltd **Trained** Newmarket, Suffolk

FOCUS
A modest maiden for 3yos. It was slowly run and the form is dubious, the third holding it down. The winner is rated 12lb off his debut effort.

758 CORAL.CO.UK H'CAP 1m 141y(P)
7:30 (7:31) (Class 5) (0-70,69) 4-Y-0+ £2,587 (£770; £384; £192) Stalls Low

Form RPR
2-14 1 **Goldstorm**[21] 478 5-9-4 66.......................................(p) WilliamCarson 2 75
(Brian Baugh) *hld up: nt clr run briefly wl over 1f out: hdwy sn after: wnt 2nd over 1f out: edgd rt and r.o ins fnl f: sn led: wl in command towards fin* 2/1[1]
0-60 2 2 ¾ **Spanish Plume**[32] 314 5-9-5 67.......................................(p) AdamKirby 8 70
(Reg Hollinshead) *led: kicked abt 3 l clr 2f out: hrd rdn ins fnl f: sn worn down: no ch w wnr towards fin* 6/1
-120 3 ¾ **Jumbo Prado (USA)**[21] 478 4-9-4 66................................ ShaneKelly 3 67
(John Stimpson) *hld up in rr: hdwy over 1f out: styd on ins fnl f: nt pce to chal* 11/2[3]
52-4 4 ½ **Hail Promenader (IRE)**[28] 376 7-9-5 67.......................(p) GrahamLee 4 67
(Anthony Carson) *trckd ldrs: effrt whn leant on rival wl over 1f out: kpt on ins fnl f: nt pce of ldrs fnl f* 9/2[2]
6150 5 3 ¼ **Lord Of The Dance (IRE)**[4] 705 7-9-0 69..................... RobertTart(7) 6 61
(Michael Mullineaux) *in tch: effrt on outer 2f out: rdn over 1f out: wknd wl ins fnl f* 8/1
1152 6 1 ¾ **Monzino (USA)**[15] 548 5-8-13 68............................... GerardGalligan(7) 5 56
(Michael Chapman) *towards rr: struggling 3f out: plugged on fnl f but nvr able to get on terms* 9/2[2]
240- 7 2 **Pearl War (USA)**[125] 7250 4-9-0 62................................... GrahamGibbons 1 46
(John Mackie) *trckd ldrs: wnt 2nd 2f out but outpcd by ldr: lost 2nd u.p over 1f out: sn wknd* 12/1
8 13 **Larghetto (USA)**[662] 1783 5-9-3 65....................................... JoeFanning 7 19
(Daniel Mark Loughnane) *sluggish s: sn prom: chsd ldr fr 7f out to 2f out: wknd over 1f out* 28/1

1m 50.39s (-0.11) **Going Correction** +0.05s/f (Slow) 8 Ran SP% **121.6**
Speed ratings (Par 103): **102,99,98,98,95 94,92,80**
toteswingers 1&2 £3.60, 1&3 £4.10, 2&3 £10.90 CSF £15.81 CT £60.73 TOTE £2.20: £1.20, £2.10, £1.70; EX 23.50 Trifecta £160.10 Pool: £1352.89 - 6.33 winning units..
Owner Magnate Racing **Bred** Andrew Bailey **Trained** Audley, Staffs

FOCUS
An open handicap for older horses. The winner is rated on the up, with the form rated around the third.

759 EXCLUSIVE FREE BETS AT BOOKMAKERS.CO.UK H'CAP 1m 1f 103y(P)
8:00 (8:00) (Class 4) (0-85,81) 4-Y-0+ £4,690 (£1,395; £697; £348) Stalls Low

Form RPR
235- 1 **Scottish Star**[154] 6445 5-9-3 77... GrahamLee 7 86
(James Eustace) *chsd ldr: rdn to ld over 1f out: r.o ins fnl f* 7/2[1]
3221 2 1 ¼ **One Scoop Or Two**[13] 593 7-8-8 75........................(p) RobertTart(7) 9 81
(Reg Hollinshead) *midfield: hdwy whn rdr dropped rein over 1f out: sn edgd lft: styd on ins fnl f: tk 2nd towards fin: nt rch wnr* 9/1
5-14 3 ¾ **Lean On Pete (IRE)**[32] 314 4-9-1 75................................... ShaneKelly 4 81
(Ollie Pears) *midfield: nt clr run over 1f out: hdwy ins fnl f: styd on: nrst fin* 6/1[3]
-222 4 hd **Knowe Head (NZ)**[11] 614 6-9-1 75........................(v) AdamBeschizza 3 79
(James Unett) *in tch: rdn and styd on ins fnl f: hld cl home* 7/2[1]
-112 5 ¾ **Berlusca (IRE)**[13] 593 4-8-13 73....................................... DanielTudhope 2 75
(David O'Meara) *led: rdn and hdd over 1f out: no ex fnl 75yds* 5/1[2]
3110 6 1 ½ **Strike Force**[6] 691 9-8-11 78...(t) PhilipPrince(7) 1 77
(Alison Hutchinson) *chsd ldrs: rdn over 1f out: one pce fnl f* 16/1
356- 7 ¾ **Brigadoon**[149] 6584 6-9-3 77.. MichaelO'Connell 8 75
(Philip Kirby) *hld up: rdn on outer over 1f out: kpt on ins fnl f: nvr a danger* 16/1
00-3 8 1 ¾ **Elspeth's Boy (USA)**[21] 476 6-8-10 70................................. JoeFanning 10 64
(Philip Kirby) *hld up: pushed along over 1f out: nvr able to trble ldrs* 25/1
133- 9 ¾ **Fabled City (USA)**[74] 8057 4-9-5 79......................................(t) AdamKirby 5 71
(Clive Cox) *chsd ldrs: u.p 3f out: wknd 1f out* 5/1[2]
330- 10 2 ¼ **Nelson's Bay**[174] 5838 4-9-4 78.. FergusSweeney 11 66
(Alan King) *hld up: u.p 3f out: nvr on terms* 11/1

2m 1.21s (-0.49) **Going Correction** +0.05s/f (Slow) 10 Ran SP% **126.0**
Speed ratings (Par 105): **104,102,102,102,101 100,99,97,97,95**
toteswingers 1&2 £10.10, 1&3 £8.90, 2&3 £3.10 CSF £39.73 CT £192.95 TOTE £3.90: £1.30, £3.00, £2.20; EX 48.90 Trifecta £502.00 Pool: £740.07 - 1.10 winning units..
Owner J C Smith **Bred** Mrs J McCreery **Trained** Newmarket, Suffolk

FOCUS
A ceompetitive handicap, though the pace was only ordinary. The winner is accorded a personal best.

760 CORAL.CO.UK MOBILE CASINO H'CAP 5f 20y(P)
8:30 (8:32) (Class 6) (0-65,71) 4-Y-0+ £1,940 (£577; £288; £144) Stalls Low

Form RPR
1-32 1 **Sunrise Dance**[14] 558 4-9-0 65.................................... GaryPhillips(7) 9 78+
(Robert Johnson) *mde all: rdn and kicked over 2 l clr over 1f out: unchal and kpt on wl after* 7/2[1]
-640 2 2 **Master Of Disguise**[32] 308 7-9-5 63.............................. WilliamCarson 6 67
(Brian Baugh) *chsd wnr thrght: rdn over 1f out: no imp fnl f* 8/1
2115 3 ¾ **Hab Reeh**[9] 645 5-8-13 64......................................(t) GemmaTutty(7) 4 65
(Ruth Carr) *chsd ldrs: rdn and kpt on ins fnl f: nvr able to mount serious chal: no imp cl home* 6/1[3]
0460 4 ¾ **Shawkantango**[14] 558 6-8-10 61..........................(v) AdamMcLean(7) 7 60+
(Derek Shaw) *midfield: rdn and outpcd 2f out: styd on ins fnl f: hld cl home* 12/1
60-1 5 ¾ **Bailadeira**[18] 516 5-8-12 56.. JamesSullivan 10 52
(Tim Etherington) *midfield: effrt over 1f out: styd on ins fnl f: nt pce to chal* 25/1
-410 6 hd **Colourbearer (IRE)**[20] 493 6-9-7 65..............................(t) GrahamLee 8 60+
(Milton Bradley) *stdd s: hld up: hdwy 1f out: kpt on ins fnl f: unable to rch ldrs* 11/2[2]
-105 7 hd **Ivestar (IRE)**[14] 558 8-9-5 63................................(bt) GrahamGibbons 5 57
(Michael Easterby) *midfield: rdn and swtchd off rail over 1f out: kpt on ins fnl f: nvr able to chal* 8/1
-460 8 ¾ **Atlantic Beach**[16] 537 8-8-12 56................................(v) RobertWinston 3 48
(Milton Bradley) *hld up: rdn and plld to outer over 1f out: kpt on: nvr able to chal* 8/1
-314 9 ½ **Whipphound**[14] 559 5-8-13 57..................................(p) RobbieFitzpatrick 12 47
(Mark Brisbourne) *in tch: rdn over 1f out: no ex fnl 75yds* 14/1
0231 10 ½ **Dickie Le Davoir**[9] 645 9-9-6 71 6ex...............................(b) PhilipPrince(7) 2 59
(Richard Guest) *bhd: pushed along thrght: nvr on terms* 8/1

2100 **11** *nk* **Lord Buffhead**[9] 640 4-8-10 **59**....(p) JasonHart(5) 13 46
(Richard Guest) *prom: pushed along over 2f out: wknd over 1f out* **40/1**
-566 **12** *5* **Perlachy**[14] 558 9-9-2 **60**....(v) KellyHarrison 1 29
(Ronald Harris) *restless in stalls: hld up: outpcd over 1f out: nvr on terms* **16/1**

1m 2.23s (-0.07) **Going Correction** +0.05s/f (Slow) 12 Ran SP% **122.9**
Speed ratings (Par 101): **102,98,97,96,95 94,94,93,92,91 91,83**
toteswingers 1&2 £9.40, 1&3 £4.30, 2&3 £14.60 CSF £32.88 CT £171.45 TOTE £4.50: £1.40, £3.70, £3.20; EX 43.20 Trifecta £359.00 Pool: £967.98 - 2.02 winning units..
Owner M Saunders **Bred** Mrs Ann Jarvis **Trained** Newburn, Tyne & Wear

FOCUS
A competitive sprint handicap but few got involved. The winner is rated back towards her better old form.
T/Plt: £133.70 to £1 stake. Pool: £84,543.60 - 461.59 winning tickets. T/Qpdt: £20.20 to £1 stake. Pool: £8464.72 -310.05 winning tickets. DO

761 - 772a (Foreign Racing) - See Raceform Interactive

608 GULFSTREAM PARK (L-H)
Friday, February 22

OFFICIAL GOING: Turf: firm

773a STARTER ALLOWANCE (ALLOWANCE) (4YO+) (TURF) 1m 110y(T)
7:09 (7:10) 4-Y-0+
£8,098 (£2,699; £1,349; £674; £134; £134)

RPR
1 **Julius Geezer (IRE)**[12] 608 5-8-7 0.... CLanerie 6 92
(Amy Weaver) *trckd ldr: led 2f out: hrd rdn whn chal fnl f: r.o wl* **121/10**
2 *3/4* **Gentleman Jackson (USA)** 6-8-7 0.... PHusbands 4 90
(Mark Casse, Canada) **9/2**
3 *1/2* **Midnite Silver (USA)**[958] 7-8-7 0....(b) LSaez 9 89
(Giuseppe Iadisernia, U.S.A) **18/5**[3]
4 *3/4* **Tom Kitten (USA)**[83] 6-8-7 0....(b) OBocachica 7 88
(Marcus J Vitali, U.S.A) **33/10**[2]
5 *3/4* **Money In Motion (USA)** 4-8-7 0.... JLezcano 1
(Philip M Serpe, U.S.A) **269/10**
6 *3/4* **Game Ball (USA)**[111] 6-8-7 0.... JRVelazquez 10 84
(Donna Green, U.S.A) **3/1**[1]
7 *2 1/4* **Stage Trip (CAN)** 5-8-3 0 ow1.... EPrado 5 75
(Roger Laurin, U.S.A) **42/10**
8 *1 1/4* **Serapi Cat (USA)**[1588] 8-8-7 0.... EduardoONunez 2
(Eduardo Mondol Jr, U.S.A) **94/1**
9 *7* **Grand Reality (ARG)** 6-8-7 0....(b) ElvisTrujillo 8 61
(Elizabeth Gray, U.S.A) **61/1**

1m 42.04s (-0.73) 9 Ran SP% **121.3**
PARI-MUTUEL (all including $2 stakes): WIN 26.20; PLACE (1-2) 13.00, 5.80; SHOW (1-2-3) 6.40, 3.40, 3.40; SF 176.20.
Owner Wildcard Racing Syndicate **Bred** Ballyhane Stud **Trained** Newmarket, Suffolk

747 LINGFIELD (L-H)
Saturday, February 23

OFFICIAL GOING: Standard
Wind: fresh, across Weather: dry

774 BET ON TODAY'S FOOTBALL AT BLUESQ.COM MAIDEN STKS 1m 4f (P)
1:20 (1:20) (Class 5) 3-Y-0 **£2,726** (£805; £402) **Stalls** Low

Form RPR
03- **1** **Brigh (IRE)**[161] 6257 3-9-0 0.... HayleyTurner 7 68+
(David Simcock) *hld up wl in tch in last pair: clsd to trck ldrs on inner 2f out: rdn and chsd ldr ent fnl f: r.o to ld wl ins fnl f: sn in command: rn green and edging rt towards fin* **9/2**[2]
322 **2** *3/4* **Aryal**[8] 663 3-9-5 73.... JoeFanning 2 71
(Mark Johnston) *led and set stdy gallop: rdn and fnd ex over 1f out: pressed and drvn ins fnl f: hdd wl ins fnl f: sn btn and eased towards fin* **2/5**[1]
00- **3** *4 1/2* **Tebee's Oasis**[64] 8201 3-9-0 0.... RobertHavlin 5 59
(John Gosden) *chsd ldrs: rdn and effrt to press ldrs 2f out: unable qck and btn ent fnl f: wknd fnl 150yds* **12/1**[3]
05- **4** *2 3/4* **Booktheband (IRE)**[107] 7642 3-9-5 0.... FrederikTylicki 1 60
(Clive Brittain) *chsd ldr: rdn and ev ch 2f out: unable qck and btn jst over 1f out: wknd fnl f* **33/1**
0 **5** *1 1/4* **Mighty Thor**[29] 373 3-9-5 0.... AdamBeschizza 4 58
(Simon Dow) *s.i.s: hld up wl in tch in last pair: pushed along and hdwy over 3f out: rdn and struggling over 2f out: wknd over 1f out* **33/1**
0-6 **6** *10* **Royal Barge (IRE)**[29] 373 3-9-0 0.... JimCrowley 3 37
(Eve Johnson Houghton) *t.k.h: hld up wl in tch in midfield: rdn and wknd over 2f out: bhd over 1f out* **16/1**

2m 36.55s (3.55) **Going Correction** +0.075s/f (Slow) 6 Ran SP% **109.1**
Speed ratings (Par 97): **91,90,87,85,84 78**
toteswingers 1&2 £1.10, 2&3 £1.60, 1&3 £2.80 CSF £6.30 TOTE £4.00: £2.10, £1.02; EX 5.80 Trifecta £20.20 Pool: £2104.69 - 77.98 winning units..
Owner H E Sheikh Sultan Bin Khalifa Al Nahyan **Bred** Sheikh Sultan Bin Khalifa Al Nayhan **Trained** Newmarket, Suffolk

FOCUS
An ordinary 3yo maiden, which was slowly run. Improvement from the winner with the second close to recent efforts.

775 BLUE SQUARE BET SPRINT SERIES GRAND FINAL (H'CAP) 6f (P)
1:55 (1:55) (Class 3) 4-Y-0+ **£11,320** (£3,368; £1,683; £841) **Stalls** Low

Form RPR
2123 **1** **Jack My Boy (IRE)**[7] 687 6-9-4 **73**....(b) ThomasBrown(5) 9 85
(David Evans) *chsd ldrs: rdn and effrt to chal 1f out: led and edgd lft ins fnl f: kpt gng lft but r.o strly and sn clr: readily* **7/1**
3110 **2** *3* **Frognal (IRE)**[14] 582 7-9-9 **73**....(bt) WilliamCarson 7 75
(Violet M Jordan) *t.k.h: hld up in midfield: hdwy u.p ins fnl f: edgd lft but r.o strly fnl 100yds to snatch 2nd last stride* **16/1**
0460 **3** *shd* **Waabel**[14] 583 6-8-12 **62**....(tp) MartinHarley 2 64
(Violet M Jordan) *chsd ldr tl 1/2-way: styd chsng ldrs: rdn and effrt to chal over 1f out: ev ch: wnt 2nd but outpcd by wnr wl ins fnl f: lost 2nd last stride* **20/1**
2004 **4** *nk* **Desert Strike**[7] 687 7-9-5 **69**....(p) HayleyTurner 1 70
(Conor Dore) *taken down early: led: rdn over 1f out: hdd and outpcd by wnr ins fnl f: lost 2 pls wl ins fnl f* **33/1**
5262 **5** *1/2* **Welease Bwian (IRE)**[7] 687 4-9-2 **66**.... AndreaAtzeni 5 65
(Stuart Williams) *hld up in tch in midfield: rdn and hdwy on inner to chse ldrs 1f out: styd on same pce fnl 100yds* **6/1**[3]
4500 **6** *shd* **My Own Way Home**[7] 687 5-8-0 **57**.... NoelGarbutt(7) 4 56
(David Evans) *chsd ldrs: wnt 2nd 1/2-way: rdn and ev ch 1f out: outpcd by wnr ins fnl f: styng same pce whn short of room wl ins fnl f* **20/1**
5042 **7** *hd* **Belle Bayardo (IRE)**[7] 688 5-9-3 **67**.... GeorgeBaker 6 65
(Ronald Harris) *chsd ldrs: rdn and effrt over 1f out: swtchd lft and styd on same pce ins fnl f* **8/1**
0631 **8** *hd* **Speak The Truth (IRE)**[21] 494 7-9-4 **68**....(p) JimCrowley 8 66
(Roger Ingram) *hld up off the pce in last quartet: rdn and effrt whn hung lft over 1f out: r.o ins fnl f: nvr trbld ldrs* **12/1**
0031 **9** *shd* **Black Cadillac (IRE)**[7] 688 5-9-1 **72**.... DanielMuscutt(7) 12 69+
(Andrew Balding) *v.s.a and lost many l: detached in last: clsd on to bk of field 4f out: rdn and effrt over 1f out: kpt on fnl f: n.d* **5/1**[2]
1-24 **10** *1* **Rich Again (IRE)**[21] 493 4-9-1 **65**.... JamieSpencer 11 59+
(James Bethell) *hld up off the pce in rr: effrt and sme hdwy over 1f out: stl plenty to do whn nt clr run ins fnl f: eased towards fin* **9/2**[1]
1-31 **11** *3/4* **Temple Road (IRE)**[14] 583 5-9-10 **74**.... RobertWinston 10 66+
(Milton Bradley) *plld v hrd: hld up in midfield: rdn and effrt over 1f out: no imp: hung lft and btn ins fnl f: eased towards fin* **9/2**[1]
4344 **12** *3 1/4* **Putin (IRE)**[10] 640 5-8-4 **54**....(bt) DavidProbert 3 35
(Phil McEntee) *rrd as stalls opened and slowly away: racd off the pce in last quartet: drvn and no hdwy over 1f out: wknd 1f out* **33/1**

1m 11.56s (-0.34) **Going Correction** +0.075s/f (Slow) 12 Ran SP% **119.9**
Speed ratings (Par 107): **105,101,100,100,99 99,99,99,99,97 96,92**
toteswingers 1&2 £14.70, 2&3 £39.00, 1&3 £27.80 CSF £108.00 CT £2156.69 TOTE £7.00: £3.00, £7.00, £5.20; EX 78.70 Trifecta £1791.20 Part won. Pool: £2388.27 - 0.30 winning units..
Owner T Earle & G Evans **Bred** Mrs Sheila Walker **Trained** Pandy, Monmouths
■ Stewards' Enquiry : William Carson one-day ban: careless riding (Mar 9)

FOCUS
The third running of this valuable and competitive series final, but relatively trouble-free and an emphatic winner. The pace held up well.

776 BLUESQUARE.COM CLEVES STKS (LISTED RACE) 6f (P)
2:30 (2:30) (Class 1) 4-Y-0+
£20,982 (£7,955; £3,981; £1,983; £995; £499) **Stalls** Low

Form RPR
002- **1** **Ladies Are Forever**[98] 7772 5-8-9 98.... WilliamTwiston-Davies 2 104
(Geoffrey Oldroyd) *chsd ldr: rdn to ld ent fnl f: edgd rt ins fnl f: r.o wl u.p* **6/1**
/0-1 **2** *1* **Farmleigh House (IRE)**[49] 78 6-9-0 104.... NGMcCullagh 5 105
(W J Martin, Ire) *chsd ldng trio: rdn and effrt wl over 1f out: hdwy to chse wnr ins fnl f: sltly hmpd fnl 100yds: kpt on but nvr looked like getting to wnr* **7/4**[1]
-545 **3** *3/4* **Fratellino**[14] 584 6-9-0 99....(t) MartinHarley 8 103
(Alan McCabe) *taken down early: led: rdn and hdd ent fnl f: styd on same pce u.p fnl 150yds* **12/1**
11-2 **4** *hd* **York Glory (USA)**[22] 480 5-9-0 102....(b) PhillipMakin 7 102+
(Kevin Ryan) *hld up in tch in last pair: hdwy on outer bnd wl over 1f out: r.o u.p ins fnl f: nt rch ldrs* **11/4**[2]
1-05 **5** *3/4* **Gorgeous Goblin (IRE)**[14] 586 6-8-9 78....(t) JoeFanning 1 95?
(David C Griffiths) *chsd ldrs: rdn and effrt over 1f out: styd on same pce u.p fnl f* **100/1**
10-3 **6** *nk* **Capone (IRE)**[22] 480 8-9-0 100.... ShaneKelly 3 99
(Garry Moss) *hld up in tch in midfield: hdwy u.p ent fnl f: kpt on but nvr gng pce to chal* **14/1**
3212 **7** *1/2* **Piscean (USA)**[14] 584 8-9-1 102 ow1.... GeorgeBaker 4 98+
(Tom Keddy) *stdd s: hld up in tch in last pair: rdn and hdwy on inner over 1f out: styd on same pce ins fnl f* **5/1**[3]
6050 **8** *1 3/4* **Swiss Cross**[14] 584 6-9-0 95....(t) DavidProbert 6 92
(Phil McEntee) *hld up in tch towards rr: rdn and no hdwy over 1f out: wl hld fnl f* **33/1**
4-26 **9** *6* **Noverre To Go (IRE)**[14] 584 7-9-0 86.... RobertWinston 9 73
(Ronald Harris) *t.k.h: hld up in tch in midfield on outer: rdn and no hdwy over 1f out: sn wknd* **50/1**

1m 10.98s (-0.92) **Going Correction** +0.075s/f (Slow) 9 Ran SP% **114.2**
Speed ratings (Par 111): **109,107,106,106,105 105,104,102,94**
toteswingers 1&2 £2.80, 2&3 £6.00, 1&3 £11.00 CSF £16.64 TOTE £9.10: £2.10, £1.10, £4.80; EX 17.40 Trifecta £134.90 Pool: £2614.38 - 14.52 winning units..
Owner R C Bond **Bred** Bond Thoroughbred Corporation **Trained** Brawby, N Yorks

FOCUS
They didn't seem to go a great pace early in this Listed sprint and the proximity of a 78-rated horse in fifth does place a slight question mark against the form. The winning time was still 0.58 seconds faster than the Blue Square Final. The form is rated around the winner and third.

777 BLUE SQUARE BET WINTER DERBY TRIAL STKS (LISTED RACE) 1m 2f (P)
3:05 (3:05) (Class 1) 4-Y-0+
£20,982 (£7,955; £3,981; £1,983; £995; £499) **Stalls** Low

Form RPR
300- **1** **Planteur (IRE)**[185] 5490 6-9-0 121.... AdamKirby 2 106
(Marco Botti) *mde all: racd keenly: rdn ent fnl 2f: 2 l clr 1f out: kpt up to work under hands and heels fnl 100yds: a gng to last home* **2/5**[1]
560- **2** *nk* **Miblish**[168] 6025 4-8-13 98....(t) FrederikTylicki 5 105
(Clive Brittain) *chsd ldrs: rdn to chse wnr jst over 2f out: 2 l down 1f out: kpt on gamely and clsng on wnr steadily fnl 100yds: nvr quite getting up* **20/1**
-336 **3** *2 1/4* **Tepmokea (IRE)**[6] 701 7-9-0 90.... ShaneKelly 6 101
(Mrs K Burke) *hld up in tch in midfield: rdn and hdwy to chse ldng pair 1f out: edgd lft and kpt on u.p fnl f* **40/1**
5314 **4** *5* **Emerald Wilderness (IRE)**[14] 585 9-9-0 99.... SebSanders 7 91
(Mark Rimmer) *stdd and dropped in bhd after s: hld up towards rr: hdwy on inner over 2f out: rdn and no ex wl over 1f out: sn wknd* **14/1**
14-6 **5** *1/2* **Tinshu (IRE)**[28] 401 7-8-9 94....(p) WilliamCarson 9 85
(Derek Haydn Jones) *in tch in midfield: rdn and effrt ent fnl 2f: outpcd and btn wl over 1f out: sn wknd* **16/1**
500- **6** *1 1/2* **Marcret (ITY)**[175] 5848 6-9-0 109....(t) JamieSpencer 3 87
(Marco Botti) *stdd s: t.k.h: hld up in rr: sme hdwy on inner over 1f out: drvn and no prog 1f out: wknd* **10/1**[3]
663- **7** *1 1/4* **Arsaadi (IRE)**[175] 5849 4-8-8 102.... AdamBeschizza 1 79
(William Haggas) *rrd as stalls opened and v.s.a: detached in last: clsd on to bk of field 5f out: wknd u.p wl over 1f out* **7/1**[2]

1141 8 17 **Harry Buckle**[7] 691 4-8-13 88 .... DavidProbert 8 50
(Philip McBride) *chsd wnr tl jst over 2f out: sn wknd: wl bhd fnl f* **10/1**[3]

0/05 9 25 **Dubawi Phantom**[14] 585 6-9-0 79 .... (b) JoeFanning 4
(David C Griffiths) *niggled along in midfield: lost pl and dropped to rr over 2f out: t.o and virtually p.u ins fnl f* **66/1**

2m 1.2s (-5.40) **Going Correction** +0.075s/f (Slow)
WFA 4 from 6yo+ 1lb **9 Ran SP% 123.4**
Speed ratings (Par 111): **124,123,121,117,117 116,115,101,81**
toteswingers 1&2 £4.00, 2&3 £31.50, 1&3 £12.40 CSF £15.59 TOTE £1.50: £1.02, £6.20, £10.90; EX 12.80 Trifecta £186.30 Pool: £3255.49 - 13.10 winning units..
Owner Mohamed Albousi Alghufli **Bred** Dayton Investments Ltd **Trained** Newmarket, Suffolk

FOCUS
Not since Eccentric in 2005 has the winner of this race gone on to win the Winter Derby itself, though the 2010 winner Gitano Hernando (already a Grade 1 winner in America) landed the following year's Group 1 Singapore Airlines International Cup at Kranji. A truly run race meant that they took 0.43 seconds off the course record. The winner did not need to match his best, with the level set around the third.

778 BET AT BLUESQ.COM FILLIES' H'CAP 7f (P)
3:40 (3:40) (Class 5) (0-70,69) 4-Y-0+ **£2,726** (£805; £402) **Stalls** Low

Form RPR

5-24 1 **Amosite**[16] 546 7-9-1 63 .... (p) JoeFanning 8 71
(J R Jenkins) *chsd ldr: rdn to ld over 1f out: hrd pressed and kpt on gamely u.p ins fnl f: rdn out* **6/1**[3]

1-21 2 ½ **Big Sylv (IRE)**[35] 271 4-8-13 61 .... (p) DavidProbert 1 69+
(James Unett) *t.k.h: hld up in tch in last trio: hdwy gng wl over 1f out: chsd ldrs and shkn up whn nt clr run and swtchd rt jst ins fnl f: rdn and r.o to chse wnr wl ins fnl f: kpt on* **1/1**[1]

5136 3 ¾ **Welsh Inlet (IRE)**[8] 665 5-8-9 62 ow2 .... WilliamTwiston-Davies(5) 4 67
(John Bridger) *hld up in rr of main gp: rdn and hdwy on inner over 1f out: drvn and chsd ldrs ins fnl f: kpt on* **8/1**

-541 4 ¾ **Chambles**[23] 446 4-8-13 61 .... FrederikTylicki 3 64
(J R Jenkins) *chsd ldrs: rdn and effrt to chal over 1f out: no ex ins fnl f: wknd towards fin* **4/1**[2]

30-0 5 2 ½ **Chevise (IRE)**[9] 650 5-9-0 62 .... (p) JimCrowley 5 58
(Steve Woodman) *hld up in tch in midfield: rdn and effrt over 1f out: styd on same pce and no imp fnl f* **14/1**

-000 6 2 **Ishiamiracle**[18] 523 4-8-3 51 ow1 .... (p) AndreaAtzeni 6 41
(Phil McEntee) *chsd ldrs: rdn over 2f out: drvn and wknd u.p over 1f out* **50/1**

00-0 7 4 ½ **Tenbridge**[45] 116 4-8-12 60 .... (p) WilliamCarson 7 38
(Derek Haydn Jones) *sn detached in last and rdn along: sme hdwy over 2f out: wknd u.p over 1f out* **25/1**

-000 8 nk **Beauty Pageant (IRE)**[19] 518 6-9-7 69 .... (v[1]) AdamKirby 2 46
(David Evans) *led: rdn ent fnl 2f: hdd over 1f out: sn btn: fdd fnl f* **14/1**

1m 23.94s (-0.86) **Going Correction** +0.075s/f (Slow) **8 Ran SP% 114.5**
Speed ratings (Par 100): **107,106,105,104,101 99,94,94**
toteswingers 1&2 £2.00, 2&3 £2.40, 1&3 £4.90 CSF £12.43 CT £48.80 TOTE £7.60: £1.50, £1.10, £2.20; EX 15.30 Trifecta £96.10 Pool: £5714.72 - 44.58 winning units..
Owner Mrs Claire Goddard **Bred** Richard Kent **Trained** Royston, Herts

FOCUS
A modest fillies' handicap, which was run at a sound pace. The winner and third set the standard.

779 ENOUGH SAID, JUST BET AT BLUESQ.COM H'CAP 1m 5f (P)
4:15 (4:15) (Class 5) (0-75,74) 4-Y-0+ **£2,726** (£805; £402) **Stalls** Low

Form RPR

1-45 1 **Scottish Boogie (IRE)**[7] 691 6-9-9 74 .... SebSanders 5 83
(Brendan Powell) *t.k.h: hld up wl in tch in last pair: rdn and hdwy ent fnl f: led fnl 100yds: r.o wl* **7/1**

0-11 2 1 ¼ **Stentorian (IRE)**[22] 475 5-9-7 72 .... (v) GeorgeBaker 1 79
(Gary Moore) *chsd ldrs: rdn and effrt on inner over 1f out: pressed ldrs and drvn jst ins fnl f: outpcd by wnr fnl 75yds: wnt 2nd last stride* **2/1**[1]

14-1 3 shd **Norfolk Sky**[23] 450 4-9-2 71 .... IanMongan 2 78
(Laura Mongan) *t.k.h: hld up wl in tch in midfield: hdwy on outer to chal ent fnl 2f: rdn to ld over 1f out: hdd and one pce fnl 100yds: lost 2nd last stride* **9/2**[3]

300- 4 1 ½ **The Holyman (IRE)**[148] 6642 5-9-9 74 .... LiamKeniry 4 79
(Jo Crowley) *led and set stdy gallop: pressed and rdn ent fnl 2f: hdd over 1f out: styng in same pce whn squeezed for room and hmpd ins fnl f* **3/1**[2]

4-1 5 ¾ **Pahente**[44] 132 5-9-2 67 .... (p) DavidProbert 3 71
(Tony Carroll) *hld up wl in tch in last pair: clsd and nt clr run jst over 2f out: swtchd ins and effrt over 1f out: styd on same pce ins fnl f* **6/1**

0-23 6 1 ½ **Where's Susie**[29] 224 8-9-7 72 .... AdamKirby 6 74
(Michael Madgwick) *chsd ldr: rdn and lost 2nd over 2f out: dropped to last and drvn over 1f out: one pce and hld fnl f* **8/1**

2m 48.36s (2.36) **Going Correction** +0.075s/f (Slow)
WFA 4 from 5yo+ 4lb **6 Ran SP% 114.4**
Speed ratings (Par 103): **95,94,94,93,92 91**
toteswingers 1&2 £3.30, 2&3 £2.70, 1&3 £4.20 CSF £22.05 TOTE £7.10: £4.10, £1.10; EX 24.70 Trifecta £121.60 Pool: £3064.57 - 18.89 winning units..
Owner A A Byrne **Bred** Littleton Stud **Trained** Upper Lambourn, Berks

FOCUS
Despite a solid early pace, the field was still closely packed turning for home.The winner is rated to last year's turf best.

780 GET STRAIGHT TO THE BET AT BLUESQ.COM H'CAP 5f (P)
4:50 (4:50) (Class 4) (0-85,85) 4-Y-0+ **£4,690** (£1,395; £697; £348) **Stalls** High

Form RPR

60-1 1 **Diamond Charlie (IRE)**[45] 113 5-9-7 85 .... SebSanders 3 94
(Simon Dow) *chsd ldrs: rdn to ld over 1f out: hld on wl u.p fnl 100yds* **5/2**[1]

1151 2 ½ **Picansort**[10] 627 6-9-3 81 .... (b) ShaneKelly 1 88
(Peter Crate) *hld up in midfield: hdwy over 1f out: swtchd lft to chse ldr ins fnl f: kpt on u.p: hld cl home* **5/1**[3]

2321 3 nk **Triple Dream**[14] 586 8-9-3 81 .... (tp) RobertWinston 8 87
(Milton Bradley) *in tch in midfield: looking to swtchd rt over 1f out: swtchd lft and hdwy 1f out: hdwy u.p to chse ldrs fnl 100yds: kpt on* **8/1**

13- 4 ½ **My Son Max**[79] 8009 5-9-5 83 .... FrannyNorton 9 90+
(P J O'Gorman) *hld up off the pce in last trio: gd hdwy on inner over 1f out: chsd ldrs whn nt clr run and swtchd rt ins fnl f: nvr enough room and one pce after* **7/2**[2]

500- 5 1 ¾ **Electric Qatar**[101] 7704 4-9-4 82 .... StephenCraine 10 80
(Tom Dascombe) *taken down early: racd wl off the pce in last pair: clsd 2f out: swtchd lft jst over 1f out: kpt on fnl f: nvr trbld ldrs* **16/1**

1-40 6 ½ **Lujeanie**[24] 443 7-8-13 77 .... EddieAhern 6 73
(Peter Crate) *hld up off the pce in rr: hdwy on inner whn nt clr run jst over 1f out: nvr enough room ins fnl f: kpt on but unable to chal* **7/1**

-524 7 hd **Le Toreador**[29] 379 8-9-4 82 .... (p) PhillipMakin 4 78
(Kevin Ryan) *chsd ldr tl over 1f out: no ex u.p: wknd ins fnl f* **8/1**

50-3 8 ¾ **Tyfos**[23] 457 8-9-2 80 .... DuranFentiman 5 73
(Brian Baugh) *racd keenly: chsd ldr over 3f out: ev ch and rdn wl over 2f out: no ex 1f out: wknd ins fnl f* **14/1**

6001 9 7 **Royal Bajan (USA)**[23] 457 5-9-4 82 .... (b) JamesSullivan 2 50
(James Given) *taken down early: led tl over 1f out: fdd ins fnl f* **16/1**

58.27s (-0.53) **Going Correction** +0.075s/f (Slow) **9 Ran SP% 120.6**
Speed ratings (Par 105): **107,106,105,104,102 101,101,99,88**
toteswingers 1&2 £2.50, 2&3 £5.80, 1&3 £6.00 CSF £16.05 CT £90.47 TOTE £3.30: £1.20, £2.20, £2.20; EX 15.60 Trifecta £89.30 Pool: £3310.11 - 27.78 winning units..
Owner David & Stanley Adams **Bred** John Malone **Trained** Epsom, Surrey
■ Stewards' Enquiry : Shane Kelly caution: careless riding.

FOCUS
The leaders went off too fast in this and the trio that forced it ended up as the last three home. The third helps set the standard.
T/Plt: £64.30 to a £1 stake. Pool of £78126.57 - 886.38 winning tickets. T/Qpdt: £6.70 to a £1 stake. Pool of £5237.34 - 577.31 winning tickets. SP

781 - (Foreign Racing) - See Raceform Interactive

[711]CAGNES-SUR-MER
Saturday, February 23
OFFICIAL GOING: Turf: soft; fibresand: standard

782a PRIX POLICEMAN (LISTED RACE) (3YO) (FIBRESAND) 1m 2f (D)
3:10 (12:00) 3-Y-O **£24,390** (£9,756; £7,317; £4,878; £2,439)

RPR

1 **Holy Warrior (IRE)**[30] 350 3-8-11 0 .... Pierre-CharlesBoudot 3 95
(Gay Kelleway) *broke wl: sent to ld: set gd pce: l clr ent st: shkn up and wnt 3 l clr 1 1/2f out: r.o wl: comf* **126/10**

2 1 ½ **Snap Call**[13] 605 3-8-11 0 .... IoritzMendizabal 9 92
(J-C Rouget, France) **5/2**[1]

3 shd **Quatorze (FR)** 3-8-11 0 .... Francois-XavierBertras 2 92
(F Rohaut, France) **78/10**

4 ¾ **Kingzar (FR)**[5] 711 3-8-11 0 .... FredericSpanu 8 90
(Mme C Barande-Barbe, France) **22/1**

5 nse **Eleuthera (FR)**[14] 3-8-8 0 .... EddyHardouin 5 87
(P Demercastel, France) **23/1**

6 ½ **Suspicieuse (FR)** 3-8-8 0 .... MickaelForest 4 86
(W Walton, France) **17/1**

7 nk **Camaretz (USA)**[26] 3-8-11 0 .... Jean-BernardEyquem 7 88
(J-C Rouget, France) **9/1**

8 hd **Sunday Dream (FR)** 3-8-11 0 .... GeraldPardon 13 88
(M Gentile, France) **50/1**

9 nse **Russian Reel (FR)**[5] 711 3-8-11 0 .... RomainAuray 11 88
(J Heloury, France) **63/1**

10 2 ½ **Mister Massagot (FR)**[98] 3-8-11 0 .... Roberto-CarlosMontenegro 1 83
(C Baillet, France) **16/1**

0 **Julius Quercus (IRE)**[36] 270 3-8-11 0 .... MaximeGuyon 12
(F Chappet, France) **7/1**[3]

0 **Le Ring (FR)**[35] 286 3-8-11 0 .... FranckBlondel 10
(F Rossi, France) **58/10**[2]

0 **Kenbella (FR)** 3-8-8 0 .... StephanePasquier 6
(J-M Capitte, France) **11/1**

2m 5.17s (125.17) **13 Ran SP% 116.3**
WIN (incl. 1 euro stake): 13.60. PLACES: 4.30, 1.80, 2.60. DF: 30.60. SF: 36.10.
Owner Robert Ng **Bred** Chris McHale And Oghill House Stud **Trained** Exning, Suffolk

[413]TURFWAY PARK (L-H)
Saturday, February 23
OFFICIAL GOING: Polytrack: fast

786a MAIDEN CLAIMING (MAIDEN) (3YO) (POLYTRACK) 5f 110y
8:56 (9:13) 3-Y-0
£3,533 (£1,177; £588; £294; £58; £58)

RPR

1 **Marchwood**[41] 3-8-10 0 .... BFayosMartin 10 69
(Amy Weaver) **9/5**[1]

2 nk **Macevil (USA)** 3-8-10 0 .... NArroyoJr 1 68
(Kellyn Gorder, U.S.A) **32/5**

3 1 ¾ **Rhythm Lake (USA)** 3-8-10 0 .... ACastanon 3 62
(William R Edwards, U.S.A) **169/10**

4 1 ¼ **Slewpy's Image (USA)** 3-8-10 0 .... (b) JZuniga 12 58
(Edward Harrison Frederick, U.S.A) **13/5**[2]

5 ½ **Shut Up Chris (USA)** 3-8-10 0 .... (b) RMorales 8 56
(Larry Demeritte, U.S.A) **23/5**[3]

6 3 ½ **Polaris (USA)** 3-8-10 0 .... ADeLeon 9 45
(Richard Budge, U.S.A) **199/10**

7 4 ¼ **Foot Patrol (USA)** 3-8-10 0 .... MStJulien 2 31
(Walter Bindner Jr, U.S.A) **29/1**

8 11 ¼ **Jenna Lee Kuma (USA)** 3-8-10 0 .... TPompell 11
(Larry Lay, U.S.A) **138/10**

9 1 **Unique Indygo (USA)** 3-8-5 0 .... RPrescott(5) 6
(Claire Reece, U.S.A) **31/1**

10 ¾ **Earned Indulgence (USA)** 3-8-10 0 .... (b) MGAdam 7
(Rowena Beck, U.S.A) **59/1**

11 3 **C J Mon (USA)** 3-8-10 0 .... AJiminez 4
(Norris Davidson, U.S.A) **45/1**

1m 6.49s (66.49) **11 Ran SP% 122.3**
PARI-MUTUEL (all including $2 stakes): WIN 5.60; PLACE (1-2) 3.20, 5.40; SHOW (1-2-3) 2.80, 3.60, 6.60; SF 32.00.Marchwood was claimed by Elliott S Logan (trainer John Rupert) for $15,000
Owner Wildcard Racing Syndicate **Bred** Mickley Stud & B Robe **Trained** Newmarket, Suffolk

The Form Book Flat, Raceform Ltd, Compton, RG20 6NL.

787 - (Foreign Racing) - See Raceform Interactive

[733]KEMPTON (A.W) (R-H)

Monday, February 25

OFFICIAL GOING: Standard
Wind: Brisk ahead Weather: Overcast

788 EASTER FAMILY FUN 30.03.13 H'CAP 1m 4f (P)
2:20 (2:21) (Class 6) (0-55,58) 4-Y-0+ **£1,940** (£577; £288; £144) **Stalls** Centre

Form RPR
00-1 **1** **Tidy Affair (IRE)**[7] 704 4-9-7 **58** 6ex ShaneKelly 5 66+
(Gary Moore) *s.i.s: sn wl in tch: gd hdwy fr 2f out: drvn to ld fnl 100yds: r.o strly* **5/4**[1]
2-20 **2** ¾ **Highly Likely (IRE)**[11] 653 4-9-4 **55** AdamKirby 4 62
(Steve Woodman) *chsd ldrs: led 2f out: styd on wl fnl f: hdd and outpcd fnl 100yds* **12/1**
3 1 **Mr Lando**[72] 4978 4-8-10 **47** JimmyQuinn 8 52
(Tony Carroll) *in rr: hdwy 2f out: drvn and styd on wl for 3rd ins fnl f but no imp on ldng duo* **10/1**
6-45 **4** ½ **Celtic Charlie (FR)**[10] 668 8-9-5 **53** IanMongan 2 57
(Pat Phelan) *in rr: hdwy over 2f out: chsng ldrs whn drvn and edgd rt over 1f out: one pce fnl f* **5/2**[2]
250/ **5** 5 **Fair Breeze**[138] 7805 6-8-12 **46** FergusSweeney 10 42
(Richard Phillips) *in rr: drvn ins fnl 3f: sme hdwy fnl f* **50/1**
U-53 **6** 3 ¾ **Crimson Monarch (USA)**[30] 406 9-8-12 **46** oh1 (b) WilliamCarson 1 39
(Peter Hiatt) *in tch: hdwy to chse ldrs whn hmpd and snatched up 2f out: no ch after* **8/1**[3]
6 **7** 2 ¾ **Numen (IRE)**[5] 724 9-9-7 **55** LiamKeniry 7 41
(Barry Brennan) *chsd ldr: chal fr 6f out tl led 3f out: hdd 2f out and sn btn* **16/1**
0-60 **8** 1 ¼ **Capellini**[12] 646 6-9-7 **55** SamTwiston-Davies 9 39
(Charles Egerton) *sn led: jnd fr 6f out: hdd 3f out: wknd fr 2f out* **20/1**
00/0 **9** 10 **Our Play (IRE)**[28] 418 5-9-5 **53** JackMitchell 6 21
(Lydia Richards) *in tch: rdn 3f out: sn wknd* **25/1**
040/ **10** 6 **Fists And Stones**[504] 6764 5-9-4 **52** EddieAhern 3 10
(Simon Hodgson) *a in rr* **66/1**

2m 35.56s (1.06) **Going Correction** +0.10s/f (Slow)
WFA 4 from 5yo+ 3lb **10** Ran SP% **118.9**
Speed ratings (Par 101): **100,99,98,98,95 92,90,90,83,79**
toteswingers 1&2 £4.20, 1&3 £3.20, 2&3 £8.90 CSF £18.27 CT £113.04 TOTE £2.00: £1.60, £2.20, £2.90; EX 20.20 Trifecta £126.60 Pool: £2758.31 - 16.33 winning units..
Owner Gallagher, O'Rourke **Bred** Jim McCormack **Trained** Lower Beeding, W Sussex
FOCUS
A low-grade handicap run at a steady pace with the front four pulling clear.

789 MIKE THE KNIGHT HERE 13.04.13 H'CAP 1m 3f (P)
2:50 (2:50) (Class 6) (0-60,60) 4-Y-0+ **£1,940** (£577; £288; £144) **Stalls** Low

Form RPR
2-61 **1** **Bridge That Gap**[22] 508 5-9-6 **60** (p) AdamKirby 3 69
(Roger Ingram) *chsd ldrs: drvn to chal fr over 1f out: led ins fnl f: kpt on wl clsng stages* **11/4**[1]
0062 **2** 1 **Amana (USA)**[5] 722 9-9-5 **59** ShaneKelly 6 68+
(Mark Brisbourne) *in tch: hdwy to trck ldrs 2f out: travelling wl on ins whn nt clr run fnl 150yds and swtchd lft: r.o to take 2nd nr fin: nt trble wnr* **8/1**
-634 **3** nk **Shirataki (IRE)**[11] 653 5-9-6 **60** ChrisCatlin 5 67
(Peter Hiatt) *chsd ldrs: drvn to take slt ld over 1f out but hrd pressed: hdd ins fnl f: one pce and lost 2nd nr fin* **4/1**[2]
-000 **4** 1 **Legal Legacy**[12] 626 7-9-4 **58** AmirQuinn 12 63+
(Richard Rowe) *s.i.s: in rr: drvn over 2f out: hdwy over 1f out: kpt on wl fnl f: nt rch ldrs* **25/1**
63-4 **5** nk **Having A Ball**[47] 112 9-9-6 **60** JohnFahy 8 64
(Geoffrey Deacon) *t.k.h: chsd ldrs: drvn over 2f out: kpt on fnl f to dispute 4th but nvr gng pce to chal* **9/1**
4661 **6** 1 ¼ **Silkee Supreme**[12] 626 4-9-4 **60** (b) SeanLevey 11 62
(Richard Hannon) *sn led: rdn 2f out: hdd over 1f out: btn ins fnl f* **7/1**[3]
0610 **7** ½ **Sir Dylan**[12] 626 4-9-2 **58** RobertWinston 13 59
(Ronald Harris) *in rr: hdwy fr 2f out: edgd lft 1f out: kpt on ins fnl f* **25/1**
60-0 **8** 1 ¼ **Scary Movie (IRE)**[32] 361 8-9-6 **60** (b[1]) JimCrowley 10 61+
(Thomas McLaughlin, Ire) *in rr: rdn and hdwy towards outer fr 2f out: nvr gng pce to rch ldrs* **12/1**
00- **9** ½ **Dicey Vows (USA)**[117] 7473 5-8-12 **59** DavidParkes(7) 2 57
(Alan Jarvis) *in tch: drvn and sme prog over 2f out: nvr gng pce to rch ldrs* **33/1**
50-3 **10** hd **Lord Golan**[3] 752 5-9-5 **59** WilliamCarson 1 57
(Violet M Jordan) *in rr: drvn over 2f out: mod prog ins fnl f* **16/1**
6/ **11** nk **Aather (IRE)**[367] 621 8-9-0 **59** WilliamTwiston-Davies(5) 9 56
(David Arbuthnot) *chsd ldrs: rdn 3f out: wknd 2f out* **10/1**
-630 **12** 1 ¼ **Dream Win**[16] 593 7-9-3 **60** (t) AshleyMorgan(3) 7 55
(Brian Ellison) *rdn and hung rt ins fnl 3f: a towards rr* **20/1**

2m 23.69s (1.79) **Going Correction** +0.10s/f (Slow)
WFA 4 from 5yo+ 2lb **12** Ran SP% **118.3**
Speed ratings (Par 101): **97,96,96,95,95 94,93,92,92,92 92,91**
toteswingers 1&2 £5.00, 2&3 £6.30, 1&3 £3.00 CSF £23.66 CT £88.97 TOTE £3.20: £1.50, £3.80, £1.20; EX 16.60 Trifecta £85.30 Pool: £2594.94 - 22.81 winning units..
Owner The Stargazers **Bred** Michael Joy **Trained** Epsom, Surrey
FOCUS
An open contest, run at a messy pace, with plenty of hard-luck stories behind the winner.

790 GET THE BETVICTOR APP FILLIES' H'CAP 6f (P)
3:20 (3:20) (Class 5) (0-70,65) 4-Y-0+ **£2,587** (£770; £384; £192) **Stalls** Low

Form RPR
2231 **1** **Climaxfortackle (IRE)**[27] 431 5-9-7 **65** JimCrowley 3 71
(Derek Shaw) *hld up in rr: drvn and gd hdwy over 1f out: str run fnl f to ld last strides* **3/1**[1]
21-4 **2** shd **Amethyst Dawn (IRE)**[5] 728 7-9-5 **63** (t) EddieAhern 8 69
(J R Jenkins) *chsd ldr: led appr fnl 2f: hrd pressed ins fnl f but kpt narrow advantage tl hdd last strides* **5/1**[3]
-326 **3** nk **Rose Garnet (IRE)**[12] 640 5-8-7 **58** RyanTate(7) 4 63
(Tony Carroll) *chsd ldrs: pushed along to chal over 1f out: styd upsides ins fnl f: edgd lft clsng stages: no ex last strides* **7/2**[2]
00-4 **4** 1 ½ **Dressed In Lace**[19] 535 4-9-7 **65** IanMongan 7 66
(Jo Crowley) *t.k.h: in tch: pushed along over 2f out: rdn and styd on to press ldrs ins fnl f: one pce whn tightened up fnl 50yds and dropped to 4th* **5/1**[3]
0-50 **5** 1 **Avonvalley**[16] 582 6-9-7 **65** AdamKirby 1 63
(Peter Grayson) *in rr: drvn over 2f out: styd on u.p fnl f: nt rch ldrs* **7/1**
556- **6** 1 ½ **Catflap (IRE)**[179] 5774 4-9-2 **60** WilliamCarson 5 53
(Derek Haydn Jones) *towards rr: hdwy over 2f out: nvr rchd ldrs: edgd lft over 1f out and sn btn* **16/1**
05-0 **7** nk **Athwaab**[5] 728 6-9-1 **59** AndreaAtzeni 2 53
(Noel Chance) *chsd ldrs: drvn and checked bnd 3f out: chsd ldrs over 2f out: hmpd and wknd over 1f out* **7/1**
00-5 **8** hd **Demoiselle Bond**[28] 421 5-9-0 **58** JackMitchell 6 50
(Lydia Richards) *sn led: t.k.h: hdd appr fnl 2f: wknd fnl f* **25/1**

1m 13.44s (0.34) **Going Correction** +0.10s/f (Slow) **8** Ran SP% **115.3**
Speed ratings (Par 100): **101,100,100,98,97 95,94,94**
toteswingers 1&2 £3.00, 1&3 £2.80, 2&3 £3.40 CSF £18.49 CT £54.38 TOTE £2.80: £1.60, £1.90, £1.90; EX 10.30 Trifecta £26.60 Pool: £2866.43 - 80.75 winning units..
Owner Shakespeare Racing **Bred** Pat Fullam **Trained** Sproxton, Leics
FOCUS
The pace was fair for this fillies' handicap, with three in a line passing the post.

791 BETVICTOR CHELTENHAM FESTIVAL ANTEPOST PIONEERS CLASSIFIED CLAIMING STKS 1m (P)
3:50 (3:51) (Class 5) 4-Y-0+ **£2,587** (£770; £384; £192) **Stalls** Low

Form RPR
3-42 **1** **Exceedexpectations (IRE)**[24] 478 4-8-11 68 WilliamTwiston-Davies(5) 3 74+
(Michael Bell) *hld up in tch: trckd ldrs: travelling wl 2f out: drvn to press ldrs between horses ins fnl f: led last strides* **11/4**[1]
6651 **2** shd **Officer In Command (USA)**[11] 652 7-8-13 66 (v) RobertWinston 6 71
(Sean Curran) *s.i.s: in rr but in tch: hdwy over 2f out: drvn to ld over 1f out: hrd pressed but kpt slt ld ins fnl f: hdd last strides* **9/2**[3]
60-3 **3** shd **Alhaban (IRE)**[3] 747 7-8-13 68 JamieSpencer 4 71
(Ronald Harris) *in rr: drvn over 2f out: hdwy over 1f out: str chal fr ins fnl f tl no ex last strides* **3/1**[2]
-223 **4** 2 ¾ **Hierarch (IRE)**[18] 546 6-8-10 66 (p) AliceHaynes(7) 7 68
(David Simcock) *towards rr but in tch: sme hdwy on outside 3f out: shkn up and one pce over 2f out: pushed along and kpt on to take 4th fnl 110yds but no ch w ldng trio* **6/1**
2345 **5** 1 ½ **Abhaath (USA)**[7] 705 4-8-11 63 WilliamCarson 1 59
(Ronald Harris) *t.k.h: chsd ldrs: rdn over 1f out: sn one pce* **12/1**
100- **6** ½ **King Vahe (IRE)**[131] 7171 4-9-2 70 MichaelJMMurphy(5) 2 68
(Alan Jarvis) *t.k.h: sn led: jnd 2f out: hdd over 1f out: wknd ins fnl f* **12/1**
-241 **7** ¾ **Gunner Will (IRE)**[12] 633 4-8-9 61 FergusSweeney 5 54
(Jamie Osborne) *sn chsng ldr: drvn to chal 2f out: wknd 1f out* **8/1**

1m 39.77s (-0.03) **Going Correction** +0.10s/f (Slow) **7** Ran SP% **110.6**
Speed ratings (Par 103): **104,103,103,101,99 99,98**
toteswingers 1&2 £2.90, 1&3 £2.50, 2&3 £3.40 CSF £14.34 TOTE £3.00: £1.70, £2.70; EX 12.10 Trifecta £40.50 Pool: £2234.14 - 41.31 winning units..Gunner Will was claimed by Mr P. T. Midgley for £4,000
Owner Malcolm Caine **Bred** R S Cockerill (farms) Ltd & Peter Dodd **Trained** Newmarket, Suffolk
FOCUS
A tight claimer that was run at a steady pace.

792 BETVICTOR NON-RUNNER FREE BET AT CHELTENHAM H'CAP (LONDON MILE QUALIFIER) 1m (P)
4:20 (4:20) (Class 4) (0-85,85) 4-Y-0+ **£4,690** (£1,395; £697; £348) **Stalls** Low

Form RPR
1033 **1** **Loyalty**[12] 644 6-9-0 **85** (v) AdamMcLean(7) 3 99
(Derek Shaw) *led 1f: styd trcking ldr: led again over 4f out: rdn over 1f out and sn jnd: strly chal fr ins fnl f: jst hld on* **10/1**
511- **2** shd **Guest Of Honour (IRE)**[67] 8181 4-9-7 **85** AdamKirby 1 99
(Marco Botti) *chsd ldrs: wnt 2nd ins fnl 3f: drvn to chal thrght fnl f: kpt on wl u.p: jst failed* **10/11**[1]
01-2 **3** 5 **Stir Trader (IRE)**[46] 133 4-9-0 **78** JimCrowley 8 81
(Philip Hide) *in tch: hdwy over 2f out: styd on for 3rd fnl f but no ch w ldng duo* **6/1**[2]
000- **4** 1 ¾ **Perfect Cracker**[205] 4805 5-8-10 **81** RyanTate(7) 6 79
(Clive Cox) *chsd ldrs: rdn and outpcd 2f out: lost 3rd fnl f* **25/1**
214- **5** ¾ **Pearl Nation (USA)**[198] 5110 4-9-2 **80** WilliamCarson 4 77
(Brian Baugh) *t.k.h in rr: drvn and hdwy fr 2f out: styd on same pce fnl f* **12/1**
10-6 **6** shd **Trois Vallees (USA)**[55] 6 4-9-1 **79** ShaneKelly 5 76
(James Tate) *in tch: chsd ldrs: drvn over 2f out: wknd over 1f out* **25/1**
10-0 **7** 1 **Brocklebank (IRE)**[12] 629 4-8-11 **75** JamieSpencer 7 69
(Simon Dow) *stdd s: in rr: pushed along over 2f out: sme hdwy fnl f* **33/1**
050- **8** 2 ½ **Dutch Old Master**[220] 4288 4-8-13 **77** FergusSweeney 11 65
(Gary Moore) *in rr: pushed along fr 2f out: sme late prog* **14/1**
00-2 **9** 3 ½ **Kindia (IRE)**[28] 415 5-8-8 **72** JimmyQuinn 10 52
(Michael Attwater) *in rr: sme hdwy and drvn over 2f out: wknd wl over 1f out* **20/1**
0-65 **10** 5 **Prince Of Burma (IRE)**[33] 345 5-9-0 **78** RobertWinston 9 47
(Jeremy Gask) *led after 1f tl hung lft over 4f out: wd bnd 3f out: wknd 2f out* **8/1**[3]
360- **11** 2 **Greensward**[191] 5342 7-9-7 **85** EddieAhern 2 49
(Mike Murphy) *in tch: hdwy 3f out: rdn over 2f out: wknd wl over 1f out* **20/1**

1m 37.99s (-1.81) **Going Correction** +0.10s/f (Slow) **11** Ran SP% **121.4**
Speed ratings (Par 105): **113,112,107,106,105 105,104,101,98,93 91**
toteswingers 1&2 £4.10, 1&3 £7.30, 2&3 £1.40 CSF £18.81 CT £67.98 TOTE £14.70: £3.50, £1.20, £1.50; EX 32.80 Trifecta £110.60 Pool: £2653.29 - 17.97 winning units..
Owner Brian Johnson (Northamptonshire) **Bred** Ecoutila Partnership **Trained** Sproxton, Leics
■ Adam McLean's first winner.
FOCUS
This fair handicap was run at a honest pace with the front two pulling clear and fighting out another thrilling finish.

793 BETVICTOR EXCLUSIVE ANTEPOST OFFER CHELTENHAM 2013 H'CAP 7f (P)
4:50 (4:50) (Class 5) (0-75,75) 3-Y-O **£2,587** (£770; £384; £192) **Stalls** Low

Form RPR
41 **1** **Poet's Prospect (IRE)**[33] 332 3-9-3 **71** AdamKirby 3 82+
(Marco Botti) *hld up in 3rd: hdwy over 2f out: drvn to ld over 1f out: pushed out fnl 50yds: comf* **5/2**[2]
1- **2** ½ **Line Of Reason (IRE)**[151] 6609 3-9-7 **75** JamieSpencer 2 83
(David Simcock) *hld up in 4th: hdwy 2f out: drvn to chse wnr 1f out: kpt on u.p fnl f: readily hld fnl 50yds* **11/10**[1]
41-4 **3** 4 ½ **Overrider**[19] 533 3-9-7 **75** (t) RobertWinston 1 71
(Charles Hills) *led: rdn along over 2f out: hdd over 1f out: wknd fnl f* **5/1**[3]

32-4 **4** 1 **Minimee**[10] 663 3-8-13 **67** JimCrowley 4 60
(Alan Bailey) *chsd ldr: rdn 2f out and sn lost 2nd: wknd fnl f* **5/1**[3]

1m 28.45s (2.45) **Going Correction** +0.10s/f (Slow) **4** Ran SP% **109.5**
Speed ratings (Par 97): **90,89,84,83**
CSF £5.77 TOTE £2.90; EX 6.30 Trifecta £8.30 Pool: £1178.34 - 105.80 winning units..
Owner Ahmed Ali **Bred** Rabbah Bloodstock Limited **Trained** Newmarket, Suffolk

FOCUS
An interesting handicap despite the small field size. It was run at a steady pace and the market leaders pulled clear.

794 FOLLOW US ON TWITTER @BETVICTORRACING H'CAP 7f (P)
5:20 (5:20) (Class 6) (0-55,55) 4-Y-O+ **£1,940** (£577; £288; £144) **Stalls** Low

Form RPR
6522 **1** **Athletic**[4] 737 4-9-5 53 (v) EddieAhern 2 62+
(J R Jenkins) *trckd ldrs: drvn to ld 1f out: styd on wl clsng stages* **7/4**[2]
0001 **2** nk **Greek Islands (IRE)**[4] 733 5-9-3 51 6ex LiamKeniry 4 60
(Ed de Giles) *hld up in rr but in tch: hdwy travelling wl appr fnl f: sn drvn to chse wnr: kpt on but a hld* **13/8**[1]
660- **3** 2 1/2 **Custom House (IRE)**[96] 7816 5-9-3 51 KirstyMilczarek 3 53
(John E Long) *led: rdn 2f out: hdd 1f out: styd on same pce* **10/1**
0050 **4** nk **Dingaan (IRE)**[11] 655 10-8-12 46 oh1 FergusSweeney 6 47
(Peter Grayson) *stdd s: towards rr: drvn and hdwy over 1f out: kpt on u.p fnl f: nt rch ldrs* **25/1**
-000 **5** 1 **Doctor Hilary**[12] 630 11-8-5 46 oh1 (v) PhilipPrince(7) 9 45
(Mark Hoad) *chsd ldrs: rdn over 2f out: wknd ins fnl f* **50/1**
3206 **6** 2 1/2 **Mataajir (USA)**[13] 618 5-8-13 54 AdamMcLean(7) 10 46
(Derek Shaw) *chsd ldrs: rdn ins fnl 2f: sn wknd* **6/1**[3]
60-0 **7** 5 **Yalding Dancer**[11] 655 4-9-2 50 RobertWinston 1 29
(John Best) *outpcd most of way* **20/1**
2-00 **8** 2 1/4 **Signora Frasi (IRE)**[11] 655 8-9-5 53 WilliamCarson 11 26
(Tony Newcombe) *s.i.s: in rr: hdwy on outside fr 4f out: rdn 3f out: wknd 2f out* **14/1**

1m 25.84s (-0.16) **Going Correction** +0.10s/f (Slow) **8** Ran SP% **115.1**
Speed ratings (Par 101): **104,103,100,100,99 96,90,88**
toteswingers 1&2 £1.10, 1&3 £3.30, 2&3 £4.70 CSF £4.88 CT £19.17 TOTE £2.10: £1.10, £1.10, £4.40; EX 4.70 Trifecta £20.20 Pool: £1305.36 - 48.31 winning units..
Owner A S Reid **Bred** A S Reid **Trained** Royston, Herts

FOCUS
A modest contest run at a fair pace with the markets leaders dominating.
T/Plt: £12.20 to a £1 stake. Pool: £56575.73 - 3360.70 winning units T/Qpdt: £5.10 to a £1 stake. Pool: £3498.12 - 505.97 winning units ST

754 WOLVERHAMPTON (A.W) (L-H)
Monday, February 25

OFFICIAL GOING: Standard
Wind: Fresh against Weather: Overcast

795 PICK THE BEST BOOKIES AT BOOKMAKERS.CO.UK H'CAP 5f 20y(P)
2:30 (2:30) (Class 5) (0-75,75) 4-Y-O+ **£2,587** (£770; £384; £192) **Stalls** Low

Form RPR
3550 **1** **Lucky Dan (IRE)**[16] 593 7-9-4 72 FrannyNorton 10 81
(Paul Green) *sn pushed along to chse ldrs: rdn to ld ins fnl f: r.o* **12/1**
2611 **2** 3/4 **Holy Angel (IRE)**[17] 558 4-8-9 70 (e) RachelRichardson(7) 7 76+
(Tim Easterby) *s.i.s: hld up: r.o wl ins fnl f: nt rch wnr* **5/2**[1]
50-3 **3** shd **Wicked Wench**[34] 316 4-8-9 70 RobertTart(7) 6 76
(Jeremy Gask) *a.p: pushed along 1/2-way: rdn over 1f out: r.o* **10/1**
11-1 **4** 1 **Monumental Man**[45] 156 4-9-5 73 (p) DavidProbert 9 75
(James Unett) *chsd ldrs: hung rt 1/2-way: rdn over 1f out: styd on same pce ins fnl f* **7/1**
555 **5** nk **Quality Art (USA)**[5] 719 5-8-13 67 RobbieFitzpatrick 4 68
(Richard Guest) *hld up: hdwy over 1f out: r.o: nrst fin* **7/1**
-044 **6** shd **Crimson Queen**[17] 558 6-8-11 68 (b) MarkCoumbe(3) 3 69
(Roy Brotherton) *chsd ldrs: rdn and ev ch ins fnl f: styd on same pce* **22/1**
-312 **7** hd **Cardinal**[24] 481 8-9-7 75 HayleyTurner 8 75
(Robert Cowell) *sn pushed along in rr: r.o wl ins fnl f: nt rch ldrs* **9/2**[3]
4111 **8** 3/4 **M J Woodward**[12] 640 4-9-1 69 JoeFanning 5 66
(Paul Green) *sn led: rdn over 1f out: hdd and unable qck ins fnl f* **4/1**[2]
00-0 **9** 3/4 **Ingleby Star (IRE)**[17] 558 8-8-4 61 oh1 (p) JulieBurke(3) 1 56
(Ian McInnes) *broke wl and stmbld s: sn hdd: chsd ldrs: rdn 1/2-way: edgd lft and no ex ins fnl f* **33/1**
0-00 **10** 1 **Elusive Hawk (IRE)**[11] 650 9-8-11 65 TomMcLaughlin 2 56
(David Evans) *in rr: pushed along 1/2-way: running on wl whn eased towards fin* **33/1**
0-06 **11** 1 **Lady Royale**[27] 431 5-9-4 72 (p) MichaelO'Connell 11 60
(Geoffrey Oldroyd) *sn outpcd* **50/1**

1m 1.72s (-0.58) **Going Correction** +0.20s/f (Slow) **11** Ran SP% **120.7**
Speed ratings (Par 103): **112,110,110,109,108 108,108,106,105,104 102**
toteswingers 1&2 £12.90, 1&3 £16.40, 2&3 £10.20 CSF £42.14 CT £327.45 TOTE £12.60: £3.40, £1.20, £3.70; EX 56.40 Trifecta £243.80 Pool: £1719.84 - 5.29 winning units..
Owner Paul Green (Oaklea) **Bred** Mountarmstrong Stud **Trained** Lydiate, Merseyside

FOCUS
They were closing well from behind at the finish but the winner had just enough left in the tank to hold them off.

796 FIND THE BEST ODDS AT BOOKMAKERS.CO.UK MAIDEN STKS 5f 216y(P)
3:00 (3:01) (Class 5) 3-Y-O+ **£2,587** (£770; £384; £192) **Stalls** Low

Form RPR
222- **1** **Flashlight (IRE)**[107] 7686 3-8-12 80 JoeFanning 2 83+
(Mark Johnston) *chsd ldr tl led 2f out: rdn and hung rt ins fnl f: r.o: readily* **1/3**[1]
3-62 **2** 5 **Loulou Vuitton**[17] 561 3-8-7 60 (p) AndrewMullen 6 61
(Brian Baugh) *chsd ldrs: rdn over 1f out: wnt 2nd ins fnl f: styd on same pce* **9/1**[3]
3 2 1/4 **Time To Begin (IRE)**[66] 8215 3-8-13 0 ow1 SebSanders 8 60
(David C Griffiths) *led 4f: sn rdn: no ex fnl f* **7/1**[2]
5- **4** 1 **Whatwehavewehold**[229] 3973 3-8-5 0 (t) GaryPhillips(7) 7 56
(Alan McCabe) *hld up: rdn over 2f out: nt trble ldrs* **10/1**
00- **5** 3 1/2 **Brynford**[173] 5932 3-8-7 0 HayleyTurner 1 41
(Chris Dwyer) *prom: rdn 1/2-way: wknd over 1f out* **33/1**
6 19 **Satwa's Sister** 3-8-0 0 HannahNunn(7) 3
(Robert Cowell) *s.i.s: outpcd: t.o* **22/1**
0 **7** 2 **Just Gwen**[16] 590 4-9-8 0 (p) DuranFentiman 5
(Brian Baugh) *hld up: wknd 1/2-way: t.o* **200/1**

1m 14.48s (-0.52) **Going Correction** +0.20s/f (Slow)
WFA 3 from 4yo 15lb **7** Ran SP% **114.4**
Speed ratings (Par 103): **111,104,101,100,95 70,67**
toteswingers 1&2 £1.30, 1&3 £1.60, 2&3 £2.30 CSF £4.26 TOTE £1.20: £1.20, £2.20; EX 4.30 Trifecta £9.60 Pool: £4037.02 - 312.65 winning units..
Owner Sheikh Hamdan Bin Mohammed Al Maktoum **Bred** Gerry Smith **Trained** Middleham Moor, N Yorks

FOCUS
This proved pretty straightforward for the favourite.

797 CORAL.CO.UK H'CAP 1m 4f 50y(P)
3:30 (3:30) (Class 5) (0-75,75) 4-Y-O+ **£2,587** (£770; £384; £192) **Stalls** Low

Form RPR
4-21 **1** **Wordiness**[21] 520 5-8-9 70 RobertTart(7) 4 79
(Brendan Powell) *mde all: set stdy pce tl qcknd over 2f out: sn clr: rdn over 1f out: styd on* **1/1**[1]
0-6P **2** 1 **All The Winds (GER)**[35] 309 8-9-7 75 (t) HayleyTurner 1 82
(Shaun Lycett) *dwlt: hld up: hdwy to go 2nd over 1f out: sn rdn: styd on: nt rch wnr* **12/1**
533- **3** 12 **Rawaafed (IRE)**[143] 6842 4-9-2 73 JoeFanning 5 61
(Keith Dalgleish) *trckd wnr to 1/2-way: rdn over 2f out: wknd over 1f out* **7/4**[2]
5-11 **4** nse **Waving**[16] 592 4-9-3 74 (t) DavidProbert 2 62
(Tony Carroll) *prom: chsd wnr 1/2-way: rdn over 2f out: wknd over 1f out* **10/3**[3]

2m 43.53s (2.43) **Going Correction** +0.20s/f (Slow)
WFA 4 from 5yo+ 3lb **4** Ran SP% **117.1**
Speed ratings (Par 103): **99,98,90,90**
CSF £12.57 TOTE £2.20; EX 18.00 Trifecta £37.30 Pool: £1718.22 - 34.53 winning units..
Owner W A Harrison-Allan **Bred** Juddmonte Farms Ltd **Trained** Upper Lambourn, Berks

FOCUS
Modest handicap form, with the first two well clear.

798 WIN MORE ON BETTING AT BOOKMAKERS.CO.UK APPRENTICE H'CAP 1m 1f 103y(P)
4:00 (4:00) (Class 5) (0-70,70) 4-Y-O+ **£2,587** (£770; £384; £192) **Stalls** Low

Form RPR
-152 **1** **Travelling**[5] 720 4-9-2 68 GeorgeDowning(3) 3 77+
(Tony Carroll) *a.p: racd keenly: chsd clr ldr over 5f out: rdn to ld 1f out: r.o* **3/1**[2]
-546 **2** 1 1/4 **Jordaura**[10] 672 7-8-0 56 oh1 JordanHibberd(7) 6 62
(Alan Berry) *racd keenly: prom: led 7f out: rdn and hung rt wl over 1f out: hdd 1f out: styd on same pce* **20/1**
0-30 **3** 2 1/2 **Cheers For Thea (IRE)**[28] 429 8-9-3 66 (bt) DarylByrne 2 67+
(Tim Easterby) *s.i.s: hld up: hdwy on outer over 2f out: rdn over 1f out: styd on* **11/2**
0/05 **4** shd **Platinum (IRE)**[10] 672 6-9-2 70 EvaMoscrop(5) 4 71
(Philip Kirby) *racd keenly: led: hdd 7f out: chsd ldr tl over 5f out: pushed along over 2f out: hung lft over 1f out: styd on* **14/1**
42-1 **5** hd **Silver Alliance**[24] 477 5-9-0 68 ShelleyBirkett(5) 5 68+
(Julia Feilden) *hld up: plld hrd: hdwy over 2f out: rdn over 1f out: styd on same pce fnl f* **9/4**[1]
5652 **6** 1 1/2 **Follow The Flag (IRE)**[6] 718 9-9-1 67 (be) RobertTart(3) 1 64
(Alan McCabe) *hld up: rdn over 2f out: nvr on terms* **4/1**[3]
3114 **7** 3/4 **Faithful Ruler (USA)**[10] 672 9-8-12 64 (p) GaryPhillips(3) 7 60
(Ronald Harris) *plld hrd and prom: rdn over 2f out: sn outpcd* **8/1**

2m 8.03s (6.33) **Going Correction** +0.20s/f (Slow) **7** Ran SP% **113.7**
Speed ratings (Par 103): **79,77,75,75,75 74,73**
toteswingers 1&2 £13.70, 1&3 £2.60, 2&3 £11.00 CSF £55.08 TOTE £4.10: £2.30, £8.60; EX 92.60 Trifecta £239.80 Pool: £2698.28 - 8.43 winning units..
Owner Longview Stud & Bloodstock Ltd **Bred** Longview Stud & Bloodstock Ltd **Trained** Cropthorne, Worcs

FOCUS
There was very little pace on early as nothing wanted to go on.

799 POKER AT CORAL.CO.UK MAIDEN STKS 1m 1f 103y(P)
4:30 (4:30) (Class 5) 3-Y-O **£2,587** (£770; £384; £192) **Stalls** Low

Form RPR
6- **1** **Majeed**[100] 7780 3-9-5 0 MartinLane 5 79
(David Simcock) *chsd ldr tl led over 2f out: shkn up and hung lft over 1f out: rdn ins fnl f: r.o* **15/8**[1]
2 1/2 **The Welsh Wizard (IRE)** 3-9-5 0 GrahamLee 1 78+
(Charles Hills) *chsd ldrs: pushed along over 3f out: chsd wnr over 1f out: rdn: hung lft and ev ch ins fnl f: r.o* **9/4**[2]
23-2 **3** 13 **He's A Striker (IRE)**[10] 673 3-9-5 78 BarryMcHugh 2 53
(Tony Coyle) *led: hdd over 2f out: rdn and wknd over 1f out* **5/2**[3]
4 24 **Ambleside** 3-9-5 0 JoeFanning 3
(Mark Johnston) *dwlt: rn green in rr: rdn 4f out: sn lost tch and eased: t.o* **6/1**

2m 3.24s (1.54) **Going Correction** +0.20s/f (Slow) **4** Ran SP% **108.4**
Speed ratings (Par 97): **101,100,89,67**
CSF £6.34 TOTE £3.00; EX 6.70 Trifecta £11.40 Pool: £1808.88 - 118.44 winning units..
Owner Khalifa Dasmal **Bred** Newsells Park Stud & Strategic B'Stock **Trained** Newmarket, Suffolk

FOCUS
A fair maiden.

800 CHOOSE THE RIGHT BOOKIE AT BOOKMAKERS.CO.UK MEDIAN AUCTION MAIDEN STKS 1m 141y(P)
5:00 (5:02) (Class 5) 3-4-Y-O **£2,587** (£770; £384; £192) **Stalls** Low

Form RPR
362- **1** **Mumeyez**[136] 7020 3-8-7 77 (p) RobertHavlin 3 73
(John Gosden) *mde all: pushed clr fr over 2f out: eased ins fnl f* **30/100**[1]
345- **2** 7 **House Of Orange (IRE)**[139] 6947 3-8-7 0 JoeFanning 2 58+
(Mark Johnston) *chsd wnr: rdn over 2f out: styd on same pce* **5/1**[2]
/4- **3** 3 **Giantstepsahead (IRE)**[110] 7625 4-10-0 0 SebSanders 5 55
(Michael Wigham) *stdd s: hld up: racd keenly and hdwy over 5f out: pushed along over 2f out: sn outpcd* **7/1**[3]
4 6 **Inigo Montoya** 3-8-4 0 [1] DeclanCannon(3) 4 36
(Alan McCabe) *prom: lost pl 5f out: rdn and wknd over 2f out* **20/1**

050- **5** *7* **Acton Jenson**[58] 8291 4-10-0 38 J-PGuillambert 1 22
(Brian Baugh) *s.i.s: racd keenly and sn trcking ldrs: rdn over 2f out: sn wknd* **100/1**

1m 53.96s (3.46) **Going Correction** +0.20s/f (Slow)
WFA 3 from 4yo 21lb 5 Ran SP% **111.8**
Speed ratings (Par 103): **92,85,83,77,71**
CSF £2.38 TOTE £1.30: £1.10, £1.90; EX 2.60 Trifecta £5.30 Pool: £2625.43 - 371.41 winning units..
Owner M Al Qatami, K M Al Mudhaf & Ms R Hood **Bred** Pollards Stables **Trained** Newmarket, Suffolk

FOCUS
This proved easy enough for the odds-on favourite.

801 CORAL.CO.UK MOBILE BETTING H'CAP 1m 141y(P)
5:30 (5:30) (Class 6) (0-60,60) 4-Y-0+ **£1,940** (£577; £288; £144) **Stalls** Low

Form RPR

-035 **1** **Chosen Forever**[27] 433 8-9-5 **58** MichaelO'Connell 11 68
(Geoffrey Oldroyd) *s.i.s: sn chsng ldrs: led over 3f out: hung rt fr over 2f out: rdn over 1f out: styd on* **14/1**

-602 **2** *¾* **John Potts**[16] 587 8-9-1 **54** (p) KellyHarrison 4 63
(Brian Baugh) *led: hdd over 5f out: chsd ldrs: rdn over 1f out: styd on* **15/2**

2100 **3** *¾* **Delightful Sleep**[4] 737 5-8-9 **55** EoinWalsh(7) 2 62
(David Evans) *hld up: edgd lft over 2f out: hdwy over 1f out: sn rdn: styd on* **10/1**

1-54 **4** *2 ¼* **Maggie Pink**[14] 617 4-9-5 **58** AndrewMullen 1 60
(Michael Appleby) *prom: rdn over 2f out: styd on same pce fnl f* **14/1**

4-40 **5** *nse* **Mr Chocolate Drop (IRE)**[41] 218 9-9-7 **60** (t) RussKennemore 9 62
(Mandy Rowland) *s.i.s: hld up: hdwy over 1f out: r.o: nt trble ldrs* **20/1**

3-53 **6** *hd* **The Noble Ord**[40] 221 4-8-10 **56** (t) JoshBaudains(7) 8 58
(Sylvester Kirk) *hld up: r.o ins fnl f: nvr nrr* **9/1**

135- **7** *½* **Tatting**[78] 8050 4-9-6 **59** (b[1]) HayleyTurner 10 60
(Chris Dwyer) *s.i.s: hld up: hdwy over 1f out: styd on: nt trble ldrs* **9/4**[1]

3222 **8** *2* **Kielty's Folly**[14] 617 9-9-3 **56** (v) GrahamGibbons 3 53
(Brian Baugh) *hld up: hdwy over 2f out: rdn over 1f out: no ex ins fnl f* **7/1**[3]

50-3 **9** *12* **Rockgoat (IRE)**[18] 545 4-9-4 **57** GrahamLee 5 28
(Ian McInnes) *prom: rdn over 2f out: sn wknd* **8/1**

006- **10** *6* **Gumnd (IRE)**[6] 6309 6-8-7 **46** oh1 (p) JoeFanning 6 5
(Chris Grant) *hld up: rdn over 3f out: wknd over 2f out* **25/1**

3214 **11** *1 ½* **Spinning Ridge (IRE)**[14] 616 8-9-0 **60** (b) GaryPhillips(7) 7 16
(Ronald Harris) *plld hrd and prom: rdn over 2f out: wknd over 1f out* **13/2**[2]

00-0 **12** *3 ¼* **King Of The Moors (USA)**[19] 530 10-8-7 **46** oh1..(b) FrannyNorton 12
(Dai Burchell) *chsd ldrs: led over 5f out: hdd over 3f out: wkng whn hmpd over 2f out* **40/1**

1m 51.39s (0.89) **Going Correction** +0.20s/f (Slow) 12 Ran SP% **122.9**
Speed ratings (Par 101): **104,103,102,100,100 100,100,98,87,82 80,78**
toteswingers 1&2 £20.10, 1&3 £33.00, 2&3 £20.30 CSF £117.05 CT £1135.75 TOTE £18.50: £5.70, £3.00, £3.50; EX 129.00 Trifecta £1103.70 Pool: £1903.91 - 1.29 winning units..
Owner R C Bond **Bred** R C Bond **Trained** Brawby, N Yorks

FOCUS
There wasn't much pace on here and it paid to be prominent.
T/Plt: £85.20 to a £1 stake. Pool: £60391.05 - 516.86 winning units T/Qpdt: £23.20 to a £1 stake. Pool: £4045.94 - 129.04 winning units CR

[774]LINGFIELD (L-H)
Tuesday, February 26

OFFICIAL GOING: Standard
Wind: medium, across Weather: overcast, dry

803 LINGFIELD PARK OWNERS GROUP APPRENTICE H'CAP 1m 2f (P)
2:10 (2:10) (Class 6) (0-65,65) 3-Y-0 **£2,045** (£603; £302) **Stalls** Low

Form RPR

051 **1** **Gabrial The Duke (IRE)**[13] 634 3-8-13 **57** AliceHaynes(3) 4 66+
(David Simcock) *t.k.h: hld up in tch in last pair: hdwy on inner over 1f out: rdn to ld jst ins fnl f: r.o strly: readily* **2/1**[1]

4-13 **2** *shd* **Flying Tempo**[35] 321 3-9-3 **58** (b) AshleyMorgan 6 63
(Ed Dunlop) *stdd s: hld up in tch in last pair: trckd ldrs and gng wl 2f out: shkn up ent fnl f: rdn and styd on same pce fnl f: fin 3rd: plcd 2nd* **9/2**

000- **3** *3* **Haverstock**[136] 7059 3-9-5 **63** RyanTate(3) 1 62
(Mark Johnston) *led: rdn and hdd 2f out: led again 1f out: sn hdd and outpcd by wnr: edgd rt ins fnl f: hld on for 2nd cl home: fin 2nd: disq: plcd 3rd* **5/2**[2]

6412 **4** *½* **Poetic Verse**[13] 634 3-9-4 **62** PatMillman(3) 3 60
(Rod Millman) *chsd ldr: rdn to chal over 2f out: led 2f out: hdd 1f out: sn outpcd by wnr and styd on same pce* **12/1**

3-31 **P** **Crystal Peaks**[20] 534 3-9-7 **65** DavidBergin(3) 2
(James Given) *chsd ldng pair: rdn and ev ch 2f out: lost action over 1f out: sn eased and p.u: fatally injured* **7/2**[3]

2m 7.87s (1.27) **Going Correction** +0.025s/f (Slow) 5 Ran SP% **110.0**
Speed ratings (Par 95): **95,92,92,92,**
CSF £11.14 TOTE £2.40: £2.80, £2.20; EX 11.40 Trifecta £34.90 Pool: £1,761.89 - 37.86 winning units..
Owner Dr Marwan Koukash **Bred** Old Carhue & Graeng Bloodstock **Trained** Newmarket, Suffolk
■ Stewards' Enquiry : Ryan Tate one-day ban: careless riding (12 Mar)

FOCUS
A modest apprentice handicap marred by the fatal injury incurred by Crystal Peaks. There was very little pace on early.

804 CYPRIUM BAR AT MARRIOTT LINGFIELD (S) STKS 1m 2f (P)
2:40 (2:40) (Class 6) 3-Y-0 **£2,045** (£603; £302) **Stalls** Low

Form RPR

-433 **1** **Entrapping**[13] 634 3-8-12 56 SeanLevey 2 61
(Richard Hannon) *chsd ldng pair tl wnt 2nd over 4f out: rdn to ld over 1f out: drvn and kpt on ins fnl f* **9/4**[2]

00-5 **2** *1 ¾* **Aphrodite Spirit (IRE)**[21] 527 3-8-7 45 JoeFanning 7 52
(Pat Eddery) *led: rdn and hdd over 1f out: styd on same pce u.p ins fnl f* **14/1**

0612 **3** *hd* **Misleading Promise (IRE)**[6] 726 3-9-4 69 (t) AdamKirby 6 63
(John Butler) *hld up in last pair: rdn and effrt ent fnl f: drvn and styd on same pce ins fnl f* **5/4**[1]

540- **4** *2 ¾* **Warrant Officer**[75] 8094 3-8-7 56 CharlesBishop(5) 3 51
(Mick Channon) *in tch: chsd ldng pair wl over 2f out tl over 1f out: 4th and btn ins fnl f: plugged on* **8/1**

535 **5** *8* **Rosie Future (IRE)**[7] 717 3-8-7 53 DavidProbert 4 30
(Rae Guest) *chsd ldr tl wl over 2f out: sn struggling u.p: wknd 2f out* **5/1**[3]

0046 **6** *1 ½* **Kalahari Breeze (IRE)**[12] 651 3-8-7 50 WilliamCarson 1 27
(William Muir) *a bhd: lost tch u.p 2f out* **50/1**

2m 5.2s (-1.40) **Going Correction** +0.025s/f (Slow) 6 Ran SP% **111.6**
Speed ratings (Par 95): **106,104,104,102,95 94**
Tote Swingers: 1&2 £3.90, 1&3 £1.10, 2&3 £4.60 CSF £30.24 TOTE £3.40: £1.20, £8.00; EX 32.40 Trifecta £96.00 Pool: £1,959.35 - 15.29 winning units..No bid for the winner.
Owner Ben CM Wong **Bred** K Snell **Trained** East Everleigh, Wilts

FOCUS
A poor seller in which the two market leaders had not convinced with their attitude in their recent starts. The pace was solid, though, and the winning time was 2.67 seconds faster than the opener.

805 FOLLOW US ON TWITTER @LINGFIELDPARK H'CAP 1m (P)
3:10 (3:10) (Class 6) (0-60,60) 4-Y-0+ **£2,045** (£603; £302) **Stalls** High

Form RPR

60-0 **1** **Indian Violet (IRE)**[23] 510 7-8-11 50 (p) LiamKeniry 1 56
(Zoe Davison) *hld up in midfield: clsd and gng wl 2f out: swtchd lft and effrt over 1f out: rdn and led wl ins fnl f: hld on cl home* **16/1**

4316 **2** *nse* **Lieutenant Dan (IRE)**[19] 546 6-9-4 57 (v) AndrewMullen 6 63
(Michael Appleby) *in tch: rdn and effrt to chse ldrs wl over 1f out: styd on u.p and ev ch wl ins fnl f: jst hld* **7/1**

0000 **3** *1* **Fairy Wing (IRE)**[10] 688 6-9-2 55 WilliamCarson 9 59
(Violet M Jordan) *taken down early: led: rdn over 1f out: drvn ins fnl f: hdd and no ex wl ins fnl f* **12/1**

5002 **4** *2 ½* **Amber Moon**[11] 664 8-8-5 49 oh1 ow3 AnnStokell(5) 10 47
(Ann Stokell) *towards rr: rdn along over 4f out: styd on wl ins fnl f: nvr trbld ldrs* **33/1**

0-41 **5** *hd* **Strategic Action (IRE)**[34] 335 4-9-3 56 RobertHavlin 8 53
(Linda Jewell) *t.k.h: chsd ldrs: rdn and effrt 2f out: no ex u.p 1f out: wknd wl ins fnl f* **11/4**[2]

5-51 **6** *shd* **Fonterutoli (IRE)**[23] 510 6-9-4 57 (e) AdamKirby 7 54
(Roger Ingram) *chsd ldr: drvn over 2f out: nt qckn over 1f out: wknd ins fnl f* **9/4**[1]

-060 **7** *2 ¼* **Menadati (USA)**[13] 626 5-9-4 57 ChrisCatlin 2 49
(Peter Hiatt) *t.k.h: chsd ldrs: rdn and unable qck over 2f out: wknd u.p over 1f out* **4/1**[3]

0560 **8** *2* **Lady Prodee**[15] 611 5-9-4 57 SebSanders 4 44
(Bill Turner) *hld up in last pair: rdn and effrt on outer wl over 1f out: no imp* **14/1**

0-00 **9** *nk* **Total Obsession**[11] 662 6-8-0 46 oh1 (v) PhilipPrince(7) 3 33
(Mark Hoad) *a towards rr: rdn 4f out: n.d:* **66/1**

-000 **10** *12* **Trip Switch**[16] 600 7-9-7 60 IanMongan 5 19
(John Butler) *a towards rr: rdn 4f out: wknd 2f out: bhd fnl f* **20/1**

1m 37.77s (-0.43) **Going Correction** +0.025s/f (Slow) 10 Ran SP% **119.4**
Speed ratings (Par 101): **103,102,101,99,99 99,96,94,94,82**
Tote Swingers: 1&2 £19.80, 1&3 £18.70, 2&3 £10.10 CSF £124.11 CT £1441.14 TOTE £20.60: £2.70, £1.90, £2.40; EX 200.20 Trifecta £1060.10 Part won. Pool: £1,413.56 - 0.28 winning units..
Owner Macable Partnership **Bred** James F Hanly **Trained** Hammerwood, E Sussex

FOCUS
A modest handicap.

806 BREATHE SPA AT MARRIOTT LINGFIELD H'CAP 7f (P)
3:40 (3:40) (Class 6) (0-60,60) 4-Y-0+ **£2,045** (£603; £302) **Stalls** Low

Form RPR

5-22 **1** **West Leake (IRE)**[33] 347 7-9-5 **58** LiamKeniry 9 66
(Paul Burgoyne) *stdd s: hld up in tch in rr: hdwy and pushed along ent fnl 2f: rdn and str run ins fnl f to ld last strides* **7/2**[2]

-243 **2** *nk* **Spin Again (IRE)**[4] 749 8-9-7 **60** MichaelO'Connell 6 67
(John Ryan) *wl in tch in midfield on outer: effrt and rdn to chse ldrs 2f out: rdn to ld ins fnl f: r.o wl tl hdd and no ex last strides* **2/1**[1]

250- **3** *1 ¼* **Mudhish (IRE)**[145] 6812 8-9-7 **60** (b) FrederikTylicki 4 64
(Clive Brittain) *hld up wl in tch in last quartet: nt clr run 2f out: rdn and hdwy ent fnl f: chsd ldng pair ins fnl f: kpt on but no imp towards fin* **7/1**

0342 **4** *hd* **Titan Diamond (IRE)**[18] 565 5-8-2 **46** oh1 RachealKneller(5) 8 49
(Mark Usher) *awkward leaving stalls: in tch in rr: c wd and effrt over 1f out: r.o wl ins fnl f: nvr trbld ldrs* **10/1**

-630 **5** *¾* **Purley Queen (IRE)**[11] 665 4-8-11 **57** JoshBaudains(7) 3 58
(Sylvester Kirk) *hld up wl in tch in last quartet: nt clr run and swtchd rt 1f out: kpt on ins fnl f: nvr trbld ldrs* **8/1**

0-43 **6** *nse* **Mack's Sister**[18] 559 6-9-5 **58** (p) JimCrowley 2 59
(Dean Ivory) *chsd ldrs: rdn and effrt to press ldrs over 1f out: no ex ins fnl f: wknd towards fin* **5/1**[3]

000- **7** *hd* **The Dancing Lord**[76] 8077 4-8-13 **59** (b[1]) RyanWhile(7) 7 59
(Bill Turner) *t.k.h: w ldr tl led over 4f out: rdn wl over 1f out: hdd & wknd ins fnl f* **33/1**

60-1 **8** *½* **Chandrayaan**[12] 655 6-8-11 **50** (v) KirstyMilczarek 1 49
(John E Long) *chsd ldrs: rdn and unable qck over 1f out: wknd u.p ins fnl f* **12/1**

6000 **9** *8* **Amenable (IRE)**[10] 687 6-9-5 **58** (e) WilliamCarson 5 35
(Violet M Jordan) *taken down down early and led to post: led tl over 4f out: w ldr tl struggling jst over 2f out: sn wknd* **20/1**

1m 25.26s (0.46) **Going Correction** +0.025s/f (Slow) 9 Ran SP% **120.3**
Speed ratings (Par 101): **98,97,96,96,95 95,94,94,85**
Tote Swingers: 1&2 £2.20, 1&3 £4.00, 2&3 £3.30 CSF £11.45 CT £47.71 TOTE £3.40: £1.70, £1.30, £2.10; EX 9.90 Trifecta £95.10 Pool: £3,267.94 - 25.76 winning units..
Owner Mrs C Leigh-Turner **Bred** Rathbarry Stud **Trained** Shepton Montague, Somerset

FOCUS
Another modest handicap and they finished in a bit of a heap.

807 PLAY GOLF AT LINGFIELD PARK RESORT MAIDEN STKS 7f (P)
4:10 (4:13) (Class 5) 3-Y-0+ **£2,726** (£805; £402) **Stalls** Low

Form RPR

53 **1** **Botteen (IRE)**[13] 636 3-8-9 0 AdamBeschizza 1 69
(William Haggas) *chsd ldr tl over 5f out: styd chsng ldrs tl rdn to ld 1f out: r.o wl: jst hld on* **5/1**[3]

2 *nse* **Storm (IRE)** 3-8-4 0 WilliamCarson 4 64+
(Charles Hills) *hld up in tch in rr of main gp: hdwy over 2f out: chsng ldrs and swtchd rt 1f out: chsd wnr fnl f: r.o strly towards fin: jst failed* **7/4**[1]

0- **3** *1 ½* **On With The Dance (IRE)**[89] 7923 3-8-9 0 JamieSpencer 7 65
(Ed Vaughan) *chsd ldrs: unable qck and sltly outpcd jst over 1f out: rallied u.p and kpt on again ins fnl f* **11/4**[2]

260- **4** *½* **The Scuttler (IRE)**[145] 6815 3-8-2 68 DanielCremin(7) 6 63+
(Mick Channon) *hld up in tch in rr od main gp: rdn and hdwy jst over 1f out: styng and swtchd rt ins fnl f: r.o but nvr trbld ldrs* **7/1**

44 5 nse **Laudation**[34] 341 3-8-9 0 JimmyQuinn 3 63
(William Jarvis) *chsd ldrs: effrt u.p over 1f out: unable qck and styd on same pce ins fnl f* **25/1**

4 6 ¾ **Floralys (USA)**[12] 651 4-9-7 73 (p) AdamKirby 10 62
(John Butler) *mde most: drvn and hdd 1f out: no ex u.p: wknd ins fnl f* **12/1**

43 7 hd **Wotabooty**[20] 532 3-7-11 0 NoelGarbutt(7) 8 56
(Hugo Palmer) *t.k.h: hld up in tch in rr of main gp: swtchd rt and wd bnd wl over 1f out: lost pl looked wl hld 1f out: styd on fnl f: nvr trbld ldrs* **20/1**

0- 8 1 **World Map (IRE)**[117] 7506 3-8-4 0 JoeFanning 9 53
(Mark Johnston) *wl in tch in midfield on outer: rdn and no prog over 1f out: styd on same pce fnl f* **12/1**

9 hd **Arjawan** 3-8-9 0 ChrisCatlin 5 58
(Clive Brittain) *awkward leaving stalls and slowly away: rn v green and detached in last early: clsd on to bk of field 4f out: rdn and no imp fr wl over 1f out* **20/1**

00- 10 nk **Boyzee**[83] 7988 5-9-12 0 RobertHavlin 2 63?
(Linda Jewell) *in tch in midfield: effrt on inner over 1f out: rdn and no hdwy 1f out: wknd ins fnl f* **100/1**

4033 11 9 **Island Express (IRE)**[11] 667 6-9-7 52 (tp) AnnStokell(5) 11 38
(Ann Stokell) *t.k.h: jnd ldr over 5f out: rdn and struggling jst over 2f out: sn wknd: bhd fnl f* **100/1**

1m 25.89s (1.09) **Going Correction** +0.025s/f (Slow)
WFA 3 from 4yo+ 17lb 11 Ran SP% 122.9
Speed ratings (Par 103): **94,93,92,91,91 90,90,89,89,88 78**
Tote Swingers: 1&2 £2.60, 1&3 £4.30, 2&3 £1.90 CSF £14.17 TOTE £6.60: £2.20, £1.50, £1.40; EX 23.50 Trifecta £73.10 Pool: £3,216.58 - 32.96 winning units..
Owner Sheikh Ahmed Al Maktoum **Bred** Mrs Chris Harrington **Trained** Newmarket, Suffolk

FOCUS
Not a strong maiden.

808 BREATHE SPA AT MARRIOTT LINGFIELD MAIDEN STKS 6f (P)
4:40 (4:41) (Class 5) 3-Y-O £2,726 (£805; £402) Stalls Low

Form RPR

4 1 **Nellie Bly**[8] 706 3-9-0 0 JoeFanning 3 68
(Mark Johnston) *chsd ldr: rdn and chal over 1f out: led jsut ins fnl f: edgd lft but kpt on wl ins fnl f: a jst gng to hold on* **12/1**

242- 2 hd **Star Of Rohm**[131] 7198 3-9-5 77 JamieSpencer 2 73
(Michael Bell) *chsd ldng pair: effrt and swtchd rt jst over 1f out: gap clsng and forced to switch further rt jst ins fnl f: r.o to chse wnr under hands and heels fnl 50yds: clsng towards fin but nvr quite getting up* **1/2**[1]

022- 3 1¼ **Silca's Dream**[120] 7434 3-9-5 69 MatthewDavies 4 69
(Mick Channon) *led: rdn and hrd pressed and rdn over 1f out: hdd jst ins fnl f and one pce after: hld whn sltly hmpd cl home* **4/1**[2]

- 4 nse **Sibaya** 3-9-0 0 JimCrowley 1 65+
(Roger Charlton) *dwlt: detached but in tch in last: rdn over 2f out: kpt on ins fnl f* **5/1**[3]

1m 13.53s (1.63) **Going Correction** +0.025s/f (Slow) 4 Ran SP% 111.0
Speed ratings (Par 97): **90,89,88,88**
CSF £19.86 TOTE £12.10; EX 24.40 Trifecta £52.60 Pool: £1,576.31 - 22.44 winning units..
Owner Sheikh Hamdan Bin Mohammed Al Maktoum **Bred** Darley **Trained** Middleham Moor, N Yorks

FOCUS
An uncompetitive maiden with two unexposed fillies up against two experienced types who had both been gelded since they were last seen.

809 LINGFIELDPARK.CO.UK H'CAP 2m (P)
5:10 (5:12) (Class 5) (0-75,74) 4-Y-O+ £3,408 (£1,006; £503) Stalls Low

Form RPR

4111 1 **Broxbourne (IRE)**[11] 675 4-9-6 74 JoeFanning 4 81
(Mark Johnston) *chsd clr ldng pair: clsd 5f out: led over 3f out: rdn over 1f out: hdd fnl f: sn led again and styd on wl towards fin* **4/5**[1]

05-3 2 ¾ **Beat Route**[48] 119 6-9-10 72 SebSanders 5 78
(Michael Attwater) *hld up wl off the pce in rr: clsd on ldrs 5f out: upsides wnr and gng wl 2f out: rdn and effrt 1f out: drvn and led fnl 75yds: sn hdd and no ex* **9/4**[2]

425- 3 3 **Ctappers**[11] 7972 4-8-2 63 DanielCremin(7) 3 66
(Mick Channon) *hld up wl off the pce in last pair: clsd on ldrs 5f out: chsd ldng pair 3f out: rdn and struggling 2f out: styd on same pce after* **14/1**

405- 4 32 **Rosewood Lad**[59] 8290 6-9-5 67 LiamKeniry 2 31
(J S Moore) *sn wl clr w ldr: rdn 8f out tl 7f out: rdn again 5f out: dropped to rr over 3f out: sn bhd: t.o over 1f out* **12/1**

22-3 5 3 **Lascaux**[38] 275 4-8-11 65 RobertHavlin 1 26
(Luke Dace) *led and sn wl clr w rival: hdd and rdn over 3f out: sn dropped out and bhd: t.o over 1f out* **7/1**[3]

3m 22.09s (-3.61) **Going Correction** +0.025s/f (Slow)
WFA 4 from 6yo 6lb 5 Ran SP% 113.2
Speed ratings (Par 103): **110,109,108,92,90**
CSF £2.96 TOTE £2.20: £1.20, £1.10; EX 3.10 Trifecta £12.60 Pool: £3,254.20 - 192.27 winning units..
Owner Ready To Run Partnership **Bred** Mount Coote Stud And M Johnston **Trained** Middleham Moor, N Yorks

FOCUS
They went a very decent pace in this, making it a true test, but the pair responsible for setting it, Lascaux and Rosewood Lad, merely succeeded in running themselves into the ground.
T/Plt: £1,099.50 to a £1 stake. Pool: £65,523.39 - 43.50 winning tickets. T/Qpdt: £111.30 to a £1 stake. Pool: £4,681.17 - 31.10 winning tickets. SP

[788]KEMPTON (A.W) (R-H)
Wednesday, February 27

OFFICIAL GOING: Standard
Wind: Modearate ahead Weather: Chilly, sunny early, getting dark

810 FREE ENTRY EVERY WEDNESDAY FOR BETDAQ MEMBERS H'CAP 1m 2f (P)
5:30 (5:30) (Class 4) (0-85,85) 4-Y-O+ £4,690 (£1,395; £697; £348) Stalls Low

Form RPR

215- 1 **Hilali (IRE)**[151] 4223 4-8-13 78 JamieSpencer 1 85+
(Gary Brown) *hld up in mid-div: drvn and hdwy over 1f out: styd on to chal ins fnl f: led fnl 50yds: kpt on wl* **5/1**[3]

0-04 2 ¾ **Askaud (IRE)**[14] 644 5-8-11 75 (b) TomMcLaughlin 8 81
(Scott Dixon) *led 2f: styd chsng ldrs: drvn to ld appr fnl f: sn jnd: hdd and nt qckn fnl 50yds* **8/1**

255- 3 nk **Jewelled**[191] 5417 7-8-8 72 MartinLane 5 78
(Lady Herries) *hld up in rr: hdwy on ins whn nt clr run and snatched up 1f out: hdd ins fnl f: rallied wl clsng stages: nt rcvr* **33/1**

6-32 4 ½ **Noguchi (IRE)**[30] 420 8-8-8 79 RobertTart(7) 4 83
(Michael Murphy) *in rr: hdwy fr 2f out: styd on ins fnl f: kpt on clsng stages* **9/4**[1]

104- 5 1¾ **Thecornishcowboy**[68] 8206 4-8-11 76 JohnFahy 7 77
(John Ryan) *chsd ldrs: led 5f out: rdn along 2f out: hdd appr fnl f: wknd fnl 50yds* **10/1**

603- 6 hd **Las Verglas Star (IRE)**[20] 7601 5-9-0 85 GeorgeChaloner(7) 6 85
(Richard Fahey) *t.k.h: chsd ldrs: drvn along fr 2f out: wknd fnl 50yds* **3/1**[2]

201- 7 hd **Monopoli**[156] 6544 4-8-7 72 RichardThomas 2 72
(Daniel Kubler) *in rr: pushed along fr 3f out: nvr gng pce to get into contention* **33/1**

1405 8 10 **Kung Hei Fat Choy (USA)**[15] 621 4-9-1 80 (b) GrahamLee 3 61
(James Given) *plld hrd: led after 2f: hdd 5f out: drvn 3f out: wknd 2f out* **13/2**

2m 8.19s (0.19) **Going Correction** +0.025s/f (Slow)
WFA 4 from 5yo+ 1lb 8 Ran SP% 111.9
Speed ratings (Par 105): **100,99,99,98,97 97,97,89**
toteswingers 1&2 £7.30, 1&3 £24.80, 2&3 £22.80 CSF £42.08 CT £1164.28 TOTE £6.60: £1.40, £2.60, £3.70; EX 45.80 Trifecta £276.20 Pool: £1939.74 - 5.26 winning units..
Owner John P McManus **Bred** Shadwell Estate Company Limited **Trained** Lambourn, Berks

FOCUS
This was a fair opening handicap, but it was run at a stop-start pace and the overall form is worth treating with a degree of caution.

811 WIN BIG WITH BETDAQ MULTIPLES H'CAP 6f (P)
6:00 (6:00) (Class 6) (0-65,65) 3-Y-O £1,940 (£577; £288; £144) Stalls Low

Form RPR

42-0 1 **Jimmy Elder**[12] 667 3-9-7 65 SeanLevey 7 69
(Richard Hannon) *stdd s: hld up in rr but in tch: str run on outside appr fnl f: qcknd to ld fnl 100yds: edgd rt: kpt on wl* **25/1**

-515 2 1½ **Roland**[15] 623 3-9-6 64 (b) PhillipMakin 5 63
(Kevin Ryan) *led: drvn 2 l clr over 1f out: hdd and outpcd fnl 100yds* **4/1**[2]

-231 3 nk **Katy Spirit (IRE)**[14] 628 3-9-7 65 LiamKeniry 4 63
(Michael Blanshard) *chsd ldr: rdn 2f out: styd on fnl f to press for 2nd clsng stages: no ch w wnr* **5/1**[3]

5-02 4 nk **Desert Donkey**[12] 667 3-9-6 64 DavidProbert 1 61
(Andrew Balding) *chsd ldrs: wnt 2nd and rdn 2f out: styd on same pce fnl f* **7/4**[1]

02-3 5 ¾ **Tregereth (IRE)**[33] 374 3-9-3 61 JohnFahy 8 56
(Jonathan Portman) *chsd ldrs: rdn over 2f out: one pce fnl f* **10/1**

6-00 6 2¼ **Iwilsayzisonlyonce**[21] 531 3-8-13 57 HayleyTurner 2 44
(Joseph Tuite) *hld up in rr but in tch: drvn and hdwy over 1f out: wknd ins fnl f* **7/1**

55-0 7 5 **Claude Greenwood**[14] 628 3-9-5 63 JamieSpencer 6 34
(David Simcock) *chsd ldrs: pushed along 2f out: wknd over 1f out* **7/1**

1m 13.68s (0.58) **Going Correction** +0.025s/f (Slow) 7 Ran SP% 111.0
Speed ratings (Par 95): **97,95,94,94,93 90,83**
toteswingers 1&2 £17.90, 1&3 £23.70, 2&3 £2.30 CSF £114.18 CT £573.78 TOTE £20.10: £5.10, £3.00; EX 223.40 Trifecta £322.10 Pool: £2179.03 - 5.07 winning units..
Owner Pineapple Stud **Bred** Mrs R Ablett **Trained** East Everleigh, Wilts

FOCUS
A moderate 3-y-o sprint handicap and it was a tight affair.

812 BACK AND LAY AT BETDAQ.COM H'CAP 6f (P)
6:30 (6:32) (Class 5) (0-75,75) 4-Y-O+ £2,587 (£770; £384; £192) Stalls Low

Form RPR

-650 1 **Gabbiano**[18] 583 4-8-11 72 RobertTart(7) 5 82+
(Jeremy Gask) *hld up in rr: pushed along over 2f out: gd hdwy over 1f out: str run to ld fnl 75yds: readily* **7/2**[1]

-136 2 1 **Alnoomaas (IRE)**[14] 627 4-9-6 74 TomMcLaughlin 7 80
(Luke Dace) *led: rdn: pushed along 2f out: kpt on fnl f: hdd and outpcd fnl 75yds* **6/1**[3]

-235 3 ¾ **The Strig**[13] 650 6-9-5 73 SeanLevey 3 77
(Stuart Williams) *in tch: drvn and kpt on to chse ldrs ins fnl f nt pce of ldng duo clsng stages* **10/1**

-042 4 hd **Haywain**[20] 546 4-9-0 68 (b) PhillipMakin 4 71+
(Kevin Ryan) *plld hrd: chsd ldrs: drvn to take 2nd over 1f out: no imp on wnr and kpt on same pce fnl f* **4/1**[2]

00-6 5 1 **Dishy Guru**[18] 582 4-8-12 66 (b[1]) LiamKeniry 8 66
(Michael Blanshard) *in tch: drvn over 2f out: styd on fnl f but nvr gng pce of ldrs* **16/1**

4-33 6 nk **Fortrose Academy (IRE)**[21] 535 4-8-12 66 DavidProbert 6 65
(Andrew Balding) *chsd ldr tl over 1f out: btn ins fnl f* **4/1**[2]

00-0 7 1¾ **Quasi Congaree (GER)**[13] 650 7-9-2 70 (tp) FergusSweeney 11 64
(Paul Fitzsimons) *in rr: pushed along over 2f out: sme prog fnl f: nvr rchd ldrs* **50/1**

5-20 8 1½ **Night Trade (IRE)**[18] 582 6-8-12 73 (p) GaryPhillips(7) 2 63
(Ronald Harris) *sn towards rr: drvn and outpcd fr over 2f out* **20/1**

-105 9 shd **Bassett Road (IRE)**[17] 603 5-9-0 68 (p) JoeFanning 9 57
(Keith Dalgleish) *t.k.h sn chsng ldrs: rdn 2f out: wknd appr fnl f* **14/1**

2310 10 4 **Dickie Le Davoir**[5] 760 9-9-1 69 (b) RobbieFitzpatrick 1 46
(Richard Guest) *s.i.s: outpcd* **20/1**

1m 12.17s (-0.93) **Going Correction** +0.025s/f (Slow) 10 Ran SP% 109.6
Speed ratings (Par 103): **107,105,104,104,103 102,100,98,98,92**
toteswingers 1&2 £4.50, 1&3 £5.70, 2&3 £12.00 CSF £21.39 CT £162.01 TOTE £2.90: £1.60, £3.20, £2.00; EX 25.30 Trifecta £141.10 Pool: £1503.04 - 7.98 winning units..
Owner Tony Bloom **Bred** Mrs R J Gallagher **Trained** Sutton Veny, Wilts

FOCUS
A modest and open-looking sprint handicap.

813 BETDAQ GAMES £50 HARD CASH BONUS H'CAP 1m (P)
7:00 (7:01) (Class 6) (0-65,66) 4-Y-O+ £1,940 (£577; £288; £144) Stalls Low

Form RPR

0311 1 **Flamborough Breeze**[6] 737 4-9-9 66 6ex (t) GeorgeBaker 5 80
(Ed Vaughan) *hld up in rr: smooth hdwy over 1f out: qcknd to ld fnl 110yds: cosily* **4/6**[1]

0-23 2 1¼ **Spirit Of Xaar (IRE)**[12] 665 7-9-3 60 (p) RobertHavlin 10 68
(Linda Jewell) *mid-div: hdwy fr 2f out: drvn to ld jst ins fnl f: hdd and outpcd fnl 110yds* **25/1**

05-1 3 1¼ **South Cape**[34] 348 10-8-12 62 NedCurtis(7) 4 67
(Gary Moore) *in rr: drvn and gd hdwy over 1f out: styd on wl fnl f to take 3rd last strides but nvr any ch w wnr* **12/1**[3]

13-2 **4** *nk* **Pastoral Jet**[34] [348] 5-8-11 **59** .... ThomasBrown(5) 6 64
(Richard Rowe) *in tch: drvn to chse ldrs 2f out: chal appr fnl f: kpt on same pce and lost 3rd last strides* **4/1**[2]

3243 **5** *1 1/4* **Arabian Flight**[9] [705] 4-9-3 **60** .... AndrewMullen 14 62
(Michael Appleby) *in rr: drvn and hdwy over 1f out: kpt on wl clsng stages but nvr a threat* **14/1**

340- **6** *1/2* **Green Earth (IRE)**[80] [8051] 6-9-2 **59** .... IanMongan 1 60
(Pat Phelan) *in rr: drvn and hdwy over 1f out: kpt on clsng stages* **20/1**

510- **7** *nk* **Karate (IRE)**[254] [3222] 5-9-0 **62** ....(t) NicoleNordblad(5) 7 62
(Hans Adielsson) *chsd ldrs: drvn to chal 2f out: slt ld over 1f out tl jst ins fnl f: sn btn* **14/1**

0560 **8** *1/2* **Final Drive (IRE)**[17] [603] 7-9-5 **62** ....(tp) LiamKeniry 12 61
(John Butler) *led: strly chal fr 2f out tl hdd over 1f out: wknd fnl f* **20/1**

50-0 **9** *2* **Navajo Charm**[7] [722] 4-8-10 **60** .... DavidParkes(7) 2 54
(Alan Jarvis) *chsd ldr: chal 2f out: wknd over 1f out* **33/1**

146U **10** *shd* **Vitznau (IRE)**[13] [652] 9-9-4 **61** .... ChrisCatlin 8 55
(K F Clutterbuck) *in rr: rdn and mod prog fnl f* **33/1**

0-40 **11** *2* **Rezwaan**[13] [652] 6-9-4 **61** ....(be) ShaneKelly 11 50
(Murty McGrath) *in tch: chsd ldrs 3f out: wknd 2f out* **33/1**

5-26 **12** *hd* **May's Boy**[51] [89] 5-9-0 **62** ....(p) RachealKneller(5) 9 51
(Mark Usher) *chsd ldrs: wknd over 2f out* **14/1**

4-25 **13** *3/4* **Blue Deer (IRE)**[11] [689] 5-9-5 **62** .... KierenFox 3 49
(Lee Carter) *t.k.h: in tch 5f* **33/1**

-000 **14** *6* **L'Hirondelle (IRE)**[27] [450] 9-9-7 **64** .... JoeFanning 13 37
(Michael Attwater) *reluctant to load: s.i.s: sn chsng ldrs: wknd 3f out* **33/1**

1m 39.89s (0.09) **Going Correction** +0.025s/f (Slow) **14** Ran SP% **135.8**
Speed ratings (Par 101): **100,98,97,97,95 95,95,94,92,92 90,90,89,83**
toteswingers 1&2 £6.20, 1&3 £4.50, 2&3 £63.00 CSF £34.02 CT £144.45 TOTE £1.70: £1.10, £8.10, £4.70; EX 27.50 Trifecta £216.00 Pool: £2073.29 - 7.19 winning units..
Owner A M Pickering **Bred** Windymains Farm Ltd **Trained** Newmarket, Suffolk

FOCUS
There was a fair pace on in this ordinary handicap and it saw plenty of chances 2f out

814 RACINGPLUS.CO.UK MAIDEN STKS (DIV I) 1m (P)
7:30 (7:31) (Class 5) 3-Y-0+ **£2,587** (£770; £384; £192) **Stalls** Low

Form RPR

35- **1** **Debdebdeb**[68] [8200] 3-8-4 0 .... DavidProbert 7 69+
(Andrew Balding) *led after 1f: drvn and hld on gamely whn chal fnl 110yds* **11/2**

430- **2** *nk* **Spring Tonic**[140] [6988] 4-10-0 70 .... JimCrowley 6 79
(Simon Dow) *chsd ldrs: drvn over 2f out: styd on to chse wnr jst ins fnl f: chal fnl 110yds but a jst hld* **4/1**[3]

26- **3** *2 1/2* **Gabrial The Thug (FR)**[138] [7033] 3-8-9 0 .... JamieSpencer 4 68
(Richard Fahey) *chsd ldrs: drvn 2f out and effrt to cl on ldng duo sn after: styd on for wl hld 3rd fnl 110yds* **3/1**[2]

-332 **4** *1 3/4* **Tanawar (IRE)**[16] [615] 3-8-9 69 ....(b) AdamBeschizza 5 64
(William Haggas) *led 1f: chsd ldrs: wnt 2nd 3f out: rdn 2f out: wknd ins fnl f* **9/4**[1]

50- **5** *5* **Handiwork**[86] [7963] 3-8-9 0 .... HayleyTurner 1 52
(Michael Bell) *s.i.s: in rr: mod prog over 1f out* **12/1**

6 *3/4* **Burgoyne (USA)** 3-8-9 0 ....(b1) RobertHavlin 2 50
(Hughie Morrison) *s.i.s: in rr: hdwy 3f out: wknd 2f out* **33/1**

7 *4* **Speed Boogie** 3-8-5 0 ow1 .... TobyAtkinson(5) 9 42
(Marco Botti) *chsd ldrs: drvn along after 2f: btn 3f out* **8/1**

8 *3/4* **Law Hill** 4-10-0 0 .... GeorgeBaker 3 45
(Michael Murphy) *slowly away: a in rr* **33/1**

6 **9** *13* **King Wood (TUR)**[30] [425] 3-8-9 0 .... RobertWinston 8
(Charles Hills) *slowly away: sn chsng ldrs on outside and wnt 2nd 4f out: wknd qckly fr 3f out* **25/1**

1m 38.68s (-1.12) **Going Correction** +0.025s/f (Slow)
WFA 3 from 4yo 19lb **9** Ran SP% **119.7**
Speed ratings (Par 103): **106,105,103,101,96 95,91,90,77**
toteswingers 1&2 £3.40, 1&3 £3.20, 2&3 £2.70 CSF £28.36 TOTE £7.40: £2.90, £1.90, £1.10; EX 30.60 Trifecta £92.00 Pool: £1654.17 - 13.48 winning units..
Owner C C Buckley **Bred** C C And Mrs D J Buckley **Trained** Kingsclere, Hants

FOCUS
An ordinary maiden and few landed a serious blow.

815 RACINGPLUS.CO.UK MAIDEN STKS (DIV II) 1m (P)
8:00 (8:03) (Class 5) 3-Y-0+ **£1,678** (£1,678; £384; £192) **Stalls** Low

Form RPR

0 **1** **Red To Amber (IRE)**[11] [685] 3-8-9 0 .... JohnFahy 7 69
(Clive Cox) *s.i.s: sn rcvrd to chse ldrs: wnt 2nd 2f out and sn hung lft: drvn to chal ins fnl f and remained upsides to force dead heat* **3/1**[2]

323- **1** *dht* **Gabrial's Wawa**[138] [7020] 3-8-9 73 .... JamieSpencer 3 69
(Richard Fahey) *chsd ldr: led over 2f out and sn wnt lft to stands' side: rdn and jnd jst ins fnl f: kpt on u.p to force dead heat* **1/1**[1]

3 *1* **Vastly (USA)** 4-10-0 0 .... LiamKeniry 1 73
(Julia Feilden) *in tch: hdwy to chse ldrs 2f out: pushed along and green fr over 1f out: kpt on but nt quite pce of ldng duo ins fnl f* **25/1**

0-2 **4** *1 1/2* **Countess Lovelace**[33] [373] 3-7-13 0 .... JemmaMarshall(5) 9 58
(Pat Phelan) *unruly bef s: chsd ldrs: drvn over 2f out: outpcd fnl f* **4/1**[3]

05- **5** *3/4* **Pearl Spice (IRE)**[160] [6412] 3-8-9 0 .... SeanLevey 4 61
(Tim Pitt) *in tch: hdwy to chse ldrs 2f out: kpt on same pce fnl f* **10/1**

45 **6** *4* **Conas Ata Tu**[9] [706] 4-9-2 0 .... AdamMcLean(7) 8 53
(Derek Shaw) *sn led: hdd over 2f out: hung lft sn after and wknd* **33/1**

7 *5* **Just Isla** 3-8-4 0 .... FrannyNorton 6 35
(Peter Makin) *reluctant to enter stalls s.i.s: outpcd most of way* **20/1**

8 *1 1/2* **Capetown Kid** 3-8-9 0 .... JDSmith 2 36
(Sylvester Kirk) *s.i.s: a outpcd* **33/1**

6 **9** *2 1/4* **Tavistock Fair**[12] [663] 3-8-3 0 ow1 .... RobertTart(7) 5 32
(Michael Squance) *s.i.s: outpcd most of way* **50/1**

1m 41.26s (1.46) **Going Correction** +0.025s/f (Slow)
WFA 3 from 4yo 19lb **9** Ran SP% **120.5**
Speed ratings (Par 103): **93,93,92,90,89 85,80,79,77**
WIN: GW £0.70, RTA £2.70; PL: GW £1.02, RTA £2.30, V £4.00; EX: GW/RTA £2.80, RTA/GW £3.90; TRI: GW/RTA/V £25.30, RTA/GW/V £53.00; CSF GW/RTA £2.05, RTA/GW 3.18.
Owner Dr Marwan Koukash **Bred** The Welcome Alliance **Trained** Musley Bank, N Yorks
Owner Mrs Olive Shaw **Bred** Tally-Ho Stud **Trained** Lambourn, Berks

FOCUS
The second division of the 1m maiden and it was markedly a slower winning time than the first. The two market leaders battled out the final furlong and were not for separating at the line.

816 MIX BUSINESS WITH PLEASURE AT KEMPTON H'CAP 1m 4f (P)
8:30 (8:30) (Class 6) (0-65,65) 4-Y-0+ **£1,940** (£577; £288; £144) **Stalls** Centre

Form RPR

6-40 **1** **Shalambar (IRE)**[35] [338] 7-9-5 **63** ....(v1) JimCrowley 11 73
(Tony Carroll) *in tch: hdwy on outer 3f out: drvn over 2f out: led over 1f out: r.o strly* **6/1**

3622 **2** *4* **Activate**[22] [524] 6-9-6 **64** ....(p) JoeFanning 9 68
(Keith Dalgleish) *chsd ldrs: drvn and kpt on to take 2nd fnl 110yds but no imp on wnr* **6/1**

3-13 **3** *3/4* **Asia Minor (IRE)**[13] [653] 4-9-1 **62** .... MartinLane 8 65
(Dr Jon Scargill) *in tch: hdwy on outer over 2f out: styd on for 3rd fnl 75yds but no ch w wnr* **5/2**[1]

-600 **4** *3/4* **Mazij**[22] [528] 5-9-2 **60** .... WilliamCarson 10 62
(Peter Hiatt) *chsd ldr: led over 2f out: hdd over 1f out: styd on same pce fnl f and lost 3rd fnl 75yds* **33/1**

0-01 **5** *3/4* **Maison Brillet (IRE)**[24] [512] 6-9-7 **65** ....(p) RobertHavlin 6 66
(Clive Drew) *chsd ldrs: drvn over 2f out: kpt on fnl f: nvr gng pce to get into contention* **12/1**

5534 **6** *1 3/4* **Thereabouts (USA)**[9] [709] 4-9-4 **65** ....(p) AndrewMullen 1 63
(Michael Appleby) *chsd ldrs: rdn over 2f out: wknd ins fnl f* **9/2**[3]

/0-1 **7** *3 1/2* **Wom**[34] [361] 5-9-4 **62** .... HayleyTurner 13 55
(Neil King) *in rr: pushed along over 2f out: mod prog fnl f* **14/1**

0-21 **8** *3/4* **Evergreen Forest (IRE)**[13] [653] 5-9-7 **65** ....(v1) GeorgeBaker 4 57
(Tom Keddy) *in rr: drvn and sme hdwy over 2f out: wknd over 1f out* **4/1**[2]

6/0- **9** *hd* **Amen (IRE)**[143] [4504] 5-8-11 **62** .... NedCurtis(7) 3 53
(Gary Moore) *led tl hdd over 2f out: sn wknd* **25/1**

-566 **10** *1 3/4* **Minority Interest**[14] [637] 4-9-4 **65** .... DavidProbert 5 54
(Brett Johnson) *bhd most of way* **16/1**

2m 35.24s (0.74) **Going Correction** +0.025s/f (Slow)
WFA 4 from 5yo+ 3lb **10** Ran SP% **122.4**
Speed ratings (Par 101): **98,95,94,94,93 92,90,89,89,88**
toteswingers 1&2 £8.40, 1&3 £4.90, 2&3 £2.90 CSF £44.14 CT £116.06 TOTE £4.30: £4.60, £2.10, £1.20; EX 51.30 Trifecta £134.60 Pool: £1004.45 - 5.59 winning units..
Owner B J Millen **Bred** His Highness The Aga Khan's Studs S C **Trained** Cropthorne, Worcs

FOCUS
This moderate handicap developed into a dash off the home turn and it's form to be wary of.

817 KEMPTON FOR WEDDINGS FILLIES' H'CAP 7f (P)
9:00 (9:01) (Class 5) (0-70,69) 3-Y-0 **£2,587** (£770; £384; £192) **Stalls** Low

Form RPR

-431 **1** **Byroness**[14] [632] 3-8-13 **68** .... RyanTate(7) 1 73+
(Heather Main) *in tch: drvn and hdwy over 1f out: led ins fnl f: readily* **13/8**[1]

350- **2** *1 3/4* **Tiger's Home**[121] [7439] 3-8-9 **57** .... AdamBeschizza 2 57
(Julia Feilden) *in rr: drvn over 2f out: styd on wl fnl 75yds: no imp* **12/1**

0-02 **3** *1 1/4* **Club Electra (IRE)**[24] [509] 3-8-8 **56** ....(b1) MartinLane 5 53
(Tobias B P Coles) *led: hdd ins fnl f: one pce and lost 2nd fnl 50yds* **14/1**

01-3 **4** *1 1/4* **Al Gharrafa**[42] [225] 3-9-7 **69** .... JimmyQuinn 3 63
(Marco Botti) *bmpd s: sn in tch: hdwy to chse ldrs fr 3f out: styd on fnl f: nt trble ldrs* **7/2**[2]

0-46 **5** *nk* **Fire Fairy (USA)**[25] [492] 3-8-9 **57** .... WilliamCarson 7 50
(Charles Hills) *sn chsng ldr: rdn and outpcd 2f out: styd on again fnl f* **16/1**

05-3 **6** *1 1/4* **Prom Dress**[35] [332] 3-8-12 **60** .... ShaneKelly 6 50
(Robert Cowell) *chsd ldrs: wnt lft and rdn over 2f out: sn hung rt: btn fnl f* **5/1**

040- **7** *1* **Seraphima**[74] [8138] 3-8-7 **62** .... RobertTart(7) 4 49
(Alan Bailey) *bmpd s: sme hdwy whn hung lft bnd 3f out: no ch after* **9/2**[3]

1m 26.26s (0.26) **Going Correction** +0.025s/f (Slow) **7** Ran SP% **115.4**
Speed ratings (Par 94): **99,97,95,94,93 92,91**
toteswingers 1&2 £6.60, 1&3 £5.00, 2&3 £9.80 CSF £23.46 TOTE £3.30: £1.40, £2.30; EX 19.50 Trifecta £395.50 Pool: £1434.07 - 2.71 winning units..
Owner Les Chevaliers **Bred** J P M Main **Trained** Kingston Lisle, Oxon

FOCUS
A weak 3-y-o fillies' handicap, run at an average pace.
T/Plt: £129.70 to a £1 stake. Pool: £73021.73 - 410.68 winning tickets. T/Qpdt: £9.20 to a £1 stake. Pool: £9287.74 - 739.10 winning tickets. ST

LYON-LA SOIE (R-H)
Wednesday, February 27

OFFICIAL GOING: Viscoride: standard

818a PRIX CARNAVAL (MAIDEN) (3YO COLTS & GELDINGS) (VISCORIDE) 1m 2f 165y
6:15 (12:00) 3-Y-0 **£6,504** (£2,601; £1,951; £1,300; £650)

RPR

1 **Papriformer (USA)**[34] 3-9-2 0 .... IoritzMendizabal 11 75
(J-C Rouget, France) **1/2**[1]

2 *1* **Super Winnie (FR)**[53] 3-9-2 0 ....(b) Pierre-CharlesBoudot 4 73
(P Cottier, France) **73/10**[2]

3 *hd* **Taiga Dream (FR)** 3-8-13 0 ....(b) MarcLerner(3) 9 73
(D Rabhi, France) **22/1**

4 *2 1/2* **Ginger Beer (FR)**[36] [331] 3-8-13 0 ....(b) RomainAuray(3) 7 68
(J Heloury, France) *fin 5th: plcd 4th* **24/1**

5 *1 1/2* **Yangoon (FR)** 3-9-2 0 ....(p) TonyPiccone 6 65
(J Bertran De Balanda, France) *fin 6th: plcd 5th* **34/1**

6 *4* **Honor Chop (FR)**[53] 3-9-2 0 .... LudovicProietti 2 57
(C Martinon, France) *fin 7th: plcd 6th* **32/1**

7 *6* **Jee Pee And Jeremy (FR)** 3-8-11 0 .... AntoineHamelin 10 41
(F Vermeulen, France) *fin 8th: plcd 7th* **16/1**

8 *4* **Mosconi (GER)** 3-8-11 0 .... MaximPecheur 3 33
(M Keller, Germany) *fin 9th: plcd 8th* **40/1**

9 *3 1/2* **Mysterieux (FR)** 3-9-2 0 ....(b) FranckForesi 8 32
(F Foresi, France) *fin 10th: plcd 9th* **42/1**

10 **Duke Jee Pee (IRE)** 3-9-2 0 .... LouisBeuzelin 12 32
(F Vermeulen, France) *fin 11th: plcd 10th* **57/1**

D *nse* **Destiny Highway (FR)**[11] 692 3-9-2 0 AnthonyCrastus 1 73
(Gay Kelleway) *racd 3rd on ins: smooth prog 3f out: led 2 1/2f out: r.o u.p fnl f: hdd 25yds out: no ex: fin 4th: disqualified - jockey weighed-in light* **15/2**[3]

2m 16.74s (136.74) 11 Ran SP% **117.1**
WIN (incl. 1 euro stake): 1.50. PLACES: 1.10, 1.50, 2.40. DF: 5.50. SF: 7.40.
Owner Joseph Allen **Bred** J Allen **Trained** Pau, France

[810]KEMPTON (A.W) (R-H)

Thursday, February 28

OFFICIAL GOING: Standard
Wind: Virtually nil Weather: Bright early, getting dark and chilly

819 GOFFS BREEZE-UP SALE 27.03.13 H'CAP 6f (P)
5:30 (5:30) (Class 7) (0-50,50) 4-Y-0+ **£1,455** (£433; £216; £108) **Stalls** Low

Form RPR
5352 **1** **Rightcar**[6] 756 6-8-11 **45** SladeO'Hara(5) 3 53
(Peter Grayson) *in tch: drvn ins fnl 3f: led ins fnl 2f: drvn out* **5/1**[3]
3035 **2** *1* **Slatey Hen (IRE)**[7] 736 5-9-5 **48** (p) WilliamCarson 4 53
(Violet M Jordan) *chsd ldrs: drvn over 2f out: styd on u.p to take 2nd last strides: no imp on wnr* **10/1**
405 **3** *hd* **Kaylee**[7] 733 4-9-5 **48** GeorgeBaker 1 54
(Gary Moore) *s.i.s: in rr: hdwy over 2f out: styd on to chse ldrs over 1f out and sn hrd drvn to dispute 2nd: one pce into 3rd in clsng stages* **7/2**[1]
0053 **4** *hd* **Illustrious Lad (IRE)**[7] 736 4-9-2 **50** (vt) NathanAlison(5) 5 54
(Jim Boyle) *t.k.h: chsd ldrs: drvn to chal wl over 1f out: disp 2nd and hung rt u.p ins fnl f: one pce in clsng stages* **4/1**[2]
0504 **5** *1 1/4* **Dingaan (IRE)**[3] 794 10-9-2 **45** FergusSweeney 8 46
(Peter Grayson) *s.i.s: in rr: hdwy over 1f out: styng on but no imp on wnr whn nt clr run in clsng stages* **6/1**
6-40 **6** *shd* **Metropolitan Chief**[14] 649 9-9-2 **45** TomMcLaughlin 9 45
(Paul Burgoyne) *chsd ldrs: drvn and one pce 2f out: styd on again fnl f* **25/1**
6-56 **7** *nk* **Rooknrasbryripple**[22] 529 4-9-2 **45** JoeFanning 10 44
(Ralph Smith) *s.i.s: in rr: hdwy over 1f out: styd on in clsng stages* **20/1**
0-00 **8** *1/2* **Minty Jones**[33] 409 4-8-9 **45** (be) RobertTart(7) 11 42
(Michael Mullineaux) *sn pressing ldr: stl upsides appr fnl 2f: outpcd and edgd rt u.p over 1f out: kpt on again in clsng stages* **20/1**
0-44 **9** *hd* **Flaxen Lake**[6] 754 6-9-7 **50** (p) JimmyQuinn 6 48
(Milton Bradley) *chsd ldrs: rdn 2f out: one pce whn nt clr run and eased in clsng stages* **6/1**
-250 **10** *9* **Adaeze (IRE)**[21] 551 5-9-3 **46** (b) JohnFahy 2 16
(Jonathan Portman) *sn led but then jnd: hdd ins fnl 2f: wkng whn bmpd appr fnl f* **16/1**

1m 12.72s (-0.38) **Going Correction** 0.0s/f (Stan) 10 Ran SP% **115.8**
Speed ratings (Par 97): **102,100,100,100,98 98,97,97,97,85**
toteswingers 1&2 £8.70, 2&3 £5.30, 1&3 £5.30 CSF £51.70 CT £176.20 TOTE £5.20: £1.60, £3.10, £1.90; EX 35.60 Trifecta £363.40 Pool: £739.57 - 1.52 winning units..
Owner Richard Teatum **Bred** J M Beever **Trained** Formby, Lancs

FOCUS
A moderate handicap run at a decent pace but very weak form.

820 MIKE THE KNIGHT HERE 13.04.13 H'CAP 1m 4f (P)
6:00 (6:01) (Class 7) (0-50,50) 4-Y-0+ **£1,455** (£433; £216; £108) **Stalls** Centre

Form RPR
6-60 **1** **Midnight Sequel**[36] 343 4-8-13 **45** MartinLane 7 52
(Michael Blake) *in tch: hdwy 3f out: led over 1f out: drvn out fnl f* **12/1**
3-44 **2** *1 1/4* **Petersboden**[25] 512 4-8-13 **45** NickyMackay 5 50
(Michael Blanshard) *chsd ldrs: led appr fnl 2f: hdd over 1f out: sn outpcd by wnr and hrd pressed into narrow 3rd ins fnl f: rallied to re-take 2nd last strides* **9/2**[1]
/400 **3** *shd* **Seaquel**[8] 724 7-9-2 **45** AdamKirby 9 50
(Tony Carroll) *in tch: hdwy 3f out: drvn to take narrow 2nd ins fnl f: no ex and dropped to 3rd last strides* **10/1**[3]
0/0- **4** *2 1/2* **Joyously**[388] 452 5-9-7 **50** (t) WilliamCarson 14 51+
(Violet M Jordan) *in rr: hdwy 3f out: sn rdn: kpt on u.p fnl f: nvr a threat* **50/1**
0-51 **5** *1* **Rollin 'n Tumblin**[15] 635 9-9-7 **50** JimmyQuinn 2 50
(Michael Attwater) *chsd ldrs: drvn along fr 3f out: wknd ins fnl f* **5/1**[2]
50-3 **6** *nse* **Fire In Babylon (IRE)**[43] 226 5-9-6 **49** (t) StevieDonohoe 6 49
(Noel Quinlan) *in rr: drvn over 2f out: hdwy appr fnl f: kpt on in clsng stages* **9/2**[1]
0553 **7** *3 1/2* **Gower Rules (IRE)**[8] 724 5-9-4 **47** (v) HayleyTurner 4 41
(John Bridger) *chsd ldeader: led appr fnl 4f: hdd appr fnl 2f: wknd appr fnl f* **5/1**[2]
0000 **8** *3/4* **Love Pegasus (USA)**[10] 703 7-9-4 **47** JoeFanning 8 40
(Paddy Butler) *s.i.s: in rr: drvn and sme hdwy over 2f out: no prog fr wl over 1f out* **20/1**
-050 **9** *4 1/2* **Dubai Emerald (USA)**[33] 406 4-9-0 **46** FrannyNorton 1 33
(Chris Dwyer) *sn led: hdd over 4f out: wknd ins fnl 2f* **20/1**
0-00 **10** *9* **High Five Prince (IRE)**[7] 737 4-8-10 **49** RobertTart(7) 3 22
(Milton Bradley) *chsd ldrs tl wknd 2f out* **33/1**
30-0 **11** *1/2* **Herschel (IRE)**[52] 94 7-8-11 **47** (be) JayneFarewell(7) 13 19
(Gary Moore) *a in rr* **33/1**
-662 **12** *nk* **Brandy Snapping**[10] 704 4-9-0 **46** (t) TomMcLaughlin 11 18
(Mark Brisbourne) *mid-div: racd wd and wknd 3f out* **10/1**[3]
065- **13** *9* **There's No Rules**[144] 6807 4-8-13 **45** (e[1]) RobbieFitzpatrick 10 3
(Richard Guest) *a in rr* **16/1**

2m 33.94s (-0.56) **Going Correction** 0.0s/f (Stan)
WFA 4 from 5yo+ 3lb 13 Ran SP% **118.8**
Speed ratings (Par 97): **101,100,100,98,97 97,95,94,91,85 85,85,79**
toteswingers 1&2 £12.70, 2&3 £7.70, 1&3 £14.60 CSF £61.08 CT £574.02 TOTE £13.40: £3.30, £2.00, £1.90; EX 72.50 Trifecta £747.70 Pool: £1531.32 - 1.53 winning units..
Owner Dajam Ltd **Bred** M Burbidge **Trained** Trowbridge, Wilts

FOCUS
A minor handicap run at fair pace and straightforward form

821 GET THE BETVICTOR APP MAIDEN FILLIES' STKS 6f (P)
6:30 (6:30) (Class 5) 3-Y-0+ **£2,587** (£770; £384; £192) **Stalls** Low

Form RPR
3-22 **1** **Bouyrin (IRE)**[31] 425 3-8-13 **66** HayleyTurner 2 77+
(Michael Bell) *trckd ldr: led: gng wl appr fnl f: pushed clr: easily* **6/4**[1]
6-3 **2** *6* **Scent Of Roses (IRE)**[10] 706 3-8-13 0 AdamKirby 3 57
(Clive Cox) *t.k.h: led: pushed along and hdd appr fnl f: sn outpcd by wnr but hld on wl for 2nd* **7/4**[2]
060- **3** *nk* **Our Golden Girl**[174] 6016 3-8-6 **50** RobertTart(7) 1 56+
(Shaun Lycett) *s.i.s: in rr: drvn and hdwy over 1f out: styd on fnl f to press for 2nd but no ch w wnr* **33/1**
4 *1 1/4* **Seymour Place** 3-8-13 0 JimCrowley 5 52
(Roger Charlton) *chsd ldrs: pushed along and green 2f out: no ex fnl f* **5/1**[3]
5 *nk* **Gift Of Silence** 4-10-0 0 MartinLane 8 55
(John Berry) *s.i.s: in rr: pushed along 3f out: styd on fr over 1f out: nt gng pce to rch ldrs* **33/1**
56 **6** *2 1/4* **Shaken Not Stirred**[13] 673 3-8-13 0 JimmyQuinn 7 45
(Milton Bradley) *sn chsng ldrs: pushed along over 2f out: wknd fnl f* **20/1**
54-2 **7** *shd* **Sally Bruce**[29] 442 3-8-6 **49** JenniferFerguson(7) 4 44
(Louise Best) *s.i.s: pushed along 1/2-way: outpcd most of way* **10/1**
8 *nk* **Meetha Achar** 3-8-8 0 NathanAlison(5) 6 44
(Jim Boyle) *s.i.s: in rr: sme hdwy over 2f out: sn wknd* **16/1**

1m 12.98s (-0.12) **Going Correction** 0.0s/f (Stan)
WFA 3 from 4yo 15lb 8 Ran SP% **118.6**
Speed ratings (Par 100): **100,92,91,89,89 86,86,86**
toteswingers 1&2 £1.10, 2&3 £12.00, 1&3 £10.20 CSF £4.47 TOTE £2.70: £1.10, £1.30, £9.30; EX 5.20 Trifecta £40.70 Pool: £1572.08 - 28.90 winning units..
Owner Saleh Al Homaizi & Imad Al Sagar **Bred** D G Hardisty Bloodstock **Trained** Newmarket, Suffolk

FOCUS
The favourite scored in smooth style in this ordinary maiden and looks capable of better. The placed horses represent the key to the form.

822 BETVICTOR GRAND NATIONAL NON RUNNER FREE BET H'CAP 7f (P)
7:00 (7:00) (Class 5) (0-75,75) 4-Y-0+ **£2,587** (£770; £384; £192) **Stalls** Low

Form RPR
0-65 **1** **The Happy Hammer (IRE)**[36] 344 7-9-0 **68** AdamKirby 1 76
(Eugene Stanford) *mde all: drvn and qcknd over 2f out: hld on wl whn strly chal fr ins fnl f* **14/1**
4-36 **2** *hd* **Chookie Avon**[15] 644 6-9-7 **75** (p) JoeFanning 3 82
(Keith Dalgleish) *chsd ldr: wnt 2nd over 1f out: str chal fnl f: no ex last strides* **11/2**[3]
-521 **3** *3/4* **Russian Ice**[14] 650 5-9-7 **75** (b) JimCrowley 6 83+
(Dean Ivory) *in rr whn hmpd after 1f: hdwy and drvn 2f out: styng on strly whn hmpd fnl 75yds: swtchd lft: rallied but nt rcvr* **7/2**[2]
3-04 **4** *1* **Avonmore Star**[14] 650 5-9-5 **73** EddieAhern 5 76
(Mike Murphy) *t.k.h: sn chsng ldrs: rdn and one pce over 2f out: styd on again u.p fnl f* **3/1**[1]
4-4 **5** *1/2* **Al Khan (IRE)**[50] 113 4-9-2 **70** WilliamCarson 10 72+
(Violet M Jordan) *s.i.s: sn in tch and t.k.h: rdn over 1f out: styd on same pce* **3/1**[1]
00-6 **6** *nse* **Perfect Mission**[36] 344 5-8-11 **72** (v) DanielMuscutt(7) 2 74
(Andrew Balding) *s.i.s: t.k.h and in tch: chsd ldrs over 2f out: rdn over 1f out: wknd ins fnl f* **7/1**
5-02 **7** *shd* **Hatta Stream (IRE)**[7] 740 7-8-12 **69** SimonPearce(3) 8 70+
(Lydia Pearce) *sn chsng ldr: rdn 2f out: wknd fnl f* **20/1**
20-6 **8** *5* **Ocean Legend (IRE)**[15] 629 8-9-5 **73** JimmyQuinn 7 61+
(Tony Carroll) *outpcd most of way* **8/1**
004/ **9** *11* **Di Stefano**[650] 2263 6-8-11 **65** LiamKeniry 4 25
(Joseph Tuite) *a outpcd* **66/1**

1m 26.1s (0.10) **Going Correction** 0.0s/f (Stan) 9 Ran SP% **124.1**
Speed ratings (Par 103): **99,98,97,96,96 96,96,90,77**
toteswingers 1&2 £11.60, 2&3 £4.30, 1&3 £10.10 CSF £95.48 CT £343.03 TOTE £22.30: £4.30, £2.30, £1.40; EX 78.90 Trifecta £594.20 Pool: £1303.50 - 1.64 winning units..
Owner Cliff Woof **Bred** Rathbarry Stud **Trained** Newmarket, Suffolk

FOCUS
They went a steady pace in this handicap and the winner had the run of things out in front. He is rated back to his best and the form is backed up by the second.

823 BETVICTOR NON RUNNER NO BET AT CHELTENHAM H'CAP 2m (P)
7:30 (7:30) (Class 4) (0-95,95) 4-Y-0+ **£4,690** (£1,395; £697; £348) **Stalls** Low

Form RPR
4-01 **1** **Thecornishcockney**[14] 654 4-10-2 **95** (t) AdamKirby 6 103+
(John Ryan) *stdd s: hld up in rr: stdy hdwy over 2f out to ld appr fnl f: easily* **6/4**[1]
34-2 **2** *1* **Tartan Jura**[16] 622 5-9-2 **75** FrannyNorton 8 80
(Mark Johnston) *chsd ldr: rdn over 2f out: styd on wl to chse wnr fnl f but nvr any ch* **5/2**[2]
503/ **3** *3/4* **Kalamill (IRE)**[752] 5260 6-8-3 **69** oh1 ow3 RobertTart(7) 3 73
(Shaun Lycett) *sn led: 7 l clr 1/2-way: rdn 3f out: hdd appr fnl f: styd on same pce for 3rd* **33/1**
00/0 **4** *1 1/4* **Topolski (IRE)**[26] 496 7-9-6 **79** (p) LiamKeniry 4 81
(David Arbuthnot) *in tch: drvn over 2f out: kpt on fnl f: nt rch ldrs* **20/1**
013/ **5** *shd* **Dr Livingstone (IRE)**[30] 7600 8-9-5 **78** SamTwiston-Davies 2 80
(Charles Egerton) *hld up towards rr: drvn and hdwy over 2f out: styd same pce ins fnl f* **7/1**[3]
100/ **6** *nk* **Bow To No One (IRE)**[344] 6690 7-8-13 **77** MichaelJMurphy(5) 7 79
(Alan Jarvis) *in rr: rdn over 2f out: kpt on ins fnl f* **16/1**
/11- **7** *3 1/4* **Kian's Delight**[194] 3953 5-9-6 **79** JimCrowley 5 77
(Peter Bowen) *chsd ldrs: rdn and wknd ins fnl 2f* **7/1**[3]
22-0 **8** *2* **Vimiero (USA)**[34] 224 6-9-3 **76** GeorgeBaker 1 72
(Jonjo O'Neill) *chsd ldrs: rdn 3f out: wknd over 2f out* **16/1**

3m 29.34s (-0.76) **Going Correction** 0.0s/f (Stan)
WFA 4 from 5yo+ 6lb 8 Ran SP% **113.0**
Speed ratings (Par 105): **101,100,100,99,99 99,97,96**
toteswingers 1&2 £1.10, 2&3 £16.80, 1&3 £15.20 CSF £5.13 CT £75.61 TOTE £3.70: £1.30, £1.50, £9.40; EX 6.10 Trifecta £227.90 Pool: £1339.79 - 4.40 winning units..
Owner C Letcher & J Ryan **Bred** D Robb **Trained** Newmarket, Suffolk

FOCUS
A decent staying handicap. It was run at a good pace and a highly progressive 4-y-o scored in good style. The winner will find things harder in future but the form behind him looks sraightforward enough.

824 BETVICTOR EXCLUSIVE ANTEPOST OFFER AINTREE 2013 H'CAP 1m (P)
8:00 (8:00) (Class 6) (0-60,60) 3-Y-0 **£1,940** (£577; £288; £144) **Stalls** Low

Form RPR
242 **1** **Shearian**[18] 599 3-8-12 **56** GeorgeDowning(5) 3 61
(Tony Carroll) *chsd ldrs: rdn and str run fnl f to ld in clsng stages* **10/1**

The Form Book Flat, Raceform Ltd, Compton, RG20 6NL.

1-24 **2** ½ **Close Together (IRE)**[15] 634 3-9-7 **60**.............................. SeanLevey 4 64
(Robert Mills) *in tch: drvn and hdwy over 1f out: slt ld ins fnl f: hdd and outpcd in clsng stages* **9/1**

-454 **3** *shd* **Rainford Glory (IRE)**[15] 632 3-9-0 **53**.............................. JimCrowley 5 57
(David Simcock) *in rr: hdwy 2f out: rdn and r.o strly ins fnl f: fin wl: nt quite get up* **5/1**[2]

0-60 **4** *1* **Alshan Fajer**[19] 580 3-9-5 **58**.............................. IanMongan 10 59+
(Paul Howling) *s.i.s: in rr: rdn and hdwy over 1f out: styd on wl fnl f: nt rch ldrs* **7/1**[3]

56-1 **5** ½ **Luv U Whatever**[9] 717 3-9-3 **56** 6ex.............................. J-PGuillambert 6 56
(Jo Hughes) *chsd ldr: rdn over 2f out: sn one pce: kpt on again ins fnl f* **9/2**[1]

6 *shd* **Our Manekineko**[34] 385 3-8-9 **48**..............................(t) LiamKeniry 11 48
(J A Nash, Ire) *chsd ldrs: drvn and one pce 2f out: rallied fnl f: kpt on cl home* **8/1**

-554 **7** ½ **Spreading**[8] 732 3-9-2 **55**.............................. NickyMackay 2 54
(Michael Blanshard) *chsd ldrs: slt ld 2f out: hdd ins fnl f: sn outpcd* **20/1**

060- **8** ½ **Whiskey N Stout (IRE)**[192] 5418 3-8-13 **52**.............. FergusSweeney 13 50+
(Jamie Osborne) *in rr: rdn 2f out: kpt on ins fnl f: gng on in clsng stages* **8/1**

0-63 **9** *hd* **World Freight Girl**[15] 632 3-8-12 **51**..............................(b) JimmyQuinn 7 48
(Dean Ivory) *s.i.s: in rr: hdwy 3f out: drvn to press ldrs fr 2f out: wknd ins fnl f* **14/1**

3213 **10** *nk* **Napinda**[12] 684 3-9-5 **58**..............................(v) WilliamCarson 1 55
(Philip McBride) *sn led: hdd u.p 2f out: wknd ins fnl f* **9/1**

0-55 **11** *shd* **Limoges**[25] 509 3-8-13 **52**.............................. EddieAhern 8 48
(Luke Dace) *in tch: pushed along over 2f out: kpt on ins fnl f: one pce in clsng stages* **33/1**

00-5 **12** 1 ¼ **Spirit Of Success**[31] 419 3-8-13 **59**.............................. RobertTart(7) 12 53
(Michael Bell) *s.i.s: in rr: hdwy over 2f out: one pce fnl f* **14/1**

050- **13** 1 ¾ **Ceekay's Girl**[145] 6893 3-8-11 **50**.............................. FrannyNorton 14 40
(Mrs K Burke) *outpcd most of way* **25/1**

0-06 **14** 1 ¼ **Exit Clause**[8] 732 3-9-4 **57**..............................(t) DavidProbert 9 44
(Tony Carroll) *outpcd most of way* **33/1**

1m 39.82s (0.02) **Going Correction** 0.0s/f (Stan) 14 Ran SP% **126.5**
Speed ratings (Par 95): **99,98,98,97,96 96,96,95,95,95 95,93,92,90**
toteswingers 1&2 £5.70, 2&3 £5.10, 1&3 £10.90 CSF £98.02 CT £393.24 TOTE £13.30: £3.90, £2.60, £1.80; EX 73.70 Trifecta £260.30 Pool: £987.58 - 2.84 winning units. .
Owner A W Carroll **Bred** Minehart Developments Ltd **Trained** Cropthorne, Worcs

FOCUS
There was a bunch finish in this moderate but competitive handicap and little of interest with the future in mind.

825 FOLLOW US ON TWITTER @BETVICTORRACING H'CAP 1m (P)
8:30 (8:30) (Class 6) (0-55,54) 4-Y-0+ **£1,940** (£577; £288; £144) **Stalls** Low

Form RPR

6054 **1** **Rapid Water**[8] 721 7-9-5 52..............................(b) LiamKeniry 6 60
(Pat Eddery) *hld up in rr: gd hdwy to ld 1f out: pushed out in clsng stages* **4/1**[2]

20-0 **2** 1 ¼ **Hill Of Dreams (IRE)**[31] 418 4-9-6 53..............................(b[1]) EddieAhern 4 58
(Dean Ivory) *s.i.s: in rr: hdwy and hmpd ins fnl 2f: hdwy and hmpd again over 1f out: styd on to take 2nd last strides* **6/1**[3]

0-00 **3** *nse* **Ensnare**[13] 665 8-9-7 54..............................(b) J-PGuillambert 5 59
(Willie Musson) *broke wl and led briefly: sn trcking ldrs: chsd wnr but no imp fnl f: ct for 2nd last strides* **8/1**

60-0 **4** 1 ¼ **The Which Doctor**[29] 441 8-9-0 47..............................(e) WilliamCarson 3 52+
(Violet M Jordan) *slowly in to stride: in rr: hdwy 2f out: hdwy whn hmpd over 1f out: styd on again fnl f but nt rcvr* **11/1**

600 **5** *1* **Olynard (IRE)**[6] 754 7-8-5 45..............................(p) RobertTart(7) 7 45
(Michael Mullineaux) *sn chsng ldr: led over 4f out: rdn over 2f out: hdd 1f out: wknd in clsng stages* **14/1**

-000 **6** *nk* **Querido (GER)**[15] 625 9-8-12 45..............................(vt) JoeFanning 10 44
(Paddy Butler) *s.i.s: in rr: hdwy fr 3f out: drvn over 2f out: kpt on fnl f: nvr a threat* **8/1**

-003 **7** *hd* **Qeethaara (USA)**[7] 737 9-9-0 52..............................(p) JackDuern(5) 9 51
(Mark Brisbourne) *t.k.h: chsd ldrs: rdn over 2f out: wknd ins fnl f* **11/4**[1]

6555 **8** *7* **Back For Tea (IRE)**[13] 667 5-8-12 45..............................(p) DavidProbert 1 27
(Phil McEntee) *chsd ldrs: rdn over 2f out: wknd over 1f out* **20/1**

0-00 **9** ½ **Jericho (IRE)**[17] 617 4-9-6 53.............................. AdamKirby 8 34
(Jamie Osborne) *sn drvn to ld: hdd over 4f out: wknd over 1f out* **8/1**

00-3 **10** 1 ½ **Hawaiian Freeze**[8] 725 4-8-12 45.............................. NickyMackay 2 23
(John Stimpson) *t.k.h: chsd ldrs: wknd 2f out* **14/1**

1m 39.81s (0.01) **Going Correction** 0.0s/f (Stan) 10 Ran SP% **120.7**
Speed ratings (Par 101): **99,97,97,96,95 95,94,87,87,85**
toteswingers 1&2 £5.20, 2&3 £14.20, 1&3 £8.10 CSF £29.49 CT £188.03 TOTE £4.20: £1.90, £2.10, £3.60; EX 34.20 Trifecta £550.00 Pool: £869.57 - 1.18 winning units. .
Owner Miss Emma L Owen **Bred** Littleton Stud **Trained** Nether Winchendon, Bucks
■ Stewards' Enquiry : J-P Guillambert ten-day ban: failed to ride out for 2nd (Mar 14-23)

FOCUS
A weak handicap, all of the runners had been beaten by at least 4l on their previous start. It was run at a muddling pace and the form should be treated with caution, with the winner the best guide rated to some of his better efforts.
T/Jkpt: Not won. T/Plt: £90.50 to a £1 stake. Pool of £84269.08 - 679.71 winning tickets. T/Qpdt: £4.60 to a £1 stake. Pool of £10057.08- 1605.85 winning tickets. ST

[712]SOUTHWELL (L-H)
Thursday, February 28

OFFICIAL GOING: Standard
Wind: Moderate across Weather: Fine and dry

826 BOOKMAKERS.CO.UK H'CAP 1m (F)
2:20 (2:20) (Class 5) (0-75,75) 3-Y-0 **£2,587** (£770; £384; £192) **Stalls** Low

Form RPR

321- **1** **Mixed Message (IRE)**[142] 6952 3-8-13 **67**.............. GrahamGibbons 6 72
(John Mackie) *cl up: rdn along wl over 1f out and sn edgd lft: drvn ent fnl f: kpt on wl u.p to ld nr fin* **16/1**

21 **2** *nk* **Kabbaas (IRE)**[18] 602 3-9-7 **75**.............................. ChrisCatlin 1 79
(Roger Varian) *dwlt and sn swtchd to outer: trckd ldng pair: hdwy 3f out and sn cl up: rdn 2f out: led over 1f out: drvn ins fnl f: hdd and no ex towards fin* **4/6**[1]

01-1 **3** *hd* **Apache Rising**[16] 623 3-8-8 **62**.............................. TomEaves 5 67
(Bryan Smart) *led: rdn along 2f out: hdd over 1f out: drvn and n.m.r ins fnl f: kpt on* **9/4**[2]

4-41 **4** 1 ¼ **Makinson Lane (IRE)**[16] 619 3-8-13 **67**.............................. TonyHamilton 3 68
(Richard Fahey) *t.k.h early: trckd ldng pair on inner: effrt wl over 2f out and sn pushed along: outpcd and swtchd rt to wd outside wl over 1f out: kpt on u.p fnl f* **7/1**[3]

1m 42.63s (-1.07) **Going Correction** -0.10s/f (Stan) 4 Ran SP% **109.1**
Speed ratings (Par 97): **101,100,100,99**
CSF £28.47 TOTE £13.50; EX 34.90 Trifecta £52.20 Pool: £1847.99 - 26.51 winning units..
Owner W I Bloomfield **Bred** J Costello **Trained** Church Broughton , Derbys

FOCUS
An ordinary 3-y-o handicap, weakened by the two non-runners, and something of a messy race. That said, the winner built on hsi previous success and the other three fit in on previous form.

827 HORSE RACING FREE BETS WITH BOOKMAKERS.CO.UK CLAIMING STKS 7f (F)
2:50 (2:50) (Class 6) 3-Y-O **£2,045** (£603; £302) **Stalls** Low

Form RPR

-113 **1** **Hiddon Coin (IRE)**[15] 643 3-9-7 75.............................. DanielTudhope 3 82+
(David O'Meara) *mde all: rdn clr 2f out: styd on strly* **7/4**[2]

5411 **2** *9* **Hillbilly Boy (IRE)**[12] 684 3-8-12 74.............................. RyanWhile(7) 1 58
(Bill Turner) *chsd wnr on inner: rdn along over 2f out: drvn wl over 1f out: no imp* **11/8**[1]

104- **3** *6* **Krupskaya (FR)**[78] 8076 3-9-0 64.............................. MichaelO'Connell 4 37
(Mrs K Burke) *chsd ldng pair: rdn along 3f out: drvn over 2f out: sn outpcd* **3/1**[3]

56-4 **4** *9* **Bix (IRE)**[21] 547 3-8-11 60.............................. TomEaves 2 10
(Alan Berry) *sn rdn along and a outpcd in rr* **20/1**

1m 29.86s (-0.44) **Going Correction** -0.10s/f (Stan) 4 Ran SP% **108.2**
Speed ratings (Par 95): **98,87,80,70**
CSF £4.54 TOTE £2.00; EX 4.50 Trifecta £3.90 Pool: £1056.16 - 201.93 winning units..
Owner Hambleton Racing Ltd - Three In One **Bred** Noel & Anthony O'Callaghan **Trained** Nawton, N Yorks

FOCUS
This modest claimer was all very straightforward. The form could be rated higher but has been treated conservatively.

828 CORAL.CO.UK H'CAP 5f (F)
3:20 (3:20) (Class 5) (0-75,71) 3-Y-O **£2,587** (£770; £384; £192) **Stalls** High

Form RPR

5-06 **1** **Miako (USA)**[10] 710 3-8-12 **62**.............................. AndrewMullen 2 74+
(Michael Appleby) *trckd ldrs: smooth hdwy over 2f out: led wl over 1f out: sn rdn and qcknd clr: readily* **7/4**[1]

1- **2** *5* **Lucies Diamond (IRE)**[306] 1671 3-9-3 **67**.............................. TomEaves 4 62
(Michael Dods) *sn outpcd and rdn along in rr: hdwy 2f out: styd on wl fnl f* **7/2**[2]

55-0 **3** *3* **Sylvia Pankhurst (IRE)**[21] 550 3-9-6 **70**..............(p) GrahamGibbons 5 53
(David C Griffiths) *chsd ldrs: hdwy over 2f out: sn rdn and one pce* **8/1**

0-62 **4** *shd* **La Sylphe**[15] 643 3-9-0 **71**.............................. AdamMcLean(7) 1 54
(Derek Shaw) *cl up: led after 2f: rdn and hdd wl over 1f out: grad wknd* **4/1**[3]

6-24 **5** *nse* **Con Leche**[12] 686 3-8-5 **55**..............................(b[1]) ChrisCatlin 7 38
(Scott Dixon) *led 2f: cl up: rdn along 2f out: grad wknd* **12/1**

4-32 **6** 4 ½ **Lexi's Beauty (IRE)**[13] 669 3-7-9 **52** oh4.............................. JoeyHaynes(7) 6 18
(Patrick Morris) *chsd ldrs: rdn along 1/2-way: sn wknd* **20/1**

56-4 **7** ¾ **Just Past Andover (IRE)**[34] 368 3-9-4 **68**..................(b[1]) KierenFox 3 32
(Bill Turner) *dwlt and in rr: sme hdwy on wd outside 1/2-way: sn rdn and wknd* **8/1**

1m 0.13s (0.43) **Going Correction** +0.20s/f (Slow) 7 Ran SP% **113.3**
Speed ratings (Par 97): **104,96,91,91,90 83,82**
toteswingers 1&2 £3.00, 1&3 £2.20, 2&3 £5.90 CSF £7.82 TOTE £2.10: £1.10, £2.80; EX 10.10 Trifecta £53.20 Pool: £1400.60 - 19.72 winning units..
Owner Rod In Pickle Partnership **Bred** Brylynn Farm Inc **Trained** Danethorpe, Notts

FOCUS
The first 5f contest here since the track reopened and few races over the trip will be won more easily. The winner took well to the surface and can go on from this.

829 CASINO AT CORAL.CO.UK MEDIAN AUCTION MAIDEN STKS 5f (F)
3:50 (3:50) (Class 5) 3-4-Y-O **£2,587** (£770; £384; £192) **Stalls** High

Form RPR

1 **My Name Is Rio (IRE)** 3-9-0 0.............................. TomEaves 1 68+
(Michael Dods) *s.i.s and wnt lft s: green and in rr: hdwy on wd outside over 1f out: sn rdn: green and edgd rt ins fnl f: styd on to ld last stride* **8/1**[3]

243- **2** *hd* **Bapak Bangsawan**[164] 6320 3-9-0 69.............................. AmyRyan 2 67+
(Kevin Ryan) *cl up: led after 1f: rdn over 1f out: drvn clr ins fnl f: hdd and no ex nr line* **6/4**[2]

2- **3** *3* **Antonio Gramsci**[253] 3286 3-9-0 0.............................. GrahamGibbons 3 56+
(David Barron) *cl up: effrt 2f out: sn rdn and ev ch tl drvn and one pce ent fnl f* **1/1**[1]

020- **4** ¾ **Pull The Pin (IRE)**[92] 7898 4-9-11 49.............................. NeilFarley(3) 5 60
(Declan Carroll) *racd nr stands' rail: chsd ldrs: hdwy 2f out: sn rdn and kpt on same pce fnl f* **16/1**

630 **5** *22* **Lady Calantha**[13] 669 3-8-9 48.............................. RobertWinston 4
(Alan Berry) *led 1f: prom: swtchd lft and rdn 2f out: sn outpcd and bhd whn eased fnl f* **50/1**

1m 1.27s (1.57) **Going Correction** +0.20s/f (Slow)
WFA 3 from 4yo 14lb 5 Ran SP% **109.0**
Speed ratings (Par 103): **95,94,89,88,53**
CSF £20.19 TOTE £12.70: £3.70, £2.00; EX 20.60 Trifecta £40.00 Pool: £2077.44 - 38.93 winning units..
Owner Kevin Kirkup **Bred** Anthony J Keane **Trained** Denton, Co Durham

FOCUS
A weak sprint maiden limited by the proximity of the fourth. The winning time was 1.14 seconds slower than the preceding 3-y-o handicap.

830 BEST HORSE RACING ODDS WITH BOOKMAKERS.CO.UK H'CAP 1m 4f (F)
4:20 (4:20) (Class 4) (0-85,85) 4-Y-0+ **£4,690** (£1,395; £697; £348) **Stalls** Low

Form RPR

0-32 **1** **Honest Deal**[15] 642 5-8-8 **72**.............................. RobertWinston 2 81
(Alan Swinbank) *mde all: rdn wl over 1f out: clr ent fnl f: kpt on* **11/4**[1]

236- **2** 4 ½ **Northside Prince (IRE)**[159] 6476 7-9-2 **85**................ GarryWhillans(5) 3 87
(Alan Swinbank) *trckd ldrs: hdwy 5f out: rdn along wl over 2f out: kpt on u.p fnl f: no ch w wnr* **4/1**[3]

0-61 **3** ½ **The Lock Master (IRE)**[15] 644 6-9-4 **82**.............................. AndrewMullen 6 84
(Michael Appleby) *trckd ldrs: hdwy to chse wnr over 4f out: rdn along over 2f out: chal and ch over 1f out: sn drvn and one pce* **11/4**[1]

23-4 **4** 2 3/4 **Ascendant**[34] 167 7-9-3 81 GrahamLee 4 78
(J R Jenkins) *hld up: hdwy to chse ldrs 4f out: rdn along wl over 2f out: sn no imp* 3/1[2]

513- **5** 6 **Mason Hindmarsh**[58] 7610 6-8-0 71 EvaMoscrop(7) 1 59
(Karen McLintock) *cl up on inner: pushed along and lost pl 5f out: bhd fnl 3f* 10/1

101- **6** 31 **Dorry K (IRE)**[50] 7444 4-8-10 77 ow1 MickyFenton 5 19
(Brian Rothwell) *in tch on wd outside: rdn along 5f out: sn outpcd and bhd fnl 3f* 25/1

2m 39.4s (-1.60) **Going Correction** -0.10s/f (Stan)
WFA 4 from 5yo+ 3lb 6 Ran SP% **111.3**
Speed ratings (Par 105): **101,98,97,95,91 71**
toteswingers 1&2 £2.40, 1&3 £2.10, 2&3 £2.60 CSF £13.78 TOTE £3.20: £1.10, £3.80; EX 11.00 Trifecta £41.90 Pool: £2356.75 - 42.10 winning units..
Owner Exors of The Late Guy Reed **Bred** G Reed **Trained** Melsonby, N Yorks

FOCUS
They went no pace in this fair middle-distance handicap, which played into the hands of the winner. It resulted in a 1-2 for the Alan Swinbank stable with the winner rated to form.

831 DOWNLOAD CORAL.CO.UK MOBILE APP H'CAP 6f (F)
4:50 (4:51) (Class 6) (0-65,65) 4-Y-0+ **£1,940** (£577; £288; £144) **Stalls** Low

Form RPR

4045 **1** **Greenhead High**[15] 640 5-9-1 59 (v[1]) AndrewMullen 10 69
(David Nicholls) *mde all: rdn wl over 1f out: drvn and kpt on wl towards fin* 8/1

4106 **2** 1/2 **Colourbearer (IRE)**[6] 760 6-9-7 65 (t) RobertWinston 7 74
(Milton Bradley) *trckd ldrs: hdwy to chse wnr over 2f out: rdn wl over 1f out: styd on fnl f* 7/1[3]

-012 **3** 2 **Hellbender (IRE)**[9] 715 7-9-5 63 (t) DuranFentiman 13 66+
(Shaun Harris) *in tch on outer: wd st: hdwy over 2f out: rdn to chse ldng pair over 1f out: drvn and no imp fnl f* 9/2[1]

5012 **4** 3 **George Fenton**[15] 640 4-9-0 65 (v) PhilipPrince(7) 4 59+
(Richard Guest) *hld up towards rr: hdwy 1/2-way: rdn to chse ldrs wl over 1f out: sn drvn and no imp fnl f* 6/1[2]

2-03 **5** 1 3/4 **Elusive Warrior (USA)**[16] 620 10-8-4 55 (p) GaryPhillips(7) 12 43
(Alan McCabe) *trckd ldrs: rdn to chse ldng pair over 2f out: drvn and one pce appr fnl f* 33/1

-414 **6** 1 1/2 **Nant Saeson (IRE)**[10] 705 4-9-2 60 (p) MichaelO'Connell 8 44
(John Quinn) *towards rr: hdwy over 2f out: sn rdn: kpt on same pce* 9/2[1]

1632 **7** 1 1/2 **Steel City Boy (IRE)**[7] 735 10-8-5 54 AnnStokell(5) 1 33
(Ann Stokell) *chsd ldrs: rdn along wl over 2f out: sn wknd* 20/1

1000 **8** hd **Lord Buffhead**[6] 760 4-9-0 58 (e[1]) KirstyMilczarek 2 37
(Richard Guest) *chsd ldrs on inner: rdn along wl over 2f out: grad wknd* 50/1

6510 **9** 2 1/4 **Lucky Mark (IRE)**[22] 535 4-9-6 64 GrahamGibbons 3 36
(Garry Moss) *reminders s and sn chsng wnr: rdn wl over 2f out: drvn wl over 1f out and grad wknd* 10/1

3610 **10** 1 **Marshall Art**[12] 687 4-8-11 62 EoinWalsh(7) 6 31
(David Evans) *chsd ldrs: rdn along wl over 2f out: sn wknd* 7/1[3]

00-5 **11** 4 1/2 **Rafaaf (IRE)**[44] 214 5-9-4 62 StephenCraine 9 17
(Richard Phillips) *nvr bttr than midfield* 16/1

40-0 **12** 2 **New Decade**[47] 187 4-9-7 65 ChrisCatlin 11 14
(Milton Bradley) *a in rr* 16/1

-436 **13** 7 **Moheebb (IRE)**[22] 347 9-8-12 56 JDSmith 5
(Robert Johnson) *sn outpcd and a bhd* 33/1

1m 15.62s (-0.88) **Going Correction** -0.10s/f (Stan) 13 Ran SP% **120.2**
Speed ratings (Par 101): **101,100,97,93,91 89,87,87,84,82 76,74,64**
toteswingers 1&2 £11.70, 1&3 £8.40, 2&3 £7.10 CSF £61.25 CT £298.91 TOTE £9.20: £2.60, £3.40, £1.50; EX 75.40 Trifecta £558.10 Pool: £2891.80 - 3.88 winning units..
Owner Charles Castle **Bred** Wyck Hall Stud Ltd **Trained** Sessay, N Yorks

FOCUS
A modest, if competitive sprint handicap contested by 13 geldings. It was crucial to be handy and the third and fourth are probably reliable guides to the form.

832 NO DEPOSIT FREE BETS WITH BOOKMAKERS.CO.UK APPRENTICE H'CAP 1m (F)
5:20 (5:20) (Class 5) (0-75,75) 4-Y-0+ **£2,587** (£770; £384; £192) **Stalls** Low

Form RPR

2-31 **1** **Caledonia Prince**[22] 540 5-9-3 71 (b) PhilipPrince 6 79
(Jo Hughes) *cl up: effrt over 2f out: rdn to ld wl over 1f out: drvn ent fnl f: kpt on wl towards fin* 3/1[2]

44-1 **2** 3/4 **Tight Lipped (IRE)**[48] 168 4-9-5 73 GaryPhillips 2 79
(James Eustace) *trckd ldrs: hdwy to ld wl over 2f out: rdn and hdd wl over 1f out: cl up and ev ch tl no ex wl ins fnl f* 7/1

-203 **3** 2 1/4 **Piceno (IRE)**[9] 715 5-9-0 75 (p) AdamMcLean(7) 1 76
(Scott Dixon) *led: rdn along and hdd wl over 2f out: cl up and drvn wl over 1f out: ev ch tl one pce ins fnl f* 12/1

1526 **4** 1 1/4 **Monzino (USA)**[6] 758 5-8-11 70 ow2 GerardGalligan(5) 5 68
(Michael Chapman) *in tch: rdn along to chse ldrs over 3f out: kpt on same pce fnl 2f* 25/1

-111 **5** 1/2 **Our Ivor**[9] 718 4-8-10 64 6ex JasonHart 3 61+
(Michael Appleby) *t.k.h: prom whn n.m.r and squeezed out after 2f: sn swtchd lft to inner and chsd ldrs: gd hdwy and cl up 3f out: rdn 2f out and ev ch tl edgd rt and wknd appr fnl f* 5/4[1]

3040 **6** 3/4 **Mazovian (USA)**[9] 715 5-8-6 67 DanielleMooney(7) 8 62
(Michael Chapman) *dwlt and towards rr: hdwy on outer 2f out: styd on fnl f: nrst fin* 33/1

1125 **7** 2 3/4 **Berlusca (IRE)**[6] 759 4-9-5 73 DavidBergin 7 62
(David O'Meara) *cl up on outer: rdn along wl over 2f out: wknd wl over 1f out* 11/2[3]

1260 **8** 16 **One Way Or Another (AUS)**[13] 672 10-8-6 67 (t) EoinWalsh(5) 4 19
(David Evans) *s.i.s: a bhd* 40/1

1m 43.99s (0.29) **Going Correction** -0.10s/f (Stan) 8 Ran SP% **114.2**
Speed ratings (Par 103): **94,93,91,89,89 88,85,69**
CSF £23.51 CT £218.92 TOTE £5.20: £1.10, £2.70, £3.30; EX 32.10 Trifecta £197.40 Pool: £2617.38 - 9.94 winning units..
Owner Isla & Colin Cage **Bred** Mrs I M Cage And C J Cage **Trained** Lambourn, Berks

FOCUS
An ordinary apprentice handicap contested entirely by geldings. The form is straightforward but limited.
T/Plt: £3040.50 to a £1 stake. Pool: £52356.22 - 12.57 winning tickets. T/Qpdt: £31.60 to a £1 stake. Pool: £5515.08 - 129.10 winning tickets. JR

741 MEYDAN (L-H)
Thursday, February 28

OFFICIAL GOING: Tapeta: standard; turf: good

833a CBD WORLD MASTERCARD (HANDICAP (TAPETA) 1m 3f
2:45 (2:45) (100-110,110) 3-Y-0+
£44,171 (£14,723; £7,361; £3,680; £2,208; £1,472)

RPR

1 **Kassiano (GER)**[14] 656 4-9-0 106 MickaelBarzalona 5 113+
(Saeed bin Suroor) *in rr of mid-div: smooth prog 3f out: led 2f out: comf* 10/11[1]

2 6 1/2 **Fattsota**[14] 661 5-9-3 107 MartinHarley 1 104
(Marco Botti) *trckd ldng: ev ch 5f out: kpt on same pce fnl 2 1/2f but no ch w wnr* 12/1

3 1/4 **In The Spotlight (IND)**[21] 555 5-8-13 102 MartinDwyer 2 100
(S Padmanabhan, India) *sn led: t.k.h: kicked clr 3 1/2f out: hdd 2f out: one pce fnl 1 1/2f* 12/1

4 1 1/4 **Bay Willow (IRE)**[21] 555 6-9-2 106 (tp) RichardMullen 7 101
(S Seemar, UAE) *s.i.s: trckd ldrs: outpcd 4f out but kpt on fnl 1 1/2f* 14/1

5 1/2 **Elderly Paradise (AUS)**[14] 659 6-9-6 110 (e) ChristopheSoumillon 8 104
(M C Tam, Macau) *trckd ldrs: ev ch 2f out: wknd fnl f* 8/1[3]

6 4 **Pisco Sour (USA)**[21] 555 5-8-13 102 (v) TedDurcan 10 90
(Saeed bin Suroor) *settled in rr: nvr able to chal but kpt on fnl 2f* 14/1

7 1 1/4 **Modun (IRE)**[14] 656 6-9-3 107 (v) KierenFallon 6 92+
(Saeed bin Suroor) *led after 1 1/2f: hdd 4f out: wknd fnl f* 5/1[2]

8 nse **Bob Le Beau (IRE)**[14] 661 6-8-11 101 (b) ShaneFoley 3 86
(Mrs John Harrington, Ire) *mid-div: rdn 5f out: sn btn* 14/1

9 5 3/4 **Adroitly (AUS)**[14] 661 6-8-13 102 PaulHanagan 9 79
(Saeed bin Suroor) *settled in rr: nvr nr to chal* 20/1

10 7 1/4 **Induna (AUS)**[14] 661 5-9-0 104 (vt) JamesDoyle 4 69
(Saeed bin Suroor) *nvr bttr than mid-div* 33/1

2m 18.06s (-0.34)
WFA 4 from 5yo+ 2lb 10 Ran SP% **123.2**
CSF: 15.04 TRICAST: 95.06 WIN: 1.70 PL: 1.40, 3.40, 2.70.
Owner Godolphin **Bred** Gestut Rottgen **Trained** Newmarket, Suffolk

FOCUS
The pace was too strong and those who raced prominently had little left at the finish. Here are the sectionals in full: 26.61 (400m) 23.95 (800m), 24.79 (1200m), 24.49 (1600m), 25.17 (2000m), before the winner ran home in a slow 13.05.

834a CBD PERSONAL LOAN (H'CAP) (TAPETA) 6f
3:20 (3:20) (100-110,110) 3-Y-0+
£44,171 (£14,723; £7,361; £3,680; £2,208; £1,472)

RPR

1 **United Color (USA)**[20] 575 4-9-3 107 (t) JamesDoyle 7 112
(D Selvaratnam, UAE) *in rr of mid-div: smooth prog 3f out: led fnl 110yds* 10/1[3]

2 3/4 **Arnold Lane (IRE)**[28] 465 4-9-0 104 MartinHarley 1 107
(Mick Channon) *mid-div: chsd ldrs 2 1/2f out: led 1f out: hdd cl home* 14/1

3 3/4 **Dubawi Sound**[14] 660 5-8-13 102 (t) JamieSpencer 12 104
(David Brown) *mid-div: smooth prog 3f out: ev ch 1 1/2f out: nt qckn fnl 110yds* 6/1[2]

4 2 1/4 **Hitchens (IRE)**[14] 660 8-9-6 110 MartinDwyer 5 104
(David Barron) *s.i.s: settled in rr: r.o fnl 2f: nrst fin*

5 1/4 **Justineo**[28] 467 4-8-10 100 PaulHanagan 2 93
(Roger Varian) *sn led: hdd 4f out: led again 2f out: hdd 1f out: kpt on same pce* 9/2[1]

6 1 1/2 **Govinda (USA)**[14] 660 6-9-0 104 TedDurcan 4 93
(Vanja Sandrup, Sweden) *mid-div: kpt on same pce fnl 1 1/2f* 18/1

7 3/4 **Red Dubawi (IRE)**[21] 557 5-8-13 102 FergalLynch 13 89
(David Marnane, Ire) *nvr able to chal* 16/1

8 1/4 **Whaileyy (IRE)**[35] 365 5-9-1 105 (b) RichardHughes 6 91
(Marco Botti) *nvr bttr than mid-div* 9/2[1]

9 3/4 **Faridat (USA)**[67] 8-9-0 104 YutakaTake 3 87
(Shigeki Matsumoto, Japan) *nvr bttr than mid-div* 6/1[2]

10 3 **Es Que Love (IRE)**[14] 660 4-8-13 102 KierenFallon 10 77
(Mark Johnston) *trckd ldrs: led 4f out: hdd & wknd 2f out* 12/1

11 1 1/2 **Global City (IRE)**[14] 660 7-8-13 102 (t) MickaelBarzalona 8 73
(Saeed bin Suroor) *nvr nr to chal* 10/1[3]

12 1 **Famous Warrior (IRE)**[7] 744 6-8-10 100 (t) PatDobbs 14 67
(Doug Watson, UAE) *chsd ldrs tl outpcd 1 1/2f out* 20/1

13 2 1/4 **Storm Ultralight (ARG)**[34] 392 7-8-10 100 RichardMullen 9 60
(S Seemar, UAE) *slowly away: nvr nr to chal* 33/1

1m 11.92s (0.32) 13 Ran SP% **125.4**
CSF: 149.56 WIN: 3.20 PL: 2.10, 3.60, 3.20 TRIFECTA: 478.10 EXACTA: 118.80.
Owner Sheikh Ahmed Al Maktoum **Bred** Adena Springs **Trained** United Arab Emirates

FOCUS
Justineo took them along in overly quick splits of 24.57 (400m), 23.03 (800m), before the winner finished in a slowing 23.70.

835a MEYDAN CLASSIC SPONSORED BY SHAHRAZAD LADIES BANKING (LISTED RACE) (TURF) 1m
3:55 (3:55) 3-Y-0
£55,214 (£18,404; £9,202; £4,601; £2,760; £1,840)

RPR

1 **Now Spun (USA)**[135] 7130 3-8-8 90 MickaelBarzalona 1 106
(Mahmood Al Zarooni) *in rr of mid-div: smooth prog 2 1/2f out: rdn to ld fnl f* 7/2[3]

2 1 1/4 **Deauville Prince (FR)**[14] 658 3-8-8 105 RichardKingscote 7 103
(Tom Dascombe) *sn led: rdn 3f out: hdd fnl f* 5/2[2]

3 1 1/4 **Tarbawi (IRE)**[21] 553 3-8-8 91 WayneSmith 2 100
(M bin Shafya, UAE) *trckd ldrs: ev ch 2 1/2f out: kpt on same pce fnl 1 1/2f* 20/1

4 1/2 **Elleval (IRE)**[21] 553 3-8-8 102 FergalLynch 3 99
(David Marnane, Ire) *settled in rr: chsd ldrs 2 1/2f out: nt qckn fnl f* 6/4[1]

5 7 1/4 **Luhaif**[21] 553 3-8-8 100 (v) MartinHarley 5 82
(Mick Channon) *trckd ldrs tl outpcd 2 1/2f out* 9/1

6 2 **Darkening (IRE)**[6] 771 3-8-8 89 AntiocoMurgia 8 78
(Ismail Mohammed) *slowly away: nvr nr to chal* 33/1

7 13 **Filfil (USA)**14 658 3-8-8 95 KierenFallon 4 48
(Mahmood Al Zarooni) *nvr bttr than mid-div* **12/1**
8 14 **Mister Big Shuffle (GER)**21 553 3-8-8 97 PaulHanagan 6 16
(Niels Petersen, Norway) *in rr of mid-div: nvr able to chal* **20/1**
1m 38.0s (98.00) **8** Ran SP% **121.0**
CSF: 13.22 WIN: 2.40 PL: 1.00,1.40, 5.20 EXACTA: 20.70 TRI: 199.00.
Owner Godolphin **Bred** Hickstead Farm **Trained** Newmarket, Suffolk

FOCUS

The sectionals show there was a slow-fast pace, set by the runner-up Deauville Prince: 27.19 (400m), 24.33 (800m), 23.31 (1200m), before the winner came home in a quick 22.86.

836a AL DANA VISA INFINITE CARD (H'CAP) (TAPETA) 1m

4:30 (4:30) (100-110,110) 3-Y-0+

£44,171 (£14,723; £7,361; £3,680; £2,208; £1,472)

RPR
1 **Mufarrh (IRE)**21 556 6-9-6 **110** PaulHanagan 4 113
(A Al Raihe, UAE) *settled in rr: led 110yds out: jst hld on* **9/1**
2 nse **Banna Boirche (IRE)**21 557 7-8-10 **100** ShaneFoley 1 103
(M Halford, Ire) *in rr of mid-div: r.o wl fnl 110yds: jst failed* **14/1**
3 1 ½ **Disa Leader (SAF)**35 367 8-9-2 **106** JGeroudis 10 106
(M F De Kock, South Africa) *trckd ldr: rdn 4f out: ev ch 110yds out: nt qckn fnl 55yds* **11/1**
4 ¼ **Modern History (IRE)**21 552 5-9-0 **104** AntiocoMurgia 11 103
(Mahmood Al Zarooni) *sn led: kicked clr 2 1/2f out: hdd fnl 110yds* **16/1**
5 ¼ **Rostrum (FR)**7 744 6-9-2 **106** DaneO'Neill 6 104
(Mahmood Al Zarooni) *mid-div: kpt on same pce fnl 1 1/2f* **10/1**
6 ¼ **Kinglet (USA)**21 557 4-9-2 **106** MickaelBarzalona 13 105
(Mahmood Al Zarooni) *mid-div: r.o fnl 1 1/2f nrst fin* **6/1**3
7 1 ½ **Sandagiyr (FR)**7 744 5-9-0 **104** PatDobbs 12 98
(Saeed bin Suroor) *mid-div: kpt on same pce fnl 1 1/2f* **10/1**
8 2 ½ **Amanee (AUS)**35 366 5-9-1 **105** ChristopheSoumillon 5 101+
(M F De Kock, South Africa) *mid-div: smooth prog 2f out: ev ch whn no room 110yds out: wknd fnl 55yds* **7/2**2
9 1 **Montmorency (IRE)**28 467 7-8-10 **100** (bt) RichardMullen 9 86
(S Seemar, UAE) *trckd ldng pair: ev ch 1 1/2f: wknd fnl 110yds* **33/1**
10 ¾ **Masteroftherolls (IRE)**14 657 5-9-0 **104** (p) KierenFallon 2 89
(Saeed bin Suroor) *nvr bttr than mid-div* **8/1**
11 2 ¼ **Producer**21 557 4-9-5 **109** RichardHughes 8 88
(Richard Hannon) *trckd ldrs tl wknd 2 1/2f out* **11/4**1
12 22 **Nordic Truce (USA)**28 465 6-9-0 **104** TedDurcan 7 33
(P Schiergen, Germany) *nvr nr to chal* **33/1**
13 19 **Le Bernardin (USA)**208 4-8-13 **102** (b) PatCosgrave 3
(Mahmood Al Zarooni) *s.i.s: sn rdn in rr: n.d* **20/1**
1m 37.85s (0.35) **13** Ran SP% **134.0**
CSF: 141.61 TRICAST: 1440.12 WIN: 13.00 PL: 3.70, 5.60, 5.30 EXACTA: 450.00.
Owner Hamdan Al Maktoum **Bred** Kenilworth House Stud **Trained** UAE

FOCUS

A strong pace helped set this up for a couple of hold-up horses. However, the long-time leader Modern History clung on for fourth, and one place ahead of him was Disa Leader, who had raced in second, and those two deserve extra credit. Here are the sectionals along with the winner's closing split: 25.53 (400m), 23.43 (800m), 24.19 (1200m) 24.08 (finish).

837a UAE OAKS SPONSORED BY AL DANA WEALTH MANAGEMENT (GROUP 3) (FILLIES) (TAPETA) 1m 1f 110y

5:05 (5:05) 3-Y-0

£92,024 (£30,674; £15,337; £7,668; £4,601; £3,067)

RPR
1 **Shuruq (USA)**21 554 3-8-9 100 (p) PaulHanagan 8 110+
(Saeed bin Suroor) *Tracked ldng trio: led 2f out: r.o wl comf* **15/2**
2 4 **Lovely Pass (IRE)**21 554 3-8-9 102 (p) KierenFallon 1 102
(Mahmood Al Zarooni) *in rr of mid-div: rdn 3f out: r.o fnl 1 1/2f: no ch w wnr* **11/4**3
3 2 ¼ **Music Chart (USA)**21 554 3-8-9 102 MickaelBarzalona 4 98
(Mahmood Al Zarooni) *settled in rr: smooth prog 2 1/2f out: ev ch 1 1/2f out: nt qckn fnl 1 1/2f* **9/4**2
4 1 ¾ **My Special J'S (USA)**21 554 3-8-9 95 RichardMullen 3 94
(John Patrick Shanahan, Ire) *trckd ldrs: led 3 1/2f out: hdd 2f out: kpt on same pce* **50/1**
5 ¼ **Emotif (ARG)**21 554 4-9-5 98 ChristopheSoumillon 2 83
(M F De Kock, South Africa) *trckd ldng trio: outpcd fnl 1 1/2f* **13/8**1
6 1 **Mar Mar (IRE)**21 554 3-8-9 97 (b) JamesDoyle 7 92
(Saeed bin Suroor) *sn led: hdd 3 1/2f out: kpt on same pce* **20/1**
7 hd **More Than Sotka (FR)**21 554 3-8-9 96 FergalLynch 6 92
(David Marnane, Ire) *settled in rr: n.d* **25/1**
8 10 **Pure Excellence**14 658 3-8-9 94 RichardHughes 9 73
(Mark Johnston) *trckd ldrs tl outpcd 3f out* **50/1**
9 ¼ **Go Angellica (IRE)**21 554 3-8-9 98 KieranO'Neill 5 72
(David Simcock) *slowly away: nvr able to chal* **50/1**
1m 58.72s (-0.28)
WFA 3 from 4yo 21lb **9** Ran SP% **121.8**
CSF: 28.87 WIN: 5.10 PL: 1.40, 1.60, 1.50 EXACTA: 17.30 TRIFECTA: 41.80.
Owner Godolphin **Bred** Darley **Trained** Newmarket, Suffolk

FOCUS

The third running of the UAE Oaks as a Group 3 (formerly Listed), but it didn't look much of a race and the pace only gradually increased. They went 26.28 (400m), 25.11 (800m), 24.85 (1200m), 23.83 (1600m). All of these had contested the 1000 Guineas (really muddling race).

838a CBD MORTGAGE LOAN (H'CAP) (TURF) 7f

5:40 (5:40) (100-111,111) 3-Y-0+

£64,417 (£21,472; £10,736; £5,368; £3,220; £2,147)

RPR
1 **Anaerobio (ARG)**14 657 6-8-9 **100** (t) PatCosgrave 7 108
(M F De Kock, South Africa) *trckd ldrs: led 1 1/2f out: r.o wl: comf* **5/1**1
2 2 ½ **Jaasoos (IRE)**28 467 9-8-6 **104** MarcMonaghan(7) 5 105
(D Selvaratnam, UAE) *trckd ldng pair: ev ch 2f out: one pce fnl f* **7/1**3
3 nse **Kenny Powers**28 467 4-9-0 **105** (vt) RichardKingscote 9 106
(Tom Dascombe) *sn led: hdd 1 1/2f out: kpt on same pce* **13/2**2
4 1 ¼ **Spirit Of Battle (USA)**12 696 5-8-9 **100** (b) HarryBentley 3 98
(A bin Huzaim, UAE) *mid-div: r.o fnl 1 1/2f but nvr nr to chal* **9/1**
5 ¾ **Field Of Dream**7 744 6-8-11 **102** (b) RichardHughes 12 98
(Jamie Osborne) *slowly away: settled in rr: r.o fnl 1 1/2f: nrst fin* **13/2**2
6 ¼ **Across The Rhine (USA)**7 745 7-8-13 **104** RichardMullen 1 99
(S Seemar, UAE) *slowly away: mid-div: kpt on same pce fnl 1 1/2f* **20/1**
7 ¼ **David Livingston (IRE)**187 5606 4-8-11 **102** PatDobbs 2 100+
(M F De Kock, South Africa) *settled in rr: nvr nr to chal* **5/1**1

8 ¼ **Pied A Terre (AUS)**28 465 5-9-0 **105** KierenFallon 4 99
(Saeed bin Suroor) *settled in rr: nvr nr to chal but kpt on same pce fnl 1 1/2f* **8/1**
9 1 ¼ **Alazeyab (USA)**14 660 7-9-0 **105** (vt) PaulHanagan 8 95
(A Al Raihe, UAE) *trckd ldng pair: nt qckn fnl 2f* **16/1**
10 ¾ **Fanunalter**28 466 7-9-6 **111** MartinHarley 11 100
(Marco Botti) *nvr nr to chal* **20/1**
11 2 ½ **Bannock (IRE)**145 6868 4-9-1 **106** (b) MickaelBarzalona 6 88
(Mahmood Al Zarooni) *trckd ldrs tl outpcd 2f out* **7/1**3
12 2 ½ **Silver Ocean (USA)**14 659 5-9-2 **107** Per-AndersGraberg 10 83
(Niels Petersen, Norway) *nvr able to chal* **33/1**
1m 24.71s (84.71) **12** Ran SP% **124.5**
CSF: 40.67, TRICAST: 238.49 WIN: 4.20 PL: 1.60, 2.90, 2.50 EXACTA: 67.20 TRIFECTA: 450.30 Placepot: £435.60 to a £1 stake. Pool: £8473.45 - 14.20 winning tickets. Quadpot: £69.40 to a £1 stake. Pool: £422.40 - 4.50 winning tickets..
Owner Mohd Khaleel Ahmed **Bred** Haras La Madrugada **Trained** South Africa

FOCUS

The pace was ordinary early on and picked up significantly just after halfway, and the first four finishers were all positioned in the top six at the 800m point. Here are the splits: 26.16 (400m), 24.32 (800m), 22.59 (1200m), 11.64 (finish).

803 LINGFIELD (L-H)

Friday, March 1

OFFICIAL GOING: Standard

Wind: Moderate, half against Weather: Overcast, chilly

839 MR LOVER LOVERIDGE FAREWELL (S) STKS 1m (P)

2:00 (2:00) (Class 6) 4-Y-0+ **£2,045** (£603; £302) **Stalls High**

Form RPR
-231 1 **Saharia (IRE)**11 707 6-9-4 77 (be) StephenCraine 5 68+
(Daniel Mark Loughnane) *stdd s: hld up in last: stl there whn ldng pair kicked on over 2f out: prog on inner over 1f out: chsd wnr fnl f: reminders and nt qckn tl lft in ld post* **11/4**3
1110 2 nse **Paphos**12 700 6-9-4 73 (v) DavidProbert 3 68+
(Charles Hills) *led: rdn whn pressed over 2f out: kpt on u.p fr over 1f out: holding on whn eased nr fin: hdd post* **1/1**1
5022 3 2 ½ **Cyflymder (IRE)**7 749 7-8-5 68 IanBurns(7) 1 55+
(David C Griffiths) *chsd ldr: rdn to chal over 2f out: hung bdly rt bnd wl over 1f out: one pce and lost 2nd fnl f* **5/2**2
0024 4 2 ¼ **Amber Moon**3 805 8-8-4 39 ow2 AnnStokell(5) 4 47
(Ann Stokell) *in tch in 4th: urged along fr 3f out: sn outpcd: n.d fnl 2f* **66/1**
0014 5 1 ½ **Fairy Mist (IRE)**9 725 6-9-4 45 (v1) AdamKirby 2 52?
(John Bridger) *chsd ldng pair: outpcd and pushed along over 2f out: reminder wl over 1f out: hld together and lost 4th fnl f* **25/1**
1m 36.99s (-1.21) **Going Correction** +0.025s/f (Slow) **5** Ran SP% **110.6**
Speed ratings (Par 101): **107,106,104,102,100**
CSF £5.97 TOTE £3.30: £1.50, £1.90; EX 6.30 Trifecta £8.80 Pool: £2682.39 - 227.77 winning units..The winner was bought in for 4,800gns. Paphos was claimed by P. D. Evans for £6000.
Owner Brooklands Racing **Bred** Woodcote Stud Ltd **Trained** Baldwin's Gate, Staffs
■ Stewards' Enquiry : David Probert 28-day ban: failed to ride out to win (Mar 15-28, 30-31, Apr 1-6,8-13)

FOCUS

The wrong horse won here, as the well-backed favourite Paphos had the race in the bag before David Probert decided to ease up on him in the final ten yards. The lowly rated fourth and fifth were closer than ideal and limit the form.

840 FOREST ROW H'CAP 1m (P)

2:30 (2:30) (Class 6) (0-65,72) 4-Y-0+ **£2,045** (£603; £302) **Stalls High**

Form RPR
6542 1 **Electrician**7 747 4-9-2 **60** (b) AndreaAtzeni 2 64
(Tim Pitt) *led at gd pce: rdn 2f out: hdd ins fnl f: rallied to ld last strides* **9/2**2
3111 2 hd **Flamborough Breeze**2 813 4-10-0 **72** 12ex (t) GeorgeBaker 6 75
(Ed Vaughan) *hld up and sn in last: stdy prog on outer fr 3f out: wnt 2nd over 1f out: rdn to ld ins fnl f: idled and urged along: hdd last strides* **1/2**1
065- 3 1 **Benandonner (USA)**64 8250 10-9-7 **65** JoeFanning 5 66
(Paddy Butler) *chsd wnr: lost 2nd and shkn up over 1f out: kpt on steadily fnl f: nvr quite chal* **16/1**
500- 4 4 ½ **Bajan Story**166 6275 4-9-2 **60** LiamKeniry 7 51
(Michael Blanshard) *stmbld s and rdr nrly fell off: hld up in 5th: rdn over 2f out: tried to cl over 1f out: wknd fnl f* **20/1**
13-4 5 ½ **Alezanna**46 200 4-8-11 **55** RobertHavlin 3 45
(James Toller) *chsd clr ldng pair to 1/2-way: rdn over 2f out: tried to cl over 1f out: sn wknd* **8/1**3
0-00 6 4 ½ **Beauchamp Xerxes**28 478 7-8-9 **58** (t) NicoleNordblad(5) 1 37
(Hans Adielsson) *s.v.s: t.k.h: prog fr last to chse ldng pair 1/2-way: wknd wl over 1f out* **16/1**
64/0 7 ½ **Tartaria**7 753 7-8-13 **57** JimmyQuinn 4 35
(Edward Creighton) *hld up in rr: pushed along 3f out: no prog 2f out: wknd on inner fnl f* **33/1**
1m 37.54s (-0.66) **Going Correction** +0.025s/f (Slow) **7** Ran SP% **115.4**
Speed ratings (Par 101): **104,103,102,98,97 93,92**
toteswingers 1&2 £1.10, 2&3 £3.50, 1&3 £4.90 CSF £7.25 TOTE £5.50: £1.80, £1.30; EX 9.10 Trifecta £56.10 Pool: £4850.97 - 64.80 winning units..
Owner Saintly Racing **Bred** Darley **Trained** Newmarket, Suffolk

FOCUS

An ordinary handicap but it was run at a solid gallop. The winner is rated to the best of last year's form.

841 LINGFIELD PARK OWNERS GROUP MAIDEN STKS 1m 4f (P)

3:05 (3:06) (Class 5) 3-Y-0+ **£2,726** (£805; £402) **Stalls Low**

Form RPR
52 1 **El Massivo (IRE)**37 333 3-8-5 0 JimmyQuinn 5 55+
(William Jarvis) *edgy in stalls: dwlt: t.k.h: hld up in tch: prog over 2f out: chsd ldr over 1f out: hrd rdn to ld last 150yds: kpt on* **4/5**1
2 2 1 ¾ **Mirth**23 541 3-8-0 0 NickyMackay 7 48
(Mark Johnston) *led: set v stdy pce to 4f out: drvn 2f out: hdd and one pce last 150yds* **3/1**2
/2 3 ½ **Fulgora**16 637 5-9-9 0 SebSanders 2 49
(Brendan Powell) *trckd ldr to 5f out: lost pl once pce lifted 4f out and sn rdn in 5th: styd on again fr over 1f out to take 3rd last 100yds* **9/2**3
00 4 1 ½ **Culture Trip**20 580 3-8-5 0 FrankieMcDonald 4 50
(Murty McGrath) *t.k.h: trckd ldng pair: wnt 2nd 5f out: drvn to chal over 2f out: fdd over 1f out* **100/1**

00-0 **5** 1/2 **Lion's Maid**49 157 4-9-7 19 RobertHavlin 6 46
(Michael Attwater) *dwlt: hld up in last pair: outpcd and pushed along 3f out: taken wd in st: kpt on ins fnl f* **66/1**

06- **6** shd **Bestfootforward**62 8291 4-9-7 0 KirstyMilczarek 1 46
(Olivia Maylam) *t.k.h: hld up in last pair: outpcd and pushed along 3f out: shkn up and kpt on fnl f* **25/1**

6 **7** 2 **Big Kahuna**49 157 6-9-7 0 IanBurns(7) 3 48
(Jane Chapple-Hyam) *edgy in stalls: dwlt: t.k.h: hld up in 5th: prog to join ldrs over 3f out: wknd over 2f out* **20/1**

2m 42.1s (9.10) **Going Correction** +0.025s/f (Slow)
WFA 3 from 4yo 23lb 4 from 5yo+ 2lb 7 Ran SP% **109.8**
Speed ratings (Par 103): **70,68,68,67,67 67,65**
toteswingers 1&2 £1.30, 2&3 £1.50, 1&3 £1.50 CSF £3.01 TOTE £1.70: £1.20, £1.60; EX 3.60 Trifecta £7.60 Pool: £6691.03 - 655.51winning units..
Owner The B A D D Partnership **Bred** Laundry Cottage Stud Farm **Trained** Newmarket, Suffolk

FOCUS
There wasn't much of a gallop on early and a race to treat negatively.

842 GRUNDFOS WATERMILL H'CAP 5f (P)
3:40 (3:40) (Class 5) (0-70,70) 4-Y-0+ **£2,726** (£805; £402) **Stalls** High

Form RPR

/211 **1** **Danziger (IRE)**9 719 4-9-6 **69** 6ex AdamKirby 5 77+
(David Evans) *w.w in last pair: taken wdst of all bnd 2f out: drvn and r.o to ld last 150yds: sn in command* **5/4**1

0044 **2** 1 1/4 **Desert Strike**6 775 7-9-1 **69** (p) ShirleyTeasdale(5) 3 73
(Conor Dore) *pressed ldr: urged along 2f out: clsd to ld briefly jst ins fnl f: outpcd after* **8/1**

0104 **3** 1/2 **Charming (IRE)**9 719 4-9-4 **67** (e) IanMongan 7 69
(Olivia Maylam) *chsd ldng pair on outer: rdn wl over 1f out: kpt on same pce fnl f* **8/1**

-060 **4** 1 1/2 **Speightowns Kid (USA)**20 583 5-9-6 **69** J-PGuillambert 2 66
(Jo Hughes) *chsd ldng pair: pushed along fr 2f out: one pce and no imp* **6/1**3

3036 **5** nk **Above The Stars**13 687 5-8-11 **60** FergusSweeney 1 55
(Jamie Osborne) *led: rdn over 1f out: hdd & wknd jst ins fnl f* **5/1**2

033- **6** 3/4 **Dreams Of Glory**131 7275 5-8-1 **57** PhilipPrince(7) 4 51
(Ron Hodges) *w.w in last pair: hmpd on inner over 2f out: struggling after* **6/1**3

59.23s (0.43) **Going Correction** +0.025s/f (Slow) 6 Ran SP% **111.9**
Speed ratings (Par 103): **97,95,94,91,91 90**
toteswingers 1&2 £2.10, 2&3 £4.90, 1&3 £2.70 CSF £11.90 CT £55.18 TOTE £1.50: £1.10, £2.90; EX 7.10 Trifecta £26.20 Pool: £4639.99 - 132.46 winning units..
Owner Mrs E Evans **Bred** Castleton Lyons & Kilboy Estate **Trained** Pandy, Monmouths

FOCUS
A good gallop was set. The winner can rate higher and the form behind is straightforward.

843 MARSH GREEN H'CAP 7f (P)
4:15 (4:15) (Class 5) (0-75,74) 3-Y-0 **£2,726** (£805; £402) **Stalls** Low

Form RPR

034- **1** **Skytrain**131 7268 3-8-10 **63** JoeFanning 1 71+
(Mark Johnston) *mde all: kicked away over 1f out: shkn up and styd on wl* **9/4**2

1146 **2** 1 1/2 **Gabrial The Boss (USA)**14 666 3-9-7 **74** (t) FergusSweeney 3 76
(David Simcock) *hld up in last effrt wl over 1f out: shkn up to take 2nd jst ins fnl f: styd on but wnr beyond recall* **5/1**3

5-21 **3** 4 **Jimmy The Snooze (IRE)**16 636 3-9-2 **69** (t) AndreaAtzeni 4 61
(Stuart Williams) *chsd wnr: rdn 2f out: lost action and wknd fnl f: broke down after r* **1/1**1

1-3 **4** 2 1/2 **Studfarmer**16 628 3-9-2 **69** AdamKirby 2 54
(David Evans) *chsd ldng pair but nvr gng that wl: rdn over 2f out: wknd over 1f out* **5/1**3

1m 24.61s (-0.19) **Going Correction** +0.025s/f (Slow) 4 Ran SP% **114.1**
Speed ratings (Par 98): **102,100,95,92**
CSF £12.93 TOTE £4.00; EX 13.20 Trifecta £18.80 Pool: £2721.37 - 108.03 winning units..
Owner A D Spence **Bred** Brook Stud Bloodstock Ltd **Trained** Middleham Moor, N Yorks

FOCUS
There was a good bit of support for the winner who can do better again and can win more races.

844 3RD BARRY GURR MEMORIAL H'CAP 7f (P)
4:50 (4:50) (Class 4) (0-85,85) 4-Y-0+ **£4,690** (£1,395; £697; £348) **Stalls** Low

Form RPR

1552 **1** **Al's Memory (IRE)**7 751 4-9-4 **82** AdamKirby 8 89
(David Evans) *mde all: wound up the pce fr 1/2-way: drvn 2f out: styd on u.p fnl f* **7/2**2

4266 **2** 3/4 **Rakaan (IRE)**13 690 6-9-7 **85** (p) FergusSweeney 1 90
(Jamie Osborne) *trckd ldng pair: effrt on inner 2f out: rdn to chse wnr fnl f: kpt on but no imp nr fin* **7/1**

34-2 **3** hd **Chokidar (IRE)**36 358 5-8-11 **75** (v) RobertWinston 6 80
(Scott Dixon) *chsd wnr: drvn to chal over 2f out: nt qckn and hld over 1f out: sn lost 2nd: kpt on again last 100yds* **7/2**2

011- **4** 3/4 **Living Leader**91 7935 4-9-1 **79** TomMcLaughlin 7 82+
(Nick Littmoden) *chsd ldng pair on outer: drvn and struggling wl over 2f out: sn lost pl: styd on again ins fnl f* **7/4**1

0-05 **5** 3/4 **Titan Triumph**7 749 9-8-7 **71** oh2 (t) JimmyQuinn 5 72
(William Knight) *hld up in tch: gng wl enough whn nt clr run on inner 2f out: rdn over 1f out: kpt on same pce* **33/1**

5421 **6** 3/4 **Showboating (IRE)**7 751 5-8-12 **81** 6ex(vt) WilliamTwiston-Davies(5) 3 80
(Alan McCabe) *s.v.s: rcvrd and in tch in rr after 2f: rdn 2f out: nt qckn and no imp on ldrs* **6/1**3

100- **7** 4 1/2 **Chiswick Bey (IRE)**136 7144 5-9-2 **80** LiamKeniry 2 67
(Noel Quinlan) *hld up and sn in last: shuffled along over 1f out: nvr remotely involved* **25/1**

1m 25.78s (0.98) **Going Correction** +0.025s/f (Slow) 7 Ran SP% **114.4**
Speed ratings (Par 105): **95,94,93,93,92 91,86**
toteswingers 1&2 £3.80, 2&3 £3.10, 1&3 £2.80 CSF £27.71 CT £90.88 TOTE £6.10: £2.50, £3.80; EX 24.30 Trifecta £112.70 Pool: £4287.30 - 28.53 winning units..
Owner Will Dawson **Bred** Brian Miller **Trained** Pandy, Monmouths

FOCUS
The Adam Kirby-David Evans partnership has been a successful one round here for a while now, but particularly this season, as they are now 10-21 when teaming up. The winner goes well here and the third helps confirm the level.

845 LINGFIELDPARK.CO.UK H'CAP 1m (P)
5:20 (5:20) (Class 6) (0-65,65) 3-Y-0 **£2,045** (£603; £302) **Stalls** High

Form RPR

21-6 **1** **Blazeofenchantment (USA)**47 195 3-9-5 **63** (p) AdamKirby 8 68
(Noel Quinlan) *led 1f: stdd into 3rd: effrt and gap appeared between rivals 2f out: led over 1f out: racd awkwardly and drvn out* **4/5**1

3113 **2** 2 **Darkest Night (IRE)**19 599 3-9-5 **63** FergusSweeney 6 63
(Jamie Osborne) *plld hrd early: hld up towards rr: prog 2f out: rdn and hanging bdly over 1f out: chsd wnr ins fnl f: nvr able to chal* **8/1**

00-4 **3** 1/2 **Zhuba (IRE)**13 685 3-9-7 **65** LiamKeniry 4 64
(John Best) *hld up in rr: pushed along fr 1/2-way: struggling over 2f out: drvn and styd on fnl f to take 3rd nr fin* **6/1**3

25-5 **4** 3/4 **Give Me High Five**58 17 3-8-13 **62** WilliamTwiston-Davies(5) 1 60
(Richard Hannon) *hld up in last: pushed along 3f out: styd on fnl f on inner to take 4th nr fin* **16/1**

-332 **5** nk **Gebayl**17 623 3-9-5 **63** (p) AndreaAtzeni 3 60
(James Tate) *mostly chsd ldr to wl over 1f out: sn rdn and fnd nil: fdd fnl f* **10/1**

230 **6** hd **Una Bella Cosa**24 527 3-8-4 **53** (v1) ShirleyTeasdale(5) 2 49
(Alan McCabe) *pushed up to ld after 1f and set gd pce: hdd over 1f out: wknd fnl f* **25/1**

33-6 **7** 4 1/2 **Scepticism (USA)**16 632 3-9-0 **58** JoeFanning 7 44
(Mark Johnston) *s.i.s: racd wd and sn wl in tch: wknd 2f out* **5/1**2

1m 37.56s (-0.64) **Going Correction** +0.025s/f (Slow) 7 Ran SP% **116.4**
Speed ratings (Par 96): **104,102,101,100,100 100,95**
toteswingers 1&2 £2.40, 2&3 £5.80, 1&3 £2.30 CSF £8.56 CT £25.34 TOTE £1.60: £1.10, £4.90; EX 9.90 Trifecta £47.00 Pool: £3468.89 - 55.35 winning units..
Owner The Unique Partnership **Bred** Gulf Coast Farms LLC **Trained** Newmarket, Suffolk

FOCUS
There was a sound gallop on here and the effort is related close to his previous course win.
T/Plt: £37.20 to a £1 stake. Pool: £55134.52 -1080.37 winning tickets. T/Qpdt: £16.80 to a £1 stake. Pool: £3922.84 - 171.91 winning tickets. JN

795 WOLVERHAMPTON (A.W) (L-H)
Friday, March 1

OFFICIAL GOING: Standard
Wind: Fresh against Weather: Overcast

846 32REDPOKER.COM APPRENTICE H'CAP 1m 4f 50y(P)
5:40 (5:41) (Class 6) (0-55,60) 4-Y-0+ **£1,940** (£577; £288; £144) **Stalls** Low

Form RPR

0-06 **1** **Smirfy's Silver**16 625 9-8-7 **46** oh1 JordanNason(5) 3 55+
(Michael Mullineaux) *hld up: plld hrd: hdwy over 2f out: led over 1f out: styd on wl* **33/1**

-536 **2** 2 1/4 **Crimson Monarch (USA)**4 788 9-8-12 **46** oh1 (b) JoshBaudains 5 51
(Peter Hiatt) *hld up: hdwy over 1f out: rdn to go 2nd wl ins fnl f: no ch w wnr* **7/2**2

1-64 **3** 1 3/4 **Tram Express (FR)**14 671 9-9-7 **55** (t) DanielMuscutt 1 58
(Shaun Lycett) *a.p: rdn over 2f out: styd on same pce fnl f* **4/1**3

60-0 **4** shd **Snowy Valley**8 737 4-9-1 **51** RyanTate 2 53
(Simon Earle) *chsd ldr over 5f: remained handy: wnt 2nd again over 2f out tl rdn over 1f out: styd on same pce fnl f* **20/1**

0-00 **5** nk **Mayan Flight (IRE)**16 625 5-8-12 **46** GaryPhillips 6 48
(Tony Carroll) *hld up: hdwy over 2f out: rdn and nt clr run over 1f out: styd on same pce fnl f* **14/1**

65-0 **6** hd **There's No Rules**1 820 4-8-10 **46** oh1 (e1) DavidBergin 4 48?
(Richard Guest) *set stdy pce tl qcknd 3f out: hdd over 1f out: no ex ins fnl f* **28/1**

3161 **7** 3/4 **Sommersturm (GER)**7 755 9-9-7 **60** 6ex (t) EoinWalsh(5) 7 60
(David Evans) *hld up: hdwy 1/2-way: rdn and lost pl over 2f out: rallied over 1f out: nt clr run ins fnl f: no ex* **7/4**1

0001 **8** 7 **Turjuman (USA)**11 703 8-9-4 **55** 6ex ConorHarrison(3) 8 44
(Simon West) *prom: chsd ldr over 6f out tl rdn over 2f out: wknd over 1f out* **11/2**

2m 45.9s (4.80) **Going Correction** +0.30s/f (Slow)
WFA 4 from 5yo+ 2lb 8 Ran SP% **111.8**
Speed ratings (Par 101): **96,94,93,93,93 92,92,87**
toteswingers 1&2 £34.80, 1&3 £17.30, 2&3 £2.30 CSF £139.14 CT £572.84 TOTE £75.40: £13.00, £1.10, £1.10; EX 220.60 Trifecta £1047.00 Pool: £2,191.30 - 1.56 winning units..
Owner Mrs Dian Plant **Bred** G S Shropshire **Trained** Alpraham, Cheshire

FOCUS
Track GallopMastered after race 4. This apprentice handicap lacked strength in depth. They went a sedate gallop and it turned into a sprint from 2f out. The form behind is straightforward but modest.

847 32RED.COM CLAIMING STKS 5f 20y(P)
6:10 (6:10) (Class 5) 3-Y-0 **£2,911** (£866; £432) **Stalls** Low

Form RPR

2143 **1** **Windforpower (IRE)**11 710 3-8-11 71 (be) WilliamCarson 3 69
(Ronald Harris) *trckd ldr: shkn up to ld wl ins fnl f: r.o* **1/2**1

3224 **2** hd **Modern Lady**11 710 3-8-8 66 RobbieFitzpatrick 4 65
(Richard Guest) *racd keenly: led at stdy pce tl qcknd 2f out: rdn and hdd wl ins fnl f: r.o* **2/1**2

0- **3** 8 **Nors The Panic**297 1949 3-8-6 0 JasonHart(5) 2 39
(Richard Guest) *trckd ldrs: plld hrd: outpcd fnl 2f* **14/1**3

1m 4.0s (1.70) **Going Correction** +0.30s/f (Slow) 3 Ran SP% **106.7**
Speed ratings (Par 98): **98,97,84**
CSF £1.76 TOTE £1.40; EX 1.80 Trifecta £1.60 Pool: £1,236.32 - 570.53 winning units..Windforpower was claimed by David Tait for £8,000.
Owner Anthony Cooke **Bred** Tally-Ho Stud **Trained** Earlswood, Monmouths

FOCUS
With the defection of Hiddon Coin, this was basically a match and the first two came away.

848 32REDBET.COM H'CAP 5f 216y(P)
6:40 (6:42) (Class 6) (0-55,55) 3-Y-0 **£1,940** (£577; £288; £144) **Stalls** Low

Form RPR

2-13 **1** **Hazard Warning (IRE)**19 598 3-9-5 **53** (b) DuranFentiman 6 67
(Tim Easterby) *hld up: hdwy over 1f out: rdn to ld ins fnl f: r.o* **5/1**3

3-53 **2** 2 1/4 **Petite Georgia (IRE)**[28] 482 3-9-7 **55**........................ GeorgeBaker 10 62
(George Baker) *s.i.s: hld up: hdwy and nt clr run over 1f out: rdn to chse wnr wl ins fnl f: r.o* **9/2[2]**

00-1 **3** 2 3/4 **Hannahs Turn**[19] 598 3-9-3 **51**........................ HayleyTurner 1 49+
(Chris Dwyer) *w ldr tl led over 2f out: sn clr: rdn: hdd and no ex ins fnl f* **11/4[1]**

-333 **4** 1 1/2 **Black Truffle (FR)**[9] 732 3-9-1 **49**........................(p) DavidProbert 9 42
(Mark Usher) *s.i.s: hld up: hdwy over 2f out: rdn over 1f out: nt trble ldrs* **8/1**

-051 **5** 1/2 **Chelsea Grey (IRE)**[30] 442 3-9-1 **49**........................(b) WilliamCarson 7 40
(Ronald Harris) *led over 3f: sn rdn: wknd ins fnl f* **16/1**

5-64 **6** nk **Daisie Cutter**[46] 207 3-9-1 **52**........................ SimonPearce(3) 4 42
(Lydia Pearce) *hmpd s: bhd: rdn and r.o ins fnl f: nvr nrr* **20/1**

2260 **7** 1 1/4 **Holding Fast (IRE)**[24] 527 3-9-7 **55**........................ MartinLane 11 41
(Tobias B P Coles) *chsd ldrs: rdn over 2f out: wknd fnl f* **8/1**

00-4 **8** nk **Southern Sapphire**[35] 374 3-9-3 **51**........................ GrahamLee 5 36
(Kristin Stubbs) *hld up: rdn and hung lft over 1f out: n.d* **14/1**

4-60 **9** 1 **Cromwell Rose (IRE)**[30] 442 3-8-7 **46**..........(b) MichaelJMMurphy(5) 8 28
(John Weymes) *prom: rdn over 2f out: wknd fnl f* **33/1**

0-25 **10** 3 1/2 **Twinwood Star (IRE)**[13] 686 3-8-12 **49**........................ MichaelMetcalfe(3) 3 20
(John Weymes) *hld up: rdn over 1f out: n.d* **66/1**

0-35 **11** 10 **Eyeline**[21] 561 3-8-13 **52**........................(p) JackDuern(5) 13
(Reg Hollinshead) *mid-div: rdn 1/2-way: wknd over 2f out* **40/1**

-305 **12** 12 **Scarlet Strand**[14] 669 3-9-6 **54**........................ GrahamGibbons 12
(Reg Hollinshead) *chsd ldrs: rdn over 2f out: wknd over 1f out* **33/1**

5-44 **U** **Jordanstown**[19] 598 3-9-5 **53**........................(p) PhillipMakin 2
(Kevin Ryan) *uns rdr leaving stalls* **13/2**

1m 15.64s (0.64) **Going Correction** +0.30s/f (Slow) **13** Ran SP% **124.2**
Speed ratings (Par 96): **107,104,100,98,97 97,95,95,93,89 75,59,**
toteswingers 1&2 £3.90, 1&3 £3.70, 2&3 £3.90 CSF £27.66 CT £79.35 TOTE £7.10: £2.10, £1.70, £1.60; EX 34.10 Trifecta £88.40 Pool: £1,666.32 - 14.13 winning units..
Owner Habton Farms **Bred** E O'Gorman **Trained** Great Habton, N Yorks

FOCUS
A competitive sprint handicap for 3-y-os. The form is rated around the first two.

849 32RED CASINO MEDIAN AUCTION MAIDEN STKS 7f 32y(P)
7:10 (7:12) (Class 5) 3-5-Y-O **£2,587** (£770; £384; £192) **Stalls** High

Form RPR

32-2 **1** **Ifan (IRE)**[17] 619 5-9-5 64........................ DanielMuscutt(7) 11 69
(Tim Vaughan) *trckd ldrs: plld hrd: led 1/2-way: clr 2f out: rdn ins fnl f: jst hld on* **3/1[2]**

3 **2** 1/2 **Green Special (ITY)**[21] 561 3-8-8 0 ow1........................ MarkCoumbe(3) 6 64
(Frank Sheridan) *a.p: nt clr run over 1f out: sn rdn: r.o* **8/1**

-033 **3** hd **Two No Bids (IRE)**[9] 729 3-8-10 64........................ DavidProbert 7 61
(Phil McEntee) *a.p: rdn over 1f out: edgd lft ins fnl f: r.o* **9/2[3]**

00- **4** 1 1/4 **Bain's Pass (IRE)**[216] 4587 3-8-7 0........................ JulieBurke(3) 9 58
(Kevin Ryan) *hld up: pushed along 1/2-way: hdwy over 1f out: r.o* **5/1**

5 1/2 **Clary (IRE)** 3-8-5 0........................ AdamBeschizza 1 52
(James Unett) *s.s: bhd: hdwy over 1f out: r.o* **20/1**

6 2 1/4 **Zainda (IRE)**[70] 8215 3-8-5 0........................ HayleyTurner 3 46
(John Wainwright) *chsd ldrs: rdn over 2f out: no ex fnl f* **5/2[1]**

0- **7** nk **Born To Run**[158] 6533 3-8-5 0........................(b[1]) MartinLane 10 46
(Hugo Palmer) *led to 1/2-way: rdn over 2f out: no ex fnl f* **25/1**

8 7 **Stoneacre Oskar** 4-9-2 0........................ SladeO'Hara(5) 8 29
(Peter Grayson) *s.s: bhd: shkn up over 1f out: nvr on terms* **80/1**

9 9 **Aura Bora (USA)**[12] 5-9-12 0........................ DuranFentiman 4 12
(Tim Easterby) *sn pushed along in rr: wknd 1/2-way* **22/1**

1m 31.08s (1.48) **Going Correction** +0.30s/f (Slow)
WFA 3 from 4yo+ 16lb **9** Ran SP% **113.7**
Speed ratings (Par 103): **103,102,102,100,100 97,97,89,79**
CSF £24.97 TOTE £3.40: £1.50, £2.20, £2.00; EX 18.70 Trifecta £43.90 Pool: £1,541.25 - 26.29 winning units..
Owner WRB Racing 61 and Derek & Jean Clee **Bred** Dr John Waldron **Trained** Aberthin, Vale of Glamorgan

FOCUS
A modest 7f maiden in which the winner scraped home and on this evidence is not much better than this.

850 32RED H'CAP 1m 1f 103y(P)
7:40 (7:41) (Class 5) (0-75,75) 4-Y-0+ **£2,911** (£866; £432; £216) **Stalls** Low

Form RPR

-535 **1** **Dakota Canyon (IRE)**[18] 614 4-9-3 **71**........................(b) FrederikTylicki 9 79
(Richard Fahey) *swtchd lft sn after s: hld up: racd keenly: hdwy over 1f out: rdn ins fnl f: r.o to ld post* **7/2[2]**

31-1 **2** shd **Ishikawa (IRE)**[58] 21 5-9-5 **73**........................ GrahamLee 1 81
(Alan King) *chsd ldrs: rdn to ld wl ins fnl f: hdd post* **5/2[1]**

143 **3** nk **Lean On Pete (IRE)**[7] 759 4-9-7 **75**........................ GrahamGibbons 3 82
(Ollie Pears) *prom: lost pl over 2f out: rallied over 1f out: rdn and ev ch ins fnl f: r.o* **5/2[1]**

0045 **4** 1/2 **Copperwood**[16] 644 8-9-2 **70**........................ FrannyNorton 2 76
(Mark Johnston) *chsd ldr: rdn to ld over 1f out: hdd wl ins fnl f: styd on* **20/1**

00-0 **5** 2 **Six Silver Lane**[51] 112 5-8-7 **68**........................(v[1]) AdamMcLean(7) 8 70+
(Derek Shaw) *racd wd: led at stdy pce: qcknd clr over 5f out: hung lft thereafter: hdd over 1f out: styd on* **28/1**

253- **6** 1/2 **McCool Bannanas**[74] 8152 5-8-13 **67**........................ DavidProbert 7 69
(James Unett) *a.p: rdn and ev ch over 1f out: styd on same pce ins fnl f* **14/1**

21-2 **7** 1 **Bert The Alert**[34] 403 5-9-4 **72**........................ GeorgeBaker 5 72
(Gary Moore) *hld up: hdwy over 2f out: rdn over 1f out: no ex ins fnl f* **8/1[3]**

00-0 **8** 11 **Mountain Range (IRE)**[18] 614 5-9-5 **73**........................ JamieMackay 6 52
(Willie Musson) *stdd s: a bhd* **12/1**

22-0 **9** 25 **Guest Book (IRE)**[58] 11 6-8-7 **66**........................ SladeO'Hara(5) 4
(Peter Grayson) *s.i.s: a bhd: t.o* **40/1**

2m 4.43s (2.73) **Going Correction** +0.30s/f (Slow) **9** Ran SP% **115.5**
Speed ratings (Par 103): **99,98,98,98,96 95,95,85,63**
toteswingers 1&2 £2.10, 1&3 £2.40, 2&3 £1.80 CSF £12.40 CT £24.94 TOTE £4.20: £1.30, £1.80, £1.40; EX 14.00 Trifecta £40.50 Pool: £1,606.71 - 29.71 winning units..
Owner Mrs Una Towell **Bred** P J Towell **Trained** Musley Bank, N Yorks
■ Stewards' Enquiry : Frederik Tylicki two-day ban: careless riding (Mar 15-16)

FOCUS
The feature handicap of the night but it was another farcical affair. The first three are all rated close to form.

851 £32 BONUS AT 32RED.COM H'CAP 2m 119y(P)
8:10 (8:10) (Class 6) (0-60,66) 4-Y-0+ **£1,940** (£577; £288; £144) **Stalls** Low

Form RPR

40-1 **1** **Hoonose**[28] 469 4-8-12 **53**........................(v) EddieAhern 6 63+
(Pat Eddery) *chsd ldr 14f out tl led over 2f out: rdn over 1f out: styd on wl* **4/1[3]**

41-1 **2** 1 3/4 **Guards Chapel**[9] 724 5-10-2 **66** 6ex........................(v) GeorgeBaker 1 74
(Gary Moore) *hld up: hdwy to chse wnr 2f out: rdn over 1f out: edgd lft: styd on same pce ins fnl f* **11/10[1]**

2412 **3** 1/2 **Scribe (IRE)**[9] 724 5-9-3 **58**........................(t) ThomasBrown(5) 2 65
(David Evans) *chsd ldr 2f: remained handy: rdn over 2f out: styd on same pce fnl f* **5/2[2]**

3-25 **4** 2 1/2 **Baan (USA)**[31] 430 10-9-5 **55**........................ GrahamLee 3 59
(James Eustace) *set stdy pce tl qcknd over 4f out: hdd over 2f out: no ex fnl f* **8/1**

3m 48.11s (6.31) **Going Correction** +0.30s/f (Slow)
WFA 4 from 5yo+ 5lb **4** Ran SP% **107.3**
Speed ratings (Par 101): **97,96,95,94**
CSF £8.84 TOTE £6.60; EX 8.70 Trifecta £13.70 Pool: £967.80 - 52.60 winning units..
Owner Miss Emma L Owen **Bred** Mrs R F Johnson Houghton **Trained** Nether Winchendon, Bucks

FOCUS
Just the four runners but a strong contest for the grade and all had their chance. The winner could have more to offer and the placed horses give the form substance.

852 JOE WRIGHT MEMORIAL H'CAP 1m 1f 103y(P)
8:40 (8:40) (Class 7) (0-50,50) 4-Y-0+ **£1,940** (£577; £288; £144) **Stalls** Low

Form RPR

0/0- **1** **Petrol**[185] 5708 4-9-2 **47**........................ DanielTudhope 2 62+
(David O'Meara) *chsd ldrs: led over 1f out: comf* **7/2[2]**

-141 **2** 1 1/2 **Lytham (IRE)**[9] 725 12-8-12 **50**........................ RyanTate(7) 4 58
(Tony Carroll) *s.i.s: hld up: hdwy on outer over 2f out: rdn over 1f out: r.o to go 2nd wl ins fnl f: no ch w wnr* **9/2[3]**

-262 **3** 1 **Angelena Ballerina (IRE)**[16] 625 6-9-4 **49**..........(b) RobertWinston 10 55
(Sean Curran) *hld up: hdwy over 5f out: rdn over 2f out: styd on* **3/1[1]**

00-0 **4** 1/2 **Chik's Dream**[53] 99 6-9-0 **45**........................ WilliamCarson 12 50
(Derek Haydn Jones) *chsd ldrs: rdn over 1f out: styd on* **66/1**

0-45 **5** nk **Hollywood All Star (IRE)**[20] 579 4-9-4 **49**........................ GrahamLee 7 54
(William Muir) *s.i.s: hld up: hdwy over 1f out: r.o: nt rch ldrs* **6/1**

00/6 **6** 1/2 **Atacama Sunrise**[29] 456 7-9-4 **49**........................(p) MickyFenton 9 53
(John Butler) *led: rdn and hdd over 1f out: no ex ins fnl f* **20/1**

620- **7** nk **Naledi**[107] 6230 9-9-2 **47**........................ GrahamGibbons 8 50
(Richard Price) *hld up: hdwy over 2f out: rdn over 1f out: styd on same pce ins fnl f* **40/1**

0/0- **8** 2 **Akarana (IRE)**[379] 578 6-9-5 **50**........................ J-PGuillambert 5 49
(Willie Musson) *hld up: shkn up and nt clr run ent fnl f: nvr nr to chal* **8/1**

006- **9** 1 **Market Puzzle (IRE)**[154] 6631 6-9-0 **45**........................(p) EddieAhern 11 42
(Mark Brisbourne) *prom: rdn over 2f out: no ex ins fnl f* **14/1**

10-0 **10** 1 1/4 **Hyde Lea Flyer**[29] 455 8-9-5 **50**........................ RussKennemore 6 45
(Barry Leavy) *prom: rdn over 2f out: wknd over 1f out* **20/1**

-505 **11** 1 **Bubbly Braveheart (IRE)**[16] 625 6-9-2 **47**..............(be) DavidProbert 3 40
(Phil McEntee) *prom: rdn over 2f out: wknd fnl f* **9/1**

00-0 **12** 14 **Kiss My Heart**[37] 335 4-9-0 **45**........................ FrannyNorton 1 11
(Eric Wheeler) *hld up: rdn over 3f out: sn wknd* **100/1**

2m 3.23s (1.53) **Going Correction** +0.30s/f (Slow) **12** Ran SP% **121.9**
Speed ratings (Par 97): **105,103,102,102,102 101,101,99,98,97 96,84**
toteswingers 1&2 £7.40, 1&3 £3.30, 2&3 £1.50 CSF £19.35 CT £54.12 TOTE £4.10: £2.20, £1.10, £1.40; EX 29.80 Trifecta £51.90 Pool: £1,133.98 - 16.37 winning units..
Owner Mrs S O'Meara & R G Fell **Bred** Fittocks Stud **Trained** Nawton, N Yorks

FOCUS
A wide-open handicap that was turned into a procession. The form looks straightforward rated around the placed horses.
T/Plt: £103.10 to a £1 stake. Pool: £80,423.30 - 568.99 winning tickets T/Qpdt: £15.50 to a £1 stake. Pool: £9,493.68 - 453.14 winning tickets CR

853 - 860a (Foreign Racing) - See Raceform Interactive

[839]LINGFIELD (L-H)
Saturday, March 2

OFFICIAL GOING: Standard
Wind: Light, across Weather: overcast, dry

861 AXA PPP INTERNATIONAL (S) STKS 5f (P)
1:40 (1:41) (Class 6) 4-Y-0+ **£2,045** (£603; £302) **Stalls** High

Form RPR

4101 **1** **Where's Reiley (USA)**[10] 727 7-9-5 70........................(v) SebSanders 1 69
(Michael Attwater) *chsd ldrs: rdn and effrt on inner over 1f out: ev ch and drvn ins fnl f: led fnl 50yds: kpt on* **7/4[2]**

200- **2** hd **Spic 'n Span**[132] 7275 8-9-0 57........................(b) WilliamCarson 3 64
(Ronald Harris) *taken down early: led: rdn over 1f out: drvn and hrd pressed ins fnl f: hdd and no ex fnl 50yds* **25/1**

3443 **3** 3/4 **Mother Jones**[11] 716 5-8-9 62........................ ThomasBrown(5) 4 61
(David Evans) *sn chsd ldr: rdn wl over 1f out: ev ch ins fnl f: styd on same pce fnl 100yds* **7/1[3]**

-025 **4** shd **Proper Charlie**[14] 688 5-9-0 68........................(p) AdamKirby 5 61
(William Knight) *hld up in tch in rr: edgd out rt and effrt over 1f out: kpt on fnl 100yds: nvr enough pce to chal* **4/6[1]**

58.9s (0.10) **Going Correction** +0.025s/f (Slow) **4** Ran SP% **112.7**
Speed ratings (Par 101): **100,99,98,98**
CSF £24.43 TOTE £2.10; EX 14.80 Trifecta £41.90 Pool: £1,181.71 - 21.12 winning units..No bid for the winner.
Owner J M Duggan & T P Duggan **Bred** Overbrook Farm **Trained** Epsom, Surrey

FOCUS
The opening seller was nearly the scene of an upset and the runner-up sets and limits the form.

862 VITABIOTICS OSTEOCARE H'CAP 5f (P)
2:15 (2:15) (Class 6) (0-55,55) 4-Y-0+ **£2,045** (£603; £302) **Stalls** High

Form RPR

0506 **1** **Speedyfix**[9] 735 6-9-5 **53**........................(t) TomMcLaughlin 6 62
(Christine Dunnett) *hld up in tch towards rr of man gp: nt clr run and travelling wl 2f out: rdn and hdwy 1f out: str run to ld wl ins fnl f: gng away at fin* **7/1**

02 **2** ¾ **Scommettitrice (IRE)**[9] 736 5-9-7 **55**........................(b) GeorgeBaker 4 61
(Mark Gillard) *chsd ldr: unable qck under over 1f out: drvn and rallied ins fnl f to go 2nd towards fin: no threat to wnr* **4/1**[2]

5640 **3** *shd* **Brandywell Boy (IRE)**[16] 649 10-8-7 **48**................ JoshBaudains(7) 7 54
(Dominic Ffrench Davis) *in tch in midfield on outer: edgd lft bnd 2f out: rdn and styd on ins fnl f: wnt 3rd nr fin* **14/1**

3-03 **4** ½ **Christopher Chua (IRE)**[29] 471 4-8-13 **52**..............(b[1]) JackDuern(5) 8 56
(Simon Dow) *pressed ldr tl led wl over 1f out: rdn ins fnl f: hdd: no ex and lost 3 pls wl ins fnl f* **3/1**[1]

0601 **5** ¾ **Chateau Lola**[8] 756 4-8-11 **52**..............................(v) AdamMcLean(7) 2 53
(Derek Shaw) *chsd ldrs: clsd and chal ent fnl f: rdn and no ex ins fnl f: wknd towards fin* **8/1**

-450 **6** ¾ **Chjimes (IRE)**[30] 449 9-9-3 **51**....................................(b) HayleyTurner 5 50
(Conor Dore) *t.k.h: hld up in tch towards rr of main gp: rdn and hdwy to press ldrs on inner 1f out: no ex fnl 150yds: wknd towards fin* **5/1**

-404 **7** 2¾ **Imaginary Diva**[39] 322 7-9-0 **55**............................ JordanVaughan(7) 1 44
(George Margarson) *pushed stall open early but v awkward leaving stall and slowly away: nt rcvr and a bhd* **9/2**[3]

060- **8** 2¾ **Miss Polly Plum**[72] 8190 6-8-13 **54**................................(p) IanBurns(7) 3 33
(Chris Dwyer) *led tl rdn and hdd wl over 1f out: wknd qckly jst ins fnl f* **20/1**

59.61s (0.81) **Going Correction** +0.025s/f (Slow) **8 Ran SP% 114.9**
Speed ratings (Par 101): **94,92,92,91,90 89,85,80**
Tote Swingers: 1&2 £8.00, 1&3 £26.30, 2&3 £21.40 CSF £35.27 CT £382.90 TOTE £9.00: £3.20, £1.50, £4.10; EX 42.50 Trifecta £1137.30 Part won. Pool: £183.91 - 0.87 winning units..
Owner Annwell Inn Syndicate **Bred** Mrs Christine Dunnett **Trained** Hingham, Norfolk

FOCUS
A wide-open sprint handicap and the form looks moderate but straightforward.

863 BROLLEY H'CAP 6f (P)
2:50 (2:51) (Class 6) (0-55,55) 4-Y-0+ **£2,045** (£603; £302) **Stalls** Low

Form RPR

0051 **1** **Red Ramesses (IRE)**[16] 649 4-9-5 **53**............................. GeorgeBaker 11 62
(John Best) *stdd and swtchd lft after s: t.k.h: hld up in last pair: swtchd rt and hdwy over 1f out: str run to chal fnl 100yds: led fnl 50yds: r.o wl* **7/2**[1]

-241 **2** ½ **Artful Lady (IRE)**[29] 471 4-9-6 **54**.................................... IanMongan 8 61
(George Margarson) *in tch in midfield: rdn and effrt over 1f out: r.o u.p to ld ins fnl f: hdd fnl 50yds: r.o but a hld* **6/1**

0352 **3** 2¼ **Slatey Hen (IRE)**[2] 819 5-8-8 **47**.......................(p) ShirleyTeasdale(5) 12 47
(Violet M Jordan) *chsd ldrs tl led 4f out: drvn wl over 1f out: hdd ins fnl f: sn outpcd by ldng pair but kpt on to hold 3rd* **14/1**

0-46 **4** *nk* **Sextons House (IRE)**[9] 736 5-8-11 **50**.....................(p) MartinHarley(5) 9 49
(Alan McCabe) *taken down early: stdd and swtchd lft s: hld up towards rr: rdn and gd hdwy on inner over 1f out: no ex and styd on same pce ins fnl f* **5/1**[3]

650- **5** ¾ **Medam**[135] 7201 4-9-7 **55**.. DuranFentiman 1 52
(Shaun Harris) *in tch in midfield: sltly hmpd wl over 1f out: hdwy 1f out: styd on ins fnl f: nt trbld ldrs* **16/1**

6512 **6** *hd* **Athaakeel (IRE)**[8] 754 7-9-0 **55**...............................(b) GaryPhillips(7) 6 52
(Ronald Harris) *in tch in midfield on outer: lost pl and rdn bnd 2f out: rallied and kpt on ins fnl f: no threat to ldrs* **7/1**

0-03 **7** 1½ **Mary's Pet**[29] 472 6-8-11 **52**...(p) AaronChave(7) 4 44
(Lee Carter) *chsd ldrs: rdn and unable qck whn edgd lft wl over 1f out: wknd ins fnl f* **12/1**

0003 **8** ¾ **Spoof Master (IRE)**[9] 735 9-8-9 **46**.............................(t) SimonPearce(3) 2 36
(Lydia Pearce) *led tl 4f out: chsd ldrs tl rdn and struggling over 2f out: wknd over 1f out* **33/1**

34-5 **9** *nse* **Kerfuffle (IRE)**[16] 649 4-8-12 **46**...............................(b) HayleyTurner 10 36
(Simon Dow) *s.i.s and swtchd lft s: sn pushed along in rr: nvr trbld ldrs* **12/1**

0330 **10** ½ **Island Express (IRE)**[4] 807 6-8-13 **52**......................(tp) AnnStokell(5) 3 40
(Ann Stokell) *rrd as stalls opened: sn in tch in midfield: lost pl and rdn ent fnl 2f: no imp* **33/1**

0003 **11** *hd* **Fairy Wing (IRE)**[4] 805 6-9-7 **55**...............................(b) WilliamCarson 5 43
(Violet M Jordan) *taken down early: chsd ldrs: wnt 2nmd over 2f out tl ent fnl f: wkng and towards rr whn hmpd ins fnl f: eased after* **9/2**[2]

1m 11.88s (-0.02) **Going Correction** +0.025s/f (Slow) **11 Ran SP% 117.7**
Speed ratings (Par 101): **101,100,97,96,95 95,93,92,92,91 91**
Tote Swingers: 1&2 £2.60, 1&3 £15.90, 2&3 £17.80 CSF £24.39 CT £259.51 TOTE £5.10: £1.40, £2.20, £4.60; EX 23.80 Trifecta £159.10 Pool: £1,062.97 - 5.00 winning units..
Owner John Best **Bred** Wardstown Stud Ltd **Trained** Hucking, Kent
■ Stewards' Enquiry : Gary Phillips caution: careless riding.
Duran Fentiman caution: careless riding.

FOCUS
Another 0-55 handicap, although this was a stronger affair. The winner is starting to fulfil promise and the form looks worth being positive about.

864 VITABIOTICS WELLWOMAN MAIDEN FILLIES' STKS 1m (P)
3:25 (3:25) (Class 5) 3-Y-0+ **£2,726** (£805; £402) **Stalls** High

Form RPR

1 **Whispering Lady (IRE)** 3-8-6 0.. MartinLane 4 70+
(David Simcock) *s.i.s: hld up in tch in last pair: stl last 2f: rdn and gd hdwy over 1f out: led jst ins fnl f: r.o wl* **9/2**[2]

3 **2** 1½ **Awattan**[21] 580 3-8-6 0.. WilliamCarson 7 69
(Ed Vaughan) *chsd ldrs: effrt to chse ldr and edgd out rt wl over 1f out: chsd wnr fnl f: r.o wl but a hld* **9/2**[2]

2 **3** 3¼ **Lady Guinevere**[14] 685 3-8-6 0...................................... DavidProbert 1 60
(Stuart Williams) *led: drvn over 1f out: hdd and no ex jst ins fnl f: wknd fnl 75yds* **4/5**[1]

303- **4** 3½ **Solvanna**[116] 7606 3-7-13 60... RyanTate(7) 8 51
(Heather Main) *hung rt thrght: broke fast: sn stdd and dropped in bhd: hdwy to chse ldrs and hung rt bnd 2f out: n.d and plugged on same pce after* **16/1**

0- **5** *hd* **Sixties Queen**[322] 1388 3-8-6 0.................................... NickyMackay 2 51
(Alan Bailey) *chsd ldrs: shkn up 3f out: rdn and unable qck wl over 1f out: sn wknd* **50/1**

2- **6** 3 **Ruff Luck**[73] 8166 3-8-8 0 ow2.................................... LiamKeniry 3 46
(Seamus Mullins) *t.k.h: chsd ldr tl 2f out: sn rdn and lost pl: wknd over 1f out* **10/1**[3]

[illegible]4s (0.34) **Going Correction** +0.025s/f (Slow) **6 Ran SP% 108.9**
[illegible]gs (Par 100): **99,97,94,90,90 87**
[illegible]s: 1&2 £1.80, 2&3 £1.50 CSF £22.97 TOTE £4.40: £3.30, £3.50; EX 31.20 Trifecta [illegible]1,706.53 - 17.14 winning units..
[illegible]ttack **Bred** Rockhart Trading Ltd **Trained** Newmarket, Suffolk

FOCUS
A fair fillies' maiden, in which all the six runners were 3-y-os. The form looks fluid.

865 CORINTHIA HOTEL LONDON H'CAP 1m (P)
4:00 (4:00) (Class 3) (0-95,91) 4-Y-0+ **£7,439** (£2,213; £1,106; £553) **Stalls** High

Form RPR

1-36 **1** **Kickingthelilly**[18] 621 4-9-2 **82**.. ChrisCatlin 5 90
(Rae Guest) *dwlt: in tch in last pair: pushed along and hdwy over 2f out: drvn and r.o wl ins fnl f to ld fnl 75yds: hld on wl* **10/1**

0331 **2** *nk* **Loyalty**[5] 792 6-9-4 **91** 6ex..(v) AdamMcLean(7) 3 99
(Derek Shaw) *hld up in tch in midfield: clr run over 1f out: swtchd rt and hdwy between horses 1f out: str chal fnl 75yds: r.o wl but a jst hld* **7/2**[2]

2001 **3** ¾ **Aquilonius (IRE)**[21] 585 4-9-6 **86**..................................(t) GeorgeBaker 7 91
(Stuart Williams) *led: shkn up over 1f out: rdn ent fnl f: hdd and one pce fnl 75yds* **5/2**[1]

63-0 **4** ¾ **Lord Ofthe Shadows (IRE)**[14] 690 4-8-12 **83**
WilliamTwiston-Davies(5) 2 87
(Richard Hannon) *chsd ldrs: rdn and effrt on inner wl over 1f out: chsd ldrs and drvn 1f out: styd on same pce ins fnl f* **5/1**

4-11 **5** ¾ **Mister Musicmaster**[27] 511 4-9-2 **82**......................... WilliamCarson 6 84
(Ron Hodges) *t.k.h: chsd ldrs tl wnt 2nd over 2f out: rdn and ev ch 2f out: drvn and unable qck over 1f out: no ex and outpcd ins fnl f* **4/1**[3]

43-3 **6** 1¼ **Dr Red Eye**[8] 751 5-9-2 **82**...(p) TomMcLaughlin 1 81
(Scott Dixon) *t.k.h: chsd ldr tl over 2f out: styd chsng ldrs: drvn over 1f out: wknd ins fnl f* **20/1**

004- **7** 1½ **Takeitfromalady (IRE)**[136] 7163 4-9-5 **85**..................(b) GrahamLee 4 81
(Lee Carter) *hld up in last pair: rdn and no prog 2f out: nvr trbld ldrs* **8/1**

1m 36.34s (-1.86) **Going Correction** +0.025s/f (Slow) **7 Ran SP% 112.4**
Speed ratings (Par 107): **110,109,108,108,107 106,104**
Tote Swingers: 1&2 £7.90, 1&3 £8.10, 2&3 £1.40 CSF £43.23 TOTE £13.20: £6.60, £1.80; EX 51.30 Trifecta £177.30 Pool: £1,916.46 - 8.10 winning units..
Owner Hailstone Piper Scott Hirschfeld & Guest **Bred** Tony Hirschfeld & L K Piggott **Trained** Newmarket, Suffolk

FOCUS
The feature on the card was a 0-95 handicap for older horses. The top weight was 4lb below the ceiling but the form looks straightforward with the placed horses the best guides.

866 VITABIOTICS WELLMAN H'CAP 1m 4f (P)
4:35 (4:35) (Class 5) (0-70,67) 4-Y-0+ **£2,726** (£805; £402) **Stalls** Low

Form RPR

0-53 **1** **Attwaal (IRE)**[12] 709 4-9-3 **65**... SebSanders 2 73+
(Neil King) *in tch in midfield: rdn and effrt on inner over 1f out: led ins fnl f: r.o strly* **2/1**[1]

634- **2** 1¼ **Marcus Antonius**[264] 2976 6-9-5 **65**............................[1] StephenCraine 1 71
(Jim Boyle) *t.k.h: chsd ldr tl 5f out: rdn to chse ldr again jst over 1f out: drvn and ev ch ins fnl f: outpcd by wnr fnl 75yds* **16/1**

60-2 **3** *nk* **Bramshill Lass**[15] 668 4-9-3 **65**...................................(b) GrahamLee 6 71
(Amanda Perrett) *led after 1f: rdn ent fnl 2f: drvn and hdd ins fnl f: styd on same pce fnl 100yds* **3/1**[2]

0323 **4** ½ **El Libertador (USA)**[15] 668 7-8-4 **57**.......................(b) JoeyHaynes(7) 7 62
(Eric Wheeler) *hld up in tch in last trio: rdn and hdwy on outer bnd 2f out: kpt on ins fnl f* **6/1**[3]

53-0 **5** 1 **Foxhaven**[29] 475 11-9-2 **67**..(v) ThomasBrown(5) 5 70
(Patrick Chamings) *in tch in midfield: rdn and effrt 2f out: unable qck u.p over 1f out: no threat to ldrs but kpt on fnl f* **6/1**[3]

-335 **6** 1 **Stylistickhill (IRE)**[8] 753 5-9-2 **62**........................(tp) TomMcLaughlin 4 64
(Scott Dixon) *t.k.h: chsd ldrs: wnt 2nd 5f out tl jst over 1f out: no ex u.p 1f out: wknd wl ins fnl f* **12/1**

-166 **7** ¾ **Temuco (IRE)**[17] 633 4-8-11 **59**.................................(b) WilliamCarson 3 60
(David Evans) *stdd s: t.k.h: hld up in tch in last pair: reminder 3f out: swtchd rt and effrt over 1f out: no imp fnl f* **14/1**

-500 **8** 9 **St Ignatius**[11] 718 6-9-7 **67**.....................................(p) AdamKirby 8 54
(Alan Bailey) *stdd s: a in rr: rdn and struggling 3f out: bhd fnl f* **10/1**

2m 32.46s (-0.54) **Going Correction** +0.025s/f (Slow)
WFA 4 from 5yo+ 2lb **8 Ran SP% 116.2**
Speed ratings (Par 103): **102,101,100,100,99 99,98,92**
Tote Swingers: 1&2 £9.80, 1&3 £2.50, 2&3 £14.90 CSF £36.82 CT £96.39 TOTE £1.90: £1.10, £6.00, £1.50; EX 35.50 Trifecta £346.80 Pool: £1,755.11 - 3.79 winning units..
Owner Dr Clive Layton **Bred** Darley **Trained** Newmarket, Suffolk

FOCUS
This fair middle-distance handicap was the scene of the performance of the day from a gelding who can graduate up from this grade. The form is straightforward rated around the first three.

867 VITABIOTICS JOINTACE H'CAP 1m 2f (P)
5:10 (5:10) (Class 5) (0-75,75) 3-Y-O **£2,726** (£805; £402) **Stalls** Low

Form RPR

201- **1** **Swing Easy**[114] 7641 3-9-7 75.. GrahamLee 3 92+
(Robert Mills) *t.k.h: chsd ldr tl led 3f out: gng best 2f out: edging rt and rn green fr over 1f out: pushed along hands and heels and a doing enough fnl f* **7/4**[2]

511 **2** 1 **Gabrial The Duke (IRE)**[4] 803 3-8-3 57..................... AndreaAtzeni 1 70
(David Simcock) *chsd ldrs: rdn to chse wnr and edgd lft over 1f out: kpt on u.p ins fnl f: a hld* **6/4**[1]

330- **3** 5 **Emulating (IRE)**[80] 8072 3-8-8 67.................. WilliamTwiston-Davies(5) 2 71
(Richard Hannon) *in tch in last pair: clsd on ldrs 3f out: rdn and unable qck 2f out: no threat to ldng pair but plugged on to go 3rd ins fnl f* **8/1**

-233 **4** 2 **Tight Knit (USA)**[24] 538 3-9-7 75..................................... AdamKirby 6 75
(James Tate) *stdd s: hld up in rr: hdwy to chse ldrs and rdn 2f out: outpcd and btn over 1f out: wknd fnl f* **7/2**[3]

04-3 **5** 21 **Lucky Mountain**[33] 428 3-8-11 65.............................. NickyMackay 4 25
(Scott Dixon) *led tl 3f out: rdn and struggling ent fnl 2f: sn wknd: wl bhd fnl f* **16/1**

2m 4.01s (-2.59) **Going Correction** +0.025s/f (Slow) **5 Ran SP% 115.6**
Speed ratings (Par 98): **111,110,106,104,87**
CSF £5.10 TOTE £4.30: £3.40, £1.02; EX 8.10 Trifecta £31.20 Pool: £1,536.73 - 36.85 winning units..
Owner Mrs B B Mills, J Harley, T Jacobs **Bred** Lady Bamford **Trained** Headley, Surrey

FOCUS
A strong 0-75 3-y-o handicap to close the card. The first two came clear and the time was decent.
T/Plt: £190. to a £1 stake. Pool: £69,760.57 - 267.98 winning tickets. T/Qpdt: £45.90 to a £1 stake. Pool: £4,630.00 - 74.60 winning tickets. SP

[833]MEYDAN (L-H)

Saturday, March 2

OFFICIAL GOING: Tapeta: standard; turf: good

868a ENERGIA ELEGANTE (H'CAP) (TURF) 6f

2:50 (12:00) (100-115,115) 3-Y-O+

£64,417 (£21,472; £10,736; £4,294; £4,294; £2,147)

RPR

1 **Kavanagh (SAF)**[16] 660 6-9-4 **112**...................(t) ChristopheSoumillon 1 119
(M F De Kock, South Africa) *trckd ldng pair: smooth prog to ld 1f out: r.o wl: comf* **5/2**[2]

2 *1* **Ballista (IRE)**[16] 660 5-8-11 **106**............................. RichardKingscote 7 109
(Tom Dascombe) *sn led: hdd 1f out: kpt on wl but no ch w wnr* **9/1**[3]

3 *2* **Invincible Ash (IRE)**[9] 746 8-8-9 **104**....................(p) JamieSpencer 12 101+
(M Halford, Ire) *slowly away: settled in rr: r.o fnl 2f: nrst fin* **12/1**

4 *1/4* **Seachantach (USA)**[14] 696 7-8-1 **102**..............(bt) MarcMonaghan(7) 2 99
(S Seemar, UAE) *trckd ldrs: ev ch 1 1/2f out: one pce fnl f* **10/1**

4 *dht* **Humidor (IRE)**[30] 464 6-9-1 **109**....................................(t) JamesDoyle 9 106
(George Baker) *mid-div: kpt on same pce fnl 1 1/2f* **9/1**[3]

6 *hd* **Rosendhal (IRE)**[30] 467 6-8-10 **105**.............................(bt) RyanMoore 6 101
(G Botti, France) *mid-div: kpt on same pce fnl 2f* **20/1**

7 *2* **Tamaathul**[16] 660 6-9-6 **115**...(t) PaulHanagan 5 105
(A Al Raihe, UAE) *a mid-div* **2/1**[1]

8 *3/4* **Desert Law (IRE)**[30] 464 5-8-8 **102**....................... MickaelBarzalona 11 90
(Saeed bin Suroor) *mid-div: chsd ldrs 2 1/2f out: nt qckn fnl f* **14/1**

9 *hd* **Es Que Love (IRE)**[2] 834 4-8-8 **102**............................ KierenFallon 4 90
(Mark Johnston) *chsd ldrs tl outpcd 1 1/2f out* **16/1**

10 *hd* **Kanaf (IRE)**[9] 746 6-8-6 **100**.. WayneSmith 3 87
(M Al Muhairi, UAE) *s.i.s: nvr bttr than mid-div* **16/1**

11 *1 1/4* **Secret Asset (IRE)**[105] 7772 8-8-9 **104**.......................... LukeMorris 10 86
(Jane Chapple-Hyam) *a in rr* **33/1**

12 *4 3/4* **Dohasa (IRE)**[8] 770 8-8-10 **105**..................................(b) TadhgO'Shea 8 73
(Ismail Mohammed) *nvr bttr than mid-div* **16/1**

1m 9.1s (69.10) **12** Ran SP% **130.7**
WIN: 2.50; PL: 1.10, 3.40, 3.60 CSF: 29.08; EXACTA: 32.70; TRIFECTA: 239.70.
Owner Wilgerbosdrift Pty Ltd **Bred** Wilgerbosdrift **Trained** South Africa

FOCUS
Rail on turf track out 15m from true position. Not a great deal of strength in depth.

869a LINTON (H'CAP) (TAPETA) 7f

3:25 (12:00) (100-111,111) 3-Y-O+

£64,417 (£21,472; £10,736; £5,368; £3,220; £2,147)

RPR

1 **Rerouted (USA)**[16] 657 5-9-6 **111**....................... ChristopheSoumillon 9 113
(M F De Kock, South Africa) *settled in rr: smooth prog 2 1/2f out: rdn 1 1/2f out: r.o wl: led fnl 110yds* **5/2**[1]

2 *3/4* **Free Wheeling (AUS)**[30] 465 5-9-3 **108**.....................(tp) KierenFallon 2 108
(Saeed bin Suroor) *mid-div: chsd ldrs 2 1/2f out: led 1f out: hdd fnl 110yds* **3/1**[2]

3 *2 1/4* **Red Duke (USA)**[23] 557 4-9-1 **106**................................... TomQueally 1 100
(David Simcock) *mid-div on rail: smooth prog 3f out: led briefly 1 1/2f out: kpt on same pce fnl f* **9/2**[3]

4 *2 3/4* **Lockwood**[30] 465 4-9-3 **108**.. RyanMoore 3 94
(Saeed bin Suroor) *settled in rr: r.o fnl 2f but nvr nr to chal* **8/1**

5 *3/4* **Final Button (SAF)**[16] 657 5-8-9 **100**.........................(bt) PatCosgrave 4 84
(M F De Kock, South Africa) *sn led: hdd 1 1/2f out: wknd fnl 110yds* **16/1**

6 *hd* **Zafeen Speed**[707] 997 6-9-1 **106**................................(vt) WayneSmith 6 90
(M Al Muhairi, UAE) *trckd ldrs: ev ch 2f out: wknd fnl f* **14/1**

7 *4 1/2* **Burj Alzain (IRE)**[30] 463 5-8-9 **100**................................ LukeMorris 5 72
(Fawzi Abdulla Nass, Bahrain) *slowly away: nvr bttr than mid-div* **20/1**

8 *1 1/2* **Smooth Operator (GER)**[9] 744 7-8-11 **102**.................(b) TedDurcan 7 70
(Mario Hofer, Germany) *nvr bttr than mid-div* **33/1**

9 *16* **Firebeam**[51] 154 5-9-3 **108**......................................(t) MickaelBarzalona 8 33
(Mahmood Al Zarooni) *trckd ldrs: ev ch 2 1/2f out: wknd fnl 1 1/2f* **11/2**

1m 25.23s (0.03) **9** Ran SP% **118.5**
WIN: 2.40; PL: 1.40, 1.70,2.00 CSF: 10.41; EXACTA: 8.00; TRIFECTA: 30.60.
Owner Mssrs Chandler, Westwood Et Al **Bred** Juddmonte Farms Inc **Trained** South Africa

FOCUS
The lead was contested by Final Button and Firebeam and neither had a hope of seeing it out. The latter, who had been off for 51 days and was trying Tapeta for the first time, with a tongue-tie added, finished really weakly even allowing for his early exertions. The sectionals were 25.49 (400m), 23.46 (800m), 24.11 (1200m), before the winner clocked 12.10 to the finish.

870a NAD AL SHEBA TROPHY SPONSORED BY HARAS ESTRELA ENERGIA (GROUP 3) (TURF) 1m 6f 11y

4:00 (12:00) 3-Y-O+

£73,619 (£24,539; £12,269; £6,134; £3,680; £2,453)

RPR

1 **Ahzeemah (IRE)**[23] 555 4-8-11 106...........................(p) KierenFallon 7 109
(Saeed bin Suroor) *mid-div: rdn 3f out: led 2f out: r.o wl: jst hld on* **6/1**

2 *1/4* **Certerach (IRE)**[23] 555 5-9-2 105................................ JamieSpencer 4 110
(M Halford, Ire) *trckd ldng trio: ev ch 1 1/2f out: kpt on fnl f out: jst failed* **13/2**

3 *3/4* **Star Empire (SAF)**[23] 555 7-9-2 106................. ChristopheSoumillon 1 109
(M F De Kock, South Africa) *trckd ldrs: ev ch 1 1/2f out: one pce fnl 55yds* **5/1**[3]

4 *3/4* **Tenenbaum**[147] 6896 4-8-11 109.............................. MickaelBarzalona 3 109+
(Mahmood Al Zarooni) *slowly away: settled in rr: nrst fin* **5/2**[1]

5 *5* **Saddler's Rock (IRE)**[133] 7235 5-9-5 113...........(t) DeclanMcDonogh 12 104+
(John M Oxx, Ire) *settled in rr: nvr nr to chal but r.o fnl 2f: nrst fin* **4/1**[2]

6 *3/4* **Ostinato (GER)**[16] 656 5-9-2 109.................................(bt) TedDurcan 9 100
(Sandor Kovacs, Hungary) *in rr of mid-div: nvr able to chal* **14/1**

7 *1/2* **Royal Diamond (IRE)**[168] 6271 7-9-7 112.................. JohnnyMurtagh 6 105
(Thomas Carmody, Ire) *sn led: hdd 2f out: kpt on same pce fnl 1 1/2f* **13/2**

8 *1 3/4* **Chicago (IRE)**[23] 555 4-8-11 99..................................... TadhgO'Shea 8 96
(John Patrick Shanahan, Ire) *trckd ldng pair: ev ch tl outpcd 2f out* **25/1**

9 *2 3/4* **Topclas (FR)**[16] 661 7-9-2 102..............................(tp) WayneSmith 5 94
(M bin Shafya, UAE) *settled in rr: nvr nr to chal* **16/1**

10 *13* **Balladry (USA)**[120] 7546 5-9-2 105................................. PaulHanagan 2 77
(Mahmood Al Zarooni) *mid-div: rdn 4 1/2f out: sn struggling* **16/1**

2m 59.26s (179.26)
WFA 4 from 5yo+ 4lb **10** Ran SP% **128.5**
WIN: 5.80; PL: 1.50, 2.40, 1.50 CSF: 49.69; EXACTA: 47.10; TRIFECTA: 145.40.
Owner Godolphin **Bred** G O'Brien **Trained** Newmarket, Suffolk

FOCUS
A trial for the Dubai Gold Cup, but misleading form as the pace was desperately slow (first 1600m covered in 1:46.30), turning the race into a relative sprint, and the well-placed front trio also had a race-fitness edge over a few of the others, notably the fourth and fifth. The top three had finished runner-up, third and first respectively in a C&D handicap last time, when separated by less than half a length, and there was again little between them.

871a GLORIA DE CAMPEAO (H'CAP) (TAPETA) 1m 2f

4:35 (12:00) (95-113,113) 3-Y-O+

£55,214 (£18,404; £9,202; £4,601; £2,760; £1,840)

RPR

1 **Plantagenet (SPA)**[9] 742 6-8-8 **101**.................................. J-LMartinez 1 101+
(G Arizkorreta Elosegui, Spain) *settled in rr: rdn 3f out: r.o wl fnl 1 1/2f: led cl home* **10/1**

2 *1/4* **Con Artist (IRE)**[9] 742 6-9-3 **110**.................................. RyanMoore 12 110
(Saeed bin Suroor) *sn led: rdn 2f out: kpt on wl: hdd fnl 55yds* **10/3**[2]

3 *1 3/4* **Out Of Bounds (USA)**[16] 659 4-9-3 **110**...................... KierenFallon 9 106
(Saeed bin Suroor) *trckd ldng trio: rdn to chal 2 1/2f out: ev ch 1f out: wknd fnl 110yds* **6/1**[3]

4 *1/4* **Daddy Long Legs (USA)**[16] 659 4-9-6 **113**...... ChristopheSoumillon 8 109
(M F De Kock, South Africa) *trckd ldng pair: rdn 2 1/2f out: kpt on same pce fnl 1 1/2f* **3/1**[1]

5 *3/4* **Dr Faustus (IRE)**[14] 698 8-8-5 **95**................................(t) TadhgO'Shea 2 92
(Doug Watson, UAE) *settled in rr: kpt on fnl 2f: nvr able to chal* **12/1**

6 *nk* **Jawhar (IRE)**[14] 698 5-8-5 **95**... PaulHanagan 5 91
(Doug Watson, UAE) *trckd ldng trio: ev ch 1 1/2f out: one pce fnl 110yds* **7/1**

7 *3* **Layali Al Andalus**[23] 552 6-8-5 **97**............................... RichardMullen 6 85
(S Seemar, UAE) *settled in rr: rdn 3 1/2f out: sn btn* **16/1**

8 *3/4* **Arthur's Tale (USA)**[23] 552 5-8-6 **99**.......................... AntiocoMurgia 4 85
(Mahmood Al Zarooni) *settled in rr: nvr nr to chal* **12/1**

9 *shd* **Universal (IRE)**[23] 552 4-8-5 **98**............................... RoystonFfrench 11 84
(Mark Johnston) *trckd ldrs tl outpcd 2 1/2f out* **7/1**

10 *1* **Art Scholar (IRE)**[23] 555 6-8-5 **98**.............................. HarryBentley 10 82
(Michael Appleby) *nvr bttr than mid-div* **12/1**

11 *8 3/4* **Bon Grain (FR)**[14] 696 8-8-5 **95** ow7...................(t) MarcMonaghan(7) 7 71
(S Seemar, UAE) *slowly away: nvr nr to chal* **66/1**

2m 5.56s (0.86) **11** Ran SP% **126.9**
WIN: 12.00; PL: 3.20, 1.60, 1.80 CSF: 46.90; EXACTA: 38.30; TRIFECTA: 281.20.
Owner Cuadra Whylar **Bred** Dehesa De Milagro **Trained** Spain

FOCUS
As usual, Trakus data helps explain how events unfolded. Here are the sectionals: 27.04 (400m), 25.08 (800m), 25.19 (1200m), 24.56 (1600m), before the winner came home in 23.23, compared to 23.75 for the runner-up. For what it's worth, the third split was set by Out Of Bounds, who ever so briefly took over.

872a ZABEEL MILE SPONSORED BY STUD ESTRELA ENERGIA (GROUP 2) (TURF) 1m

5:10 (12:00) 3-Y-O+

£92,024 (£30,674; £15,337; £7,668; £4,601; £3,067)

RPR

1 **Trade Storm**[16] 657 5-9-2 112....................................... JamieSpencer 3 116+
(David Simcock) *s.i.s: settled in rr: smooth prog 2f out: led cl home: comf* **5/2**[2]

2 *1 1/2* **Musir (AUS)**[9] 745 7-9-2 117........................... ChristopheSoumillon 1 112
(M F De Kock, South Africa) *trckd ldrs: led 1f out: hdd cl home* **9/4**[1]

3 *1* **Fulbright**[16] 659 4-9-5 113......................................(t) MickaelBarzalona 4 113
(Mahmood Al Zarooni) *mid-div: chsd ldrs 2f out: nt qckn fnl 110yds* **3/1**[3]

4 *1/4* **Don't Call Me (IRE)**[9] 745 6-9-2 107.........................(t) AdrianNicholls 7 109
(David Nicholls) *trckd ldng pair tl outpcd fnl f* **12/1**

5 *1/2* **Royal Ridge (SAF)**[23] 557 5-9-2 107............................ PaulHanagan 6 108
(M F De Kock, South Africa) *sn led: kicked clr 2 1/2f out: hdd 1f out: wknd fnl 110yds* **9/2**

6 *shd* **Mustaheel (IRE)**[16] 657 4-9-2 102............................ RoystonFfrench 2 108
(A Al Raihe, UAE) *in rr of mid-div: nvr nr to chal* **50/1**

7 *1/4* **Derbaas (USA)**[16] 659 7-9-2 113...................................(t) DaneO'Neill 5 107
(A Al Raihe, UAE) *settled in rr: nvr able to chal* **16/1**

8 *4 3/4* **Le Drakkar (AUS)**[9] 745 8-9-2 109...............................(t) TadhgO'Shea 8 97
(A bin Huzaim, UAE) *in rr of mid-div: nvr able to chal* **25/1**

1m 38.74s (98.74) **8** Ran SP% **121.9**
WIN: 3.90; PL: 1.80, 1.00, 1.50. CSF: 9.30; EXACTA: 15.70; TRIFECTA: 37.30.
Owner Universal Racing **Bred** Gt Lucas **Trained** Newmarket, Suffolk

FOCUS
The bare form doesn't tell half the story of how good Trade Storm was in taking this Group 2 prize. The race was run at a slow-fast gallop and, despite having to weave his way through from off the pace in the straight, the winner quickened up exceptionally well to take this with ease. The sectionals were 28.02 (400m), 25.20 (800m), 22.71 (1200m), before Trade Storm clocked a rapid 22.15 to the line.

873a NATAGORA (H'CAP) (TURF) 1m 2f

5:45 (5:45) (100-112,112) 3-Y-O+

£55,214 (£18,404; £9,202; £4,601; £2,760; £1,840)

RPR

1 **Quick Wit**[16] 657 6-9-0 **106**..(p) KierenFallon 11 110
(Saeed bin Suroor) *trckd ldrs: rdn to ld 2 1/2f out: r.o bravely: jst hld on* **12/1**

2 *shd* **Jutland**[16] 661 6-8-13 **105**.. PatDobbs 9 109
(Doug Watson, UAE) *mid-div: smooth prog chsd ldrs 2f out: ev ch 110yds out jst failed* **10/1**[3]

3 *1/4* **Burano (IRE)**[16] 657 4-8-8 **100**...................................... PaulHanagan 2 103
(Brian Meehan) *settled in rr: smooth prog 2f out: r.o fnl 1 1/2f nrst fin* **14/1**

4 *1/2* **Lindenthaler (GER)**[16] 661 5-9-0 **106**.............................. TedDurcan 1 108
(P Schiergen, Germany) *mid-div: chsd ldrs 2 1/2f out: ev ch 110yds out: nt qckn* **20/1**

5 *2* **Nationalism**[100] 7835 6-8-10 **102**..............................(vt) RichardMullen 6 101
(S Seemar, UAE) *settled in rr: nvr nr to chal* **25/1**

6 *2 1/2* **Bank Of Burden (USA)**[16] 661 6-8-13 **105**.......(t) Per-AndersGraberg 4 99
(Niels Petersen, Norway) *settled in rr: nvr able to chal* **25/1**

7 3/4 **Dormello (IRE)**16 661 5-8-11 **104** JamesDoyle 7 95
(D Selvaratnam, UAE) *s.i.s: mid-div: wd: rdn 3f out: sn btn* **10/1**3
8 3/4 **Without Fear (FR)**9 741 5-8-8 **100** DaneO'Neill 5 91
(Niels Petersen, Norway) *in rr of mid-div: n.d* **28/1**
9 1 1/4 **Jardim (BRZ)**16 656 7-8-9 **101** (b) WayneSmith 8 90
(M F De Kock, South Africa) *sn led: rdn 3 1/2f out: hdd: wknd 2 1/2f out* **16/1**
10 6 1/4 **Starboard**9 741 4-9-6 **112** ChristopheSoumillon 10 101
(E Charpy, UAE) *trckd ldrs: ev ch 1 1/2f out: one pce fnl 110yds* **8/1**2
11 1/2 **Royal Empire (IRE)**16 656 4-9-6 **112** MickaelBarzalona 3 102+
(Saeed bin Suroor) *trckd ldng trio: n.m.r 3f out: one pce fnl 2f* **1/2**1

2m 4.09s (124.09) **11** Ran SP% **132.1**
WIN: 9.90; PL: 2.30, 4.10, 4.20. CSF: 134.22; EXACTA: 156.30; TRIFECTA: 1,590.40. Placepot: £233.60 to a £1 stake. Pool: £7,282.44 - 22.75 winning units. Quadpot: £108.50 to a £1 stake. Pool: £366.70 - 2.50 winning units..
Owner Godolphin **Bred** Ptarmigan Bloodstock Limited **Trained** Newmarket, Suffolk
FOCUS
Not form to invest much time in, with the pace ordinary early on (27.23, 24.30, 24.73, 23.61, winner came home in 24.22) and the only progressive contender (Royal Empire) getting no sort of run.

874 - 875a (Foreign Racing) - See Raceform Interactive

819 KEMPTON (A.W) (R-H)

Monday, March 4

OFFICIAL GOING: Standard
Wind: Moderate, half against Weather: Fine

876 MIX BUSINESS WITH PLEASURE MEDIAN AUCTION MAIDEN STKS 6f (P)
2:40 (2:40) (Class 6) 3-5-Y-O **£1,940** (£577; £288; £144) **Stalls** Low

Form RPR
1 **Friendship Is Love** 3-8-9 0 LiamKeniry 3 52+
(David Elsworth) *dwlt: trckd ldr: hanging lft and lost 2nd over 1f out: continued to hang but styd on fnl f to ld last strides* **4/7**1
4-20 2 nk **Sally Bruce**4 821 3-8-3 49 ow1 JenniferFerguson(7) 4 52
(Louise Best) *s.s: hld up in last: prog 2f out: shkn up to ld ins fnl f: kpt on but hdd last strides* **9/2**2
03-4 3 1/2 **Guru Baby**11 734 3-8-9 53 RichardThomas 2 50
(John E Long) *led: hrd rdn over 1f out: hdd and one pce ins fnl f* **9/2**2
60 4 11 **Tavistock Fair**5 815 3-9-0 0 JimmyQuinn 1 22
(Michael Squance) *dwlt: chsd ldng pair: shkn up over 2f out: sn wknd qckly* **12/1**3

1m 14.3s (1.20) **Going Correction** -0.20s/f (Stan) **4** Ran SP% **107.7**
Speed ratings (Par 101): **84,83,82,68**
CSF £3.44 TOTE £1.70; EX 3.10 Trifecta £4.30 Pool: £1449.08 - 247.80 winning units..
Owner Mrs T A Foreman **Bred** Rosyground Stud **Trained** Newmarket, Suffolk
■ Stewards' Enquiry : Richard Thomas six-day ban: used whip in incorrect place (Mar 18-23)
FOCUS
A desperately weak maiden, run only at a steady pace. It served up a thrilling finish.

877 GET THE BETVICTOR APP MAIDEN STKS 1m (P)
3:15 (3:15) (Class 5) 3-Y-0+ **£2,587** (£770; £384; £192) **Stalls** Low

Form RPR
1 **Thistleandtworoses (USA)** 3-8-10 0 DavidProbert 1 77+
(Andrew Balding) *mde all: clr 1/2-way: 5 l in front over 2f out: edgd lft and pushed along fnl 2f: ld dwindled but nvr threatened* **2/1**2
2 2 **Cavalieri (IRE)** 3-8-10 0 JimmyQuinn 4 72+
(William Jarvis) *slowest away: rn green in last and pushed along after 2f: prog u.p to go 3rd over 2f out: styd on to take 2nd ins fnl f: clsd on wnr but no real ch* **11/4**3
5 3 3 **Mad About Harry (IRE)**16 685 3-8-10 0 LukeMorris 7 65
(John Best) *chsd ldrs: shkn up after 3f: drvn to chse clr wnr 3f out: no real imp and lost 2nd ins fnl f* **7/4**1
6-6 4 27 **Gunning For Glory**16 685 3-8-10 0 MartinLane 5
(Martin Bosley) *cl up: rdn after 3f: wknd rapidly 3f out: wl t.o* **14/1**
5 5 **Lalinde** 3-8-5 0 HayleyTurner 2
(Daniel Kubler) *rn green: chsd wnr to 3f out: wknd rapidly: wl t.o* **10/1**

1m 38.32s (-1.48) **Going Correction** -0.20s/f (Stan) **5** Ran SP% **112.1**
Speed ratings (Par 103): **99,97,94,67,62**
toteswingers 1&2 £8.60, 1&3 £3.10, 2&3 £8.20 CSF £8.06 TOTE £2.20: £1.90, £1.30; EX 7.40 Trifecta £12.10 Pool: £2347.17 - 144.42 winning units..
Owner Sir Alex Ferguson **Bred** Scuderia Bolgheri **Trained** Kingsclere, Hants
FOCUS
An ordinary maiden.

878 BETVICTOR EXCLUSIVE ANTEPOST OFFER AINTREE H'CAP 7f (P)
3:50 (3:51) (Class 5) (0-70,70) 4-Y-0+ **£2,587** (£770; £384; £192) **Stalls** Low

Form RPR
45 1 **Al Khan (IRE)**4 822 4-9-7 **70** WilliamCarson 1 78
(Violet M Jordan) *trckd ldrs gng easily: prog to trck ldr over 1f out: sn rdn: tk time but eventually fnd enough to go past 75yds out: drvn out* **6/1**2
643- 2 1/2 **Paradise Spectre**102 7827 6-9-7 **70** MartinHarley 5 77
(Mrs K Burke) *trckd ldng trio: prog over 2f out: rdn to ld wl over 1f out: styd on but hdd last 75yds* **5/1**1
000- 3 nk **Midnight Feast**66 8268 5-8-13 **62** (b1) LukeMorris 2 68
(Lee Carter) *trckd ldng pair: rdn to chal 2f out: pressed after but a jst hld fnl f* **20/1**
603- 4 2 **Absent Amy (IRE)**190 5625 4-9-0 **63** JamieMackay 14 64+
(Alastair Lidderdale) *forced to r wd fr outside draw: chsd ldrs: rdn over 2f out: styd on to take 4th ins fnl f: unable to chal* **12/1**
020- 5 3 1/2 **Homeward Strut**76 8159 4-9-3 **66** (b) IanMongan 12 58
(Laura Mongan) *wnt rt s: pressed ldr: led over 2f out to wl over 1f out: wknd fnl f* **25/1**
556- 6 nk **Mujaadel (USA)**155 6709 8-8-13 **62** (p) FrannyNorton 9 53
(David Nicholls) *sltly impeded s: towards rr: cajoled along and no prog over 2f out: kpt on fr over 1f out: n.d* **8/1**
-525 7 1/2 **Tidal's Baby**16 687 4-9-4 **67** JimCrowley 13 57
(Tony Carroll) *t.k.h early: hld up in last pair: rdn on outer over 2f out and no prog: kpt on fr over 1f out* **8/1**
3-12 8 1/2 **Bowstar**18 652 4-8-13 **62** (p) RobertHavlin 11 50
(Michael Attwater) *bmpd s: wl in rr: rdn and one pce fr over 2f out: no ch* **13/2**3
5-65 9 1 1/4 **Ted's Brother (IRE)**11 740 5-8-13 **62** RobbieFitzpatrick 3 47
(Richard Guest) *urged along early: nvr bttr than midfield: drvn over 2f out: fdd over 1f out* **10/1**
1-46 10 1 1/2 **Flavius Victor (IRE)**10 749 4-9-5 **68** GeorgeBaker 4 49
(Patrick Chamings) *stdd s: hld up in last pair: shkn up over 2f out: nvr involved* **8/1**
0000 11 3 1/4 **Beauty Pageant (IRE)**9 778 6-9-4 **67** TomMcLaughlin 8 40
(David Evans) *led to over 2f out: sn wknd* **50/1**
-602 12 3 **Spanish Plume**10 758 5-9-5 **68** (p) LiamKeniry 10 33
(Reg Hollinshead) *sltly impeded s: hld up wl in rr: shkn up and no prog over 2f out* **8/1**
5005 13 4 **Crowning Star (IRE)**19 638 4-9-1 **64** RobertWinston 6 18
(Gay Kelleway) *sn pushed along in midfield: u.p and no prog 3f out: wknd* **16/1**

1m 23.99s (-2.01) **Going Correction** -0.20s/f (Stan) **13** Ran SP% **122.0**
Speed ratings (Par 103): **103,102,102,99,95 95,94,94,92,91 87,84,79**
toteswingers 1&2 £4.00, 1&3 £22.10, 2&3 £20.30 CSF £36.10 CT £444.49 TOTE £6.40: £2.60, £2.90, £6.20; EX 37.60 Trifecta £790.70 Pool: £3025.78 - 2.86 winning units..
Owner Rakebackmypoker.com **Bred** Galadari Sons Stud Company Limited **Trained** Moreton Morrell, Warwicks
FOCUS
A competitive handicap, run at an honest pace.

879 BETVICTOR NON RUNNER NO BET AT CHELTENHAM H'CAP 6f (P)
4:25 (4:25) (Class 5) (0-75,75) 3-Y-0 **£2,587** (£770; £384; £192) **Stalls** Low

Form RPR
1-2 1 **Line Of Reason (IRE)**7 793 3-9-7 **75** JimCrowley 2 91+
(David Simcock) *hld up bhd ldng pair: clsd to ld wl over 1f out: reminder then pushed along and readily drew clr* **4/9**1
214 2 3 3/4 **Hard Walnut (IRE)**12 730 3-9-6 **74** WilliamCarson 3 79
(Olly Stevens) *led at gd pce: drvn and hdd wl over 1f out: one pce and no ch w wnr* **4/1**2
-024 3 3 1/2 **Desert Donkey**5 811 3-8-10 **64** DavidProbert 5 58
(Andrew Balding) *chsd ldr: rdn to chal 2f out: nt qckn over 1f out: wknd fnl f* **7/1**3
53-1 4 1 1/4 **Indian Affair**19 628 3-8-8 **69** PhilipPrince(7) 4 60
(Milton Bradley) *chsd ldng pair: rdn 1/2-way: struggling after: wl btn over 1f out* **12/1**

1m 11.46s (-1.64) **Going Correction** -0.20s/f (Stan) **4** Ran SP% **109.4**
Speed ratings (Par 98): **102,97,92,90**
toteswingers 1&2 £1.70, 1&3 £3.40, 2&3 £2.70 CSF £2.61 TOTE £1.40; EX 3.20 Trifecta £4.40 Pool: £2290.70 - 383.68 winning units..
Owner Tick Tock Partnership **Bred** Corduff Stud Ltd, J Corcoran & J Judd **Trained** Newmarket, Suffolk
FOCUS
Not a great deal of depth to this handicap.

880 BETVICTOR GRAND NATIONAL NON RUNNER FREE BET H'CAP (DIV I) 6f (P)
5:00 (5:00) (Class 4) (0-85,85) 4-Y-0+ **£4,690** (£1,395; £697; £348) **Stalls** Low

Form RPR
-401 1 **Crew Cut (IRE)**12 723 5-9-1 **79** (b) RobertWinston 4 88
(Jeremy Gask) *chsd ldrs: clsd fr 2f out: urged along after: styd on to ld last 100yds: drvn out* **5/2**1
0-51 2 1/2 **Blue Jack**23 582 8-8-10 **74** (t) AndreaAtzeni 9 81
(Stuart Williams) *pressed ldr: rdn to chal 2f out: edgd into narrow ld jst ins fnl f: hdd and nt qckn last 100yds* **5/1**3
2-00 3 1 **Elna Bright**12 723 8-9-4 **82** IanMongan 5 86
(Peter Crate) *led at gd pce: drvn and pressed 2f out: hdd and one pce jst ins fnl f* **16/1**
-122 4 1 1/2 **Hamoody (USA)**12 727 9-9-5 **83** FrannyNorton 1 82
(David Nicholls) *trckd ldng pair: rdn 2f out: tried to chal over 1f out: fdd last 100yds* **5/1**3
0434 5 nk **Forest Edge (IRE)**12 723 4-9-7 **85** (b) AdamKirby 3 83+
(David Evans) *restless stalls: dwlt: hld up in rr: shkn up and nt on terms fr over 2f out: styd on fnl f: gaining at fin* **4/1**2
1-05 6 4 1/2 **Kakatosi**39 353 6-9-6 **84** EddieAhern 6 68
(Mike Murphy) *chsd ldrs: rdn over 2f out: sn struggling* **11/2**
100- 7 7 **School Fees**184 5812 4-8-6 **77** PhilipPrince(7) 8 38
(Olly Stevens) *hld up in rr: bmpd along over 2f out: sn wknd* **25/1**
U600 8 3 1/4 **Decent Fella (IRE)**13 715 7-8-12 **76** (tp) WilliamCarson 2 27
(Violet M Jordan) *awkward s: hld up in last: brought v wd bnd 3f out: sn bhd* **14/1**

1m 10.93s (-2.17) **Going Correction** -0.20s/f (Stan) **8** Ran SP% **113.7**
Speed ratings (Par 105): **106,105,104,102,101 95,86,81**
toteswingers 1&2 £3.50, 1&3 £6.50, 2&3 £9.70 CSF £15.03 CT £162.25 TOTE £2.90: £1.40, £1.40, £4.50; EX 15.50 Trifecta £95.60 Pool: £2347.74 - 18.40 winning units..
Owner Coral Champions Club **Bred** Rathbarry Stud **Trained** Sutton Veny, Wilts
FOCUS
A competitive sprint handicap, run at a decent pace

881 BETVICTOR GRAND NATIONAL NON RUNNER FREE BET H'CAP (DIV II) 6f (P)
5:30 (5:30) (Class 4) (0-85,84) 4-Y-0+ **£4,690** (£1,395; £697; £348) **Stalls** Low

Form RPR
122- 1 **Yeeoow (IRE)**166 6368 4-9-6 **83** MartinHarley 3 93+
(Mrs K Burke) *hld up in midfield: prog 2f out: c between rivals to ld 1f out: drvn and styd on wl* **7/4**2
5-11 2 1/2 **Polar Venture**38 372 4-8-9 **72** AdamBeschizza 5 80+
(William Haggas) *sltly awkward s: hld up in last pair: plld out and shkn up over 1f out: r.o to go 2nd last 50yds and clsd on wnr: too much to do* **6/4**1
20-6 3 1 **Rowe Park**23 586 10-9-7 **84** LiamKeniry 1 89
(Linda Jewell) *trckd ldng pair: prog 2f out: rdn to chal and upsides 1f out: one pce* **20/1**
10-0 4 1 **Rylee Mooch**32 457 5-8-13 **76** (e) RobbieFitzpatrick 9 78
(Richard Guest) *led: hrd pressed fr 2f out: hdd 1f out: fdd last 100yds* **50/1**
0-12 5 1 **Burnhope**27 526 4-8-13 **76** (p) LukeMorris 6 75
(Scott Dixon) *tk fierce hold: trckd ldng pair: rdn 2f out: nt qckn over 1f out: fdd* **7/1**
000- 6 nk **Street Power (USA)**145 6979 8-9-3 **80** JimCrowley 4 78
(Jeremy Gask) *stdd s: hld up towards rr: prog on inner 2f out: tried to chal 1f out: sn wknd last 150yds* **11/2**3
2-30 7 1/2 **Clear Praise (USA)**12 723 6-9-5 **82** HayleyTurner 7 78
(Simon Dow) *t.k.h: pressed ldr to over 1f out: wknd fnl f* **12/1**

6-6 **8** *1* **Albaqaa**[12] 723 8-9-2 **79**........ J-PGuillambert 2 72
(P J O'Gorman) *c out of the stalls slowly: hld up in last: pushed along fr 2f out: nvr remotely involved* **20/1**

1m 10.92s (-2.18) **Going Correction** -0.20s/f (Stan) **8** Ran SP% **123.4**
Speed ratings (Par 105): **106,105,104,102,101 100,100,98**
toteswingers 1&2 £1.80, 1&3 £1.30, 2&3 £13.40 CSF £5.14 CT £39.26 TOTE £2.50: £1.30, £1.10, £5.00; EX 7.40 Trifecta £61.60 Pool: £2265.57 - 27.57 winning units..

Owner R Lee & Mrs E Burke **Bred** Arctic Tack Stud **Trained** Middleham Moor, N Yorks

■ Stewards' Enquiry : Robbie Fitzpatrick two-day ban: careless riding (Mar 18-19)

FOCUS
The second division of this sprint handicap was arguably a shade hotter than the first and the form looks rock solid.

882 FOLLOW US ON TWITTER @BETVICTORRACING H'CAP (LONDON MIDDLE DISTANCE QUALIFIER) 1m 3f (P)

6:00 (6:01) (Class 4) (0-85,84) 4-Y-0+ **£4,690** (£1,395; £697; £348) **Stalls** Low

Form RPR

4361 **1** **Buckland (IRE)**[12] 720 5-8-8 **78**........ RyanTate(7) 1 91+
(Hans Adielsson) *wl in tch: chsd ldr 4f out: clsd and rdn to ld over 1f out: sn drew clr* **4/1**[3]

-251 **2** *5* **Reflect (IRE)**[35] 420 5-8-13 **76**........(t) FrannyNorton 7 80
(Derek Shaw) *hld up in 6th and off the pce: nt clr run briefly over 2f out: prog on inner wl over 1f out: hrd rdn and kpt on to take 2nd last strides* **5/1**

2250 **3** *hd* **Ajeeb (USA)**[23] 585 5-9-2 **79**........(v1) JimCrowley 6 83
(Michael Scudamore) *led: kicked on 4f out: hdd over 1f out: no ch w wnr: lost 2nd last strides* **10/1**

005- **4** *1 1/4* **Right Step**[128] 7396 6-9-0 **84**........ DavidParkes(7) 4 85+
(Alan Jarvis) *hld up in detached last: rdn and stl detached 2f out: r.o fnl f: nrst fin* **7/2**[2]

3244 **5** *nk* **Sir Boss (IRE)**[16] 691 8-9-2 **79**........ TomEaves 2 80
(Michael Mullineaux) *in tch: rdn over 2f out: no imp over 1f out: wknd ins fnl f* **9/1**

-220 **6** *3 1/2* **Focail Maith**[30] 496 5-9-7 **84**........(p) AdamKirby 5 79
(John Ryan) *chsd ldrs: shkn up briefly 5f out: rdn over 2f out: steadily wknd* **9/4**[1]

/050 **7** *1 1/2* **Dubawi Phantom**[9] 777 6-9-2 **79**........(p) WilliamCarson 3 71
(David C Griffiths) *chsd ldr to 4f out: sn rdn: wknd fr over 2f out* **16/1**

2m 18.09s (-3.81) **Going Correction** -0.20s/f (Stan) **7** Ran SP% **114.6**
Speed ratings (Par 105): **105,101,101,100,100 97,96**
toteswingers 1&2 £2.50, 1&3 £7.40, 2&3 £10.70 CSF £24.21 TOTE £4.50: £2.70, £3.20; EX 15.10 Trifecta £97.40 Pool: £2259.66 - 17.38 winning units..

Owner P S McNally **Bred** Airlie Stud And Sir Thomas Pilkington **Trained** Kingston Lisle, Oxon

FOCUS
A fair handicap, run at a steady pace

883 KEMPTON FOR WEDDINGS H'CAP 1m 3f (P)

6:30 (6:30) (Class 6) (0-60,66) 4-Y-0+ **£1,940** (£577; £288; £144) **Stalls** Low

Form RPR

0-00 **1** **Scary Movie (IRE)**[7] 789 8-9-7 **60**........(b) AdamKirby 9 74+
(Thomas McLaughlin, Ire) *s.s: sn rcvrd into midfield: looking for room over 2f out: prog wl over 1f out: swept into the ld last 150yds: sn clr* **16/1**

1003 **2** *2 1/2* **Delightful Sleep**[7] 801 5-8-8 **54**........ RobJFitzpatrick(7) 6 62
(David Evans) *trckd ldrs in 6th: prog over 2f out: shkn up to ld over 1f out: hdd and outpcd last 150yds* **16/1**

-112 **3** *3/4* **Irene Kennet**[18] 653 6-9-7 **60**........ HayleyTurner 12 67
(Paul Burgoyne) *trckd ldng pair: rdn to chal 2f out: nt qckn over 1f out: one pce after* **7/2**[1]

0511 **4** *1 3/4* **Time Square (FR)**[12] 722 6-8-10 **56**........ JoeyHaynes(7) 7 60
(Tony Carroll) *t.k.h: trckd ldng trio: effrt over 2f out: cl up over 1f out: fdd ins fnl f* **9/2**[2]

6-50 **5** *hd* **Arashi**[14] 709 7-9-4 **57**........(v) JimCrowley 14 61
(Derek Shaw) *hld up towards rr: pushed along over 2f out: reminder and prog over 1f out: styd on fnl f: nrst fin* **16/1**

6233 **6** *1/2* **Divine Rule (IRE)**[19] 633 5-8-13 **57**........(v) ThomasBrown(5) 8 60
(Laura Mongan) *trckd ldrs in 5th: gng easily over 2f out: shkn up over 1f out: fnd nil and sn btn* **9/1**

6343 **7** *3/4* **Shirataki (IRE)**[7] 789 5-9-7 **60**........ ChrisCatlin 1 62
(Peter Hiatt) *t.k.h: trckd ldr: led wl over 2f out and tried to kick clr: hdd & wknd over 1f out* **5/1**[3]

0004 **8** *3/4* **Legal Legacy**[7] 789 7-9-5 **58**........ WilliamCarson 11 58
(Richard Rowe) *s.s: hld up in last pair: rdn over 2f out: hanging and no prog tl kpt on fnl f* **13/2**

1-00 **9** *3 3/4* **Rodrigo De Freitas (IRE)**[18] 653 6-9-6 **59**........(p) MatthewDavies 3 53
(Jim Boyle) *s.s: a wl in rr: rdn and no prog over 2f out* **12/1**

005- **10** *3/4* **Final Delivery**[96] 7892 4-8-10 **55**........ NathanAlison(5) 2 48
(Jim Boyle) *s.v.s: t.k.h in last pair: no prog 3f out* **16/1**

00-0 **11** *9* **Dicey Vows (USA)**[7] 789 5-8-13 **59**........ DavidParkes(7) 4 38
(Alan Jarvis) *t.k.h and sddle sn slipped: in tch in midfield tl wknd over 2f out: t.o* **33/1**

4-00 **12** *5* **On The Cusp (IRE)**[13] 718 6-9-6 **59**........(p) MartinHarley 13 30
(Violet M Jordan) *led to wl over 2f out: wknd rapidly: t.o* **33/1**

2m 19.88s (-2.02) **Going Correction** -0.20s/f (Stan)
WFA 4 from 5yo+ 1lb **12** Ran SP% **117.5**
Speed ratings (Par 101): **99,97,96,95,95 94,94,93,91,90 83,80**
toteswingers 1&2 £21.30, 1&3 £15.60, 2&3 £17.30 CSF £247.00 CT £1102.12 TOTE £22.30: £5.80, £6.30, £1.90; EX 235.50 Trifecta £1187.80 Pool: £2234.13 - 1.41 winning units..

Owner D J Dolan **Bred** Mrs T Brudenell **Trained** Rathmullan, Co Donegal

FOCUS
A fair race for the grade, which developed at a relatively early stage and that played to the strengths of the winner.

T/Plt: £37.20 to a £1 stake. Pool: £46839.68 - 917.84 winning tickets. T/Qpdt: £8.90 to a £1 stake. Pool: £4539.02 - 376.97 winning tickets. JN

[826] SOUTHWELL (L-H)

Tuesday, March 5

OFFICIAL GOING: Standard
Wind: Nil Weather: Foggy

884 32REDBINGO.COM H'CAP 7f (F)

2:10 (2:11) (Class 6) (0-52,52) 4-Y-0+ **£2,045** (£603; £302) **Stalls** Low

Form RPR

2-00 **1** **Mucky Molly**[27] 537 5-9-4 **49**........(vt) TomEaves 1 55
(Alison Hutchinson) *cl up: led wl over 1f out and sn rdn: drvn and jnd ins fnl f: jst hld on* **33/1**

04-2 **2** *nse* **Bentley**[23] 600 9-8-12 **50**........ RobertTart(7) 10 56
(Brian Baugh) *chsd ldrs on outer: pushed along and sltly outpcd after 2f: sn swtchd lft: hdwy wl over 2f out: rdn to chse wnr over 1f out: drvn to chal ins fnl f and ev ch: jst failed* **3/1**[1]

0-05 **3** *1 1/4* **Bonnie Prince Blue**[23] 600 10-9-6 **51**........ DaleSwift 5 54
(Ian McInnes) *chsd ldrs: sn rdn along: drvn wl over 1f out: sn edgd lft: kpt on wl u.p fnl f* **12/1**

6405 **4** *4* **Meydan Style (USA)**[28] 523 7-9-1 **46** oh1........ JoeFanning 3 38
(Richard Ford) *in rr: rdn along 1/2-way: hdwy on inner 2f out: styd on u.p appr fnl f: nrst fin* **4/1**[2]

0-54 **5** *1/2* **Mango Music**[21] 618 10-9-6 **51**........ BarryMcHugh 6 42
(David Thompson) *dwlt and in rr tl rdn and styd on fnl 2f: nrst fin* **7/1**

004- **6** *hd* **Mad For Fun (IRE)**[191] 5623 4-8-13 **49**........ ShirleyTeasdale(5) 2 39
(Paul Midgley) *trckd ldrs: hdwy over 2f out: rdn wl over 1f out: sn wknd* **14/1**

20-0 **7** *1 1/2* **Tenancy (IRE)**[21] 618 9-9-2 **47**........(p) DuranFentiman 8 34
(Shaun Harris) *cl up: led after 1f: rdn along 3f out: hdd wl over 1f out: sn wknd* **16/1**

600- **8** *2 1/2* **Witchry**[84] 8061 11-9-2 **52**........ ThomasBrown(5) 9 32
(Tony Newcombe) *chsd ldrs: rdn along wl over 2f out: sn wknd* **9/2**[3]

0006 **9** *9* **Ishiamiracle**[10] 778 4-9-2 **47**........(p) DavidProbert 4 4
(Phil McEntee) *led 1f: cl up: rdn along 3f out: sn wknd* **12/1**

000- **10** *31* **Prohibition (IRE)**[80] 8131 7-9-7 **52**........ AdamKirby 7
(John Butler) *dwlt: a in rr: bhd whn eased fnl f* **14/1**

1m 30.95s (0.65) **Going Correction** +0.025s/f (Slow) **10** Ran SP% **113.2**
Speed ratings (Par 101): **97,96,95,90,90 90,88,85,75,39**
toteswingers 1&2 £15.40, 1&3 £40.70, 2&3 £6.10 CSF £126.94 CT £1319.78 TOTE £28.30: £5.90, £1.50, £4.20; EX 148.10 Trifecta £622.10 Pool: £3693.18 - 4.45 winning units..

Owner Miss A L Hutchinson **Bred** Paul Sweeting **Trained** Exning, Suffolk

FOCUS
A very moderate handicap. The winner may be capable of a bit better.

885 32RED.COM H'CAP 5f (F)

2:40 (2:42) (Class 5) (0-75,74) 4-Y-0+ **£2,587** (£770; £384; £192) **Stalls** High

Form RPR

05-1 **1** **Clubland (IRE)**[33] 454 4-8-12 **68**........ MarkCoumbe(3) 1 78
(Roy Bowring) *cl up on outer: hdwy to ld after 1 1/2f: rdn and edgd rt over 1f out: drvn out* **5/1**[3]

1110 **2** *1 1/4* **M J Woodward**[8] 795 4-9-2 **69**........ JoeFanning 2 74
(Paul Green) *trckd ldrs: hdwy 1/2-way and sn chsng wnr: rdn over 1f out: drvn and kpt on same pce ins fnl f* **9/2**[2]

-113 **3** *1 3/4* **Miss Bunter**[47] 234 4-9-3 **70**........ DanielTudhope 12 69
(David O'Meara) *chsd ldrs: rdn along wl over 1f out: hung lft appr fnl f: kpt on same pce* **12/1**

000- **4** *3/4* **Oldjoesaid**[110] 7730 9-9-6 **73**........ RussKennemore 10 69
(Paul Midgley) *towards rr: hdwy 2f out: rdn and styd on fnl f: nrst fin* **33/1**

-644 **5** *1 1/4* **Hot Sugar (USA)**[20] 627 4-8-11 **64**........(t) AndrewMullen 8 56
(Michael Appleby) *towards rr: hdwy wl over 1f out: rdn whn n.m.r appr fnl f: kpt on same pce* **7/1**

43-0 **6** *1 1/4* **Sleepy Blue Ocean**[51] 196 7-9-7 **74**........(p) RobertWinston 5 61
(John Balding) *dwlt and towards rr: rdn along and hdwy wl over 1f out: kpt on fnl f: nvr nr ldrs* **6/1**

040- **7** *1* **Captain Scooby**[125] 7489 7-8-11 **69**........ JasonHart(5) 3 52
(Richard Guest) *towards rr: pushed along 1/2-way: sme hdwy on wd outside wl over 1f out: n.d* **16/1**

030- **8** *1 1/4* **Haajes**[110] 7726 9-9-5 **72**........ MickyFenton 4 51
(Paul Midgley) *a towards rr* **50/1**

310- **9** *nk* **Phoenix Clubs (IRE)**[126] 7451 4-9-7 **74**........ BarryMcHugh 7 52
(Paul Midgley) *nvr bttr than midfield* **40/1**

6112 **10** *1 1/4* **Holy Angel (IRE)**[8] 795 4-8-10 **70**........(e) RachelRichardson(7) 9 43
(Tim Easterby) *s.i.s: a in rr* **3/1**[1]

140- **11** *1/2* **Ambitious Icarus**[125] 7489 4-9-2 **69**........(e1) RobbieFitzpatrick 11 41
(Richard Guest) *a towards rr* **25/1**

060- **12** *hd* **Laura's Bairn**[134] 7299 4-9-3 **70**........(v) FrederikTylicki 6 41
(J R Jenkins) *led: hdd after 1 1/2f: chsd wnr: rdn along 2f out: sn wknd* **16/1**

3100 **13** *nk* **Dickie Le Davoir**[6] 812 9-8-8 **68**........(e1) LisaTodd(7) 13 38
(Richard Guest) *dwlt: a in rr* **33/1**

59.87s (0.17) **Going Correction** +0.125s/f (Slow) **13** Ran SP% **120.2**
Speed ratings (Par 103): **103,101,98,97,95 93,91,89,88,86 86,85,85**
toteswingers 1&2 £5.30, 1&3 £10.80, 2&3 £8.20 CSF £26.66 CT £269.89 TOTE £9.50: £4.00, £2.40, £2.10; EX 49.60 Trifecta £271.60 Pool: £3343.65 - 9.23 winning units..

Owner S R Bowring **Bred** Mrs Sharon Slattery **Trained** Edwinstowe, Notts

FOCUS
Not many got into this ordinary sprint handicap. The second helps set the level.

886 32RECBET.COM (S) STKS 1m 3f (F)

3:10 (3:10) (Class 6) 4-Y-0+ **£2,045** (£603; £302) **Stalls** Low

Form RPR

60-3 **1** **Jack Dawkins (USA)**[28] 524 8-8-11 59........ AdrianNicholls 4 72
(David Nicholls) *a.p: hdwy to ld over 3f out: rdn clr wl over 1f out: styd on* **5/1**[2]

-621 **2** *6* **Goldmadchen (GER)**[21] 624 5-8-11 66........ JoeFanning 3 62
(Keith Dalgleish) *trckd ldrs: hdwy to chse wnr 3f out: rdn wl over 1f out: drvn and one pce fr over 1f out* **2/5**[1]

5044 **3** *7* **Gay Gallivanter**[23] 601 5-8-11 46........(p) AndreaAtzeni 7 51
(Mick Quinn) *towards rr: pushed along over 4f out: hdwy on wd outside over 2f out: sn rdn and styd on appr fnl f:* **28/1**

-556 **4** *1 3/4* **Justine Time (IRE)**[23] 600 4-8-5 42........(e) JamesSullivan 9 43
(Julie Camacho) *hld up towards rr: hdwy 3f out: rdn along 2f out: sn one pce* **33/1**

-020 **5** *2 1/4* **Silver Marizah (IRE)**[15] 704 4-8-7 49 ow2..................(e) RobertHavlin 6 41
(Roger Ingram) *chsd ldng pair: rdn along 3f out: drvn 2f out and sn wknd* **16/1**

2410 **6** *3 3/4* **Gunner Will (IRE)**[8] 791 4-9-1 61.................................... MickyFenton 5 43
(Paul Midgley) *chsd ldrs: hdwy over 3f out: rdn along wl over 2f out: sn wknd* **8/1**[3]

6-04 **7** *6* **General Tufto**[23] 597 8-8-11 45.............................(b) RobbieFitzpatrick 2 29
(Charles Smith) *sn outpcd and rdn along in rr: bhd fnl 5f* **20/1**

0-30 **8** *20* **Rockgoat (IRE)**[8] 801 4-8-10 57....................................(v) LukeMorris 8
(Ian McInnes) *sn led: rdn along and hdd over 3f out: sn drvn and wknd over 2f out* **16/1**

6- **9** *21* **Ilewin Dundee**[204] 5174 7-8-6 0.................................. RachealKneller(5) 1
(Gary Brown) *dwlt and sn rdn along in rr: bhd fnl 5f* **33/1**

2m 27.86s (-0.14) **Going Correction** +0.025s/f (Slow)
WFA 4 from 5yo+ 1lb **9** Ran SP% **125.1**
Speed ratings (Par 101): **101,96,91,90,88 85,81,67,51**
toteswingers 1&2 £1.02, 1&3 £14.50, 2&3 £18.60 CSF £7.76 TOTE £4.20: £1.50, £1.02, £6.50; EX 8.30 Trifecta £139.40 Pool: £1652.42 - 8.89 winning units..There was no bid for the winner.
Owner The Three K's **Bred** Clovelly Farms **Trained** Sessay, N Yorks

FOCUS
Not as big an upset as the odds might suggest. The third and fourth give perspective.

887 32RED CASINO H'CAP 1m 6f (F)
3:40 (3:40) (Class 5) (0-75,75) 4-Y-O+ **£2,726** (£805; £402) **Stalls** Low

Form RPR

01/3 **1** **Masterful Act (USA)**[20] 642 6-9-2 65.............................. GrahamLee 7 84
(Alan McCabe) *a.p: led over 5f out: pushed clr over 2f out: styd on strly: unchal* **4/1**

4123 **2** *9* **Scribe (IRE)**[4] 851 5-8-3 59..(t) RobertTart(7) 1 64
(David Evans) *chsd ldrs on inner and sn pushed along: outpcd and lost pl 1/2-way: hdwy u.p over 3f out: drvn to chse ldng pair over 2f out: styd on to take modest 2nd ins fnl f: no ch w wnr* **7/2**[3]

-401 **3** *nk* **Mediterranean Sea (IRE)**[20] 642 7-9-12 75.............. FrederikTylicki 6 80
(J R Jenkins) *trckd ldrs: hdwy to trck wnr 5f out: rdn along wl over 2f out: sn drvn and no imp: lost 2nd ins fnl f* **11/4**[1]

310- **4** *10* **Brunello**[378] 644 5-9-1 64.. DanielTudhope 3 56
(David O'Meara) *trckd ldrs: hdwy 5f out: rdn along over 3f out: sn drvn and outpcd* **3/1**[2]

06/5 **5** *7* **Calculating (IRE)**[21] 624 9-8-7 56.................................. DavidProbert 2 39
(Mark Usher) *in tch: effrt over 4f out: sn rdn and along and outpcd fr over 3f out* **25/1**

50-3 **6** *2 1/2* **Omid**[14] 713 5-8-9 58...(vt) LukeMorris 4 38
(Nicky Vaughan) *prom: pushed along after 6f: sn lost pl and bhd fnl 4f* **7/1**

000- **7** *1 1/2* **Wells Lyrical (IRE)**[166] 6407 8-9-0 63.............................. TomEaves 5 41
(Bryan Smart) *led: rdn along and hdd over 5f out: sn wknd* **16/1**

3m 7.51s (-0.79) **Going Correction** +0.025s/f (Slow) **7** Ran SP% **116.1**
Speed ratings (Par 103): **103,97,97,91,87 86,85**
toteswingers 1&2 £15.40, 1&3 £40.70, 2&3 £6.10 CSF £18.94 TOTE £5.40: £4.10, £1.10; EX 18.00 Trifecta £25.70 Pool: £821.11 - 23.88 winning units..
Owner Universal Recycling Company **Bred** Fiona Craig & Dermot Cantillon **Trained** Averham Park, Notts

FOCUS
Clearly improved form from the winner in this ordinary handicap.

888 32REDPOKER.COM H'CAP 1m 4f (F)
4:10 (4:15) (Class 5) (0-60,59) 4-Y-O+ **£2,045** (£603; £302) **Stalls** Low

Form RPR

5/6- **1** **Amtired**[63] 8139 7-9-3 55..(be) DaleSwift 8 69
(Brian Ellison) *hld up: gd hdwy over 4f out: chsd ldr 3f out: sn chal: rdn to ld over 1f out: edgd lft ins fnl f: styd on wl* **3/1**[1]

060- **2** *2 3/4* **Linroyale Boy (USA)**[105] 7793 5-9-0 52..................... RobertWinston 10 62
(Alan Swinbank) *chsd ldrs on wd outside: hdwy over 4f out: led over 3f out: jnd and rdn wl over 2f out: hdd over 1f out: kpt on* **7/2**[2]

06 **3** *5* **Houdini Bright (USA)**[14] 714 5-8-7 45..................(b[1]) JamesSullivan 7 47
(James Given) *hld up towards rr: hdwy on wd outside over 4f out: rdn to chse ldng pair over 2f out: drvn and no imp fr wl over 1f out* **14/1**

-021 **4** *6* **Corn Maiden**[14] 714 4-8-13 53.. JoeFanning 2 46
(Mark Rimmer) *uns rdr and rn loose bef s: trckd ldrs on inner: pushed along and sltly outpcd over 4f out: rdn along over 3f out: plugged on same pce fnl 2f* **9/2**

/63- **5** *8* **Rubi Dia**[364] 811 6-9-6 58.. AdamKirby 9 39
(Sean Curran) *trckd ldrs: effrt over 3f out: rdn along wl over 2f out: sn outpcd* **4/1**[3]

3666 **6** *1 3/4* **El Bravo**[18] 671 7-8-13 56....................................(p) ShirleyTeasdale(5) 5 34
(Shaun Harris) *chsd ldrs: rdn along over 3f out: sn outpcd* **12/1**

1660 **7** *6* **Temuco (IRE)**[3] 866 4-8-12 59..(b) EoinWalsh(7) 4 28
(David Evans) *a towards rr* **14/1**

02-3 **8** *2* **Inside Knowledge (USA)**[12] 622 7-8-12 50................(b) LukeMorris 6 16
(Garry Woodward) *cl up: rdn along over 4f out: wknd 3f out* **16/1**

00-0 **9** *4 1/2* **Darwinian**[20] 633 4-8-5 45...[1] DavidProbert 3 5
(Dave Morris) *a in rr: outpcd and bhd fnl 3f* **100/1**

0210 **10** *1/2* **Maslak (IRE)**[18] 668 9-9-7 59.. ChrisCatlin 1 18
(Peter Hiatt) *slt ld: rdn along over 4f out: hdd over 3f out and sn wknd* **14/1**

2m 40.19s (-0.81) **Going Correction** +0.025s/f (Slow)
WFA 4 from 5yo+ 2lb **10** Ran SP% **120.0**
Speed ratings (Par 103): **103,101,97,93,88 87,83,82,79,78**
toteswingers 1&2 £1.80, 1&3 £0.00, 2&3 £9.10 CSF £13.99 CT £129.55 TOTE £5.80: £1.40, £1.90, £3.30; EX 40.50 Trifecta £447.40 Pool: £709.92 - 1.19 winning units..
Owner Gary Smith **Bred** Miss Dianne Hill **Trained** Norton, N Yorks

FOCUS
Viewing of this moderate handicap was restricted by fog. The winner was well on top, and the runner-up is the key.

889 32RED H'CAP 1m (F)
4:40 (4:46) (Class 4) (0-85,85) 4-Y-O+ **£4,690** (£1,395; £697; £348) **Stalls** Low

Form RPR

000- **1** **Dubai Hills**[106] 7789 7-9-4 82... TomEaves 4 102
(Bryan Smart) *trckd ldr: pushed along and sltly outpcd 3f out: hdwy 2f out: rdn to ld 1 1/2f out: styd on strly* **11/2**

-326 **2** *5* **Dubawi Island (FR)**[11] 751 4-9-0 85......................(b) RobertTart(7) 7 93
(James Tate) *sn led: rdn clr 3f out: hung rt to stands' rails and hdd 1 1/2f out: sn one pce* **9/4**[1]

-311 **3** *4 1/2* **Caledonia Prince**[5] 832 5-8-0 71.............................(b) PhilipPrince(7) 1 69
(Jo Hughes) *chsd ldng pair: rdn over 2f out: drvn and one pce fr over 1f out* **7/2**[2]

-613 **4** *1* **The Lock Master (IRE)**[5] 830 6-8-13 82.............. ShirleyTeasdale(5) 3 78
(Michael Appleby) *chsd ldrs: outpcd after 2f: hdwy wl over 2f out: sn rdn and kpt on same pce* **9/2**[3]

2033 **5** *nse* **Piceno (IRE)**[5] 832 5-8-11 75...(p) LukeMorris 8 71
(Scott Dixon) *chsd ldrs: rdn along wl over 2f out: sn one pce* **12/1**

0454 **6** *6* **Copperwood**[4] 850 8-8-7 71 oh1...................................... JoeFanning 6 53
(Mark Johnston) *chsd ldrs: rdn along wl over 2f out: sn one pce* **12/1**

56-0 **7** *12* **Brigadoon**[11] 759 6-8-12 76....................................... MichaelO'Connell 2 30
(Philip Kirby) *a towards rr* **25/1**

0/40 **8** *14* **Boom To Bust (IRE)**[25] 563 5-9-4 82.........................(b) RobertWinston 5
(Sean Curran) *in tch: rdn 3f out: sn wknd* **16/1**

434/ **9** *41* **Seattle Drive (IRE)**[140] 7155 5-9-3 84........................... PaulPickard(3) 9
(Brian Ellison) *s.i.s: a in rr: bhd fnl 3f* **20/1**

1m 41.61s (-2.09) **Going Correction** +0.025s/f (Slow) **9** Ran SP% **116.4**
Speed ratings (Par 105): **111,106,101,100,100 94,82,68,27**
toteswingers 1&2 £7.90, 1&3 £7.90, 2&3 £1.60 CSF £18.44 CT £50.01 TOTE £10.50: £4.60, £1.02, £4.00; EX 22.80 Trifecta £169.00 Pool: £694.34 - 3.08 winning units..
Owner Mrs F Denniff **Bred** A S Denniff **Trained** Hambleton, N Yorks

FOCUS
Outstanding form. The winner is a real Southwell specialist and proved himself as good as ever. The second ran a solid race in defeat.

890 £32 BONUS AT 32RED.COM H'CAP 6f (F)
5:10 (5:14) (Class 6) (0-60,65) 4-Y-O+ **£2,045** (£603; £302) **Stalls** Low

Form RPR

0451 **1** **Greenhead High**[5] 831 5-9-12 65 6ex......................... AndrewMullen 4 75
(David Nicholls) *mde all: rdn over 2f out: jnd and drvn over 1f out: styd on gamely ins fnl f* **11/4**[2]

10/1 **2** *1 1/4* **Seamster**[21] 618 6-9-6 59...(vt) GrahamLee 6 65
(Richard Ford) *prom: chsd wnr fr 1/2-way: rdn to chal wl over 1f out and ev ch tl drvn and no ex wl ins fnl f* **6/4**[1]

-601 **3** *1/2* **Masked Dance (IRE)**[14] 716 6-9-7 60.........................(bt) LukeMorris 8 65
(Scott Dixon) *in tch: hdwy to trck ldrs 1/2-way: rdn to chse ldng pair over 2f out: drvn and kpt on fnl f* **8/1**

-020 **4** *2 1/4* **Red Shadow**[21] 618 4-9-1 54.. TomEaves 5 52
(Alan Brown) *cl up: rdn along over 2f out: drvn and one pce fr over 1f out* **25/1**

6-02 **5** *nk* **Ridgeway Hawk**[21] 618 5-9-1 54..................................(v) RobertHavlin 10 51
(Mark Usher) *dwlt: sn chsng ldrs: rdn along wl over 2f out: drvn over 1f out: kpt on same pce fnl f* **10/1**

-133 **6** *7* **Romanticize**[20] 640 7-9-3 56.. DaleSwift 11 32
(Jason Ward) *towards rr: hdwy and wd st: sn rdn and n.d* **7/1**[3]

46-5 **7** *3/4* **My New Angel (IRE)**[20] 646 4-8-7 46 oh1................(b) JamesSullivan 3 20
(Paul Green) *chsd ldrs on inner: rdn along 1/2-way: sn wknd* **20/1**

1660 **8** *5* **Kai**[22] 616 4-8-12 56...(v) ShirleyTeasdale(5) 9 15
(Alan McCabe) *s.i.s: a bhd* **16/1**

1m 16.63s (0.13) **Going Correction** +0.025s/f (Slow) **8** Ran SP% **113.9**
Speed ratings (Par 101): **100,98,97,94,94 84,83,77**
toteswingers 1&2 £1.90, 1&3 £8.20, 2&3 £7.60 CSF £7.17 CT £26.78 TOTE £4.80: £1.90, £1.60, £2.10; EX 9.10 Trifecta £46.50 Pool: £463.48 - 7.47 winning units..
Owner Charles Castle **Bred** Wyck Hall Stud Ltd **Trained** Sessay, N Yorks

FOCUS
A race run in thick fog. The winner built on his recent course win.
T/Plt: £95.50 to a £1 stake. Pool: £70470.86 - 538.48 winning tickets. T/Qpdt: £14.90 to a £1 stake. Pool: £5482.38 - 271.90 winning tickets. JR

876 KEMPTON (A.W) (R-H)
Wednesday, March 6

OFFICIAL GOING: Standard
Wind: Moderate, across (towards stands) Weather: Cloudy, light race from Race 3 onwards

894 BETDAQ MEMBERS FREE ENTRY EVERY WEDNESDAY H'CAP 5f (P)
5:30 (5:30) (Class 5) (0-75,73) 3-Y-O **£2,587** (£770; £384; £192) **Stalls** Low

Form RPR

1 **1** **Riskit Fora Biskit (IRE)**[14] 729 3-9-7 73........................ HayleyTurner 1 80+
(Michael Bell) *mde all: shkn up and asserted over 1f out: pushed out firmly fnl f* **15/8**[1]

2242 **2** *1 3/4* **Modern Lady**[5] 847 3-8-7 66.. PhilipPrince(7) 5 67
(Richard Guest) *chsd wnr: rdn and nt qckn over 1f out: no imp after* **10/1**

311 **3** *1/2* **Dangerous Age**[19] 669 3-8-11 63...................................... JoeFanning 3 62
(J W Hills) *t.k.h: hld up in last: shkn up over 1f out: kpt on same pce to take 3rd last stride* **7/2**[3]

-413 **4** *shd* **Marvelino**[28] 531 3-9-2 68...(p) EddieAhern 2 67
(Pat Eddery) *chsd ldng pair: rdn and nt qckn over 1f out: no imp after: lost 3rd post* **3/1**[2]

3-14 **5** *1 3/4* **Ada Lovelace**[28] 531 3-9-5 71..JimCrowley 4 64
(Dean Ivory) *chsd ldng trio: rdn over 1f out: hanging and wknd fnl f* **4/1**

59.74s (-0.76) **Going Correction** 0.0s/f (Stan) **5** Ran SP% **111.1**
Speed ratings (Par 98): **106,103,102,102,99**
CSF £19.82 TOTE £2.00: £1.30, £3.90; EX 15.70 Trifecta £57.60 Pool: £1,623.50 - 21.10 winning units..
Owner Chris Wright & The Hon Mrs J M Corbett **Bred** Edmond Kent **Trained** Newmarket, Suffolk

FOCUS
The early leaders held their position throughout in what was a reasonable handicap for the grade. The winner should step up on this and the form makes sense.

895 WIN BIG WITH BETDAQ MULTIPLES MEDIAN AUCTION MAIDEN STKS 1m 2f (P)
6:00 (6:02) (Class 5) 3-Y-O **£2,587** (£770; £384; £192) **Stalls** Low

Form RPR

03- **1** **Barnaby Brook (CAN)**[118] 7641 3-9-5 0.................... RichardHughes 7 73
(Nick Littmoden) *hld up in 4th: pushed into 3rd 2f out: rdn to cl on ldng pair over 1f out: styd on to ld last 100yds* **5/1**[3]

3 **2** *1/2* **Incorporate**[19] 663 3-9-5 0... JoeFanning 1 72
(Pat Eddery) *led: hanging lft bnd over 2f out and jnd: rdn over 1f out: hdd and nt qckn last 100yds* **11/10**[1]

2 **3** *1 3/4* **Oratorio's Joy (IRE)**[20] 651 3-9-0 0........................ FergusSweeney 5 64+
(Jamie Osborne) *trckd ldr: rdn to chal over 2f out: stl upsides over 1f out: one pce and lost 2nd fnl f* **8/1**

4 *4* **Punditry** 3-9-5 0... NickyMackay 6 61+
(John Gosden) *rn green and pushed along thrght: mostly in last pair: lost tch w ldrs 3f out: kpt on fnl f* **4/1**[2]

0 5 ½ **Early One Morning**[20] 651 3-9-0 0 ... HayleyTurner 3 55
(Hugo Palmer) *trckd ldng pair to 2f out: sn rdn: wknd jst over 1f out: lost 4th last strides* **33/1**

6 shd **London Skolar** 3-9-5 0 ... GrahamLee 2 59
(James Eustace) *mostly in 5th: pushed along fr 1/2-way: lost tch w ldrs 3f out: kpt on fnl f* **33/1**

7 8 **Could Be (IRE)** 3-9-5 0 ... MartinLane 4 43
(David Simcock) *s.s: a in last pair: rdn 4f out: wknd over 2f out: t.o* **10/1**

2m 9.02s (1.02) **Going Correction** 0.0s/f (Stan) **7** Ran SP% **110.4**
Speed ratings (Par 98): **95,94,93,90,89 89,83**
Tote Swingers: 1&2 £2.40, 2&3 £5.20 CSF £10.14 TOTE £4.20: £2.30, £1.10; EX 12.80 Trifecta £68.00 Pool: £2,422.43 - 26.68 winning units..

Owner A A Goodman **Bred** Adena Springs **Trained** Newmarket, Suffolk

FOCUS
An ordinary maiden that run at a steady gallop.

896 BACK AND LAY AT BETDAQ.COM H'CAP 1m 2f (P)
6:30 (6:31) (Class 6) (0-65,66) 4-Y-0+ **£1,940** (£577; £288; £144) **Stalls** Low

Form RPR

-001 **1** **Scary Movie (IRE)**[2] 883 8-9-8 **66** 6ex ... (b) EddieAhern 5 74+
(Thomas McLaughlin, Ire) *hld up in midfield: smooth prog wl over 1f out: led jst ins fnl f: drvn out last 100yds* **9/2**[1]

0-00 **2** ¾ **Dream Prospector**[37] 415 4-9-4 **62** ... FergusSweeney 11 68
(James Evans) *t.k.h: hld up in last quartet: prog over 1f out: r.o to take 2nd last 75yds: nvr quite rchd wnr* **33/1**

0-33 **3** ¾ **Barachiel**[31] 508 5-9-2 **60** ... RichardHughes 8 64
(Luke Dace) *chsd ldng trio: drvn over 2f out: responded to chal 1f out: kpt on same pce* **11/2**[2]

3-45 **4** shd **Having A Ball**[9] 789 9-9-2 **60** ... JoeFanning 12 64+
(Geoffrey Deacon) *stdd s: hld up in last pair: prog jst over 1f out: r.o wl fnl f: nrst fin* **16/1**

1534 **5** ½ **Spirit Of Gondree (IRE)**[14] 722 5-9-3 **61** ... (b) RichardKingscote 4 64
(Milton Bradley) *stdd s: hld up in last pair: prog over 1f out: r.o ins fnl f: nt pce to chal* **7/1**[3]

-101 **6** 1 ¾ **Flag Of Glory**[25] 587 6-9-4 **62** ... WilliamCarson 13 62
(Peter Hiatt) *wl away fr wd draw to trck ldr: drvn to ld 2f out: hdd jst ins fnl f: wknd* **14/1**

545- **7** 1 ½ **Rockweiller**[198] 5405 6-9-2 **60** ... (v) GrahamLee 1 57
(Steve Gollings) *wl in tch in midfield: rdn to chse ldrs over 1f out: no imp: wknd ins fnl f* **11/2**[2]

000- **8** 1 **Saint Irene**[75] 8199 4-8-7 **58** ... HarryBurns(7) 2 53
(Michael Blanshard) *hld up in last quartet: tried to make prog on inner fr 2f out but nowhere to go: no ch* **50/1**

6052 **9** shd **Penbryn (USA)**[21] 626 6-9-0 **58** ... JimCrowley 3 53
(Nick Littmoden) *trckd ldng pair: drvn to chal on inner over 1f out: wknd qckly fnl f* **10/1**

60/0 **10** 1 ½ **Matraash (USA)**[25] 593 7-9-7 **65** ... LukeMorris 10 57
(Daniel Mark Loughnane) *wl away fr wd draw to ld: hdd 2f out: lost 2nd over 1f out and wknd qckly* **16/1**

1203 **11** ¾ **Jumbo Prado (USA)**[12] 758 4-9-0 **65** ... PhilipPrince(7) 7 55
(John Stimpson) *hld up towards rr: rdn over 2f out: no imp on ldrs over 1f out: wknd fnl f* **10/1**

500- **12** 3 **Lisahane Bog**[188] 4586 6-9-4 **62** ... (p) JohnFahy 6 47
(Peter Hedger) *settled in midfield: drvn and no prog 3f out: wknd over 1f out* **20/1**

05-3 **13** 1 ¾ **Elsie Bay**[12] 753 4-8-8 **57** ... RachealKneller(5) 9 38
(Mark Usher) *racd wd: prom: drvn and cl up 2f out: sn wknd qckly* **9/1**

-203 **14** 10 **Dolly Colman (IRE)**[14] 722 5-8-7 **51** oh5 ... ChrisCatlin 14 13
(Zoe Davison) *racd wd: chsd ldrs 6f: sn lost pl: t.o* **50/1**

2m 6.45s (-1.55) **Going Correction** 0.0s/f (Stan) **14** Ran SP% **119.7**
Speed ratings (Par 101): **106,105,104,104,104 102,101,100,100,99 99,96,95,87**
Tote Swingers: 1&2 £39.60, 1&3 £5.20, 2&3 £50.30 CSF £166.60 CT £840.49 TOTE £4.20: £2.30, £18.30, £2.20; EX 263.60 Trifecta £1392.10 Part won. Pool: £1,856.13 - 0.79 winning units..

Owner D J Dolan **Bred** Mrs T Brudenell **Trained** Rathmullan, Co Donegal

FOCUS
A moderate handicap and the result never looked in any doubt down the straight. The winner looks back to his best, and has more to offer.

897 BETDAQ GAMES £50 CASH BONUS H'CAP 1m 2f (P)
7:00 (7:02) (Class 2) (0-100,95) 4-Y-0+
£11,827 (£3,541; £1,770; £885; £442; £222) **Stalls** Low

Form RPR

4-31 **1** **Robin Hoods Bay**[39] 401 5-9-7 **95** ... LukeMorris 6 101+
(Ed Vaughan) *t.k.h: hld up in 4th: coped wl whn pce lifted over 2f out: clsd on ldrs over 1f out: led jst ins fnl f: drvn out last 100yds* **5/2**[1]

63-1 **2** nk **Spifer (IRE)**[46] 273 5-8-13 **87** ... (p) AndreaAtzeni 2 93+
(Marco Botti) *hld up: dropped to 5th 3f out: pce lifted sn after: prog wl over 1f out: chsd wnr ins fnl f: r.o but jst hld* **5/2**[1]

103- **3** 1 ¾ **Shamir**[86] 8056 6-8-13 **87** ... FergusSweeney 1 89
(Jo Crowley) *trckd ldng pair: rdn whn pce lifted 2f out: styd on same pce fr over 1f out* **9/1**

4-65 **4** shd **Tinshu (IRE)**[11] 777 7-9-5 **93** ... (p) WilliamCarson 5 95
(Derek Haydn Jones) *trckd ldr: rdn to chal jst over 2f out: upsides over 1f out: nt qckn and lost pl after* **8/1**[3]

5-42 **5** ¾ **George Guru**[18] 690 6-9-4 **95** ... MarkCoumbe(3) 7 96
(Michael Attwater) *t.k.h: hld up in last in slowly run event: no ch once pce lifted jst over 2f out: styd on fnl f* **6/1**[2]

01-6 **6** nse **Kaafel (IRE)**[53] 189 4-8-12 **86** ... (p) JohnFahy 4 86
(Peter Hedger) *led at stdy pce: upped the tempo over 2f out: hdd and fdd jst ins fnl f* **12/1**

212- **7** 3 ¼ **Super Say (IRE)**[74] 8228 7-9-3 **91** ... (t) GrahamLee 8 85
(Mark Rimell) *hld up in last pair: prog on outer to press ldng pair 3f out: lost pl 2f out: wknd* **8/1**[3]

2m 8.13s (0.13) **Going Correction** 0.0s/f (Stan) **7** Ran SP% **111.3**
Speed ratings (Par 109): **99,98,97,97,96 96,94**
Tote Swingers: 1&2 £1.90, 1&3 £5.60, 2&3 £4.90 CSF £7.92 CT £43.55 TOTE £2.30: £1.10, £2.30; EX 8.10 Trifecta £62.90 Pool: £1,489.72 - 17.74 winning units..

Owner A M Pickering **Bred** Palm Tree Thoroughbreds **Trained** Newmarket, Suffolk

FOCUS
They fairly dawdled through the early stages of this decent handicap, and it became a dash in the straight. The compressed finish governs the merit of the form.

898 COME DINE IN THE PANORAMIC RESTAURANT H'CAP 6f (P)
7:30 (7:30) (Class 6) (0-65,65) 4-Y-0+ **£1,940** (£577; £288; £144) **Stalls** Low

Form RPR

-115 **1** **Valdaw**[14] 728 5-9-6 **64** ... EddieAhern 8 76
(Mike Murphy) *hld up bhd ldng pair: clsd smoothly to ld over 1f out: drvn fnl f: jst hld on* **13/2**

5020 **2** shd **Haadeeth**[18] 688 6-9-4 **62** ... RichardHughes 5 74
(David Evans) *hld up in 6th: prog on wd outside 2f out: hrd rdn to chse wnr fnl f: styd on: jst failed* **7/2**[1]

5-11 **3** 3 **Homeboy (IRE)**[41] 355 5-9-7 **65** ... HayleyTurner 4 68
(Marcus Tregoning) *blasted off in front but pressed: hdd over 1f out: hung lft after but hld on for 3rd* **8/1**

1062 **4** 1 ¼ **Colourbearer (IRE)**[6] 831 6-9-6 **64** ... (t) RichardKingscote 12 63
(Milton Bradley) *rrd s: dropped in fr wdst draw and hld up in last pair: prog on inner fr 2f out: styd on to take 4th last strides: n.d* **8/1**

-056 **5** hd **Rambo Will**[14] 719 5-9-4 **62** ... FrederikTylicki 9 61
(J R Jenkins) *pressed ldr at str pce and clr of rest: lost 2nd over 1f out: carreid lft and no ex* **5/1**[3]

-002 **6** hd **Diamond Vine (IRE)**[12] 750 5-9-2 **60** ... (p) LukeMorris 1 58
(Ronald Harris) *chsd clr ldng pair to over 2f out: no imp over 1f out: fdd* **10/1**

3140 **7** shd **Whipphound**[12] 760 5-8-12 **56** ... (p) RobbieFitzpatrick 7 54
(Mark Brisbourne) *hld up in last pair and wl off the pce: carried hd high whn asked for effrt 2f out: sme prog over 1f out: n.d* **16/1**

-511 **8** ½ **Mr Optimistic**[13] 736 5-9-0 **58** ... KieranO'Neill 3 54
(Paul Howling) *chsd ldrs in 5th: rdn wl over 2f out and struggling: tried to rally over 1f out: wknd fnl f* **4/1**[2]

153- **9** 1 ¼ **Bull Bay**[65] 8304 4-8-12 **63** ... IanBurns(7) 6 56
(Jane Chapple-Hyam) *settled in 7th: rdn and no prog over 2f out: no impover 1f out: wknd* **8/1**

30-0 **10** 4 ½ **Duke Of Aricabeau (IRE)**[18] 687 4-9-2 **63** ... SimonPearce(3) 10 42
(Lydia Pearce) *hld up in last trio: struggling to go the pce fr 1/2-way: wl btn fnl 2f* **33/1**

1m 12.08s (-1.02) **Going Correction** 0.0s/f (Stan) **10** Ran SP% **123.5**
Speed ratings (Par 101): **106,105,101,100,99 99,99,98,97,91**
Tote Swingers: 1&2 £8.30, 1&3 £11.20, 2&3 £6.90 CSF £31.40 CT £192.78 TOTE £7.10: £3.00, £1.10, £2.90; EX 37.90 Trifecta £341.00 Pool: £1,095.53 - 2.40 winning units..

Owner D Spratt **Bred** Mayden Stud, J A And D S Dewhurst **Trained** Westoning, Beds

FOCUS
They appeared to go quick enough up front early. The form looks sound, with the first two capable of better in the short term.

899 GOFFS READY-TO-RUN SALE MARCH 27TH H'CAP (LONDON MILE QUALIFIER) 1m (P)
8:00 (8:00) (Class 5) (0-70,69) 4-Y-0+ **£2,587** (£770; £384; £192) **Stalls** Low

Form RPR

21 **1** **Lily Edge**[20] 651 4-9-7 **69** ... KieranO'Neill 1 76
(John Bridger) *dwlt: t.k.h: hld up in last in slowly run r: rdn whn pce lifted over 2f out: prog on outer over 1f out: drvn ahd last 100yds: edgd rt but styd on wl* **6/4**[1]

0210 **2** ½ **Diplomatic (IRE)**[20] 650 8-9-0 **69** ... (p) RobertTart(7) 3 75
(Michael Squance) *settled in 4th: rdn whn pce lifted over 2f out: clsd w others fnl f: jst outpcd last 100yds* **13/8**[2]

150- **3** hd **Lutine Charlie (IRE)**[142] 7115 6-9-2 **64** ... [1] JoeFanning 2 70
(Pat Eddery) *reluctant ldr 1f: t.k.h and restrained into 3rd: shkn up whn pce lifted over 2f out: chse ldr over 1f out and clsd: upsides 100yds out: jst outpcd* **6/1**

3130 **4** 1 ¼ **The Mongoose**[20] 652 5-9-2 **64** ... (bt) RichardHughes 5 67
(David Evans) *led after 1f and maintained slow pce: drvn 2 l clr over 2f out: hdd & wknd last 100yds* **9/2**[3]

-620 **5** 2 **Katmai River (IRE)**[23] 616 6-8-3 **56** ... (v) RachealKneller(5) 4 54
(Mark Usher) *t.k.h: trckd ldr after 2f: nudged along 2f out: lost 2nd and fdd over 1f out* **10/1**

1m 42.36s (2.56) **Going Correction** 0.0s/f (Stan) **5** Ran SP% **119.7**
Speed ratings (Par 103): **87,86,86,85,83**
Tote Swingers: 1&2 £4.81 CSF £4.81 TOTE £1.90: £1.20, £1.70; EX 5.50 Trifecta £15.50 Pool: £950.46 - 45.83 winning units..

Owner Allsorts **Bred** W J Wyatt **Trained** Liphook, Hants

■ Stewards' Enquiry : Richard Hughes two-day ban: careless riding (Mar 20-21)

FOCUS
A steadily run race. The winner improved but this is ordinary form.

900 EASTER FAMILY FUN WITH PEPPA PIG H'CAP 1m (P)
8:30 (8:31) (Class 7) (0-50,50) 4-Y-0+ **£1,533** (£452; £226) **Stalls** Low

Form RPR

0060 **1** **Rigid**[14] 725 6-9-2 **45** ... RichardHughes 6 51
(Tony Carroll) *hld up in 8th gng wl: weaved through fr 2f out: chsd ldr ins fnl f: drvn and r.o to ld post* **7/1**[3]

-640 **2** nse **Crucis Abbey (IRE)**[35] 441 5-9-2 **45** ... (p) EddieAhern 3 51
(Mark Brisbourne) *trckd ldng trio: waiting in bhd 2f out: produced to ld jst over 1f out gng strly: drvn last 100yds: hdd post* **8/1**

-036 **3** ½ **Supa Seeker (USA)**[16] 703 7-8-9 **45** ... (v[1]) RyanTate(7) 12 50
(Tony Carroll) *s.v.s: detached in last early: stl last and shkn up 2f out: gd prog over 1f out: r.o to take 3rd nr fin and cl on ldng pair* **10/1**

0556 **4** 1 ¼ **Gallantry**[13] 737 11-9-7 **50** ... JimmyQuinn 1 52
(Paul Howling) *trckd ldrs in 5th: pushed along over 2f out: effrt on inner and cl up over 1f out: kpt on same pce* **8/1**

0/66 **5** nk **Atacama Sunrise**[5] 852 7-9-6 **49** ... (p) MickyFenton 8 50
(John Butler) *led: drvn and hdd jst over 1f out: grad fdd* **16/1**

0-30 **6** 1 ½ **Hawaiian Freeze**[6] 825 4-9-2 **45** ... AndreaAtzeni 11 43
(John Stimpson) *hld up in last trio: shkn up over 2f out: kpt on fr over 1f out: n.d* **50/1**

6005 **7** nk **Olynard (IRE)**[6] 825 7-8-9 **45** ... (p) RobertTart(7) 10 42
(Michael Mullineaux) *s.s: hld up in last pair: rdn on wd outside 2f out: kpt on same pce: n.d* **12/1**

5400 **8** nk **Dvinsky (USA)**[20] 655 12-9-7 **50** ... (b) TomMcLaughlin 13 47
(Paul Howling) *trckd ldr: rdn to chal and upsides over 2f out: lost pl wl over 1f out and fdd* **25/1**

0- **9** ½ **Zaroud (IRE)**[390] 505 4-9-2 **45** ... (t) JohnFahy 7 40
(Thomas McLaughlin, Ire) *reluctant to enter stalls: chsd ldrs in 6th: rdn and effrt over 2f out: nt qckn over 1f out: wl hld after* **6/4**[1]

633- **10** ½ **Chez Vrony**[120] 7605 7-9-3 **46** .... WilliamCarson 2 40
(Dave Morris) *trckd ldng pair: rdn to chal and upsides over 1f out: wknd qckly fnl f* **6/1**[2]

00-0 **11** 1¼ **La Giaconda**[15] 714 4-9-4 **47** .... (b[1]) KirstyMilczarek 4 38
(Olivia Maylam) *hld up in 7th: shkn up wl over 2f out: no prog and btn over 1f out: wknd* **25/1**

1m 40.41s (0.61) **Going Correction** 0.0s/f (Stan) **11** Ran SP% **121.3**
Speed ratings (Par 97): **96,95,95,94,93 92,92,91,91,90 89**
Tote Swingers: 1&2 £16.20, 1&3 £3.10, 2&3 £14.60 CSF £62.83 CT £583.55 TOTE £7.90: £2.40, £2.70, £3.10; EX 55.90 Trifecta £757.60 Part won. Pool: £1,010.13 - 0.91 winning units..
Owner Mr & Mrs J B Bacciochi **Bred** Limestone And Tara Studs **Trained** Cropthorne, Worcs
■ Stewards' Enquiry : Richard Hughes two-day ban: careless riding (March 20-21)

FOCUS
Weak handicap form.
T/Plt: £18.60 to a £1 stake. Pool: £65,725.00 - 2,573.44 winning tickets, T/Qpdt: £8.90 to a £1 stake. Pool: £8,580.00 - 708.68 winning tickets, JN

861 LINGFIELD (L-H)
Wednesday, March 6

OFFICIAL GOING: Standard
Wind: virtually nil Weather: dry, bright spells

901 EXPERT GUIDE TO LINGFIELD AT LINGFIELDRACECOURSETIPS.CO.UK CLAIMING STKS 1m 4f (P)
2:00 (2:00) (Class 6) 4-Y-O+ **£2,045** (£603; £302) **Stalls** Low

Form RPR

1112 **1** **Stand Guard**[15] 713 9-9-9 87 .... LiamKeniry 4 80+
(John Butler) *hld up in tch in rr: hdwy to trck ldr 2f out: pushed into ld ent fnl f: sn clr: eased wl ins fnl f* **4/5**[1]

02-1 **2** 5 **Right Stuff (FR)**[9] 227 10-9-3 87 .... (p) GeorgeBaker 1 64+
(Gary Moore) *chsd ldrs: wnt 2nd 4f out tl led wl over 2f out: drvn over 1f out: hdd ent fnl f: sn btn* **Evs**[2]

0-53 **3** 5 **Bashama**[16] 707 5-8-0 49 .... (vt) DanielMuscutt(7) 2 44
(Nikki Evans) *chsd ldr tl 4f out: rdn and struggling 2f out: sn btn: wnt modest 3rd 1f out* **50/1**[3]

5530 **4** 1¾ **Gower Rules (IRE)**[6] 820 5-9-3 47 .... (v) KieranO'Neill 3 51
(John Bridger) *sn led: drvn and hdd wl over 2f out: wknd wl over 1f out* **50/1**[3]

2m 30.89s (-2.11) **Going Correction** +0.05s/f (Slow) **4** Ran SP% **109.5**
Speed ratings (Par 101): **109,105,102,101**
CSF £1.90 TOTE £1.70; EX 1.90 Trifecta £4.70 Pool: £1,620.46 - 255.44 winning units..
Owner J Butler **Bred** Juddmonte Farms Ltd **Trained** Newmarket, Suffolk

FOCUS
A small field, but an interesting clash between two geldings officially rated 87 and with a combined age of 19. The pace wasn't bad, with the free-running Gower Rules giving a lead to the big two until starting the home bend. The other two govern the merit of the form.

902 LINGFIELD PARK OWNERS GROUP H'CAP 5f (P)
2:30 (2:30) (Class 6) (0-65,65) 4-Y-O+ **£2,045** (£603; £302) **Stalls** High

Form RPR

-122 **1** **Dorothy's Dancing (IRE)**[14] 728 5-9-7 **65** .... (p) GeorgeBaker 6 72
(Gary Moore) *mde all: rdn and qcknd over 1f out: r.o u.p and a holding rivals fnl f* **5/2**[2]

555 **2** ¾ **Quality Art (USA)**[9] 795 5-9-7 **65** .... [1] RobbieFitzpatrick 2 69
(Richard Guest) *v.s.a: sn rcvrd and in tch in last pair: swtchd lft and effrt over 1f out: hdwy and drvn 1f out: chse wnr wl ins fnl f: no imp* **7/2**[3]

3503 **3** ½ **Pharoh Jake**[12] 750 5-8-13 **57** .... WilliamCarson 1 60
(John Bridger) *bustled along leaving stalls: nt clr run and hmpd bnd 4f out: in tch in last pair after: effrt on inner over 1f out: drvn and chsd wnr 1f out: no imp and lost 2nd wl ins fnl f* **10/1**

1-42 **4** nk **Amethyst Dawn (IRE)**[9] 790 7-9-5 **63** .... (t) EddieAhern 4 64
(J R Jenkins) *chsd ldr: rdn and unable qck over 1f out: styd on same pce ins fnl f* **6/1**

2231 **5** hd **Johnny Splash (IRE)**[12] 750 4-9-2 **60** .... (b) JimCrowley 5 61
(Roger Teal) *chsd ldrs: rdn and unable qck over 1f out: styd on same pce ins fnl f* **7/4**[1]

59.18s (0.38) **Going Correction** +0.05s/f (Slow) **5** Ran SP% **110.5**
Speed ratings (Par 101): **98,96,96,95,95**
CSF £11.49 TOTE £2.20: £1.10, £2.90; EX 10.40 Trifecta £55.40 Pool: £1,803.47 - 24.39 winning units..
Owner Tom Glynn **Bred** Patrick Carroll **Trained** Lower Beeding, W Sussex

FOCUS
A moderate sprint handicap in which the pace wasn't that strong. Straightforward form.

903 SPA BREAKS AT LINGFIELD PARK RESORT H'CAP 7f (P)
3:00 (3:00) (Class 6) (0-60,60) 4-Y-O+ **£2,045** (£603; £302) **Stalls** Low

Form RPR

0-05 **1** **Chevise (IRE)**[11] 778 5-9-6 **59** .... (p) MatthewDavies 13 66
(Steve Woodman) *chsd ldrs: rdn to ld ent fnl 2f: kpt on wl u.p fnl f: jst hld on: all out* **20/1**

-652 **2** hd **Sannibel**[19] 665 5-8-13 **59** .... RobertTart(7) 10 67
(Graeme McPherson) *taken down early: stdd s and carried lft sn after: hld up in rr: hdwy 1f out: running on whn nt clr run and swtchd rt ins fnl f: str run to press wnr cl home: jst hld* **7/1**[3]

4 03 **3** 1 **Renoir's Lady**[20] 655 5-9-1 **54** .... (b[1]) JimCrowley 7 58
(Simon Dow) *chsd ldrs: rdn and effrt on inner to chal over 1f out: drvn ins fnl f: no ex fnl 75yds* **3/1**[1]

0660 **4** hd **Outlaw Torn (IRE)**[16] 705 4-9-7 **60** .... (e) RobbieFitzpatrick 3 63
(Richard Guest) *taken down early: t.k.h: led: hdd 2f out: rdn wl over 1f out: styd on same pce u.p ins fnl f* **14/1**

1320 **5** nk **Teen Ager (FR)**[21] 631 9-8-12 **51** .... (p) JimmyQuinn 11 57
(Paul Burgoyne) *stdd and swtchd lft after s: hld up in tch in rr: hdwy on inner over 1f out: chsng ldrs but nt clr run ins fnl f: swtchd rt and styd on towards fin: unable to chal* **14/1**

2140 **6** ½ **Spinning Ridge (IRE)**[9] 801 8-9-7 **60** .... (b) LukeMorris 2 61
(Ronald Harris) *t.k.h: hld up in midfield: switching out rt and looking for run 2f out: drvn and hdwy jst over 1f out: one pce ins fnl f* **7/1**[3]

4-30 **7** hd **Miakora**[35] 440 5-8-8 **47** .... (v) AndreaAtzeni 9 48
(Mick Quinn) *chsd ldrs: rdn and unable qck over 1f out: one pce ins fnl f* **25/1**

60-3 **8** nse **Custom House (IRE)**[9] 794 5-8-12 **51** .... KirstyMilczarek 12 52
(John E Long) *in tch in midfield on outer: rdn and no imp over 1f out: kpt on fnl 100yds: nvr quite gng pce to chal* **14/1**

-040 **9** ½ **Prophet In A Dream**[37] 423 5-8-0 **46** oh1 .... (p) JoeyHaynes(7) 8 45
(Paddy Butler) *wl in tch in midfield: rdn and unable qck over 1f out: styd on same pce ins fnl f* **66/1**

5414 **10** 1¾ **Chambles**[11] 778 4-9-6 **59** .... EddieAhern 5 54
(J R Jenkins) *restless in stalls: short of room leaving stalls: in tch towards rr on outer: wdst of field bnd 2f out: rdn 1f out: kpt on but no threat to ldrs* **9/2**[2]

2230 **11** hd **Cuthbert (IRE)**[14] 725 6-8-8 **47** .... (b) RobertHavlin 4 41
(Michael Attwater) *t.k.h: hld up in midfield: effrt and nt clr run ent fnl f: no imp fnl f* **8/1**

653- **12** 7 **Trust Me Boy**[148] 6951 5-8-9 **48** .... FrankieMcDonald 1 24
(John E Long) *midfield whn hmpd and dropped to rr after 1f: sn pushed along and nvr gng wl after: rdn and lost tch 2f out* **20/1**

400- **13** 4½ **Compton Bird**[84] 8074 4-9-4 **57** .... (t) J-PGuillambert 6 21
(Hans Adielsson) *a towards rr: rdn over 3f out: lost tch 2f out* **8/1**

1m 25.04s (0.24) **Going Correction** +0.05s/f (Slow) **13** Ran SP% **125.3**
Speed ratings (Par 101): **100,99,98,98,98 97,97,97,96,94 94,86,81**
Tote Swingers: 1&2 £32.40, 1&3 £16.90, 2&3 £5.30 CSF £155.87 CT £574.44 TOTE £26.90: £7.30, £2.80, £1.60; EX 108.80 Trifecta £884.90 Pool: £2,266.25 - 1.92 winning units..
Owner The Chevise Partnership **Bred** Paul And Mrs Jenny Green **Trained** East Lavant, W Sussex
■ Stewards' Enquiry : Jimmy Quinn two-day ban: careless riding (Mar 20-21)

FOCUS
A modest handicap and typically tight Lingfield finish. The winner has plummeted in the weights and the second was unlucky not to win.

904 PLAY GOLF AT LINGFIELD PARK RESORT MAIDEN STKS 7f (P)
3:30 (3:31) (Class 5) 3-Y-O **£2,726** (£805; £402) **Stalls** Low

Form RPR

452- **1** **Red Refraction (IRE)**[191] 5661 3-9-5 75 .... RichardHughes 1 76
(Richard Hannon) *broke wl sn restrained and hdd after 1f: chsd ldr after: wnt 2nd 2f out: drvn to chal ins fnl f: led wl ins fnl f: pushed out and gng away towards fin* **4/5**[1]

023- **2** ¾ **Fraserburgh (IRE)**[146] 7007 3-9-5 75 .... JoeFanning 6 74
(Mark Johnston) *chsd ldr after 1f tl led 3f out: rdn and drew clr w wnr over 1f out: edgd rt ins fnl f: hdd and no ex wl ins fnl f: eased cl home* **5/4**[2]

53 **3** 5 **Hawaiian Dream (IRE)**[20] 651 3-9-0 0 .... JimCrowley 3 55
(Roger Teal) *chsd ldrs: 3rd and outpcd u.p over 1f out: wl hld fnl f* **14/1**[3]

0-5 **4** 5 **Douglas Pasha (IRE)**[21] 636 3-9-5 0 .... SteveDrowne 4 50
(Richard Hannon) *hld up in tch last pair: effrt to go modest 4th and hung bdly lft over 1f out: stl hanging and wknd 1f out* **25/1**

46- **5** 1 **Barbsiz (IRE)**[75] 8207 3-8-11 0 .... SimonPearce(3) 2 39
(Mark H Tompkins) *s.i.s: a bhd: outpcd wl over 1f out: no ch after* **50/1**

5-05 **6** 11 **Arabougg**[33] 479 3-9-5 44 .... FrankieMcDonald 5 15
(Nikki Evans) *chsd ldrs tl led after 1f: hdd and hanging rt fr 3f out: wknd wl over 1f out: wl bhd fnl f* **100/1**

1m 25.39s (0.59) **Going Correction** +0.05s/f (Slow) **6** Ran SP% **113.5**
Speed ratings (Par 98): **98,97,91,85,84 72**
Tote Swingers: 1&2 £1.10, 1&3 £1.80, 2&3 £1.70 CSF £2.07 TOTE £1.90: £1.10, £1.30; EX 2.60 Trifecta £5.80 Pool: £3,520.20 - 454.39 winning units..
Owner Middleham Park Racing IV & James Pak **Bred** Tally-Ho Stud **Trained** East Everleigh, Wilts

FOCUS
Only two mattered in this modest maiden and they fought out the finish. Straightforward form.

905 BREATHE SPA AT LINGFIELD MARRIOTT H'CAP 1m 5f (P)
4:00 (4:00) (Class 5) (0-70,68) 4-Y-O+ **£2,726** (£805; £402) **Stalls** Low

Form RPR

2351 **1** **Linkable**[19] 668 4-9-2 **66** .... (t) RichardHughes 1 72
(Brendan Powell) *mde all: dictated stdy gallop tl rdn and qcknd clr w rival over 2f out: sustained duel w runner-up after: forged ahd fnl 75yds* **4/1**[3]

3234 **2** ½ **El Libertador (USA)**[4] 866 7-8-3 **57** .... (b) JoeyHaynes(7) 2 62
(Eric Wheeler) *upsides wnr thrght: rdn and qcknd clr w wnr over 2f out: sustained duel and ev ch after: no ex and btn fnl 75yds* **10/1**

0-44 **3** 2¾ **Admirable Duque (IRE)**[21] 642 7-9-6 **67** .... (be) MartinLane 8 68+
(Dominic Ffrench Davis) *stdd and dropped in bhd after s: hld up in rr: lost tch w ldrs whn gallop qcknd over 2f out: hdwy 1f out: styd on wl to go 3rd ins fnl f: no threat to ldng pair* **12/1**

1-31 **4** ½ **Llamadas**[41] 351 11-9-0 **61** .... KirstyMilczarek 6 61
(Olivia Maylam) *stdd s: hld up in last pair: outpcd and lost tch w ldrs whn gallop qcknd over 2f out: hdwy 1f out: styd on wl: no threat to ldng pair* **8/1**

/00- **5** 1 **Winning Spark (USA)**[84] 8082 6-9-7 **68** .... GeorgeBaker 5 67
(Gary Moore) *hld up in midfield: outpcd whn gallop qcknd over 2f out: plenty to over 1f out: hdwy 1f out and pressing for placings ins fnl f: one pce fnl 100yds* **9/4**[1]

0422 **6** ½ **Red Mystique (IRE)**[16] 703 4-8-5 **55** .... (b) JimmyQuinn 4 53
(Philip Hide) *chsd ldng trio: rdn and outpcd whn gallop qcknd over 2f out: plugged on but no threat to ldrs fnl f* **7/2**[2]

324 **7** hd **Pullmen**[12] 752 5-8-12 **59** .... EddieAhern 3 57
(J R Jenkins) *t.k.h: chsd ldng pair: outpcd and rdn whn gallop qcknd over 2f out: kpt on but no threat to ldrs fnl f* **16/1**

0-45 **8** 1½ **Simayill**[19] 675 5-9-2 **63** .... TomMcLaughlin 7 59
(John Berry) *hld up in midfield: outpcd whn gallop qcknd over 2f out: keeping on but no threat to ldrs whn nt clr run 1f out: one pce after* **14/1**

2m 54.07s (8.07) **Going Correction** +0.05s/f (Slow)
WFA 4 from 5yo+ 3lb **8** Ran SP% **113.4**
Speed ratings (Par 103): **77,76,75,74,74 73,73,72**
Tote Swingers: 1&2 £5.20, 1&3 £9.50, 2&3 £14.60 CSF £42.14 CT £437.17 TOTE £5.20: £1.60, £2.60, £4.60; EX 29.60 Trifecta £234.90 Pool: £2,852.24 - 9.10 winning units..
Owner Jonathan H Ross **Bred** Juddmonte Farms Ltd **Trained** Upper Lambourn, Berks

FOCUS
An unsatisfactory affair, as they went no pace and that played into the hands of the front pair. Dubious form, but it does make sense.

906 FOLLOW US ON TWITTER @LINGFIELDPARK H'CAP 1m 2f (P)
4:30 (4:30) (Class 5) (0-75,73) 4-Y-O+ **£3,234** (£962; £481; £240) **Stalls** Low

Form RPR

50/ **1** **Carazam (IRE)**[357] 6-8-9 **68** .... RobertTart(7) 4 76
(William Jarvis) *t.k.h: hld up in tch: gd hdwy on inner over 1f out: swtchd rt 1f out: hung rt u.p but styd on wl to ld wl ins fnl f: hld on towards fin* **8/1**

55-3 **2** nk **Jewelled**[7] 810 7-9-6 **72** .... MartinLane 6 79
(Lady Herries) *stdd and dropped in bhd after s: hld up in rr: rdn and effrt on outer ent fnl f: str run to press wnr wl ins fnl f: hld towards fin* **5/1**[3]

6331 **3** 1 **Honey Of A Kitten (USA)**[12] 747 5-8-7 **66** .... (v) EoinWalsh(7) 3 71
(David Evans) *hld up in tch in midfield: rdn and effrt over 1f out: kpt on u.p ins fnl f* **9/2**[2]

The Form Book Flat, Raceform Ltd, Compton, RG20 6NL.

/602 **4** ½ **Gaelic Silver (FR)**[21] 639 7-9-5 **71** .... GeorgeBaker 5 76
(Gary Moore) *stdd s: t.k.h: hld up in midfield: effrt and nt clr run whn hmpd wl over 1f out: swtchd rt and hdwy jst over 1f out: styng on whn jostled ins fnl f: kpt on towards fin* **9/2**[2]

2551 **5** *hd* **Understory (USA)**[21] 639 6-9-4 **70** .... LukeMorris 7 74
(Tim McCarthy) *w ldr: rdn and ev ch 2f out: drvn to ld 1f out: hdd wl ins fnl f: no ex* **16/1**

6-46 **6** ½ **Tornado Force (IRE)**[18] 689 5-9-7 **73** .... LiamKeniry 1 76
(Chris Dwyer) *t.k.h: chsd ldrs: nt clr run over 2f out: swtchd rt and rdn wl over 1f out: styd on same pce ins fnl f* **20/1**

406- **7** 1½ **If I Were A Boy (IRE)**[145] 7027 6-9-0 **66** .... (p) JimmyQuinn 2 66
(Dominic Ffrench Davis) *led: drvn wl over 1f out: hdd 1f out: wknd ins fnl f* **20/1**

4-22 **8** 4½ **Pategonia**[36] 434 4-9-4 **70** .... WilliamBuick 9 61
(John Gosden) *t.k.h: hld up wl in tch in midfield on outer: rdn and unable qck over 2f out: wknd over 1f out* **6/4**[1]

00-0 **9** 4½ **Smokey Oakey (IRE)**[21] 639 9-8-11 **66** .... SimonPearce(3) 8 49
(Mark H Tompkins) *stdd s: hld up in last pair: swtchd to outer and effrt over 2f out: no prog: wknd over 1f out* **33/1**

2m 5.29s (-1.31) **Going Correction** +0.05s/f (Slow) **9** Ran SP% **122.5**
Speed ratings (Par 103): **107,106,105,105,105 105,103,100,96**
Tote Swingers: 1&2 £8.00, 1&3 £6.40, 2&3 £3.30 CSF £49.33 CT £208.65 TOTE £11.20: £2.70, £1.20, £1.40; EX 52.60 Trifecta £230.90 Pool: £2,400.51 - 7.79 winning units..
Owner Dr J Walker **Bred** Yeomanstown Stud **Trained** Newmarket, Suffolk

FOCUS
An ordinary handicap and a race of changing fortunes, with those held up favoured. Another compressed finish, with the second and thirds the best guides.

907 ALL WEATHER "HANDS AND HEELS" APPRENTICE SERIES H'CAP (PART OF THE RACING EXCELLENCE INITIATIVE) 1m (P)
5:00 (5:00) (Class 6) (0-55,56) 4-Y-0+ **£2,045** (£603; £302) **Stalls** High

Form RPR
-000 **1** **Total Obsession**[8] 805 6-8-9 **46** oh1 .... (v) JoeyHaynes(3) 8 54
(Mark Hoad) *hld up in last pair: rdn and effrt wl over 1f out: styd on wl to ld fnl 50yds* **50/1**

166 **2** ¾ **Sinchiroka (FR)**[43] 330 7-9-7 **55** .... RyanTate 2 61
(Ralph Smith) *in tch in midfield: hdwy to chse ldrs over 2f out: rdn and outpcd 2f out: rallied to chse wnr 1f out: ev ch last 100yds: kpt on* **9/2**[2]

0-20 **3** ¾ **Exopuntia**[21] 631 7-9-0 **51** .... (b[1]) ShelleyBirkett(3) 4 55
(Julia Feilden) *stdd s: hld up in last pair: rdn and effrt wl over 1f out: styd on wl ins fnl f: nt rch ldrs* **5/1**[3]

3113 **4** *nse* **Young Jackie**[25] 579 5-9-2 **53** .... (b) JordanVaughan(3) 1 57
(George Margarson) *in tch in midfield: hdwy to ld 2f out: rdn over 1f out: hdd last 50yds: wknd towards fin* **5/4**[1]

0-01 **5** 1¾ **Indian Violet (IRE)**[8] 805 7-9-8 **56** 6ex .... (p) RyanWhile 3 57
(Zoe Davison) *chsd ldrs: nt clr run on inner and shuffled bk over 2f out: swtchd rt wl over 1f out: kpt on ins fnl f* **8/1**

-000 **6** *nk* **Salient**[21] 631 9-8-12 **46** oh1 .... (p) RobertTart 6 45
(Michael Attwater) *in tch towards rr: pushed along and hdwy on outer to chal over 2f out: drvn and no ex over 1f out: wknd fnl f* **5/1**[3]

6042 **7** 6 **Avon Supreme**[14] 725 5-8-8 **47** .... LaurenHunter(5) 7 33
(Gay Kelleway) *led tl 2f out: btn over 1f out: fdd ins fnl f* **10/1**

-000 **8** 10 **Confirmed**[14] 722 4-9-4 **55** .... (t) AaronJones(3) 5 18
(Alison Batchelor) *dwlt: sn rcvrd and chsd ldr over 6f out tl over 2f out: wkng whn hmpd bnd 2f out: fdd over 1f out* **20/1**

1m 38.28s (0.08) **Going Correction** +0.05s/f (Slow) **8** Ran SP% **122.9**
Speed ratings (Par 101): **101,100,99,99,97 97,91,81**
Tote Swingers: 1&2 £23.60, 1&3 £28.40, 2&3 £4.10 CSF £279.35 CT £1386.03 TOTE £65.90: £15.10, £1.20, £2.70; EX 468.50 Trifecta £884.60 Pool: £2,032.21 - 1.72 winning units..
Owner Miss H Matthews **Bred** Michael E Broughton **Trained** Lewes, E Sussex
■ Stewards' Enquiry : Lauren Hunter one-day ban: failed to ride to draw (Mar 20)
Joey Haynes trainer had no explanation for the apparent improvement in form

FOCUS
A messy contest and the leaders may have gone off too quick. Straightforward low-grade form.
T/Plt: £56.80 to a £1 stake. Pool: £52,040.84 - 668.00 winning tickets. T/Qpdt: £12.80 to a £1 stake. Pool: £4,434.17 - 254.77 winning tickets. SP

884 SOUTHWELL (L-H)
Thursday, March 7

OFFICIAL GOING: Standard
Wind: Light across Weather: Heavy cloud

908 32REDBINGO.COM (S) STKS 1m 4f (F)
2:20 (2:20) (Class 6) 4-Y-0+ **£2,045** (£603; £302) **Stalls** Low

Form RPR
0-31 **1** **Jack Dawkins (USA)**[2] 886 8-9-5 **59** .... AdrianNicholls 3 71
(David Nicholls) *led 1 1/2f: prom tl led again 4f out: rdn and jnd over 2f out: hdd over 1f out: cl up and drvn ins fnl f: rallied wl to ld last 75yds* **5/4**[1]

6212 **2** *hd* **Goldmadchen (GER)**[2] 886 5-8-9 **66** .... GarryWhillans(5) 4 66
(Keith Dalgleish) *trckd ldrs: hdwy to chse ldr 3f out: rdn over 2f out: styd on to take slt ld over 1f out: sn drvn: hdd and no ex last 75yds* **7/4**[2]

04-2 **3** 3 **Xpres Maite**[17] 707 10-8-10 **69** .... (b) MarkCoumbe(3) 6 60
(Roy Bowring) *dwlt: sn chsd along and hdwy to chse ldr after 1 1/2f: rdn along wl over 3f out: drvn 2f out and kpt on same pce* **5/1**[3]

063 **4** 8 **Houdini Bright (USA)**[2] 888 5-8-13 **43** .... (b) JamesSullivan 5 47
(James Given) *in tch: reminders after 3f: rdn along on outer 1/2-way: hdwy over 3f out: drvn over 2f out and sn no imp* **10/1**

-040 **5** 12 **General Tufto**[2] 886 8-8-13 **45** .... (b) RobbieFitzpatrick 2 28
(Charles Smith) *in rr: pushed along 5f out: rdn over 3f out: n.d* **50/1**

5-06 **6** 10 **There's No Rules**[6] 846 4-8-4 **44** .... (e) PhilipPrince(7) 7 12
(Richard Guest) *chsd ldr tl led after 1 1/2f: rdn along 5f out: hdd 4f out and sn wknd* **66/1**

0-30 **7** 8 **Isola Bella**[17] 704 4-8-6 **43** .... (p) WilliamCarson 1
(Jonathan Portman) *chsd ldrs: rdn along over 5f out: sn outpcd and bhd* **40/1**

2m 40.02s (-0.98) **Going Correction** -0.025s/f (Stan)
WFA 4 from 5yo+ 2lb **7** Ran SP% **112.5**
Speed ratings (Par 101): **102,101,99,94,86 79,74**
Tote Swingers 1&2 £1.10, 2&3 £1.70 CSF £3.51 TOTE £2.10: £1.10, £1.30; EX 4.80 Trifecta £9.00 Pool: £3,018.61 - 249.63 winning tickets..There was no bid for the winner. Goldmadchen was claimed by James Given for £5,500.
Owner The Three K's **Bred** Clovelly Farms **Trained** Sessay, N Yorks

FOCUS
Four of the seven runners in this moderate seller ran here two days earlier. The form is straightforward with the third and fourth the key.

909 32REDBET.COM H'CAP 6f (F)
2:50 (2:51) (Class 6) (0-52,52) 4-Y-0+ **£2,045** (£603; £302) **Stalls** Low

Form RPR
-005 **1** **Upper Lambourn (IRE)**[23] 618 5-9-7 **52** .... (t) JoeFanning 12 62
(Christopher Kellett) *trckd ldrs on outer: hdwy over 2f out: rdn to chal over 1f out: styd on wl to ld nr line* **5/1**[3]

20-4 **2** *nk* **Pull The Pin (IRE)**[7] 829 4-9-1 **49** .... NeilFarley(3) 9 58
(Declan Carroll) *t.k.h early: cl up: rdn to chal over 2f out: led jst over 1f out: drvn ins fnl f: hdd and no ex nr line* **3/1**[1]

4400 **3** 1¾ **Ryedale Dancer (IRE)**[14] 735 5-9-7 **52** .... (e[1]) RobbieFitzpatrick 4 56
(Richard Guest) *led: rdn 2f out: drvn and hdd jst over 1f out: kpt on same pce u.p ins fnl f* **20/1**

0021 **4** 1½ **Very First Blade**[13] 754 4-9-7 **52** .... (p) FrannyNorton 5 51
(Mark Brisbourne) *t.k.h early: trckd ldrs: effrt over 2f out and sn rdn: drvn whn n.m.r and swtchd rt ent fnl f: sn one pce* **7/2**[2]

450- **5** 2¼ **Sofias Number One (USA)**[274] 2821 5-9-1 **49** ....(b) MarkCoumbe(3) 14 42
(Roy Bowring) *in tch on outer: wd st: rdn along over 2f out: kpt on u.p appr fnl f: nt rch ldrs* **10/1**

0604 **6** ¾ **Onceaponatime (IRE)**[14] 735 8-9-1 **46** .... (p) LiamJones 7 36
(Michael Squance) *chsd ldrs: rdn along over 2f out: drvn and one pce fr over 1f out* **8/1**

0030 **7** 1 **Ishi**[21] 655 4-9-1 **46** oh1 .... (b) AndreaAtzeni 2 33+
(Rod Millman) *towards rr: hdwy 2f out: sn rdn and hung lft over 1f out: sn no imp* **10/1**

03-4 **8** 1½ **Captain Cavallo**[17] 707 6-9-1 **46** oh1 .... (bt[1]) LukeMorris 10 29
(Nicky Vaughan) *prom: chsd ldng pair 1/2-way: rdn along over 2f out: sn drvn and wknd wl over 1f out* **20/1**

0534 **9** 4 **Illustrious Lad (IRE)**[7] 819 4-9-1 **51** .... (bt) NathanAlison(5) 6 22
(Jim Boyle) *awkward s and towards rr: hdwy and wd st: rdn over 2f out and sn no hdwy* **6/1**

000/ **10** 6 **Ring Of Fire**[749] 575 6-9-1 **46** oh1 .... ChrisCatlin 3
(John Spearing) *s.i.s: a in rr* **66/1**

0300 **11** 2 **Bachelor Knight (IRE)**[13] 754 5-9-1 **46** oh1 .... MichaelO'Connell 1
(Suzzanne France) *chsd ldrs on inner: rdn along 1/2-way: sn wknd* **33/1**

1m 17.04s (0.54) **Going Correction** -0.025s/f (Stan) **11** Ran SP% **121.4**
Speed ratings (Par 101): **95,94,92,90,87 86,84,82,77,69 66**
Tote Swingers 1&2 £4.30, 2&3 £16.70, 1&3 £17.00 CSF £20.26 CT £291.01 TOTE £7.30: £2.30, £1.70, £6.50; EX 24.80 Trifecta £586.00 Pool: £2,451.06 - 3.13 winning tickets..
Owner The Edwardsons **Bred** Messrs Derek Gibbons & Peter Gibbons **Trained** Appleby Magna, Derbys

FOCUS
A moderate sprint handicap and the form is ordinary, although the runner-up is improving.

910 32REDPOKER.COM H'CAP 1m (F)
3:25 (3:25) (Class 6) (0-55,53) 3-Y-O **£2,045** (£603; £302) **Stalls** Low

Form RPR
40-6 **1** **Birdy Boy (USA)**[30] 527 3-8-13 **45** .... FrannyNorton 4 63+
(Mark Johnston) *cl up: led 3f out: rdn clr 2f out: kpt on* **6/1**

00-6 **2** 8 **Conversing (USA)**[13] 757 3-9-6 **52** .... JoeFanning 7 52
(Mark Johnston) *dwlt sltly: sn pushed along in rr: rdn along 4f out: hdwy wl over 2f out: chsd wnr fr wl over 1f out: no imp* **5/1**[3]

4-33 **3** 7 **Naughtybychoice**[16] 717 3-9-0 **53** .... (p) JacobButterfield(7) 6 37
(Ollie Pears) *trckd ldrs on outer: hdwy 3f out: rdn 2f out: sn hung lft and one pce* **4/1**[2]

4543 **4** 6 **Rainford Glory (IRE)**[7] 824 3-9-7 **53** .... JimCrowley 5 23
(David Simcock) *trckd ldrs: effrt on inner wl over 2f out: sn rdn and btn* **1/1**[1]

5624 **5** 8 **Icanboogie**[32] 506 3-8-9 **48** .... RyanTate(7) 3
(Karen George) *led: pushed along and hdd 3f out: sn wknd* **14/1**

346- **6** 13 **Charlemagne Diva**[158] 6707 3-9-0 **53** .... (e[1]) PhilipPrince(7) 2
(Richard Guest) *n.m.r early: trckd ldrs on inner: swtchd wd and rdn along wl over 3f out: sn outpcd and bhd* **12/1**

1m 43.36s (-0.34) **Going Correction** -0.025s/f (Stan) **6** Ran SP% **115.3**
Speed ratings (Par 96): **100,92,85,79,71 58**
Tote Swingers 1&2 £3.50, 2&3 £2.00, 1&3 £3.00 CSF £36.14 TOTE £8.00: £3.10, £1.70; EX 22.10 Trifecta £133.10 Pool: £2,590.15 - 14.58 winning tickets..
Owner Frank Bird **Bred** Rancho San Peasea S A **Trained** Middleham Moor, N Yorks

FOCUS
They finished spread out all over Nottinghamshire in this modest handicap and it provided a 1-2 for trainer Mark Johnston. The form is very weak with not many giving their running.

911 £32 BONUS AT 32RED.COM MEDIAN AUCTION MAIDEN STKS 1m (F)
3:55 (4:00) (Class 6) 3-5-Y-O **£2,045** (£603; £302) **Stalls** Low

Form RPR
3222 **1** **Aryal**[12] 774 3-8-8 **73** .... (b[1]) JoeFanning 1 73
(Mark Johnston) *mde all: rdn clr over 2f out: kpt on* **1/1**[1]

6 **2** 2½ **Derby To Dubai**[30] 525 3-8-8 **0** .... AmyRyan 6 67+
(Kevin Ryan) *prom: hdwy to chse wnr over 2f out: rdn: green and edgd lft wl over 1f out: styd on fnl f* **3/1**[2]

0-3 **3** 14 **On With The Dance (IRE)**[9] 807 3-8-8 **0** .... LukeMorris 3 35
(Ed Vaughan) *chsd ldrs on inner: rdn along over 3f out: drvn and plugged on one pce fnl 2f* **3/1**[2]

00-4 **4** 1¼ **Munaawib**[16] 716 5-9-12 **40** .... (t) RobbieFitzpatrick 10 38
(Charles Smith) *chsd ldrs: effrt 3f out: rdn over 2f out and sn outpcd* **100/1**

5 ¾ **Solarmaite** 4-9-4 **0** .... MarkCoumbe(3) 4 31
(Roy Bowring) *s.i.s and green in rr: hdwy over 3f out: rdn and kpt on fnl 2f* **25/1**

0 **6** 9 **Aura Bora (USA)**[6] 849 5-9-7 **0** .... AdamCarter(5) 8 16
(Tim Easterby) *sn outpcd and a bhd* **25/1**

7 1 **Woodley Wonder (IRE)** 3-8-5 **0** .... DeclanCannon(3) 9 7
(Ben Haslam) *chsd ldrs on outer: pushed along and rn green home turn: sn wknd* **20/1**[3]

0- **8** 7 **Running On Faith**[113] 7712 5-9-12 **0** .... ChrisCatlin 5
(Garry Woodward) *a in rr: bhd fnl 3f* **66/1**

0-06 **9** 5 **Supastarqueen (USA)**[41] 377 5-9-7 **30** .... DuranFentiman 2
(Brian Baugh) *cl up: rdn along 1/2-way: sn lost pl and bhd fnl 3f* **100/1**

03 **10** *33* **Santorini Sunset**[22] [641] 4-9-7 0 .... FrederikTylicki 7
(J R Jenkins) *chsd ldrs: rdn along and lost pl qckly after 3f: sn bhd: t.o fnl 3f* **25/1**

1m 42.84s (-0.86) **Going Correction** -0.025s/f (Stan)
WFA 3 from 4yo+ 18lb **10** Ran SP% **119.8**
Speed ratings (Par 101): **103,100,86,85,84 75,74,67,62,29**
Tote Swingers 1&2 £1.60, 2&3 £1.70, 1&3 £1.40 CSF £4.07 TOTE £1.70: £1.10, £1.10, £1.60; EX 5.70 Trifecta £11.50 Pool: £4,044.26 - 262.87 winning tickets..
Owner Sheikh Hamdan Bin Mohammed Al Maktoum **Bred** Newsells Park Stud **Trained** Middleham Moor, N Yorks

FOCUS
They bet 20-1 bar three in this uncompetitive maiden. The winner only needed to run to his mark to score and the form is ordinary.

912 32RED CASINO H'CAP 7f (F)
4:30 (4:30) (Class 5) (0-75,74) 4-Y-O+ **£2,587** (£770; £384; £192) **Stalls** Low

Form RPR
0-50 **1** **Caldercruix (USA)**[58] [104] 6-9-3 **73** .... (v) RaulDaSilva(3) 8 82
(James Evans) *prom: chsd ldr fr 1/2-way: rdn wl over 1f out: sn chal and ev ch whn sltly hmpd ins fnl f: kpt on wl to ld last 50yds* **11/2**[3]

00-3 **2** *1 1/4* **Alpha Tauri (USA)**[22] [645] 7-9-7 **74** .... (t) RobbieFitzpatrick 9 80
(Scott Dixon) *set str pce: clr over 3f out: rdn wl over 1f out: edgd rt ent fnl f: sn drvn: hdd and no ex last 50yds* **10/1**

040- **3** *1 3/4* **Rio Cobolo (IRE)**[112] [7732] 7-8-9 **62** .... AdrianNicholls 10 63
(David Nicholls) *chsd ldrs on outer: wd st: rdn 2f out: kpt on u.p fnl f* **14/1**

6523 **4** *1* **Masai Moon**[15] [721] 9-9-0 **74** .... (b) PatMillman(7) 6 73
(Rod Millman) *dwlt: sn outpcd and rdn along in rr: hdwy 3f out: styng on whn hmpd and swtchd lft over 1f out: kpt on fnl f: nrst fin* **9/1**

2214 **5** *1/2* **Flying Pickets (IRE)**[16] [715] 4-9-3 **70** .... (be) JohnFahy 1 68
(Alan McCabe) *towards rr: hdwy 3f out: rdn to chse ldrs wl over 1f out: sn drvn and hung lft appr fnl f: one pce* **12/1**

4-12 **6** *3/4* **Tight Lipped (IRE)**[7] [832] 4-9-6 **73** .... (v) LukeMorris 5 69
(James Eustace) *in tch: rdn along and lost pl after 2f: towards rr and wd st: racd nr stands' rail and drvn to chse ldrs wl over 1f out: sn no imp* **2/1**[1]

3402 **7** *8* **Only Ten Per Cent (IRE)**[15] [721] 5-9-4 **71** .... FrederikTylicki 3 46
(J R Jenkins) *hld up in tch: hdwy 3f out: rdn along on inner 2f out: sn wknd* **9/2**[2]

3450 **8** *1 1/4* **Imprimis Tagula (IRE)**[16] [715] 9-8-10 **63** .... (v) NickyMackay 2 35
(Alan Bailey) *chsd ldrs: rdn along over 3f out: sn wknd* **14/1**

6231 **9** *3/4* **Bitaphon (IRE)**[25] [603] 4-8-8 **61** .... AndrewMullen 4 31
(Michael Appleby) *chsd ldr: rdn along bef 1/2-way: sn lost pl and bhd* **7/1**

1m 29.28s (-1.02) **Going Correction** -0.025s/f (Stan) **9** Ran SP% **119.5**
Speed ratings (Par 103): **104,102,100,99,98 98,88,87,86**
Tote Swingers 1&2 £6.00, 2&3 £20.40, 1&3 £9.90 CSF £61.02 CT £552.56 TOTE £8.20: £2.30, £3.20, £3.90; EX 57.50 Trifecta £580.10 Pool: £2,408.73 - 3.11 winning tickets..
Owner David Mantle **Bred** Bjorn Nielsen **Trained** Broadwas, Worcs

FOCUS
A fair handicap and no hanging about. The placed horses help set the level.

913 32RED H'CAP 5f (F)
5:00 (5:01) (Class 4) (0-85,84) 4-Y-O+ **£4,690** (£1,395; £697; £348) **Stalls** High

Form RPR
1211 **1** **Aubrietia**[30] [526] 4-9-7 **84** .... (b) AndrewMullen 1 102
(Alan McCabe) *cl up on outer: pushed along and sltly outpcd 2f out: rdn to ld jst ins fnl f: sn edgd lft and clr: readily* **5/2**[1]

0010 **2** *4 1/2* **Royal Bajan (USA)**[12] [780] 5-9-5 **82** .... (b) FrederikTylicki 7 84
(James Given) *awkward s: sn led: hdd after 1f: cl up: rdn to ld again wl over 1f out: drvn and hdd ent fnl f: kpt on same pce* **4/1**[3]

0-04 **3** *3/4* **Rylee Mooch**[3] [881] 5-8-13 **76** .... (e) RobbieFitzpatrick 3 75
(Richard Guest) *chsd ldrs: rdn along wl over 1f out: kpt on u.p fnl f* **7/1**

6-00 **4** *1* **Six Wives**[35] [457] 6-9-0 **77** .... (p) ChrisCatlin 4 73
(Scott Dixon) *dwlt: sn cl up: led after 1f: pushed along 2f out: sn rdn and hdd: drvn and one pce ent fnl f* **12/1**

-055 **5** *shd* **Gorgeous Goblin (IRE)**[12] [776] 6-9-3 **80** .... (t) JoeFanning 2 75
(David C Griffiths) *trckd ldrs: rdn wl over 1f out: sn no imp* **6/1**

040- **6** *2 1/4* **Crown Choice**[127] [7484] 8-8-10 **73** .... PaulMulrennan 6 60
(Paul Midgley) *a in rr* **20/1**

4434 **7** *1 1/2* **Dorback**[35] [457] 6-9-3 **80** .... FrannyNorton 8 62
(David Nicholls) *trckd ldrs: rdn wl over 1f out: sn edgd rt and wknd* **3/1**[2]

59.98s (0.28) **Going Correction** +0.20s/f (Slow) **7** Ran SP% **112.8**
Speed ratings (Par 105): **105,97,96,95,94 91,88**
Tote Swingers 1&2 £3.40, 2&3 £3.50, 1&3 £3.40 CSF £12.43 CT £59.52 TOTE £3.30: £1.90, £4.10; EX 15.70 Trifecta £88.00 Pool: £2,911.78 - 24.80 winning tickets..
Owner Shropshire Wolves 4 **Bred** C J Murfitt **Trained** Averham Park, Notts

FOCUS
A decent Fibresand sprint handicap. Another taking performance from the winner, who could rate higher.

914 32RED.COM APPRENTICE H'CAP 1m 3f (F)
5:30 (5:30) (Class 4) (0-75,75) 4-Y-O+ **£2,726** (£805; £402) **Stalls** Low

Form RPR
5-11 **1** **Dewala**[22] [646] 4-9-6 **75** .... ConorHarrison 6 82
(Michael Appleby) *set gd pce: pushed clr wl over 2f out: rdn over 1f out: kpt on wl fnl f* **4/5**[1]

-203 **2** *1 1/4* **Stanley Rigby**[30] [528] 7-8-6 **67** .... (b) EireannCagney(7) 7 72
(Richard Fahey) *hld up in rr: hdwy on outer 1/2-way: trckd ldrs 4f out: chsd wnr wl over 2f out: rdn to chal over 1f out and ev ch tl drvn and no ex ins fnl f* **7/2**[2]

660- **3** *hd* **Blades Lad**[65] [4199] 4-8-7 **67** .... KevinStott(5) 1 72
(Peter Niven) *hld up: hdwy to chse ldrs over 3f out: rdn over 2f out: chsd ldng pair ent fnl f: kpt on same pce* **16/1**

450- **4** *19* **Blue Maisey**[202] [5310] 5-8-5 **64** .... ConnorBeasley(5) 4 38
(Edwin Tuer) *trckd ldrs: hdwy to chse wnr over 5f out: rdn along 3f out: sn wknd* **33/1**

0622 **5** *14* **Amana (USA)**[10] [789] 9-8-5 **62** .... MatthewHopkins(3) 5 14
(Mark Brisbourne) *dwlt and in rr: effrt and sme hdwy 5f out: sn rdn along and outpcd fr over 3f out* **10/1**

355- **6** *13* **Light The City (IRE)**[286] [2440] 6-8-9 **66** .... JordanNason(3) 2
(Ruth Carr) *chsd ldng pair: rdn along 5f out: sn wknd and bhd whn eased over 3f out* **10/1**

35-4 **7** *99* **Toughness Danon**[26] [592] 7-8-12 **66** .... (tp) AliceHaynes 3
(Anthony Middleton) *cl up: rdn along 1/2-way: sn lost pl and bhd whn eased over 4f out: t.o* **7/1**[3]

2m 28.3s (0.30) **Going Correction** -0.025s/f (Stan)
WFA 4 from 5yo+ 1lb **7** Ran SP% **117.3**
Speed ratings (Par 105): **97,96,95,82,71 62,**
Tote Swingers 1&2 £1.60, 2&3 £7.70, 1&3 £5.10 CSF £4.05 TOTE £1.90: £1.70, £2.30; EX 3.10 Trifecta £46.50 Pool: £1,517.87 - 24.45 winning tickets..
Owner Goldform Racing **Bred** A M Wragg **Trained** Danethorpe, Notts

FOCUS
The winner made sure this fair apprentice handicap was run at a true pace. The form is straightforward rated around the first three, who finished well clear.
T/Plt: £72.80 to a £1 stake. Pool £62,508.92 - 626.71 winning tickets. T/Qpdt: £50.50 to a £1 stake. Pool £4,271.24 - 62.50 winning tickets. JR

846 WOLVERHAMPTON (A.W) (L-H)
Thursday, March 7

OFFICIAL GOING: Standard
Wind: Light against Weather: Misty

915 32RED.COM MAIDEN STKS 5f 20y(P)
5:40 (5:41) (Class 5) 3-Y-O+ **£2,587** (£770; £384; £192) **Stalls** Low

Form RPR
656- **1** **Top Boy**[176] [6139] 3-8-6 93 .... AdamMcLean(7) 5 72+
(Derek Shaw) *chsd ldr tl led over 1f out: rdn and hung lft ins fnl f: clr towards fin* **4/6**[1]

43-2 **2** *4* **Bapak Bangsawan**[7] [829] 3-8-13 69 .... PhillipMakin 4 64+
(Kevin Ryan) *s.i.s: sn prom: swtchd lft over 1f out: sn rdn to chse wnr: styng on same pce whn hmpd wl ins fnl f* **15/8**[2]

0/00 **3** *1* **Poyle Todream**[14] [733] 5-9-12 42 .... TomEaves 7 57
(Roy Brotherton) *led: rdn and hdd over 1f out: no ex ins fnl f* **125/1**

0-3 **4** *1 1/2* **Nors The Panic**[6] [847] 3-8-8 0 .... (e[1]) JasonHart(5) 3 46
(Richard Guest) *trckd ldrs: shkn up over 1f out: no ex fnl f* **25/1**

5 *1/2* **Chrisnickdave (FR)** 3-8-8 0 .... JamesSullivan 2 39
(Michael Easterby) *s.s: sn pushed along in rr: hmpd over 3f out: styd on ins fnl f: nvr nrr* **14/1**[3]

50- **6** *1 1/2* **Symphony Of Dreams**[285] [2492] 3-8-8 0 .... KierenFox 1 33
(Dai Burchell) *hld up: nt clr run over 3f out: pushed along 1/2-way: nvr on terms* **50/1**

40/0 **7** *1/2* **Anrheg**[22] [630] 5-9-7 50 .... KellyHarrison 6 38
(Dai Burchell) *chsd ldrs: pushed along 1/2-way: wknd over 1f out* **33/1**

1m 3.44s (1.14) **Going Correction** +0.075s/f (Slow)
WFA 3 from 5yo 13lb **7** Ran SP% **111.0**
Speed ratings (Par 103): **93,86,85,82,81 79,78**
toteswingers 1&2 £1.20, 2&3 £5.30, 1&3 £5.10 CSF £1.91 TOTE £1.40: £1.10, £1.30; EX 2.50 Trifecta £33.10 Pool: £2056.15 - 46.57 winning units..
Owner Brian Johnson (Northamptonshire) **Bred** Mrs C R Philipson & Mrs H G Lascelles **Trained** Sproxton, Leics

FOCUS
The winner was fully entitled to score, but ran well below his mark again rated through the runner-up.

916 £32 BONUS AT 32RED.COM (S) STKS 5f 216y(P)
6:10 (6:10) (Class 6) 4-Y-O+ **£1,940** (£577; £288; £144) **Stalls** Low

Form RPR
5245 **1** **Dark Lane**[15] [727] 7-8-13 63 .... RobJFitzpatrick(7) 3 69
(David Evans) *chsd ldrs: led over 1f out: rdn out* **5/1**[3]

0254 **2** *hd* **Proper Charlie**[5] [861] 5-8-7 68 .... RyanTate(7) 4 62
(William Knight) *chsd ldr 1f: remained handy: rdn and ev ch fr over 1f out: nt run on* **11/10**[1]

-300 **3** *1 1/4* **Whiskey Junction**[31] [516] 9-9-0 54 .... WilliamCarson 6 59
(Mick Quinn) *led: rdn and hdd over 1f out: styd on same pce ins fnl f* **16/1**

5126 **4** *hd* **Athaakeel (IRE)**[5] [863] 7-9-1 55 .... (b) DavidProbert 1 59
(Ronald Harris) *sn pushed along in rr: hdwy over 1f out: sn rdn: styd on* **8/1**

00-0 **5** *4* **The Dancing Lord**[9] [806] 4-8-7 59 .... (b) RyanWhile(7) 5 46
(Bill Turner) *chsd ldr 5f out: rdn and ev ch 2f out: no ex fnl f* **11/1**

5045 **6** *11* **Frequency**[24] [611] 6-8-9 65 .... (p) GarryWhillans(5) 2 13
(Keith Dalgleish) *hld up in tch: rdn and wknd over 1f out* **7/2**[2]

1m 15.26s (0.26) **Going Correction** +0.075s/f (Slow) **6** Ran SP% **111.8**
Speed ratings (Par 101): **101,100,99,98,93 78**
toteswingers: 1&2 £2.10, 1&3 £6.20, 2&3 £4.10 CSF £10.92 TOTE £5.90: £2.20, £2.40; EX 11.10 Trifecta £85.90 Pool: £1843.75 - 16.09 winning units..There was no bid for the winner.
Owner Jason Tucker **Bred** David Jamison Bloodstock **Trained** Pandy, Monmouths
■ The first career winner for Rob Fitzpatrick.

FOCUS
A moderate seller.

917 32REDPOKER.COM H'CAP 7f 32y(P)
6:40 (6:40) (Class 7) (0-50,50) 4-Y-O+ **£1,940** (£577; £288; £144) **Stalls** High

Form RPR
-406 **1** **Metropolitan Chief**[7] [819] 9-9-2 **45** .... (p) TomMcLaughlin 2 53
(Paul Burgoyne) *a.p: rdn to ld wl ins fnl f: hung rt: styd on* **16/1**

5066 **2** *3/4* **Jonnie Skull (IRE)**[15] [728] 7-9-0 **50** .... (vt) RyanTate(7) 4 56
(Phil McEntee) *chsd ldrs: rdn and ev ch ins fnl f: carried rt: styd on* **8/1**

-540 **3** *1 3/4* **Chester Deelyte (IRE)**[28] [551] 5-9-5 **48** .... (v) TomEaves 5 50+
(Lisa Williamson) *hld up: hdwy over 1f out: r.o to go 3rd nr fin: nt rch ldrs* **10/1**

0513 **4** *1/2* **Rise To Glory (IRE)**[14] [733] 5-9-5 **48** .... (b) DuranFentiman 10 49
(Shaun Harris) *led: rdn and hdd wl ins fnl f: styd on same pce* **11/2**

5045 **5** *3/4* **Dingaan (IRE)**[7] [819] 10-9-2 **45** .... FergusSweeney 11 44+
(Peter Grayson) *s.i.s: hld up: hung lft and r.o ins fnl f: nvr nrr* **10/1**

4342 **6** *3 1/4* **Media Jury**[14] [733] 6-9-7 **50** .... (p) DavidNolan 1 41
(John Wainwright) *s.i.s: hld up: rdn over 2f out: nvr on terms* **5/1**[3]

2022 **7** *3* **Under Par**[41] [381] 5-9-7 **50** .... (t) GrahamGibbons 6 34
(Michael Easterby) *s.i.s: sn prom: chsd ldr over 4f out: rdn over 1f out: wknd ins fnl f* **11/4**[1]

06-0 **8** *3 3/4* **Royal Envoy (IRE)**[21] [649] 10-9-2 **45** .... (p) MichaelStainton 8 19
(Paul Howling) *hld up: rdn over 2f out: n.d* **40/1**

65/0 **9** *4 1/2* **Mousie**[13] [754] 4-8-13 **47** .... ShirleyTeasdale(5) 9 10
(Alan McCabe) *prom: rdn 1/2-way: wknd 2f out* **40/1**

0-0 **10** *6* **Zaroud (IRE)**[1] 900 4-9-2 **45** (t) EddieAhern 7
(Thomas McLaughlin, Ire) *bmpd and rdr lost irons sn after s: mid-div: hdwy 1/2-way: wknd over 2f out* **9/2**[2]

1m 30.11s (0.51) **Going Correction** +0.075s/f (Slow) 10 Ran SP% **117.0**
Speed ratings (Par 97): **100,99,97,96,95 92,88,84,79,72**
toteswingers: 1&2 £23.90, 1&3 £11.40, 2&3 £20.00 CSF £138.29 CT £938.97 TOTE £19.90: £5.10, £2.60, £4.30; EX 78.40 Trifecta £502.00 Pool: £1963.69 - 2.93 winning units..
Owner Mrs C Leigh-Turner **Bred** J A Prescott And C M Oakshott **Trained** Shepton Montague, Somerset

■ Stewards' Enquiry : Tom McLaughlin three-day ban: careless riding (Mar 21-23); two-day ban: used whip above permitted level (Mar 24-25)

FOCUS
A bottom-drawer handicap that saw a messy start.

918 32REDBET.COM CLAIMING STKS 1m 141y(P)
7:10 (7:10) (Class 6) 3-Y-O **£1,940** (£577; £288; £144) **Stalls** Low

Form RPR

2-44 **1** **Minimee**[10] 793 3-8-8 67 (v[1]) RobertTart[(7)] 3 70
(Alan Bailey) *hld up: hdwy over 1f out: rdn to ld ins fnl f: r.o* **9/2**

2421 **2** *¾* **Shearian**[7] 824 3-8-10 56 LukeMorris 4 63
(Tony Carroll) *a.p: chsd ldr over 6f out: rdn over 1f out: r.o* **4/1**[3]

6123 **3** *1* **Misleading Promise (IRE)**[9] 804 3-8-10 69 (t) LiamKeniry 2 61
(John Butler) *led: rdn over 1f out: hdd ins fnl f: styd on same pce* **11/4**[2]

4112 **4** *3 ¾* **Hillbilly Boy (IRE)**[7] 827 3-8-8 74 RyanWhile[(7)] 1 58
(Bill Turner) *chsd ldr 2f: remained handy: rdn over 2f out: no ex fnl f* **11/8**[1]

1m 52.38s (1.88) **Going Correction** +0.075s/f (Slow) 4 Ran SP% **107.0**
Speed ratings (Par 96): **94,93,92,89**
CSF £19.90 TOTE £6.80; EX 20.20 Trifecta £45.00 Pool: £787.14 - 13.09 winning units..Minimee was claimed by P. S. McEntee for £10,000.
Owner John Stocker **Bred** M A Jarvis **Trained** Newmarket, Suffolk

FOCUS
An ordinary 3-y-o claimer.

919 32RED CASINO FILLIES' H'CAP 1m 141y(P)
7:40 (7:41) (Class 5) (0-70,69) 4-Y-O+ **£2,587** (£770; £384; £192) **Stalls** Low

Form RPR

1521 **1** **Travelling**[10] 798 4-9-0 **69** RyanTate[(7)] 6 81
(Tony Carroll) *hld up in tch: pushed along over 2f out: rdn to ld ins fnl f: r.o* **7/4**[1]

-212 **2** *2 ¼* **Big Sylv (IRE)**[12] 778 4-9-0 **62** (p) DavidProbert 4 69
(James Unett) *chsd ldr tl led over 3f out: rdn over 1f out: hdd and unable qck ins fnl f* **9/4**[2]

-544 **3** *1* **Maggie Pink**[10] 801 4-8-10 **58** AndrewMullen 5 63
(Michael Appleby) *a.p: chsd ldr 3f out: rdn and ev ch ins fnl f: styd on same pce* **12/1**

-341 **4** *½* **Sail Home**[13] 753 6-8-13 **68** ShelleyBirkett[(7)] 1 72
(Julia Feilden) *led 5f: outpcd 2f out: styd on ins fnl f* **11/2**

-133 **5** *½* **Spark Of Genius**[26] 589 4-9-7 **69** (p) LukeMorris 3 72
(Alan McCabe) *prom: rdn: nt clr run and stmbld 1f out: styd on same pce ins fnl f* **4/1**[3]

0 **6** *10* **Larghetto (USA)**[13] 758 5-8-12 **60** JoeFanning 7 42
(Daniel Mark Loughnane) *hld up: hdwy over 2f out: shkn up and wknd over 1f out* **40/1**

400- **7** *1 ½* **Cane Cat (IRE)**[177] 6120 6-8-13 **61** (t) LiamJones 2 40
(Tony Carroll) *hld up: pushed along over 5f out: sn lost tch* **25/1**

1m 50.13s (-0.37) **Going Correction** +0.075s/f (Slow) 7 Ran SP% **116.5**
Speed ratings (Par 100): **104,102,101,100,100 91,90**
toteswingers: 1&2 £1.30, 1&3 £7.30, 2&3 £5.60 CSF £6.17 TOTE £2.70: £2.30, £1.50; EX 5.30 Trifecta £42.50 Pool: £1266.89 - 22.31 winning units..
Owner Longview Stud & Bloodstock Ltd **Bred** Longview Stud & Bloodstock Ltd **Trained** Cropthorne, Worcs

FOCUS
Not a bad handicap for the class.

920 32RED H'CAP 1m 141y(P)
8:10 (8:10) (Class 4) (0-85,89) 3-Y-O **£4,690** (£1,395; £697; £348) **Stalls** Low

Form RPR

-221 **1** **King George River (IRE)**[20] 666 3-9-4 **89** RobertTart[(7)] 5 99+
(Alan Bailey) *hld up: hdwy 2f out: rdn whn rdr dropped whip over 1f out: led ins fnl f: r.o strly* **5/4**[1]

142- **2** *2 ½* **Sennockian Star**[134] 7335 3-8-7 **71** JoeFanning 3 75
(Mark Johnston) *led: rdn over 1f out: hdd and unable qck ins fnl f* **11/4**[2]

-13 **3** *½* **Al Raqeeb (IRE)**[29] 533 3-9-0 **78** AndreaAtzeni 2 81
(Marco Botti) *a.p: racd keenly: chsd ldr over 6f out: rdn and ev ch over 1f out: styd on same pce ins fnl f* **4/1**[3]

11-1 **4** *1 ½* **Pairumani Prince (IRE)**[52] 204 3-8-9 **73** RobertHavlin 1 73
(Ed Dunlop) *chsd ldr 2f: remained handy: rdn over 1f out: no ex ins fnl f* **8/1**

1232 **5** *1 ½* **Black Dave (IRE)**[14] 738 3-8-8 **72** WilliamCarson 4 68
(David Evans) *hld up: plld hrd: rdn over 2f out: nvr trbld ldrs* **11/1**

1m 51.2s (0.70) **Going Correction** +0.075s/f (Slow) 5 Ran SP% **110.6**
Speed ratings (Par 100): **99,96,96,95,93**
CSF £4.95 TOTE £1.50: £1.70, £1.30; EX 5.90 Trifecta £8.50 Pool: £921.63 - 80.55 winning units..
Owner John Stocker **Bred** Barronstown Stud **Trained** Newmarket, Suffolk

FOCUS
A fair 3yo handicap, run at an ordinary pace.

921 32REDBINGO.COM H'CAP 1m 1f 103y(P)
8:40 (8:43) (Class 6) (0-60,66) 4-Y-O+ **£1,940** (£577; £288; £144) **Stalls** Low

Form RPR

1 **Arabela (IRE)**[111] 7758 4-8-12 **51** DavidProbert 7 65+
(James Unett) *chsd ldr tl led over 2f out: rdn and edgd lft over 1f out: styd on wl* **16/1**

25-3 **2** *3* **Thane Of Cawdor (IRE)**[22] 631 4-9-0 **53** LiamKeniry 8 61
(Joseph Tuite) *hld up: hdwy over 2f out: rdn to chse wnr fnl f: no imp* **3/1**[2]

-305 **3** *nk* **Apache Glory (USA)**[17] 709 5-9-6 **59** (p) AndreaAtzeni 6 66
(John Stimpson) *hld up: hdwy and edgd lft over 1f out: r.o: nt rch ldrs* **15/2**[3]

0011 **4** *1 ½* **Scary Movie (IRE)**[1] 896 8-9-13 **66** 6ex (b) EddieAhern 5 70
(Thomas McLaughlin, Ire) *hld up: rdn over 2f out: hdwy over 1f out: styd on same pce fnl f* **7/4**[1]

66-0 **5** *2* **Forster Street (IRE)**[17] 709 4-9-7 **60** GrahamGibbons 11 60
(Tim Easterby) *led: rdn and hdd over 2f out: no ex fnl f* **22/1**

0/05 **6** *nk* **Gracchus (USA)**[22] 626 7-8-13 **59** (t) RyanTate[(7)] 4 58
(Tony Carroll) *hld up: pushed along over 3f out: hdwy over 1f out: nt trble ldrs* **17/2**

-405 **7** *hd* **Mr Chocolate Drop (IRE)**[10] 801 9-9-7 **60** (t) RussKennemore 3 59
(Mandy Rowland) *hld up in tch: rdn over 2f out: no ex fnl f* **16/1**

0/3 **8** *2 ¼* **Walter De La Mare (IRE)**[14] 520 6-8-13 **52** LukeMorris 2 46
(Anabel K Murphy) *chsd ldrs: rdn over 2f out: wknd fnl f* **10/1**

10/0 **9** *1 ¼* **True Pleasure (IRE)**[44] 330 6-8-10 **52** DeclanCannon[(3)] 13 43
(James Bethell) *s.s: hld up: rdn over 1f out: nvr on terms* **20/1**

103- **10** *1 ¼* **Tooley Woods (IRE)**[172] 6274 4-8-5 **51** AidenBlakemore[(7)] 1 40
(Tony Carroll) *mid-div: rdn over 2f out: wknd over 1f out* **25/1**

5050 **11** *2* **Bubbly Braveheart (IRE)**[6] 852 6-8-3 **47** RachealKneller[(5)] 10 31
(Phil McEntee) *chsd ldrs: pushed along over 3f out: wknd over 2f out* **25/1**

0-00 **12** *1 ½* **King Of Windsor (IRE)**[40] 410 6-9-1 **59** (p) AdamCarter[(5)] 12 40
(John Wainwright) *hld up: a in rr: bhd fnl 3f* **40/1**

2m 2.48s (0.78) **Going Correction** +0.075s/f (Slow) 12 Ran SP% **123.8**
Speed ratings (Par 101): **99,96,96,94,92 92,92,90,89,88 86,85**
toteswingers 1&2 £10.70, 2&3 £4.90, 1&3 £25.00 CSF £62.51 CT £412.45 TOTE £16.50: £4.80, £1.50, £2.50; EX 60.60 Trifecta £399.00 Pool: £1335.27 - 2.50 winning units..
Owner Mayne-Hamilton **Bred** His Highness The Aga Khan's Studs S C **Trained** Tedsmore Hall, Shropshire

FOCUS
A weak handicap, run at an uneven pace.
T/Plt: £196.30 to a £1 stake. Pool of £66,673.13 - 247.88 winning units. T/Qpdt: £99.00 to a £1 stake. Pool of £5,908.47 - 44.15 winning units. CR

191 DEAUVILLE (R-H)
Thursday, March 7

OFFICIAL GOING: Fibresand: standard

922a PRIX DE DOUVILLE (CLAIMER) (4YO) (FIBRESAND) 1m 4f
3:25 (12:00) 4-Y-O **£7,723** (£3,089; £2,317; £1,544; £772)

RPR

1 **Didge (FR)**[54] 4-9-1 0 Pierre-CharlesBoudot 2 71
(E Bergougnoux, France) **109/10**

2 *1* **Rich Pickings (FR)**[313] 4-8-11 0 (b) AlexandreRoussel 5 65
(P Peltier, France) **27/1**

3 *nk* **Valamar (FR)**[62] 4-9-4 0 EddyHardouin 4 72
(J-Y Artu, France) **2/1**[1]

4 *snk* **Roma Eria (FR)**[57] 4-8-11 0 (p) MathieuAndrouin 11 65
(P Monfort, France) **20/1**

5 *shd* **Don Caprice (FR)** 4-8-11 0 (p) FabriceVeron 6 65
(E Leenders, France) **14/1**

6 *1 ¼* **Priestley's Reward (IRE)**[49] 235 4-9-2 0 (p) IoritzMendizabal 10 68
(Mrs K Burke) *sn led: set mod pce: shkn up down bk st: led into st but sn u.p: hdd 2f out: rdn but no ex fnl f: styd on same pce* **3/1**[2]

7 *hd* **Ruling Pole (IRE)**[57] 4-9-1 0 ArnaudBourgeais 7 66
(N Leenders, France) **13/1**

8 *1* **Windy King**[141] 4-9-1 0 (p) MaximeGuyon 9 65
(J Bertran De Balanda, France) **13/2**[3]

9 *1 ¼* **Send For Me**[73] 4-8-6 0 (b) AntoineCoutier[(5)] 1 59
(F Chappet, France) **44/5**

10 *3* **Immigrand Child (FR)**[61] 4-8-11 0 (b) ThierryJarnet 8 54
(Mlle S-V Tarrou, France) **16/1**

2m 42.8s (162.80) 10 Ran SP% **118.3**
WIN (incl. 1 euro stake): 11.90. PLACES: 2.70, 4.90, 1.60. DF: 109.20. SF: 193.50.
Owner Eric Bergougnoux **Bred** Gfa Pre Du Roi **Trained** France

915 WOLVERHAMPTON (A.W) (L-H)
Friday, March 8

OFFICIAL GOING: Standard
Wind: Light; against Weather: Misty

923 £32 BONUS AT 32RED.COM H'CAP 5f 216y(P)
5:40 (5:40) (Class 6) (0-65,65) 3-Y-O **£1,940** (£577; £288; £144) **Stalls** Low

Form RPR

-131 **1** **Hazard Warning (IRE)**[7] 848 3-9-1 **59** 6ex (b) DuranFentiman 5 66
(Tim Easterby) *hld up: hdwy and hung lft over 1f out: rdn to ld and hung lft towards fin* **6/4**[1]

24- **2** *½* **Last Minute Lisa (IRE)**[77] 8208 3-9-6 **64** LukeMorris 4 70
(S Donohoe, Ire) *led 1f: chsd ldrs: rdn and hung lft over 1f out: ev ch wl ins fnl f: r.o* **9/1**

224- **3** *1* **Free Island**[128] 7481 3-9-6 **64** JoeFanning 10 67+
(James Tate) *chsd ldrs: led wl over 1f out: rdn and edgd lft ins fnl f: hdd towards fin* **10/1**

3U2- **4** *¾* **Grand Jipeck (IRE)**[130] 7441 3-8-12 **56** (t) PatrickMathers 2 56
(Ian McInnes) *a.p: rdn over 1f out: r.o* **33/1**

2313 **5** *3 ½* **Katy Spirit (IRE)**[9] 811 3-9-7 **65** LiamKeniry 1 54
(Michael Blanshard) *s.i.s: hld up: hdwy u.p and hung lft over 1f out: nt trble ldrs* **10/1**

-023 **6** *¾* **Club Electra (IRE)**[9] 817 3-8-12 **56** (b) MartinLane 7 43
(Tobias B P Coles) *hld up: styd on ins fnl f: nvr nrr* **14/1**

-622 **7** *1* **Loulou Vuitton**[11] 796 3-9-2 **60** (p) WilliamCarson 8 43
(Brian Baugh) *hld up: rdn over 1f out: nvr on terms* **17/2**[3]

432- **8** *1 ½* **Ayasha**[114] 7713 3-9-0 **65** RobertTart[(7)] 3 44
(Bryan Smart) *chsd ldrs: rdn over 2f out: wknd over 1f out* **7/2**[2]

0- **9** *4 ½* **Shamglas Queen**[42] 382 3-8-5 **56** (t) DavidParkes[(7)] 9 20
(J Larkin, Ire) *led 5f out: rdn and hdd wl over 1f out: wknd fnl f* **25/1**

040- **10** *3* **Baltic Prince (IRE)**[95] 7974 3-8-4 **48** FrannyNorton 6
(Paul Green) *sn pushed along and prom: wknd over 1f out* **10/1**

3050 **11** *hd* **Scarlet Strand**[7] 848 3-8-6 **55** ow1 JackDuern[(5)] 11
(Reg Hollinshead) *s.i.s: sn pushed along and a in rr* **66/1**

1m 14.27s (-0.73) **Going Correction** +0.10s/f (Slow) 11 Ran SP% **125.0**
Speed ratings (Par 96): **108,107,106,105,100 99,98,96,90,86 85**
toteswingers 1&2 £3.30, 1&3 £4.40, 2&3 £5.90 CSF £17.49 CT £114.49 TOTE £2.90: £1.90, £3.50, £4.30; EX 12.40 Trifecta £149.20 Pool: £2,139.71 - 10.74 winning units.
Owner Habton Farms **Bred** E O'Gorman **Trained** Great Habton, N Yorks

FOCUS
A modest 3yo sprint handicap in which they went an honest gallop, and the time was fair. Big improvement from the runner-up.

924 32RED.COM H'CAP 5f 20y(P)
6:10 (6:10) (Class 5) (0-70,72) 4-Y-O+ **£2,587** (£770; £384; £192) **Stalls** Low

Form RPR
5-41 **1** **Cincinnati Kit**[21] 670 4-8-8 **57**........................(t) DavidProbert 5 66
(Stuart Williams) *chsd ldrs: rdn to ld wl ins fnl f: r.o* **4/1**[1]
1133 **2** *nk* **Miss Bunter**[3] 885 4-9-0 **70**........................ DavidBergin(7) 7 78
(David O'Meara) *hld up: hdwy over 1f out: sn rdn: r.o* **4/1**[1]
1-42 **3** *½* **Novabridge**[23] 627 5-9-6 **69**........................(b) LiamKeniry 1 75
(Neil Mulholland) *led tl rdn and hdd wl ins fnl f* **9/1**[3]
4604 **4** *hd* **Shawkantango**[14] 760 6-8-4 **60**........................(v) AdamMcLean(7) 8 65
(Derek Shaw) *s.i.s: r.o ins fnl f: nt rch ldrs* **16/1**
0604 **5** *nk* **Speightowns Kid (USA)**[7] 842 5-9-6 **69**........................ J-PGuillambert 9 73
(Jo Hughes) *chsd ldrs: pushed along 1/2-way: styd on* **12/1**
0413 **6** *1 ¾* **Methaaly (IRE)**[20] 688 10-8-6 **64**........................(be) JordanNason(7) 4 62
(Michael Mullineaux) *s.i.s: rdn over 1f out: r.o ins fnl f: nvr nrr* **16/1**
2111 **7** *shd* **Danziger (IRE)**[7] 842 4-9-9 **72** 6ex........................ ShaneKelly 2 70
(David Evans) *prom: rdn over 1f out: styd on same pce fnl f* **4/1**[1]
0-33 **8** *3 ¼* **Wicked Wench**[11] 795 4-9-0 **70**........................ GaryPhillips(7) 6 56
(Jeremy Gask) *prom: rdn over 1f out: wknd fnl f* **13/2**[2]
-002 **9** *7* **Courageous (IRE)**[16] 719 7-9-0 **70**........................(t) RobertTart(7) 3 31
(Milton Bradley) *w ldr tl pushed along 3f out: rdn and wknd over 1f out* **4/1**[1]

1m 2.2s (-0.10) **Going Correction** +0.10s/f (Slow) **9** Ran SP% **122.8**
Speed ratings (Par 103): **104,103,102,102,101 99,98,93,82**
toteswingers 1&2 £4.80, 1&3 £8.80, 2&3 £4.70 CSF £21.05 CT £141.73 TOTE £6.20: £1.50, £2.70, £4.00; EX 41.80 Trifecta £205.40 Pool: £2,142.37 - 7.82 winning units.
Owner J W Parry **Bred** Old Mill Stud & S Williams & J Parry **Trained** Newmarket, Suffolk

FOCUS
A fair sprint handicap, and straightforward form.

925 THE BLACK COUNTRY'S ONLY RACECOURSE MEDIAN AUCTION MAIDEN STKS 1m 4f 50y(P)
6:40 (6:40) (Class 6) 3-5-Y-O **£1,940** (£577; £288; £144) **Stalls** Low

Form RPR
1 **Akdam (IRE)**[28] 568 3-8-5 68........................ LukeMorris 7 68
(Tony Carroll) *hld up: hdwy over 4f out: rdn and hung lft over 1f out: styd on u.p to ld wl ins fnl f* **5/2**[1]
225 **2** *hd* **Story Writer**[23] 637 4-9-12 67........................ ShaneKelly 4 70
(William Knight) *hld up: hdwy over 7f out: led over 1f out: rdn and hdd wl ins fnl f* **5/2**[1]
4 **3** *¾* **Pereira**[28] 564 3-8-0 0........................ NickyMackay 8 61
(David Simcock) *hld up: hdwy over 1f out: rdn ins fnl f: r.o* **10/1**
4 **4** *3 ¾* **Sian Gwalia** 3-8-0 0........................ MartinLane 5 55
(David Simcock) *hld up: hdwy over 2f out: no ex ins fnl f* **9/2**[3]
5 **5** *7* **Bit Windy** 4-9-3 0 ow3........................ JoshCrane(7) 3 50
(Chris Dwyer) *set stdy pce tl hdd over 7f out: remained handy: rdn whn n.m.r over 2f out: wknd over 1f out* **40/1**
53 **6** *nse* **Lacey**[32] 521 4-9-12 0........................ GrahamGibbons 2 52
(Reg Hollinshead) *chsd ldrs: led over 7f out: rdn and hdd over 1f out: wknd fnl f* **15/2**
2 **7** *½* **Lignum Vitae**[28] 564 3-8-5 0........................ PatrickMathers 9 48
(Richard Fahey) *plld hrd: trckd ldr tl over 7f out: remained handy: rdn and ev ch over 2f out: hmpd and wknd over 1f out* **4/1**[2]
450 **8** *2 ¾* **Ice Tres**[22] 651 4-9-7 0........................ DavidProbert 6 42
(Rod Millman) *prom: rdn over 2f out: wknd over 1f out* **16/1**
005- **9** *31* **Brundon**[265] 3142 4-9-4 57........................(p) MarkCoumbe(3) 1
(Ken Wingrove) *hld up: a in rr: bhd fnl 4f: t.o* **100/1**

2m 42.36s (1.26) **Going Correction** +0.10s/f (Slow)
WFA 3 from 4yo 23lb **9** Ran SP% **125.5**
Speed ratings (Par 101): **99,98,98,95,91 91,90,89,68**
toteswingers 1&2 £3.00, 1&3 £9.60, 2&3 £5.40 CSF £9.59 TOTE £5.70: £1.80, £2.90, £1.10; EX 13.90 Trifecta £74.60 Pool: £1,457.14 - 14.64 winning units.
Owner Stephen Louch **Bred** His Highness The Aga Khan's Studs S C **Trained** Cropthorne, Worcs

FOCUS
A modest maiden with a few arriving with minor form. The runner-up helps to set the level.

926 WOLVERHAMPTON-RACECOURSE.CO.UK H'CAP 1m 4f 50y(P)
7:10 (7:10) (Class 2) (0-100,91) 4-Y-O+ **£11,971** (£3,583; £1,791; £896; £446) **Stalls** Low

Form RPR
54-2 **1** **Hanoverian Baron**[55] 189 8-9-1 **85**........................ SebSanders 7 93
(Tony Newcombe) *hld up: hrd rdn: hung lft and hdwy over 1f out: styd on u.p to ld wl ins fnl f* **9/2**
1-31 **2** *¾* **Flying Power**[28] 563 5-9-5 **89**........................ PaddyAspell 3 96
(John Norton) *chsd ldrs: hmpd over 1f out: led sn after: rdn and hdd wl ins fnl f* **7/2**[2]
110- **3** *½* **The Tiger**[53] 7689 5-9-7 **91**........................ GrahamLee 8 97
(Ed Dunlop) *a.p: racd keenly: rdn over 1f out: r.o* **6/1**
051- **4** *1 ¾* **Lexington Bay (IRE)**[18] 7034 5-8-10 **80**........................(p) TonyHamilton 2 83
(Richard Fahey) *chsd ldrs: pushed along over 6f out: rdn over 3f out: styd on* **14/1**
1-12 **5** *½* **Saoi (USA)**[20] 691 6-9-3 **87**........................ JimCrowley 6 90
(William Knight) *hld up: hdwy over 1f out: sn rdn: styd on same pce ins fnl f* **4/1**[3]
1 **6** *1* **Wyborne**[32] 521 4-8-13 **85**........................ LukeMorris 1 86
(Brian Ellison) *led: rdn: hung lft and hdd over 1f out: no ex ins fnl f* **9/1**
450- **7** *¾* **Assizes**[153] 6875 4-9-0 **86**........................ JoeFanning 5 86
(Mark Johnston) *prom: chsd ldr over 7f out: rdn over 1f out: wknd ins fnl f* **3/1**[1]

2m 39.05s (-2.05) **Going Correction** +0.10s/f (Slow)
WFA 4 from 5yo+ 2lb **7** Ran SP% **116.4**
Speed ratings (Par 109): **110,109,109,108,107 107,106**
toteswingers 1&2 £3.80, 1&3 £10.30, 2&3 £4.80 CSF £21.26 CT £95.39 TOTE £5.20: £2.80, £1.10; EX 26.70 Trifecta £101.20 Pool: £1,727.40 - 12.79 winning units.
Owner Paul Moulton **Bred** S Coughlan **Trained** Yarnscombe, Devon

FOCUS
The feature on the card was a £19,000 handicap that attracted an excellent field. A slightly positive view has been taken of the form.

927 SPONSOR A RACE BY CALLING 01902 390000 H'CAP 1m 141y(P)
7:40 (7:40) (Class 7) (0-50,53) 4-Y-O+ **£1,940** (£577; £288; £144) **Stalls** Low

Form RPR
6402 **1** **Crucis Abbey (IRE)**[2] 900 5-9-2 **45**........................(p) EddieAhern 3 54
(Mark Brisbourne) *chsd ldrs: nt clr run over 1f out: led ins fnl f: edgd rt: rdn out* **9/2**[2]
5540 **2** *nk* **Lord Paget**[42] 381 4-9-0 **48**........................(p) JackDuern(5) 5 56
(Reg Hollinshead) *prom: lost pl over 6f out: hdwy over 1f out: ev ch ins fnl f: r.o* **25/1**
0530 **3** *1 ¾* **Justcallmehandsome**[15] 737 11-8-13 **47**........................(be) AmyScott(5) 8 51
(Dominic Ffrench Davis) *hld up: rdn over 1f out: r.o ins fnl f: nt rch ldrs* **20/1**
-330 **4** *¾* **Monsieur Pontaven**[28] 565 6-9-2 **45**........................(b) J-PGuillambert 13 48
(Robin Bastiman) *mid-div: hdwy over 5f out: rdn over 3f out: led over 1f out: hdd and unable qck ins fnl f* **14/1**
-300 **5** *¾* **Maz**[14] 747 5-9-0 **50**........................ RobertTart(7) 10 52
(Alan Bailey) *hld up: hdwy over 1f out: nt clr run ins fnl f: r.o* **8/1**[3]
-050 **6** *nse* **Count Ceprano (IRE)**[18] 709 9-9-4 **50**........................ SimonPearce(3) 4 51
(Lydia Pearce) *hld up: pushed along over 3f out: hdwy over 2f out: nt clr run and lost pl over 1f out: rallied ins fnl f: nvr able to chal* **20/1**
0500 **7** *½* **Dubai Emerald (USA)**[8] 820 4-9-3 **46**........................ FrannyNorton 1 46
(Chris Dwyer) *led: rdn and hdd over 1f out: edgd lft: no ex ins fnl f* **25/1**
/0-1 **8** *nk* **Petrol**[7] 852 4-9-10 **53** 6ex........................ DanielTudhope 11 53
(David O'Meara) *chsd ldrs: pushed along over 3f out: nt clr run over 2f out: sn rdn: no ex ins fnl f* **4/6**[1]
0-20 **9** *½* **Seawood**[36] 455 7-8-10 **46**........................(p) PhilipPrince(7) 6 44
(Roy Bowring) *chsd ldr: chal over 2f out: rdn over 1f out: wknd towards fin* **10/1**
/00- **10** *8* **Marina Ballerina**[301] 2048 5-9-3 **49**........................(b[1]) MarkCoumbe(3) 7 31
(Roy Bowring) *hld up: rdn and wknd over 2f out* **50/1**

1m 51.44s (0.94) **Going Correction** +0.10s/f (Slow) **10** Ran SP% **124.2**
Speed ratings (Par 97): **99,98,97,96,95 95,95,95,94,87**
toteswingers 1&2 £18.40, 1&3 £12.80, 2&3 £12.30 CSF £117.72 CT £2131.05 TOTE £12.50: £2.00, £6.40, £2.60; EX 139.30 Trifecta £1059.50 Pool: £1,525.09 - 1.07 winning units.
Owner Mark Brisbourne **Bred** M G Daly **Trained** Great Ness, Shropshire

FOCUS
Track GallopMastered after race 4. Given the grade, this was a fair contest. The winner travelled well and will be of interest in the short term.

928 DOWNLOAD OUR IPHONE APP H'CAP 2m 119y(P)
8:10 (8:10) (Class 5) (0-75,74) 4-Y-O+ **£2,587** (£770; £384; £192) **Stalls** Low

Form RPR
-541 **1** **Jezza**[21] 671 7-9-1 **63**........................ LukeMorris 1 70
(Karen George) *s.i.s: sn prom: chsd ldr 1/2-way: led over 1f out: rdn and hung lft ins fnl f: styd on* **3/1**[2]
0/0 **2** *nk* **Capellanus (IRE)**[28] 563 7-9-9 **71**........................ GrahamLee 5 79
(Brian Ellison) *hld up: hdwy 2f out: cl up whn hmpd ins fnl f: sn rdn: r.o* **7/2**[3]
620- **3** *½* **Russian George (IRE)**[315] 1640 7-9-12 **74**........................ JimCrowley 2 80
(Steve Gollings) *chsd ldr to 1/2-way: remained handy: rdn over 1f out: styd on* **4/1**
0-22 **4** *1 ½* **Broughtons Bandit**[23] 635 6-8-10 **58**........................ J-PGuillambert 3 62
(Willie Musson) *led at stdy pce tl pushed along over 3f out: hdd over 1f out: hmpd and no ex ins fnl f* **2/1**[1]
6-63 **5** *2 ½* **Brunston**[27] 592 7-9-10 **72**........................(t) ChrisCatlin 4 73
(Anthony Middleton) *hld up: rdn over 1f out: nvr on terms* **13/2**

3m 48.84s (7.04) **Going Correction** +0.10s/f (Slow) **5** Ran SP% **113.9**
Speed ratings (Par 103): **87,86,86,85,84**
CSF £14.10 TOTE £3.00: £1.20, £3.00; EX 18.40 Trifecta £34.00 Pool: £762.54 - 16.80 winning units.
Owner Kilcash Bloodstock Limited **Bred** C P Ranson **Trained** Higher Eastington, Devon

FOCUS
An average staying handicap in which the winner had the run of things. Not form to take too literally.

929 LIKE US ON FACEBOOK WOLVERHAMPTON RACECOURSE H'CAP 1m 4f 50y(P)
8:40 (8:40) (Class 6) (0-65,72) 4-Y-O+ **£1,940** (£577; £288; £144) **Stalls** Low

Form RPR
6222 **1** **Activate**[9] 816 6-9-7 **64**........................(p) JoeFanning 1 73+
(Keith Dalgleish) *chsd ldrs: pushed along over 2f out: rdn to ld wl ins fnl f: r.o* **5/4**[1]
6004 **2** *1 ½* **Mazij**[9] 816 5-9-3 **60**........................ WilliamCarson 4 66
(Peter Hiatt) *chsd ldr tl pushed along to ld over 1f out: rdn and hdd wl ins fnl f* **8/1**
0-63 **3** *nk* **Bernisdale**[21] 675 5-9-3 **60**........................ LukeMorris 3 65
(John Flint) *led at stdy pce tl qcknd over 2f out: rdn and hdd over 1f out: styd on same pce ins fnl f* **7/1**[3]
-500 **4** *shd* **Lady of Burgundy**[16] 724 7-9-1 **58**........................ DavidProbert 7 63
(Mark Usher) *s.i.s: hld up: hdwy over 1f out: sn rdn: r.o* **9/1**
000- **5** *1 ¾* **Vergrigio (IRE)**[147] 7015 4-8-10 **55**........................(b) ChrisCatlin 5 58
(David Pipe) *s.i.s: sn pushed along to chse ldrs: rdn over 2f out: styd on same pce fr over 1f out* **9/4**[2]
-556 **6** *nk* **Yeomanoftheguard**[18] 709 4-9-3 **62**........................ TonyHamilton 6 64
(Richard Fahey) *hld up: racd keenly: rdn over 1f out: nvr trbld ldrs* **8/1**

2m 43.5s (2.40) **Going Correction** +0.10s/f (Slow)
WFA 4 from 5yo+ 2lb **6** Ran SP% **119.9**
Speed ratings (Par 101): **96,95,94,94,93 93**
CSF £13.43 TOTE £3.40: £1.10, £1.40; EX 14.70 Trifecta £25.00 Pool: £1,102.96 - 33.03 winning units.
Owner Straightline Construction Ltd **Bred** Card Bloodstock **Trained** Carluke, S Lanarks

FOCUS
Ordinary form. The winner was very well in on his old form and should go well when reassessed.
T/Plt: £139.90 to a £1 stake. Pool: £82,387.33 - 429.69 winning units T/Qpdt: £36.80 to a £1 stake. Pool: £8,058.00 - 161.64 winning units CR

930 - 943a (Foreign Racing) - See Raceform Interactive

923 WOLVERHAMPTON (A.W) (L-H)

Saturday, March 9

OFFICIAL GOING: Standard

Wind: Light against Weather: Light rain

944 WILLIAMHILL.COM E B F LADY WULFRUNA STKS (LISTED RACE) 7f 32y(P)

2:20 (2:21) (Class 1) 4-Y-0+

£25,519 (£9,675; £4,842; £2,412; £1,210; £607) **Stalls** High

Form RPR

1-31 **1** **Solar Deity (IRE)**21 690 4-9-3 95 MartinHarley 7 102+
(Marco Botti) *a.p: rdn to chse ldr 1f out: r.o u.p to ld post* 7/41

-643 **2** *shd* **Kenny Powers**9 838 4-9-3 105 (vt) HayleyTurner 6 101
(Tom Dascombe) *chsd ldr tl led over 4f out: rdn and hung lft ins fnl f: hdd post* 9/42

1500 **3** *2* **Verse Of Love**21 690 4-9-3 86 RichardHughes 2 96
(David Evans) *led: hdd over 4f out: chsd ldr tl over 2f out: sn rdn: styd on same pce ins fnl f* 18/1

00-0 **4** *3/4* **Monsieur Chevalier (IRE)**21 690 6-9-3 96 TomMcLaughlin 10 94+
(P J O'Gorman) *hld up: hdwy over 1f out: r.o: nt rch ldrs* 22/1

-261 **5** *1/2* **Docofthebay (IRE)**25 621 9-9-3 87 (b) TomQueally 4 93
(Scott Dixon) *s.i.s: sn mid-div: hdwy over 1f out: styd on: nt rch ldrs* 25/1

2311 **6** *1/2* **Light From Mars**24 629 8-9-3 86 LukeMorris 3 91
(Ronald Harris) *prom: chsd ldr over 2f out: rdn over 1f out: no ex ins fnl f* 12/1

010- **7** *1 1/4* **Regal Parade**123 7624 9-9-3 108 (t) GrahamLee 9 88
(Milton Bradley) *hld up: rdn over 1f out: nvr nrr* 6/13

0-36 **8** *3/4* **Capone (IRE)**14 776 8-9-3 98 ShaneKelly 1 86
(Garry Moss) *prom: nt clr run over 2f out: rdn over 1f out: wknd fnl f* 20/1

-361 **9** *1 3/4* **Kickingthelilly**7 865 4-8-12 82 ChrisCatlin 8 76
(Rae Guest) *s.i.s: outpcd* 25/1

000- **10** *4 1/2* **King Of Eden (IRE)**140 7240 7-9-3 86 GrahamGibbons 5 69
(Eric Alston) *mid-div: pushed along 1/2-way: wknd over 2f out* 66/1

1m 27.64s (-1.96) **Going Correction** -0.025s/f (Stan) 10 Ran SP% **112.7**
Speed ratings (Par 111): **110,109,107,106,106 105,104,103,101,96**
toteswingers 1&2 £1.10, 1&3 £12.80, 2&3 £7.80 CSF £4.97 TOTE £2.80: £1.50, £1.10, £4.90; EX 6.20 Trifecta £59.90 Pool: £1,354.06 - 16.92 winning units..
Owner G Manfredini & A Tinkler **Bred** Castlemartin Stud And Skymarc Farm **Trained** Newmarket, Suffolk

FOCUS

Track GallopMastered after race 4. A decent-quality Listed race and a thrilling finish between the two market leaders. The third is the key to the form.

945 WILLIAM HILL LINCOLN TRIAL H'CAP 1m 141y(P)

2:55 (2:56) (Class 2) (0-105,97) 4-Y-0+

£28,012 (£8,388; £4,194; £2,097; £1,048; £526) **Stalls** Low

Form RPR

63-2 **1** **Strictly Silver (IRE)**42 401 4-8-12 92 RobertTart(7) 6 104+
(Alan Bailey) *s.i.s: sn prom: rdn to ld and edgd lft ins fnl f: r.o* 4/12

11-2 **2** *1/2* **Guest Of Honour (IRE)**12 792 4-9-4 91 AndreaAtzeni 8 102+
(Marco Botti) *chsd ldrs: led over 1f out: rdn: hung lft and hdd ins fnl f: r.o* 7/21

-223 **3** *2 1/4* **Chapter And Verse (IRE)**42 407 7-9-3 90 EddieAhern 11 96
(Mike Murphy) *s.i.s: hld up: hdwy over 1f out: hung lft ins fnl f: r.o* 25/1

-424 **4** *nk* **Mia's Boy**21 690 9-9-7 94 GeorgeBaker 7 100
(Chris Dwyer) *hld up: hdwy over 1f out: sn rdn: r.o* 17/2

0-02 **5** *shd* **Nazreef**25 621 6-9-10 97 (vt) JoeFanning 1 102
(Hughie Morrison) *chsd ldrs: rdn and ev ch over 1f out: styd on same pce ins fnl f* 12/1

400- **6** *1 1/2* **Global Village (IRE)**154 6868 8-9-7 94 DanielTudhope 10 96+
(Brian Ellison) *hld up: rdn over 1f out: hung lft and nt clr run ins fnl f: nt rch ldrs* 33/1

1-13 **7** *3/4* **Alfred Hutchinson**21 690 5-9-1 93 WilliamTwiston-Davies(5) 4 94
(Geoffrey Oldroyd) *prom: chsd ldr over 6f out: rdn and ev ch over 1f out: hung lft and no ex ins fnl f* 13/23

110- **8** *3/4* **Laffan (IRE)**262 3265 4-9-3 90 1 AmyRyan 3 89
(Kevin Ryan) *led: rdn and hdd over 1f out: wknd ins fnl f* 12/1

3312 **9** *nse* **Loyalty**7 865 6-8-12 92 (v) AdamMcLean(7) 9 91
(Derek Shaw) *mid-div: effrt over 1f out: no ex fnl f* 14/1

620- **10** *2 1/4* **Come On Blue Chip (IRE)**101 7904 4-8-12 90 (b) MichaelJMMurphy(5) 2 84
(Paul D'Arcy) *s.i.s: hld up: hdwy over 1f out: wknd ins fnl f* 8/1

442- **11** *12* **Pilgrims Rest (IRE)**171 6376 4-9-2 89 RichardHughes 12 58
(Richard Hannon) *prom: rdn 2f out: wknd over 1f out: eased* 9/1

000- **12** *1/2* **Memory Cloth**182 6024 6-9-10 97 DaleSwift 5 65
(Brian Ellison) *hung rt almost thrght: chsd ldr 2f: remained handy: rdn 1/2-way: wknd over 2f out* 40/1

1m 47.8s (-2.70) **Going Correction** -0.025s/f (Stan) 12 Ran SP% **118.5**
Speed ratings (Par 109): **111,110,108,108,108 106,106,105,105,103 92,92**
toteswingers 1&2 £9.40, 1&3 £56.10, 2&3 £37.20 CSF £18.03 CT £317.67 TOTE £4.40: £1.90, £1.40, £7.90; EX 17.70 Trifecta £654.50 Pool: £63,695.55 - 72.98 winning units..
Owner A J H **Bred** Langton Stud **Trained** Newmarket, Suffolk

FOCUS

A typically competitive renewal of the Lincoln Trial, run at a decent pace, and it produced another thrilling finish. Solid form, with two improvers dominating.

946 WILLIAM HILL - DOWNLOAD THE APP CLASSIFIED CLAIMING STKS 5f 20y(P)

3:30 (3:32) (Class 5) 4-Y-0+ **£2,587** (£770; £384; £192) **Stalls** Low

Form RPR

1011 **1** **Where's Reiley (USA)**7 861 7-8-8 70 (v) GrahamGibbons 6 73
(Michael Attwater) *chsd ldr: pushed along 1/2-way: r.o u.p to ld nr fin* 5/22

00-2 **2** *3/4* **Spic 'n Span**7 861 8-8-4 57 (b) LukeMorris 3 66
(Ronald Harris) *led: shkn up over 1f out: rdn and hdd nr fin* 9/1

2451 **3** *2 3/4* **Dark Lane**2 916 7-8-2 63 MartinLane 4 54
(David Evans) *hld up: hdwy and nt clr run over 1f out: nt rch ldrs* 3/13

6402 **4** *1 1/4* **Master Of Disguise**15 760 7-8-2 64 WilliamCarson 7 50
(Brian Baugh) *prom: pushed along 1/2-way: styd on same pce fr over 1f out* 9/41

5660 **5** *1 1/2* **Perlachy**15 760 9-7-13 57 (v) GaryPhillips(7) 1 49
(Ronald Harris) *chsd ldrs: pushed along 1/2-way: no ex fnl f* 20/1

030- **6** *nk* **Falasteen (IRE)**137 7309 6-8-5 70 RobertTart(7) 5 53
(Milton Bradley) *s.i.s: rdn over 1f out: nvr on terms* 7/1

00-4 **7** *1/2* **Sally's Swansong**58 142 7-8-2 53 (b) DavidProbert 2 42
(Eric Alston) *prom: rdn 1/2-way: wknd over 1f out* 20/1

1m 1.51s (-0.79) **Going Correction** -0.025s/f (Stan) 7 Ran SP% **116.4**
Speed ratings (Par 103): **105,103,99,97,95 94,93**
toteswingers 1&2 £4.70, 1&3 £1.10, 2&3 £4.30 CSF £25.64 TOTE £2.40: £1.30, £4.90; EX 8.10 Trifecta £26.50 Pool: £1,080.59 - 30.57 winning units..
Owner J M Duggan & T P Duggan **Bred** Overbrook Farm **Trained** Epsom, Surrey

FOCUS

A modest claimer and few got into it. The winner is in great form and the second is the key.

947 WILLIAM HILL - IN THE APP STORE H'CAP 5f 216y(P)

4:05 (4:09) (Class 2) (0-100,97) 4-Y-0+

£11,827 (£3,541; £1,770; £885; £442; £222) **Stalls** Low

Form RPR

-111 **1** **Tarooq (USA)**28 584 7-9-6 96 (t) SeanLevey 1 106
(Stuart Williams) *hld up in tch: shkn up over 1f out: n.m.r ins fnl f: rdn to ld nr fin* 11/41

121- **2** *hd* **Intransigent**166 6536 4-9-2 97 ThomasBrown(5) 7 106
(Andrew Balding) *a.p: rdn to ld and edgd lft wl ins fnl f: hdd nr fin* 10/32

5521 **3** *1 1/2* **Al's Memory (IRE)**8 844 4-8-8 84 RichardHughes 4 89
(David Evans) *led: rdn over 1f out: hdd and unable qck wl ins fnl f* 17/2

006- **4** *1/2* **Dubai Dynamo**178 6135 8-9-0 90 PJMcDonald 11 93
(Ruth Carr) *s.i.s: hld up: shkn up and hung lft ins fnl f: fin wl* 25/1

026- **5** *3/4* **Harrison George (IRE)**115 7704 8-8-4 87 (t) RobertTart(7) 8 88
(P J O'Gorman) *w ldr: rdn and ev ch over 1f out: no ex ins fnl f* 11/23

044- **6** *1* **Frog Hollow**186 5914 4-8-12 88 GrahamLee 12 86+
(Milton Bradley) *hld up: edgd lft and r.o ins fnl f: nvr nrr* 25/1

1233 **7** *3/4* **Profile Star (IRE)**28 584 4-8-11 87 GrahamGibbons 10 83
(David Barron) *chsd ldrs: rdn over 2f out: no ex ins fnl f* 17/2

044- **8** *shd* **Barnet Fair**128 7503 5-9-2 92 KierenFox 6 87
(Richard Guest) *hld up: rdn over 1f out: nvr on terms* 10/1

230- **9** *2* **Capaill Liath (IRE)**131 7435 5-9-2 92 PhillipMakin 2 86+
(Kevin Ryan) *hld up: effrt over 1f out: hung lft and no ex ins fnl f* 25/1

0-14 **10** *4 1/2* **Seek The Fair Land**42 405 7-8-12 88 (b) WilliamCarson 3 64
(Jim Boyle) *s.i.s: hld up: rdn over 1f out: a in rr* 16/1

606- **11** *2 1/2* **Jarrow (IRE)**148 7019 6-8-12 88 JoeFanning 5 56
(Milton Bradley) *chsd ldrs: rdn over 2f out: wknd over 1f out* 10/1

1m 13.51s (-1.49) **Going Correction** -0.025s/f (Stan) 11 Ran SP% **121.8**
Speed ratings (Par 109): **108,107,105,105,104 102,101,101,98,92 89**
toteswingers 1&2 £2.10, 1&3 £5.20, 2&3 £9.50 CSF £11.93 CT £67.93 TOTE £3.30: £1.50, £1.40, £2.10; EX 13.20 Trifecta £35.40 Pool: £1,620.71 - 34.26 winning units..
Owner H Chamberlain, I Pearce **Bred** Kirsten Rausing **Trained** Newmarket, Suffolk

FOCUS

A hot sprint handicap and it produced yet another thrilling finish. The winner is in the form of his life.

948 WILLIAM HILL - NO1 DOWNLOADED BETTING APP H'CAP 1m 5f 194y(P)

4:40 (4:40) (Class 4) (0-85,84) 4-Y-0+ **£4,690** (£1,395; £697; £348) **Stalls** Low

Form RPR

-443 **1** **Admirable Duque (IRE)**3 905 7-8-9 67 (be) MartinLane 7 74
(Dominic Ffrench Davis) *s.i.s: hld up: hdwy 8f out: rdn to ld ins fnl f: styd on* 15/2

012- **2** *3/4* **Porgy**134 5211 8-9-12 84 (b) GrahamLee 5 90
(Brian Ellison) *hld up: hdwy over 2f out: r.o to go 2nd nr fin: nt rch wnr* 4/13

1111 **3** *dht* **Broxbourne (IRE)**11 809 4-9-2 78 JoeFanning 1 84
(Mark Johnston) *chsd ldr tl shkn up over 1f out: nt clr run ins fnl f: styd on: fin dead-heat 3rd: awrdd outrt 3rd* 15/81

256- **4** *3/4* **Bathwick Street**203 5366 4-8-6 68 LukeMorris 2 73
(David Evans) *led: rdn over 1f out: hung rt and hdd ins fnl f: styd on same pce: fin dead-heat 3rd: disq & plcd 4th* 5/1

-422 **5** *4 1/2* **Tingo In The Tale (IRE)**29 562 4-8-11 73 HayleyTurner 4 71
(David Arbuthnot) *prom: rdn over 1f out: hung rt and no ex ins fnl f* 11/42

540- **6** *12* **Natural High (IRE)**133 6191 8-9-6 78 (t) WilliamCarson 6 59
(Sean Curran) *chsd ldrs: rdn over 5f out: wknd over 1f out* 33/1

00-0 **7** *25* **Grandiloquent**21 691 4-9-1 80 PatrickHills(3) 3 25
(James Given) *prom: lost pl 8f out: hdwy over 5f out: rdn and wknd over 2f out: t.o* 12/1

3m 4.6s (-1.40) **Going Correction** -0.025s/f (Stan)
WFA 4 from 7yo+ 4lb 7 Ran SP% **120.5**
Speed ratings (Par 105): **103,102,102,102,99 92,78**
toteswingers 1&2 £6.10, 1&3 £2.30, 2&3 £1.40 CSF £39.88 TOTE £6.10: £3.20, £3.60; EX 31.30 Trifecta £122.50 Pool: £1,401.13 - 8.57 winning units..
Owner Mrs J E Taylor **Bred** Airlie Stud And R N Clay **Trained** Lambourn, Berks

■ Stewards' Enquiry : Luke Morris caution; careless riding.

FOCUS

Track GallopMastered after race 4. A fair staying handicap, but the early pace was modest so not the test of stamina it might have been. Straightforward form.

949 WILLIAM HILL - DOWNLOAD THE APP H'CAP 7f 32y(P)

5:15 (5:16) (Class 4) (0-85,77) 3-Y-0 **£4,690** (£1,395; £697; £348) **Stalls** High

Form RPR

54-1 **1** **Newstead Abbey**29 561 3-9-6 76 GrahamGibbons 3 89+
(David Barron) *chsd ldrs: led 1f out: sn rdn clr* 4/13

34-1 **2** *3 1/4* **Skytrain**8 843 3-8-12 68 JoeFanning 6 72
(Mark Johnston) *chsd ldr tl led over 1f out: sn rdn and hdd: outpcd ins fnl f* 15/81

2115 **3** *nk* **Sewn Up**19 710 3-9-1 71 (tp) ShaneKelly 2 74
(Reg Hollinshead) *chsd ldrs: rdn over 1f out: styd on same pce ins fnl f* 12/1

6121 **4** *nk* **Run It Twice (IRE)**26 615 3-8-11 72 (b) ThomasBrown(5) 4 74
(David Evans) *s.i.s: hld up: nt clr run fr over 1f out tl wl ins fnl f: r.o: nvr able to chal* 8/1

1462 **5** *1/2* **Gabrial The Boss (USA)**8 843 3-9-5 75 (t) AndreaAtzeni 5 76
(David Simcock) *hld up: rdn over 1f out: styd on: nt trble ldrs* 8/1

231- **6** *3/4* **Coincidently**143 7160 3-9-7 77 RichardHughes 1 76
(Alan Bailey) *led: shkn up and hdd over 1f out: wknd ins fnl f* 11/42

1m 28.92s (-0.68) **Going Correction** -0.025s/f (Stan) 6 Ran SP% **111.4**
Speed ratings (Par 100): **102,98,97,97,97 96**
toteswingers 1&2 £2.40, 1&3 £6.70, 2&3 £6.60 CSF £11.76 TOTE £5.30: £4.40, £1.20; EX 15.80 Trifecta £96.00 Pool: £1,321.19 - 10.31 winning units..
Owner Let's Be Lucky Partnership **Bred** Grasshopper 2000 Ltd **Trained** Maunby, N Yorks

FOCUS
A small field, but some in-form 3yos lined up for this fair handicap. The early pace was good, but had slowed by the time the field reached the crown of the home bend where the field became compacted. The winner is starting to fulfil his early 2yo promise.

950 WILLIAM HILL - IPAD APP NOW AVAILABLE MAIDEN STKS 1m 141y(P)
5:45 (5:46) (Class 5) 3-Y-0+ £2,587 (£770; £384; £192) Stalls Low

Form				RPR
423-	1		**Bishop's Castle (USA)**[145] 7112 4-10-0 75 GrahamLee 4 (Brian Ellison) *chsd ldrs: shkn up to ld ins fnl f: comf* **1/2**[1]	80+
0	2	1	**Speed Boogie**[10] 814 3-8-8 0 AndreaAtzeni 6 (Marco Botti) *chsd ldr: rdn and hung rt over 1f out: styd on* **11/1**	69+
33-3	3	3/4	**Rawaafed (IRE)**[12] 797 4-10-0 72 (v[1]) RichardHughes 1 (Keith Dalgleish) *led: rdn over 1f out: hdd and unable qck ins fnl f* **9/2**[2]	73
0-0	4	1 1/2	**World Map (IRE)**[11] 807 3-8-3 0 JoeFanning 3 (Mark Johnston) *hld up: pushed along over 2f out: styd on fr over 1f out: nt trble ldrs* **16/1**	59+
50-	5	1/2	**Argaki (IRE)**[157] 6795 3-8-8 0 TomEaves 2 (Keith Dalgleish) *chsd ldrs: rdn and hung lft over 1f out: styd on same pce* **8/1**[3]	63+
65/	6	10	**Nonaynever**[479] 7440 5-10-0 0 JamesSullivan 7 (Ruth Carr) *s.i.s: hld up: shkn up over 1f out: sn wknd and eased* **50/1**	48
-54	7	6	**Silver Panther**[13] 51 5-9-11 0 MarkCoumbe(3) 5 (Aytach Sadik) *s.i.s: sn pushed along in rr: rdn and wknd over 2f out* **250/1**	36

1m 52.11s (1.61) **Going Correction** -0.025s/f (Stan)
WFA 3 from 4yo+ 20lb **7** Ran SP% **112.5**
Speed ratings (Par 103): **91,90,89,88,87 78,73**
toteswingers 1&2 £1.90, 2&3 £4.30, 1&3 £1.10 CSF £7.22 TOTE £1.40: £1.40, £5.80; EX 7.30 Trifecta £30.80 Pool: £2,661.49 - 64.75 winning units..
Owner Koo's Racing Club & Lee Keys **Bred** Darley **Trained** Norton, N Yorks
FOCUS
An uncompetitive maiden, lacking strength in depth, and run in a slow time. A mixture of abilities was on show, and the winner was well on top.
T/Plt: £67.00 to a £1 stake. Pool: £81,435.99 - 886.83 winning tickets T/Qpdt: £27.00 to a £1 stake. Pool: £3,776.97 - 103.45 winning tickets CR

951 - 952a (Foreign Racing) - See Raceform Interactive

868

MEYDAN (L-H)
Saturday, March 9

OFFICIAL GOING: Tapeta: standard; turf: good

953a AL BASTAKIYA SPONSORED BY EMIRATES SKYWARDS (LISTED RACE) (TAPETA) 1m 1f 110y
1:05 (1:05) 3-Y-0
£92,024 (£30,674; £15,337; £7,668; £4,601; £3,067)

			RPR
1		**Secret Number**[136] 7323 3-8-8 95 KierenFallon 11 (Saeed bin Suroor) *s.i.s: settled in rr: chsd ldr 3f out: rdn to ld fnl 100yds* **4/1**[2]	105
2	2	**Zahee (NZ)**[23] 658 4-9-4 100 ChristopheSoumillon 2 (M F De Kock, South Africa) *trckd ldrs: smooth prog to ld 2f out: hdd 100yds out: no ex* **5/1**[3]	104
3	1 3/4	**Snowboarder (USA)**[23] 658 3-8-8 101 MickaelBarzalona 4 (Mahmood Al Zarooni) *mid-div: n.m.r after 3f: r.o fnl 1 1/2f: nrst fin* **11/4**[1]	97
4	1/4	**Elleval (IRE)**[9] 835 3-8-8 102 FergalLynch 10 (David Marnane, Ire) *mid-div: n.m.r after 3f: dropped to rr: r.o fnl 1 1/2f: nrst fin* **12/1**	97+
5	2 1/4	**Emotif (ARG)**[9] 837 4-9-0 98 ADelpech 3 (M F De Kock, South Africa) *sn led: hdd 2f out: kpt on same pce* **14/1**	91
6	3/4	**I'm Back (IRE)**[30] 553 3-8-8 96 (t) SilvestreDeSousa 1 (Saeed bin Suroor) *trckd ldrs: ev ch 2f out: nt qckn fnl f* **5/1**[3]	91
7	8 1/2	**Deauville Prince (FR)**[9] 835 3-8-8 105 RichardKingscote 5 (Tom Dascombe) *trckd ldng trio tl outpcd 2f out* **7/1**	73
8	1 3/4	**Tarbawi (IRE)**[9] 835 3-8-8 102 (p) WayneSmith 9 (M bin Shafya, UAE) *nvr bttr than mid-div* **25/1**	70
9	2 3/4	**Darkening (IRE)**[9] 835 3-8-8 89 TadhgO'Shea 8 (Ismail Mohammed) *slowly away: a in rr* **100/1**	64
10	dist	**Stasio (USA)**[30] 553 3-8-8 90 WilliamBuick 6 (David Simcock) *a in rr* **5/1**[3]	

2m 1.35s (2.35)
WFA 3 from 4yo 20lb **10** Ran SP% **128.4**
CSF: 27.26; EX: 26.40; TRIFECTA: 65.50; WIN: 5.20; PLACE: 3.30, 1.70, 1.20..
Owner Godolphin **Bred** Darley **Trained** Newmarket, Suffolk
FOCUS
Rail on turf track sited 8m out from true position. This was a messy race contested mainly by ordinary sorts, but the winner, a latecomer to the UAE Classic scene, can rate significantly higher. The pace was slow and a few of these found trouble. Here are the splits: 28.02 (400m), 25.54 (800m), 24.59 (1200m), 24.16 (1600m).

954a MEYDAN SPRINT SPONSORED BY EMIRATES HOLIDAYS (LISTED RACE) (TURF) 5f
1:40 (1:40) 3-Y-0+
£64,417 (£21,472; £10,736; £5,368; £3,220; £2,147)

			RPR
1		**Shea Shea (SAF)**[37] 464 6-9-4 119 ChristopheSoumillon 14 (M F De Kock, South Africa) *trckd ldrs: rdn 2f out: led 1 1/2f out: easily* **10/3**[1]	122+
2	2 1/2	**Sole Power**[153] 6908 6-9-4 113 JohnnyMurtagh 6 (Edward Lynam, Ire) *mid-div: kpt on fnl 2f but no ch w wnr: nrst fin* **7/2**[2]	111
3	1	**Russian Soul (IRE)**[16] 746 5-9-4 106 (p) RyanMoore 8 (M Halford, Ire) *chsd ldrs: ev ch 1 1/2f out: nt qckn fnl 100yds* **12/1**	107
4	hd	**Russian Rock (IRE)**[1] 940 6-9-4 104 WayneSmith 9 (M Al Muhairi, UAE) *s.i.s: trckd ldrs: ev ch 1 1/2f out: one pce fnl f* **16/1**	107
5	1/4	**Spirit Quartz (IRE)**[153] 6908 5-9-4 115 JamieSpencer 4 (Robert Cowell) *chsd ldrs: ev ch 1 1/2f out: one pce fnl f* **7/1**[3]	106
6	3/4	**Medicean Man**[16] 746 7-9-4 110 (p) HarryBentley 2 (Jeremy Gask) *in rr of mid-div: r.o fnl 2f: nrst fin* **10/1**	103
7	nse	**Seachantach (USA)**[7] 868 7-9-4 102 (bt) MarcMonaghan 10 (S Seemar, UAE) *nvr bttr than mid-div* **40/1**	103
8	nse	**Monsieur Joe (IRE)**[153] 6908 6-9-4 110 WilliamBuick 3 (Robert Cowell) *chsd ldrs: ev ch 1 1/2f out: one pce fnl f* **9/1**	103
9	1/2	**Dandy Boy (ITY)**[112] 7772 7-9-4 111 PatDobbs 1 (David Marnane, Ire) *settled in rr: nvr nr to chal* **12/1**	101
10	shd	**Ballista (IRE)**[7] 868 5-9-4 106 RichardKingscote 11 (Tom Dascombe) *sn led: hdd 1 1/2f out: wknd fnl f* **14/1**	101
11	1	**Invincible Ash (IRE)**[7] 868 8-9-0 104 (p) KierenFallon 13 (M Halford, Ire) *nvr able to chal* **9/1**	93
12	1/4	**Red Dubawi (IRE)**[9] 834 5-9-4 100 PaulHanagan 5 (David Marnane, Ire) *settled in rr: trckd ldrs: ev ch 1 1/2f out: one pce fnl f* **25/1**	96
13	1 3/4	**Secret Asset (IRE)**[7] 868 8-9-4 104 JamesDoyle 7 (Jane Chapple-Hyam) *chsd ldrs tl wknd 1 1/2f out* **33/1**	90
14	2 1/2	**Vocational (USA)**[128] 7503 4-9-0 90 RoystonFfrench 15 (A Al Raihe, UAE) *nvr able to chal* **100/1**	77
15	2	**Silaah**[21] 696 9-9-4 91 (tp) SilvestreDeSousa 12 (M Ramadan, UAE) *trckd ldrs tl outpcd 2f out* **66/1**	74
16	4	**My Special J'S (USA)**[9] 837 3-8-6 105 TadhgO'Shea 16 (John Patrick Shanahan, Ire) *nvr nr to chal* **33/1**	54

57.02s (57.02)
WFA 3 from 4yo+ 13lb **16** Ran SP% **129.5**
CSF: 15.17; EX: 15.10; TRIFECTA: 83.10; WIN: 2.80; PLACE: 1.60, 1.80, 1.90..
Owner Mssrs M C Berzack & B Joffe **Bred** Klawervlei Stud **Trained** South Africa
FOCUS
Just a conditions race last year and now a Listed contest, it won't be long before this race holds Group status. Several of these were using it as a prep for the Group 1 Al Quoz Sprint, run over the same C&D on World Cup night. The time was quick.

955a MAHAB AL SHIMAAL SPONSORED BY EMIRATES SKYWARDS (GROUP 3) (TAPETA) 6f
2:15 (2:15) 3-Y-0+
£73,619 (£24,539; £12,269; £6,134; £3,680; £2,453)

			RPR
1		**Reynaldothewizard (USA)**[44] 365 7-9-0 112 (bt) RichardMullen 7 (S Seemar, UAE) *trckd ldng pair: led 1 1/2f out: r.o wl: comf* **10/1**	116
2	4	**Krypton Factor**[23] 660 5-9-0 123 (b) KierenFallon 2 (Fawzi Abdulla Nass, Bahrain) *trckd ldng pair: ev ch 3f out: kpt on same pce fnl 1 1/2f but no ch w wnr* **4/5**[1]	103+
3	1 1/2	**Balmont Mast (IRE)**[23] 660 5-9-0 110 JohnnyMurtagh 10 (Edward Lynam, Ire) *settled in last: nvr nr to chal: r.o fnl 1 1/2f: nrst fin* **8/1**[3]	98+
4	1/4	**Time Prisoner (USA)**[37] 467 6-9-0 115 MickaelBarzalona 6 (Mahmood Al Zarooni) *mid-div: kpt on fnl 1 1/2f: nrst fin* **4/1**[2]	98+
5	1/2	**Ganas (IRE)**[23] 660 5-9-0 107 TadhgO'Shea 5 (Ernst Oertel, UAE) *wl away: sn led: hdd 1 1/2f out: kpt on one pce fnl 1 1/2f* **16/1**	96
6	1/2	**Hitchens (IRE)**[9] 834 8-9-0 109 SilvestreDeSousa 4 (David Barron) *a mid-div* **12/1**	94
7	2	**Jaasoos (IRE)**[9] 838 9-9-0 104 JamesDoyle 3 (D Selvaratnam, UAE) *nvr bttr than mid-div* **16/1**	88
8	8 3/4	**August Rush (SAF)**[174] 6292 7-9-0 107 (t) RyanMoore 8 (Seth Benzel, U.S.A) *trckd ldrs tl outpcd 1 1/2f out* **16/1**	60
9	2	**Faridat (USA)**[9] 834 8-9-0 104 YutakaTake 9 (Shigeki Matsumoto, Japan) *nvr nr to chal* **33/1**	54
10	3 1/2	**Alazeyab (USA)**[9] 838 7-9-0 102 (vt) PaulHanagan 1 (A Al Raihe, UAE) *nvr nr to chal* **25/1**	42

1m 11.89s (0.29) **10** Ran SP% **127.9**
CSF: 20.21; EX: 32.700; TRIFECTA: 145.90; WIN: 12.10; PLACE: 3.00, 1.00, 2.40..
Owner Zabeel Racing International, Corp **Bred** Gibraltar Group Lp **Trained** United Arab Emirates
FOCUS
With last year's winner Krypton Factor failing to rediscover his best, this wasn't much of a race, but the winner is in the form of his life. The sectionals, set by Ganas (who was hassled by August Rush), show they went quick early before the winner came home slow: 24.39, 23.17, 24.20.

956a DUBAI CITY OF GOLD SPONSORED BY EMIRATES SKYCARGO (GROUP 2) (TURF) 1m 4f 11y
2:50 (2:50) 3-Y-0+
£92,024 (£30,674; £15,337; £7,668; £4,601; £3,067)

			RPR
1		**Jakkalberry (IRE)**[104] 7872 7-9-0 118 (t) RyanMoore 6 (Marco Botti) *trckd ldng pair: rdn 3f out: led fnl 100yds* **7/1**[2]	118
2	1/2	**Await The Dawn (USA)**[16] 741 6-9-0 120 PatCosgrave 2 (M F De Kock, South Africa) *led 2f: trckd ldrs after 2f: ev ch 2f out: nt qckn fnl 1 1/2f* **5/4**[1]	117
3	shd	**Cavalryman**[123] 7621 7-9-0 113 SilvestreDeSousa 4 (Saeed bin Suroor) *led after 2f: hdd 8f out: led again 2 1/2f out: hdd fnl 100yds* **7/1**[2]	117
4	6 1/2	**Silvaner (GER)**[23] 661 5-9-0 110 TedDurcan 3 (P Schiergen, Germany) *nvr bttr than mid-div* **25/1**	107
5	1/4	**Laajooj (IRE)**[51] 242 5-9-0 110 AhmedAjtebi 8 (Mahmood Al Zarooni) *settled in rr: nvr nr to chal but kpt on fnl 1 1/2f* **8/1**[3]	106
6	1	**Plantagenet (SPA)**[7] 871 6-9-0 105 WilliamBuick 9 (Niels Petersen, Norway) *settled in rr: nvr able to chal* **16/1**	105
7	1/4	**Burano (IRE)**[7] 873 4-8-11 102 KierenFallon 1 (Brian Meehan) *nvr bttr than mid-div* **20/1**	103
8	27	**Treble Jig (USA)**[16] 742 6-9-0 102 (t) WayneSmith 7 (M Al Muhairi, UAE) *slowly away: settled in rr: rdn to ld 8f out: rdn clr 4 1/2f out: hdd & wknd 2 1/2f out* **33/1**	61

2m 35.36s (155.36)
WFA 4 from 5yo+ 2lb **8** Ran SP% **98.0**
CSF: 10.91; EX: 11.80; TRIFECTA: 39.60; WIN: 6.10; PLACE: 1.70, 1.00, 1.80..
Owner Atb Jakkalberry Synd, Porter & Duke **Bred** Azienda Agricola Allevamento Deni **Trained** Newmarket, Suffolk

The Form Book Flat, Raceform Ltd, Compton, RG20 6NL.

FOCUS
Run over the same C&D and regarded as something of a prep race for the Sheema Classic, this promised to be an informative contest, but the second-favourite Masterstroke was withdrawn at the start, and they crawled through the first 800m in 58.78, before Treble Jig, who was surprisingly restrained leaving the gates but wouldn't settle, went to the front down the back and significantly increased the pace, leading to the following sectionals: 25.28 (1200m), 23.69 (1600m), 24.18 (2000m). The winner's split for the final 410m was 23.19, showing they finished fast. The form is probably misleading but the third and sixth help with the standard.

957a BURJ NAHAAR SPONSORED BY EMIRATES HOLIDAYS (GROUP 3) (TAPETA) 1m
3:25 (3:25) 3-Y-O+
£73,619 (£24,539; £12,269; £6,134; £3,680; £2,453)

RPR
1 **African Story**[307] [1902] 6-9-0 120 MickaelBarzalona 5 119+
(Saeed bin Suroor) *mid-div: rdn 3f out: led 1 1/2f out: comf* **11/4**[1]
2 2 1/4 **Capital Attraction (USA)**[23] [659] 6-9-0 109 TadhgO'Shea 12 113
(Ernst Oertel, UAE) *trckd ldrs: led 6f out: hdd 1 1/2f out: kpt on wl* **33/1**
3 1 3/4 **Moonwalk In Paris (FR)**[23] [659] 5-9-0 115 AhmedAjtebi 4 109
(Mahmood Al Zarooni) *trckd ldrs: ev ch 2f out: nt qckn fnl 1 1/2f* **4/1**[2]
4 3 **Disa Leader (SAF)**[9] [836] 8-9-1 107 ow1 JGeroudis 6 102+
(M F De Kock, South Africa) *mid-div: kpt on fnl 1 1/2f: nrst fin* **25/1**
5 *shd* **Saamidd**[23] [659] 5-9-0 112 (tp) WilliamBuick 14 102+
(Saeed bin Suroor) *slowly away: settled in rr: nvr nr to chal but r.o fnl 2f* **16/1**
6 1/2 **Unbridled Ocean (USA)**[16] [744] 5-9-0 105 RichardMullen 7 101+
(S Seemar, UAE) *mid-div: kpt on same pce fnl 2f* **20/1**
7 3 1/2 **Fanunalter**[9] [838] 7-9-0 108 PatDobbs 9 93
(M Hussain, UAE) *nvr able to chal* **20/1**
8 1 **Royal Ridge (SAF)**[7] [872] 5-9-0 107 PaulHanagan 1 92
(M F De Kock, South Africa) *sn led: hdd 6f out: wknd fnl f* **14/1**
9 1/4 **Nawwaar (USA)**[21] [696] 4-9-0 95 RoystonFfrench 3 90
(A Al Raihe, UAE) *chsd ldrs tl outpcd 2f out* **50/1**
10 1 1/4 **Red Jazz (USA)**[126] [7558] 6-9-0 111 RyanMoore 13 87
(Charles Hills) *settled in rr: nvr able to chal* **12/1**
11 1 1/4 **Dullahan (USA)**[126] [7573] 4-9-0 123 (t) KierenFallon 2 84
(Dale Romans, U.S.A) *slowly away: nvr bttr than mid-div* **11/2**[3]
12 1/2 **Aesop's Fables (USA)**[37] [466] 4-9-0 116 SilvestreDeSousa 8 83
(Saeed bin Suroor) *nvr bttr than mid-div* **11/2**[3]
13 2 3/4 **Barbecue Eddie (USA)**[23] [659] 9-9-0 113 (b) DaneO'Neill 11 77
(Doug Watson, UAE) *nvr nr to chal* **12/1**
14 4 1/4 **Zafeen Speed**[7] [869] 6-9-0 106 (vt) WayneSmith 10 67
(M Al Muhairi, UAE) *nvr nr to chal* **25/1**
1m 36.89s (-0.61) **14** Ran SP% **127.5**
CSF: 119.56; EX: 291.10; TRIFECTA: 1448.20; WIN: 4.10; PLACE: 1.70, 15.10, 1.70..
Owner Godolphin **Bred** Darley **Trained** Newmarket, Suffolk

FOCUS
The pace was fair enough (splits of 25.70, 23.11, 24.01 before the winner clocked 23.69). The fifth and sixth help with the standard.

958a AL MAKTOUM CHALLENGE R3 SPONSORED BY EMIRATES AIRLINE (GROUP 1) (TAPETA) 1m 2f
4:00 (4:00) 3-Y-O+
£147,239 (£49,079; £24,539; £12,269; £7,361; £4,907)

RPR
1 **Hunter's Light (IRE)**[30] [556] 5-9-0 117 SilvestreDeSousa 4 116+
(Saeed bin Suroor) *trckd ldrs: smooth prog 2f out: led 1f out: comf* **9/4**[1]
2 2 3/4 **Kassiano (GER)**[9] [833] 4-9-0 113 WilliamBuick 12 110+
(Saeed bin Suroor) *settled in rr: r.o fnl 1 1/2f: nrst fin* **6/1**[3]
3 1/4 **Prince Bishop (IRE)**[30] [556] 6-9-0 115 (v) RyanMoore 2 110
(Saeed bin Suroor) *mid-div: chsd ldrs 2f out: nt qckn fnl f* **14/1**
4 1/4 **Surfer (USA)**[30] [556] 4-9-0 111 RichardMullen 6 109
(S Seemar, UAE) *trckd ldng trio: led 2f out: hdd 1f out: kpt on same pce* **16/1**
5 1 **Jamr**[23] [656] 5-9-0 105 (v) PatCosgrave 9 107+
(M bin Shafya, UAE) *mid-div: kpt on same pce fnl 1 1/2f* **50/1**
6 1/4 **Treasure Beach**[126] [7573] 5-9-0 115 JamieSpencer 8 107+
(M F De Kock, South Africa) *s.i.s: settled in rr: nvr nr to chal* **12/1**
7 3/4 **Haatheq (USA)**[23] [659] 6-9-0 112 PaulHanagan 11 105
(A Al Raihe, UAE) *nvr bttr than mid-div* **16/1**
8 1 1/2 **Little Mike (USA)**[126] [7573] 6-9-0 123 (t) KierenFallon 1 102
(Dale Romans, U.S.A) *trckd ldrs: led 4f out: hdd 2f out: wknd fnl f* **9/2**[2]
10 5 3/4 **Monterosso**[245] [3880] 6-9-0 126 (t) MickaelBarzalona 5 91
(Mahmood Al Zarooni) *nvr bttr than mid-div* **6/1**[3]
11 2 3/4 **Trailblazer (JPN)**[76] 6-9-0 119 YutakaTake 3 85
(Yasutoshi Ikee, Japan) *trckd ldrs: ev ch 2 1/2f out: wknd fnl 1 1/2f* **12/1**
12 3 3/4 **Mendip (USA)**[30] [556] 6-9-0 113 JohnnyMurtagh 10 78
(Saeed bin Suroor) *slowly away: settled in rr: nvr able to chal* **20/1**
13 27 **Daddy Long Legs (USA)**[7] [871] 4-9-0 113 (t) ChristopheSoumillon 7 24
(M F De Kock, South Africa) *sn led: hdd & wknd 4f out* **12/1**
2m 3.65s (-1.05) **13** Ran SP% **125.8**
CSF: 16.66; EX: 17.70; TRIFECTA: 213.20; WIN: 2.80; PLACE: 1.00, 2.60, 6.10..
Owner Godolphin **Bred** Darley **Trained** Newmarket, Suffolk

FOCUS
Three horses have won this and followed up in the Dubai World Cup, namely Dubai Millennium (2000), Street Cry (2002) and Electrocutionist (2006), and last year's fourth-placed finisher Monterosso went on to take the main event. This is only the second year the race has held Group 1 status and it was a weak contest for the level, but a similar standard may be good enough come the World Cup. The finish was dominated by local, race-fit runners. They went an ordinary but even gallop: 25.72 (400m), 24.22 (800m), 24.76 (1200m), 24.76 (1600m), before winner clocked 24.01 (finish).

959a JEBEL HATTA SPONSORED BY EMIRATES AIRLINE (GROUP 1) (TURF) 1m 1f
4:35 (4:35) 3-Y-O+
£110,429 (£36,809; £18,404; £9,202; £5,521; £3,680)

RPR
1 **Sajjhaa**[16] [743] 6-8-9 112 WilliamBuick 3 115+
(Saeed bin Suroor) *trckd ldng trio: rdn 2f out: r.o wl fnl 1 1/2f: led cl home* **7/1**
2 3/4 **The Apache (SAF)**[37] [466] 6-9-0 117 ChristopheSoumillon 10 118
(M F De Kock, South Africa) *mid-div: smooth prog 2 1/2f out: led briefly 1 1/2f out: hdd 1f out: kpt on same pce* **4/1**[3]
3 1 **City Style (USA)**[37] [466] 7-9-0 115 MickaelBarzalona 4 116
(Mahmood Al Zarooni) *trckd ldrs: led 1f out: hdd fnl 100yds* **11/2**
4 3/4 **Side Glance**[140] [7238] 6-9-0 115 JamieSpencer 8 114+
(Andrew Balding) *settled in rr: nvr nr to chal but r.o fnl 1 1/2f* **14/1**
5 1/2 **Master Of Hounds (USA)**[16] [745] 5-9-0 115 (t) PatCosgrave 2 113
(M F De Kock, South Africa) *s.i.s: sn led: kicked clr 5f out: hdd 2f out: kpt on one pce fnl 1 1/2f* **9/1**
6 1/2 **Igugu (AUS)**[16] [743] 6-8-9 118 ADelpech 5 107
(M F De Kock, South Africa) *trckd ldng pair: rdn 3f out: led briefly 2f out: hdd 1 1/2f out: wknd fnl f* **11/4**[1]
7 1/2 **Sharestan (IRE)**[37] [466] 5-9-0 113 SilvestreDeSousa 7 111
(Saeed bin Suroor) *nvr bttr than mid-div* **10/3**[2]
8 1/2 **Iguazu Falls (USA)**[16] [745] 8-9-0 110 (t) JohnnyMurtagh 9 110
(M bin Shafya, UAE) *settled in rr: nvr nr to chal* **25/1**
9 3/4 **So Beautiful (FR)**[16] [741] 4-9-0 108 PaulHanagan 6 109
(Doug Watson, UAE) *in rr of mid-div: nvr nr to chal* **28/1**
10 2 **Zain Shamardal (IRE)**[16] [742] 5-9-0 105 (t) RoystonFfrench 1 104
(A Al Raihe, UAE) *nvr bttr than mid-div* **66/1**
1m 48.96s (108.96) **10** Ran SP% **123.1**
CSF: 36.74; EX: 40.30; TRIFECTA: 255.90; WIN: 8.20; PLACE: 2.10, 1.50, 1.90. PLACEPOT: £5.50. Pool of £4,072 - 537.90 winning units. QUADPOT: £3.80. Pool of £508 - 97.70 winning units..
Owner Godolphin **Bred** Darley **Trained** Newmarket, Suffolk

FOCUS
A competitive looking Group 1, and something of a private battle between Godolphin and Mike de Kock, who fielded three runners each. The pace was muddling, with Master Of Hounds going off too fast through the second section and racing well clear of the others, before inevitably coming back to his rivals, and the field were well bunched halfway up the straight. Here are the splits: 25.75 (400m), 23.41 (800m), 24.67 (1200m), 23.49 (1600m) and the winner clocked 11.39 to the finish. The first three are rated in line with their recent C&D form.

CHANTILLY (R-H)
Tuesday, March 5
OFFICIAL GOING: Polytrack: standard

960a PRIX MEYDAN RACE COURSE (H'CAP) (5YO+) (POLYTRACK) 1m 1f 110y
12:50 (12:50) 5-Y-O+
£19,869 (£8,032; £5,918; £3,804; £2,325; £1,479)

RPR
1 **Divin Leon (FR)**[71] 5-8-11 0 GregoryBenoist 3 86
(M Boutin, France) **112/10**
2 *nse* **Risquillo (FR)**[585] 7-8-10 0 IoritzMendizabal 17 85
(M Boutin, France) **11/1**
3 1/2 **Anaxis (FR)**[55] [125] 6-9-10 0 JeromeCabre 1 98
(S Wattel, France) **4/1**[1]
4 *shd* **Barlovento (FR)**[59] 7-8-5 0 (p) AnthonyCrastus 7 79
(J Rossi, France) **10/1**[3]
5 1 1/2 **Moncofar (IRE)**[75] 5-9-1 0 PaulineProd'homme 8 86
(D Prod'Homme, France) **15/1**
6 *snk* **Babel Ouest (FR)**[31] [498] 5-8-7 0 (p) AlexisBadel 12 78
(J Van Handenhove, France) **20/1**
6 *dht* **Uphold**[20] [648] 6-8-4 0 (b) MickaelForest 14 75
(Gay Kelleway) *broke wl on outside: rdn to ld after 1f: 2 l clr ent st: chal and hdd 1f out: no ex: styd on one pce* **24/1**
8 3/4 **Lemon River (FR)**[60] 5-8-13 0 BenjaminHubert 6 82
(N Leenders, France) **18/1**
9 1 3/4 **Sea Fire Salt (FR)**[71] 6-8-7 0 StephanePasquier 4 73
(D Prod'Homme, France) **9/2**[2]
10 *nk* **Jeanie Johnston (IRE)**[71] 6-8-13 0 ThierryThulliez 15 78
(P Harley, Germany) **11/1**
0 **Benadalid (FR)**[71] 6-8-9 0 Christophe-PatriceLemaire 10
(L Lallie, France) **19/1**
0 **Happy Monster (FR)**[71] 5-8-8 0 SebastienMaillot 5
(Robert Collet, France) **10/1**[3]
0 **Sacre Del Myre (FR)**[71] 7-8-8 0 AntoineHamelin 9
(J-M Jouteau, France) **30/1**
0 **Djolan (GER)**[80] 5-8-6 0 FilipMinarik 13
(N Sauer, Germany) **17/1**
0 **Close To Heaven (GER)**[181] 6-8-6 0 (b) MircoDemuro 11
(A Trybuhl, Germany) **69/1**
1m 56.2s (116.20) **15** Ran SP% **116.7**
WIN (incl. 1 euro stake): 12.20. PLACES: 3.90, 3.70, 2.20. DF: 56.00. SF: 105.40.
Owner Le Haras De La Gousserie **Bred** K Chehboub & B Chehboub **Trained** France

961a PRIX MEYDAN BEACH (CONDITIONS) (3YO+) (POLYTRACK) 6f
1:50 (1:51) 3-Y-O+ **£20,325** (£8,130; £6,097; £4,065; £2,032)

RPR
1 **Myasun (FR)**[119] [7624] 6-9-6 0 MaximeGuyon 2 107
(C Baillet, France) **7/5**[1]
2 *nse* **Onlyyouknowme (IRE)**[268] [2967] 5-8-13 0 MircoDemuro 8 100
(E Botti, Italy) **9/2**[3]
3 4 **Abu Sidra (FR)**[103] [7829] 4-9-2 0 MickaelForest 5 91
(J-F Bernard, France) **4/1**[2]
4 1 1/4 **Mon Choix (FR)**[67] [8277] 4-8-13 0 GregoryBenoist 6 84
(Y Barberot, France) **11/1**
5 1 1/4 **Kalicamix**[91] [7984] 3-8-2 0 AnthonyCrastus 3 83
(Paul Cole) *broke wl: racd 3rd under hold: wnt 2nd bef st: rdn 2f out: lost 2nd 1 1/2f out: styd on but no ex u.p fnl f* **15/1**
6 1 **Chopouest (FR)**[46] 6-9-2 0 FredericSpanu 4 80
(T Castanheira, France) **73/10**
7 2 **Robert Le Diable (FR)**[199] 4-9-2 0 IoritzMendizabal 1 74
(D Prod'Homme, France) **17/1**
8 2 **Mar Adentro (FR)**[275] [2745] 7-9-2 0 (p) ThierryJarnet 7 68
(R Chotard, France) **17/1**
1m 15.0s (75.00) **8** Ran SP% **117.6**
WFA 3 from 4yo+ 14lb
WIN (incl. 1 euro stake): 2.40. PLACES: 1.20, 1.40, 1.40. DF: 4.60. SF: 6.50.
Owner Ecurie Jarlan **Bred** Sarl Ecurie Jarlan **Trained** France

962a PRIX DU BOIS ROSIERE (CLAIMER) (3YO FILLIES) (POLYTRACK) 1m

2:20 (2:21) 3-Y-O £9,349 (£3,739; £2,804; £1,869; £934)

RPR

1 **Mahajanga (FR)**[150] 3-9-2 0 JohanVictoire 9 79
(C Boutin, France) **18/5**[2]

2 ¾ **Melivea (FR)**[75] 8193 3-8-8 0 RudyPimbonnet(6) 2 75
(C Laffon-Parias, France) **15/2**[3]

3 1 ½ **Emotionalblackmail (IRE)**[59] 3-8-13 0 ThierryThulliez 12 71
(Rod Collet, France) **33/10**[1]

4 ¾ **Slice Of Life (FR)**[52] 3-8-13 0 AlexisBadel 1 69
(Mme M Bollack-Badel, France) **18/1**

5 snk **Battante (FR)**[75] 8193 3-9-0 0 MaximeGuyon 11 69
(J-V Toux, France) **8/1**

6 1 ½ **Blue Whip (IRE)** 3-8-9 0 AnthonyCrastus 6 61
(U Suter, France) **51/1**

7 ½ **Lady Lunchalot (USA)**[17] 684 3-8-9 0 IoritzMendizabal 7 60
(J S Moore) *help up towards rr: shkn up ent st: swtchd towards outside: no ex u.p: r.o fnl f: nrest at fin* **33/10**[1]

8 snk **Candy Critic (GER)** 3-8-2 0 SebastienMartino(7) 4 60
(H-A Pantall, France) **79/1**

9 ½ **Symphony Break (IRE)**[27] 544 3-8-6 0 AntoineCoutier(3) 8 58
(N Caullery, France) **51/1**

10 ¾ **Gee Wizz (IRE)**[55] 3-8-2 0 BenjaminBoissat(7) 3 57
(Robert Collet, France) **59/1**

0 **Aziyadee (FR)**[81] 3-8-9 0 GregoryBenoist 5
(U Suter, France) **45/1**

0 **La Barbacane (FR)**[60] 3-8-13 0 MarcLerner(3) 10
(Y Barberot, France) **83/10**

1m 40.9s (100.90) 12 Ran SP% **116.1**
WIN (incl. 1 euro stake): 4.60. PLACES: 1.60, 2.30, 1.40. DF: 20.80. SF: 26.30.
Owner Bernard Sitruk **Bred** Ecurie Du Grand Chene **Trained** France

963a PRIX DU CHENE POUILLEUX (CLAIMER) (4YO) (POLYTRACK) 1m

3:55 (3:57) 4-Y-O £7,723 (£3,089; £2,317; £1,544; £772)

RPR

1 **Menyllos (GR)**[306] 4-8-13 0 RudyPimbonnet(5) 2 85
(C Laffon-Parias, France) **7/1**[3]

2 2 ½ **Majestic Oasis**[29] 4-9-2 0 StephanePasquier 14 77
(Rod Collet, France) **48/10**[2]

3 1 ½ **Dr Thibault (FR)**[67] 8277 4-9-4 0 (b) IoritzMendizabal 10 76
(U Suter, France) **33/1**

4 1 ½ **Questor (FR)**[52] 4-9-1 0 AlexandreChampenois(5) 1 74
(M Boutin, France) **41/1**

5 snk **Dellapearl (FR)**[70] 4-8-11 0 AllanBonnefoy 11 65
(F Sanchez, France) **79/1**

6 ½ **Becquanis (FR)**[52] 4-9-1 0 BriceRaballand 6 68
(E Wianny, France) **61/1**

7 1 ¼ **Enide**[188] 4-8-11 0 FilipMinarik 5 61
(P Schiergen, Germany) **36/1**

8 ¾ **Saint Louet (FR)**[120] 4-8-13 0 (b) AntoineCoutier(5) 16 66
(F Chappet, France) **48/10**[2]

9 hd **Mehitabel (FR)**[67] 4-8-5 0 MarcLerner(3) 4 56
(N Sauer, Germany) **15/1**

10 nse **Esquinade (FR)**[67] 4-8-8 0 AnthonyCrastus 3 55
(A Bonin, France) **62/1**

0 **Stormbound (IRE)**[35] 434 4-9-8 0 OlivierPeslier 13
(Paul Cole) *broke wl to r 2nd on outside: shkn up 2f out: no ex: fdd* **3/1**[1]

0 **Mr Majeika (IRE)**[67] 4-9-3 0 StephaneLaurent(5) 8
(F Vermeulen, France) **29/1**

0 **Dark Ages (IRE)**[200] 5308 4-8-11 0 ThierryJarnet 9
(E J O'Neill, France) **36/1**

0 **Gaelic Space (FR)**[119] 4-9-1 0 Pierre-CharlesBoudot 15
(J Bertran De Balanda, France) **27/1**

0 **Assinie Fix (FR)** 4-8-8 0 AntoineHamelin 7
(J-P Gallorini, France) **59/1**

0 **Astra (GER)**[166] 4-8-8 0 (b) MaximeGuyon 17
(W Hickst, Germany) **17/1**

0 **Lips Dancer (IRE)** 4-9-1 0 JohanVictoire 12
(Andreas Lowe, Germany) **11/1**

1m 38.5s (98.50) 17 Ran SP% **115.9**
WIN (incl. 1 euro stake): 8.00. PLACES: 2.70, 2.10, 9.00. DF: 28.40. SF: 73.20.
Owner Leonidas Marinopoulos **Bred** Figaia Stud **Trained** Chantilly, France

[908]SOUTHWELL (L-H)

Tuesday, March 12

OFFICIAL GOING: Standard
Wind: moderate half behind Weather: Cloudy and cold

964 CHAMPION HURDLE FREE BETS WITH BOOKMAKERS.CO.UK MAIDEN STKS 6f (F)

1:55 (1:55) (Class 5) 3-Y-O £2,726 (£805; £402) Stalls Low

Form RPR

0224 1 **Red Gift (IRE)**[19] 738 3-9-5 65 (p) TomEaves 7 72
(Brian Ellison) *trckd ldng pair: hdwy 1/2-way: cl up over 2f out: sn rdn: led over 1f out: drvn out* **8/1**

0-2 2 ½ **Moe's Place (IRE)**[35] 525 3-9-2 0 JulieBurke(3) 4 71+
(Kevin Ryan) *led: rdn along wl over 2f out: hdd and drvn over 1f out: kpt on same pce fnl f* **3/1**[2]

42-2 3 1 ½ **Star Of Rohm**[14] 808 3-9-5 75 HayleyTurner 3 66
(Michael Bell) *trckd ldrs: pushed along and n.m.r over 3f out: sn swtchd to outer and hdwy to chse ldng pair wl over 2f out: rdn and ev ch wl over 1f out: one pce ent fnl f* **1/1**[1]

6 4 2 ½ **Combustible (IRE)**[61] 148 3-9-0 0 [1] StephenCraine 1 54
(Daniel Mark Loughnane) *in tch: hdwy to chse ldrs over 2f out: sn rdn and no imp* **66/1**

2-3 5 4 **Antonio Gramsci**[12] 829 3-9-5 0 GrahamGibbons 2 47
(David Barron) *in tch: rdn along 1/2-way: sn btn* **6/1**[3]

- 6 ¾ **The Codger** 3-9-5 0 DanielTudhope 5 44+
(David O'Meara) *s.i.s and green in rr: wd st: rdn: green and wandered 2f out: n.d* **20/1**

45- 7 7 **Look On By**[196] 5715 3-9-5 0 JamesSullivan 6 23
(Ruth Carr) *chsd ldrs: rdn along wl over 2f out: sn wknd* **16/1**

1m 15.74s (-0.76) **Going Correction** -0.10s/f (Stan) 7 Ran SP% **112.5**
Speed ratings (Par 98): **101,100,98,95,89 88,79**
toteswingers 1&2 £3.20, 1&3 £2.20, 2&3 £1.20 CSF £31.15 TOTE £14.70: £3.30, £1.70; EX 33.30 Trifecta £77.30 Pool: £3548.19 - 34.40 winning units..
Owner Brian Ellison **Bred** D And Mrs D Veitch **Trained** Norton, N Yorks

FOCUS
A moderate maiden. The winner appeared pretty exposed and the second more than confirmed recent course form.

965 ENJOY THE CHELTENHAM FESTIVAL WITH BOOKMAKERS.CO.UK (S) STKS 7f (F)

2:30 (2:30) (Class 6) 3-Y-O+ £2,045 (£603; £302) Stalls Low

Form RPR

0-32 1 **Alpha Tauri (USA)**[5] 912 7-9-8 74 (t) RobbieFitzpatrick 5 68
(Scott Dixon) *led: pushed clr 3f out: rdn over 1f out: kpt on* **1/2**[1]

2310 2 2 ¼ **Bitaphon (IRE)**[5] 912 4-9-7 61 (p) RobertTart(7) 6 67
(Michael Appleby) *prom: chsd wnr over 2f out: rdn wl over 1f out: kpt on u.p fnl f* **9/2**[2]

46U0 3 3 **Vitznau (IRE)**[13] 813 9-10-0 60 ChrisCatlin 7 59
(K F Clutterbuck) *hld up: hdwy on outer wl over 2f out: rdn wl over 1f out: sn one pce* **33/1**

22-4 4 1 **River Ardeche**[21] 718 8-9-8 62 BarryMcHugh 3 51
(Tracy Waggott) *in rr on inner: swtchd rt and hdwy over 2f out: sn rdn along and one pce* **7/1**[3]

-001 5 4 ½ **Mucky Molly**[7] 884 5-9-9 49 (vt) TomEaves 1 40
(Alison Hutchinson) *trckd wnr on inner: pushed along 3f out: sn rdn and wknd fnl 2f* **22/1**

0-00 6 5 **Tenbridge**[17] 778 4-9-3 55 (b[1]) WilliamCarson 4 21
(Derek Haydn Jones) *chsd wnr: rdn along 3f out: wknd over 2f out* **33/1**

-035 7 14 **Elusive Warrior (USA)**[12] 831 10-9-1 53 (p) GaryPhillips(7) 2
(Alan McCabe) *chsd ldrs: rdn along 1/2-way: sn wknd* **25/1**

1m 29.39s (-0.91) **Going Correction** -0.10s/f (Stan) 7 Ran SP% **111.4**
Speed ratings (Par 101): **101,98,95,93,88 83,67**
toteswingers 1&2 £1.50, 1&3 £6.00, 2&3 £7.20 CSF £2.68 TOTE £1.50: £1.10, £2.00; EX 3.80 Trifecta £27.80 Pool: £3878.78 - 104.26 winning units..There were no bids.
Owner Willie McKay **Bred** Flaxman Holdings Ltd **Trained** Babworth, Notts

FOCUS
An uncompetitive seller and nothing got into it besides the hot favourite. The runner-up offers perspective.

966 COMPARE BOOKMAKERS WITH BOOKMAKERS.CO.UK H'CAP 6f (F)

3:05 (3:05) (Class 4) (0-85,90) 4-Y-O+ £4,690 (£1,395; £697; £348) Stalls Low

Form RPR

2111 1 **Aubrietia**[5] 913 4-9-13 90 6ex (b) AndrewMullen 6 98
(Alan McCabe) *cl up: led 2f out: rdn over 1f out: edgd rt ent fnl f: drvn and hung rt 100yds out: drvn and kpt on gamely* **2/1**[1]

00-4 2 1 ¼ **Sans Loi (IRE)**[35] 526 4-9-0 77 ShaneKelly 5 81
(Brian Ellison) *trckd ldng pair: hdwy on inner and cl up 2f out: rdn to chal over 1f out and ev ch tl drvn and one pce ins fnl f* **5/2**[2]

500- 3 1 ¼ **Klynch**[133] 7452 7-9-4 81 (b) PJMcDonald 8 85
(Ruth Carr) *trckd ldrs: hdwy 1/2-way: wd st and sn cl up on stands' rail: rdn to chal wl over 1f out: sn ev ch tl hmpd and one pce last 100yds* **25/1**

0-05 4 2 ¼ **Bandstand**[35] 526 7-8-11 74 TomEaves 7 68
(Bryan Smart) *towards rr and sn pushed along: rdn and hdwy 1/2-way: styd on u.p fnl 2f: edgd lft over 1f out: nrst fin* **6/1**[3]

46-6 5 3 **Advanced**[67] 60 10-8-10 80 KevinStott(7) 2 65
(Kevin Ryan) *midfield: hdwy over 2f out: sn rdn and no imp appr fnl f* **16/1**

300- 6 ½ **Beau Mistral (IRE)**[146] 7177 4-9-6 83 JoeFanning 11 66
(Paul Green) *chsd ldrs: rdn along over 2f out: sn one pce* **25/1**

304- 7 ½ **Rusty Rocket (IRE)**[133] 7451 4-9-2 79 WilliamCarson 3 61
(Paul Green) *led: rdn along 1/2-way: hdd over 2f out and sn wknd* **20/1**

050- 8 3 **Sunraider (IRE)**[152] 6999 6-8-11 74 MickyFenton 10 47
(Paul Midgley) *prom: wd st: sn rdn along and wknd fnl 2f* **25/1**

3-06 9 7 **Sound Amigo (IRE)**[21] 715 5-9-0 77 GrahamLee 1 29
(Ollie Pears) *a towards rr* **16/1**

002- 10 ½ **Victoire De Lyphar (IRE)**[152] 6999 6-9-7 84 JamesSullivan 4 34
(Ruth Carr) *rrd s: slowly away and a bhd* **7/1**

1000 11 5 **Dickie Le Davoir**[7] 885 9-7-12 68 (be) PhilipPrince(7) 9 3
(Richard Guest) *dwlt and a in rr: bhd whn eased over 1f out* **25/1**

1m 15.27s (-1.23) **Going Correction** -0.10s/f (Stan) 11 Ran SP% **120.6**
Speed ratings (Par 105): **104,102,100,97,93 93,92,88,79,78 71**
toteswingers 1&2 £2.60, 1&3 £15.30, 2&3 £14.90 CSF £6.55 CT £85.75 TOTE £2.40: £1.20, £1.50, £8.00; EX 9.50 Trifecta £207.70 Pool: £2546.68 - 9.19 winning units..
Owner Shropshire Wolves 4 **Bred** C J Murfitt **Trained** Averham Park, Notts
■ Stewards' Enquiry : Andrew Mullen two-day ban; careless riding (26th-27th March)

FOCUS
A good sprint handicap won by a filly on a roll. Decent form.

967 HORSE RACING FREE BETS WITH BOOKMAKERS.CO.UK CLASSIFIED CLAIMING STKS 1m (F)

3:45 (3:45) (Class 6) 4-Y-O+ £2,045 (£603; £302) Stalls Low

Form RPR

-032 1 **Fluctuation (IRE)**[28] 620 5-8-3 63 (v) RobertTart(7) 7 70
(Ian Williams) *prom: cl up 1/2-way: rdn to ld jst over 2f out: drvn and hdd ent fnl f: rallied u.p to ld again last 75yds* **5/4**[1]

3-44 2 1 ¼ **Bold Marc (IRE)**[34] 540 11-7-13 62 RaulDaSilva(3) 2 59
(Mrs K Burke) *led: jnd and rdn along 3f out: hdd over 2f out: drvn to take slt ld ent fnl f: hdd and no ex last 75yds* **4/1**[2]

-053 3 8 **Minortransgression (USA)**[34] 536 6-8-4 60 WilliamCarson 1 43+
(Sean Curran) *chsd ldrs on inner: rdn along 3f out: kpt on same pce u.p fnl 2f* **4/1**[2]

5145 4 hd **Michael's Nook**[41] 440 6-8-1 52 ow1 (p) FrankieMcDonald 3 39
(Alastair Lidderdale) *t.k.h early: in tch: hdwy wl over 2f out: sn rdn and no imp* **12/1**

4-40 5 4 ½ **Sir George (IRE)**[31] 587 8-8-4 57 JoeFanning 5 32
(Suzzanne France) *in tch: hdwy to chse ldrs 3f out: sn rdn and grad wknd* **12/1**

60-0 6 9 **Serjeant Buzfuz**[58] 198 4-8-8 52 [1] AndrewMullen 4 15
(Michael Appleby) *prom: pushed along after 3f: sn lost pl and rdn: bhd fr over 2f out* **20/1**

102- 7 5 **Croftamie**[157] 6885 4-8-12 62 PatrickMathers 6 8
(Tracy Waggott) *dwlt: sn chsng ldrs: rdn 3f out: sn wknd* 10/1[3]
1m 42.67s (-1.03) **Going Correction** -0.10s/f (Stan) 7 Ran SP% **113.7**
Speed ratings (Par 101): **101,99,91,91,87 78,73**
toteswingers 1&2 £1.70, 1&3 £1.40, 2&3 £3.20 CSF £6.35 TOTE £1.70: £1.10, £3.80; EX 7.80 Trifecta £16.50 Pool: £3190.42 - 144.72 winning units..
Owner J Tredwell **Bred** Corduff Stud & T J Rooney **Trained** Portway, Worcs

FOCUS
A moderate classified claimer in which the front pair had it to themselves from a long way out and the lead changed hands a couple of times up the home straight. The winner is rated to his best mile form under his useful claimer.

968 BOOKMAKERS FREE BETS AT BOOKMAKERS.CO.UK H'CAP 5f (F)
4:25 (4:25) (Class 6) (0-60,60) 4-Y-O+ **£2,045** (£603; £302) **Stalls** High

Form				RPR
6044	1		**Shawkantango**[4] 924 6-9-0 60 (v) AdamMcLean(7) 6	74
			(Derek Shaw) *chsd ldrs: swtchd lft and hdwy over 2f out: rdn to ld appr fnl f: sn edgd rt: kpt on wl* 2/1[1]	
-520	2	3 ½	**Imjin River (IRE)**[18] 750 6-8-9 55 (t) RobertTart(7) 4	56
			(William Stone) *chsd ldrs: hdwy 2f out: rdn over 1f out and sn ev ch: drvn ins fnl f and kpt on same pce* 7/2[2]	
6320	3	¾	**Steel City Boy (IRE)**[12] 831 10-8-10 54 AnnStokell(5) 2	53
			(Ann Stokell) *prom: effrt and cl up 2f out: sn rdn and ev ch tl one pce ent fnl f* 8/1	
00-6	4	1 ¼	**Nine Before Ten (IRE)**[60] 163 5-8-8 54 DavidBergin(7) 7	48
			(Charles Smith) *led: rdn along over 2f out: drvn and hdd appr fnl f: sn wknd* 14/1	
4063	5	2 ¼	**Nafa (IRE)**[29] 610 5-8-10 49 ShaneKelly 11	35
			(Daniel Mark Loughnane) *cl up: rdn along wl over 1f out: ev ch tl drvn and wknd appr fnl f* 8/1	
-300	6	2 ¼	**Molly Jones**[20] 728 4-8-11 50 (p) WilliamCarson 3	28
			(Derek Haydn Jones) *cl up: rdn 2f out: sn wknd* 7/1[3]	
0-50	7	2 ½	**Rafaaf (IRE)**[12] 831 5-9-7 60 StephenCraine 10	29
			(Richard Phillips) *a towards rr* 16/1	
0000	8	1	**Lord Buffhead**[12] 831 4-9-3 56 (e) RobbieFitzpatrick 1	21
			(Richard Guest) *chsd ldrs on wd outside: rdn along over 2f out: sn wknd* 12/1	
00-0	9	9	**Forever Janey**[63] 105 4-8-7 46 oh1 JoeFanning 9	
			(Paul Green) *a towards rr* 33/1	
-005	10	3 ¼	**Bird Dog**[21] 716 7-8-0 46 oh1 (v) RyanTate(7) 8	
			(Phil McEntee) *dwlt: a in rr* 50/1	

59.08s (-0.62) **Going Correction** -0.075s/f (Stan) 10 Ran SP% **115.4**
Speed ratings (Par 101): **101,95,94,92,88 85,81,79,65,59**
toteswingers 1&2 £2.30, 1&3 £3.80, 2&3 £5.80 CSF £8.56 CT £44.81 TOTE £2.40: £1.10, £1.30, £2.50; EX 8.40 Trifecta £35.80 Pool: £3427.15 - 71.76 winning units..
Owner Shawthing Racing Partnership **Bred** Derek Shaw **Trained** Sproxton, Leics

FOCUS
A moderate sprint handicap and there were six in a line across the track coming to the last furlong. The winner is rated back towards his best.

969 BOOKMAKER OFFERS AT BOOKMAKERS.CO.UK H'CAP 1m 4f (F)
5:05 (5:05) (Class 5) (0-75,75) 4-Y-O+ **£2,587** (£770; £384; £192) **Stalls** Low

Form				RPR
1-21	1		**Jacobs Son**[60] 161 5-9-1 69 GrahamLee 3	79
			(Robert Mills) *trckd ldrs: hdwy 4f out: chsd ldr wl over 2f out: rdn to chal wl over 1f out: led and edgd rt appr fnl f: drvn and edgd lft ins fnl f: styd on* 7/2[3]	
-111	2	1 ¼	**Dewala**[5] 914 4-9-5 75 AndrewMullen 6	83
			(Michael Appleby) *led: pushed along wl over 2f out: rdn wl over 1f out: hdd over 1f out: sn drvn and hung rt ent fnl f: kpt on same pce* 6/4[1]	
30-1	3	7	**Discay**[35] 528 4-8-13 69 JoeFanning 7	67
			(Mark Johnston) *chsd ldr: rdn along over 2f out: sn drvn and one pce* 11/4[2]	
4013	4	hd	**Mediterranean Sea (IRE)**[7] 887 7-9-7 75 FrederikTylicki 4	72
			(J R Jenkins) *hld up in rr: hdwy over 3f out: rdn to chse ldrs 2f out: sn no imp* 10/1	
2032	5	2 ¾	**Stanley Rigby**[5] 914 7-8-6 67 EireannCagney(7) 1	60
			(Richard Fahey) *hld up in tch: pushed along 3f out: rdn over 2f out: sn one pce* 9/1	
20-3	6	28	**Roc De Prince**[21] 712 4-9-2 72 DanielTudhope 5	23
			(David O'Meara) *trckd ldng pair: rdn along on inner over 4f out: sn outpcd and bhd fnl 2f* 20/1	

2m 38.71s (-2.29) **Going Correction** -0.10s/f (Stan)
WFA 4 from 5yo+ 2lb 6 Ran SP% **112.7**
Speed ratings (Par 103): **103,102,97,97,95 76**
toteswingers 1&2 £1.60, 1&3 £2.30, 2&3 £1.60 CSF £9.29 TOTE £5.30: £1.80, £1.10; EX 11.90 Trifecta £30.70 Pool: £2849.04 - 92.91 winning units..
Owner Jacobs Construction (Holdings) Limited **Bred** Stowell Park Stud **Trained** Headley, Surrey

FOCUS
An ordinary handicap, but the pace was solid enough. Straightforward form.

970 COMPARE TRUSTED BOOKMAKERS WITH BOOKMAKERS.CO.UK APPRENTICE H'CAP 1m 4f (F)
5:40 (5:40) (Class 6) (0-60,61) 4-Y-O+ **£2,045** (£603; £302) **Stalls** Low

Form				RPR
140-	1		**Neighbourhood (USA)**[82] 8189 5-8-6 48 (b1) RyanTate(3) 4	61
			(James Evans) *trckd ldng pair: hdwy 3f out: sn chsng ldr: rdn to ld wl over 1f out: styd on wl fnl f* 5/1[2]	
/6-1	2	2 ¼	**Amtired**[7] 888 7-9-5 61 6ex (be) JacobButterfield(3) 1	70+
			(Brian Ellison) *hld up: hdwy on inner 4f out: rdn to chse wnr wl over 1f out: hung rt and no imp ins fnl f* 4/7[1]	
6524	3	4 ½	**Layla's Boy**[27] 646 6-9-4 60 (bt) ShirleyTeasdale(3) 5	62
			(Simon West) *trckd ldr: cl up 1/2-way: led 3f out: sn rdn and hdd wl over 1f out: one pce* 7/1[3]	
000-	4	12	**Amazing Blue Sky**[147] 7131 7-9-4 60 DavidBergin(3) 3	43
			(Ruth Carr) *led: rdn along 4f out: hdd 3f out and sn wknd* 12/1	
355-	5	3 ½	**Dubara Reef (IRE)**[230] 4455 6-8-4 46 oh1 (p) RobertTart(3) 2	23
			(Paul Green) *trckd ldrs: pushed along 5f out: rdn 4f out: sn outpcd* 10/1	

2m 41.07s (0.07) **Going Correction** -0.10s/f (Stan) 5 Ran SP% **109.6**
Speed ratings (Par 101): **95,93,90,82,80**
CSF £8.36 TOTE £5.70: £1.70, £1.10; EX 8.80 Trifecta £22.90 Pool: £2849.04 - 92.91 winning units..
Owner James Evans Racing **Bred** Mr & Mrs Gary Middlebrook **Trained** Broadwas, Worcs

FOCUS
They dawdled for much of the way in this apprentice handicap and it developed into a sprint. The winning time was 2.36 seconds slower than the preceding contest. The winner was well on top of the in-form runner-up.

T/Plt: £21.40 to a £1 stake. Pool of £63686.46 - 2168.46 winning tickets. T/Qpdt: £2.70 to a £1 stake. Pool of £4671.44 - 1266.26 winning tickets. JR

944 WOLVERHAMPTON (A.W) (L-H)
Tuesday, March 12

OFFICIAL GOING: Standard
Wind: Fresh half-against Weather: Overcast

971 ENJOY THE CHELTENHAM FESTIVAL WITH BOOKMAKERS.CO.UK H'CAP 5f 216y(P)
5:50 (5:50) (Class 5) (0-70,67) 4-Y-O+ **£3,234** (£962; £481; £240) **Stalls** Low

Form				RPR
-505	1		**Avonvalley**[15] 790 6-8-13 64 SladeO'Hara(5) 2	72
			(Peter Grayson) *s.i.s: sn prom: rdn to ld ins fnl f: r.o* 20/1	
2600	2	¾	**One Way Or Another (AUS)**[12] 832 10-9-5 65 (t) AdamKirby 6	71
			(David Evans) *hld up: hdwy over 1f out: sn rdn: r.o* 18/1	
-000	3	nse	**Elusive Hawk (IRE)**[15] 795 9-9-3 63 TomMcLaughlin 5	69
			(David Evans) *a.p: rdn over 1f out: edgd rt: r.o* 9/2[2]	
-163	4	1 ¼	**Reginald Claude**[20] 728 5-8-12 63 RachealKneller(5) 8	65
			(Mark Usher) *mid-div: hdwy over 2f out: shkn up ins fnl f: styd on: nt trble ldrs* 4/1[1]	
3606	5	nk	**Restless Bay (IRE)**[24] 688 5-9-6 66 (b) LiamKeniry 12	67
			(Conor Dore) *sn led: rdn and edgd rt over 1f out: hdd and unable qck ins fnl f* 10/1	
0124	6	nk	**George Fenton**[12] 831 4-8-12 65 (v) PhilipPrince(7) 10	65
			(Richard Guest) *hld up: r.o ins fnl f: nvr nrr* 7/1	
1153	6	dht	**Hab Reeh**[18] 760 5-9-4 64 (t) AmyRyan 4	64
			(Ruth Carr) *chsd ldrs: rdn over 1f out: sn ev ch: styd on same pce ins fnl f* 9/1	
-030	8	½	**Little China**[34] 535 4-9-5 65 FrannyNorton 7	64
			(William Muir) *chsd ldr: rdn and ev ch over 1f out: no ex ins fnl f* 16/1	
400-	9	2 ½	**Muftarres (IRE)**[157] 6888 8-9-6 66 (t) SteveDrowne 9	57
			(Frank Sheridan) *hld up: rdn over 1f out: n.d* 33/1	
4136	10	½	**Methaaly (IRE)**[4] 924 10-8-11 64 (be) JordanNason(7) 3	54
			(Michael Mullineaux) *s.s: r.o ins fnl f: nvr nrr* 15/2	
0420	11	1 ¼	**Belle Bayardo (IRE)**[17] 775 5-9-7 67 LukeMorris 11	53
			(Ronald Harris) *chsd ldrs: rdn over 2f out: wknd over 1f out* 5/1[3]	
455-	12	2 ¼	**Satwa Laird**[116] 7743 7-9-4 67 SimonPearce(3) 13	46
			(Conor Dore) *hld up: a in rr* 22/1	

1m 14.76s (-0.24) **Going Correction** 0.0s/f (Stan) 12 Ran SP% **121.4**
Speed ratings (Par 103): **101,100,99,98,97 97,97,96,93,92 91,88**
toteswingers 1&2 £43.20, 1&3 £28.10, 2&3 £27.10 CSF £339.35 CT £1917.03 TOTE £12.60: £4.10, £6.70, £2.10; EX 226.60 Trifecta £1231.10 Part won Pool: £1641.51 - 0.28 winning units..
Owner Richard Teatum **Bred** Ercan Dogan **Trained** Formby, Lancs

FOCUS
An open handicap run at a reasonable gallop and the hold-up horses came to the fore at the business end. Ordinary form.

972 CHELTENHAM FESTIVAL FREE BETS WITH BOOKMAKERS.CO.UK MAIDEN FILLIES' STKS 1m 141y(P)
6:20 (6:20) (Class 5) 3-Y-O+ **£2,911** (£866; £432; £216) **Stalls** Low

Form				RPR
23	1		**Oratorio's Joy (IRE)**[6] 895 3-8-7 0 FergusSweeney 3	72
			(Jamie Osborne) *mde all: rdn and edgd lft ins fnl f: styd on wl* 2/1[2]	
32	2	2 ½	**Awattan**[10] 864 3-8-7 0 LukeMorris 1	67
			(Ed Vaughan) *chsd wnr: pushed along over 3f out: rdn over 1f out: styd on same pce ins fnl f* 1/1[1]	
-	3	4 ½	**Moma Lee** 3-8-7 0 NickyMackay 2	57+
			(John Gosden) *chsd ldrs: pushed along over 2f out: styd on same pce fr over 1f out* 4/1[3]	
34	4	5	**Impeccability**[18] 757 3-8-7 0 FrannyNorton 6	47
			(John Mackie) *prom: pushed along over 2f out: sn outpcd* 22/1	
	5	4	**Reiterate**[175] 4-9-13 0 RichardKingscote 5	44
			(Milton Bradley) *s.i.s: hld up: wknd over 2f out* 25/1	
00	6	1 ¾	**Bella Cinderella**[22] 706 3-8-7 0 DuranFentiman 4	35
			(George Moore) *s.i.s: plld hrd and sn prom: rdn and wknd over 1f out* 100/1	
	7	9	**Missie Snaffles** 3-8-7 0 JamesSullivan 7	16
			(Ian McInnes) *s.s: a in rr: pushed along 1/2-way: wknd wl over 2f out* 50/1	

1m 52.47s (1.97) **Going Correction** 0.0s/f (Stan)
WFA 3 from 4yo+ 20lb 7 Ran SP% **114.5**
Speed ratings (Par 100): **91,88,84,80,76 75,67**
toteswingers 1&2 £1.10, 1&3 £1.10, 2&3 £1.50 CSF £4.32 TOTE £2.40: £1.50, £1.10; EX 5.70 Trifecta £10.90 Pool: £2607.98 - 178.32 winning units..
Owner Dominic Christian **Bred** R Mahon & J Reilly **Trained** Upper Lambourn, Berks

FOCUS
There was little depth to this maiden and the principals dominated from the outset.

973 FREE HORSE RACING BETS WITH BOOKMAKERS.CO.UK H'CAP 2m 119y(P)
6:50 (6:51) (Class 6) (0-60,60) 4-Y-O+ **£1,940** (£577; £288; £144) **Stalls** Low

Form				RPR
1610	1		**Sommersturm (GER)**[11] 846 9-9-9 59 (t) AdamKirby 4	69+
			(David Evans) *hld up: hdwy and nt clr run over 2f out: shkn up to ld ins fnl f: edgd lft: styd on wl* 7/2[2]	
/3-3	2	4	**If I Had Him (IRE)**[9] 12 9-9-7 57 (v) LukeMorris 9	62
			(George Baker) *led after 1f: rdn over 2f out: hdd and unable qck ins fnl f* 5/2[1]	
-442	3	2 ¼	**Petersboden**[12] 820 4-8-5 46 NickyMackay 8	49
			(Michael Blanshard) *led 1f: remained handy: chsd ldr over 2f out: rdn over 1f out: styd on same pce* 4/1[3]	
6-22	4	shd	**Neil's Pride**[34] 542 4-8-13 54 (v) TonyHamilton 2	56
			(Richard Fahey) *prom: plld hrd: hmpd and lost pl after 1f: rdn over 3f out: styd on u.p fr over 1f out: nt trble ldrs* 4/1[3]	
156-	5	7	**Vertueux (FR)**[348] 1085 8-9-5 60 GeorgeDowning(5) 1	54
			(Tony Carroll) *prom: pushed along 6f out: rdn over 1f out: wknd fnl f* 16/1	
-005	6	1 ½	**If What And Maybe**[20] 724 5-8-7 46 (v) SimonPearce(3) 3	38
			(John Ryan) *sn drvn along to chse ldr: pushed along at various stages thrght: rdn over 3f out: lost 2nd over 2f out: sn wknd* 20/1	
63-6	7	1 ½	**Aegean Destiny**[18] 755 6-8-13 49 FrannyNorton 6	42
			(John Mackie) *prom: pushed along over 4f out: wknd 2f out* 8/1	

000/ **8** *39* **Orpen Bid (IRE)**[103] 7903 8-8-3 **46** oh1....................[1] JordanNason[(7)] 5
(Michael Mullineaux) *hld up: racd keenly: hdwy 10f out: rdn and wknd over 3f out* **50/1**

3m 40.62s (-1.18) **Going Correction** 0.0s/f (Stan)
WFA 4 from 5yo+ 5lb **8** Ran SP% **114.5**
Speed ratings (Par 101): **102,100,99,99,95 95,94,75**
toteswingers 1&2 £3.30, 1&3 £3.50, 2&3 £3.40 CSF £12.72 CT £35.31 TOTE £4.80: £1.40, £1.10, £2.10; EX 15.70 Trifecta £49.20 Pool: £1728.22 - 26.31 winning units..
Owner Ms S Howell **Bred** Gestut Schlenderhan **Trained** Pandy, Monmouths
FOCUS
A weak staying handicap but run at a reasonable gallop. Limited but straightforward form.

974 CHELTENHAM FESTIVAL FREE BETTING WITH BOOKMAKERS.CO.UK (S) STKS 1m 1f 103y(P)
7:20 (7:20) (Class 6) 4-Y-O+ **£1,940** (£577; £288; £144) **Stalls** Low

Form RPR
3313 **1** **Honey Of A Kitten (USA)**[6] 906 5-9-4 67....................(v) AdamKirby 3 75
(David Evans) *chsd ldrs: pushed along over 2f out: led and edgd lft 1f out: rdn out* **10/11**[1]
060- **2** *1 ¼* **Buaiteoir (FR)**[172] 6452 7-8-12 60.............................. FrankieMcDonald 1 67+
(Nikki Evans) *s.i.s: hld up: rdn and r.o wl ins fnl f: nt rch wnr* **28/1**
-505 **3** *1 ¾* **Availed Speaker (IRE)**[21] 718 4-8-5 63........................ LauraBarry[(7)] 7 64
(Richard Fahey) *chsd ldrs: n.m.r over 1f out: sn rdn: styd on same pce ins fnl f* **9/2**[3]
1226 **4** *1 ¼* **Yourinthewill (USA)**[18] 747 5-9-4 64................................ ShaneKelly 5 67
(Daniel Mark Loughnane) *hld up: hdwy over 1f out: nt clr run and swtchd lft 1f out: sn rdn: styd on same pce* **7/2**[2]
1140 **5** *2 ¼* **Faithful Ruler (USA)**[15] 798 9-8-11 62....................(p) GaryPhillips[(7)] 6 63
(Ronald Harris) *led: rdn over 2f out: hdd 1f out: wknd wl ins fnl f* **14/1**
-444 **6** *4 ½* **Syrian**[27] 633 6-8-12 68.. EddieAhern 4 48
(Thomas McLaughlin, Ire) *chsd ldr: rdn over 2f out: wknd fnl f* **7/1**
/0-5 **7** *3 ½* **Commerce**[22] 704 6-8-7 48....................................(p) KierenFox 2 36
(Dai Burchell) *s.i.s: a in rr: pushed along 1/2-way: wknd over 2f out* **50/1**

2m 1.55s (-0.15) **Going Correction** 0.0s/f (Stan) **7** Ran SP% **117.4**
Speed ratings (Par 101): **100,98,97,96,94 90,87**
toteswingers 1&2 £9.80, 1&3 £1.10, 2&3 £18.10 CSF £33.45 TOTE £2.00: £1.10, £10.80; EX 28.80 Trifecta £114.00 Pool: £1588.12 - 10.44 winning units..The winner was bought in for 6500gns
Owner Mrs E Evans **Bred** Kenneth L Ramsey And Sarah K Ramsey **Trained** Pandy, Monmouths
FOCUS
Low-grade form but a decent gallop to this seller. The winner is rated to form.

975 BIGGEST FREE BETS WITH BOOKMAKERS.CO.UK H'CAP 1m 141y(P)
7:50 (7:51) (Class 6) (0-60,60) 4-Y-O+ **£2,264** (£673; £336; £168) **Stalls** Low

Form RPR
6604 **1** **Outlaw Torn (IRE)**[6] 903 4-9-7 **60**........................(e) RobbieFitzpatrick 3 69
(Richard Guest) *mde all: rdn over 1f out: styd on u.p* **11/4**[1]
0363 **2** *1 ¼* **Supa Seeker (USA)**[6] 900 7-8-0 **46** oh1..................(v) JoeyHaynes[(7)] 6 53
(Tony Carroll) *pushed along in rr early: nt clr run over 2f out: hdwy over 1f out: edgd lft: r.o u.p to go 2nd nr fin: nt rch wnr* **4/1**
640- **3** *¾* **Alluring Star**[160] 6782 5-9-2 **55**...................................... JamesSullivan 2 59
(Michael Easterby) *trckd wnr: rdn over 2f out: styd on same pce ins fnl f: lost 2nd nr fin* **14/1**
00/0 **4** *2 ¼* **Valkov**[48] 334 6-8-7 **46** oh1.. LukeMorris 7 46
(Tony Carroll) *hld up: pushed along over 2f out: edgd lft and styd on u.p fnl f: nvr trbld ldrs* **40/1**
-536 **5** *1 ¼* **The Noble Ord**[15] 801 4-9-2 **55**..(t) LiamKeniry 1 52
(Sylvester Kirk) *prom: rdn over 2f out: no ex fnl f* **7/2**[3]
5352 **6** *4 ½* **Do More Business (IRE)**[39] 472 6-8-4 **50**.............(bt) PhilipPrince[(7)] 5 38
(Liam Corcoran) *plld hrd and prom: rdn: edgd lft and wknd over 1f out* **6/1**
03/ **7** *2 ¾* **Eljowzah (IRE)**[60] 174 5-9-0 **56**.................................... LeighRoche[(3)] 4 38
(Aidan Anthony Howard, Ire) *prom: rdn over 2f out: hmpd and wknd over 1f out* **3/1**[2]

1m 49.45s (-1.05) **Going Correction** 0.0s/f (Stan) **7** Ran SP% **117.3**
Speed ratings (Par 101): **104,102,102,100,99 95,92**
toteswingers 1&2 £6.10, 1&3 £3.70, 2&3 £8.80 CSF £14.79 TOTE £4.70: £2.20, £2.60; EX 19.20 Trifecta £133.40 Pool: £1140.17 - 6.40 winning units..
Owner James S Kennerley **Bred** Derek Veitch & Rory O'Brien **Trained** Wetherby, W Yorks
FOCUS
A pretty dire race, the runner-up helping with the standard.

976 COMPARE BOOKMAKERS FOR CHELTENHAM WITH BOOKMAKERS.CO.UK H'CAP 7f 32y(P)
8:20 (8:22) (Class 6) (0-65,65) 4-Y-O+ **£1,940** (£577; £288; £144) **Stalls** High

Form RPR
56-6 **1** **Mujaadel (USA)**[8] 878 8-9-4 **62**.................................(p) FrannyNorton 8 72
(David Nicholls) *s.i.s: hld up: hdwy over 1f out: r.o u.p to ld towards fin* **13/2**
0-01 **2** *1 ¾* **Prince James**[42] 436 6-9-5 **63**................................ GrahamGibbons 7 69
(Michael Easterby) *chsd ldr: rdn over 2f out: led ins fnl f: hdd toward fin* **9/2**[2]
1336 **3** *nk* **Romanticize**[7] 890 7-8-12 **56**...................................... TonyHamilton 12 61
(Jason Ward) *hld up: hdwy and nt clr run over 1f out: r.o u.p* **33/1**
00 **4** *½* **Moral Issue**[56] 218 5-9-1 **59**..(b[1]) DaleSwift 6 63
(Ian McInnes) *hld up: rdn over 1f out: r.o ins fnl f* **16/1**
40-3 **5** *2 ¼* **Rio Cobolo (IRE)**[5] 912 7-9-4 **62**............................ AdrianNicholls 3 60
(David Nicholls) *mid-div: hdwy 1/2-way: rdn over 1f out: styd on same pce* **6/1**[3]
06/ **6** *½* **Beau Amadeus (IRE)**[53] 285 4-9-7 **65**..........................(p) ShaneKelly 4 62
(S Donohoe, Ire) *chsd ldrs: rdn over 1f out: no ex ins fnl f* **11/4**[1]
1500 **7** *1 ¼* **Dhhamaan (IRE)**[33] 546 8-8-7 **51**.............................(b) JamesSullivan 1 45
(Ruth Carr) *led: rdn over 1f out: hdd and no ex ins fnl f* **25/1**
346- **8** *2 ½* **Glenridding**[172] 6455 9-9-5 **63**..................................(p) FrederikTylicki 2 51
(James Given) *chsd ldrs: rdn over 2f out: wknd ins fnl f* **8/1**
3455 **9** *½* **Abhaath (USA)**[15] 791 4-9-2 **60**...................................(p) LukeMorris 5 47
(Ronald Harris) *mid-div: rdn over 2f out: wknd over 1f out* **6/1**[3]
6100 **10** *nk* **Marshall Art**[12] 831 4-9-3 **61**...[1] AdamKirby 10 47
(David Evans) *hld up: rdn over 2f out: nvr on terms* **12/1**
0-60 **11** *4* **Victorian Bounty**[30] 603 8-8-11 **62**.......................... PhilipPrince[(7)] 11 38
(Tony Newcombe) *prom: pushed along 1/2-way: wknd over 2f out* **25/1**
2055 **12** *shd* **Resplendent Alpha**[39] 477 9-8-11 **62**.................. SemiraPashai[(7)] 9 38
(Alastair Lidderdale) *s.s: in rr: no ch whn stmbld wl over 1f out* **33/1**

1m 28.32s (-1.28) **Going Correction** 0.0s/f (Stan) **12** Ran SP% **125.0**
Speed ratings (Par 101): **107,105,104,104,101 100,99,96,96,95 91,91**
toteswingers 1&2 £8.40, 1&3 £23.40, 2&3 £24.00 CSF £36.55 CT £936.46 TOTE £8.40: £3.10, £2.30, £9.90; EX 72.60 Trifecta £868.70 Part won. Pool: £1158.28 - 0.37 winning units..
Owner W R B Racing 49 **Bred** Lawrence Goichman **Trained** Sessay, N Yorks
FOCUS
A strongly run handicap, and the winner did it well.

977 CHAMPION CHASE FREE BETS WITH BOOKMAKERS.CO.UK H'CAP 7f 32y(P)
8:50 (8:50) (Class 6) (0-60,58) 3-Y-O **£1,940** (£577; £288; £144) **Stalls** High

Form RPR
4221 **1** **Devout (IRE)**[20] 732 3-9-7 **58**.................................... FergusSweeney 3 65+
(Jamie Osborne) *chsd ldr: rdn to ld 1f out: r.o* **3/1**[2]
3-45 **2** *¾* **Sand Grouse**[27] 634 3-9-3 **54**................................(b) AndreaAtzeni 9 59
(Marco Botti) *led: rdn and hdd 1f out: styd on* **7/1**
442- **3** *3 ¼* **Panama Cat (USA)**[140] 7313 3-9-7 **58**............................ PhillipMakin 5 55
(Kevin Ryan) *trckd ldrs: racd keenly: rdn over 1f out: styd on same pce* **5/1**[3]
-350 **4** *hd* **Eyeline**[11] 848 3-8-8 **50**...(v[1]) JackDuern[(5)] 1 47
(Reg Hollinshead) *hld up: rdn over 2f out: hdwy over 1f out: styd on same pce fnl f* **33/1**
-532 **5** *½* **Petite Georgia (IRE)**[11] 848 3-9-6 **57**........................ GeorgeBaker 6 52
(George Baker) *prom: rdn over 1f out: no ex ins fnl f* **11/8**[1]
00-6 **6** *1* **Compton Silver**[61] 129 3-9-1 **57**........................ NicoleNordblad[(5)] 8 50
(Hans Adielsson) *hld up: rdn and hung lft over 1f out: nvr trbld ldrs* **16/1**
04-4 **7** *nk* **Show More Faith**[70] 5 3-9-4 **55**.................................... LiamKeniry 2 47
(Sylvester Kirk) *hld up: rdn over 2f out: n.d* **10/1**
05-5 **8** *6* **Lady Jean**[31] 588 3-8-8 **45**.. LukeMorris 7 27
(Reg Hollinshead) *s.s: in rr: rdn over 1f out: eased whn btn fnl f* **50/1**
006- **9** *22* **Lady Niramax**[199] 5586 3-9-1 **52**.................................. AdrianNicholls 10
(David Nicholls) *prom: rdn 1/2-way: hung rt and wknd over 2f out: eased* **16/1**

1m 30.73s (1.13) **Going Correction** 0.0s/f (Stan) **9** Ran SP% **122.0**
Speed ratings (Par 96): **93,92,88,88,87 86,86,79,54**
toteswingers 1&2 £5.50, 1&3 £4.80, 2&3 £2.70 CSF £26.10 CT £106.55 TOTE £5.00: £1.50, £2.10, £1.90; EX 27.00 Trifecta £57.50 Pool: £1631.85 - 21.26 winning units..
Owner Dean Margolis, Paul Hearn & Partners **Bred** Edgeridge Ltd **Trained** Upper Lambourn, Berks
FOCUS
They went much steadier than in the first division, hence the much slower time. The runner-up sets the level.
T/Plt: £156.10 to a £1 stake. Pool of £88891.10 - 415.55 winning tickets. T/Qpdt: £15.00 to a £1 stake. Pool of £7903.67 - 389.34 winning tickets. CR

894 KEMPTON (A.W) (R-H)
Wednesday, March 13

OFFICIAL GOING: Standard
Wind: light, half against Weather: dry, cold

978 GOFFS READY-TO-RUN BREEZE-UP 27.03.13 H'CAP 1m 2f (P)
5:50 (5:51) (Class 6) (0-65,65) 4-Y-O+ **£1,940** (£577; £288; £144) **Stalls** Low

Form RPR
00-4 **1** **Tenure**[46] 396 4-9-7 **65**... RyanMoore 4 77+
(Gary Moore) *t.k.h: hld up in tch and a gng wl: hdwy over 2f out: rdn to ld over 1f out: clr 1f out: r.o strly: comf* **1/1**[1]
-454 **2** *3 ½* **Having A Ball**[7] 896 9-9-1 **59**.. ChrisCatlin 5 65
(Geoffrey Deacon) *in tch in midfield: switching out lft looking for room over 2f out: rdn and hdwy over 1f out: chsd clr clr wnr ins fnl f: r.o but no imp* **10/1**[3]
40-4 **3** *hd* **Manomine**[28] 638 4-9-4 **62**.. TedDurcan 10 67
(Clive Brittain) *hld up in last quartet: rdn and hdwy over 2f out: edgd rt over 1f out but styd on u.p to press for 2nd ins fnl f: r.o but no threat to wnr* **5/1**[2]
1412 **4** *¾* **Lytham (IRE)**[12] 852 12-8-10 **54**.............................. FergusSweeney 9 57
(Tony Carroll) *stdd and dropped in bhd after s: hdwy and swtchd lft wl over 1f out: styd on u.p to press for placings ins fnl f: no threat to wnr* **14/1**
30-6 **5** *2 ¼* **Adorable Choice (IRE)**[26] 675 5-9-4 **62**..........(bt[1]) RichardKingscote 7 61
(Tom Dascombe) *led: rdn and hdd over 1f out: btn 1f out: wknd and lost 3 pls ins fnl f* **16/1**
-220 **6** *2 ¼* **Safwaan**[28] 639 6-9-2 **60**.. J-PGuillambert 1 55
(Willie Musson) *hld up in last trio: modest hdwy fnl f: n.d* **10/1**[3]
0/0- **7** *1 ¼* **Kingston Tiger**[17] 8149 5-8-13 **60**........................(vt) MarkCoumbe[(3)] 2 52
(Jo Davis) *chsd ldrs: rdn ent fnl 2f: btn over 1f out: wknd fnl f* **33/1**
0145 **8** *½* **Fairy Mist (IRE)**[12] 839 6-8-0 **51** oh5......................... PhilipPrince[(7)] 3 42
(John Bridger) *t.k.h: chsd ldr: rdn 3f out: lost 2nd 2f out: wknd over 1f out* **33/1**
0-53 **9** *2 ¼* **Landesherr (GER)**[28] 626 6-9-0 **58** ow1..........................(p) AdamKirby 8 45
(Steve Gollings) *chsd ldrs: rdn and unable qck jst over 2f out: wkng whn short of room over 1f out: fdd fnl f* **5/1**[2]
-250 **10** *6* **Blue Deer (IRE)**[14] 813 5-9-3 **61**.. KierenFox 6 37
(Lee Carter) *stdd s: hld up in rr: rdn and struggling over 2f out: sn wknd* **33/1**

2m 7.31s (-0.69) **Going Correction** -0.025s/f (Stan) **10** Ran SP% **122.9**
Speed ratings (Par 101): **101,98,98,97,95 93,92,92,90,85**
Tote Swingers: 1&2 £5.70, 1&3 £2.60, 2&3 £8.10 CSF £13.37 CT £37.41 TOTE £1.80: £1.10, £3.30, £2.70; EX 15.60 Trifecta £75.40 Pool: £1,643.11 - 16.33 winning units..
Owner R A Green **Bred** Juddmonte Farms Ltd **Trained** Lower Beeding, W Sussex
FOCUS
With the exception of the winner, these were mainly exposed performers in a modest handicap. The gallop was a steady one and the winner raced towards the far rail in the straight. The form has a very straightforward feel.

979 GETTING OUT STKS AT CHELTENHAM MEDIAN AUCTION MAIDEN STAKES 6f (P)
6:20 (6:21) (Class 6) 3-5-Y-O **£1,940** (£577; £288; £144) **Stalls** Low

Form RPR
3- **1** **Milly's Gift**[147] 7161 3-8-9 0.. JohnFahy 5 78+
(Clive Cox) *chsd ldng pair: effrt and drew clr w rival 2f out: led over 1f out: in command and r.o wl ins fnl f* **11/4**[2]
433- **2** *1 ½* **You Da One (IRE)**[151] 7067 3-9-0 80.............................. DavidProbert 4 79
(Andrew Balding) *chsd ldr: led and qcknd jst over 1f out: hdd and drvn over 1f out: kpt hanging rt and one pce fnl f* **4/11**[1]
66/ **3** *11* **Lhotse Sherpa**[453] 7783 4-10-0 0.................................. RussKennemore 7 47
(John Holt) *chsd ldng trio and wl in tch: rdn and outpcd jst over 2f out: wl hld but kpt on to hold modest 3rd ins fnl f* **50/1**

06-0 **4** *shd* **Eliya**[36] 525 3-8-2 0 ... PhilipPrince(7) 3 37
(Jo Hughes) *sn rdn along and outpcd in last trio: no ch but styd on ins fnl f and almost snatched modest 3rd* **50/1**

43 **5** *3* **Viva L'Inghilterra (IRE)**[20] 734 3-8-9 0 ... ShaneKelly 1 28
(Robert Cowell) *racd freely: led tl rdn and hdd jst over 2f out: sn outpcd and btn: wknd fnl f* **20/1**

6 *nk* **Cherry Princess** 3-8-9 0 ... SeanLevey 8 27
(Stuart Williams) *v.s.a: a in rr: n.d* **33/1**

4 **7** *8* **Belle Isle**[34] 549 3-8-9 0 ... ChrisCatlin 2
(Jeremy Noseda) *a bhd: n.d* **14/1**[3]

1m 12.25s (-0.85) **Going Correction** -0.025s/f (Stan)
WFA 3 from 4yo 14lb — 7 Ran SP% **118.3**
Speed ratings (Par 101): **104,102,87,87,83 82,72**
Tote Swingers: 1&2 £1.02, 1&3 £11.30, 2&3 £6.70 CSF £4.25 TOTE £3.50: £1.40, £1.10; EX 5.30 Trifecta £80.10 Pool: £1,749.21 - 16.35 winning units..
Owner Ken Lock Racing **Bred** Ken Lock Racing **Trained** Lambourn, Berks

FOCUS
A most uncompetitive maiden in which the two market leaders pulled a long way clear in a fair time. The pace was reasonable and the winner raced just off the inside rail passing the intersection. The form has been taken at face value.

980 BACK AND LAY AT BETDAQ.COM FILLIES' H'CAP — 7f (P)
6:50 (6:51) (Class 5) (0-75,73) 4-Y-0+ — £2,587 (£770; £384; £192) Stalls Low

Form — RPR

-112 **1** **Compton Rainbow**[31] 601 4-8-13 72 ...(t) RyanTate(7) 6 82+
(Hans Adielsson) *mde all: rdn and qcknd clr 2f out: in n.d after: rdn out* **4/5**[1]

000- **2** *7* **Perfect Ch'l (IRE)**[231] 4469 6-8-4 64 oh1 ... RobertTart(7) 3 55
(Paul Fitzsimons) *chsd ldng pair: rdn and effrt over 2f out: chsd clr wnr over 1f out: no imp but kpt on for clr 2nd* **12/1**

4414 **3** *5* **Zing Wing**[25] 689 5-9-0 73 ...(vt) EoinWalsh(7) 2 52
(David Evans) *s.i.s: grad rcvrd and wnt 4th 1/2-way: rdn and outpcd over 2f out: no ch over 1f out: wnt modest 3rd ins fnl f* **3/1**[2]

1363 **4** *3* **Welsh Inlet (IRE)**[18] 778 5-8-9 64 oh3 ... KieranO'Neill 5 32
(John Bridger) *in tch in 4th: drvn and outpcd jst over 2f out: wl btn over 1f out* **7/1**[3]

464- **5** *1 ¼* **Shahrazad (IRE)**[146] 7189 4-7-13 64 oh12 ... SimonPearce(3) 4 22
(Patrick Gilligan) *chsd ldrs: rdn and wandered u.p over 2f out: sn outpcd and btn: lost modest 3rd and wknd ins fnl f* **10/1**

1m 25.22s (-0.78) **Going Correction** -0.025s/f (Stan) — 5 Ran SP% **109.8**
Speed ratings (Par 100): **103,95,89,85,84**
CSF £11.21 TOTE £1.30: £1.02, £10.00; EX 10.60 Trifecta £28.50 Pool: £1,439.98 - 37.83 winning units..
Owner Erik Penser **Bred** Pegasus Racing Ltd **Trained** Kingston Lisle, Oxon
■ Stewards' Enquiry : Ryan Tate two-day ban: careless riding (Mar 27-28)

FOCUS
An ordinary handicap in which three of the five runners were out of the handicap to varying degrees. The gallop was fair and the winner came down the centre in the straight. She was totally dominant.

981 BETDAQ GAMES £50 CASH BONUS H'CAP — 6f (P)
7:20 (7:20) (Class 5) (0-75,73) 4-Y-0+ — £2,587 (£770; £384; £192) Stalls Low

Form — RPR

000- **1** **Pick A Little**[137] 7412 5-9-7 73 ... MartinLane 7 81
(Michael Blake) *stdd after s: hld up in tch in rr: swtchd lft over 1f out: str run 1f out: chal fnl 100yds: led fnl 50yds: r.o wl u.p* **16/1**

43-2 **2** *nk* **Paradise Spectre**[9] 878 6-9-4 70 ... MartinHarley 4 77
(Mrs K Burke) *hld up wl in tch: rdn and effrt 2f out: ev ch over 1f out: led wl ins fnl f: sn hdd: r.o wl but a jst hld* **5/4**[1]

2120 **3** *1* **Bussa**[23] 705 5-9-1 72 ...(t) ThomasBrown(5) 3 76
(David Evans) *t.k.h: hld up wl in tch: rdn and effrt to chal over 1f out: led 1f out: hdd wl ins fnl f: no ex* **4/1**[2]

6310 **4** *1* **Speak The Truth (IRE)**[18] 775 7-8-11 68 ...(p) NathanAlison(5) 1 69
(Jim Boyle) *hld up wl in tch: rdn and effrt on inner 2f out: ev ch over 1f out: no ex ins fnl f: wknd fnl 100yds* **8/1**

2353 **5** *2* **The Strig**[14] 812 6-9-7 73 ... SeanLevey 5 68
(Stuart Williams) *t.k.h: pressed ldr: rdn 2f out: ev ch over 1f out: no ex and wknd ins fnl f* **6/1**

-651 **6** *1 ¼* **The Happy Hammer (IRE)**[13] 822 7-9-4 70 ... AdamKirby 2 61
(Eugene Stanford) *led: rdn ent fnl 2f: drvn and hdd 1f out: wknd ins fnl f* **9/2**[3]

5033 **7** *3 ½* **Pharoh Jake**[7] 902 5-8-0 59 oh2 ... PhilipPrince(7) 8 40
(John Bridger) *t.k.h: pressed ldrs on outer: rdn and unable qck wl over 1f out: edgd rt and wknd ent fnl f* **33/1**

1m 12.53s (-0.57) **Going Correction** -0.025s/f (Stan) — 7 Ran SP% **116.8**
Speed ratings (Par 103): **102,101,100,98,96 94,89**
Tote Swingers: 1&2 £7.00, 1&3 £10.60, 2&3 £1.40 CSF £38.09 CT £103.37 TOTE £17.10: £4.50, £2.70; EX 42.60 Trifecta £946.10 Part won. Pool: £1,261.52 - 0.88 winning units..
Owner Michael & Sharon Blake **Bred** D R Tucker **Trained** Trowbridge, Wilts

FOCUS
A fair handicap in which just a reasonable gallop saw five horses in a line approaching the last furlong. The winner came down the centre in the straight. The second and third pin the form.

982 BETDAQ MEMBERS FREE ENTRY EVERY WEDNESDAY H'CAP — 6f (P)
7:50 (7:52) (Class 4) (0-85,83) 3-Y-O — £4,690 (£1,395; £697; £348) Stalls Low

Form — RPR

3-12 **1** **Upavon**[21] 730 3-9-0 83 ... RobertTart(7) 4 88+
(David Elsworth) *hld up wl in tch: nt clr run briefly ent fnl 2f: rdn and hdwy to chal over 1f out: led ins fnl f: r.o wl: rdn out* **5/4**[1]

22-5 **2** *½* **Fortinbrass (IRE)**[66] 85 3-9-5 81 ... JimCrowley 3 85
(Ralph Beckett) *wnt lft s: sn rcvrd and led: rdn 2f out: drvn and hrd pressed over 1f out: hdd ins fnl f: r.o wl but a hld* **7/4**[2]

600- **3** *1 ¼* **Opt Out**[133] 7478 3-9-0 76 ... FrannyNorton 5 76
(Mark Johnston) *chsd ldrs: wnt 2nd over 4f out tl unable qck over 1f out: styd on same pce ins fnl f* **8/1**

3223 **4** *2 ½* **Lager Time (IRE)**[21] 730 3-8-6 68 ... WilliamCarson 2 60
(David Evans) *s.i.s: hld up: rdn and effrt on inner over 1f out: no imp 1f out: wknd ins fnl f* **9/2**[3]

1-34 **5** *3* **Studfarmer**[12] 843 3-8-7 69 ... LukeMorris 1 52
(David Evans) *t.k.h: chsd ldr tl over 4f out: rdn and unable qck 2f out: wknd 1f out* **25/1**

1m 12.3s (-0.80) **Going Correction** -0.025s/f (Stan) — 5 Ran SP% **113.9**
Speed ratings (Par 100): **104,103,101,98,94**
CSF £3.91 TOTE £2.80: £1.60, £1.10; EX 4.20 Trifecta £12.40 Pool: £870.38 - 52.43 winning units..
Owner McPabb Racing **Bred** Major-Gen Guy Watkins **Trained** Newmarket, Suffolk

FOCUS
Only five runners but the first two home are useful types. The gallop was no more than fair and the winner came down the centre in the straight. The runner-up helps the opening level.

983 BET LATE AT CHELTENHAM H'CAP — 1m 4f (P)
8:20 (8:22) (Class 6) (0-55,55) 4-Y-0+ — £1,940 (£577; £288; £144) Stalls Centre

Form — RPR

-601 **1** **Midnight Sequel**[13] 820 4-8-13 49 ... MartinLane 6 56
(Michael Blake) *chsd ldrs: effrt u.p to chal over 1f out: led 1f out: kpt on wl fnl f: drvn out* **3/1**[1]

4-04 **2** *1* **Beggers Belief**[21] 722 5-8-13 54 ...(b) JoeyHaynes(7) 12 59
(Eric Wheeler) *chsd ldrs: wnt 2nd 3f out: drvn and pressed ldr 1f out: kpt on wl but a hld fnl 100yds* **8/1**

650- **3** *¾* **The Yank**[148] 7148 4-9-5 55 ... JimCrowley 4 59+
(Tony Carroll) *stdd s: hld up in tch towards rr: clsd smoothly ent fnl 2f: rdn and effrt to chse ldrs ins fnl f: kpt on same pce fnl 100yds* **6/1**[3]

06-0 **4** *nk* **Cozy Tiger (USA)**[49] 343 8-9-6 54 ... StevieDonohoe 2 58
(Willie Musson) *t.k.h: chsd ldrs: rdn and outpcd wl over 1f out: swtchd lft and rallied 1f out: styd on wl ins fnl f* **8/1**

/360 **5** *½* **Polarity**[28] 635 7-9-4 52 ... AdamKirby 11 55
(Gerry Enright) *chsd ldr tl led over 10f out: rdn over 1f out: hdd 1f out: no ex and wknd fnl 100yds* **16/1**

-455 **6** *2 ½* **Hollywood All Star (IRE)**[12] 852 4-8-13 49 ... LukeMorris 9 48
(William Muir) *in tch in midfield: effrt on inner 2f out: drvn and chsd ldrs over 1f out: no ex 1f out: wknd ins fnl f* **7/1**

0-40 **7** *2* **Roman Senate (IRE)**[44] 417 4-9-2 52 ...(tp) SteveDrowne 1 48
(Martin Bosley) *led tl over 10f out: chsd ldr tl 3f out: styd chsng ldrs: rdn and unable qck 2f out: wknd fnl f* **8/1**

5-30 **8** *1 ½* **Ice Apple**[27] 653 5-8-9 46 oh1 ...(p) NataliaGemelova(3) 3 39
(John E Long) *stdd s: hld up in tch in rr: rdn and hdwy 2f out: no imp over 1f out: wknd ent fnl f* **33/1**

0032 **9** *3 ½* **Delightful Sleep**[9] 883 5-9-0 55 ... RobJFitzpatrick(7) 8 43
(David Evans) *t.k.h: hld up in tch in midfield on outer: rdn and fnd little over 2f out: wknd wl over 1f out* **9/2**[2]

0 **10** *3 ½* **Gemara (USA)**[19] 750 5-9-4 52 ... LiamKeniry 5 34
(Gary Brown) *t.k.h: hld up in midfield: dropped to rr over 3f out: rdn and wknd over 2f out* **10/1**

-460 **11** *3 ¾* **Here Comes Jeanie**[21] 724 4-8-3 46 oh1 ...(v[1]) PhilipPrince(7) 7 22
(Michael Madgwick) *s.i.s and swtchd rt s: nvr gng wl in rr and rdn along: drvn over 3f out: wknd over 2f out* **14/1**

2m 36.3s (1.80) **Going Correction** -0.025s/f (Stan)
WFA 4 from 5yo+ 2lb — 11 Ran SP% **127.9**
Speed ratings (Par 101): **93,92,91,91,91 89,88,87,84,82 80**
Tote Swingers: 1&2 £3.10, 1&3 £5.60, 2&3 £14.00 CSF £30.54 CT £145.41 TOTE £4.30: £1.80, £3.30, £2.90; EX 32.30 Trifecta £303.80 Pool: £1,118.38 - 2.76 winning units..
Owner Dajam Ltd **Bred** M Burbidge **Trained** Trowbridge, Wilts

FOCUS
A moderate handicap run at a steady gallop to the home turn. The winner came down the centre to build on her recent C&D win.

984 WIN BIG WITH BETDAQ MULTIPLES H'CAP (LONDON MILE QUALIFIER) — 1m (P)
8:50 (8:53) (Class 5) (0-75,75) 4-Y-0+ — £2,587 (£770; £384; £192) Stalls Low

Form — RPR

1-06 **1** **Greyfriarschorista**[44] 415 6-8-12 73 ... RobertTart(7) 7 83+
(Tom Keddy) *chsd ldrs: rdn to chse ldr 2f out: led over 1f out: kpt on wl fnl f: rdn out* **4/1**[2]

0-00 **2** *¾* **Brocklebank (IRE)**[16] 792 4-9-5 73 ... JimCrowley 9 79
(Simon Dow) *hld up in tch in midfield: swtchd lft and effrt wl over 1f out: r.o wl u.p fnl f: snatched 2nd last stride* **10/1**

2611 **3** *shd* **Mafi (IRE)**[19] 749 5-8-11 65 ...(t) WilliamCarson 5 71
(Mark Hoad) *chsd ldrs: switching out lft over 2f out: hdwy u.p to chse wnr jst ins fnl f: kpt on but lost 2nd last stride* **14/1**

-232 **4** *1* **Spirit Of Xaar (IRE)**[14] 813 7-8-8 62 ...(p) RobertHavlin 8 66
(Linda Jewell) *in tch: effrt u.p 2f out: chsd ldng pair and drvn jst ins fnl f: kpt on same pce fnl 100yds* **12/1**

-400 **5** *¾* **Scottish Lake**[27] 650 5-9-5 73 ... KirstyMilczarek 11 75
(Olivia Maylam) *led: clr tl 6f out: rdn ent fnl 2f: hdd over 1f out: no ex u.p 1f out: wknd fnl 100yds* **12/1**

3131 **6** *hd* **Honey Of A Kitten (USA)**[1] 974 5-8-12 73 6ex ...(v) EoinWalsh(7) 6 75
(David Evans) *t.k.h: hld up in midfield: rdn and hdwy wl over 1f out: kpt on but no imp fnl 100yds* **5/1**[3]

2102 **7** *shd* **Diplomatic (IRE)**[7] 899 8-8-8 69 ...(p) RyanTate(7) 4 70
(Michael Squance) *in tch in midfield: effrt u.p over 1f out: chsd ldrs and kpt on same pce ins fnl f* **7/2**[1]

-433 **8** *nk* **Warbond**[27] 652 5-8-7 61 oh1 ...(v) LukeMorris 12 62
(Michael Madgwick) *hld up in tch towards rr: effrt u.p towards outer ent fnl 2f: kpt on u.p but nvr threatened ldrs* **10/1**

0-20 **9** *2 ¾* **Kindia (IRE)**[16] 792 5-9-4 72 ... SebSanders 2 66
(Michael Attwater) *s.i.s: hld up in rr: rdn and effrt on inner 2f out: no prog over 1f out: nvr trbld ldrs* **8/1**

000- **10** *½* **Oratory (IRE)**[126] 7640 7-9-5 73 ... AdamKirby 1 66
(Noel Quinlan) *hld up towards rr: sme hdwy u.p wl over 1f out: sn no imp: n.d* **12/1**

211- **11** *2 ½* **Cufflink**[21] 6798 4-9-7 75 ... LiamKeniry 10 62
(Charlie Longsdon) *hld up in rr: rdn and no hdwy ent fnl 2f: n.d* **20/1**

050- **12** *2 ¾* **Fugitive Motel (IRE)**[288] 2583 4-8-4 65 ... JoeyHaynes(7) 3 46
(Eric Wheeler) *chsd ldr: rdn and unable qck over 2f out: lost 2nd 2f out: wknd over 1f out* **33/1**

1m 39.81s (0.01) **Going Correction** -0.025s/f (Stan) — 12 Ran SP% **125.6**
Speed ratings (Par 103): **98,97,97,96,95 95,95,94,92,91 89,86**
Tote Swingers: 1&2 £9.60, 1&3 £16.40, 2&3 £55.90 CSF £47.01 CT £531.76 TOTE £6.50: £2.30, £3.50, £2.50; EX 70.50 Trifecta £709.30 Part won. Pool: £945.79 - 0.31 winning units..
Owner Evergreen Racing Newmarket **Bred** Castlemartin Stud And Skymarc Farm **Trained** Newmarket, Suffolk

FOCUS
Exposed performers in a fair handicap but an ordinary gallop saw those held up at a disadvantage. The winner came down the centre in the straight and the form is straightforward behind him.

T/Plt: £10.10 to a £1 stake. Pool: £73,078.70 - 5,281.90 winning tickets. T/Qpdt: £5.40 to a £1 stake. Pool: £5,708.95 - 770.60 winning tickets. SP

[964]SOUTHWELL (L-H)

Wednesday, March 13

OFFICIAL GOING: Standard

Wind: fresh behind Weather: Bright and dry

985 ENJOY THE CHELTENHAM FESTIVAL BOOKMAKERS.CO.UK H'CAP 5f (F)

1:55 (1:55) (Class 6) (0-65,57) 3-Y-O **£2,045** (£603; £302) **Stalls** High

Form RPR

0-13 **1** **Hannahs Turn**[12] 848 3-9-2 **51** HayleyTurner 6 62+
(Chris Dwyer) *cl up: led 2f out: pushed clr ent fnl f: readily* **8/11**[1]

40-0 **2** *1* **Baltic Prince (IRE)**[5] 923 3-8-13 **48** FrannyNorton 3 55+
(Paul Green) *chsd ldrs: sn rdn along and swtchd lft to outer after 1f: outpcd and bhd 1/2-way: hdwy wl over 1f out: kpt on u.p fnl f* **6/1**[3]

340- **3** *8* **Red Star Lady (IRE)**[158] 6890 3-9-0 **49** DuranFentiman 1 28
(Shaun Harris) *cl up on outer: rdn along 2f out: drvn and grad wknd appr fnl f* **25/1**

4-3 **4** *1 1/2* **Tartan Blue**[62] 137 3-9-5 **54** JoeFanning 2 27
(Robert Cowell) *sn led: rdn along and hdd 2f out: drvn and wknd appr fnl f* **9/2**[2]

305 **5** *3* **Lady Calantha**[13] 829 3-8-3 **45** JordanHibberd(7) 5 7
(Alan Berry) *a in rr: outpcd and bhd fr 1/2-way* **66/1**

205- **6** *1/2* **Megaleka**[155] 6954 3-9-7 **56** PaulMulrennan 4 17
(Chris Fairhurst) *cl up: rdn along 2f out: sn wknd* **16/1**

050- **7** *1 1/2* **Moss The Boss (IRE)**[155] 6954 3-9-1 **57** ow3 DavidSimmonson(7) 7 12
(Paul Midgley) *chsd ldrs: rdn along 1/2-way: sn outpcd* **9/1**

1m 0.33s (0.63) **Going Correction** +0.05s/f (Slow) 7 Ran SP% **111.6**

Speed ratings (Par 96): **96,94,81,79,74 73,71**

Tote Swingers: 1&2 £4.40, 1&3 £2.50, 2&3 £8.80 CSF £5.31 TOTE £1.60: £1.10, £2.60; EX 4.60 Trifecta £38.00 Pool: £1,742.59 - 34.35 winning units..

Owner Mrs K W Sneath **Bred** Wayland Stud **Trained** Newmarket, Suffolk

FOCUS

A moderate sprint handicap in which the front pair pulled a long way clear of the rest. Weak form, but the winner may do better still.

986 CHAMPION CHASE FREE BETS WITH BOOKMAKERS.CO.UK H'CAP 7f (F)

2:30 (2:30) (Class 5) (0-75,80) 4-Y-O+ **£2,587** (£770; £384; £192) **Stalls** Low

Form RPR

0-35 **1** **Rio Cobolo (IRE)**[1] 976 7-8-9 **62** AdrianNicholls 5 70
(David Nicholls) *prom: chsd wnr fr 1/2-way: led 2f out: sn rdn: styd on wl fnl f* **11/2**

0123 **2** *1* **Hellbender (IRE)**[13] 831 7-9-1 **68** (t) DuranFentiman 6 73
(Shaun Harris) *in tch: hdwy on inner 2f out: sn rdn and styd on to chse wnr ins fnl f: nrst fin* **4/1**[2]

1335 **3** *1/2* **Spark Of Genius**[6] 919 4-9-2 **69** (p) HayleyTurner 2 73+
(Alan McCabe) *dwlt: racd awkwardly and cocked jaw in kickbk on inner: sn swtchd wd and bhd: wd st and hdwy wl over 2f out: rdn to chse ldrs over 1f out: sn edgd lft and kpt on same pce towards fin* **9/2**[3]

6013 **4** *1 1/2* **Masked Dance (IRE)**[8] 890 6-8-7 **60** (bt) LukeMorris 8 60
(Scott Dixon) *prom: wd st: rdn along over 2f out: drvn and kpt on same pce appr fnl f* **6/1**

-321 **5** *1* **Alpha Tauri (USA)**[1] 965 7-9-13 **80** 6ex (t) RobbieFitzpatrick 7 77
(Scott Dixon) *set str pce: rdn along and hdd 2f out: drvn over 1f out and grad wknd* **7/2**[1]

3102 **6** *6* **Bitaphon (IRE)**[1] 965 4-8-8 **61** (p) AndrewMullen 4 43
(Michael Appleby) *chsd ldrs: rdn along 3f out: sn drvn and wknd over 2f out* **8/1**

00-0 **7** *2 3/4* **Sir Geoffrey (IRE)**[40] 481 7-8-2 **60** MichaelJMMurphy(5) 1 34
(Scott Dixon) *in tch: hdwy on inner 1/2-way: rdn along wl over 2f out: sn wknd* **50/1**

002- **8** *18* **George Benjamin**[123] 7685 6-9-1 **68** JoeFanning 3
(Christopher Kellett) *a in rr: bhd fr over 2f out* **10/1**

1m 29.29s (-1.01) **Going Correction** -0.05s/f (Stan) 8 Ran SP% **112.2**

Speed ratings (Par 103): **103,101,101,99,98 91,88,67**

Tote Swingers: 1&2 £4.40, 1&3 £5.20, 2&3 £3.40 CSF £26.67 CT £106.36 TOTE £6.00: £1.70, £1.50, £2.00; EX 28.10 Trifecta £103.60 Pool: £1,161.29 - 8.40 winning units..

Owner Claudio Michael Grech **Bred** Yvonne & Gerard Kennedy **Trained** Sessay, N Yorks

FOCUS

A fair handicap, run at a strong pace. The runner-up is the best guide to the form.

987 COMPARE BOOKMAKERS AT BOOKMAKERS.CO.UK H'CAP 1m (F)

3:05 (3:06) (Class 5) (0-70,70) 4-Y-O+ **£2,587** (£770; £384; £192) **Stalls** Low

Form RPR

-133 **1** **Frontier Fighter**[31] 603 5-9-7 **70** DanielTudhope 7 91+
(David O'Meara) *trckd ldr: cl up 1/2-way: led wl over 2f out: rdn clr appr fnl f: styd on strly* **5/4**[1]

5346 **2** *7* **Thereabouts (USA)**[14] 816 4-9-0 **63** (v[1]) AndrewMullen 2 65
(Michael Appleby) *trckd ldrs: wd st: hdwy over 2f out: rdn wl over 1f out: kpt on to take 2nd ins fnl f: no ch w wnr* **4/1**[2]

2145 **3** *1 1/4* **Flying Pickets (IRE)**[6] 912 4-9-2 **70** (be) ShirleyTeasdale(5) 1 69
(Alan McCabe) *trckd ldrs on inner: hdwy 3f out: rdn over 2f out: sn chsng wnr: drvn and one pce fnl f* **7/1**[3]

6526 **4** *6* **Follow The Flag (IRE)**[16] 798 9-9-4 **67** (be) JohnFahy 6 52
(Alan McCabe) *towards rr: pushed along after 3f: hdwy over 2f out: sn rdn and plugged on: nvr nr ldrs* **8/1**

100- **5** *3 3/4* **Thackeray**[268] 3213 6-9-3 **66** KellyHarrison 8 43
(Chris Fairhurst) *dwlt: a towards rr* **16/1**

5462 **6** *1/2* **Jordaura**[16] 798 7-8-0 **56** JordanHibberd(7) 5 31
(Alan Berry) *dwlt: a in rr* **16/1**

1505 **7** *1 1/2* **Lord Of The Dance (IRE)**[19] 758 7-9-4 **67** TomEaves 3 39
(Michael Mullineaux) *chsd ldrs on outer: rdn along over 3f out: sn wknd* **25/1**

-034 **8** *4 1/2* **Point North (IRE)**[28] 645 6-9-2 **65** GrahamGibbons 4 27
(John Balding) *dwlt: pushed along and sn led: rdn over 3f out: hdd wl over 2f out and sn wknd* **10/1**

1m 41.4s (-2.30) **Going Correction** -0.05s/f (Stan) 8 Ran SP% **112.8**

Speed ratings (Par 103): **109,102,100,94,91 90,89,84**

Tote Swingers: 1&2 £2.10, 1&3 £2.40, 2&3 £3.40 CSF £6.00 CT £23.48 TOTE £1.70: £1.10, £1.10, £3.50; EX 7.40 Trifecta £24.70 Pool: £3,335.20 - 101.10 winning units..

Owner Archibald Nichol & Partners **Bred** Darley **Trained** Nawton, N Yorks

FOCUS

Another fair handicap and they finished well spread out. A significantly improved effort from the winner.

988 HORSE RACING FREE BETS WITH BOOKMAKERS.CO.UK (S) STKS 1m (F)

3:45 (3:46) (Class 6) 3-Y-O **£2,045** (£603; £302) **Stalls** Low

Form RPR

1233 **1** **Misleading Promise (IRE)**[6] 918 3-9-4 67 (t) LiamKeniry 1 69
(John Butler) *trckd ldng pair: hdwy on bit to ld 2f out: sn clr* **5/4**[1]

544- **2** *8* **Sleepy Haven (IRE)**[209] 5254 3-8-12 61 GrahamGibbons 4 45
(David Barron) *cl up on outer: rdn along 3f out: outpcd wl over 1f out: kpt on to take mod 2nd ins fnl f* **6/4**[2]

34-0 **3** *1 1/4* **Doodles**[71] 5 3-8-7 47 AdrianNicholls 3 37
(David Nicholls) *led: rdn along 3f out: hdd 2f out: one pce appr fnl f* **14/1**

22-2 **4** *7* **Myzamour**[71] 5 3-8-13 55 (b) FrederikTylicki 2 27
(Michael Wigham) *sn chsd along in rr: rdn over 3f out and sn outpcd* **5/1**[3]

1m 45.31s (1.61) **Going Correction** -0.05s/f (Stan) 4 Ran SP% **107.8**

Speed ratings (Par 96): **89,81,79,72**

CSF £3.41 TOTE £1.70; EX 3.90 Trifecta £17.70 Pool: £1,883.94 - 79.46 winning units..The winner was bought in for £4,250.

Owner J Butler **Bred** James Waldron **Trained** Newmarket, Suffolk

FOCUS

A poor seller in which the four horses were owned by their respective trainers. The winner is the best guide to the form.

989 COMPARE FREE BETS WITH BOOKMAKERS.CO.UK H'CAP 1m 6f (F)

4:25 (4:25) (Class 5) (0-75,73) 4-Y-O+ **£2,587** (£770; £384; £192) **Stalls** Low

Form RPR

1/31 **1** **Masterful Act (USA)**[8] 887 6-9-9 **71** 6ex JoeFanning 4 93+
(Alan McCabe) *mde all: pushed clr wl over 2f out: unchal* **4/6**[1]

6-12 **2** *13* **Amtired**[1] 970 7-8-13 **61** 6ex (be) DaleSwift 5 63
(Brian Ellison) *trckd ldrs: hdwy on outer 5f out: effrt 3f out and sn chsng wnr: rdn 2f out: kpt on: no ch w wnr* **5/2**[2]

60-2 **3** *2* **Linroyale Boy (USA)**[8] 888 5-8-7 **55** oh3 AndrewMullen 2 55
(Alan Swinbank) *trckd ldrs: chsd wnr 5f out: rdn along 3f out: sn drvn and one pce* **7/1**[3]

2122 **4** *4 1/2* **Goldmadchen (GER)**[6] 908 5-9-4 **66** JamesSullivan 1 60
(James Given) *trckd wnr: pushed along over 5f out: rdn 4f out: drvn and outpcd fr over 3f out* **16/1**

01-6 **5** *28* **Dorry K (IRE)**[13] 830 4-9-7 **73** MickyFenton 3 30
(Brian Rothwell) *a in rr: rdn along 1/2-way: lost pl over 4f out: wl bhd fnl 3f* **66/1**

3m 4.8s (-3.50) **Going Correction** -0.05s/f (Stan)

WFA 4 from 5yo+ 4lb 5 Ran SP% **108.4**

Speed ratings (Par 103): **108,100,99,96,80**

CSF £2.45 TOTE £1.70: £1.10, £1.30; EX 3.80 Trifecta £5.60 Pool: £2.090.10 - 275.97 winning units..

Owner Universal Recycling Company **Bred** Fiona Craig & Dermot Cantillon **Trained** Averham Park, Notts

FOCUS

An uncompetitive staying handicap and all very straightforward for the hot-favourite. The winner is clearly a long way ahead of the handicapper but is likely to get a big increase for this.

990 LATEST ODDS AT BOOKMAKERS.CO.UK MAIDEN STKS 7f (F)

5:05 (5:05) (Class 5) 3-Y-O+ **£2,587** (£770; £384; £192) **Stalls** Low

Form RPR

23-2 **1** **Fraserburgh (IRE)**[7] 904 3-8-12 75 JoeFanning 7 74
(Mark Johnston) *trckd ldrs: hdwy 3f out: rdn to ld wl over 1f out: clr ent fnl f* **4/5**[1]

3325 **2** *6* **Gebayl**[12] 845 3-8-7 63 (p) HayleyTurner 3 51
(James Tate) *in tch: hdwy over 3f out: rdn over 2f out: kpt on fnl f* **3/1**[2]

5 **3** *1/2* **Spider House**[19] 757 3-8-12 0 DanielTudhope 5 55+
(David O'Meara) *cl up: led 3f out and sn rdn: hdd wl over 1f out: sn drvn and kpt on one pce* **20/1**

0-44 **4** *6* **Munaawib**[6] 911 5-9-7 40 (t) DavidBergin(7) 8 45
(Charles Smith) *slt ld: rdn along over 3f out: sn hdd: wknd fnl 2f* **66/1**

530/ **5** *1 1/4* **Arc Light (IRE)**[915] 5916 5-9-9 74 DarylByrne(5) 4 42
(Tim Easterby) *cl up on inner: rdn along over 3f out: sn wknd* **7/1**

23- **6** *2* **Marcus Caesar (IRE)**[134] 7450 3-8-12 0 GrahamGibbons 6 31
(David Barron) *in tch: rdn along over 3f out: sn wknd* **6/1**[3]

0- **7** *1* **Bryant Park (USA)**[73] 8295 4-10-0 0 FrederikTylicki 10 34
(Michael Wigham) *s.i.s: a in rr* **20/1**

8 *7* **Idolise (IRE)**[307] 4-10-0 0 LiamJones 1
(John Spearing) *trckd ldrs: rdn along over 3f out: sn wknd* **33/1**

1m 29.16s (-1.14) **Going Correction** -0.05s/f (Stan)

WFA 3 from 4yo+ 16lb 8 Ran SP% **121.3**

Speed ratings (Par 103): **104,97,96,89,88 86,84,76**

Tote Swingers: 1&2 £1.10, 1&3 £5.80, 2&3 £6.80 CSF £3.55 TOTE £2.30: £1.02, £1.10, £6.40; EX 3.50 Trifecta £21.50 Pool: £2,098.61 - 73.16 winning units..

Owner Sheikh Hamdan Bin Mohammed Al Maktoum **Bred** L Dettori **Trained** Middleham Moor, N Yorks

FOCUS

An uncompetitive maiden and another easy, short-priced winner. The fourth is the key to the long-term level.

991 MONEY BACK SPECIALS WITH BOOKMAKERS.CO.UK H'CAP 6f (F)

5:40 (5:40) (Class 6) (0-60,59) 4-Y-O+ **£2,045** (£603; £302) **Stalls** Low

Form RPR

0-42 **1** **Pull The Pin (IRE)**[6] 909 4-8-9 **50** (b[1]) NeilFarley(3) 8 61
(Declan Carroll) *qckly away and keen: cl up: led 1/2-way: rdn clr 2f out: drvn and hung rt ins fnl f: kpt on wl towards fin* **9/4**[1]

500- **2** *1/2* **Man Of My Word**[97] 8010 4-8-10 **53** (p) MichaelJMMurphy(5) 9 62+
(Scott Dixon) *chsd ldrs: hdwy and wd st: rdn to chse ldrs wl over 1f out: drvn to chse wnr jst ins fnl f: sn swtchd lft and kpt on* **6/1**

0/12 **3** *2 1/4* **Seamster**[8] 890 6-9-2 **59** (vt) RachealKneller(5) 3 61
(Richard Ford) *chsd ldrs: hdwy 1/2-way: rdn to chse wnr 2f out: drvn and one pce fnl f* **7/2**[3]

0051 **4** *3/4* **Upper Lambourn (IRE)**[6] 909 5-9-6 **58** 6ex (t) JoeFanning 5 58
(Christopher Kellett) *outpcd and towards rr: hdwy over 2f out: sn rdn and kpt on fnl f: nrst fin* **3/1**[2]

4003 **5** *1 1/4* **Ryedale Dancer (IRE)**[6] 909 5-9-0 **52** (e) RobbieFitzpatrick 1 48
(Richard Guest) *slt ld: hdd 1/2-way: sn rdn along and grad wknd fnl 2f* **25/1**

464 **6** *3/4* **Sextons House (IRE)**[11] 863 5-8-11 **49** (be[1]) AndrewMullen 6 42
(Alan McCabe) *hld up: hdwy over 2f out: sn rdn and no imp* **10/1**

5-60 **7** *4* **Cheyenne Red (IRE)**[50] 327 7-8-2 **45**.................. ShirleyTeasdale(5) 4 25
(Michael Herrington) *chsd ldrs: rdn along 1/2-way: sn wknd* **50/1**
5520 **8** *8* **Script**[36] 525 4-8-3 **48**.................. JordanHibberd(7) 7
(Alan Berry) *dwlt: a in rr* **40/1**
6522 **9** *23* **Sannibel**[7] 903 5-9-7 **59**.................. HayleyTurner 2
(Graeme McPherson) *a bhd* **8/1**
1m 17.1s (0.60) **Going Correction** -0.05s/f (Stan) **9** Ran SP% **120.7**
Speed ratings (Par 101): **94,93,90,89,87 86,81,70,40**
Tote Swingers: 1&2 £4.60, 1&3 £2.20, 2&3 £4.40 CSF £17.15 CT £48.04 TOTE £3.50: £2.30, £2.40, £1.10; EX 26.00 Trifecta £168.50 Pool: £1,650.15 - 7.34 wininng units..
Owner C Harding **Bred** T J Ryan **Trained** Sledmere, E Yorks
■ Stewards' Enquiry : Michael J M Murphy two-day ban; used whip above permitted level (27th-28th March)

FOCUS
A modest sprint handicap and they went very hard up front. Solid, low-grade handicap form.
T/Plt: £6.00 to a £1 stake. Pool: £53,555.00 - 6,415.60 winning tickets. T/Qpdt: £2.30 to a £1 stake. Pool: £2,450.00 - 761.17 winning tickets. JR

971 WOLVERHAMPTON (A.W) (L-H)
Thursday, March 14

OFFICIAL GOING: Standard
Wind: Fresh behind Weather: Overcast

992 GOLD CUP FREE BETS WITH BOOKMAKERS.CO.UK H'CAP 5f 20y(P)
5:45 (6:02) (Class 5) (0-75,79) 3-Y-O £2,587 (£770; £384; £192) Stalls Low

Form RPR
526- **1** **Bold Prediction (IRE)**[142] 7311 3-9-7 **74**.................. RobertWinston 3 79+
(Mrs K Burke) *edgd rt s: chsd ldrs: shkn up to ld ins fnl f: r.o* **11/2**[3]
11 **2** *3/4* **Riskit Fora Biskit (IRE)**[8] 894 3-9-12 **79** 6ex.................. HayleyTurner 2 80
(Michael Bell) *got loose prior to the s: chsd ldr: rdn to ld over 1f out: hdd ins fnl f: styd on* **1/2**[1]
2422 **3** *nk* **Modern Lady**[8] 894 3-8-6 **66**.................. PhilipPrince(7) 1 66
(Richard Guest) *led: rdn and hdd over 1f out: styd on* **15/2**
1153 **4** *nk* **Sewn Up**[5] 949 3-9-4 **71**.................. (tp) ShaneKelly 4 71
(Reg Hollinshead) *s.i.s and hmpd s: hdwy over 3f out: nt clr run over 1f out: hmpd sn after: r.o: nvr able to chal* **9/2**[2]
1m 2.15s (-0.15) **Going Correction** -0.05s/f (Stan) **4** Ran SP% **112.0**
Speed ratings (Par 98): **99,97,97,96**
CSF £9.34 TOTE £6.90; EX 18.10 Trifecta £54.90 Pool: £1357.69 - 18.54 winning units.
Owner Mrs Elaine M Burke **Bred** Mountarmstrong Stud **Trained** Middleham Moor, N Yorks
■ Stewards' Enquiry : Hayley Turner caution: careless riding.

FOCUS
This moderate sprint was run 15 minutes later than the original start time due to the long delay of the Cross Country chase at the Cheltenham Festival. The winner took this well and the next two took each other on up front.

993 GOLD CUP BEST ODDS AT BOOKMAKERS.CO.UK (S) H'CAP 1m 141y(P)
6:15 (6:23) (Class 6) (0-60,60) 4-Y-O+ £1,940 (£577; £288; £144) Stalls Low

Form RPR
3000 **1** **Daniel Thomas (IRE)**[22] 722 11-9-2 **55**.................. (tp) MartinHarley 7 62
(Violet M Jordan) *s.i.s: hld up: hdwy over 1f out: r.o u.p to ld wl ins fnl f* **9/2**[2]
02-0 **2** *3/4* **Balmoral Castle**[32] 600 4-9-3 **56**.................. JohnFahy 4 61
(Jonathan Portman) *led 1f: chsd ldrs: rdn and ev ch fr over 1f out: styd on* **10/1**
0022 **3** *shd* **Unlimited**[24] 705 11-9-7 **60**.................. LukeMorris 6 65
(Tony Carroll) *hld up: hdwy 2f out: led over 1f out: rdn and hdd wl ins fnl f* **5/2**[1]
03/0 **4** *2 3/4* **Eljowzah (IRE)**[2] 975 5-9-3 **56**.................. AdamKirby 3 55
(Aidan Anthony Howard, Ire) *prom: racd keenly: pushed along and lost pl over 2f out: rallied over 1f out: styd on same pce ins fnl f* **9/2**[2]
100- **5** *1 1/2* **Rasselas (IRE)**[150] 7095 6-9-2 **55**.................. AdrianNicholls 5 51
(David Nicholls) *sn drvn along to chse ldrs: wnt 2nd over 4f out: rdn to ld and edgd lft over 1f out: sn hdd: no ex ins fnl f* **9/2**[2]
4-22 **6** *3/4* **Bentley**[9] 884 9-8-4 **50**.................. (p) PhilipPrince(7) 2 45
(Brian Baugh) *plld hrd and prom: rdn over 1f out: no ex fnl f* **5/1**[3]
-300 **7** *3 1/4* **Rockgoat (IRE)**[9] 886 4-9-1 **54**.................. (v) GrahamLee 1 42
(Ian McInnes) *chsd ldrs: led over 7f out: rdn: hdd and bmpd over 1f out: wknd fnl f* **17/2**
-000 **8** *5* **High Five Prince (IRE)**[14] 820 4-8-7 **46** oh1.................. JoeFanning 8 23
(Milton Bradley) *prom: rdn over 3f out: wknd 2f out* **33/1**
1m 49.95s (-0.55) **Going Correction** -0.05s/f (Stan) **8** Ran SP% **122.3**
Speed ratings (Par 101): **100,99,99,96,95 94,91,87**
toteswingers 1&2 £3.80, 1&3 £5.40, 2&3 £5.60 CSF £51.56 CT £140.03 TOTE £3.80: £1.10, £4.40, £2.10; EX 59.90 Trifecta £247.70 Pool: £1721.68 - 5.21 winning units.There was no bid for the winner.
Owner Rakebackmypoker.com **Bred** Lawn Stud **Trained** Moreton Morrell, Warwicks

FOCUS
A weak handicap. The pace was firmly set up for the closers and everything went right for the closers.

994 CHELTENHAM BETTING OFFERS WITH BOOKMAKERS.CO.UK MAIDEN STKS 1m 1f 103y(P)
6:45 (6:46) (Class 5) 3-Y-O+ £2,587 (£770; £384; £192) Stalls Low

Form RPR
1 **Premium** 3-8-2 0.................. FrannyNorton 2 72+
(Charles Hills) *s.i.s: sn chsng ldrs: pushed along over 2f out: styd on to ld wl ins fnl f* **10/11**[1]
-62 **2** *1/2* **Excellent Puck (IRE)**[20] 748 3-8-7 0.................. FergusSweeney 10 76
(Jamie Osborne) *chsd ldr: pushed along over 2f out: rdn to ld and hung lft over 1f out: hdd wl ins fnl f* **7/1**[3]
3 *1 1/2* **Guising** 4-9-13 0.................. RobertWinston 1 79+
(David Brown) *led: rdn and hdd whn bmpd over 1f out: unable qck towards fin* **25/1**
0-5 **4** *7* **Autrisk (IRE)**[24] 708 3-8-7 0.................. NickyMackay 3 58
(Marco Botti) *hld up in tch: rdn over 3f out: sn outpcd: styd on ins fnl f* **25/1**
5 *4* **Peter's Friend**[96] 4-9-13 0.................. TomEaves 9 56
(Michael Herrington) *hld up: rdn over 3f out: nvr on terms* **125/1**
6- **6** *3/4* **London Bridge (USA)**[141] 7323 3-8-7 0.................. JoeFanning 5 48
(Jo Hughes) *chsd ldrs: pushed along over 3f out: edgd rt and wknd over 2f out* **7/4**[2]
02 **7** *1 1/4* **Shockingdancer (IRE)**[24] 708 3-8-7 0.................. AndreaAtzeni 6 46
(Marco Botti) *prom: rdn over 3f out: wknd over 2f out* **11/1**
0- **8** *4 1/2* **Zain Heart (IRE)**[188] 6014 3-8-2 0.................. LukeMorris 8 31
(Gerard Butler) *hld up: rdn over 3f out: sn lost tch* **33/1**
9 *15* **Chebika** 3-8-2 0.................. HayleyTurner 4
(Michael Bell) *broke wl: lost pl after 1f: sn pushed along and rn green in rr: drvn along 1/2-way: wknd over 3f out: t.o* **14/1**
1m 58.77s (-2.93) **Going Correction** -0.05s/f (Stan)
WFA 3 from 4yo 20lb **9** Ran SP% **127.7**
Speed ratings (Par 103): **111,110,109,103,99 98,97,93,80**
toteswingers 1&2 £5.00, 1&3 £12.10, 2&3 £19.80 CSF £9.62 TOTE £2.20: £1.80, £1.10, £12.40; EX 17.50 Trifecta £118.80 Pool: £1611.07 - 10.16 winning units.
Owner K Abdullah **Bred** Juddmonte Farms Ltd **Trained** Lambourn, Berks

FOCUS
This was a clear indication that maidens are about to get plenty stronger again, but few landed a blow and the principals were always up there. The first three were clear and the runner-up is the key.

995 COMPARE BOOKMAKERS AT BOOKMAKERS.CO.UK H'CAP 1m 1f 103y(P)
7:15 (7:16) (Class 4) (0-85,82) 4-Y-O+ £4,690 (£1,395; £697; £348) Stalls Low

Form RPR
11-3 **1** **Chookie Royale**[30] 621 5-9-7 **82**.................. (p) JoeFanning 1 91
(Keith Dalgleish) *trckd ldrs: racd keenly: shkn up to ld 1f out: rdn out* **3/1**[2]
433 **2** *1 1/4* **Lean On Pete (IRE)**[13] 850 4-9-0 **75**.................. ShaneKelly 5 81
(Ollie Pears) *hld up: hdwy over 1f out: rdn ins fnl f: r.o to go 2nd post: nt rch wnr* **8/1**
-341 **3** *hd* **Patriotic (IRE)**[31] 614 5-9-6 **81**.................. (p) AdamKirby 7 86
(Chris Dwyer) *chsd ldr: pushed along to ld over 2f out: rdn and hdd 1f out: styd on: lost 2nd post* **6/1**
35-1 **4** *1 1/2* **Scottish Star**[20] 759 5-9-6 **81**.................. GrahamLee 8 83
(James Eustace) *chsd ldrs: rdn over 1f out: edgd lft and styd on same pce ins fnl f* **9/4**[1]
-042 **5** *1/2* **Askaud (IRE)**[15] 810 5-9-1 **76**.................. (b) LukeMorris 3 77
(Scott Dixon) *led: rdn and hdd over 2f out: no ex ins fnl f* **10/1**
2212 **6** *1 1/4* **One Scoop Or Two**[20] 759 7-8-10 **76**.................. (p) JackDuern(5) 4 75
(Reg Hollinshead) *hld up: hdwy over 1f out: no ex fnl f* **14/1**
5351 **7** *1 1/2* **Dakota Canyon (IRE)**[13] 850 4-8-12 **73**.................. (b) FrederikTylicki 2 69
(Richard Fahey) *prom: rdn over 2f out: wknd ins fnl f* **5/1**[3]
535- **8** *nk* **Tevez**[132] 7534 8-9-4 **79**.................. DavidProbert 6 75
(John Butler) *hld up: rdn over 2f out: nvr on terms* **25/1**
1m 59.93s (-1.77) **Going Correction** -0.05s/f (Stan) **8** Ran SP% **117.4**
Speed ratings (Par 105): **105,103,103,102,101 100,99,99**
toteswingers 1&2 £6.10, 1&3 £7.00, 2&3 £3.70 CSF £27.98 CT £137.30 TOTE £5.90: £1.10, £2.70, £2.00; EX 32.60 Trifecta £226.80 Pool: £1143.78 - 3.78 winning units.
Owner Raeburn Brick Limited **Bred** D And J Raeburn **Trained** Carluke, S Lanarks

FOCUS
A competitive handicap and straightforward form. It paid to race handily.

996 FREE HORSE RACING BETS WITH BOOKMAKERS.CO.UK H'CAP 1m 141y(P)
7:45 (8:01) (Class 5) (0-70,74) 4-Y-O+ £2,587 (£770; £384; £192) Stalls Low

Form RPR
50-2 **1** **Yojojo (IRE)**[52] 313 4-8-8 **55**.................. LukeMorris 5 68+
(Gay Kelleway) *chsd ldrs: rdn to ld 1f out: r.o* **12/1**
451 **2** *2 1/4* **Al Khan (IRE)**[10] 878 4-9-13 **74** 6ex.................. MartinHarley 1 82+
(Violet M Jordan) *hld up: plld hrd: hdwy over 1f out: nt clr run sn after: rdn and r.o to go 2nd wl ins fnl f: nt trble wnr* **13/8**[1]
53-6 **3** *1 1/2* **McCool Bannanas**[13] 850 5-9-4 **65**.................. DavidProbert 3 69
(James Unett) *s.i.s: hdwy over 7f out: rdn over 1f out: styd on same pce ins fnl f* **3/1**[2]
6020 **4** *1 1/4* **Spanish Plume**[10] 878 5-9-7 **68**.................. (p) AdamKirby 4 70
(Reg Hollinshead) *led: rdn and hdd 1f out: no ex ins fnl f* **5/1**[3]
0-34 **5** *3/4* **Going Grey (IRE)**[35] 548 4-8-10 **57**.................. TonyHamilton 6 57
(Richard Fahey) *chsd ldr: rdn over 2f out: no ex fnl f* **15/2**
3213 **6** *3* **Reasons Unknown (IRE)**[27] 662 5-9-4 **65**.................. ShaneKelly 2 58
(Thomas McLaughlin, Ire) *hld up: rdn over 1f out: wknd fnl f* **5/1**[3]
1m 50.11s (-0.39) **Going Correction** -0.05s/f (Stan) **6** Ran SP% **115.9**
Speed ratings (Par 103): **99,97,95,94,93 91**
toteswingers 1&2 £4.20, 1&3 £5.20, 2&3 £1.40 CSF £33.43 TOTE £25.00: £4.40, £1.70; EX 54.80 Trifecta £111.60 Pool: £1051.47 - 7.06 winning units.
Owner Winterbeck Manor Stud **Bred** Rossenarra Bloodstock Limited **Trained** Exning, Suffolk

FOCUS
A moderate little handicap, run at an uneven pace. The winner is rated back towards the level of last year's best run.

997 ENJOY BETTING WITH BOOKMAKERS.CO.UK H'CAP 5f 20y(P)
8:15 (8:25) (Class 7) (0-50,50) 4-Y-O+ £1,940 (£577; £288; £144) Stalls Low

Form RPR
2 **1** **Majestic Timeline (IRE)**[27] 670 4-9-4 **47**.................. (t) StevieDonohoe 13 54
(Adrian Brendan Joyce, Ire) *a.p: rdn to ld 1f out: r.o* **13/2**
6044 **2** *1/2* **Ches Jicaro (IRE)**[20] 756 5-9-2 **45**.................. (v) DavidProbert 1 51
(James Unett) *chsd ldrs: nt clr run 1/2-way: rdn over 1f out: r.o* **9/1**
3521 **3** *nse* **Rightcar**[14] 819 6-9-0 **48**.................. SladeO'Hara(5) 6 53
(Peter Grayson) *hld up: hdwy over 1f out: r.o* **7/2**[1]
4 *nk* **Enter The Red (IRE)**[27] 678 4-9-2 **45**.................. (bt) AdamKirby 5 49
(Aidan Anthony Howard, Ire) *a.p: rdn over 1f out: r.o* **6/1**[3]
-405 **5** *hd* **Love Club**[20] 754 5-9-4 **47**.................. FrederikTylicki 2 50
(Brian Baugh) *led to 1/2-way: rdn over 1f out: styd on* **11/1**
3523 **6** *1 1/4* **Slatey Hen (IRE)**[12] 863 5-9-5 **48**.................. (p) MartinHarley 11 50
(Violet M Jordan) *s.s: hld up: running on whn nt clr run ins fnl f: nvr able to chal* **8/1**
030 **7** *1 3/4* **First Rebellion**[20] 754 4-9-2 **45**.................. LukeMorris 4 37
(Tony Carroll) *chsd ldrs: rdn 1/2-way: styd on same pce ins fnl f* **7/1**
0/4- **8** *1/2* **Rowayton**[204] 5497 7-9-5 **48**.................. LiamKeniry 3 44
(Gary Brown) *hld up: rdn over 1f out: nvr trbld ldrs* **14/1**
/00- **9** *1 1/2* **Red Army Blues (IRE)**[62] 170 5-8-11 **47**.................. (b) GaryPhillips(7) 10 32
(John C McConnell, Ire) *s.i.s: sn pushed along in rr: nvr nrr* **5/1**[2]
5220 **10** *1/2* **Miserere Mei (IRE)**[20] 756 4-8-13 **49**.................. (be[1]) PhilipPrince(7) 9 32
(Richard Guest) *w ldr tl led 1/2-way: rdn and hdd 1f out: wknd and eased ins fnl f* **16/1**
000- **11** *2 1/4* **Major Muscari (IRE)**[118] 7747 5-9-7 **50**.................. (e[1]) TomEaves 8 25
(Ian McInnes) *hld up: rdn over 1f out: n.d* **25/1**
0366 **12** *1 3/4* **Deveze (IRE)**[20] 756 5-9-2 **45**.................. (b) RobertWinston 7 14
(Milton Bradley) *hmpd s: sn pushed along in rr: hmpd over 3f out: n.d* **25/1**
1m 2.07s (-0.23) **Going Correction** -0.05s/f (Stan) **12** Ran SP% **128.7**
Speed ratings (Par 97): **99,98,98,97,97 95,92,91,89,88 84,82**
toteswingers 1&2 £14.50, 2&3 £5.10, 1&3 £3.50 CSF £69.78 CT £247.98 TOTE £12.20: £3.80, £3.20, £2.30; EX 99.10 Trifecta £311.70 Pool: £999.30 - 2.40 winning units.
Owner M Kerrigan **Bred** Michael Rourke **Trained** Loughview, Co Roscommon

FOCUS
This wide-open sprint handicap was another race in which it proved a disadvantage racing out the back. Straightforward, low-grade form.

998 GET BEST ODDS WITH BOOKMAKERS.CO.UK H'CAP 5f 216y(P)
8:45 (8:50) (Class 5) (0-70,70) 4-Y-O+ £2,587 (£770; £384; £192) Stalls Low

Form RPR
4511 1 **Greenhead High**[9] 890 5-9-8 70 6ex........................(v) AdrianNicholls 11 80
(David Nicholls) *mde all: rdn over 1f out: all out* **7/2**[2]
0202 2 *hd* **Haadeeth**[8] 898 6-9-0 62.. AdamKirby 4 71
(David Evans) *a.p: chsd wnr 2f out: rdn and ev ch fr over 1f out: r.o* **10/11**[1]
44-0 3 *3/4* **Jawking**[34] 560 4-8-8 56..(t) LukeMorris 8 63
(Frank Sheridan) *a.p: rdn over 1f out: r.o* **33/1**
40-0 4 *2 1/4* **Captain Scooby**[9] 885 7-9-2 69.............................. JasonHart(5) 7 69
(Richard Guest) *hld up: hdwy over 1f out: styd on same pce ins fnl f* **12/1**
0-40 5 *1* **Sweet Ovation**[20] 750 4-8-7 55.............................. DavidProbert 9 52
(Mark Usher) *sn pushed along in rr: hdwy over 1f out: nvr trbld ldrs* **12/1**
40-0 6 *1/2* **Ambitious Icarus**[9] 885 4-9-7 69..............................[1] RobbieFitzpatrick 5 65
(Richard Guest) *hld up and bhd: r.o ins fnl f:* **11/1**
6445 7 *1 1/4* **Hot Sugar (USA)**[9] 885 4-9-2 64.............................(t) AndrewMullen 10 56
(Michael Appleby) *chsd ldr tl rdn 2f out: wknd fnl f* **11/2**[3]

1m 14.59s (-0.41) **Going Correction** -0.05s/f (Stan) **7 Ran SP% 116.6**
Speed ratings (Par 103): **100,99,98,95,94 93,92**
toteswingers 1&2 £1.30, 2&3 £3.70, 1&3 £12.60 CSF £7.32 CT £85.21 TOTE £3.70: £1.90, £1.10; EX 9.10 Trifecta £76.70 Pool: £1202.63 - 11.74 winning units.
Owner Charles Castle **Bred** Wyck Hall Stud Ltd **Trained** Sessay, N Yorks

FOCUS
An ordinary sprint handicap with a solid pace on. The winner is rated back to his best.
T/Plt: £248.10 to a £1 stake. Pool of £82792.48 - 243.55 winning units T/Qpdt: £12.00 to a £1 stake. Pool of £9136.12 - 559.10 winning units CR

960 CHANTILLY (R-H)
Thursday, March 14

OFFICIAL GOING: Polytrack: standard

999a PRIX MONTENICA (LISTED RACE) (3YO COLTS & GELDINGS) (POLYTRACK) 6f 110y
2:45 (12:00) 3-Y-O £22,357 (£8,943; £6,707; £4,471; £2,235)

RPR
1 **Style Vendome (FR)**[214] 5140 3-9-2 0........................ ThierryThulliez 1 107
(N Clement, France) **41/5**
2 *1* **Complimentor (IRE)**[107] 3-9-2 0.............................. MaximeGuyon 5 104
(X Thomas-Demeaulte, France) **48/10**[2]
3 *3/4* **The Brothers War (USA)**[24] 3-9-2 0........................ IoritzMendizabal 6 102
(J-C Rouget, France) **2/1**[1]
4 *hd* **Calvin Williams (FR)**[32] 606 3-9-2 0........................ OlivierPeslier 7 101
(E Lellouche, France) **8/1**
5 *snk* **Keravnos (FR)**[144] 3-9-2 0.............................. DavidMorisson 9 101
(C Gourdain, France) **58/10**[3]
6 *snk* **Linngaro (FR)**[24] 3-9-2 0.............................. MircoDemuro 10 100
(Mario Hofer, Germany) **42/1**
7 *hd* **Annunciation**[159] 6883 3-9-2 0........................ StephanePasquier 8 100
(Richard Hannon) *racd in 4th: rdn 2f out: no ex: styd on wl fnl f* **11/1**
8 *1 1/2* **Game Mascot**[32] 606 3-9-2 0.............................. JulienAuge 2 95
(C Ferland, France) **10/1**
9 *nk* **Kalicamix**[9] 961 3-9-2 0........................ Christophe-PatriceLemaire 4 94
(Paul Cole) *broke fast: sn led: set gd pce: rdn and hdd 250yds out: no ex: wknd fnl 100yds* **23/1**
10 *4* **Local Lover (FR)**[135] 3-9-2 0.............................. FabriceVeron 3 83
(H-A Pantall, France) **19/1**

1m 17.2s (77.20) **10 Ran SP% 116.2**
WIN (incl. 1 euro stake): 9.20. PLACES: 2.20, 1.60, 1.30. DF: 18.30. SF: 38.60.
Owner Comte Andre de Ganay **Bred** G Pariente **Trained** Chantilly, France

1000a PRIX RONDE DE NUIT (LISTED RACE) (3YO FILLIES) (POLYTRACK) 6f 110y
3:55 (12:00) 3-Y-O £22,357 (£8,943; £6,707; £4,471; £2,235)

RPR
1 **Morning Frost (IRE)**[184] 3-9-0 0.............................. JulienAuge 2 100
(C Ferland, France) **17/5**[1]
2 *3/4* **Kensea (FR)**[128] 7622 3-9-0 0.............................. ThierryJarnet 10 98
(H-A Pantall, France) **17/2**
3 *3/4* **Exactement (IRE)**[132] 7518 3-9-0 0.............................. JimCrowley 8 96
(Mrs K Burke) *racd in 4th: pulling hrd: making prog towards outside whn bmpd twice by evental wnr ent fnl 1 1/2f out: rallied and r.o wl fnl f* **12/1**
4 *1/2* **Interesting (IRE)**[153] 7122 3-9-0 0.............................. FabriceVeron 11 95
(H-A Pantall, France) **48/10**
5 *1 1/4* **Flawless Beauty**[132] 7518 3-9-0 0.............................. IoritzMendizabal 5 91
(Hugo Palmer) *settled in midfield: wnt 3rd 2f out: rdn 1 1/2f out: no ex: styd on fnl f* **13/1**
6 *snk* **Jadanna (IRE)**[153] 7122 3-9-0 0........................ Christophe-PatriceLemaire 3 90
(James Given) *racd towards rr: r.o u.p fnl 1 1/2f: nrest at fin* **14/1**
7 *1/2* **Rime A Rien**[137] 7430 3-9-0 0........................ Francois-XavierBertras 6 89
(F Rohaut, France) **7/2**[2]
8 *hd* **So Oops (IRE)**[64] 126 3-9-0 0.............................. StephanePasquier 1 88
(S Wattel, France) **9/2**[3]
9 *4 1/2* **Special Reward**[142] 3-9-0 0.............................. MaximeGuyon 7 75
(H-A Pantall, France) **14/1**
10 *6* **Jollification (IRE)**[147] 7193 3-9-0 0.............................. TheoBachelot 9 58
(George Baker) *racd in 3rd towards outside: rdn 1 1/2f out: no ex: wknd: eased ins fnl f* **40/1**

1m 17.7s (77.70) **10 Ran SP% 121.5**
WIN (incl. 1 euro stake): 4.40. PLACES: 1.90, 2.60, 3.60. DF: 23.10. SF: 37.20.
Owner Mrs A G Kavanagh **Bred** J F Tuthill **Trained** France

773 GULFSTREAM PARK (L-H)
Thursday, March 14

OFFICIAL GOING: Turf: firm

1001a STARTER ALLOWANCE (ALLOWANCE) (4YO+) (TURF) 1m 1f
8:05 (12:00) 4-Y-O+
£8,098 (£2,699; £1,214; £539; £134; £134)

RPR
1 **Midnite Silver (USA)**[20] 773 7-8-7 0........................(b) PLopez 2 89
(Giuseppe Iadisernia, U.S.A) **22/5**[3]
2 *1 1/2* **Tom Kitten (USA)**[20] 773 6-8-7 0........................(b) EPrado 3 86
(Marcus J Vitali, U.S.A) **41/10**[2]
3 *3/4* **Gentleman Jackson (USA)**[20] 773 6-8-7 0........................ JRosario 6 84
(Mark Casse, Canada) **11/5**[1]
4 *nk* **Julius Geezer (IRE)**[20] 773 5-8-11 0........................ CLanerie 1 87
(Amy Weaver) *broke wl: chsd clr ldr: clsd 3f out: rdn to chal 2f out: 2nd and ev ch ent fnl f: no ex ins fnl 100yds: fdd and dropped to 4th* **83/10**
5 *3 1/2* **Don'twait Toolong (USA)**[2335] 9-8-9 0........................ JRoccoJr 5 77
(Jane Cibelli, U.S.A) **54/10**
6 *1 1/2* **Sir Rabbit (USA)**[138] 10-8-7 0........................ JBravo 8 72
(Jessica J Campitelli, U.S.A) **83/10**
7 *nk* **Mr Hadif (USA)** 6-8-0 0........................(b) EZayas(7) 7 71
(Christopher Van Culin, U.S.A) **92/1**
8 *1/2* **Valley Stream (USA)** 4-8-11 0........................ ElvisTrujillo 4 74
(Kelly Breen, U.S.A) **98/10**
9 *5 3/4* **Toh's Grey Cat (USA)**[950] 6-8-7 0........................(b) MCruz 9 57
(Manuel J Wayar, U.S.A) **57/1**
10 *7 1/4* **Century Gold (USA)** 7-8-7 0........................ JASanchez 11 40
(Rafael A Fernandez, U.S.A) **41/1**
11 *17* **Mar Bravo (USA)** 5-8-7 0........................(b) DBoraco 10 1
(Braulio Lopez Jr, U.S.A) **178/1**

1m 46.61s (106.61) **11 Ran SP% 121.5**
PARI-MUTUEL (all including $2 stakes): WIN 10.80; PLACE (1-2) 5.20, 4.80; SHOW (1-2-3) 3.60, 3.00, 3.40; SF 40.60.
Owner Run Hard Stables **Bred** Margaret Addis **Trained** USA

1002 - 1007a (Foreign Racing) - See Raceform Interactive

901 LINGFIELD (L-H)
Friday, March 15

OFFICIAL GOING: Standard
Wind: Fresh; behind Weather: Rain

1008 BIGGEST FREE BETS WITH BOOKMAKERS.CO.UK CLAIMING STKS 7f (P)
1:55 (1:55) (Class 6) 3-Y-O £2,045 (£603; £302) Stalls Low

Form RPR
2211 1 **Devout (IRE)**[3] 977 3-8-6 58........................ ChrisCatlin 3 65
(Jamie Osborne) *broke wl and led early: sn stdd and chsd ldrs: effrt on inner to ld and edgd into centre over 1f out: clr and flashed tail u.p ins fnl f: idling but a doing enough towards fin* **4/1**[2]
452- 2 *3/4* **Sublimation (IRE)**[157] 6947 3-9-7 80........................ RyanMoore 2 78+
(Richard Hannon) *in tch in rr: effrt to press ldrs whn hung rt and v wd bnd wl over 1f out: lost pl and hrd drvn over 1f out: no imp tl r.o wl under hands and heels ins fnl f: wnt 2nd: clsng on wnr towards fin* **1/2**[1]
2320 3 *1 1/4* **Lady Lunchalot (USA)**[10] 962 3-7-13 64........................(p) RyanTate(7) 1 60
(J S Moore) *in tch in last pair: rdn and effrt over 2f out: chsd clr wnr 1f out: styd on same pce after and lost 2nd ins fnl f* **14/1**
-425 4 *hd* **Ishigunnaeatit**[7] 3-8-2 61........................(v) LukeMorris 5 55
(Mrs K Burke) *t.k.h: sn chsng ldr: rdn and ev ch 2f out: outpcd u.p over 1f out: no threat to wnr but plugged on fnl 100yds* **20/1**
1-43 5 *2 1/2* **Overrider**[18] 793 3-9-7 74........................(t) RobertWinston 4 68
(Charles Hills) *t.k.h: sn led and set stdy gallop: rdn ent fnl 2f: hdd over 1f out: wknd fnl f* **6/1**[3]

1m 25.66s (0.86) **Going Correction** +0.10s/f (Slow) **5 Ran SP% 112.4**
Speed ratings (Par 96): **99,98,96,96,93**
CSF £6.65 TOTE £4.70: £2.50, £1.10; EX 8.90 Trifecta £19.10 Pool: £974.17 - 38.11 winning units.Sublimation was claimed by Mr A. W. Carroll for £12,000
Owner Dean Margolis, Paul Hearn & Partners **Bred** Edgeridge Ltd **Trained** Upper Lambourn, Berks

FOCUS
Run at a steady pace, this was a typically ordinary 3yo claimer.

1009 CHELTENHAM BETTING OFFERS WITH BOOKMAKERS.CO.UK MAIDEN STKS 1m 4f (P)
2:30 (2:30) (Class 5) 3-Y-O £2,726 (£805; £402) Stalls Low

Form RPR
4-42 1 **Masaadr**[37] 534 3-9-5 66........................(p) NeilCallan 2 69
(James Tate) *trckd ldrs: nt clr run over 2f out: rdn and effrt to chal over 1f out: led 1f out: forged clr fnl 100yds: eased cl home* **6/4**[1]
4 2 *3/4* **Ambleside**[18] 799 3-9-5 0........................ FrannyNorton 3 68+
(Mark Johnston) *s.i.s: reminder and flashed tail sn after s: nvr travelling in last pair: rdn and outpcd ent fnl 2f: rallied and flashed tail u.p 1f out: r.o strly to chse wnr and clsng towards fin* **10/1**[2]
33-2 3 *1* **Gods Gift (IRE)**[24] 712 3-9-5 72........................ ChrisCatlin 6 66
(Rae Guest) *t.k.h: chsd ldrs: wnt 2nd 7f out tl led over 2f out: hrd pressed and drvn over 1f out: hdd 1f out: styd on same pce ins fnl f* **6/4**[1]
05 4 *3/4* **Mighty Thor**[20] 774 3-9-5 0........................ GeorgeBaker 7 65?
(Simon Dow) *chsd ldr tl 7f out: styd chsng ldrs: rdn to chal 2f out: unable qck ent fnl f: outpcd fnl 150yds* **50/1**
5 5 *hd* **Kingston Eucalypt**[21] 748 3-9-0 0........................ LukeMorris 5 60?
(Ed Vaughan) *in tch in last pair: rdn along briefly 8f out: hdwy to chse ldrs and rdn 2f out: outpcd over 1f out: rallied ins fnl f: keeping on but no threat to wnr whn short of room towards fin* **33/1**[3]
22 6 *17* **Mirth**[14] 841 3-9-0 0........................ JoeFanning 1 32
(Mark Johnston) *t.k.h: led tl rdn and hdd over 2f out: racd awkwardly and fdd qckly over 1f out: eased wl ins fnl f* **10/1**[2]

The Form Book Flat, Raceform Ltd, Compton, RG20 6NL.

7 *shd* **Sheema** 3-9-0 0 .... AndreaAtzeni 4 32
(James Tate) *wl in tch in midfield: rdn and dropped to rr 4f out: lost tch over 2f out* **10/1[2]**

2m 32.46s (-0.54) **Going Correction** +0.10s/f (Slow) 7 Ran SP% **112.2**
Speed ratings (Par 98): **105,104,103,103,103 91,91**
toteswingers 1&2 £4.60, 1&3 £1.10, 2&3 £6.60 CSF £18.16 TOTE £1.80: £1.10, £9.30; EX 25.20 Trifecta £56.10 Pool: £1,883.37 - 25.16 winning units.
Owner Saeed Manana **Bred** Highfield Stud Ltd **Trained** Newmarket, Suffolk
■ Stewards' Enquiry : Franny Norton caution: careless riding.

FOCUS
A modest maiden, using the winner and third as guides.

1010 GOLD CUP FREE BETS AT BOOKMAKERS.CO.UK CLASSIFIED CLAIMING STKS 1m 2f (P)
3:05 (3:05) (Class 5) 4-Y-0+ **£2,726** (£805; £402) **Stalls** Low

Form RPR

6512 **1** **Officer In Command (USA)**[18] 791 7-8-12 66 ....(v) WilliamCarson 3 74
(Sean Curran) *chsd ldrs: rdn and effrt to chal on inner wl over 1f out: drvn to ld 1f out: sn in command but edgd lft: comf* **3/1[3]**

1134 **2** *2* **Conducting**[23] 720 5-9-2 70 .... RobertWinston 1 74
(Gay Kelleway) *wnt rt s: led: rdn and edgd rt wl over 1f out: hdd 1f out: sn outpcd and btn: kpt on to hold 2nd* **9/4[2]**

1-20 **3** *2* **Bert The Alert**[14] 850 5-9-6 72 .... RyanMoore 5 74
(Gary Moore) *chsd ldrs: effrt and pressed ldrs 2f out: unable qck and btn 1f out: plugged on same pce fnl f* **6/4[1]**

1-26 **4** *10* **Priestley's Reward (IRE)**[8] 922 4-8-12 65 ....(v) LukeMorris 2 47
(Mrs K Burke) *pushed rt s: sn rdn along to go upsides ldrs: rdn 3f out: outpcd and dropped to last wl over 1f out: sn wknd: eased wl ins fnl f* **5/1**

2m 6.87s (0.27) **Going Correction** +0.10s/f (Slow) 4 Ran SP% **112.4**
Speed ratings (Par 103): **102,100,98,90**
CSF £10.25 TOTE £3.30; EX 9.30 Trifecta £16.20 Pool: £898.86 - 41.52 winning units.
Owner P M Rich **Bred** Blooming Hills Inc **Trained** Hatford, Oxon

FOCUS
An ordinary claimer, and straightforward form.

1011 FREE BETTING TIPS WITH BOOKMAKERS.CO.UK H'CAP 1m (P)
3:45 (3:45) (Class 5) (0-75,74) 3-Y-0 **£2,726** (£805; £402) **Stalls** High

Form RPR

462- **1** **Raging Bear (USA)**[100] 7989 3-9-7 74 .... RyanMoore 2 78
(Richard Hannon) *hld up in tch in last pair: rdn and effrt 2f out: drvn and hdwy 1f out: str run ins fnl f to ld last stride* **7/4[2]**

42-2 **2** *shd* **Sennockian Star**[8] 920 3-9-4 71 .... JoeFanning 3 75
(Mark Johnston) *led: rdn wl over 1f out: hrd pressed ins fnl f: r.o gamely u.p tl hdd last stride* **6/4[1]**

1143 **3** *½* **Club House (IRE)**[44] 444 3-9-6 73 .... JimCrowley 5 76
(Robert Mills) *hld up in tch in rr: swtchd lft and effrt on inner over 1f out: rdn and hdwy to chal ins fnl f: ev ch fnl 100yds tl no ex and one pce cl home* **7/2[3]**

016- **4** *3½* **Angels Calling**[168] 6629 3-8-9 62 .... LukeMorris 1 57
(Mrs K Burke) *chsd ldrs: rdn and effrt ent fnl 2f: chsd wnr over 1f out tl jst ins fnl f: wknd fnl 100yds* **33/1**

01- **5** *3½* **Imperial Glance**[183] 6168 3-9-2 69 .... LiamKeniry 4 56
(Andrew Balding) *chsd ldr: rdn over 2f out: unable qck and lost pl u.p over 1f out: wknd 1f out: eased wl ins fnl f* **8/1**

1m 38.99s (0.79) **Going Correction** +0.10s/f (Slow) 5 Ran SP% **112.6**
Speed ratings (Par 98): **100,99,99,95,92**
CSF £4.92 TOTE £2.80: £1.30, £2.30; EX 5.70 Trifecta £13.50 Pool: £1,960.36 - 108.20 winning units.
Owner Hughes,Morecombe,Anderson,Netherthorpe **Bred** Liberation Farm **Trained** East Everleigh, Wilts

FOCUS
A fair 3-y-o handicap in which the early pace was steady, but the form should hold up.

1012 FREE HORSE RACING BETS WITH BOOKMAKERS.CO.UK MAIDEN STKS 1m (P)
4:25 (4:25) (Class 5) 3-Y-0 **£2,726** (£805; £402) **Stalls** High

Form RPR

56- **1** **Lions Arch (IRE)**[163] 6795 3-9-5 0 .... RyanMoore 1 80
(Richard Hannon) *led and set stdy gallop: rdn and qcknd ent fnl 2f: edgd rt fr 1f out: hdd ins fnl f: kpt on to ld again towards fin* **4/9[1]**

020- **2** *nk* **Limit Up**[279] 2912 3-9-5 82 .... JoeFanning 3 79
(Mark Johnston) *chsd wnr: rdn and effrt to chal wl over 1f out: edging rt and led ins fnl f: r.o tl hdd and no ex towards fin* **2/1[2]**

3 *13* **Half Turn** 3-9-5 0 .... SteveDrowne 4 49+
(Luke Dace) *s.i.s: sn rcvrd and wl in tch in last: rdn and outpcd whn gallop qcknd 2f out: sn bhd* **16/1[3]**

1m 43.47s (5.27) **Going Correction** +0.10s/f (Slow) 3 Ran SP% **108.5**
Speed ratings (Par 98): **77,76,63**
CSF £1.66 TOTE £1.80; EX 1.50 Trifecta £1.60 Pool: £793.87 - 369.36 winning units.
Owner Andrew Russell **Bred** Mrs Alice Blake **Trained** East Everleigh, Wilts

FOCUS
This was predictably a tactical affair. The runner-up's 2yo form guides the opening level.

1013 GOLD CUP ODDS AT BOOKMAKERS.CO.UK FILLIES' H'CAP 1m (P)
5:05 (5:05) (Class 5) (0-70,68) 4-Y-0+ **£2,726** (£805; £402) **Stalls** High

Form RPR

03-4 **1** **Absent Amy (IRE)**[11] 878 4-9-2 63 .... GeorgeBaker 4 69
(Alastair Lidderdale) *chsd ldr: jnd ldr ent fnl 2f: rdn to ld over 1f out: kpt on ins fnl f and a gng to hold on* **1/1[1]**

2-35 **2** *nk* **Chrissycross (IRE)**[43] 451 4-9-4 65 ....(v) RyanMoore 6 70
(Roger Teal) *hld up in tch in rr: effrt and swtchd lft over 1f out: hdwy to press ldrs ins fnl f: chsd wnr wl ins fnl f: kpt on wl but nvr quite getting to wnr* **3/1[2]**

305 **3** *½* **Purley Queen (IRE)**[17] 806 4-8-9 56 .... LiamKeniry 1 60
(Sylvester Kirk) *chsd ldrs: effrt and rdn wl over 1f out: wnt 2nd 1f out and sn pressing wnr: styd on same pce fnl 100yds* **16/1**

0001 **4** *hd* **Total Obsession**[9] 907 6-8-0 54 oh9 ....(v) JoeyHaynes(7) 3 58
(Mark Hoad) *in tch in last pair: clsd wl over 1f out: swtchd rt and rdn 1f out: kpt on ins fnl f but nvr quite gng pce to chal* **25/1**

-241 **5** *4½* **Amosite**[20] 778 7-9-4 65 ....(p) JoeFanning 2 58
(J R Jenkins) *led: jnd 2f out: rdn and hdd over 1f out: btn 1f out: sn wknd* **9/2[3]**

006- **6** *2½* **Emman Bee (IRE)**[111] 7858 4-9-7 68 .... SteveDrowne 5 56
(Luke Dace) *in tch in midfield: rdn and unable qck wl over 1f out: sn wknd* **7/1**

1m 38.82s (0.62) **Going Correction** +0.10s/f (Slow) 6 Ran SP% **115.4**
Speed ratings (Par 100): **100,99,99,99,94 92**
toteswingers 1&2 £1.60, 1&3 £2.50, 2&3 £2.90 CSF £4.45 TOTE £2.10: £1.10, £2.20; EX 5.00 Trifecta £42.00 Pool: £1,590.40 - 28.35 winning units.
Owner The Strawberries To A Donkey Partnership **Bred** Tally-Ho Stud **Trained** Lambourn, Berks

FOCUS
A steadily run fillies' handicap. Not form to place too much faith in.

1014 COMPARE BOOKMAKERS AT BOOKMAKERS.CO.UK H'CAP 7f (P)
5:40 (5:40) (Class 5) (0-70,69) 3-Y-0 **£2,726** (£805; £402) **Stalls** Low

Form RPR

60-4 **1** **The Scuttler (IRE)**[17] 807 3-8-11 68 .... DanielCremin(7) 4 72
(Mick Channon) *chsd ldrs: nt clr run jst over 2f out: rdn and effrt over 1f out: chsd wnr ins fnl f: styd on wl to ld wl ins fnl f: hld on wl cl home* **8/1**

544- **2** *nk* **Clement (IRE)**[175] 6451 3-9-2 66 .... JohnFahy 7 69
(Eve Johnson Houghton) *hld up in tch towards rr: effrt but forced wdst bnd 2f out: rallied 1f out: gd hdwy u.p to press wnr wl ins fnl f: hld cl home* **3/1[2]**

41 **3** *¾* **Nellie Bly**[17] 808 3-9-4 68 .... JoeFanning 1 69
(Mark Johnston) *led: rdn and fnd ex over 1f out: clr 1f out: drvn and edging lft u.p ins fnl f: hdd and no ex wl ins fnl f* **4/1[3]**

3-14 **4** *nk* **Indian Affair**[11] 879 3-9-5 69 .... RichardKingscote 2 69
(Milton Bradley) *chsd ldr: drvn and unable qck wl over 1f out: lost 2 pls and styd on same pce ins fnl f* **7/1**

40-0 **5** *1¾* **Echo Brava**[30] 628 3-9-3 67 ....[1] SteveDrowne 5 62
(Luke Dace) *stdd s: detached in last: rdn and clsd ent fnl f: styd on fnl f: nvr trbld ldrs* **16/1**

1-34 **6** *¾* **Al Gharrafa**[16] 817 3-9-4 68 .... AndreaAtzeni 6 61
(Marco Botti) *wl in tch in midfield: rdn and unable qck over 1f out: styd on same pce fnl f* **7/1**

445 **7** *1¼* **Laudation**[17] 807 3-9-4 68 .... RyanMoore 3 58
(William Jarvis) *chsd ldr: effrt u.p on inner 2f out: unable qck over 1f out: wknd ins fnl f* **11/4[1]**

1m 25.86s (1.06) **Going Correction** +0.10s/f (Slow) 7 Ran SP% **113.7**
Speed ratings (Par 98): **97,96,95,95,93 92,91**
toteswingers 1&2 £4.90, 1&3 £4.00, 2&3 £1.90 CSF £31.79 TOTE £9.10: £3.80, £4.00; EX 37.40 Trifecta £189.10 Pool: £2,074.59 - 8.22 winning units.
Owner Lord Ilsley Racing (Hern Syndicate) **Bred** J Hanly **Trained** West Ilsley, Berks

FOCUS
A very tight handicap. Just fair form, the winner back to his 2yo high.
T/Plt: £27.10 to a £1 stake. Pool of £49,139.16 - 1,321.95 winning units T/Qpdt: £7.80 to a £1 stake. Pool of £2,583.56 - 242.20 winning units SP

992 WOLVERHAMPTON (A.W) (L-H)
Friday, March 15

OFFICIAL GOING: Standard
Wind: Fresh behind Weather: Overcast

1015 BOOKMAKERS.CO.UK APPRENTICE H'CAP 1m 1f 103y(P)
5:25 (5:25) (Class 5) (0-70,70) 4-Y-0+ **£2,587** (£770; £384; £192) **Stalls** Low

Form RPR

662 **1** **Sinchiroka (FR)**[9] 907 7-8-2 56 oh1 .... RyanTate(5) 3 61
(Ralph Smith) *mde all: shkn up over 2f out: rdn over 1f out: r.o* **5/2[1]**

05-5 **2** *¾* **Cabal**[68] 83 6-8-4 56 oh2 ....(b) NeilFarley(3) 4 59
(Andrew Crook) *hood removed late and s.i.s: hld up: hdwy over 1f out: sn rdn: r.o* **9/1**

-421 **3** *hd* **Exceedexpectations (IRE)**[18] 791 4-9-2 70 .... PhilipPrince(5) 6 73
(Conor Dore) *trckd ldrs: racd keenly: rdn over 1f out: r.o* **5/2[1]**

000- **4** *hd* **Imtithal (IRE)**[257] 3671 4-8-11 65 .... RobertTart(5) 7 67?
(John Weymes) *prom: chsd wnr 7f out: rdn over 1f out: kpt on* **14/1**

0550 **5** *½* **Resplendent Alpha**[3] 976 9-8-8 62 .... NedCurtis(5) 1 63
(Alastair Lidderdale) *hld up: outpcd 2f out: r.o ins fnl f* **16/1**

044- **6** *hd* **Kingswinford (IRE)**[101] 7976 7-8-11 67 .... SemiraPashai(7) 2 68
(Alastair Lidderdale) *racd keenly: trckd wnr over 2f: remained handy: shkn up over 1f out: styd on same pce ins fnl f* **11/2[3]**

5424 **7** *1* **For Shia And Lula (IRE)**[21] 749 4-9-0 66 .... DarrenEgan(3) 8 65
(Daniel Mark Loughnane) *hld up: hdwy over 2f out: rdn and hung lft over 1f out: styd on same pce* **4/1[2]**

2m 3.85s (2.15) **Going Correction** +0.05s/f (Slow) 7 Ran SP% **115.1**
Speed ratings (Par 103): **92,91,91,90,90 90,89**
toteswingers 1&2 £3.10, 1&3 £2.50, 2&3 £8.90 CSF £26.38 CT £61.21 TOTE £3.30: £1.70, £4.40; EX 31.80 Trifecta £107.10 Pool: £1033.19 - 7.22 winning units.
Owner Kevin Old **Bred** Gfa Haras Du Hoguenet And Searching Sarl **Trained** Epsom, Surrey

FOCUS
Track GallopMastered after race 4. A modest apprentice handicap that lacked strength in depth. The form is clearly limited, and sensible at this level.

1016 ENJOY BETTING WITH BOOKMAKERS.CO.UK H'CAP 1m 1f 103y(P)
5:55 (5:55) (Class 6) (0-60,60) 3-Y-0 **£1,940** (£577; £288; £144) **Stalls** Low

Form RPR

-133 **1** **Flying Tempo**[17] 803 3-9-5 58 ....(b) GrahamLee 1 75+
(Ed Dunlop) *s.i.s: sn pushed along and prom: chsd ldr over 3f out: rdn to ld wl ins fnl f: r.o* **15/8[1]**

0-61 **2** *1½* **Birdy Boy (USA)**[8] 910 3-8-12 51 6ex .... MartinDwyer 5 65+
(Mark Johnston) *led: hrd rdn: edgd rt and hdd wl ins fnl f* **15/8[1]**

-363 **3** *7* **Silver Fawn (IRE)**[21] 757 3-8-9 48 ....(be) JimmyQuinn 3 49+
(John Weymes) *hld up: n.m.r 4f out: styd on u.p fr over 1f out: nvr nrr* **22/1**

000- **4** *1* **Downright Dizzie**[125] 7686 3-8-3 49 .... RobertTart(7) 7 46
(Tom Keddy) *hld up: rdn over 2f out: r.o ins fnl f: nvr nrr* **9/2[2]**

50-0 **5** *6* **Ceekay's Girl**[15] 824 3-8-2 48 ....(p) RyanTate(7) 4 32
(Mrs K Burke) *chsd ldrs: rdn over 3f out: wknd wl over 1f out* **25/1**

60-0 **6** *2¼* **Whiskey N Stout (IRE)**[15] 824 3-8-11 50 ....(p) FergusSweeney 2 30
(Jamie Osborne) *plld hrd and prom: rdn over 4f out: wknd over 2f out* **7/1[3]**

40-4 **7** *1½* **Warrant Officer**[17] 804 3-8-10 54 .... CharlesBishop(5) 6 31
(Mick Channon) *chsd ldr 6f: sn rdn: wknd wl over 1f out* **14/1**

1m 59.98s (-1.72) **Going Correction** +0.05s/f (Slow) 7 Ran SP% **115.1**
Speed ratings (Par 96): **109,107,101,100,95 93,91**
toteswingers 1&2 £1.60, 2&3 £6.80, 1&3 £2.50, 2&3 £6.80 CSF £5.39 CT £52.48 TOTE £4.90: £1.30, £1.80; EX 6.40 Trifecta £26.40 Pool: £1,366.00 - 38.71 winning units.
Owner Robert Ng **Bred** Dr Celia Marr **Trained** Newmarket, Suffolk

FOCUS
Despite this being only a 0-60 3yo handicap, there was plenty of interest. The front two pulled well clear and they'll soon be leaving this grade well behind.

1017 GET BEST ODDS WITH BOOKMAKERS.CO.UK H'CAP 1m 141y(P)
6:25 (6:26) (Class 6) (0-55,55) 4-Y-0+ £1,940 (£577; £288; £144) Stalls Low

Form RPR
030- 1 **Downtown Boy (IRE)**[146] 7248 5-8-12 **46** oh1..........(p) MartinDwyer 12 58
(Ray Craggs) *mde all: rdn and hung lft ins fnl f: styd on* **50/1**
6022 2 3 ½ **John Potts**[18] 801 8-9-7 **55**..............................(p) GrahamLee 8 60
(Brian Baugh) *chsd ldrs: rdn over 1f out: styd on same pce ins fnl f* **5/1**[3]
0-02 3 *shd* **Hill Of Dreams (IRE)**[15] 825 4-9-5 **53**..........................(b) EddieAhern 3 57
(Dean Ivory) *prom: lost pl over 4f out: hdwy over 1f out: sn rdn: styd on same pce ins fnl f* **9/1**
64/4 4 1 ¼ **William Van Gogh**[45] 435 6-9-6 **54**.............................. JamesSullivan 1 57+
(Michael Easterby) *hld up: hmpd over 7f out: hdwy u.p over 1f out: no imp fnl f* **6/4**[1]
-340 5 3 **American Lover (FR)**[49] 375 6-8-13 **47**..................... PaddyAspell 10 43
(John Wainwright) *s.i.s: hld up: hdwy 5f out: rdn over 2f out: styd on same pce fr over 1f out* **33/1**
5303 6 1 ½ **Justcallmehandsome**[7] 927 11-8-8 **47**....................(be) AmyScott(5) 4 39
(Dominic Ffrench Davis) *dwlt: hld up: hdwy on outer over 2f out: rdn over 1f out: hung lft and wknd ins fnl f* **14/1**
3005 7 *nk* **Maz**[7] 927 5-8-9 **50**.. RobertTart(7) 6 42
(Alan Bailey) *s.i.s: hld up: nvr nrr* **8/1**
4/34 8 5 **Big City Boy (IRE)**[33] 602 5-9-2 **50**.................................. AdamKirby 5 31
(Phil McEntee) *chsd ldrs: wnt 2nd over 3f out: rdn and wknd over 1f out* **40/1**
060- 9 4 **Dansili Dutch (IRE)**[101] 7982 4-9-1 **49**.......................... FrannyNorton 2 22
(Andrew Crook) *mid-div: hmpd over 7f out: nt clr run over 2f out: sn wknd* **33/1**
3000 10 ¾ **Rockgoat (IRE)**[1] 993 4-8-13 **54**.........................(v) JacobButterfield(7) 9 25
(Ian McInnes) *hld up: rdn over 2f out: n.d* **33/1**
11 5 **Musical Express (IRE)**[978] 3938 10-9-4 **52**..................(t) MartinLane 11 13
(W A Murphy, Ire) *s.i.s: rcvrd to chse ldr over 7f out tl rdn over 3f out: wknd over 1f out* **2/1**[2]

1m 50.25s (-0.25) **Going Correction** +0.05s/f (Slow) **11** Ran SP% **131.0**
Speed ratings (Par 101): **103,99,99,98,96 94,94,89,86,85 81**
toteswingers 1&2 £35.70, 1&3 £48.20, 2&3 £5.30 CSF £307.32 CT £2586.87 TOTE £80.80: £11.60, £1.90, £3.00; EX 531.80 Trifecta £1041.70 Part won. Pool: £1,388.98 - 0.04 winning units..
Owner Ray Craggs **Bred** Eclipse Thoroughbreds Inc **Trained** Sedgefield, Co Durham

FOCUS
A low-grade handicap that was notable for the gamble on the William Murphy-trained maiden Musical Express. The pace held up well and the winner proved something of a revelation.

1018 COMPARE BOOKMAKERS WITH BOOKMAKERS.CO.UK H'CAP 2m 119y(P)
7:00 (7:00) (Class 4) (0-85,76) 4-Y-0+ £4,690 (£1,395; £697; £348) Stalls Low

Form RPR
510- 1 **Foster's Road**[20] 7927 4-8-9 **69**.............................. CharlesBishop(5) 1 77
(Mick Channon) *hld up: hdwy over 3f out: rdn to ld over 1f out: styd on* **15/2**
0/02 2 1 ¼ **Capellanus (IRE)**[7] 928 7-9-7 **71**.................................... GrahamLee 5 78
(Brian Ellison) *hld up: hdwy over 1f out: sn rdn: styd on* **2/1**[2]
03/3 3 *nse* **Kalamill (IRE)**[15] 823 6-8-12 **69**.................................. RobertTart(7) 4 75
(Shaun Lycett) *led: clr 12f out tl over 4f out: rdn and hdd over 1f out: styd on* **5/1**[3]
4-22 4 2 ¼ **Tartan Jura**[15] 823 5-9-12 **76**.. FrannyNorton 2 80
(Mark Johnston) *chsd ldrs: rdn over 3f out: nt clr run over 1f out: styd on* **11/8**[1]
34-2 5 ½ **Marcus Antonius**[13] 866 6-9-2 **66**.............................. StephenCraine 3 69
(Jim Boyle) *trckd ldr: carried hd high: rdn and ev ch over 1f out: no ex ins fnl f* **14/1**

3m 41.06s (-0.74) **Going Correction** +0.05s/f (Slow)
WFA 4 from 5yo+ 5lb **5** Ran SP% **110.5**
Speed ratings (Par 105): **103,102,102,101,101**
CSF £22.93 TOTE £7.60: £3.10, £1.30; EX 19.40 Trifecta £89.80 Pool: £835.68 - 6.89 winning units.
Owner Dave and Gill Hedley **Bred** G Hedley & Mike Channon Bloodstock Limited **Trained** West Ilsley, Berks

FOCUS
A small-field staying contest but this was a notch above the earlier fare. It's hard to rate the form any higher than this.

1019 BOOKMAKERS FREE BETS WITH BOOKMAKERS.CO.UK MAIDEN FILLIES' STKS 7f 32y(P)
7:30 (7:35) (Class 5) 3-Y-0+ £2,587 (£770; £384; £192) Stalls High

Form RPR
5-52 1 **Wakeup Little Suzy (IRE)**[37] 532 3-8-10 71..............(t) MartinHarley 5 72+
(Marco Botti) *mde all: set stdy pce tl qcknd 2f out: sn clr: easily* **9/4**[2]
0 2 5 **Is This Love (IRE)**[61] 197 3-8-10 0.......................... FergusSweeney 6 60
(Jamie Osborne) *s.i.s: hld up: r.o to go 2nd wl ins fnl f: no ch w wnr* **33/1**
5 3 ¾ **Clary (IRE)**[14] 849 3-8-10 0.................................. AdamBeschizza 8 58
(James Unett) *hld up in tch: outpcd 2f out: r.o ins fnl f* **14/1**
4 ½ **Hot Right Now** 3-8-10 0.. LukeMorris 2 57
(Mrs K Burke) *prom: pushed along over 2f out: styd on same pce fr over 1f out* **12/1**
562- 5 ½ **Spiritual Girl**[172] 6541 3-8-10 72.. HayleyTurner 4 55
(Michael Bell) *plld hrd: trckd wnr 1f: remained handy: wnt 2nd again over 2f out: sn rdn: wknd ins fnl f* **11/10**[1]
46 6 1 **Floralys (USA)**[17] 807 4-9-12 68....................................(p) AdamKirby 9 59
(John Butler) *prom: chsd wnr 6f out tl 5f out: remained handy: rdn 2f out: wknd fnl f* **12/1**
7 5 **Cards** 3-8-10 0.. FrannyNorton 1 41
(Kevin Ryan) *s.i.s: rn green in rr: hmpd 3f out: nvr on terms* **7/1**[3]
00 8 11 **Just Gwen**[18] 796 4-9-12 0...................................... DuranFentiman 3 20
(Brian Baugh) *sn pushed along: hdwy to chse wnr 5f out tl rdn over 2f out: sn edgd rt and wknd* **80/1**

1m 31.21s (1.61) **Going Correction** +0.05s/f (Slow)
WFA 3 from 4yo 16lb **8** Ran SP% **117.1**
Speed ratings (Par 100): **92,86,85,84,84 83,77,64**
toteswingers 1&2 £22.40, 1&3 £7.90, 2&3 £47.30 CSF £66.53 TOTE £5.70: £1.10, £16.00, £9.50; EX 46.60 Trifecta £674.00 Pool: £1,128.14 - 1.25 winning units.
Owner Philip Newton **Bred** Philip Newton **Trained** Newmarket, Suffolk
■ Sixties Queen was withdrawn on vet's advice (R4 applies, deduct 5p in the £.)

FOCUS
The two market principals came into this fillies' maiden rated in the low 70s. The winner was another to make all, but the favourite was below form and the time slow, so it's not hard to have reservations about the form.

1020 FOOTBALL BETTING WITH BOOKMAKERS.CO.UK H'CAP (DIV I) 7f 32y(P)
8:00 (8:03) (Class 6) (0-55,55) 4-Y-0+ £1,940 (£577; £288; £144) Stalls High

Form RPR
3634 1 **Blue Noodles**[22] 733 7-8-13 **47**....................................(p) PaddyAspell 5 54
(John Wainwright) *chsd ldr tl led 5f out: hdd over 3f out: styd on u.p to ld wl ins fnl f* **14/1**
3415 2 *nk* **Harvest Mist (IRE)**[29] 655 5-8-12 **53**..........................(t) RobertTart(7) 2 59
(Shaun Lycett) *hld up: hdwy and nt clr run over 1f out: rdn and ev ch ins fnl f: r.o* **6/1**
-156 3 *shd* **Boy The Bell**[38] 523 6-9-7 **55**....................................(v[1]) FrannyNorton 6 61
(Ollie Pears) *s.i.s: plld hrd and sn trcking ldrs: rdn to ld over 1f out: edgd rt and hdd wl ins fnl f* **9/2**[3]
1454 4 1 ¼ **Michael's Nook**[3] 967 6-9-4 **52**....................................(p) LukeMorris 9 55
(Alastair Lidderdale) *hld up: hdwy over 2f out: nt clr run fr over 1f out: r.o: nvr able to chal* **7/2**[1]
5365 5 *nk* **The Noble Ord**[3] 975 4-9-2 **55**..................................(t) LeeNewnes(5) 7 57
(Sylvester Kirk) *chsd ldrs: rdn over 2f out: hung lft over 1f out: styd on* **4/1**[2]
50-5 6 3 ½ **Medam**[13] 863 4-9-6 **54**.. DuranFentiman 10 48
(Shaun Harris) *s.s: hld up: hdwy over 2f out: rdn over 1f out: wknd ins fnl f* **18/1**
4000 7 ¾ **Dvinsky (USA)**[9] 900 12-9-2 **50**....................................(b) JimmyQuinn 4 42
(Paul Howling) *led: hdd 5f out: led again over 3f out: rdn and hdd over 1f out: wknd ins fnl f* **25/1**
0024 8 2 ½ **Cadmium Loch**[28] 670 5-9-4 **52**....................................(p) AdamKirby 3 38
(Reg Hollinshead) *mid-div: rdn over 1f out: wknd ins fnl f* **11/2**
0/ 9 3 **Ros Cuire (IRE)**[832] 7709 8-8-12 **46** oh1..........................(t) MartinLane 1 24
(W A Murphy, Ire) *hld up: pushed along over 2f out: wknd wl over 1f out* **5/1**

1m 29.56s (-0.04) **Going Correction** +0.05s/f (Slow) **9** Ran SP% **122.5**
Speed ratings (Par 101): **102,101,101,100,99 95,94,92,88**
toteswingers 1&2 £16.70, 1&3 £15.60, 2&3 £7.80 CSF £101.02 CT £453.44 TOTE £17.80: £3.00, £2.60, £3.30; EX 57.60 Trifecta £524.10 Pool: £702.53 - 1.00 winning units.
Owner drawn2win.co.uk Partnership **Bred** P And Mrs A G Venner **Trained** Kennythorpe, N Yorks

FOCUS
They went a breakneck gallop in this 0-55 handicap and it's to the winner's credit that he managed to fend off all challengers given he was in the firing line from the offset. Typically modest form, but straightforward.

1021 FOOTBALL BETTING WITH BOOKMAKERS.CO.UK H'CAP (DIV II) 7f 32y(P)
8:30 (8:31) (Class 6) (0-55,55) 4-Y-0+ £1,940 (£577; £288; £144) Stalls High

Form RPR
0662 1 **Jonnie Skull (IRE)**[8] 917 7-9-2 **50**..............................(vt) LukeMorris 10 58
(Phil McEntee) *a.p: chsd ldr over 1f out: styd on u.p to ld wl ins fnl f* **9/1**
2-35 2 *nk* **Silly Billy (IRE)**[50] 348 5-8-12 **53**..................................(v) JakePayne(7) 8 60
(Bill Turner) *led early: chsd ldr tl led 1/2-way: rdn over 1f out: hdd wl ins fnl f* **7/2**[2]
414 3 3 ¾ **Fleetwoodsands (IRE)**[22] 737 6-9-4 **52**................(bt) RobertWinston 9 50
(Milton Bradley) *s.i.s: hld up: hdwy u.p over 1f out: edgd lft and styd on same pce ins fnl f* **9/2**[3]
0050 4 2 ¼ **Olynard (IRE)**[9] 900 7-8-5 **46** oh1..................................(p) RobertTart(7) 2 39
(Michael Mullineaux) *prom: rdn over 2f out: wknd ins fnl f* **20/1**
3064 5 1 ¼ **Not My Choice (IRE)**[28] 664 8-8-12 **46** oh1...........(t) TomMcLaughlin 1 36
(Paul Howling) *prom: lost pl over 4f out: n.d after* **25/1**
1-44 6 ½ **Hittin'The Skids (IRE)**[37] 537 5-9-6 **54**..........................(p) AdamKirby 3 42
(Mandy Rowland) *hld up: hdwy 1/2-way: rdn and hung lft over 1f out: wknd ins fnl f* **9/2**[3]
604- 7 ½ **Regal Acclaim (IRE)**[107] 7906 4-9-2 **55**........................(b[1]) JasonHart(5) 7 42
(Declan Carroll) *sn drvn along to ld: hdd 1/2-way: wknd fnl f* **3/1**[1]
00- 8 6 **Legal Eagle (IRE)**[126] 7673 8-9-7 **55**..........................(p) StephenCraine 5 27
(Paul Green) *sn pushed along in rr: nvr on terms* **7/1**
0/ 9 24 **Tumblecloud (IRE)**[1218] 7379 8-8-12 **46** oh1....................(t) MartinLane 6
(W A Murphy, Ire) *dwlt: outpcd* **14/1**

1m 29.2s (-0.40) **Going Correction** +0.05s/f (Slow) **9** Ran SP% **121.4**
Speed ratings (Par 101): **104,103,99,96,95 94,94,87,59**
toteswingers 1&2 £5.90, 1&3 £7.60, 2&3 £5.00 CSF £42.76 CT £152.63 TOTE £12.90: £2.80, £2.10, £1.90; EX 23.70 Trifecta £129.30 Pool: £441.09 - 2.55 winning units.
Owner Eventmaker Racehorses **Bred** Canice Farrell Jnr **Trained** Newmarket, Suffolk

FOCUS
The second division of the 7f handicap was also run at a scorching gallop. The first two were clear and this isn't bad form for the grade.

1022 BOOKMAKERS ON YOUR MOBILE WITH BOOKMAKERS.CO.UK H'CAP 1m 4f 50y(P)
9:00 (9:01) (Class 7) (0-50,50) 4-Y-0+ £1,940 (£577; £288; £144) Stalls Low

Form RPR
5362 1 **Crimson Monarch (USA)**[14] 846 9-9-3 **46**..............(b) WilliamCarson 3 52
(Peter Hiatt) *hld up: nt clr run over 2f out: hdwy over 1f out: styd on u.p to ld wl ins fnl f* **5/1**[2]
00-4 2 ¾ **Needwood Park**[25] 704 5-9-7 **50**..................................(p) MartinDwyer 2 55
(Ray Craggs) *led: rdn over 1f out: hdd wl ins fnl f* **15/2**
0-20 3 ½ **Life Of Laughter (USA)**[23] 724 5-9-7 **50**..............(b[1]) StevieDonohoe 4 54
(Willie Musson) *hld up in tch: rdn over 1f out: ev ch ins fnl f: styd on same pce* **7/2**[1]
0-04 4 2 ¼ **Snowy Valley**[14] 846 4-8-11 **49**..................................(p) RyanTate(7) 10 50
(Simon Earle) *chsd ldrs: rdn over 1f out: styd on same pce ins fnl f* **10/1**
4003 5 2 **Seaquel**[15] 820 7-9-3 **46**..(v) AdamKirby 12 44
(Tony Carroll) *chsd ldrs: wnt 2nd over 6f out: rdn over 2f out: hung lft over 1f out: no ex fnl f* **7/2**[1]
0040 6 8 **Nurse Dominatrix (IRE)**[14] 625 4-9-0 **45**.............. RobbieFitzpatrick 1 31
(Richard Guest) *hld up: plld hrd: nvr on terms* **33/1**
-066 7 1 ¼ **There's No Rules**[8] 908 4-8-7 **45**..............................(e) DavidBergin(7) 9 29
(Richard Guest) *plld hrd: trckd ldr over 5f: remained handy tl rdn and wknd over 1f out* **33/1**
0/00 8 12 **Share Option**[39] 458 11-8-9 **45**.................................. AidenBlakemore(7) 5 11
(Tony Carroll) *s.s: a in rr* **50/1**
045- 9 7 **Bandy Bob**[129] 7620 4-9-0 **45**.. JamieMackay 6
(Iain Jardine) *hld up: rdn over 3f out: sn wknd: t.o* **11/2**[3]
/0-4 10 27 **Joyously**[15] 820 5-9-7 **50**...(t) MartinHarley 11
(Violet M Jordan) *prom: rdn over 3f out: wknd 2f out: t.o* **8/1**

00/ 11 76 **Toberogan (IRE)**[1261] 6411 12-9-2 45 MartinLane 8
(W A Murphy, Ire) *hld up: a in rr: bhd fnl 5f: t.o* 14/1
2m 40.48s (-0.62) **Going Correction** +0.05s/f (Slow)
WFA 4 from 5yo+ 2lb 11 Ran SP% 123.0
Speed ratings (Par 97): **104,103,103,101,100 95,94,86,81,63 12**
toteswingers 1&2 £7.50, 1&3 £2.40, 2&3 £11.50 CSF £43.93 CT £152.44 TOTE £5.60: £1.60, £3.20, £1.90; EX 36.30 Trifecta £198.80 Pool: £611.28 - 2.30 winning units.
Owner P W Hiatt **Bred** Sun Valley Farm & Vinery Llc **Trained** Hook Norton, Oxon

FOCUS
Some poor performers in this middle-distance handicap. Weak form, rated on the negative side.
T/Plt: £105.90 to a £1 stake. Pool: £81,865.35 - 564.17 winning tickets T/Qpdt: £20.40 to a £1 stake. Pool: £8,685.16 - 314.20 winning tickets CR

1023 - 1030a (Foreign Racing) - See Raceform Interactive

1008 LINGFIELD (L-H)
Saturday, March 16

OFFICIAL GOING: Standard
Wind: Fresh, behind Weather: Rain before racing, damp

1031 BLUE SQUARE BET ALL WEATHER "HANDS AND HEELS" APPRENTICE SERIES FINAL H'CAP 1m 5f (P)
1:45 (1:45) (Class 5) (0-75,75) 4-Y-0+ **£2,726** (£805; £402) **Stalls** Low

Form RPR
-211 1 **Wordiness**[19] 797 5-9-5 72 RobertTart 2 84+
(Brendan Powell) *hld up in midfield to rr: hdwy to ld 1f out: qcknd clr: pushed out* 9/4[1]
-112 2 4 **Stentorian (IRE)**[21] 779 5-9-6 73 (p) RyanTate 7 79
(Gary Moore) *towards rr: effrt and wd into st: r.o to take 2nd ins fnl f* 7/2[2]
2342 3 3 **El Libertador (USA)**[10] 905 7-8-5 61 oh4 (b) JoeyHaynes(3) 4 63
(Eric Wheeler) *prom: rdn 2f out: one pce* 14/1
40-5 4 1 1/4 **The Ducking Stool**[71] 53 6-8-5 61 ShelleyBirkett(3) 1 61
(Julia Feilden) *s.i.s: sn led: rdn 2f out: hdd over and wknd 1f out* 25/1
5-32 5 nse **Beat Route**[18] 809 6-9-7 74 PhilipPrince 5 74
(Michael Attwater) *t.k.h: in tch: sltly lost pl 7f out: effrt and swtchd wd 2f out: unable to chal* 7/2[2]
350- 6 3 3/4 **Ostentation**[4] 7169 6-8-11 64 GaryPhillips 8 58
(Alastair Lidderdale) *hld up in rr: sme hdwy and in tch 5f out: outpcd fnl 2f* 5/1[3]
04-5 7 3/4 **Thecornishcowboy**[17] 810 4-9-0 75 (t) CarolineKelly(5) 6 68
(John Ryan) *t.k.h towards rr: hdwy on outer to join ldr 1m out: wknd over 1f out* 10/1
1/3- 8 4 **Bugsy's Boy**[218] 5051 9-8-10 66 (p) AaronJones(3) 3 53
(George Baker) *prom tl wknd 3f out* 20/1
2m 47.15s (1.15) **Going Correction** -0.05s/f (Stan)
WFA 4 from 5yo+ 3lb 8 Ran SP% 116.2
Speed ratings (Par 103): **94,91,89,88,88 86,86,83**
Tote Swingers: 1&2 £2.10, 1&3 £4.40, 2&3 £5.10 CSF £10.45 CT £87.75 TOTE £2.10: £1.10, £1.10, £3.90; EX 7.40 Trifecta £60.30 Pool: £4,021.24 - 49.95 winning units.
Owner W A Harrison-Allan **Bred** Juddmonte Farms Ltd **Trained** Upper Lambourn, Berks

FOCUS
A modest handicap, confined to apprentice riders and run at a slow pace. The form is straightforward around the second to fourth.

1032 BLUE SQUARE BET HEVER SPRINT STKS (LISTED RACE) 5f (P)
2:20 (2:21) (Class 1) 4-Y-0+ **£20,982** (£7,955; £3,981; £1,983; £995; £499) **Stalls** High

Form RPR
02-1 1 **Ladies Are Forever**[21] 776 5-8-12 99 WilliamTwiston-Davies 5 111
(Geoffrey Oldroyd) *prom: led over 1f out: rdn clr* 10/1
/03- 2 2 1/4 **Timeless Call (IRE)**[141] 7390 5-8-9 100 PaulMulrennan 1 100
(Reginald Roberts, Ire) *led: rdn and hdd over 1f out: kpt on same pce* 8/1
1111 3 1 **Tarooq (USA)**[7] 947 7-9-0 100 (t) SeanLevey 8 101
(Stuart Williams) *bhd: hdwy over 1f out: fin strly: snatched 3rd on line* 6/1[3]
5453 4 shd **Fratellino**[21] 776 6-9-0 99 (t) MartinHarley 3 101
(Alan McCabe) *chsd ldrs: rdn 2f out: one pce* 12/1
1-24 5 hd **York Glory (USA)**[21] 776 5-9-0 102 (b) NeilCallan 7 100
(Kevin Ryan) *s.s: bhd: wd on home turn: gd hdwy over 1f out: one pce ins fnl f* 9/2[2]
-334 6 1 1/4 **Bear Behind (IRE)**[23] 746 4-9-0 104 RichardKingscote 10 96
(Tom Dascombe) *ponied to s: chsd ldr tl wknd over 1f out* 7/1
21-2 7 1 **Intransigent**[7] 947 4-9-0 100 LiamKeniry 6 92
(Andrew Balding) *mid-div: rdn and no imp fnl 2f* 4/1[1]
-110 8 nk **Woolfall Sovereign (IRE)**[35] 584 7-9-0 99 IanMongan 2 91
(George Margarson) *towards rr: rdn 3f out: n.d* 20/1
0-12 9 3/4 **Farmleigh House (IRE)**[21] 776 6-9-0 104 (v[1]) NGMcCullagh 9 88
(W J Martin, Ire) *a towards rr* 8/1
230- 10 1/2 **Taajub (IRE)**[160] 6908 6-9-0 103 ShaneKelly 4 87
(Peter Crate) *mid-div tl outpcd fnl 2f* 12/1
56.67s (-2.13) **Going Correction** -0.05s/f (Stan) course record 10 Ran SP% 116.4
Speed ratings (Par 111): **115,111,109,109,109 107,105,105,104,103**
Tote Swingers: 1&2 £13.90, 1&3 £6.00, 2&3 £11.80 CSF £87.27 TOTE £12.30: £2.70, £3.00, £2.20; EX 124.20 Trifecta £730.10 Pool: £4,095.93 - 4.20 winning units.
Owner R C Bond **Bred** Bond Thoroughbred Corporation **Trained** Brawby, N Yorks

FOCUS
A competitive Listed sprint. Straightforward form, with the winner rated right back to his best.

1033 BLUESQ.COM SPRING CUP (LISTED RACE) 7f (P)
2:55 (2:56) (Class 1) 3-Y-O **£20,982** (£7,955; £3,981; £1,983; £995; £499) **Stalls** Low

Form RPR
14-1 1 **Teophilip (IRE)**[29] 674 3-9-1 89 (t) AndreaAtzeni 10 97
(Marco Botti) *swtchd to inner sn after s: hld up in tch: qcknd though on rail ent st: led 1f out: drvn out* 10/1
212- 2 1 1/4 **Emell**[140] 7400 3-9-1 100 RichardHughes 5 94+
(Richard Hannon) *hld up in midfield: rdn and hdwy over 1f out: r.o to take 2nd fnl strides* 2/1[1]
231- 3 hd **Hoarding (USA)**[143] 7331 3-9-1 93 WilliamBuick 8 95+
(John Gosden) *hld up in rr on outer: wd into st: r.o wl fnl f: nrest at fin* 7/2[2]
540- 4 nse **Shafaani**[161] 6873 3-8-10 75 (t) ChrisCatlin 3 88
(Clive Brittain) *led: rdn and hdd 1f out: kpt on: lost 2nd fnl strides* 66/1
040- 5 1/2 **Hasopop (IRE)**[140] 7404 3-9-1 97 AdamKirby 12 94+
(Marco Botti) *stdd s and swtchd lft to inner: hld up in rr: nt clr run ent st and again over 1f out: swtchd outside: r.o wl fnl f: unlucky* 8/1
460- 6 nse **Maxentius (IRE)**[140] 7404 3-9-1 104 LukeMorris 9 92
(Peter Chapple-Hyam) *stdd s and swtchd towards inner s: hld up towards rr: rdn and hdwy over 1f out: styng on whn n.m.r nr fin* 5/1[3]
-211 7 1 **Ashamaly**[38] 533 3-9-1 89 NeilCallan 2 89
(James Tate) *chsd ldrs: rdn 2f out: one pce fnl f* 14/1
2-26 8 3/4 **Lucky Di**[29] 674 3-8-10 77 JohnFahy 4 82?
(Peter Hedger) *chsd ldrs: effrt 2f out: no ex fnl f* 66/1
31-2 9 3/4 **Grilletto (USA)**[29] 674 3-9-1 75 (b) TomQueally 1 85
(James Tate) *chsd ldr: rdn 2f out: wknd fnl f* 33/1
346- 10 2 1/4 **Queen Aggie (IRE)**[130] 7622 3-8-10 94 RichardKingscote 11 74
(David Evans) *mid-div: hmpd 5f out and sn dropped to rr: mod effrt on inner over 1f out: no imp* 20/1
440- 11 3/4 **Lyric Ace (IRE)**[184] 6162 3-9-1 93 JimCrowley 7 77
(Paul D'Arcy) *t.k.h: prom on outer tl hrd rdn and wknd over 1f out* 33/1
222- 12 3 **Ask The Guru**[218] 5045 3-9-1 94 SebSanders 6 69
(Michael Attwater) *mid-div on outer tl outpcd fnl 2f* 25/1
1m 23.28s (-1.52) **Going Correction** -0.05s/f (Stan) 12 Ran SP% 116.6
Speed ratings (Par 106): **106,104,104,104,103 103,102,101,100,98 97,93**
Tote Swingers: 1&2 £5.30, 1&3 £6.40, 2&3 £2.30 CSF £28.10 TOTE £14.00: £3.50, £1.10, £1.40; EX 40.50 Trifecta £178.80 Pool: £214,397.26 - 899.13 winning units.
Owner Giuliano Manfredini **Bred** Mount Coote Stud, Richard Pegum & M Bell Racing **Trained** Newmarket, Suffolk

FOCUS
A tight 3-y-o Listed event and it was run at an uneven pace. Something of a rough race. The fourth and eighth nay be flattered but the first three are of interest going forward.

1034 BLUE SQUARE BET WINTER DERBY (GROUP 3) 1m 2f (P)
3:30 (3:30) (Class 1) 4-Y-0+
£56,710 (£21,500; £10,760; £5,360; £2,690; £1,350) **Stalls** Low

Form RPR
/31- 1 **Farraaj (IRE)**[119] 7771 4-9-0 108 AndreaAtzeni 5 107+
(Roger Varian) *trckd ldrs: rdn 2f out: led ins fnl f: hld on wl* 6/4[1]
-311 2 1/2 **Robin Hoods Bay**[10] 897 5-9-0 95 JimCrowley 1 106
(Ed Vaughan) *hld up in tch: effrt and swtchd to rail 1f out: pressed wnr ins fnl f: r.o* 12/1
026- 3 3/4 **Cai Shen (IRE)**[176] 6446 5-9-0 99 RichardHughes 8 105
(Richard Hannon) *trckd ldr: led 1f out: hrd rdn and hdd ins fnl f: kpt on* 9/2[3]
-654 4 3/4 **Tinshu (IRE)**[10] 897 7-8-11 93 (p) WilliamCarson 7 100
(Derek Haydn Jones) *towards rr: rdn and styd on fr over 1f out: nvr nrr* 33/1
013- 5 2 **Premio Loco (USA)**[169] 6634 9-9-5 111 GeorgeBaker 4 105
(Chris Wall) *trckd ldrs: nt clr run wl over 1f out: one pce fnl f* 4/1[2]
-055 6 nk **Field Of Dream**[16] 838 6-9-0 102 AdamKirby 3 99
(Jamie Osborne) *s.i.s: bhd: hrd rdn and sme hdwy over 1f out: nt rch ldrs* 16/1
113- 7 5 **Viking Storm**[129] 7630 5-9-0 106 LukeMorris 11 89
(Harry Dunlop) *on and off the bridle: a abt same pl: unable to trble ldrs fnl 2f* 6/1
8 2 1/4 **Ansgar (IRE)**[99] 8028 5-9-0 98 (t) DeclanMcDonogh 2 85
(Sabrina J Harty, Ire) *led at decent pce tl wknd qckly over 1f out* 20/1
000- 9 31 **Robin Hood (IRE)**[160] 6912 5-9-0 99 JackMitchell 9 26
(Philip Mitchell) *chsd ldrs on outer: drvn along 5f out: wknd 4f out: wl bhd fnl 2f* 50/1
2m 0.99s (-5.61) **Going Correction** -0.05s/f (Stan) 9 Ran SP% 115.7
Speed ratings (Par 113): **120,119,119,118,116 116,112,110,85**
Tote Swingers: 1&2 £5.50, 1&3 £2.60, 2&3 £9.40 CSF £21.66 TOTE £2.50: £1.10, £3.10, £1.80; EX 18.70 Trifecta £101.30 Pool: £4,360.60 - 32.27 winning units.
Owner Sheikh Ahmed Al Maktoum **Bred** Darley **Trained** Newmarket, Suffolk

FOCUS
A strong renewal of the Winter Derby with last year's first and second lining up. The winner broke the course record and this is solid Listed form. Farraaj could be rated perhaps 4lb better.

1035 BET AT BLUESQ.COM MAIDEN STKS 1m (P)
4:05 (4:08) (Class 5) 3-Y-0+ **£2,726** (£805; £402) **Stalls** High

Form RPR
034- 1 **Erodium**[191] 5963 3-8-10 75 RichardHughes 4 77+
(Richard Hannon) *trckd ldr: led 1f out: pushed out: comf* 4/5[1]
30-2 2 1 1/2 **Spring Tonic**[17] 814 4-9-13 74 NeilCallan 3 77
(Simon Dow) *sn led at modest pce: qcknd over 2f out: hdd 1f out: no ch w wnr* 7/4[2]
3 5 **Rubbamaa** 4-9-8 0 TomQueally 5 60+
(Clive Brittain) *in tch: rdn 3f out: sn outpcd by first 2: kpt on fnl f* 16/1
3 4 7 **Jolaine**[42] 492 4-9-8 0 JimCrowley 1 44
(Ralph Beckett) *chsd ldrs: rdn 3f out: sn btn* 6/1[3]
46- 5 1 1/2 **Just River**[91] 8141 4-9-13 0 (t) LiamKeniry 2 46
(Seamus Mullins) *plld hrd in rr: outpcd and lost tch over 2f out* 100/1
5 6 4 1/2 **Bit Windy**[8] 925 4-9-8 0 JDSmith 7 30
(Chris Dwyer) *plld hrd: chsd ldrs on outer: wknd over 2f out* 50/1
7 3/4 **Be Excellent** 3-8-5 0 LukeMorris 8 23
(Joseph Tuite) *hld up towards rr: outpcd and n.d fnl 2f* 33/1
1m 39.14s (0.94) **Going Correction** -0.05s/f (Stan)
WFA 3 from 4yo 17lb 7 Ran SP% 118.0
Speed ratings (Par 103): **93,91,86,79,78 73,72**
Tote Swingers: 1&2 £1.10, 2&3 £2.90 CSF £2.58 TOTE £1.80: £1.10, £1.20; EX 2.90 Trifecta £12.80 Pool: £4,187.52 - 244.00 winning units.
Owner Rockcliffe Stud **Bred** Rockcliffe Stud **Trained** East Everleigh, Wilts

FOCUS
A moderate maiden.

1036 ENOUGH SAID JUST BET AT BLUESQ.COM H'CAP 1m (P)
4:40 (4:42) (Class 2) (0-100,98) 4-Y-0+ **£12,291** (£3,657; £1,827; £913) **Stalls** High

Form RPR
321- 1 **Benzanno (IRE)**[148] 7210 4-8-8 90 ThomasBrown(5) 2 100
(Andrew Balding) *sn stdd towards rr: effrt and eased out ent st: str run to ld nr fin* 8/1
453- 2 nk **Swing Alone (IRE)**[134] 7520 4-8-7 84 oh1 LukeMorris 4 93
(Gay Kelleway) *sn rdn along towards rr: wd into st: gd hdwy fr over 1f out: styd on wl to take 2nd nr fin* 12/1
61-2 3 1/2 **Grey Mirage**[42] 495 4-8-12 89 (p) JimmyQuinn 9 97+
(Marco Botti) *sn pressing ldr: led and gng wl 2f out: hrd rdn fnl f: ct nr fin* 5/2[1]
06-4 4 1 **Dubai Dynamo**[7] 947 8-8-13 90 PJMcDonald 7 96
(Ruth Carr) *in tch: effrt over 1f out: hrd rdn ent fnl f: one pce* 5/1[2]
000- 5 3/4 **Bronze Prince**[203] 5572 6-9-7 98 RobertHavlin 1 102
(Michael Attwater) *led tl 2f out: wknd ins fnl f* 25/1

-425 **6** 1 ¼ **George Guru**[10] 897 6-9-1 **95**.................... MarkCoumbe[(3)] 6 96
(Michael Attwater) *dwlt: sn chsng ldrs: rdn over 2f out: wknd 1f out* **8/1**
4244 **7** nk **Mia's Boy**[7] 945 9-9-3 **94**.................... GeorgeBaker 3 95
(Chris Dwyer) *hld up in rr: rdn over 1f out: nvr trbld ldrs* **6/1**[3]
0-06 **8** ¾ **Mr Red Clubs (IRE)**[35] 585 4-8-12 **89**.................... ShaneKelly 5 88
(Tim Pitt) *in tch: rdn over 2f out: wknd over 1f out* **7/1**
3120 **9** 1 **Loyalty**[7] 945 6-9-1 **92**....................(v) MartinDwyer 8 89
(Derek Shaw) *prom: rdn over 2f out: 4th and btn whn n.m.r on rail over 1f out* **8/1**

1m 35.49s (-2.71) **Going Correction** -0.05s/f (Stan) 9 Ran SP% **116.9**
Speed ratings (Par 109): **111,110,110,109,108 107,106,106,105**
Tote Swingers: 1&2 £11.70, 1&3 £4.30, 2&3 £6.70 CSF £99.48 CT £312.08 TOTE £8.00: £2.60, £5.60, £1.10; EX 69.30 Trifecta £359.60 Pool: £1,686.71 - 3.51 winning units.
Owner Martin & Valerie Slade & Partner **Bred** Nanallac Stud **Trained** Kingsclere, Hants
■ Stewards' Enquiry : Mark Coumbe one-day ban: careless riding (Mar 30)

FOCUS
A competitive handicap.

1037 BET ON YOUR MOBILE AT BLUESQ.COM H'CAP 1m 4f (P)
5:15 (5:15) (Class 3) (0-95,91) 4-Y-0+ **£7,439** (£2,213; £1,106; £553) **Stalls Low**

Form RPR
3611 **1** **Buckland (IRE)**[12] 882 5-8-11 **86**.................... NicoleNordblad[(5)] 6 94
(Hans Adielsson) *t.k.h: prom: wnt 2nd over 2f out: led jst over 1f out: pushed out* **9/2**[2]
1-6 **2** ½ **Solaras Exhibition (IRE)**[28] 691 5-8-5 **82**.............. DanielMuscutt[(7)] 8 89
(Tim Vaughan) *t.k.h: chsd ldrs on outer: drvn to chal over 1f out: kpt on* **20/1**
0013 **3** 1 **Aquilonius (IRE)**[14] 865 4-9-0 **86**....................(t) JamieSpencer 5 92
(Stuart Williams) *sn led at modest pce: chsd ldr after 4f tl led again 3f out: hdd jst over 1f out: one pce* **9/2**[2]
10-3 **4** nk **The Tiger**[8] 926 5-9-7 **91**.................... GrahamLee 7 96
(Ed Dunlop) *towards rr: rdn and styd on fnl 2f: nvr nrr* **11/4**[1]
15-0 **5** ¾ **Incendo**[42] 496 7-8-11 **86**....................(t) WilliamTwiston-Davies[(5)] 2 90
(Ian Williams) *hld up towards rr: hdwy over 1f out: styd on same pce fnl f* **8/1**[3]
1-12 **6** ¾ **Cool Sky**[61] 208 4-8-8 **80**.................... LukeMorris 3 83
(William Knight) *in tch: rdn 3f out: one pce ent fnl f* **9/2**[2]
2512 **7** 2 ¼ **Reflect (IRE)**[12] 882 5-8-7 **77** oh1....................(t) MartinDwyer 4 76
(Derek Shaw) *plld hrd: chsd ldrs tl wknd over 1f out* **12/1**
560- **8** 1 ½ **Layline (IRE)**[84] 8227 6-9-4 **88**.................... NeilCallan 9 87
(Gay Kelleway) *stdd s: plld hrd in rr: rdn whn hmpd over 2f out: n.d* **12/1**
2503 **9** 13 **Ajeeb (USA)**[12] 882 5-8-9 **79**....................(v) PaulMulrennan 1 57
(Michael Scudamore) *plld hrd: prom: led 1m out and increased tempo: hdd 3f out: towards rr and wkng whn hmpd over 2f out* **20/1**

2m 30.54s (-2.46) **Going Correction** -0.05s/f (Stan)
WFA 4 from 5yo+ 2lb 9 Ran SP% **117.2**
Speed ratings (Par 107): **106,105,105,104,104 103,102,101,92**
Tote Swingers: 1&2 £9.50, 1&3 £4.20, 2&3 £10.80 CSF £88.98 CT £423.27 TOTE £5.00: £1.70, £5.00, £1.50; EX 82.70 Trifecta £340.00 Pool: £1,390.43 - 3.06 winning units.
Owner P S McNally **Bred** Airlie Stud And Sir Thomas Pilkington **Trained** Kingston Lisle, Oxon

FOCUS
A fair handicap.
T/Plt: £19.10 to a £1 stake. Pool: £114,704.00 - 4,370.49 winning tickets. T/Qpdt: £3.00 to a £1 stake. Pool: £5,450.00 - 1,330.19 winning tickets. LM

1015 WOLVERHAMPTON (A.W) (L-H)
Saturday, March 16

OFFICIAL GOING: Standard
Wind: Light behind Weather: Light rain

1038 ENJOY BETTING WITH BOOKMAKERS.CO.UK H'CAP 7f 32y(P)
5:50 (5:50) (Class 5) (0-70,76) 4-Y-0+ **£2,587** (£770; £384; £192) **Stalls High**

Form RPR
1331 **1** **Frontier Fighter**[3] 987 5-9-13 **76** 6ex.................... DanielTudhope 2 95+
(David O'Meara) *mde all: shkn up over 1f out: r.o: comf* **10/11**[1]
400- **2** 3 ¼ **Spykes Bay (USA)**[162] 6840 4-9-6 **69**.................... MartinHarley 4 75
(Mrs K Burke) *a.p: chsd wnr over 2f out: rdn over 1f out: styd on same pce ins fnl f* **4/1**[2]
5050 **3** 2 **Lord Of The Dance (IRE)**[3] 987 7-9-4 **67**.................... TomEaves 6 68
(Michael Mullineaux) *hld up: hdwy over 1f out: r.o: nt rch ldrs* **40/1**
6065 **4** ¾ **Restless Bay (IRE)**[4] 971 5-9-3 **66**....................(b) HayleyTurner 3 65
(Conor Dore) *hld up: plld hrd: hdwy over 1f out: nrst fin* **14/1**
00-1 **5** 3 **Dashwood**[33] 617 6-9-5 **68**....................(t) SteveDrowne 8 60
(Anthony Carson) *sn prom: rdn over 1f out: wknd ins fnl f* **4/1**[2]
3445 **6** ¾ **Key Ambition**[25] 715 4-9-4 **67**....................(tp) RobertWinston 5 57
(Garry Moss) *hld up: rdn over 2f out: nvr on terms* **25/1**
-600 **7** ¾ **Needwood Ridge**[37] 546 6-8-8 **60**....................(bt) RaulDaSilva[(3)] 7 48
(Frank Sheridan) *chsd wnr tl over 5f out: remained handy: rdn over 2f out: wknd over 1f out* **33/1**
-012 **8** ½ **Prince James**[4] 976 6-9-0 **63**.................... GrahamGibbons 9 50
(Michael Easterby) *prom: chsd wnr over 5f out tl rdn over 2f out: wknd fnl f* **10/1**[3]
-410 **9** 1 ½ **Prince Of Passion (CAN)**[30] 652 5-8-12 **61**............(v) FrannyNorton 1 44
(Derek Shaw) *hld up: a in rr* **25/1**

1m 27.64s (-1.96) **Going Correction** -0.125s/f (Stan) 9 Ran SP% **121.2**
Speed ratings (Par 103): **106,102,100,99,95 94,94,93,91**
toteswingers 1&2 £1.90, 1&3 £16.10, 2&3 £26.80 CSF £4.91 CT £89.85 TOTE £1.60: £1.30, £1.50, £6.90; EX 7.20 Trifecta £113.20 Pool: £1,092.90 - 7.23 winning units.
Owner Archibald Nichol & Partners **Bred** Darley **Trained** Nawton, N Yorks

FOCUS
Track GallopMastered after race 4. A one-sided handicap. The winner had no trouble reproducing his Fibresand form on Polytrack.

1039 FREE BETTING TIPS WITH BOOKMAKERS.CO.UK (S) STKS 7f 32y(P)
6:20 (6:20) (Class 6) 4-Y-0+ **£1,940** (£577; £288; £144) **Stalls High**

Form RPR
6-31 **1** **Classic Colori (IRE)**[40] 517 6-9-4 **78**....................(b) DanielTudhope 3 81
(David O'Meara) *chsd ldrs: led 1f out: rdn out* **4/6**[1]
4550 **2** 3 ½ **Abhaath (USA)**[4] 976 4-8-5 **60**.................... GaryPhillips[(7)] 4 66
(Ronald Harris) *chsd ldr tl pushed along to ld over 2f out: rdn: hung rt and hdd 1f out: styd on same pce* **9/1**
4143 **3** 2 ¾ **Zing Wing**[3] 980 5-8-13 **73**....................(v) SteveDrowne 2 60
(David Evans) *hld up: rdn over 1f out: nvr trbld ldrs* **9/2**[2]
4024 **4** shd **Master Of Disguise**[7] 946 7-8-12 **64**.................... GrahamGibbons 7 58
(Brian Baugh) *hld up: nt clr run over 2f out: rdn over 1f out: n.d* **17/2**[3]
1304 **5** 5 **The Mongoose**[10] 899 5-9-4 **62**....................(vt) MartinHarley 5 51
(David Evans) *led: rdn and hdd over 2f out: wknd fnl f* **11/1**
1406 **6** 6 **Spinning Ridge (IRE)**[10] 903 8-8-9 **58**....................(v) DarrenEgan[(3)] 1 29
(Ronald Harris) *chsd ldrs: rdn over 2f out: wknd over 1f out* **25/1**

1m 27.81s (-1.79) **Going Correction** -0.125s/f (Stan) 6 Ran SP% **110.9**
Speed ratings (Par 101): **105,101,97,97,92 85**
toteswingers 1&2 £2.50, 1&3 £1.10, 2&3 £3.80 CSF £7.37 TOTE £1.50: £1.20, £7.00; EX 7.90 Trifecta £37.30 Pool: £1,183.01 - 23.75 winning units.The winner was bought in for 3,750gns.
Owner The Classic Strollers Partnership **Bred** Frank Dunne **Trained** Nawton, N Yorks

FOCUS
The winner is a lot better than this grade. The second helps set the level.

1040 FREE HORSE RACING BETS WITH BOOKMAKERS.CO.UK H'CAP 2m 5f 194y(P)
6:50 (6:50) (Class 6) (0-60,60) 4-Y-0+ **£1,940** (£577; £288; £144) **Stalls Low**

Form RPR
-062 **1** **The Blue Dog (IRE)**[22] 755 6-9-5 **60**.................... RobertTart[(5)] 3 70
(Michael Wigham) *s.i.s: sn prom: led over 1f out: rdn and hung lft ins fnl f: styd on* **5/2**[1]
00-3 **2** 1 ¼ **Mr Plod**[22] 755 8-9-3 **53**.................... EddieAhern 1 61
(J R Jenkins) *chsd ldrs: rdn over 1f out: r.o* **11/2**
600/ **3** ½ **Star Alliance (IRE)**[645] 2874 5-9-8 **58**.................... StevieDonohoe 6 65
(Ian Williams) *prom: outpcd over 3f out: r.o ins fnl f* **5/1**[3]
-212 **4** 2 ¾ **Bold Adventure**[13] 351 9-9-8 **58**.................... TonyCulhane 4 61
(Willie Musson) *chsd ldr tl rdn over 2f out: styd on same pce fr over 1f out* **7/2**[2]
0120 **5** hd **Party Palace**[22] 755 9-8-6 **49**.................... JordanVaughan[(7)] 2 52
(Stuart Howe) *led: sddle slipped sn after s: pushed along over 2f out: rdn and hdd over 1f out: no ex ins fnl f* **7/1**
-061 **6** 3 **Smirfy's Silver**[15] 846 9-8-8 **51**.................... JordanNason[(7)] 7 50
(Michael Mullineaux) *s.i.s: hld up: hdwy over 1f out: wknd fnl f* **20/1**
/334 **7** 8 **Esteem**[12] 713 10-9-5 **55**....................(t) AdamKirby 5 43
(David Evans) *hld up: rdn over 2f out: wknd over 1f out* **8/1**

3m 4.13s (-1.87) **Going Correction** -0.125s/f (Stan) 7 Ran SP% **111.2**
Speed ratings (Par 101): **100,99,99,97,97 95,91**
toteswingers 1&2 £2.50, 1&3 £1.10, 2&3 £3.80 CSF £15.60 TOTE £2.80: £1.90, £1.70; EX 11.30 Trifecta £139.10 Pool: £924.58 - 4.98 winning units.
Owner R Carson **Bred** Mervyn Stewkesbury **Trained** Newmarket, Suffolk

FOCUS
A modest handicap.The gallop wasn't strong, the race not really beginning in earnest until the final 4f. The winner got back towards his better form.

1041 FOOTBALL ODDS WITH BOOKMAKERS.CO.UK CLAIMING STKS 5f 216y(P)
7:20 (7:21) (Class 5) 3-Y-0 **£2,587** (£770; £384; £192) **Stalls Low**

Form RPR
131 **1** **Hiddon Coin (IRE)**[16] 827 3-9-10 **81**.................... DanielTudhope 1 82
(David O'Meara) *mde virtually all: rdn over 1f out: r.o: eased nr fin* **1/1**[1]
4-15 **2** 2 ¼ **Groove On (IRE)**[24] 730 3-9-6 **73**....................(t) AdamKirby 4 70
(Marco Botti) *a.p: chsd wnr over 3f out: rdn over 1f out: hung lft and styd on same pce fnl f* **13/8**[2]
-345 **3** ¾ **Studfarmer**[3] 982 3-9-2 **68**....................(v[1]) MartinHarley 3 64
(David Evans) *sn outpcd: r.o ins fnl f: nt rch ldrs* **18/1**
-624 **4** 1 **La Sylphe**[16] 828 3-8-7 **70**.................... FrannyNorton 5 52
(Derek Shaw) *led early: plld hrd: trckd wnr tl over 3f out: rdn over 1f out: styd on same pce fnl f* **12/1**[3]
2343 **5** 1 **Princess Cammie (IRE)**[28] 686 3-8-3 **56**.................... KieranO'Neill 2 45
(Mike Murphy) *chsd ldrs: n.m.r 4f out: rdn over 1f out: styd on same pce* **16/1**

1m 14.1s (-0.90) **Going Correction** -0.125s/f (Stan) 5 Ran SP% **106.9**
Speed ratings (Par 98): **101,98,97,95,94**
CSF £2.63 TOTE £2.00: £1.20, £1.10; EX 2.20 Trifecta £11.50 Pool: £1,113.60 - 72.04 winning units.
Owner Hambleton Racing Ltd - Three In One **Bred** Noel & Anthony O'Callaghan **Trained** Nawton, N Yorks

FOCUS
The winner is consistent in these races and was always in control. The time backs up the figures.

1042 BIGGEST FREE BETS WITH BOOKMAKERS.CO.UK H'CAP (DIV I) 5f 216y(P)
7:50 (7:51) (Class 6) (0-52,58) 4-Y-0+ **£1,940** (£577; £288; £144) **Stalls Low**

Form RPR
5134 **1** **Rise To Glory (IRE)**[9] 917 5-9-2 **47**....................(b) DuranFentiman 12 55
(Shaun Harris) *w ldrs: led over 4f out: rdn over 1f out: jst hld on* **8/1**
0005 **2** nk **Doctor Hilary**[19] 794 11-8-8 **46** oh1....................(v) PhilipPrince[(7)] 3 53
(Mark Hoad) *broke wl sn lost pl: hdwy over 1f out: r.o* **20/1**
5213 **3** ½ **Rightcar**[2] 997 6-8-12 **48**.................... SladeO'Hara[(5)] 2 54
(Peter Grayson) *s.i.s: hld up: hdwy over 1f out: r.o* **9/2**[2]
0-50 **4** ½ **Almaty Express**[23] 736 11-9-2 **52**....................(b) RobertTart[(5)] 5 56+
(John Weymes) *a.p: rdn and nt clr run over 1f out: r.o* **4/1**[1]
-034 **5** ½ **Christopher Chua (IRE)**[14] 862 4-9-2 **52**....................(b) JackDuern[(5)] 4 55
(Simon Dow) *a.p: chsd wnr over 2f out: rdn over 1f out: styd on same pce ins fnl f* **7/1**
6621 **6** 1 ¼ **Jonnie Skull (IRE)**[1] 1021 7-9-13 **58** 6ex....................(vt) AdamKirby 1 57
(Phil McEntee) *chsd ldrs: rdn over 2f out: styd on same pce ins fnl f* **11/2**[3]
0455 **7** shd **Dingaan (IRE)**[9] 917 10-9-1 **46** oh1.................... FergusSweeney 9 45
(Peter Grayson) *s.i.s: r.o ins fnl f: nvr nrr* **16/1**
00-0 **8** 7 **Major Muscari (IRE)**[2] 997 5-9-5 **50**....................(e[1]) TomEaves 6 28
(Ian McInnes) *mid-div: rdn over 2f out: wknd over 1f out* **40/1**
0220 **9** 1 ¼ **Under Par**[9] 917 5-9-4 **49**....................(t) GrahamGibbons 8 23
(Michael Easterby) *dwlt: outpcd* **17/2**
60/3 **10** 1 ¾ **Spirit Of Dixie**[22] 754 6-9-1 **46** oh1.................... MartinHarley 11 15
(Alan McCabe) *led 1f: chsd ldrs: rdn over 2f out: wknd over 1f out* **20/1**
-000 **11** ½ **Minty Jones**[16] 819 4-8-8 **46** oh1....................(be) JordanNason[(7)] 10 13
(Michael Mullineaux) *led 5f out: sn hdd: chsd wnr tl rdn over 2f out: wknd over 1f out* **50/1**
4 **12** 1 ½ **Enter The Red (IRE)**[2] 997 4-9-1 **46** oh1....................(bt) ChrisCatlin 7 9
(Aidan Anthony Howard, Ire) *hld up: rdn over 1f out: sn wknd and eased* **6/1**

1m 14.59s (-0.41) **Going Correction** -0.125s/f (Stan) 12 Ran SP% **121.8**
Speed ratings (Par 101): **97,96,95,95,94 92,92,83,81,79 78,76**
toteswingers 1&2 £33.50, 1&3 £9.70, 2&3 £26.40 CSF £163.79 CT £830.35 TOTE £11.90: £2.80, £6.00, £1.40; EX 238.50 Trifecta £685.80 Part won. Pool: £914.44 - 0.24 winning units..
Owner N Blencowe,J Sunderland,M Lenton,CHarris **Bred** Bryan Ryan **Trained** Carburton, Notts

FOCUS
A low-grade sprint. The winner had the field quite well strung out by halfway and it was only late on that the pack closed in. Obviously limited form.

1043 BIGGEST FREE BETS WITH BOOKMAKERS.CO.UK H'CAP (DIV II) 5f 216y(P)
8:20 (8:22) (Class 6) (0-52,53) 4-Y-0+ £1,940 (£577; £288; £144) Stalls Low

Form				RPR
-021	1		**Flow Chart (IRE)**[37] 551 6-9-1 **51** SladeO'Hara(5) 9 (Peter Grayson) *s.i.s: sn pushed along in rr: hdwy over 1f out: rdn to ld ins fnl f: r.o* **3/1**[1]	59
0504	2	3/4	**Olynard (IRE)**[1] 1021 7-8-10 **46** oh1 (p) RobertTart(5) 6 (Michael Mullineaux) *a.p: rdn over 2f out: r.o* **9/1**	50
6341	3	nk	**Blue Noodles**[1] 1020 7-9-8 **53** 6ex (p) PaddyAspell 4 (John Wainwright) *w ldr tl rdn over 1f out: styd on* **4/1**[2]	56
646	4	1	**Sextons House (IRE)**[3] 991 5-9-4 **49** (be) MartinHarley 2 (Alan McCabe) *chsd ldrs: rdn to ld over 1f out: edgd rt and hdd ins fnl f: styd on same pce* **9/2**[3]	49
4305	5	3/4	**Fantasy Fighter (IRE)**[22] 756 8-9-1 **46** oh1 RobertWinston 10 (Ronald Harris) *s.i.s: hld up: hdwy over 1f out: sn rdn: styd on* **16/1**	44
0214	6	3/4	**Very First Blade**[9] 909 4-9-7 **52** (p) FrannyNorton 7 (Mark Brisbourne) *trckd ldrs: racd keenly: lost pl 4f out: r.o ins fnl f* **4/1**[2]	48
502	7	1/2	**Ishetoo**[52] 339 9-9-5 **50** FergusSweeney 12 (Peter Grayson) *chsd ldrs: pushed along 1/2-way: rdn over 1f out: styd on same pce ins fnl f* **11/1**	44
0-00	8	nk	**Forever Janey**[4] 968 4-8-12 **46** oh1 DarrenEgan(3) 1 (Paul Green) *hld up: rdn over 1f out: n.d* **50/1**	39
6000	9	4 1/2	**Aljosan**[36] 565 4-8-12 **46** oh1 (bt) RaulDaSilva(3) 3 (Frank Sheridan) *led: rdn: edgd rt and hdd over 1f out: wknd ins fnl f* **22/1**	26

1m 15.01s (0.01) **Going Correction** -0.125s/f (Stan) 9 Ran SP% **113.7**
Speed ratings (Par 101): **94,93,92,91,90 89,88,88,82**
toteswingers 1&2 £11.60, 1&3 £2.80, 2&3 £5.20 CSF £30.50 CT £107.97 TOTE £4.80: £1.20, £3.20, £1.80; EX 37.40 Trifecta £212.40 Pool: £811.54 - 2.86 winning units.

Owner E Grayson **Bred** John Starbuck **Trained** Formby, Lancs

FOCUS
The second division of this low-grade sprint. The winner was value for extra.

1044 COMPARE BOOKMAKERS AT BOOKMAKERS.CO.UK MEDIAN AUCTION MAIDEN STKS 1m 141y(P)
8:50 (8:50) (Class 5) 3-Y-0 £2,587 (£770; £384; £192) Stalls Low

Form				RPR
0333	1		**Two No Bids (IRE)**[15] 849 3-9-5 **63** AdamKirby 5 (Phil McEntee) *a.p: rdn to chse ldr and hung lft fr over 1f out: styd on to ld wl ins fnl f* **15/2**	65
2	2	1/2	**Off The Pulse**[22] 757 3-9-5 0 GrahamGibbons 8 (John Mackie) *led: rdn over 1f out: hdd wl ins fnl f* **7/1**[3]	64
03-	3	4	**Eric The Grey (IRE)**[167] 6708 3-8-12 0 GeorgeChaloner(7) 7 (Richard Fahey) *prom: chsd ldr over 5f out: pushed along over 3f out: styd on same pce fnl f* **9/4**[2]	56
	4	2 1/4	**Helmsley Flyer (IRE)** 3-9-5 0 DanielTudhope 4 (David O'Meara) *s.i.s: hld up: hdwy over 2f out: styd on same pce fr over 1f out* **10/1**	52+
6	5	3	**Flamingo Beat**[22] 748 3-9-5 0 ChrisCatlin 9 (Rae Guest) *s.i.s: hld up: shkn up over 2f out: styd on ins fnl f: nvr nr to chal* **22/1**	45
0-	6	8	**Ava Schmetterling**[161] 6871 3-9-0 0 RobertWinston 3 (Garry Moss) *mid-div: pushed along 5f out: nvr on terms* **33/1**	23
4	7	13	**Sharaar (IRE)**[31] 636 3-9-5 0 (p) LukeMorris 1 (Gerard Butler) *led 1f: chsd ldrs: hmpd 4f out: rdn over 2f out: sn wknd: t.o* **5/4**[1]	
00-	8	11	**Dalhousie Lassie**[138] 7433 3-9-0 0 LiamJones 6 (James Unett) *chsd ldrs: pushed along 1/2-way: wknd over 2f out: t.o* **100/1**	
	9	10	**Hartford Starts (IRE)** 3-9-5 0 PatrickMathers 2 (Ian McInnes) *sn pushed along in rr: bhd fnl 5f: t.o* **50/1**	

1m 49.5s (-1.00) **Going Correction** -0.125s/f (Stan) 9 Ran SP% **118.8**
Speed ratings (Par 98): **99,98,95,93,90 83,71,61,53**
toteswingers 1&2 £2.70, 1&3 £3.70, 2&3 £4.30 CSF £58.07 TOTE £8.30: £2.20, £2.30, £1.10; EX 32.90 Trifecta £82.60 Pool: £869.66 - 7.89 winning units.

Owner Eventmaker Racehorses **Bred** Marston & Dean Fleming Thoroughbreds **Trained** Newmarket, Suffolk

FOCUS
Just modest form at best in this maiden, the winner to his mark. It was more truly run than a lot of these sort of contests.

1045 FOOTBALL FREE BETS WITH BOOKMAKERS.CO.UK H'CAP 1m 4f 50y(P)
9:20 (9:20) (Class 5) (0-70,69) 4-Y-0+ £2,587 (£770; £384; £192) Stalls Low

Form				RPR
/412	1		**Blazing Desert**[10] 592 9-9-7 **69** LukeMorris 3 (William Kinsey) *chsd ldrs: rdn to ld over 1f out: all out* **11/10**[1]	74
10-4	2	shd	**Brunello**[11] 887 5-9-1 **63** DanielTudhope 1 (David O'Meara) *hld up in tch: chsd ldr over 2f out: sn rdn: styd on u.p* **4/1**[3]	68
223-	3	4 1/2	**Hallstatt (IRE)**[288] 2666 7-9-4 **66** (t) GrahamGibbons 4 (John Mackie) *chsd ldr tl led over 3f out: rdn and hdd over 1f out: eased whn btn ins fnl f* **11/4**[2]	64
3-	4	8	**With Hindsight (IRE)**[94] 8078 5-8-11 **64** SladeO'Hara(5) 5 (Peter Grayson) *led over 8f: rdn and wknd wl over 1f out* **6/1**	50

2m 41.53s (0.43) **Going Correction** -0.125s/f (Stan) 4 Ran SP% **108.6**
Speed ratings (Par 103): **93,92,89,84**
CSF £5.73 TOTE £1.90; EX 5.50 Trifecta £8.50 Pool: £679.25 - 59.72 winning units.

Owner W R Kinsey **Bred** Mrs Brenda Howlett-Nye **Trained** Ashton, Cheshire

FOCUS
A small field and, predictably, the pace wasn't strong. Thoroughly ordinary form.

T/Plt: £17.80 to a £1 stake. Pool: £74,429.92 - 3035.85 winning tickets T/Qpdt: £9.30 to a £1 stake. Pool: £6,813.36 - 540.84 winning tickets CR

SAINT-CLOUD (L-H)
Saturday, March 16

OFFICIAL GOING: Turf: heavy

1046a PRIX MAURICE CAILLAULT (LISTED RACE) (3YO COLTS & GELDINGS) (TURF) 1m 2f
12:30 (12:00) 3-Y-0 £22,357 (£8,943; £6,707; £4,471; £2,235)

			RPR
1		**Kapour (IRE)**[146] 3-8-11 0 Francois-XavierBertras 2 (F Rohaut, France) **17/10**[1]	99
2	nk	**Park Reel (FR)**[116] 7801 3-8-11 0 GregoryBenoist 4 (E Lellouche, France) **9/2**[3]	98
3	3	**Baradari (IRE)**[37] 3-8-11 0 Christophe-PatriceLemaire 1 (J-C Rouget, France) **2/1**[2]	92
4	1 1/4	**Kareman (FR)**[47] 445 3-8-11 0 RonanThomas 3 (T Lemer, France) **13/1**	90
5	1 1/2	**Milano Blues (FR)**[78] 3-8-11 0 ThierryThulliez 7 (B De Montzey, France) **18/1**	87?
6	3/4	**Tres Blue (IRE)**[131] 3-8-11 0 FabriceVeron 6 (H-A Pantall, France) **13/1**	85
7	1 3/4	**Glacial Age (IRE)**[164] 6780 3-8-11 0 MaximeGuyon 5 (Jo Hughes) *hld up towards rr: gng easily: rdn bef st: u.p 2 1/2f out: no ex: styng on ent fnl f tl wknd 100yds out* **44/5**	82

2m 22.79s (6.79) 7 Ran SP% **118.3**
WIN (incl. 1 euro stake): 2.70. PLACES: 1.60, 2.10. SF: 11.40.
Owner Scea Haras De Saint Pair **Bred** Scea Haras De Saint Pair **Trained** Sauvagnon, France

1048a PRIX EXBURY (GROUP 3) (4YO+) (TURF) 1m 2f
2:40 (12:00) 4-Y-0+ £32,520 (£13,008; £9,756; £6,504; £3,252)

			RPR
1		**Saga Dream (FR)**[146] 7284 7-9-2 0 ThierryJarnet 1 (F Lemercier, France) *settled in 2nd: rdn 2f out: r.o wl ent fnl f: grad clsd on ldr thrght fnl f: got up on line* **4/1**[3]	115
2	hd	**Don Bosco (FR)**[14] 6-9-0 0 MircoDemuro 3 (D Smaga, France) *sn led: wnt 2 l clr down bk st: stl clr ld ent fnl 2f: 2 l clr ent fnl f: strly chal 50yds out: hdd on line* **6/4**[1]	113
3	9	**Espero (FR)**[34] 607 4-8-9 0 GregoryBenoist 6 (J-C Rouget, France) *hld up at rr: r.o wl fr 2f out: wnt 3rd 1 1/2f out: jst hld on for 3rd fnl 50yds* **23/10**[2]	90
4	hd	**Gentle Storm (FR)**[146] 7284 4-8-11 0 (p) IoritzMendizabal 4 (Y Barberot, France) *settled in 5th: relegated to bk of field ent st: picked up wl and r.o to chal for 3rd ins fnl f: jst failed* **12/1**	91
5	7	**Pagera (FR)**[97] 8040 5-8-10 0 MaximeGuyon 2 (H-A Pantall, France) *settled in 4th on ins: rdn and no ex fr 2f out: wknd fnl f* **12/1**	76
6	9	**Nutello (USA)**[15] 4-8-11 0 FlavienPrat 5 (C Laffon-Parias, France) *settled in 3rd on outside: u.p 2 1/2f out: no rspnse and weakend fnl 1 1/2f: nt hrd rdn fnl f* **68/10**	59

2m 20.11s (4.11) 6 Ran SP% **118.5**
WIN (incl. 1 euro stake): 5.00. PLACES: 2.00, 1.50. SF: 13.40.
Owner Freddy Lemercier **Bred** A Audouinm, F Landais, A Oger & B Audouin **Trained** France

FOCUS
The first two were well clear.

1047 - 1049a (Foreign Racing) - See Raceform Interactive

1031 LINGFIELD (L-H)
Sunday, March 17

OFFICIAL GOING: Standard
Wind: light, half behind Weather: showers

1050 FURLONGS & FAIRWAYS H'CAP 5f (P)
2:15 (2:15) (Class 6) (0-60,60) 3-Y-0 £2,215 (£654; £327) Stalls High

Form				RPR
-234	1		**Batchworth Lady**[37] 561 3-9-2 **55** JimmyQuinn 6 (Dean Ivory) *chsd ldr after 1f: rdn ent fnl 2f: sustained effrt u.p fnl f to ld on post* **10/1**	59
060-	2	nse	**Balatina**[87] 8185 3-8-8 **47** HayleyTurner 3 (Chris Dwyer) *led: rdn 2f out: edgd sltly lft u.p ins fnl f: hdd on post* **5/2**[2]	51+
-256	3	1 1/4	**Marmot Bay (IRE)**[44] 470 3-8-11 **55** (e[1]) JemmaMarshall(5) 1 (David Flood) *t.k.h: chsd ldrs: effrt u.p over 1f out: no ex and btn fnl 75yds: hld on for 3rd cl home* **20/1**	54
0-04	4	nk	**Quelle Affaire**[48] 416 3-8-7 **46** oh1 LukeMorris 4 (Brendan Powell) *in tch in midfield: rdn over 2f out: drvn and unable qck over 1f out: kpt on fnl 100yds* **20/1**	44
002-	5	3/4	**Hawsies Dream**[215] 5210 3-9-0 **58** RobertTart(5) 9 (Alan Bailey) *chsd ldng trio: rdn ent fnl 2f: unable qck u.p over 1f out: one pce after* **5/1**[3]	52+
0-54	6	1/2	**Douglas Pasha (IRE)**[11] 904 3-9-2 **55** SeanLevey 2 (Richard Hannon) *in tch in last trio: pushed along 3f out: hdwy on inner over 1f out: no prog 1f out: wknd fnl 100yds* **7/1**	47
4	7	3 1/2	**Samara Jazz (IRE)**[30] 669 3-8-4 **46** DarrenEgan(3) 7 (Patrick Carey, Ire) *outpcd in last pair and sn rdn along: bhd over 1f out* **25/1**	25
000-	D	1/2	**The Manx Missile**[249] 3973 3-9-7 **60** JamieSpencer 5 (Michael Bell) *awkward leaving stalls and s.i.s: bhd: effrt but stl plenty to do wl over 1f out: drvn 1f out: styd on wl fnl 100yds: no threat to ldrs* **7/4**[1]	56+

59.4s (0.60) **Going Correction** 0.0s/f (Stan) 8 Ran SP% **116.6**
Speed ratings (Par 96): **95,94,92,92,90 89,84,91**
Tote Swingers: 1&2 £6.30, 1&3 £7.00, 2&3 £11.60 CSF £35.11 CT £508.47 TOTE £11.10: £2.70, £1.30, £3.40; EX 54.40 Trifecta £379.70 Pool: £2,883.62 - 5.69 winning units..
Owner Mrs Diana Price **Bred** Batchworth Heath Farm Stud **Trained** Radlett, Herts
■ Stewards' Enquiry : Jimmy QuinnM two-day ban: used whip above permitted level (Mar 31-Apr 1)

FOCUS
There was some heavy rain which could have quickened up the track, but it proved difficult to come from off the pace in the first. This was a low-grade handicap, but it wasn't without interest as all but two of the field were making their debuts in this sphere.

1051 LINGFIELDPARK.CO.UK MAIDEN STKS 5f (P)
2:45 (2:45) (Class 5) 3-Y-O **£3,067** (£905; £453) **Stalls** High

Form RPR
3-22 **1** **Bapak Bangsawan**[10] 915 3-9-2 69 JulieBurke(3) 1 70
(Kevin Ryan) *mde all: hung rt off bnd and drifted towards centre wl over 1f out: rdn and fnd ex ent fnl f: a gng to hold on* **7/4**[2]

22-3 **2** *nk* **Silca's Dream**[19] 808 3-9-0 69 (v1) CharlesBishop(5) 3 69
(Mick Channon) *chsd wnr thrght: rdn and sltly outpcd over 1f out: rallied u.p ins fnl f: clsng on wnr towards fin* **5/4**[1]

202- **3** *3 1/4* **Annaley My Darling (IRE)**[200] 5748 3-9-0 67 TonyCulhane 2 52
(Jo Hughes) *chsd ldng pair: rdn and no imp over 1f out: pushed along and wl hld ins fnl f* **6/1**[3]

006- **4** *2* **Sand And Deliver**[137] 7481 3-9-0 68 ShaneKelly 5 45
(Peter Crate) *hld up in tch in 4th: rdn and no prog wl over 1f out: wknd ent fnl f* **10/1**

0 **5** *1/2* **Meetha Achar**[17] 821 3-9-0 0 MatthewDavies 4 43
(Jim Boyle) *s.i.s: a outpcd in rr and sn pushed along: n.d* **25/1**

59.7s (0.90) **Going Correction** 0.0s/f (Stan) **5 Ran SP% 108.0**
Speed ratings (Par 98): **92,91,86,83,82**
CSF £4.12 TOTE £1.80: £1.10, £1.90; EX 4.10 Trifecta £7.60 Pool: £3,000.77 - 293.58 winning units..
Owner H R H Sultan Ahmad Shah **Bred** Hrh Sultan Ahmad Shah **Trained** Hambleton, N Yorks

FOCUS
A modest maiden run in a time 0.3sec slower than the preceding class 6 handicap. The order barely changed throughout.

1052 FOREST ROW FILLIES' H'CAP (THE SUNDAY £5K BONUS RACE) 6f (P)
3:15 (3:16) (Class 5) (0-75,75) 4-Y-O+ **£3,067** (£905; £453) **Stalls** Low

Form RPR
-003 **1** **Bubbly Ballerina**[32] 627 4-9-2 75 RobertTart(5) 5 80
(Alan Bailey) *chsd ldr over 4f out: rdn to ld over 1f out: pressed fnl 100yds: hld on wl towards fin* **5/4**[1]

4433 **2** *1/2* **Mother Jones**[15] 861 5-8-7 61 oh1 LukeMorris 2 64
(David Evans) *hld up in tch in rr: hdwy and swtchd out rt jst over 1f out: chsd wnr ins fnl f: chal and drvn fnl 100yds: hld towards fin* **8/1**

1110 **3** *2 1/2* **Danziger (IRE)**[9] 924 4-9-6 74 JamieSpencer 1 69
(David Evans) *led: early: sn stdd bk to chse ldrs: swtchd out rt and effrt over 1f out: no ex and btn fnl 150yds* **3/1**[3]

-560 **4** *1 3/4* **Rooknrasbryripple**[17] 819 4-8-2 63 oh16 ow2 RyanTate(7) 4 53
(Ralph Smith) *sn led: rdn ent fnl 2f: drvn and hdd over 1f out: wknd ins fnl f* **50/1**

-461 **5** *2 3/4* **Catalinas Diamond (IRE)**[25] 728 5-9-0 68 (t) SteveDrowne 6 49
(Pat Murphy) *in tch on outer: rdn and no rspnse over 1f out: wknd fnl f* **5/2**[2]

3500 **6** *1* **Hold The Star**[24] 733 7-8-5 64 oh16 ow3 AnnStokell(5) 3 42
(Ann Stokell) *wl in tch in midfield: rdn and unable qck 2f out: wknd ent fnl f* **66/1**

1m 11.51s (-0.39) **Going Correction** 0.0s/f (Stan) **6 Ran SP% 112.6**
Speed ratings (Par 100): **102,101,98,95,92 90**
Tote Swingers: 1&2 £2.40, 1&3 £1.60, 2&3 £1.80 CSF £12.48 TOTE £1.90: £1.10, £3.30; EX 11.10 Trifecta £38.30 Pool: £3,549.37 - 69.41 winning units..
Owner The Champagne Club **Bred** Whitsbury Manor Stud **Trained** Newmarket, Suffolk

FOCUS
Not a strong race, even with the Sunday bonus.

1053 SYLVIE & TIM BROWN MEMORIAL H'CAP 1m 4f (P)
3:45 (3:45) (Class 5) (0-75,74) 3-Y-O **£3,238** (£956; £478) **Stalls** Low

Form RPR
4124 **1** **Poetic Verse**[19] 803 3-8-9 62 AndreaAtzeni 1 67+
(Rod Millman) *hld up wl in tch in last pair: chsd ldrs and swtchd rt bnd wl over 1f out: drvn and led ins fnl f: r.o wl* **25/1**

531 **2** *1/2* **Edwyn Ralph**[30] 663 3-9-7 74 JimCrowley 2 79+
(David Simcock) *led for 2f: chsd ldrs after: nt clr run on inner ent fnl 2f: switching lft and rt over 1f out: hdwy between horses to chse wnr ins fnl f: kpt on wl* **5/2**[2]

4-21 **3** *1* **Silver Dixie (USA)**[25] 731 3-9-4 71 GrahamLee 4 74
(Jeremy Noseda) *t.k.h: w ldr for 2f: chsd ldr after: rdn to ld and edgd lft over 1f out: hdd 1f out: styd on same pce ins fnl f* **4/5**[1]

521 **4** *3/4* **El Massivo (IRE)**[16] 841 3-9-4 71 JimmyQuinn 3 72+
(William Jarvis) *stdd s: t.k.h: hld up wl in tch in last pair: swtchd rt and hdwy to chse ldrs over 3f out: rdn to ld 1f out: sn hdd: wknd towards fin* **8/1**[3]

62-5 **5** *3* **Raven's Tower (USA)**[25] 731 3-9-1 68 JoeFanning 6 65
(Mark Johnston) *pressed ldrs tl led 10f out: rdn and hdd over 1f out: wknd ins fnl f* **10/1**

05-5 **6** *7* **Pearl Spice (IRE)**[18] 815 3-9-0 67 SeanLevey 5 52
(Tim Pitt) *dwlt: sn pushed along and rcvrd: chsd ldrs: rdn over 4f out: dropped to rr and struggling over 3f out: lost tch over 1f out* **16/1**

2m 30.24s (-2.76) **Going Correction** 0.0s/f (Stan) **6 Ran SP% 114.1**
Speed ratings (Par 98): **109,108,108,107,105 100**
Tote Swingers: 1&2 £6.40, 1&3 £6.60, 2&3 £1.20 CSF £88.49 TOTE £22.30: £6.40, £2.10; EX 103.40 Trifecta £196.40 Pool: £3,451.78 - 13.17 winning units..
Owner The Links Partnership **Bred** The Links Partnership **Trained** Kentisbeare, Devon

FOCUS
An interesting handicap run at just an ordinary pace. It contained some lightly raced types, but went to the most experienced runner.

1054 MARSH GREEN H'CAP 1m 2f (P)
4:15 (4:16) (Class 6) (0-65,71) 4-Y-O+ **£2,045** (£603; £302) **Stalls** Low

Form RPR
-260 **1** **Scamperdale**[27] 709 11-9-4 62 (p) KierenFox 1 69
(Brian Baugh) *hld up in midfield: clsd and chsd ldrs over 2f out: rdn to ld ins fnl f: styd on wl: rdn out* **20/1**

5505 **2** *3/4* **Resplendent Alpha**[2] 1015 9-8-13 62 (p) AmyScott(5) 9 68
(Alastair Lidderdale) *stdd s: hld up in rr: clsd but stl plenty to do in 5th over 2f out: gd hdwy on inner 1f out: chsd wnr wl ins fnl f: kpt on* **20/1**

0-41 **3** *3/4* **Tenure**[4] 978 4-9-13 71 6ex GeorgeBaker 2 75
(Gary Moore) *t.k.h: chsd ldrs: chsd clr ldr over 4f out: clsd and rdn jst over 2f out: drvn and nt qckn 1f out: styd on same pce ins fnl f* **1/2**[1]

01-1 **4** *1* **Chella Thriller (SPA)**[62] 200 4-9-3 61 (b) RichardKingscote 5 63
(Alastair Lidderdale) *led: wnt clr 5f out: rdn and pressed wl over 1f out: hdd ins fnl f: no ex* **7/2**[2]

2435 **5** *4* **Arabian Flight**[18] 813 4-9-1 59 AndrewMullen 3 54
(Michael Appleby) *chsd ldrs: clsd and rdn over 2f out: no ex u.p over 1f out: wknd fnl f* **12/1**[3]

65-3 **6** *4 1/2* **Benandonner (USA)**[16] 840 10-9-6 64 JoeFanning 6 50
(Paddy Butler) *chsd ldr tl over 3f out: struggling u.p over 2f out: wknd wl over 1f out* **20/1**

00-0 **7** *86* **Lisahane Bog**[11] 896 6-9-0 58 (v) IanMongan 10
(Peter Hedger) *dwlt: pushed along early: racd in last pair: rdn and no rspnse over 4f out: lost tch over 2f out: wl t.o and virtually p.u fnl f* **33/1**

2m 4.57s (-2.03) **Going Correction** 0.0s/f (Stan) **7 Ran SP% 113.8**
Speed ratings (Par 101): **108,107,106,106,102 99,30**
Tote Swingers: 1&2 £15.70, 1&3 £3.30, 2&3 £5.30 CSF £298.44 CT £580.15 TOTE £18.00: £7.40, £5.90; EX 225.80 Trifecta £542.80 Pool: £3,076.34 - 4.25 winning units..
Owner Saddle Up Racing **Bred** Mrs J A Prescott **Trained** Audley, Staffs

FOCUS
They went a fair gallop in this modest handicap, which produced a surprise outcome.

1055 EDENBRIDGE H'CAP 7f (P)
4:45 (4:47) (Class 6) (0-55,54) 3-Y-O **£2,215** (£654; £327) **Stalls** Low

Form RPR
3334 **1** **Black Truffle (FR)**[16] 848 3-9-2 49 (v1) LiamKeniry 1 56
(Mark Usher) *t.k.h: hld up in tch in last: hdwy to chse ldrs over 1f out: nt clr run jst ins fnl f: squeezed between horses and rdn to ld fnl 50yds: r.o wl* **5/1**[3]

-452 **2** *1/2* **Sand Grouse**[5] 977 3-9-7 54 (b) AndreaAtzeni 6 60
(Marco Botti) *racd keenly: led: rdn 1f out: drvn ins fnl f: hdd and no ex fnl 50yds* **1/1**[1]

-652 **3** *1/2* **Actonetaketwo**[25] 732 3-9-1 48 HayleyTurner 3 53
(Ron Hodges) *t.k.h: hld up in tch: hdwy to chse ldr over 5f out: rdn and effrt wl over 1f out: styd on same pce ins fnl f* **9/2**[2]

5540 **4** *1/2* **Spreading**[17] 824 3-9-6 53 NickyMackay 5 56
(Michael Blanshard) *chsd ldr for 2f: rdn and ev ch jst ins fnl f: hung lft and btn towards fin* **10/1**

5046 **5** *4* **Duchess Of Dreams**[44] 482 3-8-11 51 PhilipPrince(7) 2 44
(Richard Guest) *in tch in last pair: rdn and effrt on outer bnd 2f out: outpcd over 1f out: wknd fnl f* **33/1**

000- **6** *2 1/2* **Foxy Dancer (IRE)**[145] 7306 3-9-0 47 SeanLevey 4 33
(Richard Hannon) *dwlt: rdn along thrght: hdwy into midfield after 1f out: struggling u.p 2f out: wknd ent fnl f* **9/2**[2]

1m 25.64s (0.84) **Going Correction** 0.0s/f (Stan) **6 Ran SP% 115.1**
Speed ratings (Par 96): **95,94,93,93,88 85**
Tote Swingers: 1&2 £1.50, 1&3 £2.30, 2&3 £1.80 CSF £10.87 TOTE £7.10: £2.50, £1.20; EX 13.60 Trifecta £41.60 Pool: £1,810.22 - 33.65 winning units..
Owner Ushers Court **Bred** Peter Harris **Trained** Upper Lambourn, Berks

FOCUS
This was run in heavy rain. A weak handicap, it was contested solely by maidens, and they were all fillies too except for the winner.

1056 HARTFIELD H'CAP 1m (P)
5:15 (5:15) (Class 6) (0-60,60) 4-Y-O+ **£2,045** (£603; £302) **Stalls** High

Form RPR
3162 **1** **Lieutenant Dan (IRE)**[19] 805 6-9-7 60 (v) AndrewMullen 8 68
(Michael Appleby) *sn led and mde rest: set stdy gallop: rdn and qcknd over 1f out: r.o wl and a holding rivals fnl f* **9/2**[3]

54-5 **2** *1* **Bloodsweatandtears**[69] 89 5-9-7 60 (p) SebSanders 2 66
(William Knight) *t.k.h: led: sn hdd and chsd wnr tl over 2f out: rdn to chse wnr again over 1f out: kpt on but a hld fnl f* **7/4**[1]

2336 **3** *hd* **Divine Rule (IRE)**[13] 883 5-8-12 56 (v) ThomasBrown(5) 3 61
(Laura Mongan) *in tch in midfield: hdwy to chse ldrs wl over 1f out: kpt on same pce u.p ins fnl f* **5/1**

0012 **4** *shd* **Greek Islands (IRE)**[20] 794 5-9-1 54 LiamKeniry 6 59+
(Ed de Giles) *stdd s: t.k.h: hld up in last trio: clsd and nt clr run over 1f out: rdn and hdwy 1f out: kpt on u.p ins fnl f: nt rch ldrs* **4/1**[2]

3205 **5** *1 1/4* **Teen Ager (FR)**[11] 903 9-8-12 51 (p) JimmyQuinn 7 53
(Paul Burgoyne) *stdd s: t.k.h and hld up in rr: rdn and effrt over 1f out: kpt on under hands and heels riding ins fnl f: nvr gng pce to rch ldrs* **10/1**

0244 **6** *2* **Amber Moon**[16] 839 8-8-5 49 oh1 ow3 AnnStokell(5) 1 47
(Ann Stokell) *hld up in tch in midfield: rdn and unable qck 2f out: outpcd and btn over 1f out: plugged on same pce fnl f* **20/1**

-015 **7** *3 1/2* **Indian Violet (IRE)**[11] 907 7-9-1 54 (p) LukeMorris 5 43
(Zoe Davison) *t.k.h: chsd ldr: wnt 2nd over 2f out and sn rdn: fnd little for press and lost pl over 1f out: wknd fnl f* **8/1**

050- **8** *1/2* **Trove (IRE)**[264] 3470 4-8-8 47 oh1 ow1 RobertHavlin 4 35
(Michael Attwater) *stdd s: t.k.h: hld up in rr: effrt and v wd bnd 2f out: no hdwy: n.d* **33/1**

1m 38.75s (0.55) **Going Correction** 0.0s/f (Stan) **8 Ran SP% 119.1**
Speed ratings (Par 101): **97,96,95,95,94 92,88,88**
Tote Swingers: 1&2 £3.40, 1&3 £3.50, 2&3 £2.00 CSF £13.42 CT £41.82 TOTE £4.70: £1.20, £1.60, £2.00; EX 16.00 Trifecta £57.00 Pool: £1,923.18 - 25.29 winning units..
Owner Dallas Racing **Bred** Hong Kong Breeders Club **Trained** Danethorpe, Notts

FOCUS
Very modest handicap form. It proved difficult to get into this from the rear.
T/Plt: £1,860.00 to a £1 stake. Pool: £86,760.00 - 34.05 winning tickets. T/Qpdt: £1,358.30 to a £1 stake. Pool: £6,058.00 - 3.30 winning tickets. SP

[978]KEMPTON (A.W) (R-H)

Monday, March 18

OFFICIAL GOING: Standard

Wind: Light, across Weather: Raining

1057 GET THE BETVICTOR APP NOW MEDIAN AUCTION MAIDEN STKS 1m 2f (P)

2:20 (2:23) (Class 5) 3-5-Y-0 £2,587 (£770; £384; £192) Stalls Low

Form RPR

32- 1 **Spillway**[98] 8052 3-8-8 0 LiamKeniry 7 71+
(Eve Johnson Houghton) *t.k.h: hld up towards rr: stdy prog fr 3f out: shkn up over 1f out: r.o to ld last 150yds: pushed out: comf* **15/8**[1]

3 2 1 ¼ **Vastly (USA)**[19] 815 4-10-0 0 JimCrowley 3 73
(Julia Feilden) *led 2f: trckd ldr: led again jst over 2f out: edgd lft and hdd 150yds out: outpcd* **8/1**

4 3 nk **Punditry**[12] 895 3-8-8 0 WilliamBuick 9 68+
(John Gosden) *w ldrs 2f: sn dropped to 5th: rdn and effrt over 2f out: chsd wnr over 1f out: chal fnl f but wnr sn racd past* **5/2**[2]

05 4 4 ½ **Early One Morning**[12] 895 3-8-3 0 JimmyQuinn 4 55
(Hugo Palmer) *w.w towards rr: 7th over 2f out: rdn and kpt on to take 4th fnl f: no ch w ldng trio* **50/1**

40- 5 1 ¼ **Sam Spade (IRE)**[117] 7807 3-8-8 0 SeanLevey 10 57
(Richard Hannon) *t.k.h: pressed ldrs: shkn up 2f out: nt qckn over 1f out: fdd* **7/1**

333- 6 1 **Jullundar (IRE)**[144] 7357 3-8-1 70 DanielCremin(7) 1 55
(Mick Channon) *trckd ldrs: nudged along and outpcd 2f out: effrt on inner over 1f out: no prog* **4/1**[3]

7 6 **Bold Assertion** 3-8-8 0 LukeMorris 6 44
(John Best) *dwlt: mostly in last pair: shkn up and struggling 3f out: sn no ch* **33/1**

0- 8 9 **Parsons Green**[158] 7005 4-9-9 0 RobertHavlin 8 26
(Michael Attwater) *hld up tl quick move arnd outside of rivals to ld after 2f: hdd jst over 2f out: wknd rapidly over 1f out: t.o* **100/1**

0 9 8 **Baytown Bertie**[24] 748 4-10-0 0 SteveDrowne 5 16
(Lydia Richards) *a in last pair: struggling fr 1/2-way: t.o* **100/1**

2m 9.8s (1.80) **Going Correction** 0.0s/f (Stan)
WFA 3 from 4yo 20lb 9 Ran SP% **113.8**
Speed ratings (Par 103): **92,91,90,87,86 85,80,73,66**
Tote Swingers: 1&2 £4.10, 1&3 £1.60, 2&3 £3.50 CSF £17.39 TOTE £2.70: £1.10, £2.50, £1.50; EX 12.70 Trifecta £52.30 Pool: £3,155.44 - 45.22 winning units..
Owner Mrs Virginia Neale **Bred** Cherry Park Stud **Trained** Blewbury, Oxon

FOCUS
No more than a fair maiden. Despite the ordinary gallop, the first three pulled clear, and the winner came down the centre in the straight. The form could be worth a little more.

1058 BETVICTOR CASINO ON YOUR MOBILE H'CAP 5f (P)

2:50 (2:51) (Class 5) (0-70,70) 4-Y-0+ £2,587 (£770; £384; £192) Stalls Low

Form RPR

055- 1 **Alpha Delta Whisky**[180] 6370 5-8-12 66 MichaelJMMurphy(5) 4 75
(John Gallagher) *chsd ldng pair: rdn 2f out: clsd over 1f out: led last 110yds: drvn out* **3/1**[1]

20-3 2 ½ **Steelcut**[68] 115 9-9-0 63 MartinDwyer 1 70
(Mark Buckley) *chsd ldng pair: rdn to cl over 1f out: chal and upsides ins fnl f: jst hld* **7/1**

56-6 3 ¾ **Catflap (IRE)**[21] 790 4-8-9 58 (p) LukeMorris 2 62
(Derek Haydn Jones) *s.i.s: racd in 5th and nt on terms: shoved along 1/2-way: styd on fnl f to take 3rd last strides* **12/1**

20-1 4 ½ **Love You Louis**[67] 135 7-9-4 70 PatrickHills(3) 6 73
(J R Jenkins) *pressed ldr: rdn to ld wl over 1f out: hdd & wknd last 110yds* **9/2**[3]

30-6 5 ¾ **Falasteen (IRE)**[9] 946 6-9-5 68 RobertWinston 7 68+
(Milton Bradley) *hd at awkward angle whn stalls opened and blindfold removed late: wl off the pce in last pair: pushed along fr 2f out: styd on w no recrse to the whip: nrst fin* **7/1**

0020 6 3 ¼ **Courageous (IRE)**[10] 924 7-9-7 70 (t) JimmyQuinn 3 58
(Milton Bradley) *led: rdn and hdd wl over 1f out: wknd fnl f* **6/1**

6045 7 5 **Speightowns Kid (USA)**[10] 924 5-9-5 68 TonyCulhane 5 38
(Jo Hughes) *nvr gng wl and a detached in last pair: floundering 2f out* **4/1**[2]

59.7s (-0.80) **Going Correction** 0.0s/f (Stan) 7 Ran SP% **110.2**
Speed ratings (Par 103): **106,105,104,103,102 96,88**
Tote Swingers: 1&2 £4.10, 1&3 £7.10, 2&3 £5.20 CSF £22.35 CT £201.70 TOTE £3.60: £1.50, £2.40; EX 29.10 Trifecta £242.30 Pool: £1,880.60 - 5.82 winning units..
Owner Adweb Ltd **Bred** Kentford Farm Stud Ltd **Trained** Chastleton, Oxon

FOCUS
A modest handicap run at a reasonable gallop and one that favoured those up with the pace. The winner raced in the centre in the straight.

1059 BETVICTOR EXCLUSIVE NON RUNNER FREE BET H'CAP 1m 2f (P)

3:20 (3:20) (Class 5) (0-75,75) 4-Y-0+ £2,587 (£770; £384; £192) Stalls Low

Form RPR

00-0 1 **Tadabeer**[51] 400 5-9-5 73 (t) StevieDonohoe 2 83
(Ian Williams) *sn trckd ldng pair: wnt 2nd over 2f out: led over 1f out and drvn clr: 3 l ahd ins fnl f: hld on* **7/2**[2]

1112 2 ½ **Flamborough Breeze**[17] 840 4-9-5 73 (t) JimCrowley 7 82+
(Ed Vaughan) *stdd s: hld up in last: prog on wd outside wl over 1f out: drvn to take 2nd ins fnl f: clsd on wnr fin: too much to do* **3/1**[1]

6024 3 2 **Gaelic Silver (FR)**[12] 906 7-9-3 71 TomQueally 3 76
(Gary Moore) *t.k.h: hld up towards rr: prog through rivals wl over 1f out: rdn to take 2nd briefly jst ins fnl f: styd on same pce after* **5/1**[3]

03-0 4 2 **Ashkalara**[42] 520 6-8-8 62 oh3 ow1 LiamKeniry 1 63
(Stuart Howe) *in tch in midfield: rdn and sme prog 2f out: no imp over 1f out: outpcd: fin lame* **25/1**

0-24 5 3 **Super Duplex**[33] 639 6-8-8 67 JemmaMarshall(5) 4 62
(Pat Phelan) *sn led: hdd over 1f out: wknd* **20/1**

2/2- 6 ½ **Princess Icicle**[90] 8158 5-9-0 68 IanMongan 10 62
(Jo Crowley) *hld up towards rr: rdn 2f out: outpcd and btn over 1f out* **10/1**

04-2 7 hd **Flying Trader (USA)**[65] 190 4-9-7 75 LukeMorris 8 69
(Jane Chapple-Hyam) *trckd ldrs on outer: rdn 2f out: sn wl outpcd and btn* **5/1**[3]

150- 8 1 ¾ **Rosselli (IRE)**[153] 7132 4-9-3 71 MartinHarley 5 61
(Mrs K Burke) *trckd ldrs: rdn 2f out: sn outpcd: wknd ins fnl f* **10/1**

344- 9 1 **Any Given Dream (IRE)**[96] 8082 4-8-12 66 KierenFox 6 54
(Lee Carter) *hld up in last trio: pushed along and no prog on inner wl over 1f out: wknd fnl f* **20/1**

/00- 10 2 **Turned To Gold (IRE)**[258] 3737 4-8-10 64 RobertWinston 9 52
(Alan Jarvis) *plld hrd: mostly chsd ldr to over 2f out: wknd over 1f out* **7/1**

2m 6.11s (-1.89) **Going Correction** 0.0s/f (Stan) 10 Ran SP% **124.6**
Speed ratings (Par 103): **107,106,105,103,101 100,100,99,98,96**
Tote Swingers: 1&2 £7.80, 1&3 £6.30, 2&3 £4.10 CSF £15.17 CT £55.10 TOTE £4.00: £1.80, £1.70, £1.80; EX 42.80 Trifecta £135.60 Pool: £1,490.51 - 8.24 winning units..
Owner Sir Alex Ferguson & Sotirios Hassiakos **Bred** Shadwell Estate Co Ltd **Trained** Portway, Worcs

■ Stewards' Enquiry : Liam Keniry one-day ban: careless riding (Apr 1)

FOCUS
A fair handicap in which the pace was just an ordinary one. The winner raced centre-to-far side in the straight, showing improved form. The third and fourth give perspective.

1060 GOFFS READY-TO-RUN BREEZE-UP 27.03.13 H'CAP 1m 4f (P)

3:50 (3:52) (Class 6) (0-60,60) 4-Y-0+ £1,940 (£577; £288; £144) Stalls Centre

Form RPR

-505 1 **Arashi**[14] 883 7-9-4 57 (v) MartinDwyer 3 66
(Derek Shaw) *t.k.h in midfield: prog 3f out: led 2f out: drvn and hrd pressed over 1f out: kpt on* **7/2**[2]

53-2 2 1 **Mount Abora (IRE)**[31] 662 6-9-7 60 IanMongan 8 67
(Laura Mongan) *hld up in midfield: drvn over 2f out: kpt on to take 2nd ins fnl f: tried to chal but no imp nr fin* **3/1**[1]

0320 3 2 ½ **Delightful Sleep**[5] 983 5-9-2 55 AdamKirby 9 58
(David Evans) *hld up in last trio: stdy prog fr 3f out: chsd wnr wl over 1f out and sn upsides: effrt fizzled out fnl f* **7/2**[2]

420/ 4 1 ¾ **Chapter Five**[524] 6775 6-9-4 57 StevieDonohoe 1 58
(Ian Williams) *disp 2nd pl: hrd rdn and fnd nil over 2f out: sn dropped to 5th: plugged on again fnl f* **9/1**

/0-0 5 1 ½ **Amen (IRE)**[19] 816 5-9-6 59 TomQueally 2 57
(Gary Moore) *led and untrbld in front: hdd 2f out: immediately btn* **10/1**

0-50 6 15 **Faraway Land (USA)**[45] 469 5-8-1 47 (b) ShelleyBirkett(7) 5 23
(Julia Feilden) *racd wd: hld up in last trio: lost tch w main gp 4f out: t.o* **20/1**

0-00 7 7 **Rahy's Promise (USA)**[33] 637 4-8-9 55 (vt[1]) ThomasBrown(5) 6 20
(Andrew Balding) *disp 2nd pl but needed shoving at various stages: rdn 4f out: wkng rapidly whn nudged by rival over 2f out: t.o* **5/1**[3]

0000 P **Trip Switch**[20] 805 7-9-4 57 LiamKeniry 7
(John Butler) *hld up: dropped to last bef 1/2-way: lost tch and p.u 4f out: dismntd* **33/1**

2m 33.76s (-0.74) **Going Correction** 0.0s/f (Stan)
WFA 4 from 5yo+ 2lb 8 Ran SP% **112.9**
Speed ratings (Par 101): **102,101,99,98,97 87,82,**
Tote Swingers: 1&2 £2.50, 1&3 £3.00, 2&3 £2.30 CSF £14.05 CT £37.84 TOTE £3.10: £1.10, £1.70, £1.80; EX 16.80 Trifecta £28.90 Pool: £1,637.63 - 42.46 winning units..
Owner Philip Derbyshire **Bred** Wyck Hall Stud Ltd **Trained** Sproxton, Leics

■ Stewards' Enquiry : Ian Mongan 1st incident, three-day ban: careless riding (Apr 1-3) 2nd, one-day ban: careless riding (Apr 4)

FOCUS
A moderate handicap run at a no more than a fair gallop. The winner came down the centre in the straight. The runner-up helps the opening level.

1061 BETVICTOR AINTREE GRAND NATIONAL NRFB H'CAP 7f (P)

4:20 (4:20) (Class 3) (0-95,92) 4-Y-0+ £7,439 (£2,213; £1,106; £553) Stalls Low

Form RPR

2135 1 **Atlantis Crossing (IRE)**[30] 690 4-9-2 87 MatthewDavies 1 95
(Jim Boyle) *hld up in 6th: shkn up and prog over 2f out: chsd ldr fnl f: styd on u.p to ld last strides* **5/1**[2]

400- 2 hd **Bravo Echo**[116] 7826 7-9-7 92 RobertHavlin 9 100
(Michael Attwater) *led fr wd draw and set fair pce: rdn and fought off nrest chalr over 1f out: kpt on but hdd last strides* **20/1**

-056 3 ¾ **Kakatosi**[14] 880 6-8-11 82 EddieAhern 6 88
(Mike Murphy) *hld up in midfield: rdn over 2f out: prog over 1f out: wnt 3rd fnl f: edgd rt and tried to cl: a hld* **16/1**

002- 4 2 **Galician**[142] 7408 4-9-5 90 FrannyNorton 8 91
(Mark Johnston) *chsd ldng trio: rdn over 2f out: lost pl wl over 1f out: kpt on to take 4th again nr fin* **15/2**

-140 5 ½ **Seek The Fair Land**[9] 947 7-8-11 87 (b) NathanAlison(5) 11 87
(Jim Boyle) *chsd ldr: rdn 2f out: nt qckn and hld over 1f out: fdd ins fnl f* **20/1**

000- 6 ¾ **Forceful Appeal (USA)**[116] 7826 5-8-11 82 HayleyTurner 2 80
(Simon Dow) *trckd ldng pair: gng bttr than most over 2f out: rdn and nt qckn wl over 1f out: fdd fnl f* **16/1**

5-10 7 ½ **Spirit Of Sharjah (IRE)**[44] 495 8-9-5 90 JimCrowley 7 86
(Julia Feilden) *stdd s: hld up in last pair: reminder over 1f out: kpt on but nvr remotely involved* **7/1**

-215 8 nk **Lowther**[44] 495 8-8-11 82 (b) KierenFox 4 77
(Lee Carter) *t.k.h: hld up in last pair: rdn 3f out: stl last 2f out: styd on ins fnl f* **11/1**

112/ 9 ½ **Ortac Rock (IRE)**[513] 7021 4-9-1 86 SeanLevey 5 80
(Richard Hannon) *sn in last quartet: rdn and no prog on outer over 2f out: kpt on last 150yds* **9/2**[1]

3116 10 ½ **Light From Mars**[9] 944 8-9-1 86 LukeMorris 10 79
(Ronald Harris) *hld up and swtchd fr wd draw to inner: shkn up over 2f out: no real prog over 1f out: fdd* **6/1**[3]

430- 11 2 ¼ **Roninski (IRE)**[95] 8098 5-9-2 87 AdamKirby 3 74
(Garry Moss) *chsd ldng trio: drvn over 2f out: wknd wl over 1f out* **13/2**

1m 24.39s (-1.61) **Going Correction** 0.0s/f (Stan) 11 Ran SP% **116.4**
Speed ratings (Par 107): **109,108,107,105,105 104,103,103,102,102 99**
Tote Swingers: 1&2 £31.00, 1&3 £19.60, 2&3 £23.90 CSF £98.61 CT £1492.52 TOTE £6.80: £1.80, £7.30, £5.20; EX 215.40 Trifecta £755.20 Part won. Pool: £1.006.99 - 0.22 winning units..

Owner The 'In Recovery' Partnership **Bred** J K Thoroughbreds & P Doyle Bloodstock **Trained** Epsom, Surrey

■ Stewards' Enquiry : Eddie Ahern two-day ban: used whip above permitted level (Apr 1-2)

FOCUS
A very useful handicap in which the pace was reasonable. The winner, who edged up against the inside rail in the closing stages, found a bit more improvement.

1062 BETVICTOR NON RUNNER FREE BET AT AINTREE H'CAP 2m (P)
4:50 (4:50) (Class 5) (0-70,65) 4-Y-0+ **£2,587** (£770; £384; £192) **Stalls** Low

Form RPR
-314 **1** **Llamadas**[12] [905] 11-9-8 **61** IanMongan 2 68
(Olivia Maylam) *t.k.h: hld up in 7th: prog over 2f out: drvn to ld 1f out: kpt on wl* **11/2**
0-23 **2** *1* **Bramshill Lass**[16] [866] 4-9-7 **65** (p) JimCrowley 7 71
(Amanda Perrett) *trckd ldng trio: clsd 3f out: led over 2f out: sn drvn: hdd and one pce 1f out* **5/1**[3]
0/0- **3** *nse* **Ordensritter (GER)**[9] [8082] 5-9-7 **65** JemmaMarshall(5) 6 71
(Chris Down) *trckd ldr 3f: racd in 3rd after: rdn over 2f out and sltly lost pl: kpt on fr over 1f out: pressed runner-up nr fin* **14/1**
211- **4** *nk* **Hi Note**[133] [5811] 5-9-3 **61** HarryPoulton(5) 3 66
(Sheena West) *hld up in 5th: effrt over 2f out and sn cl enough: nt qckn over 1f out: kpt on but a hld* **4/1**[2]
6-54 **5** *3 1/4* **Soweto Star (IRE)**[26] [724] 5-9-4 **57** RobertWinston 4 58
(John Best) *hld up in last in modly run event: effrt over 2f out: tried to cl over 1f out: kpt on same pce after* **8/1**
-224 **6** *1* **Broughtons Bandit**[10] [928] 6-9-4 **57** TomQueally 8 57
(Willie Musson) *hld up in 8th: prog on outer 5f out: cl enough and drvn over 2f out: steadily wknd* **3/1**[1]
25-3 **7** *1 3/4* **Ctappers**[20] [809] 4-8-11 **62** DanielCremin(7) 5 60
(Mick Channon) *hld up in 6th: shkn up 3f out: sn dropped to last: no ch after* **7/1**
0/00 **8** *1/2* **Our Play (IRE)**[21] [788] 5-8-11 **50** (b) SteveDrowne 10 48
(Lydia Richards) *trckd ldr after 3f: chal wl over 2f out and upsides: wknd over 1f out* **66/1**
031- **9** *2* **Dew Reward (IRE)**[250] [3969] 5-9-10 **63** LukeMorris 9 58
(Bill Turner) *led at modest pce: kicked on 4f out: hdd over 2f out: sn wknd* **16/1**

3m 36.87s (6.77) **Going Correction** 0.0s/f (Stan)
WFA 4 from 5yo+ 5lb **9** Ran SP% **114.7**
Speed ratings (Par 103): **83,82,82,82,80 80,79,79,78**
Tote Swingers: 1&2 £7.20, 1&3 £15.30, 2&3 £13.80 CSF £32.88 CT £364.49 TOTE £8.20: £2.70, £2.90, £5.80; EX 39.10 Trifecta £699.30 Part won. Pool: £932.45 - 0.82 winning units..
Owner K Tyre **Bred** Burton Agnes Stud Co Ltd **Trained** Epsom, Surrey

FOCUS
A modest handicap, and they went a slow pace to the intersection so the bare form is best treated with caution. The winner raced towards the far rail throughout.

1063 GOFFS READY TO WIN 27.03.13 H'CAP 6f (P)
5:20 (5:21) (Class 6) (0-65,65) 4-Y-0+ **£1,940** (£577; £288; £144) **Stalls** Low

Form RPR
0003 **1** **Elusive Hawk (IRE)**[6] [971] 9-9-5 **63** (v[1]) AdamKirby 4 83
(David Evans) *hld up in midfield: smooth prog over 2f out: led over 1f out and sn dashed wl clr: unchal* **11/4**[1]
-424 **2** *5* **Amethyst Dawn (IRE)**[12] [902] 7-9-6 **64** (t) EddieAhern 9 68
(J R Jenkins) *hld up in midfield: prog 2f out: drvn to take 2nd ins fnl f: no ch w wnr* **14/1**
0-65 **3** *1* **Dishy Guru**[19] [812] 4-9-7 **65** (b) LiamKeniry 11 66
(Michael Blanshard) *restless stalls: s.i.s: hld up in last: prog on inner over 1f out: styd on to take 3rd wl ins fnl f: no ch* **10/1**
-436 **4** *1 1/4* **Mack's Sister**[20] [806] 6-8-13 **57** (p) JimCrowley 1 54
(Dean Ivory) *chsd ldrs: rdn 2f out: chsd wnr jst over 1f out but no ch: fdd ins fnl f* **8/1**[3]
2066 **5** *shd* **Mataajir (USA)**[21] [794] 5-8-8 **52** MartinDwyer 6 48
(Derek Shaw) *hld up in last pair: shkn up 2f out: prog jst over 1f out: kpt on but no ch* **16/1**
5100 **6** *1 1/4* **Lucky Mark (IRE)**[18] [831] 4-9-5 **63** TomQueally 7 55
(Garry Moss) *led at str pce: hdd over 1f out: wknd fnl f* **10/1**
0511 **7** *1/2* **Red Ramesses (IRE)**[16] [863] 4-9-0 **58** LukeMorris 8 49
(John Best) *hld up towards rr: effrt on inner 2f out: no real prog over 1f out: one pce* **3/1**[2]
0-50 **8** *1/2* **Demoiselle Bond**[21] [790] 5-8-12 **56** SteveDrowne 2 45
(Lydia Richards) *chsd ldng pair: rdn over 2f out: steadily lost pl* **33/1**
0-44 **9** *1* **Dressed In Lace**[21] [790] 4-9-7 **65** IanMongan 3 51
(Jo Crowley) *chsd ldrs: no prog 2f out: wknd over 1f out* **10/1**
-051 **10** *1 1/2* **Chevise (IRE)**[12] [903] 5-9-3 **61** (p) MatthewDavies 5 42
(Steve Woodman) *racd on outer: chsd ldrs: lost pl wl over 2f out: struggling after* **14/1**
5006 **11** *hd* **My Own Way Home**[23] [775] 5-8-12 **56** MartinHarley 12 37
(David Evans) *chsd ldr at str pce to 2f out: sn wknd* **16/1**

1m 11.6s (-1.50) **Going Correction** 0.0s/f (Stan) **11** Ran SP% **118.1**
Speed ratings (Par 101): **110,103,102,100,100 98,97,97,95,93 93**
Tote Swingers: 1&2 £19.50, 1&3 £8.20, 2&3 £8.60 CSF £42.79 CT £348.42 TOTE £4.40: £1.90, £3.50, £4.20; EX 40.20 Trifecta £782.00 Pool: £1,196.55 - 1.14 winning units..
Owner Mrs I M Folkes **Bred** J Fike **Trained** Pandy, Monmouths

FOCUS
A modest handicap but a sound pace and a very easy winner, who raced up the centre in the straight. The form is rated on the negative side.
T/Jkpt: Part won. £18,034.30 to a £1 stake. Pool: £25,400.00 - 0.50 winning tickets. T/Plt: £59.10 to a £1 stake. Pool: £89,908.00 - 1,035.57 winning tickets. T/Qpdt: £22.30 to a £1 stake. Pool: £4,053.00 - 134.20 winning tickets. JN

1038 WOLVERHAMPTON (A.W) (L-H)
Monday, March 18

OFFICIAL GOING: Standard
Wind: Light against Weather: Overcast

1064 £32 BONUS AT 32RED.COM H'CAP 1m 141y(P)
3:00 (3:00) (Class 6) (0-65,64) 3-Y-O **£1,940** (£577; £288; £144) **Stalls** Low

Form RPR
00-4 **1** **Bain's Pass (IRE)**[17] [849] 3-9-5 **62** PhillipMakin 4 66+
(Kevin Ryan) *chsd ldrs: rdn over 2f out: led ins fnl f: styd on u.p* **11/2**[2]
605- **2** *1/2* **Mizyen (IRE)**[172] [6603] 3-9-6 **63** NeilCallan 1 68+
(James Tate) *plld hrd and prom: hmpd over 7f out: nt clr run over 2f out: rdn and r.o ins fnl f* **1/1**[1]
-060 **3** *nk* **Exit Clause**[18] [824] 3-8-5 **53** (p) RobertTart(5) 7 55
(Tony Carroll) *hld up: hdwy over 1f out: rdn and ev ch ins fnl f: styd on* **33/1**
200- **4** *1* **Eastern Dragon (IRE)**[105] [7965] 3-9-5 **62** PaulMulrennan 6 62
(Michael Scudamore) *hld up: hdwy over 2f out: rdn over 1f out: styd on* **20/1**
5434 **5** *1/2* **Rainford Glory (IRE)**[11] [910] 3-8-12 **55** JamieSpencer 2 54
(David Simcock) *hld up: r.o ins fnl f: nvr nrr* **8/1**
00-2 **6** *nse* **Haverstock**[20] [803] 3-9-6 **63** JoeFanning 8 61
(Mark Johnston) *chsd ldr tl led over 1f out: rdn and hdd ins fnl f: styd on same pce* **6/1**[3]
1132 **7** *5* **Darkest Night (IRE)**[17] [845] 3-9-7 **64** FergusSweeney 3 51
(Jamie Osborne) *chsd ldrs: rdn over 1f out: wknd fnl f* **6/1**[3]
3226 **8** *1 1/4* **Armada Bay (IRE)**[27] [717] 3-8-10 **53** TomEaves 5 37
(Bryan Smart) *led: rdn and hdd over 1f out: wknd ins fnl f* **20/1**

1m 50.57s (0.07) **Going Correction** -0.025s/f (Stan) **8** Ran SP% **117.5**
Speed ratings (Par 96): **98,97,97,96,95 95,91,90**
Tote Swingers: 1&2 £3.40, 1&3 £7.30, 2&3 £14.60 CSF £11.51 CT £171.76 TOTE £7.40: £2.70, £1.02, £7.20; EX 16.10 Trifecta £288.90 Pool: £1,191.95 - 3.09 winning units..
Owner Mrs Margaret Forsyth **Bred** Ballyreddin Stud **Trained** Hambleton, N Yorks

FOCUS
A weak handicap run at an honest pace. Straightforward form, rated around the third and fourth.

1065 32REDPOKER.COM (S) STKS 5f 20y(P)
3:30 (3:30) (Class 6) 4-Y-0+ **£1,940** (£577; £288) **Stalls** Low

Form RPR
1224 **1** **Hamoody (USA)**[14] [880] 9-9-4 **82** AdrianNicholls 5 82+
(David Nicholls) *s.i.s: sn prom: led over 1f out: shkn up and r.o: comf* **2/7**[1]
5-00 **2** *2 1/2* **Athwaab**[21] [790] 6-8-7 **57** JoeFanning 1 58
(Noel Chance) *led: rdn and hdd over 1f out: styd on same pce ins fnl f* **16/1**[3]
0111 **3** *3/4* **Where's Reiley (USA)**[9] [946] 7-9-4 **70** (v) SebSanders 4 66
(Michael Attwater) *chsd ldr: rdn 1/2-way: lost 2nd over 1f out: styd on same pce* **3/1**[2]

1m 1.85s (-0.45) **Going Correction** -0.025s/f (Stan) **3** Ran SP% **108.6**
Speed ratings (Par 101): **102,98,96**
CSF £5.06 TOTE £1.20; EX 5.60 Trifecta £5.20 Pool: £1,598.67 - 227.06 winning units..The winner was bought in for 7,500gns.
Owner Hart Inn I **Bred** Ragged Mountain Farm **Trained** Sessay, N Yorks

FOCUS
An uncompetitive seller run at a fair pace. The third was a few lengths off his recent form.

1066 32REDBET.COM H'CAP 5f 216y(P)
4:00 (4:01) (Class 6) (0-55,55) 3-Y-O **£1,940** (£577; £288; £144) **Stalls** Low

Form RPR
0-02 **1** **Baltic Prince (IRE)**[5] [985] 3-8-12 **46** oh1 JoeFanning 8 59
(Paul Green) *chsd ldrs: shkn up to ld ins fnl f: r.o* **5/2**[1]
-44U **2** *3* **Jordanstown**[17] [848] 3-9-5 **53** (p) NeilCallan 7 56
(Kevin Ryan) *led 1f: chsd ldr tl led again over 1f out: rdn and hdd ins fnl f: styd on same pce* **9/2**[2]
03-0 **3** *3 3/4* **Otto The First**[47] [442] 3-9-2 **55** RobertTart(5) 3 46
(John Best) *hld up: nt clr run wl over 1f out: r.o ins fnl f: wnt 3rd nr fin: nt trble ldrs* **8/1**[3]
U2-4 **4** *1* **Grand Jipeck (IRE)**[10] [923] 3-9-7 **55** (t) PatrickMathers 4 43
(Ian McInnes) *chsd ldrs: rdn over 2f out: styd on same pce ins fnl f* **5/2**[1]
0515 **5** *nk* **Chelsea Grey (IRE)**[17] [848] 3-9-1 **49** (b) WilliamCarson 2 36
(Ronald Harris) *s.s: hdwy over 2f out: sn rdn: styd on same pce fr over 1f out* **8/1**[3]
0236 **6** *1 3/4* **Club Electra (IRE)**[10] [923] 3-9-7 **55** (b) MartinLane 9 36
(Tobias B P Coles) *drvn along to ld 5f out: rdn and hdd over 1f out: wknd ins fnl f* **8/1**[3]
566 **7** *1 1/4* **Shaken Not Stirred**[18] [821] 3-9-1 **49** RichardKingscote 5 26
(Milton Bradley) *hld up: rdn over 2f out: wknd over 1f out* **12/1**

1m 14.88s (-0.12) **Going Correction** -0.025s/f (Stan) **7** Ran SP% **116.4**
Speed ratings (Par 96): **99,95,90,88,88 85,84**
Tote Swingers: 1&2 £2.30, 1&3 £4.00, 2&3 £6.50 CSF £14.55 CT £78.17 TOTE £2.60: £1.30, £3.60; EX 13.50 Trifecta £129.20 Pool: £1,942.91 - 11.27 winning units..
Owner A Mills **Bred** William Pilkington **Trained** Lydiate, Merseyside

FOCUS
This weak handicap was run at a sound pace. The form has been given a chance.

1067 32RED H'CAP 5f 216y(P)
4:30 (4:30) (Class 4) (0-80,80) 4-Y-0+ **£4,690** (£1,395; £697; £348) **Stalls** Low

Form RPR
-300 **1** **Clear Praise (USA)**[14] [881] 6-9-7 **80** SebSanders 2 88
(Simon Dow) *s.i.s: hdwy over 2f out: rdn over 1f out: led ins fnl f: styd on* **7/1**
0-30 **2** *1 1/4* **Tyfos**[23] [780] 8-9-7 **80** TomMcLaughlin 6 84
(Brian Baugh) *led: rdn over 1f out: hdd and unable qck ins fnl f* **12/1**
5501 **3** *hd* **Lucky Dan (IRE)**[21] [795] 7-9-2 **75** JoeFanning 8 79
(Paul Green) *prom: racd keenly: chsd ldr 4f out: rdn over 1f out: styd on same pce ins fnl f* **5/1**[3]
032- **4** *nk* **Peace Seeker**[231] [4660] 5-9-2 **75** WilliamCarson 5 80
(Anthony Carson) *stdd s: hld up: hdwya dn nt clr run over 1f out: styd on: nt trble ldrs* **3/1**[1]
1120 **5** *hd* **Holy Angel (IRE)**[13] [885] 4-8-12 **71** (e) DuranFentiman 12 73+
(Tim Easterby) *sn prom: rdn over 1f out: styd on* **6/1**
456- **6** *2* **Emiratesdotcom**[148] [7273] 7-9-4 **77** RichardKingscote 10 73+
(Milton Bradley) *hld up: rdn over 2f out: r.o ins fnl f: nvr nrr* **10/1**
00-0 **7** *shd* **Little Garcon (USA)**[73] [58] 6-9-5 **78** (e[1]) JamieSpencer 1 74
(Robert Cowell) *hld up: effrt over 1f out: nt trble ldrs* **9/2**[2]
00-0 **8** *1 1/4* **Chiswick Bey (IRE)**[17] [844] 5-9-5 **78** FergusSweeney 9 70
(Noel Quinlan) *chsd ldr 2f: remained handy: rdn over 2f out: styd on same pce fr over 1f out* **20/1**
204- **9** *1* **Thirteen Shivers**[153] [7144] 5-9-0 **80** MatthewHopkins(7) 4 69
(Michael Easterby) *chsd ldrs: rdn over 1f out: wknd ins fnl f* **9/1**

1m 14.35s (-0.65) **Going Correction** -0.025s/f (Stan) **9** Ran SP% **118.2**
Speed ratings (Par 105): **103,101,101,100,100 97,97,95,94**
Tote Swingers: 1&2 £15.50, 1&3 £7.90, 2&3 £12.00 CSF £88.53 CT £464.99 TOTE £9.70: £2.30, £4.70, £1.90; EX 91.80 Trifecta £197.50 Pool: £1,455.36 - 5.52 winning units..
Owner Racing Clear Partnership **Bred** Juddmonte Farms Inc **Trained** Epsom, Surrey

The Form Book Flat, Raceform Ltd, Compton, RG20 6NL.

FOCUS
This competitive handicap was run at a muddling pace. Things fell right for the winner.

1068 32RED.COM FILLIES' H'CAP — 1m 4f 50y(P)
5:00 (5:00) (Class 5) (0-70,70) 4-Y-0+ **£2,587** (£770; £384; £192) **Stalls** Low

Form RPR
-633 **1** **Bernisdale**[10] 929 5-8-10 **59**.......... JamieSpencer 1 68
(John Flint) *mde all: pushed clr fr over 3f out: rdr dropped whip wl over 2f out: eased nr fin* **4/1**[2]

5004 **2** *2* **Lady of Burgundy**[10] 929 7-8-8 **57**.......... FergusSweeney 3 63+
(Mark Usher) *hld up: nt clr run over 2f out: hdwy to go 2nd over 1f out: r.o: no ch w wnr* **15/2**

135- **3** *11* **Nadema Rose (IRE)**[221] 5001 4-9-5 **70**.......... JoeFanning 4 60
(Keith Dalgleish) *chsd ldrs: rdn over 2f out: wknd over 1f out* **11/8**[1]

00-0 **4** *¾* **Cane Cat (IRE)**[11] 919 6-8-10 **59**..........(t) LiamJones 5 47
(Tony Carroll) *hld up: pushed along over 3f out: rdn over 2f out: hung lft and wknd over 1f out* **28/1**

156- **5** *¾* **Passion Planet (IRE)**[17] 860 5-9-3 **66**.......... JamesSullivan 2 53
(John C McConnell, Ire) *chsd ldrs: wnt 2nd over 3f out: sn rdn: wknd over 1f out* **4/1**[2]

1/4- **6** *1 ½* **Tyrana (GER)**[200] 4189 10-8-3 **57**.......... RobertTart(5) 6 42
(Ian Williams) *chsd wnr over 8f: sn rdn: wknd wl over 1f out* **11/2**[3]

2m 39.3s (-1.80) **Going Correction** -0.025s/f (Stan)
WFA 4 from 5yo+ 2lb **6** Ran SP% **112.7**
Speed ratings (Par 100): **105,103,96,95,95 94**
Tote Swingers: 1&2 £1.60, 1&3 £1.80, 2&3 £2.60 CSF £32.47 TOTE £3.20: £1.50, £6.10; EX 16.80 Trifecta £71.60 Pool: £1,130.63 - 11.83 winning units..
Owner Roderick James & Geraint Anstee **Bred** Evelyn Duchess Of Sutherland **Trained** Kenfig Hill, Bridgend

FOCUS
Not a strong fillies' handicap, and it was run at a steady pace. The front two pulled a long way clear but not too much should be read into that.

1069 32RED CASINO MAIDEN STKS — 1m 4f 50y(P)
5:30 (5:30) (Class 5) 3-Y-0+ **£2,587** (£770; £384; £192) **Stalls** Low

Form RPR
/23 **1** **Fulgora**[17] 841 5-9-9 0.......... SebSanders 5 69
(Brendan Powell) *mde all: rdn over 1f out: styd on* **15/2**

2 *¾* **Street Artist (IRE)** 3-8-6 0.......... JoeFanning 9 70+
(Mark Johnston) *s.i.s: hld up: hdwy over 5f out: lost pl over 3f out: rallied over 2f out: styd on to go 2nd wl ins fnl f: nt rch wnr* **9/2**[3]

3 *¾* **Smalib Monterg (FR)**[170] 7-9-9 0..........(t) WilliamTwiston-Davies(5) 2 72
(Dr Richard Newland) *s.i.s: hld up: hdwy over 4f out: rdn to chse wnr over 1f out tl wl ins fnl f: styd on* **7/1**

2 **4** *1* **Keep Kicking (IRE)**[24] 752 6-10-0 0.......... RichardKingscote 3 70
(Jonjo O'Neill) *a.p: chsd wnr over 3f out tl rdn over 1f out: styd on same pce fnl f* **4/1**[2]

5-3 **5** *8* **Bin Manduro**[54] 333 3-8-6 0.......... AndreaAtzeni 6 55
(James Tate) *trckd ldr: racd keenly: lost 2nd over 5f out: remained handy: rdn over 2f out: wknd fnl f* **5/2**[1]

205- **6** *4 ½* **Drummond**[178] 6440 4-9-7 71.......... RobertWilliams(5) 7 52
(Bernard Llewellyn) *chsd ldrs: rdn over 2f out: sn wknd* **14/1**

7 *½* **Al Meezan** 3-8-6 0.......... MartinLane 8 48
(David Simcock) *sn prom: drvn along over 6f out: lost pl over 5f out: wknd over 2f out* **10/1**

8 *2* **Galway Gem (IRE)**[40] 5-9-9 0.......... StephenCraine 4 43
(John Mackie) *s.i.s: hld up: a in rr: wknd 3f out* **50/1**

9 *43* **Mickelson (IRE)**[23] 6995 7-10-0 0.......... JamieSpencer 1
(Jonjo O'Neill) *s.s: hld up: hdwy to chse wnr over 5f out tl rdn over 3f out: sn hung rt and wknd: t.o* **9/1**

2m 41.51s (0.41) **Going Correction** -0.025s/f (Stan)
WFA 3 from 4yo 22lb 4 from 5yo+ 2lb **9** Ran SP% **118.7**
Speed ratings (Par 103): **97,96,96,95,90 87,86,85,56**
CSF £42.43 TOTE £7.20: £2.10, £2.60, £2.10; EX 39.50 Trifecta £252.50 Pool: £1,572.44 - 4.67 winning units..
Owner Vino Veritas **Bred** J B W Bloodstock Ltd **Trained** Upper Lambourn, Berks

FOCUS
This weak maiden was run at a steady pace with the winner making all, under a well-judged ride. The bare form has been rated on the negative side.

1070 32REDBINGO.COM H'CAP — 1m 1f 103y(P)
6:00 (6:01) (Class 6) (0-52,52) 4-Y-0+ **£1,940** (£577; £288; £144) **Stalls** Low

Form RPR
2623 **1** **Angelena Ballerina (IRE)**[17] 852 6-9-5 **50**..........(v) WilliamCarson 5 57
(Sean Curran) *hld up: hdwy over 2f out: rdn to ld ins fnl f: edgd lft: styd on* **11/8**[1]

323- **2** *1* **Stag Hill (IRE)**[165] 6807 4-9-7 **52**.......... MartinLane 1 57
(Bernard Llewellyn) *a.p: chsd ldr over 2f out: rdn to ld and edgd lft over 1f out: hdd ins fnl f: kpt on* **3/1**[2]

-005 **3** *1 ¾* **Mayan Flight (IRE)**[17] 846 5-8-10 **46** oh1. WilliamTwiston-Davies(5) 13 48
(Tony Carroll) *hld up: hdwy over 2f out: rdn over 1f out: styd on same pce ins fnl f* **8/1**[3]

50-5 **4** *¾* **Sofias Number One (USA)**[11] 909 5-9-0 **48**......(b) MarkCoumbe(3) 12 48
(Roy Bowring) *chsd ldrs: outpcd over 2f out: rallied fnl f: r.o* **20/1**

605- **5** *¾* **Yorksters Prince (IRE)**[171] 6646 6-9-5 **50**..........(b) DanielTudhope 4 49
(Marjorie Fife) *led: rdn and hdd over 1f out: no ex ins fnl f* **10/1**

-533 **6** *3 ½* **Bashama**[12] 901 5-9-4 **49**..........(vt) AndreaAtzeni 6 41
(Nikki Evans) *mid-div: hdwy over 5f out: rdn over 1f out: no ex* **14/1**

660- **7** *3 ½* **Chapter Nine (IRE)**[131] 7629 7-9-5 **50**.......... FergusSweeney 11 36
(Tony Carroll) *s.s: hld up: rdn over 1f out: nvr on terms* **22/1**

/0-0 **8** *1 ¾* **Belle Noverre (IRE)**[48] 435 9-9-5 **50**..........(p) TomMcLaughlin 8 32
(John Butler) *hld up: rdn over 2f out: wknd over 1f out* **10/1**

9 *6* **American Kiss (SWE)**[327] 4-9-1 **46** oh1.......... SebSanders 10 17
(Robin Dickin) *hld up: rdn over 2f out: sn wknd* **28/1**

00 **10** *4* **Gemara (USA)**[5] 983 5-9-0 **52**.......... NedCurtis(7) 7 15
(Gary Brown) *sn chsng ldr tl rdn and wknd over 2f out* **25/1**

40/0 **11** *2 ¾* **Fists And Stones**[21] 788 5-8-11 **49**.......... JakePayne(7) 2 7
(Simon Hodgson) *prom: rdn over 3f out: wknd over 2f out* **66/1**

2m 1.98s (0.28) **Going Correction** -0.025s/f (Stan) **11** Ran SP% **121.0**
Speed ratings (Par 101): **97,96,94,93,93 90,87,85,80,76 74**
Tote Swingers: 1&2 £1.70, 1&3 £3.40, 2&3 £3.90 CSF £5.04 CT £24.82 TOTE £1.80: £1.10, £1.70, £3.40; EX 7.00 Trifecta £22.20 Pool: £2,182.19 - 73.71 winning units..
Owner Power Bloodstock Ltd **Bred** Waterford Hall Stud **Trained** Hatford, Oxon

FOCUS
A moderate contest run at a steady pace.
T/Plt: £183.80 to a £1 stake. Pool: £73,445.00 - 291.64 winning tickets. T/Qpdt: £32.40 to a £1 stake. Pool: £5,318.00 - 121.37 winning tickets. CR

[985] SOUTHWELL (L-H)
Tuesday, March 19

OFFICIAL GOING: Standard
Wind: light against Weather: Bright and dry

1071 32REDBET.COM APPRENTICE H'CAP — 1m (F)
2:20 (2:20) (Class 6) (0-60,60) 3-Y-0 **£2,045** (£603; £302) **Stalls** Low

Form RPR
6-15 **1** **Luv U Whatever**[19] 824 3-8-13 **55**.......... PhilipPrince(3) 4 63
(Jo Hughes) *cl up: effrt 3f out: rdn to take slt ld and edgd rt wl over 1f out: drvn and edgd lft ent fnl f: kpt on wl towards fin* **9/4**[1]

046 **2** *1* **Ivy Port**[29] 706 3-8-8 **50**.......... RyanTate(3) 1 56
(Michael Appleby) *slt ld: pushed along 3f out: rdn and edgd rt over 2f out: narrowly hdd wl over 1f out: drvn and edgd lft ent fnl f: ev ch tl no ex last 50yds* **8/1**

200- **3** *4* **Loki's Strike**[103] 8007 3-9-4 **60**..........(b) ConorHarrison(3) 6 57
(Mrs K Burke) *dwlt: hdwy on wd outside to chse ldrs over 3f out: rdn along wl over 2f out: drvn and one pce appr fnl f* **7/2**[3]

3-60 **4** *1 ¼* **Scepticism (USA)**[18] 845 3-9-3 **56**.......... MichaelJMMurphy 7 50
(Mark Johnston) *dwlt: hdwy to chse ldrs after 2f: cl up 3f out: sn rdn and wknd fnl 2f* **5/2**[2]

043- **5** *2 ¾* **Lady Raffa**[119] 7795 3-8-2 **46** oh1.......... ConnorBeasley(5) 5 33
(Michael Dods) *prom: rdn along over 3f out: wknd wl over 2f out* **16/1**

2130 **6** *1 ½* **Napinda**[19] 824 3-9-4 **57**..........(v) WilliamTwiston-Davies 3 41
(Philip McBride) *trckd ldrs: pushed along over 3f out: sn wknd* **10/1**

300- **7** *8* **Caramel Sundae**[96] 8093 3-8-11 **50**..........(b) ThomasBrown 2 15
(Robert Eddery) *chsd ldrs on inner: rdn along 3f out: sn wknd* **25/1**

1m 44.35s (0.65) **Going Correction** +0.025s/f (Slow) **7** Ran SP% **111.5**
Speed ratings (Par 96): **97,96,92,90,88 86,78**
toteswingers 1&2 £3.30, 2&3 £5.00, 1&3 £2.40 CSF £19.60 TOTE £2.70: £1.80, £4.50; EX 21.40 Trifecta £96.20 Pool: £2331.28 - 18.17 winning units..
Owner 21C Telecom.co.uk **Bred** Richard Hunt **Trained** Lambourn, Berks

FOCUS
A moderate apprentice handicap with the front two pulling well clear. Improved form from the runner-up.

1072 32REDBINGO.COM MEDIAN AUCTION MAIDEN STKS — 1m (F)
2:50 (2:51) (Class 6) 3-5-Y-0 **£2,045** (£603; £302) **Stalls** Low

Form RPR
6 **1** **Burgoyne (USA)**[20] 814 3-8-11 0..........[1] RobertHavlin 8 73+
(Hughie Morrison) *in tch on outer: green and pushed along 3f out: hdwy over 2f out: sn rdn: carried hd awkwardly and hung lft wl over 1f out: chsd ldr ins fnl f: green but kpt on wl to ld last 50yds* **7/1**

-622 **2** *1* **Excellent Puck (IRE)**[5] 994 3-8-11 0.......... FergusSweeney 7 71
(Jamie Osborne) *prom: cl up over 3f out: rdn to chal wl over 2f out: led 1 1/2f out: sn drvn and edgd lft ins fnl f: hdd and no ex last 50yds* **5/4**[1]

3-23 **3** *7* **He's A Striker (IRE)**[22] 799 3-8-11 75..........(b[1]) BarryMcHugh 3 55
(Tony Coyle) *t.k.h: led: pushed along wl over 2f out: rdn wl over 1f out: sn hdd and drvn: wknd ent fnl f* **5/1**[3]

5 **4** *1 ½* **Solarmaite**[12] 911 4-9-6 0.......... MarkCoumbe(3) 6 51
(Roy Bowring) *prom: rdn along and outpcd 1/2-way: hdwy wl over 2f out: kpt on u.p fnl f* **50/1**

06 **5** *11* **Aura Bora (USA)**[12] 911 5-9-7 0.......... RachelRichardson(7) 2 31
(Tim Easterby) *in rr: rdn along and bhd over 3f out: sme hdwy fnl 2f: nvr a factor* **16/1**

06- **6** *1* **Major Buckley (IRE)**[125] 7712 4-10-0 0.......... RussKennemore 1 24
(Alan Swinbank) *sn pushed along in rr on inner: outpcd and bhd over 3f out: nvr a factor* **33/1**

0- **7** *10* **Winter Music (IRE)**[192] 6020 3-8-11 0.......... LiamKeniry 4
(Andrew Balding) *trckd ldrs on inner: effrt 3f out: sn rdn along and wknd* **11/4**[2]

8 *11* **Harbour Captain (IRE)** 3-8-11 0.......... JoeFanning 5
(Jo Hughes) *t.k.h: trckd ldrs: pushed along 3f out: sn rdn: edgd lft to inner and wknd over 2f out* **10/1**

1m 43.75s (0.05) **Going Correction** +0.025s/f (Slow)
WFA 3 from 4yo+ 17lb **8** Ran SP% **115.3**
Speed ratings (Par 101): **100,99,92,90,79 78,68,57**
toteswingers 1&2 £2.50, 2&3 £1.50, 1&3 £3.70 CSF £16.35 TOTE £8.20: £3.10, £1.10, £1.10; EX 22.60 Trifecta £72.20 Pool: £3821.34 - 39.68 winning units..
Owner Lord Margadale H ScottBarrett & Partners **Bred** The Billabong & Fine Line Farm **Trained** East Ilsley, Berks

FOCUS
A modest maiden and they finished well spread out. The fourth and fifth offer perspective.

1073 32RED CASINO H'CAP — 6f (F)
3:20 (3:20) (Class 5) (0-70,67) 3-Y-0 **£2,587** (£770; £384; £192) **Stalls** Low

Form RPR
-131 **1** **Hannahs Turn**[6] 985 3-8-11 **57** 6ex.......... HayleyTurner 3 73+
(Chris Dwyer) *hmpd s: sn led: pushed clr 2f out: readily* **1/2**[1]

5-03 **2** *6* **Sylvia Pankhurst (IRE)**[19] 828 3-9-2 **67**..........(p) ThomasBrown(5) 5 64
(David C Griffiths) *prom: chsd wnr 2f out: sn rdn: swtchd lft over 1f out: drvn and no imp fnl f* **10/1**[3]

32-0 **3** *4 ½* **Ayasha**[11] 923 3-9-3 **63**.......... PaulMulrennan 2 47
(Bryan Smart) *hmpd s: in tch: hdwy on outer over 2f out: sn rdn and one pce* **10/1**[3]

02-6 **4** *2* **Hawsies Dream**[2] 1050 3-8-12 **58**..........(p) NickyMackay 4 36
(Alan Bailey) *wnt bdly lft s: chsd wnr: rdn along 3f out: drvn over 2f out: sn wknd* **4/1**[2]

104- **5** *12* **Poppy Bond**[132] 7635 3-9-2 **62**.......... DuranFentiman 1 4
(Chris Fairhurst) *bdly hmpd s: a in rr: bhd and eased fnl 2f* **14/1**

1m 16.42s (-0.08) **Going Correction** +0.025s/f (Slow) **5** Ran SP% **111.5**
Speed ratings (Par 98): **101,93,87,84,68**
CSF £6.64 TOTE £1.30: £1.10, £2.50; EX 6.90 Trifecta £23.10 Pool: £2578.77 - 83.64 winning units..
Owner Mrs K W Sneath **Bred** Wayland Stud **Trained** Newmarket, Suffolk

FOCUS
A fair sprint handicap contested by five fillies. The race had a messy start. The winner did it easily.

1074 £32 BONUS AT 32RED.COM (S) STKS 1m 4f (F)
3:50 (3:50) (Class 6) 4-Y-O+ £2,045 (£603; £302) Stalls Low

Form RPR
1121 1 **Stand Guard**[13] 901 9-9-5 87 AdamKirby 4 80+
(John Butler) *trckd ldng pair: hdwy and cl up 2f out: led on bit ins fnl f: readily* **2/11**[1]
-311 2 1 ½ **Jack Dawkins (USA)**[12] 908 8-9-5 65 AdrianNicholls 1 72
(David Nicholls) *led 4f: cl up tl led again 3f out: rdn over 2f out: jnd over 1f out: drvn and hdd ins fnl f: kpt on same pce* **11/2**[2]
4-23 3 1 ½ **Xpres Maite**[12] 908 10-8-10 64 (b) MarkCoumbe(3) 3 63
(Roy Bowring) *sn chsng ldr: led after 4f: pushed along 4f out: hdd 3f out: sn rdn and kpt on same pce* **20/1**[3]
2m 43.36s (2.36) **Going Correction** +0.025s/f (Slow) 3 Ran SP% **104.7**
Speed ratings (Par 101): **93,92,91**
CSF £1.44 TOTE £1.20; EX 1.40 Trifecta £1.50 Pool: £2137.23 - 1065.32 winning units..There was no bid for the winner.
Owner J Butler **Bred** Juddmonte Farms Ltd **Trained** Newmarket, Suffolk
FOCUS
A very uncompetitive seller, the winner doing it easily as he was entitled to.

1075 32RED H'CAP 5f (F)
4:20 (4:20) (Class 4) (0-85,76) 3-Y-O £4,690 (£1,395; £697; £348) Stalls High

Form RPR
1534 1 **Sewn Up**[5] 992 3-9-2 71 (tp) AdamKirby 2 78
(Reg Hollinshead) *trckd ldrs: hdwy wl over 1f out: rdn to chal ent fnl f: kpt on to ld last 100yds* **7/1**
311- 2 1 ¼ **Space Artist (IRE)**[115] 7866 3-9-2 76 WilliamTwiston-Davies(5) 3 78
(Bryan Smart) *cl up: ev ch wl over 1f out: sn rdn and kpt on ins fnl f* **4/1**[3]
-061 3 nse **Miako (USA)**[19] 828 3-9-3 72 AndrewMullen 1 74
(Michael Appleby) *led: rdn over 1f out: sn hung lft: drvn ins fnl f: hdd and one pce last 100yds: lost 2nd nr line* **5/4**[1]
4-51 4 6 **Girl At The Sands (IRE)**[34] 643 3-8-8 70 JenniferFerguson(7) 4 50
(Edward Creighton) *prom: rdn along 2f out: grad wknd over 1f out* **33/1**
010- 5 1 ½ **Welliesinthewater (IRE)**[186] 6196 3-9-6 75 MartinDwyer 5 50
(Derek Shaw) *sn pushed along in rr: rdn 1/2-way: nvr a factor* **12/1**
00-3 6 5 **Opt Out**[6] 982 3-9-7 76 JoeFanning 6 33
(Mark Johnston) *cl up: effrt over 2f out: sn rdn and wknd over 1f out* **5/2**[2]
1m 1.64s (1.94) **Going Correction** +0.475s/f (Slow) 6 Ran SP% **116.1**
Speed ratings (Par 100): **103,101,100,91,88 80**
toteswingers 1&2 £3.30, 2&3 £1.40, 1&3 £2.70 CSF £35.87 TOTE £7.30: £2.80, £2.20; EX 30.00 Trifecta £93.10 Pool: £2657.76 - 21.39 winning units..
Owner John L Marriott **Bred** M E Broughton **Trained** Upper Longdon, Staffs
FOCUS
A decent sprint handicap for 3yos with two of these having run in last season's Flying Childers. Improvement from the winner but the form has been given a chance.

1076 32RED.COM H'CAP 1m 3f (F)
4:50 (4:50) (Class 5) (0-75,74) 4-Y-O+ £2,587 (£770; £384; £192) Stalls Low

Form RPR
60-3 1 **Blades Lad**[12] 914 4-8-13 67 PaulMulrennan 6 76
(Peter Niven) *cl up: led 2f out: rdn over 1f out: hdd and drvn ins fnl f: rallied gamely to ld again towards fin* **7/4**[1]
2-46 2 nk **Royal Holiday (IRE)**[37] 603 6-8-11 64 (p) DanielTudhope 4 73
(Marjorie Fife) *led: pushed along 3f out: hdd 2f out and sn rdn: drvn and rallied to ld again ins fnl f: hdd and no ex towards fin* **5/1**[3]
600- 3 5 **Favorite Girl (GER)**[18] 5012 5-8-12 65 AndrewMullen 8 66
(Michael Appleby) *trckd ldrs on outer: rdn to chse ldng pair over 3f out: wd st and sn rdn: drvn and one pce fr wl over 1f out* **7/2**[2]
5264 4 3 **Follow The Flag (IRE)**[6] 987 9-9-0 67 (be) JohnFahy 7 63
(Alan McCabe) *in rr: pushed along 1/2-way: hdwy to chse ldrs over 3f out: wd st and sn rdn: drvn and no imp fr wl over 1f out* **6/1**
01-0 5 31 **Monopoli**[20] 810 4-9-1 69 RobertHavlin 5 16
(Daniel Kubler) *dwlt: sn chsng ldrs: rdn along over 4f out: sn outpcd and bhd* **12/1**
5264 6 9 **Monzino (USA)**[19] 832 5-9-0 67 RussKennemore 3
(Michael Chapman) *dwlt: in tch whn hmpd on inner over 8f out: rdn along in rr bef 1/2-way: bhd fnl 3f* **9/1**
460- 7 47 **Nibani (IRE)**[176] 6539 6-9-7 74 AdamKirby 2
(John Butler) *trckd ldrs on inner: rdn along 4f out: sn lost pl and bhd* **16/1**
2m 27.35s (-0.65) **Going Correction** +0.025s/f (Slow)
WFA 4 from 5yo+ 1lb 7 Ran SP% **113.1**
Speed ratings (Par 103): **103,102,99,96,74 67,33**
toteswingers 1&2 £2.40, 2&3 £9.30, 1&3 £2.60 CSF £10.59 CT £26.76 TOTE £3.00: £1.80, £3.00; EX 11.10 Trifecta £45.30 Pool: £2095.88 - 34.65 winning units..
Owner Crown Select **Bred** David Holgate **Trained** Barton-le-Street, N Yorks
FOCUS
An ordinary middle-distance handicap and a few of these found it very hard going. Straightforward form.

1077 32REDPOKER.COM H'CAP 5f (F)
5:20 (5:20) (Class 6) (0-58,53) 4-Y-O+ £2,045 (£603; £302) Stalls High

Form RPR
3-01 1 **Divertimenti (IRE)**[36] 610 9-9-3 52 (b) MarkCoumbe(3) 4 60
(Roy Bowring) *mde most: rdn wl over 1f out: drvn and edgd rt ins fnl f: hld on gamely* **6/1**
0-00 2 nk **Thorpe Bay**[68] 142 4-9-6 52 AndrewMullen 1 59
(Michael Appleby) *cl up on outer: effrt 2f out: rdn to chal over 1f out: drvn and ev ch ins fnl f: edgd rt and no ex towards fin* **7/2**[2]
05-0 3 1 ¾ **Bond Blade**[50] 423 5-8-13 45 DaleSwift 2 46
(Suzzanne France) *midfield: hdwy on outer 2f out: sn rdn and kpt on u.p fnl f* **12/1**
6015 4 1 ½ **Chateau Lola**[17] 862 4-9-6 52 (v) MartinDwyer 5 47
(Derek Shaw) *in tch: hdwy wl over 1f out: rdn and styd on fnl f: nrst fin* **9/2**[3]
0-00 5 1 ½ **Tenancy (IRE)**[14] 884 9-8-13 45 (b) DuranFentiman 6 35
(Shaun Harris) *cl up: rdn along 2f out: grad wknd* **10/1**
3300 6 nk **Island Express (IRE)**[17] 863 6-8-12 49 (tp) AnnStokell(5) 7 41+
(Ann Stokell) *s.i.s and bhd: rdn along 1/2-way: kpt on fr wl over 1f out: n.d* **16/1**
3440 7 shd **Putin (IRE)**[24] 775 5-9-7 53 (bt) AdamKirby 9 41
(Phil McEntee) *a towards rr* **3/1**[1]
026- 8 1 ¼ **Rio's Girl**[215] 5257 6-8-12 51 ow2 DavidSimmonson(7) 3 35
(Tony Coyle) *a in rr* **10/1**
000- 9 6 **Chosen One (IRE)**[183] 6314 8-9-7 53 PJMcDonald 8 15
(Ruth Carr) *prom: rdn along wl over 2f out: sn wknd* **25/1**
1m 2.31s (2.61) **Going Correction** +0.475s/f (Slow) 9 Ran SP% **115.3**
Speed ratings (Par 101): **98,97,94,92,89 89,89,87,77**
toteswingers 1&2 £6.60, 2&3 £10.90, 1&3 £15.20 CSF £27.25 CT £244.94 TOTE £9.50: £2.80, £1.90, £4.80; EX 40.00 Trifecta £352.60 Pool: £1877.10 - 3.99 winning units..
Owner K Nicholls **Bred** Airlie Stud **Trained** Edwinstowe, Notts
FOCUS
A weak sprint handicap, with the front pair dominating throughout, and there was never much between them.
T/Plt: £22.60 to a £1 stake. Pool of £52833.20 -1705.11 winning tickets. T/Qpdt: £15.40 to a £1 stake. Pool of £3349.90 -160.70 winning tickets. JR

1064 WOLVERHAMPTON (A.W) (L-H)
Tuesday, March 19

OFFICIAL GOING: Standard
Wind: Light half-against Weather: Overcast

1078 32RED.COM MAIDEN STKS 5f 216y(P)
2:10 (2:11) (Class 5) 3-Y-O+ £2,587 (£770; £384; £192) Stalls Low

Form RPR
056- 1 **Common Cents**[269] 3389 4-9-12 64 LukeMorris 3 70+
(Ronald Harris) *chsd ldr tl led over 1f out: edgd lft: rdn clr* **5/1**[2]
-4 2 3 ¼ **Sibaya**[21] 808 3-8-8 0 WilliamBuick 4 51+
(Roger Charlton) *hld up in tch: shkn up over 1f out: styd on to go 2nd wl ins fnl f: nvr nr to chal* **11/8**[1]
45 3 hd **Secret Advice**[32] 673 3-8-8 0 TomEaves 1 51
(Keith Dalgleish) *led: rdn and hdd over 1f out: styd on same pce fnl f* **14/1**[3]
4- 4 3 ½ **Evan Elpus (IRE)**[81] 8270 3-8-13 0 RichardKingscote 2 45
(Tom Dascombe) *chsd ldrs: rdn and hung lft over 1f out: wknd fnl f* **11/8**[1]
-500 5 1 ¼ **Stoneacre Hull (IRE)**[32] 670 4-9-2 44 SladeO'Hara(5) 6 40
(Peter Grayson) *dwlt: rdn over 2f out: sme hdwy over 1f out: wknd fnl f* **100/1**
6 6 2 ¼ **Satwa's Sister**[22] 796 3-8-8 0 ShaneKelly 5 30+
(Robert Cowell) *prom: rdn over 2f out: hung lft and wknd over 1f out* **66/1**
7 11 **Hares Grove (IRE)** 4-9-12 0 WilliamCarson 7
(Richard Price) *s.s: sn pushed along in rr: wknd over 2f out* **28/1**
1m 14.9s (-0.10) **Going Correction** 0.0s/f (Stan)
WFA 3 from 4yo 13lb 7 Ran SP% **113.5**
Speed ratings (Par 103): **100,95,95,90,89 86,71**
toteswingers 1&2 £1.90, 2&3 £3.10, 1&3 £3.80 CSF £12.19 TOTE £9.70: £3.00, £1.10; EX 9.40 Trifecta £65.10 Pool: £2880.65 - 33.15 winning units..
Owner S & A Mares & M Saunders **Bred** Darley **Trained** Earlswood, Monmouths
FOCUS
A weak maiden, run at a steady pace and something of an upset with the front two in the market firmly put in their place. There is possibly better to come from the winner.

1079 £32 BONUS AT 32RED.COM H'CAP 7f 32y(P)
2:40 (2:41) (Class 6) (0-60,60) 4-Y-O+ £1,940 (£577; £288; £144) Stalls High

Form RPR
5443 1 **Maggie Pink**[12] 919 4-9-4 57 TomQueally 12 64
(Michael Appleby) *chsd ldrs: led over 1f out: rdn out* **6/1**
-006 2 nk **Tenbridge**[7] 965 4-9-2 55 (b) WilliamCarson 10 61
(Derek Haydn Jones) *mid-div: hdwy over 4f out: rdn over 1f out: styd on* **50/1**
04 3 ¾ **Moral Issue**[7] 976 5-9-6 59 (b) DaleSwift 3 63
(Ian McInnes) *sn pushed along in rr: hdwy u.p over 2f out: styd on* **13/2**
0223 4 ½ **Unlimited**[5] 993 11-9-7 60 JimmyQuinn 1 65
(Tony Carroll) *prom: hmpd and lost pl over 5f out: hdwy over 1f out: sn rdn: styd on* **11/2**[3]
3363 5 ½ **Romanticize**[7] 976 7-9-3 56 TonyHamilton 4 58
(Jason Ward) *chsd ldrs: rdn over 1f out: styd on same pce ins fnl f* **5/1**[2]
4140 6 nk **Chambles**[13] 903 4-9-5 58 EddieAhern 7 59+
(J R Jenkins) *hld up: hdwy over 1f out: styd on same pce ins fnl f* **9/1**
-004 7 1 ¼ **Powerful Pierre**[25] 750 6-9-7 60 (v) ShaneKelly 5 58+
(Ian McInnes) *mid-div: lost pl over 2f out: rdn and styd on ins fnl f: nvr trbld ldrs* **4/1**[1]
0204 8 2 ¼ **Red Shadow**[14] 890 4-9-0 53 RobertWinston 6 46
(Alan Brown) *led: hdd over 5f out: led again over 2f out: rdn and hdd over 1f out: eased whn btn ins fnl f* **14/1**
52-6 9 nk **Geronimo Chief (IRE)**[74] 61 5-8-12 51 (v) FrannyNorton 8 43
(Andrew Crook) *s.i.s: plld hrd and hdwy 6f out: rdn over 1f out: wknd fnl f* **10/1**
2220 10 2 ¾ **Kielty's Folly**[22] 801 9-9-3 56 GrahamGibbons 2 45+
(Brian Baugh) *hld up: rdn over 1f out: n.d* **9/1**
6-20 11 5 **Village Green**[42] 525 4-8-13 59 (b) JacobButterfield(7) 9 32
(Ollie Pears) *chsd ldr tl led over 5f out: hdd over 2f out: wknd over 1f out* **20/1**
1m 29.92s (0.32) **Going Correction** 0.0s/f (Stan) 11 Ran SP% **122.2**
Speed ratings (Par 101): **98,97,96,96,95 95,93,91,90,87 82**
toteswingers 1&2 £49.20, 2&3 £85.60, 1&3 £5.90 CSF £264.64 CT £2065.72 TOTE £6.70: £1.90, £13.10, £3.20; EX 304.80 Trifecta £2182.50 Part won. Pool: £2910.13 - 0.82 winning units..
Owner A W Bult **Bred** Harcourt Stud **Trained** Danethorpe, Notts
FOCUS
A moderate handicap, run at a very steady pace to halfway. Things panned out well for the winner.

1080 STAY AT THE WOLVERHAMPTON HOLIDAY INN H'CAP 2m 119y(P)
3:10 (3:10) (Class 6) (0-55,55) 4-Y-O+ £1,940 (£577; £288; £144) Stalls Low

Form RPR
050- 1 **Almost Gemini (IRE)**[190] 6101 4-9-1 54 (p) JamieSpencer 10 64+
(Don Cantillon) *s.i.s: hdwy 13f out: jnd ldr over 5f out: led over 1f out: shkn up ins fnl f: shade cosily* **2/1**[1]
-450 2 nk **Perfect Shot (IRE)**[43] 515 7-8-10 49 RobertTart(5) 4 56
(Frank Sheridan) *hld up: hdwy over 1f out: rdn and ev ch ins fnl f: styd on* **10/1**
6-64 3 3 ¾ **Waldsee (GER)**[29] 703 8-8-12 46 WilliamCarson 7 49
(Sean Curran) *sn pushed along and prom: rdn over 2f out: no ex wl ins fnl f* **5/1**[2]
0/50 4 2 ¼ **Kijivu**[38] 579 8-8-12 46 oh1 (bt) LukeMorris 12 46
(Alastair Lidderdale) *chsd ldr tl led over 5f out: rdn and hdd over 1f out: edgd lft and wknd ins fnl f* **16/1**

50/5 **5** *nk* **Fair Breeze**[22] 788 6-8-12 **46** oh1 SteveDrowne 8 45
(Richard Phillips) *mid-div: hdwy u.p over 2f out: wknd ins fnl f* **22/1**
0010 **6** *3 1/2* **Turjuman (USA)**[18] 846 8-9-4 **52** PhillipMakin 6 47
(Simon West) *hld up: styd on fr over 1f out: nvr nrr* **14/1**
530 **7** *2* **Leitrim King (IRE)**[33] 653 4-9-1 **54** (tp) ShaneKelly 11 47
(Murty McGrath) *hld up: hdwy over 6f out: rdn and wknd over 1f out* **14/1**
/0-0 **8** *1/2* **I'Lldoit**[25] 755 6-8-12 **46** (v[1]) GrahamLee 9 38
(Michael Scudamore) *chsd ldrs: rdn over 4f out: wknd over 1f out* **11/1**
6/55 **9** *3/4* **Calculating (IRE)**[14] 887 9-9-4 **52** NeilCallan 1 43
(Mark Usher) *prom: n.m.r and lost pl after 2f: rdn over 4f out: n.d after* **16/1**
3240 **10** *10* **Pullmen**[13] 905 5-9-7 **55** EddieAhern 3 34
(J R Jenkins) *hld up: nvr on terms* **8/1**[3]
06-0 **11** *28* **Gumnd (IRE)**[13] 801 6-8-12 **46** oh1 (p) TomQueally 5
(Chris Grant) *led: hdd over 5f out: wknd 3f out: t.o* **40/1**
050/ **12** *59* **Paddy Partridge**[270] 2476 7-9-2 **50** TomEaves 2
(Tim Vaughan) *chsd ldrs: rdn over 4f out: wknd over 3f out: t.o* **9/1**

3m 41.67s (-0.13) **Going Correction** 0.0s/f (Stan)
WFA 4 from 5yo+ 5lb **12** Ran SP% **120.4**
Speed ratings (Par 101): **100,99,98,97,96 95,94,94,93,89 75,48**
toteswingers 1&2 £4.40, 2&3 £8.70, 1&3 £2.80 CSF £23.38 CT £92.72 TOTE £2.40: £1.10, £4.30, £1.80; EX 28.30 Trifecta £114.80 Pool: £1641.93 - 10.72 winning units..
Owner Don Cantillon **Bred** Rockhart Trading Ltd **Trained** Newmarket, Suffolk

FOCUS
A weak staying handicap. The bare form is very modest, but there's every chance the winner can do a lot better.

1081 HOTEL & CONFERENCING AT WOLVERHAMPTON RACECOURSE H'CAP 1m 141y(P)
3:40 (3:40) (Class 5) (0-75,74) 4-Y-0+ **£2,587** (£770; £384; £192) **Stalls** Low

Form RPR
-141 **1** **Goldstorm**[25] 758 5-9-6 **73** (p) WilliamCarson 1 82
(Brian Baugh) *hld up: hdwy over 1f out: r.o to ld post* **15/8**[1]
-265 **2** *nse* **California English (IRE)**[38] 593 4-9-5 **72** AndreaAtzeni 5 81
(Marco Botti) *chsd ldrs: led over 1f out: rdn and hdd post* **3/1**[2]
4546 **3** *1/2* **Copperwood**[14] 889 8-9-2 **69** FrannyNorton 3 77
(Mark Johnston) *a.p: chsd ldr over 1f out: r.o* **8/1**
4110 **4** *1 3/4* **Idol Deputy (FR)**[36] 614 7-9-1 **73** (p) RachealKneller(5) 6 77
(Mark Usher) *hld up: hdwy over 2f out: shkn up and hung lft ins fnl f: styd on* **7/1**[3]
6-00 **5** *2 1/2* **Brigadoon**[14] 889 6-9-7 **74** MichaelO'Connell 2 72
(Philip Kirby) *s.i.s: hld up: pushed along over 2f out: r.o ins fnl f: nvr nrr* **12/1**
3-33 **6** *1 1/2* **Rawaafed (IRE)**[10] 950 4-9-3 **70** (p) TomEaves 10 65
(Keith Dalgleish) *sn led: rdn and hdd over 1f out: wknd ins fnl f* **11/1**
2-44 **7** *3/4* **Hail Promenader (IRE)**[25] 758 7-8-13 **66** GrahamLee 7 59
(Anthony Carson) *chsd ldr tl rdn over 2f out: wknd fnl f* **10/1**
-300 **8** *4* **Standpoint**[57] 314 7-9-2 **72** SimonPearce(3) 8 56
(Conor Dore) *hld up: hdwy over 2f out: wknd over 1f out* **25/1**
-600 **9** *1* **Elijah Pepper (USA)**[52] 410 8-8-9 **62** LukeMorris 9 43
(Conor Dore) *hld up: rdn over 2f out: a in rr* **25/1**
0/45 **10** *18* **Ortea**[40] 548 4-9-1 **68** (t) StevieDonohoe 4
(Ian Williams) *chsd ldrs: rdn over 3f out: wknd over 2f out* **10/1**

1m 49.08s (-1.42) **Going Correction** 0.0s/f (Stan) **10** Ran SP% **125.3**
Speed ratings (Par 103): **106,105,105,103,101 100,99,96,95,79**
toteswingers 1&2 £3.20, 2&3 £5.30, 1&3 £4.90 CSF £8.06 CT £37.50 TOTE £2.10: £1.10, £1.80, £2.20; EX 12.70 Trifecta £60.90 Pool: £3137.92 - 38.62 winning units..
Owner Magnate Racing **Bred** Andrew Bailey **Trained** Audley, Staffs

FOCUS
A fair handicap for the grade. The winner should remain competitive in similar company.

1082 SPONSOR A RACE BY CALLING 01902 390000 H'CAP 1m 1f 103y(P)
4:10 (4:10) (Class 6) (0-60,60) 4-Y-0+ **£1,940** (£577; £288; £144) **Stalls** Low

Form RPR
3053 **1** **Apache Glory (USA)**[12] 921 5-9-6 **59** (p) AndreaAtzeni 7 66
(John Stimpson) *hld up: hdwy over 1f out: rdn to ld wl ins fnl f* **9/4**[1]
0-04 **2** *1/2* **Chik's Dream**[18] 852 6-8-7 **46** oh1 LukeMorris 4 52
(Derek Haydn Jones) *chsd ldrs: led over 1f out: hdd ins fnl f: styd on* **11/2**[3]
5345 **3** *nse* **Spirit Of Gondree (IRE)**[13] 896 5-9-7 **60** (b) RobertWinston 1 66
(Milton Bradley) *hld up: racd keenly: hdwy 2f out: rdn to ld ins fnl f: sn hdd and unable qck* **9/4**[1]
65/6 **4** *2 1/4* **Nonaynever**[10] 950 5-9-7 **60** JamesSullivan 6 62
(Ruth Carr) *chsd ldr: rdn and ev ch over 1f out: styd on same pce ins fnl f* **12/1**
0-60 **5** *3 3/4* **Kyle Of Bute**[38] 587 7-9-0 **53** WilliamCarson 8 48
(Brian Baugh) *led: racd keenly: rdn and hdd over 1f out: wknd ins fnl f* **5/1**[2]
00-0 **6** *1/2* **Sassi Sioux**[55] 333 4-8-2 **46** oh1 RobertTart(5) 2 40
(Tom Keddy) *hld up: rdn over 2f out: n.d* **16/1**
-540 **7** *2 1/4* **Silver Panther**[10] 950 5-8-4 **46** oh1 RaulDaSilva(3) 3 35
(Aytach Sadik) *trckd ldrs: plld hrd: rdn over 2f out: hung lft and wknd over 1f out* **66/1**
60-0 **8** *1/2* **Dansili Dutch (IRE)**[4] 1017 4-8-10 **49** FrannyNorton 5 37
(Andrew Crook) *hld up: a in rr: rdn and wknd over 1f out* **16/1**

2m 3.24s (1.54) **Going Correction** 0.0s/f (Stan) **8** Ran SP% **114.5**
Speed ratings (Par 101): **93,92,92,90,87 86,84,84**
toteswingers 1&2 £3.10, 2&3 £2.60, 1&3 £1.60 CSF £15.36 CT £29.98 TOTE £2.00: £1.10, £1.90, £1.30; EX 13.40 Trifecta £35.20 Pool: £3103.74 - 65.99 winning units..
Owner J T Stimpson **Bred** Malih Al Basti **Trained** Butterton, Staffs

FOCUS
This handicap developed from an early stage and it suited the closers. The winner is related to the balance of his better recent form.

1083 WOLVERHAMPTON-RACECOURSE.CO.UK H'CAP 1m 4f 50y(P)
4:40 (4:40) (Class 4) (0-85,85) 4-Y-0+ **£4,690** (£1,395; £697; £348) **Stalls** Low

Form RPR
-6P2 **1** **All The Winds (GER)**[22] 797 8-8-6 **75** (t) RobertTart(5) 6 84
(Shaun Lycett) *s.i.s: hld up: hdwy on outer over 2f out: led over 1f out: rdn out* **5/2**[1]
2-12 **2** *2 1/2* **Illustrious Forest**[39] 563 5-9-1 **79** GrahamGibbons 7 84
(John Mackie) *chsd ldrs: rdn over 1f out: styd on same pce ins fnl f* **7/2**[2]
061- **3** *hd* **Royal Peculiar**[87] 8228 5-9-4 **82** TomQueally 3 87
(Michael Appleby) *trckd ldrs: racd keenly: rdn over 1f out: styd on same pce ins fnl f* **4/1**[3]
160- **4** *2 1/4* **Daring Indian**[193] 6012 5-8-5 **74** MichaelJMMurphy(5) 4 75
(Ian Williams) *prom: lost pl over 4f out: rallied over 1f out: no ex ins fnl f* **12/1**
3262 **5** *6* **Dubawi Island (FR)**[14] 889 4-9-5 **85** (b) NeilCallan 1 77
(James Tate) *led: hdd over 5f out: led again over 2f out: rdn and hdd over 1f out: wknd ins fnl f* **5/1**
-321 **6** *6* **Honest Deal**[19] 830 5-9-0 **78** RobertWinston 2 60
(Alan Swinbank) *trckd ldr: plld hrd: led over 5f out: hdd over 2f out: wknd fnl f* **5/1**
364- **7** *55* **Key Gold**[167] 6784 4-8-8 **74** ShaneKelly 5
(Ian McInnes) *hld up: hdwy over 7f out: rdn and wknd over 4f out: t.o* **25/1**

2m 37.61s (-3.49) **Going Correction** 0.0s/f (Stan)
WFA 4 from 5yo+ 2lb **7** Ran SP% **115.7**
Speed ratings (Par 105): **111,109,109,107,103 99,63**
toteswingers 1&2 £2.80, 2&3 £4.60, 1&3 £3.70 CSF £11.76 TOTE £2.90: £3.60, £1.90; EX 14.40 Trifecta £55.60 Pool: £2020.10 - 27.22 winning units..
Owner Nicholls Family **Bred** Stall Tralopp **Trained** Clapton-on-the-Hill, Gloucs

FOCUS
A competitive look to this feature handicap, despite the small field. Straightforward form.

1084 LIKE US ON FACEBOOK WOLVERHAMPTON RACECOURSE H'CAP 1m 4f 50y(P)
5:10 (5:10) (Class 6) (0-65,65) 4-Y-0+ **£1,940** (£577; £288; £144) **Stalls** Low

Form RPR
0-11 **1** **Tidy Affair (IRE)**[22] 788 4-9-4 **64** ShaneKelly 8 74
(Gary Moore) *hld up: hdwy over 2f out: led 1f out: rdn out* **2/1**[1]
-622 **2** *1* **Day Of Destiny (IRE)**[35] 624 8-9-5 **63** GrahamLee 3 71
(James Given) *trckd ldrs: plld hrd: wnt 2nd over 2f out: rdn and ev ch 1f out: styd on* **3/1**[2]
/14- **3** *3 1/4* **Green To Gold (IRE)**[163] 5891 8-9-6 **64** (b) TomQueally 1 67
(Don Cantillon) *led: rdn and hdd 1f out: styd on same pce* **14/1**
1122 **4** *nk* **Easydoesit (IRE)**[18] 646 5-9-4 **62** JimmyQuinn 7 64
(Tony Carroll) *prom: nt clr run and lost pl over 2f out: rallied over 1f out: styd on* **5/1**[3]
0-10 **5** *2* **Wom**[20] 816 5-9-3 **61** (b) EddieAhern 2 60
(Neil King) *hld up: hdwy over 2f out: rdn over 1f out: wknd fnl f* **16/1**
3-00 **6** *6* **Gabrial's Hope (FR)**[32] 671 4-8-11 **57** JamieSpencer 6 47
(David Simcock) *s.i.s: hld up: nvr on terms* **10/1**
-210 **7** *1 1/2* **Evergreen Forest (IRE)**[20] 816 5-9-2 **65** (b) RobertTart(5) 5 52
(Tom Keddy) *trckd ldrs: racd keenly: rdn over 2f out: wknd over 1f out* **11/2**
006- **8** *1 1/2* **Azerodegree (IRE)**[218] 5159 4-9-4 **64** (p) GrahamGibbons 4 49
(Iain Jardine) *chsd ldr tl rdn over 2f out: wknd over 1f out* **33/1**

2m 39.32s (-1.78) **Going Correction** 0.0s/f (Stan)
WFA 4 from 5yo+ 2lb **8** Ran SP% **115.0**
Speed ratings (Par 101): **105,104,102,101,100 96,95,94**
toteswingers 1&2 £2.90, 2&3 £7.20, 1&3 £2.10 CSF £8.11 CT £62.95 TOTE £2.10: £1.40, £1.40, £2.80; EX 8.60 Trifecta £42.40 Pool: £2635.07 - 46.54 winning units..
Owner Gallagher, O'Rourke **Bred** Jim McCormack **Trained** Lower Beeding, W Sussex

FOCUS
A moderate handicap in which the first two were clear. The winner may be capable of better.
T/Jkpt: £15,829.50 to a £1 stake. Pool of £22295.16 - 1.0 winning tickets. T/Plt: £38.90 to a £1 stake. Pool of £90125.78 - 1688.96 winning tickets. T/Qpdt: £3.50 to a £1 stake. Pool of £6443.57 - 1348.18 winning tickets. CR

1085 - (Foreign Racing) - See Raceform Interactive

1057 KEMPTON (A.W) (R-H)
Wednesday, March 20

OFFICIAL GOING: Standard
Wind: Moderate, half against Weather: Overcast, cold

1086 BETDAQ MEMBERS FREE ENTRY EVERY WEDNESDAY MEDIAN AUCTION MAIDEN STKS 7f (P)
5:45 (5:48) (Class 5) 3-5-Y-0 **£2,587** (£770; £384; £192) **Stalls** Low

Form RPR
0- **1** **Endorsing (IRE)**[100] 8052 3-8-13 0 KieranO'Neill 8 70+
(Richard Hannon) *trckd ldr: rdn 2f out: led over 1f out: styd on wl* **14/1**[3]
03- **2** *1 1/4* **Hornboy**[157] 7078 3-8-13 0 WilliamBuick 5 67
(Jeremy Noseda) *chsd ldng pair: shkn up over 2f out: styd on to chse wnr jst ins fnl f: no imp* **11/8**[1]
5 **3** *nk* **Gift Of Silence**[20] 821 4-9-9 0 NeilCallan 11 66
(John Berry) *chsd ldrs: effrt over 2f out: shkn up and styd on to take 3rd ins fnl f: unable to chal* **16/1**
3- **4** *1 1/4* **Kohlaan (IRE)**[119] 7813 3-8-13 0 [1] AndreaAtzeni 13 63+
(Roger Varian) *plld hrd: hld up in last trio: stl there 2f out as ldrs wnt away: prog over 1f out: styd on to take 4th nr fin: too much to do* **6/4**[2]
5 *1/2* **Little Alice** 3-8-8 0 SeanLevey 4 57
(Stuart Williams) *hld up towards rr: outpcd over 2f out: stdy prog over 1f out: styd on fnl f* **33/1**
5 **6** *3/4* **Visual Aspect**[70] 114 3-8-13 0 JimCrowley 7 60
(Dean Ivory) *led: kicked on over 2f out: hdd over 1f out: wknd fnl f* **33/1**
4 **7** *1* **Deal Me In (IRE)**[33] 673 4-10-0 0 MichaelO'Connell 3 62+
(Ian Williams) *in tch on inner: effrt over 2f out: no imp on ldrs over 1f out: fdd ins fnl f* **33/1**
8 *1 1/4* **Florida Beat** 3-8-13 0 LiamKeniry 2 54
(Andrew Balding) *dwlt: hld up towards rr: pushed along 3f out: sn outpcd: kpt on fnl f* **14/1**[3]
9 *hd* **Hundred Acre Wood** 3-8-13 0 KirstyMilczarek 14 53
(Olivia Maylam) *wnt lft s: chsd ldrs: outpcd over 2f out: n.d after: kpt on nr fin* **33/1**
10 *4* **Kasbhom** 3-8-13 0 WilliamCarson 1 50+
(Anthony Carson) *hld up in rr: effrt over 2f out: no ch but keeping on whn twice hmpd over 1f out: eased after* **40/1**
11 *2* **Ela Goog La Mou**[127] 4-9-9 0 RobertWinston 12 38
(Peter Charalambous) *dwlt: wl in rr tl prog arnd rivals to go prom 1/2-way: wknd over 2f out* **66/1**
6 **12** *1/2* **Purford Green**[33] 667 4-9-9 0 JoeFanning 9 36
(Michael Attwater) *t.k.h early: hld up in rr: no prog over 2f out: sn wknd* **66/1**

1m 27.43s (1.43) **Going Correction** -0.025s/f (Stan)
WFA 3 from 4yo 15lb **12** Ran SP% **118.5**
Speed ratings (Par 103): **90,88,88,86,86 85,84,82,82,78 75,75**
toteswingers 1&2 £3.50, 1&3 £21.90, 2&3 £5.60 CSF £32.52 TOTE £15.30: £3.20, £1.10, £3.90; EX 36.00 Trifecta £289.90 Pool: £2970.79 - 7.68 winning units..
Owner Ben CM Wong **Bred** Paget Bloodstock **Trained** East Everleigh, Wilts

FOCUS
Probably just an ordinary maiden, run at no more than a fair tempo. The form is rated around the second.

1087 GOFFS READY-TO-RUN SALE 27.03.13 H'CAP (DIV I) 6f (P)
6:15 (6:18) (Class 6) (0-55,55) 4-Y-0+ £1,940 (£577; £288; £144) Stalls Low

Form RPR
043- 1 **Victorian Number (FR)**[90] 8184 5-9-2 **50** HayleyTurner 2 56
(Geoffrey Deacon) *trckd ldng pair: rdn 2f out: styd on to ld ins fnl f: drvn out* **4/1**[2]
5236 2 1 **Slatey Hen (IRE)**[6] 997 5-9-0 **48** (p) MartinHarley 8 51
(Violet M Jordan) *hld up in midfield: gng bttr than many 2f out: prog over 1f out: styd on to take 2nd ins fnl f: no imp on wnr* **20/1**
00-4 3 ¾ **Microlight**[27] 736 5-8-12 **46** oh1 (b) KirstyMilczarek 12 47
(John E Long) *trckd ldr: led 1/2-way: wnt for home 2f out on inner: hdd and no ex ins fnl f* **33/1**
12 4 nse **Spellmaker**[34] 649 4-9-4 **52** WilliamCarson 1 53
(Tony Newcombe) *t.k.h: hld up bhd ldrs: tried to cl fr 2f out: nt qckn over 1f out: kpt on same pce after* **4/6**[1]
-030 5 1 **Mary's Pet**[18] 863 6-9-2 **50** (p) KierenFox 3 48
(Lee Carter) *chsd ldrs: rdn sn after 1/2-way: nt qckn wl over 1f out: kpt on* **25/1**
3526 6 hd **Do More Business (IRE)**[8] 975 6-8-9 **50** (bt) PhilipPrince(7) 6 47
(Liam Corcoran) *wl in rr: rdn 2f out: kpt on fr over 1f out: n.d* **14/1**
4400 7 nse **Putin (IRE)**[1] 1077 5-9-5 **53** (bt) AdamKirby 5 50
(Phil McEntee) *led at gd pce: hdd 1/2-way: sn rdn: fdd over 1f out* **14/1**
053 8 hd **Kaylee**[20] 819 4-8-9 **48** RyanTate(5) 11 44
(Gary Moore) *hld up in last pair: shkn up over 2f out: sme prog over 1f out but nvr looked keen enough to be involved* **20/1**
6605 9 ½ **Perlachy**[11] 946 9-9-7 **55** (v) LukeMorris 10 50
(Ronald Harris) *awkward s: hld up in last pair: drvn 2f out: kpt on but n.d* **33/1**
-025 10 nk **Ridgeway Hawk**[15] 890 5-9-6 **54** (v) RobertHavlin 4 48
(Mark Usher) *dwlt: in tch in rr: sme prog 2f out: hanging and wouldn't cl on ldrs over 1f out: fdd* **25/1**
022 11 1¾ **Scommettitrice (IRE)**[18] 862 5-9-2 **55** (b) RobertTart(5) 7 44
(Mark Gillard) *racd wd: a towards rr: no ch over 1f out* **12/1**[3]
020 12 1 **Ishetoo**[4] 1043 9-8-11 **50** SladeO'Hara(5) 9 36
(Peter Grayson) *nvr beyond midfield on inner: urged along over 2f out: wknd over 1f out* **25/1**

1m 12.69s (-0.41) **Going Correction** -0.025s/f (Stan) 12 Ran SP% **128.0**
Speed ratings (Par 101): **101,99,98,98,97 97,96,96,96,95 93,91**
toteswingers 1&2 £10.80, 1&3 £22.70, 2&3 £68.10 CSF £88.04 CT £2407.61 TOTE £6.70: £1.40, £5.60, £11.30; EX 81.90 Trifecta £1407.80 Part won. Pool: £1877.19 - 0.29 winning units..
Owner Andy Pittman **Bred** Charles Barel **Trained** Compton, Berks
■ Geoffrey Deacon's first Flat winner.
■ Stewards' Enquiry : Kirsty Milczarek caution: careless riding.

FOCUS
A moderate sprint handicap. The winner might have more to offer but the bare form is only modest.

1088 GOFFS READY-TO-RUN SALE 27.03.13 H'CAP (DIV II) 6f (P)
6:45 (6:46) (Class 6) (0-55,55) 4-Y-0+ £1,940 (£577; £288; £144) Stalls Low

Form RPR
-066 1 **Mambo Spirit (IRE)**[53] 408 9-9-4 **52** SeanLevey 1 64
(Tony Newcombe) *t.k.h: hld up in rr: quick prog over 2f out to ld over 1f out: drvn and kpt on* **9/2**[3]
00 2 1 **First Rebellion**[6] 997 4-8-7 **46** oh1 (b[1]) RyanTate(5) 9 55
(Tony Carroll) *chsd clr ldr: clsd to ld 2f out: hdd over 1f out: edgd into wnr and outbattled after* **14/1**
3455 3 1½ **Sherjawy (IRE)**[27] 735 9-9-2 **50** KirstyMilczarek 2 54
(Zoe Davison) *trckd clr ldrs: taken to outer in st: rdn and kpt on to take 3rd fnl f: no imp after* **20/1**
0-56 4 nk **Medam**[5] 1020 4-9-1 **54** (t) MichaelJMMurphy(5) 7 57
(Shaun Harris) *hld up in last pair: hmpd on inner over 2f out: drvn and styd on fr over 1f out: nrst fin* **7/1**
0421 5 shd **Littlecote Lady**[27] 735 4-9-5 **53** (v) RobertHavlin 4 56
(Mark Usher) *chsd ldrs on outer: rdn 2f out: kpt on same pce after: nvr able to chal* **5/2**[1]
2133 6 ½ **Rightcar**[4] 1042 6-8-9 **48** SladeO'Hara(5) 5 49
(Peter Grayson) *awkward s: racd in last pair tl sme prog on inner fr 2f out: no hdwy fnl f* **10/3**[2]
4061 7 1¾ **Metropolitan Chief**[13] 917 9-9-1 **49** (p) TomMcLaughlin 12 44
(Paul Burgoyne) *hld up in rr: gng easily over 2f out: tried to make prog over 1f out but sn fnd nil and btn* **20/1**
-440 8 2½ **Flaxen Lake**[20] 819 6-9-0 **48** (bt) RobertWinston 3 35
(Milton Bradley) *a in midfield: shkn up and no hdwy wl over 1f out: eased ins fnl f* **12/1**
0000 9 4 **Amenable (IRE)**[22] 806 6-9-7 **55** MartinHarley 6 30
(Violet M Jordan) *chsd clr ldng pair to 2f out: wknd qckly* **8/1**
0/00 10 7 **Fantastic Smartie**[27] 735 4-9-2 **50** (b[1]) FergusSweeney 8
(Richard Phillips) *led at str pce and clr: hdd & wknd rapidly 2f out* **66/1**

1m 12.21s (-0.89) **Going Correction** -0.025s/f (Stan) 10 Ran SP% **118.8**
Speed ratings (Par 101): **104,102,100,100,100 99,97,93,88,79**
toteswingers 1&2 £12.40, 1&3 £17.10, 2&3 £40.50 CSF £64.62 CT £1183.90 TOTE £6.20: £2.50, £3.90, £2.20; EX 71.80 Trifecta £1175.60 Part won. Pool: £1567.51 - 0.62 winning units..
Owner Nigel Hardy **Bred** R Warren **Trained** Yarnscombe, Devon

FOCUS
The time was 0.48 seconds quicker than the first division. Straightforward form around the first three.

1089 GOFFS READY TO WIN MEDIAN AUCTION MAIDEN STKS 1m 4f (P)
7:15 (7:19) (Class 6) 3-5-Y-0 £1,940 (£577; £288; £144) Stalls Centre

Form RPR
352- 1 **Taglietelle**[172] 6677 4-9-7 **77** ThomasBrown(5) 5 75+
(Andrew Balding) *led 2f: trckd ldr: led again 4f out: shkn up 2f out: kpt on steadily and in command fnl f* **8/13**[1]
0 2 1¼ **Could Be (IRE)**[14] 895 3-8-6 0 MartinLane 1 71
(David Simcock) *s.s: hld up in 6th: prog 3f out: shkn up 2f out: kpt on to take 2nd ins fnl f: nvr able to chal* **25/1**
43 3 ¾ **Pereira**[12] 925 3-8-1 0 NickyMackay 3 65
(David Simcock) *t.k.h: trckd ldng pair: wnt 2nd over 3f out: rdn and nt qckn 2f out: lost 2nd and one pce ins fnl f* **9/2**[2]
6 4 8 **London Skolar**[14] 895 3-8-6 0 LukeMorris 7 57
(James Eustace) *dwlt: chsd ldrs: rdn 4f out: in tch 2f out: sn wknd* **9/1**[3]
60 5 18 **Revert (USA)**[26] 752 4-9-7 0 AdamKirby 2 25
(Gerry Enright) *in tch: rdn 4f out: wknd wl over 2f out: t.o* **100/1**
55- 6 12 **Common Courtesy**[123] 7780 3-8-1 0 HayleyTurner 6
(Michael Bell) *plld hrd and hung lft bnds: led after 2f: hdd 4f out: v wd bnd 3f out: wknd and t.o* **9/2**[2]
7 38 **Edna** 3-7-12 0 ow2 [1] NathanAlison(5) 4
(Olivia Maylam) *s.s: a bhd: lost tch 1/2-way: wl t.o* **66/1**

2m 36.12s (1.62) **Going Correction** -0.025s/f (Stan)
WFA 3 from 4yo 22lb 7 Ran SP% **114.6**
Speed ratings (Par 101): **93,92,91,86,74 66,41**
toteswingers 1&2 £4.30, 1&3 £1.10, 2&3 £9.80 CSF £21.00 TOTE £1.30: £1.10, £6.50; EX 15.30 Trifecta £57.20 Pool: £1824.51 - 23.89 winning units..
Owner Kingsclere Racing CLub **Bred** Kingsclere Stud **Trained** Kingsclere, Hants

FOCUS
A weak maiden run a slow pace. The third helps with the level and the winner didn't need to run to his best.

1090 WIN BIG WITH BETDAQ MULTIPLES H'CAP 1m 3f (P)
7:45 (7:49) (Class 6) (0-55,55) 4-Y-0+ £1,940 (£577; £216; £216) Stalls Low

Form RPR
5-32 1 **Thane Of Cawdor (IRE)**[13] 921 4-9-4 **53** LiamKeniry 8 62+
(Joseph Tuite) *hld up in midfield: angled lft quite sharply jst over 2f out: prog over 1f out: r.o to ld last 100yds: rdn out* **7/2**[1]
4124 2 ¾ **Lytham (IRE)**[7] 978 12-9-6 **54** FergusSweeney 9 61
(Tony Carroll) *t.k.h: hld up wl in rr: shkn up whn carried lft by wnr jst over 2f out: prog over 1f out: styd on wl to take 2nd last 50yds: jst hld* **10/1**
6666 3 1¼ **El Bravo**[15] 888 7-9-1 **54** (p) MichaelJMMurphy(5) 2 59
(Shaun Harris) *t.k.h: hld up and sn in midfield: rdn over 2f out: styd on fr over 1f out: nrst fin* **10/1**
5114 3 dht **Time Square (FR)**[16] 883 6-9-0 **55** JoeyHaynes(7) 3 60
(Tony Carroll) *plld hrd: hld up bhd ldrs tl prog to ld 5f out: drew 2 l clr 2f out: hdd and outpcd last 100yds* **6/1**[2]
363- 5 nse **Princess Willow**[101] 8049 5-9-4 **52** KirstyMilczarek 7 57
(John E Long) *t.k.h: led 1f: styd handy: rdn to chse ldr over 2f out to 1f out: one pce* **13/2**[3]
-042 6 2¾ **Beggers Belief**[7] 983 5-9-5 **53** (b) FrannyNorton 5 53
(Eric Wheeler) *chsd ldrs on outer: rdn whn lost footing briefly wl over 2f out: nt qckn over 1f out: wl hld after* **6/1**[2]
-044 7 nse **Snowy Valley**[5] 1022 4-8-9 **49** RyanTate(5) 4 49
(Simon Earle) *rrd several times bef stalls opened: in tch: drvn to chse ldrs over 2f out: fdd fnl f* **16/1**
000- 8 ¾ **Highway Warrior**[163] 6930 4-9-1 **50** WilliamCarson 14 49
(Sean Curran) *hld up in last pair: drvn 3f out and no hdwy: modest late prog* **25/1**
2030 9 hd **Dolly Colman (IRE)**[14] 896 5-8-12 **46** oh1 ChrisCatlin 1 44
(Zoe Davison) *hld up wl in rr: prog on inner jst over 2f out: no imp jst over 1f out: fdd* **33/1**
-000 10 nse **Burnbrake**[35] 635 8-8-12 **46** oh1 HayleyTurner 12 44
(Richard Rowe) *a wl in rr: shkn up and no prog over 2f out* **66/1**
06-0 11 3¼ **Market Puzzle (IRE)**[19] 852 6-8-12 **46** oh1 (p) EddieAhern 13 38
(Mark Brisbourne) *sn chsd ldng pair: disp 2nd over 2f out: wknd over 1f out* **25/1**
-215 12 4 **Midnight Bahia (IRE)**[34] 653 4-9-4 **53** AdamKirby 11 38
(Dean Ivory) *led after 1f to 5f out: wknd over 2f out* **7/1**
06-6 13 14 **Bestfootforward**[19] 841 4-8-11 **46** RobertWinston 10 6
(Olivia Maylam) *hld up in rr: wknd over 2f out: t.o* **20/1**

2m 21.21s (-0.69) **Going Correction** -0.025s/f (Stan)
WFA 4 from 5yo+ 1lb 13 Ran SP% **117.6**
Speed ratings (Par 101): **101,100,99,99,99 97,97,96,96,96 94,91,81**PI: EB £1.80, TS £0.60; Trifecta: TOC/L/EB £180.00, TOC/L/TS £66.10; Tricast: TOC/L/EB £161.79, TOC/L/TS £103.01; Toteswingers: TOC/L £8.10, TOC/TS £3.10, TOC/EB £4.40, L/TS £5.00, L/EB £7.20 CSF £36.22 TOTE £5.10: £2.30, £3.80; EX 39.10 TRIFECTA Pool:27 Owner.
■ Stewards' Enquiry : Liam Keniry three-day ban: careless riding (Apr 3-5)

FOCUS
This low-class handicap looked wide open and it was a lively betting heat. Straightforward form in behind the winner.

1091 BACK AND LAY AT BETDAQ.COM H'CAP 7f (P)
8:15 (8:16) (Class 4) (0-85,81) 3-Y-O £4,690 (£1,395; £697; £348) Stalls Low

Form RPR
21- 1 **Melvin The Grate (IRE)**[126] 7705 3-9-5 **79** JamieSpencer 1 85+
(Andrew Balding) *t.k.h: trckd ldng pair: clsd to ld over 1f out: edgd lft after: drvn out* **5/2**[3]
440- 2 ½ **Isis Blue**[147] 7323 3-8-9 **69** AndreaAtzeni 3 74
(Rod Millman) *hld up in last: shkn up 2f out: prog to chse wnr ins fnl f and sn swtchd rt: clsng fin: jst hld* **10/1**
1-1 3 ½ **Mystical Sapphire**[69] 129 3-9-7 **81** LiamKeniry 5 84
(Jo Crowley) *t.k.h early: hld up in 4th: hanging lft whn rdn wl over 1f out and nt qckn: swtchd rt and r.o ins fnl f: clsng at fin* **9/4**[2]
22-1 4 1½ **Flashlight (IRE)**[23] 796 3-9-6 **80** JoeFanning 4 79
(Mark Johnston) *pressed ldr: rdn 2f out: nt qckn over 1f out: sn lost pl and btn* **7/4**[1]
403- 5 nse **Hasanan**[228] 4813 3-9-4 **78** NeilCallan 6 77
(Clive Brittain) *led: tried to kick on over 2f out: hdd over 1f out: fdd ins fnl f* **8/1**

1m 25.82s (-0.18) **Going Correction** -0.025s/f (Stan) 5 Ran SP% **115.9**
Speed ratings (Par 100): **100,99,98,97,97**
CSF £25.34 TOTE £3.40: £3.10, £8.50, EX 26.60 Trifecta £92.20 Pool: £1095.90 - 8.91 winning units..
Owner Mrs Fitri Hay **Bred** Barronstown Stud **Trained** Kingsclere, Hants
■ Stewards' Enquiry : Jamie Spencer one-day ban: careless riding (Apr 3)

FOCUS
An interesting 3yo handicap. It proved tactical, but the form still looks decent for the class.

1092 BETDAQ GAMES £50 CASH BONUS H'CAP (LONDON MILE QUALIFIER) 1m (P)
8:45 (8:45) (Class 4) (0-85,85) 4-Y-0+ £4,690 (£1,395; £697; £348) Stalls Low

Form RPR
006- 1 **Ree's Rascal (IRE)**[208] 5535 5-8-11 **80** NathanAlison(5) 6 87
(Jim Boyle) *prom in chsng gp: wnt 3rd over 3f out: clsd fr 2f out: drvn to ld jst over 1f out: hld on wl* **10/1**
4-33 2 ½ **Brimstone Hill (IRE)**[37] 614 4-9-1 **79** WilliamCarson 8 85
(Anthony Carson) *s.i.s: hld up wl in rr: rdn over 2f out: prog over 1f out: r.o wl to take 2nd nr fin* **8/1**

440- 3 nk **Tigers Tale (IRE)**[144] 7407 4-9-5 **83**........................(v) RobertWinston 2 88
(Roger Teal) *chsd ldr after 2f: clr of rest 1/2-way: clsd to chal u.p over 1f out: chsd wnr fnl f: a hld: lost 2nd last strides* **5/1**[2]

-115 4 ¾ **Mister Musicmaster**[18] 865 4-9-4 **82**........................ LukeMorris 11 86
(Ron Hodges) *chsd clr ldrs: rdn 2f out: swtchd lft over 1f out: clsd steadily: nvr able to chal* **14/1**

5213 5 ½ **Russian Ice**[20] 822 5-8-12 **76**........................(b) JimCrowley 7 78
(Dean Ivory) *sn in midfield on inner: effrt and tried to chal over 1f out: one pce fnl f* **7/2**[1]

2662 6 nk **Rakaan (IRE)**[19] 844 6-9-7 **85**........................(p) FergusSweeney 4 87
(Jamie Osborne) *s.i.s: hld up wl in rr: prog and rdn 2f out: clsd on ldrs 1f out: one pce after* **11/2**[3]

00-4 7 ½ **Perfect Cracker**[23] 792 5-8-11 **80**........................ RyanTate(5) 13 81
(Clive Cox) *sn restrained into last trio: prog over 2f out: tried to cl on ldrs fr over 1f out: one pce* **14/1**

6000 8 2 ¾ **Decent Fella (IRE)**[16] 880 7-8-4 **73**........................(t) NatashaEaton(5) 5 67
(Violet M Jordan) *led and spreadeagled field after 3f: c bk to rivals fr 2f out: hdd & wknd jst over 1f out* **33/1**

50-0 9 ¾ **Dutch Old Master**[23] 792 4-8-11 **75**........................ WilliamBuick 12 68
(Gary Moore) *hld up towards rr: shkn up on outer over 2f out: no prog over 1f out: nvr a factor* **8/1**

0 10 1 **Cawett Cove (IRE)**[62] 239 5-8-9 **80**........................ IanBurns(7) 14 70
(Jane Chapple-Hyam) *sn restrained into last trio: rdn and no prog over 2f out* **66/1**

04-4 11 3 ¾ **Afkar (IRE)**[35] 629 5-8-12 **76**........................(v) ChrisCatlin 9 58
(Clive Brittain) *chsd ldr 2f: lost pl over 3f out: sn btn* **13/2**

330- 12 9 **Lady Macduff (IRE)**[141] 7461 4-9-6 **84**........................ JoeFanning 10 45
(Mark Johnston) *chsd clr ldrs tl wknd rapidly over 3f out: t.o* **10/1**

1m 37.45s (-2.35) **Going Correction** -0.025s/f (Stan) **12** Ran SP% **125.8**
Speed ratings (Par 105): **110,109,109,108,107 107,107,104,103,102 98,89**
toteswingers 1&2 £31.90, 1&3 £10.70, 2&3 £6.70 CSF £93.21 CT £468.58 TOTE £13.50: £4.10, £3.80, £2.10; EX 132.20 Trifecta £882.50 Part won. Pool: £1176.67 - 0.13 winning units..
Owner Walter Hayford **Bred** Pier House Stud **Trained** Epsom, Surrey
■ Stewards' Enquiry : Nathan Alison one-day ban: careless riding (Apr 3)

FOCUS
A modest, but competitive handicap and it was run at a solid pace. Straightforward form, the winner right to his best.

1093 FAMILY FUN WITH PEPPA PIG 30.03.13 H'CAP 1m (P)
9:15 (9:15) (Class 7) (0-50,50) 4-Y-0+ **£1,455** (£433; £216; £108) **Stalls** Low

Form RPR

0-10 1 **Chandrayaan**[22] 806 6-9-5 **50**........................(v) KirstyMilczarek 8 59
(John E Long) *led 1f: chsd ldr: rdn wl over 2f out: responded and kpt on to ld jst ins fnl f: hld on wl* **16/1**

-000 2 ½ **Signora Frasi (IRE)**[23] 794 8-9-5 **50**........................ WilliamCarson 14 58
(Tony Newcombe) *hld up wl in rr: swtchd lft over 2f out: drvn and gd prog on outer over 1f out: r.o to press wnr nr fin: nt qckn* **10/1**

4021 3 ¾ **Crucis Abbey (IRE)**[12] 927 5-9-3 **48**........................(p) EddieAhern 3 54
(Mark Brisbourne) *trckd ldng pair: gng easily over 2f out: clsd to ld over 1f out: hdd and nt qckn jst ins fnl f* **5/1**[3]

0-04 4 1 **The Which Doctor**[20] 825 8-9-2 **47**........................(e) MartinHarley 9 51
(Violet M Jordan) *hld up wl in rr: rdn and prog fr 2f out: clsd on ldrs fnl f: one pce last 100yds* **9/2**[2]

040- 5 ¾ **Wishformore (IRE)**[127] 5351 6-9-4 **49**........................ IanMongan 11 51
(Zoe Davison) *chsd ldng pair: hrd rdn over 2f out: clsd and ch over 1f out: no ex* **50/1**

0/- 6 nk **San Jose City (IRE)**[226] 4894 8-9-2 **47**........................ LiamKeniry 4 49
(Gary Brown) *hld up in midfield: prog over 2f out: rdn to chal over 1f out: fdd ins fnl f* **11/2**

50-5 7 1 ¼ **Mayforde Jack**[40] 564 4-8-12 **50**........................ JoshBaudains(7) 2 49
(Simon Hodgson) *hld up in midfield on inner: tried to make prog fr 2f out: one pce fnl f* **33/1**

3632 8 shd **Supa Seeker (USA)**[8] 975 7-8-11 **47**........................ RyanTate(5) 1 45
(Tony Carroll) *hld up wl in rr: shkn up over 2f out: prog over 1f out: one pce and no imp after* **4/1**[1]

5564 9 1 ¾ **Gallantry**[14] 900 11-9-4 **49**........................ TomMcLaughlin 6 43
(Paul Howling) *trckd ldrs in 5th: clsd 2f out: nt qckn over 1f out: fdd fnl f* **16/1**

0601 10 nk **Rigid**[14] 900 6-9-3 **48**........................ JimCrowley 12 42
(Tony Carroll) *hld up in midfield: gng bttr than many over 2f out: pushed along over 1f out and no prog: no ch after* **10/1**

455 11 nk **Miss Chardonay**[39] 590 6-9-2 **47**........................ AdamKirby 13 40
(Mandy Rowland) *hld up wl in rr: rdn and no prog 3f out: no ch after* **33/1**

-500 12 1 ¾ **The Bendy Fella (IRE)**[27] 736 5-9-5 **50**........................(p) RobertHavlin 7 39
(Mark Usher) *hld up wl in rr: shkn up and no prog over 2f out* **14/1**

/665 13 2 **Atacama Sunrise**[14] 900 7-9-3 **48**........................(p) JamieSpencer 10 32
(John Butler) *pushed up to ld after 1f: hdd over 1f out: wknd qckly* **14/1**

516/ 14 41 **Queenie's Star (IRE)**[478] 7571 6-9-5 **50**........................ SebSanders 5
(Michael Attwater) *racd wd in midfield: wknd qckly 3f out: t.o* **20/1**

1m 39.69s (-0.11) **Going Correction** -0.025s/f (Stan) **14** Ran SP% **126.1**
Speed ratings (Par 97): **99,98,97,96,96 95,94,94,92,92 92,90,88,47**
toteswingers 1&2 £76.80, 1&3 £36.60, 2&3 £20.20 CSF £169.89 CT £961.59 TOTE £30.80: £5.90, £4.80, £1.40; EX 227.90 Trifecta £1209.50 Part won. Pool: £1612.76 - 0.94 winning units..
Owner R D John **Bred** Whatton Manor Stud **Trained** Caterham, Surrey
■ Stewards' Enquiry : Kirsty Milczarek two-day ban: used whip above permitted level (Apr 3-4)

FOCUS
A bottom-drawer handicap, run at a frantic pace. Straightforward form.
T/Jkpt: Not won. T/Plt: £617.70 to a £1 stake. Pool of £109,520.10 - 129.43 winning tickets. T/Qpdt: £89.50 to a £1 stake. Pool of £10,155.80 - 83.95 winning tickets. JN

1086 KEMPTON (A.W) (R-H)
Thursday, March 21

OFFICIAL GOING: Standard
Wind: Fresh, across towards stands Weather: Overcast

1094 GOFFS READY-TO-RUN BREEZE-UP 27.03.13 CLAIMING STKS 1m (P)
6:00 (6:00) (Class 6) 4-Y-0+ **£1,940** (£577; £288) **Stalls** Low

Form RPR

1311 1 **Hurricane Spirit (IRE)**[29] 721 9-8-7 71........................ NicoleNordblad(5) 4 74+
(Hans Adielsson) *led after 1f and set modest pce: pushed clr over 1f out: a holding runner-up: comf* **5/6**[1]

5121 2 ¾ **Officer In Command (USA)**[6] 1010 7-8-13 66........................(v) WilliamCarson 1 73
(Sean Curran) *cl up in 3rd: rdn 3f out: styd on fr over 1f out: clsd on wnr fnl f: a hld* **9/4**[2]

1-04 3 8 **Mr Knightley (IRE)**[55] 370 4-9-4 74........................(b) MatthewDavies 3 61
(Jim Boyle) *led 1f: t.k.h and stdd to trck wnr: wknd 2f out* **7/2**[3]

1m 38.78s (-1.02) **Going Correction** -0.025s/f (Stan) **3** Ran SP% **107.5**
Speed ratings (Par 101): **104,103,95**
CSF £2.94 TOTE £1.70; EX 2.50 Trifecta £2.30 Pool: £532.84 - 168.61 winning units.Officer in Command was claimed by Mr H. Adielsson for £6,000
Owner Hans Adielsson A B **Bred** Knocktoran Stud **Trained** Kingston Lisle, Oxon

FOCUS
Not many runners but this was a fair claimer and the favourite scored with a bit more in hand than the winning margin under a front-running ride. The form is rated around the principals' recent efforts.

1095 GET THE BETVICTOR APP NOW MEDIAN AUCTION MAIDEN FILLIES' STKS 1m (P)
6:30 (6:34) (Class 5) 3-5-Y-O **£2,587** (£770; £384; £192) **Stalls** Low

Form RPR

2 1 **Storm (IRE)**[23] 807 3-8-11 0........................ WilliamCarson 6 63+
(Charles Hills) *broke wl: stdd to trck ldrs after 2f: wnt 2nd 2f out: shkn up and tk time to respond: pushed along to ld fnl 40yds* **2/11**[1]

03-4 2 ¾ **Solvanna**[19] 864 3-8-11 60........................ GrahamLee 7 58
(Heather Main) *led 2f: trckd ldr: led again over 2f out: kpt on u.p fr over 1f out: hdd fnl 40yds* **7/1**[2]

5- 3 2 ½ **Sweet Alabama**[301] 2407 3-8-11 0........................ AndreaAtzeni 8 52+
(Rod Millman) *chsd ldrs: rdn and outpcd over 2f out: kpt on steadily fnl f* **10/1**[3]

00- 4 2 ½ **Orla (IRE)**[216] 5309 5-9-9 0........................ MichaelJMMurphy(5) 9 47
(John Gallagher) *sn w ldrs: led after 2f tl over 2f out: sn btn: wknd over 1f out* **25/1**

0 5 1 ¾ **Just Isla**[22] 815 3-8-11 0........................ FrannyNorton 1 42
(Peter Makin) *plld hrd in 5th: rdn 3f out: sn outpcd* **16/1**

2-6 6 hd **Ruff Luck**[19] 864 3-8-11 0........................ LiamKeniry 2 42
(Seamus Mullins) *towards rr: effrt over 2f out: wknd over 1f out* **10/1**[3]

7 4 ½ **Indy Spirit (IRE)** 3-8-11 0........................ EddieAhern 3 32
(Laura Mongan) *hld up in detached last: pushed along over 2f out: nvr nr ldrs* **20/1**

1m 42.82s (3.02) **Going Correction** -0.025s/f (Stan)
WFA 3 from 5yo 17lb **7** Ran SP% **129.8**
Speed ratings (Par 100): **83,82,79,77,75 75,70**
toteswingers 1&2 £1.20, 1&3 £1.70, 2&3 £2.30 CSF £3.49 TOTE £1.10: £1.02, £3.50; EX 3.50 Trifecta £10.50 Pool: £1,393.66 - 98.76 winning units.
Owner R Morecombe, J Netherthorpe, E O'Leary **Bred** C O'Brien B McGarvey & D Everard **Trained** Lambourn, Berks

FOCUS
The hot favourite had to work quite hard to land the odds in this ordinary fillies' maiden which was run at a steady pace. The winner should get a good mark for handicaps.

1096 BETVICTOR NON RUNNER NO BET GRAND NATIONAL H'CAP 7f (P)
7:00 (7:00) (Class 5) (0-75,75) 4-Y-0+ **£2,587** (£770; £384; £192) **Stalls** Low

Form RPR

0-60 1 **Ocean Legend (IRE)**[21] 822 8-9-2 **70**........................ KierenFallon 9 80
(Tony Carroll) *hld up in 6th: hdwy 2f out: styd on to ld ins fnl f: drvn out* **8/1**

512 2 nk **Al Khan (IRE)**[7] 996 4-9-5 **73**........................ MartinHarley 5 82
(Violet M Jordan) *t.k.h: chsd ldr: led 2f out tl ins fnl f: kpt on* **5/4**[1]

0-66 3 2 **Perfect Mission**[21] 822 5-8-10 **71**........................(v) DanielMuscutt(7) 4 75
(Andrew Balding) *chsd ldrs: chal 2f out: one pce appr fnl f* **7/1**[3]

6104 4 1 ¼ **The Guru Of Gloom (IRE)**[27] 751 5-9-3 **71**........................ JackMitchell 7 72
(William Muir) *stdd s and swtchd to inner: plld hrd in rr: rdn and hdwy over 1f out: no imp fnl f* **10/1**

-104 5 1 ½ **Shaunas Spirit (IRE)**[40] 589 5-8-9 **70**........................(p) PaulBooth(7) 8 67
(Dean Ivory) *plld hrd towards rr: rdn and hdwy 2f out: wknd over 1f out* **14/1**

4005 6 ½ **Scottish Lake**[8] 984 5-9-5 **73**........................ KirstyMilczarek 1 69
(Olivia Maylam) *led: pushed along 3f out: hdd 2f out: wknd over 1f out* **5/1**[2]

-406 7 1 ½ **Lujeanie**[26] 780 7-9-7 **75**........................ ShaneKelly 6 67
(Peter Crate) *chsd ldrs tl hung rt and wknd 2f out* **10/1**

50-0 8 3 ¾ **Fugitive Motel (IRE)**[8] 984 4-8-4 **65**........................ JoeyHaynes(7) 3 47
(Eric Wheeler) *in tch tl hrd rdn and wknd over 2f out* **50/1**

1m 25.02s (-0.98) **Going Correction** -0.025s/f (Stan) **8** Ran SP% **111.5**
Speed ratings (Par 103): **104,103,101,99,98 97,95,91**
toteswingers 1&2 £1.90, 1&3 £6.60, 2&3 £2.80 CSF £17.53 CT £73.24 TOTE £5.90: £1.80, £1.10, £1.90; EX 19.70 Trifecta £113.50 Pool: £1,014.38 - 6.70 winning units.
Owner W McLuskey **Bred** Mark Commins **Trained** Cropthorne, Worcs

FOCUS
They went just a fair pace in this handicap. The well-backed favourite was just held and the first two pulled clear. The form makes plenty of sense.

1097 BETVICTOR CASINO ON YOUR MOBILE H'CAP 1m 4f (P)
7:30 (7:30) (Class 5) (0-70,70) 4-Y-0+ **£2,587** (£770; £384; £192) **Stalls** Centre

Form RPR

-016 1 **Mcbirney (USA)**[44] 528 6-8-13 **69**........................ PhilipPrince(7) 7 79
(Paul D'Arcy) *t.k.h in rr: hdwy over 2f out: led over 1f out: rdn clr: easily* **7/2**[2]

/006 2 5 **King Olav (UAE)**[29] 720 8-9-1 **64**........................ JimCrowley 3 67
(Tony Carroll) *led 2f: led again over 2f out tl over 1f out: no ch w wnr* **9/2**[3]

0/41 3 1 ¾ **Mister Bob (GER)**[36] 641 4-8-12 **63**........................ GrahamLee 2 63
(James Bethell) *t.k.h: prom: rdn 3f out: one pce fnl 2f* **2/1**[1]

15 4 2 **Pahente**[26] 779 5-8-11 **65**........................(p) WilliamTwiston-Davies(5) 8 62
(Tony Carroll) *stdd s: hld up in rr: rdn 4f out: styd on u.p fnl 2f: nt trble ldrs* **5/1**

-015 5 ¾ **Maison Brillet (IRE)**[22] 816 6-9-2 **65**........................(p) RobertHavlin 4 61
(Clive Drew) *in tch: rdn over 3f out: btn 2f out* **10/1**

-635 6 6 **Brunston**[13] 928 7-9-7 **70**........................(t) LiamKeniry 6 57
(Anthony Middleton) *chsd ldr: led after 2f tl 1m out: prom tl wknd over 2f out* **12/1**

6225 7 3 ¼ **Amana (USA)**[14] 914 9-8-12 **61**........................ ShaneKelly 5 43
(Mark Brisbourne) *hdwy to ld 1m out: hdd over 2f out: wknd wl over 1f out* **10/1**

2m 33.62s (-0.88) **Going Correction** -0.025s/f (Stan)
WFA 4 from 5yo+ 2lb **7** Ran SP% **116.3**
Speed ratings (Par 103): **101,97,96,95,94 90,88**
toteswingers 1&2 £4.90, 1&3 £2.40, 2&3 £1.60 CSF £20.19 CT £39.19 TOTE £3.30: £1.60, £4.00; EX 24.10 Trifecta £60.20 Pool: £863.91 - 10.74 winning units.

Owner Mrs Sue D'Arcy **Bred** Charles H Wacker **Trained** Newmarket, Suffolk

FOCUS

There was an emphatic winner of this middle-distance handicap. The second and third set the level.

1098 BETVICTOR NON RUNNER NO BET AT AINTREE H'CAP 1m 3f (P)

8:00 (8:01) (Class 6) (0-60,64) 3-Y-O **£1,940** (£577; £288; £144) **Stalls** Low

Form RPR

1331 **1** **Flying Tempo**[6] 1016 3-9-12 **64** 6ex.................(b) GrahamLee 3 78+
(Ed Dunlop) *a gng wl: hld up in 5th: smooth hdwy to ld over 1f out: pushed clr: easily* **6/4**[1]

-604 **2** *4* **Alshan Fajer**[21] 824 3-9-6 **58**................. IanMongan 2 63+
(Paul Howling) *towards rr: rdn over 2f out: styd on to take 2nd ins fnl f* **4/1**[2]

0-62 **3** *3½* **Conversing (USA)**[14] 910 3-9-0 **52**................. JoeFanning 5 51
(Mark Johnston) *led after 1f tl after 2f: led again over 2f out tl over 1f out: no ex* **6/1**[3]

05-4 **4** *1* **Booktheband (IRE)**[26] 774 3-9-7 **59**................. FrederikTylicki 10 57
(Clive Brittain) *towards rr: rdn 3f out: styd on fnl 2f: nvr nrr* **9/1**

00-4 **5** *1¼* **Jd Rockefeller**[46] 507 3-9-4 **56**................. SebSanders 9 51
(Paul D'Arcy) *hld up and bhd: rdn over 2f out: sme hdwy over 1f out: nt rch ldrs* **12/1**

605- **6** *1¾* **Dark Justice (IRE)**[189] 6168 3-9-6 **58**................. AndreaAtzeni 8 50
(Tim Pitt) *mid-div: effrt and hrd rdn over 2f out: wknd over 1f out* **16/1**

3-53 **7** *2* **Taming The Tweet**[43] 541 3-9-3 **55**................. EddieAhern 4 43
(J R Jenkins) *led 1f: prom: rdn 3f out: wknd over 1f out* **33/1**

0-66 **8** *nse* **Royal Barge (IRE)**[26] 774 3-8-9 **52**................. AmyScott[(5)] 6 40
(Eve Johnson Houghton) *led after 2f tl over 2f out: wknd wl over 1f out* **16/1**

6245 **9** *½* **Icanboogie**[14] 910 3-8-3 **46**................. RobertTart[(5)] 1 33
(Karen George) *stdd s: hld up and bhd: mod effrt 2f out: n.d* **25/1**

4-40 **10** *44* **Show More Faith**[9] 977 3-9-3 **55**................. LiamKeniry 7
(Sylvester Kirk) *chsd ldrs tl hrd rdn and wknd 3f out: sn bhd* **25/1**

2m 21.98s (0.08) **Going Correction** -0.025s/f (Stan) **10** Ran SP% **114.4**

Speed ratings (Par 96): **98,95,92,91,90 89,88,88,87,55**

toteswingers 1&2 £2.70, 1&3 £2.00, 2&3 £3.70 CSF £6.76 CT £27.05 TOTE £1.50: £1.02, £1.90, £2.70; EX 10.10 Trifecta £24.10 Pool: £900.01 - 27.93 winning units.

Owner Robert Ng **Bred** Dr Celia Marr **Trained** Newmarket, Suffolk

FOCUS

They went a decent pace in this handicap and the favourite delivered in great style under a hold-up ride. The form makes sense.

1099 BETVICTOR AINTREE GRAND NATIONAL NRNB H'CAP (LONDON MILE QUALIFIER) 1m (P)

8:30 (8:30) (Class 4) (0-85,80) 3-Y-O **£4,690** (£1,395; £697; £348) **Stalls** Low

Form RPR

4-41 **1** **Camachoice (IRE)**[52] 414 3-9-1 **74**.................(tp) AdamKirby 1 82
(Marco Botti) *t.k.h: prom: jnd ldrs over 1f out: led ins fnl f: drvn out* **11/4**[2]

01- **2** *nk* **Carry On Sydney**[146] 7371 3-9-7 **80**................. SeanLevey 6 87
(Richard Hannon) *prom: hrd rdn over 2f out: slt ld over 1f out tl ins fnl f: r.o* **5/4**[1]

650- **3** *½* **Jathabah (IRE)**[184] 6344 3-8-6 **65**................. ChrisCatlin 4 71
(Clive Brittain) *led: rdn over 2f out: hdd over 1f out: kpt on* **25/1**

1433 **4** *1¼* **Club House (IRE)**[6] 1011 3-8-9 **73**................. RobertTart[(5)] 3 76
(Robert Mills) *hld up in rr: hdwy to press ldrs 2f out: unable qck ins fnl f* **11/2**[3]

51 **5** *3½* **Gambolling Den (IRE)**[33] 685 3-8-10 **69**................. MartinLane 5 64
(David Simcock) *t.k.h: in tch tl wknd over 2f out* **7/1**

2325 **6** *2½* **Black Dave (IRE)**[14] 920 3-8-12 **71**................. ShaneKelly 7 60
(David Evans) *in tch: wd on bnd into st: sn wknd* **14/1**

1m 40.93s (1.13) **Going Correction** -0.025s/f (Stan) **6** Ran SP% **109.5**

Speed ratings (Par 100): **93,92,92,90,87 84**

toteswingers 1&2 £1.20, 1&3 £13.00, 2&3 £8.30 CSF £6.23 TOTE £5.00: £1.40, £1.30; EX 7.20 Trifecta £81.00 Pool: £849.27 - 7.85 winning units.

Owner Giuliano Manfredini **Bred** Doc Bloodstock **Trained** Newmarket, Suffolk

FOCUS

A decent handicap. The pace was steady and the first three were always prominent. The third is the key to the level, which could be pitched up to 4lb better.

1100 GOFFS READY TO WIN 27.03.13 H'CAP 1m (P)

9:00 (9:02) (Class 6) (0-60,60) 4-Y-O+ **£1,940** (£577; £288; £144) **Stalls** Low

Form RPR

3363 **1** **Divine Rule (IRE)**[4] 1056 5-9-3 **56**.................(v) JimCrowley 12 67
(Laura Mongan) *hld up in rr: gd hdwy over 1f out: r.o to ld ins fnl f: rdn out* **8/1**

5221 **2** *1¾* **Athletic**[24] 794 4-9-4 **57**.................(v) EddieAhern 6 64
(J R Jenkins) *hld up in tch: chal on bit 2f out: rdn and unable qck ins fnl f* **3/1**[1]

3-24 **3** *nk* **Pastoral Jet**[22] 813 5-9-1 **59**................. ThomasBrown[(5)] 3 65
(Richard Rowe) *hld up in midfield: hdwy on bit 2f out: disp 2nd 1f out: rdn and kpt on same pce* **4/1**[2]

0541 **4** *3¼* **Rapid Water**[21] 825 7-9-2 **55**.................(b) LiamKeniry 10 54
(Pat Eddery) *towards rr: hdwy over 2f out: led wl over 1f out tl wknd ins fnl f* **14/1**

4050 **5** *1¼* **Mr Chocolate Drop (IRE)**[14] 921 9-9-4 **57**.................(t) AdamKirby 9 53
(Mandy Rowland) *towards rr: gd hdwy 2f out: no ex over 1f out* **8/1**

-260 **6** *½* **May's Boy**[22] 813 5-9-2 **60**.................(p) RachealKneller[(5)] 7 55
(Mark Usher) *towards rr: pushed along over 2f out: sme late hdwy* **12/1**

0030 **7** *shd* **Qeethaara (USA)**[21] 825 9-8-7 **51**.................(p) JackDuern[(5)] 4 46
(Mark Brisbourne) *chsd ldrs: rdn over 2f out: wknd over 1f out* **16/1**

6205 **8** *2* **Katmai River (IRE)**[15] 899 6-8-9 **55**.................(v) EmilyMelbourn[(7)] 5 45
(Mark Usher) *chsd ldrs on outer tl wknd 2f out* **33/1**

22-0 **9** *¾* **Clapped**[52] 418 4-9-4 **57**.................(b[1]) IanMongan 1 45
(Ed Vaughan) *s.s: sn rdn up and prom: chal 2f out: wknd over 1f out* **9/2**[3]

0200 **10** *4* **Edgware Road**[31] 709 5-9-7 **60**................. WilliamCarson 2 39
(Sean Curran) *prom: rdn 3f out: wknd 2f out* **14/1**

4/00 **11** *nse* **Tartaria**[20] 840 7-8-13 **52**................. FrederikTylicki 8 31
(Edward Creighton) *led at gd pce tl wknd wl over 1f out* **50/1**

0/04 **12** *12* **Valkov**[9] 975 6-8-2 **46** oh1................. RyanTate[(5)] 11
(Tony Carroll) *nvr gng wl: a bhd: no ch fnl 3f* **20/1**

1m 38.71s (-1.09) **Going Correction** -0.025s/f (Stan) **12** Ran SP% **122.0**

Speed ratings (Par 101): **104,102,101,98,97 96,96,94,94,90 90,78**

toteswingers 1&2 £5.90, 1&3 £7.00, 2&3 £3.10 CSF £32.58 CT £116.59 TOTE £8.80: £3.10, £2.10, £1.60; EX 41.60 Trifecta £99.90 Pool: £1,304.40 - 9.78 winning units.

Owner Mrs L J Mongan **Bred** Car Colston Hall Stud **Trained** Epsom, Surrey

FOCUS

A low-grade handicap run at a good pace. Straightforward form, which should prove reliable, with the first three clear.

T/Plt: £8.50 to a £1 stake. Pool of £73,814.84 - 6,317.47 winning units T/Qpdt: £5.50 to a £1 stake. Pool of £7,856.62 - 1,055.14 winning units LM

1078 WOLVERHAMPTON (A.W) (L-H)

Thursday, March 21

OFFICIAL GOING: Standard

Wind: Fresh across Weather: Cloudy with sunny spells

1101 £32 BONUS AT 32RED.COM H'CAP 5f 20y(P)

2:30 (2:30) (Class 6) (0-65,66) 4-Y-O+ **£1,940** (£577; £288; £144) **Stalls** Low

Form RPR

13-3 **1** **Angelo Poliziano**[29] 727 7-9-7 **65**................. JoeFanning 9 73
(Jo Hughes) *hdwy over 3f out: shake up to ld wl ins fnl f: r.o* **4/1**[3]

5061 **2** *nk* **Speedyfix**[19] 862 6-8-12 **56**.................(t) RobertWinston 10 63
(Christine Dunnett) *chsd ldrs: led 1f out: rdn: edgd lft and hdd wl ins fnl f* **14/1**

6002 **3** *1¾* **One Way Or Another (AUS)**[9] 971 10-9-7 **65**.................(t) AdamKirby 4 66
(David Evans) *chsd ldrs: rdn over 1f out: r.o* **8/1**

0-32 **4** *nse* **Steelcut**[3] 1058 9-9-5 **63**.................(p) GrahamLee 8 63
(Mark Buckley) *hld up: hdwy over 1f out: sn rdn: r.o* **7/2**[2]

0-22 **5** *hd* **Spic 'n Span**[12] 946 8-9-2 **60**.................(b) LukeMorris 7 60
(Ronald Harris) *led: rdn and hdd 1f out: styd on same pce* **10/1**

0-00 **6** *1* **Ingleby Star (IRE)**[24] 795 8-8-11 **58**.................(p) JulieBurke[(3)] 1 54
(Ian McInnes) *chsd ldr: rdn over 1f out: no ex ins fnl f* **25/1**

-255 **7** *½* **Loyal Royal (IRE)**[47] 494 10-8-13 **57**.................(bt) RichardKingscote 11 53+
(Milton Bradley) *s.i.s: hld up: swtchd lft sn after s: r.o ins fnl f: nvr trbld ldrs* **16/1**

552 **8** *1* **Quality Art (USA)**[15] 902 5-9-7 **65**.................(b[1]) RobbieFitzpatrick 2 56
(Richard Guest) *s.i.s: hld up: plld hrd: rdn over 1f out: nvr trbld ldrs* **3/1**[1]

140- **9** *¾* **Verus Delicia (IRE)**[156] 7146 4-8-11 **55**................. ShaneKelly 6 43
(Daniel Mark Loughnane) *mid-div: rdn over 2f out: n.d* **33/1**

0441 **10** *¾* **Shawkantango**[9] 968 6-9-1 **66** 6ex.................(v) AdamMcLean[(7)] 3 51
(Derek Shaw) *s.i.s: pushed along over 3f out: a in rr* **7/1**

1m 2.45s (0.15) **Going Correction** +0.05s/f (Slow) **10** Ran SP% **119.3**

Speed ratings (Par 101): **100,99,96,96,96 94,93,92,91,89**

toteswingers 1&2 £11.00, 2&3 £18.10, 1&3 £8.70 CSF £60.09 CT £443.16 TOTE £5.20: £1.80, £4.60, £3.00; EX 80.80 Trifecta £698.10 Pool: £3591.11 - 3.85 winning units..

Owner Mrs Joanna Hughes **Bred** Bumble Bs, C Liesack & Mrs S Nicholls **Trained** Lambourn, Berks

FOCUS

A fair handicap for the grade, run at a sound pace. It paid to race handy. The winner is rated to his better form of recent years.

1102 32RED H'CAP 5f 216y(P)

3:05 (3:05) (Class 5) (0-75,73) 4-Y-O+ **£2,911** (£866; £432; £216) **Stalls** Low

Form RPR

0624 **1** **Colourbearer (IRE)**[15] 898 6-9-1 **67**.................(t) RichardKingscote 11 79
(Milton Bradley) *chsd ldr tl led over 1f out: rdn ins fnl f: r.o* **10/1**

2022 **2** *1½* **Haadeeth**[7] 998 6-9-1 **67** ow2................. AdamKirby 9 75
(David Evans) *a.p: rdn over 1f out: edgd lft ins fnl f: r.o* **7/2**[2]

1332 **3** *½* **Miss Bunter**[13] 924 4-8-13 **72**................. DavidBergin[(7)] 12 78
(David O'Meara) *hld up: hdwy over 2f out: edgd lft ins fnl f: styd on* **6/1**[3]

-053 **4** *2¼* **Song Of Parkes**[40] 583 6-9-2 **73**................. SladeO'Hara[(5)] 1 72
(Peter Grayson) *chsd ldrs: rdn and ev ch over 1f out: no ex ins fnl f* **8/1**

1634 **5** *½* **Reginald Claude**[9] 971 5-8-6 **63**................. RachealKneller[(5)] 13 60
(Mark Usher) *chsd ldrs: shkn up over 1f out: edgd lft and styd on same pce fnl f* **9/1**

246 **6** *shd* **George Fenton**[9] 971 4-8-13 **65**.................(v) RobbieFitzpatrick 7 62
(Richard Guest) *sn pushed along in rr: rdn over 1f out: swtchd lft and r.o ins fnl f: nvr nrr* **12/1**

11-4 **7** *¾* **Invigilator**[74] 86 5-8-9 **61**.................(t) JoeFanning 5 55
(Derek Shaw) *hld up: rdn and swtchd rt over 1f out: styd on same pce fnl f* **3/1**[1]

0000 **8** *½* **Beauty Pageant (IRE)**[17] 878 6-9-0 **66**................. CathyGannon 2 59
(David Evans) *sn led: rdn and hdd over 1f out: wknd ins fnl f* **25/1**

0-0 **9** *¾* **Muftarres (IRE)**[9] 971 8-9-0 **66**.................(t) LukeMorris 6 56
(Frank Sheridan) *sn pushed along in rr: n.d* **20/1**

-200 **10** *1¾* **Night Trade (IRE)**[22] 812 6-8-12 **71**.................(p) GaryPhillips[(7)] 3 56
(Ronald Harris) *mid-div: sn pushed along: hung rt over 2f out: hdwy over 1f out: hmpd and wknd ins fnl f* **14/1**

0000 **11** *3¼* **Dickie Le Davoir**[9] 966 9-8-8 **67**.................(b) PhilipPrince[(7)] 4 41
(Richard Guest) *sn pushed along and a in rr* **33/1**

1m 14.65s (-0.35) **Going Correction** +0.05s/f (Slow) **11** Ran SP% **117.6**

Speed ratings (Par 103): **104,102,101,98,97 97,96,95,94,92 88**

toteswingers 1&2 £7.00, 2&3 £4.40, 1&3 £11.50 CSF £43.96 CT £203.35 TOTE £11.60: £3.10, £2.00, £1.70; EX 53.40 Trifecta £244.40 Pool: £3474.50 - 10.65 winning units..

Owner E A Hayward **Bred** Corduff Stud & J Corcorcan **Trained** Sedbury, Gloucs

■ Stewards' Enquiry : Racheal Kneller three-day ban: careless riding (Apr 4-6)
Robbie Fitzpatrick one-day ban: careless riding (Apr 4)

FOCUS

The pace was steady and few were able to close from behind. The winner is rated to the best of this year's form.

1103 32REDPOKER.COM H'CAP 1m 4f 50y(P)

3:35 (3:35) (Class 6) (0-65,64) 3-Y-O **£1,940** (£577; £288; £144) **Stalls** Low

Form RPR

00-3 **1** **Tebee's Oasis**[26] 774 3-9-2 **59**................. WilliamBuick 1 72
(John Gosden) *mde all: shkn up over 2f out: rdn and edgd rt ins fnl f: styd on* **9/4**[2]

112 **2** *¾* **Gabrial The Duke (IRE)**[19] 867 3-9-6 **63**................. JamieSpencer 4 74
(David Simcock) *hld up: hdwy to chse wnr over 6f out: shkn up over 2f out: styd on u.p* **13/8**[1]

565- **3** *9* **Train Hard**[143] 7442 3-9-0 **57**................. FrannyNorton 3 54
(Mark Johnston) *chsd ldr 5f: remained handy tl dropped in rr over 5f out: outpcd fr over 2f out* **4/1**[3]

4125 **4** *13* **Hidden Link**[36] 632 3-9-7 **64**................. LukeMorris 6 40
(Ronald Harris) *trckd ldrs: wnt 2nd briefly 7f out: rdn over 3f out: wknd 2f out* **6/1**

The Form Book Flat, Raceform Ltd, Compton, RG20 6NL.

640- 5 hd **Moaning Butcher**[147] 7357 3-9-3 60 JoeFanning 5 36
(Mark Johnston) *s.i.s: sn pushed along and rn gren in rr: sme hdwy over 4f out: wknd over 3f out* 16/1

2m 41.73s (0.63) **Going Correction** +0.05s/f (Slow) 5 Ran SP% **109.0**
Speed ratings (Par 96): **99,98,92,83,83**
CSF £6.19 TOTE £3.30: £1.50, £2.10; EX 6.90 Trifecta £18.30 Pool: £4002.87 - 163.36 winning units..
Owner George Strawbridge **Bred** George Strawbridge **Trained** Newmarket, Suffolk

FOCUS
Three of the five were making their handicap debut. It was run at a steady pace, with the front two pulling clear. The form is rated at something like face value.

1104 32REDBET.COM (S) STKS 1m 1f 103y(P)
4:10 (4:10) (Class 6) 4-Y-0+ **£1,940** (£577; £288; £144) **Stalls** Low

Form RPR
2264 1 **Yourinthewill (USA)**[9] 974 5-9-4 64 ShaneKelly 2 71+
(Daniel Mark Loughnane) *hld up: hdwy over 5f out: shkn up to ld wl ins fnl f: comf* 13/2

5053 2 1 1/4 **Availed Speaker (IRE)**[9] 974 4-8-12 63 TonyHamilton 5 62
(Richard Fahey) *sn led at stdy pce: qcknd 2f out: rdn and hdd wl ins fnl f* 11/4[3]

0204 3 1 **Spanish Plume**[7] 996 5-8-7 67 (p) JackDuern(5) 1 60+
(Reg Hollinshead) *hld up: r.o ins fnl f: nvr nr to chal* 5/2[2]

0-33 4 1 3/4 **Alhaban (IRE)**[24] 791 7-8-12 66 LukeMorris 7 57
(Ronald Harris) *sn chsng ldr: rdn over 1f out: edgd lft and no ex ins fnl f* 9/4[1]

1405 5 2 **Faithful Ruler (USA)**[9] 974 9-8-11 62 (p) GaryPhillips(7) 6 59
(Ronald Harris) *prom: rdn over 1f out: no ex fnl f* 20/1

4626 6 1 1/4 **Jordaura**[8] 987 7-8-8 56 ow1 SladeO'Hara(5) 4 52
(Alan Berry) *hld up: rdn over 1f out: wknd fnl f* 16/1

04-6 7 3/4 **Mad For Fun (IRE)**[16] 884 4-8-2 47 ShirleyTeasdale(5) 3 44
(Paul Midgley) *chsd ldrs: pushed along over 1f out: hung lft and wknd ins fnl f* 40/1

2m 3.74s (2.04) **Going Correction** +0.05s/f (Slow) 7 Ran SP% **112.4**
Speed ratings (Par 101): **92,90,90,88,86 85,84**
toteswingers 1&2 £2.40, 2&3 £1.50, 1&3 £3.40 CSF £23.86 TOTE £5.30: £1.80, £2.20; EX 27.10 Trifecta £81.10 Pool: £4030.92 - 37.26 winning units..There was no bid for the winner.
Owner Mrs C Loughnane **Bred** Branch Equine Llc **Trained** Baldwin's Gate, Staffs

FOCUS
An open seller run at a steady pace and it developed into a sprint up the straight. The winner is rated back to his best form of recent years.

1105 32RED.COM H'CAP 1m 1f 103y(P)
4:45 (4:45) (Class 5) (0-70,70) 4-Y-0+ **£2,911** (£866; £432) **Stalls** Low

Form RPR
4213 1 **Exceedexpectations (IRE)**[6] 1015 4-9-7 70 JamieSpencer 3 78+
(Conor Dore) *led 1f: chsd ldr tl led wl over 1f out: pushed clr ins fnl f* 8/11[1]

2431 2 4 1/2 **Tyrur Ted**[16] 545 8-8-13 62 (t) CathyGannon 5 61
(Frank Sheridan) *chsd ldrs: rdn over 2f out: chsd wnr over 1f out: styd on same pce fnl f* 13/8[2]

2-00 3 13 **Guest Book (IRE)**[20] 850 6-8-9 63 SladeO'Hara(5) 4 38
(Peter Grayson) *led over 8f out: clr 5f out: pushed along over 3f out: hdd wl over 1f out: wknd fnl f* 20/1[3]

2m 2.94s (1.24) **Going Correction** +0.05s/f (Slow) 3 Ran SP% **100.8**
Speed ratings (Par 103): **96,92,80**
CSF £1.89 TOTE £1.60; EX 2.00 Trifecta £2.50 Pool: £1358.07 - 392.29 winning units..
Owner Mrs Louise Marsh **Bred** R S Cockerill (farms) Ltd & Peter Dodd **Trained** Hubbert's Bridge, Lincs

FOCUS
A virtual match on the book. The pace was honest with the well-backed favourite winning easily. Not form to take too literally.

1106 32RED CASINO MAIDEN STKS 1m 141y(P)
5:15 (5:15) (Class 5) 3-Y-0+ **£2,587** (£770; £384; £192) **Stalls** Low

Form RPR
2 1 **Back On The Trail**[28] 734 3-8-9 0 LukeMorris 3 72
(Rae Guest) *chsd ldrs: rdn over 2f out: chsd ldr over 1f out: styd on u.p to ld nr fin* 10/3[2]

0-22 2 shd **Spring Tonic**[5] 1035 4-10-0 74 NeilCallan 2 77
(Simon Dow) *chsd ldr: hmpd wl over 6f out: pushed along to ld over 1f out: rdn and edgd lft ins fnl f: hdd nr fin* 4/7[1]

44 3 10 **The Great Gabrial**[31] 708 4-10-0 0 JamieSpencer 4 59
(Ian Williams) *led: rdn over 2f out: hdd over 1f out: wknd fnl f* 10/1

53 4 14 **Spider House**[8] 990 3-8-9 0 GrahamGibbons 1 19
(David O'Meara) *outpcd: lost tch fr over 2f out* 8/1[3]

1m 50.0s (-0.50) **Going Correction** +0.05s/f (Slow)
WFA 3 from 4yo 19lb 4 Ran SP% **106.9**
Speed ratings (Par 103): **104,103,95,82**
CSF £5.69 TOTE £2.10; EX 6.70 Trifecta £12.40 Pool: £1868.16 - 112.68 winning units..
Owner Mrs Paula Smith **Bred** Mrs P Smith **Trained** Newmarket, Suffolk

FOCUS
An uncompetitive maiden run at a fair pace. The runner-up is the best guide.

1107 32REDBINGO.COM H'CAP 1m 141y(P)
5:50 (5:50) (Class 6) (0-65,62) 4-Y-0+ **£1,940** (£577; £288; £144) **Stalls** Low

Form RPR
4/44 1 **William Van Gogh**[6] 1017 6-8-13 54 GrahamGibbons 1 69+
(Michael Easterby) *s.i.s: sn chsng ldrs: wnt 2nd over 5f out tl over 3f out: shkn up to ld 1f out: r.o: comf* 9/4[1]

0351 2 1 3/4 **Chosen Forever**[24] 801 8-9-6 61 MichaelO'Connell 2 70
(Geoffrey Oldroyd) *hld up: hdwy over 1f out: r.o to go 2nd wl ins fnl f: nt trble wnr* 5/1

2122 3 1 1/4 **Big Sylv (IRE)**[14] 919 4-9-7 62 (p) RobertWinston 4 68
(James Unett) *racd keenly: trckd ldr over 3f: wnt 2nd again over 3f out: shkn up to ld over 1f out: sn hdd: styd on same pce* 3/1[2]

1016 4 3 **Flag Of Glory**[15] 896 6-9-7 62 JamieSpencer 6 62
(Peter Hiatt) *led: rdn and hdd over 1f out: no ex ins fnl f* 4/1[3]

10-0 5 2 1/4 **Karate (IRE)**[22] 813 5-9-2 62 (t) RyanTate(5) 7 57
(Hans Adielsson) *hld up: rdn over 2f out: n.d* 12/1

0/00 6 3 1/2 **Matraash (USA)**[15] 896 7-9-7 62 LukeMorris 5 50
(Daniel Mark Loughnane) *prom: rdn over 2f out: wknd fnl f* 25/1

1m 49.52s (-0.98) **Going Correction** +0.05s/f (Slow) 6 Ran SP% **104.0**
Speed ratings (Par 101): **106,104,103,100,98 95**
toteswingers 1&2 £1.90, 2&3 £1.90, 1&3 £2.00 CSF £11.58 TOTE £3.20: £2.00, £2.50; EX 11.10 Trifecta £28.10 Pool: £2193.52 - 58.36 winning units..
Owner A Morse **Bred** Stetchworth Park Stud Ltd **Trained** Sheriff Hutton, N Yorks

FOCUS
This was a decent race for the grade and the pace was honest. The winner was very well handicapped and the first two should pay their way in the short term.
T/Jkpt: £12,493.30 to a £1 stake. Pool of £17596.27 - 0.50 winning tickets. T/Plt: £155.10 to £1 stake. Pool of £86193.88 - 405.53 winning tickets. T/Qpdt: £33.10 to a £1 stake. Pool of £5476.26 - 122.24 winning tickets. CR

DONCASTER (L-H)
Friday, March 22

OFFICIAL GOING: Soft (heavy in places; 5.8)
Wind: Fresh across Weather: Heavy cloud & wintery showers

1108 WILLIAM HILL DOWNLOAD THE APP BROCKLESBY CONDITIONS STKS 5f
1:25 (1:28) (Class 4) 2-Y-0 **£6,469** (£1,925; £962; £481) **Stalls** High

Form RPR
1 **Mick's Yer Man** 2-8-10 0 RyanWhile(7) 13 89+
(Bill Turner) *mde most: rdn clr over 1f out: edgd lft and styd on strly fnl f* 5/1[2]

2 5 **Vodka Time (IRE)** 2-9-3 0 AdamKirby 4 71+
(David Evans) *trckd ldrs on outer: effrt and cl up 2f out: sn rdn to chse wnr over 1f out: kpt on same pce fnl f* 11/2[3]

3 2 3/4 **Lord Clyde** 2-9-3 0 PaulHanagan 15 61
(Richard Fahey) *cl up on stands' rail: effrt 2f out: sn rdn and ev ch tl one pce fr over 1f out* 11/2[3]

4 1 1/4 **Mops Angel** 2-8-12 0 AndrewMullen 12 52+
(Michael Appleby) *trckd ldrs: effrt and hdwy over 2f out: rdn wl over 1f out: sn one pce* 14/1

5 3 1/2 **Dovil's Duel (IRE)** 2-9-3 0 AndreaAtzeni 11 44+
(Rod Millman) *in tch: pushed along to chse ldrs 1/2-way: sn rdn and kpt on same pce fr over 1f out* 4/1[1]

6 2 1/2 **Donny Rover (IRE)** 2-9-3 0 RobbieFitzpatrick 17 35+
(Charles Smith) *s.i.s and bhd: swtchd lft and hdwy over 2f out: sn rdn and kpt on fnl f: nrst fin* 13/2

7 2 3/4 **Picks Pinta** 2-9-3 0 ShaneKelly 7 25
(Jo Hughes) *dwlt and towards rr: sme hdwy over 2f out: sn pushed along and nvr nr ldrs* 16/1

8 2 1/2 **Kraka Gym (IRE)** 2-9-3 0 GrahamGibbons 10 16
(Michael Easterby) *in tch: rdn along 1/2-way: sn wknd* 14/1

9 3 **Fuel Injection** 2-9-3 0 BarryMcHugh 16 5+
(Paul Midgley) *dwlt: sn chsng ldrs: rdn along 2f out and grad wknd* 10/1

10 8 **Bridge Of Avon** 2-8-12 0 PaulMulrennan 14
(Mel Brittain) *sn rdn along and outpcd: a bhd* 16/1

11 hd **Red Biba (IRE)** 2-8-12 0 WilliamCarson 9
(David C Griffiths) *chsd ldrs on outer: rdn along 1/2-way: sn wknd* 25/1

12 2 **Sleaford** 2-9-3 0 DuranFentiman 5
(Mel Brittain) *sn outpcd and a bhd* 33/1

1m 3.78s (3.28) **Going Correction** +0.425s/f (Yiel) 12 Ran SP% **121.7**
Speed ratings (Par 94): **90,82,77,75,70 66,61,57,52,40 39,36**
toteswingers 1&2 £6.10, 1&3 £4.50, 2&3 £7.70 CSF £33.67 TOTE £5.30: £2.70, £2.10, £1.90; EX 21.10 Trifecta £115.10 Pool: £1,143.16 - 7.44 winning units..
Owner Mrs Tracy Turner **Bred** Heather Raw **Trained** Sigwells, Somerset

FOCUS
Due to the threat of snow, the meeting had to pass three inspections before being given the go-ahead. The ground had eased slightly from that advertised and was officially described as soft, heavy in places. A field of complete unknowns, as is usual for the Brocklesby, but despite the five non-runners the draw still played its part with five of the first six berthed in double figures. Plenty of these should improve on better ground. The winner should take some beating in the short term.

1109 WILLIAM HILL IPAD, IPAD MINI H'CAP 1m 2f 60y
2:00 (2:00) (Class 3) (0-95,89) 3-Y-0 **£7,439** (£2,213; £1,106; £553) **Stalls** Low

Form RPR
451- 1 **Mister Impatience**[142] 7492 3-9-0 82 JoeFanning 2 99+
(Mark Johnston) *sn trcking ldrs: wnt 2nd over 5f out: led 3f out: wnt clr over 1f out: v easily* 7/4[1]

144- 2 9 **Allnecessaryforce (FR)**[151] 7292 3-8-10 78 PaulHanagan 3 76
(Richard Fahey) *hld up towards rr: hdwy over 4f out: sn drvn: wnt 2nd over 2f out: no ch w wnr* 7/2[3]

523- 3 7 **Arthurs Secret**[154] 7209 3-8-12 80 MichaelO'Connell 5 65
(John Quinn) *s.i.s: in rr: hdwy 5f out: kpt on one pce to take modest 3rd over 1f out* 11/2

201- 4 6 **Mister Marcasite**[162] 6997 3-8-4 72 DuranFentiman 1 47
(Mel Brittain) *led: hdd 3f out: wknd over 1f out* 10/1

161- 5 14 **Ronaldinho (IRE)**[147] 7365 3-9-7 89 RichardHughes 6 50
(Richard Hannon) *stdd s: hld up in rr: effrt over 3f out: sn rdn and no imp: wknd over 1f out: heavily eas* 3/1[2]

614- 6 49 **Mystical Man**[136] 7614 3-9-2 84 NeilCallan 7
(James Tate) *t.k.h: racd wd: chsd ldr: lost pl over 5f out: sn bhd: t.o 3f out: virtually p.u* 16/1

2m 18.31s (8.91) **Going Correction** +0.975s/f (Soft) 6 Ran SP% **113.9**
Speed ratings (Par 102): **103,95,90,85,74 35**
toteswingers 1&2 £1.70, 1&3 £2.50, 2&3 £4.00 CSF £8.40 TOTE £2.80: £1.60, £1.80; EX 7.60 Trifecta £29.30 Pool: £2,668.96 - 68.17 winning units..
Owner The Originals **Bred** The Kathryn Stud Ltd **Trained** Middleham Moor, N Yorks

FOCUS
A decent handicap, with all six runners making their seasonal reappearance, but some may have needed it more than others. The testing conditions took their toll with the field finishing spread out all over South Yorkshire. The winner could be decent but a fairly prudent view has been taken of the form in the conditions.

1110 WILLIAM HILL NO 1 DOWNLOADED BETTING APP DONCASTER SHIELD (CONDITIONS STKS) 1m 4f
2:30 (2:31) (Class 2) 4-Y-0+ **£12,938** (£3,850; £1,924; £962) **Stalls** Low

Form RPR
123- 1 **Model Pupil**[144] 7438 4-8-12 107 RyanMoore 1 106+
(Charles Hills) *trckd ldng pair: hdwy over 3f out: led 2f out: rdn clr over 1f out: styd on strly* 5/6[1]

052/ 2 8 **The Bull Hayes (IRE)**[20] 4523 7-9-0 84 (p) BarryMcHugh 4 94
(Tony Coyle) *trckd ldr: cl up 4f out: led 3f out: sn rdn and hdd 2f out: drvn and kpt on fr over 1f out: no ch w wnr* 33/1

6400 3 5 **Art Scholar (IRE)**[20] 871 6-9-0 98 TomQueally 6 87
(Michael Appleby) *hld up: hdwy to chse ldng pair 3f out: rdn 2f out: sn one pce* 9/2[3]

001- **4** *7* **Cracking Lass (IRE)**[35] 7438 6-8-13 99 PaulHanagan 2 75
(Richard Fahey) *hld up: effrt 4f out: sn pushed along: rdn 3f out and sn outpcd* **5/2**[2]

/311 **5** *4 ½* **Masterful Act (USA)**[9] 989 6-9-0 76 GrahamLee 7 69
(Alan McCabe) *led: rdn along 4f out: hdd 3f out: sn wknd* **10/1**

2m 43.82s (8.92) **Going Correction** +0.975s/f (Soft)
WFA 4 from 5yo+ 2lb **5** Ran SP% **113.3**
Speed ratings (Par 109): **109,103,100,95,92**
CSF £26.71 TOTE £1.40: £1.10, £8.10; EX 25.20 Trifecta £83.90 Pool: £2,170.84 - 19.39 winning units..
Owner K Abdullah **Bred** Juddmonte Farms Ltd **Trained** Lambourn, Berks

FOCUS
Just the five runners and on this occasion they came down the centre of the track once into the straight. The winner clearly has plenty of scope to better last year's level.

1111 CROWNHOTEL-BAWTRY.COM GENTLEMAN AMATEUR RIDERS' H'CAP 1m 4f
3:00 (3:00) (Class 5) (0-70,70) 4-Y-0+ **£2,495** (£774; £386; £193) **Stalls** Low

Form RPR

5566 **1** **Yeomanoftheguard**[14] 929 4-10-4 60 MrJHamilton(5) 8 69
(Richard Fahey) *chsd ldrs: led 2f out: drvn out: hld on wl clsng stages* **14/1**

060- **2** *¾* **Waltz Darling (IRE)**[102] 4714 5-11-4 67 MikeyEnnis 9 75
(Keith Reveley) *mid-div: hdwy over 3f out: chsng ldrs over 2f out: chsd wnr ins fnl f: no ex last 50yds* **6/1**[2]

0605 **3** *1 ½* **Boston Blue**[21] 635 6-11-2 70 MrCCarroll(5) 6 75
(Tony Carroll) *mid-div: hdwy over 3f out: chsng ldrs 2f out: kpt on same pce last 100yds* **10/1**[3]

53 **4** *nk* **Rayadour (IRE)**[39] 612 4-10-11 65 MrFMitchell(3) 7 70
(Micky Hammond) *mid-div: hdwy over 3f out: sn chsng ldrs: kpt on same pce fnl f* **20/1**

513- **5** *1 ¾* **Red Tyke (IRE)**[15] 7444 4-10-5 61 RyanHatch(5) 2 63
(John Quinn) *chsd ldrs: one pce fnl 2f* **2/1**[1]

350- **6** *2* **Royal Opera**[21] 3129 5-11-1 69 (v) MrJohnWilley(5) 13 68+
(Brian Ellison) *rrd s: swtchd lft after s: in rr: kpt on fnl 3f: nvr trbld ldrs* **16/1**

05-0 **7** *1 ½* **Frosty Berry**[52] 430 4-10-6 64 MrAFrench(7) 12 61
(John Wainwright) *in rr: drvn 4f out: hdwy over 2f out: kpt on: nvr trbld ldrs* **33/1**

512- **8** *½* **Taste The Wine (IRE)**[127] 5265 7-10-12 68 MrCWest(7) 11 64+
(Bernard Llewellyn) *hld up in rr: kpt on fnl 3f: nvr a threat* **14/1**

45-0 **9** *6* **Rockweiller**[16] 896 6-10-2 58 (v) MrCDowson(7) 4 45
(Steve Gollings) *led after 2f: hdd 2f out: sn wknd* **12/1**

650- **10** *5* **Maid Of Meft**[167] 6891 6-10-13 65 MrChrisMartin(3) 5 45
(Paul Midgley) *s.i.s: hld up in rr: effrt over 3f out: nvr a factor* **16/1**

416- **11** *6* **Tenhoo**[197] 5967 7-11-7 70 ow2 MrTomGreenway 1 39
(Eric Alston) *led 2f: chsd ldrs: lost pl over 2f out* **14/1**

120- **12** *2* **Pandorica**[172] 6735 5-11-5 68 MrFWindsorClive 14 36
(Bernard Llewellyn) *rr-div: nvr a factor* **11/1**

0-30 **13** *17* **Missionaire (USA)**[28] 510 6-10-13 65 (p) MrMJJSmith(3) 17 7
(Tony Carroll) *s.i.s: sn chsng ldrs: upsides 8f out: wknd over 2f out* **25/1**

3356 **14** *12* **Stylistickhill (IRE)**[20] 866 5-10-0 56 oh4 (t) MrKLocking(7) 16
(Scott Dixon) *in rr: wl bhd fnl 4f* **20/1**

4106 **15** *59* **Gunner Will (IRE)**[17] 886 4-10-1 59 MrJamesHughes(7) 3
(Paul Midgley) *mid-div: lost pl 7f out: bhd 4f out: sn wl t.o: virtually p.u 2f out: eventually completed* **20/1**

504- **16** *52* **Garzoni**[224] 5037 4-10-3 59 (e[1]) MrWEasterby(5) 10
(Tim Easterby) *mid-div: lost pl 7f out: bhd 4f out: t.o whn virtually p.u 2f out: eventually completed* **11/1**

2m 49.26s (14.36) **Going Correction** +0.975s/f (Soft)
WFA 4 from 5yo+ 2lb **16** Ran SP% **133.9**
Speed ratings (Par 103): **91,90,89,89,88 86,85,85,81,78 74,72,61,53,14**
toteswingers 1&2 £25.10, 1&3 £31.60, 2&3 £7.10 CSF £97.83 CT £921.34 TOTE £23.40: £5.30, £2.40, £2.50, £4.80; EX 184.10 Trifecta £2035.20 Pool: £3,066.02 - 1.12 winning units..
Owner H J P Farr **Bred** Worksop Manor Stud **Trained** Musley Bank, N Yorks
■ Jamie Hamilton's first Flat winner.
■ Stewards' Enquiry : Mr Tom Greenway one-day ban: weighed in 2lb heavy (Apr 20)
Mr C Carroll two-day ban: used whip above permitted level (Apr 20, May 13)

FOCUS
A big field for this modest amateur riders' handicap. The form makes sense with the fifth a fair guide.

1112 PARK HILL HOSPITAL H'CAP 6f
3:35 (3:35) (Class 3) (0-95,94) 3-Y-0 **£7,439** (£2,213; £1,106; £553) **Stalls** High

Form RPR

03-0 **1** **Annunciation**[8] 999 3-9-7 94 RichardHughes 2 103
(Richard Hannon) *mde all: rdn over 1f out: hung rt ins fnl f: drvn out* **6/1**

021- **2** *1 ¼* **Heaven's Guest (IRE)**[164] 6954 3-8-4 77 PaulHanagan 1 82
(Richard Fahey) *trckd ldrs on outer: hdwy wl over 2f out: rdn to chal over 1f out and ev ch tl drvn: edgd rt and one pce ins fnl f* **6/1**

51- **3** *2 ¼* **Smart Spender (IRE)**[169] 6808 3-8-7 80 JoeFanning 6 79+
(Jo Hughes) *towards rr: pushed along and hdwy over 2f out: swtchd lft and rdn to chse ldrs over 1f out: kpt on fnl f: nrst fin* **12/1**

425- **4** *nk* **Shahdaroba (IRE)**[147] 7374 3-9-1 88 AndreaAtzeni 4 86
(Rod Millman) *trckd ldrs: hdwy over 2f out: rdn to chse ldng pair over 1f out: drvn ent fnl f and sn one pce* **11/2**[3]

2-52 **5** *10* **Fortinbrass (IRE)**[9] 982 3-8-9 81 ow1 JimCrowley 3 50
(Ralph Beckett) *cl up: rdn along over 2f out: drvn and wknd wl over 1f out* **8/1**

040- **6** *3* **Threes Grand**[174] 6675 3-9-4 91 LukeMorris 9 50
(Scott Dixon) *chsd ldrs: rdn along over 2f out: sn wknd* **25/1**

313- **7** *1* **Intimidate**[146] 7399 3-8-9 82 RyanMoore 5 38
(Jeremy Noseda) *chsd ldng pair: rdn along over 2f out: sn wknd* **5/2**[1]

343- **8** *2 ¾* **Kimberella**[179] 6540 3-8-13 86 JamieSpencer 7 33
(Michael Bell) *dwlt: a in rr* **9/2**[2]

130- **9** *½* **Dream Scenario**[230] 4820 3-7-9 75 oh1 RobertDodsworth(7) 8 21
(Mel Brittain) *sn pushed along and a in rr* **28/1**

1m 15.93s (2.33) **Going Correction** +0.425s/f (Yiel) **9** Ran SP% **116.8**
Speed ratings (Par 102): **101,99,96,95,82 78,77,73,72**
toteswingers 1&2 £5.40, 1&3 £9.80, 2&3 £9.30 CSF £42.29 CT £424.75 TOTE £6.30: £1.70, £2.60, £4.70; EX 47.50 Trifecta £287.30 Pool: £3,414.84 - 8.91 winning units..
Owner Middleham Park Racing XXXIX & James Pak **Bred** Abingdon & Witney College **Trained** East Everleigh, Wilts

FOCUS
A decent sprint handicap for 3yos, in which the front four pulled miles clear of the rest. A personal best from the winner.

1113 WILLIAM HILL DOWNLOAD THE APP H'CAP (DIV I) 7f
4:10 (4:10) (Class 4) (0-85,88) 4-Y-0+ **£4,690** (£1,395; £697; £348) **Stalls** High

Form RPR

00-0 **1** **Gouray Girl (IRE)**[38] 621 6-9-2 77 DaleSwift 9 92
(Brian Ellison) *in tch: hdwy to trck ldrs 1/2-way: chal 2f out: sn led: rdn clr ent fnl f: kpt on strly* **9/2**[1]

105- **2** *5* **Fieldgunner Kirkup (GER)**[143] 7452 5-9-7 82 GrahamGibbons 6 84
(David Barron) *chsd ldrs: pushed along and sltly outpcd wl over 2f out: rdn and hdwy wl over 1f out: styd on fnl f: tk 2nd towards fin* **13/2**[3]

044- **3** *½* **Invincible Hero (IRE)**[278] 3185 6-9-0 78 NeilFarley(3) 10 79
(Declan Carroll) *cl up on outer: effrt to ld briefly 2f out: sn hdd and rdn: edgd rt and one pce fnl f: lost 2nd towards fin* **5/1**[2]

-311 **4** *3 ¼* **Classic Colori (IRE)**[6] 1039 6-9-13 88 6ex (b) DanielTudhope 2 81
(David O'Meara) *chsd ldrs: rdn along 1/2-way: plugged on one pce u.p fnl 2f* **5/1**[2]

025- **5** *4 ½* **Defence Council (IRE)**[162] 6999 5-9-7 82 DuranFentiman 4 63
(Mel Brittain) *in tch: hdwy 3f out: rdn to chse ldrs 2f out: wknd over 1f out* **8/1**

401- **6** *2* **Barkston Ash**[162] 6999 5-9-0 80 JasonHart(5) 11 56
(Eric Alston) *led: rdn along and hdd 2f out: sn wknd* **12/1**

0335 **7** *2 ¾* **Piceno (IRE)**[17] 889 5-8-13 74 (p) TomQueally 15 44
(Scott Dixon) *prom: rdn along wl over 2f out: sn wknd* **7/1**

40-6 **8** *5* **Crown Choice**[15] 913 8-8-11 72 PaulMulrennan 8 29
(Paul Midgley) *chsd ldrs: rdn along 3f out: sn wknd* **25/1**

413- **9** *3* **Day Of The Eagle (IRE)**[244] 4317 7-8-10 71 JamesSullivan 13 21
(Michael Easterby) *a in rr* **8/1**

000- **10** *15* **Viva Ronaldo (IRE)**[143] 7452 7-8-7 75 SamanthaBell(7) 12 +
(Richard Fahey) *blindfold removed late and v.s.a: a wl bhd* **11/1**

1m 31.85s (5.55) **Going Correction** +0.725s/f (Yiel) **10** Ran SP% **119.4**
Speed ratings (Par 105): **97,91,90,87,81 79,76,70,67,50**
toteswingers 1&2 £5.60, 1&3 £6.00, 2&3 £6.80 CSF £34.65 CT £154.38 TOTE £6.30: £2.00, £2.50, £1.70; EX 29.90 Trifecta £279.50 Pool: £3,248.88 - 8.71 winning units..
Owner Brian Ellison **Bred** George S O'Malley **Trained** Norton, N Yorks
■ Stewards' Enquiry : Samantha Bell Fine: £140, slow to remove blindfold.

FOCUS
A fair handicap, but again they finished well spread out. While this not form to take too literally, it does look sensible.

1114 YESSS ELECTRICAL MAIDEN STKS 7f
4:45 (4:47) (Class 5) 3-Y-0 **£2,587** (£770; £384; £192) **Stalls** High

Form RPR

1 **Aetna** 3-9-0 0 GrahamGibbons 10 76+
(Michael Easterby) *dwlt: hld up in mid-div: smooth hdwy over 2f out: chal on bit ins fnl f: shkn up: edgd rt and led nr fin* **16/1**

326- **2** *nk* **Khelman (IRE)**[167] 6880 3-9-5 77 TonyHamilton 1 77
(Richard Fahey) *w ldr: led over 2f out: hdd and no ex nr fin* **5/1**[3]

3 *1* **Munhamer (IRE)** 3-9-5 0 PaulHanagan 12 75+
(John Gosden) *dwlt: rr-div: effrt over 2f out: chsng ldrs over 1f out: styd on same pce last 100yds* **2/1**[1]

65- **4** *½* **Yul Finegold (IRE)**[184] 6371 3-9-5 0 RichardHughes 11 73
(George Baker) *w ldr: kpt on same pce last 150yds* **11/4**[2]

50- **5** *3 ¼* **Jillywinks**[147] 7364 3-9-0 0 TomQueally 8 60
(Scott Dixon) *sn trcking ldrs: effrt 2f out: wknd fnl f* **14/1**

6 *9* **Amanda Wolf (IRE)** 3-9-0 0 GrahamLee 4 38
(James Given) *dwlt: in rr and sn drvn along: bhd fnl 3f* **20/1**

40- **7** *1 ¾* **Complicator**[265] 3611 3-9-5 0 PhillipMakin 3 38
(Kevin Ryan) *led: hdd over 2f out: wknd wl over 1f out* **12/1**

5 **8** *1* **Chrisnickdave (FR)**[15] 915 3-9-0 0 JamesSullivan 9 31
(Michael Easterby) *chsd ldrs: outpcd over 2f out: sn lost pl and bhd* **25/1**

1m 32.49s (6.19) **Going Correction** +0.725s/f (Yiel) **8** Ran SP% **105.5**
Speed ratings (Par 98): **93,92,91,90,87 76,74,73**
toteswingers 1&2 £9.30, 1&3 £8.40, 2&3 £1.80 CSF £77.89 TOTE £22.80: £4.80, £1.60, £1.10; EX 157.70 Trifecta £279.00 Pool: £1,704.03 - 4.58 winning units..
Owner B Padgett **Bred** Bearstone Stud **Trained** Sheriff Hutton, N Yorks
■ Lord Ashley was withdrawn (6/1, unruly in stalls). Deduct 10p in the £ under R4.

FOCUS
Not a strong maiden by any means, but a remarkable winning debut by Aetna. She was perhaps value for a good deal more. The second appeared to match his good 2yo form.

1115 WILLIAM HILL DOWNLOAD THE APP H'CAP (DIV II) 7f
5:20 (5:21) (Class 4) (0-85,85) 4-Y-0+ **£4,690** (£1,395; £697; £348) **Stalls** High

Form RPR

463- **1** **Personal Touch**[237] 4588 4-9-0 78 PaulHanagan 1 85+
(Richard Fahey) *cl up: effrt 2f out and sn rdn: drvn ent fnl f: styd on wl to ld last 120yds* **4/1**[1]

624- **2** *¾* **Pashan Garh**[132] 7684 4-8-11 75 JoeFanning 3 80
(Pat Eddery) *dwlt: sn prom on outer: cl up 1/2-way: chal over 2f out sn rdn and ev ch: drvn ins fnl f: no ex last 75yds* **8/1**

4050 **3** *hd* **Kung Hei Fat Choy (USA)**[23] 810 4-8-9 73 (b) DaleSwift 9 78
(James Given) *prom: cl up 1/2-way: rdn to ld 2f out: drvn over 1f out: hdd ins fnl f: kpt on same pce* **16/1**

045- **4** *1* **The Osteopath (IRE)**[135] 7639 10-8-8 72 PJMcDonald 10 74+
(John Davies) *towards rr: hdwy over 2f out: rdn to chse ldrs over 1f out: kpt on wl fnl f: nrst fin* **8/1**

60/ **5** *2 ¼* **Music In The Rain (IRE)**[222] 5139 5-9-2 80 DanielTudhope 7 76
(David O'Meara) *led: rdn along 3f out: hdd 2f out and grad wknd* **13/2**[3]

461- **6** *1 ¾* **Steel Stockholder**[173] 6709 7-8-8 72 PaulMulrennan 4 64
(Mel Brittain) *chsd ldrs: rdn along 2f out: drvn and one pce fr over 1f out* **16/1**

02-0 **7** *5* **George Benjamin**[9] 986 6-8-4 71 oh3 DarrenEgan(3) 15 51
(Christopher Kellett) *in tch: rdn along wl over 2f out: sn no imp* **33/1**

532- **8** *6* **Warfare**[92] 8188 4-8-12 76 PhillipMakin 14 41
(Kevin Ryan) *towards rr: sme hdwy 3f out: sn rdn and n.d* **5/1**[2]

622- **9** *2* **Green Park (IRE)**[143] 7453 10-9-4 82 (b) DavidAllan 6 42
(Declan Carroll) *chsd ldrs: rdn along wl over 2f out: sn wknd* **16/1**

2/0- **10** *2* **Gloriam (USA)**[289] 2813 4-9-7 85 JamesSullivan 5 40
(Ruth Carr) *t.k.h: hld up: a towards rr* **33/1**

100- **11** *23* **Aerodynamic (IRE)**[200] 5888 6-9-0 78 KierenFallon 12
(Michael Easterby) *in rr and sn rdn along: bhd fr 1/2-way* **4/1**[1]

12 nk **Bankroll**[32] 1898 6-9-2 **80** HayleyTurner 11
(Jonjo O'Neill) *in tch on outer: rdn along 3f out: sn wknd* **12/1**

1m 30.4s (4.10) **Going Correction** +0.725s/f (Yiel) 12 Ran SP% **123.4**
Speed ratings (Par 105): **105,104,103,102,100 98,92,85,83,81 54,54**
toteswingers 1&2 £7.20, 1&3 £20.30, 2&3 £26.20 CSF £37.97 CT £478.14 TOTE £4.30: £1.60, £2.30, £5.40; EX 38.30 Trifecta £1276.20 Pool: £2,226.65 - 1.30 winning units..
Owner Nicholas Wrigley & Kevin Hart **Bred** Cheveley Park Stud Ltd **Trained** Musley Bank, N Yorks
FOCUS
The winning time was 1.45 seconds faster than the first division. Improvement from the first two in this reasonable handicap.
T/Jkpt: Not won. T/Plt: £66.60 to a £1 stake. Pool: £120,100.73 - 1,314.73 winning tickets
T/Qpdt: £27.00 to a £1 stake. Pool: £7,362.90 - 201.45 winning tickets JR

1101 WOLVERHAMPTON (A.W) (L-H)
Friday, March 22

OFFICIAL GOING: Standard to slow
Wind: Fresh against Weather: Snowing

1116 32REDPOKER.COM H'CAP 5f 216y(P)
5:55 (5:55) (Class 6) (0-60,60) 3-Y-O £1,940 (£577; £288) Stalls Low

Form RPR
-540 1 **Douglas Pasha (IRE)**[5] 1050 3-8-11 **55** WilliamTwiston-Davies(5) 2 59+
(Richard Hannon) *led 1f: chsd ldr tl led again over 1f out: rdn out* **6/4**[2]
326 2 1 3/4 **Lexi's Beauty (IRE)**[22] 828 3-8-9 **48** FrannyNorton 4 47
(Patrick Morris) *a.p: chsd wnr over 1f out: rdn ins fnl f: styd on same pce* **4/1**[3]
-646 3 5 **Daisie Cutter**[21] 848 3-8-9 **51** SimonPearce(3) 1 35
(Lydia Pearce) *chsd ldr tl led 5f out: rdn and hdd over 1f out: no ex fnl f* **11/10**[1]

1m 17.1s (2.10) **Going Correction** +0.15s/f (Slow) 3 Ran SP% **107.6**
Speed ratings (Par 96): **92,89,83**
CSF £6.34 TOTE £2.00; EX 4.80 Trifecta £3.30 Pool: £826.41 - 184.84 winning units..
Owner Middleham Park Racing II **Bred** John Walsh **Trained** East Everleigh, Wilts
FOCUS
With the expected short-priced favourite a late defection this was a woeful opener and was run in a blizzard. Very weak form but the winner was the most exposed.

1117 32RED.COM H'CAP 1m 5f 194y(P)
6:30 (6:30) (Class 5) (0-75,75) 4-Y-O+ £2,587 (£770; £384; £192) Stalls Low

Form RPR
4431 1 **Admirable Duque (IRE)**[13] 948 7-9-7 **69** (be) MartinLane 1 78
(Dominic Ffrench Davis) *chsd ldr: shkn up over 2f out: led over 1f out: pushed out* **6/4**[1]
5411 2 4 1/2 **Jezza**[14] 928 7-9-3 **65** LukeMorris 4 68
(Karen George) *led: rdn and hdd over 1f out: styd on same pce fnl f* **7/4**[2]
006- 3 9 **Cash Injection**[28] 6231 4-8-3 **55** oh10 (t) JamieMackay 6 45
(Karen George) *chsd ldrs: rdn over 2f out: sn wknd* **12/1**
-114 4 4 **Waving**[25] 797 4-9-2 **73** (t) GeorgeDowning(5) 5 58+
(Tony Carroll) *s.v.s: in tch 8f out: rdn and wknd 2f out* **3/1**[3]

3m 12.68s (6.68) **Going Correction** +0.15s/f (Slow)
WFA 4 from 5yo+ 4lb 4 Ran SP% **109.1**
Speed ratings (Par 103): **86,83,78,76**
CSF £4.48 TOTE £1.70; EX 3.10 Trifecta £14.30 Pool: £1141.02 - 59.44 winning units..
Owner Mrs J E Taylor **Bred** Airlie Stud And R N Clay **Trained** Lambourn, Berks
FOCUS
An unsatisfactory staying contest, with the fourth blowing the start and the pace farcical. The winner has a good chance of a hat-trick under a penalty.

1118 32REDBET.COM H'CAP 7f 32y(P)
7:00 (7:00) (Class 6) (0-60,60) 3-Y-O £1,940 (£577; £288; £144) Stalls High

Form RPR
6523 1 **Actonetaketwo**[5] 1055 3-8-2 **48** PhilipPrince(7) 5 56
(Ron Hodges) *mde all: rdn over 1f out: styd on* **8/1**
-021 2 1 1/4 **Baltic Prince (IRE)**[4] 1066 3-8-12 **51** 6ex FrannyNorton 3 56
(Paul Green) *a.p: chsd wnr over 1f out: sn rdn: styd on* **1/1**[1]
-056 3 1 3/4 **Bubbly Bailey**[41] 580 3-9-1 **59** RobertTart(5) 4 59
(Alan Bailey) *hld up: rdn over 2f out: styd on ins fnl f: nt rch ldrs* **10/3**[2]
42-3 4 shd **Panama Cat (USA)**[10] 977 3-9-5 **58** AmyRyan 6 58
(Kevin Ryan) *chsd wnr tl rdn over 1f out: styd on same pce fnl f* **11/2**[3]
5-00 5 8 **Claude Greenwood**[23] 811 3-9-7 **60** JamieSpencer 2 38
(David Simcock) *hld up: hdwy u.p over 2f out: hung lft and wknd over 1f out* **8/1**
604 6 14 **Tavistock Fair**[18] 876 3-8-7 **46** oh1 AndreaAtzeni 1
(Michael Squance) *hld up: pushed along 3f out: sn wknd* **40/1**

1m 30.77s (1.17) **Going Correction** +0.15s/f (Slow) 6 Ran SP% **113.1**
Speed ratings (Par 96): **99,97,95,95,86 70**
toteswingers 1&2 £2.10, 2&3 £1.50, 1&3 £5.00 CSF £16.90 TOTE £6.90: £5.50, £1.10; EX 22.80 Trifecta £67.30 Pool: £1568.78 - 17.47 winning units..
Owner Miss R Dobson **Bred** M Watt & Exors Of The Late Miss J John **Trained** Charlton Mackrell, Somerset
FOCUS
Stronger fare than the opener, but this was still a weak 3yo handicap. Straightforward, low-grade form.

1119 32RED CASINO H'CAP 1m 1f 103y(P)
7:30 (7:31) (Class 5) (0-75,74) 3-Y-O £2,587 (£770; £384; £192) Stalls Low

Form RPR
23-1 1 **Gabrial's Wawa**[23] 815 3-9-6 **73** JamieSpencer 3 81+
(Richard Fahey) *trckd ldr: racd keenly: led over 1f out: sn shkn up and edgd lft: styd on* **3/1**[2]
002- 2 1/2 **Khudoua**[114] 7900 3-9-7 **74** RobertHavlin 6 79+
(John Gosden) *led: pushed along over 2f out: rdn and hdd over 1f out: styd on* **4/5**[1]
1-14 3 3 3/4 **Pairumani Prince (IRE)**[15] 920 3-9-5 **72** GrahamLee 1 70
(Ed Dunlop) *stmbld s: hld up: hdwy over 5f out: rdn over 1f out: styd on same pce fnl f* **5/1**[3]
1-51 4 3/4 **Diletta Tommasa (IRE)**[39] 613 3-9-1 **68** AndreaAtzeni 5 64
(John Stimpson) *prom: pushed along over 3f out: styd on same pce fr over 1f out* **10/1**
035- 5 nk **Lady Marmelo (IRE)**[184] 6363 3-9-2 **69** MatthewDavies 4 64
(Mick Channon) *stdd s: hld up: rdn over 1f out: no ex ins fnl f* **20/1**

2m 3.84s (2.14) **Going Correction** +0.15s/f (Slow) 5 Ran SP% **111.1**
Speed ratings (Par 98): **96,95,92,91,91**
CSF £5.91 TOTE £4.40: £2.40, £1.10; EX 6.20 Trifecta £19.50 Pool: £1186.23 - 45.55 winning units..
Owner Dr Marwan Koukash **Bred** The Welcome Alliance **Trained** Musley Bank, N Yorks
FOCUS
The strongest of the 3yo handicaps on the card with decent efforts from the front pair, although both were well placed throughout on a night pace held up well.

1120 32REDBINGO.COM H'CAP 1m 1f 103y(P)
8:00 (8:00) (Class 7) (0-50,56) 4-Y-O+ £1,940 (£577; £288; £144) Stalls Low

Form RPR
0-54 1 **Sofias Number One (USA)**[4] 1070 5-9-2 **48** (b) MarkCoumbe(3) 7 59
(Roy Bowring) *mde all: clr 6f out: rdn over 1f out: eased nr fin* **9/2**
/0-0 2 3 **Akarana (IRE)**[21] 852 6-9-7 **50** TonyCulhane 3 55+
(Willie Musson) *prom: chsd wnr over 3f out tl rdn over 2f out: styd on u.p to go 2nd nr fin* **2/1**[1]
3304 3 nk **Monsieur Pontaven**[14] 927 6-9-2 **45** (b) RobertWinston 8 49
(Robin Bastiman) *hld up: hmpd over 7f out: hdwy over 4f out: chsd wnr over 2f out: rdn and edgd lft over 1f out: no ex ins fnl f: lost 2nd nr fin* **4/1**[3]
0506 4 6 **Count Ceprano (IRE)**[14] 927 9-9-4 **50** SimonPearce(3) 4 41
(Lydia Pearce) *prom: lost pl over 6f out: sn pushed along: n.d after* **10/1**
60-0 5 5 **Chapter Nine (IRE)**[4] 1070 7-9-2 **50** WilliamTwiston-Davies(5) 2 31
(Tony Carroll) *s.i.s: in rr: rdn over 3f out: nvr on terms* **14/1**
300/ 6 5 **Major Eradicator (USA)**[633] 3480 6-9-3 **46** (v) LukeMorris 10 16
(Alastair Lidderdale) *chsd ldrs: rdn over 3f out: wknd over 2f out* **3/1**[2]
-200 7 7 **Seawood**[14] 927 7-8-9 **45** (p) PhilipPrince(7) 11
(Roy Bowring) *prom tl wknd over 3f out* **9/1**

2m 2.8s (1.10) **Going Correction** +0.15s/f (Slow) 7 Ran SP% **122.3**
Speed ratings (Par 97): **101,98,98,92,88 83,77**
toteswingers 1&2 £2.50, 2&3 £2.20, 1&3 £3.30 CSF £15.26 CT £40.64 TOTE £6.40: £3.10, £2.10; EX 17.20 Trifecta £79.80 Pool: £1037.51 - 9.74 winning units..
Owner S R Bowring **Bred** Rosecrest Farm Llc **Trained** Edwinstowe, Notts
FOCUS
A basement-grade handicap that saw two big gambles go astray. The winner was well ridden from the front and this is obviously not form to trust implicitly.

1121 32RED H'CAP 5f 20y(P)
8:30 (8:30) (Class 4) (0-85,83) 4-Y-O+ £4,690 (£1,395; £697; £348) Stalls Low

Form RPR
03-4 1 **Sandfrankskipsgo**[41] 586 4-9-3 **79** JamieSpencer 7 87
(Peter Crate) *hld up: hdwy 2f out: swtchd lft 1f out: r.o to ld nr fin* **11/2**[2]
3-4 2 nk **My Son Max**[27] 780 5-9-7 **83** KierenFallon 4 90
(P J O'Gorman) *chsd ldrs: shkn up over 1f out: rdn to ld wl ins fnl f: hdd nr fin* **1/1**[1]
3213 3 shd **Triple Dream**[27] 780 8-9-5 **81** (tp) JimmyQuinn 6 88
(Milton Bradley) *chsd ldrs: rdn and ev ch ins fnl f: r.o* **9/1**
-004 4 3/4 **Six Wives**[15] 913 6-8-10 **75** (p) BillyCray(3) 5 79
(Scott Dixon) *chsd ldr tl led wl over 1f out: sn rdn: hdd wl ins fnl f* **25/1**
0102 5 6 **Royal Bajan (USA)**[15] 913 5-9-6 **82** (b) GrahamLee 2 64
(James Given) *prom: nt clr run 1/2-way: wknd fnl f* **10/1**
1330 6 1 **Roy's Legacy**[37] 627 4-8-5 **72** (t) MichaelJMMurphy(5) 9 51
(Shaun Harris) *mid-div: hdwy 1/2-way: rdn and hung lft over 1f out: wknd ins fnl f* **20/1**
00-5 7 nk **Electric Qatar**[27] 780 4-8-12 **81** MissSoniaEaton(7) 11 59+
(Tom Dascombe) *s.i.s and wnt lft s: nvr on terms* **8/1**[3]
6-60 8 1/2 **Albaqaa**[18] 881 8-9-1 **77** KieranO'Neill 8 53
(P J O'Gorman) *sn outpcd* **22/1**
630- 9 6 **Titus Gent**[97] 8143 8-9-2 **83** RobertTart(5) 10 37
(Jeremy Gask) *hmpd and rdr lost irons sn after s: outpcd* **20/1**
1-00 10 2 3/4 **Island Legend (IRE)**[50] 457 7-9-4 **80** (tp) RichardKingscote 1 24
(Milton Bradley) *led: rdn and hdd wl over 1f out: wknd fnl f* **20/1**

1m 1.48s (-0.82) **Going Correction** +0.15s/f (Slow) 10 Ran SP% **118.1**
Speed ratings (Par 105): **112,111,111,110,100 98,98,97,88,83**
toteswingers 1&2 £2.00, 2&3 £1.80, 1&3 £8.10 CSF £10.54 CT £50.44 TOTE £4.30: £2.30, £1.02, £3.10; EX 16.70 Trifecta £63.40 Pool: £1556.40 - 18.39 winning units..
Owner Peter Crate **Bred** Peter Crate **Trained** Newdigate, Surrey
FOCUS
The feature handicap saw another gamble go awry. The pace was decent and the winner maty have more to offer.

1122 £32 BONUS AT 32RED.COM MAIDEN FILLIES' STKS 5f 216y(P)
9:00 (9:01) (Class 5) 3-Y-O+ £2,587 (£770; £384; £192) Stalls Low

Form RPR
340- 1 **Polish Crown**[136] 7613 3-8-12 67 FrannyNorton 2 66
(Mark Johnston) *chsd ldr tl led 2f out: edgd rt over 1f out: rdn out* **3/1**[2]
0-5 2 1/2 **Sixties Queen**[20] 864 3-8-7 0 RobertTart(5) 3 65
(Alan Bailey) *chsd ldrs: rdn over 1f out: r.o* **20/1**
54 3 4 **Jofranka**[41] 581 3-8-12 0 GrahamGibbons 6 53
(David Barron) *s.i.s: hld up: hdwy over 1f out: styd on same pce ins fnl f* **16/1**
40- 4 1 3/4 **Hasbah (IRE)**[233] 4701 3-8-12 0 JamieSpencer 4 47
(Peter Chapple-Hyam) *hld up in tch rdn over 1f out: no ex ins fnl f* **4/6**[1]
2- 5 11 **Pastureyes**[206] 5709 3-8-12 0 LukeMorris 1 26
(Scott Dixon) *led: rdn and hdd 2f out: wknd fnl f* **11/2**[3]

1m 15.87s (0.87) **Going Correction** +0.15s/f (Slow) 5 Ran SP% **111.0**
Speed ratings (Par 100): **100,99,94,91,77**
CSF £44.46 TOTE £3.60: £2.40, £9.70; EX 58.80 Trifecta £108.60 Pool: £1097.94 - 7.58 winning units..
Owner Sheikh Hamdan Bin Mohammed Al Maktoum **Bred** L A C Ashby Newhall Estate Farm **Trained** Middleham Moor, N Yorks
FOCUS
A fair fillies' maiden to close the card. The winner did not need to reach her better 2yo form.
T/Plt: £26.50 to a £1 stake. Pool of £77566.84 - 2134.84 winning tickets. T/Qpdt: £2.20 to a £1 stake. Pol of £8131.83 - 2735.0 winning units. CR

[1071]SOUTHWELL (L-H)

Saturday, March 23

OFFICIAL GOING: Standard

An additional meeting put on at short notice.

Wind: moderate 1/2 against Weather: snow showers, cold

1145 32RED.COM H'CAP 1m 4f (F)
1:25 (1:30) (Class 4) (0-85,81) 3-Y-O **£4,851** (£1,443; £721) **Stalls** Low

Form RPR
5312 1 **Edwyn Ralph**[6] 1053 3-9-0 74 HayleyTurner 3 82
(David Simcock) *trckd ldr: effrt over 2f out: led appr fnl f: styd on strly to forge clr* **6/4**[2]
314- 2 3 **Royal Skies (IRE)**[177] 6597 3-9-7 81 JoeFanning 1 85
(Mark Johnston) *led: qcknd pce 3f out: edgd rt and hdd appr fnl f: kpt on same pce* **4/7**[1]
4-35 3 21 **Lucky Mountain**[21] 867 3-8-3 63 LukeMorris 2 38
(Scott Dixon) *trckd ldrs: pushed along 3f out: sn outpcd and hung lft: sn btn: bhd whn eased ins fnl f* **20/1**[3]

2m 38.17s (-2.83) **Going Correction** -0.125s/f (Stan) **3** Ran SP% **108.4**
Speed ratings (Par 100): **104,102,88**
CSF £2.82 TOTE £2.60; EX 3.00 Trifecta £2.60 Pool: £ 2270.98- 636.27 winning units..
Owner Gee Ceffyl Bach Club **Bred** Azienda Agricola Rosati Colarieti **Trained** Newmarket, Suffolk

FOCUS
A weakly contested handicap in which they went an honest gallop. The form is taken at face value.

1146 32REDPOKER.COM H'CAP 1m 4f (F)
2:00 (2:05) (Class 6) (0-55,55) 4-Y-O+ **£1,940** (£577; £288; £144) **Stalls** Low

Form RPR
0-23 1 **Linroyale Boy (USA)**[10] 989 5-9-6 54 RobertWinston 3 63
(Alan Swinbank) *chsd ldrs: led over 2f out: drew clr appr fnl f* **5/4**[1]
-552 2 5 **Honest Strike (USA)**[32] 714 6-9-5 53 (v[1]) ShaneKelly 4 55
(Daniel Mark Loughnane) *hld up in rr: hdwy on wd outside over 2f out: chsd wnr appr fnl f: no imp* **5/2**[2]
0500 3 3 1/2 **Bubbly Braveheart (IRE)**[8] 921 6-8-7 46 oh1 (p) RachealKneller(5) 1 42
(Phil McEntee) *led: qcknd pce over 3f out: hdd over 2f out: kpt on one pce* **33/1**
50-0 4 3/4 **Sacco D'Oro**[9] 100 7-8-12 46 oh1 EddieAhern 5 41
(Michael Mullineaux) *dwlt: sn chsng ldrs: drvn over 3f out: one pce* **25/1**
0660 5 1 1/2 **There's No Rules**[8] 1022 4-8-10 46 oh1 (e) RobbieFitzpatrick 2 39
(Richard Guest) *trckd ldrs: t.k.h: drvn 3f out: fdd over 1f out* **33/1**
0-10 6 16 **Petrol**[15] 927 4-9-5 55 DanielTudhope 6 36
(David O'Meara) *hld up: effrt over 3f out: rdn over 2f out: wknd wl over 1f out: heavily eased ins fnl f* **3/1**[3]
00/0 7 9 **Orpen Bid (IRE)**[11] 973 8-8-12 46 oh1 TomEaves 7
(Michael Mullineaux) *sn chsng ldrs: drvn over 4f out: lost pl 3f out: sn wl bhd* **100/1**

2m 39.82s (-1.18) **Going Correction** -0.125s/f (Stan)
WFA 4 from 5yo+ 2lb **7** Ran SP% **108.7**
Speed ratings (Par 101): **98,94,92,91,90 80,74**
toteswingers 1&2 £1.10, 1&3 £8.10, 2&3 £9.30 CSF £4.04 TOTE £1.90: £1.60, £1.30; EX 4.10 Trifecta £34.20 Pool: £5497.81 - 120.24 winning units..
Owner Spiral Bracken **Bred** Winstar Farm, Llc & Ashford Stud **Trained** Melsonby, N Yorks

FOCUS
A moderate middle-distance contest with the bottom four on the card racing from out of the handicap proper. Not form to get behind but this has to rate a personal best from the winner.

1147 £32 BONUS AT 32RED.COM H'CAP 6f (F)
2:35 (2:40) (Class 6) (0-58,57) 4-Y-O+ **£1,940** (£577; £288; £144) **Stalls** Low

Form RPR
0030 1 **Fairy Wing (IRE)**[21] 863 6-9-6 56 SeanLevey 1 65
(Violet M Jordan) *trckd ldrs: smooth hdwy over 2f out: led over 1f out: all out* **20/1**
-002 2 shd **Thorpe Bay**[4] 1077 4-9-2 52 AndrewMullen 9 61
(Michael Appleby) *trckd ldrs: narrow ld over 1f out: narrowly hdd over 1f out: r.o: jst failed* **4/1**[1]
0211 3 1 3/4 **Flow Chart (IRE)**[7] 1043 6-9-0 55 SladeO'Hara(5) 5 60
(Peter Grayson) *in rr: n.m.r after 1f: hdwy over 2f out: styd on to chse ldng pair jst ins fnl f: kpt on same pce* **9/2**[2]
0035 4 2 **Ryedale Dancer (IRE)**[10] 991 5-9-1 51 (e) RobbieFitzpatrick 8 49
(Richard Guest) *trckd ldrs: effrt on outer over 2f out: one pce* **14/1**
5042 5 3/4 **Olynard (IRE)**[7] 1043 7-8-11 47 (p) EddieAhern 7 43
(Michael Mullineaux) *chsd ldrs: drvn over 2f out: fdd fnl f* **14/1**
/24- 6 1 1/4 **Heidi's Delight (IRE)**[410] 455 4-8-13 56 (p) RowanScott(7) 10 48
(Ann Duffield) *dwlt: sn chsng ldrs on outer: one pce fnl 2f* **25/1**
2040 7 shd **Red Shadow**[4] 1079 4-8-10 53 (b[1]) JoshBaudains(7) 3 44
(Alan Brown) *in rr: effrt on outside over 2f out: wknd over 1f out* **7/1**
0-40 8 3/4 **Code Six (IRE)**[53] 436 4-9-5 55 TomEaves 4 44
(Bryan Smart) *led: hdd over 2f out: wknd over 1f out* **9/1**
00-2 9 3/4 **Man Of My Word**[10] 991 4-9-3 56 (p) BillyCray(3) 2 43
(Scott Dixon) *in rr: drvn over 3f out: sme hdwy on inner over 2f out: nvr a factor* **5/1**[3]
0514 10 1/2 **Upper Lambourn (IRE)**[10] 991 5-9-7 57 (t) JoeFanning 6 42
(Christopher Kellett) *s.i.s: mid-div and rdn over 3f out: nvr a threat* **9/2**[2]

1m 15.83s (-0.67) **Going Correction** -0.125s/f (Stan) **10** Ran SP% **117.5**
Speed ratings (Par 101): **99,98,96,93,92 91,91,90,89,88**
toteswingers 1&2 £19.70, 1&3 £17.50, 2&3 £4.10 CSF £99.29 CT £448.21 TOTE £23.40: £6.30, £2.10, £1.70; EX 164.60 Trifecta £1027.40 Pool: £6884.22 - 5.02 winning units..
Owner Rakebackmypoker.com **Bred** H Fitzpatrick **Trained** Moreton Morrell, Warwicks

FOCUS
A moderate sprint handicap in which they went a decent gallop. The winner has a good chance of following up here.

1148 32RED H'CAP 1m (F)
3:10 (3:15) (Class 3) (0-95,92) 4-Y-O+ **£7,439** (£2,213; £1,106; £553) **Stalls** Low

Form RPR
00-1 1 **Dubai Hills**[18] 889 7-9-7 92 TomEaves 6 102
(Bryan Smart) *w ldrs: led over 1f out: hld on gamely* **6/4**[1]
2615 2 3/4 **Docofthebay (IRE)**[14] 944 9-9-2 87 (b) LukeMorris 3 95
(Scott Dixon) *s.i.s: sn trcking ldrs: n.m.r 2f out and 1f out: kpt on to take 2nd nr fin* **7/1**[3]
501 3 hd **Caldercruix (USA)**[16] 912 6-8-4 78 (v) RaulDaSilva(3) 7 86
(James Evans) *hood removed v late: s.i.s: sn chsng ldrs: outpcd over 3f out: styd on and upsides over 1f out: styd on same pce last 50yds* **10/1**
3311 4 3/4 **Frontier Fighter**[7] 1038 5-8-13 84 DanielTudhope 1 91
(David O'Meara) *towards rr: hdwy over 4f out: nt clr run over 3f out: upsides 2f out: kpt on same pce last 100yds* **9/4**[2]
6134 5 2 3/4 **The Lock Master (IRE)**[18] 889 6-8-10 81 AndrewMullen 5 81
(Michael Appleby) *w ldrs: led over 2f out: hdd over 1f out: wknd last 100yds* **8/1**
30-0 6 7 **Roninski (IRE)**[5] 1061 5-9-2 87 RobertWinston 2 71
(Garry Moss) *sn trcking ldrs: t.k.h: upsides over 3f out: wknd over 1f out* **25/1**
3-36 7 2 **Dr Red Eye**[21] 865 5-8-6 80 (p) BillyCray(3) 4 59
(Scott Dixon) *led: hdd over 2f out: lost pl over 1f out: sn bhd* **20/1**

1m 40.86s (-2.84) **Going Correction** -0.125s/f (Stan) **7** Ran SP% **112.1**
Speed ratings (Par 107): **109,108,108,107,104 97,95**
toteswingers 1&2 £2.50, 1&3 £3.60, 2&3 £8.20 CSF £12.24 TOTE £2.30: £1.40, £2.90; EX 10.60 Trifecta £54.50 Pool: £7087.99 - 97.43 winning units..
Owner Mrs F Denniff **Bred** A S Denniff **Trained** Hambleton, N Yorks

FOCUS
The feature race of the day, and a decent 1m handicap. The winner enhanced his outstanding record here and the next two underpin this solid form.

1149 32REDBINGO.COM H'CAP 7f (F)
3:45 (3:50) (Class 6) (0-52,52) 4-Y-O+ **£1,940** (£577; £288; £144) **Stalls** Low

Form RPR
0665 1 **Mataajir (USA)**[5] 1063 5-9-0 52 AdamMcLean(7) 4 62
(Derek Shaw) *mde all: rdn over 2f out: forged clr jst ins fnl f: readily* **6/4**[1]
0015 2 5 **Mucky Molly**[11] 965 5-9-7 52 (vt) TomEaves 1 49
(Alison Hutchinson) *sn chsng ldrs: sn drvn along: kpt on to take 2nd jst ins fnl f: no ch w wnr* **4/1**[3]
4544 3 1/2 **Michael's Nook**[8] 1020 6-9-6 51 (p) LukeMorris 6 47
(Alastair Lidderdale) *in rr on outer: hdwy over 3f out: chsd wnr 2f out: kpt on same pce fnl f* **7/2**[2]
200 4 3 1/2 **Ishetoo**[3] 1087 9-8-13 49 SladeO'Hara(5) 7 36
(Peter Grayson) *sn in rr on outer: drvn and wl outpcd over 4f out: hdwy on outside over 2f out: kpt on fnl f* **20/1**
0-00 5 6 **La Giaconda**[17] 900 4-9-1 46 oh1 (b) RobertWinston 2 17
(Olivia Maylam) *chsd ldrs: hung rt and wknd 2f out: sn eased* **33/1**
-306 6 5 **Hawaiian Freeze**[17] 900 4-9-1 46 oh1 HayleyTurner 8 4
(John Stimpson) *s.i.s: sn chsng ldrs: drvn over 3f out: lost pl over 2f out* **25/1**
-6 7 shd **San Jose City (IRE)**[3] 1093 8-9-2 47 (p) EddieAhern 3 5
(Gary Brown) *chsd ldrs: drvn over 4f out: lost pl 3f out* **9/2**
6464 8 2 1/4 **Sextons House (IRE)**[7] 1043 5-9-3 48 (be) AndrewMullen 5
(Alan McCabe) *chsd ldrs: upsides over 4f out: lost pl over 2f out: sn bhd* **9/1**

1m 29.29s (-1.01) **Going Correction** -0.125s/f (Stan) **8** Ran SP% **122.0**
Speed ratings (Par 101): **100,94,93,89,82 77,77,74**
toteswingers 1&2 £2.70, 1&3 £2.00, 2&3 £3.80 CSF £8.32 CT £19.40 TOTE £2.50: £1.20, £1.50, £1.60; EX 12.90 Trifecta £35.30 Pool: £5432.28 - 115.17 winning units..
Owner Brian Johnson (Northamptonshire) **Bred** Shadwell Australia Ltd **Trained** Sproxton, Leics

FOCUS
A moderate 7f handicap in which they went a contested gallop. A race lacking depth, but straightforward form.

1150 32RED CASINO MAIDEN STKS 6f (F)
4:20 (4:20) (Class 5) 3-Y-O+ **£2,587** (£770; £384; £192) **Stalls** Low

Form RPR
222- 1 **Bispham Green**[187] 6312 3-8-13 77 TonyHamilton 2 72+
(Richard Fahey) *mde all: shkn up over 1f out: pushed out* **2/7**[1]
64 2 1 **Combustible (IRE)**[11] 964 3-8-8 0 ShaneKelly 5 58+
(Daniel Mark Loughnane) *dwlt: t.k.h: trcking ldrs whn stdd over 3f out: hdwy on inner over 2f out: chsd wnr over 1f out: no real imp* **9/2**[2]
-6 3 5 **The Codger**[11] 964 3-8-13 0 DanielTudhope 6 48+
(David O'Meara) *s.i.s: hdwy to chse ldrs over 3f out: hung lft over 1f out: kpt on to take 3rd jst ins fnl f* **8/1**[3]
3006 4 1 1/4 **Island Express (IRE)**[4] 1077 6-9-7 49 (tp) AnnStokell(5) 4 44
(Ann Stokell) *t.k.h: trckd ldrs: wknd fnl f* **20/1**
5550 5 18 **Back For Tea (IRE)**[23] 825 5-9-12 43 (b) RobertWinston 1
(Phil McEntee) *drvn to chse wnr: hung rt and lost pl over 2f out: bhd whn eased ins fnl f: t.o* **33/1**

1m 15.8s (-0.70) **Going Correction** -0.125s/f (Stan)
WFA 3 from 5yo+ 13lb **5** Ran SP% **114.8**
Speed ratings (Par 103): **99,97,91,89,65**
CSF £2.26 TOTE £1.30: £1.10, £1.50; EX 1.90 Trifecta £3.30 Pool: £5713.91 - 1268.27 winning units..
Owner David W Armstrong **Bred** Highfield Farm Llp **Trained** Musley Bank, N Yorks

FOCUS
An uncompetitive sprint maiden with only the long odds-on favourite bringing fair form to the table. The bare form is set around the second to fourth.

1151 32REDBET.COM H'CAP 1m (F)
4:50 (4:50) (Class 6) (0-58,63) 4-Y-O+ **£2,045** (£603; £302) **Stalls** Low

Form RPR
4000 1 **Putin (IRE)**[3] 1087 5-8-11 53 (tp) RachealKneller(5) 4 62
(Phil McEntee) *mde all: drvn over 2f out: styd on to pull clr last 100yds* **11/2**
4431 2 3 1/4 **Maggie Pink**[4] 1079 4-9-12 63 6ex AndrewMullen 3 65
(Michael Appleby) *trckd wnr: drvn over 2f out: chalng over 1f out: kpt on same pce jst ins fnl f* **2/1**[1]
0606 3 10 **Mcconnell (USA)**[32] 718 8-9-2 53 (b) SeanLevey 2 32
(Violet M Jordan) *hld up in rr: hdwy and modest 3rd 3f out: one pce* **9/4**[2]
456 4 3/4 **Conas Ata Tu**[24] 815 4-8-11 55 (v[1]) AdamMcLean(7) 1 32
(Derek Shaw) *dwlt: sn chsng ldrs: drvn and outpcd over 3f out: one pce* **5/1**[3]
00-5 5 12 **Rasselas (IRE)**[9] 993 6-9-4 55 (v) AdrianNicholls 5
(David Nicholls) *chsd ldrs on outside: drvn over 4f out: lost pl 3f out: bhd whn eased over 1f out* **7/1**

1m 42.12s (-1.58) **Going Correction** -0.125s/f (Stan) **5** Ran SP% **108.7**
Speed ratings (Par 101): **102,98,88,88,76**
CSF £16.43 TOTE £5.60: £1.90, £1.60; EX 14.50 Trifecta £39.00 Pool: £2461.25 - 47.31 winning units..
Owner Steve Jakes **Bred** D Llewelyn & J Runeckles **Trained** Newmarket, Suffolk

FOCUS
A very modest 1m handicap and not form to get behind.
T/Plt: £15.50 to a £1 stake. Pool: £225,707.29 - 10,603.24 winning tickets T/Qpdt: £4.50 to a £1 stake. Pool: £17,862.27 - 2,888.19 winning tickets WG

The Form Book Flat, Raceform Ltd, Compton, RG20 6NL.

1152 - 1154a (Foreign Racing) - See Raceform Interactive

1050 LINGFIELD (L-H)

Sunday, March 24

OFFICIAL GOING: Standard

Wind: Fresh; half against Weather: Overcast; cold

1155 DISCOVER RACING DAY 6TH APRIL CLAIMING STKS 6f (P)

1:40 (1:40) (Class 6) 4-Y-0+ **£2,045** (£603; £302) **Stalls** Low

Form RPR

-260 **1** **Noverre To Go (IRE)**[29] 776 7-9-3 85 LukeMorris 2 74
(Ronald Harris) *trckd ldr: drew level 2f out: led 1f out: hld on wl: drvn out* **4/6**[1]

-113 **2** *3/4* **Homeboy (IRE)**[18] 898 5-9-2 65 EddieAhern 3 71
(Marcus Tregoning) *hld up in cl 4th: hdwy on inner ent st: r.o fnl f: jst hld* **4/1**[2]

0513 **3** *nse* **Dixie Gwalia**[57] 399 5-8-4 57 (v) CathyGannon 1 59
(David Evans) *led: rdn and jnd 2f out: hdd 1f out: kpt on* **14/1**[3]

602- **4** *hd* **Bint Alzain (IRE)**[127] 7769 4-8-0 68 (tp) PhilipPrince(7) 4 61
(Gerard Butler) *t.k.h in cl 3rd: jnd ldrs on outer 2f out: kpt on wl nr fin* **4/1**[2]

1m 14.36s (2.46) **Going Correction** +0.225s/f (Slow) **4** Ran SP% **106.7**

Speed ratings (Par 101): **92,91,90,90**

CSF £3.52 TOTE £1.40; EX 3.30 Trifecta £12.70 Pool: £933.66 - 54.75 winning units.Dixie Gwalia was claimed by Mr James Michael Duggan for £2,000

Owner Robert & Nina Bailey **Bred** Gestut Gorlsdorf **Trained** Earlswood, Monmouths

FOCUS

The pace was sound in this claimer and the four runners finished in a heap. The form is straightforward rated around the second and third.

1156 ASHURSTWOOD MAIDEN STKS 5f (P)

2:10 (2:14) (Class 5) 2-Y-0 **£2,726** (£805; £402) **Stalls** High

Form RPR

1 **M'Selle (IRE)** 2-9-0 LukeMorris 8 71+
(Ronald Harris) *s.s: gd hdwy fr wdst stall to ld after 1f: rdn clr 1f out: comf* **12/1**

2 *2 1/4* **Diamond Lady** 2-9-0 J-PGuillambert 7 61
(Jo Hughes) *dwlt: hdwy to chse wnr over 3f out: unable qck appr fnl f* **20/1**

3 *nk* **Hedy** 2-9-0 MartinHarley 5 60
(Mick Channon) *mid-div: rdn 2f out: r.o fnl f: nrest at fin* **14/1**[3]

4 *3/4* **El Duque** 2-8-12 RyanWhile(7) 3 62
(Bill Turner) *towards rr: rdn and r.o fr over 1f out: nvr nrr* **7/2**[2]

5 *1 1/4* **Outback Lover (IRE)** 2-9-0 LiamKeniry 2 53+
(J S Moore) *s.s: plld hrd: rn wd 1st bnd: in rr tl rdn and r.o fr over 1f out: nt rch ldrs* **12/1**

6 *nk* **Intense Feeling (IRE)** 2-9-0 ShaneKelly 6 52
(David Evans) *plld hrd: led 1f: prom tl wknd over 1f out* **8/1**

7 *nk* **Marilyn Marquessa** 2-9-0 FrannyNorton 4 50
(Jo Hughes) *broke wl: plld hrd: chsd ldrs: rdn 2f out: wknd 1f out* **7/2**[2]

8 *7* **Smugglers Gold (IRE)** 2-9-5 AdamKirby 1 30
(David Evans) *restless in stalls: s.s: rn green: outpcd: a bhd* **3/1**[1]

1m 2.67s (3.87) **Going Correction** +0.225s/f (Slow) **8** Ran SP% **120.7**

Speed ratings (Par 92): **78,74,73,72,70 70,69,58**

toteswingers 1&2 £15.70, 1&3 £7.40, 2&3 £15.10 CSF £222.93 TOTE £10.70: £3.00, £5.20, £2.10; EX 172.30 Trifecta £868.80 Pool: £3,439.38 - 2.96 winning units.

Owner Robert & Nina Bailey **Bred** Kilshannig Stud **Trained** Earlswood, Monmouths

FOCUS

A field of unraced 2-y-os and a lively betting heat. Several showed plenty of promise and should improve for the experience, although the moderate time suggests the form is nothing special.

1157 RICHARD NORRIS 60TH BIRTHDAY H'CAP 5f (P)

2:40 (2:40) (Class 6) (0-65,62) 3-Y-0 **£2,045** (£603; £302) **Stalls** High

Form RPR

1-40 **1** **Buy Art**[34] 710 3-9-7 62 (p) RyanMoore 3 71
(Gary Moore) *dwlt: sn pressing ldr: rdn to ld 1f out: readily* **6/4**[2]

2563 **2** *3 1/2* **Marmot Bay (IRE)**[7] 1050 3-8-9 55 [1] JemmaMarshall(5) 4 51
(David Flood) *dwlt: outpcd in 3rd: styd on to take 2nd ins fnl f: nt trble wnr* **7/1**[3]

60-2 **3** *1 1/2* **Balatina**[7] 1050 3-8-6 47 HayleyTurner 2 38
(Chris Dwyer) *broke best: led: hrd rdn and hdd 1f out: wknd fnl f* **4/5**[1]

1m 0.55s (1.75) **Going Correction** +0.225s/f (Slow) **3** Ran SP% **108.1**

Speed ratings (Par 96): **95,89,87**

CSF £8.13 TOTE £2.10; EX 5.80 Trifecta £7.60 Pool: £1,389.44 - 136.98 winning units.

Owner R A Green **Bred** Mount Coote Stud & M & W Bell Racing **Trained** Lower Beeding, W Sussex

FOCUS

Only three runners but the pace was solid in this modest handicap. Nevertheless, the form is weak.

1158 LINGFIELDPARK.CO.UK H'CAP 2m (P)

3:10 (3:10) (Class 5) (0-75,74) 4-Y-0+ **£2,726** (£805; £402) **Stalls** Low

Form RPR

-325 **1** **Beat Route**[8] 1031 6-9-11 73 SebSanders 1 79
(Michael Attwater) *chsd ldrs: led ins fnl f: rdn out* **4/1**[2]

1-12 **2** *1 1/4* **Guards Chapel**[23] 851 5-9-6 68 (v) RyanMoore 5 73
(Gary Moore) *trckd ldr: led over 1f out tl ins fnl f: unable qck* **6/4**[1]

11-4 **3** *3/4* **Hi Note**[6] 1062 5-8-13 61 ChrisCatlin 8 65
(Sheena West) *led: set modest pce tl qcknd 3f out: hdd over 1f out: one pce ins fnl f* **8/1**

-333 **4** *shd* **Barachiel**[18] 896 5-8-12 60 SeanLevey 6 63
(Luke Dace) *stdd s: hld up in rr: hdwy on inner to press ldrs 1f out: styd on same pce* **12/1**

6101 **5** *3/4* **Sommersturm (GER)**[12] 973 9-9-5 67 (t) AdamKirby 3 70
(David Evans) *hld up in 6th: rdn and outpcd 3f out: styd on again fnl f* **9/2**[3]

3141 **6** *1 1/4* **Llamadas**[6] 1062 11-9-4 66 6ex IanMongan 7 67
(Olivia Maylam) *t.k.h in 5th: effrt and hrd rdn over 1f out: no ex fnl f* **7/1**

20-3 **7** *12* **Russian George (IRE)**[16] 928 7-9-12 74 (p) JamieSpencer 2 63
(Steve Gollings) *chsd ldrs tl rdn and wknd 2f out: last and btn whn eased 1f out* **10/1**

3m 29.77s (4.07) **Going Correction** +0.225s/f (Slow) **7** Ran SP% **118.6**

Speed ratings (Par 103): **98,97,97,96,96 95,89**

toteswingers 1&2 £1.70, 1&3 £6.50, 2&3 £3.80 CSF £11.04 CT £46.20 TOTE £4.90: £2.80, £1.30; EX 10.90 Trifecta £90.80 Pool: £2,723.91 - 22.49 winning units.

Owner Canisbay Bloodstock **Bred** Canisbay Bloodstock Ltd **Trained** Epsom, Surrey

FOCUS

A fair handicap in which the pace was steady which favoured those ridden prominently. The runner-up sets the level to his recent marks.

1159 BREATHE SPA AT LINGFIELD MARRIOTT H'CAP 1m 2f (P)

3:40 (3:42) (Class 3) (0-95,93) 4-Y-0+ **£7,439** (£2,213; £1,106; £553) **Stalls** Low

Form RPR

53-2 **1** **Swing Alone (IRE)**[8] 1036 4-8-13 85 LukeMorris 7 94
(Gay Kelleway) *chsd ldrs: rdn 2f out: styd on u.p to ld nr fin* **5/1**[2]

0133 **2** *nk* **Aquilonius (IRE)**[8] 1037 4-9-0 86 (t) JamieSpencer 2 94
(Stuart Williams) *led: hrd rdn and kpt on fnl f: hdd nr fin* **6/1**[3]

2440 **3** *1* **Mia's Boy**[8] 1036 9-9-2 93 RobertTart(5) 4 99
(Chris Dwyer) *dwlt: hld up towards rr: rdn and hdwy over 1f out: r.o: nrest at fin* **6/1**[3]

04-0 **4** *1* **Takeitfromalady (IRE)**[22] 865 4-8-9 84 (b) DarrenEgan(3) 9 88
(Lee Carter) *s.s: hld up in rr: hdwy 3f out: kpt on same pce fnl f* **33/1**

414- **5** *3/4* **Daghash**[176] 6677 4-8-7 79 MartinLane 1 82
(Clive Brittain) *disp 2nd pl tl no ex ins fnl f* **7/1**

050- **6** *3/4* **Fennell Bay (IRE)**[158] 7168 4-9-0 86 JoeFanning 8 87
(Mark Johnston) *disp 2nd pl tl rdn and btn 1f out* **6/1**[3]

303- **7** *nse* **John Biscuit (IRE)**[175] 6702 5-8-10 87 [1] ThomasBrown(5) 6 88
(Andrew Balding) *hld up in 6th: rdn and no hdwy fnl 2f* **5/2**[1]

434- **8** *1 1/2* **Savanna Days (IRE)**[144] 7475 4-8-7 79 FrannyNorton 3 77
(Mick Channon) *in tch: sltly outpcd over 2f out: rallied on inner ent st: wknd over 1f out* **10/1**

12-0 **9** *3/4* **Super Say (IRE)**[18] 897 7-9-4 90 (t[1]) AdamKirby 5 87
(Mark Rimell) *dwlt: bhd: mod effrt on outer over 2f out: sn btn* **14/1**

2m 4.72s (-1.88) **Going Correction** +0.225s/f (Slow) **9** Ran SP% **119.3**

Speed ratings (Par 107): **116,115,114,114,113 112,112,111,111**

toteswingers 1&2 £4.60, 1&3 £6.00, 2&3 £5.90 CSF £36.30 CT £187.17 TOTE £5.70: £1.90, £2.10, £1.60; EX 27.00 Trifecta £91.10 Pool: £3,291.89 - 27.09 winning units.

Owner Whatley, Stanbrook, Kelleway & Parr **Bred** M Sinanan **Trained** Exning, Suffolk

FOCUS

A competitive handicap in which the pace was only steady and it developed into a sprint up the straight. Straightforward form through the placed horses.

1160 LINGFIELD PARK OWNERS GROUP H'CAP (THE SUNDAY £5K BONUS RACE) 6f (P)

4:10 (4:11) (Class 4) (0-85,85) 4-Y-0+ **£4,690** (£1,395; £697; £348) **Stalls** Low

Form RPR

5213 **1** **Al's Memory (IRE)**[15] 947 4-9-6 84 CathyGannon 4 92
(David Evans) *s.i.s: sn in tch: effrt over 1f out: r.o to ld wl ins fnl f* **5/1**[2]

50-0 **2** *1/2* **Red Aggressor (IRE)**[40] 621 4-9-7 85 [1] FrederikTylicki 11 91
(Clive Brittain) *chsd ldrs on outer: rdn over 2f out: chal ins fnl f: r.o* **33/1**

4503 **3** *nse* **Sulis Minerva (IRE)**[32] 723 6-9-2 83 RyanClark(3) 3 88
(Jeremy Gask) *t.k.h in midfield: rdn and hdwy over 1f out: jnd ldrs ins fnl f: r.o* **10/1**

-512 **4** *nse* **Blue Jack**[20] 880 8-8-13 77 (t) SeanLevey 7 82
(Stuart Williams) *towards rr: rdn over 1f out: gd late hdwy* **8/1**[3]

3-22 **5** *1/2* **Free Spin (IRE)**[32] 723 4-9-5 83 GrahamGibbons 1 87
(David Barron) *in tch: rdn to chse ldrs over 1f out: kpt on* **7/4**[1]

00- **6** *nk* **Oneladyowner**[151] 7327 5-9-3 81 RobertWinston 6 84
(David Brown) *mid-div: rdn and r.o fr over 1f out: nrest at fin* **14/1**

302- **7** *1/2* **Perfect Pastime**[160] 7114 5-8-11 75 (p) JoeFanning 2 76
(Jim Boyle) *chsd ldr tl wknd ins fnl f* **8/1**[3]

0031 **8** *nk* **Bubbly Ballerina**[7] 1052 4-8-12 81 6ex RobertTart(5) 8 81
(Alan Bailey) *led: rdn 2f out: hdd & wknd wl ins fnl f* **16/1**

-003 **9** *1/2* **Elna Bright**[20] 880 8-9-4 82 ShaneKelly 9 81
(Peter Crate) *towards rr on outer: rdn over 1f out: nvr able to chal* **20/1**

0555 **10** *3/4* **Gorgeous Goblin (IRE)**[17] 913 6-8-13 77 (t) JamieSpencer 10 77
(David C Griffiths) *prom tl wknd 1f out* **20/1**

4345 **11** *3* **Forest Edge (IRE)**[20] 880 4-9-6 84 (b) AdamKirby 5 72
(David Evans) *rdn 3f out: a last* **10/1**

1m 11.8s (-0.10) **Going Correction** +0.225s/f (Slow) **11** Ran SP% **118.4**

Speed ratings (Par 105): **109,108,108,108,107 107,106,106,105,104 100**

toteswingers 1&2 £35.60, 1&3 £7.40, 2&3 £76.90 CSF £164.60 CT £1623.64 TOTE £5.40: £1.60, £10.90, £3.10; EX 182.10 Trifecta £2028.80 Pool: £3,320.97 - 1.22 winning units.

Owner Will Dawson **Bred** Brian Miller **Trained** Pandy, Monmouths

FOCUS

A typically competitive Lingfield 6f sprint and a typically tight finish. The form is straightforward.

1161 CROWHURST H'CAP (DIV I) 1m (P)

4:40 (4:42) (Class 6) (0-55,58) 4-Y-0+ **£2,045** (£603; £302) **Stalls** High

Form RPR

-003 **1** **Ensnare**[24] 825 8-9-7 55 (b) StevieDonohoe 4 63
(Willie Musson) *t.k.h: prom: led 1f out: rdn clr: readily* **5/1**[3]

0001 **2** *1 3/4* **Daniel Thomas (IRE)**[10] 993 11-9-10 58 (tp) MartinHarley 6 63
(Violet M Jordan) *stdd s: hld up in rr: rdn 2f out: hdwy over 1f out: r.o to take 2nd ins fnl f* **9/4**[1]

0006 **3** *1 1/4* **Querido (GER)**[24] 825 9-8-12 46 oh1 (tp) JoeFanning 8 47
(Paddy Butler) *s.i.s: hld up in midfield: rdn and hdwy over 1f out: styd on same pce fnl f* **8/1**

440- **4** *nk* **Bold Ring**[160] 7105 7-9-6 54 JimmyQuinn 1 54
(Edward Creighton) *chsd ldrs: rdn and one pce appr fnl f* **12/1**

0635 **5** *3 1/2* **Flying Kitty**[32] 721 4-8-12 46 oh1 KieranO'Neill 7 38
(John Bridger) *dwlt: towards rr: rdn over 2f out: nvr rchd ldrs* **33/1**

/340 **6** *hd* **Big City Boy (IRE)**[9] 1017 5-8-13 47 (tp) LukeMorris 2 39
(Phil McEntee) *led: rdn and hdd 1f out: wknd fnl f* **16/1**

045- **7** *hd* **Sunny Bank**[47] 7921 4-9-1 54 WilliamTwiston-Davies(5) 10 45
(Alan Coogan) *in tch on outer: lost pl over 3f out: rdn and n.d fnl 2f* **9/2**[2]

300- **8** *3/4* **Alfie Joe**[189] 6274 4-8-5 46 oh1 PhilipPrince(7) 3 36
(Ron Hodges) *prom: rdn over 2f out: wknd over 1f out* **20/1**

1m 39.79s (1.59) **Going Correction** +0.225s/f (Slow) **8** Ran SP% **98.0**

Speed ratings (Par 101): **101,99,98,97,94 94,93,93**

toteswingers 1&2 £1.90, 1&3 £3.80, 2&3 £3.20 CSF £12.16 CT £51.24 TOTE £4.60: £1.70, £1.10, £1.80; EX 12.10 Trifecta £31.20 Pool: £1,220.71 - 29.33 winning units.

Owner C Owen **Bred** Cheveley Park Stud Ltd **Trained** Newmarket, Suffolk

■ Avon Supreme was withdrawn on vet's advice at the s (9/2, deduct 15p in the £ under R4).

FOCUS

The steady gallop favoured those ridden handily, so not form to go overboard about.

1162 CROWHURST H'CAP (DIV II) 1m (P)

5:10 (5:11) (Class 6) (0-55,55) 4-Y-0+ **£2,045** (£603; £302) **Stalls** High

Form RPR

-006 **1** **Beauchamp Xerxes**[23] 840 7-9-2 55 (t) NicoleNordblad(5) 9 71+
(Hans Adielsson) *mde all: wnt clr over 4f out: in n.d fnl 2f: unchal* **6/1**[3]

2446 **2** *7* **Amber Moon**[7] 1056 8-8-7 **46** oh1 .... AnnStokell(5) 7 46
(Ann Stokell) *mid-div: rdn and hdwy 3f out: kpt on to take modest 2nd ins fnl f* **25/1**
0014 **3** *hd* **Total Obsession**[9] 1013 6-8-12 **53** .... (v) JoeyHaynes(7) 4 53
(Mark Hoad) *hld up in rr: hung rt fnl bnd: rdn and r.o fnl 2f: nrst fin* **4/1**[2]
3-02 **4** *2* **Teth**[49] 510 4-9-6 **54** .... WilliamCarson 6 50
(Anthony Carson) *towards rr: rdn over 2f out: sme late hdwy* **1/1**[1]
00-0 **5** *1 ½* **Boyzee**[26] 807 5-9-7 **55** .... RobertHavlin 1 46
(Linda Jewell) *mid-div: rdn and no hdwy fnl 3f* **12/1**
1450 **6** *hd* **Fairy Mist (IRE)**[11] 978 6-8-12 **46** .... SeanLevey 5 37
(John Bridger) *chsd ldrs tl lost pl fnl 3f* **8/1**
5003 **7** *nk* **Bubbly Braveheart (IRE)**[1] 1146 6-8-7 **46** oh1 .... RachealKneller(5) 2 36
(Phil McEntee) *chsd wnr tl 3f out: sn wknd* **16/1**
000 **8** *2 ½* **Surrey Dream (IRE)**[38] 655 4-8-12 **46** oh1 .... (p) KieranO'Neill 8 31
(John Bridger) *chsd ldrs: wnt modest 2nd 3f out tl wknd ins fnl f* **25/1**
0400 **9** *¾* **Prophet In A Dream**[18] 903 5-8-12 **46** oh1 .... (p) JoeFanning 3 29
(Paddy Butler) *bhd: rdn and sme hdwy 3f out: wknd 2f out* **25/1**

1m 38.19s (-0.01) **Going Correction** +0.225s/f (Slow) **9** Ran SP% **120.5**
Speed ratings (Par 101): **109,102,101,99,98 98,97,95,94**
toteswingers 1&2 £11.90, 1&3 £5.20, 2&3 £9.00 CSF £146.42 CT £672.64 TOTE £9.20: £2.10, £2.60, £1.50; EX 163.00 Trifecta £1074.20 Pool: £2,656.51 - 1.85 winning units.
Owner Erik Penser **Bred** E Penser **Trained** Kingston Lisle, Oxon

FOCUS
A low-grade handicap turned into a procession by the class-dropping winner. The time was 1.6secs faster than the preceding third division and the winner can follow up in a similar grade.
T/Jkpt: £15,832.30 to a £1 stake. Pool of £33,448.56 - 1.50 winning units T/Plt: £122.10 to a £1 stake. Pool of £98,209.13 - 586.69 winning units T/Qpdt: £30.70 to a £1 stake. Pool of £7,656.94 - 184.07 winning units LM

1163 - 1165a (Foreign Racing) - See Raceform Interactive

CURRAGH (R-H)
Sunday, March 24

OFFICIAL GOING: Heavy

1166a LODGE PARK STUD EUROPEAN BREEDERS FUND PARK EXPRESS STKS (GROUP 3) 1m
3:30 (3:30) 3-Y-O+ **£42,276** (£12,357; £5,853; £1,951)

RPR
1 **Rehn's Nest (IRE)**[148] 7418 3-8-9 99 .... (t) RoryCleary 4 103
(J S Bolger, Ire) *trckd ldr: 2nd 1/2-way: hdwy to ld narrowly under 1 1/2f out: sn extended advantage and kpt on wl u.p towards fin* **9/2**[2]
2 *1 ¾* **Yellow Rosebud (IRE)**[168] 6917 4-10-0 107 .... (b) PatSmullen 1 106
(D K Weld, Ire) *settled bhd ldrs in 3rd: rdn ent fnl f on nrside and clsd in 2nd on wnr u.p towards fin: a hld* **8/11**[1]
3 *3 ¼* **Starbright (IRE)**[175] 6717 3-8-9 99 .... ChrisHayes 5 92
(Kevin Prendergast, Ire) *wnt lft s: settled in rr: rdn in 4th ent fnl f and wnt nvr threatening 3rd fnl 150yds: kpt on* **9/2**[2]
4 *2* **More Than Sotka (FR)**[24] 837 3-8-9 96 .... FergalLynch 2 87
(David Marnane, Ire) *wnt lft s: sn led: pushed along 2f out and hdd under 1 1/2f out: dropped to 4th ins fnl f and no imp whn edgd lft fnl 100yds* **16/1**
5 *3 ¾* **Beach Of Falesa (IRE)**[159] 7155 4-9-11 89 .... JosephO'Brien 3 82
(A P O'Brien, Ire) *dwlt and settled bhd ldrs in 4th: rdn 1 1/2f out in rr and no imp ent fnl f: n.d whn sltly hmpd ins fnl 100yds: eased* **7/1**[3]

1m 56.1s (10.10) **Going Correction** +1.125s/f (Soft)
WFA 3 from 4yo 17lb **5** Ran SP% **112.6**
Speed ratings: **94,92,89,87,83**
CSF £8.55 TOTE £5.00: £1.90, £1.02; DF 8.70.
Owner Mrs J S Bolger **Bred** Ennistown Stud **Trained** Coolcullen, Co Carlow

FOCUS
A step up from the winner with the next two helping with the standard.

1168a BETVICTOR IRISH LINCOLNSHIRE (PREMIER H'CAP) 1m
4:30 (4:31) 4-Y-O+
£48,780 (£15,447; £7,317; £2,439; £1,626; £813)

RPR
1 **Sweet Lightning**[206] 5777 8-9-8 **100** .... (t) JohnnyMurtagh 15 112+
(Thomas Carmody, Ire) *hld up in mid-div: hdwy over 2f out on nrside to ld 1 1/2f out: wnt rt ent fnl f and sn extended advantage: styd on wl* **10/1**
2 *3 ¾* **Cheval Rouge (IRE)**[140] 7583 6-8-5 **83** .... (bt) BenCurtis 3 85
(H Rogers, Ire) *hld up towards rr: prog on far side fr 2f out: rdn in 4th ent fnl f and kpt on wl into nvr threatening 2nd fnl 50yds* **33/1**
3 *nk* **Bold Thady Quill (IRE)**[23] 856 6-8-6 **91** .... (p) RossCoakley(7) 12 93+
(K J Condon, Ire) *w.w towards rr: hdwy over 2f out: n.m.r 1 1/2f out: rdn into 6th 1f out and kpt on u.p to take 3rd fnl stride* **16/1**
4 *nse* **Inis Meain (USA)**[21] 6462 6-9-7 **99** .... DannyMullins 14 101
(Denis Gerard Hogan, Ire) *prom: sn led: strly pressed 2f out and sn hdd: rdn and no ex ins fnl f: dropped to 4th cl home* **9/1**
5 *nk* **Macbeth (IRE)**[148] 7423 4-8-13 **91** .... (t) ShaneFoley 19 92
(K J Condon, Ire) *towards rr: prog nrside 2f out into 3rd ins fnl f: sn no ex and dropped to 5th nr fin* **25/1**
6 *3 ¼* **Ozeta (FR)**[37] 683 5-9-4 **96** .... (t) FMBerry 18 90
(Niall Madden, Ire) *hld up in rr of mid-div: pushed along fr 1/2-way and impr to chse ldrs over 1f out: no imp in 6th ins fnl f: kpt on same pce* **20/1**
7 *2* **Hujaylea (IRE)**[343] 1402 10-9-3 **100** .... (p) ConorHoban(5) 8 89
(M Halford, Ire) *w.w in rr of mid-div: n.m.r 1 1/2f out: sn swtchd lft and rdn over 1f out: clsd u.p into nvr threatening 7th cl home* **33/1**
8 *hd* **Croi An Or (IRE)**[231] 4853 4-9-4 **96** .... (b[1]) WayneLordan 9 84
(T Stack, Ire) *chsd ldrs: 7th 1/2-way: n.m.r bhd ldrs over 1f out and edgd rt: sn rdn and no ex: kpt on same pce towards fin* **16/1**
9 *1 ¼* **Susiescot (IRE)**[140] 7581 4-8-2 **82** oh1 ow1 .... LeighRoche(3) 10 68
(W McCreery, Ire) *racd in mid-div: pushed along 1/2-way and no imp u.p in 10th ent fnl f: kpt on same pce* **25/1**
10 *shd* **Ansaab**[301] 2526 5-9-1 **93** .... ChrisHayes 1 78
(Kevin Prendergast, Ire) *chsd ldrs early: sn settled in mid-div on outer: hdwy fr 1/2-way: rdn in 4th over 1f out and sn no ex: wknd* **8/1**[3]
11 *1 ½* **Man Of Erin (IRE)**[159] 7151 5-8-6 **82** oh1 ow2 .... FergalLynch 17 66
(W T Farrell, Ire) *cl up: 3rd 1/2-way: rdn over 2f out and sn wknd* **12/1**
12 *shd* **Tandem**[186] 6386 4-9-3 **95** .... PatSmullen 13 77
(D K Weld, Ire) *hld up in mid-div: pushed along after 1/2-way and no imp 1 1/2f out: one pce fnl f* **11/2**[1]
13 *½* **Dougal Philps**[78] 6385 4-8-4 **83** ow2 .... SamJames(3) 5 65
(W P Mullins, Ire) *in rr of mid-div: 15th 1/2-way: no imp over 2f out and swtchd lft: kpt on one pce fnl f* **12/1**
14 *7* **Gunner Lindley (IRE)**[267] 3647 6-8-10 **88** .... JFEgan 16 52
(Reginald Roberts, Ire) *chsd ldrs: niggled along in 5th 1/2-way: sn rdn in 6th and no ex fr 2f out: wknd over 1f out* **8/1**[3]
15 *shd* **Campanology**[23] 856 4-8-12 **90** .... NGMcCullagh 20 54
(Thomas Carmody, Ire) *hld up in mid-div: pushed along fr 1/2-way and no imp: wknd fnl f* **12/1**
16 *1 ¾* **Custom Cut (IRE)**[23] 856 4-9-9 **104** .... RonanWhelan(3) 2 64
(George J Kent, Ire) *cl up: 2nd 1/2-way: effrt 2f out: sn no ex and wknd ent fnl f* **16/1**
17 *9 ½* **Miracle Cure (IRE)**[100] 8118 4-9-2 **94** .... KevinManning 4 32
(J S Bolger, Ire) *chsd ldrs: cl 8th bef 1/2-way: rdn 2f out and no imp whn hmpd over 1f out: eased fnl f* **14/1**
18 *3 ¾* **Shifting (IRE)**[154] 7279 4-8-4 **87** .... (b) ShaneBKelly(5) 7 17
(W McCreery, Ire) *hld up in tch: pushed along in 7th 1/2-way and sn no imp: wknd* **10/1**
19 *2 ¾* **Our Boy Jack (IRE)**[167] 6923 4-8-6 **84** .... BarryMcHugh 6 7
(Richard Fahey) *chsd ldrs: keen early: cl 3rd 1/2-way: sn pushed along and wknd over 2f out* **16/1**
20 *21* **Anton Chigurh**[176] 6670 4-9-0 **92** .... RichardKingscote 11
(Tom Dascombe) *chsd ldrs early: pushed along in 5th 1/2-way and sn no imp: wknd over 2f out* **6/1**[2]

1m 53.14s (7.14) **Going Correction** +1.125s/f (Soft) **20** Ran SP% **151.7**
Speed ratings: **109,105,104,104,104 101,99,99,97,97 96,96,95,88,88 86,77,73,70,49**
CSF £351.71 CT £5392.46 TOTE £13.20: £3.00, £9.70, £4.70, £3.10; DF 1335.00.
Owner Andrew Tinkler **Bred** Mrs M Lavell **Trained** the Curragh, Co Kildare
■ Sweet Lightning is the first horse to win both the English and Irish 'Lincolns'.

FOCUS
A very taking performance from Sweet Lightning and although he's not a young horse he won this like one that will win a good race at a higher level at some stage of the season. The winner was close to his best.

1167 - 1169a (Foreign Racing) - See Raceform Interactive

1155 LINGFIELD (L-H)
Monday, March 25

OFFICIAL GOING: Standard
Wind: Moderate, half against Weather: Overcast, cold

1170 LINGFIELD PARK OWNERS GROUP (S) STKS 1m (P)
2:10 (2:10) (Class 6) 3-Y-O+ **£2,045** (£603; £302) **Stalls High**

Form RPR
-334 **1** **Alhaban (IRE)**[4] 1104 7-9-8 66 .... LukeMorris 1 71
(Ronald Harris) *trckd ldng pair: chal fr 2f out: cajoled along to ld 1f out: hld on wl* **3/1**[2]
-650 **2** *nk* **Prince Of Burma (IRE)**[28] 792 5-9-8 78 .... (b) RobertWinston 3 70
(Jeremy Gask) *s.i.s: hld up in 4th: prog on outer to chal 2f out: drvn to chse wnr ins fnl f: clsd grad but a hld* **4/9**[1]
5502 **3** *3 ¼* **Abhaath (USA)**[9] 1039 4-9-1 60 .... GaryPhillips(7) 6 62
(Ronald Harris) *led: urged along over 2f out: styd on inner in st: hdd 1f out: sn outpcd* **8/1**[3]
3655 **4** *1 ½* **The Noble Ord**[10] 1020 4-9-8 54 .... (t) LiamKeniry 5 59
(Sylvester Kirk) *chsd ldr to 2f out: sn dropped to 4th and wl outpcd: no imp fnl f* **20/1**
600- **5** *16* **Simpson Millar**[12] 7604 4-9-8 43 .... (p) TomEaves 2 22
(Zoe Davison) *t.k.h early: hld up and sn last: wknd over 3f out: t.o* **100/1**

1m 38.75s (0.55) **Going Correction** +0.125s/f (Slow) **5** Ran SP% **111.1**
Speed ratings (Par 101): **102,101,98,96,80**
CSF £4.79 TOTE £3.70: £1.40, £1.10; EX 5.60 Trifecta £11.40 Pool: £2,792.89 - 183.56 winning units..No bid for the winner. Prince Of Burma was the suject of a friendly claim.
Owner Ridge House Stables Ltd **Bred** Eimear Mulhern **Trained** Earlswood, Monmouths

FOCUS
An uncompetitive seller, run at a steady pace, but the form makes sense at a low level.

1171 AURORA FIREWORKS H'CAP 1m (P)
2:40 (2:41) (Class 6) (0-65,64) 3-Y-O **£2,045** (£603; £302) **Stalls High**

Form RPR
1254 **1** **Hidden Link**[4] 1103 3-9-7 **64** .... LukeMorris 4 71+
(Ronald Harris) *mostly trckd ldng pair: quick move to ld jst over 1f out: urged along and sn clr: eased nr fin* **7/4**[1]
0-43 **2** *3* **Mudaawem (USA)**[42] 613 3-9-5 **62** .... JoeFanning 6 61
(Mark Johnston) *led: drvn and hdd jst over 1f out: no ch w wnr but clung on for 2nd* **11/4**[2]
0-40 **3** *½* **Warrant Officer**[10] 1016 3-8-2 **52** .... DanielCremin(7) 2 50
(Mick Channon) *hld up in last pair: rdn wl over 1f out: sn outpcd: kpt on to take 3rd nr fin* **6/1**[3]
40-3 **4** *nse* **Tebbit (USA)**[33] 726 3-9-6 **63** .... (be[1]) TomEaves 1 61
(Philip Hide) *s.i.s and rousted along early: hld up in last pair: rdn wl over 1f out: sn outpcd: kpt on to press for a pl nr fin* **8/1**
-550 **5** *½* **Limoges**[25] 824 3-8-2 **50** oh1 .... RobertTart(5) 3 47
(Luke Dace) *trckd ldr 2f: styd cl up: rdn over 2f out: tried to chal for a pl on inner 1f out: one pce* **6/1**[3]
5632 **6** *2 ¼* **Marmot Bay (IRE)**[1] 1157 3-8-7 **55** .... JemmaMarshall(5) 5 46
(David Flood) *hld up but tk fierce hold and plld way through to join ldr after 2f: wknd wl over 1f out* **8/1**

1m 40.19s (1.99) **Going Correction** +0.125s/f (Slow) **6** Ran SP% **113.8**
Speed ratings (Par 96): **95,92,91,91,90 88**
Tote Swingers: 1&2 £1.40, 1&3 £2.20, 2&3 £2.50 CSF £6.93 TOTE £2.50: £1.80, £1.80; EX 7.30 Trifecta £17.60 Pool: £3,266.81 - 138.43 winning units..
Owner Ridge House Stables Ltd **Bred** Mrs M Chaworth-Musters **Trained** Earlswood, Monmouths

FOCUS
The pace was steady for this moderate contest and the runner-up is the best guide to the level.

1172 DEMELZA HOUSE CHILDRENS HOSPICE H'CAP 7f (P)
3:10 (3:12) (Class 5) (0-70,71) 4-Y-O+ **£2,726** (£805; £402) **Stalls Low**

Form RPR
0503 **1** **Lord Of The Dance (IRE)**[9] 1038 7-9-2 **65** .... TomEaves 4 71
(Michael Mullineaux) *hld up in tch: prog 2f out: drvn to ld jst ins fnl f: styd on* **20/1**
-221 **2** *¾* **West Leake (IRE)**[27] 806 7-8-12 **61** .... LiamKeniry 5 65
(Paul Burgoyne) *t.k.h: hld up in rr: prog 2f out: rdn to chal jst over 1f out: kpt on same pce* **6/1**[3]

The Form Book Flat, Raceform Ltd, Compton, RG20 6NL.

0031 **3** ½ **Elusive Hawk (IRE)**[7] 1063 9-9-8 71 6ex.........................(v) AdamKirby 8 79+
(David Evans) *trckd ldr: trying to chal whn nrly carried off the crse bnd 2f out: lost all ch but rallied wl fnl f to take 3rd nr fin* **6/4**[1]

1151 **4** ½ **Valdaw**[19] 898 5-9-5 68.. EddieAhern 3 69
(Mike Murphy) *trckd ldng pair: lft in ld 2f out: hdd jst ins fnl f: fdd nr fin* **3/1**[2]

4-51 **5** 1 **Yankee Storm**[35] 705 8-9-5 68.......................................(v) JimCrowley 6 67
(Michael Wigham) *hld up in last: prog on inner to chal 1f out: fdd last 100yds* **8/1**

5220 **6** 2 ¾ **Sannibel**[12] 991 5-8-7 61.. RobertTart(5) 2 53
(Graeme McPherson) *trckd ldrs: rdn to chal over 1f out: wknd qckly fnl f* **8/1**

55-0 **7** 2 ½ **Satwa Laird**[13] 971 7-9-3 66... HayleyTurner 7 51+
(Conor Dore) *led at stdy pce: carried bdly rt by loose horse bnd 2f out: hdd and lost all ch* **14/1**

6516 **U** **The Happy Hammer (IRE)**[12] 981 7-9-7 70................ SteveDrowne 1
(Eugene Stanford) *stmbld and uns rdr leaving stalls* **20/1**

1m 26.08s (1.28) **Going Correction** +0.125s/f (Slow) 8 Ran SP% **117.7**
Speed ratings (Par 103): **97,96,95,95,93 90,87,**
Tote Swingers: 1&2 £13.50, 1&3 £7.20, 2&3 £3.00 CSF £137.69 CT £293.75 TOTE £30.50: £5.60, £1.80, £1.20; EX 153.60 Trifecta £648.60 Pool: £4,731.62 - 140.81 winning units..
Owner H Clewlow **Bred** Bridgewater Equine Ltd **Trained** Alpraham, Cheshire

FOCUS
Four last-time out winners in the field and an eventful race. Those held up understandably dominated and the firs two are the best guides to the form.

1173 VINES BMW FILLIES' H'CAP 6f (P)
3:40 (3:45) (Class 5) (0-75,75) 4-Y-O+ £2,726 (£805; £402) Stalls Low

Form RPR

300- **1** **Red Larkspur (IRE)**[152] 7334 4-9-7 75.......................[1] RichardHughes 3 85+
(Roger Teal) *hld up: last tl prog wl over 1f out: pushed into ld last 100yds: decisively* **4/5**[1]

0510 **2** 1 ¼ **Chevise (IRE)**[7] 1063 5-8-0 61.....................................(p) GaryPhillips(7) 4 66
(Steve Woodman) *prom: chsd ldr over 3f out: rdn to ld over 1f out: idled in front: hdd and outpcd last 100yds* **8/1**

4242 **3** 1 **Amethyst Dawn (IRE)**[7] 1063 7-8-10 64..........................(t) EddieAhern 1 66
(J R Jenkins) *wl in tch: rdn to chse ldr briefly 1f out: one pce last 150yds* **11/4**[2]

4615 **4** hd **Catalinas Diamond (IRE)**[8] 1052 5-9-0 68..................(t) SteveDrowne 5 70
(Pat Murphy) *in tch: shkn up on outer over 2f out: nt qckn over 1f out: kpt on last 150yds: n.d* **7/1**[3]

5604 **5** 3 ¼ **Rooknrasbryripple**[8] 1052 4-8-2 61 oh16........................ RyanTate(5) 6 53
(Ralph Smith) *t.k.h: led after 1f: hdd over 1f out: wknd qckly fnl f* **25/1**

5006 **6** 1 ¼ **Hold The Star**[8] 1052 7-8-5 64 oh16 ow3........................ AnnStokell(5) 2 52
(Ann Stokell) *racd freely: led 1f: lost pl fr 1/2-way: wknd wl over 1f out* **66/1**

1m 13.35s (1.45) **Going Correction** +0.125s/f (Slow) 6 Ran SP% **111.2**
Speed ratings (Par 100): **95,93,92,91,87 85**
Tote Swingers: 1&2 £2.00, 1&3 £1.20, 2&3 £2.40 CSF £8.08 TOTE £1.80: £1.20, £3.80; EX 9.60 Trifecta £27.30 Pool: £5,131.61 - 140.81 winning units..
Owner The Gracenote Partnership **Bred** Wardstown Stud Ltd **Trained** Ashtead, Surrey

FOCUS
A wide range of abilities for this fillies' handicap, with 30lb covering the six runners. The pace was honest and the form is straightforward behind the winner, who put up an improved effort in the hood.

1174 FUEL COMMUNICATIONS MAIDEN STKS 6f (P)
4:10 (4:11) (Class 5) 3-Y-O £2,726 (£805; £402) Stalls Low

Form RPR

20-2 **1** **Limit Up**[10] 1012 3-9-5 80.. JoeFanning 5 82
(Mark Johnston) *mde all and set str pce early: edgd rt briefly over 1f out: rdn out: unchal* **2/1**[2]

434- **2** 2 ¾ **Mysterial**[284] 3062 3-9-5 80... RichardHughes 4 75
(Richard Hannon) *chsd ldng pair and pushed along at various times: rdn 2f out: wnt 2nd 1f out on inner: no imp on wnr* **4/7**[1]

5- **3** 2 ¼ **Clearing**[159] 7161 3-9-0 0.. MatthewDavies 1 62
(Jim Boyle) *chsd wnr: rdn and no imp 2f out: lost 2nd 1f out: hung lft after* **20/1**[3]

64- **4** 18 **Uganda Glory (USA)**[164] 7014 3-9-0 0........................... TonyCulhane 2
(George Baker) *outpcd* **20/1**[3]

1m 11.79s (-0.11) **Going Correction** +0.125s/f (Slow) 4 Ran SP% **106.5**
Speed ratings (Par 98): **105,101,98,74**
CSF £3.44 TOTE £2.30; EX 3.20 Trifecta £5.10 Pool: £2,660.00 - 384.03 winning units..
Owner Sheikh Hamdan Bin Mohammed Al Maktoum **Bred** Minster Stud **Trained** Middleham Moor, N Yorks

FOCUS
This maiden was run at a sound pace but the winner benefited from a soft lead.

1175 "TK" BRENNAN YOU WILL BE MISSED H'CAP 1m 5f (P)
4:40 (4:41) (Class 6) (0-60,60) 4-Y-O+ £2,045 (£603; £302) Stalls Low

Form RPR

1123 **1** **Irene Kennet**[21] 883 6-9-7 60... HayleyTurner 11 67
(Paul Burgoyne) *hld up in last quartet: prog on wd outside bnd 2f out: rdn and plenty to do over 1f out: str run fnl f to ld last strides* **5/1**[2]

-515 **2** hd **Rollin 'n Tumblin**[25] 820 9-8-11 50................................. JimmyQuinn 9 57
(Michael Attwater) *hld up towards rr: prog 5f out and sn trckd ldrs: gng strly over 2f out: clsd over 1f out to ld last 120yds: hdd fnl strides* **10/1**

4423 **3** 1 ½ **Petersboden**[13] 973 4-8-4 46... NickyMackay 6 51
(Michael Blanshard) *prom and mostly in ldng trio: rdn 2f out: styd on fr over 1f out: nvr quite able to chal* **6/1**[3]

-000 **4** shd **Rodrigo De Freitas (IRE)**[21] 883 6-8-13 57.........(v) NathanAlison(5) 3 61
(Jim Boyle) *trckd ldrs: rdn and looking for room over 2f out: styd on wl fnl f but nt quite pce to chal* **20/1**

3621 **5** hd **Crimson Monarch (USA)**[10] 1022 9-8-10 49............(b) WilliamCarson 8 54
(Peter Hiatt) *hld up in last quartet: plenty to do at bk of field wl over 1f out: styd on wl fnl f: nrst fin* **16/1**

6-04 **6** ¾ **Cozy Tiger (USA)**[12] 983 8-9-1 54................................ RichardHughes 7 57
(Willie Musson) *hld up in midfield: shkn up towards outer over 2f out: sme hdwy over 1f out: wl hld whn nt clr run ins fnl f: kpt on* **4/1**[1]

4226 **7** hd **Red Mystique (IRE)**[19] 905 4-8-12 54..........................(b) TomEaves 13 57
(Philip Hide) *led after 1f tl after 3f: trckd ldr: led 3f out: kicked 2 l clr over 1f out on inner: hdd & wknd qckly last 120yds* **10/1**

046 **8** 1 ¾ **Zafaraban (IRE)**[35] 708 6-8-11 55............................... GeorgeDowning(5) 1 57
(Tony Carroll) *wl in tch on inner: shkn up over 3f out: trying to cl on inner whn nt clr run over 1f out: no hdwy after* **25/1**

3423 **9** nk **El Libertador (USA)**[9] 1031 7-8-12 58.......................(b) JoeyHaynes(7) 4 58
(Eric Wheeler) *led 1f: sn bk towards midfield: effrt on inner whn nt clr run over 2f out: no imp on ldrs over 1f out: fdd* **10/1**

3-22 **10** nk **Mount Abora (IRE)**[7] 1060 6-9-7 60..............................(p) IanMongan 2 60
(Laura Mongan) *t.k.h: trckd ldrs: prog on outer to chal wl over 2f out: nt qckn wl over 1f out: wknd fnl f* **8/1**

0040 **11** ¾ **Legal Legacy**[21] 883 7-9-4 57... AmirQuinn 12 56
(Richard Rowe) *dwlt: swtchd to inner fr wd draw and hld up in last: effrt over 2f out: one pce and no real prog over 1f out* **25/1**

3605 **12** 6 **Polarity**[12] 983 7-8-8 52 ow1.................................(p) ThomasBrown(5) 14 42
(Gerry Enright) *prog to ld after 3f: hdd 3f out: wknd 2f out* **33/1**

24-0 **13** 2 ¼ **Silver Six**[33] 724 4-8-11 53...(t) EddieAhern 5 40
(Sheena West) *a in last trio: no prog and btn over 2f out* **14/1**

/000 **14** 24 **Our Play (IRE)**[7] 1062 5-8-11 50.................................(b) SteveDrowne 10 3
(Lydia Richards) *racd wd in midfield: nt gng wl fr 1/2-way: sn eased and bhd: t.o* **50/1**

2m 47.55s (1.55) **Going Correction** +0.125s/f (Slow)
WFA 4 from 5yo+ 3lb 14 Ran SP% **119.2**
Speed ratings (Par 101): **100,99,98,98,98 98,98,97,96,96 96,92,91,76**
Tote Swingers: 1&2 £10.90, 1&3 £5.30, 2&3 £12.40 CSF £50.14 CT £311.19 TOTE £6.00: £1.90, £2.20, £2.10; EX 54.60 Trifecta £262.60 Pool: £4,057.82 - 11.58 winning units..
Owner R W Floyd **Bred** Jim Duncan And Richard William Floyd **Trained** Shepton Montague, Somerset

FOCUS
An open contest, run at a steady pace but the form is straightforward rated around the placed horses.

1176 YES EVENTS LTD H'CAP 1m 2f (P)
5:10 (5:12) (Class 5) (0-70,70) 4-Y-O+ £2,726 (£805; £402) Stalls Low

Form RPR

-111 **1** **Mubtadi**[35] 709 5-8-13 67.. ThomasBrown(5) 2 77+
(Ismail Mohammed) *trckd ldng pair: wnt 2nd wl over 2f out: upsides and cantering over 1f out: pushed along to chse new ldr ins fnl f: styd on to ld last strides* **6/4**[1]

-352 **2** hd **Chrissycross (IRE)**[10] 1013 4-9-2 65......................(v) RichardHughes 9 71
(Roger Teal) *stdd s: hld up in last trio mostly: prog on inner 2f out: drvn to ld jst over 1f out: kpt on but hdd last strides* **10/1**

126- **3** ½ **Watt Broderick (IRE)**[72] 5443 4-9-1 64.......................(t) JimCrowley 12 69
(Ian Williams) *hld up in midfield: looking for room 2f out: prog over 1f out: drvn and r.o to take 3rd last 75yds* **4/1**[2]

6331 **4** 1 **Bernisdale**[7] 1068 5-9-2 65 6ex... LukeMorris 10 68
(John Flint) *pressed ldr: rdn 3f out: sn lost 2nd and lost pl further fr 2f out: rallied fnl f: styd on* **16/1**

1342 **5** nk **Conducting**[10] 1010 5-9-6 69.. NeilCallan 7 72
(Gay Kelleway) *trckd ldrs: rdn and cl enough 2f out: nt qckn over 1f out: styd on again last 100yds* **14/1**

5515 **6** nk **Understory (USA)**[19] 906 6-9-6 69................................ HayleyTurner 5 71
(Tim McCarthy) *t.k.h: led at stdy pce: wound it up fr 3f out: hdd jst over 1f out: fdd last 100yds* **20/1**

3414 **7** 1 ¼ **Sail Home**[18] 919 6-8-12 68....................................... ShelleyBirkett(7) 11 68
(Julia Feilden) *racd on outer: trckd ldrs: lost pl and swtchd ins over 1f out: no imp after* **16/1**

0-62 **8** nk **Ogaritmo**[31] 753 4-9-2 70.. RobertTart(5) 4 69
(Alastair Lidderdale) *wl in tch in midfield: trckd ldrs fr 3f out: cl enough wl over 1f out: fdd fnl f* **14/1**

505- **9** ¾ **Laughing Jack**[166] 6988 5-8-12 66......................... GeorgeDowning(5) 8 64
(Tony Carroll) *heavily restrained s: hld up in detached last: shuffled along over 2f out: sme prog on inner over 1f out: nvr involved* **6/1**[3]

-200 **10** 1 ½ **Kindia (IRE)**[12] 984 5-9-7 70.. SebSanders 6 65
(Michael Attwater) *dwlt: hld up in last trio: shkn up over 2f out: one pce and no real prog* **20/1**

5660 **11** hd **Minority Interest**[26] 816 4-8-13 62................................ KieranO'Neill 1 56
(Brett Johnson) *a towards rr: shkn up in last pair 2f out: no prog* **50/1**

2m 6.05s (-0.55) **Going Correction** +0.125s/f (Slow) 11 Ran SP% **120.0**
Speed ratings (Par 103): **107,106,106,105,105 105,104,103,103,102 101**
Tote Swingers: 1&2 £4.90, 1&3 £2.50, 2&3 £10.60 CSF £17.93 CT £54.14 TOTE £2.30: £1.20, £2.40, £2.50; EX 19.10 Trifecta £74.90 Pool: £3,676.83 - 36.78 winning units..
Owner Abdulla Al Mansoori **Bred** Whitsbury Manor Stud **Trained** Newmarket, Suffolk

FOCUS
The pace was steady for this fair handicap but the winner is in great form and value for more than the official margin with the runner-up right up to his best.
T/Jkpt: Not won. T/Plt: £53.10 to a £1 stake. Pool: £141,011.45 - 1,936.41 winning tickets.
T/Qpdt: £33.30 to a £1 stake. Pool: £10,756.68 - 238.68 winning tickets. JN

1170 LINGFIELD (L-H)
Tuesday, March 26

OFFICIAL GOING: Standard
Wind: Moderate, half against Weather: Overcast, cold

1177 YOUR GUIDE TO LINGFIELD AT LINGFIELDRACECOURSETIPS.CO.UK H'CAP 1m 2f (P)
2:20 (2:20) (Class 6) (0-65,65) 3-Y-O £2,045 (£603; £302) Stalls Low

Form RPR

1122 **1** **Gabrial The Duke (IRE)**[5] 1103 3-9-5 63...................... JamieSpencer 6 69
(David Simcock) *won early battle for ld: mde all: drvn wl over 1f out and sn at least 2 l clr: unchal after* **4/6**[1]

0-20 **2** 1 ¼ **Hamla**[38] 685 3-9-3 61.. FrannyNorton 3 64+
(Mark Johnston) *hld up bhd ldrs: pushed along over 2f out: reminders and r.o to take 2nd last 100yds: nvr chal* **12/1**

3203 **3** ¾ **Lady Lunchalot (USA)**[11] 1008 3-9-2 60.........................(p) LiamKeniry 5 62
(J S Moore) *dwlt: rcvrd to chse wnr after 2f: rdn over 2f out: nt qckn over 1f out: lost 2nd and styd on one pce fnl 100yds* **20/1**

002- **4** 2 ¼ **Day In Day Out**[103] 8094 3-9-7 65.................................... JimCrowley 2 64
(Ralph Beckett) *hld up and sn in last: pushed along over 2f out: nt on terms after: taken to inner and rdn 1f out: one pce* **9/4**[2]

662- **5** 1 **Brick Rising**[200] 5997 3-9-5 63... JimmyFortune 4 58
(Andrew Balding) *chsd wnr 2f: cl up after: shkn up over 2f out: fdd over 1f out* **10/1**[3]

2m 6.38s (-0.22) **Going Correction** +0.075s/f (Slow) 5 Ran SP% **112.3**
Speed ratings (Par 96): **103,102,101,99,98**
CSF £10.25 TOTE £1.40: £1.10, £3.90; EX 8.80 Trifecta £31.60 Pool: £2,197.88 - 52.00 winning units..
Owner Dr Marwan Koukash **Bred** Old Carhue & Graeng Bloodstock **Trained** Newmarket, Suffolk

FOCUS
This looked a fair little race for the grade beforehand, but it turned out to be an uncompetitive affair. The third sets the level.

1178 LINGFIELD PARK OWNERS GROUP MEDIAN AUCTION MAIDEN STKS — 1m 2f (P)
2:50 (2:52) (Class 6) 3-4-Y-O — £2,045 (£603; £302) Stalls Low

Form / RPR

1 **Warrigal (IRE)** 3-8-8 0 ow1 ..... RyanMoore 3 71+
(Jeremy Noseda) *trckd ldr 2f: styd cl up: effrt to ld on inner over 1f out but sn shifted away fr rail: shkn up and styd on wl* **5/2^{2}**

3 2 1 ½ **Continental Divide (IRE)**^{61} 350 3-8-7 0 ..... FergusSweeney 6 67
(Jamie Osborne) *led: rdn and hdd over 1f out: hld whn fly-leapt 50yds out* **6/1**

3 nk **Nautilus** 3-8-7 0 ..... WilliamBuick 4 66+
(John Gosden) *trckd ldrs: tried to chal on outer 2f out but hanging and green: nt qckn over 1f out: styd on wl again last 100yds* **2/1^{1}**

4 ¾ **Maughami** 3-8-3 0 ow1 ..... AndreaAtzeni 2 61+
(Marco Botti) *difficult to load into stalls: settled in rr: pushed along over 2f out: prog to dispute 3rd 1f out: kpt on* **10/1**

4- 5 2 ¼ **Ihtikar (USA)**^{165} 7020 3-8-7 0 ..... HayleyTurner 9 60
(Ed Dunlop) *prog to trck ldr after 2f: pumped along over 2f out: steadily fdd over 1f out* **11/4^{3}**

6 2 ½ **Single Mast (USA)** 3-8-2 0 ..... WilliamCarson 8 50+
(Charles Hills) *slowly away: setted in rr: nudged rival over 2f out: outpcd wl over 1f out* **12/1**

-66 7 1 ¼ **Shirazz**^{62} 342 4-9-3 0 ..... AmyScott$^{(5)}$ 7 52
(Alastair Lidderdale) *settled in rr: effrt on outer whn nudged by rival over 2f out: wknd over 1f out* **66/1**

00 8 53 **Baytown Bertie**^{8} 1057 4-9-13 0 ..... SteveDrowne 5
(Lydia Richards) *sn in trble: t.o fr 1/2-way* **100/1**

2m 6.54s (-0.06) **Going Correction** +0.075s/f (Slow)
WFA 3 from 4yo 20lb — 8 Ran SP% **122.1**
Speed ratings (Par 101): **103,101,101,100,99 97,96,53**
CSF £19.54 TOTE £2.90: £1.20, £1.90, £1.20; EX 21.80 Trifecta £68.70 Pool: £3,187.10 - 34.74 winning units..
Owner Miss Yvonne Jacques **Bred** Newsells Park Stud **Trained** Newmarket, Suffolk

FOCUS
An interesting maiden and the form looks fair.

1179 VINES BMW CLASSIFIED CLAIMING STKS — 7f (P)
3:20 (3:21) (Class 6) 4-Y-0+ — £2,045 (£603; £302) Stalls Low

Form / RPR

-460 1 **Flavius Victor (IRE)**^{22} 878 4-8-10 67 ..... ThomasBrown$^{(5)}$ 5 72
(Patrick Chamings) *hld up: sn detached in last in strly run event: rdn and clsd over 1f out: led last 100yds: pushed out* **11/4^{2}**

5023 2 1 ¾ **Abhaath (USA)**^{1} 1170 4-8-2 60 ..... GaryPhillips$^{(7)}$ 1 61
(Ronald Harris) *cl up: chsd ldr 1/2-way: rdn to ld wl over 1f out: hdd and no ex last 100yds* **5/1**

44-6 3 1 **Kingswinford (IRE)**^{11} 1015 7-8-3 66 .....(p) NoraLooby$^{(7)}$ 6 60
(Alastair Lidderdale) *t.k.h: chsd ldr to 1/2-way: wdst of three ldrs bnd 2f out: nt qckn over 1f out: one pce after* **4/1^{3}**

5421 4 6 **Electrician**^{25} 840 4-8-9 62 .....(b) AndreaAtzeni 4 47
(Tim Pitt) *led at str pce: rdn and hdd wl over 1f out: sn btn: eased fnl f* **1/1^{1}**

1m 25.22s (0.42) **Going Correction** +0.075s/f (Slow) — 4 Ran SP% **113.3**
Speed ratings (Par 101): **100,98,96,90**
CSF £15.31 TOTE £3.70; EX 20.50 Trifecta £27.80 Pool: £1,318.77 - 35.74 winning units..
Owner P R Chamings F T Lee **Bred** Western Bloodstock **Trained** Baughurst, Hants

FOCUS
Two absentees and a soft race with the winner rated to his previous best but no higher as the third and fourth were below form.

1180 LINGFIELD PARK SUPPORTS YOUNG EPILEPSY H'CAP — 6f (P)
3:50 (3:50) (Class 6) (0-65,68) 3-Y-0 — £2,045 (£603; £302) Stalls Low

Form / RPR

55-4 1 **Little Indian**^{82} 31 3-8-8 52 ..... FrannyNorton 3 55
(J R Jenkins) *hld up in last trio off str pce: pushed along over 2f out: clsd over 1f out: styd on to ld last 75yds* **7/1**

3435 2 ¾ **Princess Cammie (IRE)**^{10} 1041 3-8-9 53 ..... KieranO'Neill 5 54
(Mike Murphy) *chsd ldng pair: rdn 2f out: clsd to chal and upsides 100yds out: jst outpcd* **16/1**

0243 3 ½ **Desert Donkey**^{22} 879 3-9-0 63 ..... ThomasBrown$^{(5)}$ 4 62
(Andrew Balding) *pressed ldr at str pce: rdn to ld jst over 1f out: hdd and no ex last 75yds* **7/2^{2}**

056- 4 shd **Idle Curiosity (IRE)**^{160} 7161 3-8-2 51 oh1 ..... NathanAlison$^{(5)}$ 6 50
(Jim Boyle) *t.k.h: racd wd: hld up in last trio: forfeited grnd whn hanging rt bnd 2f out: styd on again fnl f: gaining at fin* **14/1**

-401 5 1 ¼ **Buy Art**^{2} 1157 3-9-10 68 6ex .....(p) RyanMoore 1 63
(Gary Moore) *led at str pce but pressed: styd against rail in st: hdd and hanging jst over 1f out: wknd last 100yds* **4/5^{1}**

500- 6 10 **Mysterious Wonder**^{201} 5963 3-9-6 64 ..... LiamKeniry 2 29
(Noel Quinlan) *hld up in last trio: rdn over 2f out: sn wknd and bhd* **6/1^{3}**

1m 13.05s (1.15) **Going Correction** +0.075s/f (Slow) — 6 Ran SP% **117.1**
Speed ratings (Par 96): **95,94,93,93,91 78**
CSF £99.24 TOTE £7.10: £2.30, £3.20; EX 44.70 Trifecta £144.70 Pool: £1,743.98 - 9.03 winning units..
Owner Two Little Indians **Bred** D R Tucker **Trained** Royston, Herts

FOCUS
A moderate sprint handicap in which the lead was disputed. The form is weak.

1181 FUEL COMMUNICATIONS H'CAP — 1m (P)
4:20 (4:22) (Class 5) (0-75,75) 4-Y-0+ — £2,726 (£805; £402) Stalls High

Form / RPR

-002 1 **Brocklebank (IRE)**^{13} 984 4-9-7 75 ..... JimCrowley 8 80
(Simon Dow) *t.k.h early: trckd ldrs: shkn up over 1f out: styd on wl fnl f to ld last 50yds* **6/1^{3}**

-103 2 hd **Avertis**^{38} 689 8-9-5 73 ..... GeorgeBaker 4 78
(Alastair Lidderdale) *broke best: led but only at stdy pce and hdd over 6f out: shkn up whn ldr booted on wl over 1f out: clsd to chal last 75yds: jst outpcd* **8/1**

434- 3 nk **Xinbama (IRE)**^{152} 7358 4-9-6 74 ..... SebSanders 3 78
(J W Hills) *hld up in last: plenty to do whn shkn up over 1f out: styd on strly fnl f: too much to do* **9/2^{2}**

0-00 4 ¾ **Dutch Old Master**^{6} 1092 4-9-7 75 .....(v^{1}) RyanMoore 2 77
(Gary Moore) *t.k.h early: led over 6f out: wound it up fr 3f out: drvn more than 2 l clr over 1f out: styd agains rail and wilted fnl f: swamped last 50yds* **5/4^{1}**

6113 5 ½ **Mafi (IRE)**^{13} 984 5-8-8 67 .....(t) ThomasBrown$^{(5)}$ 1 68
(Mark Hoad) *hld up in rr: pushed along on inner fr 2f out: kpt on but nvr gng pce to rch chalng position* **10/1**

00-6 6 3 **King Vahe (IRE)**^{29} 791 4-8-8 69 ..... DavidParkes$^{(7)}$ 5 63
(Alan Jarvis) *hld up in last pair: rdn on outer over 2f out: no prog over 1f out: wknd* **25/1**

211 7 1 ¼ **Lily Edge**^{20} 899 4-9-3 71 ..... KieranO'Neill 6 62
(John Bridger) *racd wd: prog to chse ldr over 5f out: rdn wl over 2f out: wknd over 1f out* **7/1**

1m 38.98s (0.78) **Going Correction** +0.075s/f (Slow) — 7 Ran SP% **113.5**
Speed ratings (Par 103): **99,98,98,97,97 94,93**
Tote Swingers: 1&2 £5.70, 2&3 £3.10 CSF £50.67 CT £234.88 TOTE £8.20: £2.70, £4.40; EX 48.50 Trifecta £144.30 Pool: £3,023.15 - 15.70 winning units..
Owner J C G Chua **Bred** Vincent Reen **Trained** Epsom, Surrey

FOCUS
A fair handicap and straightforward form.

1182 ORPHEUS CENTRE H'CAP — 1m 5f (P)
4:50 (4:50) (Class 4) (0-80,80) 4-Y-0+ — £4,690 (£1,395; £697; £348) Stalls Low

Form / RPR

3-44 1 **Ascendant**^{26} 830 7-9-7 80 .....(v^{1}) RyanMoore 2 87+
(J R Jenkins) *trckd ldng pair: effrt to ld 1f out: sn edgd rt to centre of crse: hrd rdn and jst hld on nr fin* **9/2^{2}**

2111 2 shd **Wordiness**^{10} 1031 5-9-2 80 ..... RobertTart$^{(5)}$ 1 87+
(Brendan Powell) *hld up in last: prog between rivals over 1f out: rdn to chal fnl f: styd on nr fin: jst failed* **4/5^{1}**

500- 3 3 **Mohanad (IRE)**^{227} 5106 7-9-2 75 ..... TomEaves 4 77
(Philip Hide) *led at stdy pce: tried to kick on 2f out: hdd and outpcd 1f out* **20/1**

4311 4 2 **Admirable Duque (IRE)**^{4} 1117 7-8-9 75 6ex .....(be) JoshBaudains$^{(7)}$ 3 74
(Dominic Ffrench Davis) *hld up in 4th: effrt on outer over 2f out: nt qckn over 1f out: sn btn* **5/1^{3}**

4-13 5 1 ½ **Norfolk Sky**^{31} 779 4-8-10 72 ..... JimCrowley 5 69
(Laura Mongan) *trckd ldr: rdn wl over 1f out: sn lost pl and wknd* **6/1**

2m 50.4s (4.40) **Going Correction** +0.075s/f (Slow)
WFA 4 from 5yo+ 3lb — 5 Ran SP% **109.5**
Speed ratings (Par 105): **89,88,87,85,84**
CSF £8.55 TOTE £6.20: £3.50, £1.02; EX 7.60 Trifecta £64.90 Pool: £1,893.70 - 21.87 winning units..
Owner A S Reid **Bred** Cheveley Park Stud Ltd **Trained** Royston, Herts

FOCUS
They went a modest pace, yet the front two, who travelled equally well into the straight, drew clear and Ryan Moore just made the difference. The form is likely to have limited relevance elsewhere.

1183 AURORA FIREWORKS H'CAP — 1m 2f (P)
5:20 (5:20) (Class 6) (0-55,55) 4-Y-0+ — £2,045 (£603; £302) Stalls Low

Form / RPR

0006 1 **Salient**^{20} 907 9-8-12 46 oh1 ..... SebSanders 9 55
(Michael Attwater) *pressed ldr: drew clr w him 3f out: drvn to ld 1f out: kpt on wl* **8/1^{3}**

1134 2 1 ¼ **Young Jackie**^{20} 907 5-8-12 53 .....(v^{1}) JordanVaughan$^{(7)}$ 11 60
(George Margarson) *w.w towards rr: plenty to do whn effrt 2f out: styd on to take 2nd ins fnl f: unable to chal* **9/4^{1}**

0300 3 nk **Dolly Colman (IRE)**^{6} 1090 5-8-12 46 oh1 ..... ChrisCatlin 7 52
(Zoe Davison) *hld up in last trio: prog on wd outside over 2f out to chse ldrs over 1f out: kpt on to take 3rd and press runner-up nr fin* **25/1**

0-00 4 1 ¼ **Archelao (IRE)**^{51} 508 5-9-5 53 .....(t) AmirQuinn 3 57
(Richard Rowe) *led at stdy pce: drew clr w wnr fr 3f out: brought wd in st: hdd 1f out: fdd last 100yds* **8/1^{3}**

-400 5 3 **Roman Senate (IRE)**^{13} 983 4-9-2 50 .....(tp) SteveDrowne 10 48
(Martin Bosley) *hld up in midfield: prog to chse clr ldng pair wl over 2f out to over 1f out: fdd* **10/1**

4556 6 ½ **Hollywood All Star (IRE)**^{13} 983 4-9-0 48 ..... MartinDwyer 5 45
(William Muir) *a in midfield: nt qckn over 2f out: one pce and no imp on ldrs over 1f out* **5/1^{2}**

-353 7 3 **Frosty Friday**^{42} 619 5-9-7 55 .....(p) FrannyNorton 1 46
(J R Jenkins) *hld up in last trio: pushed along 3f out: sn lft bhd and btn* **12/1**

0-00 8 1 ½ **Yalding Dancer**^{29} 794 4-8-7 46 ..... RobertTart$^{(5)}$ 12 34
(John Best) *dwlt: t.k.h early: hld up in last trio: rdn over 3f out: sn struggling* **20/1**

500- 9 3 ¼ **Capriska**^{195} 6152 4-9-2 50 ..... TonyCulhane 2 32
(Willie Musson) *wl in tch: lost pl and rdn 3f out: sn btn* **5/1^{2}**

4506 10 2 ¼ **Fairy Mist (IRE)**^{2} 1162 6-8-12 46 ..... KieranO'Neill 4 24
(John Bridger) *t.k.h early: chsd ldng pair to wl over 2f out: wknd* **10/1**

2m 7.07s (0.47) **Going Correction** +0.075s/f (Slow) — 10 Ran SP% **120.8**
Speed ratings (Par 101): **101,100,99,98,96 95,93,92,89,87**
Tote Swingers: 1&2 £5.00, 1&3 £20.50, 2&3 £14.80 CSF £27.33 CT £450.40 TOTE £11.20: £3.00, £1.10, £7.30; EX 24.30 Trifecta £572.90 Pool: £1,679.08 - 2.19 winning units..
Owner Canisbay Bloodstock **Bred** Hesmonds Stud Ltd **Trained** Epsom, Surrey

FOCUS
The pace was steady with the time slower than the earlier races at this distance. The third sets the level.
T/Plt: £530.70 to a £1 stake. Pool: £72,031.77 - 99.07 winning tickets. T/Qpdt: £108.50 to a £1 stake. Pool: £4,809.53 - 32.80 winning tickets. JN

1145 SOUTHWELL (L-H)
Tuesday, March 26

OFFICIAL GOING: Standard
Wind: Fresh half against Weather: Cloudy with sunny periods

1184 £32 BONUS AT 32RED.COM H'CAP — 1m (F)
2:30 (2:30) (Class 6) (0-65,65) 4-Y-0+ — £2,045 (£603; £302) Stalls Low

Form / RPR

-462 1 **Royal Holiday (IRE)**^{7} 1076 6-9-6 64 .....(p) DanielTudhope 3 73
(Marjorie Fife) *mde most: rdn over 2f out: drvn and styd on wl fnl f* **6/4^{1}**

-442 2 1 ¾ **Bold Marc (IRE)**^{14} 967 11-9-0 61 ..... MichaelMetcalfe$^{(3)}$ 1 66
(Mrs K Burke) *cl up on inner: disp ld 1/2-way: rdn over 2f out: edgd lft and ev ch over 1f out: drvn and one pce ins fnl f* **9/1^{3}**

The Form Book Flat, Raceform Ltd, Compton, RG20 6NL.

3462 **3** 4 **Thereabouts (USA)**[13] 987 4-9-5 **63**....(v) LukeMorris 8 59
(Michael Appleby) *trckd ldrs: hdwy and cl up 1/2-way: chal 3f out: sn rdn and ev ch tl drvn and one pce fr over 1f out* **7/4**[2]

644- **4** 3 ½ **Keep It Dark**[131] 7729 4-9-0 **65** ow1.... DavidSimmonson(7) 6 53
(Tony Coyle) *in tch: hdwy over 3f out: rdn to chse ldrs over 2f out: sn drvn and no imp* **14/1**

-000 **5** 5 **On The Cusp (IRE)**[22] 883 6-8-12 **56**....(p) MartinHarley 4 32
(Violet M Jordan) *chsd ldrs on inner: rdn along over 3f out: sn outpcd* **16/1**

00-4 **6** 1 ½ **Imtithal (IRE)**[11] 1015 4-9-2 **65**.... MichaelJMMurphy(5) 9 38
(John Weymes) *chsd ldrs on wd outside: rdn along 3f out: sn wknd* **14/1**

541- **7** 2 ¼ **Handsome King**[286] 3051 6-9-4 **62**....(p) FrederikTylicki 7 30
(J R Jenkins) *s.i.s and a bhd* **12/1**

4- **8** 29 **Dolly Diva**[197] 6106 4-9-2 **60**.... RussKennemore 5
(Paul Midgley) *chsd ldrs: rdn along bef 1/2-way: sn lost pl and bhd fnl 3f* **20/1**

1m 41.83s (-1.87) **Going Correction** -0.10s/f (Stan) 8 Ran SP% **118.0**
Speed ratings (Par 101): **105,103,99,95,90 89,87,58**
Tote Swingers: 1&2 £2.80, 1&3 £1.40, 2&3 £3.10 CSF £16.87 CT £26.27 TOTE £1.90: £1.10, £2.10, £1.10; EX 11.40 Trifecta £30.00 Pool: £2,887.58 - 72.13 winning units..
Owner Mrs Marion Turner **Bred** E Tynan **Trained** Stillington, N Yorks

FOCUS
A modest handicap and the front pair held those positions throughout. The form is straightforward.

1185 32RED MAIDEN STKS — 1m (F)
3:00 (3:01) (Class 5) 3-Y-O — **£2,726** (£805; £402) **Stalls** Low

Form RPR

05- **1** **Corn Snow (USA)**[230] 4938 3-9-5 0.... JoeFanning 3 74+
(Mark Johnston) *dwlt: sn trcking ldr: hdwy to ld wl over 2f out: rdn and carried hd high wl over 1f out: sn clr: rdn out* **9/4**[2]

306 **2** 7 **Una Bella Cosa**[25] 845 3-9-0 52....(v) MartinHarley 4 53
(Alan McCabe) *led: rdn along 3f out: hdd wl over 2f out: drvn and one pce fr wl over 1f out* **16/1**

4 **3** 3 ¾ **Helmsley Flyer (IRE)**[10] 1044 3-9-5 0.... DanielTudhope 2 49
(David O'Meara) *chsd ldng pair: rdn along wl over 2f out: sn one pce* **3/1**[3]

0-3 **4** 2 **India's Song**[38] 685 3-9-0 0.... MartinLane 1 40
(David Simcock) *trckd ldrs: pushed along over 3f out: rdn wl over 2f out: sn drvn and one pce* **1/1**[1]

5 2 **Zaitsev (IRE)** 3-9-5 0.... ShaneKelly 5 40
(Ollie Pears) *dwlt: pushed along and green in rr: rdn over 2f out: sn no imp* **7/1**

1m 42.69s (-1.01) **Going Correction** -0.10s/f (Stan) 5 Ran SP% **124.2**
Speed ratings (Par 98): **101,94,90,88,86**
CSF £33.52 TOTE £2.90: £1.50, £5.40; EX 26.10 Trifecta £65.70 Pool: £2,431.99 - 27.74 winning units..
Owner Sheikh Hamdan Bin Mohammed Al Maktoum **Bred** Darley **Trained** Middleham Moor, N Yorks

FOCUS
A weak maiden, especially with the favourite underperforming. The runner-up is the key to the form.

1186 32REDBINGO.COM H'CAP — 5f (F)
3:30 (3:30) (Class 6) (0-60,62) 4-Y-O+ — **£2,045** (£603; £302) **Stalls** High

Form RPR

0301 **1** **Fairy Wing (IRE)**[3] 1147 6-9-9 **62** 6ex.... MartinHarley 5 72
(Violet M Jordan) *cl up: chal over 1f out: rdn to ld ins fnl f: kpt on strly towards fin* **5/1**[3]

0565 **2** 1 ¾ **Rambo Will**[20] 898 5-9-7 **60**.... FrederikTylicki 6 64
(J R Jenkins) *led: rdn along 2f out: drvn over 1f out: hdd ins fnl f: kpt on same pce* **9/4**[1]

3203 **3** nse **Steel City Boy (IRE)**[14] 968 10-8-10 **54**.... AnnStokell(5) 4 58
(Ann Stokell) *prom: rdn along wl over 1f out: kpt on u.p fnl f* **20/1**

0022 **4** hd **Thorpe Bay**[3] 1147 4-8-10 **52**.... DarrenEgan(3) 7 57
(Michael Appleby) *dwlt: sn chsng ldrs: hdwy 2f out: rdn and ev ch ent fnl f: sn drvn and one pce* **11/4**[2]

0154 **5** nse **Chateau Lola**[7] 1077 4-8-13 **52**....(v) JoeFanning 1 55
(Derek Shaw) *dwlt: hdwy on wd outside 1/2-way: rdn to chse ldrs over 1f out: ev ch ins fnl f: sn drvn and one pce* **12/1**

0-05 **6** 2 ½ **Lesley's Choice**[60] 379 7-9-7 **60**....(b) GrahamLee 8 54
(Sean Curran) *chsd ldrs: pushed along 2f out: sn rdn and wknd appr fnl f* **6/1**

1000 **7** 11 **Marshall Art**[14] 976 4-9-0 **60**.... RobJFitzpatrick(7) 9 19
(David Evans) *dwlt: sn prom: rdn along 1/2-way and sn wknd* **20/1**

-225 **8** ½ **Spic 'n Span**[5] 1101 8-9-7 **60**....(b) LukeMorris 10 20
(Ronald Harris) *racd nr stands' rail: chsd ldrs: rdn over 2f out: sn wknd* **7/1**

1m 1.6s (1.90) **Going Correction** +0.425s/f (Slow) 8 Ran SP% **118.1**
Speed ratings (Par 101): **101,98,98,97,97 93,76,75**
Tote Swingers: 1&2 £2.70, 1&3 £9.70, 2&3 £11.80 CSF £17.31 CT £202.98 TOTE £6.00: £1.90, £1.70, £3.30; EX 17.60 Trifecta £217.00 Pool: £3,507.07 - 12.11 winning units..
Owner Rakebackmypoker.com **Bred** H Fitzpatrick **Trained** Moreton Morrell, Warwicks

FOCUS
A moderate sprint handicap in which the trio berthed closest to the stands' rail filled the last three places. The third is the best guide to the level.

1187 32RED CASINO MEDIAN AUCTION MAIDEN STKS — 1m 4f (F)
4:00 (4:00) (Class 5) 3-5-Y-O — **£2,726** (£805; £402) **Stalls** Low

Form RPR

0- **1** **Glenreef**[160] 7161 3-8-0 0.... JoeFanning 4 69+
(Mark Johnston) *trckd ldr: hdwy to ld 3f out: rdn clr wl over 1f out: kpt on* **7/1**[3]

00- **2** 3 ½ **Relentless (IRE)**[153] 7332 3-8-5 0.... NickyMackay 6 68+
(John Gosden) *carried hd high: trckd ldng pair: hdwy to chse wnr wl over 2f out: effrt and hung bdly lft 1 1/2f out and sn rdn: drvn and no imp fnl f* **4/7**[1]

4 **3** 6 **Sian Gwalia**[18] 925 3-8-0 0.... MartinLane 7 55
(David Simcock) *in tch: hdwy 1/2-way: rdn along 4f out: drvn to chse ldng pair over 2f out: plugged on same pce* **11/4**[2]

56 **4** 24 **Bit Windy**[10] 1035 4-9-6 0.... KirstyMilczarek 2 18
(Chris Dwyer) *led: rdn along 4f out: hdd 3f out: sn wknd* **25/1**

5 8 **Big Thing Coming** 5-9-10 0.... MarkCoumbe(3) 1 11
(Patrick Gilligan) *a bhd: t.o fr 1/2-way* **50/1**

0 **6** 1 ½ **Galway Gem (IRE)**[8] 1069 5-9-8 0.... PJMcDonald 3
(John Mackie) *a in rr: rdn along 1/2-way: sn outpcd and bhd* **20/1**

0-0 **7** 10 **Running On Faith**[19] 911 5-9-13 0.... KellyHarrison 5
(Garry Woodward) *chsd ldrs: rdn along over 4f out: sn outpcd and bhd* **100/1**

2m 41.01s (0.01) **Going Correction** -0.10s/f (Stan)
WFA 3 from 4yo 22lb 4 from 5yo 2lb 7 Ran SP% **114.4**
Speed ratings (Par 103): **95,92,88,72,67 66,59**
Tote Swingers: 1&2 £1.40, 1&3 £1.90, 2&3 £1.10 CSF £11.61 TOTE £8.40: £2.20, £1.40; EX 15.90 Trifecta £22.80 Pool: £3,501.11 - 114.74 winning units..
Owner Wadacre Stud **Bred** Millsec Limited **Trained** Middleham Moor, N Yorks

FOCUS
A weak maiden, dominated by the three market leaders. The winner looked improved for her new yard but the level is fluid and not form to be confident about.

1188 ROSE STOCKLEY 80TH BIRTHDAY CELEBRATION H'CAP — 1m 6f (F)
4:30 (4:30) (Class 4) (0-85,85) 4-Y-O+ — **£4,690** (£1,395; £697; £348) **Stalls** Low

Form RPR

51-4 **1** **Lexington Bay (IRE)**[18] 926 5-9-6 **79**....(p) TonyHamilton 5 86
(Richard Fahey) *trckd ldrs: pushed along and sltly outpcd 3f out: swtchd rt to outer and rdn wl over 1f out: carried hd high and drvn to chal ent fnl f: styd on wl to ld last 50yds* **11/4**[2]

36-2 **2** nk **Northside Prince (IRE)**[26] 830 7-9-12 **85**.... RobertWinston 1 92
(Alan Swinbank) *hld up: hdwy 4f out: chsd ldng pair over 2f out and sn chal: rdn to take slt ld over 1f out: drvn ins fnl f: hdd and no ex last 50yds* **3/1**[3]

-211 **3** 1 **Jacobs Son**[14] 969 5-9-3 **76**.... GrahamLee 4 81
(Robert Mills) *led 3f: cl up on inner: pushed along 5f out: rdn along over 5f out: rallied u.p and ev ch fr over 1f out tl no ex wl ins fnl f* **5/4**[1]

0-64 **4** nk **Phoenix Flight (IRE)**[40] 654 8-9-1 **79**.... RyanTate(5) 6 84
(James Evans) *prom on outer: hdwy to take slt ld after 3f: rdn over 2f out: drvn and hdd over 1f out: ev ch tl one pce ins fnl f* **7/1**

55-6 **5** 28 **Light The City (IRE)**[19] 914 6-8-7 **66** oh1.... JamesSullivan 2 32
(Ruth Carr) *trckd ldrs: rdn along 4f out: outpcd fr over 2f out* **33/1**

3m 8.89s (0.59) **Going Correction** -0.10s/f (Stan)
WFA 4 from 5yo+ 4lb 5 Ran SP% **111.6**
Speed ratings (Par 105): **94,93,93,93,77**
CSF £11.43 TOTE £2.90: £1.70, £1.60; EX 8.60 Trifecta £12.20 Pool: £2,087.47 - 128.09 winning units..
Owner Keith Denham & Tony Denham **Bred** Mrs Vanessa Hutch **Trained** Musley Bank, N Yorks

FOCUS
A fair handicap and a test of stamina, but four of the five runners were in a line across the track passing the furlong pole. The form looks straightforward.

1189 32REDPOKER.COM H'CAP — 2m (F)
5:00 (5:00) (Class 6) (0-65,65) 4-Y-O+ — **£2,045** (£603; £302) **Stalls** Low

Form RPR

/550 **1** **Calculating (IRE)**[7] 1080 9-8-13 **52**.... NeilCallan 6 61
(Mark Usher) *trckd ldrs: hdwy 4f out: chsd ldr 3f out: rdn to ld over 1f out: drvn ins fnl f and kpt on strly* **20/1**

40-1 **2** 1 ¾ **Neighbourhood (USA)**[14] 970 5-8-10 **54**....(b) RyanTate(5) 2 61
(James Evans) *hld up: smooth hdwy to trck ldrs over 4f out: effrt 2f out: sn rdn: styd on fnl f to take 2nd nr fin* **6/1**

1232 **3** ¾ **Scribe (IRE)**[21] 887 5-9-6 **59**....(t) LukeMorris 3 65
(David Evans) *hld up: pushed along 1/2-way: hdwy to trck ldrs 4f out: rdn to chse ldng pair over 2f out: sn ev ch tl drvn and one pce ins fnl f* **4/1**[2]

4502 **4** 1 ½ **Perfect Shot (IRE)**[7] 1080 7-8-7 **49**.... MarkCoumbe(3) 7 53
(Frank Sheridan) *prom: hdwy to ld over 4f out: rdn along over 2f out: drvn and hdd over 1f out: one pce fnl f* **8/1**

-224 **5** 3 ½ **Neil's Pride**[14] 973 4-8-9 **53**.... TonyHamilton 8 53
(Richard Fahey) *sn led: pushed along and hdd over 4f out: rdn along 3f out: drvn and wknd wl over 1f out* **5/1**

60/3 **6** 6 **Cecily Parsley**[12] 635 7-9-2 **55**....(bt[1]) RobertHavlin 5 48
(Hughie Morrison) *prom on inner: pushed along over 6f out: rdn 5f out and sn wknd* **9/2**[3]

00-4 **7** ½ **Father Shine (IRE)**[30] 1 10-8-6 **50**.... MichaelJMMurphy(5) 9 42
(Shaun Harris) *prom: rdn along on outer over 4f out: sn wknd* **25/1**

23-1 **8** 18 **Lakota Ghost (USA)**[37] 539 5-9-12 **65**....(t) JohnFahy 1 36
(Seamus Durack) *a towards rr* **11/4**[1]

0/0- **9** 8 **Strangelittlegirl**[180] 6615 5-8-7 **46** oh1.... JamieMackay 4
(Patrick Gilligan) *t.k.h and sltly hmpd s: sn swtchd to outer and hdwy to chse ldrs: pushed along 1/2-way: rdn 6f out and sn wknd* **80/1**

3m 42.08s (-3.42) **Going Correction** -0.10s/f (Stan)
WFA 4 from 5yo+ 5lb 9 Ran SP% **116.8**
Speed ratings (Par 101): **104,103,102,102,100 97,97,88,84**
Tote Swingers: 1&2 £20.20, 1&3 £7.10, 2&3 £5.50 CSF £134.39 CT £588.65 TOTE £23.30: £3.70, £2.30, £1.60; EX 186.80 Trifecta £605.50 Pool: £2,357.30 - 2.91 winning units..
Owner Brian Rogan **Bred** Darley **Trained** Upper Lambourn, Berks
■ Stewards' Enquiry : Mark Coumbe two-day ban: use of whip (9-10 Apr)

FOCUS
Another test of stamina, but a modest contest and they didn't go much of a pace. The form is straightforward with the third the guide.

1190 32RED.COM H'CAP — 7f (F)
5:30 (5:31) (Class 5) (0-70,66) 3-Y-O — **£2,587** (£770; £384; £192) **Stalls** Low

Form RPR

0462 **1** **Ivy Port**[7] 1071 3-8-5 **50**.... LukeMorris 4 63
(Michael Appleby) *led 2f: cl up: led again over 2f out: rdn clr over 1f out: kpt on wl* **5/1**[3]

3252 **2** 5 **Gebayl**[13] 990 3-9-3 **62**....(b[1]) NeilCallan 5 62
(James Tate) *t.k.h: cl up: rdn along and ev ch 2f out: drvn and kpt on same pce appr fnl f* **8/1**

0-22 **3** ½ **Moe's Place (IRE)**[14] 964 3-9-6 **65**.... PhillipMakin 3 64
(Kevin Ryan) *dwlt: sn chsng ldrs: hdwy on outer wl over 2f out: sn rdn and kpt on same pce appr fnl f* **5/4**[1]

450- **4** 1 ¼ **Hit The Lights (IRE)**[194] 6177 3-9-7 **66**.... ShaneKelly 6 61
(Ollie Pears) *t.k.h: cl up on outer: led after 2f: rdn along and hdd over 2f out: wknd over 1f out* **6/1**

00-2 **5** 5 **Suspension**[35] 717 3-8-11 **56**.... RobertHavlin 2 38
(Hughie Morrison) *trckd ldrs on inner: pushed along over 3f out: rdn wl over 2f out: sn btn* **7/2**[2]

560- **6** 22 **Gold Roll (IRE)**[129] 7779 3-9-6 **65**.... PJMcDonald 1
(Ruth Carr) *dwlt: a in rr: bhd fr over 2f out* **25/1**

1m 29.7s (-0.60) **Going Correction** -0.10s/f (Stan) 6 Ran SP% **112.6**
Speed ratings (Par 98): **99,93,92,91,85 60**
Tote Swingers: 1&2 £3.10, 2&3 £2.00 CSF £42.01 TOTE £4.40: £2.00, £2.00; EX 23.10 Trifecta £63.80 Pool: £2,201.01 - 25.84 winning units..
Owner Goldform Racing **Bred** John Branson **Trained** Danethorpe, Notts

FOCUS
A modest 3-y-o handicap with the winner going the right way and the form behind her making sense.
T/Plt: £101.30 to a £1 stake. Pool: £79,497.84 - 572.47 winning tickets. T/Qpdt: £26.10 to a £1 stake. Pool: £6,706.48 - 189.51 winning tickets. JR

1191 - 1192a (Foreign Racing) - See Raceform Interactive

1177 LINGFIELD (L-H)

Wednesday, March 27

OFFICIAL GOING: Standard
Wind: Moderate, half against Weather: Fine but cloudy, cold

1193 H & V SERVICEPLAN H'CAP (DIV I) 7f (P)
1:30 (1:30) (Class 6) (0-60,60) 4-Y-O+ **£2,045** (£603; £302) **Stalls** Low

Form RPR
0305 **1** **Mary's Pet**[7] 1087 6-8-11 **50** .... KierenFox 5 60
(Lee Carter) *mde all: clr fr 3f out: drvn over 1f out: hld on wl* **16/1**
2212 **2** *1* **Athletic**[6] 1100 4-9-4 **57** ....(v) EddieAhern 6 64
(J R Jenkins) *hld up in 7th: prog on outer to chse wnr over 2f out and edgd lft: sn clr of rest: asked to cl over 1f out: hanging and fnd little u.str.p: nvr chal* **4/5**[1]
0062 **3** *1 ¼* **Tenbridge**[8] 1079 4-8-13 **52**........(b) WilliamCarson 8 56+
(Derek Haydn Jones) *dwlt: hld up in last pair: rdn and prog 2f out: tk modest 3rd 1f out: styd on wl: nrst fin* **6/1**[3]
3426 **4** *3 ¾* **Media Jury**[20] 917 6-8-11 **50**........(p) PaddyAspell 9 44
(John Wainwright) *cl up: outpcd fr 3f out: chsd clr ldng pair 2f out to 1f out: n.d* **14/1**
26-0 **5** *1 ½* **Royal Acclamation (IRE)**[77] 117 8-8-9 **48**........(p) ChrisCatlin 3 39
(Michael Scudamore) *hld up in last pair: no ch whn prog over 1f out: kpt on fnl f* **33/1**
66/3 **6** *1* **Lhotse Sherpa**[14] 979 4-9-1 **54**........ RussKennemore 7 42
(John Holt) *chsd wnr to over 2f out: bmpd sn after: no ch over 1f out* **14/1**
5 **7** *2 ¼* **Reiterate**[15] 972 4-9-7 **60**........ RichardKingscote 2 42
(Milton Bradley) *trckd ldrs: outpcd fr 3f out: lost pl 2f out: wl btn after* **25/1**
5505 **8** *½* **Back For Tea (IRE)**[4] 1150 5-8-3 **47** oh1 ow1........(b) RachealKneller(5) 4 28
(Phil McEntee) *chsd ldrs: outpcd whn sltly impeded over 2f out: no ch after* **66/1**
060- **9** *16* **Intomist (IRE)**[155] 7317 4-9-6 **59**........(p) WilliamBuick 1 47+
(Jim Boyle) *prom on inner: outpcd 3f out: disputing 3rd whn bdly hmpd over 2f out: eased and t.o* **9/2**[2]

1m 25.27s (0.47) **Going Correction** +0.225s/f (Slow) **9** Ran SP% **115.5**
Speed ratings (Par 101): **106,104,103,99,97 96,93,93,74**
Tote Swingers: 1&2 £4.60, 1&3 £7.70, 2&3 £1.90 CSF £29.18 CT £95.15 TOTE £15.90: £3.10, £1.10, £1.70; EX 39.10 Trifecta £137.20 Pool: £2,204.39 - 12.04 winning units..
Owner P A Allard **Bred** Green Pastures Farm **Trained** Epsom, Surrey

FOCUS
A moderate handicap run at a fair pace, with the winner making all. The form is straightforward and backed up by the time.

1194 H & V SERVICEPLAN H'CAP (DIV II) 7f (P)
2:00 (2:00) (Class 6) (0-60,60) 4-Y-O+ **£2,045** (£603; £302) **Stalls** Low

Form RPR
2055 **1** **Teen Ager (FR)**[10] 1056 9-8-12 **51**........(p) JimmyQuinn 5 61
(Paul Burgoyne) *hld up towards rr: prog over 2f out: produced to ld over 1f out gng strly: rdn and kpt on wl* **7/1**[3]
5266 **2** *1 ½* **Do More Business (IRE)**[7] 1087 6-8-6 **50**........(bt) PhilipPrince(5) 6 56
(Liam Corcoran) *t.k.h: pressed ldr: led briefly over 1f out: chsd wnr after: kpt on but a hld* **7/1**[3]
053 **3** *1 ½* **Purley Queen (IRE)**[12] 1013 4-8-10 **56**........ JoshBaudains(7) 7 58
(Sylvester Kirk) *dwlt: wl in rr: rdn on wd outside over 2f out and sme prog: nt qckn over 1f out but kpt on to take 3rd last 100yds* **5/1**[2]
41-5 **4** *½* **Patavium Prince (IRE)**[40] 665 10-9-7 **60**........ IanMongan 1 63
(Jo Crowley) *hld up in rr: trying to make prog on inner whn nt clr run over 1f out: no ch after: kpt on* **2/1**[1]
4066 **5** *1 ¼* **Spinning Ridge (IRE)**[11] 1039 8-9-1 **57**........(b) DarrenEgan(3) 8 55
(Ronald Harris) *tk fierce hold early: hld up: trckd ldrs 1/2-way: produced to chal over 1f out: emptied qckly fnl f* **8/1**
2300 **6** *1 ¼* **Cuthbert (IRE)**[21] 903 6-8-0 **46**........(b) PaigeBolton(7) 3 41
(Michael Attwater) *t.k.h: trckd ldng pair: nt clr run briefly over 1f out: pushed along and wknd* **16/1**
3413 **7** *shd* **Blue Noodles**[11] 1043 7-9-0 **53**........(p) PaddyAspell 2 47
(John Wainwright) *mde most to over 1f out: styd on inner and wknd qckly* **8/1**
0/00 **8** *11* **Fists And Stones**[9] 1070 5-8-10 **49**........(bt[1]) EddieAhern 4 15
(Simon Hodgson) *dwlt: a in rr: struggling fr 3f out: sn wl bhd* **66/1**
2500 **9** *11* **Blue Deer (IRE)**[14] 978 5-9-7 **60**........ KierenFox 9
(Lee Carter) *nvr gng wl: rousted along in rr fr s: bhd over 2f out: t.o* **8/1**

1m 25.34s (0.54) **Going Correction** +0.225s/f (Slow) **9** Ran SP% **115.7**
Speed ratings (Par 101): **105,103,101,101,99 98,98,85,72**
Tote Swingers: 1&2 £9.70, 1&3 £5.70, 2&3 £6.30 CSF £55.17 CT £268.25 TOTE £5.90: £2.20, £2.50, £1.60; EX 59.60 Trifecta £366.60 Pool: £3,250.18 - 6.64 winning units..
Owner Mrs C Leigh-Turner **Bred** Haras De Beauvoir **Trained** Shepton Montague, Somerset

FOCUS
This was not a strong contest. The pace was fair with plenty keen but the form makes sense at this level.

1195 EUROPA QUALITY PRINT (S) STKS 6f (P)
2:30 (2:31) (Class 6) 3-Y-O+ **£2,045** (£603; £302) **Stalls** Low

Form RPR
1132 **1** **Homeboy (IRE)**[3] 1155 5-10-0 65........ EddieAhern 7 68+
(Marcus Tregoning) *t.k.h: trckd ldrs: wnt 2nd 1/2-way: chal 1f out: coaxed along hands and heels to ld last 50yds* **4/5**[1]
0220 **2** *½* **Waterloo Dock**[33] 750 8-9-9 57........(v) AndreaAtzeni 8 60
(Mick Quinn) *led: drvn over 1f out: hrd pressed fnl f: kpt on but hdd last 50yds* **8/1**[3]
-002 **3** *2 ½* **Athwaab**[9] 1065 6-9-4 57........ GrahamLee 1 47
(Noel Chance) *trckd ldrs on inner: lost pl 1/2-way and 6th 2f out: effrt over 1f out: kpt on to take 3rd: n.d* **12/1**
3006 **4** *½* **Molly Jones**[15] 968 4-9-4 48........(p) WilliamCarson 3 45
(Derek Haydn Jones) *hld up off the pce in 5th: t.k.h 1/2-way and cl enough: rdn over 2f out: fdd fnl f* **25/1**
0530 **5** *nk* **Kaylee**[7] 1087 4-8-11 48........ NedCurtis(7) 6 44
(Gary Moore) *hld up off the pce in 6th: prog on outer 1/2-way: drvn 2f out: wknd fnl f* **20/1**
-352 **6** *¾* **Silly Billy (IRE)**[12] 1021 5-9-2 55........(b[1]) RyanWhile(7) 5 47
(Bill Turner) *chsd ldr to 1/2-way: steadily wknd over 1f out* **3/1**[2]
1264 **7** *4 ½* **Athaakeel (IRE)**[20] 916 7-9-2 55........(b) GaryPhillips(7) 2 33
(Ronald Harris) *s.s: wl off the pce in last: gng wl enough 1/2-way: rdn and no prog over 2f out* **16/1**

1m 12.79s (0.89) **Going Correction** +0.225s/f (Slow) **7** Ran SP% **113.8**
Speed ratings (Par 101): **103,102,99,98,97 96,90**
Tote Swingers: 1&2 £2.40, 1&3 £2.70, 2&3 £3.40 CSF £8.20 TOTE £1.90: £1.10, £3.00; EX 7.70 Trifecta £33.00 Pool: £3,493/38 - 79.36 winning units..The winner was bought in for 6,000gns. Athwaab was claimed by Mr S. P. Hodgson for £6,000.
Owner Home Marketing Limited **Bred** J Costello **Trained** Whitsbury, Hants

FOCUS
This seller, run at a fair pace, looked more open than the betting suggested. The form is straightforward rated around those immediately behind the principals.

1196 RUDRIDGE LTD H'CAP 6f (P)
3:00 (3:00) (Class 6) (0-60,60) 4-Y-O+ **£2,045** (£603; £302) **Stalls** Low

Form RPR
-405 **1** **Sweet Ovation**[13] 998 4-8-13 **52**........ WilliamBuick 7 63+
(Mark Usher) *hld up in last pair and off the pce: stoked up on outer over 1f out: str run fnl f to ld last 50yds: pushed out* **9/2**[2]
0330 **2** *¾* **Pharoh Jake**[14] 981 5-9-4 **57**........ SeanLevey 2 63
(John Bridger) *trckd ldrs: rdn to chal over 1f out: led ins fnl f: styd on but hdd last 50yds* **10/1**
2315 **3** *1* **Johnny Splash (IRE)**[21] 902 4-9-2 **60**........(b) NathanAlison(5) 12 63
(Roger Teal) *t.k.h: pressed ldr: upsides fr over 2f out to jst ins fnl f: one pce after* **5/1**[3]
2412 **4** *hd* **Artful Lady (IRE)**[25] 863 4-9-4 **57**........ IanMongan 1 59
(George Margarson) *rousted along early but unable to ld on inner: chsd ldrs: rdn over 2f out: styd on fr over 1f out: nvr able to chal* **4/1**[1]
6-63 **5** *hd* **Catflap (IRE)**[9] 1058 4-9-5 **58**........(p) WilliamCarson 9 60
(Derek Haydn Jones) *trckd ldng pair: rdn to chal over 1f out: led briefly jst ins fnl f: one pce after* **7/1**
2550 **6** *¾* **Loyal Royal (IRE)**[6] 1101 10-9-4 **57**........(bt) RichardKingscote 5 57
(Milton Bradley) *hld up in midfield on outer: rdn over 2f out: nt qckn over 1f out: kpt on last 150yds: n.d* **7/1**
4553 **7** *nk* **Sherjawy (IRE)**[7] 1088 9-8-11 **50**........ KirstyMilczarek 10 49
(Zoe Davison) *a in midfield: rdn 2f out: kpt on same pce after and nvr able to chal* **12/1**
-500 **8** *1* **Demoiselle Bond**[9] 1063 5-9-3 **56**........ SteveDrowne 11 52
(Lydia Richards) *led at decent pce but pressed: hdd & wknd jst ins fnl f* **33/1**
40-6 **9** *nk* **Green Earth (IRE)**[28] 813 6-9-0 **58**........ JemmaMarshall(5) 6 53
(Pat Phelan) *hld up in last and off the pce: shoved along fnl 2f: kpt on but nvr remotely involved* **8/1**
440- **10** *½* **Marie's Fantasy**[308] 2388 4-9-4 **57**........ LiamKeniry 4 50
(Zoe Davison) *hld up towards rr: shkn up 2f out: no prog and nvr involved* **25/1**

1m 12.71s (0.81) **Going Correction** +0.225s/f (Slow) **10** Ran SP% **114.5**
Speed ratings (Par 101): **103,102,100,100,100 99,98,97,97,96**
Tote Swingers: 1&2 £9.10, 1&3 £4.10, 2&3 £9.30 CSF £47.96 CT £238.33 TOTE £4.40: £2.00, £3.90, £1.90; EX 41.50 Trifecta £257.00 Pool: £2,873.01 - 8.38 winning units..
Owner The Ridgeway Bloodstock Company Ltd **Bred** Ridgeway Bloodstock **Trained** Upper Lambourn, Berks

FOCUS
An open if moderate handicap, run at a sound pace. The form looks reasonable at this sort of level.

1197 H & V SERVICEPLAN MEDIAN AUCTION MAIDEN STKS 5f (P)
3:30 (3:30) (Class 6) 3-Y-O **£2,045** (£603; £302) **Stalls** High

Form RPR
33-2 **1** **You Da One (IRE)**[14] 979 3-9-5 80........ LiamKeniry 3 79
(Andrew Balding) *t.k.h: w ldr: led wl over 1f out: sn clr: eased last 150yds* **1/20**[1]
5- **2** *7* **Spymistress**[96] 8208 3-9-0 0........ IanMongan 1 48
(Zoe Davison) *outpcd after 2f: no ch after: kpt on to take remote 2nd nr fin* **16/1**[2]
40-3 **3** *1 ½* **Red Star Lady (IRE)**[14] 985 3-9-0 48........ DuranFentiman 2 41
(Shaun Harris) *led: drvn and hdd on inner wl over 1f out: wknd fnl f: lost 2nd nr fin* **33/1**[3]

1m 1.2s (2.40) **Going Correction** +0.225s/f (Slow) **3** Ran SP% **104.1**
Speed ratings (Par 96): **89,77,75**
CSF £1.42 TOTE £1.10; EX 1.90 Trifecta £1.90 Pool: £2,149.38 - 833.48 winning units..
Owner Mr & Mrs R Gorell/Mr & Mrs P Pausewang **Bred** James And Joe Brannigan **Trained** Kingsclere, Hants

FOCUS
A desperately uncompetitive maiden, and the bare form is not worth much.

1198 OYSTER PARTNERSHIP H'CAP 5f (P)
4:05 (4:05) (Class 5) (0-75,75) 4-Y-O+ **£2,726** (£805; £402) **Stalls** High

Form RPR
-241 **1** **Billy Red**[39] 687 9-9-4 **72**........(b) FergusSweeney 3 78
(J R Jenkins) *mde all: hrd pressed fr over 1f out: hld on wl* **5/1**
0-65 **2** *½* **Falasteen (IRE)**[9] 1058 6-9-0 **68**........ RichardKingscote 5 72
(Milton Bradley) *cl up: chsd wnr 4f out to 1/2-way: rdn and nt qckn over 1f out: styd on again ins fnl f: tk 2nd and clsd on wnr nr fin* **5/1**
-043 **3** *½* **Rylee Mooch**[20] 913 5-9-2 **75**........(e) JasonHart(5) 4 77
(Richard Guest) *cl up: trckd wnr 1/2-way: chal and upsides jst over 1f out: styd on inner and nt qckn fnl f* **5/2**[1]
3535 **4** *¾* **The Strig**[14] 981 6-9-4 **72**........(v) SeanLevey 2 73
(Stuart Williams) *hld up in last pair: shuffled along fr over 1f out: nt clr run briefly jst ins fnl f: kpt on but nvr threatened* **4/1**[2]
253/ **5** *hd* **Go Nani Go**[526] 6932 7-9-4 **72**........ LiamKeniry 1 71
(Ed de Giles) *hld up in last pair: clsd on ldrs over 1f out: nt qckn jst ins fnl f: fdd* **7/1**
1221 **6** *4* **Dorothy's Dancing (IRE)**[21] 902 5-8-9 **70** ow3........(p) NedCurtis(7) 6 55
(Gary Moore) *racd on outer: chsd wnr 1f: hung bdly rt bnd 2f out and lost all ch* **9/2**[3]

59.18s (0.38) **Going Correction** +0.225s/f (Slow) **6** Ran SP% **112.6**
Speed ratings (Par 103): **105,104,103,102,101 95**
Tote Swingers: 1&2 £5.60, 1&3 £3.70, 2&3 £3.40 CSF £29.48 TOTE £6.40: £3.10, £3.30; EX 23.90 Trifecta £173.50 Pool: £2,652.31 - 11.46 winning units..
Owner Mrs Irene Hampson **Bred** D R Tucker **Trained** Royston, Herts

FOCUS
A trappy sprint handicap, run at a fair pace.

1199 CHARTPLAN MAIDEN STKS 7f (P)
4:40 (4:40) (Class 5) 3-Y-O £2,726 (£805; £402) Stalls Low

Form RPR
332- **1** **Bright Strike (USA)**[186] 6486 3-9-5 84 WilliamBuick 2 77+
(John Gosden) *trckd ldr: led 1/2-way and racd keenly in front: pushed clr over 1f out: eased last 100yds* **1/8**[1]
2 2 1/4 **Severiano (USA)** 3-9-5 0 AndreaAtzeni 3 66+
(Roger Varian) *t.k.h: hld up in last pair: chsd wnr over 2f out: rn green whn pushed along over 1f out: styd on but no ch* **6/1**[2]
3 **3** 5 **Half Turn**[12] 1012 3-9-5 0 SteveDrowne 5 49
(Luke Dace) *t.k.h: hld up in last pair: outpcd fr 2f out: tk modest 3rd nr fin* **66/1**[3]
0 **4** 2 **One Dark Night**[53] 492 3-8-12 0 NedCurtis(7) 1 44
(Gary Moore) *led at sedate pce: hdd 1/2-way: styd on inner and wknd over 1f out* **100/1**

1m 30.51s (5.71) **Going Correction** +0.225s/f (Slow) **4** Ran SP% **105.7**
Speed ratings (Par 98): **76,73,67,65**
CSF £1.17 TOTE £1.10; EX 1.40 Trifecta £2.00 Pool: £2,038.40 - 749.41 winning units..
Owner George Strawbridge **Bred** George Strawbridge Jr **Trained** Newmarket, Suffolk

FOCUS
Another uncompetitive maiden, run at a steady pace.

1200 CRYSTAL PALACE H'CAP 1m 4f (P)
5:15 (5:15) (Class 5) (0-75,74) 4-Y-O+ £3,408 (£1,006; £503) Stalls Low

Form RPR
4-50 **1** **Thecornishcowboy**[11] 1031 4-9-5 **74** (t) GrahamLee 4 80
(John Ryan) *trckd ldng pair: gng easily 2f out: produced on outer of four ldrs to chal ins fnl f: drvn to ld narrowly last 50yds* **8/1**
1 **2** *hd* **Kent Ragstone (USA)**[33] 752 4-9-4 **73** ShaneKelly 2 79
(William Haggas) *trckd ldng pair: shkn up 2f out: rdn to ld narrowly jst ins fnl f: styd on but hdd last 50yds* **4/5**[1]
06-0 **3** *shd* **If I Were A Boy (IRE)**[21] 906 6-8-11 **64** (be1) EddieAhern 6 70
(Dominic Ffrench Davis) *hld up in last pair: gng easily 2f out: drvn between rivals to chal ins fnl f: nt qckn last strides* **14/1**
421- **4** 3/4 **Syncopate**[105] 8080 4-9-1 **70** FergusSweeney 1 74
(Pam Sly) *rrd twice s: hld up in last pair: gng easily 2f out: produced to chal on inner and upsides jst ins fnl f: nt qcknlast 100yds* **5/1**[3]
-236 **5** 2 **Where's Susie**[32] 779 8-9-3 **70** AndreaAtzeni 5 71
(Michael Madgwick) *trckd ldr: led after 3f: jnd and rdn wl over 2f out: hdd and fdd jst ins fnl f* **20/1**
4225 **6** 5 **Tingo In The Tale (IRE)**[18] 948 4-9-4 **73** WilliamBuick 3 67
(David Arbuthnot) *led at modest pce for 3f: trckd ldr: rdn to chal 3f out: wknd over 1f out* **4/1**[2]

2m 35.46s (2.46) **Going Correction** +0.225s/f (Slow)
WFA 4 from 6yo+ 2lb **6** Ran SP% **114.8**
Speed ratings (Par 103): **100,99,99,99,97 94**
Tote Swingers: 1&2 £2.50, 1&3 £2.40, 2&3 £3.20 CSF £15.51 TOTE £7.50: £2.50, £1.20; EX 20.90 Trifecta £109.90 Pool: £2,039.19 - 13.91 winning units..
Owner C Letcher & J Ryan **Bred** Hadi Al Tajir **Trained** Newmarket, Suffolk

FOCUS
This handicap was run at a messy pace, with three in a line passing the post.
T/Jkpt: £11,797.60 to a £1 stake. Pool £74,773.92. 4.50 winning tickets. T/Plt: £39.50 to a £1 stake. Pool £67,200.47. 1,239.01 winning tickets. T/Qpdt: £12.90 to a £1 stake. Pool: £4,481.01. 255.68 winning tickets. JN

1184 SOUTHWELL (L-H)
Wednesday, March 27

OFFICIAL GOING: Standard
Wind: Moderate, across Weather: Cloudy

1201 32RED.COM CLAIMING STKS 1m 4f (F)
2:10 (2:10) (Class 6) 4-Y-O+ £2,045 (£603; £302) Stalls Low

Form RPR
-466 **1** **Tornado Force (IRE)**[21] 906 5-9-3 71 HayleyTurner 5 77
(Chris Dwyer) *hld up: hdwy over 3f out: chsd ldr over 2f out: sn chal: led wl over 1f out: pushed clr ent fnl f: readily* **10/3**[2]
3112 **2** 2 1/4 **Jack Dawkins (USA)**[8] 1074 8-9-3 65 AdrianNicholls 2 72
(David Nicholls) *trckd ldr: led 3f out: rdn and jnd 2f out: hdd wl over 1f out: kpt on same pce* **2/1**[1]
-233 **3** 1/2 **Xpres Maite**[8] 1074 10-8-12 64 (v) MarkCoumbe(3) 4 69
(Roy Bowring) *sn led: pushed along 4f out: hdd 3f out: drvn and kpt on same pce fr over 1f out* **25/1**
2-12 **4** 2 **Right Stuff (FR)**[21] 901 10-9-3 85 (be1) GeorgeBaker 1 68
(Gary Moore) *trckd ldrs: hdwy 4f out: rdn along over 2f out: drvn and no imp fr over 1f out* **2/1**[1]
3-25 **5** 2 1/4 **Priors Gold**[12] 309 6-8-12 75 LukeMorris 3 61
(George Baker) *trckd ldrs: effrt over 3f out: rdn along wl over 2f out: sn btn* **7/1**[3]

2m 40.88s (-0.12) **Going Correction** -0.05s/f (Stan) **5** Ran SP% **106.1**
Speed ratings (Par 101): **98,96,96,94,93**
CSF £9.61 TOTE £3.40: £2.20, £1.80; EX 12.00 Trifecta £71.00 Pool: £1,704.45 - 17.98 winning units..Priors Gold was claimed by Mrs L. J. Mongan £3,000.
Owner M M Foulger **Bred** Haras Du Mezeray & Ronchalon Racing **Trained** Newmarket, Suffolk

FOCUS
Clerk of the course Roderick Duncan reported before the opener that there was quite a strong wind the previous day, so he sent the tractors around to put some water on the track. The wind dries the track making it slower, so putting some water on helps keep it that bit quicker and not too testing. A tricky contest to work out but the runner-up is rated to recent form and the winner looked well suited by the surface.

1202 32RED CASINO MAIDEN STKS 7f (F)
2:40 (2:40) (Class 5) 3-Y-O+ £2,587 (£770; £384; £192) Stalls Low

Form RPR
642 **1** **Combustible (IRE)**[4] 1150 3-8-8 0 LukeMorris 7 77
(Daniel Mark Loughnane) *t.k.h: cl up: led after 1f: rdn clr wl over 1f out: readily* **7/4**[2]
2 10 **Maakirr (IRE)** 4-9-11 0 (t) MarkCoumbe(3) 2 61+
(Roy Bowring) *s.i.s and bhd: hdwy 1/2-way: rdn to chse ldng pair 2f out: edgd lft over 1f out: styd on wl fnl f* **12/1**
24-3 **3** 1 3/4 **Free Island**[19] 923 3-8-8 65 NeilCallan 1 46
(James Tate) *led 1f: cl up on inner: rdn wl over 2f out: drvn wl over 1f out: sn wknd: lost modest 2nd ins fnl f* **5/4**[1]
00- **4** 6 **Moss Hill**[249] 4341 4-9-9 0 MatthewLawson(5) 3 41
(Charles Hills) *chsd ldng pair: rdn along 3f out: sn outpcd* **9/2**[3]
0-6 **5** 1 1/4 **Ava Schmetterling**[11] 1044 3-8-5 0 BillyCray(3) 5 29
(Garry Moss) *sn rdn along in rr: outpcd and bhd fr 1/2-way* **100/1**

1m 29.05s (-1.25) **Going Correction** -0.05s/f (Stan)
WFA 3 from 4yo 15lb **5** Ran SP% **107.7**
Speed ratings (Par 103): **105,93,91,84,83**
CSF £19.10 TOTE £2.40: £1.10, £4.90; EX 17.10 Trifecta £26.80 Pool: £1,547.21 - 43.15 winning units..
Owner Mrs C Loughnane **Bred** Minch Bloodstock **Trained** Baldwin's Gate, Staffs

FOCUS
Difficult to believe this wasn't anything more than a modest event. A big step up from the winner though.

1203 THERE'S ONLY ONE BRIAN WINNEY H'CAP 1m (F)
3:10 (3:10) (Class 4) (0-80,78) 4-Y-O+ £4,690 (£1,395; £697; £348) Stalls Low

Form RPR
0-66 **1** **Trois Vallees (USA)**[30] 792 4-9-6 **77** [1] NeilCallan 1 84
(James Tate) *chsd ldrs on inner: rdn along 2f out: drvn over 1f out: styd on wl fnl f to ld last 50yds* **16/1**
5463 **2** *shd* **Copperwood**[8] 1081 8-8-12 **69** JoeFanning 7 76
(Mark Johnston) *trckd ldrs: hdwy 1/2-way: chal 2f out: rdn to ld ent fnl f: sn drvn: hdd and no ex last 50yds* **10/1**
3113 **3** *shd* **Caledonia Prince**[22] 889 5-9-3 **74** (b) FrannyNorton 6 81
(Jo Hughes) *dwlt and towards rr: hdwy on wd outside and wd st: rdn along nr stands' rail to chse ldrs wl over 1f out: drvn and ev ch ins fnl f: no ex nr fin* **7/2**[2]
0503 **4** *nk* **Kung Hei Fat Choy (USA)**[5] 1115 4-9-7 **78** (b) DaleSwift 4 84
(James Given) *t.k.h: led 2f: cl up: rdn 2f out: led briefly over 1f out: ev ch ins fnl f tl no ex last 50yds* **9/2**[3]
1115 **5** *hd* **Our Ivor**[27] 832 4-9-1 **72** LukeMorris 8 78
(Michael Appleby) *prom: effrt to chal 2f out: sn rdn and ev ch tl drvn and no ex wl ins fnl f* **5/1**
013 **6** 3/4 **Caldercruix (USA)**[4] 1148 6-9-4 **78** (v) RaulDaSilva(3) 2 82
(James Evans) *cl up: led after 2f: rdn 2f out: hdd over 1f out: ev ch tl no ex wl ins fnl f* **7/4**[1]
1453 **7** 6 **Flying Pickets (IRE)**[14] 987 4-8-12 **69** (be) JohnFahy 3 59
(Alan McCabe) *dwlt: a in rr* **25/1**
000- **8** 2 1/4 **Mutafaakir (IRE)**[175] 6789 4-8-11 **68** JamesSullivan 5 53
(Ruth Carr) *in rr: sme hdwy 3f out: sn rdn and outpcd* **50/1**

1m 42.3s (-1.40) **Going Correction** -0.05s/f (Stan) **8** Ran SP% **114.2**
Speed ratings (Par 105): **105,104,104,104,104 103,97,95**
Tote Swingers: 1&2 £11.50, 1&3 £8.70, 2&3 £6.00 CSF £161.49 CT £695.53 TOTE £16.20: £3.90, £2.50, £1.50; EX 112.00 Trifecta £723.50 Pool: £3,817.86 - 3.95 winning units..
Owner Saif Ali **Bred** Stone Farm **Trained** Newmarket, Suffolk

FOCUS
Not easy to know what to make of this form as six horses were within about a length of each other half a furlong out, and five of them not far from being in a line passing the post. The winner is rated back to form on his first try on the surface and those close behinsd give the form perspective.

1204 £32 BONUS AT 32RED.COM H'CAP 5f (F)
3:45 (3:45) (Class 5) (0-75,77) 3-Y-O £2,587 (£770; £384; £192) Stalls High

Form RPR
1311 **1** **Hannahs Turn**[8] 1073 3-8-13 64 6ex HayleyTurner 3 75+
(Chris Dwyer) *cl up: led over 2f out: rdn over 1f out: qcknd clr jst ins fnl f: readily* **10/11**[1]
5341 **2** 2 3/4 **Sewn Up**[8] 1075 3-9-12 77 6ex (tp) GeorgeBaker 2 78
(Reg Hollinshead) *trckd ldrs: hdwy 2f out: rdn to chse wnr appr fnl f: sn no imp* **4/1**[3]
0613 **3** 2 3/4 **Miako (USA)**[8] 1075 3-9-7 72 LukeMorris 1 63
(Michael Appleby) *cl up on outer: pushed along wl over 1f out: sn rdn and outpcd ent fnl f* **9/4**[2]
356- **4** 7 **Red Style (IRE)**[196] 6130 3-9-1 66 MickyFenton 4 32
(Paul Midgley) *led: rdn along and hdd over 2f out: sn wknd and eased* **22/1**

1m 1.05s (1.35) **Going Correction** +0.225s/f (Slow) **4** Ran SP% **107.5**
Speed ratings (Par 98): **98,93,89,78**
CSF £4.81 TOTE £1.40; EX 5.10 Trifecta £5.00 Pool: £2,834.70 - 424.20 winning units..
Owner Mrs K W Sneath **Bred** Wayland Stud **Trained** Newmarket, Suffolk

FOCUS
Only three of these appeared of serious interest on recent form, but it was the two penalised runners who dominated. The runner-up is rated close to his recent winning mark.

1205 32REDPOKER.COM H'CAP 6f (F)
4:20 (4:20) (Class 5) (0-70,71) 4-Y-O+ £2,587 (£770; £384; £192) Stalls Low

Form RPR
0313 **1** **Elusive Hawk (IRE)**[2] 1172 9-9-2 **71** 6ex (v) RobJFitzpatrick(7) 5 85+
(David Evans) *trckd ldrs: smooth hdwy 3f out: led wl over 1f out: pushed out* **11/8**[1]
-321 **2** 1 3/4 **Ace Master**[44] 616 5-8-12 **63** (b) MarkCoumbe(3) 3 71
(Roy Bowring) *trckd ldrs: hdwy to chse ldr after 2f: led 1/2-way: rdn over 2f out: hdd wl over 1f out: kpt on same pce fnl f* **13/2**
0442 **3** 2 3/4 **Desert Strike**[26] 842 7-9-7 **69** (p) JoeFanning 4 69
(Conor Dore) *led: rdn along and hdd 1/2-way: rdn and sltly outpcd 2f out: kpt on u.p fnl f* **20/1**
-351 **4** *nk* **Rio Cobolo (IRE)**[14] 986 7-9-2 **64** AdrianNicholls 9 63
(David Nicholls) *chsd ldrs on outer: hdwy over 2f out: sn rdn: drvn and one pce appr fnl f* **9/2**[2]
0654 **5** 3/4 **Restless Bay (IRE)**[11] 1038 5-9-2 **64** (b) HayleyTurner 1 61
(Conor Dore) *trckd ldrs on inner: pushed along over 2f out: styd on fnl f* **22/1**
41-4 **6** 3/4 **Spitfire**[72] 199 8-9-5 **67** (t) FrederikTylicki 2 61
(J R Jenkins) *dwlt: in tch on inner: rdn along wl over 2f out: sn one pce* **11/2**[3]
40-6 **7** 3/4 **Takealookatmenow (IRE)**[55] 454 4-9-5 **67** PaulQuinn 10 59
(David Nicholls) *towards rr: hdwy on wd outside wl over 2f out: sn rdn and n.d* **33/1**
000- **8** 1/2 **Baldemar**[178] 6705 8-9-0 **69** GeorgeChaloner(7) 8 60
(Richard Fahey) *in tch: rdn along 1/2-way: n.d* **12/1**

0-06 **9** *7* **Ambitious Icarus**[13] 998 4-9-3 **65**........................(e) RobbieFitzpatrick 6 35
(Richard Guest) *a in rr* **16/1**
1m 15.69s (-0.81) **Going Correction** -0.05s/f (Stan) **9** Ran SP% **114.6**
Speed ratings (Par 103): **103,100,97,96,95 94,93,92,83**
Tote Swingers: 1&2 £3.40, 1&3 £5.00, 2&3 £7.20 CSF £10.28 CT £122.17 TOTE £2.10: £1.10, £1.40, £4.40; EX 12.90 Trifecta £80.60 Pool: £3,428.25 - 31.89 winning units..
Owner Mrs I M Folkes **Bred** J Fike **Trained** Pandy, Monmouths

FOCUS
A modest sprint run at a reasonable gallop. The winner is rated right back to his best with the runner-up to his mark.

1206 32REDBET.COM H'CAP 1m (F)
4:55 (4:55) (Class 5) (0-75,73) 3-Y-O **£2,587** (£770; £384; £192) **Stalls** Low

Form RPR
1-13 **1** **Apache Rising**[27] 826 3-8-10 **62**.. TomEaves 5 77
(Bryan Smart) *led 2f: cl up tl led again 2f out: rdn and edgd rt over 1f out: clr ins fnl f: styd on strly* **5/2**[2]
-151 **2** *6* **Luv U Whatever**[8] 1071 3-8-3 **55**.. JoeFanning 6 56
(Jo Hughes) *trckd ldng pair: hdwy 3f out: rdn 2f out: chsd wnr over 1f out: sn drvn and kpt on same pce* **11/8**[1]
2334 **3** *2 1/4* **Tight Knit (USA)**[25] 867 3-9-7 **73**..(p) NeilCallan 3 69
(James Tate) *trckd ldrs: hdwy wl over 2f out: sn rdn: drvn and one pce appr fnl f* **7/2**[3]
00-3 **4** *1 1/4* **Loki's Strike**[8] 1071 3-8-8 **60**..(b) LukeMorris 2 53
(Mrs K Burke) *cl up on inner: led after 2f: rdn along 3f out: hdd 2f out: grad wknd* **14/1**
-414 **5** *4 1/2* **Makinson Lane (IRE)**[27] 826 3-9-1 **67**........................ TonyHamilton 1 50
(Richard Fahey) *chsd ldrs on inner: rdn along 3f out: sn outpcd* **12/1**
605- **6** *4* **Out Of The Blocks**[176] 6753 3-8-6 **58**........................ JamesSullivan 4 32
(Ruth Carr) *a towards rr* **33/1**
1m 41.98s (-1.72) **Going Correction** -0.05s/f (Stan) **6** Ran SP% **110.2**
Speed ratings (Par 98): **106,100,97,96,92 88**
Tote Swingers: 1&2 £1.30, 1&3 £1.60, 2&3 £1.90 CSF £6.08 TOTE £3.30: £2.20, £1.10; EX 6.80 Trifecta £13.90 Pool: £2,792.13 - 149.88 winning units..
Owner The Smart Distant Music Partnership **Bred** Southill Stud **Trained** Hambleton, N Yorks

FOCUS
The first four home got away from the other two with over 2f to go. The winning time was quicker than the older-horse handicap earlier on the card. A big step up by the winner even if rated cautiously.

1207 32REDBINGO.COM AMATEUR RIDERS' H'CAP 1m 6f (F)
5:30 (5:30) (Class 6) (0-65,64) 4-Y-O+ **£1,975** (£607; £303) **Stalls** Low

Form RPR
2100 **1** **Maslak (IRE)**[22] 888 9-10-3 **58**.. MissMEdden(5) 9 67
(Peter Hiatt) *hld up: stdy hdwy on outer 6f out: cl up over 3f out: rdn to ld wl over 1f out: sn clr: styd on* **14/1**
06-6 **2** *6* **Al Amaan**[63] 338 8-10-8 **63**..(p) MrGeorgeCrate(5) 3 64
(Gary Moore) *s.i.s and in rr: stdy hdwy 1/2-way: chsd ldrs over 3f out: rdn along over 2f out: kpt on to take 2nd ins fnl f: no ch w wnr* **4/1**[3]
1224 **3** *1* **Goldmadchen (GER)**[14] 989 5-10-10 **63**........................ NickSlatter(3) 6 63
(James Given) *a.p: led 5f out: rdn along 3f out: hdd wl over 1f out: sn one pce* **13/2**
55-5 **4** *1 1/4* **Dubara Reef (IRE)**[15] 970 6-9-2 **45**................(p) MissAimeeMKing(7) 10 43
(Paul Green) *prom on outer: rdn along 4f out: drvn wl over 2f out: plugged on same pce* **20/1**
0-04 **5** *2 1/2* **Sacco D'Oro**[4] 1146 7-9-6 **45**........................ MissMMullineaux(3) 11 40
(Michael Mullineaux) *bhd tl styd on fnl 3f: n.d* **25/1**
0205 **6** *1 1/2* **Silver Marizah (IRE)**[22] 886 4-9-1 **48**..................(e) MissRBIngram(7) 1 41
(Roger Ingram) *trckd ldrs: pushed along and outpcd 5f out: bhd and wd st: hdwy over 2f out: rdn wl over 1f out: sn no imp* **25/1**
3241 **7** *1 1/2* **Peace In Our Time**[50] 522 4-9-10 **55** ow1.......(p) MrGrahamCarson(5) 2 49
(Anthony Carson) *led: pushed along 6f out: hdd 5f out: rdn along to chse ldng pair wl over 2f out: sn wknd* **2/1**[1]
340- **8** *17* **Nippy Nikki**[127] 7800 5-9-9 **48**........................ MissJRRichards(3) 4 17
(John Norton) *trckd ldrs: pushed along over 4f out: rdn over 3f out and sn wknd* **25/1**
0/00 **9** *11* **Orpen Bid (IRE)**[4] 1146 8-9-9 **45**..(be) MissADeniel 8
(Michael Mullineaux) *chsd ldrs: rdn along 4f out: sn wknd* **66/1**
6/05 **P** **Buckie Boy (IRE)**[41] 654 7-10-11 **64**........................(b) MrFMitchell(3) 5
(Nicky Henderson) *v.s.a and rel to r: t.o and p.u after 6f* **7/2**[2]
3m 13.37s (5.07) **Going Correction** -0.05s/f (Stan)
WFA 4 from 5yo+ 4lb **10** Ran SP% **113.3**
Speed ratings (Par 101): **83,79,79,78,76 76,75,65,59,**
Tote Swingers 1&2 £10.40, 1&3 £11.00, 2&3 £4.10 CSF £63.00 CT £404.26 TOTE £21.70: £5.20, £2.00, £1.60; EX 86.30 Trifecta £609.80 Pool: £2,380.70 - 2.92 winning units..
Owner P W Hiatt **Bred** Shadwell Estate Company Limited **Trained** Hook Norton, Oxon

FOCUS
The top four in the betting looked solid enough, but two of them ran poorly. The winner is the best guide.
T/Plt: £58.20 to a £1 stake. Pool: £66,035.25. 827.06 winning tickets. T/Qpdt: £10.70 to a £1 stake. Pool: £4,683.18. 322.30 winning tickets. JR

1116 WOLVERHAMPTON (A.W) (L-H)
Wednesday, March 27

OFFICIAL GOING: Standard
Wind: Fresh against Weather: Overcast

1208 32RED.COM MAIDEN AUCTION STKS 5f 20y(P)
5:50 (5:50) (Class 5) 2-Y-O **£2,587** (£770; £384; £192) **Stalls** Low

Form RPR
5 **1** **Outback Lover (IRE)**[3] 1156 2-8-1 0........................ DarrenEgan(3) 3 69
(J S Moore) *mde all: hung rt fr over 3f out tl clr over 1f out: r.o* **5/2**[2]
2 *1 3/4* **Memory Styx** 2-8-8 0.. FrannyNorton 6 68
(Mick Channon) *a.p: pushed along 3f out: chsd wnr over 1f out: r.o* **5/2**[2]
3 *5* **Far Gaze (IRE)** 2-8-9 0.. LiamJones 5 50
(J S Moore) *s.s: outpcd: r.o ins fnl f: wnt 3rd nr fin* **10/1**[3]
4 *3/4* **Sunshine Superman** 2-8-2 0........................ JakePayne(7) 4 47
(Bill Turner) *chsd wnr tl pushed along 1/2-way: hung lft and wknd over 1f out* **15/8**[1]
5 *5* **Left Defender (IRE)** 2-8-10 0.. J-PGuillambert 2 30
(Jo Hughes) *s.i.s: sn pushed along and prom: chsd wnr 1/2-way tl rdn wl over 1f out: sn wknd* **12/1**
1m 3.42s (1.12) **Going Correction** +0.05s/f (Slow) **5** Ran SP% **108.7**
Speed ratings (Par 92): **93,90,82,81,73**
CSF £8.86 TOTE £2.80: £1.40, £1.60; EX 7.80 Trifecta £21.80 Pool: £1087.75 - 37.28 winning units..
Owner J S Moore **Bred** Christopher Maye **Trained** Upper Lambourn, Berks

FOCUS
Year in year out it pays to side with those that have a bit of experience over newcomers in these early juvenile races, and the winner confirmed that trend. Guessy form.

1209 32RED CASINO MAIDEN STKS 5f 216y(P)
6:20 (6:20) (Class 5) 3-Y-O+ **£2,587** (£770; £384; £192) **Stalls** Low

Form RPR
0- **1** **Top Trail (USA)**[167] 7007 3-8-10 0.. JamesDoyle 3 69+
(Roger Charlton) *led 1f: chsd ldr tl led again over 1f out: c clr ins fnl f: easily* **6/4**[2]
5200 **2** *4 1/2* **Script**[14] 991 4-9-2 47.. JordanHibberd(7) 5 51
(Alan Berry) *chsd wnr tl dropped to rr 5f out: nt clr run over 1f out: r.o to go 2nd towards fin* **80/1**
0424 **3** *1* **Haywain**[28] 812 4-10-0 68..(b) PhillipMakin 1 53
(Kevin Ryan) *s.i.s: rcvrd to ld 5f out: rdn over 2f out: hdd over 1f out: sn hung lft: no ex ins fnl f: fin lame* **4/5**[1]
4 *nk* **Rowlestone Lad**[12] 6-10-0 0.. RussKennemore 2 52
(John Flint) *dwlt: sn chsng ldrs: rdn over 2f out: wknd over 1f out* **20/1**[3]
1m 17.63s (2.63) **Going Correction** +0.05s/f (Slow)
WFA 3 from 4yo+ 13lb **4** Ran SP% **101.6**
Speed ratings (Par 103): **84,78,76,76**
CSF £28.83 TOTE £2.10; EX 49.50 Trifecta £53.40 Pool: £1054.07 - 14.79 winning units..
Owner K Abdullah **Bred** Juddmonte Farms Inc **Trained** Beckhampton, Wilts

FOCUS
A two-horse race on paper, but the favourite Haywain is far from straightforward, and this proved easy for the winner.

1210 32REDPOKER.COM H'CAP 7f 32y(P)
6:50 (6:50) (Class 6) (0-60,59) 3-Y-O **£1,940** (£577; £288; £144) **Stalls** High

Form RPR
0-66 **1** **Compton Silver**[15] 977 3-8-10 **53**........................(b[1]) NicoleNordblad(5) 4 62
(Hans Adielsson) *mde all: sn clr: shkn up over 1f out: unchal* **3/1**[2]
0563 **2** *3 1/2* **Bubbly Bailey**[5] 1118 3-9-2 **59**........................(p) RobertTart(5) 5 59
(Alan Bailey) *chsd ldrs: rdn to go 2nd and hung rt fr over 1f out: nt rch wnr* **5/4**[1]
004- **3** *3 1/4* **Multisure**[113] 7977 3-9-6 **58**.. PJMcDonald 6 50
(Ruth Carr) *chsd wnr who was sn clr: rdn over 2f out: lost 2nd over 1f out: styd on same pce* **14/1**
060- **4** *nk* **Niknad**[102] 8138 3-8-7 **45**.. MartinLane 2 37
(Brian Ellison) *sn outpcd: rdn over 2f out: r.o ins fnl f: nvr nrr* **5/1**[3]
000- **5** *3 1/4* **So Lyrical**[154] 7323 3-8-7 **45**.. CathyGannon 1 29
(Jo Hughes) *s.i.s: outpcd* **8/1**
025- **6** *2 1/4* **Special Report (IRE)**[174] 6826 3-8-12 **57**............ DanielleMooney(7) 3 35
(Nigel Tinkler) *chsd ldrs: rdn over 2f out: sn wknd* **14/1**
1m 30.24s (0.64) **Going Correction** +0.05s/f (Slow) **6** Ran SP% **110.6**
Speed ratings (Par 96): **98,94,90,89,86 83**
toteswingers 1&2 £1.30, 1&3 £4.90, 2&3 £4.10 CSF £6.93 TOTE £4.00: £2.90, £1.20; EX 5.90 Trifecta £34.70 Pool: £1049.96 - 22.63 winning units..
Owner Erik Penser **Bred** Stowell Hill Ltd **Trained** Kingston Lisle, Oxon

FOCUS
A weakish race, although the form could be rated a little higher.

1211 £32 BONUS AT 32RED.COM FILLIES' H'CAP 7f 32y(P)
7:20 (7:21) (Class 5) (0-70,70) 4-Y-O+ **£2,587** (£770; £384; £192) **Stalls** High

Form RPR
1223 **1** **Big Sylv (IRE)**[6] 1107 4-8-13 **62**........................(p) RobertWinston 3 69
(James Unett) *a.p: chsd ldr over 2f out: rdn over 1f out: edgd lft: styd on to ld post* **2/1**[2]
3353 **2** *hd* **Spark Of Genius**[14] 986 4-9-0 **68**..........(v[1]) WilliamTwiston-Davies(5) 5 75
(Alan McCabe) *led: shkn up over 1f out: hdd post* **15/8**[1]
3635 **3** *2* **Romanticize**[8] 1079 7-8-2 **56**.. RobertTart(5) 1 58
(Jason Ward) *prom: n.m.r and lost pl over 6f out: hdwy over 2f out: rdn over 1f out: styd on same pce ins fnl f* **7/1**
356- **4** *2 1/4* **Ssafa**[153] 7356 5-9-2 **70**.. AmyScott(5) 6 66
(Alastair Lidderdale) *hld up: hdwy over 2f out: rdn over 1f out: styd on* **17/2**
4355 **5** *1 1/2* **Arabian Flight**[10] 1054 4-8-10 **59**........................(v[1]) LukeMorris 2 52
(Michael Appleby) *prom: rdn over 2f out: no ex fnl f* **6/1**[3]
231- **6** *18* **Ozz**[320] 2030 4-9-7 **70**..(bt) CathyGannon 4 18
(Frank Sheridan) *chsd ldr tl rdn and edgd rt over 2f out: wknd over 1f out* **22/1**
1m 29.31s (-0.29) **Going Correction** +0.05s/f (Slow) **6** Ran SP% **109.8**
Speed ratings (Par 100): **103,102,100,97,96 75**
toteswingers 1&2 £1.50, 1&3 £1.80, 2&3 £2.50 CSF £5.85 TOTE £3.50: £1.50, £1.10; EX 6.80 Trifecta £21.60 Pool: £1143.50 - 39.65 winning units..
Owner Miss Ciara Doyle **Bred** John Doyle **Trained** Tedsmore Hall, Shropshire

FOCUS
Just a fair fillies' handicap. The first two were close to their best.

1212 32RED H'CAP 1m 4f 50y(P)
7:50 (7:50) (Class 4) (0-85,81) 4-Y-O+ **£4,690** (£1,395; £697; £348) **Stalls** Low

Form RPR
-122 **1** **Illustrious Forest**[8] 1083 5-9-7 **79**.. GrahamGibbons 6 87
(John Mackie) *mde all: set stdy pce tl qcknd over 3f out: rdn over 2f out: hung rt over 1f out: styd on u.p* **11/4**[3]
121 **2** *2 1/4* **Blazing Desert**[11] 1045 9-8-13 **71**.. LukeMorris 5 76
(William Kinsey) *trckd wnr: rdn and ev ch over 2f out: styd on same pce ins fnl f* **9/1**
620- **3** *hd* **Arizona John (IRE)**[199] 6076 8-9-2 **74**........................ FrannyNorton 3 78
(John Mackie) *hld up: hdwy over 2f out: rdn and edgd rt over 1f out: styd on same pce ins fnl f* **16/1**
6P21 **4** *1 1/4* **All The Winds (GER)**[8] 1083 8-9-4 **81** 6ex....................(t) RobertTart(5) 1 83
(Shaun Lycett) *s.s: hld up: hdwy over 4f out: rdn over 2f out: styd on same pce fr over 1f out* **15/8**[1]

350- **5** 3/4 **Knightly Escapade**[175] 6776 5-9-4 **76**.................................. TomEaves 2 77
(Brian Ellison) *chsd ldrs: rdn over 3f out: sn outpcd: styd on ins fnl f* **9/4**[2]

2m 39.46s (-1.64) **Going Correction** +0.05s/f (Slow)
WFA 4 from 5yo+ 2lb 5 Ran SP% **108.1**
Speed ratings (Par 105): **107,105,105,104,104**
CSF £23.46 TOTE £2.80: £1.40, £2.40; EX 12.60 Trifecta £91.60 Pool: £979.19 - 8.01 winning units..
Owner Derbyshire Racing VII **Bred** Norman A Blyth **Trained** Church Broughton , Derbys

FOCUS
This was run in a completely different way from the race in which All The Winds beat Illustrious Forest last time. Routine form.

1213 32REDBET.COM MEDIAN AUCTION MAIDEN 1m 141y(P)
8:20 (8:21) (Class 6) 3-5-Y-0 **£1,940** (£577; £288; £144) **Stalls** Low

Form RPR
0-33 **1** **On With The Dance (IRE)**[20] 911 3-8-9 67...................... LukeMorris 5 67
(Ed Vaughan) *led: hdd over 6f out: chsd ldr tl led again over 2f out: rdn and hung rt ins fnl f: styd on* **11/2**[3]

32 **2** 1 3/4 **Green Special (ITY)**[26] 849 3-8-9 0................................ CathyGannon 1 63
(Frank Sheridan) *s.s: hld up: racd keenly: nt clr run over 2f out: hdwy sn after: swtchd rt 1f out: rdn to go 2nd ins fnl f: nt rch wnr* **3/1**[2]

0 **3** 3/4 **Florida Beat**[7] 1086 3-8-9 0.. LiamKeniry 2 62
(Andrew Balding) *chsd ldrs: rdn over 2f out: styd on* **16/1**

40 **4** 1 1/4 **Deal Me In (IRE)**[7] 1086 4-10-0 0............................(p) MichaelO'Connell 6 64
(Ian Williams) *chsd ldrs: rdn over 2f out: styd on same pce ins fnl f* **40/1**

0- **5** 1 3/4 **Beautiful Life**[98] 8166 3-8-4 0...[1] MartinLane 3 50
(David Simcock) *dwlt: hld up: pushed along over 3f out: nt trble ldrs* **14/1**

426- **6** nk **Jontleman (IRE)**[197] 6114 3-8-9 72.................................. MartinHarley 4 54
(Mick Channon) *chsd wnr tl led over 6f out: rdn and hdd over 2f out: ev ch over 1f out: wknd ins fnl f* **8/11**[1]

1m 51.59s (1.09) **Going Correction** +0.05s/f (Slow)
WFA 3 from 4yo 19lb 6 Ran SP% **113.3**
Speed ratings (Par 101): **97,95,94,93,92 91**
toteswingers 1&2 £1.40, 1&3 £2.70, 2&3 £4.90 CSF £22.57 TOTE £5.30: £3.30, £1.70; EX 17.30 Trifecta £94.70 Pool: £1024.37 - 8.11 winning units..
Owner Mohammed Rashid **Bred** Rabbah Bloodstock Limited **Trained** Newmarket, Suffolk

FOCUS
Just a modest maiden, run at a slow pace. The form is rated a little negatively.

1214 32REDBINGO.COM H'CAP 1m 141y(P)
8:50 (8:50) (Class 6) (0-60,66) 4-Y-0+ **£1,940** (£577; £288; £144) **Stalls** Low

Form RPR
0520 **1** **Penbryn (USA)**[21] 896 6-9-4 **57**.. SebSanders 8 65
(Nick Littmoden) *hld up: hdwy 6f out: shkn up to ld ins fnl f: jst hld on* **9/1**

-605 **2** 1/2 **Kyle Of Bute**[8] 1082 7-9-0 **53**.. WilliamCarson 9 60
(Brian Baugh) *s.i.s: swtchd lft sn after s: hld up: rdn and r.o wl ins fnl f: nt quite get up* **25/1**

40-3 **3** 1/2 **Alluring Star**[15] 975 5-9-2 **55**...................................... GrahamGibbons 6 61
(Michael Easterby) *chsd ldr tl rdn to ld over 1f out: edgd lft and hdd ins fnl f: styd on* **7/2**[2]

1621 **4** nk **Lieutenant Dan (IRE)**[10] 1056 6-9-13 **66** 6ex.................(v) TomQueally 4 71
(Michael Appleby) *hld up: hdwy over 1f out: r.o: nt rch ldrs* **3/1**[1]

4152 **5** shd **Harvest Mist (IRE)**[12] 1020 5-8-11 **55**........... WilliamTwiston-Davies[(5)] 7 60
(Shaun Lycett) *a.p: rdn over 1f out: r.o* **12/1**

30-1 **6** 1/2 **Downtown Boy (IRE)**[12] 1017 5-9-0 **53**........................(p) MartinDwyer 1 57
(Ray Craggs) *led: rdn and hdd over 1f out: styd on same pce ins fnl f* **8/1**

3453 **7** hd **Spirit Of Gondree (IRE)**[8] 1082 5-9-7 **60**.............(b) RichardKingscote 5 65
(Milton Bradley) *hld up: pushed along over 2f out: r.o wl ins fnl f: nt trble ldrs* **4/1**[3]

0222 **8** shd **John Potts**[12] 1017 8-9-2 **55**..(p) KellyHarrison 3 58
(Brian Baugh) *chsd ldrs: pushed along over 2f out: nt clr run ins fnl f: styd on* **5/1**

231- **9** 4 **Inffiraaj (IRE)**[110] 7671 4-9-4 **57**.................................... MartinHarley 2 51
(Mick Channon) *hld up: rdn over 2f out: wknd fnl f* **6/1**

1m 50.7s (0.20) **Going Correction** +0.05s/f (Slow) 9 Ran SP% **130.8**
Speed ratings (Par 101): **101,100,100,99,99 99,99,99,95**
toteswingers 1&2 £1.40, 1&3 £2.70, 2&3 £4.90 CSF £224.46 CT £961.80 TOTE £7.80: £4.00, £4.40, £2.00; EX 136.50 Trifecta £805.10 Part won. Pool: £1073.59 - 0.16 winning units..
Owner Mrs K Graham, N Littmoden, A Highfield **Bred** Kilboy Estate Inc **Trained** Newmarket, Suffolk

FOCUS
This looked pretty open. Routine, low-grade form, but the winner was a bit better than the bare facts.
T/Plt: £33.30 to a £1 stake. Pool: £79,586.60 - 1740.37 winning tickets. T/Qpdt: £4.70 to a £1 stake. Pool: £8,465.45 - 1311.12 winning tickets. CR

[1208] WOLVERHAMPTON (A.W) (L-H)
Thursday, March 28

OFFICIAL GOING: Standard
Wind: Fresh; against Weather: Cloudy with sunny spells

1215 32RED MAIDEN STKS 5f 20y(P)
1:40 (1:40) (Class 5) 3-Y-0+ **£2,587** (£770; £384; £192) **Stalls** Low

Form RPR
2-32 **1** **Silca's Dream**[11] 1051 3-9-1 69.. MartinHarley 3 69
(Mick Channon) *led 1f: chsd ldrs: wnt 2nd 2f out: hmpd 1f out: r.o to ld towards fin* **11/10**[1]

632- **2** 3/4 **Alhaarth Beauty (IRE)**[139] 7669 3-8-10 66......................... LiamJones 6 61
(Ismail Mohammed) *edgd rt s: led 4f: rdn and hung lft fr over 1f out: hdd towards fin* **9/4**[2]

020- **3** 1 3/4 **Red Baron (IRE)**[168] 7001 4-9-13 62................................. LukeMorris 2 65
(Eric Alston) *chsd ldrs: pushed along 1/2-way: rdn and hung lft fr over 1f out: styd on same pce* **10/1**

40- **4** nse **A J Cook (IRE)**[200] 6071 3-9-1 0.................................. GrahamGibbons 1 68+
(David Barron) *prom: shkn up and running on whn hmpd 1f out: nt rcvr* **11/2**[3]

/003 **5** 6 **Poyle Todream**[21] 915 5-9-13 48... TomEaves 7 43
(Roy Brotherton) *prom: chsd ldr over 3f out tl rdn 2f out: wknd fnl f* **50/1**

66 **6** 3 3/4 **Satwa's Sister**[9] 1078 3-8-10 0.. JoeFanning 5 20
(Robert Cowell) *s.i.s: outpcd* **40/1**

0 **7** 5 **Stoneacre Oskar**[27] 849 4-9-3 0.................................... SladeO'Hara[(5)] 4
(Peter Grayson) *s.i.s: outpcd* **66/1**

1m 2.1s (-0.20) **Going Correction** +0.125s/f (Slow)
WFA 3 from 4yo+ 12lb 7 Ran SP% **108.8**
Speed ratings (Par 103): **106,104,102,101,92 86,78**
toteswingers 1&2 £1.40, 1&3 £2.30, 2&3 £2.70 CSF £3.28 TOTE £1.70: £1.10, £1.50; EX 3.30 Trifecta £13.90 Pool: £4,154.86 - 223.26 winning units..
Owner Aldridge Racing Partnership **Bred** Aldridge Racing Partnership **Trained** West Ilsley, Berks

FOCUS
A modest maiden, won in gritty fashion by the market principal. He ran right to his mark.

1216 £32 BONUS AT 32RED.COM (S) STKS 5f 20y(P)
2:10 (2:10) (Class 6) 3-Y-0 **£1,940** (£577; £288; £144) **Stalls** Low

Form RPR
6244 **1** **La Sylphe**[12] 1041 3-8-13 65... MartinDwyer 1 61
(Derek Shaw) *mde all: rdn over 1f out: r.o* **11/8**[2]

0-34 **2** 3 1/2 **Nors The Panic**[21] 915 3-8-12 48..........................(e) RobbieFitzpatrick 2 47
(Richard Guest) *a.p: rdn to chse wnr fnl f: no imp* **9/1**[3]

02-3 **3** 1 1/2 **Annaley My Darling (IRE)**[11] 1051 3-8-7 67.................. TonyCulhane 5 37
(Jo Hughes) *chsd wnr: shkn up and lost 2nd 1f out: styd on same pce* **10/11**[1]

00-0 **4** 3 1/4 **Dalhousie Lassie**[12] 1044 3-8-7 42...................................... LiamJones 4 25
(James Unett) *sn drvn along in rr: outpcd* **50/1**

1m 3.06s (0.76) **Going Correction** +0.125s/f (Slow) 4 Ran SP% **106.4**
Speed ratings (Par 96): **98,92,90,84**
CSF £11.37 TOTE £2.10; EX 9.40 Trifecta £10.90 Pool: £2,914.28 - 199.67 winning units..Annaley My Darling was claimed by Mr F J Perry for £6,000.
Owner Chris Hamilton **Bred** Denis Barry **Trained** Sproxton, Leics

FOCUS
A poor contest and, with the heavily supported favourite failing to fire, it paved the way for a straightforward success for the winner. The runner-up is the best guide.

1217 32REDPOKER.COM H'CAP 1m 4f 50y(P)
2:40 (2:40) (Class 6) (0-60,60) 4-Y-0+ **£1,940** (£577; £288; £144) **Stalls** Low

Form RPR
0042 **1** **Mazij**[20] 929 5-9-7 **60**.. LukeMorris 4 68
(Peter Hiatt) *chsd ldr over 4f: remained handy: rdn to ld over 1f out: edgd rt: all out* **4/1**[3]

000- **2** shd **Cape Alex**[175] 6807 4-8-9 **50**.. ChrisCatlin 1 58
(Clive Brittain) *hld up: pushed along over 3f out: rdn and r.o wl ins fnl f: jst failed* **14/1**

5243 **3** 1 1/4 **Layla's Boy**[16] 970 6-8-13 **57**.......................................(bt) PhilipPrince[(5)] 2 63
(Simon West) *hld up: hdwy over 2f out: rdn over 1f out: styd on* **10/1**

0042 **4** nk **Lady of Burgundy**[10] 1068 7-9-4 **57**............................... FergusSweeney 8 63
(Mark Usher) *hld up: hdwy over 2f out: rdn over 1f out: edgd lft: styd on same pce ins fnl f* **3/1**[1]

0-42 **5** 2 **Needwood Park**[13] 1022 5-8-12 **51**................................(p) MartinDwyer 9 54
(Ray Craggs) *led at stdy pce tl qcknd over 3f out: rdn and hdd over 1f out: no ex ins fnl f* **13/2**

56-5 **6** 2 3/4 **Vertueux (FR)**[16] 973 8-9-4 **57**... JimmyQuinn 3 56
(Tony Carroll) *prom: pushed along over 3f out: nt clr run and lost pl over 2f out: n.d after* **16/1**

6215 **7** 1 **Crimson Monarch (USA)**[3] 1175 9-8-10 **49**.............(b) WilliamCarson 7 46
(Peter Hiatt) *s.s: hld up: pushed along over 3f out: nvr on terms* **7/2**[2]

0-30 **8** 5 **Lord Golan**[31] 789 5-9-3 **56**..(p) CathyGannon 6 46
(Violet M Jordan) *prom: chsd ldr over 7f out tl over 5f out: rdn and wknd over 1f out* **14/1**

63-5 **9** 1 1/4 **Rubi Dia**[23] 888 6-9-3 **56**...(v) JamesDoyle 5 44
(Sean Curran) *prom: chsd ldr over 5f out tl rdn over 1f out: wknd fnl f* **12/1**

2m 43.51s (2.41) **Going Correction** +0.125s/f (Slow)
WFA 4 from 5yo+ 2lb 9 Ran SP% **116.6**
Speed ratings (Par 101): **96,95,95,94,93 91,91,87,86**
totswingers 1&2 £11.70, 1&3 £7.10, 2&3 £25.10 CSF £58.49 CT £525.95 TOTE £4.40: £1.50, £3.60, £1.60; EX 52.30 Trifecta £178.30 Pool: £1,701.19 - 7.15 winning units..
Owner Phil Kelly **Bred** The Hill Stud **Trained** Hook Norton, Oxon

FOCUS
A modest handicap, run at a very steady pace in the early stages, and that worked to the advantage of the winner. Routine form.

1218 WEATHERBYS HAMILTON INSURANCE H'CAP 2m 119y(P)
3:15 (3:15) (Class 4) (0-85,81) 4-Y-0+ **£4,690** (£1,395; £697; £348) **Stalls** Low

Form RPR
10-1 **1** **Foster's Road**[13] 1018 4-8-7 **72**.............................. CharlesBishop[(5)] 6 82+
(Mick Channon) *hld up: hdwy over 2f out: led over 1f out: rdn and edgd lft ins fnl f: styd on* **10/3**[2]

/022 **2** hd **Capellanus (IRE)**[13] 1018 7-9-3 **72**................................... GrahamLee 3 82
(Brian Ellison) *a.p: rdn and ev ch fr over 1f out: styd on* **9/2**[3]

4-30 **3** 7 **The Absent Mare**[42] 654 5-8-12 **67**.................................. LukeMorris 2 69
(Robin Dickin) *prom: pushed along over 3f out: rdn over 1f out: styd on same pce: wnt 3rd wl ins fnl f* **20/1**

/122 **4** 1/2 **Murcar**[42] 654 8-9-12 **81**...(b) LiamKeniry 4 82
(Liam Corcoran) *s.i.s: chsd ldr after 2f: led over 2f out: rdn and hdd over 1f out: no ex ins fnl f* **3/1**[1]

0161 **5** 1 **Mcbirney (USA)**[7] 1097 6-9-1 **75** 6ex.............................. PhilipPrince[(5)] 1 75
(Paul D'Arcy) *hld up: hmpd over 2f out: nvr on terms* **7/1**

061- **6** 1/2 **Marmas**[162] 7169 4-8-10 **70**... FrannyNorton 7 69
(John Mackie) *chsd ldr 2f: remained handy: rdn over 2f out: sn outpcd* **11/2**

23-3 **7** 19 **Hallstatt (IRE)**[12] 1045 7-8-10 **65**...............................(t) GrahamGibbons 5 41
(John Mackie) *led at stdy pce tl qcknd over 3f out: rdn and hdd over 2f out: wknd over 1f out* **6/1**

3m 41.72s (-0.08) **Going Correction** +0.125s/f (Slow)
WFA 4 from 5yo+ 5lb 7 Ran SP% **113.2**
Speed ratings (Par 105): **105,104,101,101,100 100,91**
toteswingers 1&2 £3.60, 1&3 £7.30, 2&3 £6.40 CSF £18.25 TOTE £3.50: £1.80, £1.70; EX 12.60 Trifecta £61.70 Pool: £2,829.90 - 34.36 winning units..
Owner Dave and Gill Hedley **Bred** G Hedley & Mike Channon Bloodstock Limited **Trained** West Ilsley, Berks

FOCUS
A competitive staying handicap, and it served up a thrilling finish between two progressive types. The form looks sound with the first pair clear.

1219 32RED.COM H'CAP 1m 1f 103y(P)
3:50 (3:50) (Class 5) (0-75,72) 3-Y-O £2,587 (£770; £384; £192) Stalls Low

Form RPR
1- **1** **Regal Hawk**[161] 7199 3-9-7 72 NeilCallan 4 84+
(James Tate) *a.p: chsd ldr over 1f out: rdn to ld and edgd rt wl ins fnl f: r.o* 11/4[2]
522- **2** *nk* **High Troja (IRE)**[149] 7468 3-9-7 72 GrahamLee 2 83+
(Ed Dunlop) *hld up: pushed along over 3f out: hdwy and nt clr run over 1f out: r.o* 7/2[3]
440- **3** *½* **Storming (IRE)**[182] 6597 3-9-6 71 FrannyNorton 3 80+
(Andrew Balding) *led: racd keenly: rdn: hung rt edgd rt and hdd wl ins fnl f* 7/4[1]
53-2 **4** *4½* **Beau Select (IRE)**[43] 632 3-8-11 67 (b) ThomasBrown(5) 1 67
(Robert Eddery) *sn chsng ldrs: rdn over 2f out: no ex fnl f* 10/1
012- **5** *2¼* **Open Letter (IRE)**[167] 7026 3-9-2 67 JoeFanning 5 62
(Mark Johnston) *chsd ldr: rdn over 2f out: wknd fnl f* 5/1

2m 1.69s (-0.01) **Going Correction** +0.125s/f (Slow) 5 Ran SP% **111.0**
Speed ratings (Par 98): **105,104,104,100,98**
CSF £12.62 TOTE £2.40: £1.10, £4.60; EX 9.80 Trifecta £23.50 Pool: £3,025.56 - 96.41 winning units..
Owner Saeed Manana **Bred** Hesmonds Stud Ltd **Trained** Newmarket, Suffolk
■ Stewards' Enquiry : Neil Callan one-day ban: careless riding (12 April)

FOCUS
An informative 3yo handicap and there was a lot to like about the performance of the winner. A positive view has been taken of the form.

1220 32RED CASINO H'CAP 1m 1f 103y(P)
4:20 (4:20) (Class 5) (0-75,76) 4-Y-O+ £2,587 (£770; £384; £192) Stalls Low

Form RPR
1-12 **1** **Ishikawa (IRE)**[27] 850 5-9-7 **74** FergusSweeney 3 81
(Alan King) *trckd ldrs: rdn and hung lft 1f out: r.o to ld wl ins fnl f* 3/1[2]
2131 **2** *½* **Exceedexpectations (IRE)**[7] 1105 4-9-9 **76** 6ex LukeMorris 5 82
(Conor Dore) *set stdy pce tl qcknd over 2f out: rdn over 1f out: hdd wl ins fnl f* 7/1
3000 **3** *1½* **Standpoint**[9] 1081 7-9-5 **72** LiamKeniry 8 75
(Conor Dore) *hld up: hdwy over 2f out: rdn and hung lft ins fnl f: styd on* 28/1
26-3 **4** *1¾* **Watt Broderick (IRE)**[3] 1176 4-8-11 **64** (t) JimCrowley 2 63
(Ian Williams) *prom: rdn over 1f out: styd on same pce ins fnl f* 2/1[1]
310- **5** *½* **Saint Thomas (IRE)**[205] 5913 6-8-13 **66** FrannyNorton 9 64
(John Mackie) *prom: chsd ldr over 7f out: rdn over 1f out: no ex ins fnl f* 14/1
1316 **6** *1¼* **Honey Of A Kitten (USA)**[15] 984 5-8-11 **71** (v) RobJFitzpatrick(7) 6 67
(David Evans) *hld up: rdn over 1f out: nvr trbld ldrs* 12/1
-043 **7** *shd* **Brown Pete (IRE)**[56] 450 5-9-0 **67** MartinHarley 10 62+
(Violet M Jordan) *hld up: rdn over 1f out: nvr nr to chal* 20/1
001- **8** *½* **Space War**[146] 7530 6-9-0 **67** (t) GrahamGibbons 4 61+
(Michael Easterby) *s.s: hld up: racd keenly: n.d* 6/1[3]
4312 **9** *¾* **Tyrur Ted**[7] 1105 8-8-5 **63** ow1 (t) JackDuern(5) 1 56
(Frank Sheridan) *chsd ldr 2f: remained handy: rdn over 2f out: wknd fnl f* 20/1
0-00 **10** *3¼* **Mountain Range (IRE)**[27] 850 5-9-3 **70** JamieMackay 7 56
(Willie Musson) *s.s: a bhd* 25/1

2m 3.58s (1.88) **Going Correction** +0.125s/f (Slow) 10 Ran SP% **116.3**
Speed ratings (Par 103): **96,95,94,92,92 91,91,90,89,87**
toteswingers 1&2 £3.60, 1&3 £17.50, 2&3 £32.40 CSF £22.67 CT £492.68 TOTE £3.00: £1.80, £1.80, £9.20; EX 14.90 Trifecta £251.20 Pool: £2,390.95 - 7.13 winning units..
Owner ROA Racing Partnership V **Bred** Ken Carroll **Trained** Barbury Castle, Wilts

FOCUS
A steadily run handicap and a good effort from the winner. Straightforward form, the winner not needing to improve.

1221 32REDBET.COM H'CAP (DIV I) 1m 141y(P)
4:55 (4:55) (Class 6) (0-52,52) 4-Y-O+ £1,940 (£577; £288; £144) Stalls Low

Form RPR
0050 **1** **Maz**[13] 1017 5-8-12 **48** NatashaEaton(5) 8 56
(Alan Bailey) *led 1f: chsd ldr: rdn to ld over 1f out: r.o* 9/2[2]
040- **2** *¾* **Local Singer (IRE)**[202] 5993 5-9-4 **52** MarkCoumbe(3) 2 58
(Frank Sheridan) *chsd ldrs: rdn and ev ch over 1f out: styd on same pce ins fnl f* 3/1[1]
0300 **3** *½* **Qeethaara (USA)**[7] 1100 9-9-6 **51** (p) LukeMorris 1 56
(Mark Brisbourne) *hld up: hdwy over 2f out: rdn over 1f out: styd on* 6/1[3]
-050 **4** *hd* **Stamp Duty (IRE)**[35] 733 5-9-1 **46** oh1 (p) RussKennemore 4 51
(Suzzanne France) *hld up: plld hrd: hdwy u.p over 1f out: r.o* 13/2
5403 **5** *2¼* **Chester Deelyte (IRE)**[21] 917 5-9-2 **47** (v) TomEaves 3 48
(Lisa Williamson) *broke wl: sn stdd and lost pl: hdwy over 1f out: sn rdn: styd on same pce ins fnl f* 13/2
0-50 **6** *1* **Mayforde Jack**[8] 1093 4-8-12 **50** JoshBaudains(7) 6 48
(Simon Hodgson) *chsd ldrs: pushed along over 3f out: no ex fnl f* 12/1
-444 **7** *½* **Munaawib**[15] 990 5-9-3 **48** (t) RobbieFitzpatrick 7 45
(Charles Smith) *s.i.s: rcvrd to ld over 7f out: rdn and hdd over 1f out: wknd ins fnl f* 12/1
03-0 **8** *1¾* **Tooley Woods (IRE)**[21] 921 4-9-4 **49** JimmyQuinn 9 42
(Tony Carroll) *stdd s: hld up: hdwy over 5f out: rdn over 1f out: wknd ins fnl f* 11/1
3405 **9** *¾* **American Lover (FR)**[13] 1017 6-9-1 **46** oh1 PaddyAspell 5 39
(John Wainwright) *hmpd sn after s: hld up: nvr on: nvr on terms* 9/1

1m 52.34s (1.84) **Going Correction** +0.125s/f (Slow) 9 Ran SP% **117.9**
Speed ratings (Par 101): **96,95,94,94,92 91,91,89,89**
toteswingers 1&2 £4.30, 1&3 £6.30, 2&3 £4.30 CSF £18.85 CT £82.87 TOTE £7.40: £2.70, £1.80, £1.80; EX 23.60 Trifecta £167.30 Pool: £2,746.36 - 12.30 winning units..
Owner AB Racing Limited **Bred** Alan Bailey **Trained** Newmarket, Suffolk

FOCUS
Not a great deal of recent form to go on in a desperately weak handicap and, as if often the case, it was the market that proved the biggest key, with the winner well supported. The pace was slow and this is not form to get behind.

1222 32REDBET.COM H'CAP (DIV II) 1m 141y(P)
5:25 (5:25) (Class 6) (0-52,52) 4-Y-O+ £1,940 (£577; £288; £144) Stalls Low

Form RPR
05-0 **1** **Final Delivery**[24] 883 4-9-7 **52** MatthewDavies 7 62+
(Jim Boyle) *hld up: hdwy 2f out: sn edgd rt: led over 1f out: rdn out* 11/2[3]
005- **2** *2* **Just Five (IRE)**[97] 8212 7-9-0 **48** (v) MichaelMetcalfe(3) 1 54
(John Weymes) *s.i.s: sn pushed along to chse ldr: rdn and hmpd over 1f out: styd on same pce ins fnl f* 10/1
3204 **3** *1¼* **This Ones For Eddy**[46] 600 8-9-5 **50** (b) RobertWinston 3 53
(John Balding) *chsd ldr: rdn and ev ch fr over 2f out: edgd lft over 1f out: styd on same pce fnl f* 12/1
3043 **4** *nk* **Monsieur Pontaven**[6] 1120 6-9-1 **46** oh1 (b) J-PGuillambert 6 49
(Robin Bastiman) *hld up: hdwy and hmpd over 1f out: sn rdn: styd on same pce fnl f* 9/2[2]
0213 **5** *shd* **Crucis Abbey (IRE)**[8] 1093 5-9-3 **48** (p) EddieAhern 4 51
(Mark Brisbourne) *chsd ldrs: rdn over 1f out: styd on same pce ins fnl f* 11/4[1]
05-5 **6** *5* **Yorksters Prince (IRE)**[10] 1070 6-9-5 **50** (b) PhillipMakin 8 42
(Marjorie Fife) *chsd ldrs: rdn over 1f out: wknd fnl f* 7/1
3036 **7** *1* **Justcallmehandsome**[13] 1017 11-8-8 **46** (be) HarryBurns(7) 5 36
(Dominic Ffrench Davis) *s.s: hld up: hdwy on outer over 2f out: wknd over 1f out* 12/1
2200 **8** *6* **Under Par**[12] 1042 5-9-3 **48** (t) GrahamGibbons 2 25
(Michael Easterby) *led: rdn and hdd over 1f out: wknd ins fnl f* 6/1
-450 **9** *6* **Kuraanda**[62] 375 4-9-1 **46** oh1 (p) PaddyAspell 9 11
(John Wainwright) *hld up: rdn over 2f out: sn wknd* 66/1

1m 50.72s (0.22) **Going Correction** +0.125s/f (Slow) 9 Ran SP% **113.0**
Speed ratings (Par 101): **104,102,101,100,100 96,95,90,84**
toteswingers 1&2 £8.10, 1&3 £8.30, 2&3 £22.40 CSF £57.48 CT £632.47 TOTE £4.40: £1.90, £3.40, £3.10; EX 65.50 Trifecta £544.90 Pool: £2,036.56 - 2.80 winning units..
Owner M Khan X2 **Bred** Mallalieu Bloodstock Ltd **Trained** Epsom, Surrey

FOCUS
The second division of this low-grade handicap looked marginally stronger than the first and it saw a commanding success for the top weight. The winner has a good chance of defying a penalty in this form.
T/Plt: £46.70 to a £1 stake. Pool: £56,125.90 - 876.22 winning units T/Qpdt: £13.50 to a £1 stake. Pool: £4,562.10 - 249.50 winning units CR

1223 - 1231a (Foreign Racing) - See Raceform Interactive

1108 DONCASTER (L-H)
Saturday, March 30

OFFICIAL GOING: Soft (7.1)
Wind: moderate 1/2 behind Weather: fine and sunny but cold

1232 WILLIAM HILL-NO 1 DOWNLOADED BETTING APP H'CAP 6f
1:20 (1:21) (Class 2) (0-100,100) 4-Y-O+ £12,938 (£3,850; £1,924; £962) Stalls High

Form RPR
-200 **1** **Thunderball**[46] 621 7-8-12 91 (p) TomQueally 6 99
(Scott Dixon) *prom: pressed ldr 1/2-way: rdn to ld appr fnl f: kpt on wl* 14/1
342- **2** *1* **Spinatrix**[188] 6515 5-8-6 92 ConnorBeasley(7) 4 97
(Michael Dods) *led narrowly: rdn whn hdd appr fnl f: kpt on: hld towards fin* 12/1
000- **3** *¾* **King Of Jazz (IRE)**[149] 7508 5-8-5 87 DarrenEgan(3) 8 90
(Michael Bell) *hld up in midfield: gd hdwy over 2f out: rdn to chse ldrs over 1f out: kpt on* 7/1[1]
006- **4** *nk* **Shropshire (IRE)**[155] 7366 5-8-12 96 MatthewLawson(5) 10 98
(Charles Hills) *hld up in midfield: pushed along 1/2-way: hdwy over 1f out: kpt on wl* 8/1[2]
142- **5** *¾* **Jamaican Bolt (IRE)**[154] 7397 5-8-11 95 WilliamTwiston-Davies(5) 1 95+
(Geoffrey Oldroyd) *prom: stl on bit over 1f out: rdn and upsides 1f out: no ex ins fnl f* 8/1[2]
231- **6** *1¼* **Another Wise Kid (IRE)**[179] 6755 5-8-8 87 MickyFenton 7 83
(Paul Midgley) *in tch: rdn over 2f out: kpt on one pce* 33/1
521- **7** *nk* **Chooseday (IRE)**[224] 5337 4-8-7 86 AmyRyan 2 81
(Kevin Ryan) *sn chsd ldrs: rdn and ev ch over 1f out: wknd ins fnl f* 20/1
030- **8** *1¼* **Mass Rally (IRE)**[140] 7690 6-9-7 100 (b) PaulMulrennan 12 91+
(Michael Dods) *hld up: rdn over 2f out: kpt on fnl f: nvr threatened* 10/1
005- **9** *nse* **Farlow (IRE)**[155] 7366 5-8-11 90 TonyHamilton 16 81
(Richard Fahey) *midfield: rdn 1/2-way: sn one pce and no imp on ldrs* 8/1[2]
610- **10** *2½* **All Or Nothin (IRE)**[92] 8272 4-8-8 87 MichaelO'Connell 9 71
(John Quinn) *in tch: rdn over 2f out: wknd ins fnl f* 16/1
005- **11** *nk* **Imperial Djay (IRE)**[182] 6659 8-8-9 88 PJMcDonald 5 71
(Ruth Carr) *midfield: rdn over 2f out: sn no imp on ldrs* 33/1
000- **12** *hd* **Trade Secret**[155] 7366 6-8-7 86 JimmyQuinn 13 68
(Mel Brittain) *trckd ldrs: rdn over 2f out: wknd over 1f out* 33/1
000- **13** *½* **Colonel Mak**[140] 7691 6-8-11 95 LMcNiff(5) 15 76
(David Barron) *in tch: rdn over 2f out: sn lost pl: wknd over 1f out* 9/1[3]
500- **14** *nk* **Fast Shot**[189] 6466 5-8-8 87 DuranFentiman 3 67
(Tim Easterby) *midfield: rdn over 2f out: nvr threatened* 20/1
440- **15** *¾* **Alejandro (IRE)**[189] 6471 4-8-2 88 SamanthaBell(7) 14 65
(Richard Fahey) *w ldr: rdn over 2f out: sn wknd* 20/1
622- **16** *1½* **Ancient Cross**[155] 7366 9-9-2 95 (t) GrahamLee 17 68
(Michael Easterby) *hld up: nvr threatened* 10/1
U00- **17** *½* **West Leake Diman (IRE)**[155] 7366 4-9-1 94 WilliamCarson 11 65
(Charles Hills) *dwlt: hld up: a towards rr* 33/1
000- **18** *6* **Chunky Diamond (IRE)**[202] 6075 4-8-9 88 DaleSwift 18 41
(Ruth Carr) *hld up: rdn 1/2-way: sn btn* 33/1

1m 13.71s (0.11) **Going Correction** +0.25s/f (Good) 18 Ran SP% **123.2**
Speed ratings (Par 109): **109,107,106,106,105 103,103,101,101,98 97,97,96,96,95 93,92,84**
Tote Swingers: 1&2 £31.00, 1&3 £23.90, 2&3 £20.20 CSF £153.72 CT £1272.12 TOTE £17.90: £3.80, £2.40, £2.70, £3.00; EX 217.80 Trifecta £1593.10 Pool: £2,947.74 - 1.38 winning units..
Owner The Doncaster Racing Club **Bred** Mrs Yvette Dixon **Trained** Babworth, Notts

FOCUS
A rescheduled card, lost to snow a week earlier. The winning jockey in the opener described the ground as "dead", and the time was 2.5sec slower than standard. They raced in one group down the middle in this competitive sprint handicap. The principals were always towards the fore and those drawn low were seen to good effect. Straightforward form, the winner rated to his best.

1233 WILLIAM HILL SPRING MILE (H'CAP) 1m (S)
1:55 (1:55) (Class 2) 4-Y-O+
£28,012 (£8,388; £4,194; £2,097; £1,048; £526) Stalls High

Form RPR
011- **1** **Educate**[169] 7032 4-9-8 88 LiamJones 16 101
(Ismail Mohammed) *mid-div: hdwy over 2f out: chsd ldr appr fnl f: bmpd last 50yds: styd on to ld nr fin* 8/1[1]
165- **2** *hd* **Boots And Spurs**[147] 7556 4-8-13 79 (v) CathyGannon 8 92
(Mrs K Burke) *trckd ldrs: led over 2f out: edgd rt ins fnl f: hdd towards fin* 20/1

3-14 **3** *1* **Haaf A Sixpence**[59] 443 4-9-3 83 JimCrowley 20 93
(Ralph Beckett) *hld up towards rr: hdwy over 2f out: edgd lft and styd on same pce ins fnl f* **12/1**

3413 **4** *2* **Patriotic (IRE)**[16] 995 5-8-5 76 5ex ow2 (p) RobertTart(5) 13 82
(Chris Dwyer) *mid-div: hdwy 2f out: sn n.m.r: styd on wl clsng stages* **11/1**[3]

101- **5** *½* **Ocean Tempest**[259] 4097 4-9-5 85 (p) MichaelO'Connell 19 90
(John Ryan) *mde most tl over 2f out: kpt on same pce fnl f* **16/1**

341- **6** *½* **Yojimbo (IRE)**[155] 7370 5-9-0 85 CharlesBishop(5) 6 89
(Mick Channon) *w ldrs: kpt on same pce fnl f* **12/1**

313- **7** *1 ½* **Gaul Wood (IRE)**[176] 6831 4-9-9 89 RichardKingscote 7 89
(Tom Dascombe) *chsd ldrs: one pce fnl 2f* **8/1**[1]

600- **8** *½* **Extraterrestrial**[150] 7493 9-8-13 82 LeeTopliss(3) 18 81
(Richard Fahey) *charged gate and broke smartly: sn in rr: hdwy over 2f out: keeping on whn hmpd appr fnl f* **20/1**

650- **9** *shd* **Satanic Beat (IRE)**[159] 7294 4-9-4 84 PJMcDonald 17 83
(Jedd O'Keeffe) *mid-div: outpcd over 2f out: kpt on fnl f* **33/1**

115- **10** *½* **Myboyalfie (USA)**[140] 7691 6-9-9 89 (v) IanMongan 5 87
(J R Jenkins) *chsd ldrs: hung rt and one pce fnl 2f* **11/1**[3]

6152 **11** *3* **Docofthebay (IRE)**[7] 1148 9-9-4 84 5ex (b) TomQueally 2 75
(Scott Dixon) *hld up in mid-div: hdwy over 2f out: wknd over 1f out* **14/1**

03-6 **12** *3 ¾* **Las Verglas Star (IRE)**[31] 810 5-9-2 89 GeorgeChaloner(7) 9 72
(Richard Fahey) *in rr: sme hdwy 2f out: nvr on terms* **16/1**

0-11 **13** *2* **Dubai Hills**[7] 1148 7-9-2 87 5ex WilliamTwiston-Davies(5) 14 66
(Bryan Smart) *trckd ldrs: effrt over 2f out: wknd over 1f out* **10/1**[2]

44-6 **14** *3* **Frog Hollow**[21] 947 4-9-8 88 GrahamLee 15 60
(Milton Bradley) *s.i.s: a in rr* **12/1**

011- **15** *1 ¼* **Nameitwhatyoulike**[143] 7639 4-9-8 88 PaulMulrennan 11 61
(Michael Easterby) *w ldrs: wkng whn hmpd over 1f out: heavily eased clsng stages* **10/1**[2]

00-0 **16** *1 ¼* **King Of Eden (IRE)**[21] 944 7-9-1 86 JasonHart(5) 4 53
(Eric Alston) *s.i.s: drvn and sme hdwy 4f out: wknd over 2f out* **66/1**

1/0- **17** *2 ½* **Garde Cotiere (USA)**[316] 2250 5-9-10 90 TonyHamilton 1 51
(Richard Fahey) *mid-div: drvn and lost pl over 2f out: sn bhd* **18/1**

025- **18** *5* **Mr Spiggott (IRE)**[148] 7520 4-8-11 80 DarrenEgan(3) 12 30
(Joseph Tuite) *in rr: drvn 3f out: sn bhd* **18/1**

1m 41.63s (2.33) **Going Correction** +0.45s/f (Yiel) **18** Ran SP% **123.1**
Speed ratings (Par 109): **106,105,104,102,102 101,100,99,99,99 96,92,90,87,86 84,82,77**
Tote Swingers: 1&2 £50.10, 1&3 £16.80, 2&3 £74.30 CSF £169.10 CT £1981.06 TOTE £6.40: £1.90, £5.50, £3.40, £3.30; EX 143.60 Trifecta £2567.30 Part won. Pool: £3,423.13 - 0.57 winning units..
Owner Sultan Ali **Bred** Lady Legard **Trained** Newmarket, Suffolk

FOCUS
Not a strong edition of this consolation event, the week's delay not helping the quality. Last year the bottom weights ran off 84 whereas this time Patriotic was off 74 while non-runner Day Of The Eagle had got in off 71. They raced in an arrowhead formation down the centre, although the first two home, who were drawn 16 and 8, ended up towards the stands' side. Straightforward form and the winner remains progressive.

1234 WILLIAM HILL - NEW IPAD APP CAMMIDGE TROPHY (LISTED RACE) 6f
2:30 (2:31) (Class 1) 3-Y-O+
£20,982 (£7,955; £3,981; £1,983; £995; £499) **Stalls** High

Form RPR

110- **1** **Jack Dexter**[140] 7690 4-9-5 102 GrahamLee 9 110
(Jim Goldie) *hld up in tch: smooth hdwy over 1f out: pushed along to ld jst ins fnl f: rdn out fnl 100yds* **15/8**[1]

0-00 **2** *½* **Captain Ramius (IRE)**[58] 467 7-9-5 106 FrannyNorton 1 109
(Kevin Ryan) *w ldr: rdn over 2f out: kpt on but a hld by wnr ins fnl f* **9/2**[3]

300- **3** *1* **Our Jonathan**[189] 6468 6-9-5 105 AndreaAtzeni 4 106
(Tim Pitt) *in tch: rdn over 2f out: kpt on* **4/1**[2]

0046 **4** *1 ¼* **Hitchens (IRE)**[21] 955 8-9-8 107 AndrewMullen 8 105
(David Barron) *hld up: rdn 2f out: kpt on one pce* **10/1**

4-00 **5** *1 ¾* **Confessional**[72] 244 6-9-5 104 (b) PaulMulrennan 2 97
(Tim Easterby) *racd keenly: trckd ldrs: led over 2f out: sn rdn: hdd jst ins fnl f: sn wknd* **10/1**

10-0 **6** *2* **Regal Parade**[21] 944 9-9-5 107 (t) DaleSwift 5 91
(Milton Bradley) *in tch: rdn 2f out: wknd fnl f* **13/2**

120- **7** *3 ½* **Effie B**[128] 7828 3-8-1 93 CathyGannon 7 75
(Mick Channon) *slowly away: hld up: rdn over 2f out: nvr threatened* **14/1**

-412 **8** *½* **Equitania**[66] 337 3-8-1 89 NickyMackay 10 74
(Alan Bailey) *racd alone towards stands' side: led: hdd over 2f out: sn drvn: wknd over 1f out* **28/1**

1m 14.51s (0.91) **Going Correction** +0.45s/f (Yiel)
WFA 3 from 4yo+ 13lb **8** Ran SP% **114.6**
Speed ratings: **111,110,109,107,105 102,97,97**
Tote Swingers: 1&2 £2.80, 1&3 £3.50, 2&3 £5.30 CSF £10.44 TOTE £2.20: £1.30, £2.00, £1.70; EX 8.40 Trifecta £25.80 Pool: £2,275.31 - 65.95 winning units..
Owner Johnnie Delta Racing **Bred** Jim Goldie **Trained** Uplawmoor, E Renfrews
■ Stewards' Enquiry : Franny Norton two-day ban: use of whip (13&15 April)

FOCUS
This event has been won in recent seasons by subsequent Group 1 winners La Cucaracha and Les Arcs, while last year's winner The Cheka was later second in the July Cup. This edition lacked a bit of depth but Jack Dexter maintained his upwardly mobile profile. The form could have been rated up to 5lb higher.

1235 WILLIAM HILL LINCOLN (HERITAGE H'CAP) 1m (S)
3:05 (3:05) (Class 2) 4-Y-O+
£62,250 (£18,640; £9,320; £4,660; £2,330; £1,170) **Stalls** High

Form RPR

260- **1** **Levitate**[182] 6674 5-8-4 90 (v) DarrenEgan(3) 3 99
(John Quinn) *chsd ldrs: styd on fnl f: led last strides* **20/1**

00-6 **2** *shd* **Global Village (IRE)**[21] 945 8-8-11 94 MartinLane 1 103
(Brian Ellison) *in rr: hdwy over 2f out: styd on strly fnl f: jst failed* **14/1**

600- **3** *nse* **Brae Hill (IRE)**[168] 7066 7-8-12 95 TonyHamilton 19 104
(Richard Fahey) *trckd ldrs: led appr fnl f: hdd and no ex nr fin* **14/1**

061- **4** *¾* **Justonefortheroad**[152] 7435 7-8-8 94 LeeTopliss(3) 10 101
(Richard Fahey) *mid-div: hdwy and prom over 2f out: chsng ldrs over 1f out: kpt on fnl 100yds* **14/1**

302- **5** *1* **Jack's Revenge (IRE)**[140] 7691 5-8-8 91 (bt) TonyCulhane 16 99+
(George Baker) *hld up towards rr: hdwy 2f out: styd on ins fnl f* **16/1**

016- **6** *1* **Chapter Seven**[98] 8227 4-9-1 98 GrahamLee 14 101
(Stuart Williams) *trckd ldrs: t.k.h: outpcd and lost pl 3f out: hdwy over 1f out: kpt on ins fnl f* **12/1**

406- **7** *½* **Majestic Myles (IRE)**[196] 6246 5-9-3 107 GeorgeChaloner(7) 11 109
(Richard Fahey) *led: hdd appr fnl f: fdd towards fin* **33/1**

3-21 **8** *shd* **Strictly Silver (IRE)**[21] 945 4-8-9 97 5ex (p) RobertTart(5) 22 98
(Alan Bailey) *hld up in tch: effrt over 2f out: kpt on same pce fnl f* **8/1**[2]

100- **9** *½* **Eshtibaak (IRE)**[251] 4365 5-8-10 93 DaneO'Neill 20 93
(John Gosden) *mid-div: hdwy over 2f out: chsng ldrs over 1f out: one pce* **8/1**[2]

30-0 **10** *3 ¼* **Capaill Liath (IRE)**[21] 947 5-8-9 92 (p) AmyRyan 18 85
(Kevin Ryan) *chsd ldrs: drvn 3f out: wknd over 1f out* **40/1**

006- **11** *¾* **Prince Of Johanne (IRE)**[140] 7691 7-9-5 102 (p) JohnFahy 21 93
(Tom Tate) *chsd ldrs: swtchd to r alone stands' side 5f out: wknd fnl f* **25/1**

65- **12** *2* **Hit The Jackpot (IRE)**[321] 2102 4-8-6 96 DavidBergin(7) 2 83
(David O'Meara) *chsd ldrs: effrt over 2f out: wknd over 1f out* **22/1**

00-0 **13** *hd* **Memory Cloth**[21] 945 6-9-0 97 (b[1]) DaleSwift 4 84
(Brian Ellison) *mid-div: drvn 3f out: wknd over 1f out* **20/1**

100- **14** *hd* **Swiftly Done (IRE)**[182] 6674 6-8-3 93 LukeLeadbitter(7) 5 79
(Declan Carroll) *in rr: hdwy over 2f out: wknd over 1f out* **20/1**

465- **15** *nse* **Bancnuanaheireann (IRE)**[110] 8056 6-8-8 91 AndrewMullen 9 77
(Michael Appleby) *mid-div: drvn and sme hdwy 3f out: wknd wl over 1f out* **16/1**

205- **16** *1 ¼* **Captain Bertie (IRE)**[175] 6868 5-8-11 94 WilliamCarson 7 77
(Charles Hills) *edgd lft s: hld up in mid-div: effrt over 2f out: nvr a factor* **10/1**[3]

112- **17** *1 ½* **Lahaag**[168] 7064 4-8-12 95 RobertHavlin 6 75
(John Gosden) *hmpd s: mid-div: hdwy over 2f out: wknd over 1f out* **13/2**[1]

112- **18** *½* **Chosen Character (IRE)**[162] 7210 5-8-4 92 (vt) NatashaEaton(5) 13 71
(Tom Dascombe) *s.i.s: sn chsng ldrs: lost pl over 1f out* **25/1**

140- **19** *1 ½* **Muffin McLeay (IRE)**[162] 7210 5-8-9 92 PaddyAspell 8 68
(David Barron) *s.i.s: nvr on terms* **100/1**

6-44 **20** *hd* **Dubai Dynamo**[14] 1036 8-8-7 90 PJMcDonald 12 65
(Ruth Carr) *mid-div: drvn over 2f out: sn wknd* **33/1**

000- **21** *5* **Anderiego (IRE)**[161] 7240 5-8-9 92 PaulMulrennan 17 56
(David O'Meara) *mid-div: effrt over 2f out: sn lost pl and bhd* **40/1**

411/ **P** **Gladys' Gal**[618] 4235 5-8-9 92 AndreaAtzeni 15
(Roger Varian) *w ldrs: lost pl 3f out: sn heavily eased and bhd: t.o whn virtually p.u over 1f out: dismntd nr line* **16/1**

1m 41.91s (2.61) **Going Correction** +0.55s/f (Yiel) **22** Ran SP% **128.1**
Speed ratings (Par 109): **108,107,107,107,106 105,104,104,104,100 100,98,97,97,97 96,94,94,92,92 87,**
Tote Swingers: 1&2 £61.30, 1&3 £91.40, 2&3 £26.70 CSF £251.01 CT £4105.96 TOTE £26.40: £6.70, £4.60, £3.20, £3.70; EX 594.00 Trifecta £5004.50 Part won. Pool: £6,672.70 - 0.10 winning units..
Owner Charles Wentworth **Bred** Cheveley Park Stud Ltd **Trained** Settrington, N Yorks

FOCUS
Snowed off a week earlier, this historic handicap was reopened to horses entered at the weights-published stage, and six horses declared to run on the original date were missing. Their absence weakened the race, while long-time ante-post favourite Nine Realms was not declared on either date. The runners formed one group although Prince Of Johanne peeled off before halfway to race on his own near the stands' side. There appeared no real draw advantage, with the winner coming from stall 3, the second from 1 and the third from 19. The time was fractionally slower than the Spring Mile, and the first four all came from Malton stables. Straightforward form, with the third helping with the level, and a personal best from Levitate.

1236 UNIVERSAL RECYCLING MAIDEN STKS 1m 2f 60y
3:40 (3:40) (Class 5) 3-Y-O **£2,911** (£866; £432; £216) **Stalls** Low

Form RPR

32 **1** **Incorporate**[24] 895 3-9-5 0 DaneO'Neill 2 86+
(Pat Eddery) *mde all: pushed along 3f out: briefly pressed 2f out: styd on wl* **4/1**[3]

434- **2** *1 ¾* **Space Ship**[184] 6596 3-9-5 78 RobertHavlin 6 82
(John Gosden) *trckd ldng pair: rdn to chal 2f out: one pce and hld by wnr fr over 1f out* **2/1**[1]

2 **3** *5* **The Welsh Wizard (IRE)**[33] 799 3-9-5 0 GrahamLee 9 73
(Charles Hills) *in tch: pushed along over 3f out: wandered u.p over 1f out: kpt on fnl f: no threat to ldng pair* **5/2**[2]

500- **4** *2 ¾* **White Coppice**[175] 6874 3-9-5 76 TonyHamilton 4 68
(Richard Fahey) *trckd ldng pair: rdn 3f out: sn one pce: wknd ins fnl f* **8/1**

432- **5** *6* **Duke Of Yorkshire**[170] 6997 3-9-2 71 NeilFarley(3) 5 57
(Declan Carroll) *hld up: rdn over 3f out: sn no imp* **8/1**

6 *8* **Hollow Beat** 3-9-0 0 DuranFentiman 8 38
(Tim Walford) *slowly away: hld up: pushed along over 3f out: nvr threatened* **50/1**

7 *11* **Moves Like Jagger (IRE)** 3-9-5 0 TomQueally 1 23
(Michael Bell) *dwlt: hld up: rdn over 3f out: a towards rr* **14/1**

4 **8** *14* **Inigo Montoya**[33] 800 3-9-5 0 JohnFahy 3
(Alan McCabe) *w ldr: rdn over 3f out: sn wknd* **100/1**

2m 16.65s (7.25) **Going Correction** +0.55s/f (Yiel) **8** Ran SP% **113.7**
Speed ratings (Par 98): **93,91,87,85,80 74,65,54**
Tote Swingers: 1&2 £4.10, 1&3 £2.50, 2&3 £1.70 CSF £12.28 TOTE £3.70: £1.20, £1.60, £1.30; EX 12.70 Trifecta £33.30 Pool: £1,243.78 - 28.01 winning units..
Owner K Abdullah **Bred** Juddmonte Farms Ltd **Trained** Nether Winchendon, Bucks

FOCUS
Quite a good maiden for the grade, run at a sound gallop. The runners came down the centre in the straight, avoiding the inside rail, and the first two were clear. It was the slowest of the four races over the trip. The first two were clear and the form is rated through the second.

1237 HARRIET POWELL H'CAP (DIV I) 1m 2f 60y
4:15 (4:15) (Class 4) (0-85,85) 4-Y-O+ **£5,175** (£1,540; £769; £384) **Stalls** Low

Form RPR

410- **1** **Eastern Destiny**[182] 6661 4-9-3 81 TonyHamilton 6 92
(Richard Fahey) *led early: trckd ldrs: led 2f out: hld on gamely* **11/2**[3]

223- **2** *hd* **Snow Trooper**[127] 7842 5-8-12 76 JimCrowley 10 87
(Dean Ivory) *mid-div: hdwy over 2f out: chal over 1f out: no ex nr fin* **9/2**[2]

1345 **3** *4 ½* **The Lock Master (IRE)**[7] 1148 6-8-13 77 AndrewMullen 4 79
(Michael Appleby) *mid-div: hdwy to chal 2f out: styd on same pce* **13/2**

521- **4** *½* **Prophesy (IRE)**[213] 5732 4-9-4 85 NeilFarley(3) 9 86
(Declan Carroll) *drvn to sn ld: hdd 9f out: styd alone on inner and led over 4f out: hdd 2f out: kpt on same pce* **8/1**

-324 **5** *¾* **Noguchi (IRE)**[31] 810 8-8-10 79 RobertTart(5) 7 79
(Michael Murphy) *in rr: hdwy on outer over 2f out: pushed wd over 1f out: kpt on one pce* **8/1**

021- **6** *nk* **Amaze**[170] 7002 5-9-7 85 DaleSwift 1 84
(Brian Ellison) *in rr: hdwy to chse ldrs over 2f out: one pce* **4/1**[1]

436- **7** 3 1/4 **Maven**[144] 7601 5-9-4 82 DuranFentiman 2 75
(Tim Easterby) *hld up in rr: smooth hdwy over 3f out: chsng ldrs and drvn over 1f out: wknd last 150yds* **14/1**

0-50 **8** 1 3/4 **Musnad (USA)**[29] 540 5-8-0 71 RichardOliver(7) 3 61
(Brian Ellison) *chsd ldrs: outpcd over 2f out: no threat after* **25/1**

0425 **9** 4 **Askaud (IRE)**[16] 995 5-9-0 78 (b) TomQueally 8 60
(Scott Dixon) *sn trcking ldrs: edgd rt and wknd over 1f out* **10/1**

021- **10** 17 **Brockfield**[155] 7369 7-8-7 71 oh1 JimmyQuinn 11 21
(Mel Brittain) *sn chsng ldrs: led 9f out: hdd over 4f out: wknd 2f out: bhd whn eased: t.o* **12/1**

11-0 **11** 7 **Cufflink**[17] 984 4-8-9 73 JamieMackay 5
(Iain Jardine) *hld up in rr: lost pl over 2f out: sn bhd: eased: t.o* **40/1**

2m 15.13s (5.73) **Going Correction** +0.55s/f (Yiel) **11** Ran SP% **118.9**
Speed ratings (Par 105): **99,98,95,94,94 94,91,90,86,73 67**
Tote Swingers: 1&2 £4.90, 1&3 £4.20, 2&3 £8.00 CSF £30.83 CT £167.40 TOTE £6.10: £1.90, £1.70, £2.50; EX 31.70 Trifecta £613.80 Pool: £1,427.59 - 1.74 winning units..
Owner B H Farr **Bred** Worksop Manor Stud **Trained** Musley Bank, N Yorks

FOCUS
Just a fair handicap. All bar one raced down the middle of the track up the straight, although the first two, who came clear, ended up near the inside rail. It was the slower division by 1.57sec. The first pair were clear and the winner is still going forward.

1238 HARRIET POWELL H'CAP (DIV II) 1m 2f 60y
4:50 (4:50) (Class 4) (0-85,85) 4-Y-0+ **£5,175** (£1,540; £769; £384) **Stalls** Low

Form RPR

236- **1** **Docs Legacy (IRE)**[55] 7842 4-8-11 75 TonyHamilton 6 89
(Richard Fahey) *mid-div: hdwy over 4f out: chal 2f out: kpt on to ld towards fin* **7/2**[2]

1- **2** hd **Star Lahib (IRE)**[215] 5679 4-8-13 77 FrannyNorton 1 91+
(Mark Johnston) *dwlt: in rr: hdwy 4f out: narrow ld over 2f out: hdd and no ex clsng stages* **11/4**[1]

200- **3** 5 **Hillview Boy (IRE)**[87] 7689 9-9-7 85 [1] GrahamLee 7 89
(Jim Goldie) *stdd s: hld up in rr: hdwy over 2f out: 3rd 1f out: kpt on one pce* **6/1**

504- **4** 1/2 **The Fun Crusher**[260] 4072 5-8-13 82 DarylByrne(5) 2 85
(Tim Easterby) *mid-div: hdwy over 3f out: chalng 2f out: 4th 1f out: kpt on one pce* **13/2**

34/0 **5** 1 1/4 **Seattle Drive (IRE)**[25] 889 5-9-1 82 PaulPickard(3) 5 83
(Brian Ellison) *hld up in rr: hdwy over 3f out: upsides 2f out: hung lft: one pce* **20/1**

000- **6** 1 **Kiwi Bay**[144] 7601 8-9-0 78 PaulMulrennan 10 77
(Michael Dods) *led after 2f: hdd over 2f out: fdd fnl f* **33/1**

0-41 **7** 6 **Canary Wharf (IRE)**[59] 439 4-8-13 77 (b) AndreaAtzeni 4 64
(Marco Botti) *mid-div: effrt over 3f out: wknd over 1f out* **5/1**[3]

554- **8** 7 **Carragold**[159] 7294 7-8-7 71 DuranFentiman 3 45
(Mel Brittain) *in rr: drvn over 3f out: wknd 2f out: bhd whn eased ins fnl f* **9/1**

26- **9** 7 **Gran Maestro (USA)**[116] 7976 4-8-8 72 (b) PJMcDonald 8 33
(Ruth Carr) *trckd ldrs: t.k.h: wknd over 2f out: sn bhd* **33/1**

156- **10** 9 **Indepub**[148] 4674 4-9-2 80 (p) AmyRyan 9 24
(Kevin Ryan) *led 2f: chsd ldr: drvn 3f out: hung lft and sn lost pl* **8/1**

2m 13.56s (4.16) **Going Correction** +0.55s/f (Yiel) **10** Ran SP% **124.9**
Speed ratings (Par 105): **105,104,100,100,99 98,93,88,82,75**
Tote Swingers: 1&2 £2.60, 1&3 £2.70, 2&3 £6.70 CSF £14.42 CT £57.88 TOTE £4.30: £1.60, £1.70, £2.60; EX 13.70 Trifecta £111.10 Pool: £499.85 - 3.37 winning units..
Owner D Bardsley **Bred** Miss Mary Davison **Trained** Musley Bank, N Yorks

FOCUS
This was run at a brisk gallop, in a time 1.57sec quicker than the first division. Ordinary handicap form with the first two clear, the winner rated to last year's Flat best.

1239 YESSS ELECTRICAL APPRENTICE H'CAP (ROUND 1 OF THE GO RACING IN YORKSHIRE FUTURE STARS SERIES) 1m 2f 60y
5:25 (5:25) (Class 5) (0-70,70) 4-Y-0+ **£2,911** (£866; £432; £216) **Stalls** Low

Form RPR

5-33 **1** **Luggers Hall (IRE)**[45] 637 5-9-7 70 CharlesBishop 10 81
(Tony Carroll) *hld up in rr: stdy hdwy over 3f out: r.o to ld last 100yds* **8/1**

240- **2** 1 **Zaplamation (IRE)**[148] 6631 8-8-11 60 WilliamTwiston-Davies 2 69
(John Quinn) *mid-div: hdwy over 3f out: led over 1f out: hdd and no ex ins fnl f* **6/1**[1]

5-00 **3** 5 **Rockweiller**[8] 1111 6-8-8 57 (v) DarrenEgan 12 57
(Steve Gollings) *chsd ldrs: led over 3f out: hdd over 1f out: one pce* **8/1**

450- **4** 6 **James Pollard (IRE)**[180] 6734 8-8-9 65 SiobhanMiller(7) 11 53
(Bernard Llewellyn) *hld up in rr: hdwy to chse ldrs 3f out: wknd fnl f* **22/1**

0532 **5** 1 **Availed Speaker (IRE)**[9] 1104 4-8-7 61 SamanthaBell(5) 15 47
(Richard Fahey) *sn chsng ldrs: one pce fnl 2f* **14/1**

030- **6** 1 1/2 **Lady Sledmere (IRE)**[158] 7314 5-8-8 60 ShirleyTeasdale(3) 5 43
(Paul Midgley) *in rr: hdwy over 3f out: one pce fnl 2f* **20/1**

2644 **7** 1 1/4 **Follow The Flag (IRE)**[11] 1076 9-8-10 62 (v) GaryPhillips(3) 1 43
(Alan McCabe) *mid-div: drvn 5f out: sn chsng ldrs: wknd over 1f out* **15/2**[3]

05-6 **8** 5 **Drummond**[12] 1069 4-9-2 68 DanielMuscutt(3) 14 39
(Bernard Llewellyn) *in rr: sme hdwy over 3f out: hung rt and wknd 2f out* **25/1**

-444 **9** shd **White Diamond**[12] 477 6-8-13 62 RobertTart 17 33
(Michael Appleby) *chsd ldrs: wknd 2f out* **9/1**

50-0 **10** nk **Rosselli (IRE)**[12] 1059 4-9-2 68 ConorHarrison(3) 7 39
(Mrs K Burke) *w ldrs: stmbld and dropped bk after 2f: drvn over 3f out: wknd 2f out* **11/1**

-002 **11** 7 **Dream Prospector**[24] 896 4-8-2 56 JoeyHaynes(5) 8 13
(James Evans) *in rr: effrt over 3f out: wknd 2f out* **7/1**[2]

00-4 **12** nk **Amazing Blue Sky**[18] 970 7-8-12 64 DavidBergin(3) 16 21
(Ruth Carr) *chsd ldrs: lost pl over 2f out* **14/1**

2-10 **13** 3 3/4 **Coastal Passage**[72] 240 5-8-7 56 oh2 (t) RachealKneller 4 6
(Charles Smith) *mid-div: effrt over 3f out: hung lft and grad wknd* **20/1**

0-05 **14** 1/2 **Six Silver Lane**[29] 850 5-8-12 66 (v) AdamMcLean(5) 3 15
(Derek Shaw) *led: hdd over 3f out: lost pl over 2f out* **10/1**

0-20 **15** 2 3/4 **Violent Velocity (IRE)**[64] 376 10-9-2 70 KevinLundie(5) 9 14
(John Quinn) *mid-div: reminders over 5f out: sn lost pl and bhd* **25/1**

00-4 **16** 39 **Oneofapear (IRE)**[50] 562 7-9-6 69 LMcNiff 13
(Ian McInnes) *in rr: bhd and drvn over 4f out: sn bhd: t.o whn virtually p.u over 1f out* **20/1**

2m 15.77s (6.37) **Going Correction** +0.65s/f (Yiel) **16** Ran SP% **127.9**
Speed ratings (Par 103): **100,99,95,90,89 88,87,83,83,83 77,77,74,73,71 40**
Tote Swingers: 1&2 £3.80, 1&3 £3.60, 2&3 £3.40 CSF £51.71 CT £409.75 TOTE £10.90: £2.50, £2.20, £7.10; EX 80.10 Trifecta £532.20 Part won. Pool: £709.61 - 0.75 winning units..
Owner M S Cooke **Bred** Knockainey Stud & Storway Ltd **Trained** Cropthorne, Worcs

FOCUS
A modest apprentice handicap in which all bar four of the field had already been out this year. The second sets the level.
T/Jkpt: Not won. T/Plt: £215.70 to a £1 stake. Pool: £194,866.10 - 659.34 winning tickets T/Qpdt: £14.10 to a £1 stake. Pool: £9,431.57 - 494.57 winning tickets WG

1094 KEMPTON (A.W) (R-H)
Saturday, March 30

OFFICIAL GOING: Standard
Wind: Brisk ahead Weather: Cloudy

1240 MIKE THE KNIGHT HERE 13.04.13 MAIDEN FILLIES' STKS 5f (P)
1:45 (1:47) (Class 4) 2-Y-0 **£3,881** (£1,155; £577; £288) **Stalls** Low

Form RPR

1 **Orton Park (IRE)** 2-9-0 0 StevieDonohoe 1 70+
(Tobias B P Coles) *trckd ldrs: effrt on ins whn n.m.r and swtchd lft 1f out: drvn and styd on wl to ld last stride* **10/1**

2 shd **Go Glamorous (IRE)** 2-9-0 0 LukeMorris 8 70+
(Ronald Harris) *chsd ldrs: drvn to ld 1f out: kpt on wl but edgd rt u.p: hdd last strides* **6/1**[2]

3 3/4 **Kodafine (IRE)** 2-9-0 0 AdamKirby 11 67+
(David Evans) *s.i.s: in rr: hdwy 2f out: styd on wl fnl f to take 3rd last strides: nt rch ldng duo* **25/1**

0 **4** 1/2 **Marilyn Marquessa**[6] 1156 2-8-9 0 PhilipPrince(5) 6 65
(Jo Hughes) *sn led: rdn 2f out: hdd 1f out: one pce whn n.m.r and dropped to 4th clsng stages* **10/1**

5 2 3/4 **Lawman's Lady (IRE)** 2-9-0 0 NeilCallan 7 55
(Mark Johnston) *chsd ldr: rdn 2f out: no ex ins fnl f* **11/2**[1]

6 3/4 **Queen Of The Tarts** 2-8-9 0 ThomasBrown(5) 2 53
(Olly Stevens) *s.i.s: in rr: hdwy on outer and hung lft over 1f out: kpt on clsng stages* **6/1**[2]

7 1 **Cafetiere** 2-9-0 0 ChrisCatlin 5 49+
(Paul Cole) *in rr: green and hanging lft after 1f: stl green and hanging over 1f out: kpt on clsng stages* **8/1**[3]

8 1 1/4 **Kindanyce (IRE)** 2-9-0 0 FrederikTylicki 9 47+
(Richard Fahey) *v green and hung bdly lft after 1f: sme prog fnl f* **8/1**[3]

9 1 1/4 **Kitty Brown (IRE)** 2-9-0 0 SeanLevey 4 40
(David Evans) *s.i.s: outpcd* **25/1**

10 93 **Jawmiener (IRE)** 2-9-0 0 TomMcLaughlin 12
(David Evans) *lost action and wknd rapidly after 2f: virtually p.u fnl f: fatally injured* **20/1**

1m 1.48s (0.98) **Going Correction** -0.075s/f (Stan) **10** Ran SP% **96.8**
Speed ratings (Par 91): **89,88,87,86,82 81,79,77,75,**
Tote Swingers: 1&2 £13.60, 2&3 £18.40 CSF £45.00 TOTE £9.40: £3.40, £2.60, £5.70; EX 53.60 Trifecta £124.80 Part won. Pool: £166.50 - 0.01 winning units..
Owner The Orton Park Partnership **Bred** Rathbarry Stud **Trained** Newmarket, Suffolk

FOCUS
In 2012 this race produced a number of subsequent winners, including runner-up Ceiling Kitty, who subsequently won the Queen Mary at Royal Ascot. The favourite Hedy refused to enter the stalls and was withdrawn (7/2, deduct 25p in the 3 under R4). Not an easy race to rate. The fourth may limit the bare form.

1241 6 PLACES EACHWAY GRAND NATIONAL AT BETVICTOR MAGNOLIA STKS (LISTED RACE) 1m 2f (P)
2:20 (2:20) (Class 1) 4-Y-0+
£20,982 (£7,955; £3,981; £1,983; £995; £499) **Stalls** Low

Form RPR

60-2 **1** **Miblish**[35] 777 4-8-13 99 (t) FrederikTylicki 1 106
(Clive Brittain) *mde all: drvn ins fnl 2f: styd on wl fnl f: unchal* **11/4**[1]

2030 **2** 1 1/4 **Burano (IRE)**[21] 956 4-8-13 100 MartinDwyer 7 103
(Brian Meehan) *hld up in rr: hdwy 2f out: hrd rdn and styd on fnl f to take 2nd fnl 110yds: no imp on wnr* **10/1**

/42- **3** 1 **Genzy (FR)**[133] 7771 5-8-13 103 NeilCallan 2 101
(Ian Williams) *chsd wnr most of way: rdn over 2f out: kpt on tl one pce into 3rd fnl 110yds* **11/2**[3]

3112 **4** 1/2 **Robin Hoods Bay**[14] 1034 5-8-13 101 LukeMorris 5 100
(Ed Vaughan) *in rr but in tch: hdwy 3f out: chsd ldrs 2f out and sn disputing 2nd: one pce ins fnl f* **11/4**[1]

26-3 **5** 6 **Cai Shen (IRE)**[14] 1034 5-8-13 99 SeanLevey 6 88
(Richard Hannon) *chsd ldrs: disp 2nd over 4f out tl 2f out: sn wknd* **4/1**[2]

6544 **6** 2 1/2 **Tinshu (IRE)**[14] 1034 7-8-8 95 (p) ShaneKelly 4 78
(Derek Haydn Jones) *in tch: rdn 3f out: wknd over 2f out* **20/1**

00-6 **7** 6 **Marcret (ITY)**[35] 777 6-8-13 103 (t) AdamKirby 3 71
(Marco Botti) *t.k.h: trckd ldrs: rdn and btn over 2f out* **10/1**

2m 4.18s (-3.82) **Going Correction** -0.075s/f (Stan) **7** Ran SP% **111.7**
Speed ratings (Par 111): **112,111,110,109,105 103,98**
Tote Swingers: 1&2 £7.00, 1&3 £3.20, 2&3 £11.80 CSF £29.38 TOTE £3.50: £2.20, £5.70; EX 29.10 Trifecta £148.90 Pool: £1,635.57 - 8.23 winning units..
Owner Saeed Manana **Bred** N E Poole And George Thornton **Trained** Newmarket, Suffolk

FOCUS
Pace held up very well on the day. Not the strongest Listed race on paper but a tightly knit affair with the whole field closely matched on official ratings. Routine form, the front pair to their marks.

1242 BETVICTOR.COM ROSEBERY H'CAP (LONDON MIDDLE DISTANCE QUALIFIER) 1m 3f (P)
2:55 (2:55) (Class 2) (0-105,98) 4-Y-0+
£28,012 (£8,388; £4,194; £2,097; £1,048; £526) **Stalls** Low

Form RPR

6111 **1** **Buckland (IRE)**[14] 1037 5-8-13 **91** NicoleNordblad(5) 1 100
(Hans Adielsson) *trckd ldrs: chal 2f out: led appr fnl f: readily* **7/1**[3]

0030 **2** 1 1/2 **Universal (IRE)**[28] 871 4-9-10 **98** NeilCallan 3 105
(Mark Johnston) *chsd ldrs: rdn over 2f out: styd on wl fnl f to take 2nd last strides but no ch w wnr* **8/1**

3363 **3** nk **Tepmokea (IRE)**[35] 777 7-9-8 **95** ShaneKelly 10 101
(Mrs K Burke) *led: rdn and jnd 2f out: hdd appr fnl f: styd on same pce and ct for 2nd last strides* **17/2**

3-12 **4** 3/4 **Spifer (IRE)**[24] 897 5-9-4 **91** (p) AdamKirby 2 96+
(Marco Botti) *in rr: hdwy over 2f out: styd on to chse ldrs over 1f out: kpt on same pce* **6/1**[1]

4-04 **5** nk **Takeitfromalady (IRE)**[6] 1159 4-8-10 **84** (b) MartinHarley 7 88+
(Lee Carter) *towards rr: hdwy over 2f out: kpt on wl clsng stages: nt rch ldrs* **25/1**

66-2 **6** *2* **Greylami (IRE)**[70] 273 8-8-8 **86** RyanTate(5) 4 87
(Clive Cox) *in tch: rdn and hdwy over 2f out: one pce u.p fnl f* **8/1**
14-5 **7** *shd* **Daghash**[6] 1159 4-8-5 **79** (b[1]) ChrisCatlin 6 79+
(Clive Brittain) *in rr: hdwy 2f out: sn edgd lft: styd on wl clsng stages* **16/1**
4-21 **8** *1 1/4* **Hanoverian Baron**[22] 926 8-9-2 **89** SebSanders 5 87
(Tony Newcombe) *in rr: hdwy over 2f out: sn hrd drvn: nvr rchd ldrs: btn ins fnl f* **10/1**
5-14 **9** *1/2* **Scottish Star**[16] 995 5-8-8 **81** LukeMorris 11 78
(James Eustace) *chsd ldrs: rdn over 2f out: btn sn after* **16/1**
2-21 **10** *nse* **Suffice (IRE)**[17] 612 4-8-2 **76** KieranO'Neill 16 73
(Richard Fahey) *chsd ldrs: rdn 3f out: wknd over 2f out* **18/1**
0/0- **11** *2 3/4* **Cry Fury**[302] 2655 5-9-9 **96** GeorgeBaker 15 88+
(Roger Charlton) *hld up in rr: effrt fr 2f out: n.m.r and wknd appr fnl f: eased* **13/2**[2]
500- **12** *2 3/4* **Life And Soul (IRE)**[29] 7396 6-9-4 **91** MartinDwyer 13 78
(Donald McCain) *chsd ldr: rdn 3f out: wknd over 2f out* **25/1**
050- **13** *42* **Vasily**[181] 6702 5-9-3 **90** (t) AdamBeschizza 9 2
(Robert Eddery) *racd wd: effrt and rdn 1/2-way: wknd over 4f out: t.o* **25/1**
03-0 **P** **John Biscuit (IRE)**[6] 1159 5-8-9 **87** ThomasBrown(5) 8
(Andrew Balding) *v.s.a: rel to r and p.u* **8/1**

2m 18.65s (-3.25) **Going Correction** -0.075s/f (Stan)
WFA 4 from 5yo+ 1lb **14** Ran SP% **121.6**
Speed ratings (Par 109): **108,106,106,106,105 104,104,103,103,103 101,99,68,**
Tote Swingers: 1&2 £18.90, 1&3 £13.10, 2&3 £17.00 CSF £61.28 CT £481.85 TOTE £6.00: £2.30, £3.60, £2.80; EX 99.80 Trifecta £1019.40 Part won. Pool: £1,359.21 - 0.65 winning units..

Owner P S McNally **Bred** Airlie Stud And Sir Thomas Pilkington **Trained** Kingston Lisle, Oxon

FOCUS
A typically competitive renewal of this long-established handicap but it fell to an improver, who was the third successive winner on the day to be drawn in stall one. The winner keeps improving and may not have stopped yet.

1243 MASCOT GRAND NATIONAL 06.05.13 MAIDEN STKS 7f (P)
3:30 (3:31) (Class 4) 3-Y-0+ **£5,175** (£1,540; £769; £384) **Stalls** Low

Form RPR
306- **1** **Country Western**[193] 6330 3-8-13 70 SteveDrowne 3 86
(Charles Hills) *mde all: pushed along and qckn wl over 1f out: styd on strly: unchal* **7/2**[3]
246- **2** *2* **Strictly Silca**[224] 5360 3-8-8 81 (v[1]) MartinHarley 1 76
(Mick Channon) *chsd ldrs: drvn to go 2nd 2f out: rdn and no imp on wnr appr fnl f* **6/1**
3 *4* **Moortahan** 3-8-13 0 SeanLevey 5 70+
(Richard Hannon) *chsd ldrs: rdn 2f out: sn tk 3rd but no imp on ldng duo fr over 1f out* **15/8**[1]
4 *2 3/4* **Artistical (IRE)** 3-8-13 0 AdamBeschizza 6 63+
(William Haggas) *s.i.s: in rr: pushed along ins fnl 3f: mod prog fnl f* **10/3**[2]
220- **5** *1 3/4* **Kept**[173] 6925 4-10-0 70 LukeMorris 4 64
(Ronald Harris) *chsd wnr: rdn and lost 2nd 2f out: sn btn* **8/1**
6 *2 1/2* **Zain Joy (CAN)** 3-8-8 0 MartinDwyer 2 47
(Gerard Butler) *s.i.s: in rr: sme hdwy over 2f out: sn btn* **14/1**

1m 24.82s (-1.18) **Going Correction** -0.075s/f (Stan)
WFA 3 from 4yo 15lb **6** Ran SP% **112.1**
Speed ratings (Par 105): **103,100,96,93,91 88**
Tote Swingers: 1&2 £1.40, 1&3 £1.20, 2&3 £2.30 CSF £23.89 TOTE £5.30: £3.10, £2.60; EX 23.10 Trifecta £55.70 Pool: £1,629.82 - 21.91 winning units..
Owner K Abdullah **Bred** Millsec Limited **Trained** Lambourn, Berks

FOCUS
A fair-looking maiden despite the small field, with a couple of interesting newcomers on breeding. Charles Hills trained the winner in 2012 and repeated the trick. Front runners did well on the day and the winner rates minor improvement on his 2yo debut form.

1244 6 PLACES AT AINTREE WITH BETVICTOR CONDITIONS STKS 7f (P)
4:05 (4:06) (Class 4) 4-Y-0+ **£5,175** (£1,540; £769; £384) **Stalls** Low

Form RPR
00-5 **1** **Bronze Prince**[14] 1036 6-9-0 97 SebSanders 6 104
(Michael Attwater) *mde all: drvn and qcknd to maintain clr advantage over 2f out: pushed along and in n.d fnl f: unchal* **10/1**
2-00 **2** *1 3/4* **Belgian Bill**[72] 241 5-9-0 102 (t) LukeMorris 1 99
(George Baker) *chsd ldrs: drvn over 2f out: wnt 2nd ins fnl f: no imp on wnr and hld on all out for 2nd* **2/1**[1]
111- **3** *shd* **Stirring Ballad**[224] 5334 4-8-9 96 LiamKeniry 5 94
(Andrew Balding) *towards rr: hdwy 2f out: sn rdn: kpt on fnl f to press for 2nd clsng stages: no ch w wnr* **4/1**[3]
120- **4** *3/4* **Shamaal Nibras (USA)**[140] 7691 4-9-2 97 SteveDrowne 2 99
(Richard Hannon) *in rr: hdwy fr 2f out: styd on fnl f but nvr gng pce to rch wnr* **7/1**
-100 **5** *1/2* **Spirit Of Sharjah (IRE)**[12] 1061 8-9-0 90 AdamKirby 4 96
(Julia Feilden) *chsd wnr: rdn and no imp fr over 1f out: wknd fnl 110yds* **25/1**
540- **6** *1 1/4* **Dance And Dance (IRE)**[147] 7558 7-9-2 104 GeorgeBaker 3 95
(Ed Vaughan) *a in last duo: rdn and no imp over 1f out* **3/1**[2]
600- **7** *1 1/4* **Redact (IRE)**[182] 6676 4-9-0 99 SeanLevey 7 89
(Richard Hannon) *a in last duo: rdn and no prog fnl 2f* **12/1**

1m 24.25s (-1.75) **Going Correction** -0.075s/f (Stan) **7** Ran SP% **111.5**
Speed ratings (Par 105): **107,105,104,104,103 102,100**
Tote Swingers: 1&2 £5.20, 1&3 £4.20, 2&3 £3.00 CSF £28.92 TOTE £12.80: £4.80, £1.10; EX 32.90 Trifecta £140.20 Pool: £2,200.49 - 11.76 winning units..
Owner Canisbay Bloodstock **Bred** Coln Valley Stud **Trained** Epsom, Surrey

FOCUS
A pretty good conditions stakes bordering on Listed level but something of a surprise result. A personal best from the winner, another to make all on the day, with the fifth offering some perspective.

1245 BETVICTOR GRAND NATIONAL 6 PLACES H'CAP 6f (P)
4:35 (4:36) (Class 3) (0-90,91) 4-Y-0+ **£8,409** (£2,502; £1,250; £625) **Stalls** Low

Form RPR
-121 **1** **Khawatim**[43] 679 5-9-5 **87** AdamKirby 11 95+
(Noel Quinlan) *stdd s: hld up in rr: stl plenty to do whn shkn up over 1f out: qcknd through field fnl 150yds to ld clsng stages: comf* **11/8**[1]
22-1 **2** *3/4* **Yeeoow (IRE)**[26] 881 4-9-6 **88** MartinHarley 2 94+
(Mrs K Burke) *t.k.h: chsd ldrs: led wl over 1f out: kpt on fnl f: hdd and outpcd clsng stages* **9/4**[2]
26-5 **3** *nk* **Harrison George (IRE)**[21] 947 8-9-4 **86** (t) SeanLevey 9 91
(P J O'Gorman) *chsd ldrs: rdn over 1f out: styd on wl to press for 2nd clsng stages but no ch w wnr* **16/1**
0-63 **4** *hd* **Rowe Park**[26] 881 10-9-2 **84** LiamKeniry 4 89
(Linda Jewell) *chsd ldrs: rdn 2f out: kpt on clsng stages but nvr any ch w wnr* **33/1**
003- **5** *shd* **Democretes**[200] 6119 4-9-5 **87** KieranO'Neill 5 91
(Richard Hannon) *s.i.s: in rr: stl plenty to do appr fnl f: str run fnl 110yds: fin wl* **14/1**
0-02 **6** *shd* **Red Aggressor (IRE)**[6] 1160 4-9-3 **85** FrederikTylicki 10 89
(Clive Brittain) *s.i.s: in rr: hdwy over 2f out and sn chsng ldrs: rdn and kpt on fnl f: no ex clsng stages* **11/1**
4011 **7** *3/4* **Crew Cut (IRE)**[26] 880 5-9-2 **84** (b) FergusSweeney 3 86
(Jeremy Gask) *in rr: rdn and hdwy over 1f out: styd on clsng stages but nvr gng pce to chal* **10/1**[3]
1405 **8** *1* **Seek The Fair Land**[12] 1061 7-8-13 **86** (b) NathanAlison(5) 1 85
(Jim Boyle) *chsd ldrs: rdn to press ldrs 2f out: outpcd fnl f* **20/1**
2601 **9** *nse* **Noverre To Go (IRE)**[6] 1155 7-9-9 **91** 6ex LukeMorris 6 90
(Ronald Harris) *towards rr but in tch: rdn over 2f out: kpt on ins fnl f: nvr rchd ldrs* **25/1**
020- **10** *3 1/4* **Arctic Feeling (IRE)**[161] 7243 5-8-12 **87** LauraBarry(7) 12 76
(Richard Fahey) *wer ldr over 4f out tl ins fnl 2f: wknd fnl f* **33/1**
06-0 **11** *2 1/4* **Jarrow (IRE)**[21] 947 6-9-3 **85** NeilCallan 8 67
(Milton Bradley) *sn led: jnd over 4f out: hdd & wknd wl over 1f out* **40/1**

1m 12.01s (-1.09) **Going Correction** -0.075s/f (Stan) **11** Ran SP% **119.8**
Speed ratings (Par 107): **104,103,102,102,102 102,101,99,99,95 92**
Tote Swingers: 1&2 £1.50, 1&3 £10.60, 2&3 £7.80 CSF £4.15 CT £33.73 TOTE £2.40: £1.10, £1.10, £4.60; EX 6.30 Trifecta £68.40 Pool: £1,065.59 - 11.67 winning units..
Owner The Unique Partnership **Bred** Baroness Bloodstock **Trained** Newmarket, Suffolk

FOCUS
A decent sprint handicap with several last-time-out winners taking part, but the market only wanted to know about two of them and they filled the first two places in a race run at a frenetic pace that produced a cracking finish. The form makes plenty of sense and the winner can get back to his old form.

1246 BETVICTOR ARE 6 PLACES ON THE NATIONAL H'CAP (LONDON MILE QUALIFIER) 1m (P)
5:10 (5:10) (Class 4) (0-85,85) 3-Y-0 **£5,175** (£1,540; £769; £384) **Stalls** Low

Form RPR
21-1 **1** **Prophets Pride**[59] 444 3-9-0 **78** SebSanders 3 87
(Jeremy Noseda) *trckd ldr: pushed along 2f out: styng on whn pushed lft ins fnl f: qcknd to ld fnl 50yds: comf* **5/4**[1]
13- **2** *1* **Hay Dude**[162] 7207 3-9-4 **85** MichaelMetcalfe(3) 1 91
(Mrs K Burke) *chsd ldrs: led ins fnl 2f: hung lft ins fnl f: hdd and outpcd fnl 50yds* **7/2**[2]
3-14 **3** *3* **Rouge Nuage (IRE)**[43] 666 3-8-10 **74** MartinDwyer 5 73
(Conrad Allen) *chsd ldrs: rdn ins fnl 3f: edgd rt u.p and styd on for 3rd ins fnl f* **20/1**
441- **4** *2* **Living The Life (IRE)**[171] 6977 3-9-0 **78** FergusSweeney 6 72
(Jamie Osborne) *in rr: pushed along and one pce fnl 2f* **10/1**
611- **5** *nk* **Ready (IRE)**[126] 7856 3-9-2 **80** AdamKirby 4 73
(Garry Moss) *in rr: hdwy over 2f out: wknd fnl f* **4/1**[3]
52-1 **6** *1 3/4* **Red Refraction (IRE)**[24] 904 3-9-1 **79** SeanLevey 2 68
(Richard Hannon) *led: hdd ins fnl 2f: wknd fnl f* **9/1**

1m 38.52s (-1.28) **Going Correction** -0.075s/f (Stan) **6** Ran SP% **110.5**
Speed ratings (Par 100): **103,102,99,97,96 94**
Tote Swingers: 1&2 £1.60, 1&3 £4.30, 2&3 £8.20 CSF £5.59 TOTE £1.80: £1.10, £3.40; EX 6.10 Trifecta £40.60 Pool: £1,086.48 - 20.08 winning units..
Owner Saeed Suhail **Bred** Rabbah Bloodstock Limited **Trained** Newmarket, Suffolk

FOCUS
A small field for this London Mile Qualifier. The market leaders had the race between them from over a furlong out. The winner has more to offer and the form could be rated higher using the third.
T/Plt: £424.70 to a £1 stake. Pool: £60,081.08 - 103.25 winning tickets T/Qpdt: £23.70 to a £1 stake. Pool: £3,676.15 - 114.40 winning tickets ST

MUSSELBURGH (R-H)
Saturday, March 30
OFFICIAL GOING: Good to soft (soft in places; 5.9)
Wind: Very light against Weather: Cloudy, sunny periods

1247 TOTEPLACEPOT RACING'S FAVOURITE BET CONDITIONS STKS 5f
1:50 (1:50) (Class 3) 2-Y-0 **£7,762** (£2,310; £1,154; £577) **Stalls** High

Form RPR
1 **1** **Mick's Yer Man**[8] 1108 2-9-0 0 RyanWhile(7) 2 86+
(Bill Turner) *cl up: led wl over 2f out: shkn up and edgd rt ent fnl f: styd on strly* **4/6**[1]
2 *2 1/2* **Skye's The Limit** 2-9-3 0 DavidNolan 5 70+
(Richard Fahey) *dwlt: sn trcking ldrs: hdwy 2f out: chsd wnr over 1f out: rdn ent fnl f: sn swtchd lft and kpt on* **4/1**[2]
6 **3** *2* **Intense Feeling (IRE)**[6] 1156 2-8-12 0 DavidAllan 1 58
(David Evans) *chsd ldng pair: rdn along: edgd lft and sltly outpcd wl over 1f out: kpt on u.p fnl f* **50/1**
4 *1* **Scargill** 2-9-3 0 MatthewDavies 3 59+
(Mick Channon) *dwlt and wnt rt s: green and sn rdn along in rr: hdwy 2f out: styd on wl fnl f: nrst fin* **12/1**
5 *1* **Vine De Nada** 2-9-3 0 JoeFanning 4 56
(Mark Johnston) *slt ld on inner: hdd wl over 2f out and sn pushed along: rdn wl over 1f out: wknd appr fnl f* **9/2**[3]
6 *15* **Lilo Lil** 2-8-12 0 TomEaves 6
(David C Griffiths) *dwlt: sn rdn along in rr: green and outpcd bef 1/2-way* **50/1**

1m 4.1s (3.70) **Going Correction** +0.70s/f (Yiel) **6** Ran SP% **109.8**
Speed ratings (Par 96): **98,94,90,89,87 63**
Tote Swingers: 1&2 £1.10, 1&3 £3.50, 2&3 £6.70 CSF £3.46 TOTE £1.50: £1.10, £2.50; EX 3.70 Trifecta £25.40 Pool: £973.67 - 23.68 winning units..
Owner Mrs Tracy Turner **Bred** Heather Raw **Trained** Sigwells, Somerset

FOCUS
Good to soft ground and these 2-y-os ran just over five seconds above RP standard. The winner set a good level on his debut win and did not need to quite match that.

1248 TOTEQUADPOT FOUR PLACES IN FOUR RACES H'CAP (DIV I) 5f
2:25 (2:25) (Class 4) (0-85,85) 4-Y-0+ **£5,175** (£1,540; £769; £384) **Stalls** High

Form RPR
00-4 **1** **Oldjoesaid**[25] 885 9-8-8 **72** RussKennemore 7 84
(Paul Midgley) *chsd ldrs: hdwy 2f out: rdn to ld ent fnl f: sn clr* **8/1**

000- **2** 2½ **Cadeaux Pearl**[126] 7859 5-8-12 **79**........(b) BillyCray(3) 2 82
(Scott Dixon) *cl up: rdn to ld wl over 1f out: drvn and hdd ent fnl f: kpt on same pce* **28/1**

3 1¾ **Gandalak (FR)**[134] 4-9-3 **81**........ JoeFanning 8 78
(David O'Meara) *led 1 1/2f: prom: effrt 2f out: sn rdn to chse ldng pair: kpt on same pce fnl f* **9/2[3]**

040- **4** ½ **Go Go Green (IRE)**[166] 7101 7-8-3 **67**........ JamesSullivan 1 62
(Jim Goldie) *in tch: hdwy 2f out: sn rdn and kpt on fnl f* **12/1**

055- **5** ½ **Lupin Pooter**[217] 5603 4-8-13 **77**........ GrahamGibbons 9 70+
(David Barron) *rrd and s.i.s: in rr tl hdwy 2f out: rdn and n.m.r jst over 1f out: swtchd to outer and styd on wl fnl f: nrst fin* **3/1[2]**

060- **6** 2¼ **Mappin Time (IRE)**[198] 6165 5-9-7 **85**........(p) DavidAllan 4 70
(Tim Easterby) *sltly hmpd s and towards rr: rdn along 1/2-way: sme late hdwy* **12/1**

04-0 **7** nk **Thirteen Shivers**[12] 1067 5-8-10 **81**........ MatthewHopkins(7) 5 65
(Michael Easterby) *wnt rt s: in tch: rdn along over 2f out: sn no hdwy* **14/1**

010- **8** 2 **Bonnie Charlie**[189] 6465 7-9-1 **79**........ PaulQuinn 10 56
(David Nicholls) *a towards rr* **9/1**

002- **9** 2 **Excel Bolt**[159] 7295 5-9-7 **85**........ TomEaves 6 55
(Bryan Smart) *cl up: led after 1 1/2f: rdn 2f out: sn hdd & wknd qckly ent fnl f* **11/4[1]**

1m 3.27s (2.87) **Going Correction** +0.70s/f (Yiel) 9 Ran SP% **116.5**
Speed ratings (Par 105): **105,101,98,97,96 93,92,89,86**
Tote Swingers: 1&2 £37.30, 2&3 £8.90 CSF £198.71 CT £1138.17 TOTE £9.10: £2.20, £7.20, £1.30; EX 144.60 Trifecta £396.50 Part won. Pool: £528.68 - 0.52 winning units..
Owner Pee Dee Tee Syndicate & T W Midgley **Bred** Mrs R D Peacock **Trained** Westow, N Yorks
■ Stewards' Enquiry : Billy Cray two-day ban: use of whip (13 & 15 Apr)

FOCUS
An open-looking sprint handicap in which they went a strong gallop with very few getting into it from off the pace. The form could be rated up to 5lb better.

1249 TOTEPOOL BORDERLESCOTT SPRINT TROPHY (CONDITIONS RACE) 5f
3:00 (3:00) (Class 2) 3-Y-O+ **£12,938** (£3,850; £1,924; £962) **Stalls** High

Form RPR

000- **1** **Tangerine Trees**[174] 6908 8-9-1 106........(v) TomEaves 1 105+
(Bryan Smart) *cl up: led after 1 1/2f: rdn 2f out: drvn ins fnl f edgd rt: hld on wl towards fin* **11/4[2]**

101- **2** nk **Kingsgate Choice (IRE)**[161] 7243 6-9-1 98........ EddieAhern 4 104+
(Ed de Giles) *trckd ldrs: hdwy 2f out: rdn to chal jst over 1f out: ev ch ins fnl f: sn drvn and no ex towards fin* **9/4[1]**

125- **3** 6 **Mary's Daughter**[168] 7065 3-8-1 95 ow1........ PatrickMathers 7 80
(Richard Fahey) *chsd ldrs: pushed along 1/2-way: swtchd rt and hdwy 2f out: rdn to chse ldng pair ent fnl f: sn one pce* **6/1**

000- **4** 4 **Silvanus (IRE)**[187] 6543 8-9-1 86........ RussKennemore 3 68
(Paul Midgley) *trckd ldrs: hdwy to chse wnr 2f out: sn rdn and one pce appr fnl f* **33/1**

033- **5** 2 **Hamish McGonagall**[174] 6908 8-10-2 113........ DavidAllan 6 76
(Tim Easterby) *led on stands' rail for 1 1/2f: cl up: rdn along wl over 2f out: sn btn* **3/1[3]**

/00- **6** 8 **Bapak Chinta (USA)**[284] 3238 4-9-1 105........ PhillipMakin 5 32
(Kevin Ryan) *a outpcd in rr* **8/1**

0-42 **7** 5 **Sans Loi (IRE)**[18] 966 4-9-1 79........ RobertWinston 2 14
(Brian Ellison) *dwlt: a outpcd in rr* **40/1**

1m 2.97s (2.57) **Going Correction** +0.70s/f (Yiel)
WFA 3 from 4yo+ 12lb 7 Ran SP% **113.2**
Speed ratings (Par 109): **107,106,96,90,87 74,66**
Tote Swingers: 1&2 £1.90, 1&3 £3.30, 2&3 £3.20 CSF £9.18 TOTE £4.20: £2.20, £1.90; EX 10.20 Trifecta £40.70 Pool: £1,788.82 - 32.88 winning units..
Owner Tangerine Trees Partnership **Bred** Mrs B A Matthews **Trained** Hambleton, N Yorks

FOCUS
A good quality conditions race and the first two came clear.

1250 TOTEPOOL.COM ROYAL MILE (H'CAP) 1m
3:35 (3:36) (Class 2) (0-100,96) 3-Y-O
£31,125 (£9,320; £4,660; £2,330; £1,165; £585) **Stalls** Low

Form RPR

4-11 **1** **Newstead Abbey**[21] 949 3-8-10 **85**........ GrahamGibbons 1 97+
(David Barron) *t.k.h: trckd ldrs: gd run through on inner home turn and sn trcking ldr: chal 2f out: led over 1f out: sn rdn clr: readily* **7/1[3]**

01-2 **2** 2¼ **Carry On Sydney**[9] 1099 3-8-8 **83**........ EddieAhern 10 88
(Richard Hannon) *hld up and bhd: reminders 3f out: hdwy over 2f out: swtchd rt to inner over 1f out: styd on to chse wnr ins fnl f: sn no imp* **11/4[2]**

311 **3** 2¼ **Hiddon Coin (IRE)**[14] 1041 3-8-4 **82**........ RaulDaSilva(3) 8 82
(David O'Meara) *led: hung lft and wd home turn: pushed along 3f out: rdn 2f out: hdd and drvn over 1f out: one pce* **18/1**

613- **4** 1¾ **Top Notch Tonto (IRE)**[159] 7292 3-9-6 **95**........ TomEaves 7 91
(Ian McInnes) *dwlt and in rr: hdwy over 3f out: rdn to chse ldrs 2f out: swtchd lft and drvn over 1f out: sn one pce* **22/1**

051- **5** 4½ **Greeleys Love (USA)**[193] 6337 3-8-3 **78**........ JoeFanning 4 64+
(Mark Johnston) *hld up towards rr: hdwy 3f out: rdn along over 2f out: nvr nr ldrs* **5/2[1]**

144- **6** 2 **Penny Rose**[155] 7365 3-8-9 **84**........ RobertWinston 2 65
(Mark Johnston) *chsd ldrs: rdn along wl over 2f out: drvn wl over 1f out and sn wknd* **8/1**

26-2 **7** 1 **Khelman (IRE)**[8] 1114 3-8-4 **79**........ PatrickMathers 3 58
(Richard Fahey) *prom: cl up whn carried wd and sltly hmpd home turn: pushed along 3f out: rdn over 2f out: sn drvn and grad wknd* **18/1**

500- **8** 12 **Fantacise**[175] 6873 3-8-7 **82**........(p) BarryMcHugh 9 33
(Richard Fahey) *chsd ldrs to 1/2-way: sn lost pl and bhd* **14/1**

3-21 **9** 10 **Fraserburgh (IRE)**[17] 990 3-8-0 **78**........ SimonPearce(3) 11 6
(Mark Johnston) *cl up on outer: carried wd home turn and sn pushed along: rdn 3f out and sn wknd* **16/1**

-000 **10** 1 **Pure Excellence**[30] 837 3-9-2 **96**........ MichaelJMMurphy(5) 6 22
(Mark Johnston) *prom: pushed along whn carried wd and sltly hmpd home turn: sn rdn and wknd: bhd fnl 2f* **9/1**

1m 46.63s (5.43) **Going Correction** +0.85s/f (Soft) 10 Ran SP% **116.3**
Speed ratings (Par 104): **106,103,101,99,95 93,92,80,70,69**
Tote Swingers: 1&2 £3.90, 1&3 £15.50, 2&3 £9.70 CSF £26.47 CT £343.55 TOTE £8.40: £2.10, £1.20, £6.50; EX 24.70 Trifecta £325.80 Pool: £1,358.51 - 3.12 winning units..
Owner Let's Be Lucky Partnership **Bred** Grasshopper 2000 Ltd **Trained** Maunby, N Yorks

FOCUS
A valuable prize and the first three home had all been plying their trade on the all-weather recently, indicating race-fitness was crucial. The winner is going the right way fast and was value for extra.

1251 YOUR FAVOURITE POOL BETS AT TOTEPOOL.COM H'CAP 1m 6f
4:10 (4:10) (Class 5) (0-70,70) 4-Y-O+ **£3,234** (£962; £481; £240) **Stalls** Low

Form RPR

00-1 **1** **Full Speed (GER)**[44] 165 8-9-3 **61**........ RussKennemore 6 71+
(Philip Kirby) *hld up in tch: smooth hdwy over 4f out: trckd ldrs on bit 3f out: effrt to chal 2f out: shkn up to ld appr fnl f: drvn and kpt on towards fin* **11/4[2]**

2221 **2** ¾ **Activate**[22] 929 6-9-10 **68**........(p) JoeFanning 9 77+
(Keith Dalgleish) *trckd ldr: led over 9f out: rdn along over 2f out: drvn and hdd appr fnl f: kpt on u.p* **2/1[1]**

06-0 **3** 7 **Azerodegree (IRE)**[11] 1084 4-8-12 **60**........(p) DavidAllan 5 60
(Iain Jardine) *trckd ldng pair: cl up 1/2-way: rdn along to chal 3f out: drvn 2f out: sn one pce* **33/1**

100- **4** 7 **Forrest Flyer (IRE)**[166] 7102 9-9-4 **62**........ PhillipMakin 10 53
(Jim Goldie) *led: hdd over 9f out: prom: rdn along 3f out: drvn 2f out and sn wknd* **20/1**

124- **5** 7 **Hawdyerwheesht**[172] 6957 5-9-2 **65**........ GeorgeDowning(5) 2 47
(Jim Goldie) *t.k.h: trckd ldr: stmbld and lost pl over 7f out and towards rr: sme hdwy on wd outside over 2f out: sn rdn along and n.d* **6/1**

030- **6** 3½ **Ad Value (IRE)**[144] 7603 5-8-13 **57**........ RobertWinston 8 34
(Alan Swinbank) *hld up in rr: hdwy 1/2-way: cl up over 5f out: rdn along 3f out: wknd over 2f out* **10/3[3]**

50-6 **7** 14 **Ostentation**[14] 1031 6-9-3 **61**........(b) EddieAhern 3 20
(Alastair Lidderdale) *hld up: effrt on inner over 4f out: sn rdn along and outpcd fnl 3f* **12/1**

00/6 **8** 3¾ **Major Eradicator (USA)**[8] 1120 6-8-2 **51** oh6........(b) AmyScott(5) 4 5
(Alastair Lidderdale) *a in rr* **33/1**

3m 17.38s (12.08) **Going Correction** +0.85s/f (Soft)
WFA 4 from 5yo+ 4lb 8 Ran SP% **115.7**
Speed ratings (Par 103): **99,98,94,90,86 84,76,74**
Tote Swingers: 1&2 £2.30, 1&3 £17.10, 2&3 £9.50 CSF £8.61 CT £136.60 TOTE £4.00: £2.60, £1.50, £15.70; EX 12.40 Trifecta £177.90 Pool: £1,151.30 - 4.85 winning units..
Owner Ryan P Hadfield **Bred** Dr K Schulte **Trained** Middleham, N Yorks

FOCUS
Again, those with recent all-weather form came to the fore. The form looks sound with the first two clear. The winner was very well treated on his old Flat form.

1252 MORE FOOTBALL THAN EVER AT TOTEPOOL.COM H'CAP 7f 30y
4:45 (4:48) (Class 3) (0-95,90) 4-Y-O+ **£8,409** (£2,502; £1,250; £625) **Stalls** Low

Form RPR

314- **1** **Hi There (IRE)**[173] 6921 4-8-11 **80**........ BarryMcHugh 9 91+
(Richard Fahey) *hld up towards rr: hdwy on inner 3f out: swtchd lft and effrt 2f out: rdn to chal whn carried lft over 1f out: led ent fnl f: kpt on strly* **7/2[2]**

10-0 **2** 3 **Laffan (IRE)**[21] 945 4-9-7 **90**........ PhillipMakin 5 94
(Kevin Ryan) *led: rdn along 2f out: hung bdly lft over 1f out: hdd ent fnl f: kpt on same pce* **9/2[3]**

02-4 **3** 2¼ **Galician**[12] 1061 4-9-7 **90**........ JoeFanning 1 88
(Mark Johnston) *dwlt: sn trcking ldrs on inner: effrt over 3f out: rdn 2f out: drvn appr fnl f and kpt on same pce* **5/2[1]**

5003 **4** 2¾ **Verse Of Love**[21] 944 4-9-7 **90**........ DavidAllan 7 81
(David Evans) *a.p: chsd ldr 1/2-way: rdn wl over 2f out: sn drvn and one pce* **10/1**

4-63 **5** 1¼ **Kingswinford (IRE)**[4] 1179 7-7-13 **71** oh5........ SimonPearce(3) 2 59
(Alastair Lidderdale) *chsd ldrs: rdn along 3f out: drvn 2f out and sn one pce* **14/1**

022- **6** 7 **Rasaman (IRE)**[131] 7790 9-8-10 **79**........ TomEaves 6 50
(Jim Goldie) *hld up in tch: hdwy 3f out: rdn to chse ldrs over 2f out: sn btn* **8/1**

440- **7** 2¾ **Shesastar**[154] 7408 5-9-2 **85**........ GrahamGibbons 8 49
(David Barron) *s.i.s: a in rr* **16/1**

00-3 **8** ¾ **Klynch**[18] 966 7-8-13 **82**........(b) JamesSullivan 4 45
(Ruth Carr) *chsd ldrs: rdn along 3f out: drvn over 2f out and sn wknd* **11/2**

4-23 **9** 7 **Chokidar (IRE)**[29] 844 5-8-3 **75**........(b) BillyCray(3) 3 20
(Scott Dixon) *s.i.s: a bhd* **14/1**

1m 33.68s (4.68) **Going Correction** +0.85s/f (Soft) 9 Ran SP% **123.8**
Speed ratings (Par 107): **107,103,101,97,96 88,85,84,76**
Tote Swingers: 1&2 £5.20, 1&3 £4.10, 2&3 £2.90 CSF £21.39 CT £48.13 TOTE £4.80: £3.30, £3.10, £1.10; EX 20.60 Trifecta £54.70 Pool: £645.38 - 8.83 winning units..
Owner Market Avenue Racing Club Ltd **Bred** J & J Waldron **Trained** Musley Bank, N Yorks

FOCUS
With the top-weight rated 5lb below the ceiling rating for the contest, this probably wasn't as strong as it could have been for the grade, but it was at least won by the most progressive runner in the field. They went a decent gallop, though.

1253 TOTEQUADPOT FOUR PLACES IN FOUR RACES H'CAP (DIV II) 5f
5:15 (5:15) (Class 4) (0-85,85) 4-Y-O+ **£5,175** (£1,540; £769; £384) **Stalls** High

Form RPR

000- **1** **Move In Time**[136] 7704 5-9-7 **85**........ DavidNolan 7 106
(David O'Meara) *cl up: led over 1f out: rdn clr ins fnl f: styd on strly* **9/4[1]**

131- **2** 5 **Come On Dave (IRE)**[175] 6886 4-9-0 **78**........ PaulQuinn 6 79
(David Nicholls) *led: rdn along 2f out: hdd over 1f out: drvn and one pce fnl f* **3/1[2]**

401- **3** 1 **Rothesay Chancer**[166] 7101 5-8-10 **74**........ JamesSullivan 10 71
(Jim Goldie) *towards rr: hdwy 2f out: rdn over 1f out: kpt on fnl f: nrst fin* **8/1**

060- **4** 1¾ **Master Rooney (IRE)**[159] 7291 7-9-0 **81**........ RaulDaSilva(3) 2 72+
(Geoffrey Harker) *chsd ldrs on outer: rdn along 2f out: drvn and one pce appr fnl f* **16/1**

-006 **5** ½ **Ingleby Star (IRE)**[9] 1101 8-8-1 **68**........(p) JulieBurke(3) 8 57
(Ian McInnes) *nvr bttr than midfield* **25/1**

000- **6** 2 **Jedward (IRE)**[161] 7243 6-9-4 **82**........ PhillipMakin 1 64+
(Kevin Ryan) *chsd ldrs on outer: hdwy over 2f out: rdn wl over 1f out: sn wknd* **6/1[3]**

400- **7** nse **Crimson Knot (IRE)**[179] 6755 5-8-9 **78**........ SladeO'Hara(5) 5 60
(Alan Berry) *nvr nr ldrs* **16/1**

U00- **8** 4½ **Flash City (ITY)**[161] 7243 5-9-3 **81**........(v) TomEaves 4 47
(Bryan Smart) *prom: rdn along 2f out: sn wknd* **13/2**

1050 9 1 1/2 **Bassett Road (IRE)**[31] 812 5-8-3 **67**............................(p) JoeFanning 3 27
(Keith Dalgleish) *chsd ldrs: rdn along over 2f out: sn wknd* **12/1**
1m 3.24s (2.84) **Going Correction** +0.70s/f (Yiel) **9** Ran SP% **117.8**
Speed ratings (Par 105): **105,97,95,92,91 88,88,81,78**
Tote Swingers: 1&2 £2.10, 1&3 £3.50, 2&3 £2.90 CSF £9.19 CT £45.51 TOTE £3.30: £2.40, £1.10, £2.00; EX 16.60 Trifecta £34.20 Pool: £1,302.32 - 28.51 winning units..
Owner A Turton, J Blackburn & R Bond **Bred** Bond Thoroughbred Corporation **Trained** Nawton, N Yorks

FOCUS
Not a particularly strong race for the grade with most having questions or fitness to prove and the market got it spot-on. The easy winner is rated right back to his best.
T/Plt: £35.60 to a £1 stake. Pool: £47,969.60 - 982.10 winning tickets T/Qpdt: £15.40 to a £1 stake. Pool: £2,514.64 - 120.81 winning tickets JR

1254 - (Foreign Racing) - See Raceform Interactive

CORK (R-H)
Saturday, March 30

OFFICIAL GOING: Sprint course - heavy (soft in places); round course - soft (soft to heavy in places)

1255a CORK STKS (LISTED RACE) 6f
3:10 (3:10) 3-Y-0+ **£21,138** (£6,178; £2,926; £975)

RPR
1 **Bold Thady Quill (IRE)**[6] 1168 6-9-7 91..............................(p) WJLee 6 104
(K J Condon, Ire) *hld up towards rr: hdwy on outer fr 1/2-way and wnt 2nd over 1f out: rdn to ld narrowly fnl 100yds and kpt on wl towards fin* **11/1**
2 1/2 **Cape Of Approval (IRE)**[196] 6270 4-9-7 93.................. WayneLordan 5 102
(T Stack, Ire) *chsd ldrs: 5th 1/2-way: prog to ld 1 1/2f out: strly pressed ins fnl f and hdd fnl 100yds: no ex cl home* **5/1**
3 9 **Red Dubawi (IRE)**[21] 954 5-9-7 100................................ PatSmullen 1 74
(David Marnane, Ire) *trckd ldrs: cl 3rd 1/2-way: sn disp: hdd 1 1/2f out and no imp on principals ent fnl f: kpt on same pce* **10/1**
4 hd **Switcher (IRE)**[175] 6870 4-9-2 .... MichaelHussey 8 68
(David O'Meara) *chsd ldrs: 4th 1/2-way: sn lost pl and swtchd: rdn in 7th over 1f out and kpt on u.p into mod 4th fnl 50yds* **5/1**
5 3/4 **Srucahan (IRE)**[6] 1165 4-9-7 90....................................(b) ChrisHayes 7 71
(P D Deegan, Ire) *w.w: 6th 1/2-way: niggled along fr 1/2-way: rdn in 5th ent fnl f: no ex* **3/1**[1]
6 3/4 **An Saighdiur (IRE)**[15] 1030 6-9-7 95................................... MACleere 2 68
(Andrew Slattery, Ire) *trckd ldr: cl 2nd 1/2-way: disp 2f out: sn rdn and no ex in 3rd ent fnl f: kpt on one pce* **9/2**[3]
7 2 **Kateeva (IRE)**[157] 7336 6-9-2 68.....................................(t) LeighRoche 3 57
(J P Fogarty, Ire) *hld up towards rr: sme hdwy on outer fr 1/2-way: outpcd fnl 2f* **66/1**
8 14 **Inxile (IRE)**[37] 746 8-9-10 ....(p) AdrianNicholls 4 20
(David Nicholls) *led: pushed along 1/2-way and sn hdd: wknd: eased under 2f out* **4/1**[2]
1m 19.75s (7.15) **8** Ran SP% **115.4**
CSF £64.20 TOTE £11.70: £2.00, £1.10, £4.70; DF 65.46.
Owner Mrs Pauline Condon **Bred** Iona Equine **Trained** The Curragh , Co Kildare
■ Stewards' Enquiry : Adrian Nicholls caution: failed to ride to draw
M A Cleere caution: failed to ride to draw

FOCUS
A Listed sprint run on very tacky ground which probably made it more like a mile race. The first two pulled a long way clear.

1002 MEYDAN (L-H)
Saturday, March 30

OFFICIAL GOING: Tapeta: standard; turf: good

1262a GODOLPHIN MILE SPONSORED BY ETISALAT (GROUP 2) (TAPETA) 1m
1:10 (1:10) 3-Y-0+
£368,098 (£122,699; £61,349; £30,674; £18,404; £12,269)

RPR
1 **Soft Falling Rain (SAF)**[44] 658 4-8-9 113.................. PaulHanagan 13 116+
(M F De Kock, South Africa) *in rr of mid-div: smooth prog 2 1/2f out: r.o wl fnl 1 1/2f: led fnl 55yds* **9/4**[1]
2 3/4 **Haatheq (USA)**[21] 958 6-9-0 110.............................. RoystonFfrench 10 114
(A Al Raihe, UAE) *mid-div: led 2f out: hdd fnl 55yds* **40/1**
3 1 **Moonwalk In Paris (FR)**[21] 957 5-9-0 115.................. AhmedAjtebi 15 112+
(Mahmood Al Zarooni) *settled in rr: r.o fnl 2f: nrst fin* **10/1**
4 1 **Sarkiyla (FR)**[149] 7515 4-8-9 108..............(t) Christophe-PatriceLemaire 7 104+
(A De Royer-Dupre, France) *mid-div: r.o fnl 2f: nrst fin* **14/1**
5 1 1/4 **Alpha (USA)**[51] 556 4-9-0 116...............................(v) SilvestreDeSousa 1 107
(Saeed bin Suroor) *trckd ldrs: led 3f out: hdd 2f out: one pce fnl f* **22/1**
6 1 **Rerouted (USA)**[28] 869 5-9-0 115.................................. WCMarwing 9 104+
(M F De Kock, South Africa) *in rr of mid-div: r.o fnl 2f but nvr nr to chal* **14/1**
7 1/4 **Surfer (USA)**[21] 958 4-9-0 111...................................... RichardMullen 6 104
(S Seemar, UAE) *mid-div: rdn 3f out: kpt on one pce fnl 1 1/2f* **7/1**[2]
8 1 3/4 **Penitent**[174] 6913 7-9-0 115... DanielTudhope 11 100
(David O'Meara) *trckd ldng trio tl outpcd 2f out* **9/1**[3]
9 2 1/4 **Saamidd**[21] 957 5-9-0 110...(tp) WilliamBuick 14 94
(Saeed bin Suroor) *slowly away: nvr nr to chal* **33/1**
10 3/4 **Capital Attraction (USA)**[21] 957 6-9-0 115................ TadhgO'Shea 12 93
(Ernst Oertel, UAE) *trckd ldng: ev ch 3f out: wknd fnl 2f* **16/1**
11 1 1/2 **Barbecue Eddie (USA)**[21] 957 9-9-0 113.....................(b) PatDobbs 16 89
(Doug Watson, UAE) *settled in rr: nvr able to chal* **33/1**
12 1 3/4 **Mufarrh (IRE)**[30] 836 6-9-0 113................................... KierenFallon 2 85
(A Al Raihe, UAE) *nvr bttr than mid-div* **12/1**
13 7 1/2 **Zazou (GER)**[28] 6-9-0 112... KUlubaev 5 68
(W Hickst, Germany) *slowly away: nvr nr to chal* **16/1**
14 1/4 **Time Prisoner (USA)**[21] 955 6-9-0 110.................. MickaelBarzalona 4 67
(Mahmood Al Zarooni) *nvr bttr than mid-div* **16/1**
15 1 1/4 **Master Of Hounds (USA)**[21] 959 5-9-0 113..(t) ChristopheSoumillon 8 64
(M F De Kock, South Africa) *slowly away: nvr bttr than mid-div* **9/1**[3]
16 3/4 **Red Jazz (USA)**[21] 957 6-9-0 111...................................... RyanMoore 3 63
(Charles Hills) *sn led: hdd & wknd 3f out* **20/1**
1m 39.97s (2.47) **16** Ran SP% **128.5**
CSF: 133.34; EX: 152.80; TRIFECTA: 980.90; TRICAST: 823.60; WIN: 2.60; PLACE: 1.20, 13.60, 3.30..
Owner Hamdan Al Maktoum **Bred** Highlands Farm Stud (pty) Ltd **Trained** South Africa

FOCUS
The Tapeta track was riding slow and proved hard work. With last year's winner African Story going for the World Cup, this wasn't a strong race. The pace was overly quick through the first half of the contest and they came home slowly, yet not many got involved from behind. Here are the sectionals: 25.22 (400m, from standing start), 22.75 (800m), 25.16 (1200m) before the winner came home in 26.49. The final time was the fifth slowest of 75 races over C&D. The winner is rated at the lower end of the race standards, with the runner-up helping with the standard.

1263a DUBAI GOLD CUP SPONSORED BY AL TAYER MOTORS (GROUP 3) (TURF) 2m
1:45 (1:45) 3-Y-0+
£368,098 (£122,699; £61,349; £30,674; £18,404; £12,269)

RPR
1 **Cavalryman**[21] 956 7-9-0 115.................................. SilvestreDeSousa 3 114+
(Saeed bin Suroor) *s.i.s: mid-div: smooth prog 2 1/2f out: led 1 1/2f: comf* **11/2**
2 3 **Ahzeemah (IRE)**[28] 870 4-8-8 111...............................(p) KierenFallon 2 109
(Saeed bin Suroor) *trckd ldng pair: rdn 4f out: kpt on same pce fnl 2f but no ch w wnr* **7/1**
3 1/4 **Verema (FR)**[153] 7431 4-8-4 105................. Christophe-PatriceLemaire 6 105
(A De Royer-Dupre, France) *settled in rr: nvr nr to chal: r.o fnl 2f* **10/1**
4 1/4 **Jutland**[13] 6-9-0 107... PatDobbs 5 109+
(Doug Watson, UAE) *settled in rr: r.o fnl 2f: nrst fin* **50/1**
5 1/2 **Star Empire (SAF)**[28] 870 7-9-0 109................ ChristopheSoumillon 10 109
(M F De Kock, South Africa) *settled in rr: nvr nr to chal* **11/1**
6 1/4 **Imperial Monarch (IRE)**[167] 7094 4-8-8 117.................... RyanMoore 1 107+
(A P O'Brien, Ire) *trckd ldng pair: ev ch 3f out: one pce fnl 2f* **5/2**[1]
7 1/4 **Saddler's Rock (IRE)**[28] 870 5-9-0 113..............(t) DeclanMcDonogh 7 108
(John M Oxx, Ire) *sddle slipped sn after s: trckd ldrs: led 14f out: hdd 2 1/2f out: n.m.r 1 1/2f out* **9/2**[2]
8 hd **Tenenbaum**[28] 870 4-8-8 109.................................. MickaelBarzalona 8 107
(Mahmood Al Zarooni) *trckd ldng pair: led 2 1/2f out: hdd 1 1/2f out: wknd fnl 110yds* **5/1**[3]
9 3 **Averroes (IRE)**[34] 6-9-0 110... TadhgO'Shea 9 105
(Ernst Oertel, UAE) *nvr bttr than mid-div* **66/1**
10 1/2 **Seismos (IRE)**[111] 5-9-0 110... MircoDemuro 4 104
(A Wohler, Germany) *sn led: hdd 14f out: chsd ldrs tl wknd 3f out* **20/1**
3m 25.31s (205.31)
WFA 4 from 5yo+ 5lb **10** Ran SP% **116.9**
CSF: 43.17; EX: 25.10; TRIFECTA: 265.90; TRICAST: 377.73; WIN: 4.70; PLACE: 1.90, 1.70, 3.70..
Owner Godolphin **Bred** Darley **Trained** Newmarket, Suffolk

FOCUS
The second running of this race, and one of the two previous Group 1 winners in the line-up came out on top. There was no pace on early (went the first 1600m in 1m48.08) and the race turned into a sprint up the straight. The form makes sense.

1264a UAE DERBY SPONSORED BY THE SAEED & MOHAMMED AL NABOODAH GROUP (GROUP 2) (TAPETA) 1m 1f 110y
2:25 (2:25) 3-Y-0
£736,196 (£245,398; £122,699; £61,349; £36,809; £24,539)

RPR
1 **Lines Of Battle (USA)**[147] 7568 3-8-9 106.....................(p) RyanMoore 4 111
(A P O'Brien, Ire) *trckd ldrs: led 2f out: r.o wl: comf* **15/2**
2 1 1/2 **Elleval (IRE)**[21] 953 3-8-9 102... FergalLynch 2 108
(David Marnane, Ire) *s.i.s: in rr of mid-div: smooth prog 2f out: nt qckn fnl 110yds* **25/1**
3 1/2 **Secret Number**[21] 953 3-8-9 112............................. SilvestreDeSousa 7 110+
(Saeed bin Suroor) *slowly away: settled in rr: rdn 3 1/2f out: r.o fnl 1 1/2f: nrst fin* **7/4**[1]
4 1 3/4 **Snowboarder (USA)**[21] 953 3-8-9 102........................ WilliamBuick 11 103
(Mahmood Al Zarooni) *mid-div: wd and t.k.h: led 4f out: hdd 2f out: wknd fnl 110yds* **25/1**
5 2 3/4 **Law Enforcement (IRE)**[168] 7076 3-8-9 110.............. RichardHughes 1 98
(Richard Hannon) *sn led: hdd 4f out: ev ch 2f out: wknd fnl 110yds* **6/1**[2]
6 hd **Zahee (NZ)**[21] 953 4-9-5 105............................... ChristopheSoumillon 8 99
(M F De Kock, South Africa) *settled in rr: nvr nr to chal but r.o fnl 2f* **14/1**
7 2 1/4 **Shuruq (USA)**[30] 837 3-8-5 112...............................(p) PaulHanagan 9 89
(Saeed bin Suroor) *trckd ldrs tl outpcd 2 1/2f out* **7/1**[3]
8 4 1/4 **Dice Flavor (USA)**[41] 3-8-9 108..(p) JValdiviaJr 5 84
(Patrick Gallagher, U.S.A) *nvr bttr than mid-div* **12/1**
9 shd **Now Spun (USA)**[30] 835 3-8-9 109...................... MickaelBarzalona 3 84
(Mahmood Al Zarooni) *trckd ldrs tl outpcd 2f out* **6/1**[2]
10 1 **Keiai Leone (JPN)**[41] 3-8-9 105..............................(b) HideakiMiyuki 10 82
(Katsuichi Nishiura, Japan) *settled in rr: nvr nr to chal* **12/1**
11 1/2 **He's Had Enough (USA)**[35] 3-8-9 110.......................(bt) MGutierrez 12 81
(Doug O'Neill, U.S.A) *settled in rr: nvr able to chal* **25/1**
12 9 1/4 **Emotif (ARG)**[21] 953 4-9-1 98....................................(b[1]) PatCosgrave 6 60
(M F De Kock, South Africa) *settled in rr: nvr nr to chal* **50/1**
2m 2.05s (3.05)
WFA 3 from 4yo 19lb **12** Ran SP% **124.8**
CSF: 191.70; EX: 203.00; TRIFECTA: 1,061.50; TRICAST: 480.71; WIN: 4.70; PLACE: 1.60, 9.20, 1.50..
Owner J Allen/Mrs J Magnier/M Tabor/D Smith **Bred** Joseph Allen **Trained** Ballydoyle, Co Tipperary

FOCUS
The form is muddling owing to a slow early pace: 26.97 (400m), 25.95 (800m), 25.08 (1200m), 24.38 (1600m). Consequently, it paid to be handy. The final time was the third slowest of 49 races over C&D. The form has been given a bit of chance with the first four improving in line with the race averages.

1265a AL QUOZ SPRINT SPONSORED BY EMIRATES NBD (GROUP 1) (TURF) 5f

3:05 (3:05) 3-Y-0+

£368,098 (£122,699; £61,349; £30,674; £18,404; £12,269)

RPR

1 **Shea Shea (SAF)**[21] 954 6-9-0 119 ChristopheSoumillon 7 123+
(M F De Kock, South Africa) *mid-div: smooth prog 2 1/2f out: rdn 1 1/2f out: led fnl 55yds* **1/1**[1]

2 3/4 **Joy And Fun (NZ)**[41] 10-9-0 113 (p) TyeAngland 11 120
(D Cruz, Hong Kong) *trckd ldrs: led 3f out: r.o: hdd fnl 55yds* **22/1**

3 3/4 **Eagle Regiment (AUS)**[62] 6-9-0 115 ODoleuze 1 117
(K L Man, Hong Kong) *mid-div: rdn 2 1/2f out: ev ch 1f out: nt qckn fnl 110yds* **6/1**[2]

4 1 **Sole Power**[21] 954 6-9-0 113 JohnnyMurtagh 15 114+
(Edward Lynam, Ire) *trckd ldrs: ev ch 1 1/2f out: nt qckn fnl f* **6/1**[2]

5 1 **Mr Big (AUS)**[90] 5-9-0 116 (bt) ZacPurton 16 110
(M Freedman, Singapore) *trckd ldrs: ev ch 1f out: one pce fnl 110yds* **20/1**

6 2 1/2 **Varsity (USA)**[56] 6-9-0 113 JBravo 6 101
(Christophe Clement, U.S.A) *trckd ldrs: ev ch 1 1/2f out: one pce fnl 110yds* **16/1**

7 1 1/4 **Dux Scholar**[37] 746 5-9-0 116 (bt) KUlubaev 4 97
(Seth Benzel, U.S.A) *chsd ldrs: ev ch 1 1/2f out: one pce fnl 110yds* **12/1**[3]

8 1/4 **Spirit Quartz (IRE)**[21] 954 5-9-0 115 JamieSpencer 5 96
(Robert Cowell) *nvr bttr than mid-div* **14/1**

9 shd **Medicean Man**[21] 954 7-9-0 110 (p) HarryBentley 14 95
(Jeremy Gask) *nvr nr to chal* **40/1**

10 shd **Invincible Ash (IRE)**[21] 954 8-8-9 104 (p) RichardHughes 12 90
(M Halford, Ire) *slowly away: n.d* **50/1**

11 1/2 **Great Attack (USA)**[56] 6-9-0 115 (bt) JRosario 13 93
(Wesley A Ward, U.S.A) *nvr bttr than mid-div* **25/1**

12 1 **Monsieur Joe (IRE)**[21] 954 6-9-0 110 WilliamBuick 2 89
(Robert Cowell) *nvr bttr than mid-div* **33/1**

13 hd **Russian Rock (IRE)**[21] 954 6-9-0 109 WayneSmith 8 89
(M Al Muhairi, UAE) *nvr bttr than mid-div* **33/1**

14 1/4 **Starspangledbanner (AUS)**[147] 7571 7-9-0 109 JosephO'Brien 10 88
(A P O'Brien, Ire) *nvr nr to chal* **20/1**

15 2 1/2 **Russian Soul (IRE)**[21] 954 5-9-0 109 (p) ShaneFoley 9 79
(M Halford, Ire) *nvr bttr than mid-div* **33/1**

16 3 3/4 **Ganas (IRE)**[21] 955 5-9-0 107 TadhgO'Shea 3 65
(Ernst Oertel, UAE) *sn led: hdd 3f out: wknd fnl 1 1/2f* **80/1**

56.41s (56.41) **16** Ran SP% **131.0**
CSF: 35.12; EX: 101.50; TRIFECTA: 476.60; TRICAST: 116.44; WIN: 1.90; PLACE: 1.00, 13.40, 3.10..

Owner Mssrs Brian Joffee & Myron C Berzack **Bred** Klawervlei Stud **Trained** South Africa

FOCUS
Not as competitive a sprint as the field size would suggest. There were only five individual Group/Grade 1 winners in the race, compared with nine last year, and they filled the first four places. The draw didn't seem to have much of an effect. The winner continued on the up and the form makes sense.

1266a DUBAI GOLDEN SHAHEEN SPONSORED BY GULF NEWS (GROUP 1) (TAPETA) 6f

3:45 (3:45) 3-Y-0+

£736,196 (£245,398; £122,699; £61,349; £36,809; £24,539)

RPR

1 **Reynaldothewizard (USA)**[21] 955 7-9-0 118 (bt) RichardMullen 5 116
(S Seemar, UAE) *trckd ldrs: rdn to ld 2 1/2f out: jst hld on* **9/1**

2 1/4 **Balmont Mast (IRE)**[21] 955 5-9-0 109 JohnnyMurtagh 6 115
(Edward Lynam, Ire) *chsd ldrs: ev ch 1 1/2f out: r.o fnl 110yds: jst failed* **33/1**

3 1/2 **Krypton Factor**[21] 955 5-9-0 117 (b) KierenFallon 13 113
(Fawzi Abdulla Nass, Bahrain) *chsd ldrs: ev ch 1 1/2f out: one pce fnl 110yds* **9/1**

4 hd **Tamaathul**[28] 868 6-9-0 115 (t) PaulHanagan 11 113
(A Al Raihe, UAE) *in rr of mid-div: r.o fnl 1 1/2f: nrst fin* **33/1**

5 3/4 **United Color (USA)**[30] 834 4-9-0 112 (t) JimmyFortune 8 110
(D Selvaratnam, UAE) *settled in rr: r.o fnl 2f: nrst fin* **33/1**

6 3/4 **Kavanagh (SAF)**[28] 868 6-9-0 116 (t) ChristopheSoumillon 7 108
(M F De Kock, South Africa) *in rr of mid-div: smooth prog 3f out: nt qckn fnl 1 1/2f* **12/1**

7 1 1/2 **Gordon Lord Byron (IRE)**[22] 936 5-9-0 118 WilliamBuick 2 103
(T Hogan, Ire) *mid-div: kpt on same pce fnl 1 1/2f* **5/1**[2]

8 3/4 **Frederick Engels**[41] 4-9-0 113 WCMarwing 1 101
(J Moore, Hong Kong) *slowly away: settled in rr: nvr nr to chal* **9/1**

9 1/4 **Private Zone (CAN)**[70] 4-9-0 113 (bt) MartinAPedroza 12 100
(Doug O'Neill, U.S.A) *sn led: hdd 2 1/2f out: wknd fnl f* **14/1**

10 1/2 **Mental (AUS)**[44] 660 5-9-0 121 (b) MickaelBarzalona 10 98
(Mahmood Al Zarooni) *nvr bttr than mid-div* **7/4**[1]

11 9 **Trinniberg (USA)**[147] 7574 4-9-0 118 (bt) WMartinez 3 69
(Shivananda Parbhoo, U.S.A) *trckd ldrs: ev ch tl outpcd 2 1/2f out* **7/1**[3]

12 nse **Taisei Legend (JPN)**[41] 6-9-0 112 (bt) RyanMoore 9 69
(Yoshito Yahagi, Japan) *trckd ldrs tl outpcd 2 1/2f out* **33/1**

13 3 1/2 **Reply (IRE)**[168] 7048 4-9-0 109 (v) JosephO'Brien 4 58
(A P O'Brien, Ire) *a in rr* **33/1**

1m 12.46s (0.86) **13** Ran SP% **124.6**
CSF: 291.24; EX: 223.50; TRIFECTA: 2,238.40; TRICAST: 2,709.85; WIN: 10.70; PLACE: 2.80, 12.30, 3.70..

Owner Zabeel Racing International, Corp **Bred** Gibraltar Group Lp **Trained** United Arab Emirates
■ Richard Mullen's first win at the top level.

FOCUS
Further evidence the Tapeta course was riding desperately slow - the final time was the 14th slowest of 57 races over C&D and the slowest this year. That played its part in making this a messy race and several of the fancied runners failed to show their best, leaving the form well short of you'd expect for an international Group 1. The sectionals were 24.55 (400m), 23.39 (800m) before the winner clocked 24.48 (finish).

1267a DUBAI DUTY FREE SPONSORED BY DUBAI DUTY FREE (GROUP 1) (TURF) 1m 1f

4:40 (4:40) 3-Y-0+

£1,840,490 (£613,496; £306,748; £153,374; £92,024; £61,349)

RPR

1 **Sajjhaa**[21] 959 6-8-9 115 SilvestreDeSousa 5 117+
(Saeed bin Suroor) *trckd ldrs: rdn to ld 1 1/2f out: r.o wl* **7/1**[3]

2 1 3/4 **The Apache (SAF)**[21] 959 6-9-0 117 ChristopheSoumillon 10 118
(M F De Kock, South Africa) *trckd ldrs: ev ch 1f out: nt qckn fnl 110yds* **10/1**

3 3/4 **Giofra**[111] 8043 5-8-9 117 (t) MaximeGuyon 9 111+
(A De Royer-Dupre, France) *mid-div: r.o fnl 1 1/2f: nrst fin* **7/1**[3]

4 1/4 **Trade Storm**[28] 872 5-9-0 116 JamieSpencer 14 116
(David Simcock) *settled in rr: r.o fnl 2f: nrst fin* **4/1**[1]

5 shd **Igugu (AUS)**[21] 959 6-8-9 115 ADelpech 6 111
(M F De Kock, South Africa) *trckd ldrs: led 2 1/2f out: hdd 1 1/2f out: wknd* **10/1**

6 1 1/2 **City Style (USA)**[21] 959 7-9-0 115 MickaelBarzalona 3 112
(Mahmood Al Zarooni) *trckd ldrs tl wknd 2 1/2f out* **16/1**

7 1 **I'm A Dreamer (IRE)**[148] 7549 6-8-9 116 HayleyTurner 2 105
(David Simcock) *mid-div: t.k.h: kpt on one pce fnl 1 1/2f* **16/1**

8 shd **Wigmore Hall (IRE)**[167] 7094 6-9-0 115 RyanMoore 12 110
(Michael Bell) *slowly away: settled in rr: nvr nr to chal* **25/1**

9 1 **French Fifteen (FR)**[28] 4-9-0 118 OlivierPeslier 13 108
(N Clement, France) *settled in rr: kpt on same pce fnl 1 1/2f but nvr able to chal* **12/1**

10 hd **Mushreq (AUS)**[37] 745 5-9-0 117 PaulHanagan 11 108
(M F De Kock, South Africa) *nvr bttr than mid-div* **12/1**

11 1/2 **Little Mike (USA)**[21] 958 6-9-0 123 (t) GaryStevens 4 107
(Dale Romans, U.S.A) *sn led: hdd & wknd 2 1/2f out* **8/1**

12 3 **Ocean Park (NZ)**[21] 5-9-0 122 (b) JohnnyMurtagh 7 100
(Gary Hennessy, New Zealand) *settled in rr: nvr nr to chal* **11/2**[2]

13 13 **Fulbright**[28] 872 4-9-0 113 (t) AhmedAjtebi 8 73
(Mahmood Al Zarooni) *settled in rr: n.d* **33/1**

14 2 1/2 **Aesop's Fables (USA)**[21] 957 4-9-0 115 (v) KierenFallon 1 68
(Saeed bin Suroor) *trckd ldrs: t.k.h: wknd 3f out* **25/1**

1m 47.93s (107.93) **14** Ran SP% **127.5**
CSF: 78.46; EX: 33.90; TRIFECTA: 557.40; TRICAST: 526.11; WIN: 5.00; PLACE: 1.40, 2.90, 4.30..

Owner Godolphin **Bred** Darley **Trained** Newmarket, Suffolk

FOCUS
A hugely competitive Group 1 featuring nine individual Group/Grade 1 winners, and no outstanding candidate. They went a pretty even gallop and it proved difficult to come from off the pace. Here are the sectional times: 25.59 (400m, from standing start), 23.61 (800m), 24.10 (1200m), 22.99 (1600m) before the winner covered the final 200m in 11.64. The Jebel Hatta has often been a key guide to this race, and no more than this year, with the winner and second finishing one-two in both races. The second and fourth help with the standard.

1268a DUBAI SHEEMA CLASSIC PRESENTED BY LONGINES (GROUP 1) (TURF) 1m 4f 11y

5:20 (5:20) 3-Y-0+

£1,840,490 (£613,496; £306,748; £153,374; £92,024; £61,349)

RPR

1 **St Nicholas Abbey (IRE)**[147] 7573 6-9-0 123 JosephO'Brien 6 121+
(A P O'Brien, Ire) *trckd ldrs: led 3f out: r.o wl* **11/4**[2]

2 2 1/4 **Gentildonna (JPN)**[125] 7872 4-8-8 122 YasunariIwata 8 114+
(Sei Ishizaka, Japan) *trckd ldrs: ev ch 1 1/2f out: kpt on same pce: jst failed* **11/8**[1]

3 1 1/4 **Very Nice Name (FR)**[30] 4-8-13 113 OlivierPeslier 9 116
(A De Mieulle, France) *settled in rr: r.o fnl 2f: nrst fin* **66/1**

4 1 1/4 **Dunaden (FR)**[111] 8040 7-9-0 122 JamieSpencer 10 113
(M Delzangles, France) *settled in rr: r.o fnl 1 1/2f: nrst fin* **10/1**

5 1 1/2 **Await The Dawn (USA)**[21] 956 6-9-0 120 PatCosgrave 11 111
(M F De Kock, South Africa) *mid-div: smooth prog 2 1/2f out: nt qckn fnl 1 1/2f* **11/1**

6 nk **Shareta (IRE)**[147] 7573 5-8-9 118 Christophe-PatriceLemaire 1 106
(A De Royer-Dupre, France) *sn led: hdd 3f out: wknd fnl 1 1/2f* **6/1**[3]

7 2 **Royal Diamond (IRE)**[28] 870 7-9-0 112 JohnnyMurtagh 2 107
(Thomas Carmody, Ire) *trckd ldrs tl outpcd 2f out* **40/1**

8 1 1/2 **Girolamo (GER)**[188] 6523 4-8-13 116 AStarke 3 106
(P Schiergen, Germany) *in rr of mid-div: nvr able to chal* **40/1**

9 1 3/4 **Sharestan (IRE)**[21] 959 5-9-0 112 SilvestreDeSousa 5 102
(Saeed bin Suroor) *slowly away: settled in rr: rdn 5f out: nvr nr able to chal* **20/1**

10 3/4 **Prince Bishop (IRE)**[21] 958 6-9-0 113 (v) MickaelBarzalona 4 101
(Saeed bin Suroor) *settled in rr: nvr able to chal* **25/1**

11 7 1/4 **Trailblazer (JPN)**[21] 958 6-9-0 119 YutakaTake 7 89
(Yasutoshi Ikee, Japan) *trckd ldrs tl wknd 2 1/2f out* **16/1**

2m 27.7s (147.70)
WFA 4 from 5yo+ 2lb **11** Ran SP% **121.3**
CSF: 6.77; EX: 12.60; TRIFECTA: 167.70; TRICAST: 201.61; WIN: 4.40; PLACE: 1.50, 1.10, 4.80..

Owner Derrick Smith & Mrs John Magnier & Michael Tabor **Bred** Barton Bloodstock & Villiers Synd **Trained** Ballydoyle, Co Tipperary

The Form Book Flat, Raceform Ltd, Compton, RG20 6NL.

FOCUS

Six Group/Grade 1 winners in the line-up, headlined by last year's runner-up St Nicholas Abbey and Japan Cup winner Gentildonna, and the pair had the race to themselves in the closing stages. Christophe Lemaire, aboard Shareta, set even fractions and the course record was lowered by the winner. Here are the sectional times: 26.5 (400m, from standing start), 24.21 (800m), 24.76 (1200m), 24.73 (1600m), 23.49 (2000m) before the winner covered the final 410m in 24.01.

1269a DUBAI WORLD CUP SPONSORED BY EMIRATES AIRLINE (GROUP 1) (TAPETA) 1m 2f

6:05 (6:05) 3-Y-O+

£3,680,981 (£1,226,993; £613,496; £306,748; £184,049; £122,699)

RPR

1 **Animal Kingdom (USA)**[49] 595 5-9-0 123......................(bt) JRosario 12 124+
(H Graham Motion, U.S.A) *trckd ldrs: led 3f out: ran on wl: cmftbly* **11/2**[3]

2 2 **Red Cadeaux**[111] 8040 7-9-0 116................................ GeraldMosse 2 119+
(Ed Dunlop) *settled in rr: r.o.wl fnl 2f but no ch w wnr* **28/1**

3 4 ¾ **Planteur (IRE)**[35] 777 6-9-0 120................................ RyanMoore 7 110
(Marco Botti) *s.s: settled in rr: r.o fnl 2f: nrst fin* **10/1**

4 ¼ **Side Glance**[21] 959 6-9-0 115.. JamieSpencer 6 109
(Andrew Balding) *trckd ldrs: ev ch 2f out: one pace fnl f* **33/1**

5 nse **African Story**[21] 957 6-9-0 120............................. MickaelBarzalona 11 109
(Saeed bin Suroor) *hld up in rr: nvr nr to chal but ran on fnl 1 1/2f* **8/1**

6 2 ¼ **Meandre (FR)**[28] 5-9-0 122.. MaximeGuyon 9 104
(A Fabre, France) *trckd ldng grp tl outpcd 3f out* **20/1**

7 2 ¼ **Hunter's Light (IRE)**[21] 958 5-9-0 117.................... SilvestreDeSousa 4 100
(Saeed bin Suroor) *trckd ldrs: ev ch 2 1/12f out: one pce fnl 1 1/2f* **5/2**[1]

8 ¾ **Treasure Beach**[21] 958 5-9-0 115.................... ChristopheSoumillon 1 98
(M F De Kock, South Africa) *trckd ldrs: rdn 3f out: sn btn* **25/1**

9 1 **Kassiano (GER)**[21] 958 4-9-0 113.............................. WilliamBuick 13 96
(Saeed bin Suroor) *settled in rr: nvr nr to chal* **16/1**

10 7 **Royal Delta (USA)**[41] 5-8-9 121.. MESmith 8 77
(William Mott, U.S.A) *sn led: hdd and wknd 3f out* **3/1**[2]

11 14 **Dullahan (USA)**[21] 957 4-9-0 123.................................(t) GaryStevens 3 54
(Dale Romans, U.S.A) *nvr bttr than mid-div* **14/1**

12 dist **Capponi (IRE)**[364] 1150 6-9-0 121...................................(t) AhmedAjtebi 5
(Mahmood Al Zarooni) *a in rr* **20/1**

2m 3.21s (-1.49) 13 Ran SP% **121.5**

CSF: 160.01; EX: 123.50; TRIFECTA: 1,895.80; TRICAST: 1,519.23; WIN: 3.70; PLACE: 1.50, 11.70, 4.00. PLACEPOT: £411.30. Pool £12,650.50 - 22.45 winning units. QUADPOT: £60.10. Pool £1,138.85 - 14.00 winning units..

Owner Arrowfield Stud & Team Valor **Bred** Team Valor **Trained** USA

FOCUS

Since the Dubai World Cup was moved to Meydan in 2010, the three runnings to date had been unsatisfactory for one reason or another (no horse at a single-figure price had made the top three), so the race badly needed a genuinely high-class winner to restore some credibility and that's exactly what it got. It helped that there a decent gallop for a change, resulting in a pretty clean race, and while there might not much depth to the form, there's no doubting this was a top performance from the tremendously versatile Animal Kingdom. On a track that had been playing slow, Royal Delta took them along in the following fractions: 26.59 (400m), 23.43 (800m), 23.61 (1200m), 25.03 (1600m), before the winner clocked 24.55. The second and third help with the form.

1247 MUSSELBURGH (R-H)

Sunday, March 31

OFFICIAL GOING: Good to soft (soft in places; 5.9)

Wind: Moderate half behind Weather: Cloudy with sunny periods

1270 BET TOTEJACKPOT TODAY AT TOTEPOOL.COM H'CAP 1m 1f

2:20 (2:20) (Class 6) (0-65,65) 4-Y-O+ **£2,587** (£770; £384; £192) **Stalls** Low

Form RPR

326- 1 **Sartingo (IRE)**[270] 3752 6-9-4 **62**.................................... RobertWinston 3 72
(Alan Swinbank) *led: qcknd clr over 3f out: rdn wl over 1f out: styd on wl fnl f* **9/2**[2]

204- 2 5 **Titus Bolt (IRE)**[23] 7117 4-9-0 **58**.. GrahamLee 7 58+
(Jim Goldie) *hld up in midfield: hdwy over 3f out: rdn to chse wnr fr wl over 1f out: drvn ent fnl f: no imp towards fin* **9/4**[1]

6663 3 6 **El Bravo**[11] 1090 7-8-5 **54**......................................(p) MichaelJMMurphy(5) 2 42
(Shaun Harris) *hld up towards rr: hdwy 3f out: rdn to chse ldrs 2f out: kpt on fnl f* **11/2**

020- 4 3 ¼ **Remember Rocky**[77] 4932 4-8-9 **53**..................................(p) TomEaves 1 35
(Lucy Normile) *trckd ldrs on inner: hdwy 1/2-way: chsd wnr over 3f out: drvn 2f out: grad wknd* **20/1**

6266 5 1 ¾ **Jordaura**[10] 1104 7-8-13 **64**.. JordanHibberd(7) 11 42
(Alan Berry) *towards rr: sme hdwy 3f out: sn rdn and nvr nr ldrs* **17/2**

04- 6 3 ¾ **One Million**[79] 6527 4-8-7 **51** oh6..................................(t) JamesSullivan 4 22
(Rose Dobbin) *a towards rr* **50/1**

420- 7 2 ½ **Flipping**[134] 7781 6-8-12 **56**.. PaulMulrennan 12 22
(Nicky Richards) *t.k.h: cl up 2f: trckd ldrs: rdn along 3f out: sn drvn and wknd* **8/1**

340- 8 2 ¾ **Cosmic Moon**[171] 7003 5-8-13 **57**.................................. TonyHamilton 5 17
(Richard Fahey) *a in rr* **5/1**[3]

45-0 9 19 **Bandy Bob**[16] 1022 4-8-4 **51** oh6.. NeilFarley(3) 10
(Iain Jardine) *t.k.h: cl up: rdn along over 3f out: sn wknd* **28/1**

0/60 10 2 ½ **Major Eradicator (USA)**[1] 1251 6-8-2 **51** oh6..............(b) AmyScott(5) 6
(Alastair Lidderdale) *s.i.s and reminders s: rapid hdwy and cl up after 2f: rdn along over 4f out: sn wknd* **28/1**

1m 59.99s (6.09) **Going Correction** +0.80s/f (Soft) 10 Ran SP% **116.3**

Speed ratings (Par 101): **104,99,94,91,89 86,84,81,64,62**

Tote Swingers: 1&2 £3.70, 1&3 £5.00, 2&3 £3.20 CSF £14.37 CT £57.96 TOTE £4.90: £1.50, £1.90, £1.60; EX 15.60 Trifecta £84.50 Pool: £1,940.12 - 17.20 winning units..

Owner Melvyn Robson **Bred** Lynch-Bages, Carhue Inv & Glenvale Stud **Trained** Melsonby, N Yorks

FOCUS

An ordinary handicap inwhich the winner had things his way up front. The form can't be taken too literally.

1271 BET TOTEEXACTA ON ALL RACES AT TOTEPOOL.COM H'CAP 7f 30y

2:50 (2:50) (Class 6) (0-65,64) 4-Y-O+ **£2,587** (£770; £384; £192) **Stalls** Low

Form RPR

1341 1 **Rise To Glory (IRE)**[15] 1042 5-8-7 **50**.......................... DuranFentiman 8 60
(Shaun Harris) *mde all: rdn clr 2f out: drvn and kpt on wl fnl f* **14/1**

44-4 2 3 ¼ **Keep It Dark**[5] 1184 4-9-0 **64**................................ DavidSimmonson(7) 2 66+
(Tony Coyle) *hld up in rr: hdwy on inner 3f out: chsd ldrs 2f out: swtchd lft and rdn to chse wnr over 1f out: edgd lft and no imp wl ins fnl f* **14/1**

4146 3 7 **Nant Saeson (IRE)**[31] 831 4-9-7 **64**......................(p) MichaelO'Connell 4 49
(John Quinn) *a.p: hdwy to chse wnr over 2f out: sn rdn and one pce appr fnl f* **7/1**

-564 4 ¾ **Medam**[11] 1088 4-8-2 **50** oh3....................................(t) ShirleyTeasdale(5) 1 33
(Shaun Harris) *chsd ldrs: hdwy over 3f out: rdn over 2f out: edgd rt and one pce fr wl over 1f out* **14/1**

024- 5 1 ¾ **Gladsome**[153] 7445 5-9-7 **64**...[1] TonyHamilton 12 43+
(Jason Ward) *hld up and bhd: hdwy on inner 2f out: sn rdn and kpt on: nvr nr ldrs* **12/1**

200- 6 ½ **Dream Walker (FR)**[134] 7776 4-9-4 **61**................................ DaleSwift 10 39
(Ian McInnes) *hld up in rr: hdwy wl over 2f out: sn rdn and plugged on one pce* **13/2**[3]

600- 7 nk **Goninodaethat**[167] 7095 5-8-11 **54**...................................... GrahamLee 3 31
(Jim Goldie) *hld up towards rr: sme hdwy wl over 2f out: sn rdn and one pce* **6/1**[2]

3514 8 8 **Rio Cobolo (IRE)**[4] 1205 7-9-7 **64**................................(v) AdrianNicholls 5 21
(David Nicholls) *prom: rdn along 1/2-way: drvn and wknd over 2f out* **4/1**[1]

355- 9 6 **Celestial Dawn**[153] 7446 4-9-4 **61**................................... JamesSullivan 9 4
(John Weymes) *midfield: hdwy 1/2-way: rdn along wl over 2f out: sn wknd* **10/1**

6041 10 shd **Outlaw Torn (IRE)**[19] 975 4-9-7 **64**.......................(e) RobbieFitzpatrick 6 6
(Richard Guest) *prom: rdn along 3f out: drvn 2f out and sn wknd* **14/1**

100- 11 4 ½ **Hoppy's Flyer (FR)**[153] 7436 5-9-7 **64**..........................(v) MickyFenton 11
(Paul Midgley) *prom: chsd wnr after 3f: rdn along over 2f out: sn wknd* **33/1**

5443 12 3 **Michael's Nook**[8] 1149 6-8-3 **51**......................................(p) AmyScott(5) 7
(Alastair Lidderdale) *chsd ldrs on outer: rdn along 3f out: sn wknd* **13/2**[3]

1m 34.81s (5.81) **Going Correction** +0.80s/f (Soft) 12 Ran SP% **119.8**

Speed ratings (Par 101): **98,94,86,85,83 82,82,73,66,66 61,57**

Tote Swingers: 1&2 £42.20, 1&3 £19.20, 2&3 £26.20 CSF £197.95 CT £1521.96 TOTE £14.10: £3.40, £5.40, £3.60; EX 523.50 Trifecta £1758.40 Part won. Pool: £2,344.65 - 0.47 winning units..

Owner N Blencowe,J Sunderland,M Lenton,CHarris **Bred** Bryan Ryan **Trained** Carburton, Notts

FOCUS

Another all-the-way winner, and the form can't be taken too seriously. The firld finished strung out and the winner is rated to his turf best.

1272 BET TOTEQUADPOT NOW AT TOTEPOOL.COM MAIDEN STKS 7f 30y

3:20 (3:20) (Class 5) 3-Y-O+ **£3,234** (£962; £481; £240) **Stalls** Low

Form RPR

434- 1 **Lightning Launch (IRE)**[219] 5534 3-8-13 **73**............... MatthewDavies 8 76
(Mick Channon) *mde all: pushed clr over 2f out: rdn and edgd lft ins fnl f: kpt on wl towards fin* **9/4**[2]

22- 2 nk **Brooke's Bounty**[152] 7450 3-8-13 0................................ TonyHamilton 1 75
(Richard Fahey) *trckd ldng pair: hdwy over 2f out: sn chsng wnr and rdn: drvn over 1f out: kpt on ins fnl f: no ex towards fin* **6/4**[1]

3 13 **Royal Duchess** 3-8-9 0 ow1.. TomEaves 2 37+
(Lucy Normile) *s.i.s: green and bhd 1/2-way: hdwy on wd outside over 2f out: rdn and kpt on fnl f: nrst fin* **50/1**

5- 4 hd **Riponian**[314] 2338 3-8-13 0... MichaelO'Connell 6 41
(Stuart Coltherd) *t.k.h: chsd ldrs: rdn along 3f out: drvn over 2f out and grad wknd* **40/1**

06- 5 3 ¾ **Carla Allegra**[208] 5919 4-9-9 0... GrahamLee 3 31
(Jim Goldie) *chsd ldrs: rdn along 3f out: sn drvn and wknd* **50/1**

-336 6 11 **Rawaafed (IRE)**[12] 1081 4-10-0 68..............................(v) FrederikTylicki 4
(Keith Dalgleish) *t.k.h: chsd wnr: rdn along 3f out: grad wknd* **5/1**

0 7 ½ **Hartford Starts (IRE)**[15] 1044 3-8-13 0................................ DaleSwift 5
(Ian McInnes) *t.k.h: a in rr* **50/1**

- 8 6 **Mojave Desert (IRE)** 3-8-8 0.. JoeFanning 7
(Mark Johnston) *s.i.s and green: a in rr* **4/1**[3]

1m 35.52s (6.52) **Going Correction** +0.90s/f (Soft)

WFA 3 from 4yo 15lb 8 Ran SP% **115.8**

Speed ratings (Par 103): **98,97,82,82,78 65,65,58**

Tote Swingers: 1&2 £1.30, 1&3 £6.90, 2&3 £8.70 CSF £6.04 TOTE £3.10: £1.10, £1.10, £6.10; EX 6.30 Trifecta £110.30 Pool: £3,533.57 - 21.01 winning units..

Owner Jaber Abdullah **Bred** Yeomanstown Lodge Stud **Trained** West Ilsley, Berks

FOCUS

Yet another winner to make all. The first two finished miles clear and are rated close to last season's 2yo form.

1273 TOTEPOOL.COM MUSSELBURGH GOLD CUP (H'CAP) 1m 6f

3:50 (3:50) (Class 3) (0-90,87) 4-Y-O+ **£16,172** (£4,812; £2,405; £1,202) **Stalls** Low

Form RPR

216- 1 **Lady Kashaan (IRE)**[155] 7396 4-9-4 **85**....................... RobertWinston 4 94
(Alan Swinbank) *trckd ldrs: hdwy over 3f out: chal 2f out and sn rdn: disp ld over 1f out: hrd drvn ins fnl f: kpt on gamely to ld nr fin* **4/1**[1]

041- 2 hd **Moidore**[116] 6517 4-9-4 **85**.. MichaelO'Connell 8 94
(John Quinn) *trckd ldng pair: hdwy to chse ldr 3f out: rdn to chal 2f out: sn led and jnd: drvn and slt advantage ent fnl f: hdd and no ex towards fin* **4/1**[1]

52/2 3 2 **The Bull Hayes (IRE)**[9] 1110 7-9-10 **87**.....................(p) BarryMcHugh 10 93
(Tony Coyle) *led: rdn along 3f out: hdd and drvn wl over 1f out: kpt on u.p fnl f* **16/1**

1-16 4 5 **Mica Mika (IRE)**[57] 496 5-9-2 **82**....................................... LeeTopliss(3) 2 82
(Richard Fahey) *in tch: hdwy to chse ldrs 3f out: rdn over 2f out: kpt on same pce* **12/1**

12-2 5 4 ½ **Porgy**[22] 948 8-9-8 **85**...(b) GrahamLee 9 79+
(Brian Ellison) *hld up in rr: hdwy wl over 2f out: sn rdn and kpt on fr over 1f out: nrst fin* **9/1**[3]

200- 6 1 ¼ **Nanton (USA)**[128] 7852 11-9-4 **86**............................ GeorgeDowning(5) 1 78+
(Jim Goldie) *hld up in rr: hdwy 3f out: rdn 2f out: kpt on: nt rch ldrs* **20/1**

1-62 7 ½ **Solaras Exhibition (IRE)**[15] 1037 5-9-7 **84**........................ TomEaves 3 75
(Tim Vaughan) *hld up: hdwy on inner wl over 2f out: sn rdn and kpt on same pce* **8/1**[2]

016- 8 2 ¾ **Los Nadis (GER)**[22] 7098 9-9-2 **82**..................................(p) NeilFarley(3) 5 70
(Jim Goldie) *towards rr: pushed along and sme hdwy on outer over 4f out: rdn along 3f out: n.d* **18/1**

324- 9 5 **Getabuzz**[190] 6472 5-9-4 **81**... DavidAllan 6 62
(Tim Easterby) *midfield: effrt and sme hdwy over 4f out: rdn along over 3f out and sn wknd* **10/1**

61-3 10 12 **Royal Peculiar**[12] 1083 5-9-5 **82**.................................... AndrewMullen 7 48
(Michael Appleby) *cl up: rdn along over 3f out: sn drvn and wknd* **9/1**[3]

160- 11 8 **Angel Gabrial (IRE)**[183] 6677 4-9-5 **86**.............................. TonyHamilton 12 41
(Ian Williams) *chsd ldrs: rdn along on outer over 3f out: sn wknd* **8/1**[2]

000- 12 26 **Cosmic Sun**[142] 7672 7-9-0 77 FrederikTylicki 11
(Richard Fahey) *a in rr: outpcd and bhd fnl 3f* **20/1**
3m 15.21s (9.91) **Going Correction** +0.90s/f (Soft)
WFA 4 from 5yo+ 4lb **12** Ran SP% **119.7**
Speed ratings (Par 107): **107,106,105,102,100 99,99,97,94,88 83,68**
Tote Swingers: 1&2 £3.00, 1&3 £19.10, 2&3 £17.90 CSF £17.97 CT £228.66 TOTE £4.60: £1.50, £1.90, £4.50; EX 16.10 Trifecta £305.20 Pool: £2,164.09 - 5.31 winning units..
Owner G Brogan **Bred** Corduff Stud Ltd & J Corcoran **Trained** Melsonby, N Yorks
■ Stewards' Enquiry : Robert Winston four-day ban: use of whip (15-18 Apr)
FOCUS
Although the winner didn't make all this time, again it paid to race prominently. Slightly improved efforts from the front pair.

1274 YOUR FAVOURITE POOL BETS AT TOTEPOOL.COM E B F MAIDEN STKS 1m 4f 100y
4:20 (4:20) (Class 4) 3-Y-0+ £5,175 (£1,540; £769; £384) Stalls Low

Form RPR
3 1 **Guising**[17] 994 4-9-11 0 RobertWinston 3 86+
(David Brown) *mde all: qcknd clr over 3f out: rdn over 1f out: styd on fnl f* **5/4**[2]
42 2 7 **Ambleside**[16] 1009 3-8-5 0 FrannyNorton 1 75+
(Mark Johnston) *hld up in rr: green and reminders 1/2-way: rdn along and edgd lft bnd 5f out: rdn to chse wnr and rn green 3f out: styd on u.p appr fnl f: no ch w wnr* **6/5**[1]
4/0- 3 23 **Wolf Heart (IRE)**[89] 7594 5-9-13 0 TomEaves 4 40
(Lucy Normile) *trckd wnr: rdn along 3f out: sn outpcd* **66/1**
4 2 **Hell Hath No Fury**[75] 4-9-6 0 AndrewMullen 2 32
(Michael Appleby) *trckd ldng pair on inner: pushed along 5f out: rdn over 3f out: sn outpcd* **11/2**[3]
56- 5 10 **Hayley**[167] 7096 3-8-0 0 [1] JamesSullivan 5 15
(Jim Goldie) *trckd ldrs: rdn along 5f out: wknd 4f out* **20/1**
2m 55.55s (13.55) **Going Correction** +1.00s/f (Soft)
WFA 3 from 4yo 22lb 4 from 5yo 2lb **5** Ran SP% **111.5**
Speed ratings (Par 105): **94,89,74,72,66**
CSF £3.14 TOTE £1.50: £1.20, £1.10; EX 3.90 Trifecta £40.40 Pool: £2,035.03 - 37.75 winning units..
Owner Peter Onslow & Ian Henderson **Bred** Peter Onslow **Trained** Averham Park, Notts
FOCUS
The fourth winner on the card to make all the running. He's rated as having shown token improvement.

1275 KINGSIZE POOLS AT TOTEPOOL.COM H'CAP (SUNDAY £5K BONUS RACE) 7f 30y
4:55 (4:56) (Class 5) (0-75,74) 3-Y-0 £3,234 (£962; £481; £240) Stalls Low

Form RPR
4-12 1 **Skytrain**[22] 949 3-9-2 69 JoeFanning 2 78
(Mark Johnston) *slt ld on inner: pushed along 3f out: rdn 2f out and sn edgd lft: drvn and edgd lft to stands' rail over 1f out: hdd ins fnl f: rallied to ld again nr fin* **2/1**[1]
2241 2 nk **Red Gift (IRE)**[19] 964 3-9-0 67 (p) TomEaves 3 75
(Brian Ellison) *trckd ldrs: pushed along over 3f out: rdn 2f out: sn chal: styd on to ld ins fnl f: hdd and no ex nr fin* **8/1**
510- 3 3 ¼ **Yorkshireman (IRE)**[141] 7687 3-9-7 74 RobertWinston 1 74
(David Brown) *trckd ldrs: hdwy 3f out: rdn to chal 2f out and ev ch tl drvn and one pce appr fnl f* **8/1**
363- 4 1 ¼ **Danehill Flyer (IRE)**[180] 6753 3-8-10 63 MichaelO'Connell 10 60
(Philip Kirby) *in tch: hdwy on outer 3f out: rdn over 2f out: drvn and kpt on same pce appr fnl f* **7/1**[3]
230- 5 3 **Someone's Darling**[135] 7745 3-8-8 61 JamesSullivan 8 51
(Jim Goldie) *stdd and swtchd rt to inner s: hdwy over 3f out: rdn to chse ldrs 2f out: sn drvn and one pce* **33/1**
0-41 6 nk **The Scuttler (IRE)**[16] 1014 3-9-4 71 MatthewDavies 7 60
(Mick Channon) *hld up towards rr: hdwy 3f out: rdn to chse ldrs 2f out: sn drvn and no imp* **15/2**
104- 7 13 **Alexandrakollontai (IRE)**[162] 7242 3-8-6 62 JulieBurke(3) 9 19
(Alistair Whillans) *s.i.s: a bhd* **25/1**
6-44 8 ¾ **Bix (IRE)**[31] 827 3-8-0 60 JordanHibberd(7) 5 15
(Alan Berry) *cl up: rdn along 1/2-way: sn wknd* **66/1**
362- 9 1 ¼ **Lexington Place**[145] 7609 3-8-12 65 TonyHamilton 6 17+
(Richard Fahey) *pushed along whn n.m.r and sltly hmpd sn after s: in tch: rdn along 1/2-way: drvn wl over 2f out and sn wknd* **3/1**[2]
005- 10 3 ¾ **Blue Clumber**[227] 5255 3-8-10 68 MichaelJMMurphy(5) 4 11
(Shaun Harris) *cl up: rdn along over 3f out: sn wknd* **33/1**
1m 36.47s (7.47) **Going Correction** +1.00s/f (Soft) **10** Ran SP% **116.0**
Speed ratings (Par 98): **97,96,92,91,88 87,72,72,70,66**
Tote Swingers: 1&2 £3.90, 1&3 £4.20, 2&3 £6.90 CSF £18.18 CT £102.55 TOTE £2.60: £1.50, £1.50, £2.20; EX 16.60 Trifecta £101.20 Pool: £3,697.85 - 27.40 winning units..
Owner A D Spence **Bred** Brook Stud Bloodstock Ltd **Trained** Middleham Moor, N Yorks
FOCUS
The winner didn't have it all his own way. The form looks sound with the first pair clear.

1276 TRY A TOTETRIFECTA AT TOTEPOOL.COM H'CAP 5f
5:25 (5:26) (Class 6) (0-60,60) 4-Y-0+ £2,587 (£770; £384; £192) Stalls High

Form RPR
5111 1 **Greenhead High**[17] 998 5-9-7 60 (v) AdrianNicholls 4 69
(David Nicholls) *mde all: rdn over 1f out: drvn ins fnl f: kpt on wl towards fin* **3/1**[2]
3306 2 1 **Roy's Legacy**[9] 1121 4-9-0 58 (t) MichaelJMMurphy(5) 8 63
(Shaun Harris) *cl up: rdn to chal over 1f out: ev ch ins fnl f: drvn and no ex last 75yds* **6/1**[3]
-421 3 1 ¾ **Pull The Pin (IRE)**[18] 991 4-8-13 55 (b) NeilFarley(3) 6 54
(Declan Carroll) *towards rr and outpcd: hdwy 1/2-way: rdn wl over 1f out: kpt on fnl f: nrst fin* **3/1**[2]
060- 4 4 ½ **Wicked Wilma (IRE)**[152] 7457 9-9-5 58 RobertWinston 1 41
(Alan Berry) *sn rdn along in rr: sme hdwy wl over 1f out: n.d* **10/1**
2200 5 1 ¼ **Miserere Mei (IRE)**[17] 997 4-8-9 48 (e) RobbieFitzpatrick 7 26
(Richard Guest) *in tch: hdwy to chse ldng pair 1/2-way: rdn wl over 1f out: sn one pce* **18/1**
040- 6 1 ¾ **Headstight (IRE)**[164] 7204 4-8-13 52 (p) MickyFenton 2 24
(Paul Midgley) *wnt rt s: chsd ldrs: rdn along 2f out: sn wknd* **9/1**
3215 7 6 **Alpha Tauri (USA)**[18] 986 7-8-7 49 (t) BillyCray(3) 3
(Scott Dixon) *chsd ldng pair: rdn along bef 1/2-way: sn btn* **5/2**[1]
1m 3.24s (2.84) **Going Correction** +0.60s/f (Yiel) **7** Ran SP% **117.2**
Speed ratings (Par 101): **101,99,96,89,87 84,75**
Tote Swingers: 1&2 £4.60, 1&3 £2.10, 2&3 £4.20 CSF £22.08 CT £58.57 TOTE £2.70: £1.10, £5.20; EX 23.50 Trifecta £65.80 Pool: £3,409.30 - 38.76 winning units..
Owner Charles Castle **Bred** Wyck Hall Stud Ltd **Trained** Sessay, N Yorks
FOCUS
Yet another all-the-way winner. He is rated closer to his sand form, with the second to his best turf figure.
T/Jkpt: Not won. T/Plt: £31.60 to a £1 stake. Pool: £75,426.24 - 1,737.89 winning tickets. T/Qpdt: £5.70 to a £1 stake. Pool: £5,501.90 - 704.05 winning tickets. JR

1277 - (Foreign Racing) - See Raceform Interactive

REDCAR (L-H)
Monday, April 1
OFFICIAL GOING: Good to soft (soft in places; 5.9)
Wind: Moderate; across Weather: Cloudy

1278 MARKET CROSS JEWELLERS FILLIES' H'CAP 5f
2:30 (2:30) (Class 5) (0-75,74) 4-Y-0+ £2,587 (£770; £384; £192) Stalls High

Form RPR
260- 1 **Foreign Rhythm (IRE)**[154] 7447 8-7-12 56 ShirleyTeasdale(5) 1 69
(Ron Barr) *trckd ldrs: hdwy to chse ldr over 2f out: rdn to ld over 1f out: kpt on* **15/2**
06-0 2 1 ¼ **Da'Quonde (IRE)**[80] 164 5-9-7 74 TomEaves 2 82
(Bryan Smart) *cl up: led 1/2-way: rdn and hdd over 1f out: drvn and one pce fnl f* **4/1**[1]
10-0 3 2 ¼ **Phoenix Clubs (IRE)**[27] 885 4-9-6 73 BarryMcHugh 9 73
(Paul Midgley) *awkward s and sn swtchd lft: hld up in rr: hdwy 2f out: rdn to chse ldng pair wl over 1f out: no imp fnl f* **5/1**[2]
220- 4 1 ¾ **Economic Crisis (IRE)**[153] 7451 4-9-4 71 PaddyAspell 3 65
(Alan Berry) *chsd ldrs: effrt 2f out: sn rdn and one pce* **10/1**
040- 5 4 ½ **See Clearly**[143] 7666 4-8-8 66 (p) AdamCarter(5) 4 43
(Tim Easterby) *towards rr: pushed along 1/2-way: sn rdn and sme late hdwy* **4/1**[1]
26-0 6 1 **Rio's Girl**[13] 1077 6-8-2 55 JamesSullivan 6 29
(Tony Coyle) *cl up: rdn along bef 1/2-way: sn wknd* **10/1**
300- 7 2 ¾ **Quaroma**[180] 6788 8-9-2 72 LeeTopliss(3) 7 36
(Paul Midgley) *wnt lft s: a towards rr* **14/1**
431- 8 ¾ **Pivotal Prospect**[180] 6783 5-9-0 67 RoystonFfrench 5 28
(Tracy Waggott) *led: pushed along 1/2-way: sn hdd & wknd* **11/2**[3]
605- 9 14 **Trust Fund Babe (IRE)**[146] 7600 4-8-3 56 DuranFentiman 8
(Tim Easterby) *sn rdn along: a outpcd and bhd* **16/1**
1m 1.04s (2.44) **Going Correction** +0.50s/f (Yiel) **9** Ran SP% **114.5**
Speed ratings (Par 100): **100,98,94,91,84 82,78,77,54**
toteswingers 1&2 £7.80, 1&3 £8.00, 2&3 £4.90 CSF £37.26 TOTE £13.00: £2.40, £2.60, £1.80; EX 30.60 Trifecta £354.80 Pool: £1922.80 - 4.06 winning units.
Owner R E Barr **Bred** Yeomanstown Stud **Trained** Seamer, N Yorks
FOCUS
Just a run-of-the-mill fillies' sprint run on ground which was described as dead. The winner is rated back to last year's reappeaance form with the second close to her mark.

1279 RACHEL TOMLINSON DESIGNED TODAY'S RACECARD COVER H'CAP 2m 4y
3:00 (3:00) (Class 6) (0-65,65) 4-Y-0+ £1,940 (£577; £288; £144) Stalls Low

Form RPR
40-2 1 **Zaplamation (IRE)**[2] 1239 8-9-7 60 BarryMcHugh 10 74+
(John Quinn) *hld up towards rr: smooth hdwy 5f out: effrt on inner over 2f out: led 1 1/2f out: readily* **7/2**[2]
500- 2 2 ¾ **Harvey's Hope**[30] 6126 7-9-7 60 (t) TomEaves 3 67
(Keith Reveley) *trckd ldrs: hdwy 4f out: sn cl up: rdn to ld over 2f out: hdd 1 1/2f out: sn drvn and kpt on: no ch w wnr* **9/4**[1]
5-54 3 3 ¼ **Dubara Reef (IRE)**[5] 1207 6-8-7 46 (p) JoeFanning 9 49
(Paul Green) *chsd ldr: hdwy to ld wl over 3f out: rdn and hdd over 2f out: sn drvn and sltly outpcd: styd on u.p to take 3rd nr line* **6/1**[3]
6222 4 nk **Day Of Destiny (IRE)**[13] 1084 8-9-12 65 GrahamLee 6 68
(James Given) *trckd ldng pair: hdwy over 3f out and sn cl up: chal 2f out: sn rdn and ev ch tl wknd appr fnl f: lost 3rd nr fin* **7/2**[2]
0-60 5 14 **Dane Cottage**[60] 458 6-8-9 48 PaulMulrennan 8 34
(Richard Ford) *hld up in rr: hdwy 4f out: sn rdn along and plugged on: nvr nr ldrs* **40/1**
0106 6 4 ½ **Turjuman (USA)**[13] 1080 8-8-7 51 NatashaEaton(5) 7 32
(Simon West) *hld up in rr: sme hdwy over 4f out: rdn along 3f out: n.d* **22/1**
231/ 7 2 ½ **Brasingaman Eric**[523] 7107 6-9-7 60 PJMcDonald 1 38
(George Moore) *in tch: hdwy to chse ldrs 4f out: rdn along 3f out: sn btn* **14/1**
505- 8 9 **Altnaharra**[168] 7102 4-8-3 46 (b) JamesSullivan 11 13
(Jim Goldie) *led: rdn along 4f out: sn hdd & wknd* **22/1**
6503 9 12 **Pirate Chest (IRE)**[42] 704 5-8-10 49 (bt) DuranFentiman 2
(Patrick Holmes) *trckd ldrs: pushed along over 4f out: sn rdn and wknd over 3f out* **22/1**
3m 43.02s (11.62) **Going Correction** +0.75s/f (Yiel)
WFA 4 from 5yo+ 4lb **9** Ran SP% **111.6**
Speed ratings (Par 101): **100,98,97,96,89 87,86,81,75**
toteswingers 1&2 £2.60, 1&3 £3.70, 2&3 £3.30 CSF £10.71 TOTE £3.80: £1.60, £1.30, £1.80; EX 13.80 Trifecta £70.20 Pool: £2211.80 - 23.61 winning units.
Owner Andrew Turton & David Barker **Bred** Mesnil Investments Ltd And Deerpark Stud **Trained** Settrington, N Yorks
FOCUS
Probably best to take a positive view of the leading pair, who pulled nicely clear of the rest. The winner is rated back to something like his previous best with the third and fourth a little below theirs.

1280 RACING UK ON SKY 432 (S) STKS 6f
3:30 (3:31) (Class 6) 3-Y-0+ £1,259 (£1,259; £288; £144) Stalls High

Form RPR
100- 1 **Tajneed (IRE)**[191] 6465 10-9-5 80 AdrianNicholls 5 72
(David Nicholls) *cl up: led 2f out: sn rdn: drvn and hdd ins fnl f: sn edgd lft: kpt on gamely to join ldr on line* **7/4**[1]
40-4 1 dht **Go Go Green (IRE)**[2] 1248 7-9-5 67 DanielTudhope 6 72
(Jim Goldie) *chsd ldrs: hdwy 2f out: rdn to chal over 1f out: slt ld ins fnl f: sn drvn and jnd on line* **2/1**[2]
366- 3 3 **Beckermet (IRE)**[153] 7453 11-9-5 79 JamesSullivan 7 62
(Ruth Carr) *led: rdn along and hdd 2f out: drvn ent fnl f: one pce* **11/4**[3]
340- 4 4 ½ **Bridge Valley**[93] 8287 6-9-5 48 JoeFanning 8 48
(Jason Ward) *chsd ldrs: rdn along over 2f out: sn drvn and one pce* **50/1**
0000 5 3 ¾ **Dickie Le Davoir**[11] 1102 9-9-11 71 (b) RobbieFitzpatrick 4 42
(Richard Guest) *sn outpcd and a in rr* **20/1**

The Form Book Flat, Raceform Ltd, Compton, RG20 6NL.

560- **6** *shd* **Charles Parnell (IRE)**[146] 7604 10-9-5 46.................. MichaelStainton 3 36
(Simon Griffiths) *dwlt: sn chsng ldrs: rdn along over 2f out: sn wknd* **100/1**

050- **7** *4* **Feel The Heat**[154] 7446 6-9-5 60.......................................(p) TomEaves 2 23
(Bryan Smart) *cl up: rdn along over 2f out: sn wknd* **14/1**

1m 15.5s (3.70) **Going Correction** +0.75s/f (Yiel) **7** Ran SP% **110.7**
Speed ratings (Par 101): **105,105,101,95,90 89,84**
WIN: Go Go Green £1.60, Tajneed £0.90 PL: GGG £1.90, TJN £1.20 EX: GGG/TJN £3.60 TJN/GGG £3.00 CSF: GGG/TJN £2.73, TJN/GGG £2.57 toteswingers: TRIFECTA 6-7-2 £7.70 7-6-2 £5.30 Pool: £3068.89 - 147.78 winning units.There was no bid for either winner.

Owner Jim Goldie Racing Club **Bred** Edmond And Richard Kent **Trained** Uplawmoor, E Renfrews

Owner Mrs Alex Nicholls **Bred** R Hodgins **Trained** Sessay, N Yorks

FOCUS
Fair efforts from the principals in this seller but not a race to be too positive about.

1281 WATCH RACING UK ON SKY 432 H'CAP (STRAIGHT-MILE CHAMPIONSHIP QUALIFIER) 1m
4:00 (4:00) (Class 4) (0-85,84) 4-Y-0+ **£6,469** (£1,925; £962; £481) **Stalls** Low

Form RPR

05-2 **1** **Fieldgunner Kirkup (GER)**[10] 1113 5-9-5 **82**............ GrahamGibbons 3 89
(David Barron) *trckd ldng pair: smooth hdwy 3f out: cl up 2f out: led jst over 1f out: shkn up ins fnl f: readily* **11/4**[1]

/0-0 **2** *1* **Gloriam (USA)**[10] 1115 4-9-3 **80**...................................... JamesSullivan 4 85
(Ruth Carr) *hld up in tch: hdwy 3f out: trckd ldrs 2f out: squeezed through to chal ent fnl f: sn rdn and edgd lft: ev ch tl nt qckn last 75yds* **50/1**

00/- **3** *2* **Destiny Blue (IRE)**[239] 6302 6-9-1 **78**.................................. DaleSwift 7 78+
(Brian Ellison) *dwlt and hld up in rr: hdwy 3f out: swtchd to outer and rdn over 1f out: styd on wl fnl f: nrst fin* **8/1**

100- **4** *2 1/4* **Solar Spirit (IRE)**[153] 7452 8-9-4 **81**................................... GrahamLee 6 76
(Tracy Waggott) *trckd ldrs: hdwy 3f out: rdn wl over 1f out: sn one pce* **33/1**

330- **5** *nk* **Gala Casino Star (IRE)**[146] 7601 8-9-0 **84**............... JordanNason(7) 10 79
(Geoffrey Harker) *trckd ldr: hdwy to ld over 3f out: rdn along and jnd 2f out: hdd jst over 1f out: hld and one pce on inner whn n.m.r ins fnl f:* **25/1**

0/4- **6** *1 1/2* **Bling King**[305] 4-9-2 **79**.. PaddyAspell 9 70
(Geoffrey Harker) *in tch: rdn along 3f out: grad wknd* **16/1**

3114 **7** *nk* **Classic Colori (IRE)**[10] 1113 6-8-12 **82**.....................(b) DavidBergin(7) 1 72
(David O'Meara) *hld up towards rr: sme hdwy on inner 4f out: rdn along 3f out: sn btn* **4/1**[2]

/13- **8** *3 1/4* **Dos Amigos (IRE)**[291] 3063 4-9-3 **80**............................ PaulMulrennan 2 63
(Michael Dods) *trckd ldrs on inner: effrt 3f out: rdn along over 2f out: sn wknd* **11/4**[1]

30-0 **9** *4* **Lady Macduff (IRE)**[12] 1092 4-9-5 **82**................................ JoeFanning 8 56
(Mark Johnston) *led: rdn along 4f out: hdd jst over 3f out: sn wknd* **13/2**[3]

1m 45.44s (8.84) **Going Correction** +0.75s/f (Yiel) **9** Ran SP% **112.4**
Speed ratings (Par 105): **104,103,101,98,98 96,96,93,89**
toteswingers 1&2 £14.80, 1&3 £7.30, 2&3 £41.70 CSF £151.97 CT £975.08 TOTE £4.00: £1.10, £9.20, £2.80; EX 88.80 Trifecta £1300.40 Pool: £1775.18 - 1.02 winning units.

Owner Kevin Kirkup **Bred** I And D Meinke **Trained** Maunby, N Yorks

FOCUS
Unusual for a 1m handicap here in that in was run on the round course. The gallop was no more than a fair one and the form is rated cautiously.

1282 WIN A VIP DAY OUT @ REDCARRACING.CO.UK MAIDEN STKS 1m 1f
4:30 (4:31) (Class 5) 3-Y-0+ **£2,587** (£770; £384; £192) **Stalls** Low

Form RPR

435- **1** **Wyldfire (IRE)**[188] 6558 3-8-9 71 ow1.............................[1] LeeTopliss(3) 5 74
(Richard Fahey) *t.k.h early: trckd ldrs: green and pushed along bnd after 3f: sltly outpcd 4f out: hdwy on wd outside over 2f out: rdn wl over 1f out: styd on strly fnl f to ld nr fin* **7/2**[2]

300- **2** *nk* **Regal Swain (IRE)**[204] 6073 5-10-0 69........................ RobertWinston 11 76
(Alan Swinbank) *chsd ldng pair: hdwy over 3f out: sn cl up: rdn to ld over 1f out: drvn and wandered ent fnl f: hdd and no ex towards fin* **4/1**[3]

306- **3** *2 1/2* **Big Johnny D (IRE)**[166] 7174 4-10-0 79........................ GrahamGibbons 4 71
(David Barron) *led: pushed along 3f out: rdn and hdd over 1f out: drvn and one pce fnl f* **9/4**[1]

30/5 **4** *3/4* **Arc Light (IRE)**[19] 990 5-9-9 70.................................... DarylByrne(5) 12 69
(Tim Easterby) *midfield: hdwy 4f out: rdn to chse ldrs wl over 2f out: drvn and one pce fr over 1f out* **40/1**

34- **5** *2 1/2* **Morocco**[319] 2196 4-10-0 0.. DanielTudhope 3 63+
(David O'Meara) *t.k.h: trckd ldrs on inner: pushed along wl over 2f out: rdn and no imp fr over 1f out* **9/2**

3- **6** *1 1/2* **Swinging Sultan**[352] 1385 6-10-0 0.................................. TomEaves 14 60+
(Keith Reveley) *hld up in rr: stdy hdwy 3f out: chsd ldrs 2f out: sn rdn and no imp appr fnl f* **20/1**

23 **7** *1 3/4* **Quintain (IRE)**[42] 708 5-9-7 0............................... RachelRichardson(7) 6 56
(Tim Easterby) *cl up: rdn along 3f out: grad wknd fr wl over 1f out* **33/1**

002- **8** *5* **Mishhar (IRE)**[305] 2626 4-9-2 67............................. DavidSimmonson(7) 2 40
(Tony Coyle) *chsd ldng pair: rdn along over 2f out: sn drvn and wknd wl over 1f out* **12/1**

5- **9** *5* **Baile Atha Cliath (IRE)**[118] 7981 4-9-7 0.................. LukeLeadbitter(7) 8 34
(Declan Carroll) *a towards rr* **50/1**

10 *3 3/4* **Rolen Sly**[129] 4-10-0 0... MickyFenton 1 26
(Brian Rothwell) *a in rr* **150/1**

11 *7* **Iktiview**[22] 5-10-0 0... MichaelO'Connell 10
(Philip Kirby) *a towards rr* **50/1**

0 **12** *1/2* **Dorlesh Way (IRE)**[42] 708 6-10-0 0.............................. PaddyAspell 15
(Patrick Holmes) *a in rr* **150/1**

60- **13** *2 1/2* **Let Me In (IRE)**[157] 7363 3-8-8 0................................. DeclanCannon(3) 9
(Nigel Tinkler) *midfield: rdn along 3f out: outpcd fr over 2f out* **66/1**

06- **14** *19* **Online**[175] 6919 3-8-11 0... RoystonFfrench 7
(Tracy Waggott) *a in rr* **100/1**

2m 0.44s (7.44) **Going Correction** +0.75s/f (Yiel)
WFA 3 from 4yo+ 17lb **14** Ran SP% **116.7**
Speed ratings (Par 103): **96,95,93,92,90 89,87,83,78,75 69,68,66,49**
toteswingers 1&2 £4.40, 1&3 £3.60, 2&3 £2.70 CSF £16.36 TOTE £4.70: £1.80, £1.80, £1.30; EX 20.80 Trifecta £75.10 Pool: £988.22 - 9.85 winning units.

Owner Mrs H Steel **Bred** Helen Smith & Sally Mullen **Trained** Musley Bank, N Yorks

FOCUS
Fair form from the leading pair in what was just an ordinary maiden overall, though a few of those in behind appeal as the types to do better in the longer term. The form is not entirely convincing with the runner-up the best guide.

1283 FOLLOW REDCARRACING ON FACEBOOK AND TWITTER H'CAP 5f
5:00 (5:01) (Class 5) (0-70,70) 4-Y-0+ **£2,587** (£770; £384; £192) **Stalls** High

Form RPR

0-04 **1** **Captain Scooby**[18] 998 7-9-6 69.. AmyRyan 4 78
(Richard Guest) *in tch: hdwy 2f out: rdn to chse ldr ent fnl f: sn drvn and styd on wl to ld nr fin* **15/2**

600- **2** *nk* **Boucher Garcon (IRE)**[215] 5739 5-8-8 60........................ NeilFarley(3) 5 68
(Declan Carroll) *cl up: led over 2f out: rdn clr over 1f out: drvn ins fnl f: hdd and no ex nr fin* **10/1**

130- **3** *1/2* **Mission Impossible**[168] 7100 8-9-3 66........................ RoystonFfrench 7 72
(Tracy Waggott) *wnt rt s: t.k.h and hld up towards rr: hdwy 2f out: rdn over 1f out: styd on ins fnl f: nrst fin* **25/1**

354- **4** *1 1/2* **Hello Stranger (IRE)**[128] 7863 4-9-5 68......................... DuranFentiman 1 69
(Tim Easterby) *chsd ldrs on wd outside: effrt 2f out: sn rdn and kpt on same pce fnl f* **9/2**[3]

1102 **5** *1 1/2* **M J Woodward**[27] 885 4-9-2 70.................................... PhilipPrince(5) 6 65
(Paul Green) *chsd ldrs: rdn along wl over 1f out: sn one pce* **7/1**

-060 **6** *2* **Ambitious Icarus**[5] 1205 4-9-5 68.........................(e) RobbieFitzpatrick 8 56
(Richard Guest) *hmpd s and in rr tl sme late hdwy* **11/1**

324- **7** *1 1/2* **Tuibama (IRE)**[186] 6605 4-8-12 61................................(p) GrahamLee 11 44
(Tracy Waggott) *led: rdn along 1/2-way: sn hdd and grad wknd* **16/1**

352- **8** *1 1/4* **Irish Girls Spirit (IRE)**[209] 5923 4-8-10 59..................... MickyFenton 10 37
(Paul Midgley) *chsd ldrs: rdn along over 2f out: sn wknd* **20/1**

550- **9** *1* **Baltic Bomber (IRE)**[156] 7395 4-8-13 62................. MichaelO'Connell 2 37
(John Quinn) *sn rdn along and a in rr* **4/1**[2]

3-31 **10** *5* **Angelo Poliziano**[11] 1101 7-9-6 69.................................... JoeFanning 9 26
(Jo Hughes) *hld up towards rr: rdn along 1/2-way: nvr a factor* **7/2**[1]

1m 2.56s (3.96) **Going Correction** +0.75s/f (Yiel) **10** Ran SP% **116.6**
Speed ratings (Par 103): **98,97,96,94,91 88,86,84,82,74**
toteswingers 1&2 £15.20, 1&3 £18.40, 2&3 £33.00 CSF £79.90 CT £1780.01 TOTE £12.80: £3.60, £4.60, £7.00; EX 99.50 Trifecta £1325.60 Part won. Pool: £1767.48 - 0.71 winning units.

Owner Resdev **Bred** Hellwood Stud Farm & Paul Davies (h'Gate) **Trained** Wetherby, W Yorks

FOCUS
Just a modest sprint and ordinary form rated around the third.

1284 REDCAR RACECOURSE GRAND NATIONAL TRIAL H'CAP 5f
5:30 (5:30) (Class 6) (0-65,64) 3-Y-0 **£1,940** (£577; £288; £144) **Stalls** High

Form RPR

033- **1** **Edith Anne**[252] 4395 3-8-13 **56**... MickyFenton 1 63
(Paul Midgley) *chsd ldrs: hdwy 1/2-way: rdn to ld over 1f out: kpt on* **9/1**

05-6 **2** *2* **Megaleka**[19] 985 3-8-10 **53**... PaulMulrennan 6 53
(Chris Fairhurst) *chsd ldrs: hdwy 2f out: rdn over 1f out: kpt on u.p fnl f* **12/1**

236- **3** *2 1/4* **Teetotal (IRE)**[171] 7031 3-9-7 **64**.. GrahamLee 4 56
(Nigel Tinkler) *dwlt and towards rr: hdwy 1/2-way: rdn wl over 1f out: kpt on fnl f* **7/2**[2]

46-6 **4** *hd* **Charlemagne Diva**[25] 910 3-8-5 **53**...........................(e) PhilipPrince(5) 2 44
(Richard Guest) *cl up: led after 2f: rdn along 2f out: hdd over 1f out: wknd fnl f* **16/1**

0212 **5** *12* **Baltic Prince (IRE)**[10] 1118 3-8-11 **54**............................... JoeFanning 8 2
(Paul Green) *in tch: rdn along 1/2-way: sn hung lft: outpcd and bhd fr wl over 1f out* **6/4**[1]

231- **6** *1 1/2* **Twilight Pearl**[166] 7176 3-9-7 **64**.................................(b) DuranFentiman 3 7
(Tim Easterby) *cl up: rdn along 2f out: sn wknd* **9/2**[3]

640- **7** *6* **Throwing Roses**[194] 6354 3-8-13 **56**..............................[1] FrederikTylicki 7
(Lawrence Mullaney) *slt ld: rdn along and hdd after 2f: sn wknd and bhd* **9/1**

1m 2.28s (3.68) **Going Correction** +0.75s/f (Yiel) **7** Ran SP% **114.0**
Speed ratings (Par 96): **100,96,93,92,73 71,61**
toteswingers 1&2 £13.70, 1&3 £4.60, 2&3 £7.50 CSF £103.75 TOTE £7.10: £2.80, £3.80; EX 73.30 Trifecta £276.10 Pool: £1258.48 - 3.41 winning units.

Owner David Mann **Bred** M Kerr-Dineen **Trained** Westow, N Yorks

FOCUS
A low-grade sprint rated through the runner-up.
T/Plt: £58.70 to a £1 stake. Pool: £46,347.59 - 575.60 winning tickets T/Qpdt: £35.50 to a £1 stake. Pool: £2,155.78 - 44.84 winning tickets JR

WARWICK (L-H)
Monday, April 1

OFFICIAL GOING: Good to soft (5.0)
Wind: Fresh; across Weather: Overcast

1285 TURFTV (S) STKS 5f
2:20 (2:20) (Class 6) 2-Y-0 **£1,940** (£577; £288; £144) **Stalls** Low

Form RPR

63 **1** **Intense Feeling (IRE)**[2] 1247 2-8-6 0............................. CathyGannon 1 60
(David Evans) *mde virtually all: rdn and edgd rt over 1f out: r.o: comf* **8/13**[1]

2 *2* **Gin Time (IRE)** 2-8-6 0.. LukeMorris 3 53+
(David Evans) *a.p: pushed along 1/2-way: rdn to chse wnr fnl f: styd on same pce* **7/1**[3]

3 *2* **Sherry For Nanny (IRE)** 2-8-6 0...................................... AndreaAtzeni 5 46+
(David Evans) *s.i.s: outpcd: styd on to go 3rd wl ins fnl f: nvr nrr* **14/1**

4 **4** *3 1/4* **Sunshine Superman**[5] 1208 2-8-4 0................................ JakePayne(7) 4 39
(Bill Turner) *w wnr: rdn and ev ch over 1f out: wknd ins fnl f* **7/2**[2]

5 *20* **Riley's Missile (IRE)** 2-8-11 0.. FrannyNorton 2
(Charles Smith) *s.s: outpcd* **14/1**

1m 5.61s (6.01) **Going Correction** +1.00s/f (Soft) **5** Ran SP% **110.0**
Speed ratings (Par 90): **91,87,84,79,47**
CSF £5.56 TOTE £1.50: £1.02, £5.20; EX 4.20 Trifecta £24.60 Pool: £487.12 - 14.82 winning units..There was no bid for the winner

Owner Mrs E Evans **Bred** R And Mrs R Hodgins **Trained** Pandy, Monmouths

FOCUS
The going was changed to Good to Soft before racing and there was a fresh breeze in the faces of the runners up the straight. The two previous winners of this juvenile seller had both scored previously. There were no previous winners in the field this time but a couple had experience and one of those got off the mark as the market expected.

1286 TURFTV H'CAP 6f
2:50 (2:50) (Class 5) (0-75,75) 4-Y-0+ £2,587 (£770; £384; £192) Stalls Low

Form RPR
460- 1 **Royal Reyah**[228] 5269 4-9-2 70 FergusSweeney 4 80
(Stuart Kittow) *chsd ldrs: rdn to ld ins fnl f: r.o: eased nr fin* 9/2[1]
040- 2 2 3/4 **Divine Call**[100] 8232 6-9-4 72 RichardKingscote 8 73
(Milton Bradley) *chsd ldrs: led 2f out: rdn: hdd and unable qck ins fnl f* 5/1[2]
601- 3 1 3/4 **Kellys Eye (IRE)**[186] 6605 6-9-5 73 (p) LiamKeniry 5 69
(Zoe Davison) *hld up: hdwy u.p over 1f out: r.o: nt rch ldrs* 20/1
136- 4 1/2 **Dutch Heritage**[184] 6665 4-9-6 74 TonyHamilton 2 68
(Richard Fahey) *s.s: hdwy over 4f out: rdn over 1f out: styd on same pce ins fnl f* 9/2[1]
0023 5 2 **One Way Or Another (AUS)**[11] 1101 10-8-13 67 (t) CathyGannon 6 55
(David Evans) *hld up: styd on ins fnl f: nvr nrr* 14/1
0222 6 1 1/4 **Haadeeth**[11] 1102 6-9-0 68 (t) AndreaAtzeni 3 52
(David Evans) *chsd ldr: ev ch 2f out: sn rdn: wknd ins fnl f* 5/1[2]
220- 7 1/2 **Mick Slates (IRE)**[180] 6789 4-8-13 72 JasonHart(5) 7 54
(Declan Carroll) *hld up: rdn over 1f out: n.d* 6/1[3]
0206 8 6 **Courageous (IRE)**[14] 1058 7-9-0 68 (t) DaneO'Neill 1 31
(Milton Bradley) *led 4f: sn rdn: wknd fnl f* 12/1
0-00 9 1 1/4 **Quasi Congaree (GER)**[33] 812 7-9-0 68 (t) LukeMorris 10 27
(Paul Fitzsimons) *hld up: rdn over 1f out: a in rr* 20/1
200- 10 12 **Rigolleto (IRE)**[154] 7437 5-9-7 75 GeorgeBaker 9
(Anabel K Murphy) *chsd ldrs: rdn over 2f out: sn wknd* 14/1
1m 17.29s (5.49) **Going Correction** +1.00s/f (Soft) 10 Ran SP% 114.5
Speed ratings (Par 103): **103,99,97,96,93 92,91,83,81,65**
toteswingers 1&2 £4.10, 2&3 £0.00, 1&3 £12.70 CSF £26.29 TOTE £6.60: £2.30, £3.10, £3.60; EX 39.90 Trifecta £423.40 Part won. Pool: £564.63 - 0.87 winning units..
Owner B Hopkins, M Harris & R Perry **Bred** Hopkins, Kittow & Mrs Perry **Trained** Blackborough, Devon

FOCUS
A modest but competitive sprint handicap rated through the runner-up.

1287 FOLLOW US ON TWITTER @WARWICKRACES CONDITIONS STKS 6f
3:20 (3:20) (Class 3) 4-Y-0+ £7,762 (£2,310; £1,154; £577) Stalls Low

Form RPR
610- 1 **Prodigality**[157] 7366 5-8-8 95 LukeMorris 4 104
(Ronald Harris) *hld up: hdwy over 2f out: jnd ldr over 1f out: sn rdn: r.o to ld wl ins fnl f* 6/4[1]
-055 2 1 1/4 **Justineo**[32] 834 4-8-8 99 AndreaAtzeni 5 100
(Roger Varian) *chsd ldr: led over 1f out: rdn and hdd wl ins fnl f* 7/4[2]
1111 3 1 **Aubrietia**[20] 966 4-8-3 95 (b) AndrewMullen 2 92
(Alan McCabe) *led: rdn and hdd over 1f out: styd on* 4/1[3]
1231 4 5 **Jack My Boy (IRE)**[37] 775 6-8-8 82 (b) CathyGannon 6 81
(David Evans) *chsd ldrs: rdn over 2f out: wknd fnl f* 16/1
014- 5 3 1/4 **Barons Spy (IRE)**[168] 7107 12-8-8 89 FrannyNorton 3 70
(Richard Price) *prom: lost pl 4f out: sn bhd* 40/1
103- 6 5 **Heartsong (IRE)**[224] 5422 4-8-3 85 MartinLane 1 49
(John Gallagher) *prom: rdn over 2f out: wknd wl over 1f out* 25/1
1m 17.31s (5.51) **Going Correction** +1.00s/f (Soft) 6 Ran SP% 108.5
Speed ratings (Par 107): **103,101,100,93,89 82**
toteswingers 1&2 £1.40, 2&3 £1.10, 1&3 £1.10 CSF £4.05 TOTE £2.40: £1.10, £1.20; EX 5.50 Trifecta £11.50 Pool: £657.25 - 42.81 winning units..
Owner Paul Moulton **Bred** Darley **Trained** Earlswood, Monmouths

FOCUS
A decent conditions stakes run fractionally slower than the preceding handicap. The market was only interested in three and they had it between them in the straight. A step up from the winner with the second to the balance of his form.

1288 REWARDS4RACING.COM MAIDEN STKS 7f 26y
3:50 (3:52) (Class 5) 3-Y-0 £2,587 (£770; £384; £192) Stalls Low

Form RPR
34-2 1 **Mysterial**[7] 1174 3-9-5 80 (b[1]) SeanLevey 2 82
(Richard Hannon) *mde all: rdn and hung lft over 1f out: edgd rt ins fnl f: styd on* 15/8[2]
245- 2 2 **Right Touch**[204] 6071 3-9-5 74 TonyHamilton 5 77
(Richard Fahey) *chsd wnr: rdn and ev ch over 1f out: styd on same pce wl ins fnl f* 2/1[3]
03- 3 1 1/4 **Guilded Spirit**[152] 7492 3-9-5 0 FergusSweeney 3 75+
(Stuart Kittow) *trckd ldrs: rdn over 1f out: styd on same pce fnl f: eased whn hld nr fin* 7/4[1]
4 20 **Abanoas (USA)** 3-9-0 0 RussKennemore 4 17
(Alan Coogan) *s.s: sme hdwy over 3f out: rdn and wknd over 2f out* 50/1
5 25 **Castell Avon** 3-9-0 0 RichardKingscote 1
(Milton Bradley) *s.s: a in rr: wknd over 2f out: t.o* 33/1
1m 30.36s (5.76) **Going Correction** +1.00s/f (Soft) 5 Ran SP% 109.4
Speed ratings (Par 98): **107,104,103,80,51**
CSF £5.94 TOTE £2.10: £1.10, £1.50; EX 3.20 Trifecta £7.00 Pool: £656.43 - 70.08 winning units..
Owner Highclere Thoroughbred Racing - Sloan **Bred** Ladyswood, Canning Down & D Farrington **Trained** East Everleigh, Wilts

FOCUS
A fair if rather uncompetitive maiden, with only three considered in the market once again. The form makes sense with the runner-up setting the standard.

1289 RACINGUK.COM H'CAP 1m 22y
4:20 (4:21) (Class 6) (0-60,60) 3-Y-0 £1,940 (£577; £288; £144) Stalls High

Form RPR
000- 1 **Astrum**[171] 7026 3-9-1 54 AndreaAtzeni 1 58
(Rod Millman) *trckd ldrs: racd keenly: rdn and n.m.r over 1f out: led and edgd lft ins fnl f: r.o* 9/2[3]
262- 2 3/4 **Alpine Mysteries (IRE)**[194] 6363 3-9-6 59 DaneO'Neill 6 61
(Harry Dunlop) *a.p: chsd ldr over 4f out: rdn to ld over 1f out: sn hung lft: hdd ins fnl f: styd on* 10/3[2]
3504 3 3/4 **Eyeline**[20] 977 3-8-4 48 (v) JackDuern(5) 4 48
(Reg Hollinshead) *led: rdn and hdd over 1f out: edgd rt: kpt on* 8/1
5-54 4 1 **Give Me High Five**[31] 845 3-9-7 60 KieranO'Neill 3 58
(Richard Hannon) *chsd ldr over 3f: remained handy: rdn over 1f out: no ex ins fnl f* 7/4[1]
030- 5 2 **Tilly T (IRE)**[133] 7786 3-8-11 50 LiamKeniry 7 43
(J S Moore) *hld up: hdwy over 1f out: no ex ins fnl f* 12/1
2450 6 3 1/2 **Icanboogie**[11] 1098 3-8-7 46 oh1 LukeMorris 5 31
(Karen George) *hld up: hdwy over 3f out: rdn over 1f out: wknd fnl f* 12/1
650- 7 17 **Cool And Clear (IRE)**[146] 7606 3-9-2 55 CathyGannon 2
(Pat Eddery) *s.i.s: hld up: wknd 3f out* 14/1
1m 49.84s (8.84) **Going Correction** +1.00s/f (Soft) 7 Ran SP% 110.8
Speed ratings (Par 96): **95,94,93,92,90 87,70**
toteswingers 1&2 £3.50, 2&3 £1.90, 1&3 £17.00 CSF £18.55 TOTE £3.50: £3.20, £1.80; EX 31.70 Trifecta £194.70 Pool: £500.34 - 1.92 winning units..
Owner The Links Partnership **Bred** Jeremy Green And Sons **Trained** Kentisbeare, Devon

FOCUS
A moderate 3-y-o handicap that went to a market springer and the first four held those positions virtually throughout. The second is rated to her AW form in a muddling race.

1290 RACING UK H'CAP 1m 2f 188y
4:50 (4:50) (Class 4) (0-85,83) 4-Y-0+ £5,175 (£1,540; £769; £384) Stalls Low

Form RPR
05-0 1 **Take Two**[63] 415 4-8-10 72 AndreaAtzeni 3 81
(Alex Hales) *chsd ldr: shkn up to ld ins fnl f: r.o* 20/1
-126 2 1 1/4 **Cool Sky**[16] 1037 4-9-4 80 JimCrowley 2 87
(William Knight) *sn led at stdy pce: qcknd 3f out: rdn over 1f out: hdd ins fnl f: styd on same pce* 5/1[3]
-331 3 2 1/4 **Luggers Hall (IRE)**[2] 1239 5-8-1 70 JoeyHaynes(7) 4 73+
(Tony Carroll) *hld up: hdwy and nt clr run over 1f out: r.o ins fnl f: nt rch ldrs* 11/8[1]
111- 4 1 3/4 **Duke Of Clarence (IRE)**[168] 7116 4-9-7 83 SeanLevey 1 83
(Richard Hannon) *chsd ldrs: pushed along over 2f out: styd on same pce fnl f* 5/2[2]
110- 5 3 **Dancing Primo**[184] 6667 7-9-2 83 JackDuern(5) 6 78
(Mark Brisbourne) *prom: rdn over 2f out: wknd ins fnl f* 16/1
300- 6 2 1/4 **Border Revia (IRE)**[261] 4082 4-8-13 75 TonyHamilton 7 66
(Richard Fahey) *chsd ldrs: rdn over 2f out: wknd over 1f out* 16/1
30-6 7 2 1/2 **Masters Blazing**[17] 668 4-8-9 71 (p) SamHitchcott 5 58
(John Ryan) *hld up: rdn over 2f out: wknd fnl f* 11/1
2m 33.07s (11.97) **Going Correction** +1.00s/f (Soft) 7 Ran SP% 112.2
Speed ratings (Par 105): **96,95,93,92,90 88,86**
toteswingers 1&2 £2.90, 2&3 £5.10, 1&3 £8.30 CSF £110.68 TOTE £21.40: £5.60, £3.60; EX 192.80 Trifecta £437.50 Pool: £657.12 - 1.12 winning units..
Owner S P Bloodstock **Bred** Steven & Petra Wallace **Trained** Edgcote, Northants

FOCUS
They went a moderate gallop in this middle-distance handicap and the first two held those positions throughout. The form is rated at face value for now.
T/Plt: £181.90 to a £1 stake. Pool of £38,311.44 - 153.73 winning tickets. T/Qpdt: £68.60 to a £1 stake. Pool of £1,487.38 - 16.04 winning tickets. CR

YARMOUTH (L-H)
Monday, April 1

OFFICIAL GOING: Good (good to soft in places; 7.0)
Wind: Fresh; across Weather: Dry; cold

1291 GRAND NATIONAL 6 PLACES WITH BETVICTOR MAIDEN STKS 1m 3y
2:05 (2:05) (Class 5) 3-Y-0+ £2,587 (£770; £384; £192) Stalls Centre

Form RPR
1 **Autspread** 3-8-12 0 NeilCallan 4 83+
(Marco Botti) *hld up in tch in midfield: effrt and rdn to ld over 1f out: sn qcknd clr and in n.d fnl f: comf* 16/1
2 4 **Unex Modigliani (IRE)** 4-9-13 0 HayleyTurner 3 76
(Michael Bell) *stdd s: hld up in tch in midfield: rdn along and rn green over 3f out: hdwy over 1f out: wnt 2nd and edgd lft ins fnl f: no threat to wnr but gng on fin* 18/1
3 3 **Naaz (IRE)** 3-8-12 0 RyanMoore 6 65
(Ed Dunlop) *t.k.h: hld up in tch in midfield: rdn and effrt 3f out: drvn and plugged on same pce fr over 1f out* 5/1[2]
3 4 1 1/4 **Munhamer (IRE)**[10] 1114 3-8-12 0 PaulHanagan 5 62
(John Gosden) *chsd ldr: rdn 3f out: led over 2f out tl drvn and hdd over 1f out: sn outpcd and no ch w wnr: lost 2 pls ins fnl f* 10/11[1]
04- 5 3 1/2 **Duke Of Orange (IRE)**[236] 4960 3-8-12 0 MartinHarley 9 54
(Mick Channon) *stdd s: hld up in rr: rdn and effrt over 2f out: drvn and no imp over 1f out: wknd fnl f* 11/2[3]
60 6 9 **Big Kahuna**[31] 841 6-9-6 0 IanBurns(7) 2 37
(Jane Chapple-Hyam) *led tl rdn and hdd over 2f out: drvn and wknd wl over 1f out: fdd fnl f* 66/1
0 7 1 **Madam Fifi**[42] 706 3-8-7 0 JohnFahy 7 26
(Alan McCabe) *chsd ldrs: rdn and hung lft over 3f out: wknd wl over 1f out: fdd over 1f out* 100/1
0 8 5 **Hares Grove (IRE)**[13] 1078 4-9-13 0 WilliamCarson 8 23
(Richard Price) *s.i.s: hld up in last trio: rdn and no hdwy 3f out: wknd 2f out: bhd fnl f* 100/1
36- 9 5 **Yahilwa (USA)**[175] 6936 3-8-8 0 ow1 WilliamBuick 10
(James Tate) *stdd s: plld hrd: hld up in last trio: rdn and short-lived effrt over 2f out: wknd 2f out: bhd fnl f* 8/1
10 13 **Araajmh (USA)** 3-8-7 0 SilvestreDeSousa 1
(James Tate) *in tch in midfield tl 1/2-way: sn struggling and dropped out: t.o fnl f* 16/1
1m 41.65s (1.05) **Going Correction** +0.125s/f (Good)
WFA 3 from 4yo+ 15lb 10 Ran SP% 116.0
Speed ratings (Par 103): **99,95,92,90,87 78,77,72,67,54**
toteswingers 1&2 £15.30, 1&3 £9.80, 2&3 £12.90 CSF £264.28 TOTE £28.40: £4.70, £4.50, £1.70; EX 306.10 Trifecta £978.20 Pool: £2343.53 - 1.79 winning units.
Owner Giuliano Manfredini **Bred** Panda Bloodstock **Trained** Newmarket, Suffolk

FOCUS
Some powerful stables in opposition for this maiden, run at a fair pace with the first three home all making their debuts. The race is rated around some pretty solid averages for the contest.

1292 BETVICTOR ARE 6 PLACES ON THE GRAND NATIONAL H'CAP 1m 3y
2:40 (2:40) (Class 5) (0-75,74) 4-Y-0+ £2,587 (£770; £384; £192) Stalls Centre

Form RPR
332 1 **Azrael**[56] 517 5-9-5 72 (p) RyanMoore 8 81
(Alan McCabe) *mde all: rdn 2f out: edgd rt u.p ins fnl f: kpt on and a holding runner-up: drvn out* 5/2[1]

-126 **2** 3/4 **Tight Lipped (IRE)**[25] 912 4-9-2 **74**................(v) RyanTate(5) 2 81
(James Eustace) *t.k.h: chsd wnr thrght: rdn over 1f out: edgd rt and styd on same pce ins fnl f* **5/1**[2]

5-45 **3** 2 1/4 **Handheld**[80] 161 6-8-5 **65**................ ShelleyBirkett(7) 6 67
(Julia Feilden) *stdd s: hld up in tch in last pair: pushed along and effrt over 1f out: rdn along hands and heels and kpt on same pce ins fnl f: wnt 3rd last strides* **12/1**

2-15 **4** nk **Silver Alliance**[35] 798 5-9-1 **68**................ AdamBeschizza 3 69
(Julia Feilden) *in tch in midfield: effrt u.p 2f out: styd on u.p to chse ldng pair ins fnl f: one pce after and lost 3rd last strides* **11/2**[3]

1020 **5** 3 **Diplomatic (IRE)**[19] 984 8-8-11 **64**................(p) NeilCallan 4 58
(Michael Squance) *in tch in midfield: rdn 1/2-way: drvn and chsd ldng pair wl over 1f out: no imp: wknd ins fnl f* **16/1**

050- **6** 8 **Aquarian Spirit**[177] 6881 6-8-13 **66**................ PaulHanagan 9 42
(Richard Fahey) *chsd ldng pair: rdn and no rspnse 2f out: sn struggling and wknd over 1f out* **5/2**[1]

41/- **7** 8 **Tweedle Dee**[605] 4761 4-8-7 **60**................ ChrisCatlin 7 17
(Noel Quinlan) *stdd s: hld up in tch in rr: rdn and edgd lft wl over 2f out: sn btn: wl bhd fnl f* **12/1**

1m 40.83s (0.23) **Going Correction** +0.125s/f (Good) **7** Ran SP% **110.5**
Speed ratings (Par 103): **103,102,100,99,96 88,80**
toteswingers 1&2 £2.00, 1&3 £6.00, 2&3 £7.20 CSF £14.22 CT £114.61 TOTE £2.70: £1.60, £3.00; EX 10.60 Trifecta £64.70 Pool: £1036.65 - 12.00 winning units.
Owner Mrs M J McCabe **Bred** Ian Neville Marks **Trained** Averham Park, Notts

FOCUS
A moderate handicap run at a steady pace, with the winner making all under a fine ride. The winner was on a good mark and the third is rated to his AW form.

1293 BETVICTOR GRAND NATIONAL 6 PLACES H'CAP 1m 3y
3:10 (3:11) (Class 4) (0-80,79) 3-Y-O **£4,690** (£1,395; £697; £348) **Stalls** Centre

Form RPR

061- **1** **Strong Conviction**[153] 7467 3-8-12 **70**................ MartinHarley 1 78
(Mick Channon) *mde most tl 3f out: styd pressing ldr tl rdn to ld again over 1f out: kpt on wl u.p fnl f: rdn out* **22/1**

034- **2** 2 1/4 **Cash Is King**[217] 5668 3-9-0 **72**................ PaulHanagan 2 75
(Richard Fahey) *t.k.h: chsd ldrs: rdn and effrt jst over 2f out: chsd wnr over 1f out: styd on same pce ins fnl f* **9/2**[2]

000- **3** 1 1/2 **Luck (IRE)**[175] 6920 3-9-5 **77**................ JamieSpencer 5 76
(Stuart Williams) *stdd s: hld up in tch in rr: hdwy 3f out: rdn and chsd ldrs over 1f out: wnt 3rd and styd on same pce ins fnl f* **10/1**

-441 **4** 1 1/4 **Minimee**[25] 918 3-8-8 **71**................(v) RobertTart(5) 11 68
(Phil McEntee) *t.k.h: hld up in tch in midfield: rdn and effrt 2f out: chsd ldng pair jst over 1f out: plugged on same pce ins fnl f* **20/1**

01- **5** 1/2 **Mandy's Boy (IRE)**[178] 6844 3-9-1 **73**................ RyanMoore 6 68
(Ed Dunlop) *hld up in tch: hdwy towards centre over 2f out: drvn and no imp over 1f out: plugged on same pce fnl f* **10/3**[1]

530- **6** 1 1/2 **Avatar Star (IRE)**[117] 7989 3-9-3 **75**................(t) AdamKirby 7 67
(Marco Botti) *hld up in tch: effrt and edgd lft 2f out: no prog: no threat: nudged along and styd on same pce fnl f* **14/1**

62-1 **7** 1 **Mumeyez**[35] 800 3-9-5 **77**................(p) WilliamBuick 12 67
(John Gosden) *t.k.h: pressed wnr tl led 3f out: rdn and hdd over 1f out: racd awkwardly u.p and sn btn: wknd ins fnl f* **9/2**[2]

451- **8** shd **Santo Prince (USA)**[174] 6946 3-9-4 **76**................ HayleyTurner 3 65
(Michael Bell) *t.k.h: hld up in rr: rdn and effrt 2f out: no imp tl plugged on ins fnl f: n.d* **10/1**

464- **9** 12 **Ocean Applause**[101] 8211 3-9-4 **79**................ RyanPowell(3) 9 41
(John Ryan) *in tch towards rr: rdn 1/2-way: lost pl and bhd whn swtchd lft 2f out: sn bhd* **16/1**

11- **10** 2 1/2 **Polar Chief**[164] 7209 3-9-5 **77**................ PatrickMathers 10 33
(Kristin Stubbs) *restless stalls: in tch in midfield: rdn and effrt over 2f out: wknd over 1f out* **6/1**[3]

304- **11** 40 **Tuffan (USA)**[231] 5155 3-8-9 **67**................(t) ChrisCatlin 4
(Clive Brittain) *w ldrs tl 1/2-way: sn lost pl and bhd: wl t.o fnl 2f* **20/1**

1m 41.41s (0.81) **Going Correction** +0.125s/f (Good) **11** Ran SP% **118.3**
Speed ratings (Par 100): **100,97,96,95,94 93,92,91,79,77 37**
toteswingers 1&2 £21.00, 1&3 £41.80, 2&3 £9.80 CSF £116.31 CT £1080.08 TOTE £43.90: £8.20, £2.20, £3.00; EX 161.60 Trifecta £1027.30 Pool: £1881.85 - 1.37 winning units.
Owner Materna, Dunleavy, Barrett **Bred** M Barrett **Trained** West Ilsley, Berks

FOCUS
This was decent enough and the pace was honest, suggesting the form is sound.

1294 6 PLACES GRAND NATIONAL AT BETVICTOR H'CAP 7f 3y
3:40 (3:41) (Class 6) (0-65,61) 4-Y-O+ **£1,940** (£577; £288; £144) **Stalls** Centre

Form RPR

0-56 **1** **Olney Lass**[68] 335 6-9-0 **57**................ SimonPearce(3) 3 69
(Lydia Pearce) *hld up wl off the pce: hdwy 3f out: rdn to chse ldrs 2f out: led ins fnl f: sn clr and r.o wl* **20/1**

-036 **2** 3 1/2 **Zaheeb**[47] 638 5-9-3 **57**................(b) TomQueally 4 60
(Dave Morris) *chsd ldrs: wnt 2nd over 2f out: rdn to ld over 1f out: hdd ins fnl f: sn btn* **13/2**[3]

3-55 **3** 1/2 **Khajaaly (IRE)**[56] 517 6-9-1 **55**................(b) AdamBeschizza 10 56
(Julia Feilden) *in tch in midfield: cajoled along and clsd 2f out: hld hd awkwardly and no imp over 1f out: plugged on ins fnl f* **16/1**

6554 **4** 3/4 **The Noble Ord**[7] 1170 4-9-0 **54**................(t) WilliamBuick 15 53
(Sylvester Kirk) *sn niggled along and wl off the pce in last quartet: hdwy past btn horses over 1f out: r.o wl ins fnl f: nvr trbld ldrs* **11/2**[2]

2432 **5** 1 1/4 **Spin Again (IRE)**[34] 806 8-9-0 **54**................ AdamKirby 12 50
(John Ryan) *racd wl off the pce towards rr: hdwy 3f out: drvn and styd on to chse ldrs over 1f out: styd on same pce ins fnl f* **7/2**[1]

0001 **6** hd **Putin (IRE)**[9] 1151 5-8-13 **58**................(tp) RachealKneller(5) 1 53
(Phil McEntee) *led: rdn and hdd over 1f out: 3rd and btn 1f out: wknd ins fnl f* **14/1**

0-34 **7** 6 **Automotive**[57] 510 5-8-13 **53**................ SilvestreDeSousa 2 32
(Julia Feilden) *v.s.a: wl detached in last: styd on past btn horses fnl f: n.d* **8/1**

5050 **8** hd **Back For Tea (IRE)**[5] 1193 5-8-4 **49** oh2 ow2................(p) RobertTart(5) 14 28
(Phil McEntee) *stdd s: hld up wl off the pce in rr: styd on past btn horses fnl f: n.d* **66/1**

0060 **9** 2 1/2 **Ishiamiracle**[27] 884 4-8-13 **53**................(p) KirstyMilczarek 7 25
(Phil McEntee) *chsd ldr tl over 2f out: sn rdn and hung lft: wknd wl over 1f out* **33/1**

50-3 **10** 2 3/4 **Mudhish (IRE)**[34] 806 8-9-6 **60**................ RyanMoore 11 24
(Clive Brittain) *racd wl off the pce towards rr: rdn and modest hdwy over 2f out: no prog 2f out: sn wknd* **8/1**

000- **11** 1 **One Kool Dude**[166] 7179 4-9-7 **61**................(v) JamieSpencer 13 23
(Michael Bell) *stdd s: t.k.h: hld up wl off the pce in rr: clsd 3f out: rdn and no hdwy 2f out: sn wknd* **14/1**

0050 **12** 10 **Bird Dog**[20] 968 7-8-2 **47** oh2................(p) RyanTate(5) 6
(Phil McEntee) *chsd ldrs: rdn 1/2-way: lost pl 3f out: bhd over 1f out* **80/1**

000- **13** hd **Princely Sum (IRE)**[300] 2788 4-9-1 **55**................(t) NeilCallan 9
(Stuart Williams) *racd wl off the pce in last quintet: rdn and no hdwy 3f out: wl bhd over 1f out* **22/1**

35-0 **14** 4 1/2 **Tatting**[35] 801 4-9-4 **58**................(b) HayleyTurner 5
(Chris Dwyer) *t.k.h: in tch in midfield: struggling whn rdn over 2f out: wknd and wl btn whn eased over 1f out: t.o* **11/2**[2]

1m 28.25s (1.65) **Going Correction** +0.125s/f (Good) **14** Ran SP% **122.5**
Speed ratings (Par 101): **95,91,90,89,88 87,81,80,77,74 73,62,62,56**
toteswingers 1&2 £2.40, 1&3 £1.80, 2&3 £1.80 CSF £142.65 CT £2214.38 TOTE £29.90: £5.90, £2.90, £5.30; EX 137.00 Trifecta £1959.80 Part won. Pool: £2613.14 - 0.66 winning units.
Owner P J Stephenson **Bred** T H Rossiter **Trained** Newmarket, Suffolk
■ Stewards' Enquiry : Kirsty Milczarek one-day ban: failed to keep straight after stalls (15 Apri)

FOCUS
An open yet moderate contest, run at a sound gallop with the front two coming with their efforts out wide. Modest form.

1295 6 PLACES AT AINTREE WITH BETVICTOR H'CAP 6f 3y
4:10 (4:11) (Class 4) (0-85,85) 3-Y-O **£4,690** (£1,395; £697; £348) **Stalls** Centre

Form RPR

416- **1** **Time And Place**[198] 6238 3-8-10 **74**................ PaulHanagan 3 83
(Richard Fahey) *t.k.h: chsd ldrs: rdn and ev ch over 1f out: led ins fnl f: r.o wl: rdn out* **9/4**[2]

041- **2** 1 **Fils Anges (IRE)**[173] 6983 3-9-7 **85**................ JamieSpencer 1 94+
(Michael Bell) *stdd and dropped in bhd after s: swtchd rt and hdwy wl over 1f out: clsng on ldrs but gap against stands' rail clsng whn stdd and swtchd lft ins fnl f: rallied and r.o to go 2nd last strides* **3/1**[3]

51-3 **3** nk **Smart Spender (IRE)**[10] 1112 3-9-2 **80**................ ShaneKelly 6 84
(Jo Hughes) *pressed ldrs tl led wl over 1f out: grad edging rt 1f out: rdn and hdd ins fnl f: no ex and lost 2nd last strides* **2/1**[1]

504- **4** 3 1/4 **Megamunch (IRE)**[190] 6511 3-8-8 **72**................ PatrickMathers 4 66
(Kristin Stubbs) *t.k.h: chsd ldrs tl stdd into last pair after 2f: rdn and effrt towards centre 2f out: no ex 1f out: wknd ins fnl f* **33/1**

245- **5** 1 **Exotic Guest**[154] 7434 3-8-10 **74**................ RyanMoore 7 65
(George Margarson) *led tl hdd and rdn wl over 1f out: wknd ins fnl f* **9/1**

155- **6** 1 1/4 **Ceelo**[191] 6491 3-9-3 **81**................ WilliamBuick 5 68
(Sylvester Kirk) *wl in tch in midfield: rdn and unable qck 2f out: wknd over 1f out* **8/1**

1m 15.62s (1.22) **Going Correction** +0.125s/f (Good) **6** Ran SP% **113.2**
Speed ratings (Par 100): **96,94,94,89,88 86**
toteswingers 1&2 £2.40, 1&3 £1.80, 2&3 £1.80 CSF £9.60 TOTE £2.80: £1.10, £3.90; EX 8.50 Trifecta £14.60 Pool: £1825.05 - 93.29 winning units.
Owner Mel Roberts & Ms Nicola Meese 1 **Bred** Worksop Manor Stud **Trained** Musley Bank, N Yorks

FOCUS
A fair handicap despite the small field size, run at a sound pace. The three in the frame behind the winner help set the level.

1296 FOLLOW US ON TWITTER @BETVICTORRACING MEDIAN AUCTION MAIDEN STKS 1m 2f 21y
4:40 (4:41) (Class 6) 3-5-Y-O **£1,940** (£577; £288; £144) **Stalls** Low

Form RPR

256- **1** **Gabrial The Master (IRE)**[170] 7057 3-8-9 68................ JamieSpencer 3 76
(Richard Fahey) *mde all: rdn and wnt 3 l clr over 3f out: drvn and kpt on 2f out: a holding rivals ins fnl f* **8/1**

32- **2** 1 **Bin Singspiel**[135] 7780 3-8-9 0................ NeilCallan 6 74
(James Tate) *hld up in tch in last trio: hdwy 4f out: sn rdn: pressing for placings but no imp on wnr 2f out: plugged on to go 2nd wl ins fnl f: clsng on wnr but lacked pce to chal* **11/10**[1]

43 **3** 1/2 **Punditry**[14] 1057 3-8-9 0................ WilliamBuick 5 73
(John Gosden) *dwlt: sn rdn along and rcvrd to chse ldrs: rdn over 3f out: chsd wnr but no imp over 1f out: plugged on ins fnl f tl n.m.r and lost 2nd wl ins fnl f* **7/2**[2]

32 **4** 4 **Vastly (USA)**[14] 1057 4-10-0 0................ RyanMoore 1 69
(Julia Feilden) *chsd wnr: rdn over 4f out: kpt on but no imp on wnr: lost 2nd over 1f out: wknd ins fnl f* **9/2**[3]

5 8 **Young Lisa** 4-9-9 0................ TomQueally 2 48
(George Margarson) *in tch in midfield: rdn and struggling 3f out: 5th and wl hld fnl 2f* **28/1**

6 10 **Jack Firefly**[29] 4-10-0 0................[1] AdamKirby 7 33
(Michael Murphy) *s.i.s: rn green in rr: rdn and lost tch over 3f out* **40/1**

64 **7** 1 **London Skolar**[12] 1089 3-8-4 0................ RyanTate(5) 4 27
(James Eustace) *in tch in midfield: lost pl and rdn 4f out: bhd fnl 3f* **40/1**

8 34 **Kaahen (USA)** 3-8-9 0................ PaulHanagan 8
(Ed Dunlop) *s.i.s: in tch in rr tl rdn and lost tch over 3f out: t.o over 1f out* **9/1**

2m 15.8s (5.30) **Going Correction** +0.475s/f (Yiel)
WFA 3 from 4yo 19lb **8** Ran SP% **117.5**
Speed ratings (Par 101): **97,96,95,92,86 78,77,50**
toteswingers 1&2 £3.00, 1&3 £4.50, 2&3 £1.90 CSF £17.67 TOTE £13.30: £2.10, £1.10, £1.20; EX 33.40 Trifecta £83.60 Pool: £3181.78 - 28.52 winning units.
Owner Dr Marwan Koukash **Bred** Paul Giles **Trained** Musley Bank, N Yorks

FOCUS
This was not a bad maiden, run at a fair pace with the winner making all to give his handler a quick double. The form is a bit fluid with the third and fourth the best guides.

1297 BETVICTOR.COM H'CAP 1m 2f 21y
5:10 (5:10) (Class 5) (0-70,67) 4-Y-O+ **£2,587** (£770; £384; £192) **Stalls** Low

Form RPR

0-54 **1** **The Ducking Stool**[16] 1031 6-8-7 **60**................ ShelleyBirkett(7) 10 69
(Julia Feilden) *chsd ldrs: jnd ldr 4f out tl led over 2f out: rdn and drew clr w rival jst over 1f out: hld on wl fnl f* **8/1**

0430 **2** hd **Brown Pete (IRE)**[4] 1220 5-9-7 **67**................ MartinHarley 2 76
(Violet M Jordan) *stdd s: hld up in rr: hdwy towards inner over 2f out: squeezed between horses 2f out: rdn and chal over 1f out: drvn and sustained duel w wnr fnl f: jst hld* **9/2**[3]

600- **3** 5 **Transfer**[163] 7251 8-8-11 **57**................ WilliamCarson 9 56
(Richard Price) *in tch in midfield: rdn and unable qck over 2f out: no ex and btn over 1f out: plugged on to go 3rd ins fnl f* **25/1**

0-00 **4** 3/4 **Smokey Oakey (IRE)**[26] 906 9-9-0 **63**..................(p) SimonPearce(3) 3 60
(Mark H Tompkins) *chsd ldrs: rdn to press wnr ent fnl 2f tl over 1f out: 3rd and btn 1f out: wknd and lost 3rd ins fnl f* **16/1**

1342 **5** 3/4 **Young Jackie**[6] 1183 5-8-0 **53**..................(v) JordanVaughan(7) 5 49
(George Margarson) *in tch in midfield: rdn and effrt jst over 2f out: no ex and btn over 1f out: wl hld and plugged on same pce fnl f* **4/1**[2]

264- **6** 1/2 **Sehnsucht (IRE)**[138] 7712 4-9-7 **67**.................................. ShaneKelly 1 62
(John Quinn) *hld up towards rr: effrt and hld hd high 2f out: hung lft and no hdwy over 1f out: nvr trbld ldrs* **7/2**[1]

0030 **7** 2 1/4 **Bubbly Braveheart (IRE)**[8] 1162 6-8-2 **53** oh8....(p) RachealKneller(5) 7 43
(Phil McEntee) *led tl rdn and hdd over 2f out: sn struggling: wknd over 1f out* **50/1**

-020 **8** 3 3/4 **Norwegian Reward (IRE)**[47] 626 5-8-10 **56**......... SilvestreDeSousa 4 39
(Michael Wigham) *in tch in midfield: rdn and effrt on inner over 2f out: no imp 2f out: sn wknd* **7/1**

3406 **9** 21 **Big City Boy (IRE)**[8] 1161 5-8-3 **55** oh6 ow1................(t) RobertTart(5) 6
(Phil McEntee) *chsd ldrs tl 3f out: lost pl u.p over 2f out: wl bhd fnl f* **40/1**

443 **10** 21 **The Great Gabrial**[11] 1106 4-8-13 **59**.............................. JamieSpencer 8
(Ian Williams) *hld up in rr: lost tch over 3f out: t.o and eased over 1f out* **9/2**[3]

2m 13.11s (2.61) **Going Correction** +0.475s/f (Yiel) **10 Ran SP% 116.3**
Speed ratings (Par 103): **36,35,31,31,30 30,28,25,8,**
toteswingers 1&2 £9.00, 1&3 £27.20, 2&3 £14.20 CSF £43.21 TOTE £6.00: £1.60, £2.30, £8.00; EX 57.20 Trifecta £765.80 Pool: £1921.11 - 1.88 winning units.
Owner Mrs S McGuiness **Bred** Cheveley Park Stud Ltd **Trained** Exning, Suffolk

FOCUS
The pace was steady for this handicap with the front two pulling clear. The winner ran close to last summer's mark with the second near to his best.
T/Plt: £1,101.60 to a £1 stake. Pool of £56,514.94 - 37.45 winning units T/Qpdt: £49.00 to a £1 stake. Pool of £3,661.39 - 55.20 winning units SP

1240 KEMPTON (A.W) (R-H)

Tuesday, April 2

OFFICIAL GOING: Standard
Wind: fresh, across Weather: dry, cold

1298 BETVICTOR AINTREE GRAND NATIONAL NRFB H'CAP 1m 2f (P)
2:00 (2:05) (Class 6) (0-60,60) 4-Y-O+ **£1,940** (£577; £288; £144) **Stalls** Low

Form RPR

1-14 **1** **Chella Thriller (SPA)**[16] 1054 4-9-7 **60**........................(b) GeorgeBaker 9 68
(Alastair Lidderdale) *chsd ldr: rdn to chal over 1f out: drvn and sustained duel w rival fnl f: led cl home* **7/2**[1]

2000 **2** shd **Edgware Road**[12] 1100 5-9-4 **57**.................................. RobertWinston 5 64
(Sean Curran) *led: jnd over 2f out: drvn and kpt on wl fr over 1f out: hdd cl home* **16/1**

0-66 **3** hd **Standing Strong (IRE)**[47] 652 5-9-7 **60**......................(p) LiamKeniry 2 67
(Zoe Davison) *t.k.h: hld up in tch in midfield: swtchd lft and effrt over 1f out: gd hdwy 1f out: chsd ldrs ins fnl f: high hd carriage but styng on wl at fin* **11/1**

000- **4** 1 **Moment In The Sun**[209] 5941 4-9-7 **60**........................ JamieSpencer 4 65
(David Flood) *hld up in tch in midfield: rdn and hdwy over 1f out: drvn and chsd ldrs ins fnl f: styd on same pce fnl 100yds* **4/1**[2]

4542 **5** 1 3/4 **Having A Ball**[20] 978 9-9-7 **60**.................................. ChrisCatlin 7 62
(Geoffrey Deacon) *hld up in last trio: rdn and effrt wl over 1f out: hdwy over 1f out: kpt on same pce ins fnl f* **9/2**[3]

6231 **6** nk **Angelena Ballerina (IRE)**[15] 1070 6-9-0 **53**..............(v) JamesDoyle 11 54
(Sean Curran) *t.k.h: chsd ldrs: rdn and unable qck over 1f out: wknd wl ins fnl f* **6/1**

4005 **7** 1 **Roman Senate (IRE)**[7] 1183 4-8-11 **50**......................(bt) MartinLane 13 49
(Martin Bosley) *t.k.h: chsd ldrs: rdn and unable qck over 1f out: wknd fnl 100yds* **16/1**

000- **8** shd **Bedibyes**[93] 8299 5-8-7 **46** oh1.................................. KirstyMilczarek 1 45
(Richard Mitchell) *s.i.s: hld up in rr: swtchd lft and hdwy over 1f out: kpt on ins fnl f: nvr trbld ldrs* **33/1**

0-04 **9** 1 **Cane Cat (IRE)**[15] 1068 6-8-12 **56**..................(t) GeorgeDowning(5) 3 53
(Tony Carroll) *hld up in last trio: c wd and effrt bnd wl over 1f out: kpt on but no real imp ins fnl f* **16/1**

1242 **10** 1 1/4 **Lytham (IRE)**[13] 1090 12-8-12 **56**.................................. RyanTate(5) 10 50
(Tony Carroll) *t.k.h: hld up in tch in midfield: rdn and no hdwy over 1f out: wknd ent fnl f* **13/2**

4564 **11** 1 1/4 **Conas Ata Tu**[10] 1151 4-9-0 **53**.................................. MartinDwyer 8 45
(Derek Shaw) *chsd ldrs: rdn and no rspnse over 1f out: wknd ent fnl f* **25/1**

00-0 **12** 8 **Saint Irene**[27] 896 4-8-9 **55**.................................. HarryBurns(7) 6 31
(Michael Blanshard) *racd wd: in tch in midfield tl dropped to rr over 2f out: lost tch over 1f out* **14/1**

2m 8.3s (0.30) **Going Correction** +0.125s/f (Slow) **12 Ran SP% 127.5**
Speed ratings (Par 101): **103,102,102,101,100 100,99,99,98,97 96,90**
Tote Swingers: 1&2 £15.20, 1&3 £8.90, 2&3 £33.60 CSF £67.12 CT £589.23 TOTE £3.30: £1.10, £7.20, £5.10; EX 71.80 Trifecta £1416.00 Pool: £3,420.53 - 1.81 winning units..
Owner The Saucy Horse Partnership **Bred** John Patrick Duffy **Trained** Lambourn, Berks

FOCUS
It paid to be handy in this moderate handicap. The winner and third set the standard.

1299 BETVICTOR CASINO ON YOUR MOBILE MAIDEN STKS 5f (P)
2:30 (2:30) (Class 5) 3-Y-O **£2,587** (£770; £384; £192) **Stalls** Low

Form RPR

63- **1** **Bluegrass Blues (IRE)**[172] 7031 3-9-5 0.................................. ChrisCatlin 3 83
(Paul Cole) *chsd ldrs: rdn over 2f out: hdwy to ld 1f out: clr fnl 100yds: r.o strly: readily* **2/1**[2]

3- **2** 2 3/4 **Pearl Bridge**[200] 6203 3-9-5 0..............................(b[1]) JamieSpencer 4 72
(Ralph Beckett) *chsd ldr: jnd ldr over 1f out: rdn to ld ent fnl f: sn hdd and drvn: racd awkwardly u.p and sn outpcd by wnr: kpt on for 2nd* **13/8**[1]

20- **3** nk **Baron Run**[227] 5367 3-9-2 0.................................. MichaelMetcalfe(3) 2 71
(Mrs K Burke) *t.k.h: chsd ldrs: rdn and swtchd lft ent fnl f: no threat to wnr but kpt on to press for 2nd towards fin* **7/2**[3]

62 **4** 1 1/2 **Irish Dream (IRE)**[69] 341 3-9-0 0.................................. SilvestreDeSousa 1 61
(Mark Johnston) *sn led: rdn and jnd over 1f out: sn hdd and unable qck: wknd ins fnl f* **6/1**

5-2 **5** 19 **Spymistress**[6] 1197 3-9-0 0.................................[1] LiamKeniry 5
(Zoe Davison) *s.i.s: in tch in rr tl rdn and outpcd 3f out: wl bhd fnl 2f* **66/1**

1m 0.28s (-0.22) **Going Correction** +0.125s/f (Slow) **5 Ran SP% 109.4**
Speed ratings (Par 98): **106,101,101,98,68**
CSF £5.58 TOTE £3.90: £1.50, £1.40; EX 6.60 Trifecta £12.30 Pool: £1,618.25 - 97.99 winning units..

Owner Mrs Fitri Hay **Bred** Yeomanstown Stud **Trained** Whatcombe, Oxon

FOCUS
A modest 3-y-o maiden but the form looks sound rated around the second and third.

1300 BETVICTOR NON-RUNNER FREE BET AT AINTREE MAIDEN STKS 1m 2f (P)
3:00 (3:01) (Class 5) 3-Y-O+ **£2,587** (£770; £384; £192) **Stalls** Low

Form RPR

02 **1** **Speed Boogie**[24] 950 3-8-9 0.................................. NeilCallan 5 74+
(Marco Botti) *mde all: rdn wl over 1f out: hrd pressed ins fnl f: hld on wl: all out* **11/4**[2]

2 shd **Gold Medal (IRE)** 3-8-9 0.................................. SeanLevey 1 74+
(Richard Hannon) *chsd ldrs: spooked and stuttered 8f out: styd chsng ldrs: rdn and effrt 2f out: str chal ins fnl f: r.o but jst hld* **7/2**[3]

05- **3** 1 **Bursledon (IRE)**[160] 7332 3-8-9 0.................................. RichardHughes 2 72+
(Richard Hannon) *dwlt: t.k.h: sn in tch in midfield: rdn and c lft wl over 1f out: hung across to r against stands' rail ins fnl f: kpt on* **7/4**[1]

4 nk **Strategic Strike (IRE)** 3-8-9 0.................................. SilvestreDeSousa 4 71
(Paul Cole) *t.k.h: hld up in tch in rr: rdn and outpcd 3f out: rallied and hdwy over 1f out: kpt on same pce ins fnl f* **8/1**

24 **5** 1 1/4 **Keep Kicking (IRE)**[15] 1069 6-10-0 0.................................. GeorgeBaker 6 73
(Jonjo O'Neill) *chsd ldr over 8f out: rdn and effrt ent fnl 2f: no ex over 1f out: one pce fnl f* **10/1**

00- **6** 9 **Loraine**[145] 7641 3-8-4 0.................................. KirstyMilczarek 3 46
(Jamie Osborne) *t.k.h: chsd wnr tl over 8f out: styd chsd ldrs tl hung lft and wknd over 1f out* **16/1**

0 **7** hd **Bold Assertion**[15] 1057 3-8-9 0.................................. SteveDrowne 8 51
(John Best) *stdd s: hld up in rr: wknd over 1f out* **50/1**

0 **8** 18 **Ela Goog La Mou**[13] 1086 4-9-9 0.................................. RobertWinston 7
(Peter Charalambous) *stdd s: t.k.h: hld up in rr: wknd 2f out: sn bhd* **66/1**

2m 9.95s (1.95) **Going Correction** +0.125s/f (Slow)
WFA 3 from 4yo+ 19lb **8 Ran SP% 114.8**
Speed ratings (Par 103): **97,96,96,95,94 87,87,73**
Tote Swingers: 1&2 £2.50, 1&3 £1.70, 2&3 £2.10 CSF £12.93 TOTE £4.50: £1.40, £1.80, £1.10; EX 13.70 Trifecta £34.90 Pool: £3,411.25 - 73.15 winning units..
Owner La Tesa Spa **Bred** La Tesa Spa **Trained** Newmarket, Suffolk

FOCUS
An average maiden in which the fifth is probably the best guide to the level.

1301 MIKE THE KNIGHT AT KEMPTON 13.04.13 CLASSIFIED STKS 7f (P)
3:30 (3:30) (Class 6) 3-Y-O **£1,940** (£577; £288; £144) **Stalls** Low

Form RPR

600- **1** **Admiralofthesea (USA)**[146] 7636 3-9-0 64................ AdamBeschizza 1 66+
(Robert Eddery) *chsd ldr: rdn to chal over 1f out: led ins fnl f: r.o wl: rdn out* **10/11**[1]

335- **2** nk **Carina Palace**[139] 7713 3-9-0 65.................................. FergusSweeney 4 65
(Jamie Osborne) *in tch in 4th: rdn and effrt on inner 2f out: ev ch ins fnl f: r.o u.p but hld fnl 75yds* **4/1**[3]

500- **3** nse **Gold Beau (FR)**[131] 7821 3-9-0 63.................................. AmyRyan 3 65?
(Kristin Stubbs) *led and set stdy gallop: rdn and qcknd jst over 2f out: hdd and styd on same pce ins fnl f* **12/1**

-242 **4** 5 **Close Together (IRE)**[33] 824 3-9-0 62.................................. SeanLevey 2 51
(Robert Mills) *chsd ldr: rdn over 2f out: outpcd and dropped to rr wl over 1f out: wknd 1f out* **11/4**[2]

1m 29.98s (3.98) **Going Correction** +0.125s/f (Slow) **4 Ran SP% 106.7**
Speed ratings (Par 96): **82,81,81,75**
CSF £4.69 TOTE £1.90; EX 4.60 Trifecta £16.60 Pool: £1,807.30 - 81.60 winning units..
Owner Mrs Pam Aitken & Ms Trisha Keane **Bred** Brushwood Stable **Trained** Newmarket, Suffolk

FOCUS
A weak affair and muddling form, so far from solid.

1302 GET THE BETVICTOR APP NOW H'CAP 1m 4f (P)
4:00 (4:00) (Class 4) (0-85,83) 4-Y-O+ **£4,690** (£1,395; £697; £348) **Stalls** Centre

Form RPR

430- **1** **Paloma's Prince (IRE)**[176] 6933 4-8-12 **75**.................. MatthewDavies 8 82
(Jim Boyle) *mde all: rdn over 2f out: edging lft over 1f out: battled v gamely u.p fnl f* **14/1**

500- **2** hd **Icebuster**[111] 8073 5-9-1 **77**.................................. JamieSpencer 2 84+
(Rod Millman) *stdd and dropped in bhd after s: wl in rr: clsd over 2f out: swtchd lft over 1f out: hdwy 1f out: chsd wnr fnl 50yds: rn in wl but nt quite get to wnr* **2/1**[1]

320- **3** 3/4 **Saint Helena (IRE)**[158] 7381 5-8-7 **69** oh1........................ ChrisCatlin 1 74
(Harry Dunlop) *chsd ldrs: rdn and pressed wnr over 1f out: chsd wnr ins fnl f: one pce and lost 2nd fnl 50yds* **14/1**

210- **4** hd **Aldwick Bay (IRE)**[153] 7487 5-9-6 **82**........................ RichardHughes 7 87
(Richard Hannon) *in tch in midfield: rdn and swtchd rt over 1f out: n.m.r and kpt on same pce ins fnl f* **7/2**[3]

111- **5** shd **Fleur De La Vie (IRE)**[225] 5430 4-9-2 **79**........................ JimCrowley 10 84
(Ralph Beckett) *chsd wnr: rdn to chal and carried lft over 1f out: lost 2nd and styd on same pce ins fnl f* **5/2**[2]

-451 **6** nk **Scottish Boogie (IRE)**[14] 779 6-9-1 **77**........................ SebSanders 5 82
(Brendan Powell) *hld up in tch in last pair: effrt to press ldrs whn sltly hmpd over 1f out: swtchd lft sn after: drvn 1f out: one pce* **12/1**

020- **7** 1 **Achalas (IRE)**[176] 6933 5-8-10 **77**........................ RyanTate(5) 4 80
(Heather Main) *in tch in midfield: rdn and effrt nrest inner over 1f out: styd on same pce ins fnl f* **11/1**

2m 35.73s (1.23) **Going Correction** +0.125s/f (Slow)
WFA 4 from 5yo+ 1lb **7 Ran SP% 113.5**
Speed ratings (Par 105): **100,99,99,99,99 98,98**
Tote Swingers: 1&2 £7.10, 1&3 £11.90, 2&3 £6.90 CSF £41.80 CT £410.84 TOTE £25.80: £7.60, £1.60; EX 55.70 Trifecta £623.90 Pool: £2,810.22 - 3.37 winning units..
Owner Serendipity Syndicate 2006 **Bred** Skymarc Farm **Trained** Epsom, Surrey

FOCUS
A competitive handicap and a tight finish. Muddling form and not a race to be confident about.

1303 BETVICTOR EXCLUSIVE NON-RUNNER FREE BET H'CAP 1m (P)
4:30 (4:31) (Class 6) (0-65,71) 4-Y-O+ **£1,940** (£577; £288; £144) **Stalls** Low

Form RPR

535- **1** **Divine Pamina (IRE)**[202] 6152 4-9-7 **65**........................ RichardHughes 4 74
(Jim Boyle) *chsd ldng trio: rdn and effrt over 1f out: chal 1f out: led ins fnl f: r.o wl: fin lame* **5/1**[2]

00-4 **2** 3/4 **Bajan Story**[32] 840 4-8-13 **57**.................................. LiamKeniry 14 64
(Michael Blanshard) *chsd ldr tl led after 1f out: rdn 2f out: kpt on wl u.p tl hdd and no ex ins fnl f* **33/1**

5031 **3** 1/2 **Lord Of The Dance (IRE)**[8] 1172 7-9-13 **71** 6ex.............. DaneO'Neill 6 77
(Michael Mullineaux) *dwlt: hld up in tch in midfield: effrt and rdn over 1f out: styd on wl u.p ins fnl f* **14/1**

2606 **4** 1 **May's Boy**[12] 1100 5-9-0 **58**......(p) MartinDwyer 1 62
(Mark Usher) *led for 1f: chsd ldrs after: rdn and effrt ent fnl 2f: styd on same pce u.p fnl f* **12/1**
-516 **5** 1 ½ **Fonterutoli (IRE)**[35] 805 6-9-0 **58** ow1......(e) AdamKirby 12 58
(Roger Ingram) *dwlt: sn rdn along to rcvr: hdwy to chse ldr after: rdn ent fnl 2f: no ex jst ins fnl f: wknd fnl 100yds* **25/1**
3631 **6** nse **Divine Rule (IRE)**[12] 1100 5-9-3 **61**......(v) JimCrowley 2 61
(Laura Mongan) *hld up in tch in midfield: rdn and no imp wl over 1f out: plugged on same pce ins fnl f* **6/1**[3]
100- **7** ¾ **Addikt (IRE)**[293] 3039 8-9-2 **65**...... WilliamTwiston-Davies(5) 5 63
(Michael Scudamore) *s.i.s: bhd: rdn and effrt jst over 2f out: styd on wl ins fnl f: nvr trbld ldrs* **50/1**
2234 **8** ½ **Unlimited**[14] 1079 11-9-2 **60**...... TomQueally 9 57
(Tony Carroll) *in tch in midfield: rdn and no imp wl over 1f out: one pce and no threat to ldrs fnl f* **20/1**
4-52 **9** hd **Bloodsweatandtears**[16] 1056 5-9-2 **60**......(p) SebSanders 7 58
(William Knight) *hld up in tch in midfield: rdn and effrt over 1f out: one pce and no real imp fnl f* **5/1**[2]
60-0 **10** 3 ¼ **Mullins Way (USA)**[90] 13 5-9-5 **63**...... J-PGuillambert 8 52
(Jo Hughes) *hld up towards rr: rdn and no hdwy jst over 2f out: nvr trbld ldrs* **8/1**
26- **11** 2 ¼ **Mister Green (FR)**[273] 3633 7-9-5 **63**...... JamieSpencer 11 47
(David Flood) *hld up in rr: rdn and no hdwy over 2f out: n.d* **12/1**
34-4 **12** ½ **Whinging Willie (IRE)**[61] 450 4-9-4 **62**...... GeorgeBaker 3 45
(Gary Moore) *stdd after s: t.k.h: hld up in rr: short-lived effrt on inner 2f out: wl hld over 1f out* **4/1**[1]
05-4 **13** 9 **Hawk Moth (IRE)**[77] 218 5-9-4 **62**...... SteveDrowne 10 24
(John Spearing) *hld up in last trio: rdn and wknd ent fnl 2f: bhd 1f out* **25/1**

1m 40.61s (0.81) **Going Correction** +0.125s/f (Slow) **13** Ran SP% **118.1**
Speed ratings (Par 101): **100,99,98,97,96 96,95,94,94,91 89,88,79**
Tote Swingers: 1&2 £49.10, 1&3 £14.30, 2&3 £58.20 CSF £170.47 CT £2244.40 TOTE £7.80: £2.60, £11.80, £5.40; EX 318.60 Trifecta £2405.70 Part won. Pool: £3,207.60 - 0.45 winning units..
Owner Sir David Prosser **Bred** Maddenstown Equine Enterprise Ltd **Trained** Epsom, Surrey

FOCUS
A steadily run handicap in which the runner-up sets the standard.

1304 MASCOT GRAND NATIONAL 06.05.13 H'CAP 6f (P)
5:00 (5:00) (Class 6) (0-65,65) 4-Y-O+ **£1,940** (£577; £288; £144) Stalls Low

Form RPR
0661 **1** **Mambo Spirit (IRE)**[13] 1088 9-8-12 **56**...... SeanLevey 6 67
(Tony Newcombe) *hld up in tch in midfield: rdn and hdwy over 1f out: led and edgd rt ins fnl f: r.o wl* **6/1**[3]
3263 **2** 1 ½ **Rose Garnet (IRE)**[36] 790 5-9-0 **58**...... RichardHughes 5 64
(Tony Carroll) *t.k.h: hld up wl in tch: rdn and ev ch ent fnl f: chsd wnr and kpt on same pce ins fnl f* **10/3**[2]
20-5 **3** ¾ **Homeward Strut**[29] 878 4-9-7 **65**......(b) JimCrowley 8 70
(Laura Mongan) *chsd ldr: rdn and ev ch 2f out: unable qck and btn whn squeezed for room ins fnl f: kpt on same pce after* **11/4**[1]
-324 **4** ½ **Steelcut**[12] 1101 9-9-5 **63**......(p) RobertWinston 4 65
(Mark Buckley) *hld up in tch in midfield: rdn and effrt wl over 1f out: kpt on ins fnl f* **10/1**
5530 **5** ½ **Sherjawy (IRE)**[6] 1196 9-8-7 **51** oh2...... KirstyMilczarek 11 52
(Zoe Davison) *chsd ldrs: rdn and unable qck over 1f out: rallied and kpt on ins fnl f* **33/1**
5000 **6** 1 **Demoiselle Bond**[6] 1196 5-8-10 **54**...... SteveDrowne 3 52
(Lydia Richards) *led: jnd and rdn 2f out: kpt on wl tl hdd ins fnl f: wknd fnl 100yds* **25/1**
1-40 **7** 1 **Invigilator**[12] 1102 5-9-3 **61**......(t) MartinDwyer 7 55
(Derek Shaw) *t.k.h: hld up in tch in last quartet: rdn and effrt on inner wl over 1f out: kpt on but nvr trbld ldrs* **7/1**
-653 **8** nk **Dishy Guru**[15] 1063 4-9-7 **65**......(b) LiamKeniry 9 58
(Michael Blanshard) *hld up in last pair: swtchd rt and effrt on inner 2f out: kpt on but nvr a threat to ldrs* **8/1**
5110 **9** shd **Mr Optimistic**[27] 898 5-9-0 **58**...... KieranO'Neill 1 51
(Paul Howling) *hld up in last trio: rdn and effrt towards inner wl over 1f out: kpt on fnl f: nvr trbld ldrs* **12/1**
-245 **10** 3 **Super Duplex**[15] 1059 6-9-2 **65**...... JemmaMarshall(5) 10 49
(Pat Phelan) *stdd and dropped in bhd after s: hld up in rr: detached last and rdn over 2f out: plugged on: n.d* **33/1**
200/ **11** nk **Sir Don (IRE)**[841] 7859 14-8-3 **54** oh6 ow3......(b) JordanNason(7) 2 37
(Michael Mullineaux) *chsd ldrs: rdn and unable qck ent fnl 2f: wknd over 1f out* **50/1**

1m 12.71s (-0.39) **Going Correction** +0.125s/f (Slow) **11** Ran SP% **116.1**
Speed ratings (Par 101): **107,105,104,103,102 101,100,99,99,95 95**
Tote Swingers: 1&2 £5.30, 1&3 £3.80, 2&3 £2.80 CSF £25.12 CT £67.64 TOTE £9.10: £2.10, £1.90, £1.40; EX 20.30 Trifecta £174.30 Pool: £3,033.17 - 13.04 winning units..
Owner Nigel Hardy **Bred** R Warren **Trained** Yarnscombe, Devon
■ Stewards' Enquiry : Sean Levey three-day ban: careless riding (16-18 Apr)

FOCUS
They went a sound pace in this ordinary sprint handicap and the form makes sense and looks straightforward, rated around the first two.
T/Plt: £88.50 to a £1 stake. Pool: £56,028.00 - 461.87 winning tickets. T/Qpdt: £38.00 to a £1 stake. Pool: £3,769.00 - 73.27 winning tickets. SP

1201 SOUTHWELL (L-H)
Tuesday, April 2

OFFICIAL GOING: Standard
Wind: Fresh across Weather: Clody with sunny periods

1305 £32 BONUS AT 32RED.COM MEDIAN AUCTION MAIDEN STKS 6f (F)
2:20 (2:20) (Class 6) 3-5-Y-O **£1,940** (£577; £288; £144) Stalls Low

Form RPR
44- **1** **Marshland**[333] 1832 3-9-0 0...... JoeFanning 4 79+
(Mark Johnston) *cl up: led 1/2-way: pushed clr 2f out: green and idling in front whn edgd rt to stands' rail: unchal* **1/2**[1]
2 7 **Guishan** 3-8-9 0...... AndrewMullen 6 50
(Michael Appleby) *dwlt: green and reminders in rr: hdwy on wd outside wl over 2f out: rdn to chse wnr over 1f out: kpt on: no imp* **12/1**[3]
00- **3** 3 ¼ **Secret Empress**[139] 7711 3-8-9 0...... TomEaves 3 39
(Bryan Smart) *cl up: rdn along wl over 2f out: kpt on same pce* **16/1**
0 **4** 7 **Woodley Wonder (IRE)**[26] 911 3-8-11 0...... DeclanCannon(3) 1 22
(Ben Haslam) *slt ld on inner: rdn along and hdd 1/2-way: drvn over 2f out and sn outpcd* **12/1**[3]
0000 **5** 9 **Minty Jones**[17] 1042 4-9-12 40......(be) JamesSullivan 5
(Michael Mullineaux) *chsd ldrs: rdn along over 3f out: sn outpcd and bhd* **100/1**
40 **6** 19 **Sharaar (IRE)**[17] 1044 3-9-0 0......(b[1]) LukeMorris 2
(Gerard Butler) *broke wl and prom 1 1/2f: sn lost pl and rdn along: bhd fr 1/2-way* **4/1**[2]

1m 17.46s (0.96) **Going Correction** +0.225s/f (Slow)
WFA 3 from 4yo 12lb **6** Ran SP% **108.9**
Speed ratings (Par 101): **102,92,88,79,67 41**
Tote Swingers: 1&2 £1.80, 1&3 £3.00, 2&3 £11.90 CSF £7.25 TOTE £1.10: £1.02, £7.40; EX 4.40 Trifecta £30.90 Pool: £2,496.68 - 60.40 winning units..
Owner Sheikh Hamdan Bin Mohammed Al Maktoum **Bred** Darley **Trained** Middleham Moor, N Yorks

FOCUS
A weak and uncompetitive maiden rated around the winner and the time.

1306 BINARY TRENDS - INVEST WITH BINARYTRENDS.CO.UK H'CAP 1m 6f (F)
2:50 (2:50) (Class 5) (0-75,74) 4-Y-O+ **£2,587** (£770; £384; £192) Stalls Low

Form RPR
1122 **1** **Stentorian (IRE)**[17] 1031 5-9-10 **74**......(v) LukeMorris 1 89+
(Gary Moore) *trckd ldr: led wl over 3f out: sn clr: unchal* **11/8**[1]
5501 **2** 9 **Calculating (IRE)**[7] 1189 9-8-6 **56** 6ex...... HayleyTurner 2 60
(Mark Usher) *set stdy pce: pushed along over 4f out: hdd wl over 3f out: sn rdn and kpt on: no ch w wnr* **9/4**[2]
0134 **3** 7 **Mediterranean Sea (IRE)**[21] 969 7-9-10 **74**...... StephenCraine 4 67
(J R Jenkins) *hld up: hdwy 4f out: rdn to chse ldng pair 3f out: sn no imp* **10/3**[3]
1015 **4** 5 **Sommersturm (GER)**[9] 1158 9-8-10 **67**...... RobJFitzpatrick(7) 5 55
(David Evans) *plld hrd: hld up in rr: hdwy on inner to trck ldng pair 1/2-way: pushed along over 4f out: sn outpcd and bhd* **7/1**

3m 14.58s (6.28) **Going Correction** +0.225s/f (Slow)
WFA 4 from 5yo+ 3lb **4** Ran SP% **108.5**
Speed ratings (Par 103): **91,85,81,79**
CSF £4.73 TOTE £1.80; EX 4.80 Trifecta £5.90 Pool: £1,635.26 - 205.10 winning units..
Owner B Homewood **Bred** Ceka Ireland Limited **Trained** Lower Beeding, W Sussex

FOCUS
A modest staying handicap, weakened further by the two non-runners, and they went no pace early. Muddling form but the runner-up sets the level to his latest mark.

1307 32RED H'CAP 7f (F)
3:20 (3:20) (Class 4) (0-80,79) 3-Y-O **£4,690** (£1,395; £697; £348) Stalls Low

Form RPR
2-14 **1** **Flashlight (IRE)**[13] 1091 3-9-7 **79**...... JoeFanning 4 91
(Mark Johnston) *cl up: led after 1f: rdn clr wl over 1f out: edgd rt ins fnl f: styd on wl* **5/2**[2]
23-1 **2** 5 **Naalatt (IRE)**[55] 541 3-9-5 **77**...... AndreaAtzeni 2 75
(Roger Varian) *trckd ldrs on inner: effrt over 2f out and sn pushed along: rdn and hdwy wl over 1f out: chsd wnr ent fnl f: sn drvn and no imp* **2/1**[1]
40-2 **3** 2 ¾ **Isis Blue**[13] 1091 3-8-7 **70**...... MichaelJMMurphy(5) 3 61
(Rod Millman) *slt ld 1f: cl up: rdn along over 2f out: sn one pce* **9/2**[3]
15 **4** 1 **Street Battle (USA)**[46] 674 3-9-5 **77**...... BarryMcHugh 6 65
(Tony Coyle) *cl up: effrt wl over 2f out: sn rdn: drvn wl over 1f out and sn one pce* **11/2**
3412 **5** 3 ¼ **Sewn Up**[6] 1204 3-9-3 **75**......(p) GrahamLee 7 54
(Reg Hollinshead) *hld up: hdwy to trck ldrs 1/2-way: effrt 2f out: sn rdn and btn over 1f out* **7/1**
164- **6** 13 **Flighty Clarets (IRE)**[187] 6611 3-8-10 **68**...... TonyHamilton 1 12
(Richard Fahey) *a in rr: rdn along over 3f out: sn outpcd and bhd* **33/1**

1m 30.34s (0.04) **Going Correction** +0.225s/f (Slow) **6** Ran SP% **110.9**
Speed ratings (Par 100): **108,102,99,98,94 79**
Tote Swingers: 1&2 £1.60, 1&3 £1.60, 2&3 £2.90 CSF £7.72 TOTE £4.20: £2.30, £1.10; EX 8.70 Trifecta £26.40 Pool: £2,619.46 - 74.38 winning units..
Owner Sheikh Hamdan Bin Mohammed Al Maktoum **Bred** Gerry Smith **Trained** Middleham Moor, N Yorks

FOCUS
A nice little handicap and an impressive winner. The runner-up sets the level.

1308 BINARY TRENDS - MAKE MONEY WITH BINARYTRENDS.CO.UK H'CAP 5f (F)
3:50 (3:51) (Class 3) (0-95,93) 4-Y-O+ **£7,439** (£2,213; £1,106; £553) Stalls High

Form RPR
113- **1** **Gladiatrix**[163] 7273 4-8-3 80...... MichaelJMMurphy(5) 5 88
(Rod Millman) *cl up: rdn to ld ent fnl f: kpt on wl towards fin* **9/1**
1025 **2** nk **Royal Bajan (USA)**[11] 1121 5-8-10 82......(b) GrahamLee 7 89
(James Given) *prom: cl up 2f out: rdn to chse wnr ins fnl f: no ex towards fin* **7/2**[1]
000- **3** hd **El Viento (FR)**[143] 7691 5-9-4 90...... TonyHamilton 3 96
(Richard Fahey) *towards rr: rdn along 2f out: hdwy on outer over 1f out: styd on wl fnl f* **17/2**[3]
04-0 **4** nk **Rusty Rocket (IRE)**[21] 966 4-8-1 78...... PhilipPrince(5) 2 83
(Paul Green) *trckd ldrs whn n.m.r and lost pl after 1f: hdwy 2f out: sn rdn to chse ldrs ent fnl f: drvn and no ex last 100yds* **9/1**
0044 **5** ½ **Six Wives**[11] 1121 6-8-3 75......(p) LukeMorris 9 78
(Scott Dixon) *led: rdn along wl over 1f out: hdd ent fnl f: sn drvn and wknd* **4/1**[2]
5013 **6** nk **Lucky Dan (IRE)**[15] 1067 7-8-3 75...... JoeFanning 8 77
(Paul Green) *chsd ldrs: rdn along and sltly outpcd 2f out: styd on fnl f: nrst fin* **10/1**
5122 **7** 1 ¾ **Al Khan (IRE)**[12] 1096 4-8-4 76...... CathyGannon 4 72
(Violet M Jordan) *s.i.s: a in rr* **7/2**[1]
000- **8** 1 ¾ **Lost In Paris (IRE)**[182] 6767 7-8-5 77......(p) DuranFentiman 1 67
(Tim Easterby) *cl up on outer: rdn along wl over 1f out: drvn and wknd appr fnl f* **20/1**
0310 **9** ¾ **Bubbly Ballerina**[9] 1160 4-8-5 77...... FrannyNorton 10 64
(Alan Bailey) *prom: rdn along over 2f out: sn wknd* **12/1**

1m 0.55s (0.85) **Going Correction** +0.35s/f (Slow) **9** Ran SP% **116.5**
Speed ratings (Par 107): **107,106,106,105,104 104,101,98,97**
Tote Swingers: 1&2 £6.60, 1&3 £12.80, 2&3 £7.00 CSF £40.97 CT £282.44 TOTE £8.30: £1.90, £1.70, £3.10; EX 46.90 Trifecta £655.40 Pool: £2,592.87 - 2.96 winning units..
Owner Harry Dutfield & Partners **Bred** H G And J R Dutfield **Trained** Kentisbeare, Devon

FOCUS
The withdrawal of the likely favourite Even Stevens left this decent sprint handicap more open than it would otherwise have been. Unusually for the straight 5f here, the stalls were against the far rail, but that didn't stop the runners ending up racing centre-to-stands' side. Straightforward form rated through the second.

1309 BINARY TRENDS - CHOOSE YOUR INCOME H'CAP — 6f (F)
4:20 (4:20) (Class 5) (0-75,79) 4-Y-0+ **£2,587** (£770; £384; £192) **Stalls** Low

Form RPR
3131 **1** **Elusive Hawk (IRE)**[6] 1205 9-9-6 **79** 6ex...............(v) RobJFitzpatrick(7) 2 94
(David Evans) *in tch: hdwy to chse ldng pair wl over 2f out: effrt to chse wnr and hung lft over 1f out: chal ent fnl f: sn led and kpt on* **8/13**[1]

224- **2** 4 1/2 **Mata Hari Blue**[272] 3749 7-9-4 **70**.................................(t) AndrewMullen 5 71
(Michael Appleby) *slt ld: rdn clr over 2f out: jnd and drvn ent fnl f: sn hdd and kpt on same pce* **14/1**

150- **3** 1 1/4 **Art Dzeko**[250] 4496 4-9-2 **68**.................................... DavidAllan 4 65
(Tim Easterby) *dwlt and in rr: hdwy 2f out: sn rdn and styd on fnl f: nrst fin* **15/2**[3]

0134 **4** 3/4 **Masked Dance (IRE)**[20] 986 6-8-7 **59**........................(bt) LukeMorris 3 53
(Scott Dixon) *in tch: rdn along and hdwy over 2f out: drvn wl over 1f out and n.d* **6/1**[2]

0000 **5** 3 1/4 **Decent Fella (IRE)**[13] 1092 7-9-4 **70**.............................(t) MartinHarley 6 54
(Violet M Jordan) *cl up: rdn along 1/2-way: wknd fnl 2f* **8/1**

0406 **6** 1/2 **Mazovian (USA)**[33] 832 5-8-12 **64**............................ RussKennemore 1 46
(Michael Chapman) *sn rdn along and a in rr* **16/1**

1m 16.73s (0.23) **Going Correction** +0.225s/f (Slow) **6** Ran SP% **111.6**
Speed ratings (Par 103): **107,101,99,98,94 93**
Tote Swingers: 1&2 £2.80, 1&3 £1.60, 2&3 £4.50 CSF £10.67 TOTE £1.30: £1.50, £2.90; EX 7.80 Trifecta £25.10 Pool: £1,869.14 - 65.65 winning units..
Owner Mrs I M Folkes **Bred** J Fike **Trained** Pandy, Monmouths

FOCUS
A modest handicap, but they went a strong early pace and the six runners were soon well spread out. The winner is rated to the best of his old form.

1310 32RED.COM H'CAP — 7f (F)
4:50 (4:50) (Class 6) (0-60,66) 4-Y-0+ **£1,940** (£577; £288; £144) **Stalls** Low

Form RPR
0045 **1** **Ace Of Spies (IRE)**[55] 537 8-8-11 **50**........................... HayleyTurner 8 60
(Conor Dore) *sn led: rdn clr over 2f out: drvn ins fnl f: kpt on gamely* **14/1**

6651 **2** 1/2 **Mataajir (USA)**[10] 1149 5-9-0 **60**................................. AdamMcLean(7) 2 69
(Derek Shaw) *trckd ldrs on inner: chsd wnr 1/2-way: rdn and sltly outpcd 2f out: drvn and styd on wl fnl f* **7/2**[3]

3011 **3** 1 3/4 **Fairy Wing (IRE)**[7] 1186 6-9-13 **66** 6ex.......................... MartinHarley 9 70
(Violet M Jordan) *trckd ldrs: hdwy 3f out: rdn to chse wnr over 1f out: drvn and one pce ins fnl f* **9/4**[1]

6U03 **4** 3 1/4 **Vitznau (IRE)**[21] 965 9-9-5 **58**.............................. DanielTudhope 6 54
(K F Clutterbuck) *chsd ldrs: hdwy over 2f out: rdn to chse wnr appr fnl f: sn drvn and wknd* **6/1**

/123 **5** 5 **Seamster**[20] 991 6-9-6 **59**...(vt) GrahamLee 3 41+
(Richard Ford) *s.i.s and bhd: wd st: sme late hdwy* **11/4**[2]

050- **6** 1 1/4 **Vogarth**[131] 5013 9-8-0 **46** oh1.................................. DanielleMooney(7) 5 25
(Michael Chapman) *prom: rdn along bef 1/2-way: sn outpcd* **80/1**

0425 **7** 28 **Olynard (IRE)**[10] 1147 7-8-3 **47**....................................(p) RobertTart(5) 4
(Michael Mullineaux) *chsd ldrs: rdn along 3f out: sn wknd* **25/1**

1m 31.99s (1.69) **Going Correction** +0.225s/f (Slow) **7** Ran SP% **105.7**
Speed ratings (Par 101): **99,98,96,92,87 85,53**
Tote Swingers: 1&2 £5.00, 1&3 £3.50, 2&3 £2.10 CSF £52.70 CT £124.72 TOTE £13.50: £3.80, £2.40; EX 34.20 Trifecta £82.80 Pool: £1,869.14 - 16.92 winning units..
Owner Mrs Louise Marsh **Bred** Gainsborough Stud Management Ltd **Trained** Hubbert's Bridge, Lincs

FOCUS
A moderate handicap that could be worth a bit more than rated.

1311 32RED CASINO H'CAP — 1m (F)
5:20 (5:20) (Class 6) (0-55,61) 4-Y-0+ **£1,940** (£577; £288; £144) **Stalls** Low

Form RPR
-541 **1** **Sofias Number One (USA)**[11] 1120 5-9-3 **54**........(b) MarkCoumbe(3) 4 68
(Roy Bowring) *in rr and pushed along after 3f: hdwy on wd outside over 3f out: chsd ldrs 2f out: rdn to ld over 1f out: kpt on strly* **9/2**[2]

6063 **2** 2 **Mcconnell (USA)**[10] 1151 8-9-2 **50**...............................(b) MartinHarley 8 59
(Violet M Jordan) *trckd ldrs: hdwy over 3f out: sn cl up: effrt and ev ch 2f out: sn rdn and chsd wnr fr over 1f out: drvn and no imp ins fnl f* **6/1**

-053 **3** 5 **Bonnie Prince Blue**[28] 884 10-9-3 **51**............................ DaleSwift 7 49
(Ian McInnes) *chsd ldrs: rdn along and outpcd over 3f out: styd on u.p fr wl over 1f out: nrst fin* **20/1**

33-0 **4** 3/4 **Chez Vrony**[27] 900 7-8-12 **46** oh1............................... WilliamCarson 5 42
(Dave Morris) *in tch: gd hdwy to chse ldrs over 3f out: led over 2f out: rdn and hdd over 1f out: sn drvn and wknd* **16/1**

-226 **5** 4 **Bentley**[19] 993 9-8-13 **52**... RobertTart(5) 2 39
(Brian Baugh) *towards rr: rdn along and sme hdwy on inner over 2f out: plugged on appr fnl f: nvr gng pce to rch ldrs* **5/1**[3]

0061 **6** 1/2 **Beauchamp Xerxes**[9] 1162 7-9-8 **61** 6ex..............(t) NicoleNordblad(5) 9 47
(Hans Adielsson) *dwlt: sn chsng ldrs: led after 3f: rdn along 3f out: hdd over 2f out and grad wknd* **13/8**[1]

0405 **7** 1 3/4 **General Tufto**[26] 908 8-8-12 **46** oh1....................(b) RobbieFitzpatrick 10 28
(Charles Smith) *sn rdn along and outpcd in rr: bhd 1/2-way: sme hdwy fnl 2f: nvr a factor* **16/1**

-005 **8** 9 **Tenancy (IRE)**[14] 1077 9-8-12 **46** oh1........................... DuranFentiman 3 7
(Shaun Harris) *slt ld 3f: chsd ldr: rdn along 3f out and sn wknd* **50/1**

100- **9** 6 **Tony Hollis**[144] 7671 5-9-4 **52**... JamesSullivan 6
(Karen Tutty) *chsd ldrs 3f: sn lost pl and bhd* **20/1**

060- **10** 8 **Slewtoo**[108] 8142 4-9-7 **55**.. GrahamLee 1
(James Given) *chsd ldrs on inner: pushed along and lost pl 1/2-way: sn bhd* **16/1**

1m 45.78s (2.08) **Going Correction** +0.225s/f (Slow) **10** Ran SP% **116.4**
Speed ratings (Par 101): **98,96,91,90,86 85,84,75,69,61**
Tote Swingers: 1&2 £6.10, 1&3 £9.10, 2&3 £8.40 CSF £30.78 CT £490.87 TOTE £6.60: £1.90, £2.10, £4.10; EX 37.80 Trifecta £152.80 Pool: £3,033.17 - 13.04 winning units..
Owner S R Bowring **Bred** Rosecrest Farm Llc **Trained** Edwinstowe, Notts

FOCUS
Another moderate handicap but the winner is rated to the best of his old form.
T/Plt: £20.80 to a £1 stake. Pool: £66,055.00 - 2,314.87 winning tickets. T/Qpdt: £10.50 to a £1 stake. Pool: £4,322.00 - 302.47 winning tickets. JR

LES LANDES
Monday, April 1

OFFICIAL GOING: Good to soft

1312a JERSEY BOOKMAKERS H'CAP STKS — 7f
3:40 (3:40) 3-Y-0+ **£1,900** (£685; £415) **Stalls** Low

RPR
1 **Pas D'Action**[217] 5-8-5 .... JemmaMarshall 9 60
(Mrs A Malzard, Jersey) **13/2**

2 5 **Toggle**[217] 5701 9-8-6 ow1... JoshBaudains 3 48
(Mrs A Corson, Jersey) **8/1**

3 1 **Lucifers Shadow (IRE)**[185] 6640 4-8-11 .... MrBenFfrenchDavis 2 50
(Mrs C Gilbert, Jersey) **5/1**

4 2 **Fast Freddie**[217] 5701 9-9-1 .... MatthewLawson 1 49
(Mrs A Corson, Jersey) **5/2**[2]

5 2 1/2 **First Cat**[217] 6-9-13 .... JamieGoldstein 5 54
(S Arthur, Jersey) **11/4**[3]

6 4 **Sutton Sid**[179] 6826 3-8-9 ow1.. TonyCulhane 7 34
(George Baker) **11/8**[1]

7 5 1/2 **Country Blue (FR)**[248] 4-9-8 .... MattieBatchelor 8 23
(Mrs A Malzard, Jersey) **11/2**

8 1/2 **Spanish Bounty**[217] 5701 8-10-12 .... HarryPoulton 4 40
(Mrs A Malzard, Jersey) **3/1**

9 12 **Cryptic Choice (IRE)**[269] 4-9-5 .... TimClark 10
(S Arthur, Jersey) **8/1**

1m 33.0s (93.00)
WFA 3 from 4yo+ 14lb **9** Ran SP% **190.0**

Owner J Jamouneau **Bred** Jenny Hall Bloodstock Ltd **Trained** St Ouen, Jersey

1313a CHANNEL ISLAND RACING AND HUNT CLUB H'CAP STKS — 1m 100y
4:50 (4:50) (0-50,) 3-Y-0+ **£1,460** (£525; £315) **Stalls** Low

RPR
1 **I'm Harry**[66] 375 4-10-12 ....(tp) TonyCulhane 3
(George Baker) **9/4**[2]

2 7 **La Verte Rue (USA)**[232] 7-10-5 .... MattieBatchelor 1
(Mrs A Malzard, Jersey) **9/2**

3 9 **Vamos (IRE)**[217] 7-9-7 .... JemmaMarshall 6
(Mrs A Malzard, Jersey) **7/2**[3]

4 3 **Grey Panel (FR)**[217] 5-10-2 .... TimClark 7
(T Le Brocq, Jersey) **6/4**[1]

5 3 **Athania (IRE)**[217] 7-10-11 .... JamieGoldstein 8
(S Arthur, Jersey) **4/1**

6 4 **Rocquaine (IRE)**[198] 6230 4-10-5 .... HarryPoulton 4
(Mrs A Malzard, Jersey) **9/1**

7 10 **Robbmaa (FR)**[232] 8-9-7 .... MrBenFfrenchDavis 2
(Mrs J L Le Brocq, Jersey) **10/1**

8 7 **Rebel Woman**[232] 7-10-0 .... MatthewLawson 5
(Mrs A Corson, Jersey) **5/1**

1m 57.0s (117.00) **8** Ran SP% **166.9**

Owner Wickfield Stud And Hartshill Stud **Bred** Wickfield Stud And Hartshill Stud **Trained** Manton, Wilts

1298 KEMPTON (A.W) (R-H)
Wednesday, April 3

OFFICIAL GOING: Standard
Wind: Strong; across (towards stands) Weather: Cloudy; very cold

1314 £200 FREE BETS AT BETDAQ H'CAP — 1m 2f (P)
5:30 (5:31) (Class 6) (0-60,60) 3-Y-0 **£1,940** (£577; £288; £144) **Stalls** Low

Form RPR
3633 **1** **Silver Fawn (IRE)**[19] 1016 3-8-9 **48**.............................(be) JimmyQuinn 7 52
(John Weymes) *stdd s: hld up in last pair: prog on outer wl over 1f out: pressed ldr fnl f: drvn to ld post* **6/1**[3]

3-42 **2** shd **Solvanna**[13] 1095 3-9-7 **60**.. TomQueally 4 64
(Heather Main) *t.k.h: hld up in 4th: clsd fr 2f out: pushed into ld over 1f out: pressed and hrd rdn fnl f: hdd post* **6/1**[3]

-623 **3** 1 3/4 **Conversing (USA)**[13] 1098 3-8-13 **52**........................ SilvestreDeSousa 6 52
(Mark Johnston) *trckd ldr: poised to chal 2f out: upsides but nt qckn over 1f out: one pce fnl f* **5/2**[2]

332- **4** 1 1/4 **Classy Trick (USA)**[109] 8132 3-9-4 **57**............................. PaulHanagan 1 55
(Richard Fahey) *trckd ldng pair: pushed along 3f out: kpt on one pce u.p fr over 1f out: nt pce to threaten* **11/8**[1]

00-6 **5** 1 3/4 **Foxy Dancer (IRE)**[17] 1055 3-8-7 **46**................................. SeanLevey 5 40
(Richard Hannon) *led at mod pce: tried to kick on 3f out: hrd rdn and hdd over 1f out: wknd* **12/1**

000- **6** 1/2 **Karl Marx (IRE)**[177] 6928 3-8-12 **51**............................ FergusSweeney 2 44
(Mark Gillard) *hld up in last pair: rdn 2f out: sn outpcd: nvr on terms after* **33/1**

2m 11.69s (3.69) **Going Correction** -0.05s/f (Stan) **6** Ran SP% **109.9**
Speed ratings (Par 96): **83,82,81,80,79 78**
toteswingers 1&2 £3.00, 1&3 £3.00, 2&3 £3.00 CSF £38.34 TOTE £7.60: £2.90, £2.10; EX 28.20 Trifecta £106.70 Pool: £31,464.93 - 221.11 winning units.
Owner Thoroughbred Partners **Bred** Bryan Ryan **Trained** Middleham Moor, N Yorks

FOCUS
A moderate handicap in which a steady gallop to the home turn resulted in a race run 7sec above Racing Post Standard and means this bare form isn't entirely reliable . The winner raced centre to far side in the straight.

1315 COMISSION FREE 1ST MONTH AT BETDAQ H'CAP — 5f (P)
6:00 (6:00) (Class 5) (0-75,67) 3-Y-0 **£2,587** (£770; £384; £192) **Stalls** Low

Form RPR
1 **1** **Secret Of Success**[47] 667 3-9-0 **60**.................................. ChrisCatlin 4 66
(Rae Guest) *trckd ldr: pushed along firmly to ld 1f out: rdn to assert last 100yds: readily* **7/4**[1]

4223 **2** 1 1/2 **Modern Lady**[20] 992 3-9-6 **66**.......................... RobbieFitzpatrick 1 67
(Richard Guest) *led: drvn and hdd 1f out: fdd nr fin* **3/1**[2]

00-4 **3** *nk* **Eastern Dragon (IRE)**16 1064 3-9-1 **61**........................ PaulMulrennan 2 61
(Michael Scudamore) *chsd ldng pair: pushed along 1/2-way and abt 2 l bhd them: stl pushed along over 1f out: fnlly clsd on runner-up nr fin: nvr chal* **6/1**3

40-1 **4** *3 ¼* **Polish Crown**12 1122 3-9-7 **67**.................................... SilvestreDeSousa 3 57
(Mark Johnston) *mostly in last: drvn after 2f: struggling after: wl btn over 1f out* **7/4**1

1m 0.24s (-0.26) **Going Correction** -0.05s/f (Stan) 4 Ran SP% **112.0**
Speed ratings (Par 98): **100,97,97,91**
CSF £7.46 TOTE £2.90; EX 7.20 Trifecta £22.00 Pool: £14,564.72 - 494.45 winning units.
Owner J H Metzger **Bred** J H Metzger **Trained** Newmarket, Suffolk

FOCUS
A modest handicap run at an ordinary gallop. The winner raced two off the inside rail throughout.

1316 MIKE THE KNIGHT 13.04.13 CLASSIFIED CLAIMING STKS 7f (P)
6:30 (6:32) (Class 6) 4-Y-0+ **£1,940** (£577; £288; £144) **Stalls** Low

Form RPR

-043 **1** **Mr Knightley (IRE)**13 1094 4-8-13 73.......................(b) MatthewDavies 5 78
(Jim Boyle) *dwlt: hld up in last pair: pushed along briefly 1/2-way: clsd over 2f out: wnt 2nd 1f out: rdn to ld last 100yds: sn asserted* **12/1**

3111 **2** *1 ½* **Hurricane Spirit (IRE)**13 1094 9-8-2 72................. NicoleNordblad(5) 3 68
(Hans Adielsson) *chsd clr ldr: clsd over 2f out: shkn up to ld over 1f out: kpt on but hdd and outpcd last 100yds* **8/11**1

11-3 **3** *4* **Commanche**79 199 4-8-11 66.................................. ThomasBrown(5) 4 66
(Patrick Chamings) *hld up in last pair: pushed along fr 1/2-way: tried to cl 2f out: outpcd fnl f but tk modest 3rd nr fin* **8/1**3

3-22 **4** *nk* **Paradise Spectre**21 981 6-9-3 72................................... MartinHarley 2 66
(Mrs K Burke) *chsd clr ldr: clsd over 2f out: rdn to try to chal over 1f out: sn wknd* **3/1**2

1102 **5** *1 ½* **Frognal (IRE)**39 775 7-8-11 74.................................(bt) CathyGannon 1 56
(Violet M Jordan) *reluctant to enter stalls: led and sn stormed at least 5 l clr: wknd and hdd over 1f out* **10/1**

1m 24.72s (-1.28) **Going Correction** -0.05s/f (Stan) 5 Ran SP% **110.8**
Speed ratings (Par 101): **105,103,98,98,96**
CSF £21.98 TOTE £11.60: £4.30, £1.10; EX 28.90 Trifecta £171.80 Pool: £23,813.16 - 103.94 winning units.Hurricane Spirit was claimed by Mr Joseph Tuite for £5,000
Owner The 'In Recovery' Partnership **Bred** Miss Deirdre Cogan **Trained** Epsom, Surrey

FOCUS
A fair classified claimer. The gallop was sound and the winner and runner-up, who pulled clear, came down the centre.

1317 BETDAQ 1ST UK RACE FREE COMISSION EVERY DAY MAIDEN STKS 1m 3f (P)
7:00 (7:00) (Class 5) 3-Y-0+ **£2,587** (£770; £384; £192) **Stalls** Low

Form RPR

40- **1** **Sizzler**154 7492 3-8-8 0.. JimCrowley 2 85
(Ralph Beckett) *hld up in tch: trckd ldng pair over 3f out: clsd over 2f out: hanging but shkn up to ld wl over 1f out: edgd rt but steadily drew clr* **3/1**2

02-2 **2** *4* **Khudoua**12 1119 3-8-8 78...(p) PaulHanagan 1 78
(John Gosden) *trckd ldng pair: pushed up to go 2nd 4f out: rdn to ld wl over 2f out: hdd and nt qckn wl over 1f out: wl hld after* **1/2**1

6/6- **3** *17* **Guardi (IRE)**333 1867 4-10-0 0... GeorgeBaker 8 50
(Dean Ivory) *led and racd freely: rdn and hdd over 2f out: hanging and sn wknd qckly: t.o* **16/1**

53- **4** *6* **Notabadgirl**94 8295 4-9-9 0... NickyMackay 5 35
(Simon Dow) *dwlt: immediately detached in last: t.o 3f out: tk remote 4th nr fin* **33/1**

5 *¾* **Reach The Beach**25 4-9-9 0.. SebSanders 4 33
(Brendan Powell) *chsd ldr to 4f out: sn rdn and wknd: t.o* **12/1**3

6 *10* **Ernie**151 6-10-0 0... ChrisCatlin 3 20
(Geoffrey Deacon) *dwlt: immediately detached in last pair: rdn and t.o fnl 3f* **33/1**

0-0 **7** *6* **Parsons Green**16 1057 4-9-9 0... RobertHavlin 6
(Michael Attwater) *in tch towards rr tl wknd 3f out: t.o* **66/1**

2m 19.84s (-2.06) **Going Correction** -0.05s/f (Stan)
WFA 3 from 4yo+ 20lb 7 Ran SP% **112.6**
Speed ratings (Par 103): **105,102,89,85,84 77,73**
toteswingers 1&2 £1.10, 1&3 £4.20, 2&3 £3.00 CSF £4.67 TOTE £3.50: £2.30, £1.20; EX 6.60 Trifecta £24.70 Pool: £20,104.22 - 609.95 winning units.
Owner Heseltine, Henley & Jones **Bred** Newsells Park Stud **Trained** Kimpton, Hants

FOCUS
An uncompetitive maiden in which the first two, who pulled clear, showed fair form. The pace was just an ordinary one to the home straight and the winner came down the centre.

1318 WINNERS ARE WELCOME AT BETDAQ H'CAP 7f (P)
7:30 (7:31) (Class 4) (0-80,80) 4-Y-0+ **£4,690** (£1,395; £697; £348) **Stalls** Low

Form RPR

111- **1** **Twenty One Choice (IRE)**193 6500 4-9-0 **73**................. TomQueally 3 88
(Ed de Giles) *wl plcd on inner: trckd ldr 3f out: quick move to ld jst over 2f out and sn 2 l clr: drvn over 1f out: styd on wl* **5/1**2

/15- **2** *2* **Flexible Flyer**302 2785 4-9-2 **75**.................................... RichardHughes 6 86
(Hughie Morrison) *awkward s: hld up towards rr: stdy prog over 2f out: chsd wnr over 1f out: drvn and nt qckn sn after: wl hld fnl f* **5/2**1

11-4 **3** *2 ¼* **Living Leader**33 844 4-9-6 **79**.................................. TomMcLaughlin 12 83
(Nick Littmoden) *rdn in last trio over 4f out: struggling after: jockey persisted and styd on fnl 2f to take 3rd last strides* **5/1**2

-663 **4** *½* **Perfect Mission**13 1096 5-8-4 **70**............................(v) DanielMuscutt(7) 4 72
(Andrew Balding) *mostly chsd ldr at str pce to 3f out: drvn to dispute 2nd again over 1f out: one pce after* **16/1**

14-5 **5** *1 ¼* **Pearl Nation (USA)**37 792 4-9-7 **80**............................ FrederikTylicki 7 79
(Brian Baugh) *wl in tch: rdn and nt qckn 2f out: kpt on one pce after and no imp on ldrs* **6/1**3

00-6 **6** *1 ¼* **Street Power (USA)**30 881 8-9-6 **79**............................... SteveDrowne 9 74
(Jeremy Gask) *hld up in last trio: stdy prog on inner over 2f out: disp 3rd jst over 1f out but no threat: wknd* **14/1**

236- **7** *2 ¼* **Dancheur (IRE)**195 6406 4-9-4 **77**.................................. MartinHarley 5 66
(Mrs K Burke) *led at str pce: hdd jst over 2f out: steadily wknd* **25/1**

1-23 **8** *1* **Stir Trader (IRE)**37 792 4-9-5 **78**...................................... TomEaves 11 65
(Philip Hide) *chsd ldrs on outer: rdn over 2f out: sn lost pl and btn* **10/1**

2135 **9** *7* **Russian Ice**14 1092 5-9-3 **76**..(b) JimCrowley 2 44
(Dean Ivory) *a in last trio: rdn sn after 1/2-way: struggling after: bhd fnl 2f* **7/1**

0335 **10** *2 ¼* **Silverware (USA)**40 751 5-9-5 **78**................................ PatrickMathers 8 40
(Kristin Stubbs) *prom on outer: rdn 1/2-way: sn wknd and bhd* **25/1**

1m 23.88s (-2.12) **Going Correction** -0.05s/f (Stan) 10 Ran SP% **118.0**
Speed ratings (Par 105): **110,107,105,104,103 101,99,98,90,87**
toteswingers 1&2 £2.80, 1&3 £6.60, 2&3 £4.70 CSF £18.12 CT £66.82 TOTE £7.00: £2.40, £1.50, £1.90; EX 22.00 Trifecta £48.80 Pool: £4,589.85 - 70.46 winning units.
Owner Penna Racing **Bred** P Byrne **Trained** Ledbury, H'fords

FOCUS
A fair handicap featuring a handful of unexposed sorts. The gallop seemed reasonable throughout and this race should throw up its share of winners. The winner came down the centre.

1319 MASCOT GRAND NATIONAL 06.05.13 H'CAP 7f (P)
8:00 (8:01) (Class 6) (0-65,65) 3-Y-0 **£1,940** (£577; £288; £144) **Stalls** Low

Form RPR

56-4 **1** **Idle Curiosity (IRE)**8 1180 3-8-7 **51** oh1......................... HayleyTurner 1 55
(Jim Boyle) *sn restrained bhd ldng pair: wnt 2nd over 2f out: carried lft but drvn to ld over 1f out: styd on wl* **2/1**1

3341 **2** *¾* **Black Truffle (FR)**17 1055 3-8-9 **53**..............................(v) RobertHavlin 5 55
(Mark Usher) *hld up in midfield: stdy prog over 2f out: wnt 2nd and chal over 1f out: nt qckn ins fnl f* **5/1**2

5231 **3** *1 ½* **Actonetaketwo**12 1118 3-8-4 **53**...................................... PhilipPrince(5) 6 51
(Ron Hodges) *chsd ldng trio: rdn over 2f out: no imp tl styd on fnl f to take 3rd nr fin* **11/2**3

640- **4** *nk* **La Luz Del Sol**109 8138 3-9-0 **58**...................................... PaulHanagan 9 55
(Richard Fahey) *chsd ldr to over 2f out: sn struggling u.p: outpcd over 1f out: kpt on again fnl f* **8/1**

333- **5** *½* **Fiducia**313 2442 3-9-5 **63**.. SebSanders 2 59
(Simon Dow) *hld up in last pair: stdy prog over 2f out: rdn to try to chal over 1f out: wknd ins fnl f* **6/1**

354- **6** *¾* **Boleyn**236 5032 3-9-7 **65**.. JamieSpencer 7 59
(Olly Stevens) *hld up towards rr: shkn up and hung lft over 2f out: no ch after: styd on quite wl nr fin* **10/1**

004- **7** *½* **Fossa**197 6332 3-8-9 **53**... JimCrowley 4 45
(Dean Ivory) *led: hung lft fr 2f out: hdd over 1f out: wknd* **8/1**

000- **8** *4* **Ropehanger**179 6871 3-8-10 **57**.. DarrenEgan(3) 8 39
(Lee Carter) *hld up in last pair: carried lft over 2f out: no ch after* **16/1**

1m 27.15s (1.15) **Going Correction** -0.05s/f (Stan) 8 Ran SP% **116.9**
Speed ratings (Par 96): **91,90,88,88,87 86,86,81**
toteswingers 1&2 £2.40, 1&3 £2.60, 2&3 £2.40 CSF £12.38 CT £48.20 TOTE £3.60: £1.40, £1.30, £1.30; EX 15.50 Trifecta £47.50 Pool: £4,579.30 - 72.21 winning units.
Owner Inside Track Racing Club **Bred** Mountarmstrong Stud **Trained** Epsom, Surrey

FOCUS
Several unexposed sorts in a modest handicap. The gallop was ordinary and, although the field fanned across the track, the winner came down the centre.

1320 FAMILY FUN 13.04.13 H'CAP 1m (P)
8:30 (8:30) (Class 6) (0-65,69) 3-Y-0 **£1,940** (£577; £288; £144) **Stalls** Low

Form RPR

0-05 **1** **Echo Brava**19 1014 3-9-6 **64**... SteveDrowne 2 68
(Luke Dace) *hld up in tch: shkn up over 2f out: grad clsd fr over 1f out: styd on fnl f to ld last 50yds* **8/1**3

40-5 **2** *nk* **Sam Spade (IRE)**16 1057 3-9-7 **65**............................... RichardHughes 4 69
(Richard Hannon) *racd wd early: led 1f: trckd ldr: rdn to chal over 1f out: upsides 75yds out: jst outpcd* **4/5**1

2541 **3** *hd* **Hidden Link**9 1171 3-9-11 **69** 6ex.. LukeMorris 3 72
(Ronald Harris) *led after 1f: wound it up fr 3f out: drvn over 1f out: kpt on but hdd and dropped to 3rd last 50yds* **7/4**2

3-03 **4** *2 ¼* **Otto The First**16 1066 3-8-4 **53**....................................... RobertTart(5) 1 51
(John Best) *trckd ldrs: rdn to chal wl over 1f out: nt qckn and fdd fnl f* **14/1**

0465 **5** *nk* **Duchess Of Dreams**17 1055 3-8-2 **51** oh3.................... PhilipPrince(5) 5 48
(Richard Guest) *sn hld up in last: rdn 2f out: one pce and nvr any imp on ldrs* **50/1**

1m 41.25s (1.45) **Going Correction** -0.05s/f (Stan) 5 Ran SP% **111.7**
Speed ratings (Par 96): **90,89,89,87,86**
CSF £15.44 TOTE £11.90: £4.80, £1.10; EX 24.00 Trifecta £43.30 Pool: £961.79 - 16.65 winning units.
Owner MCSD Racing & Mark Benton **Bred** Adweb Ltd **Trained** Five Oaks, W Sussex

FOCUS
A modest handicap in which the pace was on the steady side to the intersection and this bare form doesn't look altogether reliable. The winner came down the centre in the straight.
T/Plt: £40.80 to a £1 stake. Pool: £56,119.74 - 1,003.46 winning units T/Qpdt: £2.20 to a £1 stake. Pool: £6,302.87 - 2,058.35 winning units JN

1193 LINGFIELD (L-H)
Wednesday, April 3

OFFICIAL GOING: Standard
Wind: Fresh; half against Weather: Overcast; cold and breezy

1321 LINGFIELD PARK OWNERS GROUP FILLIES' H'CAP 1m 2f (P)
2:00 (2:01) (Class 4) (0-80,79) 3-Y-0 **£4,690** (£1,395; £697; £348) **Stalls** Low

Form RPR

50-3 **1** **Jathabah (IRE)**13 1099 3-8-9 67... RyanMoore 3 76
(Clive Brittain) *chsd ldr tl rdn to ld ent fnl 2f: clr and edging rt fr over 1f out: r.o wl: comf* **2/1**2

533 **2** *6* **Hawaiian Dream (IRE)**28 904 3-8-4 62......................... AndreaAtzeni 4 59
(Roger Teal) *in tch in last: rdn and hdwy over 2f out: 3rd and outpcd wl over 1f out: wnt 2nd fnl 100yds: no ch w wnr* **10/1**

231 **3** *1* **Oratorio's Joy (IRE)**22 972 3-9-3 75......................... FergusSweeney 2 70
(Jamie Osborne) *chsd ldng pair: rdn and effrt 2f out: chsd clr wnr over 1f out: no imp and lost 2nd fnl 100yds* **6/1**3

1- **4** *14* **Light Rose (IRE)**181 6817 3-9-7 79...................................... JoeFanning 1 53
(Mark Johnston) *led tl hdd and rdn ent fnl 2f: fnd virtually nil and sn btn: bhd and eased ins fnl f* **4/5**1

2m 5.72s (-0.88) **Going Correction** 0.0s/f (Stan) 4 Ran SP% **112.3**
Speed ratings (Par 97): **103,98,97,86**
CSF £17.34 TOTE £3.70; EX 19.80 Trifecta £31.60 Pool: £1,355.52 - 32.07 winning units.
Owner Mohammed Al Nabouda **Bred** Rabbah Bloodstock Limited **Trained** Newmarket, Suffolk

FOCUS
A disappointing turnout for a fair prize and, with the hot favourite running appallingly, the form is hard to fathom.

1322 TTS NETWORKS CLAIMING STKS 1m (P)
2:30 (2:30) (Class 6) 3-Y-O+ £2,045 (£603; £302) Stalls High

Form RPR
2311 1 **Saharia (IRE)**[33] 839 6-9-11 77 (v) ShaneKelly 6 77+
(Daniel Mark Loughnane) *hld up in tch in 3rd: hdwy to trck ldr over 2f out: cruised upsides ldr 1f out: qcknd to ld ins fnl f: sn clr: easily* **4/7**[1]
5-36 2 4 **Benandonner (USA)**[17] 1054 10-9-11 62 JoeFanning 3 66
(Paddy Butler) *chsd ldr tl over 2f out: sn rdn and unable qck: 3rd and btn 1f out: no ch w wnr but plugged on to go 2nd fnl 50yds* **10/1**
3045 3 ¾ **The Mongoose**[18] 1039 5-9-9 60 (vt) AdamKirby 5 62
(David Evans) *led: rdn 2f out: hdd and readily brushed aside ins fnl f: wknd and lost 2nd fnl 50yds* **7/2**[2]
0012 4 ¾ **Daniel Thomas (IRE)**[10] 1161 11-9-8 58 (tp) CathyGannon 4 60
(Violet M Jordan) *hld up in last: rdn and outpcd 2f out: no ch w wnr but kpt on and edgd lft fnl f* **6/1**[3]

1m 38.97s (0.77) **Going Correction** 0.0s/f (Stan) 4 Ran SP% 109.3
Speed ratings (Par 101): **96,92,91,90**
CSF £6.80 TOTE £1.30; EX 4.70 Trifecta £8.00 Pool: £1,094.00 - 101.86 winning units.
Owner Brooklands Racing **Bred** Woodcote Stud Ltd **Trained** Baldwin's Gate, Staffs

FOCUS
An uncompetitive claimer, though this time odds-on backers never had a moment's worry.

1323 YES EVENTS MEDIAN AUCTION MAIDEN STKS 7f (P)
3:00 (3:02) (Class 6) 3-5-Y-O £2,045 (£603; £302) Stalls Low

Form RPR
4- 1 **Theodore Gericault (IRE)**[250] 4539 3-8-12 0 RyanMoore 9 74+
(Sir Michael Stoute) *chsd ldr: rdn to chal and clr of field over 1f out: hanging lft 1f out: led ins fnl f: kpt on: rdn out* **6/4**[1]
025- 2 nk **Arctic Admiral (IRE)**[138] 7737 3-8-12 70 RichardHughes 1 73
(Richard Hannon) *led: jnd wl over 1f out: sn rdn and drew clr w wnr over 1f out: hdd ins fnl f: kpt on but a jst hld* **10/1**
3 1 **Secret Session (USA)** 3-8-12 0 AdamKirby 8 70+
(Marco Botti) *s.i.s: hld up towards rr: hdwy into midfield over 2f out: chsd clr ldng pair 1f out: styd on wl fnl 100yds: nt rch ldrs* **7/4**[2]
3-4 4 1½ **Kohlaan (IRE)**[14] 1086 3-8-12 0 AndreaAtzeni 7 66
(Roger Varian) *t.k.h: chsd ldrs: rdn and outpcd over 1f out: 4th and looked wl hld 1f out: edgd lft and kpt on fnl f* **9/2**[3]
0 5 6 **Logans Lad (IRE)**[47] 673 3-8-12 0 (t) ShaneKelly 3 50
(Daniel Mark Loughnane) *hld up in tch towards rr: nt clr run 2f out: bhd and swtchd rt wl over 1f out: nudged along and kpt on fnl f: no ch w ldrs* **100/1**
53 6 ½ **Gift Of Silence**[14] 1086 4-9-7 0 NeilCallan 4 49
(John Berry) *chsd ldng trio: rdn and struggling wl over 2f out: outpcd and btn wl over 1f out* **25/1**
7 ½ **Transluscent (IRE)** 3-8-5 0 DanielMuscutt[(7)] 2 47+
(Andrew Balding) *stdd s: t.k.h: hld up in rr: lost tch w ldng pair wl over 1f out: rdn and modest hdwy jst over 1f out: no imp fnl f* **33/1**
56 8 1¾ **Visual Aspect**[14] 1086 3-8-12 0 JimCrowley 6 43
(Dean Ivory) *t.k.h: hld up in tch in midfield: rdn and outpcd wl over 1f out: 5th and wl btn 1f out* **66/1**
0-0 9 ¾ **Born To Run**[33] 849 3-8-7 0 (b) MartinLane 5 36
(Hugo Palmer) *rdn along leaving stalls: midfield whn short of room sn after s: in tch towards rr after: rdn and struggling over 2f out: bhd wl over 1f out* **100/1**

1m 24.33s (-0.47) **Going Correction** 0.0s/f (Stan)
WFA 3 from 4yo 14lb 9 Ran SP% 113.9
Speed ratings (Par 101): **102,101,100,98,91 91,90,88,87**
toteswingers 1&2 £3.90, 1&3 £1.50, 2&3 £4.00 CSF £16.41 TOTE £3.20: £1.10, £2.40, £1.10; EX 11.80 Trifecta £28.90 Pool: £4,229.74 - 109.53 winning units.
Owner Ballymacoll Stud **Bred** Ballymacoll Stud Farm Ltd **Trained** Newmarket, Suffolk

FOCUS
Only four mattered in this maiden according to the market.

1324 BLYTHE HILL TAVERN H'CAP 5f (P)
3:30 (3:31) (Class 6) (0-65,65) 4-Y-O+ £2,045 (£453; £453) Stalls High

Form RPR
4513 1 **Dark Lane**[25] 946 7-9-6 64 RichardHughes 1 69
(David Evans) *chsd ldrs: swtchd rt and stl on bit over 1f out: rdn and asked for effrt 1f out: r.o u.p to ld wl ins fnl f: eased last strides* **9/2**[3]
0612 2 ½ **Speedyfix**[13] 1101 6-9-1 59 (t) TomMcLaughlin 4 62
(Christine Dunnett) *hld up in tch in last pair: nt clr run 2f out: rdn and hdwy 1f out: str burst to chal ins fnl f: unable qck towards fin* **7/1**
0000 2 dht **Beauty Pageant (IRE)**[13] 1102 6-9-5 63 (t) AdamKirby 8 66
(David Evans) *t.k.h: chsd ldr: rdn to chal 2f out: drvn to ld 1f out: hdd and no ex wl ins fnl f* **3/1**[1]
3302 4 ½ **Pharoh Jake**[7] 1196 5-8-13 57 SeanLevey 5 58
(John Bridger) *t.k.h: chsd ldrs: swtchd rt and short of room jst over 2f out: hdwy u.p 1f out: styd on same pce towards fin* **9/2**[3]
5102 5 1¼ **Chevise (IRE)**[9] 1173 5-9-3 61 (p) MatthewDavies 6 58
(Steve Woodman) *in tch in midfield: hdwy to chse ldrs and rdn jst over 1f out: unable qck ent fnl f: outpcd fnl f* **14/1**
6-00 6 1 **You'relikemefrank**[54] 560 7-8-10 54 (p) FrederikTylicki 3 47
(Richard Ford) *led: rdn and hdd 1f out: wknd fnl 100yds* **10/1**
520 7 2½ **Quality Art (USA)**[13] 1101 5-9-7 65 (b) RobbieFitzpatrick 2 49
(Richard Guest) *v.s.a: clsd and tagged on to bk of the field over 3f out: rdn and nt qckn over 1f out: wknd fnl f* **7/2**[2]

1m 0.56s (1.76) **Going Correction** 0.0s/f (Stan) 7 Ran SP% 111.8
TOTE £3.20: £1.10 TRIFECTA 2-3-5 £35.20. 2-5-3 £36.30. Pool: £2,926.27 Owner.

FOCUS
A moderate sprint handicap, but a tight finish.

1325 VINES BMW H'CAP 2m (P)
4:00 (4:01) (Class 6) (0-60,60) 4-Y-O+ £2,045 (£603; £302) Stalls Low

Form RPR
5522 1 **Honest Strike (USA)**[11] 1146 6-9-2 52 (b) ShaneKelly 7 59+
(Daniel Mark Loughnane) *stdd s: hld up in rr: clsd and stl on bit over 2f out: swtchd out rt over 1f out: pushed along and r.o wl fnl f to ld: comf* **8/1**
5152 2 1¼ **Rollin 'n Tumblin**[9] 1175 9-9-0 50 JimmyQuinn 5 55
(Michael Attwater) *hld up in tch in last trio: hdwy into midfield over 2f out: drvn and styd on fr over 1f out: led fnl 100yds tl hdd and outpcd wl ins fnl f* **2/1**[1]
3334 3 ½ **Barachiel**[10] 1158 5-9-10 60 RichardHughes 2 64
(Luke Dace) *chsd ldrs: rdn and effrt 2f out: drvn and ev ch ins fnl f: styd on same pce wl ins fnl f* **3/1**[2]
000- 4 1½ **Barnacle**[104] 8177 4-8-6 46 oh1 (v[1]) JoeFanning 3 48
(Pat Eddery) *chsd ldr: rdn and chal over 1f out: led 1f out: hdd fnl 100yds: no ex* **8/1**
-300 5 ½ **Ice Apple**[21] 983 5-8-7 46 oh1 (p) NataliaGemelova[(3)] 8 48
(John E Long) *in tch in midfield: rdn and dropped to rr but stl in tch over 2f out: kpt on u.p fnl f: nt pce to threaten ldrs* **50/1**
0-05 6 nk **Amen (IRE)**[16] 1060 5-9-6 56 RyanMoore 6 57
(Gary Moore) *led: rdn 2f out: drvn and hdd 1f out: wknd ins fnl f* **7/1**
-545 7 ½ **Soweto Star (IRE)**[16] 1062 5-9-1 56 RobertTart[(5)] 1 57
(John Best) *in tch in midfield: rdn and effrt 2f out: plugged on same pce u.p: hld whn short of room wl ins fnl f* **5/1**[3]
504- 8 1 **Irons On Fire (USA)**[37] 8153 5-9-3 53 (b) KierenFox 4 52
(Lee Carter) *t.k.h: hld up in last trio: rdn and effrt on inner over 1f out: plugging on same pce and hld whn nt clr run and eased wl ins fnl f* **25/1**

3m 25.54s (-0.16) **Going Correction** 0.0s/f (Stan)
WFA 4 from 5yo+ 4lb 8 Ran SP% 115.5
Speed ratings (Par 101): **100,99,99,98,98 97,97,97**
toteswingers 1&2 £3.00, 1&3 £3.80, 2&3 £2.00 CSF £24.72 CT £60.05 TOTE £6.80: £2.40, £1.10, £1.60; EX 21.80 Trifecta £67.40 Pool: £2,898.30 - 32.22 winning units.
Owner K Kilbane, J O'Shea & S Hunt **Bred** Juddmonte Farms Inc **Trained** Baldwin's Gate, Staffs

FOCUS
A moderate staying handicap and the whole field were still within a few lengths of each other entering the last furlong.

1326 ARUNDEL H'CAP 1m 4f (P)
4:30 (4:30) (Class 6) (0-60,59) 3-Y-O £2,045 (£603; £302) Stalls Low

Form RPR
4345 1 **Rainford Glory (IRE)**[16] 1064 3-9-2 54 JamieSpencer 3 60
(David Simcock) *hld up in tch in rr: clsd to trck ldr and swtchd rt over 1f out: rdn along hands and heels to ld and pushed rt ins fnl f: rn and a doing enough after* **4/1**[2]
50-5 2 ½ **Handiwork**[35] 814 3-9-7 59 HayleyTurner 4 64
(Michael Bell) *taken down early: chsd ldr: rdn to chal 2f out: drvn to ld ent fnl f: hdd and wnt rt u.p ins fnl f: kpt on wl but a hld* **4/6**[1]
65-3 3 4 **Train Hard**[13] 1103 3-9-3 55 JoeFanning 1 54
(Mark Johnston) *chsd ldng pair: rdn over 3f out: kpt on u.p and styd chsng ldrs tl wknd ins fnl f* **9/2**[3]
0-52 4 1½ **Aphrodite Spirit (IRE)**[36] 804 3-9-0 52 DaneO'Neill 2 48
(Pat Eddery) *led: rdn and jnd 2f out: hdd ent fnl f: wknd ins fnl f* **8/1**

2m 33.2s (0.20) **Going Correction** 0.0s/f (Stan) 4 Ran SP% 109.3
Speed ratings (Par 96): **99,98,96,95**
CSF £7.35 TOTE £3.80; EX 8.20 Trifecta £11.50 Pool: £1,407.88 - 91.71 winning units.
Owner Dr Marwan Koukash **Bred** Her Diamond Necklace **Trained** Newmarket, Suffolk

FOCUS
A moderate 3yo handicap in which all four runners were in a line across the track passing the furlong pole.

1327 LINGFIELD PARK SUPPORTS BHEST H'CAP 1m 2f (P)
5:00 (5:01) (Class 4) (0-85,81) 4-Y-O+ £4,690 (£1,395; £697; £348) Stalls Low

Form RPR
304- 1 **Fortieth And Fifth (IRE)**[244] 4741 4-9-6 80 JamieSpencer 6 89+
(Michael Bell) *chsd ldr tl led over 2f out: hld on wl u.p fnl f: rdn out* **6/4**[1]
3-04 2 hd **Lord Ofthe Shadows (IRE)**[32] 865 4-9-7 81 (b[1]) RichardHughes 5 89
(Richard Hannon) *hld up in tch in last quartet: hdwy to chse ldr jst over 2f out: ev ch and rdn 1f out: drvn and kpt on ins fnl f: a jst hld* **3/1**[2]
00-1 3 1¼ **Destiny Of Dreams**[81] 190 5-9-3 77 DaneO'Neill 7 83
(Jo Crowley) *in tch in midfield: effrt u.p to chse ldrs ent fnl f: styd on same pce fnl f* **14/1**
5-32 4 ½ **Jewelled**[28] 906 7-9-0 74 SebSanders 2 79
(Lady Herries) *hld up in tch in last quartet: hdwy u.p over 1f out: kpt on same pce u.p fnl 100yds* **6/1**[3]
-332 5 nk **Brimstone Hill (IRE)**[14] 1092 4-9-6 80 WilliamCarson 9 84+
(Anthony Carson) *stdd and dropped in bhd after s: hld up in last pair: rdn and effrt over 1f out: styd on u.p fnl f: nt rch ldrs* **8/1**
5030 6 2 **Ajeeb (USA)**[18] 1037 5-9-4 78 (v) JimCrowley 3 78
(Michael Scudamore) *chsd ldrs: drvn over 1f out: no ex 1f out: wknd fnl 100yds* **14/1**
4-20 7 hd **Flying Trader (USA)**[16] 1059 4-8-6 73 IanBurns[(7)] 8 73
(Jane Chapple-Hyam) *stdd and dropped in bhd s: hld up in last pair: hdwy and chsng ldrs whn wd bnd wl over 1f out: lost pl and bhd over 1f out: plugged on fnl f* **16/1**
1104 8 3 **Idol Deputy (FR)**[15] 1081 7-8-8 73 (v[1]) RachealKneller[(5)] 1 67
(Mark Usher) *hld up in tch in midfield: shuffled bk to rr on inner jst over 2f out: swtchd rt and tried to rally over 1f out: no real imp fnl f* **16/1**
500- 9 7 **Megalala (IRE)**[185] 6703 12-9-2 76 KieranO'Neill 4 56
(John Bridger) *led: rdn 3f out: hdd and struggling over 2f out: bhd 1f out* **50/1**

2m 4.62s (-1.98) **Going Correction** 0.0s/f (Stan) 9 Ran SP% 117.5
Speed ratings (Par 105): **107,106,105,105,105 103,103,101,95**
toteswingers 1&2 £2.20, 1&3 £5.70, 2&3 £5.60 CSF £6.04 CT £44.17 TOTE £2.80: £1.30, £2.00, £3.40; EX 10.00 Trifecta £73.60 Pool: £2,945.52 - 29.99 winning units.
Owner Colin Bryce **Bred** Airlie Stud **Trained** Newmarket, Suffolk

FOCUS
A decent handicap, run at a fair pace, and it produced a thrilling finish.

T/Plt: £65.20 to a £1 stake. Pool: £50,480.60 - 565.17 winning units T/Qpdt: £10.70 to a £1 stake. Pool: £4,228.06 - 291.20 winning units SP

1305 SOUTHWELL (L-H)

Wednesday, April 3

OFFICIAL GOING: Standard

Wind: Blustery; half against Weather: Sunny periods

1328 £32 BONUS AT 32RED.COM MAIDEN AUCTION STKS 5f (F)

2:20 (2:22) (Class 6) 2-Y-O £1,940 (£577; £288; £144) Stalls High

Form RPR

1 **Royal Warrior** 2-9-5 0 AndrewMullen 1 68+
(Alan McCabe) *cl up on outer: led 2f out: rdn: green and hung rt over 1f out: drvn and edgd rt ins fnl f: styd on wl towards fin* 6/4[1]

3 2 1 3/4 **Far Gaze (IRE)**[7] 1208 2-9-5 0 LiamJones 4 68
(J S Moore) *chsd ldrs: hdwy 2f out: rdn to chse wnr over 1f out: chal and ev ch whn n.m.r on stands' rail ent fnl f: sn rdn and kpt on same pce after* 7/1

3 5 **Tyrsal (IRE)** 2-9-5 0 AdamBeschizza 3 44
(Robert Eddery) *cl up: effrt 2f out: sn rdn and one pce appr fnl f* 5/2[2]

4 4 3 **El Duque**[10] 1156 2-8-12 0 RyanWhile(7) 2 33
(Bill Turner) *slt ld: pushed along and hdd 2f out: sn rdn and hung lft: wknd over 1f out* 3/1[3]

5 15 **Red House** 2-9-5 0 AdrianNicholls 5
(David C Griffiths) *dwlt: a in rr* 25/1

1m 4.99s (5.29) **Going Correction** +0.675s/f (Slow) 5 Ran SP% **109.9**
Speed ratings (Par 90): **84,81,73,68,44**
CSF £12.21 TOTE £1.70: £1.10, £3.90; EX 11.60 Trifecta £32.10 Pool: £2,055.89 - 47.90 winning units.
Owner Premspace Ltd **Bred** A S Denniff **Trained** Averham Park, Notts
■ Stewards' Enquiry : Andrew Mullen two-day ban: careless riding (17-18 Apr)

FOCUS
There was a stiff cross breeze during the morning which contributed to the drying out of the Fibresand. This prompted the Clerk of the course to water and harrow the surface before racing but the going remained standard. An ordinary time and modest form.

1329 BRITISH STALLION STUDS 32RED.COM EBF MAIDEN FILLIES STKS 1m (F)

2:50 (2:50) (Class 5) 3-Y-O+ £3,881 (£1,155; £577; £288) Stalls Low

Form RPR

4 1 **Hot Right Now**[19] 1019 3-8-12 0 LukeMorris 4 59
(Mrs K Burke) *chsd ldng pair: pushed along 3f out: swtchd lft and rdn over 2f out: styd on u.p to chal ent fnl f: drvn and styd on to ld last 100yds* 9/4[2]

54 2 3/4 **Solarmaite**[15] 1072 4-9-10 0 MarkCoumbe(3) 3 61
(Roy Bowring) *slt ld: rdn along 2f out: drvn over 1f out: hdd and no ex last 100yds* 8/1

0- 3 7 **Montjess (IRE)**[182] 6790 3-8-12 0 RichardKingscote 6 41
(Tom Dascombe) *dwlt: sn rdn along and outpcd in rr: bhd 1/2-way: hdwy 2f out: styd on fnl f to take 3rd nr line* 7/4[1]

50-5 4 shd **Jillywinks**[12] 1114 3-8-12 70 RobertWinston 5 41
(Scott Dixon) *cl up: disp ld 3f out: rdn over 2f out: drvn wl over 1f out: sn wknd* 7/2[3]

6 5 3 **Amanda Wolf (IRE)**[12] 1114 3-8-12 0 GrahamLee 1 34
(James Given) *chsd ldng pair on inner: rdn along over 3f out: sn wknd* 12/1

1m 45.99s (2.29) **Going Correction** +0.30s/f (Slow)
WFA 3 from 4yo 15lb 5 Ran SP% **108.2**
Speed ratings (Par 103): **100,99,92,92,89**
CSF £18.01 TOTE £3.60: £4.50, £3.70; EX 12.80 Trifecta £34.70 Pool: £2,401.95 - 51.83 winning units.
Owner Mrs Elaine M Burke **Bred** Hillwood Bloodstock **Trained** Middleham Moor, N Yorks
■ Stewards' Enquiry : Robert Winston jockey said, regarding the running and riding, that having been up with the pace until inside the final furlong, his filly weakened quickly failing to respond to a couple of smacks, so he rode her out hands and heels to the line

FOCUS
Only a modest maiden but the first two pulled clear and may be capable of better.

1330 CORRUGATED CASE CO H'CAP 1m (F)

3:20 (3:20) (Class 5) (0-70,68) 3-Y-O £2,587 (£770; £384; £192) Stalls Low

Form RPR

-131 1 **Apache Rising**[7] 1206 3-9-8 68 6ex TomEaves 1 73
(Bryan Smart) *cl up on inner: led 3f out: pushed clr wl over 1f out: kpt on* 1/4[1]

200- 2 2 1/4 **Bougaloo**[140] 7713 3-9-2 67 WilliamTwiston-Davies(5) 3 67
(Alan McCabe) *slt ld: hdd 3f out and sn rdn along: drvn wl over 1f out and kpt on same pce* 20/1[3]

-432 3 1 **Mudaawem (USA)**[9] 1171 3-9-2 62 FrannyNorton 2 60
(Mark Johnston) *cl up: rdn along after 2f: sn lost pl and rdn along in rr: styd on u.p fnl 2f: n.d* 4/1[2]

00-0 4 1 3/4 **Firstkissoflove**[79] 209 3-9-4 64 AdrianNicholls 4 58
(David C Griffiths) *t.k.h: trckd ldrs: hdwy over 2f out: sn swtchd lft and rdn: one pce fr wl over 1f out* 40/1

1m 46.14s (2.44) **Going Correction** +0.30s/f (Slow) 4 Ran SP% **107.2**
Speed ratings (Par 98): **99,96,95,94**
CSF £6.49 TOTE £1.30; EX 5.40 Trifecta £9.80 Pool: £1,520.93 - 115.34 winning units.
Owner The Smart Distant Music Partnership **Bred** Southill Stud **Trained** Hambleton, N Yorks

FOCUS
An uncompetitive handicap.

1331 BINARY TRENDS - INVEST WITH BINARYTRENDS.CO.UK H'CAP 5f (F)

3:50 (3:50) (Class 5) (0-75,74) 4-Y-O+ £2,587 (£770; £384; £192) Stalls High

Form RPR

000- 1 **Monnoyer**[219] 5662 4-8-12 65 (be[1]) LukeMorris 8 73
(Scott Dixon) *cl up: rdn over 1f out: styd on to ld last 100yds: drvn and hung lft towards fin* 13/2

4410 2 hd **Shawkantango**[13] 1101 6-8-9 69 (v) AdamMcLean(7) 5 76
(Derek Shaw) *dwlt and sn outpcd in rr: hdwy on wd outside wl over 1f out: rdn and styd on fnl f: fining wl whn sltly hmpd towards fin* 7/2[2]

0-14 3 3/4 **Love You Louis**[16] 1058 7-9-2 69 (v) AdrianNicholls 2 73
(J R Jenkins) *led: rdn wl over 1f out: drvn and edgd lft ins fnl f: hdd and no ex last 100yds* 9/2[3]

5-11 4 4 **Clubland (IRE)**[29] 885 4-9-3 73 MarkCoumbe(3) 7 63
(Roy Bowring) *dwlt and swtchd rt s: hdwy 1/2-way: rdn to chse ldng pair over 1f out: sn edgd lft and wknd* 10/11[1]

2033 5 1/2 **Steel City Boy (IRE)**[8] 1186 10-8-5 63 oh6 ow3 AnnStokell(5) 9 51
(Ann Stokell) *cl up: rdn along 1/2-way: wknd fnl 2f* 20/1

1m 1.9s (2.20) **Going Correction** +0.675s/f (Slow) 5 Ran SP% **110.9**
Speed ratings (Par 103): **109,108,107,101,100**
CSF £28.60 TOTE £13.10: £3.30, £2.10; EX 24.10 Trifecta £84.70 Pool: £2,103.45 - 18.60 winning units.
Owner Paul J Dixon **Bred** David John Brown **Trained** Babworth, Notts

FOCUS
This handicap was weakened by the four non-runners but it was run at a solid pace.

1332 BINARY TRENDS - RISK FREE INVESTMENTS APPRENTICE (S) STKS 1m 3f (F)

4:20 (4:20) (Class 6) 3-Y-O £2,045 (£603; £302) Stalls Low

Form RPR

040- 1 **Darakti (IRE)**[134] 7796 3-9-2 43 (p) WilliamTwiston-Davies 3 55
(Alan McCabe) *trckd ldrs: hdwy 3f out: swtchd rt over 2f out: led wl over 1f out: sn rdn clr: styd on* 7/1[3]

0-05 2 8 **Ceekay's Girl**[19] 1016 3-8-11 45 MichaelJMMurphy 4 36
(Mrs K Burke) *trckd ldrs: pushed along on outer and outpcd 3f out: rdn 2f out: styd on u.p fnl f: no ch w wnr* 11/4[2]

5-22 3 1 1/2 **Rakticate (IRE)**[76] 237 3-8-6 63 CharlotteJenner(5) 2 33
(J S Moore) *t.k.h: trckd ldng pair: hdwy on inner to take slt advantage after 3f: rdn along 3f out: hdd over 2f out: sn one pce* 4/7[1]

0-00 4 2 **Positive Parenting (IRE)**[46] 685 3-8-6 38 JeanVanOvermeire(5) 1 30
(Stuart Williams) *awkward s: sn led and pushed along: hdd after 3f and cl up: rdn along 3f out: led briefly over 2f out: hdd & wknd wl over 1f out* 25/1

2m 33.49s (5.49) **Going Correction** +0.30s/f (Slow) 4 Ran SP% **106.7**
Speed ratings (Par 96): **92,86,85,83**
CSF £24.22 TOTE £7.40; EX 21.50 Trifecta £44.80 Pool: £1,235.23 - 20.65 winning units.There was no bid for the winner.
Owner Mrs D E Sharp **Bred** Mrs Mary Coonan **Trained** Averham Park, Notts

FOCUS
An uncompetitive seller but a shock result all the same with the favourite underperforming.

1333 32RED CASINO H'CAP 1m 3f (F)

4:50 (4:50) (Class 5) (0-70,70) 4-Y-O+ £2,587 (£770; £384; £192) Stalls Low

Form RPR

-231 1 **Linroyale Boy (USA)**[11] 1146 5-8-10 59 RobertWinston 2 66
(Alan Swinbank) *trckd ldrs: pushed along and outpcd 5f out: hdwy on outer to chse ldrs 3f out: rdn to chal wl over 1f out: drvn and styd on wl to ld last 75yds* 13/8[1]

4623 2 3/4 **Thereabouts (USA)**[8] 1184 4-9-0 63 AndrewMullen 5 69
(Michael Appleby) *prom: hdwy to ld 3f out: rdn 2f out: jnd wl over 1f out and sn drvn: hdd and no ex last 75yds* 7/2[2]

2333 3 5 **Xpres Maite**[7] 1201 10-8-8 60 (v) MarkCoumbe(3) 7 57
(Roy Bowring) *dwlt and reminders in rr: hdwy on outer to ld after 3f: pushed along and hdd 4f out: rdn 3f out: kpt on same pce u.p fnl 2f* 11/1

0003 4 4 1/2 **Standpoint**[6] 1220 7-9-7 70 LukeMorris 3 59
(Conor Dore) *prom: rdn along over 3f out: drvn 2f out and sn one pce* 7/2[2]

0325 5 nk **Stanley Rigby**[22] 969 7-9-3 66 (b) TonyHamilton 6 54
(Richard Fahey) *sn led: hdd after 3f: cl up: led again 4f out: rdn and hdd 3f out: sn drvn and grad wknd* 5/1[3]

60-0 6 29 **Nibani (IRE)**[15] 1076 6-9-3 69 SimonPearce(3) 4 5
(John Butler) *a towards rr: bhd fnl 3f* 40/1

45-0 7 23 **Sunny Bank**[10] 1161 4-8-2 56 oh2 MichaelJMMurphy(5) 1
(Alan Coogan) *a in rr: outpcd and bhd fr 1/2-way* 50/1

2m 30.31s (2.31) **Going Correction** +0.30s/f (Slow) 7 Ran SP% **111.9**
Speed ratings (Par 103): **103,102,98,95,95 74,57**
toteswingers 1&2 £1.50, 1&3 £3.10, 2&3 £6.10 CSF £7.18 TOTE £2.60: £2.10, £2.30; EX 8.40 Trifecta £35.20 Pool: £2,762.47 - 58.83 winning units.
Owner Spiral Bracken **Bred** Winstar Farm, Llc & Ashford Stud **Trained** Melsonby, N Yorks

FOCUS
A modest handicap with the first two pulling well clear.

1334 32RED H'CAP 7f (F)

5:20 (5:20) (Class 5) (0-75,72) 4-Y-O+ £2,587 (£770; £384; £192) Stalls Low

Form RPR

3212 1 **Ace Master**[7] 1205 5-8-9 63 (b) MarkCoumbe(3) 6 77
(Roy Bowring) *sn led and clr after 2f: rdn 2f out: drvn and edgd rt ins fnl f: kpt on gamely towards fin* 5/2[1]

1232 2 1 1/2 **Hellbender (IRE)**[21] 986 7-8-12 68 (t) MichaelJMMurphy(5) 5 78
(Shaun Harris) *chsd ldrs: hdwy on outer 3f out: rdn to chse wnr 2f out: drvn and edgd lft ent fnl f: no imp towards fin* 10/3[2]

4632 3 3 1/4 **Copperwood**[7] 1203 8-9-5 70 FrannyNorton 3 71
(Mark Johnston) *chsd ldrs on inner: rdn along wl over 2f out: drvn wl over 1f out: kpt on same pce appr fnl f* 7/2[3]

3350 4 3/4 **Piceno (IRE)**[12] 1113 5-9-4 72 (p) BillyCray(3) 4 71
(Scott Dixon) *chsd wnr: rdn along wl over 2f out: drvn wl over 1f out and sn one pce* 6/1

034- 5 4 1/2 **Opus Dei**[116] 8034 6-8-11 67 (p) ShirleyTeasdale(5) 2 54
(Alan McCabe) *a towards rr* 8/1

-054 6 3/4 **Bandstand**[22] 966 7-9-2 72 WilliamTwiston-Davies(5) 1 57
(Bryan Smart) *chsd ldrs: rdn along 3f out: wknd over 2f out* 15/2

1m 31.09s (0.79) **Going Correction** +0.30s/f (Slow) 6 Ran SP% **111.0**
Speed ratings (Par 103): **107,105,101,100,95 94**
tote swingers 1&2 £2.60, 1&3 £1.80, 2&3 £1.70 CSF £10.76 TOTE £3.20: £1.80, £2.50; EX 8.50 Trifecta £29.60 Pool: £2,097.17 - 53.08 winning units.
Owner S R Bowring **Bred** S R Bowring **Trained** Edwinstowe, Notts

FOCUS
Nothing got into this handicap as the winner put the field to the sword from the off under a positive front-running ride.

T/Plt: £1,016.60 to a £1 stake. Pool: £49,369.18 - 35.45 winning units T/Qpdt: £199.00 to a £1 stake. Pool £2,985.94 - 11.10 winning units JR

1321 LINGFIELD (L-H)

Thursday, April 4

OFFICIAL GOING: Standard

Wind: fresh, half against Weather: cold, snow flurries

1342 YES EVENTS LTD APPRENTICE H'CAP — 1m 4f (P)

2:20 (2:20) (Class 6) (0-60,59) 4-Y-0+ **£2,045** (£603; £302) **Stalls** Low

Form				RPR
3430	1		**Shirataki (IRE)**[31] 883 5-9-7 **59** ... PatMillman 3 (Peter Hiatt) *chsd ldrs: wnt 2nd over 4f out: rdn to ld 1f out: kpt on wl: rdn out* **11/4**[1]	67
006	2	¾	**Gabrial's Hope (FR)**[16] 1084 4-9-2 **55** ... (t) AliceHaynes 1 (David Simcock) *t.k.h: led: rdn over 1f out: hdd 1f out: kpt on same pce u.p fnl f* **5/1**	62
0616	3	1¾	**Smirfy's Silver**[19] 1040 9-8-9 **50** ... JordanNason(3) 7 (Michael Mullineaux) *t.k.h: hld up in tch in last trio: hdwy to chse ldrs 2f out: kpt on u.p fnl f: wnt 3rd cl home* **16/1**	54
6011	4	hd	**Midnight Sequel**[22] 983 4-8-11 **53** ... JordanVaughan(3) 6 (Michael Blake) *hld up wl in tch: hdwy to chse ldrs over 2f out: styd on same pce u.p fnl f: lost 3rd cl home* **7/2**[2]	57
1143	5	9	**Time Square (FR)**[15] 1090 6-9-0 **55** ... JoeyHaynes(3) 4 (Tony Carroll) *taken down early: t.k.h: hld up wl in tch: rdn and outpcd 2f out: sn wknd* **9/2**[3]	44
3/0-	6	hd	**Madam Tessa (IRE)**[292] 3143 5-8-5 **48** ... DanielCremin(5) 2 (Tim Vaughan) *t.k.h: chsd ldr for 2f: in tch after: lost pl over 2f out: rdn and wknd 2f out* **14/1**	37
2056	7	7	**Silver Marizah (IRE)**[8] 1207 4-8-2 **48** ... (e) TomasHarrigan(7) 8 (Roger Ingram) *t.k.h: chsd ldr after 2f tl over 4f out: wknd 2f out* **33/1**	26
4-00	8	3	**Silver Six**[10] 1175 4-9-0 **53** ... (t) HannahNunn 5 (Sheena West) *a bhd: niggled along 8f out: lost tch over 2f out* **7/1**	26

2m 32.75s (-0.25) **Going Correction** +0.05s/f (Slow)

WFA 4 from 5yo+ 1lb — **8** Ran SP% **111.7**

Speed ratings (Par 101): **102,101,100,100,94 94,89,87**

Tote Swingers: 1&2 £4.00, 1&3 £10.20, 2&3 £10.10 CSF £15.94 CT £176.87 TOTE £3.50: £2.00, £1.10, £4.20; EX 20.70 Trifecta £252.40 Pool: £2,282.81 - 6.78 winning units..

Owner Carl Demczak **Bred** Deerfield Farm **Trained** Hook Norton, Oxon

FOCUS

The going was standard. Heavy snow began an hour before racing and there was a stiff breeze facing the runners in the home straight. This weak handicap, confined to apprentice riders, was run at steady pace with plenty too keen. The form looks straightforward rated around the winner and third.

1343 BLYTHE HILL TAVERN (S) STKS — 1m 2f (P)

2:55 (2:55) (Class 6) 3-Y-O **£2,045** (£603; £302) **Stalls** Low

Form				RPR
2033	1		**Lady Lunchalot (USA)**[9] 1177 3-8-8 60 ow1 ... (p) RichardHughes 2 (J S Moore) *mde all: qcknd ent fnl 2f: nudged along and in command 1f out: comf* **4/6**[1]	61
0-0	2	2	**Winter Music (IRE)**[16] 1072 3-8-5 0 ... (v[1]) DanielMuscutt(7) 3 (Andrew Balding) *chsd wnr: rdn and hung lft in bhd wnr ent fnl f: hld and one pce after* **7/4**[2]	60
-530	3	6	**Taming The Tweet**[14] 1098 3-8-4 **53** ... DarrenEgan(3) 4 (J R Jenkins) *wl in tch in 3rd: rdn and immediately struggling whn gallop qcknd 2f out: wl btn 1f out* **8/1**[3]	43

2m 12.37s (5.77) **Going Correction** +0.05s/f (Slow) — **3** Ran SP% **107.5**

Speed ratings (Par 96): **78,76,71**

CSF £2.12 TOTE £1.60; EX 2.20 Trifecta £2.20 Pool: £2,108.37 - 689.76 winning units..

Owner M Briddon **Bred** Fred W Hertrich III **Trained** Upper Lambourn, Berks

FOCUS

The snow continued to fall during this weak seller, which was run at a steady pace. The winner is rated to her latest handicap form.

1344 LINGFIELD PARK OWNERS GROUP MEDIAN AUCTION MAIDEN STKS — 5f (P)

3:30 (3:30) (Class 6) 2-Y-O **£2,045** (£603; £302) **Stalls** High

Form				RPR
32	1		**Far Gaze (IRE)**[1] 1328 2-9-5 0 ... LiamJones 5 (J S Moore) *chsd ldng pair: rdn 2f out: str run to ld 1f out: styd on strly* **9/4**[1]	68+
	2	2	**Quatuor (IRE)** 2-9-0 0 ... RichardKingscote 4 (Tom Dascombe) *led: rdn over 1f out: hdd and unable qck 1f out: styd on same pce fnl f* **3/1**[2]	56
	3	1½	**Narborough** 2-9-5 0 ... MartinHarley 2 (Mick Channon) *chsd ldng trio: rdn and effrt to chse ldng pair 1f out: no imp fnl f* **7/2**[3]	55+
2	4	¾	**Diamond Lady**[11] 1156 2-9-0 0 ... J-PGuillambert 6 (Jo Hughes) *pressed ldr: rdn 2f out: unable qck over 1f out: wknd ins fnl f* **4/1**	48
	5	2	**Brockholes Flyer (IRE)** 2-9-5 0 ... SebSanders 1 (Brendan Powell) *in tch in midfield: shkn up over 2f out: outpcd wl over 1f out: rdn and btn ent fnl f: pushed along and plugged on same pce fnl f* **16/1**	46
	6	3¼	**Sleeping Angel** 2-9-0 0 ... JimmyQuinn 7 (Milton Bradley) *s.i.s: clsd and in tch after 1f out: wknd 2f out* **66/1**	29
	7	14	**Blazing Chilli** 2-8-12 0 ... JakePayne(7) 3 (Bill Turner) *dwlt: sn outpcd and bhd: t.o fr 1/2-way* **12/1**	

1m 0.74s (1.94) **Going Correction** +0.05s/f (Slow) — **7** Ran SP% **113.1**

Speed ratings (Par 90): **86,82,80,79,76 70,48**

Tote Swingers: 1&2 £1.60, 1&3 £1.80, 2&3 £3.00 CSF £9.02 TOTE £3.30: £1.20, £2.90; EX 11.20 Trifecta £50.10 Pool: £3,419.60 - 51.18 winning units..

Owner The Moore The Merrier **Bred** Limestone & Tara Studs **Trained** Upper Lambourn, Berks

FOCUS

Only two of the field had run before. The pace was honest with the runners well strung out at the line. The winner scored well but the form looks modest, although difficult to pin down.

1345 LINGFIELD PARK SUPPORTS YOUNG EPILEPSY H'CAP — 6f (P)

4:05 (4:07) (Class 5) (0-75,73) 3-Y-O **£2,726** (£805; £402) **Stalls** Low

Form				RPR
2142	1		**Hard Walnut (IRE)**[31] 879 3-9-7 **73** ... JamieSpencer 4 (Olly Stevens) *mde all: c towards centre and rdn along over 1f out: drvn ins fnl f: jst hld on* **7/2**[2]	80
035-	2	shd	**Purcell (IRE)**[227] 5418 3-9-7 **73** ... JimmyFortune 5 (Andrew Balding) *awkward leaving stalls: in tch in midfield: rdn and hdwy to chse wnr ent fnl f: styd on wl u.p fnl 150yds: jst hld* **11/4**[1]	80+
46-1	3	1¾	**Malaysian Boleh**[62] 470 3-9-2 **68** ... PaulMulrennan 2 (Simon Dow) *hld up in tch towards rr: swtchd out rt and effrt over 1f out: hdwy to chse ldng pair but hanging lft ins fnl f: one pce fnl 100yds* **5/1**[3]	69
333-	4	¾	**Majestic Jess (IRE)**[134] 7812 3-9-2 **68** ... RyanMoore 3 (Luke Dace) *in tch in midfield: niggled along after 2f: rdn and hdwy towards inner over 1f out: styd on same pce ins fnl f* **8/1**	67
4352	5	¾	**Princess Cammie (IRE)**[9] 1180 3-8-0 **59** oh6 ... IanBurns(7) 1 (Mike Murphy) *chsd ldrs: rdn and chsd wnr briefly over 1f out: outpcd and btn whn sltly hmpd ins fnl f* **50/1**	55
2-01	6	3½	**Jimmy Elder**[36] 811 3-9-3 **69** ... RichardHughes 8 (Richard Hannon) *t.k.h: hld up in tch in rr: rdn and effrt over 1f out: no imp and wl hld fnl f* **10/1**	54
2-23	7	1½	**Star Of Rohm**[23] 964 3-8-13 **72** ... LouisSteward(7) 7 (Michael Bell) *in tch in midfield: hung rt and wd bnd 2f out: lost pl and sn rdn: wl hld 1f out* **5/1**[3]	52
413	8	nk	**Nellie Bly**[20] 1014 3-9-2 **68** ... JoeFanning 6 (Mark Johnston) *chsd wnr tl over 1f out: wknd 1f out* **8/1**	47

1m 11.82s (-0.08) **Going Correction** +0.05s/f (Slow) — **8** Ran SP% **115.5**

Speed ratings (Par 98): **102,101,99,98,97 92,90,90**

Tote Swingers: 1&2 £4.20, 1&3 £4.20, 2&3 £3.70 CSF £13.74 CT £47.15 TOTE £4.60: £1.50, £1.10, £2.20; EX 13.10 Trifecta £92.10 Pool: £4,335.76 - 35.29 winning units..

Owner Qatar Racing Limited **Bred** Barbara Prendergast **Trained** Chiddingfold, Surrey

FOCUS

This competitive handicap was run at an honest pace with the winner making all under a fine ride. The third and fifth set the standard.

1346 TTS NETWORKS H'CAP — 6f (P)

4:40 (4:40) (Class 4) (0-80,79) 4-Y-O+ **£4,690** (£1,395; £697; £348) **Stalls** Low

Form				RPR
003-	1		**The Tichborne (IRE)**[139] 7741 5-9-0 **72** ... (v) JackMitchell 5 (Roger Teal) *hld up wl in tch in midfield: rdn and effrt over 1f out: hdwy u.p 1f out: led ins fnl f: hld on wl towards fin* **14/1**	82
412-	2	½	**Nocturn**[256] 4364 4-9-7 **79** ... WilliamBuick 2 (Jeremy Noseda) *chsd ldrs: swtchd rt and n.m.r 1f out: edgd rt again and burst between horses ins fnl f: pressing wnr wl ins fnl f: hld towards fin* **6/4**[1]	87+
1362	3	1	**Alnoomaas (IRE)**[36] 812 4-9-3 **75** ... RyanMoore 3 (Luke Dace) *led: rdn and edging sltly rt ent fnl f: hdd and no ex ins fnl f* **7/2**[2]	80
-310	4	nk	**Temple Road (IRE)**[40] 775 5-9-2 **74** ... RichardKingscote 1 (Milton Bradley) *hld up in tch: stl travelling wl 2f out: clsng on ldrs whn hmpd and swtchd lft 1f out: kpt on ins fnl f* **5/1**[3]	81+
554-	5	1¾	**North Star Boy (IRE)**[147] 7646 4-9-7 **79** ... RichardHughes 6 (Richard Hannon) *chsd ldr: rdn and pressing ldr ent fnl f: stl pressing ldr but one pce whn pushed sltly rt and lost pl pl ins fnl f: nt rcvr and hld after* **5/1**[3]	81+
0-65	6	½	**Rocket Rob (IRE)**[63] 457 7-9-1 **73** ... J-PGuillambert 7 (Willie Musson) *t.k.h: hld up in last pair: rdn and hdwy ent fnl f: kpt on but nvr gng pce to threaten ldrs* **25/1**	70
56-6	7	nse	**Emiratesdotcom**[17] 1067 7-9-3 **75** ... JimmyQuinn 10 (Milton Bradley) *hld up in last trio: rdn and effrt over 1f out: kpt on ins fnl f: nvr gng pce to rch ldrs* **33/1**	72
460-	8	3½	**Batchelors Star (IRE)**[252] 4503 5-9-3 **75** ... (t) MickyFenton 4 (Seamus Durack) *taken down early and led to s: hld up in rr: rdn over 1f out: no real imp: n.d* **50/1**	61
0-00	9	nk	**Little Garcon (USA)**[17] 1067 6-8-12 **75** ... (e) MichaelJMMurphy(5) 9 (Robert Cowell) *dwlt: t.k.h and sn rcvrd to chse ldr: rdn and nt qckn wl over 1f out: wknd fnl f* **20/1**	60
00-1	9	dht	**Pick A Little**[22] 981 5-9-4 **76** ... MartinLane 8 (Michael Blake) *in tch: rdn 2f out: unable qck and btn ent fnl f: wknd fnl 150yds* **20/1**	61

1m 11.59s (-0.31) **Going Correction** +0.05s/f (Slow) — **10** Ran SP% **120.5**

Speed ratings (Par 105): **104,103,102,101,99 98,98,93,93,93**

Tote Swingers: 1&2 £5.60, 1&3 £7.70, 2&3 £2.80 CSF £34.84 CT £97.65 TOTE £15.90: £3.70, £1.20, £1.80; EX 64.60 Trifecta £343.60 Pool: £4,334.96 - 9.45 winning units..

Owner Chris Simpson & Mick Waghorn **Bred** Ms Alyson Flower And Chris Simpson **Trained** Ashtead, Surrey

FOCUS

The pace was honest for this competitive handicap. The third is the best guide to the level.

1347 TTS NETWORKS MAIDEN STKS — 1m 2f (P)

5:15 (5:15) (Class 5) 3-Y-O **£2,726** (£805; £402) **Stalls** Low

Form				RPR
0-	1		**Woodstock (IRE)**[183] 6796 3-9-5 0 ... RichardHughes 3 (Richard Hannon) *stdd s: hld up in tch: rdn and hdwy on outer to press ldrs over 2f out: drvn to ld over 1f out and sn edgd lft u.p: clr ins fnl f: kpt on and a doing enough: rdn out* **7/4**[1]	73+
	2	1	**Fantasy In Blue** 3-9-0 0 ... RyanMoore 5 (Sir Michael Stoute) *in tch in rr: rdn and rn green over 1f out: styd on f: wnt 2nd last strides and gng on fin* **3/1**[2]	66+
	3	shd	**Shalwa** 3-9-0 0 ... AdamKirby 1 (Marco Botti) *restless in stalls: led for 1f: chsd ldng pair after: drvn and effrt on inner 2f out: chsd clr wnr ins fnl f: kpt on but nvr looked like chalng wnr: lost 2nd last strides* **7/4**[1]	66+
00-	4	2¼	**Miss Tiger Lily**[148] 7636 3-9-0 0 ... LiamJones 4 (Harry Dunlop) *s.i.s: bhd: hdwy to ld 8f out: rdn and hdd over 1f out: unable qck u.p: styd on same pce and lost 2 pls ins fnl f* **33/1**	61
06-	5	7	**Jan De Heem**[126] 7924 3-9-5 0 ... JimCrowley 2 (Ralph Beckett) *rdn along at times: chsd ldr tl led after 1f: hdd 8f out: chsd ldr after tl squeezed for room bnd wl over 1f out: lost pl over 1f out: wknd 1f out* **10/1**[3]	52

2m 7.53s (0.93) **Going Correction** +0.05s/f (Slow) — **5** Ran SP% **109.8**

Speed ratings (Par 98): **98,97,97,95,89**

CSF £7.31 TOTE £2.80: £2.20, £1.30; EX 7.60 Trifecta £15.90 Pool: £2,488.62 - 116.97 winning units..

Owner Mrs J Wood **Bred** Butlersgrove Stud **Trained** East Everleigh, Wilts

The Form Book Flat, Raceform Ltd, Compton, RG20 6NL.

FOCUS
Some powerful stables took part in this maiden, which was run at a steady pace. The fourth and fifth help to set the level.

1348 VINES BMW H'CAP 2m (P)
5:45 (5:45) (Class 5) (0-70,68) 4-Y-O+ £2,726 (£805; £402) Stalls Low

Form RPR
2124 1 **Bold Adventure**[19] 1040 9-9-1 **57** KierenFallon 4 65
(Willie Musson) *racd in last pair: pushed along fr over 6f out: rdn over 4f out: clsd on ldrs over 2f out: chsd ldr over 1f out: led fnl 100yds: styd on strly* **6/1**[3]
0-40 2 2 **Dr Finley (IRE)**[32] 654 6-9-6 **65** SimonPearce(3) 6 71
(Lydia Pearce) *in tch in midfield: shkn up and hdwy to press ldr and wnt clr over 7f out: rdn to ld over 2f out: hdd and one pce fnl 100yds* **20/1**
-122 3 1 ¾ **Guards Chapel**[11] 1158 5-9-12 **68** (v) RyanMoore 2 72
(Gary Moore) *hld up in rr: rdn and clsd on ldrs over 2f out: drvn and chsd ldrs 2f out: plugged on ins fnl f: wnt 3rd cl home: nvr a threat to ldrs* **2/1**[2]
-232 4 ½ **Bramshill Lass**[17] 1062 4-9-6 **66** (p) JimCrowley 5 69
(Amanda Perrett) *chsd ldr tl over 7f out: chsd ldng pair after: clsd over 2f out: styd on same pce fr over 1f out: lost 3rd cl home* **6/1**[3]
0-11 5 13 **Hoonose**[34] 851 4-8-12 **58** (v) EddieAhern 3 45
(Pat Eddery) *chsd ldng pair tl over 7f out: 5th and struggling u.p over 3f out: wknd over 1f out: wl btn and eased ins fnl f* **6/4**[1]
-454 6 22 **Celtic Charlie (FR)**[21] 788 8-8-6 **53** (p) JemmaMarshall(5) 1 14
(Pat Phelan) *taken down early: led tl over 2f out: sn rdn and unable qck: wknd over 1f out: wl btn and eased jst ins fnl f: t.o* **12/1**

3m 25.06s (-0.64) **Going Correction** +0.05s/f (Slow)
WFA 4 from 5yo+ 4lb **6** Ran SP% **114.4**
Speed ratings (Par 103): **103,102,101,100,94 83**
Tote Swingers: 1&2 £7.30, 1&3 £1.70, 2&3 £6.10 CSF £98.16 TOTE £9.90: £4.00, £7.00; EX 133.00 Trifecta £200.30 Pool: £1,903.41 - 7.12 winning units..
Owner W J Musson **Bred** Bricklow Ltd **Trained** Newmarket, Suffolk

FOCUS
Not a bad contest for the grade, run at a messy pace, with the winner finishing strongly. The runner-up is rated in line with last year's form.
T/Plt: £19.80 to a £1 stake. Pool: £44,886.00 - 1,648.42 winning tickets. T/Qpdt: £6.20 to a £1 stake. Pool: £3,217.00 - 382.14 winning tickets. SP

1215 WOLVERHAMPTON (A.W) (L-H)
Thursday, April 4

OFFICIAL GOING: Standard
Wind: Fresh against Weather: Overcast

1349 32REDPOKER.COM H'CAP 5f 216y(P)
5:20 (5:21) (Class 6) (0-60,60) 3-Y-O £1,940 (£577; £288; £144) Stalls Low

Form RPR
44U2 1 **Jordanstown**[17] 1066 3-9-0 **53** (p) NeilCallan 6 59
(Kevin Ryan) *sn pushed along to chse ldrs: rdn to ld over 1f out: styd on* **5/1**
2-36 2 ½ **Magic Ice**[48] 669 3-9-0 **53** DaleSwift 5 56
(Brian Ellison) *chsd ldrs: pushed along over 2f out: rdn and swtchd rt over 1f out: r.o* **12/1**
00-5 3 1 **The Manx Missile**[18] 1050 3-9-7 **60** HayleyTurner 10 60
(Michael Bell) *chsd ldrs: led 4f out: rdn and hdd over 1f out: styd on same pce ins fnl f* **7/2**[2]
434- 4 shd **Not Now Blondie**[122] 7974 3-9-6 **59** LukeMorris 1 59
(Chris Dwyer) *s.i.s: sn pushed along in rr: rdn over 1f out: r.o ins fnl f: nrst fin* **9/2**[3]
-661 5 ½ **Compton Silver**[8] 1210 3-9-1 **59** 6ex (b) NicoleNordblad(5) 11 57
(Hans Adielsson) *s.i.s: hld up: hdwy over 2f out: hung lft and bmpd over 1f out: styd on: nt trble ldrs* **5/2**[1]
465- 6 nk **Beacon Tarn**[111] 8108 3-9-5 **58** TedDurcan 2 55
(Eric Alston) *s.i.s: hld up: hdwy over 2f out: nt clr run over 1f out: hung lft ins fnl f: nt trble ldrs* **12/1**
45-0 7 4 **Look On By**[23] 964 3-9-7 **60** JamesSullivan 8 45
(Ruth Carr) *led 2f: remained handy: rdn over 1f out: wknd ins fnl f* **33/1**
2-64 8 3 ½ **Hawsies Dream**[16] 1073 3-9-2 **55** GrahamLee 3 28
(Alan Bailey) *prom: rdn over 2f out: wknd fnl f* **12/1**
-342 9 2 ½ **Nors The Panic**[7] 1216 3-8-9 **48** (e) RobbieFitzpatrick 7 13
(Richard Guest) *hld up: rdn over 1f out: a in rr* **20/1**
50-6 10 9 **Symphony Of Dreams**[28] 915 3-8-7 **46** oh1 KierenFox 9
(Dai Burchell) *prom: chsd ldr 4f out: rdn: hung rt and wknd over 2f out* **80/1**

1m 16.36s (1.36) **Going Correction** +0.10s/f (Slow) **10** Ran SP% **117.7**
Speed ratings (Par 96): **94,93,92,91,91 90,85,80,77,65**
Tote Swingers: 1&2 £11.80, 1&3 £4.80, 2&3 £13.80 CSF £62.36 CT £243.84 TOTE £4.90: £1.80, £3.10, £1.60; EX 69.30 Trifecta £270.10 Pool: £2,049.29 - 5.68 winning units..
Owner Mrs Margaret Forsyth & Mrs D McAllister **Bred** Miss S E Hall **Trained** Hambleton, N Yorks

FOCUS
A moderate 3-y-o sprint handicap but improved efforts from the first three.

1350 32REDBET.COM H'CAP 1m 5f 194y(P)
5:55 (5:55) (Class 6) (0-65,65) 4-Y-O+ £1,940 (£577; £288; £144) Stalls Low

Form RPR
00-2 1 **Cape Alex**[7] 1217 4-8-6 **50** ChrisCatlin 4 61
(Clive Brittain) *a.p: racd keenly: trckd ldr tl led over 2f out: rdn and hdd ins fnl f: edgd lft: rallied to ld nr fin* **5/2**[1]
1224 2 hd **Easydoesit (IRE)**[16] 1084 5-9-7 **62** [1] GrahamLee 3 73
(Tony Carroll) *hld up: hdwy over 5f out: chsd ldr over 1f out: rdn to ld and hung lft ins fnl f: hdd nr fin* **11/4**[2]
4112 3 2 ½ **Jezza**[13] 1117 7-9-10 **65** LukeMorris 1 72
(Karen George) *hld up in tch: outpcd over 3f out: rallied over 1f out: styd on same pce ins fnl f* **6/1**
0621 4 ½ **The Blue Dog (IRE)**[19] 1040 6-9-4 **64** RobertTart(5) 5 70
(Michael Wigham) *hld up: hdwy 2f out: rdn over 1f out: styd on same pce ins fnl f* **5/1**[3]
0-42 5 6 **Brunello**[19] 1045 5-9-9 **64** DanielTudhope 9 62
(David O'Meara) *prom: pushed along 4f out: rdn over 2f out: wknd fnl f* **5/1**[3]
000- 6 2 ¼ **Absolutely Me (IRE)**[310] 2578 4-8-5 **49** JamieMackay 6 44
(Willie Musson) *sn led: rdn and hdd over 2f out: wknd fnl f* **28/1**
000 7 hd **St Ignatius**[33] 866 6-9-8 **63** (p) NickyMackay 2 57
(Alan Bailey) *chsd ldrs: rdn over 2f out: wknd over 1f out* **14/1**
0-50 8 15 **Commerce**[23] 974 6-8-6 **47** oh1 ow1 (p) KierenFox 7 20
(Dai Burchell) *s.i.s: hld up: rdn over 2f out: sn wknd* **66/1**
0/0- 9 7 **Just Jimmy (IRE)**[261] 4179 8-8-10 **51** [1] TomEaves 8 15
(George Jones) *hld up: a in rr: bhd fnl 6f* **66/1**

3m 5.33s (-0.67) **Going Correction** +0.10s/f (Slow)
WFA 4 from 5yo+ 3lb **9** Ran SP% **116.0**
Speed ratings (Par 101): **105,104,103,103,99 98,98,89,85**
Tote Swingers: 1&2 £2.20, 1&3 £3.40, 2&3 £2.80 CSF £9.56 CT £35.67 TOTE £3.20: £1.10, £1.60, £1.40; EX 11.90 Trifecta £53.30 Pool: £2,164.92 - 30.44 winning units..
Owner Saeed Manana **Bred** Castleton Lyons & Kilboy Estate **Trained** Newmarket, Suffolk

FOCUS
An ordinary staying handicap, run at an uneven pace. The form makes sense with the third and fourth setting the standard.

1351 32RED H'CAP 5f 216y(P)
6:25 (6:25) (Class 5) (0-70,70) 4-Y-O+ £2,587 (£770; £384; £192) Stalls Low

Form RPR
0-00 1 **New Decade**[35] 831 4-8-13 **62** GrahamLee 11 73
(Milton Bradley) *chsd ldr tl led over 2f out: rdn out* **20/1**
6545 2 ½ **Restless Bay (IRE)**[8] 1205 5-9-1 **64** (b) HayleyTurner 4 73
(Conor Dore) *chsd ldrs: rdn over 1f out: r.o* **6/1**[3]
1205 3 nse **Holy Angel (IRE)**[17] 1067 4-9-0 **70** (e) RachelRichardson(7) 8 79
(Tim Easterby) *mid-div: hdwy over 2f out: shkn up ins fnl f: r.o* **7/2**[2]
5051 4 2 ¼ **Avonvalley**[23] 971 6-9-0 **68** SladeO'Hara(5) 10 70
(Peter Grayson) *hld up: hdwy over 1f out: r.o: nt trble ldrs* **16/1**
466 5 ½ **George Fenton**[14] 1102 4-9-0 **63** (v) RobbieFitzpatrick 9 63
(Richard Guest) *prom: rdn over 1f out: styd on same pce ins fnl f* **14/1**
0-00 6 1 **Muftarres (IRE)**[14] 1102 8-8-9 **63** (t) AmyScott(5) 12 60
(Frank Sheridan) *s.s: bhd tl r.o ins fnl f: nvr nrr* **66/1**
360 7 hd **Methaaly (IRE)**[23] 971 10-8-9 **63** (be) RobertTart(5) 2 59
(Michael Mullineaux) *hld up: rdn over 1f out: r.o ins fnl f: nt trble ldrs* **20/1**
616- 7 dht **Iceblast**[174] 7022 5-8-9 **65** MatthewHopkins(7) 1 61
(Michael Easterby) *hld up: rdn over 1f out: r.o ins fnl f: nvr on terms* **15/2**
1536 9 1 ¾ **Hab Reeh**[23] 971 5-9-0 **63** (t) AmyRyan 6 54
(Ruth Carr) *hld up: rdn over 1f out: n.d* **20/1**
0120 10 ¾ **Prince James**[19] 1038 6-9-0 **63** JamesSullivan 5 51
(Michael Easterby) *led: rdn and hdd over 2f out: wknd fnl f* **20/1**
0450 11 ½ **Speightowns Kid (USA)**[17] 1058 5-9-5 **68** TonyCulhane 3 55
(Richard Ford) *mid-div: pushed along and lost pl 1/2-way: n.d after* **33/1**
56-1 12 2 ¼ **Common Cents**[16] 1078 4-9-7 **70** LukeMorris 7 49
(Ronald Harris) *trckd ldrs: rdn over 1f out: wknd ins fnl f* **7/4**[1]

1m 14.88s (-0.12) **Going Correction** +0.10s/f (Slow) **12** Ran SP% **120.7**
Speed ratings (Par 103): **104,103,103,100,99 98,98,98,95,94 94,91**
Tote Swingers: 1&2 £26.10, 1&3 £17.60, 2&3 £3.70 CSF £127.89 CT £543.59 TOTE £43.30: £8.70, £2.50, £1.40; EX 340.00 Trifecta £1243.70 Pool: £1,658.32 - 0.31 winning units..
Owner Darren Hudson-Wood **Bred** Cheveley Park Stud Ltd **Trained** Sedbury, Gloucs

FOCUS
A moderate sprint handicap with the winner rated to his previous personal-best and the runner-up running his best race so far. The fourth helps set the level.

1352 32RED.COM MAIDEN STKS 1m 4f 50y(P)
6:55 (6:55) (Class 5) 3-5-Y-O £2,587 (£770; £384; £192) Stalls Low

Form RPR
00- 1 **No Truth (IRE)**[152] 7552 3-8-2 0 FrannyNorton 1 66+
(Charles Hills) *mde all: rdn and edgd rt fr over 1f out: styd on* **11/10**[2]
2252 2 1 ½ **Story Writer**[27] 925 4-9-13 67 GeorgeBaker 3 69
(William Knight) *hld up: hdwy and hung lft fr over 4f out: chsd wnr over 2f out: rdn over 1f out: styd on* **10/11**[1]
3 5 **Rock Of Ages**[22] 4-9-13 0 NeilCallan 2 61
(Michael Murphy) *chsd ldrs: pushed along over 4f out: rdn over 2f out: no ex fnl f* **16/1**
4 15 **Une Des Bieffes (FR)**[36] 5-9-9 0 (v) GrahamLee 5 32
(Michael Scudamore) *s.s: sn prom: pushed along 7f out: rdn over 5f out: wknd over 4f out: t.o* **33/1**
5 10 **Always Gentle (IRE)** 3-7-13 0 RyanPowell(3) 4 14+
(George Margarson) *chsd ldr: rdn over 3f out: n.m.r and wknd over 2f out* **12/1**[3]

2m 42.48s (1.38) **Going Correction** +0.10s/f (Slow)
WFA 3 from 4yo 21lb 4 from 5yo 1lb **5** Ran SP% **116.5**
Speed ratings (Par 103): **99,98,94,84,78**
CSF £2.62 TOTE £1.50: £1.10, £1.10; EX 2.90 Trifecta £10.20 Pool: £1,694.19 - 124.00 winning units..
Owner Triermore Stud **Bred** Mrs U Schwarzenbach **Trained** Lambourn, Berks

FOCUS
A weak maiden, rated around the runner-up, although somewhat fluid.

1353 32RED CASINO CLAIMING STKS 1m 1f 103y(P)
7:25 (7:25) (Class 5) 4-Y-O+ £2,587 (£770; £384; £192) Stalls Low

Form RPR
6626 1 **Rakaan (IRE)**[15] 1092 6-9-5 85 FergusSweeney 7 75
(Jamie Osborne) *stdd s: hld up: hdwy over 1f out: rdn to ld ins fnl f: jst hld on* **11/8**[1]
4661 2 hd **Tornado Force (IRE)**[8] 1201 5-8-13 71 HayleyTurner 4 68
(Chris Dwyer) *unruly in stalls: s.s: hld up: rdn: edgd lft and r.o ins fnl f: nt quite rch wnr* **7/4**[2]
2641 3 shd **Yourinthewill (USA)**[14] 1104 5-8-10 69 ShaneKelly 1 65
(Daniel Mark Loughnane) *a.p: shkn up over 1f out: rdn and edgd lft ins fnl f: r.o* **7/1**[3]
2043 4 1 ¾ **Spanish Plume**[14] 1104 5-8-6 65 (p) JackDuern(5) 3 62
(Reg Hollinshead) *trckd ldrs: plld hrd: led over 1f out: sn hdd: styd on same pce ins fnl f* **11/1**
3341 5 ¾ **Alhaban (IRE)**[10] 1170 7-8-9 65 LukeMorris 6 59
(Ronald Harris) *chsd ldr tl led wl over 1f out: sn rdn and hdd: no ex ins fnl f* **9/1**
5336 6 2 **Bashama**[17] 1070 5-8-2 47 ow1 (bt) FrankieMcDonald 5 48?
(Nikki Evans) *led at stdy pce tl qcknd over 2f out: hdd wl over 1f out: wknd ins fnl f* **80/1**

2m 5.93s (4.23) **Going Correction** +0.10s/f (Slow) **6** Ran SP% **110.5**
Speed ratings (Par 103): **85,84,84,83,82 80**
Tote Swingers: 1&2 £1.10, 2&3 £2.60 CSF £3.87 TOTE £2.10: £1.10, £1.70; EX 3.70 Trifecta £8.30 Pool: £1,301.54 - 117.48 winning units..Tornado Force was claimed by Mr A. J. McCabe for £10,000.
Owner Leslie Marshall **Bred** L Mulryan & M Fahy **Trained** Upper Lambourn, Berks

FOCUS
A competitive affair of its type, but a slow pace turned the race into a sprint and not form to be confident about.

1354 £32 BONUS AT 32RED.COM H'CAP 1m 141y(P)
7:55 (7:55) (Class 5) (0-75,75) 4-Y-0+ £2,587 (£770; £384; £192) Stalls Low

Form RPR
1312 1 **Exceedexpectations (IRE)**[7] 1220 4-9-7 **75**................ HayleyTurner 1 85
(Conor Dore) *chsd ldr tl led over 1f out: pushed out* **11/4**[2]
45-0 2 ¾ **Rossetti**[86] 104 5-9-2 **70**...................................... GrahamLee 7 78
(Ian Williams) *hld up: hdwy over 2f out: rdn to chse wnr fnl f: r.o* **10/1**
2652 3 1 ¼ **California English (IRE)**[16] 1081 4-9-6 **74**.................... AndreaAtzeni 4 79
(Marco Botti) *stmbld s: sn chsng ldrs: rdn over 1f out: hung lft ins fnl f: styd on same pce* **9/4**[1]
320- 4 ¾ **Time To Dance**[356] 1355 4-9-0 **68**.............................. LukeMorris 2 71
(Joseph Tuite) *chsd ldrs: rdn over 1f out: styd on same pce ins fnl f* **20/1**
000- 5 1 ¾ **Cono Zur (FR)**[198] 6342 6-9-2 **70**........................ JamesSullivan 3 69
(Ruth Carr) *led: rdn and hdd over 1f out: no ex ins fnl f* **28/1**
01-0 6 hd **Space War**[7] 1220 6-8-13 **67**.......................... GrahamGibbons 5 66
(Michael Easterby) *s.s: hld up: styd on ins fnl f: nvr nrr* **5/1**
2126 7 ½ **One Scoop Or Two**[21] 995 7-9-2 **75**.......................(p) RobertTart(5) 8 73
(Reg Hollinshead) *hld up: rdn over 2f out: nvr on terms* **4/1**[3]
-440 8 ½ **Hail Promenader (IRE)**[16] 1081 7-8-5 **64**................ PhilipPrince(5) 6 60
(Anthony Carson) *hld up: nvr on terms* **16/1**

1m 49.92s (-0.58) **Going Correction** +0.10s/f (Slow) **8** Ran SP% **117.3**
Speed ratings (Par 103): **106,105,104,103,102 101,101,100**
Tote Swingers: 1&2 £3.80, 1&3 £2.00, 2&3 £4.20 CSF £31.06 CT £72.77 TOTE £4.00: £1.50, £3.40, £1.10; EX 42.90 Trifecta £120.80 Pool: £1,355.74 - 8.41 winning units..
Owner Mrs Louise Marsh **Bred** R S Cockerill (farms) Ltd & Peter Dodd **Trained** Hubbert's Bridge, Lincs

FOCUS
It paid to race handily in this moderate handicap, although the pace was sound. The runner-up, to last year's form, and the third help set the level..

1355 32REDBINGO.COM H'CAP (DIV I) 5f 20y(P)
8:25 (8:26) (Class 6) (0-55,55) 4-Y-0+ £1,940 (£577; £288; £144) Stalls Low

Form RPR
5506 1 **Loyal Royal (IRE)**[8] 1196 10-9-7 **55**..........................(bt) GrahamLee 1 63
(Milton Bradley) *mde all: plld hrd: edgd rt and shkn up over 1f out: r.o* **9/2**[2]
2362 2 1 ½ **Slatey Hen (IRE)**[15] 1087 5-9-1 **49**...........................(p) CathyGannon 2 52
(Violet M Jordan) *a.p: rdn to chse wnr over 1f out: edgd rt: styd on same pce ins fnl f* **4/1**[1]
4640 3 1 ½ **Sextons House (IRE)**[12] 1149 5-8-13 **47**................(b) GrahamGibbons 8 44
(Alan McCabe) *hld up: hdwy over 1f out: r.o to go 3rd post: nt trble ldrs* **7/1**[3]
0-15 4 nse **Bailadeira**[41] 760 5-9-7 **55**.................................... JamesSullivan 9 52
(Tim Etherington) *chsd wnr tl rdn over 1f out: styd on same pce ins fnl f: lost 3rd post* **17/2**
4440 5 2 ¼ **Munaawib**[7] 1221 5-9-0 **48**..(t) LukeMorris 7 37
(Charles Smith) *chsd ldrs: pushed along 1/2-way: rdn over 1f out: no ex fnl f* **9/1**
1545 6 ¾ **Chateau Lola**[9] 1186 4-9-4 **52**..................................(v) MartinDwyer 6 38
(Derek Shaw) *s.i.s: hld up: rdn over 1f out: nvr on terms* **7/1**[3]
433- 7 ½ **My Time**[187] 6686 4-9-0 **53**...................................... RobertTart(5) 4 37
(Michael Mullineaux) *s.i.s and hmpd s: outpcd: r.o ins fnl f: nvr nrr* **9/2**[2]
0-40 8 nk **Sally's Swansong**[26] 946 7-9-4 **52**................................(b) TedDurcan 5 35
(Eric Alston) *prom: rdn over 1f out: wknd ins fnl f* **10/1**
5-03 9 1 ½ **Bond Blade**[16] 1077 5-8-12 **46** oh1.................................... DaleSwift 3 24
(Suzzanne France) *edgd rt s: hld up: rdn 1/2-way: hdwy over 1f out: wknd fnl f* **18/1**

1m 2.83s (0.53) **Going Correction** +0.10s/f (Slow) **9** Ran SP% **116.2**
Speed ratings (Par 101): **99,96,94,94,90 89,88,88,85**
Tote Swingers: 1&2 £1.70, 1&3 £7.40, 2&3 £5.70 CSF £23.05 CT £125.31 TOTE £6.20: £1.20, £1.40, £2.40; EX 15.00 Trifecta £166.70 Pool: £1,065.70 - 4.79 winning units..
Owner Darren Hudson-Wood **Bred** J F Tuthill **Trained** Sedbury, Gloucs

FOCUS
The first division of the weak sprint handicap and another winner from the front. The form is rated around the first two to their recent marks.

1356 32REDBINGO.COM H'CAP (DIV II) 5f 20y(P)
8:55 (8:55) (Class 6) (0-55,55) 4-Y-0+ £1,940 (£577; £288; £144) Stalls Low

Form RPR
21 1 **Majestic Timeline (IRE)**[21] 997 4-9-2 **50**..............(tp) StevieDonohoe 3 61+
(Adrian Brendan Joyce, Ire) *chsd ldrs: pushed along and n.m.r over 1f out: r.o to ld wl ins fnl f* **15/8**[1]
-504 2 1 ½ **Almaty Express**[19] 1042 11-9-1 **52**..................(b) MichaelMetcalfe(3) 2 58
(John Weymes) *a.p: led over 1f out: rdn and hdd wl ins fnl f* **6/1**[3]
1336 3 nk **Rightcar**[15] 1088 6-8-10 **49**.. SladeO'Hara(5) 7 54
(Peter Grayson) *dwlt: rdn over 1f out: r.o ins fnl f: nt rch ldrs* **15/2**
0035 4 ¾ **Poyle Todream**[7] 1215 5-9-0 **48**.. TomEaves 9 50
(Roy Brotherton) *hld up: rdn over 1f out: r.o ins fnl f: nt rch ldrs* **25/1**
2005 5 ½ **Miserere Mei (IRE)**[4] 1276 4-9-0 **48**........................(e) RobbieFitzpatrick 5 49
(Richard Guest) *hld up: hdwy over 1f out: sn rdn: styd on same pce ins fnl f* **20/1**
2033 6 nk **Russian Bullet**[43] 719 4-9-2 **55**...................................... RobertTart(5) 4 54
(Jamie Osborne) *a.p: rdn over 1f out: styd on same pce ins fnl f* **11/4**[2]
4055 7 1 ¼ **Love Club**[21] 997 5-8-13 **47**... GrahamGibbons 1 42
(Brian Baugh) *sn led: rdn and hdd over 1f out: no ex ins fnl f* **12/1**
0-64 8 nse **Nine Before Ten (IRE)**[23] 968 5-9-4 **52**............................. LukeMorris 8 47
(Charles Smith) *broke wl and led early: chsd ldr: rdn and ev ch over 1f out: no ex ins fnl f* **12/1**

1m 2.45s (0.15) **Going Correction** +0.10s/f (Slow) **8** Ran SP% **111.5**
Speed ratings (Par 101): **102,99,99,97,97 96,94,94**
Tote Swingers: 1&2 £5.10, 1&3 £2.30, 2&3 £3.50 CSF £12.88 CT £65.55 TOTE £2.20: £1.10, £2.00, £1.70; EX 12.10 Trifecta £57.80 Pool: £1,129.08 - 14.64 winning units..
Owner M Kerrigan **Bred** Michael Rourke **Trained** Loughview, Co Roscommon

FOCUS
This second division of the weak sprint handicap and it was won by a progressive sprinter. The placed horses are rated around their recent form.
T/Plt: £14.60 to a £1 stake. Pool: £61,529.00 - 3,068.92 winning tickets. T/Qpdt: £5.10 to a £1 stake. Pool: £7,088.00 - 1,010.47 winning tickets. CR

MAISONS-LAFFITTE (R-H)
Thursday, April 4

OFFICIAL GOING: Turf: good to soft

1357a PRIX DJEBEL (GROUP 3) (3YO COLTS & GELDINGS) (TURF) 7f (S)
1:20 (1:20) 3-Y-0 £32,520 (£13,008; £9,756; £6,504; £3,252)

RPR
1 **Style Vendome (FR)**[21] 999 3-9-2 0............................ ThierryThulliez 1 112+
(N Clement, France) *racd in midfield on settling: swtchd towards rails 2f out: qcknd wl ent fnl f: led 150yds out: sn wnt clr: comf* **2/1**[1]
2 2 ½ **Snowday (FR)**[149] 7623 3-9-2 0................................... OlivierPeslier 7 104
(C Laffon-Parias, France) *in front rnk fr s: led 1f out: hdd 150yds out: r.o wl* **10/1**
3 snk **Penny's Picnic (IRE)**[149] 7623 3-9-2 0............................. ThierryJarnet 5 104
(D Guillemin, France) *hld up towards rr: swtchd towards outside 1 1/2f out: r.o wl ent fnl f: no ex fnl 100yds* **23/10**[2]
4 hd **Etalondes (FR)**[27] 3-9-2 0... GregoryBenoist 8 103
(J-C Rouget, France) *hld up towards rr: gd prog 1 1/2f out: r.o wl u.p fnl f* **48/10**[3]
5 ½ **My Approach (IRE)**[14] 3-9-2 0.................. Christophe-PatriceLemaire 6 102
(Robert Collet, France) *racd in 5th on settling: nt pce to go w ldrs 1 1/2f out: r.o fnl f to go 5th cl home* **12/1**
6 nk **Calvin Williams (FR)**[21] 999 3-9-2 0........................... AnthonyCrastus 2 101
(E Lellouche, France) *racd bhd ldrs: no ex u.p 1f out: styd on one pce* **16/1**
7 1 ¼ **Mazameer (IRE)**[228] 5398 3-9-2 0............................... AurelienLemaitre 9 98
(F Head, France) *hld up towards rr on outside: pulling hrd: rdn 2 1/2f out: briefly mde prog 1 1/2f out: no ex u.p ent fnl f* **10/1**
8 4 ½ **Local Lover (FR)**[21] 999 3-9-2 0................................... FabriceVeron 4 85
(H-A Pantall, France) *in front rnk on rail fr s: rdn 2 1/2f out: no ex: grad fdd* **27/1**

1m 25.98s (-2.02) **8** Ran SP% **116.2**
WIN (incl. 1 euro stake): 3.00. PLACES: 1.30, 2.00, 1.50. DF: 16.30. SF: 25.60.
Owner Comte Andre de Ganay **Bred** G Pariente **Trained** Chantilly, France

FOCUS
The winning time was 0.69sec quicker than that recorded by the fillies in the Imprudence. The runner-up and sixth help set the standard.

1358a PRIX IMPRUDENCE (GROUP 3) (3YO FILLIES) (TURF) 7f (S)
1:50 (1:50) 3-Y-0 £32,520 (£13,008; £9,756; £6,504; £3,252)

RPR
1 **What A Name (IRE)**[179] 6910 3-9-0 0......... Christophe-PatriceLemaire 4 108+
(M Delzangles, France) *a.p: rdn and sltly short of room over 1f out: sn in the clr and r.o to chal wl ins fnl f: led cl home: shade cosily* **8/5**[1]
2 nk **Holy Dazzle**[149] 7622 3-9-0 0.. RonanThomas 8 107
(J E Pease, France) *hld up in last pair: rdn and hdwy over 1f out: r.o to chal ins fnl f: w ldr and ev ch 50yds out: hld cl home* **24/1**
3 nk **Spinacre (IRE)**[186] 6717 3-9-0 0................................... GeraldMosse 9 106
(P Bary, France) *hld up in last: swtchd to wd outside and rdn to improve over 1f out: r.o to chal ins fnl f: wnt 3rd cl home: nt pce of wnr* **16/1**
4 ½ **Peace Burg (FR)**[179] 6909 3-9-0 0.......................... ChristopheSoumillon 7 104
(J-C Rouget, France) *midfield: rdn over 1f out: led ins fnl f: hdd cl home: no ex and dropped to 4th* **33/10**[2]
5 ¾ **Show Gorb (SPA)**[45] 3-9-0 0............................. Francois-XavierBertras 6 102
(P Sogorb, France) *midfield: nt clr run over 1f out: swtchd ins and rdn ent fnl f: short of room on rail 100yds out: r.o to snatch 5th post but nvr able to chal* **10/1**
6 shd **Kensea (FR)**[21] 1000 3-9-0 0... MaximeGuyon 5 102
(H-A Pantall, France) *t.k.h: trckd ldr: led 1 1/2f out: rdn ent fnl f: sn hdd: no ex and fdd* **21/1**
7 1 ¼ **Aquatinta (GER)**[149] 7622 3-9-0 0............................... OlivierPeslier 3 99
(H-A Pantall, France) *t.k.h: midfield on inner: last and looking for room 1f out: swtchd to outer and rdn ent fnl f: r.o under hands and heels but nvr a factor* **13/2**[3]
8 1 ¾ **Sara Lucille**[229] 5379 3-9-0 0...................................... ThierryJarnet 1 94
(F Head, France) *prom on inner: rdn and lost pl over 1f out: sn no ex and btn: fdd* **12/1**
9 ½ **Deux Saisons**[11] 3-9-0 0.. GregoryBenoist 10 93
(D Guillemin, France) *t.k.h: prom on outer: rdn 2f out: no ex and btn 1f out: fdd* **10/1**
10 12 **Tosca (GER)**[193] 6522 3-9-0 0...................................(b[1]) ThierryThulliez 2 60
(Mrs Ilka Gansera-Leveque) *led on rail: rdn and hdd 1 1/2f out: sn no ex and btn: wknd: eased and dropped to last: t.o* **56/1**

1m 26.67s (-1.33) **10** Ran SP% **117.1**
WIN (incl. 1 euro stake): 2.60. PLACES: 1.50, 4.40, 3.80. DF: 41.20. SF: 51.50.
Owner H H Sheikh Mohammed Bin Khalifa Al Thani **Bred** Robert B Trussell Jr **Trained** France

FOCUS
One of the principal Guineas trials for fillies run in France. Natagora won this in 2008 before scoring at Newmarket and Elusive Wave took the Pouliches after scoring here in 2009; Special Duty finished third here in 2010 before winning the 1000 Guineas in the Stewards' room. The withdrawal of the pacemaker Interesting resulted in a very steady early gallop and the field finished in a bunch.

1359 - (Foreign Racing) - See Raceform Interactive

LEICESTER (R-H)
Friday, April 5

OFFICIAL GOING: Good to soft (soft in places; 5.7)
Wind: fresh, half against Weather: dry, cold

1360 KNIGHTON MAIDEN STKS 5f 2y
2:20 (2:20) (Class 5) 2-Y-0 £2,587 (£770; £384; £192) Stalls Centre

Form RPR
1 **Master Carpenter (IRE)** 2-9-5 0.................................. AndreaAtzeni 4 82+
(Rod Millman) *rn green and pushed along in midfield: hdwy to chse ldng pair wl over 1f out: led ins fnl f: r.o strly and drew clr fnl 100yds* **9/1**
2 2 ½ **Beau Nash (IRE)** 2-9-5 0.. RichardHughes 3 73+
(Richard Hannon) *dwlt: hld up in tch in rr: hdwy ent fnl 2f: pressed ldrs ins fnl f:2nd and outpcd by wnr fnl 100yds: kpt on* **3/1**[2]
0 3 ¾ **Smugglers Gold (IRE)**[12] 1156 2-9-5 0........................(v[1]) AdamKirby 2 70
(David Evans) *chsd ldr tl rdn to ld ent fnl 2f: drvn and hrd pressed 1f out: hdd and outpcd ins fnl f* **22/1**

	4	3 1/4	**Cockney Bob** 2-9-5 0 ... CathyGannon 5 (J S Moore) *s.i.s: bhd and rdn along: hdwy into modest 5th 1f out: no threat to ldrs but styd on steadily fnl f* **12/1**		59+
4	5	1	**Scargill**[6] 1247 2-9-5 0 ... MartinHarley 7 (Mick Channon) *chsd ldng pair: chsd ldr 2f out tl ent fnl f: wknd fnl 50yds* **11/4**[1]		55
	6	9	**Posh Bounty** 2-8-7 0 ... JakePayne(7) 1 (Bill Turner) *led tl ent fnl 2f: sn hung rt and struggling: wknd over 1f out: sn bhd* **13/2**[3]		18
	7	5	**Peterkin (IRE)** 2-9-5 0 ... JoeFanning 6 (Mark Johnston) *racd freely: chsd ldrs: rn v green and wandering arnd over 2f out: lost pl qckly wl over 1f out: bhd over 1f out* **3/1**[2]		5

1m 4.03s (4.03) **Going Correction** +0.675s/f (Yiel) 7 Ran SP% **112.0**
Speed ratings (Par 92): **94,90,88,83,82 67,59**
toteswingers 1&2 £4.70, 1&3 £13.40, 2&3 £12.70 CSF £34.65 TOTE £13.70: £4.30, £1.90; EX 32.20 Trifecta £487.40 Pool: £1,268.19 - 1.95 winning units..
Owner The Links Partnership **Bred** Naiff Sa & Newtown Stud **Trained** Kentisbeare, Devon

FOCUS
False rail from top of hill on back straight to the Winning post adding 17yds to races on Round course. A fair juvenile maiden in which they went a decent gallop; the first two shaped well while the third improved on his debut effort.

1361 BURTON OVERY (S) STKS 5f 218y
2:55 (2:55) (Class 6) 3-Y-O **£1,940** (£577; £288; £144) **Stalls** High

Form				RPR
3453	1		**Studfarmer**[20] 1041 3-9-5 66 ... (v) TomQueally 5 (David Evans) *hld up in tch: rdn and effrt over 2f out: led over 1f out: kpt on and steadily forged clr fnl f* **5/2**[1]	69
2441	2	3 3/4	**La Sylphe**[8] 1216 3-9-0 65 ... MartinDwyer 3 (Derek Shaw) *taken down early: led: rdn 2f out: hdd over 1f out: btn ins fnl f: wknd fnl 100yds* **9/2**[3]	52
5401	3	4 1/2	**Douglas Pasha (IRE)**[14] 1116 3-9-5 59 ... AdrianNicholls 1 (David Nicholls) *chsd ldrs: rdn 3f out: dropped to rr over 2f out: no ch but plugged on again to go modest 3rd wl ins fnl f* **11/1**	43
	4	2 3/4	**Heyward Boy (IRE)** 3-9-0 0 ... AndreaAtzeni 4 (Robert Eddery) *s.i.s: bhd: sme hdwy u.p over 2f out: no imp and btn 1f out: wknd* **5/2**[1]	29
2433	5	5	**Desert Donkey**[10] 1180 3-9-0 63 ... (p) JimmyFortune 2 (Andrew Balding) *chsd ldr: rdn 3f out: lost 2nd wl over 1f out: and sn btn: fdd fnl f* **3/1**[2]	13

1m 18.93s (5.93) **Going Correction** +0.675s/f (Yiel) 5 Ran SP% **108.7**
Speed ratings (Par 96): **87,82,76,72,65**
CSF £13.35 TOTE £3.90: £2.00, £1.70; EX 13.00 Trifecta £40.00 Pool: £1,021.96 - 19.12 winning units..There were no bids for the winner.
Owner W T Whittle & R Kent **Bred** W T Whittle And Mickley Stud Ltd **Trained** Pandy, Monmouths

FOCUS
A modest 3-y-o seller in which the early gallop looked a solid one but the time was slow. The form is rated through the winner.

1362 LODDINGTON CONDITIONS STKS 5f 218y
3:30 (3:30) (Class 3) 3-Y-O **£7,561** (£2,263; £1,131; £566; £282) **Stalls** High

Form				RPR
060-	1		**Smoothtalkinrascal (IRE)**[175] 7028 3-9-4 92 ... DanielTudhope 1 (David O'Meara) *hld up in rr: rdn and hdwy to chse ldr wl over 1f out: kpt on wl u.p fnl f to ld last strides* **7/1**	98
122-	2	hd	**Zanetto**[195] 6491 3-9-4 94 ... WilliamBuick 2 (Andrew Balding) *t.k.h: chsd ldr and racd off of stands' rail: led 2f out: sn rdn: kpt on u.p tl hdd last strides* **7/2**[2]	97
040-	3	5	**Jillnextdoor (IRE)**[154] 7518 3-8-13 95 ... MartinHarley 3 (Mick Channon) *hld up wl in tch: 3rd and rdn wl over 1f out: 3rd and btn 1f out: wknd ins fnl f* **11/2**[3]	76
22-0	4	1 1/4	**Ask The Guru**[20] 1033 3-9-4 91 ... SebSanders 4 (Michael Attwater) *t.k.h early: chsd ldrs: rdn and effrt wl over 1f out: 4th and btn 1f out: wknd ins fnl f* **33/1**	77
153-	5	30	**El Manati (IRE)**[181] 6865 3-8-11 102 ... RyanMoore 5 (James Tate) *t.k.h: led and racd against stands' rail: rdn over 2f out: hdd 2f out and sn wl btn: wl bhd and virtually p.u ins fnl f: t.o* **4/5**[1]	

1m 16.93s (3.93) **Going Correction** +0.675s/f (Yiel) 5 Ran SP% **108.6**
Speed ratings (Par 102): **100,99,93,91,51**
CSF £29.70 TOTE £10.80: £3.50, £1.30; EX 27.90 Trifecta £124.40 Pool: £1,318.71 - 7.95 winning units..
Owner Middleham Park Racing XXXVIII **Bred** Tony Kilduff **Trained** Nawton, N Yorks

FOCUS
A decent quality 3-y-o conditions sprint best rated through the runner-up.

1363 GEORGE BEMROSE MEMORIAL H'CAP 7f 9y
4:05 (4:05) (Class 4) (0-85,84) 4-Y-O+ **£4,851** (£1,443; £721; £360) **Stalls** High

Form				RPR
60/5	1		**Music In The Rain (IRE)**[14] 1115 5-9-1 78 ... DanielTudhope 1 (David O'Meara) *chsd ldr and sn clr of field: c to r against stands' rail 1/2-way: rdn to ld over 1f out: kpt on and forged clr fnl f* **7/2**[3]	91
160-	2	2 3/4	**President Lincoln (USA)**[314] 2491 5-8-11 77 ... NeilFarley(3) 5 (Declan Carroll) *chsd clr ldng pair and clr of field: rdn over 2f out: plugged on ins fnl f: chsd wnr fnl 50yds: nvr able to chal* **13/2**	83
-342	3	2 1/2	**Haftohaf**[60] 518 4-9-0 77 ... (p) AdamKirby 2 (Marco Botti) *led and sn clr w wnr: rdn and hdd over 1f out: wknd ins fnl f: lost 2nd fnl 50yds* **5/2**[1]	76
3610	4	2 1/4	**Kickingthelilly**[27] 944 4-9-7 84 ... ChrisCatlin 8 (Rae Guest) *sn niggled along and racd off the pce in rr: drvn over 2f out: plugged on ins fnl f: nvr trbld ldrs* **11/1**	77
00-0	5	2 1/4	**Aerodynamic (IRE)**[14] 1115 6-9-0 77 ... GrahamGibbons 3 (Michael Easterby) *hld up off the pce in midfield: 4th and stl plenty to do whn asked for effrt 2f out: no prog: wknd fnl f* **20/1**	64
/06-	6	1 1/4	**Magic City (IRE)**[182] 6835 4-9-5 82 ... RichardHughes 7 (Richard Hannon) *stdd s: t.k.h: hld up off the pce in rr: rdn and no imp 2f: no ch but plugged on fnl f* **10/3**[2]	65
0-00	7	7	**Chiswick Bey (IRE)**[18] 1067 5-9-4 81 ... TomQueally 4 (Noel Quinlan) *hld up off the pce towards rr: rdn and no hdwy over 2f out: bhd over 1f out* **33/1**	45
60-0	8	3	**Greensward**[39] 792 7-9-5 82 ... EddieAhern 6 (Mike Murphy) *stdd s: hld up off the pce in rr: rdn and short-lived effrt over 2f out: sn bhd* **10/1**	38

1m 29.9s (3.70) **Going Correction** +0.675s/f (Yiel) 8 Ran SP% **112.3**
Speed ratings (Par 105): **105,101,99,96,93 92,84,81**
toteswingers 1&2 £5.90, 1&3 £1.30, 2&3 £12.30 CSF £25.40 CT £65.09 TOTE £4.60: £2.00, £3.10, £1.02; EX 29.50 Trifecta £137.70 Pool: £1,716.18 - 9.34 winning units..
Owner Colne Valley Racing **Bred** Maddenstown Equine Enterprise Ltd **Trained** Nawton, N Yorks

FOCUS
A fair handicap for older horses in which they went an even gallop. The winner is on a good mark and this is rated a personal-best, with the runner-up to form.

1364 BARKBY MAIDEN FILLIES' STKS 7f 9y
4:40 (4:42) (Class 5) 3-Y-O **£2,587** (£770; £384; £192) **Stalls** High

Form				RPR
	1		**Azenzar** 3-9-0 0 ... RyanMoore 1 (Roger Varian) *uns rdr sn after coming on the crse and galloped loose to s: t.k.h: in tch: rdn to ld and wnt clr over 1f out: kpt on* **5/2**[1]	74+
50-	2	1 1/4	**Last Hooray**[107] 8171 3-9-0 0 ... DaneO'Neill 3 (David Elsworth) *wnt rt s: chsd ldrs: rdn effrt ent fnl 2f: chsd clr wnr over 1f out: kpt on wl ins fnl f: no imp and eased towards fin* **12/1**[3]	70+
0-	3	3	**Burnt Fingers (IRE)**[161] 7371 3-9-0 0 ... AndreaAtzeni 8 (Rod Millman) *w ldr tl led over 2f out: rdn and hdd over 1f out: sn outpcd by wnr: 3rd and wknd ins fnl f* **16/1**	62
00-	4	3/4	**Dalaway (IRE)**[184] 6791 3-9-0 0 ... MartinHarley 5 (Mick Channon) *stdd s: t.k.h: hld up in tch in rr: rdn and effrt over 2f out: rn green over 1f out: no threat to wnr but kpt on ins fnl f* **20/1**	60+
0-	5	1 1/4	**Mists Of Time (IRE)**[211] 5979 3-9-0 0 ... JoeFanning 7 (Pat Eddery) *chsd ldrs: rdn and lost pl over 1f out: styd on same pce fr over 1f out* **11/4**[2]	57
	6	1 1/4	**Bill Of Rights** 3-9-0 0 ... HayleyTurner 2 (Michael Bell) *stdd and dropped in bhd after s: rdn and hdwy ent fnl 2f: no imp 1f out: wknd ins fnl f* **12/1**[3]	53
0-	7	13	**Daneglow (IRE)**[240] 4946 3-9-0 0 ... JimCrowley 6 (Mike Murphy) *led tl over 2f out: sn rdn and struggling: wknd over 1f out* **40/1**	18

1m 32.98s (6.78) **Going Correction** +0.675s/f (Yiel) 7 Ran SP% **83.7**
Speed ratings (Par 95): **88,86,83,82,80 79,64**
toteswingers 1&2 £2.40, 1&3 £4.00, 2&3 £6.00 CSF £15.69 TOTE £1.70: £1.10, £3.40; EX 9.40 Trifecta £55.90 Pool: £2,051.63 - 27.50 winning units..
Owner Saleh Al Homaizi & Imad Al Sagar **Bred** Saleh Al Homeizi **Trained** Newmarket, Suffolk

FOCUS
A ordinary 3-y-o fillies' maiden in terms of previous form and a moderate time. A nice start from the winner though.

1365 SIMON DE MONTFORT H'CAP 1m 1f 218y
5:15 (5:15) (Class 4) (0-85,78) 3-Y-O **£4,851** (£1,443; £721; £360) **Stalls** Low

Form				RPR
22-2	1		**High Troja (IRE)**[8] 1219 3-9-1 72 ... RyanMoore 3 (Ed Dunlop) *in tch: rdn to ld wl over 1f out: sn drvn clr: styd on strly: rdn out* **7/4**[1]	85
001-	2	5	**Mombasa**[161] 7373 3-9-7 78 ... JimCrowley 7 (Ralph Beckett) *chsd ldrs tl led 8f out: rdn and hdd wl over 1f out: sn outpcd by wnr and wl hld 1f out: battled on to hold 2nd fnl f* **5/2**[2]	81
201-	3	1	**Mad Jazz**[190] 6604 3-8-9 66 ... BarryMcHugh 2 (Tony Coyle) *led for 2f: chsd ldrs after: rdn and effrt jst over 2f out: no ch w wnr but battling for placings over 1f out: kpt on* **20/1**	67
162-	4	nk	**Jebril (FR)**[172] 7111 3-9-4 75 ... JamesDoyle 1 (Jonathan Portman) *hld up in tch: nt clr run and swtchd lft over 2f out: rdn and hdwy 2f out: no ch w wnr but pressing for placings 1f out: kpt on* **9/1**	75+
266-	5	2 1/4	**Dolphin Village (IRE)**[114] 8071 3-8-10 67 ... PaulHanagan 4 (Richard Fahey) *t.k.h: hld up in tch: rdn and effrt over 2f out: no imp and wl hld whn edgd rt over 1f out* **15/2**	63
341-	6	22	**East Texas Red (IRE)**[172] 7111 3-8-12 69 ... PatCosgrave 5 (Mick Quinn) *stdd s: hld up in tch in rr: rdn and no hdwy over 2f out: wknd 2f out: wl bhd and eased ins fnl f* **33/1**	21
62-1	7	1 1/2	**Raging Bear (USA)**[21] 1011 3-9-5 76 ... RichardHughes 6 (Richard Hannon) *stdd s: hld up towards rr: hdwy 8f out: chsd ldr 6f out: rdn and unable qck 3f out: lost pl over 2f out: sn wknd: wl bhd whn eased ins fnl f* **5/1**[3]	25

2m 13.9s (6.00) **Going Correction** +0.60s/f (Yiel) 7 Ran SP% **111.1**
Speed ratings (Par 100): **100,96,95,94,93 75,74**
toteswingers 1&2 £1.80, 1&3 £6.00, 2&3 £6.70 CSF £5.86 TOTE £3.30: £2.10, £1.10; EX 6.80 Trifecta £53.90 Pool: £3,015.41 - 41.95 winning units..
Owner Robert Ng **Bred** Carrigbeg Stud Co Ltd **Trained** Newmarket, Suffolk

FOCUS
A fair 3-y-o handicap rated around the third and fourth initially.

1366 GRANBY H'CAP 1m 60y
5:45 (5:45) (Class 5) (0-70,70) 4-Y-O+ **£2,587** (£770; £384; £192) **Stalls** Low

Form				RPR
0120	1		**West End Lad**[46] 709 10-8-13 65 ... (b) MarkCoumbe(3) 3 (Roy Bowring) *bhd: gd hdwy on outer to ld over 4f out: sn clr: rdn and kpt on wl fr over 2f out: in n.d 1f out: eased towards fin* **9/2**[3]	76
345-	2	3 3/4	**Skyfire**[161] 7368 6-9-1 64 ... MichaelStainton 4 (Nick Kent) *led tl hdd over 4f out: chsd wnr after: no imp u.p 2f out: wl hld after but hld on for 2nd fnl 100yds* **9/1**	66
4302	3	nk	**Brown Pete (IRE)**[4] 1297 5-9-4 67 ... MartinHarley 7 (Violet M Jordan) *hld up in last pair: rdn and effrt whn n.m.r over 2f out: hdwy u.p and modest 3rd 2f out:no ch w wnr but pressing for 2nd fnl 100yds: kpt on* **13/8**[1]	69
2-00	4	4 1/2	**George Benjamin**[14] 1115 6-9-1 67 ... DarrenEgan(3) 2 (Christopher Kellett) *stdd s: hld up in rr: swtchd lft and effrt u.p over 2f out: 4th and no imp whn edgd rt over 1f out* **20/1**	58
034-	5	2 1/4	**Illustrious Prince (IRE)**[136] 7799 6-9-2 70 ... JasonHart(5) 8 (Declan Carroll) *t.k.h: chsd ldr tl over 4f out: rdn and no hdwy over 2f out: wknd over 1f out* **8/1**	56
221-	6	1/2	**Bold Duke**[149] 7640 5-9-0 68 ... ThomasBrown(5) 5 (Edward Bevan) *in tch in midfield: rdn and unable qck over 2f out: sn struggling and btn: no ch fnl 2f* **4/1**[2]	53
00-3	7	14	**Aqua Ardens (GER)**[62] 493 5-9-2 65 ... PatCosgrave 1 (George Baker) *chsd ldrs tl 4f out: rdn and lost pl 3f out: bhd fnl 2f: eased wl ins fnl f* **8/1**	18

1m 51.3s (6.20) **Going Correction** +0.60s/f (Yiel) 7 Ran SP% **113.3**
Speed ratings (Par 103): **93,89,88,84,82 81,67**
toteswingers 1&2 £7.00, 1&3 £1.90, 2&3 £3.50 CSF £42.16 CT £91.02 TOTE £10.40: £4.40, £10.00; EX 64.70 Trifecta £184.90 Pool: £1,339.78 - 5.43 winning units..
Owner K Nicholls **Bred** Keith Nicholls **Trained** Edwinstowe, Notts

FOCUS
A modest handicap for older horses with the winner rated to last autumn's form but a bit messy otherwise.
T/Plt: £59.60 to a £1 stake. Pool: £49,662.26 - 608.14 winning tickets. T/Qpdt: £8.00 to a £1 stake. Pool: £3,137.26 - 287.60 winning tickets. SP

1349 WOLVERHAMPTON (A.W) (L-H)

Friday, April 5

OFFICIAL GOING: Standard

Wind: Fresh against Weather: Overcast

1367 32RED CASINO H'CAP 7f 32y(P)
5:55 (5:55) (Class 6) (0-60,59) 3-Y-O £1,940 (£577; £288; £144) Stalls High

Form RPR

00-5 1 **Brynford**39 796 3-9-0 52 KierenFallon 4 60+
(Chris Dwyer) *chsd ldrs: wnt 2nd 3f out: shkn up to ld ins fnl f: r.o* 9/2[3]

020- 2 1 **Clock On Tom**181 6893 3-8-7 52 MatthewHopkins(7) 1 59+
(Michael Easterby) *hld up: hdwy over 2f out: cl up whn hmpd ins fnl f: r.o to go 2nd nr fin: nvr able to chal* 6/1

2313 3 nk **Actonetaketwo**2 1319 3-8-10 53 PhilipPrince(5) 2 56
(Ron Hodges) *led: rdn over 1f out: hung lft and hdd ins fnl f: styng on same pce whn hung rt towards fin* 7/2[2]

4522 4 ¾ **Sand Grouse**19 1055 3-9-5 57 (b) AdamKirby 6 58
(Marco Botti) *s.i.s: hdwy over 5f out: rdn over 2f out: hung lft ins fnl f: styd on same pce* 2/1[1]

0-33 5 9 **Red Star Lady (IRE)**9 1197 3-8-10 48 DuranFentiman 3 25
(Shaun Harris) *hld up: rdn over 2f out: a in rr* 33/1

400- 6 6 **Ravens Nest**164 7306 3-9-7 59 RichardKingscote 5 19
(Milton Bradley) *chsd ldr tl pushed along 3f out: hung rt and wknd over 2f out* 7/2[2]

000- 7 7 **Bugsy's Babe**201 6276 3-8-9 47 TonyCulhane 7
(George Baker) *sn pushed along in rr: hdwy 5f out: wknd wl over 2f out* 16/1

1m 29.88s (0.28) **Going Correction** -0.05s/f (Stan) 7 Ran SP% **119.1**
Speed ratings (Par 96): **96,94,94,93,83 76,68**
toteswingers 1&2 £5.40, 1&3 £4.00, 2&3 £4.70 CSF £32.94 TOTE £9.60: £5.50, £6.50; EX 61.90 Trifecta £289.40 Pool: £2,494.36 - 6.46 winning units..
Owner R S G Jones **Bred** Old Suffolk Stud **Trained** Newmarket, Suffolk
■ Stewards' Enquiry : Philip Prince three-day ban: careless riding (Apr 19,20,22)

FOCUS
There was lively market for this modest handicap. The pace was steady and the first four finished clear. The form makes a fair bit of sense rated around the third and fourth to sound recent marks.

1368 £32 BONUS AT 32RED.COM CLAIMING STKS 1m 141y(P)
6:30 (6:30) (Class 6) 3-Y-O+ £1,940 (£577; £288; £144) Stalls Low

Form RPR

1140 1 **Classic Colori (IRE)**4 1281 6-10-0 78 (b) DanielTudhope 3 73
(David O'Meara) *hld up: hdwy over 2f out: led ins fnl f: shkn up and r.o* 4/7[1]

/006 2 2¾ **Matraash (USA)**15 1107 7-9-12 57 (be1) StephenCraine 2 65
(Daniel Mark Loughnane) *led and racd keenly: sn clr: stdd over 5f out: stl clr 2f out: hdd ins fnl f: styd on same pce* 33/1

446- 3 nk **Prime Exhibit**114 8081 8-9-13 81 (t) ShaneKelly 1 65
(Daniel Mark Loughnane) *hld up: rdn: edgd lft and r.o ins fnl f: nvr nr to chal* 2/1[2]

1433 4 nk **Zing Wing**20 1039 5-9-5 72 (v) AdamKirby 4 57
(David Evans) *chsd clr ldr: rdn over 2f out: tk clsr order and nt clr run over 1f out: swtchd lft: styd on same pce* 7/1[3]

1m 50.72s (0.22) **Going Correction** -0.05s/f (Stan) 4 Ran SP% **112.4**
Speed ratings (Par 101): **97,94,94,94**
CSF £16.15 TOTE £1.50; EX 10.90 Trifecta £71.60 Pool: £1,614.91 - 16.89 winning units..
Owner The Classic Strollers Partnership **Bred** Frank Dunne **Trained** Nawton, N Yorks

FOCUS
The odds-on favourite scored in good style in this fair claimer, which was run at a strong pace. With some doubts over current form the race is rated cautiously.

1369 32REDPOKER.COM H'CAP 2m 119y(P)
7:00 (7:00) (Class 6) (0-60,59) 4-Y-O+ £1,940 (£577; £288; £144) Stalls Low

Form RPR

2323 1 **Scribe (IRE)**10 1189 5-9-10 59 (vt) AdamKirby 2 69
(David Evans) *chsd ldrs tl led 2f out: rdn clr fnl f* 7/4[1]

046/ 2 6 **Simple Jim (FR)**486 7645 9-8-6 48 DavidBergin(7) 6 51
(David O'Meara) *hld up: hdwy over 2f out: chsd wnr over 1f out: no ex fnl f* 15/2[2]

40-3 3 3½ **David's Folly (IRE)**87 109 4-8-6 45 LukeMorris 7 44
(Tim Vaughan) *chsd ldr: rdn and ev ch 2f out: edgd lft and wknd fnl f* 15/2[2]

-045 4 1½ **Sacco D'Oro**9 1207 7-8-5 45 (v) RobertTart(5) 1 42
(Michael Mullineaux) *prom: rdn over 2f out: wknd over 1f out* 14/1[3]

-060 5 4½ **Newington**55 579 4-8-5 47 1 SimonPearce(3) 5 38
(Lydia Pearce) *hld up: rdn over 3f out: n.d* 18/1

000/ 6 nk **Treason Trial**14 1153 12-8-7 45 DeclanCannon(3) 8 36
(Jason Ward) *hld up: rdn and wknd 2f out* 50/1

-203 7 7 **Life Of Laughter (USA)**21 1022 5-9-1 50 KierenFallon 3 33
(Willie Musson) *chsd ldrs: pushed along over 2f out: wknd over 1f out* 7/4[1]

6605 8 4½ **There's No Rules**13 1146 4-8-6 45 (e) AndrewMullen 4 22
(Richard Guest) *sn led: clr 14f out tl 10f out: rdn and hdd 2f out: sn wknd* 25/1

3m 41.14s (-0.66) **Going Correction** -0.05s/f (Stan)
WFA 4 from 5yo+ 4lb 8 Ran SP% **114.0**
Speed ratings (Par 101): **99,96,94,93,91 91,88,86**
toteswingers 1&2 £3.40, 1&3 £3.30, 2&3 £4.60 CSF £16.40 CT £78.16 TOTE £3.20: £1.50, £1.40, £2.80; EX 17.00 Trifecta £94.60 Pool: £1,632.81 - 12.94 winning units..
Owner Shropshire Wolves/John Wilcox **Bred** Lynch Bages Ltd & Samac Ltd **Trained** Pandy, Monmouths

FOCUS
There was an emphatic winner of this low-grade staying handicap, which was run at a stop-start gallop. The winner has been rated up 4lb on recent form but there are doubts over the rest.

1370 32RED H'CAP 5f 20y(P)
7:30 (7:30) (Class 4) (0-85,84) 4-Y-O+ £4,690 (£1,395; £697; £348) Stalls Low

Form RPR

3-42 1 **My Son Max**14 1121 5-9-2 84 RobertTart(5) 5 92+
(P J O'Gorman) *hld up: hdwy over 1f out: rdn to ld wl ins fnl f: r.o* 11/10[1]

22- 2 nk **O'Gorman**127 7928 4-9-2 79 EddieAhern 10 86
(Gary Brown) *chsd ldrs: rdn over 1f out: r.o* 5/1[2]

-302 3 nk **Tyfos**18 1067 8-9-3 80 TomMcLaughlin 7 86
(Brian Baugh) *w ldr: rdn to ld ins fnl f: sn hdd: styd on* 10/1

2133 4 ¾ **Triple Dream**14 1121 8-9-5 82 (tp) JimmyQuinn 11 85
(Milton Bradley) *chsd ldrs: pushed along 1/2-way: n.m.r ins fnl f: styd on* 10/1

5033 5 hd **Sulis Minerva (IRE)**12 1160 6-9-3 83 RyanClark(3) 3 86+
(Jeremy Gask) *s.i.s: hld up: r.o wl ins fnl f: nvr nrr* 6/1[3]

000- 6 hd **Towbee**196 6427 4-9-2 79 JamesSullivan 2 81
(Michael Easterby) *a.p: pushed along 1/2-way: styd on* 50/1

343- 7 ½ **Hopes N Dreams (IRE)**148 7646 5-8-13 79 JulieBurke(3) 9 79+
(Kevin Ryan) *s.i.s: hld up: rdn over 1f out: r.o: nt rch ldrs* 12/1

-000 8 ¾ **Island Legend (IRE)**14 1121 7-9-2 79 (p) RichardKingscote 4 76
(Milton Bradley) *led: rdn: hdd and no ex ins fnl f* 20/1

00-6 9 nk **Beau Mistral (IRE)**24 966 4-9-5 82 CathyGannon 8 78
(Paul Green) *trckd ldrs: rdn over 1f out: styd on same pce* 28/1

-041 10 ¾ **Captain Scooby**4 1283 7-8-5 73 6ex JasonHart(5) 1 67
(Richard Guest) *hld up: swtchd rt over 1f out: nvr on terms* 14/1

1m 1.19s (-1.11) **Going Correction** -0.05s/f (Stan) 10 Ran SP% **121.3**
Speed ratings (Par 105): **106,105,105,103,103 103,102,101,100,99**
toteswingers 1&2 £1.60, 1&3 £6.30, 2&3 £13.80 CSF £6.90 CT £39.56 TOTE £1.70: £1.30, £1.60, £3.70; EX 7.80 Trifecta £48.50 Pool: £1,539.25 - 23.77 winning units..
Owner Racing To The Max **Bred** Mrs Fiona Denniff **Trained** Newmarket, Suffolk

FOCUS
A decent sprint handicap rated around the third and fourth. It was run at a solid pace and there was a bunch finish.

1371 32RED.COM MAIDEN FILLIES' STKS 1m 1f 103y(P)
8:00 (8:02) (Class 5) 3-Y-O+ £2,587 (£770; £384; £192) Stalls Low

Form RPR

1 **Heavenly Sound** 3-8-10 0 MartinHarley 2 78+
(Marco Botti) *led 1f: chsd ldrs: shkn up to ld over 1f out: r.o* 3/1[2]

0- 2 ¾ **Lovesome**155 7506 3-8-10 0 HayleyTurner 3 74
(Michael Bell) *a.p: chsd ldr over 7f out: shkn up and hung lft fr over 1f out: r.o* 7/2[3]

6- 3 ¾ **Permeate**184 6790 3-8-10 0 SteveDrowne 4 73
(Charles Hills) *led at stdy pce tl qcknd over 2f out: rdn: edgd lft and hdd over 1f out: styd on same pce ins fnl f* 4/5[1]

4 10 **Everlasting Dream** 3-8-10 0 MartinLane 1 52
(David Simcock) *s.i.s: hld up: rdn over 2f out: wknd over 1f out* 14/1

0 5 8 **American Kiss (SWE)**18 1070 4-9-13 30 SebSanders 5 39?
(Robin Dickin) *stdd s: hld up: rdn over 2f out: sn wknd* 66/1

2m 3.12s (1.42) **Going Correction** -0.05s/f (Stan)
WFA 3 from 4yo 17lb 5 Ran SP% **110.9**
Speed ratings (Par 100): **91,90,89,80,73**
CSF £13.69 TOTE £3.50: £1.30, £2.90; EX 16.20 Trifecta £24.50 Pool: £1,710.84 - 52.26 winning units..
Owner Newsells Park Stud **Bred** Newsells Park Stud **Trained** Newmarket, Suffolk

FOCUS
A newcomer scored with a bit more in hand than the winning margin in this fillies' maiden. Little to go on and hard to know what the form is worth.

1372 32REDBET.COM CLASSIFIED STKS 1m 1f 103y(P)
8:30 (8:30) (Class 6) 3-Y-O £1,940 (£577; £288) Stalls Low

Form RPR

05-2 1 **Mizyen (IRE)**18 1064 3-9-0 64 NeilCallan 2 74
(James Tate) *mde all: plld hrd: rdn over 1f out: edgd lft: r.o* 8/13[1]

0-41 2 2¾ **Bain's Pass (IRE)**18 1064 3-9-0 64 PhillipMakin 4 68
(Kevin Ryan) *chsd wnr: pushed along over 2f out: rdn over 1f out: no imp* 2/1[2]

45-2 3 28 **House Of Orange (IRE)**39 800 3-9-0 64 FrannyNorton 3 43
(Mark Johnston) *sn pushed along in rr: lost tch fr over 2f out: t.o* 6/1[3]

2m 1.76s (0.06) **Going Correction** -0.05s/f (Stan) 3 Ran SP% **109.5**
Speed ratings (Par 96): **97,94,69**
CSF £2.21 TOTE £1.60; EX 2.70 Trifecta £3.00 Pool: £667.89 - 166.91 winning units..
Owner Sheikh Juma Dalmook Al Maktoum **Bred** Mrs A Brudenell **Trained** Newmarket, Suffolk

FOCUS
The hot favourite made all in this small-field classified event. The winner could be better than this with the second the best guide to the level for now.

1373 32REDBINGO.COM H'CAP 1m 141y(P)
9:00 (9:00) (Class 6) (0-65,69) 3-Y-O £1,940 (£577; £288; £144) Stalls Low

Form RPR

-612 1 **Birdy Boy (USA)**21 1016 3-9-2 58 FrannyNorton 1 69
(Mark Johnston) *mde all: rdn over 1f out: r.o wl* 4/7[1]

4655 2 5 **Duchess Of Dreams**2 1320 3-8-2 49 oh1 PhilipPrince(5) 2 48
(Richard Guest) *hld up: hdwy over 3f out: rdn to chse wnr over 1f out: styd on same pce ins fnl f* 22/1

534 3 3 **Spider House**15 1106 3-9-7 63 DanielTudhope 3 55
(David O'Meara) *chsd wnr tl rdn over 1f out: no ex fnl f* 8/1[3]

050- 4 1¼ **Jawinski (IRE)**243 4837 3-9-7 63 AdamKirby 5 52
(David Evans) *s.i.s: hld up: rdn over 2f out: nvr on terms* 10/1

0603 5 1½ **Exit Clause**18 1064 3-8-6 53 (p) RobertTart(5) 6 39
(Tony Carroll) *chsd ldrs: rdn over 2f out: wknd fnl f* 11/4[2]

1m 50.5s **Going Correction** -0.05s/f (Stan) 5 Ran SP% **114.9**
Speed ratings (Par 96): **98,93,90,89,88**
CSF £15.84 TOTE £1.70: £1.10, £9.30; EX 18.90 Trifecta £41.10 Pool: £1,116.68 - 20.34 winning units..
Owner Frank Bird **Bred** Rancho San Peasea S A **Trained** Middleham Moor, N Yorks

FOCUS
The hot favourite powered clear under a trailblazing ride in this low-grade handicap. The second sets the level.
T/Plt: £103.60 to a £1 stake. Pool: £63,492.57 - 447.38 winning tickets T/Qpdt: £11.40 to a £1 stake. Pool: £6,921.47 - 447.70 winning tickets CR

1342 LINGFIELD (L-H)

Saturday, April 6

OFFICIAL GOING: Standard

Wind: medium, half against Weather: overcast, dry

1381 BRITISH HORSERACING EDUCATIONAL STANDARDS TRUST H'CAP 1m 2f (P)
1:55 (1:55) (Class 6) (0-65,66) 4-Y-O+ £2,045 (£603; £302) Stalls Low

Form RPR

0531 1 **Apache Glory (USA)**18 1082 5-9-4 61 (p) AndreaAtzeni 8 71
(John Stimpson) *in tch: rdn and hdwy to ld 1f out: r.o wl: in command whn edgd lft towards fin* 3/1[2]

-611 **2** 1 3/4 **Bridge That Gap**[40] 789 5-9-6 **63**....(p) AdamKirby 1 70+
(Roger Ingram) *hld up wl in tch: nt clr run over 1f out: rdn and hdwy 1f out: chsd clr wnr wl ins fnl f: swtchd rt towards fin: r.o but nvr gng to rch wnr* **1/1[1]**

00-4 **3** 1 1/4 **Moment In The Sun**[4] 1298 4-9-3 **60**.... JamieSpencer 3 65
(David Flood) *chsd ldrs: rdn and effrt on inner wl over 1f out: ev ch briefly 1f out: one pce and hld whn hmpd and eased towards fin* **5/1[3]**

143 **4** 1 1/4 **Total Obsession**[13] 1162 6-8-10 **53**....(v) KierenFallon 2 55
(Mark Hoad) *niggled along thrght: in tch in rr: rdn and hdwy over 2f out: no imp over 1f out: outpcd fnl f* **8/1**

4440 **5** 1/2 **Byrd In Hand (IRE)**[21] 737 6-8-7 **50** oh4.... WilliamCarson 6 51
(John Bridger) *t.k.h: chsd ldr tl over 1f out: wknd ins fnl f* **25/1**

100- **6** 2 1/4 **Cape Joy (IRE)**[213] 5942 4-9-7 **64**.... RichardHughes 5 60
(Richard Hannon) *led: hrd pressed and drvn over 1f out: hdd 1f out: sn wknd* **7/1**

2m 5.92s (-0.68) **Going Correction** 0.0s/f (Stan) **6** Ran SP% **119.1**
Speed ratings (Par 101): **102,100,99,98,98 96**
toteswingers 1&2 £1.30, 1&3 £6.00, 2&3 £1.40 CSF £6.93 CT £14.05 TOTE £4.70: £1.90, £1.50; EX 8.00 Trifecta £32.70 Pool: £1,032.29 - 23.60 winning units..

Owner J T Stimpson **Bred** Malih Al Basti **Trained** Butterton, Staffs

■ Stewards' Enquiry : Adam Kirby three-day ban: careless riding (Apr 20,22,23)

FOCUS
A modest handicap and they didn't go much of a pace, so the form is not entirely convincing. The third is the best guide for now.

1382 VINES BMW H'CAP 1m 4f (P)
2:25 (2:25) (Class 2) (0-105,101) 4-Y-0+ **£12,291** (£3,657; £1,827; £913) **Stalls** Low

Form RPR

0302 **1** **Universal (IRE)**[7] 1242 4-9-9 **101**.... JoeFanning 7 109
(Mark Johnston) *chsd ldr tl rdn to ld over 1f out: qcknd u.p and clr ins fnl f: r.o strly: readily* **3/1[2]**

3633 **2** 2 3/4 **Tepmokea (IRE)**[7] 1242 7-9-6 **97**.... ShaneKelly 3 101
(Mrs K Burke) *chsd ldr: rdn and effrt to press ldrs 2f out: drvn and outpcd by wnr over 1f out: rallied and chsd clr wnr ins fnl f: kpt on but no threat* **5/1**

223- **3** 1 1/2 **A Boy Named Suzi**[224] 5580 5-9-7 **98**.... JamieSpencer 5 100
(Andrew Balding) *stdd s: hld up in tch in last trio: rdn and effrt over 2f out: drvn and outpcd over 1f out: rallied and styd on again fnl 100yds: snatched 3rd on post: no threat to wnr* **11/4[1]**

1332 **4** *nse* **Aquilonius (IRE)**[13] 1159 4-8-10 **88**....(t) RyanMoore 1 90
(Stuart Williams) *led: drvn and hdd over 1f out: unable qck and outpcd by wnr: styd on same pce and lost 2 pls ins fnl f* **7/1**

150- **5** 1/2 **Quixote**[140] 7771 4-8-9 **87**....(t) KierenFallon 4 88
(Clive Brittain) *hld up wl in tch in midfield: swtchd and hdwy over 1f out: no threat to wnr and styd on same pce ins fnl f: lost 3rd on post* **8/1**

03/ **6** 1 1/4 **Apache (IRE)**[595] 5283 5-9-4 **95**.... GeorgeBaker 2 94
(Jane Chapple-Hyam) *t.k.h: chsd ldrs: rdn and unable qck over 1f out: wknd fnl 100yds* **4/1[3]**

00-0 **7** 1 3/4 **Robin Hood (IRE)**[21] 1034 5-8-12 **89**....[1] JackMitchell 6 85
(Philip Mitchell) *t.k.h: hld up in last pair: rdn and no imp over 1f out: nvr trbld ldrs* **50/1**

2431 **8** 5 **Wildomar**[44] 739 4-8-5 **86**.... RyanPowell(3) 8 74
(John Ryan) *s.i.s: a in rr: rdn and no hdwy ent fnl 2f: wknd over 1f out* **14/1**

2m 30.4s (-2.60) **Going Correction** 0.0s/f (Stan)
WFA 4 from 5yo+ 1lb **8** Ran SP% **120.6**
Speed ratings (Par 109): **108,106,105,105,104 103,102,99**
toteswingers 1&2 £8.20, 1&3 £4.40, 2&3 £5.00 CSF £19.67 CT £46.68 TOTE £3.50: £1.70, £2.00, £1.70; EX 20.40 Trifecta £173.30 Pool: £1,097.30 - 4.74 winning units..

Owner Abdulla Al Mansoori **Bred** Grangecon Stud **Trained** Middleham Moor, N Yorks

FOCUS
A decent handicap, though the early pace looked ordinary and a couple were keen as a result. The second sets the standard.

1383 INTERNATIONAL TRIAL STKS (LISTED RACE) 1m (P)
3:00 (3:00) (Class 1) 3-Y-O
£20,982 (£7,955; £3,981; £1,983; £995; £499) **Stalls** High

Form RPR

112- **1** **Van Der Neer**[161] 7398 3-9-0 114.... RichardHughes 7 104+
(Richard Hannon) *hld up in midfield on outer: effrt to go 3rd 2f out: chsd clr ldr 1f out: str run to ld wl ins fnl f: sn in command and eased cl home* **2/5[1]**

-035 **2** 3/4 **Luhaif**[37] 835 3-9-0 96....(v) MartinHarley 4 102?
(Mick Channon) *rdn leaving stalls and sn led: racd freely and clr 6f out: stl 5 l clr and rdn 2f out: hdd and no ex wl ins fnl f* **20/1**

11- **3** 1 **Unsinkable (IRE)**[261] 4247 3-9-0 89.... PaulHanagan 6 100
(Richard Fahey) *chsd ldr: rdn ent fnl 2f: edgd lft and lost 2nd 1f out: kpt on u.p fnl f* **8/1[3]**

60-6 **4** *nk* **Maxentius (IRE)**[21] 1033 3-9-0 104.... LukeMorris 3 99
(Peter Chapple-Hyam) *racd in midfield: rdn and chsd ldng trio 2f out: kpt on u.p ins fnl f* **14/1**

540- **5** 2 1/4 **Masarah (IRE)**[175] 7052 3-8-9 99.... RyanMoore 1 89
(Clive Brittain) *t.k.h: hld up in midfield: rdn and sme hdwy but stl plenty to do over 2f out: kpt on but no threat to ldrs fnl f* **20/1**

643- **6** 1 **Operation Chariot (IRE)**[206] 6149 3-9-0 98.... JimmyFortune 8 92
(Andrew Balding) *t.k.h: hld up in last quartet: rdn and effrt over 2f out: kpt on fnl f but nvr threatened ldrs* **25/1**

31-3 **7** 2 1/4 **Hoarding (USA)**[21] 1033 3-9-0 93.... WilliamBuick 5 86
(John Gosden) *racd in last quartet: rdn and dropped to last pair over 4f out: rdn and no rspnse over 2f out: nvr trbld ldrs* **4/1[2]**

10-5 **8** 1 1/4 **Flawless Beauty**[23] 1000 3-8-9 87.... JamesDoyle 9 78
(Hugo Palmer) *bhd: rdn and no hdwy 2f out: n.d* **33/1**

64-0 **9** 16 **Ocean Applause**[5] 1293 3-9-0 79.... KierenFallon 2 47
(John Ryan) *sn niggled along: chsd ldrs tl lost pl ent fnl 2f: sn bhd* **33/1**

1m 35.07s (-3.13) **Going Correction** 0.0s/f (Stan) **9** Ran SP% **128.5**
Speed ratings (Par 106): **115,114,113,112,110 109,107,106,90**
toteswingers 1&2 £5.40, 1&3 £2.10, 2&3 £27.70 CSF £18.79 TOTE £1.40: £1.02, £5.40, £1.80; EX 18.10 Trifecta £100.10 Pool: £1,676.89 - 12.56 winning units..

Owner Saeed Manana **Bred** Jeremy Green And Sons **Trained** East Everleigh, Wilts

FOCUS
The pace was decent for this Listed race thanks to the runner-up, who took plenty of catching. The form is a bit fluid but the runner-up is the best guide to his juvenile best.

1384 VIVIEN BLACK BIRTHDAY CELEBRATION MAIDEN STKS 6f (P)
3:40 (3:40) (Class 5) 3-Y-O **£2,587** (£770; £384; £192) **Stalls** Low

Form RPR

40-4 **1** **Shafaani**[21] 1033 3-9-0 87....(t) RyanMoore 4 79
(Clive Brittain) *mde all: rdn and qcknd clr 2f out: in command and edgd rt 1f out: rdn out* **4/7[1]**

03-2 **2** 7 **Hornboy**[17] 1086 3-9-5 71.... WilliamBuick 5 62
(Jeremy Noseda) *chsd wnr: rdn and outpcd 2f out: no ch w wnr but kpt on for 2nd fnl f* **2/1[2]**

236- **3** 1 1/4 **Puteri Nur Laila (IRE)**[159] 7433 3-9-0 67.... ChrisCatlin 2 53
(Paul Cole) *chsd ldng pair: rdn over 2f out: 3rd and wl hld over 1f out: kpt on* **16/1**

33 **4** *nk* **Half Turn**[10] 1199 3-9-5 0.... RobertHavlin 1 57
(Luke Dace) *t.k.h: hld up in last pair: outpcd by wnr 2f out: rdn and styd on same pce fr over 1f out* **100/1**

60- **5** 1 3/4 **Wildcrafting**[213] 5943 3-9-0 0.... JamieSpencer 6 46
(Michael Bell) *stdd s: hld up in rr: wd and outpcd bnd 2f out: wl hld and styd on same pce fr over 1f out* **12/1[3]**

00- **6** *nse* **Dividend Dan (IRE)**[170] 7191 3-9-5 0.... EddieAhern 3 51
(Mike Murphy) *t.k.h: hld up in midfield: outpcd 2f out: rdn and no hdwy over 1f out: wl hld and styd on same pce fnl f* **50/1**

1m 13.38s (1.48) **Going Correction** 0.0s/f (Stan) **6** Ran SP% **113.5**
Speed ratings (Par 98): **90,80,79,78,76 76**
toteswingers 1&2 £1.40, 1&3 £10.30, 2&3 £2.00 CSF £1.99 TOTE £1.40: £1.10, £1.80; EX 2.50 Trifecta £7.20 Pool: £2,117.06 - 218.67 winning units..

Owner Saeed Manana **Bred** Rabbah Bloodstock Limited **Trained** Newmarket, Suffolk

FOCUS
An uncompetitive maiden, but unlike in the previous race odds-on backers never had a moment's worry. The winner ran close to his previous form with the second helping the level.

1385 RACING TO SCHOOL H'CAP 7f (P)
4:45 (4:45) (Class 3) (0-95,95) 4-Y-0+ **£7,439** (£2,213; £1,106; £553) **Stalls** Low

Form RPR

0-04 **1** **Monsieur Chevalier (IRE)**[28] 944 6-9-6 **94**.... KierenFallon 4 106+
(P J O'Gorman) *hld up in tch in midfield: swtchd out rt and hdwy over 1f out: led 1f out: clr ins fnl f: pressed and drvn out cl home* **7/2[1]**

421- **2** *nk* **Jack Of Diamonds (IRE)**[135] 7824 4-8-8 **82**.... JamesDoyle 1 93+
(Roger Teal) *in tch: shuffled bk and nt clr run over 1f out: sn swtchd rt: rallied and str run ins fnl f: pressing wnr cl home: styd on* **7/2[1]**

2131 **3** 1 1/4 **Al's Memory (IRE)**[13] 1160 4-8-12 **86**.... CathyGannon 10 93
(David Evans) *chsd ldrs: drvn over 1f out: kpt on same pce u.p ins fnl f* **8/1[2]**

00-2 **4** 3/4 **Bravo Echo**[19] 1061 7-9-7 **95**.... RobertHavlin 13 100
(Michael Attwater) *chsd ldr tl jnd ldr 3f out: led and rdn 2f out: hdd and no ex 1f out: styd on same pce after* **14/1**

1005 **5** 3/4 **Spirit Of Sharjah (IRE)**[7] 1244 8-8-11 **92**.... ShelleyBirkett(7) 6 95
(Julia Feilden) *stdd s: hld up in tch in last trio: clsd over 1f out: swtchd lft and hdwy 1f out: styd on same pce and no imp fnl 100yds* **20/1**

1154 **6** *hd* **Mister Musicmaster**[17] 1092 4-8-8 **82**.... WilliamCarson 7 84
(Ron Hodges) *chsd ldrs: unable qck u.p over 1f out: drvn and kpt on same pce ins fnl f* **16/1**

3450 **7** 3/4 **Forest Edge (IRE)**[13] 1160 4-8-8 **82**.... SamHitchcott 9 82
(David Evans) *in tch in last trio: rdn along 4f out: sme hdwy 1f out: kpt on ins fnl f: nvr trbld ldrs* **50/1**

2-43 **8** *nk* **Galician**[7] 1252 4-9-0 **88**.... JoeFanning 2 88
(Mark Johnston) *chsd ldrs: unable qck u.p over 1f out: hld and one pce fnl f* **8/1[2]**

4-60 **9** 1/2 **Frog Hollow**[7] 1233 4-8-12 **86**.... RyanMoore 11 84
(Milton Bradley) *in tch in last quartet: rdn and styd on same pce fr over 1f out: nvr trbld ldrs* **8/1[2]**

12/0 **10** 1 **Ortac Rock (IRE)**[19] 1061 4-8-10 **84**.... RichardHughes 5 80
(Richard Hannon) *led: hdd and rdn 2f out: drvn and stl ev ch 1f out: wknd qckly ins fnl f* **7/2[1]**

33-0 **11** *nk* **Our Boy Jack (IRE)**[13] 1168 4-8-10 **84**.... PaulHanagan 8 79
(Richard Fahey) *in tch in last quartet: rdn 4f out: bhd and no imp u.p over 1f out* **12/1[3]**

1m 22.61s (-2.19) **Going Correction** 0.0s/f (Stan) **11** Ran SP% **127.0**
Speed ratings (Par 107): **112,111,110,109,108 108,107,107,106,105 105**
toteswingers 1&2 £4.80, 1&3 £9.70, 2&3 £10.70 CSF £15.85 CT £98.90 TOTE £4.30: £1.70, £2.00, £2.80; EX 19.60 Trifecta £41.00 Pool: £1,549.55 - 28.30 winning units..

Owner Racing To The Max **Bred** Tally-Ho Stud **Trained** Newmarket, Suffolk

FOCUS
A competitive handicap, run at a solid pace and the form looks sound, with the third and fourth setting the standard.

1386 CORE GROUP H'CAP 7f (P)
5:20 (5:20) (Class 5) (0-70,70) 4-Y-0+ **£2,726** (£805; £402) **Stalls** Low

Form RPR

526- **1** **Kinglami**[142] 7725 4-9-6 **69**.... RichardHughes 6 75
(Brian Gubby) *chsd ldr: rdn ent fnl 2f: drvn and stl pressing ldrs but looked hld 1f out: rallied u.p and styd on wl to ld towards fin* **5/4[1]**

3532 **2** *nk* **Spark Of Genius**[10] 1211 4-9-7 **70**....(v) RyanMoore 2 75
(Alan McCabe) *led: c towards centre and rdn wl over 1f out: drvn and looked to be holding rivals ins fnl f: hdd and no ex towards fin* **6/4[2]**

26-0 **3** *nk* **Mister Green (FR)**[4] 1303 7-9-0 **63**.... JamesDoyle 1 67
(David Flood) *chsd ldng pair: drvn to chse ldr over 1f out: ev ch ins fnl f: unable qck wl ins fnl f* **14/1**

-055 **4** 2 **Titan Triumph**[36] 844 9-9-5 **68**....(t) GeorgeBaker 5 67
(William Knight) *hld up in tch in last pair: rdn and effrt over 1f out: swtchd lft 1f out: styd on same pce fnl 100yds* **7/1[3]**

2000 **5** 3 1/4 **Kindia (IRE)**[12] 1176 5-9-4 **67**....(p) SebSanders 3 57
(Michael Attwater) *hld up in last pair: rdn and outpcd wl over 1f out: wknd ins fnl f* **10/1**

1m 24.13s (-0.67) **Going Correction** 0.0s/f (Stan) **5** Ran SP% **112.7**
Speed ratings (Par 103): **103,102,102,100,96**
CSF £3.53 TOTE £2.60: £1.10, £1.20; EX 5.10 Trifecta £22.10 Pool: £1,992.04 - 67.45 winning units..

Owner Brian Gubby **Bred** Cheveley Park Stud Ltd **Trained** Bagshot, Surrey

FOCUS
A modest handicap and ordinary but sound form rated through the runner-up.

1387 LINGFIELDPARK.CO.UK MAIDEN STKS — 7f (P)
5:55 (5:56) (Class 5) 3-Y-O — £2,726 (£805; £402) Stalls Low

Form — RPR

43- **1** **Market Town (USA)**196 6481 3-9-5 0 RyanMoore 2 88+
(Charles Hills) *chsd ldng pair tl wnt 2nd 5f out: upsides ldr 3f out tl rdn to ld wl over 1f out: asserted u.p ins fnl f: pushed out and r.o wl fnl 100yds* 1/4[1]

02- **2** 2 1/4 **Enzaal (USA)**176 7021 3-9-5 0 PaulHanagan 4 82
(Mark Johnston) *led: rdn ent fnl 2f: hdd wl over 1f out: battled on wl tl btn ins fnl f: hld on for 2nd towards fin* 8/1[3]

33- **3** nk **Secret Art (IRE)**178 6977 3-9-5 0 JamesDoyle 1 81
(Ralph Beckett) *t.k.h: chsd ldr tl 5f out: chsd ldrs after: rdn over 1f out: kpt on ins fnl f to press for 2nd towards fin* 6/1[2]

00- **4** 2 1/2 **Soul Intent (IRE)**164 7323 3-9-5 0 SebSanders 3 74
(J W Hills) *stdd s: t.k.h: hld up in tch in rr: rdn and outpcd wl over 1f out: one pce after* 20/1

1m 25.92s (1.12) **Going Correction** 0.0s/f (Stan) 4 Ran SP% 110.2
Speed ratings (Par 98): **93,90,90,87**
CSF £3.06 TOTE £1.30; EX 3.60 Trifecta £4.60 Pool: £1,027.09 - 165.93 winning units..
Owner K Abdullah **Bred** Millsec Ltd **Trained** Lambourn, Berks
FOCUS
All four of these were making their seasonal reappearances and needed this run for a handicap mark. The form is rated around the placed horses.
T/Plt: £3.50 to a £1 stake. Pool: £60,750.96 - 12,477.06 winning tickets T/Qpdt: £1.90 to a £1 stake. Pool: £2,862.38 - 1,089.82 winning tickets SP

NEWCASTLE (L-H)
Saturday, April 6

OFFICIAL GOING: Good to soft (6.1)
Wind: Almost nil Weather: Cloudy, sunny spells

1388 OPSOL UK LTD H'CAP — 5f
1:35 (1:35) (Class 6) (0-60,66) 4-Y-O+ — £1,940 (£577; £288; £144) Stalls Centre

Form — RPR

460- **1** **Dartrix**184 6806 4-8-8 54 [1] ConnorBeasley(7) 4 67
(Michael Dods) *taken early to post: hld up in tch: hdwy over 1f out: led ins fnl f: rdn out* 12/1

00-0 **2** 3/4 **Chosen One (IRE)**18 1077 8-9-0 53 PJMcDonald 5 63
(Ruth Carr) *cl up: led 1/2-way to ins fnl f: kpt on: hld nr fin* 22/1

-400 **3** 3 **Code Six (IRE)**14 1147 4-8-13 52 (p) TomEaves 7 52
(Bryan Smart) *taken early to post: in tch: rdn and edgd lft 2f out: kpt on same pce fnl f* 17/2[3]

4213 **4** 1 1/4 **Pull The Pin (IRE)**6 1276 4-8-13 55 (b) NeilFarley(3) 6 50
(Declan Carroll) *s.i.s: bhd and rdn: hdwy over 1f out: kpt on fnl f: nvr able to chal* 5/2[1]

1111 **5** 1/2 **Greenhead High**6 1276 5-9-13 66 6ex (v) AdrianNicholls 3 59
(David Nicholls) *cl up: rdn over 2f out: nt qckn appr fnl f* 5/2[1]

60-6 **6** 2 **Charles Parnell (IRE)**5 1280 10-8-7 46 RoystonFfrench 8 32
(Simon Griffiths) *bhd: rdn 1/2-way: kpt on fnl f: nvr able to chal* 33/1

3062 **7** 3 1/4 **Roy's Legacy**6 1276 4-9-0 58 (t) MichaelJMMurphy(5) 1 32
(Shaun Harris) *led to 1/2-way: sn rdn: wknd over 1f out* 10/3[2]

632- **8** 8 **Pavers Star**141 7746 4-9-4 57 (p) DuranFentiman 2
(Noel Wilson) *chsd ldrs tl wknd fr 2f out* 12/1

1m 2.96s (1.86) **Going Correction** +0.125s/f (Good) 8 Ran SP% 113.4
Speed ratings (Par 101): **90,88,84,82,81 78,72,60**
toteswingers 1&2 £12.90, 2&3 £13.80, 1&3 £13.80 CSF £225.50 CT £2341.59 TOTE £16.30: £2.50, £3.00, £2.80; EX 312.90 Trifecta £433.50 Pool: £578.13 - 0.51 winning units..
Owner K Knox **Bred** T K & Mrs P A Knox **Trained** Denton, Co Durham
FOCUS
A modest sprint handicap for older horses in which they went an even gallop on ground officially described as good to soft. The winner is rated to his best 3-y-o mark.

1389 THOMSON MAIDEN FILLIES' STKS — 1m (R)
2:10 (2:10) (Class 5) 3-4-Y-O — £2,587 (£770; £384; £192) Stalls Centre

Form — RPR

1 **Lady Artiste (IRE)** 3-8-12 0 RobertWinston 8 66+
(Alan Swinbank) *hld up on ins: shkn up 3f out: hdwy against ins rail 2f out: led ins fnl f: rdn and r.o strly* 5/2[1]

2 3 3/4 **Royal Style (IRE)** 3-8-12 0 GrahamGibbons 6 58+
(David Barron) *hld up towards rr: effrt and hdwy over 2f out: chsd wnr last 100yds: kpt on* 5/1[2]

04- **3** 3/4 **Dutch Gal**154 7552 3-8-12 0 RussKennemore 2 56
(John Holt) *plld hrd early: hld up in tch: smooth hdwy to chal over 2f out: rdn and led over 1f out to ins fnl f: one pce* 5/2[1]

02-0 **4** 2 1/2 **Mishhar (IRE)**5 1282 4-9-6 67 (p) DavidSimmonson(7) 3 50
(Tony Coyle) *led after 1f: rdn and jnd over 2f out: hdd over 1f out: outpcd ins fnl f* 5/1[2]

660- **5** 12 **Lucky Prize**245 4792 3-8-5 35 RobertDodsworth(7) 5 23
(Mel Brittain) *cl up: pushed along 1/2-way: wknd wl over 2f out* 50/1

0-46 **6** 13 **Imtithal (IRE)**11 1184 4-9-10 64 MichaelMetcalfe(3) 4
(John Weymes) *prom: effrt and ch over 2f out: sn rdn and wknd: t.o* 11/1

-0 **7** 11 **Dolly Diva**11 1184 4-9-13 60 PJMcDonald 1
(Paul Midgley) *plld hrd early: led 1f: cl up to 3f out: sn wknd: t.o* 10/1[3]

0- **8** 1 **Miss Bossy Boots**159 7445 4-9-13 0 RoystonFfrench 7
(Tracy Waggott) *s.i.s: t.k.h in rr: struggling over 3f out: sn btn: t.o* 20/1

1m 47.66s (2.36) **Going Correction** +0.375s/f (Good)
WFA 3 from 4yo 15lb 8 Ran SP% 114.6
Speed ratings (Par 100): **103,99,98,96,84 71,60,59**
toteswingers 1&2 £5.90, 2&3 £4.50, 1&3 £3.90 CSF £15.47 TOTE £3.10: £1.20, £3.10, £1.10; EX 16.50 Trifecta £55.40 Pool: £1213.66 - 16.42 winning units..
Owner Solway Stayers 2 **Bred** Lynch Bages, Samac Ltd & Longfield Stud **Trained** Melsonby, N Yorks
FOCUS
A modest fillies' maiden and the form does not look solid.

1390 F1 SIGNS & DIGITAL H'CAP — 1m 4f 93y
2:40 (2:40) (Class 5) (0-75,76) 4-Y-O+ — £2,587 (£770; £384; £192) Stalls Low

Form — RPR

600- **1** **Mohawk Ridge**158 7454 7-8-13 67 TomEaves 11 76
(Michael Dods) *mde all: rdn clr over 2f out: kpt on fnl f: unchal* 25/1

0-36 **2** 2 1/2 **Roc De Prince**25 969 4-8-13 68 DanielTudhope 10 73
(David O'Meara) *pressed wnr: drvn and outpcd over 2f out: rallied and regained 2nd last 100yds: nt gng pce of wnr* 8/1

6/3- **3** 3/4 **Graceful Descent (FR)**279 3061 8-9-2 70 FrederikTylicki 2 74
(Karen Tutty) *hld up in midfield on ins: rdn over 3f out: hdwy 2f out: kpt on fnl f: tk 3rd cl home* 25/1

2212 **4** nk **Activate**7 1251 6-9-1 74 (p) GarryWhillans(5) 8 77
(Keith Dalgleish) *in tch on outside: effrt and chsd wnr over 2f out: sn drvn: outpcd and lost two pls last 100yds* 5/2[1]

420- **5** nk **Come Here Yew (IRE)**162 7367 5-9-3 74 NeilFarley(3) 4 77+
(Declan Carroll) *hld up: rdn over 3f out: hdwy wl over 1f out: kpt on fnl f: nvr able to chal* 9/2[2]

106- **6** 8 **La Bacouetteuse (FR)**188 6712 8-9-3 71 (p) DavidAllan 5 61
(Iain Jardine) *hld up: rdn over 4f out: sme hdwy over 1f out: nt gng pce to chal* 18/1

-501 **7** 7 **Thecornishcowboy**10 1200 4-9-7 76 (t) GrahamLee 1 55
(John Ryan) *hld up towards rr: drvn over 3f out: sn no imp: btn over 1f out* 11/2[3]

5-65 **8** 1/2 **Light The City (IRE)**11 1188 6-8-11 65 JamesSullivan 7 43
(Ruth Carr) *chsd ldrs: drvn and outpcd over 2f out: sn btn* 20/1

/413 **9** 3 1/2 **Mister Bob (GER)**16 1097 4-8-6 61 RoystonFfrench 6 33
(James Bethell) *hld up in tch: struggling 3f out: sn btn* 6/1

534- **10** 2 1/4 **Beat The Shower**188 6712 7-9-1 69 PhillipMakin 9 38
(Peter Niven) *hld up: drvn and outpcd over 4f out: nvr on terms* 20/1

220- **11** 6 **Generous Dream**175 7068 5-8-10 64 PaulMulrennan 3 23
(Mel Brittain) *chsd ldrs tl rdn and wknd over 2f out* 12/1

2m 49.02s (3.42) **Going Correction** +0.375s/f (Good)
WFA 4 from 5yo+ 1lb 11 Ran SP% 117.7
Speed ratings (Par 103): **103,101,100,100,100 95,90,90,87,86 82**
toteswingers 1&2 £23.40, 2&3 £11.00, 1&3 £23.40 CSF £203.62 CT £5010.07 TOTE £37.10: £6.50, £2.10, £5.20; EX 165.90 TRIFECTA Not won..
Owner Doug Graham **Bred** Old Mill Stud Ltd And Oomswell Ltd **Trained** Denton, Co Durham
■ Stewards' Enquiry : Garry Whillans two-day ban: used whip above permitted level (Apr 20,22)
FOCUS
A fair middle-distance handicap for older horses in which a few horses were pulling early on suggesting the gallop wasn't strong. Not form to get carried away with.

1391 SENDRIG CONSTRUCTION H'CAP — 1m 2f 32y
3:15 (3:15) (Class 4) (0-85,83) 4-Y-O+ — £4,690 (£1,395; £697; £348) Stalls Low

Form — RPR

000- **1** **Beaumont's Party (IRE)**243 4879 6-9-2 78 DaleSwift 2 87+
(Brian Ellison) *t.k.h: hld up bhd ldng gp: stdy hdwy over 2f out: rdn to ld ins fnl f: kpt on wl* 4/1[3]

36-1 **2** 1 **Docs Legacy (IRE)**7 1238 4-9-5 81 TonyHamilton 3 88
(Richard Fahey) *trckd ldrs: led 2f out: rdn and hdd ins fnl f: kpt on: hld towards fin* 7/4[1]

0-31 **3** 3 1/4 **Blades Lad**18 1076 4-8-11 73 PaulMulrennan 6 74
(Peter Niven) *hld up in tch: hdwy to chse ldr over 1f out to ins fnl f: sn outpcd* 14/1

465- **4** shd **Tres Coronas (IRE)**158 7455 6-9-0 76 [1] GrahamGibbons 4 76
(David Barron) *hld up: rdn over 2f out: hdwy over 1f out: kpt on ins fnl f* 7/2[2]

21-0 **5** 8 **Brockfield**7 1237 7-8-7 70 DavidAllan 1 54
(Mel Brittain) *led: rdn over 3f out: hdd 2f out: sn outpcd* 28/1

144- **6** 1/2 **Only Orsenfoolsies**35 7455 4-8-11 73 PJMcDonald 8 56
(Micky Hammond) *chsd ldrs on outside: rdn 1/2-way: rallied 3f out: wknd over 1f out* 8/1

402- **7** 1 1/2 **Maybeagrey**166 7294 4-8-9 71 DuranFentiman 5 51
(Tim Easterby) *hld up: drvn along over 3f out: btn fnl 2f* 14/1

200- **8** 1 1/4 **Rocktherunway (IRE)**182 6884 4-9-7 83 TomEaves 7 61
(Michael Dods) *pressed ldr: rdn over 3f out: edgd lft and wknd over 2f out* 8/1

2m 14.36s (2.46) **Going Correction** +0.375s/f (Good) 8 Ran SP% 117.6
Speed ratings (Par 105): **105,104,101,101,95 94,93,92**
toteswingers 1&2 £2.40, 2&3 £6.30, 1&3 £20.80 CSF £11.80 CT £89.10 TOTE £5.70: £1.80, £1.10, £3.40; EX 17.80 Trifecta £295.10 Pool: £1109.65 - 2.81 winning units..
Owner Elliott Brothers And Peacock **Bred** Mrs Joan Murphy **Trained** Norton, N Yorks
FOCUS
A decent handicap for older horses in which they went an even gallop. The form looks sound rated around the placed horses.

1392 R F HENDERSON LTD MAIDEN STKS — 6f
3:55 (3:55) (Class 5) 3-Y-O+ — £2,587 (£770; £384; £192) Stalls Centre

Form — RPR

62-0 **1** **Lexington Place**6 1275 3-9-0 65 TonyHamilton 7 69
(Richard Fahey) *mde all against stands' rail: rdn 2f out: edgd lft ins fnl f: kpt on wl* 8/1[3]

00- **2** 3/4 **Adam's Ale**142 7729 4-9-12 0 MickyFenton 1 70
(Paul Midgley) *sn cl up: rdn and ev ch over 1f out to ins fnl f: hld towards fin* 40/1

044- **3** 2 **Bitusa (USA)**175 7067 3-9-0 69 RobertWinston 5 60
(Alan Swinbank) *trckd ldrs: drvn and outpcd 2f out: styd on fnl f: nt rch first two* 5/1[2]

2 **4** 1 **Can You Conga**45 729 3-9-0 0 PhillipMakin 2 57
(Kevin Ryan) *prom: effrt and drvn over 1f out: edgd lft ins fnl f: kpt on same pce* 8/13[1]

-63 **5** 1 **The Codger**14 1150 3-9-0 0 DanielTudhope 6 54+
(David O'Meara) *midfield: sddle slipped briefly over 2f out: effrt and drvn over 1f out: one pce fnl f* 16/1

6 4 **Compton Heights** 4-9-12 0 [1] GrahamLee 9 44
(Jim Goldie) *hld up bhd ldng gp: rdn and rn green over 2f out: n.d after* 18/1

7 1 1/4 **Burren View Lady (IRE)** 3-8-9 0 DavidAllan 8 32
(Tim Easterby) *slowly away: bhd and green: sme late hdwy: nvr on terms* 14/1

8 5 **Theatrical Dancer** 6-9-7 0 PaulMulrennan 10
(Jim Goldie) *sn pushed along towards rr: struggling 1/2-way: sn btn* 50/1

9 1 1/2 **Trixie Malone** 3-8-9 0 MichaelO'Connell 4
(Mrs K Burke) *midfield: sn rn green: rdn and wknd fr 1/2-way* 10/1

0- **10** 13 **Swift Code (IRE)**280 3638 3-9-0 0 TomEaves 3
(Nigel Tinkler) *s.i.s: bhd: no ch fr 1/2-way* 66/1

1m 16.11s (1.51) **Going Correction** +0.125s/f (Good)
WFA 3 from 4yo+ 12lb 10 Ran SP% 122.5
Speed ratings (Par 103): **94,93,90,89,87 82,80,74,72,54**
toteswingers 1&2 £26.40, 2&3 £26.40, 1&3 £4.30 CSF £280.86 TOTE £12.40: £2.80, £17.50, £2.30; EX 342.40 Trifecta £1528.10 Part won. Pool: £2037.51 - 0.01 winning units..

Owner Middleham Park Racing XXXI **Bred** Christopher & Annabelle Mason **Trained** Musley Bank, N Yorks

FOCUS
A modest maiden in which they went a decent gallop. The winner sets the level for now.

1393 D S E NORTHERN LTD H'CAP 1m 3y(S)
5:00 (5:00) (Class 6) (0-60,60) 3-Y-O £1,940 (£577; £288; £144) Stalls Centre

Form RPR
025- 1 **Mash Potato (IRE)**[171] 7173 3-9-4 **57** PaulMulrennan 1 62
(Michael Dods) *in tch: effrt and drvn 2f out: led ins fnl f: hld on wl* **7/2**[1]
04-3 2 3/4 **Multisure**[10] 1210 3-9-3 **56** PJMcDonald 3 59
(Ruth Carr) *led to over 2f out: sn rdn: rallied and chsd wnr ins fnl f: kpt on: hld nr fin* **14/1**
034- 3 3/4 **Bell'Arte (IRE)**[159] 7439 3-9-7 **60** FrannyNorton 5 61
(Mark Johnston) *hld up: rdn and hdwy wl over 1f out: styd on fnl f: nt gng pce to chal* **5/1**[2]
060- 4 nk **Multifact**[191] 6603 3-8-13 **55** LeeTopliss(3) 7 56
(Michael Dods) *plld hrd early: hld up in tch: effrt 2f out: kpt on same pce ins fnl f* **7/1**
04-3 5 1/2 **Krupskaya (FR)**[37] 827 3-9-4 **60** MichaelMetcalfe(3) 2 59
(Mrs K Burke) *cl up: led over 2f out: hung lft and hdd ins fnl f: no ex and lost two pls nr fin* **9/1**
640- 6 3 **Attansky (IRE)**[185] 6793 3-9-7 **60** DavidAllan 8 53
(Tim Easterby) *hld up: rdn and effrt over 2f out: no imp fnl f* **6/1**[3]
050- 7 1/2 **French Revolution**[185] 6793 3-8-11 **50** MichaelO'Connell 9 41
(Jedd O'Keeffe) *cl up: drvn and outpcd over 2f out: n.d after* **28/1**
004- 8 1 1/4 **Spats Colombo**[123] 7979 3-8-12 **51** TomEaves 10 40
(Micky Hammond) *hld up in tch: drvn along over 2f out: btn over 1f out* **14/1**
400- 9 2 **Captain's Dream (IRE)**[171] 7173 3-9-4 **57** GrahamLee 4 41
(Jedd O'Keeffe) *t.k.h: trckd ldrs tl rdn and wknd over 2f out* **16/1**
2-34 10 12 **Panama Cat (USA)**[15] 1118 3-9-4 **57** AmyRyan 11 13
(Kevin Ryan) *hld up: drvn over 2f out: sn struggling: t.o* **7/2**[1]

1m 45.66s (2.26) **Going Correction** +0.125s/f (Good) 10 Ran SP% **120.6**
Speed ratings (Par 96): **93,92,91,91,90 87,87,85,83,71**
toteswingers 1&2 £9.00, 2&3 £14.60, 1&3 £4.80 CSF £57.52 CT £250.95 TOTE £4.20: £2.40, £3.80, £2.70; EX 46.50 Trifecta £308.40 Pool: £3182.08 - 7.73 winning units..
Owner Bennett Potatoes & Banister **Bred** David Barry **Trained** Denton, Co Durham
■ Stewards' Enquiry : Paul Mulrennan caution: careless riding.
Michael Metcalfe four-day ban: used whip above permitted level (Apr 20,22-24)

FOCUS
A moderate 3-y-o handicap with the placed horses on fair marks on their juvenile form and this is reasoable form for the grade.

1394 COLLINGWOOD INSURANCE APPRENTICE H'CAP 7f
5:35 (5:35) (Class 6) (0-65,64) 4-Y-O+ £1,940 (£577; £288; £144) Stalls Centre

Form RPR
4-42 1 **Keep It Dark**[6] 1271 4-9-1 **63** DavidSimmonson(5) 1 74
(Tony Coyle) *hld up in midfield: gd hdwy to ld over 1f out: rdn out fnl f* **10/1**
-650 2 1 3/4 **Ted's Brother (IRE)**[33] 878 5-8-12 **60** (e[1]) JasonHart(5) 11 66+
(Richard Guest) *dwlt: bhd: plenty to do 1/2-way: gd hdwy over 1f out: styd on to take 2nd nr fin: no ch w wnr* **14/5**[1]
0-33 3 nk **Alluring Star**[10] 1214 5-8-5 **55** MatthewHopkins(7) 5 60
(Michael Easterby) *trckd ldrs: effrt over 2f out: chsd wnr appr fnl f: no ex and lost 2nd nr fin* **11/1**
3411 4 2 3/4 **Rise To Glory (IRE)**[6] 1271 5-8-10 **56** 6ex MichaelJMMurphy(3) 6 54
(Shaun Harris) *led at decent gallop: rdn and hdd over 1f out: wknd ins fnl f* **3/1**[2]
503- 5 1 3/4 **Jupiter Fidius**[151] 7599 6-8-8 **58** (p) JordanNason(7) 4 52
(Karen Tutty) *bhd and sn pushed along: hdwy over 2f out: sn edgd lft: kpt on fnl f: no imp* **20/1**
3512 6 1 1/4 **Chosen Forever**[16] 1107 8-8-11 **57** (p) WilliamTwiston-Davies(3) 10 47
(Geoffrey Oldroyd) *bhd and sn niggled along: drvn 1/2-way: styd on fnl f: nt gng pce to chal* **7/2**[3]
5000 7 12 **Dhhamaan (IRE)**[25] 976 8-8-12 **55** (b) LeeTopliss 7 14
(Ruth Carr) *w ldr tl hung lft and wknd over 1f out* **16/1**
405- 8 7 **Feeling Good**[27] 6711 4-8-7 **57** RichardOliver(7) 12
(Brian Ellison) *midfield: rdn and hung lft over 2f out: sn btn* **20/1**
2-44 9 2 1/2 **River Ardeche**[25] 965 8-8-11 **59** GeorgeChaloner(5) 8
(Tracy Waggott) *chsd ldrs tl rdn and wknd over 2f out* **16/1**
304- 10 18 **Thrust Control (IRE)**[163] 7347 6-8-10 **53** DeclanCannon 9
(Tracy Waggott) *dwlt: sn in midfield: drvn and wknd after 3f out: t.o* **16/1**
6/36 11 3 1/2 **Lhotse Sherpa**[10] 1193 4-8-4 **54** ConnorBeasley(7) 13
(John Holt) *bhd: struggling 1/2-way: sn btn: t.o* **28/1**

1m 28.47s (0.67) **Going Correction** +0.125s/f (Good) 11 Ran SP% **121.6**
Speed ratings (Par 101): **101,99,98,95,93 92,78,70,67,46 42**
toteswingers 1&2 £7.30, 2&3 £9.40, 1&3 £8.50 CSF £38.48 CT £332.79 TOTE £11.40: £3.30, £1.60, £3.50; EX 52.90 Trifecta £706.80 Pool: £1942.95 - 2.06 winning units..
Owner N Hetherton **Bred** Heather Raw **Trained** Norton, N Yorks
■ Stewards' Enquiry : David Simmonson two-day ban: used whip above permitted level (Spr 20,22)

FOCUS
A modest apprentice riders' handicap for older horses in which they went a strong pace. The third helps set the standard.
T/Plt: £1,275.80 to a £1 stake. Pool of £55315.02 - 31.65 winning tickets. T/Qpdt: £151.10 to s £1 stake. Pool of £3288.91 - 16.10 winning tickets. RY

1367 WOLVERHAMPTON (A.W) (L-H)
Saturday, April 6

OFFICIAL GOING: Standard
Wind: Light across Weather: Fine

1395 32RED.COM H'CAP (DIV I) 5f 216y(P)
5:50 (5:51) (Class 6) (0-55,55) 4-Y-O+ £1,940 (£577; £288; £144) Stalls Low

Form RPR
5042 1 **Almaty Express**[2] 1356 11-8-13 **52** (b) RobertTart(5) 12 60
(John Weymes) *chsd ldr tl led 1/2-way: clr 2f out: rdn fnl f: jst hld on* **11/2**[2]
4215 2 nk **Littlecote Lady**[17] 1088 4-9-5 **53** (v) HayleyTurner 7 60
(Mark Usher) *a.p: rdn over 2f out: r.o to go 2nd post: nt quite get there* **4/1**[1]
-360 3 shd **Prigsnov Dancer (IRE)**[54] 610 8-8-9 **46** oh1 (p) BillyCray(3) 6 53
(Deborah Sanderson) *chsd ldrs: rdn over 2f out: wnt 2nd 1f out: r.o* **33/1**
6403 4 hd **Sextons House (IRE)**[2] 1355 5-8-8 **47** (b) ShirleyTeasdale(5) 11 53
(Alan McCabe) *hld up: hdwy over 1f out: r.o wl: nt quite rch ldrs* **10/1**
3363 5 1 1/4 **Rightcar**[2] 1356 6-8-10 **49** SladeO'Hara(5) 9 51
(Peter Grayson) *hld up: rdn and r.o wl ins fnl f: nrst fin* **4/1**[1]
500- 6 1/2 **Oceana Dreamer (IRE)**[170] 7189 4-9-0 **48** (v) TedDurcan 4 49
(Ed McMahon) *s.i.s: hdwy over 2f out: rdn and hung lft over 1f out: styd on same pce* **7/1**[3]
634- 7 shd **One Last Dream**[173] 7106 4-9-7 **55** MatthewDavies 1 55
(Ron Hodges) *a.p: pushed along 1/2-way: rdn over 1f out: styd on* **7/1**[3]
2146 8 2 1/4 **Very First Blade**[21] 1043 4-8-12 **51** (p) JackDuern(5) 8 44
(Mark Brisbourne) *led to 1/2-way: rdn over 1f out: wknd ins fnl f* **12/1**
4400 9 1 3/4 **Flaxen Lake**[17] 1088 6-8-12 **46** (p) RichardKingscote 5 34
(Milton Bradley) *broke wl: lost pl 5f out: n.d after* **8/1**
24-6 10 1/2 **Heidi's Delight (IRE)**[14] 1147 4-9-0 **55** (b) RowanScott(7) 3 41
(Ann Duffield) *s.s: hld up: rdn over 1f out: a in rr* **20/1**
0000 11 nk **Aljosan**[21] 1043 4-8-12 **46** oh1 (t) MircoMimmocchi 2 31
(Frank Sheridan) *s.i.s: a in rr* **50/1**
0000 12 4 **Lord Buffhead**[25] 968 4-9-6 **54** (v) RobbieFitzpatrick 10 26
(Richard Guest) *s.i.s: sn pushed along and a in rr* **16/1**

1m 14.36s (-0.64) **Going Correction** -0.075s/f (Stan) 12 Ran SP% **123.8**
Speed ratings (Par 101): **101,100,100,100,98 97,97,94,92,91 91,86**
toteswingers 1&2 £5.10, 1&3 £23.40, 2&3 £24.10 CSF £28.61 CT £698.15 TOTE £5.00: £1.90, £1.10, £14.80; EX 24.30 Trifecta £318.40 Pool: £1,907.29 - 4.49 winning units..
Owner Highmoor Racing 4 & Tag Racing **Bred** P G Airey **Trained** Middleham Moor, N Yorks

FOCUS
Low-grade fare and this was won at the home bend. The form looks reasonable for the grade.

1396 32RED.COM H'CAP (DIV II) 5f 216y(P)
6:20 (6:20) (Class 6) (0-55,55) 4-Y-O+ £1,940 (£577; £288; £144) Stalls Low

Form RPR
002 1 **First Rebellion**[17] 1088 4-8-8 **47** (b) RyanTate(5) 8 59
(Tony Carroll) *mde all: clr 1/2-way: rdn out* **7/2**[2]
3622 2 3 **Slatey Hen (IRE)**[2] 1355 5-8-10 **49** (p) ThomasBrown(5) 5 51
(Violet M Jordan) *a.p: rdn to chse wnr over 1f out: no imp ins fnl f* **5/2**[1]
2113 3 1 1/2 **Flow Chart (IRE)**[14] 1147 6-9-2 **55** SladeO'Hara(5) 9 53+
(Peter Grayson) *hld up: hdwy over 1f out: r.o: nt rch ldrs* **11/2**[3]
-006 4 3/4 **You'relikemefrank**[3] 1324 7-9-6 **54** (p) TonyCulhane 2 49
(Richard Ford) *s.i.s: hld up: hdwy over 2f out: rdn over 1f out: no ex ins fnl f* **20/1**
6046 5 nk **Onceaponatime (IRE)**[30] 909 8-8-12 **46** oh1 (b) JimmyQuinn 6 40
(Michael Squance) *s.i.s: hld up: rdn: hung lft and r.o ins fnl f: nvr nrr* **12/1**
0610 6 1/2 **Metropolitan Chief**[17] 1088 9-9-1 **49** (p) TomMcLaughlin 7 42
(Paul Burgoyne) *hld up: shkn up over 1f out: nt trble ldrs* **8/1**
0-0 7 3/4 **Legal Eagle (IRE)**[22] 1021 8-9-4 **52** (b) SilvestreDeSousa 10 42
(Paul Green) *prom: rdn over 2f out: styd on same pce fr over 1f out* **7/1**
3003 8 shd **Whiskey Junction**[30] 916 9-9-6 **54** LukeMorris 1 44
(Mick Quinn) *prom: chsd wnr 1/2-way tl rdn over 1f out: wknd ins fnl f* **6/1**
0-00 9 1/2 **Major Muscari (IRE)**[21] 1042 5-9-0 **48** (b) DavidNolan 3 36
(Ian McInnes) *mid-div: rdn over 2f out: wknd ins fnl f* **40/1**
6-05 10 12 **Royal Acclamation (IRE)**[10] 1193 8-8-12 **46** (p) LiamKeniry 13
(Michael Scudamore) *chsd ldr to 1/2-way: sn rdn: wknd over 1f out* **25/1**

1m 14.35s (-0.65) **Going Correction** -0.075s/f (Stan) 10 Ran SP% **122.8**
Speed ratings (Par 101): **101,97,95,94,93 92,91,91,91,75**
toteswingers 1&2 £3.10, 1&3 £3.70, 2&3 £4.20 CSF £13.18 CT £49.17 TOTE £5.50: £1.90, £1.50, £2.10; EX 14.40 Trifecta £49.40 Pool: £2,520.29 - 38.25 winning units..
Owner Let's Give It A Go Racing & J Dewhurst **Bred** Mayden Stud, J A And D S Dewhurst **Trained** Cropthorne, Worcs

FOCUS
Some familiar faces in here but the race was dominated from the off by the winner. Much depends on if the winner has improved as much as the form at face value suggests.

1397 32RED CASINO (S) H'CAP 5f 216y(P)
6:50 (6:52) (Class 6) (0-60,60) 3-Y-O+ £1,940 (£577; £288; £144) Stalls Low

Form RPR
0040 1 **Powerful Pierre**[18] 1079 6-9-13 **59** (b) DavidNolan 11 68
(Ian McInnes) *hld up: hdwy over 1f out: swtchd rt wl ins fnl f: r.o to ld nr fin* **4/1**[2]
4-03 2 nk **Jawking**[23] 998 4-9-11 **57** (t) MircoMimmocchi 5 65+
(Frank Sheridan) *led: rdn over 1f out: hdd nr fin* **7/1**
-000 3 2 **Ice Trooper**[43] 750 5-9-6 **55** (p) JulieBurke(3) 10 57
(Kristin Stubbs) *a.p: chsd ldr 2f out: sn rdn: styd on same pce ins fnl f* **14/1**
060- 4 nse **Kyllachy Storm**[167] 7274 9-9-7 **58** PhilipPrince(5) 6 59
(Ron Hodges) *chsd ldrs: rdn over 2f out: styd on* **20/1**
1563 5 nk **Boy The Bell**[22] 1020 6-9-4 **57** (b) JacobButterfield(7) 1 57
(Ollie Pears) *chsd ldr tl pushed along 2f out: rdn over 1f out: styd on* **5/2**[1]
4100 6 shd **Prince Of Passion (CAN)**[21] 1038 5-10-0 **60** (v) MartinDwyer 7 60
(Derek Shaw) *sn pushed along and prom: rdn over 2f out: styd on same pce ins fnl f* **5/1**[3]
2640 7 3 1/2 **Athaakeel (IRE)**[10] 1195 7-9-5 **54** (b) DarrenEgan(3) 2 43
(Ronald Harris) *hld up: rdn over 2f out: nvr nrr* **12/1**
R-60 8 11 **Blodwen Abbey**[67] 431 4-10-0 **60** [1] LukeMorris 8 14
(Michael Mullineaux) *s.s: a bhd* **12/1**
0/5- 9 1 **Gentleman Is Back (USA)**[361] 1280 5-9-11 **57** LiamKeniry 3 8
(Ed de Giles) *s.i.s: a in rr* **7/1**

1m 14.66s (-0.34) **Going Correction** -0.075s/f (Stan)
WFA 3 from 4yo+ 12lb 9 Ran SP% **117.1**
Speed ratings (Par 101): **99,98,95,95,95 95,90,76,74**
toteswingers 1&2 £10.90, 1&3 £20.10, 2&3 £10.10 CSF £32.61 CT £360.64 TOTE £4.50: £1.70, £3.50, £5.10; EX 36.70 Trifecta £789.90 Pool: £2,480.54 - 2.35 winning units..There was no bid for the winner.
Owner Terence Elsey **Bred** Hedsor Stud **Trained** Catwick, E Yorks

FOCUS
A moderate sprint.

1398 PENNY RUSHEN'S PACESETTING 60TH BIRTHDAY FILLIES' H'CAP 5f 216y(P)
7:20 (7:21) (Class 5) (0-75,74) 4-Y-O+ £2,587 (£770; £384; £192) Stalls Low

Form RPR
2423 1 **Amethyst Dawn (IRE)**[12] 1173 7-8-5 **63** (t) RobertTart(5) 7 71
(J R Jenkins) *chsd ldr: rdn to ld 1f out: edgd lft ins fnl f: r.o* **5/1**[3]
0534 2 1/2 **Song Of Parkes**[16] 1102 6-9-0 **72** SladeO'Hara(5) 4 78
(Peter Grayson) *a.p: rdn over 1f out: edgd lft and r.o to go 2nd wl ins fnl f: nt rch wnr* **10/1**

101- **3** 1 3/4 **Finesse**[155] 7524 4-9-6 **73**.......... JimCrowley 8 73+
(Ralph Beckett) *s.i.s: hdwy over 4f out: rdn over 1f out: styd on same pce ins fnl f: wnt 3rd nr fin* **6/4**[1]

0-12 **4** 1/2 **Al Freej (IRE)**[56] 589 4-9-7 **74**.......... SilvestreDeSousa 2 76+
(Brian Ellison) *sn led: rdn and hdd 1f out: styng on same pce whn hmpd and lost 3rd nr fin* **3/1**[2]

060- **5** 3/4 **Available (IRE)**[161] 7411 4-8-11 **64**.......... NeilCallan 5 60
(John Mackie) *hld up: pushed along 1/2-way: r.o ins fnl f: nvr trbld ldrs* **25/1**

0002 **6** 2 **Beauty Pageant (IRE)**[3] 1324 6-8-10 **63**..........(vt) LukeMorris 3 53
(David Evans) *led early: chsd ldrs: rdn over 1f out: no ex fnl f* **9/1**

4334 **7** 1 1/2 **Zing Wing**[1] 1368 5-8-12 **72**..........(v) EoinWalsh(7) 1 57
(David Evans) *s.i.s: hld up: rdn over 2f out: n.d* **20/1**

0300 **8** hd **Little China**[25] 971 4-8-10 **63**..........(b[1]) MartinDwyer 6 48
(William Muir) *hld up: rdn over 1f out: n.d* **16/1**

1m 13.63s (-1.37) **Going Correction** -0.075s/f (Stan) 8 Ran SP% **115.2**
Speed ratings (Par 100): **106,105,103,102,101 98,96,96**
toteswingers 1&2 £6.20, 1&3 £1.90, 2&3 £4.70 CSF £53.46 CT £110.04 TOTE £7.20: £1.90, £1.80, £1.10; EX 54.20 Trifecta £314.30 Pool: £2,065.79 - 4.92 winning units..
Owner A S Reid **Bred** W Kane **Trained** Royston, Herts

FOCUS
A sound gallop to this fillies' handicap, but it still proved difficult to get in a blow from off the pace. The runner-up, backed up by the fourth set the level.

1399 FOLEY STEELS E.B.F MAIDEN FILLIES' STKS 5f 20y(P)
7:50 (7:50) (Class 5) 2-Y-O £2,911 (£866; £432; £216) **Stalls** Low

Form RPR

1 **Majestic Alexander (IRE)** 2-9-0 0.......... TomMcLaughlin 2 82+
(David Evans) *a.p: shkn up to ld ins fnl f: r.o wl: readily* **9/2**[2]

2 **2** 3 1/4 **Go Glamorous (IRE)**[7] 1240 2-9-0 0.......... LukeMorris 6 70
(Ronald Harris) *chsd ldrs: led 2f out: rdn and hdd ins fnl f: styd on same pce* **4/6**[1]

3 1 1/4 **Limegrove** 2-9-0 0.......... TomQueally 9 66+
(David Evans) *s.i.s: hdwy 1/2-way: rdn over 1f out: r.o to go 3rd nr fin: nt trble ldrs* **25/1**

4 1 **Shelley's Choice (IRE)** 2-9-0 0.......... RichardKingscote 5 62
(Tom Dascombe) *led 3f: wknd ins fnl f* **14/1**

04 **5** 1 1/2 **Marilyn Marquessa**[7] 1240 2-8-9 0.......... PhilipPrince(5) 1 57
(Jo Hughes) *hld up: hdwy and hung lft over 1f out: nvr on terms* **8/1**[3]

6 3 3/4 **Blithe Spirit** 2-9-0 0.......... TedDurcan 7 43
(Eric Alston) *chsd ldr tl edgd rt 1/2-way: wknd over 1f out* **25/1**

7 2 **Nomathemba (IRE)** 2-9-0 0.......... NeilCallan 4 36
(David Evans) *s.i.s: outpcd* **33/1**

8 2 1/2 **Penina (IRE)** 2-8-11 0.......... PaulPickard(3) 3 27+
(Brian Ellison) *s.i.s: outpcd* **50/1**

1m 2.06s (-0.24) **Going Correction** -0.075s/f (Stan) 8 Ran SP% **108.5**
Speed ratings (Par 89): **98,92,90,89,86 80,77,73**
toteswingers 1&2 £1.10, 1&3 £17.00, 2&3 £6.80 CSF £6.96 TOTE £5.50: £1.50, £1.02, £3.90; EX 10.40 Trifecta £188.00 Pool: £1,399.86 - 5.58 winning units..
Owner Noel O'Callaghan **Bred** Victor Stud Bloodstock & Brendan Cummins **Trained** Pandy, Monmouths

FOCUS
This form could be better than rated but perspective of previous early juvenile races here tempers enthusiasm.

1400 JULIA GAUTIER MEMORIAL H'CAP 7f 32y(P)
8:20 (8:20) (Class 5) (0-75,75) 3-Y-O £2,587 (£770; £384; £192) **Stalls** High

Form RPR

1-20 **1** **Grilletto (USA)**[21] 1033 3-9-7 **75**..........(b) NeilCallan 6 77+
(James Tate) *sn chsng ldr: shkn up to ld over 1f out: rdn and edgd lft ins fnl f: r.o* **5/6**[1]

-121 **2** 1 1/4 **Red Dragon (IRE)**[44] 738 3-9-2 **75**.......... MatthewLawson(5) 2 74
(Charles Hills) *chsd ldrs: pushed along 1/2-way: rdn over 1f out: r.o* **9/2**[2]

505- **3** hd **Pippy**[106] 8211 3-8-11 **65**.......... RichardKingscote 4 63
(Tom Dascombe) *plld hrd: led early: settled to trckd ldrs: pushed along over 2f out: rdn over 1f out: r.o* **18/1**

1214 **4** shd **Run It Twice (IRE)**[28] 949 3-8-13 **72**..........(b) ThomasBrown(5) 5 70+
(David Evans) *s.i.s: hld up: rdn and r.o wl ins fnl f: nt rch ldrs* **17/2**

003- **5** hd **Winnie Perry**[176] 7014 3-8-13 **67**.......... AndreaAtzeni 3 64
(Rod Millman) *hld up: hdwy over 1f out: r.o* **16/1**

1-61 **6** 1/2 **Blazeofenchantment (USA)**[36] 845 3-9-1 **69**..........(tp) AdamKirby 7 65
(Noel Quinlan) *s.i.s: hld up: hrd rdn and r.o ins fnl f: nt trble ldrs* **6/1**[3]

41- **7** 1 3/4 **Al Emirati (IRE)**[197] 6431 3-9-7 **75**.......... HarryBentley 1 66
(Marco Botti) *sn led: rdn and hdd over 1f out: no ex ins fnl f* **8/1**

1m 29.06s (-0.54) **Going Correction** -0.075s/f (Stan) 7 Ran SP% **119.8**
Speed ratings (Par 98): **100,98,98,98,98 97,95**
toteswingers 1&2 £2.50, 1&3 £10.50, 2&3 £6.10 CSF £5.44 TOTE £1.80: £1.10, £3.20; EX 5.50 Trifecta £65.30 Pool: £2,022.37 - 23.19 winning units..
Owner Sheikh Juma Dalmook Al Maktoum **Bred** Respite Farm Inc **Trained** Newmarket, Suffolk

FOCUS
They went quite steady in this fair handicap with the third and fifth the likely keys to the level.

1401 £32 BONUS AT 32RED.COM H'CAP 1m 141y(P)
8:50 (8:50) (Class 6) (0-60,60) 4-Y-O+ £1,940 (£577; £288; £144) **Stalls** Low

Form RPR

3203 **1** **Delightful Sleep**[19] 1060 5-9-2 **55**.......... AdamKirby 7 66
(David Evans) *a.p: rdn to ld ins fnl f: r.o* **4/1**[2]

3003 **2** 2 **Qeethaara (USA)**[9] 1221 9-8-11 **50**..........(p) LukeMorris 13 56
(Mark Brisbourne) *hld up: hdwy over 2f out: rdn over 1f out: r.o* **12/1**

5201 **3** shd **Penbryn (USA)**[10] 1214 6-9-6 **59**.......... SebSanders 8 65
(Nick Littmoden) *a.p: shkn up and ev ch ins fnl f: styd on same pce* **7/2**[1]

6052 **4** 1 **Kyle Of Bute**[10] 1214 7-9-1 **54**.......... WilliamCarson 10 57
(Brian Baugh) *s.i.s: hld up: rdn and r.o ins fnl f: nt rch ldrs* **10/1**

0232 **5** 3/4 **Abhaath (USA)**[11] 1179 4-9-3 **59**.......... DarrenEgan(3) 5 61+
(Ronald Harris) *s.s: hld up: rdn and r.o ins fnl f: nrst fin* **9/1**

3-45 **6** shd **Alezanna**[36] 840 4-9-0 **53**.......... KirstyMilczarek 2 55
(James Toller) *chsd ldr tl led over 6f out: rdn over 1f out: hdd and no ex ins fnl f* **5/1**[3]

0665 **7** 1 1/4 **Spinning Ridge (IRE)**[10] 1194 8-8-11 **57**..........(b) GaryPhillips(7) 6 56
(Ronald Harris) *s.i.s: hld up: rdn over 1f out: edgd lft ins fnl f: nvr on terms* **20/1**

43 **8** hd **Moral Issue**[18] 1079 5-9-6 **59**..........(b) DavidNolan 12 57
(Ian McInnes) *hld up: hdwy over 2f out: sn rdn: no ex fnl f* **10/1**

504/ **9** nk **Lady Tycoon**[512] 7368 4-8-9 **53**.......... JackDuern(5) 1 50
(Mark Brisbourne) *led 3f: chsd ldrs: rdn over 1f out: wknd ins fnl f* **28/1**

533- **10** 2 1/4 **Lord Franklin**[151] 7615 4-9-2 **55**.......... TedDurcan 3 47
(Eric Alston) *prom: chsd ldr over 5f out: rdn over 1f out: wknd fnl f* **7/1**

1m 51.05s (0.55) **Going Correction** -0.075s/f (Stan) 10 Ran SP% **115.5**
Speed ratings (Par 101): **94,92,92,91,90 90,89,89,88,86**
toteswingers 1&2 £12.20, 1&3 £5.20, 2&3 £10.60 CSF £50.67 CT £183.73 TOTE £2.70: £2.20, £4.00, £1.40; EX 44.90 Trifecta £255.40 Pool: £1,952.40 - 5.73 winning units..
Owner Mrs E Evans **Bred** Theresa Fitsall **Trained** Pandy, Monmouths

FOCUS
An open handicap run at a reasonable gallop and the second sets the standard with the third close to his latest winning mark.

1402 32RED H'CAP 1m 1f 103y(P)
9:20 (9:20) (Class 5) (0-75,85) 4-Y-O+ £2,587 (£770; £384; £192) **Stalls** Low

Form RPR

3166 **1** **Honey Of A Kitten (USA)**[9] 1220 5-8-9 **70**..........(b) EoinWalsh(7) 4 77
(David Evans) *mde all: rdn over 1f out: styd on wl* **5/2**[2]

0321 **2** 4 1/2 **Fluctuation (IRE)**[25] 967 5-8-11 **70**..........(v) RobertTart(5) 2 68
(Ian Williams) *chsd wnr: pushed along over 2f out: rdn over 1f out: styd on same pce fnl f* **2/1**[1]

2601 **3** hd **Scamperdale**[20] 1054 11-8-12 **66**..........(p) KierenFox 5 63
(Brian Baugh) *chsd ldrs: rdn over 1f out: styd on same pce fnl f* **3/1**

0434 **4** 6 **Spanish Plume**[2] 1353 5-8-6 **65**..........(p) JackDuern(5) 3 50
(Reg Hollinshead) *hld up: hdwy over 3f out: rdn over 1f out: wknd fnl f* **11/4**[3]

2m 0.95s (-0.75) **Going Correction** -0.075s/f (Stan) 4 Ran SP% **113.6**
Speed ratings (Par 103): **100,96,95,90**
CSF £8.20 TOTE £3.80; EX 9.40 Trifecta £19.30 Pool: £1,078.13 - 41.72 winning units..
Owner Mrs E Evans **Bred** Kenneth L Ramsey And Sarah K Ramsey **Trained** Pandy, Monmouths

FOCUS
Doubts over the form which is rated cautiously.
T/Plt: £17.90 to a £1 stake. Pool: £66,793.89 - 2,713.29 winning tickets T/Qpdt: £6.90 to a £1 stake. Pool: £7,358.70 - 788.85 winning tickets CR

1403 - 1412a (Foreign Racing) - See Raceform Interactive

1163 CURRAGH (R-H)
Sunday, April 7

OFFICIAL GOING: Straight course - good to yielding; round course - good

1413a BIG BAD BOB GLADNESS STKS (GROUP 3) 7f
3:20 (3:22) 4-Y-O+ £31,707 (£9,268; £4,390; £1,463)

RPR

1 **Custom Cut (IRE)**[14] 1168 4-9-3 102.......... RonanWhelan 5 109
(George J Kent, Ire) *mde all: over 1 l clr 1/2-way: rdn ent fnl f and styd on wl towards fin: all out* **25/1**

2 1/2 **Nephrite**[350] 1548 4-9-3 105.......... JosephO'Brien 6 108
(A P O'Brien, Ire) *w.w in rr: hdwy fr 2f out on outer into 3rd fnl 150yds: kpt on wl u.p towards fin: a hld* **7/2**[2]

3 nse **La Collina (IRE)**[190] 6673 4-9-0 109.......... DeclanMcDonogh 7 105
(Kevin Prendergast, Ire) *chsd ldrs: 5th 1/2-way: rdn into 2nd on nrside ins fnl f: kpt on wl nr fin: a hld* **7/1**

4 3/4 **Bold Thady Quill (IRE)**[8] 1255 6-9-3 100..........(p) ShaneFoley 2 106+
(K J Condon, Ire) *hld up: 7th 1/2-way: pushed along 2f out and clsd u.p into 4th fnl 150yds: kpt on same pce wout ever threatening principals* **14/1**

5 1 1/4 **Arnold Lane (IRE)**[38] 834 4-9-3.......... MartinHarley 9 102
(Mick Channon) *hld up: 8th 1/2-way: rdn over 1 1/2f out and clsd into nvr threatening 5th ins fnl f: kpt on same pce towards fin* **10/1**

6 1 1/4 **Yellow Rosebud (IRE)**[14] 1166 4-9-3 107..........(b) PatSmullen 3 99
(D K Weld, Ire) *chsd ldrs: 4th 1/2-way: effrt 1 1/2f out and sn no ex: wknd ins fnl f* **11/2**[3]

7 shd **Lily's Angel (IRE)**[45] 743 4-9-0 107.......... GaryCarroll 8 96
(G M Lyons, Ire) *trckd ldr in 2nd: 3rd 1/2-way: sn pushed along and no imp 1 1/2f out: wknd nr fin* **8/1**

8 3 **Foxtrot Romeo (IRE)**[204] 6246 4-9-3 108.......... JohnnyMurtagh 4 91
(Thomas Carmody, Ire) *prom: trckd ldr: 2nd 1/2-way: rdn over 1 1/2f out and sn no imp: wknd ent fnl f* **9/4**[1]

9 4 **Lady Wingshot (IRE)**[154] 7581 4-9-3 103.......... KevinManning 1 80
(J S Bolger, Ire) *on toes bef s: dwlt and racd towards rr: 6th 1/2-way: pushed along over 2f out and sn wknd* **7/1**

1m 32.92s (2.12) **Going Correction** +0.60s/f (Yiel) 9 Ran SP% **124.1**
Speed ratings: **111,110,110,109,108 106,106,103,98**
CSF £118.98 TOTE £16.70: £4.00, £1.20, £2.30; DF 198.90.
Owner S E Construction (Kent) Ltd **Bred** Moyglare Stud Farm Ltd **Trained** Tramore, Co Waterford

FOCUS
The winner was progressive last year and ran a small personal best from the front.

1415a IRISH OPEN ALLEGED STKS (LISTED RACE) 1m 2f
4:20 (4:21) 4-Y-O+ £22,195 (£6,487; £3,073; £1,024)

RPR

1 **Parish Hall (IRE)**[547] 6689 4-9-5 112.......... KevinManning 6 105+
(J S Bolger, Ire) *hld up towards rr: 5th 1/2-way: hdwy to get on terms ent fnl f: wandered u.p and led fnl 150yds out: styd on wl towards fin* **11/8**[1]

2 1 1/2 **Inis Meain (USA)**[14] 1168 6-9-5 100.......... DannyMullins 3 102
(Denis Gerard Hogan, Ire) *attempted to make all: 3 l clr bef 1/2-way: rdn over 2f out and sn strly pressed: hdd fnl 150yds: kpt on same pce towards fin* **12/1**

3 1/2 **Steps To Freedom (IRE)**[51] 683 7-9-5 107..........(t) FMBerry 1 101
(Mrs John Harrington, Ire) *hld up in tch: 4th 1/2-way: pushed along into st and effrt over 2f out on far side: no ex in 3rd ins fnl f: kpt on same pce* **9/2**[3]

4 1 1/4 **Ernest Hemingway (IRE)**[170] 7233 4-9-5 105.......... JosephO'Brien 4 99+
(A P O'Brien, Ire) *trckd ldr in 2nd: tk clsr order into st: rdn over 2f out and sn no imp u.p in 4th ins fnl f: kpt on same pce towards fin* **7/2**[2]

5 5 **Captain Joy (IRE)**[37] 856 4-9-5 102.......... PatSmullen 2 89
(Tracey Collins, Ire) *hld up towards rr: last 1/2-way: pushed along into st and sn no imp: n.d under 2f out: kpt on same pce ins fnl f* **10/1**

6 2 **Montebell (IRE)**[210] 6083 4-9-0 95.......... ShaneFoley 5 80
(K J Condon, Ire) *chsd ldr in 3rd: t.k.h: tk clsr order into st: sn rdn and no ex 1 1/2f out: dropped to rr ent fnl f: kpt on one pce* **5/1**

2m 14.63s (5.33) **Going Correction** +0.325s/f (Good) 6 Ran SP% **116.0**
Speed ratings: **111,109,109,108,104 102**
CSF £20.13 TOTE £2.00: £1.20, £5.20; DF 19.80.
Owner Mrs J S Bolger **Bred** J S Bolger **Trained** Coolcullen, Co Carlow

FOCUS
This developed into a sprint in the final 2f, with the winner keeping on well.

The Form Book Flat, Raceform Ltd, Compton, RG20 6NL.

1414 - 1418a (Foreign Racing) - See Raceform Interactive

LONGCHAMP (R-H)

Sunday, April 7

OFFICIAL GOING: Turf: good

1419a PRIX LA FORCE (GROUP 3) (3YO) (TURF) 1m 2f

1:30 (12:00) 3-Y-O £32,520 (£13,008; £9,756; £6,504; £3,252)

RPR

1 **Triple Threat (FR)**157 7514 3-9-2 0 MaximeGuyon 3 106+
(A Fabre, France) *swvd at s: lost several l: mde gd prog bef end of bk st: swtchd towards outside 2f out: rdn and qcknd wl ent fnl f: r.o strly fnl 100yds: led fnl 25yds: comf* **4/1**2

2 ¾ **Sefri (USA)**33 3-9-2 0 ChristopheSoumillon 7 104
(J-C Rouget, France) *settled in 2nd: rdn to ld a f out: r.o wl: hdd fnl 25yds: no answer to wnr* **4/5**1

3 1 **Ivan Grozny (FR)**19 3-9-2 0 FranckBlondel 6 102
(D Rabhi, France) *sn led: stl in front 250yds out: chal and hdd 1f out: styd on wl* **25/1**

4 snk **Onedargent (FR)**12 1192 3-9-2 0 (p) ThierryJarnet 5 102
(J-P Gallorini, France) *racd in midfield: rdn 1 1/2f out: wnt 4th 1f out: styd on wl u.p fnl f* **20/1**

5 ¾ **Ares D'Emra (FR)**148 7692 3-9-2 0 StephanePasquier 4 100
(C Delcher-Sanchez, Spain) *settled in midfield on ins: rdn 1 1/2f out to go 5th: styd on wl fnl f* **14/1**

6 1 ¼ **Ketchikan (IRE)**131 3-9-2 0 RonanThomas 2 98
(J E Pease, France) *hld up in rr: swtchd towards outside 2f out: appeared outpcd 1 1/2f out: rallied and r.o wl fnl 100yds* **14/1**

7 snk **Holy Warrior (IRE)**43 782 3-9-2 0 Pierre-CharlesBoudot 1 97
(Gay Kelleway) *broke wl: racd in 4th on rail: rdn 1 1/2f out: r.o wl ent fnl f: no ex fnl 100yds: styd on at one pce* **13/2**3

8 snk **Wight Is Wight (IRE)**22 3-9-2 0 IoritzMendizabal 8 97
(J-C Rouget, France) *racd towards rr: relegated to last 2f out: rdn but no ex enterng fnl f: styd at on one pce* **12/1**

9 4 **Pont Marie (FR)**12 1192 3-9-2 0 (p) Christophe-PatriceLemaire 9 89
(F Chappet, France) *racd towards rr: sent forward to go 3rd bef st: rdn 1 1/2f out: nt qckn: fdd fnl 150yds* **20/1**

2m 4.16s (0.16) **Going Correction** +0.225s/f (Good) 9 Ran SP% **123.3**
Speed ratings: **108,107,106,106,105 104,104,104,101**
WIN (incl. 1 euro stake): 6.50. PLACES: 1.70, 1.20, 3.70. DF: 5.30. SF: 18.40.
Owner Team Valor **Bred** Team Valour & G Barber **Trained** Chantilly, France

1420a PRIX D'HARCOURT (GROUP 2) (4YO+) (TURF) 1m 2f

2:40 (12:00) 4-Y-O+ £60,243 (£23,252; £11,097; £7,398; £3,699)

RPR

1 **Maxios**183 6898 5-8-11 0 StephanePasquier 2 115+
(J E Pease, France) *settled in 3rd: qcknd wl 1 1/2f out to chse ldr: r.o strly to ld fnl 25yds* **5/1**

2 ¾ **Don Bosco (FR)**22 1048 6-8-11 0 GregoryBenoist 3 113
(D Smaga, France) *sn led: set gd pce: clr ld 2f out: rdn 1f out: r.o wl: ct and hdd fnl 25yds: styd on wl* **3/1**2

3 1 ½ **Saga Dream (FR)**22 1048 7-9-1 0 ThierryJarnet 1 114+
(F Lemercier, France) *settled in 2nd: rdn 2f out: r.o wl: lost 2nd fnl 150yds: styd on wl* **2/1**1

4 nk **Dalkala (USA)**161 7431 4-8-11 0 Christophe-PatriceLemaire 7 109+
(A De Royer-Dupre, France) *settled in midfield on outside: rdn 2f out: r.o wl wout threatening ldrs fnl f* **4/1**3

5 ¾ **Haya Landa (FR)**160 7449 5-8-8 0 FranckBlondel 4 105+
(Mme L Audon, France) *settled in midfield: rdn 2f out: no ex: styd on u.p fnl f* **14/1**

6 shd **Top Trip**183 6896 4-9-1 0 MaximeGuyon 5 112+
(F Doumen, France) *hld up towards rr on ins: relegated to last ent st: rdn 2f out: styd on wl fnl f* **8/1**

7 2 ½ **Pagera (FR)**22 1048 5-8-10 0 ow2 OlivierPeslier 6 102+
(H-A Pantall, France) *hld up towards rr: rdn 2f out: no ex: styd on one pce fnl f* **12/1**

2m 4.48s (0.48) **Going Correction** +0.225s/f (Good) 7 Ran SP% **120.5**
Speed ratings: **107,106,105,104,104 104,102**
WIN (incl. 1 euro stake): 6.70. PLACES: 3.20, 1.90. SF: 24.40.
Owner Niarchos Family **Bred** Niarchos Family **Trained** Chantilly, France

1314 KEMPTON (A.W) (R-H)

Monday, April 8

OFFICIAL GOING: Standard

Wind: Strong, half behind Weather: Cloudy

1421 BETVICTOR.COM MAIDEN AUCTION FILLIES' STKS 5f (P)

2:20 (2:23) (Class 5) 2-Y-O £2,587 (£770; £384; £192) Stalls Low

Form RPR

1 **Alutiq (IRE)** 2-8-8 0 JohnFahy 8 80
(Eve Johnson Houghton) *trckd ldng pair: clsd on inner to ld over 1f out: clr whn edgd lft fnl f: rdn out* **2/1**2

2 2 3 **Memory Styx**12 1208 2-8-8 0 FrannyNorton 3 69
(Mick Channon) *awkward to post: led: drvn and hdd over 1f out: one pce and no ch w wnr* **13/8**1

3 ¾ **Evacusafe Lady** 2-8-2 0 RyanPowell(3) 7 63
(John Ryan) *chsd ldng trio: nt on terms fr 1/2-way: kpt on one pce to take 3rd 1f out* **33/1**

4 2 **Princess Tamay (IRE)** 2-8-8 0 SilvestreDeSousa 1 59
(Mark Johnston) *chsd ldr to 2f out: steadily wknd and lost 3rd 1f out* **12/1**

5 ¾ **Honey Meadow** 2-8-6 0 ow1 AdamBeschizza 5 54
(Robert Eddery) *s.s: wl off the pce in rr: kpt on fnl f: nrst fin* **14/1**

6 ½ **Hedge End (IRE)** 2-8-7 0 KieranO'Neill 2 54
(Richard Hannon) *dwlt: rn green in rr and outpcd: kpt on fnl f* **6/1**3

7 nk **Iseemist (IRE)** 2-8-5 0 LukeMorris 4 51
(John Gallagher) *s.s: a off the pce in rr: kpt on fnl f* **25/1**

8 33 **Luv U Honey** 2-8-2 0 PhilipPrince(5) 6
(Jo Hughes) *s.s: sn t.o* **14/1**

1m 0.93s (0.43) **Going Correction** -0.025s/f (Stan) 8 Ran SP% **113.5**
Speed ratings (Par 89): **95,90,89,85,84 83,83,30**
toteswingers 1&2 £1.80, 1&3 £18.50, 2&3 £10.70 CSF £5.52 TOTE £2.90: £1.40, £1.10, £7.70; EX 6.70 Trifecta £113.30 Pool: £3,264.51 - 21.60 winning units..
Owner Miss E Johnson Houghton **Bred** Wardstown Stud Ltd **Trained** Blewbury, Oxon
■ Stewards' Enquiry : John Fahy one-day ban: failed to ride to draw (Apr 22)

FOCUS
Only one of these fillies had run before and a few of them needed the experience.

1422 BETVICTOR.COM H'CAP 1m 2f (P)

2:50 (2:51) (Class 4) (0-85,85) 4-Y-O+ £4,690 (£1,395; £697; £348) Stalls Low

Form RPR

0-01 1 **Tadabeer**21 1059 5-8-13 77 (t) StevieDonohoe 3 91
(Ian Williams) *t.k.h early and sn restrained into 6th: prog 3f out: produced to chal 1f out: led ins fnl f: r.o wl* **4/1**2

231- 2 ½ **Aegaeus**138 7818 4-8-13 77 RyanMoore 2 90
(Ed Dunlop) *trckd ldrs: gng easily and waiting to chal 2f out: led over 1f out: rdn and hdd ins fnl f: r.o but a hld nr fin* **5/6**1

0-40 3 6 **Perfect Cracker**19 1092 5-9-0 78 AdamKirby 7 79
(Clive Cox) *stdd s: hld up in last pair: prog over 2f out: cl enough over 1f out: kpt on to take 3rd jst ins fnl f but wl outpcd by ldng pair* **12/1**

1-66 4 2 ¾ **Kaafel (IRE)**33 897 4-9-7 85 (p) DaneO'Neill 8 81
(Peter Hedger) *racd wd early: prog arnd field to trck ldr over 5f out: rdn to ld 2f out: hdd & wknd over 1f out* **12/1**

4250 5 1 ¼ **Askaud (IRE)**9 1237 5-8-11 75 (b) TomQueally 1 68
(Scott Dixon) *led to 2f out: wknd qckly* **16/1**

120- 6 4 **Sondeduro**249 4741 4-9-1 79 FergusSweeney 4 64
(Jamie Osborne) *trckd ldr to over 5f out: rdn and wknd 3f out* **10/1**3

200- 7 hd **Croquembouche (IRE)**186 6819 4-9-0 78 EddieAhern 6 63
(Ed de Giles) *prom on outer: drvn and wknd wl over 2f out* **20/1**

423- 8 1 ½ **Balady (IRE)**180 6986 4-8-12 76 SilvestreDeSousa 5 58
(Dominic Ffrench Davis) *hld up in last pair: sltly hmpd 6f out: rdn and struggling 3f out: wknd* **20/1**

2m 4.82s (-3.18) **Going Correction** -0.025s/f (Stan) 8 Ran SP% **114.4**
Speed ratings (Par 105): **111,110,105,103,102 99,99,98**
toteswingers 1&2 £1.80, 1&3 £4.30, 2&3 £3.10 CSF £7.67 CT £32.73 TOTE £4.50: £1.50, £1.10, £2.50; EX 9.30 Trifecta £46.90 Pool: £2,583.01 - 41.30 winning units..
Owner Sir Alex Ferguson & Sotirios Hassiakos **Bred** Shadwell Estate Co Ltd **Trained** Portway, Worcs

FOCUS
A decent handicap and the first two came clear of the rest.

1423 BETVICTOR.COM MAIDEN STKS 1m (P)

3:20 (3:23) (Class 5) 3-Y-O+ £2,587 (£770; £384; £192) Stalls Low

Form RPR

1 **Queensberry Rules (IRE)** 3-8-13 0 RyanMoore 3 88+
(William Haggas) *chsd ldrs in 6th: prog 2f out: pushed along firmly to chse ldr fnl f: led last 75yds: kpt on wl* **11/2**3

3/ 2 ½ **Frasers Hill**531 7082 4-10-0 0 JimmyFortune 7 91+
(Roger Varian) *trckd ldng pair: rdn to ld wl over 1f out: hung lft after: hdd and nt qckn last 75yds* **8/1**

022- 3 3 ½ **World Record (IRE)**164 7373 3-8-13 77 PatDobbs 10 79
(Richard Hannon) *trckd ldng pair: rdn to chal and upsides 2f out: one pce fr jst over 1f out* **6/1**

32/ 4 1 ½ **Key Appointment**523 7232 4-10-0 0 ChrisCatlin 9 80
(Paul Cole) *led to over 6f out: trckd ldr after: rdn to chal 2f out: fdd fnl f* **16/1**

3- 5 2 **Dalgig**198 6486 3-8-13 0 PatCosgrave 11 71
(Jamie Osborne) *prog to ld over 6f out: rdn and hdd wl over 1f out: wknd* **5/1**2

6 2 ¾ **Sedenoo** 3-8-13 0 AdamKirby 2 65+
(Marco Botti) *in tch in midfield: sltly impeded after 1f: briefly shkn up 2f out: sn outpcd and btn* **6/1**

64- 7 hd **Hands Of Time**261 4340 3-8-13 0 SeanLevey 8 64
(Richard Hannon) *chsd ldrs in 5th: shkn up wl over 2f out: steadily fdd* **7/1**

8 ½ **Yeager (USA)** 3-8-13 0 WilliamBuick 12 63+
(Jeremy Noseda) *checked sn after s: wl in rr and racd wd: pushed along over 3f out and modest prog: reminder over 2f out: no hdwy after* **3/1**1

53 9 1 ¼ **Mad About Harry (IRE)**35 877 3-8-13 0 LukeMorris 13 60
(John Best) *in tch in midfield: urged along over 3f out: no prog over 2f out: wknd* **33/1**

5- 10 4 ½ **Algorithmic (IRE)**164 7363 3-8-13 0 TomQueally 1 50
(Michael Bell) *rousted along in last trio early: nvr on terms: no ch fnl 2f* **16/1**

5-3 11 3 ¼ **Sweet Alabama**18 1095 3-8-8 0 FergusSweeney 4 37
(Rod Millman) *a wl in rr: shkn up and no prog over 2f out* **50/1**

0 12 5 **Hundred Acre Wood**19 1086 3-8-13 0 KirstyMilczarek 5 31
(Olivia Maylam) *sn in last: nvr a factor: wl bhd fnl 3f* **100/1**

4 13 8 **Rowlestone Lad**12 1209 6-10-0 0 RussKennemore 6
(John Flint) *s.s: hld up in last trio: no prog 3f out: sn wknd: t.o* **66/1**

1m 38.83s (-0.97) **Going Correction** -0.025s/f (Stan) 13 Ran SP% **128.4**
WFA 3 from 4yo+ 15lb
Speed ratings (Par 103): **103,102,99,97,95 92,92,92,90,86 83,78,70**
toteswingers 1&2 £10.00, 1&3 £9.20, 2&3 £9.80 CSF £52.60 TOTE £7.60: £2.20, £2.80, £2.40; EX 57.90 Trifecta £780.90 Pool: £2,990.71 - 2.87 winning units..
Owner Liam Sheridan **Bred** Gerard Kerin **Trained** Newmarket, Suffolk

FOCUS
An interesting maiden with some nice newcomers taking on several that had already shown promise.

1424 FOLLOW US ON TWITTER @BETVICTORACING H'CAP 1m (P)

3:50 (3:52) (Class 6) (0-65,65) 3-Y-O £1,940 (£577; £288; £144) Stalls Low

Form RPR

0-52 1 **Sam Spade (IRE)**5 1320 3-9-7 65 RyanMoore 7 68+
(Richard Hannon) *mde all: kicked on over 2f out: at least 2 l ahd over 1f out: drvn and jst hld on* **7/4**1

3-24 2 nk **Beau Select (IRE)**11 1219 3-9-7 65 (b) AdamKirby 3 67
(Robert Eddery) *dwlt but drvn to chse wnr: dropped to 3rd 1/2-way: hrd rdn to chse wnr again 2f out: clsd qckly last 100yds: jst hld* **3/1**2

322 3 1 ¼ **Green Special (ITY)**12 1213 3-9-7 65 MircoMimmocchi 6 64
(Frank Sheridan) *t.k.h: sn prom: chsd wnr 1/2-way to 2f out: hung lft u.p: unbalanced ins fnl f: kpt on* **5/1**3

560- **4** *nse* **Tagalaka (IRE)**[206] 6203 3-9-1 **59** TomQueally 5 58
(Eve Johnson Houghton) *hld up in tch: rdn 2f out: chsd ldrs over 1f out: kpt on one pce* **10/1**

055- **5** *1 3/4* **Ishisoba**[144] 7724 3-9-4 **62** GeorgeBaker 1 57
(Alastair Lidderdale) *hld up in detached last: shkn up 2f out: kpt on but nvr involved* **8/1**

50-2 **6** *1 1/2* **Tiger's Home**[40] 817 3-9-1 **59** AdamBeschizza 2 51
(Julia Feilden) *t.k.h: hld up in tch: rdn over 2f out: no imp over 1f out: wknd fnl f* **14/1**

0-06 **7** *2 1/4* **Whiskey N Stout (IRE)**[24] 1016 3-8-7 **51** oh4 KirstyMilczarek 4 37
(Jamie Osborne) *s.s: t.k.h and sn in tch: prog on wd outside 1/2-way: wknd 2f out* **16/1**

1m 41.56s (1.76) **Going Correction** -0.025s/f (Stan) 7 Ran SP% **110.8**
Speed ratings (Par 96): **90,89,88,88,86 85,82**
toteswingers 1&2 £1.80, 1&3 £2.60, 2&3 £2.50 CSF £6.57 TOTE £2.70: £1.30, £1.60; EX 8.20 Trifecta £19.00 Pool: £3,726.38 - 146.46 winning units..
Owner Mrs Valerie Hubbard **Bred** Newhall Ltd **Trained** East Everleigh, Wilts

FOCUS
A moderate handicap and a well executed front-running ride from Ryan Moore.

1425 TALK TO VICTOR H'CAP 1m 4f (P)
4:20 (4:21) (Class 6) (0-65,65) 3-Y-O **£1,940** (£577; £288; £144) **Stalls** Centre

Form RPR

1241 **1** **Poetic Verse**[22] 1053 3-9-7 **65** RyanMoore 6 73
(Rod Millman) *hld up in 6th: rdn and gd prog on outer to ld wl over 1f out: edgd rt but styd on wl* **7/2[2]**

0-52 **2** *1 3/4* **Handiwork**[5] 1326 3-9-1 **59** HayleyTurner 1 64
(Michael Bell) *mde most: tried to kick on over 3f out: hdd and nt qckn wl over 1f out: styd on but readily hld* **3/1[1]**

0-54 **3** *1 1/2* **Autrisk (IRE)**[25] 994 3-9-2 **60** AdamKirby 3 63
(Marco Botti) *cl up on inner: rdn to chal for 2nd 2f out: chsd ldng pair after: kpt on but no imp* **7/2[2]**

6233 **4** *3* **Conversing (USA)**[5] 1314 3-8-8 **52** SilvestreDeSousa 2 50
(Mark Johnston) *rrd s: trckd ldrs: looked to be gng wl enough over 2f out: sn rdn and fnd nil: one pce after* **8/1[3]**

054 **5** *1 1/2* **Mighty Thor**[24] 1009 3-9-1 **59** JimCrowley 4 54
(Simon Dow) *mostly chsd ldr to 2f out: sn wknd* **7/2[2]**

0-34 **6** *1 1/4* **Tebbit (USA)**[14] 1171 3-9-4 **62** (be) FergusSweeney 8 55
(Philip Hide) *stdd s: hld up in detached last: shkn up wl over 1f out: no prog and nvr involved* **25/1**

62-5 **7** *4 1/2* **Brick Rising**[13] 1177 3-8-9 **60** JoeyHaynes(7) 5 46
(Andrew Balding) *racd on outer: cl up tl wknd over 2f out* **16/1**

2m 36.8s (2.30) **Going Correction** -0.025s/f (Stan) 7 Ran SP% **112.5**
Speed ratings (Par 96): **91,89,88,86,85 85,82**
toteswingers 1&2 £1.90, 1&3 £3.20, 2&3 £2.90 CSF £13.94 CT £37.72 TOTE £4.40: £1.60, £2.10; EX 6.70 Trifecta £31.60 Pool: £2,839.96 - 67.20 winning units..
Owner The Links Partnership **Bred** The Links Partnership **Trained** Kentisbeare, Devon

FOCUS
Another moderate handicap in which only one of these had won a race. That remains the case.

1426 FAMILY FUN ON SATURDAY 13.04.13 H'CAP 7f (P)
4:50 (4:51) (Class 6) (0-65,64) 4-Y-O+ **£1,940** (£577; £216; £216) **Stalls** Low

Form RPR

0551 **1** **Teen Ager (FR)**[12] 1194 9-9-0 **57** (p) JimmyQuinn 2 66
(Paul Burgoyne) *t.k.h: hld up in midfield: prog on inner 2f out: shkn up to ld jst ins fnl f: pushed out and jst hld on* **16/1**

013- **2** *hd* **Duke Of Destiny (IRE)**[101] 8263 4-9-6 **63** GeorgeBaker 13 71
(Ed Walker) *dropped in fr wd draw and hld up in rr: prog over 2f out: rdn over 1f out: chsd wnr ins fnl f: clsd at fin: jst failed* **7/2[1]**

2212 **3** *1/2* **West Leake (IRE)**[14] 1172 7-9-6 **63** TomMcLaughlin 9 70
(Paul Burgoyne) *hld up in last trio: prog on inner over 2f out: rdn and styd on fr over 1f out: nrst fin* **8/1[3]**

00-3 **3** *dht* **Midnight Feast**[35] 878 5-9-6 **63** (b) LukeMorris 1 70
(Lee Carter) *chsd ldr: led 2f out: drvn and hdd jst ins fnl f: styd on same pce* **4/1[2]**

50-3 **5** *2* **Lutine Charlie (IRE)**[33] 899 6-9-7 **64** RyanMoore 5 65
(Pat Eddery) *prom: rdn over 2f out: nt qckn and outpcd over 1f out: kpt on same pce* **12/1**

00-2 **6** *2 1/4* **Perfect Ch'l (IRE)**[26] 980 6-9-0 **62** RobertTart(5) 10 57
(Paul Fitzsimons) *led to 2f out: steadily fdd* **20/1**

6-24 **7** *shd* **Arachnophobia (IRE)**[52] 665 7-9-0 **57** (b) MartinLane 7 52
(Martin Bosley) *c out of the stalls last: hld up in last trio: lft bhd over 2f out: no ch whn shkn up over 1f out: nvr involved* **16/1**

2050 **8** *3/4* **Katmai River (IRE)**[18] 1100 6-8-10 **53** (v) SteveDrowne 3 46
(Mark Usher) *a towards rr: nt gng wl fr 1/2-way: nvr a factor* **14/1**

4325 **9** *1/2* **Spin Again (IRE)**[7] 1294 8-9-5 **62** AdamKirby 8 54
(John Ryan) *hld up in rr: lft bhd whn r unfolded over 2f out: no ch whn rdn over 1f out* **10/1**

-243 **10** *hd* **Pastoral Jet**[18] 1100 5-8-13 **59** RyanPowell(3) 4 50
(Richard Rowe) *racd on outer: sn towards rr: struggling over 2f out* **8/1[3]**

000- **11** *2 1/2* **Elsie's Orphan**[135] 7857 6-9-7 **64** JimCrowley 12 48
(Patrick Chamings) *pressed ldrs tl wknd qckly over 2f out* **14/1**

5-00 **12** *3/4* **Satwa Laird**[14] 1172 7-9-7 **64** HayleyTurner 6 46
(Conor Dore) *racd wd in midfield: rdn and no prog over 2f out: sn wknd* **14/1**

1m 25.33s (-0.67) **Going Correction** -0.025s/f (Stan) 12 Ran SP% **117.8**
Speed ratings (Par 101): **102,101,101,101,98 96,96,95,94,94 91,90**
PLACE: West Leake £1.20, Midnight Feast £0.80. T/C: TA/DOD/WL £251.49, TS/DOD/MF £139.86 CSF £70.86 CT £139.86 TOTE £16.80: £4.40, £1.60, £1.20; EX 90.10 Trifecta £412.90 TA/DOD/WL: £149.50. TS/DOD/MF: £412.90.
Owner Mrs C Leigh-Turner **Bred** Haras De Beauvoir **Trained** Shepton Montague, Somerset

FOCUS
A moderate handicap, though quite a competitive one.

1427 MIKE THE KNIGHT HERE 13.04.13 CLASSIFIED STKS 6f (P)
5:20 (5:20) (Class 6) 3-Y-O **£1,940** (£577; £288; £144) **Stalls** Low

Form RPR

00-1 **1** **Admiralofthesea (USA)**[6] 1301 3-9-6 **64** AdamBeschizza 4 74+
(Robert Eddery) *hld up in 4th: trapped bhd rivals whn r unfolded wl over 1f out: squeezed through to chse ldr ins fnl f: sustained effrt to ld last 100yds: readily* **3/1[2]**

35-2 **2** *nk* **Carina Palace**[6] 1301 3-9-0 **65** FergusSweeney 5 64
(Jamie Osborne) *trckd ldr: led wl over 1f out and wnt for home: hdd last 100yds: r.o but hld after* **9/4[1]**

5224 **3** *1 1/2* **Sand Grouse**[3] 1367 3-9-0 **57** (b) MartinHarley 2 59
(Marco Botti) *trckd ldng pair: cl enough 2f out: rdn and nt qckn over 1f out: one pce after* **4/1[3]**

-640 **4** *1 1/4* **Hawsies Dream**[4] 1349 3-8-9 **55** RobertTart(5) 3 55
(Alan Bailey) *led: rdn and hdd wl over 1f out: steadily outpcd* **16/1**

040- **5** *1/2* **Royal Guinevere**[215] 5943 3-9-0 **62** JimCrowley 6 54
(Dean Ivory) *stdd s: hld up in last: plld hrd: hanging lft and looked all at sea: effrt on inner 2f out: sn no prog* **5/1**

30-6 **U** **Forceful Flame**[54] 628 3-9-0 **65** (t) NickyMackay 1
(Robert Eddery) *bucked: swvd and uns rdr s* **7/1**

1m 13.27s (0.17) **Going Correction** -0.025s/f (Stan) 6 Ran SP% **110.8**
Speed ratings (Par 96): **97,96,94,92,92**
toteswingers 1&2 £1.30, 1&3 £2.80, 2&3 £2.30 CSF £9.90 TOTE £3.70: £1.40, £1.70; EX 7.40 Trifecta £13.00 Pool: £1,959.12 - 112.85 winning units..
Owner Mrs Pam Aitken & Ms Trisha Keane **Bred** Brushwood Stable **Trained** Newmarket, Suffolk

FOCUS
This revolved around a similar event here the previous week with the first two home re-opposing. Despite the furlong-shorter trip and the weights turnaround, the result was exactly the same.
T/Jkpt: Not won. T/Plt: £11.00 to a £1 stake. Pool: £66,439.20 - 4,397.28 winning tickets T/Qpdt: £8.30 to a £1 stake. Pool: £3,644.36 - 322.24 winning tickets JN

[1395] WOLVERHAMPTON (A.W) (L-H)
Monday, April 8

OFFICIAL GOING: Standard
Wind: Fresh against Weather: Cloudy with sunny spells

1428 32RED CASINO APPRENTICE H'CAP 1m 1f 103y(P)
2:10 (2:11) (Class 6) (0-65,63) 3-Y-O **£2,102** (£625; £312; £156) **Stalls** Low

Form RPR

600- **1** **Zero Game (IRE)**[173] 7173 3-8-12 **61** (e[1]) ThomasHemsley(7) 1 66
(Michael Bell) *trckd ldrs: wnt 2nd 4f out: led 2f out: hung lft over 1f out: styd on* **7/1**

-604 **2** *2 1/4* **Scepticism (USA)**[20] 1071 3-8-7 **54** MatthewHopkins(5) 3 54
(Mark Johnston) *s.i.s: sn chsng ldrs: led 7f out: rdn and hdd 2f out: hmpd over 1f out: styd on same pce ins fnl f* **6/1[3]**

-423 **3** *3/4* **Inessa Armand (IRE)**[70] 419 3-9-1 **57** JasonHart 2 55
(J S Moore) *led early: chsd ldrs: pushed along over 3f out: rdn over 1f out: styd on* **13/2**

6331 **4** *3/4* **Silver Fawn (IRE)**[5] 1314 3-8-12 **54** 6ex (be) DavidBergin 4 51
(John Weymes) *hld up: racd keenly: hdwy over 2f out: rdn and hung lft over 1f out: styd on* **7/2[2]**

212 **5** *18* **Shearian**[32] 918 3-9-7 **63** GeorgeDowning 6 22
(Tony Carroll) *sn led: racd keenly: hdd 7f out: chsd ldr tl 4f out: pushed along over 2f out: wknd over 1f out* **3/1[1]**

-123 **6** *25* **Amelia Hull**[60] 547 3-9-1 **57** (p) RyanTate 5
(Karen George) *sn pushed along in rr: rdn over 4f out: hung rt and wknd over 2f out: eased* **3/1[1]**

2m 2.13s (0.43) **Going Correction** -0.125s/f (Stan) 6 Ran SP% **112.3**
Speed ratings (Par 96): **93,91,90,89,73 51**
toteswingers 1&2 £6.00, 1&3 £5.80, 2&3 £5.50 CSF £46.48 TOTE £8.00: £2.90, £2.50; EX 54.40 Trifecta £244.60 Pool: £2,252.27 - 6.90 winning units..
Owner Edward J Ware **Bred** Islanmore Stud **Trained** Newmarket, Suffolk
■ Thomas Hemsley's first winner.
■ Stewards' Enquiry : Thomas Hemsley one-day ban: careless riding (Apr 22)

FOCUS
A weak apprentice handicap.

1429 32RED.COM MAIDEN STKS 1m 141y(P)
2:40 (2:41) (Class 5) 3-Y-O **£2,587** (£770; £384; £192) **Stalls** Low

Form RPR

402- **1** **Fehaydi**[157] 7517 3-9-5 **83** LiamJones 4 87+
(William Haggas) *led over 7f out: hdd 4f out: chsd ldr: rdn to ld ins fnl f: r.o* **11/4[2]**

3- **2** *3* **One Pekan (IRE)**[145] 7705 3-9-5 0 AndreaAtzeni 6 80+
(Roger Varian) *a.p: pushed along over 2f out: styd on to go 2nd wl ins fnl f: nt trble wnr* **5/4[1]**

3 *1 1/4* **Nurpur (IRE)**[192] 6649 3-9-0 74 DanielTudhope 8 72
(David O'Meara) *a.p: led 4f out: shkn up and hdd ins fnl f: styd on same pce* **5/1[3]**

52-2 **4** *nk* **Sublimation (IRE)**[24] 1008 3-9-5 80 RobertWinston 1 76
(Tony Carroll) *trckd ldrs: plld hrd: rdn over 1f out: styd on same pce fnl f* **5/1[3]**

22 **5** *4 1/2* **Off The Pulse**[23] 1044 3-9-5 0 GrahamGibbons 9 66+
(John Mackie) *hld up: hdwy over 1f out: nvr nr to chal* **16/1**

6 *nk* **Wadacre Sarko** 3-9-5 0 JoeFanning 11 65
(Mark Johnston) *hld up: hdwy over 5f out: pushed along over 2f out: edgd lft and wknd fnl f* **28/1**

5 **7** *1* **Zaitsev (IRE)**[13] 1185 3-9-5 0 ShaneKelly 7 63
(Ollie Pears) *hld up: plld hrd: hdwy over 2f out: no imp fnl f* **50/1**

8 *7* **Mr Blue Nose** 3-9-0 0 RyanTate(5) 2 47
(Karen George) *s.i.s: sn pushed along and a in rr* **66/1**

43 **9** *7* **Helmsley Flyer (IRE)**[13] 1185 3-9-5 0 KierenFallon 10 31
(David O'Meara) *hld up: shkn up over 2f out: a in rr* **33/1**

0-40 **10** *1 1/2* **Dolly Bantry**[49] 708 3-8-9 30 ShirleyTeasdale(5) 3 22
(Alan McCabe) *mid-div: lost pl over 4f out: rdn and wknd over 3f out* **100/1**

5 **11** *7* **Castell Avon**[7] 1288 3-9-0 0 RichardKingscote 5
(Milton Bradley) *led 1f: chsd ldrs: rdn over 4f out: wknd over 2f out* **100/1**

1m 50.0s (-0.50) **Going Correction** -0.125s/f (Stan) 11 Ran SP% **122.1**
Speed ratings (Par 98): **97,94,93,92,88 88,87,81,75,74 67**
toteswingers 1&2 £2.00, 1&3 £3.20, 2&3 £3.00 CSF £6.70 TOTE £3.30: £1.40, £1.10, £1.60; EX 9.60 Trifecta £33.50 Pool: £2,548.72 - 57.05 winning units..
Owner Sheikh Ahmed Al Maktoum **Bred** Cheveley Park Stud Ltd **Trained** Newmarket, Suffolk

FOCUS
An informative maiden, run at strong pace.

1430 32RED H'CAP 7f 32y(P)
3:10 (3:10) (Class 5) (0-75,75) 4-Y-O+ **£3,234** (£962; £481; £240) **Stalls** High

Form RPR

21-1 **1** **Admiralty**[46] 740 4-9-2 **75** ThomasBrown(5) 1 91
(Ismail Mohammed) *led 6f out: rdn and hung rt fr over 1f out: r.o wl: eased nr fin* **13/8[1]**

The Form Book Flat, Raceform Ltd, Compton, RG20 6NL.

32-4 **2** 4 ½ **Peace Seeker**[21] 1067 5-9-7 **75** WilliamCarson 4 79
(Anthony Carson) *a.p: chsd wnr over 2f out: rdn over 1f out: styd on same pce fnl f* **3/1**[2]

1044 **3** 2 ¼ **The Guru Of Gloom (IRE)**[18] 1096 5-9-2 **70** MartinDwyer 8 68
(William Muir) *stdd s: hld up: plld hrd: hdwy over 1f out: nt trble ldrs* **8/1**

6241 **4** 1 ½ **Colourbearer (IRE)**[18] 1102 6-9-4 **72** (t) RichardKingscote 7 66
(Milton Bradley) *chsd ldrs: rdn over 1f out: styd on same pce* **9/1**

0 **5** 1 ¼ **Bankroll**[17] 1115 6-9-7 **75** (t) TedDurcan 2 66
(Jonjo O'Neill) *hld up: shkn up over 1f out: nvr nrr* **20/1**

34-5 **6** 1 **Illustrious Prince (IRE)**[3] 1366 6-8-11 **70** JasonHart(5) 3 58
(Declan Carroll) *led 1f: chsd wnr tl rdn over 2f out: wknd over 1f out* **15/2**[3]

/00- **7** nse **Easy Over (IRE)**[294] 3229 5-9-1 **69** GrahamGibbons 6 57
(Ed McMahon) *s.s: hld up: hdwy u.p over 1f out: wknd ins fnl f* **11/1**

31-6 **8** 20 **Ozz**[12] 1211 4-8-11 **65** (bt) JamesDoyle 5
(Frank Sheridan) *prom: pushed along and wknd 1/2-way* **40/1**

1m 27.64s (-1.96) **Going Correction** -0.125s/f (Stan) 8 Ran SP% **111.5**
Speed ratings (Par 103): **106,100,98,96,95 94,93,71**
toteswingers 1&2 £1.80, 1&3 £4.00, 2&3 £2.90 CSF £6.07 CT £26.86 TOTE £2.20: £1.10, £1.90, £2.80; EX 6.60 Trifecta £26.30 Pool: £2,150.12 - 61.10 winning units..
Owner Ahmad Abdulla Al Shaikh **Bred** Mrs Fiona Denniff **Trained** Newmarket, Suffolk

FOCUS
A fair race for the grade.

1431 NICOLA & STEVEN WATSON JUST MARRIED H'CAP 5f 20y(P)
3:40 (3:40) (Class 5) (0-75,75) 4-Y-O+ £2,587 (£770; £384; £192) Stalls Low

Form RPR

0136 **1** **Lucky Dan (IRE)**[6] 1308 7-9-7 **75** JoeFanning 4 83
(Paul Green) *a.p: chsd ldr 2f out: shkn up to ld wl ins fnl f: styd on* **9/4**[1]

060- **2** hd **Taurus Twins**[123] 8009 7-9-0 **68** (b) JamesDoyle 6 75
(Richard Price) *led: rdn and hung rt ins fnl f: sn hung lft and hdd: styd on* **14/1**

212- **3** 2 ½ **Another Citizen (IRE)**[100] 8285 5-9-7 **75** (b) DavidAllan 9 73
(Tim Easterby) *chsd ldrs: rdn over 1f out: styd on same pce ins fnl f* **5/2**[2]

-310 **4** nk **Angelo Poliziano**[7] 1283 7-9-1 **69** (p[1]) J-PGuillambert 2 66
(Jo Hughes) *sn pushed along in rr: hdwy u.p over 1f out: styd on same pce ins fnl f* **7/1**

0433 **5** ¾ **Rylee Mooch**[12] 1198 5-9-7 **75** (e) RobbieFitzpatrick 7 70
(Richard Guest) *chsd ldrs: pushed along 1/2-way: rdn over 1f out: no ex fnl f* **10/1**

3120 **6** nk **Cardinal**[42] 795 8-9-7 **75** TomEaves 8 68
(Robert Cowell) *s.i.s: hdwy over 1f out: wknd ins fnl f* **6/1**[3]

20- **7** 6 **Dreaming Of Rubies**[201] 6358 4-9-6 **74** (t) PJMcDonald 1 46
(Ben Haslam) *chsd ldr 3f: sn rdn: wknd fnl f* **6/1**[3]

1m 1.38s (-0.92) **Going Correction** -0.125s/f (Stan) 7 Ran SP% **116.2**
Speed ratings (Par 103): **102,101,97,97,96 95,85**
toteswingers 1&2 £9.30, 1&3 £1.70, 2&3 £8.10 CSF £34.47 CT £84.99 TOTE £3.70: £2.60, £8.40; EX 46.10 Trifecta £164.90 Pool: £1,853.90 - 8.42 winning units..
Owner Paul Green (Oaklea) **Bred** Mountarmstrong Stud **Trained** Lydiate, Merseyside

FOCUS
There was plenty of pace on in this race.

1432 £32 BONUS AT 32RED.COM MAIDEN AUCTION STKS 5f 20y(P)
4:10 (4:11) (Class 5) 2-Y-O £2,587 (£770; £384; £192) Stalls Low

Form RPR

3 **1** **Kodafine (IRE)**[9] 1240 2-8-8 0 CathyGannon 8 73+
(David Evans) *chsd ldr tl led 2f out: rdn clr fr over 1f out* **4/5**[1]

2 **2** 4 ½ **Gin Time (IRE)**[7] 1285 2-8-4 0 AndreaAtzeni 1 53
(David Evans) *prom: drvn along over 3f out: swtchd rt over 1f out: r.o to go 2nd wl ins fnl f: no ch w wnr* **9/4**[2]

3 1 ¾ **Aweebitowinker** 2-8-9 0 LiamJones 6 52
(J S Moore) *sn pushed along and prom: rdn over 1f out: no ex fnl f* **20/1**

4 5 **Vodka Chaser (IRE)** 2-8-7 0 LiamKeniry 3 32
(J S Moore) *s.i.s: sn prom: rdn over 1f out: hung lft and wknd fnl f* **12/1**

5 2 ¼ **The Bunny Catcher** 2-8-9 0 PaddyAspell 5 25+
(Sharon Watt) *dwlt: outpcd* **25/1**

0 **6** 1 **Red Biba (IRE)**[17] 1108 2-8-5 0 WilliamCarson 2 18
(David C Griffiths) *led 3f: sn rdn: wknd fnl f* **25/1**

7 4 ½ **Chilly In Rio (IRE)** 2-8-9 0 MartinDwyer 7 6
(William Muir) *s.i.s: outpcd* **7/1**[3]

1m 2.38s (0.08) **Going Correction** -0.125s/f (Stan) 7 Ran SP% **119.0**
Speed ratings (Par 92): **94,86,84,76,72 70,63**
toteswingers 1&2 £1.60, 1&3 £4.60, 2&3 £4.40 CSF £2.91 TOTE £2.20: £1.30, £1.30; EX 4.50 Trifecta £17.90 Pool: £3,114.19 - 130.43 winning units..
Owner J A Wilcox & P D Evans **Bred** Tally-Ho Stud **Trained** Pandy, Monmouths

FOCUS
Experience can often prove the key in these early season juvenile events and that was how it played out here.

1433 32REDPOKER.COM H'CAP 5f 216y(P)
4:40 (4:40) (Class 5) (0-70,69) 3-Y-O £2,587 (£770; £384; £192) Stalls Low

Form RPR

-032 **1** **Sylvia Pankhurst (IRE)**[20] 1073 3-8-12 **65** (p) ThomasBrown(5) 4 69
(David C Griffiths) *mde all: rdn over 1f out: edgd lft ins fnl f: styd on* **14/1**

-144 **2** ½ **Indian Affair**[24] 1014 3-9-7 **69** RichardKingscote 1 71
(Milton Bradley) *chsd wnr: rdn and ev ch over 1f out: kpt on* **8/1**

0-1 **3** 2 ¼ **Top Trail (USA)**[12] 1209 3-9-6 **68** JamesDoyle 5 63
(Roger Charlton) *prom: pushed along over 3f out: rdn over 1f out: styd on same pce ins fnl f* **7/4**[2]

-332 **4** ¾ **Go Far**[66] 468 3-9-6 **68** KierenFallon 2 60
(Alan Bailey) *s.i.s: sn pushed along in rr: rdn over 1f out: styd on ins fnl f: nvr nrr* **6/4**[1]

024- **5** 2 ¼ **Harrogate Fair**[99] 8293 3-9-0 **62** LiamJones 3 47
(Michael Squance) *chsd ldrs: pushed along 1/2-way: rdn over 1f out: hung lft and wknd ins fnl f* **25/1**

1311 **6** 3 ½ **Hazard Warning (IRE)**[31] 923 3-9-3 **65** (b) DuranFentiman 6 39
(Tim Easterby) *s.i.s: rdn and hung lft fr over 1f out: nvr on terms* **4/1**[3]

1m 14.57s (-0.43) **Going Correction** -0.125s/f (Stan) 6 Ran SP% **118.0**
Speed ratings (Par 98): **97,96,93,92,89 84**
toteswingers 1&2 £6.80, 1&3 £6.20, 2&3 £2.70 CSF £117.69 TOTE £20.30: £6.80, £4.60; EX 69.90 Trifecta £630.80 Pool: £2,467.42 - 2.93 winning units..
Owner Norton Common Farm Racing **Bred** T Cahalan & D Cahalan **Trained** Bawtry, S Yorks

FOCUS
An intriguing 3yo sprint handicap.

1434 32REDBET.COM H'CAP 1m 4f 50y(P)
5:10 (5:10) (Class 6) (0-65,64) 4-Y-O+ £1,940 (£577; £288; £144) Stalls Low

Form RPR

204- **1** **Rock Song**[165] 7359 4-9-5 **63** GrahamLee 4 72
(John Mackie) *hld up: hdwy and hung lft fr over 1f out: styd on to ld nr fin* **7/2**[3]

/441 **2** ½ **William Van Gogh**[18] 1107 6-9-5 **62** GrahamGibbons 8 70
(Michael Easterby) *hld up: hdwy over 2f out: led ins fnl f: rdn and hdd nr fin* **2/1**[1]

-321 **3** 1 ¾ **Thane Of Cawdor (IRE)**[19] 1090 4-8-13 **57** LiamKeniry 2 62
(Joseph Tuite) *a.p: rdn and ev ch fr over 1f out tl styd on same pce ins fnl f* **10/3**[2]

0421 **4** nk **Mazij**[11] 1217 5-9-7 **64** WilliamCarson 7 69
(Peter Hiatt) *chsd ldr tl led wl over 1f out: rdn and hdd ins fnl f: no ex towards fin* **13/2**

5 1 ¼ **Redoute Star (AUS)**[278] 7-9-3 **60** SebSanders 1 63
(Paul D'Arcy) *chsd ldrs: pushed along over 3f out: rdn and ev ch over 1f out: styd on same pce fnl f* **15/2**

400- **6** 1 ¾ **Iguacu**[153] 7620 9-8-3 **53** (p) DanielMuscutt(7) 6 53
(Richard Price) *hld up: rdn over 1f out: nvr trbld ldrs* **33/1**

3-30 **7** 1 ¼ **Hallstatt (IRE)**[11] 1218 7-9-7 **64** (t) FrannyNorton 3 62
(John Mackie) *led at stdy pce tl qcknd over 2f out: rdn and hdd wl over 1f out: wknd ins fnl f* **16/1**

-003 **8** 8 **Guest Book (IRE)**[18] 1105 6-8-10 **58** SladeO'Hara(5) 5 43
(Peter Grayson) *s.i.s: sn pushed along and prom: shkn up over 3f out: wknd 2f out* **50/1**

2m 40.79s (-0.31) **Going Correction** -0.125s/f (Stan)
WFA 4 from 5yo+ 1lb 8 Ran SP% **114.5**
Speed ratings (Par 101): **96,95,94,94,93 92,91,86**
toteswingers 1&2 £2.70, 1&3 £2.20, 2&3 £1.80 CSF £10.94 CT £24.27 TOTE £3.70: £1.30, £1.10, £1.70; EX 14.60 Trifecta £46.60 Pool: £2,345.51 - 37.71 winning units..
Owner Sotby Farming Company Limited **Bred** Shortgrove Manor Stud **Trained** Church Broughton , Derbys

FOCUS
There was very little in the way of early pace on in this and it's fair to say that worked to the strengths of the winner.
T/Plt: £347.80 to a £1 stake. Pool: £66,044.32 - 138.60 winning tickets T/Qpdt: £79.20 to a £1 stake. Pool: £6,053.17 - 56.52 winning tickets CR

1435 - 1441a (Foreign Racing) - See Raceform Interactive

PONTEFRACT (L-H)
Tuesday, April 9

OFFICIAL GOING: Good to soft (good in places; 6.8)
Wind: moderate 1/2 against Weather: fine but cold

1442 PONTEFRACT LOYALTY CARD H'CAP 1m 4y
2:10 (2:10) (Class 5) (0-75,74) 4-Y-O+ £3,234 (£962; £481; £240) Stalls Low

Form RPR

204- **1** **Dolphin Rock**[146] 7715 6-9-6 **73** DaleSwift 2 83
(Brian Ellison) *mde all: edgd rt fnl f: hld on towards fin* **9/2**[2]

50-4 **2** ½ **Blue Maisey**[33] 914 5-8-10 **63** JamesSullivan 16 72
(Edwin Tuer) *swtchd lft after s: sn chsng ldrs: hmpd 1f out: styd on same pce towards fin* **50/1**

221- **3** shd **Snooky**[146] 7712 4-9-3 **70** PaulHanagan 1 79+
(Richard Fahey) *s.s: in rr: gd hdwy over 1f out: chsd ldrs ins fnl f: kpt on same pce towards fin* **11/4**[1]

3504 **4** 3 ¼ **Piceno (IRE)**[6] 1334 5-9-5 **72** (p) TomQueally 7 73
(Scott Dixon) *chsd ldrs: one pce whn n.m.r ins fnl f* **16/1**

023- **5** nse **Falcon's Reign (FR)**[196] 6560 4-9-2 **69** AndrewMullen 11 70
(Michael Appleby) *chsd ldrs: wknd fnl 75yds* **25/1**

110- **6** 1 ¼ **Talent Scout (IRE)**[171] 7247 7-9-4 **71** DuranFentiman 4 69
(Karen Tutty) *w wnr: hmpd jst ins fnl f: sn wknd* **16/1**

056- **7** ½ **Hayek**[153] 7639 6-9-2 **74** (b) AdamCarter(5) 10 71
(Tim Easterby) *hld up in rr: hdwy on outside over 2f out: hung lft over 1f out: kpt on same pce ins fnl f* **33/1**

060- **8** 4 **Pivotman**[169] 7300 5-9-5 **72** GrahamGibbons 5 60
(Michael Easterby) *in rr-div: sme hdwy and nt clr run wl over 1f out: nvr a threat* **8/1**[3]

0-60 **9** nk **Crown Choice**[18] 1113 8-9-3 **70** PaulMulrennan 3 57
(Paul Midgley) *towards rr: t.k.h: sme hdwy over 1f out: nvr nr ldrs* **25/1**

1262 **10** ¾ **Tight Lipped (IRE)**[8] 1292 4-9-2 **74** (v) RyanTate(5) 13 60
(James Eustace) *drvn to chse ldrs on outer: hmpd 1f out: sn wknd and eased* **9/1**

-005 **11** 1 ¾ **Brigadoon**[21] 1081 6-9-5 **72** MichaelO'Connell 14 54
(Philip Kirby) *in rr: sme hdwy whn stmbld wl over 1f out: nvr a factor* **16/1**

044- **12** 2 **Buzz Law (IRE)**[235] 5322 5-9-2 **69** PhillipMakin 8 46
(Mrs K Burke) *mid-div: hdwy on outside over 3f out: one pce whn hmpd appr fnl f: fin lame* **8/1**[3]

025- **13** 1 **Merchant Of Medici**[201] 6405 6-9-6 **73** [1] PJMcDonald 9 48
(Micky Hammond) *t.k.h in rr: nvr a factor* **20/1**

0-30 **14** 12 **Elspeth's Boy (USA)**[46] 759 6-9-3 **70** AdamKirby 15 17
(Philip Kirby) *swtchd lft after s: chsd ldrs: wkng whn n.m.r 1f out: sn eased and bhd* **20/1**

430- **15** 2 ½ **King Of Paradise (IRE)**[185] 6881 4-9-1 **68** TedDurcan 12 9
(Eric Alston) *in rr-div: bhd whn eased ins fnl f* **16/1**

1-00 **16** 4 **Cufflink**[10] 1237 4-9-3 **70** (p) DavidAllan 6
(Iain Jardine) *a bhd: eased ins fnl f* **33/1**

1m 46.83s (0.93) **Going Correction** +0.325s/f (Good) 16 Ran SP% **125.7**
Speed ratings (Par 103): **108,107,107,104,104 102,102,98,98,97 95,93,92,80,78 74**
toteswingers: 1&2 £95.70, 1&3 £3.30, 2&3 £32.10 CSF £232.32 CT £780.61 TOTE £5.30: £1.80, £8.00, £1.20, £3.30; EX 326.40 Trifecta £1570.80 Part won. Pool: £2094.47 - 0.60 winning units.

Owner Mia Racing **Bred** Mia Racing **Trained** Norton, N Yorks
■ Stewards' Enquiry : Dale Swift three-day ban: careless riding (Apr 23-25)
Adam Carter two-day ban: careless riding (Apr 23-24)

FOCUS
The early lead was contested.

1443 HIGH-RISE MAIDEN STKS 1m 2f 6y
2:40 (2:41) (Class 4) 3-Y-O **£5,175** (£1,540; £769; £384) **Stalls** Low

Form RPR

1 **Libertarian** 3-9-5 0 PhillipMakin 1 83+
(Mrs K Burke) *dwlt: effrt over 2f out: nt clr run and edgd rt 1f out: hung lft and styd on to ld towards fin* **15/8**[1]

23 2 ¾ **The Welsh Wizard (IRE)**[10] 1236 3-9-5 0 GrahamLee 2 79
(Charles Hills) *sn led: hung rt thrght: increased pce after 3f: drvn 4f out: rdn over 2f out: hdd and no ex towards fin* **2/1**[2]

024- 3 nk **Elidor**[160] 7492 3-9-5 80 MartinHarley 3 78
(Mick Channon) *led early: trckd ldrs: effrt over 2f out: chal over 1f out: kpt on same pce last 50yds* **5/2**[3]

00- 4 2 ¼ **Thorpe (IRE)**[167] 7332 3-9-5 0 SebSanders 4 74
(Ralph Beckett) *s.i.s: jnd ldr 5f out: drvn and hung lft over 2f out: bmpd 1f out: sn wknd* **7/1**

2m 15.71s (2.01) **Going Correction** +0.325s/f (Good) 4 Ran SP% **109.2**
Speed ratings (Par 100): **104,103,103,101**
CSF £5.98 TOTE £3.10; EX 7.20 Trifecta £9.00 Pool: £1432.27 - 118.71 winning units..
Owner Hubert John Strecker **Bred** Serpentine Bloodstock Ltd **Trained** Middleham Moor, N Yorks
■ Stewards' Enquiry : Phillip Makin one-day ban: careless riding (Apr 23)

FOCUS
Only four runners, but an interesting maiden and it went to the sole newcomer in the line-up.

1444 DALBY STAND H'CAP 6f
3:10 (3:10) (Class 3) (0-95,94) 3-Y-O **£7,762** (£2,310; £1,154; £577) **Stalls** Low

Form RPR

001- 1 **Polski Max**[179] 7028 3-9-0 87 PaulHanagan 1 102
(Richard Fahey) *best away: led: qcknd and drvn clr over 1f out: edgd rt ins fnl f: kpt on* **11/4**[2]

-141 2 5 **Flashlight (IRE)**[7] 1307 3-8-12 85 6ex SilvestreDeSousa 2 84
(Mark Johnston) *dwlt: hdwy on ins 2f out: chsd wnr ins fnl f: no imp* **7/4**[1]

2-15 3 1 ¾ **Rangi**[67] 474 3-8-3 76 JamesSullivan 4 69
(Tony Coyle) *chsd ldrs: kpt on same pce appr fnl f* **16/1**

415- 4 ¾ **Al Udeid (IRE)**[154] 7614 3-8-6 79 AmyRyan 5 70
(Kevin Ryan) *w wnr after 1f: hung rt: styd on same pce over 1f out* **16/1**

563- 5 shd **Double Your Money (IRE)**[166] 7350 3-8-6 79 FrannyNorton 3 70
(Mark Johnston) *hld up in rr: hdwy on inner 2f out: n.m.r ins fnl f: kpt on* **12/1**

513- 6 ½ **Sanjuro (IRE)**[191] 6699 3-8-8 81 MartinHarley 9 70
(Mick Channon) *trckd ldrs: effrt 2f out: kpt on one pce* **6/1**[3]

26-1 7 1 **Bold Prediction (IRE)**[26] 992 3-8-5 78 AndreaAtzeni 10 64
(Mrs K Burke) *mid-div on outer: effrt over 2f out: nvr a threat* **16/1**

46-0 8 ¾ **Queen Aggie (IRE)**[24] 1033 3-9-2 94 WilliamTwiston-Davies(5) 7 77
(David Evans) *mid-div: lost pl after 1f: nvr a factor* **20/1**

026- 9 ½ **Blue Lotus (IRE)**[153] 7635 3-8-5 78 DuranFentiman 6 60
(Tim Easterby) *hld up in rr: effrt over 2f out: fdd fnl f* **33/1**

00-0 10 nk **Fantacise**[10] 1250 3-8-5 78 (b) PatrickMathers 8 59
(Richard Fahey) *in rr-div on outer: t.k.h: effrt over 2f out: wknd appr fnl f* **25/1**

1m 17.91s (1.01) **Going Correction** +0.325s/f (Good) 10 Ran SP% **114.2**
Speed ratings (Par 102): **106,99,97,96,95 95,93,92,92,91**
toteswingers 1&2 £1.40, 2&3 £7.70, 1&3 £8.40 CSF £7.50 CT £60.21 TOTE £3.30: £1.50, £1.10, £5.60; EX 8.00 Trifecta £80.90 Pool: £3012.64 - 27.90 winning units..
Owner Market Avenue Racing & Tremousser **Bred** Mike J Beadle **Trained** Musley Bank, N Yorks

FOCUS
Low-drawn runners dominated.

1445 JAMAICAN FLIGHT H'CAP 2m 1f 216y
3:40 (3:40) (Class 5) (0-75,74) 4-Y-O+ **£3,234** (£962; £481; £240) **Stalls** Low

Form RPR

002- 1 **Hidden Justice (IRE)**[25] 7301 4-9-6 73 MichaelO'Connell 3 85+
(John Quinn) *hld up in mid-div: smooth hdwy over 2f out: chal on bit over 1f out: shkn up to ld 1f out: v comf* **5/2**[1]

662- 2 2 ¾ **Wily Fox**[18] 7377 6-8-7 60 RyanTate(5) 2 65
(James Eustace) *led 1f: trckd ldrs: led appr fnl 2f: hdd 1f out: styd on: no ch w wnr* **10/1**

002- 3 3 ¼ **Stickleback**[67] 6567 4-8-2 55 oh5 (p) JamesSullivan 10 56
(Micky Hammond) *chsd ldrs: drvn over 4f out: kpt on ins fnl f: tk 3rd post* **25/1**

0-21 4 hd **Zaplamation (IRE)**[8] 1279 8-9-8 70 6ex BarryMcHugh 13 71+
(John Quinn) *swtchd lft s: t.k.h towards rr: hdwy over 2f out: tk 3rd last 50yds: lost 3rd post* **13/2**[3]

61-6 5 1 **Marmas**[12] 1218 4-9-3 70 FrannyNorton 12 70
(John Mackie) *t.k.h: sn trcking ldr: led briefly over 2f out: kpt on one pce fnl f* **10/1**

56-3 6 ¾ **Bathwick Street**[31] 948 4-9-1 68 AdamKirby 5 67
(David Evans) *t.k.h: sn trcking ldrs: one pce over 1f out* **5/1**[2]

5-30 7 ½ **Ctappers**[22] 1062 4-8-8 61 SamHitchcott 1 60
(Mick Channon) *hld up in rr: effrt over 2f out: chsd ldrs over 1f out: kpt on one pce* **14/1**

0-40 8 1 ½ **Father Shine (IRE)**[14] 1189 10-8-7 55 oh9 DuranFentiman 15 52
(Shaun Harris) *led after 1f: hdd over 2f out: wknd ins fnl f* **66/1**

004- 9 ¾ **My Arch**[48] 3419 11-9-12 74 GrahamLee 11 70
(Ollie Pears) *hld up in rr: effrt over 2f out: kpt on fnl f: nvr a factor* **14/1**

405- 10 1 **All That Remains (IRE)**[12] 7352 8-8-10 58 (p) DaleSwift 6 53
(Brian Ellison) *hld up in rr: effrt 4f out: nvr a factor* **20/1**

50-0 11 1 **Maid Of Meft**[18] 1111 6-8-13 64 LeeTopliss(3) 7 58
(Paul Midgley) *s.i.s: hdwy on outer over 5f out: chsd ldrs 2f out: wknd appr fnl f* **16/1**

100- 12 8 **Mr Crystal (FR)**[289] 3419 9-9-9 71 FrederikTylicki 4 56
(Micky Hammond) *hld up in rr: effrt 3f out: wknd wl over 1f out* **16/1**

3511 13 13 **Linkable**[34] 905 4-9-2 69 (t) SebSanders 14 40
(Brendan Powell) *swtchd lft s: hld up in rr: effrt over 3f out: wknd over 2f out* **14/1**

1-65 14 1 **Dorry K (IRE)**[27] 989 4-9-0 67 (b[1]) PaulHanagan 9 37
(Brian Rothwell) *mid-div: drvn over 3f out: bhd fnl 2f* **33/1**

4m 18.24s (22.04) **Going Correction** +0.325s/f (Good)
WFA 4 from 6yo+ 5lb 14 Ran SP% **121.6**
Speed ratings (Par 103): **64,62,61,61,60 60,60,59,59,58 58,54,49,48**
toteswingers: 1&2 £6.10, 1&3 £18.80, 2&3 £33.20 CSF £27.25 CT £527.37 TOTE £3.50: £1.70, £3.00, £5.90; EX 30.30 Trifecta £556.00 Pool: £2727.06 - 3.67 winning units..
Owner Highfield Racing 2 **Bred** Ballylinch Stud **Trained** Settrington, N Yorks

FOCUS
Not as demanding a test as might have been expected, the main bunch rather ignoring long-time leader Father Shine, but there's no doubting the winner was much the best.

1446 PADDOCK PACKAGE H'CAP 1m 2f 6y
4:15 (4:15) (Class 2) (0-105,98) 4-Y-O+
£12,450 (£3,728; £1,864; £932; £466; £234) **Stalls** Low

Form RPR

615- 1 **Lady Loch**[185] 6875 4-8-5 82 PaulHanagan 5 92
(Richard Fahey) *trckd ldr: upsides 7f out: effrt over 2f out: led over 1f out: edgd rt ins fnl f: styd on* **9/2**[1]

20-0 2 1 ¼ **Kingsdesire (IRE)**[68] 463 4-9-7 98 (t) AdamKirby 2 106
(Marco Botti) *trckd ldrs: wnt 2nd appr fnl f: no imp* **7/1**

3-60 3 2 **Las Verglas Star (IRE)**[10] 1233 5-8-11 88 FrederikTylicki 12 92
(Richard Fahey) *mid-div: hdwy 4f out: drvn over 2f out: kpt on to take 3rd last 100yds* **10/1**

110- 4 1 ½ **Easy Terms**[276] 3857 6-9-5 96 JamesSullivan 10 97+
(Edwin Tuer) *hld up in rr: hdwy over 1f out: styd on to take 4th ins fnl f* **16/1**

054- 5 2 **Licence To Till (USA)**[154] 7601 6-8-10 87 SilvestreDeSousa 8 84
(Mark Johnston) *chsd ldrs: one pce over 1f out* **13/2**

460- 6 nk **Spanish Duke (IRE)**[192] 6674 6-9-1 92 [1] DaleSwift 3 88+
(Brian Ellison) *s.s: hdwy on wd outside over 1f out: kpt on* **11/2**[2]

65-0 7 1 ½ **Hit The Jackpot (IRE)**[10] 1235 4-9-3 94 DanielTudhope 6 87
(David O'Meara) *led: increased pce over 2f out: hdd over 1f out: wknd last 150yds* **13/2**

000- 8 ¾ **Silvery Moon (IRE)**[192] 6674 6-8-12 89 DuranFentiman 7 80
(Tim Easterby) *trckd ldrs: drvn over 2f out: wknd over 1f out* **18/1**

446- 9 1 ¾ **Sirvino**[150] 7689 8-8-12 89 GrahamGibbons 11 77
(David Barron) *hld up in rr: nvr a factor* **6/1**[3]

306- 10 1 ¼ **Warlu Way**[200] 6445 6-8-10 87 PaulMulrennan 1 72
(Michael Easterby) *stdd s: hld up in rr: n.m.r over 1f out: nvr a factor* **14/1**

11 1 **Fluidity**[231] 5464 4-9-5 96 GrahamLee 4 79
(Nigel Tinkler) *t.k.h: mid-div: drvn over 2f out: lost pl over 1f out* **25/1**

12 1 **Moccasin (FR)**[202] 4-8-13 90 PaddyAspell 9 71
(Geoffrey Harker) *s.i.s: sme hdwy 4f out: lost pl over 1f out* **33/1**

2m 14.67s (0.97) **Going Correction** +0.325s/f (Good) 12 Ran SP% **120.7**
Speed ratings (Par 109): **109,108,106,105,103 103,102,101,100,99 98,97**
toteswingers: 1&2 £8.30, 1&3 £14.20, 2&3 £20.40 CSF £36.33 CT £306.22 TOTE £4.10: £1.60, £4.00, £3.50; EX 45.60 Trifecta £457.10 Pool: £2687.12 - 4.40 winning units..
Owner David W Armstrong **Bred** Jeremy Green And Sons **Trained** Musley Bank, N Yorks

FOCUS
This looked a good little race beforehand, but not many got into it.

1447 PONTEFRACT-RACES.CO.UK MAIDEN FILLIES' STKS 6f
4:45 (4:46) (Class 5) 3-Y-O **£3,234** (£962; £481; £240) **Stalls** Low

Form RPR

43-3 1 **Next Door (IRE)**[73] 404 3-9-0 62 GrahamGibbons 2 66
(David Barron) *chsd ldrs: effrt over 2f out: chsd ldr and edgd lft over 1f out: styd on to ld last 50yds* **13/8**[1]

3-22 2 1 ¼ **Clock Opera (IRE)**[71] 416 3-9-0 63 PaulHanagan 3 62
(William Stone) *led: hdd fnl 50yds: no ex* **10/1**

000- 3 6 **Pink Cadillac (IRE)**[213] 6049 3-9-0 41 PJMcDonald 6 43
(Ben Haslam) *chsd ldrs: kpt on to take one pce 3rd appr fnl f* **40/1**

00- 4 2 **Sorcellerie**[318] 2499 3-9-0 0 DuranFentiman 5 36
(Mel Brittain) *in rr: effrt over 2f out: n.m.r over 1f out: tk one pce 4th 1f out* **9/1**[3]

5 5 **Misty Pearl** 3-9-0 0 PaulMulrennan 9 20
(Michael Appleby) *s.i.s: bhd whn swtchd lft sn after s: hdwy over 1f out: kpt on ins fnl f* **25/1**

253- 6 1 ¼ **Ayr Missile**[266] 4173 3-9-0 67 [1] PhillipMakin 7 16
(Kevin Ryan) *restless in stalls: s.i.s: sn chsng ldrs on outer: lost pl over 2f out* **4/1**[2]

00- 7 2 **Branston Jubilee**[193] 6627 3-9-0 0 PaddyAspell 4 10
(Geoffrey Harker) *chsd ldrs: n.m.r over 1f out: wknd jst ins fnl f* **25/1**

3- 8 2 ½ **Macaabra (IRE)**[154] 7613 3-9-0 0 PatCosgrave 8
(James Tate) *s.s: sn in tch: wknd over 1f out* **4/1**[2]

0 9 2 ½ **Auntie Mildred (IRE)**[50] 706 3-9-0 0 DanielTudhope 1
(David O'Meara) *chsd ldrs: wkng whn n.m.r over 1f out* **11/1**

1m 19.8s (2.90) **Going Correction** +0.325s/f (Good) 9 Ran SP% **115.7**
Speed ratings (Par 95): **93,91,83,80,74 72,69,66,63**
toteswingers 1&2 £2.50, 2&3 £59.60, 1&3 £18.20 CSF £19.23 TOTE £2.50: £1.20, £2.20, £9.30; EX 15.70 Trifecta £520.90 Pool: £2935.32 - 4.22 winning units..
Owner Oghill House Stud & Partner **Bred** Oghill House Stud **Trained** Maunby, N Yorks

FOCUS
Modest form, but some of those in behind can do better.

1448 RACING ON MONDAY 22ND APRIL H'CAP 1m 2f 6y
5:15 (5:16) (Class 5) (0-75,75) 4-Y-O+ **£3,234** (£962; £481; £240) **Stalls** Low

Form RPR

136- 1 **Gold Show**[170] 7270 4-9-0 68 PaulMulrennan 4 78
(Edwin Tuer) *mid-div: hdwy over 2f out: styd on to ld last 75yds: drvn out* **14/1**

54-0 2 ¾ **Carragold**[10] 1238 7-9-2 70 SilvestreDeSousa 3 78
(Mel Brittain) *chsd ldrs: led on inner over 2f out: hdd last 75yds: no ex* **13/2**

00-2 3 ½ **Regal Swain (IRE)**[8] 1282 5-9-1 69 RobertWinston 10 76
(Alan Swinbank) *prom: swtchd lft bnd after 2f and mid-div: hdwy over 2f out: swtchd outside: styd on fnl f: tk 3rd last 50yds* **7/2**[1]

16-0 4 1 ¼ **Tenhoo**[18] 1111 7-8-13 67 TedDurcan 11 72
(Eric Alston) *swtchd lft after s: hld up in rr: hdwy on ins over 2f out: chsd ldrs over 1f out: kpt on to take 4th last 50yds* **33/1**

26-0 5 ¾ **Gran Maestro (USA)**[10] 1238 4-9-2 70 (b) JamesSullivan 12 73
(Ruth Carr) *swtchd lft s: in rr: hdwy over 2f out: styd on ins fnl f* **50/1**

21-4 6 ¾ **Syncopate**[13] 1200 4-9-2 70 AdamKirby 1 73
(Pam Sly) *s.i.s: sn mid-div: swtchd outside and chsd ldrs over 2f out: kpt on same pce fnl f: eased towards fin* **4/1**[2]

004- 7 4 **Kodicil (IRE)**[309] 2775 5-8-7 61 (p) DuranFentiman 8 55
(Tim Walford) *chsd ldrs: drvn over 3f out: nt clr run over 1f out: wknd fnl f* **20/1**

534 8 6 **Rayadour (IRE)**[18] 1111 4-8-12 66 PJMcDonald 7 48
(Micky Hammond) *in rr: drvn 6f out: nvr a factor* **14/1**

100- 9 1 ¼ **Sunnybridge Boy (IRE)**[179] 7032 4-9-4 75 MichaelMetcalfe(3) 13 54
(Mrs K Burke) *hld up in rr: sme hdwy 2f out: sn wknd* **12/1**

The Form Book Flat, Raceform Ltd, Compton, RG20 6NL.

050 **10** 1/2 **Six Silver Lane**[10] 1239 5-8-2 **63**...............(v) AdamMcLean(7) 2 41
(Derek Shaw) *mde most: edgd rt and hdd over 2f out: wknd over 1f out* **20/1**

000- **11** 6 **Jonny Lesters Hair (IRE)**[185] 6884 8-8-11 **70**........ AdamCarter(5) 6 36
(Tim Easterby) *sn w ldr: drvn over 3f out: lost pl over 2f out* **16/1**

3/3- **12** 1/2 **Cashpoint**[306] 2857 8-9-5 **73**........ GrahamLee 5 38
(Ian Williams) *chsd ldrs: wknd appr fnl f* **5/1**[3]

00-0 **13** 6 **Dubaianswer**[12] 644 5-9-2 **70**........ BarryMcHugh 9 23
(Tony Coyle) *rr-div: drvn over 4f out: bhd fnl 2f* **25/1**

150- **14** 1 **Warcrown (IRE)**[179] 7032 4-9-7 **75**........ PaulHanagan 14 26
(Richard Fahey) *mid-div: hdwy u.p 3f out: lost pl over 1f out* **11/1**

2m 15.1s (1.40) **Going Correction** +0.325s/f (Good) **14** Ran SP% **125.7**
Speed ratings (Par 103): **107,106,106,105,104 103,100,95,94,94 89,89,84,83**
toteswingers: 1&2 £18.40, 1&3 £17.30, 2&3 £9.50 CSF £100.55 CT £402.47 TOTE £16.70: £4.20, £2.80, £2.10; EX 109.60 Trifecta £914.70 Pool: £1977.46 - 1.62 winning units..
Owner Ontoawinner **Bred** Mr & Mrs A E Pakenham **Trained** Birkby, N Yorks

FOCUS
A modest handicap run at what looked a strong pace.
T/Jkpt: £5,336.00 to a £1 stake. Pool £165,343.78 - 22.00 winning units. T/Plt: £49.00 to a £1 stake. Pool of £79237.85 - 1,178.36 winning units. T/Qpdt: £16.70 to a £1 stake. Pool of £5,329.48 - 235.85 winning units. WG

1328 SOUTHWELL (L-H)
Tuesday, April 9

OFFICIAL GOING: Standard
Wind: Light half against Weather: Cloudy with sunny periods

1449 BRITISH STALLION STUDS E.B.F 32RED.COM MAIDEN STKS 5f (F)
2:00 (2:00) (Class 5) 2-Y-O **£2,911** (£866; £432; £216) **Stalls High**

Form RPR

1 **Split Rock** 2-9-5 0........ JoeFanning 4 70+
(Mark Johnston) *mde most: rdn over 1f out: edgd lft and styd on wl ins fnl f* **5/6**[1]

0 **2** 2 1/4 **Kitty Brown (IRE)**[10] 1240 2-9-0 0........ CathyGannon 2 57+
(David Evans) *trckd ldrs: pushed along and sltly outpcd 1/2-way: sn rdn: styd on wl fnl f: tk 2nd nr line* **5/1**[2]

3 nse **Livia Drusilla (IRE)** 2-8-11 0........ PaulPickard(3) 1 57
(Brian Ellison) *cl up: effrt 2f out: sn chal and ev ch tl wknd ins fnl f: lost 2nd nr line* **5/1**[2]

4 2 1/2 **Jaga Time** 2-9-5 0........ TonyHamilton 5 53
(Richard Fahey) *cl up: disp ld 1/2-way: rdn wl over 1f out: grad wknd* **7/1**[3]

5 10 **Claudia Octavia** 2-9-0 0........ TomEaves 3 12
(Brian Ellison) *s.i.s: a in rr* **12/1**

1m 3.93s (4.23) **Going Correction** +0.65s/f (Slow) **5** Ran SP% **108.1**
Speed ratings (Par 92): **92,88,88,84,68**
CSF £5.09 TOTE £1.60: £1.10, £3.00; EX 4.50 Trifecta £17.60 Pool: £2120.05 - 89.86 winning units..
Owner Sheikh Hamdan Bin Mohammed Al Maktoum **Bred** Darley **Trained** Middleham Moor, N Yorks

FOCUS
Probably just a modest event.

1450 BINARY TRENDS - TRIPLE YOUR INVESTMENT MEDIAN AUCTION MAIDEN STKS 7f (F)
2:30 (2:30) (Class 6) 3-4-Y-O **£2,045** (£603; £302) **Stalls Low**

Form RPR

0- **1** **Eutropius (IRE)**[223] 5753 4-9-13 0........ RussKennemore 4 76
(Alan Swinbank) *trckd ldrs: hdwy on inner 3f out: rdn to ld over 1f out: hung bdly rt to stands' rail ent fnl f: kpt on* **4/1**[2]

65 **2** 3 **Flamingo Beat**[24] 1044 3-8-13 0........ ChrisCatlin 2 63
(Rae Guest) *in rr: gd hdwy on wd outside 1/2-way: rdn to ld briefly 2f out: sn hdd and drvn: kpt on same pce fnl f* **6/1**[3]

0 **3** 8 **Harbour Captain (IRE)**[21] 1072 3-8-13 0........ J-PGuillambert 1 42
(Jo Hughes) *led 1f: cl up on inner: rdn along wl over 2f out: drvn and one pce fr wl over 1f out* **15/2**

4 3 **Mr Snooks** 3-8-13 0........ PaulQuinn 7 35
(David Nicholls) *s.i.s and in rr: rapid hdwy to chse ldrs after 3f: cl up on outer 3f out: rdn to ld briefly over 2f out: sn drvn and grad wknd* **6/1**[3]

450- **5** 1 1/4 **Another Claret**[187] 6815 3-8-13 69........ TonyHamilton 5 31
(Richard Fahey) *chsd ldrs: rdn along 1/2-way: sn outpcd* **11/8**[1]

060- **6** 7 **Queen Cassiopeia**[145] 7729 4-9-8 52........ AdrianNicholls 6
(J R Jenkins) *cl up: led over 3f out: rdn and hdd over 2f out: sn wknd* **20/1**

00/0 **7** hd **Concordia Notte (IRE)**[47] 733 4-9-8 47........(t) CathyGannon 3
(Violet M Jordan) *led after 1f: rdn along bef 1/2-way: sn hdd & wknd* **40/1**

1m 31.09s (0.79) **Going Correction** +0.15s/f (Slow)
WFA 3 from 4yo 14lb **7** Ran SP% **109.6**
Speed ratings (Par 101): **101,97,88,85,83 75,75**
toteswingers: 1&2 £3.70, 1&3 £3.80, 2&3 £7.00 CSF £25.42 TOTE £3.50: £2.20, £3.70; EX 28.50 Trifecta £107.50 Pool: £2345.40 - 16.36 winning units..
Owner Ontoawinner 2 **Bred** Grangemore Stud **Trained** Melsonby, N Yorks

FOCUS
A moderate maiden event, with pre-race doubts surrounding the favourite's ability to handle the surface seemingly playing out in the race itself.

1451 £32 BONUS AT 32RED.COM CLAIMING STKS 6f (F)
3:00 (3:00) (Class 6) 3-Y-O+ **£1,940** (£577; £288) **Stalls Low**

Form RPR

2241 **1** **Hamoody (USA)**[22] 1065 9-9-8 82........ AdrianNicholls 1 89
(David Nicholls) *slt ld: rdn and qcknd wl over 2f out: drvn over 1f out: kpt on strly ins fnl f* **9/4**[2]

1311 **2** 3 **Elusive Hawk (IRE)**[7] 1309 9-9-8 78........(v) DeclanBates(5) 2 90
(David Evans) *cl up: rdn 2f out and ev ch tl drvn and edgd lft ins fnl f: sn btn* **4/11**[1]

0064 **3** 12 **Island Express (IRE)**[17] 1150 6-9-0 48........(t) AnnStokell(5) 4 38
(Ann Stokell) *chsd ldng pair: rdn along wl over 2f out: sn outpcd* **100/1**[3]

1m 17.47s (0.97) **Going Correction** +0.15s/f (Slow) **3** Ran SP% **105.1**
Speed ratings (Par 101): **99,95,79**
CSF £3.53 TOTE £3.40; EX 2.80 Trifecta £3.50 Pool: £1782.89 - 378.74 winning units..
Owner Hart Inn I **Bred** Ragged Mountain Farm **Trained** Sessay, N Yorks
■ Stewards' Enquiry : Declan Bates two-day ban: used whip above permitted level (Apr 23-24)

FOCUS
A disappointing turnout for this claimer and something of an upset.

1452 BINARY TRENDS - MAKE MONEY WITH BINARYTRENDS.CO.UK H'CAP 6f (F)
3:30 (3:31) (Class 6) (0-60,60) 4-Y-O+ **£1,940** (£577; £288; £144) **Stalls Low**

Form RPR

2134 **1** **Pull The Pin (IRE)**[3] 1388 4-8-13 **55**........(b) NeilFarley(3) 9 68
(Declan Carroll) *cl up: led after 1f and set str pce: rdn wl over 1f out: drvn and edgd rt ins fnl f: kpt on gamely towards fin* **11/4**[1]

3051 **2** 1 3/4 **Mary's Pet**[13] 1193 6-9-3 **56**........(p) KierenFox 10 63
(Lee Carter) *chsd ldrs: hdwy wl over 2f out: sn chsng wnr: rdn and ch over 1f out: drvn whn swtchd lft ins fnl f: no imp towards fin* **5/1**[2]

0250 **3** 2 1/4 **Ridgeway Hawk**[20] 1087 5-9-0 **53**........(p) RobertHavlin 7 53
(Mark Usher) *dwlt and in rr: wd st: hdwy wl over 2f out: sn rdn and kpt on wl ins fnl f: nrst fin* **8/1**

5652 **4** 2 1/4 **Rambo Will**[14] 1186 5-9-7 **60**........ AdrianNicholls 1 53
(J R Jenkins) *towards rr: hdwy on inner wl over 2f out: sn rdn and kpt on fnl f: nrst fin* **5/1**[2]

4430 **5** 2 3/4 **Michael's Nook**[9] 1271 6-8-12 **51**........(p) LukeMorris 8 35
(Alastair Lidderdale) *chsd ldrs: hdwy over 2f out: sn rdn and no imp appr fnl f* **8/1**

0335 **6** 3 1/2 **Steel City Boy (IRE)**[6] 1331 10-8-10 **54**........ AnnStokell(5) 4 27
(Ann Stokell) *led 1f: prom: rdn along wl over 2f out and grad wknd* **20/1**

0000 **7** 3/4 **Marshall Art**[14] 1186 4-9-1 **59**........ DeclanBates(5) 3 29
(David Evans) *chsd ldrs: rdn along wl over 2f out: grad wknd* **25/1**

00-6 **8** nse **Punching**[77] 323 9-9-1 **54**........ HayleyTurner 2 24
(Conor Dore) *v.s.a: a in rr* **6/1**[3]

5644 **9** 2 1/4 **Medam**[9] 1271 4-8-8 **52**........(t) ShirleyTeasdale(5) 5 15
(Shaun Harris) *chsd ldrs: rdn along wl over 2f out: sn wknd* **16/1**

-446 **10** 10 **Hittin'The Skids (IRE)**[25] 1021 5-8-13 **52**........(p) JimmyQuinn 6
(Mandy Rowland) *dwlt: a in rr* **18/1**

1m 17.15s (0.65) **Going Correction** +0.15s/f (Slow) **10** Ran SP% **116.3**
Speed ratings (Par 101): **101,98,95,92,89 84,83,83,80,66**
toteswingers: 1&2 £2.60, 1&3 £3.80, 2&3 £8.50 CSF £16.06 CT £92.97 TOTE £3.40: £1.20, £1.80, £2.70; EX 16.10 Trifecta £133.90 Pool: £2243.11 - 12.55 winning units..
Owner C Harding **Bred** T J Ryan **Trained** Sledmere, E Yorks

FOCUS
A modest handicap, run at a furious pace.

1453 32RED CASINO H'CAP 1m 4f (F)
4:05 (4:05) (Class 5) (0-75,75) 3-Y-O **£2,587** (£770; £384; £192) **Stalls Low**

Form RPR

-112 **1** **Naru (IRE)**[57] 613 3-9-7 **75**........ RyanMoore 4 91
(James Tate) *t.k.h: sn led: pushed along 3f out and sn qcknd clr: rdn: carried hd awkwardly and hung lft wl over 1f out: wl clr ins fnl f: unchal* **11/8**[1]

-353 **2** 22 **Lucky Mountain**[17] 1145 3-8-4 **61**........ BillyCray(3) 2 46
(Scott Dixon) *hld up in tch: hdwy on inner 3f out: sn rdn and styd on same pce: tk remote 2nd ins fnl f* **16/1**

0-1 **3** 1/2 **Glenreef**[14] 1187 3-9-2 **70**........ JoeFanning 3 55
(Mark Johnston) *cl up: chal over 3f out and sn rdn: drvn over 2f out and sn one pce: lost remote 2nd ins fnl f* **3/1**[3]

61 **4** 3 **Burgoyne (USA)**[21] 1072 3-9-5 **73**........ RobertHavlin 1 53
(Hughie Morrison) *trckd ldng pair: pushed along briefly after 4f: cl up on outer 1/2-way: rdn along 3f out: sn btn* **15/8**[2]

2m 41.51s (0.51) **Going Correction** +0.15s/f (Slow) **4** Ran SP% **107.8**
Speed ratings (Par 98): **104,89,89,87**
CSF £16.92 TOTE £1.70; EX 14.70 Trifecta £28.00 Pool: £1809.99 - 48.34 winning units..
Owner Saeed Manana **Bred** Rabbah Bloodstock Limited **Trained** Newmarket, Suffolk

FOCUS
A competitive handicap on paper, but it was turned into a procession.

1454 32RED H'CAP 2m (F)
4:35 (4:35) (Class 4) (0-85,80) 4-Y-O+ **£4,690** (£1,395; £697; £348) **Stalls Low**

Form RPR

343- **1** **Anna's Arch (IRE)**[12] 4925 6-9-1 **68**........ RussKennemore 5 79+
(Alan Swinbank) *cl up: led 3f out: rdn and hdd briefly wl over 1f out: styd on to ld again appr fnl f: drvn out* **5/2**[2]

-224 **2** 1 **Tartan Jura**[25] 1018 5-9-8 **75**........(v[1]) JoeFanning 2 84
(Mark Johnston) *led: pushed along 4f out: rdn and hdd 3f out: drvn and sltly outpcd 2f out: kpt on u.p ins fnl f* **9/2**[3]

1221 **3** 2 1/4 **Stentorian (IRE)**[7] 1306 5-9-13 **80** 6ex........(v) RyanMoore 4 86
(Gary Moore) *trckd ldng pair: hdwy over 3f out: chsd wnr over 2f out: rdn to ld briefly wl over 1f out: edgd rt and hdd appr fnl f: sn drvn and one pce* **10/11**[1]

150- **4** 23 **Three White Socks (IRE)**[18] 7077 6-8-13 **69**........(p) PaulPickard(3) 6 48
(Brian Ellison) *reminders s: chsd ldrs: pushed along 6f out: rdn over 4f out: sn outpcd* **25/1**

-644 **5** 12 **Phoenix Flight (IRE)**[14] 1188 8-9-12 **79**........(b) FergusSweeney 3 43
(James Evans) *hld up: hdwy 6f out: rdn along 4f out: sn outpcd and bhd* **16/1**

110- **6** 99 **Rosairlie (IRE)**[31] 4613 5-9-4 **76**........ GarryWhillans(5) 1
(Micky Hammond) *trckd ldrs: reminders after 6f: lost pl and bhd 1/2-way: t.o fr over 4f out* **40/1**

3m 45.11s (-0.39) **Going Correction** +0.15s/f (Slow) **6** Ran SP% **111.3**
Speed ratings (Par 105): **106,105,104,92,86 37**
toteswingers 1&2 £1.30, 2&3 £1.60, 1&3 £1.30 CSF £13.76 TOTE £3.30: £1.60, £2.50; EX 14.50 Trifecta £28.30 Pool: £2554.65 - 67.50 winning units..
Owner Chris Tremewan **Bred** Arbawny Ventures 2000uc **Trained** Melsonby, N Yorks

FOCUS
A decent pace on throughout in this feature handicap and it required a strong staying performance.

1455 BINARY TRENDS - RISK FREE INVESTMENTS H'CAP 7f (F)
5:05 (5:06) (Class 6) (0-55,60) 4-Y-O+ **£1,940** (£577; £288; £144) **Stalls Low**

Form RPR

5411 **1** **Sofias Number One (USA)**[7] 1311 5-9-7 **60** 6ex......(b) PhilipPrince(5) 2 72
(Roy Bowring) *prom: rdn to chal 2f out: led appr fnl f: drvn out* **11/4**[2]

3526 **2** 3/4 **Silly Billy (IRE)**[13] 1195 5-9-0 **55**........(v) RyanWhile(7) 9 65
(Bill Turner) *trckd ldrs: hdwy wl over 2f out: swtchd rt and rdn to chal over 1f out: ev ch tl drvn and no ex last 100yds* **7/2**[3]

0152 **3** 1 **Mucky Molly**[17] 1149 5-9-4 **52**........(vt) TomEaves 8 59
(Alison Hutchinson) *slt ld: rdn along wl over 2f out: drvn over 1f out: hdd appr fnl f: kpt on same pce* **9/1**

0451 **4** *1* **Ace Of Spies (IRE)**[7] 1310 8-9-8 **56** 6ex.......................... HayleyTurner 5 60
(Conor Dore) *disp ld: rdn along and ev ch 2f out: sn drvn and one pce ent fnl f* **5/1**

0632 **5** *hd* **Mcconnell (USA)**[7] 1311 8-9-2 **50**................................(b) CathyGannon 4 54
(Violet M Jordan) *trckd ldrs: rdn along and sltly outpcd 2f out: drvn and kpt on appr fnl f* **5/2**[1]

0533 **6** *3/4* **Bonnie Prince Blue**[7] 1311 10-9-3 **51**..............................(b) AmyRyan 1 53
(Ian McInnes) *towards rr: rdn along 1/2-way: hdwy on inner 2f: out: styd on ins fnl f: nrst fin* **20/1**

50-6 **7** *5* **Vogarth**[7] 1310 9-8-5 **46** oh1..................................(v) DanielleMooney[(7)] 10 35
(Michael Chapman) *chsd ldrs on outer: rdn along over 3f out and sn outpcd* **80/1**

0/5- **8** *3 1/2* **Blue Charm**[364] 1283 9-9-2 **50**... DavidNolan 6 30
(Ian McInnes) *chsd ldrs: rdn along 3f out: sn wknd* **18/1**

05-3 **9** *2 1/2* **Dr Victoria**[58] 602 4-8-5 **46** oh1..................................(t) NoelGarbutt[(7)] 7 19
(John Norton) *a towards rr* **50/1**

250- **10** *31* **Whats For Pudding (IRE)**[175] 7126 5-8-12 **46** oh1...........[1] PaulQuinn 3
(Richard Whitaker) *s.i.s: a bhd: eased fnl 2f* **33/1**

1m 31.78s (1.48) **Going Correction** +0.15s/f (Slow) **10** Ran SP% **120.3**
Speed ratings (Par 101): **97,96,95,93,93 92,87,83,80,44**
toteswingers: 1&2 £3.20, 1&3 £5.30, 2&3 £6.90 CSF £12.98 CT £79.56 TOTE £3.00: £1.30, £2.30, £2.30; EX 14.10 Trifecta £70.10 Pool: £3368.08 - 36.01 winning units..
Owner S R Bowring **Bred** Rosecrest Farm Llc **Trained** Edwinstowe, Notts
■ Stewards' Enquiry : Philip Prince four-day ban: used whip above permitted level (Apr 23-26)

FOCUS
A hotly contested, if only modest handicap and it served up a thrilling finish.
T/Plt: £476.30 to a £1 stake. Pool of £50970.80 - 78.11 winning tickets. T/Qpdt: £42.40 to a £1 stake. Pool of £4168.81 - 72.70 winning tickets. JR

1277 SAINT-CLOUD (L-H)
Tuesday, April 9
OFFICIAL GOING: Turf: soft

1456a PRIX EDMOND BLANC (GROUP 3) (4YO+) (TURF) 1m
2:55 (2:58) 4-Y-O+ **£32,520** (£13,008; £9,756; £6,504; £3,252)

RPR

1 **Silas Marner (FR)**[38] 6-8-11 0........................... Jean-BernardEyquem 8 113
(J-C Rouget, France) *racd in midfield at outset: sent forward to 2nd after 3f: chal and led 1 1/2f out: sn established clr ld: chal 50yds out: hld on wl* **27/10**[1]

2 *snk* **Menardais (FR)**[38] 4-8-11 0...................................... StephanePasquier 3 113
(P Bary, France) *racd in midfield on settling: relegated towards rr ent st: hrd rdn 2f out: rallied wl: r.o strly fnl f: wnt 2nd 50yds out: chal ldr fnl 25yds: a being hld* **11/1**

3 *1 1/4* **Amaron**[191] 6727 4-9-4 0... MaximeGuyon 6 117
(Andreas Lowe, Germany) *racd in 2nd on settling: r.o wl u.p 2f out: no ex fnl 100yds: ct for 2nd 50yds out: r.o* **11/2**

4 *2* **Celebrissime (IRE)**[21] 1085 8-8-11 0............................... OlivierPeslier 1 105
(F Head, France) *led on settling: rdn 2f out: ct and hdd 1 1/2f out: styd on fnl f* **53/10**[3]

5 *1* **Zack Hope**[21] 1085 5-8-11 0.. TonyPiccone 5 103
(N Caullery, France) *hld up towards rr: midfield 2 1/2f out: qcknd wl u.p 1 1/2f out to go 4th: no ex fnl f* **17/2**

6 *4* **Zinabaa (FR)**[185] 6897 8-9-2 0.. GeraldMosse 2 99
(Mlle T Puitg, France) *settled in midfield on ins: rdn early in st: nt qckn: styd on one pce fnl 1 1/2f* **14/5**[2]

7 *3 1/2* **Foreign Tune**[193] 6656 4-8-8 0.. FlavienPrat 9 83
(C Laffon-Parias, France) *a towards rr: no ex u.p fnl 2f: nt hrd rdn fnl f* **22/1**

8 *3* **Takar (IRE)**[159] 7515 4-9-0 0... ThierryThulliez 7 82
(Rod Collet, France) *hld up in rr: rdn early in st: no ex: fdd: nt hrd rdn whn ch had gone* **16/1**

9 *3* **King's Hall**[142] 7784 5-9-0 0... UmbertoRispoli 4 75
(A Wohler, Germany) *racd in 3rd on settling: relegated to 4th ent st: rdn but no ex 2 1/2f out: fdd: nt hrd rdn fnl f* **34/1**

1m 48.3s (0.80) **9** Ran SP% **116.5**
WIN (incl. 1 euro stake): 3.70. PLACES: 1.80, 2.80, 2.30. DF: 16.60. SF: 27.00.
Owner Cuadra Montalban Srl **Bred** R Phillips **Trained** Pau, France

1457 - (Foreign Racing) - See Raceform Interactive

CATTERICK (L-H)
Wednesday, April 10
OFFICIAL GOING: Good (good to firm in places; 8.1)
Wind: Light, across Weather: Cloudy

1458 CATTERICK FLAT SEASON STARTS NOW H'CAP 5f
2:20 (2:20) (Class 6) (0-60,60) 3-Y-O **£2,385** (£704; £352) **Stalls** Low

Form RPR

000- **1** **Shirley's Pride**[222] 5807 3-8-7 **46**...............................(t) AndrewMullen 10 54
(Michael Appleby) *w ldr: rdn to ld over 1f out: kpt on* **12/1**

543 **2** *1/2* **Jofranka**[19] 1122 3-9-4 **57**.. GrahamGibbons 7 63
(David Barron) *chsd ldrs: rdn over 2f out: kpt on* **5/1**[2]

-362 **3** *3/4* **Magic Ice**[6] 1349 3-9-0 **53**.. DaleSwift 11 57
(Brian Ellison) *sn chsd ldrs on outer: rdn and briefly outpcd 1/2-way: kpt on fr over 1f out* **9/2**[1]

600- **4** *1/2* **Ridgeblade**[192] 6707 3-8-7 **46** oh1.............................. SilvestreDeSousa 6 48
(Noel Wilson) *w ldr: rdn over 2f out: no ex fnl 50yds* **6/1**[3]

453 **5** *1/2* **Secret Advice**[22] 1078 3-9-3 **56**.. ShaneKelly 12 56
(Keith Dalgleish) *dwlt: hld up in tch: pushed along 2f out: kpt on fnl f: nrst fin* **8/1**

6-64 **6** *hd* **Charlemagne Diva**[9] 1284 3-8-9 **53**.............................(e) PhilipPrince[(5)] 9 52
(Richard Guest) *chsd ldrs: rdn 1/2-way: one pce* **10/1**

446- **7** *1 3/4* **Princess Sheila (IRE)**[133] 7916 3-9-3 **56**........................(b[1]) LiamJones 3 49
(J S Moore) *nvr bttr than midfield* **15/2**

400- **8** *2 3/4* **Robyn**[125] 8007 3-8-8 **50**... BillyCray[(3)] 5 33
(Scott Dixon) *slowly away and hmpd sn after s: sn chsd along in rr: nvr threatened* **20/1**

50-0 **9** *shd* **Moss The Boss (IRE)**[28] 985 3-8-13 **52**..........................(p) MickyFenton 8 35
(Paul Midgley) *led narrowly: rdn whn hdd over 1f out: wknd and hung lft* **33/1**

055 **10** *2 3/4* **Lady Calantha**[28] 985 3-8-0 **46** oh1............................ JordanHibberd[(7)] 1 19
(Alan Berry) *wnt rt s: a in rr* **50/1**

-245 **11** *6* **Con Leche**[41] 828 3-8-13 **52**.......................................(p) RobertWinston 4
(Scott Dixon) *chsd ldrs: wknd over 1f out: eased* **11/1**

04-5 **12** *2 1/2* **Poppy Bond**[22] 1073 3-9-7 **60**....................................... DuranFentiman 2
(Chris Fairhurst) *hmpd s: a towards rr* **9/1**

1m 1.23s (1.43) **Going Correction** +0.225s/f (Good) **12** Ran SP% **116.8**
Speed ratings (Par 96): **97,96,95,94,93 93,90,85,85,81 71,67**
Tote Swingers: 1&2 £28.00, 1&3 £10.50, 2&3 £3.60 CSF £68.73 CT £316.79 TOTE £14.10: £5.40, £2.00, £2.20; EX 109.50 Trifecta £587.90 Part won. Pool: £783.94 - 0.24 winning tickets..
Owner M J Golding **Bred** Manor Farm Stud (rutland) **Trained** Danethorpe, Notts

FOCUS
The ground was given as good, good to firm in places (GoingStick 8.1), and Duran Fentiman reported it to be "on the quick side". Just an ordinary sprint handicap.

1459 GORACING.CO.UK CLAIMING STKS 7f
2:50 (2:51) (Class 6) 3-Y-O+ **£2,385** (£704; £352) **Stalls** Centre

Form RPR

6112 **1** **Polar Kite (IRE)**[56] 629 5-9-9 81............................ MichaelMetcalfe[(3)] 1 82
(Sean Curran) *slowly away: sn in midfield: smooth hdwy over 2f out: rdn to chal over 1f out: led 1f out: drvn out* **5/4**[1]

220- **2** *1 3/4* **Llewellyn**[131] 7935 5-9-12 70.. AdrianNicholls 4 77
(David Nicholls) *prom: rdn to ld over 2f out: hdd 1f out: kpt on* **13/2**[3]

001- **3** *3/4* **It's A Mans World**[144] 7004 7-9-9 78.............................. PaulPickard[(3)] 6 75
(Brian Ellison) *hld up in midfield: rdn and hdwy 2f out: kpt on fnl f* **4/1**[2]

66-3 **4** *1* **Beckermet (IRE)**[9] 1280 11-9-8 79.................................. JamesSullivan 8 68
(Ruth Carr) *dwlt: hld up: rdn and hdwy 2f out: kpt on* **13/2**[3]

22-0 **5** *1 1/2* **Green Park (IRE)**[19] 1115 10-9-7 82............................(b) JasonHart[(5)] 10 68
(Declan Carroll) *hld up: rdn over 2f out: hdwy over 1f out: no ex fnl 100yds* **9/1**

433- **6** *1* **No Quarter (IRE)**[35] 6479 6-9-5 58................................ RoystonFfrench 2 59
(Tracy Waggott) *trckd ldrs: rdn and outpcd by ldng pair over 2f out: no threat after* **25/1**

04-0 **7** *9* **Thrust Control (IRE)**[4] 1394 6-9-9 53...................(p) SilvestreDeSousa 3 38
(Tracy Waggott) *led: rdn whn hdd over 2f out: wknd* **33/1**

3366 **8** *nk* **Rawaafed (IRE)**[10] 1272 4-9-13 68.................................... ShaneKelly 7 41
(Keith Dalgleish) *hld up in midfield: rdn 1/2-way: sn btn* **22/1**

4264 **9** *13* **Media Jury**[14] 1193 6-9-6 49..(p) DavidNolan 9
(John Wainwright) *chsd ldrs: lost pl 1/2-way: wknd over 2f out* **100/1**

1m 26.38s (-0.62) **Going Correction** -0.05s/f (Good) **9** Ran SP% **113.2**
Speed ratings (Par 101): **101,99,98,97,95 94,83,83,68**
Tote Swingers: 1&2 £2.60, 1&3 £2.40, 2&3 £3.30 CSF £9.21 TOTE £2.00: £1.02, £3.60, £2.90; EX 9.20 Trifecta £37.80 Pool: £1,351.90 - 26.77 winning tickets..The winner was subject to a friendly claim.
Owner Power Bloodstock Ltd **Bred** Holborn Trust Co **Trained** Hatford, Oxon

FOCUS
Not too many could be fancied at the weights.

1460 EDWARD JAMES THOMPSON 84TH BIRTHDAY H'CAP (DIV I) 7f
3:20 (3:20) (Class 5) (0-75,75) 4-Y-O+ **£2,911** (£866; £432; £216) **Stalls** Centre

Form RPR

11-2 **1** **Sandy Lane (IRE)**[96] 54 4-9-0 **68**.................................. DanielTudhope 9 89+
(David O'Meara) *mde all: barely off the bridle to come clr over 2f out: v easily* **5/2**[1]

061- **2** *6* **Majestic Dream (IRE)**[176] 7142 5-8-9 **70**................ MatthewHopkins[(7)] 5 72
(Michael Easterby) *in tch: rdn over 2f out: kpt on: no ch w wnr* **6/1**[3]

50-0 **3** *shd* **Sunraider (IRE)**[29] 966 6-9-4 **72**...................................... MickyFenton 7 74
(Paul Midgley) *midfield on outer: rdn over 2f out: kpt on* **20/1**

0500 **4** *2* **Bassett Road (IRE)**[11] 1253 5-8-8 **67** ow2..............(p) GarryWhillans[(5)] 4 63
(Keith Dalgleish) *trckd ldr: rdn over 2f out: sn no ch w wnr: no ex and lost 2 pls fnl 100yds* **25/1**

201- **5** *3/4* **Sardanapalus**[214] 6048 4-9-7 **75**....................................(p) PhillipMakin 3 69
(Kevin Ryan) *hld up in tch: rdn over 2f out: nvr threatened* **3/1**[2]

46-0 **6** *1 1/2* **Glenridding**[29] 976 9-8-13 **67**...................................(p) FrederikTylicki 1 57
(James Given) *trckd ldr: rdn over 2f out: wknd over 1f out* **9/1**

112- **7** *nk* **Pravda Street**[174] 7202 8-8-11 **72**............................. RichardOliver[(7)] 2 61
(Brian Ellison) *hld up in midfield: rdn over 2f out: sn btn* **9/1**

5140 **8** *3* **Rio Cobolo (IRE)**[10] 1271 7-8-10 **64**............................(v) AdrianNicholls 8 45
(David Nicholls) *slowly away: a towards rr* **12/1**

020- **9** *3 1/4* **Hail Bold Chief (USA)**[294] 3290 6-8-12 **66**.................. RobertWinston 6 38
(Alan Swinbank) *hld up: nvr threatened* **15/2**

1m 26.09s (-0.91) **Going Correction** -0.05s/f (Good) **9** Ran SP% **115.9**
Speed ratings (Par 103): **103,96,96,93,92 91,90,87,83**
Tote Swingers: 1&2 £8.80, 1&3 £17.80, 2&3 £34.40 CSF £18.03 CT £245.28 TOTE £3.10: £1.90, £2.40, £4.90; EX 23.90 Trifecta £513.00 Pool: £1,328.86 - 1.94 winning tickets..
Owner S Laffan **Bred** John Donegan **Trained** Nawton, N Yorks

FOCUS
The winner looks well ahead of the handicapper.

1461 RACINGUK.COM MAIDEN STKS 5f 212y
3:50 (3:50) (Class 5) 3-Y-O+ **£2,911** (£866; £432; £216) **Stalls** Low

Form RPR

50-4 **1** **Hit The Lights (IRE)**[15] 1190 3-9-2 64................................ ShaneKelly 4 68
(Ollie Pears) *trckd ldr: pushed along to ld over 2f out: rdn over 1f out: kpt on* **3/1**[3]

06- **2** *2 1/4* **Bapak Muda (USA)**[151] 7686 3-9-2 0.............................. PhillipMakin 3 61
(Kevin Ryan) *in tch: rdn over 2f out: sn chsd wnr: kpt on one pce* **7/4**[1]

2002 **3** *1 1/4* **Script**[14] 1209 4-9-2 47.. JordanHibberd[(7)] 6 55
(Alan Berry) *slowly away: hld up: pushed along and hdwy over 1f out: kpt on* **33/1**

56-4 **4** *2 1/4* **Red Style (IRE)**[14] 1204 3-9-2 64.................................... MickyFenton 7 50
(Paul Midgley) *led: rdn whn hdd over 2f out: grad wknd* **11/2**

5-4 **5** *3/4* **Whatwehavewehold**[44] 796 3-9-2 0............................ DanielTudhope 5 47
(Alan McCabe) *in tch: rdn over 2f out: wknd over 1f out* **5/2**[2]

1m 13.8s (0.20) **Going Correction** -0.05s/f (Good)
WFA 3 from 4yo 12lb **5** Ran SP% **108.3**
Speed ratings (Par 103): **96,93,91,88,87**
CSF £8.37 TOTE £4.30: £1.30, £2.00; EX 11.50 Trifecta £51.80 Pool: £1,144.73 - 16.54 winning tickets..
Owner Charles Wentworth **Bred** Carrigbeg Stud **Trained** Norton, N Yorks

The Form Book Flat, Raceform Ltd, Compton, RG20 6NL.

1462 EDWARD JAMES THOMPSON 84TH BIRTHDAY H'CAP (DIV II) 7f
4:20 (4:20) (Class 5) (0-75,72) 4-Y-0+ £2,911 (£866; £432; £216) Stalls Centre

Form RPR
61-6 **1** **Steel Stockholder**[19] [1115] 7-9-7 **72**.......................... SilvestreDeSousa 1 81
(Mel Brittain) *hld up in midfield: rdn and hdwy on inner 2f out: led jst ins fnl f: kpt on* **9/2**[3]
300- **2** 2 1/4 **Snow Bay**[197] [6559] 7-9-2 **72**.......................... ShirleyTeasdale(5) 8 75
(Paul Midgley) *led: rdn over 2f out: wandered over 1f out: hdd jst ins fnl f: one pce* **8/1**
00-0 **3** *shd* **Mutafaakir (IRE)**[14] [1203] 4-9-0 **65**.......................... JamesSullivan 6 68
(Ruth Carr) *prom: rdn over 2f out: kpt on* **22/1**
6-61 **4** 2 1/2 **Mujaadel (USA)**[29] [976] 8-9-1 **66**..........................(p) AndrewMullen 3 62
(David Nicholls) *in tch: rdn over 2f out: sn one pce: nvr rchd ldrs* **10/3**[1]
504- **5** 4 1/2 **Viking Warrior (IRE)**[172] [7247] 6-8-9 **67**.......................... ConnorBeasley(7) 7 51
(Michael Dods) *chsd ldrs towards outer: rdn over 2f out: wknd over 1f out* **11/2**
105- **6** 3/4 **Summer Dancer (IRE)**[184] [6934] 9-9-4 **69**.......................... MickyFenton 5 51
(Paul Midgley) *stdd s: hld up: rdn over 2f out: nvr threatened* **22/1**
20-0 **7** 3/4 **Mick Slates (IRE)**[9] [1286] 4-9-2 **72**.......................... JasonHart(5) 9 52
(Declan Carroll) *midfield: rdn over 2f out: wknd over 1f out* **13/2**
0410 **8** 1/2 **Outlaw Torn (IRE)**[10] [1271] 4-8-13 **64**..........................(e) RobbieFitzpatrick 4 42
(Richard Guest) *chsd ldr: rdn over 2f out: sn wknd* **33/1**
044- **9** 13 **The Blue Banana (IRE)**[167] [7348] 4-8-12 **63**.......................... FrederikTylicki 2
(Edwin Tuer) *hld up: bhd 1/2-way* **7/2**[2]

1m 26.15s (-0.85) **Going Correction** -0.05s/f (Good) **9** Ran SP% **114.9**
Speed ratings (Par 103): **102,99,99,96,91 90,89,89,74**
Tote Swingers: 1&2 £7.00, 1&3 £13.10, 2&3 £20.60 CSF £38.65 CT £714.05 TOTE £4.00: £1.70, £2.90, £5.10; EX 41.30 Trifecta £667.20 Pool: £1,971.65 - 2.21 winning tickets..
Owner Mel Brittain **Bred** Mrs Joan M Langmead **Trained** Warthill, N Yorks

FOCUS
Very marginally the slower of the two divisions.

1463 2013 CATTERICK TWELVE FURLONG SERIES H'CAP (QUALIFIER) 1m 3f 214y
4:50 (4:51) (Class 4) (0-85,83) 4-Y-0+ £6,469 (£1,925; £962; £481) Stalls Low

Form RPR
010- **1** **O Ma Lad (IRE)**[113] [7051] 5-9-7 **83**.......................... MichaelO'Connell 8 92
(John Quinn) *hld up in midfield: hdwy and in tch 2f out: briefly short of room over 1f out: sn rdn: kpt on to ld fnl 100yds* **7/2**[2]
323- **2** 1 1/4 **Fly Solo**[166] [7384] 4-8-12 **75**.......................... RobertWinston 9 82
(Alan Swinbank) *trckd ldr: led over 2f out: sn rdn: strly pressed over 1f out: kpt on: hdd fnl 100yds* **4/1**[3]
20-3 **3** *nk* **Arizona John (IRE)**[14] [1212] 8-8-12 **74**.......................... GrahamGibbons 3 81
(John Mackie) *in tch: hdwy over 2f out: upsides on bit over 1f out: rdn jst ins fnl f: one pce* **13/2**
04-4 **4** 3/4 **The Fun Crusher**[11] [1238] 5-9-1 **82**.......................... DarylByrne(5) 4 88+
(Tim Easterby) *trckd ldrs: pushed along and briefly outpcd 4f out: rdn to chse ldr 2f out: n.m.r towards inner appr fnl f: angled rt ins fnl f: kpt on* **11/4**[1]
1113 **5** *nk* **Broxbourne (IRE)**[32] [948] 4-9-1 **78**.......................... SilvestreDeSousa 7 83
(Mark Johnston) *in tch: rdn over 3f out: kpt on one pce* **7/1**
606- **6** 1 **Spirit Of The Law (IRE)**[182] [6986] 4-9-4 **81**.......................... DavidNolan 12 85+
(Richard Fahey) *midfield: briefly short of room 2f out: rdn to chse ldrs over 1f out: no ex fnl 100yds: short of room nr fin* **9/1**
1/5- **7** 5 **Patavium (IRE)**[9] [1295] 10-9-0 **76**.......................... JamesSullivan 1 72
(Edwin Tuer) *hld up in midfield on inner: rdn over 2f out: wknd over 1f out* **22/1**
600- **8** 2 3/4 **Bollin Greta**[151] [7689] 8-9-0 **83**.......................... RachelRichardson(7) 11 74
(Tim Easterby) *racd keenly: trckd ldr on outer: led 4f out: rdn whn hdd over 2f out: wknd* **20/1**
260- **9** 3 1/2 **Raleigh Quay (IRE)**[145] [6706] 6-8-7 **69** oh2.......................... KellyHarrison 6 55
(Micky Hammond) *hld up: nvr threatened* **50/1**
554- **10** 2 **Hot Rod Mamma (IRE)**[192] [6710] 6-9-0 **79**.......................... LeeTopliss(3) 10 62
(Dianne Sayer) *racd keenly: hld up: nvr threatened* **25/1**
410- **11** 3 3/4 **Alsahil (USA)**[234] [5383] 7-8-8 **75**.......................... GarryWhillans(5) 5 52
(Micky Hammond) *led: hdd 4 out: wknd over 2f out* **40/1**

2m 37.88s (-1.02) **Going Correction** -0.05s/f (Good)
WFA 4 from 5yo+ 1lb **11** Ran SP% **122.1**
Speed ratings (Par 105): **101,100,99,99,99 98,95,93,91,89 87**
Tote Swingers: 1&2 £6.10, 1&3 £7.10, 2&3 £5.30 CSF £17.53 CT £90.26 TOTE £8.00: £1.90, £2.00, £2.50; EX 37.20 Trifecta £214.10 Pool: £2,064.69 - 7.22 winning tickets..
Owner Bob McMillan **Bred** Mrs Brid Cosgrove **Trained** Settrington, N Yorks

FOCUS
Yet another example on the card of a horse improving for a switch of stables.

1464 GO RACING IN YORKSHIRE H'CAP 1m 5f 175y
5:20 (5:21) (Class 5) (0-75,75) 4-Y-0+ £2,911 (£866; £432; £216) Stalls Low

Form RPR
50-6 **1** **Royal Opera**[19] [1111] 5-9-2 **68**..........................(b[1]) PaulPickard(3) 8 78
(Brian Ellison) *led: rdn over 2f out: strly pressed fr over 1f out: hdd narrowly fnl 100yds: led again post* **16/1**
/054 **2** *shd* **Platinum (IRE)**[44] [798] 6-9-1 **69**..........................(p) GarryWhillans(5) 4 79
(Philip Kirby) *trckd ldrs: rdn to chse wnr over 2f out: chal strly over 1f out: led narrowly fnl 100yds: hdd post* **12/1**
6/1- **3** 2 1/4 **Beyeh (IRE)**[39] [7472] 5-8-12 **61**.......................... AndrewMullen 10 68
(Michael Appleby) *midfield: rdn and hdwy on outer to chse ldng pair over 2f out: kpt on one pce* **15/2**[3]
50-5 **4** 1 1/2 **Knightly Escapade**[14] [1212] 5-9-12 **75**.......................... DaleSwift 3 80
(Brian Ellison) *midfield on inner: pushed along and n.m.r over 2f out: rdn and hdwy whn hmpd over 1f out: kpt on* **2/1**[1]
423- **5** *nk* **Dr Irv**[200] [6474] 4-8-10 **62**.......................... MichaelO'Connell 9 66+
(Philip Kirby) *hld up in midfield: rdn and hdwy on inner over 2f out: chsd ldng pair over 1f out: no ex fnl 100yds* **9/2**[2]
2206 **6** 1 **Focail Maith**[37] [882] 5-9-9 **72**..........................(p) FrederikTylicki 11 75
(John Ryan) *hld up in midfield: rdn and sme hdwy on outer over 2f out: one pce fr over 1f out* **11/1**
/45- **7** 2 1/2 **Danceintothelight**[35] [1598] 6-8-6 **60**.......................... JasonHart(5) 1 59
(Micky Hammond) *trckd ldr: rdn and lost pl over 3f out: btn whn hmpd over 1f out* **8/1**
506- **8** 1/2 **Sally Friday (IRE)**[184] [6940] 5-8-7 **56** oh8.......................... JamesSullivan 6 55
(Edwin Tuer) *dwlt: hld up: brief hdwy over 2f out: no further imp over 1f out* **33/1**
13-5 **9** 4 **Mason Hindmarsh**[41] [830] 6-9-7 **70**..........................(p) AdrianNicholls 13 63
(Karen McLintock) *trckd ldr: rdn 3f out: wknd over 1f out* **16/1**
400- **10** *shd* **Grand Art (IRE)**[153] [7528] 9-8-7 **56**..........................(p) SilvestreDeSousa 7 49
(Noel Wilson) *hld up: nvr threatened* **22/1**
40-6 **11** 1/2 **Natural High (IRE)**[32] [948] 8-8-9 **74**..........................(t) MichaelMetcalfe(3) 5 66
(Sean Curran) *midfield: hdwy to chse ldrs 3f out: wknd over 1f out* **25/1**
122- **12** *nk* **Pertuis (IRE)**[88] [6608] 7-8-12 **68**.......................... KatieDowson(7) 12 60
(Micky Hammond) *hld up in rr: nvr threatened* **16/1**

3m 5.13s (1.53) **Going Correction** -0.05s/f (Good)
WFA 4 from 5yo+ 3lb **12** Ran SP% **119.2**
Speed ratings (Par 103): **93,92,91,90,90 90,88,88,86,86 85,85**
Tote Swingers: 1&2 £16.30, 1&3 £16.60, 2&3 £16.20 CSF £191.54 CT £1570.76 TOTE £17.40: £3.70, £5.30, £3.50; EX 168.30 Trifecta £1148.60 Part won. Pool: £1,531.49 - 0.36 winning tickets..
Owner Dan Gilbert & Kristian Strangeway **Bred** Redmyre Bloodstock & Newhall Farm Estate **Trained** Norton, N Yorks
■ Stewards' Enquiry : Paul Pickard two-day ban: used whip above permitted level (Apr 24-25)

FOCUS
The winner dominated throughout.

1465 RACING AGAIN 24TH APRIL APPRENTICE H'CAP 5f
5:50 (5:51) (Class 6) (0-65,63) 4-Y-0+ £2,385 (£704; £352) Stalls Low

Form RPR
0-02 **1** **Chosen One (IRE)**[4] [1388] 8-8-11 **53**.......................... JulieBurke 2 65
(Ruth Carr) *w ldr: rdn to ld over 1f out: kpt on* **4/1**[2]
600- **2** 1 1/4 **Choc'A'Moca (IRE)**[162] [7457] 6-8-13 **55**..........................(v) LeeTopliss 12 62
(Paul Midgley) *chsd ldrs: rdn 1/2-way: kpt on: wnt 2nd fnl 100yds* **16/1**
24-0 **3** 1/2 **Tuibama (IRE)**[9] [1283] 4-9-0 **61**..........................(p) GeorgeChaloner(5) 5 66
(Tracy Waggott) *led: rdn whn hdd over 1f out: no ex and lost 2nd fnl 100yds* **16/1**
60-1 **4** 3/4 **Dartrix**[4] [1388] 4-8-11 **60** 6ex.......................... ConnorBeasley(7) 13 63+
(Michael Dods) *hld up: rdn 1/2-way: hdwy on wd outside over 1f out: kpt on* **3/1**[1]
0-53 **5** 1/2 **Sophie's Beau (USA)**[47] [756] 6-8-1 **50**..........................(bt) DanielleMooney(7) 7 51
(Michael Chapman) *chsd ldrs: rdn 1/2-way: kpt on same pce* **28/1**
60-4 **6** 2 1/4 **Wicked Wilma (IRE)**[10] [1276] 9-8-9 **58**.......................... JordanHibberd(7) 8 51
(Alan Berry) *midfield: rdn 1/2-way: nvr threatened ldrs* **33/1**
612- **7** 3/4 **Here Now And Why (IRE)**[152] [7673] 6-9-1 **62**..........................(p) JasonHart(5) 1 52
(Iain Jardine) *hld up in tch: rdn 1/2-way: nvr threatened* **6/1**
1006 **8** 1 1/4 **Lucky Mark (IRE)**[23] [1063] 4-9-1 **62**.......................... ShirleyTeasdale(5) 6 47
(Garry Moss) *hld up: rdn 1/2-way: minor late hdwy: nvr threatened* **14/1**
32-0 **9** 1 3/4 **Pavers Star**[4] [1388] 4-9-1 **57**..........................(p) BillyCray 9 36
(Noel Wilson) *in tch: rdn 1/2-way: wknd fnl f* **16/1**
00-2 **10** 3 1/4 **Boucher Garcon (IRE)**[9] [1283] 5-8-11 **60**.......................... LukeLeadbitter(7) 10 27
(Declan Carroll) *chsd ldrs on outer: wknd over 1f out* **5/1**[3]
-056 **11** 1 1/4 **Lesley's Choice**[15] [1186] 7-8-12 **54**..........................(b) MichaelMetcalfe 3 17
(Sean Curran) *midfield: rdn 1/2-way: sn wknd* **14/1**
000- **12** 5 **Dubai Rythm**[169] [7316] 4-8-1 **50**..........................(vt[1]) LiamDoran(7) 4
(Michael Appleby) *hld up: a in rr* **20/1**

1m 0.79s (0.99) **Going Correction** +0.225s/f (Good) **12** Ran SP% **118.1**
Speed ratings (Par 101): **101,99,98,97,96 92,91,89,86,81 79,71**
Tote Swingers: 1&2 £16.30, 1&3 £7.30, 2&3 £52.40 CSF £64.46 CT £942.94 TOTE £5.40: £1.70, £5.40, £5.50; EX 96.00 Trifecta £1118.60 Part won. Pool: £1,491.55 - 0.33 winning tickets..
Owner Bridget Houlston, Chris Jeffery & Co **Bred** Carl Holt **Trained** Huby, N Yorks

FOCUS
Modest handicap form.
T/Jkpt: Not won. T/Plt: £66.00 to a £1 stake. Pool: £61,586.21. 680.16 winning tickets. T/Qpdt: £31.50 to a £1 stake. Pool £4,411.36. 103.60 winning tickets. AS

1421 KEMPTON (A.W) (R-H)
Wednesday, April 10

OFFICIAL GOING: Standard
Wind: Moderate, half behind Weather: Overcast, rain from Race 4 onwards, becoming heavy

1466 FAMILY FUN WITH MIKE THE KNIGHT APPRENTICE H'CAP 1m 2f (P)
5:30 (5:30) (Class 6) (0-65,65) 4-Y-0+ £1,940 (£577; £288; £144) Stalls Low

Form RPR
23-2 **1** **Stag Hill (IRE)**[23] [1070] 4-8-6 **53**.......................... JoeyHaynes(3) 4 61
(Bernard Llewellyn) *trckd ldng pair: wnt 2nd 2f out: clsd on clr ldr over 1f out: led ins fnl f: rdn out* **11/4**[1]
0-43 **2** 1 1/2 **Manomine**[28] [978] 4-8-11 **62**..........................(b) LaurenHaigh(7) 6 67
(Clive Britain) *w ldr: led after 2f: drew clr 3f out: 5 l up whn wd bnd 2f out: hdd and nt qckn ins fnl f* **7/2**[3]
6064 **3** 2 3/4 **May's Boy**[8] [1303] 5-8-9 **58**..........................(p) CharlotteJenner(5) 9 58
(Mark Usher) *led 2f: w ldr to 1/2-way: outpcd 3f out: lost 2nd 2f out: one pce after* **8/1**
-453 **4** 3/4 **Handheld**[9] [1292] 6-9-7 **65**.......................... ShelleyBirkett 7 63
(Julia Feilden) *dwlt: chsd ldng pair: outpcd 3f out: pushed along over 2f out: no imp after* **5/1**
50-4 **5** *nk* **James Pollard (IRE)**[11] [1239] 8-8-13 **64**.......................... SiobhanMiller(7) 2 61
(Bernard Llewellyn) *hld up towards rr: plenty to do after ldr wnt clr 3f out: pushed along over 2f out: no imp* **14/1**
2-24 **6** 1/2 **Comedy House**[54] [668] 5-9-5 **63**.......................... PatMillman 5 59
(Michael Madgwick) *hld up towards rr: plenty to do after ldr wnt clr 3f out: rdn and no imp over 2f out* **3/1**[2]
100- **7** 3/4 **Kingscombe (USA)**[237] [3665] 4-9-5 **63**.......................... RufusVergette 8 58
(Linda Jewell) *hld up towards rr and racd wd: plenty to do after ldr wnt clr 3f out: pushed along and no imp after* **25/1**
0/0- **8** 5 **Grace And Beauty (IRE)**[42] [8079] 5-8-5 **54**.......................... AaronJones(5) 3 39
(Paul Henderson) *restrained into last: rdn 3f out: no prog: wl bhd over 1f out* **25/1**

2m 5.95s (-2.05) **Going Correction** -0.075s/f (Stan) **8** Ran SP% **116.0**
Speed ratings (Par 101): **105,103,101,101,100 100,99,95**
Tote Swingers: 1&2 £2.50, 1&3 £4.90, 2&3 £7.00 CSF £12.92 CT £65.31 TOTE £3.10: £1.40, £1.10, £2.30; EX 13.00 Trifecta £94.60 Pool: £1,984.87 - 15.72 winning units..
Owner B W Parren **Bred** Tally-Ho Stud **Trained** Fochriw, Caerphilly

FOCUS
A weak handicap, confined to apprentice riders. It was run at a sound pace yet few landed a blow.

1467 £200 FREE BETS AT BETDAQ H'CAP 5f (P)
6:00 (6:00) (Class 5) (0-70,70) 4-Y-0+ £2,587 (£770; £384; £192) Stalls Low

Form RPR
55-1 **1** **Alpha Delta Whisky**[23] [1058] 5-9-0 **68**.......................... MichaelJMMurphy(5) 6 77
(John Gallagher) *chsd ldng pair after 1f: rdn over 1f out: clsd fnl f: led last 100yds: kpt on* **6/4**[1]

53/5 **2** *nk* **Go Nani Go**[14] 1198 7-9-7 **70** .... LiamKeniry 7 78+
(Ed de Giles) *t.k.h: hld up in last: prog over 1f out: rdn fnl f: r.o to take 2nd nr fin and clsd on wnr: too much to do* **7/2**[2]
1113 **3** *¾* **Where's Reiley (USA)**[23] 1065 7-9-6 **69** ....(v) SebSanders 5 74
(Michael Attwater) *led: drvn over 1f out: hdd and no ex last 100yds* **5/1**[3]
-635 **4** *¾* **Catflap (IRE)**[14] 1196 4-8-8 **57** ....(p) WilliamCarson 8 59
(Derek Haydn Jones) *sn pressed ldr: rdn over 1f out: lost 2nd and fdd jst ins fnl f* **12/1**
5305 **5** *shd* **Sherjawy (IRE)**[8] 1304 9-8-7 **56** oh8 .... KirstyMilczarek 2 58?
(Zoe Davison) *sn lost prom pl: effrt fr midfield 2f out: tried to cl on ldrs 1f out: one pce* **25/1**
3244 **6** *1* **Steelcut**[8] 1304 9-9-0 **63** .... PaulHanagan 3 61
(Mark Buckley) *towards rr: rdn 2f out: kpt on same pce fr over 1f out: n.d* **6/1**
6000 **7** *4* **Liberal Lady**[67] 493 5-8-4 **58** .... RyanTate(5) 4 42
(Ralph Smith) *chsd ldng trio and racd wd: wknd over 1f out* **20/1**
3024 **8** *½* **Pharoh Jake**[7] 1324 5-8-10 **59** .... KieranO'Neill 1 41
(John Bridger) *rrd s: a in last pair and nvr gng wl: wknd over 1f out* **16/1**
59.22s (-1.28) **Going Correction** -0.075s/f (Stan) **8** Ran SP% **115.4**
Speed ratings (Par 103): **107,106,105,104,103 102,95,95**
Tote Swingers: 1&2 £2.60, 1&3 £3.50, 2&3 £3.20 CSF £6.84 CT £20.31 TOTE £2.40: £1.10, £1.60, £2.50; EX 10.00 Trifecta £30.30 Pool: £1,514.69 - 37.40 winning units..
Owner Adweb Ltd **Bred** Kentford Farm Stud Ltd **Trained** Chastleton, Oxon
FOCUS
A modest sprint handicap, run at a solid pace.

1468 MIKE THE KNIGHT 13.04.13 MEDIAN AUCTION MAIDEN STKS 1m 3f (P)
6:30 (6:30) (Class 6) 3-5-Y-O **£1,940** (£577; £288; £144) **Stalls** Low

Form RPR
003- **1** **King Muro**[162] 7460 3-8-8 **77** .... LiamKeniry 5 77
(Andrew Balding) *led: rdn 2f out: hdd jst over 1f out: kpt on wl to ld again last 75yds* **7/2**[3]
23- **2** *½* **High Time Too (IRE)**[156] 7592 3-8-3 **0** .... JimmyQuinn 1 72
(Hugo Palmer) *trckd ldng pair: wnt 2nd over 2f out: clsd to ld jst over 1f out: wandered and veered ins fnl f: hdd last 75yds: threw it away* **20/1**
3 *nk* **Royal Signaller** 3-8-8 **0** .... FrannyNorton 3 76+
(Amanda Perrett) *trckd ldng trio: shkn up over 2f out: wnt 3rd wl over 1f out: clsd on ldrs fnl f: nrst fin* **25/1**
0- **4** *½* **Seamless**[195] 6596 3-8-8 **0** .... WilliamCarson 7 75+
(Charles Hills) *hld up towards rr: shkn up wl over 2f out: prog into 4th over 1f out: styd on wl fnl f: nrst fin* **9/4**[2]
4-5 **5** *5* **Ihtikar (USA)**[15] 1178 3-8-8 **0** .... PaulHanagan 6 66
(Ed Dunlop) *hld up in last trio: rdn and no prog wl over 2f out: kpt on fnl f* **12/1**
3 **6** *nk* **Nautilus**[15] 1178 3-8-8 **0** .... WilliamBuick 8 66
(John Gosden) *t.k.h: trckd wnr: wandered whn rdn wl over 2f out: sn wknd tamely* **11/8**[1]
63-5 **7** *4 ½* **Princess Willow**[21] 1090 5-9-9 **52** .... KirstyMilczarek 9 55
(John E Long) *mostly chsd ldng trio to over 2f out: sn wknd* **25/1**
5 **8** *2* **Reach The Beach**[7] 1317 4-9-6 **0** .... BrendanPowell(3) 2 52
(Brendan Powell) *chsd ldrs in 5th: rdn and wknd over 2f out* **50/1**
9 *13* **Cracker Mill**[25] 4-9-7 **0** .... PatMillman(7) 4 33
(Michael Madgwick) *dwlt: hld up in last: rdn and wknd 3f out: t.o* **100/1**
2m 21.18s (-0.72) **Going Correction** -0.075s/f (Stan)
WFA 3 from 4yo+ 20lb **9** Ran SP% **118.2**
Speed ratings (Par 101): **99,98,98,98,94 94,90,89,80**
Tote Swingers: 1&2 £9.80, 1&3 £15.70, 2&3 £22.10 CSF £70.00 TOTE £4.70: £1.50, £4.50, £8.40; EX 82.20 Trifecta £1278.00 Pool: £1,915.37 - 1.12 winning units..
Owner P Brend & J Dwyer **Bred** Stourbank Stud **Trained** Kingsclere, Hants
■ Stewards' Enquiry : Jimmy Quinn eighteen-day ban (six days deffered): used whip in incorrect place, fifth whip offence since Nov 19th 2012 (Apr 26-May 8)
FOCUS
A modest maiden.

1469 FAMILY FUN ON 13.04.13 H'CAP 1m 3f (P)
7:00 (7:00) (Class 6) (0-60,60) 3-Y-O **£1,940** (£577; £288; £144) **Stalls** Low

Form RPR
000- **1** **Pivotal Silence**[160] 7505 3-9-7 **60** .... AdamKirby 2 70
(Amanda Perrett) *trckd ldng pair: wnt 2nd over 2f out: drvn to ld over 1f out: hrd pressed and edgd rt fnl f: hld on wl nr fin* **12/1**
056- **2** *nk* **Town Mouse**[153] 7641 3-9-7 **60** ....(b[1]) JimmyFortune 1 69
(Hughie Morrison) *hld up in last trio: prog jst over 2f out: drvn to press wnr fnl f: carried rt and sltly intimidated: nt qckn nr fin* **4/1**[3]
143- **3** *2 ¼* **Knight's Parade (IRE)**[177] 7111 3-9-5 **58** .... RichardHughes 3 63
(Amanda Perrett) *led at mod pce: tried to kick on over 2f out but limited rspnse: hdd over 1f out: one pce* **10/3**[2]
0-45 **4** *6* **Jd Rockefeller**[20] 1098 3-9-1 **54** .... SebSanders 8 49
(Paul D'Arcy) *s.i.s: hld up in last: rdn over 2f out: kpt on to take 4th 1f out but nt on terms: no imp after* **6/1**
006- **5** *4* **Dancing Chief (IRE)**[181] 7008 3-8-4 **50** .... DavidParkes(7) 7 37
(Alan Jarvis) *s.i.s: hld up in last pair: rapid prog on wd outside over 3f out to dispute 2nd over 2f out: wknd wl over 1f out* **33/1**
40-1 **6** *1 ¾* **Darakti (IRE)**[7] 1332 3-8-7 **46** oh1 ....(p) JohnFahy 6 30
(Alan McCabe) *chsd ldr to over 2f out: wknd qckly* **6/1**
054 **7** *8* **Early One Morning**[23] 1057 3-9-4 **57** .... JimmyQuinn 5 27
(Hugo Palmer) *trckd ldrs on outer: rdn and wknd wl over 2f out: t.o* **12/1**
5-44 **8** *2 ½* **Booktheband (IRE)**[20] 1098 3-9-4 **57** ....[1] PaulHanagan 4 22
(Clive Brittain) *trckd ldrs: rdn and no rspnse over 2f out: wknd rapidly over 1f out: t.o* **3/1**[1]
2m 21.5s (-0.40) **Going Correction** -0.075s/f (Stan) **8** Ran SP% **115.0**
Speed ratings (Par 96): **98,97,96,91,88 87,81,79**
Tote Swingers: 1&2 £10.20, 1&3 £9.30, 2&3 £3.00 CSF £59.79 CT £199.39 TOTE £15.40: £3.40, £1.50, £2.00; EX 67.10 Trifecta £472.40 Pool: £923.54 - 1.46 winning units..
Owner M H and Mrs G Tourle **Bred** M H And Mrs G Tourle **Trained** Pulborough, W Sussex
FOCUS
This was run at an uneven pace, but the form still looks fair with the principals coming clear.

1470 COMISSION FREE 1ST MONTH AT BETDAQ H'CAP 1m 4f (P)
7:30 (7:30) (Class 3) (0-95,78) 3-Y-O **£7,225** (£2,210; £1,138; £602) **Stalls** Centre

Form RPR
4-63 **1** **Blue Wave (IRE)**[68] 474 3-9-3 **77** .... WilliamBuick 4 83
(Mark Johnston) *led after 1f: mde rest: jinked lft 1/2-way: shkn up over 2f out: hrd pressed fnl f: hld on wl* **7/1**
44-2 **2** *hd* **Allnecessaryforce (FR)**[19] 1109 3-9-4 **78** .... PaulHanagan 2 84+
(Richard Fahey) *led 1f: sn in 3rd: rdn 3f out: drvn to chse wnr over 1f out: str chal fnl f: edgd lft and nt qckn nr fin* **7/1**
616- **3** *1 ¼* **Red Runaway**[207] 6247 3-9-2 **76** .... RichardHughes 1 80+
(Ed Dunlop) *hld up in last: urged along 3f out: styd on fr over 1f out to take 3rd ins fnl f: no imp last 75yds* **11/4**[2]
1 **4** *1 ¼* **Magical Kingdom (IRE)**[77] 333 3-9-3 **77** .... AdamKirby 3 79
(Marco Botti) *trckd wnr after 2f: impeded 1/2-way: rdn over 2f out: nt qckn over 1f out: fdd ins fnl f* **6/4**[1]
1 **U** **Dorfman**[50] 712 3-9-2 **76** .... FrannyNorton 5
(Mark Johnston) *hld up in 4th: jinked lft and uns rdr over 3f out* **4/1**[3]
2m 37.43s (2.93) **Going Correction** -0.075s/f (Stan) **5** Ran SP% **111.7**
Speed ratings (Par 102): **87,86,86,85,**
CSF £49.45 TOTE £11.80: £7.70, £3.60; EX 50.90 Trifecta £93.80 Pool: £796.18 - 6.36 winning units..
Owner Sheikh Hamdan Bin Mohammed Al Maktoum **Bred** Tom Darcy And Vincent McCarthy **Trained** Middleham Moor, N Yorks
FOCUS
This looked a decent little 3yo handicap, but it proved tactical.

1471 BETDAQ 1ST UK RACE COMISSION FREE-EVERYDAY H'CAP (LONDON MILE QUALIFIER) 1m (P)
8:00 (8:02) (Class 4) (0-85,85) 3-Y-O **£4,690** (£1,395; £697; £348) **Stalls** Low

Form RPR
134- **1** **Royal Prize**[183] 6972 3-8-11 **75** .... JimCrowley 8 81+
(Ralph Beckett) *hld up in last: smooth prog on wd outside over 2f out: drvn over 1f out: sn chsd ldr: chal fnl f: styd on wl to edge ahd nr fin* **12/1**
201- **2** *nk* **Intermix (IRE)**[111] 8192 3-9-7 **85** .... ChrisCatlin 7 90
(Paul Cole) *pressed ldr: led over 2f out: drvn over 1f out: styd on wl but hdd nr fin* **25/1**
34-1 **3** *2 ¾* **Erodium**[25] 1035 3-9-0 **78** .... RichardHughes 2 77
(Richard Hannon) *trckd ldrs: rdn over 2f out: wnt 2nd briefly over 1f out: lost grnd on ldng pair fnl f* **5/4**[1]
01 **4** *hd* **Red To Amber (IRE)**[42] 815 3-8-9 **73** .... JohnFahy 1 71
(Clive Cox) *s.i.s and rousted along early: in tch in rr: prog on inner 2f out: drvn and one pce over 1f out* **7/1**[3]
213- **5** *¾* **Magical Rose (IRE)**[174] 7190 3-8-11 **75** .... SebSanders 6 71
(Paul D'Arcy) *t.k.h: sn restrained bhd ldrs on outer: rdn and cl enough wl over 1f out: nt qckn and one pce after* **10/1**
041- **6** *nse* **Countryman**[169] 7304 3-8-13 **77** .... JimmyFortune 4 73
(Hughie Morrison) *hld up in tch: rdn over 2f out: nt qckn and no prog wl over 1f out: one pce after* **8/1**
046- **7** *5* **Inaugural**[166] 7371 3-8-11 **75** .... JamesDoyle 5 60
(Roger Charlton) *mde most to over 2f out: wknd over 1f out* **5/1**[2]
1m 39.45s (-0.35) **Going Correction** -0.075s/f (Stan) **7** Ran SP% **105.4**
Speed ratings (Par 100): **98,97,94,94,94 93,88**
Tote Swingers: 1&2 £13.50, 1&3 £3.50, 2&3 £7.10 CSF £196.45 CT £483.80 TOTE £13.90: £5.70, £4.90; EX 269.40 Trifecta £352.30 Pool: £846.51 - 1.80 winning units..
Owner J C Smith **Bred** Littleton Stud **Trained** Kimpton, Hants
FOCUS
A fair 3yo handicap, run at a fair enough pace.

1472 WINNERS ARE WELCOME AT BETDAQ FILLIES' H'CAP 6f (P)
8:30 (8:31) (Class 5) (0-70,69) 4-Y-O+ **£2,587** (£770; £384; £192) **Stalls** Low

Form RPR
150- **1** **Amber Heights**[175] 7179 5-8-13 **61** .... JimmyFortune 6 70
(Henry Candy) *hld up in 6th: swtchd to outer and prog wl over 1f out: r.o to chal ins fnl f: led last 75yds* **13/2**[3]
2632 **2** *½* **Rose Garnet (IRE)**[8] 1304 5-8-10 **58** ....[1] RichardHughes 4 65
(Tony Carroll) *trckd ldng trio: smooth prog over 1f out: shkn up to ld ins fnl f: drvn and hdd last 75yds* **6/4**[1]
066- **3** *2* **Camache Queen (IRE)**[110] 8202 5-9-7 **69** .... LiamKeniry 5 70
(Joseph Tuite) *led: rdn over 1f out: hdd and outpcd ins fnl f* **7/1**
466 **4** *2 ¼* **Floralys (USA)**[26] 1019 4-9-2 **64** ....(t[1]) RobertHavlin 3 57
(Amy Weaver) *hld up in last: pushed along and sme prog over 1f out: nvr remotely involved* **16/1**
20/1 **5** *1 ½* **Sister Guru**[74] 398 4-9-6 **68** .... JohnFahy 1 57
(Peter Hedger) *reluctant to enter stalls: plld hrd: hld up in 3rd: chsd ldr 2f out and tried to chal: wknd fnl f* **7/2**[2]
4051 **6** *2 ½* **Sweet Ovation**[14] 1196 4-8-10 **58** .... HayleyTurner 2 39
(Mark Usher) *t.k.h: hld up in 5th: shkn up 2f out: no prog and sn btn* **7/2**[2]
/000 **7** *¾* **Tartaria**[20] 1100 7-8-0 **55** oh8 .... CharlotteJenner(7) 7 33
(Edward Creighton) *t.k.h: pressed ldr to 2f out: wknd* **50/1**
1m 12.71s (-0.39) **Going Correction** -0.075s/f (Stan) **7** Ran SP% **118.1**
Speed ratings (Par 100): **99,98,95,92,90 87,86**
Tote Swingers: 1&2 £2.70, 1&3 £5.30, 2&3 £2.70 CSF £17.58 TOTE £5.60: £1.80, £1.80; EX 20.60 Trifecta £128.90 Pool: £1,187.63 - 6.90 winning units..
Owner Ms L Burns **Bred** Howard Barton Stud **Trained** Kingston Warren, Oxon
FOCUS
An ordinary sprint handicap.
T/Plt: £2,159.50 to a £1 stake. Pool: £60,911.12. 20.59 winning tickets. T/Qpdt: £144.30 to a £1 stake. Pool: £5,285.56. 27.10 winning tickets. JN

1381 LINGFIELD (L-H)
Wednesday, April 10
OFFICIAL GOING: Standard
Wind: Medium, behind Weather: Overcast, dry

1473 YOUR GUIDE TO LINGFIELD AT LINGFIELDRACECOURSETIPS.CO.UK H'CAP (DIV I) 1m (P)
2:00 (2:01) (Class 6) (0-55,56) 4-Y-O+ **£2,045** (£603; £302) **Stalls** High

Form RPR
-004 **1** **Archelao (IRE)**[15] 1183 5-9-4 **51** ....(t) AmirQuinn 9 59
(Richard Rowe) *hld up wl in tch in last pair: drfited rt wl over 1f out: rdn and hdwy over 1f out: led fnl 100yds: r.o wl* **7/2**[2]
0150 **2** *1 ¼* **Indian Violet (IRE)**[24] 1056 7-9-6 **53** ....(p) LiamKeniry 2 58
(Zoe Davison) *hld up wl in tch in last trio: nt clr run on inner over 2f out: rdn and gd hdwy ent fnl f: ev ch fnl 100yds: r.o but outpcd by wnr after* **8/1**
3006 **3** *1 ½* **Cuthbert (IRE)**[14] 1194 6-8-6 **46** ....(b) PaigeBolton(7) 10 48
(Michael Attwater) *dwlt: t.k.h: sn dashed up to chse ldrs: upsides ldr over 3f out tl led over 2f out: rdn and hdd fnl 100yds: no ex* **10/1**
16/0 **4** *1 ¾* **Queenie's Star (IRE)**[21] 1093 6-9-3 **50** .... SebSanders 8 48
(Michael Attwater) *stdd s: hld up wl in tch in rr: rdn and hdwy over 1f out: chsd ldrs 1f out: no ex and wknd fnl 100yds* **25/1**

The Form Book Flat, Raceform Ltd, Compton, RG20 6NL.

2135 **5** 3/4 **Crucis Abbey (IRE)**[13] 1222 5-9-1 **48**............................(p) LukeMorris 6 44
(Mark Brisbourne) *t.k.h: hld up wl in tch in midfield: rdn and unable qck over 1f out: wl hld and one pce fnl f* **7/2**[2]

-024 **6** 1 **Teth**[17] 1162 4-9-7 **54**.. WilliamCarson 3 48
(Anthony Carson) *t.k.h: led for 1f: chsd ldrs after: rdn and no rspnse wl over 1f out: wknd fnl f* **3/1**[1]

000 **7** 4 1/2 **Baytown Bertie**[15] 1178 4-8-12 **45**..............................(v[1]) RobertHavlin 4 28
(Lydia Richards) *chsd ldr tl led after 1f and set stdy gallop: hdd and rdn over 2f out: wknd over 1f out* **66/1**

4462 **8** 1 **Amber Moon**[17] 1162 8-8-7 **45**.. AnnStokell(5) 7 26
(Ann Stokell) *t.k.h: wd and wl in tch in midfield: wknd over 1f out* **16/1**

3424 **9** nk **Titan Diamond (IRE)**[43] 806 5-8-7 **45**.................... RachealKneller(5) 5 25
(Mark Usher) *t.k.h: hld up wl tch in midfield: shuffled bk to rr and n.m.r over 2f out: hmpd wl over 1f out: n.d after* **9/2**[3]

1m 38.85s (0.65) **Going Correction** +0.025s/f (Slow) **9** Ran SP% **119.0**
Speed ratings (Par 101): **97,95,94,92,91 90,86,85,84**
Tote Swingers: 1&2 £11.50, 1&3 £10.80, 2&3 £25.10 CSF £32.77 CT £262.29 TOTE £3.20: £1.50, £3.20, £3.40; EX 46.20 Trifecta £201.50 Pool: £1,069.14 - 3.97 winning tickets..
Owner Miss Victoria Baalham **Bred** Mount Coote Stud And M H Dixon **Trained** Sullington, W Sussex
■ Stewards' Enquiry : Amir Quinn one-day ban: careless riding (Apr 24)

FOCUS
A poor 46-55 handicap and the front pair came from the back of the field.

1474 YOUR GUIDE TO LINGFIELD AT LINGFIELDRACECOURSETIPS.CO.UK H'CAP (DIV II) 1m (P)
2:30 (2:30) (Class 6) (0-55,55) 4-Y-0+ **£2,045** (£603; £302) **Stalls** High

Form RPR
0032 **1** **Qeethaara (USA)**[4] 1401 9-9-2 **50**....................................(p) LukeMorris 6 60
(Mark Brisbourne) *hld up wl in tch in midfield: nt clr run ent fnl 2f: hdwy and qcknd between horses ent fnl f: led fnl 100yds: r.o strly* **11/4**[1]

5544 **2** 2 **The Noble Ord**[9] 1294 4-9-6 **54**....................................(t) RichardHughes 3 59
(Sylvester Kirk) *in tch: nt clr run and shuffled bk over 2f out: hdwy on inner over 1f out: rdn to ld 1f out: hdd and outpcd by wnr fnl 100yds* **11/4**[1]

0063 **3** 3/4 **Querido (GER)**[17] 1161 9-8-5 **46** oh1.........................(tp) JoeyHaynes(7) 1 49
(Paddy Butler) *hld up in tch in rr: swtchd lft and hdwy over 1f out: chsd ldrs and carried rt ins fnl f: styd on same pce* **16/1**

0-30 **4** 1/2 **Custom House (IRE)**[35] 903 5-9-1 **49**........................ KirstyMilczarek 4 51
(John E Long) *led tl over 2f out: drvn to ld again over 1f out: hdd 1f out: styd on same pce fnl 100yds* **7/1**[3]

400 **5** 1/2 **Legal Legacy**[16] 1175 7-9-7 **55**... AmirQuinn 2 56
(Richard Rowe) *s.i.s: hld up in tch in rr: swtchd and v wd bnd wl over 1f out: styd on ins fnl f: nvr trbld ldrs* **9/2**[2]

50-0 **6** 2 1/2 **Trove (IRE)**[24] 1056 4-8-12 **46** oh1................................(e[1]) RobertHavlin 7 41
(Michael Attwater) *stdd after s: hld up in tch in last quartet: rdn and hdwy over 1f out: styd on same pce ins fnl f* **33/1**

-044 **7** 1 **The Which Doctor**[21] 1093 8-8-13 **47**...........................(e) CathyGannon 8 40
(Violet M Jordan) *s.i.s: hld up in rr: swtchd rt and hdwy on outer over 4f out: chsd ldrs 3f out: rdn and no ex over 1f out: wknd ins fnl f* **7/1**[3]

-506 **8** 1 1/2 **Mayforde Jack**[13] 1221 4-8-6 **47**.. JakePayne(7) 9 36
(Simon Hodgson) *t.k.h: chsd ldrs after 1f tl led over 2f out: rdn and hdd over 1f out: wknd 1f out* **25/1**

0066 **9** 1/2 **Hold The Star**[16] 1173 7-8-7 **46** oh1................................ AnnStokell(5) 5 34
(Ann Stokell) *chsd ldr for 1f: styd chsng ldrs tl wknd over 1f out* **33/1**

-005 **10** 4 1/2 **La Giaconda**[18] 1149 4-8-7 **46** oh1..........................(b) NathanAlison(5) 10 24
(Olivia Maylam) *chsd ldrs: rdn and struggling ent fnl 2f: wknd over 1f out* **33/1**

1m 38.76s (0.56) **Going Correction** +0.025s/f (Slow) **10** Ran SP% **115.1**
Speed ratings (Par 101): **98,96,95,94,94 91,90,89,88,84**
Tote Swingers: 1&2 £1.10, 1&3 £6.20, 2&3 £12.40 CSF £9.41 CT £97.78 TOTE £3.40: £1.20, £1.10, £3.80; EX 12.60 Trifecta £61.90 Pool: £1,087.25 - 13.16 winning tickets..
Owner Mrs Ann Broughton **Bred** Shadwell Farm LLC **Trained** Great Ness, Shropshire

FOCUS
The winning time was 0.09 seconds faster than the first division.

1475 VINES BMW CLASSIFIED CLAIMING STKS 6f (P)
3:00 (3:01) (Class 6) 3-Y-0+ **£2,045** (£603; £302) **Stalls** Low

Form RPR
4423 **1** **Desert Strike**[14] 1205 7-9-5 69..(p) LiamKeniry 2 75
(Conor Dore) *taken down early: mde all: rdn and wnt clr over 1f out: in command fnl f: eased cl home* **5/1**[3]

1-33 **2** 2 **Commanche**[7] 1316 4-9-3 66.. AdamKirby 1 67
(Patrick Chamings) *hld up in last pair: rdn and hdwy over 1f out: chsd clr wnr 1f out: kpt on u.p but no threat to wnr* **5/4**[1]

5131 **3** 2 3/4 **Dark Lane**[7] 1324 7-9-2 64.. RichardHughes 3 57
(David Evans) *hld up in last pair: rdn and effrt wl over 1f out: no threat to wnr and kpt on same pce fnl f* **7/4**[2]

0113 **4** 1/2 **Fairy Wing (IRE)**[8] 1310 6-8-13 68................................... RobertTart(5) 4 57
(Violet M Jordan) *taken down early: chsd ldrs: drvn to chse clr wnr over 1f out: no imp: lost 2 pls fnl f* **6/1**

0023 **5** 8 **Athwaab**[14] 1195 6-8-10 56.. JakePayne(7) 5 31
(Simon Hodgson) *taken down early: t.k.h: chsd wnr tl wl over 1f out: sn wknd* **33/1**

1m 10.96s (-0.94) **Going Correction** +0.025s/f (Slow) **5** Ran SP% **114.7**
Speed ratings (Par 101): **107,104,100,100,89**
CSF £12.36 TOTE £5.00: £4.80, £2.40; EX 14.10 Trifecta £26.40 Pool: £1,230.78 - 34.89 winning tickets..The winner was subject to a friendly claim.
Owner Andrew Page **Bred** Mrs Mary Rowlands **Trained** Hubbert's Bridge, Lincs

FOCUS
A tactical classified claimer.

1476 MARTINCOLLINS.COM EQUINE SURFACES H'CAP 7f (P)
3:30 (3:31) (Class 5) (0-70,70) 3-Y-0 **£2,726** (£805; £402) **Stalls** Low

Form RPR
601- **1** **Intrigo**[163] 7432 3-9-5 **68**.. RichardHughes 7 78
(Richard Hannon) *t.k.h early: hld up in tch in midfield: hdwy to chse ldrs ent fnl 2f: rdn to press ldr and c towards centre wl over 1f out: led jst over 1f out: r.o wl* **2/1**[1]

364- **2** 1 **Lionheart**[187] 6846 3-9-5 **68**.. KirstyMilczarek 6 75
(Luca Cumani) *hld up in tch in rr: swtchd rt and hdwy over 1f out: styd on to chse wnr ins fnl f: gng on fin but no real threat to wnr* **4/1**[3]

21 **3** 1 3/4 **King Bertie (IRE)**[47] 748 3-9-7 **70**................................. WilliamBuick 3 72
(Peter Chapple-Hyam) *t.k.h: chsd ldrs: rdn and effrt against inner rail over 1f out: chsd clr wnr jst ins fnl f: no imp and lost 2nd fnl 100yds* **11/4**[2]

004- **4** 1/2 **Princess Patsky (USA)**[160] 7505 3-9-0 **63**......................... LukeMorris 5 64
(Michael Bell) *chsd ldrs: unable qck and flashed tail u.p over 1f out: styd on same pce fnl f* **10/1**

16-4 **5** 3 **Angels Calling**[26] 1011 3-8-11 **60**................................... CathyGannon 2 53
(Mrs K Burke) *led: rdn and hdd jst over 1f out: wknd fnl f* **20/1**

01- **6** 3/4 **Barbs Princess**[163] 7434 3-9-6 **69**............................... WilliamCarson 8 60
(Charles Hills) *t.k.h: in tch on outer: rdn and lost pl bnd wl over 1f out: n.d after* **4/1**[3]

00-0 **7** 18 **Ropehanger**[7] 1319 3-8-8 **57**... KierenFox 4
(Lee Carter) *t.k.h: hld up in tch in rr: hdwy on outer to press ldr 4f out: rdn over 2f out: lost pl qckly wl over 1f out: sn bhd* **66/1**

1m 24.77s (-0.03) **Going Correction** +0.025s/f (Slow) **7** Ran SP% **115.3**
Speed ratings (Par 98): **101,99,97,97,93 93,72**
Tote Swingers: 1&2 £2.90, 1&3 £1.90, 2&3 £3.80 CSF £10.66 CT £21.50 TOTE £1.90: £1.30, £2.20; EX 10.10 Trifecta £27.60 Pool: £1,394.90 - 37.89 winning tickets..
Owner Gillian, Lady Howard De Walden **Bred** Gillian Lady Howard De Walden **Trained** East Everleigh, Wilts

FOCUS
A modest 3yo handicap, but the winner looks progressive.

1477 FOLLOW US ON TWITTER @LINGFIELDPARK H'CAP 7f (P)
4:00 (4:02) (Class 4) (0-85,83) 3-Y-0 **£4,690** (£1,395; £697; £348) **Stalls** Low

Form RPR
13-0 **1** **Intimidate**[19] 1112 3-9-5 **81**..(p) WilliamBuick 6 88
(Jeremy Noseda) *chsd ldrs: wnt 2nd 5f out: rdn and ld and hung lft ent fnl f: kpt on wl u.p fnl f* **6/1**[3]

10- **2** nk **Beach Club**[209] 6162 3-9-6 **82**.. SeanLevey 2 88
(David Brown) *led: rdn and jnd whn carried lft jst over 1f out: edgd lft u.p ins fnl f: kpt on same pce towards fin* **16/1**

21-1 **3** 1 **Melvin The Grate (IRE)**[21] 1091 3-9-6 **82**..................... JimmyFortune 4 86
(Andrew Balding) *t.k.h: chsd ldrs: drvn over 1f out: kpt on same pce ins fnl f* **7/4**[1]

013- **4** 1 **Surge Ahead (IRE)**[178] 7079 3-9-3 **79**.............................. LukeMorris 1 80
(Ed Walker) *chsd ldrs: keeping on u.p whn short of room and hmpd ins fnl f: swtchd rt and styd on same pce fnl 100yds* **12/1**

060- **5** 1 3/4 **A Ladies Man (IRE)**[178] 7081 3-8-9 **71**......................... RichardHughes 3 67
(Richard Hannon) *in tch in midfield: effrt and rdn ent fnl 2f: styd on same pce fnl f* **5/2**[2]

000- **6** 1 3/4 **Saint Jerome (IRE)**[188] 6815 3-9-3 **79**....................... KirstyMilczarek 10 71
(Jamie Osborne) *in tch towards rr on outer: pushed rt and lost pl wl over 2f out: rdn and no imp over 1f out* **25/1**

-260 **7** shd **Lucky Di**[25] 1033 3-9-1 **77**... JohnFahy 7 68
(Peter Hedger) *hld up in tch towards rr: rdn and hdwy on inner over 1f out: chsng ldrs but keeping on same pce whn short of room and hmpd jst ins fnl f: n.d after* **20/1**

4334 **8** 1 **Club House (IRE)**[20] 1099 3-8-6 **73**................................ RobertTart(5) 8 62
(Robert Mills) *hld up in rr: effrt over 1f out: kpt on same pce and no imp ins fnl f* **25/1**

-525 **9** 1/2 **Fortinbrass (IRE)**[19] 1112 3-9-6 **82**......................... RichardKingscote 5 69
(Ralph Beckett) *in tch in midfield: unable qck u.p ent fnl 2f: one pce and wl hld fr over 1f out* **8/1**

04-0 **10** 7 **Jollification (IRE)**[27] 1000 3-9-7 **83**.............................(v[1]) PatCosgrave 9 51
(George Baker) *dwlt: in tch in last quartet: swtchd rt and sme hdwy on outer wl over 2f out: wknd over 1f out: fdd fnl f* **33/1**

1m 23.98s (-0.82) **Going Correction** +0.025s/f (Slow) **10** Ran SP% **119.3**
Speed ratings (Par 100): **105,104,103,102,100 98,98,97,96,88**
Tote Swingers: 1&2 £41.60, 1&3 £2.20, 2&3 £18.70 CSF £91.03 CT £239.19 TOTE £5.30: £2.00, £10.10, £1.10; EX 115.60 Trifecta £1284.60 Part won. Pool: £1,712.80 - 0.55 winning tickets..
Owner Miss Yvonne Jacques **Bred** D J And Mrs Deer **Trained** Newmarket, Suffolk

FOCUS
A decent 3yo handicap, run in a time 0.79 seconds faster than the preceding Class 5 event. Very few ever got into it, however, with the first two dominating throughout.

1478 ORPHEUS CENTRE MAIDEN STKS 1m 4f (P)
4:30 (4:30) (Class 5) 3-Y-0 **£2,726** (£805; £402) **Stalls** Low

Form RPR
333- **1** **Another Cocktail**[178] 7081 3-9-5 79.............................. RichardHughes 3 81+
(Hughie Morrison) *chsd ldrs: wnt 2nd over 5f out: rdn to ld ent fnl f: sn in command: eased towards fin* **1/2**[1]

65- **2** 3 1/2 **Divergence (IRE)**[211] 6117 3-9-0 0..................................... WilliamBuick 4 69
(Michael Bell) *chsd ldr tl led 10f out: rdn and hdd ent fnl f: sn btn but kpt on to hold 2nd* **3/1**[2]

4 **3** 1 1/2 **Strategic Strike (IRE)**[8] 1300 3-9-5 0................................. ChrisCatlin 1 72
(Paul Cole) *t.k.h: chsd ldrs: rdn 3f out: plugged on same pce fr over 1f out* **12/1**

02 **4** 1 1/4 **Could Be (IRE)**[21] 1089 3-9-5 0....................................... JimmyFortune 5 70+
(David Simcock) *led for 2f: chsd ldr tl over 5f out: rdn wl over 2f out: hung rt and btn bnd wl over 1f out* **8/1**[3]

0 **5** 3/4 **Al Meezan**[23] 1069 3-9-5 0.. LiamKeniry 2 68
(David Simcock) *rn green: a in rr: rdn over 4f out: outpcd and detached last over 3f out: no ch w wnr but kpt on again ins fnl f* **33/1**

2m 33.47s (0.47) **Going Correction** +0.025s/f (Slow) **5** Ran SP% **113.4**
Speed ratings (Par 98): **99,96,95,94,94**
CSF £2.44 TOTE £1.70: £1.10, £2.20; EX 2.30 Trifecta £11.50 Pool: £2,284.75 - 148.69 winning tickets..
Owner Michael Kerr-Dineen **Bred** Newsells Park Stud **Trained** East Ilsley, Berks

FOCUS
Not the most competitive of maidens.

1479 YES EVENTS LTD FILLIES' H'CAP 1m (P)
5:00 (5:00) (Class 5) (0-75,72) 4-Y-0+ **£2,726** (£805; £402) **Stalls** High

Form RPR
-101 **1** **Refreshestheparts (USA)**[54] 672 4-9-7 **72**............(t) RichardHughes 2 78+
(George Baker) *mde all: rdn and qcknd ent fnl 2f: r.o wl and a doing enough ins fnl f* **4/5**[1]

0-21 **2** nk **Yojojo (IRE)**[27] 996 4-8-9 **60**.. LukeMorris 4 65
(Gay Kelleway) *chsd wnr: ev ch whn edgd rt bnd wl over 1f out: kpt on u.p ins fnl f* **2/1**[2]

-253 **3** 1 3/4 **Dundrum Dancer (IRE)**[59] 601 6-8-9 **64**...................(p) RobertTart(5) 3 65
(Alex Hales) *chsd ldrs: effrt u.p 2f out: styd on same pce ins fnl f* **8/1**[3]

02-4 **4** 3 1/2 **Bint Alzain (IRE)**[17] 1155 4-9-0 **65**.. IanMongan 1 58
(Pat Phelan) *t.k.h: chsd ldrs: rdn and effrt on inner 2f out: wknd ins fnl f* **8/1**[3]

1m 39.69s (1.49) **Going Correction** +0.025s/f (Slow) **4** Ran SP% **111.1**
Speed ratings (Par 100): **93,92,90,87**
CSF £2.77 TOTE £1.70; EX 2.30 Trifecta £5.40 Pool: £1,517.44 - 209.79 winning tickets..
Owner Michel de Carvalho **Bred** Lazy Lane Farms Inc **Trained** Manton, Wilts

FOCUS
With so few runners, this fillies' handicap was always likely to be a tactical affair and so it proved.

1480 MIKE HARBRIDGE PSD AGRONOMY CONSULTANTS FILLIES' H'CAP 1m 2f (P)
5:35 (5:35) (Class 5) (0-75,72) 4-Y-0+ £2,726 (£805; £402) Stalls Low

Form RPR
6-03 1 **If I Were A Boy (IRE)**[14] 1200 6-9-0 65 (be) AdamKirby 3 70
(Dominic Ffrench Davis) *chsd ldrs: wnt 2nd and travelling wl 2f out: drvn and ev ch over 1f out: led ins fnl f: r.o wl* 6/4[1]
-532 2 ½ **Push Me (IRE)**[30] 689 6-9-2 72 RobertTart(5) 1 76
(Jamie Poulton) *hld up wl in tch in rr: rdn and hdwy on inner 2f out: led over 1f out: hdd ins fnl f: kpt on u.p* 7/4[2]
434 3 2½ **Total Obsession**[4] 1381 6-8-0 58 oh5 (v) NoelGarbutt(7) 2 57
(Mark Hoad) *hld up wl in tch: rdn and effrt 2f out: unable qck over 1f out: kpt on ins fnl f to go 3rd fnl 75yds* 10/1
00-6 4 1¼ **Cape Joy (IRE)**[4] 1381 4-8-13 64 RichardHughes 4 60
(Richard Hannon) *led: rdn and qcknd ent fnl 2f: hdd over 1f out: no ex and wknd fnl 100yds* 9/2[3]
556- 5 6 **Trulee Scrumptious**[144] 7769 4-8-3 59 oh8 ow1 RosieJessop(5) 6 43
(Peter Charalambous) *t.k.h: hld up wl in tch in midfield: rdn and unable qck 2f out: wknd over 1f out* 16/1
/0-0 6 2¼ **Rachael's Ruby**[15] 201 6-8-7 58 oh13 (v[1]) LukeMorris 5 38
(Roger Teal) *chsd ldr tl 2f out: wknd u.p over 1f out* 33/1

2m 6.84s (0.24) **Going Correction** +0.025s/f (Slow) 6 Ran SP% 112.5
Speed ratings (Par 100): **100,99,97,96,91 90**
Tote Swingers: 1&2 £1.70, 1&3 £1.80, 2&3 £3.00 CSF £4.42 TOTE £2.80: £1.90, £1.10; EX 5.00 Trifecta £23.10 Pool: £1,948.76 - 63.05 winning tickets..
Owner R F Haynes **Bred** Kilco Builders **Trained** Lambourn, Berks

FOCUS
A modest fillies' handicap with three of the six out of the weights and another already due a significant drop. The other pair dominated the finish.
T/Plt: £77.80 to a £1 stake. Pool: £59,239.38. 555.75 winning tickets. T/Qpdt: £8.30 to a £1 stake. Pool: £5,131.67. 453.20 winning tickets. SP

NOTTINGHAM (L-H)
Wednesday, April 10

OFFICIAL GOING: Good (good to soft in places; 8.1)
Wind: Virtually nil Weather: Cloudy with sunny periods

1481 BETFRED HOME OF GOALS GALORE EBF MAIDEN STKS 1m 75y
2:10 (2:10) (Class 5) 3-Y-0 £3,881 (£1,155; £577; £288) Stalls Centre

Form RPR
2- 1 **Stepping Ahead (FR)**[132] 7924 3-9-5 0 MartinHarley 8 78
(Mrs K Burke) *mde all: rdn and qcknd clr 2f out: styd on strly* 9/4[2]
002- 2 7 **Elhaame (IRE)**[216] 5962 3-9-5 82 KierenFallon 7 62
(Luca Cumani) *trckd ldng pair: niggled along over 3f out: rdn to chse wnr 2f out: no imp appr fnl f* 11/10[1]
04- 3 1¼ **Hello Sailor**[132] 7923 3-9-5 0 JimCrowley 6 59
(Ralph Beckett) *chsd wnr: rdn along wl over 2f out: sn one pce* 10/1
4 ¾ **No Win No Fee** 3-9-5 0 TomQueally 1 57
(Michael Appleby) *dwlt and towards rr: hdwy to trck ldrs on inner after 3f: rdn along over 2f out: kpt on same pce* 20/1
0- 5 1¼ **Star Of Namibia (IRE)**[133] 7900 3-9-5 0 JDSmith 5 54
(J S Moore) *chsd ldrs: rdn along over 3f out: one pce fr over 2f out* 33/1
6 nk **Magic Lando (FR)** 3-9-5 0 JoeFanning 3 54+
(Ismail Mohammed) *got loose briefly at s: s.i.s and bhd: gd hdwy on outer 1/2-way: chsd ldrs 3f out: rdn over 2f out: grad wknd* 6/1[3]
40 7 ¾ **Inigo Montoya**[11] 1236 3-9-2 0 DeclanCannon(3) 2 52
(Alan McCabe) *t.k.h: in tch: effrt 3f out: rdn along over 2f out: n.d* 100/1
8 6 **Switch On** 3-9-5 0 GeorgeBaker 4 38
(Chris Wall) *towards rr and rdn along 1/2-way: a outpcd* 14/1

1m 48.38s (-0.62) **Going Correction** -0.375s/f (Firm) 8 Ran SP% 117.1
Speed ratings (Par 98): **88,81,79,79,77 77,76,70**
Tote Swingers: 1&2 £1.20, 1&3 £3.00, 2&3 £3.90 CSF £5.14 TOTE £3.70: £1.10, £1.02, £2.40; EX 12.40 Trifecta £25.80 Pool: £2,750.88 - 79.86 winning tickets..
Owner Mark James & Mrs Elaine Burke **Bred** S C E A Haras De Manneville **Trained** Middleham Moor, N Yorks

FOCUS
Probably just a fair event but a few of those beaten should get their head to the front at some level this year. All races on Inner track.

1482 BETFRED MOBILE LOTTO H'CAP 5f 13y
2:40 (2:42) (Class 4) (0-85,85) 3-Y-0 £5,175 (£1,540; £769; £384) Stalls High

Form RPR
300- 1 **Mayfield Girl (IRE)**[186] 6883 3-9-1 79 DavidAllan 2 84
(Mel Brittain) *cl up: rdn to ld jst over 1f out: drvn ins fnl f: hld on gamely* 40/1
010- 2 hd **The Art Of Racing (IRE)**[174] 7193 3-9-0 78 (t) HarryBentley 3 82
(Olly Stevens) *trckd ldrs: hdwy 2f out: rdn to chal ins fnl f and ev ch tl nt qckn nr line* 12/1
41-2 3 nk **Fils Anges (IRE)**[9] 1295 3-9-7 85 HayleyTurner 7 88+
(Michael Bell) *wnt lft s: bhd and pushed along over 3f out: swtchd to wd outside and rdn over 1f out: styd on strly fnl f* 7/4[1]
1 4 shd **My Name Is Rio (IRE)**[41] 829 3-8-8 72 TomEaves 4 76+
(Michael Dods) *trckd ldrs: effrt and n.m.r jst over 1f out and again ent fnl f: sn swtchd rt and rdn: styd on strly nr fin* 20/1
153- 5 nse **Secret Look**[154] 7635 3-9-7 85 RyanMoore 6 88+
(Ed McMahon) *dwlt and bhd: hdwy 2f out: sn rdn: styng on wl whn n.m.r ins fnl f: nrst fin* 11/2[3]
22-1 6 nk **Bispham Green**[18] 1150 3-8-13 77 TonyHamilton 8 79
(Richard Fahey) *led: rdn along and jnd 2f out: hdd jst over 1f out: sn drvn and one pce ins fnl f* 10/1
331- 7 ½ **Secret Missile**[145] 7738 3-9-2 80 MartinDwyer 5 80
(William Muir) *towards rr: hdwy 2f out: rdn and styd on wl fnl f: nrst fin* 9/1
321- 8 1½ **Moviesta (USA)**[205] 6320 3-9-5 83 PaulMulrennan 11 77
(Bryan Smart) *towards rr: pushed along over 2f out: sn rdn and styng on whn sltly hmpd ins fnl f: nrst fin* 7/2[2]
100- 9 3½ **Starlight Angel (IRE)**[173] 7220 3-8-5 72 DarrenEgan(3) 9 54
(Ronald Harris) *prom: rdn along over 2f out: sn wknd* 66/1
025- 10 5 **Khefyn (IRE)**[151] 7687 3-8-10 74 JamesDoyle 10 38
(Ronald Harris) *prom on stands' rail: rdn along 2f out: sn wknd* 25/1
-226 11 14 **Midnight Dream (FR)**[49] 730 3-9-1 79 KierenFallon 1
(Kristin Stubbs) *prom on wd outside: pushed along 1/2-way: sn rdn and wknd over 1f out* 33/1

1m 0.47s (-1.03) **Going Correction** -0.20s/f (Firm) 11 Ran SP% 116.2
Speed ratings (Par 100): **100,99,99,99,98 98,97,95,89,81 59**
Tote Swingers: 1&2 £46.30, 1&3 £21.80, 2&3 £6.40 CSF £433.75 CT £1335.87 TOTE £56.70: £12.10, £5.50, £1.10; EX 670.10 Trifecta £1106.30 Pool: £3,200.28 - 2.16 winning tickets..
Owner Mel Brittain **Bred** Mark Commins **Trained** Warthill, N Yorks
■ Stewards' Enquiry : Tom Eaves caution: careless riding.

FOCUS
A decent handicap in which the leaders seemed to go plenty hard enough early, because both the third and fifth got well behind at one point. The winning time was only just slower than the one recorded by a 115-rated runner in the following event.

1483 BETFRED TV CONDITIONS STKS 5f 13y
3:10 (3:10) (Class 3) 3-Y-0+ £7,781 (£2,330; £1,165; £582; £291; £146) Stalls High

Form RPR
0-50 1 **Spirit Quartz (IRE)**[11] 1265 5-9-1 115 HarryBentley 8 113
(Robert Cowell) *trckd ldr: cl up 2f out: effrt on inner whn n.m.r over 1f out: squeezed through jst ins fnl f and qcknd wl to ld last 100yds* 6/5[1]
0-64 2 1¼ **Humidor (IRE)**[39] 868 6-9-1 108 (t) RyanMoore 7 108
(George Baker) *t.k.h early: trckd ldrs: swtchd lft and hdwy over 1f out: rdn to chse wnr ins fnl f: no imp towards fin* 9/4[2]
040- 3 3 **Bogart**[229] 5561 4-9-1 104 AmyRyan 5 97
(Kevin Ryan) *led: rdn and edgd rt over 1f out: drvn ent fnl f: hdd and one pce last 100yds* 9/2[3]
00-4 4 2¾ **Silvanus (IRE)**[11] 1249 8-9-1 85 RussKennemore 6 87
(Paul Midgley) *trckd ldrs: hdwy 2f out: sn rdn and one pce appr fnl f* 50/1
000- 5 nse **Stepper Point**[206] 6292 4-9-1 102 MartinDwyer 1 87
(William Muir) *wnt lft s: chsd ldrs on outer: rdn along wl over 1f out: sn one pce* 25/1
050- 6 3½ **West Coast Dream**[193] 6666 6-8-10 87 ThomasBrown(5) 2 75
(Roy Brotherton) *prom on outer: rdn along 2f out: sn wknd* 66/1
461/ 7 23 **Captain Carey**[633] 4135 7-9-1 95 TomMcLaughlin 4
(Malcolm Saunders) *towards rr: pushed along 1/2-way: sn outpcd and bhd* 14/1

1m 0.45s (-1.05) **Going Correction** -0.20s/f (Firm) 7 Ran SP% 108.4
Speed ratings (Par 107): **100,98,93,88,88 83,46**
Tote Swingers: 1&2 £1.40, 1&3 £1.70, 2&3 £1.70 CSF £3.54 TOTE £1.80: £1.10, £1.70; EX 4.20 Trifecta £6.40 Pool: £2,973.63 - 344.86 winning tickets..
Owner Qatar Racing Limited **Bred** Ballygallon Stud Limited **Trained** Six Mile Bottom, Cambs

FOCUS
Three of these looked clear of their rivals considering the betting and they dominated the outcome.

1484 E.B.F BETFRED BARRY HILLS "FURTHER FLIGHT" STKS (LISTED RACE) 1m 6f 15y
3:40 (3:40) (Class 1) 4-Y-0+ £22,684 (£8,600; £4,304; £2,144; £1,076; £540) Stalls Low

Form RPR
056- 1 **Testosterone (IRE)**[172] 7237 5-8-9 105 RyanMoore 2 101+
(Ed Dunlop) *tacked ldrs: smooth hdwy over 4f out: led 3f out: rdn clr over 2f out: readily* 6/4[1]
2 3¼ **Earth Amber**[250] 4-8-6 88 AndreaAtzeni 4 97
(Nicky Henderson) *t.k.h: hld up in tch: hdwy on outer 3f out: rdn along to chse ldrs 2f out: kpt on u.p fnl f: nrst fin* 16/1
3 ½ **Handazan (IRE)**[40] 3926 4-8-11 98 (p) TomQueally 9 101
(Alan King) *sn led: rdn along 4f out: hdd 3f out: drvn and kpt on same pce fnl 2f* 14/1
023- 4 ½ **Cavaleiro (IRE)**[187] 6833 4-8-11 97 HayleyTurner 6 100
(Marcus Tregoning) *hld up: hdwy over 4f out: chsd ldrs 3f out: rdn over 2f out: sn drvn and one pce* 4/1[3]
121- 5 6 **Sir Graham Wade (IRE)**[169] 7320 4-9-0 104 JoeFanning 7 95
(Mark Johnston) *trckd ldng pair: pushed along over 4f out: rdn 3f out: sn wknd* 9/4[2]
2/23 6 ¾ **The Bull Hayes (IRE)**[10] 1273 7-9-0 87 (p) BarryMcHugh 3 91
(Tony Coyle) *chsd ldr: rdn along 4f out: sn wknd* 25/1
045- 7 5 **Jaaryah (IRE)**[278] 3813 5-8-9 80 MartinHarley 1 79
(Mick Channon) *hld up: a towards rr* 66/1
133- 8 23 **Lily In Pink**[195] 6598 5-8-9 96 JamesDoyle 8 47
(Jonathan Portman) *hld up in tch: hdwy over 4f out: rdn along over 3f out: sn wknd* 14/1

3m 5.9s (-1.10) **Going Correction** -0.375s/f (Firm)
WFA 4 from 5yo+ 3lb 8 Ran SP% 115.3
Speed ratings (Par 111): **88,86,85,85,82 81,78,65**
Tote Swingers: 1&2 £4.40, 1&3 £5.60, 2&3 £7.10 CSF £28.52 TOTE £2.10: £1.10, £3.90, £4.10; EX 31.10 Trifecta £233.30 Pool: £2,783.62 - 8.94 winning tickets..
Owner Nurlan Bizakov **Bred** Scea La Poterie **Trained** Newmarket, Suffolk

FOCUS
A classy looking staying event won decisively by a mare whose best form entitled her to take this in the style she did.

1485 BETFRED DOUBLE DELIGHT H'CAP 1m 75y
4:10 (4:11) (Class 3) (0-95,94) 4-Y-0+ £8,086 (£2,406; £1,202; £601) Stalls Centre

Form RPR
0-20 1 **Maverik**[52] 701 5-9-0 87 JimCrowley 11 96
(Ralph Beckett) *qckly away and mde all: rdn clr wl over 1f out: kpt on strly* 11/1
204- 2 1 **Weapon Of Choice (IRE)**[163] 7435 5-9-1 88 TomQueally 1 95
(Stuart Kittow) *t.k.h early: trckd ldrs on inner: hdwy to chse wnr wl over 1f out and sn rdn: drvn and no imp fnl f* 8/1[3]
00-0 3 1¼ **Extraterrestrial**[11] 1233 9-8-7 80 BarryMcHugh 10 84
(Richard Fahey) *in tch: hdwy 4f out: rdn to chse ldrs 2f out: kpt on u.p fnl f: nrst fin* 14/1
030- 4 1¼ **Shavansky**[154] 7631 9-9-0 87 AndreaAtzeni 4 88
(Rod Millman) *trckd ldrs on inner: hdwy over 3f out: rdn along wl over 2f out: kpt on same pce appr fnl f* 8/1[3]
21-1 5 1¾ **Benzanno (IRE)**[25] 1036 4-9-0 92 ThomasBrown(5) 12 89
(Andrew Balding) *trckd ldng pair: effrt 3f out: rdn over 2f out: sn btn* 7/2[1]
05-0 6 ½ **Imperial Djay (IRE)**[11] 1232 8-9-0 87 PJMcDonald 5 83
(Ruth Carr) *towards rr: hdwy on inner wl over 2f out: rdn and styd on fnl f: nrst fin* 28/1
60-2 7 nse **President Lincoln (USA)**[5] 1363 5-8-1 77 NeilFarley(3) 7 73
(Declan Carroll) *t.k.h: chsd ldrs: rdn along wl over 3f out: grad wknd fr over 2f out* 17/2

The Form Book Flat, Raceform Ltd, Compton, RG20 6NL.

030- **8** *nse* **Osteopathic Remedy (IRE)**[151] 7691 9-9-7 **94**................. TomEaves 6 90
(Michael Dods) *chsd wnr: rdn along over 2f out: drvn and wknd wl over 1f out* **22/1**

110- **9** *½* **Discression**[210] 6143 4-9-2 **89**.. RyanMoore 13 84+
(Kevin Ryan) *stdd and swtchd lft s: hld up: hdwy on outer over 4f out: rdn to chse ldrs over 2f out: drvn wl over 1f out and sn btn* **12/1**

40-0 **10** *½* **Muffin McLeay (IRE)**[11] 1235 5-8-12 **90**............................ LMcNiff(5) 8 84
(David Barron) *dwlt: a in rr* **33/1**

155- **11** *hd* **Uppercut**[207] 6235 5-8-10 **83**.. KierenFallon 9 76
(Stuart Kittow) *in tch: hdwy to chse ldrs 3f out: sn rdn and wknd fnl 2f* **5/1**[2]

0-02 **12** *1 ¼* **Gloriam (USA)**[9] 1281 4-8-7 **80**... AmyRyan 3 70
(Ruth Carr) *dwlt: a towards rr* **16/1**

043- **13** *1* **Unex Michelangelo (IRE)**[186] 6875 4-9-2 **89**............. PaulMulrennan 2 77
(Michael Easterby) *midfield: rdn along over 3f out: sn wknd* **16/1**

1m 47.61s (-1.39) **Going Correction** -0.375s/f (Firm) **13** Ran SP% **116.8**
Speed ratings (Par 107): **91,90,88,87,85 85,85,85,84,84 83,82,81**
Tote Swingers: 1&2 £18.40, 1&3 £20.90, 2&3 £21.8 CSF £92.11 CT £1283.97 TOTE £13.70: £4.10, £1.90, £5.20; EX 119.90 Trifecta £1139.00 Part won. Pool: £1,518.78 - 0.75 winning tickets..
Owner Athos, Cooper, Quinn, EPL **Bred** J G Davis & Star Pointe Ltd **Trained** Kimpton, Hants

FOCUS
A competitive-looking race dominated by the front-running winner.

1486 BETFRED MOBILE SPORTS H'CAP 1m 75y
4:40 (4:41) (Class 5) (0-75,74) 3-Y-O **£2,726** (£805; £402) **Stalls** Centre

Form RPR

412- **1** **Ingleby Symphony (IRE)**[170] 7289 3-8-8 **61**................. TonyHamilton 4 71+
(Richard Fahey) *hld up towards rr: swtchd to outer and smooth hdwy wl over 2f out: rdn to ld appr fnl f: sn qcknd clr: readily* **14/1**

4414 **2** *4* **Minimee**[9] 1293 3-9-4 **71**.. KierenFallon 3 72
(Phil McEntee) *midfield: hdwy over 4f out: chsd ldrs over 2f out: rdn wl over 1f out: kpt on fnl f: no ch w wnr* **25/1**

01-4 **3** *1* **Mister Marcasite**[19] 1109 3-9-4 **71**..................................... DavidAllan 10 70+
(Mel Brittain) *cl up: led over 2f out: sn rdn and hdd appr fnl f: kpt on same pce* **18/1**

1- **4** *nk* **Singersongwriter**[166] 7363 3-9-7 **74**.................................. RyanMoore 6 72+
(Ed Dunlop) *s.i.s: plld hrd in rr: hdwy on outer 3f out: rdn to chse ldrs wl over 1f out: sn no imp* **5/6**[1]

665- **5** *½* **Curl (IRE)**[166] 7364 3-9-1 **68**.. TomEaves 11 65
(Michael Dods) *chsd ldrs: rdn along wl over 2f out: drvn wl over 1f out and kpt on same pce* **14/1**

562- **6** *2* **Prospera (IRE)**[144] 7779 3-9-1 **68**.. JimCrowley 1 60
(Ralph Beckett) *hld up: hdwy on inner over 3f out: rdn to chse ldrs 2f out: sn no imp* **16/1**

44-2 **7** *¾* **Clement (IRE)**[26] 1014 3-9-1 **68**.. TomQueally 13 59
(Eve Johnson Houghton) *midfield: hdwy to chse ldrs wl over 2f out: sn rdn and no imp* **20/1**

21-1 **8** *1* **Mixed Message (IRE)**[41] 826 3-9-1 **68**........................... AndreaAtzeni 5 60+
(John Mackie) *hld up: sme hdwy whn n.m.r 2f out: n.d* **9/1**[2]

4621 **9** *shd* **Ivy Port**[15] 1190 3-8-7 **60** oh2... HarryBentley 8 48
(Michael Appleby) *chsd ldng pair: pushed along over 3f out: rdn over 2f out: grad wknd* **14/1**

001- **10** *6* **Teolagi (IRE)**[147] 7708 3-9-3 **70**.. GeorgeBaker 2 44
(J S Moore) *hld up: a towards rr* **16/1**

203- **11** *1* **Dark Ocean (IRE)**[189] 6780 3-9-5 **72**............................. PJMcDonald 14 44
(Jedd O'Keeffe) *sn led: rdn along 3f out: hdd over 2f out and sn wknd* **33/1**

-14 **12** *4* **Little Dolly**[63] 538 3-8-12 **65**... MartinHarley 9 28
(Alan McCabe) *chsd ldrs: rdn along over 3f out: sn wknd* **66/1**

052- **13** *15* **Gilded Frame**[218] 5911 3-9-6 **73**....................................... HayleyTurner 12
(Marcus Tregoning) *a towards rr* **12/1**[3]

605- **14** *4 ½* **Red Four**[177] 7103 3-8-13 **66**... TedDurcan 7
(George Baker) *a in rr: bhd fnl 3f* **50/1**

1m 46.28s (-2.72) **Going Correction** -0.375s/f (Firm) **14** Ran SP% **124.3**
Speed ratings (Par 98): **98,94,93,92,92 90,89,88,88,82 81,77,62,57**
Tote Swingers: 1&2 £35.60, 1&3 £39.60, 2&3 £30.50 CSF £339.04 CT £6397.20 TOTE £21.40: £4.30, £5.30, £4.30; EX 483.70 Trifecta £2612.90 Part won. Pool: £3,483.95 - 0.25 winning tickets..
Owner Percy Green Racing 4 & Partner **Bred** Sunderland Holdings Inc **Trained** Musley Bank, N Yorks

FOCUS
The leaders went off very quickly in this, so the form should be sound.

1487 BETFRED STILL TREBLE ODDS ON LUCKYS H'CAP 1m 2f 50y
5:10 (5:11) (Class 5) (0-70,70) 3-Y-O **£2,587** (£770; £384; £192) **Stalls** Low

Form RPR

056- **1** **Sioux Chieftain (IRE)**[224] 5742 3-9-3 **66**......................... GeorgeBaker 9 76
(Tim Pitt) *trckd ldr: led over 3f out: rdn clr wl over 1f out: drvn out towards fin* **14/1**

03-3 **2** *½* **Eric The Grey (IRE)**[25] 1044 3-9-2 **65**........................... TonyHamilton 4 74+
(Richard Fahey) *hld up towards rr: swtchd to outer and hdwy wl over 2f out: sn rdn and str run fr over 1f out: edgd lft ins fnl f: kpt on wl* **5/1**[2]

35-1 **3** *4 ½* **Debdebdeb**[42] 814 3-9-7 **70**.. RyanMoore 1 71
(Andrew Balding) *led: pushed along 4f out: hdd over 3f out and sn rdn: sltly outpcd 2f out: drvn and rallied over 1f out: kpt on u.p fnl f* **7/4**[1]

400- **4** *3 ¾* **Standing Bear (IRE)**[257] 4540 3-9-2 **65**.......................... TomQueally 2 58
(Paul Cole) *chsd ldrs on inner: pushed along over 3f out: swtchd rt and rdn 2f out: sn one pce* **16/1**

500- **5** *1 ½* **Atalanta Bay (IRE)**[203] 6366 3-8-7 **56**.......................... HayleyTurner 12 47+
(Marcus Tregoning) *dwlt and in rr: hdwy over 2f out: kpt on fnl f: nrst fin* **12/1**

000- **6** *2 ¼* **Denton Skyline (IRE)**[210] 6133 3-8-7 **56**.............................. TomEaves 13 42
(Michael Dods) *prom: rdn along 3f out: wknd over 2f out* **20/1**

35-5 **7** *4 ½* **Lady Marmelo (IRE)**[19] 1119 3-9-4 **67**.......................... MatthewDavies 5 45
(Mick Channon) *dwlt and sltly hmpd s: a in rr* **16/1**

3331 **8** *¾* **Two No Bids (IRE)**[25] 1044 3-9-5 **68**.............................. KierenFallon 11 44
(Phil McEntee) *hld up towards rr: stdy hdwy over 3f out: chsd ldrs over 2f out: sn rdn and wknd* **11/1**

00-0 **9** *2* **Caramel Sundae**[22] 1071 3-8-7 **56** oh2.......................(b) AdamBeschizza 7 28
(Robert Eddery) *a towards rr* **50/1**

-514 **10** *shd* **Diletta Tommasa (IRE)**[19] 1119 3-9-4 **67**..................... AndreaAtzeni 10 39
(John Stimpson) *in tch: hdwy over 3f out: chsd ldrs over 2f out: sn rdn and wknd* **25/1**

32-5 **11** *½* **Duke Of Yorkshire**[11] 1236 3-9-4 **70**................................. NeilFarley(3) 8 41
(Declan Carroll) *nvr bttr than midfield* **12/1**

020 **12** *1 ½* **Shockingdancer (IRE)**[27] 994 3-8-11 **60**........................ MartinHarley 3 28
(Marco Botti) *t.k.h: chsd ldrs: rdn along 3f out: n.m.r and wknd 2f out* **9/1**[3]

2m 13.61s (-0.69) **Going Correction** -0.375s/f (Firm) **12** Ran SP% **115.7**
Speed ratings (Par 98): **87,86,83,80,78 77,73,72,71,71 70,69**
Tote Swingers: 1&2 £16.20, 1&3 £6.80, 2&3 £3.10 CSF £79.03 CT £186.13 TOTE £28.20: £4.20, £2.30, £1.10; EX 110.70 Trifecta £805.20 Pool: £1,835.01 - 1.70 winning tickets..
Owner Ferrybank Properties Limited **Bred** Newsells Park Stud **Trained** Newmarket, Suffolk

FOCUS
It paid to be quite handy in the finale, as both the first and third raced prominently throughout. The runner-up looked unlucky.
T/Plt: £375.90 to a £1 stake. Pool: £54,880.18. 106.55 winning tickets. T/Qpdt: £350.40 to a £1 stake. Pool: £3,836.54. 8.10 winning tickets. JR

999 CHANTILLY (R-H)
Wednesday, April 10

OFFICIAL GOING: Polytrack: standard

1495a PRIX DE LA BOISSIERE (CONDITIONS) (3YO) (POLYTRACK) 1m
6:05 (12:00) 3-Y-O **£9,756** (£3,902; £2,926; £1,951; £975)

RPR

1 **Le Deluge (FR)**[112] 8176 3-9-0 0........................ ChristopheSoumillon 11 91
(John Best) *broke wl on outside: sn led: swtchd to ins rail: r.o wl ent st: established clr ld: wandered off st line ins fnl f: a in command: kpt on wl* **8/1**

2 *2* **Damsah (USA)**[39] 3-9-3 0.. MaximeGuyon 2 90
(D De Watrigant, France) **2/1**[1]

3 *1 ¼* **You're Golden (IRE)**[111] 8192 3-8-11 0... Christophe-PatriceLemaire 12 81
(E Legrix, France) **73/10**

4 *1 ½* **Sabre Rock**[112] 8172 3-8-11 0.. SteveDrowne 6 78
(John Best) *broke wl towards ins: settled in 2nd: rdn 1 1/2f out: r.o: lost 2nd 100yds out: no ex: styd on one pce* **17/1**

5 *¾* **Gyrella (IRE)**[141] 3-9-3 0.. AllanBonnefoy 1 82
(A De Royer-Dupre, France) **63/10**[3]

6 *nk* **Ellusivance (IRE)**[19] 3-9-4 0....................................... IoritzMendizabal 10 82
(E J O'Neill, France) **4/1**[2]

7 *hd* **Linngara (FR)**[228] 5612 3-9-1 0.. TheoBachelot 3 79
(Mario Hofer, Germany) **28/1**

8 *3* **Becquarius (FR)**[262] 3-8-8 0..(p) MarcLerner(3) 4 68
(Y Fouin, France) **40/1**

9 *snk* **Iave Con (FR)** 3-8-11 0... DavidBreux 7 67
(I Endaltsev, Czech Republic) **38/1**

10 *hd* **Mountain View (GER)**[223] 5781 3-8-11 0........................ FabienLefebvre 5 67
(Frau Nina Bach, Germany) **42/1**

0 **The Monarck (FR)**[19] 3-8-11 0.. VincentVion 9
(T Lallie, France) **12/1**

1m 39.58s (99.58) **11** Ran SP% **114.2**
WIN (incl. 1 euro stake): 9.00. PLACES: 2.20, 1.30, 2.30. DF: 12.90. SF: 35.10.
Owner Longman & Malt **Bred** J F Gribomont **Trained** Hucking, Kent

1466 KEMPTON (A.W) (R-H)
Thursday, April 11

OFFICIAL GOING: Standard
Wind: light, across Weather: dry

1496 MIKE THE KNIGHT 13.04.13 CLASSIFIED CLAIMING STKS 1m (P)
4:55 (4:55) (Class 6) 4-Y-O+ **£1,940** (£577; £288; £144) **Stalls** Low

Form RPR

1212 **1** **Officer In Command (USA)**[21] 1094 7-8-4 70...(vt) NicoleNordblad(5) 3 79
(Hans Adielsson) *hld up in tch in rr: pushed along and qcknd to ld over 1f out: clr and r.o wl fnl f: comf* **5/4**[1]

0431 **2** *4* **Mr Knightley (IRE)**[8] 1316 4-8-13 73..........................(b) MatthewDavies 1 74
(Jim Boyle) *chsd ldng pair: rdn and effrt on inner 2f out: chsd clr wnr ent fnl f: no imp* **6/4**[2]

3415 **3** *2 ¾* **Alhaban (IRE)**[7] 1353 7-8-9 66... LukeMorris 5 63
(Ronald Harris) *chsd ldr: rdn to chal over 2f out: outpcd and btn over 1f out:* **5/1**[3]

-362 **4** *nk* **Benandonner (USA)**[8] 1322 10-8-6 62.......................... JoeyHaynes(7) 2 67?
(Paddy Butler) *led: jnd and rdn over 2f out: outpcd and btn over 1f out* **14/1**

1m 38.59s (-1.21) **Going Correction** 0.0s/f (Stan) **4** Ran SP% **107.8**
Speed ratings (Par 101): **106,102,99,98**
CSF £3.41 TOTE £1.90; EX 3.50 Trifecta £5.40 Pool: £1,015.59 - 140.68 winning tickets..
Owner Hans Adielsson A B **Bred** Blooming Hills Inc **Trained** Kingston Lisle, Oxon

FOCUS
With Benandonner allowed to do his own thing out in front, the pace wasn't hot, and it turned into a sprint in the straight. The winners's best form since 2011 at face value, but it's a bit shaky.

1497 MASCOT GRAND NATIONAL 06.05.13 H'CAP (DIV I) 1m (P)
5:30 (5:30) (Class 6) (0-60,60) 4-Y-O+ **£1,940** (£577; £288; £144) **Stalls** Low

Form RPR

-400 **1** **Rezwaan**[43] 813 6-9-7 **60**...(be) ShaneKelly 5 72+
(Murty McGrath) *hld up in tch: cruised up to trck ldrs 2f out: upsides ldr on bit 1f out: rdn to ld ins fnl f: sn asserted and r.o wl: comf* **6/4**[1]

4330 **2** *2 ¼* **Warbond**[29] 984 5-9-7 **60**...(v) LukeMorris 3 67
(Michael Madgwick) *chsd ldng pair: rdn to ld ent fnl f: hdd and sn brushed aside by wnr ins fnl f: kpt on* **7/2**[2]

0124 **3** *3 ¼* **Greek Islands (IRE)**[25] 1056 5-9-1 **54**............................... LiamKeniry 10 54
(Ed de Giles) *hld up in midfield: rdn and effrt 2f out: styd on to go 3rd fnl 100yds: no threat to ldrs* **5/1**[3]

0002 **4** *1* **Signora Frasi (IRE)**[22] 1093 8-8-13 **52**........................... WilliamCarson 9 49
(Tony Newcombe) *broke wl: sn stdd bk and hld up in last pair: rdn over 2f out: styd on fnl f: no threat to ldrs* **12/1**

-101 **5** *nk* **Chandrayaan**[22] 1093 6-9-0 **53**..................................(v) KirstyMilczarek 4 50
(John E Long) *chsd ldrs: rdn over 2f out: unable qck and btn over 1f out: wknd fnl f* **8/1**

0016 **6** *½* **Putin (IRE)**[10] 1294 5-9-0 **58**.......................................(tp) RachealKneller(5) 8 53
(Phil McEntee) *led tl rdn and hdd ent fnl f: wknd fnl f* **20/1**

40-5 **7** *4* **Wishformore (IRE)**[22] 1093 6-8-6 **48**.................................. RyanPowell(3) 6 34
(Zoe Davison) *t.k.h: hld up in last trio: rdn and effrt on inner 2f out: no imp: wknd fnl f* **20/1**

5414 **8** 1 3/4 **Rapid Water**[21] 1100 7-9-2 **55**..(v) JimmyFortune 7 37
(Pat Eddery) *v.s.a: clsd to bk of field after 2f: rdn and struggling over 2f out: sn wl btn* **8/1**

000- **9** 17 **Legal Pursuit**[209] 6215 4-8-4 **48** oh1 ow2................ MichaelJMurphy(5) 2
(Edward Bevan) *t.k.h: chsd ldrs tl dropped to rr qckly jst over 2f out: sn bhd* **50/1**

1m 38.64s (-1.16) **Going Correction** 0.0s/f (Stan) **9** Ran SP% **120.3**
Speed ratings (Par 101): **105,102,99,98,98 97,93,91,74**
Tote Swingers 1&2 £3.30, 2&3 £3.70, 1&3 £4.40 CSF £6.90 CT £21.91 TOTE £2.70: £1.10, £1.10, £2.10; EX 11.70 Trifecta £39.70 Pool: £1,705.89 - 32.16 winning tickets..
Owner Gallagher Equine Ltd **Bred** Shadwell Estate Company Limited **Trained** East Malling, Kent

FOCUS
A gamble was landed here. The winner was back to form off his reduced mark.

1498 MASCOT GRAND NATIONAL 06.05.13 H'CAP (DIV II) 1m (P)
6:00 (6:00) (Class 6) (0-60,60) 4-Y-0+ **£1,940** (£577; £288; £144) **Stalls** Low

Form RPR

-023 **1** **Hill Of Dreams (IRE)**[27] 1017 4-9-0 **53**....................(b) RichardHughes 1 64
(Dean Ivory) *hld up in tch in midfield: rdn and effrt to chal jst over 1f out: led jst ins fnl f: r.o wl: eased cl home* **9/2**[2]

406/ **2** 2 1/2 **Piccolo Mondo**[995] 4261 7-9-7 **60**.. TomEaves 3 65
(Philip Hide) *sn chsng ldr: rdn to ld 2f out: drvn and hdd jst ins fnl f: outpcd by wnr but battled on to hold 2nd* **12/1**

5165 **3** nse **Fonterutoli (IRE)**[9] 1303 6-9-4 **57**.................................(e) RobertHavlin 5 62
(Roger Ingram) *dwlt: sn bustled along: hdwy to chse ldrs after 2f: rdn and chal over 1f out: outpcd by wnr but battling for 2nd fnl f: kpt on* **8/1**

3003 **4** 5 **Dolly Colman (IRE)**[16] 1183 5-8-7 **46** oh1......................... ChrisCatlin 9 40
(Zoe Davison) *bhd: hdwy jst over 2f out: continued to hang lft and plugged on same pce fnl f: nvr trbld ldrs* **20/1**

-340 **5** 5 **Automotive**[10] 1294 5-8-7 **53**.. ShelleyBirkett(7) 7 35
(Julia Feilden) *in tch: hdwy to chse ldr 5f out tl 2f out: sn struggling: wknd over 1f out* **8/1**

1026 **6** hd **Bitaphon (IRE)**[29] 986 4-9-2 **60**................................ CharlesBishop(5) 8 42
(Michael Appleby) *led: rdn and hdd 2f out: sn struggling: fdd 1f out* **7/1**[3]

0501 **7** 2 **Maz**[14] 1221 5-8-6 **50**... NatashaEaton(5) 6 27
(Alan Bailey) *in tch in midfield: lost pl and rdn 4f out: bhd 2f out* **8/1**

50- **8** 5 **Charles Tyrwhitt**[253] 4709 4-9-7 **60**.................................. KierenFallon 4 26
(George Baker) *s.i.s: hld up in rr: rdn over 3f out: wknd over 2f out: bhd over 1f out* **6/4**[1]

1m 38.85s (-0.95) **Going Correction** 0.0s/f (Stan) **8** Ran SP% **116.5**
Speed ratings (Par 101): **104,101,101,96,91 91,89,84**
Tote Swingers 1&2 £5.50, 2&3 £14.80, 1&3 CSF £56.92 CT £421.70 TOTE £3.20: £1.10, £4.20, £3.00; EX 56.30 Trifecta £956.80 Part won. Pool: £1,275.79 - 0.62 winning tickets..
Owner I Gethin & R Gethin **Bred** Miss Breda Wright **Trained** Radlett, Herts

FOCUS
They appeared to go quite quick up front (winning time was 0.21sec slower than first division) and it paid to be ridden with a bit of patience. The form is rated at face value for now.

1499 GET THE BETVICTOR APP MAIDEN FILLIES' STKS 1m (P)
6:30 (6:31) (Class 5) 3-Y-O **£2,587** (£770; £384; £192) **Stalls** Low

Form RPR

60- **1** **Beat Of The Drum (IRE)**[190] 6791 3-9-0 0................. RichardHughes 8 70
(Richard Hannon) *chsd ldrs tl wnt 2nd 5f out: rdn to ld ent fnl f: hld on wl fnl 100yds* **2/1**[1]

450- **2** hd **Sinaadi (IRE)**[179] 7079 3-9-0 75................................ TomQueally 11 69
(Clive Brittain) *in tch in midfield: rdn and hdwy 2f out: str chal ins fnl f: r.o wl but hld cl home* **9/2**[3]

34 **3** 1/2 **Lady Who**[61] 580 3-9-0 0.. JimCrowley 9 68
(Ralph Beckett) *hld up in tch in last trio: swtchd lft and effrt 2f out: gd hdwy u.p over 1f out: pressed ldng pair fnl 100yds: no imp towards fin* **6/1**

54- **4** 3/4 **Jacobella**[187] 6871 3-9-0 0... JohnFahy 3 66
(Jonathan Portman) *chsd ldrs: rdn and ev ch over 1f out: styd on same pce ins fnl f* **4/1**[2]

60- **5** 3 3/4 **Whatever You Do (IRE)**[169] 7329 3-9-0 0......................... RyanMoore 1 57
(Richard Hannon) *led and set stdy gallop: rdn 2f out: hdd ent fnl f: wknd quicickly ins fnl f* **6/1**

30- **6** 3/4 **Beautiful Story (IRE)**[219] 5907 3-9-0 0........................... MartinHarley 7 56+
(Mick Channon) *stdd after s: hld up in tch in last pair: rdn and hdwy 2f out: no imp 1f out: wknd ins fnl f* **12/1**

7 3/4 **Laura Secord (CAN)** 3-8-9 0... RyanTate(5) 5 54
(Heather Main) *s.i.s: sn rcvrd and in tch in midfield: rdn and unable qck 2f out: wknd ent fnl f* **33/1**

0 **8** 1/2 **Indy Spirit (IRE)**[21] 1095 3-9-0 0.. IanMongan 4 53
(Laura Mongan) *chsd ldr tl 5f out: styd chsng ldrs: rdn and unable qck 2f out: wknd ent fnl f* **50/1**

6-5 **9** 1/2 **Bullseye Babe**[56] 651 3-9-0 0.. LiamKeniry 10 51
(Mark Usher) *t.k.h: hld up in last pair: effrt and hung lft fr 2f out: sn outpcd and n.d ent fnl f* **66/1**

10 6 **Carronade** 3-9-0 0...(t) SebSanders 6 37
(Olivia Maylam) *in tch: rdn along and hdwy to chse ldrs 3f out: unable qck 2f out: wknd over 1f out* **33/1**

1m 42.1s (2.30) **Going Correction** 0.0s/f (Stan) **10** Ran SP% **117.1**
Speed ratings (Par 95): **88,87,87,86,82 82,81,80,80,74**
Tote Swingers 1&2 £3.70, 2&3 £6.10, 1&3 £2.30 CSF £10.92 TOTE £3.90: £1.30, £2.10, £2.30; EX 13.70 Trifecta £74.70 Pool: £1,676.33 - 16.81 winning tickets..
Owner Michael Tabor, John Magnier & Derrick Smith **Bred** Atha Bloodstock **Trained** East Everleigh, Wilts

FOCUS
This didn't look a particularly strong maiden and the early gallop was fairly sedate. It was much the slowest of the five C&D times and it's hard to be too positive about the form.

1500 BETVICTOR CASINO ON YOUR MOBILE H'CAP (LONDON MILE QUALIFIER) 1m (P)
7:00 (7:00) (Class 4) (0-85,85) 4-Y-0+ **£4,690** (£1,395; £697; £348) **Stalls** Low

Form RPR

021- **1** **Rockalong (IRE)**[134] 7896 4-9-1 **79**.................................... KierenFallon 8 89+
(Luca Cumani) *t.k.h early: in tch in midfield: rdn over 2f out: hdwy to ld jst over 1f out: hdd 1f out: responded to press and led again ins fnl f: r.o wl: eased cl home* **3/1**[1]

556- **2** 1 1/4 **Cruiser**[176] 7163 5-9-5 **83**.. MartinDwyer 12 90
(William Muir) *hld up in tch in midfield: rdn and hdwy wl over 1f out: led 1f out: hdd ins fnl f: no ex and styd on same pce* **16/1**

34-0 **3** 1 **Savanna Days (IRE)**[18] 1159 4-9-0 **78**........................... MartinHarley 11 83
(Mick Channon) *chsd ldrs: rdn 2f out: drvn and sltly outpcd 1f out: rallied and kpt on again ins fnl f* **8/1**

2150 **4** nk **Lowther**[24] 1061 8-9-3 **81**.. KierenFox 7 85+
(Lee Carter) *chsd ldrs: rdn 2f out: drvn and outpcd ent fnl f: rallied and styd on again ins fnl f* **8/1**

1122 **5** 3/4 **Flamborough Breeze**[24] 1059 4-8-12 **76**..........................(t) LukeMorris 6 78+
(Ed Vaughan) *hld up in tch in last quartet: gng for run on inner whn gap clsd and forced to switch lft 1f out: styd on wl ins fnl f: unable to chal* **6/1**[3]

00-6 **6** nk **Forceful Appeal (USA)**[24] 1061 5-9-2 **80**..................... HayleyTurner 10 82
(Simon Dow) *pressed ldr: upsides and looked to be travelling wl 2f out: sn rdn and unable qck: outpcd and edgd rt 1f out: one pce after* **8/1**

312- **7** 1 **Sword In Hand**[167] 7376 4-8-7 **76**......................... MichaelJMMurphy(5) 5 75
(Alan Jarvis) *t.k.h: led tl drvn and hdd jst over 1f out: no ex and outpcd ins fnl f* **4/1**[2]

0021 **8** 2 3/4 **Brocklebank (IRE)**[16] 1181 4-8-12 **76**................................ JimCrowley 9 69
(Simon Dow) *hld up in tch in last quartet: rdn and effrt 2f out: no imp and one pce after* **14/1**

2625 **9** 1/2 **Dubawi Island (FR)**[23] 1083 4-9-7 **85**...........................(p) PatCosgrave 1 77
(James Tate) *stdd after s: hld up in tch in last trio: rdn and no prog 2f out: plugged on but nvr trbld ldrs* **8/1**

2110 **10** 1/2 **Lily Edge**[16] 1181 4-8-7 **71**... KieranO'Neill 4 62
(John Bridger) *s.i.s: hld up in tch in rr: rdn and no real imp 2f out: nvr trbld ldrs* **25/1**

1m 39.78s (-0.02) **Going Correction** 0.0s/f (Stan) **10** Ran SP% **120.1**
Speed ratings (Par 105): **100,98,97,97,96 96,95,92,92,91**
Tote Swingers 1&2 £13.50, 2&3 £26.60, 1&3 £10.80 CSF £55.50 CT £359.54 TOTE £3.70: £1.70, £5.30, £2.90; EX 47.40 Trifecta £450.60 Pool: £1,273.50 - 2.11 winning tickets..
Owner Nagy El Azar **Bred** Churchtown House Stud **Trained** Newmarket, Suffolk

FOCUS
A decent handicap, but the early gallop wasn't that strong and the time wasn't good. The bare form may not be reliable.

1501 BETVICTOR.COM H'CAP (LONDON MIDDLE DISTANCE QUALIFIER) 1m 3f (P)
7:30 (7:30) (Class 3) (0-90,90) 4-Y-0+
£7,158 (£2,143; £1,071; £535; £267; £134) **Stalls** Low

Form RPR

042- **1** **Niceofyoutotellme**[245] 5006 4-8-13 **82**............................. JimCrowley 7 96+
(Ralph Beckett) *hld up in tch in midfield: swtchd lft and effrt over 1f out: 4th and stl plenty to do 1f out: str run u.p to ld last strides* **7/2**[1]

00-2 **2** hd **Icebuster**[9] 1302 5-8-8 **77**.. AndreaAtzeni 10 88
(Rod Millman) *hld up in tch in midfield: hdwy to chse ldr over 5f out: rdn to ld jst over 2f out: edgd rt briefly but kpt on wl u.p fnl f tl hdd and no ex last strides* **9/2**[3]

101- **3** 1 **Ruscello (IRE)**[199] 6537 4-9-7 **90**...................................... GeorgeBaker 9 99
(Ed Walker) *stuck wd first bnd: chsd ldr after 2f tl over 5f out: styd chsng ldrs: rdn and effrt to chal over 1f out: no ex and styd on same pce fnl 100yds* **4/1**[2]

-011 **4** 3 1/4 **Tadabeer**[3] 1422 5-9-0 **83** 6ex...(t) StevieDonohoe 6 86
(Ian Williams) *t.k.h early: hld up in tch in midfield: drvn to chse ldng pair jst over 1f out: no ex and outpcd ins fnl f* **7/2**[1]

/21- **5** 3 **Homeric (IRE)**[191] 6770 4-9-3 **86**.. RyanMoore 4 84
(Ed Dunlop) *t.k.h early: hld up in tch in midfield: rdn and unable qck 2f out: no threat to ldrs and styd on same pce fr over 1f out* **7/1**

1-30 **6** hd **Royal Peculiar**[11] 1273 5-8-13 **82**.................................(t) AndrewMullen 8 80
(Michael Appleby) *chsd ldrs: rdn and unable qck ent fnl 2f: outpcd and plugged on same pce fr over 1f out* **25/1**

20-0 **7** 3 1/2 **Come On Blue Chip (IRE)**[33] 945 4-9-5 **88**..............(b) SebSanders 5 79
(Paul D'Arcy) *t.k.h: hld up in tch in last quartet: rdn and effrt in centre over 2f out: no prog: wknd over 1f out* **25/1**

2-00 **8** 1 **Super Say (IRE)**[18] 1159 7-9-5 **88**.....................................(t) LukeMorris 1 77
(Mark Rimell) *led tl rdn and hdd jst over 2f out: wknd over 1f out* **33/1**

414- **9** 1 1/4 **Refractor (IRE)**[197] 6584 5-8-8 **84**.............................. LouisSteward(7) 2 71
(Michael Bell) *t.k.h: hld up in tch in last quartet: rdn and no hdwy 2f out: wknd over 1f out* **25/1**

-045 **10** 9 **Takeitfromalady (IRE)**[12] 1242 4-9-1 **84**...................(b) RichardHughes 3 55
(Lee Carter) *hld up in tch in last quaret: rdn and no hdwy over 2f out: bhd and eased ins fnl f* **12/1**

2m 18.16s (-3.74) **Going Correction** 0.0s/f (Stan) **10** Ran SP% **117.3**
Speed ratings (Par 107): **113,112,112,109,107 107,104,104,103,96**
Tote Swingers 1&2 £1.50, 2&3 £4.50, 1&3 £6.40 CSF £18.63 CT £65.74 TOTE £6.40: £2.30, £2.10, £1.40; EX 25.50 Trifecta £161.60 Pool: £1,416.10 - 6.56 winning tickets..
Owner R Roberts **Bred** Minster Stud **Trained** Kimpton, Hants

FOCUS
There was a sedate early pace to this handicap but the time was not bad. The winner gave the impression he was better than the bare form.

1502 FOLLOW US ON TWITTER @BETVICTORRACING H'CAP 2m (P)
8:00 (8:00) (Class 5) (0-70,69) 4-Y-0+ **£2,587** (£770; £384; £192) **Stalls** Low

Form RPR

/0-3 **1** **Ordensritter (GER)**[24] 1062 5-9-4 **66**....................... JemmaMarshall(5) 7 74
(Chris Down) *chsd ldr: led over 2f out and rdn clr 2f out: hrd pressed fnl 100yds: jst hld on* **10/1**

2365 **2** shd **Where's Susie**[15] 1200 8-9-12 **69**.. GeorgeBaker 9 77
(Michael Madgwick) *chsd ldrs: rdn and effrt to chse clr wnr 2f out: clsd and pressed wnr fnl 100yds: grad clsng towards fin: jst hld* **8/1**

1416 **3** 3 **Llamadas**[18] 1158 11-9-7 **64**... IanMongan 5 68
(Olivia Maylam) *t.k.h: hld up in midfield: swtchd lft and effrt jst over 2f out: chsd ldng pair over 1f out: no imp ins fnl f* **13/2**[2]

-402 **4** 1 **Dr Finley (IRE)**[7] 1348 6-9-5 **65**..................................(p) SimonPearce(3) 1 68
(Lydia Pearce) *chsd ldrs: rdn over 3f out: swtchd lft over 2f out: plugged on u.p but nvr gng pce to chal* **7/1**[3]

-303 **5** 1 1/4 **The Absent Mare**[14] 1218 5-9-9 **66**....................................... LukeMorris 4 68+
(Robin Dickin) *hld up in last quartet: swtchd lft over 2f out: drvn 2f out: styd on u.p ins fnl f: nvr trbld ldrs* **7/2**[1]

31-0 **6** 1 1/2 **Inffiraaj (IRE)**[15] 1214 4-8-10 **57**...................................... MartinHarley 6 57
(Mick Channon) *stdd s: hld up in rr: rdn and hdwy ent fnl 2f: styd on same pce fnl f* **14/1**

0-10 **7** 2 1/2 **Honourable Knight (IRE)**[77] 351 5-9-12 **69**......................... LiamKeniry 3 66
(Mark Usher) *in tch in midfield: rdn and unable qck over 2f out: outpcd and wl hld fr over 1f out* **12/1**

-046 **8** 1/2 **Cozy Tiger (USA)**[17] 1175 8-8-11 **54**............................... RichardHughes 2 50
(Willie Musson) *hld up in last quartet: rdn and effrt 2f out: no real imp and wl hld 1f out: eased towards fin* **7/2**[1]

53-0 **9** 2 1/2 **Native Colony**[77] 351 5-9-7 **64**.. HayleyTurner 8 57
(Neil King) *hld up in last quartet: rdn and no hdwy over 2f out: nvr trbld ldrs* **7/1**[3]

0300 **10** 2 ½ **Bubbly Braveheart (IRE)**[10] 1297 6-8-7 **50** oh5...(t[1]) KirstyMilczarek 10 40
(Phil McEntee) *t.k.h: led and clr tl 1/2-way: rdn and hdd over 2f out: sn dropped out: bhd fnl f* **33/1**

3m 31.62s (1.52) **Going Correction** 0.0s/f (Stan)
WFA 4 from 5yo+ 4lb **10** Ran SP% **120.3**
Speed ratings (Par 103): **96,95,94,93,93 92,91,91,89,88**
Tote Swingers 1&2 £8.90, 2&3 £6.20, 1&3 £16.30 CSF £90.19 CT £569.69 TOTE £12.10: £3.10, £2.50, £2.30; EX 75.60 Trifecta £602.80 Pool: £942.93 - 1.17 winning tickets..
Owner Red Baron Racing **Bred** Gestut Karlshof **Trained** Mutterton, Devon

FOCUS
An ordinary staying handicap. The pace wasn't that strong and it was an advantage to be handy. The runner-up sets the standard.

1503 TALK TO VICTOR FILLIES' H'CAP 7f (P)
8:30 (8:30) (Class 5) (0-70,68) 4-Y-0+ **£2,587** (£770; £384; £192) **Stalls** Low

Form RPR
4312 **1** **Maggie Pink**[19] 1151 4-9-1 **62** AndrewMullen 1 74
(Michael Appleby) *taken down early: mde all: pushed clr over 1f out: in command after: tiring but nvr gng to be ct fnl 100yds* **7/2**[2]

2231 **2** 2 ¾ **Big Sylv (IRE)**[15] 1211 4-9-4 **65** (p) RobertWinston 7 70
(James Unett) *in tch on outer: lft chsng wnr but outpcd over 2f out: kpt on but no real threat to wnr ins fnl f* **9/4**[1]

1045 **3** 2 **Shaunas Spirit (IRE)**[21] 1096 5-9-0 **68** (p) PaulBooth(7) 5 67
(Dean Ivory) *t.k.h: hld up in tch in last pair: struck into rival and hmpd 3f out: rallied to go 3rd ent fnl f: kpt on but no threat to wnr* **13/2**

4664 **4** 2 ¾ **Floralys (USA)**[1] 1472 4-9-3 **64** (t) HayleyTurner 6 56
(Amy Weaver) *stdd and swtchd rt after s: hld up in last pair: rdn and effrt over 2f out: no imp: wl hld over 1f out* **20/1**

533 **5** 13 **Purley Queen (IRE)**[15] 1194 4-8-9 **56** RichardHughes 4 13
(Sylvester Kirk) *chsd ldrs: rdn and struggling over 2f out: wknd over 1f out* **4/1**[3]

2415 **P** **Amosite**[27] 1013 7-9-4 **65** (p) RyanMoore 3
(J R Jenkins) *chsd wnr tl struck into by rival and eased 3f out: p.u and dismntd* **7/2**[2]

1m 25.33s (-0.67) **Going Correction** 0.0s/f (Stan) **6** Ran SP% **113.3**
Speed ratings (Par 100): **103,99,97,94,79**
Tote Swingers 1&2 £1.60, 2&3 £5.20, 1&3 £3.70 CSF £12.03 TOTE £4.80: £2.00, £1.30; EX 16.50 Trifecta £49.70 Pool: £961.41 - 14.48 winning tickets..
Owner A W Bult **Bred** Harcourt Stud **Trained** Danethorpe, Notts

FOCUS
This proved straightforward for the all-the-way winner, who took another step forward.
T/Plt: £31.90 to a £1 stake. Pool: £51,879.41 - 1186.77 winning tickets T/Qpdt: £10.90 to a £1 stake. Pool: £7,396.57 - 499.9 winning tickets SP

1418 LONGCHAMP (R-H)
Thursday, April 11

OFFICIAL GOING: Turf: very soft

1511a PRIX DE SAINT-JAMES (MAIDEN) (3YO COLTS & GELDINGS) (TURF) 1m 2f
1:20 (12:00) 3-Y-0 **£10,162** (£4,065; £3,048; £2,032; £1,016)

RPR
1 **Tokum (FR)**[34] 3-8-10 0 CesarPasserat(6) 7 86
(N Bertran De Balanda, France) **25/1**

2 1 ½ **Vayakhan (FR)**[180] 3-9-2 0 Christophe-PatriceLemaire 6 83
(A De Royer-Dupre, France) **6/4**[1]

3 nse **Affaire Solitaire (IRE)**[23] 3-9-2 0 MaximeGuyon 9 83
(A Fabre, France) **48/10**[2]

4 nk **Lictus (FR)**[20] 3-9-2 0 Francois-XavierBertras 3 83
(F Rohaut, France) **15/2**

5 1 ¼ **Rottmayer (IRE)**[26] 3-9-2 0 OlivierPeslier 2 80
(G Botti, France) **6/1**[3]

6 nse **Majestic Power (GER)** 3-9-2 0 ChristopheSoumillon 1 80
(P Schiergen, Germany) **16/1**

7 8 **Sinndar Perfection (FR)**[182] 3-9-2 0 UmbertoRispoli 4 64
(M Delzangles, France) **7/1**

8 1 **Azabitmour (FR)**[89] 191 3-9-2 0 SteveDrowne 10 62
(John Best) *settled towards rr: rdn early in st: no ex: sn btn* **24/1**

9 nse **Huascaran (FR)**[24] 3-9-2 0 IoritzMendizabal 8 62
(F Chappet, France) **23/1**

10 5 **Ver Coquin (FR)**[21] 3-9-2 0 ThierryThulliez 5 52
(N Clement, France) **22/1**

2m 20.01s (16.01) **10** Ran SP% **118.0**
WIN (incl. 1 euro stake): 26.10. PLACES: 3.70, 1.40, 1.90. DF: 35.60. SF: 109.00.
Owner C E Stedman **Bred** Sarl Jedburgh Stud & Mme I Corbani **Trained** France

1473 LINGFIELD (L-H)
Friday, April 12

OFFICIAL GOING: Standard
Wind: Moderate, half behind Weather: Changeable with showers

1512 BHEST RACING TO SCHOOL MAIDEN AUCTION STKS 5f (P)
2:00 (2:03) (Class 6) 2-Y-0 **£2,045** (£603; £302) **Stalls** High

Form RPR
03 **1** **Smugglers Gold (IRE)**[7] 1360 2-8-11 0 TomQueally 5 76
(David Evans) *chsd ldr: pushed into ld over 1f out: reminder ins fnl f: r.o wl* **1/1**[1]

2 3 **Weisse Girl** 2-8-6 0 (b[1]) PJMcDonald 6 60+
(Noel Quinlan) *hld up bhd ldrs: wnt 3rd 2f out: green and hanging briefly over 1f out: rdn to chse wnr jst ins fnl f: r.o but no imp* **10/1**

3 2 ¼ **Kidmenot (IRE)** 2-8-6 0 LiamJones 8 52+
(J S Moore) *dwlt: pushed along in last trio: wd bnd 2f out: styd on fr over 1f out to take 3rd last 100yds* **14/1**

5 **4** 3 ¼ **Brockholes Flyer (IRE)**[8] 1344 2-8-9 0 JoeFanning 9 43
(Brendan Powell) *chsd ldng pair on outer to 2f out: sn lft bhd: plugged on towards fin* **12/1**

5 shd **Bonnie Wee Lassie** 2-8-9 0 ow1 RichardHughes 3 43
(Richard Hannon) *led: rdn and hdd over 1f out: wknd fnl f* **2/1**[2]

6 1 ½ **Flying Kyte** 2-9-0 0 ow1 IanMongan 1 43
(Pat Phelan) *s.i.s: a in last trio: pushed along 2f out: sn lft bhd: eased briefly ins fnl f* **8/1**[3]

0 **7** 4 ½ **Nomathemba (IRE)**[6] 1399 2-8-6 0 CathyGannon 2 18
(David Evans) *chsd ldrs tl wknd 1/2-way* **16/1**

58.77s (-0.03) **Going Correction** -0.025s/f (Stan) **7** Ran SP% **123.8**
Speed ratings (Par 90): **99,94,90,85,85 82,75**
Tote Swingers 1&2 £3.70, 2&3 £13.60, 1&3 £4.30 CSF £14.51 TOTE £2.80: £1.70, £4.60; EX 18.60 Trifecta £116.00 Pool: £2,199.17 - 14.21 winning tickets..
Owner T Earle, Graham Evans, P D Evans **Bred** John Graham **Trained** Pandy, Monmouths
■ Red Oasis was withdrawn (5/2, vet's advice). Deduct 25p in the £ under R4. New market formed.

FOCUS
Not an obviously strong juvenile maiden, but the form is rated towards the top end of the race averages, the winner impressing.

1513 SUMMER NIGHTS AT LINGFIELD PARK CLAIMING STKS 1m 5f (P)
2:30 (2:30) (Class 6) 4-Y-0+ **£2,045** (£603; £302) **Stalls** Low

Form RPR
1211 **1** **Stand Guard**[24] 1074 9-9-7 87 AdamKirby 2 69+
(John Butler) *hld up in last: pushed along over 3f out: clsd on ldrs and rdn over 1f out: led 150yds out: pushed out: readily* **2/5**[1]

-124 **2** 1 **Right Stuff (FR)**[16] 1201 10-8-13 83 (v[1]) RyanMoore 3 60+
(Gary Moore) *hld up in 3rd: trckd clr ldr over 2f out gng wl: rdn to cl over 1f out: upsides jst ins fnl f: one pce* **9/4**[2]

04-0 **3** 1 **Irons On Fire (USA)**[9] 1325 5-8-10 53 KierenFox 4 55
(Lee Carter) *led: clr after 6f: drvn over 2f out: hdd and one pce last 150yds* **50/1**

31-0 **4** 7 **Dew Reward (IRE)**[25] 1062 5-8-11 61 CathyGannon 1 46
(Bill Turner) *chsd ldr: rdn wl over 4f out: lost 2nd over 2f out: wknd over 1f out* **25/1**[3]

2m 47.21s (1.21) **Going Correction** -0.025s/f (Stan) **4** Ran SP% **108.0**
Speed ratings (Par 101): **95,94,93,89**
CSF £1.54 TOTE £1.30; EX 1.70 Trifecta £5.80 Pool: £2,158.03 - 276.26 winning tickets..Irons On Fire was claimed by Mr C S J Beek for £3,000.
Owner J Butler **Bred** Juddmonte Farms Ltd **Trained** Newmarket, Suffolk

FOCUS
Muddling form, with the third given an easy lead off a modest pace. The race is rated a bit cautiously.

1514 MARTINCOLLINS.COM POLYTRACK H'CAP 1m (P)
3:00 (3:00) (Class 5) (0-70,70) 4-Y-0+ **£2,726** (£805; £402) **Stalls** High

Form RPR
-635 **1** **Kingswinford (IRE)**[13] 1252 7-9-3 **66** (p) GeorgeBaker 6 74
(Alastair Lidderdale) *hld up in midfield: prog and looking for room over 1f out: r.o fnl f to ld last 75yds* **16/1**

000- **2** ½ **Poetic Lord**[106] 8252 4-9-7 **70** RyanMoore 2 77
(Sylvester Kirk) *hld up in last trio: taken to outer and drvn 1f out: r.o wl to take 2nd last stride: too late to chal* **4/1**[2]

0313 **3** shd **Lord Of The Dance (IRE)**[10] 1303 7-9-7 **70** TomEaves 9 77
(Michael Mullineaux) *trckd ldrs: rdn over 1f out: styd on w others fnl f: nt qckn last 75yds* **10/1**

6634 **4** hd **Perfect Mission**[9] 1318 5-9-0 **70** (v) DanielMuscutt(7) 10 77
(Andrew Balding) *led at decent pce: rdn and more than a l clr over 1f out: hdd last 75yds: lost 2 pls post* **10/1**

143- **5** nk **Frozen Over**[160] 7559 5-9-6 **69** RichardHughes 5 75
(Stuart Kittow) *s.i.s: settled in midfield: prog to chse ldrs 3f out: sn rdn: tried to chal w others fnl f: nt qckn last 50yds* **7/2**[1]

406- **6** nk **Cravat**[211] 6171 4-9-7 **70** LiamKeniry 1 75+
(Ed de Giles) *hld up towards rr: nt clr run over 1f out whn gng wl: gap appeared and prog fnl f: styd on same pce only* **5/1**[3]

1135 **7** 1 ½ **Mafi (IRE)**[17] 1181 5-8-13 **67** (t) ThomasBrown(5) 3 69
(Mark Hoad) *rrd s: hld up in last pair: taken to outer and rdn 1f out: kpt on same pce and nvr threatened* **14/1**

160- **8** ¾ **Siouxperhero (IRE)**[163] 7480 4-9-4 **67** MartinDwyer 7 67
(William Muir) *pressed ldrs: drvn on inner over 1f out: fdd and jst pushed along fnl f* **20/1**

6323 **9** 1 **Copperwood**[9] 1334 8-9-7 **70** JoeFanning 8 68
(Mark Johnston) *prom: chsd ldr over 4f out: rdn over 2f out: lost 2nd 1f out: wknd qckly* **6/1**

516U **10** 1 ¼ **The Happy Hammer (IRE)**[18] 1172 7-9-7 **70** SteveDrowne 12 65
(Eugene Stanford) *chsd ldr to over 4f out: styd v prom: rdn over 2f out: wknd qckly jst over 1f out* **20/1**

0554 **11** nk **Titan Triumph**[6] 1386 9-9-5 **68** (t) JimCrowley 11 62
(William Knight) *hld up in last trio: stl there 2f out: one reminder jst over 1f out: nvr remotely involved* **16/1**

1m 36.75s (-1.45) **Going Correction** -0.025s/f (Stan) **11** Ran SP% **119.3**
Speed ratings (Par 103): **106,105,105,105,104 104,103,102,101,100 99**
Tote Swingers 1&2 £17.90, 2&3 £11.00, 1&3 £31.60 CSF £80.24 CT £695.12 TOTE £28.50: £6.50, £1.10, £2.90; EX 175.10 Trifecta £1259.00 Pool: £3,152.45 - 1.87 winning tickets..
Owner C S J Beek **Bred** J Costello **Trained** Lambourn, Berks

FOCUS
A tight handicap run at what seemed a sound race. Pretty straightforward form.

1515 GOLF & RACING AT LINGFIELD MARRIOTT H'CAP 6f (P)
3:35 (3:36) (Class 5) (0-75,75) 3-Y-0 **£2,726** (£805; £402) **Stalls** Low

Form RPR
35-2 **1** **Purcell (IRE)**[8] 1345 3-9-5 **73** JimmyFortune 2 89+
(Andrew Balding) *mde all: pushed clr wl over 1f out: in n.d after: unchal* **4/5**[1]

321- **2** 3 ½ **Almalekiah (IRE)**[167] 7410 3-9-4 **72** RyanMoore 1 75
(J S Moore) *chsd ldng pair: shkn up to go 2nd over 1f out: kpt on but no ch w wnr* **9/2**[3]

043- **3** 2 ¼ **Seven Of Clubs (IRE)**[126] 8016 3-9-7 **75** StevieDonohoe 5 71
(Noel Quinlan) *in tch: outpcd fr 2f out: plugged on to take 3rd ins fnl f* **8/1**

226- **4** ¾ **Extrasolar**[177] 7164 3-9-6 **74** (t) AdamKirby 6 67+
(Amanda Perrett) *t.k.h: hld up in last: taken v wd bnd 2f out: no ch after* **4/1**[2]

200- **5** ¾ **Sadiigah**[251] 4818 3-8-10 **64** TomQueally 3 55
(Clive Brittain) *chsd wnr: rdn whn hung rt bnd 2f out: sn lost 2nd and fdd* **20/1**

600- **6** 1 1/4 **Uncomplicated**[176] 7193 3-9-4 **72** PatCosgrave 4 59
(Jim Boyle) *settled in last pair: shkn up over 2f out: no prog and wl btn over 1f out* **33/1**

1m 12.0s (0.10) **Going Correction** -0.025s/f (Stan) 6 Ran SP% **112.6**
Speed ratings (Par 98): **98,93,90,89,88 86**
Tote Swingers 1&2 £1.50, 2&3 £3.00, 1&3 £2.10 CSF £4.86 TOTE £1.80: £1.10, £2.70; EX 5.20 Trifecta £15.60 Pool: £3,954.69 - 189.76 winning tickets..
Owner Highclere Thoroughbred Racing-JohnPorter **Bred** Rathbarry Stud **Trained** Kingsclere, Hants

FOCUS
This was straightforward for the winner, who made the most of an easy lead. The form is taken at something like face value.

1516 LINGFIELD PARK SUPPORTS YOUNG EPILEPSY H'CAP 6f (P)
4:10 (4:10) (Class 5) (0-70,69) 4-Y-O+ **£2,726** (£805; £402) **Stalls** Low

Form RPR

2226 **1** **Haadeeth**[11] 1286 6-9-6 **68** (t) RichardHughes 1 76
(David Evans) *taken down early: mde all: kicked on wl over 1f out: maintained advantage after: unchal* **9/2**[1]

-652 **2** 1 1/4 **Falasteen (IRE)**[16] 1198 6-9-7 **69** JoeFanning 2 73
(Milton Bradley) *trckd ldng pair: chsd wnr 2f out: rdn and kpt on but no imp* **8/1**

6530 **3** 1 1/2 **Dishy Guru**[10] 1304 4-9-3 **65** (b) TomQueally 4 64+
(Michael Blanshard) *dwlt: hld up in last trio: prog on inner wl over 1f out: drvn and styd on to take 3rd nr fin* **7/1**

000- **4** hd **Aaranyow (IRE)**[121] 8069 5-8-7 **55** oh10 JimmyQuinn 6 54
(Clifford Lines) *chsd ldrs: rdn 2f out: outpcd over 1f out: kpt on to press for 3rd last 100yds* **33/1**

000- **5** hd **Ghostwing**[141] 7827 6-9-1 **68** (vt) NicoleNordblad(5) 8 66
(Luke Dace) *racd wd in midfield: effrt wl over 1f out: styd on to press for 3rd pl nr fin* **7/1**

0-53 **6** nk **Homeward Strut**[10] 1304 4-9-3 **65** (b) IanMongan 3 62
(Laura Mongan) *hld up in midfield on inner: effrt 2f out: drvn to dispute 3rd fnl f: fdd nr fin* **5/1**[2]

6154 **7** 1 **Catalinas Diamond (IRE)**[18] 1173 5-9-5 **67** (t) SteveDrowne 7 61
(Pat Murphy) *a in midfield: pushed along and no prog 2f out: rdn and one pce fnl f* **16/1**

1321 **8** 3/4 **Homeboy (IRE)**[16] 1195 5-9-3 **65** EddieAhern 11 56
(Marcus Tregoning) *hld up: swtchd lft after 100yds and bmpd rival: a in rr: rdn and no prog over 1f out* **6/1**[3]

600 **9** 3/4 **Methaaly (IRE)**[8] 1351 10-9-1 **63** (p) TomEaves 9 52
(Michael Mullineaux) *dwlt: bmpd then stmbld after 100yds: a in last trio: no prog over 1f out* **25/1**

2202 **9** dht **Waterloo Dock**[16] 1195 8-8-9 **57** (v) AndreaAtzeni 5 46
(Mick Quinn) *chsd wnr to 2f out: wknd fnl f: eased last 100yds* **10/1**

3153 **11** 1 **Johnny Splash (IRE)**[16] 1196 4-8-12 **60** (b) JimCrowley 10 46
(Roger Teal) *chsd ldrs tl 2f out: wknd over 1f out* **6/1**[3]

1m 11.28s (-0.62) **Going Correction** -0.025s/f (Stan) 11 Ran SP% **121.3**
Speed ratings (Par 103): **103,101,99,99,98 98,97,96,95,95 93**
Tote Swingers 1&2 £6.30, 2&3 £15.70, 1&3 £6.50 CSF £42.04 CT £212.35 TOTE £4.20: £2.00, £2.80, £2.90; EX 40.20 Trifecta £283.60 Pool: £1,856.76 - 4.90 winning tickets..
Owner Mrs I M Folkes **Bred** Bolton Grange **Trained** Pandy, Monmouths
■ Stewards' Enquiry : Nicole Nordblad one-day ban: careless riding (Apr 26)
Eddie Ahern four-day ban: careless riding (Apr 26,27,29,30)

FOCUS
A modest handicap in which the winner got an easy lead. The runner-up is rated in line with his recent form.

1517 VINES BMW H'CAP 5f (P)
4:45 (4:46) (Class 4) (0-85,82) 4-Y-O+ **£4,690** (£1,395; £697; £348) **Stalls** High

Form RPR

1512 **1** **Picansort**[48] 780 6-9-7 **82** (b) ShaneKelly 4 90
(Peter Crate) *awkward s: hld up in last: plld out wd and prog wl over 1f out: chsd ldr fnl f: edgd lft but led last 75yds: styd on* **4/1**[2]

2411 **2** 3/4 **Billy Red**[16] 1198 9-9-0 **75** (b) JoeFanning 1 80
(J R Jenkins) *led: drvn over 1f out: hdd and one pce last 75yds* **12/1**

2-2 **3** 1 **O'Gorman**[7] 1370 4-9-4 **79** EddieAhern 3 86+
(Gary Brown) *trckd ldng trio gng wl: nt clr run over 1f out: forced way through fnl f: styng on but hld whn no room last 50yds* **6/4**[1]

1334 **4** 1/2 **Triple Dream**[7] 1370 8-9-7 **82** (tp) JimmyQuinn 2 82
(Milton Bradley) *chsd ldr: rdn and stl disputing 2nd 1f out: hld whn n.m.r sn after* **6/1**

044- **5** 1 1/4 **Piazza San Pietro**[205] 6382 7-9-7 **82** RichardHughes 6 77
(Zoe Davison) *stdd s: hld up in last pair: pushed along and wd bnd 2f out: no prog after* **9/2**[3]

3100 **6** 1 3/4 **Bubbly Ballerina**[10] 1308 4-9-2 **77** RyanMoore 5 66
(Alan Bailey) *chsd ldr and racd wdst of ldng trio: rdn and hld whn squeezed out jst ins fnl f: eased* **6/1**

57.75s (-1.05) **Going Correction** -0.025s/f (Stan) 6 Ran SP% **114.4**
Speed ratings (Par 105): **107,105,104,103,101 98**
Tote Swingers 1&2 £2.50, 2&3 £3.20, 1&3 £2.60 CSF £47.17 TOTE £5.10: £1.90, £3.50; EX 28.50 Trifecta £56.10 Pool: £3,506.23 - 46.80 winning tickets..
Owner Peter Crate **Bred** Miss Brooke Sanders **Trained** Newdigate, Surrey
■ Stewards' Enquiry : Shane Kelly two-day ban: careless riding (Apr 26-27)
Eddie Ahern three-day ban: carless riding (May 1-3)

FOCUS
A fair little sprint, rated around the second who set the pace. A small personal best from the winner.

1518 JOIN LINGFIELD PARK OWNERS GROUP TODAY MAIDEN FILLIES' STKS 1m 2f (P)
5:20 (5:21) (Class 5) 3-Y-O+ **£2,726** (£805; £402) **Stalls** Low

Form RPR

0/2- **1** **Opera Box**[232] 5510 5-9-12 0 GeorgeBaker 8 80
(Marcus Tregoning) *mde all: kicked on 2f out: hrd pressed fnl f: hld on wl* **7/1**[3]

2- **2** shd **Regal Silk**[196] 6636 3-8-7 0 RyanMoore 1 76
(Jeremy Noseda) *trckd ldng pair: wnt 2nd 2f out: hrd rdn to chal fnl f: r.o but jst failed* **4/6**[1]

3 **3** 4 1/2 **Rubbamaa**[27] 1035 4-9-12 0 TomQueally 2 71
(Clive Brittain) *hld up in 5th: pushed along over 2f out: wnt 3rd over 1f out but easily outpcd by ldng pair: styd on* **10/1**

05- **4** 4 1/2 **Followeveryrainbow**[210] 6204 3-8-7 0 KieranO'Neill 7 58
(Richard Hannon) *chsd ldng trio: rdn over 2f out: sn outpcd: n.d fr over 1f out* **16/1**

5 1/2 **Tefflah** 3-8-7 0 AndreaAtzeni 4 57+
(Roger Varian) *dwlt: rn green in last: detached 3f out: no prog tl picked up a little fnl f: bttr for experience* **4/1**[2]

4 **6** 2 1/4 **Maughami**[17] 1178 3-8-7 0 JimmyQuinn 9 52
(Marco Botti) *dwlt: quick rcvry and sn chsd wnr: wknd qckly 2f out* **16/1**

7 1/2 **Celtic Legacy**[178] 6-9-12 0 ShaneKelly 5 55
(Michael Murphy) *dwlt: hld up in last pair: prog on outer to chse ldrs over 2f out: wknd qckly wl over 1f out* **100/1**

2m 7.98s (1.38) **Going Correction** -0.025s/f (Stan)
WFA 3 from 4yo+ 19lb 7 Ran SP% **114.3**
Speed ratings (Par 100): **93,92,89,85,85 83,83**
Tote Swingers 1&2 £1.90, 2&3 £3.20, 1&3 £4.10 CSF £12.14 TOTE £7.60: £2.30, £1.20; EX 15.60 Trifecta £87.20 Pool: £4,514.13 - 38.78 winning tickets..
Owner Efemera Stud **Bred** Efemera Stud **Trained** Whitsbury, Hants

FOCUS
A surprise result in this fillies' maiden but, while the odds-on favourite has to be considered a bit disappointing, this is probably still fair enough form, the winner rated in line with last year's Folkestone form. However it was slowly run.
T/Plt: £49.20 to a £1 stake. Pool: £60,457.04 - 895.96 winning tickets T/Qpdt: £21.00 to a £1 stake. Pool: £4,693.76 - 165.35 winning tickets JN

1428 WOLVERHAMPTON (A.W) (L-H)
Friday, April 12

OFFICIAL GOING: Standard
Wind: Light across Weather: Overcast

1519 £32 BONUS AT 32RED.COM MEDIAN AUCTION MAIDEN STKS 5f 216y(P)
5:50 (5:51) (Class 6) 3-5-Y-O **£1,940** (£577; £288; £144) **Stalls** Low

Form RPR

26-6 **1** **Jontleman (IRE)**[16] 1213 3-9-0 70 MartinHarley 6 62+
(Mick Channon) *chsd ldrs: led over 1f out: sn rdn and edgd lft: clr ins fnl f: comf* **11/8**[1]

0000 **2** 3 **Aljosan**[6] 1395 4-9-7 41 (bt) MircoMimmocchi 2 50
(Frank Sheridan) *sn led: rdn and hdd over 1f out: styd on same pce* **50/1**

05- **3** nk **Carrera**[161] 7525 3-9-0 0 SebSanders 7 51
(J W Hills) *hld up: hdwy 2f out: styd on to go 3rd wl ins fnl f: nvr trbld ldrs* **7/2**[3]

4 2 1/4 **Emjayem** 3-9-0 0 SeanLevey 4 44
(Ed McMahon) *broke wl: chsd ldr tl pushed along wl over 1f out: no ex ins fnl f* **3/1**[2]

00- **5** 2 1/2 **Mid Yorkshire Golf**[169] 7361 4-9-2 0 SladeO'Hara(5) 5 34
(Peter Grayson) *s.i.s: hld up: shkn up over 2f out: nvr on terms* **150/1**

525- **6** 2 1/4 **Kwanto**[182] 7014 3-8-9 65 WilliamCarson 3 24
(Malcolm Saunders) *hld up: drvn along and outpcd 1/2-way: n.d* **12/1**

- **7** 10 **Spirit Of Parkes** 3-9-0 0 TedDurcan 1
(Eric Alston) *dwlt: plld hrd and sn prom: rdn and wknd 2f out* **11/2**

1m 14.7s (-0.30) **Going Correction** -0.075s/f (Stan)
WFA 3 from 4yo 12lb 7 Ran SP% **115.0**
Speed ratings (Par 101): **99,95,94,91,88 85,71**
toteswingers 1&2 £6.80, 1&3 £1.40, 2&3 £9.80 CSF £70.29 TOTE £1.80: £1.10, £10.40; EX 53.40 Trifecta £237.30 Pool: £2,284.10 - 7.21 winning tickets..
Owner Paul Corbett **Bred** Old Carhue & Graeng Bloodstock **Trained** West Ilsley, Berks

FOCUS
A weak auction maiden, and straightforward form. The time was slow and the winner didn't need to improve.

1520 BOOK TICKETS AT WOLVERHAMPTON-RACECOURSE.CO.UK H'CAP 1m 5f 194y(P)
6:25 (6:25) (Class 6) (0-60,65) 4-Y-O+ **£1,940** (£577; £288; £144) **Stalls** Low

Form RPR

3231 **1** **Scribe (IRE)**[7] 1369 5-9-7 **65** 6ex (vt) DeclanBates(5) 4 73+
(David Evans) *prom: lost pl 6f out: pushed along over 2f out: hdwy over 1f out: styd on u.p to ld nr fin* **7/2**[1]

0-32 **2** 1/2 **Mr Plod**[27] 1040 8-8-11 **55** RobertTart(5) 12 62
(J R Jenkins) *hld up: hdwy over 5f out: rdn to ld ins fnl f: hdd nr fin* **5/1**[3]

564 **3** 3 1/4 **Bit Windy**[17] 1187 4-8-7 **49** KirstyMilczarek 11 51
(Chris Dwyer) *led: rdn and edgd lft over 1f out: hdd and no ex ins fnl f* **33/1**

3-50 **4** 1 **Rubi Dia**[15] 1217 6-9-0 **53** (vt) TedDurcan 8 54
(Sean Curran) *hld up: hdwy to chse ldr over 9f out: rdn and ev ch over 1f out: no ex ins fnl f* **25/1**

5 **5** 2 **Redoute Star (AUS)**[4] 1434 7-9-7 **60** SebSanders 7 58
(Paul D'Arcy) *prom: rdn over 2f out: wknd ins fnl f* **4/1**[2]

5221 **6** 3/4 **Honest Strike (USA)**[9] 1325 6-9-5 **58** 6ex (b) StephenCraine 6 55
(Daniel Mark Loughnane) *hld up: hdwy over 1f out: sn rdn: styd on same pce fnl f* **7/1**

4233 **7** shd **Petersboden**[18] 1175 4-8-4 **46** NickyMackay 5 43
(Michael Blanshard) *chsd ldrs: rdn over 3f out: hung lft over 1f out: no ex fnl f* **7/1**

2433 **8** 6 **Layla's Boy**[15] 1217 6-9-0 **58** (bt) PhilipPrince(5) 10 47
(Simon West) *mid-div: hdwy over 5f out: rdn over 2f out: wknd fnl f* **12/1**

00-0 **9** 1 3/4 **Highway Warrior**[23] 1090 4-8-7 **49** JohnFahy 3 35
(Sean Curran) *chsd ldr over 4f: remained handy tl rdn over 3f out: wknd over 2f out* **22/1**

2150 **10** 2 **Crimson Monarch (USA)**[15] 1217 9-8-10 **49** (b) WilliamCarson 2 32
(Peter Hiatt) *s.i.s: hld up: rdn over 3f out: sn wknd* **11/1**

0-36 **11** 28 **Fire In Babylon (IRE)**[43] 820 5-8-10 **49** (t) SeanLevey 9
(Noel Quinlan) *hld up: rdn over 3f out: wknd over 2f out: t.o* **12/1**

3m 5.91s (-0.09) **Going Correction** -0.075s/f (Stan)
WFA 4 from 5yo+ 3lb 11 Ran SP% **118.7**
Speed ratings (Par 101): **97,96,94,94,93 92,92,89,88,87 71**
toteswingers 1&2 £3.70, 1&3 £18.80, 2&3 £25.80 CSF £20.66 CT £500.85 TOTE £4.20: £1.80, £2.00, £6.40; EX 21.10 Trifecta £284.70 Pool: £2,174.79 - 5.72 winning tickets..
Owner Shropshire Wolves/John Wilcox **Bred** Lynch Bages Ltd & Samac Ltd **Trained** Pandy, Monmouths

FOCUS
A run-of-the-mill staying handicap run at an uneven pace. Few got involved and the winner more than confirmed his latest 2m effort.

1521 ONLY FOALS & HORSES H'CAP 7f 32y(P)
7:00 (7:00) (Class 5) (0-70,71) 4-Y-O+ **£2,587** (£770; £384; £192) **Stalls** High

Form RPR

2121 **1** **Ace Master**[9] 1334 5-9-5 **71** 6ex (b) MarkCoumbe(3) 3 80
(Roy Bowring) *mde all: rdn over 1f out: styd on gamely* **11/4**[1]

0-63 **2** *nk* **Imaginary World (IRE)**[80] 330 5-8-10 **59**................(p) RobertWinston 7 67
(John Balding) *s.i.s and hmpd s: hld up: hdwy over 1f out: chsd wnr ins fnl f: styd on* **10/1**

-515 **3** *¾* **Yankee Storm**[18] 1172 8-9-5 **68**................................(v) SebSanders 9 74
(Michael Wigham) *s.i.s: hld up: hdwy over 1f out: r.o: nt rch ldrs* **5/1**[3]

0235 **4** *1* **One Way Or Another (AUS)**[11] 1286 10-9-4 **67**..........(t) MartinHarley 1 70
(David Evans) *a.p: swtchd rt over 1f out: styd on* **8/1**

226- **5** *½* **Sarangoo**[208] 6277 5-9-7 **70**... TomMcLaughlin 8 72
(Malcolm Saunders) *hld up: shkn up and r.o ins fnl f: nrst fin* **25/1**

0623 **6** *nk* **Tenbridge**[16] 1193 4-8-8 **57**..(b) WilliamCarson 2 58
(Derek Haydn Jones) *mid-div: hdwy over 2f out: rdn and hmpd 1f out: nt trble ldrs* **12/1**

5-00 **7** *1¼* **Tatting**[11] 1294 4-8-9 **58**... KirstyMilczarek 4 56
(Chris Dwyer) *chsd wnr: rdn over 1f out: no ex ins fnl f* **12/1**

01-2 **8** *½* **Bang Tidy (IRE)**[95] 96 4-8-9 **58**................................(t) BarryMcHugh 6 54
(Brian Ellison) *edgd rt s: hld up: rdn over 1f out: n.d* **3/1**[2]

6512 **9** *¾* **Mataajir (USA)**[10] 1310 5-8-4 **60**............................... AdamMcLean(7) 10 54
(Derek Shaw) *hld up: rdn over 1f out: r.o ins fnl f: nvr on terms* **8/1**

055- **10** *6* **One Of Twins**[259] 4158 5-8-7 **56**...................................... JamesSullivan 5 34
(Michael Easterby) *prom: rdn 1/2-way: wknd over 2f out* **20/1**

0/00 **11** *1¾* **Anrheg**[36] 915 5-8-8 **57** oh9 ow1.......................... RobbieFitzpatrick 11 30
(Dai Burchell) *prom: rdn over 2f out: sn wknd* **66/1**

1m 28.2s (-1.40) **Going Correction** -0.075s/f (Stan) **11** Ran SP% **125.1**
Speed ratings (Par 103): **105,104,103,102,102 101,100,99,98,92 90**
toteswingers 1&2 £6.70, 1&3 £7.90, 2&3 £15.10 CSF £33.00 CT £141.41 TOTE £3.20: £1.70, £2.80, £2.90; EX 37.40 Trifecta £293.50 Pool: £2,138.03 - 5.46 winning tickets..
Owner S R Bowring **Bred** S R Bowring **Trained** Edwinstowe, Notts

FOCUS
A competitive albeit modest 7f handicap. The winner may do a bit better in the short term.

1522 32RED.COM MAIDEN STKS 1m 1f 103y(P)
7:30 (7:31) (Class 5) 3-Y-O+ **£2,587** (£770; £384; £192) **Stalls** Low

Form RPR

32 **1** **Continental Divide (IRE)**[17] 1178 3-8-10 0............... FergusSweeney 1 66+
(Jamie Osborne) *mde all: rdn and hung rt fr over 1f out: styd on* **6/1**[3]

2 **2** *3* **Maakirr (IRE)**[16] 1202 4-9-10 0.........................(t) MarkCoumbe(3) 7 65+
(Roy Bowring) *mid-div: hdwy to chse wnr 4f out: chal over 2f out: rdn and carried rt fr over 1f out tl no ex wl ins fnl f* **9/1**

5 **3** *½* **Peter's Friend**[29] 994 4-9-13 0............................... PaulMulrennan 13 63
(Michael Herrington) *prom: rdn and outpcd over 2f out: styd on fnl f* **33/1**

40 **4** *3½* **Rowlestone Lad**[4] 1423 6-9-13 0.............................. RussKennemore 8 56
(John Flint) *hld up: drvn along over 3f out: styd on fnl f: nvr trbld ldrs* **66/1**

0/0- **5** *1½* **Cherry Tree Hill (IRE)**[204] 6409 5-9-13 30................. RobertWinston 3 53
(Alan Swinbank) *prom: rdn over 2f out: sn outpcd* **40/1**

34- **6** *½* **Bahamamay**[203] 6423 3-8-10 0....................................... TonyHamilton 2 47
(Richard Fahey) *hld up in tch: plld hrd: lost pl 1/2-way: styd on ins fnl f* **9/1**

4 **7** *½* **Hell Hath No Fury**[12] 1274 4-9-8 0............................ AndrewMullen 10 45
(Michael Appleby) *hld up: rdn over 2f out: nvr nrr* **25/1**

2 **8** *½* **Unex Modigliani (IRE)**[11] 1291 4-9-13 0....................... HayleyTurner 5 49
(Michael Bell) *s.i.s: hld up: rdn over 2f out: nvr on terms* **5/2**[2]

60- **9** *nk* **Perfect Pasture**[223] 5825 3-8-10 0.............................. JamesSullivan 12 45
(Michael Easterby) *hld up: n.d* **66/1**

10 *26* **Tetbury (USA)**[215] 4-9-13 84.. DanielTudhope 6
(David O'Meara) *chsd ldrs: rdn over 2f out: sn wknd: t.o* **11/8**[1]

11 *44* **Muttley** 5-9-13 0.. TomMcLaughlin 9
(Mark Brisbourne) *s.s: a in rr: t.o* **66/1**

P **Heirgold** 6-9-13 0.. RichardKingscote 11
(Milton Bradley) *chsd wnr over 5f: sn wknd: t.o whn p.u over 2f out* **100/1**

2m 2.02s (0.32) **Going Correction** -0.075s/f (Stan)
WFA 3 from 4yo+ 17lb **12** Ran SP% **119.7**
Speed ratings (Par 103): **95,92,91,88,87 87,86,86,85,62 23,**
toteswingers 1&2 £8.40, 1&3 £21.80, 2&3 £17.10 CSF £56.73 TOTE £4.70: £2.00, £2.80, £9.90; EX 62.10 Trifecta £1465.20 Pool: £1,998.52 - 1.02 winning tickets..
Owner Michael Buckley **Bred** Limestone & Tara Studs **Trained** Upper Lambourn, Berks
■ Stewards' Enquiry : Fergus Sweeney one-day ban: careless riding (Apr 26)

FOCUS
An interesting maiden but the front pair in the market ran dreadfully. It was slowly run and the form looks weak. It has been rated cautiously.

1523 32RED H'CAP 1m 4f 50y(P)
8:00 (8:00) (Class 4) (0-80,78) 4-Y-O+ **£4,690** (£1,395; £697; £348) **Stalls** Low

Form RPR

3216 **1** **Honest Deal**[24] 1083 5-9-7 **78**.. RobertWinston 3 85
(Alan Swinbank) *mde all: rdn and edgd rt fr over 1f out: styd on* **3/1**[2]

13/5 **2** *nk* **Dr Livingstone (IRE)**[15] 823 8-9-1 **77**......... WilliamTwiston-Davies(5) 2 83
(Charles Egerton) *a.p: pushed along over 2f out: rdn and hung lft fr over 1f out: r.o* **13/2**

212 **3** *1* **Blazing Desert**[16] 1212 9-9-0 **71**.. HayleyTurner 4 76
(William Kinsey) *chsd wnr: rdn over 1f out: styd on* **11/2**[3]

52-1 **4** *½* **Taglietelle**[23] 1089 4-9-5 **77**.. TedDurcan 1 83+
(Andrew Balding) *chsd ldrs: nt clr run and short of room fr over 1f out: nvr able to chal* **2/1**[1]

1615 **5** *2¾* **Mcbirney (USA)**[15] 1218 6-9-5 **76**.. SebSanders 6 76
(Paul D'Arcy) *s.i.s: hld up: hdwy u.p over 1f out: no ex ins fnl f* **8/1**

10-5 **6** *¾* **Saint Thomas (IRE)**[15] 1220 6-8-9 **66**.............................. FrannyNorton 7 64
(John Mackie) *hld up: rdn over 1f out: nvr on terms* **11/1**

5661 **7** *3¾* **Yeomanoftheguard**[21] 1111 4-8-7 **65**.............................. BarryMcHugh 5 57
(Richard Fahey) *prom: rdn over 2f out: wknd over 1f out* **10/1**

2m 38.21s (-2.89) **Going Correction** -0.075s/f (Stan)
WFA 4 from 5yo+ 1lb **7** Ran SP% **115.6**
Speed ratings (Par 105): **106,105,105,104,102 102,99**
toteswingers 1&2 £2.40, 1&3 £4.40, 2&3 £8.20 CSF £23.10 TOTE £3.30: £2.80, £3.30; EX 25.70 Trifecta £185.20 Pool: £1,532.66 - 6.20 winning tickets..
Owner Exors of The Late Guy Reed **Bred** G Reed **Trained** Melsonby, N Yorks
■ Stewards' Enquiry : Robert Winston one-day ban: careless riding (Apr 26)

FOCUS
A fair middle-distance handicap with plenty of in-form participants. The winner enjoyed an easy lead and has to rate a personal best, but it's hard to be confident.

1524 32RED CASINO CLASSIFIED STKS 5f 216y(P)
8:30 (8:30) (Class 5) 3-Y-O **£2,587** (£770; £384; £192) **Stalls** Low

Form RPR

301- **1** **Hartwright**[190] 6822 3-9-0 70... HayleyTurner 1 73
(Michael Bell) *mde all: shkn up over 1f out: rdn out* **1/1**[1]

-221 **2** *1* **Bapak Bangsawan**[26] 1051 3-8-11 70.............................. JulieBurke(3) 2 70
(Kevin Ryan) *sn trcking ldrs: nt clr run over 2f out: rdn and ev ch ins fnl f: kpt on* **12/1**

1442 **3** *nk* **Indian Affair**[4] 1433 3-9-0 69.. RichardKingscote 3 69
(Milton Bradley) *chsd wnr tl rdn over 1f out: styd on* **9/4**[2]

-321 **4** *1½* **Silca's Dream**[15] 1215 3-9-0 70.. MartinHarley 5 64
(Mick Channon) *hld up: rdn over 1f out: nt rch ldrs* **4/1**[3]

-346 **5** *½* **Al Gharrafa**[28] 1014 3-9-0 66..(b[1]) NeilCallan 4 63
(Marco Botti) *prom: rdn over 1f out: sn hung rt: hung lft ins fnl f: no ex* **11/1**

1m 14.77s (-0.23) **Going Correction** -0.075s/f (Stan) **5** Ran SP% **116.8**
Speed ratings (Par 98): **98,96,96,94,93**
CSF £14.72 TOTE £2.30: £1.10, £3.40; EX 14.40 Trifecta £39.80 Pool: £1,308.88 - 24.65 winning tickets..
Owner Mrs L J Garton **Bred** New England Stud And Partners **Trained** Newmarket, Suffolk

FOCUS
A fair classified event restricted to 3yos. The winner was another to make all and confirmed last year's nursery improvement, but it's hard to be positive given the slow time.

1525 32REDPOKER.COM H'CAP 5f 216y(P)
9:00 (9:00) (Class 6) (0-65,65) 4-Y-O+ **£1,940** (£577; £288; £144) **Stalls** Low

Form RPR

0340 **1** **Point North (IRE)**[30] 987 6-9-4 **62**..........................(b[1]) DanielTudhope 2 79
(John Balding) *chsd ldr tl led 2f out: rdn out* **7/2**[2]

-032 **2** *2½* **Jawking**[6] 1397 4-8-13 **57**...(t) MircoMimmocchi 3 66
(Frank Sheridan) *led 4f: sn rdn: no ex fnl f* **10/1**

-400 **3** *½* **Invigilator**[10] 1304 5-8-10 **61**.....................................(t) AdamMcLean(7) 5 68+
(Derek Shaw) *s.i.s: hdwy over 2f out: r.o to go 3rd ins fnl f: nt trble ldrs* **9/1**

5452 **4** *3* **Restless Bay (IRE)**[8] 1351 5-9-4 **62**............................(b) HayleyTurner 8 60
(Conor Dore) *chsd ldrs: rdn over 2f out: styd on same pce fnl f* **13/8**[1]

665 **5** *nk* **George Fenton**[8] 1351 4-9-5 **63**..............................(v) RobbieFitzpatrick 9 60
(Richard Guest) *s.i.s: hdwy over 1f out: styd on same pce fnl f* **14/1**

00-0 **6** *1¾* **Dubai Rythm**[2] 1465 4-8-7 **51** oh1..............................(vt) AndrewMullen 1 42
(Michael Appleby) *chsd ldrs: rdn 1/2-way: wknd and eased fnl f* **40/1**

20-0 **7** *2½* **Consistant**[53] 705 5-9-3 **61**... WilliamCarson 7 44
(Brian Baugh) *s.i.s: rdn over 2f out: nvr nrr* **16/1**

0465 **8** *nk* **Onceaponatime (IRE)**[6] 1396 8-8-2 **51** oh6...............(b) PhilipPrince(5) 6 33
(Michael Squance) *prom: rdn over 2f out: wknd over 1f out* **33/1**

0005 **9** *1¼* **Dickie Le Davoir**[11] 1280 9-9-7 **65**.............................(b) KirstyMilczarek 4 43
(Richard Guest) *s.i.s: a in rr* **25/1**

023- **10** *¾* **Pelmanism**[105] 8269 6-9-6 **64**.......................................(v[1]) BarryMcHugh 12 40
(Brian Ellison) *s.i.s: hld up: drvn along 1/2-way: n.d* **4/1**[3]

1m 13.3s (-1.70) **Going Correction** -0.075s/f (Stan) **10** Ran SP% **121.2**
Speed ratings (Par 101): **108,104,104,100,99 97,93,93,91,90**
toteswingers 1&2 £8.00, 1&3 £8.80, 2&3 £10.40 CSF £39.32 CT £299.42 TOTE £3.90: £2.00, £2.60, £2.80; EX 34.20 Trifecta £335.60 Pool: £1,654.68 - 3.69 winning tickets..
Owner Billy Herring **Bred** Barronstown Stud **Trained** Scrooby, Notts

FOCUS
Another modest sprint handicap in which it once again paid to race up with the pace. The form is taken at face value with the runner-up setting the standard.
T/Plt: £191.00 to a £1 stake. Pool: £79,079.27 - 302.23 winning tickets T/Qpdt: £84.10 to a £1 stake. Pool: £7,970.82 - 70.10 winning tickets CR

1526 - 1533a (Foreign Racing) - See Raceform Interactive

[1232]DONCASTER (L-H)
Saturday, April 13

OFFICIAL GOING: Good (7.9)
Wind: Moderate half against Weather: Cloudy, sunny periods

1534 BET365 MAIDEN STKS 5f
1:50 (1:51) (Class 5) 2-Y-O **£2,911** (£866; £432; £216) **Stalls** High

Form RPR

0 **1** **Peterkin (IRE)**[8] 1360 2-9-5 0.. JoeFanning 5 77+
(Mark Johnston) *qckly away: mde all: pushed clr 2f out: green and wandered whn shkn up ins fnl f: kpt on towards fin* **2/1**[1]

2 *3¾* **Mr Dandy Man (IRE)** 2-9-5 0... LukeMorris 3 64
(Ronald Harris) *trckd ldng pair: chsd wnr bef 1/2-way: rdn along wl over 1f out: sn edgd rt and one pce* **4/1**[2]

6 **3** *¾* **Donny Rover (IRE)**[22] 1108 2-9-5 0................................. KierenFallon 2 61
(Charles Smith) *dwlt and sn pushed along in rr: rdn 1/2-way: hdwy wl over 1f out: kpt on fnl f: nrst fin* **2/1**[1]

4 *1½* **Lucky Visione** 2-9-5 0.. RobertWinston 1 55
(Gay Kelleway) *trckd ldrs: hdwy on inner 1/2-way: rdn wl over 1f out: n.m.r ent fnl f: sn one pce* **11/2**[3]

5 *19* **Bearing Kisses (IRE)** 2-9-0 0.. DuranFentiman 6
(Shaun Harris) *chsd wnr 1f: rdn along bef 1/2-way: outpcd fnl 2f* **28/1**

6 *¾* **Red Tiger Lily** 2-8-7 0... DanielleMooney(7) 4
(Nigel Tinkler) *s.i.s: sn rdn along: green and a bhd* **16/1**

1m 3.5s (3.00) **Going Correction** +0.15s/f (Good) **6** Ran SP% **111.4**
Speed ratings (Par 92): **82,76,74,72,42 40**
toteswingers 1&2 £1.60, 1&3 £1.20, 2&3 £1.60 CSF £10.25 TOTE £2.90: £2.20, £2.50; EX 9.70 Trifecta £23.10 Pool: £2398.26 - 77.74 winning tickets..
Owner Sheikh Hamdan Bin Mohammed Al Maktoum **Bred** Darley **Trained** Middleham Moor, N Yorks

FOCUS
The winning jockey in the first, which was just a modest maiden, thought that the ground was "tacky, with not a lot of good in it", but other riders thought that the ground tallied with the official description. A guessy opening level to the form.

1535 BET365 DONCASTER MILE STKS (LISTED RACE) 1m (R)
2:20 (2:20) (Class 1) 4-Y-O+ **£21,904** (£8,284; £4,140; £2,068) **Stalls** High

Form RPR

333- **1** **Gabrial (IRE)**[206] 6373 4-8-12 108.................................... KierenFallon 4 113+
(Richard Fahey) *trckd ldrs: hdwy wl over 2f out: effrt and nt clr run over 1f out: swtchd rt to outer and rdn ent fnl f: led and hung rt last 100yds: readily* **10/3**[2]

2454 **2** *1¾* **Don't Call Me (IRE)**[42] 872 6-8-12 107......................(t) AdrianNicholls 7 108
(David Nicholls) *trckd ldrs: hdwy on outer 3f out: rdn to chal over 1f out: led briefly jst ins fnl f: sn drvn: hdd and kpt on same pce last 100yds* **8/1**

000- **3** *½* **Stand My Ground (IRE)**[130] 7985 6-8-12 100............[1] DanielTudhope 2 107
(David O'Meara) *hld up in rr: swtchd rt to outer and hdwy wl over 1f out: sn rdn and styd on fnl f: nrst fin* **14/1**

205- **4** *nk* **Sovereign Debt (IRE)**[175] 7238 4-8-12 111 .... JamieSpencer 1 106
(Michael Bell) *trckd ldr: hdwy 3f out: cl up 2f out: rdn over 1f out and ev ch: drvn and edgd rt ent fnl f: kpt on same pce* **11/4**[1]

315- **5** *2* **Highland Knight (IRE)**[189] 6897 6-8-12 115 ....(t) LiamKeniry 3 102
(Andrew Balding) *set stdy pce: pushed along and qcknd over 3f out: rdn 2f out: drvn and hdd ent fnl f: sn wknd* **11/4**[1]

021/ **6** *3 ½* **Chandlery (IRE)**[626] 4424 4-8-12 108 .... RyanMoore 5 94
(Richard Hannon) *t.k.h: chsd ldng pair: rdn along wl over 2f out: wknd over 1f out* **9/2**[3]

1m 40.5s (0.80) **Going Correction** +0.15s/f (Good) **6** Ran SP% **112.4**
Speed ratings (Par 111): **102,100,99,99,97 93**
toteswingers 1&2 £3.20, 1&3 £4.90, 2&3 £7.30 CSF £28.58 TOTE £3.10: £2.40, £2.70; EX 24.00 Trifecta £158.50 Pool: £2014.45 - 9.53 winning tickets..
Owner Dr Marwan Koukash **Bred** B Kennedy **Trained** Musley Bank, N Yorks

FOCUS
A fair Listed event which was previously run at the Lincoln fixture. The pace wasn't strong. The third is perhaps the key to the form.

1536 BET365.COM H'CAP 1m 4f
2:55 (2:55) (Class 3) (0-90,90) 4-Y-0+ **£7,762** (£2,310; £1,154; £577) **Stalls** Low

Form RPR

/30- **1** **Ingleby Spirit**[63] 1605 6-8-7 **83** .... GeorgeChaloner(7) 5 96
(Richard Fahey) *trckd ldrs: hdwy over 3f out: chsd ldr wl over 1f out: rdn to ld appr fnl f: kpt on strly* **16/1**

200- **2** *3 ½* **Beyond Conceit (IRE)**[217] 6033 4-9-1 **85** .... JamieSpencer 12 92
(Andrew Balding) *t.k.h: trckd ldrs: hdwy to ld after 2 1/2f: rdn along over 2f out: hdd appr fnl f: sn drvn and kpt on same pce* **11/2**[1]

650- **3** *1 ¼* **Flashman**[147] 6834 4-8-6 **76** .... PatrickMathers 9 81
(Richard Fahey) *in tch: hdwy to chse ldrs over 3f out: rdn along 2f out: kpt on same pce u.p fnl f* **14/1**

50-6 **4** *¾* **Fennell Bay (IRE)**[20] 1159 4-9-2 **86** .... JoeFanning 10 90
(Mark Johnston) *trckd ldng pair: hdwy to chse ldr 5f out: rdn along over 2f out: drvn over 1f out: kpt on same pce* **11/2**[1]

6-22 **5** *nse* **Northside Prince (IRE)**[18] 1188 7-9-3 **86** .... RobertWinston 8 90
(Alan Swinbank) *in tch: hdwy to chse ldrs over 2f out: sn rdn along and one pce appr fnl f* **15/2**[3]

263- **6** *2 ½* **Eagle Rock (IRE)**[42] 6493 5-8-13 **82** .... MickyFenton 13 82
(Tom Tate) *sn led: hdd after 2 1/2f: chsd ldr: pushed along over 4f out: rdn on inner 3f out: grad wknd* **12/1**

420- **7** *½* **Man Of Plenty**[186] 6964 4-8-11 **81** .... RyanMoore 15 80
(Ed Dunlop) *stdd and swtchd lft s: hld up towards rr: hdwy on outer 3f out: rdn along and edgd lft wl over 1f out: sn no imp* **11/2**[1]

000- **8** *nk* **Rock A Doodle Doo (IRE)**[178] 7175 6-9-4 **87** .... GrahamLee 6 86
(Sally Hall) *hld up in rr: hdwy 3f out: rdn along 2f out: n.d* **14/1**

000- **9** *3 ½* **Merchant Of Dubai**[145] 7792 8-8-7 **76** oh3 .... PJMcDonald 14 69
(Jim Goldie) *hld up: a towards rr* **25/1**

000- **10** *1 ¼* **Franciscan**[204] 6445 5-9-7 **90** .... KierenFallon 2 84
(Luca Cumani) *midfield: hdwy to chse ldrs 3f out: sn rdn along and btn 2f out* **7/1**[2]

00-0 **11** *5* **Rocktherunway (IRE)**[7] 1391 4-8-11 **81** ....(p) TomEaves 11 64
(Michael Dods) *hld up: a towards rr* **33/1**

3453 **12** *hd* **The Lock Master (IRE)**[14] 1237 6-8-8 **77** .... AndrewMullen 3 60
(Michael Appleby) *t.k.h: led early: cl up: rdn along over 4f out: sn wknd* **16/1**

511- **13** *5* **Bowdler's Magic**[246] 5051 6-9-4 **87** .... AdrianNicholls 4 62
(David Nicholls) *hld up: a in rr* **22/1**

16 **14** *93* **Wyborne**[36] 926 4-8-11 **81** .... DaleSwift 1
(Brian Ellison) *midfield: pushed along over 4f out: rdn over 3f out: sn wknd: bhd and eased fnl 2f* **14/1**

2m 34.35s (-0.55) **Going Correction** +0.15s/f (Good)
WFA 4 from 5yo+ 1lb **14** Ran SP% **121.0**
Speed ratings (Par 107): **107,104,103,103,103 101,101,101,98,97 94,94,91,29**
toteswingers 1&2 £25.50, 1&3 £41.80, 2&3 £18.10 CSF £100.08 CT £1291.98 TOTE £25.80: £5.90, £2.20, £4.30; EX 160.10 Trifecta £2916.30 Part won. Pool: £3888.46 - 0.49 winning tickets..
Owner Percy/Green Racing **Bred** Barton Stud And Peter Botham **Trained** Musley Bank, N Yorks

FOCUS
There was a shortage of progressive types in this fair handicap, which was run at a steady initial pace. Nothing made an impact from the rear.

1537 BET365 H'CAP 6f
3:30 (3:31) (Class 2) 4-Y-0+ **£31,505** (£9,430; £4,715; £2,360; £1,175) **Stalls** High

Form RPR

00-1 **1** **Move In Time**[14] 1253 5-8-10 **95** .... DanielTudhope 18 106
(David O'Meara) *in tch: smooth hdwy over 2f out: chal wl over 1f out: rdn to ld ent fnl f: kpt on strly* **7/1**[3]

06-4 **2** *¾* **Shropshire (IRE)**[14] 1232 5-8-6 **96** .... MatthewLawson(5) 17 105
(Charles Hills) *bhd: swtchd to wd outside and gd hdwy over 2f out: rdn to chse ldrs wl over 1f out: chal ent fnl f and ev ch tl drvn and no ex last 50yds* **12/1**

0464 **3** *¾* **Hitchens (IRE)**[14] 1234 8-9-7 **106** .... GrahamGibbons 8 113
(David Barron) *hld up towards rr: gd hdwy over 2f out: rdn to chse ldrs over 1f out: ch ins fnl f: kpt on same pce* **14/1**

126- **4** *1* **Hamza (IRE)**[203] 6466 4-9-2 **101** ....(b) AmyRyan 11 104
(Kevin Ryan) *cl up: led over 3f out: rdn 2f out: drvn and hdd ent fnl f: kpt on same pce* **25/1**

?-12 **5** *shd* **Yeeoow (IRE)**[14] 1245 4-8-5 **90** .... HarryBentley 2 93
(Mrs K Burke) *in tch: hdwy 2f out: rdn to chse ldrs over 1f out: kpt on same pce ins fnl f* **14/1**

-245 **6** *1 ¼* **York Glory (USA)**[28] 1032 5-8-10 **95** ....(b) PhillipMakin 6 94
(Kevin Ryan) *in tch: hdwy to chse ldrs over 2f out: rdn over 1f out: no imp ent fnl f* **16/1**

00-3 **7** *nk* **King Of Jazz (IRE)**[14] 1232 5-7-13 **87** .... DarrenEgan(3) 14 85+
(Michael Bell) *hld up in rr: gd hdwy 2f out: chsd ldrs whn nt clr run and swtchd lft over 1f out: n.m.r and swtchd lft again ins fnl f: kpt on: nrst fin* **11/1**

-53 **8** *nk* **Harrison George (IRE)**[14] 1245 8-7-11 **87** ....(t) NatashaEaton(5) 10 84
(P J O'Gorman) *prom: rdn along and outpcd over 2f out: kpt on u.p fnl f* **25/1**

05-0 **9** *1 ½* **Farlow (IRE)**[14] 1232 5-8-4 **89** .... PatrickMathers 3 81+
(Richard Fahey) *midfield: hdwy on wd outside 2f out: sn rdn and no imp fnl f* **33/1**

265- **10** *2* **Duke Of Firenze**[190] 6835 4-8-7 **92** .... RyanMoore 15 78
(Sir Michael Stoute) *hld up towards rr: hdwy wl over 2f out: in tch and rdn wl over 1f out: sn btn* **13/2**[2]

10-1 **11** *hd* **Prodigality**[12] 1287 5-9-3 **102** .... LukeMorris 13 87
(Ronald Harris) *a towards rr* **11/1**

10-1 **12** *nk* **Jack Dexter**[14] 1234 4-9-10 **109** .... GrahamLee 9 93
(Jim Goldie) *hld up: sme hdwy over 2f out: sn rdn and n.d* **9/2**[1]

42-2 **13** *nk* **Spinatrix**[14] 1232 5-8-2 **94** ....(p) ConnorBeasley(7) 7 77
(Michael Dods) *led: hdd over 3f out: cl up tl rdn along over 2f out and grad wknd* **16/1**

350- **14** *nk* **Fitz Flyer (IRE)**[169] 7366 7-8-2 **87** .... PaulQuinn 16 69
(David Nicholls) *chsd ldrs: rdn along wl over 2f out: sn wknd* **33/1**

00-3 **15** *1* **Our Jonathan**[14] 1234 6-9-1 **105** .... RobertTart(5) 12 84
(Tim Pitt) *a in rr* **12/1**

000- **16** *nse* **Johannes (IRE)**[154] 7690 10-8-8 **93** .... TonyHamilton 4 72
(Richard Fahey) *a towards rr* **33/1**

430- **17** *3 ¾* **Xilerator (IRE)**[180] 7097 6-7-13 **89** .... ShirleyTeasdale(5) 1 56
(David Nicholls) *prom: rdn along wl over 2f out: sn wknd* **40/1**

00-0 **18** *½* **Colonel Mak**[14] 1232 6-8-9 **94** .... AndrewMullen 5 59
(David Barron) *cl up: rdn along 1/2-way: sn wknd* **25/1**

2001 **19** *4* **Thunderball**[14] 1232 7-8-11 **96** ....(p) TomQueally 20 49
(Scott Dixon) *in tch on outer: rdn along bef 1/2-way: sn wknd* **20/1**

020- **20** *18* **Tax Free (IRE)**[168] 7397 11-8-7 **92** .... AdrianNicholls 19
(David Nicholls) *in tch: rdn along wl over 2f out: sn wknd and bhd whn eased fnl f* **40/1**

1m 12.72s (-0.88) **Going Correction** +0.15s/f (Good) **20** Ran SP% **131.2**
Speed ratings (Par 109): **111,110,109,107,107 105,105,105,103,100 100,99,99,98,97 97,92,91,86,62**
toteswingers 1&2 £16.50, 1&3 £31.60, 2&3 £37.00 CSF £82.33 CT £1204.03 TOTE £7.60: £2.20, £2.80, £5.20, £7.60; EX 88.00 Trifecta £1830.50 Pool: £116,516.96 - 47.73 winning tickets..
Owner A Turton, J Blackburn & R Bond **Bred** Bond Thoroughbred Corporation **Trained** Nawton, N Yorks

■ Stewards' Enquiry : Matthew Lawson two-day ban: used whip above permitted level (Apr 27,29)

FOCUS
The prize fund for this event has been considerably boosted and the upper rating limit of 100 removed. It attracted a suitably strong field of sprinters, and this is solid handicap form. The first two were drawn high but the early pace was down the centre. There's every chance the winner can do a bit better still.

1538 STAN FOSTER CELEBRATION H'CAP 1m 2f 60y
4:05 (4:06) (Class 4) (0-85,85) 4-Y-0+ **£5,175** (£1,540; £769; £384) **Stalls** Low

Form RPR

00-1 **1** **Beaumont's Party (IRE)**[7] 1391 6-9-7 **85** .... DaleSwift 2 98+
(Brian Ellison) *trckd ldrs: hdwy 3f out: rdn to ld jst over 1f out: clr ins fnl f: kpt on* **3/1**[1]

65-4 **2** *2 ¾* **Tres Coronas (IRE)**[7] 1391 6-8-12 **76** .... GrahamGibbons 5 83
(David Barron) *in tch: hdwy 3f out: effrt whn sltly hmpd and swtchd rt over 1f out: sn rdn: chsd wnr ins fnl f: no imp* **10/1**

4134 **3** *nk* **Patriotic (IRE)**[14] 1233 5-8-5 **74** ....(p) RobertTart(5) 14 80+
(Chris Dwyer) *hld up in rr: gd hdwy on outer over 3f out: effrt to chse ldrs over 2f out: rdn to chal and ev ch whn hung bdly rt jst ins fnl f: one pce after* **12/1**

11-4 **4** *2 ¼* **Duke Of Clarence (IRE)**[12] 1290 4-9-4 **82** .... RyanMoore 11 84+
(Richard Hannon) *hld up towards rr: hdwy over 3f out: pushed along over 2f out: sn rdn and kpt on u.p fnl f: nrst fin* **17/2**

50-0 **5** *1 ¼* **Satanic Beat (IRE)**[14] 1233 4-9-4 **82** .... PJMcDonald 9 82
(Jedd O'Keeffe) *t.k.h: chsd ldrs: hdwy 3f out: rdn to chal 2f out and ch tl drvn and one pce appr fnl f* **33/1**

00-6 **6** *1 ½* **Kiwi Bay**[14] 1238 8-9-0 **78** .... TomEaves 15 75
(Michael Dods) *sn led: pushed along and jnd 2f out: sn rdn: hdd over 1f out and grad wknd* **50/1**

014- **7** *2 ¾* **Now My Sun**[246] 5044 4-8-11 **75** .... PhillipMakin 16 67
(Mrs K Burke) *stdd s and hld up in rr: hdwy on outer 3f out: rdn over 2f out: sn no imp* **33/1**

1112 **8** *nk* **Dewala**[32] 969 4-9-1 **79** .... AndrewMullen 1 70
(Michael Appleby) *trckd ldr: hdwy 3f out: rdn to chal over 2f out: sn drvn and wknd wl over 1f out* **33/1**

50/1 **9** *¾* **Carazam (IRE)**[38] 906 6-8-7 **71** .... JoeFanning 13 61
(William Jarvis) *hld up towards rr: hdwy on wd outside over 3f out: rdn along over 2f out: n.d* **20/1**

1401 **10** *2 ¼* **Classic Colori (IRE)**[8] 1368 6-9-4 **82** ....(b) DanielTudhope 3 67
(David O'Meara) *in tch: pushed along 4f out: rdn 3f out: sn no imp* **20/1**

36-0 **11** *5* **Maven**[14] 1237 5-9-4 **82** .... DavidAllan 6 58
(Tim Easterby) *midfield on inner: rdn along over 3f out: sn wknd* **25/1**

00-3 **12** *5* **Hillview Boy (IRE)**[14] 1238 9-9-5 **83** .... GrahamLee 10 49
(Jim Goldie) *hld up: a in rr* **12/1**

00 **13** *5* **Albaqaa**[22] 1121 8-8-11 **75** .... KierenFallon 12 32
(P J O'Gorman) *stdd s: hld up in rr: sme hdwy over 3f out: shkn up over 2f out: sn btn* **13/2**[3]

14- **14** *2 ¼* **Muharrer**[181] 7082 4-9-1 **79** .... PaulMulrennan 8 32
(Michael Dods) *hld up: a in rr* **11/2**[2]

000- **15** *17* **Lucky Windmill**[232] 5546 6-8-10 **74** ow1 .... RobertWinston 4
(Alan Swinbank) *a in rr* **14/1**

3510 **16** *3* **Dakota Canyon (IRE)**[30] 995 4-8-9 **73** ....(b) TonyHamilton 7
(Richard Fahey) *chsd ldrs: rdn along on inner 4f out: sn wknd* **28/1**

2m 8.8s (-0.60) **Going Correction** +0.15s/f (Good) **16** Ran SP% **123.0**
Speed ratings (Par 105): **108,105,105,103,102 101,99,99,98,96 92,88,84,82,69 66**
toteswingers 1&2 £9.10, 1&3 £12.10, 2&3 £17.50 CSF £29.72 CT £328.97 TOTE £3.80: £1.20, £2.10, £2.40, £2.00; EX 39.60 Trifecta £455.90 Pool: £2514.93 - 4.13 winning tickets..
Owner Elliott Brothers And Peacock **Bred** Mrs Joan Murphy **Trained** Norton, N Yorks

FOCUS
An ordinary handicap run in a decent time. The winner confirmed Newcastle form with the runner-up.

1539 CASINO AT BET365 MAIDEN STKS 5f
4:40 (4:40) (Class 5) 3-Y-0+ **£2,911** (£866; £432; £216) **Stalls** High

Form RPR

03- **1** **Robot Boy (IRE)**[192] 6787 3-9-1 0 .... JamieSpencer 7 81
(David Barron) *hld up in rr: hdwy 2f out: rdn wl over 1f out: drvn to chal ins fnl f: hrd drvn and kpt on gamely to ld on line* **7/4**[2]

050- **2** *nse* **Lewisham**[183] 7122 3-9-1 96 .... RyanMoore 8 81
(Ralph Beckett) *trckd ldrs: hdwy over 2f out: chal over 1f out: rdn to ld wl ins fnl f: edgd rt: drvn and hdd on line* **1/1**[1]

2- **3** *¾* **Flirtinaskirt**[312] 2783 3-8-10 0 .... SeanLevey 2 73
(Ed McMahon) *trckd ldrs: hdwy on outer 2f out: rdn to chal over 1f out: slt ld ent fnl f: sn drvn: hdd and nt qckn wl ins fnl f* **8/1**[3]

53- **4** *4 ½* **Queen Flush (IRE)**[260] 4545 3-8-10 0............................ AdrianNicholls 9 57+
(David Nicholls) *cl up: led after 1f: jnd and rdn over 1f out: hdd jst ins fnl f: wknd* **8/1**[3]

330- **5** *1* **Deepest Blue**[202] 6511 3-9-1 71.. GrahamLee 5 58
(Declan Carroll) *led 1f: cl up: rdn wl over 1f out: wknd fnl f* **14/1**

0643 **6** *2 ¾* **Island Express (IRE)**[4] 1451 6-9-7 48..........................(t) AnnStokell(5) 3 53
(Ann Stokell) *dwlt and bhd tl sme late hdwy* **100/1**

3 **7** *1 ¾* **Time To Begin (IRE)**[47] 796 3-9-1 62.............................. SebSanders 6 42
(David C Griffiths) *chsd ldrs: rdn over 2f out: sn wknd* **25/1**

05- **8** *1* **Little Eli**[133] 7953 3-8-10 0.. JasonHart(5) 11 38
(Eric Alston) *a towards rr* **50/1**

0/ **9** *shd* **Boblini**[647] 3747 5-9-7 0.. LiamKeniry 4 38
(Mark Usher) *a towards rr* **40/1**

00- **10** *10* **Supercruiser (IRE)**[297] 3286 3-9-1 0................................ TomEaves 10
(Nigel Tinkler) *chsd ldrs: rdn along over 2f out: sn wknd* **50/1**

4405 **11** *13* **Munaawib**[9] 1355 5-9-7 45..(bt) PhilipPrince(5) 1
(Charles Smith) *in tch on outer 2f: sn lost pl and bhd* **100/1**

1m 0.2s (-0.30) **Going Correction** +0.15s/f (Good)
WFA 3 from 5yo+ 11lb **11** Ran SP% **127.4**
Speed ratings (Par 103): **108,107,106,99,97 93,90,89,88,72 52**
toteswingers 1&2 £1.40, 1&3 £2.70, 2&3 £3.00 CSF £4.14 TOTE £3.20: £1.30, £1.10, £1.90; EX 4.90 Trifecta £27.10 Pool: £2,411.55 - 66.52 winning tickets..
Owner Qatar Racing Limited **Bred** Cordulf Stud Ltd **Trained** Maunby, N Yorks

FOCUS
A wide mix of abilities were on show in this sprint maiden. The first three finished clear but the sixth limits things to an extent. The runner-up was some way below his best 2yo form.

1540 BET365.COM FILLIES' H'CAP 6f
5:15 (5:15) (Class 5) (0-75,75) 4-Y-0+ **£2,911** (£866; £432; £216) **Stalls** High

Form RPR

00-0 **1** **School Fees**[40] 880 4-9-7 **75**... RyanMoore 7 83
(Olly Stevens) *in rr: hdwy 2f out: sn rdn: styd on u.p fnl f to ld nr fin* **6/1**[2]

-124 **2** *hd* **Al Freej (IRE)**[7] 1398 4-9-2 **70**.. DaleSwift 4 78
(Brian Ellison) *in rr: hdwy 2f out: rdn wl over 1f out: styd on wl u.p fnl f: ev ch towards fin: jst hld* **7/1**[3]

05-0 **3** *½* **Celtic Sixpence (IRE)**[101] 27 5-9-0 **68**................... MichaelStainton 1 74
(Nick Kent) *dwlt: sn in tch on wd outside: racd alone and hdwy 2f out: rdn over 1f out: styd on u.p fnl f to have ev ch last 50yds: no ex nr line* **20/1**

40-5 **4** *nk* **See Clearly**[12] 1278 4-8-11 **65**...(b) DavidAllan 6 70+
(Tim Easterby) *led: pushed clr wl over 1f out: sn rdn: drvn ins fnl f: wknd and hdd last 30yds* **10/1**

-640 **5** *2 ¼* **Nine Before Ten (IRE)**[9] 1356 5-8-2 **61** oh11.............(t) PhilipPrince(5) 8 59
(Charles Smith) *chsd ldrs: hdwy 2f out: rdn wl over 1f out: edgd lft and one pce ent fnl f* **50/1**

24-2 **6** *nk* **Mata Hari Blue**[11] 1309 7-9-2 **70**..................................(t) AndrewMullen 5 67
(Michael Appleby) *chsd ldrs: rdn along 1/2-way: hdwy to chse ldr over 2f out: sn drvn and one pce ent fnl f* **11/4**[1]

60-1 **7** *2 ¼* **Foreign Rhythm (IRE)**[12] 1278 8-8-2 **61**.............. ShirleyTeasdale(5) 12 51
(Ron Barr) *towards rr: rdn along wl over 2f out: sme late hdwy* **8/1**

31-0 **8** *nk* **Pivotal Prospect**[12] 1278 5-8-13 **67**........................ RoystonFfrench 9 56
(Tracy Waggott) *prom: rdn along 2f out: sn drvn and wknd over 1f out* **20/1**

5342 **9** *2 ½* **Song Of Parkes**[7] 1398 6-8-11 **70**............................ SladeO'Hara(5) 11 51
(Peter Grayson) *chsd ldrs: rdn along wl over 2f out: sn wknd* **6/1**[2]

20-4 **10** *½* **Economic Crisis (IRE)**[12] 1278 4-9-2 **70**......................... PaddyAspell 3 49
(Alan Berry) *chsd ldrs: rdn along wl over 2f out: sn wknd* **25/1**

5322 **11** *¾* **Spark Of Genius**[7] 1386 4-8-12 **71**..........(v) WilliamTwiston-Davies(5) 10 48
(Alan McCabe) *cl up: rdn along over 2f out: sn wknd* **7/1**[3]

00-0 **12** *11* **Quaroma**[12] 1278 8-8-13 **70**... LeeTopliss(3) 13 12
(Paul Midgley) *towards rr: sme hdwy 1/2-way: sn rdn along and wknd* **25/1**

6440 **13** *12* **Medam**[4] 1452 4-8-7 **61** oh14......................................(t) DuranFentiman 14
(Shaun Harris) *dwlt: fly leapt after s: sn outpcd and wl bhd fr 1/2-way* **50/1**

1m 14.32s (0.72) **Going Correction** +0.15s/f (Good) **13** Ran SP% **121.6**
Speed ratings (Par 100): **101,100,100,99,96 96,93,92,89,88 87,73,57**
toteswingers 1&2 £7.50, 1&3 £15.20, 2&3 £18.60 CSF £44.22 CT £800.83 TOTE £6.50: £2.40, £2.80, £4.60; EX 34.30 Trifecta £1546.60 Part won. Pool: £2062.18 - 0.68 winning tickets..
Owner Elias, Mitchell & Newton **Bred** Benjamin Newton And Graycroft Farm **Trained** Chiddingfold, Surrey

FOCUS
A modest fillies' handicap, run at a strong pace. The first two came from the back and they, along with the third, delivered their challenges widest out on the course. There are one or two doubts over the form.

T/Jkpt: Part won. £20,809.70 to a £1 stake. Pool: £29,309.52 - 0.50 winning tickets. T/Plt: £158.70 to a £1 stake. Pool: £134,296.62 - 617.40 winning tickets T/Qpdt: £38.30 to a £1 stake. Pool: £9,849.91 - 190.05 winning tickets JR

1496 KEMPTON (A.W) (R-H)
Saturday, April 13

OFFICIAL GOING: Standard
Wind: medium, behind Weather: dry, overcast, rain after race 4

1541 BETFRED MOBILE SPORTS/BRITISH STALLION STUDS EBF MAIDEN STKS 5f (P)
1:35 (1:36) (Class 4) 2-Y-0 **£4,075** (£1,212; £606; £303) **Stalls** Low

Form RPR

1 **Montaigne** 2-9-5 0.. JimCrowley 5 79
(Ralph Beckett) *chsd ldr: rdn to chal ent fnl f: sustained chal to ld ins fnl f: jst lasted home* **6/1**

2 *hd* **Fig Roll** 2-9-0 0.. RichardHughes 2 73
(Richard Hannon) *racd in last pair: rdn and gd hdwy on inner jst over 1f out: clsng on ldrs whn forced to swtchd lft ins fnl f: str run fnl 100yds: jst hld* **7/2**[3]

3 *1* **Meritocracy (IRE)** 2-9-5 0.. ChrisCatlin 4 75
(Paul Cole) *broke fast and led: rdn and jnd jst over 1f out: hdd ins fnl f: no ex* **22/1**

2 **4** *½* **Vodka Time (IRE)**[22] 1108 2-9-5 0... AdamKirby 1 73
(David Evans) *wl in tch in midfield: rdn and effrt over 1f out: carried sltly lft and styd on same pce ins fnl f* **9/4**[1]

2 **5** *1 ¼* **Skye's The Limit**[14] 1247 2-9-5 0....................................... PaulHanagan 3 68
(Richard Fahey) *t.k.h: hld up wl in tch in midfield: rdn and unable qck over 1f out: btn and eased cl home* **5/2**[2]

6 *¾* **Rough Courte (IRE)** 2-9-0 0.. MartinHarley 6 61
(Mick Channon) *stdd s: bhd: rdn over 1f out: styd on ins fnl f: nvr trbld ldrs* **50/1**

5 **7** *4* **Dovil's Duel (IRE)**[22] 1108 2-9-5 0...................................... AndreaAtzeni 7 51
(Rod Millman) *chsd ldrs on outer: rdn and unable qck over 1f out: wknd fnl f* **8/1**

1m 0.16s (-0.34) **Going Correction** -0.05s/f (Stan) **7** Ran SP% **113.3**
Speed ratings (Par 94): **100,99,98,97,95 94,87**
toteswingers 1&2 £5.10, 2&3 £30.90, 1&3 £30.90 CSF £26.65 TOTE £6.90: £3.60, £1.60; EX 40.10 Trifecta £466.60 Pool: £1575.61 - 2.53 winning tickets..
Owner Mr & Mrs Kevan Watts **Bred** Mr & Mrs Kevan Watts **Trained** Kimpton, Hants

FOCUS
The three with previous experience were eclipsed by three newcomers and the form looks reasonably strong for an early-season maiden.

1542 BETFRED THE HOME OF GOALS GALORE H'CAP 7f (P)
2:05 (2:05) (Class 2) (0-105,102) 4-Y-0+
£12,450 (£3,728; £1,864; £932; £466; £234) **Stalls** Low

Form RPR

1-23 **1** **Grey Mirage**[28] 1036 4-8-8 **89**.......................................(p) MartinHarley 11 103
(Marco Botti) *t.k.h: chsd ldr tl rdn to ld over 1f out: clr ins fnl f: r.o wl* **6/1**[3]

230- **2** *1 ¾* **Glen Moss (IRE)**[274] 4063 4-8-8 **89**.................................. WilliamBuick 1 98
(Charles Hills) *chsd ldrs: rdn and effrt ent fnl 2f: chsd clr wnr 1f out: kpt on but nvr threatened wnr* **11/2**[2]

0-24 **3** *1 ½* **Bravo Echo**[7] 1385 7-9-0 **95**... RobertHavlin 2 100
(Michael Attwater) *led: rdn and hdd over 1f out: 3rd and kpt on same pce ins fnl f* **14/1**

041- **4** *nk* **Head Of Steam (USA)**[131] 7966 6-8-9 **90**............................ PatDobbs 4 94+
(Amanda Perrett) *hld up in midfield: rdn and hdwy over 1f out: styd on u.p ins fnl f* **13/2**

20-4 **5** *½* **Shamaal Nibras (USA)**[14] 1244 4-9-2 **97**.................... RichardHughes 3 100
(Richard Hannon) *in tch in midfield: effrt u.p wl over 1f out: drvn and styd on same pce ins fnl f* **5/1**[1]

300- **6** *1 ½* **Lutine Bell**[184] 7010 6-8-7 **88**... EddieAhern 7 87+
(Mike Murphy) *hld up in rr: swtchd rt and hdwy but stl plenty to do 2f out: styd on ins fnl f: nvr trbld ldrs* **16/1**

350- **7** *¾* **Mabait**[184] 7010 7-8-8 **96**.. AliceHaynes(7) 14 93+
(David Simcock) *stdd and dropped in bhd after s: hld up in rr: hdwy into midfield over 3f out: rdn and clsd on ldrs over 1f out: no imp ins fnl f* **33/1**

0034 **8** *1* **Verse Of Love**[14] 1252 4-8-8 **89**.................................(v[1]) CathyGannon 12 83
(David Evans) *chsd ldrs: drvn and unable qck jst over 2f out: wknd 1f out* **33/1**

2120 **9** *½* **Piscean (USA)**[49] 776 8-9-7 **102**................................... GeorgeBaker 15 95
(Tom Keddy) *stdd and dropped in bhd after s: hld up in rr: rdn and hdwy but stl plenty to do over 1f out: styd on but n.d* **20/1**

-225 **10** *½* **Free Spin (IRE)**[20] 1160 4-8-2 **83**........................ SilvestreDeSousa 6 74
(David Barron) *t.k.h: hld up in midfield: switching out lft over 2f out: drvn and styd on same pce fr over 1f out: nvr trbld ldrs* **11/2**[2]

600- **11** *¾* **Alice's Dancer (IRE)**[189] 6870 4-7-13 **83** oh1............... RaulDaSilva(3) 9 72
(William Muir) *stdd after s: hld up in rr: stl last and rdn over 1f out: styd on but n.d* **50/1**

400- **12** *1 ½* **Mr David (USA)**[163] 7508 6-8-5 **86**................................ HayleyTurner 10 71
(Jamie Osborne) *in tch in midfield: rdn and unable qck over 2f out: wknd wl over 1f out* **33/1**

1160 **13** *1 ½* **Light From Mars**[26] 1061 8-8-5 **86**............................. WilliamCarson 13 67
(Ronald Harris) *in tch in midfield: rdn and unable qck over 2f out: wknd 2f out* **25/1**

40-0 **14** *1 ¾* **Alejandro (IRE)**[14] 1232 4-8-6 **87**..................................... PaulHanagan 8 64
(Richard Fahey) *hld up in rr: rdn and no hdwy over 2f out: n.d* **16/1**

102- **15** *11* **Amadeus Wolfe Tone (IRE)**[163] 7503 4-9-1 **96**............. JamesDoyle 5 43
(Jamie Osborne) *hld up in midfield: rdn and struggling ent fnl 2f: wknd wl over 1f out: wl bhd and eased ins fnl f* **10/1**

1m 23.78s (-2.22) **Going Correction** -0.05s/f (Stan) **15** Ran SP% **122.0**
Speed ratings (Par 109): **110,108,106,105,105 103,102,101,101,100 99,97,96,94,81**
toteswingers 1&2 £6.80, 2&3 £19.30, 1&3 £18.40 CSF £36.19 CT £463.81 TOTE £6.60: £1.90, £2.40, £4.60; EX 36.90 Trifecta £230.20 Pool: £1224.59 - 3.98 winning tickets..
Owner Scuderia Vittadini SRL 1 **Bred** Grundy Bloodstock Srl **Trained** Newmarket, Suffolk

FOCUS
The pace held up well and the first three filled those positions almost throughout. The form is taken at face value around the front-running third.

1543 BETFRED "BONUS KING BINGO" CONDITIONS STKS 1m (P)
2:40 (2:40) (Class 2) 3-Y-0
£12,450 (£3,728; £1,864; £932; £466; £234) **Stalls** Low

Form RPR

236- **1** **One Word More (IRE)**[196] 6671 3-8-12 99..................... WilliamBuick 4 100
(Charles Hills) *chsd ldrs tl wnt 2nd over 3f out: led over 2f out: rdn and edgd lft wl over 1f out: kpt on wl u.p ins fnl f* **9/2**[3]

236- **2** *½* **Glean**[168] 7404 3-8-12 102... RichardHughes 6 99+
(Richard Hannon) *t.k.h early: hld up wl in tch: rdn and qcknd to chal wl over 1f out: drvn fnl f: no ex and btn fnl 50yds* **6/4**[1]

155- **3** *2 ¾* **Georgian Bay (IRE)**[173] 7292 3-8-12 87............................ MartinHarley 1 93
(Mrs K Burke) *sn led: hdd after 1f: chsd ldr tl over 3f out: rdn and ev ch over 1f out: unable qck 1f out: outpcd fnl 150yds* **14/1**

011- **4** *1 ¾* **Code Of Honor**[168] 7399 3-8-12 90.................................. DaneO'Neill 5 89+
(Henry Candy) *in tch: niggled along after 2f: rdn over 3f out: outpcd and btn 2f out: no threat to ldrs but plugged on fnl f* **9/4**[2]

2110 **5** *2 ¾* **Ashamaly**[28] 1033 3-8-12 89.. NeilCallan 3 83
(James Tate) *stdd s: hld up in tch in rr: rdn and outpcd 2f out: n.d after* **16/1**

1 **6** *4* **Thistleandtworoses (USA)**[40] 877 3-8-12 0............. JimmyFortune 2 73
(Andrew Balding) *t.k.h: led after 1f: hdd over 2f out: rdn and no ex 2f out: wknd over 1f out* **11/1**

1m 37.92s (-1.88) **Going Correction** -0.05s/f (Stan) **6** Ran SP% **109.8**
Speed ratings (Par 104): **107,106,103,102,99 95**
toteswingers 1&2 £1.70, 1&3 £8.20, 2&3 £4.70 CSF £11.20 TOTE £5.90: £3.60, £1.10; EX 13.50 Trifecta £80.20 Pool: £1080.10 - 10.09 winning tickets..
Owner Tony Wechsler & Ann Plummer **Bred** John Fielding **Trained** Lambourn, Berks

FOCUS
The two highest rated horses in the field fought this out. The pace was steady and the race a bit muddling as a consequence. The winner is rated back to his French Flat form.

1544 BETFRED SNOWDROP FILLIES' STKS (LISTED RACE) 1m (P)
3:15 (3:16) (Class 1) 4-Y-0+

£20,982 (£7,955; £3,981; £1,983; £995; £499) **Stalls** Low

Form RPR

-140 1 **Lily's Angel (IRE)**[6] 1413 4-9-1 0 .... GaryCarroll 4 110+
(G M Lyons, Ire) *in tch in midfield: hdwy jst over 2f out: rdn to ld over 1f out: clr and r.o wl ins fnl f: eased cl home* **5/2**[1]

11-3 2 *2* **Stirring Ballad**[14] 1244 4-8-12 94 .... JimmyFortune 9 101+
(Andrew Balding) *midfield tl hmpd and lost pl over 6f out: rdn and hdwy ent fnl 2f: chsd clr wnr wl ins fnl f: r.o wl but nvr able to chal: eased cl home* **4/1**[2]

53- 3 *1 ½* **Love Your Looks**[163] 7509 5-8-12 94 .... EddieAhern 3 98
(Mike Murphy) *dwlt: sn rcvrd to r in midfield: hmpd over 5f out: hdwy over 2f out: rdn and pressed ldrs over 1f out: wnt 2nd but outpcd by wnr whn rdr dropped whip 1f out: styd on same pce after* **14/1**

002- 4 *½* **Burke's Rock**[163] 7509 4-8-12 97 .... (p) WilliamBuick 13 97+
(Jeremy Noseda) *hld up towards rr: hmpd after 1f out: n.m.r over 2f out: rdn and hdwy but plenty to do 2f out: styd on wl fnl f: nvr able to chal* **7/1**[3]

1121 5 *3 ½* **Compton Rainbow**[31] 980 4-8-12 77 .... (t) JamesDoyle 2 89
(Hans Adielsson) *taken down early: chsd ldr tl led over 2f out: rdn and hdd over 1f out: wknd ins fnl f* **33/1**

131- 6 *2 ¾* **Whimsical (IRE)**[168] 7408 4-8-12 91 .... RichardHughes 10 82+
(Richard Hannon) *stdd s: hdwy into midfield after 2f out: rdn and clsd to chse ldrs 2f out: no ex over 1f out: wknd fnl f* **10/1**

02-4 7 *1 ¼* **Switcher (IRE)**[14] 1255 4-8-12 95 .... SilvestreDeSousa 11 80
(David O'Meara) *hld up bhd: stl plenty to do but hdwy wl over 1f out: kpt on but n.d* **25/1**

100- 8 *¾* **I'm So Glad**[189] 6870 4-8-12 95 .... MartinHarley 7 78
(Mick Channon) *led tl over 2f out: wknd u.p over 1f out: fdd ins fnl f* **12/1**

211- 9 *2 ¾* **Miss Dashwood**[170] 7356 4-8-12 80 .... HayleyTurner 1 72
(James Fanshawe) *chsd ldrs: rdn and effrt on inner jst over 2f out: btn over 1f out: fdd ins fnl f* **16/1**

101- 10 *2* **Dutch Rose (IRE)**[233] 5520 4-8-12 91 .... RichardKingscote 14 67
(David O'Meara) *in tch in midfield: rdn and outpcd over 2f out: wknd 2f out: bhd fnl f* **16/1**

012- 11 *2 ½* **Four Leaves (IRE)**[148] 7740 4-8-13 83 ow1 .... (p) AdamKirby 6 62
(Marco Botti) *chsd ldrs tl lost pl 2f out: sn rdn: edgd lft and wknd qckly over 1f out* **25/1**

100- 12 *1 ½* **Chilli Green**[252] 4799 6-8-12 88 .... DaneO'Neill 12 58
(Julia Feilden) *t.k.h: hld up in rr: wd and effrt wl over 2f out: no hdwy: bhd and eased wl ins fnl f* **100/1**

505- 13 *1 ¼* **Radio Gaga**[189] 6870 4-8-12 97 .... PaulHanagan 5 55
(Ed McMahon) *in tch in midfield: rdn and lost pl over 3f out: hung rt and bhd over 2f out: bhd and eased wl ins fnl f* **9/1**

5- 14 *3* **Muzhil (IRE)**[373] 1206 4-8-12 0 .... NeilCallan 8 48
(Clive Brittain) *dwlt: sn bustled along and hdwy to r in midfield: rdn and struggling over 3f out: wknd over 2f out: bhd and eased wl ins fnl f* **50/1**

1m 36.18s (-3.62) **Going Correction** -0.05s/f (Stan) **14** Ran SP% **119.9**
Speed ratings (Par 108): **116,114,112,112,108 105,104,103,101,99 96,95,93,90**
toteswingers 1&2 £3.90, 1&3 £5.20, 2&3 £17.40 CSF £10.97 TOTE £3.30: £1.90, £2.20, £4.90; EX 15.00 Trifecta £146.10 Pool: £1719.81 - 8.82 winning tickets..
Owner Mrs Clodagh Mitchell **Bred** N And Mrs N Nugent **Trained** Dunsany, Co. Meath

FOCUS
A big field for this Listed fillies' contest, but only the penalised winner came into the race with a three-figure rating, and class told in the end. She pretty much confirmed her Dubai form, with the third fitting in. It was the pick of the four C&D times.

1545 BETFRED MOBILE LOTTO H'CAP (LONDON MILE QUALIFIER) 1m (P)
3:50 (3:52) (Class 2) (0-105,99) 4-Y-0+

£12,450 (£3,728; £1,864; £932; £466; £234) **Stalls** Low

Form RPR

0000 1 **Es Que Love (IRE)**[42] 868 4-9-7 99 .... SilvestreDeSousa 2 105
(Mark Johnston) *t.k.h: stdd after s: hld up in tch: drvn to chal over 1f out: led 1f out: r.o gamely u.p* **12/1**

302- 2 *hd* **Loving Spirit**[175] 7240 5-9-0 92 .... RobertHavlin 8 98
(James Toller) *stdd and dropped in bhd after s: hld up in rr: clsd on inner wl over 1f out: rdn and pressed ldrs 1f out: ev ch ins fnl f: nt qckning whn hung lft fnl 50yds: rdr dropped rein last strides* **9/2**[2]

-311 3 *1 ½* **Solar Deity (IRE)**[35] 944 4-9-4 96 .... MartinHarley 6 98
(Marco Botti) *chsd ldrs tl wnt 2nd 1/2-way: rdn to ld wl over 1f out: drvn and hdd 1f out: keeping on same pce whn pushed sltly lft wl ins fnl f* **11/8**[1]

2233 4 *hd* **Chapter And Verse (IRE)**[35] 945 7-8-12 90 .... EddieAhern 3 92
(Mike Murphy) *t.k.h: hld up in tch in last pair: chsd ldrs and edging rt ent fnl f: styd on fnl 100yds* **14/1**

400- 5 *¾* **Mister Music**[189] 6875 4-9-6 98 .... RichardHughes 4 99
(Richard Hannon) *chsd ldr tl 1/2-way: styd chsng ldrs: rdn and ev ch over 1f out: styng on same pce and hld whn sltly hmpd wl ins fnl f* **6/1**[3]

4256 6 *1 ½* **George Guru**[28] 1036 6-8-13 94 .... MarkCoumbe(3) 1 91
(Michael Attwater) *t.k.h: hld up wl in tch in midfield: n.m.r over 2f out: drvn and effrt jst over 1f out: styd on same pce* **11/1**

-025 7 *6* **Nazreef**[35] 945 6-9-5 97 .... (vt) JimmyFortune 5 79
(Hughie Morrison) *restless in stalls: led tl hdd and drvn wl over 1f out: wknd 1f out* **10/1**

1m 39.0s (-0.80) **Going Correction** -0.05s/f (Stan) **7** Ran SP% **106.4**
Speed ratings (Par 109): **102,101,100,100,99 97,91**
toteswingers 1&2 £7.30, 2&3 £1.90, 1&3 £4.30 CSF £55.12 CT £101.62 TOTE £15.30: £5.60, £2.90; EX 59.00 Trifecta £607.40 Pool: £1955.19 - 2.41 winning tickets..
Owner Crone Stud Farms Ltd **Bred** Newhall Ltd **Trained** Middleham Moor, N Yorks
■ Stewards' Enquiry : Robert Havlin caution: careless riding.

FOCUS
This was a messy affair and they were well bunched on straightening up. It's hard to be confident about the form.

1546 WATCH US LIVE ON BETFRED TV FILLIES' CONDITIONS STKS 1m (P)
4:25 (4:25) (Class 2) 3-Y-0

£12,450 (£3,728; £1,864; £932; £466; £234) **Stalls** Low

Form RPR

16- 1 **Zurigha (IRE)**[182] 7052 3-8-12 95 .... RichardHughes 6 100+
(Richard Hannon) *in tch: pushed along and clsd to chal ent fnl f: rdn hands and heels and qcknd to ld ins fnl f: r.o strly: comf* **1/1**[1]

311- 2 *1 ¾* **Senafe**[273] 4102 3-8-12 83 .... NeilCallan 5 92
(Marco Botti) *chsd ldr tl led over 2f out: drvn and pressed over 1f out: hdd and outpcd by wnr ins fnl f: kpt on* **10/1**

310- 3 *1* **Concise**[189] 6873 3-8-12 81 .... WilliamBuick 1 90
(Ed Dunlop) *chsd ldrs: rdn to chal over 1f out: no ex jst ins fnl f: styd on same pce fnl 100yds* **4/1**[3]

012- 4 *3 ¾* **Cocktail Queen (IRE)**[171] 7343 3-8-12 102 .... DaneO'Neill 3 81
(David Elsworth) *led tl hdd over 2f out: wknd u.p over 1f out* **10/3**[2]

1 5 *2* **Whispering Lady (IRE)**[42] 864 3-8-12 72 .... JimmyFortune 4 76+
(David Simcock) *awkward leaving stalls: hld up in rr: rdn and no imp over 2f out: plugged on* **20/1**

6- 6 *1 ¾* **Visit Copenhagen (USA)**[157] 7627 3-8-12 0 .... MartinHarley 2 72
(Mrs K Burke) *awkward leaving stalls: t.k.h: hld up in last pair: rdn and no hdwy over 2f out: bhd over 1f out* **33/1**

1m 39.18s (-0.62) **Going Correction** -0.05s/f (Stan) **6** Ran SP% **109.9**
Speed ratings (Par 101): **101,99,98,94,92 90**
toteswingers 1&2 £1.60, 1&3 £1.50, 2&3 £2.90 CSF £11.68 TOTE £1.40: £1.02, £6.90; EX 10.10 Trifecta £23.10 Pool: £3275.97 - 106.36 winning tickets..
Owner Saeed H Altayer **Bred** Sir Nicholas & Lady Nugent **Trained** East Everleigh, Wilts

FOCUS
This was won last year by Laugh Out Loud, who went on to win in Group 2 company. It was the slowest of the four C&D times and the form is a bit shaky. The winner did not need to improve as rated.

1547 BETFRED "THE BONUS KING" QUEEN'S PRIZE (H'CAP) 2m (P)
5:00 (5:00) (Class 2) (0-105,96) 4-Y-0+

£12,450 (£3,728; £1,864; £932; £466; £234) **Stalls** Low

Form RPR

/0-3 1 **Desert Recluse (IRE)**[58] 654 6-8-12 82 .... EddieAhern 2 89
(Pat Eddery) *t.k.h: hmpd and stmbld sn after s: hld up in tch in midfield tl swtchd lft and hdwy to ld 12f out: drvn over 1f out: hdd jst ins fnl f: battled on gamely to ld again last stride* **25/1**

1111 2 *shd* **Buckland (IRE)**[14] 1242 5-9-7 96 .... NicoleNordblad(5) 7 103
(Hans Adielsson) *swtchd rt leaving stalls: led for 1f: grad stdd bk and hld up in midfield: rdn and hdwy 2f out: led jst ins fnl f: kpt on u.p: hdd last stride* **9/2**[3]

1-41 3 *1 ¾* **Lexington Bay (IRE)**[18] 1188 5-8-11 81 .... (p) BarryMcHugh 4 86
(Richard Fahey) *pushed rt and hmpd sn after s: hld up in midfield: rdn and hdwy jst over 2f out: kpt on ins fnl f* **14/1**

50-5 4 *nk* **Quixote**[7] 1382 4-8-12 86 .... (t) SilvestreDeSousa 11 90
(Clive Brittain) *t.k.h: chsd ldrs: rdn ent fnl 2f: styd on same pce u.p ins fnl f* **16/1**

050/ 5 *1* **Theology**[419] 7027 6-9-9 93 .... WilliamBuick 5 96
(Steve Gollings) *stdd s: t.k.h: hld up in rr: hmpd and swtchd rt over 2f out: gd hdwy over 1f out: styd on same pce u.p ins fnl f* **25/1**

3115 6 *½* **Masterful Act (USA)**[16] 1110 6-9-3 87 .... MartinHarley 10 90
(Alan McCabe) *chsd ldrs: rdn over 2f out: unable qck u.p over 1f out: one pce fnl f* **14/1**

151- 7 *2 ½* **Mubaraza (IRE)**[245] 5106 4-9-4 92 .... PaulHanagan 1 92
(Ed Dunlop) *hmpd sn after s: hld up in last quartet: hdwy into midfield and rdn 4f out: edgd rt over 2f out: no imp and one pce fr over 1f out* **5/2**[1]

102- 8 *2 ¾* **Albert Bridge**[160] 7584 5-9-3 87 .... JimCrowley 8 83
(Ralph Beckett) *chsd ldrs: rdn and fnd virtually nil wl over 1f out: sn wknd* **7/2**[2]

0/04 9 *9* **Topolski (IRE)**[44] 823 7-8-9 78 .... (p) HayleyTurner 3 64
(David Arbuthnot) *hld up in tch: rdn and effrt on outer 3f out: sn struggling: wknd 2f out* **25/1**

0-34 10 *1 ¾* **The Tiger**[28] 1037 5-9-7 91 .... RichardHughes 6 74
(Ed Dunlop) *t.k.h: hld up in tch in last trio: rdn and effrt jst over 2f out: drvn and wknd over 1f out* **6/1**

51-1 P **Woolfall Treasure**[78] 224 8-9-6 90 .... (v) GeorgeBaker 9
(Gary Moore) *led after 1f tl 12f out: chsd ldr after tl lost action and eased over 2f out: p.u and dismntd over 1f out* **16/1**

3m 28.1s (-2.00) **Going Correction** -0.05s/f (Stan)
WFA 4 from 5yo+ 4lb **11** Ran SP% **119.9**
Speed ratings (Par 109): **103,102,102,101,101 101,99,98,94,93**
CSF £134.42 CT £1653.31 TOTE £33.90: £6.40, £1.90, £3.50; EX 281.90 Trifecta £2250.60 Pool: £3098.37 - 1.03 winning tickets..
Owner The Hill Top Partnership **Bred** John Foley & Miss Ann Aungier **Trained** Nether Winchendon, Bucks
■ Stewards' Enquiry : Eddie Ahern seven-day ban: used whip above permitted level (May 4-10)
Nicole Nordblad four-day ban: careless riding (Apr 27,29,30,May 1)

FOCUS
The top-weight was rated 9lb below the ceiling for the race, so not as classy a contest as one might have expected. A typically muddling staying hcap round here, and not form to trust too literally.
T/Plt: £164.10 to a £1 stake. Pool: £89,730.84 - 399.06 winning tickets T/Qpdt: £47.60 to a £1 stake. Pool: £5417.50 - 84.20 winning tickets SP

1554 - (Foreign Racing) - See Raceform Interactive

LEOPARDSTOWN (L-H)
Sunday, April 14

OFFICIAL GOING: Soft (good to yielding in places) changing to soft (heavy in places) after race 2 (2:35)

1555a LEOPARDSTOWN 2,000 GUINEAS TRIAL STKS (LISTED RACE) 1m
2:35 (2:36) 3-Y-0 **£21,138** (£6,178; £2,926; £975)

RPR

1 **Fort Knox**[170] 7372 3-9-3 .... JohnnyMurtagh 6 107+
(Thomas Carmody, Ire) *hld up in rr: last 1/2-way: hdwy over 2f out and wnt 4th ent fnl f: styd on wl to ld fnl 100yds: comf* **7/1**

2 *1 ¾* **Dont Bother Me (IRE)**[9] 1378 3-9-3 100 .... MartinHarley 9 102
(Niall Moran, Ire) *attempted to make all: pushed along into st and extended advantage over 1f out: sn strly pressed and hdd fnl 100yds: no ch w wnr: kpt on* **12/1**

3 *½* **High Octane**[221] 5953 3-9-3 88 .... SeamieHeffernan 7 101
(John Joseph Murphy, Ire) *chsd ldrs: hld up: 5th 1/2-way: rdn over 2f out and no imp in 6th ent fnl f: kpt on wl u.p into nvr threatening 3rd fnl 50yds: nrst fin* **16/1**

4 *½* **Dibayani (IRE)**[218] 6060 3-9-3 102 .... DeclanMcDonogh 8 100
(M Halford, Ire) *chsd ldrs: 3rd 1/2-way: rdn over 1 1/2f out and no ex ent fnl f: kpt on same pce and dropped to 4th cl home* **4/1**[3]

5 ¾ **Canary Row (IRE)**[169] 7419 3-9-3 96 ChrisHayes 4 98
(P J Prendergast, Ire) *trckd ldr: cl 2nd 1/2-way: rdn under 2f out and sn no ex: kpt on same pce in 5th towards fin* **16/1**

6 3 ¼ **The United States (IRE)**[287] 3672 3-9-3 (p) JosephO'Brien 3 91
(A P O'Brien, Ire) *chsd ldrs: 4th 1/2-way: rdn fr 2f out and nt qckn u.p ent fnl f and dropped to 6th: sn eased* **7/4**[1]

7 19 **Move To Strike (IRE)**[295] 3368 3-9-3 100 KevinManning 5 47
(J S Bolger, Ire) *chsd ldrs: racd freely: 6th 1/2-way: niggled along appr st: sn no ex in 7th: sn eased* **5/2**[2]

8 10 **Ballyorban (IRE)**[15] 1254 3-9-3 90 ShaneFoley 2 24
(K J Condon, Ire) *hld up: 7th 1/2-way: sn pushed along and no imp bef st: eased fnl f* **16/1**

1m 48.51s (7.31) **Going Correction** +1.05s/f (Soft) 8 Ran SP% **122.8**
Speed ratings: **105,103,102,102,101 98,79,69**
CSF £91.15 TOTE £9.00: £2.30, £2.30, £3.10; DF 87.60.
Owner Andrew Tinkler **Bred** A H Bennett **Trained** the Curragh, Co Kildare

FOCUS
It is hard to know what to make of this lot and this event has had little relevance to the race for which it is a trial in recent years. The form, rated around the fifth, fits the race averages.

1556a HERITAGE STKS (LISTED RACE) 1m
3:05 (3:05) 4-Y-0+ **£21,138** (£6,178; £2,926; £975)

RPR

1 **Declaration Of War (USA)**[191] 6855 4-9-10 112 JosephO'Brien 6 114+
(A P O'Brien, Ire) *cl up: sn settled bhd ldrs: 3rd 1/2-way: prog fr 2f out into cl 2nd: led narrowly ent fnl f and sn qcknd to extend advantage: easily* **6/4**[2]

2 2 ½ **Bold Thady Quill (IRE)**[7] 1413 6-9-8 103 (p) ShaneFoley 3 106
(K J Condon, Ire) *chsd ldrs: 2nd 1/2-way: hdwy to dispute into st: led narrowly 2f out: sn rdn and strly pressed: hdd ent fnl f: sn no ch w wnr: kpt on same pce* **10/1**[3]

3 2 ¾ **Windsor Palace (IRE)**[235] 5490 8-9-10 106 (p) SeamieHeffernan 5 102
(A P O'Brien, Ire) *sn led: pressed into st and hdd 2f out: sn no imp and dropped to 4th over 1f out: kpt on wl u.p towards fin to take mod 3rd fnl 50yds* **16/1**

4 ½ **Sweet Lightning**[21] 1168 8-9-5 112 (t) JohnnyMurtagh 1 96
(Thomas Carmody, Ire) *chsd ldrs: 4th 1/2-way: pushed along and clsd into 3rd 1 1/2f out: sn rdn and no ex ins fnl f: dropped to mod 4th fnl 50yds* **5/6**[1]

5 7 **Paene Magnus (IRE)**[73] 462 4-9-8 97 (tp) KevinManning 2 82
(J S Bolger, Ire) *hld up in tch: 5th 1/2-way: rdn into st and sn no imp: eased fnl f* **16/1**

1m 51.35s (10.15) **Going Correction** +1.05s/f (Soft) 5 Ran SP% **115.4**
Speed ratings: **91,88,85,85,78**
CSF £16.32 TOTE £1.90: £1.02, £2.10; DF 6.40.
Owner Mrs J Magnier & Michael Tabor & Derrick Smith & Jo **Bred** Joseph Allen **Trained** Ballydoyle, Co Tipperary

FOCUS
The very likeable Declaration of War was an easy winner despite concerns about the ground. The form makes a lot of sense.

1557a LEOPARDSTOWN 1,000 GUINEAS TRIAL STKS (GROUP 3) 7f
3:40 (3:40) 3-Y-0 **£31,707** (£9,268; £4,390; £1,463)

RPR

1 **Rawaaq**[182] 7085 3-9-0 99 PatSmullen 7 104+
(D K Weld, Ire) *hld up in tch: 5th 1/2-way: hdwy gng wl on outer to chal over 1f out: sn led and rdn clr nr fin: kpt on wl* **6/1**

2 1 ¼ **What Style (IRE)**[241] 5282 3-9-0 DeclanMcDonogh 9 100
(John M Oxx, Ire) *trckd ldr: 2nd 1/2-way: disp into st: led narrowly over 1 1/2f out: sn strly pressed and hdd 1f out: kpt on same pce towards fin* **4/1**[2]

3 nk **Snow Queen (IRE)**[175] 7278 3-9-0 99 (p) JosephO'Brien 4 99+
(A P O'Brien, Ire) *w.w towards rr: 7th 1/2-way: hdwy fr 2f out into 4th ent fnl f: styd on u.p on outer into nvr nrr 3rd cl home* **9/2**[3]

4 2 **Liberating**[9] 1378 3-9-0 96 ShaneFoley 3 94
(Mrs John Harrington, Ire) *chsd ldrs: 4th 1/2-way: rdn in 3rd on inner 1 1/2f out and sn no imp: dropped to 4th ins fnl f and kpt on same pce towards fin* **8/1**

5 1 ¾ **Bunairgead (IRE)**[161] 7578 3-9-0 90 KevinManning 5 89
(J S Bolger, Ire) *chsd ldrs: 3rd 1/2-way: rdn 2f out and sn no imp: kpt on one pce fnl f* **5/1**

6 1 **Harmonic Note**[11] 1336 3-9-0 92 (b) EmmetMcNamara 8 86
(G M Lyons, Ire) *hld up in tch: 6th 1/2-way: rdn over 2f out and no ex: kpt on one pce ins fnl f* **16/1**

7 nse **Hint Of A Tint (IRE)**[267] 4351 3-9-0 FMBerry 6 86
(David Wachman, Ire) *w.w in rr: last 1/2-way: pushed along into st and no imp over 1f out: kpt on one pce towards fin* **9/4**[1]

8 1 ¾ **Greek Goddess (IRE)**[182] 7085 3-9-0 86 SeamieHeffernan 1 82
(A P O'Brien, Ire) *led: pushed along and jnd into st: hdd over 1 1/2f out: sn wknd* **16/1**

1m 36.84s (8.14) **Going Correction** +1.05s/f (Soft) 8 Ran SP% **122.8**
Speed ratings: **95,93,93,90,88 87,87,85**
CSF £32.61 TOTE £5.80: £1.50, £1.60, £2.20; DF 32.50.
Owner Hamdan Al Maktoum **Bred** Shadwell Estate Company Limited **Trained** The Curragh, Co Kildare

FOCUS
This race lacked a wow factor but the form looks solid and there were no apparent excuses for any of them. The form, rated around the third and sixth, fits the race averages.

1558a P.W. MCGRATH MEMORIAL BALLYSAX STKS (GROUP 3) 1m 2f
4:15 (4:15) 3-Y-0 **£31,707** (£9,268; £4,390; £1,463)

RPR

1 **Battle Of Marengo (IRE)**[196] 6718 3-9-8 111 JosephO'Brien 4 114
(A P O'Brien, Ire) *prom early: sn settled in 4th on outer: clsd appr st to sn chal: led over 1 1/2f out: rdn clr ins fnl f: styd on wl* **8/13**[1]

2 1 ¾ **Sugar Boy (IRE)**[161] 7582 3-9-3 108 ChrisHayes 2 105
(P J Prendergast, Ire) *sn led: t.k.h: hdd after 2f and racd in cl 2nd on outer: brought wd into st and narrow advantage briefly over 2f out: sn hdd and no ex u.p ins fnl f: kpt on same pce* **7/2**[2]

3 1 ½ **Imperial Concorde (IRE)**[161] 7582 3-9-3 90 (b) PatSmullen 6 102
(D K Weld, Ire) *w.w in rr on outer: tk clsr order into st: rdn in 3rd over 1f out and kpt on same pce ins fnl f* **20/1**

4 4 ¾ **Beyond Thankful (IRE)**[161] 7582 3-9-3 98 (p) RoryCleary 3 93
(J S Bolger, Ire) *chsd ldrs in 3rd: hdwy between horses into st: sn rdn and no ex in 4th over 1 1/2f out: one pce fnl f* **16/1**

5 19 **Alpinist**[21] 1169 3-9-3 (t) KevinManning 1 55
(J S Bolger, Ire) *chsd ldrs early: led narrowly on inner after 2f: pushed along bef st and sn hdd: no ex 2f out: sn eased* **4/1**[3]

2m 16.58s (8.38) **Going Correction** +1.05s/f (Soft) 5 Ran SP% **114.8**
Speed ratings: **108,106,105,101,86**
CSF £3.39 TOTE £1.50: £1.02, £1.60; DF 3.40.
Owner Michael Tabor & Derrick Smith & Mrs John Magnier **Bred** Anna Karenina Syndicate **Trained** Ballydoyle, Co Tipperary

FOCUS
Foundry's defection robbed this race of its dark horse but it was a genuine Derby trial and everything was fairly straightforward for the odds-on winner. The form fits the race averages through the runner-up.

1511 LONGCHAMP (R-H)
Sunday, April 14

OFFICIAL GOING: Turf: very soft

1561a PRIX DE LA GROTTE (GROUP 3) (3YO FILLIES) (TURF) 1m
2:40 (12:00) 3-Y-0 **£32,520** (£13,008; £9,756; £6,504; £3,252)

RPR

1 **Kenhope (FR)**[14] 3-9-0 0 ThierryJarnet 3 106
(H-A Pantall, France) *settled in 4th: prog towards outside early in st: chal and led 250yds out: r.o wl u.p* **10/1**[3]

2 1 **Tasaday (USA)**[172] 7343 3-9-0 0 MaximeGuyon 2 104
(A Fabre, France) *sent to ld after 1f: set modest pce: rdn 2f out: r.o: hdd 250yds out: r.o wl u.p: jst hld 2nd on line* **1/1**[1]

3 hd **Topaze Blanche (IRE)**[189] 6909 3-9-0 0 OlivierPeslier 4 104
(C Laffon-Parias, France) *hld up in rr: swtchd to outside early in st: r.o wl ent fnl f: wnt 3rd 50yds out: fin wl: jst missed 2nd* **2/1**[2]

4 hd **Dauphine Russe (FR)**[19] 1191 3-9-0 0 IoritzMendizabal 1 103
(F Doumen, France) *racd in 3rd on ins: u.str hold: rdn 1 1/2f out: r.o wl on ins fnl f: lost 3rd 50yds out: styd on* **11/1**

5 3 ½ **Punta Stella (IRE)**[175] 7285 3-9-0 0 UmbertoRispoli 5 95
(S Kobayashi, France) *reluctant ldr for 1f: racd in 2nd on outside u.str hold: rdn 2f out: no ex: styd on fnl f* **10/1**[3]

1m 50.73s (12.33) 5 Ran SP% **109.8**
WIN (incl. 1 euro stake): 10.20. PLACES: 2.40, 1.30. SF: 25.00.
Owner Guy Pariente **Bred** Guy Pariente **Trained** France

FOCUS
The pace was steady with a sprint finish, and the time was very slow.

1562a PRIX DE FONTAINEBLEAU (GROUP 3) (3YO COLTS) (TURF) 1m
3:15 (12:00) 3-Y-0 **£32,520** (£13,008; £9,756; £6,504; £3,252)

RPR

1 **Gengis (FR)**[143] 7828 3-9-2 0 StephanePasquier 1 111+
(G Doleuze, France) *hld up in rr: swtchd towards outside 2f out: picked up wl u.p ent fnl f: fin strly to take ld 20yds out* **14/1**

2 ½ **Morandi (FR)**[155] 7693 3-9-2 0 ChristopheSoumillon 2 110+
(J-C Rouget, France) *settled in 3rd: sent forward to go 2nd bef st: chal for ld ent fnl f but wandered off st line: rallied and r.o again fnl 50yds: got up for 2nd fnl strides* **8/11**[1]

3 shd **Us Law (IRE)**[164] 7514 3-9-2 0 ThierryJarnet 7 110
(P Bary, France) *sent to ld: stl in front ent fnl f: r.o wl u.p: hdd 20yds out: lost 2nd on line* **5/1**[3]

4 1 ½ **Pilote (IRE)**[14] 3-9-2 0 OlivierPeslier 3 107
(A Fabre, France) *settled in 4th: rdn 1 1/2f out: no pce to threaten ldrs: styd on fnl f* **7/2**[2]

5 5 **Princedargent (FR)**[19] 1192 3-9-2 0 FabriceVeron 4 95+
(H-A Pantall, France) *racd in 3rd u.str hold: relegated to 4th ent st: rdn but no ex ent fnl 1 1/2f: fdd* **20/1**

6 8 **Courcy (FR)**[63] 606 3-9-2 0 GregoryBenoist 6 77
(J-C Rouget, France) *racd in 2nd on ins rail on settling: rdn early in st and sn lost pl: no ex: sn btn* **12/1**

1m 44.08s (5.68) 6 Ran SP% **115.9**
WIN (incl. 1 euro stake): 12.30. PLACES: 3.10, 1.20. SF: 27.50.
Owner Mlle Claire Stephenson **Bred** Edy S R L **Trained** France

FOCUS
The pace was steady and the form, rated around the front-running third, fits the race averages.

CAPANNELLE (R-H)
Sunday, April 14

OFFICIAL GOING: Turf: good

1563a PREMIO CARLO CHIESA (GROUP 3) (3YO+ FILLIES & MARES) (TURF) 6f
3:50 (12:00) 3-Y-0+ **£28,455** (£12,520; £6,829; £3,414)

RPR

1 **Bettolle (ITY)**[44] 4-9-3 0 MColombi 4 100
(Jessica Lari, Italy) *midfield early: trckd ldrs fr 1/2-way: rdn and hdwy to chal ldr appr fnl f: led 150yds out: sn clr: eased cl home* **154/10**

2 1 ¾ **Clorofilla (IRE)** 3-8-5 0 LManiezzi 6 91
(Marco Gasparini, Italy) *front rnk on inner: rdn and hdd over 2f out: hrd rdn in 4th and outpcd by ldrs appr fnl f: styd on wl u.p last 150yds: tk 2nd cl home but nt rch wnr* **99/10**

3 nk **Onlyyouknowme (IRE)**[40] 961 5-9-3 0 MickaelBarzalona 10 93
(E Botti, Italy) *front rnk on outside: rdn and wnt on over 2f out: u.p and chal by wnr appr fnl f: hdd 150yds out: fdd u.p fnl 50yds: lost 2nd cl home and jst hld 3rd* **19/5**[3]

4 nk **Alta Quota (IRE)**[498] 4-9-3 0 (b) SGuerrieri 1 92+
(G Vizzini, Italy) *dwlt and rdn to go early pce on inner: towards rr: one fr last and hrd rdn 1 1/2f out: styd on wl ins fnl f: jst missed 3rd* **36/1**

5 2 **Noble Hachy**[44] 4-9-5 0 AndreaMezzatesta 8 88
(L Riccardi, Italy) *front rnk between horses: hdd over 2f out: 3rd and rdn appr fnl f: nt qckn: wknd last 100yds* **7/10**[1]

6 shd **Maglietta Fina (IRE)**[28] 4-9-3 0 GMarcelli 9 86
(D Ducci, Italy) *dwlt and wnt lft s: sn towards rr on outer: prog into midfield 1/2-way: sn chsng ldrs: 5th and hrd rdn 2f out: nt qckn: plugged on at same pce ins fnl f* **60/1**

7 hd **Killachy Loose**[162] 7565 4-9-3 0 DarioVargiu 7 85
(B Grizzetti, Italy) *midfield and free early: effrt to chse ldng gp 1/2-way: rdn and nt qckn under 2f out: one pce fnl f* **7/2**[2]

8 8 **Belly To Belly (IRE)**[225] 4-9-3 0 FabioBranca 3 60
(S Botti, Italy) *towards rr: sme prog u.p to chse ldng gp 2 1/2f out: rdn and no further imp under 2f out: eased whn btn fnl f* **116/10**

9 nk **Chiara Wells (IRE)**[154] 7697 4-9-3 0 SSulas 5 59
(A Floris, Italy) *chsd ldng gp: outpcd and hrd rdn 1/2-way: eased whn btn fnl f* **17/2**

10 2 **Belliche**[63] 5-9-3 0 MEsposito 2 52
(Marco Gasparini, Italy) *a among bkmarkers: last fr 1/2-way: eased ins fnl f* **43/1**

1m 8.24s (-2.06)
WFA 3 from 4yo+ 12lb **10** Ran SP% **142.2**
WIN (incl. 1 euro stake): 16.40. PLACES: 4.00, 3.10, 2.60. DF: 152.50.
Owner Scuderia Topeeka **Bred** Dioscuri Di Alduino Et Al **Trained** Italy

DUSSELDORF (R-H)

Sunday, April 14

OFFICIAL GOING: Turf: soft

1564a WETTENLEIP FRUHJAHRSMEILE (GROUP 3) (4YO+) (TURF) 1m

4:05 (4:10) 4-Y-0+

£26,016 (£8,943; £4,471; £2,439; £1,626; £1,219)

RPR

1 **Global Thrill**[245] 4-8-11 0 ADeVries 8 107
(J Hirschberger, Germany) *midfield on outer: rdn on turn into st: r.o to chal over 1f out: led jst ins fnl f: drvn out* **49/10**

2 1 **Neatico (GER)**[210] 6291 6-8-11 0 KClijmans 6 105
(P Schiergen, Germany) *hld up towards rr on inner: rdn on turn into st: hdwy fr 2f out: nt clr run over 1f out: swtchd lft and r.o to go 2nd ins fnl f: nt rch wnr* **7/1**

3 3 1/2 **Point Blank (GER)**[147] 7784 5-8-11 0 (p) StefanieHofer 5 97
(Mario Hofer, Germany) *trckd ldr on outer: rdn to chal on turn into st: ev ch ent fnl f: sn outpcd by front pair: kpt on: wnt 3rd post* **91/10**

4 shd **Empire Storm (GER)**[231] 5651 6-9-2 0 EPedroza 7 101
(A Wohler, Germany) *led: rdn and strly pressed on turn into st: hdd jst ins fnl f: no ex and fdd: dropped to 4th post* **47/10**[3]

5 4 **Sommerabend**[164] 7515 6-8-11 0 AndreaAtzeni 4 87
(U Stoltefuss, Germany) *prom: rdn on turn into st: outpcd and btn ent fnl f: fdd* **42/10**[2]

6 7 **Konig Concorde (GER)**[162] 7565 8-9-0 0 WPanov 11 74
(C Sprengel, Germany) *hld up in rr on outer: rdn on turn into st: sn outpcd and btn: nvr a factor* **161/10**

7 2 **Amarillo (IRE)**[196] 6727 4-9-0 0 FilipMinarik 2 70
(P Schiergen, Germany) *midfield on inner: rdn on turn into st: no ex and btn over 1f out: fdd* **7/5**[1]

8 24 **Primera Vista**[120] 7-8-11 0 (b) AndreBest 3 11
(Mario Hofer, Germany) *prom on inner: rdn on turn into st: sn outpcd and btn: fdd: eased and t.o* **163/10**

9 21 **Hard Work (IRE)** 4-8-11 0 (b) SMazur 1
(Adam Wyrzyk, Poland) *midfield on inner early: lost pl rapidly over 5f out: sn detached in last: nvr a factor after: t.o* **25/1**

1m 41.0s (-0.16) **9** Ran SP% **133.3**
WIN (incl. 10 euro stake): 59. PLACES: 19, 22, 37. SF: 384.
Owner Gestut Auenquelle **Bred** Gestut Auenquelle **Trained** Germany

1388 NEWCASTLE (L-H)

Monday, April 15

OFFICIAL GOING: Good (6.8)
Wind: Fairly strong, against Weather: Cloudy

1565 BRITISH STALLION STUDS EBF MAIDEN STKS 5f

2:30 (2:30) (Class 5) 2-Y-0 **£2,911** (£866; £432; £216) **Stalls** Centre

Form RPR

1 **Pigeon Pie** 2-9-0 0 SilvestreDeSousa 5 70+
(Mark Johnston) *cl up: rdn to ld 2f out: edgd lft ins fnl f: kpt on wl towards fin* **7/2**[3]

2 nk **Princess Pheeny (IRE)** 2-9-0 0 TonyHamilton 7 69
(Richard Fahey) *led stands' rail to 2f out: rallied u.p fnl f: hld cl home* **5/2**[1]

3 1 1/4 **Lexington Rose** 2-9-0 0 RoystonFfrench 4 64+
(Bryan Smart) *cl up: ev ch over 2f out to over 1f out: kpt on same pce ins fnl f* **9/2**

4 hd **Robynelle** 2-9-0 0 GrahamLee 2 64+
(Keith Dalgleish) *cl up on outside: ev ch 1/2-way: nt qckn fnl f* **11/4**[2]

5 20 **Hebridean Princess (IRE)** 2-9-0 0 MickyFenton 3
(Paul Midgley) *s.i.s: sn rdn in rr: no ch fr 1/2-way* **9/1**

6 nse **Spring Willow (IRE)** 2-9-5 0 GrahamGibbons 1
(Eric Alston) *wnt lft s: rn green and sn outpcd: no ch fr 1/2-way* **20/1**

7 9 **Geniusinrhyme** 2-9-2 0 DeclanCannon(3) 6
(Nigel Tinkler) *cl up: drvn along 1/2-way: sn wknd* **33/1**

1m 5.27s (4.17) **Going Correction** +0.10s/f (Good) **7** Ran SP% **113.3**
Speed ratings (Par 92): **70,69,67,67,35 35,20**
toteswingers 1&2 £2.30, 2&3 £2.60, 1&3 £3.10 CSF £12.46 TOTE £3.50: £1.50, £2.00; EX 7.30 Trifecta £19.10 Pool: £2163.16 - 84.81 winning units..
Owner Hot To Trot Racing Club & Nicholas Jones **Bred** Coln Valley Stud **Trained** Middleham Moor, N Yorks

FOCUS
An informative juvenile maiden, run in blustery conditions, that was dominated by the fillies. The form looks just no more than fair at this stage, and the first two could have benefited from a rail to race against.

1566 FURNITURE CLINIC H'CAP 5f

3:00 (3:01) (Class 6) (0-65,63) 3-Y-0 **£1,940** (£577; £288; £144) **Stalls** Centre

Form RPR

5432 1 **Jofranka**[5] 1458 3-8-13 55 GrahamGibbons 1 64+
(David Barron) *pressed ldr: rdn 1/2-way: led over 1f out: edgd lft ins fnl f: pushed out* **3/1**[1]

432- 2 1 3/4 **Cracking Choice (IRE)**[171] 7379 3-9-0 63 (p) ConnorBeasley(7) 7 64
(Michael Dods) *slt ld tl rdn and hdd over 1f out: kpt on ins fnl f: nt rch wnr* **7/2**[2]

600- 3 nk **Salvatore Fury (IRE)**[156] 7687 3-8-12 54 SilvestreDeSousa 6 54+
(Keith Dalgleish) *hld up in tch: effrt and hdwy over 1f out: one pce ins fnl f* **13/2**

30-5 4 3 1/4 **Someone's Darling**[15] 1275 3-9-3 59 GrahamLee 5 47
(Jim Goldie) *hld up in tch: rdn 1/2-way: hdwy over 1f out: nvr able to chal* **7/1**

40-0 5 2 **Complicator**[24] 1114 3-9-0 56 PhillipMakin 8 37
(Kevin Ryan) *cl up: drvn 1/2-way: wknd over 1f out* **7/1**

33-1 6 2 1/4 **Edith Anne**[14] 1284 3-9-7 63 MickyFenton 2 36
(Paul Midgley) *towards rr and sn pushed along: sme hdwy over 1f out: nvr rchd ldrs* **11/2**[3]

5-62 7 2 3/4 **Megaleka**[14] 1284 3-8-12 54 PaulMulrennan 4 17
(Chris Fairhurst) *in tch: drvn along and outpcd after 2f: nvr on terms* **14/1**

4-05 8 nk **We Are City**[81] 357 3-9-2 58 RoystonFfrench 9 20
(Bryan Smart) *cl up tl rdn and wknd fr 2f out* **25/1**

060- 9 6 **Royal Jenray**[164] 7526 3-8-7 49 oh2 PJMcDonald 3
(Jedd O'Keeffe) *bhd and sn struggling: nvr on terms* **66/1**

1m 3.23s (2.13) **Going Correction** +0.10s/f (Good) **9** Ran SP% **112.9**
Speed ratings (Par 96): **86,83,82,77,74 70,66,65,56**
toteswingers 1&2 £2.40, 2&3 £4.70, 1&3 £4.80 CSF £13.16 CT £61.49 TOTE £2.90: £1.60, £1.40, £2.30; EX 8.90 Trifecta £74.40 Pool: £2380.54 - 23.96 winning units..
Owner M Dalby **Bred** Harrowgate Bloodstock Ltd **Trained** Maunby, N Yorks

FOCUS
A modest sprint handicap but a most taking success. The runner-up sets the level to previous C&D form.

1567 S.V. RUTTER LTD H'CAP (DIV I) 1m 2f 32y

3:30 (3:30) (Class 5) (0-70,70) 4-Y-0+ **£2,587** (£770; £384; £192) **Stalls** Low

Form RPR

4-02 1 **Carragold**[6] 1448 7-9-7 70 SilvestreDeSousa 7 78
(Mel Brittain) *prom: rdn over 3f out: hdwy to ld ins fnl f: rdn out* **3/1**[2]

3-66 2 3/4 **Flying Applause**[76] 435 8-9-3 69 (b) MarkCoumbe(3) 1 75
(Roy Bowring) *t.k.h: led after 1f: sn clr: rdn over 2f out: hdd ins fnl f: rallied: hld towards fin* **12/1**

04-2 3 1/2 **Titus Bolt (IRE)**[15] 1270 4-8-9 58 AndreaAtzeni 10 63
(Jim Goldie) *hld up: rdn over 2f out: hdwy over 1f out: kpt on fnl f: nvr able to chal* **9/2**[3]

0/54 4 shd **Arc Light (IRE)**[14] 1282 5-8-11 65 DarylByrne(5) 8 70
(Tim Easterby) *plld hrd towards rr: rdn and hdwy 2f out: kpt on same pce ins fnl f* **9/1**

500- 5 7 **Ma Kellys (IRE)**[73] 4397 4-8-7 56 oh3 PJMcDonald 2 47
(Micky Hammond) *in tch: rdn over 2f out: rallied: outpcd appr fnl f* **50/1**

60-2 6 2 3/4 **Waltz Darling (IRE)**[24] 1111 5-9-7 70 GrahamLee 9 55
(Keith Reveley) *hld up: rdn over 2f out: kpt on fnl f: nvr able to chal* **11/4**[1]

400- 7 1 1/2 **Running Reef (IRE)**[254] 4830 4-8-11 60 RoystonFfrench 3 42
(Tracy Waggott) *t.k.h: led 1f: chsd clr ldr: rdn over 2f out: wknd over 1f out* **40/1**

35-3 8 4 1/2 **Nadema Rose (IRE)**[28] 1068 4-9-0 68 GarryWhillans(5) 5 41
(Keith Dalgleish) *in tch: drvn and outpcd over 2f out: sn btn* **8/1**

050- 9 4 1/2 **Euston Square**[167] 7455 7-9-4 67 PaulMulrennan 4 31
(Alistair Whillans) *hld up on ins: struggling over 2f out: sn btn* **20/1**

5/64 10 7 **Nonaynever**[27] 1082 5-8-9 58 JamesSullivan 11
(Ruth Carr) *bhd: struggling over 3f out: nvr on terms* **25/1**

300- 11 4 1/2 **District Attorney (IRE)**[170] 7417 4-8-12 61 KellyHarrison 6
(Chris Fairhurst) *hld up in tch: pushed along over 2f out: sn btn* **25/1**

2m 14.67s (2.77) **Going Correction** +0.175s/f (Good) **11** Ran SP% **115.5**
Speed ratings (Par 103): **95,94,94,93,88 86,84,81,77,72 68**
toteswingers 1&2 £8.00, 2&3 £10.30, 1&3 £3.00 CSF £34.78 CT £160.59 TOTE £3.40: £1.50, £3.60, £1.20; EX 37.70 Trifecta £216.40 Pool: £2381.66 - 8.25 winning units..
Owner Mel Brittain **Bred** Darley **Trained** Warthill, N Yorks

FOCUS
A modest middle-distance handicap but it served up a thrilling finish. The third and fourth help set the level.

1568 S.V. RUTTER LTD H'CAP (DIV II) 1m 2f 32y

4:00 (4:00) (Class 5) (0-70,70) 4-Y-0+ **£2,587** (£770; £384; £192) **Stalls** Low

Form RPR

-345 1 **Going Grey (IRE)**[32] 996 4-8-8 57 oh1 ow1 TonyHamilton 5 64
(Richard Fahey) *mde virtually all: rdn whn hrd pressed over 2f out: kpt on gamely fnl f* **16/1**

000- 2 1/2 **King Kurt (IRE)**[209] 6340 5-9-7 70 [1] PhillipMakin 10 76
(Kevin Ryan) *in tch on outside: hdwy and ev ch over 2f out: tk 2nd ins fnl f: kpt on: hld nr fin* **12/1**

040- 3 hd **Seldom (IRE)**[197] 6711 7-8-8 57 SilvestreDeSousa 2 63
(Mel Brittain) *chsd wnr: ev ch and rdn over 2f out: r.o fnl f: hld towards fin* **9/1**[3]

6-05 4 nk **Gran Maestro (USA)**[6] 1448 4-9-7 70 (b) JamesSullivan 9 75
(Ruth Carr) *hld up on outside: stdy hdwy over 2f out: sn rdn: kpt on fnl f: hld towards fin* **9/1**[3]

0-23 5 1 1/4 **Regal Swain (IRE)**[6] 1448 5-9-6 69 PaddyAspell 1 72
(Alan Swinbank) *t.k.h: prom: pushed along and sltly outpcd over 2f out: kpt on ins fnl f* **6/4**[1]

340- 6 10 **Fine Altomis**[187] 6988 4-9-3 66 PaulMulrennan 3 49
(Michael Dods) *midfield: rdn and outpcd over 2f out: n.d after* **3/1**[2]

/24- 7 1 3/4 **Tropenfeuer (FR)**[252] 4869 6-8-4 56 oh6 JulieBurke(3) 11 35
(James Moffatt) *bhd: rdn over 4f out: sme late hdwy: nvr on terms* **66/1**

35-6 8 nse **Basingstoke (IRE)**[67] 548 4-9-4 67 GrahamGibbons 8 46
(Keith Dalgleish) *hld up in tch: drvn and outpcd wl over 2f out: sn btn* **11/1**

6440 9 5 **Follow The Flag (IRE)**[16] 1239 9-8-10 59 (v) FrederikTylicki 7 28
(Alan McCabe) *hld up: drvn and outpcd over 3f out: nvr on terms* **18/1**

00-0 10 6 **Turned To Gold (IRE)**[28] 1059 4-8-12 61 RussKennemore 6 18
(Robert Johnson) *plld hrd in rr: struggling over 4f out: sn btn* **50/1**

2m 14.84s (2.94) **Going Correction** +0.175s/f (Good) **10** Ran SP% **115.6**
Speed ratings (Par 103): **95,94,94,94,93 85,83,83,79,74**
toteswingers 1&2 £18.70, 2&3 £16.40, 1&3 £16.70 CSF £191.51 CT £1835.67 TOTE £14.20: £3.20, £3.70, £2.70; EX 274.30 Trifecta £881.10 Pool: £2783.86 - 2.36 winning units..
Owner Mrs H Steel **Bred** Piercetown Stud **Trained** Musley Bank, N Yorks

FOCUS
This didn't look as strong as the first division and the form should be treated with a degree of caution. The form is rated around the first four.

1569 J G PAXTON & SONS ALNWICK H'CAP 1m 3y(S)
4:30 (4:31) (Class 5) (0-75,73) 4-Y-0+ £2,587 (£770; £384; £192) Stalls Centre

Form RPR
45-4 1 **The Osteopath (IRE)**[24] 1115 10-9-6 **72**.......................... PJMcDonald 5 83+
(John Davies) *hld up: rdn and hdwy over 1f out: styd on wl ins fnl f: led last stride* **13/2**[3]
420- 2 *nse* **Le Chat D'Or**[191] 6884 5-9-7 **73**..................................(t) PaulMulrennan 11 83
(Michael Dods) *hld up in tch: stdy hdwy over 2f out: sn rdn: led ins fnl f: hdd last stride* **5/1**[2]
300- 3 *½* **Sound Advice**[224] 5888 4-9-6 **72**.................................. GrahamGibbons 2 81
(Keith Dalgleish) *led: rdn 2f out: edgd lft and hdd ins fnl f: kpt on same pce* **20/1**
00-6 4 *1 ½* **Border Revia (IRE)**[14] 1290 4-9-6 **72**............................ TonyHamilton 4 77
(Richard Fahey) *hld up in tch: effrt over 2f out: edgd rt ins fnl f: kpt on same pce* **14/1**
13-0 5 *2* **Day Of The Eagle (IRE)**[24] 1113 7-9-5 **71**........................ GrahamLee 8 72
(Michael Easterby) *hld up: shkn up and hdwy 2f out: no imp fnl f* **12/1**
000- 6 *2* **King Pin**[194] 6785 8-8-12 **64**.. RoystonFfrench 6 60
(Tracy Waggott) *hld up in midfield: stdy hdwy over 2f out: effrt over 1f out: kpt on same pce ins fnl f* **25/1**
00-5 7 *3 ¼* **Cono Zur (FR)**[11] 1354 6-9-3 **69**..................................... JamesSullivan 3 58
(Ruth Carr) *trckd ldrs: effrt and pushed along over 2f out: outpcd over 1f out* **16/1**
1201 8 *1* **West End Lad**[10] 1366 10-9-3 **72**..............................(b) MarkCoumbe(3) 7 58
(Roy Bowring) *trckd ldr tl rdn and wknd over 1f out* **7/1**
4360 9 *3 ¼* **Moheebb (IRE)**[46] 831 9-9-2 **68**.............................. RussKennemore 10 47
(Robert Johnson) *dwlt: hld up: drvn over 3f out: nvr able to chal* **28/1**
6502 10 *1* **Ted's Brother (IRE)**[9] 1394 5-8-8 **60**........................(e) FrederikTylicki 12 37
(Richard Guest) *hld up: shortlived effrt over 2f out: btn fnl f* **11/4**[1]
34-5 11 *15* **Morocco**[14] 1282 4-9-5 **71**.. DanielTudhope 1 13
(David O'Meara) *prom: shkn up over 2f out: sn wknd* **7/1**
412- 12 *8* **Social Rhythm**[249] 4996 9-8-10 **67**............................. GarryWhillans(5) 9
(Alistair Whillans) *hld up: struggling over 2f out: sn btn: t.o* **25/1**

1m 43.52s (0.12) **Going Correction** +0.10s/f (Good) 12 Ran SP% **117.8**
Speed ratings (Par 103): **103,102,102,100,98 96,93,92,89,88 73,65**
toteswingers 1&2 £6.40, 2&3 £16.20, 1&3 £26.60 CSF £36.71 CT £631.35 TOTE £7.10: £2.50, £2.30, £6.50; EX 36.40 Trifecta £783.50 Pool: £2106.05 - 2.01 winning units..
Owner Kevin Kirkup **Bred** Joe Rogers **Trained** Piercebridge, Durham

FOCUS
A steadily run 1m handicap and a bobbing finish. The runner-up is rated in line with his 3-y-o best.

1570 SENDRIG CONSTRUCTION MAIDEN STKS 7f
5:00 (5:01) (Class 5) 3-Y-0+ £2,587 (£770; £384; £192) Stalls Centre

Form RPR
06-3 1 **Big Johnny D (IRE)**[14] 1282 4-10-0 75.................... GrahamGibbons 10 77
(David Barron) *mde all stands' rail: rdn and qcknd over 1f out: kpt on wl ins fnl f* **7/2**[3]
2 *3* **Size (IRE)** 4-10-0 0.. TonyHamilton 8 69+
(Richard Fahey) *dwlt: hld up: rdn and hdwy over 2f out: chsd wnr over 1f out: kpt on fnl f: no imp* **20/1**
0- 3 *hd* **Ebony Express**[168] 7445 4-10-0 0............................. RussKennemore 11 68
(Alan Swinbank) *trckd ldrs: effrt and rdn over 2f out: kpt on same pce fr over 1f out* **40/1**
04- 4 *nk* **Rex Whistler (IRE)**[143] 7840 3-9-0 0............................ PaulMulrennan 7 63+
(Julie Camacho) *hld up in rr: plenty to do and shkn up 2f out: styd on wl fnl f: nvr nr to chal* **100/1**
5 *5* **Latin Rebel (IRE)**[62] 6-10-0 0.. GrahamLee 9 54
(Jim Goldie) *hld up: shkn up over 2f out: kpt on fnl f: nvr able to chal* **40/1**
3 6 *2 ½* **Nurpur (IRE)**[7] 1429 3-8-9 74.. DanielTudhope 1 37
(David O'Meara) *t.k.h: cl up tl rdn and wknd over 1f out* **5/2**[1]
7 *nk* **Natures Law (IRE)** 3-8-9 0... DavidAllan 5 37+
(Keith Dalgleish) *hld up bhd ldng gp: effrt and rdn over 2f out: wknd over 1f out* **10/1**
2- 8 *1 ¾* **Declamation (IRE)**[167] 7459 3-9-0 0......................... SilvestreDeSousa 3 37
(Mark Johnston) *cl up tl rdn: edgd rt and wknd over 1f out* **5/1**
06- 9 *13* **Reverberate**[132] 7978 4-9-9 0.. KellyHarrison 6
(Andrew Crook) *midfield: lost pl 1/2-way: sn struggling* **200/1**
3 10 *1 ¼* **Royal Duchess**[15] 1272 3-8-9 0....................................... FrederikTylicki 4
(Lucy Normile) *midfield: struggling over 3f out: sn btn* **66/1**
2 11 *nk* **Severiano (USA)**[19] 1199 3-9-0 0..................................... AndreaAtzeni 2
(Roger Varian) *wnt lft s: t.k.h: sn prom: pushed along and wknd 2f out* **11/4**[2]

1m 30.12s (2.32) **Going Correction** +0.10s/f (Good)
WFA 3 from 4yo+ 14lb 11 Ran SP% **115.8**
Speed ratings (Par 103): **90,86,86,86,80 77,77,75,60,58 58**
toteswingers 1&2 £11.20, 2&3 £41.90, 1&3 £24.30 CSF £73.12 TOTE £3.00: £1.10, £3.80, £11.10; EX 50.30 Trifecta £1830.10 Part won. Pool: £2440.19 - 0.76 winning units..
Owner Clive Washbourn **Bred** David McGuinness **Trained** Maunby, N Yorks

FOCUS
Plenty of interesting types in the line-up for this maiden with the winner rated to his 7f form.

1571 F1 SIGNS & DIGITAL H'CAP 7f
5:30 (5:31) (Class 4) (0-85,85) 3-Y-0+ £4,690 (£1,395; £697; £348) Stalls Centre

Form RPR
0-00 1 **King Of Eden (IRE)**[16] 1233 7-9-12 **83**..........................(b[1]) DavidAllan 8 96
(Eric Alston) *mde all stands' rail: rdn and qcknd clr 2f out: eased towards fin* **22/1**
4216 2 *5* **Showboating (IRE)**[45] 844 5-9-6 **77**............................(vt) PhillipMakin 7 76+
(Alan McCabe) *hld up: stdy hdwy 2f out: drvn to chse (clr) wnr ins fnl f: no imp* **20/1**
11-5 3 *¾* **Ready (IRE)**[16] 1246 3-8-9 **80**.. FrederikTylicki 10 72
(Garry Moss) *trckd ldrs stands' rail: chsd wnr over 2f out to ins fnl f: one pce* **17/2**[3]
1520 4 *nk* **Docofthebay (IRE)**[16] 1233 9-9-10 **81**............................(b) GrahamLee 5 77
(Scott Dixon) *t.k.h: trckd ldrs: effrt and rdn over 2f out: kpt on same pce fnl f* **10/1**
4/05 5 *hd* **Seattle Drive (IRE)**[16] 1238 5-9-4 **78**............................ PaulPickard(3) 9 74+
(Brian Ellison) *hld up: pushed along over 2f out: effrt on outside over 1f out: nvr able to chal* **11/1**
160- 6 *3 ¾* **Clockmaker (IRE)**[182] 7097 7-10-0 **85**............................ PaulMulrennan 4 71
(Tim Easterby) *hld up: rdn over 2f out: sme late hdwy: nvr able to chal* **25/1**
566- 7 *½* **Mississippi**[203] 6539 4-9-9 **80**.. GrahamGibbons 1 65
(David Barron) *trckd ldrs: drvn over 2f out: wknd over 1f out* **12/1**
1-61 8 *2* **Steel Stockholder**[5] 1462 7-9-7 **78** 6ex..................... SilvestreDeSousa 3 58
(Mel Brittain) *midfield: outpcd 1/2-way: rallied on outside 2f out: no imp fnl f* **9/2**[2]
021- 9 *15* **Dick Bos**[189] 6930 4-9-9 **80**.. DanielTudhope 2 21
(David O'Meara) *t.k.h: prom on outside: struggling over 2f out: sn btn* **5/4**[1]
000- 10 *1 ¼* **Ellaal**[194] 6789 4-9-7 **78**.. PJMcDonald 6 15
(Ruth Carr) *pressed wnr tl rdn and wknd appr fnl f* **18/1**

1m 29.03s (1.23) **Going Correction** +0.10s/f (Good)
WFA 3 from 4yo+ 14lb 10 Ran SP% **116.5**
Speed ratings (Par 105): **96,90,89,89,88 84,84,81,64,63**
toteswingers 1&2 £19.20, 2&3 £11.90, 1&3 £26.80 CSF £382.27 CT £2542.48 TOTE £22.20: £4.80, £4.60, £2.40; EX 644.60 Trifecta £1315.20 Part won. Pool: £1753.63 - 0.18 winning units..
Owner The Grumpy Old Geezers **Bred** Gainsborough Stud Management Ltd **Trained** Longton, Lancs

FOCUS
Front-running tactics have been seen to good effect on this card throughout the day and this handicap was turned into a procession. The winner is rated to his previous best with doubts about the pace bias limiting confidence.

1572 BOOKER CASH & CARRY H'CAP 1m 4f 93y
6:00 (6:00) (Class 6) (0-60,60) 4-Y-0+ £1,940 (£577; £288; £144) Stalls Low

Form RPR
301- 1 **Zarosa (IRE)**[166] 7490 4-8-9 **56**.. NoelGarbutt(7) 1 71+
(John Berry) *hld up in midfield: hdwy and swtchd rt over 2f out: led appr fnl f: kpt on same pce* **9/2**[1]
-106 2 *1 ¼* **Petrol**[23] 1146 4-9-0 **54**.. DanielTudhope 4 67+
(David O'Meara) *hld up towards rr: shkn up and hdwy over 2f out: chsd wnr ins fnl f: kpt on* **7/1**
330- 3 *1 ¾* **Naburn**[229] 5730 5-9-6 **59**.. RussKennemore 11 69
(Alan Swinbank) *in tch: effrt and drvn over 2f out: led briefly over 1f out: kpt on same pce fnl f* **7/1**
31/0 4 *nk* **Brasingaman Eric**[14] 1279 6-9-4 **57**................................ PJMcDonald 5 66
(George Moore) *hld up in midfield: effrt and pushed along over 2f out: ev ch and edgd lft over 1f out: sn one pce* **8/1**
350- 5 *2 ¾* **Operateur (IRE)**[177] 7252 5-9-2 **55**................................ PhillipMakin 14 60
(Ben Haslam) *cl up: led 3f out to over 1f out: outpcd ins fnl f* **5/1**[2]
500- 6 *hd* **Border Bandit (USA)**[212] 6262 5-8-7 **51**........................ GarryWhillans(5) 2 56
(Tracy Waggott) *plld hrd early: prom: effrt over 2f out: one pce fnl f* **20/1**
010- 7 *1 ¼* **A Southside Boy (GER)**[38] 6956 5-9-0 **53**.................... GrahamLee 13 56
(Jim Goldie) *t.k.h: led after 3f to 3f out: sn rdn and rallied: no ex appr fnl f* **11/2**[3]
055- 8 *3 ¼* **Tarantella Lady**[160] 7603 5-9-7 **60**.................................. DavidNolan 10 57
(George Moore) *hld up towards rr: rdn over 3f out: styd on fnl f: nvr able to chal* **20/1**
6-03 9 *nse* **Azerodegree (IRE)**[16] 1251 4-9-4 **58**...............................(p) DavidAllan 12 55
(Iain Jardine) *towards rr: pushed along over 3f out: nvr rchd ldrs* **11/1**
046- 10 *5* **Harare**[166] 7495 12-9-4 **57**...(v) JamesSullivan 9 46
(Karen Tutty) *bhd: pushed along over 3f out: nvr on terms* **25/1**
340- 11 *7* **Greyhope**[12] 3212 4-8-13 **53**.. FrederikTylicki 6 31
(Lucinda Russell) *cl up tl rdn and wknd 2f out* **33/1**
/0-3 12 *3 ¼* **Wolf Heart (IRE)**[15] 1274 5-9-0 **53**................................. PaulMulrennan 8 26
(Lucy Normile) *led 3f: cl up tl rdn and wknd 2f out* **40/1**
006- 13 *9* **Dean Iarracht (IRE)**[202] 6562 7-9-2 **55**........................(p) RoystonFfrench 3 14
(Tracy Waggott) *dwlt: bhd: struggling over 3f out: sn btn* **20/1**

2m 47.15s (1.55) **Going Correction** +0.175s/f (Good)
WFA 4 from 5yo+ 1lb 13 Ran SP% **118.2**
Speed ratings (Par 101): **101,100,99,98,96 96,96,93,93,90 85,83,77**
toteswingers 1&2 £8.30, 2&3 £10.20, 1&3 £31.47 CT £220.35 TOTE £5.00: £1.70, £3.70, £2.90; EX 40.60 Trifecta £156.50 Pool: £1783.00 - 8.54 winning units..
Owner Roger Vicarage **Bred** Keatly Overseas Ltd **Trained** Newmarket, Suffolk

FOCUS
A moderate staying handicap to conclude the card and it saw a clear-cut success. This form could be better than average for the grade.
T/Plt: £956.70 to a £1 stake. Pool of £64481.86 - 49.20 winning tickets. T/Qpdt: £434.70 to a £1 stake. Pool of £5522.93 - 9.40 winning tickets RY

1278 REDCAR (L-H)
Monday, April 15

OFFICIAL GOING: Good to firm (good in places; 8.5)
Wind: strong 1/2 behind Weather: fine and dry but very windy

1573 WATCH RACING UK ON SKY 432 MAIDEN AUCTION STKS 5f
2:10 (2:14) (Class 5) 2-Y-O £2,587 (£770; £384; £192) Stalls High

Form RPR
1 **One Boy (IRE)** 2-8-12 0... TomEaves 6 72+
(Michael Dods) *trckd ldrs: led over 1f out: drvn out* **9/4**[1]
6 2 *1 ¼* **Lilo Lil**[16] 1247 2-8-6 0 ow2.. AdrianNicholls 4 62
(David C Griffiths) *w ldrs: edgd lft over 1f out: kpt on same pce last 100yds* **33/1**
3 *1 ½* **Lorimer's Lot (IRE)** 2-8-4 0.. DuranFentiman 7 54
(Tim Walford) *led: hdd over 2f out: kpt on ins fnl f* **33/1**
4 *½* **Danfazi (IRE)** 2-9-2 0.. PatrickMathers 10 64+
(Kristin Stubbs) *dwlt: hdwy over 2f out: edgd lft and kpt on fnl f* **20/1**
5 *2 ¼* **Lady Mai (IRE)** 2-8-4 0... AndrewMullen 9 44+
(David Barron) *chsd ldrs: led over 2f out: hdd over 1f out: sn outpcd: styd on ins fnl f* **5/1**[2]
6 *nk* **Dotesy (IRE)** 2-8-4 0.. JimmyQuinn 8 43+
(John Quinn) *s.i.s: kpt on fnl f: nvr a threat* **11/1**[3]
0 7 *2* **Fuel Injection**[24] 1108 2-8-13 0...................................... LeeTopliss(3) 11 48
(Paul Midgley) *chsd ldrs: wknd over 1f out* **5/1**[2]
8 *1* **Lendal Bridge** 2-8-9 0... BarryMcHugh 2 37
(Tony Coyle) *dwlt: sn wl outpcd: reminders: sme hdwy and hung lft over 1f out: sn wknd* **25/1**
9 *1* **Countess Lupus (IRE)** 2-8-4 0.. AmyRyan 3 29
(Lisa Williamson) *s.i.s: in rr: sme hdwy and edgd lft over 1f out: sn wknd* **20/1**
10 *16* **Jazzy Lady (IRE)** 2-8-7 0.. CathyGannon 1
(David Evans) *slowly away and wnt lft s: sn bhd: t.o 2f out* **14/1**

58.97s (0.37) **Going Correction** -0.375s/f (Firm) 10 Ran SP% **98.4**
Speed ratings (Par 92): **82,80,77,76,73 72,69,67,66,40**
toteswingers 1&2 £11.10, 2&3 £45.20, 1&3 £19.30 CSF £69.80 TOTE £2.90: £1.30, £7.10, £7.30; EX 59.40 Trifecta £1021.00 Part won. Pool: £1361.41 - 0.83 winning units..

Owner Sekura Group **Bred** Tom Radley **Trained** Denton, Co Durham
FOCUS
An ordinary 2-y-o maiden and the form is modest.

1574 REDCAR RACECOURSE CHEAPEST ADMISSION IN BRITAIN (S) STKS 5f
2:40 (2:43) (Class 6) 2-Y-O £2,045 (£603; £302) **Stalls** High

Form RPR
45 1 **Scargill**[10] 1360 2-8-12 0 SamHitchcott 4 59
(Mick Channon) *chsd ldrs: styd on fnl f: led post* **15/8**[1]
22 2 shd **Gin Time (IRE)**[7] 1432 2-8-7 0 CathyGannon 1 54
(David Evans) *w ldr: led 3f out: kpt on fnl f: hdd last stride* **11/4**[2]
3 8 **La Ferruja (IRE)** 2-8-7 0 (b[1]) AndrewMullen 6 32+
(David Barron) *dwlt: swvd violently lft s: bhd and reminders after 1f: kpt on fnl 2f: tk modest 3rd jst ins fnl f* **11/2**
4 1 **Love's Last Adieu** 2-8-7 0 LiamJones 5 21
(J S Moore) *s.i.s: outpcd and bhd over 3f out: kpt on appr fnl f* **11/1**
5 5 6 **Riley's Missile (IRE)**[14] 1285 2-8-12 0 BarryMcHugh 2 5
(Charles Smith) *dwlt: sn chsng ldrs: drvn and outpcd over 2f out* **28/1**
6 6 **Realistically (IRE)** 2-8-12 0 AmyRyan 3
(Tony Coyle) *led 2f: wknd qckly over 1f out* **7/2**[3]
7 1 3/4 **Elualla (IRE)** 2-8-7 0 TomEaves 7
(Nigel Tinkler) *s.i.s: outpcd and a bhd* **16/1**

59.74s (1.14) **Going Correction** -0.375s/f (Firm) **7 Ran SP% 116.7**
Speed ratings (Par 90): **75,74,62,60,50 41,38**
toteswingers 1&2 £1.80, 2&3 £2.80, 1&3 £2.60 CSF £7.55 TOTE £2.50: £1.20, £1.80; EX 6.50 Trifecta £15.30 Pool: £2977.29 - 145.76 winning units..The winner was bought in 4,000gns.
Owner Bargate **Bred** Imperial **Trained** West Ilsley, Berks
FOCUS
A weak 2-y-o affair but probably about par for the grade. The first two were clear.

1575 BECOME AN ANNUAL BADGE HOLDER TODAY MEDIAN AUCTION MAIDEN STKS 7f
3:10 (3:11) (Class 5) 3-Y-O £2,587 (£770; £384; £192) **Stalls** High

Form RPR
536- 1 **Red Paladin (IRE)**[273] 4132 3-9-5 68 AmyRyan 4 72
(Kevin Ryan) *led 1f: trckd ldrs: drvn to chal over 2f out: led jst ins fnl f: hld on nr fin* **13/2**[3]
0- 2 hd **Dairam (USA)**[173] 7330 3-9-5 0 PaulHanagan 1 71
(Charles Hills) *hmpd s: led after 1f: hdd jst ins fnl f: no ex nr fin* **4/6**[1]
020- 3 7 **Serenata (IRE)**[129] 8017 3-8-11 65 (b[1]) RaulDaSilva(3) 5 48
(Paul Cole) *t.k.h: sn trcking ldrs: effrt over 2f out: edgd rt and wknd fnl 150yds* **9/1**
44-3 4 nse **Bitusa (USA)**[9] 1392 3-9-5 65 JimmyQuinn 2 52
(Alan Swinbank) *wnt lft s: chsd ldrs: drvn and hung lft 3f out: edgd rt and outpcd over 1f out* **10/3**[2]
00 5 10 **Hartford Starts (IRE)**[15] 1272 3-9-5 0 DaleSwift 3 25
(Ian McInnes) *chsd ldrs: drvn 3f out: lost pl over 1f out: sn bhd* **150/1**

1m 25.39s (0.89) **Going Correction** -0.375s/f (Firm) **5 Ran SP% 107.1**
Speed ratings (Par 98): **79,78,70,70,59**
CSF £10.89 TOTE £6.30: £3.00, £1.10; EX 12.80 Trifecta £42.50 Pool: £2401.29 - 42.33 winning units..
Owner Hambleton Racing Ltd XXII **Bred** Noel O'Callaghan **Trained** Hambleton, N Yorks
FOCUS
A modest 3-y-o maiden and not form to be too positive about.

1576 BOOK TICKETS ONLINE @ REDCARRACING.CO.UK H'CAP 1m
3:40 (3:40) (Class 4) (0-85,85) 4-Y-O+ £6,469 (£1,925; £962; £481) **Stalls** High

Form RPR
332- 1 **Oddysey (IRE)**[187] 6986 4-8-10 77 LeeTopliss(3) 7 90
(Michael Dods) *trckd ldr: led 3f out: edgd rt fnl f: hld on nr fin* **8/1**
2 hd **Two For Two (IRE)**[188] 5-9-0 85 DavidBergin(7) 6 98
(David O'Meara) *trckd ldrs: chal over 1f out: no ex nr fin* **16/1**
/4-6 3 6 **Bling King**[14] 1281 4-8-10 77 RaulDaSilva(3) 3 76
(Geoffrey Harker) *chsd ldrs: outpcd over 2f out: kpt on fnl f* **16/1**
321 4 3 1/2 **Azrael**[14] 1292 5-8-10 74 (p) PaulHanagan 9 65
(Alan McCabe) *chsd one other stands' side: effrt over 2f out: one pce* **4/1**[2]
600- 5 2 **Fazza**[171] 7370 6-8-5 76 KevinStott(7) 4 63
(Edwin Tuer) *s.i.s: in rr: hdwy over 2f out: edgd lft and wknd over 1f out* **16/1**
410- 6 shd **Ascription (IRE)**[194] 6789 4-9-0 78 (t) JimmyQuinn 1 64
(Hugo Palmer) *led: hdd 3f out: wknd over 1f out* **9/2**[3]
240- 7 nk **Kalk Bay (IRE)**[180] 7175 6-8-13 84 MatthewHopkins(7) 8 70
(Michael Easterby) *led other on stands' side: chsd ldrs: edgd lft 2f out: sn wknd* **16/1**
000- 8 4 1/2 **Barren Brook**[180] 7175 6-9-2 80 DuranFentiman 11 55
(Michael Easterby) *s.s: t.k.h: trckd ldrs after 2f: lost pl wl over 1f out* **13/2**
550- 9 4 **Hakuna Matata**[175] 7294 6-8-7 71 (p) TomEaves 2 37
(Michael Dods) *chsd ldrs: lost pl over 2f out* **7/1**
0/-3 10 1 3/4 **Destiny Blue (IRE)**[14] 1281 6-9-0 78 DaleSwift 5 40
(Brian Ellison) *sn in rr: rdn and detached 4f out* **7/2**[1]

1m 36.29s (-0.31) **Going Correction** -0.375s/f (Firm) **10 Ran SP% 120.9**
Speed ratings (Par 105): **105,104,98,95,93 93,92,88,84,82**
toteswingers 1&2 £10.00, 2&3 £18.90, 1&3 £20.80 CSF £131.60 CT £2009.88 TOTE £8.70: £2.10, £2.80, £5.20; EX 64.50 Trifecta £1795.40 Part won. Pool: £2393.90 - 0.72 winning units..
Owner Pearson & Lowthian **Bred** Darling Smile Syndicate **Trained** Denton, Co Durham
FOCUS
An open-looking handicap, run at a sound pace and sound form that could be rated higher.

1577 REDCAR RACECOURSE STRAIGHT-MILE CHAMPIONSHIP QUALIFIER (H'CAP) 1m
4:10 (4:10) (Class 5) (0-75,75) 3-Y-O £2,587 (£770; £384; £192) **Stalls** High

Form RPR
311- 1 **Lilac Lace (IRE)**[115] 8211 3-8-13 72 AdamCarter(5) 3 78
(Tim Easterby) *t.k.h: mde all: rdn and edgd lft ins fnl f: hld on wl* **9/1**
463- 2 1 **Bartack (IRE)**[167] 7458 3-9-7 75 KirstyMilczarek 4 79
(Luca Cumani) *chsd ldrs: effrt over 2f out: chsng wnr 1f out: carried lft ins fnl f: kpt on same pce* **7/2**[2]
105- 3 2 1/2 **Old Man Clegg**[205] 6469 3-8-12 73 MatthewHopkins(7) 1 71
(Michael Easterby) *chsd ldrs: upsides 4f out: styd on same pce fnl f* **20/1**
620- 4 2 **Stagweekend (IRE)**[182] 7096 3-8-11 65 MichaelO'Connell 9 58
(John Quinn) *in rr: hdwy over 2f out: kpt on same pce over 1f out* **20/1**
1311 5 nse **Apache Rising**[12] 1330 3-9-7 75 TomEaves 5 68
(Bryan Smart) *chsd ldrs: drvn over 2f out: edgd lft over 1f out: one pce* **8/1**[3]
6 1 **Excellent Addition (IRE)**[200] 6620 3-8-9 70 DavidBergin(7) 6 61
(David O'Meara) *chsd ldrs: effrt over 2f out: one pce appr fnl f* **14/1**
60-1 7 30 **Tribal Path (IRE)**[79] 396 3-9-7 75 PaulHanagan 8
(Mark Johnston) *chsd ldrs: lost pl and eased over 2f out: sn bhd: virtually p.u: t.o* **4/5**[1]
0-04 8 38 **Firstkissoflove**[12] 1330 3-8-7 61 oh1 AdrianNicholls 7
(David C Griffiths) *hung bdly lft thrght: in rr: ended up far side over 3f out: bhd and eased over 2f out: virtually p.u: hopelessly t.o* **33/1**

1m 38.55s (1.95) **Going Correction** -0.375s/f (Firm) **8 Ran SP% 118.0**
Speed ratings (Par 98): **94,93,90,88,88 87,57,19**
toteswingers 1&2 £3.90, 2&3 £11.40, 1&3 £15.10 CSF £40.80 CT £503.04 TOTE £10.00: £2.00, £1.80, £4.50; EX 43.20 Trifecta £258.00 Pool: £3183.25 - 9.25 winning units..
Owner S A Heley **Bred** Robert Ryan, Brendan Quinn & Joan Quinn **Trained** Great Habton, N Yorks
■ Stewards' Enquiry : Adam Carter two-day ban: careless riding (29-30 Apri)
FOCUS
A modest 3-y-o handicap, but it was competitive and the form looks fair. The third sets the level.

1578 RACING AGAIN ON 2ND MAY APPRENTICE CLAIMING STKS 6f
4:40 (4:42) (Class 6) 3-4-Y-O £2,045 (£603; £302) **Stalls** High

Form RPR
0-60 1 **Takealookatmenow (IRE)**[19] 1205 4-9-5 68 (v[1]) ShirleyTeasdale(4) 1 76
(David Nicholls) *w ldr: led 3f out: rdn clr over 1f out* **11/4**[2]
4531 2 4 1/2 **Studfarmer**[10] 1361 3-8-8 71 (v) EoinWalsh(4) 8 59
(David Evans) *led 3f: edgd lft and kpt on same pce appr fnl f* **13/8**[1]
40-6 3 1 1/2 **Headstight (IRE)**[15] 1276 4-9-5 50 (p) LeeTopliss 3 52
(Paul Midgley) *chsd ldrs: edgd lft over 2f out: kpt on to take 3rd 1f out* **20/1**
5-30 4 2 1/2 **First Serve (IRE)**[81] 356 3-8-3 60 NeilFarley 6 37
(David Barron) *trckd ldrs: wknd over 1f out* **8/1**
246- 5 1/2 **Liliargh (IRE)**[73] 7437 4-9-4 70 GeorgeChaloner(4) 5 46
(Ben Haslam) *half-rrd s: sn chsng ldrs: drvn over 2f out: one pce* **4/1**[3]
6 nk **Rose Of May (IRE)** 3-8-7 0 DavidBergin(4) 2 43
(David O'Meara) *in rr: outpcd and bhd after 2f: kpt on fnl f* **8/1**
5-00 7 1 1/4 **Bandy Bob**[15] 1270 4-9-2 38 [1] JasonHart(4) 7 39
(Iain Jardine) *hld up in rr: bhd and drvn after 2f: kpt on fnl f* **50/1**
000- 8 4 **Medecis Mountain**[232] 5623 4-9-6 36 (p) AdamCarter(2) 4 28
(John Wainwright) *in rr: outpcd and lost pl after 2f: sn bhd* **100/1**

1m 10.38s (-1.42) **Going Correction** -0.375s/f (Firm)
WFA 3 from 4yo 12lb **8 Ran SP% 114.7**
Speed ratings (Par 101): **94,88,86,82,82 81,79,74**
toteswingers 1&2 £1.80, 2&3 £6.00, 1&3 £7.60 CSF £7.56 TOTE £4.80: £1.90, £1.10, £3.70; EX 7.70 Trifecta £75.10 Pool: £3311.23 - 33.04 winning units..The winner was claimed by K Tutty for £10,000.
Owner D Nicholls & Mrs S J Barker **Bred** Ian W Glenton **Trained** Sessay, N Yorks
FOCUS
A weak claimer. The winner is rated back to her best with the third fitting in.

1579 FOLLOW REDCARRACING ON FACEBOOK & TWITTER FILLIES' H'CAP 1m 2f
5:10 (5:10) (Class 5) (0-70,65) 3-Y-O+ £2,587 (£770; £384; £192) **Stalls** Low

Form RPR
01-2 1 **Good Speech (IRE)**[77] 428 3-8-9 65 MickyFenton 5 68+
(Tom Tate) *mde all: pushed along over 5f out: hrd drvn over 2f out: hld on gamely: all out* **7/2**[2]
023- 2 nse **Bobs Her Uncle**[170] 7417 4-9-12 63 PaulHanagan 2 69
(James Bethell) *trckd ldrs: chal over 2f out: r.o: jst failed* **7/2**[2]
-303 3 1 **Cheers For Thea (IRE)**[49] 798 8-10-0 65 (bt) DuranFentiman 7 69
(Tim Easterby) *hld up towards rr: effrt over 3f out: chsng ldrs over 1f out: styd on same pce ins fnl f* **12/1**
306- 4 shd **Looks Like Rain**[147] 7791 4-9-11 62 DaleSwift 8 66
(Brian Ellison) *chsd ldrs: drvn and outpcd over 5f out: hdwy over 2f out: chsng ldrs over 1f out: styd on same pce ins fnl f* **11/1**
02-0 5 3 1/4 **Croftamie**[34] 967 4-9-8 59 (p) PatrickMathers 3 57
(Tracy Waggott) *t.k.h: sn trcking ldrs: effrt over 2f out: wknd jst ins fnl f* **25/1**
12-5 6 2 1/4 **Open Letter (IRE)**[18] 1219 3-8-9 65 LiamJones 1 55
(Mark Johnston) *sn drvn along: sn chsng ldrs: one pce fnl 3f: nvr a threat* **9/4**[1]
30-6 7 6 **Lady Sledmere (IRE)**[16] 1239 5-9-4 61 LeeTopliss(3) 6 39
(Paul Midgley) *hld up in rr: hdwy on inner 4f out: drvn over 2f out: hung rt wknd over 1f out: eased ins fnl f* **14/1**
640- 8 6 **Miss Blink**[124] 8082 6-9-13 64 J-PGuillambert 9 33
(Robin Bastiman) *chsd ldrs: lost pl over 1f out: eased ins fnl f* **8/1**[3]
300/ 9 3 **Keyhole Kate**[651] 3680 4-9-2 53 AmyRyan 4 16
(Tim Walford) *dwlt: a detached in last: rdn over 3f out: nvr on terms* **33/1**

2m 7.51s (0.41) **Going Correction** -0.375s/f (Firm)
WFA 3 from 4yo+ 19lb **9 Ran SP% 115.8**
Speed ratings (Par 100): **83,82,82,82,79 77,72,68,65**
toteswingers 1&2 £2.90, 2&3 £3.90, 1&3 £6.40 CSF £16.26 CT £131.03 TOTE £4.70: £1.60, £1.20, £2.30; EX 16.10 Trifecta £85.70 Pool: £2347.93 - 20.53 winning units..
Owner T T Racing **Bred** D Veitch, E McEvoy & P Costigan **Trained** Tadcaster, N Yorks
FOCUS
A modest fillies' handicap where it paid to race handy. The winner is rated slightly above her AW form.
T/Plt: £117.70 to a £1 stake. Pool of £48062.75 - 298.01 winning tickets. T/Qpdt: £48.60 to a £1 stake. Pool of £3085.30 - 46.90 winning tickets. WG

WINDSOR (R-H)

Monday, April 15

OFFICIAL GOING: Soft (good to soft in places; 5.9)

Top bend dolled out 2yds adding 7yds to races of 1m-plus. Rest of running rail at normal inner configuration and racecourse at full width.

Wind: Moderate, behind Weather: Fine but cloudy

1580 EUROPEAN BREEDERS' FUND MAIDEN STKS — 5f 10y

2:20 (2:21) (Class 5) 2-Y-O £2,911 (£866; £432; £216) Stalls Low

Form RPR

1 **Anticipated (IRE)** 2-9-5 0 RichardHughes 2 81+
(Richard Hannon) *dwlt and swvd rt s: wl off the pce and pushed along early: prog after 2f and gng much bttr: clsd against nr side rail to ld 1f out: comf* **1/1**[1]

2 1 1/2 **Rose Gloria (IRE)** 2-9-0 0 MartinHarley 6 68+
(Mick Channon) *towards rr early: prog 1/2-way: rdn 2f out: styd on to take 2nd ins fnl f: no threat* **10/1**

6 3 1 1/4 **Queen Of The Tarts**[16] 1240 2-9-0 0 NeilCallan 4 63
(Olly Stevens) *hanging lft thrght: led: rdn 2f out: hdd and one pce in centre of crse 1f out* **7/1**[3]

4 1 1/4 **Primitorio (IRE)** 2-9-5 0 JimCrowley 3 64+
(Ralph Beckett) *chsd ldng pair: clsd towards nr side and upsides over 1f out: fdd ins fnl f* **3/1**[2]

5 2 **Pennine Warrior** 2-9-5 0 TomQueally 8 56
(Scott Dixon) *pressed ldr but continually carried lft towards centre: rdn and stl chalng over 1f out: wknd fnl f* **28/1**

6 2 1/2 **Blue Anchor Bay (IRE)** 2-9-5 0 DavidProbert 7 47
(Rod Millman) *chsd ldng trio to 1/2-way: sn btn* **8/1**

7 3 **Mr Childrey (IRE)** 2-9-5 0 LiamKeniry 5 37
(J S Moore) *dwlt: sn outpcd in last: nvr a factor* **25/1**

8 17 **Little Big Man** 2-9-5 0 JamesDoyle 1
(Sylvester Kirk) *a in rr: wknd 2f out: t.o* **40/1**

1m 3.52s (3.22) **Going Correction** +0.525s/f (Yiel) 8 Ran SP% **117.4**

Speed ratings (Par 92): **95,92,90,88,85 81,76,49**

toteswingers 1&2 £4.60, 2&3 £5.20, 1&3 £3.10 CSF £12.89 TOTE £1.80: £1.10, £2.90, £1.70; EX 10.50 Trifecta £34.60 Pool: £932.02 - 20.18 winning units..

Owner Woodcock, Bull, Ivory, Hannon **Bred** M Smith & Grennanstown Stud **Trained** East Everleigh, Wilts

FOCUS

This maiden has gone to some decent sorts in recent years including Red Jazz and Zebedee. The winner can rate higher and the second can win similar.

1581 BHEST RACING TO SCHOOL H'CAP — 5f 10y

2:50 (2:52) (Class 4) (0-85,85) 4-Y-O+ £4,851 (£1,443; £721; £360) Stalls Low

Form RPR

532- 1 **Cheworee**[205] 6495 4-9-4 82 RyanMoore 11 89+
(David Elsworth) *hld up in rr: prog towards outer fr 1/2-way: drvn to chal ins fnl f: won on the nod* **4/1**[2]

210- 2 nse **Cruise Tothelimit (IRE)**[193] 6820 5-8-11 78 RyanPowell(3) 9 85
(Ian Williams) *led main gp on outer to over 3f out: styd prom: drvn to ld again ins fnl f: pipped on the post* **12/1**

421 3 3/4 **My Son Max**[10] 1370 5-8-13 82 RobertTart(5) 8 86
(P J O'Gorman) *chsd ldrs: rdn over 1f out: clsd and upsides ins fnl f: kpt on same pce* **7/2**[1]

6010 4 1 **Noverre To Go (IRE)**[16] 1245 7-9-7 85 LukeMorris 12 85
(Ronald Harris) *dwlt: chsd other rival to go far side: hrd rdn to cl on him over 1f out: led pair ins fnl f: nt quite on terms* **25/1**

00-2 5 1/2 **Cadeaux Pearl**[16] 1248 5-9-1 79 (b) NeilCallan 13 78
(Scott Dixon) *overall ldr: led pair to far side after 2f: sn relinquished ld but styd on terms: drvn over 1f out: hdd by rival ins fnl f* **14/1**

0335 6 nse **Sulis Minerva (IRE)**[10] 1370 6-8-7 74 RyanClark(3) 3 72
(Jeremy Gask) *dwlt: hld up in rr: snatched up over 3f out: prog on outer 2f out: no hdwy 1f out: kpt on* **12/1**

1206 7 shd **Cardinal**[7] 1431 8-8-10 74 JimCrowley 2 72
(Robert Cowell) *chsd ldrs: rdn over 1f out: one pce and no imp after* **9/1**

60-2 8 3/4 **Taurus Twins**[7] 1431 7-9-2 80 (b) JamesDoyle 5 75
(Richard Price) *led main gp against nr side rail over 3f out: hdd & wknd ins fnl f* **9/1**

555- 9 1 3/4 **Waseem Faris (IRE)**[167] 7451 4-9-2 80 MartinHarley 6 69
(Mick Channon) *s.s: hld up in last: pushed along 2f out: sme late prog: nvr remotely involved* **12/1**

1100 10 1 1/2 **Woolfall Sovereign (IRE)**[30] 1032 7-8-12 76 TomQueally 10 60
(George Margarson) *chsd ldrs to 2f out: steadily wknd* **8/1**[3]

6-00 11 3 1/4 **Jarrow (IRE)**[16] 1245 6-9-0 78 RichardKingscote 7 50
(Milton Bradley) *in tch nr side: rdn and no prog 2f out: wknd 1f out* **28/1**

000- 12 4 1/2 **Solemn**[185] 7019 8-9-4 82 (b) DaneO'Neill 1 38
(Milton Bradley) *rdn towards rr after 2f: no prog: wknd over 1f out: eased* **12/1**

1m 2.25s (1.95) **Going Correction** +0.525s/f (Yiel) 12 Ran SP% **118.1**

Speed ratings (Par 105): **105,104,103,102,101 101,101,99,97,94 89,82**

toteswingers 1&2 £9.30, 2&3 £10.40, 1&3 £4.40 CSF £51.43 CT £185.85 TOTE £4.30: £1.80, £4.20, £1.70; EX 70.70 Trifecta £282.30 Pool: £1143.50 - 3.03 winning units..

Owner S Stoneham,E Van Cutsem,A Hoctor-Duncan **Bred** Sarah Stoneham **Trained** Newmarket, Suffolk

FOCUS

A competitive sprint handicap in which the two highest-drawn horses ended up racing on the far side. They weren't beaten far at the line, suggesting there was no great bias. The winner and third are rated close to last year's Newmarket form.

1582 CORAL.CO.UK H'CAP — 6f

3:20 (3:21) (Class 4) (0-85,85) 3-Y-O £4,851 (£1,443; £721; £360) Stalls Low

Form RPR

350- 1 **Dominate**[171] 7374 3-9-7 85 SeanLevey 7 92
(Richard Hannon) *mde all and racd away fr nr side rail: rdn over 1f out: in command fnl f: styd on wl* **6/1**

2-16 2 2 **Red Refraction (IRE)**[16] 1246 3-8-13 77 RichardHughes 2 78
(Richard Hannon) *racd against nr side rail: cl up: pressed wnr 2f out: rdn and nt qckn over 1f out: one pce fnl f* **9/2**[2]

252- 3 1/2 **Grand Denial (IRE)**[206] 6444 3-8-12 76 JohnFahy 5 75
(Clive Cox) *trckd ldrs: short of room and nudged 3f out: sn lost pl: rallied and drvn over 1f out: chsd ldng pair fnl f: kpt on* **5/1**[3]

-315 4 3/4 **Sand Boy (IRE)**[61] 628 3-8-11 75 SteveDrowne 4 72
(Charles Hills) *hld up in tch: taken to outer and effrt 2f out: kpt on but nvr gng pce to chal* **16/1**

051- 5 nk **Fletcher Christian**[237] 5449 3-8-12 76 NeilCallan 8 72
(John Gallagher) *wnt lft s: t.k.h: mostly pressed wnr to 2f out: hanging and nt qckn over 1f out: one pce after* **20/1**

641- 6 3/4 **Benoni**[199] 6629 3-8-9 73 DaneO'Neill 1 66
(Henry Candy) *hld up in tch: shkn up 2f out: kpt on fnl f but nvr cl enough to chal* **3/1**[1]

031- 7 6 **Freddy With A Y (IRE)**[127] 8044 3-8-13 77 RyanMoore 3 51
(Gary Moore) *hld up in last: detached and rdn 1/2-way: nvr on terms after* **12/1**

106- 8 3 1/4 **Knight Charm**[237] 5450 3-8-12 76 FergusSweeney 9 40
(Eve Johnson Houghton) *impeded s: t.k.h and hld up in rr: effrt on outer over 2f out: wknd qckly over 1f out* **18/1**

41- 9 5 **Gigawatt**[188] 6945 3-9-1 79 PatCosgrave 10 27
(Jim Boyle) *chsd ldrs: nudged rival 3f out: sn wknd qckly* **5/1**[3]

1m 16.5s (3.50) **Going Correction** +0.525s/f (Yiel) 9 Ran SP% **114.4**

Speed ratings (Par 100): **97,94,93,92,92 91,83,78,72**

toteswingers 1&2 £3.80, 2&3 £4.80, 1&3 £8.40 CSF £32.81 CT £145.54 TOTE £6.20: £2.50, £1.30, £2.50; EX 29.50 Trifecta £189.80 Pool: £1142.50 - 4.51 winning units..

Owner Godfrey Wilson **Bred** Mrs C R D Wilson **Trained** East Everleigh, Wilts

■ Stewards' Enquiry : Pat Cosgrave two-day ban: careless riding (29-30 Apr)

FOCUS

A fair sprint handicap that resulted in a 1-2 for trainer Richard Hannon. It was something of a rough race, including at the start, where Fletcher Christian swerved away to his left, hampering both Knight Charm and Gigawatt. The winner is rated to his juvenile best with the placed horses and fifth fitting in.

1583 DOWNLOAD CORAL MOBILE FROM THE APP STORE H'CAP — 1m 67y

3:50 (3:51) (Class 4) (0-85,85) 4-Y-O+ £4,851 (£1,443; £541; £541) Stalls Low

Form RPR

23-2 1 **Snow Trooper**[16] 1237 5-9-2 80 JimCrowley 14 91
(Dean Ivory) *prom: trckd ldr 5f out: led over 3f out: brought to nr side rail and kicked on over 2f out: styd on wl* **9/2**[2]

21- 2 2 1/4 **Mean It (IRE)**[269] 4293 4-8-13 77 JamieSpencer 1 88+
(David Simcock) *stdd s: hld up and last early: prog fr 3f out: rdn whn nt clr run briefly over 1f out: styd on to take 2nd nr fin: too much to do* **11/4**[1]

06-1 3 1/2 **Ree's Rascal (IRE)**[26] 1092 5-9-4 82 PatCosgrave 13 87
(Jim Boyle) *chsd ldr to 5f out: sn pushed along: lost pl over 3f out: drvn and rallied fr over 1f out: edgd lft but styd on* **14/1**

220- 3 dht **Uncle Dermot (IRE)**[150] 7743 5-8-12 76 ow1 SebSanders 4 81
(Brendan Powell) *hld up towards rr: prog on outer 3f out: drvn 2f out: chsd wnr jst over 1f out: kpt on but no imp: lost 2nd nr fin* **25/1**

600- 5 1 1/2 **Starwatch**[192] 6831 6-9-2 85 WilliamTwiston-Davies(5) 6 87
(John Bridger) *led to over 3f out: styd chsng ldrs: edgd lft fr over 1f out: steadily fdd* **50/1**

425- 6 1/2 **Eurystheus (IRE)**[280] 3917 4-8-11 80 (t) PhilipPrince(5) 7 80
(Paul Nicholls) *prom: jnd ldrs over 3f out: rdn over 2f out: steadily fdd over 1f out* **16/1**

060- 7 3 1/4 **Sir Mike**[229] 5747 4-9-0 78 TomQueally 3 71
(Amanda Perrett) *hld up in midfield: in tch but rdn over 2f out: no imp: wknd fnl f* **7/1**[3]

150- 8 7 **First Post (IRE)**[150] 7751 6-9-4 82 DaneO'Neill 9 62
(Derek Haydn Jones) *prom: upsides ldr over 3f out: rdn over 2f out: hld whn hmpd over 1f out: wknd* **16/1**

65-2 9 2 1/4 **Boots And Spurs**[16] 1233 4-9-2 83 (v) MichaelMetcalfe(3) 8 55
(Mrs K Burke) *prom: lost pl and rdn 4f out: struggling fnl 3f* **9/2**[2]

461- 10 1 **Rocky Reef**[170] 7395 4-9-7 85 JackMitchell 10 54
(Philip Hide) *hld up: a in rr: rdn and struggling in last 1/2-way* **25/1**

311- 11 1 3/4 **Authoritarian**[175] 7302 4-8-12 76 RichardHughes 12 41
(Richard Hannon) *hld up in rr: rdn and no prog over 3f out on outer: no ch after* **17/2**

-061 12 3 3/4 **Greyfriarschorista**[33] 984 6-8-10 77 RyanClark(3) 11 34
(Tom Keddy) *towards rr: rdn on outer 3f out: sn wknd* **40/1**

1546 13 8 **Mister Musicmaster**[9] 1385 4-9-3 81 WilliamCarson 2 19
(Ron Hodges) *chsd ldrs early: lost pl and struggling in rr fr 1/2-way: eased over 1f out: t.o* **33/1**

1m 46.69s (1.99) **Going Correction** +0.375s/f (Good) 13 Ran SP% **119.5**

Speed ratings (Par 105): **105,102,102,102,100 100,97,90,87,86 85,81,73**Ree's Rascal £1.40 Uncle Dermot £2.50 TRICAST: Snow Trooper/Mean It/RR £84.55 ST/MI/UD £146.49 toteswingers 1&2 £3.70, 1&RR £4.90, 1&UD £13.00, 2&UD £8.50, RR&2 £5.20 CSF £16.32 TOTE £5.10: £1.90, £1.90; EX 24.30 TRIFECTA Pool of £2621.11. ST/MI/RR £38827 Owner.

■ Stewards' Enquiry : Pat Cosgrave two-day ban: careless riding (1-2 May)

FOCUS

A competitive handicap in which the third sets the standard.

1584 WINDSOR VEHICLE LEASING WVL.CO.UK MAIDEN STKS — 1m 2f 7y

4:20 (4:27) (Class 5) 3-Y-O £2,587 (£770; £384; £192) Stalls Centre

Form RPR

1 **Nearly Caught (IRE)** 3-9-5 0 GeorgeBaker 2 78+
(Hughie Morrison) *c out of the stalls slowly: hld up in last: stdy prog over 3f out fr wl off the pce: shkn up to go 2nd 1f out: clsd to ld ins fnl f: readily* **14/1**

433 2 2 **Punditry**[14] 1296 3-9-5 71 (b[1]) WilliamBuick 9 74
(John Gosden) *led: cajoled along and looked in command over 2f out: rdn over 1f out: hdd and nt qckn ins fnl f* **3/1**[2]

-233 3 2 3/4 **He's A Striker (IRE)**[27] 1072 3-9-2 73 RyanClark(3) 1 68
(Michael Blake) *t.k.h: hld up in last pair tl plld way through to chse ldr 1/2-way: rdn 2f out: lost 2nd 1f out: one pce* **12/1**

0-5 4 2 1/4 **Star Of Namibia (IRE)**[5] 1481 3-9-5 0 JDSmith 5 64
(J S Moore) *settled in midfield: shkn up and nt on terms w ldrs over 3f out: kpt on fnl 2f to take 4th nr fin* **66/1**

5 3/4 **Refer** 3-9-5 0 SteveDrowne 7 62+
(Charles Hills) *dwlt: rcvrd to chse ldr after 2f to 1/2-way: styd prom: rdn 3f out: fdd over 1f out* **9/1**

043- 6 1 1/4 **Portmonarch (IRE)**[173] 7323 3-9-5 75 TedDurcan 3 60
(David Lanigan) *trckd ldr 2f: styd prom: shkn up over 3f out: nt qckn and hld 2f out: fdd* **11/8**[1]

7 22 **Strength And Honor (IRE)** 3-9-5 0 RyanMoore 6
(Sir Michael Stoute) *prom early: dropped to rr and rdn sn after 1/2-way: t.o whn eased over 1f out* **5/1**[3]

8 6 **Xclusive** 3-9-5 0 .... LukeMorris 4
(Ronald Harris) *in tch: rdn and wknd sn after 1/2-way: t.o* **25/1**

2m 15.39s (6.69) **Going Correction** +0.575s/f (Yiel) **8 Ran SP% 113.5**
Speed ratings (Par 98): **96,94,92,90,89 88,71,66**
toteswingers 1&2 £7.10, 2&3 £4.00, 1&3 £11.10 CSF £55.09 TOTE £16.90: £3.50, £1.20, £2.50; EX 73.70 Trifecta £554.60 Pool: £3244.17 - 4.38 winning units..
Owner A N Solomons **Bred** Irish National Stud **Trained** East Ilsley, Berks

FOCUS
An ordinary maiden, but the winner has scope.

1585 READING POST H'CAP — 1m 2f 7y
4:50 (4:54) (Class 5) (0-75,75) 4-Y-0+ **£2,587** (£770; £384; £192) **Stalls** Centre

Form RPR

434- **1** **Significant Move**[165] 7511 6-9-0 **68** .... [1] NeilCallan 5 79
(Stuart Kittow) *sn trckd ldng trio: shkn up over 2f out: clsd to ld jst over 1f out: styd on wl and sn clr* **7/2**[1]

0243 **2** 3 3/4 **Gaelic Silver (FR)**[28] 1059 7-9-2 **70** .... RyanMoore 14 74
(Gary Moore) *trckd ldr: rdn to chal 2f out: upsides over 1f out: outpcd by wnr fnl f* **13/2**[2]

-135 **3** 1 3/4 **Norfolk Sky**[20] 1182 4-9-4 **72** .... JimCrowley 2 72
(Laura Mongan) *led: hrd rdn 2f out: hdd over 1f out: fdd but hld on for 3rd* **22/1**

21-6 **4** *shd* **Bold Duke**[10] 1366 5-8-9 **68** .... ThomasBrown[(5)] 16 68
(Edward Bevan) *prom early: rdn and struggling to hold pl over 4f out: rallied over 1f out: nrly snatched 3rd* **16/1**

630- **5** *nk* **Choral Festival**[171] 7375 7-8-13 **72** .... WilliamTwiston-Davies[(5)] 10 71+
(John Bridger) *hld up in midfield: prog over 3f out and gng bttr than most: rdn and nt qckn 2f out: kpt on one pce to press for 3rd nr fin* **8/1**

-240 **6** 1 1/4 **Presburg (IRE)**[65] 585 4-9-4 **75** .... DarrenEgan[(3)] 1 72+
(Joseph Tuite) *hld up wl in rr: out of tch in 11th 4f out: rdn and styd on fr over 2f out: no ch of rching ldrs* **17/2**

06-6 **7** 2 1/2 **Emman Bee (IRE)**[31] 1013 4-9-1 **69** .... RichardHughes 9 61
(Luke Dace) *a in midfield: urged along over 3f out and no imp: one pce after* **20/1**

-000 **8** 3 1/4 **Mountain Range (IRE)**[18] 1220 5-8-13 **67** .... JamieMackay 7 52
(Willie Musson) *dwlt: hld up in last pair: wl off the pce over 4f out: shkn up 3f out: kpt on but nvr involved* **14/1**

-353 **9** 1 **Whitby Jet (IRE)**[54] 720 5-9-5 **73** .... GeorgeBaker 4 56
(Ed Vaughan) *mostly chsd ldng pair to 2f out: shkn up and steadily wknd* **10/1**

50-3 **10** 17 **Fire King**[34] 403 7-8-12 **66** .... LiamKeniry 15 15
(Paul Burgoyne) *hld up in rr: wknd over 3f out: t.o* **25/1**

03-3 **11** 3/4 **Shamir**[40] 897 6-9-5 **73** .... FergusSweeney 12 21
(Jo Crowley) *hld up and a towards rr: shkn up and no prog over 3f out: sn bhd: t.o* **7/1**[3]

001- **12** 1 1/4 **Garrisson (IRE)**[108] 8267 4-9-4 **72** .... SteveDrowne 3
(Charles Hills) *chsd ldrs: drvn wl over 3f out: sn wknd: t.o* **14/1**

000 **13** 3/4 **St Ignatius**[11] 1350 6-8-7 **61** .... NickyMackay 13
(Alan Bailey) *sn hld up in last trio: rdn 1/2-way: sn btn: t.o* **33/1**

-141 **14** 3 3/4 **Chella Thriller (SPA)**[13] 1298 4-8-10 **64** ....(b) RichardKingscote 11
(Alastair Lidderdale) *dwlt: rcvrd into midfield after 3f: wknd 4f out: t.o* **16/1**

2m 13.7s (5.00) **Going Correction** +0.575s/f (Yiel) **14 Ran SP% 119.8**
Speed ratings (Par 103): **103,100,98,98,98 97,95,92,91,78 77,76,76,73**
toteswingers 1&2 £4.80, 2&3 £15.30, 1&3 £20.00 CSF £23.05 CT £443.77 TOTE £4.50: £1.50, £2.20, £7.40; EX 31.10 Trifecta £602.70 Pool: £2474.41 - 3.07 winning units..
Owner Midd Shire Racing **Bred** Juddmonte Farms Ltd **Trained** Blackborough, Devon

FOCUS
A modest handicap dominated by those that raced handily. Those in the frame behind the winner help set the level.

1586 ROYAL WINDSOR RACING CLUB H'CAP — 1m 3f 135y
5:20 (5:23) (Class 5) (0-75,75) 4-Y-0+ **£2,587** (£770; £384; £192) **Stalls** Centre

Form RPR

-531 **1** **Attwaal (IRE)**[44] 866 4-9-0 **69** .... SebSanders 13 82+
(Neil King) *hld up in midfield: prog to trck ldrs gng wl 3f out: led wl over 1f out: drvn and styd on* **11/1**

20-0 **2** 2 **Achalas (IRE)**[13] 1302 5-9-1 **74** .... RyanTate[(5)] 8 81
(Heather Main) *sn trckd ldrs: cl up 3f out: rdn over 2f out: kpt on to chse wnr jst ins fnl f: nvr able to chal* **11/1**

410- **3** 1 1/4 **Into The Wind**[175] 7301 6-8-11 **65** .... DavidProbert 9 70
(Rod Millman) *hld up in midfield: in tch at bk of ldng gp 4f out: rdn 3f out: styd on after to take 3rd nr fin* **20/1**

3314 **4** 1 **Bernisdale**[21] 1176 5-8-10 **64** .... JamieSpencer 7 67
(John Flint) *led 1f: trckd ldr: led 4f out to wl over 1f out: one pce* **6/1**[2]

226- **5** 5 **Burnham**[176] 7269 4-9-6 **75** .... RichardHughes 11 70
(Hughie Morrison) *prom: pressed ldr over 3f out tl rdn and nt qckn over 2f out: fdd over 1f out* **6/4**[1]

/50- **6** 1 3/4 **Jolly Roger (IRE)**[263] 4499 6-8-9 **70** .... AidenBlakemore[(7)] 2 62
(Tony Carroll) *v.s.i.s: hld up in last quartet: plld wd and pushed along 4f out: sme prog after but nvr on terms w ldrs: kpt on* **33/1**

433- **7** 5 **Outback (IRE)**[121] 3521 4-8-13 **68** .... EddieAhern 6 51
(Neil King) *lost prom pl after 4f: pushed along 1/2-way: no prog and btn 4f out: modest late hdwy* **25/1**

6053 **8** 2 3/4 **Boston Blue**[24] 1111 6-9-3 **71** .... JimCrowley 12 50
(Tony Carroll) *nvr bttr than midfield: rdn and out of tch 4f out: no ch after* **17/2**[3]

350- **9** 1 **April Ciel**[172] 7358 4-8-7 **65** .... DarrenEgan[(3)] 10 42
(Ronald Harris) *prom: lost pl and rdn over 4f out: sn wl btn* **16/1**

-255 **10** 2 3/4 **Priors Gold**[19] 1201 6-9-2 **73** .... SimonPearce[(3)] 14 45
(Laura Mongan) *hld up wl in rr: shkn up 4f out and sn lost all tch: bhd after* **40/1**

60-0 **11** 3 **Layline (IRE)**[30] 1037 6-9-7 **75** .... NeilCallan 3 42
(Gay Kelleway) *t.k.h: hld up in midfield: in tch 4f out: rdn and wknd qckly 3f out* **14/1**

00-0 **12** 4 1/2 **Megalala (IRE)**[12] 1327 12-9-4 **72** .... KieranO'Neill 5 32
(John Bridger) *led after 1f to 4f out: sn wknd* **50/1**

006- **13** 99 **Double Cee**[18] 7032 4-9-5 **74** .... WilliamBuick 1
(Warren Greatrex) *hld up in last pair: rdn and wknd over 4f out: t.o and all but p.u over 1f out* **14/1**

036- **P** **Eurhythmic (IRE)**[327] 2395 6-8-4 **61** oh7 ....(t) RyanPowell[(3)] 4
(Jim Old) *last whn p.u and dismntd 7f out* **50/1**

2m 35.35s (5.85) **Going Correction** +0.575s/f (Yiel) **14 Ran SP% 118.6**
WFA 4 from 5yo+ 1lb
Speed ratings (Par 103): **103,101,100,100,96 95,92,90,89,88 86,83,17,**
toteswingers 1&2 £16.50, 2&3 £35.30, 1&3 £33.90 CSF £115.88 CT £2379.48 TOTE £9.50: £3.10, £2.50, £6.70; EX 128.20 Trifecta £1049.20 Pool: £2158.30 - 1.54 winning units..
Owner Dr Clive Layton **Bred** Darley **Trained** Newmarket, Suffolk

FOCUS
Another modest handicap rated through the runner-up to last year's form.
T/Jkpt: Not won. T/Plt: £103.20 to a £1 stake. Pool of £86397.68 - 611.13 winning tickets.
T/Qpdt: £34.10 to a £1 stake. Pool of £5219.82 - 113.25 winning tickets. JN

[1554] LEOPARDSTOWN (L-H)
Monday, April 15

OFFICIAL GOING: Soft (heavy in places)

1587a BULMERS LIVE AT LEOPARDSTOWN SUMMER RACEDAYS 2013 MAIDEN — 1m 2f
4:15 (4:16) 3-Y-0 **£6,731** (£1,560; £682; £390)

RPR

1 **Indian Chief (IRE)**[173] 7337 3-9-5 .... JosephO'Brien 3 80+
(A P O'Brien, Ire) *w.w in rr: hdwy over 2f out travelling wl into 3rd over 1f out: qcknd wl to ld fnl 100yds: styd on wl: easily* **4/7**[1]

2 2 **Dubai Deer**[31] 1027 3-9-5 .... ChrisHayes 1 74
(P D Deegan, Ire) *prom: sn led: narrow advantage 1/2-way: drvn 2f out and strly pressed ent fnl f: hdd fnl 100yds: no ch w wnr: kpt on towards fin* **8/1**[3]

3 1 1/2 **Protestant (IRE)** 3-9-5 .... FMBerry 4 71
(Mrs John Harrington, Ire) *chsd ldrs in 3rd: 4th after 1/2-way: wnt 2nd under 2f out: rdn ent fnl f and sn no imp: kpt on same pce in 3rd ins fnl f* **25/1**

4 4 3/4 **Tonabrocky (IRE)**[162] 7579 3-9-5 .... KevinManning 5 62
(J S Bolger, Ire) *hld up towards rr: 6th 1/2-way: sme hdwy on outer appr st: rdn in 5th 2f out and sn no imp u.p: kpt on into mod 4th nr fin* **5/2**[2]

5 3/4 **Good On Numbers (IRE)**[173] 7339 3-9-5 .... ShaneFoley 6 60
(A Oliver, Ire) *chsd ldrs in 4th: t.k.h early: clsr in 3rd after 1/2-way: rdn on outer 2f out and sn no ex: dropped to 4th over 1f out: one pce fnl f and dropped to 5th nr fin* **16/1**

6 3 3/4 **Threat Resolved (IRE)**[150] 7756 3-9-5 .... GaryCarroll 7 53
(A Oliver, Ire) *prom: sn trckd ldr: cl 2nd 1/2-way: pushed along appr st and dropped to 4th 2f out: wknd* **40/1**

7 8 **Mouth Piece**[115] 8219 3-9-2 .... ConorHoban[(3)] 2 37
(A Oliver, Ire) *hld up in tch: 5th 1/2-way: niggled along on inner 3f out and sn dropped to rr: no ex* **50/1**

2m 19.55s (11.35) **Going Correction** +1.00s/f (Soft) **7 Ran SP% 117.5**
Speed ratings: **94,92,91,87,86 83,77**
CSF £6.67 TOTE £1.30: £1.02, £2.80; DF 5.20.
Owner Derrick Smith & Mrs John Magnier & Michael Tabor **Bred** Paget Bloodstock **Trained** Ballydoyle, Co Tipperary

FOCUS
The winner showed a nice change of gear to win.

1588 - 1593a (Foreign Racing) - See Raceform Interactive

[1357] MAISONS-LAFFITTE (R-H)
Monday, April 15

OFFICIAL GOING: Turf: very soft

1594a PRIX IDLE BOY (MAIDEN) (3YO COLTS & GELDINGS) (TURF) — 5f 110y
1:50 (12:00) 3-Y-0 **£10,162** (£4,065; £3,048; £2,032; £1,016)

RPR

1 **As De Bigorre (IRE)** 3-9-2 0 ....(b[1]) Francois-XavierBertras 7 84
(C Ferland, France) **126/10**

2 3/4 **Medeleck (FR)**[41] 3-9-2 0 .... FabienLefebvre 6 81
(Mme C De La Soudiere-Niault, France) **26/1**

3 *snk* **Xenophanes (IRE)** 3-9-2 0 .... FilipMinarik 8 81
(P Schiergen, Germany) **73/10**

4 1/2 **Lewamy (IRE)**[96] 126 3-9-2 0 .... ChristopheSoumillon 3 79
(John Best) *broke wl: racd in midfield bhd ldr on settling: rdn at 1/2-way: sn u.p: nt pce to go w ldrs: swtchd to ins rail 1 1/f out: r.o fnl f: clst at fin* **3/1**[1]

5 *hd* **Serez (IRE)**[172] 3-9-2 0 .... GregoryBenoist 5 78
(N Clement, France) **3/1**[1]

6 2 **Midnight Dancer (FR)**[25] 3-9-2 0 .... MaximeGuyon 4 72
(F Chappet, France) **15/1**

7 1 3/4 **Kukurun (FR)**[45] 3-9-2 0 .... AlexisBadel 2 66
(Mme M Bollack-Badel, France) **9/2**[3]

8 4 **Mehen (FR)**[45] 3-9-2 0 .... FabriceVeron 1 53
(H-A Pantall, France) **4/1**[2]

1m 9.4s (2.10) **8 Ran SP% 117.5**
WIN (incl. 1 euro stake): 13.60. PLACES: 4.10, 5.60, 3.00. DF: 90.80. SF: 212.90.
Owner Ecurie Tagada Sas **Bred** R Nardi **Trained** France

[1449] SOUTHWELL (L-H)
Tuesday, April 16

OFFICIAL GOING: Standard
Wind: Fresh half behind Weather: Cloudy with sunny periods

1595 BINARY TRENDS - TRIPLE YOUR INVESTMENT MEDIAN AUCTION MAIDEN STKS — 1m (F)
2:10 (2:11) (Class 6) 3-5-Y-0 **£1,940** (£577; £288; £144) **Stalls** Low

Form RPR

2-0 **1** **Glacial Age (IRE)**[31] 1046 3-8-6 0 .... HayleyTurner 6 84
(Jo Hughes) *trckd ldng pair: hdwy and cl up 3f out: led 2f out: sn pushed clr: easily* **8/11**[1]

2 11 **San Gabriel (IRE)** 3-8-6 0 .... LukeMorris 4 59
(Ed Walker) *trckd ldrs: swtchd rt to outer after 1 1/2f: rdn along and hdwy 3f out: styd on to take modest 2nd ins fnl f* **17/2**

542 **3** 1 3/4 **Solarmaite**[13] 1329 4-8-12 **65** .... MarkCoumbe[(3)] 7 54
(Roy Bowring) *led: rdn along 3f out: hdd 2f out: grad wknd* **7/1**[3]

2 **4** 11 **Guishan**[14] 1305 3-8-1 0 .... AndrewMullen 3 24
(Michael Appleby) *cl up on inner: rdn along 3f out: wknd over 2f out* **22/1**

6 **5** 18 **Wadacre Sarko**[8] 1429 3-8-6 0 .... SilvestreDeSousa 2
(Mark Johnston) *in tch: rdn along after 2f: sn outpcd and bhd* **7/2**[2]

The Form Book Flat, Raceform Ltd, Compton, RG20 6NL.

0- 6 3 1/2 **Camilla De Rossi**[169] 7433 3-7-8 0 NoelGarbutt(7) 1
(Rae Guest) *sn outpcd and a bhd* 50/1
P **Pretty Prisca** 4-8-10 0 RobertTart(5) 5
(J R Jenkins) *s.i.s: sn rdn along: a bhd: p.u 3f out: fatally injured* 66/1
1m 44.98s (1.28) **Going Correction** +0.35s/f (Slow)
WFA 3 from 4yo 14lb 7 Ran SP% **111.0**
Speed ratings (Par 101): **107,96,94,83,65 61,**
toteswingers 1&2 £2.40, 1&3 £1.80, 2&3 £3.60 CSF £7.28 TOTE £1.60: £1.30, £3.80; EX 9.00 Trifecta £26.00 Pool: £2040.14 - 58.65 winning units..
Owner James Henderson,Hugh Downs,Jo Hughes **Bred** Corduff Stud Ltd & J Corcoran **Trained** Lambourn. Berks

FOCUS
A moderate and uncompetitive maiden. The winner is rated to a literal reading of his reappearance form.

1596 32RED FILLIES' H'CAP 5f (F)
2:40 (2:40) (Class 5) (0-70,70) 4-Y-0+ **£2,587** (£770; £384; £192) **Stalls** High

Form RPR
4-26 1 **Mata Hari Blue**[3] 1540 7-9-7 **70** (t) AndrewMullen 3 86+
(Michael Appleby) *qckly away: mde all: shkn up wl over 1f out: sn clr: readily* 8/11[1]
2311 2 6 **Climaxfortackle (IRE)**[50] 790 5-9-5 **68** MartinDwyer 2 62
(Derek Shaw) *dwlt: in rr and sn swtchd lft to outer: hdwy 1/2-way: rdn to chse wnr wl over 1f out: drvn and no imp ent fnl f* 5/2[2]
0-40 3 4 **Economic Crisis (IRE)**[3] 1540 4-9-7 **70** PaddyAspell 4 50
(Alan Berry) *rrd s and dwlt: sn chsng ldng pair: rdn along 2f out: sn one pce* 9/1
040- 4 6 **Gypsy Jazz (IRE)**[274] 4143 6-8-5 **59** oh9 ow3 (p) AnnStokell(5) 1 17
(Ann Stokell) *chsd wnr: rdn along 1/2-way: sn wknd* 66/1
-154 5 5 **Bailadeira**[12] 1355 5-8-7 **56** oh1 JamesSullivan 5
(Tim Etherington) *dwlt: chsd ldrs: rdn along 1/2-way: sn outpcd* 8/1[3]
59.61s (-0.09) **Going Correction** +0.075s/f (Slow) 5 Ran SP% **109.1**
Speed ratings (Par 100): **103,93,87,77,69**
CSF £2.69 TOTE £1.60: £1.10, £1.50; EX 3.10 Trifecta £7.00 Pool: £2119.29 - 224.95 winning units..
Owner M J Golding **Bred** R T And Mrs Watson **Trained** Danethorpe, Notts

FOCUS
A one-sided contest and they finished well spread out for a 5f race. The winner is rated in line with a best view of her previous form.

1597 BINARY TRENDS - RISK FREE INVESTMENTS CLAIMING STKS 1m 3f (F)
3:15 (3:15) (Class 6) 4-Y-0+ **£1,940** (£577; £288; £144) **Stalls** Low

Form RPR
3245 1 **Noguchi (IRE)**[17] 1237 8-9-0 79 (b) NeilCallan 4 74
(Michael Murphy) *t.k.h: trckd ldrs on outer: cl up over 2f out: sn rdn and ev ch: drvn ins fnl f: sn edgd rt and styd on wl to ld last 50yds* 85/40[3]
2113 2 3/4 **Jacobs Son**[21] 1188 5-9-0 76 WilliamTwiston-Davies(5) 5 78
(Robert Mills) *cl up: slt ld 3f out: rdn jst over 2f out: drvn and hdd jst over 1f out: rallied u.p and ev ch ins fnl f: no ex towards fin* 2/1[2]
6612 3 hd **Tornado Force (IRE)**[12] 1353 5-9-3 71 HayleyTurner 3 76
(Alan McCabe) *hld up: smooth hdwy over 3f out: cl up over 2f out: effrt on inner and rdn to ld jst over 1f out: drvn ins fnl f: hdd and no ex last 50yds* 15/8[1]
4422 4 9 **Bold Marc (IRE)**[21] 1184 11-8-1 63 JoeyHaynes(7) 2 50
(Mrs K Burke) *trckd ldrs on inner: effrt over 3f out: sn rdn along and outpcd fnl 2f* 14/1
500- 5 47 **Visions Of Johanna (USA)**[190] 6940 8-8-10 54 PhilipPrince(5) 1
(Charles Smith) *set stdy pce: pushed along 4f out: rdn and hdd 3f out: sn wknd* 66/1
2m 30.13s (2.13) **Going Correction** +0.35s/f (Slow) 5 Ran SP% **108.3**
Speed ratings (Par 101): **106,105,105,98,64**
CSF £6.53 TOTE £3.20: £1.60, £1.20; EX 5.20 Trifecta £8.10 Pool: £2809.38 - 258.25 winning units..
Owner Mrs F Shaw **Bred** Cora Srl **Trained** Newmarket, Suffolk

FOCUS
They didn't go much of a pace early and the quintet remained tightly packed for the first mile. The winner did not need to match his winter best.

1598 £32 BONUS AT 32RED.COM (S) STKS 6f (F)
3:50 (3:51) (Class 6) 4-Y-0+ **£2,045** (£603; £302) **Stalls** Low

Form RPR
250- 1 **Whisky Bravo**[139] 7914 4-8-12 59 SilvestreDeSousa 6 72
(David Brown) *cl up: led over 2f out: sn rdn: drvn ins fnl f: hld on wl* 9/4[2]
00-1 2 1/2 **Tajneed (IRE)**[15] 1280 10-9-4 75 AdrianNicholls 3 76
(David Nicholls) *slt ld: rdn along and hdd over 2f out: drvn and rallied over 1f out: ev ch tl no ex last 75yds* 4/5[1]
655 3 2 3/4 **Irish Heartbeat (IRE)**[84] 317 8-8-7 72 JackDuern(5) 5 61
(Barry Leavy) *trckd ldrs: hdwy 3f out: sn swtchd wd and rdn: one pce fr over 1f out* 4/1[3]
000- 4 23 **Berrymead**[250] 5013 8-8-5 43 ow3 AnnStokell(5) 1
(Ann Stokell) *cl up on inner: rdn along 3f out: sn outpcd and bhd fnl 2f* 100/1
1m 19.07s (2.57) **Going Correction** +0.35s/f (Slow) 4 Ran SP% **107.3**
Speed ratings (Par 101): **96,95,91,61**
CSF £4.44 TOTE £3.20; EX 4.30 Trifecta £6.70 Pool: £2192.23 - 234.43 winning units..There were no bids for the winner.
Owner The Bachelor Party **Bred** Peter Onslow **Trained** Averham Park, Notts

FOCUS
A modest seller reduced to just the four runners. A slow time and shaky form.

1599 BINARY TRENDS - INVEST WITH BINARYTRENDS.CO.UK H'CAP 7f (F)
4:25 (4:26) (Class 4) (0-80,80) 4-Y-0+ **£4,690** (£1,395; £697; £348) **Stalls** Low

Form RPR
1220 1 **Al Khan (IRE)**[14] 1308 4-9-3 **76** MartinHarley 3 85
(Violet M Jordan) *cl up on inner: slt ld after 2f: rdn 2f out: styd on strly u.p fnl f* 15/2
6214 2 3/4 **Lieutenant Dan (IRE)**[20] 1214 6-8-7 **66** (v) AndrewMullen 6 73
(Michael Appleby) *cl up: chal wl over 2f out: rdn wl over 1f out and ev ch tl drvn and one pce wl ins fnl f* 16/1
2322 3 2 1/4 **Hellbender (IRE)**[13] 1334 7-8-10 **69** (t) DuranFentiman 4 70
(Shaun Harris) *chsd ldrs: rdn along and sltly outpcd wl over 2f out: styd on wl u.p fnl f* 7/1[3]
621- 4 nk **Half A Billion (IRE)**[168] 7451 4-9-0 **80** ConnorBeasley(7) 7 80
(Michael Dods) *slt ld 2f: cl up: rdn 2f out and ev ch tl wknd ent fnl f* 7/2[2]
136 5 nk **Caldercruix (USA)**[20] 1203 6-9-2 **78** (v) RaulDaSilva(3) 5 77
(James Evans) *trckd ldrs: hdwy over 2f out: sn rdn and kpt on ins fnl f* 7/2[2]
200- 6 7 **Springheel Jake**[210] 6338 4-9-2 **75** PJMcDonald 2 55
(Ann Duffield) *chsd ldrs on inner: rdn along wl over 2f out: grad wknd* 22/1
-004 7 9 **Dutch Old Master**[21] 1181 4-9-2 **75** (v) GeorgeBaker 8 31
(Gary Moore) *dwlt: t.k.h: chsd ldrs on outer: hdwy wl over 2f out: sn rdn and wknd wl over 1f out* 3/1[1]
110- 8 3 1/2 **Desert Creek (IRE)**[139] 7920 7-9-6 **79** (p) AdrianNicholls 1 26
(David Nicholls) *dwlt: a in rr* 8/1
1m 32.64s (2.34) **Going Correction** +0.35s/f (Slow) 8 Ran SP% **115.1**
Speed ratings (Par 105): **100,99,96,96,95 87,77,73**
toteswingers 1&2 £13.40, 1&3 £2.90, 2&3 £11.80 CSF £115.39 CT £875.34 TOTE £7.60: £2.80, £3.40, £2.20; EX 51.90 Trifecta £256.60 Pool: £2934.70 - 8.57 winning units..
Owner Rakebackmypoker.com **Bred** Galadari Sons Stud Company Limited **Trained** Moreton Morrell, Warwicks

FOCUS
A decent handicap, but it was crucial to be up with the pace, which was modest. A slight step up from the winner on his recent form.

1600 32RED CASINO H'CAP 1m 3f (F)
5:00 (5:00) (Class 6) (0-65,65) 4-Y-0+ **£1,940** (£577; £288; £144) **Stalls** Low

Form RPR
2224 1 **Day Of Destiny (IRE)**[15] 1279 8-9-7 **65** GrahamLee 7 73
(James Given) *a.p: cl up 4f out: chal 3f out: rdn to ld over 2f out: drvn and kpt on wl fnl f* 11/4[1]
3333 2 1 **Xpres Maite**[13] 1333 10-8-13 **60** (v) MarkCoumbe(3) 8 66
(Roy Bowring) *hmpd s and in rr: gd hdwy on outer after 4f: cl up 4f out: rdn along over 3f out and sn outpcd: drvn and styd on strly fr over 1f out: tk 2nd nr fin* 8/1
6232 3 1 **Thereabouts (USA)**[13] 1333 4-9-7 **65** (v) AndrewMullen 1 69
(Michael Appleby) *cl up: led 5f out: jnd and rdn 3f out: hdd 2f out and sn drvn: ev ch tl no ex wl ins fnl f: lost 2nd nr fin* 7/2[2]
-000 4 2 **Satwa Laird**[8] 1426 7-9-6 **64** HayleyTurner 3 65
(Conor Dore) *hld up: hdwy 4f out: rdn to chse ldrs over 2f out: sn drvn and no imp fnl f* 33/1
033- 5 2 **Dancing Paddy (IRE)**[153] 7710 5-8-4 **51** oh6 BillyCray(3) 5 48
(Alan Swinbank) *awkward s and in rr: pushed along over 5f out: rdn and hdwy 3f out: kpt on same pce fnl 2f* 8/1
2243 6 2 **Goldmadchen (GER)**[20] 1207 5-9-4 **62** JamesSullivan 2 56
(James Given) *in tch: effrt over 3f out: rdn along wl over 2f out: sn one pce* 6/1[3]
2100 7 1 1/4 **Evergreen Forest (IRE)**[28] 1084 5-9-1 **64** (p) AmyScott(5) 10 55
(Alastair Lidderdale) *hld up towards rr: sme hdwy over 3f out: sn rdn along and n.d* 8/1
6-34 8 6 **Kingaroo (IRE)**[56] 714 7-8-11 **55** LukeMorris 4 36
(Garry Woodward) *slt ld: rdn along over 5f out: sn hdd & wknd* 14/1
0443 9 1 1/2 **Gay Gallivanter**[42] 886 5-8-7 **51** oh5 (p) SilvestreDeSousa 9 29
(Mick Quinn) *chsd ldrs: rdn along over 5f out: sn wknd* 28/1
-541 10 42 **The Ducking Stool**[15] 1297 6-9-0 **65** ShelleyBirkett(7) 6
(Julia Feilden) *a in rr: bhd fnl 3f* 12/1
2m 32.09s (4.09) **Going Correction** +0.35s/f (Slow) 10 Ran SP% **117.3**
Speed ratings (Par 101): **99,98,97,96,94 93,92,87,86,56**
toteswingers 1&2 £6.70, 1&3 £3.10, 2&3 £5.70 CSF £25.62 CT £79.51 TOTE £4.30: £1.60, £2.70, £1.50; EX 34.80 Trifecta £91.40 Pool: £2689.35 - 22.05 winning units..
Owner Suzanne & Nigel Williams **Bred** Rathasker Stud **Trained** Willoughton, Lincs

FOCUS
They went a fair pace in this moderate handicap and it proved quite a test. A small step up on the winner's recent Flat form.

1601 32RED.COM APPRENTICE H'CAP 1m 6f (F)
5:35 (5:35) (Class 5) (0-70,64) 4-Y-0+ **£2,587** (£770; £384; £192) **Stalls** Low

Form RPR
043- 1 **Decana**[224] 5908 5-9-5 **62** CharlieBennett(7) 7 73
(Hughie Morrison) *dwlt: t.k.h: sn in tch: hdwy on outer 1/2-way and sn trcking ldng pair: effrt to chse ldr 3f out: rdn wl over 1f out: styd on wl to ld ins fnl f* 6/1
0-12 2 3 **Neighbourhood (USA)**[21] 1189 5-9-5 **55** (b) JoeyHaynes 1 62+
(James Evans) *hld up in rr: stdy hdwy on outer 6f out: led 4f out: pushed clr 3f out: rdn wl over 1f out: wknd and hdd ins fnl f* 7/2[2]
2311 3 10 **Linroyale Boy (USA)**[13] 1333 5-9-11 **64** BTTreanor(3) 3 57
(Alan Swinbank) *trckd ldrs: effrt 4f out: chsd ldng pair 3f out: sn rdn and one pce fnl 2f* 5/4[1]
5012 4 6 **Calculating (IRE)**[14] 1306 9-9-0 **55** CharlotteJenner(5) 5 39
(Mark Usher) *hld up towards rr: effrt 4f out: sn rdn along and nvr a factor* 5/1[3]
0056 5 nse **If What And Maybe**[35] 973 5-8-5 **48** ow2 CarolineKelly(7) 2 30
(John Ryan) *chsd ldrs: rdn along 4f out: sn outpcd* 33/1
2-30 6 1 1/4 **Inside Knowledge (USA)**[42] 888 7-8-10 **49** MatthewHopkins(3) 4 32
(Garry Woodward) *led: hdd 1/2-way: cl up on inner tl rdn along over 4f out and sn wknd* 25/1
06-3 7 12 **Royal Defence (IRE)**[44] 515 7-8-12 **48** ShelleyBirkett 6 14
(Mick Quinn) *cl up: slt ld 1/2-way: rdn along and hdd 4f out: sn wknd* 10/1
3m 11.67s (3.37) **Going Correction** +0.35s/f (Slow) 7 Ran SP% **113.5**
Speed ratings (Par 103): **104,102,96,93,93 92,85**
toteswingers 1&2 £3.20, 1&3 £2.80, 2&3 £2.00 CSF £26.76 CT £42.02 TOTE £7.80: £2.90, £1.50; EX 21.70 Trifecta £62.40 Pool: £2586.01 - 31.05 winning units..
Owner R M, S R & P J Payne **Bred** Frazer Hines & John James **Trained** East Ilsley, Berks
■ Stewards' Enquiry : Caroline Kelly two-day ban: weighed in 2lb heavy (Apr 30-May 1)

FOCUS
The tempo didn't pick up until after a mile in this modest apprentice handicap but the best time on the round course. A small personal best from the winner.

T/Plt: £84.00 to a £1 stake. Pool of £60,691.60 - 527.26 winning tickets. T/Qpdt: £41.30 to a £1 stake. Pool of £4461.59 - 79.82 winning tickets. JR

1456 SAINT-CLOUD (L-H)
Tuesday, April 16

OFFICIAL GOING: Turf: very soft

1602a PRIX PENELOPE (GROUP 3) (3YO FILLIES) (TURF) 1m 2f 110y
2:20 (2:21) 3-Y-O £32,520 (£13,008; £9,756; £6,504; £3,252)

RPR
1 **Ferevia (IRE)**20 3-9-0 0 OlivierPeslier 5 108+
(C Laffon-Parias, France) *hld up towards rr: last ent st: shkn up and qcknd wl on outside 1 1/2f out: fin strly fnl f: led 40yds out: r.o wl: comf* **91/10**
2 1 3/4 **Baltic Baroness (GER)**16 3-9-0 0 MaximeGuyon 1 104
(A Fabre, France) *sn led on ins: hdd after 4f: regained ld ent st: sn wnt clr: stl clr ent fnl f: ct and hdd 40yds out: r.o* **2/1**1
3 1 1/2 **La Banderilla (FR)**33 3-9-0 0 IoritzMendizabal 8 101
(J Heloury, France) *racd in 4th on outside: rn wd ent st: relegated to 6th 2f out: shkn up and proged to 4th ent fnl f: styd on wl: fin 4th: plcd 3rd* **15/1**
4 snk **Eleuthera (FR)**31 1047 3-9-0 0 EddyHardouin 2 101
(P Demercastel, France) *racd in midfield on ins: rdn 2f out: styng on wl on rail 1f out whn had to be snatched up after suffering interference: lost momentum: rallied fnl 50yds: fin 5th: plcd 4th* **24/1**
5 hd **Orion Love**31 3-9-0 0 FabriceVeron 7 100
(H-A Pantall, France) *racd in 2nd on outside: led after 4f: hdd ent st: r.o u.p 2f out: hung into rail 1f out causing interference to Eleuthra: styd on fnl 100yds: fin 3rd: disqualified and plcd 5th* **48/10**3
6 3 **Childa (IRE)**31 1047 3-9-0 0 StephanePasquier 6 95
(S Wattel, France) *hld up towards rr: rdn 2f out: nt qckn: styd on fnl f* **5/2**2
7 7 **Sushi Tuna**31 1047 3-9-0 0 Francois-XavierBertras 9 81
(F Rohaut, France) *prom in 3rd: rdn 2f out: no ex: sn btn* **8/1**
8 shd **Mahendranagar (FR)**33 3-9-0 0 ThierryJarnet 4 81
(J Boisnard, France) *hld up in rr: proged to 7th ent st: rdn 2 1/2f out: no ex: sn btn* **23/1**
9 12 **Chiriqui (FR)**19 3-9-0 0 TheoBachelot 3 57
(S Wattel, France) *racd in midfield on settling: rdn ent st: no ex: sn btn* **38/1**

2m 23.4s (3.80) **9 Ran SP% 117.1**
WIN (incl. 1 euro stake): 10.10. PLACES: 2.80, 1.60, 3.30. DF: 15.60. SF: 42.70.
Owner Leonidas Marinopoulos **Bred** Stilvi Compania Financiera Sa **Trained** Chantilly, France

BEVERLEY (R-H)
Wednesday, April 17

OFFICIAL GOING: Good to firm (firm in back straight; 9.3)
Wind: Fresh; across Weather: Cloudy

1603 PROMOTE YOUR HORSE PRE-AUCTION AT RACEHORSETRADER.COM (S) STKS 1m 100y
2:00 (2:00) (Class 6) 3-Y-O+ £2,264 (£673; £336; £168) Stalls Low

Form RPR
4-00 1 **Thrust Control (IRE)**7 1459 6-9-6 50 (p) FrederikTylicki 5 57
(Tracy Waggott) *mde all: pushed clr 3f out: rdn wl over 1f out: kpt on wl fnl f* **10/1**
50-0 2 1 1/2 **Firefly**45 625 4-9-3 44 MichaelMetcalfe(3) 7 54
(John Weymes) *midfield on inner: hdwy 3f out: swtchd lft and rdn 2f out: chsd ldng pair ent fnl f: sn drvn and kpt on same pce* **40/1**
305- 3 1/2 **Eeny Mac (IRE)**204 6559 6-9-3 62 JulieBurke(3) 3 53
(Neville Bycroft) *trckd ldng pair: hdwy over 2f out and sn chsng wnr: rdn wl over 1f out: drvn ins fnl f: one pce* **15/8**1
5325 4 1 1/2 **Availed Speaker (IRE)**18 1239 4-8-13 60 SamanthaBell(7) 6 49
(Richard Fahey) *trckd ldrs: hdwy 3f out: rdn along 2f out: kpt on same pce* **3/1**2
00-0 5 3/4 **Tony Hollis**15 1311 5-9-6 51 JimmyQuinn 13 48
(Karen Tutty) *chsd ldrs: hdwy wl over 2f out: rdn along wl over 1f out: drvn and one pce appr fnl f* **28/1**
-405 6 1/2 **Sir George (IRE)**36 967 8-8-13 54 JacobButterfield(7) 4 47
(Suzzanne France) *midfield: hdwy over 2f out: sn rdn and no imp fnl f* **7/1**3
000- 7 nk **City Of The Kings (IRE)**129 8051 8-9-6 60 RoystonFfrench 10 46
(Tracy Waggott) *hld up in rr: hdwy wl over 2f out: rdn and kpt on fnl f: nrst fin* **14/1**
50-0 8 2 3/4 **Kingarrick**63 646 5-9-6 53 DuranFentiman 2 40
(Noel Wilson) *in rr: sme hdwy over 2f out: sn rdn along and n.d* **14/1**
05-0 9 1/2 **Feeling Good**11 1394 4-9-3 54 PaulPickard(3) 12 38
(Brian Ellison) *hld up: a towards rr* **16/1**
4050 10 1 **American Lover (FR)**20 1221 6-8-10 43 AdamCarter(5) 8 31
(John Wainwright) *hld up and bhd: hdwy on inner whn nt clr run 1 1/2f out: no ch after: b.b.v* **28/1**
04-0 11 1 **Penderyn**66 597 6-8-10 35 PhilipPrince(5) 1 29
(Charles Smith) *chsd wnr: rdn along wl over 2f out: drvn wl over 1f out and sn wknd* **100/1**
1060 12 10 **Gunner Will (IRE)**26 1111 4-9-5 57 DavidSimmonson(7) 9 17
(Paul Midgley) *in rr: sme hdwy on wd outside 3f out: sn rdn and nvr a factor* **16/1**
4050 13 4 **General Tufto**15 1311 8-9-6 36 (b) RobbieFitzpatrick 11
(Charles Smith) *a in rr* **50/1**

1m 47.18s (-0.42) **Going Correction** -0.05s/f (Good) **13 Ran SP% 118.8**
Speed ratings (Par 101): **100,98,98,96,95 95,94,92,91,90 89,79,75**
toteswingers 1&2 £16.50, 1&3 £7.00, 2&3 £5.30 CSF £369.32 TOTE £9.20: £2.30, £14.00, £1.30; EX 437.90 Trifecta £349.00 Part won. Pool: £465.34 - 0.02 winning units..There was no bid for the winner.
Owner David Tate **Bred** Rathasker Stud **Trained** Spennymoor, Co Durham

FOCUS
On a blustery day the ground had dried out and, after the opening seller, it was described as "rattling quick" by winning rider Freddie Tylicki. Hard form to get behind with little involved from off the pace.

1604 FOLLOW US ON TWITTER @RACEHORSETRADER H'CAP 1m 1f 207y
2:35 (2:35) (Class 4) (0-80,79) 3-Y-O £4,690 (£1,395; £697; £348) Stalls Low

Form RPR
2221 1 **Aryal**41 911 3-9-1 73 (b) NeilCallan 2 82+
(Mark Johnston) *mde all: rdn clr over 2f out: styd on strly* **7/2**1
16- 2 2 1/2 **Nice Story (IRE)**221 6021 3-9-5 77 SamHitchcott 8 80+
(Mick Channon) *hld up in rr: hdwy over 4f out: chsd ldrs over 2f out: swtchd ins and rdn over 1f out: styd on fnl f* **25/1**
35-1 3 3/4 **Wyldfire (IRE)**16 1282 3-8-10 71 LeeTopliss(3) 1 73
(Richard Fahey) *trckd ldng pair on inner: hdwy to chse wnr 2f out: sn rdn: edgd lft ent fnl f and kpt on same pce* **4/1**2
441- 4 1 1/4 **Kuantan One (IRE)**154 7707 3-9-4 76 TomEaves 4 75
(Paul Cole) *chsd wnr: rdn along over 2f out: grad wknd* **9/2**3
226- 5 1 1/2 **Esteaming**177 7292 3-9-2 74 GrahamGibbons 3 70+
(David Barron) *towards rr: hdwy wl over 2f out: n.m.r on inner and swtchd lft wl over 1f out: kpt on fnl f: nrst fin* **6/1**
3311 6 2 1/2 **Flying Tempo**27 1098 3-9-3 75 (b) StevieDonohoe 7 66
(Ed Dunlop) *dwlt: a in rr* **10/1**
23-3 7 1 **Arthurs Secret**26 1109 3-9-7 79 MichaelO'Connell 6 68
(John Quinn) *chsd ldrs: rdn along wl over 2f out: sn wknd* **13/2**
1-43 8 7 **Mister Marcasite**7 1486 3-8-13 71 DavidAllan 5 46
(Mel Brittain) *t.k.h: towards rr: hdwy on outer after 3f and sn chsng ldrs: rdn along 3f out: sn drvn and wknd* **6/1**

2m 8.85s (1.85) **Going Correction** -0.05s/f (Good) **8 Ran SP% 115.2**
Speed ratings (Par 100): **90,88,87,86,85 83,82,76**
toteswingers 1&2 £14.20, 1&3 £4.40, 2&3 £34.30 CSF £86.60 CT £364.93 TOTE £3.90: £1.30, £6.30, £1.40; EX 36.60 Trifecta £300.00 Pool: £1,320.24 - 3.30 winning units..
Owner Sheikh Hamdan Bin Mohammed Al Maktoum **Bred** Newsells Park Stud **Trained** Middleham Moor, N Yorks

FOCUS
Some unexposed 3yos in this open looking 1m2f handicap. The winner made all off an easy lead but it might not pay to underestimate his effort.

1605 BATTLEFIELD STUD MAIDEN AUCTION STKS (DIV I) 5f
3:10 (3:11) (Class 5) 2-Y-O £3,234 (£962; £481; £240) Stalls Low

Form RPR
0 1 **Penina (IRE)**11 1399 2-8-6 0 PJMcDonald 9 67
(Brian Ellison) *cl up: rdn and edgd lft over 1f out: edgd rt ent fnl f: sn led: drvn and edgd lft last 100yds: jst hld on* **40/1**
2 hd **Inciting Incident (IRE)** 2-8-13 0 GrahamGibbons 2 73+
(Ed McMahon) *trckd ldrs: effrt whn n.m.r over 1f out: swtchd rt and nt clr run ent fnl f: swtchd lft and rdn to chal and ev ch whn bmpd last 100yds and again towards fin* **9/1**
3 1 **Captain Midnight (IRE)** 2-8-13 0 PhillipMakin 1 70+
(David Brown) *trckd ldrs: hdwy over 1f out: rdn to chal ent fnl f: ev ch tl no ex towards fin* **7/4**1
4 5 **Atlantic Affair (IRE)** 2-8-6 0 LiamJones 3 45+
(Mark Johnston) *led: rdn along 2f out: drvn over 1f out: hdd jst ins fnl f: wknd* **3/1**2
5 1/2 **Different Scenario** 2-8-6 0 DavidAllan 5 43
(Mel Brittain) *towards rr: hdwy wl over 1f out: styd on wl fnl f: nrst fin* **18/1**
22 6 1 1/2 **Memory Styx**9 1421 2-8-8 0 SamHitchcott 10 39
(Mick Channon) *chsd ldrs on outer: cl up 1/2-way: rdn along wl over 1f out and grad wknd* **5/1**3
7 1 1/4 **Hickster (IRE)** 2-8-11 0 NeilCallan 8 38
(Tom Dascombe) *chsd ldrs: rdn along 2f out: sn outpcd* **11/1**
8 2 1/2 **Sullivan Park** 2-8-4 0 JamesSullivan 4 22
(Ian McInnes) *in tch: rdn along 1/2-way: sn outpcd* **50/1**
9 2 1/4 **Strictly Glitz (IRE)** 2-8-8 0 MichaelO'Connell 6 18
(John Quinn) *a towards rr* **14/1**
10 15 **Doncaster Belle (IRE)** 2-8-1 0 PhilipPrince(5) 7
(Charles Smith) *sn outpcd and a bhd* **25/1**

1m 5.45s (1.95) **Going Correction** +0.30s/f (Good) **10 Ran SP% 116.5**
Speed ratings (Par 92): **96,95,94,86,85 82,80,76,73,49**
toteswingers 1&2 £30.50, 1&3 £15.20, 2&3 £4.40 CSF £361.13 TOTE £63.90: £12.60, £3.60, £1.02; EX 307.30 Trifecta £796.70 Part won. Pool: £1,062.27 - 0.03 winning units..
Owner Antonio Marucci & Brian Ellison **Bred** Lawman Syndicate & Joseph Kenny **Trained** Norton, N Yorks
■ Stewards' Enquiry : P J McDonald one-day ban: careless riding (May 1)

FOCUS
Part one of a 2yo maiden auction race. The wind had an effect, the winner and third both edged left-handed in the closing stages. The form is rated around the race average.

1606 BATTLEFIELD STUD MAIDEN AUCTION STKS (DIV II) 5f
3:45 (3:47) (Class 5) 2-Y-O £3,234 (£962; £481; £240) Stalls Low

Form RPR
5 1 **Vine De Nada**18 1247 2-8-13 0 NeilCallan 3 74+
(Mark Johnston) *wnt lft s: t.k.h and chsd ldng pair: hdwy to chal over 1f out: rdn to ld ent fnl f: green and sn hung bdly lft: jst hld on* **4/6**1
2 shd **Lily Rules (IRE)** 2-8-6 0 BarryMcHugh 1 67+
(Tony Coyle) *in tch: pushed along and sltly outpcd 1/2-way: hdwy on inner whn nt clr run over 1f out: sn swtchd lft and rdn: str run ins fnl f: jst failed* **28/1**
3 1 3/4 **Chamberlain** 2-8-11 0 1 PaulMulrennan 6 65
(Alan McCabe) *in tch: hdwy 2f out: swtchd rt to inner over 1f out: styd on and ev ch ins fnl f: one pce towards fin* **14/1**
4 5 **Hot Stock (FR)** 2-8-11 0 FrederikTylicki 4 47
(Jo Hughes) *led: rdn over 1f out: hdd jst ins fnl f: sn wknd* **14/1**
5 2 **White Flag** 2-8-6 0 DuranFentiman 8 35+
(Tim Easterby) *towards rr tl sme late hdwy* **25/1**
6 4 **Idamante** 2-8-11 0 TomEaves 9 26
(Kristin Stubbs) *chsd ldr: rdn along wl over 1f out: grad wknd* **40/1**
7 shd **Blades Boy** 2-8-9 0 ow3 LeeTopliss(3) 10 26
(Richard Fahey) *a towards rr* **6/1**3
8 nk **Princess Myla (IRE)** 2-8-4 0 JimmyQuinn 5 17
(Paul Midgley) *hmpd s: a in rr* **25/1**
3 9 hd **Tyrsal (IRE)**14 1328 2-8-9 0 AdamBeschizza 7 22
(Robert Eddery) *in tch: effrt 2f out: sn rdn and n.d* **5/1**2

0 **10** *6* **Sleaford**[26] 1108 2-8-9 0 DavidAllan 2
(Mel Brittain) *chsd ldrs: pushed along bef 1/2-way: sn wknd* **25/1**

1m 5.87s (2.37) **Going Correction** +0.30s/f (Good) **10** Ran SP% **121.7**
Speed ratings (Par 92): **93,92,90,82,78 72,72,71,71,61**
toteswingers 1&2 £10.40, 1&3 £10.90, 2&3 £35.60 CSF £34.66 TOTE £1.40: £1.02, £5.60, £3.80; EX 19.90 Trifecta £223.00 Pool: £1,528.76 - 5.14 winning units..
Owner Inner Circle Thoroughbreds - New World **Bred** Cheveley Park Stud Ltd **Trained** Middleham Moor, N Yorks

FOCUS
Part two. Little strength in depth and a slightly slower time, but the winner is probably a fair bit better than she showed on the day.

1607 RACE HORSE TRADER "COMMISSION FREE" H'CAP 5f
4:20 (4:20) (Class 3) (0-95,95) 4-Y-O+ **£7,439** (£2,213; £1,106; £553) **Stalls** Low

Form RPR

000- **1** **Mister Manannan (IRE)**[172] 7397 6-8-13 **87** AdrianNicholls 7 96
(David Nicholls) *hld up in rr: effrt over 1f out: sn swtchd lft and rdn: str run ins fnl f to ld nr fin* **14/1**

245- **2** *nk* **Last Sovereign**[127] 8066 9-8-5 **86** ow1 (b) JacobButterfield(7) 5 94
(Ollie Pears) *sltly hmpd at s: trckd ldrs: smooth hdwy to ld over 1f out: rdn clr ins fnl f: hdd and no ex nr fin* **8/1**

000- **3** *3/4* **Head Space (IRE)**[228] 5829 5-8-13 **87** JamesSullivan 1 92
(Ruth Carr) *sltly hmpd s: in tch: hdwy 2f out: rdn to chse ldr ins fnl f: kpt on same pce* **7/2**[1]

20-0 **4** *3 1/2* **Arctic Feeling (IRE)**[18] 1245 5-8-4 **85** LauraBarry(7) 6 78
(Richard Fahey) *towards rr: hdwy 2f out: sn rdn and kpt on fnl f: nrst fin* **13/2**[3]

22-0 **5** *nse* **Ancient Cross**[18] 1232 9-9-6 **94** (t) PaulMulrennan 12 87
(Michael Easterby) *trckd ldrs: hdwy 2f out: rdn to chse ldr ent fnl f: sn drvn and wknd* **8/1**

0500 **6** *1 3/4* **Swiss Cross**[53] 776 6-9-3 **91** (t) NeilCallan 4 77+
(Phil McEntee) *sltly hmpd s: chsd ldrs on inner: rdn along 2f out: sn wknd* **5/1**[2]

000- **7** *2* **Caranbola**[216] 6165 7-8-7 **81** TomEaves 9 60
(Mel Brittain) *cl up: rdn along wl over 1f out: sn wknd* **5/1**[2]

060- **8** *1 3/4* **Last Bid**[220] 6075 4-8-13 **87** DavidAllan 11 60
(Tim Easterby) *a in rr* **22/1**

000- **9** *1 1/2* **Bosun Breese**[179] 7243 8-8-13 **87** GrahamGibbons 8 54
(David Barron) *led and swtchd rt s: rdn along 2f out: hdd over 1f out and sn wknd* **7/1**

1m 4.09s (0.59) **Going Correction** +0.30s/f (Good) **9** Ran SP% **114.6**
Speed ratings (Par 107): **107,106,105,99,99 96,93,90,88**
toteswingers 1&2 £18.00, 1&3 £33.10, 2&3 £4.70 CSF £119.51 CT £485.03 TOTE £15.70: £3.50, £2.90, £1.20; EX 139.10 Trifecta £715.10 Part won. Pool: £953.47 - 0.20 winning units..
Owner Mrs M Schofield **Bred** Mull Enterprises Ltd **Trained** Sessay, N Yorks
■ Stewards' Enquiry : Graham Gibbons three-day ban: careless riding (May 1-3)

FOCUS
Plenty of pace on in this competitive sprint handicap and the winner came from behind. He was still 4lb off his 4yo best.

1608 BUY RACEHORSES ONLINE AT RACEHORSETRADER.COM 7f 100y
4:55 (4:55) (Class 5) 3-Y-O **£3,234** (£962; £481; £240) **Stalls** Low

Form RPR

221- **1** **Jabhaat (USA)**[210] 6355 3-9-7 **74** PaulMulrennan 2 87
(Ed Dunlop) *trckd ldng pair: smooth hdwy 2f out: n.m.r and swtchd rt to inner over 1f out: shkn up to ld ent fnl f: sn clr* **10/3**[2]

0-11 **2** *6* **Admiralofthesea (USA)**[9] 1427 3-9-4 **71** 6ex AdamBeschizza 1 69
(Robert Eddery) *trckd ldrs on inner: effrt 2f out: sn rdn: styd on ins fnl f: no ch w wnr* **6/1**[3]

-121 **3** *3 1/2* **Skytrain**[17] 1275 3-9-7 **74** NeilCallan 4 63
(Mark Johnston) *mde most: rdn along 2f out: drvn and hdd ent fnl f: sn wknd* **7/4**[1]

60-6 **4** *hd* **Gold Roll (IRE)**[22] 1190 3-8-9 **62** PJMcDonald 3 51
(Ruth Carr) *dwlt and towards rr: hdwy over 2f out: rdn wl over 1f out: styd on fnl f: nrst fin* **50/1**

-416 **5** *1/2* **The Scuttler (IRE)**[17] 1275 3-9-1 **68** SamHitchcott 9 56
(Mick Channon) *chsd ldrs: rdn along 2f out: sn one pce* **12/1**

630- **6** *3 1/2* **Mrs Warren**[186] 7056 3-8-7 **60** JimmyQuinn 6 39
(Charles Hills) *cl up: disp ld 1/2-way: rdn along 2f out: drvn over 1f out: sn wknd* **20/1**

556- **7** *7* **Bapak Pesta (IRE)**[209] 6404 3-8-12 **65** AmyRyan 7 26
(Kevin Ryan) *a in rr* **10/1**

10-3 **8** *7* **Yorkshireman (IRE)**[17] 1275 3-9-6 **73** PhillipMakin 5 17
(David Brown) *a outpcd and bhd fr 1/2-way* **7/1**

64-6 **9** *7* **Flighty Clarets (IRE)**[15] 1307 3-8-12 **65** FrederikTylicki 8
(Richard Fahey) *t.k.h: cl up: rdn along over 2f out: sn wknd* **20/1**

1m 33.35s (-0.45) **Going Correction** -0.05s/f (Good) **9** Ran SP% **114.5**
Speed ratings (Par 98): **100,93,89,88,88 84,76,68,60**
toteswingers 1&2 £4.10, 1&3 £2.20, 2&3 £3.10 CSF £22.76 CT £44.86 TOTE £3.40: £1.10, £2.70, £1.20; EX 21.20 Trifecta £30.30 Pool: £2,515.88 - 62.10 winning units..
Owner Hamdan Al Maktoum **Bred** Shadwell Farm LLC **Trained** Newmarket, Suffolk

FOCUS
The two leaders took each other on and the impressive winner looks sure to go on to much better things. However there were doubts over several of his opponents.

1609 SELL RACEHORSES ONLINE AT RACEHORSETRADER.COM H'CAP 1m 4f 16y
5:25 (5:25) (Class 5) (0-75,81) 3-Y-O **£3,234** (£962; £481; £240) **Stalls** Low

Form RPR

422 **1** **Ambleside**[17] 1274 3-9-2 **70** (b[1]) LiamJones 3 77
(Mark Johnston) *s.i.s: sn pushed along to go prom: trckd ldr after 4f: chal over 2f out: sn rdn and hung bdly rt over 1f out: carried hd high: sn drvn and wandered: styd on ins fnl f to ld nr line* **5/1**[3]

1121 **2** *nk* **Naru (IRE)**[8] 1453 3-9-13 **81** 6ex NeilCallan 4 87
(James Tate) *trckd ldrs: hdwy and flashed tail 3f out: chal 2f out: rdn to ld over 1f out: drvn: carried hd high and wandered ins fnl f: hdd nr line* **5/4**[1]

2-01 **3** *1 1/4* **Dali's Lover (IRE)**[75] 473 3-8-12 **66** JimmyQuinn 2 70
(Charles Hills) *hld up in rr: hdwy on outer wl over 1f out: rdn to chse ldng pair ent fnl f: no imp towards fin* **6/1**

56-1 **4** *1/2* **Gabrial The Master (IRE)**[16] 1296 3-9-3 **74** LeeTopliss(3) 5 77
(Richard Fahey) *led: rdn along over 2f out: drvn and bmpd bdly over 1f out: sn hdd and kpt on same pce* **7/2**[2]

-412 **5** *3 1/2* **Bain's Pass (IRE)**[12] 1372 3-8-10 **64** PhillipMakin 1 61
(Kevin Ryan) *trckd ldr on inner: pushed along over 3f out: rdn over 2f out: sn one pce* **7/1**

2m 39.41s (-0.39) **Going Correction** -0.05s/f (Good) **5** Ran SP% **110.1**
Speed ratings (Par 98): **99,98,97,97,95**
toteswingers 1&2 £1.70, 1&3 £3.50, 2&3 £4.00 CSF £11.83 TOTE £5.60: £2.70, £1.10; EX 14.20 Trifecta £44.70 Pool: £1,428.62 - 23.94 winning units..
Owner Sheikh Hamdan Bin Mohammed Al Maktoum **Bred** Mount Coote Partnership **Trained** Middleham Moor, N Yorks

FOCUS
A tactical and very messy 3yo 1m4f handicap. Fair form, rated around the third and fourth.

1610 SYNDICATE YOUR HORSE AT RACEHORSETRADER.COM FILLIES' STKS (H'CAP) 1m 100y
6:00 (6:00) (Class 5) (0-70,66) 4-Y-O+ **£3,234** (£962; £481; £240) **Stalls** Low

Form RPR

-333 **1** **Alluring Star**[11] 1394 5-8-3 **55** MatthewHopkins(7) 2 67
(Michael Easterby) *t.k.h: cl up: led over 3f out: rdn clr appr fnl f: kpt on: readily* **15/8**[1]

56-4 **2** *3* **Ssafa**[21] 1211 5-9-7 **66** (p) TomEaves 9 71
(Alastair Lidderdale) *wnt lft s: t.k.h: chsd ldng pair: rdn along 2f out: kpt on u.p fnl f* **7/2**[2]

0-65 **3** *1 1/4* **Adorable Choice (IRE)**[35] 978 5-9-1 **60** StephenCraine 7 62
(Tom Dascombe) *t.k.h: led: pushed along and hdd over 3f out: rdn over 2f out: drvn and one pce ent fnl f* **9/2**[3]

2-04 **4** *hd* **Mishhar (IRE)**[11] 1389 4-9-1 **60** (p) BarryMcHugh 3 62
(Tony Coyle) *t.k.h: trckd ldrs on inner: effrt over 2f out: sn rdn and one pce appr fnl f* **13/2**

3-00 **5** *4* **Kheskianto (IRE)**[63] 646 7-8-0 **52** oh3 (t) DanielleMooney(7) 1 45
(Michael Chapman) *in rr: hdwy over 2f out: sn rdn along and n.d* **16/1**

300- **6** *4* **Exclusive Dancer**[173] 7369 4-9-2 **61** PJMcDonald 4 44
(George Moore) *a in rr* **8/1**

0-00 **7** *hd* **Dansili Dutch (IRE)**[29] 1082 4-8-4 **52** oh5 [1] NeilFarley(3) 6 35
(Andrew Crook) *t.k.h: hld up: a in rr* **18/1**

1m 47.18s (-0.42) **Going Correction** -0.05s/f (Good) **7** Ran SP% **110.8**
Speed ratings (Par 100): **100,97,95,95,91 87,87**
toteswingers 1&2 £1.70, 1&3 £3.50, 2&3 £4.00 CSF £7.92 CT £22.93 TOTE £2.60: £1.90, £3.00; EX 8.00 Trifecta £21.80 Pool: £498.55 - 17.14 winning units..
Owner Jeff Hamer & Bernard Bargh **Bred** B Bargh **Trained** Sheriff Hutton, N Yorks

FOCUS
Modest fillies' form. The winner may not have needed to match last year's best.
T/Plt: £25.50 to a £1 stake. Pool of £50,484.61 - 1,444.71 winning units T/Qpdt: £8.40 to a £1 stake. Pool of £3,668.94 - 320.30 winning units JR

[1541] KEMPTON (A.W) (R-H)
Wednesday, April 17

OFFICIAL GOING: Standard
Wind: Fresh; half behind Weather: Fine

1611 KEMPTON FOR SUMMER WEDDINGS MEDIAN AUCTION MAIDEN FILLIES' STKS 1m 3f (P)
5:55 (5:56) (Class 6) 3-5-Y-O **£1,940** (£577; £288; £144) **Stalls** Low

Form RPR

1 **Abilene** 3-8-9 0 KirstyMilczarek 4 83+
(Luca Cumani) *led 1f: trckd ldr: led 2f out: pushed clr 1f out: comf* **2/1**[2]

6-3 **2** *5* **Permeate**[12] 1371 3-8-9 0 SteveDrowne 9 73
(Charles Hills) *led after 1f tl 2f out: no ex 1f out* **1/1**[1]

3 *2 1/2* **Nellie Forbush** 3-8-9 0 DavidProbert 8 68
(Andrew Balding) *chsd ldng pair: rdn 3f out: sn outpcd: kpt on fnl f* **7/1**[3]

4 *12* **Dawn Beat** 3-8-9 0 JamesDoyle 7 46
(Jonathan Portman) *s.s: towards rr: rdn 4f out: modest late hdwy* **8/1**

5 *4 1/2* **Fenton** 3-8-9 0 AndreaAtzeni 10 38
(Harry Dunlop) *v.s.a: bhd: sme hdwy 6f out: rdn 4f out: sn btn* **8/1**

0-00 **6** *9* **Parsons Green**[14] 1317 4-10-0 **40** RobertHavlin 2 25
(Michael Attwater) *a mid-div: outpcd and struggling 3f out* **100/1**

5 **7** *3 1/4* **Young Lisa**[16] 1296 4-9-7 0 JordanVaughan(7) 3 19
(George Margarson) *t.k.h: chsd ldrs tl rdn and wknd 3f out* **10/1**

5 **8** *5* **Always Gentle (IRE)**[13] 1352 3-8-6 0 RyanPowell(3) 1 7
(George Margarson) *in tch: lost pl 7f out: n.d fnl 4f* **33/1**

00 **9** *2* **Ela Goog La Mou**[15] 1300 4-10-0 0 AdamKirby 6
(Peter Charalambous) *wd: towards rr: hdwy 6f out: wknd over 3f out: btn whn hung rt in st* **66/1**

05 **10** *64* **American Kiss (SWE)**[12] 1371 4-10-0 **30** SebSanders 5
(Robin Dickin) *v.s.a: a bhd: no ch fnl 4f* **100/1**

2m 19.48s (-2.42) **Going Correction** -0.025s/f (Stan)
WFA 3 from 4yo 19lb **10** Ran SP% **133.6**
Speed ratings (Par 98): **107,103,101,92,89 83,80,77,75,29**
toteswingers 1&2 £1.60, 1&3 £1.90, 2&3 £2.80 CSF £5.15 TOTE £2.50: £1.30, £1.10, £1.50; EX 7.70 Trifecta £33.50 Pool: £1,819.48 - 40.68 winning units..
Owner Ecurie Wildenstein **Bred** Dayton Investments Ltd **Trained** Newmarket, Suffolk

FOCUS
Little depth to this low-grade maiden, run at a solid gallop. The first three were always prominent and the winner looks useful.

1612 WINNERS ARE WELCOME AT BETDAQ CLASSIFIED STKS 7f (P)
6:30 (6:30) (Class 5) 3-Y-O **£2,587** (£770; £384; £192) **Stalls** Low

Form RPR

2133 **1** **Great Demeanor (USA)**[55] 738 3-9-0 **75** LiamKeniry 6 77
(David Elsworth) *led after 2f: hrd rdn over 1f out: hld on wl fnl f* **10/1**[3]

430- **2** *3/4* **Secret Beau**[172] 7399 3-9-0 **72** (v[1]) SebSanders 8 75
(Ralph Beckett) *chsd wnr after 2f: chal over 2f out: kpt on fnl f: jst hld* **25/1**

0U3- **3** *hd* **Millers Wharf (IRE)**[140] 7894 3-9-0 **73** CathyGannon 1 74
(Richard Hannon) *mid-div: rdn and hdwy 2f out: pressed ldng pair fnl f: r.o* **20/1**

31- **4** *hd* **Leitrim Pass (USA)**[184] 7096 3-9-0 **75** ShaneKelly 9 80+
(William Haggas) *plld hrd: sn in rr of midfield: n.m.r 2f out: swtchd lft over 1f out: fin wl: unlucky* **6/4**[1]

344- **5** *1/2* **Summer Dream (IRE)**[185] 7079 3-9-0 **75** (p) AdamKirby 10 73
(Marco Botti) *mid-div on outer: rdn and hdwy over 1f out: styd on* **6/1**[2]

010- **6** *3/4* **Trapeze**[172] 7406 3-9-0 **75** RobertHavlin 2 73+
(John Gosden) *dwlt: hld up towards rr: hdwy 2f out: rdn and nt clr run on far rail 1f out: styng on whn hmpd and snatched up nr fin* **14/1**

223- **7** *1* **Swift Cedar (IRE)**[233] 5661 3-8-9 75 MichaelJMMurphy(5) 7 68
(Alan Jarvis) *dwlt: hld up in rr: rdn over 2f out: styd on fnl f: gng on at fin* **10/1**[3]

051- **8** *hd* **Shy Bride (IRE)**[167] 7506 3-8-7 75 DavidParkes(7) 4 67
(Alan Jarvis) *plld hrd: chsd ldrs: rdn over 2f out: no ex 1f out* **20/1**

100- **9** *3* **Kamchatka**[191] 6920 3-9-0 74 JamesDoyle 3 59
(Philip Hide) *led 2f: prom: rdn over 2f out: wknd 1f out: eased whn btn* **33/1**

430- **10** *6* **Harry Bosch**[175] 7324 3-9-0 72 MartinDwyer 13 43
(Brian Meehan) *rdn 3f out: a bhd* **12/1**

42-1 **11** *7* **Emperor Julius (IRE)**[55] 734 3-9-0 75 FergusSweeney 5 24
(Jo Crowley) *prom on outer: rdn 3f out: wknd over 2f out* **6/1**[2]

015- **12** *74* **Cardmaster (IRE)**[225] 5903 3-9-0 73 AndreaAtzeni 11
(Eve Johnson Houghton) *dwlt: a bhd: no ch fnl 3f* **50/1**

1m 25.65s (-0.35) **Going Correction** -0.025s/f (Stan) 12 Ran SP% **119.4**
Speed ratings (Par 98): **101,100,99,99,99 98,97,96,93,86 78,**
toteswingers 1&2 £25.90, 1&3 £38.20, 2&3 £96.60 CSF £242.72 TOTE £12.00: £2.70, £6.70, £4.20; EX 274.40 Trifecta £997.30 Part won. Pool: £1,329.86 - 0.05 winning units..
Owner Vinci Wong **Bred** Brick Kiln Stud **Trained** Newmarket, Suffolk

FOCUS
A very tight classified stakes, for horses who had won no more than once. They finished in a heap with several meeting traffic problems, and the form shouldn't be taken literally. The winner is rated back to his early form and the fourth was unlucky.

1613 £200 FREE BETS AT BETDAQ H'CAP 1m 4f (P)
7:00 (7:01) (Class 6) (0-60,60) 3-Y-O **£1,940** (£577; £288; £144) **Stalls** Centre

Form RPR

4233 **1** **Inessa Armand (IRE)**[9] 1428 3-9-4 57 (p) CathyGannon 5 63
(J S Moore) *chsd ldrs: rdn to ld 1f out: hld on wl fnl f* **10/1**

00-4 **2** *hd* **Miss Tiger Lily**[13] 1347 3-9-4 57 JamesDoyle 8 62
(Harry Dunlop) *led tl 1f out: rallied wl: jst hld* **9/1**[3]

56-2 **3** *2 1/2* **Town Mouse**[7] 1469 3-9-7 60 (b) JimmyFortune 7 61
(Hughie Morrison) *stdd s: plld hrd towards rr: stmbld 6f out: rdn and hdwy over 1f out: styd on* **5/4**[1]

226 **4** *1 1/4* **Mirth**[33] 1009 3-9-7 60 FrannyNorton 1 59
(Mark Johnston) *mid-div: n.m.r and lost pl 6f out: styd on again fnl 2f* **14/1**

2-50 **5** *5* **Brick Rising**[9] 1425 3-9-7 60 (t) DavidProbert 4 51
(Andrew Balding) *chsd ldr tl over 2f out: sn outpcd: 5th and btn whn eased fnl 100yds: sddle slipped* **25/1**

3451 **6** *4* **Rainford Glory (IRE)**[14] 1326 3-9-6 59 AndreaAtzeni 3 44
(David Simcock) *towards rr: n.m.r on bnd after 2f: last and rdn 3f out: n.d* **3/1**[2]

00-4 **7** *6* **Downright Dizzie**[33] 1016 3-8-3 47 (b[1]) JemmaMarshall(5) 2 22
(Alastair Lidderdale) *chsd ldrs: lost pl over 4f out: bhd fnl 2f* **10/1**

06-5 **8** *1 1/4* **Dancing Chief (IRE)**[7] 1469 3-8-11 50 KierenFallon 6 23
(Alan Jarvis) *stdd s: plld hrd in rr: hdwy on outer and prom over 5f out: wknd over 2f out* **16/1**

2m 36.83s (2.33) **Going Correction** -0.025s/f (Stan) 8 Ran SP% **114.0**
Speed ratings (Par 96): **91,90,89,88,85 82,78,77**
toteswingers 1&2 £15.10, 1&3 £3.70, 2&3 £4.30 CSF £94.05 CT £189.54 TOTE £13.40: £2.60, £2.10, £1.10; EX 51.40 Trifecta £340.90 Pool: £1,053.22 - 2.31 winning units..
Owner Norton Common Farm Racing **Bred** Norelands & Hugo Lascelles **Trained** Upper Lambourn, Berks

FOCUS
Modest handicap form and the pace was only steady. A couple of fillies fought out the finish and the form is not rated too positively.

1614 BETDAQ 1ST UK RACE COMMISSION FREE-EVERYDAY H'CAP 1m 3f (P)
7:30 (7:31) (Class 4) (0-85,77) 3-Y-O **£4,690** (£1,395; £697; £348) **Stalls** Low

Form RPR

32-1 **1** **Spillway**[30] 1057 3-9-4 74 JimmyFortune 7 88+
(Eve Johnson Houghton) *confidently rdn in rr: rapid hdwy over 1f out: qcknd wl to ld ins fnl f: easily* **7/1**[3]

02-1 **2** *1 1/4* **Grendisar (IRE)**[97] 141 3-9-1 71 (p) AdamKirby 5 81
(Marco Botti) *dwlt: towards rr: hdwy to ld wl over 1f out: hdd and no ch w wnr ins fnl f* **12/1**

031- **3** *1/2* **Lion Beacon**[128] 8052 3-9-0 70 JimCrowley 6 79
(Amanda Perrett) *prom: hrd rdn and sltly crossed 2f out: rallied and r.o fnl f* **7/2**[2]

0-31 **4** *1 1/2* **Jathabah (IRE)**[14] 1321 3-9-5 75 KierenFallon 3 81
(Clive Brittain) *s.s: bhd: drvn along over 2f out: styd on fr over 1f out: nrst fin* **7/1**[3]

251- **5** *1/2* **Zeus Magic**[140] 7900 3-9-7 77 LiamKeniry 2 82
(David Elsworth) *in tch: rdn over 2f out: styd on fnl f* **10/3**[1]

05-1 **6** *6* **Corn Snow (USA)**[22] 1185 3-9-2 72 FrannyNorton 4 67
(Mark Johnston) *led: edgd lft and hdd wl over 1f out: sn wknd* **8/1**

001- **7** *2 1/2* **Forced Family Fun**[196] 6793 3-9-2 72 HayleyTurner 1 62
(Michael Bell) *plld hrd: chsd ldrs: rdn over 2f out: wknd wl over 1f out* **8/1**

2-55 **8** *hd* **Raven's Tower (USA)**[31] 1053 3-8-5 66 MichaelJMMurphy(5) 8 56
(Mark Johnston) *in tch: effrt on outer over 3f out: sn rdn: wknd wl over 1f out* **15/2**

2m 20.92s (-0.98) **Going Correction** -0.025s/f (Stan) 8 Ran SP% **112.0**
Speed ratings (Par 100): **102,101,100,99,99 94,93,92**
toteswingers 1&2 £10.20, 1&3 £8.30, 2&3 £4.90 CSF £81.49 CT £340.19 TOTE £9.30: £2.50, £2.90, £1.80; EX 116.90 Trifecta £379.80 Pool: £906.32 - 1.78 winning units..
Owner Mrs Virginia Neale **Bred** Cherry Park Stud **Trained** Blewbury, Oxon

FOCUS
An interesting little handicap contested by seven last-time-out winners. The pace slowed up down the back and the time was around 1.4sec slower than in the opening fillies' maiden. A clear personal best from the winner, who looks capable of better.

1615 COMMISSION FREE 1ST MONTH AT BETDAQ H'CAP 2m (P)
8:00 (8:00) (Class 3) (0-90,90) 4-Y-0+
£7,158 (£2,143; £1,071; £535; £267; £134) **Stalls** Low

Form RPR

600- **1** **Seaside Sizzler**[208] 6428 6-9-4 82 (vt) JimCrowley 1 91
(Ralph Beckett) *chsd ldrs: sustained chal fr over 1f out: drvn to ld nr fin* **9/2**[2]

1-10 **2** *nk* **De Rigueur**[74] 496 5-9-3 81 (t) AdamKirby 6 90
(Marco Botti) *hld up in tch: led on bit 2f out: hrd rdn fnl f: hdd nr fin* **2/1**[1]

05-3 **3** *3* **Tappanappa (IRE)**[55] 739 6-9-12 90 (b) SilvestreDeSousa 10 95
(Brian Ellison) *wnt lft s: hld up towards rr: hdwy over 2f out: styd on same pce appr fnl f* **6/1**

110- **4** *1 3/4* **Porcini**[173] 7367 4-8-8 76 WilliamCarson 3 79
(Philip McBride) *chsd ldrs: led over 2f out: sn hdd: one pce* **12/1**

2242 **5** *1/2* **Tartan Jura**[8] 1454 5-8-11 75 (v) FrannyNorton 8 77
(Mark Johnston) *dwlt: towards rr: rdn 3f out: sme hdwy over 1f out: nt rch ldrs* **11/2**[3]

00/6 **6** *8* **Bow To No One (IRE)**[48] 823 7-8-12 76 KierenFallon 9 69
(Alan Jarvis) *dwlt: bhd: mod effrt on outer over 2f out: sn wknd* **10/1**

3251 **7** *2 1/2* **Beat Route**[24] 1158 6-8-12 76 SebSanders 2 66
(Michael Attwater) *mid-div: rdn and hdwy 2f out: wknd over 1f out* **10/1**

231- **8** *3 3/4* **Australia Day (IRE)**[178] 6089 10-9-11 89 MartinDwyer 7 74
(Paul Webber) *led: clr after 4f tl 4f out: hdd over 2f out: sn wknd* **20/1**

0- **9** *8* **Shelford (IRE)**[221] 6066 4-9-7 89 DavidProbert 5 65
(Tony Carroll) *plld hrd: chsd clr ldr tl 4f out: wknd qckly 2f out* **25/1**

3m 27.99s (-2.11) **Going Correction** -0.025s/f (Stan)
WFA 4 from 5yo+ 4lb 9 Ran SP% **115.7**
Speed ratings (Par 107): **104,103,102,101,101 97,95,94,90**
toteswingers 1&2 £3.50, 1&3 £8.70, 2&3 £3.90 CSF £13.92 CT £53.98 TOTE £6.00: £2.10, £2.10, £2.20; EX 18.90 Trifecta £202.40 Pool: £591.29 - 2.19 winning units..
Owner I J Heseltine **Bred** Redmyre Bloodstock And S Hillen **Trained** Kimpton, Hants

FOCUS
A decent staying handicap run at a reasonable pace. The first two came clear in the latter stages and the winner is rated close to his best.

1616 WIN BIG WITH BETDAQ MULTIPLES H'CAP 6f (P)
8:30 (8:31) (Class 5) (0-70,71) 3-Y-O **£2,587** (£770; £384; £192) **Stalls** Low

Form RPR

514- **1** **El Mirage (IRE)**[166] 7523 3-9-7 70 JimCrowley 2 76+
(Dean Ivory) *hld up in 5th: nt clr run over 2f out: hdwy over 1f out: r.o to ld 75yds out: pushed out* **7/2**[2]

5-22 **2** *1 1/4* **Carina Palace**[9] 1427 3-9-1 64 FergusSweeney 9 66
(Jamie Osborne) *hld up towards rr: hdwy over 1f out: r.o to take 2nd fnl 50yds* **9/2**[3]

0-14 **3** *3/4* **Polish Crown**[14] 1315 3-9-2 65 FrannyNorton 6 66
(Mark Johnston) *bhd: rdn over 2f out: r.o fr over 1f out: nrst fin* **11/1**

4134 **4** *shd* **Marvelino**[42] 894 3-9-4 67 (b[1]) DaneO'Neill 3 66
(Pat Eddery) *led: 4 l clr 1/2-way: wknd and hdd 75yds out* **5/1**

205- **5** *2 3/4* **Bheleyf (IRE)**[252] 4936 3-9-7 70 HarryBentley 4 60
(Joseph Tuite) *hld up in 6th: hdwy 2f out: no ex fnl f* **20/1**

252- **6** *2 1/2* **Jubilant Queen**[224] 5932 3-9-6 69 AdamKirby 8 51
(Clive Cox) *chsd ldrs: hrd rdn over 2f out: wknd jst over 1f out* **5/2**[1]

3135 **7** *2* **Katy Spirit (IRE)**[40] 923 3-9-1 64 LiamKeniry 5 40
(Michael Blanshard) *prom tl wknd over 1f out* **12/1**

05-0 **8** *3* **Blue Clumber**[17] 1275 3-8-9 63 MichaelJMMurphy(5) 1 29
(Shaun Harris) *prom tl wknd 2f out* **25/1**

1m 13.35s (0.25) **Going Correction** -0.025s/f (Stan) 8 Ran SP% **110.3**
Speed ratings (Par 98): **97,95,94,94,90 87,84,80**
toteswingers 1&2 £5.10, 1&3 £6.30, 2&3 £9.30 CSF £18.15 CT £144.05 TOTE £3.70: £1.40, £1.60, £2.80; EX 22.40 Trifecta £115.10 Pool: £611.15 - 3.97 winning units..
Owner Mrs Heather Yarrow **Bred** Jeddah Bloodstock **Trained** Radlett, Herts
■ Stewards' Enquiry : Jim Crowley one-day ban: careless riding (May 1)

FOCUS
A modest sprint handicap. The principals came from off the pace, which had been brisk. The form makes sense.

1617 MASCOT GRAND NATIONAL 06.05.13 H'CAP 1m (P)
9:00 (9:00) (Class 6) (0-60,66) 4-Y-0+ **£1,940** (£577; £288; £144) **Stalls** Low

Form RPR

4001 **1** **Rezwaan**[6] 1497 6-9-13 66 6ex (be) ShaneKelly 11 79
(Murty McGrath) *hld up towards rr: gd hdwy over 1f out: led ins fnl f: sn clr* **6/4**[1]

0231 **2** *2 3/4* **Hill Of Dreams (IRE)**[6] 1498 4-9-6 59 6ex (b) PatDobbs 3 67
(Dean Ivory) *chsd ldrs: led over 1f out and qckly wnt 2 l ahd: hdd and no ex ins fnl f* **6/1**[2]

6010 **3** *1 3/4* **Rigid**[28] 1093 6-8-4 48 RyanTate(5) 8 51
(Tony Carroll) *in tch: outpcd over 2f out: styd on again fr over 1f out* **33/1**

0-60 **4** *1/2* **Green Earth (IRE)**[21] 1196 6-9-4 57 (p) IanMongan 12 59
(Pat Phelan) *towards rr: rdn and r.o fnl 2f: nrst fin* **10/1**

03-0 **5** *1 1/2* **True Prince (USA)**[68] 559 4-9-0 53 (b) SilvestreDeSousa 6 51
(Brian Ellison) *chsd ldr: led after 3f: hrd rdn over 2f out: hdd over 1f out: sn wknd* **20/1**

500- **6** *1/2* **Norse Song**[330] 2374 4-8-11 50 LiamKeniry 5 47
(David Elsworth) *prom tl wknd over 1f out* **33/1**

124 **7** *hd* **Daniel Thomas (IRE)**[14] 1322 11-9-5 58 (tp) CathyGannon 10 55
(Violet M Jordan) *s.i.s: bhd: rdn over 2f out: styd on fr over 1f out* **25/1**

4140 **8** *hd* **Rapid Water**[6] 1497 7-9-2 55 (v) JimmyFortune 9 54
(Pat Eddery) *hld up towards rr: sme hdwy 2f out: no imp over 1f out* **25/1**

0-05 **9** *1* **Karate (IRE)**[27] 1107 5-9-2 60 (t) NicoleNordblad(5) 14 54
(Hans Adielsson) *chsd ldrs tl rdn and btn 2f out* **8/1**

0-42 **10** *1 3/4* **Bajan Story**[15] 1303 4-9-6 59 DaneO'Neill 4 49+
(Michael Blanshard) *hld up in midfield: promising hdwy 2f out: disputing 3rd whn hmpd over 1f out: nt rcvr* **6/1**[2]

005 **11** *2* **Legal Legacy**[7] 1474 7-9-2 55 (p) JimCrowley 7 40
(Richard Rowe) *v.s.a: a bhd* **7/1**[3]

055- **12** *3 1/4* **Bountiful Catch**[33] 2085 4-8-11 50 FergusSweeney 1 28
(Pam Sly) *led 3f: rdn over 2f out: wknd wl over 1f out* **66/1**

1m 39.73s (-0.07) **Going Correction** -0.025s/f (Stan) 12 Ran SP% **121.1**
Speed ratings (Par 101): **99,96,94,94,92 92,91,91,90,88 86,83**
toteswingers 1&2 £3.80, 1&3 £15.30, 2&3 £23.00 CSF £9.78 CT £222.02 TOTE £2.60: £1.60, £2.00, £10.20; EX 15.50 Trifecta £409.10 Pool: £691.88 - 1.26 winning units..
Owner Gallagher Equine Ltd **Bred** Shadwell Estate Company Limited **Trained** East Malling, Kent

FOCUS
They went a solid pace in this low-grade handicap and the form looks sound, although there wasn't much depth.
T/Plt: £144.60 to a £1 stake. Pool of £69,183.34 - 349.15 winning units T/Qpdt: £19.90 to a £1 stake. Pool of £6,944.68 - 257.30 winning units LM

NEWMARKET (R-H)

Wednesday, April 17

OFFICIAL GOING: Good (7.9)

Far side track used: Stalls on Stands side.

Wind: Strong; across Weather: bright spells

1618 ALEX SCOTT MAIDEN STKS (C&G) 7f

1:45 (1:45) (Class 4) 3-Y-O **£4,851** (£1,443; £721; £360) **Stalls** High

Form RPR

4- **1** **Music Master**[245] 5235 3-9-0 0 FergusSweeney 1 88+
(Henry Candy) *lw: chsd ldr tl rdn to ld ent fnl f: kpt on under hands and heels riding and a gng to hold on fnl 100yds* **13/2**[3]

2 *½* **Red Rocker (IRE)** 3-9-0 0 KierenFallon 9 86+
(Brian Meehan) *leggy: athletic: on toes: awkward leaving stalls and slowly away: niggled along in rr: swtchd rt and rdn 3f out: hdwy to chse ldrs over 1f out: wnt 2nd ins fnl f: kpt on wl* **25/1**

33- **3** *shd* **You're The Boss**[119] 8172 3-9-0 0 JamieSpencer 11 86
(Ed Walker) *lw: hld up wl in tch in midfield: chsd ldrs and swtchd rt jst ins fnl f: drvn and kpt on wl fnl 100yds* **7/1**

624- **4** *2 ¾* **Estifzaaz (IRE)**[214] 6237 3-9-0 79 PaulHanagan 5 79
(Charles Hills) *led: rdn and hdd ent fnl f: sn no ex and btn fnl 150yds: plugged on same pce after* **9/2**[1]

- **5** *hd* **Jammy Guest (IRE)** 3-9-0 0 SebSanders 12 78+
(George Margarson) *str: gd bodied: bit bkwd: t.k.h: stdd s: hld up in tch in midfield: rdn and effrt to chse ldng quartet jst over 1f out: swtchd rt and kpt on same pce ins fnl f* **7/1**

6 *6* **Messila Star** 3-9-0 0 RyanMoore 3 62
(Jeremy Noseda) *leggy: attr: t.k.h: chsd ldrs: rdn over 2f out: wknd u.p over 1f out: fdd fnl f* **11/1**

7 *3 ¼* **Tawtheeq (IRE)** 3-9-0 0 DaneO'Neill 2 53
(Richard Hannon) *str: lw: slowly away: t.k.h: hld up in tch towards rr: hdwy into midfield after 2f: rdn and struggling over 2f out: wknd over 1f out* **8/1**

8 *hd* **Assembly** 3-9-0 0 WilliamBuick 4 53
(William Haggas) *athletic: lw: hld up in tch: rdn and struggling over 2f out: wknd and wl btn over 1f out* **9/2**[1]

620- **9** *3 ½* **Rock Up (IRE)**[173] 7374 3-9-0 75 TedDurcan 6 43
(David Elsworth) *edgy: t.k.h: dwlt: sn rcvrd and chsd ldrs: rdn and lost pl qckly jst over 2f out: bhd fnl f* **33/1**

10 *8* **Balad (IRE)** 3-9-0 0 SilvestreDeSousa 8 21
(Saeed bin Suroor) *str: t.k.h: hld up in tch towards rr: dropped to last and struggling wl over 2f out: wl bhd fnl f* **6/1**[2]

1m 27.41s (2.01) **Going Correction** +0.125s/f (Good) **10** Ran SP% **115.2**

Speed ratings (Par 100): **93,92,92,89,88 82,78,78,74,65**

toteswingers 1&2 £59.00, 1&3 £5.30, 2&3 £24.60 CSF £150.57 TOTE £6.70: £2.10, £4.90, £3.10; EX 211.90 Trifecta £922.50 Part won. Pool: £1,230.00 - 0.59 winning units..

Owner Godfrey Wilson **Bred** Mrs C R D Wilson **Trained** Kingston Warren, Oxon

FOCUS

They didn't go that quickly early and, despite the strong wind, it paid to race up with the pace. Nevertheless, this is often a good maiden, and it should produce several winners. The fourth helps with the form.

1619 EQUESTRIANARTUK.COM CONDITIONS STKS 5f

2:20 (2:20) (Class 3) 2-Y-O **£6,469** (£1,925; £962; £481) **Stalls** High

Form RPR

24 **1** **Vodka Time (IRE)**[4] 1541 2-8-12 0 TomQueally 5 83
(David Evans) *leggy: in tch: rdn and effrt to chal ent fnl f: led ins fnl f: asserting whn edgd lft u.p fnl 100yds: styd on wl* **2/1**[1]

1 **2** *1 ¾* **M'Selle (IRE)**[24] 1156 2-8-10 0 LukeMorris 2 75
(Ronald Harris) *w'like: cl cpld: racd keenly: chsd ldr after 1f: rdn to ld over 1f out: hdd and no ex ins fnl f: tiring towards fin* **11/2**[3]

1 **3** *hd* **Split Rock**[8] 1449 2-9-1 0 JoeFanning 4 79
(Mark Johnston) *w'like: chsd ldr for 1f: chsd ldrs after: rdn and sltly outpcd 2f out: rallying and swtchd rt 1f out: no threat to wnr but kpt on and pressing for 2nd cl home* **2/1**[1]

1 **4** *1 ½* **Orton Park (IRE)**[18] 1240 2-8-10 0 JamieSpencer 3 69
(Tobias B P Coles) *w'like: led: rdn and hdd over 1f out: drvn and btn whn nt clr run and swtchd rt ins fnl f: wknd fnl 75yds* **7/2**[2]

5 *5* **Bahamian Heights** 2-8-9 0 TedDurcan 1 50+
(Clive Brittain) *leggy: wnt rt s and v.s.a: rn green and a outpcd in rr* **14/1**

1m 0.99s (1.89) **Going Correction** +0.125s/f (Good) **5** Ran SP% **110.9**

Speed ratings (Par 96): **89,86,85,83,75**

CSF £13.32 TOTE £2.80: £1.60, £2.20; EX 11.40 Trifecta £36.30 Pool: £1,336.95 - 27.56 winning units..

Owner Mrs E Evans **Bred** Rathasker Stud **Trained** Pandy, Monmouths

FOCUS

This juvenile contest has been won by some very useful performers in recent seasons, including subsequent Coventry Stakes winner Art Connoisseur and Super Sprint and Group 3 scorer Monsieur Chevalier. This looked a potentially informative contest, despite the small field, with three previous winners taking part, although overall it looked a weak renewal. It has been rated at the bottom end of the race averages.

1620 £100,000 TATTERSALLS MILLIONS 3-Y-O SPRINT 6f

2:55 (2:57) (Class 2) 3-Y-O **£55,494** (£25,223; £10,093; £5,036; £3,036; £2,020) **Stalls** High

Form RPR

22-2 **1** **Zanetto**[12] 1362 3-9-3 94 LiamKeniry 1 101
(Andrew Balding) *lw: chsd ldrs: rdn and ev ch jst over 1f out: led jst ins fnl f: styd on wl: rdn out* **7/1**[3]

6- **2** *¾* **Clancy Avenue (USA)**[40] 936 3-9-3 89 WayneLordan 9 98
(T Stack, Ire) *str: hld up in tch towards rr: gd hdwy to chse ldrs over 2f out: drvn and hdwy between horses jst over 1f out: chsd wnr fnl 100yds: kpt on but a hld* **17/2**

030- **3** *¾* **Graphic Guest**[193] 6873 3-8-12 99 MatthewDavies 11 91+
(Mick Channon) *stdd s: hld up in rr: clsng whn nt clr run 2f out: hdwy but nt clr run over 1f out: forced to switch arnd 5 rivals fr 1f out: hdwy u.p ins fnl f: wnt 3rd wl ins fnl f: styd on* **16/1**

521- **4** *1 ¼* **Bungle Inthejungle**[193] 6865 3-9-3 110 MartinHarley 5 92
(Mick Channon) *taken down early: racd keenly: led tl wl over 1f out: stl pressing ldrs and rdn jst over 1f out: no ex and outpcd fnl 100yds* **9/2**[2]

215- **5** *¾* **Tamayuz Star (IRE)**[193] 6874 3-9-3 101 PatDobbs 13 89
(Richard Hannon) *in tch in midfield: hdwy against stands' rail over 2f out: drvn and chsd ldrs over 1f out: unable qck whn nt clr run and swtchd rt jst ins fnl f: kpt on same pce fnl 100yds* **9/2**[2]

116- **6** *nk* **Victrix Ludorum (IRE)**[172] 7406 3-8-12 96 RichardHughes 4 83
(Richard Hannon) *chsd ldr tl led wl over 1f out: sn rdn: hdd jst ins fnl f: lost 2nd fnl 100yds: fdd towards fin* **7/2**[1]

0-00 **7** *¾* **Fantacise**[8] 1444 3-8-12 78 (b) PaulHanagan 7 81?
(Richard Fahey) *lw: hld up in tch in rr: swtchd rt and hdwy u.p over 1f out: styd on same pce ins fnl f* **66/1**

030- **8** *2 ¾* **Mollyvator (IRE)**[193] 6873 3-8-12 73 SilvestreDeSousa 10 72?
(Mrs K Burke) *in tch in midfield: rdn and lost pl over 2f out: no threat to ldrs but plugged on u.p fnl f* **33/1**

55-6 **9** *½* **Ceelo**[16] 1295 3-9-3 78 JamesDoyle 6 76?
(Sylvester Kirk) *hld up in tch towards rr: rdn and effrt 2f out: no real imp tl plugged on fnl f: nvr trbld ldrs* **100/1**

0-41 **10** *1* **Shafaani**[11] 1384 3-8-12 87 (t) KierenFallon 3 67
(Clive Brittain) *on toes: chsd ldrs: rdn wl over 2f out: wknd u.p over 1f out* **20/1**

025- **11** *1 ½* **Badr Al Badoor (IRE)**[193] 6873 3-8-12 84 HayleyTurner 2 63
(James Fanshawe) *on toes: s.i.s: hld up in tch towards rr: rdn and sme hdwy over 2f out: sn struggling: wknd over 1f out* **14/1**

1- **12** *2* **Amberley Heights (IRE)**[278] 4055 3-8-12 78 RyanMoore 8 56
(Richard Hannon) *s.i.s: a struggling in rr: n.d* **12/1**

0-21 **13** *11* **Limit Up**[23] 1174 3-9-3 80 JoeFanning 12 52+
(Mark Johnston) *chsd ldrs: rdn and losing pl whn hmpd 2f out: wl bhd and eased ins fnl f* **20/1**

1m 12.66s (0.46) **Going Correction** +0.125s/f (Good) **13** Ran SP% **116.8**

Speed ratings (Par 104): **101,100,99,97,96 95,94,91,90,89 87,84,69**

toteswingers 1&2 £7.70, 1&3 £19.70, 2&3 £22.50 CSF £60.33 TOTE £8.00: £2.50, £3.10, £5.80; EX 56.40 Trifecta £1074.10 Pool: £2,892.44 - 2.01 winning units..

Owner Mick and Janice Mariscotti **Bred** Aislabie Bloodstock Ltd **Trained** Kingsclere, Hants

FOCUS

Only two runners boasting a three-figure rating, but as usual a big prize on offer. The seventh to ninth help with the level.

1621 CSP EUROPEAN FREE H'CAP (LISTED RACE) 7f

3:30 (3:30) (Class 1) 3-Y-O **£20,982** (£7,955; £3,981; £1,983; £995; £499) **Stalls** High

Form RPR

412- **1** **Garswood**[193] 6865 3-9-0 **106** TonyHamilton 6 113+
(Richard Fahey) *h.d.w: stdd s: hld up in last pair: smooth hdwy 2f out: rdn to ld ins fnl f: sn in command and idling: rdn out hands and heels: comf* **5/2**[1]

12-2 **2** *2 ¼* **Emell**[32] 1033 3-8-8 **100** RichardHughes 9 98
(Richard Hannon) *hld up in tch: rdn and effrt nr stands' rail 2f out: styd on u.p ins fnl f: wnt 2nd towards fin: no threat to wnr* **4/1**[2]

435- **3** *1* **Lucky Beggar (IRE)**[172] 7400 3-8-9 **101** RyanMoore 5 96
(Charles Hills) *led: edgd rt u.p over 1f out: hdd ins fnl f: sn outpcd: edgd bk lft u.p ins fnl f* **16/1**

115- **4** *shd* **Ayaar (IRE)**[214] 6272 3-8-10 **102** MartinHarley 2 97
(Mick Channon) *stdd s: hld up in rr: rdn and effrt 2f out: hdwy u.p over 1f out: kpt on fnl f but no ch w wnr* **10/1**

102- **5** *hd* **Alhebayeb (IRE)**[172] 7404 3-9-1 **107** PaulHanagan 7 102
(Richard Hannon) *lw: chsd ldrs: rdn over 2f out: no ch w wnr and plugging on same pce u.p whn carried rt and short of room ins fnl f: kpt on* **9/2**[3]

540- **6** *nk* **Birdman (IRE)**[172] 7398 3-8-13 **105** MartinLane 8 98
(David Simcock) *chsd ldr tl jst over 1f out: sn edgd rt u.p and kpt on same pce* **20/1**

232- **7** *hd* **Well Acquainted (IRE)**[202] 6599 3-8-11 **103** JohnFahy 1 96
(Clive Cox) *chsd ldrs: rdn and unable qck ent fnl 2f: no ch w wnr and kpt on same pce u.p fnl f* **8/1**

055- **8** *14* **Chilworth Icon**[202] 6599 3-8-11 **103** MatthewDavies 3 58
(Mick Channon) *hld up in tch: rdn and struggling over 2f out: wknd wl over 1f out: bhd and eased wl ins fnl f* **28/1**

250- **9** *4 ½* **Heavy Metal**[186] 7049 3-9-4 **110** JoeFanning 4 53
(Mark Johnston) *lw: chsd ldrs tl over 2f out: sn struggling: bhd and eased wl ins fnl f* **16/1**

242- **10** *nk* **Anna's Pearl**[167] 7514 3-9-7 **113** (b) JamieSpencer 10 55
(Ralph Beckett) *chsd ldrs for 2f: sn lost pl: lost tch over 2f out: eased wl ins fnl f* **10/1**

1m 24.84s (-0.56) **Going Correction** +0.125s/f (Good) **10** Ran SP% **116.0**

Speed ratings (Par 106): **108,105,104,104,103 103,103,87,82,81**

toteswingers 1&2 £3.20, 1&3 £8.40, 2&3 £8.40 CSF £12.07 CT £130.31 TOTE £3.90: £1.80, £1.60, £5.10; EX 18.90 Trifecta £182.20 Pool: £3,134.33 - 12.89 winning units..

Owner D W Armstrong & Cheveley Park Stud **Bred** Cheveley Park Stud Ltd **Trained** Musley Bank, N Yorks

FOCUS

Not the Guineas trial that it has been in the past, but still a source of future Group performers, such as Stimulation and Red Jazz being recent winners. It produced another potentially high-class performer in Garswood, and the form seems sound.

1622 LANWADES STUD NELL GWYN STKS (GROUP 3) (FILLIES) 7f

4:05 (4:07) (Class 1) 3-Y-O **£34,026** (£12,900; £6,456; £3,216; £1,614; £810) **Stalls** High

Form RPR

1- **1** **Hot Snap**[210] 6366 3-8-12 78 TomQueally 13 113+
(Sir Henry Cecil) *tall: lengthy: scope: in tch in rr and sn pushed along: swtchd lft wl over 2f out: gd hdwy against stands' rail to ld over 1f out: stl looked green but r.o wl to assert jst ins fnl f: readily* **10/1**

210- **2** *2 ¼* **Sky Lantern (IRE)**[166] 7547 3-9-1 111 RichardHughes 14 110+
(Richard Hannon) *on toes: hld up in tch towards rr: smooth hdwy on bit 2f out: rdn and drew clr w wnr 1f out: sn outpcd by wnr and btn ins fnl f: kpt on for clr 2nd* **11/4**[1]

112- **3** *2 ½* **Winning Express (IRE)**[200] 6672 3-8-12 107 FrannyNorton 5 100+
(Ed McMahon) *hld up wl in tch: rdn and effrt wl over 1f out: short of room and jostled over 1f out: rallied and chsd clr ldng pair jst ins fnl f: styd on but no threat to wnr* **11/1**

14-3 **4** *3 ½* **Exactement (IRE)**[34] 1000 3-8-12 97 RichardKingscote 3 91
(Mrs K Burke) *in tch in midfield: rdn and hdwy over 2f out: drvn and pressing ldrs over 1f out: 3rd and btn 1f out: wknd fnl f* **25/1**

116- **5** *1 ¾* **Waterway Run (USA)**[166] 7547 3-8-12 103 JimCrowley 9 86+
(Ralph Beckett) *in tch towards rr: rdn and outpcd 3f out: rallied u.p over 1f out: no ch but plugged on fnl f* **15/2**[3]

134- **6** *3 ¾* **Reyaadah**[215] 6199 3-8-12 100 .... PaulHanagan 12 76
(Charles Hills) *lw: chsd ldrs: rdn and ev ch wl over 1f out: unable qck u.p and btn ent fnl f: fdd fnl f* **20/1**

123- **7** *½* **Sound Of Guns**[215] 6196 3-8-12 105 .... LukeMorris 11 75+
(Ed Walker) *hld up in tch towards rr: hdwy and stl wl in tch whn nt clr run: hmpd and jostled wl over 1f out: no ch after: plugged on fnl f* **20/1**

06-6 **8** *nk* **Jadanna (IRE)**[34] 1000 3-8-12 102 .... GrahamLee 4 74
(James Given) *pressed ldrs tl led 2f out: rdn and hdd over 1f out: sn btn and wknd: fdd fnl f* **50/1**

122- **9** *½* **Sorella Bella (IRE)**[178] 7285 3-8-12 104 .... MartinHarley 1 72
(Mick Channon) *chsd ldrs: rdn and unable qck ent fnl 2f: struggling whn hmpd over 1f out: sn wknd* **33/1**

223- **10** *2 ¼* **Baileys Jubilee**[200] 6672 3-8-12 107 .... JoeFanning 8 66
(Mark Johnston) *hld up wl in tch: short of room wl over 1f out: sn rdn and no hdwy: wl btn 1f out: fdd fnl f* **14/1**

1- **11** *nk* **Lady Nouf**[190] 6966 3-8-12 0 .... WilliamBuick 7 66
(William Haggas) *w'like: attr: in tch in last trio: rdn and no hdwy wl over 2f out: wknd wl over 1f out* **15/2**[3]

31-6 **12** *nk* **Coincidently**[39] 949 3-8-12 77 .... OlivierPeslier 6 65
(Alan Bailey) *hld up in tch in rr: effrt whn hmpd wl over 1f out: sn rdn and btn: wknd over 1f out* **100/1**

132- **13** *1 ¾* **Light Up My Life (IRE)**[201] 6632 3-8-12 102 .... PatDobbs 10 60
(Richard Hannon) *on toes: led tl 2f out: sn hanging rt u.p and struggling: wknd wl over 1f out* **16/1**

122- **14** *3 ¾* **Nargys (IRE)**[186] 7052 3-8-12 103 .... KierenFallon 2 50
(Luca Cumani) *lw: hld up in tch towards rr: hdwy 1/2-way: chsd ldrs but unable qck whn rdn 2f out: wknd over 1f out: bhd and eased ins fnl f* **7/2**[2]

1m 24.39s (-1.01) **Going Correction** +0.125s/f (Good) **14** Ran SP% **121.7**
Speed ratings (Par 105): **110,107,104,100,98 94,93,93,92,90 89,89,87,83**
toteswingers 1&2 £8.70, 1&3 £19.50, 2&3 £5.50 CSF £35.38 TOTE £14.40: £4.10, £1.80, £2.60; EX 50.00 Trifecta £515.20 Pool: £4,951.64 - 7.20 winning units..
Owner K Abdullah **Bred** Juddmonte Farms Ltd **Trained** Newmarket, Suffolk

FOCUS
With no standout candidate for the 1000 Guineas an impressive performance in this recognised trial was always going to cause a big reaction in the ante-post market. This was an up to scratch renewal and Hot Snap laid down a serious Guineas marker.

1623 EBM-PAPST FEILDEN STKS (LISTED RACE) 1m 1f
4:40 (4:40) (Class 1) 3-Y-O

£20,982 (£7,955; £3,981; £1,983; £995; £499) **Stalls** High

Form RPR

1 **Intello (GER)**[186] 3-8-13 0 .... OlivierPeslier 6 111+
(A Fabre, France) *chsd ldr: clsd 3f out: led gng best 2f out: rdn out hands and heels fr over 1f out: in command and r.o strly fnl f* **6/4**[1]

2211 **2** *3 ¼* **King George River (IRE)**[41] 920 3-8-13 96 .... RyanMoore 4 104
(Alan Bailey) *stdd s: hld up in rr: clsd and nt clr run over 2f out: hdwy u.p to chse wnr over 1f out: no imp 1f out and wl hld after: kpt on for clr 2nd* **8/1**

344- **3** *7* **Glory Awaits (IRE)**[186] 7053 3-8-13 95 .... HarryBentley 2 88
(Kevin Ryan) *on toes: chsd ldrs: clsd on ldr 3f out: rdn ent fnl 2f: 3rd and btn jst over 1f out: wknd fnl f* **20/1**

13- **4** *½* **Alta Lilea (IRE)**[176] 7319 3-8-8 88 .... JoeFanning 7 82+
(Mark Johnston) *lw: hld up in midfield: clsd on ldr 3f out: nt clr run and swtchd rt wl over 1f out: outpcd and btn whn bmpd 1f out: wl hld after* **12/1**

0352 **5** *4* **Luhaif**[11] 1383 3-8-13 102 .... (v) MartinHarley 3 79
(Mick Channon) *led: hdd and rdn 2f out: btn and wkng whn hung rt and bmpd rival 1f out: fdd ins fnl f* **12/1**

13- **6** *¾* **Race And Status (IRE)**[193] 6874 3-8-13 102 .... JimmyFortune 1 77
(Andrew Balding) *lw: stdd s: hld in last pair: clsd on ldr 3f out: chsd ldrs and rdn ent fnl 2f: sn struggling: wknd over 1f out* **7/2**[2]

1- **7** *7* **Kerbaaj (USA)**[266] 4472 3-8-13 82 .... PaulHanagan 5 62
(Charles Hills) *t.k.h: hld up in last trio: clsd on ldr 3f out: rdn and btn 2f out: sn lost tch* **9/2**[3]

1m 51.55s (-0.15) **Going Correction** +0.125s/f (Good) **7** Ran SP% **111.7**
Speed ratings (Par 106): **105,102,95,95,91 91,85**
toteswingers 1&2 £2.20, 1&3 £6.20, 2&3 £11.40 CSF £13.70 TOTE £1.90: £1.20, £3.60; EX 10.80 Trifecta £75.60 Pool: £6,128.64 - 60.75 winning units..
Owner Wertheimer & Frere **Bred** Wertheimer Et Frere **Trained** Chantilly, France

FOCUS
One of the lesser Derby trials and, although it has had little impact on that race in recent years, it has been won by future Group 1 winners in Campanologist and Red.wood. This looked an interesting contest and was won in style by the French raider. A decent renewal with the runner-up looking the key to the form.

1624 MONTAZ RESTAURANT EBF MAIDEN STKS 1m 2f
5:15 (5:17) (Class 4) 3-Y-O **£5,498** (£1,636; £817; £408) **Stalls** High

Form RPR

23- **1** **Improvisation (IRE)**[256] 4803 3-9-5 0 .... MickaelBarzalona 10 94+
(Mahmood Al Zarooni) *t.k.h: hld up in midfield: rdn and effrt over 2f out: chal u.p over 1f out: led ins fnl f: styd on strly* **7/4**[1]

34-2 **2** *2 ¼* **Space Ship**[18] 1236 3-9-5 79 .... WilliamBuick 4 89
(John Gosden) *chsd ldr tl led jst over 2f out: edgd lft u.p over 1f out: hdd ins fnl f and outpcd by wnr fnl 100yds: hld on for 2nd towards fin* **11/2**[3]

4- **3** *½* **Demonic**[140] 7900 3-9-5 0 .... (t) TomQueally 11 88+
(Sir Henry Cecil) *w'like: scope: str: hld up wl in tch: rdn and effrt ent fnl 2f: chsd ldrs whn n.m.r ent fnl f: kpt on ins fnl f* **7/2**[2]

2- **4** *1 ¾* **Eshtiaal (USA)**[175] 7333 3-9-5 0 .... DaneO'Neill 5 85+
(Brian Meehan) *bit bkwd: stdd s: hld up in last pair: rdn over 2f out: 7th and styng on whn switching lft jst over 1f out: styd on strly fnl 100yds: nvr trbld ldrs* **14/1**

2- **5** *½* **Tinghir (IRE)**[135] 7963 3-9-5 0 .... TedDurcan 9 84
(David Lanigan) *w'like: bit bkwd: t.k.h: chsd ldrs: rdn over 2f out: drvn and unable qck whn sltly hmpd jst over 1f out: kpt on same pceins fnl f* **9/1**

0- **6** *½* **Morpheus**[182] 7172 3-9-5 0 .... IanMongan 3 83
(Sir Henry Cecil) *str: gd bodied: bit bkwd: t.k.h: hld up in midfield: hdwy 3f out: chsng ldrs whn unable qck on downhill run over 1f out: sltly hmpd jst over 1f out: no ex fnl f* **6/1**

54- **7** *9* **Mujarrad (USA)**[182] 7172 3-9-5 0 .... PaulHanagan 7 65
(J W Hills) *racd keenly: led tl over jst over 1f out: wknd u.p over 1f out* **16/1**

8 *4 ½* **Whitefall (USA)** 3-9-0 0 .... TomMcLaughlin 6 51
(David Evans) *leggy: stdd s: hld up in rr: hdwy 4f out: rdn and struggling over 2f out: wknd wl over 1f out* **100/1**

9 *6* **Samawi (IRE)** 3-9-5 0 .... SilvestreDeSousa 8 62
(Saeed bin Suroor) *w'like: scope: lengthy: green: wl in tch in midfield: rdn and unable qck over 2f out: drvn and wknd wl over 1f out: bhd and eased wl ins fnl f* **16/1**

10 *5* **Sacred Square (GER)** 3-9-5 0 .... RichardHughes 1 34
(William Haggas) *w'like: tall: in tch in midfield: dropped and lost pl qckly over 3f out: lost tch 2f out: eased wl ins fnl f* **20/1**

2m 8.81s (3.01) **Going Correction** +0.125s/f (Good) **10** Ran SP% **122.4**
Speed ratings (Par 100): **92,90,89,88,88 87,80,76,72,68**
toteswingers 1&2 £2.60, 1&3 £2.90, 2&3 £5.00 CSF £12.49 TOTE £2.30: £1.02, £2.20, £1.70; EX 10.90 Trifecta £24.20 Pool: £2,167.13 - 66.92 winning units..
Owner Godolphin **Bred** Ennistown Stud **Trained** Newmarket, Suffolk

FOCUS
A maiden that has a habit of throwing up useful types, and on paper this looked a decent enough renewal, although it might be hard to rate the race too highly with the rather exposed 79-rated Space Ship finishing second. They didn't go that quick early. The winner is capable of improving considerably on the bare form.

1625 BLUE FROG SUPPLIED BY NP NUNN H'CAP 6f
5:45 (5:47) (Class 2) (0-100,98) 3-Y-O **£12,938** (£3,850; £1,924; £962) **Stalls** High

Form RPR

25-4 **1** **Shahdaroba (IRE)**[26] 1112 3-8-10 87 .... JamieSpencer 8 97
(Rod Millman) *lw: chsd ldrs: rdn and chal over 1f out: led 1f out: styd on wl u.p and forged ahd fnl 100yds* **6/1**[2]

531- **2** *1* **Regal Dan (IRE)**[217] 6138 3-8-8 85 .... LukeMorris 4 92
(Charles Hills) *dwlt and rdn along leaving stalls: hdwy into midfield after 2f: rdn and chsd ldrs 2f out: wnt 2nd wl ins fnl f: kpt on* **12/1**

4120 **3** *1 ¼* **Equitania**[18] 1234 3-8-7 89 .... RobertTart(5) 7 92
(Alan Bailey) *led and racd towards centre: rdn and hrd pressed wl over 1f out: hdd 1f out: no ex and btn fnl 100yds: wknd towards fin* **40/1**

451- **4** *nse* **Professor**[207] 6487 3-9-7 98 .... RichardHughes 13 101+
(Richard Hannon) *lw: bhd: rdn 1/2-way: switching rt and hdwy 2f out: kpt on wl u.p ins fnl f: nvr trbld ldrs* **4/1**[1]

011- **5** *2* **Dutch Masterpiece**[180] 7206 3-8-13 90 .... RyanMoore 2 86
(Gary Moore) *racd towards centre: hld up in midfield: rdn and hdwy 2f out: no imp 1f out: wknd wl ins fnl f* **7/1**[3]

015- **6** *1 ½* **The Taj (USA)**[193] 6865 3-9-7 98 .... PaulHanagan 9 90
(Richard Hannon) *t.k.h: chsd ldrs: drvn and unable qck over 1f out: wknd ins fnl f* **12/1**

21-2 **7** *nk* **Heaven's Guest (IRE)**[26] 1112 3-8-2 79 .... PatrickMathers 11 70+
(Richard Fahey) *in tch in midfield: rdn and outpcd ent fnl f: rallied u.p 1f out: kpt on* **8/1**

63-1 **8** *1 ¾* **Bluegrass Blues (IRE)**[15] 1299 3-8-2 79 .... SilvestreDeSousa 14 64+
(Paul Cole) *in tch in midfield: outpcd and rdn 2f out: no threat to ldrs and plugged on same pce fr over 1f out* **12/1**

550- **9** *1 ¾* **Storm Moon (USA)**[193] 6883 3-8-10 87 .... JoeFanning 16 66
(Mark Johnston) *racd against stands' rail chsd ldrs tl over 1f out: wknd ins fnl f* **16/1**

130- **10** *½* **Capo Rosso (IRE)**[207] 6487 3-8-7 84 .... RichardKingscote 12 62
(Tom Dascombe) *wl in tch: rdn 1/2-way: outpcd and btn over 1f out: wknd ins fnl f* **40/1**

-311 **11** *¾* **Panther Patrol (IRE)**[56] 730 3-8-2 79 oh2 .... JohnFahy 1 54+
(Eve Johnson Houghton) *stdd s: hld up in rr: hdwy 1/2-way: rdn and no hdwy wl over 1f out: wknd 1f out* **28/1**

61- **12** *½* **Tartary (IRE)**[167] 7498 3-8-2 79 .... HarryBentley 17 53
(Roger Charlton) *hld up in tch towards rr: n.m.r 3f out: rdn and no imp whn racd awkwardly on downhill run wl over 1f out: nvr trbld ldrs* **14/1**

16-1 **13** *nk* **Time And Place**[16] 1295 3-8-2 79 .... WilliamCarson 10 52
(Richard Fahey) *lw: wl in tch: rdn and effrt ent fnl 2f: drvn and btn over 1f out: sn wknd* **6/1**[2]

432- **14** *4* **Alcando (IRE)**[173] 7374 3-8-7 84 .... TedDurcan 6 44
(Denis Coakley) *lw: edgy: racd towards centre: in tch in midfield: rdn and btn over 1f out: bhd and eased wl ins fnl f* **20/1**

-121 **15** *7* **Upavon**[35] 982 3-8-10 87 .... WilliamBuick 15 25
(David Elsworth) *hld up in tch in midfield: dropped to rr over 2f out: lost tch 2f: bhd and eased ins fnl f* **16/1**

1m 12.35s (0.15) **Going Correction** +0.125s/f (Good) **15** Ran SP% **126.8**
Speed ratings (Par 104): **104,102,101,100,98 96,95,93,91,90 89,88,88,83,73**
toteswingers 1&2 £17.30, 1&3 £67.20, 2&3 £78.10 CSF £77.07 CT £2682.19 TOTE £5.90: £1.80, £6.50, £12.60; EX 102.80 Trifecta £1488.90 Pool: £2,519.98 - 1.26 winning units..
Owner The Links Partnership **Bred** Tinnakill Bloodstock & Forenaghts Stud **Trained** Kentisbeare, Devon

FOCUS
An interesting 3yo sprint whose best recent winner was subsequent July Cup scorer Sakhee's Secret. There were a number of recent winners and the pace was good, with the overall time 0.31secs faster than the earlier sales race over the trip. Solid, up to scratch form.
T/Plt: £381.30 to a £1 stake. Pool of £100,183.69 - 191.78 winning units T/Qpdt: £35.50 to a £1 stake. Pool of £7,046.16 - 146.50 winning units SP

1626 - 1633a (Foreign Racing) - See Raceform Interactive

1618 NEWMARKET (R-H)
Thursday, April 18

OFFICIAL GOING: Good to firm (8.5)
Far side track used: Stalls on Far side.
Wind: very strong,mainly across, slightly behind Weather: dry, windy

1634 NGK SPARK PLUGS EBF MAIDEN FILLIES' STKS 5f
1:45 (1:47) (Class 4) 2-Y-O **£4,528** (£1,347; £673; £336) **Stalls** Low

Form RPR

1 **Fire Blaze (IRE)** 2-9-0 0 .... MickaelBarzalona 12 78+
(Mahmood Al Zarooni) *w'like: dwlt: off the pce in midfield: hdwy to chse ldrs 2f out: rdn and ev ch ent fnl f: led ins fnl f: hld on wl* **11/2**[1]

2 *nk* **Blhadawa (IRE)** 2-9-0 0 .... NeilCallan 1 77+
(James Tate) *w'like: str: chsd ldrs: rdn and ev ch ent fnl f: sustained duel w wnr ins fnl f: r.o wl but a jst hld* **20/1**

3 *nk* **Twist And Shout** 2-8-7 0 .... RyanWhile(7) 14 76
(Bill Turner) *leggy: unf: chsd ldr: rdn and ev ch over 1f out: led and edgd rt ent fnl f: hdd ins fnl f: kpt on* **20/1**

4 *shd* **Kiyoshi** 2-9-0 0 .... JamieSpencer 17 76+
(Charles Hills) *w'like: scope: lw: racd off the pce in midfield: rdn and hdwy over 1f out: styd on wl ins fnl f: nt quite rch ldrs* **12/1**

5 *1 ¼* **Rizeena (IRE)** 2-9-0 0 .... FrederikTylicki 9 71+
(Clive Brittain) *w'like: on toes: v.s.a: rn green and rdn along in rr: stl plenty to do 2f out: hdwy over 1f out: str run ins fnl f: nt rch ldrs* **16/1**

The Form Book Flat, Raceform Ltd, Compton, RG20 6NL.

6 *hd* **One Chance (IRE)** 2-9-0 0 AndreaAtzeni 18 70
(Tim Pitt) *leggy: unf: wl in tch: rdn and chsd ldrs over 1f out: kpt on same pce and no imp ins fnl f* **25/1**

3 7 *1* **Limegrove**[12] 1399 2-9-0 0 TomQueally 11 67
(David Evans) *w'like: b: led: rdn and hdd whn sltly hmpd ent fnl f: no ex and wknd wl ins fnl f* **8/1**

8 *nk* **Autumns Blush (IRE)** 2-9-0 0 KierenFallon 7 66
(Jeremy Noseda) *athletic: lw: racd off the pce in midfield: effrt 2f out: hdwy over 1f out: kpt on ins fnl f: nvr gng pce to threaten ldrs* **8/1**

9 *hd* **Blockade (IRE)** 2-9-0 0 PatCosgrave 6 65
(James Tate) *w'like: in tch in midfield: rdn and hdwy 2f out: no imp whn pushed rt ent fnl f: styd on same pce after* **66/1**

10 *nse* **Dutch Courage** 2-9-0 0 PaulHanagan 16 68+
(Richard Fahey) *tall: attr: s.i.s: off the pce towards rr: hdwy 2f out: keeping on whn sltly hmpd 1f out: swtchd lft and kpt on ins fnl f: nvr trbld ldrs* **6/1**[2]

6 11 *1* **Rough Courte (IRE)**[5] 1541 2-9-0 0 MartinHarley 4 61
(Mick Channon) *w'like: in tch in midfield: rdn and no imp ent fnl 2f: kpt on ins fnl f: nvr gng pce to threaten ldrs* **7/1**[3]

12 *shd* **Lady Lydia (IRE)** 2-9-0 0 SilvestreDeSousa 13 61
(Michael Wigham) *str; scope: t.k.h: chsd ldrs: rdn and unable qck whn hung rt jst over 1f out: wknd ins fnl f* **11/1**

0 13 *8* **Cafetiere**[19] 1240 2-9-0 0 ChrisCatlin 10 32
(Paul Cole) *lengthy: on toes: racd off the pce in midfield: rdn and struggling 1/2-way: wknd wl over 1f out: bhd fnl f* **20/1**

14 *1 1/4* **Our Queenie (IRE)** 2-9-0 0 RichardHughes 8 27
(Richard Hannon) *cmpt: bit bkwd: racd off the pce in midfield: rdn and struggling 1/2-way: bhd fnl 2f* **14/1**

15 *3/4* **Mimi Luke (USA)** 2-9-0 0 GrahamLee 5 25
(Alan Bailey) *w'like: bit bkwd: slowly away: a outpcd in rr* **33/1**

16 *1* **Tubeanie (IRE)** 2-9-0 0 AdamKirby 2 21
(Clive Cox) *leggy; a towards rr: lost tch 2f out* **20/1**

17 *1 3/4* **Back On Baileys** 2-9-0 0 HayleyTurner 3 15
(Chris Dwyer) *leggy: a towards rr: rdn and struggling ent fnl 2f: wknd qckly wl over 1f out: bhd fnl f* **50/1**

59.14s (0.04) **Going Correction** -0.275s/f (Firm) **17** Ran SP% **122.3**
Speed ratings (Par 91): **88,87,87,86,84 84,82,82,82,82 80,80,67,65,64 62,59**
toteswingers 1&2 £29.80, 1&3 £21.30, 2&3 £82.60 CSF £118.42 TOTE £5.90: £1.90, £8.60, £5.70; EX 186.40 Trifecta £2372.40 Part won Pool: £3163.26 - 0.60 winning units..
Owner Godolphin **Bred** Darley **Trained** Newmarket, Suffolk

FOCUS
The stalls, on the stands' side the previous day, were this time on the far side of the track. There was a strong wind, blowing across the track from the west. The main action unfolded middle to stands' side. This can be a strong maiden, smart winners including Wunders Dream (Molecomb and Flying Childers), Flashy Wings (Queen Mary and Lowther) and Silk Blossom (Lowther), while Habaayib was third before taking the Albany.

1635 SWAN AT LAVENHAM WOOD DITTON STKS 1m
2:20 (2:22) (Class 4) 3-Y-O **£5,175** (£1,540; £769; £384) **Stalls** Low

Form RPR

1 **Ajraam (USA)** 3-9-5 0 RyanMoore 13 90
(Charles Hills) *w'like: led tl wl over 1f out: battled on u.p and led again ins fnl f: styd on wl: drvn out* **16/1**

2 *3/4* **Bustopher (USA)** 3-9-5 0 MickaelBarzalona 12 88+
(Mahmood Al Zarooni) *str: lw: t.k.h early: hld up in midfield: hdwy to chse ldr over 2f out: rdn to ld wl over 1f out: drvn and hdd ins fnl f: no ex and one pce after* **3/1**[1]

3 *nse* **String Theory (IRE)** 3-9-5 0 (t) AdamKirby 7 88+
(Marco Botti) *athletic: rrd as stalls opened: hld up in tch: hdwy 3f out: drvn and pressed ldrs 1f out: kpt on same pce fnl 100yds* **12/1**

4 *nk* **Matrooh (USA)** 3-9-5 0 DaneO'Neill 3 87
(William Haggas) *w'like: scope lw: hld up in last trio: hdwy over 2f out: 5th and styng on over 1f out: kpt on wl ins fnl f* **10/1**

5 *3/4* **Mutajally** 3-9-5 0 PaulHanagan 2 86
(Sir Michael Stoute) *w'like: attr: green: chsd ldrs: rdn ent fnl 2f: kpt on same pce u.p ins fnl f* **8/1**

6 *7* **Saskatchewan** 3-9-5 0 KierenFallon 8 70
(Luca Cumani) *w'like: scope: bit bkwd: chsd ldrs: rdn ent fnl 2f: 6th and btn over 1f out: wknd ins fnl f* **9/2**[3]

7 *1* **She's Late** 3-9-5 0 WilliamBuick 5 67+
(John Gosden) *leggy: athletic: green: in tch in midfield: rdn and no imp ent fnl 2f: wknd over 1f out* **4/1**[2]

8 *3 1/2* **Respect Me** 3-9-5 0 SilvestreDeSousa 6 59
(Saeed bin Suroor) *w'like: scope: bit bkwd: a towards rr: rdn and struggling 3f out: lost tch 2f out* **18/1**

9 *1/2* **Gerrards Cross (IRE)** 3-9-5 0 RichardHughes 1 58
(Richard Hannon) *str: chsd ldr tl over 2f out: sn struggling u.p: wknd wl over 1f out* **8/1**

10 *2 1/4* **Maraweh (IRE)** 3-9-5 0 GrahamLee 15 53
(J W Hills) *w'like: tall: a towards rr: rdn and struggling 3f out: sn bhd* **33/1**

- 11 *5* **Vanvitelli** 3-9-5 0 FrederikTylicki 10 41
(James Fanshawe) *w'like: wl in tch in midfield: rdn and no ex jst over 2f out: wknd qckly wl over 1f out* **33/1**

12 *11* **Top Banana** 3-8-12 0 JeanVanOvermeire(7) 11
(Stuart Williams) *w'like: bit bkwd: wl in tch in midfield: lost pl qckly 3f out: wl bhd over 1f out: t.o* **100/1**

1m 38.59s (-0.01) **Going Correction** -0.275s/f (Firm) **12** Ran SP% **120.2**
Speed ratings (Par 100): **89,88,88,87,87 80,79,75,75,72 67,56**
toteswingers 1&2 £13.80, 1&3 £31.60, 2&3 £9.30 CSF £64.10 TOTE £18.10: £4.00, £1.70, £3.80; EX 96.00 Trifecta £2145.40 Part won. Pool: £2860.57 - 0.92 winning units..
Owner Hamdan Al Maktoum **Bred** Shadwell Estate Co Ltd **Trained** Lambourn, Berks

FOCUS
A field of complete unknowns as usual and the runners raced up the centre early. The form is rated as average for the race for now.

1636 £200,000 TATTERSALLS MILLIONS 3-Y-O TROPHY 1m 2f
2:55 (2:57) (Class 2) 3-Y-O
£111,008 (£45,421; £20,207; £10,073; £5,046; £2,010) **Stalls** Low

Form RPR

1- 1 **Windhoek**[331] 2376 3-9-3 93 JoeFanning 8 104
(Mark Johnston) *chsd ldrs: wnt 2nd 3f out: rdn to ld over 1f out: edgd lft jst ins fnl f: tiring towards fin: jst hld on* **6/1**[2]

231- 2 *shd* **Greatwood**[176] 7324 3-9-3 84 KierenFallon 15 103+
(Luca Cumani) *lw: on toes: hld up in tch: clsng on ldrs and switching rt over 2f out: chsd ldrs and drvn over 1f out: chsd wnr wl ins fnl f: grad clsng but jst failed* **15/2**[3]

151- 3 *nk* **Ghurair (USA)**[194] 6874 3-9-3 111 PaulHanagan 11 102
(John Gosden) *hld up in midfield: effrt and rdn to chse ldrs 2f out: drvn and edgd lft jst ins fnl f tl wl ins fnl f: kpt on towards fin* **1/1**[1]

21- 4 *1 1/4* **Havana Beat (IRE)**[211] 6371 3-9-3 85 DavidProbert 3 100
(Andrew Balding) *lw: hld up in midfield: rdn and hdwy over 2f out: chsng ldrs and edgd rt on downhill run wl over 1f out: kpt on same pce ins fnl f* **9/1**

02-1 5 *1 3/4* **Fehaydi**[10] 1429 3-9-3 83 RyanMoore 1 98+
(William Haggas) *lw: chsd ldr tl led over 3f out: drvn and hdd over 1f out: stl pressing wnr whn squeezed for room and bdly hmpd jst ins fnl f: nt rcvr and one pce after* **8/1**

0- 6 *10* **Musikhani**[194] 6873 3-8-12 0 LiamKeniry 9 71
(Andrew Balding) *led tl over 3f out: struggling and btn 2f out: wknd and edgd rt on downhill run over 1f out* **100/1**

531- 7 *4* **Consign**[111] 8262 3-9-3 75 (p) WilliamBuick 5 68
(Jeremy Noseda) *hld up in rr: rdn and hdwy 3f out: no prog and btn 2f out: racd awkwardly on downhill run and wknd wl over 1f out* **50/1**

050- 8 *nk* **Discernable**[194] 6874 3-8-12 99 SilvestreDeSousa 16 62
(Mark Johnston) *lw: chsd ldrs: rdn and struggling over 2f out: wknd wl over 1f out* **22/1**

01- 9 *3 1/2* **The Gatling Boy (IRE)**[245] 5275 3-9-3 82 RichardHughes 14 60
(Richard Hannon) *noisy: on toes: chsd ldrs: rdn and lost pl 3f out: wknd over 2f out: no ch fnl 2f* **20/1**

2- 10 *hd* **A Star In My Eye (IRE)**[215] 6257 3-8-12 0 NeilCallan 12 55
(Kevin Ryan) *lengthy: in tch in midfield: lost pl and rdn 4f out: hld hd high u.p and n.d after* **100/1**

3- 11 *nk* **Enaitch (IRE)**[173] 7403 3-8-12 0 MartinHarley 7 54
(Mick Channon) *on toes: in tch in midfield: rdn and struggling 3f out: sn btn and no ch fnl 2f* **25/1**

12 *1* **Bossa Nova Baby (IRE)** 3-8-12 0 JimCrowley 10 52
(Charles Hills) *w'like: hld up in tch in rr: rdn along 4f out: wknd over 2f out* **50/1**

0- 13 *4* **Crystal Mist**[194] 6873 3-8-12 0 JamesDoyle 6 44
(Harry Dunlop) *a in rr: rdn and btn 3f out: n.d* **80/1**

60-5 14 *15* **A Ladies Man (IRE)**[8] 1477 3-9-3 71 PatDobbs 4 19
(Richard Hannon) *chsd ldrs tl rdn and struggling 3f out: sn dropped out: wl bhd over 1f out: t.o* **66/1**

00-4 15 *46* **White Coppice**[19] 1236 3-9-3 73 FrederikTylicki 13
(Richard Fahey) *on toes: in tch in midfield: rdn and lost pl over 3f out: bhd 2f out: wl t.o and virtually p.u ins fnl f* **100/1**

2m 1.45s (-4.35) **Going Correction** -0.275s/f (Firm) **15** Ran SP% **119.7**
Speed ratings (Par 104): **106,105,105,104,103 95,92,91,89,88 88,87,84,72,35**
toteswingers 1&2 £5.70, 1&3 £3.10, 2&3 £3.10 CSF £46.52 TOTE £5.30: £1.60, £2.30, £1.60; EX 61.70 Trifecta £136.60 Pool: £6164.62 - 33.83 winning units..
Owner Sheikh Hamdan Bin Mohammed Al Maktoum **Bred** Horizon Bloodstock Limited **Trained** Middleham Moor, N Yorks

FOCUS
There were a number of no hopers, but the first five pulled a long way clear off what seemed a sound enough gallop, and the form amongst the principals looks smart, although not easy to pin down. They raced stands' side.

1637 CONNAUGHT ACCESS FLOORING ABERNANT STKS (GROUP 3) 6f
3:30 (3:33) (Class 1) 3-Y-O+
£34,026 (£12,900; £6,456; £3,216; £1,614; £810) **Stalls** Low

Form RPR

/21- 1 **Tickled Pink (IRE)**[308] 3082 4-9-3 84 TomQueally 3 114
(Sir Henry Cecil) *mde all: rdn and fnd ex 1f out: in command and styd on wl ins fnl f: rdn out* **8/1**

510- 2 *2* **Jimmy Styles**[180] 7236 9-9-6 109 (p) AdamKirby 1 111
(Clive Cox) *stmbld leaving stalls: sn rcvrd and chsd ldrs: chsd wnr 1/2-way: drvn and unable qck 1f out: styd on same pce fnl f* **20/1**

0-11 3 *2 3/4* **Move In Time**[5] 1537 5-9-6 95 DanielTudhope 11 102
(David O'Meara) *broke wl: sn stdd and racd in midfield: rdn and effrt to chse ldng pair over 1f out: no imp fnl f* **9/4**[1]

002- 4 *1/2* **Hawkeyethenoo (IRE)**[180] 7236 7-9-6 112 GrahamLee 7 101
(Jim Goldie) *lw: in tch in midfield: effrt and swtchd lft over 1f out: kpt on ins fnl f: nvr trbld ldrs* **5/1**[3]

300- 5 *1 3/4* **Pandar**[152] 7772 4-9-6 104 JimCrowley 6 95
(Robert Cowell) *chsd wnr tl 1/2-way: rdn and unable qck wl over 1f out: sn btn: wknd ins fnl f* **66/1**

-002 6 *1 1/4* **Captain Ramius (IRE)**[19] 1234 7-9-6 107 RyanMoore 10 91
(Kevin Ryan) *racd in last trio: pushed along 1/2-way: rdn and struggling over 2f out: wknd wl over 1f out* **10/1**

003- 7 *1 1/4* **Angels Will Fall (IRE)**[194] 6878 4-9-3 102 RichardHughes 9 84
(Charles Hills) *stdd after s: hld up in last trio: rdn and no hdwy wl over 1f out: sn wknd* **7/1**

065- 8 *2 1/2* **The Cheka (IRE)**[159] 7690 7-9-6 107 (p) NeilCallan 5 79
(Eve Johnson Houghton) *s.i.s: sn rcvrd and racd in midfield: lost pl and drvn 2f out: sn wknd* **4/1**[2]

050- 9 *1 1/2* **Tiddliwinks**[193] 6908 7-9-6 110 JamieSpencer 8 74
(Kevin Ryan) *dwlt: hld up in tch: effrt u.p 2f out: sn struggling: wkng whn hung lft over 1f out* **12/1**

1m 9.88s (-2.32) **Going Correction** -0.275s/f (Firm) **9** Ran SP% **114.1**
Speed ratings (Par 113): **104,101,97,97,94 93,91,88,86**
toteswingers 1&2 £11.00, 1&3 £4.70, 2&3 £10.00 CSF £148.64 TOTE £7.10: £2.00, £5.20, £1.10; EX 120.20 Trifecta £726.20 Pool: £5889.36 - 6.08 winning units..
Owner Trevor C Stewart **Bred** T Stewart **Trained** Newmarket, Suffolk

FOCUS
There was a heavy shower before this contest. The first running of the Abernant since it was given Group 3 status. The race has been won by some classy sprinters in recent years, such as subsequent Group 1 winners Equiano in 2010 and Mayson last year. This looked an ordinary renewal though, with the runner-up setting the standard.

1638 NOVAE BLOODSTOCK INSURANCE CRAVEN STKS (GROUP 3) (C&G) 1m
4:05 (4:06) (Class 1) 3-Y-O **£34,026** (£12,900; £6,456; £3,216) **Stalls** Low

Form RPR

111- 1 **Toronado (IRE)**[215] 6243 3-9-1 114 RichardHughes 1 123+
(Richard Hannon) *lw: mde all: rdn and qcknd ent fnl f: drew clr 1f out and r.o strly: comf: impressive* **8/11**[1]

112- 2 *4* **Havana Gold (IRE)**[194] 6874 3-8-12 110 JamieSpencer 4 111
(Richard Hannon) *chsd ldng pair: rdn and effrt ent fnl 2f: drvn and outpcd by wnr 1f out: no ch w wnr but kpt on to go 2nd cl home* **6/1**[3]

124- 3 *nk* **Dundonnell (USA)**[166] 7568 3-8-12 113 JamesDoyle 2 110
(Roger Charlton) *ponied to s: chsd wnr: effrt u.p ent fnl 2f: drvn and outpcd 1f out: styd on same pce after: lost 2nd cl home* **11/4**[2]

211- **4** *10* **Tawhid**[173] 7404 3-8-12 111.. SilvestreDeSousa 3 87
(Saeed bin Suroor) *stdd s: t.k.h: hld up in rr: rdn and struggling over 2f out: wknd over 1f out* **8/1**

1m 35.19s (-3.41) **Going Correction** -0.275s/f (Firm) **4** Ran SP% **110.0**
Speed ratings (Par 108): **106,102,101,91**
CSF £5.59 TOTE £1.60; EX 4.40 Trifecta £8.30 Pool: £8368.90 - 754.96 winning units..
Owner HE Sh Joaan Bin Hamad Al Thani **Bred** Paul Nataf **Trained** East Everleigh, Wilts

FOCUS
Not since Haafhd in 2004 has a horse won the Craven and followed up in the Guineas, but 2009 winner Delegator was subsequently runner-up to Sea The Stars, and Native Khan, who took this in 2011, then finished third behind Frankel. Only four runners this year and it wasn't much of a contest, with the best horse in the race allowed a totally uncontested lead. They raced far side. Toronador is rated amongst the better recent winners of this with the second the guide to the level.

1639 WEATHERBYS HAMILTON INSURANCE EARL OF SEFTON STKS (GROUP 3) 1m 1f

4:40 (4:41) (Class 1) 4-Y-0+

£34,026 (£12,900; £6,456; £3,216; £1,614; £810) **Stalls** Low

Form RPR

211- **1** **Mull Of Killough (IRE)**[166] 7557 7-9-1 113........................ GeorgeBaker 3 117
(Jane Chapple-Hyam) *chsd ldr tl over 5f out: swtchd lft wl over 1f out: chal 1f out: drvn to ld fnl 100yds: sn in command: r.o wl* **3/1**[3]

643- **2** *1 ½* **Stipulate**[187] 7054 4-8-12 110.. TomQueally 4 111
(Sir Henry Cecil) *lw: t.k.h: chsd ldng pair tl wnt 2nd over 5f out: rdn and chal 2f out: led over 1f out: drvn 1f out: hdd and no ex fnl 100yds* **15/8**[1]

166- **3** *2 ¼* **Bonfire**[285] 3880 4-8-12 114.. JimmyFortune 1 106
(Andrew Balding) *lw: stdd s: hld up in rr: rdn and effrt 3f out: chsd ldrs but finding little whn edgd rt 1f out: plugged on same pce after: wnt 3rd cl home* **11/4**[2]

323- **4** *nk* **Boom And Bust (IRE)**[201] 6674 6-8-12 106.................... HayleyTurner 6 105
(Marcus Tregoning) *led: rdn and hdd over 1f out: drvn and no ex 1f out: wknd ins fnl f* **6/1**

154- **5** *4* **Proud Chieftain**[166] 7557 5-8-12 97.. JamesDoyle 5 96
(Clifford Lines) *hld up in tch in last pair: hdwy 5f out: rdn and struggling 2f out: wknd over 1f out* **66/1**

13-5 **6** *¾* **Premio Loco (USA)**[33] 1034 9-8-12 111.............................. TedDurcan 2 95
(Chris Wall) *hld up in tch: dropped to rr and rdn wl over 2f out: wknd over 1f out* **12/1**

1m 48.58s (-3.12) **Going Correction** -0.275s/f (Firm) **6** Ran SP% **109.9**
Speed ratings (Par 113): **102,100,98,98,94 94**
toteswingers 1&2 £2.00, 1&3 £2.00, 2&3 £1.80 CSF £8.65 TOTE £3.50: £1.40, £1.80; EX 8.90 Trifecta £25.60 Pool: £9644.57 - 281.76 winning units..
Owner Invictus **Bred** Owenstown Stud **Trained** Dalham, Suffolk

FOCUS
Some high-class performers have won the Earl Of Sefton in the past ten years, notably Notnowcato in 2006 and Manduro in 2007. They seemed to go an even pace here with the six runners staying against the far rail. This rates a narrow personal-best from the winner with the runner-up close to his 3-y-o form.

1640 ROSSDALES MAIDEN FILLIES' STKS 7f

5:15 (5:16) (Class 4) 3-Y-O **£4,851** (£1,443; £721; £360) **Stalls** Low

Form RPR

1 **Perfect Haven** 3-9-0 0.. JimCrowley 13 80
(Ralph Beckett) *leggy: on toes: racd in centre: chsd overall ldr: rdn and edgd lft fr wl over 1f out: led and racing aganst stands' rail ins fnl f: r.o wl: drvn out: 1st of 6 in gp* **10/1**

0- **2** *¾* **Saucy Minx (IRE)**[176] 7329 3-9-0 0..[1] PatDobbs 16 78
(Amanda Perrett) *w'like: edgy: racd in centre: midfield overall: chsd ldrs 2f out: rdn and carried lft by wnr fr wl over 1f out: pressing wnr and n.m.r ins fnl f: kpt on: 2nd of 6 in gp* **12/1**

0- **3** *3 ¼* **Sharqawiyah**[206] 6535 3-9-0 0.. KierenFallon 2 69+
(Luca Cumani) *lengthy: athletic: racd far side: chsd ldrs overall: rdn and effrt 2f out: edgd lft and kpt on ins fnl f to go 3rd fnl 75yds: 1st of 9 in gp* **10/1**

4 *½* **Call Ahead** 3-9-0 0.. RyanMoore 12 67+
(Sir Michael Stoute) *tall: lengthy: lw: racd in centre: midfield: rdn 3f out: sme hdwy over 1f out: kpt on ins fnl f: gng on fin but no threat to ldrs: 3rd of 6 in gp* **5/1**[2]

6- **5** *1 ¼* **Callmeakhab (IRE)**[191] 6966 3-9-0 0.. JamieSpencer 7 64
(Charles Hills) *w'like: attr: racd far side: overall ldr: rdn wl over 1f out: hdd ins fnl f: wknd and lost 2 pls fnl 75yds: 2nd of 9 in gp* **5/1**[2]

6 *2 ¼* **Lybica (IRE)** 3-9-0 0.. JimmyFortune 11 58
(Gary Moore) *lengthy: racd in centre: chsd ldrs overall: rdn and struggling 2f out: edgd rt and wknd over 1f out: 4th of 6 in gp* **25/1**

55- **7** *nk* **Invincible Cara (IRE)**[269] 4408 3-9-0 0........................ RichardHughes 17 57+
(Ed Dunlop) *bit bkwd: stdd and swtchd to r far side after s: hld up in rr: hdwy into midfield 1/2-way: drvn and no imp 2f out: plugged on same pce after: 3rd of 9 in gp* **3/1**[1]

-3 **8** *2 ¼* **Moma Lee**[37] 972 3-9-0 0.. WilliamBuick 8 51
(John Gosden) *lengthy: racd far side: chsd ldrs overall: rdn and unable qck 2f out: btn over 1f out and sn wknd: 4th of 9 in gp* **9/1**[3]

9 *1 ½* **Nabat Seif (USA)** 3-9-0 0.. DaneO'Neill 5 47
(Ed Dunlop) *w'like: leggy: racd far side: t.k.h: hld up towards rr: sme hdwy u.p wl over 1f out: no imp over 1f out: nvr trbld ldrs: 5th of 9 in gp* **16/1**

10 *¾* **Welsh Moonlight** 3-9-0 0.. EddieAhern 1 45
(Gerard Butler) *lengthy: attr: racd far side: s.i.s: bhd and sn rdn along: sme hdwy over 2f out: no imp over 1f out: short of room jst ins fnl f: nvr trbld ldrs: 6th of 9 in gp* **33/1**

11 *1* **Nashrah (USA)** 3-9-0 0.. PaulHanagan 6 42
(J W Hills) *w'like: attr: racd far side: bhd: rdn and no imp wl over 2f out: nvr trbld ldrs: 7th of 9 in gp* **10/1**

4 **12** *1* **Abanoas (USA)**[17] 1288 3-9-0 0.. LiamKeniry 14 40
(Alan Coogan) *lengthy: racd in centre: midfield overall: lost pl and struggling 3f out: bhd 2f out: 5th of 6 in gp* **100/1**

13 *3 ¾* **Sakhee's Alround** 3-9-0 0.. AdamKirby 15 29
(K F Clutterbuck) *w'like: lengthy: racd in centre: midfield overall: lost pl 3f out: bhd over 1f out: 6th of 6 in gp* **100/1**

6 **14** *1 ½* **Cherry Princess**[36] 979 3-9-0 0.. DavidProbert 10 25
(Stuart Williams) *w'like: leggy: racd far side: chsd ldrs tl 2f out: sn struggling: fdd fnl f: 8th of 9 in gp* **100/1**

15 *¾* **Lady Cavallo** 3-9-0 0.. MatthewDavies 3 23
(J R Jenkins) *w'like: tall: racd far side: chsd ldrs tl 3f out: wknd qckly 2f out: bhd fnl f: 9th of 9 in gp* **50/1**

1m 24.69s (-0.71) **Going Correction** -0.275s/f (Firm) **15** Ran SP% **120.9**
Speed ratings (Par 97): **93,92,88,87,86 83,83,80,79,78 77,76,71,70,69**
toteswingers 1&2 £27.70, 1&3 £20.40, 2&3 £20.30 CSF £120.44 TOTE £12.60: £3.20, £3.60, £3.10; EX 152.60 Trifecta £2116.10 Part won. Pool: £2821.57 - 0.34 winning units..
Owner Hants and Herts **Bred** Worksop Manor Stud **Trained** Kimpton, Hants

FOCUS
The bare form probably isn't that strong, although there was little to go on. There were two groups early, but the runners were spread out all over the place in the closing stages and the winner and runner-up gradually edged over to the stands' rail.

1641 PAT & PERCY GITTINGS MEMORIAL H'CAP 1m 2f

5:45 (5:50) (Class 3) (0-95,85) 3-Y-O **£9,056** (£2,695; £1,346; £673) **Stalls** Low

Form RPR

051- **1** **Soviet Rock (IRE)**[188] 7033 3-8-13 77........................ DavidProbert 6 95
(Andrew Balding) *on toes: mde all: wnt clr 1/2-way: stl 5 l clr 3f out: drvn over 1f out: pressed and looked vulnerable ins fnl f: kpt on wl u.p and holding runner-up fnl 100yds* **11/1**

41- **2** *1* **Hillstar**[184] 7127 3-9-5 83.. RyanMoore 5 99
(Sir Michael Stoute) *lw: racd in midfield: rdn 3f out: wnt 3rd over 2f out: clsd on wnr but hemmed in jst over 1f out: swtchd rt and chsd wnr ins fnl f: no imp u.p fnl 100yds* **5/4**[1]

221- **3** *1 ¾* **Heading North**[217] 6153 3-9-2 80........................ RichardHughes 4 92
(Richard Hannon) *chsd ldrs: chsd clr wnr over 3f out: clsd u.p and edging lft over 1f out: lost 2nd and no ex ins fnl f: btn and eased towards fin* **12/1**

221- **4** *7* **Van Percy**[218] 6133 3-9-3 81..[1] JimmyFortune 1 79
(Andrew Balding) *stdd and wnt rt s: hld up in rr: rdn and effrt 3f out: drvn and wnt 4th over 1f out: no ex and btn 1f out: wknd* **8/1**

31- **5** *4 ½* **Mystery Bet (IRE)**[187] 7067 3-9-4 82........................ PaulHanagan 7 71
(Richard Fahey) *chsd wnr tl over 3f out: no ex u.p over 2f out: wknd over 1f out: wl btn and eased ins fnl f* **11/2**[3]

10- **6** *7* **Glenard**[187] 7053 3-9-2 80.. WilliamBuick 2 55
(Charles Hills) *racd in midfield: rdn and effrt 3f out: no real imp: wl btn 2f out: bhd and eased ins fnl f* **4/1**[2]

213- **7** *16* **Master Ming (IRE)**[176] 7331 3-9-7 85........................ KierenFallon 3 28
(Brian Meehan) *racd in last trio: pushed along over 5f out: rdn and lost tch over 2f out: eased over 1f out: t.o* **18/1**

2m 0.39s (-5.41) **Going Correction** -0.275s/f (Firm) **7** Ran SP% **112.2**
Speed ratings (Par 102): **110,109,107,102,98 93,80**
CSF £24.42 TOTE £8.70: £4.10, £1.10; EX 26.00 Trifecta £266.70 Pool: £2821.12 - 7.93 winning units..
Owner Jackie & George Smith **Bred** Grangecon Stud **Trained** Kingsclere, Hants

FOCUS
Five of the last nine winners of this handicap went on to be successful in Group company. All of these were making their seasonal/handicap debuts and stepping up in trip, but again it looks as though this is a race to take a positive view about and has been rated as such. The pace was honest, the front three pulled well clear, and the winning time was over a second quicker than the earlier sales race.
T/Plt: £46.70 to a £1 stake. Pool of £101,950.24 - 1591.90 winning units T/Qpdt: £10.00 to a £1 stake. Pool of £5983.50 - 441.55 winning units SP

RIPON (R-H)

Thursday, April 18

OFFICIAL GOING: Good (8.1)
Rail on bend from back straight to home straight moved out 5m adding 12yds to races on Round course.
Wind: fresh, 1/2 behind Weather: fine but windy

1642 EBF EAT SLEEP & DRINK AT NAGS HEAD PICKHILL MAIDEN STKS 5f

2:10 (2:11) (Class 5) 2-Y-O **£3,881** (£1,155; £577; £288) **Stalls** High

Form RPR

6 **1** **Blithe Spirit**[12] 1399 2-8-9 0.. JasonHart(5) 7 74
(Eric Alston) *swtchd lft s: mde all: styd on wl last 100yds* **10/1**

2 *2 ½* **Muspelheim** 2-9-5 0.. PJMcDonald 3 70
(Ann Duffield) *w ldrs: kpt on same pce fnl f* **16/1**

3 *¾* **Ventura Mist** 2-9-0 0.. DuranFentiman 8 62+
(Tim Easterby) *sn chsng ldrs: kpt on ins fnl f: tk 3rd nr fin* **12/1**

4 *½* **Withernsea (IRE)** 2-9-5 0.. TonyHamilton 4 66+
(Richard Fahey) *dwlt: hdwy on outer to chse ldrs over 3f out: sn drvn: kpt on same pce fnl f* **5/2**[1]

5 *2 ¾* **Azagal (IRE)** 2-9-0 0.. DavidAllan 9 51+
(Tim Easterby) *mid-div: effrt over 2f out: kpt on: nvr a threat* **3/1**[2]

4 **6** *1 ½* **Princess Tamay (IRE)**[10] 1421 2-9-0 0........................ FrannyNorton 2 45
(Mark Johnston) *swtchd lft s: sn chsng ldrs: edgd rt and wknd over 1f out* **8/1**[3]

5 **7** *2* **Claudia Octavia**[9] 1449 2-9-0 0.. DaleSwift 5 38
(Brian Ellison) *s.s: hdwy into mid-div over 2f out: nvr a factor* **28/1**

8 *½* **Classy Lassy (IRE)** 2-8-11 0.. PaulPickard(3) 11 36+
(Brian Ellison) *dwlt: in rr: kpt on fnl f* **16/1**

9 *1 ¼* **Rokeby** 2-9-5 0.. TomEaves 1 37
(George Moore) *slowly away: hdwy into mid-div over 2f out: sn lost pl* **20/1**

10 *5* **Spirit O Goodchild** 2-9-5 0.. GrahamGibbons 10 19
(Alan McCabe) *chsd ldrs: lost pl over 1f out* **25/1**

11 *3 ¾* **Baltic Fire (IRE)** 2-9-2 0.. MichaelMetcalfe(3) 13 5
(Mrs K Burke) *sn in rr: bhd fnl 2f* **17/2**

12 *½* **Highland Princess (IRE)** 2-9-0 0.. MickyFenton 12
(Paul Midgley) *in rr: hmpd after 1f: bhd fnl 2f* **50/1**

1m 0.78s (0.78) **Going Correction** 0.0s/f (Good) **12** Ran SP% **117.8**
Speed ratings (Par 92): **93,89,87,87,82 80,77,76,74,66 60,59**
toteswingers 1&2 £21.30, 1&3 £22.60, 2&3 £24.60 CSF £150.07 TOTE £20.40: £4.40, £4.40, £4.00; EX 324.30 Trifecta £1549.50 Part won. Pool: £2066.07 - 0.38 winning units..
Owner Liam & Tony Ferguson **Bred** Liam & Tony Ferguson **Trained** Longton, Lancs

The Form Book Flat, Raceform Ltd, Compton, RG20 6NL.

FOCUS
An ordinary juvenile sprint maiden in which they went a decent gallop on ground officially described as good. The jockeys felt it was riding on the easy side.

1643 GET SET BET WITH RIPONBET CONDITIONS STKS 1m 1f 170y
2:45 (2:46) (Class 3) 4-Y-0+ £7,561 (£2,263; £1,131; £566; £282) Stalls Low

Form RPR
310- 1 St Moritz (IRE)[148] 7809 7-9-5 95 AdrianNicholls 7 98
(David Nicholls) *swtchd rt after s: led 2f: led over 3f out: rdn over 2f out: all out* 5/2[2]
0302 2 nk Burano (IRE)[19] 1241 4-9-7 103 MartinDwyer 2 99
(Brian Meehan) *s.i.s: t.k.h: hdwy to chse ldrs over 2f out: nt clr run jst ins fnl f: styd on towards fin* 10/11[1]
30-5 3 2 3/4 Gala Casino Star (IRE)[17] 1281 8-8-7 84 (p) JordanNason(7) 4 87
(Geoffrey Harker) *hld up: hdwy to trck ldrs over 2f out: upsides over 1f out: wknd fnl 100yds* 20/1
/236 4 3/4 The Bull Hayes (IRE)[8] 1484 7-9-0 89 BarryMcHugh 3 85
(Tony Coyle) *led after 2f: hdd over 3f out: lost pl over 2f out: kpt on fnl f* 4/1[3]
0 5 1 Moccasin (FR)[9] 1446 4-9-2 90 RaulDaSilva(3) 6 88?
(Geoffrey Harker) *in rr: pushed along 6f out: hdwy to chse ldrs 4f out: one pce* 25/1

2m 10.02s (4.62) **Going Correction** +0.475s/f (Yiel) 5 Ran SP% 109.6
Speed ratings (Par 107): **100,99,97,96,96**
CSF £5.12 TOTE £4.60: £1.40, £1.40; EX 6.30 Trifecta £32.50 Pool: £2504.38 - 57.73 winning units..
Owner Billy Hughes **Bred** Newsells Park Stud **Trained** Sessay, N Yorks
■ Stewards' Enquiry : Jordan Nason caution: careless riding.

FOCUS
A decent conditions stakes for older horses. Not form to place too much confidence in.

1644 PPR FOUNDATION H'CAP (DIV I) 6f
3:20 (3:23) (Class 4) (0-85,85) 4-Y-0+ £4,851 (£1,443; £721; £360) Stalls High

Form RPR
010- 1 Johnny Cavagin[192] 6939 4-8-13 77 (t) TomEaves 11 85
(Richard Guest) *dwlt: hld up: hdwy on ins 3f out: sn trcking ldrs: edgd rt ins fnl f: r.o to ld post* 15/2[3]
00-0 2 shd Baldemar[22] 1205 8-8-7 71 oh1 BarryMcHugh 12 79
(Richard Fahey) *led: edgd rt over 1f out: hdd post* 8/1
-420 3 nk Sans Loi (IRE)[19] 1249 4-9-1 79 ShaneKelly 6 86+
(Brian Ellison) *hld up in mid-div: hdwy over 2f out: sn trcking ldrs: chal over 1f out: no ex towards fin* 9/1
25-5 4 1/2 Defence Council (IRE)[27] 1113 5-9-2 80 PaulMulrennan 9 85
(Mel Brittain) *s.i.s: in rr: hdwy on inner over 2f out: chsng ldrs 1f out: styd on towards fin* 11/2[2]
4-04 5 1 1/4 Rusty Rocket (IRE)[16] 1308 4-8-7 78 JoshBaudains(7) 8 79
(Paul Green) *chsd ldrs: rdn over 2f out: chal over 1f out: kpt on same pce* 5/1[1]
60-6 6 1 1/2 Mappin Time (IRE)[19] 1248 5-9-6 84 (p) DavidAllan 5 80
(Tim Easterby) *mid-div: effrt over 2f out: one pce* 10/1
0-30 7 nk Klynch[19] 1252 7-9-4 82 (b) PJMcDonald 7 77
(Ruth Carr) *in rr: hdwy over 2f out: hung rt over 1f out: wknd last 150yds* 9/1
00-0 8 hd Chunky Diamond (IRE)[19] 1232 4-9-7 85 JamesSullivan 2 80
(Ruth Carr) *chsd ldrs: upsides over 1f out: wknd fnl 150yds* 20/1
000- 9 31 Swilly Ferry (USA)[192] 6939 6-8-11 75 AdrianNicholls 4
(David Nicholls) *t.k.h towards rr on outer: hdwy over 2f out: sn wknd: bhd whn heavily eased ins fnl f: t.o* 10/1
2330 10 4 1/2 Profile Star (IRE)[40] 947 4-9-5 83 GrahamGibbons 3
(David Barron) *chsd ldrs: lost pl over 1f out: heavily eased ins fnl f: t.o* 11/2[2]
4-00 11 2 Thirteen Shivers[19] 1248 5-8-8 79 MatthewHopkins(7) 10
(Michael Easterby) *chsd ldrs: lost pl 2f out: bhd whn heavily eased ins fnl f: t.o* 18/1

1m 14.58s (1.58) **Going Correction** +0.35s/f (Good) 11 Ran SP% 118.5
Speed ratings (Par 105): **103,102,102,101,100 98,97,97,56,50 47**
toteswingers 1&2 £16.00, 1&3 £11.30, 2&3 £14.40 CSF £66.84 CT £564.80 TOTE £11.20: £2.50, £3.50, £3.50; EX 88.80 Trifecta £1625.80 Pool: £2247.48 - 1.03 winning units..
Owner A Bell **Bred** A Bell **Trained** Wetherby, W Yorks
■ Stewards' Enquiry : Barry McHugh four-day ban: used whip above permitted level (May 2-3,6-7)

FOCUS
The first division of a good sprint handicap for older horses, and the slowest of three C&D times. The form could be rated a little higher.

1645 RIPON "COCK O'THE NORTH" H'CAP 1m
3:55 (3:56) (Class 3) (0-95,92) 3-Y-0 £7,561 (£2,263; £1,131; £566; £282) Stalls Low

Form RPR
06-1 1 Country Western[19] 1243 3-8-13 84 SteveDrowne 2 92
(Charles Hills) *s.i.s: sn trcking ldr: t.k.h: led 2f out: kpt on wl ins fnl f* 3/1[2]
34-1 2 3/4 Lightning Launch (IRE)[18] 1272 3-8-6 77 SamHitchcott 6 83
(Mick Channon) *swtchd rt s: mid-div: hdwy and pushed along over 4f out: chsd wnr appr fnl f: kpt on same pce clsng stages* 13/2[3]
462- 3 3/4 London Citizen (USA)[179] 3-8-13 87 MichaelMetcalfe(3) 5 92
(Mrs K Burke) *mid-div: effrt 3f out: chsng ldrs whn hung rt over 1f out: styd on fnl f: edgd lft towards fin* 16/1
0000 4 5 Pure Excellence[19] 1250 3-9-7 92 FrannyNorton 7 85
(Mark Johnston) *in rr: bhd and pushed along 6f out: hdwy 3f out: kpt on: nvr a threat* 10/1
224- 5 1 1/4 Dusky Queen (IRE)[208] 6469 3-8-8 79 TonyHamilton 4 69
(Richard Fahey) *chsd ldrs: drvn over 2f out: wknd over 1f out* 15/8[1]
6- 6 11 Hidden Talent[259] 3-9-3 88 PhillipMakin 8 53
(David Brown) *sn bhd: sme hdwy 3f out: lost pl over 1f out* 16/1
122- 7 2 Red Joker (IRE)[236] 5587 3-8-7 78 RussKennemore 3 38
(Alan Swinbank) *trckd ldrs: drvn over 2f out: lost pl over 1f out* 8/1
515- 8 nk Bapak Sayang (USA)[152] 7773 3-9-0 85 AmyRyan 1 45
(Kevin Ryan) *led: hdd 2f out: sn lost pl* 14/1
-210 9 1/2 Fraserburgh (IRE)[19] 1250 3-8-6 77 AdrianNicholls 9 35
(Mark Johnston) *racd wd: lost pl after 1f and sn bhd and drvn along* 16/1

1m 44.79s (3.39) **Going Correction** +0.475s/f (Yiel) 9 Ran SP% 117.6
Speed ratings (Par 102): **102,101,100,95,94 83,81,80,80**
toteswingers 1&2 £4.10, 1&3 £9.10, 2&3 £16.40 CSF £23.47 CT £272.53 TOTE £4.50: £1.60, £2.10, £3.10; EX 20.80 Trifecta £217.40 Pool: £2234.55 - 7.70 winning units..
Owner K Abdullah **Bred** Millsec Limited **Trained** Lambourn, Berks

FOCUS
A decent quality 3yo handicap which was won by Monterosso in 2010 two years before scaling Dubai World Cup heights. The pace was decent and the winner more than confirmed his reappearance improvement.

1646 PPR FOUNDATION H'CAP (DIV II) 6f
4:30 (4:32) (Class 4) (0-85,85) 4-Y-0+ £3,147 (£3,147; £721; £360) Stalls High

Form RPR
/10- 1 Baccarat (IRE)[299] 3376 4-9-6 84 TonyHamilton 4 102
(Richard Fahey) *mid-div: hdwy over 2f out: rdn and swtchd rt over 1f out: sn chsng ldr: led narrowly ins fnl f: jnd on line* 13/8[2]
1-21 1 dht Sandy Lane (IRE)[8] 1460 4-8-10 74 6ex GrahamGibbons 5 92
(David O'Meara) *chsd ldrs: rdn over 2f out: led over 1f out: narrowly hdd ins fnl f: rallied to dead-heat on line* 6/4[1]
01-6 3 6 Barkston Ash[27] 1113 5-8-11 80 (p) JasonHart(5) 9 79
(Eric Alston) *led: hdd over 1f out: kpt on same pce* 11/1[3]
1361 4 1 1/2 Lucky Dan (IRE)[10] 1431 7-8-10 81 6ex JoshBaudains(7) 12 76
(Paul Green) *hld up in rr: effrt 2f out: edgd rt over 1f out: kpt on* 20/1
000- 5 2 Queens Revenge[294] 3542 4-9-7 85 DuranFentiman 3 73
(Tim Easterby) *chsd ldrs: kpt on same pce fnl 2f* 20/1
000- 6 3 3/4 Marine Commando[201] 6665 5-8-12 76 PJMcDonald 10 52
(Ruth Carr) *t.k.h to post: w ldrs: wknd over 1f out* 16/1
02-0 7 1/2 Victoire De Lyphar (IRE)[37] 966 6-9-4 82 (e) JamesSullivan 6 57
(Ruth Carr) *dwlt: in rr: nvr a factor* 16/1
034- 8 1/2 Diamond Blue[169] 7483 5-8-7 71 oh2 AmyRyan 8 44
(Richard Whitaker) *in rr-div: hdwy on wd outside over 2f out: lost pl over 1f out* 28/1
6-65 9 3 1/2 Advanced[37] 966 10-8-7 78 PaulMcGiff(7) 2 40
(Kevin Ryan) *racd wd 1st f: sn w ldrs: rdn and wknd 2f out* 18/1
00-6 10 1 Towbee[13] 1370 4-8-8 79 MatthewHopkins(7) 7 38
(Michael Easterby) *hood removed v late: slowly away: in rr: sme hdwy over 2f out: sn wknd* 40/1

1m 14.3s (1.30) **Going Correction** +0.35s/f (Good) 10 Ran SP% 118.9
Speed ratings (Par 105): **105,105,97,95,92 87,87,86,81,80**WIN: B £1.60, SL £0.90; PL: B £2.00, SL £1.10, BA £2.10; EX: B/SL £2.70. SL/B £2.40; CSF: B/SL £2.12, SL/B £1.99; TRICAST: B/SL/BA £9.38; SL/B/BA £9.16 toteswingers B&SL £1.40, B&BA £4.20, SL&BA £3.90 TRIFECTA B27 Owner.
Owner Sir Robert Ogden **Bred** Twelve Oaks Stud **Trained** Musley Bank, N Yorks

FOCUS
The second division of a good sprint handicap for older horses. The first two stood out on recent form and came clear.

1647 HOPTON BROW H'CAP 6f
5:05 (5:05) (Class 5) (0-75,73) 3-Y-0 £3,234 (£962; £481; £240) Stalls High

Form RPR
45-2 1 Right Touch[17] 1288 3-9-0 73 GeorgeChaloner(7) 10 81+
(Richard Fahey) *chsd ldrs stands' side: drvn over 2f out: led that gp 1f out: r.o to ld overall nr fin* 9/4[1]
54- 2 nk Tumblewind[181] 7206 3-9-2 68 AmyRyan 3 75
(Richard Whitaker) *chsd ldr far side: led other three and overall ldr ins fnl f: hdd and no ex nr fin* 16/1
401- 3 1 1/2 Dream Ally (IRE)[170] 7462 3-9-5 71 PhillipMakin 14 73+
(Jedd O'Keeffe) *dwlt: sn chsng ldrs stands' side: led that gp 2f out: edgd rt and hdd 1f out: kpt on same pce* 15/2[3]
2-03 4 nk Ayasha[30] 1073 3-9-0 66 TomEaves 4 67
(Bryan Smart) *led three others and overall ldr far side: hdd ins fnl f far side gp: no ex: 2nd of 4 in that gp* 22/1
230- 5 3 3/4 Relight My Fire[212] 6337 3-8-13 65 DavidAllan 5 54
(Tim Easterby) *chsd ldng pair far side: effrt over 2f out: wknd appr fnl f: 3rd of 4 that gp* 8/1
30-0 6 1 Dream Scenario[27] 1112 3-9-6 72 PaulMulrennan 2 58
(Mel Brittain) *last of 4 far side: kpt on fnl 2f: nvr a threat: last of 4 that gp* 16/1
2412 7 hd Red Gift (IRE)[18] 1275 3-9-5 71 (p) DaleSwift 7 56
(Brian Ellison) *mid-div stands' side: outpcd over 2f out: kpt on fnl f* 11/2[2]
216- 8 3/4 Medici Dancer[159] 7687 3-9-1 72 DarylByrne(5) 11 55
(Tim Easterby) *in rr stands' side: kpt on fnl 2f: nvr a factor* 12/1
464- 9 2 1/4 Shatin Secret[173] 7410 3-8-12 67 RaulDaSilva(3) 6 43
(Noel Wilson) *chsd ldrs stands' side: lost pl over 1f out* 20/1
154 10 nk Street Battle (USA)[16] 1307 3-9-0 73 DavidSimmonson(7) 12 48
(Tony Coyle) *dwlt: sn chsng ldrs stands' side: wknd over 1f out* 12/1
421- 11 6 Red Cobra (IRE)[198] 6754 3-9-4 70 DuranFentiman 13 25
(Tim Easterby) *led stands' side gp: hdd 2f out: wkng whn hmpd over 1f out* 11/1
640- 12 8 Rat Catcher (IRE)[192] 6920 3-9-2 68 KellyHarrison 8
(Andrew Crook) *slowly away: swtchd lft after s: in rr: bhd fnl 2f: eased clsng stages* 33/1
4130 13 38 Nellie Bly[14] 1345 3-9-2 68 FrannyNorton 9
(Mark Johnston) *in rr: bhd 2f out: sn eased: virtually p.u: t.o* 14/1

1m 14.37s (1.37) **Going Correction** +0.35s/f (Good) 13 Ran SP% 123.2
Speed ratings (Par 98): **104,103,101,101,96 94,94,93,90,90 82,71,20**
toteswingers 1&2 £13.00, 1&3 £4.30, 2&3 £16.60 CSF £43.39 CT £254.73 TOTE £3.90: £1.90, £5.10, £2.80; EX 39.40 Trifecta £201.90 Pool: £1908.44 - 7.08 winning units..
Owner Nicholas Wrigley & Kevin Hart **Bred** The Athenians **Trained** Musley Bank, N Yorks

FOCUS
A fair 3yo sprint handicap in which they split into two groups, with four horses racing far side, and the remainder coming near side. There didn't appear to be any advantage either way. The initial level is set around the fourth.

1648 SIS LIVE MAIDEN STKS 1m
5:35 (5:37) (Class 5) 3-Y-0 £3,234 (£962; £481; £240) Stalls Low

Form RPR
22-2 1 Brooke's Bounty[18] 1272 3-9-5 75 TonyHamilton 1 65+
(Richard Fahey) *chsd ldr: led after 2f: drvn and styd on fnl 2f* 5/4[1]
2 2 Tinctoria 3-9-0 0 PhillipMakin 3 55
(Kevin Ryan) *led 2f: chsd ldrs: wnt 2nd over 1f out: kpt on same pce ins fnl f* 14/1
3 3/4 Samoset 3-9-5 0 RussKennemore 4 59
(Alan Swinbank) *trckd ldrs: t.k.h: stmbld over 5f out: outpcd 4f out: hdwy over 2f out: styd on to take 3rd 1f out: kpt on* 20/1
50 4 1 Chrisnickdave (FR)[27] 1114 3-9-0 0 PaulMulrennan 2 51
(Michael Easterby) *mid-div: hdwy on inner 4f out: kpt on same pce over 1f out* 66/1
6- 5 shd Jackaddock[180] 7244 3-9-5 0 TomEaves 5 56
(James Bethell) *mid-div: hdwy 4f out: sn drvn: one pce fnl 2f* 33/1

00 **6** ¾ **Madam Fifi**[17] 1291 3-9-0 0 .... DavidAllan 8 49
(Alan McCabe) *s.i.s: t.k.h in rr: hdwy on inner over 2f out: swtchd lft and kpt on fnl f* 100/1

7 ¾ **Thalweg (CAN)** 3-9-5 0 .... AhmedAjtebi 12 53+
(Mahmood Al Zarooni) *hld up in rr: hdwy on outside over 2f out: kpt on: nvr a threat* 4/1[3]

8 *shd* **Big John Cannon (IRE)** 3-9-5 0 .... GrahamGibbons 10 52+
(David Barron) *s.s: hdwy 3f out: keeping on whn nt clr run over 1f out* 12/1

035- **9** *shd* **Correggio**[208] 6486 3-9-5 80 .... PJMcDonald 9 52
(Micky Hammond) *mid-div: drvn over 3f out: one pce* 9/1

5-4 **10** 4½ **Riponian**[18] 1272 3-9-5 0 .... MichaelO'Connell 6 42
(Stuart Coltherd) *in rr-div: hdwy on ins 4f out: wkng whn n.m.r over 1f out* 66/1

00- **11** 3¼ **Fishlake Rebel**[211] 6360 3-9-5 0 .... JamesSullivan 7 34
(Ruth Carr) *in rr: t.k.h: bhd fnl 2f* 100/1

50 **12** 3½ **Zaitsev (IRE)**[10] 1429 3-9-5 0 .... ShaneKelly 13 26
(Ollie Pears) *t.k.h in rr: bhd fnl 2f* 25/1

344- **13** 3 **Future Reference (IRE)**[159] 7686 3-9-5 74 .... RobertHavlin 11 19
(Saeed bin Suroor) *t.k.h: sn w ldr: wknd qckly over 1f out: bhd whn eased clsng stages* 3/1[2]

1m 47.76s (6.36) **Going Correction** +0.475s/f (Yiel) **13 Ran SP% 130.3**
Speed ratings (Par 98): **87,85,84,83,83 82,81,81,81,76 73,70,67**
toteswingers 1&2 £6.60, 1&3 £9.40, 2&3 £31.30 CSF £25.06 TOTE £2.00: £1.10, £5.10, £10.70; EX 20.60 Trifecta £432.70 Pool: £2344.38 - 4.06 winning units..
Owner James Gaffney **Bred** East Layton Stud Ltd **Trained** Musley Bank, N Yorks

FOCUS
A fair 3yo maiden in which the gallop appeared sedate. Muddling form which has been rated cautiously.

1649 MALOSA MEDICAL APPRENTICE H'CAP (THE GO RACING IN YORKSHIRE FUTURE STARS APPRENTICE SERIES) 5f
6:05 (6:05) (Class 4) (0-80,80) 4-Y-O+ **£4,851** (£1,443; £721; £360) **Stalls** High

Form RPR

12-3 **1** **Another Citizen (IRE)**[10] 1431 5-8-6 70 .... (b) GaryMahon(8) 10 80
(Tim Easterby) *chsd ldrs: styd on to ld last 50yds: all out* 15/2[2]

0-41 **2** *shd* **Oldjoesaid**[19] 1248 9-9-9 79 .... GeorgeChaloner 1 89
(Paul Midgley) *hmpd sn after s: sn chsng ldrs on outer: styd on ins fnl f: jst denied* 8/1[3]

0445 **3** ¾ **Six Wives**[16] 1308 6-8-10 71 .... (p) AdamMcLean(5) 15 78
(Scott Dixon) *led: hdd last 50yds: no ex* 9/1

30-0 **4** ¾ **Haajes**[44] 885 9-8-11 70 .... (v) SamanthaBell(3) 8 74
(Paul Midgley) *towards rr: hdwy and edgd rt over 1f out: styd on ins fnl f* 20/1

0410 **5** *hd* **Captain Scooby**[13] 1370 7-9-3 73 .... JasonHart 4 77
(Richard Guest) *chsd ldrs on outer: one pce fnl f* 20/1

-036 **6** 1¼ **Alaskan Bullet (IRE)**[77] 457 4-9-5 80 .... ConnorBeasley(5) 13 79
(Brian Ellison) *in rr: styd on fnl f* 8/1[3]

021- **7** 3¾ **Elusive Bonus (IRE)**[189] 7001 4-9-3 76 .... DavidBergin(3) 5 62
(David O'Meara) *chsd ldrs: sn drvn along: wknd fnl f* 9/1

0-60 **8** ½ **Beau Mistral (IRE)**[13] 1370 4-9-10 80 .... JoshBaudains 6 64
(Paul Green) *in rr: sme hdwy over 1f out: nvr a factor* 22/1

006- **9** 2½ **Nomoreblondes**[194] 6887 9-9-0 70 .... (v) DavidSimmonson 14 45
(Paul Midgley) *chsd ldrs: wknd over 1f out* 40/1

31-2 **10** ¾ **Come On Dave (IRE)**[19] 1253 4-9-5 78 .... ShirleyTeasdale(3) 2 50
(David Nicholls) *chsd ldrs: wknd over 1f out* 5/2[1]

204- **11** 1 **Bronze Beau**[194] 6886 6-9-4 74 .... (t) JacobButterfield 3 42
(Kristin Stubbs) *swtchd rt s and racd alone towards far side: edgd lft over 1f out: sn wknd* 25/1

4340 **12** *nk* **Dorback**[42] 913 6-9-8 78 .... IanBurns 12 45
(David Nicholls) *mid-div: lost pl over 1f out* 16/1

420- **13** 1¼ **El McGlynn (IRE)**[169] 7489 4-9-4 74 .... GeorgeDowning 7 37
(William Kinsey) *chsd ldrs: wknd 2f out* 14/1

00-0 **14** ½ **Lost In Paris (IRE)**[16] 1308 7-8-12 76 .... (p) RachelRichardson(8) 9 37
(Tim Easterby) *mid-div: lost pl over 1f out* 25/1

59.29s (-0.71) **Going Correction** 0.0s/f (Good) **14 Ran SP% 119.1**
Speed ratings (Par 105): **105,104,103,102,102 100,94,93,89,88 86,86,84,83**
toteswingers 1&2 £17.70, 1&3 £19.40, 2&3 £17.70 CSF £58.52 CT £568.13 TOTE £9.30: £2.70, £2.40, £5.00; EX 77.30 Trifecta £555.50 Part won. Pool: £740.67 - 0.47 winning units..
Owner Middleham Park Racing V & Partners **Bred** Sandro Garavelli **Trained** Great Habton, N Yorks
■ Stewards' Enquiry : Shirley Teasdale one-day ban: careless riding (May 2); one-day ban: failed to ride to draw (May 3)

FOCUS
A fair apprentice riders' sprint handicap for older horses. The best time on the card and pretty straightforward form.
T/Plt: £264.50 to a £1 stake. Pool of £58,038.67 - 160.13 winning units T/Qpdt: £13.90 to a £1 stake. Pool of £5838.50 - 308.85 winning units WG

1519 WOLVERHAMPTON (A.W) (L-H)
Thursday, April 18

OFFICIAL GOING: Standard
Track Gallop Mastered after 4th race.
Wind: Strong behind Weather: Fine

1650 32REDPOKER.COM H'CAP 5f 216y(P)
5:20 (5:20) (Class 6) (0-65,65) 4-Y-O+ **£1,940** (£577; £288; £144) **Stalls** Low

Form RPR

4003 **1** **Invigilator**[6] 1525 5-9-3 61 .... (t) HarryBentley 3 71
(Derek Shaw) *chsd ldrs: rdn to ld ins fnl f: r.o* 9/4[1]

0050 **2** 2 **Dickie Le Davoir**[6] 1525 9-9-7 65 .... (b) RobbieFitzpatrick 4 69
(Richard Guest) *sn pushed along in rr: rdn and r.o ins fnl f: wnt 2nd nr fin: nt trble wnr* 20/1

1133 **3** ½ **Flow Chart (IRE)**[12] 1396 6-8-6 55 .... SladeO'Hara(5) 6 57
(Peter Grayson) *hld up: nt clr run over 1f out: r.o ins fnl f: nrst fin* 20/1

0322 **4** 1 **Jawking**[6] 1525 4-9-2 60 .... (t) MircoMimmocchi 2 59
(Frank Sheridan) *led 1f: chsd ldr tl led over 1f out: rdn and hdd ins fnl f: styd on same pce* 3/1[2]

60-5 **5** ½ **Available (IRE)**[12] 1398 4-9-4 62 .... StephenCraine 8 60
(John Mackie) *chsd ldrs: rdn over 2f out: styd on same pce ins fnl f* 10/1

34-5 **6** 1¼ **Opus Dei**[15] 1334 6-9-2 65 .... (p) WilliamTwiston-Davies(5) 5 59
(Alan McCabe) *prom: rdn over 1f out: no ex ins fnl f* 4/1[3]

-006 **7** ½ **Muftarres (IRE)**[14] 1351 8-9-5 63 .... (bt) LukeMorris 7 55
(Frank Sheridan) *hld up: rdn over 2f out: styd on same pce fnl f* 11/1

200 **8** 10 **Quality Art (USA)**[15] 1324 5-9-0 63 .... PhilipPrince(5) 1 23
(Richard Guest) *s.i.s: pushed along to ld 5f out: rdn and hdd over 1f out: wknd fnl f* 8/1

1m 14.34s (-0.66) **Going Correction** -0.10s/f (Stan) **8 Ran SP% 113.8**
Speed ratings (Par 101): **100,97,96,95,94 93,92,79**
Tote Swingers: 1&2 £9.70, 1&3 £5.70, 2&3 £7.40 CSF £48.18 CT £717.48 TOTE £2.80: £1.20, £3.70, £2.90; EX 37.60 Trifecta £231.10 Pool: £1,648.13 - 5.34 winning units..
Owner The Warren Partnership **Bred** Granham Farm And P Hearson Bloodstock **Trained** Sproxton, Leics

FOCUS
A couple of pace-setters went off at a decent gallop. The winner built on his latest effort to reverse form with the fourth.

1651 HOLIDAY INN WOLVERHAMPTON (S) H'CAP 5f 20y(P)
5:55 (5:55) (Class 6) (0-60,56) 3-Y-O **£1,940** (£577; £288; £144) **Stalls** Low

Form RPR

-653 **1** **Whiteflats**[62] 669 3-8-10 45 .... (v) HarryBentley 1 53
(Derek Shaw) *mde virtually all: rdn over 1f out: styd on* 9/1

042- **2** ½ **Confidential Creek**[196] 6809 3-9-7 56 .... FrederikTylicki 3 62
(Ollie Pears) *a.p: chsd wnr 2f out: rdn over 1f out: r.o* 4/5[1]

-646 **3** 4 **Charlemagne Diva**[8] 1458 3-8-8 48 .... (e) PhilipPrince(5) 6 40
(Richard Guest) *prom: rdn over 1f out: styd on same pce* 5/1[2]

420 **4** ¾ **Nors The Panic**[14] 1349 3-9-1 50 .... (e) RobbieFitzpatrick 4 39
(Richard Guest) *hmpd sn after s: pushed along in rr: hmpd 1/2-way: hdwy over 1f out: no ex ins fnl f* 20/1

262 **5** 3 **Lexi's Beauty (IRE)**[27] 1116 3-8-13 48 .... AndreaAtzeni 7 26
(Patrick Morris) *hld up: hdwy over 1f out: wknd ins fnl f* 10/1

6326 **6** 7 **Marmot Bay (IRE)**[24] 1171 3-9-0 54 .... JemmaMarshall(5) 2
(David Flood) *chsd wnr 3f: eased fnl f* 7/1[3]

1m 2.43s (0.13) **Going Correction** -0.10s/f (Stan) **6 Ran SP% 108.6**
Speed ratings (Par 96): **94,93,86,85,80 69**
Tote Swingers: 1&2 £1.90, 1&3 £4.70, 2&3 £2.30 CSF £15.78 TOTE £14.10: £5.20, £1.20; EX 37.20 Trifecta £200.50 Pool: £1,849.56 - 6.91 winning units..
Owner Houghton Bloodstock **Bred** S Birdseye **Trained** Sproxton, Leics

FOCUS
This bunch probably won't be successful at a higher level too often considering the official mark of the winner. However the first two look a bit better than their marks.

1652 32RED H'CAP 5f 20y(P)
6:25 (6:29) (Class 4) (0-85,83) 4-Y-O+ **£4,690** (£1,395; £697; £348) **Stalls** Low

Form RPR

4500 **1** **Forest Edge (IRE)**[12] 1385 4-9-1 82 .... DeclanBates(5) 1 91
(David Evans) *sn pushed along and prom: drvn along 1/2-way: chsd ldr over 1f out: styd on u.p to ld nr fin* 11/1

3023 **2** *nk* **Tyfos**[13] 1370 8-9-0 81 .... MatthewLawson(5) 4 89
(Brian Baugh) *led: pushed clr 2f out: rdn and hung rt ins fnl f: hdd nr fin* 6/1

3 **3** 1 **Gandalak (FR)**[19] 1248 4-9-5 81 .... FrederikTylicki 6 85
(David O'Meara) *chsd ldr tl rdn over 1f out: styd on* 11/4[1]

3344 **4** ½ **Triple Dream**[6] 1517 8-9-6 82 .... (tp) JimmyQuinn 7 85
(Milton Bradley) *trckd ldrs: shkn up over 1f out: styd on* 8/1

/3-0 **5** 2¾ **Lenny Bee**[68] 586 7-9-2 78 .... (t) NeilCallan 3 71
(Garry Moss) *s.i.s: hdwy over 1f out: no imp ins fnl f* 14/1

101- **6** 4 **Blanc De Chine (IRE)**[198] 6767 4-9-4 80 .... LukeMorris 2 58
(Peter Makin) *chsd ldrs: rdn 1/2-way: wknd over 1f out* 3/1[2]

0252 **7** 1½ **Royal Bajan (USA)**[16] 1308 5-9-7 83 .... (b) GrahamLee 8 56
(James Given) *hld up: pushed along 1/2-way: rdn over 1f out: n.d* 9/2[3]

1m 1.22s (-1.08) **Going Correction** -0.10s/f (Stan) **7 Ran SP% 110.2**
Speed ratings (Par 105): **104,103,101,101,96 90,87**
Tote Swingers: 1&2 £10.20, 1&3 £7.00, 2&3 £4.70 CSF £68.62 CT £220.59 TOTE £11.80: £3.90, £2.90; EX 89.10 Trifecta £443.50 Pool: £1,682.86 - 2.84 winning units..
Owner Peter Swinnerton **Bred** Alberto Panetta **Trained** Pandy, Monmouths
■ Stewards' Enquiry : Matthew Lawson caution: careless riding
Frederik Tylicki two-day ban: careless riding (May 2-3)

FOCUS
There was a slight delay to this sprint for useful AW performers when Island Legend burst out of the stalls. He took a while to stop and was withdrawn. The form is rated around the runner-up.

1653 32RED.COM MAIDEN STKS 1m 4f 50y(P)
6:55 (6:57) (Class 5) 3-Y-O+ **£2,587** (£770; £384; £192) **Stalls** Low

Form RPR

363- **1** **Requested**[168] 7501 3-8-7 78 .... SilvestreDeSousa 8 82
(Mahmood Al Zarooni) *plld hrd and prom: trckd ldr 10f out: led over 1f out: hung lft and rdn clr fnl f* 1/1[1]

34- **2** 5 **Gravitate**[364] 1479 4-9-12 0 .... MartinDwyer 11 76
(Paul Webber) *led at stdy pce tl qcknd 3f out: rdn and hdd over 1f out: no ex ins fnl f* 25/1

2 **3** 1¾ **Fantasy In Blue**[14] 1347 3-8-2 0 .... LukeMorris 5 66
(Sir Michael Stoute) *chsd ldrs: rdn over 2f out: styd on same pce fr over 1f out* 2/1[2]

3 **4** 3 **Smalib Monterg (FR)**[12] 1069 7-9-13 0 .... (t) GrahamLee 1 68
(Dr Richard Newland) *prom: rdn over 2f out: styd on same pce* 8/1[3]

6 **5** 5 **Single Mast (USA)**[23] 1178 3-8-2 0 .... WilliamCarson 4 53
(Charles Hills) *chsd ldr 2f: remained handy: rdn over 2f out: wknd over 1f out* 16/1

0/ **6** 1¾ **Between The Lines (IRE)**[547] 6954 4-9-12 0 .... FergusSweeney 3 57
(Anthony Middleton) *s.i.s: hld up: nvr nrr* 50/1

05 **7** 3½ **Al Meezan**[8] 1478 3-8-7 0 .... HarryBentley 12 50
(David Simcock) *s.i.s: hld up: rdn over 5f out: n.d* 40/1

8 3¾ **Eleanor Roosevelt (IRE)** 3-8-2 0 .... JimmyQuinn 7 39
(Jamie Osborne) *s.i.s: hld up: flashed tail smetimes: lost tch over 3f out* 14/1

9 ½ **Enchanted Garden**[46] 5-9-13 0 .... FrederikTylicki 2 45
(Malcolm Jefferson) *mid-div: rdn and wknd over 2f out* 20/1

6 **10** 2½ **Ernie**[15] 1317 6-9-13 0 .... NeilCallan 9 41
(Geoffrey Deacon) *mid-div: pushed along over 3f out: wknd over 2f out* 66/1

11 59 **Bertie Bob** 7-9-13 0 .... RobbieFitzpatrick 6
(Dai Burchell) *s.s: a in rr: bhd fnl 4f: t.o* 100/1

2m 39.18s (-1.92) **Going Correction** -0.10s/f (Stan)
WFA 3 from 4yo 20lb 4 from 5yo+ 1lb **11 Ran SP% 122.5**
Speed ratings (Par 103): **102,98,97,95,92 91,88,86,85,84 44**
Tote Swingers: 1&2 £6.00, 1&3 £1.40, 2&3 £10.50 CSF £39.96 TOTE £1.80: £1.10, £5.90, £1.50; EX 30.90 Trifecta £76.70 Pool: £1,641.94 - 16.04 winning units..
Owner Marmoom Racing **Bred** Hesmonds Stud Ltd **Trained** Newmarket, Suffolk

The Form Book Flat, Raceform Ltd, Compton, RG20 6NL.

FOCUS
Just an ordinary maiden and the first two home were in first and second throughout, suggesting the early gallop was steady. Muddling form, the winner rating a small personal best.

1654 32RED CASINO FILLIES' H'CAP 1m 4f 50y(P)
7:25 (7:25) (Class 5) (0-70,70) 4-Y-0+ **£2,587** (£770; £384; £192) **Stalls** Low

Form RPR
6214 **1** **The Blue Dog (IRE)**[14] 1350 6-8-10 **64**........................... RobertTart(5) 4 74
(Michael Wigham) *chsd ldr 3f: remained handy: led over 1f out: hung lft and rdn clr fnl f* **12/1**
4214 **2** *4* **Mazij**[10] 1434 5-9-1 **64**........................... WilliamCarson 5 67
(Peter Hiatt) *led at stdy pce tl qcknd over 3f out: rdn over 2f out: hdd over 1f out: edgd rt and no ex fnl f* **11/1**
4500 **3** *hd* **Ice Tres**[41] 925 4-8-6 **56** oh1........................... AndreaAtzeni 7 59
(Rod Millman) *s.s: hld up: nt clr run over 2f out: hdwy and hung lft over 1f out: sn rdn: styd on same pce ins fnl f* **25/1**
0-21 **4** *½* **Cape Alex**[14] 1350 4-8-6 **56** oh2........................... HarryBentley 3 58
(Clive Brittain) *prom: chsd ldr 9f out tl over 4f out: rdn over 1f out: styd on same pce* **11/4**[2]
1231 **5** *1 ¼* **Irene Kennet**[24] 1175 6-9-0 **63**........................... HayleyTurner 6 63
(Paul Burgoyne) *hld up: pushed along over 3f out: rdn over 1f out: styd on same pce* **9/2**[3]
-133 **6** *3 ¼* **Asia Minor (IRE)**[50] 816 4-8-12 **62**........................... JimmyQuinn 2 57
(Dr Jon Scargill) *hld up: pushed along over 3f out: wknd over 1f out* **9/1**
631- **7** *5* **Shea**[183] 7162 4-9-6 **70**........................... RichardKingscote 1 57
(Ralph Beckett) *chsd ldrs: wnt 2nd over 4f out: nt clr run over 2f out: wknd over 1f out* **2/1**[1]
2m 37.51s (-3.59) **Going Correction** -0.10s/f (Stan)
WFA 4 from 5yo+ 1lb 7 Ran SP% **108.1**
Speed ratings (Par 100): **107,104,104,103,103 100,97**
Tote Swingers: 1&2 £4.00, 1&3 £20.00, 2&3 £33.70 CSF £115.43 TOTE £19.60: £5.70, £5.10; EX 84.30 Trifecta £845.40 Part won. Pool: £1,127.29 - 0.18 winning units..
Owner R Carson **Bred** Mervyn Stewkesbury **Trained** Newmarket, Suffolk
FOCUS
The early gallop wasn't strong but it quickened noticeably heading to the end of the back straight. The winning time was quicker than the maiden over the same trip. The winner was better than ever.

1655 £32 BONUS AT 32RED.COM H'CAP 1m 1f 103y(P)
7:55 (7:56) (Class 5) (0-70,70) 3-Y-0 **£2,587** (£770; £384; £192) **Stalls** Low

Form RPR
6222 **1** **Excellent Puck (IRE)**[30] 1072 3-9-7 **70**........................... FergusSweeney 2 79
(Jamie Osborne) *trckd ldrs: wnt 2nd over 6f out: led over 1f out: sn rdn and hung lft: r.o* **7/2**[2]
5-21 **2** *2 ¾* **Mizyen (IRE)**[13] 1372 3-9-6 **69**........................... NeilCallan 5 72
(James Tate) *led: rdn and hdd over 1f out: styd on same pce ins fnl f* **2/1**[1]
536- **3** *¾* **Typhon (USA)**[244] 5319 3-9-6 **69**........................... TedDurcan 1 72+
(David Lanigan) *chsd ldrs: lost pl over 5f out: r.o ins fnl f* **6/1**
6121 **4** *hd* **Birdy Boy (USA)**[13] 1373 3-9-3 **66**........................... FrannyNorton 3 67
(Mark Johnston) *chsd ldr 3f: remained handy: rdn over 2f out: styd on same pce fr over 1f out* **4/1**[3]
4142 **5** *3 ¾* **Minimee**[8] 1486 3-9-7 **70**........................... LukeMorris 6 63
(Phil McEntee) *sn pushed along in rr: hdwy over 5f out: rdn over 2f out: wknd over 1f out* **9/1**
00-1 **6** *5* **Zero Game (IRE)**[10] 1428 3-8-5 **61**...........(e) ThomasHemsley(7) 4 44
(Michael Bell) *s.s: plld hrd and hdwy 7f out: wknd wl over 1f out* **12/1**
2m 0.16s (-1.54) **Going Correction** -0.10s/f (Stan) 6 Ran SP% **107.5**
Speed ratings (Par 98): **102,99,98,98,95 90**
Tote Swingers: 1&2 £1.80, 1&3 £5.30, 2&3 £3.30 CSF £9.97 TOTE £4.60: £1.10, £2.90; EX 11.50 Trifecta £50.20 Pool: £948.97 - 14.17 winning units..
Owner K J P Gundlach **Bred** Swersky & Associates **Trained** Upper Lambourn, Berks
FOCUS
It paid to race handy in this open-looking contest. The runner-up is the best guide.

1656 32REDBET.COM H'CAP (DIV I) 7f 32y(P)
8:25 (8:26) (Class 6) (0-60,60) 4-Y-0+ **£1,940** (£577; £288; £144) **Stalls** High

Form RPR
6353 **1** **Romanticize**[22] 1211 7-9-2 **55**........................... GrahamLee 9 62
(Jason Ward) *chsd ldrs: rdn over 1f out: r.o to ld nr fin* **5/1**[1]
00-4 **2** *shd* **Moss Hill**[22] 1202 4-8-10 **49**........................... FrannyNorton 6 56
(Charles Hills) *sn led: rdn over 1f out: hdd nr fin* **7/1**[2]
2340 **3** *½* **Unlimited**[16] 1303 11-9-6 **59**........................... JimmyQuinn 4 64
(Tony Carroll) *a.p: racd keenly: hrd rdn ins fnl f: r.o* **5/1**[1]
060- **4** *¾* **Rutterkin (USA)**[210] 6403 5-8-12 **51**........................... FrederikTylicki 7 54+
(Richard Ford) *hld up: hdwy over 1f out: sn rdn and swtchd lft: r.o* **8/1**[3]
4130 **5** *¾* **Blue Noodles**[22] 1194 7-9-0 **53**...........(p) PaddyAspell 10 54
(John Wainwright) *prom: rdn over 2f out: hung lft ins fnl f: styd on* **14/1**
1523 **6** *1 ¼* **Mucky Molly**[9] 1455 5-8-13 **52**...........(vt) WilliamCarson 3 50
(Alison Hutchinson) *broke wl: sn pushed along to chse ldr: rdn over 1f out: styd on same pce ins fnl f* **10/1**
2206 **7** *shd* **Sannibel**[24] 1172 5-9-2 **60**........................... RobertTart(5) 5 58
(Graeme McPherson) *dwlt: hld up: nt clr run fr over 2f out tl r.o ins fnl f: nvr nrr* **10/1**
1006 **8** *nk* **Prince Of Passion (CAN)**[12] 1397 5-9-7 **60**...........(v) MartinDwyer 8 57
(Derek Shaw) *hld up: nt clr run over 2f out: r.o ins fnl f: nrst fin* **7/1**[2]
0453 **9** *7* **The Mongoose**[15] 1322 5-9-0 **60**...........(t) RobJFitzpatrick(7) 1 38
(David Evans) *chsd ldrs: rdn over 1f out: wknd fnl f* **5/1**[1]
6600 **10** *1 ½* **Kai**[44] 890 4-8-11 **55**...........(v) WilliamTwiston-Davies(5) 11 29
(Alan McCabe) *hld up: rdn 1/2-way: a in rr* **14/1**
0500 **11** *3 ½* **Back For Tea (IRE)**[17] 1294 5-8-7 **46** oh1...........(tp) LukeMorris 2
(Phil McEntee) *hld up: hdwy 1/2-way: sn rdn: wknd over 1f out* **33/1**
1m 28.95s (-0.65) **Going Correction** -0.10s/f (Stan) 11 Ran SP% **120.6**
Speed ratings (Par 101): **99,98,98,97,96 95,95,94,86,85 81**
Tote Swingers: 1&2 £8.30, 1&3 £5.90, 2&3 £5.00 CSF £40.69 CT £191.16 TOTE £5.90: £1.90, £4.00, £2.60; EX 32.40 Trifecta £408.00 Pool: £862.79 - 1.58 winning units..
Owner Miss Vivian Pratt **Bred** Cheveley Park Stud Ltd **Trained** Middleham, N Yorks
FOCUS
The first division of a modest handicap, and sound form.

1657 32REDBET.COM H'CAP (DIV II) 7f 32y(P)
8:55 (8:56) (Class 6) (0-60,60) 4-Y-0+ **£1,940** (£577; £288; £144) **Stalls** High

Form RPR
06 **1** **Larghetto (USA)**[42] 919 5-9-2 **55**........................... ShaneKelly 11 67
(Daniel Mark Loughnane) *s.i.s: hdwy over 5f out: shkn up to ld over 1f out: r.o wl: comf* **16/1**
2662 **2** *2 ¾* **Do More Business (IRE)**[22] 1194 6-8-8 **52**...........(bt) PhilipPrince(5) 6 57
(Liam Corcoran) *hld up: rdn over 1f out: hung lft and r.o ins fnl frulrong: wnt 2nd post: nt trble wnr* **8/1**
-415 **3** *nk* **Amis Reunis**[75] 497 4-9-7 **60**...........(p) WilliamCarson 1 64
(Anthony Carson) *chsd ldrs: rdn over 2f out: styd on same pce ins fnl f* **6/1**
2640 **4** *½* **Media Jury**[8] 1459 6-8-10 **49**...........(v) PaddyAspell 5 51
(John Wainwright) *hld up: hdwy over 1f out: r.o: nt trble ldrs* **20/1**
6216 **5** *1 ¾* **Jonnie Skull (IRE)**[33] 1042 7-9-0 **53**...........(vt) GrahamLee 7 51
(Phil McEntee) *chsd ldr: rdn and ev ch over 1f out: edgd lft and no ex ins fnl f* **9/2**[2]
4114 **6** *¾* **Rise To Glory (IRE)**[12] 1394 5-9-4 **57**........................... DuranFentiman 9 53
(Shaun Harris) *sn led: rdn and hdd over 1f out: no ex ins fnl f* **7/2**[1]
5640 **7** *2 ½* **Conas Ata Tu**[16] 1298 4-8-11 **50**...........(t) MartinDwyer 2 39
(Derek Shaw) *sn pushed along in rr: nvr on terms* **14/1**
3056 **8** *1* **Compton Target (IRE)**[71] 537 4-8-7 **46** oh1...........(tp) JimmyQuinn 3 32
(Milton Bradley) *mid-div: rdn over 2f out: hung lft and wknd over 1f out* **12/1**
0-00 **9** *3 ¾* **Green Mitas (ITY)**[83] 380 4-9-7 **60**........................... LukeMorris 4 36
(Frank Sheridan) *prom: rdn over 1f out: wknd fnl f* **9/1**
-143 **10** *1 ¾* **Basle**[66] 616 6-9-6 **59**...........(t) RichardKingscote 8 30
(Michael Blake) *chsd ldrs tl rdn and wknd over 1f out* **11/2**[3]
1m 28.98s (-0.62) **Going Correction** -0.10s/f (Stan) 10 Ran SP% **116.2**
Speed ratings (Par 101): **99,95,95,94,92 92,89,88,83,81**
Tote Swingers 1&2 £24.20, 2&3 £8.80, 1&3 £22.90 CSF £137.41 CT £882.30 TOTE £24.50: £7.20, £3.10, £3.20; EX 303.90 Trifecta £812.20 Part won. Pool: £1,083.00 - 0.74 winning units..
Owner Mrs C Loughnane **Bred** Barr Inman & Giant's Causeway Syndicate **Trained** Baldwin's Gate, Staffs
FOCUS
This looked a bit weaker than the first division on paper, with the second and third limiting.
T/Plt: £304.70 to a £1 stake. Pool of £66,888.18 - 160.24 winning units T/Qpdt: £59.10 to a £1 stake. Pool of £9,808.42 - 122.70 winning units CR

1561 LONGCHAMP (R-H)
Thursday, April 18
OFFICIAL GOING: Turf: good to soft

1658a PRIX LORD SEYMOUR (LISTED RACE) (4YO+) (TURF) 1m 4f
12:15 (12:00) 4-Y-0+ **£21,138** (£8,455; £6,341; £4,227; £2,113)

RPR
1 **Now We Can**[27] 4-8-11 0........................... ThierryThulliez 1 106
(N Clement, France) **9/10**[1]
2 *1* **Gentle Storm (FR)**[33] 1048 4-9-1 0...........(p) IoritzMendizabal 4 108
(Y Barberot, France) **53/10**[3]
3 *2 ½* **Pirika (IRE)**[193] 6911 5-8-11 0........................... Pierre-CharlesBoudot 3 99
(A Fabre, France) **2/1**[2]
4 *2 ½* **Kasbah Bliss (FR)**[214] 6297 11-8-11 0........................... MaximeGuyon 2 95
(F Doumen, France) **15/2**
5 *1 ½* **Nicholascopernicus (IRE)**[159] 7689 4-8-11 0.......... TomMcLaughlin 5 94
(Ed Walker) *hld up and last thrght: rdn 3f out: sn outpcd: styd on but nvr a factor* **15/1**
2m 46.43s (16.03)
WFA 4 from 5yo+ 1lb 5 Ran SP% **119.9**
WIN (incl. 1 euro stake): 1.90. Places: 1.40, 2.10. SF: 6.30..
Owner Winfried Engelbrecht-Bresges **Bred** Gestut Zoppenbroich **Trained** Chantilly, France

BATH (L-H)
Friday, April 19
OFFICIAL GOING: Good to soft (good in places) changing to good (good to soft in places) after race 2 (5.30)
Wind: mild breeze half across Weather: cloudy

1659 BATHWICK TYRES TETBURY EBF MEDIAN AUCTION MAIDEN STKS 5f 11y
5:00 (5:01) (Class 5) 2-Y-0 **£3,067** (£905; £453) **Stalls** Centre

Form RPR
1 **Beldale Memory (IRE)** 2-9-0 0........................... AdamKirby 8 81+
(Clive Cox) *mde all: rdn clr over 1f out: r.o strly* **10/1**[3]
2 **2** *2 ½* **Beau Nash (IRE)**[14] 1360 2-9-5 0........................... PatDobbs 12 76
(Richard Hannon) *trckd ldrs: rdn to chse wnr over 1f out: kpt on but nt pce to chal* **10/11**[1]
3 *2 ¼* **Capitulate** 2-9-5 0........................... SeanLevey 13 68
(Ed McMahon) *mid-div: pushed along and hdwy 3f out: sn rdn: chsd ldng pair over 1f out: kpt on same pce* **3/1**[2]
0 **4** *1* **Iseemist (IRE)**[11] 1421 2-8-9 0........................... MichaelJMMurphy(5) 7 59
(John Gallagher) *mid-div: hdwy 2f out: rdn ent fnl f: kpt on* **50/1**
5 *hd* **Fantasy Justifier (IRE)** 2-9-5 0........................... LukeMorris 6 64
(Ronald Harris) *s.i.s: towards rr: hdwy 3f out: swtchd rt 2f out: sn rdn: kpt on wout rching ldrs* **14/1**
6 *¾* **Sartori** 2-9-5 0........................... MartinHarley 2 61
(Mick Channon) *mid-div: rdn wl over 2f out: no imp tl styd on ins fnl f* **16/1**
7 *1 ¼* **Rush** 2-9-0 0........................... SilvestreDeSousa 4 51+
(Paul Cole) *s.i.s: sn outpcd in rr: hdwy 2f out: styd on nicely fnl f: nvr able to get on terms* **20/1**
8 *3 ¼* **Dancing Sal (IRE)** 2-9-0 0........................... TomMcLaughlin 10 40
(David Evans) *sn outpcd in rr: styd on ent fnl f: nvr trbld ldrs* **66/1**
9 *1 ¾* **Caledonia Laird** 2-9-5 0........................... GrahamLee 5 38
(Jo Hughes) *towards rr: rdn and sme prog into midfield over 2f out: no further imp fnl f* **28/1**
10 *3* **Under Your Thumb (IRE)** 2-9-0 0........................... WilliamCarson 16 23
(David Evans) *sn pressing wnr: rdn over 2f out: sn wknd* **40/1**
44 **11** *1 ¼* **El Duque**[16] 1328 2-8-12 0........................... RyanWhile(7) 1 23
(Bill Turner) *chsd ldrs: rdn over 2f out: wknd wl over 1f out* **25/1**
12 *½* **Astral Rose** 2-8-11 0........................... DarrenEgan(3) 9 16
(Paul Fitzsimons) *trckd ldrs: rdn 2f out: sn wknd* **50/1**
6 **13** *1 ¾* **Sleeping Angel**[15] 1344 2-9-0 0........................... JimmyQuinn 11 10
(Milton Bradley) *mid-div tl wl over 2f out: sn towards rr* **100/1**
54 **14** *shd* **Brockholes Flyer (IRE)**[7] 1512 2-9-5 0........................... SebSanders 3 15
(Brendan Powell) *in tch: rdn whn squeezed up over 2f out: sn wknd* **66/1**

15 6 **Urban Dreamer (IRE)** 2-9-5 0 .... AndreaAtzeni 15
(Rod Millman) *sn chsng ldrs: rdn and losing pl whn sltly hmpd 2f out: sn wknd* **20/1**

1m 3.18s (0.68) **Going Correction** -0.05s/f (Good) **15 Ran SP% 126.2**
Speed ratings (Par 92): **92,88,84,82,82 81,79,74,71,66 64,63,60,60,51**
toteswingers 1&2 £4.50, 1&3 £8.30, 2&3 £1.80 CSF £18.77 TOTE £12.10: £3.60, £1.10, £1.70; EX 30.30 Trifecta £267.90 Pool: £1,653.86 - 4.62 winning units..
Owner Mrs T L Cox **Bred** Yeomanstown Stud **Trained** Lambourn, Berks

FOCUS
A debutant showed plenty of speed to win this maiden. The form looks solid with the experienced favourite in second and a well-backed newcomer in third.

1660 BATHWICK TYRES MIDSOMER NORTON MAIDEN STKS 5f 161y
5:30 (5:33) (Class 5) 3-Y-O+ **£2,587** (£770; £384; £192) **Stalls** Low

Form RPR

633- **1** **Shore Step (IRE)**[168] [7516] 3-9-1 67 .... MartinHarley 13 76
(Mick Channon) *a.p: rdn to ld wl over 1f out: in command whn idling fnl f: kpt up to work* **6/1[3]**

2 1 **Dilgura** 3-8-10 0 .... ShaneKelly 16 68
(Stuart Kittow) *mid-div: rdn and hdwy over 1f out: r.o strly fnl f: wnt 2nd nring fin* **20/1**

0- **3** 1 **Assertive Agent**[317] [2812] 3-8-10 0 .... JohnFahy 3 64
(Ben De Haan) *s.i.s: towards rr: hdwy 2f out: r.o wl fnl f: snatched 3rd fnl stride* **66/1**

23- **4** ½ **Zhiggy's Stardust**[328] [2501] 4-9-12 0 .... DaneO'Neill 7 71
(Henry Candy) *led: rdn 2f out: sn narrowly hdd: hld ent fnl f: no ex whn lost 2 pls fnl 50yds* **4/1[1]**

6- **5** 1¾ **Faluka (IRE)**[340] [2124] 3-8-10 0 .... SilvestreDeSousa 1 57
(Paul Cole) *trckd ldrs: rdn over 2f out: nt pce to chal: no ex whn lost 2 pls ins fnl f* **7/1**

6 hd **Ovatory** 3-9-1 0 .... PatDobbs 2 61+
(Amanda Perrett) *mid-div: pushed along over 2f out: nt pce to threaten ldrs but styd on wl enough fnl f* **11/2[2]**

0-3 **7** 2¼ **Burnt Fingers (IRE)**[14] [1364] 3-8-10 0 .... AndreaAtzeni 17 49+
(Rod Millman) *towards rr of midfield: hdwy wl over 1f out: sn rdn: styd on wout threatening fnl furlng* **8/1**

8 2½ **Calm Attitude (IRE)** 3-8-10 0 .... ChrisCatlin 12 41
(Rae Guest) *s.i.s: towards rr: styd on fr over 1f out: nvr a danger* **40/1**

4-4 **9** 2 **Evan Elpus (IRE)**[31] [1078] 3-9-1 0 .... RichardKingscote 4 39
(Tom Dascombe) *chsd ldrs: rdn over 2f out: wknd ent fnl f* **20/1**

10 nk **Hypnotism** 3-9-1 0 .... LukeMorris 14 38
(Ronald Harris) *dwlt: bhd and reminders: sme late prog past btn horses: nvr a factor* **33/1**

11 2¾ **The Dark Wizard (IRE)** 3-9-1 0 .... GeorgeBaker 11 29
(Roger Charlton) *v green leaving stalls: bhd: sme late prog past btn horses: nvr a factor* **8/1**

0-5 **12** 1½ **Thrasos (IRE)**[100] [123] 4-9-12 0 .... AdamKirby 9 27
(Jo Crowley) *mid-div: rdn over 2f out: no imp: wknd ent fnl f* **25/1**

50 **13** 1¾ **Castell Avon**[11] [1429] 3-8-10 0 .... JimmyQuinn 5
(Milton Bradley) *squeezed up leaving stalls and stmbld: a towards rr* **100/1**

14 shd **Miss Meticulous** 3-8-10 0 .... SeanLevey 15
(Ed McMahon) *mid-div: rdn over 2f out: wknd jst over 1f out* **14/1**

60 **15** 1¼ **Purford Green**[30] [1086] 4-9-7 0 .... RobertHavlin 6
(Michael Attwater) *sn mid-div: wknd 2f out* **66/1**

0- **16** 7 **Secret Success**[198] [6787] 3-9-1 0 .... GrahamLee 8
(Paul Cole) *in tch: rdn over 2f out: wknd 2f out* **16/1**

02 **17** 5 **Green Millionaire**[71] [549] 3-9-1 0 .... FergusSweeney 10
(Jeremy Gask) *chsd ldrs: rdn over 2f out: wkng whn squeezed up sn after* **16/1**

1m 12.2s (1.00) **Going Correction** -0.05s/f (Good)
WFA 3 from 4yo 11lb **17 Ran SP% 125.5**
Speed ratings (Par 103): **91,89,88,87,85 85,82,78,76,75 72,70,67,67,65 56,49**
toteswingers 1&2 £29.50, 1&3 £83.50, 2&3 £175.40 CSF £129.95 TOTE £4.60: £2.70, £11.50, £28.70; EX 172.60 Trifecta £1441.40 Part won. Pool: £1,921.94 - 0.13 winning units..
Owner Jon and Julia Aisbitt **Bred** Lynn Lodge Stud **Trained** West Ilsley, Berks

FOCUS
An ordinary maiden. The winner was always prominent and the placed horses finished well. The fourth sets the level.

1661 BATHWICK TYRES H'CAP 5f 11y
6:00 (6:02) (Class 4) (0-80,78) 3-Y-O **£4,690** (£1,395; £697; £348) **Stalls** Centre

Form RPR

11-2 **1** **Space Artist (IRE)**[31] [1075] 3-9-5 76 .... TomEaves 4 81
(Bryan Smart) *mde all: hld on gamely fnl f: drifted rt nring fin: all out* **11/2[3]**

212- **2** nk **Small Fury (IRE)**[119] [8204] 3-9-3 74 .... J-PGuillambert 8 78
(Jo Hughes) *played up and led to s: pressed wnr thrght: rdn 2f out: ev ch ins fnl f: kpt on but hld whn carried sltly rt nring fin* **10/1**

413- **3** nk **Shrimpton**[160] [7687] 3-9-4 75 .... MartinHarley 2 78
(Mick Channon) *trckd ldrs: rdn 2f out: swtchd sltly lft and r.o fnl 75yds* **4/1[1]**

454- **4** 1 **Hot Secret**[223] [6022] 3-8-9 71 .... ThomasBrown(5) 9 70
(Andrew Balding) *sn trcking ldrs: rdn to chal 2f out: kpt on same pce fnl f* **5/1[2]**

211 **5** 1 **Oscars Journey**[163] [7635] 3-9-1 72 .... FrederikTylicki 1 68
(J R Jenkins) *trckd ldrs: rdn 2f out: keeping on against far rails whn nt clrest of runs briefly fnl 120yds: hld after* **6/1**

4015 **6** nk **Buy Art**[24] [1180] 3-8-11 68 .... (p) FergusSweeney 5 63
(Gary Moore) *plld hrd: hld up bhd ldrs: swtchd rt and effrt 2f out: kpt on same pce fnl f* **16/1**

530- **7** 1 **Edged Out**[180] [7272] 3-8-4 66 .... RyanTate(5) 7 59+
(Christopher Mason) *hld up bhd ldrs: effrt 2f out: nt pce to chal: no ex fnl 120yds* **20/1**

25-0 **8** ¾ **Khefyn (IRE)**[9] [1482] 3-9-0 74 .... DarrenEgan(3) 6 62
(Ronald Harris) *trckd ldrs: rdn 2f out: kpt on tl no ex fnl 120yds* **10/1**

2234 **9** 12 **Lager Time (IRE)**[37] [982] 3-8-9 66 .... AndreaAtzeni 10
(David Evans) *a struggling in last but in tch: wknd jst over 1f out* **4/1[1]**

1m 2.74s (0.24) **Going Correction** -0.05s/f (Good) **9 Ran SP% 115.2**
Speed ratings (Par 100): **96,95,95,93,91 91,89,88,69**
toteswingers 1&2 £4.50, 1&3 £4.30, 2&3 £10.10 CSF £58.66 CT £244.51 TOTE £4.10: £1.90, £3.20, £2.10; EX 44.20 Trifecta £158.70 Pool: £1,556.56 - 7.35 winning units..
Owner The Smart Dame Laura Partnership **Bred** Rathasker Stud **Trained** Hambleton, N Yorks

FOCUS
The ground was drying out and the going was changed to good, good to soft in places. A fair handicap, but the pace was not very strong and there was a tight finish. The placed horses set the level.

1662 EBF AND WHITSBURY MANOR STUD LANSDOWN FILLIES' STKS (LISTED RACE) 5f 11y
6:30 (6:31) (Class 1) 3-Y-O+
£22,684 (£8,600; £4,304; £2,144; £1,076; £540) **Stalls** Centre

Form RPR

000- **1** **Place In My Heart**[160] [7690] 4-9-0 90 .... AdamKirby 4 106
(Clive Cox) *disp ld: rdn into clr advantage over 1f out: r.o wl: rdn out* **16/1**

61- **2** 1¼ **My Propeller (IRE)**[212] [6382] 4-9-0 100 .... AndreaAtzeni 1 101
(Peter Chapple-Hyam) *trckd ldrs: rdn wl over 1f out: kpt on ins fnl f: wnt 2nd fnl 120yds* **6/1**

010- **3** ½ **Caledonia Lady**[279] [4113] 4-9-0 105 .... GrahamLee 7 99
(Jo Hughes) *hld up: hdwy over 1f out: effrt on outer ent fnl f: kpt on to go 3rd towards fin* **7/2[1]**

034- **4** hd **Excelette (IRE)**[209] [6485] 4-9-0 105 .... RoystonFfrench 11 98
(Bryan Smart) *chsd ldrs: rdn over 2f out: chal briefly jst over 1f out: kpt on but no ex: lost 3rd towards fin* **8/1**

112- **5** 1 **Jwala**[219] [6140] 4-9-0 102 .... ShaneKelly 5 95
(Robert Cowell) *disp ld: rdn 2f out: hdd over 1f out: no ex fnl 120yds* **9/2[2]**

143- **6** ¾ **Swan Song**[204] [6602] 4-9-0 85 .... JimmyFortune 9 92
(Andrew Balding) *disp ld: rdn 2f out: hdd over 1f out: no ex fnl f* **6/1**

140- **7** nk **Kyleakin Lass**[174] [7397] 4-9-0 92 .... PatDobbs 13 91
(Paul Fitzsimons) *hld up: rdn to chse ldrs over 1f out: kpt on same pce fnl f* **20/1**

106- **8** ¾ **Lady Phill**[182] [7206] 3-8-4 81 .... KierenFox 10 84?
(Bill Turner) *hld up in last pair but in tch: nt pce to get involved whn rdn over 1f out* **66/1**

301- **9** ½ **Hairy Rocket**[252] [5045] 3-8-4 98 .... AdamBeschizza 6 83+
(William Haggas) *mid-div: sn pushed along: rdn to chse ldrs 2f out: fdd fnl 120yds* **5/1[3]**

40-3 **10** nse **Jillnextdoor (IRE)**[14] [1362] 3-8-4 90 .... SamHitchcott 8 86+
(Mick Channon) *chsd ldrs: gng wl enough but nvr a clr run fr over 1f out: ch gone whn stl nt clr run and eased fnl 120yds* **14/1**

6-00 **11** 8 **Queen Aggie (IRE)**[10] [1444] 3-8-4 94 .... LukeMorris 12 54
(David Evans) *sn struggling in last: wknd over 1f out* **33/1**

1m 1.21s (-1.29) **Going Correction** -0.05s/f (Good)
WFA 3 from 4yo+ 10lb **11 Ran SP% 118.5**
Speed ratings (Par 108): **108,106,105,104,103 102,101,100,99,99 86**
toteswingers 1&2 £23.10, 1&3 £15.10, 2&3 £4.50 CSF £108.21 TOTE £19.30: £4.70, £2.90, £1.60; EX 125.50 Trifecta £1104.90 Part won. Pool: £1,470.30 - 0.80 winning units..
Owner C J Harper **Bred** Whitsbury Manor Stud **Trained** Lambourn, Berks

FOCUS
They went a decent pace in this Listed fillies' event and the winner justified support at biggish prices. The time was reasonably good and the form looks sound.

1663 BATHWICK TYRES BRISTOL FILLIES' H'CAP 1m 2f 46y
7:00 (7:00) (Class 4) (0-80,80) 4-Y-O+ **£4,690** (£1,395; £697; £348) **Stalls** Low

Form RPR

106- **1** **Boonga Roogeta**[114] [8242] 4-8-13 77 .... RosieJessop(5) 1 89
(Peter Charalambous) *mde all: clr after 3f: rdn over 1f out: styd on gamely whn chal ins fnl f to assert nring fin* **7/1**

142- **2** ½ **Moment In Time (IRE)**[202] [6667] 4-9-5 78 .... MartinLane 7 89+
(David Simcock) *hld up last: pushed along and hdwy 3f out: swtchd rt and rdn 2f out: chsd wnr ent fnl f: ch fnl 120yds: hld nring fin* **4/1[2]**

20-0 **3** 4½ **Pandorica**[28] [1111] 5-8-1 67 .... DanielMuscutt(7) 6 70
(Bernard Llewellyn) *trckd ldrs: rdn 3f out: chsd wnr sn after tl ent fnl f: styd on same pce* **25/1**

0-13 **4** 2¼ **Destiny Of Dreams**[16] [1327] 5-9-5 78 .... DaneO'Neill 5 76
(Jo Crowley) *hld up in last pair: rdn and hdwy on outer over 2f out: hung lft over 1f out: styd on same pce* **7/1**

4/3- **5** 3½ **Running Deer (IRE)**[343] [2038] 4-9-1 74 .... TomQueally 4 66
(Sir Henry Cecil) *s.i.s: sn trcking ldrs: rdn 3f out: looking one-pced whn squeezed out over 1f out* **15/8[1]**

120- **6** 1½ **Shades Of Grey**[244] [5359] 6-9-2 80 .... RyanTate(5) 2 69
(Clive Cox) *trckd ldrs: rdn over 2f out: wknd ent fnl f* **9/1**

000- **7** 14 **Play Street**[186] [7116] 4-9-1 74 .... HarryBentley 3 36
(Jonathan Portman) *trckd wnr: rdn over 2f out: wknd over 1f out* **20/1**

155- **8** 13 **Magma**[170] [7475] 4-9-4 77 .... JimmyFortune 8 14
(Andrew Balding) *hld up in last pair: struggling 3f out: wknd 2f out* **13/2[3]**

2m 10.73s (-0.27) **Going Correction** +0.025s/f (Good) **8 Ran SP% 111.7**
Speed ratings (Par 102): **102,101,98,96,93 92,81,70**
toteswingers 1&2 £6.70, 1&3 £15.60, 2&3 £18.70 CSF £33.43 CT £648.54 TOTE £8.90: £3.20, £1.90, £5.60; EX 34.10 Trifecta £491.80 Pool: £1,251.29 - 1.90 winning units..
Owner P Charalambous **Bred** Peter Charles **Trained** Newmarket, Suffolk

FOCUS
The first two pulled clear in this handicap and the favourite was well held. The third helps set the standard to last year's best form.

1664 BATHWICK TYRES CHIPPENHAM H'CAP 2m 1f 34y
7:30 (7:31) (Class 6) (0-65,65) 4-Y-O+ **£1,940** (£577; £288; £144) **Stalls** Centre

Form RPR

432- **1** **Our Folly**[187] [7077] 5-9-7 65 .... (t) MichaelJMMurphy(5) 1 71+
(Stuart Kittow) *hld up towards rr: stdy prog fr 3f out: rdn over 2f out whn swtchd rt: styd on wl to ld fnl 40yds* **7/2[1]**

056- **2** nk **Fuzzy Logic (IRE)**[17] [6567] 4-8-3 46 .... MartinLane 9 51
(Bernard Llewellyn) *w ldr: led 4f out: sn rdn: styd on gamely u.str.p: hdd fnl 40yds* **14/1**

345- **3** nk **Captain Sharpe**[55] [6769] 5-9-6 64 .... (p) RobertWilliams(5) 5 69
(Bernard Llewellyn) *in tch: nt best of runs 3f out: sn rdn: swtchd rt over 1f out: styd on to go 3rd fnl 120yds* **22/1**

20/4 **4** 2½ **Chapter Five**[32] [1060] 6-9-3 56 .... StevieDonohoe 4 58
(Ian Williams) *mid-div: hdwy over 7f out to trck ldrs: rdn over 2f out: styd on same pce fnl f* **8/1**

00-0 **5** shd **Red Current**[107] [12] 9-8-12 51 .... (t) GrahamLee 16 53
(Michael Scudamore) *hld up towards rr: hdwy fr over 3f out: rdn over 2f out: ev ch briefly over 1f out: no ex fnl 120yds* **33/1**

-300 **6** nk **Ctappers**[10] [1445] 4-9-4 61 .... MartinHarley 15 63
(Mick Channon) *in tch: rdn wl over 2f out: swtchd rt to dispute 3rd over 1f out: no ex fnl f* **8/1**

410- 7 1 1/4 **Lucky Diva**200 6738 6-9-1 61..............(p) JakePayne(7) 7 61+
(Bill Turner) *hld up towards rr: hdwy whn nt clr run and snatched up jst over 2f out and again over 1f out: styd on but nvr getting to ldrs fnl f* 12/1

341- 8 2 1/2 **Tijori (IRE)**156 7377 5-9-2 62..............(p) SiobhanMiller(7) 3 60
(Bernard Llewellyn) *hld up towards rr: hdwy on inner 3f out: sn rdn: nt clr run in mid-div over 1f out: kpt on same pce fnl f* 12/1

-543 9 3 3/4 **Dubara Reef (IRE)**18 1279 6-8-7 46..............(p) SilvestreDeSousa 12 40
(Paul Green) *led tl 4f out: sn rdn: wkng whn short of room 2f out* 5/1[2]

05-3 10 3 **Galiotto (IRE)**77 469 7-9-6 59..............(v) GeorgeBaker 8 49
(Gary Moore) *trckd ldrs rdn to dispute 2nd wl over 2f out tl over 1f out: wknd fnl f* 8/1

/000 11 2 1/4 **Anrheg**7 1521 5-8-8 47.............. KellyHarrison 13 35
(Dai Burchell) *hld up bhd: swtchd out and rdn 3f out: hdwy sn after: wknd ent fnl f* 50/1

202- 12 3 1/2 **Josie's Dream (IRE)**192 6956 5-8-13 52.............. J-PGuillambert 17 36+
(Jo Hughes) *trckd ldrs: rdn to dispute 2nd wl over 2f out tl short of room briefly over 1f out: wknd* 15/2[3]

3-10 13 53 **Lakota Ghost (USA)**24 1189 5-9-12 65..............(t) JohnFahy 14
(Seamus Durack) *mid-div tl rdn 3f out: sn btn: wknd 2f out* 16/1

000/ 14 4 **Paradise Expected**345 1258 10-8-9 48..............(p) LiamKeniry 11
(Mark Gillard) *mid-div: reminders over 7f out: sn bhd: t.o* 50/1

3m 54.22s (2.32) **Going Correction** +0.025s/f (Good)
WFA 4 from 5yo+ 4lb **14** Ran SP% **123.1**
Speed ratings (Par 101): **95,94,94,93,93 93,92,91,89,88 87,85,60,58**
toteswingers 1&2 £7.60, 1&3 £15.80, 2&3 £30.00 CSF £54.79 CT £961.44 TOTE £5.30: £1.70, £3.40, £6.70; EX 62.90 Trifecta £566.80 Pool: £1,141.63 - 1.51 winning units..
Owner Midd Shire Racing **Bred** D R Tucker **Trained** Blackborough, Devon

FOCUS
The favourite scored from a long way back in this minor staying handicap. The level is set around the third running just about his best Flat race.

1665 BATHWICK TYRES TROWBRIDGE H'CAP 5f 161y
8:00 (8:03) (Class 6) (0-60,65) 4-Y-0+ **£1,940** (£577; £288; £144) **Stalls** Low

Form RPR

-021 1 **Chosen One (IRE)**9 1465 8-9-2 55.............. PJMcDonald 8 65
(Ruth Carr) *chsd ldrs: rdn 2f out: chal ins fnl f: led fnl stride* 7/1[3]

1133 2 shd **Where's Reiley (USA)**9 1467 7-9-6 59..............(v) SebSanders 7 69
(Michael Attwater) *disp ld: rdn 2f out: led narrowly ent fnl f: hdd fnl stride* 6/1[2]

0064 3 1 **Molly Jones**23 1195 4-8-9 48..............(p) LiamKeniry 3 54+
(Derek Haydn Jones) *mid-div: swtchd rt whn nt clr run over 1f out: r.o strly fnl f: wnt 3rd towards fin* 33/1

2414 4 1/2 **Colourbearer (IRE)**11 1430 6-9-3 56..............(t) GrahamLee 9 61
(Milton Bradley) *mid-div: hdwy 2f out: sn rdn: kpt on same pce fnl f* 7/1[3]

5600 5 3/4 **Lady Prodee**52 805 5-9-1 54..............(p) KierenFox 2 56
(Bill Turner) *chsd ldrs: rdn over 2f out: kpt on same pce fnl f* 33/1

00-0 6 1/2 **Kings 'n Dreams**106 35 6-8-12 51..............(b) MartinLane 15 52+
(Dean Ivory) *s.i.s: bhd: rdn and hdwy fr 2f out: kpt on far rails fnl f: nt rch ldrs* 14/1

60-4 7 nk **Kyllachy Storm**13 1397 9-9-3 56.............. GeorgeBaker 16 56
(Ron Hodges) *disp ld: rdn 2f out: hdd ent fnl f: no ex* 12/1

220 8 1/2 **Scommettitrice (IRE)**30 1087 5-9-2 55..............(b) TomQueally 4 53
(Mark Gillard) *v awkwardly away: towards rr: rdn and hdwy whn nt clr run jst over 1f out: kpt on same pce fnl f* 14/1

124 9 1 1/2 **Spellmaker**30 1087 4-8-13 52.............. WilliamCarson 5 45
(Tony Newcombe) *mid-div: rdn 3f out: sme hdwy over 2f out: fdd fnl f* 5/1[1]

55-0 10 shd **Celestial Dawn**19 1271 4-9-7 60.............. LukeMorris 12 53
(John Weymes) *towards rr: pushed along and stdy prog into midfield fr 2f out: no further imp fnl f* 8/1

511- 11 hd **Steel Rain**163 7633 5-9-6 59.............. FrankieMcDonald 6 51
(Nikki Evans) *s.i.s: rdn into midfield 3f out: swtchd rt and nt clr run over 2f out: sn hung rt: nvr trbld ldrs* 7/1[3]

00-0 12 5 **Chester'Slittlegem (IRE)**98 162 4-8-11 50.............. J-PGuillambert 1 26
(Jo Hughes) *disp ld tl rdn over 2f out: wknd over 1f out* 20/1

100- 13 shd **Greyemkay**192 6967 5-8-4 50.............. DanielMuscutt(7) 11 25
(Richard Price) *mid-div: rdn over 2f out: wknd over 1f out* 16/1

50 14 1 1/2 **Perlachy**30 1087 9-8-11 53..............(v) DarrenEgan(3) 14 23
(Ronald Harris) *a towards rr* 20/1

644- 15 3 1/4 **Jawim**180 7275 4-8-10 49.............. SamHitchcott 10 9
(Malcolm Saunders) *in tch: rdn 3f out: wkng whn hmpd over 1f out* 16/1

0354 16 10 **Poyle Todream**15 1356 5-8-8 47.............. TomEaves 13
(Roy Brotherton) *mid-div tl wknd 2f out* 33/1

1m 12.3s (1.10) **Going Correction** -0.05s/f (Good) **16** Ran SP% **130.7**
Speed ratings (Par 101): **90,89,88,87,86 86,85,85,83,83 82,76,75,73,69 56**
toteswingers 1&2 £7.60, 1&3 £15.80, 2&3 £30.00 CSF £49.02 CT £1337.10 TOTE £8.50: £1.70, £2.20, £5.50, £2.20; EX 34.90 Trifecta £834.10 Pool: £1,192.58 - 1.07 winning units..
Owner Bridget Houlston, Chris Jeffery & Co **Bred** Carl Holt **Trained** Huby, N Yorks

FOCUS
There was a tight finish to this minor sprint handicap. The form is straightforward with the runner-up the best guide.
T/Jkpt: Not won. T/Plt: £148.50 to a £1 stake. Pool: £93,929.38 - 461.45 winning tickets T/Qpdt: £32.60 to a £1 stake. Pool: £6,765.87 - 153.30 winning tickets TM

NEWBURY (L-H)
Friday, April 19

OFFICIAL GOING: Good to soft (5.8)
Wind: Moderate behind Weather: Cloudy

1666 COLN VALLEY STUD BRIDGET MAIDEN FILLIES' STKS 7f (S)
2:00 (2:01) (Class 4) 3-Y-0 **£4,851** (£1,443; £721; £360) **Stalls** Centre

Form RPR

1 **Pavlosk (USA)** 3-9-0 0.............. RyanMoore 9 80
(Sir Michael Stoute) *str: lw: trckd ldrs: slt ld 1f out: pushed along and kpt on wl fnl 110yds* 13/2[3]

2 1 **Spicy Dal** 3-9-0 0.............. KierenFallon 11 77
(Hughie Morrison) *lengthy: b.off hind: trckd ldrs: led over 2f out: sn drvn along: narrowly hdd 1f out: styd on same pce fnl 110yds* 14/1

3 1 1/2 **Grey Gazelle** 3-9-0 0.............. MartinHarley 7 73
(Mick Channon) *w'like: bit bkwd: in rr but in tch: hdwy over 2f out: drvn to take 3rd appr fnl f: kpt on but nt gng pce of ldng duo* 25/1

4 1 1/4 **Gold Chain (IRE)** 3-9-0 0.............. AdamKirby 10 70
(Clive Cox) *leggy: in tch: hdwy fr 2f out: kpt on fnl f: no imp on ldrs in clsng stages* 14/1

5 1 3/4 **Rufoof** 3-9-0 0.............. PaulHanagan 8 65+
(Charles Hills) *w'like: attr: lw: slowly away: sn in tch w main gp: hdwy and swtchd lft over 2f out: green but kpt on fnl f: no ex fnl 110yds* 9/1

6 1/2 **Marjong** 3-9-0 0.............. SebSanders 1 64
(Simon Dow) *unf: bit bkwd: stdd s: in rr: hdwy over 2f out: sn pushed lft and green: kpt on again in clsng stages* 66/1

7 3 **Rock Choir** 3-9-0 0.............. RichardHughes 6 56+
(William Haggas) *w'like: attr: on toes: in tch: trcking ldrs and pushed along whn hmpd appr fnl 2f: no ch after* 11/4[2]

8 hd **Bee Jay Kay** 3-8-9 0.............. CharlesBishop(5) 3 55
(Mick Channon) *w'like: leggy: in rr: sme hdwy 3f out: bmpd and wknd appr fnl 2f* 33/1

9 6 **Dama De La Noche (IRE)** 3-9-0 0.............. SeanLevey 4 39
(Richard Hannon) *w'like: in tch: rdn: green and wknd appr fnl 2f* 14/1

10 1 **At A Clip** 3-9-0 0.............. JimCrowley 12 36
(Ralph Beckett) *tall: athletic: lw: led tl hdd over 2f out: sn btn* 9/4[1]

11 1/2 **Finalee** 3-9-0 0.............. NeilCallan 5 35
(John Gallagher) *str: bit bkwd: chsd ldrs: rdn 3f out: wknd over 2f out* 66/1

12 13 **Map Of Love (IRE)** 3-9-0 0..............[1] JimmyFortune 2
(Jeremy Gask) *str: sn bhd* 28/1

1m 30.17s (4.47) **Going Correction** +0.275s/f (Good) **12** Ran SP% **114.0**
Speed ratings (Par 97): **85,83,82,80,78 78,74,74,67,66 65,51**
toteswingers 1&2 £13.20, 2&3 £48.40, 1&3 £14.40 CSF £84.66 TOTE £4.90: £1.40, £3.40, £6.70; EX 65.50 Trifecta £1742.10 Pool: £2928.49 - 1.26 winning units..
Owner K Abdullah **Bred** Juddmonte Farms Inc **Trained** Newmarket, Suffolk
■ Stewards' Enquiry : Paul Hanagan two-day ban: careless riding (May 3,6)

FOCUS
This maiden, for unraced fillies, has gone to a subsequent Listed or Group-race winner four times in the last nine years, notably Promising Lead (2007), who won a Group 1. The time was 3.61 seconds slower than the later handicap. They raced stands' side, but only the beaten favourite was tight against the rail throughout. This is rated slightly below average for the race for the time being.

1667 DUBAI DUTY FREE GOLF WORLD CUP EBF CONDITIONS STKS 1m 2f 6y
2:30 (2:31) (Class 3) 3-Y-O **£8,715** (£2,609; £1,304; £652; £326) **Stalls** Centre

Form RPR

61- 1 **Contributer (IRE)**154 7750 3-8-13 85.............. RyanMoore 5 100+
(Ed Dunlop) *lw: hld up in rr but in tch: stdy hdwy fr 3f out: led appr fnl f: drvn and styd on strly* 7/4[2]

121- 2 1 1/4 **Cruck Realta**292 3662 3-8-10 88.............. MartinHarley 3 94
(Mick Channon) *trckd ldrs: led 2f out: sn rdn: hdd appr fnl f: kpt on wl for 2nd but nt gng pce of wnr* 14/1

162- 3 1 1/2 **Cap O'Rushes**167 7554 3-8-13 95.............. MickaelBarzalona 4 94
(Mahmood Al Zarooni) *lw: t.k.h: pressed ldr over 6f out tl slt ld over 4f out: pushed along and hdd 2f out: kpt on same pce* 6/4[1]

321 4 6 **Incorporate**20 1236 3-8-13 83.............. DaneO'Neill 1 82
(Pat Eddery) *lw: led: jnd over 6th out: narrowly hdd over 4f out: styd chalng but rdn ins fnl 3f: hung lft 2f out: sn btn* 7/1

140- 5 12 **Mocenigo (IRE)**202 6671 3-8-13 104.............. JamieSpencer 2 58
(Peter Chapple-Hyam) *bit bkwd: trckd ldrs: rdn over 2f out: sn btn* 6/1[3]

2m 13.33s (4.53) **Going Correction** +0.75s/f (Yiel) **5** Ran SP% **109.8**
Speed ratings (Par 102): **111,110,108,104,94**
CSF £22.18 TOTE £2.60: £1.30, £4.40; EX 25.40 Trifecta £62.90 Pool: £2234.07 - 26.60 winning units..
Owner George Bolton **Bred** Petra Bloodstock Agency Ltd **Trained** Newmarket, Suffolk

FOCUS
A conditions event that has produced a number of really smart types over the years, notably Light Shift, who took this ahead of landing the Oaks in 2007. This year's race was another interesting contest and it went to a likeable type in the shape of Contributer, who stayed on from last off what looked an okay gallop for the conditions. The third and fourth help set the level.

1668 DUBAI DUTY FREE FULL OF SURPRISES H'CAP 7f (S)
3:05 (3:05) (Class 2) (0-100,99) 3-Y-O
£11,827 (£3,541; £1,770; £885; £442; £222) **Stalls** Centre

Form RPR

121- 1 **Baltic Knight (IRE)**198 6797 3-9-3 95.............. RichardHughes 6 109
(Richard Hannon) *lw: mde all: pushed along and qcknd over 1f out: drvn ins fnl f: hld on wl* 9/2[2]

14- 2 nk **Here Comes When (IRE)**259 4774 3-8-4 82..............[1] DavidProbert 1 95
(Andrew Balding) *lw: t.k.h in rr early: hdwy over 2f out: chsd wnr appr fnl f: drvn to chal fnl 110yds: kpt on but a jst hld* 6/1

40-5 3 2 **Hasopop (IRE)**34 1033 3-9-5 97.............. AdamKirby 2 105
(Marco Botti) *in tch: drvn and hdwy over 1f out: styd on to take 3rd fnl 110yds but no imp on ldng duo* 9/1

13- 4 3 **Ribaat (IRE)**219 6139 3-9-7 99.............. PaulHanagan 5 99
(Roger Varian) *lw: t.k.h: trckd ldrs: drvn ins fnl 2f: wknd fnl 110yds* 7/2[1]

420- 5 3 **Tipping Over (IRE)**193 6942 3-8-9 87.............. RyanMoore 4 79
(Hugo Palmer) *trckd wnr: rdn 2f out: wknd fnl f* 16/1

13-2 6 2 **Hay Dude**20 1246 3-8-9 90.............. MichaelMetcalfe(3) 9 76
(Mrs K Burke) *lw: chsd ldrs: rdn and btn ins fnl 2f* 11/2[3]

415- 7 1 3/4 **So Beloved**177 7331 3-8-10 88.............. JamesDoyle 3 70
(Roger Charlton) *hld up in rr: shkn up and no prog ins fnl 2f* 6/1

0-50 8 6 **Kalicamix**36 999 3-8-10 88.............. ChrisCatlin 7 53
(Paul Cole) *rdn over 2f out: a in rr* 33/1

112- 9 3/4 **Mutazamen**198 6799 3-8-11 89.............. DaneO'Neill 8 52
(Richard Hannon) *chsd ldrs: rdn 3f out: wknd over 2f out* 11/1

120- 10 2 3/4 **No Jet Lag (USA)**189 7038 3-9-7 99.............. TedDurcan 10 55
(David Lanigan) *stdd s: sn t.k.h: and in tch: rdn 2f out: sn btn* 16/1

1m 26.56s (0.86) **Going Correction** +0.275s/f (Good) **10** Ran SP% **117.4**
Speed ratings (Par 104): **106,105,103,99,96 94,92,85,84,81**
toteswingers 1&2 £4.80, 2&3 £10.70, 1&3 £7.90 CSF £31.98 CT £241.77 TOTE £4.80: £2.00, £2.70, £2.70; EX 40.40 Trifecta £257.00 Pool: £4050.96 - 11.82 winning units..
Owner Thurloe Thoroughbreds XXX **Bred** Henry O'Callaghan **Trained** East Everleigh, Wilts

FOCUS
Traditionally a really good handicap and rated as such. Indeed, the subsequent Britannia winner featured among the beaten runners in both 2008 and 2009, and the smart Aljamaaheer was only fourth last year before taking a Listed contest next time.

1669 COMPTON BEAUCHAMP ESTATES LTD E.B.F MAIDEN STKS 5f 34y
3:40 (3:41) (Class 4) 2-Y-O **£4,528** (£1,347; £673; £336) **Stalls** Centre

Form RPR

1 **Justice Day (IRE)** 2-9-5 0.............. WilliamBuick 2 89+
(David Elsworth) *cmpt: lw: sn disputing 2nd towards centre crse: led appr fnl f: pushed along and styd on wl fnl 110yds* 9/1

2 1 **Steventon Star** 2-9-5 0 .... RichardHughes 3 85+
(Richard Hannon) *disp 2nd towards centre crse: chsd wnr ins fnl f: sn rdn and edgd rt: kpt on but a hld* **5/1[3]**

3 3 5 **Meritocracy (IRE)**[6] 1541 2-9-5 0 .... ChrisCatlin 1 67
(Paul Cole) *str: lw: led towards centre crse: rdn 2f out: hdd appr fnl f sn outpcd* **3/1[1]**

4 1/2 **Green Door (IRE)** 2-9-5 0 .... JamieSpencer 10 66+
(Olly Stevens) *w'like: bit bkwd: racd towards stands' side: chsd ldrs: hung lft towards centre and hdwy fr 2f out: stl hanging and styd on same pce fnl f* **16/1**

5 1/2 **Jazz (IRE)** 2-9-5 0 .... RyanMoore 6 64
(Charles Hills) *w'like: attr: wnt lft s: sn chsng ldrs towards centre crse: rdn 2f out: styd on same pce fnl f* **11/2**

6 nk **The Smart One (IRE)** 2-9-5 0 .... MatthewDavies 4 63
(Mick Channon) *athletic: bit bkwd: chsd ldrs in centre crse: rdn over 2f out: nt qckn fnl f* **25/1**

7 nse **Neighbother** 2-9-5 0 .... PaulHanagan 5 63
(Richard Fahey) *w'like: s.i.s: in tch 1/2-way in centre crse: rdn over 2f out: kpt on same pce* **9/2[2]**

8 1/2 **Malachim Mist (IRE)** 2-9-5 0 .... DaneO'Neill 7 61+
(Richard Hannon) *unf: scope: bit bkwd: chsd ldrs towards stands' side: edgd lft towards centre and sme hdwy u.p over 2f out: nvr rchd ldrs* **22/1**

9 2 1/2 **Pastoral Witness** 2-9-0 0 .... NeilCallan 13 47+
(Clive Brittain) *unf: scope: bit bkwd: chsd ldrs towards stands' side: no ch fnl 2f* **40/1**

10 1/2 **Rosso Corsa** 2-9-0 0 .... CharlesBishop(5) 9 50+
(Mick Channon) *leggy: attr: chsd ldrs stands' side: no ch fr 1/2-way* **25/1**

11 2 3/4 **Seaham** 2-9-5 0 .... JamesDoyle 8 40+
(Rod Millman) *w'like: spd to 1/2-way on stands' side* **33/1**

12 6 **Biography** 2-9-5 0 .... JimmyFortune 11 18+
(Richard Hannon) *athletic: racd stands' side: sn outpcd* **10/1**

13 19 **Party Ruler (IRE)** 2-9-5 0 .... RichardKingscote 12 +
(Tom Dascombe) *str: bit bkwd: early spd on stands' side: sn bhd* **28/1**

1m 3.36s (1.96) **Going Correction** +0.275s/f (Good) **13** Ran SP% **121.1**
Speed ratings (Par 94): **95,93,85,84,83 83,83,82,78,77 73,63,33**
toteswingers 1&2 £9.30, 2&3 £4.40, 1&3 £7.20 CSF £49.92 TOTE £13.10: £3.70, £1.90, £1.10; EX 82.80 Trifecta £366.20 Pool: £3729.27- 7.63 winning units..
Owner D R C Elsworth **Bred** Gerry Kenny **Trained** Newmarket, Suffolk

FOCUS
Three of the last nine winners of this were subsequently successful at Group level, namely Tournedos (Molecomb), Winker Watson (Norfolk and July Stakes) and Klammer (Horris Hill). The front two pulled nicely clear and are most likely above average. The field split into two groups at around the halfway stage, and those who raced up the middle looked to be at an advantage over those positioned towards the stands' side.

1670 DREWEATTS 1759 H'CAP 2m
4:15 (4:16) (Class 4) (0-80,80) 4-Y-0+ **£5,175** (£1,540; £769; £384) **Stalls** Centre

Form RPR

633- 1 **Sign Manual**[309] 3072 4-9-0 **72** .... HayleyTurner 12 86+
(Michael Bell) *on toes: towards rr: hdwy over 3f out: rdn over 2f out: swtchd rt to outer over 1f out: styd on strly fnl f to ld last stride* **4/1[2]**

13- 2 shd **Lieutenant Miller**[130] 7522 7-9-11 **79** .... TomQueally 5 91
(Nicky Henderson) *lw: in rr: hdwy on outer and bmpd over 4f out: styd on wl to ld 2f out: kpt on wl fnl f: hdd last stride* **7/2[1]**

2/ 3 3 3/4 **Pateese (FR)**[5] 6405 8-9-4 **72** ....(b) JamieSpencer 13 79
(Philip Hobbs) *in rr and sn pushed along: hdwy: hdwy 6f out: styd on fr 2f out to take 2nd 1f out: no imp on wnr and outpcd into 3rd ins fnl f* **13/2**

456- 4 5 **Cotton King**[307] 3162 6-9-5 **73** .... RyanMoore 8 74
(Lady Herries) *chsd ldrs: drvn to chal 2f out: wknd fnl f* **9/1**

10- 5 4 **Kleitomachos (IRE)**[168] 7522 5-9-12 **80** .... RichardHughes 7 76
(Stuart Kittow) *lw: trckd clr ldr 7f out: led ins fnl 3f: rdn and hdd 2f out: wknd 1f out* **5/1[3]**

231- 6 4 1/2 **Petaluma**[180] 7271 4-8-11 **74** .... CharlesBishop(5) 14 65
(Mick Channon) *in rr: hdwy 7f out: swtchd rt over 4f out: chsd ldrs 3f out: wknd 2f out* **10/1**

03-0 7 nk **Dunhoy (IRE)**[64] 654 5-9-11 **79** .... WilliamBuick 6 69
(Tony Newcombe) *chsd ldrs: pushed along 5f out: wknd over 2f out* **22/1**

400- 8 24 **Tuscan Gold**[28] 8073 6-9-9 **77** .... IanMongan 1 39
(Laura Mongan) *in rr: hdwy to chse ldrs 7f out: wknd ins fnl 4f* **16/1**

121- 9 3 **Peachez**[164] 7617 5-9-4 **77** ....(p) AmyScott(5) 11 35
(Alastair Lidderdale) *in rr: sme hdwy 5f out: sn wknd over 3f out* **18/1**

600- 10 7 **Gilded Age**[18] 7377 7-8-13 **67** ....(tp) SamHitchcott 10 17
(Chris Gordon) *chsd clr ldr to 7f out: sn rdn: wknd qckly over 3f out* **22/1**

610- 11 1 **Knox Overstreet**[243] 5384 5-8-1 **62** .... DanielCremin(7) 9 10
(Mick Channon) *led: sn wl clr: wknd and hdd ins fnl 3f* **33/1**

-100 12 25 **Honourable Knight (IRE)**[8] 1502 5-8-11 **65** .... DavidProbert 2
(Mark Usher) *lost tch fnl 5f: t.o* **50/1**

206/ 13 2 1/2 **Kayef (GER)**[525] 6832 6-9-9 **77** .... PaulMulrennan 4
(Michael Scudamore) *prom early: wl bhd fnl 5f: t.o* **25/1**

3m 41.8s (9.80) **Going Correction** +0.75s/f (Yiel)
WFA 4 from 5yo+ 4lb **13** Ran SP% **119.9**
Speed ratings (Par 105): **105,104,103,100,98 96,96,84,82,79 78,66,64**
toteswingers 1&2 £4.10, 2&3 £4.60, 1&3 £5.50 CSF £17.19 CT £91.06 TOTE £5.80: £2.30, £1.90, £2.80; EX 23.10 Trifecta £82.10 Pool: £4032.46 - 36.80 winning units..
Owner The Queen **Bred** The Queen **Trained** Newmarket, Suffolk

FOCUS
The pace was sound thanks to Knox Overstreet, who built up a big lead before inevitably tiring. The third helps set the standard.

1671 WHITLEY STUD MAIDEN FILLIES' STKS 1m 2f 6y
4:45 (4:50) (Class 4) 3-Y-0 **£4,851** (£1,443; £721; £360) **Stalls** Centre

Form RPR

1 **Banoffee (IRE)** 3-9-0 0 .... RichardHughes 8 78
(Hughie Morrison) *mde virtually all: jnd fr 3f out: rdn to assert 1f out: r.o strly* **28/1**

2 1 1/4 **Harbinger Lass** 3-8-9 0 .... CharlesBishop(5) 10 76
(Mick Channon) *w'like: leggy: chsd ldrs: chal wnr fr 3f out: rdn over 1f out: outpcd ins fnl f but hld on wl for 2nd* **66/1**

0- 3 1 1/4 **Fanzine**[174] 7403 3-9-0 0 .... KierenFallon 9 73
(Hughie Morrison) *swtg: chsd ldrs: rdn 2f out: hung rt u.p ins fnl f: styng on but hung lft in clsng stages* **40/1**

4 nk **Whippy Cream (IRE)** 3-9-0 0 .... NeilCallan 7 72
(Marco Botti) *lengthy: chsd ldrs: drvn to chal appr fnl 2f: kpt on fnl f* **33/1**

0- 5 hd **Arbaah (USA)**[261] 4701 3-9-0 0 .... PaulHanagan 5 72
(Brian Meehan) *w'like: str: chsd ldrs: rdn and one pce 2f but styd chsng ldrs: kpt on in clsng stages* **20/1**

6 1 1/4 **Magic Of Reality (FR)** 3-9-0 0 .... TomQueally 15 70+
(Sir Henry Cecil) *athletic: attr: lw: mid-div: hdwy 3f out: styng on but hld by ldrs whn hmpd in clsng stages* **15/8[1]**

7 1 3/4 **Toast Of The Town (IRE)** 3-9-0 0 .... WilliamBuick 16 66+
(John Gosden) *w'like: scope: lw: in rr: shkn up and styd on towards outside fr over 1f out: gng on in clsng stages* **12/1**

8 nk **Bohemian Dance (IRE)** 3-9-0 0 .... RyanMoore 17 65+
(Sir Michael Stoute) *str: in rr: pushed along and hdwy fr over 2f out: sn green and hanging lft: kpt on same pce* **9/2[3]**

20- 9 1 **Motion Lass**[163] 7637 3-9-0 0 .... JimCrowley 12 65+
(Ralph Beckett) *lw: t.k.h towards rr: pushed along over 2f out: sme prog fnl f* **20/1**

3- 10 hd **Vicksburg**[175] 7373 3-9-0 0 .... JimmyFortune 11 63
(Andrew Balding) *lean: chsd ldrs: rdn over 2f out: wknd fnl f* **12/1**

000- 11 4 1/2 **Rock Diamond (IRE)**[174] 7403 3-9-0 50 .... JamesDoyle 6 54?
(Sylvester Kirk) *in rr: sme hdwy to get in tch 3f out: wknd 2f out* **100/1**

4- 12 3/4 **Just One Kiss**[209] 6489 3-9-0 0 .... IanMongan 3 53
(Sir Henry Cecil) *str: lw: chsd ldrs: rdn 3f out: wknd over 2f out* **7/2[2]**

13 3/4 **Double Accord** 3-9-0 0 .... LiamKeniry 4 51
(Anthony Honeyball) *lengthy: in rr: effrt over 3f out: sn bhd* **100/1**

33- 14 2 1/4 **Zipp (IRE)**[184] 7172 3-9-0 0 .... SteveDrowne 13 47
(Charles Hills) *lw: chsd ldrs: rdn 3f out: wknd over 2f out* **9/1**

15 nk **Dalliefour (IRE)** 3-9-0 0 .... HayleyTurner 2 46
(Michael Bell) *w'like: mid-div: effrt over 3f out: sn rdn and wknd* **33/1**

16 8 **Nepalese Pearl** 3-9-0 0 .... JamieSpencer 14 30
(Pat Eddery) *unf: a towards rr* **50/1**

2m 17.03s (8.23) **Going Correction** +0.75s/f (Yiel) **16** Ran SP% **127.3**
Speed ratings (Par 97): **97,96,95,94,94 93,92,91,91,91 87,86,86,84,84 77**
toteswingers 1&2 £89.90, 2&3 £195.40, 1&3 £98.70 CSF £1232.98 TOTE £31.80: £7.60, £18.90, £11.00; EX 3092.10 Trifecta £3787.30 Part won. Pool of £5049.76 - 0.11 winning units..
Owner M Kerr-Dineen,Hon W H Smith & Partners **Bred** P D Savill **Trained** East Ilsley, Berks

FOCUS
A fillies' maiden that has been won by a couple of subsequent Oaks winners in recent years (Eswarah, 2005) and (Dancing Rain, 2011), while both Islington (2002) and Folk Opera (2007) also took this ahead of success at the highest level. This was the first time since 2009 it hadn't been divided and the form isn't obviously strong, with big-priced runners without Group-race entries filling the first five places, and the first two raced more or less one-two throughout. The time was 3.7 seconds slower than the earlier conditions event and with little to go on the form is rated cautiously.

1672 DUBAI DUTY FREE H'CAP 5f 34y
5:15 (5:20) (Class 2) (0-110,105) 4-Y-0+
£12,450 (£3,728; £1,864; £932; £466; £234) **Stalls** Centre

Form RPR

115- 1 **Heeraat (IRE)**[188] 7066 4-9-3 **101** .... PaulHanagan 4 114
(William Haggas) *lw: mde all: drvn and qcknd appr fnl f: won gng away* **5/2[1]**

00-3 2 2 **El Viento (FR)**[17] 1308 5-8-7 **91** .... BarryMcHugh 3 96
(Richard Fahey) *lw: s.i.s: sn rcvrd to chse ldrs: wnt 2nd u.p fnl 110yds but no ch w wnr* **14/1**

01-2 3 1 1/4 **Kingsgate Choice (IRE)**[20] 1249 6-9-2 **100** .... LiamKeniry 5 101
(Ed de Giles) *hld up in rr but in tch: drvn and hdwy fnl f: styd on to take 3rd in clsng stages but nvr any ch w wnr* **9/2[2]**

-005 4 1/2 **Confessional**[20] 1234 6-9-6 **104** ....(b) PaulMulrennan 2 103
(Tim Easterby) *t.k.h: trckd ldrs: chsd wnr over 1f out but no imp: one pce and dropped to 4th fnl 110yds* **15/2**

30-0 5 11 **Taajub (IRE)**[34] 1032 6-9-2 **100** .... IanMongan 1 59
(Peter Crate) *chsd ldr: rdn over 2f out: wknd over 1f out: eased in clsng stages* **10/1**

014- 6 4 **Compton**[181] 7240 4-8-11 **95** .... WilliamBuick 6 40
(Robert Cowell) *chsd ldrs: rdn over 2f out: wknd over 1f out: eased whn no ch* **11/2[3]**

400- 7 6 **Mirza**[174] 7397 6-9-0 **98** .... RichardHughes 7 21
(Rae Guest) *chsd ldrs: swtchd lft: rdn and wknd wl over 1f out: eased* **11/2[3]**

030- 8 2 1/4 **Definightly**[194] 6908 7-9-7 **105** ....(b) JamesDoyle 9 20
(Roger Charlton) *in rr but in tch: rdn over 2f out and sn btn: eased whn no ch* **10/1**

1m 1.35s (-0.05) **Going Correction** +0.275s/f (Good) **8** Ran SP% **114.1**
Speed ratings (Par 109): **111,107,105,105,87 81,71,67**
toteswingers 1&2 £7.90, 2&3 £9.10, 1&3 £2.90 CSF £39.42 CT £149.57 TOTE £2.70: £1.50, £3.70, £1.70; EX 36.70 Trifecta £168.70 Pool: £3287.54 - 14.60 winning units..
Owner Hamdan Al Maktoum **Bred** John McEnery **Trained** Newmarket, Suffolk

FOCUS
A good sprint handicap, but nothing could live with Heeraat. They raced up the middle and the form is taken at face value with the runner-up to reappearance form.
T/Plt: £14,920.30 to a £1 stake. Pool of £85843.10 - 4.20 winning tickets. T/Qpdt: £248.90 to a £1 stake. Pool of £6122.45 - 18.20 winning tickets ST

[1666] NEWBURY (L-H)
Saturday, April 20

OFFICIAL GOING: Good to soft (good in places; 6.0)
Rail between 7f and 5f moved out 4m adding about 10m to races on Round course.
Wind: Moderate behind Weather: Sunny

1673 DUBAI DUTY FREE MILLENNIUM MILLIONAIRE H'CAP 1m 2f 6y
1:15 (1:15) (Class 4) (0-85,85) 4-Y-0+ **£5,175** (£1,540; £769; £384) **Stalls** Centre

Form RPR

5-01 1 **Take Two**[19] 1290 4-8-12 **76** .... AndreaAtzeni 16 87+
(Alex Hales) *trckd ldrs: led over 2f out: drvn clr over 1f out: n.d after* **12/1**

10-3 2 3 **Sheila's Buddy**[107] 32 4-9-0 **78** .... RichardHughes 6 82+
(J S Moore) *barged stalls: hld up towards rr: hdwy over 2f out: qcknd to chse wnr jst ins fnl f: kpt on but nvr any ch* **15/2[2]**

143- 3 nk **Ethics Girl (IRE)**[159] 6349 7-8-10 **81** ....(t) NoelGarbutt(7) 5 83
(John Berry) *in rr: hdwy on outer fr 2f out: styd on wl to press for 2nd fnl 110yds but no ch w wnr* **20/1**

132- 4 2 **Cactus Valley (IRE)**[192] 6987 4-9-7 **85** .... JamesDoyle 14 83+
(Roger Charlton) *in tch chsd ldrs 3f out: chsd wnr 2f out and sn pushed along: no imp: wknd fnl 110yds* **7/1[1]**

0-00 5 1/2 **Robin Hood (IRE)**[14] 1382 5-9-7 **85** .... JackMitchell 7 82
(Philip Mitchell) *towards rr: pushed along 3f out: styd on u.p fr 2f out: kpt on in clsng stages* **33/1**

3313 **6** 1 ¾ **Luggers Hall (IRE)**[19] 1290 5-8-7 **76** CharlesBishop(5) 9 70
(Tony Carroll) *in rr: hdwy on inner fr 3f out: kpt on fnl f: nvr rchd ldrs* **7/1**[1]
3121 **7** 1 ¼ **Exceedexpectations (IRE)**[16] 1354 4-8-9 **73** HayleyTurner 8 64
(Conor Dore) *chsd ldrs: rdn over 2f out: wknd fnl f* **12/1**
000- **8** 2 **Snow Hill**[280] 4103 5-8-9 **73** TedDurcan 4 60+
(Chris Wall) *mid-div: hdwy and n.m.r fr 2f out: kpt on same pce fnl f* **20/1**
050- **9** 1 **Alakhan (IRE)**[213] 6380 7-9-2 **80** StevieDonohoe 15 65
(Ian Williams) *in rr: pushed along 3f out: styd on fr over 1f out: nvr a threat* **33/1**
153- **10** ½ **Royal Dutch**[192] 6981 4-8-7 **71** MartinDwyer 13 55+
(Denis Coakley) *chsd ldrs on inner: n.m.r 2f out: one pce whn hmpd over 1f out: no ch after* **15/2**[2]
23-0 **11** hd **Balady (IRE)**[12] 1422 4-8-10 **74** LiamKeniry 17 58
(Dominic Ffrench Davis) *chsd ldr: rdn 3f out: wknd fr 2f out* **33/1**
003- **12** 2 ¾ **Never Perfect (IRE)**[291] 3728 4-8-7 **71** oh2 JamieSpencer 10 49
(Peter Chapple-Hyam) *stdd s: shkn up over 2f out: mod prog fnl f* **7/1**[1]
060- **13** ½ **Commitment**[188] 7082 4-9-2 **80** JimmyFortune 11 57
(Neil Mulholland) *rdn over 2f out: a towards rr* **14/1**
500- **14** 7 **Halling Dancer**[171] 7485 4-8-10 **74** KierenFox 2 37
(Lee Carter) *sn led: hdd over 2f out: sn btn* **33/1**
060- **15** 1 ½ **Dandy (GER)**[184] 7194 4-8-7 **71** oh2 DavidProbert 3 31
(Andrew Balding) *chsd ldrs: rdn 3f out: sn btn* **8/1**[3]
25-0 **16** nk **Mr Spiggott (IRE)**[21] 1233 4-9-0 **78** (v[1]) RyanMoore 1 38
(Joseph Tuite) *in tch: rdn 3f out: sn btn* **14/1**

2m 11.42s (2.62) **Going Correction** +0.40s/f (Good) **16** Ran SP% **122.1**
Speed ratings (Par 105): **105,102,102,100,100 98,97,96,95,95 95,92,92,86,85 85**
toteswingers 1&2 £18.60, 2&3 £45.20, 1&3 £81.90 CSF £91.09 CT £1777.43 TOTE £14.40: £2.80, £1.80, £5.20, £1.90; EX 102.50 Trifecta £1254.20 Part won. Pool: £1672.32 - 0.15 winning units..
Owner S P Bloodstock **Bred** Steven & Petra Wallace **Trained** Edgcote, Northants

FOCUS
This looked a competitive handicap and the placed horses help to set the standard.

1674 DUBAI DUTY FREE FINEST SURPRISE STKS (REGISTERED AS THE JOHN PORTER STAKES) (GROUP 3) 1m 4f 5y
1:50 (1:50) (Class 1) 4-Y-O+
£34,026 (£12,900; £6,456; £3,216; £1,614; £810) **Stalls** Centre

Form RPR
3021 **1** **Universal (IRE)**[14] 1382 4-8-11 107 SilvestreDeSousa 2 113
(Mark Johnston) *chsd ldr: led 3f out: rdn 2f out: sn jnd: narrowly hdd 1f out: rallied gamely u.p to chal: led again fnl 110yds: hld on wl* **11/1**[3]
410- **2** hd **Quiz Mistress**[174] 7431 5-8-9 100 RichardHughes 5 109+
(Hughie Morrison) *stdd s: in rr: hdwy fr 4f out: drvn and styd on wl fr over 1f out: fin strly to take 2nd in clsng stages: nt rch wnr* **16/1**
142- **3** hd **Noble Mission**[175] 7405 4-8-11 115 TomQueally 3 112
(Sir Henry Cecil) *trckd ldrs: wnt 2nd travelling wl 2f out: drvn to chal over 1f out: sn slt ld: fnd no ex u.p and hdd fnl 110yds: lost 2nd cl home* **5/4**[1]
23-1 **4** 5 **Model Pupil**[29] 1110 4-8-11 107 RyanMoore 4 104
(Charles Hills) *chsd ldrs: drvn along fr 3f out: styd on same pce fnl 2f* **4/1**[2]
005- **5** 2 ½ **Allied Powers (IRE)**[196] 6866 8-8-12 101 JamieSpencer 6 100
(Michael Bell) *in rr: styd on fr 3f out: nvr gng pce to rch ldrs* **33/1**
110- **6** 2 ½ **Guarantee**[217] 6245 4-8-12 105 ow1 JohnnyMurtagh 9 97
(William Haggas) *in rr: reminders over 5f out and drvn 4f out: rdn: hd high and no rspnse ins fnl 3f: no ch after* **4/1**[2]
6-02 **7** 3 **Fattsota**[51] 833 5-8-12 106 MartinHarley 1 91
(Marco Botti) *led: rdn and hdd 3f out: wknd 2f out* **11/1**[3]
300- **8** 22 **Ed De Gas**[223] 6087 4-8-11 100 ChrisCatlin 7 56
(Rae Guest) *t.k.h in rr: lost tch 3f out* **66/1**
20- **9** shd **Meganisi (IRE)**[14] 5826 6-8-12 105 LiamJones 8 56
(Rebecca Curtis) *sn drvn to chse ldrs: wknd 4f out* **40/1**

2m 37.86s (2.36) **Going Correction** +0.40s/f (Good)
WFA 4 from 5yo+ 1lb **9** Ran SP% **113.9**
Speed ratings (Par 113): **108,107,107,104,102 101,99,84,84**
toteswingers 1&2 £8.50, 2&3 £4.10, 1&3 £3.40 CSF £161.62 TOTE £10.80: £3.40, £4.00, £1.10; EX 202.10 Trifecta £817.70 Pool: £7302.66 - 6.69 winning units..
Owner Abdulla Al Mansoori **Bred** Grangecon Stud **Trained** Middleham Moor, N Yorks
■ Stewards' Enquiry : Richard Hughes four-day ban: used whip above permitted level (May 6-9)

FOCUS
It's hard to consider this strong form, but the front two are improving. personal-bests from the first two with the third rated 3lb below his highest 3-y-o mark.

1675 BERRY BROS & RUDD MAGNUM SPRING CUP (H'CAP) 1m (S)
2:20 (2:24) (Class 2) (0-105,103) 4-Y-O+
£28,012 (£8,388; £4,194; £2,097; £1,048; £526) **Stalls** Centre

Form RPR
-143 **1** **Haaf A Sixpence**[21] 1233 4-8-3 **85** AndreaAtzeni 21 97
(Ralph Beckett) *pressed ldrs: chal 2f out: slt ld over 1f out: styd on wl u.p fnl f* **10/1**[3]
1-22 **2** 1 **Guest Of Honour (IRE)**[42] 945 4-9-0 **96** (p) MartinHarley 9 105
(Marco Botti) *in tch: hdwy over 2f out: str chal fr over 1f out: stl upsides tl outpcd by wnr fnl 110yds* **16/1**
16-6 **3** nse **Chapter Seven**[21] 1235 4-9-2 **98** JamieSpencer 1 107
(Stuart Williams) *in rr: hdwy fr 2f out: hrd rdn and styd on strly fnl f: fin wl to press for 2nd cl home: nt rch wnr* **16/1**
0-62 **4** ½ **Global Village (IRE)**[21] 1235 8-9-0 **96** KierenFallon 7 104
(Brian Ellison) *in rr: hdwy fr 2f out: styd on wl u.p fnl f: gng on cl home* **9/1**[2]
125- **5** 1 **Dream Tune**[197] 6830 4-8-9 **91** JamesDoyle 16 97+
(Clive Cox) *pressed ldr tl slt ld after 2f: rdn over 2f out: narrowly hdd over 1f out but styd pressing tl no ex fnl 110yds* **16/1**
050- **6** ½ **Accession (IRE)**[203] 6676 4-8-5 **87** JohnFahy 20 92
(Clive Cox) *in tch: drvn and hdwy fr 2f out: kpt on fnl f: nt pce to rch ldrs* **33/1**
0-00 **7** 1 ¾ **Memory Cloth**[21] 1235 6-8-13 **95** TomQueally 14 96
(Brian Ellison) *in tch: hdwy to chse ldrs u.p fr 2f out: styd on same pce fnl f* **33/1**
05-0 **8** ½ **Captain Bertie (IRE)**[21] 1235 5-8-11 **93** RyanMoore 8 92
(Charles Hills) *in tch: drvn over 2f out: kpt on fnl f: nt rch ldrs* **14/1**
10-0 **9** ½ **Discression**[10] 1485 4-8-7 **89** MartinDwyer 11 87+
(Kevin Ryan) *towards rr 1/2-way: rdn over 2f out: styd on fnl f* **33/1**
0-02 **10** 3 ½ **Laffan (IRE)**[21] 1252 4-8-11 **93** ow1 NeilCallan 6 83
(Kevin Ryan) *led 2f: styd pressing ldrs tl wknd ins fnl 2f* **25/1**
0001 **11** 3 ¼ **Es Que Love (IRE)**[7] 1545 4-9-7 **103** WilliamBuick 17 86+
(Mark Johnston) *trckd ldrs: rdn 2f out: wknd qckly over 1f out* **25/1**
045- **12** ¾ **Norse Blues**[204] 6638 5-8-1 **88** RyanTate(5) 3 69
(David Barron) *chsd ldrs: rdn over 2f out: wknd fnl f* **9/1**[2]
1-31 **13** ¾ **Chookie Royale**[37] 995 5-8-4 **87** ow1 (p) AdamBeschizza 13 65
(Keith Dalgleish) *in rr: sme late prog* **33/1**
11-1 **14** ¾ **Educate**[21] 1233 4-8-11 **93** LiamJones 4 71
(Ismail Mohammed) *chsd ldrs: rdn 3f out: btn 2f out* **4/1**[1]
-002 **15** 1 **Belgian Bill**[21] 1244 5-9-5 **101** (t) PatCosgrave 5 76
(George Baker) *chsd ldrs: rdn 3f out: wknd over 2f out* **33/1**
132- **16** 1 ½ **Border Legend**[199] 6789 4-8-4 **86** HayleyTurner 15 58
(Roger Charlton) *towards rr most of way* **12/1**
41-6 **17** 6 **Yojimbo (IRE)**[21] 1233 5-8-3 **85** CathyGannon 2 43
(Mick Channon) *chsd ldrs over 5f* **33/1**
0-00 **18** ½ **Capaill Liath (IRE)**[21] 1235 5-8-5 **90** (p) JulieBurke(3) 12 47
(Kevin Ryan) *towards rr most of way* **66/1**
00-3 **19** 2 ½ **Brae Hill (IRE)**[21] 1235 7-9-1 **97** PaulHanagan 18 48
(Richard Fahey) *chsd ldrs 5f* **14/1**
600- **20** 2 ¼ **Invisible Hunter (USA)**[164] 7631 4-8-9 **91** SilvestreDeSousa 10 37
(Saeed bin Suroor) *towards rr most of way* **28/1**
60-1 **21** 1 ¾ **Levitate**[21] 1235 5-8-8 **93** (v) DarrenEgan(3) 25 35
(John Quinn) *chsd ldrs: wknd qckly over 2f out* **18/1**
606- **22** shd **Crius (IRE)**[282] 4012 4-9-3 **99** SeanLevey 22 41
(Richard Hannon) *s.i.s: a towards rr* **33/1**
61-4 **23** 3 ¾ **Justonefortheroad**[21] 1235 7-8-10 **95** LeeTopliss(3) 23 28
(Richard Fahey) *sn bhd* **25/1**
40-6 **24** 3 **Dance And Dance (IRE)**[21] 1244 7-9-7 **103** GeorgeBaker 19 29
(Ed Vaughan) *a towards rr* **25/1**
0-01 **25** 1 **Gouray Girl (IRE)**[29] 1113 6-8-4 **86** WilliamCarson 24 10
(Brian Ellison) *a towards rr* **20/1**

1m 37.74s (-1.96) **Going Correction** 0.0s/f (Good) **25** Ran SP% **138.7**
Speed ratings (Par 109): **109,108,107,107,106 105,104,103,103,99 96,95,94,94,93 91,85,85,82,80 78,78,74,71,70**
toteswingers 1&2 £33.60, 1&3 £51.30, 2&3 £147.30 CSF £146.81 CT £2632.16 TOTE £14.20: £3.70, £4.20, £5.40, £2.40; EX 254.10 Trifecta £2244.40 Part won. Pool: £2992.57 - 0.30 winning units..
Owner Melody Racing **Bred** Melody Bloodstock **Trained** Kimpton, Hants

FOCUS
A typically competitive renewal of this long-established mile handicap and solid form with the fourth a fair guide, backed up by the fifth.

1676 DUBAI DUTY FREE STKS (REGISTERED AS THE FRED DARLING STAKES) (GROUP 3) (FILLIES) 7f (S)
2:55 (2:56) (Class 1) 3-Y-O
£34,026 (£12,900; £6,456; £3,216; £1,614; £810) **Stalls** Centre

Form RPR
210- **1** **Maureen (IRE)**[203] 6672 3-9-0 106 RichardHughes 8 107+
(Richard Hannon) *t.k.h: hld up in tch: hdwy over 1f out and qcknd wl fnl f to ld fnl 120yds: pushed out* **7/2**[2]
120- **2** ¾ **Agent Allison**[195] 6909 3-9-0 101 JamieSpencer 9 103
(Peter Chapple-Hyam) *hmpd s: in rr: hdwy and swtchd rt to stands' side over 1f out: str run u.p and edging rt fnl 110yds: no imp on wnr in clsng stages* **7/1**[3]
011- **3** 1 ½ **Melbourne Memories**[169] 7518 3-9-0 97 PaulHanagan 5 99
(Clive Cox) *chsd ldrs: drvn along 2f out: styd on to take 3rd last strides but nt gng pce of ldng duo* **12/1**
111- **4** nk **Rosdhu Queen (IRE)**[203] 6672 3-9-0 110 JohnnyMurtagh 4 98
(William Haggas) *unruly stalls: led: drvn along over 1f out: hdd fnl 120yds: wknd and dropped to 4th in clsng stages* **7/4**[1]
416- **5** 2 ½ **Valais Girl**[196] 6873 3-9-0 79 (p) HayleyTurner 2 91
(Marcus Tregoning) *chsd ldrs: rdn ins fnl 2f: wknd ins fnl f* **50/1**
644- **6** 2 ¼ **City Image (IRE)**[169] 7518 3-9-0 100 RyanMoore 1 85
(Richard Hannon) *in tch: rdn over 2f out: effrt over 1f out: nvr rchd ldrs and sn btn* **12/1**
312- **7** 1 **Desert Image**[168] 7555 3-9-0 98 JamesDoyle 3 83
(Charles Hills) *trckd ldr: rdn over 2f out: wknd appr fnl f* **9/1**
520- **8** nk **Califante**[204] 6632 3-9-0 98 MartinDwyer 6 82
(William Muir) *chsd ldrs: rdn 2f out: wknd over 1f out* **50/1**
1-13 **9** 1 ½ **Mystical Sapphire**[31] 1091 3-9-0 82 LiamKeniry 7 78
(Jo Crowley) *in tch: hdwy to cl on ldrs over 2f out: sn rdn: wknd wl over 1f out* **33/1**
035- **10** 4 ½ **The Gold Cheongsam (IRE)**[169] 7547 3-9-0 105 (v[1]) WilliamBuick 10 66
(Jeremy Noseda) *in tch: rdn and effrt to cl on ldrs over 2f out: nvr on terms and wknd fnl f* **15/2**

1m 25.45s (-0.25) **Going Correction** 0.0s/f (Good) **10** Ran SP% **115.1**
Speed ratings (Par 105): **101,100,98,98,95 92,91,91,89,84**
toteswingers 1&2 £7.10, 1&3 £13.80, 2&3 £13.40 CSF £27.55 TOTE £5.20: £1.50, £2.30, £4.20; EX 26.90 Trifecta £419.10 Pool: £106515.85 - 190.61 winning units..
Owner Ahmad Alkhallafi **Bred** Colm McEvoy **Trained** East Everleigh, Wilts

FOCUS
All bar Valais Girl came into this with a 1000 Guineas entry, but not since Wince in 1999 has a filly won this and followed up in the Newmarket Classic, and that probably won't change this year. The favourite blatantly didn't stay after going off too fast, and the fifth came into this officially rated just 79. They raced up the middle and the form looks ordinary, although the winner ran to her juvenile best, with the placed horses and fifth all recording personal-bests.

1677 AON GREENHAM STKS (GROUP 3) (C&G) 7f (S)
3:30 (3:30) (Class 1) 3-Y-O **£34,026** (£12,900; £6,456; £3,216; £1,614) **Stalls** Centre

Form RPR
111- **1** **Olympic Glory (IRE)**[195] 6910 3-9-0 117 RichardHughes 2 109+
(Richard Hannon) *hld up in tch: drvn over 2f out: rdn to chse ldr appr fnl f: led fnl 150yds: pushed out* **8/11**[1]
266- **2** 1 **Sir Patrick Moore (FR)**[175] 7398 3-9-0 100 RyanMoore 5 106
(Harry Dunlop) *led after 1f: drvn and styd alone in centre of crse fr 2f out: hdd and outpcd by wnr fnl 150yds but hld on wl for 2nd* **20/1**
512- **3** ¾ **Moohaajim (IRE)**[189] 7049 3-9-0 116 MartinHarley 1 104+
(Marco Botti) *hld up in rr: smooth hdwy over 1f out: drvn and qcknd to cl on ldng duo jst ins fnl f: no ex and styd on same pce fnl 110yds* **13/8**[2]
011- **4** 9 **Correspondent**[169] 7523 3-9-0 92 EddieAhern 4 81
(Brian Meehan) *sn trcking ldr: rdn 2f out: wknd over 1f out* **14/1**[3]
113 **5** 10 **Hiddon Coin (IRE)**[21] 1250 3-9-0 82 KierenFallon 3 57
(David O'Meara) *led 1f: styd chsng ldrs: rdn along 3f out: wknd 2f out* **50/1**

1m 26.14s (0.44) **Going Correction** 0.0s/f (Good) **5** Ran SP% **109.4**
Speed ratings (Par 108): **97,95,95,84,73**
CSF £15.79 TOTE £1.40: £1.02, £4.40; EX 7.80 Trifecta £19.00 Pool: £14603.14 - 574.12 winning units..
Owner HE Sh Joaan Bin Hamad Al Thani **Bred** Denis McDonnell **Trained** East Everleigh, Wilts

FOCUS
Muddling form as both the winner and third came into this with 21lb in hand of the runner-up judged on RPRs. The time was 0.69 seconds slower than the Fred Darling. The runners started off up the middle but most ended up stands' side.

1678 DUBAI DUTY FREE TENNIS CHAMPIONSHIPS MAIDEN STKS 1m (S)
4:05 (4:11) (Class 4) 3-Y-O £5,175 (£1,540; £769; £384) Stalls Centre

Form				RPR
3-	1		**Cape Peron**161 7686 3-9-5 0 DaneO'Neill 5 (Henry Candy) *s.i.s: in rr: pushed along and gd hdwy over 2f out: str run to ld fnl 110yds: styd on strly* 8/13	92+
4-	2	1 1/2	**Kyllachy Rise**259 4803 3-9-5 0 TomQueally 10 (Sir Henry Cecil) *trckd ldrs: led appr fnl 2f: pushed along over 1f out: hdd and outpcd fnl 110yds* 6/41	89
63-	3	nk	**Number One London (IRE)**196 6876 3-9-5 0 KierenFallon 3 (Brian Meehan) *chsd ldrs: drvn to chal wl over 1f out and stl upsides ins fnl f kpt pressing for 2nd in clsng stages but nt gng pce of wnr* 12/1	88
6-	4	1/2	**Glorious Protector (IRE)**205 6596 3-9-5 0 JamieSpencer 4 (Ed Walker) *chsd ldrs: drvn 2f out: styd on wl fnl f: nver quite gng pce to chal* 7/22	87
	5	5	**Prince's Trust** 3-9-5 0 RichardHughes 6 (Richard Hannon) *in tch: drvn and effrt over 1f out: nvr rchd ldrs and sn outpcd* 16/1	76
	6	1/2	**Aldborough (IRE)** 3-9-5 0 RichardThomas 1 (Ralph Beckett) *towards rr: drvn over 2f out: kpt on fnl f but nvr a threat* 33/1	75+
	7	3 1/4	**Bold Sniper** 3-9-5 0 RyanMoore 13 (Sir Michael Stoute) *s.i.s: towards rr: pushed along over 2f out: kpt on ins fnl f: nvr a threat* 12/1	67+
0-	8	1 3/4	**Switcharooney (IRE)**113 8262 3-9-5 0 StephenCraine 9 (Tom Dascombe) *chsd ldrs: rdn over 2f out: wknd over 1f out* 100/1	63
40-	9	1/2	**Llaregyb (IRE)**164 7637 3-9-5 0 LiamKeniry 14 (David Elsworth) *t.k.h: chsd ldrs: shkn up 2f out: wknd over 1f out* 33/1	62
04-	10	2 1/4	**Epic Charm**198 6817 3-8-9 0 CharlesBishop(5) 15 (Mick Channon) *led 5f out: hdd over 2f out: wknd wl over 1f out* 100/1	52
	11	3 1/4	**Fitzwilly** 3-9-5 0 CathyGannon 8 (Mick Channon) *s.i.s: in rr and outpcd most of way* 33/1	49
6-	12	1 1/2	**Tonor (IRE)**197 6845 3-9-5 0 JimmyFortune 11 (Roger Varian) *led 2f: styd pressing ldrs tl wknd 2f out* 40/1	46
	13	1	**Kazak** 3-9-5 0 JamesDoyle 2 (Roger Charlton) *s.i.s: bhd most of way* 40/1	43
26-	14	3 1/4	**Rock God (IRE)**232 5792 3-9-5 0 1 JohnFahy 12 (Eve Johnson Houghton) *s.i.s: sn wl in tch: wknd over 2f out* 14/1	36
3	15	1	**Secret Session (USA)**17 1323 3-9-5 0 MartinHarley 16 (Marco Botti) *pressed ldrs tl wknd qujckly 2f out* 8/13	34
	16	9	**Brave Acclaim (IRE)** 3-9-5 0 GeorgeBaker 7 (Tom Dascombe) *s.i.s: a in rr* 80/1	13

1m 41.24s (1.54) **Going Correction** 0.0s/f (Good) **16** Ran SP% **129.3**
Speed ratings (Par 100): **92,90,90,89,84 84,80,79,78,76 73,71,70,67,66 57**
toteswingers 1&2 £4.90, 2&3 £7.20, 1&3 £17.30 CSF £20.73 TOTE £10.30: £3.10, £1.30, £3.30; EX 28.90 Trifecta £322.50 Pool: £4145.82 - 9.63 winning units..
Owner The Earl Cadogan **Bred** The Earl Cadogan **Trained** Kingston Warren, Oxon

FOCUS
This is often a good maiden and has thrown up a couple of subsequent Group 3 winners and a Listed scorer in the last ten years. Four came clear of the rest and the form is rated around the race averages, with the first four all improving on their juvenile marks.

1679 BATHWICK TYRES MAIDEN STKS 1m 3f 5y
4:40 (4:43) (Class 4) 3-Y-O £5,175 (£1,540; £769; £384) Stalls Centre

Form				RPR
	1		**Feel Like Dancing** 3-9-5 0 WilliamBuick 8 (John Gosden) *pushed along to trck ldrs: drvn over 2f out: styd on to chse ldr 1f out: str run ins fnl f to ld on line* 5/13	90+
4-	2	nse	**Boite (IRE)**164 7637 3-9-5 0 JamieSpencer 14 (Peter Chapple-Hyam) *led after 2f: pushed along 2f out: hrd rdn and hung rt fnl f: kpt on wl: ct on line* 13/2	89
6-	3	2 3/4	**Shwaiman (IRE)**164 7636 3-9-5 0 JamesDoyle 5 (James Fanshawe) *in rr: hdwy over 2f out: swtchd lft and styd on ins fnl f to take 3rd fnl 110yds no imp on ldng duo* 40/1	84+
3-	4	2 1/4	**Squire Osbaldeston (IRE)**246 5321 3-9-5 0 TomQueally 7 (Sir Henry Cecil) *t.k.h: chsd ldrs: drvn along 2f out: styd on one pce fnl f* 2/11	80+
6-	5	1 1/2	**Dragon City**176 7373 3-9-5 0 DaneO'Neill 13 (Harry Dunlop) *chsd ldrs: rdn and n.m.r 1f out: styd on same pce* 25/1	78
4-	6	1 1/2	**Chief Executive (IRE)**147 7868 3-9-5 0 PaulHanagan 9 (Jo Hughes) *chsd ldrs: drvn to chal fr 2f out: wknd ins fnl f* 20/1	75
	7	1 1/2	**Hamelin (IRE)** 3-9-5 0 EddieAhern 11 (Sir Henry Cecil) *in rr: pushed along over 3f out: hdwy 2f out: nvr rchd ldrs and one same pce* 14/1	72+
05-	8	3 1/4	**White Month**171 7492 3-9-5 0 LiamKeniry 6 (Andrew Balding) *led 2f: chsd ldrs to 3f out: wknd 2f out* 40/1	66
34-	9	1/2	**Excellent Result (IRE)**188 7081 3-9-5 0 SilvestreDeSousa 2 (Saeed bin Suroor) *in tch: pushed along and sme hdwy over 3f out: wknd fr 2f out* 7/22	66
	10	2 1/4	**Federal (IRE)** 3-9-5 0 RobertWinston 12 (Roger Teal) *in tch: pushed along over 2f out: sn wknd* 25/1	62
	11	1 1/4	**Dalaklear (IRE)** 3-9-5 0 TedDurcan 10 (David Lanigan) *towards rr most of way* 50/1	59
	12	12	**Circus Turn (USA)** 3-9-5 0 RyanMoore 3 (Sir Michael Stoute) *towards rr: sme prog over 3f out: sn wknd* 10/1	38
	13	1 1/4	**Strawberry Jam** 3-9-5 0 ChrisCatlin 1 (Paul Cole) *s.i.s: a in rr* 28/1	35

2m 26.77s (5.57) **Going Correction** +0.40s/f (Good) **13** Ran SP% **124.1**
Speed ratings (Par 100): **95,94,92,91,90 89,88,85,85,83 82,74,73**
toteswingers 1&2 £12.20, 2&3 £55.20, 1&3 £50.40 CSF £36.09 TOTE £5.10: £1.80, £2.20, £9.00; EX 40.10 Trifecta £2001.40 Pool: £6064.08 - 2.27 winning units..
Owner Lady Bamford **Bred** Lady Bamford **Trained** Newmarket, Suffolk

FOCUS
An interesting maiden in which they raced middle to stands' side in the straight. The field were relatively bunched at the finish and this is rated as one of the lower recent renewals.
T/Plt: £47.90 to a £1 stake. Pool of £116314.59 - 1772.20 winning tickets. T/Qpdt: £10.10 to a £1 stake. Pool of £6918.89 - 502.61 winning tickets. ST

1481 NOTTINGHAM (L-H)
Saturday, April 20

OFFICIAL GOING: Good (good to firm in places; 8.6)
All races on Inner track and home bend moved in 2m.
Wind: Light half against Weather: Fine and dry

1680 J C FRETWELL RACING MAIDEN STKS 5f 13y
5:30 (5:31) (Class 5) 2-Y-O £3,234 (£962; £481; £240) Stalls High

Form				RPR
	1		**Extortionist (IRE)** 2-9-5 0 JimCrowley 7 (Olly Stevens) *cl up: led bef 1/2-way: shkn up and qcknd clr over 1f out: edgd lft ins fnl f: readily* 10/32	81+
	2	2 3/4	**Red Pike (IRE)** 2-9-5 0 RoystonFfrench 2 (Bryan Smart) *dwlt and pushed lft s: sn trcking ldrs: hdwy to chse wnr wl over 1f out: rdn and no imp ins fnl f* 8/1	71
	3	3 1/4	**Bounty Hunter (IRE)** 2-9-5 0 RichardKingscote 6 (Tom Dascombe) *trckd ldrs: hdwy wl over 1f out: styd on to chse ldng pair ins fnl f: no imp* 12/1	59
	4	2 3/4	**Bandolier** 2-9-5 0 FrederikTylicki 8 (Richard Fahey) *dwlt and in rr: pushed along over 2f out: kpt on fnl f* 11/1	50
	5	3/4	**Wickhambrook (IRE)** 2-9-5 0 MickaelBarzalona 3 (Mahmood Al Zarooni) *wnt lft s: sn trcking ldrs: effrt over 2f out: rdn wl over 1f out: wknd ent fnl f* 5/21	47
	6	3/4	**Zalzilah** 2-9-5 0 PatCosgrave 1 (James Tate) *wnt lft s: towards rr: sme hdwy on wd outside over 2f out: sn rdn and n.d* 4/13	44
3	7	3 1/4	**Hedy**27 1156 2-9-0 0 MatthewDavies 9 (Mick Channon) *led: hdd bef 1/2-way and sn pushed along: rdn over 2f out: sn wknd* 5/1	27

1m 0.31s (-1.19) **Going Correction** -0.325s/f (Firm) **7** Ran SP% **115.5**
Speed ratings (Par 92): **96,91,86,82,80 79,74**
toteswingers 1&2 £5.80, 1&3 £9.20, 2&3 £18.10 CSF £30.06 TOTE £4.20: £1.60, £4.80; EX 35.40 Trifecta £243.40 Pool: £1872.13- 5.76 winning units..
Owner Sheikh Suhaim Al Thani **Bred** Mrs Louise Lyons **Trained** Chiddingfold, Surrey

FOCUS
Dry and bright and the ground was drying out all the time which led to quite a few non-runners throughout the card. Jim Crowley reported that it was riding on the quick side after the first race. All bar Hedy were making their racecourse debuts and this has the potential to be quite a smart piece of juvenile form.

1681 LODGE FARM STUD, CHRIS AND MAY MULLIN H'CAP 5f 13y
6:00 (6:01) (Class 6) (0-65,65) 4-Y-O+
£1,940 (£577; £288; £48; £48; £48) Stalls High

Form				RPR
430-	1		**Gowanharry (IRE)**196 6886 4-9-5 63 PaulMulrennan 13 (Michael Dods) *trckd ldrs: gd hdwy over 2f out: led 1 1/2f out: sn rdn: drvn and edgd lft ins fnl f: kpt on strly* 8/12	73
6122	2	3/4	**Speedyfix**17 1324 6-9-1 59 (t) TomMcLaughlin 4 (Christine Dunnett) *in tch on wd outside: hdwy over 1f out: rdn and str run ins fnl f: no ex towards fin* 10/1	66
050-	3	shd	**Black Annis Bower**247 5257 5-8-8 59 MatthewHopkins(7) 2 (Michael Easterby) *trckd ldrs: hdwy 2f out: effrt whn n.m.r ent fnl f: sn swtchd rt and rdn: kpt on same pce* 22/1	66
0224	4	nk	**Thorpe Bay**25 1186 4-8-11 55 MickaelBarzalona 1 (Michael Appleby) *midfield: hdwy 2f out: rdn to chse ldrs jst ins fnl f: kpt on* 12/1	61
500-	4	dht	**Majestic Manannan (IRE)**185 7178 4-9-5 63 PaulQuinn 8 (David Nicholls) *prom: effrt to chal 2f out and ev ch: rdn and edgd rt ent fnl f: kpt on same pce* 9/13	69
33-0	4	dht	**My Time**16 1355 4-8-8 52 (p) RichardKingscote 6 (Michael Mullineaux) *hld up in midfield: hdwy wl over 1f out: rdn to chse ldrs whn n.m.r ins fnl f: kpt on* 22/1	58
003-	7	1 1/4	**Errigal Lad**164 7634 8-8-8 52 KellyHarrison 11 (Garry Woodward) *outpcd and towards rr: hdwy over 1f out: styd on wl fnl f: nrst fin* 18/1	53+
-114	8	1 3/4	**Clubland (IRE)**17 1331 4-9-4 65 MarkCoumbe(3) 10 (Roy Bowring) *cl up: rdn and slt ld over 2f out: hdd and drvn 1 1/2f out: grad wknd* 7/11	60
3325	9	shd	**Spartic**87 346 5-8-8 52 (p) SeanLevey 14 (Alan McCabe) *chsd ldrs: rdn along wl over 1f out: grad wknd* 16/1	47
600-	10	3/4	**Two Turtle Doves (IRE)**172 7457 7-8-8 57 RobertTart(5) 7 (Michael Mullineaux) *nvr bttr than midfield* 14/1	49
4034	11	1/2	**Sextons House (IRE)**14 1395 5-8-7 51 oh3 (b) AndreaAtzeni 5 (Alan McCabe) *towards rr tl sme late hdwy* 12/1	41
4/	12	1	**Mr Man In The Moon (IRE)**710 2011 5-9-7 65 FergusSweeney 9 (Mandy Rowland) *a towards rr* 25/1	52
0-30	13	nk	**Aqua Ardens (GER)**15 1366 5-9-4 62 (t) PatCosgrave 16 (George Baker) *a in rr* 20/1	48
52-0	14	1	**Irish Girls Spirit (IRE)**19 1283 4-9-0 58 MickyFenton 17 (Paul Midgley) *cl up: rdn along 1/2-way: sn wknd* 8/12	40
0620	15	2	**Roy's Legacy**14 1388 4-8-9 58 (t) MichaelJMMurphy(5) 12 (Shaun Harris) *slt ld: rdn along 1/2-way: sn hdd & wknd wl over 1f out* 11/1	33
4500	16	3 3/4	**Speightowns Kid (USA)**16 1351 5-9-3 61 J-PGuillambert 15 (Richard Ford) *a in rr* 20/1	22
-011	17	16	**Divertimenti (IRE)**32 1077 9-8-7 56 (b) ThomasBrown(5) 3 (Roy Bowring) *blind removed v late: v.s.a: a t.o* 7/11	

59.66s (-1.84) **Going Correction** -0.325s/f (Firm) **17** Ran SP% **129.9**
Speed ratings (Par 101): **101,99,99,99,99 99,97,94,94,93 92,90,90,88,85 79,53**
tote place: MT £2.10, MM £1.00, TB £0.80; toteswingers 1&2 £22.80, 1&3 £83.00, 2&3 £69.40 CSF £83.41 CT £1796.61 TOTE £11.30: £2.40, £3.30, £6.20; EX 119.70 Trifecta £623.50 Part won. Pool: £831.40 - 0.68 winning units..
Owner Les Waugh **Bred** L Waugh **Trained** Denton, Co Durham

The Form Book Flat, Raceform Ltd, Compton, RG20 6NL.

FOCUS
The front few finished in a heap but they went quite a strong gallop from the start and quite a few were taken off their feet in the first half of the race. The form is straightforward rated around the first two.

1682 CAR COLSTON HALL STUD FILLIES' H'CAP 5f 13y
6:30 (6:31) (Class 5) (0-75,74) 3-Y-O **£2,587** (£770; £384; £192) **Stalls** High

Form RPR
40-5 **1** **Royal Guinevere**[12] 1427 3-8-7 **60** JimmyQuinn 1 70
(Dean Ivory) *t.k.h: cl up on outer: chal over 1f out: rdn ent fnl f: led last 100yds: kpt on strly* **16/1**
U1 **2** 1 ¾ **Holley Shiftwell**[63] 686 3-9-0 **67** AndreaAtzeni 3 71
(Stuart Williams) *led: rdn wl over 1f out: drvn ent fnl f: hdd and one pce last 100yds* **7/1**
445- **3** *nk* **Chasing Dreams**[190] 7028 3-9-4 **74** JulieBurke(3) 4 77
(Kevin Ryan) *trckd ldrs: hdwy 2f out: sn rdn and kpt on fnl f* **7/2**[2]
1- **4** 2 ¾ **Gift Of Music (IRE)**[141] 7931 3-9-1 **68** LukeMorris 10 61+
(James Eustace) *towards rr: hdwy 2f out: swtchd lft and rdn over 1f out: styd on fnl f* **11/2**[3]
51- **5** 2 **Exotic Isle**[206] 6579 3-9-4 **71** JimCrowley 9 57
(Ralph Beckett) *cl up: rdn along 2f out: drvn and wknd appr fnl f* **2/1**[1]
6-32 **6** *nk* **Scent Of Roses (IRE)**[51] 821 3-8-9 **67** RyanTate(5) 8 52
(Clive Cox) *in tch: hdwy 2f out: swtchd lft and rdn over 1f out: sn no imp* **14/1**
425- **7** 1 **Clean Blow (USA)**[216] 6284 3-9-3 **70** SeanLevey 6 51
(David Brown) *cl up: rdn along 2f out: sn wknd* **6/1**
460- **8** 2 **Betty Boo (IRE)**[216] 6283 3-7-11 **55** oh10 NatashaEaton(5) 5 29
(Shaun Harris) *hmpd and squeezed out after s: a bhd* **40/1**

59.92s (-1.58) **Going Correction** -0.325s/f (Firm) **8** Ran SP% **112.7**
Speed ratings (Par 95): **99,96,95,91,88 87,86,82**
toteswingers 1&2 £15.30, 1&3 £5.80, 2&3 £6.10 CSF £118.42 CT £403.78 TOTE £22.30: £3.90, £2.30, £2.40; EX 241.60 Trifecta £710.40 Part won. Pool: £947.27 - 0.05 winning units..
Owner M J Yarrow **Bred** Plantation Stud **Trained** Radlett, Herts

FOCUS
Not many got into this. The winner is capable of better and the placed horses set the level.

1683 DICK WHITE REFERRALS H'CAP 1m 75y
7:00 (7:01) (Class 4) (0-80,80) 3-Y-O **£5,175** (£1,540; £769; £384) **Stalls** Centre

Form RPR
415- **1** **Al Mukhdam**[212] 6414 3-9-2 **75** PaulMulrennan 5 84
(Peter Chapple-Hyam) *mde all: rdn clr wl over 1f out: styd on strly* **12/1**
61-1 **2** 2 ¾ **Strong Conviction**[19] 1293 3-9-3 **76** MatthewDavies 6 79
(Mick Channon) *chsd wnr: rdn along over 2f out: drvn and sltly outpcd over 1f out: styd on u.p fnl f* **12/1**
32-1 **3** ½ **Emerging**[98] 184 3-9-2 **75** SebSanders 12 77
(David Elsworth) *prom: effrt to chse wnr 3f out: rdn along 2f out: drvn and one pce appr fnl f* **12/1**
231- **4** 1 ¼ **Lilac Tree**[164] 7628 3-9-6 **79** MickaelBarzalona 3 79+
(Mahmood Al Zarooni) *t.k.h: trckd ldng pair whn n.m.r and snatched up on inner: plld hrd after: chsd ldrs: effrt 2f out: sn rdn along and one pce* **5/2**[1]
01- **5** ¾ **Rottingdean**[164] 7627 3-9-3 **76** RobertHavlin 13 73+
(John Gosden) *s.i.s: t.k.h in rr: hdwy on inner over 3f out: rdn to chse ldrs 2f out: no imp appr fnl f* **8/1**
41-4 **6** *nk* **Living The Life (IRE)**[21] 1246 3-9-4 **77** FergusSweeney 11 74+
(Jamie Osborne) *s.i.s and bhd: hdwy on wd outside 3f out: rdn to chse ldrs 2f out: edgd lft and no imp appr fnl f* **9/1**
-411 **7** 3 ½ **Camachoice (IRE)**[30] 1099 3-9-6 **79** (tp) AndreaAtzeni 4 68
(Marco Botti) *hld up in tch: hdwy 3f out: rdn along 2f out: sn btn* **10/1**
332- **8** *nk* **Loch Moy**[205] 6603 3-9-1 **74** FrederikTylicki 2 62
(Richard Fahey) *sltly hmpd s: sn in tch: rdn along over 4f out: sn wknd* **6/1**[2]
361- **9** 4 **Iberis**[198] 6816 3-9-2 **75** IanMongan 7 54
(Sir Henry Cecil) *hld up: hdwy on outer and in tch 1/2-way: chsd ldrs 3f out: sn rdn and wknd over 2f out* **7/1**[3]
1 **10** 5 **Aetna**[29] 1114 3-9-4 **77** GrahamGibbons 1 44
(Michael Easterby) *dwlt: hdwy and in tch 1/2-way: effrt and hdwy over 3f out: rdn wl over 2f out and sn wknd* **11/1**

1m 43.41s (-5.59) **Going Correction** -0.675s/f (Hard) course record **10** Ran SP% **117.0**
Speed ratings (Par 100): **100,97,96,95,94 94,90,90,86,81**
toteswingers 1&2 £38.00, 1&3 £25.30, 2&3 £10.20 CSF £147.04 CT £1767.76 TOTE £16.00: £4.10, £2.80, £4.40; EX 88.50 Trifecta £529.00 Pool: £790.62 - 1.12 winning units..
Owner Ziad A Galadari **Bred** Galadari Sons Stud Company Limited **Trained** Newmarket, Suffolk

FOCUS
As can often be the case on the round course, it proved hard to make an impact from off the pace and this was won by a fine front-running ride. The winner is unexposed while the three in the frame behind him help to set the level.

1684 NORMANDIE STUD WITH LODGE FARM STUD MAIDEN STKS 1m 2f 50y
7:30 (7:33) (Class 5) 3-Y-O **£3,234** (£962; £481; £240) **Stalls** Low

Form RPR
1 **Centurius** 3-9-5 0 AndreaAtzeni 9 95+
(Marco Botti) *hld up in midfield: hdwy 4f out: swtchd lft 3f out: chsd ldrs 2f out: rdn to chse ldr over 1f out: styd on to ld ins fnl f* **8/1**
2-24 **2** ¾ **Sublimation (IRE)**[12] 1429 3-9-0 79 GeorgeDowning(5) 2 88
(Tony Carroll) *led: rdn along wl over 2f out: drvn over 1f out: hdd ins fnl f: kpt on* **20/1**
3- **3** 2 ¾ **Emperical**[170] 7507 3-9-5 0 IanMongan 1 83+
(Sir Henry Cecil) *trckd ldrs: hdwy 1/2-way: chsd ldng pair 4f out: rdn along wl over 2f out: drvn and kpt on same pce appr fnl f* **4/1**[3]
2- **4** 2 ¼ **Thouwra (IRE)**[155] 7750 3-9-5 0 MickaelBarzalona 12 79
(Saeed bin Suroor) *dwlt and hld up in rr: hdwy on outer 4f out: chsd ldrs over 2f out: sn rdn and no imp appr fnl f* **10/3**[2]
5 1 ½ **Brass Ring** 3-9-5 0 RobertHavlin 8 76+
(John Gosden) *s.i.s and bhd tl styd on fnl 2f: nrst fin* **13/2**
0- **6** ½ **Shades Of Silver**[269] 4472 3-9-5 0 SeanLevey 11 75
(Sir Michael Stoute) *trckd ldrs: effrt on inner 4f out: rdn along over 2f out: sn one pce* **20/1**
6- **7** *hd* **Lemon Pearl**[176] 7364 3-9-0 0 JimCrowley 10 70
(Ralph Beckett) *trckd ldrs: pushed along and sltly outpcd over 3f out: rdn and kpt on same pce fnl 2f* **3/1**[1]
052- **8** 3 **Song Light**[164] 7637 3-9-5 73 SebSanders 4 69
(David Elsworth) *t.k.h: hld up in rr: hdwy over 4f out: rdn along 3f out: n.d* **10/1**
000- **9** 4 **Rutherglen**[224] 6020 3-9-5 67 PatCosgrave 6 61
(George Baker) *t.k.h: hld up towards rr: pushed along over 3f out: n.d* **40/1**
4- **10** 8 **Himalayan Peak**[172] 7468 3-9-5 0 LukeMorris 3 46
(James Eustace) *trckd ldrs: hdwy 6f out: rdn along over 3f out: sn wknd* **20/1**
6 **11** 60 **Hollow Beat**[21] 1236 3-9-0 0 GrahamGibbons 7
(Tim Walford) *cl up: rdn along over 3f out: sn wknd* **50/1**

2m 9.4s (-4.90) **Going Correction** -0.675s/f (Hard) course record **11** Ran SP% **120.3**
Speed ratings (Par 98): **92,91,89,87,86 85,85,83,80,73 25**
toteswingers 1&2 £24.20, 1&3 £11.80, 2&3 £11.00 CSF £160.50 TOTE £9.10: £3.30, £3.40, £1.80; EX 153.80 Trifecta £734.00 Part won. Pool: £978.74 - 0.31 winning units..
Owner Mohamed Albousi Alghufli **Bred** D J Bloodstock, G Roddick & Wrottesley Ltd **Trained** Newmarket, Suffolk

FOCUS
Some potentially nice horses on show here and this might turn out to be a reasonable maiden. The runner-up is the key to the form.

1685 RACING WELFARE H'CAP 1m 2f 50y
8:00 (8:00) (Class 6) (0-65,64) 3-Y-O **£1,940** (£577; £288; £144) **Stalls** Low

Form RPR
640- **1** **Love Marmalade (IRE)**[154] 7779 3-9-7 **64** JoeFanning 13 72+
(Mark Johnston) *hld up in midfield: stdy hdwy on outer 3f out: rdn to ld appr fnl f: styd on* **6/1**[2]
003- **2** 2 **Thwart**[198] 6817 3-9-4 **61** JimCrowley 10 65+
(Ralph Beckett) *cl up: rdn to ld 2f out: drvn and hdd appr fnl f: kpt on same pce* **9/4**[1]
00-1 **3** *shd* **Astrum**[19] 1289 3-9-0 **57** AndreaAtzeni 5 61
(Rod Millman) *trckd ldrs: hdwy 3f out: rdn to chse ldng pair over 1f out: kpt on u.p fnl f* **7/1**[3]
0331 **4** 3 **Lady Lunchalot (USA)**[16] 1343 3-9-3 **60** (p) LiamJones 1 58
(J S Moore) *trckd ldrs on inner: pushed along 3f out: rdn and n.m.r 2f out: sn swtchd rt and kpt on same pce* **14/1**
00-4 **5** ½ **Standing Bear (IRE)**[10] 1487 3-9-6 **63** IanMongan 4 60
(Paul Cole) *sn led: rdn along 3f out: hdd 2f out and grad wknd* **9/1**
344 **6** 1 ¾ **Impeccability**[39] 972 3-8-9 **52** GrahamGibbons 7 46
(John Mackie) *dwlt and hld up in rr: hdwy on inner 3f out: chsd ldrs over 2f out: sn rdn and one pce* **25/1**
-543 **7** *hd* **Autrisk (IRE)**[12] 1425 3-9-4 **61** NickyMackay 14 54
(Marco Botti) *hld up in rr: sme hdwy 3f out: rdn along 2f out: n.d* **17/2**
30-5 **8** *hd* **Tilly T (IRE)**[19] 1289 3-8-7 **50** oh3 LukeMorris 3 43
(J S Moore) *in tch on inner: effrt and nt clr run 3f out: swtchd rt and rdn 2f out: n.d* **33/1**
1512 **9** 1 ¼ **Luv U Whatever**[24] 1206 3-9-2 **59** J-PGuillambert 11 50
(Jo Hughes) *trckd ldrs on outer: effrt 3f out: sn rdn along and wknd fnl 2f* **11/1**
005- **10** 2 ¾ **Hurricane John (IRE)**[194] 6919 3-8-13 **56** PaulQuinn 9 41
(David Nicholls) *a in rr* **14/1**
32-4 **11** 20 **Classy Trick (USA)**[17] 1314 3-9-0 **57** FrederikTylicki 6
(Richard Fahey) *chsd ldrs: rdn along over 3f out: sn wknd and eased* **8/1**

2m 10.74s (-3.56) **Going Correction** -0.675s/f (Hard) **11** Ran SP% **117.6**
Speed ratings (Par 96): **87,85,85,82,82 81,80,80,79,77 61**
toteswingers 1&2 £6.60, 1&3 £4.70, 2&3 £4.70 CSF £19.80 CT £98.63 TOTE £5.40: £3.00, £1.40, £1.80; EX 30.70 Trifecta £289.40 Pool: £769.68 - 1.99 winning units..
Owner Crone Stud Farms Ltd **Bred** Stonethorn Stud Farms Ltd **Trained** Middleham Moor, N Yorks

FOCUS
Low-grade fare but a few in here have the potential to improve this year. The form looks sound with the fourth and fifth the best guides.
T/Plt: £642.80 to a £1 stake. Pool of £40594.29 - 46.10 winning tickets. T/Qpdt: £150.40 to a £1 stake. Pool of £3924.10 - 19.30 winning tickets. JR

THIRSK (L-H)
Saturday, April 20

OFFICIAL GOING: Good (8.4)
Both bends dolled out 3-4 yards adding circa 20yds to 7f races and circa 30yds to 12f race.
Wind: light across Weather: sunny

1686 THIRSKRACECOURSE.NET FOR DISCOUNTED TICKETS ONLINE H'CAP (DIV I) 7f
2:15 (2:16) (Class 5) (0-75,75) 4-Y-O+ **£2,726** (£805; £402) **Stalls** Low

Form RPR
00-2 **1** **Snow Bay**[10] 1462 7-9-0 **73** ShirleyTeasdale(5) 5 84
(Paul Midgley) *mde all: rdn clr over 1f out: comf* **7/2**[2]
1242 **2** 2 ¾ **Al Freej (IRE)**[7] 1540 4-9-4 **72** DaleSwift 6 76
(Brian Ellison) *midfield: rdn and hdwy over 2f out: kpt on: wnt 2nd fnl 100yds: no ch w wnr* **11/4**[1]
0-03 **3** ½ **Mutafaakir (IRE)**[10] 1462 4-8-12 **66** JamesSullivan 9 68
(Ruth Carr) *in tch: hdwy over 2f out: rdn to chse wnr 2f out: one pce: lost 2nd fnl 100yds* **17/2**
-614 **4** ½ **Mujaadel (USA)**[10] 1462 8-8-11 **65** (p) FrannyNorton 3 66
(David Nicholls) *hld up: rdn over 2f out: hdwy over 1f out: kpt on fnl f* **7/1**
01-5 **5** 2 ¼ **Sardanapalus**[10] 1460 4-9-7 **75** (p) PhillipMakin 10 70
(Kevin Ryan) *s.i.s: hld up: rdn and sme hdwy over 2f out: kpt on one pce: nvr threatened* **4/1**[3]
00-0 **6** 1 ¼ **Orwellian**[66] 640 4-8-10 **64** (p) TomEaves 4 55
(Bryan Smart) *nvr bttr than midfield* **40/1**
4-56 **7** ½ **Illustrious Prince (IRE)**[12] 1430 6-8-12 **69** NeilFarley(3) 1 59
(Declan Carroll) *midfield: rdn over 2f out: sn no imp* **14/1**
0-05 **8** 2 ¼ **Aerodynamic (IRE)**[15] 1363 6-9-7 **75** GrahamGibbons 7 59
(Michael Easterby) *dwlt: hld up: pushed along over 2f out: nvr threatened* **16/1**
254- **9** 3 ¾ **Shamrocked (IRE)**[98] 7246 4-9-2 **70** SamHitchcott 8 44
(Mick Channon) *trckd ldr: rdn over 2f out: wknd over 1f out* **18/1**
033- **10** *nk* **Windygoul Lad**[165] 7604 4-8-7 **61** oh2 (p) AndrewMullen 2 34
(Michael Smith) *t.k.h early: trckd ldr: rdn over 2f out: wknd over 1f out* **22/1**

1m 25.51s (-1.69) **Going Correction** -0.125s/f (Firm) **10** Ran SP% **116.5**
Speed ratings (Par 103): **104,100,100,99,97 95,95,92,88,87**
toteswingers 1&2 £2.80, 1&3 £7.80, 2&3 £4.80 CSF £13.54 CT £75.28 TOTE £6.40: £2.50, £1.10, £3.40; EX 15.20 Trifecta £69.20 Pool: £1666.49 - 14.00 winning units..
Owner Snow Bay Partnership **Bred** West Dereham Abbey Stud **Trained** Westow, N Yorks

FOCUS
A fair handicap with the placed horses close to their marks.

1687 THIRSK RACECOURSE - A GREAT CONFERENCE VENUE MEDIAN AUCTION MAIDEN STKS 6f
2:50 (2:51) (Class 5) 3-4-Y-0 £2,587 (£770; £384; £192) Stalls High

Form RPR
4- **1** **Lord Ashley (IRE)**[372] 1352 3-9-0 0 RichardKingscote 1 81
(Tom Dascombe) *midfield towards outer: hdwy over 2f out: pushed along to ld 1f out: kpt on to go clr: easily* 13/2[2]
20-3 **2** 5 **Red Baron (IRE)**[23] 1215 4-9-11 62 (b[1]) LukeMorris 9 68
(Eric Alston) *w ldr: led over 3f out: rdn 2f out: hdd 1f out: sn no ch w wnr* 9/1[3]
523- **3** 1 **Nordikhab (IRE)**[245] 5367 3-9-0 81 GrahamLee 11 62
(Kevin Ryan) *chsd ldrs: pushed along over 2f out: drvn appr fnl f: sn one pce in 3rd* 4/6[1]
6 **4** 1 **Compton Heights**[14] 1392 4-9-11 0 TomEaves 3 62
(Jim Goldie) *hld up in rr: pushed along and hdwy over 1f out: kpt on fnl f: nrst fin* 33/1
00-2 **5** ½ **Adam's Ale**[14] 1392 4-9-11 67 MickyFenton 4 60
(Paul Midgley) *in tch: pushed along and hung lft over 2f out: rdn and one pce fr over 1f out* 11/1
000- **6** 1 ¼ **Grey Destiny**[266] 4612 3-9-0 0 PaulMulrennan 7 53
(Mel Brittain) *slowly away: hld up: pushed along over 2f out: hdwy whn short of room jst ins fnl f: kpt on: nvr threatened* 66/1
36-3 **7** ¾ **Teetotal (IRE)**[19] 1284 3-9-0 62 PhillipMakin 10 51
(Nigel Tinkler) *led narrowly: hdd over 3f out: rdn 2f out: wknd fnl f* 12/1
4 **8** 1 ½ **Mr Snooks**[11] 1450 3-9-0 0 AdrianNicholls 12 46
(David Nicholls) *midfield: rdn over 2f out: wandered u.p jst ins fnl f: wknd fnl 100yds* 10/1
9 hd **The Nifty Blaze** 3-9-0 0 DavidAllan 2 54+
(Tim Easterby) *s.i.s: swtchd rt s: hld up towards inner: pushed along and sme hdwy over 1f out: short of room ins fnl f: nvr threatened* 25/1
65 **10** 7 **Amanda Wolf (IRE)**[17] 1329 3-8-9 0 JamesSullivan 13
(James Given) *hld up: a towards rr* 66/1
500- **11** 1 ½ **Val's Diamond (IRE)**[175] 7410 3-8-9 45 PJMcDonald 5
(Ann Duffield) *midfield: rdn 3f out: sn wknd* 80/1

1m 11.42s (-1.28) **Going Correction** -0.25s/f (Firm)
WFA 3 from 4yo 11lb 11 Ran SP% 119.1
Speed ratings (Par 103): **98,91,90,88,88 86,85,83,83,73 71**
toteswingers 1&2 £6.00, 1&3 £2.50, 2&3 £2.60 CSF £62.05 TOTE £10.20: £2.20, £2.40, £1.10; EX 67.30 Trifecta £181.80 Pool: £3081.16 - 12.70 winning units..
Owner D R Passant **Bred** Ms A Lynam **Trained** Malpas, Cheshire

FOCUS
The smart Jack Dexter took this maiden last year and it seems unlikely this field contained anything quite as good. The form is a bit fluid with the runner-up rated to form for now.

1688 DAVID KERFOOT CHILL-OUT H'CAP 7f
3:25 (3:26) (Class 3) (0-95,94) 4-Y-0+ £7,439 (£2,213; £1,106; £553) Stalls Low

Form RPR
-440 **1** **Dubai Dynamo**[21] 1235 8-9-1 88 PJMcDonald 5 95
(Ruth Carr) *mid-div: hdwy over 2f out: styd on wl fnl f: led nr fin* 9/2[1]
30-0 **2** nk **Xilerator (IRE)**[7] 1537 6-9-1 88 AdrianNicholls 8 94
(David Nicholls) *w ldrs: chal over 2f out: led over 1f out: hdd and no ex nr fin* 16/1
003- **3** hd **Lightning Cloud (IRE)**[182] 7240 5-9-6 93 AmyRyan 11 98+
(Kevin Ryan) *s.s: in rr: gd hdwy on outside over 2f out: styd on wl fnl f* 5/1[2]
010- **4** 1 **Wannabe King**[161] 7691 7-8-11 91 JordanNason[(7)] 10 94
(Geoffrey Harker) *chsd ldrs: drvn over 2f out: kpt on same pce last 150yds* 28/1
000- **5** 1 ¾ **Powerful Presence (IRE)**[187] 7097 7-9-0 87 GrahamGibbons 4 85
(David O'Meara) *led: hdd over 1f out: grad wknd* 8/1
210- **6** ½ **Zacynthus (IRE)**[182] 7240 5-9-1 91 [1] PatrickHills[(3)] 13 88
(Luca Cumani) *s.i.s: swtchd lft after s: in rr: hdwy over 2f out: styd on fnl f* 8/1
30-0 **7** hd **Osteopathic Remedy (IRE)**[10] 1485 9-9-7 94 TomEaves 7 90
(Michael Dods) *chsd ldrs: effrt over 2f out: fdd appr fnl f* 20/1
400- **8** 1 ¾ **Mehdi (IRE)**[197] 6835 4-9-4 91 (t) FrannyNorton 3 82
(David Nicholls) *mid-div: effrt on ins over 2f out: nvr threatened* 15/2[3]
236- **9** ½ **Toto Skyllachy**[173] 7435 8-9-0 87 DavidNolan 9 77
(David O'Meara) *mid-div: nvr a threat* 25/1
12-0 **10** nk **Chosen Character (IRE)**[21] 1235 5-9-2 92 (t) RossAtkinson[(3)] 6 81
(Tom Dascombe) *mid-div: effrt over 2f out: sn wknd* 16/1
002- **11** hd **Ardmay (IRE)**[194] 6921 4-9-1 88 PhillipMakin 1 77
(Kevin Ryan) *chsd ldrs: effrt over 2f out: wknd wl over 1f out* 8/1
11-0 **12** shd **Nameitwhatyoulike**[21] 1233 4-9-1 88 PaulMulrennan 12 76
(Michael Easterby) *s.i.s: swtchd lft after s: in rr: nvr on terms* 14/1
00-0 **13** 1 ½ **Fast Shot**[21] 1232 5-8-13 86 DavidAllan 14 70
(Tim Easterby) *a in rr* 33/1
114- **14** 1 ½ **No Poppy (IRE)**[178] 7334 5-9-0 92 AdamCarter[(5)] 2 72
(Tim Easterby) *a towards rr* 12/1

1m 25.07s (-2.13) **Going Correction** -0.125s/f (Firm) 14 Ran SP% 121.1
Speed ratings (Par 107): **107,106,106,105,103 102,102,100,99,99 99,99,97,95**
toteswingers 1&2 £30.10, 1&3 £5.30, 2&3 £28.20 CSF £73.95 CT £389.84 TOTE £5.00: £2.30, £7.00, £2.30; EX 98.70 Trifecta £732.50 Pool: £1828.53 - 1.87 winning units..
Owner The Bottom Liners **Bred** T K & Mrs P A Knox **Trained** Huby, N Yorks

FOCUS
A competitive and decent handicap, though the feeling is that the best horse didn't win. The form is rated through the runner-up backed up by the third.

1689 JAMES HERRIOT HALL - IDEAL PARTY VENUE H'CAP 1m 4f
4:00 (4:02) (Class 2) (0-100,96) 4-Y-0+ £12,938 (£2,887; £2,887; £962) Stalls Low

Form RPR
300- **1** **Itlaaq**[187] 7098 7-9-2 88 (t) GrahamGibbons 6 96
(Michael Easterby) *in tch: rdn to chal over 1f out: kpt on: led post* 28/1
100- **2** hd **Entihaa**[265] 4621 5-8-6 78 RussKennemore 8 86
(Alan Swinbank) *trckd ldr: rdn to ld over 2f out: strly pressed thrght fnl f: kpt on: hdd post* 8/1
061- **2** dht **Handsome Man (IRE)**[212] 6415 4-9-5 92 HarryBentley 7 100
(Saeed bin Suroor) *midfield: rdn and hdwy to chse ldrs 2f out: drvn and kpt on fnl f: jst failed* 5/1[3]
221- **4** nse **Suegioo (FR)**[155] 7739 4-8-12 85 (p) JimmyQuinn 3 93
(Marco Botti) *led at stdy pce: rdn whn hdd over 2f out: rallied and upsides jst ins fnl f: kpt on: jst hld* 11/4[1]
4/ **5** 1 ¾ **Oriental Fox (GER)**[202] 5-9-9 95 JoeFanning 1 100
(Mark Johnston) *trckd ldrs: rdn over 2f out: one pce* 18/1
-164 **6** nk **Mica Mika (IRE)**[20] 1273 5-8-9 81 TonyHamilton 12 86
(Richard Fahey) *prom: rdn over 2f out: ev ch tl wknd fnl 100yds* 10/1
-131 **7** 1 ¼ **Noble Silk**[77] 496 4-9-2 89 (p) LukeMorris 2 92
(Lucy Wadham) *midfield: rdn over 2f out: one pce and nvr threatened ldrs* 9/2[2]
10-4 **8** ¾ **Easy Terms**[11] 1446 6-9-10 96 JamesSullivan 5 97
(Edwin Tuer) *hld up in tch: pushed along over 2f out: nvr threatened* 7/1
00-6 **9** 1 ¼ **Nanton (USA)**[20] 1273 11-8-12 84 GrahamLee 10 83
(Jim Goldie) *hld up: pushed along over 2f out: nvr threatened* 20/1
-210 **10** 1 ½ **Suffice (IRE)**[21] 1242 4-8-4 77 oh2 PatrickMathers 9 74
(Richard Fahey) *hld up: rdn over 3f out: nvr threatened* 16/1
24-0 **11** 9 **Getabuzz**[20] 1273 5-8-8 80 DuranFentiman 11 63
(Tim Easterby) *hld up: rdn over 2f out: wknd over 1f out* 28/1

2m 36.56s (0.36) **Going Correction** -0.125s/f (Firm)
WFA 4 from 5yo+ 1lb 11 Ran SP% 117.0
Speed ratings (Par 109): **93,92,92,92,91 91,90,90,89,88 82**PL: I £7.80, H £2.10, E £3.90; EX: I/HM £8.90, I/E £178.10; CSF: I/HM £79.63, I/E £116.05; TRIFECTA: I/HM/E £796.80, I/E/HM £796.80; TRICAST: I/HM/E £621.56, I/E/HM £658.31; toteswingers I&HM £34.80, I&E £48.70, HM&E £9.80 TOTE £30.50 0.027 Trifecta £Owner Mrs Jean Turpin Bred.
■ Stewards' Enquiry : Russ Kennemore two-day ban: used whip above permitted level (May 6-7)
Jimmy Quinn two-day ban: used whip above permitted level (May 9-10)

FOCUS
Another decent handicap, but they didn't go much of a pace early and that probably contributed to a thrilling four-way photo finish. Those that raced towards the back of the field early never got a look in. The form makes sense through the winner.

1690 JW 4X4 NORTHALLERTON - LILY'S 8 TODAY H'CAP 5f
4:35 (4:35) (Class 3) (0-95,93) 3-Y-0 £7,439 (£2,213; £1,106; £553) Stalls High

Form RPR
00-1 **1** **Mayfield Girl (IRE)**[10] 1482 3-8-9 81 DavidAllan 4 87
(Mel Brittain) *chsd ldrs towards outer: rdn to chal over 1f out: led narrowly ins fnl f: kpt on* 11/2[3]
2-16 **2** hd **Bispham Green**[10] 1482 3-8-5 77 BarryMcHugh 6 82
(Richard Fahey) *w ldr: rdn to ld wl over 1f out: sn strly pressed: hdd ins fnl f: kpt on: jst hld* 11/4[2]
202- **3** 3 **Satsuma**[280] 4093 3-9-3 89 NickyMackay 5 83+
(David Brown) *trckd ldrs: rdn 2f out: kpt on one pce* 2/1[1]
411- **4** 1 **Rhagori Aur**[183] 7220 3-8-11 83 TomEaves 3 74
(Bryan Smart) *hld up in tch: pushed along 1/2-way: kpt on fnl f: nvr threatened* 8/1
050- **5** ¾ **Dream Maker (IRE)**[226] 5979 3-9-4 90 DuranFentiman 1 78
(Tim Easterby) *hld up: pushed along 1/2-way: kpt on fnl f: nvr threatened* 25/1
030- **6** ½ **Lady Poppy**[190] 7028 3-8-6 78 AndrewMullen 8 64
(George Moore) *led narrowly: rdn whn hdd wl over 1f out: wknd fnl f* 10/1
021- **7** nk **Star Up In The Sky (USA)**[237] 5620 3-8-5 77 AmyRyan 7 62
(Kevin Ryan) *w ldr: rdn 1/2-way: wknd fnl f* 9/1
20-0 **8** 2 **Effie B**[21] 1234 3-9-7 93 SamHitchcott 2 71
(Mick Channon) *s.i.s: hld up: a towards rr* 20/1

58.05s (-1.55) **Going Correction** -0.25s/f (Firm) 8 Ran SP% 114.2
Speed ratings (Par 102): **102,101,96,95,94 93,92,89**
CSF £20.97 CT £39.97 TOTE £7.90: £2.20, £1.10, £1.40; EX 26.00 Trifecta £81.00 Pool: £1197.76 - 11.07 winning units..
Owner Mel Brittain **Bred** Mark Commins **Trained** Warthill, N Yorks

FOCUS
One colt against seven fillies in this decent 3yo sprint handicap. The first two came nicely clear and the winner is rated as recording a personal-best.

1691 MICHAEL FOSTER MEMORIAL E B F CONDITIONS STKS 7f
5:10 (5:10) (Class 3) 4-Y-0+
£9,337 (£2,796; £1,398; £699; £349; £175) Stalls Low

Form RPR
0625 **1** **Arnold Lane (IRE)**[13] 1413 4-9-0 105 SamHitchcott 3 97
(Mick Channon) *trckd ldr: rdn to chal 2f out: led narrowly appr fnl f: drvn and kpt on* 10/3[2]
06-0 **2** ¾ **Majestic Myles (IRE)**[21] 1235 5-9-7 107 TonyHamilton 7 102
(Richard Fahey) *prom: led after 2f: rdn whn hdd appr fnl f: drvn ins fnl f: kpt on but a jst hld* 2/1[1]
000- **3** 1 ½ **Rodrigo De Torres**[149] 7826 6-9-7 92 FrannyNorton 2 98
(David Nicholls) *led for 2f: in tch: rdn and hdwy to chse ldng pair over 1f out: kpt on one pce* 25/1
410- **4** 1 ¼ **Set The Trend**[196] 6868 7-9-5 105 DavidNolan 1 93
(David O'Meara) *hld up in tch: rdn over 2f out: kpt on fnl f: wnt 4th post* 9/1
-110 **5** shd **Dubai Hills**[21] 1233 7-9-0 87 TomEaves 8 87
(Bryan Smart) *trckd ldrs: rdn over 2f out: drvn over 1f out: sn one pce: lost 4th post* 16/1
0-06 **6** 3 ¼ **Regal Parade**[21] 1234 9-9-0 106 (t) GrahamLee 6 79
(Milton Bradley) *hld up in tch: rdn and sme hdwy over 1f out: wknd ins fnl f* 9/1
104- **7** 2 ¼ **Pintura**[195] 6913 6-9-0 108 PhillipMakin 5 72
(Kevin Ryan) *hld up in rr: rdn over 2f out: nvr threatened* 4/1[3]
032- **8** 3 ¾ **Beacon Lodge (IRE)**[196] 6879 8-9-0 103 AdrianNicholls 4 62
(David Nicholls) *racd keenly: trckd ldr: rdn over 2f out: wknd over 1f out* 12/1

1m 24.75s (-2.45) **Going Correction** -0.125s/f (Firm) 8 Ran SP% 113.8
Speed ratings (Par 107): **109,108,106,105,104 101,98,94**
toteswingers 1&2 £2.90, 1&3 £18.60, 2&3 £12.50 CSF £10.31 TOTE £4.90: £1.80, £1.40, £4.10; EX 11.20 Trifecta £186.90 Pool: £1782.87 - 7.15 winning units..
Owner Nick & Olga Dhandsa & John & Zoe Webster **Bred** Lynn Lodge Stud **Trained** West Ilsley, Berks

FOCUS
Recent winners of this conditions race include the Group-class sprinters Tax Free, Utmost Respect, Hitchens and Markab, though the distance was increased from 6f to 7f last year. They went just a fair pace and several still had a chance coming to the last furlong. The third looks the best guide to the level.

1692 THOMAS LORD H'CAP 6f
5:45 (5:50) (Class 5) (0-75,75) 4-Y-0+ £2,587 (£770; £384; £192) Stalls High

Form RPR
30-3 **1** **Mission Impossible**[19] 1283 8-8-13 67 PatrickMathers 4 79
(Tracy Waggott) *chsd ldrs far side: rdn over 2f out: hdwy and overall ldr over 1f out: kpt on* 18/1

The Form Book Flat, Raceform Ltd, Compton, RG20 6NL.

134- **2** *nk* **Chester Aristocrat**[186] 7141 4-8-11 **70** .... JasonHart(5) 6 81
(Eric Alston) *led far side: rdn over 2f out: hdd over 1f out: kpt on: jst hld: 2nd of 7 in gp* **12/1**[3]

000- **3** *1 3/4* **Azzurra Du Caprio (IRE)**[224] 6044 5-9-7 **75** .... PJMcDonald 2 80
(Ben Haslam) *hld up far side: rdn 1/2-way: hdwy to chse ldng pair over 1f out: kpt on: 3rd of 7 in gp* **20/1**

-125 **4** *1 1/2* **Burnhope**[47] 881 4-9-4 **75** .... (p) BillyCray(3) 16 76
(Scott Dixon) *led stands' side: rdn 1/2-way: kpt on: 1st of 10 in gp* **14/1**

656- **5** *nk* **Mercers Row**[187] 7100 6-9-2 **70** .... BarryMcHugh 13 70+
(Karen Tutty) *chsd ldrs stands' side: rdn over 2f out: kpt on: 2nd of 10 in gp* **33/1**

001- **6** *nk* **Indian Trail**[213] 6358 13-8-12 **71** .... ShirleyTeasdale(5) 10 70
(David Nicholls) *hld up stands'side: rdn and hdwy over 1f out: kpt on fnl f: 3rd of 10 in gp* **33/1**

600- **7** *1* **Indego Blues**[172] 7451 4-9-6 **74** .... AdrianNicholls 14 69
(David Nicholls) *prom stands' side: rdn over 2f out: no ex fnl 100yds: 4th of 10 in gp* **12/1**[3]

0-46 **8** *nse* **Tango Sky (IRE)**[97] 196 4-9-7 **75** .... FrannyNorton 18 70
(David Nicholls) *prom stands' side: rdn over 2f out: no ex fnl f: 5th of 10 in gp* **12/1**[3]

320- **9** *1/2* **Breezolini**[180] 7291 5-9-4 **75** .... RaulDaSilva(3) 1 69
(Geoffrey Harker) *racd far side: hld up in rr: rdn 1/2-way: hdwy over 1f out: nvr threatened ldrs: 4th of 7 in gp* **14/1**

030- **10** *3/4* **Nasharra (IRE)**[165] 7607 5-9-0 **68** .... (tp) AmyRyan 15 59
(Kevin Ryan) *slowly away: hld up in rr stands' side: rdn and hdwy over 2f out: wknd fnl 100yds: 6th of 10 in gp* **18/1**

5034 **11** *1/2* **Kung Hei Fat Choy (USA)**[24] 1203 4-9-7 **75** .... (b) GrahamLee 12 65
(James Given) *hld up stands' side: rdn over 2f out: nvr threatened: 7th of 10 in gp* **5/1**[2]

-000 **12** *1* **Little Garcon (USA)**[16] 1346 6-9-4 **72** .... (p) TonyHamilton 19 59
(Robert Cowell) *chsd ldrs stands' side: rdn over 2f out: wknd fnl f: 8th of 10 in gp* **16/1**

103- **13** *1/2* **Blue Shoes (IRE)**[172] 7451 4-9-1 **69** .... DavidAllan 5 54
(Tim Easterby) *racd far side: w ldr: rdn over 2f out: wknd over 1f out: 5th of 7 in gp* **14/1**

030- **14** *3 1/2* **Planetex (IRE)**[180] 7291 4-9-6 **74** .... MichaelO'Connell 7 48
(John Quinn) *chsd ldrs far side: wknd fnl 2f: 6th of 7 in gp* **12/1**[3]

54-4 **15** *3/4* **Hello Stranger (IRE)**[19] 1283 4-8-13 **67** .... DuranFentiman 17 38
(Tim Easterby) *dwlt: hld up stands' side: rdn 1/2-way: nvr threatened: 9th of 10 in gp* **4/1**[1]

230- **16** *4* **Commanche Raider (IRE)**[190] 7023 6-9-4 **72** .... (p) TomEaves 9 31
(Michael Dods) *dwlt: sn in tch far side: wknd over 1f out: last of 7 in gp* **18/1**

550- **17** *14* **Lady Del Sol**[182] 7247 5-8-13 **67** .... PhillipMakin 11
(Marjorie Fife) *hld up stands' side: a towards rr: last of 10 in gp* **28/1**

1m 11.46s (-1.24) **Going Correction** -0.25s/f (Firm) 17 Ran SP% **123.2**
Speed ratings (Par 103): **98,97,95,93,92 92,91,91,90,89 88,87,86,82,81 75,57**
toteswingers 1&2 £46.60, 1&3 £73.30, 2&3 £48.40 CSF £211.99 CT £2424.51 TOTE £19.10: £4.70, £2.70, £4.80, £3.70; EX 316.30 Trifecta £1345.10 Part won. Pool: £1793.59 - 0.29 winning units..

Owner H Conlon **Bred** Rodney Meredith **Trained** Spennymoor, Co Durham

FOCUS
An open sprint handicap. Ten horses came stands' side, while seven went far side and the smaller group produced the first three home. The first three all stepped up on recent form.

1693 THIRSKRACECOURSE.NET FOR DISCOUNTED TICKETS ONLINE H'CAP (DIV II) 7f
6:10 (6:15) (Class 5) (0-75,75) 4-Y-0+ **£2,726** (£805; £402) **Stalls** Low

Form RPR

000- **1** **Whispered Times (USA)**[217] 6258 6-8-7 **61** oh4 .... (p) FrannyNorton 2 69
(Tracy Waggott) *trckd ldrs: t.k.h: swtchd rt over 1f out: styd on to ld last 50yds* **16/1**

20-2 **2** *nk* **Llewellyn**[10] 1459 5-9-2 **70** .... AdrianNicholls 1 77
(David Nicholls) *led rdrless to s: uns rdr s: led: edgd rt over 1f out: edgd lft ins fnl f: hdd and no ex last 50yds* **9/4**[1]

/20- **3** *1/2* **Dialogue**[385] 1135 7-8-9 **66** .... RaulDaSilva(3) 9 72
(Geoffrey Harker) *s.i.s: hdwy over 4f out: styd on fnl 2f: tk 3rd last 50yds* **11/1**

060- **4** *1/2* **Paramour**[157] 7715 6-8-13 **74** .... DavidBergin(7) 5 81+
(David O'Meara) *hld up in midfield: hdwy on ins over 2f out: nt clr run: nt clr run whn poised to chal over 1f out to post: nt rcvr* **4/1**[2]

051- **5** *3 1/2* **Star City (IRE)**[194] 6941 4-8-8 **62** .... TomEaves 7 57
(Michael Dods) *trckd ldrs: t.k.h: wknd appr fnl f* **15/2**[3]

00-0 **6** *1/2* **Viva Ronaldo (IRE)**[29] 1113 7-9-0 **75** .... SamanthaBell(7) 3 69+
(Richard Fahey) *dwlt: hdwy on ins over 2f out: nt clr run over 1f out: nvr a factor* **15/2**[3]

-200 **7** *2 1/4* **Violent Velocity (IRE)**[21] 1239 10-8-8 **69** .... KevinLundie(7) 8 56
(John Quinn) *chsd ldrs: effrt on outside over 3f out: outpcd fnl 2f* **25/1**

12-0 **8** *3/4* **Pravda Street**[10] 1460 8-9-4 **72** .... DaleSwift 4 57
(Brian Ellison) *s.i.s: hdwy over 4f out: n.m.r and swtchd rt over 1f out: nvr a factor* **17/2**

50-3 **9** *1 1/2* **Art Dzeko**[18] 1309 4-9-0 **68** .... DavidAllan 6 49
(Tim Easterby) *chsd ldrs: wknd appr fnl f* **12/1**

6-06 **10** *9* **Glenridding**[10] 1460 9-8-11 **65** .... (p) GrahamLee 10 22
(James Given) *chsd ldrs: lost pl over 1f out: bhd whn eased clsng stages* **14/1**

1m 26.17s (-1.03) **Going Correction** -0.125s/f (Firm) 10 Ran SP% **117.2**
Speed ratings (Par 103): **100,99,99,98,94 93,91,90,88,78**
toteswingers 1&2 £30.50, 1&3 £58.50, 2&3 £6.50 CSF £52.47 CT £442.48 TOTE £21.70: £5.60, £1.60, £4.00; EX 108.30 Trifecta £657.50 Part won. Pool: £876.68 - 0.10 winning units..

Owner Miss T Waggott **Bred** Hetrich-McCarthy Livestock **Trained** Spennymoor, Co Durham

FOCUS
The first four came clear of the rest and the winning time was 0.66 seconds slower than the first division. The form is rated at face value through the runner-up.

T/Plt: £60.30 to a £1 stake. Pool of £54020.51 - 653.74 winning tickets. T/Qpdt: £52.50 to a £1 stake. Pool of £2366.9 - 33.30 winning tickets. AS

1650 WOLVERHAMPTON (A.W) (L-H)
Saturday, April 20

OFFICIAL GOING: Standard
Track Gallop Mastered after 4th race.
Wind: Fresh behind Weather: Cloudy

1694 £32 BONUS AT 32RED.COM AMATEUR RIDERS' H'CAP 5f 216y(P)
6:15 (6:17) (Class 5) 4-Y-0+ **£2,495** (£774; £386; £193) **Stalls** Low

Form RPR

065- **1** **Magical Speedfit (IRE)**[211] 6439 8-10-1 **65** .... MissKMargarson(5) 3 77
(George Margarson) *broke wl: sn lost pl: hdwy over 1f out: r.o to ld wl ins fnl f* **40/1**

4524 **2** *1 1/2* **Restless Bay (IRE)**[8] 1525 5-10-2 **66** .... (b) MrDLevey(5) 1 73
(Conor Dore) *chsd ldrs: pushed along over 2f out: rdn to ld ins fnl f: sn hdd and unable qck* **8/1**[3]

461- **3** *nk* **Going French (IRE)**[218] 6195 6-10-4 **70** .... MissSLewis(7) 5 76
(Dai Burchell) *a.p: swtchd lft over 4f out: chsd ldr 1/2-way: rdn and ev ch over 1f out: edgd rt ins fnl f: styd on same pce* **16/1**

4060 **4** *hd* **Lujeanie**[30] 1096 7-10-9 **73** .... (b[1]) MrGeorgeCrate(5) 4 78
(Peter Crate) *plld hrd: led 5f out: clr 1/2-way: hung rt over 1f out: hdd ins fnl f: styd on same pce* **8/1**[3]

-141 **5** *1* **Captain Kendall (IRE)**[73] 535 4-10-13 **72** .... MrSWalker 2 74+
(David Evans) *prom: hmpd and lost pl over 4f out: hdwy over 2f out: rdn whn hmpd ins fnl f: styd on same pce* **15/8**[1]

000 **6** *nk* **Methaaly (IRE)**[8] 1516 10-9-13 **61** .... (be) MissMMullineaux(3) 8 62
(Michael Mullineaux) *hld up: rdn and r.o ins fnl f: nvr nrr* **25/1**

2625 **7** *3/4* **Welease Bwian (IRE)**[56] 775 4-9-13 **65** .... NatalieHambling-Yates(7) 12 64
(Stuart Williams) *hld up: racd wd ent st: hdwy over 1f out: edgd lft: nt trble ldrs* **11/1**

3104 **8** *2* **Angelo Poliziano**[12] 1431 7-10-2 **68** .... MrJamesHughes(7) 11 60
(Jo Hughes) *hld up: hdwy over 1f out: nvr trbld ldrs* **25/1**

-146 **9** *1/2* **Gaelic Wizard (IRE)**[66] 645 5-9-12 **64** .... MrBenFfrenchDavis(7) 7 55
(Dominic Ffrench Davis) *led 1f: chsd ldrs: rdn over 1f out: wknd fnl f* **20/1**

00-0 **10** *2* **Rigolleto (IRE)**[19] 1286 5-10-8 **72** .... MissJoannaMason(5) 6 56
(Anabel K Murphy) *prom: pushed along 1/2-way: wknd over 1f out* **50/1**

2053 **11** *1 1/2* **Holy Angel (IRE)**[16] 1351 4-10-8 **72** .... (e) MrWEasterby(5) 13 52
(Tim Easterby) *mid-div: effrt over 2f out: sn wknd* **4/1**[2]

1025 **12** *2 1/4* **M J Woodward**[19] 1283 4-10-4 **70** .... MissAimeeMKing(7) 10 42
(Paul Green) *chsd ldrs: rdn over 2f out: wknd over 1f out* **16/1**

1m 14.92s (-0.08) **Going Correction** -0.05s/f (Stan) 12 Ran SP% **114.0**
Speed ratings (Par 103): **98,96,95,95,94 93,92,89,89,86 84,81**
toteswingers 1&2 £33.20, 1&3 £88.50, 2&3 £29.90 CSF £308.85 CT £5273.99 TOTE £36.00: £16.10, £2.30, £5.20; EX 146.30 Trifecta £777.90 Part won. Pool: £1037.27 - 0.64 winning units..

Owner Graham Lodge Partnership **Bred** John Malone **Trained** Newmarket, Suffolk

FOCUS
A furiously run sprint handicap and, with plenty of these running wide off the home turn, it was those ridden towards the inside that held a definite advantage.

1695 FOLEY STEELS H'CAP 5f 216y(P)
6:45 (6:45) (Class 6) (0-60,60) 3-Y-0 **£1,940** (£577; £288; £144) **Stalls** Low

Form RPR

0-43 **1** **Eastern Dragon (IRE)**[17] 1315 3-9-4 **60** .... LeeTopliss(3) 4 69
(Michael Scudamore) *sn outpcd: hdwy over 2f out: led over 1f out: rdn out* **4/1**[2]

5325 **2** *1 1/2* **Petite Georgia (IRE)**[39] 977 3-9-4 **57** .... TonyCulhane 7 61
(George Baker) *prom: pushed along over 2f out: nt clr run over 1f out: rdn to chse wnr ins fnl f: styd on* **5/1**[3]

-005 **3** *2* **Claude Greenwood**[29] 1118 3-9-1 **57** .... (p) DarrenEgan(3) 5 55
(David Simcock) *sn outpcd: rdn over 1f out: nt clr run and swtchd rt ins fnl f: r.o to go 3rd post: nt rch ldrs* **16/1**

60-5 **4** *nk* **Wildcrafting**[14] 1384 3-9-4 **57** .... HayleyTurner 3 54+
(Michael Bell) *trckd ldrs: shkn up over 1f out: styd on* **7/1**

4U21 **5** *hd* **Jordanstown**[16] 1349 3-9-4 **57** .... (p) NeilCallan 8 53
(Kevin Ryan) *chsd ldrs: rdn over 2f out: styd on same pce ins fnl f* **9/4**[1]

3525 **6** *1/2* **Princess Cammie (IRE)**[16] 1345 3-8-8 **54** .... IanBurns(7) 6 49
(Mike Murphy) *led 1f: chsd ldr: rdn and ev ch over 1f out: no ex ins fnl f* **8/1**

3266 **7** *3 1/4* **Marmot Bay (IRE)**[2] 1651 3-8-10 **54** .... (b[1]) JemmaMarshall(5) 2 38
(David Flood) *led 5f out: rdn and hdd over 1f out: wknd ins fnl f* **16/1**

004- **8** *2 1/4* **Shes Ellie**[216] 6276 3-9-6 **59** .... ShaneKelly 1 36
(Jo Hughes) *broke wl: lost pl 5f out: n.d after* **7/1**

1m 14.9s (-0.10) **Going Correction** -0.05s/f (Stan) 8 Ran SP% **115.3**
Speed ratings (Par 96): **98,96,93,92,92 92,87,84**
toteswingers 1&2 £5.60, 1&3 £8.60, 2&3 £21.40 CSF £24.52 CT £287.20 TOTE £5.30: £2.00, £1.70, £3.80; EX 24.80 Trifecta £259.80 Pool: £1130.93 - 3.26 winning units..

Owner Chua Ong Salthouse **Bred** James Mahon **Trained** Bromsash, H'fords

1696 SPEC LTD (S) STKS 1m 141y(P)
7:15 (7:15) (Class 6) 3-Y-0+ **£1,940** (£577; £288; £144) **Stalls** Low

Form RPR

3111 **1** **Saharia (IRE)**[17] 1322 6-10-0 77 .... (v) ShaneKelly 3 67+
(Daniel Mark Loughnane) *hld up: hdwy over 1f out: led on bit wl ins fnl f: comf* **4/9**[1]

0004 **2** *nk* **Satwa Laird**[4] 1600 7-9-9 62 .... HayleyTurner 2 61
(Conor Dore) *a.p: chsd ldr over 1f out: sn edgd lft: rdn and ev ch ins fnl f: styd on* **4/1**[2]

040- **3** *1 3/4* **Shomberg**[147] 7867 4-9-9 51 .... DavidProbert 5 57
(Dai Burchell) *led at stdy pce tl qcknd 3f out: rdn clr 2f out: edgd lft and hdd wl ins fnl f* **25/1**

00/ **4** *4* **Mr Opulence**[46] 6951 4-9-9 0 .... RenatoSouza 1 48?
(Jo Hughes) *s.i.s: sn chsng ldrs: rdn over 2f out: styd on same pce fr over 1f out* **28/1**

063- **5** *1 3/4* **Aciano (IRE)**[14] 8047 5-9-9 66 .... (tp) SteveDrowne 4 44
(Brendan Powell) *chsd ldr: rdn over 2f out: lost 2nd over 1f out: wknd ins fnl f* **13/2**[3]

1m 51.75s (1.25) **Going Correction** -0.05s/f (Stan) 5 Ran SP% **109.9**
Speed ratings (Par 101): **92,91,90,86,85**
CSF £2.55 TOTE £1.40: £1.02, £2.40; EX 2.70 Trifecta £18.40 Pool: £1894.55 - 77.19 winning units..The winner was bought in for 7,500gns

Owner Brooklands Racing **Bred** Woodcote Stud Ltd **Trained** Baldwin's Gate, Staffs

1697 32RED FILLIES' H'CAP 1m 141y(P)

7:45 (7:47) (Class 5) (0-70,70) 3-Y-0 £2,587 (£770; £384; £192) Stalls Low

Form RPR

404- 1 Of Course Darling[179] 7312 3-9-6 69 RyanMoore 10 74
(Ed Dunlop) *led: hdd over 7f out: led again over 6f out: hdd over 5f out: chsd ldr: rdn to ld 1f out: r.o* 3/1[1]

01- 2 ½ Oilinda[168] 7552 3-9-4 67 HayleyTurner 5 71
(Michael Bell) *racd keenly: trckd ldr tl led over 7f out: hdd over 6f out: led again over 5f out: rdn and hdd 1f out: edgd lft: styd on* 3/1[1]

0-51 3 1¾ Brynford[15] 1367 3-8-4 56 DarrenEgan(3) 6 56
(Chris Dwyer) *chsd ldrs: rdn and edgd lft over 1f out: styd on* 9/1

00-4 4 ½ Dalaway (IRE)[15] 1364 3-8-12 61 MartinHarley 3 60+
(Mick Channon) *hld up: hdwy and nt clr run over 1f out: r.o: nt trble ldrs* 7/1

1- 5 nk Elle Rebelle[306] 3208 3-9-5 68 EddieAhern 8 66
(Mark Brisbourne) *trckd ldrs: plld hrd: rdn over 1f out: styd on same pce ins fnl f* 14/1

1-44 6 1¾ Azma (USA)[59] 731 3-9-7 70 (b[1]) MartinDwyer 2 64
(Conrad Allen) *s.i.s and hmpd s: outpcd: r.o ins fnl f: nvr nrr* 11/2[2]

441- 7 1½ Aeronwyn Bryn (IRE)[215] 6318 3-8-13 65 (t) LeeTopliss(3) 7 56
(Michael Dods) *s.i.s: sn pushed along and prom: rdn over 1f out: wknd ins fnl f* 6/1[3]

54-6 8 hd Boleyn[17] 1319 3-9-0 63 LiamKeniry 1 53
(Olly Stevens) *wnt rt s: hld up: rdn over 1f out: nvr on terms* 14/1

1m 50.3s (-0.20) **Going Correction** -0.05s/f (Stan) 8 Ran SP% **115.5**
Speed ratings (Par 95): **98,97,96,95,95 93,92,92**
toteswingers 1&2 £2.40, 1&3 £7.50, 2&3 £4.40 CSF £11.75 CT £71.69 TOTE £3.80: £1.60, £1.50, £2.50; EX 15.20 Trifecta £93.10 Pool: £1599.17 - 12.87 winning units..
Owner Gredley, Hurley, ORS & Stanley **Bred** New England Stud & Middle Park Stud Ltd **Trained** Newmarket, Suffolk

FOCUS
An informative fillies' handicap, dominated by the market principals who were allowed to set some very modest fractions out in front.

1698 32RED.COM MAIDEN FILLIES' STKS 1m 1f 103y(P)

8:15 (8:17) (Class 5) 3-Y-0+ £2,587 (£770; £384; £192) Stalls Low

Form RPR

- 1 Woodland Aria 3-8-11 0 WilliamBuick 4 86+
(John Gosden) *s.i.s: hld up: swtchd rt and hdwy over 1f out: shkn up to ld wl ins fnl f: readily* 4/1[2]

03- 2 ½ Elik (IRE)[179] 7312 3-8-11 0 RyanMoore 6 83
(Sir Michael Stoute) *trckd ldrs: racd keenly: wnt 2nd over 6f out: shkn up to ld 1f out: rdn and hdd wl ins fnl f* 5/6[1]

3 1¼ Speckled (USA) 3-8-11 0 AhmedAjtebi 1 80
(Mahmood Al Zarooni) *led 1f: chsd ldrs: rdn over 1f out: styd on same pce ins fnl f* 12/1

04- 4 2½ Waverunner[156] 7721 3-8-11 0 SilvestreDeSousa 8 75
(Mahmood Al Zarooni) *a.p: shkn up over 1f out: no ex ins fnl f* 5/1[3]

0-2 5 nk Lovesome[15] 1371 3-8-11 0 HayleyTurner 3 74
(Michael Bell) *w ldr tl led over 8f out: rdn and hdd 1f out: no ex ins fnl f* 8/1

0 6 13 Whitefall (USA)[3] 1624 3-8-11 0 SteveDrowne 7 47
(David Evans) *s.i.s: a bhd* 50/1

64-4 7 1¾ Uganda Glory (USA)[26] 1174 3-8-11 58 TonyCulhane 5 44
(George Baker) *stdd s: hld up: bhd fnl 6f* 50/1

1m 59.56s (-2.14) **Going Correction** -0.05s/f (Stan) 7 Ran SP% **113.9**
Speed ratings (Par 100): **107,106,105,103,102 91,89**
toteswingers 1&2 £1.70, 1&3 £9.10, 2&3 £7.60 CSF £7.65 TOTE £6.30: £2.70, £1.30; EX 11.80 Trifecta £71.30 Pool: £2458.29 - 25.85 winning units..
Owner R J H Geffen **Bred** Wardall Bloodstock **Trained** Newmarket, Suffolk

FOCUS
A potentially decent maiden for the track.

1699 32RED CASINO H'CAP 1m 1f 103y(P)

8:45 (8:46) (Class 5) (0-75,75) 4-Y-0+ £2,587 (£770; £384; £192) Stalls Low

Form RPR

1040 1 Idol Deputy (FR)[17] 1327 7-9-5 73 (p) KirstyMilczarek 8 83
(James Bennett) *hld up: hdwy over 1f out: rdn to ld wl ins fnl f: r.o* 20/1

1-46 2 ¾ Syncopate[11] 1448 4-9-1 69 LiamKeniry 6 77
(Pam Sly) *chsd ldr tl lft in ld over 6f out: rdn: edgd rt and hdd wl ins fnl f* 7/2[1]

2031 3 ¾ Delightful Sleep[14] 1401 5-8-7 61 oh1 SilvestreDeSousa 4 67
(David Evans) *hld up: hdwy over 5f out: rdn over 1f out: r.o* 5/1[3]

205- 4 ¾ Hurakan (IRE)[162] 7672 7-8-11 70 (p) ThomasBrown(5) 5 75
(Richard Price) *a.p: rdn over 1f out: styd on* 8/1

2121 5 1½ Officer In Command (USA)[9] 1496 7-9-2 75 (vt) NicoleNordblad(5) 3 77
(Hans Adielsson) *s.s: hld up: hdwy over 1f out: nt rch ldrs* 4/1[2]

0034 6 2½ Standpoint[17] 1333 7-9-4 72 HayleyTurner 11 68
(Conor Dore) *chsd ldrs: lft 2nd over 6f out: rdn over 1f out: wknd ins fnl f* 14/1

6413 7 2¼ Yourinthewill (USA)[16] 1353 5-9-1 69 ShaneKelly 10 61
(Daniel Mark Loughnane) *hld up: hdwy over 5f out: rdn over 2f out: edgd lft and styd on same pce fr over 1f out* 12/1

20-4 8 1 Time To Dance[16] 1354 4-8-12 66 EddieAhern 9 56
(Joseph Tuite) *prom: rdn over 1f out: wknd fnl f* 11/2

342- 9 2¼ Bold Cross (IRE)[182] 7250 10-8-8 65 MarkCoumbe(3) 2 50
(Edward Bevan) *s.s: hld up: rdn over 2f out: wknd over 1f out* 12/1

00-0 10 3½ Oratory (IRE)[38] 984 7-9-3 71 MartinHarley 7 49
(Noel Quinlan) *s.s: hld up: a in rr: rdn and wknd over 2f out* 16/1

5-60 P Hurricane Hymnbook (USA)[84] 403 8-8-9 63 JamieMackay 1
(Willie Musson) *led: wnt wrong and hdd over 6f out: sn p.u* 20/1

1m 59.69s (-2.01) **Going Correction** -0.05s/f (Stan) 11 Ran SP% **122.8**
Speed ratings (Par 103): **106,105,104,104,102 100,98,97,95,92**
toteswingers 1&2 £23.40, 1&3 £25.60, 2&3 £5.20 CSF £93.00 CT £419.13 TOTE £13.50: £4.40, £2.00, £2.00; EX 139.20 Trifecta £1305.30 Part won. Pool: £1740.49 - 0.49 winning units..
Owner Miss J C Blackwell **Bred** Sheikh Sultan Bin Khalifa Al Nayan **Trained** Letcombe Bassett, Oxon

FOCUS
A fair handicap, run at a decent pace and it saw a career-best effort from a course specialist.

1700 32REDPOKER.COM H'CAP 1m 4f 50y(P)

9:15 (9:15) (Class 6) (0-60,57) 4-Y-0+ £1,940 (£577; £288; £72; £72) Stalls Low

Form RPR

062 1 Gabrial's Hope (FR)[16] 1342 4-9-3 57 (t) DarrenEgan(3) 1 64
(David Simcock) *led: hdd over 10f out: trckd ldr: plld hrd: led wl over 1f out: sn rdn: edgd lft ins fnl f: styd on* 15/8[1]

00-6 2 2¼ Iguacu[12] 1434 9-8-11 52 (p) ThomasBrown(5) 7 55
(Richard Price) *hld up: rdn over 2f out: swtchd rt and hdwy over 1f out: r.o to go 2nd post: nt rch wnr* 14/1

4-03 3 nk Irons On Fire (USA)[8] 1513 5-8-13 49 [1] MartinDwyer 6 52
(Alastair Lidderdale) *led at stdy pce over 10f out: qcknd over 2f out: rdn and hdd wl over 1f out: styd on same pce ins fnl f* 9/2[3]

000- 4 nk Kian's Joy[127] 6807 4-8-5 45 DeclanCannon(3) 4 47
(Jedd O'Keeffe) *chsd ldrs: rdn over 1f out: styd on same pce ins fnl f* 18/1

3005 4 dht Aviso (GER)[23] 747 9-9-0 55 (p) DeclanBates(5) 9 57
(David Evans) *hld up: rdn over 1f out: r.o ins fnl f: nvr nrr* 14/1

6- 6 ½ Lac Sacre (FR)[13] 4-8-8 45 (p) DavidProbert 8 47
(Tony Carroll) *hld up: hdwy over 4f out: rdn over 2f out: styd on same pce fnl f* 11/4[2]

-504 7 ½ Rubi Dia[8] 1520 6-9-1 51 (vt) LiamKeniry 2 52
(Sean Curran) *chsd ldrs: rdn over 1f out: no ex ins fnl f* 8/1

0-06 8 5 Sassi Sioux[32] 1082 4-8-1 45 NoelGarbutt(7) 3 38
(Tom Keddy) *plld hrd and prom: stdd and lost pl over 10f out: rdn and wknd fnl 2f* 40/1

2m 40.68s (-0.42) **Going Correction** -0.05s/f (Stan)
WFA 4 from 5yo+ 1lb 8 Ran SP% **111.8**
Speed ratings (Par 101): **99,97,97,97,97 96,96,93**
toteswingers 1&2 £8.70, 1&3 £2.10, 2&3 £14.10 CSF £28.54 CT £102.16 TOTE £2.90: £1.10, £3.70, £1.60; EX 41.10 Trifecta £282.60 Pool: £1699.98 - 4.51 winning units..
Owner Dr Marwan Koukash **Bred** Mrs G Forien & G Forien **Trained** Newmarket, Suffolk

FOCUS
A tactically run and moderate affair but plenty to like about the effort of the winner.
T/Plt: £93.70 to a £1 stake. Pool of £68,440.46 - 532.70 winning tickets. T/Qpdt: £3.60 to a £1 stake. Pool of £5651.90 - 1153.30 winning tickets. CR

1701 - 1703a (Foreign Racing) - See Raceform Interactive

NAAS (L-H)

Saturday, April 20

OFFICIAL GOING: Soft (soft to heavy for 100yds by furlong pole)

1704a WOODLANDS STKS (LISTED RACE) 5f

3:55 (3:57) 3-Y-0+ £21,138 (£6,178; £2,926; £325; £325)

RPR

1 Maarek[165] 7624 6-10-0 114 SeamieHeffernan 2 118+
(David Peter Nagle, Ire) *trckd ldr on far side tl swtchd to join main gp in centre of trck bef 1/2-way: pushed along to ld ent fnl f: sn qcknd clr: comf* 5/2[1]

2 1½ Scream Blue Murder (IRE)[288] 3835 3-8-8 95 ShaneGray 7 98
(T Stack, Ire) *chsd ldrs in main centre gp: pushed along in 5th appr fnl f: styd on wl to go 2nd fnl 100yds wout troubling wnr* 16/1

3 1½ Red Dubawi (IRE)[21] 1255 5-9-9 100 FergalLynch 5 101
(David Marnane, Ire) *w.w in rr: tk clsr order over 1f out but nt pce to chal: styd on wl to go 3rd on line* 20/1

4 hd Doc Hay (USA)[161] 7690 6-9-12 DanielTudhope 3 103
(David O'Meara) *bit slowly away and racd towards rr: pushed along to take cl order appr fnl f in 4th: no ex fnl 100yds* 4/1[3]

4 dht Roseraie (IRE)[190] 7038 3-8-8 94 ChrisHayes 6 91
(Kevin Prendergast, Ire) *broke wl and sn settled jst bhd ldrs: pushed along and nt qckn ins fnl 2f then kpt on wl again clsng stages* 25/1

6 ½ Leitir Mor (IRE)[189] 7050 3-9-2 117 (tp) KevinManning 9 98
(J S Bolger, Ire) *broke wl and sn led centre trck gp: 2nd 1/2-way: pushed along and wknd ent fnl f* 9/2

7 2½ Cape Of Approval (IRE)[21] 1255 4-9-9 102 WayneLordan 8 90
(T Stack, Ire) *bit slowly away: a in rr: no threat over 1f out* 10/3[2]

8 2 My Girl Anna (IRE)[196] 6869 6-9-7 105 RoryCleary 4 80
(Muredach Kelly, Ire) *trckd ldr of centre trck gp: 3rd 1/2-way: sn pushed along: wknd 1f out* 8/1

9 6 Nero Emperor (IRE)[176] 7390 4-9-9 95 (e[1]) WJLee 1 61
(T Stack, Ire) *broke wl and led on far side: jnd main gp in centre bef 1/2-way: hdd ent fnl f and wknd qckly: eased* 20/1

1m 5.34s (3.34)
WFA 3 from 4yo+ 10lb 9 Ran SP% **120.2**
CSF £44.98 TOTE £3.40: £1.40, £3.30, £3.40; DF 50.00.
Owner Lisbunny Syndicate **Bred** New England Stud & P J & P M Vela **Trained** Fethard, Co Tipperary

FOCUS
This was fairly straightforward for the winner.

1705 - 1707a (Foreign Racing) - See Raceform Interactive

KREFELD (R-H)

Sunday, April 21

OFFICIAL GOING: Turf: good

1708a GROSSER EHRMANN CUP - DR BUSCH-MEMORIAL (GROUP 3) (3YO) (TURF) 1m 110y

4:30 (5:30) 3-Y-0

£26,016 (£8,943; £4,471; £2,439; £1,626; £1,219)

RPR

1 Chopin (GER)[154] 3-9-2 0 AStarke 4 114+
(A Wohler, Germany) *trckd ldr on inner: rdn on turn into st: r.o to ld 2f out: drew clr ent fnl f: drvn rt out: impressive* 16/5[2]

2 8 Global Bang (GER)[184] 3-9-2 0 AndreaAtzeni 5 96
(Mario Hofer, Germany) *hld up in last: rdn and hdwy fr 3f out: hung rt u.p but r.o to go 2nd cl home: no ch w wnr* 19/5

3 nk Ideal (GER)[20] 3-9-2 0 LennartHammer-Hansen 3 96
(Ferdinand J Leve, Germany) *hld up towards rr: rdn on turn into st: r.o to go 3rd fnl strides: no ch w wnr* 104/10

4 *nk* **Wake Forest (GER)**[184] 3-9-2 0 EPedroza 1 95
(A Wohler, Germany) *midfield on inner: rdn and ev ch 2f out: outpcd by wnr over 1f out: kpt on but dropped to 4th fnl strides* **8/5**[1]
5 *1 ¾* **Limario (GER)**[189] 7091 3-9-2 0 APietsch 2 91
(R Dzubasz, Germany) *led: rdn and strly pressed on turn into st: hdd 2f out: sn outpcd by wnr: kpt on: dropped to 5th ins fnl f* **17/5**[3]
6 *shd* **Anatol Artist (GER)**[161] 7698 3-9-2 0 ADeVries 7 91
(J Hirschberger, Germany) *trckd ldr on outer: rdn to chal on turn into st: ev ch 2f out: outpcd over 1f out: plugged on u.p* **32/5**
7 *8* **Maurice (GER)**[167] 7597 3-9-2 0 THellier 6 73
(S Smrczek, Germany) *midfield on outer: rdn and outpcd over 2f out: last and btn ent fnl f: eased* **236/10**

1m 43.71s (-2.89) 7 Ran SP% **132.2**
WIN (incl. 10 euro stake): 42. PLACES: 23, 28. SF: 223.
Owner Gestut Graditz **Bred** Gestut Graditz **Trained** Germany

SAN SIRO (R-H)
Sunday, April 21

OFFICIAL GOING: Turf: heavy

1709a PREMIO AMBROSIANO (GROUP 3) (4YO+) (TURF) 1m 2f
3:40 (12:00) 4-Y-0+ **£22,764** (£10,016; £5,463; £2,731)

RPR
1 **Orpello (IRE)**[210] 6554 4-8-11 0 (b) FabioBranca 6 107
(S Botti, Italy) *mde all: rdn 2f out: styd on wl u.p and drew clr ins fnl f: v readily* **19/10**[2]
2 *4* **Vola E Va**[14] 4-8-11 0 DarioVargiu 7 99
(B Grizzetti, Italy) *trckd ldr in 2nd: rdn 2f out: chsd wnr thrght fnl 1 1/2f: styd on but nvr on terms* **11/4**[3]
3 *3* **Delicatezza**[301] 3426 4-8-8 0 NicolaPinna 2 90+
(E Botti, Italy) *hld up in tch: rdn 3f out: wnt 3rd 2f out: styd on but nvr remotely dangerous* **13/10**[1]
4 *2* **Storming Loose**[203] 6727 6-8-11 0 GArena 5 89
(B Grizzetti, Italy) *hld up in tch: rdn 3f out: sn outpcd: plugged on for n.d 4th* **11/4**[3]
5 *4* **Mister Sandro (ITY)**[28] 4-8-11 0 LManiezzi 4 81
(S Botti, Italy) *midfield: rdn over 2f out: outpcd and btn over 1f out: fdd* **29/10**
6 *5* **Pattaya (ITY)**[14] 5-9-0 0 MEsposito 3 74
(S Botti, Italy) *dwlt: hld up and last thrght: rdn 3f out: sn outpcd and btn: nvr a factor* **29/10**

2m 20.5s (13.80) 6 Ran SP% **182.6**
WIN (incl. 1 euro stake): 2.91. PLACES: 2.23, 2.28. DF: 13.46.
Owner Effevi **Bred** Deni Srl & Effevi Snc **Trained** Italy

1611 KEMPTON (A.W) (R-H)
Monday, April 22

OFFICIAL GOING: Standard
Wind: medium, behind Weather: dry,cloudy with bright spells

1710 MASCOT GRAND NATIONAL 06.05.13 CLASSIFIED STKS 7f (P)
2:20 (2:22) (Class 6) 3-Y-0+ **£1,940** (£577; £288; £144) **Stalls** Low

Form RPR
64-5 **1** **Shahrazad (IRE)**[40] 980 4-9-8 50 (t) SilvestreDeSousa 5 59
(Patrick Gilligan) *mde all: rdn wl over 1f out: styd on wl fnl f* **12/1**
3412 **2** *½* **Black Truffle (FR)**[19] 1319 3-8-9 55 (v) RichardHughes 7 53
(Mark Usher) *hld up in tch in midfield: travelled wl tl asked for effrt and hdwy over 1f out: pressed wnr and drvn wl ins fnl f: kpt on cl home* **3/1**[1]
-034 **3** *½* **Otto The First**[19] 1320 3-8-9 50 MickaelBarzalona 6 52
(John Best) *chsd ldrs: effrt u.p and chsd wnr 1f out: lost 2nd and styd on same pce fnl 100yds* **20/1**
000- **4** *1 ½* **Thomasina**[210] 6533 3-8-9 52 TedDurcan 2 48
(Denis Coakley) *in tch in midfield: drvn and unable qck over 1f out: kpt on u.p ins fnl f* **7/1**
6-41 **5** *¾* **Idle Curiosity (IRE)**[19] 1319 3-8-9 55 HayleyTurner 1 46
(Jim Boyle) *chsd ldrs: drvn and effrt 2f out: no ex 1f out: wknd wl ins fnl f* **7/2**[2]
606- **6** *1* **Poetic Belle**[191] 7056 3-8-9 55 (v[1]) KierenFallon 13 43
(Alan Jarvis) *chsd wnr: drvn and unable qck over 1f out: lost 2nd 1f out: wknd fnl 100yds* **8/1**
0000 **7** *½* **Tartaria**[12] 1472 7-9-8 47 MarcHalford 9 47
(Edward Creighton) *stdd s and dropped out in rr: stl plenty to do and hdwy 1f out: styd on wl fnl f: nvr trbld ldrs* **66/1**
404- **8** *shd* **Men Don't Cry (IRE)**[152] 7816 4-9-8 54 (b) LiamKeniry 12 46
(Ed de Giles) *t.k.h: hld up towards rr: hdwy on inner jst over 2f out: racd awkwardly u.p but kpt on ins fnl f* **6/1**[3]
00-0 **9** *¾* **Princely Sum (IRE)**[21] 1294 4-9-8 50 (t) AndreaAtzeni 8 44
(Stuart Williams) *dwlt: sn rdn along towards rr: hdwy into midfield: drvn 3f out: kpt on ins fnl f: nvr trbld ldrs* **33/1**
40-0 **10** *hd* **Marie's Fantasy**[26] 1196 4-9-8 54 IanMongan 10 44
(Zoe Davison) *hld up in midfield: drvn and effrt wl over 1f out: kpt on but nvr threatened ldrs* **33/1**
40-4 **11** *2* **Bubblina**[89] 332 6-9-8 53 MartinHarley 4 38
(Alastair Lidderdale) *hld up towards rr: rdn and effrt wl over 1f out: keeping on but n.d whn nt clr run 1f out: n.d* **10/1**
600- **12** *shd* **Foie Gras**[208] 6583 3-8-9 55 MartinDwyer 11 33
(William Muir) *hld up in last quartet: rdn and no imp 2f out: n.d* **16/1**
0-05 **13** *23* **Boyzee**[29] 1162 5-9-8 53 SteveDrowne 14
(Linda Jewell) *stdd and dropped in bhd after s: lost tch wl over 2f out: sn t.o* **33/1**

1m 26.62s (0.62) **Going Correction** 0.0s/f (Stan)
WFA 3 from 4yo+ 13lb 13 Ran SP% **122.9**
Speed ratings (Par 101): **96,95,94,93,92 91,90,90,89,89 87,86,60**
toteswingers 1&2 £8.40, 1&3 £20.10, 2&3 £8.70 CSF £47.21 TOTE £14.80: £4.50, £1.80, £4.40; EX 73.50 Trifecta £981.00 Pool: £2740.38 - 2.09 winning units..
Owner Linton Doolan **Bred** Shadwell Estate Company Limited **Trained** Newmarket, Suffolk

FOCUS
A moderate classified stakes in which it paid to be ridden prominently, as the first six turning for home occupied those positions at the line. The winner's early maiden form could be rated this high.

1711 BETVICTOR.COM MEDIAN AUCTION MAIDEN STKS 7f (P)
2:50 (2:52) (Class 5) 3-4-Y-0 **£2,587** (£770; £384; £192) **Stalls** Low

Form RPR
2- **1** **Secret Talent**[156] 7773 3-9-1 0 RyanMoore 5 91
(Hughie Morrison) *mde all: rdn and qcknd clr 2f out: sn wl clr: r.o wl: easily* **4/5**[1]
0- **2** *7* **Nelson Quay (IRE)**[206] 6636 3-9-1 0 SteveDrowne 1 72
(Jeremy Gask) *chsd ldrs: rdn and wnt 2nd but outpcd by wnr 2f out: wl hld after but kpt on for clr 2nd* **16/1**[3]
4- **3** *7* **Perfect Calm (USA)**[195] 6966 3-8-10 0 RichardHughes 6 48
(Richard Hannon) *chsd wnr tl 2f out: sn outpcd and wl btn: jst hld on to 3rd* **7/4**[2]
00- **4** *nse* **Bertie Moon**[180] 7324 3-9-1 0 LiamKeniry 4 53
(Geoffrey Deacon) *t.k.h: hld up in midfield: no ch w wnr but hdwy over 1f out: kpt on to press for 3rd cl home: n.d* **66/1**
05 **5** *1 ½* **Meetha Achar**[36] 1051 3-8-5 0 NathanAlison(5) 2 44
(Jim Boyle) *t.k.h: hld up in midfield: rdn and outpcd jst over 2f out: wnt modest 4th over 1f out: no imp* **50/1**
04- **6** *¾* **The Ginger Berry**[124] 8172 3-9-1 0 SeanLevey 8 47
(Dr Jon Scargill) *hld up in last quartet: rdn and outpcd over 2f out: no ch fnl 2f: plugged on* **33/1**
4- **7** *¾* **Certavi (IRE)**[310] 3155 4-10-0 0 KirstyMilczarek 9 50
(Brendan Powell) *t.k.h: chsd ldrs: rdn and outpcd jst over 2f out: no ch wl over 1f out* **33/1**
0/6 **8** *¾* **South Kenter (USA)**[88] 350 4-10-0 0 (t) TomQueally 10 48
(Heather Main) *in tch in midfield: rdn and outpcd jst over 2f out: wl hld whn edgd rt over 1f out* **50/1**
4- **9** *6* **Ningbo Express (IRE)**[175] 7433 3-8-10 0 J-PGuillambert 11 22
(Rae Guest) *stdd and dropped in bhd after s: a bhd: lost tch 2f out* **16/1**[3]
10 *4* **Let's Rhumba** 3-8-10 0 ChrisCatlin 7
(Rae Guest) *s.i.s: a bhd: lost tch 2f out* **16/1**[3]

1m 26.77s (0.77) **Going Correction** 0.0s/f (Stan)
WFA 3 from 4yo 13lb 10 Ran SP% **120.9**
Speed ratings (Par 103): **95,87,79,78,77 76,75,74,67,63**
toteswingers 1&2 £3.50, 1&3 £1.10, 2&3 £3.60 CSF £17.40 TOTE £1.70: £1.10, £3.60, £1.10; EX 16.60 Trifecta £42.90 Pool: £3745.78 - 65.46 winning units..
Owner Wood Street Syndicate IV **Bred** J P Repard **Trained** East Ilsley, Berks

FOCUS
This maiden appeared to be a match on paper, although in the end it was a procession for the favourite. The time was 0.15secs slower than the preceding contest, otherwise the winner could be rated higher.

1712 DOWNLOAD THE BETVICTOR SPINCAST APP H'CAP 1m (P)
3:20 (3:20) (Class 6) (0-65,65) 3-Y-0 **£1,940** (£577; £288; £144) **Stalls** Low

Form RPR
040- **1** **Order Of Service**[248] 5325 3-9-5 **63** SeanLevey 8 70
(David Brown) *sn led and mde rest: rdn and wnt clr w rival 2f out: forged ahd ins fnl f: kpt on wl u.p: drvn out* **5/1**[3]
125 **2** *½* **Shearian**[14] 1428 3-8-13 **62** WilliamTwiston-Davies(5) 2 68
(Tony Carroll) *hld up in last quartet: rdn and hdwy over 2f out: chsd clr ldng pair 1f out: swtchd rt and r.o strly ins fnl f: wnt 2nd last stride: nt quite rch wnr* **20/1**
011- **3** *shd* **Mushaakis (IRE)**[186] 7190 3-9-6 **64** DaneO'Neill 3 70
(Mark Johnston) *chsd ldrs: rdn and effrt to chal and drew clr w wnr 2f out: sustained duel w wnr tl no ex fnl 100yds: lost 2nd last stride* **10/3**[1]
00-6 **4** *1 ¾* **Loraine**[20] 1300 3-9-0 **58** FergusSweeney 14 60+
(Jamie Osborne) *t.k.h: hld up in rr: rdn and gd hdwy over 1f out: styd on strly ins fnl f: nt rch ldrs* **33/1**
000- **5** *1* **Bountiful Bess**[140] 7965 3-9-4 **62** LiamKeniry 1 61
(Pam Sly) *in tch in midfield: rdn and effrt on inner 2f out: chsd clr ldng pair over 1f out: styd on same pce ins fnl f* **33/1**
525- **6** *2 ¼* **Red Tulip**[144] 7924 3-9-3 **61** MartinLane 12 55+
(James Fanshawe) *stdd after s: hld up in last quartet: rdn and hdwy on inner 2f out: styd on same pce and no imp fnl f* **12/1**
55-5 **7** *3 ½* **Ishisoba**[14] 1424 3-9-2 **60** MartinHarley 5 46
(Alastair Lidderdale) *hld up in midfield: rdn and effrt jst over 2f out: no imp u.p over 1f out: plugged on fnl f* **20/1**
02-4 **8** *nk* **Day In Day Out**[27] 1177 3-9-7 **65** JimCrowley 6 51
(Ralph Beckett) *chsd ldr tl jst over 2f out: wknd u.p over 1f out* **4/1**[2]
343- **9** *2 ¼* **Secretori**[209] 6564 3-9-5 **63** J-PGuillambert 13 43
(Jo Hughes) *t.k.h: hld up in last quartet: rdn and effrt ent fnl 2f: no imp: n.d* **33/1**
2424 **10** *¾* **Close Together (IRE)**[20] 1301 3-9-4 **62** (b[1]) RyanMoore 9 41
(Robert Mills) *in tch in midfield: rdn and outpcd ent fnl 2f: wknd over 1f out* **12/1**
065- **11** *nk* **Hot Mustard**[185] 7223 3-9-4 **62** HayleyTurner 4 40
(Michael Bell) *in tch in midfield: rdn and struggling over 2f out: wknd u.p over 1f out* **20/1**
01-6 **12** *½* **Sutton Sid**[21] 1312 3-9-4 **62** (b[1]) PatCosgrave 10 39
(George Baker) *dwlt: sn pushed along and rcvrd: hdwy to chse ldrs 6f out: drvn and struggling jst over 2f out: wknd wl over 1f out* **16/1**
-544 **13** *4 ½* **Give Me High Five**[21] 1289 3-9-1 **59** RichardHughes 11 25
(Richard Hannon) *a towards rr: rdn over 3f out: no hdwy: bhd over 1f out* **7/1**
334 **14** *8* **Half Turn**[16] 1384 3-9-5 **63** SteveDrowne 7 11
(Luke Dace) *t.k.h: w wnr for 1f: snatched up and chsd ldrs fr 6f out tl lost pl over 2f out: wl bhd fnl f* **16/1**

1m 39.97s (0.17) **Going Correction** 0.0s/f (Stan) 14 Ran SP% **122.5**
Speed ratings (Par 96): **99,98,98,96,95 93,89,89,87,86 86,85,81,73**
toteswingers 1&2 £26.90, 1&3 £5.00, 2&3 £8.10 CSF £110.04 CT £392.31 TOTE £8.50: £1.80, £6.80, £1.90; EX 100.30 Trifecta £779.00 Pool: £1608.87 - 1.54 winning units..
Owner J C Fretwell **Bred** Cheveley Park Stud Ltd **Trained** Averham Park, Notts

FOCUS
A modest but competitive handicap with the whole field covered by just 7lb. There are some positives to be taken from the form.

1713 GET THE BETVICTOR APP/BRITISH STALLION STUDS E.B.F MAIDEN STKS 1m (P)
3:50 (3:50) (Class 5) 3-Y-0 **£3,881** (£1,155; £577; £288) **Stalls** Low

Form RPR
02- **1** **Pether's Moon (IRE)**[180] 7323 3-9-5 0 RichardHughes 11 87
(Richard Hannon) *mde all: rdn over 1f out: kpt on wl ins fnl f: rdn out* **7/4**[1]

6- **2** *1* **Thatchmaster (USA)**[296] 3611 3-9-5 0 MickaelBarzalona 2 84
(Mahmood Al Zarooni) *chsd ldr for 2f: chsd ldrs after: rdn and effrt on inner 2f out: chsd wnr 1f out: kpt on same pce u.p ins fnl f* **9/2**[3]

03- **3** *2* **Evangelist**[256] 5005 3-9-5 0 RyanMoore 14 80
(Sir Michael Stoute) *chsd ldrs tl wnt 2nd 6f out: drvn and ev ch 2f out: 3rd and outpcd 1f out: kpt on same pce after* **7/2**[2]

6 **4** *3 ½* **Sedenoo**[14] 1423 3-9-5 0 MartinHarley 10 72
(Marco Botti) *chsd ldrs: rdn and outpcd ent fnl 2f: 4th and wl hld fnl f: kpt on* **6/1**

5 *½* **Love Excel** 3-9-5 0 WilliamCarson 4 70
(Charles Hills) *in tch in midfield: rdn and unable qck 2f out: styd on same pce and no threat to ldrs fr over 1f out* **33/1**

6 *1 ¼* **Atlantic Isle (GER)** 3-9-0 0 TomQueally 6 63
(Sir Henry Cecil) *hld up in midfield: rdn and outpcd jst over 2f out: no threat to ldrs and kpt on same pce fr over 1f out* **16/1**

7 *hd* **Midaz** 3-9-5 0 JimmyFortune 5 67+
(Hughie Morrison) *s.i.s: hld up towards rr: sme hdwy wl over 1f out: no threat to ldrs but kpt on steadily fnl f* **16/1**

8 *½* **Masquerading (IRE)** 3-9-5 0 TedDurcan 12 66+
(David Lanigan) *stdd s: hld up in tch in rr: effrt and edging rt 2f out: no imp over 1f out: n.d but kpt on ins fnl f: eased cl home* **50/1**

5-0 **9** *4 ½* **Algorithmic (IRE)**[14] 1423 3-9-5 0 MartinLane 3 56+
(Michael Bell) *s.i.s: a in rr: outpcd and rdn over 2f out: n.d and styd on same pce fr over 1f out* **50/1**

10 *½* **Investment Expert (IRE)** 3-9-5 0 WilliamBuick 1 55
(Jeremy Noseda) *hld up in tch in last quartet: effrt jst over 2f out: green and carried hd high u.p: wknd over 1f out* **25/1**

3 **11** *2* **Naaz (IRE)**[21] 1291 3-9-2 0 AshleyMorgan(3) 9 50
(Ed Dunlop) *t.k.h: hld up in midfield: rdn and dropped to rr over 2f out: n.d fnl 2f* **20/1**

-0 **12** *7* **Mojave Desert (IRE)**[22] 1272 3-9-0 0 KierenFallon 7 45
(Mark Johnston) *chsd ldrs: rdn and lost pl over 2f out: wl bhd and virtually p.u ins fnl f* **25/1**

1m 39.53s (-0.27) **Going Correction** 0.0s/f (Stan) 12 Ran SP% **122.1**
Speed ratings (Par 98): **101,100,98,94,94 92,92,92,87,87 85,78**
toteswingers 1&2 £2.90, 1&3 £2.90, 2&3 £3.10 CSF £9.17 TOTE £2.30: £2.20, £1.40, £1.10; EX 10.20 Trifecta £31.80 Pool: £2341.87 - 55.14 winning units..
Owner John Manley **Bred** Michael G Daly **Trained** East Everleigh, Wilts

FOCUS
Another maiden and again the winner made all with nothing coming from off the pace. The time was 0.44secs faster than the preceding contest. The favourite set a good standard and the form is rated around him.

1714 BETVICTOR CASINO ON YOUR MOBILE H'CAP 7f (P)
4:20 (4:21) (Class 4) (0-85,84) 3-Y-O **£4,690** (£1,395; £697; £348) **Stalls** Low

Form RPR

32-1 **1** **Bright Strike (USA)**[26] 1199 3-9-7 **84** WilliamBuick 9 97+
(John Gosden) *hld up in tch in rr: hdwy 2f out: rdn and qcknd to ld ent fnl f: clr and idling ins fnl f: comf* **9/4**[1]

01-1 **2** *2 ¾* **Intrigo**[12] 1476 3-8-11 **74** RichardHughes 5 79
(Richard Hannon) *chsd ldr tl wnt upsides over 2f out: rdn to ld wl over 1f out: hdd and outpcd by wnr ent fnl f: kpt on for clr 2nd* **7/2**[2]

43-0 **3** *1 ¾* **Kimberella**[31] 1112 3-9-7 **84** TomQueally 4 84
(Michael Bell) *t.k.h: hld up in midfield: hdwy u.p over 1f out: wnt 3rd jst ins fnl f: kpt on but no imp after* **16/1**

021- **4** *½* **Excuse To Linger**[221] 6177 3-9-3 **80** RyanMoore 7 79+
(Jeremy Noseda) *hld up in rr: effrt and rdn jst over 2f out: hdwy over 1f out: kpt on ins fnl f: no threat to wnr* **6/1**

221- **5** *nk* **Nenge Mboko**[165] 7653 3-9-0 **77** (p) PatCosgrave 8 75
(George Baker) *in tch in midfield: rdn and unable qck wl over 1f out: kpt on same pce u.p fnl f* **25/1**

4311 **6** *1 ¼* **Byroness**[5] 817 3-8-7 **75** RyanTate(5) 1 70
(Heather Main) *chsd ldrs: rdn and effrt to press ldrs wl over 1f out: no ex and outpcd jst over 1f out: wknd ins fnl f* **16/1**

14- **7** *¾* **Plunder**[121] 8223 3-9-2 **79** PhillipMakin 2 72
(Kevin Ryan) *t.k.h: led: rdn and hdd wl over 1f out: wknd fnl f* **9/2**[3]

0-23 **8** *nk* **Isis Blue**[20] 1307 3-8-7 **70** AndreaAtzeni 6 62+
(Rod Millman) *t.k.h: hld up in tch: rdn and outpcd jst over 2f out: wl hld but kpt on ins fnl f* **5/1**

010- **9** *6* **Complexity**[212] 6469 3-9-4 **81** WilliamCarson 3 57
(Charles Hills) *t.k.h: hld up in tch towards rr: rdn and btn wl over 1f out: bhd fnl f* **33/1**

1m 25.45s (-0.55) **Going Correction** 0.0s/f (Stan) 9 Ran SP% **120.7**
Speed ratings (Par 100): **103,99,97,97,96 95,94,94,87**
CSF £10.71 CT £104.48 TOTE £2.90: £1.70, £1.40, £3.00; EX 9.90 Trifecta £149.60 Pool: £3003.57 - 15.05 winning units..
Owner George Strawbridge **Bred** George Strawbridge Jr **Trained** Newmarket, Suffolk

FOCUS
The principal race of the meeting and a decent 3yo handicap. The time was unsurprisingly 1.17secs faster than the quicker of the earlier races over the trip. Three of the first four were unexposed or progressive.

1715 FOLLOW US ON TWITTER @BETVICTORRACING H'CAP (DIV I) 1m 3f (P)
4:50 (4:50) (Class 6) (0-65,65) 4-Y-O+ **£1,940** (£577; £288; £144) **Stalls** Low

Form RPR

3-05 **1** **Foxhaven**[51] 866 11-9-2 **65** (v) ThomasBrown(5) 4 73
(Patrick Chamings) *chsd ldr: rdn to ld wl over 1f out: styd on wl ins fnl f: rdn out* **5/1**[3]

4301 **2** *1 ¾* **Shirataki (IRE)**[18] 1342 5-8-12 **63** PatMillman(7) 8 68
(Peter Hiatt) *in tch in midfield: swtchd lft and effrt jst over 2f out: chsd wnr jst ins fnl f: kpt on but no imp* **4/1**[2]

3213 **3** *1* **Thane Of Cawdor (IRE)**[14] 1434 4-8-13 **57** LiamKeniry 10 60
(Joseph Tuite) *hld up in rr: hdwy u.p ent fnl f: styd on wl to go 3rd cl home* **4/1**[2]

6-03 **4** *hd* **Mister Green (FR)**[16] 1386 7-9-0 **63** WilliamTwiston-Davies(5) 1 66
(David Flood) *chsd ldrs: rdn and effrt over 1f out: no ex and styd on same pce fnl 100yds* **10/1**

0426 **5** *3* **Beggers Belief**[33] 1090 5-8-4 **55** (b) JoeyHaynes(7) 9 52
(Eric Wheeler) *chsd ldrs: rdn and effrt ent fnl 2f: keeping on same pce whn rdr dropped reins briefly ent fnl f: wknd fnl 100yds* **12/1**

1-05 **6** *hd* **Monopoli**[34] 1076 4-9-7 **65** RichardThomas 6 62
(Daniel Kubler) *hld up in last trio: swtchd lft and effrt u.p wl over 1f out: kpt on fnl f: nvr trbld ldrs* **12/1**

404 **7** *¾* **Rowlestone Lad**[10] 1522 6-9-2 **60** RussKennemore 7 56
(John Flint) *taken down early: hld up in tch in rr: effrt on inner ent fnl 2f: no imp u.p over 1f out* **20/1**

6-62 **8** *¾* **Al Amaan**[26] 1207 8-9-4 **62** (p) RyanMoore 5 56
(Gary Moore) *in tch in midfield: drvn and unable qck ent fnl 2f: wknd 1f out* **11/4**[1]

0-64 **9** *5* **Cape Joy (IRE)**[12] 1480 4-8-13 **57** PatDobbs 3 42
(Richard Hannon) *led tl rdn and hdd wl over 1f out: sn btn: wknd 1f out* **16/1**

2m 22.64s (0.74) **Going Correction** 0.0s/f (Stan) 9 Ran SP% **118.5**
Speed ratings (Par 101): **97,95,95,94,92 92,91,91,87**
toteswingers 1&2 £4.80, 1&3 £3.90, 2&3 £2.70 CSF £26.06 CT £88.97 TOTE £6.00: £2.10, £1.90, £1.40; EX 29.60 Trifecta £101.80 Pool: £2657.27 - 19.56 winning units..
Owner The Foxford House Partnership **Bred** Highclere Stud Ltd **Trained** Baughurst, Hants

FOCUS
The first division of this modest handicap was run much slower than the second, and the form is muddling.

1716 FOLLOW US ON TWITTER @BETVICTORRACING H'CAP (DIV II) 1m 3f (P)
5:20 (5:20) (Class 6) (0-65,65) 4-Y-O+ **£1,940** (£577; £288; £144) **Stalls** Low

Form RPR

0062 **1** **King Olav (UAE)**[32] 1097 8-9-6 **64** KirstyMilczarek 10 78+
(Tony Carroll) *pushed along leaving stalls and sn led: mde rest: rdn and qcknd clr 2f out: in n.d after: easily* **5/1**[3]

220 **2** *6* **Mount Abora (IRE)**[28] 1175 6-9-4 **62** IanMongan 4 63
(Laura Mongan) *t.k.h: hld up in rr: hdwy u.p over 1f out: styd on wl u.p to go 2nd last strides: no ch w wnr* **15/2**

053- **3** *hd* **Glens Wobbly**[334] 2395 5-8-2 **51** oh6 RyanTate(5) 3 52
(Jonathan Geake) *chsd ldrs: rdn to chse wnr but outpcd ent fnl 2f: no imp and kpt on same pce fnl f: lost 2nd last strides* **50/1**

3-21 **4** *¾* **Stag Hill (IRE)**[12] 1466 4-8-6 **57** JoeyHaynes(7) 1 56
(Bernard Llewellyn) *hld up towards rr: hdwy on inner over 2f out: no ch w wnr but pressing for placings over 1f out: styd on same pce* **9/4**[1]

1653 **5** *1 ½* **Fonterutoli (IRE)**[11] 1498 6-8-13 **57** (e) AdamBeschizza 2 54
(Roger Ingram) *in tch in midfield: effrt over 2f out: outpcd by wnr but pressing for placings over 1f out: wknd ins fnl f* **10/1**

-663 **6** *½* **Standing Strong (IRE)**[20] 1298 5-9-5 **63** (p) LiamKeniry 7 59
(Zoe Davison) *t.k.h: hld up in tch in last quartet: hdwy over 2f out: sn outpcd by wnr and rdn: no threat and kpt on one pce after* **9/2**[2]

00-0 **7** *4 ½* **Kingscombe (USA)**[12] 1466 4-9-2 **60** SteveDrowne 5 48
(Linda Jewell) *hld up in tch in midfield: hung rt and lost pl jst over 2f out: continued to hang and wl btn over 1f out* **25/1**

/6-3 **8** *1* **Guardi (IRE)**[19] 1317 4-9-4 **62** TedDurcan 8 48
(Dean Ivory) *hld up in tch in rr: outpcd and rdn jst over 2f out: wl hld after* **5/1**[3]

5-60 **9** *5* **Drummond**[23] 1239 4-9-0 **65** DanielMuscutt(7) 9 42
(Bernard Llewellyn) *chsd wnr tl ent fnl 2f: sn lost pl and bhd over 1f out* **14/1**

3-4 **10** *21* **With Hindsight (IRE)**[37] 1045 5-8-13 **62** SladeO'Hara(5) 6
(Peter Grayson) *styd wd: chsd ldrs tl lost pl qckly wl over 2f out: t.o over 1f out* **25/1**

2m 19.9s (-2.00) **Going Correction** 0.0s/f (Stan) 10 Ran SP% **119.5**
Speed ratings (Par 101): **107,102,102,101,100 100,97,96,92,77**
toteswingers 1&2 £5.50, 1&3 £38.00, 2&3 £25.00, CSF £42.52 CT £1692.59 TOTE £5.50: £1.40, £3.10, £11.70; EX 53.30 Trifecta £1850.60 Part won..
Owner Cover Point Racing **Bred** Darley **Trained** Cropthorne, Worcs
■ Stewards' Enquiry : Adam Beschizza two-day ban: careless riding (May 6-7)

FOCUS
The second leg of this Class 6 handicap was run 2.7secs faster than the first. The form is rated around the second and is believable, despite the third being out of the wights.

1717 BOOK KEMPTON TICKETS ON 0844 579 3008 H'CAP 7f (P)
5:55 (5:55) (Class 6) (0-65,64) 4-Y-O+ **£1,940** (£577; £288; £144) **Stalls** Low

Form RPR

0-33 **1** **Midnight Feast**[14] 1426 5-9-7 **64** (v[1]) KierenFox 4 72
(Lee Carter) *stdd s: t.k.h: hld up in rr: hmpd and swtchd lft over 1f out: str run ins fnl f to ld last stride* **9/4**[1]

-536 **2** *shd* **Homeward Strut**[10] 1516 4-9-7 **64** (b) IanMongan 9 71
(Laura Mongan) *chsd ldrs: ev ch and pushed lft 2f out: drvn to ld over 1f out: kpt on u.p tl hdd last stride* **8/1**

5-13 **3** *½* **South Cape**[54] 813 10-8-12 **62** NedCurtis(7) 6 68
(Gary Moore) *hld up in tch in rr: hdwy on inner 2f out: chsd ldrs 1f out: kpt on u.p fnl 100yds* **6/1**[3]

000- **4** *hd* **Mishrif (USA)**[115] 8268 7-9-6 **63** (b) PatDobbs 10 68
(J R Jenkins) *t.k.h: w ldr: ev ch and rdn whn pushed rt 2f out: no ex and styd on same pce ins fnl f* **16/1**

60-0 **5** *¾* **Intomist (IRE)**[26] 1193 4-8-11 **59** NathanAlison(5) 5 62
(Jim Boyle) *in tch in midfield: rdn and ev ch 1f out: no ex and one pce fnl 100yds* **14/1**

2123 **6** *nse* **West Leake (IRE)**[14] 1426 7-9-7 **64** LiamKeniry 7 67+
(Paul Burgoyne) *t.k.h: hld up in tch in midfield: nt clr run 2f out: rdn and effrt over 1f out: kpt on same pce ins fnl f* **4/1**[2]

3634 **7** *1 ½* **Welsh Inlet (IRE)**[40] 980 5-8-12 **60** WilliamTwiston-Davies(5) 8 59
(John Bridger) *in tch in midfield: nt clr run over 1f out: drvn and one pce ins fnl f* **14/1**

260- **8** *¾* **Darnathean**[115] 8263 4-9-2 **59** (b) WilliamCarson 2 58+
(Paul D'Arcy) *t.k.h: hld up in tch towards rr: effrt over 1f out: nt clr run and swtchd rt jst ins fnl f: nvr able to chal* **6/1**[3]

0-26 **9** *hd* **Perfect Ch'l (IRE)**[14] 1426 6-9-3 **60** (p) JimmyFortune 1 56
(Paul Fitzsimons) *chsd ldrs: rdn and led over 1f out: sn hdd and no ex: losing pl and sltly hmpd ins fnl f* **12/1**

0006 **10** *10* **Demoiselle Bond**[20] 1304 5-8-9 **52** SteveDrowne 3 21
(Lydia Richards) *sn led: rdn and wnt lft 2f out: hdd over 1f out: sn wknd* **33/1**

1m 26.51s (0.51) **Going Correction** 0.0s/f (Stan) 10 Ran SP% **120.3**
Speed ratings (Par 101): **97,96,96,96,95 95,93,92,92,80**
toteswingers 1&2 £5.40, 1&3 £3.80, 2&3 £10.30 CSF £21.94 CT £101.33 TOTE £3.00: £1.30, £1.70, £3.30; EX 27.50 Trifecta £85.60 Pool: £1502.05 - 13.15 winning units..
Owner One More Bid Partnership **Bred** Whitsbury Manor Stud **Trained** Epsom, Surrey
■ Stewards' Enquiry : Pat Dobbs four-day ban: used whip above permitted level (May 6-9)

FOCUS
The fourth race of the afternoon run over 7f and the time compared well with the first two races. The winner is rated up slightly on recent form.
T/Plt: £11.70 to a £1 stake. Pool of £50,294.81 - 3115.91 winning tickets. T/Qpdt: £4.90 to a £1 stake. Pool of £2570.70 - 388 winning tickets. SP

1442 PONTEFRACT (L-H)

Monday, April 22

OFFICIAL GOING: Good (7.9)

Wind: Moderarte across Weather: Grey cloud

1718 BHEST RACING TO SCHOOL MAIDEN FILLIES' STKS 5f

2:10 (2:11) (Class 5) 2-Y-O **£3,234** (£962; £481; £240) **Stalls** Low

Form RPR

4 **1** **Mops Angel**[31] 1108 2-9-0 0 AndrewMullen 6 72+
(Michael Appleby) *trckd ldrs on inner: hdwy 2f out: swtchd rt and rdn to chse ldr over 1f out: led ins fnl f: styd on wl* **4/1**[2]

2 1¾ **Hello Beautiful (IRE)** 2-9-0 0 PJMcDonald 2 66+
(Ann Duffield) *trckd ldng pair: smooth hdwy 1/2-way: chal 2f out: led 1 1/2f out: rdn and hdd ins fnl f: kpt on same pce* **9/2**[3]

3 2¾ **Heskin (IRE)** 2-9-0 0 PaulHanagan 7 59+
(Richard Fahey) *dwlt and towards rr: hdwy 2f out: rdn to chse ldrs over 1f out: kpt on wl* **10/3**[1]

6 **4** 1¾ **Dotesy (IRE)**[7] 1573 2-9-0 0 MichaelO'Connell 8 50
(John Quinn) *in tch: hdwy 2f out: rdn over 1f out: kpt on same pce* **12/1**

4 **5** 8 **Shelley's Choice (IRE)**[16] 1399 2-9-0 0 StephenCraine 4 21
(Tom Dascombe) *qckly away: led: rdn and edgd lft wl over 1f out: sn hdd & wknd* **13/2**

6 2 **Lady Captain (IRE)** 2-9-0 0 AmyRyan 12 22+
(Kevin Ryan) *hmpd s: sn swtchd lft and in rr: hdwy whn hmpd and swtchd lft wl over 1f out: nt clr run on inner and swtchd rt ent fnl f: green and kpt on: nrst fin* **16/1**

7 1½ **Madame Mirasol (IRE)** 2-9-0 0 NeilCallan 5 8
(Kevin Ryan) *cl up: rdn along 1/2-way: grad wknd* **10/1**

8 1¾ **She's A Lucky Lady** 2-8-7 0 JakePayne(7) 11 2
(Bill Turner) *a towards rr* **18/1**

0 **9** 2¾ **Jazzy Lady (IRE)**[7] 1573 2-9-0 0 LukeMorris 9
(David Evans) *a towards rr* **66/1**

10 1¼ **Queenie's Home** 2-9-0 0 GrahamLee 10
(James Given) *chsd ldrs: rdn along 2f out: sn wknd* **11/1**

0 **11** 4½ **Doncaster Belle (IRE)**[5] 1605 2-9-0 0 DanielTudhope 16
(Charles Smith) *in tch on outer: rdn along 1/2-way: sn outpcd* **100/1**

12 1¼ **Red Dakota (IRE)** 2-9-0 0 AdrianNicholls 14
(David C Griffiths) *wnt lft s: chsd ldrs on wd outside: rdn along over 2f out: sn wknd* **50/1**

13 5 **Lady Liz** 2-9-0 0 TomEaves 1
(George Moore) *sn rdn along: a outpcd and bhd* **33/1**

1m 4.56s (1.26) **Going Correction** +0.05s/f (Good) 13 Ran SP% **118.2**
Speed ratings (Par 89): **91,88,83,81,68 65,62,59,55,53 46,44,36**
toteswingers 1&2 £5.60, 1&3 £3.70, 2&3 £4.60 CSF £21.82 TOTE £4.70: £1.90, £2.40, £1.50; EX 30.20 Trifecta £96.70 Pool: £2473.14 - 19.17 winning units..
Owner Sarnian Racing **Bred** Michael Appleby **Trained** Danethorpe, Notts

FOCUS
An informative juvenile event. The first four were well clear and the form, already rated at the top end of the race averages, could be rated higher.

1719 PONTEFRACT'S GOT TALENT NIGHT ON 7TH JUNE H'CAP 1m 4f 8y

2:40 (2:40) (Class 4) (0-80,78) 3-Y-O **£5,175** (£1,540; £769; £384) **Stalls** Low

Form RPR

-631 **1** **Blue Wave (IRE)**[12] 1470 3-9-7 **78** JoeFanning 2 89
(Mark Johnston) *set stdy pce: qcknd over 4f out: rdn and qcknd clr wl over 1f out: styd on strly* **2/1**[1]

416- **2** 8 **Noble Bull (IRE)**[234] 5786 3-9-4 **75** RobertWinston 1 73
(Charles Hills) *t.k.h: hld up: swtchd rt and rdn over 2f out: styd on u.p ent fnl f: no ch w wnr* **6/1**[3]

26-3 **3** 3¼ **Gabrial The Thug (FR)**[54] 814 3-8-13 **70** PaulHanagan 5 63
(Richard Fahey) *cl up: effrt over 2f out: sn rdn along and one pce fr wl over 1f out* **9/4**[2]

-421 **4** 22 **Masaadr**[38] 1009 3-9-0 **71** (p) NeilCallan 4 51
(James Tate) *trckd ldng pair: hdwy over 2f out: rdn to chse wnr wl over 1f out: wknd ent fnl f: sn bhd and eased* **9/4**[2]

2m 42.73s (1.93) **Going Correction** -0.075s/f (Good) 4 Ran SP% **109.2**
Speed ratings (Par 100): **90,84,82,67**
CSF £12.67 TOTE £2.20; EX 13.20 Trifecta £15.90 Pool: £1032.12 - 48.62 winning units..
Owner Sheikh Hamdan Bin Mohammed Al Maktoum **Bred** Tom Darcy And Vincent McCarthy **Trained** Middleham Moor, N Yorks
■ Dorfman was withdrawn after spreading a plate at the start.

FOCUS
This had looked competitive handicap on paper and, with three of the four runners sharing favouritism just moments before the off, punters clearly found it difficult to split them. However, the race itself proved very different and was turned into a procession by the winner. The form is taken at something like face value.

1720 RIU PALACE MELONERAS H'CAP 6f

3:10 (3:12) (Class 2) (0-100,100) 4-Y-O+

£12,450 (£3,728; £1,398; £1,398; £466; £234) **Stalls** Low

Form RPR

2456 **1** **York Glory (USA)**[9] 1537 5-9-1 **94** (b) NeilCallan 14 103+
(Kevin Ryan) *stdd and swtchd lft s: hld up towards rr: stdy hdwy on inner over 2f out: trckd ldrs whn nt clr run and swtchd rt jst over 1f out: rdn to chal ins fnl f: led last 100yds: kpt on wl* **17/2**

-430 **2** nk **Galician**[16] 1385 4-8-9 **88** FrannyNorton 1 96
(Mark Johnston) *trckd ldrs on inner: hdwy to chse ldr 1/2-way: rdn to ld appr fnl f: drvn and hdd last 100yds: kpt on* **4/1**[2]

0660 **3** ¾ **Santefisio**[60] 744 7-9-7 **100** (b) JoeFanning 12 106
(Keith Dalgleish) *stdd and swtchd lft s: hld up in rr: hdwy on inner 2f out: chsd ldrs ent fnl f: sn rdn and kpt on: nrst fin* **25/1**

1313 **3** dht **Al's Memory (IRE)**[16] 1385 4-8-7 **86** LukeMorris 2 92
(David Evans) *chsd ldrs: hdwy 1/2-way: rdn and ev ch over 1f out: drvn ins fnl f: kpt on same pce* **17/2**

050- **5** 1 **Singeur (IRE)**[191] 7063 6-8-13 **92** RobertWinston 4 94
(Robin Bastiman) *in tch: hdwy over 2f out: rdn to chse ldrs over 1f out: drvn and one pce ins fnl f* **20/1**

140- **6** ½ **Misplaced Fortune**[184] 7240 8-8-9 **93** JasonHart(5) 10 94
(Nigel Tinkler) *midfield: hdwy 2f out: rdn to chse ldrs over 1f out: sn swtchd rt and kpt on wl towards fin* **33/1**

0-00 **7** 2½ **Colonel Mak**[9] 1537 6-8-13 **92** GrahamGibbons 7 85
(David Barron) *led: rdn along wl over 1f out: hdd appr fnl f and sn wknd* **16/1**

00-3 **8** 2¼ **Head Space (IRE)**[5] 1607 5-8-8 **87** JamesSullivan 6 73+
(Ruth Carr) *midfield: hdwy 2f out: sn rdn and no imp* **15/2**[3]

314- **9** 3¼ **Escape To Glory (USA)**[213] 6432 5-8-10 **89** PaulMulrennan 8 64
(Michael Dods) *a towards rr* **14/1**

000- **10** 8 **Sir Reginald**[184] 7240 5-8-9 **88** PaulHanagan 9 38+
(Richard Fahey) *prom: rdn along wl over 2f out: sn wknd* **7/2**[1]

10-0 **11** 1¾ **All Or Nothin (IRE)**[23] 1232 4-8-4 **86** JulieBurke(3) 11 30+
(John Quinn) *a towards rr* **16/1**

3423 **12** 1 **Haftohaf**[17] 1363 4-8-7 **86** oh9 (p) NickyMackay 5 27+
(Marco Botti) *cl up: rdn along over 2f out: sn wknd* **17/2**

0010 **13** 3¾ **Thunderball**[9] 1537 7-8-13 **95** (p) BillyCray(3) 13 24+
(Scott Dixon) *prom on wd outside: rdn along wl over 2f out: sn wknd* **40/1**

-026 **14** 1¾ **Red Aggressor (IRE)**[23] 1245 4-8-0 **86** oh1 IanBurns(7) 3
(Clive Brittain) *midfield: hdwy to chse ldrs 1/2-way: sn rdn along and wknd wl over 1f out* **25/1**

1m 15.76s (-1.14) **Going Correction** +0.05s/f (Good) 14 Ran SP% **121.8**
Speed ratings (Par 109): **109,108,107,107,106 105,102,99,94,84 81,80,75,73**
PL: S £3.30, AM £1.60; TRIFECTA: YG/G/S £1088.40, YG/G/AM £77.60; TRICAST: YG/G/S £432.94, YG/G/AM £158.58; toteswingers YG&G £6.80, G&S £15.20, YG&S £21.50, G&AM £3.10, YG&AM £6.10 CSF £40.23 TOTE £8.50: £2.40, £2.20; EX 60.50 TRIFECTA Part won..

FOCUS
A strong turnout for the feature sprint handicap. The second and dead-heater Al's Memory set the level.

1721 PONTEFRACT MARATHON H'CAP 2m 5f 122y

3:40 (3:41) (Class 5) (0-75,75) 4-Y-O+ **£3,234** (£962; £481; £240) **Stalls** Low

Form RPR

6-11 **1** **Kazbow (IRE)**[62] 713 7-9-12 **75** (t) FrederikTylicki 8 86+
(Richard Ford) *mde all: set stdy pce: qcknd over 3f out: rdn clr 2f out: styd on wl* **4/1**[2]

02-3 **2** 4½ **Stickleback**[13] 1445 4-8-1 **56** oh1 (p) JamesSullivan 2 63
(Micky Hammond) *hld up towards rr: hdwy over 4f out: rdn along wl over 2f out: chsd wnr ent fnl f: no imp* **7/2**[1]

030- **3** 1½ **Riptide**[107] 6493 7-9-10 **73** (p) PaulMulrennan 1 78
(Michael Scudamore) *in tch: pushed along 4f out: rdn to chse wnr 2f out: sn drvn and plugged on same pce* **6/1**

04-0 **4** 3¼ **My Arch**[13] 1445 11-9-8 **71** GrahamLee 9 73
(Ollie Pears) *towards rr: hdwy and in tch 1/2-way: rdn along and outpcd 3f out: kpt on u.p fnl f: tk 4th nr fin* **17/2**

000- **5** 1½ **Jeu De Roseau (IRE)**[165] 4590 9-9-0 **63** PaulHanagan 5 64
(Chris Grant) *in tch: pushed along 5f out: rdn to chse ldrs 3f out: plugged on one pce fnl 2f: lost 4th towards fin* **9/2**[3]

-400 **6** 10 **Father Shine (IRE)**[3] 1445 10-8-7 **56** oh7 DuranFentiman 12 48
(Shaun Harris) *trckd ldrs: hdwy to trck wnr after 6f: rdn along 4f out: drvn 3f out and sn wknd* **33/1**

300/ **7** 7 **Galley Slave (IRE)**[55] 2874 8-8-0 **56** oh11 (t) DanielleMooney(7) 4 42
(Michael Chapman) *hld up: a bhd* **80/1**

3/33 **8** 1¾ **Kalamill (IRE)**[38] 1018 6-9-7 **70** LukeMorris 10 54
(Shaun Lycett) *trckd ldrs: hdwy 7f out: rdn along 4f out: grad wknd* **8/1**

0-00 **9** 2¾ **Maid Of Meft**[13] 1445 6-8-13 **62** MickyFenton 3 44
(Paul Midgley) *hld up in rr: hdwy 5f out: chsd ldrs over 3f out: sn rdn and wknd wl over 1f out* **12/1**

230- **10** 29 **Bijou Dan**[195] 6956 12-8-7 **56** oh1 PJMcDonald 6 12
(George Moore) *prom: rdn along over 4f out: drvn 3f out: sn wknd* **18/1**

0/0- **11** 13 **Go Amwell**[40] 6769 10-8-4 **56** oh10 (v) JulieBurke(3) 7
(J R Jenkins) *hld up towards rr: hdwy over 5f out: rdn along 4f out: sn wknd* **33/1**

4m 55.33s (4.33) **Going Correction** -0.075s/f (Good)
WFA 4 from 6yo+ 6lb 11 Ran SP% **116.4**
Speed ratings (Par 103): **89,87,86,85,85 81,78,78,77,66 62**
toteswingers 1&2 £1.60, 1&3 £5.50, 2&3 £4.80 CSF £17.98 CT £83.10 TOTE £5.90: £1.50, £1.70, £2.80; EX 18.30 Trifecta £100.50 Pool: £2244.48 - 16.74 winning units..
Owner The Most Wanted Partnership **Bred** Airlie Stud **Trained** Garstang, Lancs

FOCUS
A decent renewal of this marathon handicap and it was hard not be impressed by the performance of the winner. The relevance of the form is limited with the second and third not sure to repeat this over shorter.

1722 SUBSCRIBE ONLINE @ RACINGUK.COM MAIDEN STKS 6f

4:10 (4:15) (Class 5) 3-Y-O+ **£3,234** (£962; £481; £240) **Stalls** Low

Form RPR

424- **1** **Mayaasem**[270] 4507 3-9-0 77 PaulHanagan 4 84
(Charles Hills) *trckd ldng pair: hdwy on outer 2f out: rdn to ld and hung lft over 1f out: edgd lft ins fnl f: styd on* **3/1**[3]

0- **2** 1½ **Bastion (USA)**[172] 7497 3-9-0 0 GrahamLee 1 79
(Roger Varian) *t.k.h: trckd ldng pair on inner: effrt 2f out and sn ev ch: rdn over 1f out: hld whn n.m.r and one pce ins fnl f* **5/2**[2]

432- **3** 1¾ **Anderton (IRE)**[192] 7031 3-9-0 72 TonyHamilton 2 74
(Richard Fahey) *slt ld: rdn 2f out: drvn whn hdd and hmpd over 1f out: one pce after* **15/8**[1]

0 **4** 3¼ **Burren View Lady (IRE)**[16] 1392 3-8-9 0 DavidAllan 3 58
(Tim Easterby) *in rr: pushed along 3f out: sn rdn: kpt on appr fnl f: n.d* **50/1**

5 nk **Sarjinsky (IRE)**[256] 3-9-0 0 RobertWinston 5 62
(Peter Chapple-Hyam) *cl up: rdn along over 2f out: wknd over 1f out* **4/1**

0 **6** 9 **Trixie Malone**[16] 1392 3-8-9 0 MichaelO'Connell 6 28
(Mrs K Burke) *t.k.h: hld up in rr: pushed along 3f out: sn rdn and outpcd* **66/1**

1m 17.1s (0.20) **Going Correction** +0.05s/f (Good) 6 Ran SP% **111.8**
Speed ratings (Par 103): **100,98,95,91,90 78**
toteswingers 1&2 £2.40, 1&3 £2.40, 2&3 £1.40 CSF £10.83 TOTE £3.70: £1.80, £1.80; EX 14.90 Trifecta £24.20 Pool: £3437.95 - 106.11 winning units..
Owner Hamdan Al Maktoum **Bred** Leydens Farm Stud **Trained** Lambourn, Berks
■ Stewards' Enquiry : Paul Hanagan one-day ban: careless riding (May 7)

FOCUS
Some powerful stables were represented and a likeable performance from the winner. He and the third set an ordinary standard on 2yo form but were entitled to improve.

1723 BIRTHDAY PACKAGE - NEW FOR 2013 H'CAP 1m 4y

4:40 (4:40) (Class 4) (0-85,85) 4-Y-O+ **£5,175** (£1,540; £769; £384) **Stalls** Low

Form RPR

3114 **1** **Frontier Fighter**[30] 1148 5-9-6 **84** DanielTudhope 7 95+
(David O'Meara) *trckd ldng pair: hdwy 2f out: rdn to ld over 1f out: edgd lft ins fnl f: styd on wl* **7/2**[2]

010- 2 1 1/4 **Shadowtime**[209] 6559 8-8-12 **76** BarryMcHugh 1 84
(Tracy Waggott) *hld up in rr: hdwy 3f out: effrt on inner to chal ent fnl f: sn rdn and ev ch tl no ex last 75yds* **17/2**
04-1 3 1 3/4 **Dolphin Rock**[13] 1442 6-8-12 **76** DaleSwift 5 80
(Brian Ellison) *slt ld: rdn along 2f out: hdd jst over 1f out: sn swtchd rt and kpt on same pce* **10/3**[1]
415- 4 1 1/4 **Green Howard**[189] 7097 5-9-7 **85** RobertWinston 2 86
(Robin Bastiman) *in tch: hdwy to chse ldrs over 2f out: swtchd rt to outer and rdn over 1f out: one pce ent fnl f* **4/1**[3]
5-02 5 4 1/2 **Rossetti**[18] 1354 5-8-8 **72** PaulHanagan 4 63
(Ian Williams) *in tch: hdwy to chse ldrs 3f out: rdn wl over 1f out: sn no imp* **13/2**
1155 6 1/2 **Our Ivor**[26] 1203 4-8-8 **72** AndrewMullen 6 62
(Michael Appleby) *cl up: disp ld 1/2-way: rdn along 2f out: wknd over 1f out* **16/1**
56-0 7 nk **Hayek**[13] 1442 6-8-1 **72** (b) RachelRichardson(7) 3 61
(Tim Easterby) *hld up: a towards rr* **9/1**
5044 8 10 **Piceno (IRE)**[13] 1442 5-8-4 **71** oh1 (p) BillyCray(3) 9 37
(Scott Dixon) *chsd ldng pair: rdn along 3f out: wknd over 2f out* **20/1**
445- 9 12 **Al Muheer (IRE)**[185] 7210 8-9-6 **84** (b) JamesSullivan 8 22
(Ruth Carr) *a in rr* **20/1**

1m 44.25s (-1.65) **Going Correction** -0.075s/f (Good) **9** Ran SP% **114.6**
Speed ratings (Par 105): **105,103,102,100,96 95,95,85,73**
toteswingers 1&2 £10.90, 1&3 £2.30, 2&3 £7.90 CSF £32.99 CT £105.72 TOTE £4.10: £1.80, £2.70, £1.40; EX 49.70 Trifecta £178.90 Pool: £2446.63 - 10.25 winning units..
Owner Archibald Nichol & Partners **Bred** Darley **Trained** Nawton, N Yorks

FOCUS
Plenty of early pace on in this handicap and it required a strong staying effort from the winner. He has a progressive profile and still looks on the up.
T/Plt: £45.20 to a £1 stake. Pool of £53,548.74 - 863.78 winning tickets. T/Qpdt: £10.00 to a £1 stake. Pool of £3289.33 - 241.10 winning tickets. JR

1580 WINDSOR (R-H)

Monday, April 22

OFFICIAL GOING: Good (8.4)
Wind: Light, behind Weather: Overcast

1724 FUNRAISING MAIDEN AUCTION FILLIES' STKS 5f 10y
5:30 (5:32) (Class 5) 2-Y-O **£2,587** (£770; £384; £192) **Stalls** Low

Form RPR
2 1 **Quatuor (IRE)**[18] 1344 2-8-10 0 RichardKingscote 5 77
(Tom Dascombe) *mde all: hung lft over 1f out: drvn and styd on wl* **5/1**[3]
3 2 3/4 **Kidmenot (IRE)**[10] 1512 2-8-4 0 LiamJones 12 68
(J S Moore) *wl in tch: rdn to chse wnr 1f out: styd on towards fin but a hld* **12/1**
3 3/4 **Hoku (IRE)** 2-8-10 0 JamieSpencer 11 72+
(Olly Stevens) *slowest away: wl in rr tl prog on outer fr 1/2-way: clsd and looked dangerous 1f out: one pce last 100yds* **2/1**[1]
5 4 2 **Honey Meadow**[14] 1421 2-8-4 0 AndreaAtzeni 7 58
(Robert Eddery) *restless in stalls: prom: chsd wnr after 2f to 1f out: edgd lft and one pce* **17/2**
5 3/4 **Jive** 2-8-8 0 RichardHughes 3 60
(Richard Hannon) *trckd ldrs: shkn up 2f out: one pce and no imp on ldrs* **3/1**[2]
3 6 1 1/2 **Evacusafe Lady**[14] 1421 2-8-1 0 RyanPowell(3) 8 50
(John Ryan) *outpcd in last quartet: prog on outer 2f out: rdn and kpt on fr over 1f out: n.d* **16/1**
7 1 1/2 **Zac's Princess** 2-8-4 0 DavidProbert 4 45
(Milton Bradley) *chsd wnr 2f: steadily wknd fr 2f out* **100/1**
4 8 1 1/4 **Vodka Chaser (IRE)**[14] 1432 2-8-3 0 DarrenEgan(3) 6 42
(J S Moore) *hld up in midfield: rdn over 1f out: steadily wknd* **33/1**
5 9 hd **Bonnie Wee Lassie**[10] 1512 2-8-6 0 KieranO'Neill 2 42
(Richard Hannon) *chsd ldrs: rdn 2f out: steadily wknd over 1f out* **14/1**
10 2 3/4 **Faye Belle** 2-7-13 0 ow2 AdamMcLean(7) 10 32
(Derek Shaw) *rn green in last quartet: nvr a factor* **33/1**
0 11 nk **Chilly In Rio (IRE)**[14] 1432 2-8-8 0 MartinDwyer 1 33
(William Muir) *dwlt: a in last quartet: wl btn fnl 2f* **40/1**
12 nk **Liefie** 2-8-4 0 SilvestreDeSousa 9 28
(Jo Hughes) *dwlt: rn green and a wl in rr* **50/1**

59.84s (-0.46) **Going Correction** -0.225s/f (Firm) **12** Ran SP% **117.0**
Speed ratings (Par 89): **94,92,91,88,87 84,82,80,80,75 75,74**
toteswingers 1&2 £9.40, 1&3 £2.30, 2&3 £6.90 CSF £60.06 TOTE £5.70: £2.40, £3.30, £1.10; EX 54.40 Trifecta £247.60 Pool: £2144.42 - 6.49 winning units..
Owner Edwards Hughes Jenkins Roberts **Bred** Ecurie La Cauviniere **Trained** Malpas, Cheshire

FOCUS
Top bend dolled out 5yds from normal configuration adding 20yds to races of 1m and beyond. Inner of straight dolled out 6yds at 6f and 3yds at Winning Post. A moderate fillies' maiden, rated at the bottom end of the race standard.

1725 CORAL.CO.UK H'CAP 1m 67y
6:00 (6:04) (Class 4) (0-85,81) 3-Y-O **£4,851** (£1,443; £721; £360) **Stalls** Low

Form RPR
203- 1 **Sea Shanty (USA)**[178] 7372 3-8-13 **73** RichardHughes 2 82
(Richard Hannon) *hld up in last quartet: stdy prog fr 3f out: rdn to cl on ldrs over 1f out: led ins fnl f: styd on wl* **11/4**[1]
3-12 2 1 1/2 **Naalatt (IRE)**[20] 1307 3-9-1 **75** AndreaAtzeni 1 80
(Roger Varian) *pressed ldr: upsides fr 1/2-way: rdn to ld 2f out: hdd and outpcd ins fnl f* **10/1**
315- 3 1/2 **Pompeia**[201] 6775 3-9-4 **78** JimCrowley 12 82
(Ralph Beckett) *trckd ldrs disputing 5th: clsd 2f out: drvn to chal 1f out: styd on same pce* **10/1**
01- 4 nse **Zamoyski**[208] 6571 3-9-6 **80** RyanMoore 7 84
(Jeremy Noseda) *hld up in last quartet: prog on wd outside fr 3f out: clsd on ldrs 1f out: kpt on u.p* **7/2**[2]
016- 5 3 1/4 **Pearl Castle (IRE)**[212] 6469 3-9-7 **81** JamieSpencer 11 77
(Andrew Balding) *led to 2f out: wknd fnl f* **13/2**
65-4 6 nk **Yul Finegold (IRE)**[31] 1114 3-9-4 **78** PatCosgrave 8 74
(George Baker) *t.k.h: trckd ldng pair: rdn over 2f out: hanging and lost pl over 1f out: no imp after* **28/1**
01- 7 1/2 **St Paul De Vence (IRE)**[123] 8178 3-9-6 **80** SilvestreDeSousa 10 75
(Paul Cole) *hld up in last pair: pushed along 3f out: kpt on one pce fnl 2f: nvr on terms* **11/2**[3]
1212 8 3 1/4 **Red Dragon (IRE)**[16] 1400 3-9-2 **76** WilliamBuick 5 63
(Charles Hills) *chsd ldng pair: shkn up 3f out: lost pl over 2f out: n.d after* **10/1**
242- 9 shd **Khelac**[205] 6669 3-8-12 **72** FergusSweeney 9 59
(Philip Hide) *in tch: rdn on outer over 2f out: no prog over 1f out: wknd fnl f* **66/1**
414- 10 1/2 **Exzachary**[185] 7207 3-9-1 **75** J-PGuillambert 3 61
(Jo Hughes) *snatched up sn after s and hld up in last: pushed along over 3f out: hanging and no great prog* **50/1**
446- 11 5 **Choral Prince (IRE)**[172] 7501 3-8-12 **72** MartinDwyer 4 46
(Mike Murphy) *free to post: t.k.h: hld up in midfield: drvn over 3f out: sn wknd* **40/1**
3343 12 10 **Tight Knit (USA)**[26] 1206 3-8-12 **72** (b) KierenFallon 6 23
(James Tate) *chsd ldrs disputing 5th: drvn 3f out: sn wknd: t.o* **20/1**

1m 41.54s (-3.16) **Going Correction** -0.225s/f (Firm) **12** Ran SP% **119.0**
Speed ratings (Par 100): **106,104,104,103,100 100,99,96,96,96 91,81**
toteswingers 1&2 £6.40, 1&3 £5.10, 2&3 £11.40 CSF £29.98 CT £249.35 TOTE £3.10: £1.30, £3.30, £3.20; EX 29.50 Trifecta £391.60 Pool: £1411.16 - 2.70 winning units..
Owner The Queen **Bred** Her Majesty The Queen **Trained** East Everleigh, Wilts

FOCUS
An informative 3-y-o handicap, run in a good time. Plenty of positives to be taken from the form.

1726 SBOBET.COM H'CAP 6f
6:30 (6:31) (Class 3) (0-90,90) 4-Y-O+ **£7,439** (£2,213; £1,106; £553) **Stalls** Low

Form RPR
12-2 1 **Nocturn**[18] 1346 4-8-13 **82** (p) WilliamBuick 7 91
(Jeremy Noseda) *pressed ldr: cajoled along fr 2f out: pressed new ldr 1f out: inclined to hang but hrd rdn and styd on to ld post* **4/1**[1]
020- 2 nse **Poole Harbour (IRE)**[199] 6835 4-9-5 **88** SeanLevey 14 97
(Richard Hannon) *pressed ldng pair and racd on outer: drvn to ld over 1f out: hrd pressed fnl f: hdd post* **20/1**
03-5 3 nk **Democretes**[23] 1245 4-9-4 **87** RichardHughes 12 95+
(Richard Hannon) *in tch in midfield: prog 2f out: clsd on ldrs 1f out: swtchd lft ins fnl f: fin wl* **9/2**[2]
-530 4 1 **Harrison George (IRE)**[9] 1537 8-9-2 **85** (t) KierenFallon 2 90
(P J O'Gorman) *t.k.h early: hld up bhd ldrs: rdn and nt qckn 2f out: styd on again ins fnl f* **10/1**
-600 5 1 1/4 **Frog Hollow**[16] 1385 4-8-9 **83** MatthewLawson(5) 10 84+
(Milton Bradley) *wl in rr: prog on outer fr over 2f out: tried to cl 1f out: one pce after* **25/1**
030- 6 shd **Charlotte Rosina**[199] 6835 4-9-3 **86** DaneO'Neill 1 87
(Roger Teal) *led: edgd lft and hdd over 1f out: fdd last 150yds* **14/1**
012- 7 3/4 **Ashpan Sam**[174] 7451 4-8-13 **82** LiamJones 8 80
(John Spearing) *cl up bhd ldrs: rdn over 2f out: trying to chal whn squeezed out wl over 1f out: nt rcvr* **33/1**
165- 8 1 1/4 **Links Drive Lady**[165] 7645 5-8-13 **82** SilvestreDeSousa 11 76+
(Dean Ivory) *wl in rr: prog on outer 2f out: unable to cl 1f out: fdd nr fin* **12/1**
13-1 9 nk **Gladiatrix**[20] 1308 4-8-8 **82** MichaelJMMurphy(5) 6 75
(Rod Millman) *trckd ldrs: lost pl fr 2f out: pushed along and no hdwy fnl f* **7/1**
062- 10 1/2 **Elusive Flame**[172] 7508 4-9-7 **90** RyanMoore 13 82
(David Elsworth) *hld up wl in rr: drvn over 2f out: sme prog over 1f out: no hdwy fnl f* **8/1**
2314 11 3 3/4 **Jack My Boy (IRE)**[21] 1287 6-8-8 **82** (v) DeclanBates(5) 5 62
(David Evans) *sn pushed along towards rr: nvr on terms w ldrs* **33/1**
336- 12 3/4 **Italian Tom (IRE)**[115] 8266 6-8-10 **82** DarrenEgan(3) 4 59
(Ronald Harris) *n.m.r sn after s: hld up in last pair: rdn and no great prog 2f out* **50/1**
000- 13 1 1/4 **My Kingdom (IRE)**[180] 7327 7-8-10 **79** (t) DavidProbert 3 52
(Stuart Williams) *nvr beyond midfield against rail: rdn 2f out: no prog* **20/1**
003- 14 1 1/4 **Lexi's Hero (IRE)**[210] 6543 5-9-3 **86** JamieSpencer 9 59
(Ed Dunlop) *stdd s: hld up in last pair: shkn up 2f out: no prog* **6/1**[3]
14-5 15 3 3/4 **Barons Spy (IRE)**[21] 1287 12-9-4 **87** JimCrowley 15 44
(Richard Price) *chsd ldrs on outer to 1/2-way: sn wknd* **66/1**

1m 10.6s (-2.40) **Going Correction** -0.225s/f (Firm) **15** Ran SP% **122.2**
Speed ratings (Par 107): **107,106,106,105,103 103,102,100,100,99 94,93,92,90,85**
toteswingers 1&2 £24.70, 1&3 £4.70, 2&3 £9.60 CSF £89.91 CT £393.36 TOTE £4.30: £2.00, £6.40, £2.40; EX 113.70 Trifecta £380.70 Pool: £1635.14 - 3.22 winning units..
Owner Miss Yvonne Jacques **Bred** J Ellis **Trained** Newmarket, Suffolk
■ Stewards' Enquiry : Matthew Lawson four-day ban: used whip above permitted level (May 6-9)

FOCUS
It paid to race handily in this fair sprint handicap and the main action developed down the centre late on. The winner is progressive and the Hannon pair both improved too.

1727 SBOBET LIVE CASINO MAIDEN STKS 1m 2f 7y
7:00 (7:03) (Class 5) 3-Y-O **£2,587** (£770; £384; £192) **Stalls** Centre

Form RPR
0- 1 **Powder Hound**[173] 7492 3-9-5 0 DavidProbert 8 87
(Andrew Balding) *racd freely early: mde virtually all: rdn and pressed over 2f out: flashed tail but hld on wl* **14/1**
52- 2 1/2 **Persepolis (IRE)**[187] 7167 3-9-5 0 RyanMoore 10 86
(Sir Michael Stoute) *mostly trckd wnr: rdn over 2f out: persistent chal after: nt qckn ins fnl f* **2/1**[1]
4- 3 2 3/4 **Thomas Hobson**[131] 8071 3-9-5 0 WilliamBuick 1 80
(John Gosden) *sn trckd ldng trio: shkn up to chse ldng pair 2f out: styd on but nvr able to land a blow* **3/1**[2]
4 7 **Conquestadim** 3-9-5 0 JimmyFortune 4 66
(Hughie Morrison) *hld up towards rr: outpcd over 3f out: pushed along fr over 2f out: styd on steadily to take 4th nr fin* **12/1**
5 2 **Satwa Story** 3-9-5 0 (t) MickaelBarzalona 5 62
(Mahmood Al Zarooni) *t.k.h: trckd ldng pair: wnt 2nd briefly 1/2-way: wknd 2f out* **7/2**[3]
0- 6 2 1/2 **King's Request (IRE)**[206] 6636 3-9-5 0 PatDobbs 3 57
(Sir Michael Stoute) *hld up in rr: outpcd and pushed along over 3f out: no ch after: kpt on fnl f* **11/2**
7 1 1/4 **Brave Helios** 3-9-5 0 RichardKingscote 2 55
(Jonathan Portman) *in tch: pushed along 4f out: sn outpcd: n.d after: kpt on fnl f* **66/1**
06- 8 5 **Furibondo**[166] 7637 3-9-5 0 TedDurcan 9 45
(David Lanigan) *hld up in rr: outpcd over 3f out: nvr on terms after* **25/1**
00- 9 3/4 **Noor Al Haya (IRE)**[150] 7840 3-9-0 0 JohnFahy 7 38
(Mark Usher) *t.k.h: sn hld up in 5th: rdn 4f out: wknd 3f out* **100/1**

0- 10 *11* **Endura**170 7552 3-9-0 0 DaneO'Neill 6 16
(Harry Dunlop) *hld up: a last: t.o* **66/1**

2m 6.08s (-2.62) **Going Correction** -0.225s/f (Firm) **10** Ran SP% **118.1**
Speed ratings (Par 98): **101,100,98,92,91 89,88,84,83,74**
toteswingers 1&2 £5.20, 1&3 £13.20, 2&3 £2.40 CSF £42.67 TOTE £12.00: £3.30, £1.40, £1.50; EX 55.60 Trifecta £512.70 Pool: £1699.67 - 2.48 winning units..
Owner George Strawbridge **Bred** George Strawbridge **Trained** Kingsclere, Hants

FOCUS
This is usually a fair 3-y-o maiden and the form is rated around the race averages. Improvement from the winner with the form pair second and third, the first three clear.

1728 150 BONUS AT SBOBET.COM H'CAP 1m 3f 135y
7:30 (7:31) (Class 4) (0-85,85) 4-Y-O+ **£4,851** (£1,443; £721; £360) **Stalls** Centre

Form RPR
31 1 **Guising**22 1274 4-8-13 **78** SilvestreDeSousa 2 88+
(David Brown) *mde all: hung lft and racd awkwardly u.p fr over 2f out: kpt on fr over 1f out: jst hld on* **7/2**1

60-0 2 *hd* **Angel Gabrial (IRE)**22 1273 4-9-5 **84** JamieSpencer 3 93+
(Ian Williams) *hld up in last: prog jst over 2f out: hrd rdn to chse wnr fnl f: clsd nr fin: jst failed* **17/2**

010- 3 *1 ¼* **Abundantly**171 7519 4-8-8 **73** WilliamBuick 4 80+
(Hughie Morrison) *hld up in last pair early: rchd midfield over 3f out: shkn up over 2f out: styd on fnl f to take 3rd last strides: nvr nr to chal* **7/2**1

1262 4 *hd* **Cool Sky**21 1290 4-9-2 **81** JimCrowley 8 88
(William Knight) *taken down early: trckd ldng pair to over 4f out: styd in tch: renewed effrt 2f out: chsd ldng pair fnl f: one pce and lost 3rd last strides* **8/1**3

-000 5 *2* **Super Say (IRE)**11 1501 7-9-2 **85** (t) WilliamTwiston-Davies(5) 1 89
(Mark Rimell) *taken down early: trckd ldng pair: wnt 2nd 5f out: poised to chal gng strly 3f out: rdn and nt qckn jst over 2f out: wknd fnl f* **33/1**

2066 6 *nse* **Focail Maith**12 1464 5-8-7 **71** oh1 (p) FergusSweeney 6 75
(John Ryan) *hld up: shkn up and last 2f out: rdn and kpt on fr over 1f out: no ch* **25/1**

10-4 7 *2 ¾* **Aldwick Bay (IRE)**20 1302 5-9-4 **82** RichardHughes 7 81
(Richard Hannon) *trckd ldrs: wnt 3rd 4f out: rdn and cl enough 2f out: wknd over 1f out* **7/2**1

20-0 8 *2 ¾* **Man Of Plenty**9 1536 4-9-0 **79** (b1) RyanMoore 9 73
(Ed Dunlop) *chsd wnr to 5f out: hrd rdn and no rspnse 4f out: hanging and wknd fr 2f out: eased* **5/1**2

511- 9 *1 ¼* **Mafeteng**225 6074 5-8-9 **73** TedDurcan 10 65
(Roger Charlton) *hld up in rr: shkn up over 2f out: no prog whn bmpd over 1f out* **16/1**

2m 26.53s (-2.97) **Going Correction** -0.225s/f (Firm)
WFA 4 from 5yo+ 1lb **9** Ran SP% **117.6**
Speed ratings (Par 105): **100,99,99,98,97 97,95,93,93**
toteswingers 1&2 £7.00, 1&3 £3.90, 2&3 £7.60 CSF £35.19 CT £112.56 TOTE £3.90: £1.50, £2.90, £1.60; EX 46.60 Trifecta £324.10 Pool: £1348.44 - 3.12 winning units..
Owner Peter Onslow & Ian Henderson **Bred** Peter Onslow **Trained** Averham Park, Notts

FOCUS
A fair handicap and another winner from the front. The winner was unexposed and the form is rated around the fourth.

1729 SBOBET GAMES H'CAP 1m 3f 135y
8:00 (8:01) (Class 5) (0-75,75) 3-Y-O **£2,587** (£770; £288; £288) **Stalls** Centre

Form RPR
2411 1 **Poetic Verse**14 1425 3-9-3 **71** AndreaAtzeni 1 75+
(Rod Millman) *hld up and last tl over 5f out: smooth prog over 2f out: led over 1f out gng easily: pushed out fnl f* **7/2**1

5214 2 *2* **El Massivo (IRE)**36 1053 3-9-2 **70** KierenFallon 4 70
(William Jarvis) *hld up: quick move to chse ldr 5f out: shkn up over 3f out: upsides sn after tl wnr cruised by over 1f out: kpt on* **7/2**1

62-4 3 *½* **Jebril (FR)**17 1365 3-9-7 **75** RichardKingscote 5 74
(Jonathan Portman) *trckd ldr to 5f out: stl cl up 2f out: rdn and one pce after* **4/1**2

00-2 3 *dht* **Relentless (IRE)**27 1187 3-9-1 **69** (b1) WilliamBuick 3 68
(John Gosden) *racd v keenly early: led: drvn and jnd 3f out: hdd and nt qckn over 1f out: one pce* **9/2**3

005- 5 *40* **Tigerish**159 7706 3-9-0 **68** JimCrowley 7
(Amanda Perrett) *cl up tl wknd qckly over 3f out: t.o* **9/2**3

211- 6 *81* **Paddy's Saltantes (IRE)**135 8032 3-9-3 **71** LiamJones 6
(J S Moore) *nvr gng wl: drvn and lost tch 5f out: wl t.o* **17/2**

2m 28.58s (-0.92) **Going Correction** -0.225s/f (Firm) **6** Ran SP% **111.3**
Speed ratings (Par 98): **94,92,92,92,65 11**
TRIFECTA: PV/EM/J £22.40, PV/EM/R £13.50; toteswingers PV&EM £1.10, PV&J £2.60, PV&R £2.00, EM&R £1.30, EM&J £1.30 CSF £15.61 TOTE £4.30: £2.30, £2.50; EX 13.00 TRIFECTA Pool: £986.56 - 16.48 winning units..
Owner The Links Partnership **Bred** The Links Partnership **Trained** Kentisbeare, Devon

FOCUS
This looked toght, but the progressive winner hosed up. The time was reasonable compared with the previous race.
T/Jkpt: Not won. T/Plt: £33.50 to a £1 stake. Pool of £81,450.44 - 1774.83 winning tickets. T/Qpdt: £6.70 to a £1 stake. Pool of £6616.79 - 724.04 winning tickets. JN

1694 WOLVERHAMPTON (A.W) (L-H)
Monday, April 22

OFFICIAL GOING: Standard
Wind: Fresh behind Weather: Overcast

1730 £32 BONUS AT 32RED.COM APPRENTICE H'CAP 1m 1f 103y(P)
5:50 (5:50) (Class 6) (0-55,55) 4-Y-O+ **£1,940** (£577; £288; £144) **Stalls** Low

Form RPR
0-16 1 **Downtown Boy (IRE)**26 1214 5-9-5 **53** (p) GeorgeChaloner 8 61
(Ray Craggs) *trckd ldr: racd keenly: led 4f out: rdn clr 2f out: jst hld on* **6/1**3

2316 2 *nk* **Angelena Ballerina (IRE)**20 1298 6-9-5 **53** (v) NoelGarbutt 1 62+
(Sean Curran) *hld up: rdn over 1f out: hung lft and r.o wl ins fnl f: nt quite get up* **9/2**2

2- 3 *1 ¼* **Dustland Fairytale (IRE)**19 1337 5-8-9 **48** RobJFitzpatrick(5) 11 53
(R McGlinchey, Ire) *hld up: hdwy over 2f out: rdn to chse wnr over 1f out: hung rt ins fnl f: styd on* **16/1**

50-3 4 *1 ¾* **The Yank**40 983 4-9-7 **55** GeorgeDowning 4 56
(Tony Carroll) *s.i.s: hld up: hdwy over 1f out: sn rdn: styd on: nt trble ldrs* **3/1**1

05-2 5 *nk* **Just Five (IRE)**25 1222 7-9-0 **48** (v) ConorHarrison 5 48
(John Weymes) *a.p: rdn over 1f out: styd on same pce ins fnl f* **9/2**2

440- 6 *nk* **Belle Park**150 7841 6-9-4 **52** RyanWhile 3 52
(Karen George) *mid-div: rdn over 2f out: n.m.r ins fnl f: nt trble ldrs* **12/1**

2665 7 *nk* **Jordaura**22 1270 7-8-13 **54** JordanHibberd(7) 9 53
(Alan Berry) *s.i.s: hld up: rdn over 1f out: nvr on terms* **10/1**

6-00 8 *1 ¼* **Market Puzzle (IRE)**33 1090 6-8-12 **46** oh1 (p) JackDuern 7 43
(Mark Brisbourne) *prom: rdn over 2f out: no ex fnl f* **16/1**

5010 9 *6* **Maz**11 1498 5-9-2 **50** TimClark 6 34
(Alan Bailey) *chsd ldrs: rdn over 1f out: wknd fnl f* **10/1**

4550 10 *8* **Miss Chardonay**33 1093 6-8-12 **46** oh1 DavidBergin 2 13
(Mandy Rowland) *chsd ldrs tl wknd over 2f out* **33/1**

406/ 11 *4 ½* **Ernest Speak (IRE)**623 4867 4-8-13 **50** (t) EoinWalsh(3) 10
(David Evans) *led over 5f: n.m.r sn after: wknd over 2f out* **25/1**

1m 59.72s (-1.98) **Going Correction** -0.15s/f (Stan) **11** Ran SP% **120.1**
Speed ratings (Par 101): **102,101,100,99,98 98,98,97,91,84 80**
toteswingers 1&2 £5.50, 1&3 £18.90, 2&3 £11.20 CSF £33.93 CT £419.99 TOTE £11.00: £2.30, £1.80, £3.30; EX 41.80 Trifecta £855.00 Part won..
Owner Ray Craggs **Bred** Eclipse Thoroughbreds Inc **Trained** Sedgefield, Co Durham
■ Stewards' Enquiry : Rob J Fitzpatrick four-day ban: used whip above permitted level (May 6-9)

FOCUS
A low-grade apprentice handicap and the winner stole a march on his rivals turning in.

1731 32REDPOKER.COM H'CAP 5f 20y(P)
6:20 (6:20) (Class 6) (0-60,59) 4-Y-O+ **£1,940** (£577; £288; £144) **Stalls** Low

Form RPR
0635 1 **Nafa (IRE)**41 968 5-8-10 **48** ShaneKelly 7 58
(Daniel Mark Loughnane) *trckd ldrs: shkn up to ld ins fnl f: rdn out* **10/1**

6322 2 *1 ¾* **Rose Garnet (IRE)**12 1472 5-9-2 **59** GeorgeDowning(5) 5 63+
(Tony Carroll) *s.i.s and hmpd s: hld up: hdwy over 1f out: sn rdn: styd on* **11/4**1

0000 3 *nk* **Lord Buffhead**16 1395 4-9-2 **54** (v) RobbieFitzpatrick 4 57
(Richard Guest) *mid-div: drvn along 1/2-way: hdwy over 1f out: r.o* **14/1**

6222 4 *1 ¼* **Slatey Hen (IRE)**16 1396 5-8-12 **50** (p) CathyGannon 6 48+
(Violet M Jordan) *hld up: nt clr run 1/2-way: hdwy over 1f out: r.o: nt trble ldrs* **7/1**

0-00 5 *1 ¾* **Volcanic Dust (IRE)**87 369 5-9-4 **56** (t) NeilCallan 3 48
(Milton Bradley) *led: rdn over 1f out: hdd and no ex ins fnl f* **12/1**

0110 6 *nk* **Divertimenti (IRE)**2 1681 9-9-1 **56** (b) MarkCoumbe(3) 13 47
(Roy Bowring) *hld up: rdn over 1f out: edgd lft and r.o ins fnl f: nvr nrr* **13/2**

2250 7 *¾* **Spic 'n Span**27 1186 8-9-6 **58** (b) LukeMorris 9 46
(Ronald Harris) *prom: chsd ldr 1/2-way: rdn and ev ch over 1f out: wknd ins fnl f* **16/1**

0421 8 *nse* **Almaty Express**16 1395 11-8-12 **55** (b) RobertTart(5) 12 43+
(John Weymes) *hmpd in rr sn after s: r.o ins fnl f: nvr on terms* **11/2**3

540- 9 *½* **See Vermont**236 5739 5-8-9 **47** HayleyTurner 1 33
(Robin Bastiman) *w ldr 2f: sn rdn: wknd fnl f* **5/1**2

0560 10 *2 ½* **Lesley's Choice**12 1465 7-9-4 **56** (p) JamesDoyle 8 33
(Sean Curran) *chsd ldrs: drvn along 1/2-way: nt clr run and wknd over 1f out* **14/1**

005- 11 *nk* **Mandy's Hero**415 783 5-9-0 **52** (b) SebSanders 10 28
(Olivia Maylam) *prom: rdn 1/2-way: wknd over 1f out* **33/1**

1m 1.32s (-0.98) **Going Correction** -0.15s/f (Stan) **11** Ran SP% **123.5**
Speed ratings (Par 101): **101,98,97,95,92 92,91,91,90,86 85**
toteswingers 1&2 £10.00, 1&3 £50.90, 2&3 £19.20 CSF £39.59 CT £406.56 TOTE £11.40: £3.60, £1.70, £5.60; EX 67.70 Trifecta £909.30 Part won..
Owner Ian O'Connor **Bred** Basil Brindley **Trained** Baldwin's Gate, Staffs

1732 32RED.COM MAIDEN STKS 5f 216y(P)
6:50 (6:52) (Class 5) 3-Y-O+ **£2,587** (£770; £384; £192) **Stalls** Low

Form RPR
4- 1 **Smokethatthunders (IRE)**171 7516 3-9-3 0 RobertHavlin 2 73
(James Toller) *chsd ldr tl led over 3f out: rdn out* **9/2**3

5- 2 *¾* **Aglaophonos**193 7006 3-9-3 0 NeilCallan 1 71
(Roger Varian) *sn prom: rdn to chse wnr over 1f out: r.o* **2/1**2

3 *½* **Realize** 3-9-3 0 HayleyTurner 6 69+
(Hughie Morrison) *s.i.s: bhd: swtchd rt over 1f out: shkn up: edgd lft and r.o wl ins fnl f: improve* **8/1**

62- 4 *5* **Abated**187 7161 3-8-12 0 JamesDoyle 5 48
(Roger Charlton) *chsd ldrs: shkn up and hung lft over 1f out: wknd fnl f* **11/8**1

6 5 *½* **Zain Joy (CAN)**23 1243 3-8-12 0 LukeMorris 4 47
(Gerard Butler) *chsd ldrs: rdn over 1f out: wknd fnl f* **20/1**

0023 6 *¾* **Script**12 1461 4-9-2 48 JordanHibberd(7) 8 47
(Alan Berry) *hld up: nt clr run over 2f out: hdwy over 1f out: wknd ins fnl f* **50/1**

0- 7 *2 ¾* **Carneades (IRE)**129 8102 3-9-3 0 TomMcLaughlin 7 41
(Ed Walker) *hld up: pushed along over 2f out: nvr on terms* **33/1**

04 8 *nse* **Lady Farah**78 509 3-8-12 0 HarryBentley 3 35
(Robert Cowell) *led: hdd over 3f out: rdn and wknd over 1f out* **22/1**

1m 13.88s (-1.12) **Going Correction** -0.15s/f (Stan)
WFA 3 from 4yo 11lb **8** Ran SP% **118.7**
Speed ratings (Par 103): **101,100,99,92,92 91,87,87**
toteswingers 1&2 £2.00, 1&3 £4.80, 2&3 £3.50 CSF £14.03 TOTE £6.30: £2.40, £1.10, £3.60; EX 16.40 Trifecta £71.30 Pool: £1909.05 - 20.06 winning units..
Owner M E Wates **Bred** P Doyle Bloodstock & J K Thoroughbred **Trained** Newmarket, Suffolk

FOCUS
An interesting maiden and it again paid to race up with the pace.

1733 32RED H'CAP 1m 5f 194y(P)
7:20 (7:20) (Class 4) (0-85,85) 4-Y-O+ **£4,690** (£1,395; £697; £348) **Stalls** Low

Form RPR
11-5 1 **Fleur De La Vie (IRE)**20 1302 4-9-2 **79** JamesDoyle 9 89+
(Ralph Beckett) *hld up: hdwy over 1f out: rdn to ld ins fnl f: r.o* **9/1**

2-25 2 *nk* **Porgy**22 1273 8-9-9 **84** (b) GrahamLee 4 93
(Brian Ellison) *hld up: hdwy and nt clr run over 1f out: rdn and ev ch ins fnl f: r.o* **7/1**

021- 3 *4* **Red Orator**199 6834 4-9-8 **85** JoeFanning 2 88+
(Mark Johnston) *sn led: rdn and hdd ins fnl f: styd on same pce* **7/2**1

3114 4 *hd* **Admirable Duque (IRE)**27 1182 7-8-13 **74** (be) MartinLane 7 77
(Dominic Ffrench Davis) *hld up: hdwy over 1f out: nt trble ldrs* **20/1**

220/ 5 *½* **Eshtyaaq**583 6171 6-8-12 **73** TomQueally 8 75
(David Evans) *chsd ldrs: swtchd lft over 1f out: no ex ins fnl f* **16/1**

400- **6** *shd* **Cosimo de Medici**[117] 7367 6-9-5 **80**..........................(t) RobertHavlin 11 82+
(Hughie Morrison) *s.s: bhd: hdwy over 6f out: rdn over 1f out: no ex ins fnl f* **4/1**[2]

0154 **7** *3/4* **Sommersturm (GER)**[20] 1306 9-8-5 **66**..........................(t) LukeMorris 6 67
(David Evans) *hld up: rdn and edgd lft fnl f: nvr trbld ldrs* **25/1**

60-4 **8** *nk* **Daring Indian**[34] 1083 5-8-12 **73**.................................. FrederikTylicki 10 73
(Ian Williams) *chsd ldrs: nt clr run over 1f out: wknd ins fnl f* **9/1**

1112 **9** *1 1/4* **Wordiness**[27] 1182 5-9-2 **82**.................................. RobertTart(5) 1 81
(Brendan Powell) *chsd ldrs: rdn over 1f out: wknd ins fnl f* **11/2**[3]

140- **10** *4 1/2* **Galleon**[210] 6537 4-9-7 **84**..(t) HayleyTurner 5 76
(Michael Bell) *got loose prior to the s: chsd ldr: rdn over 3f out: wknd fnl f* **7/1**

/231 **11** *1/2* **Fulgora**[35] 1069 5-8-10 **71** ow1.. SebSanders 3 63
(Brendan Powell) *prom: rdn over 3f out: wknd over 1f out* **16/1**

2m 59.65s (-6.35) **Going Correction** -0.15s/f (Stan)
WFA 4 from 5yo+ 2lb **11** Ran SP% **123.0**
Speed ratings (Par 105): **112,111,109,109,109 109,108,108,107,105 104**
toteswingers 1&2 £14.10, 1&3 £9.80, 2&3 £4.60 CSF £74.05 CT £269.93 TOTE £7.60: £2.00, £2.80, £1.80; EX 46.40 Trifecta £132.60 Pool: £985.71 - 5.57 winning units..
Owner Prime Of Life 3 **Bred** Edward & Scarlet Leatham **Trained** Kimpton, Hants

FOCUS
A good class stayers' handicap and the complexion changed dramatically in the final furlong.

1734 ENJOY THE PUNTERS PACKAGE GROUP OFFER H'CAP 7f 32y(P)
7:50 (7:50) (Class 6) (0-55,61) 4-Y-O+ **£1,940** (£577; £288; £144) **Stalls** High

Form RPR

6000 **1** **Needwood Ridge**[37] 1038 6-9-7 **55**..............................(bt) LukeMorris 12 63
(Frank Sheridan) *mid-div: hdwy over 1f out: rdn to ld wl ins fnl f: r.o u.p* **11/2**[3]

006- **2** *shd* **High On The Hog (IRE)**[285] 3964 5-9-7 **55**............... TomMcLaughlin 5 63
(Mark Brisbourne) *mid-div: hdwy over 1f out: ev ch wl ins fnl f: r.o* **14/1**

021 **3** *1 3/4* **First Rebellion**[16] 1396 4-9-2 **55**........................(b) GeorgeDowning(5) 10 58
(Tony Carroll) *led: clr over 1f out: rdn: edgd rt and hdd wl ins fnl f* **10/1**

4460 **4** *nk* **Hittin'The Skids (IRE)**[13] 1452 5-9-2 **50**..........................(p) JimmyQuinn 8 52
(Mandy Rowland) *s.i.s: hld up: rdn and r.o ins fnl f: nt rch ldrs* **20/1**

2152 **5** *1/2* **Littlecote Lady**[16] 1395 4-9-6 **54**..........................(v) HayleyTurner 7 55
(Mark Usher) *hld up: pushed along over 2f out: r.o ins fnl f: nrst fin* **5/1**[2]

061 **6** *shd* **Larghetto (USA)**[4] 1657 5-9-13 **61** 6ex.......................... ShaneKelly 11 61
(Daniel Mark Loughnane) *hld up in tch: rdn over 1f out: styd on same pce ins fnl f* **11/8**[1]

2503 **7** *1 3/4* **Ridgeway Hawk**[13] 1452 5-9-5 **53**..........................(v) RobertHavlin 9 49
(Mark Usher) *s.i.s and hmpd s: in rr and rdn 1/2-way: r.o ins fnl f: nvr nrr* **10/1**

6405 **8** *2 1/4* **Nine Before Ten (IRE)**[9] 1540 5-9-7 **55**..........................(t) NeilCallan 6 45
(Charles Smith) *chsd ldrs: rdn over 2f out: wknd ins fnl f* **16/1**

04-0 **9** *2* **Regal Acclaim (IRE)**[38] 1021 4-9-7 **55**.......................... DavidNolan 2 39
(Ian McInnes) *chsd ldrs: rdn over 2f out: wknd over 1f out* **16/1**

0000 **10** *6* **Dhhamaan (IRE)**[16] 1394 8-9-2 **50**..........................(b) JamesSullivan 3 18
(Ruth Carr) *trckd ldr: plld hrd: rdn over 1f out: wknd and eased fnl f* **12/1**

1m 28.83s (-0.77) **Going Correction** -0.15s/f (Stan) **10** Ran SP% **123.2**
Speed ratings (Par 101): **98,97,95,95,94 94,92,90,88,81**
toteswingers 1&2 £18.20, 1&3 £7.60, 2&3 £39.00 CSF £84.01 CT £784.15 TOTE £9.60: £2.40, £5.30, £1.90; EX 137.90 Trifecta £898.80 Part won..
Owner Wood Bank Racing **Bred** Mrs Joy Maund-Powell **Trained** Wolverhampton, W Midlands

1735 32REDBET.COM MEDIAN AUCTION MAIDEN STKS 1m 141y(P)
8:20 (8:21) (Class 6) 3-5-Y-O **£1,940** (£577; £288; £144) **Stalls** Low

Form RPR

02-2 **1** **Enzaal (USA)**[16] 1387 3-8-13 **79**.. PaulHanagan 5 77
(Mark Johnston) *mde all: shkn up over 2f out: rdn and edgd rt ins fnl f: styd on gamely* **11/4**[2]

0- **2** *hd* **Arms (IRE)**[212] 6481 3-8-13 **0**.. SebSanders 7 76
(J W Hills) *a.p: chsd wnr over 6f out: rdn and ev ch ins fnl f: styd on* **3/1**[3]

02- **3** *2 1/2* **Misfer**[144] 7923 3-8-13 **0**..(b[1]) TomQueally 3 70
(Sir Henry Cecil) *chsd wnr 2f: remained handy: shkn up over 1f out: styd on same pce ins fnl f* **6/4**[1]

36 **4** *9* **Nautilus**[12] 1468 3-8-13 **0**.. RobertHavlin 6 49
(John Gosden) *s.i.s: plld hrd and hdwy over 6f out: rdn and hung rt over 2f out: sn wknd* **7/1**

/4-3 **5** *1/2* **Giantstepsahead (IRE)**[56] 800 4-10-0 **0**................. TomMcLaughlin 1 51
(Michael Wigham) *hld up: shkn up over 1f out: nvr nr to chal* **25/1**

6 *1* **Silver Forest (IRE)** 3-8-8 **0**.. JimmyQuinn 4 41
(John Weymes) *chsd ldrs tl pushed along and wknd over 2f out* **50/1**

7 *33* **Illshowya (IRE)** 4-9-9 **0**.. LMcNiff(5) 2
(Michael McElhone, Ire) *s.i.s: hld up: pushed along over 3f out: sn wknd: t.o* **40/1**

1m 49.51s (-0.99) **Going Correction** -0.15s/f (Stan)
WFA 3 from 4yo 15lb **7** Ran SP% **112.4**
Speed ratings (Par 101): **98,97,95,87,87 86,56**
toteswingers 1&2 £3.00, 1&3 £1.70, 2&3 £2.10 CSF £10.96 TOTE £3.10: £2.60, £1.90; EX 10.20 Trifecta £34.40 Pool: £1441.80 - 31.34 winning units..
Owner Hamdan Al Maktoum **Bred** Shadwell Farm LLC **Trained** Middleham Moor, N Yorks

FOCUS
A fair maiden. The first three were clear.

1736 32RED CASINO FILLIES' H'CAP 1m 141y(P)
8:50 (8:50) (Class 5) (0-70,69) 4-Y-O+ **£2,587** (£770; £384; £192) **Stalls** Low

Form RPR

6-42 **1** **Ssafa**[5] 1610 5-9-7 **69**..(p) PaulHanagan 4 76
(Alastair Lidderdale) *chsd ldrs: pushed along over 3f out: rdn to ld ins fnl f: edgd lft: r.o* **5/2**[1]

304- **2** *shd* **Waveguide (IRE)**[189] 7112 4-9-4 **66**.......................... MartinLane 5 73
(David Simcock) *led: hdd 6f out: chsd ldrs: led again over 1f out: rdn and hdd ins fnl f: r.o* **11/4**[2]

-212 **3** *2 3/4* **Yojojo (IRE)**[12] 1479 4-9-0 **62**.. LiamKeniry 2 62
(Gay Kelleway) *trckd ldrs: racd keenly: lost pl over 5f out: rdn over 1f out: r.o to go 3rd wl ins fnl f* **9/2**[3]

3560 **4** *1 1/2* **Stylistickhill (IRE)**[31] 1111 5-8-9 **60**..........................(t) BillyCray(3) 7 57
(Scott Dixon) *s.i.s: hld up: plld hrd: hdwy over 6f out: chsd ldr over 5f out: led over 2f out: rdn and hdd over 1f out: no ex ins fnl f* **9/1**

0321 **5** *1/2* **Qeethaara (USA)**[12] 1474 9-8-8 **56**..........................(p) LukeMorris 3 52
(Mark Brisbourne) *hld up: plld hrd: hdwy over 6f out: rdn over 1f out: no ex ins fnl f* **9/2**[3]

500- **6** *4 1/2* **Vale Of Clara (IRE)**[149] 7863 5-9-3 **65**.......................... PaulMulrennan 1 50
(Peter Niven) *s.i.s: hld up: rdn over 1f out: nt trble ldrs* **8/1**

-466 **7** *7* **Imtithal (IRE)**[16] 1389 4-8-11 **64**..........................[1] RobertTart(5) 6 33
(John Weymes) *chsd ldrs: led 6f out: rdn and hdd over 2f out: ev ch over 1f out: wknd fnl f* **14/1**

1m 49.03s (-1.47) **Going Correction** -0.15s/f (Stan) **7** Ran SP% **119.4**
Speed ratings (Par 100): **100,99,97,96,95 91,85**
toteswingers 1&2 £2.00, 1&3 £1.60, 2&3 £3.50 CSF £10.35 TOTE £5.00: £2.40, £1.70; EX 14.30 Trifecta £51.00 Pool: £1381.65 - 20.30 winning units..
Owner The Ssafa Partnership **Bred** Newsells Park Stud **Trained** Lambourn, Berks

FOCUS
The pace was not strong and it developed into a three-furlong dash with four horses almost in a line a furlong out
T/Plt: £1108.40 to a £1 stake. Pool of £52,689.67 - 34.70 winning tickets. T/Qpdt: £90.10 to a £1 stake. Pool of £6163.00 - 50.60 winning tickets. CR

1658 LONGCHAMP (R-H)
Monday, April 22

OFFICIAL GOING: Turf: good to soft

1737a PRIX NOAILLES (GROUP 2) (3YO COLTS & FILLIES) (TURF) 1m 2f 110y
1:20 (1:20) 3-Y-O **£60,243** (£23,252; £11,097; £7,398; £3,699)

RPR

1 **Tableaux (USA)**[19] 3-9-2 **0**.. MaximeGuyon 2 106+
(A Fabre, France) *racd in 4th towards outside on settling: rdn 2f out: r.o wl u.p ent fnl f: chal for ld 50yds out: led 25yds out: r.o wl* **29/10**[2]

2 *1/2* **Kapour (IRE)**[37] 1046 3-9-2 **0**.......................... Francois-XavierBertras 5 105
(F Rohaut, France) *sn led: rdn 1 1/2f out whn chal: rallied and r.o wl u.p ent fnl f: hdd 25yds out: r.o wl* **9/5**[1]

3 *snk* **Art Contemporain (USA)**[21] 3-9-2 **0**.................. ChristopheSoumillon 6 105+
(P Bary, France) *racd in cl 2nd on settling: rdn 2f out: r.o wl: chal for ld 1 1/2f out: nt qckn: styd on wl u.p fnl 100yds: jst hld on for 3rd on line* **3/1**[3]

4 *nse* **Max Dynamite (FR)**[22] 1277 3-9-2 **0**.......................... AntoineHamelin 3 105
(J Van Handenhove, France) *hld up towards rr on ins: swtchd away fr rail 1 1/2f out: qcknd wl ent fnl f: fin strly fnl 50yds: jst missed 3rd* **10/1**

5 *1 3/4* **Garrogorille (FR)**[34] 3-9-2 **0**.. OlivierPeslier 1 102
(Y Durepaire, France) *settled in 3rd towards ins: full of running 1 1/2f out: short of room 1f out whn beginning to chal between ldrs: swtchd to rail: no ex fnl 100yds: nt hrd rdn whn ch gone* **13/1**

6 *snk* **Camaretz (USA)**[22] 1277 3-9-2 **0**.......................... IoritzMendizabal 4 101
(J-C Rouget, France) *hld up towards rr: mde prog towards outside 1 1/2f out: rdn but no ex ent fnl f: styd on fnl f* **10/1**

7 *1 1/2* **Niente Paura (IRE)**[34] 3-9-2 **0**.. MarcLerner 7 98
(C Lerner, France) *hld up at rr of field: rdn but no ex 1 1/2f out: styd on fnl f* **18/1**

2m 19.07s (8.87) **7** Ran SP% **116.9**
WIN (incl. 1 euro stake): 3.90. PLACES: 1.90, 1.60. SF: 12.90.
Owner Derrick Smith & Michael Tabor **Bred** Galleria Bloodstock **Trained** Chantilly, France

1312 LES LANDES
Sunday, April 21

OFFICIAL GOING: Good

1738a HER MAJESTY THE QUEEN'S BIRTHDAY H'CAP 5f 100y
3:05 (3:09) (0-60,) 3-Y-O+ **£760** (£270; £170)

RPR

1 **Fast Freddie**[20] 1312 9-10-12..........................(p) MatthewLawson 2
(Mrs A Corson, Jersey) **9/2**

2 *2* **Toggle**[20] 1312 9-9-2..........................(p) JoshBaudains 5
(Mrs A Corson, Jersey) **10/11**[1]

3 *1/2* **Kersivay**[266] 7-10-5.. MattieBatchelor 7
(Mrs A Malzard, Jersey) **5/2**[2]

4 *10* **Nordic Light (USA)**[183] 7254 9-8-13.......................... JemmaMarshall 3
(Mrs A Malzard, Jersey) **12/1**

5 *dist* **Copper Falls**[51] 7378 4-10-9.. JohnLawson 4
(Brendan Powell) **3/1**[3]

1m 10.0s (1.00) **5** Ran SP% **131.8**

Owner The Crawford Family **Bred** New Hall Stud **Trained** Jersey

1739a JERSEY GUINEAS 1m 100y
3:40 (3:42) 3-Y-O+ **£1,460** (£525; £315)

RPR

1 **Major Maximus**[20] 6-10-5.. DavidCuthbert 7
(Mrs C Gilbert, Jersey) **7/2**[3]

2 *1/2* **Spanish Bounty**[20] 1312 8-10-5.. HarryPoulton 6
(Mrs A Malzard, Jersey) **5/1**

3 *1* **I'm Harry**[20] 1313 4-10-5..........................(tp) TonyCulhane 5
(George Baker) **5/2**[2]

4 *4* **First Cat**[20] 1312 6-10-5.. JamieGoldstein 3
(S Arthur, Jersey) **6/1**

5 *hd* **Good Luck Charm**[157] 7725 4-10-5.. NedCurtis 1
(Gary Moore) **8/11**[1]

6 *2* **King Kenny**[20] 8-10-5.. MatthewLawson 8
(Mrs A Corson, Jersey) **9/2**

7 *10* **Athania (IRE)**[20] 1313 7-10-2.. MrPCollington 9
(S Arthur, Jersey) **10/1**

8 *8* **Country Blue (FR)**[20] 1312 4-9-9.. MattieBatchelor 4
(Mrs A Malzard, Jersey) **7/1**

1m 55.0s (115.00) **8** Ran SP% **179.4**

Owner Rushmore Racing **Bred** Mrs S M Roy **Trained** Jersey

1740a LAST RACE H'CAP 1m 1f
4:50 (4:53) (0-55,) 3-Y-O+ **£760** (£270; £170)

RPR

1 **Grey Panel (FR)**[20] 1313 5-9-10.. TimClark 2
(T Le Brocq, Jersey) **2/1**[2]

The Form Book Flat, Raceform Ltd, Compton, RG20 6NL.

2 7 **Vamos (IRE)**[20] 1313 7-9-2 ... JemmaMarshall 1
(Mrs A Malzard, Jersey) **3/1**[3]
3 nk **Red Lago (IRE)**[252] 5-10-9 ... MrPCollington 5
(S Arthur, Jersey) **9/1**
4 5 **Rocquaine (IRE)**[20] 1313 4-9-12 ... HarryPoulton 6
(Mrs A Malzard, Jersey) **10/1**
5 1 **La Verte Rue (USA)**[20] 1313 7-10-1 ... MattieBatchelor 7
(Mrs A Malzard, Jersey) **3/1**[3]
6 2 **Rebel Woman**[20] 1313 7-9-7 ... MatthewLawson 4
(Mrs A Corson, Jersey) **9/2**
7 nk **Lightning Spirit**[138] 7983 5-10-12 ...(p) NedCurtis 3
(Gary Moore) **1/1**[1]
2m 7.0s (127.00) 7 Ran SP% **170.6**

Owner The Le Brocq Boys **Bred** John Berry **Trained** Jersey

[1730] WOLVERHAMPTON (A.W) (L-H)

Tuesday, April 23

OFFICIAL GOING: Standard
Wind: Light behind Weather: Cloudy with sunny spells

1741 32REDPOKER.COM MEDIAN AUCTION MAIDEN STKS 1m 1f 103y(P)
2:20 (2:23) (Class 6) 3-Y-O £1,940 (£577; £288; £144) Stalls Low

Form RPR
43 1 **Strategic Strike (IRE)**[13] 1478 3-9-5 0 ... GrahamLee 1 70
(Paul Cole) *mde all: pushed clr over 1f out: styd on* **15/8**[2]
00 2 1 **Bold Assertion**[21] 1300 3-9-5 0 ... LukeMorris 4 68
(John Best) *a.p: chsd wnr over 3f out tl rdn over 1f out: styd on to go 2nd again nr fin* **50/1**
33-6 3 nk **Jullundar (IRE)**[36] 1057 3-9-5 67 ... MartinHarley 7 67
(Mick Channon) *a.p: rdn to chse wnr over 1f out: styd on: lost 2nd nr fin* **13/8**[1]
03 4 11 **Florida Beat**[27] 1213 3-9-5 0 ... LiamKeniry 8 44
(Andrew Balding) *chsd wnr tl pushed along over 3f out: rdn and wknd over 1f out* **10/3**[3]
43 5 4 **Sian Gwalia**[28] 1187 3-9-0 0 ... MartinLane 3 31
(David Simcock) *prom tl rdn and wknd over 2f out* **8/1**
0 5 dht **Carronade**[12] 1499 3-9-0 0 ... NeilCallan 9 31
(Olivia Maylam) *hld up: pushed along 6f out: bhd fnl 5f* **50/1**
0 7 nk **Mr Blue Nose**[15] 1429 3-9-5 0 ... JamieMackay 6 35
(Karen George) *s.i.s: a in rr: bhd fnl 6f* **50/1**
2m 0.52s (-1.18) **Going Correction** -0.225s/f (Stan) 7 Ran SP% **113.0**
Speed ratings (Par 96): **96,95,94,85,81 81,81**
Tote Swingers 1&2 £9.10, 2&3 £9.50, 1&3 £1.40 CSF £75.21 TOTE £2.80: £1.70, £7.10; EX 69.40 Trifecta £235.60 Pool: £2,552.61 - 8.12 winning tickets..
Owner H R H Sultan Ahmad Shah **Bred** Hrh Sultan Ahmad Shah **Trained** Whatcombe, Oxon
FOCUS
Gallop Mastered after race four. A weak maiden.

1742 32REDBINGO.COM H'CAP 5f 20y(P)
2:50 (2:50) (Class 6) (0-60,60) 3-Y-O £1,940 (£577; £288; £144) Stalls Low

Form RPR
0-23 1 **Balatina**[30] 1157 3-8-6 50 ow1 ... RobertTart(5) 13 59
(Chris Dwyer) *chsd ldrs: led 4f out: clr 2f out: rdn and edgd rt fnl f: r.o* **12/1**
24-5 2 1 3/4 **Harrogate Fair**[15] 1433 3-9-7 60 ... RobertWinston 4 63
(Michael Squance) *sn led: hdd 4f out: chsd wnr: rdn over 1f out: edgd rt: kpt on* **4/1**[2]
164- 3 3 1/4 **Chloe's Dream (IRE)**[180] 7355 3-9-7 60 ...(p) PJMcDonald 2 51
(Ann Duffield) *prom: rdn over 1f out: styd on same pce* **6/1**[3]
0-53 4 hd **The Manx Missile**[19] 1349 3-9-7 60 ... JamieSpencer 1 51
(Michael Bell) *chsd ldrs: rdn over 1f out: styd on same pce* **7/2**[1]
6463 5 1 1/2 **Charlemagne Diva**[5] 1651 3-8-11 50 ...(e) KellyHarrison 5 35
(Richard Guest) *chsd ldrs: rdn over 1f out: no ex fnl f* **20/1**
061- 6 1 3/4 **Constant Dream**[168] 7609 3-9-5 58 ... GrahamLee 7 37+
(James Given) *hld up: styd on ins fnl f: nvr trbld ldrs* **15/2**
30 7 3/4 **Time To Begin (IRE)**[10] 1539 3-9-2 60 ...(tp) ThomasBrown(5) 3 36+
(David C Griffiths) *s.i.s: sn pushed along in rr: nvr nrr* **4/1**[2]
5155 8 1 3/4 **Chelsea Grey (IRE)**[36] 1066 3-8-10 49 ... LukeMorris 8 19
(Ronald Harris) *mid-div: drvn along 1/2-way: wknd over 1f out* **18/1**
204 9 1 1/4 **Nors The Panic**[5] 1651 3-8-11 50 ...(e) RobbieFitzpatrick 11 15
(Richard Guest) *s.i.s: hmpd wl over 3f out: nvr on terms* **33/1**
443- 10 3/4 **Tristessa**[225] 6093 3-9-3 56 ... LiamKeniry 10 19
(Derek Haydn Jones) *sn outpcd* **25/1**
0-00 11 3/4 **Moss The Boss (IRE)**[13] 1458 3-8-10 49 ... MickyFenton 6 9
(Paul Midgley) *prom tl rdn and wknd over 1f out* **66/1**
504- 12 hd **Borough Boy (IRE)**[227] 6054 3-9-7 60 ... MartinDwyer 9 19
(Derek Shaw) *s.s: a bhd* **16/1**
1m 1.54s (-0.76) **Going Correction** -0.225s/f (Stan) 12 Ran SP% **120.2**
Speed ratings (Par 96): **97,94,89,88,86 83,82,79,77,76 75,74**
Tote Swingers 1&2 £12.30, 2&3 £7.30, 1&3 £14.30 CSF £58.35 CT £330.81 TOTE £14.70: £4.00, £1.60, £2.10; EX 80.30 Trifecta £599.10 Pool: £1,795.79 - 2.24 winning tickets..
Owner Mrs K W Sneath **Bred** K W Sneath **Trained** Newmarket, Suffolk
FOCUS
A moderate sprint handicap for 3yos and few got into it.

1743 32RED CASINO H'CAP 1m 4f 50y(P)
3:20 (3:23) (Class 6) (0-65,65) 3-Y-O £1,940 (£577; £288; £144) Stalls Low

Form RPR
621- 1 **Nine Iron (IRE)**[193] 7026 3-9-7 65 ... MartinHarley 7 68+
(Mick Channon) *hld up: hdwy over 2f out: rdn to ld wl ins fnl f* **11/4**[2]
4125 2 1 **Bain's Pass (IRE)**[6] 1609 3-9-3 64 ... JulieBurke(3) 4 65
(Kevin Ryan) *led: pushed clr over 2f out: rdn over 1f out: hdd wl ins fnl f* **11/2**[3]
0-04 3 1 1/4 **World Map (IRE)**[45] 950 3-9-4 62 ... JoeFanning 1 61
(Mark Johnston) *chsd ldrs: pushed along 7f out: chsd wnr over 2f out: sn rdn: styd on same pce ins fnl f* **15/2**
50-4 4 1/2 **Jawinski (IRE)**[18] 1373 3-9-2 60 ... LukeMorris 3 58
(David Evans) *hld up: hdwy over 4f out: rdn over 2f out: styd on: nt trble ldrs* **12/1**
4516 5 9 **Rainford Glory (IRE)**[6] 1613 3-9-1 59 ... JamieSpencer 6 43
(David Simcock) *stdd s: hld up: hdwy over 1f out: sn rdn: wknd fnl f* **11/2**[3]
00-1 6 7 **No Truth (IRE)**[19] 1352 3-9-6 64 ... RobertWinston 5 37
(Charles Hills) *chsd ldr tl rdn over 2f out: sn wknd* **5/2**[1]
005- 7 3/4 **Hi Candy (IRE)**[202] 6793 3-8-7 51 oh3 ... PJMcDonald 8 22
(Ben Haslam) *prom: rdn over 4f out: wknd over 2f out* **9/1**
3532 8 7 **Lucky Mountain**[14] 1453 3-8-12 59 ... BillyCray(3) 2 19
(Scott Dixon) *plld hrd and prom: stdd and lost pl after 2f: rdn over 3f out: wknd over 2f out* **20/1**
2m 38.37s (-2.73) **Going Correction** -0.225s/f (Stan) 8 Ran SP% **120.2**
Speed ratings (Par 96): **100,99,98,92 87,87,82**
Tote Swingers 1&2 £4.30, 2&3 £5.20, 1&3 £3.70 CSF £19.51 CT £104.80 TOTE £3.20: £1.10, £2.60, £2.70; EX 13.70 Trifecta £126.10 Pool: £2,930.48 - 17.42 winning tickets..
Owner The Hon Mrs J M Corbett & C Wright **Bred** Patrick F Kelly **Trained** West Ilsley, Berks
■ Stewards' Enquiry : Julie Burke two-day ban: used whip above permitted level (May 7-8)
FOCUS
A moderate middle-distance handicap for 3yos.

1744 £32 BONUS AT 32RED.COM H'CAP 2m 119y(P)
3:55 (3:55) (Class 6) (0-65,65) 4-Y-O+ £1,940 (£577; £288; £144) Stalls Low

Form RPR
50-1 1 **Almost Gemini (IRE)**[35] 1080 4-9-4 61 ...(p) JamieSpencer 5 71+
(Don Cantillon) *chsd ldr tl led on bit 3f out: rdn over 1f out: hdd ins fnl f: rallied to ld nr fin* **8/13**[1]
2242 2 nk **Easydoesit (IRE)**[19] 1350 5-9-12 65 ... GrahamLee 3 74
(Tony Carroll) *a.p: chsd wnr over 2f out: rdn over 1f out: led ins fnl f: hdd nr fin* **11/2**[2]
1123 3 12 **Jezza**[19] 1350 7-9-12 65 ... LukeMorris 1 60
(Karen George) *chsd ldrs: rdn over 2f out: wknd fnl f* **8/1**[3]
00-4 4 1/2 **Barnacle**[20] 1325 4-8-3 46 oh1 ...(v) JoeFanning 6 40
(Pat Eddery) *hld up: hdwy over 2f out: wknd over 1f out* **12/1**
06-3 5 10 **Cash Injection**[32] 1117 4-8-3 46 oh1 ...(t) JamieMackay 4 28
(Karen George) *s.i.s: hld up: rdn and wknd over 2f out* **40/1**
0124 6 6 **Calculating (IRE)**[7] 1601 9-9-2 55 ... DavidProbert 2 30
(Mark Usher) *set stdy pce tl qcknd 4f out: rdn and hdd 3f out: sn wknd* **25/1**
3m 39.06s (-2.74) **Going Correction** -0.225s/f (Stan)
WFA 4 from 5yo+ 4lb 6 Ran SP% **102.4**
Speed ratings (Par 101): **97,96,91,90,86 83**
Tote Swingers 1&2 £1.90, 2&3 £1.30, 1&3 £1.80 CSF £3.25 TOTE £1.70: £1.60, £1.10; EX 2.80 Trifecta £6.10 Pool: £2,133.71 - 260.88 winning tickets..
Owner Don Cantillon **Bred** Rockhart Trading Ltd **Trained** Newmarket, Suffolk
FOCUS
A moderate staying handicap and nearly a turn-up.

1745 32RED H'CAP 1m 141y(P)
4:30 (4:30) (Class 3) (0-95,93) 4-Y-O+ £7,439 (£2,213; £1,106; £553) Stalls Low

Form RPR
6250 1 **Dubawi Island (FR)**[12] 1500 4-8-11 83 ...(b) NeilCallan 2 92
(James Tate) *mde all: clr 5f out: rdn and hung rt ins fnl f: styd on* **8/1**[3]
0340 2 1 **Verse Of Love**[10] 1542 4-9-3 89 ... MartinHarley 4 96
(David Evans) *chsd wnr: rdn over 1f out: r.o* **8/1**[3]
4403 3 3 **Mia's Boy**[30] 1159 9-9-2 93 ... RobertTart(5) 6 93+
(Chris Dwyer) *hld up: hdwy over 1f out: sn rdn: r.o: too much to do* **4/1**[2]
405- 4 1 3/4 **Good Authority (IRE)**[141] 7966 6-8-10 82 ... LukeMorris 8 78
(Karen George) *hld up: rdn over 2f out: styd on: nt trble ldrs* **11/1**
010- 5 1/2 **Postscript (IRE)**[206] 6674 5-9-6 92 ... JamieSpencer 3 87
(David Simcock) *chsd ldrs: rdn over 2f out: wknd ins fnl f* **11/4**[1]
36-3 6 1 **Kingscroft (IRE)**[112] 6 5-9-2 88 ... JoeFanning 1 80
(Mark Johnston) *prom: rdn over 1f out: wknd fnl f* **4/1**[2]
3112 7 1/2 **Elusive Hawk (IRE)**[14] 1451 9-8-6 85 ... EoinWalsh(7) 9 76
(David Evans) *hld up: n.d* **20/1**
/00- 8 4 **Newnton Lodge**[235] 5794 4-8-8 80 ... TomEaves 7 62
(Ian Williams) *s.i.s: hld up: n.d* **16/1**
060- 9 1 3/4 **Springinmystep (IRE)**[186] 7229 4-9-0 86 ... LiamKeniry 5 64
(Ed de Giles) *prom: racd keenly: wknd 2f out* **22/1**
1m 46.99s (-3.51) **Going Correction** -0.225s/f (Stan) 9 Ran SP% **112.2**
Speed ratings (Par 107): **106,105,102,100,100 99,99,95,94**
Tote Swingers 1&2 £5.10, 2&3 £10.10, 1&3 £5.60 CSF £67.50 CT £294.05 TOTE £8.90: £2.60, £2.60, £1.80; EX 77.00 Trifecta £328.90 Pool: £2,652.44 - 6.04 winning tickets..
Owner Saif Ali **Bred** Darley Stud Management Co Ltd **Trained** Newmarket, Suffolk
FOCUS
A decent handicap run at a good pace, but the front pair held those positions throughout.

1746 32RED.COM H'CAP 7f 32y(P)
5:05 (5:05) (Class 4) (0-80,79) 4-Y-O+ £4,690 (£1,395; £697; £348) Stalls High

Form RPR
-360 1 **Dr Red Eye**[31] 1148 5-9-3 78 ...(p) BillyCray(3) 3 89
(Scott Dixon) *mde all: rdn clr over 1f out: eased nr fin* **14/1**
3350 2 2 3/4 **Silverware (USA)**[20] 1318 5-9-5 77 ... PatrickMathers 8 81
(Kristin Stubbs) *a.p: chsd wnr over 5f out: rdn over 1f out: styd on same pce fnl f* **16/1**
16- 3 1 1/2 **An Cat Dubh (IRE)**[213] 6488 4-9-7 79 ... JoeFanning 2 79
(Ian Williams) *chsd ldrs: rdn over 2f out: styd on same pce fnl f* **3/1**[1]
-060 4 2 1/4 **Sound Amigo (IRE)**[42] 966 5-9-2 74 ... GrahamLee 5 68
(Ollie Pears) *prom: rdn over 2f out: styd on but no ex fnl f* **4/1**[2]
0443 5 1/2 **The Guru Of Gloom (IRE)**[15] 1430 5-8-11 69 ... MartinDwyer 7 62
(William Muir) *hld up: plld hrd: hdwy over 1f out: nt trble ldrs* **15/2**
3133 6 1 **Lord Of The Dance (IRE)**[11] 1514 7-8-13 71 ... TomEaves 11 61
(Michael Mullineaux) *s.i.s: hld up: hdwy over 2f out: rdn and hung lft over 1f out: wknd ins fnl f* **14/1**
2142 7 6 **Lieutenant Dan (IRE)**[7] 1599 6-8-8 66 ...(v) AndrewMullen 9 40
(Michael Appleby) *hld up: hdwy u.p 1/2-way: wknd over 2f out* **7/1**
000- 8 nk **Sea Soldier (IRE)**[195] 6979 5-9-6 78 ... DavidProbert 1 51
(Andrew Balding) *prom: pushed along 1/2-way: wknd 2f out* **12/1**
005 9 1 1/2 **Decent Fella (IRE)**[21] 1309 7-8-4 67 ...(t) NatashaEaton(5) 10 36
(Violet M Jordan) *hld up: hdwy over 2f out: sn wknd* **16/1**
102 10 1/2 **Paphos**[53] 839 6-8-12 77 ... EoinWalsh(7) 4 44
(David Evans) *prom: lost pl 4f out: wknd over 2f out* **6/1**[3]
1m 27.43s (-2.17) **Going Correction** -0.225s/f (Stan) 10 Ran SP% **116.3**
Speed ratings (Par 105): **103,99,98,95,95 93,87,86,84,84**
Tote Swingers 1&2 £42.50, 2&3 £11.00, 1&3 £12.30 CSF £215.48 CT £876.71 TOTE £23.30: £5.80, £7.10, £1.20; EX 232.70 Trifecta £1621.70 Part won. Pool: £2,162.32 - 0.86 winning tickets..
Owner The Red Eye Partnership **Bred** G E Amey **Trained** Babworth, Notts

FOCUS
A fair handicap and another race dominated by the pace-setters.

1747 32REDBET.COM H'CAP 1m 1f 103y(P)
5:35 (5:38) (Class 6) (0-60,58) 3-Y-0 £1,940 (£577; £288; £144) Stalls Low

Form RPR
60-4 **1** **Niknad**[27] 1210 3-8-8 **45** MartinLane 5 49
(Brian Ellison) *hld up: hdwy u.p over 1f out: styd on to ld wl ins fnl f* **10/1**
6042 **2** ¾ **Scepticism (USA)**[15] 1428 3-9-3 **54** JoeFanning 4 56
(Mark Johnston) *led: clr 6f out: rdn over 1f out: hdd wl ins fnl f* **11/4**[2]
3314 **3** ¾ **Silver Fawn (IRE)**[15] 1428 3-9-1 **52** (be) JimmyQuinn 6 52
(John Weymes) *hld up: hdwy over 2f out: rdn over 1f out: unable qck nr fin* **10/1**
33-5 **4** 1 ¾ **Sweet Vintage (IRE)**[104] 122 3-9-7 **58** EddieAhern 3 55
(Mark Brisbourne) *a.p: chsd ldr 3f out: rdn over 1f out: styd on same pce ins fnl f* **9/1**[3]
5-30 **5** 6 **Sweet Alabama**[15] 1423 3-9-4 **55** JamieSpencer 1 39
(Rod Millman) *chsd ldrs: rdn over 2f out: eased whn btn fnl f* **9/1**[3]
60-6 **6** 2 ¼ **By A Wiska**[96] 237 3-9-1 **52** (t) PJMcDonald 2 31
(Ann Duffield) *chsd ldr tl rdn 3f out: wknd 2f out* **33/1**
6035 **7** ¾ **Exit Clause**[18] 1373 3-8-11 **53** (p) RobertTart(5) 9 31
(Tony Carroll) *hld up: rdn over 2f out: n.d* **14/1**
600- **8** 59 **Maisie's Moon (USA)**[153] 7813 3-9-7 **58** MartinHarley 8
(Hughie Morrison) *chsd ldrs: lost pl 6f out: bhd fnl 4f: t.o* **7/4**[1]
5043 **9** 4 ½ **Eyeline**[22] 1289 3-8-11 **48** (v) MartinDwyer 7
(Reg Hollinshead) *hld up: bhd fnl 5f: t.o* **16/1**

2m 1.53s (-0.17) **Going Correction** -0.225s/f (Stan) 9 Ran SP% **116.7**
Speed ratings (Par 96): **91,90,89,88,82 80,80,27,23**
Tote Swingers 1&2 £7.50, 2&3 £3.30, 1&3 £9.20 CSF £38.16 CT £289.90 TOTE £12.80: £3.30, £1.30, £1.90; EX 41.10 Trifecta £231.30 Pool: £2,013.28 - 6.52 winning tickets..
Owner Market Avenue Racing Club Ltd **Bred** Miss D Fleming **Trained** Norton, N Yorks

FOCUS
A moderate 3yo handicap.
T/Jkpt: Not won. T/Plt: £221.90 to a £1 stake. Pool: £59,498.67 - 195.65 winning tickets. T/Qpdt: £21.00 to a £1 stake. Pool: £4,859.38 - 170.92 winning tickets. CR

1291 YARMOUTH (L-H)
Tuesday, April 23

OFFICIAL GOING: Good to firm (good in places; 7.6)
Wind: fairly light, across Weather: dry and sunny

1748 JOHN KEMP LTD 4X4 SPECIALIST OF NORWICH APPRENTICE H'CAP 6f 3y
4:40 (4:40) (Class 6) (0-60,65) 4-Y-0+ £1,940 (£577; £288; £144) Stalls Centre

Form RPR
50-1 **1** **Whisky Bravo**[7] 1598 4-9-4 **65** 6ex ClaireMurray(8) 8 72
(David Brown) *chsd ldrs: wnt 2nd over 2f out tl rdn to ld wl over 1f out: hld on wl fnl 100yds* **9/2**[2]
0166 **2** hd **Putin (IRE)**[12] 1497 5-9-0 **58** (bt) SiobhanMiller(5) 6 64
(Phil McEntee) *led tl hdd wl over 1f out: rallied u.p and ev ch fnl 100yds: kpt on but jst hld* **7/1**
4124 **3** 1 ¾ **Artful Lady (IRE)**[27] 1196 4-8-12 **54** JordanVaughan(3) 5 54+
(George Margarson) *hld up in last trio: stl plenty to do whn asked for effrt and hdwy against stands' rail over 1f out: chsd ldrs and edgd lft ins fnl f: no imp fnl 100yds* **5/1**[3]
0340 **4** 1 ½ **Sextons House (IRE)**[3] 1681 5-8-9 **48** (b) AaronJones 4 44
(Alan McCabe) *s.i.s: bhd: rdn and hdwy over 2f out: chsd ldrs 1f out: no imp ins fnl f* **6/1**
00-0 **5** ¾ **One Kool Dude**[22] 1294 4-9-4 **60** (v) LouisSteward(3) 3 53
(Michael Bell) *chsd ldrs: rdn over 2f out: no ex u.p and outpcd over 1f out: wknd ins fnl f* **12/1**
0600 **6** 2 ¼ **Ishiamiracle**[22] 1294 4-8-6 **50** (p) KirstenSmith(5) 1 36
(Phil McEntee) *racd alone in centre: chsd ldr tl over 2f out: btn over 1f out: wknd fnl f* **25/1**
-020 **7** ¾ **Hatta Stream (IRE)**[54] 822 7-9-4 **57** CharlotteJenner 7 41
(Lydia Pearce) *in tch in midfield: lost pl and rdn 2f out: sme hdwy over 1f out: no imp 1f out and wknd ins fnl f* **10/3**[1]
-300 **8** nse **Miakora**[48] 903 5-8-7 **46** oh1 (v) DanielCremin 9 29
(Mick Quinn) *in tch in midfield: rdn and unable qck 2f out: hung lft and btn over 1f out: wknd ins fnl f* **10/1**
-000 **9** 4 ½ **Major Muscari (IRE)**[17] 1396 5-8-7 **46** oh1 KevinStott 2 15
(Ian McInnes) *s.i.s: in rr: rdn and effrt 2f out: sn no imp: wknd 1f out* **20/1**

1m 13.58s (-0.82) **Going Correction** -0.35s/f (Firm) 9 Ran SP% **110.1**
Speed ratings (Par 101): **91,90,88,86,85 82,81,81,75**
Tote Swingers 1&2 £5.10, 2&3 £7.30, 1&3 £2.70 CSF £33.19 CT £150.97 TOTE £7.40: £2.10, £3.10, £1.20; EX 43.00 Trifecta £168.90 Pool: £535.44 - 2.37 winning tickets..
Owner The Bachelor Party **Bred** Peter Onslow **Trained** Averham Park, Notts
■ Claire Murray's first winner.

FOCUS
A dry run up to a meeting run on ground that had been "selectively watered". Not much to dwell on in just an ordinary handicap. The gallop was a reasonable one but not many figured.

1749 HAVEN SEASHORE HOLIDAY PARK AT GREAT YARMOUTH MAIDEN AUCTION STKS 5f 43y
5:10 (5:11) (Class 6) 2-Y-0 £1,940 (£577; £288; £144) Stalls Centre

Form RPR
1 **Der Blaue Reiter (IRE)** 2-8-13 0 PatCosgrave 5 74+
(George Baker) *in tch: rdn to chse ldr 2f out: drvn and led 1f out: rn green and hung rt ins fnl f: stened and styd on wl towards fin* **12/1**
4 **2** 1 ¼ **Cockney Bob**[18] 1360 2-8-9 0 CathyGannon 4 66+
(J S Moore) *s.i.s: rn green and sn rdn along in rr: hdwy 1/2-way: drvn and hdwy to chse ldrs over 1f out: styng on whn carried rt and sightly hmpd ins fnl f: wnt 2nd wl ins fnl f* **13/8**[1]
045 **3** 1 ¼ **Marilyn Marquessa**[17] 1399 2-8-5 0 HayleyTurner 1 57
(Jo Hughes) *led: rdn wl over 1f out: hdd 1f out: sn drvn and stl ev ch tl no ex and wknd fnl 75yds* **5/1**[3]
4 4 ½ **Anfield** 2-8-5 0 AndreaAtzeni 7 41
(Mick Quinn) *chsd ldr tl over 2f out: sn rdn and no ex: 4th and btn over 1f out: wknd fnl f* **11/1**
4 **5** 4 **Jaga Time**[14] 1449 2-8-11 0 PaulHanagan 6 32
(Richard Fahey) *chsd ldrs: rdn and lost pl ent fnl 2f: wknd over 1f out* **4/1**[2]
3 **6** 1 **Aweebitowinker**[15] 1432 2-8-9 0 LiamJones 2 27+
(J S Moore) *v.s.a: sn rdn along: clsd 3f out: struggling u.p 2f out: sn wknd* **12/1**
7 ½ **Applejack Lad** 2-8-11 0 KierenFallon 3 27
(John Ryan) *pushed along in last trio: hdwy 1/2-way: btn over 1f out: nt given and hrd time after and wknd fnl f* **7/1**

1m 3.16s (0.46) **Going Correction** -0.35s/f (Firm) 7 Ran SP% **111.0**
Speed ratings (Par 90): **82,80,78,70,64 62,62**
Tote Swingers 1&2 £4.30, 2&3 £2.70, 1&3 £8.20 CSF £30.19 TOTE £16.10: £7.40, £1.10; EX 47.60 Trifecta £182.80 Pool: £1659.16 - 6.80 winning tickets..
Owner Clive Washbourn **Bred** Mrs Ann Kennedy **Trained** Manton, Wilts

FOCUS
A couple that had shown ability and a couple of interestingly bred newcomers in an ordinary maiden. The gallop was sound and this form looks reliable. The second and third help set the level.

1750 WEDDINGS AT GREAT YARMOUTH RACECOURSE MEDIAN AUCTION MAIDEN STKS 6f 3y
5:40 (5:42) (Class 5) 3-4-Y-0 £2,587 (£770; £384; £192) Stalls Centre

Form RPR
6-20 **1** **Khelman (IRE)**[24] 1250 3-9-1 78 PaulHanagan 5 74
(Richard Fahey) *chsd ldrs: rdn to ld 1f out: styd on wl to draw clr fnl f* **11/8**[1]
2 4 **Chester Row** 3-9-1 0 KirstyMilczarek 6 61+
(James Toller) *in tch: rdn and effrt over 1f out: no threat to wnr but edgd lft and kpt on ins fnl f to go 2nd on post* **15/8**[2]
03 **3** nse **Harbour Captain (IRE)**[14] 1450 3-9-1 0 J-PGuillambert 4 61
(Jo Hughes) *chsd ldr tl led 2f out: awkward hd carriage whn rdn: hdd 1f out: sn outpcd and btn: lost 2nd on post* **40/1**
0- **4** 1 **Oh So Sassy**[217] 6343 3-8-10 0 TedDurcan 1 53
(Chris Wall) *in tch: rdn and effrt 2f out: outpcd u.p jst ins fnl f: plugged on same pce after* **14/1**
240- **5** 3 ¾ **Speedfit Boy (IRE)**[215] 6411 3-9-1 68 (b[1]) TomQueally 3 46
(George Margarson) *sn rdn along and detached in last: n.d* **13/2**[3]
5-3 **6** ½ **Clearing**[29] 1174 3-8-11 0 ow1 PatCosgrave 2 43
(Jim Boyle) *led tl hdd 2f out: hung bdly lft and sn wknd: eased whn wl btn ins fnl f* **10/1**

1m 11.85s (-2.55) **Going Correction** -0.35s/f (Firm) 6 Ran SP% **108.4**
Speed ratings (Par 103): **103,97,97,96,91 90**
Tote Swingers 1&2 £2.20, 2&3 £20.50, 1&3 £3.20 CSF £3.82 TOTE £2.10: £1.50, £2.00; EX 3.30 Trifecta £25.90 Pool: £903.28 - 26.15 winning tickets..
Owner S & G Clayton **Bred** Oghill House Stud & Jimmy Hyland **Trained** Musley Bank, N Yorks

FOCUS
An uncompetitive maiden in which the gallop was sound.

1751 GOLD & SILVER EXCHANGE OF GREAT YARMOUTH H'CAP 1m 3y
6:15 (6:17) (Class 4) (0-85,83) 4-Y-0+ £4,690 (£1,395; £697; £348) Stalls Centre

Form RPR
21-3 **1** **Snooky**[14] 1442 4-8-10 **72** PaulHanagan 3 82+
(Richard Fahey) *mde all: rdn and qcknd over 2f out: r.o strly and drew clr fnl f: readily* **11/4**[2]
2162 **2** 2 ¼ **Showboating (IRE)**[8] 1571 5-9-1 **77** (v) KierenFallon 5 82
(Alan McCabe) *v.s.a: in tch in rr: swtchd lft and hdwy over 4f out: chsd wnr over 3f out: drvn 2f out: no ex and outpcd ins fnl f: kpt on* **12/1**
350- **3** nk **Haylaman (IRE)**[221] 6202 5-9-7 **83** TomQueally 4 87
(David Simcock) *chsd ldrs: rdn ent fnl f: sltly outpcd over 1f out: rallied u.p and kpt on again ins fnl f: no threat to wnr* **11/2**[3]
502- **4** 2 ¼ **Great Expectations**[164] 7684 5-8-11 **73** FrederikTylicki 1 72
(J R Jenkins) *t.k.h: hld up in tch in midfield: rdn and effrt ent fnl 2f: no threat to wnr and styd on same pce fnl f* **15/2**
003- **5** 1 ½ **Shamdarley (IRE)**[207] 6638 5-9-3 **79** AndreaAtzeni 7 75+
(Marco Botti) *chsd wnr tl over 3f out: sn rdn and lost pl over 2f out: plugged on same pce fr over 1f out* **15/8**[1]
346- **6** 1 **Barwick**[216] 6381 5-9-0 **79** SimonPearce(3) 2 72
(Mark H Tompkins) *hld up in tch in rr: hdwy to chse ldrs 3f out: sn rdn and hung lft: wknd over 1f out* **9/1**
124- **7** 5 **Macchiara**[246] 5409 4-8-11 **73** SilvestreDeSousa 6 55
(Rae Guest) *t.k.h: hld up in tch: rdn and outpcd 2f out: wknd over 1f out* **18/1**

1m 39.82s (-0.78) **Going Correction** -0.35s/f (Firm) 7 Ran SP% **111.6**
Speed ratings (Par 105): **89,86,86,84,82 81,76**
Tote Swingers 1&2 £4.20, 2&3 £5.60, 1&3 £2.30 CSF £32.46 TOTE £3.90: £2.80, £2.30; EX 13.50 Trifecta £48.80 Pool: £1321.29 - 20.27 winning tickets..
Owner Mrs Janis Macpherson **Bred** Dunchurch Lodge Stud Co **Trained** Musley Bank, N Yorks

FOCUS
A fair handicap but a steady pace favoured those at the head of the field and this bare form doesn't look totally reliable.

1752 MOUGHTON ENGINEERING H'CAP 1m 3y
6:50 (6:50) (Class 6) (0-65,65) 4-Y-0+ £1,940 (£577; £288; £144) Stalls Centre

Form RPR
2165 **1** **Jonnie Skull (IRE)**[5] 1657 7-8-10 **54** ow1 (vt) KierenFallon 4 65
(Phil McEntee) *racd keenly: mde all: rdn over 1f out: kpt on wl ins fnl f: rdn out* **12/1**
064- **2** 3 **Pat's Legacy (USA)**[237] 5741 7-9-7 **65** RyanMoore 2 69
(Gary Moore) *chsd ldrs: chsd wnr over 2f out: rdn 2f out: drvn and styd on same pce fr over 1f out* **9/4**[1]
1133 **3** 1 ¾ **Caledonia Prince**[27] 1203 5-8-11 **55** (b) HayleyTurner 3 55
(Jo Hughes) *hld up in midfield: hdwy over 2f out: drvn to chse ldng pair wl over 1f out: kpt on same pce fnl f* **3/1**[2]
00-6 **4** 7 **Dream Walker (FR)**[23] 1271 4-9-1 **59** DavidNolan 8 43
(Ian McInnes) *chsd ldrs: rdn over 2f out: 4th and btn over 1f out: wknd ins fnl f* **12/1**
0362 **5** 1 ¾ **Zaheeb**[22] 1294 5-8-13 **57** (b) TomQueally 9 37
(Dave Morris) *chsd wnr tl over 2f out: racd awkwardky u.p and nt qckn 2f out: wknd over 1f out* **9/2**[3]
306/ **6** 4 ½ **Laugh Or Cry**[565] 6653 5-8-13 **57** SebSanders 6 27
(Dean Ivory) *t.k.h: hld up in midfield: rdn and struggling over 2f out: wknd wl over 1f out* **25/1**
-004 **7** hd **Smokey Oakey (IRE)**[11] 1297 9-8-13 **60** (p) SimonPearce(3) 1 29
(Mark H Tompkins) *hld up in rr: sme hdwy 1/2-way: rdn and no imp 2f out: nvr trbld ldrs* **18/1**
3000 **8** 14 **Bubbly Braveheart (IRE)**[12] 1502 6-8-7 **51** oh6 (t) KirstyMilczarek 7
(Phil McEntee) *s.i.s: a bhd: lost tch 3f out: t.o* **66/1**
010- **9** dist **Lady Layla**[159] 7732 4-9-5 **63** WilliamBuick 5
(Lady Herries) *sn bhd and nvr gng: lost tch 5f out: eased fnl 3f and wl t.o* **6/1**

1m 37.56s (-3.04) **Going Correction** -0.35s/f (Firm) 9 Ran SP% **114.2**
Speed ratings (Par 101): **101,98,96,89,87 83,82,68,**
Tote Swingers 1&2 £7.20, 2&3 £3.30, 1&3 £5.40 CSF £38.87 CT £104.52 TOTE £12.10: £2.90, £1.80, £1.20; EX 44.00 Trifecta £171.50 Pool: £726.56 - 3.17 winning tickets..

The Form Book Flat, Raceform Ltd, Compton, RG20 6NL.

Owner Eventmaker Racehorses **Bred** Canice Farrell Jnr **Trained** Newmarket, Suffolk

FOCUS

A modest handicap run at a reasonable gallop but another race in which very few figured. The first three pulled clear.

1753 BURLINGTON PALM HOTEL H'CAP — 1m 2f 21y

7:25 (7:25) (Class 4) (0-80,80) 4-Y-O+ — **£4,690** (£1,395; £697; £348) **Stalls** Low

Form — RPR

06-6 **1** **Spirit Of The Law (IRE)**[13] 1463 4-9-0 **80**............. GeorgeChaloner(7) 8 — 89
(Richard Fahey) *in tch in midfield: n.m.r 4f out: swtchd rt and hdwy between horses over 1f out: led ins fnl f: r.o wl* **7/2**[1]

-413 **2** ¾ **Tenure**[37] 1054 4-8-13 **72**........................ RyanMoore 9 — 80
(Gary Moore) *hld up in last pair: hdwy 3f out: drvn and ev ch 1f out: styd on same pce fnl 100yds* **4/1**[2]

00 **3** *nk* **Cawett Cove (IRE)**[34] 1092 5-8-9 **75**.................... IanBurns(7) 2 — 82?
(Jane Chapple-Hyam) *led: clr 1/2-way: rdn 2f out: drvn and hdd ins fnl f: kpt on same pce after* **40/1**

5010 **4** 3 **Thecornishcowboy**[17] 1390 4-9-0 **73**........................(tp) TomQueally 3 — 74
(John Ryan) *in tch in midfield: rdn and effrt to chse ldrs 2f out: drvn and unable qck 1f out: one pce after* **12/1**

-324 **5** *nk* **Jewelled**[20] 1327 7-9-1 **74**........................ SebSanders 5 — 74
(Lady Herries) *in tch in midfield: hdwy 4f out: chsd ldr over 3f out: rdn and ev ch over 1f out: unable qck and btn ins fnl f: wknd fnl f* **7/1**

-200 **6** 2 **Flying Trader (USA)**[20] 1327 4-8-13 **72**........................ WilliamBuick 4 — 68
(Jane Chapple-Hyam) *chsd ldrs: rdn and unable qck wl over 1f out: btn 1f out: wknd ins fnl f* **11/2**[3]

0-00 **7** *hd* **Lady Macduff (IRE)**[22] 1281 4-9-5 **78**........................ SilvestreDeSousa 7 — 74
(Mark Johnston) *in tch in last trio: effrt u.p over 2f out: drvn and plugged on same pce fr over 1f out: nvr trble ldrs* **17/2**

000- **8** 7 **My Guardian Angel**[132] 8082 4-8-9 **71**.................... AshleyMorgan(3) 11 — 53
(Mark H Tompkins) *hld up in last pair: rdn and short-lived effrt 2f out: sn btn and wknd over 1f out* **33/1**

060- **9** *hd* **Handsome Ransom**[216] 6376 4-9-5 **78**........................ TedDurcan 6 — 62
(David Lanigan) *chsd ldr tl over 2f out: sn outpcd and lost pl: wknd over 1f out* **6/1**

000- **10** 14 **Chain Of Events**[9] 6819 6-9-4 **77**........................(t) HayleyTurner 10 — 40
(Sarah Humphrey) *in tch in midfield tl dropped to rr over 2f out: sn lost tch* **16/1**

2m 7.38s (-3.12) **Going Correction** -0.175s/f (Firm) — **10** Ran SP% **113.9**

Speed ratings (Par 105): **105,104,104,101,101 99,99,94,94,82**

Tote Swingers 1&2 £3.80, 2&3 £16.00, 1&3 £21.70 CSF £16.90 CT £466.43 TOTE £3.50: £1.10, £2.40, £11.80; EX 19.20 Trifecta £632.20 Part won. Pool: £842.95 - 0.36 winning tickets..

Owner The Matthewman One Partnership **Bred** Georgestown Stud **Trained** Musley Bank, N Yorks

FOCUS

A fair handicap run at just an ordinary gallop.

1754 VISITENGLAND.COM H'CAP — 1m 2f 21y

7:55 (7:55) (Class 5) (0-75,75) 3-Y-O — **£2,587** (£770; £384; £192) **Stalls** Low

Form — RPR

22-1 **1** **Iridescence**[88] 377 3-9-7 **75**........................ RyanMoore 2 — 82+
(Jeremy Noseda) *chsd ldrs: clsd to join ldr 3f out: rdn to ld wl over 1f out: drvn and hld on wl fnl f: all out* **11/4**[1]

021 **2** *nk* **Speed Boogie**[21] 1300 3-9-4 **72**........................ AndreaAtzeni 1 — 78+
(Marco Botti) *led: hung rt bnd 6f out: rdn over 2f out: hdd wl over 1f out: kpt on wl u.p and sustained duel w wnr: a jst hld* **3/1**[2]

443- **3** 1 ½ **Interior Minister**[146] 7899 3-9-6 **74**........................ HayleyTurner 9 — 77+
(Jo Hughes) *stdd s: hld up in last pair: rdn and effrt 2f out: hdwy u.p ins fnl f: r.o to go 3rd fnl 75yds: nt pce to rch ldrs* **11/2**

000- **4** ¾ **Funky Cold Medina**[213] 6489 3-9-3 **71**........................ PaulHanagan 7 — 72
(Charles Hills) *in tch in midfield: rdn and effrt 2f out: drvn and styd on same pce fr over 1f out* **6/1**

104- **5** *hd* **Topamichi**[183] 7289 3-8-4 **61** oh2.................... SimonPearce(3) 8 — 63
(Mark H Tompkins) *t.k.h: stdd and dropped in bhd after s: hld up in last pair: rdn and effrt on inner 2f out: disputing 3rd and styng on same pce whn rdr lost iron ins fnl f: lost 2 pls towards fin* **20/1**

304- **6** 1 ½ **Kelvingrove (IRE)**[132] 8070 3-9-6 **74**........................ TomQueally 6 — 72
(Ed Vaughan) *chsd ldr tl 3f out: stl pressing ldrs and rdn over 2f out: outpcd and edgd lft over 1f out: btn and one pce fnl f* **10/3**[3]

2m 9.51s (-0.99) **Going Correction** -0.175s/f (Firm) — **6** Ran SP% **109.2**

Speed ratings (Par 98): **96,95,94,93,93 92**

Tote Swingers 1&2 £2.30, 2&3 £1.40, 1&3 £4.40 CSF £10.61 CT £35.95 TOTE £3.60: £2.10, £2.70; EX 10.40 Trifecta £20.70 Pool: £1043.26 - 37.78 winning tickets..

Owner Cheveley Park Stud **Bred** Cheveley Park Stud Ltd **Trained** Newmarket, Suffolk

FOCUS

Several unexposed sorts in a fair handicap. The gallop was a modest one and the field finished in a bit of a heap.

T/Plt: £20.70 to a £1 stake. Pool: £45,139.26 - 1585.36 winning tickets. T/Qpdt: £5.70 to a £1 stake. Pool: £4,269.00 - 549.4 winning tickets. SP

1755 - (Foreign Racing) - See Raceform Interactive

1594 MAISONS-LAFFITTE (R-H)

Tuesday, April 23

OFFICIAL GOING: Turf: soft

1756a PRIX DE BEAUVAL (H'CAP) (3YO) (TURF) — 1m 2f (S)

4:20 (4:23) 3-Y-O — **£12,195** (£4,878; £3,658; £2,439; £1,219)

RPR

1 **Polo (GER)**[108] 3-9-4 **0**........................ GregoryBenoist 7 — 80
(D Smaga, France) **41/10**[1]

2 1 ½ **Varing (FR)**[35] 3-9-3 **0**........................(b) FabriceVeron 11 — 76
(P Chatelain, France) **11/1**

3 1 ½ **Chene Boppe (FR)**[22] 3-9-1 **0**........................ CesarPasserat(3) 5 — 74
(F-X De Chevigny, France) **11/1**

4 ½ **Missing Ones (FR)**[12] 3-8-10 **0**........................ ChristopheSoumillon 2 — 65
(P Chatelain, France) **11/2**[2]

5 *snk* **Haya Kan (FR)**[26] 3-9-3 **0**........................(b[1]) FranckBlondel 4 — 72
(Mme L Audon, France) **8/1**[3]

6 ½ **Destiny Highway (FR)**[55] 818 3-9-2 **0**........................ MaximeGuyon 1 — 70
(Gay Kelleway) *racd in 4th on ins: pulling hrd early stages: lost pl 3f out: dropped bk into midfield: rallied and r.o again u.p fnl 1 1/2f* **23/1**

7 ¾ **Guilla (FR)**[32] 3-9-4 **0**........................ RonanThomas 13 — 70
(P Van De Poele, France) **24/1**

8 *snk* **Tom Mix (FR)**[22] 3-9-2 **0**........................(p) ThierryThulliez 9 — 68
(F-X De Chevigny, France) **25/1**

9 *hd* **Sweni Hill (IRE)**[46] 3-8-13 **0**........................ AntoineHamelin 8 — 65
(Y De Nicolay, France) **26/1**

10 2 ½ **Sakina (FR)**[47] 3-7-13 **0**........................ JimmyTastayre(4) 16 — 50
(G Brillet, France) **31/1**

0 **Royalitta (FR)**[14] 3-8-11 **0**........................ StephanePasquier 12
(M Boutin, France) **11/1**

0 **Bahaa (FR)**[32] 3-9-4 **0**........................ ThierryJarnet 10
(F Head, France) **13/1**

0 **Amigo Tonio (FR)**[8] 3-9-4 **0**........................ OlivierPeslier 6
(Robert Collet, France) **15/1**

0 **Good Game (IRE)**[164] 3-8-5 **0**.................... Christophe-PatriceLemaire 3
(Y De Nicolay, France) **50/1**

0 **Ciel D'Automne (FR)**[91] 331 3-8-5 **0**....................(b) AnthonyCrastus 14
(J-P Delaporte, France) **23/1**

0 **Brakina (FR)**[38] 3-9-3 **0**........................ UmbertoRispoli 15
(J Heloury, France) **16/1**

2m 12.87s (10.47) — **16** Ran SP% **115.3**

WIN (incl. 1 euro stake): 5.10. PLACES: 2.30, 4.00, 3.30. DF: 30.60. SF: 52.60.

Owner Gerard Augustin-Normand **Bred** Gestut Etzean **Trained** Lamorlaye, France

1458 CATTERICK (L-H)

Wednesday, April 24

OFFICIAL GOING: Good to firm (good in places; 8.3)

Wind: Moderate across Weather: Heavy cloud

1757 RACINGUK.COM APPRENTICE H'CAP — 7f

1:35 (1:35) (Class 6) (0-65,65) 4-Y-O+ — **£2,385** (£704; £352) **Stalls** Centre

Form — RPR

-001 **1** **Thrust Control (IRE)**[7] 1603 6-8-12 **56** 6ex.............(p) GeorgeChaloner 3 — 64
(Tracy Waggott) *led: hdd 1/2-way: cl up tl rdn to ld again 1 1/2f out: drvn ins fnl f and kpt on wl* **9/2**[1]

000- **2** ½ **Secret City (IRE)**[177] 7447 7-9-5 **63**........................ ConorHarrison 1 — 70
(Robin Bastiman) *trckd ldrs on inner: n.m.r 4f out and again 3f out: hdwy to chse ldrs 2f out: rdn to chse wnr ent fnl f: sn edgd rt and ev ch tl no ex towards fin* **28/1**

353- **3** 1 ½ **Eastlands Lad (IRE)**[211] 6562 4-8-8 **59**.................... KatieDowson(7) 13 — 62+
(Micky Hammond) *towards rr: sme hdwy on inner whn n.m.r over 4f out: hdwy on inner 2f out: rdn wl over 1f out: styd on fnl f: nrst fin* **20/1**

100- **4** 1 ½ **Drive Home (USA)**[166] 7670 6-9-2 **60**........................(p) IanBurns 2 — 59
(Noel Wilson) *trckd ldrs: hdwy 3f out: chsd ldng pair 2f out: sn rdn and one pce fnl f* **8/1**[3]

-044 **5** 1 ¾ **Mishhar (IRE)**[7] 1610 4-9-2 **60**........................(v[1]) DavidSimmonson 5 — 54+
(Tony Coyle) *towards rr whn squeezed out after 1f: hdwy whn n.m.r on inner over 4f out: rdn along wl over 2f out: kpt on appr fnl f: nrst fin* **10/1**

04-5 **6** ½ **Viking Warrior (IRE)**[14] 1462 6-9-2 **65**.................... ConnorBeasley(5) 7 — 58
(Michael Dods) *towards rr: hdwy over 2f out: rdn and kpt on fnl f: nrst fin* **5/1**[2]

5635 **7** 1 **Boy The Bell**[18] 1397 6-8-13 **57**........................(v) JacobButterfield 4 — 47
(Ollie Pears) *dwlt: sn chsng ldrs: rdn along over 2f out: kpt on same pce* **12/1**

1341 **8** ¾ **Pull The Pin (IRE)**[15] 1452 4-8-6 **55**....................(b) LukeLeadbitter(5) 10 — 43
(Declan Carroll) *cl up: led 1/2-way: rdn along 2f out: hdd 1 1/2f out: drvn appr fnl f: sn hung rt and wknd* **8/1**[3]

300- **9** ¾ **West Leake Hare (IRE)**[222] 6211 4-9-0 **65**................ CarolineKelly(7) 11 — 51+
(David Nicholls) *n.m.r and squeezed out 1st f: in rr tl sme late hdwy* **10/1**

1200 **10** *nk* **Prince James**[20] 1351 6-9-1 **62**........................ MatthewHopkins(3) 6 — 47
(Michael Easterby) *prom: rdn along 3f out: wknd fnl 2f* **12/1**

5360 **11** *shd* **Hab Reeh**[20] 1351 5-8-12 **56**........................(t) DavidBergin 15 — 41
(Ruth Carr) *midfield: hdwy on outer over 2f out: sn rdn along and no imp* **16/1**

0060 **12** *nse* **Muftarres (IRE)**[6] 1650 8-9-5 **63**........................(p) NedCurtis 9 — 48
(Frank Sheridan) *dwlt: a in rr* **14/1**

00-0 **13** 1 **Hoppy's Flyer (FR)**[24] 1271 5-9-1 **62**....................(v) SamanthaBell(3) 12 — 44
(Paul Midgley) *towards rr: sme hdwy on wd outside 2f out: sn rdn along: wknd over 1f out* **20/1**

33-6 **14** 2 **No Quarter (IRE)**[14] 1459 6-8-9 **58**........................ DanielCremin(5) 8 — 35
(Tracy Waggott) *in tch: effrt 3f out: rdn along over 2f out: sn wknd* **8/1**[3]

0-50 **15** 8 **Sairaam (IRE)**[111] 42 7-9-2 **60**........................ RyanWhile 14 — 15
(Charles Smith) *dwlt: a bhd: fin lame* **33/1**

1m 27.24s (0.24) **Going Correction** +0.10s/f (Good) — **15** Ran SP% **130.2**

Speed ratings (Par 101): **102,101,99,98,96 95,94,93,92,92 92,92,90,88,79**

toteswingers 1&2 £30.70, 2&3 £184.30, 1&3 £25.30 CSF £146.88 CT £2424.26 TOTE £4.50: £2.00, £7.80, £3.90; EX 160.20 Trifecta £1081.60 Part won. Pool of £1442.17 - 0.36 winning units..

Owner David Tate **Bred** Rathasker Stud **Trained** Spennymoor, Co Durham

FOCUS

A wide-open apprentice handicap, run at a sound pace. It paid to race prominently.

1758 INTERACTIVE PLANNING H'CAP — 5f

2:05 (2:05) (Class 5) (0-70,70) 4-Y-O+ — **£2,587** (£770; £384; £192) **Stalls** Low

Form — RPR

210- **1** **Mr Mo Jo**[189] 7179 5-9-0 63........................(b[1]) DanielTudhope 4 — 75
(Lawrence Mullaney) *qckly away: sn clr: mde all: rdn over 1f out: kpt on wl towards fin* **13/2**[3]

4-03 **2** 2 ¾ **Tuibama (IRE)**[14] 1465 4-8-12 61........................(p) RoystonFfrench 9 — 63
(Tracy Waggott) *a chsng wnr: hdwy wl over 1f out: rdn and hung lft ins fnl f: one pce* **6/1**[2]

1115 **3** 2 ¾ **Greenhead High**[18] 1388 5-9-0 63........................(v) AdrianNicholls 3 — 55
(David Nicholls) *chsd ldng pair: rdn along 1/2-way: drvn wl over 1f out: no imp* **3/1**[1]

0065 **4** 2 **Ingleby Star (IRE)**[25] 1253 8-8-12 66........................(p) LMcNiff(5) 8 — 51
(Ian McInnes) *in tch: hdwy 2f out: rdn to chse ldrs over 1f out: sn no imp* **16/1**

530- **5** ½ **Novalist**[183] 7316 5-8-11 60........................ RobertWinston 2 — 43
(Robin Bastiman) *dwlt: hdwy 1/2-way: rdn along wl over 1f out: kpt on fnl f: nt rch ldrs* **6/1**[2]

0-46 **6** 1 ¾ **Wicked Wilma (IRE)**[14] 1465 9-8-0 56.................... JordanHibberd(7) 5 — 33
(Alan Berry) *dwlt and towards rr: hdwy 2f out: sn rdn and nt rch ldrs* **20/1**

-535 **7** 1 ½ **Sophie's Beau (USA)**[14] 1465 6-8-0 56 oh7.....(tp) DanielleMooney(7) 12 — 28
(Michael Chapman) *chsd ldrs on wd outside: rdn along 2f out: grad wknd* **33/1**

0250 **8** ½ **M J Woodward**[4] 1694 4-9-4 67........................ JamesSullivan 10 — 37
(Paul Green) *dwlt: a in rr* **8/1**

0606 **9** ½ **Ambitious Icarus**[23] 1283 4-9-3 66 (e) RobbieFitzpatrick 6 34
(Richard Guest) *dwlt: a in rr* **10/1**

006- **10** 3½ **Tongalooma**[238] 5739 7-8-13 62 PJMcDonald 7 17
(James Moffatt) *nvr nr ldrs* **10/1**

000- **11** 2¾ **Invincible Force (IRE)**[203] 6788 9-9-2 65 DavidAllan 1 11
(Paul Green) *dwlt and towards rr: bhd fr 1/2-way* **25/1**

06-0 **12** 1¾ **Nomoreblondes**[6] 1649 9-9-7 70 (v) MickyFenton 11 9
(Paul Midgley) *chsd ldrs on outer: rdn along 1/2-way: sn wknd* **9/1**

59.89s (0.09) **Going Correction** +0.10s/f (Good) **12** Ran SP% **123.6**
Speed ratings (Par 103): **103,98,94,91,90 87,85,84,83,77 73,70**
toteswingers 1&2 £4.90, 2&3 £2.40, 1&3 £5.70 CSF £46.30 CT £147.01 TOTE £10.40: £3.10, £1.40, £1.30; EX 45.90 Trifecta £117.20 Pool: £2081.48 - 13.31 winning units..
Owner Ontoawinner 3 **Bred** D A Flavell **Trained** Great Habton, N Yorks

FOCUS
Plenty of pace on for this sprint handicap, with those racing prominently dominating from the off and the winner making all.

1759 WE RACE AGAIN ON 7TH MAY H'CAP (DIV I) 7f
2:35 (2:37) (Class 6) (0-60,66) 3-Y-O £2,385 (£704; £352) **Stalls** Centre

Form RPR

560- **1** **Loucal**[176] 7459 3-9-2 **55** (b[1]) StevieDonohoe 2 64
(Noel Quinlan) *in tch on inner: n.m.r and sltly outpcd after 3f: swtchd rt to outer and hdwy wl over 2f out: rdn to chse ldrs over 1f out: styd on wl fnl f to ld nr fin* **10/1**

20-2 **2** *hd* **Clock On Tom**[19] 1367 3-8-8 **54** MatthewHopkins(7) 7 62
(Michael Easterby) *in tch: gd hdwy on outer to trck ldrs 3f out: rdn over 1f out: led ent fnl f: sn drvn and edgd rt: hdd and no ex nr fin* **7/1**

060- **3** *1* **Rocket Ronnie (IRE)**[218] 6337 3-9-3 **56** AdrianNicholls 12 61+
(David Nicholls) *prom on outer: hdwy to chse ldr 2f out: rdn to ld over 1f out: hdd and drvn ent fnl f: kpt on same pce* **4/1**[2]

-431 **4** 2½ **Eastern Dragon (IRE)**[4] 1695 3-9-13 **66** 6ex PaulMulrennan 1 65
(Michael Scudamore) *trckd ldrs: hdwy on inner 1/2-way: rdn along wl over 1f out: drvn and one pce fnl f* **7/2**[1]

035- **5** 2¼ **Just Paul (IRE)**[197] 6952 3-9-6 **59** MichaelO'Connell 8 51
(Philip Kirby) *chsd ldrs: rdn along 2f out: sn one pce* **11/2**[3]

04-0 **6** 3¼ **Alexandrakollontai (IRE)**[24] 1275 3-9-7 **60** (b) JamesSullivan 5 44
(Alistair Whillans) *sn led: rdn along 2f out: drvn over 1f out: sn hdd & wknd* **25/1**

60-0 **7** 1¾ **Let Me In (IRE)**[23] 1282 3-8-5 **47** DeclanCannon(3) 3 26
(Nigel Tinkler) *midfield: hdwy on inner over 2f out: sn rdn along and nvr nr ldrs* **28/1**

-340 **8** *nk* **Panama Cat (USA)**[18] 1393 3-9-4 **57** AmyRyan 14 35
(Kevin Ryan) *towards rr tl sme late hdwy* **16/1**

40-0 **9** 1½ **Throwing Roses**[23] 1284 3-9-0 **53** DanielTudhope 15 27
(Lawrence Mullaney) *nvr bttr than midfield* **40/1**

604- **10** ½ **Diddy Eric**[176] 7450 3-8-13 **52** PJMcDonald 6 25
(Micky Hammond) *a in rr* **33/1**

603- **11** *shd* **Bernardino**[211] 6556 3-9-5 **58** GrahamGibbons 9 30
(David Barron) *midfield: hdwy and in tch 3f out: rdn along over 2f out: sn wknd* **7/1**

43-5 **12** ¾ **Lady Raffa**[36] 1071 3-8-0 **46** oh1 ConnorBeasley(7) 4 16
(Michael Dods) *a in rr* **28/1**

005- **13** *18* **Superoo (IRE)**[176] 7450 3-8-11 **50** FrannyNorton 10
(Mark Johnston) *prom: rdn along 1/2-way: sn wknd and bhd fnl 2f* **9/1**

0655 **14** *1* **Jonny Wombat**[73] 598 3-8-7 **46** oh1 (p) AndrewMullen 11
(Richard Ford) *dwlt: a in rr: bhd fnl 2f* **66/1**

5632 **15** *4* **Bubbly Bailey**[28] 1210 3-9-1 **59** RobertTart(5) 13
(Alan Bailey) *a in rr: bhd fnl 2f* **10/1**

1m 27.5s (0.50) **Going Correction** +0.10s/f (Good) **15** Ran SP% **134.3**
Speed ratings (Par 96): **101,100,99,96,94 90,88,88,86,85 85,84,64,63,58**
toteswingers 1&2 £17.90, 2&3 £9.90, 1&3 £18.40 CSF £82.47 CT £350.83 TOTE £15.20: £5.90, £2.30, £2.40; EX 84.40 Trifecta £1023.10 Pool: £2270.69 - 1.66 winning units..
Owner Brian Dick **Bred** Burns Farm Stud **Trained** Newmarket, Suffolk
■ Stewards' Enquiry : Adrian Nicholls four-day ban: used whip above permitted level (May 8-11)

FOCUS
Another open contest with five handicap debutants in the field. The pace was sound with the prominent racers again favoured and the front two coming wide down the straight.

1760 GO RACING IN YORKSHIRE MAIDEN STKS 7f
3:10 (3:10) (Class 5) 3-Y-O £2,911 (£866; £432; £216) **Stalls** Centre

Form RPR

3-0 **1** **Macaabra (IRE)**[15] 1447 3-9-0 0 PaulMulrennan 7 66
(James Tate) *t.k.h: mde all: rdn and edgd rt wl over 1f out: drvn ins fnl f: hld on wl* **14/1**

3324 **2** *shd* **Go Far**[16] 1433 3-9-0 67 RobertTart(5) 6 71
(Alan Bailey) *chsd ldr: rdn along 2f out: drvn ent fnl f: styd on wl towards fin: jst failed* **7/2**[3]

36 **3** 1½ **Nurpur (IRE)**[9] 1570 3-9-0 74 DanielTudhope 2 62
(David O'Meara) *trckd wnr: effrt 2f out: swtchd lft 1 1/2f out and sn rdn: ev ch ent fnl f: sn drvn and one pce* **6/5**[1]

4 *7* **Tom's Anna (IRE)** 3-9-0 0 DavidAllan 1 43+
(Tim Easterby) *s.i.s and bhd: hdwy wl over 2f out: styd on appr fnl f: nrst fin* **20/1**

00 **5** 4½ **Auntie Mildred (IRE)**[15] 1447 3-9-0 0 DavidNolan 4 31
(David O'Meara) *chsd ldrs: rdn along wl over 2f out: n.d* **33/1**

0- **6** *2* **My Claire**[189] 7161 3-9-0 56 KellyHarrison 8 26
(Nigel Tinkler) *a towards rr* **50/1**

-223 **7** *shd* **Moe's Place (IRE)**[29] 1190 3-9-5 65 AmyRyan 3 30
(Kevin Ryan) *towards rr: pushed along and sme hdwy wl over 2f out: sn rdn and n.d* **11/4**[2]

\- **8** *hd* **Ground Ginger** 3-9-2 0 DeclanCannon(3) 5 30
(James Bethell) *dwlt and a in rr* **25/1**

1m 28.19s (1.19) **Going Correction** +0.10s/f (Good) **8** Ran SP% **114.5**
Speed ratings (Par 98): **97,96,95,87,82 79,79,79**
toteswingers 1&2 £5.60, 2&3 £1.40, 1&3 £4.90 CSF £59.88 TOTE £14.50: £3.60, £1.30, £1.10; EX 61.70 Trifecta £171.10 Pool: £2579.06 - 11.30 winning units..
Owner Saif Ali **Bred** Rabbah Bloodstock Limited **Trained** Newmarket, Suffolk
■ Stewards' Enquiry : Paul Mulrennan two-day ban: careless riding (May 8-9)

FOCUS
This was not a strong maiden, but run at a sound pace with the front three always occupying those positions.

1761 BRITISH STALLION STUDS E B F RICHMOND CONDITIONS STKS 1m 3f 214y
3:40 (3:46) (Class 3) 3-Y-O £9,337 (£2,796; £1,398; £699) **Stalls** Low

Form RPR

13-4 **1** **Alta Lilea (IRE)**[7] 1623 3-8-13 88 FrannyNorton 1 78+
(Mark Johnston) *trckd clr ldr: cl up over 4f out: led over 3f out: pushed clr over 1f out: readily* **2/7**[1]

6-14 **2** *3* **Gabrial The Master (IRE)**[7] 1609 3-8-12 74 TonyHamilton 3 69+
(Richard Fahey) *trckd ldng pair: pushed along 4f out: rdn to chse wnr wl over 2f out: no imp fnl f* **11/4**[2]

-440 **3** *11* **Bix (IRE)**[24] 1275 3-8-11 55 JordanHibberd(7) 2 57?
(Alan Berry) *led and clr: pushed along 4f out: rdn and hdd over 3f out: sn one pce* **100/1**

0-40 **4** *11* **Downright Dizzie**[7] 1613 3-8-7 47 (b) FrankieMcDonald 4 28
(Alastair Lidderdale) *a in rr: rdn along 4f out: sn outpcd* **80/1**[3]

2m 41.39s (2.49) **Going Correction** +0.10s/f (Good) **4** Ran SP% **106.7**
Speed ratings (Par 102): **95,93,85,78**
CSF £1.30 TOTE £1.10; EX 1.10 Trifecta £3.00 Pool: £2049.68 - 498.72 winning units..
Owner Mrs S Bianco & Ms J Bianco **Bred** Rockhart Trading Ltd **Trained** Middleham Moor, N Yorks

FOCUS
A disappointing turnout for the money. The pace was honest with the short-priced favourite winning easily.

1762 PIN POINT RECRUITMENT H'CAP 5f
4:15 (4:16) (Class 6) (0-65,65) 3-Y-O £2,385 (£704; £352) **Stalls** Low

Form RPR

25- **1** **Rangooned**[151] 7855 3-9-7 **65** PJMcDonald 2 74
(Ann Duffield) *in tch on inner: hdwy 2f out: rdn to ld ins fnl f: kpt on* **10/1**

00-1 **2** 2½ **Shirley's Pride**[14] 1458 3-8-8 **52** (t) AndrewMullen 10 52
(Michael Appleby) *chsd ldrs: hdwy 1/2-way: led wl over 1f out and sn rdn: hdd ins fnl f: sn drvn and edgd lft: one pce* **13/2**[3]

42-2 **3** 1¼ **Confidential Creek**[6] 1651 3-8-5 **56** (v[1]) JacobButterfield(7) 8 52
(Ollie Pears) *chsd ldrs: hdwy and cl up over 2f out: sn ev ch: rdn over 1f out and kpt on same pce* **4/1**[2]

4-33 **4** *3* **Free Island**[28] 1202 3-9-6 **64** (p) PaulMulrennan 6 49
(James Tate) *cl up: ev ch 2f out: sn rdn and wknd appr fnl f* **4/1**[2]

000- **5** 2¼ **Ichimoku**[144] 7953 3-8-7 **51** oh1 (t) TomEaves 11 28
(Bryan Smart) *dwlt and towards rr tl styd on appr fnl f: nrst fin* **12/1**

525- **6** *nk* **Perfect Words (IRE)**[177] 7441 3-9-7 **65** DanielTudhope 9 41
(Marjorie Fife) *chsd ldrs: rdn along 2f out: sn no imp* **7/1**

32-2 **7** *hd* **Alhaarth Beauty (IRE)**[27] 1215 3-9-2 **65** ThomasBrown(5) 7 40
(Ismail Mohammed) *cl up: led 1/2-way: rdn and hdd wl over 1f out: sn wknd* **3/1**[1]

5-00 **8** ¾ **Look On By**[20] 1349 3-9-0 **58** JamesSullivan 4 30
(Ruth Carr) *prom: rdn along 1/2-way: sn wknd* **20/1**

00-4 **9** 1¾ **Ridgeblade**[14] 1458 3-8-7 **51** oh4 DuranFentiman 3 17
(Noel Wilson) *led: rdn along 1/2-way: sn hdd & wknd* **14/1**

-250 **10** 1½ **Twinwood Star (IRE)**[54] 848 3-8-7 **51** oh4 JimmyQuinn 12 11
(John Weymes) *a in rr* **33/1**

00-0 **11** *5* **Supercruiser (IRE)**[11] 1539 3-8-4 **51** oh3 DeclanCannon(3) 5
(Nigel Tinkler) *cl up: rdn along 1/2-way: sn wknd* **50/1**

1m 2.02s (2.22) **Going Correction** +0.10s/f (Good) **11** Ran SP% **123.9**
Speed ratings (Par 96): **86,82,80,75,71 71,70,69,66,64 56**
toteswingers 1&2 £11.90, 2&3 £6.40, 1&3 £8.60 CSF £76.37 CT £320.02 TOTE £8.70: £1.90, £2.60, £2.00; EX 91.10 Trifecta £395.40 Pool: £2376.57 - 4.50 winning units..
Owner Morecool Racing & David Redvers **Bred** Simon Tindall **Trained** Constable Burton, N Yorks

FOCUS
A moderate sprint handicap run at a sound pace, with the winner racing up the far rail.

1763 2013 CATTERICK TWELVE FURLONG SERIES H'CAP (QUALIFIER) 1m 3f 214y
4:45 (4:45) (Class 5) (0-70,70) 4-Y-O+ £2,911 (£866; £432; £216) **Stalls** Low

Form RPR

004- **1** **Bright Applause**[127] 7245 5-9-3 **66** BarryMcHugh 2 75
(Tracy Waggott) *trckd ldrs on inner: n.m.r and pushed along over 3f out: swtchd rt over 2f out: rdn to chse ldrs over 1f out: styd on u.p fnl f to ld nr fin* **7/2**[2]

260- **2** ½ **Eijaaz (IRE)**[186] 7245 12-8-5 **57** (p) RaulDaSilva(3) 3 65
(Geoffrey Harker) *hld up towards rr: hdwy over 3f out: chsd ldrs wl over 1f out: rdn to ld ins fnl f: hdd and no ex nr fin* **20/1**

-362 **3** 1¼ **Roc De Prince**[18] 1390 4-9-5 **69** (v[1]) DanielTudhope 12 75
(David O'Meara) *led: clr after 4f: rdn along wl over 1f out: drvn and tired ent fnl f: sn hdd and one pce* **7/2**[2]

-425 **4** 2½ **Brunello**[20] 1350 5-8-7 **63** (p) DavidBergin(7) 6 65
(David O'Meara) *trckd ldrs: hdwy 4f out: rdn wl over 2f out: drvn to chse ldrs over 1f out: kpt on same pce* **10/1**

443- **5** *nk* **Tinseltown**[105] 6626 7-9-5 **68** (p) MickyFenton 10 70
(Brian Rothwell) *chsd ldr: rdn along over 3f out: drvn 2f out and kpt on same pce appr fnl f* **10/1**

00-2 **6** 1¾ **King Kurt (IRE)**[9] 1568 5-9-7 **70** PhillipMakin 9 69
(Kevin Ryan) *trckd ldrs: hdwy 4f out: rdn to chse ldrs on outer over 2f out: drvn and edgd lft over 1f out: sn btn* **3/1**[1]

1000 **7** 1¼ **Evergreen Forest (IRE)**[8] 1600 5-9-1 **64** FrankieMcDonald 4 61
(Alastair Lidderdale) *hld up: hdwy and in tch 1/2-way: rdn along 3f out: sn one pce* **18/1**

100- **8** 1¼ **Silver Tigress**[197] 6957 5-8-12 **61** PJMcDonald 14 56
(George Moore) *hld up: hdwy 4f out: rdn along wl over 2f out: n.d* **33/1**

1066 **9** *shd* **Turjuman (USA)**[23] 1279 8-8-0 **56** oh6 EvaMoscrop(7) 8 51
(Simon West) *a towards rr* **33/1**

510- **10** 3¾ **Fine Kingdom**[46] 5054 4-8-6 **56** oh1 (b) JamesSullivan 1 45
(Brian Ellison) *hld up: a towards rr* **15/2**[3]

4330 **11** 2¾ **Layla's Boy**[12] 1520 6-8-8 **57** (bt) AmyRyan 7 41
(Simon West) *a in rr* **25/1**

350- **12** *2* **Amir Pasha (UAE)**[72] 6956 8-8-7 **56** oh8 (p) TomEaves 13 37
(Micky Hammond) *prom: chsd ldr after 4f: rdn along 3f out: wknd fnl 2f* **40/1**

-000 **13** *11* **Cufflink**[15] 1442 4-9-1 **65** (p) DavidAllan 11 29
(Iain Jardine) *hld up: a in rr* **50/1**

006- **14** 1¾ **Paramythi (IRE)**[57] 4601 4-8-9 **64** (b[1]) ShirleyTeasdale(5) 5 25
(Marjorie Fife) *chsd ldrs: rdn along over 4f out: sn wknd* **33/1**

2m 39.23s (0.33) **Going Correction** +0.10s/f (Good)
WFA 4 from 5yo+ 1lb **14** Ran SP% **126.5**
Speed ratings (Par 103): **102,101,100,99,98 97,96,96,96,93 91,90,83,81**
toteswingers 1&2 £19.20, 2&3 £18.60, 1&3 £4.00 CSF £80.17 CT £275.46 TOTE £4.90: £1.40, £7.90, £1.60; EX 129.80 Trifecta £1021.50 Part won. Pool of £1362.03 - 0.69 winning units..

Owner Littlethorpe Park Racing **Bred** Old Mill Stud **Trained** Spennymoor, Co Durham
FOCUS
The pace was sound for this competitive handicap.

1764 WE RACE AGAIN ON 7TH MAY H'CAP (DIV II) 7f
5:15 (5:18) (Class 6) (0-60,60) 3-Y-O **£2,385** (£704; £352) **Stalls** Centre

Form RPR

40-4 **1** **La Luz Del Sol**[21] [1319] 3-9-4 **57** TonyHamilton 10 64
(Richard Fahey) *towards rr: hdwy over 2f out: swtchd wd and rdn over 1f out: str run fnl f to ld nr fin* **7/1**[2]

500- **2** *1 1/4* **Surround Sound**[204] [6753] 3-9-5 **58** DavidAllan 15 62
(Tim Easterby) *stdd s and hld up: hdwy on outer over 2f out: rdn to chse ldrs over 1f out: drvn and ev ch whn hung lft wl ins fnl f: kpt on* **10/1**

0-05 **3** *hd* **Complicator**[9] [1566] 3-9-3 **56** PhillipMakin 8 59
(Kevin Ryan) *trckd ldrs: hdwy 3f out: rdn to chse ldng pair wl over 1f out: drvn and ev ch ins fnl f: kpt on* **14/1**

23-6 **4** *shd* **Marcus Caesar (IRE)**[42] [990] 3-9-6 **59** GrahamGibbons 12 62
(David Barron) *led 3f: cl up tl rdn to ld again wl over 1f out: drvn ins fnl f: hdd and no ex last 50yds* **8/1**[3]

05-6 **5** *2 1/4* **Out Of The Blocks**[28] [1206] 3-9-2 **55** PJMcDonald 13 57+
(Ruth Carr) *towards rr: hdwy 1/2-way: rdn and str run on outer over 1f out: ev ch ins fnl f: hmpd last 50yds: nt rcvr* **8/1**[3]

6-44 **6** *1/2* **Red Style (IRE)**[14] [1461] 3-9-7 **60** MickyFenton 5 59+
(Paul Midgley) *cl up on inner: led after 3f: rdn along 2f out: hdd and drvn over 1f out: hld whn hmpd last 50yds: nt rcvr* **14/1**

25-6 **7** *3/4* **Special Report (IRE)**[28] [1210] 3-9-2 **55** AndrewMullen 14 49
(Nigel Tinkler) *midfield: hdwy on inner 3f out: rdn 2f out: styd on to chse ldrs ent fnl f: sn drvn and no imp* **33/1**

2260 **8** *1* **Armada Bay (IRE)**[37] [1064] 3-8-12 **51** TomEaves 2 42
(Bryan Smart) *hld up towards rr: effrt over 2f out: sn pushed along and kpt on appr fnl f: nrst fin* **22/1**

346- **9** *3/4* **Amelia Jay**[177] [7432] 3-8-13 **52** JamesSullivan 1 41
(Danielle McCormick) *dwlt and towards rr tl sme late hdwy* **18/1**

00-3 **10** *nk* **Pink Cadillac (IRE)**[15] [1447] 3-8-11 **50** PaulMulrennan 3 38
(Ben Haslam) *chsd ldrs: rdn along wl over 2f out: sn wknd* **12/1**

005- **11** *1* **Silvio Dante (USA)**[187] [7208] 3-9-7 **60** DanielTudhope 6 49+
(David O'Meara) *trckd ldrs: hdwy to chse ldng pair 2f out: sn rdn: drvn appr fnl f and sn wknd* **7/4**[1]

-600 **12** *2 1/4* **Cromwell Rose (IRE)**[54] [848] 3-8-7 **46** oh1 (b) JimmyQuinn 11 25
(John Weymes) *chsd ldrs: rdn over 2f out: sn wknd: b.b.v* **25/1**

2125 **13** *1* **Baltic Prince (IRE)**[23] [1284] 3-9-1 **54** FrannyNorton 9 31
(Paul Green) *a towards rr* **10/1**

060- **14** *7* **Jomari (IRE)**[217] [6356] 3-8-4 **46** oh1 NeilFarley(3) 7
(Declan Carroll) *dwlt: a towards rr* **50/1**

60-0 **15** *24* **Royal Jenray**[9] [1566] 3-8-8 **47** (p) MichaelO'Connell 4
(Jedd O'Keeffe) *midfield: n.m.r on inner after 3f: sn lost pl and bhd* **66/1**

1m 29.18s (2.18) **Going Correction** +0.10s/f (Good) **15** Ran SP% **130.1**
Speed ratings (Par 96): **91,89,89,89,86 86,85,84,83,82 81,79,78,70,42**
toteswingers 1&2 £9.60, 2&3 £22.90, 1&3 £19.80 CSF £77.66 CT £1013.74 TOTE £7.20: £3.90, £5.00, £6.70; EX 110.10 Trifecta £815.40 Pool: £1304.26 - 1.19 winning units..
Owner R A Fahey **Bred** P W Pool **Trained** Musley Bank, N Yorks
■ Stewards' Enquiry : Phillip Makin caution: entered wrong stall.
FOCUS
Only one previous winner in this modest contest which was run at a fierce pace.
T/Plt: £45.80 to a £1 stake. Pool of £42988.94 - 684.87 winning tickets. T/Qpdt: £9.00 to a £1 stake. Pool of £2954.56 - 241.05 winning tickets. JR

EPSOM (L-H)
Wednesday, April 24

OFFICIAL GOING: Good (good to firm in places; derby course 8.3, 5f course 8.5)
Wind: Moderate, half against Weather: Fine but cloudy

1765 INVESTEC WEALTH & INVESTMENT H'CAP 5f
2:20 (2:21) (Class 3) (0-95,95) 4-Y-O+ **£12,450** (£3,728; £1,864; £932; £466; £234) **Stalls** Low

Form RPR

353- **1** **Ajjaadd (USA)**[134] [8066] 7-9-2 **95** WilliamTwiston-Davies(5) 1 104
(Ted Powell) *racd towards centre: hld up in midfield: prog 2f out: chsd ldng pair fnl f: drvn and r.o to ld post* **12/1**

456- **2** *shd* **La Fortunata**[209] [6602] 6-8-8 **87** CharlesBishop(5) 7 96
(Mike Murphy) *led and racd towards centre: hung lft fr wl over 1f out and ended nr far rail: kpt on fnl f: hdd post* **10/1**

0-44 **3** *1* **Silvanus (IRE)**[14] [1483] 8-8-13 **87** PaulHanagan 9 92
(Paul Midgley) *swtg: pressed ldr: hung lft fr wl over 1f out and ended towards far rail: nt qckn fnl f: lost 2nd nr fin* **14/1**

006 **4** *1/2* **Swiss Cross**[7] [1607] 6-9-3 **91** (t) KierenFallon 5 95+
(Phil McEntee) *lw: hmpd and snatched up sn after s: wl off the pce in rr: prog 2f out: styd on fnl f: nrst fin* **7/1**[3]

3-41 **5** *nk* **Sandfrankskipsgo**[33] [1121] 4-8-7 **81** ShaneKelly 2 84
(Peter Crate) *prom towards centre: rdn to chse ldng pair wl over 1f out: one pce fnl f* **11/2**[1]

43-0 **6** *1 1/4* **Hopes N Dreams (IRE)**[19] [1370] 5-8-4 **81** oh2 JulieBurke(3) 13 79+
(Kevin Ryan) *s.v.s: wl bhd towards nr side rail: styd on fr over 1f out: nvr nrr* **14/1**

0-11 **7** *1 1/4* **Diamond Charlie (IRE)**[60] [780] 5-9-0 **88** SebSanders 10 82+
(Simon Dow) *chsd ldrs and r towards nr side: pressed for a pl over 1f out: hanging lft after and steadily lost position* **8/1**

356- **8** *1/2* **Lady Gibraltar**[212] [6536] 4-8-8 **87** MichaelJMMurphy(5) 3 79+
(Alan Jarvis) *lw: bmpd sn after s: in tch: nt qckn and lost pl over 1f out: eased whn no ch* **11/1**

001- **9** *hd* **Church Music (IRE)**[170] [7595] 4-8-10 **84** GrahamLee 12 75
(Michael Scudamore) *racd towards nr side: nvr on terms w ldrs: hanging lft and no prog over 1f out* **14/1**

50-6 **10** *nk* **West Coast Dream**[14] [1483] 6-8-8 **85** MarkCoumbe(3) 8 75
(Roy Brotherton) *chsd ldng pair to wl over 1f out: sn wknd* **22/1**

0-20 **11** *1 1/4* **Taurus Twins**[9] [1581] 7-8-7 **81** oh1 (b) AndreaAtzeni 6 66
(Richard Price) *chsd ldrs to 2f out: sn lost pl and btn* **14/1**

601- **12** *1 1/2* **Sacrosanctus**[239] [5703] 5-9-4 **92** (p) TomQueally 11 72+
(Scott Dixon) *b.hind: s.i.s: nvr on terms w ldrs: wl btn fnl 2f* **6/1**[2]

400- **13** *3 1/4* **Racy**[285] [4073] 6-9-3 **91** (b[1]) SeanLevey 4 59+
(Ed McMahon) *swtg: taken down early: sweating: propped as stalls opened and jockey couldn't remove blindfold: lost all ch though briefly ct up at rr of field 1/2-way: sn wknd* **10/1**

55.48s (-0.22) **Going Correction** +0.15s/f (Good) **13** Ran SP% **118.5**
Speed ratings (Par 107): **107,106,105,104,103 101,99,99,98,98 96,93,88**
toteswingers 1&2 £89.00, 2&3 £52.60, 1&3 £29.50 CSF £125.84 CT £1758.71 TOTE £13.50: £4.80, £4.00, £4.10; EX 202.80 Trifecta £904.90 Part won. Pool: £1206.61 - 0.01 winning units..
Owner Katy & Lol Pratt **Bred** Darley **Trained** Reigate, Surrey
■ Stewards' Enquiry : Shane Kelly three-day ban: careless riding (May 8-10)
FOCUS
Rail dolled out from 1m to Winning Post adding approximately 15yds to races on Round course. The ground was given as good, good to firm in places (GoingStick: Derby course 8.3, 5f course 8.5). There appeared to be a distinct advantage to racing towards the middle, rather than on the stands' rail, which is usually the best place to be over this sharp 5f, and they were making quite a print.

1766 INVESTEC GREAT METROPOLITAN H'CAP 1m 4f 10y
2:50 (2:54) (Class 3) (0-95,94) 4-Y-O+ **£12,450** (£3,728; £1,864; £932; £466; £234) **Stalls** Centre

Form RPR

00-2 **1** **Beyond Conceit (IRE)**[11] [1536] 4-8-13 **87** JamieSpencer 10 96
(Andrew Balding) *lw: mde all at decent pce: shkn up over 2f out: hrd pressed and drvn wl over 1f out: hld on wl* **3/1**[1]

325- **2** *hd* **Kuda Huraa (IRE)**[23] [6584] 5-8-12 **85** RichardHughes 11 93
(Alan King) *lw: trckd ldng pair: wnt 2nd 4f out: rdn to chal fr 2f out: kpt trying fnl f: jst hld* **8/1**[3]

214- **3** *1 1/4* **Novirak (IRE)**[215] [6445] 5-8-7 **80** EddieAhern 2 86
(James Fanshawe) *wl in tch: 4th st: rdn over 2f out: tended to hang but chsd ldng pair 1f out: styd on but nvr able to chal* **11/1**

605- **4** *1/2* **Scatter Dice (IRE)**[221] [6248] 4-9-3 **91** JoeFanning 4 96
(Mark Johnston) *lw: trckd wnr to 4f out: styd cl up: shkn up over 2f out: kpt on but lost 3rd fnl f* **11/1**

6- **5** *1 1/2* **Moldowney**[201] [6856] 4-9-1 **89** KierenFallon 9 93+
(Luca Cumani) *swtg: taken bk to last sn after s: in tch: prog and 6th st: sn rdn: kpt on same pce and nvr able to chal* **9/2**[2]

365- **6** *1 3/4* **Perennial**[207] [6677] 4-9-6 **94** RyanMoore 6 94
(Charles Hills) *sn taken bk towards rr: 7th st: shkn up and no prog over 2f out: kpt on fnl f: no ch* **9/2**[2]

4-50 **7** *1* **Daghash**[25] [1242] 4-8-6 **80** oh2 [1] MartinLane 3 78
(Clive Brittain) *chsd ldrs: rdn 4f out: 5th st: struggling over 2f out: wl btn after* **20/1**

113- **8** *1/2* **Brockwell**[207] [6677] 4-9-3 **91** RichardKingscote 7 89+
(Tom Dascombe) *swtg: hld up in last trio: 8th and wd into st: edgd lft and no prog 2f out: wl btn after: kpt on* **12/1**

05-4 **9** *6* **Right Step**[51] [882] 6-8-10 **83** JimCrowley 5 71
(Alan Jarvis) *hld up in last trio: 9th st: no prog and btn 2f out: wknd* **12/1**

4532 **10** *6* **Mawaakef (IRE)**[62] [739] 5-9-1 **88** FrederikTylicki 8 66
(J R Jenkins) *hld up in last trio: last st: no prog: wknd 2f out* **25/1**

2m 37.54s (-1.36) **Going Correction** +0.075s/f (Good)
WFA 4 from 5yo+ 1lb **10** Ran SP% **113.1**
Speed ratings (Par 107): **107,106,106,105,104 103,102,102,98,94**
toteswingers 1&2 £4.20, 2&3 £13.00, 1&3 £6.20 CSF £26.49 CT £228.94 TOTE £3.30: £1.60, £3.00, £2.90; EX 33.50 Trifecta £240.40 Pool: £1610.82 - 5.02 winning units..
Owner Mrs Fitri Hay **Bred** Barronstown Stud **Trained** Kingsclere, Hants
FOCUS
The rail was dolled out from the 1m marker to the winning post, adding approximately 15 yards to the Derby course distances. This looked fairly competitive on paper.

1767 INVESTEC DERBY TRIAL (CONDITIONS RACE) 1m 2f 18y
3:20 (3:24) (Class 2) 3-Y-O **£31,125** (£9,320; £4,660; £2,330; £1,165; £585) **Stalls** Low

Form RPR

130- **1** **Mirsaale**[200] [6874] 3-8-13 95 NeilCallan 9 101
(James Tate) *led 2f: w ldr after: drvn to ld wl over 1f out: styd on wl to assert fnl f* **5/1**[3]

33-1 **2** *1 1/2* **Another Cocktail**[14] [1478] 3-8-13 83 RichardHughes 1 98
(Hughie Morrison) *lw: trckd ldrs: wnt 3rd st: drvn over 2f out: styd on to take 2nd ins fnl f: nvr able to chal* **7/1**

11- **3** *2 1/4* **Gabrial's Kaka (IRE)**[206] [6700] 3-9-1 89 PaulHanagan 2 96
(Richard Fahey) *led after 2f but pressed thrght: drvn and hdd wl over 1f out: one pce and lost 2nd ins fnl f* **9/2**[2]

51-1 **4** *7* **Mister Impatience**[33] [1109] 3-8-13 93 JoeFanning 8 80
(Mark Johnston) *trckd ldng pair tl 4th st: shkn up and no rspnse wl over 2f out: wl btn after* **6/5**[1]

1-30 **5** *nk* **Hoarding (USA)**[18] [1383] 3-9-3 93 (p) WilliamBuick 4 83+
(John Gosden) *t.k.h: hld up in midfield: lost pl downhill and 7th st: sn bhd: kpt on to press for modest 4th nr fin* **10/1**

43-6 **6** *hd* **Operation Chariot (IRE)**[18] [1383] 3-8-13 97 JimmyFortune 7 79
(Andrew Balding) *hld up in last pair: prog and 5th st: no imp on ldrs over 2f out: fdd* **16/1**

612- **7** *1 1/2* **Canadian Run (IRE)**[133] [8072] 3-8-13 81 GrahamLee 6 76
(Robert Mills) *hld up in rr: 6th st: lost tch and hung lft over 2f out: n.d after* **33/1**

4-00 **8** *23* **Ocean Applause**[18] [1383] 3-8-13 77 KierenFallon 5 30
(John Ryan) *detached in last early and pushed along: nvr a factor: wknd over 2f out: t.o* **66/1**

2m 8.35s (-1.35) **Going Correction** +0.075s/f (Good) **8** Ran SP% **112.2**
Speed ratings (Par 104): **108,106,105,99,99 99,97,79**
toteswingers 1&2 £6.30, 2&3 £3.40, 1&3 £4.80 CSF £37.95 TOTE £6.60: £1.70, £1.70, £1.30; EX 38.80 Trifecta £129.90 Pool: £2815.56 - 16.25 winning units..
Owner Saif Ali **Bred** Mr & Mrs A E Pakenham **Trained** Newmarket, Suffolk
FOCUS
This Derby trial had the carrot of win-and-you're-in, but the winner is already engaged in the Derby.

1768 INVESTEC PROPERTY INVESTMENTS CITY AND SUBURBAN STKS (H'CAP) 1m 2f 18y
3:55 (3:56) (Class 2) (0-105,105) 4-Y-O+ **£31,125** (£9,320; £4,660; £2,330; £1,165; £585) **Stalls** Low

Form RPR

650- **1** **Area Fifty One**[214] [6484] 5-8-13 **97** JamieSpencer 3 105
(Richard Fahey) *sn pressed ldr: cajoled along to ld over 1f out: edgd lft ins fnl f: styd on* **10/1**

260- 2 ¾ **Clayton**[165] 7689 4-8-9 **93** .... NeilCallan 6 99
(Kevin Ryan) *lw: trckd ldng trio: rdn over 2f out: disp 3rd but no imp on ldng pair fnl f: sltly checked 75yds out then inherited 2nd nr fin* **11/2**[1]

50-0 3 ½ **Vasily**[25] 1242 5-8-4 **88** .... AndreaAtzeni 9 95+
(Robert Eddery) *led: rdn and hdd over 1f out: keeping on but hld whn hmpd 75yds out and sn lost 2nd* **20/1**

010- 4 1 **King's Warrior (FR)**[207] 6674 6-9-3 **101** .... RobertHavlin 8 104+
(Peter Chapple-Hyam) *dwlt: hld up in last pair: 9th st: tried to make prog over 2f out but stl only 8th over 1f out: styd on fnl f to take 4th nr fin* **16/1**

-124 5 1 ½ **Spifer (IRE)**[25] 1242 5-8-8 **92** ....(p) MartinHarley 1 94+
(Marco Botti) *hld up: prog and 5th st: looking for room 2f out: nt qckn wl over 1f out: wl hld whn sltly checked last 75yds* **9/1**[3]

/15- 6 hd **Validus**[154] 7809 4-9-3 **101** .... KierenFallon 4 107+
(Luca Cumani) *chsd ldng pair: drvn over 2f out and tended to hang lft: stl battling for 3rd but hld whn hmpd 75yds out and eased* **11/2**[1]

3-0P 7 nk **John Biscuit (IRE)**[25] 1242 5-8-3 **87** .... DavidProbert 2 86
(Andrew Balding) *hld up: prog and 6th st: hanging and no imp on ldrs 2f out: kpt on nr fin* **11/1**

112- 8 hd **Rhagori**[175] 7475 4-8-2 **86** .... MartinLane 7 84
(Ralph Beckett) *lw: hld up towards rr: nt handle downhill that wl and 7th st: sme prog over 1f out: no hdwy and btn over 1f out* **13/2**[2]

15-1 9 6 **Lady Loch**[15] 1446 4-8-3 **87** .... PaulHanagan 10 73+
(Richard Fahey) *prom early: lost pl bdly downhill and 8th st: sn bhd* **11/2**[1]

60-6 10 10 **Spanish Duke (IRE)**[15] 1446 6-8-8 **92** .... WilliamBuick 11 77
(Brian Ellison) *nvr appeared to handle the trck: a in last pair: wl bhd over 2f out* **11/2**[1]

2m 8.1s (-1.60) **Going Correction** +0.075s/f (Good) **10** Ran SP% **112.9**
Speed ratings (Par 109): **109,108,108,107,106 105,105,105,100,92**
toteswingers 1&2 £7.90, 2&3 £36.00, 1&3 £9.80 CSF £62.08 CT £1076.57 TOTE £12.90: £4.00, £2.20, £7.40; EX 88.50 Trifecta £1248.10 Pool: £1664.19 - 0.34 winning units..
Owner Dr Marwan Koukash **Bred** Carmel Stud **Trained** Musley Bank, N Yorks

FOCUS
They didn't go a great pace early on and once again it paid to race handily.

1769 INVESTEC SPECIALIST CASH PRODUCTS MAIDEN STKS 1m 114y
4:30 (4:30) (Class 4) 3-4-Y-O **£4,851** (£1,443; £721; £360) **Stalls** Low

Form RPR

3-2 1 **One Pekan (IRE)**[16] 1429 3-8-11 0 .... RyanMoore 8 83+
(Roger Varian) *pressed ldr: shkn up to ld over 2f out: asserted over 1f out: drvn out fnl f* **4/1**[2]

2- 2 1 ¼ **Legal Waves (IRE)**[182] 7330 3-8-11 0 .... KierenFallon 3 85+
(Brian Meehan) *lw: awkward s: rn green in last trio: 6th st: plld out and prog 2f out: styd on fnl f to take 2nd last 75yds: no ch to chal* **1/1**[1]

0- 3 ¾ **Ghost Runner (IRE)**[234] 5851 3-8-11 0 .... TomQueally 2 79
(Sir Henry Cecil) *leggy: angular: chsd ldrs: 5th st: clsd over 2f out: drvn to chse wnr over 1f out: kpt on but no real imp: lost 2nd last 75yds* **16/1**

3- 4 2 **Double Discount (IRE)**[133] 8070 3-8-11 0 .... RichardKingscote 1 74+
(Tom Dascombe) *lw: trckd ldng pair: shkn up and nt qckn over 2f out: wl hld after: kpt on fnl f* **15/2**

40-3 5 3 ¼ **Storming (IRE)**[27] 1219 3-8-11 73 .... DavidProbert 4 67
(Andrew Balding) *trckd ldng pair: rdn wl over 2f out: no imp: wknd fnl f* **5/1**[3]

25-2 6 10 **Arctic Admiral (IRE)**[21] 1323 3-8-11 72 .... RichardHughes 7 53+
(Richard Hannon) *led to over 2f out: lost 2nd and wknd over 1f out: heavily eased* **10/1**

006- 7 10 **Dawn Rock**[240] 5661 3-8-6 49 .... HayleyTurner 5 16
(Simon Dow) *a in last trio: 7th st: sn wknd* **66/1**

04 8 10 **One Dark Night**[28] 1199 3-8-11 0 .... FergusSweeney 6
(Gary Moore) *awkward s: a in last: t.o* **66/1**

1m 45.69s (-0.41) **Going Correction** +0.075s/f (Good) **8** Ran SP% **116.4**
Speed ratings (Par 105): **104,102,102,100,97 88,79,70**
toteswingers 1&2 £1.90, 2&3 £5.40, 1&3 £7.70 CSF £8.53 TOTE £4.30: £1.90, £1.10, £4.80; EX 9.30 Trifecta £94.80 Pool: £3315.70 - 26.22 winning units..
Owner H R H Sultan Ahmad Shah **Bred** Chris & James McHale **Trained** Newmarket, Suffolk

FOCUS
A fair maiden, although it's debatable whether the best horse won.

1770 INVESTEC SPECIALIST BANK H'CAP 1m 114y
5:00 (5:02) (Class 4) (0-80,80) 3-Y-O **£4,851** (£1,443; £721; £360) **Stalls** Low

Form RPR

023- 1 **Aint Got A Scooby (IRE)**[180] 7365 3-8-8 **67** .... JohnFahy 11 76
(Clive Cox) *awkward to load into stalls: chsd ldr to 7f out: 4th st: effrt and squeezed through to go 2nd again over 1f out: r.o wl to ld nr fin* **14/1**

2-22 2 ½ **Sennockian Star**[40] 1011 3-8-13 **72** .... JoeFanning 7 80
(Mark Johnston) *led: rdn over 1f out: kpt on wl but hdd and outpcd nr fin* **7/2**[2]

044- 3 3 **Couloir Extreme (IRE)**[161] 7707 3-8-8 **67** .... FergusSweeney 6 68
(Gary Moore) *prog out wd to chse ldr 7f out: rdn and hanging 2f out: lost 2nd and one pce over 1f out* **16/1**

23-0 4 1 ¼ **Swift Cedar (IRE)**[7] 1612 3-8-11 **75** .... MichaelJMMurphy(5) 8 73
(Alan Jarvis) *forced to r v wd early: prom: 3rd st: nt qckn over 2f out: wl hld whn nudged by rival over 1f out* **6/1**

2-10 5 ½ **Mumeyez**[23] 1293 3-9-2 **75** .... WilliamBuick 2 72
(John Gosden) *hld up in rr: 8th st: prog over 2f out: rdn to dispute 4th over 1f out and edgd rt: no hdwy after* **7/1**

41-6 6 1 ¾ **East Texas Red (IRE)**[19] 1365 3-8-10 **69** .... AndreaAtzeni 1 62
(Mick Quinn) *swtg: sn hld up in midfield: 7th st: rdn and no prog over 2f out: wl hld after* **40/1**

13-5 7 ½ **Magical Rose (IRE)**[14] 1471 3-9-1 **74** .... SebSanders 3 66+
(Paul D'Arcy) *wl in rr: nt handle downhill and 9th st: struggling over 2f out: modest late prog* **14/1**

64-2 8 1 ¾ **Lionheart**[14] 1476 3-9-0 **73** .... KierenFallon 4 61
(Luca Cumani) *lw: t.k.h: hld up in 5th: shkn up and lost pl over 2f out: wl btn after* **11/4**[1]

3340 9 2 ½ **Club House (IRE)**[14] 1477 3-8-13 **72** .... GrahamLee 5 54
(Robert Mills) *hld up: last st: jst pushed along and no prog fnl 3f* **33/1**

106- 10 4 ½ **Colmar Kid (IRE)**[192] 7079 3-9-6 **79** .... RichardHughes 9 51
(Richard Hannon) *lw: stdd s: racd wd in midfield: 6th st: no prog over 2f out: wknd over 1f out* **5/1**[3]

1m 46.99s (0.89) **Going Correction** +0.075s/f (Good) **10** Ran SP% **116.9**
Speed ratings (Par 100): **99,98,95,94,94 92,92,90,88,84**
toteswingers 1&2 £7.90, 2&3 £17.00, 1&3 £25.30 CSF £62.86 CT £812.04 TOTE £9.60: £2.50, £1.80, £6.20; EX 40.00 Trifecta £1038.40 Pool: £2172.52 - 1.56 winning units..
Owner Mrs Olive Shaw **Bred** D Veitch & R O'Callaghan **Trained** Lambourn, Berks

FOCUS
Another race run at a fairly steady early pace, and little got into it from behind.

T/Jkpt: Not won. T/Plt: £1,058.60 to a £1 stake. Pool of £85067.88 -58.66 winning tickets T/Qpdt: £53.80 to a £1 stake. Poo of £5797.35 - 79.62 winning tickets. JN

1603 BEVERLEY (R-H)
Thursday, April 25

OFFICIAL GOING: Good to firm (9.5)
Wind: Light, against Weather: Cloudy

1771 BEVERLEY MINSTER CLAIMING STKS 5f
2:05 (2:05) (Class 6) 3-Y-O **£2,264** (£673; £336; £168) **Stalls** Low

Form RPR

4412 1 **La Sylphe**[20] 1361 3-8-4 64 .... FrannyNorton 5 57
(Derek Shaw) *qckly away: mde all: rdn over 1f out: kpt on wl towards fin* **3/1**[2]

035- 2 ¾ **Tatlisu (IRE)**[240] 5710 3-9-5 78 .... PaulHanagan 3 69
(Richard Fahey) *trckd wnr: effrt wl over 1f out: sn rdn: rdr dropped reins appr fnl f: sn drvn and kpt on* **10/11**[1]

6-30 3 nse **Teetotal (IRE)**[5] 1687 3-8-6 62 .... JasonHart(5) 1 61
(Nigel Tinkler) *hld up in rr: hdwy 2f out: sn swtchd lft and rdn over 1f out: styd on and ch ins fnl f: drvn and one pce towards fin* **13/2**

421- 4 3 ½ **Dream Vale (IRE)**[178] 7441 3-8-4 67 .... DuranFentiman 2 41
(Tim Easterby) *trckd wnr on inner: pushed along wl over 1f out: sn rdn and wknd ent fnl f* **9/2**[3]

0-40 5 12 **Southern Sapphire**[55] 848 3-8-7 50 .... JamesSullivan 4
(Kristin Stubbs) *sltly hmpd s: sn chsng ldrs: rdn along 2f out: sn wknd and eased* **33/1**

1m 3.2s (-0.30) **Going Correction** -0.05s/f (Good) **5** Ran SP% **111.8**
Speed ratings (Par 96): **100,98,98,93,73**
CSF £6.30 TOTE £4.60: £2.10, £1.10; EX 6.70 Trifecta £18.30 Pool: £2,302.47 - 94.05 winning units..
Owner Chris Hamilton **Bred** Denis Barry **Trained** Sproxton, Leics

FOCUS
The going was good to firm (watered), with the GoingStick reading 9.5. An honest pace for this claimer, with the winner making all under a well-judged ride. The form looks a little shaky.

1772 MAYDAY RACEDAY HERE MONDAY 6TH MAY H'CAP 7f 100y
2:35 (2:37) (Class 5) (0-70,70) 3-Y-O **£3,234** (£962; £481; £240) **Stalls** Low

Form RPR

1- 1 **How's Life**[195] 7021 3-9-7 **70** .... AndreaAtzeni 9 82+
(Rae Guest) *trckd ldr: cl up 1/2-way: shkn up to ld appr fnl f: sn qcknd clr: easily* **4/1**[3]

464- 2 4 ½ **Byron's Dream**[188] 7223 3-8-10 **59** .... MichaelO'Connell 12 62+
(Jedd O'Keeffe) *in rr and hmpd after 1f: bhd tl hdwy over 2f out: swtchd rt to inner and rdn over 1f out: fin wl: no ch w wnr* **20/1**

1- 3 ¾ **Cinderslipper (IRE)**[170] 7598 3-9-4 **67** .... PJMcDonald 3 66
(Ann Duffield) *in tch: hdwy on inner to chse ldrs wl over 2f out: swtchd lft and rdn over 1f out: drvn and one pce fnl f* **3/1**[1]

4-32 4 shd **Multisure**[19] 1393 3-8-9 **58** .... JamesSullivan 2 57
(Ruth Carr) *t.k.h: led: rdn along 2f out: hdd and edgd lft appr fnl f: kpt on same pce* **8/1**

4013 5 2 **Douglas Pasha (IRE)**[20] 1361 3-8-9 **58** .... AdrianNicholls 1 52
(David Nicholls) *chsd ldrs: hdwy over 2f out: sn rdn: drvn and one pce fr over 1f out* **25/1**

510- 6 nk **Emperatriz**[210] 6597 3-9-4 **67** ....[1] FrannyNorton 6 62+
(John Holt) *hld up in rr: hdwy wl over 2f out: sn swtchd rt to chse ldrs on inner: nt clr run and hmpd over 1f out: no imp after* **11/1**

300- 7 1 **Bayan Kasirga (IRE)**[226] 6121 3-9-4 **67** .... PaulHanagan 7 58+
(Richard Fahey) *in tch: effrt 3f out: sn rdn along and one pce fnl 2f* **12/1**

406- 8 nk **Izzy Boy (USA)**[214] 6511 3-9-4 **67** .... JoeFanning 4 57
(Mark Johnston) *hld up in midfield: hdwy wl over 2f out: rdn along wl over 1f out: n.d* **10/3**[2]

00-2 9 10 **Bougaloo**[22] 1330 3-8-8 **57** .... GrahamGibbons 10 22
(Alan McCabe) *chsd ldng pair: rdn along 3f out: wknd over 2f out* **16/1**

560- 10 1 **Inovate (IRE)**[241] 5668 3-8-10 **59** .... DuranFentiman 11 22
(Tim Easterby) *chsd ldrs on outer: rdn along 1/2-way: drvn over 2f out and sn wknd* **25/1**

400- 11 ¾ **Antonius**[168] 7649 3-9-0 **63** .... TomEaves 8 24
(Kristin Stubbs) *in tch: rdn along wl over 2f out: sn wknd* **50/1**

-040 12 dist **Firstkissoflove**[10] 1577 3-8-11 **60** ....(b[1]) MartinHarley 5
(David C Griffiths) *hld up in rr: plld hrd and rapid hdwy after 1f: sn hung bdly lft to wd outside: sddle slipped and rdr lost irons after 2f: hit outer rail and stmbld over 4f out: sn bhd and virtually p.u over 3f out* **33/1**

1m 32.45s (-1.35) **Going Correction** -0.40s/f (Firm) **12** Ran SP% **118.5**
Speed ratings (Par 98): **91,85,85,84,82 82,81,80,69,68 67,**
toteswingers: 1&2 £22.70, 1&3 £3.80, 2&3 £17.80 CSF £87.72 CT £278.74 TOTE £6.70: £1.90, £4.10, £1.80; EX 100.20 Trifecta £887.20 Pool: £1,811.44 - 1.53 winning units..
Owner J H Metzger **Bred** John-Henry Metzger **Trained** Newmarket, Suffolk

FOCUS
This was a fair 3-y-o handicap run at a sound pace, and the winner scored impressively. The third and fourth help set the level.

1773 HAPPY BIRTHDAY PAT ROBERTS STKS (H'CAP) 7f 100y
3:05 (3:06) (Class 3) (0-95,83) 3-Y-O **£7,439** (£2,213; £1,106; £553) **Stalls** Low

Form RPR

310- 1 **Shebebi (USA)**[193] 7079 3-9-3 **79** .... PaulHanagan 7 95+
(Mark Johnston) *disp ld tl slt advantage over 4f out: rdn wl over 1f out: sn clr: styd on strly* **13/8**[1]

250- 2 4 ½ **Asgardella (IRE)**[201] 6873 3-8-13 **78** .... LeeTopliss(3) 3 82
(Richard Fahey) *trckd ldrs: effrt wl over 2f out and sn rdn along: swtchd lft to outer over 1f out: styd on u.p fnl f: no ch w wnr* **2/1**[2]

445- 3 4 **Talqaa**[224] 6167 3-9-2 **78** .... MartinHarley 2 72
(Mick Channon) *disp ld 3f: cl up on inner: rdn and ev ch 2f out: sn drvn and grad wknd* **10/1**

44-1 4 ½ **Marshland**[23] 1305 3-9-2 **78** .... JoeFanning 4 71
(Mark Johnston) *trckd ldng pair: hdwy 3f out: rdn 2f out and sn one pce* **7/2**[3]

113- 5 1 ½ **Delores Rocket**[187] 7242 3-9-4 **83** .... JulieBurke(3) 1 72
(Kevin Ryan) *hld up in rr: hdwy wl over 2f out: rdn and hung rt wl over 1f out: one pce* **16/1**

1m 30.94s (-2.86) **Going Correction** -0.40s/f (Firm) **5** Ran SP% **108.6**
Speed ratings (Par 102): **100,94,90,89,88**
CSF £5.01 TOTE £2.80: £1.90, £1.10; EX 4.40 Trifecta £20.20 Pool: £2,165.56 - 80.08 winning units..
Owner Hamdan Al Maktoum **Bred** Shadwell Farm LLC **Trained** Middleham Moor, N Yorks

The Form Book Flat, Raceform Ltd, Compton, RG20 6NL.

FOCUS
This was not a bad contest. It was run at an honest pace, with the winner scoring impressively. The runner-up gives the form some substance.

1774 MOORENDS HOTEL H'CAP 1m 4f 16y
3:35 (3:35) (Class 4) (0-85,85) 4-Y-O+ £4,690 (£1,395; £697; £348) Stalls Low

Form RPR
0-64 1 **Fennell Bay (IRE)**12 1536 4-9-6 85 JoeFanning 2 94+
(Mark Johnston) *a.p: effrt 2f out and n.m.r: nt clr run ent fnl f: sn swtchd lft and rdn: styd on wl to ld nr line* 7/4[1]
0-33 2 hd **Arizona John (IRE)**15 1463 8-8-10 74 FrannyNorton 3 81
(John Mackie) *trckd ldrs: hdwy over 3f out: cl up 2f out: sn chal: rdn to ld jst ins fnl f: drvn and hdd nr line* 6/1[3]
003- 3 ¾ **High Office**215 6472 7-9-2 80 PaulHanagan 6 86
(Richard Fahey) *trckd ldrs: hdwy to chse ldr 4f out: chal over 2f out: sn rdn and led wl over 1f out: drvn and hdd jst ins fnl f: kpt on* 9/4[2]
304- 4 1 ½ **Palazzo Bianco**254 5200 5-9-4 85 LeeTopliss(3) 1 88
(Brian Ellison) *in tch: hdwy over 2f out: sn rdn and kpt on fnl f* 9/1
2445 5 ½ **Sir Boss (IRE)**52 882 8-9-0 78 TomEaves 5 81
(Michael Mullineaux) *hld up in rr: hdwy on inner over 2f out: nt clr run and swtchd lft over 1f out: rdn and styd on wl fnl f* 28/1
000- 6 ½ **Tartan Gigha (IRE)**177 7455 8-8-9 76 RaulDaSilva(3) 4 78
(Geoffrey Harker) *hld up in rr: hdwy over 3f out: rdn 2f out: kpt on same pce appr fnl f* 16/1
0-61 7 2 ½ **Royal Opera**15 1464 5-8-8 72 (b) PJMcDonald 8 70
(Brian Ellison) *sn led and clr: pushed along over 3f out: rdn over 2f out: hdd wl over 1f out and sn wknd* 10/1
02-0 8 2 ½ **Maybeagrey**19 1391 4-8-6 71 DuranFentiman 7 65
(Tim Easterby) *hld up in rr: hdwy on outer over 3f out: sn rdn and chsd ldrs 2f out: sn wknd* 25/1

2m 35.23s (-4.57) **Going Correction** -0.40s/f (Firm)
WFA 4 from 5yo+ 1lb 8 Ran SP% **113.7**
Speed ratings (Par 105): **99,98,98,97,97 96,95,93**
toteswingers: 1&2 £3.10, 1&3 £1.70, 2&3 £3.50 CSF £12.74 CT £23.59 TOTE £2.70: £1.40, £1.80, £1.30; EX 12.70 Trifecta £35.20 Pool: £2,932.73 - 62.31 winning units..
Owner Sheikh Hamdan Bin Mohammed Al Maktoum **Bred** J R Wills **Trained** Middleham Moor, N Yorks

FOCUS
This fair handicap was run at a sound early pace but the bare form is ordinary judging by the proximity of the second.

1775 RAPID LAD H'CAP 1m 1f 207y
4:05 (4:05) (Class 5) (0-70,69) 4-Y-O+ £3,234 (£962; £481; £240) Stalls Low

Form RPR
5311 1 **Apache Glory (USA)**19 1381 5-9-5 67 (p) AndreaAtzeni 3 76+
(John Stimpson) *hld up in rr: gd hdwy wl over 2f out: chsd ldrs over 1f out: rdn to chal ent fnl f: styd on wl to ld nr fin* 7/1
0-56 2 hd **Saint Thomas (IRE)**13 1523 6-9-2 64 FrannyNorton 4 73
(John Mackie) *trckd ldrs: hdwy over 2f out: rdn to chal over 1f out: slt ld ins fnl f: drvn: hdd and no ex nr fin* 9/2[2]
400- 3 ¾ **Ailsa Craig (IRE)**227 6103 7-8-9 57 PaulHanagan 6 64
(Edwin Tuer) *trckd ldrs: hdwy over 2f out: rdn to chal over 1f out: ev ch tl drvn and one pce wl ins fnl f* 9/2[2]
-003 4 ½ **Rockweiller**26 1239 6-8-8 56 (v) JoeFanning 5 62
(Steve Gollings) *cl up: led 2f out: sn rdn: drvn and hdd jst ins fnl f: wknd last 50yds* 4/1[1]
600- 5 nk **Meetings Man (IRE)**54 6957 6-9-0 62 (p) PJMcDonald 11 67+
(Micky Hammond) *hld up towards rr: hdwy on outer wl over 2f out: rdn to chse ldrs over 1f out: drvn and edgd rt ins fnl f: kpt on* 25/1
1-05 6 5 **Brockfield**19 1391 7-9-6 68 DuranFentiman 7 63
(Mel Brittain) *hld up towards rr: hdwy on inner 3f out: effrt and n.m.r wl over 1f out: sn rdn 1f out and no imp* 12/1
00-0 7 2 **Jonny Lesters Hair (IRE)**16 1448 8-9-6 68 TomEaves 9 59
(Tim Easterby) *trckd ldrs: effrt 3f out: rdn along over 2f out: sn one pce* 20/1
230 8 1 ¼ **Quintain (IRE)**24 1282 5-8-3 58 GaryMahon(7) 8 47
(Tim Easterby) *hld up in tch: hdwy to chse ldrs over 2f out: sn rdn and wknd over 1f out* 28/1
0-40 9 2 **Amazing Blue Sky**26 1239 7-9-0 62 JamesSullivan 1 47
(Ruth Carr) *led: rdn along 3f out: hdd 2f out and sn wknd* 14/1
234- 10 3 ½ **Tribal Myth (IRE)**242 5622 6-8-13 64 (p) JulieBurke(3) 12 42
(Kevin Ryan) *chsd ldrs: rdn along on outer wl over 2f out: sn wknd* 6/1[3]
-662 11 21 **Flying Applause**10 1567 8-9-4 69 (bt) MarkCoumbe(3) 10
(Roy Bowring) *s.i.s: a in rr: fin lame* 11/1

2m 2.24s (-4.76) **Going Correction** -0.40s/f (Firm) 11 Ran SP% **117.9**
Speed ratings (Par 103): **103,102,102,101,101 97,96,95,93,90 73**
toteswingers: 1&2 £6.40, 1&3 £6.80, 2&3 £5.50 CSF £37.66 CT £159.95 TOTE £8.00: £2.50, £1.90, £1.50; EX 39.10 Trifecta £150.00 Pool: £3,113.47 - 15.55 winning units..
Owner J T Stimpson **Bred** Malih Al Basti **Trained** Butterton, Staffs

FOCUS
An open looking contest, run at a decent pace and the second is rated close to last season's course form.

1776 FOLLOW US ON TWITTER @BEVERLEY_RACES H'CAP 1m 1f 207y
4:35 (4:37) (Class 5) (0-70,71) 3-Y-O £3,234 (£962; £481; £240) Stalls Low

Form RPR
-535 1 **Ofcoursewecan (USA)**73 615 3-9-7 68 JoeFanning 5 73+
(Mark Johnston) *mde all: set stdy pce qcknd wl over 2f out: jnd and rdn over 1f out: drvn and kpt on gamely fnl f* 8/1[3]
66-5 2 1 ¼ **Dolphin Village (IRE)**20 1365 3-9-4 65 PaulHanagan 7 67+
(Richard Fahey) *hld up in tch: hdwy on outer over 2f out: rdn to chse ldrs over 1f out: styd on u.p fnl f: tk 2nd nr line* 5/2[2]
21-1 3 shd **Nine Iron (IRE)**2 1743 3-9-10 71 6ex MartinHarley 3 73
(Mick Channon) *trckd ldrs: hdwy over 2f out: chal over 1f out: sn rdn and ev ch tl drvn and one pce ins fnl f: lost 2nd nr line* 11/10[1]
402- 4 1 ½ **Chant (IRE)**182 7357 3-9-5 66 PJMcDonald 2 65
(Ann Duffield) *trckd ldng pair on inner: effrt 2f out: nt clr run over 1f out: sn swtchd lft and rdn: no imp ins fnl f* 11/1
040- 5 2 ½ **Red Charmer (IRE)**187 7244 3-9-7 68 (p) TomEaves 1 62
(Ann Duffield) *t.k.h: chsd ldrs on inner: rdn along wl over 2f out: sn one pce* 33/1
350- 6 ½ **Causeway Foot (USA)**183 7325 3-9-5 66 (t) MichaelO'Connell 6 59
(Jedd O'Keeffe) *cl up: rdn along over 2f out: keeping on u.p whn nt clr run and squeezed out 1 1/2f out: no ch after* 12/1
004- 7 1 ¾ **Marble Silver (IRE)**222 6257 3-9-1 62 DuranFentiman 4 52
(Tim Easterby) *hld up in rr: hdwy over 2f out: sn rdn and hung bdly lft wl over 1f out: n.d* 28/1

2m 9.07s (2.07) **Going Correction** -0.40s/f (Firm) 7 Ran SP% **109.7**
Speed ratings (Par 98): **75,74,73,72,70 70,68**
toteswingers: 1&2 £2.40, 1&3 £2.20, 2&3 £1.60 CSF £26.04 TOTE £6.20: £3.10, £1.10; EX 17.40 Trifecta £35.60 Pool: £3,239.06 - 68.17 winning units..
Owner Douglas Livingston **Bred** Robert Raphaelson **Trained** Middleham Moor, N Yorks

FOCUS
The pace was very steady for this moderate handicap and the winner made all. The fourth is the best guide to the level.

1777 THE PROCLAIMERS PLAY LIVE HERE ON 22 JUNE MAIDEN STKS 1m 100y
5:10 (5:10) (Class 5) 3-Y-O+ £3,234 (£962; £481; £240) Stalls Low

Form RPR
255- 1 **Awake My Soul (IRE)**195 7016 4-9-5 82 DavidBergin(7) 6 73+
(David O'Meara) *cl up: led on bit wl over 1f out: shkn up ent fnl f: kpt on wl* 5/6[1]
0- 2 2 ¾ **Manchester**177 7459 3-8-12 0 PaulHanagan 1 63+
(Richard Fahey) *t.k.h early: trckd ldng pair: hdwy 2f out: rdn to chse wnr ent fnl f: sn no imp* 9/4[2]
53 3 3 ¼ **Peter's Friend**13 1522 4-9-12 0 TomEaves 7 60
(Michael Herrington) *led: rdn along 3f out: hdd wl over 1f out: one pce* 5/1[3]
4 hd **Bonnie Echo**136 6-9-4 0 [1] LeeTopliss(3) 2 54
(Michael Dods) *dwlt and green: pushed along and in tch after 1f: hdwy over 2f out: rdn and green wl over 1f out: styd on fnl f: nrst fin* 22/1
0- 5 10 **Rapid Rabbit Foot**197 6977 3-8-7 0 FrannyNorton 3 31
(John Holt) *chsd ldrs: rdn along wl over 2f out: sn wknd* 28/1
6 12 **Moonlight Dreamer**11 4-9-4 0 JulieBurke(3) 5
(David C Griffiths) *s.i.s: a in rr* 66/1
0 7 12 **Rolen Sly**24 1282 4-9-12 0 JoeFanning 4
(Brian Rothwell) *v s.i.s: a wl bhd* 66/1

1m 44.66s (-2.94) **Going Correction** -0.40s/f (Firm)
WFA 3 from 4yo+ 14lb 7 Ran SP% **112.8**
Speed ratings (Par 103): **98,95,92,91,81 69,57**
toteswingers: 1&2 £1.10, 1&3 £1.30, 2&3 £1.40 CSF £2.78 TOTE £1.50: £1.10, £1.80; EX 3.10 Trifecta £7.00 Pool: £1,586.73 - 168.10 winning units..
Owner K Nicholson **Bred** Grundy Bloodstock Srl **Trained** Nawton, N Yorks

FOCUS
A weak maiden run at a fair pace. The winner is rated below his official mark and the third is the best guide to the form.
T/Plt: £18.90 to a £1 stake. Pool: £44,700.47. 1,718.51 winning tickets. T/Qpdt: £13.50 to a £1 stake. Pool: £2,614.50. 142.70 winning tickets. JR

1512 LINGFIELD (L-H)
Thursday, April 25

OFFICIAL GOING: Standard
Wind: Fresh, behind Weather: Fine and warm

1778 HOLLOW LANE MEDIAN AUCTION MAIDEN STKS 5f (P)
4:55 (4:56) (Class 5) 2-Y-O £2,587 (£770; £384; £192) Stalls High

Form RPR
30 1 **Limegrove**7 1634 2-9-0 0 TomQueally 4 80
(David Evans) *mde all: rdn over 1f out: holding runner-up fnl 150yds* 5/4[1]
2 2 ¾ **Fine 'n Dandy (IRE)** 2-9-5 0 RichardKingscote 5 75
(Tom Dascombe) *trckd wnr: rdn over 1f out: no ex ins fnl f* 6/4[2]
4 3 8 **Lucky Visione**12 1534 2-9-5 0 DavidProbert 1 46
(Gay Kelleway) *a 3rd: rdn 3f out: wknd wl over 1f out* 12/1
4 5 **Quinta Feira (IRE)** 2-9-5 0 LiamKeniry 3 28
(Ed de Giles) *dwlt: outpcd: a last: n.d fnl 3f* 5/1[3]

58.54s (-0.26) **Going Correction** -0.05s/f (Stan) 4 Ran SP% **108.8**
Speed ratings (Par 92): **100,95,82,74**
CSF £3.46 TOTE £1.50; EX 2.90 Trifecta £8.70 Pool: £1,057.89 - 90.23 winning units..
Owner Mark Windsor **Bred** Mark Windsor **Trained** Pandy, Monmouths

FOCUS
Probably just modest form. The first two finished well clear.

1779 LINGFIELD PARK OWNERS CLUB H'CAP 1m 2f (P)
5:25 (5:25) (Class 6) (0-60,60) 4-Y-O+ £1,940 (£577; £288; £144) Stalls Low

Form RPR
6600 1 **Minority Interest**31 1176 4-9-5 58 (v[1]) GeorgeBaker 4 64
(Brett Johnson) *led: hrd rdn and narrowly hdd over 1f out: rallied and led again ins fnl f: gamely* 9/2[3]
6/04 2 nk **Queenie's Star (IRE)**15 1473 6-8-9 48 RobertHavlin 3 53
(Michael Attwater) *hld up in midfield: hdwy over 2f out: chal ins fnl f: nt qckn nr fin* 20/1
6535 3 nk **Fonterutoli (IRE)**3 1716 6-9-4 57 (e) AdamBeschizza 5 62
(Roger Ingram) *s.i.s and rdn in rr early: cajoled along over 3f out: gd hdwy fnl 2f: fin wl* 7/2[2]
-300 4 1 ¼ **Missionaire (USA)**34 1111 6-9-0 53 (b[1]) JimmyQuinn 8 55
(Tony Carroll) *chsd ldrs: wnt 2nd 3f out: slt ld over 1f out tl ins fnl f: no ex* 8/1
0633 5 3 ¼ **Querido (GER)**15 1474 9-8-0 46 oh1 (bt[1]) JoeyHaynes(7) 9 42
(Paddy Butler) *hld up in midfield: hdwy over 2f out: hrd rdn over 1f out: no imp* 14/1
0034 6 2 ¼ **Dolly Colman (IRE)**14 1498 5-8-7 46 oh1 ChrisCatlin 11 37
(Zoe Davison) *towards rr: rdn 3f out: nvr rchd ldrs* 16/1
-520 7 4 ½ **Bloodsweatandtears**23 1303 5-9-7 60 [1] SebSanders 7 42
(William Knight) *s.i.s: sn rcvrd and hld up in 6th: wnt handy 4f out: rdn and btn over 2f out* 3/1[1]
8 ¾ **Metropolis (IRE)**627 4832 8-8-7 46 oh1 (p) LiamJones 10 27
(Adrian Brendan Joyce, Ire) *prom: chsd wnr 4f out tl 3f out: wknd 2f out* 7/1
/040 9 ½ **Valkov**35 1100 6-8-2 46 oh1 RyanTate(5) 2 26
(Tony Carroll) *towards rr: dropped to last over 4f out: rdn and n.d fnl 3f* 33/1
0-06 10 4 **Nibani (IRE)**22 1333 6-9-6 59 TomQueally 1 31
(John Butler) *chsd wnr tl 4f out: sn drvn along and wknd* 7/1

2m 5.48s (-1.12) **Going Correction** -0.05s/f (Stan) 10 Ran SP% **121.8**
Speed ratings (Par 101): **102,101,101,100,97 96,92,91,91,88**
toteswingers: 1&2 £21.60, 1&3 £4.50, 2&3 £17.90 CSF £93.46 CT £358.34 TOTE £4.90: £2.90, £12.10, £2.30; EX 103.60 Trifecta £937.30 Part won. Pool: £1,249.77 - 0.71 winning units..
Owner J Daniels **Bred** Juddmonte Farms Ltd **Trained** Epsom, Surrey

FOCUS
A race that contained quite a few horses with questions to answer, so this won't be strong form.

1780 MARRIOTTLINGFIELD.CO.UK H'CAP 1m (P)
5:55 (5:55) (Class 5) (0-70,73) 4-Y-0+ £2,587 (£770; £384; £192) Stalls High

Form RPR
00-2 1 **Poetic Lord**[13] [1514] 4-9-7 70 RyanMoore 10 78
(Sylvester Kirk) *bhd: hrd rdn and hdwy over 1f out: str run fnl f: led on line* **11/4**[1]
0011 2 *nse* **Rezwaan**[8] [1617] 6-9-10 73 6ex (be) JamieSpencer 6 81
(Murty McGrath) *towards rr: hmpd on rail 5f out: hdwy over 1f out: led ins fnl f: jst ct* **5/1**[3]
1350 3 *1 ¾* **Mafi (IRE)**[13] [1514] 5-9-3 66 (t) RobertHavlin 5 70
(Mark Hoad) *dwlt: sn prom: led jst ins fnl f: sn hdd: one pce* **25/1**
232- 4 *½* **Tenessee**[176] [7474] 6-9-3 66 (t) PatCosgrave 2 69
(Ben De Haan) *pressed ldr: rdn over 3f out: unable qck fnl f* **12/1**
06-6 5 *½* **Cravat**[13] [1514] 4-9-7 70 LiamKeniry 9 72
(Ed de Giles) *hld up in tch: pressed ldrs 3f out: one pce appr fnl f* **4/1**[2]
00-5 6 *1* **Ghostwing**[13] [1516] 6-8-13 67 (vt) NicoleNordblad(5) 1 66
(Luke Dace) *t.k.h: led tl wknd jst ins fnl f* **20/1**
311- 7 *¾* **Dana's Present**[198] [6968] 4-9-7 70 RichardHughes 12 68+
(George Baker) *dwlt: hld up in rr: fnd room on inner and hdwy to chse ldrs 1f out: no ex fnl 100yds* **5/1**[3]
3210 8 *½* **Homeboy (IRE)**[13] [1516] 5-9-0 63 EddieAhern 8 59
(Marcus Tregoning) *plld hrd: prom tl wknd 1f out* **16/1**
3624 9 *nk* **Benandonner (USA)**[14] [1496] 10-8-8 64 JoeyHaynes(7) 4 60
(Paddy Butler) *anticipated s and burst out of stalls in front: chsd ldrs: n.m.r and lost pl 5f out: rdn and btn 3f out* **66/1**
4601 10 *4* **Flavius Victor (IRE)**[30] [1179] 4-9-2 70 ThomasBrown(5) 7 56
(Patrick Chamings) *towards rr: rdn and n.d fnl 3f* **12/1**

1m 37.2s (-1.00) **Going Correction** -0.05s/f (Stan) **10** Ran SP% **111.4**
Speed ratings (Par 103): **103,102,101,100,100 99,98,97,97,93**
toteswingers: 1&2 £4.40, 1&3 £15.50, 2&3 £32.70 CSF £14.64 CT £245.31 TOTE £3.60: £1.30, £4.60, £9.70; EX 15.60 Trifecta £260.60 Pool: £1,032.68 - 2.97 winning units..
Owner Mrs John Lee **Bred** Howard Barton Stud **Trained** Upper Lambourn, Berks

FOCUS
A fair handicap in which it paid to be held up.

1781 LINGFIELDPARK.CO.UK CLASSIFIED STKS 1m (P)
6:30 (6:30) (Class 6) 3-Y-0+ £1,940 (£577; £288; £144) Stalls High

Form RPR
300- 1 **Poetry Writer**[160] [7752] 4-9-6 45 LiamKeniry 9 61
(Michael Blanshard) *chsd ldrs: effrt 2f out: led ins fnl f: rdn out* **5/1**[3]
343 2 *1 ¼* **Total Obsession**[15] [1480] 6-9-6 53 (v) KierenFallon 12 58
(Mark Hoad) *chsd ldr: led over 3f out tl ins fnl f: unable qck* **5/1**[3]
1306 3 *2 ¼* **Napinda**[37] [1071] 3-8-6 55 (v) WilliamCarson 7 49
(Philip McBride) *towards rr: rdn along over 4f out: gd hdwy fnl f: catching tiring ldrs fast at fin* **4/1**[2]
0-00 4 *½* **Born To Run**[22] [1323] 3-8-6 49 (b) MartinLane 11 48
(Hugo Palmer) *led and sn crossed to rail: hdd and drvn along over 3f out: one pce fnl 2f* **20/1**
00-5 5 *4 ½* **So Lyrical**[29] [1210] 3-8-6 42 KieranO'Neill 6 47
(Jo Hughes) *mid-div: rdn 4f out: nvr rchd ldrs* **20/1**
220- 6 *1* **Ermyn Flyer**[126] [8180] 4-9-6 53 IanMongan 5 39
(Pat Phelan) *in tch: rdn 3f out: sn btn* **3/1**[1]
5505 7 *2* **Limoges**[31] [1171] 3-8-6 47 (v[1]) CathyGannon 3 30
(Luke Dace) *s.i.s and rdn s: sn prom: wknd 2f out* **10/1**
060- 8 *1 ½* **Cosmic Dream**[215] [6473] 3-8-6 42 SamHitchcott 4 27
(Garry Moss) *plld hrd: in tch: outpcd 3f out: sn btn* **8/1**
0-06 9 *nk* **Trove (IRE)**[15] [1474] 4-9-6 40 (b[1]) RobertHavlin 2 30
(Michael Attwater) *t.k.h: hld up in midfield: rdn over 2f out: fnd little* **33/1**
600- 10 *hd* **Batchworth Firefly**[134] [8069] 5-9-6 52 (p) JimmyQuinn 10 30
(Dean Ivory) *s.i.s: rdn 3f out: a bhd* **14/1**
-000 11 *4 ½* **Yalding Dancer**[30] [1183] 4-9-6 43 GeorgeBaker 8 19
(John Best) *stdd in rr and t.k.h early: pushed along 3f out: a bhd* **20/1**

1m 38.24s (0.04) **Going Correction** -0.05s/f (Stan)
WFA 3 from 4yo+ 14lb **11** Ran SP% **122.4**
Speed ratings (Par 101): **97,95,93,93,88 87,85,84,83,83 79**
toteswingers: 1&2 £9.00, 1&3 £5.70, 2&3 £4.30 CSF £29.82 TOTE £5.80: £1.70, £2.80, £1.40; EX 44.30 Trifecta £447.20 Pool: £1,214.56 - 2.03 winning units..
Owner John H W Finch **Bred** Catridge Farm Stud Ltd **Trained** Upper Lambourn, Berks

FOCUS
A shocker of a race, worthy of the level, which saw a gamble landed.

1782 LINGFIELDPARK.CO.UK H'CAP 7f (P)
7:00 (7:00) (Class 4) (0-85,85) 4-Y-0+ £4,690 (£1,395; £697; £348) Stalls Low

Form RPR
0-06 1 **Roninski (IRE)**[33] [1148] 5-9-6 84 JimCrowley 2 92
(Garry Moss) *chsd ldrs: effrt 2f out: clsd on ldr fnl f: led on line* **10/1**
-601 2 *nse* **Ocean Legend (IRE)**[35] [1096] 8-8-10 74 KierenFallon 3 82
(Tony Carroll) *t.k.h: pressed ldr: led wl over 1f out: rdn along fnl f: jst ct* **16/1**
2/00 3 *1* **Ortac Rock (IRE)**[19] [1385] 4-9-6 84 RichardHughes 9 89
(Richard Hannon) *dwlt: hld up in rr: rdn and hdwy over 1f out: r.o fnl f* **5/1**[3]
35-1 4 *1* **Light Burst (USA)**[65] [715] 4-9-1 84 ThomasBrown(5) 5 86
(Ismail Mohammed) *plld hrd: in tch: n.m.r 3f out: rdn over 2f out: styd on fnl f* **9/4**[1]
00-0 5 *½* **Mr David (USA)**[12] [1542] 6-9-6 84 (b) GeorgeBaker 7 85
(Jamie Osborne) *stdd s: hld up towards rr: rdn over 2f out: styd on fnl f* **16/1**
104- 6 *nse* **Johnno**[259] [5004] 4-9-6 84 SebSanders 1 85
(J W Hills) *led tl wl over 1f out: wknd fnl f* **7/2**[2]
4-40 7 *nk* **Afkar (IRE)**[36] [1092] 5-8-10 74 TomQueally 8 74
(Clive Brittain) *prom on outer: rdn over 2f out: sn btn* **14/1**
552- 8 *nk* **Jungle Bay**[157] [7789] 6-8-6 77 IanBurns(7) 6 76
(Jane Chapple-Hyam) *t.k.h in midfield: rdn and outpcd 3f out: nvr able to chal* **10/1**
4050 9 *1 ¼* **Seek The Fair Land**[26] [1245] 7-9-7 85 (b) WilliamCarson 4 81
(Jim Boyle) *towards rr: rdn to chse ldrs on inner ent st: wknd over 1f out* **8/1**

1m 24.66s (-0.14) **Going Correction** -0.05s/f (Stan) **9** Ran SP% **117.4**
Speed ratings (Par 105): **98,97,96,95,95 95,94,94,92**
toteswingers 1&2 £31.40, 1&3 £7.00, 2&3 £2.30 CSF £156.90 CT £906.11 TOTE £11.00: £3.00, £2.20, £1.70; EX 92.40 Trifecta £556.50 Pool: £1,183.60 - 1.59 winning units..
Owner Ron Hull **Bred** Peter Hodgson & Star Pointe Ltd **Trained** Tickhill, S Yorks

FOCUS
A decent contest but the whole field finished close together, suggesting this isn't strong form.

1783 BREATHE SPA AT MARRIOTT LINGFIELD H'CAP 7f (P)
7:30 (7:32) (Class 6) (0-60,60) 4-Y-0+ £1,940 (£577; £288; £144) Stalls Low

Form RPR
0-05 1 **Intomist (IRE)**[3] [1717] 4-9-6 59 (p) PatCosgrave 7 71
(Jim Boyle) *trckd ldrs: wnt 2nd over 1f out: led ins fnl f: comf* **6/1**[2]
40-4 2 *2 ¾* **Bold Ring**[32] [1161] 7-8-13 52 JimmyQuinn 10 57
(Edward Creighton) *hld up in tch: effrt 2f out: r.o to take 2nd ins fnl f* **14/1**
5262 3 *hd* **Silly Billy (IRE)**[16] [1455] 5-8-11 57 (v) RyanWhile(7) 8 61
(Bill Turner) *led tl ins fnl f: no ex* **7/1**[3]
4153 4 *¾* **Amis Reunis**[7] [1657] 4-9-7 60 (p) WilliamCarson 1 62
(Anthony Carson) *mid-div: hdwy over 1f out: kpt on fnl f* **7/1**[3]
0040 5 *½* **Jackie Love (IRE)**[69] [665] 5-8-4 48 (v) NathanAlison(5) 14 51
(Olivia Maylam) *towards rr: r.o fr over 1f out: nrest at fin* **16/1**
0-30 6 *2 ½* **Mudhish (IRE)**[24] [1294] 8-8-13 59 LaurenHaigh(7) 11 53
(Clive Brittain) *mid-div on outer: hdwy 3f out: wknd over 1f out* **25/1**
0-66 7 *nk* **Shared Moment (IRE)**[92] [334] 7-9-0 53 (v) RichardHughes 2 46
(Luke Dace) *mid-div: rdn 2f out: styd on same pce* **7/1**[3]
6045 8 *½* **Rooknrasbryripple**[31] [1173] 4-8-3 47 RyanTate(5) 4 39
(Ralph Smith) *stdd s: t.k.h in rr: gd hdwy on inner over 1f out: no ex fnl f* **25/1**
202 9 *2 ¾* **Imjin River (IRE)**[44] [968] 6-8-11 55 (t) NatashaEaton(5) 12 39
(William Stone) *stdd s: hld up in rr: styd on fnl f: nvr nrr* **14/1**
0063 10 *½* **Cuthbert (IRE)**[15] [1473] 6-8-0 46 (b) PaigeBolton(7) 3 29
(Michael Attwater) *t.k.h in midfield: effrt on outer over 2f out: btn wl over 1f out* **14/1**
0512 11 *¾* **Mary's Pet**[16] [1452] 6-9-4 57 CathyGannon 9 38
(Lee Carter) *w ldrs tl wknd over 1f out* **8/1**
03-6 12 *1 ¾* **Comadoir (IRE)**[62] [750] 7-9-5 58 (p) IanMongan 5 34
(Jo Crowley) *nvr gng wl: sn outpcd towards rr* **5/1**[1]
200- 13 *nk* **Fault**[338] [2366] 7-9-1 54 ChrisCatlin 6 29
(Zoe Davison) *chsd ldrs tl wknd 2f out* **33/1**
-000 14 *16* **Ziefhd**[78] [535] 4-9-5 58 (p) TomQueally 13
(Tim McCarthy) *w ldrs tl wknd over 2f out* **12/1**

1m 24.32s (-0.48) **Going Correction** -0.05s/f (Stan) **14** Ran SP% **123.8**
Speed ratings (Par 101): **100,96,96,95,95 92,92,91,88,87 86,84,84,66**
totewingers 1&2 £23.90, 1&3 £11.50, 2&3 £24.50 CSF £88.15 CT £615.55 TOTE £6.80: £2.40, £5.00, £2.20; EX 107.40 Trifecta £559.60 Part won. Pool: £746.15 - 0.15 winning units..
Owner The Clueless Syndicate **Bred** P M Guerin **Trained** Epsom, Surrey

FOCUS
The early fractions set by the leader didn't look too quick, and one felt this developed into a bit of a sprint to the line. That said, the winning time was quicker than the preceding 0-85 handicap over the same distance.

1784 CYPRIUM BAR AT MARRIOTT LINGFIELD H'CAP 6f (P)
8:00 (8:01) (Class 5) (0-70,70) 3-Y-O £2,587 (£770; £384; £192) Stalls Low

Form RPR
33-4 1 **Majestic Jess (IRE)**[21] [1345] 3-9-4 67 JimCrowley 6 73
(Luke Dace) *chsd ldr: led 1f out: hld on wl* **4/1**[3]
0-22 2 *hd* **Firmdecisions (IRE)**[68] [686] 3-9-5 68 DavidProbert 2 73
(Brett Johnson) *racd keenly: led: pushed along 2f out: hdd 1f out: rallied gamely* **8/1**
36-0 3 *2* **Yahilwa (USA)**[24] [1291] 3-9-1 64 TomQueally 3 63
(James Tate) *hld up: effrt and hung lft wl over 1f out: styd on fnl f* **7/1**
36-3 4 *½* **Puteri Nur Laila (IRE)**[19] [1384] 3-8-10 64 (b) RyanTate(5) 1 61
(Paul Cole) *in tch: rdn to chse ldrs over 1f out: one pce* **16/1**
00-6 5 *1 ¼* **Dividend Dan (IRE)**[19] [1384] 3-8-9 58 EddieAhern 5 51
(Mike Murphy) *s.s: bhd tl styd on fnl f* **16/1**
11 6 *2* **Secret Of Success**[22] [1315] 3-9-3 66 ChrisCatlin 7 53
(Rae Guest) *chsd ldrs: rdn 2f out: wknd over 1f out* **9/4**[1]
351- 7 *1 ¼* **Keep The Dream**[186] [7268] 3-9-7 70 (t) JamieSpencer 4 53
(Paul Cole) *in tch tl outpcd fnl 2f* **5/2**[2]

1m 11.76s (-0.14) **Going Correction** -0.05s/f (Stan) **7** Ran SP% **114.7**
Speed ratings (Par 98): **98,97,95,94,92 90,88**
toteswingers 1&2 £3.50, 1&3 £5.00, 2&3 £6.80 CSF £35.21 CT £216.46 TOTE £5.10: £3.80, £3.70; EX 39.20 Trifecta £444.70 Pool: £1,096.75 - 1.84 winning units..
Owner Mark Benton **Bred** Mrs Eileen Comer **Trained** Five Oaks, W Sussex

FOCUS
The first two home were first and second throughout, and one felt the runner-up's jockey controlled the pace really well.
T/Plt: £150.80 to a £1 stake. Pool: £46,312.15. 224.19 winning tickets. T/Qpdt: £27.30 to a £1 stake. Pool: £4,740.50. 128.40 winning tickets. LM

[1565]NEWCASTLE (L-H)
Thursday, April 25

OFFICIAL GOING: Good to firm (good in places; 7.4) changing to good (good to firm in places) after race 1 (5.15)
Wind: Fresh, half against Weather: Cloudy

1785 ESH GROUP/E.B.F. NOVICE STKS 5f
5:15 (5:15) (Class 4) 2-Y-O £4,075 (£1,212; £606; £303) Stalls Centre

Form RPR
1 **Eastern Impact (IRE)** 2-9-0 0 TonyHamilton 3 85+
(Richard Fahey) *cl up in 3rd: led gng wl appr fnl f: pushed clr ins fnl f: comf* **11/4**[2]
2 2 *3 ½* **Lily Rules (IRE)**[8] [1606] 2-8-9 0 BarryMcHugh 4 67
(Tony Coyle) *led narrowly: rdn 2f out: hdd appr fnl f: one pce and sn no ch w wnr* **4/1**[3]
12 3 *nk* **M'Selle (IRE)**[8] [1619] 2-9-0 0 LukeMorris 1 71
(Ronald Harris) *hld up in tch: rdn 1/2-way: sn one pce: briefly carried lft appr fnl f: wnt 3rd ins fnl f: nvr threatened* **11/4**[2]
51 4 *1 ½* **Vine De Nada**[8] [1606] 2-9-2 0 SilvestreDeSousa 2 68
(Mark Johnston) *w ldr: rdn over 1f out: wandered and outpcd appr fnl f: wknd fnl 100yds* **15/8**[1]

1m 3.56s (2.46) **Going Correction** +0.15s/f (Good) **4** Ran SP% **108.1**
Speed ratings (Par 94): **86,80,79,77**
CSF £12.78 TOTE £5.20; EX 16.80 Trifecta £50.00 Pool: £534.46 - 8.00 winning units..
Owner D W Barker **Bred** Airlie Stud **Trained** Musley Bank, N Yorks
■ Stewards' Enquiry : Barry McHugh one-day ban: failed to ride to draw (May 9)

FOCUS
After just 5mm of rain during the day on a fine evening the ground was changed to good, good to firm in places. A fair maiden with a taking winner and the runner-up the best guide.

1786 NORTHUMBRIAN WATER CLAIMING STKS 1m 3y(S)
5:45 (5:47) (Class 6) 3-Y-O+ £1,940 (£577; £288; £144) Stalls Low

Form RPR
00-6 **1** **King Pin**[10] 1569 8-9-9 64 BarryMcHugh 1 74
(Tracy Waggott) *hld up in rr: smooth hdwy over 2f out: rdn over 1f out: led ins fnl f: kpt on* **9/1**
4010 **2** 3/4 **Classic Colori (IRE)**[12] 1538 6-9-12 80 (v) DanielTudhope 3 75
(David O'Meara) *hld up: swtchd rt to r alone against stands' rail over 3f out: gd hdwy to ld over 2f out: sn rdn: hdd ins fnl f: kpt on* **3/1**[2]
01-3 **3** 1 1/2 **It's A Mans World**[15] 1459 7-9-11 78 GrahamLee 5 71
(Brian Ellison) *dwlt: hld up in tch: pushed along 2f out: edgd rt and hdwy to chse ldr appr fnl f: one pce ins fnl f* **4/1**[3]
62 **4** 6 **Derby To Dubai**[49] 911 3-8-11 0 AmyRyan 9 53
(Kevin Ryan) *in tch: rdn 3f out: ev ch wl over 1f out: wknd fnl f* **7/1**
0-03 **5** 6 **Extraterrestrial**[15] 1485 9-9-10 80 FrederikTylicki 8 42
(Richard Fahey) *trckd ldr: rdn over 2f out: wknd wl over 1f out* **7/4**[1]
6650 **6** 7 **Spinning Ridge (IRE)**[19] 1401 8-9-8 56 (v) LukeMorris 7 24
(Ronald Harris) *trckd ldrs: rdn over 2f out: sn wknd* **66/1**
060- **7** 7 **Tropical Duke (IRE)**[222] 6259 7-9-8 48 DavidAllan 2
(Ron Barr) *in tch: rdn 3f out: wknd fnl 2f* **100/1**
323 **8** 11 **Miami Gator (IRE)**[65] 718 6-9-3 69 (v) ConorHarrison(7) 6
(Mrs K Burke) *sn led: rdn whn hdd over 2f out: wknd* **16/1**
5-00 **9** 1/2 **Blue Clumber**[8] 1616 3-8-4 63 (p) KellyHarrison 4
(Shaun Harris) *w ldr: rdn over 3f out: sn wknd* **66/1**

1m 44.45s (1.05) **Going Correction** +0.15s/f (Good)
WFA 3 from 6yo+ 14lb **9** Ran SP% **113.7**
Speed ratings (Par 101): **100,99,97,91,85 78,71,60,60**
toteswingers: 1&2 £4.50, 1&3 £7.00, 2&3 £3.20 CSF £35.69 TOTE £9.20: £2.30, £2.10, £1.80; EX 45.50 Trifecta £302.00 Pool: £1,245.68 - 3.09 winning units..
Owner H Conlon **Bred** Cheveley Park Stud Ltd **Trained** Spennymoor, Co Durham

FOCUS
They set off racing in one group towards the centre in this one-mile claimer in which official ratings went out of the window. The placed horses to recent marks set the level.

1787 JEWSON DURHAM H'CAP 6f
6:20 (6:21) (Class 4) (0-85,89) 4-Y-O+ £4,690 (£1,395; £697; £348) Stalls Centre

Form RPR
33 **1** **Gandalak (FR)**[7] 1652 4-9-3 81 DanielTudhope 16 97
(David O'Meara) *racd stands' side: mde all: rdn clr over 1f out: kpt on wl* **5/1**[2]
-001 **2** 2 3/4 **King Of Eden (IRE)**[10] 1571 7-9-11 89 6ex (b) DavidAllan 11 96+
(Eric Alston) *racd stands' side: hld up: hdwy whn n.m.r against rail over 1f out: swtchd lft: kpt on to go 2nd fnl 75yds: 2nd of 10 in gp* **9/2**[1]
400- **3** 1 1/4 **New Leyf (IRE)**[192] 7097 7-9-3 81 PaulQuinn 13 84
(David Nicholls) *awkward s: racd stands' side: midfield: hdwy to chse clr ldr over 1f out: kpt on one pce: lost 2nd fnl 75yds: 3rd of 10 in gp* **14/1**
2-00 **4** 3 3/4 **Victoire De Lyphar (IRE)**[7] 1646 6-9-4 82 (e) AmyRyan 3 73
(Ruth Carr) *led far side pair: in tch overall: merged w pair in centre 1/2-way: rdn over 2f out: kpt on one pce* **25/1**
10-1 **5** 3/4 **Johnny Cavagin**[7] 1644 4-9-5 83 6ex (t) RobertWinston 10 72
(Richard Guest) *racd stands' side: midfield: rdn over 2f out: one pce and nvr threatened: 4th of 10 in gp* **11/2**[3]
0-6 **6** nk **Oneladyowner**[32] 1160 5-9-3 81 PhillipMakin 1 69
(David Brown) *dwlt: hld up in centre: merged w far side pair 1/2-way: rdn over 2f out: one pce and nvr threatened* **11/1**
0-00 **7** 1 1/4 **Alejandro (IRE)**[12] 1542 4-9-7 85 TonyHamilton 4 69
(Richard Fahey) *led centre pair: prom overall: merged w far side pair 1/2-way: rdn over 2f out: wknd over 1f out* **12/1**
420- **8** 1/2 **Barney McGrew (IRE)**[248] 5412 10-9-1 79 PaulMulrennan 7 61
(Michael Dods) *racd stands' side: midfield: rdn over 2f out: sn no imp: 5th of 10 in gp* **20/1**
024- **9** 4 1/2 **Dark Castle**[213] 6536 4-9-3 81 FrederikTylicki 14 49
(Micky Hammond) *racd stands' side: trckd ldr: rdn over 2f out: wknd over 1f out: 6th of 10 in gp* **10/1**
00-4 **10** 1 3/4 **Solar Spirit (IRE)**[24] 1281 8-9-3 81 RussKennemore 2 43
(Tracy Waggott) *hld up far side: hld up: merged w pair in centre 1/2-way: nvr threatened* **11/1**
200- **11** hd **Partner (IRE)**[171] 7595 7-9-3 81 (p) GrahamLee 9 42
(Noel Wilson) *hld up stands' side: nvr threatened: 7th of 10 in gp* **16/1**
0104 **12** 1 3/4 **Noverre To Go (IRE)**[10] 1581 7-9-7 85 LukeMorris 8 41
(Ronald Harris) *racd stands' side: midfield: rdn over 2f out: wknd over 1f out: 8th of 10 in gp* **25/1**
320- **13** 1 1/2 **Best Trip (IRE)**[166] 7690 6-9-3 81 BarryMcHugh 12 32
(Brian Ellison) *racd stands' side: trckd ldr: rdn over 2f out: sn wknd: 9th of 10 in gp* **7/1**
400- **14** nse **Roker Park (IRE)**[177] 7453 8-8-11 82 JoshDoyle(7) 6 33
(David O'Meara) *hld up stands' side: rdn over 2f out: sn btn* **33/1**

1m 14.36s (-0.24) **Going Correction** +0.15s/f (Good) **14** Ran SP% **124.1**
Speed ratings (Par 105): **107,103,101,96,95 95,93,92,86,84 84,82,80,79**
toteswingers 1&2 £4.80, 1&3 £27.50, 2&3 £22.90 CSF £27.29 CT £252.07 TOTE £6.80: £3.60, £1.60, £5.10; EX 28.80 Trifecta £240.70 Pool: £947.04 - 2.95 winning units..
Owner Middleham Park Racing LIII & Partners **Bred** Haras De Son Altesse L'Aga Khan S C E A **Trained** Nawton, N Yorks
■ Stewards' Enquiry : David Allan one-day ban: careless riding (May 9)

FOCUS
Two raced towards the far side, two more up the middle, but the other ten raced towards the stands' side. The runner-up sets the standard rated close to his latest C&D mark.

1788 SWINBURNE MADDISON LLP H'CAP 1m 3y(S)
6:50 (6:52) (Class 6) (0-65,65) 4-Y-O+ £1,940 (£577; £288; £144) Stalls Centre

Form RPR
005- **1** **Spavento (IRE)**[269] 4641 7-9-5 63 DavidAllan 10 73
(Eric Alston) *hld up in rr stands' side: rdn over 2f out: stl plenty to do wl over 1f out: r.o strly towards rail to ld fnl 75yds* **16/1**
150- **2** nk **Cross The Boss (IRE)**[187] 7256 6-8-11 55 DanielTudhope 12 64+
(David O'Meara) *hld up on stands' side: gd hdwy 2f out: rdn to chse overall ldr appr fnl f: kpt on ins fnl f: jst hld: 2nd of 10 in gp* **3/1**[1]
110- **3** 1/2 **Dandarrell**[153] 7841 6-9-1 59 FrederikTylicki 7 67+
(Julie Camacho) *racd alone centre: prom: overall ldr 1/2-way: rdn over 2f out: hdd fnl 75yds: no ex* **10/1**
4100 **4** 5 **Outlaw Torn (IRE)**[15] 1462 4-9-2 60 (e) RobbieFitzpatrick 9 57
(Richard Guest) *hld up stands' side: rdn over 2f out: plugged on: nvr threatened ldrs: 3rd of 10 in gp* **25/1**
00-0 **5** nk **Running Reef (IRE)**[10] 1567 4-9-2 60 RussKennemore 14 56
(Tracy Waggott) *midfield: rdn and hdwy to ld stands' side gp 2f out: wknd fnl f: 4th of 10 in gp* **10/1**
4153 **6** 3 3/4 **Alhaban (IRE)**[14] 1496 7-9-7 65 LukeMorris 13 52
(Ronald Harris) *racd stands' side: midfield: rdn over 2f out: sn no imp on ldrs: 5th of 10 in gp* **28/1**
0-55 **7** 7 **Rasselas (IRE)**[33] 1151 6-8-13 57 (v) PaulQuinn 5 28
(David Nicholls) *racd far side: in tch: led gp 1/2-way but a bhd overall ldrs: 1st of 4 in gp* **33/1**
45-6 **8** 3 3/4 **Koo And The Gang (IRE)**[108] 98 6-8-9 53 SilvestreDeSousa 3 16
(Brian Ellison) *led far side: hdd in gp 1/2-way: a wl bhd overall ldrs: 2nd of 4 in gp* **10/1**
50-6 **9** 1/2 **Aquarian Spirit**[24] 1292 6-8-13 64 SamanthaBell(7) 6 25
(Richard Fahey) *swtchd rt sn after s: chsd ldrs stands' side: rdn over 2f out: sn btn: 6th of 10 in gp* **20/1**
1- **10** 1/2 **Dance For Georgie**[258] 5036 4-9-6 64 PhillipMakin 11 24
(Ben Haslam) *prom stands' side: wknd over 2f out: 7th of 10 in gp* **7/1**[3]
00-0 **11** 2 3/4 **District Attorney (IRE)**[10] 1567 4-9-3 61 KellyHarrison 15 15
(Chris Fairhurst) *led stands' side gp: overall ldr tl 1 1/2-way: hdd in gp 2f out: wknd: 8th of 10 in gp* **33/1**
24-5 **12** 1 1/2 **Gladsome**[25] 1271 5-9-4 62 TonyHamilton 2 13
(Jason Ward) *hld up far side: nvr threatened: 3rd of 4 in gp* **20/1**
050- **13** 8 **Pelican Rock (IRE)**[141] 6105 4-8-4 51 oh2 NeilFarley(3) 16
(Andrew Crook) *racd stands' side: midfield: wknd over 2f out: 9th of 10 in gp* **33/1**
4412 **14** 7 **William Van Gogh**[17] 1434 6-9-7 65 GrahamGibbons 8
(Michael Easterby) *chsd ldr stands' side: rdn 3f out: sn wknd: last of 10 in gp* **4/1**[2]
000- **15** 10 **Icy Blue**[182] 7348 5-8-12 56 AmyRyan 4
(Richard Whitaker) *dwlt: hld up far side: a towards rr: last of 4 in gp* **16/1**

1m 43.88s (0.48) **Going Correction** +0.15s/f (Good) **15** Ran SP% **122.2**
Speed ratings (Par 101): **103,102,102,97,96 93,86,82,81,81 78,77,69,62,52**
toteswingers: 1&2 £17.60, 1&3 £21.40, 2&3 £6.30 CSF £58.79 CT £520.55 TOTE £15.60: £6.30, £1.70, £2.60; EX 117.90 Trifecta £674.10 Part won. Pool: £898.86 - 0.13 winning units..
Owner Whitehills Racing Syndicate **Bred** E Prosser, J Singh, & N & E Kent **Trained** Longton, Lancs
■ Stewards' Enquiry : Graham Gibbons three-day ban: careless riding (May 9-11)
Russ Kennemore one-day ban: careless riding (May 9)

FOCUS
Four raced towards the far side, one alone up the centre and the remainder stuck to the stands' side. The winner is ratred back to his best with the second to last year's AW form.

1789 LAFARGE TARMAC H'CAP 1m 4f 93y
7:20 (7:24) (Class 6) (0-60,60) 4-Y-O+ £1,940 (£577; £288; £144) Stalls Low

Form RPR
30-3 **1** **Naburn**[10] 1572 5-9-6 59 RobertWinston 9 67
(Alan Swinbank) *trckd ldng pair: rdn to chse ldr over 2f out: led jst ins fnl f: kpt on* **7/2**[2]
050- **2** 1 1/2 **Al Furat (USA)**[176] 7496 5-9-5 58 DavidAllan 10 64
(Ron Barr) *trckd ldng pair: led 3f out: sn rdn: hdd jst ins fnl f: one pce* **12/1**
50-5 **3** 1 1/4 **Operateur (IRE)**[10] 1572 5-9-2 55 PhillipMakin 11 59
(Ben Haslam) *in tch: rdn to chse ldng pair over 2f out: kpt on one pce* **8/1**[3]
1062 **4** 1 1/2 **Petrol**[10] 1572 4-9-0 54 DanielTudhope 7 56
(David O'Meara) *midfield: rdn over 3f out: kpt on* **9/4**[1]
0-00 **5** 1 **Kingarrick**[8] 1603 5-8-11 53 NeilFarley(3) 12 53
(Noel Wilson) *midfield: rdn over 3f out: kpt on one pce* **40/1**
0P0- **6** 3 **Jan Smuts (IRE)**[53] 7454 5-9-0 53 (tp) GrahamLee 5 48
(Wilf Storey) *hld up: rdn 3f out: kpt on one pce: nvr threatened* **40/1**
002- **7** 6 **Maska Pony (IRE)**[170] 7603 9-9-1 54 TonyHamilton 1 40
(George Moore) *hld up: rdn over 3f out: minor late hdwy: nvr threatened* **16/1**
04-0 **8** 3/4 **Kodicil (IRE)**[16] 1448 5-9-6 59 PaddyAspell 2 43
(Tim Walford) *midfield: rdn over 3f out: sn btn* **8/1**[3]
0-04 **9** nk **Lyric Poet (USA)**[78] 542 6-9-4 57 (t) BarryMcHugh 14 41
(David Thompson) *hld up: rdn over 3f out: nvr threatened* **33/1**
050- **10** 10 **Valantino Oyster (IRE)**[192] 7095 6-9-5 58 (p) PatrickMathers 3 26
(Tracy Waggott) *w ldr: rdn 3f out: sn wknd* **11/1**
-650 **11** 4 **Dorry K (IRE)**[16] 1445 4-9-6 60 (p) MickyFenton 4 22
(Brian Rothwell) *midfield: rdn over 3f out: sn wknd* **33/1**
546- **12** 7 **Petella**[217] 6407 7-9-7 60 PJMcDonald 6 10
(George Moore) *hld up: pushed along over 4f out: a towards rr* **20/1**
6633 **13** 3 1/4 **El Bravo**[25] 1270 7-9-1 54 (p) RussKennemore 8
(Shaun Harris) *led narrowly: hdd 3f out: wknd* **12/1**

2m 45.51s (-0.09) **Going Correction** +0.025s/f (Good)
WFA 4 from 5yo+ 1lb **13** Ran SP% **120.3**
Speed ratings (Par 101): **101,100,99,98,97 95,91,91,90,84 81,76,74**
totewingers 1&2 £6.60, 1&3 £5.80, 2&3 £27.20 CSF £42.87 CT £318.46 TOTE £4.00: £1.20, £4.90, £3.00; EX 61.50 Trifecta £567.10 Pool: £1,112.17 - 1.47 winning units..
Owner Elsa Crankshaw & G Allan **Bred** Old Mill Stud **Trained** Melsonby, N Yorks

FOCUS
They went a sound gallop here in this low-grade 1m4f handicap. The first three home were prominent throughout and the form looks pretty sound.

1790 ARMS LENGTH H'CAP 1m 2f 32y
7:50 (7:52) (Class 6) (0-65,65) 4-Y-O+ £1,940 (£577; £288; £144) Stalls Centre

Form RPR
4-23 **1** **Titus Bolt (IRE)**[10] 1567 4-9-0 58 GrahamLee 12 72+
(Jim Goldie) *midfield: smooth hdwy over 3f out: led gng wl over 2f out: rdn over 1f out: kpt on wl* **5/2**[1]
620- **2** 3 **Mr Snoozy**[199] 6924 4-9-6 64 (p) PaddyAspell 6 72
(Tim Walford) *prom: rdn over 2f out: kpt on but no ch w wnr fnl f* **12/1**
440- **3** 2 1/4 **Politbureau**[187] 7245 6-8-7 51 GrahamGibbons 4 55
(Michael Easterby) *midfield: rdn over 2f out: kpt on* **13/2**[3]
230- **4** hd **Barton Bounty**[152] 7869 6-8-8 52 TomEaves 8 55
(Peter Niven) *hld up in midfield: rdn and hdwy over 2f out: kpt on one pce* **11/1**
00-6 **5** 2 1/2 **Border Bandit (USA)**[10] 1572 5-8-7 51 RussKennemore 5 56+
(Tracy Waggott) *hld up in rr: hdwy on inner whn n.m.r over 2f out: n.m.r again 1f out: kpt on: nrst fin* **9/2**[2]
2-05 **6** nk **Croftamie**[10] 1579 4-9-1 59 (p) RoystonFfrench 11 57
(Tracy Waggott) *led after 1f: rdn whn hdd over 2f out: wknd fnl f* **14/1**

40-0 **7** ¾ **Cosmic Moon**[25] 1270 5-8-12 **56** .... TonyHamilton 14 52
(Richard Fahey) *s.i.s: hld up in rr: sme hdwy on bit over 2f out: rdn 2f out: no further imp* **9/1**

030- **8** ¾ **Madame Blavatsky (FR)**[192] 7095 5-8-12 **56** .... PaulMulrennan 9 51
(Karen McLintock) *hld up: rdn 2f out: sn no imp* **20/1**

20-4 **9** 1 **Remember Rocky**[25] 1270 4-8-8 **52** .... (p) JamesSullivan 1 45
(Lucy Normile) *midfield: rdn over 3f out: sn wknd* **25/1**

44-0 **10** 18 **The Blue Banana (IRE)**[15] 1462 4-9-2 **60** .... FrederikTylicki 16 17
(Edwin Tuer) *midfield: rdn over 3f out: wknd over 1f out* **9/1**

0-00 **11** 14 **Turned To Gold (IRE)**[10] 1568 4-9-3 **61** ....[1] RobertWinston 10
(Robert Johnson) *midfield on outer: wnt prom 1/2-way: hung lft and lost pl over 2f out: wknd and eased* **33/1**

0-40 **12** 1½ **Oneofapear (IRE)**[26] 1239 7-9-7 **65** .... DavidNolan 3
(Ian McInnes) *led for 1f: in tch: rdn over 4f out: sn btn* **16/1**

2m 13.31s (1.41) **Going Correction** +0.025s/f (Good) 12 Ran SP% **120.2**
Speed ratings (Par 101): **95,92,90,90,88 88,87,87,86,72 60,59**
toteswingers: 1&2 £10.30, 1&3 £3.90, 2&3 £17.70 CSF £34.16 CT £181.55 TOTE £3.00: £1.10, £4.20, £2.20; EX 35.90 Trifecta £477.60 Part won. Pool: £636.89 - 0.54 winning units..
Owner Ian G M Dalgleish **Bred** Patrick Brady **Trained** Uplawmoor, E Renfrews

FOCUS
A modest handicap and no great depth. The runner-up sets the level.

1791 NEWCASTLE EAGLES "FAB" H'CAP 5f
8:20 (8:20) (Class 5) (0-75,75) 3-Y-O **£2,587** (£770; £384; £192) **Stalls** Centre

Form RPR

221- **1** **Bogsnog (IRE)**[232] 5932 3-9-7 **75** .... GrahamLee 7 80+
(Kristin Stubbs) *hld up in tch: pushed along and hdwy appr fnl f: squeezed through narrow gap jst ins fnl f: kpt on wl to ld post* **7/1**

32-2 **2** nk **Cracking Choice (IRE)**[10] 1566 3-8-9 **63** .... (p) PaulMulrennan 2 67
(Michael Dods) *led: sn swtchd rt to r against rail: rdn over 1f out: strly pressed jst ins fnl f: kpt on: hdd post* **5/1**[3]

4-2 **3** 1¾ **Tumblewind**[7] 1647 3-9-0 **68** .... AmyRyan 3 65+
(Richard Whitaker) *in tch: smooth hdwy 2f out: rdn over 1f out: chal strly jst ins fnl f: no ex fnl 75yds* **9/4**[1]

664- **4** 1½ **Our Diane (IRE)**[258] 5055 3-8-13 **67** .... DanielTudhope 8 59
(David O'Meara) *racd keenly: in tch: rdn over 1f out: one pce ins fnl f* **4/1**[2]

-621 **5** ½ **Boxing Shadows**[66] 710 3-9-7 **75** .... TomEaves 6 65
(Bryan Smart) *chsd ldr: rdn over 1f out: wknd ins fnl f* **6/1**

2212 **6** 1 **Bapak Bangsawan**[13] 1524 3-8-9 **70** .... KevinStott[(7)] 4 57+
(Kevin Ryan) *hld up: hdwy on outer 1/2-way: rdn over 1f out: edgd lft and wknd ins fnl f* **14/1**

650- **7** 5 **Lucky Lodge**[166] 7687 3-8-12 **66** .... DavidAllan 5 35
(Mel Brittain) *hld up: a towards rr* **8/1**

1m 1.65s (0.55) **Going Correction** +0.15s/f (Good) 7 Ran SP% **112.0**
Speed ratings (Par 98): **101,100,97,95,94 92,84**
toteswingers: 1&2 £5.20, 1&3 £4.20, 2&3 £2.90 CSF £39.59 CT £102.47 TOTE £7.50: £3.80, £3.10; EX 41.00 Trifecta £125.20 Pool: £1,169.40 - 6.99 winning units..
Owner Facts & Figures **Bred** J R Weston **Trained** Norton, N Yorks
■ A first winner as a trainer for Kristin Stubbs since she took over the licence from her mother Linda.

FOCUS
A tight 3-y-o sprint handicap in which the runner-up is the best guide, backed up by the third.
T/Jkpt: Not won. T/Plt: £353.50 to a £1 stake. Pool £54,160.64. 111.82 winning tickets. T/Qpdt: £22.30 to a £1 stake. Pool: £6,978.20. 230.90 winning tickets. AS

1741 WOLVERHAMPTON (A.W) (L-H)
Thursday, April 25

OFFICIAL GOING: Standard
Wind: Light, behind Weather: Overcast

1792 MORRIS SITE MACHINERY/IRISH STALLION FARMS EBF MAIDEN STKS 5f 20y(P)
2:25 (2:26) (Class 5) 2-Y-O **£2,911** (£866; £432; £216) **Stalls** Low

Form RPR

1 **Lady Frances** 2-9-0 0 .... NeilCallan 2 73+
(Mark Johnston) *chsd ldr: shkn up to ld over 1f out: r.o wl: readily* **4/5**[1]

62 **2** 2¾ **Lilo Lil**[10] 1573 2-9-0 0 .... JamesDoyle 1 63
(David C Griffiths) *led: rdn and hdd over 1f out: edgd lft and styd on same pce ins fnl f* **2/1**[2]

3 16 **Will To Survive (IRE)** 2-9-5 0 .... AndrewMullen 4 10
(Richard Guest) *s.s: hdwy over 3f out: rdn and wknd 1/2-way* **25/1**

4 nk **Pixmiester** 2-9-5 0 .... AdamKirby 3 9
(James Unett) *s.i.s: rn green in rr: rdn and wknd 1/2-way* **10/1**

5 4½ **Caesars Gift (IRE)** 2-9-5 0 .... MartinDwyer 5
(Derek Shaw) *chsd ldrs: rn green: wknd 1/2-way* **9/1**[3]

1m 2.05s (-0.25) **Going Correction** -0.25s/f (Stan) 5 Ran SP% **111.8**
Speed ratings (Par 92): **92,87,62,61,54**
CSF £2.69 TOTE £1.60: £1.30, £1.10; EX 3.00 Trifecta £19.50 Pool: £2,297.85 - 88.18 winning units..
Owner Sheikh Hamdan Bin Mohammed Al Maktoum **Bred** Darley **Trained** Middleham Moor, N Yorks

FOCUS
Gallop Mastered after race four. This uncompetitive maiden only ever involved the two market leaders and the form looks straightforward.

1793 ARCGEN WELDER GENERATOR (S) STKS 5f 216y(P)
2:55 (2:55) (Class 6) 3-Y-O+ **£1,940** (£577; £288; £144) **Stalls** Low

Form RPR

234 **1** **Jake The Snake (IRE)**[63] 740 12-9-2 71 .... AmyBaker[(3)] 2 59
(Tony Carroll) *s.i.s: hld up: hdwy over 1f out: rdn ins fnl f: r.o to ld nr fin* **5/2**[2]

1460 **2** nk **Gaelic Wizard (IRE)**[5] 1694 5-9-4 64 .... JoshBaudains[(7)] 4 64
(Dominic Ffrench Davis) *chsd ldr: rdn to ld wl ins fnl f: hdd nr fin* **6/1**[3]

2020 **3** 1 **Waterloo Dock**[13] 1516 8-9-0 55 .... (v) RobertTart[(5)] 3 55
(Mick Quinn) *led: rdn over 1f out: hdd wl ins fnl f* **14/1**

2261 **4** 1½ **Haadeeth**[13] 1516 6-9-11 73 .... (t) AdamKirby 1 56
(David Evans) *chsd ldrs: pushed along over 2f out: rdn and hung lft over 1f out: styd on same pce* **4/6**[1]

1m 14.04s (-0.96) **Going Correction** -0.25s/f (Stan) 4 Ran SP% **109.5**
Speed ratings (Par 101): **96,95,94,92**
CSF £15.21 TOTE £3.50; EX 19.30 Trifecta £39.40 Pool: £2,458.89 - 46.80 winning units..The winner was bought in for 4,750gns.
Owner T P Ramsden **Bred** J F Tuthill **Trained** Cropthorne, Worcs
■ Stewards' Enquiry : Amy Baker two-day ban: used whip above permitted level (May 9-10)

FOCUS
A modest seller limited by the second and third.

1794 HILTA PUMPS & POWER WASHERS H'CAP 1m 5f 194y(P)
3:25 (3:26) (Class 6) (0-65,64) 4-Y-O+ **£1,940** (£577; £288; £144) **Stalls** Low

Form RPR

-300 **1** **Hallstatt (IRE)**[17] 1434 7-9-6 **60** .... (t) StephenCraine 3 69
(John Mackie) *chsd ldr after 2f: shkn up to ld over 1f out: drvn out* **10/1**

-322 **2** hd **Mr Plod**[13] 1520 8-8-12 **57** .... RobertTart[(5)] 5 65
(J R Jenkins) *a.p: rdn to chse wnr fnl f: r.o* **3/1**[2]

1500 **3** 1¾ **Crimson Monarch (USA)**[13] 1520 9-8-8 **48** .... (b) KirstyMilczarek 10 54
(Peter Hiatt) *hld up: hdwy over 2f out: nt clr run over 1f out: styd on* **10/1**

53-3 **4** 3½ **Glens Wobbly**[3] 1716 5-8-5 **45** .... HayleyTurner 4 46
(Jonathan Geake) *chsd ldr tl led at stdy pce after 2f: rdn and hdd over 1f out: no ex ins fnl f* **9/2**[3]

0-43 **5** ¾ **Moment In The Sun**[19] 1381 4-9-5 **61** .... JamesDoyle 2 61
(David Flood) *racd keenly: led 2f: chsd ldrs: rdn over 2f out: styd on same pce fnl f* **12/1**

260/ **6** 1½ **Layla's Dancer**[453] 4389 6-9-10 **64** .... AndrewMullen 6 62
(Michael Appleby) *prom: rdn over 2f out: edgd lft and wknd ins fnl f* **11/4**[1]

000- **7** 3 **Blackstone Vegas**[165] 7293 7-9-7 **61** .... MartinDwyer 9 55
(Derek Shaw) *hld up: pushed along over 3f out: nvr on terms* **11/1**

600- **8** 6 **Action Front (USA)**[201] 6891 5-8-13 **60** .... AdamMcLean[(7)] 7 45
(Derek Shaw) *s.i.s: hld up and a in rr* **7/1**

3m 2.44s (-3.56) **Going Correction** -0.25s/f (Stan)
WFA 4 from 5yo+ 2lb 8 Ran SP% **116.6**
Speed ratings (Par 101): **100,99,98,96,96 95,93,90**
toteswingers: 1&2 £4.90, 1&3 £16.30, 2&3 £8.10 CSF £41.00 CT £315.36 TOTE £18.60: £4.10, £1.80, £2.00; EX 53.70 Trifecta £804.00 Pool: £3,262.82 - 3.04 winning units..
Owner A B Hill **Bred** Darley **Trained** Church Broughton , Derbys

FOCUS
The pace wasn't that strong in this moderate handicap but the form looks reasonably sound for the grade, rated around the placed horses.

1795 DENYO ULTRA SILENT GENERATOR CLAIMING STKS 1m 4f 50y(P)
3:55 (3:55) (Class 6) 4-Y-O+ **£1,940** (£577; £288; £144) **Stalls** Low

Form RPR

2451 **1** **Noguchi (IRE)**[9] 1597 8-9-1 79 .... (b) NeilCallan 3 82
(Michael Murphy) *chsd ldrs tl led over 3f out: sn clr: comf* **8/13**[1]

114- **2** 5 **Just Lille (IRE)**[203] 6828 10-8-5 76 .... (p) RowanScott[(7)] 2 71
(Ann Duffield) *led: racd keenly: sddle slipped after 1f: hdd over 3f out: sn outpcd* **5/2**[2]

4/3- **3** 6 **Dontpaytheferryman (USA)**[26] 1950 8-8-13 80 .... JamesDoyle 1 62
(Brian Ellison) *hld up: hdwy to join ldr over 7f out: pushed along over 3f out: wknd over 2f out* **11/2**[3]

4 ¾ **Thewestwalian (USA)**[11] 5-8-2 0 .... DanielMuscutt[(7)] 4 57?
(Keith Goldsworthy) *chsd ldr tl over 7f out: remained handy tl rdn and wknd over 2f out* **50/1**

2m 38.65s (-2.45) **Going Correction** -0.25s/f (Stan) 4 Ran SP% **107.8**
Speed ratings (Par 101): **98,94,90,90**
CSF £2.40 TOTE £1.30; EX 2.30 Trifecta £4.10 Pool: £1,828.36 - 327.01 winning units..Thewestwalian was claimed by Mr P. W. Hiatt for £4,000.
Owner Mrs F Shaw **Bred** Cora Srl **Trained** Newmarket, Suffolk

FOCUS
An uncompetitive claimer with the winner rated to his winter handicap form.

1796 SMC LIGHTING TOWER H'CAP 1m 141y(P)
4:30 (4:30) (Class 4) (0-85,89) 4-Y-O+ **£4,690** (£1,395; £697; £348) **Stalls** Low

Form RPR

1504 **1** **Lowther**[14] 1500 8-9-3 **81** .... (v) KierenFox 7 91
(Lee Carter) *a.p: chsd ldr over 2f out: rdn to ld over 1f out: edgd lft ins fnl f: jst hld on* **5/1**[3]

0401 **2** nk **Idol Deputy (FR)**[5] 1699 7-8-10 **79** 6ex .... (p) RachealKneller[(5)] 4 88
(James Bennett) *hld up: hdwy over 1f out: rdn to chse wnr ins fnl f: r.o* **12/1**

332 **3** 2¾ **Lean On Pete (IRE)**[42] 995 4-8-12 **76** .... ShaneKelly 2 79
(Ollie Pears) *a.p: nt clr run over 1f out: rdn and edgd lft ins fnl f: styd on* **4/1**[2]

1210 **4** 1 **Exceedexpectations (IRE)**[5] 1673 4-9-1 **79** .... HayleyTurner 1 79
(Conor Dore) *chsd ldrs: rdn and ev ch over 1f out: no ex ins fnl f* **11/2**

2501 **5** 1¼ **Dubawi Island (FR)**[2] 1745 4-9-11 **89** 6ex .... (b) NeilCallan 5 87
(James Tate) *led: hdd over 6f out: led again 4f out: rdn and hdd over 1f out: no ex ins fnl f* **15/8**[1]

6261 **6** 7 **Rakaan (IRE)**[21] 1353 6-9-7 **85** .... (p) FergusSweeney 3 66
(Jamie Osborne) *s.i.s: outpcd: hdwy over 2f out: rdn over 1f out: hung lft and wknd fnl f* **9/1**

46-3 **7** 10 **Prime Exhibit**[20] 1368 8-9-1 **79** .... (be[1]) StephenCraine 8 37
(Daniel Mark Loughnane) *hld up: pushed along over 3f out: wknd over 2f out* **25/1**

00-0 **8** 4½ **Croquembouche (IRE)**[17] 1422 4-8-13 **77** .... DaneO'Neill 6 25
(Ed de Giles) *chsd ldrs: rdn over 3f out: wknd over 2f out* **25/1**

60-4 **9** 17 **Outpost (IRE)**[111] 60 5-9-2 **85** .... RobertTart[(5)] 9
(Alan Bailey) *hood removed late and s.i.s: hdwy to ld over 6f out: hdd 4f out: sn rdn: wknd over 2f out: t.o* **16/1**

1m 46.69s (-3.81) **Going Correction** -0.25s/f (Stan) 9 Ran SP% **118.1**
Speed ratings (Par 105): **106,105,103,102,101 95,86,82,67**
toteswingers: 1&2 £11.10, 1&3 £5.70, 2&3 £7.90 CSF £64.23 CT £263.56 TOTE £9.40: £4.60, £5.40, £1.90; EX 84.30 Trifecta £274.40 Pool. £3,099.67 - 8.47 winning units..
Owner P G Marsh **Bred** L J Barratt **Trained** Epsom, Surrey

FOCUS
A decent handicap and the pace was solid. An improvement from the winner and second with the third just below recent form.

1797 ARCGEN 40TH ANNIVERSARY H'CAP 1m 141y(P)
5:00 (5:06) (Class 6) (0-60,60) 4-Y-O+ **£1,940** (£577; £288; £144) **Stalls** Low

Form RPR

-01 **1** **Final Delivery**[28] 1222 4-9-5 **58** .... MatthewDavies 5 67
(Jim Boyle) *pushed along in rr early: hld up: hdwy over 1f out: hit over hd by rivals whip ins fnl f: led sn after: r.o wl* **4/1**[2]

544- **2** 1¼ **Zenafire**[159] 7781 4-9-0 **58** .... JackDuern[(5)] 11 64
(Reg Hollinshead) *led: rdn over 1f out: edgd rt and hdd wl ins fnl f: styd on same pce* **7/1**[3]

0062 **3** nk **Matraash (USA)**[20] 1368 7-9-7 **60** .... (be) ShaneKelly 2 65
(Daniel Mark Loughnane) *chsd ldrs: hmpd over 7f out and over 6f out: rdn and ev ch ins fnl f: unable qck nr fin* **8/1**

0313 **4** 3/4 **Delightful Sleep**[5] 1699 5-9-7 **60** .... AdamKirby 1 65
(David Evans) *hld up: hdwy over 1f out: sn rdn: unable qck towards fin* **15/8**[1]

55-0 **5** *nk* **One Of Twins**[13] 1521 5-8-8 **54** .... (b) MatthewHopkins(7) 3 57
(Michael Easterby) *prom: n.m.r and lost pl 7f out: hdwy over 2f out: rdn over 1f out: r.o* **18/1**

-042 **6** 1 1/4 **Chik's Dream**[37] 1082 6-8-2 **46** .... ShirleyTeasdale(5) 9 46
(Derek Haydn Jones) *chsd ldr: edgd lft over 6f out: rdn and ev ch over 1f out: styd on same pce fnl f* **12/1**

2013 **7** 1 1/2 **Penbryn (USA)**[19] 1401 6-9-6 **59** .... SteveDrowne 6 56
(Nick Littmoden) *prom: rdn over 1f out: no ex ins fnl f* **15/2**

6000 **8** *6* **Elijah Pepper (USA)**[37] 1081 8-9-6 **59** .... (p) HayleyTurner 13 42
(Conor Dore) *s.i.s: a in rr* **16/1**

0360 **9** 1/2 **Justcallmehandsome**[28] 1222 11-8-4 **46** oh1 .... (v) BillyCray(3) 10 28
(Dominic Ffrench Davis) *dwlt: hld up: hdwy over 3f out: wknd fnl f* **25/1**

400- **10** *2* **Son Vida (IRE)**[161] 7733 5-9-3 **56** .... NickyMackay 4 33
(Alan Bailey) *chsd ldrs: hmpd over 6f out: rdn over 2f out: sn wknd* **16/1**

1m 48.74s (-1.76) **Going Correction** -0.25s/f (Stan) **10** Ran SP% **118.7**
Speed ratings (Par 101): **97,95,95,94,94 93,92,86,86,84**
toteswingers: 1&2 £7.00, 1&3 £7.10, 2&3 £8.40 CSF £32.91 CT £222.59 TOTE £3.50: £1.10, £2.40, £3.20; EX 40.10 Trifecta £329.50 Pool: £3,040.54 - 6.91 winning units..
Owner M Khan X2 **Bred** Mallalieu Bloodstock Ltd **Trained** Epsom, Surrey
■ Stewards' Enquiry : Shirley Teasdale two-day ban: careless riding (May 9-10)
Jack Duern one-day ban: careless riding (May 9)

FOCUS
A moderate handicap, but a tight finish. The form is a bit fluid with the third and fourth the best guides.

1798 ALCON HEAVY DUTY PUMPS APPRENTICE H'CAP 5f 216y(P)
5:35 (5:35) (Class 5) (0-75,74) 4-Y-0+ **£2,587** (£770; £384; £192) **Stalls** Low

Form RPR

1514 **1** **Valdaw**[31] 1172 5-9-1 **68** .... WilliamTwiston-Davies 7 80+
(Mike Murphy) *a.p: chsd ldr over 1f out: led ins fnl f: r.o* **4/1**[2]

3112 **2** 3/4 **Climaxfortackle (IRE)**[9] 1596 5-8-10 **68** .... AdamMcLean(5) 9 77
(Derek Shaw) *s.s: hdwy over 1f out: rdn to go 2nd wl ins fnl f: r.o: nt rch wnr* **12/1**

1313 **3** 1 1/2 **Dark Lane**[15] 1475 7-8-8 **66** .... RobJFitzpatrick(5) 1 71
(David Evans) *a.p: rdn over 1f out: edgd rt and styd on same pce ins fnl f* **14/1**

000- **4** 1 3/4 **Diamondhead (IRE)**[205] 6768 4-9-4 **74** .... NedCurtis(3) 5 73+
(Ed de Giles) *w ldr tl rdn 2f out: styd on same pce fnl f* **7/2**[1]

3401 **5** 1 1/4 **Point North (IRE)**[13] 1525 6-9-3 **70** .... (b) LMcNiff 4 65
(John Balding) *led: rdn over 1f out: hdd and no ex ins fnl f* **7/2**[1]

6345 **6** *shd* **Reginald Claude**[35] 1102 5-8-4 **62** .... CharlotteJenner(5) 2 57
(Mark Usher) *hld up: styd on ins fnl f: nvr nrr* **12/1**

0502 **7** *2* **Dickie Le Davoir**[7] 1650 9-8-10 **63** .... (b) CharlesBishop 3 51
(Richard Guest) *s.i.s: outpcd: nvr on terms* **14/1**

5242 **8** 3/4 **Restless Bay (IRE)**[5] 1694 5-8-13 **66** .... (b) ShirleyTeasdale 11 52
(Conor Dore) *chsd ldrs: rdn over 2f out: wknd over 1f out* **7/1**[3]

640- **9** *shd* **Tom Sawyer**[146] 7937 5-8-12 **70** .... MatthewHopkins(5) 10 56
(Julie Camacho) *w ldrs tl rdn over 2f out: wknd over 1f out* **20/1**

4231 **10** 3 1/2 **Amethyst Dawn (IRE)**[19] 1398 7-9-0 **67** .... (t) RobertTart 6 41
(Andrew Reid) *w ldrs to 1/2-way: sn rdn: wknd 2f out* **8/1**

1m 13.04s (-1.96) **Going Correction** -0.25s/f (Stan) **10** Ran SP% **121.5**
Speed ratings (Par 103): **103,102,100,97,96 95,93,92,92,87**
toteswingers 1&2 £10.70, 1&3 £7.90, 2&3 £7.50 CSF £53.67 CT £642.43 TOTE £4.10: £1.40, £4.10, £3.10; EX 49.90 Trifecta £302.70 Pool: £1,752.27 - 4.34 winning units..
Owner D Spratt **Bred** Mayden Stud, J A And D S Dewhurst **Trained** Westoning, Beds

FOCUS
A modest apprentice handicap, but there was a five-way battle for the early lead. The runner-up, to recent form, is the best guide.
T/Plt: £81.70 to a £1 stake. Pool: £43,609.22. 389.24 winning tickets. T/Qpdt: £30.10 to a £1 stake. Pool £2,676.15. 65.70 winning tickets. CR

1737 LONGCHAMP (R-H)
Thursday, April 25

OFFICIAL GOING: Turf: good

1799a PRIX DE NANTERRE (CONDITIONS) (3YO COLTS & GELDINGS) (TURF) 1m 1f 165y
11:15 (12:00) 3-Y-0 **£11,788** (£4,715; £3,536; £2,357; £1,178)

RPR

1 **Sky Hunter**[170] 3-8-13 0 .... MaximeGuyon 2 98
(A Fabre, France) **1/2**[1]

2 1 1/4 **Excellentissime (IRE)**[186] 3-8-13 0 .... OlivierPeslier 5 95
(C Ferland, France) **68/10**[2]

3 *hd* **Aarhus (SPA)**[25] 3-9-3 0 .... StephanePasquier 4 99
(M Delcher Sanchez, France) **23/1**

4 1 3/4 **Rottmayer (IRE)**[14] 1511 3-8-9 0 .... UmbertoRispoli 7 87
(G Botti, France) **27/1**

5 *1* **Nervi (FR)** 3-8-13 0 .... ChristopheSoumillon 3 89
(P Bary, France) **17/2**[3]

6 1/2 **Efteos (FR)**[55] 3-8-9 0 .... JeromeClaudic 6 84
(C Laffon-Parias, France) **20/1**

7 4 1/2 **Habeshia**[111] 72 3-8-9 0 .... IoritzMendizabal 1 75
(John Best) *broke wl on ins: racd 3rd: rdn 2 1/2f out: no ex u.p: sn relagated to bk of field: styd on one pce fnl f* **33/1**

2m 9.19s (6.29) **7** Ran SP% **105.5**
WIN (incl. 1 euro stake): 1.50. PLACES: 1.10, 1.40. SF: 4.40.
Owner Sheikh Mohammed **Bred** Darley Stud Management Co Ltd **Trained** Chantilly, France

1534 DONCASTER (L-H)
Friday, April 26

OFFICIAL GOING: Good to firm (9.5)
Wind: Light half against Weather: Cloudy

1800 32RED ON APP STORE H'CAP (DIV I) 7f
1:30 (1:31) (Class 5) (0-70,70) 4-Y-0+ **£2,587** (£770; £384; £192) **Stalls** High

Form RPR

460 **1** **Creek Falcon (IRE)**[79] 540 4-8-10 **66** .... DavidBergin(7) 13 81+
(David O'Meara) *midfield: smooth hdwy over 3f out: led over 2f out: sn asserted: pushed out fnl f: shade cosily* **6/1**[2]

503- **2** 1 1/2 **It's My Time**[158] 7787 4-8-13 **62** .... TonyHamilton 15 71
(Richard Fahey) *hld up: smooth hdwy 3f out: rdn to chse wnr over 1f out: kpt on wl but a hld* **7/1**[3]

16U0 **3** 3 1/4 **The Happy Hammer (IRE)**[14] 1514 7-8-10 **59** .... WilliamCarson 8 59
(Eugene Stanford) *midfield: rdn over 3f out: kpt on: wnt 3rd 1f out: nvr threatened ldng pair* **14/1**

655 **4** *hd* **George Fenton**[14] 1525 4-8-12 **61** .... (p) RobbieFitzpatrick 4 61
(Richard Guest) *s.i.s: hld up: rdn over 3f out: kpt on fr over 1f out* **14/1**

040- **5** 3 1/4 **Offbeat Safaris (IRE)**[191] 7166 5-8-9 **61** .... DarrenEgan(3) 10 52
(Ronald Harris) *midfield: rdn over 3f out: plugged on: nvr threatened* **22/1**

6-06 **6** *nk* **Fred Willetts (IRE)**[35] 104 5-9-2 **70** .... (v) DeclanBates(5) 3 60
(David Evans) *prom: rdn to ld narrowly over 3f out: hdd over 2f out: grad wknd* **7/1**[3]

240- **7** 3/4 **Tamara Bay**[199] 6961 5-8-9 **58** .... PJMcDonald 11 46
(John Davies) *slowly away: hld up: rdn over 3f out: sn no imp on ldrs* **11/2**[1]

500- **8** *3* **Rough Rock (IRE)**[167] 7685 8-8-13 **67** .... RobertTart(5) 14 47
(Chris Dwyer) *in tch: rdn over 3f out: sn wknd* **11/1**

4243 **9** 1 1/4 **Haywain**[30] 1209 4-9-4 **67** .... (b) NeilCallan 1 44
(Kevin Ryan) *prom: rdn over 3f out: wknd over 2f out* **9/1**

34-0 **10** *5* **Diamond Blue**[8] 1646 5-9-6 **69** .... AmyRyan 7 32
(Richard Whitaker) *hld up: rdn over 2f out: sn btn* **25/1**

23-0 **11** 2 3/4 **Pelmanism**[14] 1525 6-9-0 **63** .... (v) TomEaves 6 19
(Brian Ellison) *trckd ldrs: wknd over 3f out* **16/1**

05-0 **12** *9* **Trust Fund Babe (IRE)**[25] 1278 4-8-7 **56** oh2 ....[1] DuranFentiman 9
(Tim Easterby) *chsd ldrs: lost pl 1/2-way: bhd fnl 3f* **50/1**

00/0 **13** *9* **Youhavecontrol (IRE)**[67] 705 5-9-4 **67** .... (t[1]) JamesDoyle 12
(Nicky Vaughan) *chsd ldrs: lost pl 1/2-way: sn bhd* **25/1**

-001 **14** *7* **New Decade**[22] 1351 4-9-3 **66** .... GrahamLee 5
(Milton Bradley) *led: hdd over 3f out: wknd* **9/1**

1m 26.3s **Going Correction** +0.025s/f (Good) **14** Ran SP% **116.2**
Speed ratings (Par 103): **101,99,95,95,91 91,90,87,85,79 76,66,56,48**
toteswingers 1&2 £14.00, 1&3 £0.00, 2&3 £0.00 CSF £43.79 CT £578.29 TOTE £7.90: £2.60, £3.00, £5.90; EX 55.00 Trifecta £481.20 Part won. Pool: £641.67 - 0.01 winning units..
Owner Direct Racing Partnership **Bred** Shadwell Estate Company Limited **Trained** Nawton, N Yorks

FOCUS
Rail on round course from 9f to where it joins straight moved out 5yds to provide fresh ground adding about 18yds to races on Round course. A wide-open 7f handicap, but the first two pulled clear.

1801 32RED ON APP STORE H'CAP (DIV II) 7f
2:00 (2:01) (Class 5) (0-70,69) 4-Y-0+ **£2,587** (£770; £384; £192) **Stalls** High

Form RPR

1-20 **1** **Bang Tidy (IRE)**[14] 1521 4-8-10 **58** .... (t) TomEaves 14 67
(Brian Ellison) *racd nr stands' rail: a.p: rdn to chal jst over 1f out: led jst ins fnl f: drvn out* **16/1**

-033 **2** *1* **Mutafaakir (IRE)**[6] 1686 4-9-4 **66** .... JamesSullivan 7 72
(Ruth Carr) *hld up in midfield: hdwy 3f out and sn trcking ldrs: rdn and slt ld over 1f out: hdd jst ins fnl f: sn drvn and kpt on same pce towards fin* **9/2**[2]

5020 **3** *nk* **Ted's Brother (IRE)**[11] 1569 5-8-12 **60** .... (e) RobbieFitzpatrick 10 65
(Richard Guest) *in tch: pushed along over 2f out: rdn to chse ldrs and n.m.r over 1f out: kpt on u.p fnl f* **8/1**

3660 **4** 3/4 **Rawaafed (IRE)**[16] 1459 4-9-0 **62** .... JoeFanning 12 65
(Keith Dalgleish) *hld up in rr: hdwy 2f out: rdn over 1f out: styd on fnl f: nrst fin* **25/1**

-421 **5** 1/2 **Keep It Dark**[20] 1394 4-8-12 **67** .... DavidSimmonson(7) 8 69
(Tony Coyle) *midfield: hdwy wl over 2f out: rdn to chse ldrs over 1f out: drvn and one pce fnl f* **7/2**[1]

0244 **6** 3/4 **Master Of Disguise**[41] 1039 7-9-1 **63** .... WilliamCarson 13 63
(Brian Baugh) *hld up and bhd: swtchd lft 3f out: hdwy 2f out: rdn to chse ldrs over 1f out: kpt on fnl f: nrst fin* **40/1**

20-5 **7** *2* **Kept**[27] 1243 4-9-5 **67** .... LukeMorris 2 61
(Ronald Harris) *led: rdn along 2f out: hdd over 1f out and grad wknd* **25/1**

055- **8** *nk* **Relentless Harry (IRE)**[142] 7997 4-9-6 **68** .... (t) PatCosgrave 3 61
(George Baker) *prom on wd outside: effrt and cl up over 2f out: sn rdn and wknd over 1f out* **9/1**

00-2 **9** 1 1/2 **Spykes Bay (USA)**[41] 1038 4-9-7 **69** .... JimCrowley 5 58
(Mrs K Burke) *trckd ldrs: hdwy over 2f out: rdn and ch wl over 1f out: sn wknd* **5/1**[3]

040- **10** 1/2 **Last Destination (IRE)**[228] 6105 5-8-1 **56** .... DanielleMooney(7) 9 44
(Nigel Tinkler) *hld up in rr: effrt and pushed along 2f out: sn rdn and one pce* **50/1**

105- **11** 3 1/2 **First Class**[177] 7484 5-9-2 **64** .... TedDurcan 11 43
(Rae Guest) *in tch: rdn along 3f out: sn wknd* **10/1**

500- **12** *2* **Ptolemy**[256] 5170 4-8-12 **60** .... GrahamGibbons 6 33
(David Barron) *dwlt: sn prom: cl up 1/2-way: rdn along wl over 2f out and sn wknd* **14/1**

060- **13** *shd* **Little Jimmy Odsox (IRE)**[204] 6824 5-9-3 **65** ....[1] DavidAllan 1 38
(Tim Easterby) *dwlt: a in rr* **14/1**

1m 27.82s (1.52) **Going Correction** +0.025s/f (Good) **13** Ran SP% **118.6**
Speed ratings (Par 103): **92,90,90,89,89 88,85,85,83,83 79,77,76**
toteswingers 1&2 £31.10, 1&3 £48.50, 2&3 £10.60 CSF £83.41 CT £658.89 TOTE £17.00: £4.90, £2.20, £2.30; EX 108.10 Trifecta £579.10 Part won. Pool: £772.19 - 0.03 winning units..
Owner Koo's Racing Club **Bred** James And Sarah Mulcahy **Trained** Norton, N Yorks

FOCUS
More of the same and plenty still in contention entering the final furlong.

1802 REWARD CAPITAL LLP FILLIES' H'CAP — 6f
2:30 (2:30) (Class 5) (0-70,70) 4-Y-O+ £2,587 (£770; £384; £192) Stalls High

Form RPR
0-55 **1** **Available (IRE)**[8] 1650 4-9-7 **70**....................(p) FrannyNorton 6 83
(John Mackie) *prom: rdn over 2f out: led appr fnl f: kpt on wl* **12/1**
030- **2** *2* **Tahlia Ree (IRE)**[171] 7600 4-9-0 **70**.................. LouisSteward(7) 13 77
(Michael Bell) *hld up in midfield: rdn and hdwy over 1f out: chsd wnr ins fnl f: kpt on* **8/1**[3]
300- **3** *hd* **Big Wave (IRE)**[155] 7827 5-9-4 **67**....................(e[1]) TomEaves 9 73
(Alison Hutchinson) *trckd ldrs: led 2f out: sn rdn: hdd appr fnl f: one pce* **20/1**
0060 **4** *1 1/4* **My Own Way Home**[39] 1063 5-8-7 **56** oh1.................. LukeMorris 5 58
(David Evans) *midfield: rdn over 2f out: hdwy to chse ldrs over 1f out: no ex fnl 100yds* **12/1**
3000 **5** *2* **Little China**[20] 1398 4-8-7 **56** oh1.................. WilliamCarson 10 52
(William Muir) *led narrowly: rdn whn hdd 2f out: wknd fnl f* **20/1**
5-03 **6** *3/4* **Celtic Sixpence (IRE)**[13] 1540 5-9-6 **69**.................. MichaelStainton 4 62
(Nick Kent) *chsd ldrs on outside: rdn over 2f out: edgd lft over 1f out: wknd fnl f* **6/1**[2]
625- **7** *nk* **Ficelle (IRE)**[179] 7437 4-8-9 **61**.................. DarrenEgan(3) 7 53
(Ronald Harris) *hld up: rdn over 3f out: minor late hdwy: nvr threatened* **22/1**
0-66 **8** *1/2* **Dancing Welcome**[97] 271 7-8-13 **62**..................(b) GrahamLee 12 53
(Milton Bradley) *midfield: pushed along over 3f out: nvr threatened* **14/1**
-601 **9** *1 1/2* **Takealookatmenow (IRE)**[11] 1578 4-9-0 **68**.......(v) ShirleyTeasdale(5) 1 54
(David Nicholls) *w ldr on outer: rdn over 2f out: wknd over 1f out* **4/1**[1]
0-54 **10** *nk* **See Clearly**[13] 1540 4-9-2 **65**..................(p) DavidAllan 11 50
(Tim Easterby) *chsd ldrs: rdn 1/2-way: wknd fnl f* **4/1**[1]
604- **11** *1/2* **Loukoumi**[205] 6783 5-8-1 **57**.................. GaryMahon(7) 2 40
(Tim Easterby) *stdd s: hld up: nvr threatened* **16/1**
-060 **12** *1/2* **Lady Royale**[60] 795 5-9-5 **68**..................(p) MichaelO'Connell 14 50
(Geoffrey Oldroyd) *hld up: rdn 1/2-way: nvr threatened* **25/1**
22-0 **13** *3 3/4* **Mey Blossom**[109] 101 8-8-11 **60**..................(p) JimCrowley 8 30
(Richard Whitaker) *hld up: a towards rr* **25/1**
600- **14** *1/2* **Misty Eyes**[192] 7126 4-8-4 **56** oh11.................. RaulDaSilva(3) 3 24
(Geoffrey Harker) *hld up: rdn 1/2-way: sn btn* **100/1**

1m 13.66s (0.06) **Going Correction** +0.025s/f (Good) 14 Ran SP% **115.9**
Speed ratings (Par 100): **100,97,97,95,92 91,91,90,88,88 87,86,81,81**
toteswingers 1&2 £25.20, 1&3 £41.00, 2&3 £41.00 CSF £91.02 CT £1949.25 TOTE £17.10: £5.30, £1.70, £7.70; EX 153.20 Trifecta £761.90 Part won. Pool: £1015.90 - 0.45 winning units..
Owner Derbyshire Racing V **Bred** Carrigbeg Stud & David Powell **Trained** Church Broughton , Derbys

FOCUS
An open-looking fillies' sprint handicap, but a clear-cut winner.

1803 32RED CASINO H'CAP — 1m 2f 60y
3:05 (3:05) (Class 4) (0-80,80) 3-Y-O £4,690 (£1,395; £697; £348) Stalls Low

Form RPR
321- **1** **Disclaimer**[179] 7442 3-9-7 **79**.................. IanMongan 5 92+
(Sir Henry Cecil) *trckd ldng pair: led gng wl over 1f out: pushed clr: easily* **7/2**[2]
026- **2** *5* **Orions Hero (IRE)**[178] 7458 3-8-12 **70**.................. TonyHamilton 2 73
(Richard Fahey) *hld up: rdn and hdwy over 2f out: kpt on: wnt 2nd fnl 100yds: no threat to wnr* **12/1**
2211 **3** *1* **Aryal**[9] 1604 3-9-7 **79** 6ex..................(b) JoeFanning 6 80
(Mark Johnston) *trckd ldr: led 3f out: rdn whn hdd over 1f out: sn no ch w wnr: no ex and lost 2nd fnl 100yds* **5/2**[1]
506- **4** *2 1/4* **Color Shades**[234] 5907 3-8-13 **71**.................. JohnFahy 3 68
(Clive Cox) *trckd ldng pair: rdn and outpcd 3f out: no threat after* **12/1**
002- **5** *shd* **Short Squeeze (IRE)**[163] 7705 3-9-3 **75**.................. JamesDoyle 4 72
(Hugo Palmer) *dwlt: hld up: hung rt on bnd over 5f out: rdn and hdwy on wd outside over 2f out: wknd fnl f* **10/1**
1 **6** *8* **Warrigal (IRE)**[31] 1178 3-9-5 **77**.................. GrahamLee 1 58
(Jeremy Noseda) *hld up: rdn 3f out: sn btn* **7/2**[2]
021- **7** *21* **Makin (IRE)**[130] 8147 3-9-1 **73**..................(t) NeilCallan 8
(Marco Botti) *racd keenly: sn led: hdd 3f out: wknd and eased* **5/1**[3]

2m 10.25s (0.85) **Going Correction** +0.025s/f (Good) 7 Ran SP% **114.2**
Speed ratings (Par 100): **97,93,92,90,90 83,67**
toteswingers 1&2 £23.70, 1&3 £1.10, 2&3 £23.70 CSF £42.64 CT £121.64 TOTE £4.20: £2.60, £6.10; EX 45.70 Trifecta £283.60 Pool: £1411.56 - 3.73 winning units..
Owner K Abdullah **Bred** Juddmonte Farms Ltd **Trained** Newmarket, Suffolk

FOCUS
Some unexposed 3yos in this 1m2f handicap and a wide-margin winner who will hold his own in much strong company.

1804 £32 BONUS AT 32RED.COM MAIDEN STKS — 1m 4f
3:35 (3:36) (Class 5) 3-Y-O+ £2,587 (£770; £384; £192) Stalls Low

Form RPR
1 **Mad Moose (IRE)**[21] 9-9-8 0.................. WilliamTwiston-Davies(5) 9 94+
(Nigel Twiston-Davies) *trckd ldrs: hdwy over 3f out: chal wl over 1f out: rdn to ld ent fnl f: kpt on wl* **28/1**
24-3 **2** *nk* **Elidor**[17] 1443 3-8-7 78.................. SamHitchcott 5 91+
(Mick Channon) *trckd ldrs: effrt and nt clr run over 1f out: swtchd rt and rdn ins fnl f: styd on wl: jst hld* **11/4**[2]
0-4 **3** *2 1/2* **Seamless**[16] 1468 3-8-7 0.................. JamieSpencer 8 87
(Charles Hills) *trckd ldr: cl up 4f out: rdn to ld over 1f out: drvn and hdd ent fnl f: one pce* **11/8**[1]
3-6 **4** *2 1/4* **Swinging Sultan**[25] 1282 6-9-13 0.................. TomEaves 10 86
(Keith Reveley) *hld up in rr: stdy hdwy over 5f out: chsd ldrs over 2f out: sn rdn and no imp appr fnl f* **25/1**
2-22 **5** *3 1/2* **Khudoua**[23] 1317 3-8-7 78..................(b[1]) RobertHavlin 11 78
(John Gosden) *led: pushed along over 3f out: rdn over 2f out: hdd over 1f out: wknd* **9/2**[3]
20 **6** *10* **Unex Modigliani (IRE)**[14] 1522 4-9-12 0.................. LukeMorris 7 64
(Michael Bell) *chsd ldrs: rdn along over 5f out: wknd over 3f out* **10/1**
- **7** *8* **Woodacre**[226] 6-9-13 0.................. AmyRyan 3 51
(Richard Whitaker) *hld up in rr: sme hdwy over 4f out: sn rdn along and n.d* **16/1**
8 *1 1/2* **Sammyman**[413] 6-9-13 0.................. JimCrowley 6 49
(Michael Blanshard) *a in rr* **28/1**
0 **9** *11* **Celtic Legacy**[14] 1518 6-9-8 0.................. NeilCallan 2
(Michael Murphy) *in tch: effrt 5f out: sn rdn along and btn over 3f out* **50/1**
55 **10** *13* **Lil Sophella (IRE)**[105] 168 4-9-7 0.................. DuranFentiman 1
(Patrick Holmes) *chsd ldrs: rdn along over 4f out: sn wknd* **125/1**
3 **11** *4 1/2* **Rock Of Ages**[22] 1352 4-9-12 0.................. LiamJones 4
(Michael Murphy) *a in rr: rdn along over 4f out: sn bhd* **66/1**

2m 33.07s (-1.83) **Going Correction** +0.025s/f (Good)
WFA 3 from 4yo 20lb 4 from 6yo+ 1lb 11 Ran SP% **116.9**
Speed ratings (Par 103): **107,106,105,103,101 94,89,88,80,72 69**
toteswingers 1&2 £21.30, 1&3 £21.30, 2&3 £1.60 CSF £100.97 TOTE £35.70: £6.10, £1.30, £1.40; EX 99.10 Trifecta £1062.50 Pool: £1834.88 - 1.29 winning units..
Owner Middleham Park Racing XXXV & Partner **Bred** Miss E And Miss M Murphy **Trained** Naunton, Gloucs

FOCUS
Plenty of dead wood in this 1m4f maiden. A talented but temperamental jumper put the classic generation in the shade. The placed horses set the level.

1805 32RED.COM H'CAP — 2m 110y
4:10 (4:10) (Class 4) (0-85,85) 4-Y-O+ £4,690 (£1,395; £697; £348) Stalls Low

Form RPR
13-2 **1** **Lieutenant Miller**[7] 1670 7-9-6 **79**.................. GrahamLee 6 89+
(Nicky Henderson) *trckd ldrs: hdwy on outer 3f out: rdn over 1f out: led ent fnl f: styd on strly* **13/8**[1]
1135 **2** *1 1/4* **Broxbourne (IRE)**[16] 1463 4-9-1 **78**.................. JoeFanning 14 87
(Mark Johnston) *prom: hdwy 4f out: rdn to ld over 2f out: drvn and hdd ent fnl f: kpt on* **10/1**
5-33 **3** *1 1/4* **Tappanappa (IRE)**[9] 1615 6-9-9 **82**..................(b) DaneO'Neill 8 89
(Brian Ellison) *hld up in midfield: hdwy 3f out: chsd ldrs 2f out: rdn to chal over 1f out and ev ch tl drvn and one pce ins fnl f* **14/1**
63-6 **4** *1 1/4* **Eagle Rock (IRE)**[13] 1536 5-9-7 **80**.................. MickyFenton 4 86
(Tom Tate) *trckd ldr: tk clsr order 4f out: chal wl over 2f out: sn rdn and ev ch tl drvn and one pce ins fnl f* **5/1**[2]
545- **5** *nk* **Gabrial's Star**[210] 6625 4-9-6 **83**.................. JamieSpencer 11 88
(Ed Dunlop) *hld up in midfield: hdwy on outer over 3f out: rdn to chse ldrs whn edgd lft over 1f out: one pce after* **5/1**[2]
-214 **6** *2 1/2* **Zaplamation (IRE)**[17] 1445 8-8-11 **70**.................. MichaelO'Connell 12 72
(John Quinn) *hld up towards rr: gd hdwy over 3f out: chsd ldrs 2f out: n.m.r and swtchd lft over 1f out: sn rdn and no imp* **9/1**[3]
/21- **7** *3 3/4* **Categorical**[30] 7603 10-9-1 **74**.................. PJMcDonald 2 72
(Keith Reveley) *trckd ldrs: rdn along 4f out: grad wknd fnl 2f* **40/1**
1-65 **8** *4 1/2* **Marmas**[17] 1445 4-8-7 **70**.................. FrannyNorton 5 62+
(John Mackie) *trckd ldrs: pushed along 4f out: rdn 3f out: sn wknd* **20/1**
0-11 **9** *2 1/2* **Foster's Road**[19] 1218 4-8-8 **76**.................. CharlesBishop(5) 13 65
(Mick Channon) *hld up: a in rr* **16/1**
00-0 **10** *7* **Bollin Greta**[16] 1463 8-9-6 **79**.................. DavidAllan 3 60+
(Tim Easterby) *hld up: a in rr* **33/1**
34-0 **11** *6* **Beat The Shower**[20] 1390 7-8-7 **66**.................. TomEaves 1 40
(Peter Niven) *hld up: a in rr* **66/1**
11-0 **12** *11* **Bowdler's Magic**[13] 1536 6-9-12 **85**.................. AdrianNicholls 9 45
(David Nicholls) *led: clr after 3f: rdn along 4f out: hdd over 2f out and sn wknd* **33/1**

3m 41.16s (0.76) **Going Correction** +0.025s/f (Good)
WFA 4 from 5yo+ 4lb 12 Ran SP% **117.6**
Speed ratings (Par 105): **99,98,97,97,97 95,94,92,90,87 84,79**
toteswingers 1&2 £7.20, 1&3 £11.00, 2&3 £31.20 CSF £17.99 CT £175.31 TOTE £2.50: £1.50, £3.30, £3.60; EX 23.50 Trifecta £236.90 Pool: £1478.22 - 4.67 winning units..
Owner W H Ponsonby **Bred** M J Langdell **Trained** Upper Lambourn, Berks

FOCUS
Bowdler's Magic made this 2m handicap a true test and the form should stand up well. The fourth and fifth are the best guides to the level.

1806 32RED H'CAP — 6f
4:45 (4:45) (Class 3) (0-90,88) 3-Y-O £7,439 (£2,213; £1,106; £553) Stalls High

Form RPR
21-0 **1** **Moviesta (USA)**[16] 1482 3-9-2 **83**.................. PaulMulrennan 11 89
(Bryan Smart) *t.k.h: trckd ldrs: hdwy and cl up 2f out: rdn ent fnl f: led last 100yds* **5/1**[3]
1-21 **2** *nk* **Line Of Reason (IRE)**[53] 879 3-9-2 **83**.................. JamieSpencer 10 88+
(David Simcock) *stdd s and sn swtchd lft: hdwy on outer over 2f out: sn chsng ldrs: rdn to chal and edgd rt ent fnl f: sn drvn and ev ch tl no ex towards fin* **10/3**[2]
40-6 **3** *1* **Threes Grand**[35] 1112 3-9-7 **88**.................. LukeMorris 1 90
(Scott Dixon) *led: rdn along 2f out: drvn ent fnl f: hdd and no ex last 100yds* **40/1**
301- **4** *1 1/4* **Rivellino**[149] 7894 3-9-1 **82**.................. NeilCallan 7 80+
(Mrs K Burke) *hld up in tch: hdwy whn nt clr run and hmpd 2f out: rdn and styng on wl whn hmpd ent fnl f: kpt on towards fin* **11/4**[1]
310- **5** *1 1/4* **Sejalaat (IRE)**[216] 6487 3-9-2 **83**.................. DaneO'Neill 5 77
(Ed Dunlop) *t.k.h early: chsd ldrs: rdn along and edgd rt 2f out: drvn and one pce ent fnl f* **14/1**
11-1 **6** *1 1/4* **Foxtrot Jubilee (IRE)**[93] 337 3-9-3 **84**.................. JimCrowley 4 74
(Ralph Beckett) *chsd ldrs: rdn along 2f out: sn drvn and grad wknd* **13/2**
551- **7** *nse* **Tommy's Secret**[162] 7723 3-8-13 **87**.................. IanBurns(7) 8 77
(Jane Chapple-Hyam) *in rr: rdn along over 2f out: sn swtchd lft and styd on fnl f: nrst fin* **33/1**
13-6 **8** *shd* **Sanjuro (IRE)**[17] 1444 3-8-7 **79**.................. CharlesBishop(5) 6 69
(Mick Channon) *t.k.h early: hld up towards rr: swtchd lft to outer and hdwy wl over 1f out: rdn and kpt on fnl f: nrst fin* **10/1**
63-5 **9** *hd* **Double Your Money (IRE)**[17] 1444 3-8-10 **77**.................. JoeFanning 3 66
(Mark Johnston) *dwlt: sn chsng ldrs: cl up 1/2-way: rdn along 2f out: wknd over 1f out* **16/1**
102- **10** *nk* **Penny Garcia**[200] 6920 3-8-12 **79**.................. DuranFentiman 12 67
(Tim Easterby) *midfield: hdwy to chse ldrs 2f out: sn rdn and wknd over 1f out* **33/1**
210- **11** *1 1/2* **Avec Rose**[202] 6883 3-8-2 **76**.................. SamanthaBell(7) 2 59
(Richard Fahey) *cl up: rdn along over 2f out: sn wknd* **16/1**
3-10 **12** *2 1/2* **Tanghan (IRE)**[78] 550 3-8-8 **75**.................. TonyHamilton 9 50
(Richard Fahey) *a towards rr* **25/1**

1m 13.36s (-0.24) **Going Correction** +0.025s/f (Good) 12 Ran SP% **119.4**
Speed ratings (Par 102): **102,101,100,98,96 95,95,95,94,94 92,89**
toteswingers 1&2 £7.40, 1&3 £34.10, 2&3 £34.10 CSF £21.42 CT £619.38 TOTE £6.30: £1.70, £1.40, £8.30; EX 23.10 Trifecta £726.10 Part won. Pool: £968.14 - 0.20 winning units..
Owner Redknapp, Salthouse & Fiddes **Bred** John D Gunther **Trained** Hambleton, N Yorks

FOCUS
A good-quality 3-y-o sprint handicap that should throw up a few winners. Thye exposed third is the best guide to the form.

1807 32REDPOKER.COM H'CAP 5f
5:15 (5:16) (Class 4) (0-85,85) 4-Y-0+ £4,690 (£1,395; £697; £348) Stalls High

Form RPR
145- **1** **Love Island**[175] 7521 4-8-12 **76**............ PaulQuinn 3 86+
(Richard Whitaker) *in tch: trckd ldrs 2f out: rdn to chal ent fnl f: sn led: drvn and edgd rt last 75yds: jst hld on* **33/1**
45-2 **2** *shd* **Last Sovereign**[9] 1607 9-9-0 **85**............(b) JacobButterfield(7) 9 95
(Ollie Pears) *midfield: hdwy to trck ldrs 2f out: n.m.r and swtchd lft over 1f out: rdn ent fnl f: styd on strly: jst failed* **8/1**
-360 **3** *1* **Moorhouse Lad**[76] 586 10-9-4 **82**............ JimCrowley 10 88
(Garry Moss) *cl up: disp ld 2f out: rdn to ld over 1f out: drvn and hdd ins fnl f: no ex towards fin* **14/1**
100- **4** *1 1/4* **Bedloe's Island (IRE)**[315] 3127 8-9-5 **83**............ DavidNolan 16 85+
(David O'Meara) *trckd ldrs: hdwy 2f out: sn cl up: rdn and ev ch ent fnl f: sn drvn and kpt on same pce* **9/2**[1]
0-03 **5** *3/4* **Phoenix Clubs (IRE)**[25] 1278 4-8-8 **72**............ BarryMcHugh 6 71
(Paul Midgley) *trckd ldrs: hdwy and cl up 2f out: rdn over 1f out: hld whn n.m.r ins fnl f: kpt on same pce* **40/1**
31-6 **6** *1/2* **Another Wise Kid (IRE)**[27] 1232 5-9-7 **85**............ MickyFenton 1 82+
(Paul Midgley) *in rr: hdwy whn nt clr run over 1f out: swtchd rt and rdn ent fnl f: styng on whn hmpd last 100yds: kpt on nr fin* **10/1**
02-0 **7** *1/2* **Excel Bolt**[27] 1248 5-9-1 **84**............ LMcNiff(5) 7 80
(Bryan Smart) *cl up: rdn and ev ch over 1f out: drvn and wknd fnl f* **14/1**
1103 **8** *2* **Danziger (IRE)**[40] 1052 4-8-9 **73**............ LukeMorris 2 61
(David Evans) *in tch: hdwy on wd outside to chse ldrs over 2f out: rdn wl over 1f out: wknd appr fnl f* **33/1**
2-31 **9** *hd* **Another Citizen (IRE)**[8] 1649 5-8-0 **71** oh1............(b) GaryMahon(7) 8 59
(Tim Easterby) *chsd ldrs: rdn along wl over 1f out: grad wknd* **7/1**
012- **10** *shd* **We'll Deal Again**[196] 7023 6-9-3 **81**............(b) GrahamGibbons 13 68
(Michael Easterby) *awkward s: in rr tl sme late hdwy* **10/1**
205- **11** *nse* **Pea Shooter**[172] 7595 4-9-4 **82**............ AmyRyan 17 69
(Kevin Ryan) *chsd ldrs: rdn along wl over 1f out: grad wknd* **6/1**[3]
4453 **12** *1 1/4* **Six Wives**[8] 1649 6-8-4 **71**............(p) BillyCray(3) 14 54
(Scott Dixon) *led: rdn along 2f out: hdd over 1f out and sn wknd* **11/2**[2]
050- **13** *3/4* **Noodles Blue Boy**[186] 7291 7-9-1 **79**............ TonyHamilton 11 59
(Ollie Pears) *a towards rr* **20/1**
053- **14** *1/2* **Wild Sauce**[186] 7295 4-8-13 **77**............ TomEaves 4 55
(Bryan Smart) *cl up on outer: rdn along 2f out: sn wknd* **25/1**
100- **15** *nk* **Medici Time**[225] 6165 8-9-5 **83**............(v) TedDurcan 12 60
(Tim Easterby) *dwlt: a in rr* **25/1**

59.88s (-0.62) **Going Correction** +0.025s/f (Good) 15 Ran SP% **123.8**
Speed ratings (Par 105): **105,104,103,101,100 99,98,95,94,94 94,92,91,90,90**
toteswingers 1&2 £29.80, 1&3 £31.90, 2&3 £31.90 CSF £268.99 CT £3972.30 TOTE £42.60: £9.70, £2.40, £7.30; EX 564.10 TRIFECTA Not won..
Owner J Barry Pemberton **Bred** Hellwood Farm And J B Pemberton **Trained** Scarcroft, W Yorks

FOCUS
A fiercely competitive sprint handicap and a very tight finish. The placed horses set the level.
T/Jkpt: Not won. T/Plt: £1460.90 to a £1 stake. Pool: £68,043.91 - 34.0 winning tickets. T/Qpdt: £236.90 to a £1 stake. Pool: £5314.75 - 16.6 winning tickets. JR

SANDOWN (R-H)
Friday, April 26
OFFICIAL GOING: Good (good to soft in places; 7.3)
Wind: Moderate, half against Weather: Fine but cloudy

1808 BET365.COM H'CAP 5f 6y
1:40 (1:40) (Class 2) (0-100,98) 3-Y-0 £12,450 (£3,728; £1,864; £932; £466; £234) Stalls High

Form RPR
112 **1** **Riskit Fora Biskit (IRE)**[43] 992 3-8-3 **80**............ HayleyTurner 4 88
(Michael Bell) *mde virtually all: kicked on 2f out: 2 l clr over 1f out: drvn out* **12/1**
60-1 **2** *3/4* **Smoothtalkinrascal (IRE)**[21] 1362 3-9-4 **95**............ DanielTudhope 7 105+
(David O'Meara) *hld up towards rr and racd against rail: prog but nvr a clr run fr 2f out: r.o fnl f to take 2nd last 75yds: clsd on wnr but nvr gng to get there* **9/2**[1]
110- **3** *3/4* **Barracuda Boy (IRE)**[246] 5515 3-8-10 **87**............ RichardKingscote 3 90
(Tom Dascombe) *lw: racd against rail: chsd ldrs but sn pushed along: prog 2f out: chsd wnr 1f out: styd on but no real imp: lost 2nd last 75yds* **6/1**[2]
230- **4** *1 1/4* **Normal Equilibrium**[216] 6487 3-8-11 **88**............ WilliamBuick 6 87+
(Robert Cowell) *chsd ldrs: nt clr run over 1f out and n.m.r sn after: styd on but nt pce to chal* **8/1**
31-0 **5** *1/2* **Secret Missile**[16] 1482 3-8-2 **79**............ SilvestreDeSousa 14 76+
(William Muir) *lw: hld up in rr and racd wdst of all: prog fr 2f out: kpt on same pce fnl f* **8/1**
56-1 **6** *3/4* **Top Boy**[50] 915 3-9-2 **93**............ MartinDwyer 13 87
(Derek Shaw) *hld up in last pair: nt clr run fr 2f out: styd on fnl f: nrst fin but n.d* **20/1**
2-04 **7** *1/2* **Ask The Guru**[21] 1362 3-8-10 **87**............ KierenFallon 2 79
(Michael Attwater) *chsd ldng pair: rdn and stl disputing 2nd jst over 1f out: fdd* **20/1**
0-30 **8** *hd* **Jillnextdoor (IRE)**[7] 1662 3-8-13 **90**............ MartinHarley 12 81
(Mick Channon) *towards rr on outer: rdn 2f out: kpt on one pce fr over 1f out: n.d* **16/1**
513- **9** *1* **New Fforest**[223] 6238 3-8-8 **85**............ DavidProbert 1 73
(Andrew Balding) *racd against rail: w wnr to 2f out: steadily wknd jst over 1f out* **7/1**[3]
030- **10** *1 1/2* **Lasilia (IRE)**[216] 6467 3-8-13 **90**............ PhillipMakin 11 72+
(Kevin Ryan) *lost midfield pl bef 1/2-way: nt clr run fr over 1f out: no ch fnl f* **40/1**
1203 **11** *1/2* **Equitania**[9] 1625 3-8-12 **89**............ RyanMoore 9 70
(Alan Bailey) *chsd ldrs: lost pl sn after 1/2-way: struggling fnl 2f* **12/1**
15-6 **12** *1/2* **The Taj (USA)**[9] 1625 3-9-7 **98**............ PaulHanagan 10 77
(Richard Hannon) *racd towards outer: chsd ldrs tl wknd over 1f out* **9/1**
234- **13** *3/4* **Miss Diva**[252] 5307 3-8-11 **88**............ RichardHughes 8 64
(Richard Hannon) *a in last pair: no prog fnl 2f* **14/1**

1m 1.19s (-0.41) **Going Correction** +0.125s/f (Good) 13 Ran SP% **117.1**
Speed ratings (Par 104): **108,106,105,103,102 101,100,100,98,96 95,94,93**
toteswingers 1&2 £4.80, 1&3 £7.60, 2&3 £5.90 CSF £62.32 CT £363.77 TOTE £7.10: £3.00, £1.80, £2.40; EX 43.30 Trifecta £143.90 Pool: £2971.47 - 15.48 winning units..
Owner Chris Wright & The Hon Mrs J M Corbett **Bred** Edmond Kent **Trained** Newmarket, Suffolk

FOCUS
Sprint track at full width. Home bend at outermost configuration which added about 8yds to distances on Round course. Following 3mm of overnight rain the ground was good. A decent 3yo sprint handicap that has been won by decent sorts such as Corrybrough and Night Carnation. There was a large field and it paid to be close to the pace and near the far rail, as is often the case. The unlucky second is rated as the winner, while the third and fourth fit in.

1809 BET365.COM ESHER CUP (H'CAP) 1m 14y
2:10 (2:11) (Class 2) (0-100,95) 3-Y-0 £15,562 (£4,660; £2,330; £1,165; £582; £292) Stalls Low

Form RPR
13- **1** **Haafaguinea**[225] 6162 3-9-4 **92**............ AdamKirby 2 102
(Clive Cox) *lw: hld up in last pair: rdn over 2f out: prog over 1f out at same time as runner-up: drvn to ld ins fnl f: styd on wl* **11/2**[3]
43-1 **2** *nk* **Market Town (USA)**[20] 1387 3-8-10 **84**............[1] WilliamBuick 4 93
(Charles Hills) *t.k.h early: hld up in last: prog and squeezed through rivals over 1f out: rdn to ld briefly jst ins fnl f: nt qckn last 100yds* **7/1**
112- **3** *1 3/4* **Yarroom (IRE)**[125] 8223 3-9-2 **90**............ AndreaAtzeni 3 95
(Roger Varian) *wl in tch: shkn up over 2f out: tried to cl on ldrs over 1f out: chsd ldng pair last 150yds: styd on but no imp* **15/2**
1412 **4** *3* **Flashlight (IRE)**[17] 1444 3-8-13 **87**............ SilvestreDeSousa 7 85
(Mark Johnston) *led: kicked on over 2f out: hdd & wknd jst ins fnl f* **17/2**
2-15 **5** *nse* **Fehaydi**[8] 1636 3-9-0 **88**............ RyanMoore 6 86
(William Haggas) *lw: t.k.h early: trckd ldr after 3f: rdn and no imp over 2f out: lost 2nd and fdd jst over 1f out* **13/8**[1]
13-4 **6** *3 3/4* **Top Notch Tonto (IRE)**[27] 1250 3-9-7 **95**............ DaleSwift 5 84
(Ian McInnes) *t.k.h: hld up bhd ldrs: rdn on outer over 2f out: wknd over 1f out* **33/1**
121- **7** *14* **Red Avenger (USA)**[211] 6597 3-9-4 **92**............ RichardHughes 1 49
(Ed Dunlop) *chsd ldr 3f: styd prom: rdn over 2f out: wknd rapidly over 1f out: eased and t.o* **4/1**[2]

1m 45.32s (2.02) **Going Correction** +0.375s/f (Good) 7 Ran SP% **111.2**
Speed ratings (Par 104): **104,103,101,98,98 95,81**
toteswingers 1&2 £4.40,1&3 £5.90, 2&3 £7.10 CSF £40.24 TOTE £6.10: £3.80, £3.50; EX 30.20 Trifecta £318.60 Pool: £3252.12 - 7.65 winning units..
Owner Mrs Olive Shaw **Bred** Bishop Wilton Stud **Trained** Lambourn, Berks

FOCUS
Usually a very decent handicap with a couple of recent winners going on to score at Listed level at the May meeting back here. Despite the small field this looked a reasonable contest and it produced a good finish between two relatively unexposed colts. The third sets the level rated to the best of his AW form.

1810 BET365 MILE (GROUP 2) 1m 14y
2:45 (2:45) (Class 1) 4-Y-0+ £51,039 (£19,350; £9,684; £4,824; £2,421; £1,215) Stalls Low

Form RPR
150- **1** **Trumpet Major (IRE)**[210] 6634 4-9-0 114............ RichardHughes 1 117+
(Richard Hannon) *trckd ldng pair: wnt 2nd wl over 1f out and sn clsd on ldr: rdn to ld ins fnl f: pushed out: readily* **3/1**[2]
15-5 **2** *1 1/4* **Highland Knight (IRE)**[13] 1535 6-9-0 113............(t) DavidProbert 3 114
(Andrew Balding) *led and sn spread field out: kicked on 3f out: edgd lft over 2f out: collared ins fnl f: no ex* **7/1**
610- **3** *1 1/4* **Chil The Kite**[176] 7515 4-9-0 104............ RyanMoore 6 111+
(Hughie Morrison) *hld up in 5th and off the pce: prog over 2f out: wnt 3rd over 1f out but hanging rt: nt qckn fnl f* **7/2**[3]
100- **4** *5* **Libranno**[188] 7236 5-9-4 112............ KierenFallon 4 104
(Richard Hannon) *hld up in 4th and off the pce: shkn up and no prog over 2f out: wl btn after* **12/1**
31-1 **5** *3/4* **Farraaj (IRE)**[41] 1034 4-9-0 108............ AndreaAtzeni 7 98
(Roger Varian) *lw: chsd ldr: rdn wl over 2f out: lost 2nd and wknd wl over 1f out* **9/4**[1]
00-3 **6** *2* **Stand My Ground (IRE)**[13] 1535 6-9-0 106............ DanielTudhope 2 93
(David O'Meara) *t.k.h: hld up in last and wl off the pce: shkn up and no prog over 2f out: wl btn after* **12/1**
-063 **7** *5* **Red Duke (USA)**[55] 869 4-9-0 105............ TomQueally 5 82
(David Simcock) *taken down early: hld up in 6th and off the pce: rdn and no prog over 2f out: wknd over 1f out* **14/1**

1m 45.34s (2.04) **Going Correction** +0.375s/f (Good) 7 Ran SP% **112.5**
Speed ratings (Par 115): **104,102,101,96,95 93,88**
toteswingers 1&2 £3.80, 1&3 £3.20, 2&3 £4.00 CSF £23.13 TOTE £3.70: £2.30, £3.20; EX 20.60 Trifecta £84.20 Pool: £3514.39 - 31.27 winning units..
Owner John Manley **Bred** John Cullinan **Trained** East Everleigh, Wilts

FOCUS
Richard Hannon had dominated recent renewals of this Group 2, winning six of the last ten, with such as Paco Boy (twice) and Dick Turpin. He extended that sequence thanks to Trumpet Major. The time was fractionally slower than the preceding 3-y-o handicap. The runner-up sets the standard.

1811 BET365 CLASSIC TRIAL (GROUP 3) 1m 2f 7y
3:15 (3:15) (Class 1) 3-Y-0 £34,026 (£12,900; £6,456; £3,216; £1,614; £810) Stalls Low

Form RPR
2 **1** **Sugar Boy (IRE)**[12] 1558 3-9-0 107............ ChrisHayes 7 111
(P J Prendergast, Ire) *led: shkn up and hdd jst over 2f out: rallied wl u.p fr over 1f out to ld again ins fnl f: hld on* **4/1**[3]
3- **2** *hd* **Eye Of The Storm (IRE)**[195] 7053 3-9-0 99............ RyanMoore 4 110
(A P O'Brien, Ire) *lw: trckd ldr: shkn up to ld jst over 2f out: drvn over 1f out: hdd ins fnl f: kpt on but jst hld* **2/1**[1]
5- **3** *1/2* **Galileo Rock (IRE)**[195] 7053 3-9-0 97............ WayneLordan 6 109
(David Wachman, Ire) *t.k.h: hld up in tch: rdn to chse ldng pair 2f out: styd on and grad clsd gap fnl f: a hld* **8/1**
1 **4** *8* **Libertarian**[17] 1443 3-9-0 82............ PhillipMakin 5 100+
(Mrs K Burke) *w'like: str: scope: lw: hld up in last trio: brought wd in st then carried to centre of crse: lost all ch and nrly t.o over 2f out: styd on fnl f to snatch 4th last strides* **14/1**
150- **5** *nk* **Fantastic Moon**[174] 7568 3-9-2 109............ WilliamBuick 2 95
(Jeremy Noseda) *lw: t.k.h: hld up in last trio: shkn up and no prog over 2f out: wl btn after: wknd fnl f* **11/2**
123- **6** *3/4* **Al Waab (IRE)**[209] 6671 3-9-0 103............ TomQueally 1 91
(Sir Henry Cecil) *chsd ldr to 1/2-way and fr over 3f out to 2f out: wknd over 1f out* **7/2**[2]

0-1 7 44 **Woodstock (IRE)**[22] 1347 3-9-0 0 RichardHughes 3
(Richard Hannon) *w'like: str: hld up in last: quick move to go 3rd 1/2-way to over 3f out: hung lft and wknd sn after: t.o* 33/1

2m 12.26s (1.76) **Going Correction** +0.375s/f (Good) 7 Ran SP% **111.7**
Speed ratings (Par 108): **107,106,106,100,99 99,64**
toteswingers 1&2 £2.50, 1&3 £5.30, 2&3 £5.50 CSF £11.83 TOTE £4.10: £1.80, £2.00; EX 10.40 Trifecta £41.50 Pool: £2423.83 - 43.77 winning units..
Owner Rick Barnes **Bred** Grangecon Stud **Trained** Melitta Lodge, Co Kildare
■ Stewards' Enquiry : Chris Hayes four-day ban: use of whip (10-14 May)

FOCUS
This Classic Trial has not had much impact on the Derby recently, although Fracas went on to finish fourth in 2005, but Imperial Monarch took the Grand Prix de Paris after winning last season. There were three Irish challengers and they dominated the finish, coming well clear of the home contingent. This is rated one of the lesser recent renewals.

1812 CASINO AT BET365.COM CONDITIONS STKS 1m 14y
3:50 (3:52) (Class 3) 3-Y-O £7,470 (£1,677; £1,677; £559; £279) Stalls Low

Form RPR
1 1 **Queensberry Rules (IRE)**[18] 1423 3-9-2 89 RyanMoore 4 103+
(William Haggas) *lw: mde all: set stdy pce tl grad wound it up fr 3f out: asserted over 1f out: rdn out* 11/8[1]

51- 2 1 ¼ **Mujazif (IRE)**[184] 7332 3-9-2 85 (t) KierenFallon 3 100+
(Brian Meehan) *trckd ldng pair: shkn up over 2f out: nt qckn wl over 1f out: styd on fnl f to dead-heat for 2nd* 7/4[2]

2-01 2 dht **Glacial Age (IRE)**[10] 1595 3-8-12 0 HayleyTurner 5 96
(Jo Hughes) *trckd wnr: rdn and nt qckn wl over 1f out: styd on same pce after* 8/1

10- 4 5 **Jalaa (IRE)**[307] 3368 3-9-2 0 PaulHanagan 1 89
(Richard Hannon) *lw: hld up in last pair: shkn up over 2f out: no imp on ldng trio over 1f out: wknd fnl f* 11/2[3]

01-1 5 9 **Smileswithhiseyes (IRE)**[109] 91 3-8-12 75 RobertWinston 2 64
(Gay Kelleway) *hld up in last pair: wknd over 2f out: t.o* 25/1

1m 49.78s (6.48) **Going Correction** +0.375s/f (Good) 5 Ran SP% **108.8**
Speed ratings (Par 102): **82,80,80,75,66**
PL: GA £2.00, M £0.60; EX: QR/GA £5.40, QR/M £1.80; CSF: QR/GA £6.06, QR/M £1.97; Trifecta: QR/M/GA £5.20, QR/GA/M £9.50 TOTE £2.20: £1.30 TRIFECTA Pool: £2021.23 - 143.43 winning units..
Owner Liam Sheridan **Bred** Gerard Kerin **Trained** Newmarket, Suffolk

FOCUS
A decent conditions stakes with seven going on to Listed success after scoring here, but the best recent winner was Plea Bargain, who subsequently scored at Group 2 level. All of these were previous winners but the pace was very steady, being 4.46secs slower than the earlier handicap over the trip and not form to be totally confident about.

1813 BET365 MAIDEN FILLIES' STKS 1m 2f 7y
4:25 (4:26) (Class 4) 3-Y-O £6,469 (£1,925; £962; £481) Stalls Low

Form RPR
0- 1 **Waila**[205] 6791 3-9-0 0 KierenFallon 9 94+
(Sir Michael Stoute) *hld up in tch: prog on outer over 2f out: led wl over 1f out: shkn up and edgd rt but wl in command fnl f* 8/1

2 1 ½ **Riposte** 3-9-0 0 TomQueally 1 91+
(Sir Henry Cecil) *w'like: bit bkwd: dwlt: sn trckd ldng trio: lost pl sltly and shkn up over 2f out: prog over 1f out: tk 2nd last 150yds: styd on but unable to threaten wnr* 5/1

2- 3 1 ¾ **Auld Alliance (IRE)**[162] 7720 3-9-0 0 RyanMoore 7 88+
(Sir Michael Stoute) *w'like: str: hld up in last trio: outpcd and urged along wl over 2f out: plld out and prog over 1f out: styd on to take 3rd last 75yds* 10/3[2]

32- 4 1 **Muthmera (USA)**[205] 6791 3-9-0 0 PaulHanagan 4 86
(Roger Varian) *lw: trckd ldng pair: clsd to chal over 2f out: w wnr briefly wl over 1f out: sn outpcd: lost 2 pls ins fnl f* 4/1[3]

032- 5 5 **Cushion**[205] 6790 3-9-0 81 WilliamBuick 6 76
(John Gosden) *w ldr: led after 3f: hdd & wknd wl over 1f out* 3/1[1]

6 2 **Near Time** 3-9-0 0 JimmyFortune 8 72+
(Andrew Balding) *unf: scope: tall: s.s: rn green in last pair and often t.k.h: outpcd fr 3f out: nvr on terms after* 16/1

2-2 7 1 ¼ **Regal Silk**[14] 1518 3-9-0 0 RichardHughes 3 69
(Jeremy Noseda) *lw: led 3f: trckd ldr: chal over 2f out: wknd qckly over 1f out* 13/2

0- 8 14 **Penang Power**[191] 7160 3-9-0 0 RobertWinston 10 41
(Michael Bell) *w'like: leggy: hld up in last trio: rdn and in tch over 2f out: sn wknd rapidly: t.o* 40/1

2m 13.52s (3.02) **Going Correction** +0.375s/f (Good) 8 Ran SP% **117.5**
Speed ratings (Par 97): **102,100,99,98,94 93,92,80**
toteswingers 1&2 £9.40, 1&3 £5.70, 2&3 £4.40 CSF £48.88 TOTE £10.40: £2.80, £2.60, £1.80; EX 74.40 Trifecta £320.00 Pool: £2376.61 - 5.56 winning units..
Owner Sir Evelyn De Rothschild **Bred** Southcourt Stud **Trained** Newmarket, Suffolk

FOCUS
An above-average race of its type rated around race averages.

1814 NORDOFF ROBBINS WILLIE ROBERTSON MEMORIAL H'CAP 5f 6y
5:00 (5:00) (Class 4) (0-80,79) 4-Y-0+ £6,469 (£1,925; £962; £481) Stalls High

Form RPR
600- 1 **Tagula Night (IRE)**[193] 7114 7-9-2 74 (t[1]) RobertWinston 9 84
(Dean Ivory) *wl away fr middle draw: mde virtually all and sn crossed to rail: drvn to assert 2f out: hung lft fnl f: styd on* 14/1

-656 2 1 **Rocket Rob (IRE)**[22] 1346 7-9-0 72 J-PGuillambert 11 78+
(Willie Musson) *dwlt: hld up in last pair: plld to wd outside fr 1/2-way: pushed along and gd prog over 1f out: r.o fnl f to take 2nd nr fin: unable to chal* 12/1

663- 3 nk **Rebecca Romero**[185] 7309 6-9-2 74 RichardHughes 12 79+
(Denis Coakley) *dwlt: hld up towards rr: prog towards outer wl over 1f out: r.o to dispute 2nd nr fin: nvr nrr* 14/1

30-0 4 shd **Titus Gent**[35] 1121 8-9-4 79 RyanClark(3) 5 84
(Jeremy Gask) *racd against rail: chsd ldrs but sn shoved along to hold pl: drvn over 1f out: chsd wnr jst ins fnl f: a hld: lost 2 pls nr fin* 33/1

201- 5 ½ **Lupo D'Oro (IRE)**[177] 7489 4-9-7 79 SteveDrowne 16 82
(John Best) *dwlt: sn in midfield: prog towards outer 2f: rdn to dispute 2nd ins fnl f: one pce* 20/1

5-11 6 ½ **Alpha Delta Whisky**[16] 1467 5-9-0 72 TomQueally 10 73
(John Gallagher) *chsd ldng pair: rdn 2f out: disp 2nd briefly 1f out: fdd* 12/1

223- 7 ½ **Macdillon**[196] 7019 7-8-10 73 MichaelJMMurphy(5) 3 72
(Stuart Kittow) *settled in midfield: rdn 2f out: checked over 1f out: styd on same pce fnl f* 4/1[1]

10-2 8 1 **Cruise Tothelimit (IRE)**[11] 1581 5-9-6 78 KierenFallon 13 74
(Ian Williams) *w wnr to 2f out: lost 2nd and wknd 1f out* 13/2[2]

3001 9 hd **Clear Praise (USA)**[39] 1067 6-9-7 79 SebSanders 4 74
(Simon Dow) *s.i.s: wl in rr against rail: rdn 2f out: kpt on same pce fnl f: no ch* 12/1

414- 10 nk **Generalyse**[147] 7937 4-8-13 71 (b) PaulHanagan 2 65
(Ben De Haan) *chsd ldrs: rdn 1/2-way: lost pl and struggling over 1f out* 16/1

3104 11 nk **Temple Road (IRE)**[22] 1346 5-9-2 74 RichardKingscote 8 67+
(Milton Bradley) *trckd ldrs gng wl: drvn to try to cl over 1f out: wknd qckly fnl f* 14/1

02-0 12 ½ **Perfect Pastime**[33] 1160 5-9-7 79 (p) WilliamBuick 17 70
(Jim Boyle) *racd wd towards rr: effrt 2f out: no imp on ldrs fnl f* 16/1

5124 13 hd **Blue Jack**[33] 1160 8-9-5 77 (t) RyanMoore 6 67
(Stuart Williams) *pushed along early but unable to gain gd position and sn in rr: shkn up 2f out: rn into trble more than once after: eased ins fnl f* 4/1[1]

01-3 14 nse **Kellys Eye (IRE)**[25] 1286 6-9-1 73 LiamKeniry 1 63
(Zoe Davison) *nvr bttr than midfield: rdn 1/2-way: no prog over 1f out: wknd* 10/1[3]

246- 15 ¾ **Interakt**[221] 6303 6-8-7 72 NoraLooby(7) 7 59
(Joseph Tuite) *dwlt: outpcd and a bhd* 33/1

014- 16 1 ¼ **Whitecrest**[177] 7489 5-9-1 73 CathyGannon 15 56
(John Spearing) *prom on outer 3f: wknd qckly* 33/1

1m 1.57s (-0.03) **Going Correction** +0.125s/f (Good) 16 Ran SP% **130.9**
Speed ratings (Par 105): **105,103,102,102,101 101,100,98,98,97 97,96,96,96,95 93**
toteswingers 1&2 £77.90, 1&3 £37.90, 2&3 £54.20 CSF £178.44 CT £2419.98 TOTE £19.70: £3.90, £3.80, £3.60, £12.10; EX 264.10 Trifecta £1734.00 Part won. Pool: £2312.04 - 0.21 winning units..
Owner Hufford & Papworth **Bred** Carpet Lady Partnership **Trained** Radlett, Herts

FOCUS
Another competitive sprint handicap, but the time was 0.38secs slower than the opening 3-y-o handicap. The placed horses are rated close to their best at face value.
T/Plt: £91.70 to a £1 stake. Pool: £86,228.54 - 686.22 winning tickets. T/Qpdt: £10.40 to a £1 stake. Pool: £5957.30 - 421.80 winning tickets. JN

1800 DONCASTER (L-H)
Saturday, April 27

OFFICIAL GOING: Good to firm (9.4) changing to good after race 2 (5.40)
Wind: Moderate behind Weather: Cloudy with showers

1819 CROWNHOTEL-BAWTRY.COM AJA LADY RIDERS' H'CAP (LADY AMATEUR RIDERS) 7f
5:10 (5:11) (Class 4) (0-80,78) 4-Y-0+ £4,991 (£1,548; £773; £387) Stalls High

Form RPR
000- 1 **Karaka Jack**[196] 7069 6-10-2 73 MissADeniel 12 84
(David Nicholls) *in tch: pushed along and hdwy 2f out: rdn over 1f out: led appr fnl f: kpt on* 4/1[2]

500- 2 1 ¾ **Meandmyshadow**[178] 7483 5-9-11 71 MissJRRichards(3) 10 77
(Alan Brown) *mde most tl rdn along and hdd jst over 1f out: edgd lft ent fnl f: kpt on same pce* 33/1

54-0 3 ¾ **Shamrocked (IRE)**[7] 1686 4-9-6 68 MissSMDoolan(5) 7 72
(Mick Channon) *trckd ldrs: pushed along and outpcd 3f out: swtchd lft and rdn over 2f out: styd on wl fnl f: tk 3rd nr line* 20/1

546- 4 hd **Mitchum**[224] 6261 4-9-3 65 MrsVDavies(5) 6 68
(Ron Barr) *trckd ldrs: cl up 3f out: effrt 2f out: sn rdn and ev ch tl one pce fnl f: lost 3rd nr line* 25/1

1-06 5 ¾ **Space War**[23] 1354 6-9-2 66 (t) AnnaHesketh(7) 4 67
(Michael Easterby) *trckd ldrs on outer: hdwy and cl up 1/2-way: rdn along 2f out: one pce appr fnl f* 9/1[3]

22-6 6 ½ **Rasaman (IRE)**[28] 1252 9-10-6 77 MrsCBartley 3 77
(Jim Goldie) *trckd ldrs: hdwy 2f out: rdn over 1f out: kpt on same pce fnl f* 12/1

0050 7 1 **Brigadoon**[18] 1442 6-9-10 70 MissHBethell(3) 8 67
(Philip Kirby) *dwlt and bhd tl sme late hdwy* 10/1

4-55 8 1 **Pearl Nation (USA)**[24] 1318 4-10-7 78 MissSBrotherton 11 73
(Brian Baugh) *chsd ldrs: rdn along over 2f out: sn drvn and wknd* 9/4[1]

-560 9 1 ¾ **Illustrious Prince (IRE)**[7] 1686 6-9-5 67 MissJoannaMason(5) 9 57
(Declan Carroll) *dwlt and a in rr* 12/1

214 10 2 **Azrael**[12] 1576 5-10-3 74 (p) MissZoeLilly 2 59
(Alan McCabe) *cl up: disp ld 1/2-way: rdn along wl over 2f out: sn wknd* 9/1[3]

54-0 11 4 **Hot Rod Mamma (IRE)**[17] 1463 6-10-4 75 EmmaSayer 5 49
(Dianne Sayer) *s.i.s: a in rr* 12/1

1m 26.18s (-0.12) **Going Correction** -0.025s/f (Good) 11 Ran SP% **114.5**
Speed ratings (Par 105): **99,97,96,95,95 94,93,92,90,87 83**
Tote Swingers: 1&2 £20.20, 1&3 £14.20, 2&3 £42.90 CSF £131.14 CT £2366.30 TOTE £3.80: £1.90, £6.00, £4.50; EX 75.50 Trifecta £499.90 Pool: £760.98 - 1.14 winning units..
Owner M Mackay & S Bruce **Bred** Tarworth Bloodstock Investments Ltd **Trained** Sessay, N Yorks
■ Stewards' Enquiry : Anna Hesketh two-day ban: use of whip (11, 13 May)

FOCUS
Rail on round course from 9f to where it joins straight moved out 5yds to provide fresh ground adding about 18yds to races on Round course. Ground officially on the quick side of good and although a shower beforehand appeared to have eased conditions a touch, the time of the opening heat was 0.12sec quicker than the 7f opener on Friday.

1820 ROBINSONS OF BAWTRY MAIDEN STKS 5f
5:40 (5:41) (Class 5) 2-Y-O £2,911 (£866; £432; £216) Stalls High

Form RPR
1 **Haikbidiac (IRE)** 2-9-5 0 LiamJones 5 81+
(William Haggas) *trckd ldrs: hdwy over 2f out: sn swtchd lft to chal and led 1 1/2f out: rdn and edgd rt fnl f: kpt on wl* 11/4[2]

4 2 2 ¾ **Robynelle**[12] 1565 2-9-0 0 PaulMulrennan 6 65
(Keith Dalgleish) *led: rdn along 2f out: hdd 1 1/2f out: sn drvn and kpt on same pce* 15/8[1]

4 3 1 ¼ **Danfazi (IRE)**[12] 1573 2-9-5 0 PatrickMathers 3 66
(Kristin Stubbs) *trckd ldr: effrt and cl up 2f out: sn rdn and kpt on same pce* 11/2

63 4 1 ¼ **Donny Rover (IRE)**[14] 1534 2-9-5 0 HayleyTurner 7 61
(David C Griffiths) *chsd ldrs: rdn along over 2f out: drvn and one pce fr wl over 1f out* 13/2

5 hd **Ocean Storm (IRE)** 2-9-5 0 NeilCallan 4 60
(James Tate) *s.i.s and green in rr: hdwy wl over 1f out: kpt on fnl f: bttr for r* 5/1[3]

The Form Book Flat, Raceform Ltd, Compton, RG20 6NL.

55 **6** *4 1/2* **Riley's Missile (IRE)**[12] 1574 2-9-0 0........................ RachealKneller(5) 2 44
(Charles Smith) *chsd ldrs: rdn along 1/2-way: sn outpcd* **66/1**
7 *2 3/4* **Pavers Bounty** 2-9-5 0.. DuranFentiman 1 34
(Noel Wilson) *dwlt: sn in tch: rdn along 1/2-way: sn outpcd* **33/1**
00 **8** *25* **Doncaster Belle (IRE)**[5] 1718 2-9-0 0................................ IanMongan 8
(Charles Smith) *sn outpcd and a in rr: bhd fr 1/2-way* **66/1**
1m 0.52s (0.02) **Going Correction** -0.025s/f (Good) **8** Ran SP% **112.8**
Speed ratings (Par 92): **98,93,91,89,89 82,77,37**
Tote Swingers: 1&2 £2.20, 1&3 £4.90, 2&3 £5.40 CSF £8.05 TOTE £5.00: £1.30, £1.40, £1.60; EX 13.40 Trifecta £54.50 Pool: £971.81 - 13.36 winning units..
Owner Sheikh Juma Dalmook Al Maktoum **Bred** Silk Fan Syndicate **Trained** Newmarket, Suffolk
FOCUS
This might not be a bad little maiden. The form makes sense in behind the taking winner.

1821 CHINA ROSE OF BAWTRY MAIDEN FILLIES' STKS 6f
6:15 (6:16) (Class 5) 3-Y-0+ **£2,911** (£866; £432; £216) **Stalls** High

Form RPR
32- **1** **Jubilante**[226] 6167 3-8-13 0... RichardHughes 7 76
(Hughie Morrison) *t.k.h early: hdwy to trck ldr after 2f: effrt wl over 1f out: rdn to ld ent fnl f: kpt on* **1/1[1]**
5- **2** *1 1/2* **Tomintoul Magic (IRE)**[177] 7506 3-8-13 0......................... IanMongan 1 71
(Sir Henry Cecil) *plld hrd and sn led: pushed along 2f out: rdn over 1f out: hdd ent fnl f: kpt on same pce* **13/8[2]**
3 *nse* **Be Lucky** 3-8-13 0.. PaulMulrennan 3 71
(Michael Easterby) *stdd and wnt lft s: keen and hld up and bhd: smooth hdwy to trck ldrs over 2f out: cl up and ev ch over 1f out: tenderly rdn and kpt on same pce fnl f* **16/1**
64- **4** *5* **Hayyona**[269] 4704 3-8-13 0... MartinHarley 2 55
(Mick Channon) *led early: prom: rdn along over 2f out: sn one pce* **10/1[3]**
5 *8* **Moonvale (IRE)** 3-8-13 0.. TedDurcan 6 29
(Tony Carroll) *t.k.h early: chsd ldrs: rdn along wl over 2f out: sn wknd* **50/1**
30- **6** *1 1/4* **Sugar Blaze**[308] 3378 3-8-13 0... HayleyTurner 8 25
(Jim Goldie) *t.k.h early: in tch: rdn along wl over 2f out: sn outpcd* **20/1**
7 *2 3/4* **Delicious Patrica** 4-9-10 0....................................... MichaelO'Connell 4 17
(Tony Carroll) *in rr: outpcd and bhd fr 1/2-way* **66/1**
1m 13.48s (-0.12) **Going Correction** -0.025s/f (Good)
WFA 3 from 4yo 11lb **7** Ran SP% **111.3**
Speed ratings (Par 100): **99,97,96,90,79 77,74**
Tote Swingers: 1&2 £1.10, 1&3 £3.70, 2&3 £4.00 CSF £2.60 TOTE £1.90: £1.10, £2.20; EX 3.00 Trifecta £18.90 Pool: £2,506.27 - 99.10 winning units..
Owner S de Zoete & Partners **Bred** Wellsummers Stud **Trained** East Ilsley, Berks
FOCUS
Not too much depth here.

1822 GLENDINNINGS OF BAWTRY H'CAP 1m (S)
6:45 (6:45) (Class 3) (0-90,84) 3-Y-0 **£7,762** (£2,310; £1,154; £577) **Stalls** High

Form RPR
56-1 **1** **Lions Arch (IRE)**[43] 1012 3-9-3 **80**................................ RichardHughes 6 85+
(Richard Hannon) *trckd ldrs whn sltly hmpd after 1f and t.k.h after: hdwy wl over 1f out: rdn and qcknd to chal ins fnl f: led nr fin: readily* **3/1[1]**
1- **2** *1/2* **Love Magic**[253] 5300 3-9-4 **81**.. NeilCallan 1 85
(Sir Michael Stoute) *trckd ldng pair: hdwy and cl up 3f out: led wl over 1f out: rdn ent fnl f: hdd and no ex nr fin* **3/1[1]**
12-1 **3** *1* **Ingleby Symphony (IRE)**[17] 1486 3-7-13 **69**............. SamanthaBell(7) 7 71
(Richard Fahey) *hld up towards rr: swtchd lft and hdwy over 2f out: chal on outer wl over 1f out: sn rdn and ev ch tl one pce ins fnl f* **4/1[2]**
510- **4** *nk* **Starlight Symphony (IRE)**[252] 5361 3-8-12 **75**............... TedDurcan 4 76
(Eve Johnson Houghton) *trckd ldrs: effrt 2f out: sn rdn and ch tl drvn ent fnl f and kpt on same pce* **14/1**
110- **5** *1* **Lady Of The House (IRE)**[199] 6980 3-9-7 **84**...................(p) AmyRyan 3 83
(Kevin Ryan) *t.k.h: sn led and set stdy pce: qcknd 3f out: rdn along and hdd wl over 1f out: sn drvn and grad wknd* **10/1**
352- **6** *5* **Mowhoob**[200] 6946 3-8-11 **74**... HayleyTurner 2 61
(Jim Goldie) *hld up: a in rr* **12/1**
156- **7** *5* **Hunting Rights (USA)**[227] 6138 3-9-3 **80**....................... FrannyNorton 5 56
(Mark Johnston) *t.k.h: led early: sn hdd: trckd ldr: pushed along 3f out: rdn 2f out: wknd wl over 1f out* **9/2[3]**
1m 39.87s (0.57) **Going Correction** -0.025s/f (Good) **7** Ran SP% **111.6**
Speed ratings (Par 102): **96,95,94,94,93 88,83**
Tote Swingers: 1&2 £2.60, 1&3 £4.10, 2&3 £2.90 CSF £11.45 TOTE £2.80: £1.90, £2.20; EX 10.10 Trifecta £26.50 Pool: £1,749.20 - 49.43 winning units..
Owner Miss Donna Boyle **Bred** Mrs Alice Blake **Trained** East Everleigh, Wilts
FOCUS
Some interesting 3yos in opposition here and the finish was fought out by the two with arguably the most potential this season.

1823 CAVIARS OF BAWTRY & PROSPECT HOUSE FARM FILLIES' H'CAP 1m (S)
7:15 (7:15) (Class 4) (0-80,83) 4-Y-0+ **£5,175** (£1,540; £769; £384) **Stalls** High

Form RPR
434- **1** **Westwiththenight (IRE)**[248] 5474 4-9-6 **79**................. RichardHughes 5 97+
(William Haggas) *stdd s and hld up in rr: hdwy on bit 2f out: trckd ldrs over 1f out: shkn up to ld ins fnl f: sn qcknd clr: easily* **5/2[1]**
4-03 **2** *5* **Savanna Days (IRE)**[16] 1500 4-9-5 **78**........................... MartinHarley 8 82
(Mick Channon) *trckd ldrs: hdwy wl over 2f out: rdn along and ev ch over 1f out: kpt on same pce u.p fnl f* **8/1**
3 *3/4* **Modern Romance (IRE)**[260] 5070 4-9-5 **78**....................... NeilCallan 4 80
(Marco Botti) *trckd ldrs: hdwy over 2f out: sn n.m.r and swtchd lft: qcknd to ld jst over 1f out: sn rdn: hdd ins fnl f: one pce* **11/2[3]**
32-1 **4** *1/2* **Oddysey (IRE)**[12] 1576 4-9-7 **83**..................................... LeeTopliss(3) 1 84
(Michael Dods) *trckd ldng pair: hdwy on outer and cl up 3f out: rdn and ev ch over 1f out tl drvn and one pce fnl f* **11/4[2]**
502- **5** *nk* **Lisiere (IRE)**[201] 6923 4-9-3 **79**.........................(b) MichaelMetcalfe(3) 7 79
(Mrs K Burke) *chsd ldr: hdwy and cl up over 3f out: led wl over 2f out: sn rdn and edgd rt: hdd over 1f out: wknd ins fnl f* **20/1**
1411 **6** *3* **Goldstorm**[39] 1081 5-9-3 **76**...(p) WilliamCarson 2 70
(Brian Baugh) *dwlt and a in rr* **6/1**
2505 **7** *nk* **Askaud (IRE)**[19] 1422 5-9-0 **76**..(b) BillyCray(3) 9 69
(Scott Dixon) *led: rdn along 3f out: sn hdd & wknd* **12/1**
524- **8** *4 1/2* **Dubious Escapade (IRE)**[145] 7975 4-8-11 **70**............... PJMcDonald 3 52
(Ann Duffield) *chsd ldrs: rdn along wl over 2f out: sn wknd* **20/1**
1m 38.63s (-0.67) **Going Correction** -0.025s/f (Good) **8** Ran SP% **113.2**
Speed ratings (Par 102): **102,97,96,95,95 92,92,87**
Tote Swingers: 1&2 £6.50, 1&3 £1.60, 2&3 £6.60 CSF £22.57 CT £98.45 TOTE £3.70: £1.40, £3.00, £2.20; EX 22.00 Trifecta £108.10 Pool: £1,918.64 - 13.30 winning units..
Owner A E Oppenheimer **Bred** Hascombe And Valiant Studs **Trained** Newmarket, Suffolk
FOCUS
This looked an open race on paper.

1824 FINE AND COUNTRY-BAWTRY'S PREMIER AGENT H'CAP 1m 2f 60y
7:45 (7:46) (Class 3) (0-95,89) 4-Y-0+ **£7,762** (£2,310; £1,154; £577) **Stalls** Low

Form RPR
335- **1** **Sheikhzayedroad**[210] 6661 4-9-2 **84**.................................. MartinLane 5 96
(David Simcock) *hld up in rr: smooth hdwy on outer over 3f out: chal on bit wl over 1f out: shkn up to ld 1f out: rdn clr ins fnl f* **3/1[2]**
560- **2** *4* **Lucky Henry**[217] 6484 4-9-0 **82**..(p) AdamKirby 9 88+
(Clive Cox) *hld up in rr: hdwy over 3f out: chsd ldrs whn n.m.r wl over 1f out: sn swtchd rt and rdn to chse wnr ent fnl f: kpt on: no ch w wnr* **5/4[1]**
0/0- **3** *1 3/4* **Status Symbol (IRE)**[45] 427 8-9-7 **89**........................(t) WilliamCarson 4 90
(Anthony Carson) *trckd ldrs: hdwy 4f out: led wl over 2f out: sn rdn: hdd over 1f out: kpt on same pce* **40/1**
46-0 **4** *1 3/4* **Sirvino**[18] 1446 8-9-1 **88**.. LMcNiff(5) 8 86
(David Barron) *hld up in tch: pushed along over 3f out: rdn over 2f out: sn no imp* **11/2[3]**
-603 **5** *3/4* **Las Verglas Star (IRE)**[18] 1446 5-9-3 **88**........................ LeeTopliss(3) 1 84
(Richard Fahey) *trckd ldng pair: hdwy on inner 4f out: chal 3f out: rdn and ev ch wl over 1f out: wknd appr fnl f* **11/2[3]**
011/ **6** *2 1/4* **San Cassiano (IRE)**[57] 4818 6-9-3 **85**............................. PJMcDonald 2 77
(Ruth Carr) *led: rdn along 4f out: hdd 3f out and sn wknd* **16/1**
0- **7** *25* **Demolition**[182] 7415 9-9-3 **85**.. DuranFentiman 7
(Noel Wilson) *chsd ldr: rdn along over 3f out: sn wknd* **25/1**
2m 9.01s (-0.39) **Going Correction** +0.15s/f (Good) **7** Ran SP% **112.4**
Speed ratings (Par 107): **107,103,102,101,100 98,78**
Tote Swingers: 1&2 £1.10, 1&3 £50.20, 2&3 £16.70 CSF £6.86 CT £109.59 TOTE £3.80: £2.00, £1.90; EX 10.00 Trifecta £198.90 Pool: £2,068.70 - 7.79 winning units..
Owner Mohammed Jaber **Bred** Rabbah Bloodstock Limited **Trained** Newmarket, Suffolk
FOCUS
Another stylish winner.

1825 COOPER & GRIFFIN WINE BAR OF BAWTRY FILLIES' H'CAP 1m 2f 60y
8:15 (8:15) (Class 4) (0-85,83) 4-Y-0+ **£5,175** (£1,540; £769; £384) **Stalls** Low

Form RPR
06-1 **1** **Boonga Roogeta**[8] 1663 4-9-0 **81**................................... RosieJessop(5) 4 94
(Peter Charalambous) *sn chsng clr ldr: tk clsr order 4f out: led 3f out and sn rdn clr: drvn fnl f and hld on wl* **9/2[3]**
/2-1 **2** *1/2* **Opera Box**[15] 1518 5-9-3 **79**.. GeorgeBaker 6 91+
(Marcus Tregoning) *hld up bhd ldng pair: hdwy 3f out: rdn to chse wnr fr wl over 1f out: drvn and clsd strly ins fnl f: edgd lft and no ex towards fin* **7/2[2]**
12-0 **3** *11* **Four Leaves (IRE)**[14] 1544 4-9-7 **83**................................... AdamKirby 2 74
(Marco Botti) *hld up: hdwy 3f out: rdn along 2f out: no imp fnl f* **7/1**
45-0 **4** *8* **Jaaryah (IRE)**[17] 1484 5-9-4 **80**.. MartinHarley 3 56
(Mick Channon) *hld up: a in rr* **14/1**
300- **5** *nk* **Candycakes (IRE)**[210] 6667 4-9-1 **77**.............................. HayleyTurner 1 52
(Michael Bell) *sn led and clr: rdn along and hdd 3f out: wknd fnl 2f* **9/2[3]**
1- **6** *29* **Estemaala (IRE)**[219] 6408 4-8-11 **73**..................................... KierenFallon 5
(David O'Meara) *dwlt and in rr: niggled along bef 1/2-way: rdn over 3f out: bhd and eased fnl 2f* **2/1[1]**
2m 9.07s (-0.33) **Going Correction** +0.15s/f (Good) **6** Ran SP% **111.1**
Speed ratings (Par 102): **107,106,97,91,91 67**
Tote Swingers: 1&2 £1.80, 1&3 £4.80, 2&3 £5.50 CSF £19.95 TOTE £4.60: £2.80, £1.90; EX 18.60 Trifecta £37.80 Pool: £2,152.31 - 42.62 winning units..
Owner P Charalambous **Bred** Peter Charles **Trained** Newmarket, Suffolk
FOCUS
A strong gallop, and useful efforts from the first two who finished well clear.
T/Plt: £30.50 to a £1 stake. Pool: £54,086.76 - 1,293.97 winning units. T/Qpdt: £4.20 to a £1 stake. Pool: £5,990.10 - 1,044.60 winning units. JR

HAYDOCK (L-H)
Saturday, April 27

OFFICIAL GOING: Good to firm (7.8)
Wind: fresh behind Weather: Cloudy, showers

1826 GPWRECRUITMENT.COM MAIDEN STKS 1m 3f 200y
5:25 (5:27) (Class 5) 3-Y-0+ **£2,911** (£866; £432; £216) **Stalls** Low

Form RPR
5 **1** **Brass Ring**[7] 1684 3-8-8 0.. RobertHavlin 2 88+
(John Gosden) *reluctant to go in stall: s.i.s: hld up in tch: gd hdwy 3f out: rdn 2f out: led appr fnl f: kpt on* **7/4[2]**
53- **2** *2* **Prairie Ranger**[185] 7333 3-8-8 0... DavidProbert 9 85
(Andrew Balding) *trckd ldr: led over 3f out: sn rdn: strly pressed over 2f out: hdd appr fnl f: one pce* **4/1[3]**
22- **3** *2 1/2* **Chancery (USA)**[207] 6770 5-10-0 0............................... DanielTudhope 6 83
(David O'Meara) *hld up in tch: smooth hdwy 4f out: rdn and upsides over 2f out: no ex ins fnl f* **5/4[1]**
40 **4** *15* **Hell Hath No Fury**[15] 1522 4-9-8 0..................................... CathyGannon 7 54
(Michael Appleby) *dwlt: hld up: rdn over 3f out: sn no imp: wnt poor 4th over 1f out* **25/1**
0 **5** *2 1/2* **Gerrards Cross (IRE)**[9] 1635 3-8-8 0................................... SeanLevey 4 53
(Richard Hannon) *trckd ldr: rdn over 3f out: wknd over 2f out* **12/1**
0 **6** *1 1/2* **Enchanted Garden**[9] 1653 5-9-9 0.............................. GeorgeChaloner(5) 8 53
(Malcolm Jefferson) *s.i.s: hld up: a towards rr* **20/1**
00- **7** *3 3/4* **Primo Blanca**[133] 8135 4-9-13 0..............................(v[1]) RichardKingscote 1 47
(Michael Mullineaux) *led: hdd over 3f out: wknd* **100/1**
000- **8** *29* **Urbonite (IRE)**[201] 6925 4-9-13 0.................................. RussKennemore 5
(Alan Swinbank) *midfield: rdn 4f out: sn wknd: t.o* **66/1**
2m 32.67s (-1.13) **Going Correction** 0.0s/f (Good)
WFA 3 from 4yo 20lb 4 from 5yo 1lb **8** Ran SP% **119.6**
Speed ratings (Par 103): **103,101,100,90,88 87,84,65**
Tote Swingers: 1&2 £1.70, 1&3 £1.60, 2&3 £1.80 CSF £9.50 TOTE £2.40: £1.10, £1.40, £1.10; EX 11.90 Trifecta £17.70 Pool: £1,676.07 - 70.70 winning units..
Owner K Abdullah **Bred** Millsec Limited **Trained** Newmarket, Suffolk

FOCUS
All races on Stands side track and all races run over 37yds more than advertised. Run at just a fair gallop, this was an interesting maiden, in which the first three were all lightly raced with plenty of potential.

1827 FIND STAFF AT GPWRECRUITMENT.COM H'CAP — 1m
5:55 (5:55) (Class 5) (0-75,75) 4-Y-O+ £2,911 (£866; £432; £216) Stalls Low

Form RPR
1336 1 **Lord Of The Dance (IRE)**4 [1746] 7-8-12 71 RobertTart(5) 7 82
(Michael Mullineaux) *hld up: rdn and gd hdwy 2f out: led ins fnl f: kpt on wl* 16/1
112- 2 2 **No Dominion (IRE)**158 [7799] 4-9-1 69 RichardKingscote 6 75
(James Given) *in tch: hdwy over 3f out: led over 2f out: sn rdn: hdd ins fnl f: one pce* 14/1
3-63 3 2 **McCool Bannanas**44 [996] 5-8-7 61 DavidProbert 13 63
(James Unett) *hld up in midfield: rdn and hdwy on outer over 2f out: wnt 3rd ins fnl f: kpt on* 12/1
60-4 4 3 1/4 **Paramour**7 [1693] 6-9-6 74 DanielTudhope 9 68
(David O'Meara) *trckd ldr: rdn and upsides over 2f out: wknd fnl f* 11/4[1]
0-66 5 3/4 **King Vahe (IRE)**32 [1181] 4-8-7 66 (v1) MichaelJMMurphy(5) 12 59
(Alan Jarvis) *hld up: rdn over 2f out: no imp tl kpt on ins fnl f* 40/1
414- 6 1/2 **Sky Crossing**204 [6840] 4-8-11 65 MickyFenton 11 56
(Tom Tate) *led after 1f: rdn whn hdd over 2f out: wknd fnl f* 16/1
1260 7 1 1/4 **One Scoop Or Two**23 [1354] 7-9-1 74 (p) JackDuern(5) 5 63
(Reg Hollinshead) *midfield: rdn over 2f out: wknd ins fnl f* 20/1
0-64 8 3/4 **Border Revia (IRE)**12 [1569] 4-8-12 71 GeorgeChaloner(5) 4 58
(Richard Fahey) *midfield: rdn over 2f out: wknd over 1f out* 6/1[3]
0-50 9 shd **Cono Zur (FR)**12 [1569] 6-8-13 67 JamesSullivan 2 54
(Ruth Carr) *led for 1f: trckd ldr: rdn 3f out: wknd over 1f out* 13/2
0346 10 nse **Standpoint**7 [1699] 7-9-2 70 PhillipMakin 10 57
(Conor Dore) *in tch: rdn over 2f out: wknd over 1f out* 25/1
3230 11 nk **Copperwood**15 [1514] 8-9-1 69 JoeFanning 1 55
(Mark Johnston) *in tch: rdn 3f out: already wkng whn sltly short of room appr fnl f* 9/1
34-3 12 1 1/2 **Xinbama (IRE)**32 [1181] 4-9-6 74 SebSanders 3 56
(J W Hills) *midfield on inner: rdn 3f out: wknd over 1f out* 5/1[2]
1m 43.29s (-0.41) **Going Correction** 0.0s/f (Good) 12 Ran SP% 118.1
Speed ratings (Par 103): **102,100,98,94,94 93,92,91,91,91 91,89**
Tote Swingers: 1&2 £22.00, 1&3 £6.90, 2&3 £15.40 CSF £216.22 CT £2817.04 TOTE £17.60: £4.20, £3.20, £3.90; EX 293.20 Trifecta £1326.00 Part won. Pool: £1,768.11 - 0.76 winning units..
Owner H Clewlow **Bred** Bridgewater Equine Ltd **Trained** Alpraham, Cheshire

FOCUS
This was a middling handicap, run at a medium tempo, with the first three all showing that they are just as capable on turf as they are on sand. The winner is rated better than ever.

1828 FIND JOBS AT GPWRECRUITMENT.COM MAIDEN FILLIES' STKS — 1m
6:30 (6:30) (Class 5) 3-Y-O+ £2,911 (£866; £432; £216) Stalls Low

Form RPR
1 **Valtina (IRE)** 3-9-0 0 GrahamLee 12 83+
(William Haggas) *dwlt: hld up in midfield: stdy hdwy fr 4f out: led wl over 1f out: pushed along to assert: rdn fnl 100yds: jst hld on* 9/2[2]
5- 2 hd **Iffraaj Pink (IRE)**192 [7160] 3-9-0 0 RobertHavlin 6 82+
(Roger Varian) *in tch: pushed along over 3f out: rdn to chse wnr jst ins fnl f: kpt on wl fnl 100yds: jst hld* 9/4[1]
3 3/4 **Wall Of Sound** 3-9-0 0 RichardKingscote 2 80+
(Tom Dascombe) *trckd ldr: rdn to ld over 2f out: hdd wl over 1f out: kpt on* 11/1
4 2 3/4 **Odeliz (IRE)** 3-9-0 0 DanielTudhope 9 74+
(Mrs K Burke) *dwlt: hld up: pushed along and stl plenty to do over 2f out: kpt on wl fr over 1f out: nrst fin* 16/1
003- 5 3 3/4 **Azelle**218 [6444] 3-9-0 70 SeanLevey 11 65
(Richard Hannon) *trckd ldrs: rdn 3f out: wknd fnl f* 11/1
0- 6 1/2 **Mesmerized (IRE)**141 [8017] 3-8-9 0 RobertTart(5) 10 64
(Marco Botti) *hld up: pushed along over 3f out: sme hdwy over 1f out: kpt on one pce* 14/1
7 hd **Beep** 3-9-0 0 DavidProbert 8 64
(Sir Michael Stoute) *midfield: rdn and hdwy to chse ldrs over 2f out: wknd ins fnl f* 5/1[3]
0- 8 1 1/4 **Bousatet (FR)**208 [6751] 3-9-0 0 PhillipMakin 4 61
(Kevin Ryan) *led: rdn whn hdd over 2f out: grad wknd* 25/1
9 2 **Lexi's Dancer** 3-9-0 0 StevieDonohoe 1 56
(Ed Dunlop) *trckd ldr: rdn 3f out: wknd over 1f out* 12/1
- 10 6 **Speedy Utmost Meg** 3-9-0 0 JamesSullivan 5 42
(William Kinsey) *midfield: rdn over 3f out: sn wknd* 50/1
2 11 4 **Royal Style (IRE)**21 [1389] 3-9-0 0 GrahamGibbons 13 33
(David Barron) *slowly away: hld up: pushed along over 3f out: nvr threatened* 10/1
5 12 2 1/4 **Misty Pearl**18 [1447] 3-9-0 0 CathyGannon 14 28
(Michael Appleby) *midfield: rdn 4f out: sn wknd* 50/1
06- 13 22 **Poste Restante**141 [8018] 3-9-0 0 JoeFanning 3
(David Simcock) *s.i.s: hld up: a towards rr* 33/1
0 14 4 1/2 **Theatrical Dancer**21 [1392] 6-10-0 0 TomEaves 7
(Jim Goldie) *slowly away: a in rr* 100/1
1m 43.73s (0.03) **Going Correction** 0.0s/f (Good)
WFA 3 from 6yo 14lb 14 Ran SP% 123.3
Speed ratings (Par 100): **99,98,98,95,91 91,90,89,87,81 77,75,53,48**
Tote Swingers: 1&2 £2.30, 1&3 £8.20, 2&3 £6.80 CSF £14.86 TOTE £5.80: £2.10, £1.30, £3.60; EX 19.00 Trifecta £132.60 Pool: £1,184.41 - 6.69 winning units..
Owner M J & L A Taylor **Bred** Celbridge Estates Ltd **Trained** Newmarket, Suffolk

FOCUS
Some expensive and well-bred fillies were involved in the finish, giving this the look of an above-average race of its type. The fifth gives the form some substance. The pace was strong.

1829 SEND YOUR CV TO JOBS@GPWRECRUITMENT.COM H'CAP — 1m
7:00 (7:03) (Class 5) (0-75,75) 3-Y-O £2,911 (£866; £432; £216) Stalls Low

Form RPR
41- 1 **Danat Al Atheer**206 [6781] 3-9-5 73 [1] GrahamLee 13 80+
(William Haggas) *stdd s and swtchd lft: hld up: pushed along and hdwy 2f out: angled out to chse ldr appr fnl f: kpt on: led nr fin* 9/2[1]
0-1 2 hd **Endorsing (IRE)**38 [1086] 3-9-5 73 SeanLevey 1 79
(Richard Hannon) *midfield: sn trckd ldr: rdn to ld 2f out: kpt on: hdd nr fin* 8/1
6223 3 2 1/2 **Dha Chara (IRE)**70 [692] 3-9-7 75 GrahamGibbons 6 76
(Reg Hollinshead) *led narrowly: rdn whn hdd over 2f out: one pce* 33/1
400- 4 nk **Star Of Mayfair (USA)**183 [7373] 3-8-7 66 MichaelJMMurphy(5) 12 66+
(Alan Jarvis) *hld up in rr: rdn and hdwy on outer over 2f out: kpt on fnl f* 14/1
200- 5 2 1/4 **Woody Bay**171 [7637] 3-9-2 70 JamesSullivan 11 65
(James Given) *in tch: rdn over 2f out: no ex ins fnl f* 33/1
435- 6 1 3/4 **Hazzaat (IRE)**237 [5851] 3-9-4 72 RobertHavlin 7 63
(Roger Varian) *dwlt: midfield: rdn over 2f out: briefly chsd ldrs: no ex fnl f* 6/1[3]
05-3 7 nk **Pippy**21 [1400] 3-8-11 65 RichardKingscote 3 55
(Tom Dascombe) *midfield: rdn over 2f out: n.m.r wl over 1f out: one pce fnl f* 9/1
01-5 8 nse **Mandy's Boy (IRE)**26 [1293] 3-9-5 73 StevieDonohoe 9 63
(Ed Dunlop) *dwlt: hld up: rdn over 2f out: one pce: nvr threatened* 9/1
400- 9 4 1/2 **Fife Jo**168 [7687] 3-8-7 61 oh3 DavidProbert 2 41
(Jim Goldie) *midfield on inner: rdn over 3f out: wknd over 1f out* 33/1
355- 10 3/4 **Rocky Two (IRE)**206 [6780] 3-9-3 71 TomEaves 10 49
(Michael Dods) *w ldr: rdn 3f out: wknd appr fnl f* 16/1
50-5 11 2 3/4 **Another Claret**18 [1450] 3-8-6 65 GeorgeChaloner(5) 5 37
(Richard Fahey) *hld up in midfield: rdn 3f out: sn btn* 25/1
215- 12 1 1/4 **Marhaba Malayeen (IRE)**212 [6597] 3-9-4 72 HarryBentley 8 41
(Kevin Ryan) *trckd ldrs: rdn and lost pl 3f out: wknd over 1f out* 5/1[2]
0-10 13 9 **Tribal Path (IRE)**12 [1577] 3-9-7 75 JoeFanning 4 23
(Mark Johnston) *in tch: rdn over 3f out: wknd 2f out* 13/2
1m 44.65s (0.95) **Going Correction** 0.0s/f (Good) 13 Ran SP% 118.8
Speed ratings (Par 98): **95,94,92,92,89 88,87,87,83,82 79,78,69**
Tote Swingers: 1&2 £7.70, 1&3 £27.50, 2&3 £46.30 CSF £38.54 CT £1076.52 TOTE £4.60: £1.90, £3.60, £7.90; EX 29.30 Trifecta £717.30 Part won. Pool: £956.43 - 0.68 winning units..
Owner Jaber Abdullah **Bred** Rabbah Bloodstock Limited **Trained** Newmarket, Suffolk

FOCUS
This was better than most races in this rating band. The first two were unexposed and likely to make up into decent sorts this season. The third is the key to the form.

1830 GPW RECRUITMENT 40TH ANNIVERSARY H'CAP — 7f
7:30 (7:31) (Class 2) (0-105,103) 4-Y-O+ £12,938 (£3,850; £1,924; £962) Stalls Low

Form RPR
031- 1 **Tartiflette**168 [7691] 4-8-7 89 ow1 GrahamGibbons 11 101+
(Ed McMahon) *midfield: stl on bit 2f out: qcknd to ld ins fnl f: pushed out: shade cosily* 10/1[3]
5-20 2 3/4 **Summerinthecity (IRE)**102 [217] 6-7-11 84 oh1 ShirleyTeasdale(5) 10 92
(David Nicholls) *trckd ldrs: rdn over 2f out: led over 1f out: hdd ins fnl f: kpt on but a hld* 33/1
106- 3 1 **Cape Classic (IRE)**203 [6868] 5-9-1 97 GrahamLee 3 102
(William Haggas) *trckd ldrs: rdn over 2f out: kpt on* 7/2[1]
200- 4 3/4 **Highland Colori (IRE)**168 [7691] 5-8-12 94 DavidProbert 1 97
(Andrew Balding) *led narrowly: rdn over 2f out: hdd over 1f out: no ex ins fnl f* 7/2[1]
0/51 5 shd **Music In The Rain (IRE)**22 [1363] 5-8-4 86 AndrewMullen 5 89
(David O'Meara) *midfield: rdn over 2f out: kpt on one pce* 8/1[2]
0010 6 1 3/4 **Es Que Love (IRE)**7 [1675] 4-9-7 103 JoeFanning 6 101
(Mark Johnston) *in tch: rdn over 2f out: one pce and nvr threatened ldrs* 12/1
14-1 7 nk **Hi There (IRE)**28 [1252] 4-8-7 89 BarryMcHugh 7 86+
(Richard Fahey) *dwlt: hld up: rdn over 2f out: hdwy whn n.m.r ins fnl f: kpt on fnl 75yds* 7/2[1]
5204 8 hd **Docofthebay (IRE)**12 [1571] 9-7-13 84 oh4 (b) RaulDaSilva(3) 2 81
(Scott Dixon) *racd keenly: w ldr: rdn over 2f out: wknd fnl f* 16/1
000- 9 1 3/4 **Balty Boys (IRE)**210 [6676] 4-8-10 92 TomEaves 9 84
(Jamie Osborne) *hld up in midfield: rdn 3f out: sn struggling* 25/1
060- 10 1/2 **Smarty Socks (IRE)**189 [7240] 9-8-11 93 ow1 DanielTudhope 4 84
(David O'Meara) *dwlt: hld up in rr: rdn over 2f out: nvr threatened* 16/1
5-06 11 nk **Imperial Djay (IRE)**17 [1485] 8-8-3 85 JamesSullivan 8 75
(Ruth Carr) *hld up: rdn over 2f out: nvr threatened* 12/1
1m 29.7s (-1.00) **Going Correction** 0.0s/f (Good) 11 Ran SP% 120.8
Speed ratings (Par 109): **105,104,103,102,102 100,99,99,97,96 96**
Tote Swingers: 1&2 £68.60, 1&3 £13.50, 2&3 £36.30 CSF £297.88 CT £1418.81 TOTE £11.50: £3.50, £10.80, £1.40; EX 280.50 Trifecta £889.90 Part won. Pool: £1,186.65 - 0.02 winning units..
Owner A Buxton **Bred** Andrew Buxton **Trained** Lichfield, Staffs

FOCUS
This was a competitive race, with some smart handicappers contesting a good prize, run at a decent pace that suited the winner. The runner-up looks the key to the form longer term.

1831 THANK YOU TO GPW RECRUITMENT STAFF H'CAP — 1m 2f 95y
8:00 (8:00) (Class 4) (0-80,80) 4-Y-O+ £5,175 (£1,540; £769; £384) Stalls Low

Form RPR
0-22 1 **Icebuster**16 [1501] 5-9-7 80 DanielTudhope 5 92
(Rod Millman) *hld up: pushed along and hdwy over 2f out: swtchd rt over 1f out: sn rdn: kpt on wl: led nr fin* 7/2[2]
5-42 2 hd **Tres Coronas (IRE)**14 [1538] 6-9-5 78 GrahamGibbons 12 90
(David Barron) *midfield: hdwy over 2f out: rdn to ld over 1f out: kpt on: hdd nr fin* 7/2[2]
14-0 3 3 **Now My Sun**14 [1538] 4-9-1 74 PhillipMakin 3 80
(Mrs K Burke) *dwlt: hld up in rr: hdwy on wd outside 3f out: rdn to chse ldrs over 1f out: one pce fnl f* 6/1[3]
0-66 4 nk **Kiwi Bay**14 [1538] 8-9-4 77 TomEaves 10 82
(Michael Dods) *led: rdn over 2f out: hdd over 1f out: no ex ins fnl f* 20/1
0500 5 hd **Dubawi Phantom**54 [882] 6-9-4 77 (b) MartinDwyer 8 82
(David C Griffiths) *hld up in midfield: hdwy over 2f out: rdn and ev ch wl over 1f out: no ex ins fnl f* 25/1
2454 6 4 1/2 **Dazzling Valentine**64 [753] 5-8-5 69 NatashaEaton(5) 6 65
(Alan Bailey) *midfield on inner: pushed along fr over 4f out: one pce and nvr threatened ldrs* 25/1
2224 7 3/4 **Knowe Head (NZ)**64 [759] 6-9-5 78 (p) DavidProbert 7 73
(James Unett) *hld up in midfield: rdn and hdwy on outer over 2f out: wknd ins fnl f* 14/1
210- 8 2 1/4 **Another For Joe**168 [6638] 5-9-4 77 GrahamLee 2 68
(Jim Goldie) *hld up: rdn over 2f out: nvr threatened* 12/1
123 9 3/4 **Blazing Desert**15 [1523] 9-8-7 71 RobertTart(5) 11 60
(William Kinsey) *trckd ldr: rdn over 2f out: wknd over 1f out* 20/1
23-2 10 4 1/2 **Fly Solo**17 [1463] 4-9-3 76 RobertWinston 9 57
(Alan Swinbank) *t.k.h: midfield: rdn over 2f out: wknd over 1f out* 3/1[1]
56-0 11 3/4 **Indepub**28 [1238] 4-9-0 80 (b) KevinStott(7) 1 59
(Kevin Ryan) *trckd ldrs: rdn over 2f out: sn wknd* 33/1

The Form Book Flat, Raceform Ltd, Compton, RG20 6NL.

4530 **12** 4 1/2 **The Lock Master (IRE)**[14] 1536 6-8-10 **74**........ ShirleyTeasdale(5) 4 45
(Michael Appleby) *in tch: rdn 3f out: sn wknd* **14/1**

2m 14.06s (-1.44) **Going Correction** 0.0s/f (Good) **12** Ran SP% **124.9**
Speed ratings (Par 105): **105,104,102,102,102 98,97,96,95,91 91,87**
Tote Swingers: 1&2 £4.90, 1&3 £5.20, 2&3 £6.80 CSF £15.83 CT £75.05 TOTE £5.10: £2.40, £1.90, £3.20; EX 22.60 Trifecta £203.80 Pool: £922.54 - 3.39 winning units..
Owner The Links Partnership **Bred** Cheveley Park Stud Ltd **Trained** Kentisbeare, Devon

FOCUS
They were soon going a solid pace in this middling handicap. The relatively unexposed favourite was well beaten and the winner built on his AW latest.
T/Plt: £237.40 to a £1 stake. Pool: £56,519.10 - 173.75 winning units. T/Qpdt: £33.60 to a £1 stake. Pool: £5,383.19 - 118.52 winning units. AS

1360 LEICESTER (R-H)
Saturday, April 27

OFFICIAL GOING: Good to firm (9.7)
Wind: Light against Weather: Overcast

1832 BET TOTEJACKPOT AT TOTEPOOL.COM H'CAP 7f 9y
2:10 (2:10) (Class 5) (0-75,75) 3-Y-O **£3,234** (£962; £481; £240) **Stalls High**

Form RPR
1-12 **1** **Intrigo**[5] 1714 3-9-6 **74**........ RichardHughes 7 85+
(Richard Hannon) *chsd ldrs: led 4f out: qcknd clr fnl f: easily* **9/4**[1]
353- **2** 2 **Gravitational (IRE)**[196] 7059 3-9-5 **73**........ SebSanders 5 73+
(Chris Wall) *hld up: plld hrd: n.m.r 1/2-way: swtchd rt over 2f out: hdwy over 1f out: r.o to take 2nd nr fin: no ch w wnr* **14/1**
130- **3** 1/2 **Entwined (IRE)**[210] 6675 3-9-3 **71**........ AdamKirby 2 70
(Clive Cox) *hld up: swtchd rt over 2f out: hdwy over 1f out: chsd wnr fnl f: styd on same pce: lost 2nd nr fin* **17/2**
41-6 **4** 2 **Benoni**[12] 1582 3-9-5 **73**........ FergusSweeney 3 67
(Henry Candy) *s.i.s: hld up: hdwy 1/2-way: pushed along over 2f out: n.m.r ins fnl f: styd on: nt trble ldrs* **8/1**
-112 **5** 3/4 **Admiralofthesea (USA)**[10] 1608 3-9-2 **70**........ AdamBeschizza 4 62
(Robert Eddery) *chsd ldr: rdn over 1f out: no ex ins fnl f* **7/1**[3]
1 **6** 1 3/4 **Repetition**[81] 525 3-9-3 **71**........ PhillipMakin 9 58
(Kevin Ryan) *prom: pushed along 1/2-way: rdn over 2f out: hung rt and no ex ins fnl f: eased nr fin* **9/2**[2]
51-0 **7** 1 1/4 **Santo Prince (USA)**[26] 1293 3-9-7 **75**........ HayleyTurner 12 58
(Michael Bell) *s.i.s: hld up: r.o towards fin: nvr nrr* **14/1**
6-61 **8** 3/4 **Jontleman (IRE)**[15] 1519 3-9-2 **70**........ MartinHarley 1 51
(Mick Channon) *s.i.s: hld up: hdwy 1/2-way: rdn over 1f out: wknd ins fnl f* **16/1**
01-6 **9** 5 **Barbs Princess**[17] 1476 3-9-1 **69**........ PaulHanagan 6 37
(Charles Hills) *prom: rdn over 2f out: wknd fnl f* **22/1**
3256 **10** 4 **Black Dave (IRE)**[37] 1099 3-8-10 **69**........ DeclanBates(5) 10 26
(David Evans) *led 3f: rdn over 2f out: wknd over 1f out* **33/1**
-616 **11** 3 **Blazeofenchantment (USA)**[21] 1400 3-9-0 **68**........(tp) ChrisCatlin 11 17
(Noel Quinlan) *s.i.s: a in rr: wknd over 2f out* **33/1**
05-1 **12** 22 **Striking Echo**[71] 673 3-9-4 **72**........ GeorgeBaker 8
(Reg Hollinshead) *chsd ldrs: pushed along 1/2-way: wknd over 2f out: t.o* **33/1**

1m 28.07s (1.87) **Going Correction** +0.125s/f (Good) **12** Ran SP% **115.5**
Speed ratings (Par 98): **94,91,91,88,88 86,84,83,78,73 70,44**
Tote Swingers: 1&2 £9.80, 1&3 £16.60, 2&3 £34.50 CSF £33.94 CT £226.81 TOTE £2.60: £1.10, £6.20, £3.70; EX 40.50 Trifecta £210.00 Pool: £292.87 - 1.04 winning units..
Owner Gillian, Lady Howard De Walden **Bred** Gillian Lady Howard De Walden **Trained** East Everleigh, Wilts

FOCUS
False rail from top of hill on back straight all the way to Winning post added circa 17yds to races on Round course. A fair 3yo handicap in which they went a decent gallop.

1833 BET TOTESCOOP6 AT TOTEPOOL.COM MEDIAN AUCTION MAIDEN STKS 5f 2y
2:45 (2:45) (Class 5) 2-Y-O **£2,587** (£770; £384; £192) **Stalls High**

Form RPR
1 **Sleepy Joe (IRE)** 2-9-5 0........ MartinHarley 7 70+
(Mick Channon) *chsd ldrs: shkn up to ld and hung rt ins fnl f: r.o* **5/2**[2]
2 1 1/4 **Larsen Bay (IRE)** 2-9-5 0........ RichardKingscote 4 66
(Tom Dascombe) *led: rdn and hdd ins fnl f: styd on same pce: wnt rt towards fin* **11/2**[3]
3 1 1/2 **Trinity Boy** 2-9-5 0........ AdamKirby 3 60
(Clive Cox) *s.i.s: sn chsng ldrs: rdn over 1f out: styd on same pce ins fnl f* **11/8**[1]
4 2 1/2 **Nonagon** 2-9-5 0........ StevieDonohoe 5 51
(Noel Quinlan) *s.i.s: hld up: rn green in rr: hdwy over 1f out: nt trble ldrs* **18/1**
5 nk **Shot In The Sun (IRE)** 2-9-0 0........ WilliamCarson 1 45
(David Evans) *in tch: sn pushed along: styd on same pce fr over 1f out* **12/1**
00 **6** 1/2 **Nomathemba (IRE)**[15] 1512 2-8-9 0........ DeclanBates(5) 2 43
(David Evans) *w ldr: rdn 1/2-way: wknd ins fnl f* **40/1**
7 1 3/4 **Earl's Bridge** 2-8-12 0........ JakePayne(7) 6 42+
(Bill Turner) *s.s: hdwy 2f out: wknd fnl f* **9/1**

1m 3.99s (3.99) **Going Correction** +0.125s/f (Good) **7** Ran SP% **111.5**
Speed ratings (Par 92): **73,71,68,64,64 63,60**
Tote Swingers: 1&2 £9.60, 1&3 £1.02, 2&3 £1.20 CSF £15.70 TOTE £3.00: £2.10, £2.60; EX 14.00 Trifecta £30.40 Pool: £578.09 - 14.22 winning units..
Owner Nick & Olga Dhandsa & John & Zoe Webster **Bred** Wardstown Stud Ltd **Trained** West Ilsley, Berks

FOCUS
An ordinary juvenile maiden sprint in which they went an honest gallop. The form has been rated at the lower end of the race averages.

1834 LIVE TOTESCOOP6 INFORMATION AT TOTEPOOL.COM H'CAP 1m 3f 183y
3:20 (3:21) (Class 3) (0-95,83) 3-Y-O **£7,561** (£2,263; £1,131; £566) **Stalls Low**

Form RPR
16-3 **1** **Red Runaway**[17] 1470 3-9-2 **76**........ PaulHanagan 4 85
(Ed Dunlop) *hld up: pushed along over 3f out: hdwy over 1f out: rdn and r.o to ld post* **4/1**[3]
1- **2** hd **Cafe Society (FR)**[196] 7057 3-9-2 **76**........ RichardHughes 3 85+
(David Simcock) *chsd ldr: rdn to ld 1f out: sn hung rt: hdd post* **9/4**[2]
6311 **3** 2 1/2 **Blue Wave (IRE)**[5] 1719 3-9-9 **83** 5ex........ JoeFanning 1 88
(Mark Johnston) *led at stdy pce tl qiuckened over 3f out: rdn and hdd 1f out: styng on same pce whn nt clr run wl ins fnl f* **1/1**[1]
1U **4** 11 **Dorfman**[17] 1470 3-9-2 **76**........(b[1]) MartinDwyer 2 68
(Mark Johnston) *chsd ldrs: rdn over 2f out: wknd over 1f out* **11/1**

2m 38.1s (4.20) **Going Correction** +0.225s/f (Good) **4** Ran SP% **109.1**
Speed ratings (Par 102): **95,94,93,85**
CSF £13.01 TOTE £4.20; EX 15.70 Trifecta £28.50 Pool: £637.65 - 16.57 winning units..
Owner The Hon R J Arculli **Bred** Lofts Hall, M Philipson & Cheveley Park **Trained** Newmarket, Suffolk

FOCUS
A fair small-field 3yo middle-distance handicap in which the early gallop appeared a modest one.

1835 EBF TOTEPOOL.COM KING RICHARD III STKS (LISTED RACE) 7f 9y
3:55 (3:59) (Class 1) 4-Y-O+ **£25,519** (£9,675; £4,842; £2,412; £1,210) **Stalls High**

Form RPR
4-20 **1** **Producer**[58] 836 4-9-2 108........ RichardHughes 4 114
(Richard Hannon) *a.p: shkn up over 2f out: chsd ldr over 1f out: sn rdn: r.o u.p to ld nr fin* **11/4**[2]
333- **2** hd **Aljamaaheer (IRE)**[245] 5573 4-9-2 110........ PaulHanagan 9 113
(Roger Varian) *led: rdn over 1f out: hdd nr fin* **4/5**[1]
/34- **3** 9 **Burwaaz**[344] 2236 4-9-2 108........ PaulMulrennan 1 89
(Ed Dunlop) *hld up in tch: racd keenly: rdn over 1f out: wknd fnl f* **12/1**
6-02 **4** 1 1/2 **Majestic Myles (IRE)**[7] 1691 5-9-2 106........ DavidNolan 2 85
(Richard Fahey) *trckd ldr: racd keenly and edgd rt thrght: rdn over 2f out: wknd fnl f* **9/2**[3]
00-0 **5** 3/4 **Chilli Green**[14] 1544 6-8-11 87........ MartinHarley 6 78
(Julia Feilden) *dwlt: hld up: plld hrd: rdn and wknd over 1f out* **80/1**

1m 25.29s (-0.91) **Going Correction** +0.125s/f (Good) **5** Ran SP% **109.3**
Speed ratings (Par 111): **110,109,99,97,96**
CSF £5.29 TOTE £2.90: £1.40, £1.10; EX 6.00 Trifecta £21.40 Pool: £1,421.64 - 49.68 winning units..
Owner J Palmer-Brown **Bred** Cheveley Park Stud Ltd **Trained** East Everleigh, Wilts
■ A new name for this event, formerly called the Leicestershire Stakes.

FOCUS
A good quality Listed race for older horses in which they went an even gallop.

1836 PLAY TEN TO FOLLOW AT TOTEPOOL.COM H'CAP 1m 1f 218y
4:30 (4:30) (Class 5) (0-70,71) 4-Y-O+ **£3,234** (£962; £481; £240) **Stalls Low**

Form RPR
043- **1** **Tafawuk (USA)**[317] 3088 4-9-3 **66**........ RichardHughes 13 79
(Roger Varian) *a.p: led over 1f out: pushed out* **11/4**[1]
033- **2** 2 **Curly Come Home**[256] 5219 4-9-3 **66**........ GeorgeBaker 7 75
(Chris Wall) *hld up: hdwy 2f out: chsd wnr fnl f: edgd rt: styd on same pce* **10/1**
6112 **3** 2 1/4 **Bridge That Gap**[21] 1381 5-9-2 **65**........(p) AdamKirby 2 69
(Roger Ingram) *hld up: hdwy over 3f out: rdn over 1f out: styd on same pce* **8/1**[3]
624- **4** hd **Breaking The Bank**[193] 7129 4-9-5 **68**........ MartinDwyer 12 72
(William Muir) *prom: chsd ldr 6f out: rdn and ev ch over 1f out: no ex ins fnl f* **14/1**
4440 **5** 3/4 **White Diamond**[28] 1239 6-8-11 **60**........(p) LukeMorris 10 63
(Michael Appleby) *led: rdn and hdd over 1f out: no ex ins fnl f* **16/1**
6-04 **6** 1 **Tenhoo**[18] 1448 7-8-13 **67**........ JasonHart(5) 3 71+
(Eric Alston) *hld up: outpcd over 3f out: hdwy u.p over 1f out: nt clr run ins fnl f: nvr trbld ldrs* **9/2**[2]
0-50 **7** 1 3/4 **Zafranagar (IRE)**[56] 403 8-9-1 **69**........ GeorgeDowning(5) 5 66
(Tony Carroll) *hld up: hdwy over 4f out: rdn and ev ch over 1f out: wknd ins fnl f* **28/1**
312- **8** nk **Tawseef (IRE)**[178] 7495 5-9-2 **68**........ MarkCoumbe(3) 9 64+
(Roy Brotherton) *hld up: rdn over 3f out: hdwy over 1f out: nt trble ldrs* **11/1**
/640 **9** 13 **Nonaynever**[12] 1567 5-8-4 **56** oh1........ JulieBurke(3) 4 26
(Ruth Carr) *chsd ldrs: rdn over 3f out: wknd 2f out* **40/1**
3451 **10** 7 **Going Grey (IRE)**[12] 1568 4-8-11 **60**........ PaulHanagan 6 16
(Richard Fahey) *chsd ldr 4f: remained handy: rdn over 3f out: wknd 2f out* **9/2**[2]
000- **11** hd **Divea**[253] 5309 4-9-4 **67**........ WilliamCarson 8 23
(Anthony Carson) *stdd s: hld up: shkn up 1/2-way: sn lost tch* **33/1**
05-0 **12** 10 **Glass Mountain (IRE)**[111] 83 5-8-11 **60**........(v) SteveDrowne 1
(John Mackie) *hld up: wknd and eased over 2f out: t.o* **16/1**

2m 9.26s (1.36) **Going Correction** +0.225s/f (Good) **12** Ran SP% **118.8**
Speed ratings (Par 103): **103,101,99,99,98 98,96,96,86,80 80,72**
Tote Swingers: 1&2 £6.80, 1&3 £5.60, 2&3 £8.70 CSF £31.09 CT £201.14 TOTE £3.20: £1.10, £2.00, £3.60; EX 42.20 Trifecta £299.00 Pool: £999.21 - 2.50 winning units..
Owner Michael Hill **Bred** Shadwell Farm LLC **Trained** Newmarket, Suffolk

FOCUS
A modest handicap for older horses in which they went a steady gallop.

1837 YOUR FAVOURITE POOL BETS AT TOTEPOOL.COM MAIDEN STKS 1m 1f 218y
5:05 (5:09) (Class 5) 3-Y-O+ **£3,234** (£962; £481; £240) **Stalls Low**

Form RPR
54- **1** **Unmoothaj**[220] 6371 3-8-10 0........ PaulHanagan 9 70+
(Charles Hills) *s.i.s: sn trcking ldrs: shkn up to ld over 2f out: rdn and hung rt over 1f out: jst hld on* **6/5**[1]
- **2** hd **Continuum** 4-9-13 0........[1] GeorgeBaker 2 72+
(Sir Henry Cecil) *s.i.s: hld up: hdwy over 2f out: rdn to chse wnr ins fnl f: r.o* **11/4**[2]
34 **3** 1 1/2 **Smalib Monterg (FR)**[9] 1653 7-9-10 0........ JulieBurke(3) 1 69
(Dr Richard Newland) *a.p: rdn over 1f out: styd on same pce ins fnl f* **11/1**
00- **4** 1 **Kalily**[229] 6102 4-9-8 0........ WilliamTwiston-Davies(5) 6 67
(Rae Guest) *s.i.s: hld up: hdwy over 1f out: edgd rt: styd on: nt rch ldrs* **14/1**
0- **5** hd **Just Darcy**[234] 5947 3-8-5 0........ KieranO'Neill 4 59+
(Sir Michael Stoute) *chsd ldrs: rdn over 1f out: styd on* **7/2**[3]
50 **6** 1 1/4 **Reach The Beach**[17] 1468 4-9-8 0........ SteveDrowne 7 59
(Brendan Powell) *led at stdy pce tl qckná over 3f out: hdd over 2f out: no ex ins fnl f* **50/1**
06 **7** 2 3/4 **Whitefall (USA)**[7] 1698 3-8-5 0........ WilliamCarson 5 51
(David Evans) *s.i.s: hld up: hdwy over 1f out: styd on same pce fnl f* **80/1**
00- **8** 1 1/2 **Tallaay (IRE)**[171] 7637 3-8-10 0........ MartinDwyer 10 53
(Mark Johnston) *chsd ldr tl pushed along over 3f out: wknd over 1f out* **22/1**

2m 15.35s (7.45) **Going Correction** +0.225s/f (Good)
WFA 3 from 4yo+ 17lb **8** Ran SP% **116.9**
Speed ratings (Par 103): **79,78,77,76,76 75,73,72**
Tote Swingers: 1&2 £1.70, 1&3 £3.30, 2&3 £5.90 CSF £4.75 TOTE £2.20: £1.10, £1.80, £2.60; EX 5.30 Trifecta £32.10 Pool: £3,171.38 - 74.03 winning units..
Owner Hamdan Al Maktoum **Bred** Shadwell Estate Company Limited **Trained** Lambourn, Berks

FOCUS
A fair maiden for 3yos and up which includes 2008 Derby second Tartan Bearer and last year's Melbourne Cup winner Green Moon on its roll of honour in recent years. The gallop was sedate early on.

1838 FOLLOW TOTEPOOL ON FACEBOOK AND TWITTER H'CAP — 5f 218y
5:35 (5:36) (Class 4) (0-85,85) 4-Y-0+ — **£5,175** (£1,540; £769; £384) **Stalls** High

Form — RPR

34-4 **1** **Seeking Magic**[106] 164 5-9-6 **84** ....(t) AdamKirby 1 — 98
(Clive Cox) *trckd ldrs: racd keenly: rdn to ld over 1f out: r.o* **7/2**[1]

0110 **2** *2 ½* **Crew Cut (IRE)**[28] 1245 5-9-5 **83** ....(b) GeorgeBaker 10 — 89+
(Jeremy Gask) *hld up: hdwy over 1f out: r.o to go 2nd post: nt rch wnr* **9/1**

-300 **3** *hd* **Klynch**[9] 1644 7-9-0 **81** ....(b) JulieBurke(3) 13 — 86
(Ruth Carr) *s.i.s: hld up: hdwy over 1f out: rdn to chse wnr wl ins fnl f: styd on same pce* **12/1**

/04- **4** *nk* **Shamahan**[324] 2854 4-8-13 **77** .... LukeMorris 3 — 81
(Gary Moore) *a.p: rdn over 1f out: styd on same pce ins fnl f* **14/1**

54-5 **5** *1* **North Star Boy (IRE)**[23] 1346 4-8-9 **78** .... WilliamTwiston-Davies(5) 12 — 79
(Richard Hannon) *led: rdn and hdd over 1f out: no ex ins fnl f* **11/2**[2]

1-63 **6** *2* **Barkston Ash**[9] 1646 5-8-11 **80** ....(p) JasonHart(5) 14 — 75
(Eric Alston) *chsd ldr tl rdn over 1f out: wknd ins fnl f* **7/1**

36-4 **7** *shd* **Dutch Heritage**[26] 1286 4-8-10 **74** .... PaulHanagan 11 — 68
(Richard Fahey) *prom: rdn over 2f out: no ex fnl f* **13/2**[3]

1025 **8** *3 ¼* **Frognal (IRE)**[24] 1316 7-8-7 **74** ....(bt) DarrenEgan(3) 9 — 58
(Violet M Jordan) *hld up: hdwy over 2f out: rdn over 1f out: wknd ins fnl f* **20/1**

312- **9** *3* **Lunar Deity**[222] 6303 4-9-2 **80** ....(p) JohnFahy 15 — 54
(Eve Johnson Houghton) *chsd ldrs: rdn over 2f out: wknd ins fnl f* **9/1**

113- **10** *½* **Clear Spring (IRE)**[194] 7114 5-8-13 **77** .... NickyMackay 7 — 50
(John Spearing) *hood removed late and s.i.s: hld up: hdwy over 1f out: wknd fnl f* **10/1**

116- **11** *½* **Capitol Gain (IRE)**[183] 7376 4-8-9 **73** .... MartinLane 6 — 44
(Brian Meehan) *hood removed late: s.i.s: rdn over 2f out: wknd over 1f out* **14/1**

-000 **12** *5* **Chiswick Bey (IRE)**[22] 1363 5-9-2 **80** .... ChrisCatlin 4 — 35
(Noel Quinlan) *hld up: rdn over 2f out: sn wknd* **33/1**

1m 12.93s (-0.07) **Going Correction** +0.125s/f (Good) — **12** Ran SP% **121.3**
Speed ratings (Par 105): **105,101,101,101,99 97,96,92,88,87 87,80**
Tote Swingers: 1&2 £6.10, 1&3 £11.50, 2&3 £25.30 CSF £36.23 CT £354.79 TOTE £4.20: £1.30, £2.70, £3.70; EX 42.00 Trifecta £231.90 Pool: £414.64 - 1.34 winning units..
Owner The Seekers **Bred** R, J D & M R Bromley Gardner **Trained** Lambourn, Berks

FOCUS
A decent sprint handicap for older horses in which they went a proper gallop.
T/Plt: £78.80 to a £1 stake. Pool: £54,375.63 - 503.45 winning tickets. T/Qpdt: £16.70 to a £1 stake. Pool: £3,218.50 - 142.40 winning tickets. CR

1642 RIPON (R-H)
Saturday, April 27

OFFICIAL GOING: Good (8.2)
Wind: Fresh, half against Weather: Overcast

1839 GET SET BET WITH RIPONBET MAIDEN AUCTION FILLIES' STKS — 5f
1:50 (1:53) (Class 5) 2-Y-0 — **£3,234** (£962; £481; £240) **Stalls** High

Form — RPR

3 **1** **Lexington Rose**[12] 1565 2-8-8 0 .... RoystonFfrench 3 — 75+
(Bryan Smart) *mde all far side: drifted lft but overall ldr over 1f out: kpt on strly fnl f: 1st of 4 in gp* **8/1**

226 **2** *1 ½* **Memory Styx**[10] 1605 2-8-6 0 ow3 .... CharlesBishop(5) 10 — 73
(Mick Channon) *hld up in midfield stands' side: hdwy wl over 1f out: led that gp ins fnl f: kpt on: nt rch far side wnr: 1st of 9 in gp* **16/1**

3 **3** *1 ¾* **Ventura Mist**[9] 1642 2-8-10 0 .... DuranFentiman 8 — 66
(Tim Easterby) *prom stands' side: effrt over 1f out: disp ld that gp ins fnl f: kpt on same pce: 2nd of 9 in gp* **13/2**

4 **4** *1 ¾* **Atlantic Affair (IRE)**[10] 1605 2-8-6 0 .... FrannyNorton 11 — 55
(Mark Johnston) *led stands' side: rdn over 1f out: hdd ins fnl f: kpt on same pce: 3rd of 9 in gp* **5/1**[3]

3 **5** *nk* **Lorimer's Lot (IRE)**[12] 1573 2-8-4 0 .... JamesSullivan 12 — 52
(Tim Walford) *in tch stands' side: rdn and edgd rt fr over 1f out: kpt on same pce fnl f: 4th of 9 in gp* **22/1**

6 *nk* **Woodland Girl** 2-8-10 0 .... TonyHamilton 1 — 57
(Richard Fahey) *chsd wnr far side: pushed along 2f out: kpt on fnl f: no imp: 2nd of 4 in gp* **9/2**[2]

60 **7** *1 ½* **Rough Courte (IRE)**[9] 1634 2-8-8 0 .... SamHitchcott 7 — 50
(Mick Channon) *in tch stands' side: effrt and cl up that gp over 1f out: rdn and outpcd fnl f: 5th of 9 in gp* **11/1**

8 *nk* **Shamouti (IRE)** 2-8-8 0 .... AmyRyan 6 — 49
(Kevin Ryan) *slowly away: bhd stands' side: rdn and hdwy over 1f out: kpt on: nvr able to chal: 6th of 9 in gp* **20/1**

9 *1 ¾* **Rosebay Coral (IRE)** 2-8-8 0 .... BarryMcHugh 2 — 42
(Tony Coyle) *chsd far side ldrs: pushed along 2f out: sn no imp: 3rd of 4 in gp* **66/1**

2 **10** *2 ¼* **Hello Beautiful (IRE)**[5] 1718 2-8-6 0 .... PJMcDonald 5 — 32
(Ann Duffield) *chsd stands' side ldrs tl rdn and wknd over 1f out: 7th of 9 in gp* **5/2**[1]

11 *nk* **Lady Montenegro** 2-7-11 0 .... RowanScott(7) 9 — 29
(Ann Duffield) *hld up stands' side: hdwy on outside of that gp 2f out: sn btn: 8th of 9 in gp* **40/1**

12 *1 ¾* **Parisian Melody** 2-8-1 0 .... NeilFarley(3) 4 — 23
(Mel Brittain) *slowly away: a bhd far side: last of 4 in gp* **33/1**

6 **13** *2 ½* **Red Tiger Lily**[14] 1534 2-8-3 0 .... DeclanCannon(3) 13 — 16
(Nigel Tinkler) *hld up stands' side: struggling 2f out: sn btn: last of 9 in gp* **80/1**

1m 2.07s (2.07) **Going Correction** +0.275s/f (Good) — **13** Ran SP% **119.3**
Speed ratings (Par 89): **94,91,88,86,85 85,82,82,79,75 75,72,68**
Tote Swingers: 1&2 £28.90, 1&3 £8.90, 2&3 £13.30 CSF £117.96 TOTE £11.20: £3.40, £5.90, £1.10; EX 147.10 Trifecta £1091.60 Part won. Pool: £1,455.49 - 0.13 winning units..
Owner Middleham Park Racing VIII & Partners **Bred** Mickley Stud & Richard Kent **Trained** Hambleton, N Yorks

FOCUS
The field split into two groups in this modest maiden, and it was from the four that raced on the far side that the winner came. It's hard to say she benefited from a track bias given where her companions on that side finished, although all three of them were newcomers. It was a Racing Post Yearling Bonus and BOBIS race, so the form has been rated a shade positively.

1840 ATTHERACES.COM WILLIAM BUICK EXCLUSIVE BLOG H'CAP — 1m
2:20 (2:20) (Class 3) (0-90,92) 4-Y-0+
£9,337 (£2,796; £1,398; £699; £349; £175) **Stalls** Low

Form — RPR

2 **1** **Two For Two (IRE)**[12] 1576 5-9-7 **90** .... DanielTudhope 5 — 104
(David O'Meara) *t.k.h early: prom: hdwy over 2f out: led over 1f out: sn rdn: qcknd clr fnl f* **5/1**[2]

533- **2** *3 ¾* **Lord Aeryn (IRE)**[197] 7030 6-9-6 **89** .... TonyHamilton 9 — 94
(Richard Fahey) *trckd ldrs: effrt whn nt clr run over 2f out: hdwy over 1f out: chsd (clr) wnr ins fnl f: kpt on: no imp* **9/1**

21-6 **3** *shd* **Amaze**[28] 1237 5-9-2 **85** .... DaleSwift 4 — 90
(Brian Ellison) *prom: pushed along 3f out: rallied over 1f out: kpt on ins fnl f* **14/1**

4401 **4** *½* **Dubai Dynamo**[7] 1688 8-9-9 **92** .... PJMcDonald 11 — 96
(Ruth Carr) *hld up: pushed along over 2f out: hdwy over 1f out: kpt on fnl f: nrst fin* **8/1**[3]

041- **5** *1* **Ginger Jack**[203] 6881 6-9-0 **86** .... RaulDaSilva(3) 1 — 88+
(Geoffrey Harker) *hld up last: shkn up and stdy hdwy whn nt clr run over 1f out to ins fnl f: nvr nr ldrs* **8/1**[3]

65-0 **6** *hd* **Bancnuanaheireann (IRE)**[28] 1235 6-9-6 **89** .... AndrewMullen 7 — 90
(Michael Appleby) *hld up in midfield: hdwy on outside to ld over 2f out: hdd over 1f out: sn outpcd* **10/1**

3-21 **7** *nse* **Snow Trooper**[12] 1583 5-9-2 **85** .... KierenFallon 3 — 86
(Dean Ivory) *hld up: pushed along and effrt over 2f out: hdwy over 1f out: no imp fnl f: eased nr fin* **9/4**[1]

0-00 **8** *½* **Muffin McLeay (IRE)**[17] 1485 5-9-0 **88** .... LMcNiff(5) 2 — 88
(David Barron) *hld up: n.m.r and lost grnd on ins 3f out: hdwy over 1f out: no imp* **11/1**

10-0 **9** *3 ¼* **Desert Creek (IRE)**[11] 1599 7-8-5 **79** ....(p) ShirleyTeasdale(5) 8 — 72
(David Nicholls) *t.k.h: led to over 2f out: sn btn* **40/1**

44-3 **10** *1 ¼* **Invincible Hero (IRE)**[36] 1113 6-8-6 **78** .... NeilFarley(3) 6 — 68
(Declan Carroll) *dwlt: hld up: hdwy on outside over 2f out: rdn and wknd over 1f out* **14/1**

0-02 **11** *8* **Xilerator (IRE)**[7] 1688 6-9-8 **91** .... AdrianNicholls 12 — 73
(David Nicholls) *t.k.h early: chsd ldr tl wknd over 2f out: eased whn no ch fnl f* **20/1**

1m 42.02s (0.62) **Going Correction** +0.275s/f (Good) — **11** Ran SP% **117.6**
Speed ratings (Par 107): **107,103,103,102,101 101,101,100,97,96 88**
Tote Swingers: 1&2 £6.50, 1&3 £19.50, 2&3 £20.80 CSF £49.61 CT £606.17 TOTE £3.10: £1.60, £3.50, £3.80; EX 53.00 Trifecta £294.20 Pool: £1,661.93 - 4.23 winning units..
Owner High Hopes Partnership **Bred** Patrick Fahey **Trained** Nawton, N Yorks
■ Stewards' Enquiry : Raul Da Silva 14-day ban: failed to take all reasonable and permissable measures to obtain best possible placing (Jun 14-27)
Kieren Fallon two-day ban: failed to ride out 6th place (11-13 May)

FOCUS
Rail on bend from back straight to home straight moved out 5m adding 12yds to races on Round course. There was a decent gallop on here once Desert Creek went to the front and that suited the winner.

1841 AT THE RACES H'CAP — 2m
2:55 (2:55) (Class 2) (0-105,96) 4-Y-0+
£15,562 (£4,660; £2,330; £1,165; £582; £292) **Stalls** High

Form — RPR

221- **1** **Ardlui (IRE)**[92] 7522 5-9-11 **95** .... NeilCallan 3 — 101
(Alan King) *pressed ldr: led over 3f out: rdn and hrd pressed fnl f: hld on gamely* **9/2**[2]

16-1 **2** *nk* **Lady Kashaan (IRE)**[27] 1273 4-9-3 **91** .... RobertWinston 5 — 96+
(Alan Swinbank) *prom: nt clr run and swtchd lft over 2f out: drvn and chsd wnr over 1f out: kpt on wl fnl f: jst hld* **4/1**[1]

-413 **3** *1 ½* **Lexington Bay (IRE)**[14] 1547 5-8-11 **81** ....(p) TonyHamilton 2 — 85
(Richard Fahey) *trckd ldrs: drvn over 2f out: kpt on ins fnl f* **14/1**

430- **4** *1* **Dazinski**[217] 6493 7-9-3 **87** .... TedDurcan 10 — 89
(Mark H Tompkins) *in tch on outside: drvn over 2f out: hung rt: kpt on fr over 1f out: nt pce to chal* **20/1**

000- **5** *2 ¼* **Montaff**[196] 7051 7-9-1 **85** .... SamHitchcott 6 — 85
(Mick Channon) *hld up: pushed along over 3f out: hdwy over 1f out: nrst fin* **12/1**

210- **6** *½* **Party Line**[168] 7689 4-9-4 **92** .... KierenFallon 9 — 91
(Mark Johnston) *hld up in tch: hdwy to chse ldrs over 3f out: sn rdn: no ex over 1f out* **8/1**[3]

162/ **7** *2 ¼* **Manyriverstocross (IRE)**[22] 5823 8-9-11 **95** .... GrahamLee 4 — 92
(Alan King) *hld up: pushed along 3f out: no imp fr 2f out* **4/1**[1]

640- **8** *nse* **Good Morning Star (IRE)**[177] 7510 4-9-6 **94** .... FrannyNorton 7 — 91
(Mark Johnston) *prom: drvn over 3f out: outpcd fnl 2f* **20/1**

41-2 **9** *6* **Moidore**[27] 1273 4-9-2 **90** .... MichaelO'Connell 1 — 79
(John Quinn) *led at modest gallop: rdn and hdd over 3f out: wkd 2f out* **4/1**[1]

000- **10** *26* **Crackentorp**[182] 7396 8-9-12 **96** .... DavidAllan 11 — 54
(Tim Easterby) *hld up: rdn along over 3f out: struggling fnl 2f: t.o* **33/1**

3m 36.74s (4.94) **Going Correction** +0.275s/f (Good)
WFA 4 from 5yo+ 4lb — **10** Ran SP% **116.1**
Speed ratings (Par 109): **98,97,97,96,95 95,94,94,91,78**
Tote Swingers: 1&2 £4.10, 1&3 £5.60, 2&3 £8.40 CSF £22.11 CT £233.32 TOTE £4.20: £2.30, £1.30, £2.50; EX 25.20 Trifecta £226.50 Pool: £1,451.61 - 4.80 winning units..
Owner Thomas Barr **Bred** Sunderland Holdings Ltd **Trained** Barbury Castle, Wilts

FOCUS
The top weight weighed in 9lb below the ceiling for the race. The early pace wasn't hectic.

1842 RIPONBET YANKEE (S) STKS — 1m 1f 170y
3:30 (3:31) (Class 6) 3-4-Y-0 — **£2,587** (£770; £384; £192) **Stalls** Low

Form — RPR

1252 **1** **Shearian**[5] 1712 3-8-11 **62** .... GrahamLee 5 — 65
(Tony Carroll) *midfield on ins: hdwy to ld over 1f out: rdn and r.o wl fnl f* **11/4**[2]

353- **2** *1* **Idyllic Star (IRE)**[234] 5950 4-9-5 **61** ....(p) NeilCallan 9 — 57
(Bernard Llewellyn) *t.k.h: cl up: led 3f out to over 1f out: kpt on same pce ins fnl f* **2/1**[1]

3 3 **Munro Bagger (IRE)**[24] 4-9-10 0 MichaelO'Connell 3 56
(John Quinn) *in tch: hdwy and cl up over 2f out: sn rdn: outpcd ins fnl f* **11/2**

-052 4 ½ **Ceekay's Girl**[24] 1332 3-7-9 43 (p) JoeyHaynes(7) 1 47
(Mrs K Burke) *prom: rdn over 2f out: one pce fr over 1f out* **20/1**

3254 5 1 **Availed Speaker (IRE)**[10] 1603 4-9-3 58 LauraBarry(7) 11 53
(Richard Fahey) *midfield on outside: effrt over 2f out: edgd rt and outpcd over 1f out* **4/1**[3]

5-00 6 1 **Feeling Good**[10] 1603 4-9-7 52 PaulPickard(3) 7 51
(Brian Ellison) *missed break: bhd tl styd on fr 2f out: nvr rchd ldrs* **20/1**

0600 7 3½ **Gunner Will (IRE)**[10] 1603 4-9-7 53 (v[1]) DavidSimmonson(7) 6 48
(Paul Midgley) *hld up: rdn over 2f out: sme hdwy over 1f out: nvr able to chal* **33/1**

4-60 8 1¾ **Mad For Fun (IRE)**[37] 1104 4-9-0 45 (v[1]) ShirleyTeasdale(5) 13 35
(Paul Midgley) *t.k.h: led after 2f: hdd 3f out: rdn and wknd wl over 1f out* **40/1**

0-66 9 6 **By A Wiska**[4] 1747 3-8-7 52 (b[1]) PJMcDonald 12 25
(Ann Duffield) *hld up towards rr: drvn along over 3f out: btn fnl 2f* **25/1**

000- 10 8 **Windsor Rose (IRE)**[145] 7974 3-8-3 50 ow1 FrannyNorton 10
(Mark Brisbourne) *t.k.h: hld up: rdn over 3f out: btn 2f out* **25/1**

0-0 11 19 **Miss Bossy Boots**[21] 1389 4-9-5 0 RoystonFfrench 2
(Tracy Waggott) *t.k.h: led 2f: cl up tl rdn and wknd wl over 2f out* **33/1**

2m 8.21s (2.81) **Going Correction** +0.275s/f (Good)
WFA 3 from 4yo 17lb **11** Ran SP% **120.9**
Speed ratings (Par 101): **99,98,95,95,94 93,91,89,84,78 63**
Tote Swingers: 1&2 £5.90, 1&3 £7.10, 2&3 £21.00 CSF £8.08 TOTE £4.00: £2.30, £1.10, £1.50; EX 10.90 Trifecta £49.10 Pool: £1,118.92 - 17.08 winning units..Winner sold to Mr D. Tate for £6,000. Idyllic Star was bought by Mr Keith Dalgleish for £6,000.
Owner A W Carroll **Bred** Minehart Developments Ltd **Trained** Cropthorne, Worcs

FOCUS
Plenty failed to settle off a moderate gallop in this seller.

1843 RIPONBET PATENT CONDITIONS STKS 1m 4f 10y
4:05 (4:05) (Class 3) 4-Y-O+
£8,092 (£2,423; £1,211; £605; £302; £152) **Stalls** Low

Form RPR

343- 1 **Voodoo Prince**[168] 7689 5-8-9 97 GrahamLee 2 93
(Ed Dunlop) *prom: smooth hdwy to ld 2f out: rdn and hung rt appr fnl f: kpt on wl last 100yds* **11/8**[1]

-225 2 1 **Northside Prince (IRE)**[14] 1536 7-8-10 85 ow1 RobertWinston 6 92
(Alan Swinbank) *t.k.h: pressed ldr: effrt and ev ch over 2f out: sn rdn: kpt on ins fnl f: hld towards fin* **12/1**

3-00 3 ½ **Be Perfect (USA)**[77] 585 4-8-8 92 AdrianNicholls 1 90
(David Nicholls) *trckd ldrs: effrt and edgd lft 2f out: rdn and edgd rt over 1f out: kpt on fnl f: hld towards fin* **16/1**

012/ 4 1¼ **Highland Castle**[575] 6498 5-8-9 103 TedDurcan 5 88+
(David Elsworth) *hld up in tch: pushed along and hdwy 2f out: kpt on fnl f: bttr for r* **5/1**[3]

333- 5 ½ **Cardinal Walter (IRE)**[213] 6576 4-8-12 91 KierenFallon 7 91+
(David Simcock) *plld hrd: hld up in tch: hdwy to ld over 6f out: rdn and hdd 2f out: outpcd fnl f* **9/4**[2]

2364 6 1¼ **The Bull Hayes (IRE)**[9] 1643 7-8-9 89 BarryMcHugh 4 85
(Tony Coyle) *in tch: rdn and outpcd over 2f out: sme late hdwy: nvr able to chal* **33/1**

7 1 **Fort Belvedere**[739] 9001 5-8-9 0 TomEaves 3 84
(Keith Dalgleish) *led to over 6f out: rdn over 2f out: wknd over 1f out* **16/1**

2m 39.09s (2.39) **Going Correction** +0.275s/f (Good)
WFA 4 from 5yo+ 1lb **7** Ran SP% **111.9**
Speed ratings (Par 107): **103,102,102,101,100 100,99**
Tote Swingers: 1&2 £3.60, 1&3 £13.50, 2&3 £18.30 CSF £18.53 TOTE £2.40: £2.20, £1.80; EX 13.80 Trifecta £75.50 Pool: £1,539.80 - 15.29 winning units..
Owner Lord Derby **Bred** Stanley Estate And Stud Co **Trained** Newmarket, Suffolk

FOCUS
There wasn't much pace on early, but things picked up once Cardinal Walter went to the front down the back.

1844 RIPONBET PLACE6 H'CAP 5f
4:40 (4:40) (Class 4) (0-80,80) 3-Y-O **£5,175** (£1,540; £769; £384) **Stalls** High

Form RPR

10-2 1 **The Art Of Racing (IRE)**[17] 1482 3-9-7 **79** (t) HarryBentley 3 82+
(Olly Stevens) *trckd ldrs gng wl: hdwy to ld ent fnl f: sn drvn: hld on wl* **5/4**[1]

15- 2 hd **Angus Og**[199] 6984 3-9-1 **80** ow1 ConorHarrison(7) 4 82+
(Mrs K Burke) *hld up in tch on outside: rdn and hdwy over 1f out: kpt on fnl f: jst hld* **13/2**[3]

3214 3 ¾ **Silca's Dream**[15] 1524 3-8-6 **69** CharlesBishop(5) 9 68
(Mick Channon) *led stands' rail: rdn over 1f out: hdd ent fnl f: kpt on same pce* **9/1**

30-5 4 ½ **Deepest Blue**[14] 1539 3-8-12 **70** DavidAllan 1 68
(Declan Carroll) *chsd ldr: rdn over 1f out: kpt on same pce ins fnl f* **22/1**

1431 5 4 **Windforpower (IRE)**[57] 847 3-8-8 **66** (be) RoystonFfrench 2 49
(Tracy Waggott) *prom: rdn over 2f out: wknd over 1f out* **16/1**

140- 6 2 **Lord Avonbrook**[228] 6121 3-8-5 **70** RowanScott(7) 7 46
(Andrew Crook) *towards rr: drvn along over 2f out: sn n.d* **40/1**

41- 7 2¾ **Royal Acquisition**[154] 7855 3-8-5 **70** GaryPhillips(7) 8 36
(Robert Cowell) *dwlt: sn prom: rdn 1/2-way: wknd over 1f out* **13/2**[3]

50-0 8 2¾ **Lucky Lodge**[2] 1791 3-8-1 **66** RobertDodsworth(7) 5 22
(Mel Brittain) *bhd and sn outpcd: nvr on terms* **28/1**

53-4 9 6 **Queen Flush (IRE)**[14] 1539 3-8-9 **67** AdrianNicholls 6
(David Nicholls) *towards rr on ins: n.m.r over 4f out: rdn and outpcd whn nt clr run over 1f out: sn btn* **9/2**[2]

1m 1.33s (1.33) **Going Correction** +0.275s/f (Good) **9** Ran SP% **115.4**
Speed ratings (Par 100): **100,99,98,97,91 88,83,79,69**
Tote Swingers: 1&2 £3.10, 1&3 £3.50, 2&3 £7.30 CSF £9.59 CT £52.09 TOTE £1.90: £1.80, £1.60, £1.80; EX 10.00 Trifecta £77.20 Pool: £3,697.49 - 35.89 winning units..
Owner Qatar Racing Limited **Bred** Carrigbeg Stud & David Powell **Trained** Chiddingfold, Surrey
■ Stewards' Enquiry : David Allan three-day ban: careless riding (11, 13, 14 May)

FOCUS
A smaller field than the opening maiden over this trip, so they all stayed on the stands' side.

1845 RIPONBET FORECAST MAIDEN STKS 1m 1f 170y
5:15 (5:15) (Class 5) 3-Y-O **£3,234** (£962; £481; £240) **Stalls** Low

Form RPR

2- 1 **Havana Cooler (IRE)**[185] 7332 3-9-5 0 KierenFallon 5 77+
(Luca Cumani) *hld up in tch: hdwy to ld 2f out: sn rdn and hung rt: hrd pressed fnl f: kpt on* **6/4**[1]

3- 2 ¾ **Heroine Required (FR)**[197] 7033 3-9-0 0 AdamBeschizza 2 70+
(William Haggas) *led and sn clr: rdn and hdd 2f out: rallied fnl f: hld towards fin* **13/8**[2]

2 3 2¾ **Harbinger Lass**[8] 1671 3-9-0 0 SamHitchcott 7 65
(Mick Channon) *chsd ldrs: effrt whn n.m.r and outpcd over 2f out: rallied fnl f: nt rch first two* **7/1**[3]

4 1½ **Aramist (IRE)** 3-9-5 0 RobertWinston 4 67
(Alan Swinbank) *hld up: rdn over 3f out: styd on fnl f: nrst fin* **16/1**

5 ½ **Cupertino** 3-9-5 0 PJMcDonald 6 66+
(Kevin Ryan) *t.k.h: chsd clr ldr: ev ch over 2f out: sn rdn: wknd fnl f* **10/1**

4 6 shd **No Win No Fee**[17] 1481 3-9-5 0 AndrewMullen 1 66
(Michael Appleby) *prom: rdn and outpcd over 2f out: n.d after* **28/1**

7 43 **Bannockburn Boy** 3-9-5 0 DavidAllan 3
(Tim Easterby) *s.i.s: bhd: struggling over 3f out: sn lost tch: t.o* **22/1**

2m 7.13s (1.73) **Going Correction** +0.275s/f (Good) **7** Ran SP% **113.4**
Speed ratings (Par 98): **104,103,101,100,99 99,65**
CSF £4.12 TOTE £1.90: £2.60, £1.10; EX 4.20 Trifecta £9.20 Pool: £1,637.82 - 133.01 winning units..
Owner Leonidas Marinopoulos **Bred** Ammerland Verwaltung Gmbh **Trained** Newmarket, Suffolk

FOCUS
There was a good gallop on here and that suited the winner.
T/Plt: £59.40 to a £1 stake. Pool: £80,046.48 - 982.69 winning tickets. T/Qpdt: £6.80 to a £1 stake. Pool: £4,888.90 - 531.80 winning tickets. RY

1808 SANDOWN (R-H)
Saturday, April 27

OFFICIAL GOING: Jumps courses - good (chs 7.4; hdl 7.2); flat course - good (good to soft in places; 7.5) changing to good to soft after race 6 (4.25)
Wind: Medium; across Weather: Overcast

1846 BET365 GORDON RICHARDS STKS (GROUP 3) 1m 2f 7y
3:15 (3:15) (Class 1) 4-Y-O+
£34,026 (£12,900; £6,456; £3,216; £1,614; £810) **Stalls** Low

Form RPR

2/1- 1 **Al Kazeem**[357] 1855 5-9-0 117 JamesDoyle 3 117+
(Roger Charlton) *hld up in tch: swtchd lft and clsd to press ldrs gng wl 2f out: rdn to ld 1f out: r.o wl and in command whn edgd rt u.p towards fin* **9/4**[1]

150- 2 1 **Thomas Chippendale (IRE)**[224] 6245 4-9-0 111 TomQueally 7 115
(Sir Henry Cecil) *hld up in tch in last pair: hdwy on outer to press ldrs 3f out: rdn ent fnl 2f: 3rd and kpt on same pce u.p ins fnl f: wnt 2nd towards fin* **3/1**[2]

202- 3 nk **Ektihaam (IRE)**[213] 6575 4-9-0 112 DaneO'Neill 6 115
(Roger Varian) *t.k.h: chsd ldr tl led after 2f: rdn jst over 2f out: hdd 1f out: kpt on same pce u.p and hld whn hmpd and lost 2nd towards fin* **10/3**[3]

3022 4 4½ **Burano (IRE)**[9] 1643 4-9-0 103 JimmyFortune 4 105
(Brian Meehan) *led for 2f: chsd ldrs after tl drvn and outpcd wl over 1f out: no threat to ldrs after but plugged on* **25/1**

001- 5 nk **Dick Doughtywylie**[225] 6202 5-9-0 89 WilliamBuick 8 104
(John Gosden) *chsd ldrs: wnt 2nd 8f out: rdn and pressing ldr over 2f out: no ex and btn 1f out: wknd ins fnl f* **16/1**

0/1- 6 ½ **Eagles Peak**[213] 6576 5-9-0 99 RyanMoore 5 103+
(Sir Michael Stoute) *t.k.h: hld up wl in tch: rdn and effrt over 3f out: outpcd and btn 2f out: wl hld after* **7/2**

034 7 21 **Mister Green (FR)**[5] 1715 7-9-0 60 JemmaMarshall 2 61
(David Flood) *in tch in rr tl 3f out: sn bhd* **150/1**

2m 10.18s (-0.32) **Going Correction** +0.30s/f (Good) **7** Ran SP% **111.5**
Speed ratings (Par 113): **113,112,111,108,108 107,90**
toteswingers 1&2 £2.40, 1&3 £2.50, 2&3 £3.20 CSF £8.77 TOTE £2.90: £1.70, £2.60; EX 9.40 Trifecta £24.20 Pool: £2,642.62 - 81.76 winning units..
Owner D J Deer **Bred** D J And Mrs Deer **Trained** Beckhampton, Wilts

FOCUS
Home bend at outermost configuration which added about 8yds to distances on Round course. An interesting running of this Group 3 contest and, while the bare form is nothing special, this was a pleasing comeback from the winner. He did not need to repweat his best form of last year, the second and third setting the standard.

1847 BET365 H'CAP 1m 2f 7y
4:25 (4:26) (Class 3) (0-95,87) 3-Y-O
£9,337 (£2,796; £1,398; £699; £349; £175) **Stalls** Low

Form RPR

2-11 1 **Spillway**[10] 1614 3-9-2 **82** TomQueally 8 92
(Eve Johnson Houghton) *stdd after s: hld up in last pair: rdn and gd hdwy on outer over 2f out: led over 1f out: styd on wl ins fnl f: rdn out* **5/1**[3]

1-22 2 1 **Carry On Sydney**[28] 1250 3-9-4 **84** RyanMoore 3 92
(Richard Hannon) *hld up in tch in last trio: rdn and effrt jst over 2f out: chalng and edgd rt ent fnl f: r.o but nt pce of wnr fnl 100yds* **11/4**[1]

231- 3 3 **Nichols Canyon**[195] 7081 3-9-5 **85** WilliamBuick 2 90+
(John Gosden) *in tch: chsd ldng pair 8f out: hmpd and swtchd lft 3f out: pressing ldrs but unable qck whn short of room ent fnl f: styd on same pce after* **11/4**[1]

150- 4 ¾ **Pasaka Boy**[203] 6871 3-9-7 **87** MatthewDavies 4 87
(Jonathan Portman) *hld up in last pair: rdn and outpcd over 2f out: rallied and stdy on ins fnl f: no threat to ldrs* **33/1**

031- 5 nk **Dashing Star**[171] 7636 3-9-3 **83** LiamKeniry 7 85+
(David Elsworth) *t.k.h: chsd ldr after 1f: hung lft 3f out: pressed ldrs 2f out: outpcd and n.m.r jst over 1f out: wl hld and one pce fnl f* **4/1**[2]

313- 6 nk **Linguine (FR)**[175] 7554 3-9-5 **85** DaneO'Neill 5 84
(Seamus Durack) *t.k.h: chsd ldr for 1f: in tch after: rdn and outpcd 3f out: rallied ins fnl f: kpt on* **20/1**

14-2 7 nk **Royal Skies (IRE)**[35] 1145 3-9-0 **80** JimCrowley 1 78
(Mark Johnston) *led: rdn over 2f out: hdd over 1f out: sn outpcd and btn jst ins fnl f: wknd fnl 100yds* **11/2**

2m 13.62s (3.12) **Going Correction** +0.40s/f (Good) **7** Ran SP% **113.1**
Speed ratings (Par 102): **103,102,99,99,98 98,98**
toteswingers 1&2 £3.30, 1&3 £3.10, 2&3 £2.60 CSF £18.71 CT £44.37 TOTE £5.80: £2.80, £1.90; EX 20.40 Trifecta £75.00 Pool: £3,111.63 - 31.07 winning units..
Owner Mrs Virginia Neale **Bred** Cherry Park Stud **Trained** Blewbury, Oxon

FOCUS
This race was run in a heavy shower and afterwards the going was changed to good to soft all over. Usually a good handicap and the first two continued to progress. The sixth is a decent guide.

1848 POKER AT BET365.COM H'CAP — 1m 14y
4:55 (4:59) (Class 2) (0-105,99) 4-Y-0+

£15,562 (£4,660; £2,330; £1,165; £582; £292) **Stalls** Low

Form — RPR

030- **1** — **Directorship**[175] 7556 7-8-12 **90** .... DaneO'Neill 7 — 97
(Patrick Chamings) *hld up in tch in rr: rdn and effrt over 2f out: hdwy u.p over 1f out: edgd rt but styd on strly fnl f to ld last stride* **12/1**

060- **2** *shd* **Spa's Dancer (IRE)**[184] 6674 6-8-13 **91** .... TomQueally 6 — 98
(James Eustace) *t.k.h: chsd ldr tl jnd ldr 5f out: stl on bit 2f out: rdn to ld ins fnl f: drvn and kpt on tl hdd last stride* **6/1**[3]

-201 **3** *1* **Maverik**[17] 1485 5-9-0 **92** .... JimCrowley 2 — 96
(Ralph Beckett) *led: jnd 5f out: rdn over 2f out: drvn and hdd ins fnl f: one pce fnl 100yds* **7/1**

100- **4** *1* **Forgotten Hero (IRE)**[189] 7240 4-8-11 **89** ....[1] RyanMoore 4 — 92
(Charles Hills) *t.k.h: hld up wl in tch in midfield: rdn and effrt over 2f out: styd on u.p to press ldrs ins fnl f: carried rt and eventually short of room and hmpd fnl 50yds* **9/4**[1]

113- **5** *3/4* **Fire Ship**[175] 7558 4-9-7 **99** .... WilliamBuick 8 — 99
(William Knight) *chsd ldrs: rdn over 2f out: drvn and stl cl enough 1f out: carried rt and one pce ins fnl f: hld whn nt clr run fnl 50yds* **9/2**[2]

413- **6** *4 1/2* **Jake's Destiny (IRE)**[175] 7556 4-9-1 **93** ....(t) PatCosgrave 5 — 83
(George Baker) *awkward leaving stalls: in tch in midfield: rdn and effrt over 2f out: sn drvn and outpcd: wknd 1f out* **6/1**[3]

00-5 **7** *8* **Mister Music**[14] 1545 4-9-6 **98** .... PatDobbs 3 — 70
(Richard Hannon) *in tch in last trio: rdn and struggling over 2f out: bhd over 1f out* **8/1**

106- **8** *2 1/2* **Embankment**[118] 8296 4-8-5 **83** .... KirstyMilczarek 1 — 49
(William Jarvis) *hld up in tch in rr: rdn and no prog 3f out: sn struggling: bhd over 1f out* **20/1**

1m 44.7s (1.40) **Going Correction** +0.40s/f (Good) — **8** Ran SP% **113.6**
Speed ratings (Par 109): **109,108,107,106,106 101,93,91**
toteswingers 1&2 £11.90, 1&3 £12.30, 2&3 £8.30 CSF £80.37 CT £546.20 TOTE £15.70: £3.20, £2.00, £2.00; EX 106.90 Trifecta £1568.10 Pool: £3,789.84 - 1.81 winning units..
Owner Mrs R Lyon,Mrs P Hayton,P R Chamings **Bred** Mrs D O Joly **Trained** Baughurst, Hants

FOCUS
An ordinary handicap for the class. The runner-up and third helped set the pace, while the winner was held up. Few looked well treated and the winner is rated to last May's C&D form.

1849 CASINO AT BET365.COM FLAT V JUMP JOCKEYS H'CAP — 1m 14y
5:30 (5:33) (Class 4) (0-80,79) 4-Y-0+ — **£6,469** (£1,925; £962; £481) **Stalls** Low

Form — RPR

0/10 **1** — **Carazam (IRE)**[14] 1538 6-10-9 **70** .... DaneO'Neill 13 — 80
(William Jarvis) *hld up in last pair: rdn and hdwy on outer wl over 1f out: str run fnl f to ld fnl 75yds: gng away at fin* **9/1**

020- **2** *3/4* **Charitable Act (FR)**[184] 7359 4-11-0 **75** .... RyanMoore 9 — 83
(Gary Moore) *t.k.h: chsd ldrs: rdn to ld over 1f out: kpt on u.p tl hdd and no ex fnl 75yds* **4/1**[1]

310- **3** *1 1/2* **Restaurateur (IRE)**[159] 7789 4-11-3 **78** .... JimmyFortune 7 — 83
(Andrew Balding) *stdd s: hld up in last trio: gd hdwy on inner over 2f out: swtchd lft and drvn to chse ldrs 1f out: one pce ins fnl f* **8/1**

4111 **4** *1* **Ancient Greece**[69] 702 6-11-2 **77** ....(t) WayneHutchinson 4 — 80
(George Baker) *wl in tch in midfield: rdn and effrt to chse ldr 2f out: no ex u.p 1f out: one pce and lost 2 pls fnl f* **9/1**

32/4 **5** *hd* **Key Appointment**[19] 1423 4-11-3 **78** .... JoeTizzard 11 — 80
(Paul Cole) *wl in tch in midfield: effrt u.p to chse ldrs wl over 1f out: edgd rt and styd on same pce fnl f* **8/1**

360- **6** *1 1/2* **Red Seventy**[156] 7823 4-11-2 **77** .... TomQueally 1 — 76
(Harry Dunlop) *mde most tl rdn and hdd over 1f out: no ex and wknd ins fnl f* **16/1**

-222 **7** *nk* **Spring Tonic**[37] 1106 4-10-13 **74** .... WilliamBuick 12 — 72
(Simon Dow) *racd off the pce towards rr: rdn and effrt on outer ent fnl 2f: no real imp tl styd on ins fnl f* **13/2**[3]

1365 **8** *1* **Caldercruix (USA)**[11] 1599 6-11-2 **77** ....(v) RichardJohnson 14 — 73
(James Evans) *chsd ldrs: rdn and hdwy u.p to chse ldrs 2f out: no ex ent fnl f: wknd ins fnl f* **16/1**

111- **9** *2 1/2* **Grand Liaison**[194] 7108 4-10-10 **71** .... JamesDoyle 8 — 61
(John Berry) *racd off the pce in last trio: rdn and effrt jst over 2f out: kpt on but no real imp: nvr trbld ldrs* **9/2**[2]

33-0 **10** *1 1/4* **Fabled City (USA)**[64] 759 4-11-4 **79** ....(t) NickScholfield 2 — 66
(Clive Cox) *t.k.h: hld up wl in tch in midfield: rdn and unable qck 2f out: wknd ent fnl f* **10/1**

0610 **11** *4* **Greyfriarschorista**[12] 1583 6-10-13 **74** .... SamTwiston-Davies 3 — 52
(Tom Keddy) *chsd ldrs tl lost pl qckly 2f out: bhd 1f out* **25/1**

0306 **12** *2* **Ajeeb (USA)**[24] 1327 5-11-1 **76** ....(v) AidanColeman 6 — 49
(Michael Scudamore) *t.k.h: chsd ldr: jnd ldr 5f out tl rdn and lost pl 2f out: bhd 1f out* **16/1**

1m 45.87s (2.57) **Going Correction** +0.40s/f (Good) — **12** Ran SP% **124.3**
Speed ratings (Par 105): **103,102,100,99,99 98,97,96,94,93 89,87**
toteswingers 1&2 £14.90, 1&3 £21.40, 2&3 £10.20 CSF £47.14 CT £313.54 TOTE £13.90: £4.50, £2.00, £2.60; EX 68.90 Trifecta £548.60 Pool: £2,179.70 - 2.97 winning units..
Owner Dr J Walker **Bred** Yeomanstown Stud **Trained** Newmarket, Suffolk

FOCUS
A competitive handicap, which was strong run. The winner was on a good mark based on his old Irish form.
T/Jkpt: Not won. T/Plt: £117.00 to a £1 stake. Pool of £175,574.31 - 1,094.95 winning units
T/Qpdt: £18.10 to a £1 stake. Pool of £11,812.90 - 480.80 winning units SP

1633 CHANTILLY (R-H)
Saturday, April 27

OFFICIAL GOING: Turf: good: polytrack: standard

1850a PRIX DU CHEMIN DES OFFICIERS (CONDITIONS) (3YO COLTS & GELDINGS) (POLYTRACK) — 1m 1f 110y
7:00 (12:00) 3-Y-0 — **£6,504** (£2,601; £1,951; £1,300; £650)

RPR

1 — **Masiyann (FR)**[20] 3-8-11 0 .... Christophe-PatriceLemaire 8 — 76
(A De Royer-Dupre, France) **26/5**[3]

2 *2* **Taboule**[26] 3-8-6 0 .... NicolasLarenaudie(5) 3 — 72
(G Martin, Austria) **11/1**

3 *snk* **Murillo (FR)** 3-8-9 0 .... FlavienPrat 2 — 70
(J-M Beguigne, France) **41/1**

4 *snk* **Court Politics**[188] 3-8-11 0 .... Pierre-CharlesBoudot 7 — 71
(A Fabre, France) **43/10**[2]

5 *3/4* **Rodion Raskolnikov (FR)**[129] 8176 3-8-9 0...... ChristopheSoumillon 4 — 68
(C Lerner, France) **2/1**[1]

6 *hd* **Stormy Coast (FR)** 3-8-9 0 ....(p) ThierryThulliez 5 — 67
(N Clement, France) **25/1**

7 *1/2* **Livento (FR)**[16] 3-8-11 0 .... AnthonyCrastus 6 — 68
(A Bonin, France) **16/1**

8 *1 3/4* **Barsam (FR)**[36] 3-8-9 0 .... StephanePasquier 11 — 63
(P Bary, France) **53/10**

9 *3 1/2* **Azabitmour (FR)**[16] 1511 3-8-11 0 .... JohanVictoire 9 — 58
(John Best) *broke fast towards outside: racd in cl 2nd on settling: chal for ld 2f out: sn rdn: no ex: qckly fdd* **13/1**

10 *nk* **Ally Pally (FR)**[183] 3-9-0 0 .... IoritzMendizabal 1 — 60
(G Botti, France) **16/1**

1m 58.95s (118.95) — **10** Ran SP% **117.7**
WIN (incl. 1 euro stake): 6.20. PLACES: 2.50, 3.40, 8.60. DF: 34.60. SF: 63.20.
Owner H H Aga Khan **Bred** S.A. Aga Khan **Trained** Chantilly, France

1851 - 1861a (Foreign Racing) - See Raceform Interactive

1435 GOWRAN PARK (R-H)
Sunday, April 28

OFFICIAL GOING: Soft (yielding to soft in places)

1862a IRISH STALLION FARMS EUROPEAN BREEDERS FUND VICTOR MCCALMONT MEMORIAL STKS (LISTED RACE) — 1m 1f 100y
4:40 (4:41) 3-Y-0+ — **£26,422** (£7,723; £3,658; £1,219)

RPR

1 — **Caponata (USA)**[217] 6518 4-9-12 110 .... PatSmullen 4 — 111+
(D K Weld, Ire) *chsd ldrs in 4th: prog into 3rd early in st: drvn along to ld over 1f out: pushed out to maintain narrow advantage* **5/4**[1]

2 *1/2* **We'll Go Walking (IRE)**[20] 1439 3-8-9 .... KevinManning 6 — 105+
(J S Bolger, Ire) *attempted to make all: strly pressed and hdd over 1f out: rallied gamely: clr of remainder* **11/4**[2]

3 *8* **Aloof (IRE)**[205] 6855 4-9-12 107 .... WayneLordan 7 — 94
(David Wachman, Ire) *racd in 3rd tl chsd ldr in 2nd 5f out: pushed along and dropped to 3rd over 1f out: sn no ex w principals* **6/1**[3]

4 *2 1/4* **Cleofila (IRE)**[29] 1257 4-9-9 96 .... RonanWhelan 3 — 86
(J S Bolger, Ire) *slowly away and racd in rr: jnd rr of field 4f out: strly drvn and no imp fr 2f out: kpt on one pce into 4th ins fnl f* **25/1**

5 *2 1/2* **Euphrasia (IRE)**[20] 1438 4-9-9 81 .... GaryCarroll 2 — 81
(Joseph G Murphy, Ire) *trckd ldr in 2nd tl dropped to 3rd 5f out: rdn and no ex ent fnl 2f: passed for 4th ins fnl f* **16/1**

6 *12* **Coolibah (IRE)**[175] 7582 3-8-9 93 .... DeclanMcDonogh 1 — 54
(Charles O'Brien, Ire) *w.w in 5th: pushed along home turn: sn no imp* **8/1**

7 *3 1/2* **Starbright (IRE)**[35] 1166 3-8-9 99 .... ChrisHayes 5 — 47
(Kevin Prendergast, Ire) *racd in 6th: pushed along and dropped to 7th over 3f out: sn no ex* **9/1**

2m 4.17s (-2.83)
WFA 3 from 4yo 15lb — **7** Ran SP% **116.2**
CSF £5.00 TOTE £1.70: £1.02, £2.30; DF 6.50.
Owner K Abdullah **Bred** Juddmonte Farms Inc **Trained** The Curragh, Co Kildare

FOCUS
Two very good fillies lit up an otherwise mundane card and it is likely we will hear plenty more of the pair as the season progresses.

1863 - 1864a (Foreign Racing) - See Raceform Interactive

1563 CAPANNELLE (R-H)
Sunday, April 28

OFFICIAL GOING: Turf: good to soft

1865a PREMIO PARIOLI SISAL MATCHPOINT (GROUP 3) (3YO COLTS) (TURF) — 1m
3:50 (12:00) 3-Y-0 — **£48,780** (£21,463; £11,707; £5,853)

RPR

1 — **Best Tango (ITY)**[178] 7513 3-9-2 0 .... UmbertoRispoli 13 — 103
(Gianluca Bietolini, Italy) *trckd ldr on outer: shkn up and led 2f out: sn rdn and r.o: asserted fnl 50yds* **44/5**

2 *1/2* **Fairy Nayef**[21] 3-9-2 0 .... DarioVargiu 6 — 102
(B Grizzetti, Italy) *broke wl: led: hdd 2f out: rallied u.p: pressed ldr thrght fnl f: no ex fnl 50yds* **14/5**[1]

3 *1 1/4* **Lodovico Il Moro (IRE)** 3-9-2 0 .... MickaelBarzalona 12 — 99
(L Riccardi, Italy) *midfield on outer: shkn up and hdwy over 3f out: wnt 3rd under 2f out: sn rdn: kpt on at one pce fnl f: edgd rt last 75yds* **66/10**

4 *hd* **Porsenna (IRE)**[189] 3-9-2 0 .... DPerovic 4 — 99
(S Botti, Italy) *midfield on inner: hrd rdn 3f out: styd on ins fnl 1 1/2f: nt pce to chal* **214/10**

5 *3/4* **Nabucco (GER)**[21] 3-9-2 0 .... LManiezzi 1 — 97
(R Rohne, Germany) *hld up towards rr: swtchd outside and rdn 2 1/2f out: no immediate imp: styd on u.p fr over 1f out: nrest at fin* **79/10**

6 *1/2* **Bastiani (IRE)** 3-9-2 0 .... SSulas 11 — 96
(L Racco, Italy) *hld up towards rr: hdwy fr 2f out: styd on fnl f tl hmpd by eventual 3rd fnl 75yds: nt rcvr* **105/10**

7 *2* **Zamiro (IRE)** 3-9-2 0 .... PierantonioConvertino 5 — 91
(Sebastiano Latina, Italy) *broke wl and trckd ldrs: 3rd and rdn 3f out but no imp: wknd fnl f* **204/10**

8 *3* **Lord Unfuwain**[141] 3-9-2 0 .... IoritzMendizabal 3 — 84
(M Sardelli, Italy) *followed ldr on inner: rdn and nt qckn over 2 1/2f out: wknd fnl f* **31/1**

9 *3/4* **Never Say Never (ITY)**[178] 7513 3-9-2 0 .... CColombi 2 — 83
(S Botti, Italy) *midfield: rdn and nt qckn 2f out: eased whn btn appr fnl f* **8/1**

10 *2 1/2* **Dark Dream (IRE)**[35] 3-9-2 0 .... MEsposito 8 — 77
(Agostino Affe', Italy) *v.s.a and detached in last: jnd rr of field 1/2-way: hdwy on outside over 3f out: sn rdn and no further imp over 2f out: wknd and eased fnl 1 1/2f* **39/10**[2]

11 *2* **Battier (ITY)** 3-9-2 0 CFiocchi 7 72
(L Polito, Italy) *trckd ldng gp: lost pl and midfield appr 1/2-way: wknd fr 2f out* **89/1**
12 *1* **Gordol Du Mes (USA)**[35] 3-9-2 0 GBietolini 10 70
(Gianluca Bietolini, Italy) *midfield: rdn and no imp over 2f out: sn btn: eased fnl f* **42/10**[3]
13 *6* **Freetown (USA)**[140] 3-9-2 0 FabioBranca 9 56
(S Botti, Italy) *hld up towards rr: short-lived effrt 2f out but sn btn: heavily eased fnl f* **125/10**
1m 38.4s (-1.40) **13** Ran SP% **141.1**
WIN (incl. 1 euro stake): 9.82. PLACES: 2.69, 1.65, 2.37. DF: 32.45.
Owner Elia Tanghetti **Bred** Elia Tanghetti **Trained** Italy

1866a PREMIO REGINA ELENA (GROUP 3) (3YO FILLIES) (TURF) 1m
4:25 (12:00) 3-Y-0 **£48,780** (£21,463; £11,707; £5,853)

RPR
1 **Dancer Destination** 3-8-11 0 DarioVargiu 11 100
(B Grizzetti, Italy) *prom on inner: rdn over 3f out: r.o to chal ent fnl f: led ins fnl 150yds: drvn and asserted cl home* **7/1**[3]
2 *1 ½* **Grand Treasure (IRE)**[175] 7585 3-8-11 0 IoritzMendizabal 3 97
(G Colella, Italy) *midfield: smooth hdwy on to heels of ldrs over 2f out: swtchd lft and rdn over 1 1/2f out: r.o to go 2nd post* **79/10**
3 *nse* **Clorofilla (IRE)**[14] 1563 3-8-11 0 LManiezzi 7 97
(Marco Gasparini, Italy) *trckd ldr: led gng wl 3f out: rdn 2f out: strly pressed ent fnl f: hdd ins fnl 150yds: no ex and lost 2nd cl home* **127/10**
4 *1* **Collusiva (IRE)**[21] 1418 3-8-11 0 MickaelBarzalona 4 95
(G Botti, France) *hld up towards rr on inner: rdn and hdwy fr over 3f out: r.o to go 4th fnl strides: nvr able to chal* **71/10**
5 *shd* **Lear Oile Oile (IRE)**[148] 3-8-11 0 GiuseppeCannarella 5 94
(S Cannavo', Italy) *midfield on inner: rdn over 2f out: 3rd and ev ch ent fnl f: kpt on but dropped to 5th fnl strides* **7/1**[3]
6 *1 ½* **Shirley's Kitten (USA)**[49] 3-8-11 0 GBietolini 8 91
(Gianluca Bietolini, Italy) *midfield: rdn 3f out: kpt on steadily but nvr able to chal* **9/2**[2]
7 *½* **Punta Stella (IRE)**[14] 1561 3-8-11 0 UmbertoRispoli 19 90
(S Kobayashi, France) *hld up towards rr: rdn 3f out: r.o: gd late hdwy but n.d* **2/1**[1]
8 *½* **Mangiapregaama (ITY)**[21] 3-8-11 0 GArena 9 89
(B Grizzetti, Italy) *hld up: rdn over 3f out: r.o but n.d* **7/1**[3]
9 *1 ½* **Al Jar (IRE)** 3-8-11 0 SSulas 10 85
(S Sordi, Italy) *prom: rdn and outpcd 3f out: kpt on wout threatening* **35/1**
10 *1 ½* **Night Of Light (IRE)**[49] 3-8-11 0 CFiocchi 12 82
(F Camici, Italy) *midfield: nt clr run 3f out: swtchd lft and rdn over 2f out: kpt on wout ever threatening* **60/1**
11 *hd* **Must Be Me**[201] 6946 3-8-11 0 MKolmarkaj 6 81
(D Grilli, Italy) *midfield: rdn 3f out: outpcd 2f out: plugged on u.p but n.d* **28/1**
12 *4* **Fulgetta (ITY)** 3-8-11 0 PBorrelli 14 72
(Gianluca Bietolini, Italy) *hld up towards rr: rdn over 3f out: no ex over 1f out: eased whn btn* **31/1**
13 *shd* **Avomcic (IRE)**[224] 3-8-11 0 MSanna 20 72
(M Maroni, Italy) *hld up towards rr on outer: rdn 3f out: no ex over 1f out: eased whn btn* **64/1**
14 *½* **Deflection (IRE)**[189] 7285 3-8-11 0 MEsposito 2 71
(S Botti, Italy) *hld up in last: rdn 3f out: kpt on tl no ex and btn ent fnl f: eased* **92/10**
15 *2* **Roman Dream (IRE)**[140] 3-8-11 0 NicolaPinna 17 66
(Giada Ligas, Italy) *prom: rdn over 3f out: no ex and btn 2f out: fdd and eased* **66/1**
16 *2* **Reina Cross (ITY)**[21] 3-8-11 0 CColombi 1 61
(S Botti, Italy) *led: rdn and hdd 3f out: no ex and btn 2f out: fdd and eased* **114/10**
17 *3* **Lady Silvy (IRE)**[21] 3-8-11 0 PierantonioConvertino 16 55
(A Marcialis, Italy) *hld up towards rr: rdn and btn 2f out: nvr a factor* **59/1**
18 *2* **Nina Nosei (IRE)** 3-8-11 0 SDiana 13 50
(M Oppo, Italy) *midfield: rdn and dropped to rr 3f out: sn btn and eased* **99/1**
19 *1 ½* **Dream Can True (IRE)** 3-8-11 0 FabioBranca 18 47
(L Riccardi, Italy) *prom on outer: rdn over 3f out: no ex and btn 2f out: eased and fdd* **159/10**
20 *6* **Dark Woman** 3-8-11 0 DPerovic 15 33
(S Botti, Italy) *midfield on outer: rdn and reminders 4f out: last and btn 2f out: eased and t.o* **248/10**
1m 37.96s (-1.84) **20** Ran SP% **164.2**
WIN (incl. 1 euro stake): 7.98 (Dancer Destination coupled with Mangiapregaama). PLACES: 3.71, 3.38, 4.51. DF: 92.69.
Owner Scuderia Blueberry **Bred** Scuderia Blueberry Srl **Trained** Italy

FRANKFURT (L-H)
Sunday, April 28
OFFICIAL GOING: Turf: soft

1867a FRUHJAHRS-PREIS DES BANKHAUSES METZLER (GROUP 3) (3YO) (TURF) 1m 2f
4:00 (12:00) 3-Y-0
£26,016 (£8,943; £4,471; £2,439; £1,626; £1,219)

RPR
1 **Vif Monsieur (GER)**[178] 3-9-2 0 KClijmans 1 103
(J Hirschberger, Germany) *sn led and mde rest: rdn clr 2f out: styd on strly u.p: readily* **165/10**
2 *2 ½* **Lucky Speed (IRE)** 3-9-2 0 AStarke 3 98
(P Schiergen, Germany) *dwlt: pushed along to rcvr and sn racing in midfield on inner: smooth hdwy fr 3f out: rdn 2f out: wnt 2nd over 1f out: chsd wnr thrght fnl f but no imp* **5/2**[1]
3 *3 ½* **Noble Galileo (GER)**[190] 3-9-2 0 FredericSpanu 5 91
(Mario Hofer, Germany) *prom: rdn over 3f out: outpcd by ldrs over 1f out: swtchd rt ins fnl f and styd on to go 3rd post* **4/1**[2]
4 *nk* **Stellato**[168] 7698 3-9-2 0 EPedroza 7 90
(A Wohler, Germany) *midfield on outer: rdn over 2f out: styd on to go 4th post: nt pce to chal* **54/10**
5 *shd* **Erlkonig (GER)** 3-9-2 0 DPorcu 4 90
(Markus Klug, Germany) *trckd ldr on outer: rdn to chal 2f out: outpcd by wnr over 1f out: styd on but dropped to 5th post* **22/5**[3]
6 *1 ¾* **Empire Hurricane (GER)**[196] 7091 3-9-2 0 RJuracek 8 86
(A Wohler, Germany) *hld up in last pair on inner: rdn over 2f out: styd on steadily but n.d* **115/10**
7 *2 ½* **Orsello (GER)** 3-9-2 0 MrDennisSchiergen 6 81
(N Sauer, Germany) *midfield: rdn and outpcd 3f out: plugged on but n.d* **5/1**
8 *10* **Balu** 3-9-2 0 ADeVries 9 61
(J Hirschberger, Germany) *hld up in last: rdn and sme hdwy fr 3f out: no ex and btn ins fnl f: eased* **91/10**
9 *½* **Flamingo Star (GER)**[168] 7698 3-9-2 0 RobertHavlin 2 60
(R Dzubasz, Germany) *prom on inner: rdn and lost pl 3f out: last and toiling 2f out: sn btn: eased* **19/2**
2m 14.1s (5.53) **9** Ran SP% **132.5**
WIN (incl. 10 euro stake): 175. PLACES: 41, 18, 21. SF: 489.
Owner F Van Gorp **Bred** Frau Ursula Herberts **Trained** Germany

KYOTO (R-H)
Sunday, April 28
OFFICIAL GOING: Turf: firm

1868a TENNO SHO (SPRING) (GRADE 1) (4YO+) (TURF) 2m
7:40 (12:00) 4-Y-O+ **£963,686** (£383,794; £238,016; £141,904; £93,656)

RPR
1 **Fenomeno (JPN)**[36] 4-9-2 0 MasayoshiEbina 6 123
(Hirofumi Toda, Japan) *settled in midfield: stdy hdwy fr over 3f out: rdn to chal on turn into st: led 2f out: edgd rt and qckng clr: styd on strly: drvn out: readily* **26/5**[2]
2 *1 ¼* **Tosen Ra (JPN)**[77] 5-9-2 0 YutakaTake 1 117
(Hideaki Fujiwara, Japan) *midfield: stdy hdwy fr over 3f out: rdn to chal on turn into st: wnt 2nd over 1f out: styd on ins fnl f but no real imp on wnr* **126/10**[3]
3 *2* **Red Cadeaux**[29] 1269 7-9-2 0 GeraldMosse 13 115
(Ed Dunlop) *midfield: hdwy fr over 3f out: rdn on turn into st: wnt 3rd jst ins fnl f: styd on wl but nt pce to chal* **28/1**
4 *1 ¾* **Admire Rakti (JPN)**[71] 5-9-2 0 YasunariIwata 7 113
(Tomoyuki Umeda, Japan) *midfield: rdn and towards rr 3f out: styd on to go 4th wl ins fnl f: fin wl but n.d* **207/10**
5 *nk* **Gold Ship (JPN)**[42] 4-9-2 0 HiroyukiUchida 8 117
(Naosuke Sugai, Japan) *hld up towards rr early: prog into midfield over 6f out: rdn and rapid hdwy on outer over 3f out: outpcd by ldrs on turn into st: sltly hmpd and swtchd lft over 1f out: styd on to go 5th cl home* **30/100**[1]
6 *¾* **Jaguar Mail (JPN)**[71] 9-9-2 0 (b) KeitaTosaki 4 112
(Noriyuki Hori, Japan) *hld up towards rr: rdn and hdwy on wd outside over 3f out: hung rt and sltly hmpd rival over 1f out: 5th ent fnl f: styd on but dropped to 6th cl home* **47/1**
7 *2 ½* **Meiner Kitz (JPN)**[36] 10-9-2 0 (b) CristianDemuro 5 109
(Sakae Kunieda, Japan) *midfield: rdn over 3f out: styd on to go 7th post: nt pce to chal* **117/1**
8 *nse* **Tokai Paradise (JPN)**[28] 6-9-2 0 YuichiShibayama 16 109
(Hidetaka Tadokoro, Japan) *trckd ldr: led 3f out: rdn and strly pressed on turn into st: hdd 2f out: no ex ent fnl f: fdd and dropped to 8th post* **136/1**
9 *2* **Desperado (JPN)**[42] 5-9-2 0 SuguruHamanaka 3 107
(Akio Adachi, Japan) *hld up in last: rdn 3f out: plugged on ins fnl 2f but nvr a factor* **243/10**
10 *nse* **Forgettable (JPN)**[42] 7-9-2 0 (b) RyujiWada 12 107
(Yasutoshi Ikee, Japan) *midfield: rdn over 3f out: sn outpcd: plugged on but nvr a factor* **71/1**
11 *1 ¾* **Tokai Trick (JPN)**[42] 11-9-2 0 HiroshiKitamura 11 105
(Kenji Nonaka, Japan) *hld up: rdn in rr 3f out: plugged on and sme late hdwy but nvr a factor* **197/1**
12 *2* **Red Davis (JPN)**[183] 5-9-2 0 YuichiKitamura 17 103
(Hidetaka Otonashi, Japan) *midfield: rdn over 3f out: outpcd and btn over 2f out: fdd* **128/1**
13 *¾* **Universal Bank (JPN)**[217] 5-9-2 0 YugaKawada 9 102
(Hiroyoshi Matsuda, Japan) *prom: rdn 3f out: sn lost pl: no ex and btn ent fnl f: fdd* **187/1**
14 *nk* **Meisho Kampaku (JPN)**[36] 6-9-2 0 ShinjiFujita 10 102
(Yoshiyuki Arakawa, Japan) *hld up towards rr: rdn and hdwy on outer 3f out: sn outpcd: no ex and btn ent fnl f: fdd* **230/1**
15 *dist* **Capote Star (JPN)**[36] 4-9-2 0 RyoTakakura 15
(Yoshito Yahagi, Japan) *prom: rdn and lost pl over 4f out: no ex and btn 2f out: eased and t.o* **50/1**
16 *5* **Mousquetaire (JPN)**[36] 5-9-2 0 YuichiFukunaga 18
(Yasuo Tomomichi, Japan) *trckd ldr: lost pl over 3f out: sn in rr and btn: eased and t.o* **47/1**
17 *½* **Copano Jingu (JPN)**[28] 8-9-2 0 KyosukeKokubun 14
(Toru Miya, Japan) *prom: lost pl over 4f out: rdn in rr and btn over 2f out: eased and t.o* **327/1**
18 *dist* **Satono Shuren (JPN)**[722] 5-9-2 0 HidekiMiyuki 2
(Akira Murayama, Japan) *led: set strr pce: 10 l clr 5f out: rapidly diminishing advantage and hdd 3f out: rdn and immediately btn: wknd and dropped to last: eased and tailed rt off* **123/1**
3m 14.2s (194.20)
WFA 4 from 5yo+ 4lb **18** Ran SP% **124.9**
PARI-MUTUEL (all including 100 ypj stake): WIN 620; SHOW 300, 650, 1540; DF 3190; SF 6500.
Owner Sunday Racing Co Ltd **Bred** Oiwake Farm **Trained** Japan

1799 LONGCHAMP (R-H)

Sunday, April 28

OFFICIAL GOING: Turf: good

1869a PRIX VANTEAUX (GROUP 3) (3YO FILLIES) (TURF) 1m 1f 55y

1:30 (12:00) 3-Y-0 **£32,520** (£13,008; £9,756; £6,504; £3,252)

RPR

1 **Esoterique (IRE)**[19] 3-9-0 0 .... MaximeGuyon 6 112
(A Fabre, France) *racd in cl 2nd: rdn 1 1/2 out: chal 250yds out: led 1f out: r.o wl: wnt clr: comf* **13/8**[1]

2 1 ½ **Silasol (IRE)**[203] 6909 3-9-0 0 .... OlivierPeslier 3 109
(C Laffon-Parias, France) *broke fast: sent to ld: rdn 1 1/2f out: hdd 1f out: r.o wl: jst hld 2nd fnl strides* **9/4**[2]

3 shd **Pearlside (FR)**[35] 3-9-0 0 .... StephanePasquier 2 109+
(M Delcher Sanchez, France) *hld up in 5th: rdn 1 1/2f out: r.o wl u.p ent fnl f: fin strly: jst missed 2nd* **14/1**

4 shd **Parle Moi (IRE)**[178] 3-9-0 0 .... ChristopheSoumillon 1 109+
(P Bary, France) *racd in 3rd on ins: rdn 1 1/2f out: relegated to 4th 1f out: rallied and r.o strly fnl 50yds: jst missed 3rd* **9/2**[3]

5 hd **Ighraa (IRE)**[21] 1418 3-9-0 0 .... AntoineHamelin 5 108+
(F-H Graffard, France) *hld up at rr of field: swtchd to outside of field 1 1/2f out: r.o wl fnl f: jst missed 4th* **14/1**

6 7 **Aquatinta (GER)**[24] 1358 3-9-0 0 .... FabriceVeron 4 93
(H-A Pantall, France) *prom early: 4th ent st: rdn over 1 1/2f out: no ex: fdd: eased fnl 100yds* **7/1**

1m 53.72s (-1.58) **6 Ran SP% 112.9**

WIN (incl. 1 euro stake): 2.20. PLACES: 1.20, 1.50. SF: 5.00.

Owner Baron Edouard De Rothschild **Bred** Societe Civile De L'Ecurie De Meautry **Trained** Chantilly, France

1870a PRIX GANAY (GROUP 1) (4YO+) (TURF) 1m 2f 110y

2:40 (12:00) 4-Y-0+ **£139,365** (£55,756; £27,878; £13,926; £6,975)

RPR

1 **Pastorius (GER)**[190] 7239 4-9-2 0 .... OlivierPeslier 3 121
(Mario Hofer, Germany) *racd 3rd: qcknd wl 2f out: r.o strly to ld 250yds out: styd on wl* **7/2**[3]

2 1 **Maxios**[21] 1420 5-9-2 0 .... StephanePasquier 2 119
(J E Pease, France) *racd in midfield: qcknd wl 2f out: chal and led 1 1/2f out: hdd 250yds out: r.o wl* **9/2**

3 1 **Dunaden (FR)**[29] 1268 7-9-2 0 .... JamieSpencer 5 117+
(M Delzangles, France) *hld up at rr of field: swtchd arnd field 2f out: r.o wl: fin strly: clst at fin* **9/1**

4 2 **Giofra**[29] 1267 5-8-13 0 .... ChristopheSoumillon 1 110
(A De Royer-Dupre, France) *racd in 4th on ins: rdn and r.o wl 1 1/2f out: no ex ins fnl f: nt hrd rdn whn ch gone fnl 50yds* **11/4**[1]

5 ¾ **Saonois (FR)**[140] 8043 4-9-2 0 .... AntoineHamelin 8 112
(J-P Gauvin, France) *hld up towards rr on ins: gd prog 2f out: r.o fnl f wout threatening ldrs* **8/1**

6 ½ **Ridasiyna (FR)**[177] 7549 4-8-13 0 .... Christophe-PatriceLemaire 6 108
(M Delzangles, France) *hld up towards rr: plld hrd: rdn 1 1/2f out: r.o fnl f* **3/1**[2]

7 1 ¾ **Haya Landa (FR)**[21] 1420 5-8-13 0 .... FranckBlondel 7 104
(Mme L Audon, France) *racd in 7th on ins: rdn early in st: no ex: styd on one pce fnl f* **40/1**

8 1 ¾ **Point Blank (GER)**[14] 1564 5-9-2 0 .... (p) StefanieHofer 4 104
(Mario Hofer, Germany) *sn led: stl in front 2f out: hdd 1 1/2f out: no ex: styd on one pce fnl f* **100/1**

9 10 **Mandistana (FR)**[176] 4-8-13 0 .... GregoryBenoist 9 81
(M Delzangles, France) *racd in 2nd: rdn 2f out: no ex: sn wknd* **50/1**

2m 8.39s (-1.81) **9 Ran SP% 118.6**

WIN (incl. 1 euro stake): 7.20 (Pastorius coupled with Point Blank. PLACES: 2.70, 2.30, 3.20. DF: 15.40. SF: 37.00.

Owner Stall Antanando **Bred** Franz Prinz Von Auersperg Et Al **Trained** Germany

FOCUS

With two pacemakers in the field, one for Ridasiyna and the other for Pastorius, there promised to be a good pace on here, but in the event they set no more than a fair gallop.

1871a PRIX DE BARBEVILLE (GROUP 3) (4YO+) (TURF) 1m 7f 110y

3:10 (12:00) 4-Y-0+ **£32,520** (£13,008; £9,756; £6,504; £3,252)

RPR

1 **Last Train**[57] 4-8-13 0 .... MaximeGuyon 1 109+
(A Fabre, France) *settled in 2nd: clsd on ldr bef st: rdn 2f out: r.o wl ent fnl f: chal eventual 3rd 100yds out: led 50yds out: all out to jst hold on* **3/1**[2]

2 hd **Verema (FR)**[29] 1263 4-8-11 0 .... Christophe-PatriceLemaire 6 108+
(A De Royer-Dupre, France) *racd in midfield: qcknd wl 1 1/2f out: r.o strly to chal ldrs wl ins fnl f: wnt 2nd cl home: jst failed to get up on line* **10/3**[3]

3 snk **Domeside**[28] 7-8-11 0 .... AnthonyCrastus 2 104+
(M Delcher Sanchez, France) *racd in 3rd: clsd on ldrs bef st: rdn and qcknd wl to chal 1 1/2f out: led u.str.p 250yds out: r.o wl: hdd 50yds out: styd on wl: lost 2nd cl home* **20/1**

4 1 ½ **Ivory Land (FR)**[224] 6297 6-9-5 0 .... StephanePasquier 4 110+
(A De Royer-Dupre, France) *hld up towards rr: gd prog bhd ldrs 1 1/2f out: short of room to chal 1f out: styd on wl* **9/2**

5 ¾ **Les Beaufs (FR)**[19] 1457 4-9-5 0 .... JulienGuillochon 3 116+
(Mme V Seignoux, France) *broke slowly: sn mde up grnd and rdn to ld: rdn 2f out: u.p and hdd 250yds out: r.o tl fdd fnl 50yds* **7/4**[1]

6 3 ½ **Silver Valny (FR)**[164] 7735 7-9-1 0 .... ThomasMessina 5 104+
(Mlle M-L Mortier, France) *hld up at rr of field: wl bhd ent fnl 2f: sme late prog fnl f* **12/1**

3m 30.44s (8.94)

WFA 4 from 6yo+ 3lb **6 Ran SP% 115.1**

WIN (incl. 1 euro stake): 4.30. PLACES: 2.80, 2.30. SF: 13.60.

Owner K Abdullah **Bred** Juddmonte Farms Ltd **Trained** Chantilly, France

787 SHA TIN (R-H)

Sunday, April 28

OFFICIAL GOING: Turf: good

1872a AUDEMARS PIGUET QEII CUP (GROUP 1) (3YO+) (TURF) 1m 2f

9:35 (12:00) 3-Y-0+

£633,836 (£244,638; £111,199; £63,542; £36,536; £22,239)

RPR

1 **Military Attack (IRE)**[35] 5-9-0 0 .... TommyBerry 3 123
(J Moore, Hong Kong) *midfield: rdn 2f out: r.o to chal over 1f out: led ent fnl f: drvn clr: readily* **105/10**

2 1 ¾ **California Memory (USA)**[63] 787 7-9-0 0 .... MatthewChadwick 1 119
(A S Cruz, Hong Kong) *midfield on inner: swtchd out and rdn 2f out: lugged lft and bmpd rival over 1f out: w ldrs and ev ch ent fnl f: sn outpcd by wnr: kpt on and jst hld on for 2nd* **13/1**

3 shd **Eishin Flash (JPN)**[28] 6-9-0 0 .... MircoDemuro 13 119+
(Hideaki Fujiwara, Japan) *dropped in fr wd draw and hld up in last: stl gng wl and looking for room 2f out: swtchd ins and rdn over 1f out: r.o to go 3rd cl home: almost snatched 2nd post* **10/1**

4 nk **Sajjhaa**[29] 1267 6-8-10 0 .... SilvestreDeSousa 8 114+
(Saeed bin Suroor) *dwlt: sn rcvrd and racd in midfield: rdn over 2f out: drifted rt u.p: r.o to go 3rd wl ins fnl f: dropped to 4th cl home* **54/10**[3]

5 ¾ **Akeed Mofeed**[42] 4-9-0 0 .... DouglasWhyte 4 117
(R Gibson, Hong Kong) *t.k.h early: prom on inner: rdn to chal 2f out: led 1 1/2f out: hdd ent fnl f: fdd and dropped to 5th* **19/10**[1]

6 ½ **Ambitious Dragon (NZ)**[42] 7-9-0 0 .... (b) ZacPurton 6 117+
(A T Millard, Hong Kong) *hld up in midfield: rdn and hdwy fr 2f out: bmpd by rival and hmpd over 1f out: r.o but nvr able to chal* **2/1**[2]

7 ½ **Thumbs Up (NZ)**[21] 9-9-0 0 .... BrettPrebble 9 115
(C Fownes, Hong Kong) *hld up in last pair: rdn in last 2f out: styd on down wd outside to go 7th cl home but n.d* **54/1**

8 1 **Igugu (AUS)**[29] 1267 6-8-10 0 .... ADelpech 10 109
(M F De Kock, South Africa) *prom: rapid hdwy to ld 6f out: rdn and hdd 1 1/2f out: no ex and btn ins fnl f: fdd* **36/1**

9 shd **Irian (GER)**[35] 7-9-0 0 .... ODoleuze 5 113
(J Moore, Hong Kong) *hld up: hdwy on outer over 3f out: rdn 2f out: styd on but nt pce to chal* **54/1**

10 ¾ **Wrath of Fire (NZ)**[35] 6-9-0 0 .... TyeAngland 7 111
(D Cruz, Hong Kong) *hld up towards rr: rdn 2f out: sn outpcd: plugged on but nvr a factor* **191/1**

11 ½ **Treasure Beach**[29] 1269 5-9-0 0 .... CO'Donoghue 12 110
(M F De Kock, South Africa) *midfield: rdn 3f out: outpcd 2f out: plugged on* **182/1**

12 ¾ **Zaidan (USA)**[35] 5-9-0 0 .... (t) RFourie 14 109
(A S Cruz, Hong Kong) *got across fr wdst draw and trckd ldr: rdn and brief effrt to chal 2f out: no ex and btn ent fnl f: fdd* **35/1**

13 5 ½ **Ashkiyr (FR)**[42] 4-9-0 0 .... [1] WCMarwing 11 98
(J Moore, Hong Kong) *sent forward and sn led: hdd 6f out and trckd ldr: rdn 2f out: sn no ex and btn: fdd* **29/1**

14 5 ¾ **Crackerjack (FR)**[70] 4-9-0 0 .... (t) ASuborics 2 86
(D Cruz, Hong Kong) *midfield on inner: rdn 2f out: last and btn ent fnl f: eased* **301/1**

2m 2.15s (0.75) **14 Ran SP% 122.2**

PARI-MUTUEL (all including HK$10 stake): WIN 111.50; PLACE 27.00, 37.00, 27.50; DF 595.50.

Owner Mr & Mrs Steven Lo Kit Sing **Bred** P E Banahan **Trained** Hong Kong

FOCUS

This looked an average Group 1. The pace slowed quite a bit down the far side so they were well bunched turning in.

1778 LINGFIELD (L-H)

Monday, April 29

OFFICIAL GOING: Standard

Wind: medium, across Weather: dry, bright spells

1873 YOUR GUIDE TO LINGFIELD AT LINGFIELDRACECOURSETIPS.CO.UK H'CAP 1m (P)

4:55 (4:56) (Class 6) (0-60,60) 4-Y-0+ **£1,940** (£577; £288; £144) **Stalls** High

Form RPR

0-42 1 **Bold Ring**[4] 1783 7-8-13 **52** .... MarcHalford 6 61
(Edward Creighton) *chsd ldng pair tl wnt 2nd 2f out: pushed along to ld 1f out: drvn and r.o wl ins fnl f* **8/1**

06/2 2 nk **Piccolo Mondo**[18] 1498 7-9-7 **60** .... TomEaves 7 68
(Philip Hide) *led: rdn wl over 1f out: hdd 1f out: sustained duel w wnr after: r.o but a jst hld* **3/1**[1]

-415 3 2 ¾ **Strategic Action (IRE)**[62] 805 4-9-3 **56** .... RobertHavlin 3 58
(Linda Jewell) *hld up wl in tch in midfield: rdn and effrt 2f out: drvn to chse ldng pair 1f out: no ex and one pce fnl f* **6/1**[3]

-304 4 1 ¼ **Custom House (IRE)**[19] 1474 5-8-9 **48** .... (b) KirstyMilczarek 5 47
(John E Long) *dwlt: sn pushed along and rcvrd to chse ldr: lost 2nd and drvn 2f out: nt qckn over 1f out: outpcd fnl f* **8/1**

54-4 5 ½ **Rock Anthem (IRE)**[117] 13 9-9-6 **59** .... KieranO'Neill 4 57
(Mike Murphy) *wl in tch in midfield: rdn and effrt 2f out: drvn and unable qck over 1f out: one pce fnl f* **4/1**[2]

000- 6 1 **Zammy**[129] 8205 4-8-11 **50** .... SilvestreDeSousa 2 46
(Michael Wigham) *t.k.h: hld up in last pair: rdn and effrt ent fnl 2f: no prog* **4/1**[2]

1502 7 hd **Indian Violet (IRE)**[19] 1473 7-9-3 **56** .... (p) LiamKeniry 1 51
(Zoe Davison) *broke wl: stdd bk and hld up in rr: rdn and effrt 2f out: swtchd lft over 1f out: no prog* **8/1**

1m 38.28s (0.08) **Going Correction** +0.025s/f (Slow) **7 Ran SP% 112.6**

Speed ratings (Par 101): **100,99,96,95,95 94,94**

toteswingers 1&2 £3.70, 1&3 £10.10, 2&3 £2.70 CSF £31.19 TOTE £8.90: £3.80, £2.20; EX 30.40 Trifecta £79.00 Pool: £969.51 - 9.19 winning units..

Owner Miss Charlotte Harper **Bred** J A Pickering & T Pears **Trained** Wormshill, Kent

■ Edward Creighton's first winner back after a year out of training.

The Form Book Flat, Raceform Ltd, Compton, RG20 6NL.

FOCUS
This low-grade handicap looked open beforehand. The pace was steady and nothing became involved from the rear.

1874 LINGFIELDPARK.CO.UK CLASSIFIED STKS 6f (P)
5:25 (5:26) (Class 6) 3-Y-O £2,045 (£603; £302) Stalls Low

Form RPR
650- 1 **Elusive Gold (IRE)**[179] 7506 3-9-0 65 SebSanders 7 67
(J W Hills) *hld up in rr: rdn and effrt over 1f out: r.o wl to ld fnl 100yds: gng away at fin* 9/2[2]
-222 2 1 1/4 **Carina Palace**[12] 1616 3-9-0 65 FergusSweeney 5 63
(Jamie Osborne) *hld up in midfield: effrt u.p over 1f out: chal ins fnl f: outpcd by wnr fnl 75yds* 2/1[1]
60-5 3 shd **Whatever You Do (IRE)**[18] 1499 3-9-0 65 RyanMoore 2 63
(Richard Hannon) *dwlt: pushed along and sn rcvrd to chse ldng pair: rdn ent fnl 2f: styd on to press ldrs ins fnl f: one pce fnl 75yds* 6/1[3]
3340 4 3/4 **Half Turn**[7] 1712 3-9-0 63 SteveDrowne 6 60
(Luke Dace) *stdd s: hld up in last pair: rdn and effrt over 1f out: pressed ldrs ins fnl f: styd on same pce fnl 100yds* 16/1
560 5 2 1/4 **Visual Aspect**[26] 1323 3-9-0 62 AdamKirby 3 55+
(Dean Ivory) *led and clr for 2f: stdd gallop tl rdn and qcknd clr again 2f out: edgd rt and hdd fnl 100yds: sn btn and eased* 16/1
624 6 3/4 **Irish Dream (IRE)**[27] 1299 3-9-0 65 SilvestreDeSousa 4 57+
(Mark Johnston) *chsd ldr: rdn ent fnl 2f: styd on to press ldrs whn squeezed for room and bdly hmpd ins fnl f: nt rcvr and eased after* 2/1[1]

1m 12.73s (0.83) **Going Correction** +0.025s/f (Slow) 6 Ran SP% **110.9**
Speed ratings (Par 96): **95,93,93,92,89 88**
toteswingers 1&2 £1.50, 1&3 £3.70, 2&3 £2.10 CSF £13.60 TOTE £4.60: £2.60, £1.50; EX 11.70 Trifecta £64.70 Pool: £1905.26 - 22.07 winning units..
Owner Gold, Clark, McDonagh, Stopp & Tofts **Bred** Airlie Stud **Trained** Upper Lambourn, Berks

FOCUS
A typically tight classified stakes on the ratings.

1875 VINES BMW MAIDEN FILLIES' STKS 6f (P)
5:55 (5:55) (Class 5) 3-Y-O £2,726 (£805; £402) Stalls Low

Form RPR
00- 1 **Reqaaba**[194] 7160 3-9-0 0 PaulHanagan 4 80+
(John Gosden) *taken down early: in tch in midfield: rdn and outpcd by ldrs 2f out: hung lft over 1f out: str run fnl f to ld fnl 50yds: gng away at fin* 5/4[1]
420- 2 1 1/2 **Bountybeamadam**[275] 4574 3-9-0 78 JamesDoyle 2 72
(George Baker) *led and set stdy gallop: rdn and qcknd 2f out: hdd and no ex fnl 50yds* 7/1
42- 3 2 1/2 **Little Choosey**[141] 8044 3-9-0 0 AdamKirby 6 64
(Clive Cox) *chsd ldr: rdn and qcknd clr w ldr 2f out: btn and lost 2nd ins fnl f: wknd fnl 100yds* 2/1[2]
0- 4 1/2 **Speronella**[166] 7705 3-9-0 0 RobertHavlin 3 62+
(Hughie Morrison) *dwlt: hld up in last pair: wnt 4th but outpcd by ldrs 2f out: no threat to ldrs but kpt on ins fnl f* 6/1[3]
5 8 **High Tone** 3-9-0 0 KieranO'Neill 5 37
(Dean Ivory) *stdd s: in tch in last pair: rdn and struggling whn wd bnd 2f out: sn wknd* 25/1
0- 6 6 **Pastoral Symphony**[220] 6438 3-9-0 0 SteveDrowne 1 18
(John Best) *t.k.h: chsd ldrs: rdn and lost pl over 2f out: lost tch over 1f out* 66/1

1m 13.31s (1.41) **Going Correction** +0.025s/f (Slow) 6 Ran SP% **109.9**
Speed ratings (Par 95): **91,89,85,85,74 66**
toteswingers 1&2 £1.80, 1&3 £1.10, 2&3 £1.40 CSF £10.27 TOTE £1.70: £1.20, £1.90; EX 6.60 Trifecta £16.00 Pool: £2067.22 - 96.62 winning units..
Owner Hamdan Al Maktoum **Bred** Manor Farm Stud (rutland) **Trained** Newmarket, Suffolk

FOCUS
An ordinary fillies' maiden, but a taking display from the winner.

1876 LINGFIELD PARK SUPPORTS BHEST MAIDEN FILLIES' STKS 1m (P)
6:25 (6:27) (Class 5) 3-Y-O+ £2,726 (£805; £402) Stalls High

Form RPR
1 **Dream Wild** 3-8-9 0 RyanMoore 12 79+
(Sir Michael Stoute) *in tch: rdn and clsd on ldrs jst over 2f out: chsd wnr over 1f out: led fnl 150yds: r.o wl and gng on at fin* 1/1[1]
5- 2 1 3/4 **Sunbula (USA)**[187] 7329 3-8-9 0 PaulHanagan 8 74
(Charles Hills) *led and set stdy gallop: rdn and qcknd 2f out: hdd fnl 150yds: no ex but hld on for 2nd* 9/4[2]
4- 3 1/2 **Clear Pearl (USA)**[217] 6534 3-8-9 0 JamieSpencer 3 73
(Ed Vaughan) *t.k.h: hld up wl in tch: rdn and effrt on inner to chal jst over 1f out: no ex and one pce fnl 150yds* 8/1[3]
4 3 3/4 **Sultanah Heyam** 3-8-9 0 AdamBeschizza 4 64+
(William Haggas) *s.i.s: hld up in rr of main gp: stl plenty to do and rdn over 1f out: styd on wl ins fnl f: nvr trbld ldrs* 8/1[3]
0- 5 1/2 **Point Of Control**[165] 7720 3-8-9 0 LiamKeniry 2 63+
(Michael Bell) *hld up in tch towards rr of main gp: rdn and no imp 2f out: swtchd rt over 1f out: styd on wl ins fnl f: nvr trbld ldrs* 50/1
-30 6 nse **Moma Lee**[11] 1640 3-8-9 0 NickyMackay 1 63
(John Gosden) *chsd ldrs: rdn wl over 1f out: no ex and btn 1f out: wknd ins fnl f* 16/1
0 7 1/2 **Dama De La Noche (IRE)**[10] 1666 3-8-9 0 SeanLevey 7 61
(Richard Hannon) *hld up in tch towards rr of main gp: hdwy u.p on inner over 1f out: no ch w ldrs but kpt on ins fnl f* 25/1
8 3 1/4 **A Good Year (IRE)** 3-8-9 0 SteveDrowne 9 54
(J W Hills) *s.i.s: flashing tail and in tch towards rr of main gp: rdn and hung rt bnd 2f out: n.d after* 33/1
0/ 9 hd **Princess Spirit**[558] 6954 4-9-9 0 MarcHalford 10 57?
(Edward Creighton) *hld up in tch in midfield: rdn and unable qck whn edgd lft over 1f out: wknd 1f out* 100/1
46 10 1/2 **Maughami**[17] 1518 3-8-4 0 TobyAtkinson(5) 11 52
(Marco Botti) *t.k.h: chsd ldr tl over 1f out: sn drvn and no ex: fdd fnl f* 25/1
0- 11 4 1/2 **Jessica's Gold**[235] 5970 4-9-2 0 DanielMuscutt(7) 6 45
(Christine Dunnett) *t.k.h: hld up in tch in midfield: rdn and struggling 2f out: wknd over 1f out* 100/1
12 20 **Fleur De Fortune** 6-9-2 0 JoeyHaynes(7) 5
(Eric Wheeler) *slowly away and sn detached in last and much tail flashing: clsd and in tch 1/2-way: lost tch over 2f out: t.o* 100/1

1m 38.22s (0.02) **Going Correction** +0.025s/f (Slow)
WFA 3 from 4yo+ 14lb 12 Ran SP% **124.4**
Speed ratings (Par 100): **100,98,97,94,93 93,92,89,89,89 84,64**
toteswingers 1&2 £1.50, 1&3 £2.70, 2&3 £2.40 CSF £3.33 TOTE £2.00: £1.10, £1.10, £2.70; EX 5.50 Trifecta £12.70 Pool: £2280.93 - 134.30 winning units..
Owner K Abdullah **Bred** Juddmonte Farms Ltd **Trained** Newmarket, Suffolk

FOCUS
An interesting maiden which featured a wide range of abilities.

1877 LINGFIELD PARK OWNERS GROUP H'CAP 1m 5f (P)
6:55 (6:56) (Class 6) (0-60,58) 4-Y-O+ £2,045 (£603; £302) Stalls Low

Form RPR
-202 1 **Highly Likely (IRE)**[63] 788 4-9-6 58 JamesDoyle 4 64
(Steve Woodman) *chsd ldr: rdn and wnt clr w ldr ent fnl 2f: led ins fnl f: forged ahd fnl 50yds: styd on* 5/1[2]
050- 2 1 1/2 **Gladstone (IRE)**[180] 7479 5-8-11 48 LiamKeniry 1 52
(Polly Gundry) *chsd ldrs: 3rd and outpcd by ldng pair jst over 2f out: swtchd rt over 1f out and then hung rt: styd on wl fnl 100yds: snatched 2nd last stride* 6/1[3]
4230 3 shd **El Libertador (USA)**[35] 1175 7-9-0 58 (b) JoeyHaynes(7) 2 62
(Eric Wheeler) *led: rdn and clr w wnr ent fnl 2f: hdd ins fnl f: no ex and wknd towards fin: lost 2nd last stride* 8/1
0004 4 3 **Rodrigo De Freitas (IRE)**[35] 1175 6-9-1 57 (v) NathanAlison(5) 5 56
(Jim Boyle) *hld up in last quartet: rdn and effrt on outer 3f out: stl plenty to do but styng on whn wd bnd 2f out: styd on wl fnl f: nvr trbld ldrs* 6/1[3]
040- 5 1/2 **Icebreaker Two**[194] 7162 4-9-2 54 KirstyMilczarek 6 52
(John E Long) *in tch in midfield: reminder and rdn 6f out: outpcd over 3f out and looked wl hld over 2f out: rallied u.p over 1f out: styd on wl ins fnl f* 20/1
3-34 6 5 **Glens Wobbly**[4] 1794 5-8-8 45 (p) RichardThomas 10 36
(Jonathan Geake) *chsd ldrs: drvn and outpcd over 2f out: 4th and wl btn over 1f out: wknd fnl f* 16/1
53-4 7 2 **Notabadgirl**[26] 1317 4-9-5 57 NickyMackay 3 45
(Simon Dow) *s.i.s: bhd: no ch but sme hdwy on inner over 1f out: plugged on but n.d* 16/1
-033 8 1 1/2 **Irons On Fire (USA)**[9] 1700 5-8-11 48 RyanMoore 7 34
(Alastair Lidderdale) *chsd ldrs: drvn and outpcd over 2f out: wknd wl over 1f out: fdd ins fnl f* 3/1[1]
4600 9 1 **Here Comes Jeanie**[47] 983 4-8-2 45 NatashaEaton(5) 8 29
(Michael Madgwick) *stdd and dropped in bhd after s: hld up wl off the pce in rr: rdn over 4f out: n.d* 25/1
2330 10 6 **Petersboden**[17] 1520 4-8-7 45 RobertHavlin 9 20
(Michael Blanshard) *chsd ldrs tl rdn and lost pl 3f out: sn wknd* 5/1[2]
000- 11 1 3/4 **The Ploughman**[159] 7811 4-8-7 45 KieranO'Neill 11 17
(John Bridger) *in tch in midfield: drvn and struggling 4f out: sn wknd* 66/1

2m 45.06s (-0.94) **Going Correction** +0.025s/f (Slow)
WFA 4 from 5yo+ 1lb 11 Ran SP% **119.9**
Speed ratings (Par 101): **103,102,102,100,99 96,95,94,94,90 89**
toteswingers 1&2 £6.30, 1&3 £8.70, 2&3 £11.30 CSF £35.16 CT £241.19 TOTE £3.80: £1.60, £2.40, £3.30; EX 62.40 Trifecta £566.90 Pool: £1665.45 - 2.20 winning units..
Owner Mrs Sally Woodman **Bred** Windflower Overseas **Trained** East Lavant, W Sussex

FOCUS
The pace was only steady and few got into this very modest handicap.

1878 LINGFIELD PARK SUPPORTS YOUNG EPILEPSY H'CAP 7f (P)
7:25 (7:26) (Class 4) (0-85,85) 4-Y-O+ £4,690 (£1,395; £697; £348) Stalls Low

Form RPR
0-66 1 **Forceful Appeal (USA)**[18] 1500 5-9-0 78 JamieSpencer 8 86
(Simon Dow) *hld up in tch in midfield: effrt and rdn 2f out: r.o wl u.p ins fnl f to ld towards fin: jst hld on* 8/1[3]
21-2 2 shd **Jack Of Diamonds (IRE)**[23] 1385 4-9-7 85 RobertWinston 1 95+
(Roger Teal) *hld up in tch in midfield: shuffled bk and hmpd ent fnl 2f: swtchd rt and hdwy over 1f out: str run u.p fnl f: jst failed* 11/4[2]
4230 3 1/2 **Haftohaf**[7] 1720 4-8-13 77 (p) MartinHarley 4 83
(Marco Botti) *led: rdn and fnd ex wl over 1f out: kpt on wl u.p tl hdd and no ex towards fin* 8/1[3]
/15- 4 nk **Net Whizz (USA)**[173] 7631 4-9-6 84 RyanMoore 6 90
(Jeremy Noseda) *dwlt: sn rcvrd and chsd ldrs after 2f: rdn and hung lft over 1f out: nt qckn u.p 1f out: styd on same pce fnl 100yds* 5/4[1]
26-1 5 3/4 **Kinglami**[23] 1386 4-8-7 71 SilvestreDeSousa 9 75
(Brian Gubby) *chsd ldrs: rdn wl over 1f out: kpt on tl no ex and lost 3 pls wl ins fnl f* 16/1
00-4 6 1 1/2 **Wilfred Pickles (IRE)**[116] 32 7-8-12 76 IanMongan 11 75
(Jo Crowley) *hld up wl in tch: rdn and effrt on inner to chse ldrs 1f out: no imp and btn fnl 100yds* 25/1
500- 7 1 **Mingun Bell (USA)**[166] 7715 6-9-6 84 LiamKeniry 10 81
(Ed de Giles) *hld up in tch in last trio: swtchd rt and effrt over 1f out: styd on fnl f: nvr trbld ldrs* 50/1
00-0 8 3/4 **Alice's Dancer (IRE)**[16] 1542 4-9-1 82 RaulDaSilva(3) 3 77
(William Muir) *hld up in tch towards rr: c wd and effrt over 1f out: kpt on but nvr trbld ldrs* 25/1
356 9 3/4 **Sulis Minerva (IRE)**[14] 1581 6-8-11 82 JoeyHaynes(7) 7 75
(Jeremy Gask) *s.i.s: swtchd lft after s and hld up in last pair: c wd and effrt over 1f out: kpt on but nvr gng pce to threaten ldrs* 33/1
1032 10 1 **Avertis**[34] 1181 8-8-9 73 PaulHanagan 5 63
(Alastair Lidderdale) *awkward leaving stalls and slowly away: hld up in rr: rdn and effrt over 1f out: styd on but nvr trbld ldrs* 25/1
-210 11 3 3/4 **Lastkingofscotland (IRE)**[95] 353 7-8-13 80 (b) SimonPearce(3) 2 60
(Conor Dore) *chsd ldrs: rdn and lost pl over 2f out: bhd 1f out* 33/1

1m 24.07s (-0.73) **Going Correction** +0.025s/f (Slow) 11 Ran SP% **118.6**
Speed ratings (Par 105): **105,104,104,103,103 101,100,99,98,97 93**
toteswingers 1&2 £4.90, 1&3 £7.80, 2&3 £4.60 CSF £28.47 CT £191.51 TOTE £9.70: £3.20, £1.30, £3.70; EX 38.20 Trifecta £179.70 Pool: £2103.92 - 8.70 winning units..
Owner Simon Caunce **Bred** Juddmonte Farms Inc **Trained** Epsom, Surrey

FOCUS
A competitive handicap which produced a blanket finish.

1879 AURORA FIREWORKS H'CAP 1m 2f (P)
7:55 (7:56) (Class 6) (0-60,60) 3-Y-O £2,045 (£603; £302) Stalls Low

Form RPR
650- 1 **Chocolate Block (IRE)**[177] 7553 3-8-11 50 AdamBeschizza 5 57+
(William Haggas) *dwlt: t.k.h: hld up in tch in rr: swtchd rt and gd hdwy on outer 3f out: led ent fnl 2f: rn green and hung rt ins fnl f: stened and r.o towards fin* 5/2[1]
43-3 2 1 3/4 **Knight's Parade (IRE)**[19] 1469 3-9-6 59 (p) PatDobbs 9 63+
(Amanda Perrett) *hld up in tch in last trio: hdwy to chse ldrs whn n.m.r jst over 2f out: drvn to chse wnr 1f out: pressing wnr whn carried rt and hmpd fnl 75yds: one pce after* 5/1[3]
62-2 3 2 **Alpine Mysteries (IRE)**[28] 1289 3-9-7 60 RyanMoore 2 62+
(Harry Dunlop) *t.k.h: chsd ldrs: rdn and effrt 2f out: chsd ldng pair and styng on whn pushed rt and bdly hmpd fnl 100yds: nt rcvr and one pce after* 5/1[3]

000- **4** ½ **Kastini**[166] 7708 3-9-1 **54** TedDurcan 4 54+
(Denis Coakley) *t.k.h: chsd ldrs: rdn and effrt wl over 1f out: 4th and keeping on whn pushed rt and bdly hmpd fnl 100yds: nt rcvr and one pce* **8/1**

00-0 **5** *hd* **Rock Diamond (IRE)**[10] 1671 3-8-11 **50** JamesDoyle 7 48
(Sylvester Kirk) *broke wl: t.k.h: pressed ldr tl led over 2f out: sn hdd and rdn: drvn and unable qck over 1f out: one pce fnl f* **25/1**

652 **6** ¾ **Flamingo Beat**[20] 1450 3-9-7 **60** StevieDonohoe 8 57+
(Rae Guest) *in tch in midfield: swtchd rt and effrt over 2f out: styd on same pce fr over 1f out* **8/1**

0422 **7** 1¼ **Scepticism (USA)**[6] 1747 3-9-1 **54** SilvestreDeSousa 6 48+
(Mark Johnston) *t.k.h: hld up in tch in midfield: shuffled bk towards rr over 2f out: rdn and trying to rally whn hmpd and swtchd lft 1f out: one pce after* **3/1**[2]

-346 **8** 2½ **Tebbit (USA)**[21] 1425 3-9-6 **59** (bt) TomEaves 1 48
(Philip Hide) *t.k.h: hld up wl in tch in midfield: rdn and edging rt over 1f out: no imp* **33/1**

-300 **8** *dht* **Hanga Roa (IRE)**[83] 527 3-8-12 **51** LiamKeniry 3 40
(Gary Moore) *t.k.h: hld up in tch in rr: rdn and effrt over 1f out: no imp* **50/1**

-465 **10** 8 **Fire Fairy (USA)**[61] 817 3-9-1 **54** RobertWinston 10 27
(Charles Hills) *sn rdn along to ld: hdd and rdn over 2f out: wknd wl over 1f out: bhd fnl f* **16/1**

2m 7.56s (0.96) **Going Correction** +0.025s/f (Slow) **10** Ran SP% **123.8**
Speed ratings (Par 96): **97,95,94,93,93 92,91,89,89,83**
toteswingers 1&2 £3.80, 1&3 £5.10, 2&3 £5.40 CSF £16.34 CT £61.47 TOTE £3.70: £1.20, £2.20, £2.20; EX 21.30 Trifecta £61.50 Pool: £1572.44 - 19.16 winning units..
Owner Wood Hall Stud Limited **Bred** Wood Hall Stud Limited **Trained** Newmarket, Suffolk
■ Stewards' Enquiry : Adam Beschizza four-day ban: careless riding (May 13-16)

FOCUS
A very moderate handicap, but not without interest.
T/Plt: £34.90 to a £1 stake. Pool of £49,972.04 - 1044.78 winning units T/Qpdt: £9.30 to a £1 stake. Pool of £4923.10 - 391.70 winning units SP

1724 WINDSOR (R-H)

Monday, April 29

OFFICIAL GOING: Good (good to soft in places) changing to good after race 2 (6.10)
Wind: Moderate, behind Weather: Fine

1880 IRISH STALLION FARMS EBF MAIDEN STKS 5f 10y
5:40 (5:41) (Class 5) 2-Y-O **£2,911** (£866; £432; £216) **Stalls** Low

Form RPR

2 **1** **Steventon Star**[10] 1669 2-9-5 0 RichardHughes 2 81+
(Richard Hannon) *w ldr against rail: shkn up briefly to ld jst ins fnl f: sn in command: eased nr fin* **1/10**[1]

2 ¾ **Culdaff (IRE)** 2-9-5 0 DaneO'Neill 5 72+
(Charles Hills) *s.s: rcvrd after 2f: prog and rdn 2f out: tried to chal fnl f: kpt on to take 2nd last 75yds: no real ch w wnr* **5/1**[2]

0 **3** ½ **Mimi Luke (USA)**[11] 1634 2-9-0 0 SamHitchcott 6 65
(Alan Bailey) *narrow ldr: drvn over 1f out: hdd jst ins fnl f: kpt on wl but lost 2nd last 75yds* **33/1**

4 2¼ **Ding Ding** 2-9-0 0 MartinHarley 3 57
(Mick Channon) *chsd ldrs: rdn 2f out: no imp over 1f out: kpt on one pce* **12/1**[3]

6 **5** 7 **Flying Kyte**[17] 1512 2-9-5 0 IanMongan 1 37
(Pat Phelan) *chsd ldrs: nt on terms fr 1/2-way: no ch over 1f out: eased last 100yds* **25/1**

6 1½ **Bold Max** 2-9-5 0 ChrisCatlin 4 31
(Zoe Davison) *s.i.s: outpcd and bhd after 2f* **50/1**

1m 1.49s (1.19) **Going Correction** +0.075s/f (Good) **6** Ran SP% **124.0**
Speed ratings (Par 92): **93,91,91,87,76 73**
toteswingers 1&2 £1.20, 1&3 £3.70, 2&3 £14.40 CSF £1.69 TOTE £1.10: £1.02, £2.10; EX 2.10 Trifecta £12.10 Pool: £2182.20 - 134.58 winning units..
Owner Robert Tyrrell **Bred** The National Stud **Trained** East Everleigh, Wilts

FOCUS
The inner of the straight was dolled out six yards at 6f and three yards at the winning post, with the top bend dolled out five yards from the normal inner configuration to add 20 yards to races of 1m-plus. Conditions remained as dry, as they had all day.

1881 FAMILY FUN DAY MAY 6TH MAIDEN STKS 1m 67y
6:10 (6:11) (Class 5) 3-Y-O **£2,587** (£770; £384; £192) **Stalls** Low

Form RPR

1 **Ogbourne Downs** 3-9-5 0 DaneO'Neill 12 79+
(Charles Hills) *hld up in midfield: prog on wd outside fr 3f out: clsd on ldrs over 1f out: drvn to ld jst ins fnl f: jst hld on* **33/1**

0 **2** *shd* **Yeager (USA)**[21] 1423 3-9-5 0 WilliamBuick 8 79+
(Jeremy Noseda) *trckd ldrs: cl up fr 2f out: produced to chal fnl f: drvn and styd on: jst failed* **7/2**[3]

323- **3** 1¼ **Caramack**[220] 6443 3-9-5 76 RichardHughes 5 76
(Richard Hannon) *taken down early: led: pushed along and hdd over 2f out: kpt on to ld again jst over 1f out: hdd and one pce jst ins fnl f* **7/4**[1]

4 1¼ **Defendant** 3-9-5 0 DavidProbert 9 74+
(Sir Michael Stoute) *pressed ldr: pushed along to ld over 2f out: hdd and fdd jst over 1f out* **14/1**

0- **5** ½ **Saxon Soldier**[194] 7167 3-9-5 0 StevieDonohoe 2 72
(Ed Dunlop) *trckd ldrs: pushed along over 2f out: no imp but kpt on steadily fr over 1f out* **66/1**

6 ½ **Orbison (IRE)** 3-9-5 0 NeilCallan 11 71
(Roger Varian) *wl in tch: prog towards outer to chal 2f out: wknd jst over 1f out* **16/1**

7 3¼ **Evident (IRE)** 3-9-5 0 JimmyFortune 6 63
(Jeremy Noseda) *trckd ldng pair: effrt on outer to chal 2f out: wknd over 1f out* **16/1**

0- **8** 4 **Sonnetation (IRE)**[194] 7160 3-9-0 0 MatthewDavies 1 49
(Jim Boyle) *in tch tl wknd u.p over 2f out* **80/1**

9 *nk* **Delicious Poison** 3-9-5 0 (t) MartinLane 4 53
(James Fanshawe) *settled in rr: pushed along and outpcd over 2f out: nvr on terms after* **33/1**

10 3¼ **Violet Dancer** 3-9-5 0 GeorgeBaker 10 46
(Gary Moore) *a in last trio: shkn up and struggling over 3f out* **33/1**

11 *nk* **Pembroke (IRE)** 3-9-5 0 KierenFallon 3 50+
(William Haggas) *dwlt: rn green and pushed along in rr: nvr on terms: wknd 2f out* **11/4**[2]

12 ¾ **Elusive Bleu (IRE)** 3-9-5 0 RichardKingscote 7 44
(Tom Dascombe) *dwlt: a last and struggling* **33/1**

1m 44.28s (-0.42) **Going Correction** -0.225s/f (Firm) **12** Ran SP% **118.2**
Speed ratings (Par 98): **93,92,91,90,89 89,86,82,81,78 78,77**
toteswingers 1&2 £14.20, 1&3 £11.90, 2&3 £2.10 CSF £141.86 TOTE £36.10: £9.10, £1.50, £1.20; EX 253.80 Trifecta £1234.70 Part won. Pool: £1646.34 - 0.13 winning units..
Owner S W Group Logistics Limited **Bred** Bumble Bloodstock & Mrs S Nicholls **Trained** Lambourn, Berks

FOCUS
At least five were in line with over a furlong to travel of this mile maiden.

1882 WINDSOR VEHICLE LEASING WVL.CO.UK MAIDEN STKS 1m 2f 7y
6:40 (6:42) (Class 5) 3-Y-O+ **£2,587** (£770; £384; £192) **Stalls** Centre

Form RPR

66/ **1** **Sir Bedivere (IRE)**[556] 6994 4-10-0 0 WilliamBuick 2 83
(Brian Meehan) *trckd ldr: led 3f out and kicked on: rdn and asserted wl over 1f out: styd on wl* **17/2**

0- **2** 3¼ **Bedouin Invader (IRE)**[195] 7130 3-8-11 0 DavidProbert 7 73
(Sir Michael Stoute) *trckd ldng pair: rdn to chse wnr over 1f out: styd on but no imp* **6/1**[3]

0 **3** 3 **Strawberry Jam**[9] 1679 3-8-11 0 JackMitchell 11 67
(Paul Cole) *led to 3f out: chsd wnr to over 1f out: steadily outpcd* **66/1**

4 3 **Jazz Master** 3-8-11 0 KierenFallon 8 61+
(Luca Cumani) *towards rr: pushed along 1/2-way: prog to go 4th 3f out: no imp and wl hld fnl 2f* **3/1**[2]

5 1¼ **Pursivere** 3-8-11 0 RichardKingscote 1 59
(Hughie Morrison) *trckd ldrs: shkn up 4f out: hung lft and btn over 2f out* **14/1**

2- **6** *nk* **Aficionado**[172] 7641 3-8-11 0 RichardHughes 5 58
(Ed Dunlop) *hld up in midfield: pushed along and no prog over 3f out: struggling after: modest hdwy fnl f* **6/4**[1]

00- **7** *nse* **Dusky Lark**[138] 8070 3-8-11 0 NeilCallan 13 58
(Hughie Morrison) *nvr beyond midfield: rdn and no imp on ldrs 3f out: one pce after* **10/1**

0 **8** ¾ **Eleanor Roosevelt (IRE)**[11] 1653 3-8-6 0 ChrisCatlin 3 53+
(Jamie Osborne) *rn green in last and adrift: pushed along and prog on outer 3f out: keeping on and pressing for 5th whn heavily eased last 50yds* **66/1**

9 1½ **Bombardier** 3-8-11 0 (t) MartinLane 6 53+
(James Fanshawe) *rn green in last pair: no prog 4f out: nvr on terms after* **20/1**

0/6 **10** 1½ **Between The Lines (IRE)**[11] 1653 4-10-0 0 JohnFahy 9 53
(Anthony Middleton) *dwlt: nvr beyond midfield: no prog 3f out: wl btn after* **33/1**

60 **11** 3½ **Ernie**[11] 1653 6-10-0 0 DaneO'Neill 4 46
(Geoffrey Deacon) *a in rr: jst pushed along fr 3f out: no prog* **100/1**

/34- **12** 9 **Atmanna**[223] 6345 4-9-9 51 [1] SamHitchcott 12 23
(Zoe Davison) *wl in rr: rdn and brief effrt on outer 4f out: wknd 3f out: t.o* **125/1**

2m 9.75s (1.05) **Going Correction** -0.225s/f (Firm)
WFA 3 from 4yo+ 17lb **12** Ran SP% **118.0**
Speed ratings (Par 103): **86,83,81,78,77 77,77,76,75,74 71,64**
toteswingers 1&2 £8.80, 1&3 £79.80, 2&3 £71.30 CSF £56.39 TOTE £9.20: £1.90, £1.80, £8.70; EX 67.70 Trifecta £530.70 Pool: £1624.23 - 2.29 winning units..
Owner Trelawny II **Bred** Car Colston Hall Stud **Trained** Manton, Wilts

FOCUS
Not that frenetically run and it proved too hard for anything to make significant progress from the rear as a result.

1883 SYDNEY ARMS PUB CHELSEA & RACING CLUB H'CAP 1m 2f 7y
7:10 (7:11) (Class 4) (0-85,84) 4-Y-O+ **£4,851** (£1,443; £721; £360) **Stalls** Centre

Form RPR

1-44 **1** **Duke Of Clarence (IRE)**[16] 1538 4-9-4 **81** RichardHughes 3 90+
(Richard Hannon) *trckd ldr: led 2f out: shkn up over 1f out: hrd pressed fnl f: pushed out firmly and a holding on* **9/4**[2]

1- **2** *nk* **Hanseatic**[172] 7647 4-9-3 **80** WilliamBuick 6 88+
(John Gosden) *t.k.h early: trckd ldng trio: prog to go 2nd wl over 1f out: drvn to chal fnl f: stl green and nt qckn nr fin* **13/8**[1]

6-26 **3** 1¾ **Greylami (IRE)**[30] 1242 8-8-8 **76** RyanTate(5) 4 81
(Clive Cox) *trckd ldrs in 5th: rdn 2f out: styd on fnl f to take 3rd last 75yds: unable to chal* **5/1**[3]

2-5 **4** ¾ **Cayuga**[97] 318 4-9-5 **82** DavidProbert 8 85
(Brett Johnson) *hld up in last trio: prog on outer fr 3f out: chsd ldng pair jst over 1f out but edgd lft: fdd last 100yds* **16/1**

6104 **5** 1½ **Kickingthelilly**[24] 1363 4-9-3 **80** ChrisCatlin 9 80
(Rae Guest) *stdd s: detached in last early: pushed along and sme prog over 2f out: shkn up and one pce fr over 1f out* **33/1**

0450 **6** 5 **Takeitfromalady (IRE)**[18] 1501 4-9-7 **84** (b) KierenFox 7 74
(Lee Carter) *led: drvn and hdd 2f out: wknd over 1f out* **20/1**

-121 **7** 6 **Ishikawa (IRE)**[32] 1220 5-8-12 **75** FergusSweeney 5 53
(Alan King) *t.k.h early: hld up in last trio: shkn up over 3f out: wknd over 2f out* **12/1**

00-5 **8** ¾ **Starwatch**[14] 1583 6-9-2 **84** WilliamTwiston-Davies(5) 2 61
(John Bridger) *trckd ldng pair tl wknd qckly over 2f out* **14/1**

2m 5.11s (-3.59) **Going Correction** -0.225s/f (Firm) **8** Ran SP% **113.5**
Speed ratings (Par 105): **105,104,103,102,101 97,92,92**
toteswingers 1&2 £2.10, 1&3 £2.20, 2&3 £1.90 CSF £6.17 CT £14.67 TOTE £3.30: £1.40, £1.10, £1.70; EX 7.40 Trifecta £26.50 Pool: £1781.85 - 50.35 winning units..
Owner D Dixon J Stunt J Fiyaz **Bred** Corduff Stud Ltd & J F Gribomont **Trained** East Everleigh, Wilts

FOCUS
A fair event which largely revolved around the once-raced favourite.

1884 CORAL.CO.UK H'CAP 1m 3f 135y
7:40 (7:42) (Class 4) (0-80,79) 4-Y-O+ **£4,851** (£1,443; £721; £360) **Stalls** Centre

Form RPR

5311 **1** **Attwaal (IRE)**[14] 1586 4-9-2 **75** SebSanders 9 83
(Neil King) *settled in midfield: rdn 3f out: prog over 2f out: drvn to ld over 1f out: kpt on wl* **4/1**[2]

0666 **2** ½ **Focail Maith**[7] 1728 5-8-12 **70** KierenFallon 4 77
(John Ryan) *wl in tch: cl up but pushed along 4f out: drvn over 2f out: burst through to take 2nd last 100yds and cl on wnr: jst hld* **16/1**

330- **3** 1 **Sula Two**[211] 6703 6-9-2 **79** PhilipPrince(5) 12 84
(Ron Hodges) *t.k.h: hld up towards rr: rdn 3f out: prog on outer 2f out: styd on fnl f to take 3rd nr fin* **25/1**

The Form Book Flat, Raceform Ltd, Compton, RG20 6NL.

21 **4** 1 1/4 **Cousin Khee**[75] 637 6-9-7 **79**.. GeorgeBaker 10 82
(Hughie Morrison) *trckd ldrs: smooth prog to ld over 2f out: hdd over 1f out: fnd nil and sn btn* **3/1**[1]

30-1 **5** 1 3/4 **Paloma's Prince (IRE)**[27] 1302 4-9-4 **77**..................... MatthewDavies 8 77
(Jim Boyle) *prom: rdn to try to chal 2f out: fdd jst over 1f out* **8/1**

666- **6** nse **Perfect Delight**[130] 8182 4-9-1 **79**.............................. RyanTate(5) 1 79
(Clive Cox) *hld up in last quartet: sme prog into midfield over 2f out: rdn over 1f out: kpt on but nvr rchd ldrs* **11/1**

3023 **7** 2 **Brown Pete (IRE)**[24] 1366 5-8-13 **71**.............................. CathyGannon 6 68
(Violet M Jordan) *dwlt: hld up in last quartet: sme prog on wd outside fr 3f out: nvr able to threaten* **33/1**

30-5 **8** shd **Choral Festival**[14] 1585 7-8-8 **71**.................. WilliamTwiston-Davies(5) 3 68
(John Bridger) *wnt to post wout zest: trckd ldrs: cl enough and rdn over 2f out: fdd over 1f out* **7/1**[3]

000- **9** 1 **Star Date (IRE)**[143] 8020 4-8-12 **71**.............................. DavidProbert 13 66
(Michael Attwater) *hld up in last quartet: rdn over 3f out: sme prog 2f out: no imp over 1f out* **20/1**

3/52 **10** 1/2 **Dr Livingstone (IRE)**[17] 1523 8-9-6 **78**.................... RichardHughes 2 72
(Charles Egerton) *hld up and sn in last quartet: pushed along 3f out: sme prog 2f out: keeping on but no ch whn eased fnl f* **12/1**

1132 **11** 3 3/4 **Jacobs Son**[13] 1597 5-9-4 **76**.. JimmyFortune 14 64
(Robert Mills) *led to 5f out: styd prom tl wknd wl over 2f out* **25/1**

14-0 **12** 17 **Refractor (IRE)**[18] 1501 5-9-3 **75**.................................. WilliamBuick 11 34
(Michael Bell) *hld up in midfield tl quick prog to ld 5f out: hdd & wknd rapidly over 2f out: t.o* **12/1**

20-6 **13** 1 **Sondeduro**[21] 1422 4-9-4 **77**.. FergusSweeney 7 34
(Jamie Osborne) *prom 5f: sn lost pl and bhd: t.o* **28/1**

2m 28.05s (-1.45) **Going Correction** -0.225s/f (Firm)
WFA 4 from 5yo+ 1lb 13 Ran SP% **117.1**
Speed ratings (Par 105): **95,94,94,93,92 91,90,90,89,89 87,75,75**
toteswingers 1&2 £17.90, 1&3 £28.30, 2&3 £115.50 CSF £59.29 CT £1418.39 TOTE £5.00: £1.60, £5.90, £8.90; EX 86.30 Trifecta £876.30 Part won. Pool: £1168.42 - 0.03 winning units..
Owner Dr & Mrs Clive Layton **Bred** Darley **Trained** Newmarket, Suffolk
■ Stewards' Enquiry : Seb Sanders two-day ban: used whip above permitted level (May 13-14)

FOCUS
A fair handicap.

1885 DOWNLOAD CORAL MOBILE FROM THE APP STORE H'CAP 1m 3f 135y
8:10 (8:12) (Class 5) (0-70,70) 3-Y-O **£2,587** (£770; £384; £192) **Stalls** Centre

Form RPR

-505 **1** **Brick Rising**[12] 1613 3-8-7 **56** oh1.................................(t) DavidProbert 7 61
(Andrew Balding) *led at slow pce for 2f: styd prom: rdn to press ldng pair 3f out: sustained effrt to ld 1f out: drvn out* **16/1**

04-3 **2** 1/2 **Hello Sailor**[19] 1481 3-8-11 **60**.. JimCrowley 4 64
(Ralph Beckett) *led after 2f tl after 4f: pressed ldr after: rdn 3f out: upsides fr 2f out tl nt qckn ins fnl f* **11/4**[1]

00-1 **3** hd **Pivotal Silence**[19] 1469 3-9-2 **65**...................................... AdamKirby 6 69
(Amanda Perrett) *t.k.h early: hld up tl led after 4f: rdn and pressed 3f out: hdd and one pce 1f out* **5/1**[3]

1 **4** 1/2 **Akdam (IRE)**[52] 925 3-9-5 **68**.. LukeMorris 5 71
(Tony Carroll) *hld up in last trio: rdn 3f out: swtchd lft to outer 2f out: tried to cl on ldrs but one pce* **6/1**

002- **5** 3/4 **Mallory Heights (IRE)**[138] 8071 3-9-7 **70**.................... KierenFallon 3 73+
(Luca Cumani) *hld up in cl tch: rdn over 3f out: styd pressing ldrs but hanging and nt qckn over 1f out: one pce after* **3/1**[2]

163- **6** shd **Getaway Car**[184] 7414 3-8-12 **61**.. NeilCallan 1 63
(Gerard Butler) *trckd ldrs: rdn 3f out: kpt on same pce u.p fnl 2f and nvr able to chal seriously* **6/1**

2331 **7** 9 **Inessa Armand (IRE)**[12] 1613 3-8-12 **61**.....................(p) CathyGannon 2 47
(J S Moore) *nt gng wl in last bef 1/2-way despite modest pce: t.o over 2f out* **12/1**

420- **8** 14 **Just A Pound (IRE)**[210] 6732 3-8-13 **62**........................ J-PGuillambert 8 31
(Jo Hughes) *a in rr: pushed along over 4f out: sn btn* **33/1**

2m 30.55s (1.05) **Going Correction** -0.225s/f (Firm) 8 Ran SP% **113.4**
Speed ratings (Par 98): **87,86,86,86,85 85,79,70**
toteswingers 1&2 £11.00, 1&3 £13.60, 2&3 £3.60 CSF £59.04 CT £258.37 TOTE £12.70: £4.70, £1.60, £2.30; EX 72.40 Trifecta £280.20 Pool: £1912.12 - 5.11 winning units..
Owner Brick Racing **Bred** Winterbeck Manor Stud **Trained** Kingsclere, Hants
■ Stewards' Enquiry : David Probert four-day ban: used whip above permitted level (May 13-16)

FOCUS
A stop-start pace gave way to a sprint for home past the intersection, and the winning time was 2.5 seconds slower than that of the winner in the preceding contest.
T/Plt: £58.60 to a £1 stake. Pool of £71,568.96 - 890.98 winning units T/Qpdt: £24.50 to a £1 stake. Pool of £6102.30 - 184.10 winning units JN

1792 WOLVERHAMPTON (A.W) (L-H)
Monday, April 29

OFFICIAL GOING: Standard
Wind: Fresh behind Weather: Cloudy with sunny spells

1886 £32 BONUS AT 32RED.COM H'CAP (DIV I) 7f 32y(P)
1:50 (1:51) (Class 6) (0-60,60) 4-Y-0+ **£1,940** (£577; £288; £144) **Stalls** High

Form RPR

2325 **1** **Abhaath (USA)**[23] 1401 4-9-6 **59**.. LukeMorris 6 67
(Ronald Harris) *hld up: hdwy over 2f out: rdn to ld ins fnl f: r.o* **3/1**[1]

1305 **2** 1 1/4 **Blue Noodles**[11] 1656 7-8-13 **52**.................................(v) PaddyAspell 2 57
(John Wainwright) *led: clr 5f out: rdn and hung rt fr over 1f out: hdd ins fnl f: styd on same pce* **11/1**

0060 **3** hd **Prince Of Passion (CAN)**[11] 1656 5-9-6 **59**...............(v) MartinDwyer 5 63
(Derek Shaw) *s.i.s: sn hld up in tch and racd keenly: rdn over 2f out: ev ch ins fnl f: styd on same pce* **7/1**[3]

0000 **4** 3/4 **Marshall Art**[20] 1452 4-9-1 **57**...............................(tp) MarkCoumbe(3) 3 59
(Ken Wingrove) *chsd ldr: rdn over 2f out: edgd rt and styd on same pce ins fnl f* **50/1**

4604 **5** 3/4 **Hittin'The Skids (IRE)**[7] 1734 5-8-11 **50**.................(p) TomMcLaughlin 7 50
(Mandy Rowland) *s.i.s: hld up: hdwy over 1f out: sn rdn: no ex towards fin* **10/1**

3531 **6** nk **Romanticize**[11] 1656 7-9-5 **58**.. TomQueally 8 57
(Jason Ward) *prom: racd keenly: rdn over 1f out: edgd rt ins fnl f: styd on same pce* **3/1**[1]

2060 **7** 5 **Sannibel**[11] 1656 5-9-6 **59**.. WilliamCarson 9 45
(Graeme McPherson) *mid-div: drvn along 1/2-way: wknd over 2f out* **16/1**

305- **8** 1/2 **Striker Torres (IRE)**[135] 8137 7-9-7 **60**.....................(v) GrahamLee 4 44
(Ian McInnes) *hld up: rdn and wknd over 2f out* **10/3**[2]

000- **9** hd **Remix (IRE)**[308] 3454 4-9-2 **60**.. JackDuern(5) 1 44
(Reg Hollinshead) *prom: pushed along over 4f out: lost pl whn hmpd wl over 3f out: sn wknd* **14/1**

1m 27.45s (-2.15) **Going Correction** -0.30s/f (Stan) 9 Ran SP% **117.5**
Speed ratings (Par 101): **100,98,98,97,96 96,90,90,89**
toteswingers 1&2 £6.00, 1&3 £4.70, 2&3 £14.60 CSF £37.67 CT £218.23 TOTE £3.50: £1.10, £3.40, £3.40; EX 31.40 Trifecta £260.30 Pool: £1936.31 - 5.57 winning units..
Owner Ridge House Stables Ltd **Bred** Santa Rosa Partners **Trained** Earlswood, Monmouths

FOCUS
A moderate handicap.

1887 £32 BONUS AT 32RED.COM H'CAP (DIV II) 7f 32y(P)
2:20 (2:21) (Class 6) (0-60,60) 4-Y-0+ **£1,940** (£577; £216; £216) **Stalls** High

Form RPR

0600 **1** **Muftarres (IRE)**[5] 1757 8-9-7 **60**....................................(t) GeorgeBaker 4 69
(Frank Sheridan) *hld up: hdwy over 1f out: rdn and hung lft ins fnl f: r.o to ld nr fin* **10/1**

0-42 **2** 3/4 **Moss Hill**[11] 1656 4-8-12 **51**.. FrannyNorton 5 58
(Charles Hills) *chsd ldr: rdn over 2f out: styd on to ld wl ins fnl f: hdd nr fin* **15/8**[1]

-060 **3** 1 3/4 **Glenridding**[9] 1693 9-9-6 **59**..(p) GrahamLee 2 61
(James Given) *sn pushed along to ld: clr over 2f out: rdn over 1f out: hdd and unable qck wl ins fnl f* **14/1**

2623 **3** dht **Silly Billy (IRE)**[4] 1783 5-8-11 **57**.................................(v) RyanWhile(7) 8 61+
(Bill Turner) *chsd ldrs: nt clr run over 2f out: rdn over 1f out: styd on* **4/1**[2]

600- **5** hd **Heart Beat Song**[243] 5734 5-8-7 **46** oh1.............................. LiamJones 6 48
(Richard Ford) *chsd ldrs: rdn and hung lft over 1f out: styd on* **28/1**

3403 **6** 1 1/4 **Unlimited**[11] 1656 11-9-7 **60**.. TomQueally 3 58
(Tony Carroll) *mid-div: rdn and r.o ins fnl f: nt trble ldrs* **13/2**

1430 **7** 1/2 **Basle**[11] 1657 6-9-6 **59**..(t) RichardKingscote 1 56
(Michael Blake) *hld up: r.o ins fnl f: nvr nrr* **14/1**

000- **8** 1 **Farmers Dream (IRE)**[424] 744 6-8-0 **46** oh1........... AdamMcLean(7) 7 40
(Derek Shaw) *mid-div: rdn over 1f out: hung lft and no ex ins fnl f* **40/1**

0266 **9** 1 1/2 **Bitaphon (IRE)**[18] 1498 4-9-1 **59**.................................... RobertTart(5) 9 49
(Michael Appleby) *prom: rdn over 2f out: wknd fnl f* **6/1**[3]

6236 **10** 6 **Tenbridge**[17] 1521 4-9-4 **57**..(b) WilliamCarson 10 31
(Derek Haydn Jones) *s.i.s: sn pushed along in rr: nvr on terms* **10/1**

1m 27.37s (-2.23) **Going Correction** -0.30s/f (Stan) 10 Ran SP% **119.8**
Speed ratings (Par 101): **100,99,97,97,96 95,94,93,92,85**PL: G £2.30, SB £0.80; Trifecta: M/MH/G £242.40, M/MH/SB £97.10; Tricast: M/MH/G £138.79, M/MH/SB £46.29; toteswingers M/MH £4.50, M/G £11.10, M/SB £3.90, MH/G £3.70, MH/SB £1.10 CSF £29.91 TOTE £11.90: £4.00, £1.10; EX 33.10 TRIFECTA Pool; £2637.53 - 427 Owner.

FOCUS
The winning time was marginally quicker than the first division.

1888 32REDPOKER.COM CLASSIFIED CLAIMING STKS 5f 20y(P)
2:50 (2:50) (Class 6) 3-Y-0+ **£1,940** (£577; £288; £144) **Stalls** Low

Form RPR

-460 **1** **Tango Sky (IRE)**[9] 1692 4-9-9 73.. FrannyNorton 2 74
(David Nicholls) *led 1f: chsd ldr: rdn ins fnl f: r.o to ld post* **5/6**[1]

2500 **2** nk **Spic 'n Span**[7] 1731 8-8-13 58...(be) LukeMorris 5 63
(Ronald Harris) *led 4f out: clr 1/2-way: rdn over 1f out: hdd post* **16/1**

3133 **3** hd **Dark Lane**[4] 1798 7-8-6 66.. RobJFitzpatrick(7) 1 62
(David Evans) *chsd ldrs: rdn over 1f out: r.o* **7/4**[2]

032/ **4** 2 1/4 **Desert Icon (IRE)**[489] 7883 7-8-10 70...................... GeorgeChaloner(5) 6 56
(Alastair Lidderdale) *dwlt: drvn along 1/2-way: hdwy over 1f out: r.o: nt rch ldrs* **11/1**[3]

6404 **5** 5 **Hawsies Dream**[21] 1427 3-8-6 56.. TimClark(7) 4 46
(Alan Bailey) *s.i.s: sn pushed along in rr: wknd wl over 1f out* **25/1**

0-06 **6** 6 **Dubai Rythm**[17] 1525 4-8-11 47..................................(bt) AndrewMullen 3 13
(Michael Appleby) *chsd ldrs: rdn 1/2-way: wknd 2f out* **40/1**

1m 0.84s (-1.46) **Going Correction** -0.30s/f (Stan)
WFA 3 from 4yo+ 10lb 6 Ran SP% **111.4**
Speed ratings (Par 101): **99,98,98,94,86 77**
toteswingers 1&2 £2.30, 1&3 £1.10, 2&3 £2.70 CSF £15.86 TOTE £1.80: £1.10, £6.90; EX 14.80 Trifecta £30.50 Pool: £3277.43 - 80.46 winning units..There were no claims.
Owner Dr Marwan Koukash **Bred** L Mulryan **Trained** Sessay, N Yorks

FOCUS
An ordinary claimer, but the pace was decent.

1889 32RED.COM H'CAP 1m 4f 50y(P)
3:20 (3:20) (Class 5) (0-70,70) 4-Y-0+ **£2,587** (£770; £384; £192) **Stalls** Low

Form RPR

233- **1** **Singzak**[199] 7024 5-9-6 **69**.. GrahamGibbons 6 76
(Michael Easterby) *mde all: rdn over 1f out: styd on gamely* **15/8**[1]

2141 **2** nk **The Blue Dog (IRE)**[11] 1654 6-9-2 **70**............................ RobertTart(5) 5 76
(Phil McEntee) *chsd ldrs: lost pl over 3f out: hdwy 2f out: rdn ins fnl f: styd on* **11/2**[3]

04-1 **3** hd **Rock Song**[21] 1434 4-9-4 **68**.. GrahamLee 4 74
(John Mackie) *hld up: hdwy over 2f out: swtchd lft over 1f out: ev ch ins fnl f: sn rdn: unable qck nr fin* **2/1**[2]

245 **4** 11 **Keep Kicking (IRE)**[27] 1300 6-9-6 **69**............................ GeorgeBaker 1 57
(Jonjo O'Neill) *hld up: hdwy over 4f out: chsd wnr 3f out tl rdn over 1f out: wknd fnl f* **11/2**[3]

1-64 **5** 3 1/2 **Bold Duke**[14] 1585 5-8-13 **67**.. ThomasBrown(5) 2 50
(Edward Bevan) *prom: rdn over 3f out: hmpd over 2f out: sn wknd* **12/1**

60/6 **6** 8 **Layla's Dancer**[4] 1794 6-9-1 **64**.. AndrewMullen 3 34
(Michael Appleby) *chsd wnr tl rdn 3f out: edgd lft over 2f out: wknd over 1f out* **12/1**

2m 35.87s (-5.23) **Going Correction** -0.30s/f (Stan)
WFA 4 from 5yo+ 1lb 6 Ran SP% **114.3**
Speed ratings (Par 103): **105,104,104,97,95 89**
toteswingers 1&2 £2.40, 1&3 £1.20, 2&3 £2.60 CSF £12.97 TOTE £2.50: £2.00, £1.80; EX 11.50 Trifecta £30.30 Pool: £2291.84 - 56.65 winning units..
Owner Clark Industrial Services Partnership **Bred** Clark Industrial Services Partnership **Trained** Sheriff Hutton, N Yorks

FOCUS
An ordinary handicap.

1890 WOLVERHAMPTON-RACECOURSE.CO.UK CLAIMING STKS 1m 1f 103y(P)
3:50 (3:51) (Class 6) 4-Y-0+ **£2,045** (£603; £302) **Stalls** Low

Form RPR

1661 **1** **Honey Of A Kitten (USA)**[23] 1402 5-8-6 76.................(v) EoinWalsh(7) 8 77
(David Evans) *mde all: clr 3f out: rdn over 1f out: edgd rt ins fnl f: kpt on* **6/1**[3]

1215 **2** 1 1/2 **Officer In Command (USA)**[9] 1699 7-8-4 75..............(vt) RyanTate(5) 6 70
(Hans Adielsson) *s.s: sn prom: rdn over 2f out: chsd wnr over 1f out: sn hung lft: styd on* **7/2**[2]

0102 **3** *nk* **Classic Colori (IRE)**[4] 1786 6-9-7 76..........................(v) DanielTudhope 1 81
(David O'Meara) *a.p: rdn over 1f out: styd on: nt trble ldrs* **7/4**[1]

1112 **4** 2 1/2 **Hurricane Spirit (IRE)**[26] 1316 9-8-4 72.............. DarrenEgan(3) 4 62
(Joseph Tuite) *chsd ldrs: rdn over 1f out: styd on same pce fnl f* **7/2**[2]

60-2 **5** 2 1/4 **Buaiteoir (FR)**[48] 974 7-8-7 62.............................. FrankieMcDonald 2 57
(Nikki Evans) *s.i.s: hld up: rdn over 1f out: nvr on terms* **20/1**

330/ **6** 3 3/4 **Viva Vettori**[548] 7168 9-9-3 93.. LukeMorris 3 59
(Brian Forsey) *chsd wnr tl rdn over 1f out: wknd fnl f* **7/1**

7 *10* **Ghost Opera**[32] 5-8-4 0... WilliamCarson 5 25
(Philip McBride) *s.s: hld up: rdn over 3f out: wknd over 2f out* **33/1**

1m 58.28s (-3.42) **Going Correction** -0.30s/f (Stan) **7 Ran SP% 115.3**
Speed ratings (Par 101): **103,101,101,99,97 93,84**
toteswingers 1&2 £3.40, 1&3 £2.70, 2&3 £1.90 CSF £27.65 TOTE £8.60: £4.10, £2.40; EX 30.40 Trifecta £96.30 Pool: £2872.27 - 22.36 winning units..Officer in Command was claimed by Mr J Butler for £6,000.
Owner Mrs E Evans **Bred** Kenneth L Ramsey And Sarah K Ramsey **Trained** Pandy, Monmouths

FOCUS
An unsatisfactory claimer with the winner being handed it on a plate.

1891 32RED CASINO MEDIAN AUCTION MAIDEN STKS 1m 141y(P)
4:20 (4:21) (Class 5) 3-5-Y-O **£2,587** (£770; £384; £192) **Stalls** Low

Form RPR

225 **1** **Off The Pulse**[21] 1429 3-8-12 0.................................. GrahamGibbons 5 77
(John Mackie) *hld up: racd keenly: hdwy over 2f out: chsd ldr and hmpd over 1f out: shkn up to ld nr fin* **14/1**

02- **2** *hd* **Aneedh**[193] 7199 3-8-12 0... LiamJones 7 76
(William Haggas) *led: rdn and hung rt over 1f out: hdd nr fin* **6/4**[1]

2 **3** 2 1/4 **San Gabriel (IRE)**[13] 1595 3-8-12 0.......................... TomMcLaughlin 8 71
(Ed Walker) *chsd ldrs: rdn over 2f out: styd on same pce ins fnl f* **20/1**

2 **4** *shd* **Cavalieri (IRE)**[56] 877 3-8-12 0.................................. GrahamLee 3 71
(William Jarvis) *prom: rdn and hung rt over 2f out: styd on same pce ins fnl f* **4/1**[3]

4 **5** *3* **Call Ahead**[11] 1640 3-8-7 0.. PatDobbs 4 59
(Sir Michael Stoute) *chsd ldr: rdn over 2f out: wknd fnl f* **5/2**[2]

6 *nk* **Loved One** 3-8-7 0.. HayleyTurner 2 58
(James Fanshawe) *chsd ldrs: pushed along over 2f out: wknd fnl f* **7/1**

7 3 1/4 **Keene** 3-8-12 0.. WilliamCarson 1 56
(Philip McBride) *pushed along in rr: rdn and wknd over 2f out* **33/1**

8 *5* **Need To Be Bold** 4-9-8 0.. LukeMorris 6 42
(Derek Haydn Jones) *sn pushed along and a in rr: rdn over 3f out: sn wknd* **66/1**

1m 47.77s (-2.73) **Going Correction** -0.30s/f (Stan)
WFA 3 from 4yo 15lb **8 Ran SP% 116.9**
Speed ratings (Par 103): **100,99,97,97,95 94,91,87**
toteswingers 1&2 £3.50, 1&3 £7.60, 2&3 £7.00 CSF £36.07 TOTE £14.50: £1.90, £1.10, £3.80; EX 45.50 Trifecta £450.20 Pool: £2939.23 - 4.89 winning units..
Owner G B Maher **Bred** Mrs V E Hughes **Trained** Church Broughton , Derbys

FOCUS
This looked a strong maiden for the track with several already having shown ability, but it went to the horse with most experience.

1892 32RED H'CAP 5f 216y(P)
4:50 (4:54) (Class 4) (0-80,79) 3-Y-O **£4,690** (£1,395; £697; £348) **Stalls** Low

Form RPR

3-10 **1** **Bluegrass Blues (IRE)**[12] 1625 3-9-7 79......................... GrahamLee 10 85+
(Paul Cole) *hld up: hdwy over 2f out: rdn over 1f out: r.o to ld wl ins fnl f* **4/1**[2]

1- **2** 1/2 **Equity Risk (USA)**[174] 7613 3-9-3 75............................... PhillipMakin 13 80+
(Kevin Ryan) *hld up: outpcd 1/2-way: hdwy over 1f out: r.o wl: nt rch wnr* **7/2**[1]

6-10 **3** *hd* **Bold Prediction (IRE)**[20] 1444 3-9-3 78.............. MichaelMetcalfe(3) 2 82
(Mrs K Burke) *hld up: hdwy 2f out: rdn and ev ch ins fnl f: styd on: hung rt towards fin* **12/1**

321 **4** *1* **Sylvia Pankhurst (IRE)**[21] 1433 3-8-10 68..............(p) GrahamGibbons 1 69
(David C Griffiths) *led: rdn over 1f out: edgd rt: hdd and unable qck wl ins fnl f: nt clr run towards fin* **12/1**

2260 **5** *nk* **Midnight Dream (FR)**[19] 1482 3-9-7 79......................... PatrickMathers 9 79
(Kristin Stubbs) *chsd ldr: rdn and ev ch ins fnl f: styd on same pce* **33/1**

4125 **6** *1* **Sewn Up**[27] 1307 3-9-5 77..(tp) ShaneKelly 12 74
(Reg Hollinshead) *hld up: r.o ins fnl f: nvr nrr* **25/1**

632- **7** *nk* **Bellitudo (IRE)**[145] 7987 3-8-12 70................................... AndreaAtzeni 5 66
(Marco Botti) *chsd ldrs: rdn over 1f out: styd on same pce ins fnl f* **10/1**

033- **8** 1/2 **Sharaarah (IRE)**[212] 6658 3-9-5 77................................. DanielTudhope 7 71
(David O'Meara) *mid-div: hdwy over 2f out: rdn over 1f out: sn hung lft: styd on same pce ins fnl f* **9/2**[3]

3111 **9** 2 3/4 **Hannahs Turn**[33] 1204 3-9-1 73... HayleyTurner 3 58
(Chris Dwyer) *chsd ldrs: rdn over 1f out: wknd ins fnl f* **8/1**

4-16 **10** 3/4 **Blazing Knight (IRE)**[81] 550 3-9-4 76................................ JimCrowley 6 59
(Ralph Beckett) *s.i.s: in rr and drvn along 1/2-way: nvr on terms* **8/1**

36- **11** 1 1/4 **Mandy Lexi (IRE)**[212] 6658 3-8-4 65 oh1......................... DarrenEgan(3) 4 44
(Patrick Morris) *hld up: plld hrd: rdn over 1f out: wknd fnl f* **40/1**

2340 **12** *1* **Lager Time (IRE)**[10] 1661 3-8-8 66...............................(v[1]) WilliamCarson 11 42
(David Evans) *s.s: swtchd lft sn after s: a bhd* **33/1**

1m 12.87s (-2.13) **Going Correction** -0.30s/f (Stan) **12 Ran SP% 119.3**
Speed ratings (Par 100): **102,101,101,99,99 98,97,96,93,92 90,89**
toteswingers 1&2 £4.60, 1&3 £12.30, 2&3 £12.20 CSF £17.86 CT £159.35 TOTE £3.50: £1.40, £2.50, £3.00; EX 22.00 Trifecta £496.50 Pool: £3665.23 - 5.53 winning units..
Owner Mrs Fitri Hay **Bred** Yeomanstown Stud **Trained** Whatcombe, Oxon

FOCUS
A decent sprint handicap for 3yos and this is form to take a positive view of. The pace was strong.

1893 32REDBET.COM APPRENTICE H'CAP 1m 141y(P)
5:20 (5:20) (Class 6) (0-55,55) 4-Y-O+ **£1,940** (£577; £288; £144) **Stalls** Low

Form RPR

0434 **1** **Monsieur Pontaven**[32] 1222 6-8-7 46 oh1...............(b) GaryMahon(5) 10 52
(Robin Bastiman) *chsd ldr tl led over 5f out: rdn over 1f out: edgd lft: jst hld on* **11/2**[3]

-040 **2** *nk* **Cane Cat (IRE)**[27] 1298 6-9-5 53..(t) EoinWalsh 3 58+
(Tony Carroll) *hld up: rdn over 1f out: r.o wl ins fnl f: nt quite get up* **13/2**

0504 **3** *nse* **Stamp Duty (IRE)**[32] 1221 5-8-9 46 oh1..............(p) JordanVaughan(3) 9 51
(Suzzanne France) *a.p: chsd ldr 2f out: rdn and ev ch ins fnl f: r.o* **13/2**

1355 **4** *nk* **Crucis Abbey (IRE)**[19] 1473 5-9-0 48....................(p) MatthewHopkins 8 53
(Mark Brisbourne) *chsd ldrs: rdn over 1f out: r.o* **7/1**

060- **5** 1/2 **Attain**[181] 7470 4-9-7 55... ShelleyBirkett 4 58
(Julia Feilden) *led 3f: chsd ldr: rdn and ev ch over 1f out: styd on same pce ins fnl f* **3/1**[1]

/0-0 **6** *2* **Just Jimmy (IRE)**[25] 1350 8-8-5 46 oh1.................. DanielleMooney(7) 6 45
(George Jones) *hld up: hdwy over 2f out: rdn over 1f out: styd on same pce fnl f* **50/1**

00-0 **7** *nk* **Medecis Mountain**[14] 1578 4-8-7 46 oh1.......................(p) KevinStott(5) 2 44
(John Wainwright) *hld up: rdn over 1f out: nvr trbld ldrs* **50/1**

5442 **8** *1* **The Noble Ord**[19] 1474 4-9-2 55...................................(t) LouisSteward(5) 1 51
(Sylvester Kirk) *mid-div: pushed along over 3f out: rdn over 1f out: styd on same pce fnl f* **4/1**[2]

00-0 **9** 2 3/4 **Alfie Joe**[36] 1161 4-8-7 46 oh1................................... ThomasHemsley(5) 11 35
(Ron Hodges) *hld up: nvr on terms* **28/1**

5402 **10** 1 1/4 **Lord Paget**[52] 927 4-9-2 50..(p) HannahNunn 5 37
(Reg Hollinshead) *hld up in tch: racd keenly: wknd over 1f out* **7/1**

1m 50.09s (-0.41) **Going Correction** -0.30s/f (Stan) **10 Ran SP% 119.4**
Speed ratings (Par 101): **89,88,88,88,87 86,85,85,82,81**
toteswingers 1&2 £7.70, 1&3 £6.20, 2&3 £12.60 CSF £41.67 CT £244.29 TOTE £4.90: £2.70, £4.00, £2.40; EX 57.60 Trifecta £520.50 Pool: £2164.81 - 3.11 winning units..
Owner E N Barber **Bred** Whitsbury Manor Stud **Trained** Cowthorpe, N Yorks

FOCUS
A moderate apprentice handicap and the time was 2.32 seconds slower than the earlier maiden. It produced a tight finish between the front five.
T/Plt: £101.80 to a £1 stake. Pool of £54,207.02 - 388.71 winning units T/Qpdt: £25.80 to a £1 stake. Pool of £3703.50 - 106.10 winning units CR

1850 CHANTILLY (R-H)
Monday, April 29

OFFICIAL GOING: Turf: good

1894a PRIX CARAVELLE (CONDITIONS) (2YO FILLIES) (TURF) 5f
2:20 (12:00) 2-Y-0 **£13,821** (£5,528; £4,146; £2,764; £1,382)

RPR

1 **Vorda (FR)** 2-8-9 0.. Francois-XavierBertras 5 86
(P Sogorb, France) **136/10**

2 1 1/2 **Aventure Love (FR)** 2-8-13 0............................. AntoineCoutier(3) 6 87
(M Gentile, France) **12/1**

3 1 1/4 **Early Prime (FR)**[18] 2-9-2 0.. MarcNobili 4 83
(Rod Collet, France) **43/10**[2]

4 *1* **Orton Park (IRE)**[12] 1619 2-9-2 0.. OlivierPeslier 7 79
(Tobias B P Coles) *broke wl on outside: racd in cl 2nd: shkn up 2f out: rdn 1 1/2f out: no ex: dropped bk to midfield: raillied and styd on wl clsng stages: wnt 4th fnl strides* **14/5**[1]

5 *hd* **Benodet (FR)**[44] 2-9-2 0.. ChristopheSoumillon 1 78
(C Boutin, France) **63/10**

6 *snk* **Skiperia (FR)**[18] 2-8-13 0.. FabriceVeron 3 75
(H-A Pantall, France) **6/1**

7 *shd* **New Elite (FR)**[14] 2-9-2 0.. MaximeGuyon 2 77
(C Boutin, France) **48/10**[3]

8 *7* **Yemaya (FR)**[34] 2-9-2 0.. AntoineHamelin 8 52
(U Suter, France) **17/2**

59.6s (1.30) **8 Ran SP% 115.5**
WIN (incl. 1 euro stake): 14.60. PLACES: 3.40, 3.10, 2.00. DF: 44.10. SF: 158.00.
Owner Remy Picamau **Bred** Edy S.R.L. **Trained** France

1895a PRIX ALLEZ FRANCE (GROUP 3) (4YO+ FILLIES & MARES) (TURF) 1m 2f
2:55 (12:00) 4-Y-0+ **£32,520** (£13,008; £9,756; £6,504; £3,252)

RPR

1 **Romantica**[225] 6295 4-9-2 0... MaximeGuyon 10 111
(A Fabre, France) *prom in 4th on outside: rdn to chal lf out: r.o wl to ld 100yds out: styd on wl* **16/5**[2]

2 1/2 **Harem Lady (FR)**[29] 4-8-7 0.. GregoryBenoist 5 101
(D Smaga, France) *sn led: stl in front 1f out: rdn and r.o wl: hdd 100yds out: styd on wl* **15/2**

3 *1* **Victorinna (FR)**[29] 5-8-7 0.. AnthonyCrastus 2 99
(C Laffon-Parias, France) *racd in midfield: rdn 1f out: nt pce to go w ldr: rallied and styd on wl fnl 100yds* **19/1**

4 *hd* **Sediciosa (IRE)**[190] 7284 4-9-0 0.. OlivierPeslier 9 106
(Y Barberot, France) *racd in midfield: rdn 1f out: r.o wl u.p fnl 100yds* **13/2**[3]

5 *1* **Pearls Or Passion (FR)**[22] 4-8-7 0................ Francois-XavierBertras 7 97
(F Rohaut, France) *swvd awkwardly at s: hld up towards rr: u.p 1f out: no ex: rallied u.p styd on wl at fin* **17/1**

6 *nse* **Fairly Fairy (FR)**[29] 4-8-7 0.. AntoineHamelin 4 97
(A De Royer-Dupre, France) *hld up in rr: u.p 1f out: no ex: styd on wl fnl 150yds* **5/2**[1]

7 *hd* **Sargasses (FR)**[25] 1359 7-8-10 0 ow3................. ChristopheSoumillon 6 100
(Mlle V Dissaux, France) *prom in cl 2nd fr s: rdn 1 1/2f out: r.o wl tl no ex 100yds out: fdd* **14/1**

8 *nk* **Omana (FR)**[165] 7734 4-8-9 0.. FabriceVeron 1 98
(H-A Pantall, France) *racd in 3rd on ins: plld hrd: dropped bk to midfield 1f out: rdn but no ex u.p: styd on one pce* **30/1**

9 *shd* **Grace Lady (FR)**[25] 1359 4-8-7 0.. ThierryJarnet 3 96
(Mlle T Puitg, France) *racd in midfield on ins: rdn 1 1/2f out: short of room to make chal 150yds out: styd on one pce* **73/10**

10 *1* **La Pomme D'Amour**[191] 7237 5-9-2 0.............................. MlleAmelieFoulon 8 103
(A Fabre, France) *hld up at rr of field: swtchd to wd outside ent st: no ex fnl f: styd on at fin* **12/1**

2m 4.3s (-0.50) **10 Ran SP% 117.7**
WIN (incl. 1 euro stake): 4.20. PLACES: 1.90, 2.90, 4.10. DF: 20.70. SF: 41.70.
Owner K Abdullah **Bred** Juddmonte Farms Ltd **Trained** Chantilly, France

The Form Book Flat, Raceform Ltd, Compton, RG20 6NL.

[1659]BATH (L-H)

Tuesday, April 30

OFFICIAL GOING: Good to firm (good in places)

Wind: Moderate across Weather: Sunny spells

1896 CORK BAR MAIDEN STKS 5f 161y
2:20 (2:20) (Class 5) 3-Y-O+ £2,587 (£770; £384; £192) Stalls Low

Form RPR
422- 1 **Asian Trader**[250] 5505 4-9-12 67.....................................(t) KellyHarrison 6 88
(William Haggas) *mde virtually all: c clr appr fnl f: comf* 7/2[2]
623- 2 4 ½ **Silverrica (IRE)**[257] 5260 3-8-10 68.............................. TomMcLaughlin 3 65
(Malcolm Saunders) *chsd ldrs: wnt 2nd 2f out: sn drvn: kpt on but nvr any ch w wnr* 10/1
0 3 2 ¼ **The Dark Wizard (IRE)**[11] 1660 3-9-1 0........................ SteveDrowne 8 63
(Roger Charlton) *in tch: hdwy fr 2f out: pushed along to take 3rd 1f out: nvr any imp on ldng duo* 16/1
0-3 4 2 ½ **Assertive Agent**[11] 1660 3-8-10 0.. JohnFahy 5 49
(Ben De Haan) *towards rr: drvn over 2f out: kpt on fnl f but nvr any ch* 5/1[3]
053- 5 2 ½ **Imperial Spirit**[124] 8258 3-9-1 65...................................... MartinHarley 1 46
(Mick Channon) *chsd wnr tl ins fnl 3f: wknd 2f out* 7/1
0 6 1 ½ **Hypnotism**[11] 1660 3-9-1 0.. LukeMorris 2 41
(Ronald Harris) *slowly away: sn drvn: kpt on past btn horses fnl f* 33/1
4- 7 1 ½ **Marishi Ten (IRE)**[347] 2234 3-8-10 0..........................[1] DavidProbert 10 31
(Andrew Balding) *prom: chsd wnr ins fnl 3f to 2f out: sn wknd* 5/4[1]
045 8 10 **Don't Be Scilly**[80] 581 5-9-0 40.................................... JoeyHaynes(7) 4
(Eric Wheeler) *spd to 1/2-way* 100/1
9 20 **Never A Quarrel (IRE)** 3-8-10 0.................................... HarryBentley 7
(Jeremy Gask) *chsd ldrs: wknd qckly 2f out* 40/1

1m 10.06s (-1.14) **Going Correction** -0.35s/f (Firm)
WFA 3 from 4yo+ 11lb 9 Ran SP% **117.2**
Speed ratings (Par 103): **93,87,84,80,77 75,73,60,33**
toteswingers 1&2 £3.70, 2&3 £13.10, 1&3 £9.80 CSF £38.12 TOTE £3.90: £1.20, £2.20, £3.80; EX 29.00 Trifecta £237.40 Pool: £1205.47 - 3.80 winning units..
Owner M S Bloodstock Ltd **Bred** Mike Smith **Trained** Newmarket, Suffolk

FOCUS
Just a modest sprint maiden. The favourite disappointed and it's hard to gauge what the winner achieved, but he is clearly improved.

1897 32RED CASINO H'CAP 1m 3f 144y
2:50 (2:50) (Class 6) (0-60,60) 3-Y-O £1,940 (£577; £288; £144) Stalls Low

Form RPR
000- 1 **Instinctual**[143] 8033 3-8-7 46 oh1.................................(b[1]) CathyGannon 7 54
(Brendan Powell) *in rr: hdwy 3f out: sn drvn to chse ldrs: wnt 2nd appr fnl f: styd wl on to ld fnl 30yds* 10/1[3]
0-02 2 1 ½ **Winter Music (IRE)**[26] 1343 3-8-12 58.................(v) DanielMuscutt(7) 11 63
(Andrew Balding) *chsd ldr: chal fr 4f out tl led over 2f out: drvn over 1f out: hdd and one pce fnl 30yds* 5/1[1]
00-6 3 2 ¼ **Karl Marx (IRE)**[27] 1314 3-8-8 47................................ FergusSweeney 3 48
(Mark Gillard) *in rr: pushed along and detached 6f out: hdwy over 2f out: kpt in for 3rd ins fnl f but no imp on ldng duo* 25/1
001- 4 5 **Pink Mischief**[221] 6435 3-9-1 54... LukeMorris 2 47
(Harry Dunlop) *in rr: hdwy 3f out: sn pushed along: hung lft u.p and one pce fr over 1f out* 5/1[1]
3314 5 shd **Lady Lunchalot (USA)**[10] 1685 3-9-0 60...........(p) CharlotteJenner(7) 10 53
(J S Moore) *led: jnd 4f out: hdd over 2f out: wknd fnl f* 7/1[2]
0-44 6 8 **Jawinski (IRE)**[7] 1743 3-9-2 60...................................... DeclanBates(5) 1 39
(David Evans) *in tch: chsd ldrs 6f out: wknd ins fnl 3f* 5/1[1]
0-50 7 ½ **Tilly T (IRE)**[10] 1685 3-8-5 47.. RyanPowell(3) 9 25
(J S Moore) *chsd ldrs: wknd over 2f out* 12/1
-524 8 1 **Aphrodite Spirit (IRE)**[27] 1326 3-8-5 49............ MichaelJMMurphy(5) 4 25
(Pat Eddery) *chsd ldrs: wknd fr 3f out* 5/1[1]
00-5 9 7 **Impertinent**[113] 90 3-8-13 52.. JohnFahy 8 16
(Jonathan Portman) *in tch: rdn along 6f out: wknd over 3f out* 5/1[1]
000- 10 3 ¾ **Greenfordgirl (IRE)**[182] 7460 3-8-4 46 oh1................. RaulDaSilva(3) 5
(John Weymes) *chsd ldrs: wknd 4f out* 33/1

2m 33.7s (3.10) **Going Correction** -0.025s/f (Good) 10 Ran SP% **119.4**
Speed ratings (Par 96): **88,87,85,82,82 76,76,75,71,68**
toteswingers 1&2 £15.70, 2&3 £13.30, 1&3 £42.00 CSF £60.89 CT £1236.46 TOTE £13.00: £3.20, £3.00, £7.50; EX 119.50 Trifecta £771.60 Pool: £1937.32 - 1.88 winning units..
Owner Nigel M Davies **Bred** Juddmonte Farms Ltd **Trained** Upper Lambourn, Berks

FOCUS
A really moderate contest with little convincing form to go on. Rated as average for the grade.

1898 32RED MEDIAN AUCTION MAIDEN STKS 1m 3f 144y
3:20 (3:21) (Class 5) 3-4-Y-O £2,587 (£770; £384; £192) Stalls Low

Form RPR
5 1 **Refer**[15] 1584 3-8-9 0.. SteveDrowne 2 74+
(Charles Hills) *mde all: pushed along 2f out: drvn and styd on strly ins fnl f* 9/4[1]
024 2 ¾ **Could Be (IRE)**[20] 1478 3-8-9 71... MartinLane 7 73
(David Simcock) *chsd wnr most of way: rdn fr ins fnl 2f: kpt on in clsng stages but a hld* 7/2[3]
00- 3 4 **Ballinderry Boy**[165] 7750 3-8-9 0..................................... DavidProbert 3 66
(Andrew Balding) *t.k.h early: chsd ldrs: rdn 3f out: btn ins fnl 2f* 12/1
3-63 4 7 **Jullundar (IRE)**[7] 1741 3-8-9 67.. MartinHarley 5 54
(Mick Channon) *in rr: hdwy over 6f out: chsd ldrs 3f out: sn rdn: wknd ins fnl 2f* 3/1[2]
020- 5 7 **Checkpoint**[269] 4797 4-10-0 81.. GeorgeBaker 6 44
(Gary Moore) *t.k.h early: disp 2nd 7f out tl over 2f out: sn wknd* 3/1[2]
0 6 46 **Cracker Mill**[20] 1468 4-10-0 0.. AdamKirby 1
(Michael Madgwick) *s.i.s: a in rr: lost tch fnl 3f: t.o* 100/1

2m 33.02s (2.42) **Going Correction** -0.025s/f (Good)
WFA 3 from 4yo 20lb 6 Ran SP% **111.7**
Speed ratings (Par 103): **90,89,86,82,77 46**
toteswingers 1&2 £1.50, 2&3 £5.70, 1&3 £4.10 CSF £10.38 TOTE £3.40: £2.10, £1.50; EX 9.60 Trifecta £46.70 Pool: £1949.35 - 31.24 winning units..
Owner K Abdullah **Bred** Juddmonte Farms Ltd **Trained** Lambourn, Berks

FOCUS
Not much of a race and they finished spread out. The runner-up is the best guide to the form.

1899 32RED.COM H'CAP 1m 5f 22y
3:50 (3:50) (Class 5) (0-70,69) 4-Y-O+ £2,587 (£770; £384; £192) Stalls High

Form RPR
6-36 1 **Bathwick Street**[21] 1445 4-9-4 67... MartinHarley 4 79+
(David Evans) *chsd ldrs: wnt 2nd over 3f out: drvn to take narrow ld 1f out: pushed clr fnl 110yds* 7/2[2]
136- 2 1 ¾ **Silver Samba**[203] 6971 4-9-6 69.. DavidProbert 7 77
(Andrew Balding) *chsd ldr: led 6f out: rdn 2f out: narrowly hdd 1f out: sn outpcd by wnr but kpt on wl for 2nd* 4/1[3]
023- 3 4 ½ **Sunny Future (IRE)**[191] 7269 7-9-6 68.....................[1] TomMcLaughlin 5 69+
(Malcolm Saunders) *in rr: drvn along 2f out: hdwy over 1f out: styd on to take 3rd in clsng stages: nvr a threat* 16/1
50-6 4 1 **Jolly Roger (IRE)**[15] 1586 6-9-6 68.................................... CathyGannon 3 68
(Tony Carroll) *in tch: rdn 3f out: hdwy to dispute one pce 3rd fr 2f out: no ch fnl f and wknd into 4th in clsng stages* 10/3[1]
2324 5 2 ¾ **Bramshill Lass**[26] 1348 4-8-7 56...(p) MartinLane 6 52
(Amanda Perrett) *chsd ldrs: rdden 3f out: sn disputing one pce 3rd fr 2f out: wknd over 1f out* 8/1
-246 6 4 **Comedy House**[20] 1466 5-9-1 63..(p) AdamKirby 8 53
(Michael Madgwick) *in rr: reminders 6f out: sme hdwy 3f out: wknd over 2f out* 9/1
2522 7 ¾ **Story Writer**[26] 1352 4-9-4 67...(p) ShaneKelly 2 56
(William Knight) *in tch: rdn 3f out: sn btn* 12/1
330- 8 20 **Steely**[264] 4983 5-9-7 69.. GeorgeBaker 1 28
(Gary Moore) *led: hdd 6f out: wknd 3f out* 11/2

2m 50.58s (-1.42) **Going Correction** -0.025s/f (Good)
WFA 4 from 5yo+ 1lb 8 Ran SP% **115.4**
Speed ratings (Par 103): **103,101,99,98,96 94,93,81**
toteswingers 1&2 £3.40, 2&3 £10.40, 1&3 £9.80 CSF £18.13 CT £195.67 TOTE £4.90: £1.80, £2.10, £2.90; EX 22.30 Trifecta £168.30 Pool: £2339.50 - 10.42 winning units..
Owner Wayne Clifford **Bred** Mrs D Du Feu **Trained** Pandy, Monmouths

FOCUS
A modest staying handicap with little depth. The winner is rated back to his best.

1900 GRASSROOTS RACING H'CAP 1m 5y
4:20 (4:21) (Class 5) (0-70,70) 3-Y-O £2,587 (£770; £384; £192) Stalls Low

Form RPR
-051 1 **Echo Brava**[27] 1320 3-9-3 66.. SteveDrowne 10 71+
(Luke Dace) *in rr: hdwy towards outside over 2f out: drvn and str run fnl f to ld cl home* 17/2[3]
204- 2 ½ **Poor Duke (IRE)**[197] 7103 3-9-5 68............................... FergusSweeney 3 72
(Jamie Osborne) *sn slt ld but hrd pressed tl asserted fr 2f out: styd on u.p fnl f: hdd cl home* 20/1
5413 3 1 ¼ **Hidden Link**[27] 1320 3-9-7 70... LukeMorris 1 71
(Ronald Harris) *chsd ldrs: drvn along fr 3f out: styd on u.p fr 2f out to take 3rd fnl f: kpt on but nvr gng pce of ldng duo* 12/1
040- 4 hd **Roanne (USA)**[186] 7364 3-9-4 67... AdamKirby 7 68
(Clive Cox) *chsd ldrs: drvn to dispute 3rd fr 2f out: nvr gng pce to chal: one pce fnl f* 7/2[1]
30-0 5 nse **Harry Bosch**[13] 1612 3-9-7 70... MartinLane 9 70
(Brian Meehan) *sn disputing ld: rdn 2f out: one pce u.p fnl f* 8/1[2]
330- 6 1 ½ **Muskat Link**[206] 6871 3-9-4 67... CathyGannon 5 64
(Henry Candy) *chsd ldrs: rdn over 2f out: one pce fnl f* 8/1[2]
52-0 7 ½ **Gilded Frame**[20] 1486 3-9-7 70.. GeorgeBaker 12 66
(Marcus Tregoning) *s.i.s: in rr: swtchd rt and hdwy 2f out: styd on fnl f: nvr a threat* 14/1
01-5 8 hd **Imperial Glance**[46] 1011 3-9-5 68..................................... DavidProbert 4 63
(Andrew Balding) *in tch: drvn to chse ldrs 4f out: styd on same pce u.p fnl 2f* 10/1
325- 9 ¾ **Ivanhoe**[160] 7814 3-9-5 68... LiamKeniry 11 62
(Michael Blanshard) *chsd ldrs: rdn over 2f out: wknd fnl f* 14/1
515 10 ½ **Gambolling Den (IRE)**[40] 1099 3-9-6 69............................... ShaneKelly 2 61
(David Simcock) *in rr: hdwy 4f out: chsd ldrs and rdn 3f out: wknd ins fnl 2f* 22/1
60-4 11 nk **Tagalaka (IRE)**[22] 1424 3-8-10 59.. JohnFahy 14 51
(Eve Johnson Houghton) *in tch: rdn 3f out: sn outpcd: styd on again u.p fnl f* 20/1
4165 12 ½ **The Scuttler (IRE)**[13] 1608 3-9-3 66.................................. MartinHarley 8 57
(Mick Channon) *in rr: rdn and sme hdwy 3f out: btn fnl 2f* 11/1
254- 13 9 **Rioja Day (IRE)**[197] 7111 3-9-4 67..................................... SebSanders 13 37
(J W Hills) *in rr: sme hdwy 3f out wknd 2f out* 14/1
03-5 14 dist **Winnie Perry**[24] 1400 3-8-13 67............................ MichaelJMMurphy(5) 6
(Rod Millman) *t.o fnl 3f: virtually p.u fnl 2f* 10/1

1m 41.44s (0.64) **Going Correction** -0.025s/f (Good) 14 Ran SP% **123.0**
Speed ratings (Par 98): **95,94,93,93,93 91,91,90,90,89 89,88,79,**
toteswingers 1&2 £55.60, 2&3 £23.70, 1&3 £9.50 CSF £174.07 CT £2114.08 TOTE £12.90: £3.70, £6.60, £3.40; EX 233.30 Trifecta £1893.00 Part won. Pool: £2524.00 - 0.59 winning units..
Owner MCSD Racing & Mark Benton **Bred** Adweb Ltd **Trained** Five Oaks, W Sussex

FOCUS
Just a modest, if open, handicap. The pace held up. The winner may do better yet.

1901 CB SECURITY H'CAP 1m 5y
4:50 (4:50) (Class 5) (0-75,75) 4-Y-O+ £2,749 (£818; £408; £204) Stalls Low

Form RPR
1111 1 **Mubtadi**[36] 1176 5-9-0 73.. ThomasBrown(5) 9 81+
(Ismail Mohammed) *stdd towards rr: hdwy on outer over 2f out: led appr fnl f: kpt on wl under hands and heels: a jst doing enough* 5/2[1]
2234 2 shd **Hierarch (IRE)**[64] 791 6-8-5 66...................................... SiobhanMiller(7) 8 73
(David Simcock) *chsd ldrs: drvn to chse wnr 1f out: rallied and str chal in clsng stages: nt quite get up* 12/1
6502 3 1 ¾ **Prince Of Burma (IRE)**[36] 1170 5-9-7 75.........................(bt) AdamKirby 1 78
(Jeremy Gask) *in rr: hdwy fr 2f out: drvn and styd on to take 3rd ins fnl f: kpt on same pce* 7/2[2]
-210 4 3 **Stormbound (IRE)**[56] 963 4-8-13 67.................................. DavidProbert 5 63
(Paul Cole) *chsd ldr: drvn to ld over 2f out: hdd appr fnl f: wknd fnl 110yds* 4/1[3]
6012 5 nk **Ocean Legend (IRE)**[5] 1782 8-9-6 74................................ CathyGannon 6 69
(Tony Carroll) *t.k.h: chsd ldrs: rdn ins fnl 2f: wknd fnl f* 6/1
0-30 6 1 ½ **Fire King**[15] 1585 7-8-11 65...(p) LiamKeniry 7 57
(Paul Burgoyne) *in rr: pushed along over 1f out: sme late prog* 16/1
60-0 7 1 ¼ **Siouxperhero (IRE)**[18] 1514 4-9-2 70............................(b) MartinHarley 2 59
(William Muir) *led: hdd over 2f out: wknd appr fnl f* 10/1

0-50 8 1 **Kept**[4] 1801 4-8-13 **67** .... LukeMorris 4 54
(Ronald Harris) *chsd ldrs: rdn and btn 2f out* **14/1**
0/0- 9 ¾ **Ebony Song (USA)**[276] 4586 5-8-8 **62** .... FergusSweeney 3 47
(Jo Crowley) *chsd ldrs: rdn over 2f out: sn btn* **33/1**
1m 40.09s (-0.71) **Going Correction** -0.025s/f (Good) **9** Ran SP% **117.4**
Speed ratings (Par 103): **102,101,100,97,96 95,94,93,92**
toteswingers 1&2 £5.40, 2&3 £7.50, 1&3 £2.60 CSF £35.03 CT £107.63 TOTE £3.30: £1.90, £3.10, £1.20; EX 24.10 Trifecta £154.30 Pool: £2439.98 - 11.85 winning units..
Owner Abdulla Al Mansoori **Bred** Whitsbury Manor Stud **Trained** Newmarket, Suffolk
■ Stewards' Enquiry : Siobhan Miller one-day ban: careless riding (May 14)
FOCUS
An ordinary handicap. The winner is edging towards his old form and can't get hit hard for this.

1902 £32 BONUS AT 32RED.COM H'CAP 5f 11y
5:20 (5:21) (Class 6) (0-65,65) 4-Y-O+ **£1,940** (£577; £288; £144) **Stalls** Centre

Form RPR
33-6 1 **Dreams Of Glory**[60] 842 5-8-13 **57** .... DavidProbert 12 73
(Ron Hodges) *mde all: drvn clr appr fnl f: unchal* **8/1**
0-40 2 4 **Kyllachy Storm**[11] 1665 9-8-6 **55** .... PhilipPrince(5) 7 57
(Ron Hodges) *chsd ldrs: rdn over 2f out: styd on to dispute 2nd over 1f out: chsd wnr cl home but nvr any ch* **10/1**
1332 3 nk **Where's Reiley (USA)**[11] 1665 7-9-4 **62** ....(v) SebSanders 13 63
(Michael Attwater) *chsd wnr: no imp fr 2f out: one pce fnl f and dropped to 3rd cl home* **7/2**[2]
5121 4 2¾ **Picansort**[18] 1517 6-9-5 **63** ....(b) ShaneKelly 3 54
(Peter Crate) *chsd ldrs: rdn and one pce fnl 2f* **9/4**[1]
-005 5 2¾ **Volcanic Dust (IRE)**[8] 1731 5-8-12 **56** ....(t) MartinHarley 6 38
(Milton Bradley) *in rr: drvn and styd on fr 2f out: nvr rchd ldrs* **25/1**
560- 6 1 **The Name Is Frank**[197] 7105 8-8-8 **52** ....(t) FergusSweeney 15 30
(Mark Gillard) *in rr: pushed along over 2f out: styd on fnl f* **20/1**
50-0 7 ¾ **Jolly Ranch**[85] 516 7-8-8 **52** .... MartinLane 1 28
(Tony Newcombe) *chsd ldrs: rdn over 2f out: wknd wl over 1f out* **22/1**
2060 8 1¼ **Courageous (IRE)**[29] 1286 7-9-2 **65** ....(t) MatthewLawson(5) 14 36
(Milton Bradley) *in tch 3f* **16/1**
0235 9 hd **Athwaab**[20] 1475 6-8-12 **63** .... JakePayne(7) 2 34
(Simon Hodgson) *chsd ldrs to 1/2-way* **33/1**
04-0 10 ½ **Even Bolder**[69] 719 10-8-6 **57** ....(b) JoeyHaynes(7) 10 26
(Eric Wheeler) *spd to 1/2-way* **20/1**
453- 11 1½ **Trending (IRE)**[129] 8231 4-9-4 **62** ....(b) HarryBentley 5 26
(Jeremy Gask) *sn outpcd* **6/1**[3]
00/0 12 1¾ **Sir Don (IRE)**[28] 1304 14-8-3 **54** oh6 ow3............(b) JordanNason(7) 4
(Michael Mullineaux) *sn outpcd* **66/1**
5061 13 5 **Loyal Royal (IRE)**[26] 1355 10-8-7 **51** oh1............(bt) ChrisCatlin 9
(Milton Bradley) *s.i.s: a outpcd* **20/1**
05-0 14 hd **Mandy's Hero**[8] 1731 5-8-8 **52** ....(b) CathyGannon 8
(Olivia Maylam) *a outpcd* **50/1**
1m 0.59s (-1.91) **Going Correction** -0.35s/f (Firm) **14** Ran SP% **122.2**
Speed ratings (Par 101): **101,94,94,89,85 83,82,80,80,79 77,74,66,65**
toteswingers 1&2 £18.60, 2&3 £11.70, 1&3 £5.00 CSF £76.70 CT £337.61 TOTE £10.20: £2.70, £5.00, £2.40; EX 102.70 Trifecta £411.20 Pool: £1753.54 - 3.19 winning units..
Owner P E Axon **Bred** P E Axon **Trained** Charlton Mackrell, Somerset
FOCUS
A moderate sprint handicap and nothing could live with the winner, who would be hard to beat under a penalty. It was a one-two for Ron Hodges.
T/Plt: £430.70 to a £1 stake. Pool of £54361.26 - 92.12 winning tickets. T/Qpdt: £26.30 to a £1 stake. Pool of £4261.50 - 119.80 winning tickets. ST

[1873]LINGFIELD (L-H)
Tuesday, April 30

OFFICIAL GOING: Standard
Wind: Moderate, half against Weather: Sunny spells

1903 YOUR GUIDE TO LINGFIELD AT LINGFIELDRACECOURSETIPS.CO.UK CLAIMING STKS 7f (P)
2:00 (2:00) (Class 6) 3-Y-O **£2,045** (£603; £302) **Stalls** Low

Form RPR
0-50 1 **A Ladies Man (IRE)**[12] 1636 3-9-7 67............ RichardHughes 6 74
(Richard Hannon) *mde all: pushed clr over 1f out: comf* **1/1**[1]
5256 2 2¼ **Princess Cammie (IRE)**[10] 1695 3-8-0 53............ KieranO'Neill 2 47
(Mike Murphy) *plld hrd: disp 2nd: chsd wnr fnl 2f: one pce: jst hld on for 2nd* **12/1**
21 3 nse **Back On The Trail**[40] 1106 3-9-13 75............ StevieDonohoe 3 74
(Rae Guest) *dwlt: sn in tch: outpcd 2f out: rallied and r.o wl fnl f* **3/1**[2]
33-5 4 shd **Fiducia**[27] 1319 3-8-11 62............ RobertTart(5) 8 63
(Simon Dow) *stdd s: hld up in rr: shkn up and hdwy over 1f out: r.o wl fnl f: clsng at fin* **10/1**
6320 5 2¼ **Bubbly Bailey**[6] 1759 3-8-13 59............(b[1]) PaulHanagan 5 54
(Alan Bailey) *disp 2nd tl 2f out: wknd fnl f* **7/1**[3]
0053 6 3½ **Claude Greenwood**[10] 1695 3-8-11 57............(p) TomQueally 1 42
(David Simcock) *a abt same pl: outpcd and btn 2f out* **14/1**
060- 7 7 **Everreadyneddy**[194] 7191 3-8-9 57............ LiamJones 7 21
(J S Moore) *in tch on outer: hrd rdn 3f out: sn wknd* **33/1**
1m 25.32s (0.52) **Going Correction** 0.0s/f (Stan) **7** Ran SP% **113.9**
Speed ratings (Par 96): **97,94,94,94,91 87,79**
toteswingers 1&2 £5.70, 2&3 £4.80, 1&3 £2.30 CSF £14.89 TOTE £1.80: £1.30, £4.90; EX 17.10 Trifecta £75.00 Pool: £1884.03 - 18.82 winning units..Back On The Trail was claimed by M Blake for £13,000. Princess Cammie was claimed by J Bridger for £2,000.
Owner Mrs J Wood **Bred** Bloomsbury Stud **Trained** East Everleigh, Wilts
FOCUS
A modest claimer which was all about the winner, who posted a fair time and rates a personal best.

1904 COWDEN MEDIAN AUCTION MAIDEN STKS 1m (P)
2:30 (2:32) (Class 6) 3-Y-O **£2,045** (£603; £302) **Stalls** High

Form RPR
22-3 1 **World Record (IRE)**[22] 1423 3-9-5 79............ RichardHughes 2 76+
(Richard Hannon) *mde virtually all: smoothly drew clr over 1f out: easily* **1/2**[1]
- 2 1¾ **Mawj Tamy (USA)** 3-9-5 0............ PaulHanagan 1 69
(Charles Hills) *dwlt: sn chsng ldrs: wnt 2nd 2f out: one pce appr fnl f* **5/1**[2]
0- 3 nk **Liberty Jack (IRE)**[220] 6486 3-9-5 0............ JamesDoyle 9 68+
(Roger Charlton) *stdd s: hld up towards rr: shkn up and hdwy fr over 1f out: gng on at fin* **6/1**[3]

32- 4 nk **Banreenahreenkah (IRE)**[221] 6431 3-9-0 0............ TomQueally 11 62
(Denis Coakley) *trckd ldrs: shkn up over 1f out: kpt on fnl f* **12/1**
0 5 1¾ **Bee Jay Kay**[11] 1666 3-9-0 0............ MatthewDavies 8 58
(Mick Channon) *mid-div: rdn over 4f out: outpcd 3f out: styd on fnl f* **33/1**
0- 6 hd **Cherry Tiger**[167] 7707 3-9-5 0............ RobertHavlin 10 63
(James Toller) *sn stdd bk to rr: hld up: shkn up and hdwy over 1f out: nrest at fin* **20/1**
0 7 ½ **Welsh Moonlight**[12] 1640 3-9-0 0............ WilliamBuick 5 56
(Gerard Butler) *dwlt: sn in tch: wnt 3rd over 1f out: wknd fnl f* **25/1**
0P6- 8 5 **Smart Alice**[158] 7840 3-9-0 0............ TedDurcan 12 44
(Chris Wall) *bhd: pushed along over 2f out: nvr trbld ldrs* **66/1**
0-0 9 hd **I Need A Dollar**[111] 114 3-9-0 0............ DannyBrock(5) 7 49
(J R Jenkins) *pressed wnr on outer tl wknd 2f out* **100/1**
00 10 5 **Hundred Acre Wood**[22] 1423 3-9-5 0............ IanMongan 6 37
(Olivia Maylam) *prom: rdn 3f out: wknd 2f out* **100/1**
11 24 **We'Re In The Red (IRE)** 3-9-5 0............ WilliamCarson 3
(Mark Hoad) *s.s: rn green: a bhd: no ch fnl 3f* **100/1**
1m 38.86s (0.66) **Going Correction** 0.0s/f (Stan) **11** Ran SP% **121.3**
Speed ratings (Par 96): **96,94,93,93,91 91,91,86,86,81 57**
toteswingers 1&2 £1.80, 2&3 £2.50, 1&3 £2.90 CSF £3.34 TOTE £1.60: £1.02, £2.70, £1.80; EX 3.80 Trifecta £11.50 Pool: £2702.83 - 176.13 winning units..
Owner Mrs J Wood **Bred** Roy W Tector **Trained** East Everleigh, Wilts
FOCUS
This maiden has gone to some decent sorts in recent years including Premio Loco in 2007 and Beachfire three years ago. It's wasn't the most competitive of races, but there were some eye-catching performances. The winner won with a bit in hand and the form is rated around him, with the fourth fitting in.

1905 LINGFIELDPARK.CO.UK H'CAP 1m (P)
3:00 (3:00) (Class 3) (0-95,93) 4-Y-O+ **£7,439** (£2,213; £1,106; £553) **Stalls** High

Form RPR
4033 1 **Mia's Boy**[7] 1745 9-9-2 93............ RobertTart(5) 1 100
(Chris Dwyer) *s.s: hld up in rr: rdn over 2f out: str run fnl f: led nr fin* **8/1**
56-2 2 nk **Cruiser**[19] 1500 5-8-13 85............ MartinDwyer 5 91
(William Muir) *in tch: outpcd 3f out: rallied fnl f: r.o wl to take 2nd fnl strides* **8/1**
5041 3 nk **Lowther**[5] 1796 8-9-1 87 6ex............(v) KierenFox 6 92
(Lee Carter) *in tch: jnd ldrs on outer 2f out: led ins fnl f: hdd and no ex nr fin* **4/1**[3]
120- 4 ½ **Roserrow**[307] 3508 4-9-1 87............ JimmyFortune 4 91+
(Andrew Balding) *t.k.h: pressed ldrs: led over 1f out tl ins fnl f: one pce* **6/1**
13-0 5 ½ **Gaul Wood (IRE)**[31] 1233 4-9-3 89............ RichardKingscote 2 92
(Tom Dascombe) *sn w ldr: led over 6f out tl over 1f out: one pce ins fnl f* **9/4**[1]
3402 6 nk **Verse Of Love**[7] 1745 4-9-3 89............(v) RichardHughes 3 91
(David Evans) *led over 1f: chsd ldrs after: rdn over 2f out: styd on same pce fnl f* **3/1**[2]
1m 36.21s (-1.99) **Going Correction** 0.0s/f (Stan) **6** Ran SP% **112.3**
Speed ratings (Par 107): **109,108,108,107,107 107**
toteswingers 1&2 £1.70, 2&3 £14.60, 1&3 £12.50 CSF £65.42 TOTE £7.30: £2.00, £3.70; EX 34.90 Trifecta £193.40 Pool: £1330.67 - 5.15 winning units..
Owner Mrs Shelley Dwyer **Bred** Sir Eric Parker **Trained** Newmarket, Suffolk
FOCUS
A decent handicap but, despite the small field, the pace was strong which played right into the hands of the winner. The winner is rated to his winter form.

1906 PLAWHATCH H'CAP 6f (P)
3:30 (3:30) (Class 6) (0-60,60) 3-Y-O **£2,045** (£603; £302) **Stalls** Low

Form RPR
04-0 1 **Fossa**[27] 1319 3-8-11 **50**............ RichardHughes 9 57+
(Dean Ivory) *hld up towards rr: hdwy over 1f out: qcknd to ld ins fnl f: comf* **7/2**[2]
6-45 2 1¼ **Angels Calling**[20] 1476 3-9-4 **57**............ RobertWinston 4 57
(Mrs K Burke) *in tch: rdn to chse ldrs over 1f out: kpt on to take 2nd ins fnl f* **3/1**[1]
06-6 3 hd **Poetic Belle**[8] 1710 3-8-9 **55**............(v) DavidParkes(7) 8 54
(Alan Jarvis) *chsd ldrs: led over 1f out: hdd and one pce ins fnl f* **10/1**
004- 4 3 **Trymyluck**[189] 7313 3-9-2 **55**............ DaneO'Neill 7 45
(Pam Sly) *sltly outpcd in rr: effrt on outer 2f out: styd on fnl f* **6/1**[3]
2-33 5 hd **Annaley My Darling (IRE)**[33] 1216 3-9-7 **60**............ JoeFanning 1 49
(Mark Rimmer) *broke wl: chsd ldrs: effrt over 1f out: styd on same pce fnl f* **10/1**
4045 6 hd **Hawsies Dream**[1] 1888 3-9-3 **56**............ PaulHanagan 10 44
(Alan Bailey) *pressed ldr: slt ld over 1f out: sn hdd & wknd* **7/1**
050- 7 ¾ **Royal Betty**[224] 6330 3-8-10 **49**............ KierenFox 3 35
(Lee Carter) *towards rr: rdn 2f out: n.d* **16/1**
-202 8 1 **Sally Bruce**[57] 876 3-8-9 **55**............ JenniferFerguson(7) 6 38
(Louise Best) *s.s: t.k.h in rr: nt clr run on inner over 2f out: mod effrt ent st: unable to chal* **25/1**
5-36 9 1¾ **Prom Dress**[62] 817 3-9-0 **60**............ GaryPhillips(7) 2 37
(Robert Cowell) *prom tl wknd over 1f out* **7/1**
00-6 10 1½ **Eton Miss (IRE)**[69] 729 3-8-7 **46** oh1............ MartinDwyer 5 18
(Mike Murphy) *sn led: hdd & wknd over 1f out* **33/1**
1m 13.91s (2.01) **Going Correction** 0.0s/f (Stan) **10** Ran SP% **117.4**
Speed ratings (Par 96): **86,84,84,80,79 79,78,77,74,72**
toteswingers 1&2 £4.20, 2&3 £9.10, 1&3 £20.10 CSF £14.55 CT £97.50 TOTE £4.50: £1.80, £1.20, £4.30; EX 15.60 Trifecta £173.00 Pool: £906.94 - 3.93 winning units..
Owner Geoff Copp **Bred** G B Turnbull Ltd **Trained** Radlett, Herts
FOCUS
Nine of the ten runners came into this moderate handicap as maidens. The winner was value for a bit extra, with the second helping to set the standard.

1907 CROWHURST FILLIES' H'CAP 7f (P)
4:00 (4:01) (Class 5) (0-70,67) 3-Y-O **£2,726** (£805; £402) **Stalls** Low

Form RPR
023- 1 **Girl Of Cadiz**[137] 8103 3-9-2 **67**............ WilliamTwiston-Davies(5) 9 71
(Richard Hannon) *prom: wnt 2nd 3f out: led ins fnl f: rdn out to hold on fr clsng rivals* **6/1**[3]
030- 2 nk **Tight Fit**[188] 7329 3-9-1 **61**............ DaneO'Neill 8 64+
(Henry Candy) *racd wd: mid-div: effrt 2f out: r.o wl fnl f: wnt 2nd and clsng on wnr nr fin: a hld* **7/4**[1]
6-03 3 nse **Yahilwa (USA)**[5] 1784 3-9-4 **64**............ TomQueally 7 67+
(James Tate) *plld hrd towards rr: effrt and wd into st: fin wl* **8/1**
04-4 4 ½ **Princess Patsky (USA)**[20] 1476 3-9-2 **62**............(v[1]) WilliamBuick 10 64
(Michael Bell) *t.k.h: chsd ldrs on outer: rdn 2f out: kpt on fnl f* **7/1**

1300 **5** *nk* **Nellie Bly**[12] 1647 3-9-6 **66** JoeFanning 4 67
(Mark Johnston) *led: rdn and hdd ins fnl f: one pce* **16/1**
034- **6** *2 ¾* **Mojo Bear**[164] 7777 3-9-5 **65** JDSmith 6 58
(Sylvester Kirk) *hld up in rr: stdy late hdwy: sddle slipped* **50/1**
34-4 **7** *½* **Not Now Blondie**[26] 1349 3-8-8 **59** (p) RobertTart(5) 5 51
(Chris Dwyer) *in tch: rdn 2f out: sn outpcd* **8/1**
20-3 **8** *1 ¼* **Serenata (IRE)**[15] 1575 3-9-0 **60** (p) JamesDoyle 3 49
(Paul Cole) *towards rr: rdn 2f out: n.d* **25/1**
04-0 **9** *1 ¼* **Epic Charm**[10] 1678 3-8-13 **59** MatthewDavies 1 44
(Mick Channon) *in tch: rdn over 2f out: sn btn* **5/1**[2]
056- **10** *nk* **Something Magic**[165] 7737 3-9-5 **65** RichardHughes 2 50
(Sylvester Kirk) *chsd ldr tl 3f out: wknd 2f out* **12/1**

1m 25.8s (1.00) **Going Correction** 0.0s/f (Stan) **10** Ran SP% **121.4**
Speed ratings (Par 95): **94,93,93,93,92 89,88,87,86,85**
toteswingers 1&2 £2.20, 2&3 £3.20, 1&3 £2.10 CSF £17.61 CT £89.08 TOTE £7.40: £2.20, £1.60, £2.20; EX 23.00 Trifecta £136.20 Pool: £1319.75 - 7.26 winning units..
Owner Mrs J K Powell **Bred** Mrs J K Powell **Trained** East Everleigh, Wilts

FOCUS
A modest fillies' handicap and there was little covering the front five at the line. Ordinary form but it does make sense.

1908 BRITISH STALLION STUDS SUPPORTING BRITISH RACING EBF MAIDEN STKS 7f (P)
4:30 (4:33) (Class 5) 3-Y-O **£3,881** (£1,155; £577; £288) **Stalls** Low

Form RPR
6 **1** **Messila Star**[13] 1618 3-9-5 WilliamBuick 7 84+
(Jeremy Noseda) *trckd ldr: rdn 2f out: led ins fnl f: comf* **7/1**
06- **2** *½* **Shaishee (USA)**[220] 6486 3-9-5 PaulHanagan 6 82
(Charles Hills) *trckd ldrs: rdn 2f out: r.o to take 2nd fnl 50yds* **6/4**[1]
23- **3** *nk* **Hanzada (USA)**[195] 7159 3-9-0 JamesDoyle 9 76
(Ed Dunlop) *prom: rdn to chal over 1f out: kpt on* **3/1**[2]
230- **4** *2 ¼* **Living Desert**[206] 6874 3-9-5 79 RobertHavlin 4 75+
(James Toller) *hld up in rr: rdn and r.o fr over 1f out: nrest at fin* **16/1**
032- **5** *½* **Mac's Superstar (FR)**[152] 7926 3-9-5 77 TomQueally 3 74
(James Fanshawe) *prom: hrd rdn over 1f out: one pce* **10/1**
2-0 **6** *½* **Declamation (IRE)**[15] 1570 3-9-5 JoeFanning 1 73
(Mark Johnston) *led: rdn and hdd ins fnl f: wknd fnl 100yds* **14/1**
\- **7** *1 ½* **Candy Kitten** 3-9-0 RichardKingscote 2 64
(Alastair Lidderdale) *s.i.s: towards rr: brief effrt on inner ent st: nvr able to chal* **100/1**
3 **8** *shd* **Moortahan**[31] 1243 3-9-5 DaneO'Neill 8 68
(Richard Hannon) *s.i.s: towards rr: hrd rdn over 1f out: n.d* **5/1**[3]
0 **9** *2 ¾* **Kasbhom**[41] 1086 3-9-5 WilliamCarson 5 61
(Anthony Carson) *in tch: hrd rdn over 2f out: sn outpcd* **66/1**

1m 25.34s (0.54) **Going Correction** 0.0s/f (Stan) **9** Ran SP% **118.3**
Speed ratings (Par 98): **96,95,95,92,91 91,89,89,86**
toteswingers 1&2 £10.10, 2&3 £1.80, 1&3 £4.40 CSF £18.36 TOTE £6.80: £2.40, £1.30, £1.20; EX 26.10 Trifecta £105.40 Pool: £1868.80 - 13.28 winning units..
Owner Sheikh Khaled Duaij Al Sabah **Bred** Cheveley Park Stud Ltd **Trained** Newmarket, Suffolk

FOCUS
An interesting maiden including three who were very expensive yearlings and that trio dominated the finish. Above-average form for the grade.

1909 LINGFIELD PARK OWNERS GROUP H'CAP 1m 2f (P)
5:00 (5:02) (Class 6) (0-60,64) 4-Y-O+ **£2,045** (£603; £302) **Stalls** Low

Form RPR
0061 **1** **Salient**[35] 1183 9-8-10 **48** JoeFanning 10 55
(Michael Attwater) *prom: wnt 2nd after 3f: drvn to ld 1f out: hld on gamely* **5/1**[3]
2410 **2** *nk* **Peace In Our Time**[34] 1207 4-9-2 **54** (p) WilliamCarson 8 60
(Anthony Carson) *led 2f: prom: led briefly over 1f out: ev ch fnl f: kpt on wl: jst hld* **6/1**
100- **3** *½* **Penang Pegasus**[179] 7527 4-8-13 **51** RobertWinston 6 56
(Roger Teal) *in tch: rdn to press ldrs 2f out: kpt on fnl f* **3/1**[1]
0346 **4** *1 ½* **Dolly Colman (IRE)**[5] 1779 5-8-7 **45** (p) RichardKingscote 7 47
(Zoe Davison) *towards rr: hdwy over 2f out: styd on fnl f* **12/1**
2206 **5** *2 ¼* **Safwaan**[48] 978 6-9-7 **59** JamieMackay 2 57
(Willie Musson) *mid-div: dropped towards rr 5f out: rdn and sme hdwy over 1f out: no imp* **6/1**
3405 **6** *1* **Automotive**[19] 1498 5-8-13 **51** JamesDoyle 3 47
(Julia Feilden) *chsd ldr: led after 2f tl hdd & wknd over 1f out* **8/1**
0-20 **7** *4 ½* **Tinkerbell Will**[69] 722 6-8-12 **50** KirstyMilczarek 5 37
(John E Long) *mid-div on outer: rdn 3f out: n.d fnl 2f* **10/1**
030- **8** *¾* **Highlife Dancer**[181] 7474 5-9-2 **59** CharlesBishop(5) 1 44
(Mick Channon) *chsd ldrs: rdn 3f out: sn wknd* **4/1**[2]
00-0 **9** *1 ½* **Capriska**[35] 1183 4-8-11 **49** J-PGuillambert 4 31
(Willie Musson) *a bhd* **33/1**

2m 5.93s (-0.67) **Going Correction** 0.0s/f (Stan) **9** Ran SP% **121.1**
Speed ratings (Par 101): **102,101,101,100,98 97,93,93,92**
toteswingers 1&2 £2.50, 2&3 £5.20, 1&3 £5.50 CSF £36.90 CT £107.80 TOTE £5.30: £3.10, £1.70, £1.10; EX 16.40 Trifecta £57.40 Pool: £1435.30 - 18.73 winning units..
Owner Canisbay Bloodstock **Bred** Hesmonds Stud Ltd **Trained** Epsom, Surrey

FOCUS
A weak handicap but the pace looked reasonable. Hard to enthuse over the form.
T/Plt: £34.40 to a £1 stake. Pool of £53835.30 - 1142.13 winning tickets. T/Qpdt: £25.00 to a £1 stake. Pool of £3680.30 - 108.80 winning tickets. LM

1748 YARMOUTH (L-H)
Tuesday, April 30

OFFICIAL GOING: Good to firm (7.5)
Wind: medium, behind Weather: bright and breezy

1910 WEATHERBYS HAMILTON INSURANCE MAIDEN AUCTION STKS 5f 43y
2:10 (2:11) (Class 5) 2-Y-O **£2,587** (£770; £384; £192) **Stalls** Centre

Form RPR
0 **1** **Lady Lydia (IRE)**[12] 1634 2-8-4 0 SilvestreDeSousa 4 68
(Michael Wigham) *dwlt: in tch in last pair: pushed along after 1f: hdwy 1/2-way: chsd ldr and rdn over 1f out: rn green and wandered ent fnl f: hanging lft but r.o fnl 100yds to ld cl home* **4/5**[1]
622 **2** *½* **Lilo Lil**[5] 1792 2-8-1 0 DarrenEgan(3) 1 66
(David C Griffiths) *dwlt: sn rcvrd to chse ldr after 1f tl led wl over 1f out: drvn ins fnl f: hdd and no ex cl home* **9/2**[3]
3 *3* **Sunningdale Rose (IRE)** 2-8-9 0 HayleyTurner 5 60
(Michael Bell) *dwlt: rn green and sn pushed along in rr: rdn 1/2-way: styd on fr over 1f out: wnt 3rd fnl 100yds: no threat to ldrs* **3/1**[2]
30 **4** *1 ¾* **Tyrsal (IRE)**[13] 1606 2-8-9 0 AndreaAtzeni 3 54
(Robert Eddery) *chsd ldr for 1f: rdn and struggling 1/2-way: rallied u.p to chse ldrs over 1f out: no ex and no imp ins fnl f* **25/1**
4 **5** *8* **Anfield**[7] 1749 2-8-5 0 NickyMackay 2 21
(Mick Quinn) *led tl rdn and hdd wl over 1f out: sn btn: fdd fnl f* **20/1**

1m 1.5s (-1.20) **Going Correction** -0.325s/f (Firm) **5** Ran SP% **107.3**
Speed ratings (Par 92): **96,95,90,87,74**
CSF £4.50 TOTE £1.40: £1.20, £1.70; EX 3.80 Trifecta £6.50 Pool: £2323.83 - 266.95 winning units..
Owner V Smith **Bred** Albert Conneally **Trained** Newmarket, Suffolk

FOCUS
A small field for a modest juvenile maiden.

1911 RIVERSIDE-RENTALS.CO.UK MEDIAN AUCTION MAIDEN STKS 5f 43y
2:40 (2:40) (Class 6) 3-Y-O **£1,940** (£577; £288; £144) **Stalls** Centre

Form RPR
6- **1** **Different**[277] 4545 3-9-0 0 TomEaves 6 71
(Bryan Smart) *mde all: rdn over 1f out: kpt on wl ins fnl f: rdn out* **9/4**[1]
20-3 **2** *1 ¼* **Baron Run**[28] 1299 3-9-2 70 MichaelMetcalfe(3) 4 71
(Mrs K Burke) *taken down early: chsd ldrs: rdn 2f out: wnt 2nd fnl 100yds: kpt on but no imp on wnr* **5/2**[2]
\- **3** *1 ¼* **Sixty Minutes** 3-9-5 0 (t) SeanLevey 1 67
(David Brown) *in tch in midfield: rdn and hdwy 2f out: chsd wnr ent fnl f: styd on same pce and lost 2nd fnl 100yds* **10/3**[3]
-222 **4** *2 ¼* **Clock Opera (IRE)**[21] 1447 3-9-0 63 KierenFallon 7 53
(William Stone) *racd towards stands' rail: chsd wnr tl ent fnl f: wknd* **6/1**
6-5 **5** *3* **Faluka (IRE)**[11] 1660 3-9-0 0 SilvestreDeSousa 2 43
(Paul Cole) *chsd ldrs for 2f: sn rdn and struggling: wl hld over 1f out* **8/1**
40 **6** *3 ¼* **Abanoas (USA)**[12] 1640 3-8-7 0 ShelleyBirkett(7) 5 31
(Alan Coogan) *sn outpcd in rr: n.d* **100/1**
7 *4* **Lily The Dragon (IRE)** 3-9-0 0 AndreaAtzeni 3 17
(Mick Quinn) *s.i.s: a outpcd in rr* **40/1**

1m 1.49s (-1.21) **Going Correction** -0.325s/f (Firm) **7** Ran SP% **111.2**
Speed ratings (Par 96): **96,94,92,88,83 78,72**
toteswingers 1&2 £2.00, 2&3 £1.90, 1&3 £2.00 CSF £7.69 TOTE £3.50: £1.80, £1.70; EX 8.80 Trifecta £27.20 Pool: £ 2700.19 - 74.30 winning units..
Owner Mrs F Denniff **Bred** A S Denniff **Trained** Hambleton, N Yorks

FOCUS
Another modest maiden over the minimum trip. The runner-up is the best guide.

1912 PLEASUREWOOD HILLS THEME PARK H'CAP 1m 3y
3:10 (3:10) (Class 4) (0-85,85) 3-Y-O **£4,690** (£1,395; £697; £348) **Stalls** Centre

Form RPR
163- **1** **Dark Emerald (IRE)**[196] 7125 3-9-7 **85** KierenFallon 2 91
(Brendan Powell) *mde all: rdn ent fnl 2f: styd on wl and a doing enough ins fnl f: rdn out* **12/1**
433- **2** *nk* **Yourartisonfire**[208] 6815 3-8-13 **80** MichaelMetcalfe(3) 1 85
(Mrs K Burke) *t.k.h: chsd ldrs: rdn and effrt 2f out: drvn and pressed wnr ent fnl f: sustained effrt fnl f but a jst hld* **4/1**[3]
2100 **3** *2 ¼* **Fraserburgh (IRE)**[12] 1645 3-8-9 **73** SilvestreDeSousa 5 73
(Mark Johnston) *chsd wnr: rdn 2f out: 3rd and styd on same pce fnl f* **12/1**
612- **4** *nk* **George Cinq**[202] 6980 3-9-1 **79** HayleyTurner 6 78
(Michael Bell) *hld up in last pair: rdn and effrt to chse ldng trio 2f out: no imp over 1f out: kpt on ins fnl f* **3/1**[2]
614- **5** *6* **Claim (IRE)**[224] 6344 3-8-13 **77** RyanMoore 4 63
(Sir Michael Stoute) *t.k.h: hld up in tch in midfield: rdn and no hdwy wl over 1f out: wknd 1f out* **5/2**[1]
00-3 **6** *3* **Luck (IRE)**[29] 1293 3-8-13 **77** JamieSpencer 3 56
(Stuart Williams) *v.s.a: detached in last: clsd and in tch whn reminders 1/2-way: drvn and no prog over 1f out: wknd fnl f* **11/2**
1425 **7** *1 ½* **Minimee**[12] 1655 3-8-4 **71** DarrenEgan(3) 7 46
(Phil McEntee) *racd towards stands' rail: in tch in midfield: rdn and effrt over 2f out: sn struggling: bhd over 1f out* **14/1**

1m 37.66s (-2.94) **Going Correction** -0.325s/f (Firm) **7** Ran SP% **111.0**
Speed ratings (Par 100): **101,100,98,98,92 89,87**
toteswingers 1&2 £6.90, 2&3 £8.70, 1&3 £8.90 CSF £55.61 TOTE £10.70: £3.90, £1.70; EX 65.80 Trifecta £667.40 Pool: £2469.54 - 2.77 winning units..
Owner K Rhatigan **Bred** Olive O'Connor **Trained** Upper Lambourn, Berks
■ Stewards' Enquiry : Michael Metcalfe two-day ban: used whip above permitted level (May 14-15)

FOCUS
A fair handicap where a case could be made for all seven runners. Much like the preceding sprint races they stuck to the centre of the course. The winner rates a personal best.

1913 WEATHERBYS HAMILTON INSURANCE H'CAP 7f 3y
3:40 (3:40) (Class 3) (0-95,94) 4-Y-O+ **£7,246** (£2,168; £1,084; £542; £270) **Stalls** Centre

Form RPR
2-26 **1** **Fast Finian (IRE)**[94] 400 4-8-12 **85** (b[1]) NeilCallan 4 95
(Paul D'Arcy) *t.k.h: mde all: rdn and forged clr ent fnl f: styd on wl: rdn out* **10/1**
240- **2** *1 ½* **Khubala (IRE)**[175] 7624 4-9-7 **94** RyanMoore 1 100
(Hugo Palmer) *t.k.h: chsd ldrs: rdn and effrt 2f out: chsd wnr ins fnl f: kpt on same pce after* **7/2**[2]
0-30 **3** *1* **King Of Jazz (IRE)**[17] 1537 5-8-11 **87** DarrenEgan(3) 3 90
(Michael Bell) *t.k.h: chsd ldrs: effrt u.p 2f out: kpt on ins fnl f: wnt 3rd cl home* **5/1**[3]
130- **4** *nk* **Comrade Bond**[178] 7559 5-8-4 **80** oh2 SimonPearce(3) 7 82
(Mark H Tompkins) *chsd wnr tl drvn and no ex ent fnl f: kpt on same pce and lost 2 pls ins fnl f* **28/1**
064 **5** *¾* **Swiss Cross**[6] 1765 6-9-2 **89** (t) KierenFallon 9 89
(Phil McEntee) *wl in tch in midfield: rdn and unable qck wl over 1f out: kpt on same pce ins fnl f* **5/1**[3]
060/ **6** *½* **Karam Albaari (IRE)**[524] 7516 5-9-3 **90** FrederikTylicki 5 89+
(J R Jenkins) *in tch tl dropped to rr 4f out: looked wl hld 2f out: hdwy and swtchd rt 1f out: styd on wl* **40/1**
100- **7** *½* **Princess Of Orange**[214] 6633 4-9-4 **91** JamieSpencer 6 89+
(Rae Guest) *v.s.a: hld up in rr: hdwy into midfield 2f out: drvn and styd on 1f out: nvr gng pce to rch ldrs: eased cl home* **16/1**
420- **8** *1 ¼* **Noble Citizen (USA)**[201] 7010 8-8-9 **89** (b) AliceHaynes(7) 2 83
(David Simcock) *in tch in midfield: rdn and effrt over 1f out: no real imp: plugged on same pce fnl f* **25/1**

0055 **9** 3 ½ **Spirit Of Sharjah (IRE)**[24] 1385 8-8-10 **90**............. ShelleyBirkett(7) 10 75
(Julia Feilden) *in tch in midfield: rdn and lost pl ent fnl 2f: bhd 1f out* **16/1**

06-5 **10** 2 ¼ **Bayleyf (IRE)**[111] 121 4-8-9 **82**...............................(t) AndreaAtzeni 8 61
(John Best) *stdd s: hld up in tch in midfield: rdn and lost pl over 2f out: wknd wl over 1f out* **28/1**

4302 **11** 13 **Galician**[8] 1720 4-9-1 **88**........................... SilvestreDeSousa 11 32
(Mark Johnston) *a towards rr: rdn and struggling 5f out: lost tch over 2f out: bhd and eased fnl f* **5/2**[1]

1m 23.71s (-2.89) **Going Correction** -0.325s/f (Firm) **11** Ran SP% **118.2**
Speed ratings (Par 107): **103,101,100,99,98 98,97,96,92,89 74**
toteswingers 1&2 £6.10, 2&3 £5.50, 1&3 £8.40 CSF £43.63 CT £179.09 TOTE £9.20: £2.30, £1.40, £2.00; EX 48.40 Trifecta £345.70 Pool: £3251.00 - 7.05 winning units..
Owner John W Kennedy **Bred** N Hartery **Trained** Newmarket, Suffolk

FOCUS
The feature race on the card and it looked to be a good, competitive handicap. However, it paid to race prominently again and few ever got involved. A number took a keen hold early but the time was quicker than standard. The winner showed he is every bit as good on turf as the AW.

1914 BBC RADIO NORFOLK FILLIES' H'CAP 7f 3y
4:10 (4:10) (Class 5) (0-70,70) 4-Y-O+ **£2,587** (£770; £384; £192) **Stalls** Centre

Form RPR

500- **1** **Alice Rose (IRE)**[175] 7600 4-8-13 **62**.............................. NickyMackay 3 71
(Rae Guest) *mde virtually all: rdn and clr over 1f out: in command and kpt on wl fnl f* **8/1**

536 **2** 1 ¾ **Gift Of Silence**[27] 1323 4-9-1 **64**.. NeilCallan 9 68
(John Berry) *t.k.h: hld up in last trio: rdn and effrt 2f out: hdwy to chse ldrs 1f out: kpt on u.p to go 2nd last strides: no threat to wnr* **8/1**

30-2 **3** hd **Tahlia Ree (IRE)**[4] 1802 4-9-0 **70**............................. LouisSteward(7) 6 73
(Michael Bell) *t.k.h early: chsd ldrs: wnt 2nd over 2f out: rdn and tried to chal over 1f out: styd on same pce fnl f: lost 2nd last strides* **11/4**[2]

-561 **4** 2 ½ **Olney Lass**[29] 1294 6-8-12 **64**.................................... SimonPearce(3) 5 61
(Lydia Pearce) *in tch in midfield: pushed along 1/2-way: rdn and effrt 2f out: drvn and styd on to chse ldng trio 1f out: kpt on same pce after* **5/1**[3]

041- **5** 4 ½ **Malekat Jamal (IRE)**[225] 6306 4-9-4 **67**.......................... KierenFallon 1 52
(David Simcock) *t.k.h: hld up in tch in midfield: rdn ent fnl 3f: drvn and wknd over 1f out* **9/4**[1]

1/-0 **6** ¾ **Tweedle Dee**[29] 1292 4-8-8 **57**.. JackMitchell 7 40
(Noel Quinlan) *s.i.s: hld up in rr: rdn and no hdwy 2f out: wl hld over 1f out* **25/1**

5-60 **7** ¾ **Caramelita**[79] 603 6-9-7 **70**.......................................(v) FrederikTylicki 2 51
(J R Jenkins) *stdd and awkward leaving stalls: t.k.h: hld up in last trio: rdn and no hdwy 2f out: nvr trbld ldrs* **9/1**

3000 **8** 2 ¼ **Miakora**[7] 1748 5-8-7 **56** oh11.. AndreaAtzeni 8 30
(Mick Quinn) *chsd wnr tl over 2f out: sn struggling: wknd wl over 1f out: bhd fnl f* **66/1**

1m 24.97s (-1.63) **Going Correction** -0.325s/f (Firm) **8** Ran SP% **111.7**
Speed ratings (Par 100): **96,94,93,90,85 84,84,81**
toteswingers 1&2 £8.10, 2&3 £3.10, 1&3 £4.70 CSF £66.05 CT £219.38 TOTE £8.40: £2.80, £1.90, £1.30; EX 70.20 Trifecta £286.10 Pool: £899.13 - 2.35 winning units..
Owner O T Lury **Bred** Kevin & Meta Cullen **Trained** Newmarket, Suffolk

FOCUS
Just a modest fillies' handicap where the winner, once again, made all down the centre of the track. The time was over a second slower than the preceding Class 3 event. The winner took advantage of a career-low mark.

1915 SCROBY SANDS WINDFARM H'CAP 1m 1f
4:40 (4:41) (Class 5) (0-70,69) 4-Y-O+ **£2,587** (£770; £384; £192) **Stalls** Low

Form RPR

-154 **1** **Silver Alliance**[29] 1292 5-8-12 **67**..........................(p) ShelleyBirkett(7) 6 74
(Julia Feilden) *stdd and dropped in bhd after s: t.k.h: hld up in rr: hdwy to chal and rdn wl over 1f out: led wl ins fnl f: rdn out* **9/4**[2]

05-0 **2** hd **Laughing Jack**[36] 1176 5-8-13 **66**........................ GeorgeDowning(5) 3 72
(Tony Carroll) *t.k.h: hld up in tch in last pair: swtchd rt and hdwy to chal 2f out: rdn to ld 1f out: hdd wl ins fnl f: kpt on* **85/40**[1]

55 **3** 1 ¼ **Redoute Star (AUS)**[18] 1520 7-8-10 **58**............................(b) NeilCallan 1 61
(Paul D'Arcy) *t.k.h: ev ch 2f out: sn rdn and ev ch after tl no ex and outpcd fnl 75yds* **3/1**[3]

000- **4** 4 **Saskia's Dream**[141] 8059 5-9-0 **69**.................................... IanBurns(7) 4 63
(Jane Chapple-Hyam) *chsd ldrs tl rdn to ld over 2f out: drvn and hdd 1f out: wknd qckly fnl 100yds* **8/1**

000- **5** 15 **King Of Wing (IRE)**[43] 7474 4-9-0 **62**..........................(t[1]) KierenFallon 2 32
(Phil McEntee) *led and set stdy gallop: rdn 3f out: hdd over 2f out and sn btn: bhd and eased ins fnl f* **11/1**

1m 59.13s (3.33) **Going Correction** 0.0s/f (Good) **5** Ran SP% **107.2**
Speed ratings (Par 103): **85,84,83,80,66**
CSF £7.00 TOTE £3.10: £1.70, £1.10; EX 6.50 Trifecta £13.50 Pool: £2013.99 - 111.13 winning units..
Owner In It To Win Partnership **Bred** Peter Harris **Trained** Exning, Suffolk

FOCUS
A small field for another modest affair but all five looked to have a chance. This was the first race on the round course and they stuck to the far rail. The early pace was sedate and the time was well outside of standard. Muddling form.

1916 CONFERENCES AT GREAT YARMOUTH RACECOURSE H'CAP 1m 3f 101y
5:10 (5:10) (Class 6) (0-55,55) 4-Y-O+ **£1,940** (£577; £288; £144) **Stalls** Low

Form RPR

0214 **1** **Corn Maiden**[56] 888 4-9-5 **53**.. FrederikTylicki 6 62+
(Mark Rimmer) *chsd ldrs: nt clr run and travelling wl over 2f out: rdn to ld jst over 1f out: styd on wl: rdn out* **5/1**[2]

-530 **2** 2 **Landesherr (GER)**[48] 978 6-9-4 **55**............................ DarrenEgan(3) 11 60
(Steve Gollings) *hld up in midfield: hdwy on outer travelling wl 3f out: drvn and ev ch over 1f out: no ex and one pce ins fnl f* **6/1**[3]

00P- **3** ¾ **Wasabi (IRE)**[270] 4776 4-9-2 **50**.. NeilCallan 8 54
(John Berry) *in tch in midfield: chsng ldrs and drvn whn nt clr run over 1f out: swtchd rt and rallied 1f out: kpt on* **12/1**

626- **4** ½ **Medieval Bishop (IRE)**[192] 7248 4-9-2 **50**.................. DuranFentiman 12 53
(Tim Walford) *chsd ldrs: drvn and effrt 2f out: kpt on same pce ins fnl f* **8/1**

0460 **5** 1 ¾ **Zafaraban (IRE)**[36] 1175 6-9-0 **53**.......................... GeorgeDowning(5) 4 53
(Tony Carroll) *hld up wl in rr: hdwy on outer 4f out: chsd ldrs and drvn 2f out: no ex 1f out: one pce ins fnl f* **9/2**[1]

-300 **6** hd **Lord Golan**[33] 1217 5-8-12 **53**...................................(b[1]) EDLinehan(7) 1 53
(Violet M Jordan) *hld up towards rr: hdwy on inner over 3f out: swtchd rt jst over 1f out: kpt on u.p ins fnl f* **20/1**

050- **7** 4 **Omega Omega**[247] 5637 4-8-13 **47**.............................. AdamBeschizza 5 40
(Julia Feilden) *chsd ldrs: wnt 2nd over 3f out: rdn and ev ch jst over 2f out: no ex ent fnl f: wknd ins fnl f* **12/1**

500- **8** hd **Chankillo**[153] 7921 4-9-4 **55**..................................... AshleyMorgan(3) 7 48
(Mark H Tompkins) *hld up in tch in last quartet: rdn and effrt 2f out: plugged on fnl f but nvr gng pce to threaten ldrs* **10/1**

6-60 **9** 5 **Bestfootforward**[41] 1090 4-8-12 **46** oh1...............(p) SilvestreDeSousa 2 33
(Olivia Maylam) *led: rdn and hrd pressed 2f out: hdd jst over 1f out: btn and heavily eased ins fnl f* **40/1**

4-60 **10** 15 **Gangsterbanksters (FR)**[103] 238 4-8-9 **46** oh1. MichaelMetcalfe(3) 10
(Mrs K Burke) *in tch in midfield: lost pl u.p over 3f out: bhd fnl 2f* **9/1**

4430 **11** 1 ½ **Gay Gallivanter**[14] 1600 5-8-12 **46** oh1............................ AndreaAtzeni 9
(Mick Quinn) *nvr gng wl and sn rdn along in midfield: dropped to rr 4f out: bhd fnl 2f* **16/1**

50-6 **12** shd **Merchants Return**[116] 62 4-8-9 **46** oh1.................... SimonPearce(3) 3
(Lydia Pearce) *hld up in tch in midfield: rdn and no hdwy 3f out: wknd 2f out* **14/1**

5-00 **13** 2 ½ **Sunny Bank**[27] 1333 4-8-12 **46**..(t) TomEaves 14
(Alan Coogan) *chsd ldr tl over 3f out: sn lost pl and bhd fnl 2f* **40/1**

2m 28.26s (-0.44) **Going Correction** 0.0s/f (Good) **13** Ran SP% **116.9**
Speed ratings (Par 101): **101,99,99,98,97 97,94,94,90,79 78,78,76**
toteswingers 1&2 £4.90, 2&3 £23.20, 1&3 £9.40 CSF £33.58 CT £339.92 TOTE £4.40: £1.30, £2.00, £4.60; EX 18.90 Trifecta £330.60 Pool: £1891.04 - 4.28 winning units..
Owner Ms Johanna McHugh **Bred** G B Turnbull Ltd **Trained** Newmarket, Suffolk
■ Stewards' Enquiry : George Downing caution: entered wrong stall

FOCUS
A poor affair to close the card which, despite the size of field, didn't take much winning. Another personal best from the winner.
T/Plt: £60.40 to a £1 stake. Pool of £50027.61 - 603.80 winning tickets. T/Qpdt: £44.20 to a £1 stake. Pool of £3297.10 - 55.10 winning tickets. SP

ASCOT (R-H)
Wednesday, May 1

OFFICIAL GOING: Good (str 8.3; rnd 9.2)
Wind: Moderate across Weather: Sunny

1917 ALDERMORE CONDITIONS STKS 5f
2:00 (2:03) (Class 2) 2-Y-O **£8,715** (£2,609; £1,304; £652; £326) **Stalls** Centre

Form RPR

1 **1** **Anticipated (IRE)**[16] 1580 2-9-1 0.............................. RichardHughes 3 94+
(Richard Hannon) *hld up towards rr but in tch tl quickned to ld 2f out: pushed along and styd on strly fnl f: readily* **5/2**[2]

1 **2** ¾ **Justice Day (IRE)**[12] 1669 2-9-1 0.............................. WilliamBuick 2 91+
(David Elsworth) *trckd ldrs: qckn to press wnr ins fnl 2f: drvn and nt qckn ins fnl f* **11/8**[1]

1 **3** 3 **Master Carpenter (IRE)**[26] 1360 2-9-1 0........................ AndreaAtzeni 1 80
(Rod Millman) *led to 2f out: sn drvn and one pce: kpt on again ins fnl f* **9/2**[3]

1 **4** ¾ **Montaigne**[18] 1541 2-9-1 0.. JimCrowley 5 78
(Ralph Beckett) *in tch: drvn 2f out: one pce fnl f* **9/2**[3]

321 **5** nse **Far Gaze (IRE)**[27] 1344 2-8-11 0.................................... LiamJones 4 73
(J S Moore) *chsd ldr 3f: outpcd over 1f out* **40/1**

1m 2.47s (1.97) **Going Correction** -0.025s/f (Good) **5** Ran SP% **109.5**
Speed ratings (Par 99): **83,81,77,75,75**
CSF £6.29 TOTE £3.40: £1.80, £1.30; EX 5.40 Trifecta £8.40 Pool: £3214.55 - 386.34 winning units..
Owner Woodcock, Bull, Ivory, Hannon **Bred** M Smith & Grennanstown Stud **Trained** East Everleigh, Wilts

FOCUS
With four unbeaten colts in attendance, this had the appearance of a smart contest but the early pace wasn't quick and it developed in a 2f sprint.

1918 ACTIVE NAVIGATION EBF STKS (CONDITIONS RACE) (FILLIES) 1m (R)
2:30 (2:32) (Class 3) 3-Y-O **£9,337** (£2,796; £1,398; £699; £349) **Stalls** Centre

Form RPR

40-5 **1** **Masarah (IRE)**[25] 1383 3-8-12 95.................................. RyanMoore 4 95
(Clive Brittain) *set modest early pce: drvn and quickned 2f out: styd on wl in clsng stages* **8/1**

150- **2** 1 **Pearl Sea (IRE)**[180] 7518 3-8-12 92.............................. JamieSpencer 3 93
(David Brown) *chsd wnr 4f out: rdn and qcknd to chal wl over 1f out: no ex and out styd ins fnl f* **3/1**[2]

21-2 **3** shd **Cruck Realta**[12] 1667 3-9-1 93...................................... MartinHarley 2 95
(Mick Channon) *trckd wnr 4f: styd cl up: nt clr run and swtchd rt to rail jst ins fnl f: kpt on to press for 2nd but no imp on wnr* **3/1**[2]

4 hd **Typhoon Lily (USA)**[28] 1336 3-8-12 94........................(t) RichardHughes 5 92
(M D O'Callaghan, Ire) *hld up on outer and in tch: drvn wl over 1f out: styd on fnl f to press for 2nd in clsng stages but no imp on wnr* **7/2**[3]

1- **5** 11 **Chat (USA)**[322] 3034 3-8-12 87.................................... WilliamBuick 1 78
(John Gosden) *in tch: pushed along 2f out and sn dropped away: eased whn no ch ins fnl f* **5/2**[1]

1m 42.92s (2.22) **Going Correction** +0.25s/f (Good) **5** Ran SP% **111.9**
Speed ratings (Par 100): **98,97,96,96,85**
CSF £31.87 TOTE £11.10: £3.40, £2.00; EX 30.00 Trifecta £91.30 Pool: £2510.25 - 20.61 winning units..
Owner Mohammed Al Nabouda **Bred** Rabbah Bloodstock Limited **Trained** Newmarket, Suffolk

FOCUS
Historically this hasn't been a contest for producing really classy types, with the notable exception of Fallen For You last year, albeit that success came on Kempton's Polytrack when the meeting was transferred. This result isn't reliable as the early gallop was ordinary.

1919 BATTERSEA DOGS & CATS HOME PARADISE STKS (LISTED RACE) 1m (S)
3:00 (3:04) (Class 1) 4-Y-O+
£20,982 (£7,955; £3,981; £1,983; £995; £499) **Stalls** Centre

Form RPR

304- **1** **Fencing (USA)**[200] 7048 4-9-0 106.............................. WilliamBuick 3 115
(John Gosden) *trckd ldrs: qcknd to ld 2f out: drvn clr fnl f: readily* **9/2**[3]

05-4 **2** 2 ½ **Sovereign Debt (IRE)**[18] 1535 4-9-0 111.................... JamieSpencer 8 109+
(Michael Bell) *in tch: drvn and hung rt fr 2f out: kpt on u.p ins fnl f to take 2nd last strides but nvr any ch w wnr* **9/2**[3]

43-2 **3** shd **Stipulate**[13] 1639 4-9-0 110.. TomQueally 7 109
(Sir Henry Cecil) *in tch: pushed along and outpcd 2f out: rdn and kpt on to chse wnr fnl 110yds: no imp and ct for 2nd last strides* **11/4**[1]

-041 **4** 1 ½ **Monsieur Chevalier (IRE)**[25] 1385 6-9-0 98.................... KierenFallon 9 106
(P J O'Gorman) *chsd ldrs: rdn to go 2nd jst ins fnl f but no ch w wnr: wknd into 4th fnl 110yds* **25/1**
23-4 **5** *nk* **Boom And Bust (IRE)**[13] 1639 6-9-0 106........................ HayleyTurner 5 105
(Marcus Tregoning) *slt ld tl over 5f out: styd pressing ldr: rdn and ev ch 2f out: wknd ins fnl f* **8/1**
4542 **6** 2 **Don't Call Me (IRE)**[18] 1535 6-9-0 107........................(t) AdrianNicholls 2 100
(David Nicholls) *in rr: drvn and hdwy over 1f out: swtchd rt and styd on in clsng stages: nvr a threat* **12/1**
252- **7** 2 **Pastoral Player**[228] 6246 6-9-0 111.................................... GeorgeBaker 1 96
(Hughie Morrison) *reluctant to post: t.k.h in rr: hdwy 3f out: wknd 1f out* **7/2**[2]
21/6 **8** *shd* **Chandlery (IRE)**[18] 1535 4-9-0 105.............................. RichardHughes 6 95
(Richard Hannon) *w ldr: led over 5f out: hdd 2f out: kpt on tl wknd fnl 110yds* **20/1**

1m 39.7s (-1.10) **Going Correction** -0.025s/f (Good) **8** Ran SP% **112.7**
Speed ratings (Par 111): **104,101,101,99,99 97,95,95**
toteswingers 1&2 £5.30, 2&3 £2.90, 1&3 £3.80 CSF £24.24 TOTE £5.80: £1.80, £1.80, £1.40; EX 29.40 Trifecta £82.80 Pool: £5060.30 - 45.78 winning units..
Owner George Strawbridge **Bred** George Strawbridge Jr **Trained** Newmarket, Suffolk

FOCUS
A strong race for the level when considering the best form of some of these, but the winning time was marginally slower than the later 1m handicap.

1920 LONGINES SAGARO STKS (GROUP 3) 2m
3:35 (3:37) (Class 1) 4-Y-O+
£34,026 (£12,900; £6,456; £3,216; £1,614; £810) **Stalls** Low

Form RPR
133- **1** **Estimate (IRE)**[230] 6163 4-8-9 108...................................... RyanMoore 9 109
(Sir Michael Stoute) *trckd ldrs: drvn to ld over 1f out: styd on strly* **2/1**[1]
001- **2** 1 ¾ **Caucus**[216] 6600 6-9-1 105.. WilliamBuick 6 110
(John Gosden) *in tch: hdwy 3f out: drvn and styd on wl fnl 2f: chsd wnr fnl f: kpt on but no imp* **6/1**[3]
21-5 **3** ½ **Sir Graham Wade (IRE)**[21] 1484 4-8-12 104.................. KierenFallon 4 109
(Mark Johnston) *t.k.h: trckd ldrs: drvn to ld over 2f out: hdd over 1f out: styd on same pce into 3rd fnl f* **6/1**[3]
1112 **4** 2 ½ **Buckland (IRE)**[18] 1547 5-9-1 94....................................... JimCrowley 7 106?
(Hans Adielsson) *in rr: hdwy 3f out: styd on u.p to take 4th ins fnl f: nt trble ldng trio* **33/1**
60-3 **5** ¾ **Steps To Freedom (IRE)**[24] 1415 7-9-1 107...........(t) RichardHughes 2 105
(Mrs John Harrington, Ire) *t.k.h in rr: hdwy 3f out to chse ldrs over 2f out: wknd ins fnl f* **9/2**[2]
3 **6** 7 **Handazan (IRE)**[21] 1484 4-8-12 98...............................(p) TomQueally 5 97
(Alan King) *chsd ldr: drvn and slt ld 3f out: hdd over 2f out: wknd wl over 1f out* **25/1**
2 **7** 6 **Earth Amber**[21] 1484 4-8-9 94.. JamieSpencer 3 87
(Nicky Henderson) *chsd ldrs: rdn and wknd qckly 2f out* **10/1**
630- **8** 4 ½ **Solar Sky**[249] 5599 5-9-1 105..(p) LiamKeniry 10 84
(David Elsworth) *t.k.h in rr: rdn and btn 3f out* **25/1**
663- **9** ½ **Askar Tau (FR)**[193] 7235 8-9-1 111.............................(v) GeorgeBaker 1 84
(Marcus Tregoning) *t.k.h: hld up in rr: rdn and sme hdwy on ins whn hung rt and wknd wl over 2f out* **8/1**
140- **10** 6 **Tres Rock Danon (FR)**[255] 5400 7-9-1 111..............(b[1]) FrederikTylicki 8 77
(Gerald Geisler, Germany) *led to 3f out: wknd qckly 2f out* **20/1**

3m 28.32s (-0.68) **Going Correction** +0.25s/f (Good) **10** Ran SP% **115.7**
WFA 4 from 5yo+ 3lb
Speed ratings (Par 113): **111,110,109,108,108 104,101,99,99,96**
toteswingers 1&2 £3.40, 2&3 £3.70, 1&3 £4.30 CSF £13.19 TOTE £3.00: £1.20, £2.20, £2.30; EX 13.90 Trifecta £79.90 Pool: £6127.36 - 57.51 winning units..
Owner The Queen **Bred** His Highness The Aga Khan's Studs S C **Trained** Newmarket, Suffolk

FOCUS
This well-established staying event looked right up to the standard you'd hope to see, and it produced a filly destined for better things.

1921 BATTERSEA DOGS & CATS HOME PAVILION STKS (LISTED RACE) 6f
4:10 (4:12) (Class 1) 3-Y-O
£20,982 (£7,955; £3,981; £1,983; £995; £499) **Stalls** Centre

Form RPR
411- **1** **Ninjago**[180] 7521 3-8-11 95... RichardHughes 13 107+
(Richard Hannon) *stdd s: hld up in rr: swtchd rt and qcknd appr fnl f: pushed along to ld fnl 110yds: confortably* **7/1**
110- **2** 1 ½ **Intibaah**[235] 6038 3-8-11 90.. PaulHanagan 9 101
(Brian Meehan) *chsd ldrs: rdn and kpt on wl to take 2nd fnl 110yds: kpt on to hold that position: no imp on wnr* **25/1**
0-53 **3** *nk* **Hasopop (IRE)**[12] 1668 3-8-11 100.................................. RyanMoore 10 100
(Marco Botti) *in tch: drvn 2f out: kpt on fnl f to take 3rd nr fin and gaining on 2nd cl home but no imp on wnr* **5/1**[2]
2-21 **4** 1 ¼ **Zanetto**[14] 1620 3-8-11 100.. LiamKeniry 5 96
(Andrew Balding) *trckd ldr tl led over 2f out: sn rdn: hdd and outpcd fnl 110yds* **5/1**[2]
30-3 **5** ½ **Graphic Guest**[14] 1620 3-8-6 99...................................... FrannyNorton 6 89
(Mick Channon) *chsd ldrs: rdn 2f out: wknd ins fnl f* **10/1**
30-4 **6** *nk* **Liberating**[17] 1557 3-8-6 96... LukeMorris 8 88
(Mrs John Harrington, Ire) *mid-div: hrd rdn wl over 1f out: kpt on u.p ins fnl f* **16/1**
010- **7** 1 ¼ **Tassel**[180] 7518 3-8-6 89... KieranO'Neill 3 84
(Richard Hannon) *in rr: drvn over 2f out: kpt on fnl f: nt rch ldrs* **66/1**
155- **8** ¾ **Pearl Acclaim (IRE)**[235] 6038 3-8-11 103............................ HarryBentley 12 87
(Robert Cowell) *in rr: drvn over 2f out: styd on fnl f: nvr a threat* **10/1**
06-0 **9** ¾ **Lady Phill**[12] 1662 3-8-6 89.. KierenFox 7 80?
(Bill Turner) *mde most tl hdd over 2f out: wknd fnl f* **100/1**
361- **10** 1 **Sandreamer (IRE)**[234] 6090 3-8-9 101............................ MartinHarley 1 79
(Mick Channon) *chsd ldrs: rdn 3f out: wknd over 1f out* **14/1**
6-60 **11** 1 ¾ **Jadanna (IRE)**[14] 1622 3-8-6 100.................................. JamesSullivan 11 71
(James Given) *chsd ldrs: rdn over 2f out: wknd over 1f out* **16/1**
530- **12** 5 **Ahern**[272] 4736 3-8-11 103... JamieSpencer 2 67
(David Barron) *in rr: drvn and sme hdwy 3f out: sn btn* **13/2**[3]
10- **13** ½ **Snow King (USA)**[179] 7567 3-8-11 0................................. WilliamBuick 4 58
(John Gosden) *pushed along 1/2-way: a in rr* **4/1**[1]

1m 12.1s (-2.40) **Going Correction** -0.025s/f (Good) **13** Ran SP% **122.1**
Speed ratings (Par 107): **115,113,112,110,110 109,108,107,106,104 102,95,95**
toteswingers 1&2 £17.40, 2&3 £26.50, 1&3 £8.00 CSF £174.09 TOTE £7.60: £2.60, £8.80, £2.20; EX 204.60 Trifecta £1021.70 Pool: £4968.12 - 3.64 winning units..
Owner J Palmer-Brown & Potensis Ltd **Bred** Newsells Park Stud **Trained** East Everleigh, Wilts

FOCUS
This has the potential to produce plenty of nice types, and the winner could easily be a Group performer if following the trend of the likes of Society Rock (2010) and Total Gallery (2009). The winning time was quick.

1922 REDCENTRIC H'CAP 1m (S)
4:45 (4:47) (Class 4) (0-85,85) 4-Y-O+ **£6,469** (£1,925; £962; £481) **Stalls** Centre

Form RPR
21-1 **1** **Rockalong (IRE)**[20] 1500 4-9-6 **84**..................................... KierenFallon 17 96+
(Luca Cumani) *in tch: drvn to ld ins fnl 2f: hrd pressed ins fnl f: a jst doing enough* **10/3**[1]
00-1 **2** ½ **Karaka Jack**[4] 1819 6-9-1 **79** 6ex.................................... AdrianNicholls 6 89
(David Nicholls) *in rr: rdn over 2f out: styd on u.p fnl f to take 2nd last strides but nt rch wnr* **10/1**
05-4 **3** *hd* **Good Authority (IRE)**[8] 1745 6-9-4 **82**............................... LukeMorris 5 92
(Karen George) *in tch: drvn to chal over 1f out: styd on fnl f but nvr quite gng pce of wnr: lost 2nd last strides* **25/1**
55-0 **4** ½ **Uppercut**[21] 1485 5-9-4 **82**.. NeilCallan 18 91
(Stuart Kittow) *in tch: hrd rdn fr 2f out: styd on wl fnl f: nt rch ldrs* **16/1**
11-1 **5** *hd* **Twenty One Choice (IRE)**[28] 1318 4-9-3 **81**..................... LiamKeniry 1 89
(Ed de Giles) *chsd ldrs: chal fr 2f out tl outpcd fnl 110yds* **15/2**[2]
40-3 **6** 1 ¾ **Tigers Tale (IRE)**[42] 1092 4-9-5 **83**..............................(v) JamesDoyle 13 87
(Roger Teal) *chsd ldrs: rdn 2f out: wknd ins fnl f* **16/1**
2334 **7** 1 ¾ **Chapter And Verse (IRE)**[18] 1545 7-9-2 **80**................ RichardHughes 7 80
(Mike Murphy) *stdd s: bhd: drvn and qcknd over 1f out: kpt on fnl f: nt rch ldrs* **8/1**[3]
-111 **8** 3 **Toga Tiger (IRE)**[74] 689 6-8-11 **80**.. RobertTart[(5)] 3 73
(Jeremy Gask) *in rr: hdwy to chse ldrs 2f out: wknd appr fnl f* **10/1**
000- **9** 2 **Poisson D'Or**[189] 7334 4-8-13 **77**.. TomQueally 8 66
(Rae Guest) *chsd ldrs: rdn 2f out: sn btn* **25/1**
456- **10** *nse* **Another Try (IRE)**[174] 7646 8-8-11 **82**........................... DavidParkes[(7)] 4 71
(Alan Jarvis) *in rr: pushed along and hdwy 3f out: chse ldrs 2f out: wknd over 1f out* **50/1**
130- **11** 1 ¼ **Hurricane Lady (IRE)**[189] 7334 5-9-2 **80**.......................... RyanMoore 20 66
(Mike Murphy) *in rr: rdn and sme hdwy over 2f out: no further prog and sn btn* **20/1**
-140 **12** 1 ¼ **Scottish Star**[32] 1242 5-8-11 **80**.. RyanTate[(5)] 9 63
(James Eustace) *chsd ldrs: wknd u.p ins fnl 2f* **16/1**
-664 **13** 1 **Kaafel (IRE)**[23] 1422 4-9-5 **83**......................................(v[1]) IanMongan 10 64
(Peter Hedger) *led tl hdd ins fnl 2f: sn wknd* **33/1**
000- **14** 5 **Forest Row**[248] 5626 4-9-1 **79**... AdamKirby 11 48
(Clive Cox) *in tch: rdn 3f out: wknd fr 2f out* **9/1**
61-0 **15** 1 ½ **Rocky Reef**[16] 1583 4-9-5 **83**.. JackMitchell 14 49
(Philip Hide) *outpcd most of way* **33/1**
6005 **16** 2 ¼ **Frog Hollow**[9] 1726 4-9-0 **83**................................. MatthewLawson[(5)] 15 44
(Milton Bradley) *chsd ldrs to 1/2-way* **16/1**
1-60 **17** ½ **Yojimbo (IRE)**[11] 1675 5-9-6 **84**................................... MatthewDavies 12 43
(Mick Channon) *chsd ldrs tl wknd over 2f out* **25/1**
50-0 **18** 14 **First Post (IRE)**[16] 1583 6-9-3 **81**.. DaneO'Neill 19
(Derek Haydn Jones) *early spd: bhd fr 1/2-way* **14/1**

1m 39.51s (-1.29) **Going Correction** -0.025s/f (Good) **18** Ran SP% **128.5**
Speed ratings (Par 105): **105,104,104,103,103 101,100,97,95,95 93,92,91,86,85 82,82,68**
toteswingers 1&2 £9.60, 2&3 £65.30, 1&3 £32.10 CSF £33.94 CT £778.28 TOTE £3.40: £1.50, £2.80, £6.30, £3.40; EX 40.90 Trifecta £1344.60 Pool: £5457.31 - 3.04 winning units..
Owner Nagy El Azar **Bred** Churchtown House Stud **Trained** Newmarket, Suffolk

FOCUS
A hugely competitive handicap in which the field mainly came in a line across the track and there didn't appear to be any significant bias.
T/Jkpt: Part won. £31,526.30 to a £1 stake. Pool of £44403.33 - 0.50 winning units. T/Plt: £58.90 to a £1 stake. Pool of £114798.48 - 1421.49 winning tickets T/Qpdt: £14.30 to a £1 stake. Pool of £8579.10 - 442.30 winning tickets. ST

1710 KEMPTON (A.W) (R-H)
Wednesday, May 1

OFFICIAL GOING: Standard
Wind: Light, across Weather: Sunny

1923 £200 FREE BETS AT BETDAQ CLASSIFIED STKS 1m 2f (P)
5:50 (5:51) (Class 5) 3-Y-O **£2,587** (£770; £384; £192) **Stalls** Low

Form RPR
536- **1** **Lamusawama**[213] 6699 3-9-0 70.. PaulHanagan 9 82
(Ed Dunlop) *stdd s: hld up in last pair: gd hdwy on inner over 1f out: led ins fnl f: r.o strly: easily* **11/2**[3]
40-1 **2** 3 ¾ **Love Marmalade (IRE)**[11] 1685 3-9-0 70......................... FrannyNorton 1 74
(Mark Johnston) *chsd ldr: rdn and ev ch over 1f out: led 1f out: sn hdd and brushed aside by wnr: kpt on same pce for clr 2nd* **3/1**[1]
5-13 **3** 2 ¼ **Debdebdeb**[21] 1487 3-9-0 70.. DavidProbert 6 70
(Andrew Balding) *sn pushed along: hdwy to ld after 1f: hung lft bnd over 3f out tl 2f out: hdd u.p 1f out: sn outpcd* **3/1**[1]
41- **4** ¾ **Magika**[137] 8134 3-9-0 66.. AndreaAtzeni 5 68
(Marco Botti) *hld up in last trio: effrt u.p over 1f out: no threat to ldrs but styd on fnl f* **20/1**
5-35 **5** 2 ¼ **Bin Manduro**[44] 1069 3-9-0 69... NeilCallan 8 64
(James Tate) *s.i.s: hld up in rr: rdn and hdwy jst over 2f out: chsd ldng trio and no imp over 1f out: wknd fnl f* **25/1**
653- **6** *nse* **Shamaheart (IRE)**[165] 7779 3-9-0 68.................................. SeanLevey 2 63
(Richard Hannon) *led for 1f: stdd bk to chse ldrs: forced wdst bnd 2f out: sme hdwy u.p over 1f out: kpt on but no ch* **7/2**[2]
052- **7** 6 **Codebreaker**[188] 7349 3-9-0 69...................................... JimmyFortune 7 51
(Hughie Morrison) *s.i.s: sn rcvrd and in tch in midfield: wknd u.p over 1f out* **10/1**
01-0 **8** 1 ¼ **Forced Family Fun**[14] 1614 3-9-0 70................................ HayleyTurner 4 49
(Michael Bell) *hld up towards rr: stuck bhd horses over 2f out: rdn and effrt over 1f out: no prog and wl hld fnl f* **20/1**
36-3 **9** 15 **Typhon (USA)**[13] 1655 3-9-0 69.. TedDurcan 3 33
(David Lanigan) *chsd ldrs: rdn and lost pl over 2f out: bhd and eased 1f out: t.o* **10/1**

2m 5.98s (-2.02) **Going Correction** -0.075s/f (Stan) **9** Ran SP% **119.2**
Speed ratings (Par 99): **105,102,100,99,97 97,92,91,79**
toteswingers 1&2 £6.30, 1&3 £7.90, 2&3 £7.90. CSF £22.51 TOTE £9.50: £1.80, £1.70, £1.20; EX 43.60 Trifecta £121.90 Pool: £1,323.87 - 8.14 winning units..
Owner Hamdan Al Maktoum **Bred** Mrs C Regalado-Gonzalez **Trained** Newmarket, Suffolk

FOCUS
A modest but competitive classified stakes, with just 4lb covering the entire field on official ratings.

1924 NEW CUSTOMERS COMMISSION FREE 1ST MONTH MAIDEN FILLIES' STKS 5f (P)
6:25 (6:25) (Class 5) 2-Y-O **£2,749** (£818; £408; £204) **Stalls** Low

Form RPR
1 **Suite (IRE)** 2-9-0 0 RichardHughes 1 80+
(Richard Hannon) *chsd ldrs: swtchd lft and effrt to chal jst over 1f out: rdn to ld wl ins fnl f: r.o wl and gng away at fin* **7/4**[1]

22 2 ¾ **Go Glamorous (IRE)**[25] [1399] 2-9-0 0 LukeMorris 2 77
(Ronald Harris) *led: rdn over 1f out: drvn and hdd wl ins fnl f: no ex and one pce after* **9/2**[3]

0 3 1 **Blockade (IRE)**[13] [1634] 2-9-0 0 NeilCallan 4 73
(James Tate) *chsd ldrs: hdwy u.p over 1f out: chsd ldng pair 1f out: kpt on same pce ins fnl f* **9/2**[3]

3 4 1¼ **Twist And Shout**[13] [1634] 2-8-7 0 RyanWhile(7) 7 69
(Bill Turner) *chsd ldrs: unable qck u.p over 1f out: lost 2nd 1f out and kpt on same pce after* **7/2**[2]

5 5 **Touch Paper (IRE)** 2-9-0 0 RyanMoore 5 51+
(Richard Hannon) *in tch in rr of main gp: rn green and wd bnd over 3f out: lost pl and sn rdn: n.d after* **6/1**

6 8 **Danetimeranger (IRE)** 2-8-11 0 DarrenEgan(3) 6 22+
(Ronald Harris) *rn green and sn totally outpcd and detached in last: n.d* **25/1**

7 ¾ **Packet Station** 2-9-0 0 DavidProbert 3 19+
(Alan McCabe) *in tch in rr of main gp: rn green bnd and lost pl over 3f out: a struggling after: lost tch over 1f out* **33/1**

59.99s (-0.51) **Going Correction** -0.075s/f (Stan) **7** Ran SP% **116.0**
Speed ratings (Par 90): **101,99,98,96,88 75,74**
toteswingers: 1&2 £1.70, 1&3 £1.90, 2&3 £2.90. CSF £10.40 TOTE £2.50: £1.40, £2.70; EX 12.20 Trifecta £28.10 Pool: £1,176.49 - 31.35 winning units..
Owner Mrs J Wood **Bred** Mogeely Stud **Trained** East Everleigh, Wilts
■ Stewards' Enquiry : Ryan While two-day ban: careless riding (May 15-16)

FOCUS
A fair juvenile maiden.

1925 MASCOT GRAND NATIONAL 06.05.13 H'CAP 1m (P)
7:00 (7:00) (Class 6) (0-65,65) 4-Y-O+ **£1,940** (£577; £288; £144) **Stalls** Low

Form RPR
0340 1 **Mister Green (FR)**[4] [1846] 7-9-5 **63** (b) JamesDoyle 5 72
(David Flood) *hld up wl in tch: rdn and effrt over 1f out: chsd wnr ins fnl f: r.o wl to ld fnl 75yds* **8/1**

000- 2 ¾ **Kakapuka**[167] [7725] 6-9-7 **65** GeorgeBaker 11 73
(Anabel K Murphy) *led and set stdy gallop: rdn and qcknd clr wl over 1f out: hdd and no ex fnl 75yds* **12/1**

00-4 3 2½ **Mishrif (USA)**[9] [1717] 7-9-5 **63** (b) RichardHughes 9 65
(J R Jenkins) *chsd ldrs: rdn and effrt 2f out: unable qck w ldr over 1f out: styd on same pce fnl f* **8/1**

02-2 4 ½ **Grand Theft Equine**[118] [33] 5-9-7 **65** StephenCraine 1 66
(Jim Boyle) *chsd ldr: drvn and unable qck w ldr over 1f out: styd on same pce ins fnl f* **12/1**

1536 5 nk **Alhaban (IRE)**[6] [1788] 7-9-7 **65** LukeMorris 6 65
(Ronald Harris) *hld up wl in tch towards rr: rdn and hdwy on inner over 1f out: kpt on ins fnl f* **16/1**

2324 6 ½ **Spirit Of Xaar (IRE)**[49] [984] 7-9-4 **62** JimmyFortune 3 61
(Linda Jewell) *dwlt: sn rcvrd and wl in tch in midfield: rdn and effrt over 1f out: styd on same pce fnl f* **12/1**

1236 7 ¾ **West Leake (IRE)**[9] [1717] 7-9-6 **64** LiamKeniry 10 61
(Paul Burgoyne) *t.k.h: stdd after s: hld up wl in tch towards rr: swtchd lft and effrt wl over 1f out: no imp fnl f* **12/1**

6316 8 ½ **Divine Rule (IRE)**[29] [1303] 5-9-3 **61** (v) IanMongan 2 57
(Laura Mongan) *t.k.h: chsd ldrs: rdn ent fnl 2f: drvn and unable qck over 1f out: one pce fnl f* **12/1**

4-40 9 ½ **Whinging Willie (IRE)**[29] [1303] 4-9-3 **61** RyanMoore 8 56
(Gary Moore) *chsd ldrs on outer: rdn and unable qck 2f out: outpcd and btn 1f out: plugged on* **7/1**[3]

560- 10 nk **Uncle Fred**[161] [7805] 8-9-7 **65** JimCrowley 13 59+
(Patrick Chamings) *stdd s: hld up in tch in last pair: switching lft but nt clr run enteriing fnl 2f: looking for run but gaps nvr c: rdr eased off ins fnl f: nvr able to chal* **11/2**[1]

006- 11 1¾ **Catchanova (IRE)**[198] [7115] 6-9-4 **62** NeilCallan 14 52
(Eve Johnson Houghton) *hld up in tch in last pair: clsng and nt clr run 2f out: no imp after* **14/1**

3302 12 2 **Warbond**[20] [1497] 5-9-3 **61** (v) DaneO'Neill 12 47
(Michael Madgwick) *in tch towards rr on outer: hdwy u.p over 2f out: wknd over 1f out* **6/1**[2]

141- 13 ¾ **Whitstable Native**[241] [5850] 5-8-9 **60** NoraLooby(7) 4 44
(Joseph Tuite) *t.k.h: hld up in midfield: rdn and wkng whn squeezed for room wl over 1f out: bhd fnl f* **33/1**

1m 39.34s (-0.46) **Going Correction** -0.075s/f (Stan) **13** Ran SP% **118.3**
Speed ratings (Par 101): **99,98,95,95,94 94,93,93,92,92 90,88,87**
toteswingers: 1&2 £28.90, 1&3 £9.40, 2&3 £13.00. CSF £99.53 CT £799.70 TOTE £10.60: £3.30, £4.20, £3.00; EX 126.00 Trifecta £596.30 Pool: £1,029.58 - 1.29 winning units..
Owner Flood Family Racing Limited **Bred** Gainsborough Stud Management Ltd **Trained** Exning, Suffolk

FOCUS
A modest but tightly knit handicap with only 5lb covering the entire field. However, they went a moderate gallop and nothing got involved from off the pace.

1926 KEMPTON FOR WEDDINGS MAIDEN STKS 1m (P)
7:35 (7:35) (Class 5) 3-4-Y-O **£2,587** (£770; £384; £192) **Stalls** Low

Form RPR
3 1 **String Theory (IRE)**[13] [1635] 3-9-0 0 (t) AdamKirby 1 92+
(Marco Botti) *chsd ldr for 1f: chsd ldrs after tl cruised upsides ldr over 2f out: rdn to ld over 1f out: qcknd wl clr fnl f: eased cl home: easily* **9/4**[1]

2 6 **Reminisce (IRE)** 3-9-0 0 NeilCallan 12 78
(Marco Botti) *chsd ldrs: swtchd lft and effrt jst over 2f out: chsd clr wnr over 1f out: wl outpcd fnl f but kpt on for clr 2nd* **14/1**

24- 3 1½ **Lucanin**[342] [2430] 4-9-13 0 RyanMoore 8 78
(Sir Michael Stoute) *hld up off the pce in midfield: rdn and effrt to chse ldng pair over 1f out: kpt on but no ch w wnr* **5/2**[2]

4 2¼ **Mutanaweb (IRE)** 3-9-0 0 PaulHanagan 4 69+
(John Gosden) *dwlt: sn outpcd in last trio and rdn along: hdwy 2f out: wnt modest 4th ins fnl f: kpt on: nvr trbld ldrs* **7/2**[3]

56- 5 1½ **On My Own (TUR)**[357] [1976] 4-9-13 0 SebSanders 10 63+
(J W Hills) *stdd after s: hld up off the pce in last quartet: rdn and hdwy wl over 1f out: styd on same pce fnl f: nvr trbld ldrs* **33/1**

54- 6 2¼ **Duke Of Perth**[189] [7333] 3-9-0 0 KierenFallon 11 61+
(Luca Cumani) *hld up off the pce in midfield: rdn and no prog ent fnl 2f: nvr trbld ldrs* **8/1**

7 ¾ **Bravestar (IRE)** 3-9-0 0 TedDurcan 2 59
(David Lanigan) *in tch: rdn and unable qck over 2f out: wknd over 1f out* **33/1**

8 shd **Mrs Mann (USA)** 3-8-9 0 J-PGuillambert 13 54
(Jo Hughes) *dwlt: rcvrd to chse ldr after 1f tl 2f out: wknd u.p over 1f out* **50/1**

60- 9 nse **Marlborough House**[142] [8052] 3-9-0 0 JamesSullivan 6 59
(James Given) *led: rdn and hdd over 1f out: sn btn: fdd fnl f* **50/1**

10 1 **La Rosiere (USA)** 4-9-8 0 GeorgeBaker 5 54
(Jo Hughes) *stdd after s: a bhd* **66/1**

11 4½ **Al Baahi (IRE)** 3-9-0 0 AndreaAtzeni 9 46+
(Roger Varian) *dwlt: sn pushed along in last pair: n.d* **12/1**

1m 39.04s (-0.76) **Going Correction** -0.075s/f (Stan)
WFA 3 from 4yo 13lb **11** Ran SP% **118.3**
Speed ratings (Par 103): **100,94,92,90,88 86,85,85,85,84 80**
toteswingers: 1&2 £7.00, 1&3 £2.40, 2&3 £8.80. CSF £34.04 TOTE £3.60: £1.50, £4.60, £1.10; EX 29.20 Trifecta £171.70 Pool: £797.59 - 3.48 winning units..
Owner Prince A A Faisal **Bred** Minch Bloodstock **Trained** Newmarket, Suffolk

FOCUS
A number of major yards were represented in this maiden, the time was 0.30secs faster than the preceding handicap.

1927 BETDAQ 1ST UK RACE COMMISSION FREE H'CAP 2m (P)
8:05 (8:05) (Class 5) (0-75,72) 4-Y-O+ **£2,587** (£770; £384; £192) **Stalls** Low

Form RPR
631- 1 **Albonny (IRE)**[228] [6255] 4-8-10 **66** MichaelJMMurphy(5) 8 76
(Alan Jarvis) *in tch in midfield: rdn and effrt over 2f out: led over 1f out: sn hrd pressed and drew clr w rival 1f out: forged ahd fnl 75yds: rdn out* **3/1**[1]

4163 2 1½ **Llamadas**[20] [1502] 11-9-2 **64** RyanMoore 6 72
(Olivia Maylam) *hld up in midfield: swtchd lft and effrt over 2f out: str chal over 1f out: drew clr w wnr 1f out: sustained effrt fnl f tl no ex and btn fnl 75yds* **3/1**[1]

1540 3 5 **Sommersturm (GER)**[9] [1733] 9-9-4 **66** (t) RichardHughes 5 68
(David Evans) *stdd s: hld up in rr: hdwy over 3f out: rdn and outpcd 2f out: rallied and styd on again ins fnl f: no ch w ldrs* **7/2**[2]

43-5 4 2¾ **Ginger Fizz**[97] [351] 6-9-7 **69** (t) MartinDwyer 7 68
(Ben Case) *t.k.h: chsd ldr: rdn and ev ch 2f out: no ex and btn 1f out: wknd fnl f* **6/1**

/0-0 5 hd **Bahrain Storm (IRE)**[24] [654] 10-9-8 **70** (b) StevieDonohoe 2 68
(Noel Quinlan) *hld up in last pair: rdn and outpcd ent fnl 2f: no ch but styd on past btn horses fnl f* **20/1**

02/0 6 4½ **Watergate (IRE)**[56] [119] 7-9-6 **68** JimCrowley 3 61
(Richard Rowe) *led: rdn over 2f out: hdd over 1f out: no ex and btn 1f out: sn fdd* **16/1**

3652 7 4½ **Where's Susie**[20] [1502] 8-9-10 **72** (t) GeorgeBaker 4 60
(Michael Madgwick) *chsd ldrs: rdn and effrt 2f out: unable qck over 1f out: btn 1f out: fdd fnl f* **11/2**[3]

0/0- 8 3¾ **Bin End**[73] [296] 7-8-9 **57** (p) LiamKeniry 1 40
(Barry Brennan) *hld up in last trio: rdn and struggling over 2f out: wknd 2f out and sn bhd* **25/1**

3m 29.88s (-0.22) **Going Correction** -0.075s/f (Stan)
WFA 4 from 6yo+ 3lb **8** Ran SP% **116.4**
Speed ratings (Par 103): **97,96,93,92,92 90,87,85**
toteswingers: 1&2 £2.90, 1&3 £1.30, 2&3 £4.40. CSF £12.42 CT £32.24 TOTE £4.70: £1.10, £1.30, £1.90; EX 18.50 Trifecta £50.60 Pool: £788.58 - 11.68 winning units..
Owner M&J Partnership **Bred** J Costello **Trained** Twyford, Bucks

FOCUS
A modest staying handicap and the pace was very steady until halfway.

1928 WINNERS ARE WELCOME AT BETDAQ H'CAP 7f (P)
8:35 (8:36) (Class 5) (0-70,70) 3-Y-O **£2,587** (£770; £384; £192) **Stalls** Low

Form RPR
4-20 1 **Clement (IRE)**[21] [1486] 3-9-4 **67** JohnFahy 6 69
(Eve Johnson Houghton) *t.k.h: chsd ldrs: rdn and ev ch over 1f out: r.o wl u.p to ld last strides* **8/1**

3223 2 hd **Green Special (ITY)**[23] [1424] 3-9-2 **65** (b[1]) LukeMorris 2 67
(Frank Sheridan) *t.k.h: hld up wl in tch: rdn and effrt to chal on inner 1f out: edgd lft and led wl ins fnl f: hdd last strides* **12/1**

003- 3 hd **Knight Owl**[149] [7963] 3-9-1 **64** TomQueally 7 65+
(James Fanshawe) *hld up in tch towards rr: swtchd rt and effrt over 1f out: swtchd rt again and str run ins fnl f: nt quite rch ldrs* **7/1**[3]

042- 4 ¾ **Dark Templar**[124] [8262] 3-9-7 **70** JamieSpencer 13 69+
(Ed Vaughan) *stdd s: t.k.h and hld up in rr: clsd on ldrs 2f out: drvn and chsd ldrs 1f out: styd on same pce ins fnl f* **5/1**[2]

30-6 5 shd **Beautiful Story (IRE)**[20] [1499] 3-8-13 **62** MartinHarley 5 61
(Mick Channon) *chsd ldrs: effrt u.p and ev ch over 1f out: no ex and one pce wl ins fnl f* **25/1**

605- 6 nse **Raven's Rock (IRE)**[190] [7311] 3-9-1 **64** NeilCallan 10 63+
(Roger Varian) *t.k.h: hld up wl in tch in midfield on outer: rdn and effrt ent fnl 2f: kpt on ins fnl f: nt quite pce to chal* **8/1**

64-0 7 shd **Hands Of Time**[23] [1423] 3-9-6 **69** RichardHughes 8 70+
(Richard Hannon) *sn led: rdn and hrd pressed ent fnl 2f: kpt on wl u.p tl hdd wl ins fnl f: no ex and eased cl home* **5/4**[1]

5-41 8 ½ **Little Indian**[36] [1180] 3-8-7 **56** FrannyNorton 11 53+
(J R Jenkins) *in tch in last trio: pushed along 5f out: rdn and no hdwy 2f out tl styd on wl ins fnl f: nt rch ldrs* **25/1**

235- 9 ¾ **Miss Mocca**[203] [6977] 3-9-4 **67** JamesDoyle 1 62
(Paul Fitzsimons) *t.k.h: pressed ldr: ev ch and drvn 2f out: no ex jst ins fnl f: outpcd fnl 100yds* **33/1**

020- 10 nse **Royal Caper**[131] [8203] 3-8-13 **62** KierenFallon 4 60+
(John Ryan) *t.k.h: hld up wl in tch: rdn and chsd ldrs ent fnl f: nvr enough room ins fnl f: eased towards fin* **25/1**

60-3 11 nk **Our Golden Girl**[62] [821] 3-8-7 **56** HayleyTurner 9 53+
(Shaun Lycett) *in tch in last trio: rdn and sltly outpcd jst over 2f out: rallied 1f out: styd on wl and clsng on ldrs whn nt clr run and eased towards fin* **33/1**

1m 27.45s (1.45) **Going Correction** -0.075s/f (Stan) **11** Ran SP% **120.9**
Speed ratings (Par 99): **88,87,87,86,86 86,86,85,84,84 84**
toteswingers: 1&2 £14.90, 1&3 £6.20, 2&3 £23.90. CSF £93.95 CT £710.57 TOTE £13.40: £4.10, £3.30, £3.90; EX 123.70 Trifecta £613.50 Part won. Pool: £818.10 - 0.47 winning units..

The Form Book Flat, Raceform Ltd, Compton, RG20 6NL.

Owner Mrs R F Johnson Houghton **Bred** P Kelly **Trained** Blewbury, Oxon
■ Stewards' Enquiry : Luke Morris two-day ban: careless riding (May 15-16)
FOCUS
A modest handicap in which they went slowly early and the whole field finished in a heap, as a result a couple had hard-luck stories.

1929 BOOK KEMPTON TICKETS ON 0844 579 3008 H'CAP 6f (P)
9:05 (9:07) (Class 6) (0-65,62) 4-Y-0+ **£1,940** (£577; £288; £144) **Stalls** Low

Form RPR
000- **1** **Commandingpresence (USA)**[134] 8160 7-9-2 **57**......... KieranO'Neill 3 65
(John Bridger) *chsd ldrs: rdn to ld 1f out: kpt on wl u.p fnl f* **33/1**
00-4 **2** *hd* **Aaranyow (IRE)**[19] 1516 5-8-4 **50**......................... RobertTart(5) 2 58
(Clifford Lines) *led: rdn and hdd 1f out: drvn and kpt on wl fnl f: a jst hld* **9/2**[3]
6611 **3** *½* **Mambo Spirit (IRE)**[29] 1304 9-9-7 **62**......................... SeanLevey 10 68+
(Tony Newcombe) *hld up in tch in midfield: rdn and effrt over 1f out: kpt on wl u.p ins fnl f* **3/1**[2]
1525 **4** *nk* **Littlecote Lady**[9] 1734 4-8-13 **54**.........................(v) HayleyTurner 1 59+
(Mark Usher) *in tch in midfield: rdn and effrt on inner over 1f out: chsd ldrs and drvn 1f out: kpt on* **5/1**
3055 **5** *hd* **Sherjawy (IRE)**[21] 1467 9-8-9 **50**......................... KirstyMilczarek 8 54
(Laura Mongan) *chsd ldrs: rdn and effrt wl over 1f out: kpt on same pce ins fnl f* **9/1**
406- **6** *2* **Volito**[335] 2629 7-9-7 **62**......................... GeorgeBaker 5 60
(Anabel K Murphy) *stdd s: hld up in rr: rdn and hdwy over 1f out: no imp ins fnl f* **8/1**
3222 **7** *½* **Rose Garnet (IRE)**[9] 1731 5-9-4 **59**......................... RichardHughes 9 55+
(Tony Carroll) *t.k.h: hld up in last pair: rdn and effrt wl over 1f out: no imp tl kpt on ins fnl f* **5/2**[1]
0002 **8** *1 ¼* **Aljosan**[19] 1519 4-8-9 **50**.........................(bt) LukeMorris 4 42
(Frank Sheridan) *chsd ldr tl over 1f out: wknd fnl f* **33/1**
0003 **9** *5* **Lord Buffhead**[9] 1731 4-8-13 **54**.........................(v) RobbieFitzpatrick 6 30
(Richard Guest) *taken down early: s.i.s: rdn along leaving stalls: a in rr: drvn and struggling over 2f out: bhd 1f out* **14/1**

1m 12.13s (-0.97) **Going Correction** -0.075s/f (Stan) **9** Ran SP% **122.1**
Speed ratings (Par 101): **103,102,102,101,101 98,98,96,89**
toteswingers: 1&2 £25.60, 1&3 £37.00, 2&3 £3.20. CSF £185.27 CT £600.68 TOTE £48.90: £11.60, £2.30, £2.00; EX 241.80 Trifecta £1175.90 Part won. Pool: £1,567.87 - 0.09 winning units..
Owner T Wallace & J J Bridger **Bred** Lazy Lane Farms Inc **Trained** Liphook, Hants
■ Stewards' Enquiry : Kieran O'Neill two-day ban: used whip above permitted level (May 15-16)
FOCUS
A moderate sprint handicap and a shock result.
T/Plt: £47.90 to a £1 stake. Pool of £55,495.87 - 844.01 winning tickets. T/Qpdt: £24.00 to a £1 stake. Pool of 5,335.70 - 164.30 winning tickets. SP

1718 PONTEFRACT (L-H)
Wednesday, May 1
OFFICIAL GOING: Good to firm (good in places; 8.4)
Wind: Light half behind Weather: Cloudy with sunny periods

1930 WILLIAM HILL/ BRITISH STALLION STUDS EBF MAIDEN STKS 5f
2:20 (2:21) (Class 4) 2-Y-0 **£4,528** (£1,347; £673; £336) **Stalls** Low

Form RPR
1 **Peniaphobia (IRE)** 2-9-5 0......................... TonyHamilton 6 81+
(Richard Fahey) *sn cl up: rdn to ld ent fnl f: kpt on wl* **17/2**
6 **2** *2 ¼* **Sartori**[12] 1659 2-9-0 0......................... CharlesBishop(5) 2 73
(Mick Channon) *sn led: rdn along 2f out: hdd ent fnl f: kpt on wl u.p* **11/2**[3]
33 **3** *¾* **Meritocracy (IRE)**[12] 1669 2-9-5 0......................... GrahamLee 8 70
(Paul Cole) *trckd ldrs: hdwy to chse ldng pair 2f out: rdn wl over 1f out: kpt on same pce ins fnl f* **4/1**[2]
4 *1 ¼* **Al Baz** 2-9-5 0......................... PaulMulrennan 3 66
(James Tate) *sn chsng ldrs on inner: rdn along wl over 1f out: kpt on same pce* **12/1**
5 *2 ½* **Ifwecan** 2-9-5 0......................... JoeFanning 9 57+
(Mark Johnston) *dwlt and green: hdwy into midfield whn n.m.r 1/2-way: t.k.h after: effrt to chse ldrs 2f out: rdn wl over 1f out: sn no imp* **7/4**[1]
6 *½* **New Bidder** 2-9-5 0......................... MichaelO'Connell 11 55+
(Jedd O'Keeffe) *towards rr: green and pushed along 1/2-way: hdwy wl over 1f out: swtchd lft and rdn appr fnl f: kpt on: nrst fin* **50/1**
3 **7** *2 ¾* **Chamberlain**[14] 1606 2-9-5 0......................... SilvestreDeSousa 12 45
(Alan McCabe) *midfield: sme hdwy on wd outside 2f out: sn rdn and n.d* **20/1**
0 **8** *2* **Princess Myla (IRE)**[14] 1606 2-9-0 0......................... MickyFenton 1 36+
(Paul Midgley) *s.i.s and in rr: sme hdwy on inner 2f out: sn rdn along and n.d* **100/1**
0 **9** *1 ¼* **Hickster (IRE)**[14] 1605 2-9-5 0......................... RichardKingscote 10 33
(Tom Dascombe) *chsd ldrs: rdn along 1/2-way: sn wknd* **50/1**
50 **10** *2 ¼* **Claudia Octavia**[13] 1642 2-8-11 0......................... PaulPickard(3) 4 20
(Brian Ellison) *a in rr* **80/1**
11 *2 ½* **Sirpertan** 2-9-5 0......................... DuranFentiman 14 16
(Tim Walford) *a in rr* **100/1**
12 *1 ½* **Native Falls (IRE)** 2-9-5 0......................... RobertWinston 5 11
(Alan Swinbank) *midfield: rdn along on inner 1/2-way: sn wknd* **7/1**
0 **13** *1 ¼* **Rokeby**[13] 1642 2-9-5 0......................... TomEaves 15 6
(George Moore) *s.i.s: a in rr* **50/1**

1m 3.38s (0.08) **Going Correction** -0.20s/f (Firm) **13** Ran SP% **116.3**
Speed ratings (Par 95): **91,87,86,84,80 79,75,71,69,66 62,59,57**
totewingers 1&2 £8.70, 2&3 £4.00, 1&3 £5.60 CSF £51.65 TOTE £7.30: £2.30, £2.10, £1.40; EX 61.70 Trifecta £315.30 Pool: £4804.94- 11.42 winning units..
Owner P Timmins & A Rhodes Haulage **Bred** Aidan Fogarty **Trained** Musley Bank, N Yorks
FOCUS
Probably quite a decent juvenile maiden, using the third as a guide.

1931 TOTEPOOL SUPPORTS THENRC/BRITISH STALLION STUDS EBF MAIDEN STKS 1m 2f 6y
2:50 (2:53) (Class 5) 3-Y-0 **£3,881** (£1,155; £577; £288) **Stalls** Low

Form RPR
4-2 **1** **Boite (IRE)**[11] 1679 3-9-5 0......................... RobertWinston 1 84+
(Peter Chapple-Hyam) *mde all: rdn wl over 1f out: kpt on* **8/13**[1]
-00 **2** *3 ¼* **Mojave Desert (IRE)**[9] 1713 3-9-0 0......................... JoeFanning 2 72
(Mark Johnston) *trckd ldrs: hdwy 3f out: pushed along 2f out: sn rdn and chsd wnr whn hung lft ins fnl f: no imp* **66/1**
3 *3 ¾* **Remote** 3-9-5 0......................... NickyMackay 5 70+
(John Gosden) *trckd ldng pair: effrt 3f out: rdn along wl over 1f out: one pce appr fnl f* **2/1**[2]
05- **4** *1 ¼* **Perpetual Ambition**[154] 7900 3-9-5 0.........................(b) SebSanders 3 67
(Paul D'Arcy) *trckd ldrs: effrt 3f out: sn rdn along and plugged on one pce* **33/1**
264- **5** *3* **Marsh Dragon**[202] 7006 3-8-11 74......................... SimonPearce(3) 4 56
(Mark H Tompkins) *trckd wnr: cl up 4f out: rdn along 3f out: wknd fnl 2f* **20/1**
6 *26* **Kattaf (IRE)** 3-9-5 0......................... SilvestreDeSousa 6
(Marco Botti) *hld up in rr: pushed along over 3f out: rdn wl over 2f out: sn outpcd* **9/1**[3]

2m 12.41s (-1.29) **Going Correction** -0.20s/f (Firm) **6** Ran SP% **114.4**
Speed ratings (Par 99): **97,94,91,90,88 67**
toteswingers 1&2 £6.80, 2&3 £12.50, 1&3 £1.10 CSF £60.08 TOTE £1.60: £1.10, £10.30; EX 23.50 Trifecta £86.00 Pool: £4103.74 - 35.77 winning units..
Owner Eledy Srl **Bred** Eledy Srl **Trained** Newmarket, Suffolk
FOCUS
No great depth to this maiden.

1932 BETFRED SUPPORTS THE NRC H'CAP 1m 4y
3:20 (3:21) (Class 5) (0-75,72) 4-Y-0+ **£3,234** (£962; £481; £240) **Stalls** Low

Form RPR
0-1 **1** **Eutropius (IRE)**[22] 1450 4-9-3 **68**......................... RobertWinston 3 79
(Alan Swinbank) *in tch: gd hdwy to chse ldng pair wl over 2f out: chsd ldr over 1f out: rdn to ld ent fnl f: edgd rt and kpt on* **8/1**
3331 **2** *1 ¼* **Alluring Star**[14] 1610 5-8-4 **62**......................... MatthewHopkins(7) 2 69
(Michael Easterby) *led: pushed clr over 2f out: rdn wl over 1f out: hdd and drvn ent fnl f: kpt on* **3/1**[1]
64-6 **3** *¾* **Sehnsucht (IRE)**[30] 1297 4-9-0 **65**.........................(p) ShaneKelly 6 70
(John Quinn) *in tch: hdwy wl over 2f out: rdn wl over 1f out: kpt on fnl f: nrst fin* **14/1**
5100 **4** *½* **Dakota Canyon (IRE)**[18] 1538 4-9-4 **72**.........................(b) LeeTopliss(3) 7 76
(Richard Fahey) *midfield: pushed along 3f out: rdn 2f out: kpt on fnl f: nrst fin* **16/1**
314/ **5** *3 ¾* **Makbullet**[25] 7074 6-9-0 **65**......................... GrahamLee 9 60
(Michael Smith) *hld up in rr: hdwy over 2f out: rdn along wl over 1f out: kpt on: nrst fin* **22/1**
0-42 **6** *shd* **Blue Maisey**[22] 1442 5-9-0 **65**......................... PaulMulrennan 10 60
(Edwin Tuer) *stdd s and hld up in rr: sme hdwy over 2f out: rdn along wl over 1f out: kpt on: nrst fin* **6/1**[3]
005- **7** *nk* **Eastward Ho**[210] 6785 5-9-3 **68**......................... TonyHamilton 5 62
(Jason Ward) *in tch: rdn along to chse ldng pair wl over 2f out: drvn wl over 1f out and sn btn* **11/1**
504- **8** *1 ¼* **Save The Bees**[218] 6559 5-8-13 **67**......................... NeilFarley(3) 4 58
(Declan Carroll) *nvr bttr than midfield* **8/1**
20-3 **9** *1 ¼* **Dialogue**[11] 1693 7-8-12 **66**......................... RaulDaSilva(3) 1 55
(Geoffrey Harker) *s.i.s and in rr: sme hdwy on to midfield 1/2-way: rdn along 3f out: sn btn* **4/1**[2]
10-6 **10** *13* **Talent Scout (IRE)**[22] 1442 7-9-6 **71**......................... DuranFentiman 8 43
(Karen Tutty) *cl up: rdn along 3f out: wknd 2f out* **12/1**

1m 43.54s (-2.36) **Going Correction** -0.20s/f (Firm) **10** Ran SP% **114.4**
Speed ratings (Par 103): **103,101,101,100,96 96,96,95,93,80**
toteswingers 1&2 £5.50, 2&3 £11.70, 1&3 £23.90 CSF £31.59 CT £333.31 TOTE £10.70: £3.30, £1.60, £3.50; EX 25.90 Trifecta £337.30 Pool: £2221.83 - 4.93 winning units..
Owner Ontoawinner 2 **Bred** Grangemore Stud **Trained** Melsonby, N Yorks
FOCUS
No hanging around here, with Alluring Star and Talent Scout racing clear from an early stage. Little got into the race from off the pace, though, and it looks fair form for the level.

1933 LADBROKES MOBILE FILLIES' H'CAP 1m 2f 6y
3:55 (3:55) (Class 3) (0-90,87) 3-Y-0+
£9,337 (£2,796; £1,398; £699; £349; £175) **Stalls** Low

Form RPR
362- **1** **Centred (IRE)**[167] 7721 3-8-0 **74** oh1......................... SilvestreDeSousa 2 87+
(Sir Michael Stoute) *rn in snatches: pushed along over 3f out: chsd ldrs on outer 2f out: rdn to chal over 1f out: styd on to ld ins fnl f: sn edgd lft and kpt on wl towards fin* **5/1**[3]
21-3 **2** *1 ¾* **Heading North**[13] 1641 3-8-9 **83**......................... PatDobbs 4 92
(Richard Hannon) *t.k.h early: sn led: rdn wl over 1f out: drvn and hdd ins fnl f: kpt on same pce towards fin* **5/2**[1]
1 **3** *1 ¾* **Abilene**[14] 1611 3-8-13 **87**......................... KirstyMilczarek 1 93+
(Luca Cumani) *led early: trckd ldr on inner: hdwy 3f out: rdn 2f out and ev ch tl drvn appr fnl f and kpt on same pce* **9/2**[2]
-421 **4** *5* **Ssafa**[9] 1736 5-8-12 **71** 6ex.........................(p) TomEaves 3 68
(Alastair Lidderdale) *hld up in rr: hdwy on inner 2f out: sn rdn to chse ldrs tl wknd appr fnl f* **28/1**
10-1 **5** *8* **Eastern Destiny**[32] 1237 4-9-8 **86**......................... GeorgeChaloner(5) 6 67
(Richard Fahey) *trckd ldrs: cl up on outer 4f out: effrt and ev ch 2f out: sn rdn and wknd qckly wl over 1f out* **13/2**
1-2 **6** *39* **Star Lahib (IRE)**[32] 1238 4-9-9 **82**......................... JoeFanning 5
(Mark Johnston) *dwlt: sn chsng ldr: pushed along whn n.m.r and squeezed out wl over 2f out: no ch and eased after* **5/2**[1]

2m 11.29s (-2.41) **Going Correction** -0.20s/f (Firm)
WFA 3 from 4yo+ 15lb **6** Ran SP% **108.8**
Speed ratings (Par 104): **101,99,98,94,87 56**
toteswingers 1&2 £2.80, 2&3 £3.00, 1&3 £3.30 CSF £16.73 TOTE £6.70: £3.00, £1.50; EX 18.40 Trifecta £54.10 Pool: £2356.48 - 32.62 winning units..
Owner Ballymacoll Stud **Bred** Ballymacoll Stud Farm Ltd **Trained** Newmarket, Suffolk
FOCUS
An interesting fillies' handicap, with a handful of progressive types in the field, and it was pleasing to see the 3yo's come to the fore.

1934 BETVICTOR.COM H'CAP 1m 2f 6y
4:30 (4:31) (Class 4) (0-85,78) 3-Y-0 **£5,175** (£1,540; £769; £384) **Stalls** Low

Form RPR
4-1 **1** **Theodore Gericault (IRE)**[28] 1323 3-9-7 **78**......................... PatDobbs 5 89+
(Sir Michael Stoute) *hld up in tch: hdwy over 2f out: effrt whn nt clr run and hmpd over 1f out: squeezed through and rdn to ld ins fnl f: styd on* **7/2**[2]
1- **2** *2 ½* **Gioia Di Vita**[188] 7357 3-9-2 **73**......................... SilvestreDeSousa 8 77
(Marco Botti) *trckd ldr: cl up 1/2-way: rdn to ld wl over 1f out: drvn: hdd and edgd lft ins fnl f: edgd rt and kpt on towards fin* **9/2**[3]
31- **3** *shd* **Buckstay (IRE)**[229] 6214 3-9-6 **77**......................... PaulMulrennan 7 82+
(Peter Chapple-Hyam) *trckd ldrs: hdwy over 2f out: sn chal on outer and rdn wl over 1f out: sn hmpd and drvn: kpt on same pce fnl f* **13/2**

3-32 **4** *nk* **Eric The Grey (IRE)**[21] 1487 3-9-1 **72** TonyHamilton 4 77+
(Richard Fahey) *hld up towards rr: hdwy over 2f out: swtchd rt to outer and rdn over 1f out: str run fnl f: nrst fin* **3/1**[1]

26-5 **5** *1* **Esteaming**[14] 1604 3-9-1 **72** PhillipMakin 2 75+
(David Barron) *trckd ldrs: effrt whn sltly hmpd over 1f out: swtchd lft and nt clr run on inner ins fnl f: swtchd rt and keeping on whn n.m.r towards fin* **9/1**

220- **6** *8* **Astrosapphire**[204] 6972 3-8-13 **73** SimonPearce(3) 6 58
(Mark H Tompkins) *a towards rr: outpcd and bhd fnl 2f* **40/1**

100- **7** *1 3/4* **Grey Blue (IRE)**[204] 6972 3-9-4 **75** JoeFanning 1 57
(Mark Johnston) *led: rdn along 2f out: drvn on inner and hdd wl over 1f out: wkng whn sltly hmpd after* **12/1**

41-4 **8** *7* **Kuantan One (IRE)**[14] 1604 3-9-5 **76** GrahamLee 9 44
(Paul Cole) *chsd ldrs: rdn along 3f out: sn wknd* **9/1**

05-3 **9** *11* **Old Man Clegg**[16] 1577 3-8-7 **71** MatthewHopkins(7) 3 17
(Michael Easterby) *s.i.s: a in rr* **16/1**

2m 11.99s (-1.71) **Going Correction** -0.20s/f (Firm) **9** Ran SP% **114.8**
Speed ratings (Par 101): **98,96,95,95,94 88,87,81,72**
toteswingers 1&2 £3.90, 2&3 £5.80, 1&3 £4.50 CSF £19.55 CT £96.95 TOTE £3.90: £2.00, £2.40, £1.90; EX 17.90 Trifecta £96.10 Pool: £2895.12 - 22.58 winning units..

Owner Ballymacoll Stud **Bred** Ballymacoll Stud Farm Ltd **Trained** Newmarket, Suffolk

■ Stewards' Enquiry : Pat Dobbs one-day ban: careless riding (May 15)

FOCUS
They went just a steady gallop, but the right horses came to the fore and it's fair form for the grade.

1935 CORAL.CO.UK H'CAP 6f
5:00 (5:00) (Class 5) (0-75,75) 3-Y-O **£3,234** (£962; £481; £240) **Stalls** Low

Form RPR

0-41 **1** **Hit The Lights (IRE)**[21] 1461 3-8-11 **65** ShaneKelly 7 76
(Ollie Pears) *mde virtually all: rdn and qcknd clr wl over 1f out: drvn ins fnl f: edgd rt and hld on wl* **15/2**[3]

4-60 **2** *1/2* **Flighty Clarets (IRE)**[14] 1608 3-8-8 **62** TonyHamilton 1 71
(Richard Fahey) *towards rr: pushed along 2f out: gd hdwy over 1f out: rdn ins fnl f: styd on wl towards fin* **20/1**

326- **3** *nk* **Bondesire**[276] 4618 3-9-0 **68** DanielTudhope 5 76
(David O'Meara) *cl up: rdn along and sltly outpcd 2f out: styd on to chse wnr ins fnl f: kpt on wl towards fin* **8/1**

-153 **4** *4 1/2* **Rangi**[22] 1444 3-9-0 **75** DavidSimmonson(7) 8 69
(Tony Coyle) *t.k.h early: trckd ldrs: hdwy 2f out: rdn over 1f out: drvn and one pce ent fnl f* **9/1**

3154 **5** *nk* **Sand Boy (IRE)**[16] 1582 3-9-6 **74** RobertWinston 10 67
(Charles Hills) *hld up in tch: hdwy 2f out: effrt and n.m.r over 1f: out: sn rdn and no imp* **15/2**[3]

01-3 **6** *1 1/2* **Dream Ally (IRE)**[13] 1647 3-9-3 **71** PhillipMakin 4 59
(Jedd O'Keeffe) *trckd ldrs: hdwy on inner over 2f out: rdn along wl over 1f out: sn wknd* **9/4**[1]

01-1 **7** *1/2* **Hartwright**[19] 1524 3-9-5 **73** GrahamLee 9 59
(Michael Bell) *t.k.h: trckd ldng pair: hdwy over 2f out: rdn wl over 1f out: sn drvn and wknd* **4/1**[2]

-334 **8** *3 1/4* **Free Island**[7] 1762 3-8-10 **64** (p) PaulMulrennan 11 40
(James Tate) *hld up: effrt 3f out: a towards rr* **20/1**

035- **9** *1/2* **Dewi Chinta (IRE)**[184] 7433 3-8-7 **61** AmyRyan 6 35
(Kevin Ryan) *a towards rr* **20/1**

3116 **10** *4* **Hazard Warning (IRE)**[23] 1433 3-8-11 **65** (b) DuranFentiman 3 26
(Tim Easterby) *dwlt: a in rr* **25/1**

1m 15.3s (-1.60) **Going Correction** -0.20s/f (Firm) **10** Ran SP% **113.5**
Speed ratings (Par 99): **102,101,100,94,94 92,91,87,86,81**
toteswingers 1&2 £3.90, 2&3 £5.80, 1&3 £4.50 CSF £145.55 CT £1249.99 TOTE £10.00: £2.80, £8.10, £1.90; EX 211.50 Trifecta £1350.10 Part won. Pool of: £1800.25 - 0.69 winning units..

Owner Charles Wentworth **Bred** Carrigbeg Stud **Trained** Norton, N Yorks

FOCUS
An open-looking 3yo sprint.

1936 GO RACING IN YORKSHIRE FUTURE STARS APPRENTICE H'CAP (ROUND 3) 1m 2f 6y
5:35 (5:36) (Class 5) (0-75,73) 4-Y-O+ **£3,234** (£962; £481; £240) **Stalls** Low

Form RPR

520- **1** **Special Mix**[26] 6410 5-8-12 **67** MatthewHopkins(3) 1 75
(Michael Easterby) *in tch: hdwy to chse ldrs wl over 2f out: rdn along wl over 1f out: styd on u.p ins fnl f to ld nr fin* **10/1**

00-0 **2** *1/2* **Sunnybridge Boy (IRE)**[22] 1448 4-9-3 **72** JoeyHaynes(3) 4 79
(Mrs K Burke) *led: rdn clr over 2f out: drvn ins fnl f: edgd rt and tired last 50yds: hdd nr fin* **9/2**[2]

22-0 **3** *3/4* **Pertuis (IRE)**[21] 1464 7-8-6 **65** KatieDowson(7) 6 71
(Micky Hammond) *hld up in rr: hdwy wl over 1f out: rdn and styd on wl fnl f: nrst fin* **10/1**

36-1 **4** *1 1/2* **Gold Show**[22] 1448 4-9-6 **72** JacobButterfield 2 75
(Edwin Tuer) *trckd ldrs: hdwy over 2f out: chsd clr ldr over 1f out: sn rdn and one pce ins fnl f* **7/4**[1]

556- **5** *8* **Free Art**[207] 6885 5-8-4 **61** JordanNason(5) 7 48
(Geoffrey Harker) *chsd ldrs: rdn along over 2f out: wknd over 1f out* **20/1**

011- **6** *11* **Kuwait Star**[176] 7600 4-9-6 **72** JoshBaudains 3 37
(Jason Ward) *a towards rr: outpcd and bhd fr over 2f out* **11/2**

-313 **7** *1 1/4* **Blades Lad**[25] 1391 4-9-7 **73** DavidSimmonson 5 35
(Peter Niven) *trckd ldr: rdn along wl over 2f out: wknd wl over 1f out* **5/1**[3]

2m 11.03s (-2.67) **Going Correction** -0.20s/f (Firm) **7** Ran SP% **109.5**
Speed ratings (Par 103): **102,101,101,99,93 84,83**
toteswingers 1&2 £6.90, 2&3 £6.80, 1&3 £11.20 CSF £49.47 TOTE £10.50: £4.80, £2.60; EX 67.10 Trifecta £313.30 Pool: £1427.13 - 3.41 winning units..

Owner E A Brook **Bred** W J Wyatt **Trained** Sheriff Hutton, N Yorks

FOCUS
This was run at a fair gallop.

T/Plt: £198.60 to a £1 stake. Pool of £46583.02 -171.19 winning tickets. T/Qpdt: £113.20 to a £1 stake. Pool of £3106.50 - 20.30 winning tickets. JR

MUNICH (L-H)
Wednesday, May 1

OFFICIAL GOING: Turf: good

1944a BETHMANN BANK - SILBERNE PEITSCHE (GROUP 3) (3YO+) (TURF) 6f 110y
4:00 (12:00) 3-Y-O+

£26,016 (£8,943; £4,471; £2,439; £1,626; £1,219)

RPR

1 **Arnold Lane (IRE)**[11] 1691 4-9-6 0 SamHitchcott 1 107
(Mick Channon) *trckd ldng pair on inner: rdn on turn into st: r.o to chal ent fnl f: led ins fnl 150yds: drvn clr* **2/1**[1]

2 *2* **Gracia Directa (GER)**[11] 5-9-3 0 OliverWilson 2 98
(D Moser, Germany) *disp ld on inner: rdn to ld on turn into st and qcknd clr: reeled in and strly pressed ent fnl f: hdd ins fnl 150yds: no ex and jst hld on for 2nd* **11/1**

3 *1/2* **Smooth Operator (GER)**[60] 869 7-9-6 0 (b) StefanieHofer 7 100
(Mario Hofer, Germany) *hld up towards rr: rdn on turn into st: hdwy fr over 1f out: wnt 3rd ins fnl f: r.o and almost snatched 2nd but no threat to wnr* **13/2**

4 *1 1/2* **Konig Concorde (GER)**[17] 1564 8-9-6 0 FilipMinarik 9 95
(C Sprengel, Germany) *midfield on outer: towards rr and rdn on turn into st: hung lft u.p: r.o to go 4th cl home: n.d* **26/5**[2]

5 *1/2* **Nordic Truce (USA)**[62] 836 6-9-6 0 MrDennisSchiergen 8 94
(P Schiergen, Germany) *hld up in last: rdn and hdwy on turn into st: 3rd ent fnl f: kpt on but dropped to 5th cl home* **94/10**

6 *1 1/2* **Ferro Sensation (GER)**[176] 7624 7-9-6 0 ADeVries 3 89
(D Klomp, Holland) *hld up towards rr on inner: rdn and hdwy on turn into st: outpcd ent fnl f: fdd* **63/10**

7 *5* **Walero (GER)**[227] 7-9-6 0 KClijmans 5 75
(J Hirschberger, Germany) *trckd ldng pair on outer: rdn on turn into st: outpcd and btn 1f out: fdd* **84/10**

8 *3* **Lipocco**[73] 700 9-9-6 0 KKerekes 6 66
(J D Hillis, Germany) *disp ld on outer: rdn and hdd on turn into st: sn no ex and btn: steadily fdd* **184/10**

9 *nk* **Elenya (IRE)**[24] 4-9-3 0 JohanVictoire 4 62
(M Cesandri, France) *trckd ldng pair: rdn and lost pl over 2f out: last and btn over 1f out* **58/10**[3]

1m 15.56s (-4.44) **9** Ran SP% **124.9**
WIN (incl. 10 euro stake): 30. PLACES: 15, 26, 22. SF: 231.
Owner Nick & Olga Dhandsa & John & Zoe Webster **Bred** Lynn Lodge Stud **Trained** West Ilsley, Berks

[1602]SAINT-CLOUD (L-H)
Wednesday, May 1

OFFICIAL GOING: Turf: good to soft

1945a PRIX DU MUGUET (GROUP 2) (4YO+) (TURF) 1m
2:20 (12:00) 4-Y-O+ **£60,243** (£23,252; £11,097; £7,398; £3,699)

RPR

1 **Don Bosco (FR)**[24] 1420 6-8-11 0 GregoryBenoist 8 113
(D Smaga, France) *sn led: clr ld ent st and 2l's clr 1 1/2f out: rdn 1f out: r.o wl fnl f: all out to jst hold on* **23/10**[1]

2 *hd* **Sarkiyla (FR)**[32] 1262 4-8-8 0 AntoineHamelin 1 110+
(A De Royer-Dupre, France) *racd 5th: gng easily whn swtchd to ins rail 1f out: r.o strly fnl 100yds: jst failed* **15/2**[3]

3 *snk* **Sofast (FR)**[248] 5649 4-8-11 0 (b[1]) OlivierPeslier 9 112+
(F Head, France) *hld up towards rr: swtchd towards outside 2f out: picked up wl ent fnl 1 1/2f: r.o strly to go 3rd fnl 100yds* **11/1**

4 *nk* **Zinabaa (FR)**[22] 1456 8-9-1 0 Francois-XavierBertras 5 116
(Mlle T Puitg, France) *settled in midfield: rdn 2f out: wnt 4th 1 1/2f out: r.o wl to go 3rd 1f out: styd on wl: lost 3rd 100yds out: styd on wl* **12/1**

5 *1 1/4* **Menardais (FR)**[22] 1456 4-8-11 0 StephanePasquier 3 109
(P Bary, France) *a.p in 4th: rdn 2f out: r.o wl to go 3rd 1 1/2f out: lost pl 1f out: styd on wl u.p fnl 100yds* **4/1**[2]

6 *1 1/4* **Coup De Theatre (FR)**[25] 4-8-11 0 RonanThomas 2 106
(P Van De Poele, France) *prom fr s: racd in 3rd: wnt 2nd u.p over 1 1/2f out: sn lost pl: no ex u.p fnl f* **12/1**

7 *nse* **Zack Hope**[22] 1456 5-8-11 0 TonyPiccone 12 106
(N Caullery, France) *slowly away: r.o wl fr rr fnl 1 1/2f: clst at fin* **24/1**

8 *1/2* **Sir Oscar (GER)**[23] 6-9-1 0 AurelienLemaitre 6 108
(Christina Bucher, Switzerland) *racd midfield: u.p 2f out: nt qckn: rallied and styng on wl fnl f* **70/1**

9 *1* **Foreign Tune**[22] 1456 4-8-8 0 FlavienPrat 11 99
(C Laffon-Parias, France) *hld up towards rr: nt qckn in st: styng on fnl f: clst at fin* **50/1**

10 *4* **Blue Soave (FR)**[171] 7697 5-8-11 0 ThierryThulliez 10 93
(F Chappet, France) *sn prom in 2nd: u.p 2f out: no ex: sn fdd: eased fnl f* **53/1**

11 **Laugh Out Loud**[214] 6673 4-8-11 0 ChristopheSoumillon 4 93
(J-C Rouget, France) *racd in midfield: rdn 2f out: no ex: fdd fnl f* **4/1**[2]

12 **King Air (FR)**[60] 6-9-1 0 MickaelBarzalona 7 97
(R Pritchard-Gordon, France) *racd in midfield: rdn 2f out: no ex: wknd fr 1 1/2f out* **37/1**

1m 39.0s (-8.50) **12** Ran SP% **117.6**
WIN (incl. 1 euro stake): 3.30. PLACES: 1.40, 2.20, 2.90. DF: 12.70. SF: 20.50.
Owner Omar El Sharif **Bred** Haras D`etreham & Vision Bloodstock Ltd **Trained** Lamorlaye, France

CHEPSTOW (L-H)
Thursday, May 2

OFFICIAL GOING: Good (good to firm in places; 8.5)
Meeting switched from Brighton.
Wind: vitrually nil Weather: dry and sunny

1946 FOSTERS EBF MAIDEN STKS 5f 16y
5:05 (5:05) (Class 5) 2-Y-O **£2,911** (£866; £432; £216) **Stalls** Centre

Form RPR
6 **1** **Hedge End (IRE)**[24] 1421 2-9-0 0 PatDobbs 1 64
(Richard Hannon) *hld up in tch in midfield: hdwy 2f out: rdn and pressed ldrs 1f out: led fnl 100yds: r.o wl* **7/2**[2]
0 **2** *nk* **Urban Dreamer (IRE)**[13] 1659 2-9-5 0 AndreaAtzeni 6 68
(Rod Millman) *t.k.h: chsd ldrs: ev ch and rdn over 1f out: led jst ins fnl f: hdd fnl 100yds: r.o but a jst hld* **8/1**
3 **3** *3 ¾* **Sherry For Nanny (IRE)**[31] 1285 2-9-0 0 MartinHarley 9 49
(David Evans) *in tch: rdn and outpcd wl over 1f out: kpt on ins fnl f but no threat to ldng pair* **7/1**[3]
0 **4** *1 ½* **Countess Lupus (IRE)**[17] 1573 2-9-0 0 GrahamLee 7 44
(Lisa Williamson) *s.i.s: outpcd in last trio: hdwy and swtchd rt wl over 1f out: kpt on steadily fnl f: nvr trbld ldrs* **33/1**
2 **5** *nk* **Mr Dandy Man (IRE)**[19] 1534 2-9-5 0 LukeMorris 5 48
(Ronald Harris) *chsd ldr tl led 2f out: hung bdly lft over 1f out: hdd jst ins fnl f: sn wknd* **7/2**[2]
0 **6** *2* **Dancing Sal (IRE)**[13] 1659 2-9-0 0 TomMcLaughlin 8 36
(David Evans) *chsd ldrs: rdn and unable qck wl over 1f out: wknd fnl f* **14/1**
7 *hd* **Centrality** 2-9-5 0 KierenFallon 4 42+
(Mark Johnston) *s.i.s: pushed along and wl outpcd in last pair: styd on ins fnl f: n.d* **9/4**[1]
8 *3 ½* **Heavens Edge** 2-9-0 0 DavidProbert 2 22
(Christopher Mason) *wnt lft s and slowly away: rn green and sn wl bhd: no ch but kpt on ins fnl f: n.d* **12/1**
0 **9** *5* **Under Your Thumb (IRE)**[13] 1659 2-9-0 0 WilliamCarson 3 4
(David Evans) *sn led: hdd 2f out: sn wknd: fdd fnl f* **50/1**

59.81s (0.51) **Going Correction** -0.125s/f (Firm) **9** Ran SP% **118.1**
Speed ratings (Par 93): **90,89,83,81,80 77,77,71,63**
Tote Swingers: 1&2 £4.80, 1&3 £6.50, 2&3 £8.00 CSF £32.46 TOTE £4.70: £1.30, £3.60, £2.40; EX 47.50 Trifecta £427.60 Pool: £1,427.51 - 2.50 winning units..
Owner Grimes, Ivory, Bull, Hannon **Bred** Airlie Stud **Trained** East Everleigh, Wilts

FOCUS
Pat Dobbs described the ground as good while Andrea Atzeni felt it was "just about good to firm". The front pair drew clear in what was an ordinary juvenile maiden. The form is fluid and will take time to settle.

1947 HEINEKEN H'CAP 7f 16y
5:40 (5:41) (Class 5) (0-75,72) 4-Y-0+ **£2,587** (£770; £384; £192) **Stalls** Centre

Form RPR
0-15 **1** **Dashwood**[47] 1038 6-9-2 67 (t) WilliamCarson 3 77
(Anthony Carson) *in tch in last trio: effrt and clsd on ldrs over 2f out: rdn to ld over 1f out: r.o wl ins fnl f: rdn out* **7/1**
-066 **2** *2* **Fred Willetts (IRE)**[6] 1800 5-9-0 70 DeclanBates(5) 2 75
(David Evans) *chsd ldrs: rdn and effrt to chal 2f out: chsd wnr over 1f out: styd on same pce ins fnl f* **4/1**[2]
640- **3** *nk* **Lady Bayside**[193] 7273 5-9-2 67 TomMcLaughlin 4 71
(Malcolm Saunders) *t.k.h: hld up in tch in last trio: hdwy into midfield 1/2-way: swtchd rt 2f out: hdwy u.p to chse ldrs 1f out: kpt on same pce after* **3/1**[1]
1134 **4** *1 ½* **Fairy Wing (IRE)**[22] 1475 6-9-2 67 MartinHarley 5 67
(Violet M Jordan) *taken down early: led for 1f: chsd ldr after tl led again over 2f out: drvn and hdd over 1f out: styd on same pce fnl f* **8/1**
6-60 **5** *1 ½* **Emiratesdotcom**[28] 1346 7-9-3 68 RobertWinston 6 64
(Milton Bradley) *in tch in rr: rdn and hdwy 2f out: drvn and unable qck over 1f out: wknd ins fnl f* **4/1**[2]
-004 **6** *2 ¼* **George Benjamin**[27] 1366 6-8-11 65 DarrenEgan(3) 1 55
(Christopher Kellett) *t.k.h: chsd ldrs: rdn and pressed ldrs 2f out: edgd lft and btn 1f out: wknd* **10/1**
5-3 **7** *3 ¾* **Macdonald Mor (IRE)**[70] 740 4-9-7 72 (b[1]) GrahamLee 8 52
(Michael Wigham) *dwlt: t.k.h and rcvrd to ld after 1f: hdd over 2f out: rdn and btn over 1f out: wknd 1f out* **6/1**[3]

1m 22.93s (-0.27) **Going Correction** -0.125s/f (Firm) **7** Ran SP% **112.0**
Speed ratings (Par 103): **96,93,93,91,89 87,83**
Tote Swingers: 1&2 £4.60, 1&3 £3.50, 2&3 £1.50 CSF £33.40 CT £100.83 TOTE £10.10: £3.30, £2.50; EX 51.00 Trifecta £269.30 Pool: £990.08 - 2.75 winning units..
Owner Macattack, William Lea Screed & Form IT **Bred** Darley **Trained** Newmarket, Suffolk
■ Stewards' Enquiry : Tom McLaughlin one-day ban: careless riding (May 16)

FOCUS
Modest handicap form and rated cautiously, with the winner close to his former best and the second rated to his autumn AW form for now.

1948 BULMERS H'CAP 1m 2f 36y
6:10 (6:10) (Class 6) (0-65,65) 4-Y-0+ **£1,940** (£577; £288; £144) **Stalls** Low

Form RPR
50-0 **1** **April Ciel**[17] 1586 4-9-1 62 DarrenEgan(3) 14 71
(Ronald Harris) *chsd ldr tl led over 3f out: kpt on wl u.p fr over 1f out: rdn out* **6/1**[2]
-214 **2** *nk* **Stag Hill (IRE)**[10] 1716 4-8-9 53 MartinLane 2 61
(Bernard Llewellyn) *chsd ldrs: rdn and effrt 2f out: chsd wnr fnl 100yds: kpt on wl towards fin* **9/2**[1]
0-45 **3** *hd* **James Pollard (IRE)**[22] 1466 8-8-11 62 (t) SiobhanMiller(7) 13 70
(Bernard Llewellyn) *hld up wl in tch in midfield: effrt u.p over 1f out: styd on wl fnl 100yds* **10/1**
42-0 **4** *1 ¾* **Bold Cross (IRE)**[12] 1699 10-9-2 65 ThomasBrown(5) 4 69
(Edward Bevan) *hld up in tch in last trio: hdwy over 2f out: drvn over 1f out: kpt on same pce ins fnl f* **8/1**[3]
400- **5** *nk* **Present Day**[166] 7781 4-8-7 51 (b) JohnFahy 5 55
(Clive Cox) *led tl over 3f out: styd chsng ldr: drvn over 1f out: lost 2nd fnl 100yds: kpt on same pce after* **16/1**
335- **6** *1 ¾* **Eightfold**[19] 6626 4-9-3 61 (t) PatDobbs 3 61
(Seamus Durack) *stdd after s: hld up in last trio: hdwy 1/2-way: rdn and no imp over 2f out: no threat to ldrs but kpt on ins fnl f* **9/2**[1]
0-62 **7** *1* **Iguacu**[12] 1700 9-8-1 52 (p) DanielMuscutt(7) 11 50
(Richard Price) *wl in tch in midfield: effrt u.p over 2f out: no ex and btn ent fnl f: one pce after* **10/1**
130- **8** *2 ½* **Wyndham Wave**[155] 7917 4-8-12 56 AndreaAtzeni 1 49
(Rod Millman) *t.k.h: hld up in midfield: hdwy 4f out: rdn and no ex 1f out: wknd fnl f* **9/2**[1]
000- **9** *1 ¾* **Operettist**[199] 7108 4-8-11 60 RyanTate(5) 6 50
(Tony Carroll) *hld up in tch in midfield: rdn and lost pl 3f out: plugged on but no ch fnl 2f* **12/1**
-016 **10** *4* **Royal Sea (IRE)**[90] 477 4-9-4 62 GrahamLee 9 44
(Barry Leavy) *hld up in last trio: rdn and struggling over 3f out: no ch fnl 2f* **14/1**
-100 **11** *13* **Lakota Ghost (USA)**[13] 1664 5-9-5 63 (t) DaneO'Neill 15 19
(Seamus Durack) *hld up wl in tch in midfield: rdn and struggling 3f out: wknd over 2f out: bhd and eased ins fnl f* **20/1**
50 **12** *50* **Reiterate**[36] 1193 4-8-11 55 (p) RobertWinston 12
(Milton Bradley) *t.k.h: chsd ldrs tl 1/2-way: bhd 4f out: sn lost tch: t.o* **33/1**

2m 8.89s (-1.71) **Going Correction** -0.125s/f (Firm) **12** Ran SP% **126.1**
Speed ratings (Par 101): **101,100,100,99,98 97,96,94,93,90 79,39**
Tote Swingers: 1&2 £7.50, 1&3 £16.80, 2&3 £6.40 CSF £35.43 CT £278.47 TOTE £7.60: £2.40, £2.00, £3.30; EX 52.70 Trifecta £423.60 Pool: £837.02 - 1.48 winning units..
Owner Paul & Ann de Weck **Bred** Paul And Ann De Weck **Trained** Earlswood, Monmouths

FOCUS
Low-grade stuff, but it was certainly an open handicap, and one that should produce winners at a similar level. The winner is rated close to his 3-y-o for with the second to recent AW form.

1949 STRONGBOW H'CAP 1m 4f 23y
6:40 (6:40) (Class 6) (0-60,59) 4-Y-0+ **£1,940** (£577; £288; £144) **Stalls** Low

Form RPR
000- **1** **Jewelled Dagger (IRE)**[335] 2669 9-8-12 50 (t) GrahamLee 6 60
(Sharon Watt) *chsd ldr tl led after 2f: mde rest: kpt finding ex u.p fr over 2f out: styd on wl: rdn out* **12/1**
1144 **2** *1 ¼* **Admirable Duque (IRE)**[10] 1733 7-9-7 59 (b) MartinLane 14 67
(Dominic Ffrench Davis) *towards rr early: hdwy into midfield 8f out: rdn and effrt to chse ldr 2f out: kpt on u.p but no imp ins fnl f* **8/1**[3]
600- **3** *½* **Minstrel Lad**[19] 5974 5-9-0 52 RichardKingscote 15 59
(Jonjo O'Neill) *hld up in midfield: nt clr run over 3f out: hdwy on inner to chse ldng pair wl over 1f out: kpt on same pce ins fnl f* **12/1**
5003 **4** *2 ½* **Ice Tres**[14] 1654 4-9-4 56 AndreaAtzeni 8 59
(Rod Millman) *hld up in midfield: effrt u.p over 2f out: 4th and kpt on same pce ins fnl f* **7/1**[2]
0054 **5** *nse* **Aviso (GER)**[4] 1700 9-8-11 54 (p) DeclanBates(5) 1 57
(David Evans) *hld up in tch towards rr: nt clr run 2f out: sn swtchd lft and hdwy u.p over 1f out: kpt on but nvr threatened ldrs* **20/1**
0020 **6** *hd* **Dream Prospector**[33] 1239 4-9-1 53 FergusSweeney 10 56
(James Evans) *stdd s: t.k.h: hld up in last trio: rdn and effrt over 2f out: hdwy u.p over 1f out: kpt on ins fnl f: nvr trbld ldrs* **16/1**
/0-6 **7** *1 ¾* **Madam Tessa (IRE)**[28] 1342 5-8-8 46 DavidProbert 11 46
(Tim Vaughan) *chsd ldrs: drvn and chsd wnr briefly over 2f out: unable qck u.p wl over 1f out: wknd ins fnl f* **33/1**
0053 **8** *2* **Mayan Flight (IRE)**[45] 1070 5-8-2 45 RyanTate(5) 7 42
(Tony Carroll) *wl in tch in midfield: rdn and effrt over 2f out: drvn and no imp 2f out: wknd over 1f out* **7/1**[2]
043- **9** *½* **Descaro (USA)**[21] 7102 7-9-5 57 LukeMorris 3 53
(John O'Shea) *chsd ldrs: wnt 2nd over 3f out tl over 2f out: sn drvn and nt qckn: wknd 1f out* **7/2**[1]
00-0 **10** *½* **Maccabees**[13] 704 4-8-9 54 NedCurtis(7) 4 49
(Roger Curtis) *stdd s: t.k.h: hld up in rr: effrt and drvn over 2f out: plugged on but nvr trbld ldrs* **33/1**
142- **11** *2 ¾* **Beacon Lady**[205] 6948 4-8-11 54 NicoleNordblad(5) 2 45
(William Knight) *a towards rr: dropped to last and detached 1/2-way: n.d* **7/2**[1]
0-05 **12** *10* **Chapter Nine (IRE)**[41] 1120 7-8-10 48 (t) LiamKeniry 13 23
(Tony Carroll) *stdd s: t.k.h: hld up towards rr: hdwy into midfield 6f out: rdn and lost pl 3f out: bhd over 1f out* **25/1**
-110 **P** **Kyllachykov (IRE)**[93] 435 5-9-4 56 RobertWinston 9
(Robin Bastiman) *led for 2f: chsd ldr tl over 3f out: lost pl 2f out: heavily eased and wl bhd whn p.u ins fnl f: sddle slipped* **16/1**

2m 37.75s (-1.25) **Going Correction** -0.125s/f (Firm) **13** Ran SP% **122.2**
Speed ratings (Par 101): **99,98,97,96,96 96,94,93,93,92 91,84,**
Tote Swingers: 1&2 £22.90, 1&3 £50.20, 2&3 £32.80 CSF £102.74 CT £1191.91 TOTE £17.50: £4.60, £2.30, £3.60; EX 343.90 Trifecta £667.00 Part won. Pool: £889.36 - 0.49 winning units..
Owner Rosey Hill Partnership **Bred** Ballyhane Stud **Trained** Brompton-on-Swale, N Yorks

FOCUS
Few got into this weak handicap from off the pace. Graham Lee dominated from the front and the third and fourth offer the best guides to the form.

1950 FOSTERS H'CAP 1m 14y
7:10 (7:11) (Class 5) (0-70,70) 4-Y-0+ **£2,587** (£770; £384; £192) **Stalls** Centre

Form RPR
1 **Sharp And Smart (IRE)**[242] 5861 4-9-4 67 KierenFallon 9 83+
(Hughie Morrison) *chsd ldrs tl hdwy to ld 3f out: rdn and wnt clr 2f out: in command fr over 1f out: r.o: comf* **9/4**[1]
4400 **2** *3 ¾* **Hail Promenader (IRE)**[28] 1354 7-8-8 62 (p) PhilipPrince(5) 6 67
(Anthony Carson) *led tl hdd 3f out: drvn and outpcd by wnr 2f out: wl hld after but kpt on for clr 2nd* **5/1**[3]
43-5 **3** *2* **Frozen Over**[20] 1514 5-9-6 69 IanMongan 7 69+
(Stuart Kittow) *hld up wl off the pce in rr: plenty to do but hdwy 2f out: edgd lft over 1f out: styd on to go 3rd cl home: no ch w wnr* **9/2**[2]
6636 **4** *nk* **Standing Strong (IRE)**[10] 1716 5-9-0 63 (b[1]) LiamKeniry 4 63
(Zoe Davison) *hld up in tch in midfield: effrt u.p and racing awkwardly 2f out: kpt on ins fnl f: no ch w wnr* **16/1**
522- **5** *3* **Derfenna Art (IRE)**[125] 8263 4-9-2 65 (t) MickyFenton 3 58
(Seamus Durack) *towards rr: hdwy and chsd ldrs 1/2-way: drvn and unable qck over 2f out: 3rd and btn over 1f out: wknd fnl f* **10/1**
020- **6** *hd* **Graylyn Valentino**[132] 8213 4-9-3 66 (t) AndreaAtzeni 5 58
(Robin Dickin) *in tch in midfield: rdn and struggling 3f out: n.d after but plugged on ins fnl f* **25/1**
4530 **7** *4 ½* **The Mongoose**[14] 1656 5-8-10 59 (t) MartinHarley 1 41
(David Evans) *chsd ldrs: drvn and outpcd 2f out: btn over 1f out: wknd fnl f* **25/1**
23-5 **8** *shd* **Falcon's Reign (FR)**[23] 1442 4-9-6 69 AndrewMullen 2 51
(Michael Appleby) *chsd ldr tl over 3f out: sn drvn and lost pl: no threat to ldrs fnl 2f* **8/1**

0-00 **9** *1* **Saint Irene**[30] 1298 4-8-5 61 .... HarryBurns(7) 10 40
(Michael Blanshard) *bhd: struggling and lost tch 1/2-way: no ch but plugged on ins fnl f* **33/1**

600- **10** *3* **Hamis Al Bin (IRE)**[202] 7027 4-9-0 63 .... GrahamLee 12 36
(Milton Bradley) *chsd ldrs tl 3f out: sn struggling: bhd 1f out* **25/1**

306- **11** *7* **Loyal N Trusted**[181] 7530 5-8-10 59 .... LukeMorris 13 15
(Richard Price) *stdd s: hld up towards rr: hdwy into midfield 1/2-way: wknd u.p over 2f out: bhd and eased ins fnl f* **12/1**

4530 **12** *16* **Spirit Of Gondree (IRE)**[36] 1214 5-8-11 60 ....(b) RobertWinston 11
(Milton Bradley) *t.k.h: hld up in rr: lost tch 3f out: t.o and eased fnl f* **12/1**

1m 33.65s (-2.55) **Going Correction** -0.125s/f (Firm) **12** Ran SP% **121.6**
Speed ratings (Par 103): **107,103,101,100,97 97,93,93,92,89 82,66**
Tote Swingers: 1&2 £4.10, 1&3 £3.60, 2&3 £7.00 CSF £12.75 CT £48.84 TOTE £3.30: £2.10, £2.80, £2.00; EX 13.10 Trifecta £35.00 Pool: £865.10 - 18.51 winning units..
Owner The Caledonian Racing Society **Bred** Piercetown Stud **Trained** East Ilsley, Berks

FOCUS
This moderate handicap was taken apart by the well-backed ex-Irish winner, who made a big step forward, with the runner-up rated to recent AW form for now.

1951 JOHN SMITHS H'CAP — 7f 16y
7:40 (7:40) (Class 6) (0-55,55) 4-Y-0+ **£1,940** (£577; £288; £144) **Stalls** Centre

Form RPR

3-00 **1** **Tooley Woods (IRE)**[35] 1221 4-8-13 47 .... CathyGannon 4 57
(Tony Carroll) *chsd ldr and a gng wl: led wl over 1f out: rdn ent fnl f: a in command fnl f: r.o wl* **8/1**

040- **2** *1* **Cheers Big Ears (IRE)**[199] 7105 7-8-5 46 oh1 .... DanielMuscutt(7) 3 53
(Richard Price) *hld up in tch in midfield: hdwy u.p 2f out: styd on wl ins fnl f to chse wnr fnl 75yds: nt quite pce to chal* **33/1**

0405 **3** *3/4* **Jackie Love (IRE)**[7] 1783 5-8-11 52 ....(v) IanBurns(7) 9 57
(Olivia Maylam) *chsd ldrs: rdn and swtchd lft wl over 1f out: chsd wnr ins fnl f: kpt on same pce fnl 100yds* **10/1**

4306 **4** *shd* **Peak Storm**[80] 611 4-9-7 55 .... LukeMorris 16 60
(John O'Shea) *hld up in tch towards rr: hdwy u.p over 1f out: kpt on wl ins fnl f: nt rch ldrs* **6/1**[2]

030- **5** *1 1/4* **Jack Barker**[246] 5728 4-9-7 55 .... RobertWinston 1 57
(Robin Bastiman) *chsd ldrs: rdn to chse wnr over 1f out: no ex 1f out: wknd fnl 100yds* **12/1**

60-4 **6** *1* **Rutterkin (USA)**[14] 1656 5-9-3 51 .... AndrewMullen 13 50
(Richard Ford) *hld up in midfield: hdwy to chse ldrs 1/2-way: drvn and unable qck 2f out: no ex 1f out: wknd ins fnl f* **5/1**[1]

6005 **7** *3/4* **Lady Prodee**[13] 1665 5-9-5 53 ....(p) KierenFox 15 50
(Bill Turner) *hld up in tch towards rr: effrt u.p 2f out: drvn and sme hdwy over 1f out: styd on same pce and no imp fnl f* **7/1**[3]

0440 **8** *1/2* **The Which Doctor**[22] 1474 8-8-12 46 oh1 ....(b) MartinHarley 10 42
(Violet M Jordan) *stdd s: hld up in rr: rdn and effrt but stl plenty to do over 1f out: kpt on ins fnl f: nvr trbld ldrs* **14/1**

0-60 **9** *1 1/2* **Quan (IRE)**[112] 147 4-9-3 51 .... GrahamLee 7 43
(Milton Bradley) *led tl wl over 1f out: sn rdn and no ex: btn 1f out: fdd fnl f* **8/1**

0-00 **10** *1* **Marie's Fantasy**[10] 1710 4-9-6 54 .... IanMongan 14 43
(Zoe Davison) *hld up in tch in midfield: rdn and effrt 2f out: edgd lft and no hdwy over 1f out: nvr trbld ldrs* **25/1**

06/0 **11** *5* **Ernest Speak (IRE)**[10] 1730 4-8-9 50 ....(t) EoinWalsh(7) 5 25
(David Evans) *in tch in midfield: rdn and no rspnse 3f out: wknd 2f out: wl btn fnl f* **50/1**

0-20 **12** *3* **Man Of My Word**[40] 1147 4-9-5 53 ....(p) TomMcLaughlin 6 20
(Scott Dixon) *chsd ldrs: rdn and lost pl 3f out: bhd 1f out* **12/1**

0560 **13** *2 3/4* **Compton Target (IRE)**[14] 1657 4-8-12 46 oh1 ....(tp) LiamKeniry 2
(Milton Bradley) *a bhd: n.d* **16/1**

3066 **14** *hd* **Hawaiian Freeze**[40] 1149 4-8-12 46 oh1 ....(p) AndreaAtzeni 17
(John Stimpson) *towards rr: hdwy to chse ldrs 1/2-way: wknd u.p 2f out: bhd fnl f* **33/1**

4000 **15** *9* **Flaxen Lake**[26] 1395 6-8-12 46 oh1 ....(p) ChrisCatlin 11
(Milton Bradley) *stdd s: t.k.h early: a bhd: lost tch over 2f out* **20/1**

5140 **16** *6* **Upper Lambourn (IRE)**[40] 1147 5-9-2 53 ....(t) DarrenEgan(3) 12
(Christopher Kellett) *in tch in midfield tl lost pl 4f out: bhd fnl 2f: t.o* **18/1**

1m 22.85s (-0.35) **Going Correction** -0.125s/f (Firm) **16** Ran SP% **124.4**
Speed ratings (Par 101): **97,95,95,94,93 92,91,90,89,88 82,78,75,75,65 58**
Tote Swingers: 1&2 £36.30, 1&3 £24.70, 2&3 £67.10 CSF £266.31 CT £2682.23 TOTE £9.00: £2.80, £9.10, £3.00, £1.50; EX 329.20 Trifecta £378.80 Part won. Pool: £505.07 - 0.01 winning units..
Owner Jason Tucker **Bred** Mount Coote Stud & M & W Bell Racing **Trained** Cropthorne, Worcs

FOCUS
Quite a poor handicap, and another race in which the winner raced prominently. The form looks sound at around this level.

1952 KRONENBOURG H'CAP — 5f 16y
8:10 (8:11) (Class 5) (0-70,70) 4-Y-0+ **£2,587** (£770; £384; £192) **Stalls** Centre

Form RPR

1333 **1** **Dark Lane**[3] 1888 7-8-10 66 .... RobJFitzpatrick(7) 5 76
(David Evans) *chsd ldrs: rdn and effrt ent fnl f: drvn and styd on wl to ld fnl 75yds* **7/1**

062- **2** *3/4* **Superior Edge**[311] 3435 6-8-12 61 ....(p) DavidProbert 1 68
(Christopher Mason) *led tl 2f out: battled on wl u.p and stl ev ch after tl no ex towards fin* **16/1**

-466 **3** *1 3/4* **Swendab (IRE)**[80] 616 5-9-3 66 ....(b) MartinHarley 4 67
(John O'Shea) *chsd ldr tl led 2f out: edgd lft u.p over 1f out: hdd fnl 75yds: wknd towards fin* **9/2**[1]

00-1 **4** *shd* **Monnoyer**[29] 1331 4-9-4 67 ....(bc) LukeMorris 10 68
(Scott Dixon) *chsd ldrs: rdn and sltly outpcd over 1f out: kpt on same pce ins fnl f* **10/1**

-235 **5** *nk* **Sole Danser (IRE)**[82] 582 5-9-7 70 .... RobertWinston 2 70+
(Milton Bradley) *taken down early: racd in midfield: clsd on ldrs and rdn 2f out: swtchd lft and unable qck over 1f out: one pce ins fnl f* **5/1**[2]

050 **6** *nse* **Decent Fella (IRE)**[9] 1746 7-9-4 67 ....(tp) CathyGannon 9 66
(Violet M Jordan) *stdd s: wl bhd in rr: pushed along and hdwy ent fnl f: r.o wl: nvr trbld ldrs* **8/1**

221- **7** *1/2* **Dear Maurice**[287] 4238 9-9-6 69 ....(t) MartinLane 8 67
(Tobias B P Coles) *sn outpcd in last quartet: wl bhd and u.p 1/2-way: hdwy 1f out: styd on wl fnl f: nvr trbld ldrs* **8/1**

25-0 **8** *nk* **Ficelle (IRE)**[6] 1802 4-8-9 61 .... DarrenEgan(3) 11 58
(Ronald Harris) *sn outpcd in last quartet: wl bhd and rdn 1/2-way: hdwy 1f out: styd on wl: nvr trbld ldrs* **8/1**

1043 **9** *1 1/2* **Charming (IRE)**[62] 842 4-9-3 66 ....(e) IanMongan 6 57
(Olivia Maylam) *taken down early: racd off the pce in midfield: rdn and effrt 2f out: no real prog: wl btn and eased wl ins fnl f* **14/1**

2000 **10** *2 1/4* **Night Trade (IRE)**[42] 1102 6-9-6 69 ....(p) WilliamCarson 13 52
(Ronald Harris) *a outpcd in last quartet: n.d* **16/1**

6522 **11** *3/4* **Falasteen (IRE)**[20] 1516 6-9-6 69 .... GrahamLee 3 49
(Milton Bradley) *awkward leaving stalls: racd off the pce in midfield: rdn and no hdwy 2f out: wknd 1f out* **6/1**[3]

58.57s (-0.73) **Going Correction** -0.125s/f (Firm) **11** Ran SP% **122.5**
Speed ratings (Par 103): **100,98,96,95,95 95,94,94,91,88 86**
Tote Swingers: 1&2 £14.30, 1&3 £10.20, 2&3 £24.80 CSF £117.68 CT £569.47 TOTE £7.90: £2.60, £6.60, £2.10; EX 125.00 Trifecta £391.60 Part won. Pool: £522.26 - 0.09 winning units..Laura's Bairn (33-1) was withdrawn. Rule 4 does not apply.
Owner Mrs E Evans **Bred** David Jamison Bloodstock **Trained** Pandy, Monmouths

FOCUS
They went hard in this sprint, but again it paid to be up there. This was the winner's best effort for a couple of years, with the runner-up rated similar to last summer's form.
T/Jkpt: Not won. T/Plt: £608.90 to a £1 stake. Pool: £72,781.42 - 87.25 winning tickets. T/Qpdt: £56.70 to a £1 stake. Pool: £7,444.85 - 97.00 winning tickets. SP

1903 LINGFIELD (L-H)
Thursday, May 2

OFFICIAL GOING: Standard
Wind: Light, half against Weather: Sunny, warm

1953 LINGFIELD PARK SUPPORTS YOUNG EPILEPSY H'CAP — 2m (P)
2:20 (2:22) (Class 6) (0-60,60) 4-Y-0+ **£2,045** (£603; £302) **Stalls** Low

Form RPR

2216 **1** **Honest Strike (USA)**[20] 1520 6-9-3 **56** ....(b) ShaneKelly 7 64+
(Daniel Mark Loughnane) *hld up in last: gng easily whn nt clr run wl over 1f out: swtchd rt to wd outside: mde up plenty of grnd under hands and heels to ld last 50yds* **2/1**[1]

2246 **2** *1/2* **Broughtons Bandit**[31] 1062 6-9-3 **56** .... J-PGuillambert 3 61
(Willie Musson) *hld up in 5th: urged along over 1f out: prog to ld jst ins fnl f: idled in front: hdd and outpcd last 50yds* **3/1**[2]

3006 **3** *1 1/2* **Ctappers**[13] 1664 4-8-13 **60** .... CharlesBishop(5) 8 63
(Mick Channon) *hld up in 7th: rdn 2f out: prog to chse ldr briefly ins fnl f: kpt on same pce* **7/2**[3]

0565 **4** *3 1/4* **If What And Maybe**[16] 1601 5-8-4 **46** oh1 .... RyanPowell(3) 6 45
(John Ryan) *uns rdr and rn loose bef r: trckd ldng pair: rdn 5f out: drvn on outer to ld 2f out: hdd & wknd jst ins fnl f* **20/1**

-254 **5** *1 1/4* **Baan (USA)**[62] 851 10-8-9 **53** .... RyanTate(5) 1 51
(James Eustace) *trckd ldng pair: pushed along 4f out: effrt u.p on inner over 1f out: wknd fnl f* **5/1**

3005 **6** *3/4* **Ice Apple**[29] 1325 5-8-7 **46** oh1 .... KirstyMilczarek 4 43
(John E Long) *led: set mod pce to 1/2-way: drvn and hdd 2f out: wknd fnl f* **20/1**

5-00 **7** *1/2* **Superstición**[13] 579 4-8-1 **46** oh1 .... SimonPearce(3) 5 42
(Michael Madgwick) *pressed ldr: rdn 5f out: stl pressing 2f out: wknd over 1f out* **50/1**

0/0- **8** *3 1/2* **Balaton**[329] 2848 4-8-4 **46** oh1 .... KieranO'Neill 2 38
(William Muir) *hld up in 6th: rdn 6f out: last and lost tch 3f out* **33/1**

3m 28.65s (2.95) **Going Correction** +0.05s/f (Slow)
WFA 4 from 5yo+ 3lb **8** Ran SP% **111.6**
Speed ratings (Par 101): **94,93,93,91,90 90,90,88**
toteswingers 1&2 £1.80, 2&3 £3.00, 1&3 £2.10 CSF £7.51 CT £17.92 TOTE £2.80: £1.10, £1.40, £1.40; EX 8.00 Trifecta £19.60 Pool: £ 3624.50 - 138.04 winning units..
Owner K Kilbane, J O'Shea & S Hunt **Bred** Juddmonte Farms Inc **Trained** Baldwin's Gate, Staffs

FOCUS
A moderate staying handicap with half the field running from out of the weights. The placed horses are rated close to form.

1954 LINGFIELD PARK SUPPORTS BHEST CLAIMING STKS — 6f (P)
2:50 (2:50) (Class 6) 3-Y-0+ **£2,045** (£603; £302) **Stalls** Low

Form RPR

4-55 **1** **North Star Boy (IRE)**[5] 1838 4-9-10 78 .... SeanLevey 2 83
(Richard Hannon) *mde all: rdn wl clr fr over 1f out: kpt up to work thrght fnl f* **1/2**[1]

2100 **2** *8* **Homeboy (IRE)**[7] 1780 5-9-6 63 .... GeorgeBaker 4 53
(Marcus Tregoning) *hld up in last: asked for effrt 2f out: hanging bdly and fnd nil: eventually rdn to take 2nd last 100yds* **11/4**[2]

100- **3** *1 1/4* **Al Aqabah (IRE)**[155] 7901 8-8-12 67 ....(b) NeilCallan 1 41
(Brian Gubby) *tried to match strides w wnr but couldn't: disp 2nd: rdn 1/2-way: lft bhd fr over 1f out: b.b.v* **7/1**[3]

0-43 **4** *3/4* **Microlight**[43] 1087 5-9-4 45 ....(b) KirstyMilczarek 3 45
(John E Long) *tried to match strides w wnr but coudn't: disp 2nd: rdn 1/2-way: lft bhd over 1f out* **33/1**

1m 11.94s (0.04) **Going Correction** +0.05s/f (Slow) **4** Ran SP% **108.8**
Speed ratings (Par 101): **101,90,88,87**
CSF £2.17 TOTE £1.40; EX 2.40 Trifecta £3.00 Pool: £1910.86 - 466.64 winning units..
Owner Robert Tyrrell **Bred** Hascombe And Valiant Studs **Trained** East Everleigh, Wilts

FOCUS
A small field and mixed levels of ability in this claimer. The winner is rated around his winter form.

1955 AURORA FIREWORKS MEDIAN AUCTION MAIDEN STKS — 1m 2f (P)
3:20 (3:26) (Class 6) 3-4-Y-0 **£2,045** (£603; £302) **Stalls** Low

Form RPR

0-5 **1** **Arbaah (USA)**[13] 1671 3-8-8 0 .... PaulHanagan 2 75+
(Brian Meehan) *led: rdn whn hung rt bnd 2f out and sn hdd: drvn to chal again fnl f: styd on to ld last strides* **9/4**[1]

6- **2** *hd* **Playbill**[220] 6535 3-8-8 0 .... RyanMoore 5 72
(Sir Michael Stoute) *trckd ldng pair: tk advantage of large gap on inner to ld wl over 1f out: hrd rdn and strly pressed fnl f: kpt on but hdd last strides* **3/1**[3]

6- **3** *1/2* **Velvetina (IRE)**[301] 3783 3-8-8 0 .... TedDurcan 8 71+
(Harry Dunlop) *hld up in midfield: effrt whn carried v wd bnd 2f out: shkn up and prog to chse ldng pair ins fnl f: clsng at fin* **8/1**

4 *1 1/4* **Optical** 3-8-8 0 .... TomQueally 3 69
(Sir Henry Cecil) *free to post: t.k.h: hld up in tch: 5th 3f out: effrt on inner 2f out: tried to cl 1f out: one pce* **7/1**

4332 **5** *1 1/4* **Punditry**[17] 1584 3-8-13 72 ....(b) WilliamBuick 9 71
(John Gosden) *trckd ldr after 3f: pushed along to chal over 2f out: fnd nil then carried wd bnd sn after: one pce fr over 1f out* **5/2**[2]

00- **6** *10* **Al Zein**[220] 6533 3-8-13 0 .... KieranO'Neill 4 51
(Richard Hannon) *w ldr for 3f: sn lost pl: wknd 3f out: t.o* **25/1**

7 *3 3/4* **Money Talks** 3-8-10 0 .... SimonPearce(3) 6 44
(Michael Madgwick) *rn green in rr: lost tch over 3f out: t.o* **66/1**

0 **8** 1 3/4 **Sakhee's Alround**14 1640 3-8-8 0 SamHitchcott 1 35
(K F Clutterbuck) *s.s: t.k.h in rr: wknd and hung rt over 3f out: t.o* **66/1**

0 **9** 1/2 **Fitzwilly**12 1678 3-8-8 0 CharlesBishop(5) 7 39
(Mick Channon) *dwlt: rn green and a in rr: lost tch over 3f out: t.o* **33/1**

2m 5.34s (-1.26) **Going Correction** +0.05s/f (Slow) **9** Ran SP% **117.7**
Speed ratings (Par 101): **107,106,106,105,104 96,93,92,91**
toteswingers 1&2 £2.10, 2&3 £4.80, 1&3 £4.20 CSF £9.35 TOTE £3.60: £1.10, £1.40, £2.90; EX 11.00 Trifecta £63.70 Pool: £3334.33 - 39.25 winning units..
Owner Hamdan Al Maktoum **Bred** Shadwell Farm LLC **Trained** Manton, Wilts

FOCUS
Several major yards represented in this maiden. The winner is rated close to her Newbury reappearance form.

1956 VINES BMW H'CAP 1m 2f (P)
3:50 (3:53) (Class 5) (0-75,72) 4-Y-0+ **£2,726** (£805; £402) **Stalls** Low

Form RPR

5156 **1** **Understory (USA)**38 1176 6-9-3 **68** (b1) NeilCallan 6 75
(Tim McCarthy) *mde all: stretched on fr 3f out: drvn and hrd pressed fnl f: hld on gamely* **8/1**

-462 **2** *shd* **Syncopate**12 1699 4-9-6 **71** AdamKirby 5 78
(Pam Sly) *trckd wnr: clr w him over 2f out: drvn over 1f out: chal fnl f: jst hld* **11/4**2

-031 **3** 1 1/4 **If I Were A Boy (IRE)**22 1480 6-9-1 **66** (be) JamesDoyle 7 70
(Dominic Ffrench Davis) *hld up in 6th: outpcd and shkn up 3f out: drvn and styd on fr over 1f out to take 3rd last 50yds: no ch to chal* **14/1**

0042 **4** 1/2 **Satwa Laird**12 1696 7-8-11 **62** HayleyTurner 3 65
(Conor Dore) *hld up in 4th: outpcd 3f out: pushed along over 2f out: styd on fr over 1f out to take 3rd briefly 75yds out: one pce* **25/1**

/00- **5** 1/2 **Mr Maynard**348 2265 4-9-7 **72** RyanMoore 2 74
(Sir Michael Stoute) *chsd ldng pair: rdn and outpcd by them 3f out: no imp after: lost 3rd last 75yds* **6/4**1

6123 **6** 3/4 **Tornado Force (IRE)**16 1597 5-9-6 **71** JimCrowley 4 72
(Alan McCabe) *hld up in last: stl there and wl off the pce 2f out: pushed along and sme prog over 1f out: rdn and no imp fnl f* **4/1**3

6013 **7** 4 **Scamperdale**26 1402 11-9-1 **66** (p) KierenFox 1 59
(Brian Baugh) *hld up in 5th: shkn up and outpcd wl over 2f out: wknd over 1f out* **16/1**

2m 5.47s (-1.13) **Going Correction** +0.05s/f (Slow) 7 Ran SP% **114.2**
Speed ratings (Par 103): **106,105,104,104,104 103,100**
toteswingers 1&2 £4.30, 2&3 £4.50, 1&3 £6.60 CSF £30.18 CT £305.45 TOTE £9.80: £3.40, £2.20; EX 40.10 Trifecta £268.10 Pool: £3059.25 - 8.55 winning units..
Owner Homecroft Wealth Racing **Bred** Darley **Trained** Godstone, Surrey

FOCUS
Quite a competitive handicap on paper, run in a time 0.13secs slower than the preceding maiden. The first two are rated slight improvers with the third and fourth fitting in.

1957 VINES BMW FILLIES' H'CAP 6f (P)
4:20 (4:22) (Class 5) (0-70,68) 4-Y-0+ **£2,726** (£805; £402) **Stalls** Low

Form RPR

313- **1** **If So**205 6961 4-9-6 **67** HayleyTurner 2 76+
(James Fanshawe) *fast away: trckd ldr 2f and again 2f out gng easily: led jst over 1f out: nudged along and in command after* **1/1**1

1540 **2** 1 **Catalinas Diamond (IRE)**20 1516 5-9-5 **66** (t) SteveDrowne 5 72
(Pat Murphy) *hld up in 4th in slowly run event: shkn up over 1f out: styd on to take 2nd nr fin: no ch w wnr* **6/1**3

1025 **3** *nk* **Chevise (IRE)**29 1324 5-9-0 **61** (p) MatthewDavies 1 66
(Steve Woodman) *led at modest pce: tried to poach a decisive ld 2f out: drvn and hdd jst over 1f out: one pce* **12/1**

50-1 **4** *nk* **Amber Heights**22 1472 5-8-12 **64** AmyScott(5) 4 68
(Henry Candy) *s.s: hld up in last in slowly run event: effrt on inner over 1f out: disp 2nd fnl f: no ch w wnr* **2/1**2

0514 **5** 2 1/4 **Avonvalley**28 1351 6-9-2 **68** SladeO'Hara(5) 6 65
(Peter Grayson) *chsd ldr after 2f to 2f out: sn wknd* **14/1**

1m 14.78s (2.88) **Going Correction** +0.05s/f (Slow) 5 Ran SP% **112.0**
Speed ratings (Par 100): **82,80,80,79,76**
CSF £7.78 TOTE £1.60: £1.30, £2.20; EX 6.60 Trifecta £22.80 Pool: £2937.72 - 96.36 winning units..
Owner Hopper, Grundy, Handscombe **Bred** Mr & Mrs K W Grundy, Mr & Mrs P Hopper **Trained** Newmarket, Suffolk

FOCUS
A modest but quite competitive fillies' sprint judged on the ratings. The placed horses set an ordinary level but the winner can improve on this.

1958 DERBY TRIAL COMING SOON H'CAP 7f (P)
4:50 (4:51) (Class 4) (0-80,79) 3-Y-0 **£4,690** (£1,395; £697; £348) **Stalls** Low

Form RPR

021- **1** **Mission Approved**210 6818 3-9-5 **77** RyanMoore 10 86+
(Sir Michael Stoute) *hld up in last trio: gd prog jst over 1f out: urged along and r.o to ld last 75yds: readily* **5/4**1

1- **2** 1/2 **Khobaraa**148 7987 3-9-4 **76** PaulHanagan 3 82+
(John Gosden) *trckd ldng pair: rdn to go 2nd 1f out: led v briefly 100yds out: outpcd nr fin* **9/2**2

-201 **3** 1/2 **Grilletto (USA)**26 1400 3-9-7 **79** (b) NeilCallan 12 82
(James Tate) *chsd ldr: rdn 2f out: lost 2nd 1f out: styd on but a hld after* **8/1**3

1213 **4** *nk* **Skytrain**15 1608 3-9-1 **73** JoeFanning 9 75
(Mark Johnston) *led: drvn over 1f out: hdd and fdd last 75yds* **8/1**3

210- **5** 1/2 **Labienus**239 5946 3-9-6 **78** TedDurcan 2 81+
(David Lanigan) *hld up in midfield: pushed along over 2f out: prog on inner over 1f out: styng on but unlikely to win whn nowhere to go 100yds out: kpt on* **16/1**

145- **6** *hd* **African Oil (FR)**210 6815 3-9-5 **77** JimCrowley 4 81+
(Charles Hills) *t.k.h early: trckd ldng trio: mounting an effrt whn nt clr run 1f out and sn lost pl: nt rcvr* **10/1**

50-2 **7** 3/4 **Sinaadi (IRE)**21 1499 3-9-0 **72** TomQueally 7 70
(Clive Brittain) *towards rr: rdn over 2f out: nudged by rival over 1f out and struggling: styd on again ins fnl f: nrst fin* **25/1**

30-6 **8** 2 1/2 **Avatar Star (IRE)**31 1293 3-9-1 **73** (tp) AdamKirby 8 64
(Marco Botti) *racd wd: chsd ldrs: drvn to try to chal 2f out: wknd u.p jst over 1f out* **20/1**

1-53 **9** 1 3/4 **Ready (IRE)**17 1571 3-9-7 **79** HayleyTurner 6 66
(Garry Moss) *hld up: a in last pair: jst pushed along and no prog fr 2f out* **8/1**3

214- **10** 5 **King Of Kudos (IRE)**148 7994 3-8-9 **70** BillyCray(3) 5 43
(Scott Dixon) *a in last trio: wknd over 2f out* **33/1**

1m 24.85s (0.05) **Going Correction** +0.05s/f (Slow) **10** Ran SP% **122.5**
Speed ratings (Par 101): **101,100,99,99,98 98,97,95,93,87**
toteswingers 1&2 £2.50, 2&3 £6.90, 1&3 £3.40 CSF £7.09 CT £35.32 TOTE £2.30: £1.20, £1.80, £2.30; EX 8.80 Trifecta £39.60 Pool: £4000.87 - 75.63 winning units..
Owner K Abdullah **Bred** Juddmonte Farms Ltd **Trained** Newmarket, Suffolk

FOCUS
The best race of the day, a tightly knit 3-y-o handicap that produced a close finish with a couple of hard-luck stories. The third and fourth help set the initial standard.

1959 LINGFIELD PARK OWNERS GROUP H'CAP 1m 4f (P)
5:25 (5:27) (Class 5) (0-75,75) 3-Y-0 **£2,726** (£805; £402) **Stalls** Low

Form RPR

0-23 **1** **Relentless (IRE)**10 1729 3-9-1 **69** (p1) WilliamBuick 5 76
(John Gosden) *trckd ldr: rdn to chal over 2f out: hanging and nt finding anything over 1f out: urged along to cl fnl f: forced ahd last strides* **5/1**3

05-0 **2** *nk* **White Month**12 1679 3-9-0 **68** JimmyFortune 3 74
(Andrew Balding) *led: rdn over 2f out: kpt on wl on inner fr over 1f out: hdd last strides* **6/1**

43-6 **3** *nk* **Portmonarch (IRE)**17 1584 3-9-7 **75** TedDurcan 2 81
(David Lanigan) *hld up in 4th: chsd ldng pair over 2f out but wd bnd sn after and looked awkward: styd on fr over 1f out: gaining at fin* **4/1**2

62-6 **4** 4 1/2 **Prospera (IRE)**22 1486 3-8-13 **67** JimCrowley 1 66
(Ralph Beckett) *chsd ldng pair: shkn up over 3f out: lost 3rd and struggling over 2f out: n.d after* **3/1**1

3116 **5** 1 **Flying Tempo**15 1604 3-9-7 **75** RyanMoore 6 72
(Ed Dunlop) *hld up in last: urged along over 3f out: sn lost tch w ldrs: no ch after* **3/1**1

-043 **6** *hd* **World Map (IRE)**9 1743 3-8-8 **62** JoeFanning 4 59
(Mark Johnston) *hld up in 5th: outpcd fr 3f out: no prog and wl btn 2f out* **8/1**

2m 33.55s (0.55) **Going Correction** +0.05s/f (Slow) **6** Ran SP% **112.1**
Speed ratings (Par 99): **100,99,99,96,95 95**
toteswingers 1&2 £4.90, 2&3 £3.80, 1&3 £2.60 CSF £33.49 TOTE £4.00: £2.40, £3.90; EX 34.20 Trifecta £81.60 Pool: £1619.26 - 14.87 winning units..
Owner Eric N Kronfeld **Bred** Basil Brindley **Trained** Newmarket, Suffolk

FOCUS
An ordinary middle-distance 3-y-o handicap but not a race to be with.
T/Plt: £21.60 to a £1 stake. Pool of £52464.86 - 1769.73 winning tickets. T/Qpdt: £14.80 to a £1 stake. Pool of £3416.92 - 170.65 winning tickets. JN

1573 REDCAR (L-H)
Thursday, May 2

OFFICIAL GOING: Good to firm (9.1)
Wind: moderate 1/2 against Weather: fine and sunny

1960 BUY YOUR TICKETS ON-LINE @ REDCARRACING.CO.UK MAIDEN AUCTION STKS 5f
2:00 (2:00) (Class 6) 2-Y-0 **£2,045** (£603; £302) **Stalls** Centre

Form RPR

1 **Innocently (IRE)** 2-9-5 0 DanielTudhope 1 72+
(David O'Meara) *mde all: racd keenly: pushed out: readily* **5/1**3

2 1 1/4 **Kirtling Belle** 2-9-0 0 SilvestreDeSousa 5 60
(Keith Dalgleish) *s.s: effrt and nt clr run over 2f out: swtchd lft: styd on to chse wnr 1f out: no imp* **17/2**

6 **3** 2 3/4 **Idamante**15 1606 2-9-5 0 TomEaves 2 55
(Kristin Stubbs) *dwlt: hdwy on outer 2f out: edgd rt: kpt on fnl f* **33/1**

2 **4** 2 **Princess Pheeny (IRE)**17 1565 2-9-0 0 TonyHamilton 4 43
(Richard Fahey) *chsd ldrs: drvn 2f out: fdd appr fnl f* **4/5**1

0 **5** 1 1/2 **Baltic Fire (IRE)**14 1642 2-9-2 0 MichaelMetcalfe(3) 3 43
(Mrs K Burke) *w ldrs: edgd rt over 2f out: wknd appr fnl f* **20/1**

6 **6** 1/2 **Lady Captain (IRE)**10 1718 2-9-0 0 AmyRyan 6 36
(Kevin Ryan) *sn chsng ldrs: drvn 3f out: wknd over 1f out* **4/1**2

0 **7** 7 **Sullivan Park**15 1605 2-9-0 0 JamesSullivan 7 11
(Ian McInnes) *chsd ldrs: outpcd over 2f out: lost pl over 1f out* **100/1**

59.9s (1.30) **Going Correction** -0.025s/f (Good) 7 Ran SP% **111.4**
Speed ratings (Par 91): **88,86,81,78,76 75,64**
toteswingers 1&2 £3.70, 2&3 £10.70, 1&3 £10.10 CSF £41.52 TOTE £5.30: £2.20, £3.50; EX 48.90 Trifecta £460.10 Pool: £4305.54 -7.01 winning units..
Owner Direct Racing Partnership **Bred** Longfort Stud **Trained** Nawton, N Yorks

FOCUS
The going was good to firm (watered). The pace was honest for this uncompetitive maiden, with the finish dominated by the two debutants in the field. The winner was the stable's first 2-y-o runner of 2013 and there should be more to come.

1961 ENJOY HOSPITALITY AT REDCAR RACECOURSE (S) STKS 5f
2:30 (2:30) (Class 6) 3-Y-0+ **£2,045** (£603; £302) **Stalls** Centre

Form RPR

0-04 **1** **Haajes**14 1649 9-9-7 70 (v) ShirleyTeasdale(5) 4 76
(Paul Midgley) *chsd ldrs: led 1f out: drvn out* **7/4**1

3400 **2** 1 1/2 **Dorback**14 1649 6-9-12 76 AdrianNicholls 7 71
(David Nicholls) *trckd ldrs: nt clr run over 2f out tl swtchd lft over 1f out: sn chsng wnr: hung lft and swtchd lft jst ins fnl f: no imp* **2/1**2

64-3 **3** 6 **Chloe's Dream (IRE)**9 1742 3-8-12 68 (p) PJMcDonald 9 40
(Ann Duffield) *w ldrs: led over 1f out: hdd 1f out: kpt on same pce* **7/2**3

520- **4** *nse* **Captain Royale (IRE)**163 7794 8-9-7 59 (p) GeorgeChaloner(5) 8 49
(Tracy Waggott) *w ldrs: kpt on same pce appr fnl f* **11/1**

0055 **5** 3 **Miserere Mei (IRE)**28 1356 4-9-7 46 RobbieFitzpatrick 3 33
(Richard Guest) *dwlt: in rr: effrt and sme hdwy over 2f out: wknd fnl 75yds* **25/1**

400- **6** 1 1/4 **Triskaidekaphobia**205 6959 10-9-12 43 (t) AmyRyan 5 31
(Wilf Storey) *sn outpcd: a in rr* **66/1**

00-0 **7** 1 1/4 **Branston Jubilee**23 1447 3-8-9 40 (v1) RaulDaSilva(3) 1 17
(Geoffrey Harker) *led over 2f: edgd lft and wknd over 1f out* **25/1**

244- **D** 3/4 **Rio Sands**167 7746 8-9-5 45 DanielleMooney(7) 2 46
(Richard Whitaker) *in rr: effrt over 2f out: kpt on: nvr a threat* **25/1**

58.88s (0.28) **Going Correction** -0.025s/f (Good)
WFA 3 from 4yo+ 9lb **8** Ran SP% **113.3**
Speed ratings (Par 101): **96,93,84,83,77 75,73,82**
toteswingers 1&2 £1.80, 2&3 £2.20, 1&3 £2.20 CSF £5.20 TOTE £3.10: £1.50, £1.10, £1.10; EX 9.40 Trifecta £20.60 Pool: £3413.28 - 123.74 winning units..There was no bid for the winner. Dorback was claimed by S Arnold for £6,000.
Owner Sandfield Racing **Bred** Irish National Stud **Trained** Westow, N Yorks

FOCUS
A weak contest even for the grade, run at a fair pace. The winner is rated to his best since last summer.

1962 VOLTIGEUR 2 COURSE SPECIAL MENU £10.95 MAIDEN FILLIES' STKS 6f
3:00 (3:06) (Class 5) 3-Y-O+ **£2,587** (£770; £384; £192) **Stalls** Centre

Form RPR
0 **1** **Natures Law (IRE)**[17] 1570 3-9-0 0 SilvestreDeSousa 9 61+
(Keith Dalgleish) *chsd ldrs: led over 1f out: styd on wl to forge clr ins fnl f: readily* **9/2**[2]
04 **2** 2 ¼ **Burren View Lady (IRE)**[10] 1722 3-9-0 0 DavidAllan 10 54+
(Tim Easterby) *chsd ldr: led over 2f out: hdd 1f out: kpt on wl towards fin* **14/1**
0236 **3** nk **Script**[10] 1732 4-9-3 48 JordanHibberd[(7)] 6 53
(Alan Berry) *in rr: hdwy over 2f out: chsng ldrs over 1f out: kpt on same pce* **16/1**
240- **4** nse **Karate Queen**[205] 6959 8-9-10 48 (p) AmyRyan 4 52
(Ron Barr) *in rr: hdwy over 2f out: chsng ldrs over 1f out: kpt on same pce* **20/1**
6 **5** ¾ **Rose Of May (IRE)**[17] 1578 3-9-0 0 DanielTudhope 1 47
(David O'Meara) *mid-div: hdwy to chse ldrs over 1f out: kpt on one pce* **7/1**[3]
000- **6** 3 ½ **Shesnotforturning (IRE)**[219] 6556 3-9-0 35 PhillipMakin 7 36
(Ben Haslam) *chsd ldrs: wknd appr fnl f* **66/1**
5- **7** nk **Cara Gina**[204] 6983 3-9-0 0 LiamJones 13 35
(William Haggas) *mid-div: drvn over 2f out: styd on fnl f* **4/1**[1]
5-30 **8** ¾ **Dr Victoria**[23] 1455 4-9-10 36 PaddyAspell 5 35
(John Norton) *rn wout declared tongue strap: gave problems gng to s: in rr: hdwy over 2f out: nvr trbld ldrs* **100/1**
65-6 **9** 3 ¼ **Beacon Tarn**[28] 1349 3-9-0 57 TomEaves 11 24
(Eric Alston) *trckd ldrs: wknd over 1f out* **7/1**[3]
3623 **10** 2 ¼ **Magic Ice**[22] 1458 3-8-9 56 WilliamTwiston-Davies[(5)] 16 15
(Brian Ellison) *trckd ldrs: wknd over 1f out* **9/2**[2]
11 1 ½ **Cannons Hall (IRE)** 4-9-3 0 DavidSimmonson[(7)] 14 13
(Paul Midgley) *uns rdr and rn loose to post: dwlt: a in rr* **100/1**
550- **12** 2 ¾ **Sound Affects**[246] 5748 3-9-0 43 DaleSwift 12
(Alan Brown) *in tch: drvn over 2f out: sn outpcd* **50/1**
-620 **13** 5 **Megaleka**[17] 1566 3-9-0 53 PaulMulrennan 3
(Chris Fairhurst) *mid-div: hdwy over 2f out: nt clr run over 1f out: hung lft and sn wknd: eased* **18/1**
65 **14** 2 **Zain Joy (CAN)**[10] 1732 3-9-0 0 NickyMackay 2
(Gerard Butler) *mid-div: drvn over 2f out: sn lost pl: eased fnl f* **16/1**
15 nk **Cantara** 3-8-9 0 JasonHart[(5)] 15
(Eric Alston) *dwlt: a bhd* **33/1**
000- **16** 2 ¾ **Cara's Delight (AUS)**[233] 6125 6-9-10 26 (t) DuranFentiman 8
(Frederick Watson) *led: hung lft and hdd over 2f out: sn lost pl: bhd whn eased in clsng stages* **100/1**

1m 11.8s **Going Correction** -0.025s/f (Good)
WFA 3 from 4yo+ 10lb **16** Ran SP% **119.2**
Speed ratings (Par 100): **99,96,95,95,94 89,89,88,84,81 79,75,68,66,65 62**
toteswingers 1&2 £12.40, 2&3 £18.30, 1&3 £18.90 CSF £62.22 TOTE £5.40: £2.30, £3.50, £6.70; EX 64.80 Trifecta £1458.20 Pool: £4376.02 - 2.25 winning units..
Owner Prestige Thoroughbred Racing **Bred** Paul Hensey **Trained** Carluke, S Lanarks

FOCUS
A moderate fillies' maiden. It looked to favour those racing towards the far rail. The form is limited by the proximity of the third and fourth.

1963 REDCAR RACECOURSE CONFERENCE & WEDDING VENUE H'CAP 7f
3:30 (3:31) (Class 4) (0-85,85) 3-Y-O+ **£6,469** (£1,925; £962; £481) **Stalls** Centre

Form RPR
330- **1** **Mont Ras (IRE)**[202] 7030 6-10-0 85 DanielTudhope 7 97
(David O'Meara) *mde all: drvn over 1f out: kpt on wl* **9/4**[1]
1-55 **2** 1 ¾ **Sardanapalus**[12] 1686 4-9-3 74 (p) PhillipMakin 4 81
(Kevin Ryan) *mid-div: hdwy over 2f out: chsng ldrs over 1f out: hung lft: styd on same pce* **14/1**
-202 **3** ½ **Summerinthecity (IRE)**[5] 1830 6-9-12 83 FrannyNorton 5 89
(David Nicholls) *chsd ldrs: drvn 2f out: kpt on same pce fnl f* **3/1**[2]
1622 **4** ½ **Showboating (IRE)**[9] 1751 5-9-6 77 (vt) SebSanders 3 81
(Alan McCabe) *hld up in rr: effrt over 2f out: kpt on fnl f* **9/1**
435- **5** 2 ½ **My Single Malt (IRE)**[153] 7935 5-9-0 71 PaulMulrennan 9 69
(Julie Camacho) *hld up towards rr: t.k.h: hdwy over 2f out: nt clr run and swtchd rt over 1f out: one pce* **9/1**
343- **6** 1 ¾ **Flynn's Boy**[276] 4661 5-9-4 75 SilvestreDeSousa 8 68
(Rae Guest) *trckd ldrs: t.k.h: effrt 2f out: hung lft over 1f out: one pce* **13/2**[3]
3502 **7** 8 **Silverware (USA)**[9] 1746 5-9-6 77 PatrickMathers 6 53
(Kristin Stubbs) *chsd ldrs: drvn 4f out: lost pl over 1f out: eased* **14/1**
00-0 **8** 6 **Ellaal**[17] 1571 4-9-4 75 JamesSullivan 2 30
(Ruth Carr) *hld up in rr: effrt over 2f out: hung lft and sn lost pl* **50/1**
051- **9** shd **Diman Waters (IRE)**[174] 7666 6-8-11 73 (b) JasonHart[(5)] 1 28
(Eric Alston) *t.k.h: sn hung bdly lft and racd alone far side: sn trcking ldrs: lost pl and eased over 1f out* **22/1**
64/- **10** 7 **Jessie's Spirit (IRE)**[573] 6670 4-9-7 78 PJMcDonald 10 14
(Ann Duffield) *stdd s: t.k.h: sn trcking ldrs: reminder 3f out: sn lost pl* **16/1**

1m 23.3s (-1.20) **Going Correction** -0.025s/f (Good) **10** Ran SP% **114.6**
Speed ratings (Par 105): **105,103,102,101,99 97,87,81,80,72**
toteswingers 1&2 £4.40, 2&3 £10.50, 1&3 £2.10 CSF £35.23 CT £96.04 TOTE £2.50: £1.50, £3.50, £1.20; EX 52.90 Trifecta £637.30 Pool: £1125.37 - 1.32 winning units..
Owner Colne Valley Racing **Bred** Patrick M Ryan **Trained** Nawton, N Yorks

FOCUS
This was competitive enough and is best rated through the runner-up to his 3-y-o best, backed up by the third. The pace was steady with the winner making all.

1964 WIN A VIP DAY @ REDCARRACING.CO.UK CLAIMING STKS 6f
4:00 (4:00) (Class 6) 3-Y-O+ **£2,045** (£603; £302) **Stalls** Centre

Form RPR
6-34 **1** **Beckermet (IRE)**[22] 1459 11-9-4 72 JamesSullivan 2 73
(Ruth Carr) *racd wd towards far side: mde virtually all: edgd rt over 1f out: hld on gamely* **4/1**[3]
366 **2** hd **Alaskan Bullet (IRE)**[14] 1649 4-9-10 79 SilvestreDeSousa 4 78
(Brian Ellison) *t.k.h: racd alone towards stands' side: sn upsides: rdn and edgd lft over 1f out: no ex towards fin* **5/4**[1]
5020 **3** 3 ½ **Dickie Le Davoir**[7] 1798 9-9-4 69 (b) RobbieFitzpatrick 5 61
(Richard Guest) *in rr: effrt over 2f out: styd on wl last 150yds: tk 3rd nr fin* **20/1**
2411 **4** ¾ **Hamoody (USA)**[23] 1451 9-9-10 83 AdrianNicholls 1 65
(David Nicholls) *trckd ldrs: upsides over 2f out: rdn over 1f out: wknd last 75yds* **2/1**[2]
4-56 **5** 3 ½ **Opus Dei**[14] 1650 6-8-12 63 (v) WilliamTwiston-Davies[(5)] 3 47
(Alan McCabe) *dwlt: in rr: effrt over 2f out: nvr a factor* **16/1**

1m 11.91s (0.11) **Going Correction** -0.025s/f (Good) **5** Ran SP% **108.4**
Speed ratings (Par 101): **98,97,93,92,87**
CSF £9.21 TOTE £5.50: £2.90, £2.20; EX 10.50 Trifecta £82.90 Pool: £2380.33 - 21.51 winning units..
Owner Mrs Marion Chapman **Bred** Fritz Von Ball Moss **Trained** Huby, N Yorks

FOCUS
Not a bad claimer despite the small field size. It was run at a sound pace and the winner ran his best race since last summer, while the second is rated close to the balance of his recent form.

1965 DOWNLOAD THE FREE RACING UK APP H'CAP 1m 1f
4:30 (4:30) (Class 5) (0-70,70) 3-Y-O **£2,587** (£770; £384; £192) **Stalls** Low

Form RPR
5-16 **1** **Corn Snow (USA)**[15] 1614 3-9-7 70 FrannyNorton 4 77+
(Mark Johnston) *chsd ldr: led over 3f out: drvn out* **10/3**[1]
1-10 **2** ¾ **Mixed Message (IRE)**[22] 1486 3-9-0 68 RobertTart[(5)] 6 73+
(John Mackie) *sn in rr: hdwy on ins 4f out: nt clr run and swtchd rt over 2f out: styd on wl to take 2nd last 50yds* **4/1**[3]
50-5 **3** 1 ½ **Argaki (IRE)**[54] 950 3-9-4 67 SilvestreDeSousa 5 68
(Keith Dalgleish) *chsd ldrs: drvn and outpcd over 4f out: edgd lft and chsd wnr over 2f out: kpt on same pce fnl f* **5/1**
02-4 **4** 1 **Chant (IRE)**[7] 1776 3-9-3 66 PJMcDonald 1 65
(Ann Duffield) *half-rrd s: sn trcking ldrs on inner: nt clr run over 3f out tl swtchd rt 2f out: kpt on same pce* **9/1**
65-5 **5** ½ **Curl (IRE)**[22] 1486 3-9-4 67 TomEaves 7 65
(Michael Dods) *chsd ldrs: drvn and outpcd over 5f out: hdwy 4f out: chsng ldrs over 2f out: one pce* **7/2**[2]
000- **6** 9 **Bapak Besar (CAN)**[182] 7497 3-8-10 59 AmyRyan 8 37
(Kevin Ryan) *s.s: detached in last: drvn 4f out: sme hdwy over 2f out: edgd lft and sn lost pl* **25/1**
016- **7** nk **Red Eight (USA)**[127] 8240 3-9-7 70 PaulMulrennan 2 47
(John Butler) *led tl over 3f out: lost pl over 1f out* **12/1**
4-34 **8** hd **Bitusa (USA)**[17] 1575 3-8-13 62 RussKennemore 3 39
(Alan Swinbank) *chsd ldrs: drvn over 4f out: chsng ldrs whn nt clr run over 2f out: hung lft and lost pl wl over 1f out* **12/1**

1m 52.46s (-0.54) **Going Correction** -0.025s/f (Good) **8** Ran SP% **111.2**
Speed ratings (Par 99): **101,100,99,98,97 89,89,89**
toteswingers 1&2 £3.10, 2&3 £3.50, 1&3 £4.00 CSF £15.92 CT £61.75 TOTE £4.20: £1.70, £1.10, £1.40; EX 18.20 Trifecta £90.30 Pool: £3279.76 - 27.21 winning units..
Owner Sheikh Hamdan Bin Mohammed Al Maktoum **Bred** Darley **Trained** Middleham Moor, N Yorks
■ Stewards' Enquiry : Silvestre De Sousa caution: careless riding

FOCUS
A number of unexposed types in this handicap, which was run at a steady pace. The form is rated at face value around the third, fourth and fifth.

1966 WATCH RACING UK ON SKY 432 H'CAP (STRAIGHT-MILE CHAMPIONSHIP QUALIFIER) (DIV I) 1m
5:00 (5:01) (Class 6) (0-60,60) 3-Y-O **£2,045** (£603; £302) **Stalls** Low

Form RPR
00-2 **1** **Surround Sound**[8] 1764 3-9-5 58 DavidAllan 5 72+
(Tim Easterby) *hld up towards rr: t.k.h: hdwy 3f out: swtchd rt and led over 1f out: forged clr* **6/1**[3]
026- **2** 4 ½ **Darkside**[211] 6780 3-9-1 54 (b) RoystonFfrench 11 58
(Tracy Waggott) *hmpd s: towards rr: hdwy over 3f out: hung rt and ended up stands' side: kpt on to take 2nd towards fin* **20/1**
60-3 **3** 1 ½ **Rocket Ronnie (IRE)**[8] 1759 3-9-3 56 AdrianNicholls 1 57
(David Nicholls) *hld up in mid-div: hdwy 3f out: chsng ldrs over 1f out: kpt on same pce* **15/8**[1]
040- **4** ½ **Pour La Victoire (IRE)**[197] 7173 3-8-11 50 SilvestreDeSousa 4 49
(Nigel Tinkler) *trckd ldrs: t.k.h: effrt over 2f out: one pce over 1f out* **20/1**
650- **5** 1 ¼ **Lexington Blue**[255] 5410 3-9-2 55 DanielTudhope 12 52
(David O'Meara) *wnt lft s: trckd ldrs: effrt over 2f out: one pce over 1f out* **12/1**
3400 **6** 3 ¼ **Panama Cat (USA)**[8] 1759 3-9-4 57 (b[1]) PhillipMakin 8 46
(Kevin Ryan) *w ldrs: led after 2f: hdd over 1f out: sn wknd* **16/1**
6552 **7** 1 ¾ **Duchess Of Dreams**[27] 1373 3-8-8 47 RobbieFitzpatrick 6 32
(Richard Guest) *in rr: drvn over 3f out: sme late hdwy: nvr a factor* **33/1**
4323 **8** ½ **Mudaawem (USA)**[29] 1330 3-9-7 60 (b[1]) FrannyNorton 7 44
(Mark Johnston) *chsd ldrs: drvn over 2f out: lost pl over 1f out* **8/1**
35-5 **9** ¾ **Just Paul (IRE)**[8] 1759 3-9-6 59 MichaelO'Connell 2 41
(Philip Kirby) *t.k.h: led 2f: w ldrs: wknd over 1f out* **5/1**[2]
000- **10** nk **Halfwaytocootehill (IRE)**[177] 7598 3-8-12 51 TomEaves 9 32
(Ollie Pears) *prom: lost pl over 3f out and sn bhd: sme late hdwy* **16/1**
000- **11** 21 **Threepence**[177] 7598 3-9-2 55 PaulQuinn 3
(Richard Whitaker) *s.s: drvn over 3f out: sn bhd: eased fnl f: t.o* **33/1**
-434 **12** 8 **Faither**[72] 717 3-8-9 48 PaulMulrennan 10
(Keith Dalgleish) *trckd ldrs: rdn and lost pl over 3f out: sn bhd: eased fnl f: t.o* **20/1**

1m 37.61s (1.01) **Going Correction** -0.35s/f (Firm) **12** Ran SP% **116.5**
Speed ratings (Par 97): **99,94,93,92,91 88,86,85,85,84 63,55**
toteswingers 1&2 £10.40, 2&3 £11.10, 1&3 £3.70 CSF £123.97 CT £311.19 TOTE £6.10: £1.20, £5.10, £1.70; EX 59.30 Trifecta £154.00 Pool: £2828.02 - 13.77 winning units..
Owner Craig Wilson **Bred** D & N Leggate, R Kent & I Henderson **Trained** Great Habton, N Yorks

FOCUS
This ordinary handicap was run at a fair pace, and the winner scored impressively. The second is getting back to his juvenile form but is not straigfhtforward and there are doubts about those behind.

1967 WATCH RACING UK ON SKY 432 H'CAP (STRAIGHT-MILE CHAMPIONSHIP QUALIFIER) (DIV II) 1m
5:35 (5:36) (Class 6) (0-60,60) 3-Y-O **£2,045** (£603; £302) **Stalls** Low

Form RPR
-635 **1** **The Codger**[26] 1392 3-9-4 57 DanielTudhope 11 66+
(David O'Meara) *hld up in rr: gd hdwy 3f out: led 1f out: rdn and styd on wl* **4/1**[2]
0-22 **2** 1 ¾ **Clock On Tom**[8] 1759 3-9-1 54 JamesSullivan 6 59
(Michael Easterby) *rrd s: in rr: swtchd lft over 3f out: rdn to join ldrs over 1f out: edgd rt: kpt on same pce last 100yds* **2/1**[1]
00-0 **3** ½ **Fishlake Rebel**[14] 1648 3-8-9 48 PJMcDonald 9 51
(Ruth Carr) *led: edgd rt and hdd 1f out: kpt on same pce* **33/1**

000- 4 3 **Vision Of Judgment**[268] 4907 3-8-8 47 .... PaulMulrennan 3 43
(Ollie Pears) *w ldr: rdn over 2f out: keeping on same pce whn nt clr run ins fnl f* **33/1**

0-20 5 ½ **Bougaloo**[7] 1772 3-8-13 57 ....(v) WilliamTwiston-Davies(5) 8 52
(Alan McCabe) *half-rrd s: in rr: edgd rt 4f out: kpt on fnl f* **14/1**

00-4 6 ½ **Sorcellerie**[23] 1447 3-9-6 59 .... DuranFentiman 2 53
(Mel Brittain) *dwlt: sn chsng ldrs: drvn 2f out: one pce* **7/1**[3]

2600 7 8 **Armada Bay (IRE)**[8] 1764 3-8-12 51 .... TomEaves 10 26
(Bryan Smart) *chsd ldrs: drvn over 2f out: lost pl over 1f out* **14/1**

60-4 8 4 ½ **Multifact**[26] 1393 3-8-13 55 .... LeeTopliss(3) 4 19
(Michael Dods) *in rr: edgd lft over 2f out: sn wknd* **4/1**[2]

050- 9 3 ½ **Spivey Cove**[266] 4991 3-9-7 60 .... TonyHamilton 1 15
(Karen Tutty) *t.k.h: sn w ldrs: lost pl 3f out* **16/1**

5-40 10 3 ½ **Riponian**[14] 1648 3-9-2 55 .... MichaelO'Connell 5
(Stuart Coltherd) *trckd ldrs: t.k.h: wknd 2f out: sn bhd* **16/1**

1m 37.38s (0.78) **Going Correction** -0.35s/f (Firm) **10** Ran SP% **116.8**
Speed ratings (Par 97): **101,99,98,95,95 94,86,82,78,75**
toteswingers 1&2 £2.30, 2&3 £16.30, 1&3 £25.70 CSF £12.39 CT £223.37 TOTE £5.10: £1.30, £1.70, £13.30; EX 14.40 Trifecta £398.30 Pool: £2563.92 - 4.82 winning units..
Owner Middleham Park Racing Xxvi **Bred** Woodcote Stud Ltd **Trained** Nawton, N Yorks

FOCUS
A modest handicap run at a sound pace. The runner-up is rated close to his recent Catterick form and sets the level.
T/Plt: £154.00 to a £1 stake. Pool of £51322.54 - 243.15 winning tickets. T/Qpdt: £16.40 to a £1 stake. Pool of £5031.00 - 226.90 winning tickets. WG

1968 - 1971a (Foreign Racing) - See Raceform Interactive

1869 LONGCHAMP (R-H)
Thursday, May 2

OFFICIAL GOING: Turf: soft

1972a PRIX DU PORT DE BERCY (CONDITIONS) (3YO) (TURF) 1m
11:45 (12:00) 3-Y-O £9,756 (£3,902; £2,926; £1,951; £975)

RPR

1 **Indigo (FR)** 3-9-1 0 ....(b) OlivierPeslier 4 96
(C Ferland, France) **63/10**

2 3 **Quiet Diplomacy**[41] 3-9-0 0 .... MaximeGuyon 6 88
(A Fabre, France) **19/5**[2]

3 shd **You're Golden (IRE)**[22] 1495 3-8-11 0 .... JohanVictoire 2 85
(E Legrix, France) **78/10**

4 nse **Arsheef (USA)**[32] 3-9-3 0 .... IoritzMendizabal 7 91
(J-C Rouget, France) **9/5**[1]

5 1 ½ **Claudiniho (FR)**[41] 3-9-0 0 .... StephanePasquier 3 84
(C Ferland, France) **63/10**

6 ¾ **So Oops (IRE)**[49] 1000 3-8-11 0 .... CesarPasserat(6) 5 85
(S Wattel, France) **6/1**[3]

7 ¾ **Sabre Rock**[22] 1495 3-8-11 0 .... MickaelBarzalona 1 78
(John Best) *sn led on ins: set stdy pce: rdn 2f out: hdd 1 1/2f out: no ex u.p: styd on one pce fnl f* **16/1**

1m 44.93s (6.53) **7** Ran SP% **115.5**
WIN (incl. 1 euro stake): 7.30. PLACES: 2.30, 2.10, 2.30. DF: 13.20. SF: 29.70.
Owner Wertheimer & Frere **Bred** Ecurie Du Sud **Trained** France

1946 CHEPSTOW (L-H)
Friday, May 3

OFFICIAL GOING: Good to firm (8.6)
Wind: Moderate across Weather: Sunny invtervals

1973 £32 BONUS AT 32RED.COM H'CAP 1m 4f 23y
2:20 (2:21) (Class 5) (0-75,74) 4-Y-0+ £2,587 (£770; £384; £192) Stalls Low

Form RPR

003- 1 **Jupiter Storm**[224] 6441 4-9-6 73 .... GeorgeBaker 11 81
(Gary Moore) *led after 3f: t.k.h: styd on wl fr 2f out: hrd drvn and edgd lft ins fnl f: hld on all out* **5/1**[3]

10-3 2 shd **Abundantly**[11] 1728 4-9-6 73 .... RichardHughes 3 81
(Hughie Morrison) *in rr: pushed along and hdwy over 2f out: chsd wnr 1f out: styd on wl u.p: fin wl: jst failed* **6/4**[1]

00-4 3 1 **The Holyman (IRE)**[69] 779 5-9-4 71 .... IanMongan 6 77
(Jo Crowley) *chsd wnr after 3f: rdn 2f out: styd on same pce ins fnl f* **25/1**

05-4 4 nse **Hurakan (IRE)**[13] 1699 7-8-10 70 ....(p) DanielMuscutt(7) 4 76
(Richard Price) *chsd ldrs: disp 2nd fr 2f out: sn rdn: styd on same pce ins fnl f* **12/1**

12-0 5 ½ **Taste The Wine (IRE)**[16] 1111 7-9-0 67 .... MartinLane 1 72
(Bernard Llewellyn) *in rr: hdwy 4f out: rdn 3f out: kpt on u.p fnl 2f but nvr gng pce to chal* **16/1**

1- 6 3 ¼ **Kayalar (IRE)**[72] 569 5-9-7 74 .... GrahamLee 5 74
(Evan Williams) *slowly away: in rr: hdwy 4f out: sn rdn and outpcd: styd on again fnl f* **20/1**

43-1 7 13 **Tafawuk (USA)**[6] 1836 4-9-5 72 6ex .... AndreaAtzeni 8 51
(Roger Varian) *chsd ldrs: rdn over 3f out: wknd over 2f out* **7/4**[2]

00/ 8 13 **William Hogarth**[7] 5909 8-8-9 62 .... LukeMorris 9 20
(Keith Goldsworthy) *chsd ldrs: rdn over 5f out: wknd 4f out* **50/1**

500- 9 11 **Look Left**[19] 3610 5-8-12 70 ....(t) RyanTate(5) 2 11
(Nikki Evans) *led 3f: styd chsng ldrs: wknd 4f out* **100/1**

2m 36.54s (-2.46) **Going Correction** -0.175s/f (Firm) **9** Ran SP% **118.2**
Speed ratings (Par 103): **101,100,100,100,99 97,89,80,73**
toteswingers 1&2 £4.80, 1&3 £11.60, 2&3 £9.10 CSF £12.93 CT £174.26 TOTE £7.10: £1.80, £1.10, £5.80; EX 15.40 Trifecta £210.90 Pool: £2193.65 - 7.79 winning units..
Owner Heart Of The South Racing **Bred** Breeding Capital, Watership Down, Farish **Trained** Lower Beeding, W Sussex

FOCUS
Modest handicap form, with the first five finishing in a heap. The winner is rated to the best of his 2012 form and it looks straghtforward judged on those immediately behind.

1974 32RED CASINO FILLIES' H'CAP 1m 2f 36y
2:50 (2:50) (Class 5) (0-75,75) 4-Y-0+ £2,587 (£770; £384; £192) Stalls Low

Form RPR

105- 1 **Our Phylli Vera (IRE)**[30] 6667 4-9-2 70 .... FergusSweeney 1 80
(Alan King) *hld up in rr: hdwy 3f out: led jst ins fnl 2f: kpt on strly fnl f* **4/1**[2]

00-0 2 3 ¾ **Play Street**[14] 1663 4-9-4 72 .... HarryBentley 5 75
(Jonathan Portman) *chsd ldrs: pushed along 2f out: hdwy on inner whn nt clr run and swtchd rt 1f out: styd on to take 2nd last strides but no ch w wnr* **10/1**

600- 3 nk **Berwin (IRE)**[153] 7954 4-8-13 67 .... JamesDoyle 2 69
(Sylvester Kirk) *in rr: hdwy to cl on ldrs 4f out: styd on to chse wnr 1f out but no imp: ct for 2nd last strides* **9/2**[3]

0-03 4 2 **Pandorica**[14] 1663 5-8-12 66 ....(p) MartinLane 8 65+
(Bernard Llewellyn) *chsd ldrs: led over 2f out: sn hdd: wknd ins fnl f* **7/2**[1]

3144 5 1 ½ **Bernisdale**[18] 1586 5-8-10 64 .... LukeMorris 6 60+
(John Flint) *chsd ldr: chal between horses and slt ld 3f out: hdd over 2f out: wknd fnl f* **7/2**[1]

0000 6 26 **Anrheg**[14] 1664 5-8-7 61 oh16 .... KellyHarrison 4 7
(Dai Burchell) *s.i.s: a bhd: lost tch fnl 3f* **66/1**

-640 7 ½ **Cape Joy (IRE)**[11] 1715 4-9-0 68 .... RichardHughes 9 13+
(Richard Hannon) *led: hdd 3f out: sn btn: eased fnl 2f* **4/1**[2]

2m 9.26s (-1.34) **Going Correction** -0.175s/f (Firm) **7** Ran SP% **113.2**
Speed ratings (Par 100): **98,95,94,93,91 71,70**
toteswingers 1&2 £2.90, 1&3 £2.00, 2&3 £14.10 CSF £41.01 CT £184.95 TOTE £3.60: £1.50, £4.00; EX 30.40 Trifecta £202.10 Pool: £1889.09 - 7.00 winning units..
Owner Let's Live Racing **Bred** Awbeg Stud **Trained** Barbury Castle, Wilts

FOCUS
An ordinary fillies' handicap, run at a sound pace which suited the winner, who produced an improved effort.

1975 32RED.COM MAIDEN STKS 1m 2f 36y
3:20 (3:20) (Class 5) 3-Y-0+ £2,587 (£770; £384; £192) Stalls Low

Form RPR

50- 1 **Flashheart (IRE)**[209] 6872 3-8-12 0 .... HarryBentley 7 81
(Marcus Tregoning) *trckd ldrs: hdwy to chal 3f out: led 2f out: pushed along and hrd pressed ins fnl f but a doing enough and kpt on strly clsng stages* **3/1**[2]

0-6 2 1 **Musikhani**[15] 1636 3-8-7 0 .... DavidProbert 3 74
(Andrew Balding) *t.k.h: led: jnd 3f out: hdd 2f out: rallied to press wnr ins fnl f but a hld* **7/4**[1]

3-0 3 3 **Enaitch (IRE)**[15] 1636 3-8-7 0 .... SamHitchcott 8 68+
(Mick Channon) *in rr: pushed along 3f out: drvn to take wl-hld 3rd ins fnl f* **5/1**[3]

4 2 ¾ **Sleeping Giant (GER)** 3-8-12 0 .... KierenFallon 9 68
(Luca Cumani) *chsd ldrs: chal 3f out: sn rdn: btn fr ins fnl 2f* **7/4**[1]

0 5 hd **Xclusive**[18] 1584 3-8-12 0 .... LukeMorris 6 68?
(Ronald Harris) *t.k.h: chsd ldr: rdn to chal 3f out: btn fr ins fnl 2f* **40/1**

2m 10.19s (-0.41) **Going Correction** -0.175s/f (Firm)
WFA 3 from 9yo 15lb **5** Ran SP% **116.8**
Speed ratings (Par 103): **94,93,90,88,88**
CSF £9.33 TOTE £5.00: £1.40, £1.80; EX 10.30 Trifecta £22.90 Pool: £1429.35 - 46.64 winning units..
Owner Guy Brook **Bred** Corduff Stud Ltd & D Egan **Trained** Whitsbury, Hants

FOCUS
This maiden was not without interest, although the time was around 0.8sec slower than the preceding fillies' handicap. The winner is rated back to his debut form, backed up by the runner-up.

1976 32RED VETERANS' H'CAP 5f 16y
3:50 (3:50) (Class 5) (0-75,75) 6-Y-0+ £2,587 (£770; £384; £192) Stalls Centre

Form RPR

3/52 1 **Go Nani Go**[23] 1467 7-9-5 73 .... LiamKeniry 1 81
(Ed de Giles) *t.k.h: trckd ldrs: led wl over 1f out and sn edging rt: pushed out: comf* **7/4**[1]

540- 2 1 ¾ **Stonecrabstomorrow (IRE)**[168] 7742 10-8-9 66 .... MarkCoumbe(3) 5 68
(Roy Brotherton) *chsd ldrs: drvn and styd on to press ldrs fr 2f out: chsd wnr fnl f: no imp* **10/1**

336- 3 nk **Comptonspirit**[212] 6788 9-8-10 69 .... MatthewLawson(5) 8 70
(Brian Baugh) *pressed ldr: drvn and ev ch fr over 2f out: nt qckn ins fnl f* **8/1**

-000 4 ½ **Jarrow (IRE)**[18] 1581 6-9-7 75 .... SilvestreDeSousa 7 77
(Milton Bradley) *trckd ldrs: styng on whn hmpd and snatched up over 1f out: kpt on again clsng stages: nt rcvr* **4/1**[3]

21-0 5 nk **Dear Maurice**[1] 1952 9-9-1 69 ....(t) MartinLane 2 67
(Tobias B P Coles) *chsd ldrs: drvn along fr 1/2-way: one pce fnl f* **3/1**[2]

006- 6 ½ **Wooden King (IRE)**[197] 7197 8-9-3 71 .... TomMcLaughlin 4 67
(Malcolm Saunders) *slt ld tl hdd wl over 1f out: outpcd fnl f* **6/1**

59.05s (-0.25) **Going Correction** -0.175s/f (Firm) **6** Ran SP% **115.9**
Speed ratings: **95,92,91,90,90 89**
toteswingers 1&2 £5.00, 1&3 £2.10, 2&3 £8.00 CSF £20.77 CT £113.47 TOTE £1.70: £1.10, £7.80; EX 18.60 Trifecta £83.10 Pool: £2265.95 - 20.44 winning units..
Owner T Gould **Bred** D J And Mrs Deer **Trained** Ledbury, H'fords
■ Stewards' Enquiry : Liam Keniry three-day ban: careless riding (May 17,19,20)

FOCUS
A moderate handicap for old-timers. The winner is rated back to his 2011 form and the race could rate a few pounds higher.

1977 BREWIN DOLPHIN H'CAP 1m 14y
4:20 (4:21) (Class 4) (0-80,78) 3-Y-0 £4,690 (£1,395; £697; £348) Stalls Centre

Form RPR

-222 1 **Sennockian Star**[9] 1770 3-9-1 72 ....(b[1]) SilvestreDeSousa 5 78
(Mark Johnston) *trckd ldr: chal over 2f out: shkn up and rdr dropped whip appr fnl f: sn led: pushed out and hld on wl* **11/4**[1]

33-3 2 nk **Secret Art (IRE)**[27] 1387 3-9-6 77 .... JimCrowley 4 82
(Ralph Beckett) *in tch: hdwy over 1f out: styd on wl fnl f: clsng on wnr nr fin but a hld* **6/1**[3]

4-13 3 1 ¼ **Erodium**[23] 1471 3-9-7 78 .... RichardHughes 3 80
(Richard Hannon) *trckd ldrs: hdwy to chse ldrs 1f out: nvr quite gng pce to chal and one pce fnl 110yds* **4/1**[2]

00-6 4 ½ **Saint Jerome (IRE)**[23] 1477 3-9-6 77 .... FergusSweeney 1 78
(Jamie Osborne) *led: jnd over 2f out: hdd 1f out: stl ev ch ins fnl f: no ex fnl 110yds* **16/1**

03-3 5 4 ½ **Guilded Spirit**[32] 1288 3-9-1 72 .... IanMongan 7 64
(Stuart Kittow) *s.i.s: sn outpcd: drvn 3f out: sme hdwy over 2f out: nvr on terms and styd on same pce* **4/1**[2]

1-12 6 1 **Strong Conviction**[13] 1683 3-9-6 77 .... MartinHarley 2 66
(Mick Channon) *chsd ldrs: rdn over 2f out: wknd appr fnl f* **10/1**

333- **7** *5* **David's Secret**[176] 7642 3-8-11 **68**.................................... KierenFallon 6 45
(Hughie Morrison) *in tch: rdn and sme hdwy 3f out: wknd 2f out: eased whn no ch fnl f* **4/1**[2]

1m 34.05s (-2.15) **Going Correction** -0.175s/f (Firm) **7** Ran SP% **115.9**
Speed ratings (Par 101): **103,102,101,100,96 95,90**
toteswingers 1&2 £3.80, 1&3 £2.70, 2&3 £4.30 CSF £20.30 CT £65.35 TOTE £2.50: £2.10, £3.00; EX 14.40 Trifecta £61.00 Pool: £3333.30 - 40.92 winning units..
Owner The Vine Accord **Bred** Cheveley Park Stud Ltd **Trained** Middleham Moor, N Yorks

FOCUS
Quite an interesting handicap contested by some potential improvers and rated at face value around the first three.

1978 32REDPOKER.COM H'CAP 6f 16y
4:50 (4:50) (Class 6) (0-65,65) 3-Y-0 **£1,940** (£577; £288; £144) **Stalls** Centre

Form				RPR
30-0	**1**		**Edged Out**[14] 1661 3-9-6 **64**.................................... DavidProbert 2 (Christopher Mason) *mde all: drvn along over 2f out: styd on wl fnl f* **6/1**[3]	71
04-5	**2**	*1 ¾*	**Duke Of Orange (IRE)**[32] 1291 3-9-5 **63**.......................... MartinHarley 3 (Mick Channon) *chsd ldrs: rdn to chse wnr over 1f out: kpt on but no imp: hld on wl for 2nd* **7/4**[1]	65
402-	**3**	*hd*	**Baltic Gin (IRE)**[194] 7272 3-9-4 **62**.......................... TomMcLaughlin 6 (Malcolm Saunders) *in rr: pushed along over 2f out: str run fnl f to press for 2nd cl home but no imp on wnr* **8/1**	63
-143	**4**	*nse*	**Polish Crown**[16] 1616 3-9-7 **65**.......................... SilvestreDeSousa 7 (Mark Johnston) *racd in 2nd: rdn fr 1/2-way: rallied and kpt on fnl f to press for 2nd again cl home but no imp on wnr* **3/1**[2]	66
4122	**5**	*2*	**Black Truffle (FR)**[11] 1710 3-8-11 **55**.......................... RichardHughes 1 (Mark Usher) *in rr: drvn: swtchd lft and sme hdwy appr fnl f: nvr gng pce to rch ldrs* **3/1**[2]	50
1350	**6**	*hd*	**Katy Spirit (IRE)**[16] 1616 3-9-5 **63**.......................... LiamKeniry 5 (Michael Blanshard) *chsd ldrs: drvn 1/2-way: outpcd fr over 1f out* **16/1**	58

1m 11.38s (-0.62) **Going Correction** -0.175s/f (Firm) **6** Ran SP% **117.6**
Speed ratings (Par 97): **97,94,94,94,91 91**
toteswingers 1&2 £2.50, 1&3 £5.80, 2&3 £4.40 CSF £18.01 TOTE £8.40: £3.70, £1.30; EX 27.40 Trifecta £129.00 Pool: £3228.38 - 18.76 winning units..
Owner Christopher & Annabelle Mason **Bred** Christopher & Annabelle Mason **Trained** Caewent, Monmouthshire

FOCUS
A modest little handicap, but a taking performance from the winner. The fourth helps to set the level.

1979 32REDBINGO.COM H'CAP (DIV I) 2m 49y
5:20 (5:23) (Class 6) (0-65,65) 4-Y-0+ **£1,940** (£577; £288; £144) **Stalls** Low

Form				RPR
515-	**1**		**Filatore (IRE)**[194] 7271 4-9-7 **65**.......................(p) MartinLane 3 (Bernard Llewellyn) *trckd ldr: upsides fr 1/2-way tl led over 6f out: drvn over 3f out: styd on wl fnl 2f* **7/2**	75
/1-3	**2**	*4*	**Beyeh (IRE)**[23] 1464 5-9-6 **61**.......................... AndrewMullen 2 (Michael Appleby) *chsd ldrs: drvn to chse wnr 2f out but sn no imp and wl hld* **9/4**[1]	66
-122	**3**	*3*	**Neighbourhood (USA)**[17] 1601 5-9-1 **56**................(b) RichardHughes 7 (James Evans) *sn led: jnd 1/2-way: hdd over 6f out: styd chsng wnr: rdn over 3f out and no imp: btn into 3rd 2f out* **11/4**[3]	57
43-0	**4**	*shd*	**Descaro (USA)**[1] 1949 7-9-2 **57**.......................... LukeMorris 9 (John O'Shea) *chsd ldrs: rdn and one pce fnl 3f* **5/2**[2]	58
266-	**5**	*8*	**Micquus (IRE)**[302] 3781 4-8-6 **50**.......................... RichardThomas 10 (Jonathan Geake) *in rr: pushed along and sme hdwy over 4f out: wknd over 2f out* **14/1**	42
0400	**6**	*7*	**Valkov**[8] 1779 6-8-5 **46** oh1.......................... DavidProbert 4 (Tony Carroll) *reluctant to enter stalls: a in rr: rdn and wknd over 2f out* **33/1**	29

3m 35.67s (-3.23) **Going Correction** -0.175s/f (Firm)
WFA 4 from 5yo+ 3lb **6** Ran SP% **117.8**
Speed ratings (Par 101): **101,99,97,97,93 89**
toteswingers 1&2 £2.50, 1&3 £2.80, 2&3 £2.00 CSF £12.59 CT £24.49 TOTE £3.00: £1.40, £2.70; EX 14.80 Trifecta £33.60 Pool: £1979.18 - 44.07 winning units..
Owner B J Llewellyn **Bred** Ballymacoll Stud Farm Ltd **Trained** Fochriw, Caerphilly

FOCUS
A low-grade staying handicap and, for what it's worth, it was the quicker division to the tune of ten seconds. The winner could be rated a few pounds higher.

1980 32REDBINGO.COM H'CAP (DIV II) 2m 49y
5:55 (5:55) (Class 6) (0-65,65) 4-Y-0+ **£1,940** (£577; £288; £144) **Stalls** Low

Form				RPR
10-0	**1**		**Knox Overstreet**[14] 1670 5-9-7 **62**.......................... MartinHarley 2 (Mick Channon) *hld up in rr: stdy hdwy 3f out: chal 2f out: led appr fnl f: pushed out* **3/1**[1]	69+
6-56	**2**	*3*	**Vertueux (FR)**[36] 1217 8-9-0 **55**.......................... GrahamLee 5 (Tony Carroll) *disp 2nd tl chsd ldr 4f out: drvn to chal fr 3f out: slt ld 2f out: hdd u.p appr fnl f: sn one pce and jst hld on for 2nd clsng stages* **5/1**[3]	58
350-	**3**	*nk*	**Spinning Waters**[7] 5196 7-8-5 **46** oh1.......................(p) KellyHarrison 4 (Dai Burchell) *chsd ldrs: rdn 3f out: styd on fnl f to cl on 2nd but no ch w wnr* **8/1**	49
56-2	**4**	*2 ¼*	**Fuzzy Logic (IRE)**[14] 1664 4-8-4 **48**.......................(p) MartinLane 8 (Bernard Llewellyn) *led: drvn along 5f out: jnd 3f out: hdd 2f out: wknd fnl f* **3/1**[1]	48
10-0	**5**	*5*	**Lucky Diva**[14] 1664 6-8-13 **61**.......................(p) JakePayne(7) 3 (Bill Turner) *in rr: rdn and sme hdwy 4f out: btn fr 3f out* **9/2**[2]	55
45-3	**6**	*2*	**Captain Sharpe**[14] 1664 5-9-5 **65**.......................(p) RobertWilliams(5) 1 (Bernard Llewellyn) *disp 2nd to 4f out: wknd fr 3f out* **5/1**[3]	57

3m 45.72s (6.82) **Going Correction** -0.175s/f (Firm)
WFA 4 from 5yo+ 3lb **6** Ran SP% **112.6**
Speed ratings (Par 101): **75,73,73,72,69 68**
toteswingers 1&2 £2.50, 1&3 £3.80, 2&3 £7.60 CSF £18.27 CT £105.85 TOTE £4.00: £2.30, £2.20; EX 24.50 Trifecta £114.60 Pool: £1001.67 - 6.55 winning units..
Owner M Channon **Bred** Bearstone Stud **Trained** West Ilsley, Berks

FOCUS
This division was run in a time ten seconds slower than the first. The runner-up is rated to his best form of the previous year.

T/Jkpt: £13,640.60 to a £1 stake. Pool: £115,272.93 - 6.00 winning tickets. T/Plt: £139.60 to a £1 stake. Pool: £85,549.38 - 447.04 winning tickets. T/Qpdt: £13.50 to a £1 stake. Pool: £5024.55 - 275.10 winning tickets. ST

[1953] LINGFIELD (L-H)
Friday, May 3

OFFICIAL GOING: Standard
Wind: Moderate, across (towards stands) Weather: Sunny, warm

1981 PENSHURST H'CAP 1m (P)
2:10 (2:10) (Class 6) (0-60,58) 4-Y-0+ **£2,045** (£603; £302) **Stalls** High

Form				RPR
0630	**1**		**Cuthbert (IRE)**[8] 1783 6-8-9 **46**.......................(b) RobertHavlin 2 (Michael Attwater) *hld up: prog on outer 2f out: clsd to ld jst ins fnl f: shkn up and styd on wl* **8/1**	54
-050	**2**	*1 ¾*	**Karate (IRE)**[16] 1617 5-9-2 **58**.......................(vt[1]) NicoleNordblad(5) 6 (Hans Adielsson) *t.k.h: lost pl after 1f and dropped to last after 3f: effrt on wd outside 2f out: styd on to take 2nd last 75yds: no ch to threaten wnr* **2/1**[1]	62
5020	**3**	*1 ¼*	**Indian Violet (IRE)**[4] 1873 7-9-2 **56**.......................(p) DarrenEgan(3) 4 (Zoe Davison) *in tch: rdn on inner 2f out: tried to chal 1f out but sn outpcd* **5/1**	57
1015	**4**	*¾*	**Chandrayaan**[22] 1497 6-9-2 **53**.......................(v) KirstyMilczarek 5 (John E Long) *led: rdn 2f out: hdd & wknd jst ins fnl f* **7/2**[2]	52
3432	**5**	*2 ¾*	**Total Obsession**[8] 1781 6-9-2 **53**.......................(v) WilliamCarson 7 (Mark Hoad) *dwlt and routed along early: sn cl up: chsd ldr 3f out: hrd rdn and wknd jst over 1f out* **9/2**[3]	46
4240	**6**	*1*	**Titan Diamond (IRE)**[23] 1473 5-8-5 **47** ow2.......... RachealKneller(5) 1 (Mark Usher) *in tch: rdn against ins rail 2f out: no prog over 1f out* **10/1**	38
00-4	**7**	*21*	**Orla (IRE)**[43] 1095 5-8-13 **50**.......................... NeilCallan 8 (John Gallagher) *dwlt: rdn to rcvr and sn chsd ldr: lost 2nd 3f out: wkng whn hmpd 2f out: t.o* **14/1**	

1m 38.09s (-0.11) **Going Correction** +0.05s/f (Slow) **7** Ran SP% **117.3**
Speed ratings (Par 101): **102,100,99,98,95 94,73**
toteswingers 1&2 £4.90, 1&3 £12.00, 2&3 £3.90 CSF £25.47 CT £91.05 TOTE £10.30: £5.70, £1.90; EX 42.10 Trifecta £190.90 Pool: £1641.49 - 6.44 winning units..
Owner Canisbay Bloodstock **Bred** Gerard Callanan **Trained** Epsom, Surrey

FOCUS
A poor 1m handicap run at a steady pace. The runner-up is rated to this year's form.

1982 EVERGREEN (S) STKS 1m (P)
2:40 (2:40) (Class 6) 3-Y-0 **£2,045** (£603; £302) **Stalls** High

Form				RPR
1-60	**1**		**Sutton Sid**[11] 1712 3-8-12 62.......................... PatCosgrave 4 (George Baker) *trckd clr ldr: clsd 3f out: chal on outer 2f out: led over 1f out: drvn and kpt on* **4/6**[1]	57
-654	**2**	*1 ¼*	**Handsome Stranger (IRE)**[95] 427 3-8-5 56.............(p) EoinWalsh(7) 1 (David Evans) *t.k.h: hld up in 3rd: clsd 3f out: chal on inner and led briefly wl over 1f out: nt qckn fnl f* **9/4**[2]	54
60-0	**3**	*8*	**Everreadyneddy**[3] 1903 3-8-12 57.......................(b[1]) LiamJones 3 (J S Moore) *led and allowed 5 l advantage by others: rdn wl over 2f out: hdd & wknd wl over 1f out* **7/1**[3]	36
000-	**4**	*9*	**Lilly May (IRE)**[192] 7313 3-8-5 46 ow3.......................... RachealKneller(5) 2 (Phil McEntee) *stdd s: hld up: a last: pushed along and lost tch over 3f out: t.o* **12/1**	13

1m 39.92s (1.72) **Going Correction** +0.05s/f (Slow) **4** Ran SP% **110.9**
Speed ratings (Par 97): **93,91,83,74**
CSF £2.53 TOTE £1.40; EX 2.30 Trifecta £3.20 Pool: £1242.71 - 286.53 winning units..There were no bids.
Owner P Bowden **Bred** Peter Hunt & Mrs Sally Hunt **Trained** Manton, Wilts

FOCUS
A desperately weak race that took little winning and the form is moderate.

1983 JIM BURDEN'S 70TH BIRTHDAY H'CAP 1m 4f (P)
3:10 (3:10) (Class 6) (0-65,70) 4-Y-0+ **£2,045** (£603; £302) **Stalls** Low

Form				RPR
0621	**1**		**Gabrial's Hope (FR)**[13] 1700 4-9-0 **61**.......................(t) DarrenEgan(3) 8 (David Simcock) *trckd ldr: drvn to chal 2f out: carried hd awkwardly after but styd on to grad gain advantage last 100yds* **6/1**[3]	70
0621	**2**	*nk*	**King Olav (UAE)**[11] 1716 8-9-7 **70** 6ex.......... WilliamTwiston-Davies(5) 2 (Tony Carroll) *led: rdn and pressed 2f out: kpt on wl but hdd and jst hld last 100yds* **7/4**[1]	78
435	**3**	*2 ¾*	**Moment In The Sun**[8] 1794 4-9-3 **61**.......................... WilliamBuick 1 (David Flood) *hld up in last: lot to do whn shkn up 2f out: styd on fr over 1f out to take 3rd nr fin: hopeless task* **20/1**	64
3012	**4**	*1*	**Shirataki (IRE)**[11] 1715 5-9-0 **65**.......................... PatMillman(7) 6 (Peter Hiatt) *s.s: rcvrd to trck ldng trio: rdn to chse ldng pair 2f out: edgd lft and no imp over 1f out: lost 3rd nr fin* **6/1**[3]	67
331-	**5**	*shd*	**Kittens**[188] 7417 4-9-7 **65**.......................... MartinDwyer 4 (William Muir) *hld up in 6th: drvn over 3f out: kpt on one pce fnl 2f: n.d* **4/1**[2]	66
22-5	**6**	*6*	**Elegant Ophelia**[112] 165 4-9-7 **65**.......................... AdamKirby 5 (Dean Ivory) *trckd ldng pair to 2f out: sn wknd* **4/1**[2]	57
0-40	**7**	*4 ½*	**Time To Dance**[13] 1699 4-9-7 **65**.......................... CathyGannon 3 (Joseph Tuite) *hld up in 5th: rdn 3f out: sn wknd* **16/1**	50

2m 32.09s (-0.91) **Going Correction** +0.05s/f (Slow) **7** Ran SP% **115.6**
Speed ratings (Par 101): **105,104,102,102,102 98,95**
toteswingers 1&2 £4.20, 1&3 £3.80, 2&3 £6.50 CSF £17.37 CT £198.91 TOTE £7.60: £2.80, £1.50; EX 20.30 Trifecta £120.30 Pool: £2297.04 - 14.30 winning units..
Owner Dr Marwan Koukash **Bred** Mrs G Forien & G Forien **Trained** Newmarket, Suffolk

FOCUS
A competitive race for the grade and it produced a thrilling finish between two leading apprentices. The third tends to limit the form.

1984 DFSK CUTIE CAMPERVAN H'CAP 5f (P)
3:40 (3:40) (Class 4) (0-85,84) 4-Y-0+ **£4,690** (£1,395; £697; £348) **Stalls** High

Form				RPR
1-14	**1**		**Monumental Man**[67] 795 4-8-9 **72**.......................(p) HayleyTurner 1 (James Unett) *trckd ldng pair: urged along to take 2nd 1f out: clsd to ld last 120yds: drvn out* **4/1**[2]	80
040-	**2**	*½*	**Decision By One**[179] 7595 4-9-5 **82**.......................(t) RichardKingscote 3 (Tom Dascombe) *chsd ldr to 1f out: drvn and kpt on wl to regain 2nd last 50yds: a hld* **7/2**[1]	88
3420	**3**	*½*	**Song Of Parkes**[20] 1540 6-8-7 **75** ow1.......................... SladeO'Hara(5) 5 (Peter Grayson) *hld up in last trio: shkn up and prog over 1f out: styd on to take 3rd nr fin* **16/1**	79

104- **4** nk **Arctic Lynx (IRE)**[155] 7928 6-9-1 **83**.................... MichaelJMMurphy(5) 2 86
(Robert Cowell) *hld up in last trio: effrt on inner wl over 1f out: styd on fnl f to press for 3rd nr fin* **6/1**

310- **5** ½ **Howyadoingnotsobad (IRE)**[230] 6226 5-9-1 **78**................ NeilCallan 7 80
(Karen George) *led: tried to kick away over 1f out: hdd & wknd last 120yds* **5/1**[3]

634 **6** 1 **Rowe Park**[34] 1245 10-9-7 **84**..(p) SteveDrowne 4 82
(Linda Jewell) *chsd ldng trio: rdn 2f out: lost pl and btn over 1f out: one pce* **5/1**[3]

0604 **7** hd **Lujeanie**[13] 1694 7-8-10 **73**.. ShaneKelly 6 70
(Peter Crate) *dwlt: hld up in last trio: rdn on outer 2f out: nt qckn and no prog fnl f* **4/1**[2]

58.42s (-0.38) **Going Correction** +0.05s/f (Slow) **7** Ran SP% **115.7**
Speed ratings (Par 105): **105,104,103,102,102 100,100**
toteswingers 1&2 £4.30, 1&3 £9.00, 2&3 £16.20 CSF £18.85 TOTE £3.40: £2.40, £3.50; EX 20.60 Trifecta £164.60 Pool: £2874.50 - 13.09 winning units..
Owner P Fetherston-Godley **Bred** Christopher Chell **Trained** Tedsmore Hall, Shropshire

FOCUS
Pace was never going to be at a shortage in this sprint handicap and, with Howyadoingnotsobad setting off like a bullet from a gun, it played right into the hands of Monumental Man. The runner-up is rated to his best recent course form.

1985 HANNAH BURDEN IS 18 H'CAP — 6f (P)
4:10 (4:12) (Class 5) (0-75,75) 4-Y-0+ **£2,726** (£805; £402) **Stalls** Low

Form RPR
414- **1** **Langley Vale**[249] 5662 4-8-11 **65**... SebSanders 1 76+
(Roger Teal) *trckd ldng pair: wnt 2nd over 2f out: clsd to ld over 1f out: rdn out but nvr in serious danger* **14/1**

2-42 **2** ½ **Peace Seeker**[25] 1430 5-9-7 **75**...................................... WilliamCarson 7 85
(Anthony Carson) *chsd ldng trio: pushed along 2f out: styd on fr over 1f out to take 2nd last 100yds: clsd on wnr but nvr able to chal* **3/1**[2]

4231 **3** 1½ **Desert Strike**[23] 1475 7-9-2 **70**..(p) HayleyTurner 5 75
(Conor Dore) *led: rdn and hdd over 1f out: lost 2nd last 100yds: fdd nr fin* **14/1**

5141 **4** 1 **Valdaw**[8] 1798 5-8-9 **68**.................................... WilliamTwiston-Davies(5) 2 70
(Mike Murphy) *trckd ldrs in 5th: n.m.r over 2f out and sn rdn: kpt on same pce fr over 1f out: n.d* **5/2**[1]

0250 **5** nk **Frognal (IRE)**[6] 1838 7-9-6 **74**......................................(bt) CathyGannon 9 75+
(Violet M Jordan) *dropped in fr wd draw and hld up in last pair: shkn up on inner 2f out: kpt on same pce fr over 1f out: nvr threatened* **16/1**

-332 **6** nk **Commanche**[23] 1475 4-8-7 **66**..................................... ThomasBrown(5) 3 67
(Patrick Chamings) *hld up in last trio: shkn up 2f out: kpt on same pce fr over 1f out: nvr threatened* **5/1**

23-4 **7** 3 **Zhiggy's Stardust**[14] 1660 4-9-2 **70**................................. DaneO'Neill 10 60
(Henry Candy) *racd wd: nvr beyond midfield: struggling 2f out* **9/2**[3]

2450 **8** 6 **Super Duplex**[31] 1304 6-8-4 **63**................................ JemmaMarshall(5) 4 34
(Pat Phelan) *mostly in last: lost tch w rest 1/2-way: t.o* **33/1**

4112 **9** ¾ **Billy Red**[21] 1517 9-9-7 **75**..(b) WilliamBuick 6 44
(J R Jenkins) *chsd ldr to over 2f out: wknd rapidly: eased over 1f out: t.o* **10/1**

1m 10.83s (-1.07) **Going Correction** +0.05s/f (Slow) **9** Ran SP% **119.7**
Speed ratings (Par 103): **109,108,106,105,104 104,100,92,91**
toteswingers 1&2 £8.40, 1&3 £8.40, 2&3 £9.30 CSF £58.02 CT £624.99 TOTE £9.10: £2.50, £2.20, £2.70; EX 93.40 Trifecta £1043.50 Pool: £4675.56 - 3.36 winning units..
Owner Dr G F Forward & F C Taylor **Bred** Miss Brooke Sanders **Trained** Ashtead, Surrey

FOCUS
Some in-form sprinters lined up for this handicap at the form looks solid, with the placed horses giving the race perspective.

1986 GOATS CROSS MAIDEN FILLIES' STKS — 7f (P)
4:40 (4:40) (Class 5) 3-Y-0+ **£2,726** (£805; £402) **Stalls** Low

Form RPR
533- **1** **Auction (IRE)**[189] 7364 3-8-10 73.. WilliamBuick 3 77
(Ed Dunlop) *mde all: set modest pce tl qcknd 1/2-way: hrd rdn over 1f out: jst hld on* **5/4**[1]

240- **2** hd **Thakana**[169] 7720 3-8-10 72.. DaneO'Neill 8 76
(J W Hills) *chsd ldng pair: wd bnd 2f out: drvn to go 2nd jst over 1f out: clsd on wnr nr fin: jst failed* **6/1**

2 **3** 4 **Spicy Dal**[14] 1666 3-8-10 0.. RobertHavlin 1 65
(Hughie Morrison) *chsd ldng pair: drvn to dispute 2nd on inner 2f out: fdd ins fnl f* **5/2**[2]

5-0 **4** 1¼ **Muzhil (IRE)**[20] 1544 4-9-8 0.. NeilCallan 11 66
(Clive Brittain) *trckd wnr: rdn over 2f out: lost 2nd and wknd jst over 1f out* **12/1**

5 4½ **Greek Spirit (IRE)** 3-8-10 0... JimmyFortune 9 50+
(Jeremy Noseda) *hld up in midfield: outpcd fr 1/2-way: trying to make grnd whn v wd bnd 2f out: modest 5th fr over 1f out* **5/1**[3]

6 **6** 1½ **Bill Of Rights**[28] 1364 3-8-10 0.. HayleyTurner 10 46+
(Michael Bell) *c out of stalls slowly and swtchd to inner: hld up in last quartet: wl bhd once pce lifted 1/2-way: sme hdwy fnl 2f: do bttr* **20/1**

7 shd **Persian Patriot** 3-8-10 0... CathyGannon 4 46+
(William Jarvis) *hld up in last trio: wl bhd once pce lifted 1/2-way: sme prog fr over 2f out: pushed along and kpt on: nt disgracd* **33/1**

0-6 **8** 4 **Made It (IRE)**[89] 509 3-8-10 0.. WilliamCarson 2 35
(Anthony Carson) *chsd ldng quartet: drvn 1/2-way: sn wknd and bhd* **50/1**

9 8 **Serendippidy** 3-8-10 0.. AdamBeschizza 6 13
(James Unett) *s.s: a in last trio: wl bhd once pce lifted 1/2-way: t.o* **66/1**

0-0 **10** 6 **Daneglow (IRE)**[28] 1364 3-8-10 0.. ShaneKelly 7
(Mike Murphy) *t.k.h: sn restrained into midfield: wknd sn after 1/2-way: t.o* **100/1**

11 3¼ **Tcharmeddotorg** 3-8-5 0... RachealKneller(5) 5
(Phil McEntee) *a in last trio: wl bhd fr 1/2-way: t.o* **66/1**

1m 24.77s (-0.03) **Going Correction** +0.05s/f (Slow)
WFA 3 from 4yo 12lb **11** Ran SP% **125.3**
Speed ratings (Par 100): **102,101,97,95,90 88,88,84,75,68 64**
toteswingers 1&2 £2.70, 1&3 £1.60, 2&3 £3.70 CSF £10.14 TOTE £1.70: £1.40, £1.50, £1.30; EX 13.60 Trifecta £35.50 Pool: £4267.88 - 89.98 winning units..
Owner Highclere Thoroughbred Racing - Coventry **Bred** Edy Srl And Societa Agricola Gem Srl **Trained** Newmarket, Suffolk

FOCUS
An informative fillies' maiden but, with the race developing into nothing more than a 2f dash for home, it remains to be seen how well the form will work out. The third and fourth are key to the level of the form.

1987 SHOVELSTRODE RACING STABLES H'CAP — 1m 2f (P)
5:10 (5:10) (Class 6) (0-60,60) 4-Y-0+ **£2,045** (£603; £302) **Stalls** Low

Form RPR
0623 **1** **Matraash (USA)**[8] 1797 7-9-7 **60**......................................(be) ShaneKelly 8 74
(Daniel Mark Loughnane) *trckd ldr: led over 3f out: kicked on over 2f out: drvn and styd on wl fr over 1f out* **5/2**[1]

3162 **2** 2¾ **Angelena Ballerina (IRE)**[11] 1730 6-9-0 **53**...................(v) AdamKirby 1 61
(Sean Curran) *trckd ldng pair: chsd wnr over 2f out: styd on wl fr over 1f out but no imp* **5/2**[1]

3464 **3** 4 **Dolly Colman (IRE)**[3] 1909 5-8-7 **46** oh1....................(p) CathyGannon 7 46
(Zoe Davison) *hld up in midfield: rdn and outpcd over 2f out: kpt on to take mod 3rd ins fnl f* **10/1**

5353 **4** 1¾ **Fonterutoli (IRE)**[8] 1779 6-9-4 **57**..........................(e) AdamBeschizza 4 54
(Roger Ingram) *drvn early to get gng: sn chsd ldrs: wnt 2nd u.p over 3f out to over 2f out: sn lft bhd* **5/1**[2]

/042 **5** 1¼ **Queenie's Star (IRE)**[8] 1779 6-8-9 **48**............................ RobertHavlin 2 42
(Michael Attwater) *hld up in last trio: gng wl enough whn taken fr inner to outer bnd 2f out and lft bhd: shkn up over 1f out: nvr involved* **8/1**

06-6 **6** 1½ **Major Buckley (IRE)**[45] 1072 4-8-7 **46** oh1.................. WilliamCarson 5 37
(David Evans) *a in rr: lft bhd fr 3f out: no ch after* **6/1**[3]

2420 **7** ¾ **Lytham (IRE)**[31] 1298 12-9-2 **55**.. HayleyTurner 3 45
(Tony Carroll) *stdd s: hld up in last pair: outpcd fr over 3f out: nvr on terms after* **10/1**

000- **8** 2¼ **Frosty Secret**[184] 7473 4-9-6 **59**.. MartinDwyer 6 44
(Jane Chapple-Hyam) *led: set mod pce to 1/2-way: hdd over 3f out: wknd rapidly sn after* **16/1**

2m 7.85s (1.25) **Going Correction** +0.05s/f (Slow) **8** Ran SP% **123.3**
Speed ratings (Par 101): **97,94,91,90,89 88,87,85**
toteswingers 1&2 £1.90, 1&3 £3.20, 2&3 £4.30 CSF £9.30 CT £55.52 TOTE £3.60: £1.10, £1.60, £4.20; EX 17.10 Trifecta £74.50 Pool: £2633.06 - 26.47 winning units..
Owner Mrs C Loughnane **Bred** Shadwell Farm LLC **Trained** Baldwin's Gate, Staffs

FOCUS
A tactical affair best rated through the runner-up to the balance of his recent form.
T/Plt: £61.70 to a £1 stake. Pool: £59,685.67 - 705.19 winning tickets. T/Qpdt: £14.60 to a £1 stake. Pool: £4565.20 - 230.95 winning tickets. JN

1270 MUSSELBURGH (R-H)
Friday, May 3

OFFICIAL GOING: Good to soft (7.4)
Wind: Moderate across Weather: Cloudy and rain

1988 BREWIN DOLPHIN H'CAP — 5f
2:00 (2:00) (Class 6) (0-65,71) 3-Y-0 **£2,587** (£770; £384; £192) **Stalls** High

Form RPR
2-35 **1** **Antonio Gramsci**[52] 964 3-8-13 **62**...................................... LMcNiff(5) 4 81
(David Barron) *trckd ldrs: hdwy wl over 1f out: swtchd rt and rdn to ld ent fnl f: carried hd high: drvn out* **3/1**[2]

0-54 **2** 2¾ **Someone's Darling**[18] 1566 3-8-13 **57**.......................(p) DanielTudhope 5 66
(Jim Goldie) *hld up in rr: swtchd to outer and gd hdwy 2f out: rdn to chal ent fnl f: ev ch tl drvn and nt qckn towards fin* **8/1**

00-5 **3** 1¾ **Ichimoku**[9] 1762 3-8-6 **50**...(t) RoystonFfrench 8 53
(Bryan Smart) *hld up in rr: hdwy wl over 1f out: swtchd rt and rdn ent fnl f: styd on: nrst fin* **16/1**

2-22 **4** 1¾ **Cracking Choice (IRE)**[8] 1791 3-9-5 **63**..................(p) PaulMulrennan 1 59
(Michael Dods) *qckly away and led: rdn over 1f out: hdd and drvn ent fnl f: sn wknd* **5/2**[1]

2040 **5** 2¾ **Nors The Panic**[10] 1742 3-8-2 **49** ow1..............................(e) BillyCray(3) 9 36
(Richard Guest) *prom: rdn along over 2f out: grad wknd* **50/1**

00-3 **6** 1 **Salvatore Fury (IRE)**[18] 1566 3-8-10 **54**..........................(p) JoeFanning 7 39
(Keith Dalgleish) *hld up: hdwy 2f out: rdn to chse ldrs whn nt clr run ent fnl f: one pce after* **11/2**[3]

60-0 **7** 1 **Betty Boo (IRE)**[13] 1682 3-8-2 **46** oh1........................ DuranFentiman 10 25
(Shaun Harris) *cl up: rdn along 1/2-way: sn wknd* **40/1**

25-1 **8** shd **Rangooned**[9] 1762 3-9-13 **71** 6ex.. PJMcDonald 6 50
(Ann Duffield) *chsd ldrs: rdn wl over 1f out: sn drvn and wknd* **6/1**

4535 **9** 5 **Secret Advice**[23] 1458 3-8-12 **56**... TomEaves 3 17
(Keith Dalgleish) *in tch: chsd ldrs 1/2-way: sn rdn along and wkng whn sltly hmpd over 1f out* **10/1**

-000 **10** 2¼ **Moss The Boss (IRE)**[10] 1742 3-8-0 **49**............(b[1]) ShirleyTeasdale(5) 2
(Paul Midgley) *cl up: chal 2f out: sn rdn and wknd over 1f out* **50/1**

1m 1.92s (1.52) **Going Correction** +0.25s/f (Good) **10** Ran SP% **115.7**
Speed ratings (Par 97): **97,92,89,87,82 81,79,79,71,67**
toteswingers 1&2 £7.30, 1&3 £15.40, 2&3 £15.60 CSF £26.83 CT £325.48 TOTE £5.00: £1.90, £2.30, £5.00; EX 32.10 Trifecta £700.90 Pool: £1947.74 - 2.08 winning units..
Owner Norton Common Farm Racing **Bred** A C M Spalding **Trained** Maunby, N Yorks

FOCUS
The ground, given as good overnight, had been watered, and following 1mm of rain prior to the start of the meeting conditions eased to good to soft. After the first, Danny Tudhope said: "It is good to soft, soft in places" and Tom Eaves said: "It is soft." They went pretty hard up front and the first two came from behind, finishing up the centre of the track away from the normally favoured stands' rail. The runner-up goes well here and sets the level.

1989 BAILLIE GIFFORD EUROPEAN BREEDERS' FUND MAIDEN STKS — 5f
2:30 (2:30) (Class 4) 2-Y-0 **£4,204** (£1,251; £625; £312) **Stalls** High

Form RPR
4 **1** **Withernsea (IRE)**[15] 1642 2-9-5 0.................................... TonyHamilton 6 79+
(Richard Fahey) *racd nr stands' rail: mde all: rdn clr ent fnl f: sn edgd rt and kpt on strly* **7/4**[1]

2 1¾ **Tanseeb** 2-9-5 0.. PaulMulrennan 4 73+
(Mark Johnston) *prom: pushed along: green and outpcd after 1f: sn detached fr ldrs: gd hdwy on inner wl over 1f out: styd on to chse wnr ins fnl f: kpt on* **16/1**

3 **3** 3¼ **Captain Midnight (IRE)**[16] 1605 2-9-5 0...................... RobertWinston 2 61
(David Brown) *prom on outer: hdwy to chse wnr appr fnl f: sn rdn and one pce* **15/8**[2]

4 1½ **Lyn Valley** 2-9-5 0.. JoeFanning 5 56+
(Mark Johnston) *cl up: rdn along 2f out: wknd over 1f out* **11/1**

2 5 nk **Muspelheim**[15] 1642 2-9-5 0 .... PJMcDonald 1 55
(Ann Duffield) *wnt rt s: sn outpcd and bhd: hdwy on wd outside and chsd ldrs 2f out: sn rdn and wknd* 11/2[3]
6 9 **Disclosure** 2-9-5 0 .... TomEaves 3 22
(Bryan Smart) *cl up: rdn along 2f out: wkng whn n.m.r and hmpd over 1f out: bhd after* 11/1
1m 3.56s (3.16) **Going Correction** +0.25s/f (Good) 6 Ran SP% **109.1**
Speed ratings (Par 95): **84,81,76,73,73 58**
toteswingers 1&2 £7.40, 1&3 £1.30, 2&3 £6.60 CSF £26.24 TOTE £2.20: £1.80, £4.30; EX 35.10 Trifecta £55.40 Pool: £2458.21 - 33.25 winning units..
Owner City Vaults Racing 1 **Bred** Yeomanstown Stud **Trained** Musley Bank, N Yorks
FOCUS
No more than a fair looking maiden and the form is fluid.

1990 WEATHERBYS BANK H'CAP — 1m 1f
3:00 (3:00) (Class 4) (0-85,90) 4-Y-0+ **£6,469** (£1,925; £962; £481) **Stalls** Low

Form RPR
650- 1 **Next Edition (IRE)**[211] 6124 5-8-6 **76** .... EvaMoscrop(7) 5 88
(Philip Kirby) *hld up in rr: stdy hdwy on inner: over 3f out: cl up wl over 2f out: sn led and rdn: edgd lft jst over 1f out: kpt on wl* 10/1
1141 2 3 1/4 **Frontier Fighter**[11] 1723 5-9-13 **90** 6ex .... DanielTudhope 6 95
(David O'Meara) *trckd ldrs: hdwy to ld 3f out: sn rdn and hdd over 2f out: sn drvn: swtchd rt jst ins fnl f: no imp after* 7/5[1]
0-53 3 4 **Gala Casino Star (IRE)**[15] 1643 8-9-0 **84** ....(v) JordanNason(7) 7 81
(Geoffrey Harker) *hld up towards rr: hdwy on outer over 3f out: chsd ldrs over 2f out: sn rdn and edgd rt over 1f out: kpt on one pce* 12/1
0-05 4 3/4 **Satanic Beat (IRE)**[20] 1538 4-9-4 **81** .... PJMcDonald 2 76
(Jedd O'Keeffe) *trckd ldng pair: hdwy and cl up 3f out: sn rdn and one pce fnl 2f* 11/4[2]
100- 5 1 **Nemushka**[202] 7069 4-9-2 **79** ....(p) TonyHamilton 4 72
(Richard Fahey) *hld up: hdwy into midfield 4f out: rdn along over 2f out: sn no imp* 12/1
333/ 6 8 **Nimiety**[587] 6340 4-8-7 **70** .... JoeFanning 1 46
(Mark Johnston) *cl up on inner: led 1/2-way: rdn along and hdd 3f out: sn wknd* 7/1[3]
000- 7 1/2 **Reve De Nuit (USA)**[189] 1654 7-8-11 **77** .... MichaelMetcalfe(3) 3 52
(Mrs K Burke) *in tch on inner: rdn along over 3f out: sn wknd* 16/1
524- 8 nk **Act Your Shoe Size**[204] 7002 4-9-3 **80** .... TomEaves 8 55
(Keith Dalgleish) *slt ld: hdd 1/2-way: cl up tl rdn along 3f out and sn wknd* 25/1
500- 9 21 **Royal Straight**[215] 6706 8-8-5 **71** ....(t) JulieBurke(3) 9
(Linda Perratt) *s.i.s: a bhd* 33/1
1m 57.47s (3.57) **Going Correction** +0.55s/f (Yiel) 9 Ran SP% **118.0**
Speed ratings (Par 105): **106,103,99,98,98 90,90,90,71**
toteswingers 1&2 £5.10, 1&3 £9.70, 2&3 £6.70 CSF £24.98 CT £180.38 TOTE £16.50: £3.70, £1.10, £3.10; EX 38.80 Trifecta £294.50 Pool: £2878.11 - 7.32 winning units..
Owner The Dibble Bridge Partnership **Bred** Manister House Stud **Trained** Middleham, N Yorks
FOCUS
The leaders went off too quick here and it paid to be held up off the gallop. The winner is rated back to his best with the runner-up to his Pontefract form.

1991 WEATHERBYS PRIVATE BANKING H'CAP — 1m 1f
3:30 (3:30) (Class 3) (0-90,89) 3-Y-O **£7,762** (£2,310; £1,154; £577) **Stalls** Low

Form RPR
241- 1 **Romantic Settings**[239] 5962 3-8-9 **77** .... TonyHamilton 1 89+
(Richard Fahey) *trckd ldrs on inner: hdwy 3f out: swtchd lft and rdn to chal 2f out: carried lft over 1f out: drvn to ld ins fnl f: styd on* 7/2[3]
001- 2 1 1/2 **King Of The Danes**[135] 8172 3-8-3 **71** .... JoeFanning 5 81
(Mark Johnston) *led: pushed along 3f out: jnd and rdn 2f out: hung lft over 1f out: drvn and hdd ins fnl f: one pce* 10/3[2]
1 3 6 **Lady Artiste (IRE)**[27] 1389 3-8-4 **72** .... NickyMackay 2 68
(Alan Swinbank) *in tch: hdwy 3f out: rdn to chse ldrs over 2f out: sn drvn and plugged on same pce* 5/1
62-3 4 shd **London Citizen (USA)**[15] 1645 3-9-4 **89** .... MichaelMetcalfe(3) 4 85
(Mrs K Burke) *hld up: hdwy on outer over 3f out: rdn along over 2f out: sn drvn and no imp* 5/2[1]
130- 5 shd **Lazarus Bell**[205] 6980 3-9-3 **85** .... DaleSwift 8 81
(Alan Brown) *trckd ldng pair: effrt 3f out: sn rdn and one pce fr wl over 1f out* 25/1
15-0 6 nk **Marhaba Malayeen (IRE)**[6] 1829 3-8-4 **72** ....(b) AmyRyan 3 67
(Kevin Ryan) *dwlt and sn rdn along: a in rr* 10/1
3115 7 1/2 **Apache Rising**[18] 1577 3-8-5 **73** ow1 .... RoystonFfrench 7 68
(Bryan Smart) *trckd ldr: hdwy and cl up 3f out: sn rdn and hld whn n.m.r 2f out: sn swtchd rt and drvn: sn wknd* 12/1
2m 0.25s (6.35) **Going Correction** +0.55s/f (Yiel) 7 Ran SP% **111.2**
Speed ratings (Par 103): **93,91,86,86,86 85,85**
toteswingers 1&2 £3.30, 1&3 £2.50, 2&3 £3.30 CSF £14.66 CT £54.23 TOTE £5.00: £3.40, £3.70; EX 18.40 Trifecta £50.20 Pool: £1998.05 - 29.82 winning units..
Owner Mel Roberts & Ms Nicola Meese 1 **Bred** Newsells Park Stud **Trained** Musley Bank, N Yorks
FOCUS
Two handicap debutants came clear in this fairly decent handicap. The pace wasn't overly strong and an improved effort from the winner, although the ground probably contributed to the first two finishing clear.

1992 CORE (OIL AND GAS) LTD H'CAP — 7f 30y
4:00 (4:01) (Class 3) (0-90,87) 4-Y-0+ **£7,762** (£2,310; £1,154; £577) **Stalls** Low

Form RPR
331 1 **Gandalak (FR)**[8] 1787 4-9-6 **86** 6ex .... DanielTudhope 4 98
(David O'Meara) *mde all: sn clr and set str pce: rdn 2f out and styd on strly: unchal* 11/8[1]
0-00 2 4 1/2 **Discression**[13] 1675 4-9-7 **87** .... PhillipMakin 2 86
(Kevin Ryan) *trckd ldng pair: effrt wl over 2f out and sn rdn: drvn ent fnl f and no imp* 2/1[2]
3-00 3 1/2 **Our Boy Jack (IRE)**[27] 1385 4-9-1 **81** .... TonyHamilton 6 79
(Richard Fahey) *trckd ldrs: hdwy 3f out: rdn along over 2f out: drvn and no imp fr over 1f out* 7/1
00-5 4 3 3/4 **Powerful Presence (IRE)**[13] 1688 7-9-2 **87** .... DavidBergin(5) 3 75
(David O'Meara) *chsd wnr: rdn along wl over 2f out: sn drvn and btn wl over 1f out* 4/1[3]
200- 5 19 **Silver Rime (FR)**[174] 7685 8-8-2 **71** .... JulieBurke(3) 5 10
(Linda Perratt) *s.i.s: a bhd* 33/1
1m 33.37s (4.37) **Going Correction** +0.70s/f (Yiel) 5 Ran SP% **110.9**
Speed ratings (Par 107): **103,97,97,93,71**
CSF £4.45 TOTE £1.90: £1.10, £2.00; EX 5.00 Trifecta £17.50 Pool: £2906.56 - 124.40 winning units..
Owner Middleham Park Racing LIII & Partners **Bred** Haras De Son Altesse L'Aga Khan S C E A **Trained** Nawton, N Yorks

FOCUS
The placed horses rated to rwecent form look the best guides.

1993 BRUCE STEVENSON INSURANCE BROKERS H'CAP — 1m 6f
4:30 (4:30) (Class 5) (0-70,70) 4-Y-0+ **£3,234** (£962; £481; £240) **Stalls** Low

Form RPR
-005 1 **Kingarrick**[8] 1789 5-8-2 **51** .... NeilFarley(3) 3 64
(Noel Wilson) *trckd ldrs: hdwy 5f out: cl up over 3f out: rdn to ld 2f out: drvn ent fnl f: jst hld on* 8/1
1/04 2 hd **Brasingaman Eric**[18] 1572 6-8-11 **57** .... PJMcDonald 11 70
(George Moore) *led: rdn along 3f out: hdd 2f out: cl up and drvn over 1f out: rallied gamely u.p ins fnl f: jst hld* 4/1[1]
06-6 3 10 **La Bacouetteuse (FR)**[27] 1390 8-9-10 **70** ....(v) DavidAllan 5 70+
(Iain Jardine) *hld up in rr: pushed along and hdwy 3f out: rdn over 2f out: swtchd lft and styd on wl fnl f* 8/1
60-0 4 3/4 **Raleigh Quay (IRE)**[23] 1463 6-9-5 **65** .... PhillipMakin 7 64
(Micky Hammond) *hld up towards rr: hdwy over 4f out: rdn along wl over 2f out: kpt on u.p fnl f* 25/1
600/ 5 1 1/4 **Spiekeroog**[34] 6988 7-9-2 **67** ....(v[1]) DavidBergin(5) 4 64
(David O'Meara) *in tch: hdwy on wd outside 3f out: rdn over 2f out: sn drvn and one pce* 10/1
0-13 6 1/2 **Discay**[52] 969 4-9-7 **68** .... JoeFanning 6 64
(Mark Johnston) *cl up: rdn along 3f out: drvn 2f out: grad wknd* 9/2[2]
440- 7 6 **Madrasa (IRE)**[126] 6076 5-9-5 **65** ....(t) TomEaves 8 54
(Keith Reveley) *hld up: nvr bttr than midfield* 11/1
5-30 8 1/2 **Nadema Rose (IRE)**[18] 1567 4-8-13 **65** .... GarryWhillans(5) 1 53
(Keith Dalgleish) *chsd ldrs: rdn along over 3f out: sn wknd* 15/2
9 nk **Badged**[349] 2292 4-9-2 **63** .... PaulMulrennan 2 51
(Lucy Normile) *trckd ldrs on inner: rdn along 4f out: drvn 3f out: wknd fnl 2f* 14/1
/3-3 10 19 **Graceful Descent (FR)**[27] 1390 8-9-10 **70** .... DuranFentiman 10 33
(Karen Tutty) *a towards rr: bhd fnl 3f* 13/2[3]
05-0 11 7 **Altnaharra**[32] 1279 4-8-4 **51** oh6 ....(b) NickyMackay 9
(Jim Goldie) *chsd ldrs: pushed along and lost pl 1/2-way: sn bhd* 50/1
3m 13.91s (8.61) **Going Correction** +0.70s/f (Yiel)
WFA 4 from 5yo+ 1lb 11 Ran SP% **115.4**
Speed ratings (Par 103): **103,102,97,96,96 95,92,92,91,81 77**
toteswingers 1&2 £7.90, 1&3 £12.00, 2&3 £7.90 CSF £39.21 CT £267.07 TOTE £7.50: £3.10, £1.50, £3.40; EX 51.40 Trifecta £738.20 Pool: £3028.93 - 3.07 winning units..
Owner Hurn Racing Club **Bred** Southcourt Stud **Trained** Middleham, N Yorks
■ Stewards' Enquiry : P J McDonald two-day ban: used whip above permitted level (May 17,19)
FOCUS
An ordinary handicap. The pace wasn't particularly strong and the first two were up there throughout. The third is probably the best guide, despite being beaten a fair way.

1994 OAK H'CAP (DIV I) — 7f 30y
5:05 (5:05) (Class 6) (0-65,65) 4-Y-0+ **£2,587** (£770; £384; £192) **Stalls** Low

Form RPR
000- 1 **Cara's Request (AUS)**[186] 7447 8-8-7 **51** oh3 .... TomEaves 4 69
(Michael Dods) *mde all: pushed clr 2f out: rdn jst ins fnl f: kpt on wl* 4/1[2]
0-05 2 6 **Tony Hollis**[16] 1603 5-8-7 **51** oh1 .... DuranFentiman 1 51
(Karen Tutty) *trckd ldrs: hdwy 3f out: rdn to chse wnr wl over 1f out: drvn and no imp fnl f* 9/1
00-0 3 2 **West Leake Hare (IRE)**[9] 1757 4-9-7 **65** .... AdrianNicholls 7 60
(David Nicholls) *in tch: reminders over 3f out: rdn over 2f out: sn one pce* 7/1
010- 4 7 **Lothair (IRE)**[164] 7798 4-8-9 **53** ow1 .... RobertWinston 8 30
(Alan Swinbank) *chsd wnr: rdn along wl over 2f out: drvn and wknd wl over 1f out* 12/1
16-0 5 nse **Iceblast**[29] 1351 5-9-1 **59** .... PaulMulrennan 5 35
(Michael Easterby) *midfield: pushed along 3f out: rdn 2f out: nvr nr ldrs* 7/2[1]
0-30 6 4 **North Central (USA)**[110] 194 6-8-10 **54** ....(e) JamesSullivan 10 20
(Ruth Carr) *chsd ldng pair: rdn along 3f out: drvn over 2f out: sn wknd* 28/1
6554 7 4 1/2 **George Fenton**[7] 1800 4-9-3 **61** ....(v) RobbieFitzpatrick 6 15+
(Richard Guest) *dwlt: a in rr* 9/2[3]
603- 8 11 **Berbice (IRE)**[165] 7788 8-8-12 **56** .... PhillipMakin 2
(Linda Perratt) *nvr bttr than midfield* 16/1
06-5 9 1 **Carla Allegra**[33] 1272 4-8-7 **51** oh6 .... NickyMackay 3
(Jim Goldie) *a in rr* 40/1
000/ 10 2 **Sunnandaeg**[711] 2369 6-9-7 **65** .... JoeFanning 9 +
(Keith Dalgleish) *hld up: a in rr* 7/1
1m 34.62s (5.62) **Going Correction** +0.85s/f (Soft) 10 Ran SP% **114.9**
Speed ratings (Par 101): **101,94,91,83,83 79,74,61,60,58**
toteswingers 1&2 £6.20, 1&3 £4.70, 2&3 £11.10 CSF £39.26 CT £250.90 TOTE £5.60: £2.00, £3.30, £2.30; EX 47.60 Trifecta £353.10 Pool: £1499.43 - 3.18 winning units..
Owner Stewart Aitken **Bred** S Aitken **Trained** Denton, Co Durham
FOCUS
A moderate handicap but the winner looks well handicapped and can score under a penalty.

1995 OAK H'CAP (DIV II) — 7f 30y
5:35 (5:36) (Class 6) (0-65,65) 4-Y-0+ **£2,587** (£770; £384; £192) **Stalls** Low

Form RPR
434- 1 **Jebel Tara**[213] 6756 8-8-7 **51** oh2 ....(bt) TomEaves 4 58
(Alan Brown) *trckd ldrs: smooth hdwy wl over 2f out: led over 1f out: rdn ins fnl f: kpt on* 12/1
320- 2 1 1/4 **Just The Tonic**[195] 7247 6-9-1 **64** .... ShirleyTeasdale(5) 2 68
(Marjorie Fife) *chsd ldrs on inner: effrt 3f out and sn rdn along: drvn over 1f out: styd on fnl f* 4/1[3]
00-0 3 1/2 **Goninodaethat**[33] 1271 5-8-8 **52** .... NickyMackay 10 54
(Jim Goldie) *trckd ldng pair: cl up over 3f out: rdn to ld over 2f out: drvn and hdd over 1f out: kpt on same pce* 7/1
5004 4 3/4 **Bassett Road (IRE)**[23] 1460 5-9-7 **65** ....(p) JoeFanning 9 66
(Keith Dalgleish) *hld up: hdwy 3f out: rdn to chse ldrs 2f out: kpt on fnl f: nrst fin* 4/1[3]
03-5 5 3/4 **Jupiter Fidius**[27] 1394 6-9-0 **58** ....(p) DaleSwift 5 57
(Karen Tutty) *s.i.s and bhd: rdn along 3f out: hdwy on wd outside over 2f out: kpt on u.p fnl f: nrst fin* 7/2[2]
1146 6 17 **Rise To Glory (IRE)**[15] 1657 5-8-12 **56** .... DuranFentiman 8 10
(Shaun Harris) *trckd ldr: cl up 3f out: rdn over 2f out: drvn wl over 1f out and sn btn* 10/3[1]
0000 7 1 3/4 **Dhhamaan (IRE)**[11] 1734 8-8-9 **53** ....(b) PJMcDonald 3
(Ruth Carr) *slt ld: rdn along over 3f out: hdd over 2f out and sn wknd* **12/1**

055- 8 9 **Mr Khan**[362] 1876 5-8-4 **51** oh5.. JulieBurke(3) 6
(Linda Perratt) *a towards rr: rdn along and wknd fnl 2f* **40/1**

1m 35.41s (6.41) **Going Correction** +0.85s/f (Soft) **8** Ran SP% **115.6**
Speed ratings (Par 101): **97,95,95,94,93 73,71,61**
toteswingers 1&2 £5.90, 1&3 £7.10, 2&3 £7.80 CSF £60.13 CT £370.94 TOTE £11.00: £2.50, £2.00, £2.80; EX 38.20 Trifecta £423.60 Pool: £1069.42 - 1.89 winning units..
Owner Miss E Johnston **Bred** Mrs G P Booth And J Porteous **Trained** Yedingham, N Yorks

FOCUS
The slower of the two divisions by 0.79sec and the fom is modest with the first two the best guides.
T/Plt: £69.50 to a £1 stake. Pool: £60,763.65 - 637.86 winning tickets. T/Qpdt: £10.10 to a £1 stake. Pool: £4227.00 - 308.50 winning tickets. JR

1996 - 2003a (Foreign Racing) - See Raceform Interactive

1819 DONCASTER (L-H)
Saturday, May 4

OFFICIAL GOING: Good to firm (9.9)
Wind: Moderate; half against Weather: Cloudy with sunny periods

2004 CROWNHOTEL-BAWTRY.COM APPRENTICE FILLIES' H'CAP 1m 4f
5:05 (5:05) (Class 4) (0-85,81) 4-Y-0+ **£5,175** (£1,540; £769; £384) **Stalls** Low

Form RPR

42-2 1 **Moment In Time (IRE)**[15] 1663 4-8-13 **80**.................. SiobhanMiller(7) 3 98
(David Simcock) *trckd ldrs: smooth hdwy over 3f out: led wl over 2f out: rdn clr wl over 1f out: unchal* **13/8**[1]

1353 2 11 **Norfolk Sky**[19] 1585 4-8-8 **71**.. ThomasBrown(3) 2 71
(Laura Mongan) *hld up in rr: hdwy over 4f out: effrt to chse wnr wl over 2f out and sn rdn: drvn and no imp fr wl over 1f out* **7/1**

20-3 3 16 **Saint Helena (IRE)**[32] 1302 5-8-11 **76**............................... NedCurtis(5) 6 51
(Harry Dunlop) *led: jnd 1/2-way: rdn along over 3f out: hdd and drvn wl over 2f out: plugged on one pce* **9/2**[3]

1412 4 7 **The Blue Dog (IRE)**[5] 1889 6-8-7 **70**............................... RobertTart(3) 1 34
(Phil McEntee) *trckd ldng pair on inner: pushed along over 4f out: rdn over 3f out: outpcd fr wl over 2f out* **3/1**[2]

10-5 5 3 1/4 **Dancing Primo**[33] 1290 7-9-2 **81**.. JackDuern(5) 4 39
(Mark Brisbourne) *trckd ldr: cl up 1/2-way: rdn along over 3f out: sn wknd* **6/1**

/000 6 34 **Catawollow**[6] 417 6-8-2 **67** oh22.................................(v) PhilipPrince(5) 5
(Richard Guest) *a in rr: t.o fnl 3f* **40/1**

2m 30.35s (-4.55) **Going Correction** -0.325s/f (Firm) **6** Ran SP% **110.5**
Speed ratings (Par 102): **102,94,84,79,77 54**
toteswingers 1&2 £3.00, 1&3 £2.70, 2&3 £3.60 CSF £13.16 TOTE £2.30: £1.30, £3.60; EX 11.60 Trifecta £29.20 Pool: £1,630.84 - 41.82 winning units..
Owner Mrs Julia Annable **Bred** L K I Bloodstock Ltd **Trained** Newmarket, Suffolk
■ Stewards' Enquiry : Siobhan Miller two-day ban: used whip when clearly winning (May 19-20)

FOCUS
Rail on round course from 9f to where it joins straight moved out 5yds to provide fresh ground adding about 18yds to races on Round course. A fillies' handicap for apprentice riders. The winner scored easily but the form behind is pretty weak.

2005 POLYPIPE MAIDEN STKS 5f
5:40 (5:41) (Class 5) 2-Y-0 **£2,911** (£866; £432; £216) **Stalls** High

Form RPR

1 **Thunder Strike** 2-9-5 0.. SeanLevey 5 77+
(Richard Hannon) *cl up: shkn up to ld ent fnl f: sn rdn clr: edgd rt and kpt on* **13/8**[1]

2 2 1/4 **Musical Molly (IRE)** 2-9-0 0... TomEaves 4 61+
(Brian Ellison) *trckd ldrs: effrt over 1f out: swtchd lft and nt clr run ent fnl f: squeezed through and kpt on wl towards fin* **15/2**

0 3 1/2 **Party Ruler (IRE)**[15] 1669 2-9-5 0............................ RichardKingscote 6 65
(Tom Dascombe) *slt ld: rdn along wl over 1f out: hdd ent fnl f: sn edgd lft and one pce* **4/1**[3]

4 4 1 **Bandolier**[14] 1680 2-9-5 0.. FrederikTylicki 2 61
(Richard Fahey) *cl up: rdn along over 2f out: drvn appr fnl f: kpt on same pce* **2/1**[2]

556 5 4 **Riley's Missile (IRE)**[7] 1820 2-9-0 0........................ RachealKneller(5) 1 47
(Charles Smith) *dwlt: chsd ldrs: rdn along over 2f out: sn wknd* **40/1**

6 9 **Orient Sky** 2-9-5 0.. MickyFenton 3 14
(Paul Midgley) *s.i.s: green and rdn along in rr: a outpcd* **20/1**

1m 0.75s (0.25) **Going Correction** -0.125s/f (Firm) **6** Ran SP% **110.4**
Speed ratings (Par 93): **93,89,88,87,80 66**
toteswingers 1&2 £2.00, 1&3 £1.90, 2&3 £5.30 CSF £13.82 TOTE £2.20: £1.40, £2.60; EX 10.20 Trifecta £41.60 Pool: £1,258.72 - 22.68 winning units..
Owner Mohamed Saeed Al Shahi **Bred** Southill Stud **Trained** East Everleigh, Wilts

FOCUS
Not a bad 2-y-o maiden and the winner looks to have more to offer.

2006 PARK HILL HOSPITAL MAIDEN STKS 6f
6:10 (6:11) (Class 5) 3-4-Y-0 **£2,911** (£866; £432; £216) **Stalls** High

Form RPR

24 1 **Can You Conga**[28] 1392 3-9-2 0.. PhillipMakin 4 84
(Kevin Ryan) *mde all: slt ld whn jinked rt and hit rail after 2f: rdn wl over 1f out: styd on gamely u.p ins fnl f* **11/2**[3]

42- 2 3/4 **Floating Along (IRE)**[184] 7497 3-8-11 0............................ LiamJones 5 77
(William Haggas) *cl up: rdn to chal over 1f out: ev ch tl drvn and nt qckn ins fnl f* **10/11**[1]

3 3 1/4 **Timeless** 3-8-11 0.. MartinLane 6 66
(Tobias B P Coles) *trckd ldrs: hdwy 2f out: sn rdn: kpt on fnl f* **25/1**

30 4 nk **Secret Session (USA)**[14] 1678 3-9-2 0............................... JamesDoyle 2 70
(Marco Botti) *trckd ldrs: hdwy wl over 2f out: rdn along wl over 1f out: one pce* **10/3**[2]

05- 5 3/4 **Emerald Sea**[268] 5016 3-8-11 0.. TedDurcan 1 63
(Chris Wall) *in tch: effrt wl over 2f out: sn rdn and no imp* **7/1**

65- 6 7 **Wotalad**[183] 7516 3-9-2 0.. TomEaves 7 45
(Richard Whitaker) *trckd ldng pair: pushed along 1/2-way: sn rdn and wknd 2f out* **33/1**

06- P **Copper To Gold**[166] 7787 4-9-7 0................................. RobertWinston 3
(Robin Bastiman) *rrd s: fly j. and bucked thrght first f: sddle slipped and t.o: p.u over 1f out* **66/1**

1m 13.08s (-0.52) **Going Correction** -0.125s/f (Firm)
WFA 3 from 4yo 10lb **7** Ran SP% **111.6**
Speed ratings (Par 103): **98,97,92,92,91 81,**
toteswingers 1&2 £1.60, 1&3 £20.70, 2&3 £8.20 CSF £10.46 TOTE £5.70: £2.30, £1.10; EX 13.60 Trifecta £70.70 Pool: £1,477.51 - 15.66 winning units..
Owner Exors of The Late Guy Reed **Bred** G Reed **Trained** Hambleton, N Yorks

FOCUS
A modest maiden where the first pair dominated. The runner-up is rated in line with his best juvenile form.

2007 32RED H'CAP 6f
6:45 (6:45) (Class 3) (0-90,90) 4-Y-0+ **£8,409** (£2,502; £1,250; £625) **Stalls** High

Form RPR

311- 1 **Enrol**[204] 7023 4-8-13 **82**.. JamesDoyle 6 95+
(Sir Michael Stoute) *hld up in tch: smooth hdwy 2f out: led ent fnl f: sn rdn and edgd rt: kpt on wl towards fin* **6/4**[1]

66-0 2 nk **Mississippi**[19] 1571 4-8-9 **78**.. GrahamGibbons 10 90
(David Barron) *hld up in tch: hdwy over 1f out: rdn to chal jst ins fnl f: ev ch tl drvn: edgd lft and no ex last 75yds* **16/1**

1-66 3 2 1/2 **Another Wise Kid (IRE)**[8] 1807 5-9-2 **85**........................ MickyFenton 1 89
(Paul Midgley) *hld up towards rr: gd hdwy on outer wl over 1f out: rdn and ch ins fnl f: sn drvn and one pce* **12/1**

3003 4 nk **Klynch**[7] 1838 7-8-12 **81**..(b) JamesSullivan 12 84
(Ruth Carr) *in tch: pushed along and lost pl 1/2-way: hdwy over 1f out: sn rdn and kpt on fnl f: nrst fin* **12/1**

-004 5 1 3/4 **Victoire De Lyphar (IRE)**[9] 1787 6-8-11 **80**........................(e) DaleSwift 9 77
(Ruth Carr) *cl up: rdn along 2f out: drvn over 1f out: kpt on same pce* **12/1**

14-0 6 hd **Escape To Glory (USA)**[12] 1720 5-9-5 **88**.................. PaulMulrennan 3 85
(Michael Dods) *broke wl: stdd and trckd ldrs: effrt wl over 1f out: sn rdn and no imp* **20/1**

3-06 7 hd **Hopes N Dreams (IRE)**[10] 1765 5-8-7 **79**........................ JulieBurke(3) 2 75
(Kevin Ryan) *prom: cl up 1/2-way: led over 2f out: rdn over 1f out: hdd ent fnl f: sn n.m.r and one pce* **10/1**[3]

20-0 8 3/4 **Tax Free (IRE)**[21] 1537 11-9-7 **90**.................................. AdrianNicholls 13 84
(David Nicholls) *chsd ldrs: rdn along wl over 1f out: wknd ent fnl f* **25/1**

00-3 9 nse **New Leyf (IRE)**[9] 1787 7-8-9 **81**.............................. MichaelMetcalfe(3) 17 75
(David Nicholls) *towards rr: hdwy 2f out: sn rdn and n.d* **9/1**[2]

0-66 10 nk **Mappin Time (IRE)**[16] 1644 5-8-13 **82**..............................(p) DavidAllan 11 75+
(Tim Easterby) *hld up and bhd: hdwy and nt clr run wl over 1f out: sn swtchd lft: rdn and kpt on fnl f: nrst fin* **20/1**

24-0 11 1/2 **Dark Castle**[9] 1787 4-8-9 **78**.. FrederikTylicki 14 69
(Micky Hammond) *towards rr: hdwy over 1f out: kpt on ins fnl f: n.d* **40/1**

1/0- 12 3/4 **Loki's Revenge**[364] 1844 5-8-9 **83**..................................(b) RobertTart(5) 15 72
(William Jarvis) *hld up and bhd: sme hdwy wl over 1f out: n.d* **33/1**

10-0 13 hd **Bonnie Charlie**[35] 1248 7-8-9 **78**... TedDurcan 4 66
(David Nicholls) *a towards rr* **25/1**

4203 14 1 3/4 **Sans Loi (IRE)**[16] 1644 4-8-12 **81**... ShaneKelly 5 63+
(Brian Ellison) *chsd ldrs: rdn along over 2f out: hld and n.m.r whn wknd over 1f out* **16/1**

000- 15 5 **Hazelrigg (IRE)**[217] 6666 8-9-5 **88**...................................... TomEaves 16 54
(Tim Easterby) *hld up: a in rr* **50/1**

1254 16 21 **Burnhope**[14] 1692 4-8-7 **76** oh1.......................................(p) PaulHanagan 7
(Scott Dixon) *led: rdn along and hdd over 2f out: sn wknd* **14/1**

1m 11.77s (-1.83) **Going Correction** -0.125s/f (Firm) **16** Ran SP% **125.2**
Speed ratings (Par 107): **107,106,103,102,100 100,100,99,98,98 97,96,96,94,87 59**
toteswingers 1&2 £17.80, 1&3 £4.60, 2&3 £56.40 CSF £25.76 CT £246.61 TOTE £2.10: £1.10, £4.10, £3.70, £3.10; EX 34.20 Trifecta £939.40 Part won. Pool: £1,252.53 - 0.52 winning units..
Owner Cheveley Park Stud **Bred** Cheveley Park Stud Ltd **Trained** Newmarket, Suffolk
■ Stewards' Enquiry : James Doyle one-day ban: careless riding (May 19)

FOCUS
They raced up the centre at a solid pace in this competitive sprint handicap and the winner remains progressive. The form looks sound with the third and fourth the best guides.

2008 32RED.COM CONDITIONS STKS 7f
7:20 (7:21) (Class 3) 3-Y-0 **£8,092** (£2,423; £1,211; £605) **Stalls** High

Form RPR

144- 1 **Ebn Arab (USA)**[219] 6599 3-9-0 **99**................................... PaulHanagan 4 103
(Charles Hills) *trckd ldng pair on inner: swtchd lft and hdwy 2f out: effrt and qcknd to ld appr fnl f: sn clr* **4/5**[1]

110- 2 3 1/4 **Flyman**[233] 6162 3-9-2 **95**.. FrederikTylicki 1 96
(Richard Fahey) *cl up: led wl over 1f out: rdn and hdd appr fnl f: kpt on same pce* **7/2**[3]

40-6 3 1 3/4 **Birdman (IRE)**[17] 1621 3-9-2 **105**.. MartinLane 3 91
(David Simcock) *set stdy pce: qcknd 2 1/2f out: sn rdn and hdd wl over 1f out: one pce appr fnl f* **11/4**[2]

6 4 8 **Zainda (IRE)**[64] 849 3-8-7 **60**.. PaddyAspell 2 61?
(John Wainwright) *trckd ldrs: rdn along over 2f out: sn outpcd* **100/1**

1m 25.88s (-0.42) **Going Correction** -0.125s/f (Firm) **4** Ran SP% **105.4**
Speed ratings (Par 103): **97,93,91,82**
CSF £3.71 TOTE £1.60; EX 3.70 Trifecta £6.10 Pool: £937.36 - 113.67 winning units..
Owner Hamdan Al Maktoum **Bred** Shadwell Farm LLC **Trained** Lambourn, Berks

FOCUS
An interesting 3-y-o conditions event in which the winner stepped up again while the second is rated to his Nottingham figure, backed up by the third.

2009 32RED CASINO H'CAP 1m 6f 132y
7:50 (7:50) (Class 4) (0-85,77) 4-Y-0+ **£5,175** (£1,540; £769; £384) **Stalls** Low

Form RPR

0-00 1 **Rocktherunway (IRE)**[21] 1536 4-9-7 **77**..........................(p) TomEaves 8 86
(Michael Dods) *hld up in rr: swtchd to outer and gd hdwy 3f out: rdn to ld 1 1/2f out: edgd lft ent fnl f: kpt on* **25/1**

0-54 2 1 **Knightly Escapade**[24] 1464 5-9-7 **75**.................................... DaleSwift 4 83
(Brian Ellison) *hld up in tch: hdwy over 3f out: rdn along to chse ldrs and n.m.r 2f out: swtchd rt and drvn to chse wnr ins fnl f: kpt on* **4/1**[2]

50-3 3 1/2 **Flashman**[21] 1536 4-9-6 **76**.. PaulHanagan 2 83
(Richard Fahey) *led: rdn along 3f out: drvn 2f out: hdd 1 1/2f out: kpt on u.p fnl f* **11/8**[1]

/10- 4 4 **Astromagick**[219] 6600 5-9-9 **77**.. NeilCallan 7 79
(Mark H Tompkins) *trckd ldrs: hdwy over 3f out: rdn to chal 2f out: ev ch tl drvn and one pce ent fnl f* **14/1**

10- 5 5 **No Such Number**[164] 7810 5-9-6 **74**................................ JamesDoyle 6 70
(Julia Feilden) *trckd ldng pair: hdwy and cl up 4f out: rdn along wl over 2f out: sn drvn and wknd wl over 1f out* **9/1**

223- 6 2 **Up Ten Down Two (IRE)**[207] 6971 4-9-2 **72**..............(t) JamesSullivan 5 65
(Michael Easterby) *trckd ldr: cl up over 4f out: rdn along over 3f out: sn wknd* **8/1**

5340 7 3/4 **Rayadour (IRE)**[25] 1448 4-8-9 **65**..................................... PJMcDonald 1 57
(Micky Hammond) *trckd ldrs on inner: rdn along over 3f out: sn wknd* **40/1**

2425 **8** 2 **Tartan Jura**^{17} [1615] 5-9-7 **75**.................................(v) SilvestreDeSousa 3 64
(Mark Johnston) *reminders s: rn in snatches: in tch: rdn along 1/2-way: sme hdwy 4f out: rdn 3f out and sn btn* **5/1**^{3}

3m 6.04s (-1.36) **Going Correction** -0.325s/f (Firm)
WFA 4 from 5yo 2lb **8** Ran SP% **112.8**
Speed ratings (Par 105): **90,89,89,87,84 83,82,81**
toteswingers 1&2 £35.20, 1&3 £10.40, 2&3 £1.20 CSF £119.00 CT £235.07 TOTE £28.30: £5.80, £2.20, £1.02; EX 148.60 Trifecta £649.00 Part won. Pool: £865.43 - 0.42 winning units..
Owner Sedgewick,Dods,Sunley Racing Partnership **Bred** J Hanly, A Stroud And T Stewart **Trained** Denton, Co Durham

FOCUS
A fair staying handicap and the form looks straightforward rated around the three in the frame behind the winner.

2010 £32 BONUS AT 32RED.COM H'CAP 6f 110y
8:20 (8:23) (Class 5) (0-75,75) 3-Y-O **£2,587** (£770; £384; £192) **Stalls** High

Form RPR

240- **1** **Hoofalong**^{212} [6808] 3-9-2 **70**.................................(p) PaulMulrennan 8 84
(Michael Easterby) *sn led: mde most: rdn and qcknd wl over 1f out: kpt on strly fnl f* **11/4**^{1}

26-4 **2** 2¼ **Extrasolar**^{22} [1515] 3-9-5 **73**.................................(t) JamesDoyle 10 81
(Amanda Perrett) *trckd ldrs: hdwy 2f out: rdn to chse wnr ent fnl f: sn edgd lft and no imp* **15/2**

110- **3** 2 **Reconsider Baby (IRE)**^{237} [6070] 3-8-13 **70**......... MichaelMetcalfe$^{(3)}$ 3 72
(Mrs K Burke) *dwlt and in rr: pushed along 3f out: swtchd lft to over 2f out: sn rdn and styd on fnl f: nrst fin* **16/1**

3-31 **4** 2 **Next Door (IRE)**^{25} [1447] 3-8-12 **66**........................ GrahamGibbons 2 62
(David Barron) *trckd ldrs: hdwy over 2f out: rdn to chse wnr wl over 1f out: drvn appr fnl f: sn one pce* **5/1**^{3}

2-01 **5** 3 **Lexington Place**^{28} [1392] 3-8-13 **67**........................ PaulHanagan 4 54
(Richard Fahey) *trckd wnr: rdn along 2f out: wknd appr fnl f* **11/2**

056- **6** 6 **Unassailable**^{264} [5168] 3-8-4 **61** oh1........................ JulieBurke$^{(3)}$ 1 31
(Kevin Ryan) *a towards rr* **12/1**

44-5 **7** 1½ **Summer Dream (IRE)**^{17} [1612] 3-9-6 **74**.......................(p) NeilCallan 9 40
(Marco Botti) *in tch: chsd ldrs 1/2-way: rdn over 2f out and sn wknd* **9/2**^{2}

14-1 **8** 1½ **El Mirage (IRE)**^{17} [1616] 3-9-7 **75**........................ RobertWinston 5 36
(Dean Ivory) *t.k.h early: hld up: a in rr* **9/1**

53-6 **9** 11 **Ayr Missile**^{25} [1447] 3-8-9 **63**........................ FrederikTylicki 6
(Kevin Ryan) *chsd ldrs: rdn along wl over 2f out: sn wknd* **20/1**

1m 18.65s (-1.25) **Going Correction** -0.125s/f (Firm) **9** Ran SP% **117.0**
Speed ratings (Par 99): **102,99,97,94,91 84,82,81,68**
toteswingers 1&2 £6.90, 1&3 £12.90, 2&3 £26.90 CSF £24.40 CT £281.92 TOTE £3.60: £1.30, £3.60, £4.80; EX 30.00 Trifecta £393.60 Pool: £1,116.43 - 2.12 winning units..
Owner A Chandler, L Westwood, D & Y Blunt **Bred** D F Spence **Trained** Sheriff Hutton, N Yorks

FOCUS
A modest 3-y-o handicap but the winner looks capable of better. The placed horses help to set the level.
T/Plt: £8.70 to a £1 stake. Pool: £56,722.65 - 4,706.91 winning units T/Qpdt: £3.80 to a £1 stake. Pool: £5,448.30 - 1,052.50 winning units JR

GOODWOOD (R-H)
Saturday, May 4

OFFICIAL GOING: Good (good to firm in places on round course; 8.1)
Wind: Brisk, half against Weather: Overcast becoming bright

2011 BETFRED TV E.B.F MAIDEN STKS 5f
1:50 (1:50) (Class 5) 2-Y-O **£3,881** (£1,155; £577; £288) **Stalls** High

Form RPR

04 **1** **Iseemist (IRE)**^{15} [1659] 2-8-9 0........................ MichaelJMMurphy$^{(5)}$ 5 73
(John Gallagher) *racd against nr side rail: mde virtually all: shkn up over 1f out: hrd pressed fnl f: hld on wl* **8/1**

42 **2** ½ **Cockney Bob**^{11} [1749] 2-9-5 0........................ CathyGannon 4 76
(J S Moore) *sn w ldng pair: shkn up to chal fr 2f out: nrly upsides fnl f: nt qckn* **3/1**^{2}

2 **3** 5 **Larsen Bay (IRE)**^{7} [1833] 2-9-5 0........................ GeorgeBaker 3 58
(Tom Dascombe) *racd on outer of ldng trio: on terms w wnr tl wavered and wknd jst over 1f out* **1/1**^{1}

4 3½ **Redlorryellowlorry (IRE)** 2-9-5 0........................ PatCosgrave 1 46+
(George Baker) *s.s: outpcd in last: pushed along and lost no further grnd tl wknd fnl f* **7/2**^{3}

1m 0.9s (0.70) **Going Correction** -0.20s/f (Firm) **4** Ran SP% **108.3**
Speed ratings (Par 93): **86,85,77,71**
CSF £29.46 TOTE £9.50; EX 26.50 Trifecta £62.60 Pool: £860.06 - 10.30 winning units..
Owner J-P Lim & Keith Marsden **Bred** J P Lim,K Marsden & South Hatch Racing **Trained** Chastleton, Oxon

FOCUS
First 2f of Mile course dolled out 5yds which added circa 15yds to races on that course. Almost certainly not a strong race, in which it may have paid to come up the stands' rail. The level looks fluid with the favourite below form.

2012 BETFRED THE BONUS KING EBF DAISY WARWICK STKS (LISTED RACE) 1m 4f
2:20 (2:21) (Class 1) 4-Y-O+ **£23,680** (£8,956; £4,476; £2,236) **Stalls** Low

Form RPR

354- **1** **Khione**^{189} [7405] 4-8-12 102........................ KierenFallon 1 104+
(Luca Cumani) *t.k.h: hld up in 5th: prog to trck ldng pair 1/2-way: wnt 2nd 4f out: led wl over 2f out: pushed along and won convincingly* **4/1**^{3}

405- **2** 1¾ **Jehannedarc (IRE)**^{170} [7735] 5-8-12 102........................ GrahamLee 3 101
(Ed Dunlop) *hld up in rr: trckd ldrs fr 3f out: shkn up to chse wnr 2f out: kpt on but no imp at all* **6/1**

3 ½ **Souviens Toi**^{174} 4-9-1 96........................ CathyGannon 2 104+
(Marco Botti) *hld up in last: prog and cl up on inner whn nt clr run 3f out: lost pl and sn rdn: 6th 2f out: styd on again fr over 1f out to take 3rd ins fnl f: pressed runner-up nr fin* **11/1**

146- **4** 2 **Bite Of The Cherry**^{233} [6163] 4-8-12 97........................ DaneO'Neill 7 97
(Michael Bell) *led: clr after 3f: hdd wl over 2f out: steadily outpcd: short of room briefly fnl f* **9/1**

1/3- **5** 1¾ **Reckoning (IRE)**^{175} [7688] 4-8-12 99........................ MickaelBarzalona 6 94
(Jeremy Noseda) *trckd ldrs: lost pl 1/2-way: last 4f out: prog on outer 3f out: drvn to dispute 2nd wl over 1f out: sn wknd* **9/4**^{1}

630- **6** 3¾ **Coquet**^{210} [6899] 4-8-12 104........................ JimmyFortune 4 88
(Hughie Morrison) *trckd ldng pair to 1/2-way: styd cl up: rdn to dispute 2nd over 2f out: wknd wl over 1f out* **3/1**^{2}

33-0 **7** 25 **Lily In Pink**^{24} [1484] 5-8-12 95........................ JimCrowley 5
(Jonathan Portman) *chsd ldr to 4f out: sn wknd: t.o* **20/1**

2m 39.4s (1.00) **Going Correction** +0.15s/f (Good) **7** Ran SP% **113.2**
Speed ratings (Par 111): **102,100,100,99,98 95,78**
CSF £27.18 TOTE £4.80: £2.60, £4.10; EX 24.50 Trifecta £217.50 Pool: £1698.84 - 5.85 winning units..
Owner Aston House Stud **Bred** Aston House Stud **Trained** Newmarket, Suffolk
■ Stewards' Enquiry : Dane O'Neill one-day ban: careless riding (May 19)
Cathy Gannon one-day ban: careless riding (May 19)

FOCUS
This looked a fair contest for the level, in which all but one of the runners was making their seasonal debut. The early gallop appeared modest and the second and fourth help set the standard.

2013 BETFRED MOBILE LOTTO STKS (H'CAP) 7f
2:55 (2:56) (Class 2) (0-100,98) 4-Y-O+ **£19,407** (£5,775; £2,886; £1,443) **Stalls** Low

Form RPR

2566 **1** **George Guru**^{21} [1545] 6-8-10 **87**........................ KierenFallon 7 100
(Michael Attwater) *hld up in rr: clsd on ldrs fr 3f out: prog to ld jst over 1f out: drvn and in command fnl f* **10/1**

3-53 **2** 1¾ **Democretes**^{12} [1726] 4-8-11 **88**........................ PatDobbs 6 98+
(Richard Hannon) *hld up disputing 6th: clsng on ldrs whn bmpd over 2f out and lost pl: renewed effrt over 1f out: styd on wl fnl f to take 2nd last strides* **6/1**^{3}

300- **3** nk **The Confessor**^{196} [7240] 6-8-13 **90**........................ CathyGannon 4 97
(Henry Candy) *trckd clr ldng trio: clsd 3f out: wnt 2nd over 2f out: rdn to ld briefly over 1f out: no ch w wnr after: lost 2nd last strides* **11/2**^{2}

0563 **4** ¾ **Kakatosi**^{47} [1061] 6-8-7 **84**........................ AndreaAtzeni 2 89
(Mike Murphy) *pushed along in midfield after 2f: prog over 2f out: drvn and styd on fr over 1f out: nvr able to threaten* **22/1**

0-45 **5** 1 **Shamaal Nibras (USA)**^{21} [1542] 4-9-1 **97**.. WilliamTwiston-Davies$^{(5)}$ 13 99+
(Richard Hannon) *hld up in last quartet fr wdst draw: rdn 3f out: styd on u.p fnl 2f: nrst fin* **12/1**

-243 **6** 1¼ **Bravo Echo**^{21} [1542] 7-8-7 **84** oh1........................ RobertHavlin 1 83
(Michael Attwater) *w ldng pair: led 1/2-way: hdd over 1f out: wknd fnl f: fared best of trio that blasted off* **9/1**

213- **7** ¾ **Silverheels (IRE)**^{127} [8277] 4-8-13 **90**........................ JackMitchell 5 87
(Paul Cole) *hld up in rr: prog on outer and rdn over 2f out: no imp on ldrs over 1f out: fdd* **10/1**

50-6 **8** ¾ **Accession (IRE)**^{14} [1675] 4-8-9 **86**........................ JohnFahy 3 81
(Clive Cox) *s.i.s and rousted along to chse clr ldng trio: wnt 2nd 3f out to over 2f out: wknd jst over 1f out* **9/2**^{1}

41-4 **9** nk **Head Of Steam (USA)**^{21} [1542] 6-8-13 **90**........................ GrahamLee 12 84
(Amanda Perrett) *a in rr: shkn up and no prog over 2f out: plugged on* **12/1**

1200 **10** 2¾ **Piscean (USA)**^{21} [1542] 8-8-13 **90**........................ JimCrowley 11 77
(Tom Keddy) *stdd s: hld up in last: sme prog on inner 3f out: nt clr run 2f out: sn wknd* **20/1**

0552 **11** 1¾ **Justineo**^{33} [1287] 4-9-7 **98**........................(b^{1}) JimmyFortune 10 80
(Roger Varian) *w ldr at str pce: led after 2f to 1/2-way: wknd over 2f out* **16/1**

50-0 **12** nse **Mabait**^{21} [1542] 7-8-11 **95**........................ AliceHaynes$^{(7)}$ 9 77
(David Simcock) *hld up in last quartet: rdn and no prog whn short of room 2f out: no ch after* **10/1**

00-0 **13** 39 **I'm So Glad**^{21} [1544] 4-8-13 **95**........................ CharlesBishop$^{(5)}$ 8
(Mick Channon) *led at fast pce but hdd after 2f: losing pl whn bmpd over 2f out: wknd and virtually p.u* **14/1**

1m 26.44s (-0.56) **Going Correction** +0.15s/f (Good) **13** Ran SP% **122.2**
Speed ratings (Par 109): **109,107,106,105,104 103,102,101,101,98 96,95,51**
toteswingers 1&2 £15.10, 1&3 £9.80, 2&3 £6.90 CSF £70.50 CT £374.03 TOTE £8.50: £3.10, £2.20, £2.40; EX 73.00 Trifecta £343.00 Pool: £1966.10 - 4.29 winning units..
Owner T M Jones **Bred** T M Jones **Trained** Epsom, Surrey

FOCUS
A competitive handicap run at a strong gallop. The winner ran to his AW best, while the third provides a fair line to the form.

2014 BETFRED MOBILE SPORTS STKS (H'CAP) 5f
3:30 (3:31) (Class 3) (0-95,95) 4-Y-O+ **£9,703** (£2,887; £1,443; £721) **Stalls** High

Form RPR

65-0 **1** **Duke Of Firenze**^{21} [1537] 4-9-3 **91**........................ KierenFallon 1 102+
(Sir Michael Stoute) *w.w bhd ldrs: prog to go 2nd over 1f out: shkn up to ld ins fnl f: only pushed out and jst hld on* **6/4**^{1}

40-0 **2** shd **Kyleakin Lass**^{15} [1662] 4-9-4 **92**........................ GeorgeBaker 5 102+
(Paul Fitzsimons) *stdd s: hld up in last gng wl: prog 2f out: had to wait for gap tl 1f out: str burst to press wnr nr fin: jst failed* **14/1**

200- **3** 1½ **Fair Value (IRE)**^{219} [6602] 5-9-2 **90**........................ SebSanders 6 95
(Simon Dow) *led: rdn over 1f out: hdd and outpcd ins fnl f* **15/2**

000- **4** nk **Top Cop**^{280} [4598] 4-9-0 **88**........................ JimmyFortune 4 92
(Andrew Balding) *in tch in midfield: effrt 2f out: inclined to hang fr over 1f out: kpt on but nt pce to chal* **7/1**^{3}

500- **5** ¾ **Steps (IRE)**^{189} [7397] 5-9-2 **90**........................ AndreaAtzeni 9 91
(Roger Varian) *lost midfield pl 1/2-way: hanging in last pair 2f out: styd on again against rail fnl f* **7/1**^{3}

56-0 **6** nk **Lady Gibraltar**^{10} [1765] 4-8-7 **86**........................ MichaelJMMurphy$^{(5)}$ 2 86
(Alan Jarvis) *prom: chsd ldr 1/2-way to over 1f out: fdd* **6/1**^{2}

621- **7** ¾ **Naabegha**^{321} [3188] 6-9-7 **95**........................ LiamKeniry 8 92
(Ed de Giles) *dwlt: rcvrd to chse ldr to 1/2-way: styd cl up tl wknd fnl f* **9/1**

0-25 **8** 8 **Cadeaux Pearl**^{19} [1581] 5-8-4 **81** oh2........................(b) BillyCray$^{(3)}$ 7 50
(Scott Dixon) *prom early but rdn: sn lost pl: bhd 2f out: t.o* **20/1**

61/0 **9** 3½ **Captain Carey**^{24} [1483] 7-9-4 **92**........................ TomMcLaughlin 3 48
(Malcolm Saunders) *s.s: racd on outer: nvr on terms w ldrs: hanging rt and wknd fr 2f out: t.o* **50/1**

58.3s (-1.90) **Going Correction** -0.20s/f (Firm) **9** Ran SP% **114.4**
Speed ratings (Par 107): **107,106,104,103,102 102,101,88,82**
toteswingers 1&2 £4.50, 1&3 £4.90, 2&3 £53.50 CSF £25.06 CT £123.35 TOTE £2.10: £1.10, £3.50, £2.90; EX 26.90 Trifecta £181.10 Pool: £1962.10 - 8.12 winning units..
Owner Cheveley Park Stud **Bred** Cheveley Park Stud Ltd **Trained** Newmarket, Suffolk

FOCUS
Probably just ordinary form for the level with the third the best guide.

2015 BETFRED MOBILE CASINO BRITISH STALLION STUDS E.B.F CONQUEROR STKS (LISTED RACE) 1m
4:05 (4:05) (Class 1) 3-Y-0+

£22,684 (£8,600; £4,304; £2,144; £1,076; £540) **Stalls** Low

Form RPR
02-4 **1** **Burke's Rock**[21] 1544 4-9-7 97................................(p) MickaelBarzalona 5 103
(Jeremy Noseda) *trckd ldng pair: rdn 2f out: lcd jst over 1f out: drvn and styd on wl* **12/1**
531- **2** ½ **Sentaril**[184] 7509 4-9-10 103................................ GrahamLee 1 104+
(William Haggas) *trckd leding pair: waiting for a run 2f out: gap appeared 1f out and rdn to press wnr ins fnl f: nt qckn last 75yds* **2/1**[1]
324- **3** ½ **Oojooba**[217] 6667 4-9-7 90................................ AndreaAtzeni 2 100
(Roger Varian) *led to over 6f out: trckd ldr: led again 2f out: rdn and hd high over 1f out: sn hdd and nt qckn* **12/1**
1-32 **4** ½ **Stirring Ballad**[21] 1544 4-9-7 98................................ JimmyFortune 3 99+
(Andrew Balding) *hld up in last trio: waiting for room 2f out: rdn and nt qckn over 1f out: styd on but nvr able to chal* **5/2**[2]
31-6 **5** ½ **Whimsical (IRE)**[21] 1544 4-9-7 91................................ PatDobbs 4 98
(Richard Hannon) *hld up in last trio: waiting for room 2f out: swtchd lft over 1f out: styd on fnl f but n.d* **25/1**
201- **6** 4 **Hippy Hippy Shake**[192] 7334 4-9-7 95................................ KierenFallon 7 89
(Luca Cumani) *wnt lft s: racd in last trio: shoved along 3f out: no prog and btn 2f out* **7/2**[3]
000- **7** 1 **Making Eyes (IRE)**[204] 7124 5-9-7 98................................ GeorgeBaker 6 87
(Hugo Palmer) *racd wd early: led over 6f out: hdd & wknd 2f out* **16/1**

1m 40.8s (0.90) **Going Correction** +0.15s/f (Good) **7** Ran SP% **109.2**
Speed ratings (Par 111): **101,100,100,99,99 95,94**
toteswingers 1&2 £3.30, 1&3 £21.20, 2&3 £8.20 CSF £33.23 TOTE £13.60: £4.20, £1.90; EX 36.40 Trifecta £456.60 Pool: £1284.42 - 2.10 winning units..
Owner S E Construction (Kent) Ltd **Bred** Brook Stud Bloodstock Ltd **Trained** Newmarket, Suffolk

FOCUS
A sound-looking contest but whether this is strong form is open to debate. \the winner recorded a persoanl-best with the second just below hers.

2016 BETFRED "STILL TREBLE ODDS ON LUCKY'S" MEDIAN AUCTION MAIDEN STKS 7f
4:40 (4:41) (Class 5) 3-Y-O **£3,234** (£962; £481; £240) **Stalls** Low

Form RPR
-222 **1** **Firmdecisions (IRE)**[9] 1784 3-9-5 70................................ GeorgeBaker 6 75
(Brett Johnson) *trckd ldrs: prog to go 2nd wl over 1f out: rdn to ld 1f out: tended to idle and jst hld on* **8/1**[3]
52-3 **2** nk **Grand Denial (IRE)**[19] 1582 3-9-5 76................................ JohnFahy 8 74
(Clive Cox) *led: wnt for home over 2f out: rdn and hd high after: hdd 1f out: rallied: jst hld* **1/1**[1]
05 **3** 3½ **Bee Jay Kay**[4] 1904 3-8-9 0................................ CharlesBishop(5) 2 60
(Mick Channon) *hld up in rr: pushed along 3f out: styd on fnl 2f to take 3rd ins fnl f* **8/1**[3]
4 1½ **Baltic Blade (IRE)** 3-9-5 0................................ JimmyFortune 3 61
(Gary Moore) *slowly away: settled in last: rdn and prog 2f out: kpt on to take modest 4th nr fin* **12/1**
5 ½ **Czech It Out (IRE)** 3-9-5 0................................ JimCrowley 5 59+
(Amanda Perrett) *trckd ldrs: wnt 2nd wl over 2f out gng wl: rdn and wknd wl over 1f out* **7/2**[2]
0 **6** 1¾ **Transluscent (IRE)**[31] 1323 3-8-12 0......................[1] DanielMuscutt(7) 4 55
(Andrew Balding) *plld v hrd early in rr: effrt on outer over 2f out: wknd over 1f out* **20/1**
5 **7** 8 **Little Alice**[45] 1086 3-9-0 0................................ AndreaAtzeni 1 28
(Stuart Williams) *slowly away: a in rr: wknd over 2f out: t.o* **16/1**
0 **8** 1 **Lady Cavallo**[16] 1640 3-8-9 0................................ DannyBrock(5) 7 25
(J R Jenkins) *t.k.h: w ldr to 3f out: wknd qckly: t.o* **40/1**

1m 29.48s (2.48) **Going Correction** +0.15s/f (Good) **8** Ran SP% **115.2**
Speed ratings (Par 99): **91,90,86,84,84 82,73,72**
toteswingers 1&2 £1.60, 1&3 £4.80, 2&3 £3.50 CSF £16.60 TOTE £7.50: £2.20, £1.02, £2.70; EX 17.00 Trifecta £72.00 Pool: £3501.35 - 36.46 winning units..
Owner White Bear Racing **Bred** Thomas O'Meara **Trained** Epsom, Surrey

FOCUS
A very ordinary-looking maiden with a small persoan-best from the winner and the third seemingly running to her Lingfield mark.

2017 COLLECT TOTEPOOL BETS AT BETFRED SHOPS STKS (H'CAP) 1m 1f 192y
5:15 (5:20) (Class 5) (0-70,70) 3-Y-O **£3,234** (£962; £481; £240) **Stalls** Low

Form RPR
06-5 **1** **Jan De Heem**[30] 1347 3-8-11 **60**................................(v[1]) JimCrowley 3 69+
(Ralph Beckett) *wl in tch: looking for room fr over 2f out: effrt and n.m.r wl over 1f out: prog after to ld ins fnl f: r.o wl* **16/1**
3-32 **2** 1¼ **Knight's Parade (IRE)**[5] 1879 3-8-10 **59**................................(p) PatDobbs 6 65
(Amanda Perrett) *prom: trckd ldng pair 6f out: chal 2f out: rdn to ld jst over 1f out: hdd and outpcd ins fnl f* **7/2**[1]
320- **3** 1¼ **Contradict**[248] 5742 3-9-7 **70**................................ SamHitchcott 9 74+
(Mick Channon) *hld up in last trio: prog on inner fr 3f out: shkn up 2f out: styd on to take 3rd ins fnl f: nt pce to chal* **20/1**
44-3 **4** 1¾ **Couloir Extreme (IRE)**[10] 1770 3-9-4 **67**................................ GeorgeBaker 11 67
(Gary Moore) *racd wd early: led after 1f: rdn and pressed 2f out: hdd jst over 1f out: wknd* **8/1**
550- **5** 1 **Fair Comment**[134] 8200 3-8-13 **62**................................ LiamKeniry 1 60
(Michael Blanshard) *t.k.h: sn hld up towards rr: prog 3f out: nt clr run briefly over 2f out: pressed ldrs over 1f out: wknd fnl f* **28/1**
00-4 **6** 2¼ **Star Of Mayfair (USA)**[7] 1829 3-8-12 **66**........... MichaelJMMurphy(5) 7 60+
(Alan Jarvis) *slowly away: hld up in last: tried to make prog 3f out: nt clr run and swtchd rt 2f out: nt clr run over 1f out and no ch after* **5/1**[3]
003- **7** ¾ **Eton Rambler (USA)**[208] 6928 3-9-4 **67**................................(b[1]) PatCosgrave 4 59
(George Baker) *trckd ldr after 1f: rdn 3f out: lost 2nd and wknd wl over 1f out* **9/1**
600- **8** 6 **Halling's Wish**[145] 8052 3-8-12 **61**................................(t) MickaelBarzalona 12 41
(John Best) *hld up in rr: tried to cl on ldrs over 2f out: short of room briefly wl over 1f out: wknd* **4/1**[2]
-422 **9** ¾ **Solvanna**[31] 1314 3-9-0 **63**................................ GrahamLee 2 42
(Heather Main) *led 1f: styd prom: rdn 2f out: wknd over 1f out* **20/1**
004- **10** 3 **Platinum Proof (USA)**[140] 8134 3-9-0 **63**................................ KierenFallon 13 36
(John Berry) *hld up towards rr: prog and prom 4f out: wknd 3f out: eased over 1f out* **5/1**[3]
300- **11** 1¼ **Classic Art**[241] 5946 3-9-3 **66**................................ SebSanders 10 36
(Roger Teal) *a in rr: reminder sn after 1/2-way: struggling over 3f out: sn bhd* **20/1**

2m 11.65s (3.55) **Going Correction** +0.15s/f (Good) **11** Ran SP% **120.3**
Speed ratings (Par 99): **91,90,89,87,86 85,84,79,79,76 75**
toteswingers 1&2 £11.70, 1&3 £24.60, 2&3 £8.20 CSF £69.30 CT £1164.97 TOTE £21.00: £4.80, £2.00, £5.50; EX 83.40 Trifecta £187.00 Pool: £1528.91 - 6.13 winning units..
Owner Larksborough Stud Limited **Bred** Larksborough Stud Limited **Trained** Kimpton, Hants
■ Stewards' Enquiry : Michael J M Murphy one-day ban: careless riding (May 19)

FOCUS
They didn't appear to go that quickly early on, so this probably isn't reliable form, with the runner-up probably the best guide.
T/Plt: £512.80 to a £1 stake. Pool: £85,188.76 - 121.25 winning tickets T/Qpdt: £12.90 to a £1 stake. Pool: £6,253.20 - 357.95 winning tickets JN

1634 NEWMARKET (R-H)
Saturday, May 4

OFFICIAL GOING: Good to firm (9.0)
Wind: Fresh; half behind Weather: Dry and breezy, shower before and during 2000 Guineas

2018 MAKFI SUFFOLK STKS (H'CAP) 1m 1f
2:05 (2:06) (Class 2) 3-Y-O+

£28,012 (£8,388; £4,194; £2,097; £1,048; £526) **Stalls** High

Form RPR
6-11 **1** **Boonga Roogeta**[7] 1825 4-8-5 **86**................................ RosieJessop(5) 8 99
(Peter Charalambous) *pressed ldrs tl led after 1f: rdn wl over 1f out: edgd lft 1f out: battled on gamely and a jst holding rival fnl f* **10/1**
/15- **2** ¾ **Danchai**[202] 7082 4-8-7 **83**................................ PaulHanagan 11 94+
(William Haggas) *t.k.h: hld up wl in tch: rdn and effrt to chse wnr wl over 1f out: ev ch 1f out: kpt on but a jst hld* **5/1**[1]
54-5 **3** 2¾ **Proud Chieftain**[16] 1639 5-9-7 **97**................................ JamesDoyle 10 102
(Clifford Lines) *hld up towards rr: nt clr run over 3f out: hdwy u.p 2f out: chsd ldng pair over 1f out: styd on same pce ins fnl f* **18/1**
-221 **4** 1¼ **Icebuster**[7] 1831 5-8-10 **86**................................ RoystonFfrench 7 89+
(Rod Millman) *stdd and dropped in bhd after s: rdn and effrt ent fnl 2f: swtchd rt 1f out: kpt on fnl f* **9/1**[3]
012- **5** nk **Basseterre (IRE)**[184] 7502 4-8-10 **86**................................ JamieSpencer 2 88
(Charles Hills) *lw: hld up in tch in midfield: effrt u.p jst over 2f out: no imp and styd on same pce fnl f* **5/1**[1]
1-11 **6** ¾ **Whispering Warrior (IRE)**[93] 451 4-7-12 **77**.............. DarrenEgan(3) 5 77+
(David Simcock) *lw: hld up in last quartet: nt clr run over 2f out: styng on and swtchd rt over 1f out: kpt on ins fnl f: nvr trbld ldrs* **8/1**[2]
01-5 **7** ½ **Ocean Tempest**[35] 1233 4-8-9 **85**................................(p) NickyMackay 6 84
(John Ryan) *pressed ldrs: drvn and unable qck 2f out: btn ent fnl f: wknd ins fnl f* **16/1**
1343 **8** 1½ **Patriotic (IRE)**[21] 1538 5-7-7 **76**................................(p) NoelGarbutt(7) 12 72
(Chris Dwyer) *in tch in midfield: lost pl and rdn ent fnl 2f: rallied and hdwy over 1f out: styd on same pce fnl f* **12/1**
54-5 **9** ½ **Licence To Till (USA)**[25] 1446 6-8-10 **86**................................ JoeFanning 13 80
(Mark Johnston) *led for 1f: chsd ldrs after tl drvn and unable qck wl over 1f out: wknd 1f out* **8/1**[2]
1-15 **10** nk **Benzanno (IRE)**[24] 1485 4-9-2 **92**................................ DavidProbert 3 86
(Andrew Balding) *t.k.h: hld up wl in tch: rdn and unable qck 2f out: wknd ent fnl f* **16/1**
0-60 **11** nk **Dance And Dance (IRE)**[14] 1675 7-9-10 **100**................. WilliamBuick 4 93
(Ed Vaughan) *lw: stdd s: hld up in last quartet: hdwy over 2f out: no ex u.p over 1f out: wknd fnl f* **10/1**
-000 **12** 21 **Memory Cloth**[14] 1675 6-9-3 **93**................................ TomQueally 1
(Brian Ellison) *t.k.h: chsd ldrs: rdn 4f out: dropped to rr u.p 2f out: wl bhd and eased ins fnl f* **10/1**

1m 48.85s (-2.85) **Going Correction** -0.075s/f (Good) **12** Ran SP% **117.5**
Speed ratings (Par 109): **109,108,105,104,104 103,103,102,101,101 101,82**
toteswingers 1&2 £6.50, 1&3 £24.30, 2&3 £17.90 CSF £58.85 CT £899.97 TOTE £8.90: £2.50, £2.40, £3.50; EX 67.60 Trifecta £2120.40 Pool: £4,387.29 - 1.55 winning units..
Owner P Charalambous **Bred** Peter Charles **Trained** Newmarket, Suffolk

FOCUS
Stands' side track used with stalls on stands' side except 3.10 &3.50: Centre. Despite being well watered the ground was good to firm, with the GoingStick 9.0 (Stands' side 9.1; Centre 9.0; Far side 9.0). Although the wind was slightly behind, it was blowing across the track and into the stands. A fairly competitive handicap, but probably lacking the future Group horse of some previous renewals. The winner continued her remarkable progress and the second can do better still.

2019 PEARL BLOODSTOCK PALACE HOUSE STKS (GROUP 3) 5f
2:35 (2:37) (Class 1) 3-Y-O+

£34,026 (£12,900; £6,456; £3,216; £1,614; £810) **Stalls** High

Form RPR
5-24 **1** **Sole Power**[35] 1265 6-9-0 113................................ JohnnyMurtagh 9 117
(Edward Lynam, Ire) *hld up in midfield: hdwy 1/2-way: swtchd lft and effrt over 1f out: rdn to ld ins fnl f: r.o strly* **7/2**[1]
200- **2** 1 **Kingsgate Native (IRE)**[190] 7390 8-9-0 107................................ ShaneKelly 11 114
(Robert Cowell) *swtg: hld up towards rr: hdwy u.p over 1f out: chsd wnr wl ins fnl f: kpt on but a hld* **25/1**
00-1 **3** 1¼ **Tangerine Trees**[35] 1249 8-9-0 106................................(v) TomEaves 10 109
(Bryan Smart) *prom: led wl over 1f out: drvn over 1f out: hdd ins fnl f: no ex* **9/1**[3]
15-1 **4** shd **Heeraat (IRE)**[15] 1672 4-9-0 108................................ PaulHanagan 7 109
(William Haggas) *lw: chsd ldr: rdn and ev ch over 1f out: no ex and one pce ins fnl f* **7/2**[1]
-501 **5** 1 **Spirit Quartz (IRE)**[24] 1483 5-9-0 115................................ JosephO'Brien 15 105
(Robert Cowell) *chsd ldrs: rdn 2f out: kpt on same pce fnl f* **6/1**[2]
000- **6** 2 **Elusivity (IRE)**[196] 7236 5-9-0 103................................ JamesDoyle 14 98
(David O'Meara) *chsd ldrs: rdn and unable qck 2f out: outpcd and btn 1f out: one pce fnl f* **20/1**
43-6 **7** ½ **Swan Song**[15] 1662 4-8-11 93................................ DavidProbert 1 93
(Andrew Balding) *lw: pressed ldr: rdn and ev ch ent fnl 2f: btn 1f out and wknd ins fnl f* **50/1**
150- **8** ¾ **Hoyam**[217] 6672 3-8-2 103................................ HayleyTurner 18 91
(Michael Bell) *lw: taken down early: bhd: sme hdwy u.p over 1f out: kpt on fnl f: nvr trbld ldrs* **25/1**

00-5 **9** *hd* **Stepper Point**[24] 1483 4-9-0 98 MartinDwyer 16 93
(William Muir) *s.i.s: racd off the pce in midfield: sme hdwy u.p wl over 1f out: styd on same pce fnl f* **100/1**

352- **10** *hd* **Free Zone**[210] 6869 4-9-0 105 RoystonFfrench 17 92
(Bryan Smart) *racd off the pce in midfield: rdn and effrt ent fnl 2f: kpt on but no real imp* **28/1**

00-4 **11** *nk* **Doc Hay (USA)**[14] 1704 6-9-0 104 TomQueally 5 91
(David O'Meara) *sn outpcd in rr and rdn along: styd on fnl f: nvr trbld ldrs* **16/1**

10-3 **12** *½* **Caledonia Lady**[15] 1662 4-8-11 104 JoeFanning 4 86
(Jo Hughes) *stdd s: wl bhd in rr: sme hdwy over 1f out: styd on fnl f: nvr trbld ldrs* **25/1**

61-2 **13** *¾* **My Propeller (IRE)**[15] 1662 4-8-11 100 WilliamBuick 3 84
(Peter Chapple-Hyam) *racd off the pce in midfield: rdn and no imp wl over 1f out: nvr trbld ldrs* **20/1**

21-4 **14** *1 ¼* **Bungle Inthejungle**[17] 1620 3-8-8 110 MartinHarley 2 85
(Mick Channon) *taken down early: led tl wl over 1f out: wknd ent fnl f* **12/1**

03-0 **15** *½* **Angels Will Fall (IRE)**[16] 1637 4-8-11 102 RichardHughes 8 77
(Charles Hills) *racd off the pce in midfield: effrt and rdn 2f out: no prog ent fnl f: wknd ins fnl f* **20/1**

120- **16** *2 ½* **Fire Eyes**[232] 6196 3-8-5 101 NickyMackay 12 71
(David Brown) *lw: a towards rr: n.d* **25/1**

40-3 **17** *2 ¼* **Bogart**[24] 1483 4-9-0 101 AmyRyan 6 63
(Kevin Ryan) *chsd ldrs tl wknd jst over 2f out: bhd fnl f* **33/1**

57.02s (-2.08) **Going Correction** -0.075s/f (Good)
WFA 3 from 4yo+ 9lb **17** Ran SP% **121.3**
Speed ratings (Par 113): **113,111,109,109,107 104,103,102,102,101 101,100,99,97,96 92,88**
toteswingers 1&2 £25.10, 1&3 £9.90, 2&3 £91.90 CSF £101.36 TOTE £4.00: £2.10, £9.60, £3.30; EX 103.50 Trifecta £1553.50 Pool: £66,549.05 - 32.12 winning units..
Owner Mrs S Power **Bred** G Russell **Trained** Dunshaughlin, Co Meath

FOCUS
The last three winners of this race subsequently won at the highest level, Equiano (King's Stand) in 2010, Tangerine Trees (Prix de l'Abbaye) in 2011 and Mayson (July Cup) last year. With the first three home this time all former Group 1 winners, the race looks well worthy of an upgrade. The first two are rated in line with last year's form. The field were spread out from the middle of the course to the stands' rail and, while the main players emerged from the centre of the bunch, they were probably just best on the day. The time was only 0.21 seconds outside the track record.

2020 QATAR BLOODSTOCK JOCKEY CLUB STKS (GROUP 2) 1m 4f
3:10 (3:10) (Class 1) 4-Y-O+ **£56,710** (£21,500; £10,760; £5,360) **Stalls** Centre

Form RPR

0211 **1** **Universal (IRE)**[14] 1674 4-8-12 110 JoeFanning 1 114
(Mark Johnston) *led: hdd over 2f out: rdn and stl ev ch 2f out: led again ins fnl f: r.o gamely* **11/4**[3]

120- **2** *nk* **Dandino**[146] 8040 6-8-12 114 JohnnyMurtagh 2 113
(Marco Botti) *t.k.h: chsd ldr tl rdn to ld over 2f out: edgd rt and hdd ins fnl f: r.o wl but a jst hld after* **9/4**[2]

14-0 **3** *2 ½* **Wigmore Hall (IRE)**[35] 1267 6-9-3 115 JamieSpencer 3 114
(Michael Bell) *hld up in tch in 3rd: rdn and effrt wl over 1f out: styd on same pce and no imp fnl f* **13/2**

42-3 **4** *nk* **Noble Mission**[14] 1674 4-8-12 113 TomQueally 4 109
(Sir Henry Cecil) *swtg: stdd s: t.k.h: hld up in rr: rdn and effrt wl over 1f out: styd on but no imp on ldng pair fnl f* **7/4**[1]

2m 32.83s (0.83) **Going Correction** -0.075s/f (Good) **4** Ran SP% **107.1**
Speed ratings (Par 115): **94,93,92,91**
CSF £8.97 TOTE £4.30; EX 8.90 Trifecta £30.90 Pool: £3,093.61 - 74.94 winning units..
Owner Abdulla Al Mansoori **Bred** Grangecon Stud **Trained** Middleham Moor, N Yorks

FOCUS
A weak race for the class, and with just the four runners it always promised to be tactical. Universal is perhaps the best guide to the form.

2021 QIPCO 2000 GUINEAS STKS (205TH RUNNING) (BRITISH CHAMPIONS SERIES) (GROUP 1) (C&F) 1m
3:50 (3:50) (Class 1) 3-Y-O
£226,840 (£86,000; £43,040; £21,440; £10,760; £5,400) **Stalls** Centre

Form RPR

111- **1** **Dawn Approach (IRE)**[203] 7050 3-9-0 124 KevinManning 6 127
(J S Bolger, Ire) *lw: chsd ldr: clsd over 2f out: rdn and ev ch wl over 1f out: drvn ahd jst over 1f out: styd on strly and drew clr fnl f* **11/8**[1]

44-3 **2** *5* **Glory Awaits (IRE)**[17] 1623 3-9-0 95 (b[1]) JamieSpencer 4 115
(Kevin Ryan) *racd alone centre to far side: chsd ldrs: 3rd and hung lft u.p over 1f out: chsd wnr ins fnl f: no imp but hld on for 2nd* **150/1**

12-1 **3** *2 ¼* **Van Der Neer**[28] 1383 3-9-0 114 WilliamBuick 1 110
(Richard Hannon) *racd off the pce in midfield: rdn and effrt over 2f out: wnt modest 4th over 1f out: kpt on to go 3rd nr fin: no ch w wnr* **20/1**

11-1 **4** *nk* **Toronado (IRE)**[16] 1638 3-9-0 121 RichardHughes 12 109
(Richard Hannon) *lw: chsd ldrs: clsd to ld but pressed by wnr 2f out: sn rdn: hdd jst over 1f out: no ex: lost 2nd fnl 150yds: wknd and lost 3rd nr fin* **11/4**[2]

2S4- **5** *¾* **Cristoforo Colombo (USA)**[203] 7049 3-9-0 112 (p) JosephO'Brien 11 107+
(A P O'Brien, Ire) *racd off the pce in midfield: drvn and no imp over 2f out: outpcd 2f out: hrd drvn over 1f out: no ch but kpt on ins fnl f* **10/1**

1- **6** *½* **Mars (IRE)**[292] 4161 3-9-0 0 SeamieHeffernan 3 106+
(A P O'Brien, Ire) *tall: angular: racd off the pce towards rr: rdn and hdwy into midfield 3f out: outpcd 2f out: no ch but kpt on ins fnl f* **9/1**[3]

12-1 **7** *¾* **Garswood**[17] 1621 3-9-0 115 TonyHamilton 8 104+
(Richard Fahey) *lw: stdd and sltly hmpd sn after s: hld up in rr: rdn and effrt but plenty to do 2f out: swtchd lft and hdwy over 1f out: kpt on fnl f: n.d* **12/1**

65-2 **8** *½* **Dont Bother Me (IRE)**[20] 1555 3-9-0 103 MartinHarley 2 103
(Niall Moran, Ire) *racd off the pce in midfield: rdn and lost pl over 2f out: wl hld but rallied u.p over 1f out: plugged on but no ch* **100/1**

32-6 **9** *2 ½* **Leitir Mor (IRE)**[14] 1704 3-9-0 115 (tp) RonanWhelan 13 97
(J S Bolger, Ire) *led: rdn and hdd 2f out: sn outpcd and wl btn 5th over 1f out: wknd fnl f* **50/1**

631- **10** *2 ¼* **George Vancouver (USA)**[182] 7568 3-9-0 117 CO'Donoghue 10 91
(A P O'Brien, Ire) *racd off fthe pce in midfield: drvn and outpcd over 2f out: bhd over 1f out* **20/1**

11-4 **11** *nk* **Correspondent**[14] 1677 3-9-0 92 PaulHanagan 7 91
(Brian Meehan) *stdd s: t.k.h: hld up in rr: rdn and btn over 2f out: bhd wl over 1f out* **150/1**

12-3 **12** *7* **Moohaajim (IRE)**[14] 1677 3-9-0 116 AdamKirby 5 74
(Marco Botti) *racd off the pce in midfield: rdn and lost pl over 2f out: lost tch wl over 1f out* **20/1**

4-2 **13** *4 ½* **Kyllachy Rise**[14] 1678 3-9-0 0 TomQueally 9 63
(Sir Henry Cecil) *hmpd sn after s: hld up in rr: rdn and lost tch 2f out* **50/1**

1m 35.84s (-2.76) **Going Correction** -0.075s/f (Good) **13** Ran SP% **116.1**
Speed ratings (Par 113): **110,105,102,102,101 101,100,99,97,95 94,87,83**
toteswingers 1&2 £32.10, 1&3 £7.60, 2&3 £86.20 CSF £350.73 CT £2980.58 TOTE £2.50: £1.40, £12.50, £2.90; EX 201.50 Trifecta £2525.00 Pool: £23,250.20 - 6.90 winning units..
Owner Godolphin **Bred** J S Bolger **Trained** Coolcullen, Co Carlow

FOCUS
The field started off up the middle of the track, but gradually edged over towards the stands' rail. While the performance of the 150-1 shot Glory Awaits (best RPR in eight previous starts just 96) takes some believing, clearly that one has run way above himself and the time was almost three seconds quicker than the 100-rated Glean managed later on the card. There were several disappointments among the beaten runners, confirming the pre-race impression this year's 2,000 Guineas lacked depth. Perhaps the underfoot conditions go some way to explaining why so many of the beaten runners struggled to get involved as there was a heavy shower shortly before the off, and the track had already been watered. The runners were kicking the top off the ground and it was surprising how many of them were beaten by around halfway, even allowing for what the on-screen sectionals showed was a good pace. Dawn Approach, though, rates up with the best winners of the past decade bar Frankel.

2022 HARBOUR WATCH TIMEFORM "EUROPEAN CHAMPION TWO-YEAR-OLD" H'CAP 6f
4:25 (4:26) (Class 2) (0-100,94) 3-Y-O **£12,938** (£3,850; £1,924; £962) **Stalls** High

Form RPR

11- **1** **Secretinthepark**[185] 7478 3-8-11 84 RichardHughes 3 97
(Ed McMahon) *lw: hld up wl in tch: rdn and effrt 2f out: chsd ldr 1f out: styd on wl to ld wl ins fnl f: sn in command* **9/2**[1]

513- **2** *1 ½* **Brazen**[224] 6487 3-8-6 82 DarrenEgan(3) 7 90
(David Simcock) *t.k.h: hld up wl in tch: clsd to chse ldr 2f out: rdn to ld but edging rt over 1f out: 2 l clr but stl gng rt 1f out: hdd wl ins fnl f: no ex* **9/1**

5-21 **3** *1 ¼* **Purcell (IRE)**[22] 1515 3-8-11 84 DavidProbert 12 88
(Andrew Balding) *stdd s: hld up in midfield: hdwy 1/2-way: chsd ldr wl over 1f out: hung fire and ducked lft ent fnl f: 3rd and one pce fnl f* **10/1**

5-41 **4** *2 ¼* **Shahdaroba (IRE)**[17] 1625 3-9-7 94 TomQueally 10 91
(Rod Millman) *chsd ldrs: rdn and unable qck ent fnl 2f: kpt on same pce u.p and no threat to ldrs fr over 1f out* **6/1**[2]

15-0 **5** *½* **Bapak Sayang (USA)**[16] 1645 3-8-11 84 AmyRyan 9 79
(Kevin Ryan) *lw: taken down early: led: drvn and hdd wl over 1f out: no ex and btn over 1f out: plugged on same pce fnl f* **33/1**

631- **6** *1* **Vallarta (IRE)**[225] 6443 3-8-10 83 MartinHarley 11 75+
(Mick Channon) *s.i.s: bhd: rdn and hdwy over 1f out: kpt on ins fnl f: nvr trbld ldrs* **6/1**[2]

03-1 **7** *½* **Robot Boy (IRE)**[21] 1539 3-8-11 84 JamieSpencer 2 74+
(David Barron) *str: bhd: rdn and struggling over 2f out: hrd drvn and hdwy over 1f out: styd on fnl f: nvr trbld ldrs* **7/1**[3]

122- **8** *nk* **Dance With Dragons (IRE)**[127] 8276 3-8-8 81 ChrisCatlin 8 70
(William Stone) *s.i.s: sn rdn along and outpcd in rr: styd on ins fnl f: nvr trbld ldrs* **40/1**

216- **9** *½* **Jamesbo's Girl**[218] 6632 3-9-2 89 TonyHamilton 6 77
(Richard Fahey) *chsd ldr tl over 2f out: sn struggling u.p: wknd over 1f out* **16/1**

1-23 **10** *1 ¼* **Fils Anges (IRE)**[24] 1482 3-9-2 89 HayleyTurner 1 73
(Michael Bell) *taken down early: racd off the pce in midfield: rdn and struggling over 2f out: n.d fnl 2f* **6/1**[2]

-210 **11** *¾* **Limit Up**[17] 1620 3-8-7 80 JoeFanning 13 61
(Mark Johnston) *lw: leaving stalls: sn rcvrd and in tch: effrt and hung rt 2f out: no prog and btn over 1f out: wknd* **33/1**

1-05 **12** *1 ¾* **Secret Missile**[8] 1808 3-8-6 79 MartinDwyer 5 55
(William Muir) *a towards rr: rdn and struggling 1/2-way: no ch fnl 2f* **14/1**

512- **13** *11* **Agerzam**[198] 7193 3-9-0 87 WilliamBuick 4 28
(Roger Varian) *lw: a towards rr: rdn and effrt ent fnl 2f: no hdwy: bhd and eased ins fnl f* **12/1**

1m 11.0s (-1.20) **Going Correction** -0.075s/f (Good) **13** Ran SP% **121.2**
Speed ratings (Par 105): **105,103,101,98,97 96,95,95,94,92 91,89,74**
toteswingers 1&2 £7.90, 1&3 £8.30, 2&3 £18.40 CSF £45.13 CT £405.25 TOTE £4.80: £2.00, £3.70, £3.00; EX 60.10 Trifecta £644.20 Pool: £3,737.69 - 4.35 winning units..
Owner Mia Racing **Bred** Mia Racing **Trained** Lichfield, Staffs

FOCUS
Although the top-weight was rated 6lb below the ceiling for the race this looked a good, competitive heat and it's likely to throw up plenty of future winners. The early pace was pretty strong (the second furlong was the quickest sectional) and they got gradually slower as the race went on, but the time was relatively good. The bare form could rate a bit higher.

2023 QATAR RACING NEWMARKET STKS (LISTED RACE) (C&G) 1m 2f
5:00 (5:00) (Class 1) 3-Y-O
£22,684 (£8,600; £4,304; £2,144; £1,076; £540) **Stalls** High

Form RPR

1-1 **1** **Windhoek**[16] 1636 3-8-12 104 JoeFanning 2 107+
(Mark Johnston) *lw: mde all and dictated stdy gallop: rdn and readily wnt clr over 1f out: in command whn ducked lft ins fnl f: sn stened and r.o wl: comf* **4/5**[1]

1 **2** *3 ¼* **Centurius**[14] 1684 3-8-12 83 MartinHarley 1 100
(Marco Botti) *w'like: scope: t.k.h: chsd ldrs: rdn and chsd cleae wnr over 1f out: styd on same pce fnl f* **15/2**[3]

-305 **3** *¾* **Hoarding (USA)**[10] 1767 3-8-12 92 (p) WilliamBuick 6 99
(John Gosden) *lw: hld up in tch in midfield: rdn and effrt over 2f out: 4th and edgd lft u.p jst ins fnl f: kpt on but no threat to wnr* **18/1**

11-3 **4** *½* **Unsinkable (IRE)**[28] 1383 3-8-12 100 TonyHamilton 5 98
(Richard Fahey) *t.k.h: chsd ldrs: rdn and unable qck over 1f out: styd on same pce and no threat to wnr fnl f* **10/1**

-3 **5** *3 ¾* **High Octane**[20] 1555 3-8-12 0 SeamieHeffernan 4 90
(John Joseph Murphy, Ire) *hld up in tch in rr: hdwy 4f out: rdn 2f out: outpcd and btn whn sltly hmpd 1f out: wknd ins fnl f* **7/2**[2]

0-64 **6** *12* **Maxentius (IRE)**[28] 1383 3-8-12 100 RichardHughes 3 66
(Peter Chapple-Hyam) *t.k.h: hld up in tch in last pair: rdn over 2f out: no hdwy 2f out: sn wknd: bhd and eased ins fnl f* **16/1**

2m 5.35s (-0.45) **Going Correction** -0.075s/f (Good) **6** Ran SP% **109.8**
Speed ratings (Par 107): **98,95,94,94,91 81**
toteswingers 1&2 £1.70, 1&3 £4.10, 2&3 £7.40 CSF £7.14 TOTE £1.90: £1.40, £3.20; EX 10.00 Trifecta £54.50 Pool: £27,502.71 - 378.05 winning units..
Owner Sheikh Hamdan Bin Mohammed Al Maktoum **Bred** Horizon Bloodstock Limited **Trained** Middleham Moor, N Yorks

FOCUS
A race that rarely has an impact on the Derby. The winner had an easy lead but still rates an up-to-scratch winner of the race, and can rate higher. The next two both improved.

2024 QIPCO SUPPORTS RACING WELFARE H'CAP 1m
5:35 (5:35) (Class 2) (0-105,102) 3-Y-O **£12,938** (£3,850; £1,924; £962) **Stalls** High

Form RPR
36-2 **1** **Glean**[21] 1543 3-9-5 **100**.................... RichardHughes 7 107
(Richard Hannon) *chsd ldr: rdn to lchal over 1f out: led jst ins fnl f: styd on wl: eased cl home* **10/3**[2]
21-0 **2** 2 1/2 **Red Avenger (USA)**[8] 1809 3-8-11 **92**.................... WilliamBuick 6 93
(Ed Dunlop) *t.k.h: hld up in tch: effrt u.p wl over 1f out: kpt on ins fnl f: wnt 2nd last strides* **15/2**
50-0 **3** hd **Discernable**[16] 1636 3-8-13 **94**.................... JoeFanning 1 95
(Mark Johnston) *led: rdn and jnd over 1f out: hdd jst ins fnl f: no ex and one pce after: lost 2nd last strides* **25/1**
6-11 **4** 2 1/4 **Country Western**[16] 1645 3-8-8 **89**.................... SteveDrowne 4 85
(Charles Hills) *lw: t.k.h: chsd ldrs: rdn wl over 1f out: outpcd and drvn over 1f out: styd on same pce fnl f* **7/2**[3]
4124 **5** nse **Flashlight (IRE)**[8] 1809 3-8-6 **87**.................... RoystonFfrench 5 83+
(Mark Johnston) *stdd s: t.k.h: hld up in last pair: rdn and wandered 2f out: kpt on ins fnl f: no threat to wnr* **12/1**
15-4 **6** 1 **Ayaar (IRE)**[17] 1621 3-9-7 **102**.................... MartinHarley 2 95
(Mick Channon) *stdd s: hld up in tch in last pair: rdn and effrt wl over 1f out: no imp and wl hld fnl f* **8/1**
16- **7** 2 3/4 **Azrur (IRE)**[238] 6027 3-8-6 **87**.................... JamieSpencer 3 77
(Michael Bell) *stdd s: in tch in midfield: rdn and no hdwy 2f out: wknd ent fnl f* **2/1**[1]

1m 38.7s (0.10) **Going Correction** -0.075s/f (Good) **7 Ran SP% 113.0**
Speed ratings (Par 105): **96,93,93,91,91 90,87**
toteswingers 1&2 £4.20, 1&3 £14.10, 2&3 £26.50 CSF £27.28 TOTE £4.10: £2.40, £2.20; EX 27.10 Trifecta £185.70 Pool: £4,182.17 - 16.88 winning units..
Owner Lady Rothschild **Bred** The Rt Hon Lord Rothschild **Trained** East Everleigh, Wilts

FOCUS
A decent little handicap for 3yos, but they went a modest early pace and very few got seriously involved. Doubts over the form, but the winner improved from his reappearance.
T/Jkpt: £3,039.30 to a £1 stake. Pool: £25,000.00 - 5.84 winning units T/Plt: £337.10 to a £1 stake. Pool: £203,496.07 - 440.61 winning units T/Qpdt: £35.70 to a £1 stake. Pool: £7,402.60 - 153.10 winning units SP

1686 THIRSK (L-H)
Saturday, May 4

OFFICIAL GOING: Good to firm (good in places; 9.5)
Wind: Fresh; behind Weather: Cloudy

2025 BET TOTEJACKPOT AT TOTEPOOL.COM MAIDEN AUCTION STKS 5f
2:15 (2:16) (Class 5) 2-Y-O **£3,234** (£962; £481; £240) **Stalls** High

Form RPR
1 **Champagne Babe** 2-9-0 0.................... SilvestreDeSousa 8 73+
(Keith Dalgleish) *mde all: pushed along over 1f out: kpt on to go clr ins fnl f: edgd lft nr fin: comf* **11/4**[1]
0 **2** 3 **Classy Lassy (IRE)**[16] 1642 2-8-11 0.................... PaulPickard(3) 2 62
(Brian Ellison) *prom: rdn 2f out: kpt on but no ch w wnr fnl f* **3/1**[2]
3 2 1/4 **Secret Applause** 2-9-0 0.................... PaulMulrennan 4 54+
(Michael Dods) *chsd ldng pair: pushed along 1/2-way: sn one pce in 3rd* **7/2**[3]
0 **4** 2 3/4 **Blades Boy**[17] 1606 2-9-2 0.................... LeeTopliss(3) 1 49
(Richard Fahey) *slowly away: hld up in rr: pushed along 1/2-way: sme hdwy over 1f out: kpt on: nvr threatened* **11/2**
5 1 1/2 **Miguela McGuire** 2-8-9 0.................... JasonHart(5) 5 39
(Eric Alston) *hld up: pushed along 1/2-way: nvr threatened* **10/1**
6 nk **Noble Reach** 2-8-7 0.................... JordanNason(7) 7 38
(Geoffrey Harker) *dwlt: hld up: pushed along 1/2-way: edgd lft over 1f out: nvr threatened* **25/1**
5 **7** 2 1/4 **The Bunny Catcher**[26] 1432 2-9-0 0.................... PaddyAspell 6 30
(Sharon Watt) *dwlt: sn chsd ldng pair: rdn 2f out: wknd fnl f* **14/1**
8 21 **Paparima (IRE)** 2-9-0 0.................... LukeMorris 3
(Paul Green) *v.s.a: a bdly outpcd in rr* **18/1**

58.74s (-0.86) **Going Correction** -0.30s/f (Firm) **8 Ran SP% 114.1**
Speed ratings (Par 93): **94,89,85,81,78 78,74,41**
toteswingers 1&2 £2.00, 1&3 £6.10, 2&3 £3.70 CSF £11.19 TOTE £4.00: £1.60, £1.10, £1.60; EX 12.60 Trifecta £35.90 Pool: £1,239.65 - 25.88 winning units..
Owner Straightline Construction Ltd **Bred** Bishopswood Bloodstock **Trained** Carluke, S Lanarks

FOCUS
One colt against seven fillies in this ordinary maiden for cheaply bought horses, and the front pair dominated throughout. The winner was much the best on the day and the time was decent.

2026 BET TOTESCOOP6 AT TOTEPOOL.COM FILLIES' H'CAP 1m
2:45 (2:45) (Class 4) (0-85,84) 3-Y-O+ **£4,851** (£1,443; £721; £360) **Stalls** Low

Form RPR
11-1 **1** **Lilac Lace (IRE)**[19] 1577 3-8-8 **77**.................... DuranFentiman 5 80
(Tim Easterby) *t.k.h early: prom: rdn over 2f out: led narrowly wl over 1f out: jnd by runner-up ins fnl f: hld on all out* **4/1**[2]
100- **2** nse **Tussie Mussie**[217] 6675 3-8-6 **75**.................... SilvestreDeSousa 7 78
(Mark Johnston) *prom: led over 6f out: rdn 3f out: hdd narrowly wl over 1f out: rallied and bk upsides ins fnl f: kpt on: jst failed* **7/1**
1- **3** nk **Ice Pie**[134] 8200 3-8-4 **73**.................... FrannyNorton 1 75+
(Tom Dascombe) *s.i.s: hld up in tch: pushed along and rn green over 2f out: kpt on strly fnl f: fin wl* **6/4**[1]
10-5 **4** 1 **Lady Of The House (IRE)**[7] 1822 3-9-1 **84**.................... PhillipMakin 2 84
(Kevin Ryan) *led: hdd over 6f out: trckd ldr: rdn over 2f out: kpt on one pce* **5/1**[3]
200- **5** 2 3/4 **Sareeah (IRE)**[341] 2544 4-8-9 **70** oh4.................... DavidBergin(5) 8 66
(David O'Meara) *in tch: rdn over 2f out: wknd fnl 100yds* **20/1**
40-0 **6** 3 1/4 **Shesastar**[35] 1252 5-10-0 **84**.................... GrahamGibbons 4 73
(David Barron) *slowly away: hld up in rr: rdn over 2f out: nvr threatened* **14/1**
010- **7** nk **New Falcon (IRE)**[233] 6160 3-8-8 **77** ow1.................... (p) PaulMulrennan 3 62
(James Tate) *hld up: rdn over 2f out: nvr threatened* **8/1**

1m 39.74s (-0.36) **Going Correction** -0.05s/f (Good)
WFA 3 from 4yo+ 13lb **7 Ran SP% 111.7**
Speed ratings (Par 102): **99,98,98,97,94 91,91**
toteswingers 1&2 £2.20, 1&3 £1.90, 2&3 £1.90 CSF £29.92 CT £57.75 TOTE £3.60: £2.30, £3.70; EX 17.30 Trifecta £47.10 Pool: £1,471.10 - 23.41 winning units..
Owner S A Heley **Bred** Robert Ryan, Brendan Quinn & Joan Quinn **Trained** Great Habton, N Yorks

FOCUS
A thrilling finish to this fillies' handicap. The form has been given a bit of a chance, with the winner continuing to progress.

2027 LIVE TOTESCOOP6 INFORMATION AT TOTEPOOL.COM MAIDEN STKS 7f
3:20 (3:22) (Class 4) 3-Y-O **£4,851** (£1,443; £721; £360) **Stalls** Low

Form RPR
5- **1** **Off Art**[349] 2308 3-9-5 0.................... DavidAllan 8 81
(Tim Easterby) *mde all: rdn 2f out: strly pressed appr fnl f: kpt on wl to assert towards fin* **7/1**[3]
33-3 **2** 1 **You're The Boss**[17] 1618 3-9-5 82.................... LukeMorris 2 78
(Ed Walker) *trckd ldrs: hdwy to chal 2f out: drvn and ev ch appr fnl f: one pce and hld towards fin* **4/7**[1]
305- **3** 7 **Midnight Warrior**[186] 7458 3-9-5 70.................... DaleSwift 5 59
(Ron Barr) *trckd ldrs: rdn over 2f out: one pce and no ch w ldng pair fnl 2f* **12/1**
3- **4** 3/4 **Chevalgris**[179] 7598 3-9-5 0.................... RobertWinston 6 57
(Alan Swinbank) *hld up: pushed along wl over 3f out: stl only 8th 2f out: kpt on wl fnl f* **4/1**[2]
5 3 1/4 **Absolute Diamond** 3-9-0 0.................... MichaelO'Connell 1 43
(John Quinn) *dwlt: sn in tch: rdn over 2f out: wknd ins fnl f* **16/1**
225- **6** 1 1/2 **Lady Margaeux (IRE)**[284] 4427 3-8-9 72.................... DavidBergin(5) 9 39
(David O'Meara) *hld up: rdn over 2f out: nvr threatened* **8/1**
00- **7** 1/2 **Erica Starprincess**[228] 6335 3-9-0 0.................... PJMcDonald 10 38
(George Moore) *prom: rdn over 2f out: wknd over 1f out* **100/1**
6 **8** 4 1/2 **Silver Forest (IRE)**[12] 1735 3-8-11 0.................... MichaelMetcalfe(3) 4 26
(John Weymes) *midfield: rdn over 2f out: wknd over 1f out* **50/1**
9 36 **The Troyster** 3-9-5 0.................... PaulMulrennan 7
(Julie Camacho) *slowly away: a in rr* **100/1**

1m 27.05s (-0.15) **Going Correction** -0.05s/f (Good) **9 Ran SP% 124.8**
Speed ratings (Par 101): **98,96,88,88,84 82,82,76,35**
toteswingers 1&2 £3.10, 1&3 £12.90, 2&3 £4.00 CSF £12.41 TOTE £8.90: £2.20, £1.10, £2.80; EX 18.10 Trifecta £139.20 Pool: £1,961.23 - 10.56 winning units..
Owner D B Lamplough **Bred** D B Lamplough **Trained** Great Habton, N Yorks

FOCUS
Not a particularly competitive maiden and the first two pulled clear. The time was ordinary and the form is not entirely convincing.

2028 KING SIZE POOLS AT TOTEPOOL.COM H'CAP 7f
4:00 (4:00) (Class 4) (0-85,91) 4-Y-O+ **£6,469** (£1,925; £962; £481) **Stalls** Low

Form RPR
000- **1** **Yair Hill (IRE)**[217] 6676 5-9-7 **85**.................... PhillipMakin 3 96
(Kevin Ryan) *hld up: gd hdwy on outer fr over 2f out: rdn to ld ins fnl f: edgd lft: kpt on* **17/2**[3]
0-22 **2** 3/4 **Llewellyn**[14] 1693 5-8-7 **71**.................... AdrianNicholls 7 80
(David Nicholls) *in tch: rdn over 2f out: hdwy and ev ch appr fnl f: kpt on* **6/1**[2]
34-2 **3** 2 **Chester Aristocrat**[14] 1692 4-8-5 **74**.................... JasonHart(5) 14 78
(Eric Alston) *led: clr 5f out tl over 2f out: hdd ins fnl f: no ex* **11/1**
-061 **4** 3/4 **Roninski (IRE)**[9] 1782 5-9-9 **87**.................... AndrewElliott 4 89
(Garry Moss) *midfield: swtchd rt 2f out: sn rdn and hdwy: kpt on fnl f* **16/1**
0-40 **5** nk **Solar Spirit (IRE)**[9] 1787 8-9-1 **79**.................... RobertWinston 5 80
(Tracy Waggott) *hld up in midfield: rdn over 2f out: hdwy over 1f out: kpt on* **20/1**
30-1 **6** 1 1/4 **Mont Ras (IRE)**[2] 1963 6-9-8 **91** 6ex.................... DavidBergin(5) 13 88
(David O'Meara) *sn prom: rdn to chse ldr 2f out: wknd ins fnl f* **2/1**[1]
32-0 **7** 3 **Warfare**[43] 1115 4-8-12 **76**.................... (p) FrannyNorton 6 65
(Kevin Ryan) *hld up in midfield: pushed along whn n.m.r over 1f out: no threat after* **20/1**
-060 **8** 1 **Imperial Djay (IRE)**[7] 1830 8-9-7 **85**.................... PJMcDonald 2 72
(Ruth Carr) *hld up: rdn over 3f out: nvr threatened* **6/1**[2]
/50- **9** nk **Ceremonial Jade (UAE)**[184] 7508 10-8-13 **77**.................... (t) NeilCallan 1 63
(Marco Botti) *hld up: rdn over 2f out: nvr threatened* **20/1**
40-0 **10** 4 **Kalk Bay (IRE)**[19] 1576 6-9-6 **84**.................... (t) JamesSullivan 12 59
(Michael Easterby) *hld up: nvr threatened* **33/1**
-600 **11** nk **Beau Mistral (IRE)**[16] 1649 4-9-0 **78**.................... LukeMorris 9 52
(Paul Green) *chsd ldrs: rdn 3f out: wknd over 1f out* **50/1**
000- **12** 2 **Evervescent (IRE)**[166] 7790 4-9-0 **78**.................... LiamJones 8 47
(J S Moore) *in tch: rdn over 3f out: wknd over 1f out* **14/1**
503- **13** 3 1/4 **Orbit The Moon (IRE)**[200] 7144 5-9-1 **79**.................... (t) PaulMulrennan 10 39
(Michael Dods) *chsd ldr: wknd fnl 2f* **16/1**

1m 25.52s (-1.68) **Going Correction** -0.05s/f (Good) **13 Ran SP% 118.4**
Speed ratings (Par 105): **107,106,103,103,102 101,97,96,96,91 91,89,85**
toteswingers 1&2 £4.20, 1&3 £43.60, 2&3 £3.90 CSF £53.97 CT £591.34 TOTE £9.00: £2.70, £1.80, £2.60; EX 56.40 Trifecta £252.90 Pool: £908.34 - 2.69 winning units..
Owner D J Emsley **Bred** The Earl Cadogan **Trained** Hambleton, N Yorks

FOCUS
A competitive handicap, run at a decent pace, and the form looks sound.

2029 TOTEPOOL.COM THIRSK HUNT CUP (H'CAP) 1m
4:35 (4:36) (Class 2) (0-100,100) 4-Y-O+ **£16,172** (£4,812; £2,405; £1,202) **Stalls** Low

Form RPR
45-0 **1** **Norse Blues**[14] 1675 5-8-8 **87**.................... GrahamGibbons 7 98
(David Barron) *mde all: rdn over 2f out: strly pressed ins fnl f: hld on wl* **7/2**[1]
00-0 **2** hd **Anderiego (IRE)**[35] 1235 5-8-6 **90**.................... DavidBergin(5) 8 101
(David O'Meara) *hld up in midfield: rdn and gd hdwy on outside 2f out: edgd lft appr fnl f: chal strly ins fnl f: kpt on: jst hld* **16/1**
21 **3** 2 1/4 **Two For Two (IRE)**[7] 1840 5-9-6 **99**.................... SilvestreDeSousa 14 104+
(David O'Meara) *hld up: hmpd 6f out: rdn and stl plenty to do 2f out: r.o strly fnl f: nrst fin* **7/2**[1]
10-4 **4** 1 1/2 **Wannabe King**[14] 1688 7-8-10 **92**.................... (p) RaulDaSilva(3) 10 94
(Geoffrey Harker) *chsd ldrs: rdn 3f out: kpt on one pce* **22/1**
33-2 **5** nk **Lord Aeryn (IRE)**[7] 1840 6-8-10 **89**.................... BarryMcHugh 2 90
(Richard Fahey) *in tch on inner: rdn 3f out: kpt on one pce* **7/1**[3]
0-00 **6** 1/2 **Osteopathic Remedy (IRE)**[14] 1688 9-8-6 **92**.................... ConnorBeasley(7) 1 92
(Michael Dods) *chsd ldrs: rdn 3f out: one pce* **25/1**
4014 **7** nk **Dubai Dynamo**[7] 1840 8-8-13 **92**.................... PJMcDonald 9 91
(Ruth Carr) *hld up: rdn over 2f out: kpt on fnl f: nvr threatened* **10/1**
215- **8** 3/4 **Trail Blaze (IRE)**[225] 6426 4-8-12 **91**.................... PhillipMakin 6 89
(Kevin Ryan) *prom: rdn over 2f out: grad wknd fnl f* **14/1**
6603 **9** 1 **Santefisio**[12] 1720 7-9-7 **100**.................... (b) NeilCallan 4 95
(Keith Dalgleish) *dwlt: sn midfield: hmpd 6f out: rdn over 2f out: one pce and nvr threatened ldrs* **14/1**

5-21 **10** ½ **Fieldgunner Kirkup (GER)**[33] 1281 5-8-8 **87**............ AndrewMullen 13 81
(David Barron) *in tch towards outer: rdn 3f out: wknd ins fnl f* **20/1**

-130 **11** 1 **Alfred Hutchinson**[56] 945 5-9-0 **93**........................ MichaelO'Connell 3 85
(Geoffrey Oldroyd) *midfield: rdn 3f out: wknd fnl f* **22/1**

00-3 **12** 6 **Rodrigo De Torres**[14] 1691 6-9-3 **96**........................ FrannyNorton 12 74
(David Nicholls) *prom: rdn 3f out: wknd over 1f out* **22/1**

14-0 **13** 1 **No Poppy (IRE)**[14] 1688 5-8-8 **92**.............................. AdamCarter(5) 11 68
(Tim Easterby) *hld up in rr: a bhd* **33/1**

431- **14** 2 **Jacob Cats**[224] 6494 4-9-3 **96**... HarryBentley 16 67
(Olly Stevens) *hld up: a towards rr* **13/2**[2]

10-1 **15** 8 **St Moritz (IRE)**[16] 1643 7-9-2 **95**.................................. AdrianNicholls 5 48
(David Nicholls) *midfield on outer: hmpd 6f out: rdn 3f out: wknd over 1f out: eased* **20/1**

1m 37.83s (-2.27) **Going Correction** -0.05s/f (Good) **15** Ran SP% **127.9**
Speed ratings (Par 109): **109,108,106,105,104 104,103,103,102,101 100,94,93,91,83**
toteswingers 1&2 £19.00, 1&3 £4.20, 2&3 £16.50 CSF £62.08 CT £226.42 TOTE £4.70: £1.60, £5.90, £2.00; EX 86.90 Trifecta £741.00 Pool: £3,196.20 - 3.23 winning units..
Owner J Bollington & Partners **Bred** Littleton Stud **Trained** Maunby, N Yorks

FOCUS
A typically hot renewal of the Thirsk Hunt Cup, won last year by Farhh before he placed in five consecutive Group 1s. The winner looks better than ever on the face of things, and the second and third can do better.

2030 MORE FOOTBALL THAN EVER AT TOTEPOOL.COM MAIDEN STKS 1m 4f
5:10 (5:15) (Class 5) 3-Y-0+ **£3,234** (£962; £481; £240) **Stalls** High

Form RPR

1 **Renew (IRE)**[228] 6351 3-8-9 0.. NeilCallan 7 81+
(Marco Botti) *trckd ldr: led over 3f out: rdn over 1f out: kpt on to go clr fnl f* **5/2**[2]

2 **2** 4 ½ **Street Artist (IRE)**[47] 1069 3-8-9 0.......................... SilvestreDeSousa 5 73+
(Mark Johnston) *s.i.s: hld up in rr: wnt a little in snatches: rdn over 3f out: hdwy 2f out: wandered u.p: styd on wl to go 2nd fnl 50yds: no ch w wnr* **5/2**[2]

22-3 **3** ¾ **Chancery (USA)**[7] 1826 5-10-0 81.................................... DavidNolan 1 74
(David O'Meara) *trckd ldr: rdn to chse wnr over 2f out: one pce fnl f: lost 2nd fnl 50yds* **9/4**[1]

0 **4** 2 ½ **Tetbury (USA)**[22] 1522 4-9-9 82.................................. DavidBergin(5) 11 70
(David O'Meara) *midfield: rdn and hdwy over 2f out: one pce fr over 1f out* **12/1**

4-6 **5** 7 **Chief Executive (IRE)**[14] 1679 3-8-9 0........................ J-PGuillambert 2 58
(Jo Hughes) *in tch: rdn over 3f out: wknd over 1f out* **6/1**[3]

-0 **6** 1 **Woodacre**[8] 1804 6-10-0 0.. PaulMulrennan 6 57
(Richard Whitaker) *trckd ldrs: rdn 3f out: wknd over 1f out* **33/1**

060- **7** nk **Shirls Son Sam**[179] 7603 5-10-0 43........................... MichaelStainton 3 56?
(Chris Fairhurst) *hld up: rdn over 3f out: nvr threatened ldrs* **80/1**

00 **8** 30 **Rolen Sly**[9] 1777 4-10-0 0.. BarryMcHugh 4
(Brian Rothwell) *hld up: a towards rr* **200/1**

0/ **9** 2 ¼ **Regy From Sedgy**[687] 3138 6-9-9 0............................... AdamCarter(5) 8
(Frederick Watson) *hld up: a bhd* **200/1**

00/0 **10** 9 **Keyhole Kate**[19] 1579 4-9-9 47................................(b[1]) DuranFentiman 10
(Tim Walford) *led: rdn whn hdd over 3f out: wknd* **66/1**

2m 35.49s (-0.71) **Going Correction** -0.05s/f (Good)
WFA 3 from 4yo+ 19lb **10** Ran SP% **116.6**
Speed ratings (Par 103): **100,97,96,94,90 89,89,69,67,61**
toteswingers 1&2 £2.60, 1&3 £2.30, 2&3 £1.90 CSF £9.20 TOTE £3.50: £1.50, £1.30, £1.20; EX 12.40 Trifecta £26.20 Pool: £2,694.96 - 76.96 winning units..
Owner Giuliano Manfredini **Bred** Premier Bloodstock **Trained** Newmarket, Suffolk

FOCUS
Not much depth to this maiden and they dawdled early, but the overall time wasn't bad. The seventh casts doubt but the winner did it emphatically.

2031 FOLLOW TOTEPOOL ON FACEBOOK AND TWITTER H'CAP 5f
5:45 (5:48) (Class 4) (0-85,85) 4-Y-0+ **£6,469** (£1,925; £962; £481) **Stalls** High

Form RPR

00-4 **1** **Bedloe's Island (IRE)**[8] 1807 8-9-4 **82**.......................... DavidNolan 19 93
(David O'Meara) *dwlt: hld up stands' side: swtchd lft wl over 1f out: sn rdn and gd hdwy: led ins fnl f: kpt on wl: jst hld on* **4/1**[1]

113- **2** nk **Angelito**[217] 6689 4-8-12 **76**... FrannyNorton 13 86
(Ed McMahon) *hld up stands' side: rdn and hdwy over 1f out: kpt on wl fnl f: edgd lft fnl 100yds: jst hld: 2nd of 10 in gp* **8/1**[2]

3603 **3** ½ **Moorhouse Lad**[8] 1807 10-9-5 **83**................................. AndrewElliott 18 91
(Garry Moss) *racd stands' side: chsd ldr: rdn 2f out: ev ch ins fnl f: kpt on: 3rd of 10 in gp* **16/1**

55-0 **4** 1 **Waseem Faris (IRE)**[19] 1581 4-9-0 **78**.................... MatthewDavies 16 83
(Mick Channon) *hld up stands' side: rdn 2f out: swtchd lft ins fnl f: kpt on wl: nrst fin: 4th of 10 in gp* **17/2**[3]

01-3 **5** ½ **Rothesay Chancer**[35] 1253 5-8-10 **74**.......................... BarryMcHugh 7 77
(Jim Goldie) *chsd ldrs far side: rdn 2f out: kpt on to ld gp fnl 100yds: 1st of 9 in gp* **33/1**

05-0 **5** dht **Pea Shooter**[8] 1807 4-9-2 **80**...(b[1]) NeilCallan 15 83
(Kevin Ryan) *chsd ldr stands' side: rdn 1/2-way: one pce ins fnl f: 5th of 10 in gp* **9/1**

1-20 **7** ¾ **Come On Dave (IRE)**[16] 1649 4-9-0 **78**................. MichaelO'Connell 11 78
(David Nicholls) *racd stands 'side: overall ldr: rdn 2f out: hdd ins fnl f: wknd: 6th of 10 in gp* **12/1**

45-1 **8** hd **Love Island**[8] 1807 4-9-3 **81**.. PaulQuinn 5 80
(Richard Whitaker) *hld up far side: rdn and hdwy over 1f out: kpt on: 2nd of 0 in gp* **11/1**

00-0 **9** 1 **Bosun Breese**[17] 1607 8-9-2 **85**...................................... LMcNiff(5) 2 81
(David Barron) *w ldr far side: rdn 1/2-way: no ex fnl 100yds: 3rd of 9 in gp* **25/1**

2-00 **10** nk **Excel Bolt**[8] 1807 5-9-2 **83**.. LeeTopliss(3) 3 78
(Bryan Smart) *led far side: rdn 2f out: hdd in gp fnl 100yds: no ex: 4th of 9 in gp* **16/1**

-045 **11** 2 ¼ **Rusty Rocket (IRE)**[16] 1644 4-9-0 **78**............................ LukeMorris 9 65
(Paul Green) *chsd ldrs far side: wknd ins fnl f: 5th of 9 in gp* **33/1**

0-00 **12** 1 ½ **Lost In Paris (IRE)**[16] 1649 7-8-9 **73**.....................(p) DuranFentiman 12 54
(Tim Easterby) *chsd ldrs stands' side: wknd fnl f: 7th of 10 in gp* **33/1**

340- **13** hd **Kuanyao (IRE)**[227] 6368 7-8-9 **80**.............................. CarolineKelly(7) 10 60
(David Nicholls) *chsd ldrs stands' side: wknd over 1f out: 8th of 10 in gp* **33/1**

55-5 **14** 1 ¼ **Lupin Pooter**[35] 1248 4-8-13 **77**.................................... AndrewMullen 6 53
(David Barron) *slowly away: hld up far side: nvr threatened: 6th of 9 in gp* **14/1**

20-0 **15** ½ **Breezolini**[14] 1692 5-8-10 **74**.................................. SilvestreDeSousa 17 48
(Geoffrey Harker) *a towards rr stands' side: 9th of 10 in gp* **12/1**

50-0 **16** 1 **Noodles Blue Boy**[8] 1807 7-8-7 **78**.......................... JacobButterfield(7) 1 49
(Ollie Pears) *dwlt: hld up far side: nvr threatened: 7th of 9 in gp* **25/1**

106- **17** nk **Whozthecat (IRE)**[157] 7918 6-9-2 **85**..........................(v) JasonHart(5) 14 54
(Declan Carroll) *a towards rr stands' side: last of 10 in gp* **20/1**

003- **18** ¾ **The Nifty Fox**[205] 7000 9-8-8 **77**.................................... AdamCarter(5) 4 44
(Tim Easterby) *hld up far side: nvr threatened: 8th of 9 in gp* **40/1**

0-00 **19** 6 **Chunky Diamond (IRE)**[16] 1644 4-9-5 **83**...................... PJMcDonald 8 28
(Ruth Carr) *prom far side: wknd fnl 2f* **12/1**

57.43s (-2.17) **Going Correction** -0.30s/f (Firm) **19** Ran SP% **128.1**
Speed ratings (Par 105): **105,104,103,102,101 101,100,99,98,97 94,91,91,89,88 87,86,85,75**
toteswingers 1&2 £7.60, 1&3 £16.20, 2&3 £53.30 CSF £30.81 CT £487.76 TOTE £5.00: £1.40, £2.20, £6.30, £3.50; EX 40.60 Trifecta £322.20 Pool: £1,386.45 - 3.22 winning units..
Owner J G Lumsden & M F Hogan **Bred** Dr Dean Harron **Trained** Nawton, N Yorks

FOCUS
A competitive sprint handicap in which ten raced stands' side and nine went far side. The nearside group held sway. Pretty straightforward form.
T/Plt: £22.20 to a £1 stake. Pool of £55,822.28 - 1,831.85 winning units T/Qpdt: £6.40 to a £1 stake. Pool of £3,116.60 - 358.00 winning units AS

2003 CHURCHILL DOWNS (L-H)
Saturday, May 4

OFFICIAL GOING: Dirt: sloppy; turf: yielding

2033a KENTUCKY DERBY PRESENTED BY YUM! BRANDS (GRADE 1) (3YO) (DIRT) 1m 2f (D)
11:24 (12:00) 3-Y-0 **£867,975** (£245,398; £122,699; £61,349; £36,809)

RPR

1 **Orb (USA)**[35] 1261 3-9-0 0.. JRosario 16 122+
(Claude McGaughey III, U.S.A) *hld up towards rr on outer: hdwy fr over 3f out: drifted lft and rdn to chal over 1f out: led jst ins fnl f: drvn and styd on strly: forged clr* **11/2**[1]

2 2 ½ **Golden Soul (USA)**[35] 3-9-0 0.. RAlbarado 4 116
(Dallas Stewart, U.S.A) *hld up towards rr on inner: hdwy on rail fr 3f out: rdn over 2f out: swtchd out and styd on to go 2nd wl ins fnl f: nt pce of wnr* **35/1**

3 1 **Revolutionary (USA)**[35] 3-9-0 0.. CHBorel 3 114
(Todd Pletcher, U.S.A) *hld up in last trio on inner: stdy hdwy on rail fr 3f out: rdn 2f out: angled out ent fnl f: styd on to go 3rd post* **32/5**[2]

4 hd **Normandy Invasion (USA)**[28] 1404 3-9-0 0................... JJCastellano 5 114
(Chad C Brown, U.S.A) *midfield on inner: hdwy and prom over 4f out: swtchd out and rdn to chal 2 1/2f out: led 2f out: strly pressed and hdd jst ins fnl f: qckly outpcd by wnr: no ex and dropped to 4th post* **93/10**

5 hd **Mylute (USA)**[35] 3-9-0 0.. RosieNapravnik 6 114
(Thomas Amoss, U.S.A) *stdd and hld up in last trio on outer: rdn and hdwy fr 3f out: sn 5th ins fnl f: styd on but nt pce to chal* **153/10**

6 6 **Oxbow (USA)**[21] 1552 3-9-0 0..................................... GaryStevens 2 102+
(D Wayne Lukas, U.S.A) *broke wl fr ins gate: prom on inner: rdn to chal 2f out: no ex ent fnl f: steadily fdd* **249/10**

7 2 **Lines Of Battle (USA)**[35] 1264 3-9-0 0.......................(p) RyanMoore 11 98
(A P O'Brien, Ire) *rn in snatches: racd towards rr: rdn and hdwy fr over 2f out: swtchd to wd outside in st and styd on to go 7th cl home: no threat to ldrs* **32/1**

8 ½ **Will Take Charge (USA)**[49] 3-9-0 0..............................(b) JKCourt 17 97
(D Wayne Lukas, U.S.A) *midfield: rdn and hdwy 3f out: sltly hmpd and lost pl on turn into st: swtchd ins and plugged on u.p but nvr able to chal* **36/1**

9 1 **Charming Kitten (USA)**[21] 1550 3-9-0 0................................ EPrado 15 95
(Todd Pletcher, U.S.A) *midfield on inner: rdn over 2f out: plugged on but sn outpcd and btn* **33/1**

10 hd **Giant Finish (USA)**[42] 3-9-0 0... JLEspinoza 7 94
(Anthony Dutrow, U.S.A) *midfield: rdn 3f out: sn outpcd: plugged on under heavy press but n.d* **39/1**

11 hd **Overanalyze (USA)**[21] 1552 3-9-0 0..................................... RBejarano 9 94
(Todd Pletcher, U.S.A) *towards rr on inner: rdn 3f out: plugged on but nvr a factor* **162/10**

12 hd **Palace Malice (USA)**[21] 1550 3-9-0 0............................(b[1]) MESmith 10 93+
(Todd Pletcher, U.S.A) *led: set fast pce: rdn and hdd 2f out: sn no ex and btn: steadily fdd* **237/10**

13 2 **Java's War (USA)**[21] 1550 3-9-0 0.................................... JRLeparoux 19 89
(Kenneth McPeek, U.S.A) *s.v.s: hld up in last: rdn 3f out: swtchd to outer and plugged on in st but nvr a factor* **215/10**

14 nk **Verrazano (USA)**[28] 1404 3-9-0 0................................... JRVelazquez 14 89+
(Todd Pletcher, U.S.A) *trckd ldr: rdn 3f out: stl ev ch 2f out: no ex and btn ent fnl f: fdd and eased* **87/10**

15 6 ½ **Itsmyluckyday (USA)**[35] 1261 3-9-0 0.................................. ElvisTrujillo 12 76
(Edward Plesa Jr, U.S.A) *prom in midfield: rdn 3f out: no ex and btn over 1f out: fdd and eased* **19/2**

16 2 **Frac Daddy (USA)**[21] 1552 3-9-0 0....................................... VLebron 18 72
(Kenneth McPeek, U.S.A) *midfield on outer: rdn and outpcd 3f out: sn towards rr and btn* **25/1**

17 25 **Goldencents (USA)**[27] 3-9-0 0.. KKrigger 8 72+
(Doug O'Neill, U.S.A) *broke wl and w ldr early: sn stdd bk but remained prom on inner: rdn and btn over 2f out: wknd and eased: t.o* **79/10**[3]

18 3 ¼ **Vyjack (USA)**[28] 1404 3-9-0 0... GKGomez 20 65+
(Rudy Rodriguez, U.S.A) *trckd ldr on outer: rdn and lost pl rapidly 3f out: sn bhd and btn: eased 2f out and t.o* **188/10**

19 nk **Falling Sky (USA)**[21] 1552 3-9-0 0.. LSaez 13 65
(John Terranova II, U.S.A) *prom early: sn relegated to midfield: rdn and lost pl 3f out: sn in rr and btn: eased and dropped to last: t.o* **40/1**

2m 2.89s (1.70) **19** Ran SP% **119.3**
PARI-MUTUEL (all including $2 stakes): WIN 12.80; PLACE (1-2) 7.40, 38.60; SHOW (1-2-3) 5.40, 19.40, 5.40; SF 981.60.
Owner Stuart S Janney III & Phipps Stable **Bred** Stuart S Janney III & Phipps Stable **Trained** USA

FOCUS
The track was officially sloppy on a very wet day. When Bodemeister took the field along in last year's Kentucky Derby, his half-mile split of 45.39 was reported as the fifth fastest in the history of the race, and the 1:09.80 he clocked at the 6f point was given as the fourth quickest. This year, under vastly different conditions, Palace Malice, in blinkers first for the first time and under the same rider as Bodemeister, went even quicker, going 45.33 before matching that 6f split. While Bodemeister clung on for a most gallant second, this time around the pace completely collapsed. Here are the track positions of the first six home at the 6f point: winner (17th), second (15th), third (18th), fourth (6th), fifth (16th) and sixth (2nd).

818 LYON-LA SOIE (R-H)

Saturday, May 4

OFFICIAL GOING: Viscoride: standard

2034a PRIX YAKOBA (H'CAP) (3YO) (VISCORIDE) 1m 2f 165y(P)
12:15 (12:00) 3-Y-0 £7,723 (£3,089; £2,317; £1,544; £772)

RPR

1 **Shabaka (FR)**75 711 3-9-1 0 (p) FranckForesi 14 75
(F Foresi, France) **117/10**

2 2 **Baz (FR)** 3-9-8 0 (p) UmbertoRispoli 11 78
(F-H Graffard, France) **83/10**3

3 3/4 **Varing (FR)**11 1756 3-9-5 0 (b) EddyHardouin 5 74
(P Chatelain, France) **5/1**1

4 1 1/2 **Destiny Highway (FR)**11 1756 3-9-4 0 SylvainRuis 12 70
(Gay Kelleway) *rdn to be prom: racd in cl 2nd on settling: rdn bef st: relegated to 5th 1 1/2f out: rallied u.p and r.o fnl f: got up to be 4th fnl strides* **14/1**

5 snk **Chef Chaudard (FR)**100 3-9-6 0 (b) GregoryBenoist 13 71
(J-C Rouget, France) **5/1**1

6 2 1/2 **Bien Determinee (FR)**51 3-8-0 0 PamelaBoehm(6) 7 53
(X Betron, France) **12/1**

7 1 **Eyebreak (FR)** 3-8-3 0 (b) AlexisDoncieux(5) 15 53
(B Goudot, France) **36/1**

8 2 1/2 **Casa Tua (FR)**14 3-9-0 0 (b) Francois-XavierBertras 10 54
(F Rohaut, France) **44/5**

9 3/4 **Primadonna Girl (IRE)**33 3-8-4 0 JimmyTastayre(3) 4 45
(C Boutin, France) **73/1**

10 3/4 **Echion (IRE)**112 3-9-5 0 NicolasGauffenic(3) 8 59
(F Vermeulen, France) **19/1**

0 **Wilholden (FR)**236 3-7-11 0 (p) SarahCallac(3) 2
(P Nador, France) **89/1**

0 **Maria Kristina (FR)**14 3-8-6 0 TheoBachelot 3
(S Wattel, France) **9/1**

0 **Honor Chop (FR)**47 3-7-11 0 MlleCindyBento(3) 1
(C Martinon, France) **59/1**

0 **Saphir Nonantais (FR)**75 711 3-8-8 0 (b) MickaelForest 6
(W Walton, France) **7/1**2

0 **Vacoas (IRE)**64 3-8-13 0 AurelienLemaitre 9
(F Head, France) **15/1**

2m 16.87s (-1.13) **15** Ran SP% **117.1**
WIN (incl. 1 euro stake): 12.70. PLACES: 3.00, 2.90, 1.90. DF: 46.10. SF: 118.70.
Owner Claude Memran **Bred** San Gabriel Inv. Inc. & R Geringer **Trained** France

1945 SAINT-CLOUD (L-H)

Saturday, May 4

OFFICIAL GOING: Turf: good to soft

2035a PRIX GREFFULHE (GROUP 2) (3YO COLTS & FILLIES) (TURF) 1m 2f
5:55 (12:00) 3-Y-0 £60,243 (£23,252; £11,097; £7,398; £3,699)

RPR

1 **Ocovango**34 1277 3-9-2 0 Pierre-CharlesBoudot 1 112+
(A Fabre, France) *sn led: set gd pce: r.o wl in st: established 2 l ld 2f out: r.o wl fnl f: briefly threatened 100yds out: r.o wl: a on command* **4/5**1

2 1/2 **Bravodino (USA)**31 3-9-2 0 StephanePasquier 3 111+
(J E Pease, France) *settled in 3rd: swtchd to outside early in st: rdn 2 1/2f out: r.o wl u.p 1 1/2f out: fin wl and briefly threatened ldr ent fnl 100yds: no ex fnl 50yds* **33/10**3

3 2 1/2 **Wire To Wire (FR)**39 1192 3-9-2 0 ChristopheSoumillon 5 106
(J-C Rouget, France) *hld up at rr: wnt 4th at end of bk st: slipped through on rail to go 2nd 2f out: travelling easily: rdn 1 1/2f out: no ex: styd on fnl f: jst hld 3rd* **3/1**2

4 shd **Superplex (FR)**16 3-9-2 0 IoritzMendizabal 2 106+
(M Figge, Germany) *hld up in 4th: relegated to 5th bef st: picked up wl 1 1/2f out: r.o wl fnl 100yds: jst missed 3rd* **11/1**

5 1 1/4 **Ivan Grozny (FR)**27 1419 3-9-2 0 FranckBlondel 4 103
(D Rabhi, France) *racd in 2nd: under hold: rdn 2 1/2f out: r.o: no ex fnl 1 1/2f: fdd fnl f* **16/1**

2m 6.96s (-9.04) **5** Ran SP% **118.0**
WIN (incl. 1 euro stake): 1.80. PLACES: 1.10, 1.30. SF: 2.70.
Owner Prince A A Faisal **Bred** Watership Down Stud **Trained** Chantilly, France

FOCUS
The form fits the race averages.

HAMILTON (R-H)

Sunday, May 5

OFFICIAL GOING: Soft (good to soft in places; 7.2)
Wind: Fresh, half behind Weather: Cloudy, bright

2036 TOTEPOOL MOBILE TEXT TOTE TO 89660 H'CAP (DIV I) 6f 5y
1:40 (1:42) (Class 5) (0-70,68) 4-Y-0+ £3,881 (£1,155; £577; £288) Stalls High

Form RPR

30-0 1 **Nasharra (IRE)**15 1692 5-9-5 66 (tp) AmyRyan 3 75
(Kevin Ryan) *dwlt: sn prom on outside: smooth hdwy to ld over 1f out: rdn out fnl f* **7/2**2

050- 2 1 3/4 **Mandalay King (IRE)**197 7246 8-9-3 64 (p) PhillipMakin 6 67
(Marjorie Fife) *in tch: effrt and pushed along over 2f out: chsd wnr over 1f out: kpt on ins fnl f* **12/1**

3-00 3 hd **Pelmanism**9 1800 6-8-13 60 DaleSwift 4 62
(Brian Ellison) *in tch: drvn along 1/2-way: hdwy and edgd rt over 1f out: one pce ins fnl f* **9/1**

33-0 4 2 **Windygoul Lad**15 1686 4-8-12 59 (p) AndrewMullen 1 55
(Michael Smith) *led tl rdn and hdd over 2f out: outpcd fnl f* **11/2**

614- 5 7 **Legal Bond**224 6514 4-9-1 62 (v1) DavidNolan 5 36
(David O'Meara) *t.k.h early: chsd ldr: led over 2f out to over 1f out: sn rdn: wandered and wknd* **7/4**1

0-11 6 9 **Whisky Bravo**12 1748 4-9-7 68 RobertWinston 7 13
(David Brown) *prom: pushed along 1/2-way: wknd wl over 1f out* **4/1**3

1m 15.04s (2.84) **Going Correction** +0.55s/f (Yiel) **6** Ran SP% **111.7**
Speed ratings (Par 103): **103,100,100,97,88 76**
toteswingers 1&2 £5.30, 1&3 £4.40, 2&3 £9.00 CSF £40.21 CT £339.54 TOTE £4.80: £2.60, £5.10; EX 47.40 Trifecta £203.10 Pool: £1,565.78 - 5.78 winning units..
Owner Mr & Mrs Julian And Rosie Richer **Bred** P McCutcheon **Trained** Hambleton, N Yorks

FOCUS
Races on round course increased in distance by approximately 25yds. The first division of a modest sprint saw three horses taken out during the morning and Ambitious Icarus withdrawn close to the off. The winning time was quickest of the three races over the distance on the card. The first three were all on good marks on last year's form.

2037 TOTEPOOL MOBILE TEXT TOTE TO 89660 H'CAP (DIV II) 6f 5y
2:15 (2:15) (Class 5) (0-70,67) 4-Y-0+ £3,881 (£1,155; £577; £288) Stalls High

Form RPR

-403 1 **Economic Crisis (IRE)**19 1596 4-9-7 67 PaddyAspell 10 77
(Alan Berry) *prom: hdwy to ld 2f out: edgd rt and sn rdn clr* **14/1**

1153 2 2 1/2 **Greenhead High**11 1758 5-9-3 63 (v) AdrianNicholls 5 65
(David Nicholls) *led: hrd rdn and hdd 2f out: edgd lft: kpt on ins fnl f: nt pce of wnr* **5/1**3

5-00 3 1 1/4 **Celestial Dawn**16 1665 4-8-13 59 JamesSullivan 2 57
(John Weymes) *dwlt: bhd and outpcd: hdwy on outside 2f out: r.o fnl f: nrst fin* **10/1**

1463 4 nse **Nant Saeson (IRE)**35 1271 4-9-4 64 (p) MichaelO'Connell 6 62
(John Quinn) *cl up: drvn and outpcd wl over 1f out: r.o fnl f: no imp* **7/1**

4215 5 nk **Keep It Dark**9 1801 4-9-0 67 DavidSimmonson(7) 4 64
(Tony Coyle) *t.k.h: hld up in tch: effrt and hdwy over 2f out: rdn and no imp over 1f out* **9/4**1

0044 6 3 1/2 **Bassett Road (IRE)**2 1995 5-9-0 65 (p) GarryWhillans(5) 8 51
(Keith Dalgleish) *chsd ldng gp: hdwy over 2f out: rdn and wknd over 1f out* **9/2**2

20-0 7 2 **Flipping**35 1270 6-8-9 55 PaulMulrennan 1 34
(Nicky Richards) *in tch tl rdn and wknd fr 2f out* **8/1**

050- 8 4 1/2 **Tadalavil**180 7604 8-8-12 58 TomEaves 3 23
(Linda Perratt) *prom: struggling over 2f out: sn lost pl* **14/1**

4250 9 7 **Olynard (IRE)**33 1310 7-8-7 53 oh7 (p) AmyRyan 9
(Michael Mullineaux) *in tch: drvn along and outpcd over 2f out: sn btn* **50/1**

1m 15.66s (3.46) **Going Correction** +0.55s/f (Yiel) **9** Ran SP% **113.6**
Speed ratings (Par 103): **98,94,93,92,92 87,85,79,69**
toteswingers 1&2 £10.40, 1&3 £18.70, 2&3 £8.00 CSF £81.10 CT £744.93 TOTE £19.50: £4.30, £1.90, £2.70; EX 98.00 Trifecta £974.80 Pool: £1,499.17 - 1.15 winning units..
Owner Mr & Mrs T Blane **Bred** Philip Hore Jnr **Trained** Cockerham, Lancs

FOCUS
The second division of the sprint had more runners but clocked a 10lb slower time than the opener. A weak race, with the winner rated back to his 3yo form.

2038 CANCER RESEARCH UK CLAIMING STKS 6f 5y
2:45 (2:45) (Class 6) 4-6-Y-0 £2,045 (£603; £302) Stalls High

Form RPR

6010 1 **Takealookatmenow (IRE)**9 1802 4-8-8 70 (v) AdrianNicholls 4 71
(David Nicholls) *led tl rdn and hdd over 1f out: rallied u.p fnl f: led cl home* **1/1**1

-224 2 hd **Paradise Spectre**32 1316 6-8-13 72 MichaelO'Connell 1 75
(Mrs K Burke) *w ldr: drvn and led over 1f out: edgd lft and kpt on fnl f: hdd cl home* **5/4**2

5-00 3 7 **Spread Boy (IRE)**89 523 6-8-6 48 JordanHibberd(7) 5 53
(Alan Berry) *sn outpcd: sme hdwy wl over 1f out: no ch w first two* **33/1**

1/ 4 14 **Pitt Rivers**595 6186 4-9-5 70 TomEaves 3 14
(Linda Perratt) *taken early to post: rrd s: sn outpcd: no ch fr 1/2-way* **7/1**3

1m 16.3s (4.10) **Going Correction** +0.55s/f (Yiel) **4** Ran SP% **109.9**
Speed ratings: **94,93,84,65**
CSF £2.60 TOTE £1.90; EX 2.60 Trifecta £11.50 Pool: £1,406.33 - 91.21 winning units..
Owner D Nicholls & Mrs S J Barker **Bred** Ian W Glenton **Trained** Sessay, N Yorks

FOCUS
A weak race that concerned only two.

2039 TOTEPOOL MOBILE TANGERINE TREES CONDITIONS STKS (THE SUNDAY £5K BONUS RACE) 5f 4y
3:25 (3:25) (Class 3) 3-Y-0 £9,703 (£2,887; £1,443; £721) Stalls High

Form RPR

01-1 1 **Polski Max**26 1444 3-9-0 97 TonyHamilton 8 102
(Richard Fahey) *in tch: sn pushed along: hdwy to ld appr fnl f: rdn and r.o wl* **7/2**3

35-3 2 3/4 **Lucky Beggar (IRE)**18 1621 3-9-0 101 WilliamCarson 6 99
(Charles Hills) *towards rr: rdn and hdwy over 1f out: chsd wnr ins fnl f: r.o* **6/1**

0-12 3 1 3/4 **Smoothtalkinrascal (IRE)**9 1808 3-8-12 99 DavidBergin(5) 1 96+
(David O'Meara) *hld up in tch: smooth hdwy on outside to ld briefly over 1f out: kpt on same pce ins fnl f* **3/1**2

510- 4 1/2 **Lady Ibrox**184 7518 3-9-0 88 DaleSwift 9 91
(Alan Brown) *cl up stands' rail: effrt and rdn 2f out: kpt on same pce ins fnl f* **28/1**

6-16 5 2 **Top Boy**9 1808 3-9-0 90 MartinDwyer 3 84
(Derek Shaw) *dwlt: sn in tch: rdn over 2f out: outpcd over 1f out: n.d after* **16/1**

01-0 6 1/2 **Hairy Rocket**16 1662 3-8-9 98 1 AdamBeschizza 7 77
(William Haggas) *taken early to post: bhd and sn outpcd: hdwy and swtchd rt over 2f out: rdn and no imp fnl f* **8/1**

3-01 7 2 1/2 **Annunciation**44 1112 3-9-0 99 AdrianNicholls 5 73
(Richard Hannon) *chsd ldrs: rdn over 2f out: wknd over 1f out* **11/4**1

02-3 8 5 **Satsuma**15 1690 3-8-9 89 RobertWinston 2 50
(David Brown) *w ldr tl rdn and wknd over 1f out* **12/1**

11-4 9 1 1/4 **Rhagori Aur**15 1690 3-8-9 83 TomEaves 4 45
(Bryan Smart) *taken early to post: led to over 1f out: sn wknd* **40/1**

1m 1.42s (1.42) **Going Correction** +0.55s/f (Yiel) **9** Ran SP% **118.7**
Speed ratings (Par 103): **110,108,106,105,102 101,97,89,87**
toteswingers 1&2 £4.90, 1&3 £2.80, 2&3 £4.90 CSF £25.70 TOTE £4.00: £1.30, £2.20, £1.70; EX 25.90 Trifecta £102.80 Pool: £2,948.76 - 21.49 winning units..
Owner Market Avenue Racing & Tremousser **Bred** Mike J Beadle **Trained** Musley Bank, N Yorks

FOCUS
A classy event, which had only attracted four and five runners the previous two times it had been staged. It may have been an advantage to be close to the rail early, as the first two raced close to it. The winner built on his Pontefract win.

2040 TOTEPOOL.COM BUTTONHOOK H'CAP — 1m 5f 9y
4:00 (4:03) (Class 3) (0-90,90) 4-Y-0+ **£9,703** (£2,887; £1,443; £721) **Stalls** High

Form RPR
10-1 **1** **O Ma Lad (IRE)**[25] 1463 5-9-4 **87** ... MichaelO'Connell 10 97
(John Quinn) *hld up in tch: smooth hdwy to ld over 2f out: drvn over 1f out: hld on wl fnl f* **4/1**[1]
-340 **2** ¾ **The Tiger**[22] 1547 5-9-7 **90** ... PaulMulrennan 6 99
(Ed Dunlop) *t.k.h: hld up: hdwy and prom over 3f out: drvn over 2f out: styd on to chse wnr wl ins fnl f: r.o* **6/1**[3]
1646 **3** ¾ **Mica Mika (IRE)**[15] 1689 5-8-12 **81** ... TonyHamilton 11 89
(Richard Fahey) *prom: hdwy and ev ch over 2f out: sn drvn: kpt on fnl f* **10/1**
000- **4** 10 **Bolivia (GER)**[226] 6428 7-9-2 **85** ...(be[1]) PhillipMakin 8 78
(Lucy Wadham) *t.k.h early: cl up: led over 5f out to over 2f out: wknd over 1f out* **20/1**
3646 **5** ½ **The Bull Hayes (IRE)**[8] 1843 7-8-9 **85** ow1 ... DavidSimmonson(7) 14 77
(Tony Coyle) *hld up: drvn and hung rt over 4f out: sn outpcd: styd on fnl 2f: nvr rchd ldrs* **14/1**
040- **6** 4½ **Ultimate**[18] 6031 7-8-5 **74** ...(b) BarryMcHugh 7 60
(Brian Ellison) *hld up in tch: rdn and outpcd over 3f out: rallied 2f out: nt pce to chal* **33/1**
0-30 **7** 9 **Hillview Boy (IRE)**[22] 1538 9-8-13 **82** ... TomEaves 12 54
(Jim Goldie) *hld up: stdy hdwy over 3f out: sn rdn: no imp fr 2f out* **8/1**
00-0 **8** 1¼ **Rock A Doodle Doo (IRE)**[22] 1536 6-9-1 **84** ... MartinDwyer 1 54
(Sally Hall) *hld up: drvn along 4f out: no imp fr 3f out* **15/2**
020- **9** 2¼ **Lady Amakhala**[353] 2214 5-8-6 **75** ... PJMcDonald 4 42
(George Moore) *midfield on ins: outpcd over 4f out: sn struggling* **40/1**
00-2 **10** 3½ **Entihaa**[15] 1689 5-8-12 **81** ... RobertWinston 3 43
(Alan Swinbank) *hld up: hdwy and in tch over 3f out: edgd rt and wknd 2f out* **9/2**[2]
251- **11** 11 **Aleksandar**[191] 7380 4-8-0 **72** ... RaulDaSilva(3) 2 17
(Jim Goldie) *prom tl rdn and wknd over 3f out* **22/1**
000- **12** 7 **Persian Peril**[187] 7455 9-9-0 **83** ... RussKennemore 13 18
(Alan Swinbank) *hld up: rdn and edgd rt over 4f out: nvr rchd ldrs* **25/1**
341- **13** 2 **Narcissist (IRE)**[251] 5680 4-8-10 **79** ... JamesSullivan 9 11
(Michael Easterby) *led at decent gallop to over 5f out: rdn and wknd over 3f out* **12/1**
00-0 **14** 89 **Merchant Of Dubai**[22] 1536 8-8-3 **72** ... DuranFentiman 5
(Jim Goldie) *cl up to 1/2-way: sn rdn and wknd: t.o* **16/1**

2m 57.69s (3.79) **Going Correction** +0.475s/f (Yiel) **14 Ran SP% 123.0**
Speed ratings (Par 107): **107,106,106,99,99 96,91,90,89,87 80,75,74,19**
toteswingers 1&2 £6.10, 1&3 £8.40, 2&3 £14.90 CSF £26.28 CT £232.33 TOTE £4.20: £1.60, £3.50, £3.80; EX 35.20 Trifecta £270.80 Pool: £1,860.39 - 5.15 winning units..
Owner Bob McMillan **Bred** Mrs Brid Cosgrove **Trained** Settrington, N Yorks

FOCUS
Plenty took part in this decent staying event but very few made much impression. The pace sorted them out and the third is the best guide.

2041 CASINO ROYALE RACENIGHT NEXT WEEK OPEN MAIDEN STKS — 1m 65y
4:35 (4:37) (Class 5) 3-5-Y-0 **£3,881** (£1,155; £577; £288) **Stalls** Low

Form RPR
2- **1** **Maputo**[350] 2308 3-9-1 0 ... J-PGuillambert 9 88+
(Mark Johnston) *mde all: pushed along 3f out: drvn clr fr 2f out: kpt on wl* **11/4**[2]
443- **2** 3¼ **Pacific Heights (IRE)**[181] 7594 4-10-0 74 ... DaleSwift 1 78
(Brian Ellison) *prom: effrt over 3f out: drvn and chsd (clr) wnr over 1f out: edgd lft: no imp fnl f* **7/1**[3]
03-0 **3** 1½ **Dark Ocean (IRE)**[25] 1486 3-9-1 69 ... PJMcDonald 7 72
(Jedd O'Keeffe) *hld up: stdy hdwy over 3f out: rdn and kpt on fnl f: nvr able to chal* **33/1**
0- **4** 1½ **Carthaginian (IRE)**[370] 1703 4-10-0 0 ... TonyHamilton 10 72
(Richard Fahey) *prom: rdn and outpcd over 3f out: rallied over 1f out: no imp fnl f* **14/1**
0-3 **5** 2 **Ebony Express**[20] 1570 4-10-0 0 ... RobertWinston 6 69
(Alan Swinbank) *cl up: drvn over 3f out: wknd over 1f out* **16/1**
3/2 **6** 13 **Frasers Hill**[27] 1423 4-10-0 0 ... PhillipMakin 4 48
(Roger Varian) *t.k.h: hld up in tch: smooth hdwy and cl up 3f out: chsd wnr and rdn wl over 1f out: edgd lft and fnd little: wknd fnl f* **8/11**[1]
30 **7** 1½ **Naaz (IRE)**[13] 1713 3-9-1 0 ... PaulMulrennan 3 31
(Ed Dunlop) *hld up on ins: struggling over 3f out: btn fnl 2f* **33/1**
8 1½ **Nos Da** 3-8-10 0 ... TomEaves 8 22
(Bryan Smart) *hld up: effrt on outside over 3f out: sn rdn: wknd 2f out* **28/1**
4/ **9** 9 **Born To Shine (USA)**[522] 2785 5-10-0 0 ... RussKennemore 5
(Alan Swinbank) *hld up: struggling over 3f out: sn btn* **66/1**

1m 53.14s (4.74) **Going Correction** +0.475s/f (Yiel)
WFA 3 from 4yo+ 13lb **9 Ran SP% 120.4**
Speed ratings (Par 103): **95,91,90,88,86 73,72,70,61**
toteswingers 1&2 £2.60, 1&3 £9.80, 2&3 £11.20 CSF £22.59 TOTE £4.10: £1.60, £1.30, £6.30; EX 21.00 Trifecta £278.30 Pool: £4,052.61 - 10.91 winning units..
Owner Sheikh Hamdan Bin Mohammed Al Maktoum **Bred** Darley **Trained** Middleham Moor, N Yorks

FOCUS
Probably a fair maiden, from which a few subsequent winners should emerge. The form is rated around the second and third.

2042 FX SIGNS H'CAP — 1m 65y
5:10 (5:10) (Class 5) (0-70,74) 4-Y-0+ **£3,881** (£1,155; £577; £288) **Stalls** Low

Form RPR
006- **1** **Coral Sands (IRE)**[299] 3939 5-8-7 **56** oh4 ... AndrewMullen 1 64
(Alan Swinbank) *t.k.h: chsd ldrs: drvn over 2f out: rallied to ld ins fnl f: edgd lft: drvn out* **25/1**
2-00 **2** 1 **Pravda Street**[15] 1693 8-9-7 **70** ... TomEaves 8 76
(Brian Ellison) *t.k.h: cl up: led gng wl over 2f out: rdn and hdd ins fnl f: kpt on: hld nr fin* **14/1**
0-11 **3** nk **Eutropius (IRE)**[4] 1932 4-9-11 **74** 6ex ... RobertWinston 7 79
(Alan Swinbank) *in tch on outside: hdwy 3f out: rdn and ev ch over 1f out: one pce towards fin* **11/8**[1]
5-60 **4** 2½ **Koo And The Gang (IRE)**[10] 1788 6-8-7 **56** oh5 ...(p) DaleSwift 6 56
(Brian Ellison) *led: rdn and hdd over 2f out: one pce over 1f out* **14/1**
060- **5** ¾ **Just Fabulous**[236] 6124 4-9-4 **67** ... PJMcDonald 3 65
(George Moore) *missed break: t.k.h in rr: hdwy over 2f out: kpt on fnl f: no imp* **7/2**[2]
30-0 **6** 9 **King Of Paradise (IRE)**[26] 1442 4-8-12 **66** ... JasonHart(5) 2 43
(Eric Alston) *plld hrd: in tch: drvn over 2f out: sn btn* **9/1**[3]
12- **7** shd **Uncle Brit**[235] 6131 7-8-13 **62** ... PhillipMakin 5 39
(Malcolm Jefferson) *hld up towards rr: effrt over 3f out: rdn and wknd 2f out* **7/2**[2]
530- **8** 2¼ **Joshua The First**[165] 7203 4-9-7 **70** ... PaulMulrennan 9 42
(Keith Dalgleish) *hld up: drvn over 2f out: sn btn* **12/1**

1m 53.51s (5.11) **Going Correction** +0.475s/f (Yiel) **8 Ran SP% 121.4**
Speed ratings (Par 103): **93,92,91,89,88 79,79,77**
toteswingers 1&2 £17.90, 1&3 £9.00, 2&3 £4.30 CSF £337.82 CT £821.78 TOTE £33.90: £5.40, £3.90, £1.20; EX 142.40 Trifecta £1857.00 Part won. Pool: £2,476.01 - 0.92 winning units..
Owner Mrs J M Penney **Bred** Ger Hayes **Trained** Melsonby, N Yorks
■ Stewards' Enquiry : Andrew Mullen caution: careless riding.

FOCUS
Probably just ordinary form for the level, with the winner and fourth both out of the handicap. The pace seemed uneven and the time was relatively slow.

2043 RED HOT CHILLI PIPERS ON BRAVEHEART H'CAP — 5f 4y
5:45 (5:48) (Class 6) (0-60,60) 4-Y-0+ **£2,045** (£603; £302) **Stalls** High

Form RPR
00-0 **1** **Two Turtle Doves (IRE)**[15] 1681 7-8-10 **54** ... SladeO'Hara(5) 13 64
(Michael Mullineaux) *bhd stands' side: rdn and hdwy over 1f out: edgd rt and led ins fnl f: drvn out* **17/2**
4003 **2** ¾ **Code Six (IRE)**[29] 1388 4-8-12 **51** ...(p) TomEaves 4 58
(Bryan Smart) *w ldr: led over 1f out to ins fnl f: kpt on: hld nr fin* **4/1**[1]
12-0 **3** 1¼ **Here Now And Why (IRE)**[25] 1465 6-9-7 **60** ...(p) DavidAllan 15 63
(Iain Jardine) *in tch: effrt and rdn over 1f out: kpt on ins fnl f* **4/1**[1]
0030 **4** nse **Lord Buffhead**[4] 1929 4-9-3 **56** ...(b[1]) RobbieFitzpatrick 2 58
(Richard Guest) *hld up: hdwy on outside over 1f out: rdn and r.o ins fnl f* **17/2**
-466 **5** ¾ **Wicked Wilma (IRE)**[11] 1758 9-9-1 **54** ... PaddyAspell 7 54
(Alan Berry) *midfield: effrt and hdwy over 1f out: rdn and no imp fnl f* **6/1**[3]
054- **6** 2¼ **Lees Anthem**[180] 7604 6-8-11 **50** ... AndrewMullen 3 42
(Michael Smith) *reluctant to enter stalls: cl up tl rdn and no ex over 1f out* **9/2**[2]
-400 **7** ½ **Sally's Swansong**[31] 1355 7-8-6 **50** ...(b) JasonHart(5) 12 40
(Eric Alston) *s.i.s: bhd and outpcd: hdwy over 1f out: r.o fnl f: n.d* **12/1**
0050 **8** nk **Tenancy (IRE)**[33] 1311 9-8-11 **50** ...(b) DuranFentiman 14 39
(Shaun Harris) *cl up tl rdn and wknd wl over 1f out* **25/1**
40-0 **9** 1 **Verus Delicia (IRE)**[45] 1101 4-9-2 **55** ... StephenCraine 9 40
(Daniel Mark Loughnane) *rrd s: bhd and outpcd: hdwy over 1f out: nvr able to chal* **9/1**
040- **10** ¾ **Cayman Fox**[306] 3730 8-9-0 **53** ... PJMcDonald 11 35
(Linda Perratt) *led to over 1f out: sn rdn and wknd* **33/1**
300- **11** 1 **Ballinargh Girl (IRE)**[180] 7604 5-9-1 **54** ... RobertWinston 10 33
(Danielle McCormick) *in tch: drvn along 1/2-way: wknd over 1f out* **10/1**

1m 3.03s (3.03) **Going Correction** +0.55s/f (Yiel) **11 Ran SP% 127.1**
Speed ratings (Par 101): **97,95,93,93,92 88,88,87,86,84 83**
toteswingers 1&2 £9.20, 1&3 £10.20, 2&3 £6.30 CSF £46.08 CT £167.51 TOTE £12.20: £3.10, £1.70, £2.00; EX 60.30 Trifecta £322.50 Pool: £1,607.76 - 3.73 winning units..
Owner George Cornes **Bred** M Sharkey **Trained** Alpraham, Cheshire
■ Stewards' Enquiry : Slade O'Hara five-day ban: used whip above permitted level without giving mare time to respond (May 19-23)

FOCUS
Considering there was evidence earlier on the card that making your bid close to the stands' rail had been beneficial, it was surprising that the majority of jockeys drawn high didn't utilise a potential bias. Modest form, the winner rated to last year's Chepstow win.
T/Plt: £429.60 to a £1 stake. Pool of £58,293.03 - 99.05 winning units T/Qpdt: £30.30 to a £1 stake. Pool of £3,651.70 - 89.10 winning units RY

2018 NEWMARKET (R-H)
Sunday, May 5

OFFICIAL GOING: Good to firm (9.0)
Wind: Light; half behind Weather: Bright and sunny

2044 QIPCO SUPPORTING BRITISH RACING STKS (H'CAP) — 1m 4f
2:05 (2:06) (Class 2) (0-105,98) 4-Y-0+
£28,012 (£8,388; £4,194; £2,097; £1,048; £526) **Stalls** Centre

Form RPR
213- **1** **No Heretic**[233] 6197 5-9-1 **89** ... WilliamBuick 11 101
(David Simcock) *in tch in midfield: rdn and effrt to chse ldr 2f out: led wl over 1f out: edgd rt jst ins fnl f: styd on wl: drvn out* **12/1**
21-4 **2** 1¼ **Suegioo (FR)**[15] 1689 4-9-0 **88** ...(p) MartinHarley 4 98+
(Marco Botti) *hld up in tch in midfield: effrt whn nt clr run and sltly hmpd 2f out: swtchd lft over 1f out: styd on wl u.p ins fnl f to go 2nd towards fin* **12/1**
010- **3** nk **Opinion (IRE)**[239] 6025 4-9-6 **94** ... RyanMoore 3 104
(Sir Michael Stoute) *chsd ldr: rdn and ev ch wl over 1f out: unable qck u.p ent fnl f: styd on same pce after* **8/1**[3]
103- **4** 2½ **Silver Lime (USA)**[239] 6025 4-9-5 **93** ... JamesDoyle 14 99
(Roger Charlton) *hld up in tch towards rr: hdwy to chse ldrs and pushed rt 2f out: styd on same pce u.p fr over 1f out* **8/1**[3]
51-0 **5** 2¼ **Mubaraza (IRE)**[22] 1547 4-9-3 **91** ... PaulHanagan 10 93+
(Ed Dunlop) *lw: in tch in midfield: drvn and outpcd over 2f out: kpt on again u.p ins fnl f but no threat to ldrs* **12/1**
122- **6** ½ **Stencive**[239] 6025 4-9-10 **98** ... RichardHughes 8 103+
(William Haggas) *lw: stdd s: hld up towards rr: hdwy 4f out: chsd ldrs whn nt clr run and swtchd rt 2f out: no ex u.p over 1f out: wknd ins fnl f: eased cl home: lame* **5/2**[1]
043- **7** 2 **Willie Wag Tail (USA)**[229] 6348 4-9-3 **91** ... JamieSpencer 13 89
(Ed Walker) *lw: stdd and dropped in bhd after s: t.k.h: rdn and effrt over 2f out: no imp u.p fr over 1f out* **9/2**[2]
03/6 **8** 2½ **Apache (IRE)**[29] 1382 5-9-5 **93** ... JosephO'Brien 6 87
(Jane Chapple-Hyam) *swtg: led and clr early: rdn and hdd wl over 1f out: sn btn and lost pl: wknd fnl f* **14/1**
403/ **9** 1½ **All The Aces (IRE)**[29] 6301 8-9-7 **95** ... NeilCallan 12 87
(Nicky Henderson) *in tch in midfield: lost pl and struggling u.p over 3f out: plugged on same pce and wl hld fnl 2f* **40/1**
-641 **10** 4 **Fennell Bay (IRE)**[10] 1774 4-9-0 **88** ... JoeFanning 5 73
(Mark Johnston) *swtg: chsd ldrs: rdn 3f out: lost pl and btn 2f out: wknd over 1f out* **8/1**[3]

The Form Book Flat, Raceform Ltd, Compton, RG20 6NL.

4310 **11** *55* **Wildomar**[29] 1382 4-8-12 **86**.. StevieDonohoe 9
(John Ryan) *hld up in tch in rr: rdn and struggling over 3f out: lost tch over 2f out: t.o and virtually p.u ins fnl f* **100/1**

520- **12** *63* **Nordic Quest (IRE)**[178] 7655 4-8-7 **81**..............................(p) LukeMorris 1
(Gerard Butler) *in tch in midfield: rdn and lost pl over 4f out: wl t.o and virtually p.u over 1f out* **33/1**

2m 30.06s (-1.94) **Going Correction** -0.025s/f (Good) **12** Ran SP% **116.2**
Speed ratings (Par 109): **105,104,103,102,100 100,99,97,96,93 57,15**
toteswingers 1&2 £9.70, 1&3 £15.80, 2&3 £15.70 CSF £143.63 CT £1225.49 TOTE £14.40: £3.90, £3.40, £2.70; EX 124.30 Trifecta £1979.40 Pool: £3,995.26 - 1.51 winning units..
Owner Mrs Fitri Hay **Bred** Belgrave Bloodstock Ltd **Trained** Newmarket, Suffolk
■ Stewards' Enquiry : Richard Hughes one-day ban: careless riding (May 19)

FOCUS
Stands' side track used with stalls on stands' side, except 3.05 & 3.50: Centre. Despite the heavy shower in the middle of racing the previous day, a further 3mm was added overnight and the ground remained Good to Firm; the wind had also dropped significantly. The jockeys reported it was riding fast, but safe enough. A good handicap despite the top weight being rated 7lb below the race ceiling. They went an even gallop and came centre to stands' side in the straight. The form looks set to work out well and has been rated on the positive side.

2045 QATAR BLOODSTOCK DAHLIA STKS (GROUP 3) (F&M) 1m 1f
2:35 (2:35) (Class 1) 4-Y-0+

£34,026 (£12,900; £6,456; £3,216; £1,614; £810) **Stalls** High

Form RPR

215- **1** **Dank**[219] 6633 4-9-1 104.. RyanMoore 4 113
(Sir Michael Stoute) *chsd ldrs: rdn 3f out: pressing ldrs and drvn over 1f out: led fnl 100yds: hld on cl home: all out* **4/1**

611- **2** *shd* **Chigun**[219] 6633 4-8-12 108.. TomQueally 5 110
(Sir Henry Cecil) *t.k.h: chsd ldrs: rdn 2f out: led over 1f out: racd awkwardly u.p and hdd fnl 100yds: kpt on again towards fin: jst hld* **7/2**[3]

212- **3** *3* **Thistle Bird**[219] 6633 5-8-12 107.. JamesDoyle 7 104
(Roger Charlton) *lw: wnt rt s: t.k.h: pressed ldr tl led 7f out: rdn: hung rt and hdd over 1f out: no ex and outpcd ins fnl f* **3/1**[2]

310- **4** *nk* **Bana Wu**[220] 6598 4-8-12 98.. DavidProbert 6 103
(Andrew Balding) *stdd s: hld up in tch in last pair: rdn and effrt over 2f out: outpcd wl over 1f out: rallied and kpt on ins fnl f* **25/1**

422- **5** *3* **Shirocco Star**[197] 7237 4-8-12 112...................................... KierenFallon 2 96
(Hughie Morrison) *t.k.h: chsd ldrs: drvn and effrt 2f out: no ex and outpcd over 1f out: wknd fnl f* **5/2**[1]

-111 **6** *7* **Boonga Roogeta**[1] 2018 4-8-12 86... RosieJessop 1 81
(Peter Charalambous) *led tl 7f out: styd chsng ldr tl over 2f out: struggling whn sltly hmpd 2f out: sn wknd* **16/1**

615- **7** *6* **Semayyel (IRE)**[197] 7237 4-8-12 105............................(b) FrederikTylicki 3 68
(Clive Brittain) *in tch in last pair: rdn and struggling 3f out: wknd over 2f out: wl bhd fnl f* **16/1**

1m 49.69s (-2.01) **Going Correction** -0.025s/f (Good) **7** Ran SP% **111.4**
Speed ratings (Par 113): **107,106,104,103,101 95,89**
toteswingers 1&2 £2.50, 1&3 £2.60, 2&3 £3.10 CSF £17.36 TOTE £4.60: £2.40, £2.30; EX 15.90 Trifecta £50.90 Pool: £5,380.53 - 79.23 winning units..
Owner James Wigan **Bred** London Thoroughbred Services Ltd **Trained** Newmarket, Suffolk

FOCUS
Both Echelon in 2007 and Izzi Top last year took this before enjoying success at Group 1 level, while the 2011 winner I'm A Dreamer landed the 2012 Grade 1 Beverley D. Several of these were expected to come on for the run, including the winner. She posted above-average figures in winning and can rate higher.

2046 TIMEFORM "EUROPEAN CHAMPION TWO-YEAR-OLD" - HARBOUR WATCH H'CAP 6f
3:10 (3:11) (Class 2) 4-Y-0+

£28,012 (£8,388; £4,194; £2,097; £1,048; £526) **Stalls** High

Form RPR

26-4 **1** **Hamza (IRE)**[22] 1537 4-9-4 **101**..(b) NeilCallan 6 113
(Kevin Ryan) *mde all: rdn and 2 l clr over 1f out: styd on wl fnl f: drvn out* **5/1**[1]

231- **2** *2 3/4* **Gabriel's Lad (IRE)**[212] 6835 4-8-12 **95**.............................. KierenFallon 8 98+
(Denis Coakley) *in tch in midfield: rdn and effrt 2f out: hdwy over 1f out: chsd wnr and edgd lft ins fnl f: no imp: kpt on* **5/1**[1]

20-2 **3** *3/4* **Poole Harbour (IRE)**[13] 1726 4-8-7 **90**................................. SeanLevey 5 91
(Richard Hannon) *taken down early: chsd ldrs: rdn and effrt 2f out: chsd wnr over 1f out: lost 2nd and carried lft ins fnl f: styd on same pce* **12/1**

6-42 **4** *1* **Shropshire (IRE)**[22] 1537 5-8-11 **99**........................ MatthewLawson(5) 7 102+
(Charles Hills) *swtg: stdd s: t.k.h: hld up in tch in rr: hdwy and nt clr run over 1f out: swtchd lft and stl n.m.r 1f out: gap opened and styd on fnl 100yds: nt threaten ldrs* **8/1**

516- **5** *hd* **Doctor Parkes**[128] 8272 7-8-5 **88**....................................... DavidProbert 15 85
(Stuart Williams) *swtg: chsd wnr tl over 1f out: no ex u.p and one pce fnl f* **50/1**

645 **6** *1 1/4* **Swiss Cross**[5] 1913 6-8-7 **90**...(t) PaulHanagan 10 83
(Phil McEntee) *swtg: chsd ldrs: drvn 2f out: unable qck over 1f out: styng on same pce and hld whn nt clr run and hmpd ins fnl f* **25/1**

4643 **7** *3/4* **Hitchens (IRE)**[22] 1537 8-9-10 **107**..................................... RichardHughes 4 98
(David Barron) *lw: stdd s: hld up in tch in rr: rdn and hdwy over 1f out: no imp ins fnl f* **11/2**[2]

313- **8** *1 1/4* **Goldream**[234] 6165 4-8-7 **90**.. WilliamBuick 3 77
(Robert Cowell) *in tch in midfield: clsd to chse ldrs 2f: rdn and no hdwy over 1f out: wknd ins fnl f* **14/1**

202- **9** *1 1/2* **Ladyship**[220] 6602 4-8-13 **96**... RyanMoore 13 89+
(Sir Michael Stoute) *in tch in midfield: effrt against stands' rail but nvr enough room fr over 1f out: unable to make prog and btn whn hmpd and eased ins fnl f* **6/1**[3]

00-0 **10** *hd* **Johannes (IRE)**[22] 1537 10-8-4 **92**............................ GeorgeChaloner(5) 2 73
(Richard Fahey) *taken down early: bhd: rdn over 2f out: no hdwy tl swtchd rt jst over 1f out: kpt on ins fnl f: nvr trbld ldrs* **33/1**

-2U0 **11** *1* **Whaileyy (IRE)**[66] 834 5-9-1 **98**...(b) AdamKirby 12 76
(Marco Botti) *in tch in midfield: rdn and no rspnse over 1f out: drvn and wknd 1f out* **20/1**

000- **12** *1/2* **Pearl Ice**[225] 6468 5-8-12 **95**.. GrahamGibbons 9 71
(David Barron) *chsd ldrs: rdn 2f out: wknd u.p ent fnl f* **16/1**

2201 **13** *2* **Al Khan (IRE)**[19] 1599 4-8-0 **83** oh2..................................(p) LukeMorris 1 53
(Violet M Jordan) *swtg: stdd s: hld up in rr: rdn and no hdwy wl over 1f out* **50/1**

02-0 **14** *2 1/2* **Amadeus Wolfe Tone (IRE)**[22] 1542 4-8-13 **96**.....(p) JamieSpencer 11 58
(Jamie Osborne) *in tch in midfield: rdn and struggling whn swtchd rt over 1f out: wknd over 1f out* **16/1**

1-43 **15** *1* **Living Leader**[32] 1318 4-7-11 **83** oh4................................ DarrenEgan(3) 14 42
(Nick Littmoden) *in tch in rr against stands' rail: rdn and no hdwy whn hung rt wl over 1f out: sn wknd* **28/1**

1m 10.39s (-1.81) **Going Correction** -0.025s/f (Good) **15** Ran SP% **119.2**
Speed ratings (Par 109): **111,107,106,105,104 103,102,100,98,98 96,96,93,90,88**
toteswingers 1&2 £5.60, 1&3 £9.00, 2&3 £7.00 CSF £26.38 CT £286.95 TOTE £5.60: £2.10, £2.20, £3.30; EX 28.40 Trifecta £190.90 Pool: £6,242.63 - 24.51 winning units..
Owner Mubarak Al Naemi **Bred** Castlemartin Stud And Skymarc Farm **Trained** Hambleton, N Yorks
■ Stewards' Enquiry : Kieren Fallon four-day ban: careless riding (May 19-22)

FOCUS
A hot sprint handicap and the form looks solid, for all that the winner had the run of things.

2047 QIPCO 1000 GUINEAS STKS (THE 200TH RUNNING) (BRITISH CHAMPIONS SERIES) (GROUP 1) (FILLIES) 1m
3:50 (3:52) (Class 1) 3-Y-O

£241,584 (£91,590; £45,837; £22,833; £11,459; £5,751) **Stalls** Centre

Form RPR

10-2 **1** **Sky Lantern (IRE)**[18] 1622 3-9-0 111.............................. RichardHughes 7 112
(Richard Hannon) *t.k.h: hld up in tch in midfield: rdn and gd hdwy over 1f out: drvn to chal ins fnl f: r.o wl to ld fnl 50yds* **9/1**

111- **2** *1/2* **Just The Judge (IRE)**[204] 7052 3-9-0 107.................... JamieSpencer 13 111+
(Charles Hills) *lw: travelled wl: chsd ldrs: jnd ldr gng wl 2f out: rdn over 1f out: drvn to ld ins fnl f: hdd and no ex fnl 50yds* **7/1**[3]

3 *1 1/2* **Moth (IRE)**[28] 1412 3-9-0 0... JosephO'Brien 11 108+
(A P O'Brien, Ire) *w'like: leggy: stdd s: hld up in rr: rdn and effrt but stl plenty to do 2f out: hdwy and swtchd lft over 1f out: n.m.r and wnt between horses 1f out: r.o strly fnl f: snatched 3rd on post* **9/1**

12-3 **4** *nse* **Winning Express (IRE)**[18] 1622 3-9-0 104.................... FrannyNorton 2 107
(Ed McMahon) *lw: travelled wl: chsd ldr tl led 2f out: sn pressed and rdn: battled on wl tl hdd ins fnl f: no ex and btn fnl 75yds: lost 3rd on post* **33/1**

50-3 **5** *nk* **Snow Queen (IRE)**[21] 1557 3-9-0 100...........................(p) RyanMoore 15 106
(A P O'Brien, Ire) *lw: stdd s: bhd: pushed along 1/2-way: stl 14th wl over 1f out: hdwy past btn horses jst over 1f out: r.o strly ins fnl f: nt rch ldrs* **20/1**

10-1 **6** *shd* **Maureen (IRE)**[15] 1676 3-9-0 106...................................... OlivierPeslier 10 106
(Richard Hannon) *stdd after s: hld up in last quartet: nt clr run over 2f out: stl only 11th whn rdn wl over 1f out: hdwy and edging rt over 1f out: r.o strly ins fnl f: nt rch ldrs* **16/1**

12-1 **7** *2* **What A Name (IRE)**[31] 1358 3-9-0 111..... Christophe-PatriceLemaire 12 101
(M Delzangles, France) *lengthy: lw: hld up in tch: rdn and unable qck wl over 1f out: no imp and plugged on same pce fnl f* **7/2**[2]

0-51 **8** *3/4* **Masarah (IRE)**[4] 1918 3-9-0 95.. FrederikTylicki 5 99
(Clive Brittain) *led tl 2f out: sn drvn and no ex: outpcd and btn over 1f out: wknd ins fnl f* **100/1**

1-1 **9** *1/2* **Hot Snap**[18] 1622 3-9-0 113.. TomQueally 14 98
(Sir Henry Cecil) *in tch in midfield: rdn 3f out: drvn and no imp over 2f out: changing legs on downhill run over 1f out: plugged on but no threat to ldrs fnl f* **5/2**[1]

112- **10** *8* **Roz**[219] 6635 3-9-0 104... JimCrowley 3 79
(Harry Dunlop) *hld up wl in tch in midfield: rdn over 2f out: sn struggling: wknd over 1f out:* **33/1**

20-2 **11** *2 1/4* **Agent Allison**[15] 1676 3-9-0 103.. WilliamBuick 9 74
(Peter Chapple-Hyam) *hld up in tch in last quartet: rdn and short-lived effrt jst over 2f out: btn wl over 1f out: wknd fnl f* **25/1**

16- **12** *nk* **Ollie Olga (USA)**[219] 6635 3-9-0 104.................................. MartinHarley 1 73
(Mick Channon) *wl in tch in midfield: rdn over 2f out: drvn and btn over 1f out: fdd fnl f* **40/1**

1 **13** *3 1/2* **Celtic Filly (IRE)**[19] 3-9-0 89.. MickaelBarzalona 6 64
(E J O'Neill, France) *str: chsd ldrs tl rdn and lost pl jst over 2f out: bhd over 1f out* **100/1**

3- **14** *29* **Rasmeyaa (IRE)**[190] 7418 3-9-0 0.. PatSmullen 4
(D K Weld, Ire) *tall: str: t.k.h: chsd ldrs tl rdn and lost pl over 2f out: wl bhd over 1f out: t.o* **9/1**

214- **15** *10* **Diaminda (IRE)**[241] 5979 3-9-0 99..................................... PaulHanagan 8
(Alan Jarvis) *in tch in midfield: rdn 3f out: sn dropped out: t.o over 1f out: burst blood vessel* **50/1**

1m 36.38s (-2.22) **Going Correction** -0.025s/f (Good) **15** Ran SP% **120.0**
Speed ratings (Par 110): **110,109,108,107,107 107,105,104,104,96 94,93,90,61,51**
toteswingers 1&2 £9.20, 1&3 £12.10, 2&3 £9.80 CSF £65.37 CT £603.44 TOTE £10.00: £2.70, £3.40, £3.10; EX 92.50 Trifecta £597.80 Pool: £15,975.31 - 20.04 winning units..
Owner B Keswick **Bred** Tally-Ho Stud **Trained** East Everleigh, Wilts
■ Stewards' Enquiry : Jamie Spencer three-day ban: used whip with giving filly time to respond (May 19-21)

FOCUS
The 200th running of the first fillies' Classic of the season and, apart from Rosdhu Queen and Certify, most of the winners of the big juvenile races and significant trials this season took their chance. The field raced in the centre of the track and the pace was fairly even. There was depth to the race and the form looks up to scratch, although the favourite disappointed. The form is set around the race averages and the sixth.

2048 MAKFI FUTURE STARS MAIDEN STKS 5f
4:25 (4:26) (Class 4) 2-Y-O **£9,703** (£2,887; £1,443; £721) **Stalls** High

Form RPR

4 **1** **Green Door (IRE)**[16] 1669 2-9-5 0.. JimCrowley 4 85
(Olly Stevens) *lw: mde all: rdn and fnd ex over 1f out: in command and styd on wl fnl f: rdn out* **9/2**[3]

2 *1 1/4* **Windfast (IRE)** 2-9-5 0.. KierenFallon 9 81+
(Brian Meehan) *w'like: scope: lw: chsd ldrs: rdn and effrt over 1f out: styng on whn rn green and wnt rt ins fnl f: chsd wnr fnl 100yds: kpt on but no threat to wnr* **7/2**[2]

3 *1 1/4* **Nathr (USA)** 2-9-5 0... RyanMoore 7 76+
(Charles Hills) *w'like: in tch in midfield: pushed along but nt enough room against stands' rail over 1f out: hdwy ins fnl f: wnt 3rd wl ins fnl f: kpt on* **11/2**

4 *1 1/2* **Wind Fire (USA)** 2-9-0 0.. JamieSpencer 3 66+
(David Brown) *cmpt: chsd ldrs: short of room and shuffled bk towards rr ent fnl 2f: rallied and hdwy 1f out: swtchd rt ins fnl f: styd on wl towards fin* **10/1**

5 *nk* **Crowdmania** 2-9-5 0... JoeFanning 10 70+
(Mark Johnston) *str: awkward leaving stalls and slowly away: in tch in last: nt clr run on stands' rail tl ins fnl f: styd on wl fnl 100yds: nvr trbld ldrs* **12/1**

6 **6** *1/2* **The Smart One (IRE)**[16] 1669 2-9-5 0.................................. MartinHarley 2 68
(Mick Channon) *lw: chsd wnr: drvn and unable qck over 1f out: lost 2nd ins fnl f: wknd wl ins fnl f* **11/1**

7 2 3/4 **Piazon** 2-9-5 0 WilliamBuick 8 58+
(Michael Bell) *str: bit bkwd: rn green and pushed along in rr early: hdwy over 2f out: rdn and unable qck over 1f out: wknd ins fnl f* **14/1**

8 *shd* **Anjaal** 2-9-5 0 PaulHanagan 6 57
(Richard Hannon) *w'like: scope: tall: lengthy: jostled sn after s: in tch towards rr: rdn and hdwy wl over 1f out: no imp ent fnl f: wknd ins fnl f* **11/4**[1]

9 3/4 **Zain Zone (IRE)** 2-9-5 0 LukeMorris 5 55
(Gerard Butler) *lw: in tch: chsd ldrs 3f out: n.m.r wl over 1f out: sn drvn and outpcd over 1f out: wknd ins fnl f* **50/1**

10 2 1/4 **Wiki Tiki** 2-9-0 0 DavidProbert 1 42
(Stuart Williams) *leggy: tall: unruly in paddock: chsd ldrs: rdn 2f out: lost 3rd and btn ent fnl f: wknd and edgd lft ins fnl f* **50/1**

59.7s (0.60) **Going Correction** -0.025s/f (Good) **10** Ran SP% **118.2**
Speed ratings (Par 95): **94,92,90,87,87 86,81,81,80,76**
toteswingers 1&2 £4.00, 1&3 £6.00, 2&3 £4.20 CSF £20.96 TOTE £6.00: £2.40, £2.00, £1.70; EX 21.50 Trifecta £118.80 Pool: £3,356.29 - 21.17 winning units..
Owner David Redvers **Bred** Mrs Sue Lenehan **Trained** Chiddingfold, Surrey
■ Stewards' Enquiry : Jim Crowley one-day ban: failed to ride to draw (May 19)

FOCUS
An interesting maiden with previous experience proving the key. The form may not prove quite up to the race standard, but winnes should come out of it.

2049 TWEENHILLS PRETTY POLLY STKS (LISTED RACE) 1m 2f
5:00 (5:00) (Class 1) 3-Y-O
£22,684 (£8,600; £4,304; £2,144; £1,076; £540) **Stalls High**

Form RPR

31- **1** **Talent**[240] [6017] 3-8-12 82 JimCrowley 3 99
(Ralph Beckett) *t.k.h: chsd ldrs: drvn and chsd ldr over 1f out: sustained effrt u.p to ld wl ins fnl f: styd on wl: rdn out* **11/1**

1-0 **2** 1/2 **Lady Nouf**[18] [1622] 3-8-12 88 RichardHughes 1 98
(William Haggas) *lw: led: rdn and edgd lft fr over 1f out and racing against stands' rail ins fnl f: hdd and no ex wl ins fnl f* **7/2**[2]

1- **3** 2 1/4 **Madame Defarge (IRE)**[194] [7312] 3-8-12 80 JamieSpencer 7 93
(Michael Bell) *w'like: scope: tall: lengthy: stdd s: hld up in tch in rr: rdn and effrt to wl over 1f out: chsd ldrs whn nt clr run and swtchd rt jst ins fnl f: styd on same pce after* **5/1**

6 **4** 2 **Magic Of Reality (FR)**[16] [1671] 3-8-12 0 TomQueally 8 89
(Sir Henry Cecil) *t.k.h: hld up in tch in midfield: rdn and chsng ldrs over 1f out: keeping on same pce whn carried rt jst ins fnl f: no ex and wknd towards fin* **6/1**

1-23 **5** 2 3/4 **Cruck Realta**[4] [1918] 3-8-12 93 MartinHarley 2 87+
(Mick Channon) *t.k.h: hld up in tch in midfield: hdwy to chse ldrs 4f out: rdn and unable qck wl over 1f out: wknd ins fnl f: sddle slipped* **4/1**[3]

62- **6** 4 **Vanity Rules**[225] [6489] 3-8-12 0 WilliamBuick 6 79+
(John Gosden) *lw: t.k.h: sn chsng ldr: rdn: carried rt: lost 2nd and hmpd over 1f out: sn btn: wl hld and eased ins fnl f* **10/3**[1]

503- **7** 5 **Poitin**[172] [7706] 3-8-12 67 PaulHanagan 5 66?
(Harry Dunlop) *t.k.h: hld ip in tch: rdn and struggling over 2f out: wknd 2f out: bhd fnl f* **66/1**

10-3 **8** 59 **Concise**[22] [1546] 3-8-12 84 RyanMoore 4
(Ed Dunlop) *t.k.h: chsd ldrs tl rdn and lost pl over 2f out: sn bhd: virtually p.u ins fnl f: t.o* **12/1**

2m 4.14s (-1.66) **Going Correction** -0.025s/f (Good) **8** Ran SP% **113.8**
Speed ratings (Par 107): **105,104,102,101,99 95,91,44**
toteswingers 1&2 £6.90, 1&3 £7.90, 2&3 £3.90 CSF £48.87 TOTE £8.90: £2.80, £1.40, £2.00; EX 71.10 Trifecta £395.50 Pool: £4,351.48 - 8.25 winning units..
Owner J L Rowsell & M H Dixon **Bred** Ashbrittle Stud & M H Dixon **Trained** Kimpton, Hants

FOCUS
The best recent winner of this Listed contest by far was Ouija Board and this year's line-up looked unlikely to reach the heights of that prolific winning mare. The pace was steady but the race did throw up a couple of promising performances with the future in mind. The form is rated around the race averages.

2050 QATAR RACING H'CAP (THE SUNDAY £5K BONUS RACE) 1m 2f
5:35 (5:35) (Class 2) (0-100,90) 3-Y-O
£12,450 (£3,728; £1,864; £932; £466; £234) **Stalls High**

Form RPR

51-1 **1** **Soviet Rock (IRE)**[17] [1641] 3-9-3 86 DavidProbert 6 97
(Andrew Balding) *mde all: rdn: edging lft but kpt finding ex u.p over 1f out: hld on gamely fnl f: rdn out* **15/8**[1]

600- **2** 3/4 **Salutation (IRE)**[213] [6815] 3-8-12 81 FrannyNorton 8 91
(Mark Johnston) *lw: t.k.h: chsd ldrs: rdn and effrt ent fnl 2f: drvn and chsd wnr ins fnl f: kpt on* **25/1**

2-21 **3** 2 1/4 **High Troja (IRE)**[30] [1365] 3-8-12 81 RyanMoore 5 86
(Ed Dunlop) *chsd ldrs: rdn to chse ldr 2f out: no ex jst ins fnl f: wknd wl ins fnl f* **7/2**[3]

250- **4** *nse* **Makafeh**[204] [7053] 3-9-5 88 [1] KierenFallon 2 93
(Luca Cumani) *ponied to s and taken down early: hld up in tch in midfield: rdn and effrt 2f out: chsd ldrs 1f out: styd on same pce ins fnl f* **11/1**

-222 **5** 1 1/4 **Carry On Sydney**[8] [1847] 3-9-4 87 RichardHughes 7 91
(Richard Hannon) *lw: stdd s: hld up in tch in rr: rdn and effrt nrest stands' rail jst over 2f out: keeping on same pce and swtchd rt over 1f out: plugged on but wl hld fnl 100yds* **11/4**[2]

1212 **6** 9 **Naru (IRE)**[10] [1609] 3-9-0 83 NeilCallan 4 68
(James Tate) *chsd ldr tl 2f out: sn drvn and btn: wknd over 1f out* **12/1**

0004 **7** 27 **Pure Excellence**[17] [1645] 3-9-7 90 JoeFanning 1 21
(Mark Johnston) *in tch in midfield: rdn 2f out: fnd nil and sn btn: wl bhd and eased ins fnl f: t.o* **16/1**

03-1 **8** 42 **Barnaby Brook (CAN)**[60] [895] 3-8-6 75 LukeMorris 3
(Nick Littmoden) *hld up in tch in rr: rdn 3f out: sn lost tch: t.o and eased fnl 2f* **14/1**

2m 3.97s (-1.83) **Going Correction** -0.025s/f (Good) **8** Ran SP% **116.1**
Speed ratings (Par 105): **106,105,103,103,102 95,73,40**
toteswingers 1&2 £11.70, 1&3 £2.10, 2&3 £15.30 CSF £52.36 CT £157.13 TOTE £2.70: £1.20, £4.90, £1.50; EX 56.10 Trifecta £379.40 Pool: £3,889.75 - 7.68 winning units..
Owner Jackie & George Smith **Bred** Grangecon Stud **Trained** Kingsclere, Hants

FOCUS
A decent 3yo handicap in which the pace was fair and the time was 0.17 seconds faster than the Pretty Polly. The winner should continue to progress.
T/Jkpt: Not won. T/Plt: £539.90 to a £1 stake. Pool of £198,117.59 - 267.86 winning units
T/Qpdt: £67.30 to a £1 stake. Pool of £11,907.70 - 130.90 - winning units SP

SALISBURY (R-H)
Sunday, May 5

OFFICIAL GOING: Good to firm (9.2)
Wind: Virtually nil Weather: Cloudy with sunny periods

2051 BETFRED "GOALS GALORE" MAIDEN STKS 6f
1:50 (1:51) (Class 5) 3-Y-O+
£4,204 (£1,251; £625; £312) **Stalls Low**

Form RPR

43- **1** **Secondo (FR)**[202] [7110] 3-9-3 0 GeorgeBaker 10 84+
(Roger Charlton) *stdd in rr: smooth hdwy but nt best of runs fr jst over 2f out: swtchd lft and qcknd up wl jst over 1f out: led fnl 100yds: comf* **4/1**[1]

6 **2** 3/4 **Marjong**[16] [1666] 3-8-13 0 ow1 SebSanders 1 75
(Simon Dow) *mid-div: hdwy over 2f out: rdn wl over 1f out: led ent fnl f: hdd fnl 100yds: kpt on but nt pce of wnr* **20/1**

0- **3** 1 1/4 **Royal Challis**[316] [3397] 3-9-3 0 PatDobbs 7 75
(Richard Hannon) *prom: rdn wl over 1f out: ev ch ent fnl f: kpt on same pce fnl 120yds* **10/1**[3]

2- **4** 3 1/4 **Secretly**[260] [5352] 3-8-12 0 CathyGannon 2 60+
(Henry Candy) *trckd ldrs: rdn 2f out: kpt on same pce* **4/1**[1]

64- **5** *hd* **Apricot Sky**[185] [7498] 3-9-3 0 DaneO'Neill 5 64
(Henry Candy) *led: rdn 2f out: hdd ent fnl f: fdd fnl 120yds* **5/1**[2]

6 1 1/2 **Mediska** 3-8-12 0 FergusSweeney 12 55
(Henry Candy) *s.i.s: towards rr: styd on fr over 1f out: nvr threatened* **40/1**

-42 **7** *nse* **Sibaya**[47] [1078] 3-8-7 0 RobertTart[(5)] 9 54
(Roger Charlton) *trckd ldrs: rdn and ev ch 2f out: sn drifted lft and one pce* **20/1**

6 **8** 1/2 **Ovatory**[16] [1660] 3-9-3 0 GrahamLee 13 58
(Amanda Perrett) *mid-div: rdn over 2f out: no imp* **14/1**

65- **9** *nk* **Lady Vermeer**[274] [4792] 3-8-12 0 RichardKingscote 3 52+
(Ralph Beckett) *mid-div: pushed along over 3f out: sn rdn: nvr any imp* **4/1**[1]

45-3 **10** 2 **Talqaa**[10] [1773] 3-8-12 76 SamHitchcott 8 45
(Mick Channon) *prom: rdn 2f out: wknd fnl f* **12/1**

0000 **11** 2 3/4 **Surrey Dream (IRE)**[42] [1162] 4-9-13 40 (p) KieranO'Neill 11 42
(John Bridger) *mid-div: rdn over 2f out: wknd jst over 1f out* **200/1**

12 1 **Shikamoo** 3-8-12 0 RichardThomas 6 33
(Dr Jeremy Naylor) *s.i.s: a towards rr* **200/1**

13 6 **Light Catcher** 3-8-12 0 JimmyFortune 4 14
(Andrew Balding) *mid-div: struggling over 3f out: sn in rr* **12/1**

1m 14.43s (-0.37) **Going Correction** -0.10s/f (Good)
WFA 3 from 4yo 10lb **13** Ran SP% **120.8**
Speed ratings (Par 103): **98,97,95,91,90 88,88,88,87,84 81,79,71**
toteswingers 1&2 £13.50, 1&3 £16.90, 2&3 £24.70 CSF £91.79 TOTE £4.90: £1.70, £4.40, £4.50; EX 87.10 Trifecta £491.30 Part won. Pool: £655.07 - 0.42 winning units..
Owner D J Deer **Bred** John Deer **Trained** Beckhampton, Wilts

FOCUS
A total of 10mm of water had been put on the track between Wednesday and Saturday and the going was given as good to firm (GoingStick 9.2). Probably a fair maiden, but there are mixed messages about the form. The winner was value for a bit extra.

2052 BETFRED "CITY BOWL" H'CAP 1m 6f 21y
2:20 (2:20) (Class 3) (0-95,93) 4-Y-O+
£13,695 (£4,100; £2,050; £1,025; £512; £257)

Form RPR

210- **1** **Sun Central (IRE)**[239] [6025] 4-9-7 92 SebSanders 12 101+
(William Haggas) *in tch: tk clsr order over 5f out: rdn to dispute 2nd over 2f out: no imp on ldr tl str run fnl 120yds: drifted rt nring fin: led fnl strides* **4/1**[1]

140- **2** *shd* **Mysterious Man (IRE)**[211] [6896] 4-8-13 84 JimmyFortune 3 93+
(Andrew Balding) *racd keenly: trckd ldrs: rdn to chse ldr over 2f out: edgd lft ins fnl f: str run to ld fnl 75yds: slt bump whn hdd fnl strides* **9/2**[2]

05-4 **3** 1 1/2 **Scatter Dice (IRE)**[11] [1766] 4-9-1 91 MichaelJMMurphy[(5)] 8 98
(Mark Johnston) *led: kicked 2 l clr wl over 1f out: rdn ent fnl f: no ex whn hdd fnl 75yds* **8/1**

00-1 **4** 1 3/4 **Seaside Sizzler**[18] [1615] 6-9-2 86 (vt) RichardKingscote 1 91
(Ralph Beckett) *mid-div: rdn and hdwy over 2f out: styd on same pce fnl f* **10/1**

101- **5** 1 3/4 **Castilo Del Diablo (IRE)**[199] [7195] 4-9-1 86 GrahamLee 4 88+
(David Simcock) *mid-div: rdn 3f out: styd on but nt pce to get involved* **5/1**[3]

124- **6** 2 3/4 **Mawaqeet (USA)**[227] [6415] 4-9-6 91 (v) DaneO'Neill 10 89+
(Sir Michael Stoute) *hld up towards rr: rdn into midfield 3f out: no further imp fnl 2f* **8/1**

000- **7** 1 3/4 **Spice Fair**[261] [5306] 6-8-13 83 LiamKeniry 13 79+
(Mark Usher) *hld up bhd: hdwy over 3f out: rdn over 2f out: nvr rchd ldrs: styd on same pce fr over 1f out* **28/1**

441 **8** 6 **Ascendant**[40] [1182] 7-8-8 83 (v) RobertTart[(5)] 5 70
(J R Jenkins) *mid-div: effrt 3f out: nvr threatened: fdd fnl f* **28/1**

-110 **9** 1/2 **Foster's Road**[9] [1805] 4-8-5 76 SamHitchcott 11 63
(Mick Channon) *mid-div: rdn wl over 3f out: wknd 2f out* **33/1**

121- **10** 4 1/2 **Lady Rosamunde**[317] [3341] 5-9-2 86 (p) TedDurcan 2 66
(Marcus Tregoning) *towards rr: hdwy to trck ldrs after 2f: rdn wl over 2f out: wknd over 1f out: eased ins fnl f* **10/1**

010- **11** 2 **The Betchworth Kid**[64] [7367] 8-9-9 93 HayleyTurner 7 71
(Michael Bell) *hld up towards rr: pushed along over 4f out: rdn over 3f out: nvr any imp* **20/1**

241- **12** 1 3/4 **Al Saham**[274] [4796] 4-9-3 88 HarryBentley 9 63
(Saeed bin Suroor) *racd keenly: trckd ldrs: wnt 2nd after 5f tl rdn over 3f out: wknd 2f out* **9/1**

050- **13** 1/2 **Rosslyn Castle**[65] [6875] 4-9-6 91 GeorgeBaker 6 65
(Gary Brown) *w ldr for 5f: trckd ldrs: rdn 3f out: wknd 2f out: eased fnl f* **33/1**

3m 1.83s (-5.57) **Going Correction** -0.20s/f (Firm)
WFA 4 from 5yo+ 1lb **13** Ran SP% **122.8**
Speed ratings (Par 107): **107,106,106,105,104 102,101,98,97,95 94,93,92**
toteswingers 1&2 £4.30, 1&3 £10.20, 2&3 £9.90 CSF £20.83 CT £140.44 TOTE £5.00: £2.20, £2.30, £3.20; EX 23.10 Trifecta £110.80 Pool: £783.86 - 5.30 winning units..
Owner Lael Stable **Bred** Lael Stables **Trained** Newmarket, Suffolk
■ Stewards' Enquiry : Seb Sanders one-day ban: careless riding (May 19)

FOCUS
Flip start. There wasn't much pace on early. The third sets the standard with the first two improving.

2053 BETFRED "THE BONUS KING" FILLIES' CONDITIONS STKS 5f
2:55 (2:55) (Class 3) 2-Y-O £7,762 (£2,310; £1,154; £577) Stalls Low

Form				RPR
2	1		**Fig Roll**22 1541 2-8-11 0 PatDobbs 7 (Richard Hannon) *outpcd in last pair: hdwy over 2f out: chsng ldrs whn gap appeared ent fnl f: led fnl 120yds: r.o strly* **2/1**1	84+
301	2	1 1/4	**Limegrove**10 1778 2-8-11 0 JimmyFortune 1 (David Evans) *led: rdn whn drifted lft 2f out: kpt on but no ex whn hdd fnl 120yds* **7/1**3	79
1	3	nse	**Alutiq (IRE)**27 1421 2-8-11 0 HarryBentley 6 (Eve Johnson Houghton) *in tch: chsd ldrs 2f out: sn rdn: kpt on ins fnl f* **2/1**1	79
32	4	2 1/2	**Kidmenot (IRE)**13 1724 2-8-11 0 LiamJones 3 (J S Moore) *chsd ldr: rdn and ev ch whn edgd rt 1f out: no ex fnl 120yds* **25/1**	70
	5	hd	**Got To Dance** 2-8-8 0 RichardKingscote 8 (Ralph Beckett) *racd green: s.i.s: outpcd in last: kpt on nicely fnl f: n.d* **20/1**	66+
631	6	3/4	**Intense Feeling (IRE)**34 1285 2-8-11 0 CathyGannon 5 (David Evans) *chsd ldr: rdn over 2f out: no ex fnl 120yds* **25/1**	66
51	7	3 1/4	**Outback Lover (IRE)**39 1208 2-8-11 0 LiamKeniry 4 (J S Moore) *stdd bhd ldrs after 1f: rdn over 2f out: wknd ent fnl f* **40/1**	55
1	8	8	**Lady Frances**10 1792 2-9-0 0 SilvestreDeSousa 2 (Mark Johnston) *s.i.s: in tch: stmbld over 3f out: sn struggling: swtchd lft and wknd 2f out* **4/1**2	65+

1m 0.63s (-0.37) **Going Correction** -0.10s/f (Good) 8 Ran SP% **114.1**
Speed ratings (Par 94): **98,96,95,91,91 90,85,72**
toteswingers 1&2 £5.10, 1&3 £1.20, 2&3 £3.60 CSF £16.08 TOTE £2.40: £1.50, £1.20, £1.30; EX 19.00 Trifecta £54.40 Pool: £2,126.48 - 29.31 winning units..
Owner Des Anderson **Bred** D J Anderson **Trained** East Everleigh, Wilts

■ Stewards' Enquiry : Liam Jones two-day ban: used whip down shoulder in the forehand (May 19-20)

FOCUS
A competitive looking event for juvenile fillies and a very pleasing performance from the winner, whose dam, Cake, won this race in 2007. The form fits with the race averages.

2054 BETFRED TV H'CAP 1m 1f 198y
3:35 (3:36) (Class 4) (0-85,83) 3-Y-O £5,175 (£1,540; £769; £384) Stalls Low

Form				RPR
01-1	1		**Swing Easy**64 867 3-9-7 83 GrahamLee 3 (Robert Mills) *mde all: qcknd 3 l clr 3f out: rdn over 1f out: jnd fnl 100yds: kpt on gamely: hld on: all out* **7/2**2	95
02-1	2	hd	**Pether's Moon (IRE)**13 1713 3-9-7 83 PatDobbs 7 (Richard Hannon) *trckd ldr: rdn over 2f out: steadily clsd on wnr fr over 1f out: drew upsides u.p fnl 100yds: styd on: jst hld* **9/2**3	94
21-	3	6	**Lady Pimpernel**214 6791 3-8-13 75 DaneO'Neill 8 (Henry Candy) *cl up: rdn wl over 2f out: sn chsng ldng pair but nvr gng pce to chal* **3/1**1	76
2-13	4	9	**Emerging**15 1683 3-8-13 75 LiamKeniry 2 (David Elsworth) *trckd wnr tl rdn wl over 2f out: lost 3rd sn after: wknd over 1f out* **10/1**	56
101-	5	5	**Felix Fabulla**216 6732 3-9-1 77 NickyMackay 1 (Hughie Morrison) *in tch: rdn wl over 2f out: wknd over 1f out* **14/1**	48
1-	6	2 1/4	**Al Jamal**171 7720 3-9-2 78 SilvestreDeSousa 6 (Saeed bin Suroor) *in tch: dropped to last 4f out: sn drvn: little imp: wknd over 1f out* **5/1**	45
34-1	7	5	**Royal Prize**25 1471 3-9-5 81 RichardKingscote 4 (Ralph Beckett) *hld up: rdn wl over 2f out: nvr any imp: wknd over 1f out* **13/2**	38
16-2	8	71	**Nice Story (IRE)**18 1604 3-9-3 79 SamHitchcott 5 (Mick Channon) *hld up: hdwy over 5f out: rdn 4f out: wknd wl over 2f out: virtually p.u fnl f* **16/1**	

2m 5.3s (-4.60) **Going Correction** -0.20s/f (Firm) 8 Ran SP% **117.0**
Speed ratings (Par 101): **110,109,105,97,93 92,88,31**
toteswingers 1&2 £5.40, 1&3 £3.20, 2&3 £3.50 CSF £20.21 CT £52.51 TOTE £5.10: £1.90, £2.80, £1.10; EX 26.60 Trifecta £71.90 Pool: £2,210.11 - 23.02 winning units..
Owner Mrs B B Mills, J Harley, T Jacobs **Bred** Lady Bamford **Trained** Headley, Surrey

FOCUS
This looked an interesting little handicap. It was run at what looked a steady early pace, but they clocked a good time and the form looks strong. It has been rated on the positive side, with the first two clear.

2055 BETFRED MOBILE LOTTO E.B.F MAIDEN STKS 1m 4f
4:10 (4:10) (Class 5) 3-Y-O £4,851 (£1,443; £721; £360) Stalls Low

Form				RPR
	1		**Deira Phantom (IRE)** 3-9-5 0 HarryBentley 3 (David Simcock) *trckd ldrs: wnt 2nd 4f out: led over 2f out: sn rdn: styd on gamely whn pressed fnl 75yds: jst hld on* **7/2**3	77
	2	shd	**Baihas** 3-9-5 0 DaneO'Neill 4 (Sir Michael Stoute) *hld up bhd ldrs: wnt cl 4th 3f out: sn rdn: clsd on wnr ent fnl f: nrly upsides fnl 75yds: styd on: jst failed* **2/1**1	77
5	3	1 3/4	**Tefflah**23 1518 3-9-0 0 AndreaAtzeni 5 (Roger Varian) *led: rdn and hdd over 2f out: kpt pressing wnr tl no ex fnl 75yds* **9/4**2	69
05	4	4 1/2	**Gerrards Cross (IRE)**8 1826 3-9-5 0 PatDobbs 1 (Richard Hannon) *trckd ldr tl 4f out: swtchd lft for effrt 2f out: sn rdn: fdd fnl 120yds* **7/2**3	67
	5	28	**Dark Rumour (IRE)** 3-9-0 0 KieranO'Neill 2 (John Bridger) *trckd ldrs: rdn 3f out: wknd 2f out* **25/1**	30

2m 42.97s (4.97) **Going Correction** -0.20s/f (Firm) 5 Ran SP% **112.4**
Speed ratings (Par 99): **75,74,73,70,52**
CSF £11.18 TOTE £5.30: £2.30, £1.10; EX 13.70 Trifecta £27.30 Pool: £1,474.45 - 40.49 winning units..
Owner A & A **Bred** Hascombe And Valiant Studs **Trained** Newmarket, Suffolk

FOCUS
There was quite a tight finish to this middle-distance maiden, which was slowly run. Hard to be too confident about the level of the form.

2056 BETFRED "STILL TREBLE ODDS ON LUCKY'S" H'CAP 6f 212y
4:45 (4:45) (Class 3) (0-95,89) 3-Y-O £8,086 (£2,406; £1,202; £601) Stalls Low

Form				RPR
302-	1		**Fleeting Smile (USA)**218 6675 3-9-7 89 DaneO'Neill 2 (Richard Hannon) *little slowly away: led after 1f: kpt on wl to assert fnl 120yds: rdn out* **15/8**1	98
4-12	2	3	**Lightning Launch (IRE)**17 1645 3-8-12 80 SamHitchcott 3 (Mick Channon) *trckd ldrs: rdn to chse wnr over 2f out: kpt on but nt pce to chal* **3/1**2	81
104-	3	2	**Tantshi (IRE)**190 7406 3-9-6 88 AndreaAtzeni 6 (Roger Varian) *stdd s: last but wl in tch: tk clsr order 3f out: sn rdn: kpt on same pce fnl f* **11/2**3	84
13-4	4	1 1/4	**Surge Ahead (IRE)**25 1477 3-8-11 79 HayleyTurner 5 (Ed Walker) *trckd ldrs: rdn over 2f out: kpt on same pce fr over 1f out* **3/1**2	71
4-14	5	7	**Marshland**10 1773 3-8-8 76 SilvestreDeSousa 4 (Mark Johnston) *led for 1f: trckd wnr tl rdn over 2f out: wknd over 1f out* **15/2**	49

1m 27.21s (-1.39) **Going Correction** -0.10s/f (Good) 5 Ran SP% **111.9**
Speed ratings (Par 103): **103,99,97,95,87**
CSF £7.92 TOTE £2.20: £1.40, £1.80; EX 3.80 Trifecta £17.70 Pool: £1,829.97 - 77.24 winning units..
Owner Hamdan Al Maktoum **Bred** Summer Wind Farm **Trained** East Everleigh, Wilts

FOCUS
Perhaps not as good a race as the ratings band would suggest, with the top-weight rated 6lb below the ceiling, but a pleasing performance nevertheless from the winner, who is still improving.

2057 BETFRED MOBILE SPORTS LADY RIDERS' H'CAP (FOR LADY AMATEUR RIDERS) 6f 212y
5:20 (5:20) (Class 6) (0-65,65) 4-Y-O+ £2,495 (£774; £386; £193) Stalls Low

Form				RPR
5300	1		**The Mongoose**3 1950 5-9-8 59 (t) MissHDoyle(7) 13 (David Evans) *a.p: led over 3f out: drifted lft: hld on: all out* **8/1**	67
4405	2	1/2	**Byrd In Hand (IRE)**29 1381 6-9-7 51 oh3 MissADeniel 5 (John Bridger) *prom early: trcking ldrs whn swtchd rt over 3f out: ev ch thrght fnl f: kpt on: hld nring fin* **14/1**	58
060-	3	1/2	**Takitwo**137 8167 10-9-7 58 MissKatyLyons(7) 2 (Geoffrey Deacon) *a.p: rdn and ev ch fr 2f out: kpt on fnl f: hld towards fin* **12/1**	63
025-	4	3 3/4	**Gaelic Ice**171 7719 4-9-11 58 MissCBoxall(3) 11 (Rod Millman) *hld up towards rr: styd on u.p fr over 1f out: wnt 4th ins fnl f: nt rch ldrs* **7/1**	53
34-0	5	3 3/4	**One Last Dream**29 1395 4-9-10 54 MissSBrotherton 6 (Ron Hodges) *led for 1f: prom tl lost pl 3f out: one pce fnl 2f* **4/1**1	39
6-30	6	3/4	**Guardi (IRE)**13 1716 4-9-7 58 MissECrossman(7) 14 (Dean Ivory) *nvr bttr than mid-div* **10/1**	41
63-5	7	nk	**Aciano (IRE)**15 1696 5-10-0 65 (bt) MissJenniferPowell(7) 3 (Brendan Powell) *s.i.s: sn pushed along in tch: rdn over 2f out: kpt on same pce tl fdd ins fnl f* **8/1**	47
0-00	8	1	**Alfie Joe**6 1893 4-9-0 51 oh6 MissMorganKerr(7) 1 (Ron Hodges) *chsd ldrs for 3f: sn towards rr* **33/1**	31
6240	9	1 1/4	**Benandonner (USA)**10 1780 10-9-8 57 ow3 (t) MissMBryant(5) 8 (Paddy Butler) *hld up towards rr: sme prog u.p into midfield over 2f out: wknd fnl f* **12/1**	33
060	10	1/2	**Fairy Mist (IRE)**40 1183 6-9-4 51 oh6 (v) MissLMasterton(3) 10 (John Bridger) *bolted to s: chsd ldrs tl rdn over 2f out: sn btn* **25/1**	26
6126	11	nse	**Storm Runner (IRE)**91 511 5-10-0 63 MissKMargarson(5) 7 (George Margarson) *mid-div: struggling 4f out: wknd over 1f out* **6/1**3	38
023-	12	4 1/2	**Billion Dollar Kid**240 5998 8-10-7 65 (p) MissEJJones 4 (Jo Davis) *mid-div: rdn and no imp fr over 2f out: wknd ent fnl f* **11/2**2	28
4000	13	10	**Prophet In A Dream**42 1162 5-9-7 51 oh6 (v1) MissZoeLilly 12 (Paddy Butler) *a towards rr* **50/1**	

1m 29.39s (0.79) **Going Correction** -0.10s/f (Good) 13 Ran SP% **124.3**
Speed ratings (Par 101): **91,90,89,85,81 80,80,78,77,76 76,71,60**
toteswingers 1&2 £27.80, 1&3 £14.30, 2&3 £34.20 CSF £117.80 CT £1407.35 TOTE £11.40: £3.10, £4.70, £3.90; EX 144.60 Trifecta £1501.60 Part won. Pool: £2,002.24 - 0.28 winning units..
Owner G Evans & P D Evans **Bred** Kincorth Investments Inc **Trained** Pandy, Monmouths

FOCUS
Ordinary form and most of the principals were on the pace throughout. The winner is rated close to his recent AW form.
T/Plt: £10.60 to a £1 stake. Pool of £58,309.75 - 3,995.49 winning units T/Qpdt: £2.60 to a £1 stake. Pool of £3,856.30 - 1,087.10 winning units TM

2058 - 2064a (Foreign Racing) - See Raceform Interactive

COLOGNE (R-H)
Sunday, May 5

OFFICIAL GOING: Turf: good

2065a KARIN BARONIN VON ULLMANN - SCHWARZGOLD-RENNEN (GROUP 3) (3YO FILLIES) (TURF) 1m
4:15 (4:17) 3-Y-O
£26,016 (£8,943; £4,471; £2,439; £1,626; £1,219)

			RPR
1		**Beatrice**40 1191 3-9-2 0 FabriceVeron 1 (H-A Pantall, France) *sn led: rdn and strly pressed fr 2f out: jnd ent fnl f: r.o and jst prevailed on hd bob in driving fin* **48/10**	98
2	shd	**Red Lips (GER)**21 3-9-2 0 DPorcu 8 (Andreas Lowe, Germany) *sn prom on outer: rdn 3f out: jnd ldr ent fnl f: r.o but jst denied on hd bob in driving fin* **15/2**	97
3	1 1/2	**Calyxa**21 3-9-2 0 LennartHammer-Hansen 4 (Ferdinand J Leve, Germany) *hld up in tch: rdn 3f out: r.o to go 3rd ins fnl f: nt pce of front pair* **37/10**2	94
4	1/2	**Ars Nova (GER)**21 3-9-2 0 JohanVictoire 7 (W Figge, Germany) *midfield: rdn and hdwy fr 3f out: ev ch 2f out: outpcd by ldrs ent fnl f: r.o* **124/10**	93
5	1	**Molly Mara (GER)**21 3-9-2 0 SHellyn 9 (J Hirschberger, Germany) *hld up in tch on outer: rdn over 2f out: towards rr and outpcd ent fnl f: styd on to go 5th cl home but nvr able to chal* **7/1**	91

6 *nk* **Artemisia (IRE)** 3-9-2 0 AStarke 10 90
(P Schiergen, Germany) *trckd ldr on outer: rdn to chal 2f out: outpcd over 1f out: no ex ins fnl f: fdd* **17/5**1
7 ½ **Akua'da (GER)**196 7281 3-9-2 0 EPedroza 2 89
(A Wohler, Germany) *midfield on inner: rdn over 2f out: kpt on tl no ex ins fnl f: fdd* **43/10**3
8 *nk* **Legenda Aurea (GER)** 3-9-2 0 MrDennisSchiergen 3 88
(P Schiergen, Germany) *trckd ldr on inner: rdn to chal 3f out: ev ch 2f out: kpt on tl no ex ins fnl f: fdd* **205/10**
9 *2* **You Will See (FR)**25 3-9-2 0 ADeVries 5 83
(Mario Hofer, Germany) *hld up in last pair on inner: rdn 3f out: hdwy and ev ch 2f out: kpt on tl no ex and btn ins fnl f: eased* **13/1**
10 *8* **Isioma**21 3-9-2 0 StefanieHofer 6 65
(Mario Hofer, Germany) *hld up in last pair on outer: rdn 3f out: last and btn ent fnl f: eased* **157/10**

1m 36.31s (-2.08) **10** Ran SP% **129.6**
WIN (incl. 10 euro stake): 58. PLACES: 23, 24, 20. SF: 488.
Owner Alexandre Pereira **Bred** Alexandre Pereira **Trained** France

1872 SHA TIN (R-H)
Sunday, May 5

OFFICIAL GOING: Turf: good

2066a CHAMPIONS MILE (GROUP 1) (3YO+) (TURF) 1m
9:35 (12:00) 3-Y-0+
£543,288 (£209,690; £95,313; £54,011; £31,771; £19,062)

RPR
1 **Dan Excel (IRE)**28 5-9-0 0 (t) WCMarwing 1 119
(J Moore, Hong Kong) *prom on inner: rdn 2f out: r.o to chal ent fnl f: led ins fnl 100yds: drvn out* **23/5**3
2 *shd* **Helene Spirit (IRE)**28 6-9-0 0 (t) MatthewChadwick 3 119
(C Fownes, Hong Kong) *led: rdn 2f out: strly pressed ent fnl f: hdd ins fnl 100yds: kpt on: jst hld* **74/1**
3 *1½* **Packing Whiz (IRE)**28 5-9-0 0 BrettPrebble 9 116+
(C Fownes, Hong Kong) *hld up in last pair on inner: rdn 2f out: r.o to go 3rd cl home: nvr able to chal* **27/10**2
4 *nk* **Glorious Days (AUS)**49 6-9-0 0 (b) DouglasWhyte 2 115+
(J Size, Hong Kong) *midfield on inner: swtchd out and rdn 2f out: 3rd and ev ch ent fnl f: kpt on but nt pce to chal: dropped to 4th cl home* **7/5**1
5 *1½* **Gold-Fun (IRE)**49 4-9-0 0 (b1) ODoleuze 6 111+
(R Gibson, Hong Kong) *hld up in last pair on outer: rdn over 2f out: r.o to take n.d 5th cl home* **5/1**
6 *¾* **Xtension (IRE)**28 6-9-0 0 JamesMcDonald 4 110+
(J Moore, Hong Kong) *midfield: rdn 3f out: kpt on wout threatening* **10/1**
7 *nk* **Penitent**36 1262 7-9-0 0 DanielTudhope 7 109+
(David O'Meara) *hld up in last trio on outer: rdn over 2f out: kpt on u.p but n.d* **98/1**
8 *1* **Pure Champion (IRE)**28 6-9-0 0 (t) GeraldMosse 8 107+
(A S Cruz, Hong Kong) *midfield on outer: rdn over 2f out: sn outpcd: kpt on wout threatening* **15/1**
9 *19* **King Mufhasa (NZ)**29 9-9-0 0 (b) MichaelRodd 5 63
(Bruce Wallace, New Zealand) *trckd ldr on outer: rdn 2f out: qckly lost pl and btn: eased and dropped to last: t.o* **34/1**

1m 33.42s (-1.28) **9** Ran SP% **123.8**
PARI-MUTUEL (all including HK$10 stake): WIN 56.00; PLACE 17.00, 92.00, 14.50; DF 1,787.00.
Owner David Philip Boehm **Bred** John Connaughton **Trained** Hong Kong

1896 BATH (L-H)
Monday, May 6

OFFICIAL GOING: Firm (good to firm in places; 10.7)
Wind: mild breeze across Weather: sunny

2067 BATHWICK TYRES MIDSOMER NORTON MEDIAN AUCTION MAIDEN STKS 5f 11y
2:10 (2:11) (Class 6) 2-Y-0 **£1,940** (£577; £288; £144) **Stalls** Centre

Form RPR
1 **Bird Of Light (IRE)** 2-9-0 0 KieranO'Neill 1 69+
(Richard Hannon) *trckd ldrs: swtchd rt 2f out: sn rdn: r.o wl to ld fnl 75yds* **2/1**1
30 2 *1* **Hedy**16 1680 2-9-0 0 SamHitchcott 6 64
(Mick Channon) *led: rdn wl over 1f out: kpt on but no ex whn hdd fnl 75yds* **8/1**3
0 3 *4* **Earl's Bridge**9 1833 2-8-12 0 RyanWhile(7) 5 55
(Bill Turner) *chsd ldrs: rdn over 2f out: ch over 1f out: hung lft ins fnl f: kpt on same pce* **25/1**
6 4 *2½* **Blue Anchor Bay (IRE)**21 1580 2-9-5 0 WilliamCarson 3 46
(Rod Millman) *prom early: chsd wnr: rdn over 2f out: hld in one pce 4th whn squeezed up on rails ins fnl f* **5/2**2
5 *1¾* **Unfashionable (IRE)** 2-9-0 0 ShaneKelly 8 34
(Stuart Kittow) *struggling in last 3f out: sme late prog but nvr a threat* **14/1**
6 *1¾* **Mister Mayday (IRE)** 2-9-5 0 PatCosgrave 4 33
(George Baker) *s.i.s: bhd: sme prog wl over 2f out: wknd ent fnl f* **5/2**2
7 *8* **Sarlat** 2-9-0 0 TomMcLaughlin 7
(Mark Brisbourne) *in tch: rdn over 2f out: wknd over 1f out* **16/1**

1m 2.87s (0.37) **Going Correction** -0.20s/f (Firm) **7** Ran SP% **118.0**
Speed ratings (Par 91): **89,87,81,77,74 71,58**
Tote Swingers 1&2 £3.10, 2&3 £9.50, 1&3 £7.80 CSF £19.92 TOTE £2.30: £1.70, £3.30; EX 9.50 Trifecta £99.30 Pool: £1,885.45 - 14.23 winning units..
Owner Rockcliffe Stud **Bred** Airlie Stud **Trained** East Everleigh, Wilts
■ Stewards' Enquiry : Ryan While one-day ban: careless riding (May 20)

FOCUS
The market can often prove the best guide in these juvenile contests and that proved the case again here. It was over a stone slower than the seller and has to be rated on the negative side.

2068 BATHWICK TYRES TROWBRIDGE (S) STKS 5f 11y
2:40 (2:40) (Class 6) 2-Y-0 **£2,045** (£603; £302) **Stalls** Centre

Form RPR
24 1 **Diamond Lady**32 1344 2-8-6 0 CathyGannon 2 67
(Jo Hughes) *mde all: kpt on strly: rdn out* **6/1**
451 2 *2½* **Scargill**21 1574 2-9-2 0 SebSanders 6 68
(Brian Ellison) *trckd ldrs: rdn to chse wnr over 1f out: kpt on but a being hld* **2/1**1
222 3 *2* **Gin Time (IRE)**21 1574 2-8-6 0 WilliamCarson 9 51
(David Evans) *in tch: rdn wl over 2f out: kpt on same pce fnl f* **10/3**3
4 *2¼* **Marti's Girl** 2-8-3 0 RyanPowell(3) 7 43
(J S Moore) *towards rr: hdwy over 2f out: sn rdn: styd on same pce fnl f* **50/1**
00 5 *1¼* **Chilly In Rio (IRE)**14 1724 2-8-6 0 FrannyNorton 8 38
(William Muir) *chsd wnr tl rdn wl over 1f out: fdd ins fnl f* **33/1**
4 6 *1¼* **Love's Last Adieu**21 1574 2-8-6 0 LiamJones 1 34
(J S Moore) *s.i.s: sn outpcd: nvr a factor* **33/1**
6 7 *1¼* **Posh Bounty**31 1360 2-8-6 0 KieranO'Neill 4 29
(Bill Turner) *mid-div tl outpcd over 2f out* **14/1**
00 8 *2¾* **Under Your Thumb (IRE)**4 1946 2-8-6 0 LukeMorris 10 19
(David Evans) *trckd ldrs: rdn over 2f out: wknd over 1f out* **66/1**
4 9 *4* **Ding Ding**7 1880 2-8-7 0 ow1 SamHitchcott 5 6
(Mick Channon) *rdn 3f out: a towards rr* **11/4**2

1m 1.43s (-1.07) **Going Correction** -0.20s/f (Firm) **9** Ran SP% **113.4**
Speed ratings (Par 91): **100,96,92,89,87 85,83,78,72**
Tote Swingers 1&2 £3.00, 2&3 £2.20, 1&3 £3.40 CSF £17.77 TOTE £6.50: £1.90, £1.10, £2.10; EX 23.00 Trifecta £68.40 Pool: £1,661.55 - 18.19 winning units..There was no bid for the winner. There were no claims.
Owner B Bedford, P Hanly, J Hughes **Bred** Mickley Stud **Trained** Lambourn. Berks

FOCUS
Juvenile sellers at this time of year take very little winning but the time was decent for the grade. The winner is rated roughly to her debut form. The next two went different ways from Redcar.

2069 BATHWICK TYRES TETBURY H'CAP 2m 1f 34y
3:10 (3:10) (Class 4) (0-85,85) 4-Y-0+ **£4,690** (£1,395; £697; £348) **Stalls** Low

Form RPR
112- 1 **Callisto Moon**17 4756 9-9-1 76 (p) CathyGannon 6 83
(Jo Hughes) *mde all: pushed along 2f out: styd on v gamely ins fnl f: hld on: drvn out* **5/1**
21-3 2 *½* **Red Orator**14 1733 4-9-7 85 FrannyNorton 3 91
(Mark Johnston) *trckd wnr: rdn jst over 2f out: styd on to cl on wnr ins fnl f but a jst hld* **6/4**1
5403 3 *3* **Sommersturm (GER)**5 1927 9-8-5 66 oh4 (t) LukeMorris 5 69
(David Evans) *trckd ldrs: rdn over 2f out: styd on same pce* **9/1**
0222 4 *2¼* **Capellanus (IRE)**37 1218 7-9-0 75 ShaneKelly 4 75
(Brian Ellison) *hld up: hdwy over 2f out to chse ldrs: sn rdn: styd on same pce fnl f* **3/1**2
31-6 5 *7* **Petaluma**17 1670 4-8-10 74 SamHitchcott 7 66
(Mick Channon) *trckd ldrs: rdn over 2f out: wknd ent fnl f* **4/1**3

3m 49.05s (-2.85) **Going Correction** -0.025s/f (Good)
WFA 4 from 5yo+ 3lb **5** Ran SP% **111.7**
Speed ratings (Par 105): **105,104,103,102,99**
Tote Swinger 1&2 £5.70 CSF £13.24 TOTE £6.90: £3.10, £1.50; EX 14.40 Trifecta £45.50 Pool: £1,249.34 - 20.57 winning units..
Owner B Bedford & Mrs Gill White **Bred** Barton Stud **Trained** Lambourn. Berks

FOCUS
A fair staying handicap. It's doubtful if the winner had to find much on last year's form to gain his third C&D victory.

2070 BATHWICK TYRES FILLIES' H'CAP 1m 5y
3:45 (3:45) (Class 5) (0-75,75) 4-Y-0+ **£2,726** (£805; £402) **Stalls** High

Form RPR
1 1 **Sharp And Smart (IRE)**4 1950 4-9-5 73 6ex DaneO'Neill 3 81
(Hughie Morrison) *mde all: clr 5f out: 2 l up whn rdn ent fnl f: a holding on* **2/9**1
26-5 2 *¾* **Sarangoo**24 1521 5-9-0 68 TomMcLaughlin 1 74
(Malcolm Saunders) *hld up last of 4: rdn to chal for 2nd over 2f out: styd on wl fnl 100yds: a being hld* **12/1**3
3245 3 *1¼* **Jewelled**13 1753 7-9-5 73 (p) SebSanders 5 76
(Lady Herries) *trckd ldng pair: wnt 2nd over 2f out: sn rdn and jnd: styd on but a being hld by wnr: no ex fnl 75yds* **6/1**2
030- 4 *11* **Silvas Romana (IRE)**193 7356 4-9-4 75 RyanClark(3) 2 53
(Mark Brisbourne) *trckd wnr tl rdn over 2f out: wknd ent fnl f* **25/1**

1m 40.77s (-0.03) **Going Correction** -0.025s/f (Good) **4** Ran SP% **107.7**
Speed ratings (Par 100): **99,98,97,86**
CSF £3.72 TOTE £1.10; EX 3.10 Trifecta £5.70 Pool: £617.15 - 80.62 winning units..
Owner The Caledonian Racing Society **Bred** Piercetown Stud **Trained** East Ilsley, Berks

FOCUS
A one-horse race according the market, but the winner was not particularly impressive in the end off an easy lead. Unconvincing form.

2071 BATHWICK TYRES BRISTOL CLASSIFIED STKS 1m 5y
4:15 (4:16) (Class 5) 3-Y-0 **£2,726** (£805; £402) **Stalls** High

Form RPR
202- 1 **Reggae Star**240 6043 3-9-0 70 FrannyNorton 4 76
(Mark Johnston) *mde all: pushed clr ent fnl f: comf* **7/4**1
035- 2 *6* **Snoqualmie Chief**145 8071 3-9-0 67 SebSanders 3 62
(David Elsworth) *trckd wnr: rdn 2f out: kpt on but nt pce to chal comfortable wnr* **9/2**2
05-4 3 *7* **Followeveryrainbow**24 1518 3-9-0 68 KieranO'Neill 2 46
(Richard Hannon) *chsd ldng pair: rdn over 3f out: wknd fnl f* **8/1**3
1-5 S **Elle Rebelle**16 1697 3-9-0 66 TomMcLaughlin 1
(Mark Brisbourne) *trcking ldng trio whn short of room and slipped up ins first f* **10/1**

1m 40.88s (0.08) **Going Correction** -0.025s/f (Good) **4** Ran SP% **74.7**
Speed ratings (Par 91): **98,92,85,**
CSF £3.99 TOTE £1.70; EX 5.10 Trifecta £12.80 Pool: £114.98 - 6.70 winning units..
Owner Hugh Hart **Bred** Mrs P Hart **Trained** Middleham Moor, N Yorks
■ Estiqaama was withdrawn after becoming fractious in the stalls (13-8F, deduct 35p in the £ under R4).

FOCUS
It's unlikely that the form amounts to a great deal and the race has been rated cautiously. The winner was another to make all.

2072 BATHWICK TYRES DEVIZES H'CAP (DIV I) 1m 5y
4:45 (4:45) (Class 6) (0-55,55) 4-Y-0+ £1,940 (£577; £288; £144) Stalls High

Form RPR
6506 1 **Spinning Ridge (IRE)**[11] 1786 8-9-6 54 (b) LukeMorris 8 62
(Ronald Harris) *hld up: hdwy fr over 2f out: shkn up to ld jst ins fnl f: r.o wl* 8/1
060- 2 1 1/2 **Mr Udagawa**[206] 7015 7-8-6 47 (p) DanielMuscutt(7) 4 52
(Bernard Llewellyn) *sn pushed into ld: rdn 2f out: hdd jst ins fnl f: kpt on same pce* 14/1
5-04 3 1/2 **Finlodex**[82] 631 6-9-7 55 ShaneKelly 3 58
(Murty McGrath) *trckd ldr: rdn to chal 2f out tl jst ins fnl f: kpt on but no ex* 9/4[1]
3554 4 3/4 **Crucis Abbey (IRE)**[7] 1893 5-8-12 46 (p) TomMcLaughlin 6 48
(Mark Brisbourne) *t.k.h: hld up in tch: rdn 2f out to chse ldrs: styng on whn short of room and bmpd ins fnl f: kpt on towards fin* 6/1
0103 5 hd **Rigid**[19] 1617 6-8-10 47 AmyBaker(3) 7 48
(Tony Carroll) *hld up: nt clr run on rails 3f out: sn swtchd rt and rdn: chsd ldrs on outer over 1f out: styd on same pce* 13/2
0-02 6 1 **Firefly**[19] 1603 4-9-1 52 MichaelMetcalfe(3) 5 51
(John Weymes) *in tch: rdn over 2f out: kpt on same pce* 7/2[2]
2-3 7 1/2 **Dustland Fairytale (IRE)**[14] 1730 5-9-7 55 KieranO'Neill 1 53
(R McGlinchey, Ire) *trckd ldr: rdn over 2f out: nt clr run briefly wl over 1f out: styd on same pce fnl f* 4/1[3]

1m 43.39s (2.59) **Going Correction** -0.025s/f (Good) 7 Ran SP% **118.4**
Speed ratings (Par 101): **86,84,84,83,83 82,81**
Tote Swingers 1&2 £16.00, 2&3 £13.00, 1&3 £5.00 CSF £109.93 CT £337.47 TOTE £9.70: £3.90, £8.80; EX 82.20 Trifecta £257.50 Part won. Pool: £343.39 - 0.31 winning units..
Owner Ridge House Stables Ltd **Bred** Eddie O'Leary **Trained** Earlswood, Monmouths

FOCUS
A low-grade handicap run about 5sec slower than the second division. Weak form.

2073 BATHWICK TYRES DEVIZES H'CAP (DIV II) 1m 5y
5:15 (5:15) (Class 6) (0-55,55) 4-Y-0+ £1,940 (£577; £288; £144) Stalls High

Form RPR
4240 1 **For Shia And Lula (IRE)**[52] 1015 4-9-7 55 ShaneKelly 2 61+
(Daniel Mark Loughnane) *trckd ldrs: swtchd rt over 1f out: led ent fnl f: drvn rt out* 7/2[2]
560- 2 1/2 **Perfect Outlook**[25] 8212 5-8-12 46 SamHitchcott 8 51
(Charlie Longsdon) *hld up: rdn and hdwy over 2f out: chsd ldrs over 1f out: styd on wl fnl 120yds: wnt 2nd towards fin: nt quite rch wnr* 20/1
00-0 3 nk **Fushicho**[123] 41 4-9-0 48 SebSanders 6 53+
(Brendan Powell) *awkward leaving stalls: bhd: pushed along fr 3f out: hdwy over 1f out: styng on wl whn nt clr run twice in the clsng stages: snatched 3rd nr fin: unlucky* 25/1
-001 4 1/2 **Tooley Woods (IRE)**[4] 1951 4-9-5 53 6ex CathyGannon 5 56
(Tony Carroll) *racd keenly: led: rdn over 2f out: hdd jst ins fnl f: kpt on but no ex whn lost 2 pls nr fin* 5/2[1]
4420 5 1 1/2 **The Noble Ord**[7] 1893 4-9-6 54 (t) DaneO'Neill 3 54
(Sylvester Kirk) *hld up: pushed along over 5f out: styd on fnl f: nvr threatened ldrs* 9/2[3]
-600 6 3/4 **Mad For Fun (IRE)**[9] 1842 4-8-7 46 oh1 (v) ShirleyTeasdale(5) 1 44
(Paul Midgley) *trckd ldr: rdn and ch wl over 1f out: slt bump sn after: no ex ins fnl f* 20/1
2406 7 1 3/4 **Titan Diamond (IRE)**[3] 1981 5-8-8 47 RachealKneller(5) 4 42+
(Mark Usher) *mid-div: pushed along over 3f out: rdn to chse ldrs over 2f out: one pce fnl f* 8/1
3215 8 1 3/4 **Qeethaara (USA)**[14] 1736 9-9-3 51 (p) LukeMorris 9 41
(Mark Brisbourne) *hld up: rdn 3f out: short-lived effrt sn after: wknd ins fnl f* 5/1
04/0 9 20 **Lady Tycoon**[30] 1401 4-9-3 51 TomMcLaughlin 7
(Mark Brisbourne) *trckd ldrs: rdn 5f out: wknd 2f out: eased fnl f* 16/1

1m 40.17s (-0.63) **Going Correction** -0.025s/f (Good) 9 Ran SP% **116.0**
Speed ratings (Par 101): **102,101,101,100,99 98,96,94,74**
Tote Swingers 1&2 £22.60, 2&3 £23.20, 1&3 £14.20 CSF £72.40 CT £1524.20 TOTE £3.60: £1.50, £6.00, £6.50; EX 109.60 Trifecta £880.30 Part won. Pool: £1,173.82 - 0.12 winning units..

Owner Loughnane,Fletcher,Ward & Ebanks-Blake **Bred** A M F Persse **Trained** Baldwin's Gate, Staffs

FOCUS
This looked marginally stronger than the first division of this weak handicap and the form could very well hold up at a similar lowly level given the furious early pace. It was the quicker division.

2074 BATHWICK TYRES SWINDON H'CAP 5f 11y
5:45 (5:46) (Class 6) (0-60,63) 4-Y-0+ £2,045 (£603; £302) Stalls Centre

Form RPR
0365 1 **Above The Stars**[66] 842 5-9-0 58 RachealKneller(5) 13 71
(Jamie Osborne) *bhd: pushed along over 3f out: hdwy on outer 2f out: drifted lft but str run to ld fnl 120yds: drew clr: readily* 14/1
0643 2 2 1/4 **Molly Jones**[17] 1665 4-8-10 49 (p) WilliamCarson 10 54
(Derek Haydn Jones) *mid-div: pushed along wl over 2f out: hdwy over 1f out: swtchd lft ins fnl f: led briefly fnl 130yds: nt pce of wnr* 10/1[3]
0-00 3 1 **Chester'Slittlegem (IRE)**[17] 1665 4-8-9 48 CathyGannon 14 49
(Jo Hughes) *mid-div: pushed along 3f out: rdn and hdwy 2f out: squeezed up ent fnl f: drifted lft: r.o* 25/1
6351 4 1 1/2 **Nafa (IRE)**[14] 1731 5-9-0 53 ShaneKelly 1 49
(Daniel Mark Loughnane) *chsd ldr: chal over 1f out: sn rdn: kpt on same pce ins fnl f* 14/1
5002 5 hd **Spic 'n Span**[7] 1888 8-8-13 52 (b) LukeMorris 3 47
(Ronald Harris) *wnt to s early: prom: rdn 2f out: led ent fnl f: hdd fnl 130yds: no ex* 8/1[2]
230- 6 1 1/4 **Arch Walker (IRE)**[178] 7673 6-9-4 60 (b) MichaelMetcalfe(3) 8 51
(John Weymes) *chsd ldrs: rdn over 2f out: nt clr run over 1f out: hld after: kpt on same pce* 14/1
3-61 7 nk **Dreams Of Glory**[6] 1902 5-9-3 63 6ex DanielMuscutt(7) 12 53
(Ron Hodges) *chsd ldrs: rdn and ch whn squeezed up jst over 1f out: one pce fnl f* 5/4[1]
0336 8 1 **Russian Bullet**[32] 1356 4-8-8 47 (b) KieranO'Neill 2 33
(Jamie Osborne) *chsd ldrs: rdn over 2f out: ch over 1f out: wknd fnl f* 14/1
2200 9 shd **Scommettitrice (IRE)**[17] 1665 5-9-1 54 (p) DaneO'Neill 11 40
(Mark Gillard) *rrd leaving stalls: bhd: r.o ins fnl f: nvr threatened ldrs* 14/1
0005 10 1 **Little China**[10] 1802 4-9-2 55 FrannyNorton 7 37
(William Muir) *chsd ldrs: rdn over 2f out: nt best of runs over 1f out: fdd fnl f* 10/1[3]
2-00 11 hd **Irish Girls Spirit (IRE)**[16] 1681 4-8-13 57 (b[1]) ShirleyTeasdale(5) 5 38
(Paul Midgley) *led: rdn over 2f out: hdd ent fnl f: wknd* 8/1[2]
12 3/4 **Ferocious Fran (IRE)**[579] 6636 5-8-7 46 oh1 FrankieMcDonald 9 25
(R McGlinchey, Ire) *mid-div: rdn wl over 2f out: hdwy over 1f out: wknd fnl 120yds* 25/1
3-40 13 1 1/4 **Captain Cavallo**[60] 909 6-8-0 46 oh1 (bt) NoelGarbutt(7) 6 20
(Nicky Vaughan) *wnt rt and s.i.s: a towards rr* 66/1
600- 14 1 3/4 **Choisirez (IRE)**[12] 6305 4-8-4 46 oh1 (b[1]) AmyBaker(3) 4 14
(John Panvert) *sn outpcd in rr* 100/1

1m 1.27s (-1.23) **Going Correction** -0.20s/f (Firm) 14 Ran SP% **128.4**
Speed ratings (Par 101): **101,97,95,93,93 91,90,89,88,87 86,85,83,80**
Tote Swingers 1&2 £24.40, 2&3 £52.00, 1&3 £69.80 CSF £153.60 CT £2114.39 TOTE £20.90: £5.70, £3.50, £11.50; EX 174.70 Trifecta £1102.80 Part won. Pool: £1,470.50 - 0.30 winning units..
Owner Morsethehorse Syndicate **Bred** Manor Farm Stud (rutland) **Trained** Upper Lambourn, Berks

FOCUS
A lopsided market for a race of this nature. The pace from good and the first two came from a long way back. The winner was not far off the balance of her 4yo form.
T/Plt: £84.30 to a £1 stake. Pool: £50,349.38 - 435.53 winning tickets. T/Qpdt: £45.00 to a £1 stake. Pool: £2,459.70 - 40.40 winning tickets. TM

1771 BEVERLEY (R-H)
Monday, May 6

OFFICIAL GOING: Good to firm (9.7)
Wind: Light; half against Weather: Fine and dry

2075 RACING UK ON SKY 432 MEDIAN AUCTION MAIDEN STKS 5f
2:25 (2:25) (Class 6) 2-Y-0 £2,264 (£673; £336; £168) Stalls Low

Form RPR
6 1 **Zalzilah**[16] 1680 2-9-5 0 NeilCallan 10 80
(James Tate) *qckly away: mde all: rdn clr wl over 1f out: styd on wl* 11/2[3]
0 2 6 **Kraka Gym (IRE)**[45] 1108 2-9-5 0 GrahamGibbons 3 58
(Michael Easterby) *sltly hmpd s and sn pushed along: hdwy over 2f out: rdn over 1f out: kpt on to take 2nd ins fnl f* 11/1
3 1/2 **Augusta Ada** 2-9-0 0 PaulMulrennan 11 52+
(Ollie Pears) *s.i.s and bhd: stdy hdwy 1/2-way: swtchd lft and effrt over 1f out: kpt on fnl f: tk 3rd nr fin* 25/1
4 shd **Spiceupyourlife (IRE)** 2-9-0 0 TonyHamilton 4 51
(Richard Fahey) *cl up on inner: rdn along 2f out: drvn over 1f out and sn one pce* 11/4[1]
22 5 1 1/4 **Lily Rules (IRE)**[11] 1785 2-8-9 0 ow2 DavidSimmonson(7) 6 49
(Tony Coyle) *chsd ldrs: rdn along 2f out: sn one pce* 7/2[2]
5 6 1 **Different Scenario**[19] 1605 2-9-0 0 DavidAllan 1 43
(Mel Brittain) *chsd ldrs: rdn along 2f out: sn drvn and wknd over 1f out* 9/1
7 7 **Scoreline** 2-9-5 0 DanielTudhope 9 23
(David O'Meara) *chsd ldrs: rdn along 1/2-way: sn wknd* 7/2[2]
8 3 **Barleycorn** 2-9-0 0 DarylByrne(5) 2
(Tim Easterby) *sltly hmpd s: sn outpcd and green: a in rr* 16/1
9 3 1/2 **San Remo Rose (IRE)** 2-8-7 0 DanielleMooney(7) 7
(Nigel Tinkler) *green and sn outpcd in rr* 50/1

1m 2.83s (-0.67) **Going Correction** -0.225s/f (Firm) 9 Ran SP% **116.5**
Speed ratings (Par 91): **96,86,85,85,83 81,70,65,60**
Tote Swingers 1&2 £8.90, 2&3 £8.70, 1&3 £8.90 CSF £64.39 TOTE £8.50: £2.60, £3.50, £5.30; EX 68.40 TRIFECTA Not won..
Owner Sheikh Juma Dalmook Al Maktoum **Bred** Heather Raw **Trained** Newmarket, Suffolk

FOCUS
An uncompetitive maiden with an easy winner. The standard is questionable in behind.

2076 MAYDAY RACEDAY STKS (H'CAP) 5f
2:55 (2:56) (Class 5) (0-75,73) 3-Y-0 £3,234 (£962; £481; £240) Stalls Low

Form RPR
4-23 1 **Tumblewind**[11] 1791 3-9-1 72 GeorgeChaloner(5) 8 83
(Richard Whitaker) *trckd ldrs: hdwy wl over 1f out: rdn to ld ins fnl f: kpt on wl* 4/1[1]
6215 2 1 3/4 **Boxing Shadows**[11] 1791 3-9-4 73 LeeTopliss(3) 12 78
(Bryan Smart) *towards rr: hdwy wl over 1f out: rdn and styd on wl fnl f* 10/1
2126 3 nk **Bapak Bangsawan**[11] 1791 3-8-13 68 (b[1]) JulieBurke(3) 10 72
(Kevin Ryan) *sn led: rdn over 1f out: edgd rt ent fnl f: sn hdd and one pce* 8/1
-303 4 1 3/4 **Teetotal (IRE)**[11] 1771 3-8-10 62 PaulMulrennan 11 60
(Nigel Tinkler) *towards rr: hdwy wl over 1f out: sn rdn and styd on fnl f: nrst fin* 22/1
64-4 5 1/2 **Our Diane (IRE)**[11] 1791 3-8-13 65 DanielTudhope 6 61
(David O'Meara) *cl up: rdn along 2f out: drvn and wknd appr fnl f* 5/1[2]
25-6 6 1 **Perfect Words (IRE)**[12] 1762 3-8-8 63 RaulDaSilva(3) 1 55
(Marjorie Fife) *chsd ldrs: rdn along wl over 1f out: sn one pce* 14/1
051- 7 1/2 **Monsieur Royale**[179] 7649 3-9-5 71 (b) MichaelO'Connell 7 61
(Geoffrey Oldroyd) *s.i.s and in rr tl sme late hdwy* 12/1
40-4 8 1/2 **A J Cook (IRE)**[39] 1215 3-8-13 65 GrahamGibbons 13 54
(David Barron) *dwlt: a in rr* 9/1
130- 9 nk **Balinka**[180] 7635 3-9-3 69 DavidAllan 5 57
(Mel Brittain) *midfield: hdwy on inner to chse ldrs over 1f out: sn rdn and n.d* 10/1
4315 10 2 1/4 **Windforpower (IRE)**[9] 1844 3-8-11 63 (be) RoystonFfrench 9 42
(Tracy Waggott) *chsd ldrs: rdn along over 2f out: sn wknd* 16/1
064- 11 3 1/2 **Knockamany Bends (IRE)**[240] 6049 3-8-11 63 PaddyAspell 3 30
(John Wainwright) *a in rr* 25/1
-034 12 3/4 **Ayasha**[18] 1647 3-9-0 66 TomEaves 2 30
(Bryan Smart) *chsd ldng pair: rdn along 2f out: sn wknd* 11/2[3]

1m 2.4s (-1.10) **Going Correction** -0.225s/f (Firm) 12 Ran SP% **119.8**
Speed ratings (Par 99): **99,96,95,92,92 90,89,88,88,84 79,78**
Tote Swingers 1&2 £15.00, 2&3 £10.60, 1&3 £2.80 CSF £44.96 CT £311.81 TOTE £4.60: £1.80, £3.70, £2.50; EX 49.00 Trifecta £409.80 Part won. Pool: £546.42 - 0.40 winning units..
Owner Nice Day Out Partnership **Bred** Hellwood Stud Farm **Trained** Scarcroft, W Yorks

FOCUS
The two leaders seemed to go off very quick in this 3yo 5f handicap. The winner confirmed her Newcastle superiority over the second, third and fifth.

2077 ARTHUR MUDD MEMORIAL H'CAP — 1m 1f 207y
3:25 (3:26) (Class 4) (0-80,80) 4-Y-O+ — **£3,042** (£3,042; £697; £348) **Stalls** Low

Form — RPR

066- **1** **Classic Punch (IRE)**[234] 6202 10-9-7 **80** ...... DanielTudhope 6 — 87
(Tim Etherington) *set stdy pce: qcknd over 2f out: rdn and qcknd again ent fnl f: drvn and jnd on line* **11/2**[3]

-562 **1** *dht* **Saint Thomas (IRE)**[11] 1775 6-8-7 **66** ...... GrahamGibbons 1 — 73
(John Mackie) *trckd ldr: cl up 2f out: effrt wl over 1f out and sn rdn: drvn ins fnl f: kpt on wl towards fin to join ldr on line* **15/8**[1]

00-6 **3** *1 1/2* **Tartan Gigha (IRE)**[11] 1774 8-8-12 **74** ...... RaulDaSilva(3) 5 — 79+
(Geoffrey Harker) *hld up in tch: hdwy on inner 2f out: effrt over 1f out: swtchd lft and rdn to cl whn nt clr run ins fnl f: nt rcvr* **8/1**

4-10 **4** *2* **Exning Halt**[84] 614 4-9-0 **73** ...... MichaelO'Connell 2 — 73
(John Quinn) *trckd ldng pair: effrt on outer over 2f out: sn rdn and one pce ent fnl f* **7/2**[2]

50-0 **5** *3/4* **Warcrown (IRE)**[27] 1448 4-8-13 **72** ......(t) TonyHamilton 3 — 71
(Richard Fahey) *trckd ldrs: effrt over 2f out: sn rdn along and no imp fr over 1f out* **11/2**[3]

-054 **6** *9* **Gran Maestro (USA)**[21] 1568 4-8-12 **71** ......(b) JamesSullivan 4 — 52
(Ruth Carr) *dwlt: hld up in rr: sme hdwy over 2f out: sn rdn along and btn* **13/2**

2m 3.83s (-3.17) **Going Correction** -0.325s/f (Firm) **6** Ran SP% **112.2**
Speed ratings (Par 105): **99,99,97,96,95 88**WIN: CP £1.00, ST £4.00; PL: CP £2.00, ST £1.70; EX: CP & ST £10.60, ST & CP £6.70; TRIF: CP, ST & TG £30.90, ST, CP & TG £11.30; Tote Swingers: CP & TG £2.50, CP & ST £1.10, ST & TG £1.10 TRIFECTA Pool: £848.00 - 10.27 w27 Owner.
Owner P Riley **Bred** S Coughlan **Trained** Church Broughton , Derbys

FOCUS
Just a steady pace until the final 3f. Classic Punch was a few pounds off last year's form, with fellow dead-heater Saint Thomas pretty much to form.

2078 SWAN INDUSTRIAL DRIVES H'CAP — 1m 100y
4:00 (4:01) (Class 4) (0-85,85) 4-Y-O+ — **£6,469** (£1,925; £962; £481) **Stalls** Low

Form — RPR

36-0 **1** **Toto Skyllachy**[16] 1688 8-9-7 **85** ...... DanielTudhope 6 — 97
(David O'Meara) *trckd ldrs: hdwy on outer over 2f out: led over 1f out: sn rdn: clr whn edgd rt ins fnl f* **7/2**[2]

4-63 **2** *4 1/2* **Bling King**[21] 1576 4-8-10 **77** ......(p) RaulDaSilva(3) 7 — 79
(Geoffrey Harker) *trckd ldr: hdwy to ld over 2f out: rdn and hdd over 1f out: drvn and kpt on same pce fnl f* **7/1**

10-2 **3** *shd* **Shadowtime**[14] 1723 8-9-1 **79** ...... DaleSwift 3 — 81+
(Tracy Waggott) *trckd ldrs on inner: hdwy 2f out: effrt whn nt clr run over 1f out: sn rdn and kpt on fnl f* **3/1**[1]

-000 **4** *1/2* **Lady Macduff (IRE)**[13] 1753 4-8-11 **75** ...... JoeFanning 4 — 76
(Mark Johnston) *trckd ldr on inner: swtchd lft and effrt over 2f out: rdn wl over 1f out: kpt on same pce* **5/1**

-020 **5** *1* **Gloriam (USA)**[26] 1485 4-9-4 **82** ...... PJMcDonald 1 — 80
(Ruth Carr) *hld up in rr: hdwy over 2f out and sn rdn along: drvn and edgd rt ent fnl f: sn no imp* **13/2**

/055 **6** *nk* **Seattle Drive (IRE)**[21] 1571 5-8-12 **76** ...... TomEaves 5 — 74
(Brian Ellison) *sn pushed along to ld: rdn and hdd over 2f out: wknd over 1f out* **4/1**[3]

45-0 **7** *hd* **Al Muheer (IRE)**[14] 1723 8-9-5 **83** ......(b) JamesSullivan 2 — 81
(Ruth Carr) *hld up in rr: hdwy 2f out: rdn over 1f out: styng on whn nt clr run ins fnl f: n.d* **16/1**

1m 44.68s (-2.92) **Going Correction** -0.325s/f (Firm) **7** Ran SP% **115.6**
Speed ratings (Par 105): **101,96,96,95,94 94,94**
Tote Swingers 1&2 £2.80, 2&3 £4.00, 1&3 £1.80 CSF £28.34 TOTE £4.20: £2.00, £2.70; EX 23.70 Trifecta £69.30 Pool: £1,223.61 - 13.23 winning units..
Owner Richard Walker **Bred** Mrs G Slater **Trained** Nawton, N Yorks

FOCUS
An open-looking handicap run at a sound, level pace and in the end a most convincing winner. He looks better than ever.

2079 CHECK OUT OUR RACEDAY PACKAGES H'CAP — 1m 4f 16y
4:30 (4:30) (Class 5) (0-75,71) 3-Y-O — **£3,408** (£1,006; £503) **Stalls** Low

Form — RPR

31-3 **1** **Lion Beacon**[19] 1614 3-9-7 **71** ...... PaulMulrennan 6 — 80+
(Amanda Perrett) *t.k.h early: hld up in rr: pushed along over 4f out: rdn 2f out: swtchd rt to inner ent fnl f: drvn and styd on wl to ld last 30yds* **6/4**[1]

1-21 **2** *1/2* **Good Speech (IRE)**[21] 1579 3-9-4 **68** ...... MickyFenton 1 — 75
(Tom Tate) *dwlt: trckd ldrs on inner: hdwy 2f out: rdn and squeezed through to ld ins fnl f: sn drvn and hung lft: hdd and no ex last 30yds* **13/2**

1252 **3** *3 3/4* **Bain's Pass (IRE)**[13] 1743 3-8-9 **62** ...... JulieBurke(3) 2 — 63
(Kevin Ryan) *cl up whn led and hung lft bnd after 1f: pushed along over 2f out: rdn over 1f out: drvn and hdd ins fnl f: kpt on same pce* **5/1**[3]

5351 **4** *2 3/4* **Ofcoursewecan (USA)**[11] 1776 3-9-7 **71** ...... JoeFanning 3 — 68
(Mark Johnston) *slt ld whn carried wd bnd after 1f: trckd ldr: effrt over 2f out: rdn wl over 1f out: drvn appr fnl f and sn wknd* **11/4**[2]

0-13 **5** *11* **Glenreef**[27] 1453 3-9-5 **69** ...... NeilCallan 4 — 53
(Mark Johnston) *trckd ldrs whn carried wd bnd after 1f: trckd ldng pair: effrt over 2f out and sn rdn: drvn wl over 1f out and sn wknd* **15/2**

2m 36.83s (-2.97) **Going Correction** -0.325s/f (Firm) **5** Ran SP% **108.4**
Speed ratings (Par 99): **96,95,93,91,84**
Tote Swinger 1&2 £12.60 CSF £11.06 TOTE £2.20: £1.40, £1.90; EX 10.10 Trifecta £35.10 Pool: £880.50 - 18.79 winning units..
Owner Mrs Alexandra J Chandris **Bred** The Late A M Jenkins & J Chandris **Trained** Pulborough, W Sussex

FOCUS
Quite a messy 1m4f 3yo handicap but the form makes sense. The winner looks capable of better.

2080 WHITE RABBIT H'CAP — 7f 100y
5:00 (5:00) (Class 6) (0-65,65) 3-Y-O — **£2,264** (£673; £336; £168) **Stalls** Low

Form — RPR

1250 **1** **Baltic Prince (IRE)**[12] 1764 3-8-6 **53** ...... RaulDaSilva(3) 8 — 65
(Paul Green) *mde all: rdn clr wl over 1f out: styd on strly fnl f* **33/1**

-222 **2** *2 1/2* **Clock On Tom**[4] 1967 3-9-1 **59** ...... GrahamGibbons 13 — 65
(Michael Easterby) *hld up in midfield: hdwy whn n.m.r over 2f out: swtchd rt and rdn over 1f out: styd on wl on inner ent fnl f: sn chsng wnr: no imp* **7/2**[1]

005- **3** *1* **Reggie Bond**[212] 6893 3-8-10 **54** ...... FrederikTylicki 7 — 57
(Geoffrey Oldroyd) *hld up towards rr: hdwy over 2f out: rdn wl over 1f out: styd on wl fnl f: nrst fin* **12/1**

5343 **4** *nk* **Spider House**[31] 1373 3-9-2 **60** ...... DanielTudhope 5 — 63
(David O'Meara) *trckd ldng pair: hdwy on inner over 2f out: rdn wl over 1f out: sn drvn and kpt on same pce* **16/1**

41-0 **5** *6* **Aeronwyn Bryn (IRE)**[16] 1697 3-9-7 **65** ......(t) PaulMulrennan 10 — 53
(Michael Dods) *chsd ldrs: hdwy over 2f out: rdn and edgd rt over 1f out: sn drvn and no imp* **18/1**

446- **6** *1/2* **Art Mistress (IRE)**[293] 4178 3-9-7 **65** ...... DavidAllan 2 — 51
(Tim Easterby) *hld up in rr: hdwy wl over 2f out: kpt on fr over 1f out: nrst fin* **8/1**

1214 **7** *1 1/4* **Birdy Boy (USA)**[18] 1655 3-9-7 **65** ...... JoeFanning 9 — 48
(Mark Johnston) *trckd ldr: effrt and cl up over 2f out: sn rdn and wknd wl over 1f out* **5/1**[3]

0-33 **8** *nk* **Rocket Ronnie (IRE)**[4] 1966 3-9-1 **59** ...... AdrianNicholls 11 — 41+
(David Nicholls) *stdd s and hld up towards rr: sme hdwy on wd outside over 2f out: sn rdn and n.d* **9/2**[2]

20-4 **9** *3 3/4* **Stagweekend (IRE)**[21] 1577 3-9-4 **62** ...... MichaelO'Connell 6 — 35
(John Quinn) *a towards rr* **12/1**

-324 **10** *1/2* **Multisure**[11] 1772 3-9-0 **58** ...... PJMcDonald 15 — 30
(Ruth Carr) *chsd ldrs on outer: rdn along over 2f out: sn edgd rt and grad wknd* **16/1**

U215 **11** *2 3/4* **Jordanstown**[16] 1695 3-8-12 **56** ......(p) NeilCallan 3 — 26
(Kevin Ryan) *chsd ldrs on inner: rdn along wl over 2f out: sn wknd* **8/1**

006 **12** *1/2* **Madam Fifi**[18] 1648 3-9-3 **61** ...... TomEaves 4 — 25
(Alan McCabe) *a in rr* **20/1**

5-60 **13** *1/2* **Special Report (IRE)**[12] 1764 3-8-6 **53** ...... DeclanCannon(3) 14 — 15
(Nigel Tinkler) *a towards rr* **50/1**

1m 31.27s (-2.53) **Going Correction** -0.325s/f (Firm) **13** Ran SP% **121.4**
Speed ratings (Par 97): **101,98,97,96,89 89,87,87,83,82 79,78,78**
Tote Swingers 1&2 £31.60, 2&3 £31.60, 1&3 £69.60 CSF £146.21 CT £1528.01 TOTE £41.30: £9.30, £1.20, £4.00; EX 344.20 Trifecta £789.50 Part won. Pool: £1,052.71 - 0.08 winning units..
Owner A Mills **Bred** William Pilkington **Trained** Lydiate, Merseyside

FOCUS
A modest 3yo handicap and a surprise all-the-way winner. The first four finished clear and possibly showed form above the usual standard for the grade.

2081 RACING AGAIN ON TUESDAY 14 MAY H'CAP — 7f 100y
5:30 (5:30) (Class 5) (0-75,73) 4-Y-O+ — **£3,234** (£962; £481; £240) **Stalls** Low

Form — RPR

6144 **1** **Mujaadel (USA)**[16] 1686 8-8-12 **64** ......(p) PaulMulrennan 10 — 73
(David Nicholls) *hld up in tch: hdwy over 2f out: rdn over 1f out: styd on along inner to ld ins fnl f: kpt on wl* **8/1**[3]

61-2 **2** *1 1/2* **Majestic Dream (IRE)**[26] 1460 5-9-4 **70** ......(v) JamesSullivan 2 — 75
(Michael Easterby) *prom: effrt 2f out: rdn to chal ent fnl f: ev ch tl drvn and one pce last 100yds* **9/2**[1]

0011 **3** *2 1/4* **Thrust Control (IRE)**[12] 1757 6-8-9 **61** ......(p) FrederikTylicki 6 — 60
(Tracy Waggott) *set str pce: rdn along wl over 1f out: drvn ent fnl f: sn hdd and one pce* **9/2**[1]

05-3 **4** *nk* **Eeny Mac (IRE)**[19] 1603 6-8-9 **61** ...... DaleSwift 4 — 59
(Neville Bycroft) *prom: chsd ldr after 3f: rdn to chal wl over 1f out: drvn and ev ch ent fnl f: sn one pce* **6/1**[2]

05-6 **5** *3/4* **Summer Dancer (IRE)**[26] 1462 9-9-1 **67** ...... MickyFenton 9 — 63
(Paul Midgley) *hld up: hdwy 3f out: rdn to chse ldrs wl over 1f out: sn swtchd to outer and kpt on fnl f* **11/1**

-050 **6** *1 3/4* **Aerodynamic (IRE)**[16] 1686 6-9-7 **73** ...... GrahamGibbons 8 — 65
(Michael Easterby) *stdd s: hld up and bhd tl styd on fnl 2f* **10/1**

4-50 **7** *1* **Morocco**[21] 1569 4-9-2 **68** ...... DanielTudhope 1 — 57
(David O'Meara) *trckd ldrs: hdwy 3f out: rdn 2f out: drvn and wknd over 1f out* **6/1**[2]

6-00 **8** *shd* **Hayek**[14] 1723 6-8-11 **70** ......(b) RachelRichardson(7) 7 — 59
(Tim Easterby) *a towards rr* **10/1**

313- **9** *2 3/4* **Fayr Fall (IRE)**[157] 7936 4-9-2 **73** ......(p) DarylByrne(5) 5 — 55
(Tim Easterby) *chsd ldrs: hdwy on outer 3f out: rdn over 2f out: wknd over 1f out* **8/1**[3]

2646 **10** *2 1/2* **Monzino (USA)**[48] 1076 5-8-0 **59** oh4...... DanielleMooney(7) 3 — 34
(Michael Chapman) *s.i.s: a in rr* **25/1**

1m 30.88s (-2.92) **Going Correction** -0.325s/f (Firm) **10** Ran SP% **117.5**
Speed ratings (Par 103): **103,101,98,98,97 95,94,94,91,88**
Tote Swingers 1&2 £9.60, 2&3 £2.10, 1&3 £2.90 CSF £44.29 CT £189.42 TOTE £10.40: £2.70, £2.40, £2.40; EX 68.80 Trifecta £274.00 Pool: £869.65 - 2.38 winning units..
Owner W R B Racing 49 **Bred** Lawrence Goichman **Trained** Sessay, N Yorks

FOCUS
The leader went off very strongly and the field was soon well strung out. The winner is rated back to his March AW win.
T/Jkpt: Not won. T/Plt: £448.30 to a £1 stake. Pool: £54,078.34 - 88.05 winning tickets. T/Qpdt: £26.50 to a £1 stake. Pool: £3,208.70 - 89.55 winning tickets. JR

1923 KEMPTON (A.W) (R-H)
Monday, May 6

OFFICIAL GOING: Standard
Wind: Light across Weather: Sunny

2082 BRITISH STALLION STUDS E.B.F MAIDEN STKS — 5f (P)
2:15 (2:15) (Class 5) 2-Y-O — **£2,911** (£866; £432; £216) **Stalls** Low

Form — RPR

333 **1** **Meritocracy (IRE)**[5] 1930 2-9-5 0 ...... JamieSpencer 5 — 80
(Paul Cole) *mde all: rdn 2f out: sn qcknd clr: kpt on* **15/8**[2]

4 **2** *4 1/2* **Primitorio (IRE)**[21] 1580 2-9-5 0 ...... JimCrowley 2 — 64
(Ralph Beckett) *chsd ldr: sn pushed along: one pce and no ch w wnr fr over 1f out* **11/10**[1]

5 **3** *1* **Touch Paper (IRE)**[5] 1924 2-9-0 0 ...... RyanMoore 1 — 55
(Richard Hannon) *hld up in tch: pushed along 1/2-way: one pce and nvr threatened* **9/2**[3]

4 **4** *3/4* **Hot Stock (FR)**[19] 1606 2-9-5 0 ...... AdamKirby 4 — 58
(Jo Hughes) *trckd ldr: rdn 2f out: no ex ins fnl f* **20/1**

5 **5** *78* **Caesars Gift (IRE)**[11] 1792 2-9-5 0 ...... MartinDwyer 3
(Derek Shaw) *s.i.s: sn wl bhd* **100/1**

1m 0.14s (-0.36) **Going Correction** -0.075s/f (Stan) **5** Ran SP% **106.3**
Speed ratings (Par 93): **99,91,90,89,**
CSF £3.96 TOTE £3.00: £1.10, £1.20; EX 3.90 Trifecta £4.10 Pool: £339.84 - 61.16 winning units..
Owner Mrs Fitri Hay **Bred** Oghill House Stud **Trained** Whatcombe, Oxon

FOCUS
Not the most competitive of races but fair form from the winner. The gallop was on the steady side to the straight and the winner edged into the centre late on. He showed useful form.

2083 BETVICTOR.COM H'CAP 5f (P)
2:45 (2:45) (Class 4) (0-85,85) 3-Y-O **£4,690** (£1,395; £697; £348) **Stalls** Low

Form RPR
50-0 **1** **Storm Moon (USA)**[19] 1625 3-9-7 **85** WilliamBuick 2 93+
(Mark Johnston) *hld up in tch: nudged along and hdwy over 1f out: led jst ins fnl f: pushed out: cosily* **11/10**[1]
54-4 **2** 1 ½ **Hot Secret**[17] 1661 3-8-7 **71** DavidProbert 1 73
(Andrew Balding) *trckd ldr: rdn over 1f out: kpt on: wnt 2nd post* **7/1**[3]
15-2 **3** *nk* **Angus Og**[9] 1844 3-9-4 **82** JimCrowley 5 83+
(Mrs K Burke) *hld up in rr: rdn 2f out: kpt on wl fnl f: nrst fin* **15/8**[2]
12-2 **4** *nse* **Small Fury (IRE)**[17] 1661 3-8-13 **77** J-PGuillambert 3 78
(Jo Hughes) *led: rdn 2f out: hdd jst ins fnl f: one pce: lost 2 pls post* **11/1**
-040 **5** 2 ½ **Ask The Guru**[10] 1808 3-9-7 **85** RobertHavlin 4 77
(Michael Attwater) *trckd ldr: rdn 2f out: wknd ins fnl f* **9/1**
59.5s (-1.00) **Going Correction** -0.075s/f (Stan) **5** Ran SP% **113.2**
Speed ratings (Par 101): **105,102,102,102,98**
CSF £9.71 TOTE £2.30: £1.10, £1.80; EX 9.90 Trifecta £15.80 Pool: £284.00 - 13.39 winning units..
Owner Sheikh Hamdan Bin Mohammed Al Maktoum **Bred** Darley **Trained** Middleham Moor, N Yorks

FOCUS
Only five runners but a useful handicap in which the gallop was no more than fair. The winner raced centre to far side in the closing stages. The time was nothing special but the form makes a fair bit of sense.

2084 £25 FREE BET AT BETVICTOR.COM STUDS E.B.F MAIDEN FILLIES' STKS 1m (P)
3:15 (3:18) (Class 5) 3-Y-O **£3,881** (£1,155; £577; £288) **Stalls** Low

Form RPR
2- **1** **Mango Diva**[229] 6366 3-9-0 0 RyanMoore 8 91+
(Sir Michael Stoute) *midfield: angled lft 2f out: str run on outer to ld jst ins fnl f: kpt on wl* **4/5**[1]
03- **2** 2 **Stresa**[243] 5947 3-9-0 0 WilliamBuick 3 86
(John Gosden) *trckd ldrs: rdn 3f out: led 1f out: sn hdd: kpt on but sn no ch w wnr* **15/2**[3]
3 3 **International Love (IRE)** 3-9-0 0 DavidProbert 9 79+
(Andrew Balding) *s.i.s: sn in midfield: rdn and hdwy over 1f out: kpt on to go 3rd ins fnl f* **33/1**
26- **4** 2 ¾ **Hidden Belief (IRE)**[186] 7506 3-9-0 0 JimCrowley 11 72+
(Ralph Beckett) *prom: led 3f out: rdn and briefly clr 2f out: hdd 1f out: wknd* **5/1**[2]
0-2 **5** 1 **Saucy Minx (IRE)**[18] 1640 3-9-0 0 RobertHavlin 12 70
(Amanda Perrett) *trckd ldrs: rdn over 2f out: one pce: grad wknd fnl f* **8/1**
6 *shd* **Rail Star** 3-9-0 0 JamesDoyle 10 69+
(Roger Charlton) *hld up in midfield: pushed along over 2f out: kpt on fnl f: nvr threatened* **25/1**
0- **7** 1 ½ **Jareeda (USA)**[194] 7329 3-9-0 0 MartinDwyer 14 66+
(Sir Michael Stoute) *s.i.s: hld up: pushed along over 2f out: kpt on fnl f: nvr threatened* **50/1**
- **8** 1 ¼ **Salford Excel** 3-9-0 0 AdamKirby 2 63+
(Marco Botti) *hld up in midfield: rdn over 2f out: nvr threatened* **16/1**
9 2 **Cape Appeal** 3-8-9 0 WilliamTwiston-Davies(5) 4 58
(Richard Hannon) *trckd ldrs: rdn over 3f out: wknd over 1f out* **25/1**
10 ¾ **Simply Elegant (IRE)** 3-9-0 0 J-PGuillambert 1 56
(Amanda Perrett) *dwlt: hld up: nvr threatened* **50/1**
50-2 **11** 3 ¾ **Last Hooray**[31] 1364 3-9-0 68 LiamKeniry 5 47
(David Elsworth) *midfield: rdn 3f out: wknd over 1f out* **25/1**
6 **12** 12 **Atlantic Isle (GER)**[14] 1713 3-9-0 0 TomQueally 13 18
(Sir Henry Cecil) *midfield towards outer: rdn 3f out: sn wknd* **16/1**
3-40 **13** 1 **Lincolnrose (IRE)**[94] 482 3-9-0 50 (p) KirstyMilczarek 6 16
(Alan McCabe) *led: hdd 3f out: sn wknd* **100/1**
14 3 ¾ **Faustinatheyounger (IRE)** 3-8-9 0 MichaelJMMurphy(5) 7
(David Elsworth) *sn pushed along in rr: a bhd* **50/1**
1m 38.74s (-1.06) **Going Correction** -0.075s/f (Stan) **14** Ran SP% **128.2**
Speed ratings (Par 96): **102,100,97,94,93 93,91,90,88,87 83,71,70,67**
toteswingers 1&2 £3.60, 1&3 £17.70, 2&3 Not won CSF £7.43 TOTE £1.80: £1.10, £3.00, £7.80; EX 10.00 Trifecta £312.90 Part won. Pool: £417.28 - 0.66 winning units..
Owner Antoniades Family **Bred** A G Antoniades **Trained** Newmarket, Suffolk

FOCUS
A useful maiden featuring several unexposed sorts from good yards and a race that should throw up its share of winners. The gallop was no more than fair, so some may be flattered, and the winner came down the centre.

2085 DOWNLOAD THE BETVICTOR APP NOW JUBILEE H'CAP (LONDON MILE SERIES QUALIFIER) 1m (P)
3:50 (3:50) (Class 3) (0-90,87) 4-Y-O+
£7,158 (£2,143; £1,071; £535; £267; £134) **Stalls** Low

Form RPR
55-0 **1** **Magma**[17] 1663 4-8-9 **75** (b1) DavidProbert 6 82
(Andrew Balding) *racd keenly: in tch: rdn over 2f out: drvn over 1f out: kpt on: edgd rt fnl 100yds: led fnl 50yds: hld on all out* **12/1**
30-4 **2** *nk* **Shavansky**[26] 1485 9-9-0 **87** PatMillman(7) 3 93
(Rod Millman) *s.i.s: hld up in midfield: angled lft over 2f out: sn rdn and hdwy: kpt on fnl f: wnt 2nd nr fin* **9/2**[3]
00-0 **3** ½ **Halling Dancer**[16] 1673 4-8-7 **73** oh1 MartinDwyer 1 78
(Lee Carter) *trckd ldr: rdn to ld wl over 1f out: hdd fnl 50yds: no ex and lost 3rd nr fin* **20/1**
6-13 **4** *nk* **Ree's Rascal (IRE)**[21] 1583 5-8-11 **82** NathanAlison(5) 7 86
(Jim Boyle) *hld up: dropped to rr 1/2-way: rdn over 2f out: hdwy on wd outside over 1f out: kpt on fnl f* **5/2**[1]
4012 **5** 2 ¼ **Idol Deputy (FR)**[11] 1796 7-9-3 **83** (p) KirstyMilczarek 5 82
(James Bennett) *hld up in rr: rdn over 2f out: nvr threatened ldrs* **10/1**
-230 **6** ¾ **Stir Trader (IRE)**[33] 1318 4-8-12 **78** ow2 WilliamBuick 4 75
(Philip Hide) *midfield: rdn over 2f out: one pce and no imp on ldrs* **5/1**
06-0 **7** ½ **Embankment**[9] 1848 4-9-0 **80** RobertHavlin 2 76
(William Jarvis) *in tch: rdn over 2f out: wknd ins fnl f* **11/1**
1215 **8** *hd* **Compton Rainbow**[23] 1544 4-9-1 **86** (t) NicoleNordblad(5) 8 81
(Hans Adielsson) *led: rdn whn hdd wl over 1f out: wknd ins fnl f* **4/1**[2]
1m 38.53s (-1.27) **Going Correction** -0.075s/f (Stan) **8** Ran SP% **113.3**
Speed ratings (Par 107): **103,102,102,101,99 98,98,98**
toteswingers 1&2 £6.00, 1&3 £20.20, 2&3 £20.20 CSF £63.84 CT £1082.64 TOTE £18.90: £3.30, £1.50, £3.20; EX 58.30 Trifecta £418.80 Part won. Pool: £558.47 - 0.77 winning units..
Owner A H Robinson **Bred** H & Mrs C Robinson **Trained** Kingsclere, Hants
■ Stewards' Enquiry : William Buick two-day ban: weighed in 2lb heavy (May 20-21)

FOCUS
Mainly exposed performers in a useful handicap, and the form is ordinary for the grade. The gallop was rather muddling and the winner came down the centre in the straight.

2086 BETVICTOR CASINO ON YOUR MOBILE H'CAP (LONDON MIDDLE DISTANCE QUALIFIER) 1m 3f (P)
4:20 (4:22) (Class 3) (0-95,90) 3-Y-O **£7,158** (£2,143; £1,071; £535; £267) **Stalls** Low

Form RPR
21-1 **1** **Disclaimer**[10] 1803 3-9-7 **90** TomQueally 4 102+
(Sir Henry Cecil) *trckd ldr: pushed along to ld over 1f out: rdn to assert ins fnl f: shade cosily* **5/4**[1]
0-1 **2** 1 ¾ **Powder Hound**[14] 1727 3-9-0 **83** DavidProbert 1 89
(Andrew Balding) *led: rdn whn hdd over 1f out: kpt on but a hld by wnr ins fnl f* **10/3**[3]
51-5 **3** *hd* **Zeus Magic**[19] 1614 3-8-7 **76** LiamKeniry 2 82
(David Elsworth) *in tch in 3rd: rdn over 2f out: kpt on* **5/1**
40-1 **4** 7 **Sizzler**[33] 1317 3-9-1 **84** JimCrowley 5 77
(Ralph Beckett) *hld up in rr: rdn over 2f out: nvr threatened* **3/1**[2]
61-5 **5** 3 ¾ **Ronaldinho (IRE)**[45] 1109 3-9-5 **88** RyanMoore 3 74
(Richard Hannon) *hld up in tch in 4th: rdn over 3f out: wknd over 1f out* **12/1**
2m 21.15s (-0.75) **Going Correction** -0.075s/f (Stan) **5** Ran SP% **116.9**
Speed ratings (Par 103): **99,97,97,92,89**
CSF £6.28 TOTE £1.90: £1.30, £2.40; EX 6.40 Trifecta £11.00 Pool: £283.15 - 19.23 winning units..
Owner K Abdullah **Bred** Juddmonte Farms Ltd **Trained** Newmarket, Suffolk
■ Aryal was withdrawn on vet's advice (9/1, deduct 10p in the £ under R4). New market formed.

FOCUS
Several last-time out winners in a useful handicap but a steady gallop means this bare form isn't entirely reliable. Another step forward from the winner, who came down the centre in the straight.

2087 CONOR MAYNARD AT KEMPTON 14.09.13 H'CAP 2m (P)
4:50 (4:50) (Class 5) (0-75,74) 4-Y-O+ **£2,587** (£770; £384; £192) **Stalls** Low

Form RPR
5051 **1** **Arashi**[49] 1060 7-8-12 **62** (v) MartinDwyer 7 70
(Derek Shaw) *hld up: hdwy over 2f out: rdn to ld over 1f out: edgd lft: kpt on wl* **8/1**
2-00 **2** 2 ¼ **Vimiero (USA)**[67] 823 6-9-9 **73** RyanMoore 4 78
(Jonjo O'Neill) *trckd ldr: rdn to chal over 1f out: one pce and a hld by wnr fnl f* **4/1**[2]
/330 **3** ½ **Kalamill (IRE)**[14] 1721 6-8-13 **68** WilliamTwiston-Davies(5) 2 72
(Shaun Lycett) *led: rdn whn hdd over 2f out: kpt on one pce* **11/4**[1]
0-30 **4** ¾ **Russian George (IRE)**[43] 1158 7-9-10 **74** (p) AdamKirby 5 78
(Steve Gollings) *midfield: rdn 4f out: kpt on one pce* **11/1**
2311 **5** ½ **Scribe (IRE)**[24] 1520 5-9-1 **70** (vt) DeclanBates(5) 6 73
(David Evans) *trckd ldr: rdn to ld over 2f out: hdd over 1f out: wknd ins fnl f* **4/1**[2]
00-0 **6** 3 ¾ **Blackstone Vegas**[11] 1794 7-8-8 **58** DavidProbert 1 56
(Derek Shaw) *midfield: rdn 4f out: sn no imp on ldrs* **12/1**
0-01 **7** 5 **Knox Overstreet**[3] 1980 5-8-11 **68** 6ex DanielCremin(7) 3 60
(Mick Channon) *hld up in rr: rdn over 3f out: sn btn* **9/2**[3]
3m 31.25s (1.15) **Going Correction** -0.075s/f (Stan) **7** Ran SP% **112.0**
Speed ratings (Par 103): **94,92,92,92,92 90,87**
toteswingers 1&2 £14.90, 1&3 £14.90, 2&3 £14.90 CSF £38.05 TOTE £9.50: £2.70, £2.20; EX 43.40 Trifecta £212.80 Part won. Pool: £283.76 - 0.04 winning units..
Owner Philip Derbyshire **Bred** Wyck Hall Stud Ltd **Trained** Sproxton, Leics

FOCUS
A fair handicap run at a gallop that soon steadied. Muddling form. The winner came down the centre in the straight.

2088 BETVICTOR.COM FILLIES' H'CAP 6f (P)
5:20 (5:20) (Class 4) (0-85,85) 4-Y-O+ **£4,690** (£1,395; £697; £348) **Stalls** Low

Form RPR
30-6 **1** **Charlotte Rosina**[14] 1726 4-9-7 **85** RyanMoore 3 95
(Roger Teal) *trckd clr ldr: rdn over 2f out: kpt on: led ins fnl f* **6/5**[1]
36-0 **2** 1 ½ **Dancheur (IRE)**[33] 1318 4-8-11 **75** JimCrowley 2 80
(Mrs K Burke) *led: clr 4f out tl over 1f out: hdd ins fnl f: no ex* **3/1**[2]
3-10 **3** 2 ½ **Gladiatrix**[14] 1726 4-8-13 **82** MichaelJMMurphy(5) 5 79
(Rod Millman) *in tch: rdn over 2f out: briefly chsd appr fnl f: no ex ins fnl f* **9/2**[3]
235- **4** ¾ **Ray Of Joy**[254] 5576 7-9-5 **83** TomQueally 4 78
(J R Jenkins) *in tch: rdn over 2f out: sn no imp on ldrs* **8/1**
1122 **5** 3 **Climaxfortackle (IRE)**[11] 1798 5-8-0 **71** oh1 AdamMcLean(7) 1 56
(Derek Shaw) *hld up in rr: s.i.s: a bhd* **8/1**
1m 11.72s (-1.38) **Going Correction** -0.075s/f (Stan) **5** Ran SP% **110.9**
Speed ratings (Par 102): **106,104,100,99,95**
CSF £5.08 TOTE £1.90: £2.30, £3.50; EX 6.10 Trifecta £18.90 Pool: £452.12 - 17.92 winning units..
Owner Homecroft Wealth Racing **Bred** Edward Hyde **Trained** Ashtead, Surrey

FOCUS
Exposed sorts in a useful handicap. The gallop increased before halfway but only the winner and runner-up figured. The winner came down the centre in the straight.
T/Plt: £128.20 to a £1 stake. Pool: £45,651.77 - 259.82 winning tickets T/Qpdt: £50.50 to a £1 stake. Pool: £1,994.80 - 29.20 winning tickets AS

1285 WARWICK (L-H)
Monday, May 6

OFFICIAL GOING: Good to firm (firm in places; 7.6)
Wind: Light; behind Weather: Fine

2089 JOIN TODAY AT REWARDS4RACING.COM APPRENTICE H'CAP 1m 22y
2:05 (2:06) (Class 6) (0-65,65) 4-Y-O+ **£1,940** (£577; £288; £144) **Stalls** Low

Form RPR
0000 **1** **Evergreen Forest (IRE)**[12] 1763 5-9-0 **61** NoraLooby(3) 2 73
(Alastair Lidderdale) *hld up: hdwy 2f out: shkn up to ld wl ins fnl f: styd on* **12/1**
2-02 **2** ½ **Balmoral Castle**[53] 993 4-8-7 **56** DavidCoyle(5) 9 67
(Jonathan Portman) *a.p: led 2f out: shkn up and hdd wl ins fnl f: kpt on* **20/1**
6001 **3** *hd* **Muftarres (IRE)**[7] 1887 8-9-7 **65** 6ex (t) ThomasBrown 4 76
(Frank Sheridan) *hld up: hdwy over 1f out: rdn ins fnl f: styd on* **8/1**

13-2 **4** 1 ¾ **Duke Of Destiny (IRE)**[28] 1426 4-9-0 **65**................ BradleyBosley(7) 10 76+
(Ed Walker) *prom: stdd and lost pl over 6f out: stmbld over 5f out: nt clr run over 2f out tl swtchd lft over 1f out: r.o: nt rch ldrs* **6/1**[3]

44-2 **5** 2 **Zenafire**[11] 1797 4-8-11 **58**................................ JackDuern(3) 1 60
(Reg Hollinshead) *a.p: rdn over 2f out: styd on same pce fnl f* **4/1**[1]

0524 **6** nk **Kyle Of Bute**[30] 1401 7-8-5 **54**............................. MatthewHopkins(5) 5 55
(Brian Baugh) *hld up: pushed along over 3f out: hdwy u.p over 1f out: nt rch ldrs* **14/1**

-201 **7** 1 ¼ **Bang Tidy (IRE)**[10] 1801 4-9-0 **61**......................(t) JacobButterfield(3) 11 59
(Brian Ellison) *racd keenly: w ldr tl pushed along 3f out: no ex fnl f* **9/2**[2]

33-0 **8** 3 ½ **Lord Franklin**[30] 1401 4-8-10 **54**.. JasonHart 8 44
(Eric Alston) *led: rdn and hdd 2f out: wknd fnl f* **12/1**

-660 **9** ¾ **Shared Moment (IRE)**[11] 1783 7-8-2 **51**................(v) EvaMoscrop(5) 12 40
(Luke Dace) *dwlt: hdwy over 6f out: pushed along over 2f out: wknd fnl f* **16/1**

000- **10** 1 **Jay Kay**[214] 6813 4-8-4 **51** oh1.. IanBurns(3) 3 37
(Danielle McCormick) *hld up in tch: racd keenly: pushed along over 3f out: wknd over 1f out* **50/1**

60-0 **11** 7 **Master Of Song**[119] 98 6-9-0 **58**.................................(p) RobertTart 7 28
(Roy Bowring) *s.i.s: racd keenly: hdwy over 5f out: rdn and wknd over 1f out* **7/1**

260- **12** 20 **Beaumont Cooper**[203] 7108 4-9-2 **63**.................. GeorgeDowning(3) 13
(Anabel K Murphy) *mid-div: rdn over 2f out: sn wknd: t.o* **18/1**

1m 39.14s (-1.86) **Going Correction** -0.175s/f (Firm) **12** Ran SP% **116.0**
Speed ratings (Par 101): **102,101,101,99,97 97,96,92,91,90 83,63**
toteswingers 1&2 £62.60, 1&3 £28.70, 2&3 £15.20 CSF £224.86 CT £2054.31 TOTE £21.90: £4.90, £5.40, £2.20; EX 365.60 Trifecta £799.50 Part won. Pool: £1,066.07 - 0.08 winning units..

Owner C S J Beek **Bred** Shadwell Estate Company Limited **Trained** Lambourn, Berks

FOCUS
A low-grade apprentice handicap.

2090 BRITISH STALLION STUDS SUPPORTING BRITISH RACING E.B.F MAIDEN FILLIES' STKS 5f

2:35 (2:36) (Class 5) 2-Y-O **£2,911** (£866; £432; £216) **Stalls** Low

Form RPR

6 **1** **One Chance (IRE)**[18] 1634 2-9-0 0.............................. AndreaAtzeni 6 77+
(Tim Pitt) *mde all: rdn over 1f out: r.o: comf* **9/4**[1]

2262 **2** 1 ¼ **Memory Styx**[9] 1839 2-9-0 0.. MartinHarley 3 73
(Mick Channon) *hld up: hdwy 1/2-way: chsd wnr over 1f out: styd on* **11/2**

3 1 **Princess Rose** 2-9-0 0.. KellyHarrison 7 69+
(William Haggas) *chsd ldrs: lost pl over 3f out: hdwy over 1f out: r.o* **9/2**[3]

63 **4** 1 **Queen Of The Tarts**[21] 1580 2-8-9 0................................ RobertTart(5) 8 65
(Olly Stevens) *wnt rt s: sn chsng ldr: rdn over 1f out: styd on same pce fnl f* **5/1**

5 nk **A Childs Dream (IRE)** 2-9-0 0.. SeanLevey 4 64
(Richard Hannon) *hld up: racd keenly: hdwy over 3f out: no ex ins fnl f* **10/3**[2]

6 4 **Dandy Maid** 2-9-0 0.. AndrewMullen 5 50
(Michael Appleby) *s.s: rdn and hung lft over 1f out: n.d* **40/1**

7 ¾ **Sleeping Princess (IRE)** 2-9-0 0..................................... TedDurcan 1 47
(Clive Brittain) *s.i.s: sn prom: rdn over 1f out: wknd fnl f* **28/1**

1m 0.66s (1.06) **Going Correction** +0.075s/f (Good) **7** Ran SP% **110.0**
Speed ratings (Par 90): **94,92,90,88,88 81,80**
toteswingers 1&2 £1.60, 1&3 £2.30, 2&3 £4.40 CSF £13.85 TOTE £3.00: £1.90, £2.70; EX 11.50 Trifecta £37.90 Pool: £1,073.88 - 21.24 winning units..
Owner Recycled Products Limited **Bred** Mrs C Regalado-Gonzalez **Trained** Newmarket, Suffolk

FOCUS
A modest juvenile contest for fillies. The runner-up, the time and the race averages help with the level of the form.

2091 QUANTUM MANUFACTURING H'CAP 5f

3:05 (3:07) (Class 6) (0-60,60) 3-Y-O **£1,940** (£577; £288; £144) **Stalls** Low

Form RPR

0-12 **1** **Shirley's Pride**[12] 1762 3-8-13 **52**..............................(t) AndrewMullen 3 68
(Michael Appleby) *sn pushed along in rr: hdwy 1/2-way: rdn to ld 1f out: sn clr* **5/1**[2]

2341 **2** 3 ¼ **Batchworth Lady**[50] 1050 3-9-5 **58**...................................[1] KierenFallon 5 62
(Dean Ivory) *sn pushed along in rr: hdwy over 1f out: r.o to go 2nd nr fin: nt trble wnr* **9/2**[1]

05-0 **3** ½ **Little Eli**[23] 1539 3-8-8 **52**.. JasonHart(5) 8 54
(Eric Alston) *w ldr tl rdn to ld and hung lft 2f out: hdd 1f out: no ex ins fnl f* **17/2**

330- **4** 1 **Millie N Aire**[192] 7379 3-9-0 **60**............................. MatthewHopkins(7) 4 59
(Danielle McCormick) *s.s: outpcd: r.o ins fnl f: nvr nrr* **14/1**

-231 **5** 1 ½ **Balatina**[13] 1742 3-9-0 **58**.. RobertTart(5) 6 51
(Chris Dwyer) *led: hmpd and hdd 2f out: no ex fnl f* **9/2**[1]

2-35 **6** hd **Tregereth (IRE)**[68] 811 3-9-7 **60**...................................... JohnFahy 1 52
(Jonathan Portman) *chsd ldrs: rdn over 1f out: no ex fnl f* **15/2**

034- **7** ¾ **Fidget**[250] 5733 3-9-5 **58**.. SeanLevey 7 48
(David Brown) *mid-div: pushed along and lost pl 3f out: n.d after* **7/1**[3]

040- **8** 3 ¼ **Symboline**[296] 4116 3-9-7 **60**... MartinHarley 9 38
(Mick Channon) *sn pushed along in rr: n.d* **5/1**[2]

06-4 **9** 7 **Sand And Deliver**[50] 1051 3-9-7 **60**............................[1] FergusSweeney 2
(Peter Crate) *chsd ldrs: rdn 1/2-way: wkng whn hmpd wl over 1f out* **22/1**

1m 0.3s (0.70) **Going Correction** +0.075s/f (Good) **9** Ran SP% **115.5**
Speed ratings (Par 97): **97,91,91,89,87 86,85,80,69**
toteswingers 1&2 £4.30, 1&3 £12.00, 2&3 £12.90 CSF £27.78 CT £188.41 TOTE £6.50: £1.60, £1.80, £1.80; EX 13.40 Trifecta £242.30 Pool: £955.11 - 2.95 winning units..
Owner M Golding & H Singh Birah **Bred** Manor Farm Stud (rutland) **Trained** Danethorpe, Notts
■ Stewards' Enquiry : John Fahy caution: careless riding.

FOCUS
Moderate handicap form. They went fast up front early.

2092 102 TOUCH FM - THE LOCAL FAVOURITE FILLIES' H'CAP 7f 26y

3:40 (3:42) (Class 5) (0-70,69) 3-Y-O+ **£2,587** (£770; £384; £192) **Stalls** Low

Form RPR

415P **1** **Amosite**[25] 1503 7-9-10 **65**.............................(p) SilvestreDeSousa 9 72
(J R Jenkins) *mde all: rdn and edgd rt over 1f out: styd on wl* **10/1**

3121 **2** ¾ **Maggie Pink**[25] 1503 4-9-13 **68**................................... AndrewMullen 3 73
(Michael Appleby) *chsd wnr: rdn and ev chancxe over 1f out: styd on* **3/1**[1]

23-1 **3** nk **Dutch Mistress**[116] 148 4-9-9 **64**............................... FergusSweeney 6 68+
(James Unett) *hld up: hdwy over 1f out: r.o: nt rch ldrs* **11/2**

00-6 **4** ½ **Uncomplicated**[24] 1515 3-9-2 **69**..........................(b[1]) MatthewDavies 5 68
(Jim Boyle) *chsd ldrs: rdn over 2f out: hung lft ins fnl f: styd on same pce* **17/2**

00-0 **5** 2 ¾ **Remix (IRE)**[7] 1886 4-9-0 **60**......................................(p) JackDuern(5) 4 55
(Reg Hollinshead) *mid-div: rdn over 1f out: no ex ins fnl f* **33/1**

0-52 **6** 1 ¼ **Sixties Queen**[45] 1122 3-8-10 **63**.................................. KierenFallon 7 51
(Alan Bailey) *hld up: shkn up 3f out: styng on whn eased ins fnl f: nvr nr to chal* **9/2**[2]

54-4 **7** ¾ **Jacobella**[25] 1499 3-9-1 **68**... JohnFahy 2 54
(Jonathan Portman) *s.i.s: nvr nrr* **11/2**

0-53 **8** hd **Whatever You Do (IRE)**[7] 1874 3-8-12 **65**..................... SeanLevey 1 50
(Richard Hannon) *prom: rdn over 2f out: wknd fnl f* **5/1**[3]

1m 24.3s (-0.30) **Going Correction** -0.175s/f (Firm)
WFA 3 from 4yo+ 12lb **8** Ran SP% **113.2**
Speed ratings (Par 100): **94,93,92,92,89 87,86,86**
toteswingers 1&2 £6.20, 1&3 £10.90, 2&3 £2.30 CSF £39.34 CT £184.49 TOTE £7.30: £2.80, £1.20, £2.30; EX 64.00 Trifecta £289.80 Pool: £2,571.97 - 6.65 winning units..
Owner Mrs Claire Goddard **Bred** Richard Kent **Trained** Royston, Herts

FOCUS
Little got into this.

2093 BIG LOCAL APP WARWICK MAIDEN STKS 1m 22y

4:10 (4:14) (Class 5) 3-Y-O+ **£2,587** (£770; £384; £192) **Stalls** Low

Form RPR

0- **1** **Pleasure Bent**[220] 6636 3-9-1 0.................................... KierenFallon 1 74+
(Luca Cumani) *a.p: shkn up over 2f out: rdn to ld wl ins fnl f: readily* **13/8**[1]

400- **2** ½ **Mazaaher**[180] 7627 3-9-1 67..................................... SteveDrowne 11 73
(J W Hills) *chsd ldrs: led over 1f out: rdn: hung lft and hdd wl ins fnl f* **10/1**

0- **3** ¾ **Paris Rose**[192] 7364 3-8-10 0.......................... SilvestreDeSousa 15 66
(William Haggas) *chsd ldr 7f out: pushed along to ld 2f out: hdd over 1f out: nt clr run ins fnl f: r.o* **3/1**[2]

6-0 **4** ½ **Tenor (IRE)**[16] 1678 3-9-1 0.. AndreaAtzeni 9 70+
(Roger Varian) *mid-div: hdwy u.p over 1f out: r.o: nt trble ldrs* **14/1**

5 hd **Velox** 3-8-12 0.. PatrickHills(3) 7 73+
(Luca Cumani) *s.i.s: hld up: shkn up over 1f out: r.o wl ins fnl f: nrst fin* **22/1**

6 1 ¼ **Breccbennach**[199] 7228 3-9-1 80.................................... JohnFahy 10 67
(Seamus Durack) *chsd ldrs: rdn and ev ch over 1f out: no ex ins fnl f* **7/1**[3]

6-6 **7** ½ **London Bridge (USA)**[53] 994 3-9-1 0........................... RenatoSouza 2 66+
(Jo Hughes) *hld up: rdn over 1f out: nt trble ldrs* **12/1**

0 **8** 2 ½ **Dalliefour (IRE)**[17] 1671 3-8-10 0................................ MartinHarley 12 55+
(Michael Bell) *hld up: pushed along over 2f out: nt clr run over 1f out: n.d* **33/1**

9 1 **Jimmy Sewell (IRE)**[83] 4-10-0 0................................ AndrewMullen 3 61
(Michael Appleby) *hld up: rdn over 2f out: nvr on terms* **28/1**

00 **10** ¾ **Eleanor Roosevelt (IRE)**[7] 1882 3-8-10 0................ FergusSweeney 4 51
(Jamie Osborne) *s.i.s: swished tail in rr: effrt over 2f out: n.d* **33/1**

0- **11** 7 **Peninsula**[324] 3161 4-9-9 0..[1] SeanLevey 14 38
(Tobias B P Coles) *led: rdn and hdd 2f out: wknd over 1f out* **25/1**

05 **12** ½ **Just Isla**[46] 1095 3-8-10 0.. ChrisCatlin 8 34
(Peter Makin) *plld hrd: trckd ldrs: rdn over 1f out: wknd fnl f* **66/1**

13 4 ½ **Memorize (IRE)** 3-9-1 0.. TedDurcan 5 28
(Ed Walker) *s.i.s: a in rr* **33/1**

14 ½ **Shameless Man (IRE)**[22] 6-9-11 0.........................(t) SimonPearce(3) 6 30
(Anthony Middleton) *s.i.s: a in rr* **66/1**

1m 40.96s (-0.04) **Going Correction** -0.175s/f (Firm)
WFA 3 from 4yo+ 13lb **14** Ran SP% **122.5**
Speed ratings (Par 103): **93,92,91,91,91 89,89,86,85,85 78,77,73,72**
toteswingers 1&2 £6.40, 1&3 £2.50, 2&3 £7.80 CSF £17.96 TOTE £3.20: £1.60, £2.70, £1.90; EX 26.10 Trifecta £101.20 Pool: £2,096.54 - 15.52 winning units..
Owner Craig Bennett **Bred** Whitley Stud **Trained** Newmarket, Suffolk
■ Stewards' Enquiry : Steve Drowne one-day ban: careless riding (May 20)

FOCUS
They went quite steady in this, but it's a race that should throw up winners.

2094 AMBER SECURITY LTD H'CAP (LONDON MILE QUALIFIER) 1m 22y

4:40 (4:43) (Class 5) (0-70,70) 3-Y-O **£2,587** (£770; £384; £192) **Stalls** Low

Form RPR

3-44 **1** **Kohlaan (IRE)**[33] 1323 3-9-7 **70**.................................. AndreaAtzeni 8 78+
(Roger Varian) *a.p: racd keenly: trckd ldr over 5f out: rdn and hmpd over 1f out: r.o to ld and edgd lft wl ins fnl f* **4/1**[2]

40-1 **2** nk **Order Of Service**[14] 1712 3-9-5 **68**................................ SeanLevey 1 74
(David Brown) *led: rdn and edgd rt over 1f out: hdd wl ins fnl f* **2/1**[1]

-230 **3** 1 ¾ **Isis Blue**[14] 1714 3-9-5 **68**.. SteveDrowne 5 70+
(Rod Millman) *hld up: hdwy over 1f out: r.o to go 3rd nr fin: nt rch ldrs* **9/2**[3]

063- **4** nk **Posh Boy (IRE)**[170] 7780 3-9-1 **64**................................... TedDurcan 2 65
(Chris Wall) *chsd ldrs: rdn over 1f out: no ex wl ins fnl f* **6/1**

1-66 **5** nk **East Texas Red (IRE)**[12] 1770 3-8-13 **67**....................... RobertTart(5) 6 68
(Mick Quinn) *hld up: hdwy over 2f out: rdn over 1f out: r.o* **16/1**

2232 **6** 9 **Green Special (ITY)**[5] 1928 3-9-2 **65**..................(v[1]) SilvestreDeSousa 4 52
(Frank Sheridan) *s.i.s: hld up: hdwy over 3f out: rdn and hung lft over 2f out: wknd over 1f out* **5/1**

5-50 **7** 8 **Lady Marmelo (IRE)**[26] 1487 3-9-2 **65**......................... MatthewDavies 7 26
(Mick Channon) *chsd ldr over 2f: rdn and wknd over 2f out* **20/1**

5-10 **8** 4 **Striking Echo**[9] 1832 3-9-7 **70**................................... FergusSweeney 3 22
(Reg Hollinshead) *broke wl: lost pl 6f out: n.d after: bhd whn hung lft wl over 1f out* **50/1**

1m 39.56s (-1.44) **Going Correction** -0.175s/f (Firm) **8** Ran SP% **115.1**
Speed ratings (Par 99): **100,99,97,97,97 88,80,76**
toteswingers 1&2 £3.10, 1&3 £4.00, 2&3 £2.70 CSF £12.52 CT £36.88 TOTE £3.50: £1.50, £1.50, £1.80; EX 13.60 Trifecta £54.90 Pool: £2,482.94 - 33.88 winning units..
Owner Sheikh Ahmed Al Maktoum **Bred** Old Carhue Stud **Trained** Newmarket, Suffolk

FOCUS
A competitive little heat and no surprise to see it produce a close finish. It paid to race prominently.

2095 CRESCENT PRESS LTD H'CAP 1m 2f 188y

5:10 (5:10) (Class 6) (0-60,60) 3-Y-O **£1,940** (£577; £288; £144) **Stalls** Low

Form RPR

0-13 **1** **Astrum**[16] 1685 3-9-6 **59**... AndreaAtzeni 7 66+
(Rod Millman) *a.p: rdn to ld 2f out: sn edgd rt: styd on wl* **7/2**[1]

600- **2** 1 ¾ **Nateeja (IRE)**[180] 7628 3-9-7 **60**.................................. SteveDrowne 1 63
(J W Hills) *s.i.s: sn pushed along and prom: rdn over 2f out: r.o to go 2nd wl ins fnl f: nt trble wnr* **5/1**

000- **3** ½ **Burma Days (USA)**[173] 7705 3-8-11 **50**.......................... MartinHarley 6 52+
(Sylvester Kirk) *hld up: hdwy over 1f out: styd on* **14/1**

064- 4 ½ **Exclusion (USA)**[140] 8147 3-9-2 **55**..........................(b[1]) StevieDonohoe 2 56
(Noel Quinlan) *chsd ldrs: rdn and ev ch 2f out: styd on same pce ins fnl f* **7/1**

0-64 5 2¼ **Loraine**[14] 1712 3-9-6 **59**.. FergusSweeney 5 56+
(Jamie Osborne) *hld up: rdn over 2f out: nt trble ldrs* **4/1[2]**

5165 6 ½ **Rainford Glory (IRE)**[13] 1743 3-9-5 **58**................................ SeanLevey 9 55
(David Simcock) *hld up: rdn over 2f out: hung lft over 1f out: n.d* **11/1**

5050 7 ½ **Limoges**[11] 1781 3-8-7 **46**...(v) ChrisCatlin 3 42
(Luke Dace) *led: rdn and hdd 2f out: no ex fnl f* **50/1**

0350 8 6 **Exit Clause**[13] 1747 3-8-8 **52**..(p) RobertTart(5) 4 38
(Tony Carroll) *prom: rdn over 2f out: wknd over 1f out* **25/1**

36- 9 3½ **Laughing Rock (IRE)**[172] 7724 3-9-6 **59**................... AndrewMullen 8 39
(Michael Appleby) *hld up: hung rt and wknd over 3f out* **9/2[3]**

05-0 10 1 **Superoo (IRE)**[12] 1759 3-8-8 **47**.................................. SilvestreDeSousa 10 29
(Mark Johnston) *trckd ldrs: racd keenly: rdn over 2f out: wknd over 1f out* **12/1**

2m 24.29s (3.19) **Going Correction** -0.175s/f (Firm) **10** Ran SP% **118.1**
Speed ratings (Par 97): **81,79,79,79,77 77,76,72,69,69**
toteswingers 1&2 £3.80, 1&3 £19.50, 2&3 £17.80 CSF £21.42 CT £220.31 TOTE £3.70: £1.20, £2.30, £4.90; EX 10.60 Trifecta £144.40 Pool: £1,261.48 - 6.54 winning units..
Owner The Links Partnership **Bred** Jeremy Green And Sons **Trained** Kentisbeare, Devon

FOCUS
Solid form for the grade. They went just a steady pace.
T/Plt: £120.20 to a £1 stake. Pool: £45,572.24 - 276.68 winning units T/Qpdt: £8.10 to a £1 stake. Pool: £2,537.80 - 231.30 winning units CR

1880 WINDSOR (R-H)
Monday, May 6
OFFICIAL GOING: Good to firm (good in places; 8.9)
Wind: Virtually nil Weather: Sunny

2096 YOUNG HOOVES KIDS CLUB APPRENTICE TRAINING SERIES H'CAP (RACING EXCELLENCE INITIATIVE) 6f
2:30 (2:31) (Class 6) (0-65,65) 4-Y-0+ **£1,940** (£577; £288; £144) **Stalls** Low

Form RPR
006 1 **Methaaly (IRE)**[16] 1694 10-8-8 **55**..............................(be) JoeyHaynes(3) 2 63
(Michael Mullineaux) *in rr: rdn 2f out: hdwy 1f out: styd on wl to ld fnl 25yds: pushed out* **9/1**

0213 2 nk **First Rebellion**[14] 1734 4-8-4 **55**...........................(b) AidenBlakemore(7) 9 62
(Tony Carroll) *led on stands' rail: drvn 2f out: hrd pressed 1f out: kpt on tl hdd and no ex fnl 25yds* **15/2[2]**

5600 3 hd **Illustrious Prince (IRE)**[9] 1819 6-9-2 **65**............... LukeLeadbitter(5) 12 71
(Declan Carroll) *chsd ldrs: drvn to chal appr fnl f: stl ev ch fnl 110yds: no ex clsng stages* **6/1[1]**

430- 4 2½ **Maria Montez**[241] 6002 4-8-10 **57**............................... ShelleyBirkett(3) 7 55
(J W Hills) *chsd ldr: drvn 2f out: stl v ch whn hit over hd fnl 110yds: sn btn* **20/1**

020 5 1¼ **Imjin River (IRE)**[11] 1783 6-8-7 **51** oh2............................(t) NoelGarbutt 3 45
(William Stone) *s.i.s: in rr: hdwy to press ldrs 1f out: wknd fnl 110yds* **16/1**

0345 6 ¾ **Christopher Chua (IRE)**[51] 1042 4-8-2 **51**............... DanielCremin(5) 1 43
(Simon Dow) *in tch: rdn and sme hdwy over 1f out: one pce ins fnl f* **15/2[2]**

-660 7 hd **Dancing Welcome**[10] 1802 7-9-2 **60**..................................(b) NedCurtis 8 51
(Milton Bradley) *chsd ldrs: rdn 2f out: wknd ins fnl f* **17/2[3]**

3456 8 ½ **Reginald Claude**[11] 1798 5-8-10 **61**........................ EmilyMelbourn(7) 13 51
(Mark Usher) *in rr: hdwy over 1f out: wknd ins fnl f* **12/1**

06/6 9 1 **Laugh Or Cry**[13] 1752 5-8-4 **53**..[1] PaulBooth(5) 6 40
(Dean Ivory) *in rr: pushed along and sme prog 2f out: sn btn* **14/1**

600- 10 1¼ **Cocohatchee**[210] 6932 5-9-7 **65**... JakePayne 4 48
(Pat Phelan) *chsd ldrs: rdn 2f out: wknd over 1f out* **25/1**

0600 11 ¾ **Courageous (IRE)**[6] 1902 7-9-4 **65**................................. EoinWalsh(3) 5 45
(Milton Bradley) *chsd ldrs: rdn 2f out: wknd over 1f out* **15/2[2]**

060- 12 2¾ **Madame Kintyre**[143] 8115 5-8-10 **57**............................ PatMillman(3) 11 28
(Rod Millman) *outpcd most of way* **12/1**

1m 13.15s (0.15) **Going Correction** -0.075s/f (Good) **12** Ran SP% **112.8**
Speed ratings (Par 101): **96,95,95,92,90 89,89,88,87,85 84,80**
Tote Swingers 1&2 £6.60, 2&3 £4.30, 1&3 £12.40 CSF £71.21 CT £442.83 TOTE £13.00: £3.80, £1.50, £1.90; EX 60.60 Trifecta £254.80 Pool: £1,773.44 - 5.21 winning units..
Owner S A Pritchard **Bred** Scuderia Golden Horse S R L **Trained** Alpraham, Cheshire
■ Stewards' Enquiry : Luke Leadbitter two-day ban: used whip above permitted level (May 20-21)

FOCUS
The ground, which had been watered, was given as good to firm, good in places (GoingStick: 8.9). Ian Mongan said after the second race, "It's quick ground without any jar." The inner of the straight was dolled out 6yds at the 6f pole and 3yds at the winning post. The top bend was dolled out 5yds from the normal inner configuration, adding 20yds to races over 1m and more. They looked to go an even pace in this apprentices' handicap. Modest form, but the winner's best turf run for a couple of years.

2097 MAGNUM INFINITY H'CAP 6f
3:00 (3:02) (Class 4) (0-85,85) 4-Y-0+ **£4,851** (£1,443; £721; £360) **Stalls** Low

Form RPR
2-21 1 **Nocturn**[14] 1726 4-9-7 **85**...(p) GrahamLee 2 99+
(Jeremy Noseda) *mde all: hung lft over 3f out: pushed along and hung bdly lft again ins fnl f but a doing enough* **2/1[1]**

1240 2 nk **Blue Jack**[10] 1814 8-8-13 **77**..(t) MickaelBarzalona 7 90
(Stuart Williams) *in tch: hdwy to chse wnr over 1f out: chal ins fnl f: sn pushed lft: kpt on but a readily hld* **15/2[3]**

12-0 3 4½ **Ashpan Sam**[14] 1726 4-9-4 **82**.. NickyMackay 8 81
(John Spearing) *chsd ldrs: wnt 2nd over 2f out: no imp over 1f out: sn outpcd into 3rd* **12/1**

-23 4 ¾ **O'Gorman**[24] 1517 4-9-3 **81**.. GeorgeBaker 9 77
(Gary Brown) *in rr: nt clr run over 2f out: hdwy over 1f out: kpt on for wl-hld 4th ins fnl f* **9/1**

15-2 5 1½ **Flexible Flyer**[33] 1318 4-9-0 **78**....................................... JimmyFortune 10 69+
(Hughie Morrison) *stdd s and c rt towards stands' rail: t.k.h: hdwy over 1f out: no prog fnl f* **10/3[2]**

03-0 6 1¼ **Lexi's Hero (IRE)**[14] 1726 5-9-7 **85**................................. HayleyTurner 3 72
(Ed Dunlop) *chsd ldrs: bmpd over 3f out: wknd over 1f out* **14/1**

65-0 7 2 **Links Drive Lady**[14] 1726 5-9-4 **82**...................................... PatDobbs 1 63
(Dean Ivory) *chsd ldrs: rdn 2f out: wknd over 1f out* **17/2**

44-5 8 8 **Piazza San Pietro**[24] 1517 7-9-7 **85**.................................. IanMongan 5 40
(Zoe Davison) *rdn over 2f out: a outpcd in rr* **25/1**

000- 9 2 **Nasri**[192] 7366 7-9-7 **85**... RichardKingscote 6 34
(Milton Bradley) *chsd ldrs: rdn over 2f out: sn btn* **25/1**

1040 10 6 **Noverre To Go (IRE)**[11] 1787 7-9-6 **84**........................ RobertWinston 4 14
(Ronald Harris) *chsd ldrs whn bmpd over 3f out: sn btn* **33/1**

1m 11.64s (-1.36) **Going Correction** -0.075s/f (Good) **10** Ran SP% **113.7**
Speed ratings (Par 105): **106,105,99,98,96 94,92,81,78,70**
Tote Swingers 1&2 £4.10, 2&3 £14.20, 1&3 £4.50 CSF £16.59 CT £143.88 TOTE £2.60: £1.10, £2.60, £4.30; EX 13.90 Trifecta £116.00 Pool: £2,612.85 - 16.88 winning units..
Owner Miss Yvonne Jacques **Bred** J Ellis **Trained** Newmarket, Suffolk

FOCUS
Two came clear here and both look ahead of the handicapper. The time was good and the winner is obviously progressing.

2098 SOLERO H'CAP 5f 10y
3:30 (3:32) (Class 5) (0-70,70) 3-Y-0 **£2,587** (£770; £384; £192) **Stalls** Low

Form RPR
51-5 1 **Exotic Isle**[16] 1682 3-9-7 **70**.. JamieSpencer 11 79+
(Ralph Beckett) *hld up in rr: hdwy 2f out: led over 1f out and hung lft: drvn out ins fnl f: readily* **11/1**

0-51 2 1½ **Royal Guinevere**[16] 1682 3-9-3 **66**....................................... PatDobbs 15 70
(Dean Ivory) *chsd ldrs: wnt 2nd over 1f out: kpt on but nvr any ch w wnr* **11/2[2]**

0156 3 nk **Buy Art**[17] 1661 3-9-4 **67**...(p) GeorgeBaker 8 70
(Gary Moore) *s.i.s: in rr: hdwy over 1f out to take 3rd ins fnl f: clsng nr fin but nvr any ch w ldrs* **11/1**

00-0 4 ½ **Starlight Angel (IRE)**[26] 1482 3-9-4 **70**........................ DarrenEgan(3) 6 71
(Ronald Harris) *in rr: hdwy 2f out: styd on to take 4th ins fnl f* **20/1**

2143 5 1½ **Silca's Dream**[9] 1844 3-9-1 **69**................................... CharlesBishop(5) 10 65
(Mick Channon) *chsd ldrs: rdn and edgd rt ins fnl f: sn wknd* **11/2[2]**

6-13 6 hd **Malaysian Boleh**[32] 1345 3-9-5 **68**........................... MickaelBarzalona 5 63
(Simon Dow) *in rr: hdwy on ins over 2f out: squeezed through to chse ldrs ins fnl f: sn one pce* **6/1[3]**

0-54 7 2¾ **Deepest Blue**[9] 1844 3-8-12 **68**................................ LukeLeadbitter(7) 13 53
(Declan Carroll) *pressed ldrs: rdn 2f out: edgd rt ins fnl f and sn wknd* **14/1**

300- 8 nk **Risky Rizkova**[208] 6984 3-9-1 **64**.............................. RichardKingscote 9 48
(Jonathan Portman) *chsd ldrs: rdn and btn whn nt clr run ins fnl f* **25/1**

213- 9 shd **Gallena**[198] 7241 3-9-6 **69**.. GrahamLee 12 53+
(William Haggas) *trckd ldrs: wl there whn nt clr run fr over 1f out and ins fnl f: nt rcvr* **7/2[1]**

1344 10 1¼ **Marvelino**[19] 1616 3-9-3 **66**...(v) IanMongan 1 50+
(Pat Eddery) *led tl hdd over 1f out: wkng whn hmpd ins fnl f* **9/1**

05-5 11 2 **Bheleyf (IRE)**[19] 1616 3-9-4 **67**... HayleyTurner 2 39
(Joseph Tuite) *s.i.s: outpcd and only mod prog clsng stages* **22/1**

25-0 12 1¾ **Clean Blow (USA)**[16] 1682 3-9-4 **67**............................... JimmyFortune 7 51+
(David Brown) *chsd ldrs: rdn and one pce whn bdly hmpd ins fnl f: nt rcvr* **16/1**

1m 0.21s (-0.09) **Going Correction** -0.075s/f (Good) **12** Ran SP% **119.4**
Speed ratings (Par 99): **97,94,94,93,90 90,86,85,85,83 80,77**
Tote Swingers 1&2 £9.50, 2&3 £11.70, 1&3 £14.70 CSF £69.09 CT £704.33 TOTE £10.60: £3.00, £2.10, £3.70; EX 57.30 Trifecta £1081.60 Pool: £2,032.81 - 1.40 winning units..
Owner Pearl Bloodstock Ltd & N H Wrigley **Bred** T R G Vestey **Trained** Kimpton, Hants

FOCUS
There was a bit of trouble on the inside in the closing stages, but the principals raced away from the rail and dominated. The winner showed her Nottingham run to be all wrong.

2099 MAGNUM MEDIAN AUCTION MAIDEN STKS 1m 67y
4:05 (4:05) (Class 5) 3-4-Y-0 **£2,587** (£770; £384; £192) **Stalls** Low

Form RPR
0-3 1 **Ghost Runner (IRE)**[12] 1769 3-9-1 0.................................. IanMongan 3 82+
(Sir Henry Cecil) *trckd ldrs: led ins fnl 2f: pushed out fnl f: comf* **7/4[2]**

30- 2 ¾ **Da Do Run Run**[212] 6872 3-9-1 0.. MartinLane 2 80+
(Brian Meehan) *led: hdd ins fnl 2f: edgd lft u.p ins fnl f: kpt on but a comf hld* **11/2[3]**

33- 3 3¼ **Capella's Song (IRE)**[194] 7329 3-8-10 0.......................(t) HayleyTurner 7 68
(Michael Bell) *chsd ldr tl over 2f out: rdn and swtchd lft wl over 1f out: kpt on same pce for 3rd* **6/4[1]**

4 7 **Viennese Verse** 3-9-1 0... PatDobbs 8 56
(Henry Candy) *in rr: drvn over 4f out: hdwy 3f out but nvr on terms w ldrs and wknd ins fnl 2f* **13/2**

040- 5 1½ **Perseverent Pete (USA)**[195] 7313 3-8-12 51............... DarrenEgan(3) 1 53?
(Christine Dunnett) *in rr: hdwy and rdn over 3f out: nvr on terms w ldrs: wknd and hung lft fr 2f out* **66/1**

0- 6 7 **Bella Michelle**[235] 6153 3-8-10 0.................................. RichardKingscote 5 32
(Sylvester Kirk) *chsd ldrs: rdn over 3f out: wknd over 2f out* **33/1**

0 7 1½ **Be Excellent**[51] 1035 3-8-10 0... HarryBentley 6 28
(Joseph Tuite) *in rr: rdn over 4f out: sme hdwy 3f out: sn wknd* **33/1**

1m 45.34s (0.64) **Going Correction** -0.15s/f (Firm) **7** Ran SP% **112.5**
Speed ratings (Par 103): **90,89,86,79,77 70,69**
Tote Swingers 1&2 £1.90, 2&3 £2.00, 1&3 £1.20 CSF £11.27 TOTE £3.00: £1.60, £2.50; EX 9.50 Trifecta £21.00 Pool: £2,415.63 - 86.14 winning units..
Owner Middleham Park Racing L **Bred** D And Mrs D Veitch **Trained** Newmarket, Suffolk

FOCUS
This didn't look a particularly strong maiden and the pace was muddling. The favourite was below form but the winner progressed.

2100 MR WHIPPY H'CAP 1m 67y
4:35 (4:35) (Class 3) (0-90,88) 3-Y-0 **£7,439** (£2,213; £1,106) **Stalls** Low

Form RPR
03-1 1 **Sea Shanty (USA)**[14] 1725 3-8-12 **79**.................................... PatDobbs 2 88+
(Richard Hannon) *trckd ldr: pushed along 3f out: led 2f out: styd on strly fnl f to assert fnl 110yds: readily* **8/11[1]**

21-4 2 1¾ **Excuse To Linger**[14] 1714 3-8-13 **80**.................................. GrahamLee 1 84
(Jeremy Noseda) *plld hrd in cl 3rd: swtchd lft to outside over 2f out and sn hanging lft and chsng wnr: continued to hang and styd on same pce fnl f* **4/1[3]**

13-1 3 6 **Hipster**[102] 359 3-9-7 **88**...(v) RichardKingscote 3 78
(Ralph Beckett) *sn drvn to ld: hdd 2f out: btn appr fnl f* **5/2[2]**

1m 42.67s (-2.03) **Going Correction** -0.15s/f (Firm) **3** Ran SP% **106.5**
Speed ratings (Par 103): **104,102,96**
CSF £3.65 TOTE £1.60; EX 3.40 Trifecta £4.60 Pool: £1,083.78 - 174.70 winning units..
Owner The Queen **Bred** Her Majesty The Queen **Trained** East Everleigh, Wilts

FOCUS
Just a small field, but three interesting runners. The pace was decent and the winner built on his reappearance win.

2101 CORNETTO H'CAP 1m 2f 7y
5:05 (5:05) (Class 4) (0-85,85) 4-Y-0+ £4,851 (£1,443; £721; £360) Stalls Centre

Form RPR
0-00 1 **Come On Blue Chip (IRE)**25 1501 4-9-1 79..........(p) RobertWinston 6 89
(Paul D'Arcy) *in rr: drvn and hdwy over 2f out: pressed ldr u.p ins fnl f: led last strides* **15/2**
104- 2 *hd* **Highland Duke (IRE)**227 6450 4-8-4 73.......................... RyanTate(5) 2 83
(Clive Cox) *t.k.h: led after 3f: rdn over 2f out: hrd pressed ins fnl f: hdd last strides* **7/2**2
0-32 3 3 1/4 **Sheila's Buddy**16 1673 4-9-1 79.......................... LiamJones 1 82
(J S Moore) *in tch: rdn to chse ldrs over 2f out: styd on for one pce 3rd fnl f* **11/2**3
0104 4 3/4 **Thecornishcowboy**13 1753 4-8-8 72..........................(t) JackMitchell 4 74
(John Ryan) *chsd ldrs: rdn over 2f out: effrt over 1f out: no ex ins fnl f* **14/1**
340- 5 4 1/2 **Open Water (FR)**319 3296 4-9-7 85.......................... JimmyFortune 9 78
(Andrew Balding) *t.k.h: led 3f: styd chsng ldr: rdn ins fnl 3f: wknd ins fnl 2f* **7/4**1
0-21 6 3 3/4 **Poetic Lord**11 1780 4-8-11 75.......................... JamesDoyle 8 60
(Sylvester Kirk) *in rr: rdn and sme prog ins fnl 3f: nvr rchd ldrs and wknd appr fnl 2f* **6/1**
0210 7 2 **Brocklebank (IRE)**25 1500 4-8-12 76.......................... GrahamLee 3 57
(Simon Dow) *s.i.s: rdn wl over 2f out: a bhd* **16/1**

2m 5.57s (-3.13) **Going Correction** -0.15s/f (Firm) 7 Ran SP% **112.6**
Speed ratings (Par 105): **106,105,103,102,99 96,94**
Tote Swingers 1&2 £2.90, 2&3 £4.80, 1&3 £9.50 CSF £32.70 CT £155.35 TOTE £8.00: £4.20, £2.10; EX 44.40 Trifecta £202.50 Pool: £3,124.20 - 10.25 winning units..
Owner Blue Chip Feed Ltd **Bred** Gerry Flannery Developments **Trained** Newmarket, Suffolk

FOCUS
There was a strong pace on here and that eventually set the race up for one of those more patiently ridden. Straightforward form.

2102 FIREMAN SAM FAMILY FUN DAY - MAY 27 H'CAP 1m 3f 135y
5:35 (5:38) (Class 4) (0-85,80) 4-Y-0+ £4,851 (£1,443; £721; £360) Stalls Centre

Form RPR
0-33 1 **Saint Helena (IRE)**2 2004 5-9-3 76.......................... JamesDoyle 3 82
(Harry Dunlop) *s.i.s: hld up in rr: hdwy over 2f out: rdn to ld and edgd rt 1f out: rdn ins fnl f: on top fnl 50yds* **4/1**2
2 1 1/2 **Duaiseoir (IRE)**16 3423 7-9-1 74.......................... HayleyTurner 5 77
(Venetia Williams) *chsd ldr: led appr fnl 2f: styd on u.p: hdd 1f out: no ex fnl 50yds* **12/1**
316/ 3 2 1/4 **Crimson Knight**669 3772 5-8-13 72.......................... MartinLane 7 72+
(Brian Meehan) *chsd ldrs: chal fr over 2f out and stl ev ch whn bmpd 1f out: wknd fnl 110yds* **7/2**1
4455 4 2 **Sir Boss (IRE)**11 1774 8-9-4 77.......................... RichardKingscote 4 73
(Michael Mullineaux) *chsd ldrs: rdn over 2f out: wknd appr fnl f* **12/1**
0-02 5 3 1/4 **Achalas (IRE)**21 1586 5-8-13 77.......................... RyanTate(5) 8 68
(Heather Main) *led: hdd appr fnl 2f: wknd over 1f out* **5/1**3
114- 6 4 1/2 **Presto Volante (IRE)**204 7077 5-8-13 72..........................(p) PatDobbs 2 55
(Amanda Perrett) *chsd ldrs: rdn and wknd over 2f out* **7/2**1
130- 7 12 **The Quarterjack**204 7082 4-9-2 75.......................... GrahamLee 6 38
(Ron Hodges) *rdn 3f out: a in rr* **5/1**3

2m 26.68s (-2.82) **Going Correction** -0.15s/f (Firm) 7 Ran SP% **113.2**
Speed ratings (Par 105): **103,102,100,99,97 94,86**
Tote Swingers 1&2 £7.10, 2&3 £7.60, 1&3 £2.60 CSF £47.45 CT £181.77 TOTE £3.80: £1.90, £4.80; EX 42.20 Trifecta £148.00 Pool: £2,172.34 - 11.00 winning units..
Owner W R B Racing 47 **Bred** Frank O'Malley **Trained** Lambourn, Berks
■ Stewards' Enquiry : James Doyle caution: careless riding.

FOCUS
This looked quite competitive and it was run in a decent time, but there are one or two doubts over the form. The winner is rated back to her 3yo best.
T/Plt: £1,038.30 to a £1 stake. Pool: £68,058.86 - 47.85 winning tickets. T/Qpdt: £225.50 to a £1 stake. Pool: £3,124.20 - 10.25 winning tickets. ST

2103 - 2104a (Foreign Racing) - See Raceform Interactive

1411 CURRAGH (R-H)
Monday, May 6

OFFICIAL GOING: Round course - good to yielding; straight course - yielding (soft in places)

2105a HIGH CHAPARRAL EUROPEAN BREEDERS FUND MOORESBRIDGE STKS (GROUP 3) 1m 2f
3:15 (3:17) 4-Y-0+ £38,313 (£11,199; £5,304; £1,768)

RPR
1 **Camelot**211 6912 4-9-8 124.......................... JosephO'Brien 4 112+
(A P O'Brien, Ire) *w.w in rr tl tk clsr order in 4th 3f out: qcknd to ld 1f out: pushed out: comf* **1/3**1
2 1 3/4 **Triumphant (IRE)**227 6462 4-9-3 100..........................(v1) SeamieHeffernan 2 102+
(A P O'Brien, Ire) *sn clr ldr: reduced advantage appr fnl 2f: hdd 1f out: kpt on same pce* **20/1**3
3 *hd* **Parish Hall (IRE)**29 1415 4-9-3 112.......................... KevinManning 5 102+
(J S Bolger, Ire) *racd in 3rd: pushed along 3f out: nt qckn w wnr 1f out: kpt on for press into 3rd ins fnl f* **5/2**2
4 1 1/2 **Macbeth (IRE)**21 1592 4-9-3 91..........................(v1) ShaneFoley 1 99?
(K J Condon, Ire) *chsd clr ldr in 2nd tl reduced deficit over 1f out: sn no ex and dropped to 4th: one pce* **40/1**
5 4 1/2 **Negotiate**21 1592 5-9-0 88.......................... PatSmullen 3 87?
(Ms Joanna Morgan, Ire) *hld up in 4th: dropped to rr 3f out: no imp over 1f out* **66/1**

2m 16.27s (6.97) **Going Correction** +0.025s/f (Good) 5 Ran SP% **112.3**
Speed ratings: **93,91,91,90,86**
CSF £9.56 TOTE £1.20: £1.02, £6.60; DF 10.00.
Owner Derrick Smith & Michael Tabor & Mrs John Magnier **Bred** Sheikh Abdulla Bin Isa Al-Khalifa **Trained** Ballydoyle, Co Tipperary

FOCUS
The winning time was 3sec slower than the 50-80 handicap. The front-running second has been rated close to hise best.

2108a CANFORD CLIFFS EUROPEAN BREEDERS FUND ATHASI STKS (GROUP 3) (FILLIES) 7f
4:50 (4:50) 3-Y-0+ £38,313 (£11,199; £5,304; £1,768)

RPR
1 **Viztoria (IRE)**181 7623 3-8-12 111 ow1.......................... JohnnyMurtagh 1 102+
(Edward Lynam, Ire) *w.w tl tk clsr order under 2f out: swtchd rt and qcknd to ld fnl 150yds: sn clr under hands and heels: comf* **1/1**1
2 1 **Bunairgead (IRE)**8 1858 3-8-11 92..........................(b1) KevinManning 6 98
(J S Bolger, Ire) *chsd ldr in 2nd: clsd and led briefly 1f out: sn hdd and outpcd by wnr* **10/1**3
3 1 3/4 **Moonstone Magic**365 1884 4-9-9.......................... PatSmullen 4 98
(Ralph Beckett) *chsd ldrs in 4th: pushed along 2f out where nt qckn: kpt on same pce fnl f* **5/2**2
4 *hd* **Caprella**249 5777 4-9-9 96.......................... CO'Donoghue 5 97
(P D Deegan, Ire) *led tl strly-pressed and hdd 1f out: sn one pce* **16/1**
5 *nk* **Roseraie (IRE)**16 1704 3-8-11 94.......................... DeclanMcDonogh 7 92
(Kevin Prendergast, Ire) *trckd ldrs in 3rd tl pushed along over 2f out: sn no imp: kpt on one pce* **10/1**3
6 1 **Dubaya**191 7419 3-8-11 92.......................... ChrisHayes 8 90
(A Oliver, Ire) *w.w in 5th: pushed along and swtchd rt 1f out: sn no imp* **14/1**
7 2 **Bethany Bay (IRE)**25 1504 3-8-11 73.......................... TadhgO'Shea 2 84?
(John Patrick Shanahan, Ire) *t.k.h in rr: niggled along over 2f out: nvr gng pce to chal: kpt on one pce* **25/1**
8 1 3/4 **Infanta Branca (USA)**33 1336 3-8-11 95.......................... SeamieHeffernan 3 79
(A P O'Brien, Ire) *hld up in rr: pushed along and nt qckn over 1f out* **10/1**3

1m 30.53s (-0.27) **Going Correction** -0.05s/f (Good)
WFA 3 from 4yo 12lb 8 Ran SP% **122.2**
Speed ratings: **99,97,95,95,95 94,91,89**
CSF £14.17 TOTE £1.80: £1.02, £1.30, £2.10; DF 5.50.
Owner Mrs K Lavery **Bred** Airlie Stud **Trained** Dunshaughlin, Co Meath

FOCUS
A comfortable win for the highest-rated runner. It proved hard to make up ground but the winner did, and won cosily. The fourth, fifth and sixth help set the standard.

2109 - (Foreign Racing) - See Raceform Interactive

AYR (L-H)
Tuesday, May 7

2110 Meeting Abandoned - course unfit

1757 CATTERICK (L-H)
Tuesday, May 7

OFFICIAL GOING: Good to firm (firm in places; 9.0)
Wind: Light; half behind Weather: Fine; sunny

2117 RACINGUK.COM MAIDEN AUCTION STKS 5f
6:10 (6:12) (Class 6) 2-Y-O £2,385 (£704; £352) Stalls Low

Form RPR
35 1 **Lorimer's Lot (IRE)**10 1839 2-8-4 0.......................... DuranFentiman 1 60
(Tim Walford) *w ldr: led over 4f out: hung rt over 2f out: fnd ex whn chal clsng stages* **5/1**
2 *nk* **Bajan Rebel** 2-8-6 0.......................... GrahamGibbons 3 61
(Michael Easterby) *dwlt: sn chsng ldrs: outpcd over 2f out: hdwy to chse wnr last 100yds: no ex towards fin* **3/1**2
2 3 2 1/4 **Weisse Girl**25 1512 2-8-8 0..........................(b) PJMcDonald 5 55
(Noel Quinlan) *led for 1f: chsd ldr: swtchd lft over 1f out: hung lft and one pce* **2/1**1
4 1 1/2 **Porsh Herrik** 2-8-11 0.......................... MichaelO'Connell 2 52
(John Quinn) *dwlt: sn chsng ldrs: outpcd over 2f out: hdwy over 1f out: keeping on same pce whn hmpd wl ins fnl f* **7/1**
5 *hd* **Music Stop** 2-8-6 0.......................... JoeFanning 4 47+
(Mark Johnston) *dwlt: sn chsng ldrs on outer: hung lft and lost pl 3f out: hmpd and swtchd rt wl ins fnl f: nvr threatened* **7/2**3

1m 0.07s (0.27) **Going Correction** -0.20s/f (Firm) 5 Ran SP% **109.7**
Speed ratings (Par 91): **89,88,84,82,82**
CSF £19.77 TOTE £5.50: £1.60, £1.30; EX 18.30 Trifecta £57.20 Pool: £1132.73 - 14.84 winning units..
Owner Lorimer Walford **Bred** Roundhill Stud & Gleadhill House Stud Ltd **Trained** Sheriff Hutton, N Yorks
■ Stewards' Enquiry : P J McDonald two-day ban: careless riding (May 21-22)

FOCUS
Far bend dolled out 3yds, increasing distance of races between 6f-1m4ff by 12yds and 2m race by 24yds. A weak juvenile maiden.

2118 RACING AGAIN ON FRIDAY 24TH MAY CLAIMING STKS 1m 3f 214y
6:40 (6:40) (Class 6) 4-Y-0+ £2,385 (£704; £352) Stalls Low

Form RPR
14-2 1 **Just Lille (IRE)**12 1795 10-8-12 75..........................(p) PJMcDonald 2 67
(Ann Duffield) *trckd ldrs: pushed along 4f out: chsd ldr over 2f out: led appr fnl f: styd on wl* **3/1**1
-610 2 1 1/4 **Royal Opera**12 1774 5-8-6 72..........................(b) PaulPickard(3) 9 61
(Brian Ellison) *drvn to ld after 1f: hdd appr fnl f: kpt on same pce* **5/1**3
06-0 3 *nk* **Sally Friday (IRE)**27 1464 5-8-2 48 ow3..........................(p) KevinStott(7) 3 61
(Edwin Tuer) *in rr-div: hdwy over 3f out: swtchd rt 2f out: kpt on to take 3rd ins fnl f: styng on at fin* **33/1**
600- 4 2 **Sinatramania**213 6885 6-8-7 52.......................... FrannyNorton 4 56
(Tracy Waggott) *t.k.h towards rr: hdwy over 3f out: chsng ldrs over 2f out: 3rd and swtchd rt over 1f out: kpt on same pce* **14/1**
60-2 5 2 1/2 **Eijaaz (IRE)**13 1763 12-8-4 59..........................(p) RaulDaSilva(3) 5 52
(Geoffrey Harker) *dwlt: in rr: drvn 6f out: kpt on fnl 2f: nvr a factor* **6/1**
430- 6 2 1/2 **Blue Top**32 6361 4-8-9 51.......................... GrahamGibbons 6 50
(Tim Walford) *chsd ldrs: drvn over 3f out: wknd over 1f out* **33/1**
600- 7 1 **Hawk Mountain (UAE)**283 4613 8-9-13 80.......... MichaelO'Connell 10 66
(John Quinn) *hld up in rr: effrt 3f out: nvr a threat* **6/1**
600/ 8 7 **Party Doctor**726 2031 6-9-3 85.......................... GrahamLee 12 45
(Martin Todhunter) *wnt rt s: t.k.h in rr: pushed along 6f out: lost pl over 3f out* **12/1**

The Form Book Flat, Raceform Ltd, Compton, RG20 6NL.

3623 **9** *10* **Roc De Prince**[13] 1763 4-9-7 69....(v) DanielTudhope 8 40
(David O'Meara) *chsd ldrs: effrt over 3f out: lost pl over 1f out: eased whn bhd clsng stages* **10/3**[2]

0 **10** *40* **Wesleydale (IRE)**[112] 215 6-8-7 0.... DuranFentiman 11
(Simon West) *sn chsng ldrs: lost pl over 3f out: sn bhd: t.o* **200/1**

00- **11** *59* **Fa'Side Castle (IRE)**[13] 908 4-8-7 0....(t) AndrewMullen 7
(Maurice Barnes) *led 1f: chsd ldrs: lost pl over 3f out: sn wl bhd: t.o over 2f out: virtually p.u: eventually completed* **200/1**

2m 34.06s (-4.84) **Going Correction** -0.20s/f (Firm) **11** Ran SP% **114.6**
Speed ratings (Par 101): **108,107,106,105,103 102,101,96,90,63 24**
toteswingers 1&2 £4.50, 1&3 £13.00, 2&3 £40.30 CSF £17.53 TOTE £4.10: £1.20, £1.90, £10.50; EX 15.30 Trifecta £557.30 Pool: £1096.78 - 1.47 winning units..
Owner MPR,Warrender,Baines,Farrington,Kay **Bred** Sweetmans Bloodstock **Trained** Constable Burton, N Yorks

FOCUS
The bare form is weak, and the time slow, and the first two did not need to perform near their marks.

2119 YORKSHIRE-OUTDOORS.CO.UK H'CAP 7f
7:10 (7:13) (Class 4) (0-80,80) 4-Y-O+ **£6,469** (£1,925; £962; £481) **Stalls** Centre

Form RPR

20-0 **1** **Best Trip (IRE)**[12] 1787 6-9-3 **79**....(t) PaulPickard(3) 5 88
(Brian Ellison) *trckd ldrs: wnt 2nd over 4f out: styd on fnl f: led last stride* **8/1**

0-21 **2** *nse* **Snow Bay**[17] 1686 7-9-2 **80**.... ShirleyTeasdale(5) 3 89
(Paul Midgley) *led: rdn over 1f out: kpt on: hdd post* **5/2**[2]

-406 **3** *1 ½* **Smalljohn**[92] 518 7-8-8 **67**....(v) TomEaves 2 72
(Bryan Smart) *w ldr tl over 4f out: drvn 3f out: swtchd rt 1f out: kpt on same pce* **20/1**

200- **4** *5* **Orpsie Boy (IRE)**[189] 7453 10-9-4 **77**.... PJMcDonald 7 69+
(Ruth Carr) *dwlt: in rr: drvn 3f out: tk modest 4th appr fnl f* **12/1**

-405 **5** *7* **Solar Spirit (IRE)**[3] 2028 8-9-6 **79**.... GrahamLee 8 53+
(Tracy Waggott) *hld up towards rr: effrt 3f out: edgd lft and wknd appr fnl f* **5/1**[3]

-222 **6** *4* **Llewellyn**[3] 2028 5-8-12 **71**.... AdrianNicholls 1 34+
(David Nicholls) *trckd ldrs: effrt over 3f out: sn hrd drvn: wknd appr fnl f* **11/8**[1]

1m 24.9s (-2.10) **Going Correction** -0.20s/f (Firm) **6** Ran SP% **110.9**
Speed ratings (Par 105): **104,103,102,96,88 83**
toteswingers 1&2 £5.60, 1&3 £13.80, 2&3 £7.90 CSF £27.57 CT £370.73 TOTE £6.90: £5.40, £5.50; EX 38.90 Trifecta £244.60 Pool: £1045.66 - 3.20 winning units..
Owner Koo's Racing Club **Bred** Limetree Stud **Trained** Norton, N Yorks
■ Stewards' Enquiry : Shirley Teasdale two-day ban: used whip above permitted level (May 21-22)
Paul Pickard two-day ban: used whip above permitted level (May 21-22)

FOCUS
Few got involved, with the pace holding up well and the order changing little. The winner basically ran to his best.

2120 GO RACING IN YORKSHIRE H'CAP 1m 7f 177y
7:40 (7:40) (Class 6) (0-65,62) 4-Y-O+ **£2,385** (£704; £352) **Stalls** Centre

Form RPR

P0-6 **1** **Jan Smuts (IRE)**[12] 1789 5-8-13 **51**....(tp) GrahamLee 10 60
(Wilf Storey) *mid-div: hdwy 4f out: edgd lft 2f out: led on ins jst ins fnl f: hld on towards fin* **10/1**

4-00 **2** *¾* **Kodicil (IRE)**[12] 1789 5-9-4 **56**.... GrahamGibbons 9 64
(Tim Walford) *w ldrs: led over 2f out: hdd over 1f out: styd on towards fin* **6/1**[3]

50-0 **3** *nk* **Amir Pasha (UAE)**[13] 1763 8-8-10 **48**....(p) TomEaves 2 56
(Micky Hammond) *trckd ldrs: upsides over 1f out: kpt on towards fin* **28/1**

4254 **4** *1 ½* **Brunello**[13] 1763 5-9-5 **62**....(p) DavidBergin(5) 7 68
(David O'Meara) *trckd ldrs: slt ld over 1f out: hdd jst ins fnl f: kpt on same pce* **9/2**[2]

-000 **5** *1 ¼* **Maid Of Meft**[15] 1721 6-9-8 **60**.... MickyFenton 8 64
(Paul Midgley) *s.s: in rr: hdwy 3f out: kpt on one pce over 1f out* **15/2**

30-0 **6** *2 ¼* **Bijou Dan**[15] 1721 12-9-0 **52**.... PJMcDonald 1 53
(George Moore) *in rr: drvn 6f out: hdwy over 3f out: one pce fnl 2f* **16/1**

45-0 **7** *nk* **Danceintothelight**[13] 1464 6-9-6 **58**.... KellyHarrison 3 59
(Micky Hammond) *chsd ldrs: rdn and outpcd over 2f out: hung rt and one pce over 1f out* **10/1**

0/6- **8** *1 ½* **Heart Of Dubai (USA)**[339] 2698 8-8-13 **51**.... PaulMulrennan 13 50+
(Micky Hammond) *stdd s: hld up in rr: kpt on fnl 2f: nvr nr to chal* **25/1**

0-53 **9** *8* **Operateur (IRE)**[12] 1789 5-9-3 **55**....(p) PhillipMakin 5 44
(Ben Haslam) *led after 1f: qcknd pce over 4f out: hdd over 2f out: wknd over 1f out* **4/1**[1]

026- **10** *3 ¼* **Sea Cliff (IRE)**[62] 7717 9-8-10 **48**.... RoystonFfrench 15 33
(Andrew Crook) *sn mid-div: effrt over 3f out: sn lost pl* **33/1**

626- **11** *nk* **Hi Dancer**[170] 6101 10-8-10 **53**.... GeorgeChaloner(5) 12 38
(Ben Haslam) *mid-div: lost pl over 3f out* **9/1**

00-0 **12** *8* **Grand Art (IRE)**[27] 1464 9-8-11 **52**....(p) RaulDaSilva(3) 6 27
(Noel Wilson) *in rr: drvn 6f out: bhd fnl 3f* **12/1**

564- **13** *26* **Ferney Boy**[189] 7454 7-8-10 **48**.... MichaelStainton 14
(Chris Fairhurst) *led 1f: chsd ldrs: drvn over 4f out: sn lost pl and bhd: t.o* **28/1**

3m 28.14s (-3.86) **Going Correction** -0.20s/f (Firm) **13** Ran SP% **119.7**
Speed ratings (Par 101): **101,100,100,99,99 97,97,97,93,91 91,87,74**
toteswingers 1&2 £17.40, 1&3 £80.10, 2&3 £43.10 CSF £66.35 CT £1647.62 TOTE £14.50: £3.70, £2.10, £8.60; EX 86.40 Trifecta £510.60 Part won. Pool: £680.89 - 0.11 winning units..
Owner H S Hutchinson & W Storey **Bred** Tipper House Stud **Trained** Muggleswick, Co Durham

FOCUS
A really moderate staying handicap. The pace held up well and the winner, down to his last winning mark, built on a fair run last time.

2121 CATTERICKBRIDGE.CO.UK MAIDEN STKS 7f
8:10 (8:21) (Class 5) 3-Y-O+ **£2,911** (£866; £432; £216) **Stalls** Centre

Form RPR

4 **1** *hd* **Tom's Anna (IRE)**[13] 1760 3-8-9 0.... DavidAllan 11 67+
(Tim Easterby) *dwlt in rr: sn pushed along: hdwy 3f out: swtchd ins 2f out: sn hmpd: swtchd rt appr fnl f: sn chsng ldr: styd on towards fin: jst hld: fin 2nd, hd: awrdd r* **10/1**[3]

35-0 **2** **Correggio**[19] 1648 3-9-0 78.... PJMcDonald 1 70
(Micky Hammond) *trckd ldrs: led over 2f out: edgd lft over 1f out: jst hld on: fin 1st: disq & plcd 2nd* **5/1**[2]

2 **3** *4 ½* **Size (IRE)**[22] 1570 4-9-12 0.... TonyHamilton 9 63
(Richard Fahey) *chsd ldrs: drvn over 3f out: upsides over 2f out: one pce fnl f* **2/1**[1]

000- **4** *4* **Don't Tell**[189] 7450 3-8-9 36.... AndrewMullen 7 43
(George Moore) *led 1f: chsd ldrs: wknd appr fnl f* **100/1**

000- **5** *2* **Synphonic Air (IRE)**[238] 6115 3-8-6 46.... RaulDaSilva(3) 8 38
(John Weymes) *chsd ldrs: lost pl after 1f: hdwy 3f out: one pce* **66/1**

400- **6** *5* **Stormont Bridge**[245] 5917 5-9-12 58....(t) MichaelO'Connell 3 34
(Maurice Barnes) *in rr: hdwy 4f out: chsng ldrs over 2f out: wknd over 1f out* **50/1**

0- **7** *1 ¾* **High Flame (IRE)**[213] 6880 3-8-2 0.... RachelRichardson(7) 10 20
(Tim Easterby) *chsd ldrs: lost pl over 3f out* **20/1**

000- **8** *23* **Tomasini**[230] 6361 4-9-12 35....(b[1]) PaulMulrennan 6
(John Weymes) *led after 1f: hdd over 2f out: sn lost pl and bhd: eased: t.o* **100/1**

1m 26.86s (-0.14) **Going Correction** -0.20s/f (Firm)
WFA 3 from 4yo+ 12lb **8** Ran SP% **69.3**
Speed ratings (Par 103): **91,92,86,82,79 74,72,45**
toteswingers 1&2 £3.40, 1&3 £2.00, 2&3 £1.10 CSF £16.59 TOTE £7.20: £1.40, £1.90, £1.02; EX 13.80 Trifecta £26.80 Pool: £575.43 - 16.05 winning units..
Owner Mrs S Johnson **Bred** Chesters Stud Ltd **Trained** Great Habton, N Yorks
■ Stewards' Enquiry : P J McDonald two-day ban: careless riding (May 23-24)
David Allan one-day ban: careless riding (May 21)

FOCUS
Eium Mac reared up in his stall and then Reverberate went down in hers. Both were withdrawn, and so too was one of the leading fancies, Noble Deed, who was in the gate next to Reverberate and was taken out on vet's advice. There was further drama in the race itself but the form is modest, with obvious limitations.

2122 DON'T MISS SATURDAY 8TH JUNE H'CAP 5f
8:40 (8:47) (Class 5) (0-75,75) 4-Y-O+ **£3,067** (£905; £453) **Stalls** Low

Form RPR

0211 **1** **Chosen One (IRE)**[18] 1665 8-8-7 **61** oh2.... PJMcDonald 3 71
(Ruth Carr) *chsd ldrs: drvn over 2f out: led over 1f out: styd on strly: eased towards fin* **13/2**

10-1 **2** *1 ¾* **Mr Mo Jo**[13] 1758 5-9-2 **70**....(b) DanielTudhope 6 74
(Lawrence Mullaney) *led tl over 2f out: wnt 2nd jst ins fnl f: no real imp* **2/1**[1]

-032 **3** *¾* **Tuibama (IRE)**[13] 1758 4-8-7 **61**....(p) RoystonFfrench 2 62
(Tracy Waggott) *w ldr: led over 2f out: hdd over 1f out: kpt on same pce* **7/1**

04-0 **4** *3 ¾* **Bronze Beau**[19] 1649 6-8-10 **71**....(t) JacobButterfield(7) 4 59
(Kristin Stubbs) *chsd ldrs: fdd fnl f* **5/1**[2]

062- **5** *6* **Just Like Heaven (IRE)**[230] 6357 4-8-10 **64**.... DuranFentiman 5 30
(Tim Easterby) *dwlt: sn w ldrs: wknd fnl f* **18/1**

304- **6** *1 ½* **Almond Branches**[230] 6357 4-9-6 **74**....(t) PaddyAspell 7 35
(Sharon Watt) *dwlt: sn detached in last: nvr on terms* **10/1**

106- **7** *1* **Imperial Legend (IRE)**[189] 7451 4-9-2 **75**....(p) ShirleyTeasdale(5) 1 32
(David Nicholls) *dwlt: sn in tch: wknd wl over 1f out* **11/2**[3]

2520 **8** *1 ½* **Royal Bajan (USA)**[19] 1652 5-9-4 **72**....(b) GrahamLee 9 24
(James Given) *chsd ldrs on outer: lost pl over 2f out* **9/1**

58.41s (-1.39) **Going Correction** -0.20s/f (Firm) **8** Ran SP% **115.6**
Speed ratings (Par 103): **103,100,99,93,83 81,79,77**
toteswingers 1&2 £2.20, 1&3 £3.90, 2&3 £4.30 CSF £20.18 CT £95.45 TOTE £7.50: £1.80, £1.10, £2.20; EX 13.30 Trifecta £82.40 Pool: £962.35 - 8.75 winning units..
Owner Bridget Houlston, Chris Jeffery & Co **Bred** Carl Holt **Trained** Huby, N Yorks

FOCUS
A modest sprint handicap where pace was dominant. The winner was back to his 2011 level.
T/Jkpt: Not won. T/Plt: £489.00 to a £1 stake. Pool of £69,459.83 - 103.69 winning units T/Qpdt: £100.40 to a £1 stake. Pool of £5,554.47 - 40.90 winning units WG

2082 KEMPTON (A.W) (R-H)
Tuesday, May 7

OFFICIAL GOING: Standard
Wind: Slight; behind Weather: Hot; sunny

2123 CONOR MAYNARD LIVE AT KEMPTON PARK 14.09.13 MEDIAN AUCTION MAIDEN STKS 6f (P)
2:10 (2:10) (Class 6) 3-5-Y-O **£1,940** (£577; £288; £144) **Stalls** Low

Form RPR

50-2 **1** **Lewisham**[24] 1539 3-9-3 92.... JimCrowley 4 74
(Ralph Beckett) *t.k.h: pressed ldr: shkn up briefly to ld appr fnl f: easily* **1/20**[1]

0 **2** *1 ½* **Nepalese Pearl**[18] 1671 3-8-12 0.... NeilCallan 2 56
(Pat Eddery) *led: rdn and qcknd 2f out: hdd appr fnl f: kpt on: no ch w wnr* **20/1**

2020 **3** *2 ¼* **Sally Bruce**[7] 1906 3-8-5 55.... JenniferFerguson(7) 1 49
(Louise Best) *t.k.h: trckd ldrs: effrt and shkn up wl over 1f out: sn one pce* **8/1**[2]

0/0 **4** *3* **Boblini**[24] 1539 5-9-8 0.... LiamKeniry 5 43
(Mark Usher) *t.k.h: in tch: rdn and outpcd 2f out: no imp fnl f* **20/1**

3-43 **5** *1 ¾* **Guru Baby**[64] 876 3-8-12 53.... KirstyMilczarek 3 35
(John E Long) *prom on outside: outpcd whn hung lft wl over 1f out: sn btn* **10/1**[3]

1m 14.33s (1.23) **Going Correction** +0.075s/f (Slow)
WFA 3 from 5yo 10lb **5** Ran SP% **125.0**
Speed ratings (Par 101): **94,92,89,85,82**
CSF £6.02 TOTE £1.10: £1.02, £4.80; EX 3.80 Trifecta £17.90 Pool: £2,233.68 - 93.42 winning units..
Owner Raymond Tooth **Bred** Whitwell Bloodstock **Trained** Kimpton, Hants

FOCUS
As one-sided a race as you are ever likely to see. The winner is decent but this form may not be as good as rated.

2124 LADIES DAY WITH TOBY ANSTIS 07.09.13 H'CAP 1m 4f (P)
2:40 (2:41) (Class 6) (0-60,60) 3-Y-O **£1,940** (£577; £288; £144) **Stalls** Centre

Form RPR

0-42 **1** **Miss Tiger Lily**[20] 1613 3-9-7 60.... JamesDoyle 4 66
(Harry Dunlop) *hld up on outside: pushed along and prom over 3f out: kpt on wl u.p fnl f to ld towards fin* **5/1**[3]

2334 **2** *shd* **Conversing (USA)**[29] 1425 3-8-12 51.... SilvestreDeSousa 7 57
(Mark Johnston) *pressed ldr: led and rdn over 2f out: kpt on u.p fnl f: hdd towards fin* **7/1**

0-41 **3** *nk* **Niknad**[14] 1747 3-8-9 48.... DaleSwift 5 54
(Brian Ellison) *hld up towards rr: drvn and outpcd over 3f out: rallied and ev ch ins fnl f: kpt on: hld cl home* **10/1**

-322 **4** *1½* **Knight's Parade (IRE)**[3] 2017 3-9-6 59..............................(p) PatDobbs 3 62
(Amanda Perrett) *hld up: smooth hdwy over 3f out: effrt and drvn 2f out: kpt on same pce wl ins fnl f* **9/4**[2]

-305 **5** *3* **Sweet Alabama**[14] 1747 3-8-13 52.............................. FergusSweeney 8 51
(Rod Millman) *prom: effrt and rdn over 2f out: outpcd appr fnl f* **33/1**

000- **6** *4½* **Noble Bacchus (IRE)**[227] 6486 3-9-7 60.................. RichardKingscote 6 52
(Tom Dascombe) *trckd ldrs: drvn and outpcd over 2f out: btn whn edgd rt over 1f out* **2/1**[1]

-004 **7** *9* **Born To Run**[12] 1781 3-8-9 48..(b) NeilCallan 1 27
(Hugo Palmer) *led and sn stdd pce: rdn and hdd over 2f out: rallied: wknd over 1f out* **20/1**

2-40 **8** *6* **Classy Trick (USA)**[17] 1685 3-9-1 57.............................. LeeTopliss(3) 2 27
(Richard Fahey) *in tch on ins: drvn and struggling over 3f out: sn btn* **20/1**

2m 35.1s (0.60) **Going Correction** +0.075s/f (Slow) **8** Ran SP% **114.8**
Speed ratings (Par 97): **101,100,100,99,97 94,88,84**
toteswingers 1&2 £3.00, 1&3 £6.20, 2&3 £6.00 CSF £38.11 CT £336.28 TOTE £4.60: £1.30, £2.80, £3.20; EX 28.40 Trifecta £234.90 Pool: £3,402.17 - 10.86 winning units..
Owner Mr & Mrs D Hearson **Bred** Granham Farm Partnership **Trained** Lambourn, Berks
■ Stewards' Enquiry : Pat Dobbs two-day ban: used whip in incorrect place (May 21-22)
James Doyle two-day ban: used whip above permitted level (May 21-22)

FOCUS
A moderate handicap and the pace was steady. The form looks quite straightforward.

2125 IRISH NIGHT ON 10.07.13 H'CAP (DIV I) 7f (P)
3:10 (3:13) (Class 6) (0-55,58) 4-Y-0+ **£1,940** (£577; £288; £144) **Stalls** Low

Form RPR

-421 **1** **Bold Ring**[8] 1873 7-9-11 58 6ex.. MarcHalford 5 68
(Edward Creighton) *hld up in midfield: hdwy to ld over 1f out: kpt on wl u.p fnl f: jst hld on* **7/1**

3-05 **2** *nse* **True Prince (USA)**[20] 1617 4-9-4 51......................(b) SilvestreDeSousa 3 61
(Brian Ellison) *prom: drvn and outpcd 3f out: rallied u.p over 1f out: kpt on wl fnl f: jst failed* **11/4**[1]

0000 **3** *6* **Dvinsky (USA)**[53] 1020 12-9-0 47..(b) AdamKirby 4 41
(Roger Ingram) *pressed ldr: led over 2f out to over 1f out: drvn and outpcd by ldng pair fnl f* **16/1**

6404 **4** *1½* **Media Jury**[19] 1657 6-9-1 48..(v) PaddyAspell 10 38
(John Wainwright) *walked to post: prom on outside: drvn over 2f out: no ex over 1f out* **10/1**

00-0 **5** *hd* **Farmers Dream (IRE)**[8] 1887 6-8-5 45..................... AdamMcLean(7) 2 35
(Derek Shaw) *trckd ldrs on ins: rdn and ev ch over 2f out to wl over 1f out: sn outpcd* **20/1**

5254 **6** *hd* **Littlecote Lady**[6] 1929 4-9-6 53......................................(v) HayleyTurner 9 42
(Mark Usher) *hld up: drvn along 3f out: hdwy over 1f out: kpt on fnl f: nvr able to chal* **4/1**[2]

1333 **7** *4* **Flow Chart (IRE)**[19] 1650 6-9-2 54................................ SladeO'Hara(5) 8 33
(Peter Grayson) *hld up: drvn and outpcd over 3f out: n.d after* **6/1**[3]

0000 **8** *½* **Dhhamaan (IRE)**[4] 1995 8-9-1 48..................................(b) JamesSullivan 1 26
(Ruth Carr) *led tl edgd lft and hdd over 2f out: rdn and wknd wl over 1f out* **6/1**[3]

6355 **9** *¾* **Flying Kitty**[44] 1161 4-8-12 45.. KieranO'Neill 6 21
(John Bridger) *towards rr: struggling over 3f out: sn btn* **20/1**

0-06 **10** *17* **Fleeting Indian (IRE)**[94] 491 4-8-12 45....................(t) SaleemGolam 7
(Linda Jewell) *bhd: struggling over 3f out: sn btn: t.o* **33/1**

1m 25.92s (-0.08) **Going Correction** +0.075s/f (Slow) **10** Ran SP% **115.2**
Speed ratings (Par 101): **103,102,96,94,94 93,89,88,87,68**
toteswingers 1&2 £5.00, 1&3 £14.20, 2&3 £9.40 CSF £25.52 CT £299.73 TOTE £6.70: £2.50, £1.50, £4.30; EX 25.80 Trifecta £564.70 Pool: £3,761.47 - 4.99 winning units..
Owner Miss Charlotte Harper **Bred** J A Pickering & T Pears **Trained** Wormshill, Kent
■ Stewards' Enquiry : Adam McLean four-day ban: used whip above permitted level (May 21-24)

FOCUS
A moderate handicap run at just a fair pace. The first pair were well clear and the winner was back towards her best 2012 figure.

2126 IRISH NIGHT ON 10.07.13 H'CAP (DIV II) 7f (P)
3:40 (3:40) (Class 6) (0-55,55) 4-Y-0+ **£1,940** (£577; £288; £144) **Stalls** Low

Form RPR

43-1 **1** **Victorian Number (FR)**[48] 1087 5-9-6 54...................... HayleyTurner 4 61
(Geoffrey Deacon) *chsd ldr: rdn and hdwy to ld appr fnl f: sn hrd pressed: hld on gamely fnl f* **6/4**[1]

3052 **2** *shd* **Blue Noodles**[8] 1886 7-9-4 52..(v) PaddyAspell 1 59
(John Wainwright) *led: clr over 3f out: rdn over 2f out: hdd appr fnl f: str chal fnl f: jst hld* **11/2**[3]

0500 **3** *3½* **Katmai River (IRE)**[29] 1426 6-8-10 51........................(v) EmilyMelbourn(7) 9 49
(Mark Usher) *hld up: rdn and hdwy on wd outside over 1f out: kpt on fnl f: no ch w first two* **14/1**

0030 **4** *½* **Guest Book (IRE)**[29] 1434 6-8-9 48............................ SladeO'Hara(5) 6 45
(Peter Grayson) *hld up: rdn and outpcd over 3f out: rallied over 1f out: kpt on fnl f: no imp* **11/2**[3]

00-0 **5** *½* **Batchworth Firefly**[12] 1781 5-8-13 47...........................(b[1]) NeilCallan 3 42
(Dean Ivory) *trckd ldrs: rdn over 2f out: edgd rt and outpcd fr wl over 1f out* **16/1**

2350 **6** *2* **Athwaab**[7] 1902 6-9-7 55.. GeorgeBaker 5 45
(Simon Hodgson) *hld up: rdn and effrt over 2f out: hung rt: no imp over 1f out* **14/1**

3044 **7** *9* **Custom House (IRE)**[8] 1873 5-9-0 48.......................... KirstyMilczarek 2 15
(John E Long) *towards rr on ins: struggling over 3f out: sn btn* **5/1**[2]

050 **8** *3¼* **Royal Acclamation (IRE)**[31] 1396 8-8-12 46 oh1.........(p) JimCrowley 8
(Michael Scudamore) *trckd ldrs tl rdn and wknd fr 2f out* **25/1**

1m 26.45s (0.45) **Going Correction** +0.075s/f (Slow) **8** Ran SP% **110.5**
Speed ratings (Par 101): **100,99,95,95,94 92,82,78**
toteswingers 1&2 £2.90, 1&3 £5.70, 2&3 £11.10 CSF £9.14 CT £75.37 TOTE £2.20: £1.10, £1.50, £4.40; EX 7.10 Trifecta £50.80 Pool: £2,925.17 - 43.10 winning units..
Owner Andy Pittman **Bred** Charles Barel **Trained** Compton, Berks
■ Stewards' Enquiry : Hayley Turner two-day ban: used whip above permitted level (May 21-22)

FOCUS
The front pair dominated this race and they pulled clear. The winning time was over half a second slower than the first division. Straightforward, limited form.

2127 LONDON'S RACE TRACKS RACINGANDMUSIC.CO.UK FILLIES' H'CAP 1m 3f (P)
4:10 (4:10) (Class 5) (0-75,73) 3-Y-0 **£2,587** (£770; £384; £192) **Stalls** Low

Form RPR

03-2 **1** **Thwart**[17] 1685 3-8-11 63.. JimCrowley 4 70+
(Ralph Beckett) *t.k.h: trckd ldrs on ins: pushed along and hdwy to ld over 1f out: edgd lft ins fnl f: kpt on wl* **7/2**[2]

633- **2** *1* **Neamour**[220] 6657 3-9-4 70.. HayleyTurner 2 74
(David Simcock) *hld up in tch: effrt and pushed along over 2f out: hdwy to chse wnr 1f out: kpt on same pce towards fin* **7/1**[3]

23-2 **3** *1¼* **High Time Too (IRE)**[27] 1468 3-9-5 71............................ JamesDoyle 6 73
(Hugo Palmer) *hld up: rdn and hdwy on outside 2f out: kpt on same pce ins fnl f* **10/1**

221- **4** *hd* **Magique (IRE)**[130] 8270 3-9-7 73.................................... WilliamBuick 5 75
(Jeremy Noseda) *t.k.h: trckd ldrs: effrt and rdn 2f out: no ex ins fnl f* **11/8**[1]

06-4 **5** *2¼* **Color Shades**[11] 1803 3-9-4 70.. AdamKirby 8 68
(Clive Cox) *cl up: led 1/2-way: rdn and hdd over 1f out: sn outpcd* **7/1**[3]

541- **6** *shd* **Mandy The Nag (USA)**[168] 7796 3-9-3 69................... StevieDonohoe 3 67
(Ed Dunlop) *hld up last: drvn and outpcd 3f out: rallied over 1f out: no imp* **10/1**

2-56 **7** *½* **Open Letter (IRE)**[22] 1579 3-8-12 64........................ SilvestreDeSousa 7 61
(Mark Johnston) *led at stdy gallop: hdd 1/2-way: rdn over 3f out: wknd over 1f out* **14/1**

2m 22.42s (0.52) **Going Correction** +0.075s/f (Slow) **7** Ran SP% **114.2**
Speed ratings (Par 96): **101,100,99,99,97 97,97**
toteswingers 1&2 £2.50, 1&3 £3.30, 2&3 £5.30 CSF £27.60 CT £221.76 TOTE £4.50: £1.90, £5.20; EX 19.40 Trifecta £93.10 Pool: £1,718.85 - 13.83 winning units..
Owner M H Dixon **Bred** M H Dixon **Trained** Kimpton, Hants

FOCUS
The pace didn't look strong in this fillies' handicap. The winner looks to have more to offer, as does the second.

2128 KEMPTON.CO.UK H'CAP 6f (P)
4:40 (4:40) (Class 4) (0-80,80) 4-Y-0+ **£4,690** (£1,395; £697; £348) **Stalls** Low

Form RPR

000- **1** **Apollo D'Negro (IRE)**[204] 7114 5-9-2 75........................(v) AdamKirby 4 82
(Clive Cox) *in tch: effrt and swtchd lft wl over 1f out: qcknd to ld ins fnl f: drvn out* **5/2**[1]

300- **2** *1* **We Have A Dream**[159] 7928 8-9-0 73.............................. MartinDwyer 2 77
(William Muir) *led: rdn over 1f out: hdd ins fnl f: kpt on same pce* **14/1**

1-30 **3** *½* **Kellys Eye (IRE)**[11] 1814 6-9-0 73.................................... LiamKeniry 1 75
(Zoe Davison) *trckd ldrs: effrt and rdn wl over 1f out: one pce ins fnl f* **20/1**

542- **4** *1* **Dream Catcher (FR)**[198] 7274 5-8-11 75......................... AmyScott(5) 7 74
(Henry Candy) *disp ld to 2f out: sn rdn: kpt on same pce fnl f* **6/1**[3]

0-10 **5** *nk* **Pick A Little**[33] 1346 5-8-12 76..................... WilliamTwiston-Davies(5) 5 74
(Michael Blake) *trckd ldrs: effrt and drvn over 2f out: kpt on same pce fnl f* **8/1**

0-66 **6** *1¼* **Street Power (USA)**[34] 1318 8-9-4 77............................... SteveDrowne 6 71
(Jeremy Gask) *stdd s: hld up towards rr: rdn and outpcd 2f out: styd on fnl f: no imp* **3/1**[2]

2100 **7** *½* **Lastkingofscotland (IRE)**[8] 1878 7-9-7 80.................(b) HayleyTurner 3 73
(Conor Dore) *hld up towards rr: drvn along wl over 2f out: no imp fr over 1f out* **10/1**

00-1 **8** *1* **Red Larkspur (IRE)**[43] 1173 4-9-7 80............................... JamesDoyle 8 69
(Roger Teal) *hld up last: rdn along 1/2-way: nvr able to chal* **3/1**[2]

1m 12.5s (-0.60) **Going Correction** +0.075s/f (Slow) **8** Ran SP% **124.5**
Speed ratings (Par 105): **107,105,105,103,103 101,100,99**
toteswingers 1&2 £7.20, 1&3 £10.00, 2&3 £12.50 CSF £42.64 CT £607.45 TOTE £2.70: £1.10, £7.00, £5.90; EX 48.00 Trifecta £515.00 Pool: £2,783.55 - 4.05 winning units..
Owner Gwyn Powell and Peter Ridgers **Bred** Patrick Cummins **Trained** Lambourn, Berks

FOCUS
A fair sprint handicap and the pace was good thanks to a disputed lead. The winner was well backed.

2129 MIX BUSINESS WITH PLEASURE H'CAP 7f (P)
5:10 (5:10) (Class 6) (0-65,64) 3-Y-0 **£1,940** (£577; £288; £144) **Stalls** Low

Form RPR

042- **1** **Bright Glow**[171] 7778 3-9-7 64.. TedDurcan 5 74+
(David Lanigan) *trckd ldrs: rdn and hdwy to ld over 1f out: kpt on wl fnl f* **5/2**[1]

0536 **2** *¾* **Claude Greenwood**[7] 1903 3-9-0 57..............................(b[1]) AdamKirby 1 63
(David Simcock) *led: rdn and jnd 2f out: edgd rt and hdd over 1f out: kpt on ins fnl f* **10/1**

-033 **3** *¾* **Yahilwa (USA)**[7] 1907 3-9-6 63.. TomQueally 2 67
(James Tate) *t.k.h: trckd ldr: effrt and led briefly over 1f out: kpt on same pce fnl f* **7/2**[2]

0-30 **4** *¾* **Our Golden Girl**[6] 1928 3-8-13 56........................... SilvestreDeSousa 3 58
(Shaun Lycett) *prom: effrt and rdn over 2f out: one pce appr fnl f* **16/1**

60-1 **5** *2* **Loucal**[13] 1759 3-9-4 61..(b) StevieDonohoe 9 59+
(Noel Quinlan) *t.k.h: hld up towards rr: drvn and outpcd over 2f out: rallied 1f out: nvr rchd ldrs* **4/1**[3]

05-3 **6** *1¾* **Carrera**[25] 1519 3-9-6 63.. SebSanders 8 55
(J W Hills) *in tch on outside: rdn and outpcd over 2f out: rallied over 1f out: no imp fnl f* **8/1**

3404 **7** *3¾* **Half Turn**[8] 1874 3-9-3 60.. SteveDrowne 7 43
(Luke Dace) *hld up in midfield on ins: drvn over 2f out: btn appr fnl f* **20/1**

4-52 **8** *2¼* **Harrogate Fair**[14] 1742 3-9-5 62.. LiamJones 4 39
(Michael Squance) *in tch: drvn and outpcd over 2f out: n.d after* **12/1**

0343 **9** *2¼* **Otto The First**[15] 1710 3-8-11 54..................................(e[1]) HayleyTurner 10 25
(John Best) *t.k.h: hld up: outpcd over 2f out: sn btn* **25/1**

0-50 **10** *nk* **Lively Little Lady**[81] 667 3-8-10 53.................................... ShaneKelly 6 23
(Tim Pitt) *hld up: struggling over 2f out: sn btn* **33/1**

1m 27.3s (1.30) **Going Correction** +0.075s/f (Slow) **10** Ran SP% **116.1**
Speed ratings (Par 97): **95,94,93,92,90 88,83,81,78,78**
toteswingers 1&2 £7.80, 1&3 £3.30, 2&3 £6.50 CSF £27.90 CT £88.23 TOTE £3.20: £1.10, £2.50, £1.90; EX 36.20 Trifecta £228.70 Pool: £2,844.90 - 9.32 winning units..
Owner Bjorn Nielsen & Lord Lloyd Webber **Bred** Watership Down Stud **Trained** Upper Lambourn, Berks

FOCUS
A moderate handicap dominated by those who raced handily. The third and fourth set the standard.

2130 KEMPTON FOR WEDDINGS H'CAP 1m (P)
5:40 (5:40) (Class 6) (0-60,60) 4-Y-0+ **£1,940** (£577; £288; £144) **Stalls** Low

Form RPR

0002 **1** **Edgware Road**[35] 1298 5-9-7 60.. JamesDoyle 8 67
(Sean Curran) *pressed ldr: led and rdn over 2f out: hld on wl u.p fnl f* **4/1**[2]

06-2 **2** *¾* **High On The Hog (IRE)**[15] 1734 5-9-5 58......................... ShaneKelly 7 63
(Mark Brisbourne) *in tch: rdn over 2f out: hdwy to chse wnr ins fnl f: kpt on fin* **3/1**[1]

1400 **3** *1* **Rapid Water**[20] 1617 7-8-10 54..................(b) WilliamTwiston-Davies(5) 9 57
(Pat Eddery) *trckd ldrs gng wl: effrt and rdn over 1f out: edgd lft and no ex ins fnl f* **9/2**[3]

41-0 **4** *2* **Whitstable Native**[6] 1925 5-9-7 60 .... LiamKeniry 1 58
(Joseph Tuite) *chsd ldrs: drvn over 2f out: one pce over 1f out* **12/1**

0600 **5** *¾* **Sannibel**[8] 1886 5-9-6 59 .... AdamKirby 4 56
(Graeme McPherson) *hld up towards rr: rdn over 2f out: sme hdwy over 1f out: sn no imp* **10/1**

0000 **6** *1 ¼* **Tartaria**[15] 1710 7-8-8 47 .... MarcHalford 5 41
(Edward Creighton) *hld up on ins: effrt and rdn 2f out: no imp appr fnl f* **14/1**

6335 **7** *2* **Querido (GER)**[12] 1779 9-8-2 46 oh1 ....(tp) MichaelJMMurphy(5) 10 35
(Paddy Butler) *hld up: drvn and outpcd over 2f out: n.d after* **12/1**

6400 **8** *4* **Nonaynever**[10] 1836 5-8-13 52 ....(b[1]) JamesSullivan 2 32
(Ruth Carr) *t.k.h: led to over 2f out: rdn and wknd over 1f out* **6/1**

4040 **9** *13* **Rowlestone Lad**[15] 1715 6-9-5 58 .... TedDurcan 3 8
(John Flint) *missed break: bhd and a struggling: nvr on terms* **14/1**

1m 40.96s (1.16) **Going Correction** +0.075s/f (Slow) **9** Ran SP% **115.3**
Speed ratings (Par 101): **97,96,95,93,92 91,89,85,72**
toteswingers 1&2 £2.60, 1&3 £4.00, 2&3 £3.90 CSF £16.39 CT £55.42 TOTE £5.00: £2.30, £1.90, £1.10; EX 12.20 Trifecta £60.70 Pool: £1,832.69 - 22.61 winning units..
Owner Power Bloodstock Ltd **Bred** Juddmonte Farms Ltd **Trained** Hatford, Oxon

FOCUS
A moderate handicap and another race where it paid to be handy. Slightly improved form from the winner.
T/Plt: £69.40 to a £1 stake. Pool of £45,047.41 - 473.60 winning units T/Qpdt: £37.90 to a £1 stake. Pool of £3,073.32 - 60.00 winning units RY

1910 YARMOUTH (L-H)
Tuesday, May 7

OFFICIAL GOING: Good to firm (7.5)
Wind: Light; across Weather: Sunny

2131 EUROPEAN BREEDERS' FUND MAIDEN STKS — 5f 43y
2:20 (2:21) (Class 5) 2-Y-O — **£2,911** (£866; £432; £216) **Stalls** Centre

Form — RPR

0 **1** **Autumns Blush (IRE)**[19] 1634 2-9-0 0 .... KierenFallon 4 77+
(Jeremy Noseda) *trckd ldrs: effrt and qcknd to ld 1f out: r.o wl: comf* **30/100**[1]

2 *1 ¼* **Bush Beauty (IRE)** 2-9-0 0 .... FrederikTylicki 1 70+
(Clive Brittain) *chsd ldr: rdn and ev ch over 1f out: chsd wnr and kpt on same pce ins fnl f* **6/1**[2]

03 **3** *2 ¾* **Mimi Luke (USA)**[8] 1880 2-9-0 0 .... SamHitchcott 2 60
(Alan Bailey) *led: rdn 2f out: hdd 1f out: wknd ins fnl f* **6/1**[2]

4 *13* **My Little Friend** 2-9-2 0 .... AshleyMorgan(3) 3 18
(Mark H Tompkins) *dwlt: a in rr: rdn and struggling over 3f out: lost tch u.p 2f out* **25/1**[3]

1m 3.08s (0.38) **Going Correction** -0.20s/f (Firm) **4** Ran SP% **109.3**
Speed ratings (Par 93): **88,86,81,60**
CSF £2.66 TOTE £1.30; EX 2.60 Trifecta £4.20 Pool: £1,274.99 - 224.64 winning units..
Owner Fawzi Abdulla Nass **Bred** Lodge Park Stud **Trained** Newmarket, Suffolk

FOCUS
Just the four runners, but probably fair form. The winner was value for a bit extra.

2132 EASTERN DAILY PRESS H'CAP — 5f 43y
2:50 (2:50) (Class 5) (0-70,70) 4-Y-0+ — **£2,587** (£770; £384; £192) **Stalls** Centre

Form — RPR

1-52 **1** **Danzoe (IRE)**[103] 360 6-9-4 70 .... DarrenEgan(3) 5 77
(Christine Dunnett) *chsd ldrs: shkn up to chse ldr 2f out: rdn and chal ins fnl f: led wl ins fnl f: r.o wl* **8/1**

143 **2** *1 ¼* **Love You Louis**[34] 1331 7-9-6 69 ....(v) FrederikTylicki 7 72
(J R Jenkins) *led: rdn over 1f out: drvn and hdd wl ins fnl f: no ex* **8/1**

1222 **3** *¾* **Speedyfix**[17] 1681 6-8-11 60 ....(t) TomMcLaughlin 6 61
(Christine Dunnett) *hld up in tch: rdn and hdwy over 1f out: pressing ldng pair and keeping on whn squeezed for room and hmpd wl ins fnl f: nt rcvr and one pce after* **9/2**[3]

40-0 **4** *½* **Tom Sawyer**[12] 1798 5-9-5 68 ....(b) LukeMorris 4 66
(Julie Camacho) *in tch in midfield: rdn and effrt to chse ldrs wl over 1f out: styd on same pce ins fnl f* **4/1**[2]

0026 **5** *1 ¼* **Beauty Pageant (IRE)**[31] 1398 6-9-0 63 .... SeanLevey 9 57
(David Brown) *chsd ldr tl 2f out: sn drvn and outpcd over 1f out: kpt on same pce ins fnl f* **11/4**[1]

0030 **6** *3 ¾* **Whiskey Junction**[31] 1396 9-8-7 56 oh2 .... WilliamCarson 8 36
(Mick Quinn) *sn rdn along in midfield: drvn and struggling 1/2-way: plugged on but no threat to ldrs fnl 2f* **25/1**

-315 **7** *2 ¾* **Liberty Ship**[112] 213 8-8-13 62 .... RobertWinston 2 32
(Mark Buckley) *stdd s: hld up in tch in rr: shkn up and effrt wl over 1f out: no imp 1f out: wknd ins fnl f* **16/1**

000- **8** *2* **Irish Boy (IRE)**[194] 7351 5-8-13 62 .... MartinHarley 1 25
(Christine Dunnett) *hld up in last pair: rdn and no imp wl over 1f out: wknd fnl f* **20/1**

0-05 **9** *11* **One Kool Dude**[14] 1748 4-8-9 58 ....(v) JamieSpencer 3
(Michael Bell) *chsd ldrs but sn pushed along: wknd 2f out: eased fnl f* **6/1**

1m 1.9s (-0.80) **Going Correction** -0.20s/f (Firm) **9** Ran SP% **115.8**
Speed ratings (Par 103): **98,96,94,94,92 86,81,78,60**
toteswingers 1&2 £5.00, 1&3 £4.30, 2&3 £3.50 CSF £70.22 CT £325.11 TOTE £16.90: £4.50, £3.30, £2.50; EX 42.60 Trifecta £115.70 Pool: £1,591.11 - 10.30 winning units..
Owner One For All **Bred** Miss Anne Ormsby **Trained** Hingham, Norfolk

FOCUS
A typically modest sprint for the grade, but limited, straightforward form.

2133 NORFOLK & SUFFOLK ANIMAL TRUST CLASSIFIED STKS — 6f 3y
3:20 (3:20) (Class 6) 3-Y-0+ — **£1,940** (£577; £288; £144) **Stalls** Centre

Form — RPR

051- **1** **Resonare**[144] 8109 4-9-5 55 .... DavidProbert 2 59+
(Stuart Williams) *chsd ldrs and travelled wl: ev ch 2f out: rdn over 1f out: drvn to ld ins fnl f: styd on: drvn out* **6/4**[1]

4635 **2** *½* **Charlemagne Diva**[14] 1742 3-8-4 53 .... PhilipPrince(5) 1 52
(Richard Guest) *w ldrs tl led 2f out: sn rdn: hdd ins fnl f: kpt on wl but a jst hld after* **5/1**[3]

0450 **3** *¾* **Rooknrasbryripple**[12] 1783 4-9-0 45 .... RyanTate(5) 7 53
(Ralph Smith) *hld up in tch in last trio: rdn and hdwy wl over 1f out: chsd ldrs over 1f out: styd on ins fnl f tl no imp fnl 50yds* **16/1**

0000 **4** *1* **Miakora**[7] 1914 5-9-5 44 .... WilliamCarson 3 50
(Mick Quinn) *led for 1f: chsd ldrs tl rdn and sltly outpcd 1/2-way: rallied and drvn to chse ldrs over 1f out: one pce ins fnl f* **25/1**

30-5 **5** *8* **Jack Barker**[5] 1951 4-9-5 55 .... RobertWinston 4 26
(Robin Bastiman) *pushed along leaving stalls: t.k.h and led after 1f: rdn and hdd 2f out: wknd over 1f out: wl btn and eased towards fin* **9/4**[2]

600- **6** *½* **Marvelous Miss (IRE)**[295] 4152 3-8-6 36 .... DarrenEgan(3) 6 22
(Christine Dunnett) *in tch in midfield: rdn and no hdwy 2f out: wknd over 1f out* **33/1**

6463 **7** *nk* **Daisie Cutter**[46] 1116 3-8-6 49 .... SimonPearce(3) 8 21
(Lydia Pearce) *a bhd: rdn 1/2-way: lost tch 2f out* **9/1**

60-6 **8** *1 ½* **Queen Cassiopeia**[28] 1450 4-9-0 50 .... DannyBrock(5) 5 19
(J R Jenkins) *chsd ldrs tl rdn and dropped out qckly wl over 1f out: bhd fnl f* **16/1**

1m 13.5s (-0.90) **Going Correction** -0.20s/f (Firm)
WFA 3 from 4yo+ 10lb **8** Ran SP% **116.0**
Speed ratings (Par 101): **98,97,96,95,84 83,83,81**
toteswingers 1&2 £2.00, 1&3 £4.30, 2&3 £9.20 CSF £9.77 TOTE £2.90: £1.10, £1.20, £3.60; EX 10.70 Trifecta £120.10 Pool: £2,510.85 - 15.66 winning units..
Owner G D Thompson **Bred** Old Mill Stud **Trained** Newmarket, Suffolk

FOCUS
Pretty poor stuff and no surprise to see it go to the well-backed favourite. He can rate a good bit higher in time.

2134 GREATER YARMOUTH TOURIST AUTHORITY H'CAP — 7f 3y
3:50 (3:51) (Class 6) (0-60,58) 4-Y-0+ — **£1,940** (£577; £288; £144) **Stalls** Centre

Form — RPR

1651 **1** **Jonnie Skull (IRE)**[14] 1752 7-9-7 58 ....(vt) KierenFallon 5 68
(Phil McEntee) *mde all: rdn and clr over 1f out: stl 2 l clr ins fnl f: all out cl home: jst hld on* **11/4**[1]

400- **2** *shd* **Pink Lips**[167] 7815 5-8-12 49 .... DavidProbert 7 59
(J R Jenkins) *in tch in midfield: hdwy u.p over 1f out: chsd wnr but stl 2 l down ins fnl f: r.o wl u.p: jst failed* **14/1**

35-6 **3** *4* **Give Us A Belle (IRE)**[97] 441 4-8-6 46 ....(t) DarrenEgan(3) 6 45
(Christine Dunnett) *hld up wl in tch: chsd wnr and rdn 2f out: no imp over 1f out: lost 2nd and outpcd ins fnl f: plugged on to hold 3rd* **25/1**

123/ **4** *1 ¾* **Hamble**[80] 4-9-7 58 ....(t) AndreaAtzeni 10 52
(Marco Botti) *in tch in midfield: rdn and hdwy wl over 1f out: no ex and btn 1f out: edgd lft and wknd ins fnl f* **4/1**[2]

60-4 **5** *½* **Katy's Secret**[105] 317 6-9-5 56 .... LukeMorris 2 49
(William Jarvis) *dwlt and pushed along leaving stalls: sn in tch in midfield: drvn and effrt to chse ldrs over 1f out: sn no imp: wknd ins fnl f* **12/1**

00-6 **6** *nk* **Norse Song**[20] 1617 4-8-10 47 .... JamieSpencer 12 39
(David Elsworth) *hld up in last trio: rdn and hdwy u.p over 1f out: no imp 1f out: wknd ins fnl f* **7/1**

3250 **7** *nk* **Spin Again (IRE)**[29] 1426 8-9-2 53 .... MartinHarley 3 45
(John Ryan) *in tch in midfield: effrt u.p over 2f out: no ex over 1f out: wknd fnl f* **11/1**

U60- **8** *¾* **Coach Montana (IRE)**[131] 8257 4-8-12 49 .... FrederikTylicki 1 38
(Jane Chapple-Hyam) *hld up in last trio: rdn and hdwy over 2f out: no ex and btn over 1f out: wknd fnl f* **20/1**

2122 **9** *1 ½* **Athletic**[41] 1193 4-8-13 55 ....(v) RobertTart(5) 8 40
(Andrew Reid) *t.k.h: chsd ldrs: rdn and racd awkwardly u.p over 2f out: wknd over 1f out* **5/1**[3]

-553 **10** *2 ½* **Khajaaly (IRE)**[36] 1294 6-8-11 55 ....(b) ShelleyBirkett(7) 11 34
(Julia Feilden) *stdd s: hld up in rr: rdn and no hdwy wl over 1f out: sn wl btn: bhd fnl f* **11/1**

-260 **11** *2* **Perfect Ch'l (IRE)**[15] 1717 6-9-7 58 .... TomMcLaughlin 4 34
(Paul Fitzsimons) *chsd ldrs: rdn and struggling over 2f out: wknd wl over 1f out: bhd fnl f* **20/1**

-500 **12** *3 ¼* **Sairaam (IRE)**[13] 1757 7-9-6 57 .... MartinLane 9 22
(Charles Smith) *chsd wnr tl 2f out: sn dropped out u.p: bhd fnl f* **20/1**

1m 24.9s (-1.70) **Going Correction** -0.20s/f (Firm) **12** Ran SP% **125.0**
Speed ratings (Par 101): **101,100,96,94,93 93,93,92,90,87 85,81**
toteswingers 1&2 £13.00, 1&3 £14.70, 2&3 £59.70 CSF £43.89 CT £840.55 TOTE £2.90: £1.10, £5.00, £10.40; EX 66.70 Trifecta £961.50 Pool: £3,255.27 - 2.53 winning units..
Owner Eventmaker Racehorses **Bred** Canice Farrell Jnr **Trained** Newmarket, Suffolk

FOCUS
The front pair drew a little way on in what was a weak handicap. The winner was back to his 2012 high.

2135 TRAFALGAR RESTAURANT AT GREAT YARMOUTH RACECOURSE H'CAP — 6f 3y
4:20 (4:21) (Class 5) (0-70,70) 3-Y-0 — **£2,587** (£770; £384; £192) **Stalls** Centre

Form — RPR

244- **1** **Burning Dawn (USA)**[231] 6335 3-9-5 68 .... JamieSpencer 7 75+
(David Brown) *broke wl: sn stdd into midfield: pushed along and off the pce 1/2-way: rdn and styd on over 1f out: pressed ldr 1f out: drvn to ld fnl 100yds: styd on wl and sn in command* **11/4**[2]

4450 **2** *1 ¾* **Laudation**[53] 1014 3-8-12 66 .... RobertTart(5) 6 68
(William Jarvis) *racd off the pce in last trio: effrt but stl plenty to do whn sltly hmpd wl over 1f out: hdwy u.p over 1f out: pressed ldr 1f out: plugged on same pce fnl 100yds: wnt 2nd last strides* **20/1**

42-4 **3** *hd* **Pixilated**[122] 75 3-9-5 68 .... DavidProbert 9 69
(Gay Kelleway) *led: rdn over 1f out: kpt on wl tl hdd fnl 100yds: no ex and lost 2nd last strides* **25/1**

531- **4** *7* **Cross My Heart**[229] 6404 3-9-7 70 ....(t) KierenFallon 1 50
(William Haggas) *chsd ldr: rdn and no ex over 1f out: lost 2nd jst ins fnl f: fdd* **11/10**[1]

555- **5** *5* **Spicy (IRE)**[147] 8065 3-9-5 68 .... AndreaAtzeni 4 33
(Marco Botti) *racd off the pce in last trio: effrt and hung lft over 2f out: sn wl btn and bhd* **10/1**[3]

0-54 **6** *nk* **Wildcrafting**[17] 1695 3-8-0 56 .... LouisSteward(7) 3 20
(Michael Bell) *chsd ldrs: effrt and edgd lft 2f out: 5th and btn over 1f out: fdd ins fnl f* **20/1**

4-52 **7** *4 ½* **Duke Of Orange (IRE)**[4] 1978 3-9-0 63 .... MartinHarley 8 14
(Mick Channon) *sn outpcd in rr: nvr on terms* **11/4**[2]

-335 **8** *12* **Annaley My Darling (IRE)**[7] 1906 3-8-11 60 ....(b[1]) FrederikTylicki 2
(Mark Rimmer) *chsd ldrs: rdn and struggling 2f out: bhd 2f out: lost tch over 1f out: t.o* **25/1**

1m 12.02s (-2.38) **Going Correction** -0.20s/f (Firm) **8** Ran SP% **127.3**
Speed ratings (Par 99): **107,104,104,95,88 88,82,66**
toteswingers 1&2 £10.10, 1&3 £5.10, 2&3 £16.10 CSF £60.21 CT £1190.06 TOTE £3.30: £1.80, £5.20, £5.70; EX 61.50 Trifecta £611.60 Pool: £3,995.92 - 4.89 winning units..
Owner Qatar Racing Limited **Bred** Clearsky Farms **Trained** Averham Park, Notts

FOCUS
They appeared to go fast enough up front early and the race set up for the closers. The winner was back to the level her debut promised.

2136 INJURED JOCKEYS FUND H'CAP 1m 3f 101y
4:50 (4:50) (Class 5) (0-70,69) 4-Y-O+ £2,587 (£770; £384; £192) Stalls Low

Form RPR
6662 1 **Focail Maith**[8] [1884] 5-9-7 69 (p) KierenFallon 3 77
(John Ryan) *in tch in last pair: rdn and effrt to ld over 2f out: pressed and drew clr w rival 1f out: kpt on and a jst doing enough fnl f* 10/11[1]
4546 2 *hd* **Dazzling Valentine**[10] [1831] 5-9-0 67 NatashaEaton(5) 1 75
(Alan Bailey) *chsd ldr tl 1/2-way: stmbld bnd over 5f out: swtchd rt 2f out: rdn and chal 1f out: r.o wl but a jst hld fnl f* 11/2[3]
/46- 3 7 **Astrogold**[340] [2668] 4-8-4 55 SimonPearce(3) 6 51
(Mark H Tompkins) *led tl over 2f out: sn rdn: outpcd and btn 1f out: wknd* 25/1
0155 4 1 **Maison Brillet (IRE)**[47] [1097] 6-9-2 64 (p) RobertHavlin 4 59
(Clive Drew) *in tch in last pair: effrt u.p 2f out: pressing ldrs and drvn over 1f out: btn 1f out: wknd ins fnl f* 14/1
6211 5 *hd* **Gabrial's Hope (FR)**[4] [1983] 4-9-2 67 6ex (t) DarrenEgan(3) 7 62
(David Simcock) *t.k.h: sn chsng ldng pair: wnt 2nd 1/2-way: ev ch u.p wl over 1f out: btn 1f out: wknd ins fnl f* 5/2[2]

2m 28.44s (-0.26) **Going Correction** -0.20s/f (Firm) 5 Ran SP% **106.9**
Speed ratings (Par 103): **92,91,86,86,85**
CSF £5.94 TOTE £1.90: £1.10, £3.40; EX 3.50 Trifecta £25.20 Pool: £2,405.29 - 71.55 winning units..
Owner Cathal Fegan **Bred** D Robb **Trained** Newmarket, Suffolk
FOCUS
The front pair drew clear in this modest handicap, and it was a clear-cut case of swap the jockeys, change the result. Just ordinary form.

2137 NORFOLK CHAMBER OF COMMERCE APPRENTICE H'CAP 1m 2f 21y
5:20 (5:20) (Class 6) (0-65,65) 4-Y-O+ £1,940 (£577; £288; £144) Stalls Low

Form RPR
-432 1 **Manomine**[27] [1466] 4-8-12 63 (b) LaurenHaigh(7) 4 72
(Clive Brittain) *t.k.h: mde virtually all: wnt wl clr 1/2-way: urged along ins fnl f: nvr gng to be threatened* 9/2[2]
553 2 3¾ **Redoute Star (AUS)**[7] [1915] 7-9-0 58 (b) PhilipPrince 9 60
(Paul D'Arcy) *t.k.h: sn pressing wnr tl let wnr go clr 1/2-way: rdn over 2f out: drvn over 1f out: kpt on but nvr gng to get to wnr* 11/2[3]
5410 3 ¾ **The Ducking Stool**[21] [1600] 6-9-4 65 ShelleyBirkett(3) 3 65
(Julia Feilden) *chsd ldrs: let ldng pair go clr 1/2-way: rdn and effrt 2f out: kpt on ins fnl f: nvr threatened wnr* 7/1
5302 4 ¾ **Landesherr (GER)**[7] [1916] 6-8-11 55 RyanTate 7 54
(Steve Gollings) *racd off the pce in midfield: rdn 4f out: drvn fnl 2f: kpt on ins fnl f: nvr threatened wnr* 7/2[1]
40-0 5 4 **Miss Blink**[22] [1579] 6-9-4 62 ConorHarrison 8 53
(Robin Bastiman) *stdd s: hld up wl off the pce in rr: rdn and sme hdwy on inner over 3f out: nvr nr wnr: wknd over 1f out* 7/1
11 6 1½ **Final Delivery**[12] [1797] 4-9-0 61 JoeyHaynes(3) 2 50
(Jim Boyle) *hld up off the pce in last pair: rdn and effrt over 2f out: no real imp: n.d* 7/2[1]
30-0 7 1½ **Highlife Dancer**[7] [1909] 5-8-10 59 DanielCremin(5) 1 45
(Mick Channon) *racd off the pce in last trio: rdn and no hdwy 3f out: bhd fnl 2f* 9/1

2m 8.11s (-2.39) **Going Correction** -0.20s/f (Firm) 7 Ran SP% **113.0**
Speed ratings (Par 101): **101,98,97,96,93 92,91**
toteswingers 1&2 £3.10, 1&3 £4.70, 2&3 £6.30 CSF £28.34 CT £168.61 TOTE £4.00: £1.40, £3.40; EX 27.00 Trifecta £118.40 Pool: £2,364.60 - 14.96 winning units..
Owner Mrs C E Brittain **Bred** C R Mason **Trained** Newmarket, Suffolk
FOCUS
It looked as though they'd gone quite hard in this, with the front pair racing clear. Not form to take too literally, but a personal best from the winner on the bare form.
T/Plt: £146.00 to a £1 stake. Pool of £52,444.88 - 262.12 winning units T/Qpdt: £46.00 to a £1 stake. Pool of £3,658.06 - 58.77 winning units SP

JAGERSRO (R-H)
Tuesday, May 7
OFFICIAL GOING: Dirt: standard

2145a LANWADES STUD JAGERSRO SPRINT (LISTED RACE) (3YO+) (DIRT) 6f (D)
6:32 (12:00) 3-Y-O+ £18,921 (£9,460; £4,541; £3,027; £1,892)

RPR
1 **Beat Baby (IRE)**[75] [746] 6-9-6 0 Per-AndersGraberg 5 96
(Niels Petersen, Norway) 207/100[2]
2 *nse* **Alcohuaz (CHI)**[222] 8-9-6 0 ElioneChaves 4 96
(Lennart Reuterskiold Jr, Sweden) 4/5[1]
3 1 **Match Point (FR)**[285] 7-9-3 0 RafaelSchistl 1 90
(Niels Petersen, Norway) 219/10
4 1 **Let'sgoforit (IRE)**[240] 5-9-6 0 EspenSki 8 90
(Bodil Hallencreutz, Sweden) 37/1
5 ½ **Govinda (USA)**[68] [834] 6-9-6 0 ValmirDeAzeredo 3 88
(Vanja Sandrup, Sweden) 104/10
6 ¾ **Dingle View (IRE)**[17] 5-9-3 0 JacobJohansen 6 83
(Bent Olsen, Denmark) 16/1
7 ½ **Timeless Stride (IRE)**[268] 6-9-6 0 MadeleineSmith 7 84
(Madeleine Smith, Sweden) 66/1
8 3 **Aubrietia**[36] [1287] 4-9-3 0 (b) ManuelMartinez 2 72
(Alan McCabe) *slow to stride: in rr: last and outpcd 1/2-way: rdn and no imp fr over 1 1/2f out: eased fnl 50yds* 57/10[3]

1m 11.8s (71.80) 8 Ran SP% **126.2**
PARI-MUTUEL (all including 1sek stake): WIN 3.07; PLACE 1.30, 1.20, 2.03; SF 5.81.
Owner Atle & Hege Walgren **Bred** Paget Bloodstock **Trained** Norway

2146a IKC FONDER PRAMMS MEMORIAL (GROUP 3) (4YO+) (DIRT) 1m 143y(D)
8:06 (12:00) 4-Y-O+ £47,303 (£23,651; £11,352; £7,568; £4,730)

RPR
1 **Plantagenet (SPA)**[59] [956] 6-9-4 0 Per-AndersGraberg 12 105
(Niels Petersen, Norway) *swtiched ins fr wd draw: in rr: hdwy on outside 3f out: led under 1 1/2f out: rdn clr fnl f: won easing down* 69/20[3]
2 1½ **Energia Colonial (BRZ)**[184] 6-9-4 0 CarlosLopez 2 102
(Fabricio Borges, Sweden) *midfield: rdn to hold pl under 4f out: gd prog on outside fr 2f out: styd on wl u.p fr 1 1/2f out to go 2nd ins fnl f: nrest at fin but no ch w wnr* 36/5
3 5 **Lindenthaler (GER)**[66] [873] 5-9-4 0 ElioneChaves 11 91
(Fredrik Reuterskiold, Sweden) *midfield: short of room and squeezed out after 2f: sn rcvrd into midfield: 6th and scrubbed along to hold pl 2 1/2f out: styd on u.p fr 1 1/2f out to take 3rd fnl 100yds: nt pce to chal* 152/10
4 3 **Copper Canyon**[365] [1939] 5-9-4 0 OliverWilson 10 84
(Vanja Sandrup, Sweden) *midfield on outer: rdn and no imp over 2f out: styd on u.p fnl 1 1/2f: nvr on terms* 43/1
5 ¾ **Falmouth Bay (USA)**[240] 5-9-4 0 RafaeldeOliveira 8 82
(Catharina Vang, Sweden) *prom: disp ld 1/2-way: rdn and hdd over 1 1/2f out: one pce til wknd ins fnl f* 191/10
6 7 **Funinthesand (IRE)**[254] 4-9-4 0 EspenSki 9 67
(Wido Neuroth, Norway) *chsd ldrs on outer: rdn and nt qckn under 2 1/2f out: one pce til wknd ins fnl f* 32/1
7 7 **Sir Freddie (USA)**[268] 4-9-4 0 RafaelSchistl 6 52
(Fredrik Reuterskiold, Sweden) *led or disp ld: hdd ins fnl 1 1/2f: wknd qckly fr 1f out* 184/10
8 7 **Empire Storm (GER)**[23] [1564] 6-9-4 0 EPedroza 5 36
(A Wohler, Germany) *prom early: sn settled on heels of ldrs: rdn in 4th and nt qckn 2f out: wknd over 1f out: btn whn eased fnl 100yds* 9/5[1]
9 1¾ **Luca Brasi (FR)**[205] 9-9-4 0 ValmirDeAzeredo 4 32
(Francisco Castro, Sweden) *rdn to go early pce: chsd ldrs on inner: rdn and lost pl over 3f out: wl bhd fnl 2f* 13/5[2]
10 1¼ **East Meets West (IRE)**[10] 4-9-4 0 JacobJohansen 7 30
(Bent Olsen, Denmark) *pressed ldrs til lost pl over 3f out: sn btn* 64/1
11 2 **Weald**[10] 8-9-4 0 ShaneKarlsson 1 25
(Hans-Inge Larsen, Sweden) *dwlt: towards rr: rdn and no imp fr 3f out: nvr figured* 31/1
12 2½ **Nova Valorem (IRE)**[227] [6506] 5-9-4 0 ManuelMartinez 3 25
(Bent Olsen, Denmark) *towards rr: rdn and no imp fr over 3f out: nvr in contention* 57/1

1m 47.1s (107.10) 12 Ran SP% **126.2**
PARI-MUTUEL (all including 1sek stake): WIN 4.43; PLACE 2.12, 3.16, 4.67; SF 29.39.
Owner Rune Vidar Nordum & Atle Walgren **Bred** Dehesa De Milagro **Trained** Norway

CHESTER (L-H)
Wednesday, May 8
OFFICIAL GOING: Good to firm (8.0)
Wind: Fairly strong, direction changeable Weather: Fine, turned overcast

2147 MANOR HOUSE STABLES LILY AGNES CONDITIONS STKS 5f 16y
1:45 (1:47) (Class 2) 2-Y-O £12,602 (£3,772; £1,886; £944; £470) Stalls Low

Form RPR
21 1 **Quatuor (IRE)**[16] [1724] 2-8-7 0 RichardKingscote 8 85+
(Tom Dascombe) *mde all: rdn and edgd rt ent fnl f: r.o wl: drew clr ins fnl 100yds* 9/2[1]
61 2 4 **Blithe Spirit**[20] [1642] 2-8-10 0 JasonHart 9 74
(Eric Alston) *w wnr: rdn over 1f out: nt qckn ins fnl f: sn no ch* 13/2[3]
6316 3 ½ **Intense Feeling (IRE)**[3] [2053] 2-8-7 0 DavidAllan 10 69
(David Evans) *outpcd and bhd: hdwy 2f out: r.o ins fnl f: gng on at fin: no ch w wnr* 40/1
3012 4 1¼ **Limegrove**[3] [2053] 2-8-7 0 JFEgan 12 65
(David Evans) *chsd ldrs: rdn over 1f out: kpt on same pce fnl 100yds* 9/1
0453 5 1½ **Marilyn Marquessa**[15] [1749] 2-8-7 0 PaulHanagan 6 59
(Jo Hughes) *chsd ldrs: rdn over 1f out: wknd fnl 100yds* 25/1
031 6 ½ **Smugglers Gold (IRE)**[26] [1512] 2-8-12 0 (v) TomQueally 2 62
(David Evans) *chsd ldrs on inner tl lost pl after 1f: no bttr than midfield tl hdwy over 2f out: chsd ldrs over 1f out: kpt on same pce ins fnl f* 5/1[2]
6222 7 1½ **Lilo Lil**[8] [1910] 2-8-7 0 FrannyNorton 5 52
(David C Griffiths) *towards rr: rdn and hdwy over 1f out: unable to chal: eased whn nt clr run ins fnl 100yds* 9/1
510 8 3 **Outback Lover (IRE)**[3] [2053] 2-8-7 0 LiamKeniry 3 41
(J S Moore) *hld up: n.m.r under 3f out: rdn over 1f out: no imp* 20/1
5 9 ¾ **Bearing Kisses (IRE)**[25] [1534] 2-8-7 0 HarryBentley 4 38
(Shaun Harris) *in tch: rdn and wknd over 1f out* 100/1
1 10 1¾ **Sleepy Joe (IRE)**[11] [1833] 2-8-12 0 MartinHarley 7 37
(Mick Channon) *in tch: u.p and lost pl over 2f out: bhd over 1f out* 15/2
123 11 *hd* **M'Selle (IRE)**[13] [1785] 2-8-10 0 LukeMorris 1 34+
(Ronald Harris) *s.i.s: bhd and outpcd: nvr a threat* 9/2[1]
31 12 *hd* **Kodafine (IRE)**[30] [1432] 2-8-7 0 DavidProbert 11 31
(David Evans) *restless in stalls: midfield: u.p on outer and lost pl over 2f out: bhd fnl 2f* 12/1

1m 0.44s (-0.56) **Going Correction** -0.025s/f (Good) 12 Ran SP% **117.9**
Speed ratings (Par 99): **103,96,95,93,91 90,88,83,82,79 79,78**
toteswingers 1&2 £6.10, 1&3 £42.10, 2&3 £23.90 CSF £32.24 TOTE £4.70: £2.00, £2.00, £14.00; EX 38.90 Trifecta £349.20 Pool: £1,502.93 - 3.22 winning units..
Owner Edwards Hughes Jenkins Roberts **Bred** Ecurie La Cauviniere **Trained** Malpas, Cheshire
FOCUS
Course at normal configuration and all distances as advertised. After just 1mm of early-morning rain the ground was riding as advertised. A bigger field than usual for this conditions event, despite the three non-runners who were drawn, incidentally, in the highest three stalls. It was perhaps not the strongest of renewals. Fillies had won the last two runnings, the smart Lily's Angel taking it two years ago, and they made up all but two of the field this time, filling the first five places. Pace proved dominant and the winner did it well, but the bare form can't be rated much higher.

2148 WEATHERBYS BANK CHESHIRE OAKS (FOR THE ROBERT SANGSTER MEMORIAL CUP) (LISTED RACE) 1m 3f 79y
2:15 (2:16) (Class 1) 3-Y-O
£22,684 (£8,600; £4,304; £2,144; £1,076; £540) Stalls Low

Form RPR
1 1 **Banoffee (IRE)**[19] [1671] 3-8-12 0 KierenFallon 7 93+
(Hughie Morrison) *dwlt: hld up in rr: flashed tail early on: nt clr run under 2f out: hdwy on inner over 1f out: r.o to ld ins fnl 75yds: in command cl home* 9/1
3-21 2 1¼ **Gertrude Versed**[109] [275] 3-8-12 78 WilliamBuick 9 91+
(John Gosden) *chsd ldr: led over 2f out: rdn and hung rt ins fnl f: hdd ins fnl 75yds: no ex cl home and jst hld on for 2nd* 12/1
-314 3 *shd* **Jathabah (IRE)**[21] [1614] 3-8-12 74 FrederikTylicki 6 91
(Clive Brittain) *midfield: rdn and hdwy on outer over 1f out: r.o ins fnl f: jst failed to get up for 2nd* 50/1

03-2 **4** 1 ¾ **Elik (IRE)**[18] 1698 3-8-12 76 RyanMoore 5 88
(Sir Michael Stoute) *hld up: bmpd over 1f out: styd on ins fnl f: nvr able to mount serious chal* **9/1**

14- **5** ½ **Hollowina**[186] 7555 3-8-12 85 RobertWinston 4 87+
(David Brown) *midfield: nt clr run 2f out: effrt whn hmpd jst over 1f out: kpt on ins fnl f* **16/1**

1 **6** ½ **Premium**[55] 994 3-8-12 73 JohnnyMurtagh 11 86+
(Charles Hills) *hld up in rr: nt clr run over 1f out: sn swtchd lft: kpt on ins fnl f but unable to get to ldrs* **6/1**[3]

7 ½ **Salhooda (IRE)**[220] 6714 3-8-12 0 PatSmullen 3 85
(D K Weld, Ire) *dwlt: trckd ldrs: stmbld over 7f out: rdn over 2f out: wknd fnl 75yds* **5/2**[1]

8 2 ¾ **Keeping (IRE)**[21] 1630 3-8-12 0 GaryCarroll 2 80
(G M Lyons, Ire) *led: hdd over 2f out: rdn and wknd 1f out* **4/1**[2]

23 **9** 1 ¾ **Harbinger Lass**[11] 1845 3-8-12 0 MartinHarley 1 77
(Mick Channon) *racd keenly: trckd ldrs: rdn over 2f out: wknd 1f out* **40/1**

34-6 **10** 54 **Reyaadah**[21] 1622 3-8-12 98 PaulHanagan 10
(Charles Hills) *in tch: lost pl 6f out: wknd over 3f out: t.o* **7/1**

2m 23.77s (-1.03) **Going Correction** -0.025s/f (Good) **10** Ran SP% **113.3**
Speed ratings (Par 107): **102,101,101,99,99 99,98,96,95,56**
toteswingers 1&2 £5.70, 1&3 £20.90, 2&3 £11.10 CSF £108.11 TOTE £8.00: £3.20, £4.30, £9.80; EX 62.80 TRIFECTA Not won..
Owner M Kerr-Dineen,Lord Hambleden & Partners **Bred** P D Savill **Trained** East Ilsley, Berks

FOCUS
An interesting edition of this Listed event. Light Shift in 2007 was the last winner to go on and take the Oaks, but Wonder Of Wonders was second at Epsom two years ago. The latter's trainer Aidan O'Brien has dominated this race in recent years, but was unrepresented this time. The pace was solid. The form is not quite up to standard for the race but there are plenty of potential improvers.

2149 STANJAMES.COM CHESTER CUP (HERITAGE H'CAP) 2m 2f 147y
2:45 (2:50) (Class 2) 4-Y-0+
£74,700 (£22,368; £11,184; £5,592; £2,796; £1,404) **Stalls** High

Form RPR

130- **1** **Address Unknown**[242] 6031 6-9-0 97 JamieSpencer 2 104
(Richard Fahey) *broke wl: prom: wnt 2nd over 1f out: r.o to ld jst ins fnl f: sn jinked rt: drvn out and styd on gamely: edgd lft cl home* **12/1**

30-1 **2** ½ **Ingleby Spirit**[25] 1536 6-8-3 91 GeorgeChaloner(5) 7 97
(Richard Fahey) *in tch: rdn to chse ldrs over 2f out: r.o ins fnl f: gng on at fin* **22/1**

143- **3** hd **Tominator**[60] 7051 6-9-3 100 TomQueally 11 106
(Jonjo O'Neill) *dwlt: midfield: hdwy 3f out: rdn to chse ldrs over 1f out: r.o ins fnl f: gng on at fin* **11/1**[3]

655- **4** ½ **Simenon (IRE)**[128] 6271 6-9-10 107 JohnnyMurtagh 14 112+
(W P Mullins, Ire) *midfield: nt clr run and swtchd rt off rail over 3f out: nt clr run again over 2f out: hdwy over 1f out: r.o ins fnl f: fin wl* **16/1**

/12- **5** hd **Countrywide Flame**[34] 7051 5-8-9 92 MichaelO'Connell 4 97
(John Quinn) *racd keenly: sn led: hdd after 1f: chsd ldr after 2f: led over 3f out: rdn over 2f out: hdd jst ins fnl f: no ex cl home: eased and lost one pl* **7/2**[1]

40-0 **6** 1 ¾ **Good Morning Star (IRE)**[11] 1841 4-8-7 94 JoeFanning 12 97
(Mark Johnston) *chsd ldrs: wnt 2nd over 3f out: rdn and ev ch over 2f out: stl wl there ins fnl f: no ex towards fin* **33/1**

7 1 ¼ **Justification**[24] 1560 5-8-8 91 RyanMoore 3 93+
(A P O'Brien, Ire) *midfield: nt clr run and hmpd wl over 2f out: hdwy over 1f out: styd on wout threatening ins fnl f* **7/2**[1]

0/0- **8** 1 **Softsong (FR)**[39] 1697 5-9-0 97 AdamKirby 19 98
(Philip Hobbs) *hld up: hdwy over 3f out: rdn to chse ldrs over 1f out: one pce and no imp ins fnl f* **66/1**

033/ **9** 6 **Investissement**[127] 5285 7-8-9 97 WilliamTwiston-Davies(5) 1 91
(David Pipe) *chsd ldrs: rdn and outpcd over 2f out: wknd fnl f* **20/1**

163- **10** ½ **Suraj**[175] 6668 4-8-10 97 HayleyTurner 15 91
(Michael Bell) *hld up in rr: styd on fnl f: nvr able to chal* **20/1**

020- **11** 4 ½ **Very Good Day (FR)**[207] 7051 6-8-9 92 KierenFallon 13 81
(Mick Channon) *s.i.s: hld up: hdwy u.p over 1f out: nvr able to trble ldrs* **16/1**

1124 **12** 9 **Buckland (IRE)**[7] 1920 5-8-11 94 WilliamBuick 10 73
(Hans Adielsson) *hld up in midfield: struggling over 2f out: nvr able to get on terms w ldrs* **14/1**

110- **13** 2 ½ **Ile De Re (FR)**[165] 7235 7-9-8 105 JimCrowley 16 81
(Donald McCain) *hld up in midfield: rdn and wknd over 2f out* **16/1**

005- **14** 7 **Kiama Bay (IRE)**[263] 5333 7-8-4 90 DarrenEgan(3) 18 58
(John Quinn) *hld up: hdwy wl over 7f out: in tch 5f out: rdn and wknd over 2f out* **40/1**

50/5 **15** ½ **Theology**[25] 1547 6-8-10 93 PaulHanagan 8 61
(Steve Gollings) *racd keenly: racd wout cover in midfield: tk clsr order 8f out: rdn and wknd 2f out* **16/1**

550- **16** 7 **Thimaar (USA)**[19] 5599 5-9-10 107 (b[1]) GrahamLee 6 67
(Donald McCain) *led after 1f: rdn 4f out: sn hdd: wknd qckly* **25/1**

10- **17** 2 ½ **Olympiad (IRE)**[207] 7051 5-8-12 95 PatSmullen 17 52
(D K Weld, Ire) *hld up in rr: struggling 3f out: wl btn* **9/1**[2]

4m 5.31s (0.51) **Going Correction** -0.025s/f (Good)
WFA 4 from 5yo+ 4lb **17** Ran SP% **125.3**
Speed ratings (Par 109): **97,96,96,96,96 95,95,94,92,91 90,86,85,82,82 79,78**
toteswingers 1&2 £41.80, 1&3 £41.40, 2&3 £37.30 CSF £261.99 CT £2996.11 TOTE £17.40: £4.50, £4.60, £3.60, £4.00; EX 371.00 Trifecta £3105.90 Part won. Pool: £4,140.30 - 0.40 winning units..
Owner Dr Marwan Koukash **Bred** Juddmonte Farms Ltd **Trained** Musley Bank, N Yorks

FOCUS
A competitive edition of this historic handicap. It proved an advantage to race prominently from a low draw and was a triumph for the Richard Fahey stable, who had the first two. Thwe form makes plenty of sense, with the winner at least as good as ever, but there are doubts about this working out.

2150 STELLAR GROUP H'CAP 5f 16y
3:15 (3:20) (Class 2) (0-105,100) 4**£16,762** (£4,715; £2,357; £1,180; £587) **Stalls** Low

Form RPR

5001 **1** **Forest Edge (IRE)**[20] 1652 4-8-6 85 (b) JFEgan 3 97
(David Evans) *chsd ldrs: rdn over 1f out: wnt 2nd ins fnl f: led fnl 75yds: sn sprinted clr* **12/1**

020- **2** 2 ¼ **Captain Dunne (IRE)**[193] 7397 8-9-2 95 DavidAllan 5 99
(Tim Easterby) *led: rdn over 1f out: hdd fnl 75yds outpcd by wnr towards fin* **9/1**

1-23 **3** nk **Kingsgate Choice (IRE)**[19] 1672 6-9-7 100 LiamKeniry 8 103
(Ed de Giles) *chsd ldrs: rdn and hung lft over 1f out: swtchd rt ins fnl f: r.o: fin wl* **8/1**[3]

500- **4** 1 ¼ **Noble Storm (USA)**[238] 6140 7-9-6 99 GrahamLee 6 97
(Ed McMahon) *chsd ldr: rdn and lost 2nd ins fnl f: one pce towards fin* **9/1**

50-0 **5** nk **Fitz Flyer (IRE)**[25] 1537 7-8-7 86 (v) JoeFanning 11 83
(David Nicholls) *midfield: hdwy over 1f out: styd on ins fnl f: nt rch ldrs* **20/1**

00-1 **6** 1 ¼ **Mister Manannan (IRE)**[21] 1607 6-8-12 91 KierenFallon 12 84+
(David Nicholls) *in rr: nt clr run over 1f out: styd on ins fnl f: eased whn no ch towards fin* **16/1**

-443 **7** ¾ **Silvanus (IRE)**[14] 1765 8-8-8 87 PaulHanagan 9 77
(Paul Midgley) *chsd ldrs: rdn over 1f out: no imp: no ex fnl 100yds* **16/1**

5-22 **8** nk **Last Sovereign**[12] 1807 9-8-10 89 (b) FrannyNorton 1 78+
(Ollie Pears) *s.i.s: in rr: kpt on fnl f: nvr a threat* **9/2**[2]

050- **9** 1 ¼ **Gatepost (IRE)**[194] 7366 4-8-11 90 JamieSpencer 4 74+
(Richard Fahey) *midfield: rdn over 1f out: nvr able to get on terms* **3/1**[1]

610- **10** shd **Ubetterbegood (ARG)**[161] 7897 5-9-3 96 JimCrowley 2 80
(Robert Cowell) *midfield: outpcd 2f out: nvr a threat* **10/1**

0-30 **11** ¾ **Head Space (IRE)**[16] 1720 5-8-9 88 (e[1]) JamesSullivan 7 69+
(Ruth Carr) *hld up: rdn and outpcd 2f out: nvr a threat* **12/1**

40-2 **12** ¾ **Decision By One**[5] 1984 4-8-3 82 (t) HarryBentley 13 61
(Tom Dascombe) *in tch: wknd 2f out* **33/1**

060- **13** 2 **Foxy Music**[174] 7726 9-8-2 81 DavidProbert 10 53
(Eric Alston) *chsd ldrs: rdn and hung rt on bnd wl over 1f out: sn wknd* **20/1**

59.55s (-1.45) **Going Correction** -0.025s/f (Good) **13** Ran SP% **123.0**
Speed ratings (Par 109): **110,106,105,103,103 101,100,99,97,97 96,95,92**
toteswingers 1&2 £29.30, 1&3 £11.60, 2&3 £14.30 CSF £116.32 CT £934.92 TOTE £14.00: £5.40, £2.50, £2.60; EX 208.60 Trifecta £1570.10 Part won. Pool: £2,093.53 - 0.01 winning units..
Owner Peter Swinnerton **Bred** Alberto Panetta **Trained** Pandy, Monmouths

FOCUS
A decent sprint handicap, but a race in which few were involved. The time was inside the standard. The winner is rated back to his AW best.

2151 BOODLES DIAMOND MAIDEN STKS 1m 2f 75y
3:50 (3:50) (Class 3) 3-Y-0 **£7,762** (£2,310; £1,154; £577) **Stalls** High

Form RPR

4-22 **1** **Space Ship**[21] 1624 3-9-5 80 WilliamBuick 7 90
(John Gosden) *trckd ldrs: wnt 2nd over 2f out: led ins fnl f: r.o: pushed out towards fin* **5/1**[3]

2- **2** 2 ¼ **Butterfly McQueen (USA)**[201] 7208 3-9-0 0 DavidProbert 11 81
(Andrew Balding) *racd keenly: w ldr: led over 2f out: rdn over 1f out: hdd ins fnl f: outpcd by wnr towards fin* **9/1**

63-3 **3** 3 **Number One London (IRE)**[18] 1678 3-9-5 82 KierenFallon 6 80+
(Brian Meehan) *midfield: hdwy over 1f out: styd on ins fnl f: nt rch front two* **4/1**[2]

3-5 **4** ½ **Dalgig**[30] 1423 3-9-5 0 GeorgeBaker 1 79
(Jamie Osborne) *led early: trckd ldrs after: rdn over 1f out: outpcd by ldrs fnl f: kpt on same pce* **14/1**

5 nk **Battalion (IRE)** 3-9-5 0 GrahamLee 3 79+
(William Haggas) *midfield: rdn and hdwy over 1f out: styd on but no imp on ldrs: one pce towards fin* **10/1**

3-4 **6** 1 **Double Discount (IRE)**[14] 1769 3-9-5 0 RichardKingscote 5 77+
(Tom Dascombe) *towards rr: hdwy over 1f out: kpt on ins fnl f: nvr able to chal* **20/1**

55- **7** 1 ¼ **Revise (IRE)**[173] 7750 3-9-5 0 [1] AdamKirby 2 74
(Marco Botti) *trckd ldrs: rdn over 1f out: wknd ins fnl f* **40/1**

4- **8** ½ **Hasheem**[196] 7332 3-9-5 0 PaulHanagan 8 73+
(Roger Varian) *midfield: rdn over 1f out: sn wknd* **8/1**

3- **9** 1 ¾ **Russian Realm**[236] 6204 3-9-5 0 RyanMoore 10 70+
(Sir Michael Stoute) *hld up: rdn over 1f out: nt clr run ins fnl f: no imp* **15/8**[1]

0 **10** 2 **Maraweh (IRE)**[20] 1635 3-9-5 0 JimCrowley 4 66+
(J W Hills) *s.s: hld up: struggling fnl 2f: nvr a threat* **66/1**

11 1 ½ **Konzert (ITY)** 3-9-5 0 TomQueally 12 63
(Reg Hollinshead) *hld up: struggling fnl 2f: nvr a threat* **100/1**

05- **12** 7 **Doctor's Gift**[160] 7922 3-9-5 0 LiamKeniry 9 50
(Pat Eddery) *sn led: rdn and hdd over 2f out: wknd over 1f out* **100/1**

2m 13.02s (1.82) **Going Correction** -0.025s/f (Good) **12** Ran SP% **119.0**
Speed ratings (Par 103): **91,89,86,86,86 85,84,83,82,80 79,74**
toteswingers 1&2 £14.00, 1&3 £8.00, 2&3 £11.00 CSF £48.08 TOTE £4.40: £1.90, £3.60, £1.10; EX 28.80 Trifecta £150.90 Pool: £2,294.24 - 11.40 winning units..
Owner Lady Rothschild **Bred** Kincorth Investments Inc **Trained** Newmarket, Suffolk

FOCUS
The brilliant Harbinger won this race four years ago, while Mountain High and Colombian are other high-class winners in recent seasons. Mixed messages from the form, but the winner looks to have improved.

2152 HILL DICKINSON CONDITIONS STKS 5f 16y
4:25 (4:26) (Class 3) 3-Y-0+ **£10,350** (£3,080; £1,539; £769) **Stalls** Low

Form RPR

0020 **1** **Ballista (IRE)**[60] 954 5-10-0 109 RichardKingscote 3 113
(Tom Dascombe) *mde all: rdn over 1f out: kpt on gamely towards fin* **7/1**

025- **2** 1 **Masamah (IRE)**[238] 6140 7-9-4 107 JamieSpencer 2 99
(Marco Botti) *chsd wnr: rdn over 1f out: styd on u.p ins fnl f whn trying to chal: jst hld towards fin* **6/4**[1]

0-00 **3** ¾ **Secret Asset (IRE)**[60] 954 8-9-4 100 GeorgeBaker 1 97
(Jane Chapple-Hyam) *hld up in tch: effrt over 1f out: styd on same pce ins fnl f* **12/1**

215- **4** nk **Face The Problem (IRE)**[214] 6869 5-9-4 108 KierenFallon 5 96
(Jamie Osborne) *s.i.s: in rr: effrt and hdwy on inner over 1f out: kpt on ins fnl f* **9/2**[2]

235/ **5** hd **Miss Lahar**[558] 7135 4-8-13 94 MartinHarley 4 90
(Mick Channon) *in tch: rdn over 1f out: kpt on ins fnl f: nt pce to chal* **33/1**

0054 **6** ¾ **Confessional**[19] 1672 6-9-4 102 (b) PaulHanagan 6 92
(Tim Easterby) *hld up: pushed along over 1f out: kpt on ins fnl f: nvr able to chal* **5/1**[3]

12-5 **7** 1 ¾ **Jwala**[19] 1662 4-8-13 102 WilliamBuick 7 81
(Robert Cowell) *chsd ldrs: pushed along and outpcd over 1f out: n.d after* **7/1**

59.75s (-1.25) **Going Correction** -0.025s/f (Good) **7** Ran SP% **110.5**
Speed ratings (Par 107): **109,107,106,105,105 104,101**
toteswingers 1&2 £3.00, 1&3 £5.40, 2&3 £3.40 CSF £16.76 TOTE £10.40: £3.60, £1.30; EX 20.10 Trifecta £91.80 Pool: £4,291.99 - 35.05 winning units..
Owner Well Done Top Man Partnership **Bred** Sj Partnership **Trained** Malpas, Cheshire

FOCUS
A decent conditions event run in a good time, only marginally slower than the earlier handicap. The first two occupied the same placings throughout. A good effort from Ballista on the face of it, but not form to get carried away with.

2153 IRISH THOROUGHBRED MARKETING H'CAP — 1m 4f 66y
5:00 (5:01) (Class 3) (0-90,79) 3-Y-O — **£10,350** (£3,080; £1,539; £769) **Stalls** Low

Form — RPR

-013 **1** — **Dali's Lover (IRE)**[21] 1609 3-8-8 **66** .... PaulHanagan 6 — 73
(Charles Hills) *in tch: rdn to ld over 1f out: edgd lft ent fnl f: r.o and in command after* — **12/1**

-241 **2** 2 **Good Evans**[88] 591 3-8-10 **68** .... RichardKingscote 7 — 72
(Tom Dascombe) *led: rdn and hdd over 1f out: hld by wnr ins fnl f* — **10/1**

4040 **3** nk **Snowy Dawn**[79] 711 3-8-12 **70** .... TomQueally 8 — 74
(Reg Hollinshead) *midfield: pushed along over 3f out: hdwy 2f out: styd on ins fnl f* — **33/1**

6-1 **4** nk **Majeed**[72] 799 3-9-7 **79** .... WilliamBuick 4 — 82+
(David Simcock) *sn dropped to midfield: pushed along briefly wl over 7f out: swtchd rt over 1f out: r.o ins fnl f: gng on at fin* — **7/2**[2]

4221 **5** 1 3/4 **Ambleside**[21] 1609 3-9-1 **73** ....(b) FrannyNorton 5 — 73
(Mark Johnston) *s.i.s: towards rr: pushed along and swtchd lft over 1f out: kpt on ins fnl f: nvr able to chal* — **10/3**[1]

-142 **6** 1/2 **Gabrial The Master (IRE)**[14] 1761 3-9-2 **74** .... JamieSpencer 3 — 73
(Richard Fahey) *hld up: rdn over 1f out: one pce fnl f: nvr able to chal* — **6/1**

2221 **7** hd **Excellent Puck (IRE)**[20] 1655 3-9-4 **76** .... FergusSweeney 10 — 75
(Jamie Osborne) *in rr: pushed along over 1f out: kpt on ins fnl f: nvr able to chal* — **12/1**

16-2 **8** 4 1/2 **Noble Bull (IRE)**[16] 1719 3-9-3 **75** .... RyanMoore 2 — 67
(Charles Hills) *racd keenly: prom: rdn over 1f out: wknd fnl f* — **9/2**[3]

03-1 **9** 7 **King Muro**[28] 1468 3-9-5 **77** .... DavidProbert 9 — 58
(Andrew Balding) *racd keenly: prom: ev ch 2f out: rdn and wknd over 1f out: eased whn wl btn ins fnl f* — **9/1**

2m 38.19s (-0.31) **Going Correction** -0.025s/f (Good) — **9** Ran SP% **115.2**
Speed ratings (Par 103): **100,98,98,98,97 96,96,93,88**
toteswingers 1&2 £13.20, 1&3 £34.80, 2&3 £40.80 CSF £124.33 CT £3805.77 TOTE £12.90: £3.70, £3.80, £8.30; EX 118.90 Trifecta £657.90 Pool: £2,592.11 - 2.95 winning units..
Owner Triermore Stud **Bred** W Maxwell Ervine **Trained** Lambourn, Berks

FOCUS
Not a strong handicap for the grade, the topweight rated 11lb below the race maximum, and it was run at just a fair gallop. It lacked unexposed types and the first two were always well placed.
T/Plt: £1,492.00 to a £1 stake. Pool: £183,700.14 - 89.88 winning tickets T/Qpdt: £66.90 to a £1 stake. Pool: £11,353.1 - 125.40 winning tickets DO

2123 KEMPTON (A.W) (R-H)
Wednesday, May 8

OFFICIAL GOING: Standard
Wind: Fresh, across (away from stands) Weather: Fine but cloudy

2154 RACINGANDMUSIC.CO.UK H'CAP — 1m (P)
5:40 (5:40) (Class 6) (0-60,60) 3-Y-O — **£1,940** (£577; £288; £144) **Stalls** Low

Form — RPR

0-40 **1** — **Tagalaka (IRE)**[8] 1900 3-9-6 **59** .... JohnFahy 7 — 66
(Eve Johnson Houghton) *trckd ldrs: prog jst over 2f out: led over 1f out: drvn out* — **6/1**[3]

00-4 **2** 1 **Bertie Moon**[16] 1711 3-9-4 **57** .... JamesDoyle 4 — 62
(Geoffrey Deacon) *trckd ldng pair: led wl over 2f out: drvn and hdd over 1f out: kpt on* — **8/1**

606- **3** 3/4 **Sovereign Power**[175] 7708 3-9-7 **60** .... JackMitchell 2 — 63
(Paul Cole) *slowly away: hld up in last: c wd bnd 3f out: edgd lft after and ended against nr side rail: prog 2f out: styd on to take 3rd fnl f: nrst fin* — **7/2**[2]

5520 **4** 2 1/4 **Duchess Of Dreams**[6] 1966 3-8-8 **47** .... RobbieFitzpatrick 1 — 45
(Richard Guest) *taken down early: hld up in rr: rdn and prog over 2f out: kpt on same pce fr over 1f out: n.d* — **25/1**

6-50 **5** 2 1/4 **Bullseye Babe**[27] 1499 3-9-2 **55** .... RobertHavlin 11 — 48
(Mark Usher) *s.i.s: towards rr: rdn over 2f out: hung lft to nr side rail after: no imp on ldrs fnl 2f* — **33/1**

502- **6** 1/2 **Many Elements**[161] 7891 3-9-0 **53** .... LukeMorris 10 — 45
(Lee Carter) *wl in rr: rdn 3f out: no prog 2f out and no ch after* — **16/1**

4331 **7** 3/4 **Entrapping**[71] 804 3-9-7 **60** .... RichardThomas 8 — 50
(John E Long) *t.k.h: trckd ldrs on outer: chal over 2f out: wknd qckly over 1f out* — **8/1**

006- **8** 2 3/4 **Index Waiter**[233] 6318 3-9-1 **54** .... DaneO'Neill 3 — 38
(Brian Meehan) *pushed along in midfield bef 1/2-way: brief effrt over 2f out: sn btn u.p* — **5/2**[1]

500- **9** 1 3/4 **Whiskeymack**[165] 7854 3-9-0 **53** ....(v[1]) SamHitchcott 6 — 33
(Mick Channon) *mde most to wl over 2f out: wknd qckly over 1f out* — **7/1**

6-04 **10** 9 **Eliya**[56] 979 3-8-8 **47** .... RenatoSouza 9
(Jo Hughes) *w ldr to 3f out: sn wknd rapidly: t.o* — **33/1**

1m 41.29s (1.49) **Going Correction** +0.10s/f (Slow) — **10** Ran SP% **115.4**
Speed ratings (Par 97): **96,95,94,92,89 89,88,85,84,75**
toteswingers 1&2 £6.30, 1&3 £5.60, 2&3 £6.90 CSF £51.48 CT £191.49 TOTE £6.60: £2.80, £3.00, £1.50; EX 61.30 Trifecta £275.10 Pool: £1,742.88 - 4.75 winning units..
Owner Eden Racing IV **Bred** Fergus O'Neill **Trained** Blewbury, Oxon

FOCUS
A moderate 3yo handicap and the first two had it between them through the last quarter-mile.

2155 NEW CUSTOMERS COMMISSION FREE 1ST MONTH FILLIES' H'CAP — 1m (P)
6:10 (6:10) (Class 5) (0-70,70) 4-Y-O+ — **£2,587** (£770; £384; £192) **Stalls** Low

Form — RPR

2123 **1** — **Yojojo (IRE)**[16] 1736 4-8-12 **61** .... LukeMorris 7 — 73
(Gay Kelleway) *trckd ldr: led gng wl 2f out: drvn and steadily drew clr fr over 1f out* — **9/2**[2]

/2-6 **2** 2 1/2 **Princess Icicle**[51] 1059 5-9-4 **67** .... IanMongan 1 — 73
(Jo Crowley) *trckd ldr: chal and upsides 2f out: chsd wnr after: one pce fnl f* — **7/2**[1]

-632 **3** 2 1/4 **Imaginary World (IRE)**[26] 1521 5-8-8 **62**........(p) MichaelJMMurphy[(5)] 4 — 63
(John Balding) *hld up bhd ldng trio: tried to cl 2f out: kpt on one pce to take 3rd ins fnl f* — **9/2**[2]

3-00 **4** 1 **Balady (IRE)**[18] 1673 4-9-7 **70** .... JamesDoyle 8 — 69
(Dominic Ffrench Davis) *led: drvn and hdd 2f out: nt qckn and sn btn: fdd fnl f* — **7/2**[1]

0005 **5** 1 **Kindia (IRE)**[32] 1386 5-9-1 **64**........(p) SebSanders 5 — 60
(Michael Attwater) *s.i.s: hld up in last: hanging whn asked for effrt jst over 2f out: one pce after* — **6/1**[3]

554/ **6** 1 **Thewinningmachine**[569] 6921 4-8-8 **57** .... LiamJones 3 — 51
(Jo Hughes) *hld up bhd ldng trio: rdn wl over 2f out: nt qckn and sn btn* — **20/1**

1100 **7** 1 1/2 **Lily Edge**[27] 1500 4-9-7 **70** .... KieranO'Neill 6 — 61
(John Bridger) *hld up in last trio: urged along wl over 2f out: no prog and btn after* — **12/1**

4660 **8** 15 **Imtithal (IRE)**[16] 1736 4-8-11 **60** .... WilliamCarson 2 — 16
(John Weymes) *t.k.h: hld up in last trio: rdn 3f out: sn wknd: t.o* — **25/1**

1m 41.43s (1.63) **Going Correction** +0.10s/f (Slow) — **8** Ran SP% **111.4**
Speed ratings (Par 100): **95,92,90,89,88 87,85,70**
toteswingers 1&2 £3.70, 1&3 £2.20, 2&3 £4.80 CSF £19.51 CT £72.04 TOTE £4.50: £1.10, £1.40, £1.60; EX 19.60 Trifecta £41.70 Pool: £1,41.50 - 25.45 winning units..
Owner Winterbeck Manor Stud **Bred** Rossenarra Bloodstock Limited **Trained** Exning, Suffolk

FOCUS
A modest handicap for older fillies and the time was 0.14secs slower than the opening contest.

2156 CONOR MAYNARD AT KEMPTON 14.09.13 H'CAP — 1m 3f (P)
6:40 (6:42) (Class 6) (0-65,65) 3-Y-O — **£1,940** (£577; £288; £144) **Stalls** Low

Form — RPR

003- **1** — **Tajheez (IRE)**[182] 7636 3-9-4 **62** .... DaneO'Neill 11 — 73+
(Roger Varian) *w.w towards rr: 8th over 3f out: smooth prog over 2f out to ld over 1f out: rdn and kpt on* — **6/4**[1]

530 **2** 1 1/4 **Mad About Harry (IRE)**[30] 1423 3-9-7 **65** .... GrahamLee 2 — 71
(John Best) *chsd ldrs: drvn over 3f out: prog on inner over 2f out: led briefly wl over 1f out: chsd wnr after: kpt on but readily hld* — **7/1**

6042 **3** 1 3/4 **Alshan Fajer**[48] 1098 3-9-3 **61** .... JamesDoyle 10 — 64
(Roger Ingram) *hld up: hmpd in rr over 8f out: brought wd and drvn bnd 3f out: prog over 2f out: styd on to take 3rd over 1f out* — **9/2**[2]

1- **4** 1 1/4 **Streak**[152] 8018 3-9-7 **65** .... TedDurcan 8 — 66
(David Lanigan) *prog to trck ldrs 8f out: rdn in 6th over 3f out: tried to cl 2f out: one pce* — **6/1**[3]

U33- **5** nk **Super Cookie**[193] 7414 3-9-6 **64** .... WilliamCarson 7 — 64
(Philip McBride) *hmpd over 8f out: racd in last trio after: impeded and swtchd lft over 2f out: styd on fnl 2f: n.d* — **25/1**

00-5 **6** 3 **Bountiful Bess**[16] 1712 3-9-2 **60** .... SamHitchcott 6 — 55
(Pam Sly) *n.m.r after 150yds and dropped to last: rdn wl over 2f out: plugged on fnl 2f: no ch* — **16/1**

-454 **7** shd **Jd Rockefeller**[28] 1469 3-8-8 **52** .... LiamJones 4 — 47
(Paul D'Arcy) *trckd ldr: led after 5f: hrd rdn over 2f out: hd in air and no rspnse: hdd & wknd wl over 1f out* — **16/1**

5-23 **8** 1 3/4 **House Of Orange (IRE)**[33] 1372 3-8-13 **62**...(b[1]) MichaelJMMurphy[(5)] 1 — 53
(Mark Johnston) *dwlt and rousted to take decent position: drvn over 3f out: wknd over 2f out* — **33/1**

41 **9** 1 **Hot Right Now**[35] 1329 3-9-7 **65** .... LukeMorris 9 — 55
(Mrs K Burke) *chsd ldrs: drvn over 3f out: wknd 2f out* — **20/1**

0-45 **10** 7 **Standing Bear (IRE)**[18] 1685 3-9-4 **62** .... IanMongan 3 — 39
(Paul Cole) *led: racd awkwardly and jinked after 5f: hdd and sharp reminders: chsd ldr after: tried to chal u.p over 2f out: sn wknd: virtually p.u last 100yds* — **16/1**

3143 **11** 3/4 **Silver Fawn (IRE)**[15] 1747 3-8-8 **52**........(be) KieranO'Neill 5 — 28
(John Weymes) *impeded over 8f out: n.m.r on inner sn after: nvr really a factor: wknd over 2f out* — **20/1**

2m 22.58s (0.68) **Going Correction** +0.10s/f (Slow) — **11** Ran SP% **118.9**
Speed ratings (Par 97): **101,100,98,97,97 95,95,94,93,88 87**
toteswingers 1&2 £4.50, 1&3 £3.00, 2&3 £5.40 CSF £11.68 CT £40.77 TOTE £2.70: £1.20, £1.60, £2.00; EX 18.40 Trifecta £68.90 Pool: £1,457.54 - 15.86 winning units..
Owner Hamdan Al Maktoum **Bred** Shadwell Estate Company Limited **Trained** Newmarket, Suffolk
■ Stewards' Enquiry : Ian Mongan two-day ban: used whip with excessive force (May 22-23)

FOCUS
A competitive 3-y-o handicap on paper but only four mattered in the market and they filled the frame.

2157 WINNERS ARE WELCOME AT BETDAQ MEDIAN AUCTION MAIDEN STKS — 1m 3f (P)
7:10 (7:13) (Class 5) 3-5-Y-O — **£2,587** (£770; £384; £192) **Stalls** Low

Form — RPR

0 **1** — **Masquerading (IRE)**[16] 1713 3-8-11 0 .... TedDurcan 2 — 80+
(David Lanigan) *hld up in 5th: prog over 2f out: shkn up to ld over 1f out: 2 l clr and wl in command fnl f: eased last 75yds* — **13/2**[3]

3 **2** 3/4 **Royal Signaller**[28] 1468 3-8-11 0 .... PatDobbs 5 — 74
(Amanda Perrett) *trckd ldr: drvn over 2f out: chal and upsides wl over 1f out: chsd wnr after: kpt on but flattered by proximity* — **5/1**[2]

3- **3** 2 1/4 **Hold On Tight (IRE)**[228] 6489 3-8-7 0 ow1 .... JimCrowley 3 — 66
(Ralph Beckett) *trckd ldng pair: rdn and nt qckn jst over 2f out: pushed along and kpt on one pce to take 3rd ins fnl f* — **8/11**[1]

4 **4** 1 **Conquestadim**[16] 1727 3-8-11 0 .... JimmyFortune 10 — 68
(Hughie Morrison) *led: rdn over 2f out: hdd over 1f out: grad fdd* — **12/1**

4-0 **5** 4 **Himalayan Peak**[18] 1684 3-8-11 0 .... LukeMorris 1 — 61
(James Eustace) *settled in 7th and off the pce: shkn up over 2f out: sn wnt 5th but nt on terms w ldrs: no imp after* — **33/1**

4 **6** 2 **Dawn Beat**[21] 1611 3-8-6 0 .... JohnFahy 7 — 52
(Jonathan Portman) *a abt same pl: shkn up and outpcd fr over 2f out: nvr on terms after* — **50/1**

7 hd **This Is Me**[60] 5-10-0 0 .... DaneO'Neill 12 — 58
(Don Cantillon) *dwlt: hld up in 8th and off the pce: shkn up and no prog over 2f out: no ch after* — **14/1**

5 **8** 4 **Fenton**[21] 1611 3-8-6 0 .... LiamJones 9 — 45
(Harry Dunlop) *chsd ldng trio tl wknd over 2f out* — **50/1**

00- **9** 1 1/4 **Katie Gale**[172] 7780 3-8-6 0 .... WilliamCarson 11 — 43
(Tim Pitt) *stdd s: hld up in last pair: pushed along over 3f out: sn struggling* — **100/1**

10 1 **Ardaal** 3-8-11 0 ....(t) JamesDoyle 8 — 46
(James Fanshawe) *dwlt: a in last trio: urged along over 3f out: no prog* — **20/1**

11 55 **Echoe Beach** 3-8-6 0 .... ChrisCatlin 4
(Olivia Maylam) *dwlt: rn v green: a in last: t.o 4f out* — **66/1**

2m 24.18s (2.28) **Going Correction** +0.10s/f (Slow)
WFA 3 from 5yo 17lb — **11** Ran SP% **116.4**
Speed ratings (Par 103): **95,94,92,92,89 87,87,84,83,83 43**
toteswingers 1&2 £5.70, 2&3 £2.60, 1&3 £2.20 CSF £36.63 TOTE £6.10: £2.40, £1.70, £1.02; EX 42.40 Trifecta £104.80 Pool: £1,690.08 - 12.08 winning units..
Owner B E Nielsen **Bred** Bjorn Nielsen **Trained** Upper Lambourn, Berks

FOCUS
This auction maiden was run 1.18secs slower than the preceding handicap.

2158 BETDAQ 1ST UK RACE COMMISSION FREE-EVERYDAY H'CAP 6f (P)
7:40 (7:41) (Class 4) (0-85,83) 3-Y-O £4,690 (£1,395; £697; £348) Stalls Low

Form RPR
01-4 1 **Rivellino**[12] 1806 3-9-6 **82** LukeMorris 1 94
(Mrs K Burke) *t.k.h: trckd ldr: led over 2f out and kicked on: drifted lft fr over 1f out but wl on top after* **10/11**[1]
1-16 2 3½ **Foxtrot Jubilee (IRE)**[12] 1806 3-9-7 **83** JimCrowley 6 84
(Ralph Beckett) *in tch: rdn over 2f out: chsd wnr over 1f out: no ch and jst hld on for 2nd* **7/2**[2]
61-0 3 shd **Tartary (IRE)**[21] 1625 3-9-1 **77** JamesDoyle 2 77
(Roger Charlton) *dwlt: t.k.h: in tch: pushed along and sme prog 2f out: shkn up fnl f: pressed for 2nd nr fin* **4/1**[3]
140- 4 shd **Strictly Ballroom (IRE)**[277] 4820 3-8-8 **75** MichaelJMMurphy(5) 3 75
(Mark Johnston) *hld up in last pair: prog 2f out: drvn and kpt on to press for 2nd nr fin* **25/1**
06-0 5 1 **Knight Charm**[23] 1582 3-8-11 **73** JohnFahy 5 70
(Eve Johnson Houghton) *t.k.h: trckd ldng pair: rdn over 2f out: lost pl over 1f out* **33/1**
1256 6 ¾ **Sewn Up**[9] 1892 3-9-1 **77** (tp) GrahamLee 7 72
(Reg Hollinshead) *hld up in last pair: wd bnd 3f out: pushed along and no imp on ldrs fnl 2f* **25/1**
51-5 7 1 **Fletcher Christian**[23] 1582 3-8-13 **75** PatCosgrave 4 66
(John Gallagher) *led to over 2f out: wknd over 1f out* **16/1**
1m 14.22s (1.12) **Going Correction** +0.10s/f (Slow) 7 Ran SP% **111.1**
Speed ratings (Par 101): **96,91,91,91,89 88,87**
toteswingers 1&2 £1.60, 1&3 £1.10, 2&3 £2.00 CSF £3.95 TOTE £2.20: £1.10, £1.30; EX 4.20 Trifecta £7.80 Pool: £1,445.77 - 137.71 winning units..
Owner Mrs Melba Bryce **Bred** Castlemartin Sky & Skymarc Farm **Trained** Middleham Moor, N Yorks

FOCUS
The two previous runnings of this handicap were won by unexposed, lightly raced sorts and this year's scorer to some extent has a similar profile.

2159 MIX BUSINESS WITH PLEASURE H'CAP 1m 4f (P)
8:10 (8:13) (Class 6) (0-60,60) 4-Y-0+ £1,940 (£577; £288; £144) Stalls Low

Form RPR
-214 1 **Cape Alex**[20] 1654 4-9-2 **55** ChrisCatlin 10 65
(Clive Brittain) *trckd ldr after 1f: clsd to chal 2f out: drvn ahd over 1f out: styd on* **8/1**[3]
3-50 2 2 **Princess Willow**[28] 1468 5-8-13 **52** KirstyMilczarek 9 59
(John E Long) *trckd ldng trio after 4f: clsd to chal 2f out: upsides over 1f out: chsd wnr after: kpt on one pce* **10/1**
1435 3 3 **Time Square (FR)**[34] 1342 6-9-1 **54** (t) GrahamLee 1 56
(Tony Carroll) *racd freely: led at gd pce: hdd over 1f out: one pce* **8/1**[3]
4353 4 2¼ **Moment In The Sun**[5] 1983 4-9-7 **60** JamesDoyle 5 58
(David Flood) *hld up in last pair: prog fr 3f out to go 5th jst over 2f out but nt on terms w ldrs: plugged on to take 4th fnl f* **9/2**[2]
024- 5 ½ **Gucci D'Oro (USA)**[230] 6399 4-9-3 **56** (p) JimCrowley 2 54
(David Simcock) *sn trckd ldng pair: drvn over 3f out: lost pl over 2f out: steadily wknd* **6/4**[1]
5003 6 1½ **Crimson Monarch (USA)**[13] 1794 9-8-9 **48** (b) WilliamCarson 7 43
(Peter Hiatt) *hld up in last trio: rdn wl over 2f out: no ch after but kpt on fnl f* **16/1**
5425 7 1½ **Having A Ball**[36] 1298 9-9-7 **60** DaneO'Neill 6 53
(Geoffrey Deacon) *hld up in midfield: rdr looking down after 5f: drvn 3f out: no imp on ldrs: no ch over 1f out* **8/1**[3]
4265 8 1 **Beggers Belief**[16] 1715 5-8-8 **54** (b) JoeyHaynes(7) 8 45
(Eric Wheeler) *chsd ldr 1f: dropped to 5th after 4f: rdn and no imp wl over 2f out: fdd* **16/1**
0000 9 ¾ **Burnbrake**[49] 1090 8-8-7 **46** oh1 (b) LukeMorris 4 36
(Richard Rowe) *hld up in last trio: jst pushed along fr over 2f out: nvr involved* **20/1**
0560 10 shd **Silver Marizah (IRE)**[34] 1342 4-8-0 **46** oh1 (e) TomasHarrigan(7) 3 36
(Roger Ingram) *hld up in midfield: unbalanced whn rdn over 2f out: sn wknd* **33/1**
000- 11 18 **Suhailah**[197] 7303 7-8-7 **46** oh1 (p) RobertHavlin 11
(Michael Attwater) *nvr bttr than midfield: wknd 3f out: t.o* **25/1**
2m 33.27s (-1.23) **Going Correction** +0.10s/f (Slow) 11 Ran SP% **123.9**
Speed ratings (Par 101): **108,106,104,103,102 101,100,100,99,99 87**
toteswingers 1&2 £8.40, 1&3 £7.40, 2&3 £17.50 CSF £87.80 CT £676.75 TOTE £10.20: £1.70, £4.80, £2.40; EX 106.40 Trifecta £886.40 Part won. Pool: £1,181.97 - 0.11 winning units..
Owner Saeed Manana **Bred** Castleton Lyons & Kilboy Estate **Trained** Newmarket, Suffolk

FOCUS
A moderate handicap but they went a good pace.

2160 £200 FREE BETS AT BETDAQ CLASSIFIED STKS 7f (P)
8:40 (8:40) (Class 5) 3-Y-O £2,587 (£770; £384; £192) Stalls Low

Form RPR
3-50 1 **Double Your Money (IRE)**[12] 1806 3-8-9 75 MichaelJMMurphy(5) 4 81
(Mark Johnston) *mde all: stretched clr fr wl over 1f out: 3 l ahd fnl f: tired nr fin but nvr in danger* **5/1**[3]
6-14 2 1¼ **Keene's Pointe**[90] 550 3-9-0 75 SebSanders 3 78
(J W Hills) *chsd wnr: shkn up 2f out: sn outpcd: n.d after but hld on for 2nd and clsd nr fin* **20/1**
212 3 shd **Kabbaas (IRE)**[69] 826 3-9-0 75 DaneO'Neill 2 78
(Roger Varian) *hld up in 4th: rdn wl over 1f out: nt qckn and wl hld after: kpt on to press for 2nd nr fin* **3/1**[2]
1-4 4 shd **Singersongwriter**[28] 1486 3-9-0 74 GrahamLee 5 77
(Ed Dunlop) *t.k.h: hld up in last: tried to cl on ldrs over 1f out: sn rdn and nt qckn: kpt on to press for 2nd nr fin* **10/11**[1]
221- 5 9 **Midnight Flower (IRE)**[138] 8208 3-9-0 75 JamesDoyle 1 61
(David Simcock) *t.k.h: trckd ldng pair: shkn up wl over 1f out: sn wknd and eased* **8/1**
1m 25.41s (-0.59) **Going Correction** +0.10s/f (Slow) 5 Ran SP% **109.9**
Speed ratings (Par 99): **107,105,105,105,95**
CSF £68.87 TOTE £6.20: £1.60, £2.70; EX 50.30 Trifecta £340.90 Pool: £879.78 - 1.93 winning units..
Owner A D Spence **Bred** Twelve Oaks Stud **Trained** Middleham Moor, N Yorks

FOCUS
A tight-looking classified stakes, despite the small field, but an all-the-way winner.
T/Jkpt: £14,053.00 to a £1 stake. Pool: £128654.73 - 6.50 winning tickets T/Plt: £28.30 to a £1 stake. Pool: £52769.04 - 1359.20 winning tickets T/Qpdt: £6.70 to a £1 stake. Pool: £4962.12 - 542.14 winning tickets JN

1785 NEWCASTLE (L-H)
Wednesday, May 8

OFFICIAL GOING: Good to firm (firm in places; 8.2)
Wind: moderate half against Weather: showers beforehand then sunny

2161 BET365 BRITISH STALLION STUDS E B F MAIDEN STKS 5f
5:30 (5:30) (Class 5) 2-Y-O £2,911 (£866; £432; £216) Stalls Low

Form RPR
1 **Sleeping Shadow** 2-9-0 0 GrahamGibbons 5 67
(Keith Dalgleish) *w ldr: rdn 2f out: led narrowly 1f out: kpt on* **11/4**[2]
43 2 nk **Danfazi (IRE)**[11] 1820 2-9-5 0 PatrickMathers 3 71
(Kristin Stubbs) *led narrowly: rdn 2f out: hdd 1f out: kpt on but a jst hld* **2/1**[1]
3 ¾ **Abisko (IRE)** 2-8-11 0 PaulPickard(3) 6 63+
(Brian Ellison) *trckd ldrs: rdn 2f out: hdwy to chal strly ins fnl f: no ex towards fin* **7/1**
45 4 5 **Jaga Time**[15] 1749 2-9-2 0 LeeTopliss(3) 2 50
(Richard Fahey) *hld up in tch: pushed along 1/2-way: nvr threatened* **12/1**
5 2¼ **By The Light (IRE)** 2-9-5 0 SilvestreDeSousa 7 42
(Mark Johnston) *trckd ldrs: rdn 1/2-way: wknd over 1f out* **3/1**[3]
6 2¼ **Wolfwood** 2-9-5 0 PJMcDonald 4 34
(John Davies) *s.i.s: sn pushed along in rr: a bhd* **33/1**
1m 1.72s (0.62) **Going Correction** -0.10s/f (Good) 6 Ran SP% **108.1**
Speed ratings (Par 93): **91,90,89,81,77 74**
toteswingers 1&2 £1.70, 1&3 £4.60, 2&3 £3.80 CSF £7.98 TOTE £4.10: £2.70, £2.00; EX 15.10 Trifecta £50.70 Pool: £1,359.59 - 20.10 winning units..
Owner Straightline Construction Ltd **Bred** D R Tucker **Trained** Carluke, S Lanarks

FOCUS
Fresh bend into the home straight. Probably just an ordinary juvenile maiden. Guessy form.

2162 BET365.COM H'CAP 7f
6:00 (6:00) (Class 6) (0-65,62) 4-Y-0+ £1,940 (£577; £288; £144) Stalls Low

Form RPR
560- 1 **Never Forever**[240] 6100 4-9-4 **59** PJMcDonald 3 72
(George Moore) *dwlt: midfield on inner: rdn and hdwy over 2f out: led over 1f out: kpt on wl* **8/1**
6604 2 2½ **Rawaafed (IRE)**[12] 1801 4-9-7 **62** SilvestreDeSousa 6 68
(Keith Dalgleish) *hld up: rdn 3f out: hdwy over 1f out: wnt 2nd ins fnl f: kpt on but a hld by wnr* **5/1**[2]
640- 3 3 **Mcmonagle (USA)**[169] 7799 5-9-7 **62** (bt) DaleSwift 13 60
(Alan Brown) *w ldr: rdn over 2f out: one pce fr over 1f out* **7/1**[3]
3600 4 3¼ **Hab Reeh**[14] 1757 5-8-12 **53** (t) AmyRyan 2 42
(Ruth Carr) *w ldr: rdn to ld over 2f out: hdd over 1f out: wknd fnl f* **22/1**
0-60 5 ¾ **Lady Sledmere (IRE)**[23] 1579 5-8-13 **54** (v[1]) MickyFenton 1 41
(Paul Midgley) *hld up: rdn over 2f out: minor late hdwy: nvr threatened* **25/1**
04-0 6 hd **Garzoni**[47] 1111 4-9-2 **57** (e) DuranFentiman 11 44
(Tim Easterby) *chsd ldrs: rdn 3f out: grad wknd over 1f out* **20/1**
3-60 7 nk **No Quarter (IRE)**[14] 1757 6-9-1 **56** BarryMcHugh 4 42
(Tracy Waggott) *in tch: rdn 3f out: grad wknd over 1f out* **12/1**
3312 8 1¼ **Alluring Star**[7] 1932 5-9-0 **62** MatthewHopkins(7) 7 44
(Michael Easterby) *led narrowly: rdn whn hdd over 2f out: sn wknd* **5/4**[1]
-000 9 4½ **Turned To Gold (IRE)**[13] 1790 4-8-11 **52** MartinLane 9 22
(Robert Johnson) *prom: lost pl 4f out: wknd over 2f out* **28/1**
-00 10 2 **Dolly Diva**[32] 1389 4-9-2 **60** LeeTopliss(3) 10 25
(Paul Midgley) *s.i.s: sn in tch: wknd over 2f out* **28/1**
1m 27.28s (-0.52) **Going Correction** -0.10s/f (Good) 10 Ran SP% **112.3**
Speed ratings (Par 101): **98,95,91,88,87 86,86,85,80,77**
toteswingers 1&2 £4.10, 1&3 £5.40, 2&3 £5.00 CSF £41.90 CT £303.06 TOTE £8.10: £1.80, £2.00, £1.30; EX 55.80 Trifecta £180.20 Pool: £1,139.04 - 4.73 winning units..
Owner Northern Premier Partnership **Bred** Millsec Limited **Trained** Middleham Moor, N Yorks

FOCUS
Weak form especially as the short-priced favourite Alluring Star was beaten out of sight.

2163 BET365 H'CAP 1m 3y(S)
6:30 (6:30) (Class 5) (0-75,75) 4-Y-0+ £2,587 (£770; £384; £192) Stalls Low

Form RPR
00-3 1 **Sound Advice**[23] 1569 4-9-6 **74** GrahamGibbons 2 85
(Keith Dalgleish) *mde all: pushed along 2f out: kpt on to go clr ins fnl f* **9/4**[1]
2300 2 4 **Copperwood**[11] 1827 8-8-13 **67** SilvestreDeSousa 6 69
(Mark Johnston) *trckd ldr: rdn over 2f out: one pce and no ch w wnr fnl f* **7/1**
206- 3 ½ **I'm Super Too (IRE)**[251] 5759 6-9-7 **75** RobertWinston 7 76
(Alan Swinbank) *midfield: rdn 3f out: kpt on one pce: wnt 3rd post: nvr threatened* **13/2**
0-61 4 nse **King Pin**[13] 1786 8-9-2 **70** BarryMcHugh 4 71
(Tracy Waggott) *hld up: rdn over 2f out: hdwy over 1f out: kpt on one pce: briefly short of room ins fnl f* **9/2**[3]
2342 5 2 **Hierarch (IRE)**[8] 1901 6-8-5 **66** SiobhanMiller(7) 3 62
(David Simcock) *trckd ldr: rdn over 2f out: grad wknd over 1f out* **10/3**[2]
50-0 6 1¼ **Hakuna Matata**[23] 1576 6-9-2 **70** (b) TomEaves 9 63
(Michael Dods) *in tch: rdn over 2f out: briefly chsd wnr over 1f out: wknd ins fnl f* **11/1**
3600 7 4½ **Moheebb (IRE)**[23] 1569 9-8-6 **65** NathanAlison(5) 8 48
(Robert Johnson) *s.i.s: hld up: a towards rr* **28/1**
0/0- 8 27 **Conjuror's Bluff**[256] 5585 5-8-8 **62** DuranFentiman 5
(Frederick Watson) *midfield: wknd over 2f out: eased ins fnl f* **66/1**
1m 42.02s (-1.38) **Going Correction** -0.10s/f (Good) 8 Ran SP% **111.1**
Speed ratings (Par 103): **102,98,97,97,95 94,89,62**
toteswingers 1&2 £3.90, 1&3 £2.60, 2&3 £5.70 CSF £17.57 CT £84.74 TOTE £2.40: £1.10, £1.90, £2.30; EX 19.80 Trifecta £98.30 Pool: £1,450.98 - 11.06 winning units..
Owner G L S Partnership **Bred** G L S Partnership **Trained** Carluke, S Lanarks

FOCUS
This was a good bit of riding by Graham Gibbons, who firstly grabbed what seemed a favoured rail and then dictated matters at the head of affairs.

2164 BET365.COM MAIDEN FILLIES' STKS 1m 4f 93y
7:00 (7:02) (Class 5) 3-Y-0+ £2,587 (£770; £384; £192) Stalls Low

Form RPR
65-2 1 **Divergence (IRE)**[28] 1478 3-8-7 71 HayleyTurner 10 74
(Michael Bell) *mde all: t.k.h early: clr 9f out tl 1f out: drvn out: a holding on* **7/2**

3 **2** *1 ½* **Shalwa**[34] 1347 3-8-7 0 NickyMackay 2 72
(Marco Botti) *racd in 4th: pushed along and stl wl adrift of clr ldr over 3f out: kpt on fnl 2f: wnt 2nd fnl 50yds* **3/1**[2]

2 **3** *½* **Huffoof (IRE)**[88] 580 3-8-7 0 AndreaAtzeni 6 71
(Roger Varian) *racd in 3rd: pushed along and stl wl adrift of clr ldr over 3f out: wnt 2nd over 2f out: kpt on: lost 2nd fnl 50yds* **15/8**[1]

3- **4** *7* **Zeva**[203] 7160 3-8-7 0 MartinLane 1 60
(David Simcock) *hld up in rr: pushed along and hdwy over 3f out: wnt 4th over 1f out: wknd ins fnl f* **10/3**[3]

5 *5* **Attention Seaker** 3-8-7 0 DuranFentiman 5 52
(Tim Easterby) *hld up in midfield: rdn over 3f out: wknd over 1f out* **25/1**

006- **6** *5* **Miss Mohawk (IRE)**[216] 6807 4-9-9 42 PaulPickard(3) 3 44
(Alan Brown) *trckd clr ldr: rdn over 3f out: wknd fnl 2f* **100/1**

000- **7** *17* **Under Ambition**[254] 5679 5-9-7 36 AdamCarter(5) 7 17
(Frederick Watson) *midfield: rdn over 4f out: sn wknd* **150/1**

5 **8** *1 ½* **Sweetie Royale (IRE)**[84] 641 4-9-12 0 DavidNolan 4 14
(John Wainwright) *hld up: a in rr* **100/1**

2m 41.59s (-4.01) **Going Correction** -0.10s/f (Good)
WFA 3 from 4yo+ 19lb **8 Ran SP% 111.6**
Speed ratings (Par 100): **109,108,107,103,99 96,85,84**
toteswingers 1&2 £1.60, 1&3 £1.70, 2&3 £1.50 CSF £13.60 TOTE £4.40: £1.30, £1.30, £1.10; EX 12.70 Trifecta £26.70 Pool: £1,496.79 - 41.94 winning units..
Owner Lawrie Inman **Bred** L K I Bloodstock Ltd **Trained** Newmarket, Suffolk

FOCUS
The winner set a decent gallop in front and has enough in reserve to hang on.

2165 CASINO AT BET365 H'CAP 1m 4f 93y
7:30 (7:30) (Class 5) (0-75,72) 4-Y-0+ **£2,587** (£770; £384; £192) **Stalls** Low

Form RPR

04-1 **1** **Bright Applause**[14] 1763 5-9-5 **70** BarryMcHugh 2 78
(Tracy Waggott) *hld up in tch: hdwy over 2f out: rdn to chal over 1f out: led ins fnl f: drvn out* **4/1**[2]

00-0 **2** *½* **Silver Tigress**[14] 1763 5-8-9 **60** PJMcDonald 7 67
(George Moore) *hld up in midfield: hdwy on bit over 2f out: led narrowly 2f out: sn rdn: hdd ins fnl f: one pce and a jst hld* **20/1**

06-4 **3** *shd* **Looks Like Rain**[23] 1579 4-8-11 **62** DaleSwift 8 69+
(Brian Ellison) *in tch: rdn and briefly outpcd over 2f out: kpt on fr over 1f out: clsng at fin* **9/2**[3]

6610 **4** *1 ¾* **Yeomanoftheguard**[26] 1523 4-8-10 **64** LeeTopliss(3) 10 68
(Richard Fahey) *hld up in tch: rdn over 2f out: kpt on one pce* **9/1**

0-31 **5** *6* **Naburn**[13] 1789 5-8-13 **64** RobertWinston 4 58
(Alan Swinbank) *trckd ldrs: rdn and upsides 2f out: wknd appr fnl f* **6/5**[1]

-650 **6** *nk* **Light The City (IRE)**[32] 1390 6-8-11 **62** AmyRyan 3 56
(Ruth Carr) *trckd ldrs: rdn over 2f out: wknd over 1f out* **28/1**

/5-0 **7** *6* **Patavium (IRE)**[28] 1463 10-9-7 **72** FrederikTylicki 9 56
(Edwin Tuer) *sn led: rdn whn hdd 2f out: wknd* **18/1**

200- **8** *9* **Falcun**[274] 4908 6-8-7 **58** oh1 (v) SilvestreDeSousa 1 28
(Micky Hammond) *v.s.a: hld up: rdn over 3f out: a towards rr* **20/1**

2m 43.36s (-2.24) **Going Correction** -0.10s/f (Good) **8 Ran SP% 111.9**
Speed ratings (Par 103): **103,102,102,101,97 97,93,87**
toteswingers 1&2 £1.60, 1&3 £1.10, 2&3 £2.00 CSF £76.69 CT £367.55 TOTE £3.80: £1.40, £5.00, £2.70; EX 62.20 Trifecta £215.10 Pool: £997.94 - 3.47 winning units..
Owner Littlethorpe Park Racing **Bred** Old Mill Stud **Trained** Spennymoor, Co Durham
■ Stewards' Enquiry : Frederik Tylicki two-day ban: careless riding (May 22-23)

FOCUS
A modest contest.

2166 BET365.COM FILLIES' H'CAP 6f
8:00 (8:00) (Class 5) (0-75,75) 3-Y-0+ **£2,587** (£770; £384; £192) **Stalls** Low

Form RPR

00-3 **1** **Azzurra Du Caprio (IRE)**[18] 1692 5-10-0 **75** PJMcDonald 5 85
(Ben Haslam) *hld up: rdn and hdwy over 1f out: led fnl 100yds: kpt on* **5/2**[1]

00-2 **2** *1 ¼* **Meandmyshadow**[11] 1819 5-9-12 **73** DaleSwift 6 79
(Alan Brown) *w ldr: rdn 2f out: led 1f out: hdd fnl 100yds: one pce* **7/2**[2]

0-10 **3** *1 ¼* **Foreign Rhythm (IRE)**[25] 1540 8-8-9 **61** ShirleyTeasdale(5) 3 63
(Ron Barr) *trckd ldrs: rdn 2f out: kpt on* **14/1**

45-3 **4** *2 ¾* **Chasing Dreams**[18] 1682 3-9-3 **74** AmyRyan 2 64+
(Kevin Ryan) *s.i.s: hld up in tch by 1/2-way: short of room on inner fr over 1f out tl tl jst ins fnl f: no ch after* **5/2**[1]

-321 **5** *1* **Sunrise Dance**[75] 760 4-9-10 **71** RobertWinston 4 61
(Robert Johnson) *led narrowly: rdn whn hdd 1f out: wknd* **12/1**

440- **6** *nk* **Jeannie Galloway (IRE)**[237] 6176 6-10-0 **75** SilvestreDeSousa 7 64
(Keith Dalgleish) *t.k.h early: trckd ldrs: rdn 2f out: wknd fnl f: sddle slipped* **11/2**[3]

1m 14.02s (-0.58) **Going Correction** -0.10s/f (Good)
WFA 3 from 4yo+ 10lb **6 Ran SP% 109.1**
Speed ratings (Par 100): **99,97,95,92,90 90**
toteswingers 1&2 £1.02, 1&3 £11.00, 2&3 £16.80 CSF £10.78 TOTE £3.20: £1.90, £3.40; EX 9.70 Trifecta £118.00 Pool: £767.79 - 4.87 winning units..
Owner Blue Lion Racing IX **Bred** Glending Bloodstock **Trained** Middleham Moor, N Yorks

FOCUS
Only six runners but a good pace was set by Sunrise Dance, returning to turf after a 75-day absence, before she faded. She stays 6f but might be better over 5f.

2167 POKER AT BET365 H'CAP 1m 3y(S)
8:30 (8:30) (Class 5) (0-75,75) 3-Y-0 **£2,587** (£770; £384; £192) **Stalls** Low

Form RPR

012- **1** **Grandorio (IRE)**[247] 5890 3-9-6 **74** DanielTudhope 7 83
(David O'Meara) *mde all: set stdy pce: pushed clr over 1f out: comf* **10/3**[2]

100- **2** *2 ¾* **Grey Street**[212] 6920 3-9-3 **71** DavidNolan 4 74
(Richard Fahey) *hld up in tch: rdn and hdwy 2f out: kpt on: wnt 2nd ins fnl f: no ch w wnr* **10/1**

063- **3** *1 ¾* **Ersaal**[173] 7750 3-9-2 **70** AndreaAtzeni 3 69
(Roger Varian) *trckd ldrs: rdn to chse wnr over 1f out: lost 2nd ins fnl f: no ex* **2/1**[1]

521- **4** *4* **Corton Lad**[156] 7973 3-8-9 **63** (p) GrahamGibbons 1 53
(Keith Dalgleish) *in tch: rdn 2f out: sn btn in 4th* **9/1**

041- **5** *8* **Mandeville (IRE)**[263] 5331 3-9-7 **75** TomEaves 2 46
(Michael Dods) *w ldr: rdn over 2f out: sn wknd* **15/2**

06-2 **6** *1 ¾* **Bapak Muda (USA)**[28] 1461 3-8-8 **62** AmyRyan 8 29
(Kevin Ryan) *in tch: rdn over 2f out: sn wknd* **7/2**[3]

1m 41.74s (-1.66) **Going Correction** -0.10s/f (Good) **6 Ran SP% 109.5**
Speed ratings (Par 99): **104,101,99,95,87 85**
toteswingers 1&2 £5.80, 1&3 £2.50, 2&3 £4.00 CSF £32.15 CT £74.45 TOTE £2.80: £1.20, £3.50; EX 27.50 Trifecta £59.60 Pool: £760.47 - 9.56 winning units..
Owner Hambleton Racing Ltd - Three In One **Bred** The Grand Splendour Partnership **Trained** Nawton, N Yorks
■ Stewards' Enquiry : David Nolan caution: careless riding.

FOCUS
Far from frenetic stuff early and this developed into a bit of a 3f dash to the line.
T/Plt: £43.00 to a £1 stake. Pool: £52,259.53 - 886.57 winning tickets T/Qpdt: £10.10 to a £1 stake. Pool: £5,275.42 - 386.40 winning tickets AS

1595 SOUTHWELL (L-H)
Wednesday, May 8

OFFICIAL GOING: Standard
Wind: Moderate across Weather: Cloudy with sunny periods

2168 BINARY TRENDS - BINARYTRENDS.CO.UK H'CAP (DIV I) 1m (F)
1:25 (1:27) (Class 6) (0-60,60) 4-Y-0+ **£1,940** (£577; £288; £144) **Stalls** Low

Form RPR

0-00 **1** **Kingscombe (USA)**[16] 1716 4-9-3 **56** SteveDrowne 10 67
(Linda Jewell) *trckd ldrs: hdwy on outer 3f out: led 2f out: sn rdn: kpt on wl fnl f* **7/2**[1]

6325 **2** *2* **Mcconnell (USA)**[29] 1455 8-9-0 **53** (b) CathyGannon 9 59
(Violet M Jordan) *towards rr: hdwy 3f out: rdn to chse ldrs over 1f out: kpt on u.p fnl f* **7/2**[1]

0000 **3** *1* **Rockgoat (IRE)**[54] 1017 4-8-9 **48** AndreaAtzeni 6 52
(Ian McInnes) *in tch: hdwy on outer to chse ldrs 1/2-way: rdn 2f out: drvn to chse wnr ent fnl f: sn edgd lft and one pce* **16/1**

4400 **4** *1* **Follow The Flag (IRE)**[23] 1568 9-9-7 **60** (be) SeanLevey 1 62
(Alan McCabe) *in rr: hdwy 2f out: sn rdn and kpt on fnl f: nrst fin* **6/1**[2]

4514 **5** *nk* **Ace Of Spies (IRE)**[29] 1455 8-8-10 **54** PhilipPrince(5) 2 55
(Conor Dore) *led 1f: prom: effrt over 2f out: rdn to chse wnr over 1f out: wknd fnl f* **10/1**

00-0 **6** *3* **Marina Ballerina**[61] 927 5-8-7 **49** oh1 ow3 MarkCoumbe(3) 4 43
(Roy Bowring) *in and sn pushed along: hdwy 2f out: styd on appr fnl f: nrst fin* **25/1**

00-6 **7** *2* **Zammy**[9] 1873 4-8-11 **50** (b[1]) WilliamCarson 11 40
(Michael Wigham) *dwlt: hdwy to chse ldrs after 1f and sn cl up: led wl over 3f out: rdn and hdd 2f out: grad wknd* **7/1**[3]

534- **8** *5* **Blackamoor Harry**[190] 7470 4-8-0 **46** oh1 VictorSantos(7) 3 24
(Richard Ford) *trckd ldrs: smooth hdwy 3f out: effrt 2f out: sn rdn and wknd over 1f out* **10/1**

/55- **9** *8* **Oakwell (IRE)**[31] 6408 5-8-10 **49** MartinDwyer 5
(Sally Hall) *prom: rdn along 1/2-way: sn wknd* **10/1**

0-60 **10** *½* **Vogarth**[29] 1455 9-8-0 **46** oh1 (v) DanielleMooney(7) 7
(Michael Chapman) *cl up: led after 1f: pushed along and hdd wl over 3f out: sn wknd* **100/1**

50-0 **11** *15* **Pelican Rock (IRE)**[13] 1788 4-8-8 **47** ChrisCatlin 8
(Andrew Crook) *sn swtchd to wd outside: a outpcd and bhd: t.o fnl 3f* **10/1**

1m 44.9s (1.20) **Going Correction** +0.275s/f (Slow) **11 Ran SP% 118.3**
Speed ratings (Par 101): **105,103,102,101,100 97,95,90,82,82 67**
toteswingers 1&2 £3.50, 1&3 £13.10, 2&3 £11.30 CSF £14.73 CT £174.46 TOTE £4.90: £2.00, £1.30, £6.00; EX 19.80 Trifecta £216.40 Pool: £1,986.31 - 6.88 winning units..
Owner Peter Oppenheimer **Bred** Juddmonte Farms Inc **Trained** Sutton Valence, Kent

FOCUS
A moderate handicap to kick-off the card.

2169 BINARY TRENDS - TRIPLE YOUR INVESTMENT MAIDEN STKS 5f (F)
1:55 (1:56) (Class 5) 3-Y-0+ **£2,587** (£770; £384; £192) **Stalls** High

Form RPR

2-3 **1** **Flirtinaskirt**[25] 1539 3-8-12 0 SeanLevey 5 68
(Ed McMahon) *in tch: hdwy 2f out: rdn over 1f out: chal ent fnl f: kpt on to ld last 100yds: drvn towards fin and jst hld on* **5/4**[1]

3 **2** *shd* **Be Lucky**[11] 1821 3-8-12 0 GrahamGibbons 6 67
(Michael Easterby) *cl up: led wl over 1f out: sn rdn: hdd last 100yds: rallied gamely nr fin: jst failed* **5/2**[2]

22- **3** *½* **Charter (IRE)**[140] 8165 3-9-3 0 WilliamCarson 3 70
(Michael Wigham) *s.i.s and bhd: hdwy 1/2-way: rdn to chal on wd outside ent fnl f: ev ch tl drvn and no ex nr fin* **7/2**[3]

6436 **4** *4 ½* **Island Express (IRE)**[25] 1539 6-9-7 48 (tp) AnnStokell(5) 8 58?
(Ann Stokell) *chsd ldrs: rdn along 2f out: sn one pce* **66/1**

6-34 **5** *½* **Puteri Nur Laila (IRE)**[13] 1784 3-8-12 62 (t) NeilCallan 2 47
(Paul Cole) *prom: cl up 2f out: sn rdn and grad wknd appr fnl f* **10/1**

00-0 **6** *4 ½* **Robyn**[28] 1458 3-8-9 49 BillyCray(3) 10 31
(Scott Dixon) *dwlt: racd nr stands' rail: a towards rr* **40/1**

426- **7** *1* **Itum**[150] 8046 6-9-12 50 TomMcLaughlin 7 36
(Christine Dunnett) *cl up: led after 2f: rdn along and hdd wl over 1f out: sn wknd* **25/1**

-066 **8** *1 ¼* **Dubai Rythm**[9] 1888 4-9-12 47 (b) AndrewMullen 4 32
(Michael Appleby) *slt ld 2f: cl up tl rdn along wl over 1f out and sn wknd* **40/1**

9 *1* **Bowlands Legacy** 4-9-0 0 VictorSantos(7) 1 23
(Richard Ford) *a towards rr* **66/1**

00-5 **10** *1 ½* **Mid Yorkshire Golf**[26] 1519 4-9-2 47 SladeO'Hara(5) 9 18
(Peter Grayson) *a in rr* **100/1**

1m 0.61s (0.91) **Going Correction** +0.175s/f (Slow)
WFA 3 from 4yo+ 9lb **10 Ran SP% 117.0**
Speed ratings (Par 103): **99,98,98,90,90 82,81,79,77,75**
toteswingers 1&2 £1.80, 1&3 £1.80, 2&3 £1.90 CSF £4.37 TOTE £2.30: £1.10, £1.10, £1.80; EX 5.50 Trifecta £13.60 Pool: £2,719.94 - 149.59 winning units..
Owner Philip Wilkins **Bred** Alvediston Stud **Trained** Lichfield, Staffs

FOCUS
A maiden with a mix between a few promising types and some exposed, modest performers. The right horses came to the fore and it was good to see the first three pull clear.

2170 BINARY TRENDS - CHOOSE YOUR INCOME H'CAP 6f (F)
2:25 (2:25) (Class 6) (0-55,55) 4-Y-0+ **£1,940** (£577; £288; £144) **Stalls** Low

Form RPR

2244 **1** **Thorpe Bay**[18] 1681 4-9-7 **55** AndrewMullen 14 64
(Michael Appleby) *sn cl up: chal 1/2-way: led wl over 2f out: rdn wl over 1f out: drvn ins fnl f: kpt on wl* **9/2**[1]

5236 **2** *¾* **Mucky Molly**[20] 1656 5-9-4 **52** (vt) PhillipMakin 12 59
(Alison Hutchinson) *prom: rdn 2f out: styd on to chal ins fnl f: ev ch tl drvn: edgd lft and no ex last 50yds* **7/1**

5030 **3** *nk* **Ridgeway Hawk**[16] 1734 5-9-2 **50**..............(v) RobertHavlin 1 56+
(Mark Usher) *dwlt and in rr: rdn along over 2f out: hdwy wl over 1f out: swtchd lft to inner ent fnl f: fin strly* **6/1**

1460 **4** *nk* **Very First Blade**[32] 1395 4-9-2 **50**..............(p) TomMcLaughlin 13 55
(Mark Brisbourne) *chsd ldrs: hdwy 2f out: rdn over 1f out: styng on whn n.m.r ins fnl f: kpt on* **16/1**

0-60 **5** *shd* **Punching**[29] 1452 9-9-6 **54**.............. NeilCallan 11 58
(Conor Dore) *sn led: hdd wl over 2f out: cl up and sn rdn: drvn ent fnl f and ev ch tl no ex last 100yds* **11/2**[3]

052 **6** *1 1/4* **Doctor Hilary**[53] 1042 11-8-9 **48**..............(v) PhilipPrince(5) 8 48
(Mark Hoad) *dwlt and towards rr: hdwy wl over 2f out: sn rdn and edgd lft over 1f out: kpt on: nrst fin* **16/1**

100 **7** *2 1/4* **Coastal Passage**[39] 1239 5-9-5 **53**.............. MartinDwyer 2 46
(Charles Smith) *in tch on inner: rdn along over 2f out: no imp fr over 1f out* **16/1**

050- **8** *3 3/4* **Gracie's Games**[191] 7447 7-8-7 **48**..............(v) JacobButterfield(7) 7 29
(John Spearing) *prom: rdn along 1/2-way: wknd 2f out* **25/1**

2004 **9** *1/2* **Ishetoo**[46] 1149 9-8-8 **47**.............. SladeO'Hara(5) 10 27
(Peter Grayson) *a towards rr* **20/1**

0000 **10** *nk* **Amenable (IRE)**[49] 1088 6-9-4 **52**.............. CathyGannon 4 31
(Violet M Jordan) *dwlt: a towards rr* **5/1**[2]

4050 **11** *2 3/4* **Munaawib**[25] 1539 5-8-12 **46** oh1..............(t) ChrisCatlin 6 16
(Charles Smith) *a towards rr* **50/1**

0555 **12** *1/2* **Sherjawy (IRE)**[7] 1929 9-9-2 **50**.............. KirstyMilczarek 5 18
(Laura Mongan) *nvr bttr than midfield* **10/1**

000- **13** *1* **Toothache**[195] 7354 5-8-12 **49**..............(b[1]) BillyCray(3) 9 14
(Garry Woodward) *chsd ldrs: rdn along over 2f out: sn wknd* **33/1**

255- **14** *shd* **Emily Hall**[255] 5621 4-9-1 **49**.............. RussKennemore 3 14
(Bryan Smart) *dwlt: a in rr* **12/1**

1m 19.02s (2.52) **Going Correction** +0.275s/f (Slow) **14** Ran SP% **125.0**
Speed ratings (Par 101): **94,93,92,92,92 90,87,82,81,81 77,77,75,75**
toteswingers 1&2 £5.70, 1&3 £4.30, 2&3 £6.70 CSF £35.71 CT £202.37 TOTE £4.80: £1.80, £2.40, £2.20; EX 28.90 Trifecta £88.90 Pool: £1,952.36 - 16.45 winning units..
Owner Dallas Racing **Bred** Clive Dennett **Trained** Danethorpe, Notts
■ Stewards' Enquiry : Slade O'Hara 1st incident; caution: careless riding; 2nd, two-day ban: careless riding (May 24-25)

FOCUS
A weak race featuring a number of horses with declining handicap marks. The pace was solid.

2171 BINARY TRENDS - BINARYTRENDS.CO.UK H'CAP (DIV II) 1m (F)

2:55 (2:55) (Class 6) (0-60,60) 4-Y-0+ **£1,940** (£577; £288; £144) **Stalls** Low

Form RPR

5-25 **1** **Just Five (IRE)**[16] 1730 7-8-6 **48**..............(v) RaulDaSilva(3) 5 57
(John Weymes) *in tch: pushed along after 2f: hdwy over 2f out: trckd ldng pair over 2f out: swtchd rt and rdn over 1f out: led appr fnl f: kpt on* **9/2**[3]

0005 **2** *2* **On The Cusp (IRE)**[43] 1184 6-8-13 **52**..............(p) CathyGannon 6 56
(Violet M Jordan) *sn cl up: chal 1/2-way: led over 2f out and sn rdn: drvn and hdd appr fnl f: kpt on same pce* **5/1**

1662 **3** *5* **Putin (IRE)**[15] 1748 5-9-2 **60**..............(tp) RachealKneller(5) 10 53
(Phil McEntee) *led: rdn along 3f out: hdd over 2f out: cl up tl drvn and wknd ent fnl f* **4/1**[2]

432- **4** *6* **Monte Cassino (IRE)**[161] 7917 8-9-1 **54**..............(e) RoystonFfrench 3 33
(Bryan Smart) *chsd ldrs: rdn along 3f out: swtchd rt and drvn over 2f out: sn wknd* **6/1**

5336 **5** *1/2* **Bonnie Prince Blue**[29] 1455 10-8-11 **50**..............(v) AndrewElliott 1 28
(Ian McInnes) *broke wl and led early: sn hdd and pushed along: outpcd 1/2-way: rdn 3f out: plugged on along inner* **16/1**

2000 **6** *3 3/4* **Seawood**[47] 1120 7-8-7 **49** oh1 ow3..............(p) MarkCoumbe(3) 7 18
(Roy Bowring) *dwlt: hdwy on outer to chse ldrs 1/2-way: rdn along 3f out: sn wknd* **9/1**

606 **7** *22* **Big Kahuna**[37] 1291 6-8-2 **48**.............. IanBurns(7) 2
(Jane Chapple-Hyam) *dwlt: a in rr* **16/1**

000- **8** *1 1/4* **Plus Fours (USA)**[173] 7752 4-8-7 **46** oh1..............(p) AndrewMullen 8
(Michael Appleby) *cl up: pushed along after 2f: lost pl bef 1/2-way and sn bhd* **3/1**[1]

1m 45.22s (1.52) **Going Correction** +0.275s/f (Slow) **8** Ran SP% **115.9**
Speed ratings (Par 101): **103,101,96,90,89 85,63,62**
toteswingers 1&2 £4.00, 1&3 £4.50, 2&3 £6.40 CSF £27.62 CT £98.07 TOTE £6.80: £2.40, £1.40, £1.30; EX 27.10 Trifecta £92.20 Pool: £1,522.17 - 12.37 winning units..
Owner Thoroughbred Racing Club **Bred** Rathbarry Stud **Trained** Middleham Moor, N Yorks

FOCUS
Another weak affair.

2172 BINARY TRENDS - INVESTMENT TROPHY MEDIAN AUCTION MAIDEN STKS 7f (F)

3:25 (3:26) (Class 6) 3-4-Y-0 **£1,940** (£577; £288; £144) **Stalls** Low

Form RPR

620- **1** **Testamatta**[277] 4820 3-8-9 76.............. AndreaAtzeni 10 71+
(Marco Botti) *in tch: hdwy to trck ldrs 1/2-way: chal over 2f out: led on bit wl over 1f out: sn clr: easily* **10/11**[1]

23-3 **2** *3 3/4* **Nordikhab (IRE)**[18] 1687 3-9-0 78.............. PhillipMakin 8 60
(Kevin Ryan) *slt ld: rdn wl over 2f out: hdd wl over 1f out: sn drvn and kpt on same pce* **6/4**[2]

062 **3** *nk* **Una Bella Cosa**[43] 1185 3-8-9 52..............(v) SeanLevey 6 54
(Alan McCabe) *cl up: rdn along 3f out: drvn wl over 1f out and kpt on same pce* **10/1**

5423 **4** *4* **Solarmaite**[22] 1595 4-9-4 63..............(p) MarkCoumbe(3) 1 48
(Roy Bowring) *cl up on inner: rdn along 3f out: sn one pce* **8/1**[3]

00 **5** *3 1/4* **Stoneacre Oskar**[41] 1215 4-9-2 0.............. SladeO'Hara(5) 9 39
(Peter Grayson) *chsd ldrs: rdn along over 3f out: n.d* **40/1**

6 *6* **Grivola (GER)** 3-8-9 0.............. MartinDwyer 7 20
(Conrad Allen) *dwlt and in rr: sme hdwy on wd outside wl over 2f out: sn rdn along and nvr a factor* **14/1**

6/ **7** *nk* **Mr Mallo**[720] 2234 4-9-12 0.............. StephenCraine 2 28
(John Stimpson) *a towards rr* **40/1**

6 **8** *12* **Moonlight Dreamer**[13] 1777 4-9-0 0..............(p) AliRawlinson(7) 4
(David C Griffiths) *dwlt: a in rr: bhd fr 1/2-way* **40/1**

6 **9** *2 1/4* **Jack Firefly**[37] 1296 4-9-7 0.............. TobyAtkinson(5) 3
(Michael Murphy) *dwlt: a in rr: bhd fr 1/2-way* **33/1**

0- **10** *9* **Poppanella (IRE)**[249] 5823 4-9-4 0.............. DeclanCannon(3) 5
(Lawrence Mullaney) *a in rr: bhd fr 1/2-way* **50/1**

1m 34.26s (3.96) **Going Correction** +0.275s/f (Slow)
WFA 3 from 4yo 12lb **10** Ran SP% **131.5**
Speed ratings (Par 101): **88,83,83,78,75 68,67,54,51,41**
toteswingers 1&2 £1.20, 1&3 £2.30, 2&3 £3.20 CSF £2.85 TOTE £1.70: £1.10, £1.10, £2.50; EX 3.60 Trifecta £11.80 Pool: £3,137.34 - 198.80 winning units..
Owner Immobiliare Casa Paola SRL **Bred** Motivator Syndicate And Grovewood Stud **Trained** Newmarket, Suffolk
■ Stewards' Enquiry : Phillip Makin three-day ban: careless riding (May 22-24)

FOCUS
The two that dominated the market in this maiden had been assigned marks in the high 70s. Arguably only one was able to run to such a mark and she ran out an easy victor.

2173 E B F BINARYTRENDS - TOO GOOD TO BE TRUE-INVESTMENTS FILLIES' H'CAP 5f (F)

4:00 (4:01) (Class 4) (0-80,80) 4-Y-0+ **£6,469** (£1,925; £962; £481) **Stalls** High

Form RPR

122- **1** **Silken Express (IRE)**[221] 6689 4-9-5 **78**.............. NeilCallan 2 94+
(Robert Cowell) *dwlt and swtchd lft to outer after s: gd hdwy 1/2-way: rdn to ld and edgd rt over 1f out: sn hung lft: drvn out* **9/4**[1]

311- **2** *1 3/4* **Demora**[203] 7177 4-9-7 **80**.............. AndrewMullen 1 90
(Michael Appleby) *prom on outer: cl up 1/2-way: rdn and ev ch whn sltly hmpd over 1f out: drvn and kpt on same pce ins fnl f* **7/2**[2]

-261 **3** *1/2* **Mata Hari Blue**[22] 1596 7-9-5 **78**..............(t) PhillipMakin 3 86
(Michael Appleby) *chsd ldrs: hdwy and cl up 2f out: rdn and ev ch ent fnl f: sn drvn and kpt on same pce* **7/2**[2]

-330 **4** *2 3/4* **Wicked Wench**[61] 924 4-8-11 **70**.............. SteveDrowne 4 68
(Jeremy Gask) *chsd ldrs: hdwy 2f out: sn rdn and one pce appr fnl f* **7/1**[3]

4203 **5** *1 1/2* **Song Of Parkes**[5] 1984 6-8-10 **74**.............. SladeO'Hara(5) 8 67
(Peter Grayson) *sn pushed along and outpcd towards rr: hdwy 2f out: sn rdn and no imp appr fnl f* **20/1**

4530 **6** *1 1/2* **Six Wives**[12] 1807 6-8-12 **74**..............(p) BillyCray(3) 5 61
(Scott Dixon) *led: rdn 2f out: drvn and hdd over 1f out: sn wknd* **9/1**

53-0 **7** *3* **Wild Sauce**[12] 1807 4-9-2 **75**..............(b) RoystonFfrench 6 51
(Bryan Smart) *cl up: rdn along 2f out: sn drvn and grad wknd* **12/1**

21-0 **8** *1* **Elusive Bonus (IRE)**[20] 1649 4-8-12 **76**.............. DavidBergin(5) 10 49
(David O'Meara) *in tch: rdn along 1/2-way: sn outpcd* **16/1**

20-0 **9** *5* **El McGlynn (IRE)**[20] 1649 4-8-9 **73**.............. CharlesBishop(5) 9 28
(William Kinsey) *chsd ldrs to 1/2-way: sn outpcd and bhd* **33/1**

0/0- **10** *4 1/2* **Royal Award**[392] 1317 4-9-7 **80**.............. StephenCraine 7 19
(Jonathan Portman) *a towards rr* **25/1**

59.37s (-0.33) **Going Correction** +0.175s/f (Slow) **10** Ran SP% **122.8**
Speed ratings (Par 102): **109,106,105,101,98 96,91,89,81,74**
toteswingers 1&2 £2.20, 1&3 £2.60, 2&3 £3.80 CSF £10.46 CT £28.05 TOTE £4.80: £1.90, £2.90, £1.10; EX 14.10 Trifecta £19.80 Pool: £2,507.41 - 94.84 winning units..
Owner Malih Lahej Al Basti **Bred** Redpender Stud Ltd **Trained** Six Mile Bottom, Cambs

FOCUS
The feature race on the card was a fair fillies' handicap. Everything broke on terms, the first-four in the market were the first-four home, the time was good and the winner is potentially useful.

2174 BINARY TRENDS - MAKE MONEY WITH BINARYTRENDS.CO.UK H'CAP 1m 6f (F)

4:35 (4:35) (Class 5) (0-75,70) 4-Y-0+ **£2,587** (£770; £384; £192) **Stalls** Low

Form RPR

1223 **1** **Neighbourhood (USA)**[5] 1979 5-8-5 **56**..............(b) RyanTate(5) 2 71+
(James Evans) *trckd ldrs: hdwy to ld 3f out: rdn clr 2f out: drvn and kpt on wl fnl f* **2/1**[2]

10-0 **2** *6* **Fine Kingdom**[14] 1763 4-8-1 **53**..............(b) PhilipPrince(5) 7 59
(Brian Ellison) *prom: led after 6f: rdn along over 3f out: sn hdd: drvn wl over 1f out: kpt on u.p fnl f* **25/1**

43-1 **3** *4* **Decana**[22] 1601 5-9-0 **67**.............. CharlieBennett(7) 5 69
(Hughie Morrison) *hld up in rr: stdy hdwy 4f out: trckd ldrs 3f out: effrt to chse wnr 2f out: sn rdn and hung lft ent fnl f: one pce* **1/1**[1]

1230 **4** *6* **Blazing Desert**[11] 1831 9-9-5 **70**.............. CharlesBishop(5) 4 62
(William Kinsey) *trckd ldr: cl up 1/2-way: rdn along over 3f out: sn outpcd* **10/1**

1246 **5** *8* **Calculating (IRE)**[15] 1744 9-8-6 **52**.............. MartinDwyer 6 33
(Mark Usher) *in tch: pushed along 5f out: sn outpcd and bhd fnl 3f* **14/1**

3332 **6** *nk* **Xpres Maite**[22] 1600 10-8-13 **62**..............(v) MarkCoumbe(3) 3 43
(Roy Bowring) *reminders and rdn along after s: sn swtchd to outer: cl up 1/2-way: rdn along 4f out: sn outpcd* **8/1**[3]

-340 **7** *99* **Kingaroo (IRE)**[22] 1600 7-8-3 **52**.............. BillyCray(3) 1
(Garry Woodward) *led: hdd after 6f and sn pushed along: rdn over 5f out: sn outpcd and bhd: t.o whn virtually p.u wl over 1f out* **40/1**

3m 11.18s (2.88) **Going Correction** +0.275s/f (Slow)
WFA 4 from 5yo+ 1lb **7** Ran SP% **116.5**
Speed ratings (Par 103): **102,98,96,92,88 88,31**
toteswingers 1&2 £7.10, 1&3 £1.40, 2&3 £7.70 CSF £47.91 TOTE £2.10: £1.10, £9.20; EX 58.70 Trifecta £210.80 Pool: £3,337.39 - 11.87 winning units..
Owner James Evans Racing **Bred** Mr & Mrs Gary Middlebrook **Trained** Broadwas, Worcs

FOCUS
A poorly contested staying handicap and they only wanted to know two of them in the betting.

2175 NEW KIA CEE'D H'CAP 1m 3f (F)

5:10 (5:10) (Class 5) (0-70,62) 3-Y-0 **£2,587** (£770; £384; £192) **Stalls** Low

Form RPR

5120 **1** **Luv U Whatever**[18] 1685 3-9-4 **59**.............. J-PGuillambert 2 73
(Jo Hughes) *cl up: led over 4f out: sn jnd: rdn wl over 2f out: drvn and edgd rt ent fnl f: kpt on wl* **3/1**[3]

63-4 **2** *3* **Danehill Flyer (IRE)**[38] 1275 3-9-7 **62**.............. RussKennemore 6 71
(Philip Kirby) *hld up in rr: hdwy 4f out and sn cl up: chal 3f out: rdn 2f out: drvn over 1f out and ev ch tl one pce fnl f* **9/4**[1]

0-16 **3** *19* **Darakti (IRE)**[28] 1469 3-9-0 **55**..............(p) AndrewMullen 5 30
(Alan McCabe) *dwlt and in rr: hdwy over 3f out: sn chsng ldng pair: drvn over 2f out and plugged on same pce* **10/1**

040- **4** *5* **Angilina**[172] 7780 3-9-2 **57** ow2..............(b[1]) PhillipMakin 3 21
(Kevin Ryan) *chsd ldrs: rdn along 5f out: outpcd fr over 3f out* **11/2**

5320 **5** *10* **Lucky Mountain**[15] 1743 3-8-11 **55**.............. BillyCray(3) 1
(Scott Dixon) *led: pushed along and hdd over 4f out: sn rdn and wknd* **20/1**

34-3 **6** *10* **Bell'Arte (IRE)**[32] 1393 3-9-5 **60**..............(b[1]) NeilCallan 4
(Mark Johnston) *t.k.h early: chsd ldng pair: pushed along 4f out: rdn over 3f out and sn wknd* **11/4**[2]

2m 29.77s (1.77) **Going Correction** +0.275s/f (Slow) **6** Ran SP% **111.7**
Speed ratings (Par 99): **104,101,88,84,77 69**
toteswingers 1&2 £2.00, 1&3 £3.70, 2&3 £4.30 CSF £10.07 TOTE £4.10: £1.20, £2.60; EX 16.00 Trifecta £95.80 Pool: £2,752.09 - 21.52 winning units..
Owner 21C Telecom.co.uk **Bred** Richard Hunt **Trained** Lambourn, Berks
■ Stewards' Enquiry : Phillip Makin three-day ban: weighed in 2lb heavy (May 25,27,28)

FOCUS
A modest race to end the card. It looked competitive enough on paper, but only two horses ever got involved.

T/Plt: £9.40 to a £1 stake. Pool: £49,538.05 - 3,824.38 winning tickets T/Qpdt: £5.10 to a £1 stake. Pool: £3,277.67 - 466.80 winning tickets JR

2176 - 2183a (Foreign Racing) - See Raceform Interactive

1972 LONGCHAMP (R-H)

Wednesday, May 8

OFFICIAL GOING: Turf: good to soft

2184a PRIX D'HEDOUVILLE (GROUP 3) (4YO+) (TURF) 1m 4f

2:50 (12:00) 4-Y-0+ **£32,520** (£13,008; £9,756; £6,504; £3,252)

RPR

1 **Pirika (IRE)**[20] 1658 5-8-8 0 Pierre-CharlesBoudot 4 108
(A Fabre, France) *hld up towards rr: qcknd strly 1 1/2f out on wd outside: sn chal for ld: tk ld 1f out: r.o wl* **12/5**[1]

2 ½ **Haya Landa (FR)**[10] 1870 5-8-8 0 FranckBlondel 3 107
(Mme L Audon, France) *settled in midfield on ins: rdn 1 1/2f out: r.o wl fnl f to go 2nd 100yds out: fin strly: a being hld* **19/1**

3 2 **Remus De La Tour (FR)**[38] 4-9-2 0 NicolasPerret 8 112
(K Borgel, France) *led on settling: r.o wl u.p 1 1/2f out: hdd 1f out: styd on wl* **16/1**

4 1 ¼ **Slow Pace (USA)**[38] 5-8-9 0 OlivierPeslier 2 103
(F Head, France) *settled in 4th towards ins: rdn 2f out: wandered off st line 1 1/2f out: causing interfernce: r.o again ins fnl f* **11/2**[3]

5 hd **Allied Powers (IRE)**[18] 1674 8-9-2 0 ChristopheSoumillon 6 109
(Michael Bell) *settled in midfield towards outside: rdn 2f out: nt qckn: styd on wl fnl f* **7/1**

6 nse **Meleagros (IRE)**[38] 4-8-9 0 AdrienFouassier 5 102
(A Couetil, France) *settled towards rr: rdn 2f out: short of room whn beginning forward move over 1 1/2f out: had to be stdd and swtchd to outside: rallied and r.o wl fnl 100yds: unlucky* **15/2**

7 1 **Gentle Storm (FR)**[20] 1658 4-8-11 0 (p) IoritzMendizabal 9 103
(Y Barberot, France) *settled in cl 2nd: rdn 2 1/2f out: chal ldr 2f out: no ex: styd on one pce fnl f* **68/10**

8 2 **Testosterone (IRE)**[28] 1484 5-8-6 0 Christophe-PatriceLemaire 7 95
(Ed Dunlop) *prom early: settled in 4th towards ins: u.p 2f out: no ex: suffered minor interference 1 1/2f out: fdd fnl f* **9/2**[2]

9 3 ½ **Rollex Borget (FR)**[66] 7431 4-8-11 0 ThierryJarnet 1 94
(J Bertran De Balanda, France) *a at rr: no prog u.p 2f out: nvr a factor* **17/1**

2m 37.52s (7.12) 9 Ran SP% **116.5**
WIN (incl. 1 euro stake): 3.40. PLACES: 1.90, 4.20, 3.80. DF: 25.60. SF: 46.70.
Owner Teruya Yoshida **Bred** Shadai Farm **Trained** Chantilly, France

2147 CHESTER (L-H)

Thursday, May 9

OFFICIAL GOING: Good to firm changing to good after race 1 (1.45) changing to good to soft after race 4 (3.15)
Wind: Strong, half behind Weather: Rain

2185 CRABBIE'S ALCOHOLIC GINGER BEER H'CAP 1m 2f 75y

1:45 (1:47) (Class 2) (0-105,103) 4-Y-0+ **£16,762** (£4,715; £2,357; £1,180; £587) **Stalls High**

Form RPR

104- 1 **Sir John Hawkwood (IRE)**[194] 7407 4-9-1 **97** RyanMoore 11 107+
(Sir Michael Stoute) *rdn along early to get position: sn wnt cl 2nd: rdn to ld ins fnl f: styd on nicely* **10/3**[2]

00-0 2 ¾ **Eshtibaak (IRE)**[40] 1235 5-8-10 **92** PaulHanagan 9 101+
(John Gosden) *towards rr: hdwy on outer over 2f out: styd on to take 2nd wl ins fnl f: clsd at fin but unable to chal wnr* **5/1**[3]

0-11 3 1 ¼ **Beaumont's Party (IRE)**[26] 1538 6-8-12 **94** DaleSwift 2 100
(Brian Ellison) *midfield: niggled along over 3f out: rdn over 2f out: hdwy to chse ldrs over 1f out: styd on towards fin: nt gng pce to chal front two* **3/1**[1]

50-1 4 ¾ **Area Fifty One**[15] 1768 5-9-6 **102** JamieSpencer 8 107
(Richard Fahey) *led: rdn over 1f out: hdd ins fnl f: no ex fnl 50yds* **8/1**

-150 5 2 ¼ **Benzanno (IRE)**[5] 2018 4-8-10 **92** DavidProbert 6 92
(Andrew Balding) *towards rr: rdn over 1f out: styd on ins fnl f: nt trble ldrs* **22/1**

0/ 6 1 ½ **Tellovoi (IRE)**[341] 5-8-10 **92** RobertWinston 4 89
(Andrew Hollinshead) *s.i.s: in rr: rdn and hung rt on bnd wl over 1f out: kpt on ins fnl f: no imp* **40/1**

50-0 7 14 **Assizes**[62] 926 4-8-2 **84** JoeFanning 1 53
(Mark Johnston) *racd keenly: prom tl pushed along and wknd over 1f out* **6/1**

-312 8 3 ¾ **Flying Power**[62] 926 5-8-8 **90** PaddyAspell 7 52
(John Norton) *in tch: pushed along and lost pl 2f out: sn wl btn* **14/1**

650- 9 10 **Halfsin (IRE)**[327] 3164 5-8-13 **95** KierenFallon 5 37
(Marco Botti) *racd keenly: trckd ldrs: pushed along over 3f out: sn lost pl: bhd over 1f out* **10/1**

2m 11.15s (-0.05) **Going Correction** +0.225s/f (Good) 9 Ran SP% **112.7**
Speed ratings (Par 109): **109,108,107,106,105 103,92,89,81**
toteswingers 1&2 £3.80, 2&3 £4.30, 1&3 £2.90 CSF £19.81 CT £53.53 TOTE £4.00: £1.20, £1.80, £2.00; EX 17.30 Trifecta £59.50 Pool: £2894.10 - 36.47 winning units..
Owner Ballymacoll Stud **Bred** Ballymacoll Stud Farm Ltd **Trained** Newmarket, Suffolk

FOCUS
Rail moved out 3yds from 6f to 1.5f with drop in. Races 1, 2, &7 increased in distance by 14yds, race 3 by 20yds, race 4 & 6 by 13yds and race 5 by 10yds. The watered ground was given as good to firm (GoingStick 7.7) at 8am, but it started raining at 10am and it had got in to some extent by the time of the first race, and the going was changed to good soon afterwards. There was a tailwind in the straight. The winning time of the opener, run at a decent gallop, was 2.95sec outside standard, and Ryan Moore described the ground as "good, a bit slow and a bit slick in places.", while Dale Swift said "It's on the easy side of good and is loose on top." A good handicap, the form rated around the third and fourth.

2186 STELLA ARTOIS HUXLEY STKS (FOR THE TRADESMAN'S CUP) (GROUP 3) 1m 2f 75y

2:15 (2:16) (Class 1) 4-Y-0+

£34,026 (£12,900; £6,456; £3,216; £1,614; £810) **Stalls High**

Form RPR

101- 1 **Danadana (IRE)**[260] 5492 5-9-0 109 KierenFallon 3 111+
(Luca Cumani) *towards rr: in last pl wl over 7f out: nvr travelled wl after: hdwy over 1f out: r.o to ld wl ins fnl f: in command cl home* **10/3**[1]

5-52 2 ¾ **Highland Knight (IRE)**[13] 1810 6-9-0 113 (t) DavidProbert 6 109
(Andrew Balding) *led: rdn 2f out: hdd wl ins fnl f: kpt on but nt gng pce of wnr* **4/1**[3]

33-1 3 nk **Gabrial (IRE)**[26] 1535 4-9-0 111 JamieSpencer 7 108
(Richard Fahey) *dwlt: hld up: hdwy over 1f out: sn hung lft: ev ch ent fnl f: continued to hang lft: kpt on u.p but nt gng pce of wnr and hld* **7/2**[2]

0-21 4 2 **Miblish**[40] 1241 4-9-0 103 (t) FrederikTylicki 4 106+
(Clive Brittain) *in tch: effrt whn n.m.r and hmpd over 1f out: sn lost pl: unable to get on terms w ldrs after* **8/1**

01-5 5 shd **Dick Doughtywylie**[12] 1846 5-9-0 100 WilliamBuick 2 104
(John Gosden) *dwlt: chsd ldrs: rdn over 1f out: hung lft ins fnl f: one pce fnl 150yds* **8/1**

400- 6 shd **Rewarded**[222] 6674 4-9-0 99 KirstyMilczarek 1 104
(James Toller) *hld up: pushed along over 1f out: kpt on ins fnl f on inner: nvr able to chal* **16/1**

66-3 7 5 **Bonfire**[21] 1639 4-9-0 110 JimmyFortune 5 95
(Andrew Balding) *sn chsd ldr: pushed along and ev ch 2f out: rdn and wandered over 1f out: sn lost 2nd: wknd ins fnl f* **4/1**[3]

2m 11.61s (0.41) **Going Correction** +0.225s/f (Good) 7 Ran SP% **113.4**
Speed ratings (Par 113): **107,106,106,104,104 104,100**
toteswingers 1&2 £3.20, 2&3 £3.50, 1&3 £2.70 CSF £16.65 TOTE £3.90: £2.10, £2.90; EX 18.40 Trifecta £90.60 Pool: £3866.97 - 31.98 winning units..
Owner Sheikh Mohammed Obaid Al Maktoum **Bred** Darley **Trained** Newmarket, Suffolk

FOCUS
Most of these had questions to answer, either on stamina, class or fitness grounds, while the easing conditions was another variable. Once again there was a good gallop on, and on this occasion the leaders did come back to one more patiently ridden. The winner didn't need to improve but has more to offer.

2187 MBNA CHESTER VASE (GROUP 3) (C&G) 1m 4f 66y

2:45 (2:46) (Class 1) 3-Y-O **£34,026** (£12,900; £6,456; £3,216) **Stalls Low**

Form RPR

1 **Ruler Of The World (IRE)**[32] 1417 3-8-12 0 (p) RyanMoore 4 112
(A P O'Brien, Ire) *chsd ldr: led over 1f out: r.o wl to draw clr ins fnl f* **10/11**[1]

1-14 2 6 **Mister Impatience**[15] 1767 3-8-12 93 JoeFanning 5 102
(Mark Johnston) *led: rdn and hdd over 1f out: unable to go w wnr and no ch ins fnl f* **11/1**

21-4 3 1 ½ **Havana Beat (IRE)**[21] 1636 3-8-12 100 DavidProbert 1 100
(Andrew Balding) *racd keenly: chsd ldrs: rdn over 2f out: one pce fnl f: nvr able to chal* **11/4**[2]

1 4 2 **Feel Like Dancing**[19] 1679 3-8-12 89 WilliamBuick 2 96+
(John Gosden) *dwlt: racd keenly: hld up in rr: pushed along 3f out: rdn over 1f out: outpcd thrght fnl f* **4/1**[3]

2m 40.29s (1.79) **Going Correction** +0.225s/f (Good) 4 Ran SP% **107.4**
Speed ratings (Par 109): **103,99,98,96**
CSF £10.17 TOTE £1.60; EX 10.40 Trifecta £20.80 Pool: £2533.51 - 91.33 winning units..
Owner Mrs John Magnier & Michael Tabor & Derrick Smith **Bred** Southern Bloodstock **Trained** Ballydoyle, Co Tipperary

FOCUS
It's a long time since this Derby trial produced the winner at Epsom (Shergar in 1981), but Aidan O'Brien's winners in recent years have tended to run well in defeat at Epsom afterwards - Soldier Of Fortune and Golden Sword both finished fifth, and Treasure Beach only found Pour Moi too good - so there's a good chance Ruler Of The World will at least be in the mix at Epsom. Not a great deal to go on, but Ruler Of The World is rated on a par with O'Brien's previous Vase winners.

2188 BOODLES DIAMOND H'CAP 7f 122y

3:15 (3:15) (Class 2) (0-100,100) 3-Y-O **£16,752** (£4,715; £2,357; £1,180; £587) **Stalls Low**

Form RPR

14-2 1 **Here Comes When (IRE)**[20] 1668 3-8-10 **89** DavidProbert 1 102+
(Andrew Balding) *chsd ldrs: led over 1f out: sn qcknd up: r.o: edgd lft fnl 100yds: rdn out* **9/4**[1]

11- 2 1 **Breton Rock (IRE)**[218] 6799 3-8-7 **86** oh1 MartinLane 7 96+
(David Simcock) *rrd s: in rr: pushed along and hdwy 2f out: rdn over 1f out whn chsng ldrs: sn swtchd rt: prog to take 2nd wl ins fnl f: r.o and clsd nr fin: nt quite rch wnr* **15/2**

1245 3 4 ½ **Flashlight (IRE)**[5] 2024 3-8-8 **87** JoeFanning 4 86
(Mark Johnston) *chsd ldrs: effrt and ev ch over 1f out: kpt on same pce ins fnl f: no ch w front two fnl 100yds* **13/2**[3]

22-0 4 nk **Sorella Bella (IRE)**[22] 1622 3-9-7 **100** MartinHarley 2 98
(Mick Channon) *chsd ldr: rdn and ev ch over 1f out: kpt on same pce ins fnl f: no ch w front two fnl 100yds* **8/1**

13-4 5 4 **Ribaat (IRE)**[20] 1668 3-9-6 **99** PaulHanagan 6 87
(Roger Varian) *s.i.s: racd keenly in midfield: u.p over 1f out: sn outpcd* **4/1**[2]

14- 6 2 **Baddilini**[215] 6883 3-9-0 **93** GrahamLee 5 76
(Alan Bailey) *hld up: pushed along over 3f out: outpcd fnl 2f* **20/1**

462- 7 hd **Dashing David (IRE)**[190] 7478 3-9-0 **93** RyanMoore 3 76
(Richard Hannon) *towards rr: bhd over 4f out: pushed along over 3f out: nvr on terms* **7/1**

235- 8 1 **Fat Gary**[166] 7856 3-8-7 **86** oh1 (v[1]) RichardKingscote 8 66
(Tom Dascombe) *led: rdn and hdd over 1f out: wknd ins fnl f* **12/1**

1m 35.95s (2.15) **Going Correction** +0.225s/f (Good) 8 Ran SP% **111.9**
Speed ratings (Par 105): **98,97,92,92,88 86,86,85**
CSF £18.81 CT £93.48 TOTE £2.80: £1.60, £2.90, £1.80; EX 21.40 Trifecta £145.10 Pool: £2549.96 - 13.17 winning units..
Owner Mrs Fitri Hay **Bred** Old Carhue & Graeng Bloodstock **Trained** Kingsclere, Hants

FOCUS
The deteriorating ground perhaps played its part in this, but the pace looked good. This proved straightforward for the winner, who took another biggish step forward. The first two were clear.

2189 LIVERPOOL ONE EBF MAIDEN STKS 5f 16y

3:50 (3:54) (Class 3) 2-Y-O **£9,056** (£2,695; £1,346; £673) **Stalls Low**

Form RPR

2 1 **Fine 'n Dandy (IRE)**[14] 1778 2-9-5 0 RichardKingscote 3 93+
(Tom Dascombe) *mde all: drew clr over 1f out: r.o wl and in command after* **13/8**[1]

2 2 8 **Inciting Incident (IRE)**[22] 1605 2-9-5 0 PaulHanagan 4 64
(Ed McMahon) *chsd ldrs: n.m.r and snatched up 2f out: wnt 2nd wl over 1f out: unable to go w wnr and no ch fnl f* **11/4**[2]

3 1 ¼ **Salford Red Devil** 2-9-5 0 JamieSpencer 12 60+
(Richard Fahey) *dwlt: rn green: bhd: hdwy over 1f out: styd on ins fnl f: nt rch ldrs* **14/1**

2223 4 hd **Gin Time (IRE)**[3] 2068 2-8-9 0 DeclanBates(5) 1 54
(David Evans) *midfield: sn pushed along: chsd ldrs 2f out: styd on ins fnl f: nvr able to chal* **11/1**

5 **5** *nk* **Jive**[17] 1724 2-9-0 0 RyanMoore 7 53
(Richard Hannon) *towards rr: pushed along whn nt clr run and swtchd rt over 1f out: styd on ins fnl f* **5/1**[3]
6 *1 3/4* **Quincel** 2-9-5 0 LukeMorris 5 52
(Tom Dascombe) *missed break: in rr: hdwy over 1f out: kpt on ins fnl f: nvr able to chal* **20/1**
7 *3/4* **Red Forever** 2-9-0 0 SladeO'Hara(5) 10 49
(Alan Berry) *dwlt: towards rr: sme hdwy whn hung lft 1f out: no ex fnl 150yds* **100/1**
8 *3 1/4* **Anytimeatall (IRE)** 2-9-0 0 FrannyNorton 9 36
(Alan Bailey) *displayed gd spd to chse wnr: lost 2nd and outpcd wl over 1f out: wknd ins fnl f* **20/1**
9 *1 1/2* **Brave Imp** 2-9-5 0 PhillipMakin 2 32
(Kevin Ryan) *dwlt: hld up: pushed along and no imp 1f out: bhd after* **11/1**
04 **10** *1* **Countess Lupus (IRE)**[7] 1946 2-9-0 0 TomEaves 6 23
(Lisa Williamson) *chsd ldrs: no imp whn hmpd 1f out: bhd after* **80/1**

1m 3.41s (2.41) **Going Correction** +0.40s/f (Good) **10** Ran SP% **116.5**
Speed ratings (Par 97): **96,83,81,80,80 77,76,71,68,67**
toteswingers 1&2 £2.20, 2&3 £5.60, 1&3 £6.50 CSF £5.79 TOTE £2.40: £1.10, £1.30, £3.70; EX 7.00 Trifecta £49.50 Pool: £4282.01 - 64.76 winning units..
Owner The United Rocks **Bred** G Flannery Developments **Trained** Malpas, Cheshire

FOCUS
The going was changed to good to soft before this race. Tom Dascombe sent out the winner of this race last year, and Fine 'n Dandy did the business for the stable this time.

2190 INVESTEC STRUCTURED PRODUCTS H'CAP 6f 18y
4:25 (4:26) (Class 3) (0-90,90) 3-Y-O **£10,350** (£3,080; £1,539; £769) **Stalls** Low

Form RPR
0-00 **1** **Effie B**[19] 1690 3-9-6 **89** MartinHarley 2 96
(Mick Channon) *chsd ldrs: rdn to ld over 1f out: kpt on gamely ins fnl f* **12/1**
24-1 **2** *3/4* **Mayaasem**[17] 1722 3-8-10 **79** PaulHanagan 5 84+
(Charles Hills) *s.i.s: sn pushed along: impr into midfield over 4f out: prog 2f out: rdn over 1f out: r.o to take 2nd wl ins fnl f: hld cl home* **10/3**[1]
3-21 **3** *hd* **You Da One (IRE)**[43] 1197 3-8-11 **80** [1] DavidProbert 3 84
(Andrew Balding) *disp ld: pushed along 2f out: hdd over 1f out: stl ev ch ins fnl f: nt qckn cl home* **9/2**[3]
-162 **4** *3/4* **Red Refraction (IRE)**[24] 1582 3-8-8 **77** WilliamBuick 13 79+
(Richard Hannon) *in tch: rdn over 1f out: styd on to press ldrs ins fnl f: one pce fnl strides* **10/1**
5 **5** *1 3/4* **Your Pal Tal**[40] 1254 3-8-12 **81** KierenFallon 1 77
(T Stack, Ire) *disp ld: rdn and hdd over 1f out: kpt on u.p ins fnl f: one pce fnl 75yds* **4/1**[2]
-000 **6** *1 1/2* **Queen Aggie (IRE)**[20] 1662 3-8-13 **87** DeclanBates(5) 4 78
(David Evans) *chsd ldrs: pushed along over 2f out: rdn over 1f out: one pce fnl 150yds* **20/1**
01-1 **7** *2* **Rene Mathis (GER)**[123] 85 3-8-13 **82** JamieSpencer 12 67
(Richard Fahey) *stdd s: hld up: effrt into midfield 2f out: no imp on ldrs* **8/1**
1-12 **8** *1 1/4* **Archie Stevens**[123] 85 3-8-12 **81** RichardKingscote 15 62
(Tom Dascombe) *dwlt: hld up: u.p over 1f out: styd on ins fnl f: nt trble ldrs* **33/1**
0-36 **9** *2 1/2* **Opt Out**[51] 1075 3-8-9 **78** JoeFanning 8 51
(Mark Johnston) *chsd ldrs: u.p over 1f out: wknd ins fnl f* **16/1**
35-2 **10** *3/4* **Tatlisu (IRE)**[14] 1771 3-8-2 **76** oh1 GeorgeChaloner(5) 7 46
(Richard Fahey) *midfield: u.p 2f out: outpcd whn hmpd over 1f out: nvr a threat* **20/1**
15-4 **11** *hd* **Al Udeid (IRE)**[30] 1444 3-8-8 **77** AmyRyan 9 47
(Kevin Ryan) *hld up early: pushed along and bhd over 4f out: nvr a threat* **12/1**
3110 **12** *nk* **Panther Patrol (IRE)**[22] 1625 3-8-8 **77** JohnFahy 10 46
(Eve Johnson Houghton) *sn niggled along towards rr: struggling fnl 2f: nvr on terms* **25/1**

1m 17.56s (3.76) **Going Correction** +0.40s/f (Good) **12** Ran SP% **119.0**
Speed ratings (Par 103): **90,89,88,87,85 83,80,79,75,74 74,74**
toteswingers 1&2 £8.70, 2&3 £3.80, 1&3 £7.00 CSF £49.51 CT £214.74 TOTE £14.00: £3.50, £2.20, £1.70; EX 52.40 Trifecta £241.60 Pool: £3424.32 - 10.62 winning units..
Owner R Bastian **Bred** R Bastian **Trained** West Ilsley, Berks
■ Stewards' Enquiry : Jamie Spencer caution: careless riding

FOCUS
Once again there was a good gallop on and, not for the first time round here, saving ground on the inside proved key. The form isn't rated as positively as it might have been.

2191 MERSEYRAIL DAY SAVER TICKET H'CAP 1m 2f 75y
5:00 (5:00) (Class 3) (0-90,89) 4-Y-0+ **£10,350** (£3,080; £1,539; £769) **Stalls** High

Form RPR
-422 **1** **Tres Coronas (IRE)**[12] 1831 6-9-1 **83** PhillipMakin 11 92
(David Barron) *towards rr: hdwy over 1f out: rdn to ld ent fnl f: edgd rt fnl 100yds: kpt on wl cl home* **9/1**
50-3 **2** *3/4* **Haylaman (IRE)**[16] 1751 5-9-1 **83** JamieSpencer 6 91
(David Simcock) *midfield: hdwy on outer over 3f out: led 2f out: rdn and c wd ent st wl over 1f out: sn hdd: rallied ins fnl f: sn pressed wnr: hld cl home* **13/2**[3]
10- **3** *2* **Proofreader**[194] 7396 4-9-7 **89** WilliamBuick 12 93+
(John Gosden) *hld up: wnt wd and unbalanced on bnd wl over 7f out: n.m.r and hmpd 2f out: hdwy whn nt clr run over 1f out: chsd ldrs ins fnl f: styd on: nt rch front two* **4/1**[1]
3-21 **4** *1 1/4* **Swing Alone (IRE)**[46] 1159 4-9-6 **88** LukeMorris 9 89
(Gay Kelleway) *hld up: hdwy into midfield 6f out: effrt 2f out: kpt on ins fnl f: nvr able to chal ldrs* **12/1**
3- **5** *1/2* **Break Rank (USA)**[221] 6704 4-8-10 **78** JohnFahy 13 78+
(Ed de Giles) *hld up bhd: hdwy on outer 2f out: led over 1f out: hdd ent fnl f: no ex fnl 75yds* **50/1**
3-05 **6** *3/4* **Gaul Wood (IRE)**[9] 1905 4-9-7 **89** RichardKingscote 2 88
(Tom Dascombe) *led: hdd over 6f out: continued to chse ldrs: rdn and ev ch 1f out: fdd fnl 100yds* **7/1**
6035 **7** *3 1/4* **Las Verglas Star (IRE)**[12] 1824 5-9-5 **87** PaulHanagan 1 80
(Richard Fahey) *midfield: effrt on inner over 1f out: wknd fnl 100yds* **10/1**
1-63 **8** *1 3/4* **Amaze**[12] 1840 5-9-3 **85** DaleSwift 10 75
(Brian Ellison) *midfield: niggled along over 5f out: wknd over 1f out* **10/1**
6-61 **9** *3* **Spirit Of The Law (IRE)**[16] 1753 4-8-11 **84** GeorgeChaloner(5) 4 68
(Richard Fahey) *s.i.s: sn chsd ldrs: rdn and wknd 2f out* **11/2**[2]
110- **10** *1 3/4* **Star Links (USA)**[4] 2061 7-8-10 **78** (b) RobertWinston 3 59
(S Donohoe, Ire) *racd keenly: prom: ev ch 2f out: rdn and wknd over 1f out: eased whn btn ins fnl f* **14/1**
003 **11** *2 3/4* **Cawett Cove (IRE)**[16] 1753 5-8-9 **77** FrannyNorton 5 52
(Jane Chapple-Hyam) *racd keenly: chsd ldrs: led over 6f out: rdn and hdd 2f out: wknd over 1f out: eased whn btn ins fnl f* **16/1**
140- **12** *21* **Modernism**[120] 6415 4-9-2 **84** KierenFallon 8 19
(Alan McCabe) *chsd ldrs: pushed along 4f out: bdly hmpd and shuffled bk 2f out: bhd after* **14/1**

2m 14.06s (2.86) **Going Correction** +0.40s/f (Good) **12** Ran SP% **118.3**
Speed ratings (Par 107): **104,103,101,100,100 99,97,95,93,92 89,73**
toteswingers 1&2 £12.30, 2&3 £5.20, 1&3 CSF £66.31 CT £275.28 TOTE £12.70: £3.90, £1.80, £1.80; EX 95.00 Trifecta £418.70 Pool: £2711.61 - 4.85 winning units..
Owner D Pryde & J Cringan **Bred** Denis McDonnell **Trained** Maunby, N Yorks
■ Stewards' Enquiry : John Fahy caution: careless riding

FOCUS
The early pace set by Gaul Wood wasn't great, but Cawett Cove, who raced freely, took over in front heading down the back, and things picked up from there. On the turn in, however, those two, along with Star Links, who was also prominent but hadn't settled early on, and Modernism, who lost his footing on the turn, fell back into the pack, hampering one or two of those in behind in the process. A straightforward level for the form, with the first two back to their best.
T/Plt: £16.40 to a £1 stake. Pool of £160892.38 - 7160.63 winning tickets. T/Qpdt: £4.20 to a £1 stake. Pool of £7053.50 -1221.72 winning tickets. DO

2011 GOODWOOD (R-H)
Thursday, May 9

OFFICIAL GOING: Good changing to good (good to firm in places) after race 1 (1.55)
Wind: strong, against Weather: windy, showers and bright spells

2192 GOODWOOD BUSINESS CLUB MAIDEN STKS 1m
1:55 (1:56) (Class 5) 3-Y-0+ **£3,234** (£962; £481; £240) **Stalls** Low

Form RPR
3- **1** **Enobled**[197] 7324 3-9-0 0 HayleyTurner 9 92+
(Sir Michael Stoute) *stdd s: hld up in tch towards rr: gd hdwy to chse ldr over 1f out: led ins fnl f: r.o wl: comf* **6/4**[1]
0-6 **2** *1 1/4* **Morpheus**[22] 1624 3-9-0 0 TomQueally 1 87
(Sir Henry Cecil) *pressed ldr tl led 2f out: sn rdn: hdd and no ex ins fnl f: kpt on same pce after* **5/2**[2]
5 **3** *1/2* **Prince's Trust**[19] 1678 3-9-0 0 PatDobbs 6 89+
(Richard Hannon) *t.k.h: hld up in tch in midfield: stl travelling wl 2f out: hdwy over 1f out: swtchd lft and hmpd ins fnl f: sn chsng ldng pair and gng on wl at fin* **5/1**[3]
02- **4** *3 1/2* **Sweet Martoni**[206] 7103 3-8-10 0 ow1 NeilCallan 3 74
(William Knight) *in tch in midfield: rdn and effrt jst over 2f out: chsd wnr briefly over 1f out: 3rd and btn 1f out: wknd ins fnl f* **33/1**
-0 **5** *2* **Vanvitelli**[21] 1635 3-9-0 0 (t) JamesDoyle 7 73+
(James Fanshawe) *hld up off the pce in rr of main gp: outpcd over 2f out: hdwy but stl plenty to do over 1f out: kpt on fnl f: nvr trbld ldrs* **50/1**
6 *6* **Bosham** 3-8-9 0 MichaelJMMurphy(5) 5 59
(William Jarvis) *led tl 2f out: sn rdn and no ex: btn over 1f out: fdd fnl f* **50/1**
0-2 **7** *1 3/4* **Arms (IRE)**[17] 1735 3-9-0 0 SebSanders 10 55
(J W Hills) *chsd ldng pair: rdn and no ex 2f out: btn over 1f out: fdd fnl f* **10/1**
02- **8** *8* **Harwoods Star (IRE)**[217] 6818 3-9-0 0 JimCrowley 8 37
(Amanda Perrett) *stdd after s: hld up off the pce in rr of main gp: rdn and no hdwy 3f out: lost tch 2f out* **10/1**
6 **9** *1 3/4* **Lybica (IRE)**[21] 1640 3-8-9 0 FergusSweeney 4 28
(Gary Moore) *broke wl: chsd ldrs: rdn and struggling over 2f out: sn dropped out: bhd over 1f out* **66/1**
00 **10** *6* **Fitzwilly**[7] 1955 3-9-0 0 SamHitchcott 2 19
(Mick Channon) *s.i.s: sn rdn and outpcd in detached last: t.o* **100/1**

1m 40.59s (0.69) **Going Correction** +0.325s/f (Good) **10** Ran SP% **112.8**
Speed ratings (Par 103): **109,107,107,103,101 95,94,86,84,78**
toteswingers 1&2 £1.90, 2&3 £2.80, 1&3 £2.50 CSF £4.92 TOTE £2.40: £1.10, £2.00, £1.50; EX 6.80 Trifecta £17.50 Pool: £2617.56 - 112.05 winning units..
Owner Cheveley Park Stud **Bred** Cheveley Park Stud Ltd **Trained** Newmarket, Suffolk

FOCUS
First 2f of Mile course dolled out 5yds which added circa 15yds to races on that course. This looked an ordinary maiden, but there were a couple of eyecatchers.

2193 32RED STKS (H'CAP) 1m 1f
2:30 (2:31) (Class 3) (0-90,88) 3-Y-0+ **£9,703** (£2,887; £1,443; £721) **Stalls** Low

Form RPR
5-06 **1** **Bancnuanaheireann (IRE)**[12] 1840 6-10-0 **88** TomQueally 4 97
(Michael Appleby) *in tch in last pair: swtchd to outer over 3f out: rdn and hdwy 2f out: edgd rt and chsd ldrs ent fnl f: led ins fnl f: r.o wl: eased nr fin* **9/2**[1]
42-0 **2** *1* **Pilgrims Rest (IRE)**[61] 945 4-9-13 **87** PatDobbs 9 94
(Richard Hannon) *led: hrd pressed and drvn ent fnl 2f: battled on wl u.p: hdd ins fnl f and kpt on same pce fnl 100yds* **10/1**
2-21 **3** *nk* **Enzaal (USA)**[17] 1735 3-8-5 **79** SilvestreDeSousa 6 83
(Mark Johnston) *chsd ldr: ev ch and rdn ent fnl 2f: battled on wl u.p: styd on same pce fnl 100yds* **5/1**[2]
60-2 **4** *1* **Lucky Henry**[12] 1824 4-9-8 **82** (b[1]) AdamKirby 1 86
(Clive Cox) *in tch in midfield: reminder 4f out: rdn and effrt to chse ldrs 2f out: edgd lft 1f out: kpt on same pce ins fnl f* **9/2**[1]
60-0 **5** *1* **Sir Mike**[24] 1583 4-9-2 **76** JimCrowley 3 78
(Amanda Perrett) *chsd ldrs: stl travelling wl on inner 2f out: sn rdn and ev ch 1f out: no ex ins fnl f: wknd towards fin* **13/2**[3]
643- **6** *3* **Aussie Reigns (IRE)**[190] 7478 3-7-11 **74** oh2 DarrenEgan(3) 2 67
(William Knight) *in tch in last trio: rdn 3f out: keeping on same pce and looked hld whn carried rt and sltly hmpd ent fnl f: wknd fnl 150yds* **12/1**
0-50 **7** *3/4* **Starwatch**[10] 1883 6-9-5 **84** WilliamTwiston-Davies(5) 7 77
(John Bridger) *chsd ldrs: rdn and effrt ent fnl 2f: unable qck and btn whn carried rt and hmpd ent fnl f: plugged on same pce and wl hld after* **33/1**
20-2 **8** *42* **Charitable Act (FR)**[12] 1849 4-9-4 **78** GeorgeBaker 5
(Gary Moore) *stdd s: t.k.h: hld up in last pair: rdn and no hdwy ent fnl 2f: sn btn: virtually p.u fnl f* **7/1**

1m 57.9s (1.60) **Going Correction** +0.325s/f (Good)
WFA 3 from 4yo+ 14lb **8** Ran SP% **98.6**
Speed ratings (Par 107): **105,104,103,102,102 99,98,61**
toteswingers 1&2 £5.30, 2&3 £4.70, 1&3 £4.30 CSF £35.60 CT £143.47 TOTE £4.20: £1.30, £2.40, £1.50; EX 41.10 Trifecta £315.20 Pool: £1460.27 - 3.47 winning units..
Owner Dallas Racing & Stephen Almond **Bred** J S Bolger **Trained** Danethorpe, Notts
■ Stewards' Enquiry : Adam Kirby one-day ban: careless riding (May 23)

FOCUS
The going was changed to good, good to firm in places before this race. They didn't go a great pace in this decent handicap and five horses were still within a length of his each other half a furlong from home.

2194 BRITISH STALLION STUDS SUPPORTING BRITISH RACING EBF MAIDEN STKS 6f
3:00 (3:02) (Class 5) 2-Y-O £3,881 (£1,155; £577; £288) Stalls High

Form RPR

0 1 **Malachim Mist (IRE)**[20] 1669 2-9-5 0 SeanLevey 6 86
(Richard Hannon) *mde all and sn crossed to r against stands' rail: rdn over 1f out: styd on strly: eased towards fin* 5/1

2 2 3/4 **Lanark (IRE)** 2-9-5 0 SilvestreDeSousa 4 78
(Mark Johnston) *chsd wnr thrght: rdn 1/2-way: drvn and unable qck over 1f out: no threat to wnr but kpt on for 2nd fnl f* 9/2[3]

0 3 1 1/4 **Rosso Corsa**[20] 1669 2-9-0 0 CharlesBishop(5) 11 74
(Mick Channon) *racd against stands' rail: in tch in midfield: edgd rt and nt clr run 2f out: swtchd bk lft and stl n.m.r wl over 1f out: hdwy to chse ldng pair 1f out: kpt on* 20/1

5 4 2 1/4 **Ocean Storm (IRE)**[12] 1820 2-9-5 0 NeilCallan 3 67+
(James Tate) *chsd ldrs: rdn 1/2-way: outpcd and btn over 1f out: plugged on same pce fnl f* 12/1

2 5 1/2 **Culdaff (IRE)**[10] 1880 2-9-5 0 SteveDrowne 7 66
(Charles Hills) *racd off the pce in midfield: pushed along and stdy hdwy but edging lft fr 1/2-way: racing against stands' rail and kpt on ins fnl f: nvr trbld ldrs* 4/1[2]

6 2 3/4 **Hatha Hooh** 2-9-5 0 PatDobbs 10 58+
(Richard Hannon) *in tch: effrt to chse ldrs and rn green over 1f out: no ex and btn 1f out: wknd ins fnl f* 2/1[1]

7 7 **Ravenous** 2-9-5 0 JimCrowley 2 37
(Ralph Beckett) *in tch in midfield: rdn and struggling 1/2-way: sn lost pl: bhd over 2f out* 12/1

8 hd **Faintly (USA)** 2-9-5 0 JamesDoyle 1 36+
(Amanda Perrett) *off the pce towards rr of main gp: hdwy 1/2-way: 6th and btn over 1f out: wknd* 33/1

9 2 3/4 **Deeds Not Words (IRE)** 2-9-5 0 SamHitchcott 5 28
(Mick Channon) *s.i.s: outpcd and bhd thrght* 40/1

10 3/4 **Ghasaq (IRE)** 2-9-5 0 DaneO'Neill 8 25
(Brian Meehan) *s.i.s: outpcd and a bhd* 25/1

1m 12.59s (0.39) **Going Correction** +0.025s/f (Good) 10 Ran SP% 117.6
Speed ratings (Par 93): **98,94,92,89,89 85,76,75,72,71**
toteswingers 1&2 £4.50, 2&3 £15.50, 1&3 £17.40 CSF £26.79 TOTE £6.20: £2.20, £1.60, £7.20; EX 27.60 Trifecta £629.50 Pool: £3098.84 - 3.69 winning units..
Owner Michael Daniels **Bred** Guy O'Callaghan **Trained** East Everleigh, Wilts
■ Stewards' Enquiry : James Doyle caution: eased colt prematurely.

FOCUS
The first 6f race of the season for 2yos in Britain.

2195 NISSAN INNOVATION AND EXCITEMENT FILLIES' STKS (H'CAP) 1m
3:30 (3:31) (Class 4) (0-85,83) 3-Y-O £6,469 (£1,925; £962; £481) Stalls Low

Form RPR

1- 1 **Ribbons**[175] 7721 3-8-13 75 HayleyTurner 4 84+
(James Fanshawe) *hld up in tch in last trio: rdn: edgd rt and hdwy to chse ldrs 2f out: wnt between horses and drvn to ld 1f out: r.o wl fnl f* 3/1[2]

10-6 2 1 **Trapeze**[22] 1612 3-8-13 75 RobertHavlin 7 83+
(John Gosden) *dropped in after s: hld up in rr: hdwy on inner over 2f out: nt clr run 2f out: hdwy u.p 1f out: running on whn nt clr run and snatched up ins fnl f: swtchd lft and r.o strly fnl 75yds* 8/1

-521 3 nse **Wakeup Little Suzy (IRE)**[55] 1019 3-8-11 73 (t) NeilCallan 2 76
(Marco Botti) *chsd ldrs: rdn over 3f out: drvn and ev ch over 1f out: styd on same pce ins fnl f: lost 2nd on post* 14/1

210- 4 1/2 **Miss Marjurie (IRE)**[211] 6980 3-9-1 77 TomQueally 1 79
(Denis Coakley) *hld up in tch in last trio: hdwy over 2f out: rdn and led over 1f out: sn hdd and styd on same pce ins fnl f* 8/1

044- 5 1 **Everleigh**[197] 7325 3-9-0 76 SeanLevey 3 76
(Richard Hannon) *wl in tch in midfield: rdn and effrt 2f out: chsd ldrs over 1f out: styd on same pce ins fnl f* 10/1

141- 6 4 1/2 **Annecdote**[222] 6675 3-9-7 83 JamesDoyle 9 74+
(Jonathan Portman) *t.k.h: chsd ldrs: rdn to ld 2f out: hdd over 1f out and no ex: btn whn bdly hmpd and snatched up ins fnl f: wknd* 9/2[3]

-122 7 2 **Naalatt (IRE)**[17] 1725 3-9-0 76 AndreaAtzeni 6 61
(Roger Varian) *chsd ldr: rdn and unable qck over 2f out: lost pl 2f out: wknd over 1f out* 11/4[1]

540- 8 8 **Mystical Moment**[211] 6980 3-9-7 83 JimCrowley 5 61
(Richard Hannon) *led tl rdn and hdd 2f out: wkng whn sltly hmpd over 1f out: sn bhd and eased ins fnl f* 25/1

1m 41.52s (1.62) **Going Correction** +0.325s/f (Good) 8 Ran SP% 111.7
Speed ratings (Par 98): **104,103,102,102,101 96,94,86**
toteswingers 1&2 £7.00, 2&3 £8.10, 1&3 £5.20 CSF £25.72 CT £283.09 TOTE £4.30: £1.30, £2.40, £2.90; EX 33.60 Trifecta £139.50 Pool: £3588.03 - 19.27 winning units..
Owner Elite Racing Club **Bred** Elite Racing Club **Trained** Newmarket, Suffolk

FOCUS
This fair fillies' handicap proved to be quite a rough race.

2196 GOLF AT GOODWOOD STKS (H'CAP) 6f
4:05 (4:05) (Class 5) (0-75,75) 4-Y-O+ £3,234 (£962; £481; £240) Stalls High

Form RPR

446- 1 **Aye Aye Digby (IRE)**[225] 6570 8-9-6 74 GeorgeBaker 2 83
(Patrick Chamings) *mde all: hrd pressed and rdn along mainly hands and heels fr over 1f out: kpt on and a jst doing enough fnl f* 6/1[3]

3323 2 1/2 **Where's Reiley (USA)**[9] 1902 7-8-8 62 (v) TomQueally 10 69
(Michael Attwater) *chsd ldrs: rdn 2f out: pressed wnr u.p fr over 1f out: kpt on same pce ins fnl f* 11/2[2]

14-0 3 nse **Generalyse**[13] 1814 4-9-2 70 (b) AdamKirby 3 77
(Ben De Haan) *chsd ldrs: wnt 2nd after 2f: rdn and pressed wnr over 1f out: kpt on same pce ins fnl f* 5/1[1]

0030 4 nk **Elna Bright**[46] 1160 8-9-2 70 IanMongan 6 76
(Peter Crate) *hld up in midfield: hdwy 1/2-way: chsd ldng trio and drvn over 1f out: edgd rt 1f out: kpt on same pce ins fnl f* 7/1

000- 5 7 **Orders From Rome (IRE)**[187] 7559 4-9-2 75 AmyScott(5) 8 58+
(Eve Johnson Houghton) *wl off pce in last quartet: rdn 2f out: styd on past btn horses fnl f: n.d* 12/1

1040 6 1/2 **Temple Road (IRE)**[13] 1814 5-9-6 74 SilvestreDeSousa 4 56
(Milton Bradley) *hld up in midfield: rdn and effrt wl over 1f out: hung rt and no imp over 1f out: wknd fnl f* 8/1

-000 7 3/4 **Quasi Congaree (GER)**[38] 1286 7-8-11 65 (t) PatDobbs 9 44+
(Paul Fitzsimons) *wl off the pce in rr: styd on past btn horses ins fnl f: n.d* 20/1

2355 8 3/4 **Sole Danser (IRE)**[7] 1952 5-9-2 70 NeilCallan 12 47
(Milton Bradley) *chsd ldrs: rdn and edgd rt 2f out: wknd ent fnl f* 6/1[3]

16-0 9 3 **Capitol Gain (IRE)**[12] 1838 4-9-4 72 JamieMackay 13 39
(Brian Meehan) *s.i.s: sn outpcd and wl bhd: kpt shifting rt and racing in centre whn styd on and swtchd rt ins fnl f: n.d* 20/1

46-0 10 hd **Interakt**[13] 1814 6-9-2 70 HarryBentley 5 37
(Joseph Tuite) *s.i.s: wl outpcd in rr: sme hdwy but stl wl off the pce whn edgd rt over 2f out: n.d* 16/1

6340 11 1 3/4 **Welsh Inlet (IRE)**[17] 1717 5-8-8 62 KieranO'Neill 1 23
(John Bridger) *in tch in midfield: rdn and struggling over 2f out: wknd and edgd rt 2f out* 33/1

000- 12 1 3/4 **Bermondsey Bob (IRE)**[241] 6094 7-8-7 61 ChrisCatlin 11 17
(John Spearing) *chsd wnr for 2f: sn struggling and steadily lost pl: bhd fnl f* 33/1

235- 13 1 1/4 **Leadenhall Lass (IRE)**[238] 6171 7-8-2 61 JemmaMarshall(5) 7 13
(Pat Phelan) *taken down early: a wl off the pce in last quartet: n.d* 25/1

1m 12.61s (0.41) **Going Correction** +0.025s/f (Good) 13 Ran SP% 117.1
Speed ratings (Par 103): **98,97,97,96,87 86,85,84,80,80 78,75,74**
toteswingers 1&2 £3.50, 2&3 £4.50, 1&3 £6.10 CSF £35.14 CT £182.18 TOTE £8.00: £2.70, £2.00, £2.10; EX 20.60 Trifecta £111.30 Pool: £2303.13 - 15.50 winning units..
Owner Trolley Action **Bred** G J King **Trained** Baughurst, Hants

FOCUS
Very few ever got into this ordinary sprint handicap.

2197 MOLECOMB BLUE STKS (H'CAP) 2m
4:40 (4:40) (Class 5) (0-70,70) 4-Y-O+ £3,234 (£962; £481; £240) Stalls Low

Form RPR

32-1 1 **Our Folly**[20] 1664 5-9-3 68 (t) MichaelJMMurphy(5) 11 76+
(Stuart Kittow) *hld up in last pair: hdwy on outer 3f out: rdn and chsd ldr ent fnl f: edging rt after: led ins fnl f: kpt on wl* 5/2[1]

2550 2 nk **Priors Gold**[24] 1586 6-9-10 70 IanMongan 5 77
(Laura Mongan) *hld up in tch in midfield: rdn to ld over 1f out: hdd ins fnl f: kpt on wl u.p but a jst hld* 20/1

2510 3 2 1/4 **Beat Route**[22] 1615 6-9-7 67 SebSanders 12 71
(Michael Attwater) *stdd after s: hld up in last trio: hdwy towards inner over 2f out: rdn and effrt 2f out: chsd ldng pair ent fnl f: one pce after* 6/1

06/0 4 nk **Kayef (GER)**[20] 1670 6-9-5 70 WilliamTwiston-Davies(5) 2 74
(Michael Scudamore) *chsd ldrs: drvn and edging rt over 1f out: styd on same pce ins fnl f* 8/1

3245 5 3/4 **Bramshill Lass**[9] 1899 4-8-9 58 ow2 (p) JimCrowley 6 61
(Amanda Perrett) *hld up in tch in midfield: effrt u.p jst over 2f out: chsng ldrs but unable qck whn carried lft ent fnl f: no ex and one pce fnl f* 11/2[3]

322- 6 4 1/2 **Queen's Star**[190] 7490 4-9-1 64 LiamKeniry 9 62
(Andrew Balding) *chsd ldrs: chsd ldr 10f out tl over 1f out: sn struggling and wknd 1f out* 11/4[2]

0-05 7 1 1/2 **Bahrain Storm (IRE)**[8] 1927 10-9-10 70 (b) StevieDonohoe 10 66
(Noel Quinlan) *hld up in tch in rr: rdn and no rspnse over 3f out: bhd and wl hld 2f out: no ch but kpt on ins fnl f* 28/1

5/0- 8 1/2 **Torran Sound**[19] 2468 6-8-2 53 RyanTate(5) 3 48
(James Eustace) *led tl hdd 2f out: sn rdn and struggling: wknd qckly over 1f out* 16/1

4024 9 2 1/2 **Dr Finley (IRE)**[28] 1502 6-9-2 65 (p) SimonPearce(3) 8 57
(Lydia Pearce) *chsd ldr tl 10f out: styd chsng ldrs tl lost pl u.p 3f out: bhd over 1f out* 20/1

3m 38.17s (9.17) **Going Correction** +0.325s/f (Good)
WFA 4 from 5yo+ 3lb 9 Ran SP% 114.9
Speed ratings (Par 103): **90,89,88,88,88 85,85,84,83**
toteswingers 1&2 £8.60, 2&3 £10.70, 1&3 £4.00 CSF £55.26 CT £274.12 TOTE £3.50: £1.40, £4.20, £2.40; EX 52.60 Trifecta £240.50 Pool: £2981.68 - 9.29 winning units..
Owner Midd Shire Racing **Bred** D R Tucker **Trained** Blackborough, Devon

FOCUS
They only went a modest pace in this staying handicap.

2198 THREE FRIDAY NIGHTS MAIDEN STKS 1m 4f
5:15 (5:16) (Class 5) 3-Y-O+ £3,234 (£962; £481; £240) Stalls Low

Form RPR

2-4 1 **Eshtiaal (USA)**[22] 1624 3-8-9 0 DaneO'Neill 8 92+
(Brian Meehan) *in tch in midfield: hdwy to chse ldrs 3f out: edging rt u.p over 1f out: styd on wl and sustained duel w rival fnl f: led last stride* 9/4[1]

0-43 2 shd **Seamless**[13] 1804 3-8-9 75 SteveDrowne 2 91
(Charles Hills) *chsd ldrs: nt clr run over 3f out: swtchd rt and led on inner 3f out: edgd lft u.p over 1f out: hrd pressed and battled on wl fnl f tl hdd last stride* 8/1

6-3 3 3/4 **Shwaiman (IRE)**[19] 1679 3-8-9 0 JamesDoyle 5 90+
(James Fanshawe) *hld up in last pair: hdwy but kpt wanting to edge rt fnl 2f: styd on wl ins fnl f: wnt 3rd last stride* 7/2[3]

3-4 4 shd **Squire Osbaldeston (IRE)**[19] 1679 3-8-9 0 TomQueally 3 92+
(Sir Henry Cecil) *t.k.h: hld up in tch in midfield: chsng ldrs and trying to switch lft whn hmpd over 1f out: stl chsng ldrs whn nt clr run and swtchd lft ins fnl f: kpt on: lost 3rd last stride* 11/4[2]

0 5 7 **Hamelin (IRE)**[19] 1679 3-8-9 0 SilvestreDeSousa 10 85+
(Sir Henry Cecil) *t.k.h: chsd ldrs: jnd ldrs gng wl 5f out: rdn and chsd ldr wl over 2f out: stl pressing ldrs but struggling whn squeezed for room and hmpd over 1f out: sn wknd* 8/1

0- 6 6 **Shemaal (IRE)**[197] 7333 3-8-9 0 AndreaAtzeni 7 69+
(Roger Varian) *in tch in last trio: effrt on inner 3f out: struggling ent fnl 2f: 6th and wl btn over 1f out: wknd fnl f* 12/1

46 7 22 **No Win No Fee**[12] 1845 3-8-9 0 LiamKeniry 4 34
(Michael Appleby) *hld up in rr: lost tch 3f out: t.o* 50/1

0 8 4 **Double Accord**[20] 1671 3-8-4 0 ChrisCatlin 9 22
(Anthony Honeyball) *chsd ldr tl over 3f out: sn lost pl and bhd: t.o fnl 2f* 66/1

4 9 3/4 **Thewestwalian (USA)**[14] 1795 5-10-0 0 WilliamCarson 1 26
(Peter Hiatt) *racd keenly: led tl edgd lft and hdd 3f out: sn lost pl: t.o* 100/1

2m 41.49s (3.09) **Going Correction** +0.325s/f (Good)
WFA 3 from 5yo 19lb 9 Ran SP% 114.0
Speed ratings (Par 103): **102,101,101,101,96 92,78,75,74**
toteswingers 1&2 £3.80, 2&3 £5.10, 1&3 £2.40 CSF £20.85 TOTE £3.10: £1.70, £1.90, £1.50; EX 18.30 Trifecta £51.10 Pool: £3537.30 - 51.88 winning units..
Owner Hamdan Al Maktoum **Bred** Shadwell Farm LLC **Trained** Manton, Wilts

FOCUS
An interesting maiden, though a modest pace resulted in some trouble.

T/Jkpt: Not won. T/Plt: £98.80 to a £1 stake. Pool of £69834.44 - 515.54 winning tickets. T/Qpdt: £30.30 to a £1 stake. Pool of £3889.94 - 94.98 winning tickets. SP

2199 - 2201a (Foreign Racing) - See Raceform Interactive

BADEN-BADEN (L-H)

Thursday, May 9

OFFICIAL GOING: Turf: good to soft

2202a BADENER MEILE (GROUP 3) (3YO+) (TURF) 1m

3:50 (12:00) 3-Y-0+

£26,016 (£8,943; £4,471; £2,439; £1,626; £1,219)

RPR

1 **Felician (GER)**[214] 6906 5-9-0 0 LennartHammer-Hansen 1 106
(Ferdinand J Leve, Germany) *hld up towards rr: rdn and hdwy over 1f out: r.o to ld wl ins fnl f: drvn out* **155/10**

2 ½ **Neatico (GER)**[25] 1564 6-9-0 0 AStarke 2 105
(P Schiergen, Germany) *midfield on inner: shuffled bk and lost pl over 2f out: rdn over 1f out: nt clr run briefly ent fnl f: sn in the clr and r.o to go 2nd cl home* **18/5**[1]

3 1 **Combat Zone (IRE)**[186] 7587 7-9-6 0 NRichter 11 109
(Mario Hofer, Germany) *prom on outer: rdn 2f out: kpt on but nt pce of front pair: wnt 3rd fnl strides* **217/10**

4 hd **Amarillo (IRE)**[25] 1564 4-9-2 0 FilipMinarik 9 104
(P Schiergen, Germany) *trckd ldr: rdn to chal over 1f out: r.o and led briefly wl ins fnl f: immediately hdd: no ex and dropped to 4th fnl strides* **15/2**

5 nk **Point Blank (GER)**[11] 1870 5-9-0 0 (p) StefanieHofer 5 102
(Mario Hofer, Germany) *sn led: rdn 2f out: strly pressed fr over 1f out: kpt on tl no ex and hdd wl ins fnl f: fdd and dropped to 5th* **142/10**

6 ¾ **Indomito (GER)**[201] 7238 7-9-2 0 EPedroza 10 102
(A Wohler, Germany) *dwlt: sn rcvrd into midfield on outer: rdn and ev ch 2f out: nt qckn over 1f out: kpt on one pce ins fnl f* **53/10**[3]

7 nk **Sommerabend**[25] 1564 6-9-0 0 GaetanMasure 4 99
(U Stoltefuss, Germany) *midfield: rdn 2f out: keeping on and stl ev ch whn nt clr run briefly ins fnl f: nt rcvr* **79/10**

8 shd **Global Thrill**[25] 1564 4-9-4 0 ADeVries 8 103
(J Hirschberger, Germany) *trckd ldr on inner: rdn 2f out: kpt on one pce ins fnl f* **9/2**[2]

9 ½ **Zazou (GER)**[40] 1262 6-9-2 0 APietsch 6 100
(W Hickst, Germany) *midfield: rdn 2f out: kpt on but nt pce to chal* **18/5**[1]

10 hd **Samba Brazil (GER)**[208] 7075 4-8-13 0 MircoDemuro 7 96
(A Wohler, Germany) *hld up: rdn and hdwy on outer over 2f out: kpt on but sn outpcd* **104/10**

11 1 ¼ **King's Hall**[30] 1456 5-9-4 0 (b) DPorcu 3 98
(A Wohler, Germany) *hld up and last thrght: rdn over 2f out: plugged on but nvr a factor* **32/1**

1m 40.9s (1.79) 11 Ran SP% **129.4**
WIN (incl. 10 euro stake): 165. PLACES: 44, 18, 52. SF: 607.
Owner Gestut Haus Ittlingen **Bred** Gestut Haus Ittlingen **Trained** Germany

2203 - (Foreign Racing) - See Raceform Interactive

[1917]ASCOT (R-H)

Friday, May 10

OFFICIAL GOING: Good to firm (stands' side 9.1; centre 9.0; far side 8.9; round 9.4)

Wind: Moderate ahead Weather: Cloudy

2204 IRISH STALLION FARMS EBF MAIDEN FILLIES' STKS 5f

5:30 (5:31) (Class 4) 2-Y-0

£5,175 (£1,540; £769; £384) **Stalls** Centre

Form RPR

5 1 **Rizeena (IRE)**[22] 1634 2-9-0 0 FrederikTylicki 7 84
(Clive Brittain) *trckd ldr: led over 1f out: styd on strly ins fnl f* **7/2**[2]

2 1 ¾ **Oriel** 2-9-0 0 RichardHughes 4 78+
(Richard Hannon) *trckd ldrs: swtchd lft and qcknd to chse wnr 1f out: kpt on wl but a readily hld* **10/11**[1]

3 1 ¾ **Caletta Bay** 2-9-0 0 MartinHarley 3 71
(Mick Channon) *in tch: pushed along 1/2-way: hdwy ins fnl 2f: sn drvn: styd on wl in clsng stages to take 3rd but no ch w ldng duo* **25/1**

44 4 nse **Atlantic Affair (IRE)**[13] 1839 2-9-0 0 FrannyNorton 5 71
(Mark Johnston) *led: rdn and kpt on fr 2f out: hdd over 1f out: styd on same pce and ct for 3rd last strides* **25/1**

5 1 ½ **Corncockle** 2-9-0 0 KieranO'Neill 2 66+
(Richard Hannon) *wnt rt s: bhd: hdwy 2f out: chsd ldrs over 1f out: one pce ins fnl f* **33/1**

6 ½ **Lady In Blue (IRE)** 2-9-0 0 PaulHanagan 6 64
(William Haggas) *s.i.s: in rr: sme hdwy over 1f out: nvr gng pce to rch ldrs* **20/1**

7 1 **Simple Magic (IRE)** 2-9-0 0 WilliamBuick 8 60
(John Gosden) *trckd ldrs: pushed along ins fnl 2f: wknd ins fnl f* **5/1**[3]

8 3 ¼ **Prize** 2-9-0 0 PatDobbs 9 49
(Richard Hannon) *chsd ldrs: rdn 1/2-way: wknd ins fnl 2f* **16/1**

9 11 **Red Lady (IRE)** 2-9-0 0 KierenFallon 1 9
(Brian Meehan) *hmpd s: a outpcd in rr* **20/1**

1m 0.82s (0.32) **Going Correction** -0.025s/f (Good) **9 Ran SP% 117.3**
Speed ratings (Par 92): **96,93,90,90,87 87,85,80,62**
toteswingers 1&2 £1.60, 2&3 £9.10, 1&3 £20.40 CSF £6.64 TOTE £4.10: £1.30, £1.30, £6.20; EX 7.70 Trifecta £146.30 Pool: £3793.04 - 19.44 winning units..
Owner Sheikh Rashid Dalmook Al Maktoum **Bred** Round Hill Stud **Trained** Newmarket, Suffolk

FOCUS
Rail on Round course positioned 3m inside from 12f to entrance to home straight increasing 10f race by 9yds and 2m race by 16yds. An experienced runner held off a heavily-backed Richard Hannon-trained newcomer in this fillies' maiden. The form is rated slightly positively, the winner giving another boost to Fire Blaze's Newmarket maiden.

2205 TWO CIRCLES H'CAP 2m

6:00 (6:01) (Class 3) (0-90,88) 4-Y-0+

£7,470 (£2,236; £1,118; £559; £279; £140) **Stalls** Low

Form RPR

21-5 1 **Homeric (IRE)**[29] 1501 4-9-4 85 RyanMoore 3 93
(Ed Dunlop) *in rr: hdwy 4f out: drvn over 2f out: led wl over 1f out but hrd pressed thrght fnl f but a jst doing enough* **9/1**

0-54 2 shd **Quixote**[27] 1547 4-9-5 86 (t) KierenFallon 1 94
(Clive Brittain) *loose briefly bef s: in rr: hdwy over 3f out: drvn between horse to chal fr over 1f out: styd upsides thrght fnl f: nt quite get up* **14/1**

36-2 3 2 ¼ **Silver Samba**[10] 1899 4-8-2 69 CathyGannon 11 75+
(Andrew Balding) *chsd ldrs: pressing whn bmpd and lost momentum bnd ins fnl 3f: rallied u.p fr over 1f out and kpt on to take 3rd in clsng stages but no imp on ldng duo* **6/1**[3]

0/66 4 ½ **Bow To No One (IRE)**[19] 1615 7-8-5 74 MichaelJMMurphy(5) 8 79
(Alan Jarvis) *in rr: hdwy on outside fr over 3f out: styd on wl fnl f but nvr gng pce to rch ldrs* **25/1**

-333 5 ¾ **Tappanappa (IRE)**[14] 1805 6-9-5 83 (b) WilliamBuick 6 87
(Brian Ellison) *hld up in rr: hdwy on ins over 2f out: drvn and kpt on wl fnl f: nt rch ldrs* **12/1**

56-4 6 1 ¼ **Cotton King**[21] 1670 6-8-8 72 PaulHanagan 10 74
(Lady Herries) *chsd ldrs: drvn to chal fr over 2f out: wknd 1f out* **25/1**

00-5 7 2 **Montaff**[13] 1841 7-9-6 84 MartinHarley 9 84
(Mick Channon) *in tch: hdwy to chse ldrs fr 5f out: chalng whn bmpd bnd ins fnl 3f: led u.p appr fnl 2f: hdd over 1f out: sn wknd* **10/1**

435- 8 nk **Toptempo**[189] 7522 4-8-2 72 SimonPearce(3) 7 72
(Mark H Tompkins) *chsd ldrs: rdn 3f out: styd on same pce fnl 2f* **25/1**

25-2 9 3 ½ **Kuda Huraa (IRE)**[16] 1766 5-9-10 88 RichardHughes 13 83
(Alan King) *chsd ldr to 1/2-way: chalng whn bmpd bnd ins fnl 3f: str chal fr over 2f out: wkng whn n.m.r appr fnl f* **9/2**[2]

30-3 10 5 **Riptide**[18] 1721 7-8-8 72 (p) FrederikTylicki 2 61
(Michael Scudamore) *in tch: dropped in rr 5f out: styd on same pce fnl 3f* **33/1**

33-1 11 2 ¾ **Sign Manual**[21] 1670 4-8-13 80 HayleyTurner 4 66
(Michael Bell) *in rr: rdn 4f out: little rspnse and no prog* **10/3**[1]

000- 12 ½ **Ermyn Lodge**[209] 7051 7-9-10 88 (v) IanMongan 5 73
(Pat Phelan) *chsd ldrs: wnt 2nd 1/2-way: rdn over 4f out: wknd fr 3f out* **25/1**

45-5 13 2 ½ **Gabrial's Star**[14] 1805 4-9-1 82 JamieSpencer 12 64
(Ed Dunlop) *sn led: rdn and hung lft bnd ins fnl 3f: hdd & wknd qckly over 2f out* **7/1**

3m 30.59s (1.59) **Going Correction** +0.025s/f (Good)
WFA 4 from 5yo+ 3lb **13 Ran SP% 119.8**
Speed ratings (Par 107): **97,96,95,95,95 94,93,93,91,89 87,87,86**
toteswingers 1&2 £27.90, 2&3 £19.20, 1&3 £11.80 CSF £119.18 CT £825.47 TOTE £10.00: £3.10, £4.80, £2.00; EX 136.60 Trifecta £1119.50 Pool: £2442.55 - 1.63 winning units..
Owner Highclere Thoroughbred Racing - Jackson **Bred** Lynch Bages Ltd **Trained** Newmarket, Suffolk

FOCUS
There was a tight finish to this decent staying handicap which was run at a fair pace. Ordinary form for the grade in all probability.

2206 FEDERATION OF BLOODSTOCK AGENTS MAIDEN FILLIES' STKS 1m 2f

6:30 (6:35) (Class 4) 3-Y-0+

£5,175 (£1,540; £769; £384) **Stalls** Low

Form RPR

1 **Sea Meets Sky (FR)** 3-8-12 0 IanMongan 7 87+
(Sir Henry Cecil) *in rr: pushed along 5f out: drvn and swtchd lft to outside over 2f out but stl plenty to do: str run fnl f: styd on to ld last stride* **20/1**

0 2 nk **Toast Of The Town (IRE)**[21] 1671 3-8-12 0 WilliamBuick 5 86+
(John Gosden) *chsd ldrs: drvn over 2f out: styd on wl to ld fnl 130yds: ct last stride* **7/2**[2]

3 ½ **Fersah (USA)** 3-8-12 0 PaulHanagan 9 85+
(William Haggas) *sn trcking ldr: chal wl over 1f out: stl upsides fnl 110yds: no ex in clsng stages* **8/1**[3]

0-3 4 1 ½ **Sharqawiyah**[22] 1640 3-8-12 0 KierenFallon 3 82
(Luca Cumani) *t.k.h: trckd ldrs: chal fr 2f out tl led over 1f out: hdd fnl 130yds: no ex in clsng stages* **7/2**[2]

4-0 5 2 ¼ **Just One Kiss**[21] 1671 3-8-12 0 TomQueally 2 78
(Sir Henry Cecil) *sn led: rdn over 2f out: hdd over 1f out: wknd ins fnl f* **10/1**

6 6 **Okavango** 3-8-12 0 HayleyTurner 12 66+
(James Fanshawe) *s.i.s and bhd: pushed along and styd on fnl 2f: nvr a threat* **66/1**

0-3 7 hd **Montjess (IRE)**[37] 1329 3-8-12 0 HarryBentley 6 65
(Tom Dascombe) *in tch: pushed along and outpcd 5f out: hung rt u.p over 2f out: mod late prog* **66/1**

46- 8 hd **Janie Runaway (IRE)**[224] 6644 3-8-12 0 MartinLane 8 65
(Brian Meehan) *in tch: pushed along 3f out: wknd fr 2f out* **33/1**

9 ¾ **Wolfs Breath (TUR)** 3-8-12 0 RichardHughes 11 63
(Charles Hills) *in tch: drvn along over 3f out: edgd rt: green and flashed tail over 2f out: sn wknd* **16/1**

0 10 3 ¾ **Bohemian Dance (IRE)**[21] 1671 3-8-12 0 RyanMoore 4 56
(Sir Michael Stoute) *chsd ldrs: rdn over 2f out: sn btn* **5/2**[1]

0- 11 12 **Granule**[265] 5339 3-8-12 0 JamieSpencer 1 32
(Peter Chapple-Hyam) *t.k.h: a in rr* **10/1**

2m 7.59s (0.19) **Going Correction** +0.025s/f (Good) **11 Ran SP% 118.9**
Speed ratings (Par 102): **100,99,99,98,96 91,91,91,90,87 78**
toteswingers 1&2 £17.20, 2&3 £8.10, 1&3 £27.30 CSF £88.41 TOTE £21.80: £3.70, £1.70, £2.60; EX 94.30 Trifecta £683.60 Pool: £3230.01 - 3.54 winning units..
Owner Niarchos Family **Bred** Suc S Niarchos **Trained** Newmarket, Suffolk

FOCUS
A decent fillies' maiden but a mixture of abilities and profiles. It was run at a fair pace and a newcomer scored from a long way back. The winner looks a very nic prospect and there were other likely improvers behind.

2207 ROYAL ASCOT RACING CLUB 15TH BIRTHDAY CELEBRATION H'CAP 6f

7:05 (7:05) (Class 3) (0-95,95) 4-Y-0+

£7,762 (£2,310; £1,154; £577) **Stalls** Centre

Form RPR

-125 1 **Yeeoow (IRE)**[27] 1537 4-9-2 90 MartinHarley 1 99+
(Mrs K Burke) *in rr: gd hdwy over 1f out: squeezed between horses 1f out: qcknd to ld fnl 100yds: hld on wl* **8/1**[3]

-532 2 nk **Democretes**[6] 2013 4-9-0 88 RichardHughes 9 96
(Richard Hannon) *trckd ldrs: drvn to chal fnl 110yds: nt quite gng pce of wnr in clsng stages* **3/1**[1]

1102 3 ½ **Crew Cut (IRE)**[13] 1838 5-8-10 84 (b) JamieSpencer 12 91
(Jeremy Gask) *in rr: swtchd rt and hdwy ins fnl 2f: str run to chal fnl 100yds: nt qckn in clsng stages* **20/1**

041- 4 nk **Emilio Largo**[265] 5356 5-9-7 95 TomQueally 16 101
(James Fanshawe) *in rr: drvn and hdwy appr fnl f: fin strly: gng on cl home* **15/2**[2]

02- **5** *hd* **Nassau Storm**[211] 7010 4-9-3 **91** JimCrowley 4 96
(William Knight) *chsd ldrs: drvn over 1f out: chal fnl 100yds: no ex in clsng stages* **16/1**

6-06 **6** *1/2* **Lady Gibraltar**[6] 2014 4-8-12 **86** KierenFallon 10 90
(Alan Jarvis) *chsd ldrs: pushed along and one pce 2f out: styd on in clsng stages nt rch ldrs* **33/1**

213- **7** *nk* **Tropics (USA)**[169] 7823 5-8-10 **84** PaulHanagan 7 87
(Dean Ivory) *trckd ldrs: led over 1f out: hdd fnl 100yds: wknd nr fin* **8/1**[3]

300- **8** *1/2* **Tioman Legend**[243] 6075 4-9-4 **92** JamesDoyle 15 96
(Roger Charlton) *in rr: pushed along over 1f out: styd on wl fnl 120yds: gng on cl home* **25/1**

1-20 **9** *nk* **Intransigent**[55] 1032 4-9-5 **93** JimmyFortune 8 93
(Andrew Balding) *t.k.h: chsd ldrs: rdn over 1f out: one pce whn sltly hmpd ins fnl f* **10/1**

2436 **10** *nk* **Bravo Echo**[6] 2013 7-8-9 **83** RobertHavlin 13 82
(Michael Attwater) *chsd ldrs: rdn 2f out: outpcd fnl f* **16/1**

44-0 **11** *1 1/4* **Barnet Fair**[62] 947 5-9-4 **92** KierenFox 3 88
(Richard Guest) *hdwy to chse ldrs over 2f out: wknd fnl 100yds* **20/1**

600- **12** *1 1/2* **B Fifty Two (IRE)**[243] 6075 4-9-6 **94** SebSanders 14 85
(J W Hills) *chsd ldrs: rdn 2f out: wknd fnl 100yds* **33/1**

025- **13** *1 1/4* **L'Ami Louis (IRE)**[265] 5368 5-9-1 **89** FergusSweeney 2 76
(Henry Candy) *racd in centre of crse: led tl hdd over 1f out: sn btn* **14/1**

-000 **14** *3 3/4* **Colonel Mak**[18] 1720 6-9-2 **90** RyanMoore 11 81
(David Barron) *chsd ldr: wknd and eased over 1f out* **15/2**[2]

01-0 **15** *3/4* **Church Music (IRE)**[16] 1765 4-8-9 **83** HayleyTurner 6 57
(Michael Scudamore) *in rr: rdn and sme prog over 2f out: nvr rchd ldrs and sn wknd* **50/1**

1m 13.29s (-1.21) **Going Correction** -0.025s/f (Good) **15 Ran SP% 119.5**
Speed ratings (Par 107): **107,106,105,105,105 104,104,103,103,102 101,99,97,92,91**
toteswingers 1&2 £2.30, 2&3 £14.10, 1&3 £28.50 CSF £28.81 TOTE £7.70: £2.80, £1.20, £6.70; EX 32.20 Trifecta £564.50 Pool: £2234.64 - 2.96 winning units..
Owner R Lee & Mrs E Burke **Bred** Arctic Tack Stud **Trained** Middleham Moor, N Yorks

FOCUS
There was a bunch finish to this good sprint handicap. The bare form looks fairly sound.

2208 ASCOT RACECOURSE H'CAP 7f
7:40 (7:40) (Class 2) (0-105,98) 3-Y-O **£12,938** (£3,850; £1,924; £962) **Stalls** Centre

Form RPR

51-4 **1** **Professor**[23] 1625 3-9-7 **98** RichardHughes 3 107+
(Richard Hannon) *hld up in tch: qcknd smartly to ld fnl 100yds: cosily* **7/2**[2]

2-1 **2** *1* **Secret Talent**[18] 1711 3-8-10 **87** RyanMoore 7 93+
(Hughie Morrison) *hld up in tch: hdwy to chal appr fnl f: slt ld sn after: hdd and outpcd fnl 100yds* **5/2**[1]

502- **3** *3/4* **Pay Freeze (IRE)**[230] 6487 3-9-5 **96** JamieSpencer 2 100
(Mick Channon) *hld up in rr: hdwy fnl f: kpt on to take 3rd in clsng stages: no imp on ldng duo* **14/1**

55-3 **4** *1* **Georgian Bay (IRE)**[27] 1543 3-9-2 **93** MartinHarley 5 95
(Mrs K Burke) *chsd ldrs: rdn to chal over 1f out: outpcd fnl 110yds* **20/1**

31-2 **5** *1/2* **Regal Dan (IRE)**[23] 1625 3-8-12 **89** WilliamBuick 1 90
(Charles Hills) *chsd ldrs: rdn over 1f out: sn outpcd* **4/1**[3]

221- **6** *1* **Huntsmans Close**[199] 7311 3-8-9 **86** HayleyTurner 6 84
(Michael Bell) *led: rdn over 2f out: kpt slt advantage tl hdd 1f out: wknd fnl 110yds* **8/1**

10-1 **7** *shd* **Shebebi (USA)**[15] 1773 3-8-12 **89** PaulHanagan 4 87
(Mark Johnston) *chsd ldr: chal 2f out: wknd u.p fnl 110yds* **4/1**[3]

1m 26.39s (-1.21) **Going Correction** -0.025s/f (Good) **7 Ran SP% 113.3**
Speed ratings (Par 105): **105,103,103,101,101 100,100**
toteswingers 1&2 £2.80, 2&3 £4.60, 1&3 £6.90 CSF £12.46 TOTE £4.40: £2.50, £1.80; EX 10.30 Trifecta £116.70 Pool: £1688.26 - 10.84 winning units..
Owner Mrs P Good **Bred** Exors Of The Late J R Good **Trained** East Everleigh, Wilts

FOCUS
A useful handicap. The pace was decent and the winner scored in good style under a hold-up ride. The form is rated on the positive side.

2209 RACE, RATTLE 'N' ROLL H'CAP 1m (S)
8:15 (8:15) (Class 4) (0-85,85) 3-Y-O **£5,175** (£1,540; £769; £384) **Stalls** Centre

Form RPR

01-2 **1** **King Of The Danes**[7] 1991 3-8-7 **71** FrannyNorton 8 81
(Mark Johnston) *mde all: pushed along over 2f out: styd on strly fr over 1f out: unchal* **6/1**[3]

12-4 **2** *3/4* **George Cinq**[10] 1912 3-9-1 **79** HayleyTurner 4 87
(Michael Bell) *in rr: drvn and hdwy over 2f out: chsd wnr 1f out but no imp* **16/1**

413- **3** *1/2* **Ajmany (IRE)**[237] 6247 3-9-7 **85** (b[1]) KierenFallon 6 92
(Luca Cumani) *chsd ldrs: rdn over 2f out: styd on same pce fr 3rd ins fnl f* **9/2**[2]

522- **4** *1 3/4* **Swift Bounty**[184] 7628 3-8-10 **79** MichaelJMMurphy(5) 9 84+
(Alan Jarvis) *in rr: hdwy fr 2f out: kpt on wl fnl f: nt rch ldrs* **33/1**

01-5 **5** *1/2* **Rottingdean**[20] 1683 3-8-12 **76** WilliamBuick 10 78
(John Gosden) *disp 2nd fr 1/2-way: pushed along over 2f out: outpcd fnl f* **9/2**[2]

41-6 **6** *3/4* **Countryman**[30] 1471 3-8-12 **76** JimmyFortune 11 76
(Hughie Morrison) *chsd ldrs: rdn over 2f out: no ex ins fnl f* **25/1**

-121 **7** *nse* **Intrigo**[13] 1832 3-9-4 **82** RichardHughes 13 83
(Richard Hannon) *t.k.h: in tch: pushed along over 2f out: styd on same pce ins fnl f* **2/1**[1]

014 **8** *1* **Red To Amber (IRE)**[30] 1471 3-8-9 **73** JohnFahy 14 71
(Clive Cox) *in tch: rdn 3f out: wknd over 1f out* **25/1**

614- **9** *1* **Etijaah (USA)**[231] 6447 3-9-6 **84** PaulHanagan 5 80
(Brian Meehan) *chsd ldrs: disp 2nd fr 1/2-way: wknd ins fnl f* **10/1**

212- **10** *3* **Tobacco Road (IRE)**[248] 5903 3-9-0 **83** WilliamTwiston-Davies(5) 2 72
(Richard Hannon) *t.k.h: chsd ldrs: wknd ins fnl 2f* **11/1**

2144 **11** *shd* **Run It Twice (IRE)**[34] 1400 3-8-8 **72** (b) CathyGannon 1 60
(David Evans) *in rr: sme hdwy 3f out: wknd 2f out* **33/1**

3400 **12** *9* **Club House (IRE)**[16] 1770 3-8-2 **71** oh1 RyanTate(5) 12 39
(Robert Mills) *in rr: pushed along 1/2-way: no rspnse* **66/1**

1m 40.63s (-0.17) **Going Correction** -0.025s/f (Good) **12 Ran SP% 122.4**
Speed ratings (Par 101): **99,98,97,96,95 94,94,93,92,89 89,80**
toteswingers 1&2 £25.60, 2&3 £18.50, 1&3 £3.50 CSF £93.92 CT £481.82 TOTE £6.20: £2.10, £3.60, £1.90; EX 74.70 Trifecta £340.50 Pool: £2085.46 - 4.59 winning units..
Owner Newsells Park Stud **Bred** Newsells Park Stud **Trained** Middleham Moor, N Yorks

FOCUS
There was a gutsy front-running winner of this fair handicap. The winner was obviously well treated and confirmed last week's good Musselburgh effort. A race that should throw up winners.
T/Jkpt: Not won. T/Plt: £175.90 to a £1 stake. Pool of £113986.56 - 472.95 winning tickets. T/Qpdt: £24.00 to a £1 stake. Pool of £5508.21 - 169.55 winning tickets. ST

2185 CHESTER (L-H)
Friday, May 10

OFFICIAL GOING: Good to soft (7.4)
Wind: Fresh, half against Weather: Sunny intervals

2210 SPORTINGBET.COM EARL GROSVENOR H'CAP 7f 122y
1:45 (1:48) (Class 2) (0-105,100) 4-Y-O+ **£15,762** (£4,715; £2,357; £1,180; £587) **Stalls** Low

Form RPR

5-00 **1** **Captain Bertie (IRE)**[20] 1675 5-8-12 **91** RyanMoore 2 100
(Charles Hills) *chsd ldrs: rdn over 1f out: wnt 2nd ent fnl f: r.o to get up fnl strides* **9/4**[1]

2-00 **2** *nk* **Chosen Character (IRE)**[20] 1688 5-8-12 **91** (vt) StephenCraine 1 99
(Tom Dascombe) *s.i.s: rdn along to sn rcvr and chse ldr: led 2f out: abt 2 l clr over 1f out: all out ins fnl 100yds: ct fnl strides* **15/2**[3]

100- **3** *3 3/4* **Hefner (IRE)**[36] 6601 4-8-10 **89** AndreaAtzeni 13 88
(Marco Botti) *hld up: pushed along over 1f out: styd on and prog ins fnl f: gng on and tk 3rd towards fin: nt rch front pair* **20/1**

3311 **4** *3/4* **Gandalak (FR)**[7] 1992 4-9-2 **95** 6ex DanielTudhope 5 92
(David O'Meara) *led: pushed along and hdd 2f out: lost 2nd ent fnl f: no ex fnl 100yds: lost 3rd towards fin* **10/3**[2]

04-2 **5** *1 1/2* **Weapon Of Choice (IRE)**[30] 1485 5-8-11 **90** NeilCallan 12 83
(Stuart Kittow) *s.i.s: rdn along in rr early: sn hld up: hdwy 2f out: rdn to chse ldrs over 1f out: kpt on one pce ins fnl f* **17/2**

0140 **6** *2 3/4* **Dubai Dynamo**[6] 2029 8-8-13 **92** PJMcDonald 14 78
(Ruth Carr) *in rr: pushed along 3f out: hrd at work after: plugged on wout threatening ins fnl f* **16/1**

4026 **7** *1* **Verse Of Love**[10] 1905 4-8-7 **89** (p) DarrenEgan(3) 11 73
(David Evans) *chsd ldrs: forced wd 6f out: rdn over 2f out: wknd over 1f out* **28/1**

500- **8** *2* **Seanie (IRE)**[20] 1706 4-9-0 **93** GrahamLee 4 72
(David Marnane, Ire) *midfield: n.m.r 6f out: effrt 2f out: chsd ldrs over 1f out: wknd ins fnl f* **9/1**

00-0 **9** *4 1/2* **Balty Boys (IRE)**[13] 1830 4-8-11 **90** MartinDwyer 7 57
(Jamie Osborne) *chsd ldrs: rdn and lost pl 4f out: bhd sn after* **33/1**

10-5 **10** *3* **Postscript (IRE)**[17] 1745 5-8-12 **91** JamieSpencer 6 51
(David Simcock) *hld up in midfield: hmpd 6f out: effrt 2f out: no imp on ldrs: wknd ins fnl f* **8/1**

1m 35.46s (1.66) **Going Correction** +0.425s/f (Yiel) **10 Ran SP% 114.3**
Speed ratings (Par 109): **108,107,103,103,101 98,97,95,91,88**
toteswingers 1&2 £4.50, 2&3 £23.10, 1&3 £12.50 CSF £18.70 CT £271.56 TOTE £3.30: £1.40, £2.50, £6.10; EX 17.40 Trifecta £230.70 Pool: £3835.97 - 12.46 winning units..
Owner A L R Morton **Bred** Glending Bloodstock **Trained** Lambourn, Berks

■ Stewards' Enquiry : Stephen Craine two-day ban: used whip in incorrect place (May 24-25)

FOCUS
Rail moved out 6yds from 6f to 1.5f with drop in. Races 1, 5 & 6 increased in distance by 24yds, race 2 by 26yds, race 3 by 44yds, race 4 by 20yds and race 7 by 38yds. There was always likely to be plenty of pace on in this good-quality handicap, but it proved hard to make up ground. Straightforward Chester form, rated around the first two.

2211 BETVICTOR.COM DEE STKS (GROUP 3) (C&G) 1m 2f 75y
2:15 (2:15) (Class 1) 3-Y-O **£34,026** (£12,900; £6,456; £3,216; £1,614) **Stalls** High

Form RPR

0- **1** **Magician (IRE)**[195] 7419 3-8-12 93 RyanMoore 3 113+
(A P O'Brien, Ire) *chsd ldr: effrt 2f out: sn led and c wd ent st: r.o wl and powered clr fnl 150yds* **13/8**[1]

61-1 **2** *4* **Contributer (IRE)**[21] 1667 3-8-12 99 GrahamLee 6 105+
(Ed Dunlop) *hld up in rr: hdwy on inner over 1f out: sn in 2nd and ev ch: edgd rt ins fnl f: sn outpcd: no ch w wnr fnl 150yds* **9/4**[2]

-012 **3** *4* **Glacial Age (IRE)**[14] 1812 3-8-12 89 JoeFanning 4 97
(Jo Hughes) *hld up in tch: effrt 2f out: wl there over 1f out: kpt on same pce ins fnl f: no ch fnl 150yds* **25/1**

112- **4** *nse* **Willie The Whipper**[181] 7693 3-8-12 101 JamieSpencer 1 97
(Ann Duffield) *chsd ldrs: wl there whn got unbalanced and nt qckn over 1f out: kpt on same pce ins fnl f: no ch fnl 150yds* **3/1**[3]

11-3 **5** *10* **Gabrial's Kaka (IRE)**[16] 1767 3-8-12 91 TonyHamilton 2 78
(Richard Fahey) *led: rdn and hdd wl over 1f out: sn wknd* **15/2**

2m 12.96s (1.76) **Going Correction** +0.425s/f (Yiel) **5 Ran SP% 109.5**
Speed ratings (Par 109): **109,105,102,102,94**
CSF £5.50 TOTE £2.40: £1.60, £1.40; EX 5.80 Trifecta £47.90 Pool: £3190.98 - 49.95 winning units..
Owner Michael Tabor & Derrick Smith & Mrs John Magnier **Bred** Absolutelyfabulous Syndicate **Trained** Ballydoyle, Co Tipperary

FOCUS
There was little depth to this, a race that over the years has been one of the more recognised Derby trials but has lost some of its lustre in recent times and is now in danger of losing its Group 3 status. They went just a steady pace early, but it was hard not to be taken with Magician's performance. There is a bit of doubt over the form, which has been rated around the race averages.

2212 BOODLES DIAMOND ORMONDE STKS (GROUP 3) 1m 5f 89y
2:45 (2:48) (Class 1) 4-Y-O+
£42,532 (£16,125; £8,070; £4,020; £2,017; £1,012) **Stalls** Low

Form RPR

150- **1** **Mount Athos (IRE)**[166] 7872 6-9-0 117 JamieSpencer 5 114+
(Luca Cumani) *mde all: effrtlessly drew clr fr over 3f out: shkn up whn hung rt and c wd ent st wl over 1f out: eased down wl ins fnl f: easily* **11/8**[2]

1 **2** *9* **Mad Moose (IRE)**[14] 1804 9-9-0 79 DanielTudhope 6 98
(Nigel Twiston-Davies) *hld up: hdwy over 3f out: pushed along and wnt 2nd wl over 2f out: no imp: kpt on in vain ins fnl f: no ch* **20/1**

224- **3** *14* **Communicator**[163] 7895 5-9-0 98 DavidProbert 2 77
(Andrew Balding) *chsd ldrs: pushed along to take 2nd wl over 3f out: no imp on wnr: lost 2nd wl over 2f out: sn wknd* **13/2**[3]

/10- **4** *12* **Memphis Tennessee (IRE)**[321] 3369 5-9-0 117 RyanMoore 3 59
(A P O'Brien, Ire) *chsd wnr: pushed along over 4f out: rdn and wknd over 3f out* **6/5**[1]

5 *21* **Zafarqand (IRE)**[393] 1351 5-9-0 0 JoeFanning 4 27
(Patrick O Brady, Ire) *chsd ldrs: pushed along over 4f out: wknd over 3f out: t.o* **50/1**

The Form Book Flat, Raceform Ltd, Compton, RG20 6NL.

600/ **6** *81* **Luthien (IRE)**[633] 7369 7-8-11 47........................ NickyMackay 1
(Alex Hales) *hld up in rr: pushed along over 7f out: struggling 5f out: lost tch 4f out: t.o* **100/1**

2m 56.13s (3.43) **Going Correction** +0.425s/f (Yiel) **6** Ran SP% **108.6**
Speed ratings (Par 113): **106,100,91,84,71 21**
toteswingers 1&2 £3.80, 2&3 £3.50, 1&3 £1.30 CSF £22.15 TOTE £3.70: £1.70, £5.70; EX 33.80 Trifecta £66.10 Pool: £29125.85 - 330.39 winning units..
Owner Dr Marwan Koukash **Bred** David Magnier And Cobra Bloodstock **Trained** Newmarket, Suffolk

FOCUS
The expected duel between last year's winner Memphis Tennessee and Mount Athos failed to materialise, with the former stopping quickly and looking like a horse with a problem.

2213 SUSTAINABLE GROUP UK LTD EBF H'CAP 5f 16y
3:15 (3:19) (Class 2) (0-105,99) 3-Y£15,752 (£4,715; £2,357; £1,180; £587) **Stalls** Low

Form RPR

30-4 **1** **Normal Equilibrium**[14] 1808 3-8-9 **87**........................ JamieSpencer 8 96
(Robert Cowell) *hld up: c wd ent st and hdwy over 1f out: r.o to ld wl ins fnl f: in command cl home* **5/1**[3]

-162 **2** *1½* **Bispham Green**[20] 1690 3-8-4 **82**........................ BarryMcHugh 5 86
(Richard Fahey) *chsd ldrs: rdn and sltly outpcd over 1f out: r.o to take 2nd wl ins fnl f: no match for wnr towards fin* **9/2**[2]

13-0 **3** *1½* **New Fforest**[14] 1808 3-8-6 **84**........................ DavidProbert 9 83
(Andrew Balding) *chsd ldrs: rdn to ld over 1f out: hdd wl ins fnl f and edgd rt: styd on same pce towards fin* **12/1**

2030 **4** *¾* **Equitania**[14] 1808 3-8-11 **89**........................ LiamJones 2 85
(Alan Bailey) *prom: n.m.r and hmpd after nrly 1f: dropped to midfield: kpt on u.p ins fnl f: nt quite gng pce of ldrs* **12/1**

2-30 **5** *¾* **Satsuma**[5] 2039 3-8-11 **89**........................ NickyMackay 7 82
(David Brown) *chsd ldr: rdn and ev ch 1f out: nt qckn: kpt on same pce fnl 100yds* **16/1**

-300 **6** *1* **Jillnextdoor (IRE)**[14] 1808 3-8-12 **90**........................ SamHitchcott 3 80
(Mick Channon) *towards rr: pushed along 2f out: kpt on ins fnl f: nvr able to chal* **7/1**

0-01 **7** *hd* **Storm Moon (USA)**[4] 2083 3-8-13 **91** 6ex........................ JoeFanning 1 80+
(Mark Johnston) *chsd ldrs: effrt and ch over 1f out: no ex fnl and wl btn fnl 100yds* **9/4**[1]

40-0 **8** *1½* **Lyric Ace (IRE)**[55] 1033 3-8-7 **88**........................(b[1]) DarrenEgan(3) 4 71
(Paul D'Arcy) *n.m.r s: bhd: u.p over 1f out: nvr on terms* **12/1**

36- **9** *½* **Almanack**[224] 6648 3-8-7 **90**........................(t) ShaneGray(5) 11 72
(T Stack, Ire) *a bhd: outpcd over 2f out: nvr on terms* **20/1**

10 *½* **All Ablaze (IRE)**[56] 1030 3-8-6 **84**........................ RoryCleary 12 64
(Damian Joseph English, Ire) *led and displayed plenty of spd: rdn and hdd over 1f out: wknd ins fnl f* **16/1**

1m 2.17s (1.17) **Going Correction** +0.425s/f (Yiel) **10** Ran SP% **117.7**
Speed ratings (Par 105): **107,104,102,101,99 98,97,95,94,93**
toteswingers 1&2 £4.40, 2&3 £4.60, 1&3 £9.70 CSF £28.10 CT £259.00 TOTE £5.20: £1.70, £1.70, £2.90; EX 27.30 Trifecta £184.90 Pool: £3826.86 - 15.51 winning units..
Owner Qatar Racing Limited **Bred** D R Tucker **Trained** Six Mile Bottom, Cambs

FOCUS
They went hard up front early in what looked an open sprint handicap and the race set up nicely for the closers. A personal best from the winner.

2214 CRUISE NIGHTSPOT H'CAP 7f 2y
3:50 (3:51) (Class 4) (0-85,91) 4-Y-0+ **£7,762** (£2,310; £1,154; £577) **Stalls** Low

Form RPR

3601 **1** **Dr Red Eye**[17] 1746 5-9-3 **85**........................(p) BillyCray(3) 2 94
(Scott Dixon) *mde all: rdn over 2f out: pressed ins fnl f: r.o gamely towards fin* **7/1**[2]

1121 **2** *1* **Polar Kite (IRE)**[30] 1459 5-8-13 **81**........................ MichaelMetcalfe(3) 6 87
(Sean Curran) *hld up in midfield: effrt and hdwy over 1f out: r.o to chal ins fnl f: hld cl home* **7/1**[2]

3 *hd* **Cash Or Casualty (IRE)**[20] 1706 5-9-6 **85**........................(t) RoryCleary 12 91
(Damian Joseph English, Ire) *chsd wnr: rdn over 2f out: chalng ins fnl f: styd on same pce and hld towards fin* **16/1**

2010 **4** *1¼* **Al Khan (IRE)**[5] 2046 4-9-2 **81**........................(p) SteveDrowne 1 83
(Violet M Jordan) *in tch: effrt to chse ldrs 2f out: kpt on ins fnl f: nt quite able to chal* **20/1**

63-1 **5** *1* **Personal Touch**[49] 1115 4-9-3 **82**........................ TonyHamilton 3 82
(Richard Fahey) *chsd ldrs: rdn over 1f out: nt qckn ins fnl f: kpt on same pce towards fin* **9/4**[1]

60-6 **6** *3* **Clockmaker (IRE)**[25] 1571 7-9-5 **84**........................ PhillipMakin 9 76+
(Tim Easterby) *midfield: pushed along over 2f out: one pce fnl f* **8/1**[3]

0011 **7** *6* **Forest Edge (IRE)**[2] 2150 4-9-7 **91** 6ex........................(b) DeclanBates(5) 5 66
(David Evans) *bmpd early: towards rr: pushed along and hdwy into midfield over 2f out: no imp fnl 2f* **12/1**

00-5 **8** *1¼* **Queens Revenge**[22] 1646 4-9-4 **83**........................ J-PGuillambert 14 55
(Tim Easterby) *chsd ldrs: pushed along and lost pl over 3f out: outpcd over 2f out: no imp after* **50/1**

100- **9** *¾* **Baby Strange**[176] 7730 9-9-4 **83**........................ AndrewElliott 10 53
(Derek Shaw) *hld up: sme prog into midfield over 1f out: no imp on ldrs* **33/1**

6-36 **10** *2¼* **Kingscroft (IRE)**[17] 1745 5-9-5 **84**........................ JoeFanning 11 48
(Mark Johnston) *hld up in rr: u.p over 2f out: nvr on terms* **10/1**

4-50 **11** *½* **Barons Spy (IRE)**[18] 1726 12-9-5 **84**........................ DavidProbert 8 47
(Richard Price) *midfield: pushed along over 3f out: sn outpcd* **50/1**

0-05 **12** *shd* **Mr David (USA)**[15] 1782 6-8-12 **82**........................(b) RachealKneller(5) 7 44
(Jamie Osborne) *bmpd early: hld up: u.p over 2f out: nvr on terms* **20/1**

0-00 **13** *½* **All Or Nothin (IRE)**[18] 1720 4-9-2 **84**........................ DarrenEgan(3) 4 45
(John Quinn) *bmpd early: in midfield: pushed along over 3f out: outpcd over 2f out: nvr a threat* **7/1**[2]

1120 **14** *13* **Elusive Hawk (IRE)**[17] 1745 9-8-12 **84**........................(v) RobJFitzpatrick(7) 13
(David Evans) *towards rr: u.p and bhd over 2f out: nvr a threat* **50/1**

1m 29.02s (2.52) **Going Correction** +0.425s/f (Yiel) **14** Ran SP% **120.4**
Speed ratings (Par 105): **102,100,100,99,98 94,87,86,85,82 82,82,81,66**
toteswingers 1&2 £14.20, 2&3 £10.10, 1&3 £18.90 CSF £51.47 CT £778.90 TOTE £10.60: £2.50, £2.20, £7.10; EX 67.70 Trifecta £944.90 Pool: £1606.89 - 1.27 winning units..
Owner The Red Eye Partnership **Bred** G E Amey **Trained** Babworth, Notts
■ Stewards' Enquiry : Rory Cleary seven-day ban: used whip above permitted level (May 24,25,27-31)

FOCUS
The early pace appeared pretty generous, yet little got into this from off the pace, with the first five being up there more or less throughout. The form horses came to the fore, with the winner a proven 'Chester horse'.

2215 HIGHSTREETVOUCHERS.COM MAIDEN FILLIES' STKS 7f 2y
4:25 (4:28) (Class 3) 3-Y-0 **£7,762** (£2,310; £1,154; £577) **Stalls** Low

Form RPR

6-5 **1** **Callmeakhab (IRE)**[22] 1640 3-9-0 0........................ SteveDrowne 7 71
(Charles Hills) *w ldr: led 2f out: rdn over 1f out: pushed out and r.o towards fin* **4/1**[2]

53 **2** *1¾* **Clary (IRE)**[56] 1019 3-8-11 0........................ DarrenEgan(3) 9 66
(James Unett) *taken out of stalls and checked by vet bef s: hld up: hdwy over 2f out: chsd ldrs over 1f out: r.o to take 2nd ins fnl f: no imp on wnr towards fin* **28/1**

-526 **3** *¾* **Sixties Queen**[4] 2092 3-9-0 63........................ LiamJones 2 64
(Alan Bailey) *hld up: pushed along over 2f out: u.p over 1f out to get on terms w ldrs: styd on ins fnl f: nrst fin* **12/1**

30- **4** *hd* **Arbeel**[258] 5571 3-9-0 0........................ JoeFanning 11 64
(Peter Chapple-Hyam) *hld up: hdwy over 3f out: rdn and tried to chal over 1f out: one pce fnl 75yds* **6/4**[1]

0 **5** *3¼* **Lexi's Dancer**[13] 1828 3-9-0 0........................(b[1]) TonyHamilton 6 55
(Ed Dunlop) *racd keenly in tch: pushed along over 2f out: rdn over 1f out: kpt on but no imp fnl f* **8/1**[3]

20- **6** *½* **Shamiana**[162] 7924 3-9-0 0........................ NickyMackay 4 54
(Gerard Butler) *led: pushed along 3f out: hdd 2f out: rdn over 1f out: wknd fnl 100yds* **8/1**[3]

0- **7** *16* **Zarla**[214] 6936 3-9-0 0........................ StephenCraine 3 10
(Tom Dascombe) *chsd ldrs: pushed along over 3f out: wknd over 2f out* **20/1**

006- **8** *9* **Wicked Tara**[223] 6664 3-8-7 0........................(t) CharlieBennett(7) 8
(Frank Sheridan) *in tch: rdn and wknd over 2f out* **100/1**

1m 31.86s (5.36) **Going Correction** +0.425s/f (Yiel) **8** Ran SP% **99.1**
Speed ratings (Par 100): **86,84,83,82,79 78,60,50**
toteswingers 1&2 £8.60, 2&3 £10.60, 1&3 £4.70 CSF £76.27 TOTE £4.40: £1.20, £4.70, £2.70; EX 82.60 Trifecta £408.30 Pool: £2418.43 - 4.44 winning units..
Owner AEGIS Partnership **Bred** Oak Hill Stud **Trained** Lambourn, Berks

FOCUS
A moderate maiden in truth, and Oasis Spirit, one of the more interesting runners, had to be withdrawn at the start. The time was slow. The winner is rated up 7lb.

2216 GLEVENTS OWEN BROWN H'CAP 1m 4f 66y
5:00 (5:00) (Class 2) (0-105,86) 3-Y£15,752 (£4,715; £2,357; £1,180; £587) **Stalls** Low

Form RPR

6-31 **1** **Red Runaway**[13] 1834 3-8-13 **78**........................ PhillipMakin 4 86+
(Ed Dunlop) *hld up in rr: pushed along 2f out: rdn over 1f out: prog on outer ins fnl f: str run to ld ins fnl 75yds* **5/2**[2]

21-4 **2** *½* **Van Percy**[22] 1641 3-9-2 **81**........................ DavidProbert 3 88
(Andrew Balding) *racd keenly: trckd ldrs: rdn over 1f out: chalng and r.o ins fnl f: nt match pce of wnr cl home* **2/1**[1]

2412 **3** *nk* **Good Evans**[2] 2153 3-7-12 **68**........................ NatashaEaton(5) 1 75
(Tom Dascombe) *led: rdn and hdd over 1f out: stl chalng ins fnl f: sn regained ld briefly: one pce fnl strides* **7/2**[3]

3-11 **4** *2¾* **Gabrial's Wawa**[49] 1119 3-8-13 **78**........................ TonyHamilton 6 81
(Richard Fahey) *chsd ldr: rdn to ld over 1f out: hdd wl ins fnl f: no ex fnl 50yds* **11/2**

3113 **5** *9* **Blue Wave (IRE)**[13] 1834 3-9-7 **86**........................ JoeFanning 5 74
(Mark Johnston) *hld up in tch: pushed along over 2f out: wknd over 1f out: eased whn btn ins fnl f* **7/1**

2m 45.46s (6.96) **Going Correction** +0.425s/f (Yiel) **5** Ran SP% **112.0**
Speed ratings (Par 105): **93,92,92,90,84**
CSF £8.09 TOTE £3.30: £1.50, £1.40; EX 6.90 Trifecta £30.40 Pool: £2781.64 - 68.59 winning units..
Owner The Hon R J Arculli **Bred** Lofts Hall, M Philipson & Cheveley Park **Trained** Newmarket, Suffolk

FOCUS
Quite an ordinary handicap for the grade and, following just a steady pace, it developed into a bit of a dash in the straight. The form is rated around the third.
T/Plt: £129.80 to a £1 stake. Pool of £166234.83 - 934.85 winning tickets. T/Qpdt: £37.30 to a £1 stake. Pool of £6557.05 -129.94 winning tickets. DO

2036 HAMILTON (R-H)
Friday, May 10

OFFICIAL GOING: Good to soft (good in places; 8.2)
Wind: Breezy, half behind Weather: overcast

2217 FOLLOW @HAMILTONPARKRC ON TWITTER APPRENTICE H'CAP (ROUND 1 OF HAMILTON PARK APPRENTICE SERIES) 5f 4y
6:05 (6:05) (Class 6) (0-65,64) 4-Y-0+ **£2,045** (£603; £302) **Stalls** High

Form RPR

0-14 **1** **Dartrix**[30] 1465 4-8-12 **59**........................ ConnorBeasley(7) 3 73+
(Michael Dods) *sn pushed along bhd ldng gp: effrt and hdwy over 1f out: led ins fnl f: kpt on strly* **5/2**[1]

50-2 **2** *1½* **Mandalay King (IRE)**[5] 2036 8-9-5 **64**........................(p) DavidSimmonson(3) 1 72
(Marjorie Fife) *chsd ldrs: hdwy to ld over 1f out: hdd ins fnl f: kpt on same pce nr fin* **7/2**[3]

4665 **3** *2* **Wicked Wilma (IRE)**[5] 2043 9-8-7 **54**........................ JordanHibberd(7) 5 55
(Alan Berry) *led to over 1f out: sn rdn: kpt on same pce ins fnl f* **7/1**

000- **4** *¾* **Bondi Beach Boy**[193] 7445 4-8-1 **48** ow3........................ JordanNason(7) 4 46
(James Turner) *t.k.h: chsd ldrs: rdn and outpcd over 1f out: kpt on ins fnl f* **20/1**

600- **5** *hd* **Rock Canyon (IRE)**[222] 6713 4-8-8 **53**........................ DavidBergin(5) 6 51
(Linda Perratt) *chsd ldrs: pushed along wl over 1f out: one pce appr fnl f* **22/1**

401- **6** *1¼* **Weetentherty**[207] 7099 6-8-9 **54**........................(p) LauraBarry(5) 2 47
(Keith Dalgleish) *dwlt: sn pushed along in rr: shortlived effrt on outside 2f out: sn n.d* **13/2**

0304 **7** *shd* **Lord Buffhead**[5] 2043 4-8-13 **56**........................(p) JasonHart(3) 7 49
(Richard Guest) *dwlt: sn chsng ldrs: rdn and outpcd 2f out: no imp whn rdr dropped whip ins fnl f* **3/1**[2]

1m 1.3s (1.30) **Going Correction** +0.30s/f (Good) **7** Ran SP% **110.7**
Speed ratings (Par 101): **101,98,95,94,93 91,91**
toteswingers 1&2 £1.10, 2&3 £7.00, 1&3 £8.50 CSF £10.72 CT £48.91 TOTE £3.40: £1.40, £2.30; EX 9.00 Trifecta £72.50 Pool: £181.02 - 1.87 winning units..
Owner K Knox **Bred** T K & Mrs P A Knox **Trained** Denton, Co Durham

■ Stewards' Enquiry : Connor Beasley one-day ban: careless riding (May 24)

FOCUS

Races on round course increased in distance by approximately 25yds. Despite 0.4mm of rain overnight, a drying wind meant the conditions were good to soft, good in places with a GoingStick reading of 8.2. Light drizzle greeted the runners in the opener and there was a fairly stiff breeze behind the runners up the straight. A weak apprentices' handicap but run at a decent pace. They came up the stands' side. The winner progressed and the runner-up is on a good mark at present.

2218 THOMSON OPEN MAIDEN STKS — 6f 5y

6:40 (6:41) (Class 5) 3-Y-O+ **£3,234** (£962; £481; £240) **Stalls** High

Form RPR

2363 **1** **Script**^{8} 1962 4-9-8 48 PaddyAspell 2 58
(Alan Berry) *cl up on outside: hdwy to ld over 1f out: rdn and drifted lft ins fnl f: jst hld on* **12/1**

0-40 **2** *hd* **A J Cook (IRE)**^{4} 2076 3-9-3 65 RobertWinston 4 59
(David Barron) *t.k.h early: cl up: effrt and ev ch over 1f out: sn rdn: kpt on fnl f: jst hld* **11/10**^{1}

245- **3** *3* **Pastoral Prey**^{283} 4670 3-9-3 68 PaulMulrennan 8 50
(Ian Semple) *chsd ldrs: rdn 2f out: kpt on ins fnl f: nt rch first two* **7/1**

64 **4** *nse* **Compton Heights**^{20} 1687 4-9-13 0 GrahamLee 5 53
(Jim Goldie) *t.k.h: chsd ldrs: hdwy over 2f out: rdn and one pce fnl f* **7/2**^{2}

0-36 **5** *1 1/4* **Salvatore Fury (IRE)**^{7} 1988 3-8-12 54 (p) GarryWhillans(5) 7 46
(Keith Dalgleish) *led to over 1f out: drvn and outpcd fnl f* **13/2**^{3}

6 *2 3/4* **Anan**^{1533} 7-9-13 0 DavidNolan 1 40
(Kevin Morgan) *in tch on outside: rdn and outpcd 2f out: n.d after* **10/1**

45- **7** *23* **Princess Cayan (IRE)**^{300} 4083 3-8-7 0 GeorgeChaloner(5) 3
(Linda Perratt) *awkward s: in tch: drvn and struggling after 2f: sn lost tch: t.o* **66/1**

1m 14.86s (2.66) **Going Correction** +0.30s/f (Good)
WFA 3 from 4yo+ 10lb **7 Ran SP% 114.0**
Speed ratings (Par 103): **94,93,89,89,88 84,53**
toteswingers 1&2 £1.80, 2&3 £1.80, 1&3 £10.90 CSF £25.69 TOTE £12.80: £5.50, £1.10; EX 32.10 Trifecta £60.40 Pool: £657.19 - 8.16 winning units..
Owner Alan Berry **Bred** Bearstone Stud **Trained** Cockerham, Lancs

FOCUS

A poor maiden run at a modest pace on easing ground. The stalls were stands' side but again the winner came up the centre of the track before edging towards the stands' rail. The winner is the most likely guide.

2219 ALEX FERGUSSON MEMORIAL H'CAP (QUALIFIER FOR THE £15000 BETFAIR SCOTTISH MILE SERIES FINAL) — 1m 65y

7:15 (7:15) (Class 6) (0-65,65) 4-Y-O+ **£2,264** (£673; £336; £168) **Stalls** Low

Form RPR

0203 **1** **Ted's Brother (IRE)**^{14} 1801 5-9-2 60 (e) RobbieFitzpatrick 3 70
(Richard Guest) *dwlt: t.k.h early: hld up in tch: smooth hdwy on outside over 2f out: led 1f out: edgd rt: rdn out* **4/1**^{3}

006- **2** *1/2* **Tectonic (IRE)**^{228} 6530 4-8-4 51 oh2 JulieBurke(3) 9 60
(Keith Dalgleish) *t.k.h: trckd ldrs: smooth hdwy to ld 2f out: hdd 1f out: rallied: kpt on: hld cl home* **25/1**

540- **3** *nk* **Raamz (IRE)**^{392} 1363 6-9-2 65 GeorgeChaloner(5) 8 73
(Kevin Morgan) *sn towards rr: hdwy over 3f out: rdn and drifted lft fr over 2f out: styd on wl fnl f: nrst fin* **16/1**

6042 **4** *7* **Rawaafed (IRE)**^{2} 2162 4-8-13 62 GarryWhillans(5) 6 54
(Keith Dalgleish) *in tch: checked after 2f: rdn and outpcd over 3f out: rallied over 1f out: nt gng pce to chal* **7/2**^{2}

50-0 **5** *1* **Euston Square**^{25} 1567 7-9-6 64 PaddyAspell 4 54
(Alistair Whillans) *hld up: effrt and pushed along over 3f out: no imp fr 2f out* **11/1**

0000 **6** *2* **Cufflink**^{16} 1763 4-8-8 57 (p) JasonHart(5) 2 42
(Iain Jardine) *hld up: hmpd after 2f: rdn over 3f out: nvr able to chal* **22/1**

606- **7** *nk* **Last Supper**^{197} 7361 4-9-7 65 GrahamLee 1 50
(James Bethell) *trckd ldrs: rdn over 3f out: wknd wl over 1f out* **14/1**

40-6 **8** *2 1/2* **Fine Altomis**^{25} 1568 4-9-5 63 (p) PaulMulrennan 7 42
(Michael Dods) *midfield: rushed up to join ldr after 2f: rdn over 2f out: edgd rt and sn wknd* **3/1**^{1}

3230 **9** *7* **Miami Gator (IRE)**^{15} 1786 6-9-7 65 (v) RobertWinston 5 35
(Mrs K Burke) *led tl hung lft and hdd 2f out: sn wknd* **5/1**

1m 51.72s (3.32) **Going Correction** +0.40s/f (Good) **9 Ran SP% 113.0**
Speed ratings (Par 101): **99,98,98,91,90 88,87,85,78**
toteswingers 1&2 £15.10, 2&3 £15.10, 1&3 £15.10 CSF £92.50 CT £1436.77 TOTE £3.80: £1.20, £11.90, £6.70; EX 64.50 Trifecta £358.50 Part won. Pool: £478.04 - 0.18 winning units..
Owner Mrs Alison Guest **Bred** T Counihan **Trained** Wetherby, W Yorks

FOCUS

A weak handicap run at a muddling pace and they spread out across the track for the last 3f. The winner took advantage of a reduced mark.

2220 THOMSON.CO.UK H'CAP — 1m 1f 36y

7:50 (7:50) (Class 4) (0-80,80) 4-Y-O+ **£6,145** (£1,828; £913; £456) **Stalls** Low

Form RPR

0-12 **1** **Karaka Jack**^{9} 1922 6-9-5 78 PaddyAspell 9 87
(David Nicholls) *in tch: smooth hdwy over 2f out: led and hrd pressed over 1f out: hld on wl fnl f* **11/4**^{2}

001/ **2** *nk* **Spes Nostra**^{499} 7901 5-8-4 68 JasonHart(5) 7 76
(David Barron) *hld up towards rr: pushed along over 3f out: hdwy on outside and ev ch over 1f out: kpt on fnl f* **11/1**

0230 **3** *2 1/4* **Brown Pete (IRE)**^{11} 1884 5-8-12 71 SaleemGolam 1 74
(Violet M Jordan) *hld up: rdn over 2f out: swtiched lft over 1f out: styd on wl fnl f: nt rch first two* **18/1**

20-2 **4** *3/4* **Le Chat D'Or**^{25} 1569 5-9-3 76 (tp) PaulMulrennan 2 78
(Michael Dods) *midfield on ins: hdwy over 3f out: effrt and drvn 2f out: one pce fnl f* **5/2**^{1}

010- **5** *1/2* **High Resolution**^{202} 7250 6-8-8 72 GeorgeChaloner(5) 10 73
(Linda Perratt) *hld up in midfield: stdy hdwy and cl up over 2f out: rdn and one pce fr over 1f out* **16/1**

24-0 **6** *1* **Act Your Shoe Size**^{7} 1990 4-9-2 80 GarryWhillans(5) 4 78
(Keith Dalgleish) *led to over 2f out: rdn and outpcd over 1f out* **16/1**

10-0 **7** *1/2* **Another For Joe**^{13} 1831 5-9-3 76 GrahamLee 8 73
(Jim Goldie) *cl up: led over 2f out to over 1f out: sn no ex* **5/1**^{3}

410- **8** *nk* **Supreme Luxury (IRE)**^{212} 6986 4-9-1 74 DavidNolan 3 71
(Kevin Ryan) *t.k.h early: trckd ldrs: rdn over 2f out: wknd over 1f out* **16/1**

064- **9** *7* **Painted Tail (IRE)**^{119} 5731 6-8-10 69 RobertWinston 5 50
(Alan Swinbank) *cl up: effrt and rdn over 3f out: wknd over 1f out* **11/1**

12-0 **10** *5* **Social Rhythm**^{25} 1569 9-8-5 67 JulieBurke(3) 6 37
(Alistair Whillans) *hld up: struggling 4f out: n.d after* **33/1**

2m 1.43s (1.73) **Going Correction** +0.40s/f (Good) **10 Ran SP% 114.4**
Speed ratings (Par 105): **108,107,105,105,104 103,103,103,96,92**
toteswingers 1&2 £10.10, 2&3 £0.00, 1&3 £3.40 CSF £32.59 CT £454.39 TOTE £3.60: £1.30, £4.00, £5.10; EX 44.60 Trifecta £200.90 Pool: £609.32 - 2.27 winning units..
Owner M Mackay & S Bruce **Bred** Tarworth Bloodstock Investments Ltd **Trained** Sessay, N Yorks

FOCUS

A reasonably competitive handicap run at a fair pace, with plenty still having a chance with a furlong and a half to run. The form looks solid enough. Pretty straightforward form.

2221 THOMSON CLAIMING STKS — 1m 3f 16y

8:25 (8:25) (Class 6) 4-Y-O+ **£2,045** (£603; £302) **Stalls** High

Form RPR

6650 **1** **Jordaura**^{18} 1730 7-8-12 60 PaddyAspell 4 63
(Alan Berry) *hld up in last pl: stdy hdwy over 2f out: shkn up to ld appr fnl f: kpt on strly* **10/1**

2124 **2** *3 1/4* **Activate**^{34} 1390 6-9-7 74 (p) PaulMulrennan 1 66
(Keith Dalgleish) *led at stdy pce 5f: chsd ldr: led on bit over 3f out: rdn over 2f out: hdd appr fnl f: one pce* **4/9**^{1}

4224 **3** *hd* **Bold Marc (IRE)**^{24} 1597 11-8-9 56 RobertWinston 6 54
(Mrs K Burke) *t.k.h: chsd ldrs: rdn and wnt 2nd over 2f out: one pce fnl f* **6/1**^{3}

/00- **4** *9* **Kaolak (USA)**^{397} 1239 7-8-12 77 (v) GrahamLee 5 41
(Jim Goldie) *plld hrd: in tch: rdn and outpcd over 3f out: n.d after* **9/2**^{2}

006- **5** *20* **Lochluichart (IRE)**^{229} 6516 4-8-6 13 (p) RaulDaSilva(3) 3
(Ian Semple) *t.k.h: chsd ldr: led after 5f to over 2f out: sn drvn and wknd* **66/1**

2m 32.07s (6.47) **Going Correction** +0.40s/f (Good) **5 Ran SP% 112.3**
Speed ratings (Par 101): **92,89,89,82,68**
CSF £15.73 TOTE £17.00: £3.90, £1.10; EX 21.30 Trifecta £71.00 Pool: £440.75 - 4.65 winning units..
Owner Alan Berry **Bred** Pendley Farm **Trained** Cockerham, Lancs

FOCUS

A paucity of runners for this weak claimer. The result saw something of a surprise, especially given the ease of the win. It's hard to be confident about the form.

2222 GINGER GROUSE BRAVEHEART NIGHT H'CAP (QUALIFIER FOR £15000 BETFAIR SCOTTISH SPRINT SERIES FINAL) — 6f 5y

8:55 (8:55) (Class 5) (0-70,73) 4-Y-O+ **£3,408** (£1,006; £503) **Stalls** High

Form RPR

0-01 **1** **Nasharra (IRE)**^{5} 2036 5-9-4 72 6ex (tp) KevinStott(7) 2 82
(Kevin Ryan) *in tch: stdy hdwy over 2f out: rdn to ld ins fnl f: kpt on wl* **5/2**^{2}

1532 **2** *2* **Greenhead High**^{5} 2037 5-9-2 63 (v) PaulMulrennan 7 67
(David Nicholls) *led: rdn wl over 1f out: hdd ins fnl f: kpt on same pce* **9/4**^{1}

1344 **3** *1 1/4* **Fairy Wing (IRE)**^{8} 1947 6-9-6 67 SaleemGolam 4 67
(Violet M Jordan) *fly-jmpd s: sn trcking ldrs: effrt and rdn 2f out: one pce fnl f* **14/1**

4031 **4** *1 3/4* **Economic Crisis (IRE)**^{5} 2037 4-9-12 73 6ex PaddyAspell 8 67
(Alan Berry) *t.k.h: trckd ldr: drvn over 2f out: no ex fr over 1f out* **5/2**^{2}

6060 **5** *1/2* **Ambitious Icarus**^{16} 1758 4-9-3 64 (e) RobbieFitzpatrick 1 57
(Richard Guest) *t.k.h: hld up in tch: drvn along over 2f out: no imp over 1f out* **12/1**

040- **6** *nk* **Black Douglas**^{199} 7316 4-8-10 57 GrahamLee 5 49
(Jim Goldie) *plld hrd: in tch: drvn over 2f out: no ex over 1f out* **10/1**^{3}

1m 13.55s (1.35) **Going Correction** +0.30s/f (Good) **6 Ran SP% 111.4**
Speed ratings (Par 103): **103,100,98,96,95 95**
toteswingers 1&2 £1.90, 2&3 £2.60, 1&3 £4.70 CSF £8.41 CT £58.24 TOTE £3.90: £2.40, £1.10; EX 10.70 Trifecta £181.90 Pool: £637.78 - 2.62 winning units..
Owner Mr & Mrs Julian And Rosie Richer **Bred** P McCutcheon **Trained** Hambleton, N Yorks

FOCUS

A run-of-the-mill sprint handicap but the time was good for the conditions. The winner is rated back to his 2yo C&D win.

T/Plt: £32.80 to a £1 stake. Pool of £39180.27 - 870.52 winning tickets. T/Qpdt: £10.20 to a £1 stake. Pool of £2375.10 - 172.10 winning tickets. RY

1981 LINGFIELD (L-H)

Friday, May 10

OFFICIAL GOING: Turf - good; all-weather - standard

Wind: Fresh, half behind Weather: Fine

2223 LADBROKES CLASSIFIED STKS — 1m 2f

2:05 (2:05) (Class 5) 3-Y-O **£2,726** (£805; £402) **Stalls** Low

Form RPR

0-1 **1** **Ray Ward (IRE)**^{105} 373 3-9-0 74 MartinLane 3 86+
(David Simcock) *hld up in last: gd prog on outer 3f out to ld 2f out: shkn up over 1f out: styd on wl: readily* **5/2**^{1}

04-1 **2** *1 1/2* **Of Course Darling**^{20} 1697 3-9-0 74 WilliamBuick 1 83
(Ed Dunlop) *chsd ldng pair: pushed along 4f out: clsd towards outer to chal 2f out: chsd wnr after: styd on but a hld* **7/2**^{3}

-143 **3** *3 1/2* **Rouge Nuage (IRE)**^{41} 1246 3-8-9 74 RyanTate(5) 4 76
(Conrad Allen) *hld up in 4th: rdn and nt qckn 3f out: sn outpcd: kpt on to take 3rd 1f out but racd awkwardly: no imp* **9/2**

60-1 **4** *8* **Beat Of The Drum (IRE)**^{29} 1499 3-9-0 73 RichardHughes 6 61
(Richard Hannon) *trckd ldr: shkn up over 2f out: nt qckn and btn wl over 1f out: wknd fnl f* **3/1**^{2}

1-46 **5** *3* **Living The Life (IRE)**^{20} 1683 3-9-0 75 (p) FergusSweeney 2 55
(Jamie Osborne) *s.i.s: t.k.h: hld up in 5th: styd on inner in st: no prog over 2f out: sn wknd* **7/1**

3-50 **6** *1 1/2* **Magical Rose (IRE)**^{16} 1770 3-9-0 73 SebSanders 5 52
(Paul D'Arcy) *led: rdn and hdd 2f out: styd on inner and wknd qckly* **16/1**

2m 11.87s (1.37) **Going Correction** +0.025s/f (Good) **6 Ran SP% 112.4**
Speed ratings (Par 99): **95,93,91,84,82 81**
toteswingers 1&2 £1.40, 2&3 £6.70, 1&3 £4.60 CSF £11.56 TOTE £4.50: £1.80, £2.50; EX 10.90 Trifecta £39.60 Pool: £1522.63 - 28.82 winning units..
Owner Mrs Fitri Hay **Bred** Churchtown House Stud **Trained** Newmarket, Suffolk

The Form Book Flat, Raceform Ltd, Compton, RG20 6NL.

FOCUS
Not that a strong a contest, but the front two are progressive and the form is rated positively.

2224 LADBROKES MAIDEN STKS 7f
2:35 (2:37) (Class 5) 3-Y-O+ **£2,726** (£805; £402) **Stalls** High

Form RPR
-5 **1** **Jammy Guest (IRE)**[23] 1618 3-9-0 0 SebSanders 5 84+
(George Margarson) *mde all and sn crossed to nr side rail: pushed along firmly to assert over 1f out: styd on wl* **2/1**[1]
23-3 **2** 2 ¼ **Caramack**[11] 1881 3-9-0 76 RichardHughes 1 78
(Richard Hannon) *prom: trckd wnr after 3f: shkn up 2f out: styd on but no imp* **3/1**[3]
3 **3** 2 ½ **Realize**[18] 1732 3-9-0 0 HayleyTurner 3 72
(Hughie Morrison) *hld up in midfield: prog to chse ldng pair 2f out: shkn up and styd on same pce* **9/2**
45- **4** ½ **Cloudwalker (USA)**[188] 7555 3-8-9 0 WilliamBuick 10 65+
(Ed Vaughan) *hld up in midfield: pushed along over 2f out: tk 4th fnl f: shkn up and kpt on* **11/4**[2]
00- **5** 10 **Tychaios**[189] 7517 3-8-7 0 JeanVanOvermeire(7) 8 44
(Stuart Williams) *racd against rail: chsd wnr 3f: styd handy tl wknd rapidly over 1f out* **100/1**
0-0 **6** 1 **Sonnetation (IRE)**[11] 1881 3-8-4 0 NathanAlison(5) 4 37
(Jim Boyle) *t.k.h: hld up in midfield: no prog over 2f out: wknd over 1f out* **100/1**
7 1 ½ **Gone Dutch** 3-9-0 0 MartinLane 2 38+
(James Fanshawe) *dwlt: hld up in rr: pushed along over 2f out: wknd wl over 1f out* **33/1**
8 6 **Cauberg** 3-9-0 0 JimCrowley 11 22
(Roger Varian) *hld up in rr: pushed along and no prog over 2f out: sn wknd qckly* **16/1**
9 3 ¾ **Echoes Of War** 4-9-9 0 MarkCoumbe(3) 9 16
(Michael Attwater) *dwlt: rn green in rr: reminder and hung lft over 2f out: wknd and bhd after* **100/1**
0- **10** 12 **Later In Life**[246] 5970 4-9-7 0 TomMcLaughlin 6
(Christine Dunnett) *racd on outer: in tch in rr tl wknd rapidly over 2f out: t.o* **200/1**

1m 22.88s (-0.42) **Going Correction** +0.025s/f (Good)
WFA 3 from 4yo 12lb 10 Ran SP% **115.5**
Speed ratings (Par 103): **103,100,97,97,85 84,82,75,71,57**
toteswingers 1&2 £1.10, 2&3 £1.60, 1&3 £2.10 CSF £8.19 TOTE £3.00: £1.50, £1.20, £1.50; EX 7.30 Trifecta £20.80 Pool: £2334.70 - 84.09 winning units..
Owner John Guest Racing **Bred** Robert Power Bloodstock Ltd **Trained** Newmarket, Suffolk

FOCUS
The stands' side is often the place to be on the straight track here, but it might be worth noting the rail had been moved in a little since last season, presumably in an attempt to reduce the bias. The winner of this race was positioned tight against the fence, but was basically just the best horse on the day. The second gives the form perspective.

2225 LADBROKES H'CAP (LADY AMATEUR RIDERS) 7f
3:05 (3:07) (Class 5) (0-75,73) 4-Y-O+ **£2,634** (£810; £405) **Stalls** High

Form RPR
-065 **1** **Space War**[13] 1819 6-9-7 66 (t) AnnaHesketh(7) 3 75
(Michael Easterby) *s.s: swtchd to nr side and hld up in last: detached early: stdy prog fr 1/2-way: trckd ldrs and waiting for a gap 1f out: urged along and styd on to ld last 75yds* **5/1**[2]
6100 **2** nk **Greyfriarschorista**[13] 1849 6-10-1 70 (p) MissCBoxall(3) 10 78
(Tom Keddy) *racd one off rail: w ldr: rdn 2f out: stl upsides 100yds out: jst outpcd nr fin* **10/1**
0-56 **3** ½ **Ghostwing**[15] 1780 6-9-13 65 (vt) MissSBrotherton 5 72
(Luke Dace) *trckd ldng quintet: clsd against rail fr 2f out: led over 1f out: fnd little in front and hdd last 75yds* **8/1**
300/ **4** 3 ½ **Kilburn**[649] 1269 9-10-4 70 MissZoeLilly 9 68
(Alastair Lidderdale) *hld up in midfield and nt on terms: urged along furiously fr over 2f out: styd on fr over 1f out to take 4th nr fin* **16/1**
0-00 **5** ½ **Rigolleto (IRE)**[20] 1694 5-9-12 69 MissJoannaMason(5) 11 66
(Anabel K Murphy) *racd against rail: led to over 1f out: wknd fnl f* **20/1**
52- **6** ½ **Rulesn'regulations**[169] 7827 7-9-11 70 MissJenniferPowell(7) 4 65
(Alastair Lidderdale) *racd wdst of five ldrs: lost pl and urged along wl over 2f out: n.d over 1f out* **6/1**[3]
0040 **7** ¾ **Dutch Old Master**[24] 1599 4-10-4 73 MissHayleyMoore(3) 1 66
(Gary Moore) *hld up in last trio: stdy prog on wd outside fr 3f out: no hdwy over 1f out* **8/1**
2310 **8** 3 ¼ **Amethyst Dawn (IRE)**[15] 1798 7-9-10 67 (t) MissPhillipaTutty(5) 8 52
(Andrew Reid) *t.k.h: racd three off rail: w ldrs to 3f out: sn lost pl and btn* **16/1**
0662 **9** hd **Fred Willetts (IRE)**[8] 1947 5-9-11 68 MissHDoyle(5) 6 52
(David Evans) *racd four off rail: w ldrs 2f: lost pl sharply and reminder: tried to rally over 2f out: wknd over 1f out* **11/4**[1]
3160 **10** 1 ½ **Divine Rule (IRE)**[9] 1925 5-9-0 59 oh6 (v) MissRBIngram(7) 2 39
(Laura Mongan) *racd on outer: hld up in last trio: no prog 3f out: wl btn after* **25/1**
65-1 **11** 2 ¼ **Magical Speedfit (IRE)**[20] 1694 8-9-13 70 MissKMargarson(5) 7 45
(George Margarson) *hld up in midfield: pushed along and lost pl 3f out: wl in rr after* **10/1**

1m 24.04s (0.74) **Going Correction** +0.025s/f (Good) 11 Ran SP% **118.4**
Speed ratings (Par 103): **96,95,95,91,90 89,89,85,85,83 80**
toteswingers 1&2 £0.00, 2&3 £30.10, 1&3 £7.90 CSF £54.74 CT £406.88 TOTE £5.50: £2.10, £5.00, £2.60; EX 83.70 Trifecta £722.80 Pool: £1953.63 - 2.02 winning units..
Owner R F H Partnership & Brian Padgett **Bred** Shutford Stud And O F Waller **Trained** Sheriff Hutton, N Yorks
■ Anna Hesketh's first winner.
■ Stewards' Enquiry : Miss Zoe Lilly seven-day ban: used whip above permitted level (May 24,28,31,Jun 1,8,12,14)

FOCUS
The lead was contested and the pace looked good. The winner is capable of doing good bit better on this evidence.

2226 LADBROKES MAIDEN FILLIES' STKS 6f
3:40 (3:43) (Class 5) 3-Y-O **£2,726** (£805; £402) **Stalls** High

Form RPR
0 **1** **At A Clip**[21] 1666 3-9-0 0 JimCrowley 4 71+
(Ralph Beckett) *w ldr and three off the rail: rdn 2f out: narrow ld 1f out: drvn out* **5/4**[1]
40-4 **2** 1 **Hasbah (IRE)**[49] 1122 3-9-0 64 WilliamBuick 2 68
(Peter Chapple-Hyam) *chsd ldng quartet but sn pushed along: rdn 2f out: styd on to take 2nd nr fin* **8/1**
340- **3** hd **It's Taboo**[239] 6160 3-9-0 75 JimmyFortune 6 67
(Mark Usher) *led against rail but pressed: hrd rdn and hdd 1f out: kpt on but lost 2nd nr fin* **3/1**[2]
30-6 **4** 1 ¼ **Mrs Warren**[23] 1608 3-9-0 57 WilliamCarson 10 64
(Charles Hills) *chsd ldng trio: shkn up 2f out: kpt on but nvr able to chal* **6/1**[3]
6- **5** ¾ **Birdie Queen**[364] 2039 3-9-0 0 TedDurcan 7 61+
(John Best) *hld up in 6th and sn sme way off the pce: nudged along fr 2f out: kpt on steadily after: nrst fin* **33/1**
02 **6** 4 ½ **Is This Love (IRE)**[56] 1019 3-9-0 0 FergusSweeney 3 48
(Jamie Osborne) *stdd s: hld up in 7th and sme way off the pce: nudged along and no real prog fnl 2f* **20/1**
6- **7** 2 ¾ **Dee Aitch Dove**[190] 7498 3-9-0 0 PatCosgrave 5 43+
(George Baker) *w ldng pair tl sed to wobble 2f out: wknd qckly over 1f out* **25/1**
64- **8** 8 **Speed Date**[247] 5943 3-9-0 0 MartinLane 1 16
(Tobias B P Coles) *hld up: a wl in rr: bhd fnl 2f* **16/1**
9 nk **Toffee Shot** 3-9-0 0 SebSanders 9 15
(J W Hills) *outpcd in last trio: a bhd* **10/1**
10 11 **Raymond's Dream** 3-8-9 0 DannyBrock(5) 8
(J R Jenkins) *outpcd in last trio: a bhd: t.o* **66/1**

1m 11.03s (-0.17) **Going Correction** +0.025s/f (Good) 10 Ran SP% **122.9**
Speed ratings (Par 96): **102,100,100,98,97 91,88,77,77,62**
toteswingers 1&2 £2.80, 2&3 £3.90, 1&3 £4.00 CSF £12.85 TOTE £1.90: £1.10, £3.00, £1.30; EX 18.50 Trifecta £38.00 Pool: £1733.44 - 34.13 winning units..
Owner Lady Cobham **Bred** Lady Cobham **Trained** Kimpton, Hants
■ Stewards' Enquiry : Jim Crowley caution: careless riding.

FOCUS
A weak race of its type, but at least one or two of these can do better, particularly the winner.

2227 LADBROKES DOWNLOAD THE APP H'CAP 5f
4:15 (4:16) (Class 4) (0-85,85) 4-Y-O+ **£4,690** (£1,395; £697; £348) **Stalls** High

Form RPR
01-6 **1** **Blanc De Chine (IRE)**[22] 1652 4-9-2 80 JimmyFortune 3 89
(Peter Makin) *mde all and crossed sharply to rail after 1f: rdn fnl f: hld on nr fin* **12/1**
0-04 **2** ½ **Titus Gent**[14] 1814 8-8-13 80 RyanClark(3) 9 87+
(Jeremy Gask) *racd against rail: hmpd by wnr after 1f: chsng after: drvn and tk 2nd ins fnl f: clsng at fin* **5/1**[3]
-415 **3** ¾ **Sandfrankskipsgo**[16] 1765 4-9-1 79 IanMongan 2 84
(Peter Crate) *mostly chsd wnr: rdn over 1f out: kpt on but lost 2nd nr fin* **7/2**[1]
-110 **4** ½ **Diamond Charlie (IRE)**[16] 1765 5-9-7 85 SebSanders 7 88
(Simon Dow) *chsd ldrs and sn swtchd towards outer: drvn over 1f out: nt qckn and hld fnl f* **7/2**[1]
020- **5** ½ **First In Command (IRE)**[222] 6716 8-8-11 82 (t) EoinWalsh(7) 6 83
(Daniel Mark Loughnane) *hld up in last pair: vigorously drvn and fair burst to cl on ldrs fnl f: hopeless task* **6/1**
1000 **6** 1 ½ **Woolfall Sovereign (IRE)**[25] 1581 7-8-9 73 TomQueally 8 69
(George Margarson) *a towards rr: rdn and no prog sn after 1/2-way* **9/2**[2]
000- **7** ¾ **Best Be Careful (IRE)**[191] 7483 5-8-7 71 HarryBentley 4 64
(Mark Usher) *prom whn hmpd by wnr after 1f and lost pl: rdn over 1f out: fdd* **12/1**
-034 **8** ¾ **Gung Ho Jack**[105] 372 4-8-8 72 LiamKeniry 5 62
(John Best) *hld up in last pair: shkn up and no prog 2f out* **16/1**

57.4s (-0.80) **Going Correction** +0.025s/f (Good) 8 Ran SP% **114.8**
Speed ratings (Par 105): **107,106,105,104,103 101,99,98**
toteswingers 1&2 £14.90, 2&3 £4.40, 1&3 £5.70 CSF £70.90 CT £259.21 TOTE £8.30: £3.10, £3.10, £1.60; EX 51.90 Trifecta £161.90 Pool: £2515.19 - 11.64 winning units..
Owner R P Marchant & Mrs E Lee **Bred** Newlands House Stud **Trained** Ogbourne Maisey, Wilts
■ Stewards' Enquiry : Jimmy Fortune two-day ban: careless riding (May 24-25)

FOCUS
This race was won in the first furlong when Jimmy Fortune (two-day careless riding ban) switched the front-running Blanc De Chine onto the stands' rail, forcing Titus Gent to be snatched up and leaving that one with little room to make a challenge until it was too late. Straightforward form.

2228 LADBROKES BET ON YOUR MOBILE H'CAP 1m (P)
4:50 (4:51) (Class 5) (0-70,70) 4-Y-O+ **£2,726** (£805; £402) **Stalls** High

Form RPR
-331 **1** **Midnight Feast**[18] 1717 5-9-3 66 (v) KierenFox 1 74
(Lee Carter) *t.k.h: trckd ldng pair: clsd towards inner over 1f out: drvn to ld ins fnl f: styd on* **9/2**[2]
-420 **2** ½ **Bajan Story**[23] 1617 4-8-10 59 LiamKeniry 8 66
(Michael Blanshard) *trckd ldr: chal and upsides 1f out: nt qckn but kpt on to press wnr nr fin* **16/1**
3503 **3** ½ **Mafi (IRE)**[15] 1780 5-9-3 66 (t) RobertHavlin 7 72
(Mark Hoad) *trckd ldng pair: rdn 2f out: cl enough but nt qckn jst over 1f out: styd on fnl f* **7/1**
6/22 **4** ½ **Piccolo Mondo**[11] 1873 7-8-11 60 FergusSweeney 4 65
(Philip Hide) *led: rdn 2f out: hdd and one pce ins fnl f* **9/2**[2]
2360 **5** hd **West Leake (IRE)**[9] 1925 7-9-1 64 TomMcLaughlin 2 68
(Paul Burgoyne) *t.k.h: hld up in last trio: gd prog jst over 1f out: chsd ldrs ins fnl f: styd on same pce* **12/1**
000- **6** 2 **May Be Some Time**[184] 7639 5-9-7 70 (t) TomQueally 6 69+
(Stuart Kittow) *hld up in last trio: rdn and struggling in last over 2f out: kpt on fnl f* **7/1**
3401 **7** hd **Mister Green (FR)**[9] 1925 7-9-1 69 6ex (b) JemmaMarshall(5) 3 68
(David Flood) *hld up in midfield: effrt on inner 2f out: nt qckn over 1f out: no prog after* **10/1**
5362 **8** shd **Homeward Strut**[18] 1717 4-9-2 65 (b) JimCrowley 5 64
(Laura Mongan) *hld up in midfield: rdn and nt qckn over 1f out: wl btn after* **4/1**[1]
60-0 **9** 2 ½ **Uncle Fred**[9] 1925 8-9-2 65 GeorgeBaker 10 58
(Patrick Chamings) *stdd s fr wd draw: hld up in last trio: effrt on outer 3f out: no prog over 1f out: wknd* **5/1**[3]

1m 37.95s (-0.25) **Going Correction** +0.001s/f 9 Ran SP% **120.7**
Speed ratings (Par 103): **101,100,100,99,99 97,97,97,94**
toteswingers 1&2 £12.90, 2&3 £17.60, 1&3 £6.40 CSF £75.98 CT £511.00 TOTE £7.40: £2.00, £5.50, £2.00; EX 99.30 Trifecta £637.08 Pool: £2587.78 - 3.04 winning units..
Owner One More Bid Partnership **Bred** Whitsbury Manor Stud **Trained** Epsom, Surrey

FOCUS
A modest handicap run at just a fair pace. The second and third offer perspective.

2229 LADBROKES MOBILE H'CAP 7f (P)
5:20 (5:20) (Class 5) (0-75,75) 3-Y-O **£2,726** (£805; £402) **Stalls** Low

Form RPR
5-26 1 **Arctic Admiral (IRE)**[16] 1769 3-8-11 **70**...... WilliamTwiston-Davies(5) 1 81
(Richard Hannon) *trckd ldr: shkn up 2f out: clsd to ld last 150yds: rdn clr* **9/4**[1]
43-3 2 3 ¼ **Seven Of Clubs (IRE)**[28] 1515 3-9-7 **75**.................(b) StevieDonohoe 5 76
(Noel Quinlan) *led: kicked on 2f out: hdd last 150yds: fdd nr fin* **7/1**
221- 3 2 ¼ **Maid A Million**[155] 8006 3-9-3 **71**................................ SebSanders 2 66
(David Elsworth) *t.k.h: hld up: bmpd over 5f out: rdn over 2f out: kpt on one pce to take 3rd ins fnl f* **3/1**[3]
531 4 1 **Botteen (IRE)**[73] 807 3-9-3 **71**................................ AdamBeschizza 4 63
(William Haggas) *scratchy to post: trckd ldng pair: rdn on inner 2f out: nt qckn and sn btn: wknd fnl f* **5/2**[2]
55-0 5 1 ¾ **Invincible Cara (IRE)**[22] 1640 3-9-7 **75**................................ TedDurcan 6 63+
(Ed Dunlop) *stdd s: tk fierce hold and bmpd rival over 5f out: effrt in 4th 1/2-way: rdn and no prog 2f out: wl btn over 1f out* **10/1**
20-0 6 6 **Royal Caper**[9] 1928 3-8-8 **62**................................ JohnFahy 3 33+
(John Ryan) *t.k.h: hld up: meat in sandwich over 5f out and dropped to last: struggling over 2f out: sn bhd* **20/1**

1m 24.49s (-0.31) **Going Correction** +0.001s/f **6** Ran SP% **110.7**
Speed ratings (Par 99): **101,97,94,93,91 84**
toteswingers 1&2 £5.00, 2&3 £3.80, 1&3 £1.70 CSF £17.56 TOTE £3.00: £2.30, £2.70; EX 25.80 Trifecta £56.00 Pool: £1393.99 - 18.66 winning units..
Owner P D Merritt **Bred** Miss Adelaide Foley & Brian Gordon **Trained** East Everleigh, Wilts

FOCUS
This modest race rather fell apart. The winner did it in good style and the runner-up and time offer perspective.
T/Plt: £63.40 to a £1 stake. Pool of £55960.41 -643.96 winning tickets. T/Qpdt: £33.30 to a £1 stake. Pool of £3698.76 - 82.0 winning tickets. JN

1680 NOTTINGHAM (L-H)
Friday, May 10

OFFICIAL GOING: Good to firm changing to good after race 2 (5:40)
Wind: Moderate half against Weather: Cloudy with sunny periods

2230 FREEBETS.CO.UK FREE BETS ON YOUR MOBILE MEDIAN AUCTION MAIDEN FILLIES' STKS 5f 13y
5:10 (5:11) (Class 5) 2-Y-O **£3,234** (£962; £481; £240) **Stalls** High

Form RPR
1 **Sandiva (IRE)** 2-9-0 0................................ TomEaves 4 92+
(Richard Fahey) *trckd ldng pair: green and pushed along 2f out: hdwy and nt clr run over 1f out: sn swtchd lft to outer: rdn and qcknd wl to ld ins fnl f: sn clr* **15/8**[1]
2 6 **Stepping Out (IRE)** 2-9-0 0................................ NeilCallan 1 69
(Tom Dascombe) *qckly away and disp ld tl led over 1f out: sn rdn and edgd rt: hdd ins fnl f: kpt on same pce* **10/3**[2]
3 1 ½ **Misty Sparkler** 2-9-0 0................................ DaneO'Neill 7 63
(Brian Meehan) *disp ld: rdn along wl over 1f out: one pce ent fnl f* **11/1**
3 4 2 ¼ **Sunningdale Rose (IRE)**[10] 1910 2-9-0 0................................ LukeMorris 3 55
(Michael Bell) *chsd ldng pair: rdn along over 2f out: sn one pce* **9/2**[3]
5 4 ½ **Chance Of Romance (IRE)** 2-9-0 0................................ AdamKirby 5 39
(Clive Cox) *green and sn pushed along in rr: sme hdwy 2f out: nvr a factor* **9/2**[3]
6 7 **Hustle Bustle (IRE)** 2-9-0 0................................ SeanLevey 2 14
(David Brown) *chsd ldrs: green and rdn along bef 1/2-way: sn outpcd* **16/1**

1m 1.28s (-0.22) **Going Correction** -0.275s/f (Firm) **6** Ran SP% **108.4**
Speed ratings (Par 90): **90,80,78,74,67 56**
toteswingers 1&2 £1.60, 1&3 £4.90, 2&3 £3.50 CSF £7.65 TOTE £3.00: £2.20, £1.60; EX 8.60 Trifecta £51.80 Pool: £2204.42 - 31.88 winning units..
Owner Middleham Park Racing XXX **Bred** Denis McDonnell **Trained** Musley Bank, N Yorks

FOCUS
Outer track used. Ground on the fast side of good although there was quite a heavy shower just before racing, on ground that had already been watered. This fillies' maiden has thrown up some useful types in recent years, notably subsequent Albany Stakes winner Habaayib and Hilary Needler winner Dozy. The winner impressed and looks a very useful 2yo.

2231 FREEBETTINGTIPS.CO.UK FREE BETTING TIPS MAIDEN FILLIES' STKS 1m 75y
5:40 (5:41) (Class 5) 3-Y-O **£3,234** (£962; £481; £240) **Stalls** Centre

Form RPR
5-2 1 **Iffraaj Pink (IRE)**[13] 1828 3-9-0 0................................ AndreaAtzeni 12 78+
(Roger Varian) *trckd ldrs on outer: hdwy and cl up 4f out: rdn wl over 1f out: styd on to ld ins fnl f: edgd lft and kpt on wl towards fin* **7/4**[1]
3 2 nk **Wall Of Sound**[13] 1828 3-9-0 0................................ SeanLevey 3 77
(Tom Dascombe) *sn led: rdn along and hdd wl over 2f out: cl up on inner and ev ch ins fnl f: drvn: edgd rt and no ex towards fin* **5/2**[2]
2-0 3 2 **A Star In My Eye (IRE)**[22] 1636 3-9-0 0................................ NeilCallan 6 74+
(Kevin Ryan) *a.p: cl up 4f out: led wl over 2f out: rdn wl over 1f out: hdd ins fnl f: hld whn n.m.r towards fin* **10/1**
55 4 3 ¼ **Kingston Eucalypt**[56] 1009 3-9-0 0................................ MickyFenton 11 65+
(Ed Vaughan) *towards rr: hdwy over 2f out: nt clr run and swtchd rt over 1f out: rdn and styd on strly fnl f: nrst fin* **100/1**
24 5 1 ¾ **Guishan**[24] 1595 3-9-0 0................................ AndrewMullen 10 61
(Michael Appleby) *chsd ldrs: hdwy 3f out: rdn over 2f out: sn no imp* **100/1**
6 shd **Meddling** 3-9-0 0................................ SilvestreDeSousa 2 61
(Sir Michael Stoute) *in tch: hdwy on inner to chse ldrs 3f out: rdn along 2f out: kpt on one pce* **15/2**[3]
7 nk **Kenny's Girl (IRE)** 3-9-0 0................................ MartinDwyer 8 60
(William Muir) *towards rr: hdwy wl over 1f out: kpt on appr fnl f: nrst fin* **28/1**
- 8 ¾ **Crave** 3-8-9 0................................ RobertTart(5) 5 58+
(William Jarvis) *hld up in midfield: hdwy over 3f out: swtchd rt to outer and chsd ldrs 2f out: sn rdn: edgd rt and no imp appr fnl f* **33/1**
9 1 **Cosseted** 3-9-0 0................................ LukeMorris 7 56
(James Fanshawe) *s.i.s: a in rr* **33/1**
0 10 3 **Nashrah (USA)**[22] 1640 3-9-0 0................................ DaneO'Neill 13 49
(J W Hills) *s.i.s: a in rr* **50/1**
6- 11 1 **Vega Dance (IRE)**[195] 7403 3-9-0 0................................ AdamKirby 1 47
(Clive Cox) *chsd ldrs: hdwy on inner and cl up after 3f: rdn along over 2f out: grad wknd* **17/2**
0- 12 2 ½ **Sugar Coated (IRE)**[188] 7553 3-9-0 0................................ TomEaves 14 41
(Michael Bell) *a towards rr* **33/1**
0-20 13 1 **Sinaadi (IRE)**[8] 1958 3-9-0 72................................ ChrisCatlin 9 39
(Clive Brittain) *nvr bttr than midfield* **14/1**
0-5 14 3 ¼ **Rapid Rabbit Foot**[15] 1777 3-8-7 0................................ IanBurns(7) 4 31
(John Holt) *chsd ldrs: rdn along over 3f out: sn wknd* **100/1**

1m 46.23s (-2.77) **Going Correction** -0.275s/f (Firm) **14** Ran SP% **120.2**
Speed ratings (Par 96): **102,101,99,96,94 94,94,93,92,89 88,86,85,81**
toteswingers 1&2 £2.20, 1&3 £3.90, 2&3 £4.90 CSF £5.58 TOTE £2.70: £1.10, £1.10, £3.00; EX 5.90 Trifecta £38.70 Pool: £2216.12 - 42.86 winning units..
Owner Mrs Fitri Hay **Bred** Stock Vale Ltd **Trained** Newmarket, Suffolk

FOCUS
This could be quite a useful piece of maiden form given the front two had shown already shown significant promise in the same race last time and there was also real encouragement from a few in behind. Winners will come out of this race, but the fourth and fifth are slight doubts over the form.

2232 FREEBETS.CO.UK FREE BETS H'CAP 1m 75y
6:15 (6:15) (Class 4) (0-80,79) 4-Y-O+ **£5,175** (£1,540; £769; £384) **Stalls** Centre

Form RPR
4-30 1 **Invincible Hero (IRE)**[13] 1840 6-9-1 **76**................................ NeilFarley(3) 6 89
(Declan Carroll) *set gd pce: rdn along and hdd wl over 1f out: chsd ldr and drvn over 1f out: styd on gamely u.p fnl f to ld again last 50yds* **14/1**
10-6 2 ½ **Ascription (IRE)**[25] 1576 4-9-6 **78**................................(t[1]) MartinDwyer 1 90+
(Hugo Palmer) *towards rr early: hdwy into midfield 1/2-way: effrt on inner to ld wl over 2f out and sn rdn clr: drvn ins fnl f: hdd and no ex last 50yds* **9/1**
-664 3 6 **Kiwi Bay**[13] 1831 8-9-5 **77**................................ TomEaves 4 75
(Michael Dods) *t.k.h early: trckd wnr: effrt over 2f out: sn rdn and one pce* **9/2**[1]
050- 4 1 **Stellar Express (IRE)**[204] 7202 4-9-3 **75**................................ AndrewMullen 5 71
(Michael Appleby) *chsd ldrs: hdwy on inner over 3f out: rdn over 2f out: kpt on same pce* **8/1**[3]
3361 5 nk **Lord Of The Dance (IRE)**[13] 1827 7-8-13 **76**................................ RobertTart(5) 9 71+
(Michael Mullineaux) *towards rr: hdwy wl over 2f out: rdn and styd on appr fnl f: nrst fin* **12/1**
451- 6 1 ½ **Self Employed**[234] 6341 6-9-1 **73**................................ MickyFenton 3 65
(Garry Woodward) *chsd ldng pair: rdn along wl over 2f out: grad wknd* **25/1**
12-0 7 1 ½ **Sword In Hand**[29] 1500 4-9-4 **76**................................ NeilCallan 13 64
(Alan Jarvis) *in tch: hdwy on outer 3f out: rdn to chse ldrs over 2f out: drvn and wknd over 1f out* **6/1**[2]
100- 8 5 **Woolston Ferry (IRE)**[214] 6931 7-9-3 **75**................................ DaneO'Neill 14 52
(Henry Candy) *s.i.s: a towards rr* **20/1**
325- 9 1 **Qanan**[219] 6792 4-9-0 **72**................................ AndreaAtzeni 8 46
(Chris Wall) *a towards rr* **8/1**[3]
500- 10 1 **Legendary**[258] 5588 4-9-3 **75**................................ LukeMorris 10 47
(Ed Vaughan) *nvr bttr than midfield* **22/1**
20-3 11 2 ½ **Uncle Dermot (IRE)**[25] 1583 5-9-3 **75**................................ ChrisCatlin 7 41
(Brendan Powell) *chsd ldrs: rdn along 3f out: wknd over 2f out* **10/1**
3-00 12 ¾ **Fabled City (USA)**[13] 1849 4-9-5 **77**................................(t) AdamKirby 2 42
(Clive Cox) *chsd ldrs: rdn along 3f out: wknd over 2f out* **12/1**
-025 13 nk **Rossetti**[18] 1723 5-9-0 **72**................................ SilvestreDeSousa 12 36
(Ian Williams) *a towards rr* **11/1**

1m 45.13s (-3.87) **Going Correction** -0.225s/f (Firm) **13** Ran SP% **117.1**
Speed ratings (Par 105): **110,109,103,102,102 100,99,94,93,92 89,88,88**
toteswingers 1&2 £21.30, 1&3 £13.10, 2&3 £10.40 CSF £128.29 CT £665.50 TOTE £19.40: £5.30, £4.20, £2.40; EX 120.80 Trifecta £814.40 Part won. Pool: £1085.97 - 0.70 winning units..
Owner Mrs Sarah Bryan **Bred** Fortbarrington Stud **Trained** Sledmere, E Yorks

FOCUS
The persistent rain changed the ground from good to firm to good before this race. The winner set a decent gallop but the time was only 8lb faster than the preceding maiden so the winner may not have improved that much.

2233 UWIN.CO.UK FREE GAMES & FREE PRIZES H'CAP 1m 6f 15y
6:50 (6:50) (Class 5) (0-75,72) 3-Y-O **£2,587** (£770; £384; £192) **Stalls** Low

Form RPR
044- 1 **Argent Knight**[158] 7963 3-8-12 **63**................................ TomEaves 2 69+
(William Jarvis) *trckd ldng pair on inner: effrt and nt clr run wl over 1f out: sn swtchd rt and rdn: styd on to ld jst ins fnl f: rdn out* **15/8**[1]
40-5 2 2 **Moaning Butcher**[50] 1103 3-8-6 **57**................................ SilvestreDeSousa 1 58
(Mark Johnston) *set stdy pce: niggled along bef 1/2-way: rdn over 4f out: jnd 3f out: drvn wl over 1f out: hdd jst ins fnl f: kpt on u.p* **11/2**[2]
002 3 4 ½ **Bold Assertion**[17] 1741 3-9-5 **70**................................ LukeMorris 3 65
(John Best) *trckd ldr: pushed along over 3f out: rdn over 2f out: sn wknd* **7/1**[3]
05-6 4 ½ **Dark Justice (IRE)**[50] 1098 3-8-4 **55**................................ AndreaAtzeni 8 49
(Tim Pitt) *trckd ldrs: hdwy on outer 4f out: cl up 3f out: rdn and edgd lft wl over 1f out: sn drvn and wknd* **8/1**
1-13 5 3 **Nine Iron (IRE)**[15] 1776 3-9-2 **72**................................ CharlesBishop(5) 5 62
(Mick Channon) *hld up in rr: effrt and hdwy on outer 3f out: rdn along over 2f out: sn btn* **15/8**[1]

3m 10.7s (3.70) **Going Correction** -0.225s/f (Firm) **5** Ran SP% **108.6**
Speed ratings (Par 99): **80,78,76,76,74**
CSF £12.12 TOTE £3.70: £2.00, £5.80; EX 7.80 Trifecta £39.10 Pool: £1151.14 - 22.07 winning units..
Owner Dr J Walker **Bred** Mr & Mrs A E Pakenham **Trained** Newmarket, Suffolk

FOCUS
The slow time of this contest was probably a result of the rain getting into the ground as the pace looked fairly even. The market got it spot on. The form is not conclusive but the winner should do better.

2234 CONGRATULATIONS SCARBOROUGH AFC H'CAP (JOCKEY CLUB GRASSROOTS MIDDLE DISTANCE SERIES) 1m 2f 50y
7:25 (7:26) (Class 5) (0-75,79) 4-Y-O+ **£2,587** (£770; £384; £192) **Stalls** Low

Form RPR
00-5 1 **Meetings Man (IRE)**[15] 1775 6-8-8 **62**................................(p) TomEaves 6 73
(Micky Hammond) *t.k.h early: trckd ldrs: hdwy 3f out: rdn to ld 1 1/2f out: clr whn edgd rt ins fnl f: kpt on wl* **15/2**
154- 2 3 ¼ **Ashdown Lad**[213] 6964 4-9-0 **73**................................ RobertTart(5) 7 78+
(William Jarvis) *hld up towards rr: stdy hdwy on wd outside over 3f out: rdn to chse ldrs 2f out and sn edgd lft: n.m.r whn swtchd lft ent fnl f: sn drvn and kpt on same pce* **3/1**[2]

The Form Book Flat, Raceform Ltd, Compton, RG20 6NL.

214/ **3** 2 **West Brit (IRE)**224 6409 5-9-7 **75**...(t) SamHitchcott 3 76
(Charlie Longsdon) *cl up: led 1/2-way: rdn wl over 2f out: hdd 1 1/2f out: sn drvn and one pce fnl f* **25/1**

1111 **4** 3/4 **Mubtadi**10 1901 5-9-6 **79** 6ex... ThomasBrown(5) 10 79+
(Ismail Mohammed) *stdd s and hld up in rr: stdy hdwy 1/2-way: trckd ldrs over 2f out: rdn and n.m.r ent fnl f: sn swtchd lft and no imp* **9/4**1

2142 **5** 1 1/4 **Mazij**22 1654 5-8-10 **64**... LukeMorris 8 61
(Peter Hiatt) *led: hdd 1/2-way: cl up: rdn over 3f out: drvn over 2f out and grad wknd* **11/1**

24-4 **6** 1 1/4 **Breaking The Bank**13 1836 4-9-0 **68**... MartinDwyer 9 63
(William Muir) *chsd ldrs: rdn along over 3f out: drvn 2f out and sn one pce* **13/2**3

2010 **7** 9 **West End Lad**25 1569 10-9-1 **72**...(b) MarkCoumbe(3) 5 50
(Roy Bowring) *towards rr: gd hdwy to join ldrs on outer after 3f: cl up 4f out: rdn along 3f out: drvn and wknd over 2f out* **20/1**

324 **8** 6 **Vastly (USA)**39 1296 4-9-2 **70**... DaneO'Neill 1 36
(Julia Feilden) *in tch: rdn along over 3f out: sn wknd* **12/1**

000/ **9** 12 **Seven Summits (IRE)**671 3867 6-9-2 **70**... MickyFenton 2 14
(Sophie Leech) *in tch: rdn along 4f out: sn wknd* **50/1**

-665 **10** 61 **King Vahe (IRE)**13 1827 4-8-10 **64**...(v) NeilCallan 11
(Alan Jarvis) *a in rr: bhd fnl 3f* **16/1**

2m 12.08s (-2.22) **Going Correction** -0.225s/f (Firm) **10** Ran SP% **113.3**
Speed ratings (Par 103): **99,96,94,94,93 92,85,80,70,21**
toteswingers 1&2 £3.70, 1&3 £32.00, 2&3 £11.60 CSF £28.75 CT £534.23 TOTE £10.10: £1.70, £1.50, £8.50; EX 40.00 Trifecta £1054.30 Part won. Pool: £1405.82 - 0.98 winning units..

Owner Paul,Vicky,Gabby,Tom & Hattie Snook **Bred** Hakan Keles **Trained** Middleham Moor, N Yorks

FOCUS
They went a decent gallop here but the two market leaders, who were both held up at the back, found it very difficult to land a telling blow, which can often be the case for hold-up horses at this venue. The winner is rated to last year's form.

2235 BONUS.CO.UK CASINO BONUS H'CAP 1m 2f 50y
8:00 (8:00) (Class 5) (0-75,75) 3-Y-O **£2,587** (£770; £384; £192) **Stalls** Low

Form RPR
0-12 **1** **Love Marmalade (IRE)**9 1923 3-9-2 **70**... SilvestreDeSousa 6 83
(Mark Johnston) *trckd ldr: hdwy and cl up over 3f out: led 2 1/2f out: rdn wl over 1f out: styd on strly fnl f* **11/8**1

02-5 **2** 3 1/2 **Short Squeeze (IRE)**14 1803 3-9-7 **75**... MartinDwyer 2 81
(Hugo Palmer) *hld up in rr: hdwy on inner 3f out: swtchd rt 2f out: sn rdn to chse wnr: drvn: edgd lft and one pce ins fnl f* **11/4**2

-212 **3** 5 **Mizyen (IRE)**22 1655 3-9-2 **70**... NeilCallan 3 67
(James Tate) *led: rdn along and jnd 3f out: hdd 2 1/2f out: sn drvn and grad wknd* **7/2**3

126- **4** 5 **Kolonel Kirkup**213 6955 3-9-6 **74**... TomEaves 5 61
(Michael Dods) *trckd ldng pair: effrt 3f out: rdn along 2f out: sn wknd* **16/1**

-102 **5** hd **Mixed Message (IRE)**8 1965 3-9-0 **68**... AndrewMullen 8 55
(John Mackie) *trckd ldng pair on outer: pushed along wl over 3f out: rdn wl over 2f out: sn btn* **13/2**

2m 12.77s (-1.53) **Going Correction** -0.225s/f (Firm) **5** Ran SP% **110.2**
Speed ratings (Par 99): **97,94,90,86,86**
CSF £5.42 TOTE £2.20: £1.40, £1.70; EX 6.80 Trifecta £11.00 Pool: £1025.72 - 99.46 winning units..

Owner Crone Stud Farms Ltd **Bred** Stonethorn Stud Farms Ltd **Trained** Middleham Moor, N Yorks

FOCUS
A sound run handicap and a decent time. The winner took advantage of a good mark.

2236 FREEBETS.CO.UK DOWNLOAD OUR APP APPRENTICE H'CAP 6f 15y
8:35 (8:36) (Class 6) (0-60,61) 4-Y-O+ **£1,940** (£577; £288; £144) **Stalls** High

Form RPR
1106 **1** **Divertimenti (IRE)**18 1731 9-8-12 **56**...(b) AdamMcLean(5) 15 69
(Roy Bowring) *qckly away: mde all: rdn clr wl over 1f out: unchal* **14/1**

3603 **2** 9 **Prigsnov Dancer (IRE)**34 1395 8-8-7 **46**...(p) TobyAtkinson 7 30
(Deborah Sanderson) *trckd ldrs: hdwy 2f out: sn rdn to chse wnr: drvn and no imp fnl f* **20/1**

0005 **3** 1 3/4 **Minty Jones**38 1305 4-8-7 **46** oh1...(v) RobertTart 16 25
(Michael Mullineaux) *towards rr: hdwy 2f out: swtchd lft and rdn over 1f out: kpt on fnl f* **33/1**

43-0 **4** 1 1/4 **Dancing Maite**124 86 8-8-11 **53**...(b) NoelGarbutt(3) 6 28
(Roy Bowring) *chsd ldrs: rdn along 2f out: sn drvn and one pce* **12/1**

1211 **5** 1 **Ace Master**28 1521 5-9-7 **60**...(b) DeclanBates 4 31
(Roy Bowring) *chsd wnr: rdn along wl over 2f out: drvn wl over 1f out and grad wknd* **4/1**2

6644 **6** 3/4 **Floralys (USA)**29 1503 4-9-4 **60**...1 DannyBrock(3) 13 29
(Amy Weaver) *in rr: swtchd to wd outside and hdwy to chse ldrs over 2f out: sn rdn and n.d* **16/1**

2441 **7** 5 **Thorpe Bay**2 2170 4-9-8 **61** 6ex... CharlesBishop 3 14
(Michael Appleby) *chsd ldrs on outer: rdn along 2f out: sn drvn and wknd* **11/4**1

3404 **8** 3/4 **Sextons House (IRE)**17 1748 5-8-3 **47**...(b) AaronJones(5) 14
(Alan McCabe) *a in rr* **8/1**3

0-00 **9** 3/4 **Hinton Admiral**120 143 9-8-13 **55**... RyanWhile(3) 10
(Pat Eddery) *chsd ldrs: rdn along wl over 2f out: sn wknd* **16/1**

-200 **10** 4 **Village Green**52 1079 4-8-13 **55**...(v1) JacobButterfield(3) 1
(Ollie Pears) *a in rr* **16/1**

1m 15.3s (0.60) **Going Correction** -0.15s/f (Firm) **10** Ran SP% **97.5**
Speed ratings (Par 101): **90,78,75,74,72 71,65,64,63,57**
toteswingers 1&2 £41.40, 2&3 £23.00, 1&3 £95.80 CSF £176.07 CT £4636.08 TOTE £13.40: £3.00, £6.00, £7.90; EX 149.40 Trifecta £325.40 Part won. Pool: £433.94 - 0.01 winning units..

Owner K Nicholls **Bred** Airlie Stud **Trained** Edwinstowe, Notts

FOCUS
A depleted field. Most of these usually ply their trade on the all-weather. The winner is rated back to last May's form.

T/Plt: £51.70 to a £1 stake. Pool of £29148.09 - 411.31 winning tickets. T/Qpdt: £66.10 to a £1 stake. Pool of £1852.62 - 20.74 winning tickets. JR

1839 RIPON (R-H)
Friday, May 10

OFFICIAL GOING: Good (8.4)
Wind: fresh across Weather: cloudy, odd shower

2237 SIS LIVE (S) STKS 1m 1f 170y
5:50 (5:50) (Class 6) 3-4-Y-O **£2,587** (£770; £384; £192) **Stalls** Low

Form RPR
44-2 **1** **Sleepy Haven (IRE)**58 988 3-8-9 **59**... DavidAllan 6 62
(David Barron) *trckd ldr: rdn to ld over 2f out: hdd jst ins fnl f: rallied to ld again nr fin* **2/1**1

030- **2** shd **Her Nibbs**140 8213 4-9-5 **60**... PJMcDonald 9 57
(Micky Hammond) *trckd ldrs: rdn to chal 2f out: led narrowly jst ins fnl f: one pce: hdd nr fin* **5/1**3

550 **3** 3 **Lil Sophella (IRE)**14 1804 4-9-5 **40**... DuranFentiman 5 51
(Patrick Holmes) *hld up in midfield: rdn over 2f out: kpt on to go 3rd ins fnl f: nvr threatened ldng pair* **33/1**

3 **4** hd **Munro Bagger (IRE)**13 1842 4-9-10 **0**... MichaelO'Connell 4 56
(John Quinn) *midfield: trckd ldrs over 3f out: rdn over 2f out: no ex ins fnl f* **10/3**2

5566 **5** 5 **Hollywood All Star (IRE)**45 1183 4-9-10 **47**... JackMitchell 1 45
(William Muir) *hld up in tch: rdn 3f out: wknd over 1f out* **8/1**

403 **6** 3/4 **Bix (IRE)**16 1761 3-8-9 **55**... RoystonFfrench 10 43
(Alan Berry) *sn led: rdn whn hdd over 2f out: sn wknd* **8/1**

0524 **7** 2 3/4 **Ceekay's Girl**13 1842 3-7-11 **49**...(b1) JoeyHaynes(7) 2 32
(Mrs K Burke) *midfield: rdn over 3f out: nvr threatened* **8/1**

60-0 **8** shd **Jomari (IRE)**16 1764 3-8-9 **41**... JamesSullivan 8 37
(Declan Carroll) *trckd ldrs: rdn over 2f out: wknd over 1f out* **50/1**

9 57 **Son Of Neptune** 3-8-6 **0**... DeclanCannon(3) 3
(Nigel Tinkler) *s.i.s: hld up: a bhd: t.o fnl 3f* **28/1**

2m 8.38s (2.98) **Going Correction** +0.30s/f (Good)
WFA 3 from 4yo 15lb **9** Ran SP% **114.8**
Speed ratings (Par 101): **100,99,97,97,93 92,90,90,44**
toteswingers 1&2 £9.10, 2&3 £16.30, 1&3 £5.80 CSF £11.99 TOTE £2.40: £1.02, £4.70, £13.70; EX 17.70 Trifecta £161.90 Pool: £1560.69 - 7.22 winning units..There was no bid for the winner.

Owner T D Barron **Bred** Equine Associates Fr **Trained** Maunby, N Yorks

■ Stewards' Enquiry : David Allan four-day ban: used whip above permitted level (May 24,25,27,28)

FOCUS
The rail on the bend from the back straight to home straight was moved out 5m, adding an additional 12yds to races on the round course. This pace was steady for this weak seller with those prominent always in command. The proximity of the third limits the form.

2238 SIS EARLY MORNING PRODUCT MAIDEN AUCTION STKS 5f
6:20 (6:20) (Class 5) 2-Y-O **£3,234** (£962; £481; £240) **Stalls** High

Form RPR
0 **1** **Rosebay Coral (IRE)**13 1839 2-8-8 **0**... BarryMcHugh 1 66
(Tony Coyle) *mde all: sn swtchd lft to r against stands' rail: rdn over 1f out: kpt on and a holding runner-up* **8/1**3

64 **2** nk **Dotesy (IRE)**18 1718 2-8-5 **0**... PatrickMathers 2 62
(John Quinn) *w ldr: rdn 2f out: kpt on but a jst hld* **15/8**1

3 2 **Tears And Rain (IRE)** 2-8-5 **0**... DuranFentiman 4 55+
(Tim Easterby) *trckd ldng pair: rdn 2f out: no ex ins fnl f* **14/1**

4 1/2 **Talksalot (IRE)** 2-8-10 **0**... JDSmith 3 58
(J S Moore) *s.i.s: sn in tch towards outer: rdn 2f out: no ex ins fnl f* **3/1**2

5 2 1/2 **The Hooded Claw (IRE)** 2-9-0 **0**... DavidAllan 5 55+
(Tim Easterby) *dwlt: hld up in rr: pushed along 1/2-way: nvr threatened* **15/8**1

1m 0.86s (0.86) **Going Correction** -0.075s/f (Good) **5** Ran SP% **112.3**
Speed ratings (Par 93): **90,89,86,85,81**
toteswingers 1&2 £3.10, 2&3 £7.60, 1&3 £10.20 CSF £23.89 TOTE £17.40: £4.40, £1.10; EX 35.20 Trifecta £90.60 Pool: £654.64 - 5.41 winning units..

Owner John L Marriott **Bred** Gerry Cumiskey **Trained** Norton, N Yorks

FOCUS
A modest maiden run at a fair pace, with the two runners with experience dominating. All five showed promise.

2239 SIS - FIRST FOR LATIN AMERICAN RACING H'CAP 6f
6:55 (6:58) (Class 4) (0-85,85) 4-Y-O+ **£4,851** (£1,443; £721; £360) **Stalls** High

Form RPR
0034 **1** **Klynch**6 2007 7-9-3 **81**...(b) JamesSullivan 5 93
(Ruth Carr) *prom: rdn to ld 2f out: edgd rt ins fnl f: kpt on* **6/1**2

21-0 **2** 1 1/2 **Dick Bos**25 1571 4-9-2 **80**... DanielTudhope 6 87+
(David O'Meara) *chsd ldrs: rdn to chse wnr over 1f out: kpt on but a hld* **7/2**1

0-00 **3** 3/4 **Fast Shot**20 1688 5-9-6 **84**... DavidAllan 12 89
(Tim Easterby) *w ldr: rdn over 2f out: kpt on one pce* **15/2**

21-0 **4** 2 **Chooseday (IRE)**41 1232 4-9-7 **85**...(p) AmyRyan 8 84+
(Kevin Ryan) *s.i.s: hld up: pushed along 1/2-way: kpt on fr over 1f out: nvr threatened ldrs* **13/2**3

0530 **5** 1 **Holy Angel (IRE)**20 1694 4-8-1 **72**...(e) RachelRichardson(7) 10 67
(Tim Easterby) *hld up in midfield: pushed along 1/2-way: kpt on fr over 1f out: nvr threatened ldrs* **33/1**

5-54 **6** 2 1/4 **Defence Council (IRE)**22 1644 5-9-3 **81**... DuranFentiman 3 69
(Mel Brittain) *chsd ldrs: rdn over 2f out: wknd fnl f* **12/1**

00-0 **7** 2 3/4 **Indego Blues**20 1692 4-8-8 **72**... PaulQuinn 7 51
(David Nicholls) *dwlt: hld up: pushed along 1/2-way: nvr threatened* **14/1**

2-05 **8** 1 1/4 **Green Park (IRE)**30 1459 10-8-9 **80**...(b) LukeLeadbitter(7) 11 55
(Declan Carroll) *hld up: pushed along 1/2-way: nvr threatened* **40/1**

21-4 **9** 1 1/4 **Half A Billion (IRE)**24 1599 4-8-13 **80**... LeeTopliss(3) 1 51
(Michael Dods) *racd alone far side: a bhd ldrs in main gp* **8/1**

30-0 **9** dht **Planetex (IRE)**20 1692 4-8-9 **73**... MichaelO'Connell 13 44
(John Quinn) *led narrowly: rdn whn hdd 2f out: wknd* **14/1**

110- **11** 4 **Henry Bee**279 4829 4-8-6 **77**... EireannCagney(7) 4 36
(Richard Fahey) *midfield towards outer: wknd fnl 2f* **40/1**

0-02 **12** 1/2 **Baldemar**22 1644 8-8-10 **74**... BarryMcHugh 9 31
(Richard Fahey) *midfield: wknd fnl 2f: eased* **8/1**

1m 11.59s (-1.41) **Going Correction** -0.075s/f (Good) **12** Ran SP% **112.7**
Speed ratings (Par 105): **106,104,103,100,99 96,92,90,89,89 83,83**
toteswingers 1&2 £3.10, 2&3 £7.60, 1&3 £10.20 CSF £24.39 CT £139.49 TOTE £8.10: £2.50, £1.60, £2.70; EX 28.50 Trifecta £184.40 Pool: £864.66 - 3.51 winning units..

Owner Douglas Renton **Bred** J C S Wilson Bloodstock **Trained** Huby, N Yorks

FOCUS
We'll Deal Again broke through the stalls and had to be withdrawn. Plenty of speed on for this competitive, decent handicap, which again favoured those up with the pace. The winner built on this year's form.

2240 SIS INTERNATIONAL H'CAP 1m 1f 170y
7:30 (7:30) (Class 3) (0-90,88) 4-Y-0 **£7,561** (£2,263; £1,131; £566; £282) **Stalls** Low

Form RPR

55-1 **1** **Awake My Soul (IRE)**[15] 1777 4-9-1 **82**....................... DanielTudhope 7 93
(David O'Meara) *mde all: briefly pressed over 2f out: rdn to assert over 1f out: kpt on: shade cosily* **4/1**[1]

-000 **2** *1 ¼* **Muffin McLeay (IRE)**[13] 1840 5-9-0 **86**............................. LMcNiff(5) 4 94
(David Barron) *trckd ldr: rdn over 2f out: kpt on but a hld by wnr* **9/2**[2]

50-1 **3** *2 ½* **Next Edition (IRE)**[7] 1990 5-8-7 **81** 5ex........................ EvaMoscrop(7) 2 84
(Philip Kirby) *hld up in midfield on inner: rdn over 2f out: kpt on to go 3rd fnl 100yds* **9/2**[2]

-003 **4** *1 ½* **Be Perfect (USA)**[13] 1843 4-9-7 **88**.............................. DavidAllan 3 88
(David Nicholls) *in tch: rdn 3f out: one pce and nvr threatened ldrs* **5/1**[3]

1-31 **5** *¾* **Snooky**[17] 1751 4-8-9 **79** ow1.. LeeTopliss(3) 9 77
(Richard Fahey) *trckd ldr: rdn to chal over 2f out: wknd fnl f* **4/1**[1]

4-00 **6** *1 ¼* **Hot Rod Mamma (IRE)**[13] 1819 6-8-7 **74** oh1................ PJMcDonald 1 70
(Dianne Sayer) *s.i.s: hld up in rr: angled lft to outer 2f out: sn rdn and no imp on ldrs* **28/1**

040- **7** *3 ½* **Rio's Rosanna (IRE)**[189] 7519 6-9-6 **87**............................ AmyRyan 8 76
(Richard Whitaker) *racd keenly: in tch on outer: rdn over 3f out: wknd over 1f out* **16/1**

-310 **8** *3 ¾* **Chookie Royale**[20] 1675 5-9-5 **86**...............................(p) BarryMcHugh 5 67
(Keith Dalgleish) *racd keenly: hld up: rdn 3f out: sn btn* **10/1**

43-0 **9** *8* **Unex Michelangelo (IRE)**[30] 1485 4-9-6 **87**................ JamesSullivan 6 51
(Michael Easterby) *hld up: rdn over 3f out: sn wknd* **22/1**

2m 6.59s (1.19) **Going Correction** +0.30s/f (Good) **9** Ran SP% **115.8**
Speed ratings (Par 107): **107,106,104,102,102 101,98,95,89**
toteswingers 1&2 £11.30, 2&3 £5.50, 1&3 £7.50 CSF £22.15 CT £83.85 TOTE £3.20: £1.80, £1.60, £1.70; EX 29.80 Trifecta £82.90 Pool: £293.61 - 2.65 winning units..
Owner K Nicholson **Bred** Grundy Bloodstock Srl **Trained** Nawton, N Yorks

FOCUS
This was a decent contest run at a fair pace. Once again those up with the pace dominated. The unexposed winner built on his maiden win.

2241 SIS VIRTUAL BETTING CHANNEL MAIDEN STKS 6f
8:05 (8:06) (Class 5) 3-Y-0 £3,234 (£962; £481; £240) **Stalls** High

Form RPR

4-2 **1** **Rapscallion Deep (IRE)**[123] 102 3-9-5 0.......................... AmyRyan 7 66+
(Kevin Ryan) *w ldr: led narrowly over 2f out: rdn 2f out: kpt on to assert towards fin* **5/2**[1]

350- **2** *1* **Annie Gogh**[241] 6121 3-9-0 62.. DavidAllan 6 57
(Tim Easterby) *trckd ldrs: rdn to chal over 1f out: kpt on: hld towards fin* **7/2**[3]

550 **3** *2 ½* **Lady Calantha**[30] 1458 3-8-9 41.................................... SladeO'Hara(5) 1 49
(Alan Berry) *hld up in tch towards outer: rdn over 2f out: kpt on to go 3rd ins fnl f: no threat to ldng pair* **150/1**

0 **4** *nk* **Calm Attitude (IRE)**[21] 1660 3-8-11 0.............................. LeeTopliss(3) 3 48+
(Rae Guest) *s.i.s and sltly hmpd s: sn swtchd lft to r against rail: hld up in rr: rdn and hdwy over 1f out: kpt on fnl f* **9/1**

65 **5** *¾* **Rose Of May (IRE)**[8] 1962 3-9-0 0.................................. DanielTudhope 5 46
(David O'Meara) *chsd ldrs: rdn over 2f out: no ex and lost 2 pls ins fnl f* **15/2**

623- **6** *9* **Showtime Girl (IRE)**[284] 4651 3-9-0 67........................ DuranFentiman 4 17
(Tim Easterby) *chsd ldrs: wknd over 1f out* **7/1**

40 **7** *6* **Mr Snooks**[20] 1687 3-9-5 0.. PaulQuinn 2
(David Nicholls) *sltly hmpd s: hld up: n.m.r 2f out: wknd appr fnl f: eased* **33/1**

- **8** *1 ½* **Level Best** 3-9-5 0.. MichaelStainton 8
(Mark Johnston) *ponied to s: led narrowly: rdn whn hdd over 2f out: wknd* **11/4**[2]

1m 13.17s (0.17) **Going Correction** -0.075s/f (Good) **8** Ran SP% **115.3**
Speed ratings (Par 99): **95,93,90,89,88 76,68,66**
toteswingers 1&2 £1.20, 2&3 £9.90, 1&3 £9.90 CSF £11.73 TOTE £2.90: £1.10, £2.30, £23.30; EX 10.80 Trifecta £170.80 Pool: £994.40 - 4.36 winning units..
Owner P Brosnan **Bred** Epona Bloodstock Ltd **Trained** Hambleton, N Yorks

FOCUS
Some fair stables in opposition for this maiden, which was run at an honest pace. A modest maiden, with the third a hole in the form, and the race is rated cautiously.

2242 SIS SERVING INTERNATIONAL BOOKMAKERS H'CAP 2m
8:40 (8:41) (Class 5) (0-75,71) 4-Y-0+ £3,234 (£962; £481; £240) **Stalls** Low

Form RPR

3-50 **1** **Mason Hindmarsh**[19] 1464 6-9-5 **66**.............................. PhillipMakin 3 71
(Karen McLintock) *trckd ldr: led 9f out: hdd 5f out: sn outpcd by ldr: clsd on eased ldr over 1f out: led again fnl 100yds: hld on all out* **17/2**

2146 **2** *shd* **Zaplamation (IRE)**[14] 1805 8-9-8 **69**......................... MichaelO'Connell 6 74
(John Quinn) *racd keenly: hld up in midfield: pushed along and hdwy 3f out: clsd on eased ldr over 1f out: ev ch fnl 100yds: kpt on: jst hld* **7/2**[2]

23-5 **3** *nk* **Dr Irv**[30] 1464 4-8-4 **61**... EvaMoscrop(7) 4 73+
(Philip Kirby) *tk str hold in midfield: plld way to front 5f out: sn rn wd on bnd: rdn 6 to 7 l clr 3f out: rdr looked bhd and eased over 1f out: hdd fnl 100yds: rdn again and rallied: should have won: rdr fell off sn after line* **5/2**[1]

4-00 **4** *nk* **Beat The Shower**[14] 1805 7-9-1 **62**.............................. DaleSwift 10 66
(Peter Niven) *midfield: rdn over 3f out: hdwy over 2f out: kpt on wl fnl f* **16/1**

55-0 **5** *3 ½* **Tarantella Lady**[25] 1572 5-8-12 **59**............................... TonyHamilton 9 59
(George Moore) *sn led: hdd 9f out: rdn and outpcd over 4f out: plugged on fnl 2f* **12/1**

46-0 **6** *2 ¼* **Petella**[15] 1789 7-8-10 **57**.. PJMcDonald 5 54
(George Moore) *hld up: rdn 3f out: sme late hdwy: nvr threatened* **6/1**[3]

006- **7** *nk* **Golden Future**[132] 8290 10-8-10 **57**.............................. RoystonFfrench 7 54
(Peter Niven) *hld up in midfield: rdn over 3f out: nvr threatened* **16/1**

00-0 **8** *½* **Mr Crystal (FR)**[31] 1445 9-9-8 **69**.............................. MichaelStainton 1 65
(Micky Hammond) *trckd ldrs: rdn over 3f out: wknd over 1f out* **25/1**

10-6 **9** *hd* **Rosairlie (IRE)**[31] 1454 5-9-7 **71**................................. LeeTopliss(3) 2 67
(Micky Hammond) *trckd ldrs: rdn over 3f out: wknd over 1f out* **8/1**

6-14 **10** *1 ½* **Sohcahtoa (IRE)**[15] 309 7-9-5 **71**................................... LMcNiff(5) 8 65
(Andrew Crook) *hld up: pushed along over 3f out: nvr threatened* **20/1**

0660 **11** *¾* **Turjuman (USA)**[16] 1763 8-7-12 **52** oh2................. DanielleMooney(7) 11 45
(Simon West) *hld up: a towards rr* **40/1**

3m 41.45s (9.65) **Going Correction** +0.30s/f (Good)
WFA 4 from 5yo+ 3lb **11** Ran SP% **117.2**
Speed ratings (Par 103): **87,86,86,86,84 83,83,83,83,82 82**
toteswingers 1&2 £8.80, 2&3 £1.10, 1&3 £15.20 CSF £37.38 CT £98.11 TOTE £12.20: £3.20, £1.10, £1.40; EX 37.30 Trifecta £148.20 Pool: £646.96 - 3.27 winning units..
Owner Brian Chicken **Bred** Newsells Park Stud **Trained** Ingoe, Northumberland
■ Stewards' Enquiry : Eva Moscrop ten-day ban: failed to ride out for first (May 24,25,27-31,Jun 1,3,4)

FOCUS
A weak staying handicap run at a steady pace, with an extraordinary finish. The level is set around the winner and second.
T/Plt: £26.90 to a £1 stake. Pool of £45335.55 - 1226.64 winning tickets. T/Qpdt: £9.70 to £1 stake. Pool of £3317.40 - 252.90 winning tickets. AS

2204 ASCOT (R-H)
Saturday, May 11

OFFICIAL GOING: Good to firm (stands' side 9.3; centre 9.2; far side 9.4; round 9.2)
Wind: Virtually nil Weather: Overcast

2250 BETFRED MOBILE MAIDEN STKS 5f
1:30 (1:30) (Class 3) 2-Y-0 **£7,762** (£2,310; £1,154; £577) **Stalls** Centre

Form RPR

5 **1** **Ifwecan**[10] 1930 2-9-3 0.. JoeFanning 9 82+
(Mark Johnston) *mde virtually all: hrd pressed fr over 2f out: hung lft u.p fr 1f out: hld on wl in clsng stages: jinked and uns rdr after fin* **11/4**[1]

2 *½* **Finflash (IRE)** 2-9-3 0.. MartinHarley 5 80+
(Mick Channon) *in tch: hdwy over 1f out: styd on wl fnl f to take 2nd in clsng stages: nt rch wnr* **9/1**

3 *1* **Langavat (IRE)** 2-9-3 0... RichardHughes 10 77+
(Richard Hannon) *chsd ldrs: chal fr 2f out tl outpcd wl ins fnl f and lost 2nd in clsng stages* **3/1**[2]

4 *shd* **Royal Mezyan (IRE)** 2-9-3 0.. LiamJones 2 76+
(William Haggas) *chsd ldrs: chal fr 2f out tl wl ins fnl f: styd on same pce cl home* **9/2**

5 *2 ¼* **Costa Filey** 2-9-3 0.. TomQueally 3 68+
(Ed Vaughan) *hld up in rr: shkn up and hdwy fnl f: styd on wl in clsng stages* **50/1**

5 **6** *nse* **Jazz (IRE)**[22] 1669 2-9-3 0.. SteveDrowne 6 68
(Charles Hills) *chsd ldr: chal over 2f out tl appr fnl f: wknd fnl 150yds* **7/2**[3]

7 *nk* **Highland Acclaim (IRE)** 2-9-3 0.......................................[1] DavidProbert 1 67
(Andrew Balding) *s.i.s: in rr: hdwy to chse ldrs 1/2-way: wknd ins fnl f* **16/1**

8 *2* **Stormy Paradise (IRE)** 2-9-3 0...................................... PaulHanagan 4 60
(Brian Meehan) *outpcd 1/2-way: pushed along and kpt on fr over 1f out: nvr a threat* **25/1**

9 *3 ½* **Flying Author (IRE)** 2-9-3 0...................................... KirstyMilczarek 7 47
(Phil McEntee) *s.i.s: a outpcd* **100/1**

1m 2.62s (2.12) **Going Correction** +0.325s/f (Good) **9** Ran SP% **114.8**
Speed ratings (Par 97): **96,95,93,93,89 89,89,86,80**
toteswingers 1&2 £12.20, 1&3 £2.00, 2&3 £5.50 CSF £27.68 TOTE £4.00: £1.40, £2.20, £1.60; EX 32.10 Trifecta £153.40 Pool: £1303.42 - 6.37 winning units..
Owner Douglas Livingston **Bred** P T Tellwright **Trained** Middleham Moor, N Yorks

FOCUS
The round course rail was positioned approximately three metres inside from the 1m4f start to the home straight, increasing distances by approximately the following: 1m2f - 9yds, 1m4f - 12yds, 2m - 16yds. The ground was given as good to firm, but there was rain around. A few of these were fancied and this was probably quite a strong maiden. The form is rated in line with the race average. They raced up the middle for most of the way, but the winner ended up against the stands' rail.

2251 LEO BANCROFT SIGNATURE HAIRCARE H'CAP 1m 4f
2:05 (2:05) (Class 3) (0-95,95) 4-Y-0+ **£8,409** (£2,502; £1,250; £625) **Stalls** Low

Form RPR

0-02 **1** **Angel Gabrial (IRE)**[19] 1728 4-8-13 **87**.......................... TomQueally 11 96+
(Ian Williams) *hld up in rr: hdwy on outside fr 3f out: str run fr 2f out to ld 1f out: pushed out* **13/2**

301- **2** *¾* **Noble Alan (GER)**[235] 6339 10-9-0 **88**.......................... PaulHanagan 7 95
(Nicky Richards) *t.k.h early: chsd ldrs: led over 2f out: sn rdn: hdd 1f out: kpt on but nt gng pce of wnr* **14/1**

/45- **3** *1 ¼* **Harvard N Yale (USA)**[245] 6025 4-8-12 **86**...................(t) MartinHarley 5 93+
(Jeremy Noseda) *in tch: hdwy fr 4f out: rdn and styd on fr over 1f out: tk 3rd ins fnl f: styd on wl in clsng stages but nt rch ldng duo* **4/1**[2]

264- **4** *1* **Maria's Choice (IRE)**[206] 7168 4-8-9 **83**........................ DavidProbert 12 86
(Sir Michael Stoute) *t.k.h in tch: hdwy to chse ldrs 3f out: styd on same pce for 4th fnl f* **11/2**[3]

22/- **5** *1 ½* **Tahaamah**[420] 949 5-9-7 **95**...(t) MickaelBarzalona 6 96
(Saeed bin Suroor) *hld up in rr: hdwy fr 4f out: chsd ldr briefly 2f out: rdn over 1f out: wknd ins fnl f* **9/1**

6 *1* **Mexicali (IRE)**[390] 5-8-10 **84**.. TedDurcan 10 83
(Dean Ivory) *in rr: hdwy and edgd rt over 1f out: kpt on in clsng stages but nvr a threat* **16/1**

-005 **7** *2 ¼* **Robin Hood (IRE)**[21] 1673 5-8-9 **83**.............................. JackMitchell 8 79
(Philip Mitchell) *in rr: pushed along over 2f out: styd on ins fnl f* **20/1**

5446 **8** *1* **Tinshu (IRE)**[42] 1241 7-8-12 **86**....................................(p) WilliamCarson 3 80
(Derek Haydn Jones) *in rr: pushed along and styd on same pce fnl 2f* **14/1**

3324 **9** *2 ¾* **Aquilonius (IRE)**[35] 1382 4-9-0 **88**...............................(t) SaleemGolam 4 78
(Stuart Williams) *chsd ldr: rdn over 2f out: sn btn* **25/1**

31-0 **10** *1 ¾* **Australia Day (IRE)**[9] 1615 10-8-11 **85**........................ JimmyFortune 2 72
(Paul Webber) *led: rdn 3f out: hdd over 2f out: sn wknd* **9/1**

5-43 **11** *8* **Scatter Dice (IRE)**[6] 2052 4-9-3 **91**.............................. JoeFanning 1 65
(Mark Johnston) *chsd ldrs: rdn 3f out: wknd 2f out* **7/2**[1]

2m 32.04s (-0.46) **Going Correction** +0.20s/f (Good) **11** Ran SP% **118.8**
Speed ratings (Par 107): **109,108,107,107,106 105,103,103,101,100 94**
toteswingers 1&2 £34.60, 2&3 £19.80, 1&3 £5.10 CSF £94.62 CT £414.58 TOTE £6.50: £2.10, £5.00, £1.80; EX 137.30 Trifecta £872.60 Pool: £1221.67 - 1.05 winning units..
Owner Dr Marwan Koukash **Bred** K And Mrs Cullen **Trained** Portway, Worcs

FOCUS
A good handicap run at what looked a sound pace. The winner built on his latest Windsor form.

2252 BUCKHOUNDS STKS (LISTED RACE) 1m 4f
2:40 (2:40) (Class 1) 4-Y-0+ **£20,982** (£7,955; £3,981; £1,983; £995) **Stalls** Low

Form RPR

02-3 **1** **Ektihaam (IRE)**[14] 1846 4-8-12 112 PaulHanagan 5 121
(Roger Varian) *mde all: drvn and qcknd 3f out: styd on strly fnl f: unchal* **11/4**[3]

50-2 **2** *6* **Thomas Chippendale (IRE)**[14] 1846 4-8-12 111 TomQueally 3 111
(Sir Henry Cecil) *stdd s: hld up in rr and t.k.h: hdwy to cl 4f out: chsd wnr appr fnl 2f: sn rdn and no imp: one pce fnl f* **9/4**[2]

425- **3** *4 1/2* **Main Sequence (USA)**[238] 6245 4-8-12 115 TedDurcan 6 107
(David Lanigan) *t.k.h and sn chsng wnr: rdn and no imp over 2f out and sn dropped to 3rd: wknd fnl f* **7/4**[1]

130- **4** *6* **Number Theory**[239] 6197 5-8-12 99 FrannyNorton 1 95
(John Holt) *chsd ldrs in 3rd tl outpcd and dropped to 5th over 3f out: no ch after and kpt on for modest 4th again over 1f out* **16/1**

12/4 **5** *8* **Highland Castle**[14] 1843 5-8-12 95 RichardHughes 4 90
(David Elsworth) *in rr: mod hdwy to take 4th over 3f out: nvr any ch: dropped to poor 5th over 1f out* **12/1**

2m 32.0s (-0.50) **Going Correction** +0.20s/f (Good) **5** Ran SP% **107.4**
Speed ratings (Par 111): **109,105,102,98,92**
CSF £8.82 TOTE £4.00: £1.50, £1.70; EX 8.00 Trifecta £11.40 Pool: £1991.89 - 129.99 winning units..
Owner Hamdan Al Maktoum **Bred** Bernard Cooke **Trained** Newmarket, Suffolk

FOCUS
In theory a good race for the grade with the first three all dropping down from Group company, but none of them really convince and it might be unwise to get carried away. A clear best from the winner at face value but the form is rated cautiously.

2253 BOVIS HOMES FILLIES' H'CAP 1m (S)
3:15 (3:16) (Class 2) 3-Y-0+ **£29,110** (£8,662; £4,329; £2,164) **Stalls** Centre

Form RPR

261- **1** **Gifted Girl (IRE)**[168] 7858 4-9-0 92 TomQueally 11 108
(Paul Cole) *in tch: smooth hdwy to ld ins fnl 2f: clr 1f out: easily* **11/1**

34-1 **2** *5* **Westwiththenight (IRE)**[14] 1823 4-8-12 90 RichardHughes 5 95
(William Haggas) *stdd s: hld up in rr: hdwy and n.m.r 2f out: drvn and styd on to chse wnr ins fnl f but nvr any ch* **11/8**[1]

00-0 **3** *1 1/2* **Princess Of Orange**[11] 1913 4-8-13 91 TedDurcan 2 92
(Rae Guest) *in rr: hdwy over 2f out: chsd wnr over 1f out: no imp and styd on same pce for 3rd fnl f* **20/1**

212- **4** *1 1/4* **Lizzie Tudor**[220] 6775 3-8-0 91 oh13 DavidProbert 3 86
(Andrew Balding) *chsd ldrs: led appr fnl 2f: hdd sn after: styd on same pce fnl f* **16/1**

20-5 **5** *3 3/4* **Tipping Over (IRE)**[22] 1668 3-7-7 91 oh5 NoelGarbutt(7) 9 78
(Hugo Palmer) *in tch: rdn over 2f out: kpt on same pce* **40/1**

11 **6** *1/2* **Sharp And Smart (IRE)**[5] 2070 4-8-3 81 6ex PaulHanagan 8 69
(Hughie Morrison) *towards rr: rdn and sme hdwy fr 2f out: one pce fr over 1f out* **5/1**[2]

3 **7** *7* **Modern Romance (IRE)**[14] 1823 4-8-2 80 ow2 AndreaAtzeni 7 52
(Marco Botti) *chsd ldrs: rdn and wknd 2f out* **8/1**[3]

00-5 **8** *1 1/2* **Candycakes (IRE)**[14] 1825 4-7-11 78 oh1 DarrenEgan(3) 1 47
(Michael Bell) *in tch drvn to chal over 2f out: wknd qckly over 1f out* **33/1**

63-0 **9** *2 3/4* **Arsaadi (IRE)**[77] 777 4-9-10 102 (p) LiamJones 10 65
(William Haggas) *pressed ldrs: rdn over 2f out: btn sn after* **9/1**

312- **10** *5* **Fulney**[234] 6375 4-8-3 81 CathyGannon 6 32
(James Eustace) *slt ld tl hdd appr fnl 2f: sn wknd* **14/1**

110- **11** *52* **Shena's Dream (IRE)**[199] 7334 4-8-2 80 FrannyNorton 4
(Stuart Williams) *pressed ldrs 5f: wknd rapidly over 2f out: eased* **20/1**

1m 42.19s (1.39) **Going Correction** +0.325s/f (Good)
WFA 3 from 4yo 13lb **11** Ran SP% **115.7**
Speed ratings (Par 96): **106,101,99,98,94 94,87,85,82,77 25**
toteswingers 1&2 £8.00, 2&3 £16.20, 1&3 £7.50 CSF £24.92 CT £320.47 TOTE £10.60: £3.00, £1.10, £5.40; EX 42.20 Trifecta £312.30 Pool: £1811.53 - 4.35 winning units..
Owner A D Spence **Bred** Airlie Stud **Trained** Whatcombe, Oxon

FOCUS
This looked a good fillies' handicap. The winner impressed in posting a clear best.

2254 BETFRED VICTORIA CUP (H'CAP) 7f
3:50 (3:54) (Class 2) 4-Y-0+
£52,912 (£15,844; £7,922; £3,961; £1,980; £994) **Stalls** Centre

Form RPR

000- **1** **Excellent Guest**[224] 6674 6-8-10 93 TomQueally 13 104
(George Margarson) *in tch: stdy hdwy fr 2f out: led fnl 120yds: drvn out* **25/1**

046- **2** *1/2* **Bertiewhittle**[203] 7240 5-8-10 93 RichardHughes 27 103
(David Barron) *hld up in rr: hdwy fr 2f out: drvn and qcknd to chse wnr fnl 110yds: no imp cl home* **12/1**

06-3 **3** *nk* **Cape Classic (IRE)**[14] 1830 5-9-0 97 AdamBeschizza 16 106
(William Haggas) *chsd ldrs: impr 2f out: rdn to ld 1f out: hdd fnl 120yds: styd on same pce to hold 3rd* **16/1**

325- **4** *1 3/4* **Redvers (IRE)**[203] 7240 5-8-6 89 (b) JoeFanning 21 93
(Ed Vaughan) *in rr: hdwy over 1f out: styd on to take 4th in clsng stages: no imp on ldng trio* **25/1**

25-5 **5** *nk* **Dream Tune**[21] 1675 4-8-3 91 RyanTate(5) 2 94+
(Clive Cox) *racd alone far side tl c to join main gp 3f out and pressed ldrs: stl upsides over 1f out: no ex fnl 110yds* **9/1**[2]

31-1 **6** *1/2* **Tartiflette**[14] 1830 4-8-11 94 FrannyNorton 7 96+
(Ed McMahon) *in tch towards centre of crse: chsd ldrs over 1f out: one pce ins fnl f* **12/1**

660- **7** *1* **Jamesie (IRE)**[38] 1338 5-8-13 96 PatDobbs 14 95
(David Marnane, Ire) *s.i.s: in rr: hdwy and nt clr run over 2f out: kpt on fnl f: nt rch ldrs* **10/1**[3]

02-2 **8** *1/2* **Loving Spirit**[28] 1545 5-8-12 95 RobertHavlin 26 96+
(James Toller) *in rr: hdwy over 1f out: styd on wl in clsng stages: nt each ldrs* **16/1**

62-0 **9** *1 1/4* **Elusive Flame**[19] 1726 4-8-7 90 CathyGannon 4 85
(David Elsworth) *mede most towards centre of crse tl hdd 1f out: sn wknd* **50/1**

00-4 **10** *1/2* **Highland Colori (IRE)**[14] 1830 5-8-9 92 DavidProbert 24 85
(Andrew Balding) *pressed ldrs: rdn over 2f out: wknd fnl f* **14/1**

0-00 **11** *1 1/2* **Mabait**[7] 2013 7-8-10 93 PatCosgrave 11 82
(David Simcock) *in rr: hdwy over 1f out: kpt on in clsng stages* **25/1**

30-2 **12** *3/4* **Glen Moss (IRE)**[28] 1542 4-8-6 89 WilliamCarson 12 76
(Charles Hills) *in tch: chsd ldrs and rdn over 2f out: styd on same pce fnl f* **16/1**

010- **13** *1/2* **Born To Surprise**[218] 6835 4-8-10 96 DarrenEgan(3) 29 82
(Michael Bell) *towards rr: rdn and sme hdwy fnl 2f: nt rch ldrs* **16/1**

03-3 **14** *3/4* **Lightning Cloud (IRE)**[21] 1688 5-8-12 95 AmyRyan 22 79
(Kevin Ryan) *chsd ldrs: rdn over 2f out: wknd fnl f* **10/1**[3]

400- **15** *3/4* **Rebellious Guest**[302] 4063 4-8-11 97 RyanPowell(3) 23 79
(George Margarson) *chsd ldrs: rdn 3f out: wknd fr 2f out* **33/1**

40-2 **16** *hd* **Khubala (IRE)**[11] 1913 4-8-12 95 JimmyFortune 6 76
(Hugo Palmer) *in rr: hdwy to cl on ldrs over 2f out: wknd ins fnl f* **16/1**

0012 **17** *2 1/2* **King Of Eden (IRE)**[16] 1787 7-8-7 90 (b) JimmyQuinn 20 64
(Eric Alston) *s.i.s: in rr: n.m.r over 2f out: sme prog in clsng stages* **33/1**

-261 **18** *nk* **Fast Finian (IRE)**[11] 1913 4-8-6 89 (b) LiamJones 5 63
(Paul D'Arcy) *chsd ldrs: rdn over 2f out: wknd wl over 1f out* **33/1**

010- **19** *1/2* **Bubbly Bellini (IRE)**[10] 1937 6-8-8 94 (p) IJBrennan(3) 18 66
(Adrian McGuinness, Ire) *chsd ldrs: rdn and n.m.r over 1f out: sn wknd* **40/1**

1431 **20** *9* **Haaf A Sixpence**[21] 1675 4-8-7 90 SteveDrowne 19 38
(Ralph Beckett) *chsd ldrs: rdn over 2f out: sn wknd* **7/1**[1]

0-51 **21** *3* **Bronze Prince**[42] 1244 6-8-11 94 J-PGuillambert 17 34
(Michael Attwater) *chsd ldrs: btn whn n.m.r over 1f out* **33/1**

0260 **22** *2 1/4* **Verse Of Love**[1] 2210 4-7-13 89 (p) NoelGarbutt(7) 15 23
(David Evans) *chsd ldrs over 4f* **66/1**

2000 **23** *4 1/2* **Piscean (USA)**[7] 2013 8-8-5 88 NickyMackay 8 10
(Tom Keddy) *chsd ldrs in centre of crse over 4f* **66/1**

60-0 **24** *3/4* **Smarty Socks (IRE)**[14] 1830 9-8-3 91 DavidBergin(5) 10 11
(David O'Meara) *s.i.s: towards rr most of way* **33/1**

3113 **25** *1/2* **Solar Deity (IRE)**[28] 1545 4-8-13 96 AndreaAtzeni 1 14
(Marco Botti) *chsd ldrs towards centre of crse over 4f* **16/1**

500- **26** *6* **Well Painted (IRE)**[182] 7691 4-8-10 93 (t) PaulHanagan 9
(William Haggas) *towards rr most of way* **16/1**

1m 28.26s (0.66) **Going Correction** +0.325s/f (Good) **26** Ran SP% **137.5**
Speed ratings (Par 109): **109,108,108,106,105 105,104,103,102,101 99,98,98,97,96 96,93,93,92,82 78,76,71,70,69 62**
toteswingers 1&2 £28.70, 2&3 £21.10, 1&3 £134.60 CSF £293.97 CT £4998.30 TOTE £35.10: £8.00, £4.10, £5.60, £6.80; EX 496.40 Trifecta £4944.20 Part won. Pool: £6592.30 - 0.70 winning units..
Owner John Guest Racing **Bred** John Guest Racing Ltd **Trained** Newmarket, Suffolk

FOCUS
There was loads of good course form on offer in this competitive, historic handicap. Straightforward form.

2255 ESPIRITO SANTO INVESTMENT BANK H'CAP 6f
4:25 (4:30) (Class 4) (0-80,81) 4-Y-0+ **£5,175** (£1,540; £769; £384) **Stalls** Centre

Form RPR

6501 **1** **Gabbiano**[73] 812 4-8-13 77 RobertTart(5) 3 88
(Jeremy Gask) *racd far side: hdwy appr fnl f: str run to ld cl home* **14/1**

5106 **2** *1* **Waking Warrior**[95] 526 5-9-1 74 (tp) AmyRyan 2 82
(Kevin Ryan) *racd far side: in tch: hdwy 1f out: rdn to ld fnl 110yds: hdd cl home* **33/1**

4002 **3** *hd* **Dorback**[9] 1961 6-8-12 71 CathyGannon 6 78
(Violet M Jordan) *mde most on far side: hdd and no ex fnl 110yds* **40/1**

0-01 **4** *1/2* **School Fees**[28] 1540 4-9-5 78 RichardHughes 1 83
(Olly Stevens) *racd far side: hdwy over 1f out: styd on: nt rch ldrs* **8/1**[2]

00-1 **5** *1/2* **Apollo D'Negro (IRE)**[4] 2128 5-9-3 81 6ex (v) RyanTate(5) 12 85
(Clive Cox) *racd far side: chsd ldrs fr 1/2-way: rdn 2f out: styd on same pce fnl f* **12/1**[3]

112- **6** *1 3/4* **Saloomy**[233] 6417 4-9-6 79 MartinHarley 22 77+
(John Butler) *racd stands' side and led that grnd: nt gng pce of far side fr 2f out but fin first stands' side* **14/1**

6562 **7** *nk* **Rocket Rob (IRE)**[15] 1814 7-9-1 74 J-PGuillambert 9 71
(Willie Musson) *racd far side: in rr: hdwy fnl f: nt rch ldrs: fin 6th in gp* **20/1**

340- **8** *nse* **Uprise**[231] 6488 4-9-0 73 TomQueally 4 70
(George Margarson) *racd far side: in tch: chsd ldrs 2f out: kpt on same pce: fin 7th in gp* **16/1**

12-0 **9** *hd* **Lunar Deity**[14] 1838 4-9-7 80 (p) JimmyFortune 8 76
(Eve Johnson Houghton) *racd far side: chsd ldrs: rdn and hld whn n.m.r over 1f out: fin 8th in gp* **20/1**

500- **10** *1/2* **Sir Pedro**[220] 6800 4-9-7 80 WilliamCarson 16 75
(Charles Hills) *chsd ldrs far side: rdn over 2f out: no ex ins fnl f: fin 9th in gp* **16/1**

211- **11** *1 1/4* **Muhdiq (USA)**[184] 7646 4-9-7 80 PatDobbs 14 71+
(Mike Murphy) *racd stands' side: in rr: hdwy over 1f out: kpt on wl to fin 2nd in gp but no ch w far side* **16/1**

0010 **12** *3/4* **Clear Praise (USA)**[15] 1814 6-9-5 78 SteveDrowne 13 66
(Simon Dow) *racd far side: in tch tl outpcd fnl 2f: fin 10th in gp* **33/1**

241- **13** *nk* **Pettochside**[240] 6173 4-8-8 67 (t) SaleemGolam 21 54
(Stuart Williams) *racd stands' side: chsd ldrs: styd on fnl f: fin 3rd in gp* **33/1**

4601 **13** *dht* **Creek Falcon (IRE)**[15] 1800 4-8-9 73 DavidBergin(5) 10 60
(David O'Meara) *racd far side: in tch 4f: fin 11th in gp* **5/1**[1]

00-1 **15** *1* **Tagula Night (IRE)**[15] 1814 7-9-6 79 (t) PaulHanagan 11 63
(Dean Ivory) *chsd ldrs far side: wknd fnl f: fin 12th in gp* **12/1**[3]

200- **16** *3/4* **Picture Dealer**[220] 6800 4-9-7 80 PatCosgrave 7 62
(Gary Moore) *chsd ldr far side tl wknd fnl f: fin 13th in gp* **33/1**

00-0 **17** *shd* **My Kingdom (IRE)**[19] 1726 7-9-4 77 (t) AndreaAtzeni 18 59
(Stuart Williams) *chsd ldrs stands' side: one pce fnl f: fin 4th in gp* **20/1**

-551 **18** *nse* **Available (IRE)**[15] 1802 4-9-3 76 (p) FrannyNorton 17 57
(John Mackie) *chsd ldrs stands' side: one pce fnl f: fin 5th in gp* **16/1**

351- **19** *3/4* **Annes Rocket (IRE)**[237] 6277 8-9-0 73 (p) JimmyQuinn 19 52
(Jimmy Fox) *racd stands' side: in rr: sme hdwy fnl f: fin 6th in gp* **33/1**

-105 **20** *hd* **Pick A Little**[4] 2128 5-9-3 76 DavidProbert 15 54
(Michael Blake) *in tch stands' side: one pce fnl f: fin 7th in gp* **40/1**

03-1 **21** *1/2* **The Tichborne (IRE)**[37] 1346 5-9-4 77 (v) JackMitchell 24 54
(Roger Teal) *chsd ldrs stands' side: wknd fnl f: fin 8th in gp* **12/1**[3]

13-0 **22** *nse* **Clear Spring (IRE)**[14] 1838 5-9-4 77 NickyMackay 20 54
(John Spearing) *in tch stands' side: outpcd over 1f out: fin 9th in gp* **25/1**

36-0 **23** *9* **Italian Tom (IRE)**[19] 1726 6-9-4 80 DarrenEgan(3) 26 28
(Ronald Harris) *racd stands' side: chsd ldrs 4f: fin 10th in gp* **12/1**[3]

2-00 **24** *2 1/2* **Perfect Pastime**[15] 1814 5-9-6 79 (p) JoeFanning 23 19
(Jim Boyle) *chsd ldrs stands' side 4f: fin 11th in gp* **25/1**

316- **25** *26* **Charity Box**[276] 4965 4-8-12 71 TedDurcan 25
(Chris Wall) *racd stands' side: in tch: wknd rapidly 2f out: fin 12th and last in gp* **25/1**

1m 15.58s (1.08) **Going Correction** +0.325s/f (Good) **25** Ran SP% **140.8**
Speed ratings (Par 105): **105,103,103,102,102 99,99,99,99,98 96,95,95,95,93 92,92,92,91,91 90,90,78,75,40**
toteswingers 1&2 £0.00, 2&3 £0.00, 1&3 £0.00 CSF £439.62 CT £8152.81 TOTE £24.30: £6.20, £10.90, £10.30, £2.40; EX 586.80 TRIFECTA Not won..
Owner Tony Bloom **Bred** Mrs R J Gallagher **Trained** Sutton Veny, Wilts

FOCUS
They raced in two groups and those on the far side looked at a significant advantage over those on the stands' side, providing the first five home, as well as ten of the first 12. Consequently, it's worth treating this as two separate races. The first three had all posted their best recent form on Polytrack.
T/Jkpt: Not won. T/Plt: £504.70 to a £1 stake. Pool of £175825.12 - 254.28 winning tickets.
T/Qpdt: £175.10 to a £1 stake. Pool of £9394.68 - 39.70 winning tickets. ST

1826 HAYDOCK (L-H)
Saturday, May 11

OFFICIAL GOING: Flat course - good to firm (good in places) changing to good to soft after race 2 (2.25); jumps courses - good
Wind: Moderate, half against Weather: Overcast

2256 PERTEMPS NETWORK H'CAP — 1m 2f 95y
2:25 (2:26) (Class 4) (0-85,83) 4-Y-0+ — **£5,175** (£1,540; £769; £384) **Stalls** Centre

Form — RPR

1-2 **1** **Hanseatic**[12] 1883 4-9-7 83 WilliamBuick 2 97+
(John Gosden) *mde all: rdn over 1f out: styd on wl thrght fnl f* **4/6**[1]

14-0 **2** *3* **Muharrer**[28] 1538 4-9-2 78 PaulMulrennan 3 86
(Michael Dods) *chsd ldrs: pushed along over 2f out: rdn to chse wnr over 1f out: no imp ins fnl f* **16/1**

34-1 **3** *2* **Significant Move**[26] 1585 6-8-12 74 NeilCallan 7 78
(Stuart Kittow) *chsd wnr: effrt over 2f out: lost 2nd over 1f out: kpt on same pce ins fnl f* **5/1**[2]

2100 **4** *nk* **Suffice (IRE)**[21] 1689 4-8-10 72 TonyHamilton 4 75
(Richard Fahey) *hld up: pushed along 2f out: rdn over 1f out: kpt on u.p ins fnl f: nvr able to chal* **18/1**

4-03 **5** *6* **Now My Sun**[14] 1831 4-8-12 74 PhillipMakin 1 66
(Mrs K Burke) *hld up in rr: hdwy on outer to chse ldrs over 2f out: wknd over 1f out* **5/1**[2]

25-6 **6** *2* **Eurystheus (IRE)**[26] 1583 4-8-12 79 (t) PhilipPrince(5) 5 67
(Paul Nicholls) *hld up in tch: pushed along 3f out: rdn and wknd ent fnl 2f* **12/1**[3]

2m 17.37s (1.87) **Going Correction** +0.325s/f (Good) **6** Ran SP% **112.2**
Speed ratings (Par 105): **105,102,101,100,95 94**
toteswingers 1&2 £3.30, 1&3 £1.10, 2&3 £3.30 CSF £13.31 TOTE £1.60: £1.10, £6.20; EX 11.90 Trifecta £27.70 Pool: £864.63 - 23.38 winning units..
Owner K Abdullah **Bred** Juddmonte Farms Ltd **Trained** Newmarket, Suffolk

FOCUS
Stands' side track used and distances increased by 43yds. The ground on the Flat course was riding soft according to the riders in this, considerably easier than the official description. Just a fair handicap but the first pair were unexposed and the form could be rated a bit higher..

2257 PERTEMPS NETWORK CONDITIONS STKS — 6f
3:00 (3:00) (Class 2) 3-Y-0+
£12,450 (£3,728; £1,864; £932; £466; £234) **Stalls** Centre

Form — RPR

-066 **1** **Regal Parade**[21] 1691 9-9-0 103 (t) MatthewLawson 3 102
(Milton Bradley) *hld up in rr: effrt 2f out: edgd lft over 1f out whn chalng: led narrowly ins fnl f: all out fnl strides* **14/1**

560- **2** *nse* **Royal Rock**[203] 7236 9-9-0 105 GeorgeBaker 1 104+
(Chris Wall) *hld up: pushed along whn nt clr run and swtchd rt over 1f out: chsd ldrs ins fnl f: r.o cl home: jst failed* **9/2**

433- **3** *nk* **Boomerang Bob (IRE)**[258] 5647 4-9-0 105 SebSanders 6 101
(J W Hills) *chsd ldr tl over 3f out: rdn to ld narrowly over 1f out: hdd ins fnl f: r.o u.p: hld fnl strides* **5/2**[1]

00-5 **4** *hd* **Pandar**[23] 1637 4-9-0 100 NeilCallan 5 100
(Robert Cowell) *led: rdn and hdd over 1f out: continued to chal ins fnl f: hld ins fnl 50yds* **7/1**

101/ **5** *1 ¾* **Mezmaar**[600] 6221 4-9-0 90 WilliamBuick 4 95+
(Charles Hills) *s.s: racd keenly: hld up: impr to go 2nd over 3f out: pushed along and losing pl whn n.m.r and hmpd over 1f out: no imp ins fnl f* **3/1**[2]

34-3 **6** *nse* **Burwaaz**[14] 1835 4-9-0 103 DaneO'Neill 2 94
(Ed Dunlop) *chsd ldrs: rdn over 1f out: one pce fnl 100yds* **4/1**[3]

1m 16.24s (2.44) **Going Correction** +0.625s/f (Yiel) **6** Ran SP% **110.9**
Speed ratings (Par 109): **108,107,107,107,104 104**
toteswingers 1&2 £5.40, 1&3 £3.50, 2&3 £4.90 CSF £71.90 TOTE £14.80: £4.70, £1.90; EX 67.20 Trifecta £349.60 Pool: £725.03 - 1.55 winning units..
Owner Dab Hand Racing **Bred** Highclere Stud And Harry Herbert **Trained** Sedbury, Gloucs
■ Stewards' Enquiry : Neil Callan caution: careless riding.

FOCUS
The ground on the Flat was officially amended to good to soft before this race. A decent conditions event, albeit not as strong as the 2011 edition in which Bated Breath beat Society Rock (Royal Rock third). The pace was not strong and the first four were covered by a mere half length at the line. Muddling conditions form.

2258 PERTEMPS NETWORK SPRING TROPHY STKS (LISTED RACE) — 7f
4:05 (4:05) (Class 1) 3-Y-0+
£20,982 (£7,955; £3,981; £1,983; £995; £499) **Stalls** Low

Form — RPR

001- **1** **Eton Forever (IRE)**[217] 6882 6-9-11 111 NeilCallan 5 115
(Roger Varian) *chsd ldrs: wnt 2nd 2f out: led over 1f out: drvn out towards fin: jst hld on* **9/2**[3]

012- **2** *hd* **Gregorian (IRE)**[208] 7107 4-9-7 114 WilliamBuick 7 110
(John Gosden) *hld up: effrt and hdwy on outer over 1f out: styd on to take 2nd ins fnl f: clsd to press wnr towards fin* **3/1**[2]

2-00 **3** *1 ¼* **Red Jazz (USA)**[42] 1262 6-9-7 111 RobertWinston 4 107
(Charles Hills) *led: pushed along 2f out: rdn and hdd over 1f out: kpt on same pce fnl 100yds* **9/2**[3]

52-0 **4** *hd* **Pastoral Player**[10] 1919 6-9-7 111 GeorgeBaker 1 106+
(Hughie Morrison) *stdd s: hld up: nt clr run on inner over 1f out: effrt to chse ldrs ins fnl f: kpt on u.p but unable to chal front pair* **15/8**[1]

2-22 **5** *1 ¼* **Emell**[24] 1621 3-8-9 101 DaneO'Neill 3 99
(Richard Hannon) *chsd ldrs: effrt over 2f out: one pce ins fnl f* **13/2**

04-0 **6** *5* **Pintura**[21] 1691 6-9-7 108 PhillipMakin 6 90
(Kevin Ryan) *chsd ldr tl rdn over 2f out: wknd 1f out* **16/1**

1m 32.01s (1.31) **Going Correction** +0.475s/f (Yiel)
WFA 3 from 4yo+ 12lb **6** Ran SP% **115.4**
Speed ratings (Par 111): **111,110,109,109,107 101**
toteswingers 1&2 £5.00, 1&3 £4.10, 2&3 £3.80 CSF £18.98 TOTE £7.50: £3.60, £1.90; EX 23.90 Trifecta £40.30 Pool: £796.56 - 14.80 winning units..
Owner H R H Sultan Ahmad Shah **Bred** Mrs Brid Cosgrove **Trained** Newmarket, Suffolk

FOCUS
A fair Listed race. The form is a bit muddling, but the winner ran a personal best at face value. The runner-up was 4lb off his 1m form.

2259 PERTEMPS H'CAP — 1m
5:15 (5:17) (Class 3) (0-95,92) 3-Y-0 — **£8,086** (£2,406; £1,202; £601) **Stalls** Low

Form — RPR

3-26 **1** **Hay Dude**[22] 1668 3-9-2 90 MichaelMetcalfe(3) 4 97
(Mrs K Burke) *wnt sideways s: hld up: hdwy 2f out: wnt 2nd over 1f out: led ins fnl f: all out cl home* **11/2**

15-1 **2** *nse* **Al Mukhdam**[21] 1683 3-8-11 82 NeilCallan 2 89
(Peter Chapple-Hyam) *racd keenly: led: rdn over 1f out: hdd ins fnl f: rallied cl home: jst hld* **7/2**[2]

01-4 **3** *2 ¼* **Zamoyski**[19] 1725 3-8-9 80 WilliamBuick 1 82
(Jeremy Noseda) *racd keenly: trckd ldrs: rdn over 2f out: nt qckn over 1f out: no imp on ldrs ins fnl f* **13/8**[1]

13-0 **4** *nk* **Master Ming (IRE)**[23] 1641 3-8-12 83 DaneO'Neill 6 84
(Brian Meehan) *in tch: rdn over 2f out: kpt on u.p but no imp on ldrs ins fnl f* **20/1**

3-46 **5** *1 ½* **Top Notch Tonto (IRE)**[15] 1809 3-9-2 92 GarryWhillans(5) 3 90
(Ian McInnes) *bmpd s: hld up: pushed along 2f out: nvr able to chal* **16/1**

2-21 **6** *6* **Brooke's Bounty**[23] 1648 3-8-1 75 NeilFarley(3) 7 59
(Richard Fahey) *chsd ldr: rdn over 2f out: lost 2nd over 1f out: wknd ins fnl f* **10/1**

6-11 **7** *nk* **Lions Arch (IRE)**[14] 1822 3-8-9 85 WilliamTwiston-Davies(5) 5 68
(Richard Hannon) *in tch tl rdn and wknd over 1f out* **9/2**[3]

1m 46.96s (3.26) **Going Correction** +0.475s/f (Yiel) **7** Ran SP% **113.6**
Speed ratings (Par 103): **102,101,99,99,97 91,91**
toteswingers 1&2 £5.20, 1&3 £8.80, 2&3 £1.50 CSF £24.65 TOTE £6.10: £1.90, £2.00; EX 34.20 Trifecta £85.10 Pool: £1901.67 - 16.74 winning units..
Owner Ray Bailey **Bred** Ray Bailey **Trained** Middleham Moor, N Yorks

FOCUS
An interesting 3yo handicap, run at a fair pace. Decent form, rated around the third.
T/Plt: £87.60 to a £1 stake. Pool: £111803.03 - 931.10 winning tickets T/Qpdt: £32.50 to a £1 stake. Pool: £5167.96 - 117.50 winning tickets DO

2223 LINGFIELD (L-H)
Saturday, May 11

OFFICIAL GOING: Good (good to soft down the hill) changing to good to soft after race 1 (1.45) and soft after race 2 (2.20)
Wind: Gusty, half behind Weather: breezy, bright spells and showers

2260 BETFRED MOBILE LOTTO/BRITISH STALLION STUDS EBF MAIDEN STKS — 5f
1:45 (1:46) (Class 4) 2-Y-0 — **£4,075** (£1,212; £606; £303) **Stalls** High

Form — RPR

1 **Cool Bahamian (IRE)** 2-9-5 0 JohnFahy 5 76
(Eve Johnson Houghton) *in tch in midfield: swtchd out lft and effrt over 1f out: chalng whn rdr dropped whip fnl 100yds: r.o to ld cl home* **16/1**

02 **2** *nk* **Urban Dreamer (IRE)**[9] 1946 2-9-5 0 JamieSpencer 2 75
(Rod Millman) *chsd ldr: rdn and ev ch 2f out: drvn to ld ins fnl f: hdd and no ex cl home* **3/1**[2]

62 **3** *1 ½* **Sartori**[10] 1930 2-9-5 0 SamHitchcott 6 70
(Mick Channon) *led: drvn and pressed over 1f out: hdd ins fnl f: no ex and one pce towards fin* **7/4**[1]

5 **4** *2 ¾* **Fantasy Justifier (IRE)**[22] 1659 2-9-5 0 HarryBentley 3 60
(Ronald Harris) *chsd ldng pair: rdn and effrt 2f out: no ex u.p 1f out: wknd ins fnl f* **7/2**[3]

5 *21* **Red Oasis** 2-9-5 0 (v[1]) RyanMoore 4
(Robert Eddery) *chsd ldrs: rdn 1/2-way: struggling and btn wl over 1f out: eased ins fnl f: t.o* **3/1**[2]

6 *3 ½* **Movie Magic** 2-9-0 0 KierenFox 1
(John Bridger) *v.s.a: sn t.o* **66/1**

59.31s (1.11) **Going Correction** +0.10s/f (Good) **6** Ran SP% **116.0**
Speed ratings (Par 95): **95,94,92,87,54 48**
toteswingers 1&2 £4.30, 1&3 £4.20, 2&3 £1.30 CSF £65.47 TOTE £17.10: £6.20, £2.40; EX 62.70 Trifecta £258.10 Pool: £2515.74 - 7.31 winning units..
Owner L R Godfrey & R F Johnson Houghton **Bred** Kildaragh Stud **Trained** Blewbury, Oxon

FOCUS
After 6.2mm of rain overnight the going was changed to good, good to soft down the hill (GoingStick: Straight 8.6; Round 8.4). Returning after the first, Sam Hitchcott said "it's soft", and Jamie Spencer said "it's on the soft side". The wind was behind them up the straight. This looked a fair early-season maiden, the second and third helping with the level.

2261 BETFRED "THE BONUS KING" OAKS TRIAL STKS (LISTED RACE) — 1m 3f 106y
2:20 (2:21) (Class 1) 3-Y-0
£22,684 (£8,600; £4,304; £2,144; £1,076; £540) **Stalls** High

Form — RPR

21- **1** **Secret Gesture**[196] 7403 3-8-12 0 JimCrowley 5 110+
(Ralph Beckett) *a travelling wl: in tch in midfield: chsd ldr over 2f out: led on bit 2f out: shkn up and readily qck
nd clr over 1f out: nt extended: impressive* **1/1**[1]

423- **2** *10* **Miss You Too**[182] 7693 3-8-12 93 IanMongan 4 90
(David Simcock) *stdd s: plld v hrd: hld up in rr tl swtchd rt and hdwy to chse ldr 7f out: led 6f out: rdn and hdd 2f out: no ch w wnr after but kpt on for 2nd* **9/2**[3]

4 **3** *1 ½* **Whippy Cream (IRE)**[22] 1671 3-8-13 0 ow1 AdamKirby 7 88
(Marco Botti) *hld up in tch towards rr: rdn and sme hdwy over 2f out: wnt modest 3rd over 1f out: kpt on but no ch w wnr* **14/1**

3-41 **4** *4 ½* **Alta Lilea (IRE)**[17] 1761 3-8-12 88 SilvestreDeSousa 6 79
(Mark Johnston) *t.k.h early: chsd ldr after 1f tl led 10f out: hdd 6f out: rdn and struggling over 2f out: 4th and wl btn over 1f out* **3/1**[2]

3-03 **5** ¾ **Enaitch (IRE)**[8] 1975 3-8-12 73 SamHitchcott 3 78
(Mick Channon) *t.k.h: hld up in tch in rr: rdn and effrt wl over 2f out: outpcd and wl btn 2f out* **50/1**

3-2 **6** 5 **Heroine Required (FR)**[14] 1845 3-8-12 0 RyanMoore 2 70
(William Haggas) *pushed along leaving stalls: led after 1f tl 10f out: chsd ldr tl 6f out: rdn and effrt 3f out: sn struggling: wl bhd over 1f out* **7/1**

402- **7** 2¾ **Northern Star (IRE)**[224] 6664 3-8-12 0 RichardKingscote 1 65
(Tom Dascombe) *hld up in tch in midfield: pushed along 4f out: rdn and short-lived effrt 3f out: wl bhd over 1f out* **16/1**

2m 33.82s (2.32) **Going Correction** +0.425s/f (Yiel) **7 Ran SP% 120.2**
Speed ratings (Par 107): **108,100,99,96,95 92,90**
toteswingers 1&2 £2.30, 2&3 £6.30, 1&3 £4.20 CSF £6.60 TOTE £2.10: £1.30, £2.50; EX 6.20 Trifecta £45.30 Pool: £3221.32 - 53.24 winning units..
Owner Newsells Park Stud **Bred** Newsells Park Stud **Trained** Kimpton, Hants

FOCUS
Only one horse came into this Oaks Trial with the potential to shake up the market for Epsom and that was the favourite. She was an impressive, wide-margin winner, and rates up with the best winners of this, but the race did rather fall apart and the overall form is not up to scratch.

2262 BETFRED DERBY TRIAL STKS (LISTED RACE) (C&G) 1m 3f 106y
2:55 (2:55) (Class 1) 3-Y-O **£35,520** (£13,434; £6,714; £3,354) **Stalls High**

Form RPR
6- **1** **Nevis (IRE)**[238] 6272 3-8-12 98 RyanMoore 5 108+
(A P O'Brien, Ire) *mde virtually all: rdn and readily asserted ent fnl 2f: styd on strly: rdn out: easily* **4/9**[1]

4-32 **2** 9 **Elidor**[15] 1804 3-8-12 78 SamHitchcott 1 93
(Mick Channon) *chsd wnr tl over 6f out: rdn and chsd clr wnr again over 2f out: plugged on but no imp* **8/1**[3]

50-4 **3** 6 **Pasaka Boy**[14] 1847 3-8-12 86 RichardKingscote 4 83
(Jonathan Portman) *hld up wl in tch in last: rdn and effrt over 3f out: struggling over 2f out: 3rd and wl btn fnl 2f* **20/1**

3-12 **4** 15 **Another Cocktail**[17] 1767 3-8-12 93 JimCrowley 2 69
(Hughie Morrison) *chsd ldng pair tl wnt 2nd over 6f out tl over 2f out: sn dropped out and bhd: t.o and eased fnl f* **11/4**[2]

2m 40.09s (8.59) **Going Correction** +0.925s/f (Soft) **4 Ran SP% 111.8**
Speed ratings (Par 107): **105,98,94,83**
CSF £5.00 TOTE £1.30; EX 5.40 Trifecta £16.60 Pool: £1801.51 - 81.13 winning units..
Owner Mrs John Magnier & Michael Tabor & Derrick Smith **Bred** Orpendale, Chelston & Wynatt **Trained** Ballydoyle, Co Tipperary

FOCUS
Heavy rain saw a change in the going to soft before this Derby trial and, with the morning favourite Greatwood a late withdrawal, the race was left at the mercy of Nevis. It's hard to rate him up with the O'Brien yard's Chester winners, with this race rather falling apart.

2263 WEATHERBYS HAMILTON INSURANCE H'CAP 1m 2f
3:25 (3:25) (Class 2) (0-100,98) 4-Y-O+ **£12,291** (£3,657; £1,827) **Stalls Low**

Form RPR
1-10 **1** **Educate**[21] 1675 4-9-2 93 JamieSpencer 1 106+
(Ismail Mohammed) *dwlt: hld up in last: clsd over 2f out: rdn to ld 1f out: hung lft but r.o wl fnl f* **1/1**[1]

35-1 **2** 2 **Sheikhzayedroad**[14] 1824 4-9-1 92 MartinLane 4 101
(David Simcock) *chsd ldr: rdn and effrt over 2f out: led 2f out: hdd 1f out: hung lft and no ex ins fnl f* **6/4**[2]

6332 **3** 9 **Tepmokea (IRE)**[35] 1382 7-9-7 98 ShaneKelly 6 96
(Mrs K Burke) *led: rdn and hdd 2f out: btn 1f out: eased ins fnl f* **7/2**[3]

2m 18.54s (8.04) **Going Correction** +0.925s/f (Soft) **3 Ran SP% 112.2**
Speed ratings (Par 109): **104,102,95**
CSF £2.98 TOTE £1.70; EX 3.10 Trifecta £3.10 Pool: £1273.45 - 301.62 winning units..
Owner Sultan Ali **Bred** Lady Legard **Trained** Newmarket, Suffolk

FOCUS
Three of the declared runners were taken out and the time was slow. It's hard to be confident about the level of the form, which could be rated higher.

2264 BETFRED.COM CHARTWELL FILLIES' STKS (GROUP 3) 7f
4:00 (4:01) (Class 1) 3-Y-O+
£34,026 (£12,900; £6,456; £3,216; £1,614; £810) **Stalls High**

Form RPR
1401 **1** **Lily's Angel (IRE)**[28] 1544 4-9-3 106 GaryCarroll 7 109
(G M Lyons, Ire) *racd off the pce in midfield: clsd on ldrs over 2f out: rdn and outpcd 2f out: rallied u.p and edging out lft over 1f out: r.o wl u.p to ld last stride* **4/1**[3]

033- **2** shd **Kendam (FR)**[34] 4-9-3 107 ThierryJarnet 5 108
(H-A Pantall, France) *racd off the pce in midfield: clsd on ldrs and wnt 2nd 2f out: rdn and led ins fnl f: kpt on wl tl hdd last stride* **11/4**[2]

001- **3** ½ **Intense Pink**[217] 6870 4-9-3 98 JimCrowley 11 107
(Chris Wall) *led: clr w rival 4f out: rdn over 1f out: hdd and styd on same pce ins fnl f* **6/1**

222- **4** 4½ **Ultrasonic (USA)**[182] 7690 4-9-3 102 RyanMoore 8 95
(Sir Michael Stoute) *s.i.s: pushed along and wl in rr: hdwy and in tch in midfield over 2f out: keeping on whn nt clr run and swtchd lft jst over 1f out: no imp fnl f* **7/4**[1]

0- **5** 3 **Pleine Forme (USA)**[148] 8130 5-9-3 101 AdamKirby 10 88
(Marco Botti) *chsd clr ldrs: clsd over 2f out: chsng ldrs whn rdn and unable qck over 1f out: wknd ins fnl f* **8/1**

10-0 **6** 5 **Tassel**[10] 1921 3-8-5 89 KieranO'Neill 2 71
(Richard Hannon) *racd off the pce in midfield: clsd on ldrs over 2f out: rdn and effrt 2f out: btn ent fnl f: wknd* **33/1**

2 **7** 11 **Majestic Oasis**[67] 963 4-9-3 86 JamieSpencer 6 46
(Robert Cowell) *racd wl off the pce in last pair: sme hdwy over 2f out: struggling and btn 2f out: wl bhd and eased fnl f* **20/1**

1421 **8** 4 **Hard Walnut (IRE)**[37] 1345 3-8-5 76 HarryBentley 3 32
(Olly Stevens) *pressed ldr and clr of field tl rdn and lost pl qckly over 2f out: t.o fnl f* **33/1**

1m 25.41s (2.11) **Going Correction** +0.525s/f (Yiel)
WFA 3 from 4yo+ 12lb **8 Ran SP% 119.1**
Speed ratings (Par 110): **108,107,107,102,98 93,80,75**
toteswingers 1&2 £3.40, 2&3 £5.00, 1&3 £4.80 CSF £15.85 TOTE £5.30: £2.30, £1.30, £2.00; EX 14.10 Trifecta £101.00 Pool: £3646.39 - 27.05 winning units..
Owner Mrs Clodagh Mitchell **Bred** N And Mrs N Nugent **Trained** Dunsany, Co. Meath
■ Stewards' Enquiry : Gary Carroll one-day ban: careless riding (May 25)

FOCUS
There was only one previous Group race winner in this line-up, but three others with Listed level successes to their names. The pace looked decent for the conditions and the form is rated around the second.

2265 BETFRED TV H'CAP 7f 140y
4:35 (4:35) (Class 3) (0-95,90) 4-Y-O+ **£7,439** (£2,213; £1,106; £553) **Stalls Centre**

Form RPR
5-20 **1** **Boots And Spurs**[26] 1583 4-9-0 83 (v) RichardKingscote 1 92
(Mrs K Burke) *pressed ldr and crossed to r nr stands' rail: rdn and ev ch 2f out: drvn to ld ins fnl f: kpt on u.p* **11/4**[2]

3020 **2** ½ **Galician**[11] 1913 4-9-7 90 SilvestreDeSousa 8 98
(Mark Johnston) *led: drvn ent fnl 2f: hdd ins fnl f: battled on wl u.p but a jst hld* **7/2**[3]

1-22 **3** 1¾ **Jack Of Diamonds (IRE)**[12] 1878 4-8-13 82 RyanMoore 3 86+
(Roger Teal) *chsd ldrs: pushed along 1/2-way: drvn and ev ch ent fnl f: no ex and btn fnl 100yds* **7/4**[1]

30-5 **4** 2¼ **Corporal Maddox**[127] 60 6-9-2 85 HarryBentley 6 83
(Ronald Harris) *hld up wl in tch: rdn and effrt wl over 1f out: drvn and no ex 1f out: hung rt and wknd ins fnl f* **16/1**

0413 **5** 4½ **Lowther**[11] 1905 8-9-4 87 (v) KierenFox 9 74
(Lee Carter) *t.k.h: chsd ldrs: rdn and no rspnse ent fnl 2f: wknd over 1f out* **8/1**

00-6 **6** 1 **Lutine Bell**[28] 1542 6-9-2 85 EddieAhern 4 69
(Mike Murphy) *hld up wl in tch in last pair: rdn and no hdwy wl over 1f out: sn wknd* **8/1**

044- **7** 2¼ **Fanrouge (IRE)**[224] 6685 4-9-0 83 TomMcLaughlin 5 62
(Malcolm Saunders) *t.k.h: hld up in tch: stdd bk in to last pair over 5f out: rdn and effrt 2f out: sn struggling: wknd over 1f out* **25/1**

1m 35.04s (2.74) **Going Correction** +0.525s/f (Yiel) **7 Ran SP% 117.2**
Speed ratings (Par 107): **107,106,104,102,98 97,94**
toteswingers 1&2 £3.00, 2&3 £1.80, 1&3 £1.90 CSF £13.42 CT £20.89 TOTE £4.00: £2.50, £2.20; EX 16.80 Trifecta £41.60 Pool: £2283.00 - 41.11 winning units..
Owner Colin Bryce **Bred** Miss G Abbey **Trained** Middleham Moor, N Yorks

FOCUS
The early pace was only modest and as a result those at the head of affairs were not for passing. The winner is rated in line with his Spring Mile second, with the second back to form.

2266 BETFRED MOBILE SPORTS H'CAP 7f
5:10 (5:11) (Class 4) (0-85,85) 4-Y-O+ **£4,690** (£1,395; £697; £348) **Stalls High**

Form RPR
02-4 **1** **Great Expectations**[18] 1751 5-8-9 73 SilvestreDeSousa 4 82
(J R Jenkins) *dwlt: in tch in rr: hdwy 1/2-way: chsd ldrs and swtchd rt over 1f out: racing against stands' rail ins fnl f: r.o wl to ld fnl 50yds* **8/1**

5304 **2** ¾ **Harrison George (IRE)**[19] 1726 8-9-1 84 (t) NatashaEaton(5) 14 91
(P J O'Gorman) *chsd ldrs: rdn and ev ch over 1f out: led fnl 100yds: sn hdd and no ex* **3/1**[2]

52-0 **3** ¾ **Jungle Bay**[16] 1782 6-8-13 77 (p) AdamKirby 7 82
(Jane Chapple-Hyam) *chsd ldrs: wnt 2nd ent fnl 2f: drvn to ld over 1f out: kpt on wl u.p tl hdd and one pce fnl 100yds* **12/1**

31-5 **4** nk **Good Luck Charm**[20] 1739 4-8-5 76 NedCurtis(7) 11 80+
(Gary Moore) *hld up in tch in last pair: hdwy against stands' rail over 2f out: chsng ldng trio and clsng whn nt clr run and swtchd lft ins fnl f: r.o* **20/1**

5-14 **5** 7 **Light Burst (USA)**[16] 1782 4-9-1 84 ThomasBrown(5) 15 70
(Ismail Mohammed) *w ldr tl led over 2f out: drvn and hdd over 1f out: wknd fnl f* **8/1**

000- **6** ¾ **Shifting Star (IRE)**[159] 7966 8-8-13 77 SamHitchcott 1 61
(John Bridger) *in tch in midfield: drvn and no imp 3f out: outpcd and btn over 1f out: plugged on fnl f* **33/1**

16- **7** 2½ **Selkie's Friend**[170] 7824 4-9-0 78 IanMongan 10 56
(Henry Candy) *taken down early: in tch in midfield: dropped towards rr and rdn 1/2-way: bhd u.p 2f out: no ch but plugged on fnl f* **8/1**

310- **8** ½ **Ginzan**[211] 7019 5-8-12 76 TomMcLaughlin 6 52
(Malcolm Saunders) *chsd ldrs: rdn ent fnl 2f: no ex u.p and btn over 1f out: wknd* **33/1**

0500 **9** 2¾ **Seek The Fair Land**[16] 1782 7-9-3 81 (b) ShaneKelly 9 50
(Jim Boyle) *hld up in tch in last trio: rdn and no hdwy over 2f out: nvr trbld ldrs* **25/1**

-032 **10** 8 **Savanna Days (IRE)**[14] 1823 4-9-0 78 MatthewDavies 13 26
(Mick Channon) *led tl over 2f out: sn dropped out: wl bhd fnl f* **6/1**[3]

/003 **11** shd **Ortac Rock (IRE)**[16] 1782 4-9-6 84 (t) RyanMoore 16 64
(Richard Hannon) *pushed along leaving stalls: in tch in midfield: edgd out lft and chsd ldrs u.p wl over 1f out: no ex: btn 1f out: heavily eased ins fnl f* **11/4**[1]

1m 27.35s (4.05) **Going Correction** +0.525s/f (Yiel) **11 Ran SP% 121.5**
Speed ratings (Par 105): **97,96,95,94,86 86,83,82,79,70 70**
toteswingers 1&2 £9.00, 2&3 £8.00, 1&3 £18.10 CSF £32.02 CT £298.77 TOTE £11.40: £3.80, £1.70, £2.50; EX 36.70 Trifecta £293.10 Pool: £1628.74 - 4.16 winning units..
Owner The Great Expectations Partnership **Bred** R B Hill **Trained** Royston, Herts
■ Stewards' Enquiry : Ryan Moore one-day ban: careless riding (May 25)

FOCUS
There was a good gallop on here. The favourite disappointed but the second and third help with the standard.
T/Plt: £110.30 to a £1 stake. Pool of £70893.11 - 468.80 winning tickets. T/Qpdt: £27.70 to a £1 stake. Pool of £4408.48 - 117.36 winning tickets. SP

2230 NOTTINGHAM (L-H)
Saturday, May 11
OFFICIAL GOING: Good changing to good to soft after race 4 (3.55)
Wind: Moderate half against Weather: Grey c;loud and showers

2267 ODDS ON FAVOURITE DG TAXIS 01159 500500 MAIDEN STKS 6f 15y
2:15 (2:17) (Class 5) 3-Y-O **£3,234** (£962; £481; £240) **Stalls High**

Form RPR
-230 **1** **Star Of Rohm**[37] 1345 3-9-5 75 HayleyTurner 6 77
(Michael Bell) *led over 1 1/2f: trckd ldr: swtchd lft and hdwy to chal over 1f out: rdn to ld ins fnl f: kpt on* **5/2**[2]

2 nk **Duke Cosimo** 3-9-5 0 TomEaves 5 76+
(Sir Michael Stoute) *trckd ldrs: hdwy and cl up 1/2-way: effrt to chal over 1f out and ev ch: green and rdn ent fnl f: kpt on wl towards fin* **9/4**[1]

03 **3** 1 **The Dark Wizard (IRE)**[11] 1896 3-9-5 0 JamesDoyle 1 73
(Roger Charlton) *sn cl up: led over 4f out: jnd and rdn 2f out: drvn and hdd ins fnl f: kpt on* **10/3**[3]

0-0 **4** *13* **Carneades (IRE)**[19] 1732 3-9-5 0 LukeMorris 7 31
(Ed Walker) *towards rr and rdn along 1/2-way: sme hdwy over 2f out: n.d* **50/1**

5-0 **5** *6* **Cara Gina**[9] 1962 3-9-0 0 GrahamLee 3
(William Haggas) *chsd ldrs on wd outside: rdn along wl over 2f out: sn wknd* **9/1**

0- **6** *5* **Green Monkey**[212] 7006 3-9-5 0 FrederikTylicki 4
(James Fanshawe) *chsd ldrs: rdn along over 2f out: sn wknd* **13/2**

7 *18* **Dropping Zone** 3-9-5 0 MickyFenton 2
(Des Donovan) *s.i.s: a bhd* **33/1**

1m 15.44s (0.74) **Going Correction** +0.15s/f (Good) **7** Ran SP% **110.7**
Speed ratings (Par 99): **101,100,99,81,73 67,43**
toteswingers 1&2 £1.30, 2&3 £1.10, 1&3 £3.30 CSF £7.95 TOTE £2.90: £2.00, £1.80; EX 7.80 Trifecta £27.60 Pool: £1419.30 - 38.43 winning units..
Owner Mrs Louise Whitehead & Chris Lomas **Bred** C J Murfitt **Trained** Newmarket, Suffolk

FOCUS
Outer track used. The rain came just before racing and, after riding in the opener, Luke Morris described the ground as somewhere between good to soft and soft. This looks pretty ordinary maiden form, rated a little cautiously.

2268 MCARTHURGLEN EAST MIDLANDS DESIGNER OUTLET H'CAP (JOCKEY CLUB GRASSROOTS SPRINT SERIES QUALIFIER) 5f 13y

2:45 (2:45) (Class 5) (0-75,75) 4-Y-0+ **£3,234** (£962; £481; £240) **Stalls** High

Form RPR

14-0 **1** **Whitecrest**[15] 1814 5-9-3 **71** LukeMorris 5 81
(John Spearing) *chsd ldrs: hdwy 2f out: n.m.r and swtchd lft over 1f out: sn rdn: led jst ins fnl f: drvn and kpt on wl towards fin* **10/1**

-035 **2** *½* **Phoenix Clubs (IRE)**[15] 1807 4-9-3 **71** BarryMcHugh 8 79
(Paul Midgley) *in tch: hdwy whn nt clr run and swtchd rt over 1f out: rdn and ev ch whn wandered ins fnl f: kpt on* **4/1**[1]

3331 **3** *1½* **Dark Lane**[9] 1952 7-8-11 **72** RobJFitzpatrick(7) 9 75
(David Evans) *towards rr: hdwy 2f out: sn rdn: styng on whn n.m.r over 1f out: drvn and kpt on fnl f* **6/1**[3]

000 **4** *1¼* **Quality Art (USA)**[23] 1650 5-8-7 **61** oh1 KellyHarrison 3 59
(Richard Guest) *chsd ldrs on outer: hdwy 2f out: rdn and ev ch ent fnl f: sn drvn and one pce* **28/1**

4105 **5** *hd* **Captain Scooby**[23] 1649 7-9-5 **73** RobbieFitzpatrick 10 71
(Richard Guest) *bhd: rdn along over 2f out: styd on appr fnl f: nrst fin* **7/1**

-310 **6** *½* **Another Citizen (IRE)**[15] 1807 5-8-13 **74** (b) GaryMahon(7) 6 70
(Tim Easterby) *chsd ldrs: hdwy 2f out: rdn and edgd lft over 1f out: sn drvn and btn* **4/1**[1]

2446 **7** *2½* **Steelcut**[31] 1467 9-8-7 **61** MartinDwyer 7 48
(Mark Buckley) *a towards rr* **14/1**

00-4 **8** *1* **Majestic Manannan (IRE)**[21] 1681 4-8-9 **63** PaulQuinn 4 46
(David Nicholls) *broke wl and led early: sn hdd and trckd ldr: rdn along 2f out: sn wknd* **9/2**[2]

020- **9** *1* **Powerful Wind (IRE)**[157] 7995 4-9-7 **75** JamesDoyle 1 55
(Ronald Harris) *sn led: clr 1/2-way: rdn over 1f out: hdd jst ins fnl f and wknd qckly* **12/1**

1m 2.09s (0.59) **Going Correction** +0.15s/f (Good) **9** Ran SP% **111.9**
Speed ratings (Par 103): **101,100,97,95,95 94,90,89,87**
toteswingers 1&2 £7.80, 2&3 £4.20, 1&3 £8.60 CSF £47.72 CT £262.10 TOTE £3.80: £7.30, £1.80, £1.40; EX 98.90 Trifecta £696.50 Part won. Pool: £928.74 - 0.20 winning units..
Owner G M Eales **Bred** J Spearing And Kate Ive **Trained** Kinnersley, Worcs

FOCUS
They congregated down the middle of the track this time and the early gallop was frenetic, with those to the fore early dropping away at the business end and the principals coming from off the pace. The form is rated around the winner.

2269 WEATHERBYS HAMILTON INSURANCE H'CAP 1m 6f 15y

3:20 (3:20) (Class 4) (0-85,85) 4-Y-0+ **£5,175** (£1,540; £769; £384) **Stalls** Low

Form RPR

3001 **1** **Hallstatt (IRE)**[16] 1794 7-8-2 **66** oh3 (t) RaulDaSilva(3) 5 74
(John Mackie) *trckd ldrs: hdwy 3f out: rdn to chse clr ldr 2f out: drvn ins fnl f: led last 50yds: hld on wl* **8/1**

331- **2** *hd* **Twelve Strings (IRE)**[202] 7269 4-9-4 **80** JamesDoyle 4 88
(Brian Ellison) *hld up in rr: stdy hdwy on wd outside wl over 2f out: rdn to chal over 1f out: drvn and ev ch ins fnl f: no ex towards fin* **5/2**[1]

162- **3** *½* **Stock Hill Fair**[208] 7109 5-9-4 **79** LiamKeniry 6 86
(Brendan Powell) *led: qcknd clr over 3f out: rdn along wl over 1f out: drvn ins fnl f: hdd and no ex last 50yds* **9/2**[3]

P20- **4** *4* **Danvilla**[198] 3241 6-9-8 **83** MartinDwyer 2 84
(Paul Webber) *trckd ldng pair: hdwy over 3f out: rdn 2f out: sn one pce* **9/1**

04-4 **5** *1¼* **Palazzo Bianco**[16] 1774 5-9-7 **85** LeeTopliss(3) 7 85
(Brian Ellison) *trckd ldrs: effrt over 3f out: sn rdn along and wknd over 2f out* **7/2**[2]

20/5 **6** *3¼* **Eshtyaaq**[19] 1733 6-8-11 **72** LukeMorris 3 67
(David Evans) *trckd ldr: rdn along 3f out: drvn over 2f out: grad wknd* **9/2**[3]

0-00 **7** *4½* **Bollin Greta**[15] 1805 8-8-9 **75** DarylByrne(5) 8 64
(Tim Easterby) *hld up: a in rr* **16/1**

3m 8.51s (1.51) **Going Correction** +0.15s/f (Good)
WFA 4 from 5yo+ 1lb **7** Ran SP% **114.2**
Speed ratings (Par 105): **101,100,100,98,97 95,93**
toteswingers 1&2 £22.20, 2&3 £1.50, 1&3 £5.50 CSF £28.25 CT £101.99 TOTE £11.20: £2.60, £1.90; EX 35.40 Trifecta £79.70 Pool: £566.31 - 5.32 winning units..
Owner A B Hill **Bred** Darley **Trained** Church Broughton , Derbys

FOCUS
This looks reasonable form for the grade and there are reasons for thinking most of these can win races this season. The winner is rated back to last year's C&D form.

2270 E B F WEATHERBYS HAMILTON INSURANCE KILVINGTON FILLIES' STKS (LISTED RACE) 6f 15y

3:55 (3:58) (Class 1) 3-Y-0+

£22,684 (£8,600; £4,304; £2,144; £1,076; £540) **Stalls** High

Form RPR

5-2 **1** **Scream Blue Murder (IRE)**[21] 1704 3-8-7 98 WayneLordan 2 106
(T Stack, Ire) *racd towards centre: trckd ldrs: hdwy over 2f out: swtchd rt towards stands' rail wl over 1f out: sn rdn to chal: drvn ins fnl f: kpt on wl to ld nr fin* **85/40**[2]

50-0 **2** *nk* **Hoyam**[7] 2019 3-8-7 101 HayleyTurner 7 105
(Michael Bell) *trckd ldr on stands' rail: hdwy over 2f out: rdn to ld over 1f out: drvn ins fnl f: hdd and nt qckn towards fin* **5/1**[3]

600- **3** *6* **Restiadargent (FR)**[186] 7624 4-9-3 111 GrahamLee 1 89
(William Haggas) *dwlt: hdwy 3f out: trckd ldrs towards centre: hdwy 2f out: edgd rt towards rails and rdn to chse ldng pair ent fnl f: sn no imp* **11/10**[1]

30-0 **4** *5* **Lasilia (IRE)**[15] 1808 3-8-7 87 FrederikTylicki 8 70
(Kevin Ryan) *led on stands' rail: pushed along 2f out: rdn and hdd over 1f out: wknd ent fnl f* **33/1**

110- **5** *nse* **Picabo (IRE)**[238] 6244 5-9-3 92 FergusSweeney 6 73
(Henry Candy) *chsd ldrs towards centre: rdn along over 2f out: sn one pce* **10/1**

0-05 **6** *5* **Chilli Green**[14] 1835 6-9-3 87 LiamKeniry 4 57
(Julia Feilden) *prom centre: rdn along over 2f out: sn wknd* **80/1**

34-0 **7** *1¼* **Miss Diva**[15] 1808 3-8-7 85 ChrisCatlin 5 50
(Richard Hannon) *racd towards centre: prom: rdn along 1/2-way: sn wknd* **33/1**

1m 14.5s (-0.20) **Going Correction** +0.15s/f (Good)
WFA 3 from 4yo+ 10lb **7** Ran SP% **112.5**
Speed ratings (Par 108): **107,106,98,91,91 85,83**
toteswingers 1&2 £3.00, 2&3 £2.30, 1&3 £1.10 CSF £12.56 TOTE £3.40: £1.40, £2.10; EX 14.50 Trifecta £15.60 Pool: £1140.15 - 54.56 winning units..
Owner Mrs G A Rupert **Bred** Annalee Bloodstock & Rockhart Trading Ltd **Trained** Golden, Co Tipperary

FOCUS
Not a great deal of depth to this fillies' Listed contest, especially with clear form pick Restiadargent not running anywhere near to her official rating of 111. The form is rated around the runner-up.

2271 WEATHERBYS BANK H'CAP 1m 2f 50y

4:30 (4:31) (Class 3) (0-90,81) 3-Y-0 **£9,703** (£2,887; £1,443; £721) **Stalls** Low

Form RPR

00-2 **1** **Salutation (IRE)**[6] 2050 3-9-2 **81** MichaelJMMurphy(5) 3 91
(Mark Johnston) *mde all: rdn and qcknd over 2f out: styd on strly fnl f* **11/8**[1]

1- **2** *1¾* **Magog**[220] 6796 3-9-1 **75** JamesDoyle 1 82+
(Roger Charlton) *hld up in rr: stdy hdwy on outer wl over 2f out: rdn wl over 1f out: styd on fnl f: tk 2nd nr fin* **13/8**[2]

50-2 **3** *nk* **Asgardella (IRE)**[16] 1773 3-9-0 **79** GeorgeChaloner(5) 2 85
(Richard Fahey) *t.k.h: trckd wnr on inner: pushed along 3f out: effrt and nt clr run 2f out: rdn to chse wnr over 1f out: sn drvn and kpt on same pce: lost 2nd nr fin* **6/1**[3]

540- **4** *7* **Arlecchino (IRE)**[226] 6597 3-9-3 **77** RoystonFfrench 4 70
(Ed McMahon) *trckd wnr: effrt 3f out: rdn along 2f out: drvn and wknd over 1f out* **15/2**

2m 15.57s (1.27) **Going Correction** +0.15s/f (Good) **4** Ran SP% **106.3**
Speed ratings (Par 103): **100,98,98,92**
CSF £3.77 TOTE £1.80; EX 3.30 Trifecta £5.60 Pool: £926.88 - 122.78 winning units..
Owner Sheikh Hamdan Bin Mohammed Al Maktoum **Bred** Foursome Thoroughbreds, Muir & Waldron **Trained** Middleham Moor, N Yorks

FOCUS
An intriguing race despite just four runners. The winner was well in and is rated to his Newmarket form.

2272 MOST RELIABLE BET DG TAXIS H'CAP 1m 75y

5:05 (5:05) (Class 5) (0-75,75) 3-Y-0 **£3,234** (£962; £481; £240) **Stalls** Centre

Form RPR

01- **1** **Noble Gift**[208] 7103 3-9-7 **75** HayleyTurner 1 81+
(William Knight) *t.k.h: hld up in rr: stdy hdwy 3f out: swtchd outside and effrt wl over 1f out: rdn to ld ent fnl f: styd on* **5/1**[3]

34-2 **2** *1½* **Cash Is King**[40] 1293 3-9-0 **73** GeorgeChaloner(5) 2 75+
(Richard Fahey) *t.k.h: trckd ldng pair: hdwy 3f out: effrt and n.m.r over 1f out: sn swtchd rt and rdn: kpt on fnl f* **3/1**[1]

-242 **3** *hd* **Beau Select (IRE)**[33] 1424 3-8-13 **67** (b) LukeMorris 7 67
(Robert Eddery) *trckd ldrs: hdwy 3f out: effrt to chal 2f out: rdn to ld and hung bdly lft jst over 1f out: hdd and drvn ent fnl f: edgd lft and one pce* **20/1**

022- **4** *½* **Soaring Spirits (IRE)**[164] 7899 3-9-1 **74** MichaelJMMurphy(5) 4 76+
(Roger Varian) *trckd ldrs: hdwy over 3f out: effrt whn nt clr run over 1f out: sn rdn and kpt on fnl f* **7/2**[2]

-161 **5** *7* **Corn Snow (USA)**[9] 1965 3-9-7 **75** RoystonFfrench 6 58
(Mark Johnston) *trckd ldr: cl up over 4f out: led over 3f out: rdn along and hdd whn hmpd over 1f out: sn wknd* **5/1**[3]

00-5 **6** *¾* **Woody Bay**[14] 1829 3-9-0 **68** GrahamLee 3 49
(James Given) *sn led: rdn along 4f out: hdd over 3f out: wkng whn n.m.r over 1f out* **9/1**

202- **7** *hd* **Danz Choice (IRE)**[168] 7856 3-9-7 **75** JamesDoyle 8 56
(Richard Hannon) *hld up: hdwy 3f out: rdn along 2f out: sn btn* **6/1**

6160 **8** *19* **Blazeofenchantment (USA)**[14] 1832 3-8-10 **64** (p) ChrisCatlin 5
(Noel Quinlan) *a in rr: outpcd and bhd fnl 3f* **40/1**

1m 49.79s (0.79) **Going Correction** +0.15s/f (Good) **8** Ran SP% **112.0**
Speed ratings (Par 99): **102,100,100,99,92 92,91,72**
toteswingers 1&2 £4.00, 2&3 £6.30, 1&3 £13.70 CSF £19.53 CT £271.13 TOTE £7.70: £2.40, £1.30, £3.30; EX 21.20 Trifecta £250.50 Pool: £2627.55 - 7.86 winning units..
Owner Gail Brown Racing (V) **Bred** Theakston Stud **Trained** Patching, W Sussex

FOCUS
They went a good gallop but it became quite messy as the pacesetters weakened. The third looks the key to the form.

2273 SAFE BET DG TAXIS 01159 500500 APPRENTICE TRAINING SERIES H'CAP (RACING EXCELLENCE INITIATIVE) 1m 75y

5:35 (5:36) (Class 6) (0-65,64) 4-Y-0+ **£1,940** (£577; £288; £144) **Stalls** Centre

Form RPR

4534 **1** **Handheld**[31] 1466 6-9-3 **63** (p) ShelleyBirkett(3) 9 71
(Julia Feilden) *in tch: hdwy over 2f out: rdn to chse ldrs wl over 1f out: styd on wl fnl f to ld on line* **7/1**[3]

45-2 **2** *shd* **Skyfire**[36] 1366 6-9-2 **64** KevinStott(5) 8 72
(Nick Kent) *trckd ldrs: hdwy over 3f out: led wl over 1f out: rdn appr fnl f: hdd on line* **6/1**[2]

1004 **3** *shd* **Outlaw Torn (IRE)**[16] 1788 4-8-11 **57** (e) EoinWalsh(3) 5 65+
(Richard Guest) *hld up in rr: stdy hdwy 3f out: chsd ldrs 2f out: sn rdn: swtchd rt to outer over 1f out and rdn: styd on strly fnl f: jst failed* **10/1**

0445 **4** *2* **Mishhar (IRE)**[17] 1757 4-9-0 **57** (v) DavidSimmonson 3 60
(Tony Coyle) *dwlt and in rr: stdy hdwy 3f out: rdn to chse ldrs wl over 1f out: drvn and kpt on fnl f* **10/1**

4-56 **5** *1¼* **Viking Warrior (IRE)**[17] 1757 6-9-1 **63** ConnorBeasley(5) 13 63
(Michael Dods) *prom: hdwy 3f out and sn cl up: chal 2f out: sn rdn and ev ch tl drvn and one pce wl ins fnl f* **10/1**

4002 **6** 1 ½ **Hail Promenader (IRE)**[9] [1950] 7-9-0 **62**............(p) RobJFitzpatrick(5) 12 59
(Anthony Carson) *prom: led over 3f out: rdn along 2f out: sn hdd: drvn over 1f out and grad wknd* **5/2**[1]
0600 **7** 1 ¼ **Menadati (USA)**[74] [805] 5-8-9 **55**.................................. PatMillman(3) 11 49
(Peter Hiatt) *dwlt and in rr: sme hdwy over 2f out: sn rdn and n.d* **14/1**
2300 **8** 2 **Quintain (IRE)**[16] [1775] 5-8-7 **55**...................................... GaryMahon(5) 4 44
(Tim Easterby) *a towards rr* **16/1**
5-05 **9** 4 **One Of Twins**[16] [1797] 5-8-7 **53**...........................(p) MatthewHopkins(3) 2 33
(Michael Easterby) *led: rdn along and hdd over 3f out: wknd wl over 2f out* **12/1**
00-5 **10** ¾ **Ma Kellys (IRE)**[26] [1567] 4-8-3 **53**................................ KatieDowson(7) 7 31
(Micky Hammond) *nvr bttr than midfield* **22/1**
-005 **11** 1 ¼ **Kheskianto (IRE)**[24] [1610] 7-8-0 **50** oh3...............(t) DanielleMooney(7) 10 25
(Michael Chapman) *a towards rr* **50/1**
6350 **12** *nk* **Boy The Bell**[17] [1757] 6-8-12 **55**................................(p) JacobButterfield 6 30
(Ollie Pears) *chsd ldrs: rdn along wl over 3f out: sn wknd* **25/1**
5120 **13** 1 ¾ **Mataajir (USA)**[29] [1521] 5-8-11 **59**............................. AdamMcLean(5) 1 30
(Derek Shaw) *chsd ldrs: rdn along over 3f out: sn wknd* **16/1**

1m 48.64s (-0.36) **Going Correction** +0.15s/f (Good) **13** Ran SP% **118.9**
Speed ratings (Par 101): **107,106,106,104,103 102,100,98,94,94 92,92,90**
toteswingers 1&2 £3.10, 2&3 £11.70, 1&3 £9.20 CSF £47.44 CT £426.31 TOTE £7.40: £2.20, £2.00, £4.10; EX 37.50 Trifecta £339.90 Pool: £1590.11 - 3.50 winning units..
Owner Miss J Feilden **Bred** Juddmonte Farms Ltd **Trained** Exning, Suffolk

FOCUS
A cracking finish to this apprentice riders' race, which was run at a good pace. The winner is rated in line with last year's turf form.
T/Plt: £82.80 to a £1 stake. Pool of £48585.05 - 428.27 winning tickets. T/Qpdt: £23.60 to a £1 stake. Pool of £1793.12 - 56.20 winning tickets. JR

2025 THIRSK (L-H)
Saturday, May 11

OFFICIAL GOING: Good (good to firm in places; 8.8)
Wind: fresh 1/2 behind Weather: finw but breezy

2274 BET & WATCH WITH RACINGUK'S APP H'CAP 1m
5:45 (5:47) (Class 6) (0-60,60) 3-Y-O **£2,045** (£603; £302) **Stalls** Low

Form RPR
604- **1** **War Lord (IRE)**[197] [7363] 3-9-4 **58**................................ DanielTudhope 11 72
(David O'Meara) *led 1f: trckd ldrs: led wl over 1f out: hrd rdn ins fnl f: hld on towards fin* **13/8**[1]
4-35 **2** *nk* **Krupskaya (FR)**[35] [1393] 3-8-13 **60**................................ JoeyHaynes(7) 4 73
(Mrs K Burke) *trckd ldrs: chal jst ins fnl f: no extr nr fin* **14/1**
3-64 **3** 6 **Marcus Caesar (IRE)**[17] [1764] 3-9-0 **59**.............................. LMcNiff(5) 6 58
(David Barron) *t.k.h: led after 1f: hdd wl over 1f out: grad wknd* **5/1**[2]
4511 **4** 4 **Precision Strike**[97] [507] 3-9-2 **56**..............................(p) KellyHarrison 13 46
(Richard Guest) *in rr: hdwy on outside over 2f out: edgd lft over 1f out: nvr trbld ldrs* **14/1**
3-54 **5** 2 **Sweet Vintage (IRE)**[18] [1747] 3-9-0 **57**............................ RyanClark(3) 5 42
(Mark Brisbourne) *chsd ldrs effrt over 2f out: kpt on one pce* **16/1**
334- **6** *nse* **Baraboy (IRE)**[221] [6753] 3-9-5 **59**.................................. JamesSullivan 12 44
(Barry Murtagh) *mid-div: effrt over 2f out: one pce* **16/1**
400- **7** 2 ¾ **Ella Motiva (IRE)**[164] [7919] 3-9-5 **59**.............................. MickyFenton 2 38
(Mark Brisbourne) *s.i.s: kpt on fnl 2f: nvr a factor* **33/1**
04-0 **8** 3 ¼ **Marble Silver (IRE)**[16] [1776] 3-9-5 **59**............................ DuranFentiman 3 30
(Tim Easterby) *in tch: effrt over 2f out: wknd over 1f out* **50/1**
000- **9** 1 ½ **Artful Prince**[217] [6880] 3-9-2 **56**.................................... DaleSwift 8 24
(James Given) *mid-div: drvn and lost pl after 2f* **10/1**
00-6 **10** *shd* **Grey Destiny**[21] [1687] 3-9-4 **58**..................................... PaulMulrennan 1 26
(Mel Brittain) *dwlt: hdwy into mid-div after 2f: drvn over 2f out: wknd over 1f out* **18/1**
4-65 **11** 2 ¾ **Polar Forest**[94] [538] 3-9-4 **58**................................ RobbieFitzpatrick 7 19
(Richard Guest) *s.i.s: t.k.h in rr: nvr on terms* **50/1**
0-64 **12** 3 ¼ **Gold Roll (IRE)**[24] [1608] 3-9-6 **60**................................ PJMcDonald 9 14
(Ruth Carr) *s.i.s: a bhd* **6/1**[3]
500- **13** 31 **Noosa Sound**[235] [6337] 3-9-3 **60**.................................... LeeTopliss(3) 14
(John Davies) *chsd ldrs: wd bnd over 4f out: lost pl over 2f out: bhd whn eased: t.o* **50/1**
00-0 **14** ¾ **Antonius**[16] [1772] 3-9-4 **58**.. TomEaves 10
(Kristin Stubbs) *chsd ldrs: lost pl over 2f out: bhd whn eased: t.o* **40/1**

1m 42.4s (2.30) **Going Correction** +0.225s/f (Good) **14** Ran SP% **119.8**
Speed ratings (Par 97): **97,96,90,86,84 84,81,78,77,77 74,71,40,39**
toteswingers 1&2 £66.70, 1&3 £9.40, 2&3 £28.20 CSF £26.29 CT £99.91 TOTE £3.00: £1.20, £3.50, £2.00; EX 29.90 Trifecta £56.70 Pool: £1170.33 - 15.48 winning units..
Owner Geoff & Sandra Turnbull **Bred** Mrs Brid Cosgrove **Trained** Nawton, N Yorks

FOCUS
An opener run on ground which jockeys' described as being on the easy side. It was just an ordinary handicap overall but it's best to take a positive view of the leading pair, who pulled clear. The time was relatively good too. In common with many races here it paid to race handily.

2275 DICK PEACOCK SPRINT H'CAP 6f
6:15 (6:16) (Class 5) (0-75,75) 4-Y-O+ **£3,234** (£962; £481; £240) **Stalls** High

Form RPR
00-2 **1** **Secret City (IRE)**[17] [1757] 7-8-13 **67**...........................(b) FrederikTylicki 9 76
(Robin Bastiman) *towards rr: hdwy over 2f out: styd on wl fnl f: led nr fin* **10/1**
3-05 **2** *nk* **Lenny Bee**[23] [1652] 7-9-7 **75**.......................................(t) PhillipMakin 7 83
(Garry Moss) *chsd ldr: led jst ins fnl f: hdd nr fin* **22/1**
0-20 **3** 2 ¾ **Spykes Bay (USA)**[15] [1801] 4-9-1 **69**......................(b[1]) RobertWinston 15 68
(Mrs K Burke) *led: hdd jst ins fnl f: kpt on same pce* **6/1**[3]
-341 **4** ½ **Beckermet (IRE)**[9] [1964] 11-9-4 **72**.............................. JamesSullivan 3 70+
(Ruth Carr) *racd wd: chsd ldrs: edgd rt and kpt on fnl f* **11/1**
006- **5** *shd* **Mon Brav**[178] [7716] 6-9-7 **75**... DaleSwift 14 72
(Brian Ellison) *sn drvn along in mid-div: hdwy over 2f out: kpt on fnl f* **5/1**[2]
6003 **6** ½ **Illustrious Prince (IRE)**[5] [2096] 6-8-4 **65**.............. LukeLeadbitter(7) 13 61
(Declan Carroll) *mid-div: hdwy over 2f out: nvr nr ldrs* **15/2**
56-5 **7** 4 ½ **Mercers Row**[21] [1692] 6-9-2 **70**.................................... BarryMcHugh 6 51
(Karen Tutty) *dwlt: sme hdwy over 2f out: nvr a factor* **14/1**
0203 **8** ½ **Dickie Le Davoir**[9] [1964] 9-8-13 **67**......................(b) RobbieFitzpatrick 8 47
(Richard Guest) *s.i.s: kpt on fnl 2f: nvr a factor* **25/1**
4-00 **9** ½ **Diamond Blue**[15] [1800] 5-8-13 **67**...............................(v) PaulQuinn 10 45
(Richard Whitaker) *mid-div: effrt over 2f out: sn wknd* **28/1**
3-06 **10** ½ **Sleepy Blue Ocean**[67] [885] 7-8-13 **67**......................(p) DanielTudhope 12 44
(John Balding) *w ldr: wknd appr fnl f* **12/1**
0-31 **11** *hd* **Mission Impossible**[21] [1692] 8-9-4 **72**........................ PatrickMathers 11 48
(Tracy Waggott) *mid-div: effrt over 2f out: wknd over 1f out* **9/2**[1]
30-0 **12** 6 **Commanche Raider (IRE)**[21] [1692] 6-9-3 **71**..................(p) TomEaves 1 28
(Michael Dods) *racd wd: chsd ldrs: lost pl over 2f out* **33/1**
13 1 ¼ **Storm Lightning**[199] [7336] 4-9-4 **75**.............................. RyanClark(3) 2 28
(Mark Brisbourne) *racd wd: chsd ldrs: wknd 2f out* **33/1**
134- **14** 2 **Half A Crown (IRE)**[152] [8059] 8-9-1 **69**.................... MichaelStainton 5 15
(Nick Kent) *in rr: bhd fnl 2f* **18/1**
00-0 **15** 1 ¾ **Swilly Ferry (USA)**[23] [1644] 6-9-4 **72**........................(v[1]) MartinDwyer 4 13
(David Nicholls) *racd wd: chsd ldrs: lost pl 2f out* **28/1**

1m 11.33s (-1.37) **Going Correction** -0.125s/f (Firm) **15** Ran SP% **118.9**
Speed ratings (Par 103): **104,103,99,99,99 98,92,91,91,90 90,82,80,77,75**
toteswingers 1&2 £66.70, 1&3 £9.40, 2&3 £28.20 CSF £220.90 CT £1460.97 TOTE £8.50: £3.10, £6.20, £2.50; EX 318.30 Trifecta £769.30 Part won. Pool: £1025.77 - 0.06 winning units..
Owner Ms M Austerfield **Bred** Miss Karen Theobald **Trained** Cowthorpe, N Yorks

FOCUS
A fair sprint. They went a good pace, setting it up to some extent for the winner, who came from well back. The main action unfolded towards the stands' rail, the quartet who raced more towards the centre always struggling to keep tabs on the main group. Straightforward form.

2276 ABF SOLDIERS' CHARITY (S) STKS 6f
6:45 (6:46) (Class 6) 3-Y-O+ **£1,940** (£577; £288; £144) **Stalls** High

Form RPR
0-12 **1** **Tajneed (IRE)**[25] [1598] 10-9-11 72.............................. PaulMulrennan 9 70
(David Nicholls) *mid-div: hdwy over 2f out: styd on to ld ins fnl f: drvn out* **9/4**[1]
0-63 **2** 2 **Headstight (IRE)**[26] [1578] 4-9-1 50..............................(p) MickyFenton 10 54
(Paul Midgley) *in rr: hdwy over 2f out: styd on to take 2nd nr fin* **33/1**
0-41 **3** *hd* **Go Go Green (IRE)**[40] [1280] 7-9-11 72......................... DanielTudhope 4 63
(Jim Goldie) *in rr: hdwy over 2f out: styd on ins fnl f* **7/2**[2]
40-4 **4** *nk* **Karate Queen**[9] [1962] 8-8-10 48..........................(p) ShirleyTeasdale(5) 11 52
(Ron Barr) *towards rr: hdwy over 2f out: kpt on same pce fnl f* **40/1**
520- **5** ½ **Red Cape (FR)**[140] [8232] 10-9-6 70................................ JamesSullivan 8 56
(Ruth Carr) *led: hdd ins fnl f: kpt on one pce* **8/1**[3]
20-4 **5** *dht* **Captain Royale (IRE)**[9] [1961] 8-9-6 59......................(p) BarryMcHugh 1 56
(Tracy Waggott) *w ldrs: kpt on same pce fnl f* **28/1**
2230 **7** 3 **Moe's Place (IRE)**[17] [1760] 3-8-10 65..........................(b[1]) PhillipMakin 7 46
(Kevin Ryan) *w ldrs: wkng whn n.m.r jst ins fnl f* **11/1**
401- **8** 3 ¼ **Ryedane (IRE)**[233] [6403] 11-8-13 64.................(b) RachelRichardson(7) 6 36
(Tim Easterby) *mid-div: wknd fnl 2f* **20/1**
40-4 **8** *dht* **Bridge Valley**[40] [1280] 6-8-13 48.............................. KieranSchofield(7) 12 36
(Jason Ward) *a in rr* **66/1**
2242 **10** 47 **Paradise Spectre**[6] [2038] 6-9-6 72................................ RobertWinston 5
(Mrs K Burke) *in rr: heavily eased over 1f out: virtually p.u: t.o* **9/4**[1]

1m 11.95s (-0.75) **Going Correction** -0.125s/f (Firm)
WFA 3 from 4yo+ 10lb **10** Ran SP% **118.3**
Speed ratings (Par 101): **100,97,97,96,96 96,92,87,87,25**
toteswingers 1&2 £3.20, 1&3 £2.50, 2&3 £17.70 CSF £91.45 TOTE £3.10: £1.50, £9.10, £2.10; EX 64.00 Trifecta £572.80 Pool: £795.35 - 1.04 winning units..There was no bid for the winner.
Owner Mrs Alex Nicholls **Bred** R Hodgins **Trained** Sessay, N Yorks

FOCUS
Probably best to take a low view of the overall form, the likes of the second and fourth certainly holding it down.

2277 GT GROUP H'CAP 1m 4f
7:15 (7:15) (Class 4) (0-80,80) 4-Y-O+ **£5,175** (£1,540; £769; £384) **Stalls** High

Form RPR
3 **1** **Roman Flight (IRE)**[42] [563] 5-9-5 **78**........................(v) DanielTudhope 7 93+
(David O'Meara) *trckd ldrs: led 2f out: wnt clr fnl f: eased nr fin* **11/4**[1]
5120 **2** 6 **Reflect (IRE)**[56] [1037] 5-9-3 **76**..............................(t) MartinDwyer 15 79
(Derek Shaw) *swtchd lft after s: in rr: hdwy on outside over 2f out: edgd lft over 1f out: kpt on to take 2nd nr fin* **16/1**
-332 **3** *nk* **Arizona John (IRE)**[16] [1774] 8-9-2 **75**........................ StephenCraine 13 78
(John Mackie) *mid-div: hdwy on outside to trck ldrs 6f out: effrt 2f out: styd on same pce* **12/1**
43-5 **4** ½ **Tinseltown**[17] [1763] 7-8-3 **67**................................(p) ShirleyTeasdale(5) 8 69
(Brian Rothwell) *led hdd 2f out: kpt on one pce* **20/1**
-021 **5** ½ **Carragold**[26] [1567] 7-9-1 **74**.. DuranFentiman 1 75
(Mel Brittain) *mid-div: effrt over 3f out: one pce fnl 2f* **25/1**
0-2 **6** *nk* **Mr Snoozy**[16] [1790] 4-8-7 **66** oh1....................................(p) PaddyAspell 9 67
(Tim Walford) *chsd ldr: drvn over 3f out: one pce fnl 2f* **12/1**
-231 **7** ½ **Titus Bolt (IRE)**[16] [1790] 4-8-9 **68** oh1 ow2......................... GrahamLee 5 71+
(Jim Goldie) *in rr: hdwy over 3f out: swtchd rt 2f out: kpt on one pce fnl 2f* **7/1**[3]
11/6 **8** *nk* **San Cassiano (IRE)**[14] [1824] 6-9-7 **80**............................ PJMcDonald 4 79
(Ruth Carr) *mid-div: hdwy 4f out: keeping on whn nt clr run on inner 2f out: nvr a threat* **16/1**
505- **9** *nk* **Scarlet Whispers**[197] [7367] 4-9-4 **77**............................ MickyFenton 14 76
(Pam Sly) *in rr: hdwy on outside over 2f out: nvr nr ldrs* **22/1**
102- **10** *hd* **Villa Royale**[202] [7269] 4-9-1 **74**.................................... DavidNolan 12 72
(David O'Meara) *chsd ldrs: drvn over 4f out: one pce fnl 2f* **9/1**
321- **11** 3 ¾ **Major Domo (FR)**[144] [6126] 5-8-10 **69**........................ RussKennemore 6 61
(Micky Hammond) *s.i.s: in rr: sme hdwy over 2f out: sn lost pl* **33/1**
6-14 **12** 3 ¾ **Gold Show**[10] [1936] 4-8-13 **72**.................................... PaulMulrennan 3 58+
(Edwin Tuer) *mid-div: sme hdwy whn nt clr run 2f out: sn eased* **11/1**
531- **13** *nk* **Nashville (IRE)**[143] [8170] 4-8-11 **70**............................ FrederikTylicki 2 56
(Richard Fahey) *trckd ldrs: wkng whn hmpd over 1f out* **6/1**[2]
420- **14** 17 **Dark Dune (IRE)**[207] [7147] 5-9-4 **77**................................ TomEaves 10 36
(Tim Easterby) *chsd ldrs: wnt 2nd over 3f out: lost pl 2f out: bhd whn eased: t.o* **28/1**

2m 37.84s (1.64) **Going Correction** +0.225s/f (Good) **14** Ran SP% **118.3**
Speed ratings (Par 105): **103,99,98,98,98 97,97,97,97,97 94,92,91,80**
toteswingers 1&2 £7.70, 1&3 £5.50, 2&3 £16.60 CSF £45.58 CT £464.42 TOTE £3.00: £1.30, £5.50, £2.30; EX 53.70 Trifecta £542.60 Part won. Pool: £723.51 - 0.67 winning units..
Owner Favourites Racing **Bred** Jim Cockburn **Trained** Nawton, N Yorks

FOCUS
This looked to be a competitive handicap beforehand but turned out to be anything but. The level is set around the second to sixth.

2278 CALVERTS CARPETS H'CAP 1m
7:45 (7:45) (Class 5) (0-75,75) 4-Y-O+ **£3,234** (£962; £481; £240) **Stalls** Low

Form RPR
12-2 **1** **No Dominion (IRE)**[14] [1827] 4-9-2 **70**................................ GrahamLee 6 81+
(James Given) *s.i.s: hdwy on outer over 2f out: styd on to ld nr fin* **11/2**[1]
-500 **2** ¾ **Cono Zur (FR)**[14] [1827] 6-8-11 **65**............................... JamesSullivan 4 74
(Ruth Carr) *led: hdd and no ex towards fin* **12/1**

2104 **3** *5* **Exceedexpectations (IRE)**16 1796 4-9-1 **69**........... DanielTudhope 13 67
(Conor Dore) *chsd ldrs: kpt on same pce fnl f* **9/1**3

-426 **4** *1* **Blue Maisey**10 1932 5-8-11 **65**.................... PaulMulrennan 14 60
(Edwin Tuer) *chsd ldrs: effrt over 2f out: kpt on same pce appr fnl f* **11/1**

-552 **5** *shd* **Sardanapalus**9 1963 4-9-7 **75**...........................(p) PhillipMakin 9 70
(Kevin Ryan) *in rr-div: hdwy on outside over 2f out: kpt on fnl f* **11/2**1

0500 **6** *nk* **Brigadoon**14 1819 6-9-2 **70**.......................... MichaelO'Connell 2 65+
(Philip Kirby) *stdd s: hld up in rr: hdwy whn nt clr run 2f out: swtchd rt nt rchd ldrs* **14/1**

6-22 **7** *1* **Cruiser**11 1905 5-9-7 **75**.......................... MartinDwyer 12 67
(William Muir) *towards rr: hdwy on outer over 2f out: kpt on fnl f* **11/2**1

0-03 **8** *shd* **West Leake Hare (IRE)**8 1994 4-8-9 **63**.................... PaulQuinn 11 55
(David Nicholls) *mid-div: effrt over 2f out: kpt on same pce* **22/1**

11-6 **9** *½* **Kuwait Star**10 1936 4-9-1 **72**.................... RaulDaSilva(3) 8 63
(Jason Ward) *chsd ldrs: drvn over 3f out: one pce fnl 2f* **33/1**

1-33 **10** *hd* **It's A Mans World**16 1786 7-9-4 **75**.................... PaulPickard(3) 5 65+
(Brian Ellison) *mid-div: hdwy on inner over 2f out: one pce whn nt clr run over 1f out* **7/1**2

0-00 **11** *2* **Ellaal**9 1963 4-9-4 **72**.......................... PJMcDonald 10 58
(Ruth Carr) *in rr: sme hdwy over 2f out: nvr on terms* **50/1**

354- **12** *nse* **Who's Shirl**190 7524 7-9-0 **68**.......................... KellyHarrison 7 54
(Chris Fairhurst) *in rr: nvr on terms* **25/1**

0-60 **13** *1* **Aquarian Spirit**16 1788 6-8-7 **61**....................(b1) FrederikTylicki 3 44
(Richard Fahey) *in tch: effrt 3f out: wknd over 1f out* **16/1**

51-5 **14** *2½* **Star City (IRE)**21 1693 4-8-8 **62**.................... TomEaves 1 40
(Michael Dods) *dwlt: t.k.h: sn trcking ldrs: lost pl over 1f out* **14/1**

00/ **15** *22* **Fred Archer (IRE)**45 5086 5-9-7 **75**.................... RobertWinston 15
(Sue Smith) *s.i.s: in rr: bhd whn eased over 1f out: virtually p.u: virtually p.u* **50/1**

1m 42.46s (2.36) **Going Correction** +0.225s/f (Good) **15** Ran SP% **119.0**
Speed ratings (Par 103): **97,96,95,94,94 93,92,92,92,92 90,90,89,86,64**
toteswingers 1&2 £7.70, 1&3 £5.20, 2&3 £9.90 CSF £66.71 CT £599.99 TOTE £4.20: £2.10, £3.50, £2.90; EX 48.40 Trifecta £319.40 Pool: £561.01 - 1.31 winning units..
Owner J Barson **Bred** N Cable & M Smith **Trained** Willoughton, Lincs

FOCUS
Essentially a run-of-the-mill handicap, but it was competitive and the first two were clear. The winner is generally progressive.

2279 LADIES FROM FOUNDATION MAIDEN STKS 1m
8:15 (8:17) (Class 5) 3-Y-O+ £2,587 (£770; £384; £192) Stalls Low

Form RPR

00- **1** **Forging The Path (USA)**206 7167 3-8-13 0................ FrederikTylicki 8 79
(Richard Fahey) *chsd ldrs: led over 2f out: styd on wl to forge clr fnl f: readily* **13/2**2

52-6 **2** *3¼* **Mowhoob**14 1822 3-8-13 72.......................... GrahamLee 10 72
(Jim Goldie) *trckd ldrs: upsides over 2f out: kpt on same pce appr fnl f: no imp* **8/1**3

5 **3** *2* **Cupertino**14 1845 3-8-13 0.......................... PhillipMakin 1 67
(Kevin Ryan) *led: hdd over 2f out: styd on same pce over 1f out* **2/1**1

54-0 **4** *shd* **Mujarrad (USA)**24 1624 3-8-13 74.......................... DaneO'Neill 2 67
(J W Hills) *trckd ldrs: upsides over 2f out: one pce over 1f out* **2/1**1

5 *3¼* **Hussar Ballad (USA)**220 4-9-12 0.................... PaulMulrennan 4 63
(Mel Brittain) *in rr: hdwy over 2f out: nvr a factor* **50/1**

0- **6** *1* **Finn Mac**197 7363 3-8-13 0.......................... PaddyAspell 11 57
(John Norton) *rr-div: hdwy over 2f out: kpt on fnl f* **200/1**

4 **7** *½* **Bonnie Echo**16 1777 6-9-7 0.......................... TomEaves 14 54
(Michael Dods) *in rr: hdwy over 2f out: kpt on fnl f* **28/1**

0- **8** *½* **Three Glasses (IRE)**245 6043 3-8-13 0.................... DuranFentiman 3 55
(Tim Easterby) *prom: effrt over 2f out: fdd over 1f out* **50/1**

0- **9** *nk* **Fab Lolly (IRE)**197 7364 3-8-5 0.................... DeclanCannon(3) 9 49
(James Bethell) *mid-div: drvn and outpcd over 4f out: lost pl over 2f out* **100/1**

0 **10** *¾* **Big John Cannon (IRE)**23 1648 3-8-13 0................ AndrewMullen 15 53
(David Barron) *mid-div: effrt over 2f out: wandered: nvrr a factor* **9/1**

-0 **11** *2¾* **Ground Ginger**17 1760 3-8-13 0.................... AndrewElliott 13 46
(James Bethell) *in tch: effrt over 2f out: sn wknd* **66/1**

12 *1¾* **Whistle We Go (GER)**162 5-9-7 0.................... MichaelStainton 5 40
(Nick Kent) *s.i.s: t.k.h in rr: nvr on terms* **80/1**

13 *2½* **Aryizad (IRE)** 4-9-7 0.......................... RobertWinston 7 35
(Alan Swinbank) *mid-div: hung lft and lost pl over 2f out: sn bhd* **20/1**

60 **14** *5* **Moonlight Dreamer**3 2172 4-9-0 0....................(v1) AliRawlinson(7) 12 23
(David C Griffiths) *prom: lost pl over 1f out: eased* **150/1**

15 *17* **Snap Crackle (IRE)** 3-8-1 0.......................... JoeyHaynes(7) 6
(Mrs K Burke) *s.v.s and green: a detached in rr: t.o 3f out* **20/1**

1m 43.6s (3.50) **Going Correction** +0.225s/f (Good)
WFA 3 from 4yo+ 13lb **15** Ran SP% **122.9**
Speed ratings (Par 103): **91,87,85,85,82 81,80,80,80,79 76,74,72,67,50**
CSF £55.06 TOTE £7.40: £2.60, £2.40, £1.30; EX 30.40 Trifecta £266.30 Pool: £814.31 - 2.29 winning units..
Owner Peter O'Callaghan **Bred** Galleria Bloodstock **Trained** Musley Bank, N Yorks

FOCUS
Fair form from the principals in this maiden. The first four were always prominent off an ordinary pace and the time was moderate. The winner was up a stone on his 2yo form.

2280 WATCH RACING UK ON FREEVIEW 231 H'CAP 7f
8:45 (8:47) (Class 6) (0-60,62) 4-Y-O+ £1,940 (£577; £288; £144) Stalls Low

Form RPR

-600 **1** **No Quarter (IRE)**3 2162 6-9-3 **56**.......................... BarryMcHugh 3 68+
(Tracy Waggott) *trckd ldrs: t.k.h: effrt over 2f out: led over 1f out: styd on wl: readily* **11/2**3

4-50 **2** *1¾* **Gladsome**16 1788 5-9-3 **59**.......................... RaulDaSilva(3) 13 65
(Jason Ward) *in rr: hdwy on outer over 2f out: styd on to chse wnr ins fnl f: no imp* **20/1**

4-00 **3** *2* **The Blue Banana (IRE)**16 1790 4-9-4 **57**..............(p) PaulMulrennan 11 58
(Edwin Tuer) *in rr: hdwy over 2f out: hung lft over 1f out: styd on to take 3rd nr fin* **25/1**

00-1 **4** *½* **Cara's Request (AUS)**8 1994 8-9-9 **62**.................... TomEaves 7 61
(Michael Dods) *w ldr: led after 1f: hdd over 1f out: edgd rt: kpt on same pce* **15/8**1

53-3 **5** *hd* **Eastlands Lad (IRE)**17 1757 4-9-7 **60**....................(p) PJMcDonald 12 59
(Micky Hammond) *chsd ldrs: effrt over 2f out: kpt on same pce fnl f* **5/1**2

0-00 **6** *¾* **Hoppy's Flyer (FR)**17 1757 5-9-7 **60**....................(v) MickyFenton 4 57
(Paul Midgley) *in tch: effrt over 2f out: one pce* **40/1**

-003 **7** *1* **Pelmanism**6 2036 6-9-4 **60**.......................... PaulPickard(3) 2 54
(Brian Ellison) *s.i.s: hdwy over 2f out: kpt on: nvr a threat* **6/1**

0060 **8** *1¾* **Lucky Mark (IRE)**31 1465 4-9-6 **59**.................... RobertWinston 9 48
(Garry Moss) *t.k.h: led 1f: trckd ldr: wknd fnl f* **20/1**

04-0 **9** *1* **Loukoumi**15 1802 5-8-9 **55**.................... RachelRichardson(7) 5 42
(Tim Easterby) *in rr: hdwy and swtchd outside over 1f out: nvr a factor* **33/1**

0603 **10** *½* **Prince Of Passion (CAN)**12 1886 5-9-4 **57**.................... MartinDwyer 1 42
(Derek Shaw) *chsd ldrs: drvn 3f out: lost pl over 1f out* **11/1**

00-6 **11** *3¼* **Exclusive Dancer**24 1610 4-9-5 **58**.................... AndrewMullen 8 34
(George Moore) *s.i.s: a towards rr* **16/1**

0/5- **12** *4½* **First Phase**220 6783 4-9-7 **60**.................... DuranFentiman 6 24
(Mel Brittain) *in tch: hdwy to chse ldrs over 4f out: lost pl 2f out* **40/1**

400/ **13** *3¼* **Storey Hill (USA)**1529 757 8-9-2 **55**.................... RobbieFitzpatrick 14 11
(Charles Smith) *s.i.s and swtchd lft after s: in rr: bhd fnl 2f* **100/1**

1m 29.55s (2.35) **Going Correction** +0.225s/f (Good) **13** Ran SP% **117.5**
Speed ratings (Par 101): **95,93,90,90,89 89,87,85,84,84 80,75,71**
toteswingers 1&2 £69.90, 1&3 £39.00, 2&3 £65.00 CSF £112.59 CT £2618.62 TOTE £8.00: £2.30, £7.60, £6.80; EX 129.50 Trifecta £700.20 Part won. Pool: £933.71 - 0.01 winning units..
Owner Miss T Waggott **Bred** Mrs T V Ryan **Trained** Spennymoor, Co Durham

FOCUS
A modest handicap run at a good pace. The winner goes well here and his yard is in good form.
T/Plt: £87.20 to a £1 stake. Pool: £55270.01 - 462.23 winning tickets T/Qpdt: £14.00 to a £1 stake. Pool: £4132.89 - 217.16 winning tickets WG

2089 WARWICK (L-H)
Saturday, May 11

OFFICIAL GOING: Good to firm (8.6)
Wind: Strong behind Weather: Sunshine and showers

2281 KINGSTONE PRESS CHAMPIONSHIPS H'CAP (FOR LADY AMATEUR RIDERS) 6f
6:05 (6:05) (Class 6) (0-65,63) 4-Y-O+ £1,871 (£580; £290; £145) Stalls Low

Form RPR

1243 **1** **Artful Lady (IRE)**18 1748 4-9-7 **54**.................... MissKMargarson(5) 6 62
(George Margarson) *hld up: pushed along over 2f out: hdwy over 1f out: r.o to ld wl ins fnl f* **10/1**

2446 **2** *hd* **Master Of Disguise**15 1801 7-10-6 **62**.................... MissSBrotherton 8 69
(Brian Baugh) *mid-div: pushed along 1/2-way: hdwy u.p over 1f out: r.o* **6/1**

0-01 **3** *1¼* **Two Turtle Doves (IRE)**6 2043 7-10-1 **60** 6ex.... MissMMullineaux(3) 4 63
(Michael Mullineaux) *prom: pushed along over 2f out: r.o to go 3rd nr fin* **11/2**3

3410 **4** *½* **Pull The Pin (IRE)**17 1757 4-9-4 **53**.................... MissCLWhitehead(7) 7 54
(Declan Carroll) *led: rdn over 1f out: hdd and unable qck wl ins fnl f* **5/1**2

3001 **5** *1¾* **The Mongoose**6 2057 5-10-2 **63** 6ex..............(t) MissHDoyle(5) 11 59
(David Evans) *sn prom: rdn and ev ch fr over 1f out tl no ex wl ins fnl f* **9/2**1

6113 **6** *shd* **Mambo Spirit (IRE)**10 1929 9-10-2 **63**.................... MissNDumelow(5) 5 58
(Tony Newcombe) *hld up: hdwy over 1f out: styd on: nt trble ldrs* **11/2**3

2220 **7** *hd* **Rose Garnet (IRE)**10 1929 5-10-0 **59**.................... MissSallyRandell(3) 10 54
(Tony Carroll) *w ldr: rdn and ev ch over 1f out: styd on same pce ins fnl f* **10/1**

306- **8** *¾* **Insolenceofoffice (IRE)**278 4866 5-10-0 **56**..............(p) MissEJJones 3 48
(Richard Ford) *chsd ldrs: rdn and ev ch over 1f out: no ex ins fnl f* **10/1**

06-6 **9** *¾* **Volito**10 1929 7-9-13 **60**.................... MissJoannaMason(5) 9 50
(Anabel K Murphy) *s.i.s: hld up: bhd 1/2-way: r.o ins fnl f: nvr on terms* **18/1**

00-0 **10** *16* **Invincible Force (IRE)**17 1758 9-9-13 **62**.........(b) MissAimeeMKing(7) 2
(Paul Green) *prom: pushed along 1/2-way: hung lft and wknd 2f out* **40/1**

1m 12.05s (0.25) **Going Correction** +0.025s/f (Good) **10** Ran SP% **114.9**
Speed ratings (Par 101): **99,98,97,96,94 93,93,92,91,70**
toteswingers 1&2 £4.70, 1&3 £4.40, 2&3 £10.40 CSF £67.82 CT £366.59 TOTE £8.50: £2.20, £1.80, £2.30; EX 59.80 Trifecta £449.70 Pool: £1358.80 - 2.26 winning units..
Owner Graham Lodge Partnership **Bred** Michael Begley **Trained** Newmarket, Suffolk

FOCUS
Races of this type are usually weak, but this wasn't a bad one, with several runners in decent form. There wasn't much between the first nine. The winner's first real turf form.

2282 PSA PEUGEOT CITROEN MAIDEN AUCTION STKS 5f 110y
6:35 (6:38) (Class 5) 2-Y-O £2,587 (£770; £384; £192) Stalls Low

Form RPR

324 **1** **Kidmenot (IRE)**6 2053 2-8-6 0.......................... LiamJones 4 69
(J S Moore) *chsd ldrs: pushed along 1/2-way: rdn over 1f out: edgd rt and styd on to ld wl ins fnl f* **7/4**1

2 *½* **Mr Matthews (IRE)** 2-8-9 0.......................... MartinHarley 5 70
(Mrs K Burke) *led: rdn and edgd rt over 1f out: hdd wl ins fnl f* **5/1**3

3 *nse* **Ixelles Diamond (IRE)** 2-8-8 0.......................... TonyHamilton 6 69
(Richard Fahey) *wnt rt s: sn chsng ldr: rdn over 1f out: styd on* **9/1**

4 *2¾* **Thewandaofu (IRE)** 2-8-11 0.......................... FergusSweeney 2 63+
(Jamie Osborne) *s.i.s: sn prom: rdn over 1f out: styd on same pce fnl f* **20/1**

5 **5** *2½* **Shot In The Sun (IRE)**14 1833 2-8-4 0.................... WilliamCarson 3 48+
(David Evans) *sn pushed along in rr: rdn over 1f out: nvr nrr* **28/1**

6 **6** *1½* **Bold Max**12 1880 2-8-11 0.......................... RichardThomas 7 50
(Zoe Davison) *hmpd s: sn chsng ldrs: rdn 1/2-way: wknd over 1f out* **100/1**

7 *hd* **Kopkap** 2-8-9 0.......................... FrannyNorton 8 47+
(Ed McMahon) *hmpd s: a in rr* **14/1**

8 *nk* **Jana** 2-8-9 0 ow3.......................... RichardHughes 1 52+
(Richard Hannon) *edgd rt s: hld up: shkn up 2f out: wknd fnl f* **15/8**2

1m 7.17s (1.27) **Going Correction** +0.025s/f (Good) **8** Ran SP% **113.7**
Speed ratings (Par 93): **92,91,91,87,84 82,82,81**
toteswingers 1&2 £2.30, 1&3 £4.40, 2&3 £8.50 CSF £10.76 TOTE £2.70: £1.10, £2.10, £2.70; EX 12.50 Trifecta £82.10 Pool: £1918.50 - 17.51 winning units..
Owner Ever Equine & J S Moore **Bred** Lynnlodge Stud & Arthur Finnan **Trained** Upper Lambourn, Berks

FOCUS
With the exception of the winner, this looked a routine maiden judged on the sales prices of the newcomers and what little earlier form there was on offer. However, the proximity of the placed horses suggests they are good enough to win at this level.

2283 E.B.F CUT THE MUSTARD WITH MUSTARD PRESENTATIONS MAIDEN STKS 5f
7:05 (7:06) (Class 5) 2-Y-O **£2,911** (£866; £432; £216) **Stalls** Low

Form RPR
0 **1** **Neighbother**[22] 1669 2-9-5 0 TonyHamilton 2 72+
(Richard Fahey) *mde all: shkn up over 1f out: hung rt ins fnl f: r.o* **4/6**[1]
2 *3/4* **Midnite Angel (IRE)** 2-9-0 0 RichardHughes 6 64+
(Richard Hannon) *chsd wnr: shkn up and edgd rt over 1f out: r.o* **5/2**[2]
0 **3** *shd* **Seaham**[22] 1669 2-9-5 0 AndreaAtzeni 5 72+
(Rod Millman) *chsd ldrs: rdn over 1f out: nt clr run and swtchd lft ins fnl f: r.o wl* **6/1**[3]
4 *6* **Sweet Alibi (IRE)** 2-9-0 0 LiamJones 3 42
(J S Moore) *s.s: rn green in rr: rdn 1/2-way: hung rt and lft ins fnl f: nvr on terms* **28/1**
5 *6* **Oakley Dancer** 2-9-0 0 LukeMorris 1 21
(Tony Carroll) *prom: lost pl 3f out: sn bhd* **66/1**
6 *13* **Roodee Lady** 2-8-11 0 JulieBurke(3) 4
(Lisa Williamson) *sn outpcd* **66/1**

1m 0.67s (1.07) **Going Correction** +0.025s/f (Good) **6** Ran SP% **109.3**
Speed ratings (Par 93): **92,90,90,81,71 50**
toteswingers 1&2 £1.10, 1&3 £1.10, 2&3 £1.60 CSF £2.36 TOTE £1.60: £1.20, £1.40; EX 2.40 Trifecta £5.00 Pool: £1192.32 - 176.96 winning units..
Owner Mrs H Steel **Bred** Mrs P K O'Rourke **Trained** Musley Bank, N Yorks

FOCUS
The first three in this maiden are likely to prove above-average, with the winner likely to do a good bit better.

2284 BAM CONSTRUCTION H'CAP 1m 6f 213y
7:35 (7:35) (Class 5) (0-75,73) 4-Y-0+ **£2,587** (£770; £384; £192) **Stalls** Low

Form RPR
-361 **1** **Bathwick Street**[11] 1899 4-9-8 73 MartinHarley 3 80+
(David Evans) *chsd ldr over 4f: remained handy: wnt 2nd again over 1f out: rdn to ld ins fnl f: styd on wl: eased nr fin* **7/4**[1]
2454 **2** *1* **Keep Kicking (IRE)**[12] 1889 6-9-4 67 (p) GeorgeBaker 6 71
(Jonjo O'Neill) *set stdy pce tl qcknd over 5f out: rdn over 1f out: hdd ins fnl f: styd on same pce* **8/1**
23-3 **3** *1 3/4* **Thundering Home**[25] 309 6-8-8 57 KirstyMilczarek 2 59
(Richard Mitchell) *hld up: hdwy over 1f out: sn rdn: nt rch ldrs* **6/1**[3]
2422 **4** *3* **Easydoesit (IRE)**[18] 1744 5-9-5 68 LukeMorris 7 66
(Tony Carroll) *hld up: hdwy 8f out: rdn over 3f out: styd on same pce fr over 1f out* **6/1**[3]
-401 **5** *1 1/4* **Shalambar (IRE)**[62] 816 7-9-5 68 (v) RichardHughes 4 64
(Tony Carroll) *prom: chsd ldr over 9f out: rdn 3f out: lost 2nd over 1f out: wknd ins fnl f* **5/2**[2]
0044 **6** *4* **Rodrigo De Freitas (IRE)**[12] 1877 6-8-2 56 (v) NathanAlison(5) 1 47
(Jim Boyle) *dwlt: sn drvn along: wnt prom and racd keenly after 2f: rdn over 3f out: wknd over 1f out* **14/1**

3m 23.1s (4.10) **Going Correction** +0.025s/f (Good)
WFA 4 from 5yo+ 2lb **6** Ran SP% **111.3**
Speed ratings (Par 103): **90,89,88,86,86 84**
toteswingers 1&2 £3.20, 1&3 £3.10, 2&3 £5.20 CSF £15.89 TOTE £2.50: £1.50, £3.90; EX 15.00 Trifecta £75.10 Pool: £962.66 - 9.60 winning units..
Owner Wayne Clifford **Bred** Mrs D Du Feu **Trained** Pandy, Monmouths

FOCUS
This didn't have much depth, but most of the runners were in decent form beforehand. The pace was modest. It's doubtful the winner had to improve much.

2285 ASTON MANOR 30TH ANNIVERSARY H'CAP 7f 26y
8:05 (8:07) (Class 4) (0-85,85) 3-Y-O **£4,690** (£1,395; £697; £348) **Stalls** Low

Form RPR
30-0 **1** **Capo Rosso (IRE)**[24] 1625 3-9-4 82 RichardKingscote 8 91
(Tom Dascombe) *chsd ldr: rdn to ld ins fnl f: edgd rt: r.o wl* **8/1**
33-1 **2** *1 1/4* **Shore Step (IRE)**[22] 1660 3-8-11 75 MartinHarley 5 81
(Mick Channon) *led: rdn over 1f out: hdd and unable qck ins fnl f* **12/1**
140- **3** *nk* **Majestic Moon (IRE)**[232] 6425 3-8-13 77 TonyHamilton 3 82+
(Richard Fahey) *hld up in tch: rdn to go 3rd and hung rt ins fnl f: r.o* **3/1**[1]
364- **4** *3 3/4* **Prince Regal**[197] 7374 3-8-7 78 DavidParkes(7) 10 73
(Alan Jarvis) *s.i.s: racd keenly and hdwy over 4f out: wknd ins fnl f* **20/1**
2013 **5** *2 3/4* **Grilletto (USA)**[9] 1958 3-9-2 80 (b) NeilCallan 7 67
(James Tate) *chsd ldrs: rdn over 2f out: wknd over 1f out* **7/1**
210- **6** *1/2* **Banovallum**[217] 6874 3-9-4 82 RichardHughes 4 68+
(Sylvester Kirk) *prom: lost pl over 4f out: n.d after* **7/2**[2]
10-5 **7** *1 1/4* **Sejalaat (IRE)**[15] 1806 3-9-3 81 PaulHanagan 9 64
(Ed Dunlop) *hld up: plld hrd: nvr on terms* **6/1**[3]
10-2 **8** *1 3/4* **Beach Club**[31] 1477 3-9-7 85 FrannyNorton 12 63
(David Brown) *prom: racd keenly: rdn over 2f out: wknd over 1f out* **14/1**
13-5 **9** *nk* **Delores Rocket**[16] 1773 3-9-0 81 JulieBurke(3) 6 58
(Kevin Ryan) *mid-div: lost pl over 5f out: n.d after* **50/1**
41-0 **10** *2 3/4* **Gigawatt**[26] 1582 3-9-1 79 PatCosgrave 2 49
(Jim Boyle) *hld up: racd keenly: a in rr* **25/1**

1m 23.32s (-1.28) **Going Correction** -0.15s/f (Firm) **10** Ran SP% **117.7**
Speed ratings (Par 101): **101,99,99,94,91 91,89,87,87,84**
toteswingers 1&2 £12.30, 1&3 £8.70, 2&3 £8.90 CSF £97.34 CT £362.43 TOTE £10.40: £2.60, £2.70, £1.90; EX 94.50 Trifecta £315.00 Pool: £2015.39 - 4.79 winning units..
Owner Deva Racing Red Clubs Partnership **Bred** Michael Wiley **Trained** Malpas, Cheshire

FOCUS
This was contested by a number of second-season horses who had shown decent form as juveniles, as well as several in good recent AW form. Few got involved. The winner is rated up a length.

2286 OFFICIAL LADIES NIGHT AFTERPARTY AT ALTORIA H'CAP 7f 26y
8:35 (8:35) (Class 5) (0-75,79) 4-Y-O+ **£2,587** (£770; £384; £192) **Stalls** Low

Form RPR
01-3 **1** **Finesse**[35] 1398 4-9-5 73 RichardKingscote 2 79+
(Ralph Beckett) *mde all: rdn and hung lft over 1f out: styd on* **9/2**[2]
600- **2** *3/4* **Wise Venture (IRE)**[238] 6251 4-8-7 61 KirstyMilczarek 7 65
(Alan Jarvis) *chsd ldrs: rdn over 1f out: r.o* **16/1**
140- **3** *1/2* **George Baker (IRE)**[142] 8181 6-9-7 75 RichardHughes 4 78
(George Baker) *chsd ldr: rdn over 1f out: styd on same pce ins fnl f* **14/1**
-422 **4** *hd* **Peace Seeker**[8] 1985 5-9-11 79 (p) WilliamCarson 6 81
(Anthony Carson) *chsd ldrs: rdn over 1f out: edgd lft ins fnl f: styd on* **9/1**
151- **5** *3/4* **Scottish Glen**[258] 5625 7-9-4 72 GeorgeBaker 5 72+
(Patrick Chamings) *hld up: hdwy u.p over 1f out: nt rch ldrs* **8/1**[3]
03-2 **6** *shd* **It's My Time**[15] 1800 4-8-11 65 TonyHamilton 8 65+
(Richard Fahey) *hld up: rdn over 1f out: r.o ins fnl f: nvr nrr* **7/2**[1]
4435 **7** *1/2* **The Guru Of Gloom (IRE)**[18] 1746 5-9-0 68 LukeMorris 3 68
(William Muir) *trckd ldrs: racd keenly: rdn over 1f out: styng on same pce whn nt clr run wl ins fnl f* **20/1**
00-4 **8** *hd* **Diamondhead (IRE)**[16] 1798 4-9-5 73 LiamKeniry 1 71
(Ed de Giles) *prom: racd keenly: rdn over 1f out: styd on same pce fnl f* **9/1**
6U03 **9** *1 1/2* **The Happy Hammer (IRE)**[15] 1800 7-8-7 61 oh3 PaulHanagan 12 55
(Eugene Stanford) *s.i.s: hld up: rdn over 2f out: n.d* **16/1**
00-0 **10** *hd* **Easy Over (IRE)**[33] 1430 5-8-11 65 FrannyNorton 11 59
(Ed McMahon) *hld up: rdn over 2f out: n.d* **12/1**
000 **11** *nk* **Albaqaa**[28] 1538 8-9-5 73 PatCosgrave 9 66
(P J O'Gorman) *s.i.s: hld up: racd keenly: shkn up over 1f out: nvr nr to chal* **12/1**
052- **12** *1* **Excellent Jem**[150] 8069 4-9-0 68 TedDurcan 10 58
(Jane Chapple-Hyam) *hld up: rdn over 2f out: n.d* **14/1**

1m 23.88s (-0.72) **Going Correction** -0.15s/f (Firm) **12** Ran SP% **116.8**
Speed ratings (Par 103): **98,97,96,96,95 95,94,94,92,92 92,91**
toteswingers 1&2 £39.20, 1&3 £8.50, 2&3 £53.40 CSF £73.37 CT £950.80 TOTE £4.70: £2.40, £6.70, £2.50; EX 121.70 Trifecta £966.90 Part won. Pool: £1289.24 - 0.86 winning units..
Owner P K Gardner **Bred** Springcombe Park Stud **Trained** Kimpton, Hants

FOCUS
This was a middling handicap for older horses, in which the first three are all worth keeping an eye on. The first eight were covered by just three lengths but the form makes sense.
T/Plt: £85.40 to a £1 stake. Pool: £50512.35 - 431.50 winning tickets T/Qpdt: £17.50 to a £1 stake. Pool: £3060.24 -129.34 winning tickets CR

2287 - (Foreign Racing) - See Raceform Interactive

1587 LEOPARDSTOWN (L-H)
Sunday, May 12

OFFICIAL GOING: Yielding (yielding to soft in places)

2288a AMETHYST STKS (GROUP 3) 1m
2:55 (2:56) 3-Y-O+ **£31,707** (£9,268; £4,390; £1,463)

RPR
1 **Duntle (IRE)**[246] 6061 4-9-9 113 WayneLordan 5 110+
(David Wachman, Ire) *settled in 3rd tl qcknd to ld over 1f out: pushed out clsng stages to maintain advantage* **8/13**[1]
2 *3/4* **Custom Cut (IRE)**[35] 1413 4-9-12 106 RonanWhelan 2 111
(George J Kent, Ire) *chsd ldr in 2nd tl briefly dropped to 3rd over 1f out: narrowly regained 2nd: kpt on wl wout getting on terms w wnr* **10/1**
3 *hd* **Sweet Lightning**[28] 1556 8-9-9 112 (t) JohnnyMurtagh 3 108
(Thomas Carmody, Ire) *led tl hdd over 1f out: nt match wnr but rallied wl: only jst hld for 2nd* **3/1**[2]
4 *1 1/2* **Bold Thady Quill (IRE)**[28] 1556 6-9-9 103 (p) ShaneFoley 4 104+
(K J Condon, Ire) *w.w in 4th: pushed along under 3f out and nt qckn over 1f out: kpt on clsng stages* **6/1**[3]
5 *3 3/4* **Elusive Ridge (IRE)**[30] 1530 7-9-9 96 PatSmullen 1 96+
(H Rogers, Ire) *a in rr: kpt on same pce fnl f* **20/1**

1m 42.5s (1.30) **Going Correction** +0.20s/f (Good) **5** Ran SP% **115.1**
Speed ratings: **101,100,100,98,94**
CSF £8.50 TOTE £1.30: £1.10, £3.10; DF 7.00.
Owner Flaxman Stables Ireland Ltd **Bred** Airlie Stud **Trained** Goolds Cross, Co Tipperary

FOCUS
The time was slow so this Group 3 is hard to weigh up. The progressive runner-up has been rated as running another personal best, while the fourth has been rated close to his previous C&D effort.

2289a DERRINSTOWN STUD 1,000 GUINEAS TRIAL (GROUP 3) 1m
3:25 (3:28) 3-Y-O **£33,028** (£9,654; £4,573; £1,524)

RPR
1 **Just Pretending (USA)**[5] 2140 3-9-0 87 JosephO'Brien 5 103
(A P O'Brien, Ire) *chsd ldrs in 4th tl qcknd to ld under 2f out: pressed ins fnl f: styd on wl* **6/1**[3]
2 *nk* **Hint Of A Tint (IRE)**[28] 1557 3-9-0 FMBerry 6 102
(David Wachman, Ire) *w.w in 5th tl tk clsr order in 4th 2f out: sn chsd wnr in 2nd: kpt on wl to chal ent fnl f: nvr quite on terms* **6/1**[3]
3 *2 1/4* **Mizzava (IRE)**[31] 1504 3-9-0 87 ShaneFoley 10 97
(M Halford, Ire) *hld up in rr: tk clsr order 2f out to chse ldrs: pushed along in 3rd ent fnl f: kpt on but no imp on principals fnl 100yds* **14/1**
4 *1/2* **Uleavemebreathless**[6] 2107 3-9-0 96 GaryCarroll 9 96
(A Oliver, Ire) *w.w in 7th: c wd in st and sn pushed along: nt qckn over 1f out: kpt on wl ins fnl f to go 4th* **20/1**
5 *1/2* **Wannabe Better (IRE)**[6] 2104 3-9-0 80 WayneLordan 3 95?
(T Stack, Ire) *bit slowly away and racd towards rr: pushed along in last appr home turn: kpt on wl ins fnl f: nvr nrr* **16/1**
6 *3* **Talitha Kum (IRE)**[22] 1702 3-9-0 89 SeamieHeffernan 7 88
(P D Deegan, Ire) *chsd ldr in 2nd: disp early in st: nt qckn over 1f out: sn one pce* **25/1**
7 *4 3/4* **Rawaaq**[28] 1557 3-9-0 103 PatSmullen 8 80
(D K Weld, Ire) *hld up towards rr: tk clsr order 2f out to chse ldrs: wknd and wandering fnl f* **2/1**[2]
8 *1 3/4* **Ramsa (FR)**[22] 1707 3-9-0 JFEgan 1 73
(John Francis Egan, Ire) *chsd ldrs in 3rd: n.m.r on inner under 2f out: sn one pce* **33/1**
9 *4 3/4* **We'll Go Walking (IRE)**[14] 1862 3-9-0 107 KevinManning 2 62
(J S Bolger, Ire) *led tl hdd under 2f out: wknd qckly: eased* **13/8**[1]

1m 41.46s (0.26) **Going Correction** +0.20s/f (Good) **9** Ran SP% **124.1**
Speed ratings: **106,105,103,102,102 99,94,92,88**
CSF £43.91 TOTE £7.60: £1.90, £2.20, £3.00; DF 53.80.
Owner Michael Tabor & Derrick Smith & Mrs John Magnier **Bred** Eagle Holdings **Trained** Ballydoyle, Co Tipperary

FOCUS
Probably not the strongest renewal of this trial. The fourth, rated to the pick of her juvenile efforts, is the best guide, along with the sixth and eighth.

2290a DERRINSTOWN STUD DERBY TRIAL STKS (GROUP 2) 1m 2f
3:55 (3:55) 3-Y-O **£52,845** (£15,447; £7,317; £2,439)

RPR
1 **Battle Of Marengo (IRE)**[28] 1558 3-9-6 115 JosephO'Brien 4 116
(A P O'Brien, Ire) *racd in 2nd tl led after 4f: qcknd clr under 2f out: pushed out ins fnl f: comf* **2/13**[1]

2 1 3/4 **Loch Garman (IRE)**[192] 7514 3-9-6 114........................ KevinManning 5 112
(J S Bolger, Ire) *settled in 3rd tl improvement to chse ldr 4f out: sn pushed along and nt qckn 2f out: kpt on fnl f to reduce deficit cl home* **9/2**[2]

3 1 1/4 **Little White Cloud (IRE)**[177] 7756 3-9-3 91............ DeclanMcDonogh 1 106
(John M Oxx, Ire) *hld up in rr: tk clsr order over 2f out: rn green in 3rd and no imp appr fnl f: kpt on again clsng stages* **33/1**

4 7 **Dont Bother Me (IRE)**[8] 2021 3-9-3 105.......................... MartinHarley 3 92
(Niall Moran, Ire) *led tl hdd after 4f: dropped to 3rd 4f out: sn pushed along and dropped to 4th over 1f out: no ex* **25/1**[3]

2m 7.79s (-0.41) **Going Correction** +0.20s/f (Good) **4** Ran SP% **111.6**
Speed ratings: **109,107,106,101**
CSF £1.41; DF 1.30.
Owner Michael Tabor & Derrick Smith & Mrs John Magnier **Bred** Anna Karenina Syndicate **Trained** Ballydoyle, Co Tipperary

FOCUS
All eyes will be on the Dante, but for now the Irish grip on the Derby is tighter at the end of a week that witnessed an excellent haul of trial races for Aidan O'Brien. With all due respect to the two Chester winners and to wide-margin Lingfield winner Nevis, this is the colt who truly matters from a Derby perspective. The winner has been rated in the middle of the averages for this race.

2202 BADEN-BADEN (L-H)
Sunday, May 12

OFFICIAL GOING: Turf: good to soft

2294a GROSSER PREIS DER BADISCHEN UNTERNEHMER (GROUP 2) (4YO+) (TURF) 1m 3f
3:50 (12:00) 4-Y-0+ **£32,520** (£12,601; £5,284; £3,252; £2,032; £1,219)

RPR

1 **Novellist (IRE)**[203] 7287 4-9-6 0.................................. EPedroza 8 121
(A Wohler, Germany) *t.k.h: hld up in last pair on outer: rapid hdwy on turn into st: rdn to ld 2f out: jnd ent fnl f: styd on wl u.p: jst prevailed* **9/10**[1]

2 hd **Waldpark (GER)**[21] 5-9-0 0.. JBojko 3 115
(A Wohler, Germany) *dwlt: hld up in last pair on inner: rdn and hdwy on turn into st: jnd ldr ent fnl f: styd on but hung lft u.p cl home and jst denied* **71/10**

3 2 1/2 **Technokrat (IRE)**[21] 5-9-0 0......................................(b) APietsch 2 111
(W Hickst, Germany) *settled in midfield: rdn and lost pl 3f out: rallied u.p and styd on to go 3rd ins fnl f: no imp on front pair* **32/5**[3]

4 2 **Girolamo (GER)**[43] 1268 4-9-6 0.................................... AStarke 6 113
(P Schiergen, Germany) *hld up in last trio: rdn 3f out: 3rd and ev ch 2f out: outpcd by front pair ent fnl f: sn dropped to 4th: plugged on* **37/10**[2]

5 hd **Seismos (IRE)**[43] 1263 5-9-0 0................................. HarryBentley 7 107
(A Wohler, Germany) *slow to stride and pushed along to rcvr: sn prom on outer: rdn 3f out: lost pl whn short of room and hmpd 2f out: rallied u.p and styd on to go 5th fnl strides* **92/10**

6 hd **Salon Soldier (GER)**[41] 4-9-0 0................................ FilipMinarik 4 106
(P Schiergen, Germany) *prom on inner: rdn over 2f out: outpcd by ldrs over 1f out: plugged on but dropped to 6th fnl strides* **97/10**

7 11 **Sir Lando**[41] 6-9-0 0..........................(p) LennartHammer-Hansen 5 86
(Wido Neuroth, Norway) *trckd ldr: rdn and lost pl 3f out: last and btn ent fnl f: eased* **18/1**

8 4 **Silvaner (GER)**[41] 5-9-0 0.. ADeVries 1 79
(P Schiergen, Germany) *led: rdn and hdd 2f out: sn no ex and btn: fdd: eased and dropped to last ins fnl f* **174/10**

2m 24.65s (5.38) **8** Ran SP% **129.6**
WIN (incl. 10 euro stake): 19. PLACES: 13, 16, 16. SF: 100.
Owner Dr Christoph Berglar **Bred** Christoph Berglar **Trained** Germany

1865 CAPANNELLE (R-H)
Sunday, May 12

OFFICIAL GOING: Turf: good

2295a PREMIO PRESIDENTE DELLA REPUBBLICA GBI RACING (GROUP 1) (4YO+) (TURF) 1m 2f
4:50 (12:00) 4-Y-0+ **£77,235** (£33,983; £18,536; £9,268)

RPR

1 **Vedelago (IRE)**[41] 4-9-2 0.................................... MEsposito 2 108
(S Botti, Italy) *hld up towards rr: short of room 2 1/2f out: hdwy 2f out: 2nd and shkn up appr 1f out: rdn and r.o ins fnl f: led 100yds out: pushed out* **7/4**[1]

2 1/2 **Orpello (IRE)**[21] 1709 4-9-2 0.............................(b) FabioBranca 6 107
(S Botti, Italy) *trckd ldr: led 2 1/2f out: sn rdn: pressed appr 1f out: kpt on u.p fnl f and drifted lft: hdd 100yds out: no ex* **16/5**[2]

3 hd **Pattaya (ITY)**[21] 1709 5-9-2 0................................ GBietolini 7 107
(S Botti, Italy) *hld up in rr: hdwy on outside over 2f out: r.o u.p fnl f: wnt 3rd 100yds out: nrest at fin* **43/5**

4 2 **Vola E Va**[21] 1709 4-9-2 0.................................... DarioVargiu 4 103
(B Grizzetti, Italy) *midfield: rdn and outpcd 2f out: styd on u.p fnl f: nt pce to chal* **37/10**[3]

5 nse **Bedetti**[35] 5-9-2 0.. AFiori 9 103
(F Brogi, Italy) *midfield: outpcd and dropped to last 2f out: styd on ins fnl f: nvr on terms* **35/1**

6 1 1/2 **Principe Adepto (USA)**[14] 5-9-2 0........................ MircoDemuro 3 100
(E Botti, Italy) *trckd ldrs on inner: rdn and nt qckn over 2f out: wknd ins fnl f* **43/10**

7 1/2 **Storming Loose**[14] 6-9-2 0.................................... GArena 8 99
(B Grizzetti, Italy) *towards rr: last into st 4f out: effrt on ins but blocked over 2f out: swtchd outside appr fnl f and kpt on: nt pce to chal* **37/10**[3]

8 5 **Teixidor (ITY)**[35] 4-9-2 0.................................. JimmyFortune 1 89
(Ottavio Di Paolo, Italy) *dwlt: sn rcvrd and settled in midfield: 5th and rdn over 2 1/2f out: wknd u.p fr 2f out* **12/1**

9 dist **Branderburgo (IRE)**[189] 7586 6-9-2 0........................ CFiocchi 5
(M Grassi, Italy) *led: qcknd 4f out: rdn and hdd 2 1/2f out: sn wknd: wl bhd whn heavily eased fnl f* **36/5**

2m 1.5s (-1.80) **9** Ran SP% **154.7**
WIN (incl. 1 euro stake): 2.73. PLACES: 1.56, 1.58, 2.33. DF: 6.25.
Owner G T A **Bred** G T A Srl **Trained** Italy

2296 - (Foreign Racing) - See Raceform Interactive

2183 LONGCHAMP (R-H)
Sunday, May 12

OFFICIAL GOING: Turf: good

2297a PRIX HOCQUART CHINA HORSE CLUB (GROUP 2) (3YO COLTS & FILLIES) (TURF) 1m 3f
1:30 (12:00) 3-Y-0 **£52,845** (£21,138; £15,853; £10,569; £5,284)

RPR

1 **Tableaux (USA)**[20] 1737 3-9-2 0.............................. MaximeGuyon 4 110+
(A Fabre, France) *broke wl: trckd ldr: scrubbed along whn ldr qcknd 2 1/2f out: rdn to chal on outer fr 1 1/2f out: led narrowly appr fnl f: r.o u.p* **7/2**[2]

2 shd **Park Reel (FR)**[42] 1277 3-9-2 0.......................... GregoryBenoist 8 110+
(E Lellouche, France) *sn led and swtchd to inner rail: set stdy gallop tl qcknd over 2 1/2f out: hdd appr fnl f: rdn and rallied gamely: r.o u.p fnl f* **14/1**

3 shd **Festive Cheer (FR)**[258] 5690 3-9-2 0.......................... RyanMoore 2 110+
(A P O'Brien, Ire) *trckd ldrs: 3rd on outer and ev ch 2 1/2f out: sn pushed along and nt qckn immediately: rdn and responded 1 1/2f out: r.o u.p fnl f: clsng wl cl home* **2/1**[1]

4 1 1/4 **Art Contemporain (USA)**[20] 1737 3-9-2 0......... ChristopheSoumillon 7 107+
(P Bary, France) *midfield on outer: rdn over 2f out: nt qckn tl styd on fnl f: nt pce to chal* **8/1**

5 hd **Ferevia (IRE)**[26] 1602 3-8-13 0.............................. OlivierPeslier 1 104+
(C Laffon-Parias, France) *broke wl and led briefly: sn trcking ldr on inner: rdn and briefly short of room 2f out: styd on u.p over 1f out: one pce fnl 110yds* **11/2**[3]

6 1/2 **Golden Bowl (FR)**[33] 3-9-2 0................................ ThierryJarnet 6 106+
(J Bertran De Balanda, France) *towards rr: pushed along 2f out: rdn under 1 1/2f out: no imp tl kpt on u.p fnl 100yds: nvr on terms* **25/1**

7 hd **Max Dynamite (FR)**[20] 1737 3-9-2 0...................... AntoineHamelin 5 106+
(J Van Handenhove, France) *midfield: rdn and nt qckn fr 2f out: kpt on at same pce u.p fnl f: n.d* **14/1**

8 3/4 **Zaidiyn (FR)**[31] 3-9-2 0.................. Christophe-PatriceLemaire 3 104+
(M Delzangles, France) *dwlt: t.k.h early in rr: last and shkn up on outer 2f out: rdn appr fnl f: kpt on under hands and heels: nvr on terms* **7/2**[2]

2m 17.42s (-2.48) **Going Correction** -0.125s/f (Firm) **8** Ran SP% **121.5**
Speed ratings: **104,103,103,102,102 102,102,101**
WIN (incl. 1 euro stake): 4.30. PLACES: 1.50, 2.60, 2.50. DF: 19.00. SF: 25.80.
Owner Derrick Smith & Michael Tabor **Bred** Galleria Bloodstock **Trained** Chantilly, France

FOCUS
There was a bunched finish and the time was nothing special. The positions hardly changed but the distances condensed near the line, and it's likely that something is flattered.

2298a POULE D'ESSAI DES POULAINS (LE PARISIEN) (GROUP 1) (3YO COLTS) (TURF) 1m
2:08 (12:00) 3-Y-0 **£255,504** (£102,219; £51,109; £25,532; £12,788)

RPR

1 **Style Vendome (FR)**[38] 1357 3-9-2 0.......................... ThierryThulliez 3 115
(N Clement, France) *broke wl enough but squeezed out early: chsd ldng gp on inner: 5th and travelling wl enough over 2 1/2f out: swtchd outside and shkn up 2f out: rdn 1 1/2f out: r.o wl u.p fnl f to ld 75yds out: rdn out* **9/2**[2]

2 nk **Dastarhon (IRE)**[20] 3-9-2 0.............................. UmbertoRispoli 13 114+
(Mme Pia Brandt, France) *midfield: rdn and short of room 2f out: swtchd outside and on heels of wnr under 1 1/2f out: r.o u.p fnl f: a hld by wnr* **50/1**

3 hd **Intello (GER)**[25] 1623 3-9-2 0............................ MaximeGuyon 17 114+
(A Fabre, France) *towards rr: rdn and nowhere to go 2 1/2f out and again 2f out: swtchd outside under 1 1/2f out: styd on strly u.p fnl f: nrest at fin* **7/1**[3]

4 hd **Gale Force Ten**[37] 1378 3-9-2 0................................(p) RyanMoore 5 113
(A P O'Brien, Ire) *chsd ldng gp: in share of 6th and pushed along 2 1/2f out: rdn outpcd over 2f out: styd on u.p appr 1f out: r.o fnl f but nvr quite on terms* **10/1**

5 shd **Havana Gold (IRE)**[24] 1638 3-9-2 0.......................... JamieSpencer 11 113
(Richard Hannon) *hld up towards rr: last 3f out: hdwy on inner 2 1/2f out: 5th and styng on appr fnl f: r.o u.p to ld 150yds out: hdd and no ex 75yds out: dropped to 5th fnl strides* **20/1**

6 1 **Morandi (FR)**[28] 1562 3-9-2 0........................ ChristopheSoumillon 9 111
(J-C Rouget, France) *midfield: towards rr 3f out: hdwy tl short of room and swtchd outside 1 1/2f out: rdn and styd on appr 1f out: r.o fnl f: nrest at fin* **8/1**

7 3/4 **Anodin (IRE)**[20] 3-9-2 0......................................(b) OlivierPeslier 8 109
(F Head, France) *tk a gd hold in midfield: swtchd outside and hdwy 2f out: styd on ins fnl f: nt pce to chal* **9/1**

8 hd **Gengis (FR)**[28] 1562 3-9-2 0............................ StephanePasquier 18 109
(G Doleuze, France) *dwlt: towards rr and keen early: awkward and wnt wd first bnd: rdn and prog over 2f out: styd on u.p to chal 1f out: sn outpcd and fdd fnl 100yds* **16/1**

9 3/4 **Flying The Flag (IRE)**[239] 6272 3-9-2 0...................... CO'Donoghue 10 107
(A P O'Brien, Ire) *towards rr: last 2 1/2f out: styd on fr over 2f out: kpt on ins fnl f: nvr on terms* **40/1**

10 1 **Bright Strike (USA)**[20] 1714 3-9-2 0.......................... WilliamBuick 2 105
(John Gosden) *led briefly: sn hdd: prom tl rdn and nt qckn fr 2f out: one pce fnl f* **20/1**

11 1/2 **Olympic Glory (IRE)**[22] 1677 3-9-2 0...................... RichardHughes 12 104
(Richard Hannon) *towards rr on outer: pushed along and c wd fnl bnd into st 2 1/2f out: rdn and nt qckn 1 1/2f out: styd on fnl 100yds: nvr plcd to chal* **3/1**[1]

12 hd **Princedargent (FR)**[28] 1562 3-9-2 0.......................... FabriceVeron 4 103
(H-A Pantall, France) *sn led: pushed along and hdd appr fnl 2f: rallied and pressed ldr under 1 1/2f out: regained ld appr 1f out: hdd 150yds out and wknd* **100/1**

13 3/4 **Lion D'Anvers (FR)**[16] 1815 3-9-2 0.......................... RonanThomas 1 101
(J Van Handenhove, France) *midfield on inner: rdn and hdwy to chse ldrs over 1f out: wknd ins fnl f* **50/1**

14 3/4 **Pearl Flute (IRE)**[192] 7514 3-9-2 0...................... MickaelBarzalona 15 100
(F-H Graffard, France) *trckd ldr: led appr 2f out: sn rdn: hdd over 1f out: wknd ins fnl f* **50/1**

The Form Book Flat, Raceform Ltd, Compton, RG20 6NL.

15 *8* **My Approach (IRE)**[38] 1357 3-9-2 0 GeraldMosse 7 81
(Robert Collet, France) *prom: 4th and pushed along 2 1/2f out: sn rdn and wknd ins fnl 1 1/2f* **50/1**

16 *½* **Etalondes (FR)**[38] 1357 3-9-2 0 GregoryBenoist 16 80
(J-C Rouget, France) *played up in stalls: dwlt: towards rr: rdn and no imp fr 2f out: nvr in contention* **50/1**

17 *½* **Us Law (IRE)**[28] 1562 3-9-2 0 Christophe-PatriceLemaire 6 79
(P Bary, France) *midfield: rdn to hold pl over 2 1/2f out: wkng whn twice sltly hmpd under 2f out: eased ins fnl f* **12/1**

18 *20* **Penny's Picnic (IRE)**[38] 1357 3-9-2 0 ThierryJarnet 14 33
(D Guillemin, France) *midfield on outer: rdn and wknd over 2f out: eased fnl f* **25/1**

1m 34.68s (-3.72) **Going Correction** -0.125s/f (Firm) **18** Ran SP% **126.1**
Speed ratings: **113,112,112,112,112 111,110,110,109,108 108,107,107,106,98 97,97,77**
WIN (incl. 1 euro stake): 6.80. PLACES: 2.80, 8.90, 3.60. DF: 132.60. SF: 214.40.
Owner Comte A De Ganay & C-B Baillet **Bred** G Pariente **Trained** Chantilly, France

FOCUS
A race that's thrown up some questionable winners in recent times and it was again quite a muddling affair, despite the good gallop, with the draw playing a big part given the size of the field. Still, the winner arrived with a reputation, and there were one or two eyecatching performances in behind. It's been rated around the averages for the placed horses.

2299a POULE D'ESSAI DES POULICHES (GROUP 1) (3YO FILLIES) (TURF) 1m
2:40 (12:00) 3-Y-0 **£209,048** (£83,634; £41,817; £20,890; £10,463)

RPR

1 **Flotilla (FR)**[191] 7547 3-9-0 0 Christophe-PatriceLemaire 5 115+
(M Delzangles, France) *midfield: hdwy fr 2f out: rdn over 1f out: r.o to chal wl ins fnl f: led cl home: drvn out* **7/1**[3]

2 *nk* **Esoterique (IRE)**[14] 1869 3-9-0 0 MaximeGuyon 6 114
(A Fabre, France) *dwlt: qckly rcvrd and racd in midfield: hdwy fr 3f out: angled out and rdn to chal 2f out: led ent fnl f: r.o but hdd cl home* **2/1**[1]

3 *4* **Tasaday (USA)**[28] 1561 3-9-0 0 MickaelBarzalona 14 105
(A Fabre, France) *prom: smooth hdwy to chal 3f out: rdn to ld over 2f out: strly pressed and hdd ent fnl f: sn dropped to 3rd and outpcd by front pair: fdd* **14/1**

4 *snk* **Zurigha (IRE)**[29] 1546 3-9-0 0 RichardHughes 17 104
(Richard Hannon) *dropped in fr wd draw and hld up in last trio on inner: stdy hdwy fr over 3f out: rdn 2f out: r.o to go 4th cl home: n.d to front pair* **25/1**

5 *1* **Dauphine Russe (FR)**[28] 1561 3-9-0 0 WilliamBuick 3 102
(F Doumen, France) *midfield on inner: rdn 2f out: nt clrest of runs over 1f out: swtchd lft ent fnl f and r.o to go 5th post* **25/1**

6 *nse* **Waterway Run (USA)**[25] 1622 3-9-0 0 JimCrowley 7 102
(Ralph Beckett) *prom: rdn 3f out: kpt on same pce u.p: dropped to 6th post* **25/1**

7 *1 ½* **Melbourne Memories**[22] 1676 3-9-0 0 RyanMoore 4 99
(Clive Cox) *stdd and hld up towards rr on inner: rdn 3f out: r.o to go 7th cl home: n.d* **33/1**

8 *hd* **Vaunoise (IRE)**[35] 1418 3-9-0 0 GregoryBenoist 19 98
(J-C Rouget, France) *dropped in fr wd draw and hld up in last trio on outer: rdn 3f out: edgd rt u.p but styd on down wd outside to go 8th fnl strides: n.d* **40/1**

9 *½* **Spinacre (IRE)**[38] 1358 3-9-0 0 GeraldMosse 18 97
(P Bary, France) *hld up towards rr on outer: rdn 3f out: r.o to go 9th post: n.d* **33/1**

10 *snk* **Alterite (FR)**[47] 1191 3-9-0 0 ChristopheSoumillon 2 97
(J-C Rouget, France) *midfield on inner: cl up whn hmpd on rail over 2f out: rdn to chal and ev ch 1 1/2f out: no ex ins fnl f: fdd and lost multiple pls ins fnl 100yds* **6/1**[2]

11 *snk* **Baie D'Honneur (FR)**[16] 1818 3-9-0 0 IoritzMendizabal 1 96
(D De Watrigant, France) *trckd ldr on inner: hmpd 2f out as ldr wknd: rdn 1 1/2f out: kpt on one pce ins fnl f* **12/1**

12 *nk* **Show Gorb (SPA)**[38] 1358 3-9-0 0 Francois-XavierBertras 9 96
(P Sogorb, France) *dwlt: qckly rcvrd and sn trcking ldr: w ldrs and ev ch 2f out: sn rdn and outpcd: steadily fdd* **25/1**

13 *1* **Topaze Blanche (IRE)**[28] 1561 3-9-0 0 OlivierPeslier 11 93
(C Laffon-Parias, France) *dwlt: t.k.h: midfield on outer: rdn 2f out: outpcd over 1f out: fdd* **8/1**

14 *¾* **Meri Shika (FR)**[35] 1418 3-9-0 0 AntoineHamelin 20 92
(J Bertran De Balanda, France) *dwlt: hld up towards rr: rdn 2f out: kpt on but nvr a factor* **66/1**

15 *nk* **Kenhope (FR)**[28] 1561 3-9-0 0 ThierryJarnet 16 91
(H-A Pantall, France) *prom on outer: rdn and ev ch 2f out: outpcd and btn over 1f out: fdd* **16/1**

16 *3 ½* **Morning Frost (IRE)**[59] 1000 3-9-0 0 JulienAuge 13 83
(C Ferland, France) *midfield: rdn 2f out: sn outpcd and btn: eased ent fnl f* **40/1**

17 *4* **Cocktail Queen (IRE)**[29] 1546 3-9-0 0 JamieSpencer 8 74
(David Elsworth) *stdd and hld up in last trio: rdn and detached in last 3f out: sn btn: nvr a factor* **33/1**

18 *4* **Sage Melody (FR)**[171] 7828 3-9-0 0 UmbertoRispoli 10 64
(M Delzangles, France) *led: rdn and hdd over 2f out: immediately btn and wknd: eased over 1f out* **66/1**

19 *1 ½* **Tuna Papita (USA)**[42] 3-9-0 0 ThierryThulliez 12 61
(F Rohaut, France) *t.k.h: midfield: rdn over 2f out: no ex and btn over 1f out: fdd and eased* **25/1**

20 *15* **Kensea (FR)**[25] 1633 3-9-0 0 FabriceVeron 15 26
(H-A Pantall, France) *t.k.h: trckd ldr on outer: rdn 3f out: awkward u.p and fdd: eased 2f out and dropped to last: t.o* **50/1**

1m 34.77s (-3.63) **Going Correction** -0.125s/f (Firm) **20** Ran SP% **129.3**
Speed ratings: **113,112,108,108,107 107,106,105,105,105 105,104,103,102,102 99,95,91,89,74**
WIN (incl. 1 euro stake): 5.50 ((Flotilla coupled with Sage Melody & Topaze Blanche). PLACES: 3.20, 1.60, 2.60. DF: 18.30. SF: 30.80.
Owner H H Sheikh Mohammed Bin Khalifa Al Thani **Bred** E Puerari, Oceanic Bloodstock Inc & Mme A Graverea **Trained** France

FOCUS
A more reliable race than the colts equivalent in recent years, with some real top-notchers adding their names to the roll of honour. The presence of pacemakers ensured there was no hanging around and the form looks strong, with the right pair drawing right away inside the final furlong. The runner-up, third, fifth, sixth and seventh help set the standard.

2300a PRIX DE SAINT-GEORGES (GROUP 3) (3YO+) (TURF) 5f (S)
3:40 (12:00) 3-Y-0+ **£32,520** (£13,008; £9,756; £6,504; £3,252)

RPR

1 **Catcall (FR)**[44] 1231 4-9-0 0 Francois-XavierBertras 7 106
(P Sogorb, France) *dwlt: hld up towards rr on outer: rdn and hdwy fr 2f out: r.o to chal ins fnl f: led cl home: drvn out* **11/1**

2 *hd* **Move In Time**[24] 1637 5-9-2 0 DanielTudhope 8 107
(David O'Meara) *midfield: rdn 2f out: r.o to chal ins fnl f: wnt 2nd cl home: jst hld* **9/2**[2]

3 *snk* **Place In My Heart**[23] 1662 4-8-10 0 GeraldMosse 9 100
(Clive Cox) *midfield on outer: rdn 2f out: r.o to chal ins fnl f: wnt 3rd cl home* **13/2**

4 *hd* **Stepper Point**[8] 2019 4-9-2 0 ChristopheSoumillon 10 106
(William Muir) *led: 1 l in front and gng best 1 1/2f out: rdn over 1f out: r.o but hdd cl home and dropped to 4th* **14/1**

5 *1 ¼* **Bear Behind (IRE)**[57] 1032 4-9-0 0 RichardKingscote 5 99
(Tom Dascombe) *trckd ldr on inner: rdn 2f out: nt qckn ins fnl f: jst hld on for 5th* **10/1**

6 *nse* **Tulips (IRE)**[30] 4-8-10 0 MaximeGuyon 4 95
(A Fabre, France) *towards rr and outpcd: rdn in last 3f out: r.o to go 6th post: fin wl but n.d* **13/2**

7 *nse* **Humidor (IRE)**[32] 1483 6-9-0 0 RichardHughes 3 99
(George Baker) *dwlt: hld up: rdn 2f out: r.o but nvr able to chal* **5/1**[3]

8 *1 ½* **Monsieur Joe (IRE)**[43] 1265 6-9-6 0 OlivierPeslier 6 99
(Robert Cowell) *trckd ldr on outer: rdn 2f out: no ex ins fnl f: fdd* **7/2**[1]

9 *5* **Gammarth (FR)**[19] 1755 5-9-2 0 FabriceVeron 1 77
(H-A Pantall, France) *midfield on inner: rdn over 2f out: keeping on and ev ch whn nt clr run on rail over 1f out: nt rcvr and sn dropped to last: eased* **7/1**

55.57s (-0.73) **Going Correction** +0.20s/f (Good) **9** Ran SP% **120.3**
Speed ratings: **113,112,112,112,110 110,109,107,99**
WIN (incl. 1 euro stake): 6.50. PLACES: 2.30, 3.50, 4.00. DF: 37.70. SF: 75.00.
Owner Mme Gerard Samama **Bred** Fern. Krief **Trained** France

FOCUS
The fourth was quickly away and has been rated back to his best, while the runner-up has been rated in line with a better view of his old form.

L'ANCRESSE
Monday, May 6
OFFICIAL GOING: Good (good to firm in places)

2301a E P MINOGUE H'CAP 1m 6f
2:15 (2:15) 3-Y-0+ **£1,800** (£750; £450)

RPR

1 **Pass The Time**[25] 226 4-10-4 (p) RichardEvans 4 53
(Neil Mulholland) **5/2**[3]

2 *2* **If I Had Him (IRE)**[15] 973 9-10-12 (v) MattieBatchelor 1 57
(George Baker) **1/2**[1]

3 *10* **Iron Duke**[60] 109 7-9-10 (bt) PhilipPrince 5 27
(Liam Corcoran) **4/1**

P **Fine The World**[15] 9-8-6 JoshBaudains 2
(Mrs A Corson, Jersey) **2/1**[2]

3m 5.0s (185.00)
WFA 4 from 7yo+ 1lb **4** Ran SP% **148.6**

Owner Dajam Ltd **Bred** M Burbidge **Trained** Limpley Stoke, Wilts

2302a RANDALLS OF GUERNSEY H'CAP 1m 2f
2:50 (2:50) 3-Y-0+ **£1,800** (£750; £450)

RPR

1 **I'm Harry**[15] 1739 4-10-11 (tp) MattieBatchelor 5
(George Baker) **2/1**[2]

2 *2* **Beck's Bolero (IRE)**[15] 7-10-12 (p) JoshBaudains 4
(Mrs A Corson, Jersey) **2/1**[2]

3 *1* **Rocquaine (IRE)**[15] 1740 4-9-9 MrFTett 3
(Mrs A Malzard, Jersey) **6/1**

4 *½* **Delightful Sleep**[11] 1797 5-10-12 RichardEvans 1
(David Evans) **4/5**[1]

5 *6* **Lang Shining (IRE)**[35] 9-10-12 JemmaMarshall 2
(Mrs A Malzard, Jersey) **5/2**[3]

2m 10.0s (130.00) **5** Ran SP% **165.1**

Owner Wickfield Stud And Hartshill Stud **Bred** Wickfield Stud And Hartshill Stud **Trained** Manton, Wilts

2303a CENKOS CHANNEL ISLANDS H'CAP 6f
3:25 (3:25) 3-Y-0+ **£3,100** (£1,200; £700)

RPR

1 **Haadeeth**[11] 1793 6-10-12 (t) RichardEvans 4
(David Evans) **4/5**[1]

2 *3* **Do More Business (IRE)**[18] 1657 6-9-11 (bt) PhilipPrince 5
(Liam Corcoran) **6/1**

3 *½* **Fast Freddie**[15] 1738 9-10-1 (p) JoshBaudains 3
(Mrs A Corson, Jersey) **2/1**[3]

4 *4* **Kersivay**[15] 1738 7-9-5 JemmaMarshall 2
(Mrs A Malzard, Jersey) **6/1**

5 *3* **Nenge Mboko**[14] 1714 3-10-12 (p) MattieBatchelor 1
(George Baker) **6/4**[2]

1m 10.0s (70.00)
WFA 3 from 6yo+ 10lb **5** Ran SP% **157.5**

Owner Mrs I M Folkes **Bred** Bolton Grange **Trained** Pandy, Monmouths

2304a GUERNSEY RACE CLUB H'CAP — 1m 4f
4:00 (4:00) (0-70,) 3-Y-O+ £1,800 (£750)

RPR

1 **Blue Pencil**[77] 703 4-9-12 .... MrFTett 2
(Roger Curtis) 2/1[2]

2 8 **Penang Cinta**[269] 5038 10-10-12 .... RichardEvans 1
(Mrs A Malzard, Jersey) 1/3[1]

2m 38.0s (158.00) 2 Ran SP% 108.4

Owner The Racing 4 Fun Partnership **Bred** Robin Ellerbeck (bloodstock) Ltd **Trained** Lambourn, Berks

2305a HUNSCOTE STUD H'CAP — 1m
4:35 (4:35) (0-50,) 3-Y-O+ £1,800 (£750; £450)

RPR

1 **Pas D'Action**[35] 1312 5-10-7 .... JemmaMarshall 2
(Mrs A Malzard, Jersey) 4/6[1]

2 1 **The Bay Bandit**[30] 6396 6-10-12 .... MattieBatchelor 4
(Neil Mulholland) 5/4[2]

3 2 **Rainbow Riches (IRE)**[74] 736 4-10-2 .... MrFTett 1
(Roger Curtis) 3/1[3]

1m 43.0s (103.00) 3 Ran SP% 129.4

Owner J Jamouneau **Bred** Jenny Hall Bloodstock Ltd **Trained** St Ouen, Jersey

2004 DONCASTER (L-H)
Monday, May 13

OFFICIAL GOING: Good to firm (9.9)
Wind: Mderate against Weather: Cloudy with sunny periods

2306 32REDPOKER.COM MAIDEN STKS — 1m (S)
2:10 (2:13) (Class 5) 3-Y-O £2,587 (£770; £384; £192) Stalls Low

Form RPR

4 1 **Matrooh (USA)**[25] 1635 3-9-5 0 .... PaulHanagan 3 86+
(William Haggas) *cl up: led over 3f out: rdn clr over 1f out: kpt on* 2/1[1]

2 1 **Stableford** 3-9-5 0 .... JimmyFortune 6 83+
(Brian Meehan) *dwlt and towards rr: gd hdwy over 2f out: rdn wl over 1f out: styd on strly fnl f: nt rch wnr* 33/1

4 3 2 **Defendant**[14] 1881 3-9-5 0 .... RyanMoore 12 78
(Sir Michael Stoute) *trckd ldrs: hdwy 3f out: rdn to chal wl over 1f out: one pce appr fnl f* 11/4[2]

5 4 nk **Mutajally**[25] 1635 3-9-5 0 .... DaneO'Neill 9 77+
(Sir Michael Stoute) *hld up towards rr: swtchd lft to outer and hdwy 3f out: rdn wl over 1f out: styd on fnl f: nrst fin* 11/2[3]

5 ¾ **Spirit Rider (USA)** 3-9-5 0 .... NickyMackay 1 75+
(John Gosden) *dwlt and towards rr: hdwy and in tch after 2f: trckd ldrs 1/2-way: rdn over 2f out: kpt on same pce appr fnl f* 25/1

64 6 ½ **Sedenoo**[21] 1713 3-9-5 0 .... AdamKirby 18 74
(Marco Botti) *trckd ldrs: hdwy 3f out: rdn over 2f out: one pce appr fnl f* 11/1

0 7 1 **Kazak**[23] 1678 3-9-5 0 .... JamesDoyle 7 72+
(Roger Charlton) *dwlt and rr tl styd on fnl 2f: nrst fin* 33/1

8 2¼ **Canon Law (IRE)** 3-9-2 0 .... PatrickHills(3) 14 66+
(Luca Cumani) *towards rr whn sltly hmpd after 2f: sme hdwy fnl 2f: nvr nr ldrs* 20/1

24 9 hd **Cavalieri (IRE)**[14] 1891 3-9-5 0 .... JimmyQuinn 13 66
(William Jarvis) *nvr bttr than midfield* 25/1

0-0 10 hd **Switcharooney (IRE)**[23] 1678 3-9-5 0 .... RichardKingscote 5 66
(Tom Dascombe) *in tch: pushed along wl over 2f out: sn rdn and no imp* 50/1

0-2 11 4½ **Nelson Quay (IRE)**[21] 1711 3-9-5 0 .... SteveDrowne 2 55
(Jeremy Gask) *chsd ldrs: rdn along 3f out: grad wknd* 25/1

6 12 1¼ **Orbison (IRE)**[14] 1881 3-9-5 0 .... RichardHughes 10 69+
(Roger Varian) *stdd s: t.k.h and hld up bhd: swtchd rt and smooth hdwy wl over 2f out: pushed along and in tch on wd outside wl over 1f out: sn eased* 11/1

13 3¾ **Miss Chuckles** 3-9-0 0 .... GrahamGibbons 4 38
(Tim Easterby) *a in rr* 100/1

14 4½ **West Beat**[182] 3-9-0 0 .... DanielTudhope 11 27
(David O'Meara) *midfield: whn hung rt after 2f: pushed along over 3f out: sn wknd* 100/1

6-5 15 5 **Jackaddock**[25] 1648 3-9-5 0 .... TomEaves 16 20
(James Bethell) *a towards rr* 80/1

16 hd **Rocky Couloir** 3-8-12 0 .... MatthewHopkins(7) 15 19
(Michael Easterby) *led: rdn along 1/2-way: sn hdd & wknd* 100/1

0 17 1½ **Evident (IRE)**[14] 1881 3-9-5 0 .... MickaelBarzalona 17 16
(Jeremy Noseda) *chsd ldrs: rdn along 3f out: sn wknd* 20/1

1m 42.24s (2.94) **Going Correction** +0.30s/f (Good) 17 Ran SP% 125.2
Speed ratings (Par 99): **97,96,94,93,92 92,91,89,89,88 84,83,79,74,69 69,68**
Tote Swingers: 1&2 £24.80, 1&3 £2.70, 2&3 £34.10 CSF £86.51 TOTE £2.70: £1.30, £11.80, £1.40; EX 121.30 Trifecta £689.20 Pool: £2,606.03 - 2.83 winning units..
Owner Hamdan Al Maktoum **Bred** WinStar Farm LLC **Trained** Newmarket, Suffolk

FOCUS
Round course railed out from 9f to where it joins straight adding circa 18yds to races on that course. Probably an above average 3yo maiden run over the straight mile. The time was ordinary but the form makes a fair bit of sense.

2307 £32 BONUS AT 32RED.COM MAIDEN STKS — 5f 140y
2:40 (2:41) (Class 5) 2-Y-O £2,587 (£770; £384) Stalls Low

Form RPR

1 **Canyari (IRE)** 2-9-5 0 .... PaulHanagan 4 86+
(Richard Fahey) *cl up: disp ld 1/2-way: slt ld wl over 1f out: rdn and edgd lft ent fnl f: sn qcknd clr: styd on wl* 7/4[2]

2 5 **Legend Rising (IRE)** 2-9-5 0 .... RichardHughes 2 69
(Richard Hannon) *slt ld: jnd 1/2-way: hdd wl over 1f out: cl up and ev ch appr fnl f: sn rdn and one pce* 8/11[1]

3 5 **Howz The Family (IRE)** 2-9-5 0 .... RichardKingscote 5 52
(Tom Dascombe) *pushed along and sltly outpcd in rr: hdwy over 2f out: sn rdn and no imp* 7/1[3]

1m 10.37s (1.57) **Going Correction** +0.30s/f (Good) 3 Ran SP% 106.8
Speed ratings (Par 93): **101,94,87**
CSF £3.44 TOTE £1.80; EX 3.30 Trifecta £3.50 Pool: £1,168.44 - 249.30 winning units..
Owner M A Leatham & G H Leatham **Bred** John Malone **Trained** Musley Bank, N Yorks

FOCUS
Three newcomers in this 2yo maiden run over the split Portland distance. The time was reasonable and the winner produced a taking performance.

2308 32RED CASINO H'CAP — 7f
3:15 (3:18) (Class 5) (0-70,70) 3-Y-O £3,234 (£962; £481; £240) Stalls Low

Form RPR

-344 1 **Black Rider (IRE)**[97] 525 3-8-13 **62** .... PaulMulrennan 14 69
(Julie Camacho) *hld up in rr: stdy hdwy on outer over 2f out: chsd ldrs over 1f out: rdn to chal ent fnl f: sn led and hung lft: kpt on* 40/1

03-3 2 1½ **Knight Owl**[12] 1928 3-9-3 **66** .... FrederikTylicki 6 71+
(James Fanshawe) *trckd ldrs: hdwy 2f out: rdn over 1f out: ev ch ins fnl f: keeping on same pce whn n.m.r nr line: jst hld 2nd* 5/1[2]

36-1 3 nse **Red Paladin (IRE)**[28] 1575 3-9-7 **70** .... AmyRyan 3 73
(Kevin Ryan) *cl up: led 1/2-way: rdn wl over 1f out: drvn and edgd rt ent fnl f: sn hdd: kpt on wl u.p towards fin* 9/1

16-0 4 ¾ **Medici Dancer**[25] 1647 3-9-2 **70** .... DarylByrne(5) 9 71
(Tim Easterby) *midfield and pushed along whn n.m.r after 2f: sn swtchd lft to outer and hdwy to chse ldrs 3f out: rdn over 2f out: kpt on fnl f: nrst fin* 33/1

65-0 5 hd **Hot Mustard**[21] 1712 3-8-8 **57** .... HayleyTurner 4 57
(Michael Bell) *hld up in tch: hdwy to chse ldrs wl over 1f out: sn rdn and kpt on fnl f* 20/1

5-30 6 1 **Pippy**[16] 1829 3-9-2 **65** .... RichardKingscote 13 62
(Tom Dascombe) *prom: rdn along 2f out: drvn over 1f out: hld whn n.m.r ent fnl f* 9/1

4-00 7 ½ **Epic Charm**[13] 1907 3-8-8 **57** .... PaulHanagan 10 53
(Mick Channon) *hld up in rr: swtchd rt to outer 2f out: rdn over 1f out: kpt on fnl f: nrst fin* 25/1

321- 8 1 **Glossy Posse**[196] 7439 3-9-3 **66** .... RichardHughes 11 59+
(Richard Hannon) *hld up: hdwy over 2f out: effrt whn nt clr run over 1f out and again jst ins fnl f: no ch after* 5/1[2]

2560 9 ¾ **Black Dave (IRE)**[16] 1832 3-8-11 **65** .... DeclanBates(5) 16 56
(David Evans) *trckd ldrs on outer: hdwy over 2f out: rdn over 1f out: n.m.r and one pce ent fnl f* 40/1

3242 10 1¾ **Go Far**[19] 1760 3-9-5 **68** .... LiamKeniry 7 55
(Alan Bailey) *trckd ldrs: effrt wl over 2f out: sn rdn along and wknd over 1f out* 6/1[3]

21 11 1¾ **Iggy**[116] 236 3-9-7 **70** .... GrahamGibbons 8 52
(Michael Easterby) *hld up: sme hdwy over 2f out: rdn along whn n.m.r wl over 1f out: sn wknd* 9/1

12 ½ **Aminah**[80] 765 3-9-1 **64** .... JamesDoyle 15 44
(Robert Cowell) *chsd ldrs: rdn along 2f out: sn wknd* 33/1

135 13 nse **Hazza The Jazza**[95] 550 3-9-0 **63** .... (e[1]) RobbieFitzpatrick 2 43
(Richard Guest) *s.i.s: a in rr* 50/1

04-3 14 8 **Dutch Gal**[37] 1389 3-8-13 **62** .... RyanMoore 5 21
(John Holt) *led: shkn up and hdd 1/2-way: wknd qckly* 4/1[1]

050- 15 nk **Stand N Applaude**[206] 7223 3-8-9 **58** .... AndrewMullen 1 16
(David Nicholls) *cl up: rdn along wl over 2f out: sn wknd* 50/1

1m 29.86s (3.56) **Going Correction** +0.30s/f (Good) 15 Ran SP% 120.9
Speed ratings (Par 99): **91,89,89,88,88 87,86,85,84,82 80,79,79,70,70**
Tote Swingers: 1&2 £31.30, 1&3 £47.10, 2&3 £12.20 CSF £218.57 CT £2048.53 TOTE £51.30: £11.50, £1.50, £3.00; EX 330.90 Trifecta £193.10 Pool: £2,782.85 - 1.09 winning units..
Owner Nigel Gravett **Bred** Patrick A Cassidy **Trained** Norton, N Yorks

FOCUS
A competitive 3yo handicap. They raced in one group towards the centre. A surprise winner, and the fifth and sixth are the best guides.

2309 32RED.COM H'CAP — 1m (S)
3:50 (3:52) (Class 4) (0-80,80) 3-Y-O £4,690 (£1,395; £697; £348) Stalls Low

Form RPR

200- 1 **Derwent (USA)**[233] 6487 3-9-7 **80** .... JamesDoyle 1 88
(Roger Charlton) *hld up in rr: hdwy 3f out: trckd ldrs 2f out: rdn to chal ent fnl f: led last 100yds: drvn out* 10/1

63-2 2 hd **Bartack (IRE)**[28] 1577 3-9-2 **78** .... PatrickHills(3) 8 85
(Luca Cumani) *trckd ldrs: cl up on outer 1/2-way: edgd rt 3f out: chal 2f out: rdn to ld jst ins fnl f: sn edgd lft: hdd and no ex last 100yds* 3/1[2]

12-1 3 ½ **Grandorio (IRE)**[5] 2167 3-9-6 **79** 5ex .... DanielTudhope 6 85
(David O'Meara) *trckd ldr: cl up 1/2-way: led 3f out: sn rdn and hdd over 2f out: drvn and rallied ins fnl f: kpt on towards fin* 1/1[1]

24-5 4 1½ **Dusky Queen (IRE)**[25] 1645 3-9-1 **79** .... GeorgeChaloner(5) 7 82
(Richard Fahey) *trckd ldrs: hdwy 1/2-way: led over 2f out: sn rdn: drvn and hdd ins fnl f: wknd* 11/2[3]

1003 5 18 **Fraserburgh (IRE)**[13] 1912 3-9-0 **73** .... JoeFanning 4 34
(Mark Johnston) *trckd ldrs: effrt and pushed along whn hmpd and squeezed out 3f out: sn wknd* 12/1

1331 6 24 **Great Demeanor (USA)**[26] 1612 3-9-3 **76** .... LiamKeniry 2
(David Elsworth) *led: pushed along 1/2-way: hdd 3f out and sn wknd* 22/1

1m 41.5s (2.20) **Going Correction** +0.30s/f (Good) 6 Ran SP% 111.5
Speed ratings (Par 101): **101,100,100,98,80 56**
Tote Swingers: 1&2 £3.60, 1&3 £2.40, 2&3 £1.30 CSF £39.24 CT £55.39 TOTE £10.10: £4.50, £2.20; EX 52.30 Trifecta £92.90 Pool: £2,929.32 - 23.62 winning units..
Owner K Abdullah **Bred** Juddmonte Farms Inc **Trained** Beckhampton, Wilts

FOCUS
The first four home all had their chance in the closing stages of this 3yo handicap run on the straight course. They set off towards the far side before edging nearer the stands' side. The pace increased markedly soon after the halfway mark. The first two showed improvement.

2310 32RED H'CAP — 7f
4:25 (4:27) (Class 3) (0-95,91) 4-Y-O+ £7,439 (£2,213; £1,106; £553) Stalls Low

Form RPR

05-0 1 **Mezzotint (IRE)**[128] 78 4-9-3 **87** .... AdamKirby 13 99
(Marco Botti) *hld up in rr: hdwy wl over 2f out: chsd ldrs over 1f out: rdn to chal ent fnl f: squeezed through and drvn to ld last 100yds: edgd lft: kpt on* 12/1

655- 2 hd **Poetic Dancer**[151] 8098 4-8-10 **85** .... RyanTate(5) 8 96
(Clive Cox) *trckd ldrs: cl up 1/2-way: led 3f out: rdn wl over 1f out: drvn ent fnl f: hdd last 100yds: no ex towards fin* 8/1[3]

10-6 **3** 2 ¾ **Zacynthus (IRE)**[23] 1688 5-9-3 **90**........ PatrickHills(3) 9 94
(Luca Cumani) *hld up towards rr: hdwy over 2f out: swtchd lft and rdn to chse ldrs over 1f out: ev ch ent fnl f: sn one pce* **9/2**[1]

1105 **4** *shd* **Dubai Hills**[23] 1691 7-9-3 **87**........ TomEaves 3 90
(Bryan Smart) *a.p: effrt 2f out: sn rdn to chal and ev ch tl drvn and one pce ins fnl f* **20/1**

-303 **5** *2* **King Of Jazz (IRE)**[13] 1913 5-9-0 **87**........ DarrenEgan(3) 10 85
(Michael Bell) *in tch: trckd ldrs 1/2-way: effrt 2f out: sn rdn to chal and ev ch tl drvn ent fnl f and sn one pce* **5/1**[2]

2040 **6** 3 ¼ **Docofthebay (IRE)**[16] 1830 9-8-7 **80**........(b) BillyCray(3) 11 69
(Scott Dixon) *in rr: swtchd wd to outer and hdwy wl over 1f out: sn rdn and styd on fnl f: nrst fin* **20/1**

-000 **7** 1 ¼ **Alejandro (IRE)**[18] 1787 4-8-12 **82**........ PaulHanagan 4 68
(Richard Fahey) *chsd ldrs: rdn along over 2f out: sn one pce* **12/1**

4-06 **8** 2 ¼ **Escape To Glory (USA)**[9] 2007 5-9-2 **86**........ PaulMulrennan 12 66
(Michael Dods) *chsd ldrs: rdn along over 2f out: sn one pce* **14/1**

410- **9** ½ **Sam Nombulist**[184] 7691 5-9-2 **86**........ RobertWinston 5 64
(Richard Whitaker) *led: rdn along 1/2-way: hdd 3f out and sn wknd* **25/1**

226- **10** *nk* **Able Master (IRE)**[213] 7030 7-9-7 **91**........ DanielTudhope 14 69
(David O'Meara) *chsd ldrs on wd outside: rdn along over 2f out: sn btn* **9/1**

0614 **11** 3 ½ **Roninski (IRE)**[9] 2028 5-9-1 **85**........ FrederikTylicki 1 53
(Garry Moss) *cl up: rdn along over 2f out: grad wknd* **10/1**

3133 **12** *11* **Al's Memory (IRE)**[21] 1720 4-8-11 **86**........ DeclanBates(5) 6 24
(David Evans) *dwlt: sn trcking ldrs: prom 1/2-way: rdn along wl over 2f out and sn wknd* **12/1**

0-00 **13** 4 ½ **Kalk Bay (IRE)**[9] 2028 6-8-5 **82**........(t) MatthewHopkins(7) 2
(Michael Easterby) *dwlt: a in rr* **50/1**

0-06 **14** *8* **Shesastar**[9] 2026 5-8-11 **81**........ GrahamGibbons 7
(David Barron) *dwlt: a in rr* **17/2**

1m 28.2s (1.90) **Going Correction** +0.30s/f (Good) **14** Ran SP% **120.7**
Speed ratings (Par 107): **101,100,97,97,95 91,90,87,86,86 82,70,64,55**
Tote Swingers: 1&2 £36.10, 1&3 £11.10, 2&3 £11.30 CSF £100.27 CT £507.50 TOTE £12.50: £3.50, £2.60, £2.40; EX 198.60 Trifecta £2236.80 Part won. Pool: £2,982.44 - 0.96 winning units..
Owner GIB Bloodstock Ltd & J Allison **Bred** David Barry **Trained** Newmarket, Suffolk

FOCUS
A competitive-looking 7f handicap, but only the first five were seriously involved in the closing stages. The form is rated around the first two.

2311 1STSECURITYSOLUTIONS.CO.UK FILLIES' H'CAP 1m 2f 60y
5:00 (5:00) (Class 5) (0-70,70) 4-Y-0+ **£2,911** (£866; £432; £216) **Stalls** Low

Form RPR

53-2 **1** **Cosmic Halo**[125] 107 4-8-12 **66**........ GeorgeChaloner(5) 4 77
(Richard Fahey) *trckd ldrs: hdwy 3f out: led appr fnl f: sn rdn and kpt on wl towards fin* **9/2**[2]

3111 **2** *1* **Apache Glory (USA)**[18] 1775 5-9-7 **70**........(p) AndreaAtzeni 6 79
(John Stimpson) *hld up in rr: stdy hdwy 3f out: chsd ldrs over 1f out: rdn to chse wnr ins fnl f: sn drvn and kpt on* **9/2**[2]

23-2 **3** *4* **Bobs Her Uncle**[28] 1579 4-9-2 **65**........ PaulHanagan 3 66
(James Bethell) *chsd ldr: hdwy to ld over 3f out: rdn 2f out: hdd and drvn appr fnl f: kpt on same pce* **7/2**[1]

33-2 **4** *nk* **Curly Come Home**[16] 1836 4-9-7 **70**........ GeorgeBaker 7 71
(Chris Wall) *hld up in tch: hdwy on outer to chse ldrs 3f out: rdn 2f out: drvn and one pce ent fnl f* **7/2**[1]

5462 **5** ½ **Dazzling Valentine**[6] 2136 5-8-13 **67**........ NatashaEaton(5) 1 67
(Alan Bailey) *chsd ldng pair: rdn along and outpcd wl over 2f out: kpt on fnl f* **7/1**[3]

1410 **6** 1 ½ **Chella Thriller (SPA)**[28] 1585 4-8-12 **61**........(b) RichardKingscote 2 58
(Alastair Lidderdale) *awkward s: sn trcking ldrs: effrt over 3f out: rdn along wl over 2f out: sn no imp* **16/1**

3033 **7** 2 ¾ **Cheers For Thea (IRE)**[28] 1579 8-9-2 **65**........(bt) GrahamGibbons 5 57
(Tim Easterby) *dwlt: hld up towards rr: hdwy 3f out: chsd ldrs 2f out: sn rdn: n.m.r and wknd appr fnl f* **14/1**

4405 **8** 3 ¾ **White Diamond**[16] 1836 6-8-10 **59**........ AndrewMullen 8 44
(Michael Appleby) *led: rdn along over 4f out: hdd over 3f out and sn wknd* **11/1**

2m 11.9s (2.50) **Going Correction** +0.30s/f (Good) **8** Ran SP% **114.2**
Speed ratings (Par 100): **102,101,98,97,97 96,93,90**
Tote Swingers: 1&2 £5.00, 1&3 £3.50, 2&3 £3.80 CSF £24.95 CT £77.99 TOTE £5.10: £1.80, £2.10, £2.00; EX 31.30 Trifecta £128.60 Pool: £2,806.42 - 16.36 winning units..
Owner The Cosmic Cases **Bred** The Cosmic Cases **Trained** Musley Bank, N Yorks

FOCUS
The front pair drew clear in what was a reasonable race for the grade. A personal best from the winner, with the second getting closer to old form.

2312 AJA GENTLEMAN AMATEUR RIDERS' H'CAP 1m 4f
5:35 (5:35) (Class 5) (0-70,70) 3-Y-0 **£2,495** (£774; £386; £193) **Stalls** Low

Form RPR

-163 **1** **Darakti (IRE)**[5] 2175 3-10-0 **56** oh1........(v[1]) MrBenFfrenchDavis(7) 1 59
(Alan McCabe) *in rr: pushed along and outpcd bef 1/2-way: hdwy and in tch on inner 3f out: swtchd rt to wd outside wl over 1f out: styd on to ld ins fnl f: kpt on* **16/1**

052- **2** ¾ **Khotan**[212] 7057 3-11-4 **70**........ MrFMitchell(3) 5 72+
(Sir Mark Prescott Bt) *racd wd: trckd ldrs: hdwy 3f out: chal 2f out: sn rdn and hung bdly lft: drvn and wandered ins fnl f: kpt on* **4/6**[1]

14 **3** 1 ¼ **Akdam (IRE)**[14] 1885 3-11-2 **68**........ MrMJJSmith(3) 3 68+
(Tony Carroll) *chsd ldrs: hdwy over 2f out: rdn whn bdly hmpd 1 1/2f out: kpt on u.p fnl f* **9/2**[3]

-522 **4** 2 ¼ **Handiwork**[35] 1425 3-10-8 **62**........ MrRGSpencer(5) 2 58+
(Michael Bell) *trckd ldrs: hdwy on inner over 3f out: rdn whn bdly hmpd 1 1/2f out: swtchd rt and kpt on fnl f* **4/1**[2]

-446 **5** *nse* **Jawinski (IRE)**[13] 1897 3-10-8 **57**........ MrTomGreenway 4 53
(David Evans) *led: rdn along wl over 2f out: hdd ent fnl f: wknd* **12/1**

2m 40.32s (5.42) **Going Correction** +0.30s/f (Good) **5** Ran SP% **111.7**
Speed ratings (Par 99): **93,92,91,90,90**
CSF £28.50 TOTE £19.10: £5.90, £1.30; EX 35.80 Trifecta £151.00 Pool: £2,130.65 - 10.57 winning units..
Owner Mrs D E Sharp **Bred** Mrs Mary Coonan **Trained** Averham Park, Notts
■ Stewards' Enquiry : Mr Tom Greenway four-day ban: failed to ride out for fourth (May 28,Jun 8,12,13)
Mr F Mitchell three-day ban: careless riding (May 28, Jun 8,12)

FOCUS
The rain had eased the ground ahead of this most unsatisfactory amateur riders' handicap, which was run at a strong pace. A messy race, tricky to assess.
T/Plt: £193.00 to a £1 stake. Pool: £67,805.90 - 256.36 winning tickets. T/Qpdt: £41.10 to a £1 stake. Pool: £4,526.88 - 256.36 winning tickets. JR

1988 MUSSELBURGH (R-H)
Monday, May 13

OFFICIAL GOING: Good (good to soft in places; 7.6)
Wind: Fairly strong, half against Weather: Cloudy, showers

2313 32RED H'CAP (FOR AMATEUR RIDERS) 2m
2:00 (2:00) (Class 6) (0-65,62) 4-Y-0+ **£2,495** (£774; £386; £193) **Stalls** Low

Form RPR

0-61 **1** **Jan Smuts (IRE)**[6] 2120 5-10-4 **57** 6ex........(tp) MissSMDoolan(5) 7 66+
(Wilf Storey) *hld up: stdy hdwy over 4f out: c wd 3f out: led over 1f out: pushed out* **4/1**[2]

/042 **2** 1 ¼ **Brasingaman Eric**[10] 1993 6-10-9 **62**........ MrRSmith(5) 6 69
(George Moore) *cl up: rdn and led centre over 2f out: hdd over 1f out: edgd lft and kpt on fnl f: hld nr fin* **13/8**[1]

300- **3** 4 ½ **Talk Of Saafend (IRE)**[15] 6315 8-10-4 **57**........ MissRobynGray(5) 2 59
(Dianne Sayer) *hld up: hdwy on wd outside and prom 1/2-way: effrt and ev ch over 2f out: one pce over 1f out* **12/1**

02/ **4** 1 ¼ **Summerlea (IRE)**[710] 2666 7-10-0 **55**........ MissAChadwick(7) 10 56
(Patrick Holmes) *prom: effrt and ev ch in centre over 2f out: nt qckn over 1f out* **50/1**

5-00 **5** *1* **Frosty Berry**[52] 1111 4-10-3 **61**........ MrAFrench(7) 3 60
(John Wainwright) *hld up: hdwy and prom 1/2-way: effrt over 2f out: edgd rt and outpcd wl over 1f out* **20/1**

260- **6** ½ **Goodlukin Lucy**[40] 7102 6-9-8 **45**........ MrJHamilton(3) 8 44
(Dianne Sayer) *led: rdn and hdd over 2f out: wknd over 1f out* **9/1**

50-4 **7** 1 ½ **Three White Socks (IRE)**[34] 1454 6-10-7 **62**........ MissNHayes(7) 12 59
(Brian Ellison) *midfield: drvn and outpcd over 2f out: rallied far side 2f out: kpt on: nvr able to chal* **15/2**[3]

0-00 **8** 3 ¼ **Grand Art (IRE)**[6] 2120 9-10-4 **52**........(p) MissCWalton 1 45
(Noel Wilson) *t.k.h: prom: styd far side in st: wknd fr over 2f out* **22/1**

644- **9** 4 ½ **Terenzium (IRE)**[136] 7102 11-9-8 **47**........(p) MissBeckySmith(5) 11 35
(Micky Hammond) *bhd and sn detached: shkn up and sme late hdwy far side: nvr nr ldrs* **12/1**

160/ **10** *10* **Grandad Bill (IRE)**[606] 6082 10-9-13 **54**........ MrsLGoldie(7) 9 30
(Jim Goldie) *in tch: rdn far side over 3f out: sn wknd* **25/1**

000- **11** *15* **Rare Coincidence**[15] 7255 12-9-4 **45**........(t) MrJamesHughes(7) 4
(Alan Berry) *prom tl rdn and wknd fr over 5f out: t.o* **50/1**

-040 **12** *166* **Lyric Poet (USA)**[18] 1789 6-10-1 **54**........(tp) MrGrahamCarson(5) 5
(David Thompson) *hld up: struggling over 6f out: sn btn: t.o* **20/1**

3m 42.12s (8.62) **Going Correction** +0.425s/f (Yiel)
WFA 4 from 5yo+ 3lb **12** Ran SP% **116.9**
Speed ratings (Par 101): **95,94,92,91,91 90,90,88,86,81 73,**
Tote Swingers: 1&2 £2.00, 2&3 £5.60 CSF £9.63 CT £69.68 TOTE £5.40: £1.50, £1.10, £3.10; EX 11.80 Trifecta £78.10 Pool: £1,197.34 - 11.49 winning units..
Owner H S Hutchinson & W Storey **Bred** Tipper House Stud **Trained** Muggleswick, Co Durham
■ Stewards' Enquiry : Miss Becky Smith ten-day ban: failed to take all reasonable and permissable measures to obtain best possible placing (May 28,31,Jun 1,8,12,14,14,17,20,24)

FOCUS
Franny Norton described the ground as being "on the soft side of good". This modest amateur riders' handicap was run at a fair pace. The first two home finished near the stands' side rail. The second helps set the standard.

2314 BRITISH STALLION STUDS EUROPEAN BREEDERS' FUND MEDIAN AUCTION MAIDEN STKS 5f
2:30 (2:30) (Class 5) 2-Y-0 **£3,234** (£962; £481; £240) **Stalls** High

Form RPR

1 **Suzi's Connoisseur** 2-9-5 0........ FrannyNorton 5 76+
(Mark Johnston) *noisy in paddock: cl up: led 1/2-way: pushed along over 1f out: styd on strly* **9/2**[3]

2 2 ¼ **Meadway** 2-9-5 0........ RoystonFfrench 3 68
(Bryan Smart) *n.m.r sn after s: sn pushed along and cl up on outside: effrt and rdn 2f out: one pce whn edgd lft ins fnl f* **10/11**[1]

0 **3** 3 ½ **Lendal Bridge**[28] 1573 2-8-12 0........ DavidSimmonson(7) 4 55
(Tony Coyle) *chsd ldrs: rdn and outpcd 1/2-way: plugged on fnl f: no imp* **18/1**

4 *3* **Alaskan Night (IRE)** 2-9-5 0........ PhillipMakin 2 45
(Kevin Ryan) *led to 1/2-way: sn drvn: wknd over 1f out* **2/1**[2]

1m 3.03s (2.63) **Going Correction** +0.425s/f (Yiel) **4** Ran SP% **109.2**
Speed ratings (Par 93): **95,91,85,81**
CSF £9.28 TOTE £4.70; EX 9.90 Trifecta £29.80 Pool: £1,036.69 - 26.04 winning units..
Owner Greenstead Hall Racing Ltd **Bred** Greenstead Hall Racing Ltd **Trained** Middleham Moor, N Yorks

FOCUS
Only one of the four runners had experience for this maiden, which was run at an honest pace. The bare form is very ordinary.

2315 32RED CASINO H'CAP 1m
3:05 (3:05) (Class 5) (0-70,70) 4-Y-0+ **£3,234** (£962; £481; £240) **Stalls** Low

Form RPR

000- **1** **Staff Sergeant**[132] 7203 6-9-7 **70**........ GrahamLee 4 83
(Iain Jardine) *t.k.h: mde all: pushed along and qcknd over 2f out: kpt on strly fnl f* **5/1**[3]

05-0 **2** 2 ¾ **Eastward Ho**[12] 1932 5-9-1 **67**........ RaulDaSilva(3) 1 74
(Jason Ward) *trckd ldrs: drvn over 2f out: chsd (clr) wnr appr fnl f: no imp* **11/4**[2]

005- **3** 2 ¾ **Rex Romanorum (IRE)**[225] 6709 5-9-2 **65**........ PJMcDonald 8 65
(Patrick Holmes) *w wnr: rdn over 2f out: one pce fr over 1f out* **6/1**

3002 **4** ¾ **Copperwood**[5] 2163 8-9-4 **67**........ FrannyNorton 3 66
(Mark Johnston) *t.k.h: trckd ldrs: drvn along over 2f out: edgd rt and no imp over 1f out* **9/4**[1]

143- **5** *nse* **Edas**[225] 6711 11-8-6 **60**........ JasonHart(5) 7 59
(Thomas Cuthbert) *dwlt: hld up in tch: smooth hdwy on outside wl over 2f out: rdn and nt qckn over 1f out* **15/2**

00-5 **6** *15* **Silver Rime (FR)**[10] 1992 8-9-5 **68**........ PhillipMakin 6 32
(Linda Perratt) *hld up: rdn and struggling over 2f out: sn btn* **20/1**

00-0 **7** ¾ **Royal Straight**[10] 1990 8-9-1 **69**........(t) GarryWhillans(5) 2 31
(Linda Perratt) *s.i.s: hld up in tch: rdn over 3f out: wknd over 2f out* **33/1**

1m 43.92s (2.72) **Going Correction** +0.425s/f (Yiel) **7** Ran SP% **107.9**
Speed ratings (Par 103): **103,100,97,96,96 81,80**
Tote Swingers: 1&2 £3.10, 1&3 £5.50, 2&3 £3.00 CSF £16.91 CT £71.13 TOTE £5.40: £2.70, £1.90; EX 20.50 Trifecta £118.40 Pool: £2,499.43 - 15.81 winning units..
Owner Derek Walpole & Iain Jardine **Bred** Darley **Trained** Bonchester Bridge, Borders

FOCUS
Plenty of out-of-form performers in this handicap, which was run at a steady pace. Once again the winner made all, and there are doubts about him repeating this.

2316 TURCAN CONNELL H'CAP — 1m 4f 100y
3:40 (3:40) (Class 5) (0-75,75) 4-Y-O+ **£3,234** (£962; £481; £240) **Stalls** Low

Form — RPR

00-1 **1** **Mohawk Ridge**[37] 1390 7-8-11 **72** ConnorBeasley(7) 5 80
(Michael Dods) *mde all: rdn 2f out: kpt on wl fnl f: unchal* **5/1**[3]

24-5 **2** 1 1/4 **Hawdyerwheesht**[44] 1251 5-8-10 **64** GrahamLee 1 70
(Jim Goldie) *t.k.h: chsd ldrs: effrt and wnt 2nd over 2f out: rdn and edgd rt over 1f out: kpt on same pce ins fnl f* **5/1**[3]

40-0 **3** 2 1/4 **Madrasa (IRE)**[10] 1993 5-8-8 **62** (t) MickyFenton 2 65+
(Keith Reveley) *hld up: shkn up and effrt on outside over 2f out: chsd (clr) ldng pair appr fnl f: kpt on: nvr nr ldrs* **10/1**

2224 **4** 5 **Capellanus (IRE)**[7] 2069 7-9-4 **75** PaulPickard(3) 3 70+
(Brian Ellison) *dwlt: sn pushed along in rr: drvn and effrt 3f out: kpt on fnl f: nvr able to chal* **9/2**[2]

016- **5** 1 1/4 **Schmooze (IRE)**[205] 7252 4-8-5 **59** RoystonFfrench 11 52
(Linda Perratt) *bhd: pushed along over 4f out: styd on fr 2f out: nvr rchd ldrs* **25/1**

055- **6** 3/4 **Vittachi**[160] 7980 6-7-11 **58** RowanScott(7) 8 50
(Alistair Whillans) *hld up in tch: effrt and drvn 3f out: outpcd 2f out* **20/1**

600- **7** nk **Call Of Duty (IRE)**[243] 6131 8-8-7 **66** GarryWhillans(5) 7 57
(Dianne Sayer) *midfield: rdn along wl over 2f out: no imp fr over 1f out* **10/1**

10-0 **8** 1 1/4 **Alsahil (USA)**[33] 1463 7-9-3 **71** PJMcDonald 9 60
(Micky Hammond) *chsd wnr to over 2f out: drvn and wknd over 1f out* **14/1**

30-0 **9** 2 **Madame Blavatsky (FR)**[18] 1790 5-8-2 **56** oh3 JamesSullivan 4 42
(Karen McLintock) *in tch: drvn along 3f out: wknd wl over 1f out* **20/1**

-054 **10** 3/4 **Torero**[90] 624 4-8-6 **60** FrannyNorton 10 45
(Kevin Ryan) *hld up in tch: drvn along over 2f out: sn btn* **4/1**[1]

336- **11** 12 **Miss Ella Jade**[178] 7752 4-8-2 **56** oh4 PaulQuinn 12 22
(Richard Whitaker) *t.k.h: hld up: rdn over 3f out: sn struggling* **16/1**

200- **12** 29 **Geanie Mac (IRE)**[175] 7791 4-8-3 **60** (b) JulieBurke(3) 6
(Linda Perratt) *t.k.h: prom tl rdn and wknd over 2f out: t.o* **50/1**

2m 51.54s (9.54) **Going Correction** +0.425s/f (Yiel) 12 Ran SP% **117.6**
Speed ratings (Par 103): **85,84,82,79,78 78,77,76,75,75 67,47**
Tote Swingers: 1&2 £7.10, 1&3 £12.90, 2&3 £9.60 CSF £28.40 CT £243.29 TOTE £5.40: £1.60, £1.80, £4.50; EX 31.10 Trifecta £410.00 Pool: £2,243.81- 4.10 winning units..
Owner Doug Graham **Bred** Old Mill Stud Ltd And Oomswell Ltd **Trained** Denton, Co Durham

FOCUS
It started raining heavily prior to this contest. The pace was sound with the winner again making every yard of the running. He confirmed his Newcastle run to be no fluke.

2317 RACING UK - YOUR RACING HOME FROM HOME MAIDEN STKS — 5f
4:15 (4:15) (Class 5) 3-Y-O+ **£3,234** (£962; £481; £240) **Stalls** High

Form — RPR

1 **Algar Lad** 3-9-5 0 GrahamLee 7 74+
(Jim Goldie) *bhd and sn pushed along: hdwy 2f out: qcknd to ld ins fnl f: sn clr* **20/1**

0-32 **2** 2 1/4 **Red Baron (IRE)**[23] 1687 4-9-9 64 (b) JasonHart(5) 6 68
(Eric Alston) *chsd ldrs: hdwy to ld over 1f out: rdn: carried hd high and hung lft ins fnl f: sn hdd: kpt on same pce* **7/1**

65-6 **3** 1 3/4 **Wotalad**[9] 2006 3-9-5 56 FrannyNorton 8 58
(Richard Whitaker) *prom: drvn and outpcd 1/2-way: styd on fnl f: nvr able to chal* **22/1**

5-60 **4** 1/2 **Beacon Tarn**[11] 1962 3-9-0 55 (b[1]) PhillipMakin 3 51
(Eric Alston) *in tch: effrt on outside 2f out: sn rdn: one pce fnl f* **12/1**

32-3 **5** 2 1/2 **Anderton (IRE)**[21] 1722 3-9-5 72 TonyHamilton 1 47
(Richard Fahey) *cl up: rdn and ev ch over 1f out: outpcd fnl f* **6/4**[1]

-224 **6** 4 **Cracking Choice (IRE)**[10] 1988 3-8-12 65 (p) ConnorBeasley(7) 4 33
(Michael Dods) *cl up: rdn and ev ch over 1f out: sn wknd* **3/1**[2]

3-40 **7** 3/4 **Queen Flush (IRE)**[16] 1844 3-9-0 65 PaulQuinn 9 25
(David Nicholls) *led at decent gallop: rdn and hdd over 1f out: sn wknd* **4/1**[3]

0 **8** 3 1/2 **Busy Bimbo (IRE)**[91] 610 4-9-9 40 (b) PaddyAspell 2 16
(Alan Berry) *dwlt and wnt rt s: bhd: struggling 1/2-way: btn over 1f out* **100/1**

1m 2.23s (1.83) **Going Correction** +0.425s/f (Yiel)
WFA 3 from 4yo 9lb 8 Ran SP% **115.3**
Speed ratings (Par 103): **102,98,95,94,90 84,83,77**
Tote Swingers: 1&2 £5.60, 1&3 £19.00, 2&3 £11.10 CSF £150.06 TOTE £15.40: £3.60, £1.90, £5.10; EX 99.10 Trifecta £912.20 Pool: £3,579.38 - 2.94 winning units..
Owner Great Northern Partnership **Bred** Highclere Stud **Trained** Uplawmoor, E Renfrews

FOCUS
This was not a strong maiden, although the pace was fair. Improvement from the winner, but the form picks were below par.

2318 32RED.COM H'CAP — 7f 30y
4:50 (4:51) (Class 5) (0-75,73) 3-Y-O **£3,234** (£962; £481; £240) **Stalls** Low

Form — RPR

2134 **1** **Skytrain**[11] 1958 3-9-7 **73** FrannyNorton 6 78+
(Mark Johnston) *pressed ldr: rdn over 2f out: led and edgd rt over 1f out: hld on wl fnl f* **9/4**[1]

2-62 **2** nk **Mowhoob**[2] 2279 3-9-6 **72** GrahamLee 3 76
(Jim Goldie) *led at ordinary gallop: shkn up and hdd over 1f out: rdn fnl f: kpt on: hld nr fin* **7/2**[2]

0-41 **3** 2 **La Luz Del Sol**[19] 1764 3-8-8 **60** TonyHamilton 2 59+
(Richard Fahey) *trckd ldrs: effrt and ev ch whn blkd appr fnl f: one pce last 100yds* **7/2**[2]

1534 **4** 6 **Rangi**[12] 1935 3-9-0 **73** DavidSimmonson(7) 4 56
(Tony Coyle) *hld up in tch: rdn and hung lft wl over 1f out: sn outpcd* **4/1**[3]

3-60 **5** 1/2 **Ayr Missile**[9] 2010 3-8-5 **60** JulieBurke(3) 1 41
(Kevin Ryan) *dwlt: bhd on ins: effrt and pushed along wl over 2f out: no imp fnl 2f* **33/1**

5-65 **6** 7 **Out Of The Blocks**[19] 1764 3-8-2 **54** JamesSullivan 5 17
(Ruth Carr) *hld up on outside: effrt and rdn wl over 2f out: wknd over 1f out* **8/1**

313- **7** 28 **Findog**[276] 5055 3-9-6 **72** PhillipMakin 7
(Linda Perratt) *t.k.h: trckd ldrs tl rdn and wknd over 1f out: eased whn no ch ins fnl f* **22/1**

1m 34.0s (5.00) **Going Correction** +0.425s/f (Yiel) 7 Ran SP% **113.6**
Speed ratings (Par 99): **88,87,85,78,77 69,37**
Tote Swingers: 1&2 £2.80, 1&3 £2.80, 2&3 £3.00 CSF £10.22 TOTE £2.80: £2.00, £2.10; EX 12.60 Trifecta £33.00 Pool: £3,005.66 - 68.18 winning units..
Owner A D Spence **Bred** Brook Stud Bloodstock Ltd **Trained** Middleham Moor, N Yorks

FOCUS
A fair pace on for this handicap, with the first three home always in command. The winner is rated up a length on his 2yo form.

2319 32REDPOKER.COM H'CAP — 7f 30y
5:20 (5:20) (Class 6) (0-60,59) 4-Y-O+ **£2,587** (£770; £384; £192) **Stalls** Low

Form — RPR

34-1 **1** **Jebel Tara**[10] 1995 8-9-2 **54** (bt) TonyHamilton 12 70+
(Alan Brown) *trckd ldrs: short of room over 2f out: effrt whn bdly hmpd 2f out and no room over 1f out: swtchd lft and qcknd to ld ins fnl f: sn clr: readily* **7/2**[1]

00-0 **2** 4 1/2 **Ptolemy**[17] 1801 4-9-1 **58** LMcNiff(5) 1 59
(David Barron) *hld up: rdn and hdwy whn nt clr run over 2f out: effrt over 1f out: styd on fnl f to take 2nd nr fin: no ch w wnr* **8/1**

6004 **3** hd **Hab Reeh**[5] 2162 5-8-12 **53** (t) JulieBurke(3) 2 53
(Ruth Carr) *midfield: rdn 3f out: hdwy on outside to ld briefly ent fnl f: kpt on same pce: lost 2nd cl home* **9/2**[2]

-003 **4** nk **Spread Boy (IRE)**[8] 2038 6-8-10 **48** PaddyAspell 9 48
(Alan Berry) *hld up: rdn over 2f out: hdwy on outside over 1f out: kpt on fnl f: nvr able to chal* **22/1**

035- **5** 1 1/2 **Amno Dancer (IRE)**[242] 6179 6-8-4 **47** JasonHart(5) 3 53+
(Keith Dalgleish) *hld up: pushed along and hdwy over 2f out: trcking ldrs on ins whn no room fr over 1f out to ins fnl f: nt rcvr* **15/2**

-306 **6** 2 1/4 **North Central (USA)**[10] 1994 6-9-0 **52** (e) JamesSullivan 8 42
(Ruth Carr) *trckd ldrs: effrt over 2f out: led over 1f out to ent fnl f: sn outpcd* **25/1**

0-03 **7** 2 **Goninodaethat**[10] 1995 5-9-0 **52** GrahamLee 6 37
(Jim Goldie) *t.k.h: sit ld to over 1f out: sn wknd* **7/2**[1]

4104 **8** 2 **Pull The Pin (IRE)**[2] 2281 4-8-8 **53** (b) LukeLeadbitter(7) 7 33
(Declan Carroll) *t.k.h: disp ld: rdn and wandered over 2f out: wknd over 1f out* **5/1**[3]

03-0 **9** 5 **Berbice (IRE)**[10] 1994 8-9-2 **54** PhillipMakin 4 21
(Linda Perratt) *hld up: hdwy on outside over 2f out: wknd over 1f out* **18/1**

1m 35.0s (6.00) **Going Correction** +0.425s/f (Yiel) 9 Ran SP% **115.6**
Speed ratings (Par 101): **82,76,76,76,74 72,69,67,61**
Tote Swingers: 1&2 £8.50, 1&3 £6.00, 2&3 £8.90 CSF £32.26 CT £128.85 TOTE £3.90: £1.60, £2.60, £1.70; EX 34.80 Trifecta £198.80 Pool: £1,087.00 - 4.10 winning units..
Owner Miss E Johnston **Bred** Mrs G P Booth And J Porteous **Trained** Yedingham, N Yorks

FOCUS
A moderate handicap run at a solid pace with plenty of trouble in running, as the field grouped up at the 2f pole. The winner is rated close to his 2009 form.
T/Plt: £1,071.10 to a £1 stake. Pool: £41,013.53 - 27.95 winning tickets. T/Qpdt: £88.30 to a £1 stake. Pool: £3,577.58 - 29.98 winning tickets. RY

2096 WINDSOR (R-H)
Monday, May 13

OFFICIAL GOING: Good (8.2)
Wind: Blustery/strong, mostly behind Weather: Sunshine and showers

2320 LEE ROBINSON MAIDEN FILLIES' STKS — 5f 10y
5:50 (5:50) (Class 5) 2-Y-O **£2,587** (£770; £384; £192) **Stalls** Low

Form — RPR

00 **1** **Cafetiere**[25] 1634 2-9-0 0 [1] ChrisCatlin 1 76
(Paul Cole) *led to over 3f out: rdn over 1f out: rallied and clsd to ld last 75yds: pushed out* **8/1**[3]

2 1/2 **Weisse Socken (IRE)** 2-9-0 0 JimCrowley 4 74
(Ralph Beckett) *dwlt sltly: rcvrd to ld over 3f out: edgd lft fr over 1f out: rdn and hdd last 75yds: nt qckn* **8/11**[1]

3 3 1/2 **Senorita Guest (IRE)** 2-9-0 0 MartinHarley 5 62+
(Mick Channon) *in tch in last: effrt over 2f out: fdd over 1f out* **2/1**[2]

4 10 **Paradise Child** 2-8-7 0 RyanWhile(7) 2 26
(Bill Turner) *chsd ldr 1f: in tch to 1/2-way: rn green and wknd* **16/1**

1m 0.51s (0.21) **Going Correction** -0.05s/f (Good) 4 Ran SP% **108.2**
Speed ratings (Par 90): **96,95,89,73**
CSF £14.74 TOTE £5.90; EX 9.70 Trifecta £10.20 Pool: £605.23 - 44.24 winning units..
Owner A H Robinson **Bred** A H And C E Robinson Partnership **Trained** Whatcombe, Oxon

FOCUS
Top bend dolled out 8yds from normal configuration adding 29yds to races of 1m and beyond. Inner of straight dolled out 10yds at 6f and 5yds at winning post. Not a bad little fillies' maiden, but the winner may not rate much higher.

2321 DOWNLOAD CORAL MOBILE FROM THE APP STORE MEDIAN AUCTION MAIDEN STKS — 1m 2f 7y
6:20 (6:22) (Class 5) 3-5-Y-O **£2,587** (£770; £384; £192) **Stalls** Centre

Form — RPR

6-4 **1** **Glorious Protector (IRE)**[23] 1678 3-8-13 0 JamieSpencer 2 86+
(Ed Walker) *mde virtually all: shkn up 2f out: edgd lft and pressed 1f out: drvn to assert fnl f* **11/4**[2]

2-2 **2** 2 **Legal Waves (IRE)**[19] 1769 3-8-13 0 RichardHughes 12 84+
(Brian Meehan) *mostly chsd wnr: urged along 5f out: drvn 3f out: clsd to chal 1f out: nt qckn* **4/7**[1]

4 **3** 4 **Jazz Master**[14] 1882 3-8-13 0 KirstyMilczarek 10 74
(Luca Cumani) *chsd ldng pair: cl enough but u.p fr over 3f out: steadily outpcd fnl 2f* **20/1**

4 3/4 **Northern Meeting (IRE)** 3-8-8 0 RyanMoore 11 68
(Sir Michael Stoute) *sn chsd ldng trio: drvn 3f and cl enough: steadily outpcd fnl 2f* **16/1**

5 13 **Gertrude Gray (IRE)** 3-8-8 0 TomQueally 3 42+
(Sir Henry Cecil) *rn green in midfield: urged along and nt on terms over 4f out: tried to cl on chsng gp 3f out: kpt on to do best of those fr off the pce* **14/1**[3]

6 2 **Dumbfounded (FR)**[436] 5-10-0 0 MartinLane 16 43
(Lady Herries) *hld up wl in rr: pushed along 4f out: sn lft bhd by ldrs: kpt on fnl 2f* **100/1**

0 **7** 1/2 **Bombardier**[14] 1882 3-8-13 0 EddieAhern 6 42+
(James Fanshawe) *hld up in rr: lft bhd by ldrs 4f out: nudged along and kpt on steadily fnl 2f* **66/1**

0 **8** nk **This Is Me**[5] 2157 5-10-0 0 DaneO'Neill 14 41+
(Don Cantillon) *dwlt: t.k.h: hld up in last trio: outpcd by ldrs fr 4f out: nudged along and kpt on steadily fnl 2f* **40/1**

5 **9** 1 1/4 **Pursivere**[14] 1882 3-8-13 0 JimmyFortune 8 38
(Hughie Morrison) *nvr bttr than midfield: pushed along and lft bhd over 3f out: nvr on terms after* **33/1**

10 1 1/4 **Sun And Stars**[36] 5-9-11 0 BrendanPowell(3) 7 36
(Brendan Powell) *in tch in midfield: hung lft u.p and outpcd over 3f out: steadily wknd* **100/1**

11 3/4 **Royal Marskell** 4-9-9 0 LauraPike(5) 1 34
(K F Clutterbuck) *hld up wl in rr: pushed along and lft bhd by ldrs fr 4f out: sme hdwy 2f out: eased fnl f* **100/1**

0- 12 2 **Admirable Art (IRE)**[273] 5162 3-8-13 0 PatDobbs 9 30
(Tony Carroll) *t.k.h early: trckd ldrs in 6th: rdn and lft bhd fr 4f out: sn wknd* **100/1**

13 20 **Halling's Treasure** 3-8-13 0 JimCrowley 15
(Andrew Balding) *dwlt: rn green in last trio: bhd fr 1/2-way: t.o* **50/1**

0 14 2 1/2 **Brave Helios**[21] 1727 3-8-13 0 TedDurcan 13
(Jonathan Portman) *a towards rr: lost tch w ldrs 4f out: t.o* **66/1**

0 15 27 **Top Banana**[25] 1635 3-8-13 0 SaleemGolam 5
(Stuart Williams) *chsd ldrs in 5th: wknd rapidly 4f out: wl t.o* **100/1**

2m 7.58s (-1.12) **Going Correction** -0.05s/f (Good)
WFA 3 from 4yo+ 15lb **15** Ran SP% **122.9**
Speed ratings (Par 103): **102,100,97,96,86 84,84,83,82,81 81,79,63,61,40**
Tote Swingers: 1&2 £1.20, 1&3 £5.40, 2&3 £3.30 CSF £4.43 TOTE £2.60: £1.10, £1.10, £3.70; EX 5.40 Trifecta £24.40 Pool: £1,603.49 - 49.24 winning units..
Owner Ms A A Yap **Bred** T Boylan **Trained** Newmarket, Suffolk

FOCUS
A fair maiden where the first two set a good standard and were always 1-2. The front four pulled a long way clear.

2322 CORAL.CO.UK H'CAP 1m 2f 7y
6:50 (6:53) (Class 4) (0-80,79) 3-Y-O **£4,851** (£1,443; £721; £360) **Stalls** Centre

Form RPR

2333 1 **He's A Striker (IRE)**[28] 1584 3-8-8 69 RyanClark(3) 5 78
(Michael Blake) *s.s: hld up in last: taken to wd outside and gd prog fr 3f out: rdn to ld jst over 1f out: styd on wl* **10/1**

51-5 2 nk **Greeleys Love (USA)**[44] 1250 3-9-6 78 SilvestreDeSousa 9 86
(Mark Johnston) *mde most: pressed and shkn up over 3f out: drvn 2f out: hdd jst over 1f out: edgd lft but battled on wl: jst hld* **7/2**[1]

011- 3 5 **Keep Calm**[175] 7785 3-8-11 69 PatDobbs 6 67
(Richard Hannon) *hld up bhd ldrs: pushed along 4f out: drvn and tried to cl 2f out: plugged on to take 3rd nr fin* **14/1**

303- 4 3/4 **Monsieur Rieussec**[201] 7335 3-9-5 77 TedDurcan 2 74+
(Jonathan Portman) *hld up in midfield: gng bttr than most 4f out: rdn and prog to dispute 2nd briefly 2f out: nt qckn and sn btn: wknd ins fnl f* **13/2**[2]

02-3 5 2 **Misfer**[21] 1735 3-9-1 73 (b) TomQueally 3 66
(Sir Henry Cecil) *hld up towards rr: shkn up 4f out: tried to make prog on outer 3f out: no hdwy and btn over 1f out* **7/1**[3]

23-1 6 3/4 **Aint Got A Scooby (IRE)**[19] 1770 3-9-1 73 JohnFahy 8 64
(Clive Cox) *trckd ldng pair: pressed ldr 4f out gng wl: rdn 3f out: lost 2nd and wknd 2f out* **13/2**[2]

2-31 7 3 3/4 **World Record (IRE)**[13] 1904 3-9-7 79 RichardHughes 4 66
(Richard Hannon) *hld up in 8th but in front of eventual wnr: shkn up 3f out: no prog 2f out: eased fnl f* **7/2**[1]

1-40 8 13 **Kuantan One (IRE)**[12] 1934 3-9-3 75 JamieSpencer 7 42
(Paul Cole) *mostly chsd ldr to 4f out: sn wknd: bhd fnl 2f* **9/1**

614 9 21 **Burgoyne (USA)**[34] 1453 3-9-0 72 (b) RyanMoore 1
(Hughie Morrison) *prom early: wknd over 4f out: t.o* **14/1**

2m 7.76s (-0.94) **Going Correction** -0.05s/f (Good) **9** Ran SP% **116.0**
Speed ratings (Par 101): **101,100,96,96,94 93,90,80,63**
Tote Swingers: 1&2 £8.60, 1&3 £20.00, 2&3 £10.60 CSF £45.24 CT £498.68 TOTE £14.00: £3.90, £1.40, £3.30; EX 52.10 Trifecta £1132.40 Part won. Pool: £1,509.93 - 0.98 winning units..

Owner B Dunn & J Pierce **Bred** Kildare Racing Syndicate **Trained** Trowbridge, Wilts

FOCUS
A fair 3-y-o handicap, run at a solid gallop and the first pair came nicely clear. The winner is rated back to his early 2yo form.

2323 BRITISH STALLION STUDS SUPPORTING BRITISH RACING EBF STKS (ROYAL WINDSOR STAKES) (LISTED) (C&G) 1m 67y
7:20 (7:20) (Class 1) 3-Y-O+
£22,684 (£8,600; £4,304; £2,144; £1,076; £540) **Stalls** Low

Form RPR

-222 1 **Guest Of Honour (IRE)**[23] 1675 4-9-2 98 (p) MartinHarley 1 113
(Marco Botti) *trckd ldr: gng strly 3f out: led 2f out: sn drvn: styd on wl and in command fnl f* **9/2**[3]

5426 2 2 1/4 **Don't Call Me (IRE)**[12] 1919 6-9-2 107 (t) AdrianNicholls 2 108
(David Nicholls) *trckd ldng pair: rdn over 3f out: clsd to go 2nd wl over 1f out: kpt on but no imp on wnr* **25/1**

112- 3 nk **Montiridge (IRE)**[212] 7053 3-8-3 104 KieranO'Neill 4 104
(Richard Hannon) *stdd s: t.k.h in last pair: prog over 2f out: rdn over 1f out: pressed runner-up fnl f but effrt flattened out* **8/11**[1]

050- 4 1 3/4 **Fury**[226] 6674 5-9-2 104 RyanMoore 6 103
(William Haggas) *led: kicked on 4f out: rdn and hdd 2f out: outpcd after* **4/1**[2]

0414 5 3 1/4 **Monsieur Chevalier (IRE)**[12] 1919 6-9-2 106 RichardHughes 3 96
(P J O'Gorman) *trckd ldng trio: shkn up wl over 2f out: no prog and btn over 1f out: fdd* **14/1**

0630 6 3 **Red Duke (USA)**[17] 1810 4-9-2 103 TomQueally 5 89
(David Simcock) *stdd s: t.k.h in last pair: rdn and no prog over 2f out: fdd* **33/1**

1m 42.69s (-2.01) **Going Correction** -0.05s/f (Good)
WFA 3 from 4yo+ 13lb **6** Ran SP% **109.5**
Speed ratings (Par 111): **108,105,105,103,100 97**
Tote Swingers: 1&2 £7.30, 1&3 £3.60, 2&3 £1.70 CSF £81.97 TOTE £5.00: £2.20, £6.90; EX 47.80 Trifecta £118.30 Pool: £1,129.58 - 7.16 winning units..
Owner Giuliano Manfredini **Bred** Azienda Agricola Gennaro Stimola **Trained** Newmarket, Suffolk

FOCUS
This looked a tight heat, but the winner proved too classy. The time was only ordinary and the favourite disappointed. The level is set by the runner-up.

2324 SIS RACING WELFARE H'CAP 1m 67y
7:50 (7:50) (Class 5) (0-70,70) 3-Y-O **£2,587** (£770; £384; £192) **Stalls** Low

Form RPR

30-3 1 **Emulating (IRE)**[72] 867 3-9-3 66 RichardHughes 7 77
(Richard Hannon) *mde all: 2 l clr and gng best 3f out: hld together tl drvn out fnl f* **3/1**[1]

04-2 2 1 3/4 **Poor Duke (IRE)**[13] 1900 3-9-7 70 FergusSweeney 2 76
(Jamie Osborne) *trckd ldng pair: rdn to chse wnr over 2f out: styd on fr over 1f out: a hld* **7/1**

0-05 3 1 1/4 **Harry Bosch**[13] 1900 3-9-7 70 (b[1]) JamieSpencer 13 73+
(Brian Meehan) *t.k.h: hld up in last trio: stdy prog on wd outside fr 3f out: hrd rdn over 1f out: styd on to take 3rd ins fnl f* **8/1**

-521 4 1/2 **Sam Spade (IRE)**[35] 1424 3-9-0 68 WilliamTwiston-Davies(5) 8 70
(Richard Hannon) *hld up in 9th: prog on outer over 3f out: rdn to chse ldng pair 2f out: no imp over 1f out: lost 3rd ins fnl f* **9/1**

35-0 5 3 3/4 **Miss Mocca**[12] 1928 3-8-11 65 AmyScott(5) 6 58
(Paul Fitzsimons) *w.w in midfield: shkn up and nt qckn 3f out: n.d over 1f out: one pce* **33/1**

504- 6 nk **Plenum (GER)**[156] 8033 3-9-7 70 TedDurcan 5 63+
(David Lanigan) *hld up in 9th: jst pushed along fr 3f out: n.d fnl 2f: modest late prog: nvr involved* **7/2**[2]

2423 7 nk **Beau Select (IRE)**[2] 2272 3-8-13 67 (b) ThomasBrown(5) 12 59
(Robert Eddery) *hld up in last trio: jst pushed along fr 3f out: n.d 2f out: modest late prog: nvr involved* **6/1**[3]

000- 8 nk **Haatefina**[211] 7079 3-9-5 68 TomQueally 10 59
(Mark Usher) *trckd ldrs: pushed along 3f out: no imp on ldrs 2f out: sn wknd* **20/1**

33-0 9 3 **David's Secret**[10] 1977 3-9-3 66 JimmyFortune 1 50
(Hughie Morrison) *chsd ldng pair: hrd rdn 2f out: wknd* **20/1**

30-6 10 2 1/4 **Muskat Link**[13] 1900 3-9-2 65 DaneO'Neill 3 44
(Henry Candy) *hld up in last trio: shkn up and struggling 4f out: sn no ch* **14/1**

0-65 11 8 **Beautiful Story (IRE)**[12] 1928 3-8-13 62 MartinHarley 9 23
(Mick Channon) *trckd ldrs in 5th: cl enough 3f out: lost pl and wknd qckly over 2f out* **20/1**

0-6U 12 19 **Forceful Flame**[35] 1427 3-9-2 65 MartinLane 11
(Robert Eddery) *restless in stalls: dwlt: quick move to press wnr after 1f: rdn over 3f out: wknd rapidly over 2f out: t.o* **66/1**

1m 44.18s (-0.52) **Going Correction** -0.05s/f (Good) **12** Ran SP% **120.5**
Speed ratings (Par 99): **100,98,97,96,92 92,92,91,88,86 78,59**
Tote Swingers: 1&2 £6.10, 1&3 £3.60, 2&3 £11.50 CSF £22.91 CT £159.30 TOTE £4.10: £1.70, £2.70, £3.10; EX 27.20 Trifecta £125.30 Pool: £1,167.53 - 6.98 winning units..
Owner Ben CM Wong **Bred** Mrs E J O'Grady **Trained** East Everleigh, Wilts

FOCUS
A modest 3-y-o handicap where it paid to be handy although it was sound run. The first two were the form pair.

2325 CORAL.CO.UK BEST PRICE ON HORSE RACING H'CAP 1m 3f 135y
8:20 (8:21) (Class 5) (0-75,73) 3-Y-O **£2,587** (£770; £384; £192) **Stalls** Centre

Form RPR

060- 1 **Plutocracy (IRE)**[193] 7507 3-9-4 70 TedDurcan 3 83+
(David Lanigan) *trckd ldrs: wnt 2nd over 3f out: shkn up to ld 2f out: styd on wl: comf* **11/4**[1]

25-0 2 3 **Ivanhoe**[13] 1900 3-9-0 66 DaneO'Neill 5 71
(Michael Blanshard) *hld up in last trio: rdn and prog fr 3f out: sustained effrt to take 2nd ins fnl f: no ch w wnr* **14/1**

333- 3 2 **Duroble Man**[159] 7989 3-9-6 72 RyanMoore 8 74
(Roger Varian) *led: stdd pce 7f out to over 4f out: rdn and hdd over 1f out: one pce* **10/3**[2]

431 4 1/2 **Strategic Strike (IRE)**[20] 1741 3-9-7 73 TomQueally 7 74
(Paul Cole) *hld up in last trio: rdn 3f out: sme prog on outer over 2f out: kpt on one pce over 1f out* **8/1**

321 5 4 1/2 **Continental Divide (IRE)**[31] 1522 3-9-5 71 JamieSpencer 9 66
(Jamie Osborne) *trckd ldrs: rdn and nt qckn wl over 2f out: ch of a pl jst over 1f out: wknd* **8/1**

0-10 6 7 **Woodstock (IRE)**[17] 1811 3-9-6 72 RichardHughes 4 57
(Richard Hannon) *trckd ldrs: rdn over 3f out: lost pl over 2f out: eased whn no ch fnl f* **5/1**[3]

51 7 18 **Refer**[13] 1898 3-9-7 73 SteveDrowne 1 24
(Charles Hills) *trckd ldr to 1/2-way: wknd over 3f out: eased over 1f out: t.o* **7/1**

0-24 8 19 **Countess Lovelace**[75] 815 3-8-13 65 IanMongan 2
(Pat Phelan) *prom: pressed ldr 1/2-way to over 3f out: wknd rapidly: wl t.o* **20/1**

-230 9 2 1/2 **House Of Orange (IRE)**[5] 2156 3-8-10 62 SilvestreDeSousa 6
(Mark Johnston) *a in last trio: u.str.p and struggling in last 5f out: wl t.o* **25/1**

2m 30.58s (1.08) **Going Correction** -0.05s/f (Good) **9** Ran SP% **116.4**
Speed ratings (Par 99): **94,92,90,90,87 82,70,58,56**
Tote Swingers: 1&2 £6.20, 1&3 £2.90, 2&3 £11.30 CSF £43.06 CT £134.05 TOTE £3.90: £1.60, £4.10, £1.60; EX 45.60 Trifecta £180.50 Pool: £1,288.56 - 5.35 winning units..
Owner B E Nielsen **Bred** Bjorn Nielsen **Trained** Upper Lambourn, Berks

FOCUS
Not a bad 3-y-o handicap for the class. The second and third set the standard.
T/Plt: £568.90 to a £1 stake. Pool: £86,403.06 - 110.87 winning units. T/Qpdt: £114.20 to a £1 stake. Pool: £7,904.95 - 51.20 winning units. JN

1886 WOLVERHAMPTON (A.W) (L-H)
Monday, May 13

OFFICIAL GOING: Standard
Wind: Fresh behind Weather: Cloudy with sunny spells

2326 FOLLOW US ON TWITTER @BETVICTORRACING H'CAP 5f 20y(P)
1:50 (1:53) (Class 6) (0-65,58) 4-Y-O+ **£2,045** (£603; £302) **Stalls** Low

Form RPR

3514 1 **Nafa (IRE)**[7] 2074 5-9-2 53 ShaneKelly 8 59
(Daniel Mark Loughnane) *hld up in tch: racd keenly: shkn up over 1f out: r.o u.p to ld nr fin* **3/1**[1]

2224 2 hd **Slatey Hen (IRE)**[21] 1731 5-8-13 50 (p) NeilCallan 3 55
(Violet M Jordan) *chsd ldr tl over 3f out: wnt 2nd again 1/2-way: rdn over 1f out: ev ch ins fnl f: r.o* **7/2**[2]

0025 3 shd **Spic 'n Span**[7] 2074 8-9-7 58 (be) LukeMorris 2 63
(Ronald Harris) *sn led: shkn up over 1f out: hdd nr fin* **9/2**[3]

3360 4 2 1/4 **Russian Bullet**[7] 2074 4-8-11 53 (b) RachealKneller(5) 1 50
(Jamie Osborne) *chsd ldrs: rdn over 1f out: styd on same pce ins fnl f* **9/2**[3]

5600 5 3 1/4 **Lesley's Choice**[21] 1731 7-9-1 52 WilliamCarson 4 37
(Sean Curran) *mid-div: drvn along and outpcd 1/2-way: rdn after* **12/1**

0442 6 2 **Ches Jicaro (IRE)**[60] 997 5-8-9 46 (v) KirstyMilczarek 10 24
(James Unett) *prom: chsd ldr over 3f out tl pushed along 1/2-way: rdn and wknd over 1f out* **6/1**

0064 7 nk **You'relikemefrank**[37] 1396 7-9-0 51 (p) LiamJones 9 28
(Richard Ford) *s.s: nvr nrr* **16/1**

5456 **8** *2¼* **Chateau Lola**[39] 1355 4-9-0 **51**..(v) MartinDwyer 7 20
(Derek Shaw) *mid-div: rdn 1/2-way: wknd over 1f out* **20/1**

-000 **9** *2* **Forever Janey**[58] 1043 4-8-8 **45**..(b) CathyGannon 5
(Paul Green) *sn outpcd* **50/1**

1m 1.36s (-0.94) **Going Correction** -0.125s/f (Stan) **9** Ran SP% **118.2**
Speed ratings (Par 101): **102,101,101,97,92 89,89,85,82**
Tote Swingers: 1&2 £3.00, 1&3 £3.70, 2&3 £2.60 CSF £13.99 CT £46.96 TOTE £4.90: £1.50, £1.70, £1.90; EX 12.20 Trifecta £24.70 Pool: £931.54 - 28.23 winning units..
Owner Ian O'Connor **Bred** Basil Brindley **Trained** Baldwin's Gate, Staffs

FOCUS
A run-of-the-mill sprint handicap with little separating the front three at the finish. It's been rated around the second and third to recent form.

2327 DOWNLOAD THE BETVICTOR APP NOW MAIDEN AUCTION FILLIES' STKS — 5f 20y(P)

2:20 (2:20) (Class 5) 2-Y-O **£2,587** (£770; £384; £192) **Stalls** Low

Form RPR

03 **1** **Blockade (IRE)**[12] 1924 2-8-10 0.. NeilCallan 5 73
(James Tate) *mde all: pushed clr over 1f out: rdn ins fnl f: jst hld on* **1/3**[1]

2 *shd* **Rural Celebration** 2-8-5 0.. DavidBergin(5) 3 73+
(David O'Meara) *dwlt: hld up: hdwy to chse wnr over 1f out: r.o wl* **11/2**[2]

4 **3** *3¾* **Marti's Girl**[7] 2068 2-8-4 0.. LiamJones 1 53
(J S Moore) *prom: rdn over 1f out: edgd lft and styd on same pce fnl f* **20/1**

4 *2¼* **Sandsman's Girl (IRE)** 2-8-10 0.. DaleSwift 6 51
(James Given) *sn pushed along in rr: lost tch 1/2-way: r.o ins fnl f* **9/1**[3]

0 **5** *1½* **Zac's Princess**[21] 1724 2-8-4 0.. CathyGannon 2 40
(Milton Bradley) *chsd ldrs: sn pushed along: wknd ins fnl f* **18/1**

6 **6** *3¼* **Danetimeranger (IRE)**[12] 1924 2-8-11 0.. LukeMorris 4 35
(Ronald Harris) *chsd wnr tl rdn over 1f out: wknd fnl f* **33/1**

1m 2.34s (0.04) **Going Correction** -0.125s/f (Stan) **6** Ran SP% **113.4**
Speed ratings (Par 90): **94,93,87,84,81 76**
Tote Swingers: 1&2 £1.50, 1&3 £1.60, 2&3 £5.90 CSF £2.77 TOTE £1.10: £1.02, £4.40; EX 2.40 Trifecta £13.70 Pool: £1,273.79 - 69.66 winning units..
Owner Saeed Manana **Bred** Patrick A Cassidy **Trained** Newmarket, Suffolk

FOCUS
An uncompetitive maiden and the odds-on favourite only just held on. She's rated to her Kempton form, with the first pair clear.

2328 £25 FREE BET AT BETVICTOR.COM H'CAP — 1m 5f 194y(P)

2:50 (2:51) (Class 6) (0-65,69) 4-Y-O+ **£1,940** (£577; £288; £144) **Stalls** Low

Form RPR

5430 **1** **Dubara Reef (IRE)**[24] 1664 6-8-5 **46** oh1..(p) LukeMorris 2 52
(Paul Green) *a.p: chsd ldr over 5f out: pushed along over 3f out: rdn to ld over 1f out: styd on* **7/1**[3]

26-4 **2** *½* **Medieval Bishop (IRE)**[13] 1916 4-8-8 **50**..(p) DuranFentiman 9 55
(Tim Walford) *sn led: rdn and hdd over 1f out: styd on* **3/1**[1]

0160 **3** *hd* **Royal Sea (IRE)**[11] 1948 4-9-5 **61**..(p) NeilCallan 1 66
(Barry Leavy) *chsd ldrs: rdn over 1f out: styd on* **7/1**[3]

2-31 **4** *nk* **Goldan Jess (IRE)**[102] 458 9-8-8 **56**.. EvaMoscrop(7) 3 60
(Philip Kirby) *chsd ldr over 8f: remained handy: rdn over 1f out: styd on* **3/1**[1]

0206 **5** *nse* **Dream Prospector**[11] 1949 4-9-7 **63**.. FergusSweeney 8 67
(James Evans) *s.i.s: hld up: hdwy on outer over 2f out: rdn and ev ch over 1f out: styd on* **10/1**

4033 **6** *hd* **Sommersturm (GER)**[7] 2069 9-9-3 **65**..(t) EoinWalsh(7) 4 69+
(David Evans) *s.s: hld up and bhd: travelled wl: rdn over 1f out: r.o wl ins fnl f: nvr nr to chal* **10/3**[2]

/56- **7** *3¾* **The Winged Assasin (USA)**[416] 1003 7-9-5 **65**..(t) RobertTart(5) 6 64
(Shaun Lycett) *hld up: rdn over 1f out: styd on same pce* **16/1**

00/0 **8** *½* **William Hogarth**[10] 1973 8-8-7 **55**.. DanielMuscutt(7) 5 53
(Keith Goldsworthy) *prom: rdn over 3f out: no ex fnl f* **40/1**

3m 3.54s (-2.46) **Going Correction** -0.125s/f (Stan)
WFA 4 from 6yo+ 1lb **8** Ran SP% **115.5**
Speed ratings (Par 101): **102,101,101,101,101 101,99,98**
Tote Swingers: 1&2 £2.80, 1&3 £3.70, 2&3 £2.20 CSF £28.64 CT £154.09 TOTE £7.00: £2.90, £1.40, £2.60; EX 34.40 Trifecta £343.80 Pool: £1,489.07 - 3.24 winning units..
Owner Oaklea Aces **Bred** M Duffy **Trained** Lydiate, Merseyside

FOCUS
The front six finished in a bunch in this low-grade staying handicap. A messy race to assess.

2329 BETVICTOR CASINO ON YOUR MOBILE H'CAP — 5f 216y(P)

3:25 (3:28) (Class 5) (0-70,70) 3-Y-O **£2,911** (£866; £432; £216) **Stalls** Low

Form RPR

214 **1** **Sylvia Pankhurst (IRE)**[14] 1892 3-9-0 **68**..(p) ThomasBrown(5) 6 77
(David C Griffiths) *led 1f: chsd ldrs: led again over 2f out: r.o wl* **7/2**[2]

4423 **2** *2* **Indian Affair**[31] 1524 3-9-7 **70**.. CathyGannon 9 72
(Milton Bradley) *a.p: racd keenly: rdn over 2f out: chsd wnr fnl f: no imp* **7/1**

1-4 **3** *nk* **Gift Of Music (IRE)**[23] 1682 3-9-5 **68**.. LukeMorris 8 69
(James Eustace) *hld up: nt clr run 2f out: hdwy and swtchd rt over 1f out: sn rdn: r.o* **4/1**[3]

04-4 **4** *¾* **Megamunch (IRE)**[42] 1295 3-9-7 **70**.. PatrickMathers 4 69+
(Kristin Stubbs) *s.i.s: pushed along in rr early: travelling wl whn n.m.r and hit rails 3f out: hdwy over 1f out: r.o: nt rch ldrs* **10/1**

060- **5** *1* **Ishi Honest**[231] 6541 3-9-5 **68**.. MartinDwyer 7 63
(Mark Usher) *chsd ldrs: rdn over 1f out: no ex ins fnl f* **25/1**

1160 **6** *4½* **Hazard Warning (IRE)**[12] 1935 3-9-2 **65**..(b) DuranFentiman 1 46
(Tim Easterby) *s.s: nvr on terms* **12/1**

3-01 **7** *3¼* **Macaabra (IRE)**[19] 1760 3-9-1 **64**.. NeilCallan 2 35
(James Tate) *led 5f out: hdd 2f out: wknd fnl f* **7/4**[1]

3005 **8** *7* **Nellie Bly**[13] 1907 3-9-2 **65**.. MichaelO'Connell 5 13
(Mark Johnston) *chsd ldrs: rdn over 2f out: wknd over 1f out* **12/1**

1m 14.04s (-0.96) **Going Correction** -0.125s/f (Stan) **8** Ran SP% **119.4**
Speed ratings (Par 99): **101,98,97,96,95 89,85,75**
Tote Swingers: 1&2 £2.70, 1&3 £1.90, 2&3 £4.60 CSF £29.52 CT £103.87 TOTE £6.50: £1.80, £1.30, £1.30; EX 21.60 Trifecta £59.80 Pool: £1,788.73 - 22.41 winning units..
Owner Norton Common Farm Racing **Bred** T Cahalan & D Cahalan **Trained** Bawtry, S Yorks

FOCUS
A modest 3yo sprint handicap. It was well run and the form is sound despite the favourite flopping.

2330 TALK TO VICTOR H'CAP — 7f 32y(P)

4:00 (4:02) (Class 6) (0-60,60) 3-Y-O **£1,940** (£577; £288; £144) **Stalls** High

Form RPR

-306 **1** **Moma Lee**[14] 1876 3-9-7 **60**.. WilliamBuick 2 69+
(John Gosden) *hld up: hdwy over 1f out: rdn to ld ins fnl f: sn clr* **2/1**[1]

40-4 **2** *2¾* **Pour La Victoire (IRE)**[11] 1966 3-8-9 **48**.. DaleSwift 11 50
(Nigel Tinkler) *hld up: hdwy over 1f out: rdn to ld ins fnl f: sn hdd and unable qck* **20/1**

25-6 **3** *2¼* **Red Tulip**[21] 1712 3-9-6 **59**.. LukeMorris 6 55
(James Fanshawe) *s.i.s: hdwy over 5f out: rdn over 1f out: styd on same pce ins fnl f* **9/2**[3]

0-25 **4** *1* **Suspension**[48] 1190 3-8-11 **55**.. RachealKneller(5) 9 48
(Hughie Morrison) *prom: rdn over 1f out: no ex ins fnl f* **10/1**

2501 **5** *½* **Baltic Prince (IRE)**[7] 2080 3-9-1 **59** 6ex.. ThomasBrown(5) 4 51
(Paul Green) *chsd ldr tl led 2f out: sn rdn: hdd and no ex ins fnl f* **4/1**[2]

05-0 **6** *¾* **Silvio Dante (USA)**[19] 1764 3-9-6 **59**.. DavidNolan 3 49
(David O'Meara) *led: rdn and hdd 2f out: ev ch 1f out: no ex ins fnl f* **14/1**

-513 **7** *2¼* **Brynford**[23] 1697 3-8-12 **56**.. RobertTart(5) 8 40
(Chris Dwyer) *chsd ldrs: rdn and ev ch over 1f out: wknd ins fnl f* **4/1**[2]

-600 **8** *10* **Special Report (IRE)**[7] 2080 3-8-7 **53**.. DanielleMooney(7) 10 10
(Nigel Tinkler) *hld up: nvr on terms* **66/1**

00-6 **9** *4½* **Bapak Besar (CAN)**[11] 1965 3-9-2 **55**..(p) StephenCraine 1
(Kevin Ryan) *sn pushed along and prom: rdn and wknd 1/2-way* **33/1**

40 **10** *18* **Lady Farah**[21] 1732 3-8-13 **52**.. NeilCallan 7
(Robert Cowell) *hld up: rdn 1/2-way: wknd over 2f out* **20/1**

1m 28.99s (-0.61) **Going Correction** -0.125s/f (Stan) **10** Ran SP% **121.2**
Speed ratings (Par 97): **98,94,92,91,90 89,87,75,70,50**
Tote Swingers: 1&2 £9.30, 1&3 £3.40, 2&3 £13.70 CSF £51.79 CT £175.77 TOTE £2.80: £1.20, £4.80, £1.90; EX 39.70 Trifecta £317.10 Pool: £2,977.59 - 7.04 winning units..
Owner Magnolia Racing LLC & Ms Rachel Hood **Bred** Newsells Park Stud **Trained** Newmarket, Suffolk

FOCUS
A modest 3yo handicap, the pace was solid and the principals all came from mid-division or further back. The winner is entitled to do better from here.

2331 DOWNLOAD THE BETVICTOR APP NOW FILLIES' H'CAP — 1m 141y(P)

4:35 (4:36) (Class 5) (0-70,66) 3-Y-O **£2,911** (£866; £432; £216) **Stalls** Low

Form RPR

0-16 **1** **Zero Game (IRE)**[25] 1655 3-9-6 **65**..(e) LukeMorris 5 70
(Michael Bell) *chsd ldrs: shkn up to ld ins fnl f: pushed out* **5/1**

1434 **2** *¾* **Polish Crown**[10] 1978 3-9-5 **64**.. MichaelO'Connell 4 68
(Mark Johnston) *sn led: clr 2f out: rdn and hdd ins fnl f: styd on* **3/1**[1]

34-6 **3** *2½* **Mojo Bear**[13] 1907 3-9-6 **65**.. WilliamBuick 1 63
(Sylvester Kirk) *chsd ldrs: rdn over 1f out: styd on same pce ins fnl f* **5/1**

434- **4** *5* **Al Thumama**[214] 6997 3-9-3 **62**.. NeilCallan 7 49
(Kevin Ryan) *sn chsng ldr: rdn over 2f out: wknd ins fnl f* **4/1**[2]

5140 **5** *nk* **Diletta Tommasa (IRE)**[33] 1487 3-9-7 **66**..(t) ShaneKelly 2 52
(John Stimpson) *hld up: hdwy 2f out: sn rdn: no ex fnl f* **9/2**[3]

05-0 **6** *1¼* **Red Four**[33] 1486 3-9-3 **62**.. PatCosgrave 3 45
(George Baker) *sn pushed along in mid-div: rdn over 3f out: wknd over 1f out* **14/1**

0-26 **7** *1* **Tiger's Home**[35] 1424 3-8-7 **59**.. ShelleyBirkett(7) 8 40
(Julia Feilden) *s.i.s: effrt on outer over 2f out: n.d* **18/1**

000- **8** *9* **Aphrodite's Dream**[238] 6320 3-8-0 **52** oh7.. AdamMcLean(7) 6 12
(Derek Shaw) *hld up: wknd over 2f out* **50/1**

40 **9** *1½* **Little Dolly**[33] 1486 3-9-3 **62**..(p) RobertHavlin 9 18
(Alan McCabe) *prom: rdn over 3f out: wknd over 2f out* **12/1**

1m 48.96s (-1.54) **Going Correction** -0.125s/f (Stan) **9** Ran SP% **118.1**
Speed ratings (Par 96): **101,100,98,93,93 92,91,83,82**
Tote Swingers: 1&2 £3.90, 1&3 £4.10, 2&3 £3.80 CSF £20.91 CT £80.52 TOTE £7.50: £2.30, £1.70, £2.30; EX 22.70 Trifecta £92.90 Pool: £3,006.17 - 24.24 winning units..
Owner Edward J Ware **Bred** Islanmore Stud **Trained** Newmarket, Suffolk

FOCUS
The front three pulled clear in this modest fillies' handicap. The form seems sound enough.

2332 BETVICTOR.COM AMATEUR RIDERS' H'CAP (DIV I) — 1m 4f 50y(P)

5:10 (5:15) (Class 6) (0-55,55) 4-Y-O+ **£1,871** (£580; £290; £145) **Stalls** Low

Form RPR

6330 **1** **El Bravo**[18] 1789 7-10-3 **51**.. WilliamFeatherstone(7) 3 63
(Shaun Harris) *led: hdd over 8f out: chsd ldr tl led again over 3f out: rdn clr fr over 1f out* **5/1**

40-3 **2** *8* **Politbureau**[18] 1790 6-10-7 **48**.. MissSBrotherton 8 47
(Michael Easterby) *chsd ldrs: rdn over 2f out: styd on same pce: wnt 2nd wl ins fnl f* **5/2**[1]

/0-5 **3** *1¾* **Cherry Tree Hill (IRE)**[31] 1522 5-11-0 **55**.. MrSWalker 9 51
(Alan Swinbank) *prom: rdn over 2f out: wknd ins fnl f* **11/4**[2]

40-0 **4** *¾* **Heading To First**[97] 522 6-10-0 **46** oh1..(p) MissMBryant(5) 1 41
(Paddy Butler) *hld up: plld hrd: hdwy over 3f out: rdn to chse wnr over 1f out: wknd ins fnl f* **66/1**

6600 **5** *½* **Turjuman (USA)**[3] 2242 8-10-9 **50**.. NicodeBoinville 6 44+
(Simon West) *hld up: rdn over 2f out: styd on ins fnl f: nvr nrr* **8/1**

00-0 **6** *1¼* **Son Vida (IRE)**[18] 1797 5-10-5 **53**..(p) MrDSMcLaughlin(7) 7 45
(Alan Bailey) *chsd ldr tl led over 8f out: hdd over 3f out: wknd over 1f out* **16/1**

000/ **7** *1½* **Bernix**[531] 6235 11-10-2 **48**..(p) MissLWilson(5) 11 38
(Julie Camacho) *hld up: hdwy over 5f out: wknd over 2f out* **25/1**

50-0 **8** *2¼* **Omega Omega**[13] 1916 4-10-5 **46** oh1.. MrRossBirkett 10 32
(Julia Feilden) *s.i.s: hld up: pushed along over 3f out: hdwy over 2f out: rdn and wknd over 1f out* **14/1**

5300 **9** *2¼* **Leitrim King (IRE)**[55] 1080 4-10-6 **52**.. MrGeorgeCrate(5) 5 35
(Murty McGrath) *hld up: rdn over 2f out: a in rr* **4/1**[3]

/000 **10** *2½* **Jakeys Girl**[97] 522 6-9-12 **46** oh1.. MissLWilliams(7) 2 25
(Pat Phelan) *prom tl wknd over 2f out* **40/1**

2m 41.61s (0.51) **Going Correction** -0.125s/f (Stan) **10** Ran SP% **123.3**
Speed ratings (Par 101): **93,87,86,86,85 84,83,82,80,79**
Tote Swingers: 1&2 £3.60, 1&3 £4.00, 2&3 £1.90 CSF £18.86 CT £43.12 TOTE £9.10: £2.60, £1.40, £1.40; EX 24.00 Trifecta £54.70 Pool: £2,500.68 - 34.23 winning units..
Owner www.nottinghamshireracing.co.uk (2) **Bred** D J And Mrs Deer **Trained** Carburton, Notts

FOCUS
They didn't go particularly quick in this amateur riders' handicap, the winner making all. He's rated back to December's C&D level.

2333 BETVICTOR.COM AMATEUR RIDERS' H'CAP (DIV II) — 1m 4f 50y(P)

5:45 (5:45) (Class 6) (0-55,53) 4-Y-O+ **£1,871** (£580; £290; £145) **Stalls** Low

Form RPR

50-2 **1** **Gladstone (IRE)**[14] 1877 5-10-10 **49**.. MissRachelKing 1 57+
(Polly Gundry) *prom: lost pl 7f out: hdwy over 1f out: r.o to ld nr fin* **9/4**[1]

30-6 **2** *nk* **Blue Top**[6] 2118 4-10-12 **51**.. MissJCoward 8 56
(Tim Walford) *led: rdn over 1f out: hdd nr fin* **3/1**[2]

3425 **3** 1 3/4 **Young Jackie**[42] 1297 5-10-9 **53**..........................(b) MissKMargarson(5) 5 55
(George Margarson) *s.i.s: hld up: hdwy over 5f out: pushed along and rn wd over 2f out: styd on* **3/1**[2]
0530 **4** *hd* **Mayan Flight (IRE)**[11] 1949 5-10-6 **45**................................ MrSWalker 6 47
(Tony Carroll) *hld up: hdwy 3f out: rdn over 1f out: styd on* **9/2**[3]
0/0- **5** 1 1/2 **Celebrian**[314] 3721 6-10-6 **52**.................................(t) MrJGoss(7) 2 52
(Alex Hales) *chsd ldrs: rdn over 1f out: styd on same pce fnl f* **25/1**
010/ **6** 1 1/2 **Windpfeil (IRE)**[601] 4703 7-10-4 **46**.............................. MissCBoxall(3) 9 43
(Dominic Ffrench Davis) *chsd ldr: rdn over 2f out: no ex ins fnl f* **18/1**
0000 **7** 2 1/4 **Love Pegasus (USA)**[43] 820 7-10-1 **45**...................(t) MissMBryant(5) 4 39
(Paddy Butler) *s.i.s: hld up: hdwy over 3f out: outpcd over 2f out: n.d after* **20/1**
60 **8** 3/4 **Numen (IRE)**[61] 788 9-10-11 **53**................................ MrChrisMartin(3) 3 45
(Barry Brennan) *hld up: rdn over 1f out: n.d* **12/1**
/000 **9** 18 **Orpen Bid (IRE)**[47] 1207 8-10-3 **45**....................(b) MissMMullineaux(3) 7
(Michael Mullineaux) *prom: rdn over 3f out: sn wknd* **40/1**

2m 44.87s (3.77) **Going Correction** -0.125s/f (Stan) **9** Ran SP% **123.0**
Speed ratings (Par 101): **82,81,80,80,79 78,77,76,64**
Tote Swingers: 1&2 £2.30, 1&3 £2.60, 2&3 £3.60 CSF £9.71 CT £21.30 TOTE £4.20: £1.80, £1.90, £1.10; EX 10.70 Trifecta £34.50 Pool: £1,360.06 - 29.51 winning units..
Owner G Carstairs **Bred** Hascombe And Valiant Studs **Trained** Ottery St Mary, Devon

FOCUS
The second division of the amateur riders' handicap and again the pace was modest. The slower division. The winner is batter than the bare form.
T/Plt: £26.20 to a £1 stake. Pool: £54,765.34 - 1,523.46 winning tickets. T/Qpdt: £11.50 to a £1 stake. Pool: £3,120.86 - 200.07 winning tickets. CR

1755 MAISONS-LAFFITTE (R-H)
Monday, May 13

OFFICIAL GOING: Turf: good

2334a PRIX TEXANITA (LISTED RACE) (3YO) (TURF) 5f 110y
2:20 (12:00) 3-Y-O **£22,357** (£8,943; £6,707; £4,471; £2,235)

RPR
1 **Mazameer (IRE)**[20] 1755 3-8-11 0..............................(b1) ThierryJarnet 4 101
(F Head, France) **14/5**[2]
2 *nk* **Wedge Trust (IRE)**[172] 7828 3-8-8 0.......................... IoritzMendizabal 8 97
(J-C Rouget, France) **53/10**
3 *shd* **Via Chope (FR)**[16] 3-8-8 0.................................... MaximeGuyon 7 97
(C Boutin, France) **11/1**
4 *nk* **Faithfilly (IRE)**[192] 7518 3-8-8 0.......................... AntoineHamelin 6 96
(F Rohaut, France) **18/1**
5 2 **Artplace (IRE)**[39] 3-8-11 0.......................................(b) JulienAuge 2 92
(C Ferland, France) **48/10**[3]
6 3/4 **Asteria (FR)**[26] 1633 3-8-8 0.................................. RonanThomas 5 87
(J E Pease, France) **10/1**
7 3 1/2 **Blaine**[212] 7049 3-8-11 0.. OlivierPeslier 3 78
(Kevin Ryan) *trckd ldng gp: 3rd and scrubbed along 1/2-way: rdn and outpcd 2f out: btn whn eased ins fnl f* **21/10**[1]
8 10 **Spellbound (FR)**[183] 7698 3-8-8 0.............................. FilipMinarik 1 42
(M Munch, Germany) **40/1**

1m 3.9s (-3.40) **8** Ran SP% **116.8**
WIN (incl. 1 euro stake): 3.80. PLACES: 1.80, 1.90, 2.70. DF: 11.10. SF: 18.10.
Owner Hamdan Al Maktoum **Bred** S Kennedy & P Carmody **Trained** France

2335a PRIX DE LA VASTINE (H'CAP) (3YO) (TURF) 6f (S)
3:55 (12:00) 3-Y-O **£12,195** (£4,878; £3,658; £2,439; £1,219)

RPR
1 **Jo De Vati (FR)**[12] 3-9-4 **0**................................ TheoBachelot 4 93
(S Wattel, France) **171/10**
2 1 1/2 **Tiberio (SPA)**[21] 3-8-10 **0**..............................(b) UmbertoRispoli 6 80
(M Delzangles, France) **83/10**[3]
3 3/4 **La Sage (FR)**[28] 3-8-9 **0**................................ ThierryJarnet 13 77
(J Heloury, France) **11/1**
4 3 1/2 **Bontoni (FR)**[16] 3-8-6 **0**................................ AntoineWerle(5) 7 67
(H-A Pantall, France) **36/1**
5 *nse* **Dummy Traou Land (FR)**[12] 3-8-0 0..........(p) AntoineCoutier 14 56
(P Costes, France) **106/1**
6 *hd* **As De Bigorre (IRE)**[28] 1594 3-9-3 **0**......................(b) JulienAuge 11 73
(C Ferland, France) **63/10**[2]
7 *nk* **Midnight Dancer (FR)**[16] 3-8-4 **0**.......................... AnthonyCrastus 8 59
(F Chappet, France) **11/1**
8 *shd* **Ruby Wedding (FR)**[39] 3-9-2 **0**.............................. IoritzMendizabal 2 70
(C Baillet, France) **11/1**
9 *hd* **Salinas Road (FR)**[26] 1633 3-9-11 **0**........................ MircoDemuro 12 79
(M Figge, Germany) **40/1**
10 *shd* **Lewamy (IRE)**[28] 1594 3-9-0 0.......................... ChristopheSoumillon 1 67
(John Best) *towards rr: rdn and hdwy on rail over 1 1/2f out: kpt on fnl f: nt pce to chal* **4/1**[1]
0 **Asian Rocket (FR)**[35] 3-7-11 **0**.............................. JimmyTastayre(3) 10
(C Boutin, France) **15/1**
0 **Jimmy Chop (FR)**[6] 3-8-7 **0**..........................(p) AlexandreChampenois 5
(C Boutin, France) **39/1**
0 **Contesurmoi (FR)**[16] 3-8-7 **0**................................ RonanThomas 9
(A Bonin, France) **14/1**
0 **Mehen (FR)**[28] 1594 3-9-2 **0**.................................. FabriceVeron 17
(H-A Pantall, France) **32/1**
0 **Ysper (FR)**[28] 3-8-9 **0**.. AlexisBadel 3
(M Nigge, France) **16/1**
0 **Babaway (FR)**[136] 3-8-11 **0**.................................. MaximeGuyon 15
(Mlle M Henry, France) **29/1**
0 **Trois Voeux (FR)**[21] 3-8-0 **0**..............................(b) SylvainRuis 18
(P Monfort, France) **36/1**
0 **Blacksou (FR)**[52] 3-8-0 0.............................. NicolasLarenaudie(4) 16
(P Adda, France) **82/1**
0 **Decision (FR)** 3-8-10 **0**.. BriceRaballand 19
(Mme C Head-Maarek, France) **30/1**

1m 11.2s (-2.20) **19** Ran SP% **115.8**
WIN (incl. 1 euro stake): 18.10. PLACES: 5.80, 3.50, 3.60. DF: 82.20. SF: 163.00.
Owner Guy Amsaleg **Bred** G Amsaleg **Trained** France

2075 BEVERLEY (R-H)
Tuesday, May 14

OFFICIAL GOING: Good to firm (9.7)
Wind: moderate half against Weather: Cloudy with sunny periods

2336 FANTASTIC PRIZES AT LUCKY IN LOVE (S) STKS 5f
2:10 (2:16) (Class 6) 3-Y-O **£2,264** (£673; £336; £168) **Stalls** Low

Form RPR
005 **1** **Auntie Mildred (IRE)**[20] 1760 3-8-6 38.................... SilvestreDeSousa 2 58+
(David O'Meara) *hld up towards rr: swtchd lft and hdwy wl over 1f out: rdn and str run ins fnl f to ld last 40yds* **10/1**
-365 **2** 3/4 **Salvatore Fury (IRE)**[4] 2218 3-8-11 54..........................(p) JoeFanning 1 60
(Keith Dalgleish) *hld up towards rr: swtchd lft and gd hdwy 2f out: rdn to chal ent fnl f: sn slt ld: drvn and hdd last 40yds* **3/1**[2]
4-33 **3** 1/2 **Chloe's Dream (IRE)**[12] 1961 3-8-6 64........................(p) PJMcDonald 6 53
(Ann Duffield) *led: rdn along and jnd over 1f out: drvn and hdd ins fnl f: no ex last 50yds* **10/3**[3]
2-23 **4** 3 **Confidential Creek**[20] 1762 3-8-11 56.......................... FrederikTylicki 7 47
(Ollie Pears) *sn trcking ldr: hdwy and cl up 2f out: rdn and ev ch over 1f out: wknd ent fnl f* **2/1**[1]
0405 **5** 4 1/2 **Nors The Panic**[11] 1988 3-8-11 47..........................(e) RobbieFitzpatrick 4 31
(Richard Guest) *cl up: pushed along bef 1/2-way: sn rdn and wknd 2f out* **33/1**
2500 **6** 3/4 **Twinwood Star (IRE)**[20] 1762 3-8-3 46........................ RaulDaSilva(3) 5 24
(John Weymes) *chsd ldrs: rdn along 1/2-way: sn wknd* **25/1**
-446 **7** 1 3/4 **Red Style (IRE)**[20] 1764 3-8-11 59..............................(b1) MickyFenton 8 22
(Paul Midgley) *chsd ldrs on outer: rdn along 2f out: sn wknd* **4/1**

1m 3.08s (-0.42) **Going Correction** -0.175s/f (Firm) **7** Ran SP% **117.3**
Speed ratings (Par 97): **96,94,94,89,82 80,78**
toteswingers 1&2 £4.20, 1&3 £4.20, 2&3 £3.10 CSF £41.64 TOTE £9.20: £3.50, £2.40; EX 50.60 Trifecta £225.70 Pool: £2005.71 - 6.66 winning units..There were no bids.
Owner Direct Racing Partnership **Bred** D G Iceton **Trained** Nawton, N Yorks

FOCUS
Weak selling form, rated around the runner-up. The winner can rate higher.

2337 RACING UK ON CHANNEL 432 MAIDEN STKS 5f
2:40 (2:41) (Class 5) 2-Y-O **£3,408** (£1,006; £503) **Stalls** Low

Form RPR
1 **Supplicant** 2-9-5 0.. TonyHamilton 1 82+
(Richard Fahey) *qckly away: mde all: rdn clr ent fnl f: styd on wl* **15/8**[1]
2 2 **Jacquotte Delahaye** 2-9-0 0.................................... TomEaves 6 70
(Bryan Smart) *wnt rt and hmpd s: green and towards rr: hdwy 2f out: rdn over 1f out: styd on strly fnl f* **11/2**[3]
3 2 1/2 **Tamayuz Magic (IRE)** 2-9-5 0.................................. JoeFanning 3 66
(Mark Johnston) *wnt lft s: sn trcking ldrs: effrt and green wl over 1f out: rdn to chse wnr ins fnl f: sn one pce* **7/2**[2]
4 3 1/2 **Uncle Bobby** 2-9-5 0.. JamesSullivan 5 54+
(Michael Easterby) *hmpd s and bhd: hdwy wl over 1f out: rdn and styd on wl fnl f: nrst fin* **25/1**
02 **5** 1 **Kraka Gym (IRE)**[8] 2075 2-9-5 0.............................. GrahamGibbons 8 50
(Michael Easterby) *cl up: rdn to chal over 1f out: drvn and wknd fnl f* **7/2**[2]
0 **6** 3/4 **Highland Princess (IRE)**[26] 1642 2-9-0 0................ RussKennemore 7 42
(Paul Midgley) *trckd ldng pair: pushed along over 2f out: rdn wl over 1f out: sn one pce* **66/1**
6 **7** 1 1/2 **Orient Sky**[10] 2005 2-9-5 0.................................... MickyFenton 4 42
(Paul Midgley) *hmpd s: a in rr* **28/1**
8 3/4 **Gerdani** 2-9-0 0.. PaulMulrennan 2 34
(Michael Easterby) *chsd ldrs: rdn along bef 1/2-way: sn outpcd* **8/1**

1m 4.58s (1.08) **Going Correction** -0.175s/f (Firm) **8** Ran SP% **114.5**
Speed ratings (Par 93): **84,80,76,71,69 68,66,64**
toteswingers 1&2 £3.10, 1&3 £2.60, 2&3 £2.70 CSF £12.59 TOTE £2.80: £1.10, £2.10, £1.60; EX 13.00 Trifecta £33.00 Pool: £1751.31 - 39.75 winning units..
Owner Cheveley Park Stud **Bred** Cheveley Park Stud Ltd **Trained** Musley Bank, N Yorks

FOCUS
A fair juvenile maiden that was dominated by the newcomers. The winner can do better.

2338 ANNIE OXTOBY MEMORIAL H'CAP (DIV I) 5f
3:10 (3:10) (Class 5) (0-70,70) 4-Y-O+ **£3,234** (£962; £481; £240) **Stalls** Low

Form RPR
2-00 **1** **Mey Blossom**[18] 1802 8-8-4 **58** ow1...................(p) GeorgeChaloner(5) 6 66
(Richard Whitaker) *trckd ldrs: swtchd lft and hdwy wl over 1f out: rdn to chal ins fnl f: kpt on wl u.p to ld nr fin* **14/1**
00-0 **2** *nk* **Irish Boy (IRE)**[7] 2132 5-8-13 **62**..............................(t) RoystonFfrench 7 69
(Christine Dunnett) *trckd ldrs: hdwy and cl up 2f out: rdn to ld ent fnl f: sn drvn and hdd nr fin* **20/1**
0-30 **3** 1/2 **Art Dzeko**[24] 1693 4-9-3 **66**.................................. DuranFentiman 5 71
(Tim Easterby) *hld up: hdwy on inner 2f out: swtchd lft and rdn over 1f out: chal ent fnl f: drvn and ev ch tl no ex last 50yds* **14/1**
1061 **4** *nk* **Divertimenti (IRE)**[4] 2236 9-8-0 **56**........................(b) AdamMcLean(7) 8 60
(Roy Bowring) *dwlt: sn in tch on outer: pushed along and sltly outpcd 2f out: sn rdn and kpt on fnl f: nrst fin* **11/4**[1]
00-3 **5** 2 1/2 **Big Wave (IRE)**[18] 1802 5-9-4 **67**..............................(t1) TomEaves 1 62
(Alison Hutchinson) *prom: cl up 1/2-way: rdn and ev ch over 1f out: drvn and wknd fnl f* **11/4**[1]
15- **6** *nk* **Ingenti**[226] 6713 5-8-11 **60**.................................... PaddyAspell 9 54
(Christopher Wilson) *sn led: rdn along wl over 1f out: hdd ent fnl f: sn wknd* **10/1**
30-6 **7** 2 **Arch Walker (IRE)**[8] 2074 6-8-8 **60**........................(b) RaulDaSilva(3) 2 47
(John Weymes) *towards rr: swtchd lft 1/2-way: sn rdn along and n.d* **7/2**[2]
0654 **8** 2 1/4 **Ingleby Star (IRE)**[20] 1758 8-8-11 **65**........................(p) LMcNiff(5) 4 44
(Ian McInnes) *t.k.h: prom: pushed along over 2f out: sn rdn and wknd* **13/2**[3]

1m 2.82s (-0.68) **Going Correction** -0.175s/f (Firm) **8** Ran SP% **116.1**
Speed ratings (Par 103): **98,97,96,96,92 91,88,84**
toteswingers 1&2 £27.90, 1&3 £11.80, 2&3 £10.20 CSF £248.89 CT £3937.67 TOTE £17.30: £3.20, £4.50, £2.80; EX 204.70 Trifecta £867.50 Pool: £1768.28 - 1.52 winning units..
Owner Waz Developments Ltd **Bred** Hellwood Stud Farm **Trained** Scarcroft, W Yorks
■ Stewards' Enquiry : Royston Ffrench two-day ban: used whip above permitted level (May 28-29)

FOCUS
An open sprint handicap with a compressed finish. The winner ran basically to her best 2012 form.

2339 JOHN JACKSON H'CAP 1m 100y
3:40 (3:40) (Class 4) (0-85,91) 4-Y-0+ **£6,469** (£1,925; £962; £481) **Stalls** Low

Form RPR
6-01 1 **Toto Skyllachy**[8] 2078 8-9-13 **91** 6ex DanielTudhope 1 99
(David O'Meara) *trckd ldng pair: effrt wl over 1f out: sn swtchd lft and rdn to chse ldr ins fnl f: kpt on wl to ld nr fin* **5/2**[1]
0 2 ½ **Fort Belvedere**[17] 1843 5-9-7 **85** SilvestreDeSousa 5 92
(Keith Dalgleish) *trckd ldr: cl up 3f out: rdn to ld wl over 1f out: edgd rt and drvn ent fnl f: hdd and no ex nr fin* **13/2**[3]
0-23 3 2½ **Shadowtime**[8] 2078 8-9-1 **79** BarryMcHugh 4 81
(Tracy Waggott) *hld up towards rr: hdwy on outer wl over 2f out: rdn to chal and ev ch over 1f out: drvn and edgd lft ins fnl f: one pce* **7/1**
-632 4 ½ **Bling King**[8] 2078 4-8-10 **77** (p) RaulDaSilva(3) 7 78
(Geoffrey Harker) *hld up in rr: hdwy on wd outside 2f out: rdn to chse ldrs appr fnl f: no imp* **9/1**
0004 5 *shd* **Lady Macduff (IRE)**[8] 2078 4-8-11 **75** JoeFanning 2 76
(Mark Johnston) *led: rdn along 2f out: sn hdd and grad wknd* **10/1**
1441 6 1½ **Mujaadel (USA)**[8] 2081 8-8-7 **71** 6ex (p) PaulMulrennan 3 68
(David Nicholls) *chsd ldrs: rdn along wl over 2f out: sn one pce* **8/1**
/101 7 2 **Carazam (IRE)**[17] 1849 6-8-11 **75** TomEaves 6 68
(William Jarvis) *trckd ldrs: hdwy 3f out: rdn along 2f out: sn btn* **11/4**[2]
1m 44.88s (-2.72) **Going Correction** -0.325s/f (Firm) 7 Ran SP% **111.3**
Speed ratings (Par 105): **100,99,97,96,96 94,92**
toteswingers 1&2 £2.90, 1&3 £3.90, 2&3 £4.80 CSF £17.97 TOTE £2.90: £2.10, £2.30; EX 19.30 Trifecta £42.10 Pool: £2612.66 - 46.45 winning units..
Owner Richard Walker **Bred** Mrs G Slater **Trained** Nawton, N Yorks

FOCUS
They went a decent gallop and the form looks fair for the grade. The winner confirmed himself an improved performer.

2340 BEVERLEY DRIFTWOOD HORSE MAIDEN STKS 7f 100y
4:10 (4:10) (Class 5) 3-Y-O **£3,234** (£962; £481; £240) **Stalls** Low

Form RPR
2-06 1 **Declamation (IRE)**[14] 1908 3-9-5 72 JoeFanning 2 76
(Mark Johnston) *mde all: rdn clr over 1f out: kpt on strly* **5/2**[2]
6 2 6 **Excellent Addition (IRE)**[29] 1577 3-9-5 68 DanielTudhope 3 61
(David O'Meara) *trckd ldrs: hdwy on inner 3f out: rdn wl over 1f out: n.m.r ins fnl f: kpt on to take 2nd nr fin* **9/4**[1]
0 3 *nk* **Assembly**[27] 1618 3-9-5 0 GrahamGibbons 6 60
(William Haggas) *trckd wnr: effrt over 2f out: sn rdn: drvn and one pce fr over 1f out: lost 2nd nr fin* **9/4**[1]
0- 4 1¼ **Rosie Hall (IRE)**[291] 4546 3-9-0 0 RoystonFfrench 7 52+
(Bryan Smart) *trckd ldng pair: rdn along over 3f out: drvn 2f out: plugged on one pce* **40/1**
0 5 7 **Delicious Poison**[15] 1881 3-9-5 0 (t) SilvestreDeSousa 5 40
(James Fanshawe) *a in rr* **6/1**[3]
0 6 9 **Bannockburn Boy**[17] 1845 3-9-5 0 DuranFentiman 1 17
(Tim Easterby) *a outpcd in rr* **50/1**
60 7 99 **Silver Forest (IRE)**[10] 2027 3-8-11 0 RaulDaSilva(3) 4
(John Weymes) *towards rr and fly-leaping: hung violently lft to outer rail after 1 1/2f: sn t.o and virtually p.u over 4f out* **66/1**
1m 30.67s (-3.13) **Going Correction** -0.325s/f (Firm) 7 Ran SP% **110.3**
Speed ratings (Par 99): **104,97,96,95,87 77,**
toteswingers 1&2 £1.90, 1&3 £1.80, 2&3 £1.60 CSF £7.88 TOTE £3.60: £1.90, £1.60; EX 11.00 Trifecta £22.10 Pool: £2763.55 - 93.67 winning units..
Owner Sheikh Hamdan Bin Mohammed Al Maktoum **Bred** Darley **Trained** Middleham Moor, N Yorks

FOCUS
Just an ordinary maiden. An improved effort from the winner, who set his own pace.

2341 BEVERLEY MIDDLE DISTANCE SERIES H'CAP 1m 4f 16y
4:40 (4:42) (Class 6) (0-60,59) 3-Y-O **£2,587** (£770; £384; £192) **Stalls** Low

Form RPR
6526 1 **Flamingo Beat**[15] 1879 3-9-7 **59** SilvestreDeSousa 9 68
(Rae Guest) *trckd ldr: cl up 4f out: rdn to ld 1 1/2f out: drvn ins fnl f: kpt on wl towards fin* **3/1**[2]
3342 2 ¾ **Conversing (USA)**[7] 2124 3-8-13 **51** JoeFanning 4 59
(Mark Johnston) *led: jnd 4f out: rdn along 2f out: hdd 1 1/2f out: rallied u.p and ev ch ins fnl f: no ex towards fin* **11/4**[1]
00-0 3 3 **Halfwaytocootehill (IRE)**[12] 1966 3-8-12 **50** (t) TomEaves 7 53+
(Ollie Pears) *hld up towards rr: stdy hdwy on outer over 5f out: effrt over 2f out: rdn to chse ldng pair ins fnl f: kpt on* **8/1**
6602 4 4 **Dutch Delight**[94] 591 3-8-11 **49** BarryMcHugh 2 46
(Tony Coyle) *in tch on inner: hdwy 3f out: rdn to chse ldrs 2f out: sn drvn and one pce* **15/2**[3]
50-0 5 1¾ **French Revolution**[38] 1393 3-8-9 **47** MichaelO'Connell 1 41
(Jedd O'Keeffe) *chsd ldng pair: rdn along 3f out: drvn and wknd 2f out* **20/1**
05-0 6 2¼ **Hurricane John (IRE)**[24] 1685 3-9-0 **52** AdrianNicholls 8 43
(David Nicholls) *trckd ldrs: hdwy over 5f out: rdn along 3f out: drvn 2f out and sn wknd* **8/1**
0540 7 *hd* **Early One Morning**[34] 1469 3-8-10 **55** NoelGarbutt(7) 5 45
(Hugo Palmer) *in tch: pushed along 1/2-way: rdn 5f out and sn wknd* **16/1**
540- 8 4½ **Princess Hollow**[201] 7349 3-8-9 **54** LauraBarry(7) 6 37
(Tony Coyle) *in tch: rdn along over 4f out: sn wknd* **22/1**
0-06 9 ¾ **Annalova**[100] 507 3-8-0 **45** SamanthaBell(7) 10 27
(Richard Fahey) *hld up: a in rr* **28/1**
5-64 10 6 **Dark Justice (IRE)**[4] 2233 3-8-10 **55** GeorgeBuckell(7) 3 27
(Tim Pitt) *dwlt: a in rr* **10/1**
005 11 32 **Hartford Starts (IRE)**[29] 1575 3-8-7 **45** JamesSullivan 11
(Ian McInnes) *s.i.s: a in rr* **50/1**
2m 39.09s (-0.71) **Going Correction** -0.325s/f (Firm) 11 Ran SP% **115.1**
Speed ratings (Par 97): **89,88,86,83,82 81,81,78,77,73 52**
toteswingers 1&2 £2.10, 1&3 £7.60, 2&3 £6.80 CSF £10.78 CT £58.26 TOTE £4.80: £1.60, £1.60, £2.10; EX 12.30 Trifecta £98.60 Pool: £3286.78 - 24.97 winning units..
Owner The Storm Again Syndicate **Bred** York Stut & Stald Rainbow **Trained** Newmarket, Suffolk

FOCUS
Little got into this weak handicap. The first two both posted personal bests.

2342 BEST UK RACECOURSES ON TURFTV H'CAP 1m 1f 207y
5:10 (5:10) (Class 5) (0-70,70) 3-Y-O **£3,234** (£962; £481; £240) **Stalls** Low

Form RPR
5-06 1 **Marhaba Malayeen (IRE)**[11] 1991 3-9-7 **70** HarryBentley 1 74
(Kevin Ryan) *trckd ldrs on inner: hdwy over 2f out: rdn over 1f out: led ent fnl f: drvn out* **9/2**[3]
604- 2 ½ **Wellingrove (IRE)**[217] 6955 3-9-5 **68** JoeFanning 3 71
(Mark Johnston) *in tch: hdwy wl over 2f out: rdn to chse ldrs over 1f out: styd on wl fnl f* **9/2**[3]
2-13 3 *shd* **Ingleby Symphony (IRE)**[17] 1822 3-9-3 **69** LeeTopliss(3) 6 72+
(Richard Fahey) *trckd ldrs on outer: edgd lft and niggled along over 4f out: pushed wd 3f out: rdn along on wd outside 2f out: styd on wl u.p fnl f* **5/2**[1]
2521 4 1¾ **Shearian**[17] 1842 3-9-3 **66** BarryMcHugh 4 66
(Tracy Waggott) *trckd ldrs: smooth hdwy and cl up over 3f out: led over 2f out: rdn over 1f out: drvn and hdd ent fnl f: kpt on same pce* **8/1**
40-5 5 *nk* **Red Charmer (IRE)**[19] 1776 3-9-2 **65** PJMcDonald 7 64
(Ann Duffield) *led: pushed along 3f out: hdd over 2f out and sn rdn: drvn and ev ch appr fnl f: kpt on same pce* **22/1**
430 6 ½ **Helmsley Flyer (IRE)**[36] 1429 3-8-7 **56** oh1 AndrewMullen 5 54
(David O'Meara) *hld up in rr: hdwy over 2f out: rdn to chse ldrs over 1f out: n.m.r and swtchd rt ent fnl f: kpt on towards fin* **11/1**
0-53 7 2¼ **Argaki (IRE)**[12] 1965 3-9-4 **67** SilvestreDeSousa 8 62
(Keith Dalgleish) *trckd ldr: cl up 1/2-way: pushed along 3f out: rdn over 2f out: drvn and wknd over 1f out* **7/2**[2]
00-0 8 18 **Threepence**[12] 1966 3-8-7 **56** oh4 (v[1]) PaulQuinn 2 16
(Richard Whitaker) *dwlt: a in rr* **50/1**
2m 4.14s (-2.86) **Going Correction** -0.325s/f (Firm) 8 Ran SP% **112.9**
Speed ratings (Par 99): **98,97,97,96,95 95,93,79**
toteswingers 1&2 £4.90, 1&3 £2.90, 2&3 £2.40 CSF £24.35 CT £60.21 TOTE £4.60: £1.20, £1.70, £2.60; EX 30.90 Trifecta £97.70 Pool: £2617.62 - 20.08 winning units..
Owner Ahmad Abdulla Al Shaikh **Bred** Cecil And Miss Alison Wiggins **Trained** Hambleton, N Yorks

FOCUS
A number held their chance inside the final 2f in what was a modest handicap run at an ordinary gallop. The form makes sense.

2343 ANNIE OXTOBY MEMORIAL H'CAP (DIV II) 5f
5:40 (5:40) (Class 5) (0-70,70) 4-Y-O+ **£3,234** (£962; £481; £240) **Stalls** Low

Form RPR
50-3 1 **Black Annis Bower**[24] 1681 5-8-11 **60** JamesSullivan 5 68
(Michael Easterby) *trckd ldrs: hdwy and cl up on outer 2f out: rdn to chal ent fnl f: sn led: drvn and kpt on wl towards fin* **9/1**
01-6 2 ½ **Indian Trail**[24] 1692 13-9-2 **70** (b) ShirleyTeasdale(5) 4 76
(David Nicholls) *in tch: hdwy 2f out: chsd ldrs over 1f out: effrt and str run to chal ins fnl f: ev ch tl drvn and nt qckn nr fin* **13/2**[3]
-000 3 ½ **Diamond Blue**[3] 2275 5-9-4 **67** (p) AmyRyan 9 71+
(Richard Whitaker) *dwlt and wnt lft s: sn swtchd rt to inner and bhd: hdwy 2f out: sn rdn and swtchd lft to outer over 1f out: styd on strly fnl f: nrst fin* **13/2**[3]
50-0 4 *shd* **Baltic Bomber (IRE)**[43] 1283 4-8-12 **61** (v[1]) MichaelO'Connell 6 65
(John Quinn) *towards rr and sn pushed along: rdn along on inner 1/2-way: hdwy over 1f out: n.m.r and swtchd rt wl ins fnl f: kpt on: nrst fin* **16/1**
1140 5 1 **Clubland (IRE)**[24] 1681 4-8-9 **63** PhilipPrince(5) 7 63
(Roy Bowring) *cl up: rdn to ld over 1f out: drvn and hdd ins fnl f: one pce* **9/2**[2]
060- 6 3 **Red Roar (IRE)**[197] 7447 6-8-8 **60** JulieBurke(3) 2 51
(Alan Berry) *chsd ldrs: rdn along 2f out: sn drvn and wknd* **8/1**
2111 7 ¾ **Chosen One (IRE)**[7] 2122 8-9-2 **65** 6ex PJMcDonald 1 52
(Ruth Carr) *slt ld: rdn 2f out: drvn and hdd over 1f out: wknd* **2/1**[1]
363- 8 3½ **Sharp Shoes**[196] 7457 6-8-4 **56** oh5 RaulDaSilva(3) 3 30
(Christopher Wilson) *cl up: rdn wl 2f out: sn wknd* **20/1**
2-00 9 5 **Pavers Star**[34] 1465 4-8-7 **56** oh1 [1] DuranFentiman 8 12
(Noel Wilson) *a in rr* **20/1**
1m 2.38s (-1.12) **Going Correction** -0.175s/f (Firm) 9 Ran SP% **114.7**
Speed ratings (Par 103): **101,100,99,99,97 92,91,86,78**
toteswingers 1&2 £4.10, 1&3 £6.70, 2&3 £5.10 CSF £65.65 CT £406.83 TOTE £10.30: £2.30, £1.90, £2.20; EX 29.20 Trifecta £214.70 Pool: £3223.17 - 11.25 winning units..
Owner Mrs A Jarvis **Bred** Mrs A Jarvis **Trained** Sheriff Hutton, N Yorks

FOCUS
Like division one, this looked quite open and it was run in a slightly faster time. The second and fourth set the level.
T/Plt: £879.70 to a £1 stake. Pool: £59,120.02 - 49.05 winning tickets. T/Qpdt: £176.70 to a £1 stake. Pool: £4125.24 - 17.27 winning tickets. JR

1973 CHEPSTOW (L-H)
Tuesday, May 14

OFFICIAL GOING: Soft
Wind: Moderate across Weather: Rain

2344 EBF/BATHWICK TYRES MAIDEN STKS 5f 16y
5:30 (5:30) (Class 5) 2-Y-O **£2,911** (£866; £432; £216) **Stalls** Centre

Form RPR
1 **Fast (IRE)** 2-9-0 0 RichardHughes 3 90+
(Richard Hannon) *led after 1f: shkn up to go clr appr fnl f: v easily* **7/4**[1]
302 2 7 **Hedy**[8] 2067 2-9-0 0 MartinHarley 7 64
(Mick Channon) *led 1f: styd chsng wnr tl easily outpcd appr fnl f* **3/1**[2]
3 2 **Lyrical** 2-9-5 0 WilliamCarson 5 62
(Derek Haydn Jones) *outpcd in rr tl hdwy fr 2f out to take wl hld 3rd fnl f* **20/1**
4 6 **Severnwind (IRE)** 2-9-5 0 LukeMorris 1 40
(Ronald Harris) *chsd ldrs: rdn 3f out: wknd fr 2f out* **8/1**
5 *nk* **Island Kingdom (IRE)** 2-9-5 0 LiamKeniry 4 39+
(J S Moore) *spd to 1/2-way* **16/1**
6 21 **Denby Dale** 2-8-12 0 JakePayne(7) 6
(Bill Turner) *chsd ldrs to 1/2-way: wknd qckly 2f out: eased ins fnl f* **4/1**[3]
7 3 **Mannerist** 2-9-5 0 ShaneKelly 2
(Daniel Mark Loughnane) *sn bhd: eased whn wl bhd fnl f* **8/1**
1m 3.02s (3.72) **Going Correction** +0.65s/f (Yiel) 7 Ran SP% **114.2**
Speed ratings (Par 93): **96,84,81,72,71 37,33**
toteswingers 1&2 £2.10, 1&3 £4.40, 2&3 £20.60 CSF £7.13 TOTE £2.40: £1.80, £2.70; EX 4.20 Trifecta £78.10 Pool: £711.10 - 6.82 winning units..

Owner Mrs J Wood **Bred** Ringfort Stud **Trained** East Everleigh, Wilts
FOCUS
With significant rain throughout the day the opening 2yo maiden was run on soft ground. The winner impressed and the second gives a tentative guide to the form.

2345 PETESMITHCARSALES.CO.UK & JOHNOSHEARACING.CO.UK CLASSIFIED STKS 7f 16y
6:00 (6:01) (Class 6) 3-Y-0+ **£1,940** (£577; £288; £144) **Stalls** Centre

Form RPR
3064 **1** **Peak Storm**[12] 1951 4-9-7 54 LukeMorris 13 67
(John O'Shea) *in tch: rdn and styd on fr over 1f out: kpt on u.p to ld fnl 50yds: kpt on wl* **3/1**[1]
2360 **2** *1 1/4* **Tenbridge**[15] 1887 4-9-7 55 (b) WilliamCarson 7 64
(Derek Haydn Jones) *pressed ldrs tl led over 4f out: rdn over 1f out: hdd fnl 50yds: no ex but styd on wl for clr 2nd* **6/1**[2]
6045 **3** *4* **Hittin'The Skids (IRE)**[15] 1886 5-9-7 49 (p) JimmyQuinn 3 54+
(Mandy Rowland) *mid-div: hdwy u.p over 1f out: kpt on fnl f to take 3rd clsng stages but no ch w ldng duo* **25/1**
1525 **4** *1/2* **Harvest Mist (IRE)**[48] 1214 5-9-2 55 WilliamTwiston-Davies(5) 15 53
(Shaun Lycett) *in tch: hdwy over 1f out: styd on fnl f: nvr a threat* **8/1**
40-3 **5** *nse* **Shomberg**[24] 1696 4-9-7 55 DaneO'Neill 10 53
(Dai Burchell) *chsd ldrs: rdn to go 2nd over 2f out but no imp on ldr: wknd fnl f* **7/1**[3]
446- **6** *3* **Annie Besant**[241] 6237 3-8-2 53 JoeyHaynes(7) 9 45
(Michael Mullineaux) *disp ld 3f: rdn over 3f out: wknd fr 2f out* **14/1**
0-40 **7** *3* **Orla (IRE)**[11] 1981 5-9-2 47 MichaelJMMurphy(5) 1 38
(John Gallagher) *in tch: rdn over 2f out: sn btn* **66/1**
5335 **8** *3/4* **Brown Volcano (IRE)**[92] 617 4-9-4 54 DarrenEgan(3) 6 36
(John O'Shea) *disp ld 3f: wknd fr 3f out* **10/1**
050- **9** *nk* **All Right Now**[210] 7142 6-9-7 50 MartinHarley 11 35+
(Tony Newcombe) *stdd in rr: rdn and styd on fnl 2f: nt rch ldrs* **14/1**
014- **10** *5* **Cristaliyev**[218] 6926 5-9-2 50 (p) ThomasBrown(5) 5 22
(John Flint) *chsd ldrs to 1/2-way* **25/1**
00-0 **11** *4 1/2* **Foie Gras**[22] 1710 3-8-9 52 MartinDwyer 14 11
(William Muir) *rdn and bhd fr 1/2-way* **33/1**
0-05 **12** *nk* **Batchworth Firefly**[7] 2126 5-9-7 47 (b) JohnFahy 2 10
(Dean Ivory) *bhd fr 1/2-way* **66/1**
005- **13** *4* **Lady Bonanova (IRE)**[260] 5661 3-8-4 55 JemmaMarshall(5) 12
(Pat Phelan) *sn bhd* **20/1**
6/60 **14** *3/4* **Laugh Or Cry**[8] 2096 5-9-7 53 RichardHughes 8 36
(Dean Ivory) *chsd ldrs to 1/2-way* **8/1**
46-0 **15** *3 3/4* **Princess Sheila (IRE)**[34] 1458 3-8-9 54 LiamJones 16
(J S Moore) *sn bhd* **14/1**
00-0 **16** *9* **Whiskeymack**[6] 2154 3-8-9 53 (v) SamHitchcott 4
(Mick Channon) *sn bhd* **16/1**

1m 29.32s (6.12) **Going Correction** +0.75s/f (Yiel)
WFA 3 from 4yo+ 12lb **16** Ran SP% **127.4**
Speed ratings (Par 101): **95,93,89,88,88 84,81,80,80,74 69,69,64,63,59 49**
toteswingers 1&2 £7.30, 1&3 £23.70, 2&3 £57.40 CSF £19.09 TOTE £4.20: £1.60, £2.50, £10.60; EX 27.50 Trifecta £417.20 Pool: £1105.88 - 1.98 winning units..
Owner The Cross Racing Club **Bred** Redhill Bloodstock Limited **Trained** Elton, Gloucs
FOCUS
A poor classified event with very little winning form on offer. Only the front three gave their running.

2346 THANK YOU TO CHEPSTOW RACECOURSE MEDIAN AUCTION MAIDEN STKS 1m 14y
6:35 (6:35) (Class 5) 3-5-Y-0 **£2,587** (£770; £384; £192) **Stalls** Centre

Form RPR
2-2 **1** **Rosie Rebel**[124] 148 3-8-9 0 ChrisCatlin 3 74+
(Rae Guest) *hld up in rr: pushed along and hdwy fr 2f out: chsd ldr 1f out: led fnl 110yds: kpt on strly* **5/1**
0-2 **2** *1 1/4* **Dairam (USA)**[29] 1575 3-9-0 0 DaneO'Neill 8 76
(Charles Hills) *trckd ldrs: led over 3f out: rdn 2f out: edgd lft fnl f: hdd and no ex fnl 110yds* **7/2**[2]
0-3 **3** *3 1/2* **Liberty Jack (IRE)**[14] 1904 3-9-0 0 JamesDoyle 9 68
(Roger Charlton) *in tch: stdy hdwy to trck ldr 2f out: rdn over 1f out: sn btn* **6/4**[1]
4 *7* **Miss Mitigate** 3-8-9 0 LiamKeniry 4 48
(Andrew Balding) *s.i.s: in rr: rdn and edgd lft over 2f out: mod prog ins fnl f* **10/1**
23 **5** *13* **San Gabriel (IRE)**[15] 1891 3-9-0 0 TomMcLaughlin 6 24
(Ed Walker) *chsd ldrs: rdn 3f out: wknd over 2f out* **4/1**[3]
400- **6** *9* **My Stroppy Poppy**[217] 6967 4-9-8 50 (tp) MircoMimmocchi 5
(Frank Sheridan) *led: hdd over 3f out: sn btn: eased fnl f* **66/1**
00- **7** *56* **Atilia**[232] 6533 3-8-9 0 LukeMorris 2
(Harry Dunlop) *chsd ldrs to 1/2-way: sn bhd: t.o fnl 2f* **33/1**

1m 42.42s (6.22) **Going Correction** +0.85s/f (Soft)
WFA 3 from 4yo 13lb **7** Ran SP% **112.4**
Speed ratings (Par 103): **102,100,97,90,77 68,12**
toteswingers 1&2 £3.30, 1&3 £1.10, 2&3 £2.30 CSF £21.97 TOTE £5.60: £2.60, £2.40; EX 19.20 Trifecta £60.40 Pool: £614.98 - 16.61 winning units..
Owner P W Saunders, R Guest & O Lury **Bred** Miss Deborah Wisbey **Trained** Newmarket, Suffolk
FOCUS
The underfoot conditions played their part in this mile maiden. Weak form, the winner building on her AW promise.

2347 BETFRED MOBILE SPORTS H'CAP 5f 16y
7:05 (7:05) (Class 6) (0-60,60) 3-Y-0 **£1,940** (£577; £288; £144) **Stalls** Centre

Form RPR
3412 **1** **Batchworth Lady**[8] 2091 3-9-5 58 JimmyQuinn 7 65
(Dean Ivory) *trckd ldrs: led wl over 1f out: drvn and styd on strly ins fnl f* **3/1**[1]
660- **2** *1 1/2* **Senora Lobo (IRE)**[159] 8007 3-9-2 55 FrederikTylicki 10 57
(Lisa Williamson) *in rr but in tch: hdwy over 1f out: styd on to chse wnr ins fnl f but a readily hld* **16/1**
614- **3** *3/4* **My Sweet Lord**[144] 8203 3-9-2 55 RichardKingscote 2 54
(Mark Usher) *chsd ldrs: chal fr 2f out tl 1f out: one pce into 3rd ins fnl f* **3/1**[1]
-006 **4** *3/4* **Vergality Ridge (IRE)**[110] 357 3-8-13 52 (be) LukeMorris 5 48
(Ronald Harris) *sn led: rdn 1/2-way: hdd wl over 1f out: outpcd ins fnl f* **10/1**[3]
04-0 **5** *5* **Borough Boy (IRE)**[21] 1742 3-9-4 57 (v[1]) MartinDwyer 3 35
(Derek Shaw) *in rr but in tch: hdwy to chse ldrs 2f out: wknd appr fnl f* **12/1**
04-6 **6** *20* **Copper Leyf**[110] 356 3-9-1 54 LiamKeniry 1
(Jeremy Gask) *chsd ldr 2f: wknd rapidly ins fnl 2f: eased ins fnl f* **6/1**[2]
5605 **7** *16* **Visual Aspect**[15] 1874 3-9-7 60 RichardHughes 8
(Dean Ivory) *racd alone stands' side: spd to 1/2-way: sn wknd: virtually p.u fnl 110yds* **3/1**[1]

1m 4.07s (4.77) **Going Correction** +0.95s/f (Soft) **7** Ran SP% **112.0**
Speed ratings (Par 97): **99,96,95,94,86 54,28**
toteswingers 1&2 £8.90, 1&3 £1.50, 2&3 £7.60 CSF £50.44 CT £152.72 TOTE £3.20: £1.50, £8.00; EX 49.90 Trifecta £124.60 Pool: £594.32 - 3.57 winning units..
Owner Mrs Diana Price **Bred** Batchworth Heath Farm Stud **Trained** Radlett, Herts
FOCUS
A very modest sprint handicap for 3yos, run in softening ground. The second highlights the limitations of the bare form.

2348 BETFRED MOBILE LOTTO H'CAP 1m 2f 36y
7:40 (7:40) (Class 5) (0-70,70) 4-Y-0+ **£2,587** (£770; £384; £192) **Stalls** Low

Form RPR
12-0 **1** **Tawseef (IRE)**[17] 1836 5-9-1 67 MarkCoumbe(3) 16 76
(Roy Brotherton) *in rr: hdwy over 4f out: drvn over 2f out: led 1f out: drvn out* **5/1**[1]
0-01 **2** *1* **April Ciel**[12] 1948 4-9-0 66 DarrenEgan(3) 9 73
(Ronald Harris) *chsd ldrs: chal 3f out: sn led: hrd drvn 2f out: hdd 1f out: styd on same pce* **5/1**[1]
20 **3** *1/2* **Tyrur Ted**[47] 1220 8-8-4 58 (t) MichaelJMMurphy(5) 15 64
(Frank Sheridan) *in rr: drvn and hdwy over 2f out: styd on to chse ldrs fnl f: no ex clsng stages* **16/1**[3]
-600 **4** *1* **Drummond**[22] 1716 4-8-3 59 JoeyHaynes(7) 13 64
(Bernard Llewellyn) *chsd ldr: led briefly appr fnl 3f: sn hdd: no ex fnl f* **16/1**[3]
6/5- **5** *1 1/2* **Secret Dancer (IRE)**[108] 7211 8-9-7 70 SteveDrowne 1 76+
(Alan Jones) *hld up in rr: stl plenty to do over 2f out: styd on strly fnl f: nt rch ldrs* **20/1**
-453 **6** *6* **James Pollard (IRE)**[12] 1948 8-8-9 65 (t) DanielMuscutt(7) 4 56
(Bernard Llewellyn) *chsd ldrs: rdn over 2f out: wknd wl over 1f out* **5/1**[1]
500 **7** *6* **Six Silver Lane**[35] 1448 5-8-12 61 (v) MartinDwyer 11 41
(Derek Shaw) *led tl hdd appr fnl 3f: wknd sn after* **20/1**
2142 **8** *1 1/4* **Stag Hill (IRE)**[12] 1948 4-8-7 56 MartinLane 2 34
(Bernard Llewellyn) *chsd ldrs: rdn and btn 3f out* **6/1**[2]
2432 **9** *21* **Gaelic Silver (FR)**[18] 1585 7-9-7 70 GeorgeBaker 6 10
(Gary Moore) *bhd: brief effrt over 3f out: sn wknd* **5/1**[1]
2-56 **10** *77* **Elegant Ophelia**[11] 1983 4-9-0 63 (t) RichardHughes 14
(Dean Ivory) *a in rr: rdn 4f out: sn lost tch: eased whn no ch* **5/1**[1]

2m 20.18s (9.58) **Going Correction** +1.05s/f (Soft) **10** Ran SP% **118.9**
Speed ratings (Par 103): **103,102,101,101,99 95,90,89,72,10**
toteswingers 1&2 £6.30, 1&3 £23.80, 2&3 £18.70 CSF £30.32 CT £369.50 TOTE £8.20: £3.50, £1.90, £3.70; EX 31.10 Trifecta £538.60 Part won. Pool: £718.15 - 0.66 winning units..
Owner Millend Racing Club **Bred** Shadwell Estate Company Limited **Trained** Elmley Castle, Worcs
FOCUS
The mud was flying in the 1m2f handicap in which they started racing well over 3f out. The form has a sound feel to it.

2349 SACRAMENTO EVENTS FILLIES' H'CAP 1m 4f 23y
8:10 (8:10) (Class 5) (0-75,75) 4-Y-0+ **£3,072** (£914; £456; £228) **Stalls** Low

Form RPR
632- **1** **Astra Hall**[188] 7640 4-8-12 66 JimCrowley 7 76
(Ralph Beckett) *in tch: hdwy over 2f out: sn drvn to chal: led appr fnl f: styd on strly clsng stages* **1/1**[1]
-034 **2** *3/4* **Pandorica**[11] 1974 5-8-4 65 (p) DanielMuscutt(7) 2 74
(Bernard Llewellyn) *chsd ldrs: chal fr 2f out and stl pressing wnr 1f out: no ex clsng stages* **9/2**[3]
240- **3** *8* **Miss Fortywinks**[192] 7557 4-9-2 70 LiamKeniry 4 67
(Joseph Tuite) *in rr but in tch: drvn and hdwy over 2f out: styd on for wl hld 3rd ins fnl f* **14/1**
0-02 **4** *4* **Play Street**[11] 1974 4-9-4 72 RichardKingscote 5 63
(Jonathan Portman) *chsd ldr: led appr fnl 3f: jnd 2f out: hdd appr fnl f: wknd qckly* **4/1**[2]
1343 **5** *5* **Mediterranean Sea (IRE)**[42] 1306 7-9-5 73 FrederikTylicki 3 57
(J R Jenkins) *in rr but in tch: rdn and sme hdwy over 3f out: sn btn* **12/1**
1/5- **6** *36* **Carinya (IRE)**[389] 1491 5-9-7 75 RichardHughes 8
(Amy Weaver) *sn led: hdd appr fnl 3f: wknd qckly: eased* **8/1**

2m 52.57s (13.57) **Going Correction** +1.15s/f (Soft) **6** Ran SP% **113.7**
Speed ratings (Par 100): **100,99,94,91,88 64**
toteswingers 1&2 £1.80, 1&3 £4.30, 2&3 £11.10 CSF £6.03 CT £36.97 TOTE £1.50: £1.40, £2.10; EX 5.40 Trifecta £56.40 Pool: £656.34 - 8.72 winning units..
Owner G B Balding **Bred** Miss B Swire **Trained** Kimpton, Hants
FOCUS
Handling the conditions and staying were the name of the game in this 1m4f fillies' handicap. Only the front pair gave their running. The winner showed marginal improvement on last year's form.

2350 BETFRED H'CAP 1m 4f 23y
8:40 (8:40) (Class 6) (0-65,63) 4-Y-0+ **£1,940** (£577; £288; £144) **Stalls** Low

Form RPR
010/ **1** **Acapulco Bay**[31] 5379 9-8-2 49 oh4 (p) AmyScott(5) 8 56
(Dai Burchell) *led after 2f: rdn along 3f out: kpt on wl fnl f: all out* **20/1**
600- **2** *nk* **On Stage**[256] 5795 4-8-6 53 MichaelJMMurphy(5) 2 60
(Stuart Kittow) *chsd ldrs: wnt 2nd over 3f out: styd on u.p to cl on wnr thrght fnl f: nt quite get up* **11/4**[1]
41-0 **3** *1* **Tijori (IRE)**[25] 1664 5-9-6 62 (p) MartinLane 12 67
(Bernard Llewellyn) *chsd ldrs: drvn along fr 5f out: outpcd over 2f out: styd on again thrght fnl f: nt quite rch ldng duo* **3/1**[2]
060- **4** *11* **Golden Jubilee (USA)**[16] 7015 4-8-10 57 WilliamTwiston-Davies(5) 7 46
(Nigel Twiston-Davies) *in rr but in tch: hrd drvn fr 3f out: nvr rchd ldrs and no ch fnl 2f* **7/1**
105- **5** *7* **Cuckoo Rock (IRE)**[75] 7301 6-9-5 61 (p) RichardKingscote 1 39
(Jonathan Portman) *chsd ldrs: rdn over 3f out: sn wknd* **9/2**[3]
526- **6** *10* **Kashgar**[208] 7196 4-8-12 61 DanielMuscutt(7) 3 24
(Bernard Llewellyn) *chsd ldrs: wknd qckly 3f out* **3/1**[2]
400/ **7** *7* **Feeling (IRE)**[31] 4952 9-8-0 49 oh4 OisinMurphy(7) 6
(Dai Burchell) *led 2f: styd chsng ldrs tl wknd 4f out* **33/1**

2m 54.66s (15.66) **Going Correction** +1.25s/f (Soft) **7** Ran SP% **115.1**
Speed ratings (Par 101): **97,96,96,88,84 77,72**
toteswingers 1&2 £17.20, 1&3 £6.60, 2&3 £4.40 CSF £75.42 CT £219.33 TOTE £19.30: £5.90, £2.80; EX 112.30 Trifecta £461.20 Part won. Pool: £614.98 - 0.61 winning units..
Owner J Parfitt **Bred** Mrs S Camacho **Trained** Briery Hill, Blaenau Gwent
FOCUS
The gloom had set in for the closing 1m4f handicap, a decidedly Welsh contest with the majority of the field trained locally. Limited form, only the front three giving their running.

T/Jkpt: £3,957.90 to a £1 stake. Pool: £356,771.70 - 64.00 winning tickets. T/Plt: £63.90 to a £1 stake. Pool: £73,516.44 - 838.77 winning tickets. T/Qpdt: £29.50 to a £1 stake. Pool: £5807.89 - 145.30 winning tickets. ST

1894 CHANTILLY (R-H)

Tuesday, May 14

OFFICIAL GOING: Turf: good; polytrack: standard

2355a PRIX DE GUICHE (GROUP 3) (3YO COLTS) (TURF) 1m 1f

2:20 (12:00) 3-Y-O £32,520 (£13,008; £9,756; £6,504; £3,252)

RPR

1 **Dalwari (USA)**[26] 3-9-2 0 Christophe-PatriceLemaire 3 110+
(J-C Rouget, France) *trckd ldr: led ins fnl 2f: r.o wl fnl f: a holding runner-up* **47/10**

2 1 3/4 **Mshawish (USA)**[28] 3-9-2 0 UmbertoRispoli 4 106
(M Delzangles, France) *trckd ldrs: rdn and chsd ldr over 1f out: kpt on fnl f: a hld by wnr* **19/5**[2]

3 1 **Triple Threat (FR)**[37] 1419 3-9-2 0 MaximeGuyon 2 104+
(A Fabre, France) *v slow to s: in rr: shkn up and swtchd outside over 2f out: r.o u.p fnl f: nvr on terms* **4/5**[1]

4 snk **Diyamindar (FR)**[18] 1815 3-9-2 0 (p) ThierryJarnet 5 104
(J Boisnard, France) *trckd ldrs: rdn and nt qckn 1 1/2f out: one pce fnl f* **17/1**

5 1 1/4 **Spiritjim (FR)**[30] 3-9-2 0 ChristopheSoumillon 1 101
(P Bary, France) *led: set stdy pce: qcknd tempo after 4f: hdd under 2f out: wknd u.p fnl f* **9/2**[3]

1m 51.74s (0.64) **5 Ran SP% 117.7**
WIN (incl. 1 euro stake): 5.70. PLACES: 2.80, 2.30. SF: 21.60.
Owner H H Aga Khan **Bred** S A Aga Khan **Trained** Pau, France

FOCUS
This was run at a steady pace and the winner scored with a bit to spare.

2357 - (Foreign Racing) - See Raceform Interactive

2067 BATH (L-H)

Wednesday, May 15

OFFICIAL GOING: Good to soft (good in places)
Wind: Moderate across Weather: Sunny spells, showers

2358 BRITISH STALLION STUDS EBF MAIDEN STKS 5f 161y

5:40 (5:41) (Class 5) 2-Y-O £3,067 (£905; £453) Stalls Centre

Form RPR

1 **Riverboat Springs (IRE)** 2-9-5 0 MartinHarley 3 83+
(Mick Channon) *in tch: drvn along wl over 1f out: qcknd nicely ins fnl f to ld fnl 50yds: readily* **5/1**

2 2 1/4 **Money Team (IRE)** 2-9-0 0 MichaelJMMurphy(5) 7 76
(Bill Turner) *in tch: pushed along to ld ins fnl 2f: kpt on fnl f: hdd and outpcd fnl 50yds: drvn out to hold on to 2nd* **12/1**

422 3 nk **Cockney Bob**[11] 2011 2-9-5 0 (p) CathyGannon 1 75
(J S Moore) *slt ld tl narrowly hdd ins fnl 3f: sn drvn along: styd on again clsng stages* **3/1**[2]

4 1 3/4 **Expert (IRE)** 2-9-5 0 PatDobbs 6 69
(Richard Hannon) *chsd ldrs: rdn and one pce over 2f out: kpt on ins fnl f* **7/2**[3]

0 5 6 **Centrality**[13] 1946 2-9-5 0 JoeFanning 4 49
(Mark Johnston) *t.k.h: pressed ldr: slt ld ins fnl 3f: hdd over 2f out: wknd over 1f out* **7/4**[1]

25 6 3/4 **Mr Dandy Man (IRE)**[13] 1946 2-9-2 0 DarrenEgan(3) 5 47
(Ronald Harris) *chsd ldrs: led over 2 out: hdd ins fnl 2f: wknd over 1f out* **16/1**

1m 13.77s (2.57) **Going Correction** +0.125s/f (Good) **6 Ran SP% 113.8**
Speed ratings (Par 93): **87,84,83,81,73 72**
toteswingers 1&2 £7.40, 1&3 £2.00, 2&3 £6.90 CSF £57.72 TOTE £6.60: £3.00, £6.80; EX 79.00 Trifecta £320.60 Pool: £1592.94 - 3.72 winning units..
Owner Chris Wright & The Hon Mrs J M Corbett **Bred** Cecil And Martin McCracken **Trained** West Ilsley, Berks

FOCUS
There was 23mm of rain in the previous 24 hours and the going was good to soft, good in places. They went a fair pace in this 2yo maiden and a newcomer surged clear. The third and fifth help with the level.

2359 WINTERSTOKE DECORATORS SUPPLY LTD MAIDEN AUCTION STKS 5f 11y

6:10 (6:12) (Class 6) 2-Y-O £2,045 (£603; £302) Stalls Centre

Form RPR

1 **Lilbourne Lass** 2-8-10 0 PatDobbs 4 85+
(Richard Hannon) *fractious bef s: in tch: n.m.r ins fnl 2f: qcknd between horses to ld 1f out: drvn clr fnl 110yds* **11/10**[1]

2 4 **Disko (IRE)** 2-8-3 0 DarrenEgan(3) 5 67+
(Daniel Kubler) *in rr but in tch: hdwy over 1f out: edgd lft and green but styd on wl fnl f to take 2nd clsng stages but no ch w wnr* **20/1**

3 1/2 **Bonjour Steve** 2-8-9 0 LiamKeniry 3 68
(J S Moore) *chsd ldr: led 2f out: sn rdn: hdd 1f out: sn outpcd by wnr: ct for 2nd clsng stages* **8/1**[3]

5 4 1 1/2 **Left Defender (IRE)**[49] 1208 2-8-9 0 CathyGannon 6 62
(Jo Hughes) *sn chsng ldrs: rdn over 2f out: wknd ins fnl f* **25/1**

50 5 2 3/4 **Dovil's Duel (IRE)**[32] 1541 2-8-9 0 FergusSweeney 2 53
(Rod Millman) *sn slt ld: hdd 2f out: wknd fnl f* **11/4**[2]

6 3 1/2 **Captain Ryan** 2-8-11 0 SteveDrowne 1 42
(Peter Makin) *wnt lft s: pressed ldrs to 1/2-way* **10/1**

7 3 3/4 **Zafraaj** 2-8-11 0 WilliamCarson 7 28
(Ronald Harris) *sn drvn along: chsd ldrs 3f out: wknd qckly ins fnl 2f* **12/1**

8 2 1/2 **Connaught Water (IRE)** 2-8-9 0 JohnFahy 8 17
(Jonathan Portman) *in rr: swtchd rt to outside and sme hdwy over 2f out: sn rdn and wknd* **25/1**

1m 4.24s (1.74) **Going Correction** +0.125s/f (Good) **8 Ran SP% 114.6**
Speed ratings (Par 91): **91,84,83,81,77 71,65,61**
toteswingers 1&2 £10.20, 1&3 £1.80, 2&3 £20.50 CSF £29.23 TOTE £1.80: £1.10, £4.70, £1.70; EX 41.10 Trifecta £250.90 Pool: £1640.70 - 4.90 winning units..
Owner Hon Mrs Sarah Ensor **Bred** Alvediston Stud **Trained** East Everleigh, Wilts

FOCUS
The hot favourite delivered in impressive style for Richard Hannon in this maiden which involved a majority of newcomers. A guessy level of form but the winner could be decent.

2360 FOSTER REFRIGERATOR FILLIES' H'CAP 1m 5f 22y

6:40 (6:40) (Class 5) (0-70,69) 4-Y-0+ £2,726 (£805; £402) Stalls Centre

Form RPR

2315 1 **Irene Kennet**[27] 1654 6-9-0 62 JimmyQuinn 4 74+
(Paul Burgoyne) *hld up in tch: hdwy over 2f out: led 1f out: drvn out fnl 110yds* **4/1**[2]

651- 2 1 **Passion Play**[265] 5507 5-9-6 68 JoeFanning 9 78
(William Knight) *chsd ldrs: chal fr 7f out tl led 3f out: rdn and hdd 1f out: kpt on fnl f but no imp on wnr* **3/1**[1]

3 8 **Danisa**[227] 4-9-0 62 RobbieFitzpatrick 5 60
(David Bridgwater) *chsd ldrs: wnt 2nd ins fnl 3f: sn rdn: wknd 1f out* **10/1**

0-05 4 4 1/2 **Red Current**[26] 1664 9-8-4 55 oh5 (tp) DarrenEgan(3) 2 46
(Michael Scudamore) *slowly away: in rr: hdwy to cl on ldrs over 3f out: rdn over 2f out: wknd over 1f out* **14/1**

-620 5 shd **Ogaritmo**[51] 1176 4-9-2 69 AmyScott(5) 8 60
(Alastair Lidderdale) *in rr: clsd on ldrs 6f out: rdn over 2f out: wknd wl over 1f out* **8/1**

2310 6 1 3/4 **Fulgora**[23] 1733 5-9-7 69 SebSanders 6 57
(Brendan Powell) *pressed ldr to 7f out: rdn 3f out: wknd fr 2f out* **6/1**[3]

31-5 7 1 1/4 **Kittens**[12] 1983 4-9-2 64 MartinDwyer 3 51
(William Muir) *rdn 4f out: a in rr* **3/1**[1]

13-0 8 19 **Bondi Mist (IRE)**[82] 753 4-9-2 64 RichardThomas 1 22
(Jonathan Geake) *chsd ldrs: rdn and wknd ins fnl 3f* **25/1**

0006 9 12 **Anrheg**[12] 1974 5-8-0 55 oh10 OisinMurphy(7) 7
(Dai Burchell) *sn slt ld: rdn and hdd 3f out: wknd rapidly* **50/1**

2m 53.59s (1.59) **Going Correction** +0.125s/f (Good) **9 Ran SP% 117.0**
Speed ratings (Par 100): **100,99,94,91,91 90,89,78,70**
toteswingers 1&2 £3.40, 1&3 £9.60, 2&3 £7.10 CSF £16.68 CT £112.17 TOTE £4.90: £2.80, £1.20, £3.10; EX 20.10 Trifecta £52.80 Pool: £624.69 - 8.86 winning units..
Owner R W Floyd **Bred** Jim Duncan And Richard William Floyd **Trained** Shepton Montague, Somerset

FOCUS
The went a stop-start gallop in this fillies' handicap and the first two pulled clear. The winner carried over her AW progress.

2361 BBC RADIO BRISTOL FILLIES' H'CAP 1m 5y

7:10 (7:10) (Class 5) (0-75,69) 4-Y-0+ £2,587 (£770; £384; £192) Stalls Low

Form RPR

33/6 1 **Nimiety**[12] 1990 4-9-5 67 JoeFanning 8 75+
(Mark Johnston) *led tl hdd over 2f out: styd pressing tl led again ins fnl f: styd on strly* **2/1**[1]

04-2 2 3/4 **Waveguide (IRE)**[23] 1736 4-9-7 69 MartinLane 1 75
(David Simcock) *trckd ldr: drvn to ld over 2f out: hdd ins fnl f: kpt on same pce* **7/2**

6-52 3 2 1/2 **Sarangoo**[9] 2070 5-9-6 68 TomMcLaughlin 4 68
(Malcolm Saunders) *s.i.s: in rr but sn in tch: chsd ldrs 3f out: rdn and ev ch 2f out: outpcd fnl f* **3/1**[3]

4214 4 hd **Ssafa**[14] 1933 5-9-4 66 (p) JimmyFortune 2 66
(Alastair Lidderdale) *chsd ldrs in cl 3rd: chal u.p 2f out: no ex and outpcd fnl f* **9/4**[2]

1m 44.58s (3.78) **Going Correction** +0.125s/f (Good) **4 Ran SP% 111.3**
Speed ratings (Par 100): **86,85,82,82**
CSF £9.16 TOTE £2.90; EX 11.40 Trifecta £36.60 Pool: £330.82 - 6.76 winning units..
Owner Miss K Rausing **Bred** Miss K Rausing **Trained** Middleham Moor, N Yorks

FOCUS
The was a tight market for this small-field handicap. The pace increased some way out and the winner rallied well. Hard to be confident given the slow pace but the winner may yet build on her 2yo form.

2362 LIBERTY MUTUAL INSURANCE H'CAP 1m 5y

7:40 (7:43) (Class 6) (0-60,60) 3-Y-O £1,940 (£577; £288; £144) Stalls Low

Form RPR

00-0 1 **Noor Al Haya (IRE)**[23] 1727 3-8-0 46 oh1 DanielMuscutt(7) 4 52
(Mark Usher) *in tch: hdwy 3f out: pushed along to ld fnl 110yds: readily* **25/1**

50-5 2 1 1/4 **Fair Comment**[11] 2017 3-9-6 59 LiamKeniry 2 62
(Michael Blanshard) *chsd ldrs: rdn over 2f out: slt ld 1f out: hdd and outpcd fnl 110yds* **6/1**[3]

0430 3 2 **Eyeline**[22] 1747 3-8-9 48 (v) MartinDwyer 11 46
(Andrew Hollinshead) *t.k.h: sn led: hrd rdn and hdd 2f out: sn outpcd* **8/1**

406 4 3 **Abanoas (USA)**[15] 1911 3-8-13 52 MartinLane 5 44
(Alan Coogan) *chsd ldrs: drvn 2f out: wknd appr fnl f* **25/1**

00-4 5 1/2 **Thomasina**[23] 1710 3-8-13 52 ShaneKelly 13 42
(Denis Coakley) *chsd ldr: led 2f out: hdd 1f out and sn wknd* **5/1**[2]

000- 6 1 **Choral Rhythm (IRE)**[272] 5267 3-8-7 46 oh1 JimmyQuinn 1 34
(Tony Carroll) *in rr: hdwy and nt clr run appr fnl f: sn btn* **16/1**

00-6 7 nse **Al Zein**[13] 1955 3-9-6 59 PatDobbs 9 47
(Richard Hannon) *chsd ldrs: rdn over 2f out: wknd 1f out* **4/1**[1]

4240 8 1 1/2 **Close Together (IRE)**[23] 1712 3-9-2 60 RobertTart(5) 7 44
(Robert Mills) *rdn over 2f out: a towards rr* **6/1**[3]

050- 9 1/2 **Boogie De Bispo**[201] 7364 3-8-7 46 oh1 ChrisCatlin 14 29
(Stuart Kittow) *slowly away: wl bhd and rdn 3f out: sme prog fr 2f out* **12/1**

3133 10 14 **Actonetaketwo**[40] 1367 3-8-9 53 PhilipPrince(5) 10
(Ron Hodges) *s.i.s: in rr: hdwy 3f out: drvn to chse ldrs over 2f out: wknd sn after* **7/1**

1m 44.21s (3.41) **Going Correction** +0.125s/f (Good) **10 Ran SP% 110.1**
Speed ratings (Par 97): **87,85,83,80,80 79,79,77,77,63**
toteswingers 1&2 £46.60, 1&3 £26.20, 2&3 £5.70 CSF £151.88 CT £1167.53 TOTE £60.10: £11.20, £1.60, £3.80; EX 294.70 Trifecta £529.80 Part won. Pool: £706.49 - 0.05 winning units..
Owner Imran Butt & High Five Racing **Bred** Victor Stud Bloodstock Ltd **Trained** Upper Lambourn, Berks

FOCUS
They went a decent pace in this low-grade handicap and there was a big-priced winner. Market springer Dawn Rock refused to enter the stalls. Unconvincing form, rated around the first two.

2363 ALLEN FORD H'CAP 5f 11y

8:10 (8:10) (Class 5) (0-75,72) 3-Y-O £2,726 (£805; £402) Stalls Centre

Form RPR

033 1 **Harbour Captain (IRE)**[22] 1750 3-8-9 60 CathyGannon 7 73
(Jo Hughes) *pressed ldr: led 2f out: rdn and edgd lft appr fnl f: readily* **7/4**[1]

23-2 **2** 3 ¼ **Silverrica (IRE)**[15] 1896 3-9-1 **66** .... TomMcLaughlin 4 67
(Malcolm Saunders) *t.k.h: chsd ldrs: disp 2nd wl over 1f out: tk 2nd ins fnl f but nvr gng pce to trble wnr* **6/1**[2]

4-42 **3** *nk* **Hot Secret**[9] 2083 3-9-6 **71** .... JimmyFortune 1 71
(Andrew Balding) *chsd ldrs: disp 2nd wl over 1f out: nvr gng pce of wnr and one pce into 3rd ins fnl f* **7/4**[1]

53-5 **4** 6 **Imperial Spirit**[15] 1896 3-8-12 **63** .... MartinHarley 3 41
(Mick Channon) *led tl hdd 2f out: wknd over 1f out* **6/1**[2]

000- **5** 3 ¼ **Majestic Red (IRE)**[244] 6155 3-8-12 **63** .... WilliamCarson 2 30
(Malcolm Saunders) *s.i.s: rdn to get in tch over 2f out: sn btn* **9/1**[3]

1m 2.82s (0.32) **Going Correction** +0.125s/f (Good) **5** Ran SP% **111.3**
Speed ratings (Par 99): **102,96,96,86,81**
CSF £12.85 TOTE £3.00: £1.10, £3.70; EX 14.50 Trifecta £17.80 Pool: £437.31 - 18.40 winning units..
Owner James Hearne **Bred** Paul Kavanagh **Trained** Lambourn, Berks

FOCUS
An unexposed type powered clear in this sprint handicap, clocking the best sprint time on the card. The form is rated a bit cautiously.

2364 CO-OPERATIVE BANKING GROUP H'CAP 5f 161y
8:40 (8:40) (Class 5) (0-70,70) 4-Y-0+ **£2,587** (£770; £384; £192) **Stalls** Centre

Form RPR

3651 **1** **Above The Stars**[9] 2074 5-8-10 **64** 6ex .... RachealKneller(5) 7 75
(Jamie Osborne) *in tch: trckd ldrs 2f out: led gng wl appr fnl f: pushed out* **9/2**[1]

4300 **2** 1 ¾ **Basle**[16] 1887 6-8-9 **58** ....(t) MartinLane 1 63
(Michael Blake) *s.i.s: in rr: hdwy over 1f out: styd on u.p to take 2nd fnl 110yds: no imp* **10/1**

-605 **3** ¾ **Emiratesdotcom**[13] 1947 7-9-3 **66** .... CathyGannon 9 69
(Milton Bradley) *in rr: rdn over 2f out: hdwy over 1f out: styd on fnl f to take 3rd clsng stages* **9/2**[1]

0010 **4** ½ **New Decade**[19] 1800 4-9-3 **66** .... JoeFanning 14 67
(Milton Bradley) *w ldr: led over 3f out: hdd appr fnl f: no ex fnl 110yds* **6/1**[3]

50-6 **5** *nk* **Monsieur Jamie**[128] 95 5-9-3 **66** ....(v[1]) PatDobbs 6 66
(J R Jenkins) *in tch: hdwy over 1f out: styd on fnl f: nt rch ldrs* **16/1**

-402 **6** 3 ¼ **Kyllachy Storm**[15] 1902 9-8-2 **56** oh1 .... PhilipPrince(5) 15 45
(Ron Hodges) *chsd ldrs: rdn 3f out: wknd ins fnl f* **5/1**[2]

6000 **7** 1 ¼ **Courageous (IRE)**[9] 2096 7-8-13 **62** .... SteveDrowne 2 47
(Milton Bradley) *chsd ldrs: rdn over 2f out: wknd over 1f out* **25/1**

40-2 **8** 1 ½ **Stonecrabstomorrow (IRE)**[12] 1976 10-9-0 **66** .... MarkCoumbe(3) 5 46
(Roy Brotherton) *in tch: rdn to chse ldrs over 2f out: wknd over 1f out* **10/1**

000- **9** 2 ½ **Courtland Avenue (IRE)**[205] 7299 4-8-13 **62** .... ShaneKelly 10 34
(Jonathan Portman) *outpcd most of way* **20/1**

62-2 **10** 1 ¾ **Superior Edge**[13] 1952 6-9-1 **64** ....(p) FergusSweeney 17 30
(Christopher Mason) *led tl hdd over 3f out: wknd fr 2f out* **10/1**

2132 **11** 4 **First Rebellion**[9] 2096 4-8-2 **56** oh1 ....(b) RyanTate(5) 8 +
(Tony Carroll) *rrd stalls and slowly away: a in rr* **7/1**

1m 12.38s (1.18) **Going Correction** +0.125s/f (Good) **11** Ran SP% **121.6**
Speed ratings (Par 103): **97,94,93,93,92 88,86,84,81,78 73**
toteswingers 1&2 £18.50, 1&3 £8.10, 2&3 £18.80 CSF £51.75 CT £223.76 TOTE £6.40: £1.90, £2.50, £2.40; EX 87.70 Trifecta £463.70 Part won. Pool: £618.27 - 0.89 winning units..
Owner Morsethehorse Syndicate **Bred** Manor Farm Stud (rutland) **Trained** Upper Lambourn, Berks

FOCUS
They went a decent pace in this minor sprint handicap. The winner is rated to last year's turf form.
T/Plt: £1413.90 to a £1 stake. Pool: £62,659.71 - 32.35 winning tickets. T/Qpdt: £55.90 to a £1 stake. Pool: £7362.70 - 97.30 winning tickets. ST

YORK (L-H)
Wednesday, May 15

OFFICIAL GOING: Good to soft (good in places)
Wind: fresh 1/2 against Weather: overcast, light rain

2365 INFINITY TYRES STKS (H'CAP) 1m 2f 88y
1:45 (1:45) (Class 2) (0-100,100) 4-Y-0+**£16,172** (£4,812; £2,405; £1,202) **Stalls** Low

Form RPR

110- **1** **First Mohican**[186] 7689 5-9-7 **100** .... TomQueally 3 113+
(Sir Henry Cecil) *lw: hld up in midfield: smooth hdwy over 2f out: nt clr run and swtchd outside over 1f out: r.o to ld towards fin* **3/1**[1]

12-0 **2** *nk* **Lahaag**[46] 1235 4-9-2 **95** .... PaulHanagan 6 106+
(John Gosden) *mid-div: effrt on outer over 3f out: led over 1f out: hdd and no ex towards fin* **9/2**[2]

0-15 **3** 5 **Eastern Destiny**[14] 1933 4-8-7 **86** .... BarryMcHugh 11 88
(Richard Fahey) *lw: chsd ldrs on outer: led over 2f out: hdd over 1f out: kpt on same pce* **16/1**

6410 **4** 1 **Fennell Bay (IRE)**[10] 2044 4-8-9 **88** .... SilvestreDeSousa 14 88
(Mark Johnston) *chsd ldrs: one pce fnl 2f* **16/1**

-0P0 **5** 1 **John Biscuit (IRE)**[21] 1768 5-8-7 **86** oh1 .... HayleyTurner 12 84
(Andrew Balding) *rrd s: in rr: hdwy on outside over 2f out: kpt on fnl f* **20/1**

60-2 **6** ½ **Clayton**[21] 1768 4-9-1 **94** .... NeilCallan 5 91
(Kevin Ryan) *lw: trckd ldrs: led 3f out: sn hdd: wknd fnl f* **6/1**[3]

003/ **7** ½ **Prompter**[216] 5250 6-9-1 **94** .... RyanMoore 7 90
(Jonjo O'Neill) *t.k.h towards rr: hdwy 3f out: chsng ldrs over 1f out: sn wknd* **16/1**

00-1 **8** 1 ¾ **Itlaaq**[25] 1689 7-8-13 **92** ....(t) GrahamGibbons 10 85
(Michael Easterby) *lw: chsd ldrs: effrt 3f out: hung lft and wknd over 1f out* **20/1**

110- **9** 6 **Bridle Belle**[186] 7689 5-8-9 **88** .... TonyHamilton 2 70
(Richard Fahey) *chsd ldrs: wknd over 1f out* **8/1**

01-3 **9** *dht* **Ruscello (IRE)**[34] 1501 4-8-13 **92** .... WilliamBuick 8 74
(Ed Walker) *lw: hld up in rr: hdwy on outside over 3f out: drvn over 2f out: sn wknd (dht 9th)* **7/1**

1300 **11** 2 ¼ **Alfred Hutchinson**[11] 2029 5-8-8 **92** .... WilliamTwiston-Davies(5) 4 69
(Geoffrey Oldroyd) *hld up in mid-div: hdwy on inner 3f out: wknd over 1f out* **33/1**

00-0 **12** 15 **Silvery Moon (IRE)**[36] 1446 6-8-9 **88** .... TedDurcan 1 37
(Tim Easterby) *led: hdd 3f out: lost pl over 1f out: sn bhd and eased* **20/1**

0 **13** *hd* **Fluidity**[36] 1446 4-9-1 **94** .... GrahamLee 9 42
(Nigel Tinkler) *unruly and hit hd on stalls: s.i.s: in rr: reminders over 3f out: sn lost pl: eased whn bhd fnl f* **50/1**

2m 11.01s (-1.49) **Going Correction** +0.10s/f (Good) **13** Ran SP% **117.9**
Speed ratings (Par 109): **109,108,104,103,103 102,102,100,96,96 94,82,82**
toteswingers 1&2 £2.50, 1&3 £15.50, 2&3 £31.70 CSF £14.10 CT £186.66 TOTE £3.60: £1.50, £1.90, £6.30; EX 14.50 Trifecta £287.10 Pool: £3020.30 - 7.88 winning units..
Owner W H Ponsonby **Bred** Bottisham Heath Stud **Trained** Newmarket, Suffolk

FOCUS
Course at normal configuration and all distances as advertised. With the horses declared at the 48-hour stage on good to firm ground, conditions were slower than had perhaps been expected, with a total of 18mm of rain having fallen overnight and during the morning. There was a strong headwind in the straight as well, but the winning time of the opener wasn't at all bad, being 3.51sec slower than standard, and jockeys' descriptions of the ground on returning after the opener generally suggested the going was on the soft side of good. They went a solid gallop here and two unexposed types drew clear in a handicap that often pays to follow. The winner is rated better than the bare form.

2366 INFINITY ECOSIS TYRES STKS (H'CAP) 6f
2:15 (2:17) (Class 2) (0-105,103) 4-Y-0+**£16,172** (£4,812; £2,405; £1,202) **Stalls** Centre

Form RPR

30-0 **1** **Mass Rally (IRE)**[46] 1232 6-9-3 **99** ....(b) PaulMulrennan 18 109
(Michael Dods) *stdd s and hld up in rr: stdy hdwy into midfield over 1f out: trckd ldrs over 1f out: swtchd rt and effrt ent fnl f: rdn to ld last 75yds: edgd lft and kpt on* **14/1**

-211 **2** ½ **Nocturn**[9] 2097 4-8-9 **91** 6ex ....(p) WilliamBuick 3 99+
(Jeremy Noseda) *lw: racd wd: a.p: cl up 1/2-way: led wl over 1f out: rdn ent fnl f: hdd and no ex last 75yds* **4/1**[1]

0-10 **3** 1 ¼ **Prodigality**[32] 1537 5-9-4 **100** .... GrahamLee 5 104
(Ronald Harris) *in tch: hdwy 2f out: rdn and ev ch over 1f out tl drvn and one pce wl ins fnl f* **7/1**

4561 **4** ½ **York Glory (USA)**[23] 1720 5-9-2 **98** ....(b) NeilCallan 11 100+
(Kevin Ryan) *trckd ldrs: hdwy 2f out: cl up over 1f out: rdn and ev ch ins fnl f: one pce last 100yds* **6/1**[3]

5-00 **5** 1 **Farlow (IRE)**[32] 1537 5-8-5 **87** .... PaulHanagan 16 86
(Richard Fahey) *chsd ldrs on wd outside: rdn along wl over 1f out: kpt on u.p fnl f* **15/2**

020- **6** 1 ¼ **Louis The Pious**[186] 7691 5-9-4 **100** .... DanielTudhope 8 95
(David O'Meara) *in tch: effrt over 2f out: sn swtchd lft and rdn: kpt on same pce fnl f* **9/2**[2]

14-6 **7** 2 **Compton**[26] 1672 4-8-8 **95** .... WilliamTwiston-Davies(5) 17 84
(Robert Cowell) *trckd ldrs: smooth hdwy 2f out: cl up and ev ch over 1f out: sn rdn and wknd ins fnl f* **14/1**

0-32 **8** 1 ¼ **El Viento (FR)**[26] 1672 5-8-5 **92** .... GeorgeChaloner(5) 1 77
(Richard Fahey) *trckd ldrs: hdwy to ld briefly 2f out: sn rdn and hdd wl over 1f out: wknd appr fnl f* **14/1**

00-6 **9** 1 ¾ **Bapak Chinta (USA)**[46] 1249 4-9-3 **99** .... PhillipMakin 14 78
(Kevin Ryan) *hld up towards rr: sme hdwy 2f out: n.d* **33/1**

644/ **10** ¾ **Evens And Odds (IRE)**[559] 7253 9-8-10 **97** .... SladeO'Hara(5) 9 74
(Peter Grayson) *a towards rr* **100/1**

0-00 **11** 2 **Tax Free (IRE)**[11] 2007 11-8-6 **88** .... AdrianNicholls 13 58
(David Nicholls) *led: rdn along and hdd 2f out: sn wknd* **20/1**

610- **12** *nk* **Cheveton**[201] 7366 9-8-7 **89** ow1 .... DaleSwift 15 58
(Richard Price) *half-rrd and awkward s: s.i.s: sn in tch: rdn along over 2f out and sn wknd: b.b.v* **33/1**

000- **13** 3 ½ **Secret Witness**[200] 7397 7-9-7 **103** ....(b) JamesDoyle 2 61
(Ronald Harris) *prom: rdn along 2f out: sn edgd lft and wknd over 1f out* **25/1**

0-04 **14** 2 **Arctic Feeling (IRE)**[28] 1607 5-8-2 **84** oh1 .... PatrickMathers 12 36
(Richard Fahey) *prom: rdn along wl over 2f out: sn wknd* **40/1**

50-5 **15** ¾ **Singeur (IRE)**[23] 1720 6-8-10 **92** .... RobertWinston 6 41
(Robin Bastiman) *t.k.h: chsd ldrs: rdn along and hld whn n.m.r and sltly hmpd 2f out: sn wknd* **14/1**

1m 12.48s (0.58) **Going Correction** +0.325s/f (Good) **15** Ran SP% **121.3**
Speed ratings (Par 109): **109,108,106,106,104 103,100,98,96,95 92,92,87,84,83**
toteswingers 1&2 £12.60, 1&3 £19.60, 2&3 £6.90 CSF £65.10 CT £450.75 TOTE £19.40: £5.20, £1.80, £3.30; EX 123.70 Trifecta £720.80 Pool: £3919.25 - 4.07 winning units..
Owner Business Development Consultants Limited **Bred** Round Hill Stud **Trained** Denton, Co Durham

FOCUS
A fiercely competitive sprint handicap and, into a strong headwind, they certainly didn't hang about. The main action was predictably down the centre of the track and the form looks strong as there was no obvious bias in the draw. A personal best from the winner to beat the progressive runner-up.

2367 TATTERSALLS MUSIDORA STKS (GROUP 3) (FILLIES) 1m 2f 88y
2:45 (2:46) (Class 1) 3-Y-0
£42,532 (£16,125; £8,070; £4,020; £2,017; £1,012) **Stalls** Low

Form RPR

1- **1** **Liber Nauticus (IRE)**[253] 5902 3-8-12 86 .... RyanMoore 1 101+
(Sir Michael Stoute) *h.d.w: hld up: drvn and hdwy over 3f out: led over 2f out: styd on wl fnl f* **4/6**[1]

41-1 **2** 1 ½ **Romantic Settings**[12] 1991 3-8-12 85 .... PaulHanagan 4 98
(Richard Fahey) *hld up: hdwy over 3f out: rdn over 1f out: kpt on to take 2nd last 50yds* **11/1**

-1 **3** 1 ½ **Woodland Aria**[25] 1698 3-8-12 79 .... WilliamBuick 2 95+
(John Gosden) *lw: hld up: drvn over 3f out: hdwy over 2f out: upsides over 1f out: kpt on same pce* **4/1**[2]

513- **4** 3 ¾ **Indigo Lady**[246] 6129 3-8-12 104 .... JamieSpencer 3 88
(Peter Chapple-Hyam) *half-rrd s: sn trcking ldrs: drvn over 3f out: wl outpcd over 2f out: kpt on fnl f* **8/1**[3]

14-5 **5** ¾ **Hollowina**[7] 2148 3-8-12 85 .... RobertWinston 5 87
(David Brown) *chsd ldrs: drvn over 3f out: wl outpcd over 2f out: kpt on fnl f* **14/1**

0-03 **6** 9 **Discernable**[11] 2024 3-8-12 94 .... SilvestreDeSousa 6 75
(Mark Johnston) *led: qcknd pce over 4f out: hdd over 2f out: lost pl over 1f out: eased ins fnl f* **20/1**

2m 14.58s (2.08) **Going Correction** +0.10s/f (Good) **6** Ran SP% **110.9**
Speed ratings (Par 106): **95,93,92,89,89 81**
toteswingers 1&2 £2.40, 1&3 £1.40, 2&3 £3.20 CSF £8.97 TOTE £1.50: £1.10, £3.20; EX 9.50 Trifecta £18.80 Pool: £4343.57 - 172.43 winning units..
Owner Ballymacoll Stud **Bred** Ballymacoll Stud Farm Ltd **Trained** Newmarket, Suffolk

FOCUS
This trial has had a fair record in recent years for pinpointing Oaks winners, with Alexandrova finishing second here in 2006 before going one better at Epsom, Sariska doing the double in 2009, and arguably last year's winner The Fugue an unlucky loser in the Oaks afterwards. Improvement from Liber Nauticus but doubts over the bare form. The winner rates a bit below the race averages.

2368 DUKE OF YORK CLIPPER LOGISTICS STKS (GROUP 2) 6f
3:15 (3:20) (Class 1) 3-Y-O+
£60,481 (£22,929; £11,475; £5,716; £2,868; £1,439) **Stalls** Centre

Form RPR

315- **1** **Society Rock (IRE)**[207] [7236] 6-9-13 117........................ KierenFallon 18 122
(James Fanshawe) *dwlt: hld up in mid-div stands' side: hdwy over 2f out: led over 1f out: hld on wl towards fin* **10/1**

130- **2** *hd* **Lethal Force (IRE)**[220] [6913] 4-9-8 111............................ AdamKirby 15 116
(Clive Cox) *chsd ldrs stands' side: upsides over 1f out: no ex nr fin* **16/1**

14-0 **3** *1 1/4* **Gordon Lord Byron (IRE)**[46] [1266] 5-9-13 118................ RyanMoore 4 117+
(T Hogan, Ire) *lw: in rr: hdwy far side over 2f out: styd on wl fnl f* **7/1**

02-4 **4** *nse* **Hawkeyethenoo (IRE)**[27] [1637] 7-9-8 112........................ GrahamLee 14 112+
(Jim Goldie) *lw: dwlt: sn chsng ldrs: nt clr run 2f out tl 1f out: styd on wl* **14/1**

12-1 **5** *1 1/4* **Maarek**[25] [1704] 6-9-11 114.. PaulHanagan 3 111
(David Peter Nagle, Ire) *s.i.s: hdwy far side over 2f out: kpt on fnl f* **7/2**[1]

0-10 **6** *nk* **Jack Dexter**[32] [1537] 4-9-8 109.................................... DanielTudhope 6 107+
(Jim Goldie) *hld up towards rr: hdwy and nt clr run 2f out: swtchd lft: styd on wl fnl f* **12/1**

510- **7** *3/4* **Swiss Spirit**[220] [6908] 4-9-8 107.. WilliamBuick 5 105
(John Gosden) *mid-div: effrt over 2f out: kpt on same pce over 1f out* **12/1**

0-30 **8** *1 1/2* **Bogart**[11] [2019] 4-9-8 99... AmyRyan 8 100
(Kevin Ryan) *led 1f: w ldrs: led over 2f out: hdd over 1f out: fdd fnl 150yds* **50/1**

21-1 **9** *nk* **Tickled Pink (IRE)**[27] [1637] 4-9-5 109.............................. TomQueally 7 96
(Sir Henry Cecil) *trckd ldrs: effrt over 1f out: sn wknd* **6/1**[2]

111- **10** *1 3/4* **Mince**[221] [6867] 4-9-5 113.. JamesDoyle 11 90
(Roger Charlton) *w ldr: led after 1f: hdd over 2f out: wknd fnl f* **13/2**[3]

343- **11** *hd* **Sirius Prospect (USA)**[175] [7809] 5-9-8 107.................... JimCrowley 12 93
(Dean Ivory) *lw: mid-div: effrt over 2f out: nvr a threat* **20/1**

2-11 **12** *4 1/2* **Ladies Are Forever**[60] [1032] 5-9-5 108............ WilliamTwiston-Davies 2 75
(Geoffrey Oldroyd) *mid-div towards far side: lost pl over 1f out* **20/1**

15-4 **13** *5* **Face The Problem (IRE)**[7] [2152] 5-9-8 108.................. GeorgeBaker 1 62
(Jamie Osborne) *t.k.h in midfield far side: lost pl over 1f out* **40/1**

361- **14** *7* **Royal Rascal**[214] [7065] 3-8-9 101..................................... DavidAllan 10 37
(Tim Easterby) *hmpd s: in rr: eased whn bhd* **50/1**

65-0 **15** *1/2* **The Cheka (IRE)**[27] [1637] 7-9-8 106............................(v) NeilCallan 17 38
(Eve Johnson Houghton) *chsd ldrs stands' side: sn drvn along: lost pl wl over 1f out: eased* **28/1**

3-00 **16** *3/4* **Angels Will Fall (IRE)**[11] [2019] 4-9-5 100..................... RobertWinston 13 33
(Charles Hills) *chsd ldrs: drvn over 2f out: lost pl over 1f out: eased* **66/1**

50-0 **17** *99* **Tiddliwinks**[27] [1637] 7-9-8 109.. JamieSpencer 9
(Kevin Ryan) *hood removed v late: wnt rt s: towards rr: sme hdwy stands' side over 2f out: lost pl over 1f out: heavily eased: virtually p.u: dismntd after line (btn 99+)* **20/1**

1m 11.44s (-0.46) **Going Correction** +0.325s/f (Good)
WFA 3 from 4yo+ 10lb **17 Ran SP% 125.0**
Speed ratings (Par 115): **116,115,114,114,112 111,110,108,108,106 105,99,93,83,83 82,**
toteswingers 1&2 £33.60, 1&3 £12.10, 2&3 £25.80 CSF £148.42 TOTE £13.20: £3.90, £7.50, £3.90; EX 189.30 Trifecta £2801.40 Pool: £8445.20 - 2.26 winning units..
Owner Simon Gibson **Bred** San Gabriel Investments **Trained** Newmarket, Suffolk
■ Stewards' Enquiry : Amy Ryan two-day ban: used whip above permitted level (May 29-30)

FOCUS
A classy Group 2 sprint where the headwind facing runners meant it was tricky for those forcing the pace. They went a strong early gallop down the centre, ignoring both rails, but the first pair drew clear late nearest the stands' side. It was understandably a second quicker than the earlier C&D handicap and the ground looked near perfect. This was a strong renewal and Society Rock rates better than ever.

2369 CONSTANT SECURITY STKS (H'CAP) 1m 4f
3:50 (3:51) (Class 4) (0-85,85) 4-Y-O+ **£9,703** (£2,887; £1,443; £721) **Stalls** Low

Form RPR

214 **1** **Cousin Khee**[16] [1884] 6-9-1 79.. RyanMoore 19 87
(Hughie Morrison) *lw: stdd s: hld up and bhd: pushed along and hdwy on wd outside over 2f out: sn chsng ldrs: rdn to ld ent fnl f: drvn and edgd rt: kpt on wl towards fin* **14/1**

252 **2** *3/4* **Northside Prince (IRE)**[18] [1843] 7-9-7 85......................... JimCrowley 9 91
(Alan Swinbank) *a.p: wd st: hdwy 3f out and sn cl up: rdn over 1f out and ev ch tl drvn and no ex wl ins fnl f* **25/1**

14-3 **3** *hd* **Novirak (IRE)**[21] [1766] 5-9-3 81..................................... EddieAhern 14 87
(James Fanshawe) *trckd ldrs: wd st to stands' rail: cl up 3f out: led over 2f out: rdn wl over 1f out: drvn and edgd lft ent fnl f: sn hdd and kpt on same pce last 100yds* **10/1**

-000 **4** *nse* **Bollin Greta**[4] [2269] 8-8-11 75... DavidAllan 2 81
(Tim Easterby) *hld up in rr: hdwy over 3f out: rdn to chse ldrs and n.m.r wl over 1f out: sn swtchd lft and rdn: kpt on wl: nrst fin* **25/1**

063- **5** *1/2* **Eltheeb**[290] [4621] 6-9-5 83.. DanielTudhope 5 88
(David O'Meara) *hld up in midfield: stdy hdwy on inner over 4f out: chsd ldrs 3f out: rdn along 2f out: drvn ent fnl f: kpt on same pce* **14/1**

053- **6** *1* **Cockney Sparrow**[39] [6964] 4-9-0 78.......................... MichaelO'Connell 8 82+
(John Quinn) *midfield: hdwy and in tch 5f out: effrt and nt clr run over 2f out and again over 1f out: swtchd lft and rdn appr fnl f: kpt on: nrst fin* **7/2**[1]

6-13 **7** *hd* **Discovery Bay**[26] [691] 5-8-7 71.................................. SilvestreDeSousa 3 74+
(Brian Ellison) *lw: in tch: hdwy 3f out: n.m.r 2f out: chsd ldrs whn nt clr run over 1f out and again jst ins fnl f: swtchd lft and kpt on wl towards fin* **6/1**[2]

000- **8** *nse* **Herostatus**[158] [7098] 6-9-6 84.. KierenFallon 18 87
(Jason Ward) *prom: cl up over 4f out: rdn along wl over 2f out: drvn over 1f out and grad wknd ent fnl f* **40/1**

03-3 **9** *hd* **High Office**[20] [1774] 7-8-13 80.................................. LeeTopliss[(3)] 13 83
(Richard Fahey) *hld up in midfield: wd st to stands' rail and sn trcking ldrs: effrt and nt clr run 2f out tl ent fnl f: rdn and kpt on towards fin* **10/1**

0-60 **10** *1 1/4* **Nanton (USA)**[25] [1689] 11-9-4 82................................... GrahamLee 16 83+
(Jim Goldie) *hld up towards rr: effrt wl over 2f out: sn n.m.r: effrt and nt clr run wl over 1f out: swtchd lft and kpt on fnl f: nrst fin* **20/1**

6-04 **11** *1/2* **Sirvino**[18] [1824] 8-9-7 85.. RichardHughes 15 85+
(David Barron) *hld up towards rr: hdwy 3f out: nt clr run 2f out and again over 1f out: no ch after* **9/1**

301- **12** *nk* **Pintrada**[323] [3459] 5-8-11 75... JamieSpencer 11 75+
(James Bethell) *wnt rt s: hld up and bhd: hdwy wl over 2f out: swtchd rt to rail and effrt wl over 1f out: sn nt clr run and no ch after* **40/1**

00-0 **13** *1* **Cosmic Sun**[45] [1273] 7-8-9 73......................................(t) PaulHanagan 17 71
(Richard Fahey) *hld up towards rr: hdwy on outer 3f out: rdn along 2f out: grad wknd* **33/1**

0215 **14** *1* **Carragold**[4] [2277] 7-8-10 74... PaulMulrennan 10 70
(Mel Brittain) *cl up: rdn along wl over 3f out: drvn over 2f out: edgd rt and wknd over 1f out* **40/1**

2-12 **15** *2* **Opera Box**[18] [1825] 5-9-5 83... GeorgeBaker 7 76
(Marcus Tregoning) *hld up towards rr: hdwy 3f out: n.m.r fr over 2f out tl over 1f out: no hdwy after* **8/1**[3]

311 **16** *18* **Guising**[23] [1728] 4-9-5 83... RobertWinston 1 47
(David Brown) *set stdy pce: swtchd towards stands' rail and qcknd wl over 3f out: rdn along and hdd over 2f out: sn drvn and wknd wl over 1f out* **8/1**[3]

503- **17** *10* **Choisan (IRE)**[249] [6045] 4-8-13 77................................. DuranFentiman 6 25
(Tim Easterby) *lw: trckd ldrs on inner: hdwy to chse ldng pair over 4f out: rdn along wl over 2f out: sn wknd* **50/1**

1-00 **18** *13* **Bowdler's Magic**[19] [1805] 6-9-3 81.............................. AdrianNicholls 12
(David Nicholls) *in rr: rdn along 3f out: sn bhd* **66/1**

2m 35.88s (2.68) **Going Correction** +0.10s/f (Good) **18 Ran SP% 126.4**
Speed ratings (Par 105): **95,94,94,94,94 93,93,93,93,92 91,91,91,90,89 77,70,61**
toteswingers 1&2 £22.80, 1&3 £28.20, 2&3 £25.60 CSF £340.90 CT £3653.11 TOTE £16.80: £3.20, £5.20, £2.80, £6.60; EX 267.10 Trifecta £2104.70 Part won. Pool: £2806.28 - 0.26 winning units..
Owner Raymond Tooth **Bred** Miss B Swire **Trained** East Ilsley, Berks

FOCUS
The early pace didn't look that strong and it became very messy as several were caught up in trouble on the stands' rail in the closing stages. The unexposed winner avoided the trouble.

2370 THERIPLEYCOLLECTION.COM EBF NOVICE STKS 5f
4:25 (4:25) (Class 3) 2-Y-O **£9,703** (£2,887; £1,443; £721) **Stalls** Centre

Form RPR

21 **1** **Steventon Star**[16] [1880] 2-9-5 0.................................... RichardHughes 4 91
(Richard Hannon) *lw: w ldrs gng wl: shkn up to ld 1f out: rdn ins fnl f: all out* **9/4**[1]

1 **2** *nk* **Peniaphobia (IRE)**[14] [1930] 2-9-5 0................................ TonyHamilton 1 90
(Richard Fahey) *unf: scope: w ldrs: drvn over 2f out: kpt on wl fnl f: jst hld* **7/2**[3]

1 **3** *3/4* **Haikbidiac (IRE)**[18] [1820] 2-9-5 0..................................... LiamJones 5 87
(William Haggas) *w'like: str: chsd ldrs: drvn over 2f out: styd on last 150yds* **5/1**

1 **4** *1 1/2* **Extortionist (IRE)**[25] [1680] 2-9-5 0................................ HarryBentley 6 82
(Olly Stevens) *str: w ldr: led over 2f out: hdd 1f out: wknd clsng stages* **5/2**[2]

1 **5** *7* **One Boy (IRE)**[30] [1573] 2-9-2 0....................................... TomEaves 3 54
(Michael Dods) *leggy: chsd ldrs: drvn over 2f out: lost pl over 1f out* **20/1**

1 **6** *3 1/4* **Innocently (IRE)**[13] [1960] 2-9-2 0.................................. DanielTudhope 7 42
(David O'Meara) *w'like: led tl over 2f out: lost pl over 1f out* **20/1**

10 **7** *4 1/2* **Lady Frances**[10] [2053] 2-9-0 0................................. SilvestreDeSousa 8 24
(Mark Johnston) *w'like: swvd rt s: sn w ldrs: lost pl over 2f out: sn bhd* **20/1**

59.86s (0.56) **Going Correction** +0.325s/f (Good) **7 Ran SP% 112.5**
Speed ratings (Par 97): **108,107,106,103,92 87,80**
toteswingers 1&2 £2.30, 1&3 £2.80, 2&3 £3.80 CSF £10.00 TOTE £2.60: £1.80, £3.00; EX 10.00 Trifecta £31.70 Pool: £4865.83 - 114.86 winning units..
Owner Robert Tyrrell **Bred** The National Stud **Trained** East Everleigh, Wilts

FOCUS
The strongest novice race run so far this year. The time reads well and the form could be rated 5lb higher. They went a good pace and, rather predictably, came more towards the stands' side. The first four were clear and the form should prove reliable.

2371 COOPERS MARQUEES STKS (H'CAP) 7f
5:00 (5:01) (Class 3) (0-90,89) 3-Y-O **£9,703** (£2,887; £1,443; £721) **Stalls** Low

Form RPR

022- **1** **Lancelot Du Lac (ITY)**[214] [7067] 3-9-1 83........................ RyanMoore 13 87+
(Dean Ivory) *in rr: hdwy over 2f out: styd on wl to ld last 50yds* **8/1**

30-5 **2** *2* **Lazarus Bell**[12] [1991] 3-9-2 84.. DaleSwift 4 82
(Alan Brown) *chsd ldrs: led jst ins fnl f: hdd and no ex last 50yds* **25/1**

5-30 **3** *shd* **Old Man Clegg**[14] [1934] 3-8-7 75 oh4............................. JamesSullivan 2 73
(Michael Easterby) *led tl over 1f out: kpt on same pce wl ins fnl f* **20/1**

41- **4** *shd* **Unknown Villain (IRE)**[197] [7458] 3-8-8 76.................. RichardKingscote 5 74
(Tom Dascombe) *lw: in rr: hdwy on outer over 2f out: chsng ldrs and n.m.r 1f out: kpt on same pce* **7/1**[3]

61- **5** *shd* **Steelriver (IRE)**[217] [6978] 3-9-6 88.................................. TedDurcan 15 85+
(James Bethell) *hld up in rr: effrt over 2f out: styd on wl fnl f* **20/1**

50-5 **6** *shd* **Dream Maker (IRE)**[25] [1690] 3-9-7 89.................................[1] DavidAllan 8 86
(Tim Easterby) *mid-div: nt clr run over 2f out: styd on fnl f* **20/1**

211- **7** *shd* **George Rooke (IRE)**[218] [6955] 3-9-0 82............................. AmyRyan 12 79+
(Kevin Ryan) *sn chsng ldrs: drvn over 2f out: nt clr run on ins over 1f out: styd on fnl 150yds* **8/1**

10 **8** *hd* **Aetna**[25] [1683] 3-8-7 75... GrahamGibbons 3 71
(Michael Easterby) *chsd ldr: upsides over 1f out: kpt on same pce last 100yds* **25/1**

5-21 **9** *3/4* **Right Touch**[27] [1647] 3-8-5 78.................................. GeorgeChaloner[(5)] 6 72
(Richard Fahey) *chsd ldrs: upsides over 1f out: wknd fnl 50yds* **7/1**[3]

3-10 **10** *2 1/2* **Robot Boy (IRE)**[11] [2022] 3-9-1 83.................................. JamieSpencer 1 71
(David Barron) *lw: mid-div: hdwy on outer over 2f out: chsng ldrs over 1f out: wknd fnl 150yds* **11/2**[2]

321- **11** *nk* **Mundahesh (IRE)**[197] [7459] 3-9-1 83.................................[1] PaulHanagan 7 70
(William Haggas) *in rr: effrt far side over 2f out: chsng ldrs 1f out: wknd ins fnl f* **5/1**[1]

26-0 **12** *1 1/2* **Blue Lotus (IRE)**[36] [1444] 3-8-8 76.............................. DuranFentiman 11 59
(Tim Easterby) *in rr: sme hdwy 2f out: nvr on terms* **40/1**

-201 **13** *3/4* **Khelman (IRE)**[22] [1750] 3-8-9 77................................... TonyHamilton 17 58
(Richard Fahey) *swtchd lft after 100yds: sn chsng ldrs: wknd fnl 150yds* **16/1**

-000 **14** *1/2* **Fantacise**[28] [1620] 3-8-8 76.......................................(b) TomEaves 9 55
(Richard Fahey) *chsd ldrs drvn over 2f out: lost pl over 1f out* **25/1**

-212 **15** *1/2* **Line Of Reason (IRE)**[19] [1806] 3-9-4 86.......................... GrahamLee 10 64
(Paul Midgley) *lw: mid-div: hdwy and nt clr run 2f out: wknd over 1f out* **10/1**

1210 16 23 **Upavon**[28] 1625 3-9-3 **85** RichardHughes 14
(David Elsworth) *s.i.s: in rr: bhd and eased over 1f out: t.o* **25/1**
1m 26.33s (1.03) **Going Correction** +0.225s/f (Good) **16** Ran SP% **126.4**
Speed ratings (Par 103): **103,100,100,100,100 100,100,99,99,96 95,94,93,92,92 65**
toteswingers 1&2 £41.20, 1&3 £48.80, 2&3 £119.70 CSF £202.57 CT £4019.62 TOTE £9.00: £2.60, £6.30, £5.20, £1.80; EX 311.40 Trifecta £3185.00 Part won. Pool: £4246.74 - 0.40 winning units..
Owner M J Yarrow **Bred** Elektra Di Fausto Martellozzo & C Sas **Trained** Radlett, Herts
FOCUS
This looked fiercely competitive beforehand, and there was indeed a bunched finish for the places. The race lacked obvious improvers but the winner created a good impression.
T/Jkpt: Not won. T/Plt: £305.20 to a £1 stake. Pool: £195,967.81 - 468.62 winning tickets.
T/Qpdt: £54.90 to a £1 stake. Pool: £9557.52 - 128.82 winning tickets. WG

[1701]NAAS (L-H)
Wednesday, May 15

OFFICIAL GOING: Yielding to soft

2374a WOODLANDS 100 CLUB H'CAP (PREMIER HANDICAP) 6f
6:20 (6:21) 3-Y-O
£24,390 (£7,723; £3,658; £1,016; £1,016; £406)

RPR

1 **Gathering Power (IRE)**[46] 1254 3-8-8 **81** FergalLynch 2 91
(Edward Lynam, Ire) *towards rr tl prog after 1/2-way: chsd ldrs 2f out: pressed ldr in 2nd ent fnl f: qcknd to ld fnl 100yds* **8/1**[3]
2 1 ½ **Boston Rocker (IRE)**[227] 6715 3-9-10 **97** DeclanMcDonogh 8 102
(Edward Lynam, Ire) *chsd ldrs far side: 3rd 1/2-way: pressed ldr in 2nd 2f out: kpt on wl tl nt qckn w wnr ins fnl 100yds* **20/1**
3 ½ **Scotland Forever (IRE)**[9] 2104 3-9-1 **91** RonanWhelan(3) 12 94
(John Patrick Shanahan, Ire) *trckd ldrs tl pushed along over 2f out: 5th appr fnl f: styd on wl to go 3rd clsng strides* **10/1**
4 nk **Abstraction (IRE)**[173] 7845 3-8-13 **86** SeamieHeffernan 10 89
(Sarah Dawson, Ire) *disp to beyond 1/2-way: remained cl 4th: one pce ins fnl f* **20/1**
4 dht **Boom And Bloom (IRE)**[9] 2109 3-8-4 **77** oh4 WayneLordan 4 80
(W McCreery, Ire) *chsd ldrs far side: led over 2f out tl hdd fnl 100yds: no ex* **33/1**
6 ½ **Toccata Blue (IRE)**[52] 1167 3-8-1 **77** oh2 IJBrennan(3) 9 78
(G M Lyons, Ire) *racd towards rr: plenty to do 2f out: 10th 1f out: styd on strly clsng stages: nrst fin* **33/1**
7 ½ **Roseraie (IRE)**[9] 2108 3-9-8 **95** ChrisHayes 15 94
(Kevin Prendergast, Ire) *trckd ldrs towards stands' side: pushed along 2f out: nt qckn appr fnl f: kpt on same pce* **6/1**[1]
8 shd **Wexford Opera (IRE)**[9] 2104 3-9-3 **90** (t) KevinManning 16 89
(J S Bolger, Ire) *racd in mid-div: kpt on wl fr over 1f out: nvr nrr* **7/1**[2]
9 2 **Versilia Gal (IRE)**[28] 1628 3-8-2 **78** ConorHoban(3) 7 71
(Patrick Martin, Ire) *hld up towards rr: swtchd lft 2f out: kpt on wl fnl f: nvr nrr* **14/1**
10 hd **Yulong Baoju (IRE)**[269] 5391 3-9-2 **89** FMBerry 11 81
(Edward Lynam, Ire) *chsd ldrs in centre of trck: gd prog appr fnl f: no imp fnl 100yds* **6/1**[1]
11 1 ½ **Ask Dad**[263] 5591 3-9-10 **97** JohnnyMurtagh 18 84
(Thomas Carmody, Ire) *hld up towards rr on stands' side: sme late hdwy wout ever threatening* **7/1**[2]
12 2 ¾ **Sword Of Light (IRE)**[96] 567 3-7-11 **77** oh2 (b) ConnorKing(7) 13 55
(David Marnane, Ire) *nvr bttr than mid-div: no imp over 1f out* **14/1**
13 nk **Lightnin Hopkins (IRE)**[206] 7278 3-8-13 **86** GaryCarroll 5 63
(G M Lyons, Ire) *nvr bttr than mid-div: no imp over 1f out* **16/1**
14 ¾ **Vinson Massif (USA)**[8] 2139 3-9-3 **90** (p) JosephO'Brien 17 65
(A P O'Brien, Ire) *trckd ldrs stands' side tl wknd appr fnl f* **10/1**
15 1 ¼ **Hazy Glow (IRE)**[42] 1336 3-9-5 **92** PatSmullen 1 63
(D K Weld, Ire) *racd alone far side early: chsd ldrs 1/2-way tl wknd appr fnl f* **16/1**
16 1 ¼ **Katchy Lady**[8] 2139 3-8-9 **82** (b) CO'Donoghue 3 49
(P J Prendergast, Ire) *chsd ldrs tl wknd appr fnl f* **18/1**
17 shd **Plunder**[23] 1714 3-8-6 **79** (b[1]) RoryCleary 14 46
(Kevin Ryan) *disp to beyond 1/2-way: wknd under 2f out* **10/1**
18 18 **Hard Core Debt**[25] 1702 3-8-9 **82** ShaneFoley 6
(A Oliver, Ire) *towards rr fr 1/2-way: adrift fnl 2f: eased* **25/1**
1m 11.75s (-1.45) **18** Ran SP% **141.6**
Tote place: Abstraction £3.20, Boom And Bloom £4.50 CSF £179.19 CT £1717.93 TOTE £5.10: £1.60, £4.20, £2.60; DF 139.30.
Owner Mrs S Power **Bred** D G Iceton **Trained** Dunshaughlin, Co Meath
FOCUS
A competitive handicap. The winner, third and fifth have been rated as running personal bests, with the standard being set by the second and fourth to their best.

2375a IRISH STALLION FARMS EUROPEAN BREEDERS FUND BLUE WIND STKS (GROUP 3) 1m 2f
6:50 (6:50) 3-Y-O+
£40,955 (£11,971; £5,670; £1,890)

RPR

1 **Euphrasia (IRE)**[10] 2062 4-9-9 85 GaryCarroll 1 101
(Joseph G Murphy, Ire) *mde all: qcknd over 2f out: 2 l advantage appr fnl f: styd on wl* **33/1**
2 2 **La Collina (IRE)**[38] 1413 4-9-9 108 ChrisHayes 2 97+
(Kevin Prendergast, Ire) *settled in 3rd: nt qckn w wnr under 2f out: kpt on wl ins fnl f to get up clsng stages for 2nd* **5/2**[2]
3 ½ **Princess Highway (USA)**[213] 7093 4-10-0 117 PatSmullen 3 101+
(D K Weld, Ire) *trckd ldr in 2nd tl nt qckn under 2f out: kpt on same pce fnl f and passed clsng stages for 2nd* **8/13**[1]
4 ½ **Rehn's Nest (IRE)**[52] 1166 3-8-12 102 (t) KevinManning 4 98+
(J S Bolger, Ire) *w.w in rr: nt qckn 2f out and sn pushed along: kpt on wl clsng stages: nvr nrr* **9/2**[3]
2m 21.19s (5.59)
WFA 3 from 4yo 15lb **4** Ran SP% **111.6**
CSF £108.06 TOTE £19.80; DF 65.10.
Owner Joseph G Murphy **Bred** Tally-Ho Stud **Trained** Fethard, Co Tipperary
FOCUS
A major upset here. The time was slow and the winner was best placed in the sprint to the line. She has been rated as running a big personal best, but the form is clearly unreliable.

2376 - 2379a (Foreign Racing) - See Raceform Interactive

LA ZARZUELA (R-H)
Wednesday, May 15

OFFICIAL GOING: Turf: good

2380a PREMIO HECTOR LICUDI (CONDITIONS) (3YO+) (AMATEUR RIDERS) (TURF) 1m 1f
4:40 (12:00) 3-Y-O+ **£3,252** (£1,300; £650; £325)

RPR

1 **Karluv Most (FR)**[325] 7-9-8 0 MrMarcosCarmena-Garcia 1 77
(J L Maroto, Spain) **4/5**[1]
2 4 ¼ **Avon Ferry**[936] 7069 6-9-3 0 MissCBoville(9) 5 72
(F Perez, Spain) **138/10**
3 ¾ **Ancient Greece**[18] 1849 6-10-11 0 MrFMitchell 6 83
(George Baker) *midfield on outer: rdn and outpcd 3f out: rallied u.p and styd on to go 3rd fnl strides: no ch w wnr* **14/5**[2]
4 nk **Tafadhali (SPA)** 5-9-5 0 MrNicolasDeJulianAlonso 2 62
(J A Lopez, Spain) **7/1**
5 7 **Arsalan**[612] 4-10-8 0 MrDiegoSarabia 7 65
(F Rodriguez Puertas, Spain) **5/1**
6 ¾ **Steeler (SPA)** 4-9-8 0 (b) MrRMartinArranz 4 49
(R Martin, Spain) **192/10**
7 8 ¾ **Happy Few** 5-10-8 0 MrRAguilera 3 45
(R H Huayas, Spain) **42/10**[3]
1m 53.06s (113.06) **7** Ran SP% **142.0**
DIVIDENDS (all including 1 euro stakes): WIN 1.80; PLACE 1.90, 5.40; DF 15.60.
Owner Cuadra Cholaica **Bred** Dr Jean-Pierre Colombu **Trained** Spain

[2035]SAINT-CLOUD (L-H)
Wednesday, May 15

OFFICIAL GOING: Turf: good

2381a PRIX CLEOPATRE (GROUP 3) (3YO FILLIES) (TURF) 1m 2f 110y
1:05 (12:00) 3-Y-O **£32,520** (£13,008; £9,756; £6,504; £3,252)

RPR

1 **Baltic Baroness (GER)**[29] 1602 3-8-9 0 MaximeGuyon 8 106
(A Fabre, France) *trckd ldr: rdn to chal 2f out: led over 1f out: qcknd clr ent fnl f: drvn out: rapidly diminishing advantage cl home but a holding on* **17/10**[1]
2 snk **Santa Ponsa (FR)**[19] 1816 3-8-9 0 FranckBlondel 5 106
(F Rossi, France) *hld up in last trio on outer: rdn over 2f out: styd on to go 2nd ins fnl f: clsng rapidly on wnr cl home but nvr getting there* **5/2**[2]
3 1 ¼ **Eleuthera (FR)**[29] 1602 3-8-9 0 EddyHardouin 4 104
(P Demercastel, France) *midfield on outer: rdn to chal 2f out: outpcd by wnr ent fnl f: styd on* **12/1**
4 nk **Melodique (FR)**[19] 1816 3-8-9 0 OlivierPeslier 7 103+
(C Laffon-Parias, France) *t.k.h: hld up in last: rdn 2f out: stl last 100yds out: r.o to go 4th cl home: fin v strly but nvr able to chal* **18/1**
5 hd **Shahad (IRE)**[48] 3-8-9 0 (b) AurelienLemaitre 6 103+
(F Head, France) *hld up in last pair on inner: rdn over 2f out: styd on u.p but n.d* **21/1**
6 ½ **Piana (FR)**[42] 3-8-9 0 ChristopheSoumillon 3 102
(Y Durepaire, France) *led: rdn and hdd over 1f out: sn no ex and btn: fdd* **19/5**[3]
7 ¾ **Childa (IRE)**[29] 1602 3-8-9 0 Christophe-PatriceLemaire 1 100
(S Wattel, France) *midfield on inner: rdn 2f out: outpcd ins fnl f: fdd* **13/1**
8 1 **Siljan's Saga (FR)**[23] 3-8-9 0 AntoineHamelin 2 98
(J-P Gauvin, France) *prom on inner: rdn 2f out: sn outpcd: fdd and dropped to last* **20/1**
2m 16.09s (-3.51) **8** Ran SP% **115.8**
WIN (incl. 1 euro stake): 2.70. PLACES: 1.10, 1.20, 1.70. DF: 3.60. SF: 6.50.
Owner Gestut Ammerland **Bred** Gestut Ammerland **Trained** Chantilly, France

[2044]NEWMARKET (R-H)
Thursday, May 16

OFFICIAL GOING: Good (7.9)

2382 HOMESTORE AND SAFEPAC MAIDEN AUCTION STKS 6f
5:20 (5:23) (Class 5) 2-Y-O **£3,234** (£962; £481; £240) **Stalls** Low

Form RPR

1 **Lucky Kristale** 2-8-10 0 TomQueally 4 83
(George Margarson) *mde all: rdn and drew wl clr w runner-up over 1f out: battled on gamely fnl f* **8/1**[3]
0 2 shd **Our Queenie (IRE)**[28] 1634 2-8-10 0 JimmyQuinn 8 83
(Richard Hannon) *w wnr thrght: rdn and drew wl clr w wnr over 1f out: sustained effrt fnl f: a jst hld* **10/1**
3 11 **Rizal Park (IRE)** 2-8-11 0 MartinDwyer 9 51+
(Andrew Balding) *s.i.s: rn green in rr: hdwy and squeezed between horses wl over 1f out: no ch w ldng pair but kpt on to go 3rd wl ins fnl f* **9/2**[2]
4 ½ **Razor Quest** 2-8-9 0 WilliamCarson 7 47+
(Philip McBride) *hld up in last trio: swtchd lft and hdwy over 2f out: no ch w ldng pair but battling for 3rd fnl f: kpt on* **12/1**
5 ½ **Plucky Dip** 2-8-6 0 RyanPowell(3) 6 46
(John Ryan) *chsd ldrs: 3rd and wl outpcd by ldng pair over 1f out: lost 2 pls wl ins fnl f* **33/1**
0 6 nk **Flying Author (IRE)**[5] 2250 2-8-13 0 KirstyMilczarek 12 49
(Phil McEntee) *s.i.s: hdwy to chse ldrs after 2f: rdn and outpcd by ldng pair over 1f out: batling for 3rd and kpt on same pce fnl f* **16/1**
4 7 3 ¾ **Sweet Alibi (IRE)**[5] 2283 2-8-4 0 LiamJones 11 29
(J S Moore) *hld up in tch in midfield: rdn and effrt ent fnl 2f: outpcd and wl btn over 1f out: wknd* **16/1**
8 5 **Mount Cheiron (USA)** 2-9-1 0 MickaelBarzalona 2 25
(Brian Meehan) *hld up in tch in midfield: rdn and no rspnse ent fnl 2f: sltly hmpd and wknd wl over 1f out* **4/1**[1]

9 *nk* **Scooping (IRE)** 2-8-8 0 SeanLevey 1 17
(Richard Hannon) *in tch in midfield: rdn and btn ent fnl 2f: wknd and wl btn whn n.m.r over 1f out* 9/2[2]

10 *2 ¾* **Nip A Bear** 2-8-11 0 SebSanders 10 11
(John Holt) *chsd ldrs tl 2f out: sn struggling and wkng whn short of room wl over 1f out: fdd* 25/1

11 *18* **Bushy Glade (IRE)** 2-8-6 0 NickyMackay 5
(Julia Feilden) *t.k.h and hld up in midfield early: short of room and lost pl after 2f: lost tch over 2f out: t.o* 33/1

1m 14.66s (2.46) **Going Correction** +0.30s/f (Good) **11** Ran SP% **105.8**
Speed ratings (Par 93): **95,94,80,79,78 78,73,66,66,62 38**
Tote Swingers: 1&2 £7.90, 1&3 £8.40, 2&3 £7.00 CSF £64.09 TOTE £7.40: £1.90, £2.60, £2.60; EX 44.10 Trifecta £162.00 Pool: £879.92 - 4.07 winning units..
Owner Graham Lodge Partnership **Bred** Lilac Bloodstock & Redmyre Bloodstock **Trained** Newmarket, Suffolk
■ Honey Meadow was withdrawn (5/1, unruly in the stalls). Deduct 15p in the 3 under R4.

FOCUS
Stands' side track used. Stalls far side except 1m4f: centre. Hard to believe this was a strong Newmarket maiden overall but the leading pair clearly deserve some credit for pulling so far clear of the rest.

2383 REDBOURN ENGINEERING LTD H'CAP 1m 2f
5:55 (5:58) (Class 5) (0-75,74) 4-Y-O+ **£3,234** (£962; £481; £240) **Stalls** Low

Form RPR

3-53 **1** **Frozen Over**[14] [1950] 5-9-2 **69** MickaelBarzalona 4 79
(Stuart Kittow) *stdd and swtchd lft after s: hld up in rr: pushed along briefly 5f out: stdy hdwy 4f out: rdn to ld over 1f out: kpt on u.p: jst hld on* 5/1[3]

53-0 **2** *nse* **Royal Dutch**[26] [1673] 4-9-3 **70** TomQueally 13 80
(Denis Coakley) *hld up in tch: hdwy 3f out: drvn to chse wnr over 1f out: ev ch ins fnl f: kpt on u.p cl home: jst failed* 7/2[1]

2620 **3** *¾* **Tight Lipped (IRE)**[37] [1442] 4-9-2 **74** RyanTate(5) 2 82
(James Eustace) *chsd ldrs: rdn and effrt ent fnl 2f: pressed ldrs and drvn 1f out: kpt on same pce fnl 100yds* 9/1

4-13 **4** *½* **Rock Song**[17] [1889] 4-9-3 **70** FrannyNorton 10 77
(John Mackie) *t.k.h: hld up in tch in midfield: shuffled bk to rr 5f out: rdn and hdwy to ld 2f out: hdd over 1f out: styd pressing ldrs tl no ex wl ins fnl f* 15/2

163- **5** *5* **Laconicos (IRE)**[236] [6503] 11-8-4 **62** ow2 (t) RobertTart(5) 7 59
(William Stone) *in tch in midfield: drvn and unable qck wl over 1f out: plugged on same pce fnl f* 25/1

00-4 **6** *shd* **Kalily**[19] [1837] 4-9-1 **68** LiamJones 6 65
(Rae Guest) *chsd ldrs: rdn ent fnl 2f: unable qck ent fnl f: wknd fnl 100yds* 12/1

213- **7** *7* **Geeaitch**[205] [7317] 4-9-0 **67** WilliamCarson 12 50
(Anthony Carson) *hld up in tch in last trio: rdn and effrt over 2f out: no imp 2f out and sn wknd* 14/1

1106 **8** *1* **Strike Force**[83] [759] 9-9-0 **72** (t) NatashaEaton(5) 8 53
(Alison Hutchinson) *in tch in midfield: rdn and unable qck over 2f out: wknd over 1f out* 33/1

0-00 **9** *10* **Layline (IRE)**[31] [1586] 6-9-5 **72** JimmyQuinn 3 33
(Gay Kelleway) *hld up in tch towards rr: rdn 3f out: sn struggling: wknd wl over 1f out: bhd and eased ins fnl f* 20/1

1044 **10** *nk* **Thecornishcowboy**[10] [2101] 4-9-5 **72** (t) KierenFallon 9 32
(John Ryan) *chsd ldr tl led 1/2-way: hdd 2f out: sn wknd: bhd and eased ins fnl f* 11/1

003- **11** *1* **Flash Crash**[77] [6639] 4-8-12 **65** HayleyTurner 11 23
(Robert Cowell) *t.k.h: led tl 1/2-way: chsd ldrs tl rdn and wknd ent fnl 2f: wl bhd and eased ins fnl f* 20/1

000- **12** *23* **Judicious**[190] [7639] 6-9-6 **73** AdamKirby 14
(Noel Quinlan) *t.k.h: chsd ldrs tl wknd over 2f out: t.o and eased fnl f: b.b.v* 9/2[2]

/35- **P** **Sacrilege**[130] [3589] 8-8-11 **67** (v) RyanPowell(3) 1
(Daniel O'Brien) *v.s.a and rel to r: plld himself up after 100yds* 25/1

2m 8.6s (2.80) **Going Correction** +0.30s/f (Good) **13** Ran SP% **121.7**
Speed ratings (Par 103): **100,99,99,98,94 94,89,88,80,80 79,61,**
Tote Swingers: 1&2 £4.80, 1&3 £14.00, 2&3 £8.40 CSF £21.41 CT £158.46 TOTE £5.60: £1.90, £2.40, £2.80; EX 26.90 Trifecta £302.00 Pool: £1,608.87 - 3.99 winning units..
Owner P A & M J Reditt **Bred** Manor Farm Packers Ltd **Trained** Blackborough, Devon

FOCUS
A fair handicap. The front four came clear off what looked a sound enough gallop. Straightforward form, taken at face value.

2384 JANE RUTHERFORD MEMORIAL EBF MAIDEN STKS 1m 2f
6:25 (6:31) (Class 5) 3-Y-O **£3,881** (£1,155; £577; £288) **Stalls** Low

Form RPR

42- **1** **Elkaayed (USA)**[231] [6596] 3-9-5 0 PaulHanagan 12 98+
(Roger Varian) *t.k.h: hld up wl in tch in midfield: effrt to press ldr 2f out: led over 1f out: edgd rt but clr 1f out: r.o wl: comf* 2/1[2]

2 *2 ½* **Arab Spring (IRE)** 3-9-5 0 RyanMoore 11 95+
(Sir Michael Stoute) *t.k.h: hld up in tch towards rr: rdn and effrt 3f out: chsd clr ldng pair over 1f out: wnt 2nd ins fnl f: styd on wl but no threat to wnr* 12/1

3 *1 ¼* **Royal Flag** 3-9-5 0 MickaelBarzalona 6 91
(Saeed bin Suroor) *t.k.h: led: rdn 2f out: hdd over 1f out: no ex and btn 1f out: one pce and lost 2nd ins fnl f* 7/1[3]

4-3 **4** *¾* **Demonic**[29] [1624] 3-9-5 0 (t) TomQueally 2 92+
(Sir Henry Cecil) *chsd ldrs: rdn and effrt over 2f out: nt clr run and shuffled bk ent fnl 2f: sn swtchd lft and rdn: swtchd rt again over 1f out: rallied and styd on wl ins fnl f: no threat to wnr* 15/8[1]

5- **5** *1 ¼* **Dance King**[204] [7333] 3-9-5 0 TedDurcan 8 87+
(David Lanigan) *in tch in midfield: rdn and effrt wl over 2f out: keeping on but no threat to ldrs whn short of room over 1f out: kpt on fnl f* 16/1

0- **6** *1 ½* **Great Hall**[239] [6371] 3-9-5 0 KierenFallon 15 84
(Brian Meehan) *in tch in midfield: rdn and effrt to chse clr ldng pair 2f out: edgd rt and no imp over 1f out: wknd ins fnl f* 11/1

- **7** *½* **Fledged** 3-9-5 0 WilliamBuick 9 83+
(John Gosden) *chsd ldr tl over 2f out: outpcd and rdn 2f out: wl hld and n.m.r over 1f out: plugged on* 20/1

8 *3 ¼* **Soho Dancer** 3-9-0 0 KirstyMilczarek 14 71
(James Toller) *stdd s: t.k.h: hld up in tch towards rr: rdn and effrt 3f out: wknd 2f out* 50/1

9 *6* **Caperina (IRE)** 3-9-0 0 JimCrowley 3 59
(Ralph Beckett) *hld up in tch towards rr: rdn and outpcd 3f out: sn wknd* 33/1

10 *1 ½* **Fanny Squeers** 3-9-0 0 HayleyTurner 7 56
(Michael Bell) *stdd s: t.k.h: hld up in tch in midfield: rdn and struggling 3f out: sn wknd* 50/1

6 **11** *1 ¾* **Kattaf (IRE)**[15] [1931] 3-9-5 0 AdamKirby 1 58
(Marco Botti) *hld up: rdn 3f out: sn struggling and wl btn* 80/1

6- **12** *1 ¾* **Don Padeja**[169] [7899] 3-9-2 0 PatrickHills(3) 10 54
(Luca Cumani) *chsd ldrs: rdn and wkng whn bdly hmpd 2f out: bhd 1f out* 25/1

13 *17* **Phosphorescence (IRE)** 3-9-5 0 EddieAhern 5 65
(Sir Henry Cecil) *in tch in midfield: rdn wl over 2f out: bhd and nt clr run wl over 1f out: wl bhd and eased ins fnl f: t.o* 25/1

00 **14** *53* **Sakhee's Alround**[14] [1955] 3-9-0 0 ChrisCatlin 4
(K F Clutterbuck) *virtually ref to r and t.o thrght* 150/1

2m 8.84s (3.04) **Going Correction** +0.30s/f (Good) **14** Ran SP% **123.7**
Speed ratings (Par 99): **99,97,96,95,94 93,92,90,85,84 82,81,67,25**
Tote Swingers: 1&2 £6.90, 1&3 £4.30, 2&3 £8.90 CSF £25.25 TOTE £2.80: £1.20, £2.70, £2.50; EX 24.10 Trifecta £75.90 Pool: £2,145.35 - 21.18 winning units..
Owner Hamdan Al Maktoum **Bred** Shadwell Farm LLC **Trained** Newmarket, Suffolk

FOCUS
A maiden which is sure to throw up plenty of winners. It was steadily run but looks a decent renewal with plenty of depth.

2385 CHASSIS CAB DAF H'CAP 1m 4f
7:00 (7:02) (Class 4) (0-85,85) 4-Y-O+ **£5,175** (£1,540; £769; £384) **Stalls** Centre

Form RPR

231- **1** **Arch Villain (IRE)**[210] [7194] 4-8-13 **77** RyanMoore 4 89
(Amanda Perrett) *chsd ldrs: effrt to ld 2f out: styd on strly and drew clr fnl f: comf* 7/2[1]

43-3 **2** *5* **Ethics Girl (IRE)**[26] [1673] 7-8-10 **81** (t) NoelGarbutt(7) 2 85
(John Berry) *in tch in midfield: effrt and swtchd lft over 1f out: kpt on to go 2nd fnl 100yds: no threat to wnr* 10/1

6155 **3** *2 ¼* **Mcbirney (USA)**[34] [1523] 6-8-6 **75** RobertTart(5) 9 75
(Paul D'Arcy) *stdd s: hld up in tch in rr: swtchd lft and hdwy 3f out: rdn to press wnr over 1f out: no ex 1f out: wknd ins fnl f* 25/1

2112 **4** *nk* **English Summer**[103] [496] 6-9-0 **85** (t) AliceHaynes(7) 6 85
(David Simcock) *hld up in tch in midfield: rdn and effrt wl over 1f out: chsd ldrs and drvn over 1f out: styd on same pce fnl f* 12/1

3136 **5** *1* **Luggers Hall (IRE)**[26] [1673] 5-8-11 **75** TomQueally 5 73
(Tony Carroll) *stdd s: hld up in tch in rr: rdn and effrt 2f out: edging rt over 1f out: swtchd lft ent fnl f: styd on same pce u.p fnl f* 11/1

343- **6** *nk* **Kiwayu**[202] [7367] 4-9-4 **82** (t) StevieDonohoe 7 80
(Ian Williams) *hld up in tch towards rr: rdn and effrt 2f out: keeping on but no threat to wnr whn pushed lft ent fnl f: no imp after* 7/1

3111 **7** *¾* **Attwaal (IRE)**[17] [1884] 4-9-2 **80** SebSanders 10 77
(Neil King) *led tl 2f out: sn rdn and unable qck: wknd fnl f* 9/2[2]

66/1 **8** *12* **Sir Bedivere (IRE)**[17] [1882] 4-9-6 **84** KierenFallon 8 69
(Brian Meehan) *chsd ldr: rdn 3f out: lost pl and btn 2f out: bhd and eased ins fnl f* 5/1[3]

231- **9** *24* **Omar Khayyam**[159] [8037] 4-9-2 **80** (t) WilliamBuick 3 19
(Andrew Balding) *chsd ldrs: rdn and struggling wl over 2f out: wl bhd and eased fnl f: t.o* 9/2[2]

2m 34.53s (2.53) **Going Correction** +0.30s/f (Good) **9** Ran SP% **116.7**
Speed ratings (Par 105): **103,99,98,97,97 97,96,88,72**
Tote Swingers: 1&2 £6.80, 1&3 £14.80, 2&3 £22.10 CSF £39.90 CT £760.05 TOTE £3.70: £2.00, £2.60, £8.30; EX 41.80 Trifecta £433.20 Pool: £1,427.83 - 2.47 winning units..
Owner F Cotton, P Conway **Bred** Summerhill Bloodstock **Trained** Pulborough, W Sussex

FOCUS
This looked quite a competitive beforehand but the winner did it comfortably. He matched last year's turf best.

2386 ORBITAL FOOD MACHINERY CLASSIFIED STKS 1m 4f
7:35 (7:36) (Class 5) 3-Y-O **£3,408** (£1,006; £503) **Stalls** Centre

Form RPR

52-0 **1** **Song Light**[26] [1684] 3-9-0 72 SebSanders 1 76
(David Elsworth) *stdd s: t.k.h: hld up in tch in last: rdn and str run to ld 1f out: r.o wl* 6/1[3]

00-4 **2** *1 ¾* **Thorpe (IRE)**[37] [1443] 3-9-0 74 JimCrowley 5 73
(Ralph Beckett) *chsd ldr tl 7f out: styd chsng ldrs: rdn and pressing ldrs 2f out: kpt on same pce ins fnl f* 9/4[1]

051- **3** *½* **Rhombus (IRE)**[209] [7205] 3-9-0 75 [1] RyanMoore 2 72
(William Haggas) *t.k.h: in tch: hdwy to chse ldr 7f out: led 5f out: drvn 2f out: hdd 1f out: kpt on same pce and lost 2nd wl ins fnl f* 11/4[2]

20-6 **4** *1 ½* **Astrosapphire**[15] [1934] 3-9-0 71 TomQueally 3 70?
(Mark H Tompkins) *t.k.h: chsd ldrs: rdn and effrt 2f out: nt clr run and swtchd lft jst ins fnl f: one pce after* 12/1

0212 **5** *2 ¼* **Speed Boogie**[23] [1754] 3-9-0 74 AdamKirby 4 66
(Marco Botti) *led tl 5f out: chsd ldr: drvn 2f out: outpcd and btn 1f out: wknd fnl 100yds* 9/4[1]

2m 42.01s (10.01) **Going Correction** +0.30s/f (Good) **5** Ran SP% **110.2**
Speed ratings (Par 99): **78,76,76,75,74**
CSF £19.77 TOTE £6.30: £3.40, £1.30; EX 17.70 Trifecta £49.00 Pool: £765.80 - 11.69 winning units..
Owner D and C Bloodstock **Bred** D & C Bloodstock **Trained** Newmarket, Suffolk

FOCUS
Fair form in this conditions event. With just the five runners it wasn't a surprise that the pace was pretty sedate for a long way. The second to fourth were rated close to their marks.

2387 SIMON GIBSON FILLIES' H'CAP (JOCKEY CLUB GRASSROOTS MIDDLE DISTANCE SERIES QUALIFIER) 1m
8:05 (8:05) (Class 5) (0-75,76) 3-Y-O **£3,234** (£962; £481; £240) **Stalls** Low

Form RPR

33-1 **1** **Auction (IRE)**[13] [1986] 3-9-5 **73** RyanMoore 8 89+
(Ed Dunlop) *stdd s: hld up in tch in midfield: hdwy ent fnl 2f: led over 1f out: sn stormed clr: r.o wl: readily* 2/1[2]

2-13 **2** *4 ½* **Tilstarr (IRE)**[122] [204] 3-8-8 **67** RobertTart(5) 7 73
(Roger Teal) *stdd s: hld up in tch in last trio: effrt ent fnl 2f: styng on whn nt clr run and swtchd lft ent fnl f: r.o wl to go 2nd fnl 100yds: no ch w wnr* 50/1

-446 **3** *1* **Azma (USA)**[26] [1697] 3-9-1 **69** MartinDwyer 6 72
(Conrad Allen) *in tch in midfield: rdn and effrt ent fnl 2f: styd on u.p fnl f to go 3rd towards fin: no ch w wnr* 40/1

30-2 **4** *¾* **Tight Fit**[16] [1907] 3-8-3 **62** AmyScott(5) 9 63
(Henry Candy) *w ldr tl led 1/2-way: rdn and hdd over 1f out: sn outpcd by wnr: styd on same pce after and lost 2 pls fnl 100yds* 12/1

10-4 **5** *shd* **Starlight Symphony (IRE)**[19] 1822 3-9-7 **75**.................. TedDurcan 10 76
(Eve Johnson Houghton) *stdd s: hld up in tch in last trio: rdn and effrt 2f out: no threat to wnr and kpt on same pce ins fnl f* **16/1**

10-6 **6** *3/4* **Emperatriz**[21] 1772 3-8-13 **67**.................. SebSanders 4 66+
(John Holt) *hld up in tch in last trio: hdwy on far rail wl over 1f out: nt clr run and swtchd lft 1f out: styd on ins fnl f: nvr trbld ldrs* **33/1**

01-2 **7** *nk* **Oilinda**[26] 1697 3-9-3 **71**.................. HayleyTurner 1 70
(Michael Bell) *t.k.h: chsd ldrs: nt clr run and outpcd whn swtchd lft over 1f out: n.d and kpt on same pce fnl f* **14/1**

1-3 **8** *nk* **Ice Pie**[12] 2026 3-9-5 **73**.................. RichardKingscote 11 71
(Tom Dascombe) *t.k.h: chsd ldrs: rdn and unable qck 2f out: outpcd and btn over 1f out: wknd ins fnl f* **15/8**[1]

64-5 **9** *1 3/4* **Marsh Dragon**[15] 1931 3-8-13 **67**.................. TomQueally 12 61
(Mark H Tompkins) *stdd s: hld up in tch in last trio: rdn and effrt 2f out: sn no imp: nvr trbld ldrs* **33/1**

2600 **10** *4 1/2* **Lucky Di**[36] 1477 3-9-7 **75**.................. JimCrowley 5 58
(Peter Hedger) *chsd ldrs: rdn and outpcd 2f out: btn over 1f out and wknd fnl f* **33/1**

02-1 **11** *3/4* **Reggae Star**[10] 2071 3-9-8 **76** 6ex.................. FrannyNorton 3 57
(Mark Johnston) *led tl 1/2-way: rdn and struggling 2f out: wknd over 1f out* **11/2**[3]

23-1 **12** *15* **Girl Of Cadiz**[16] 1907 3-8-10 **69**.................. WilliamTwiston-Davies(5) 2
(Richard Hannon) *chsd ldrs: rdn and losing pl whn bdly hmpd wl over 1f out: sn bhd* **25/1**

1m 40.23s (1.63) **Going Correction** +0.30s/f (Good) 12 Ran SP% **120.8**
Speed ratings (Par 96): **103,98,97,96,96 95,95,95,93,89 88,73**
Tote Swingers: 1&2 £58.30, 1&3 £18.90, 2&3 £27.60 CSF £119.96 CT £3172.86 TOTE £2.80: £1.60, £12.40, £8.90; EX 176.70 Trifecta £803.40 Part won. Pool: £1,071.25 - 0.04 winning units..
Owner Highclere Thoroughbred Racing - Coventry **Bred** Edy Srl And Societa Agricola Gem Srl **Trained** Newmarket, Suffolk

FOCUS
This looked quite competitive beforehand but turned out to be anything but. The pace was decent and the form is rated around the second and third.

2388 EAST ANGLIAN DAILY TIMES H'CAP 5f
8:35 (8:35) (Class 4) (0-85,84) 4-Y-0+ **£5,175** (£1,154; £1,154; £384) **Stalls** Low

Form RPR

303- **1** **Sir Maximilian (IRE)**[239] 6368 4-9-7 **84**.................. StevieDonohoe 3 94
(Ian Williams) *hld up in tch in last trio: hdwy on far rail wl over 1f out: r.o wl to ld fnl 100yds: edgd lft but styd on wl towards fin* **12/1**

63-3 **2** *3/4* **Rebecca Romero**[20] 1814 6-8-12 **75**.................. RyanMoore 8 82+
(Denis Coakley) *t.k.h: hld up in midfield: bdly hmpd and dropped to rr over 3f out: stl last and swtchd lft ent fnl f: r.o strly fnl 150yds: nt quite rch ldrs* **15/2**

4335 **2** *dht* **Rylee Mooch**[38] 1431 5-8-12 **75**..................(e) RobbieFitzpatrick 1 82
(Richard Guest) *chsd ldr: rdn over 1f out: led ins fnl f: hdd and one pce fnl 100yds* **33/1**

01-5 **4** *nk* **Lupo D'Oro (IRE)**[20] 1814 4-9-2 **79**.................. SteveDrowne 7 85
(John Best) *in tch in midfield: jostled wl over 1f out: rdn and hdwy over 1f out: ev ch ins fnl f: styd on same pce towards fin* **6/1**[3]

23-0 **5** *1 1/2* **Macdillon**[20] 1814 7-8-10 **73**.................. LiamKeniry 2 74
(Stuart Kittow) *chsd ldrs: rdn over 1f out: drvn and unable qck 1f out: styd on same pce after* **16/1**

2402 **6** *nse* **Blue Jack**[10] 2097 8-9-0 **77**..................(t) MickaelBarzalona 4 77
(Stuart Williams) *in tch in midfield: hdwy u.p over 1f out: styd on same pce fnl 100yds* **3/1**[1]

5-04 **7** *shd* **Waseem Faris (IRE)**[12] 2031 4-9-0 **77**.................. MartinHarley 10 77
(Mick Channon) *in tch: effrt and drvn to chse ldrs 1f out: no ex and one pce ins fnl f* **17/2**

04-4 **8** *hd* **Arctic Lynx (IRE)**[13] 1984 6-9-1 **83**.................. MichaelJMMurphy(5) 11 82
(Robert Cowell) *taken down early: towards rr: rdn and hdwy 1/2-way: drvn over 1f out: styd on same pce ins fnl f* **14/1**

0232 **9** *1/2* **Tyfos**[28] 1652 8-9-1 **83**.................. MatthewLawson(5) 6 80
(Brian Baugh) *led: rdn over 1f out: hdd ins fnl f: wknd fnl 100yds* **16/1**

213 **10** *1 1/2* **My Son Max**[31] 1581 5-9-6 **83**.................. KierenFallon 9 75
(P J O'Gorman) *in tch towards rr: effrt and rdn over 1f out: no imp 1f out: wknd ins fnl f* **10/3**[2]

6033 **11** *5* **Moorhouse Lad**[12] 2031 10-9-7 **84**.................. JimCrowley 5 58
(Garry Moss) *taken down early: chsd ldrs: rdn and struggling over 1f out: wknd fnl f* **12/1**

59.89s (0.79) **Going Correction** +0.30s/f (Good) 11 Ran SP% **121.4**
Speed ratings (Par 105): **105,103,103,103,100 100,100,100,99,97 89**PL: RM £7.10, RR £2.80. EX: SM/RR £65.70, SM/RR £180.70. CSF: SM/RR £51.17, SM/RM £176.43. Tricast: SM, RR, RM £1,478.65, SM, RM, RR £1,604.62. TRIFECTA: £424.70 TOTE £12.00: £3.00 TRIFECTA Tote Swingers: 1&RR £7.60, 1&RM £28.60, R27 Owner.

FOCUS
A fairly useful sprint. The leaders went hard and the form is straightforward.
T/Plt: £777.50 to a £1 stake. Pool: £52,044.55 - 48.86 winning tickets. T/Qpdt: £99.40 to a £1 stake. Pool: £4,665.48 - 34.70 winning tickets. SP

2051 SALISBURY (R-H)
Thursday, May 16

OFFICIAL GOING: Good to soft (good in places; 7.9)
Wind: Virtually nil Weather: Sunny spells

2389 CASTLEPOINT SHOPPING PARK A3060 BOURNEMOUTH MAIDEN FILLIES' STKS (DIV I) 1m 1f 198y
1:30 (1:30) (Class 5) 3-Y-0+ **£3,234** (£962; £481; £240) **Stalls** High

Form RPR

1 **Songbird (IRE)** 4-9-12 0.................. IanMongan 5 91+
(Sir Henry Cecil) *chsd ldrs: led 2f out: pushed clr fnl f: comf* **6/1**

32-5 **2** *5* **Cushion**[20] 1813 3-8-12 81.................. RobertHavlin 6 81+
(John Gosden) *led 1f: trckd ldrs: pushed along and one pce over 2f out: pushed along and styd on to chse wnr fnl 110yds but nvr any ch* **3/1**[1]

3-0 **3** *1 1/2* **Vicksburg**[27] 1671 3-8-12 0.................. JimmyFortune 12 76
(Andrew Balding) *led after 1f: rdn over 3f out: jnd over 2f out and sn hdd: kpt on wl to hold 3rd ins fnl f but no ch w ldng duo* **9/1**

446- **4** *shd* **Society Pearl (IRE)**[194] 7553 3-8-12 71.................. HarryBentley 1 76
(Charles Hills) *chsd ldrs: rdn over 2f out: kpt on fnl f but nvr any ch w wnr* **9/1**

0-3 **5** *1/2* **Fanzine**[27] 1671 3-8-12 0.................. DaneO'Neill 4 75
(Hughie Morrison) *in tch: pushed along 3f out: styd on ins fnl f: nt rch ldrs* **11/2**[3]

54- **6** *1/2* **Fast Pace**[160] 8017 3-8-12 0.................. PatDobbs 8 74
(Amanda Perrett) *chsd ldrs: chal over 2f out tl jst ins fnl 2f: wknd ins fnl f* **10/1**

7 *shd* **Oscilate Wildly (IRE)** 3-8-12 0.................. PatCosgrave 9 74
(Peter Chapple-Hyam) *in rr: pushed along 3f out: hdwy fr 2f out: styd on same pce fnl f* **40/1**

8 *1 1/2* **Madame Vestris (IRE)** 3-8-12 0.................. RichardHughes 3 71+
(Sir Michael Stoute) *s.i.s: in rr: hdwy to cl on ldrs 3f out: wknd over 1f out* **4/1**[2]

9 *3* **Sureness (IRE)** 3-8-12 0.................. NeilCallan 2 65
(Marco Botti) *in tch: pushed along over 2f out: wknd appr fnl f* **33/1**

10 *11* **Heavenly Prospect** 3-8-12 0.................. JackMitchell 7 43
(William Muir) *in rr: wd bnd 7f out: sn running green and styd bhd* **50/1**

11 *4* **Dance**[22] 4-9-5 0..................(t) PatMillman(7) 10 36
(Rod Millman) *s.i.s: a in rr* **66/1**

12 *3/4* **Pure Mischief (IRE)** 3-8-12 0.................. FrankieMcDonald 11 33
(David Lanigan) *rdn over 4f out: a in rr* **33/1**

0 **13** *19* **Fleur De Fortune**[17] 1876 6-9-5 0..................(b[1]) JoeyHaynes(7) 14
(Eric Wheeler) *a in rr* **200/1**

5 **14** *16* **Dark Rumour (IRE)**[11] 2055 3-8-12 0.................. KierenFox 13
(John Bridger) *t.k.h: rdn 5f out: a wl bhd* **200/1**

2m 10.45s (0.55) **Going Correction** +0.10s/f (Good)
WFA 3 from 4yo+ 14lb 14 Ran SP% **116.5**
Speed ratings (Par 100): **101,97,95,95,95 94,94,93,91,82 79,78,63,50**
toteswingers 1&2 £5.10, 1&3 £9.90, 2&3 £5.60 CSF £22.85 TOTE £7.90: £2.30, £1.10, £3.20; EX 26.00 Trifecta £151.00 Pool: £2333.87 - 11.58 winning units..
Owner Sir Robert Ogden **Bred** Mine Excavation Syndicate **Trained** Newmarket, Suffolk

FOCUS
There was no overnight rain and the ground was officially described as good to soft, good in places. The first division of this fillies' maiden was run 2.16secs faster than the second leg and it looked a fair heat which included a couple of expensive debutantes from high-profile stables. The pace was good and the principals raced handily. Better form than division II.

2390 BATHWICK TYRES BRITISH STALLION STUDS EBF FILLIES' H'CAP 1m 1f 198y
2:00 (2:00) (Class 4) (0-85,85) 3-Y-0 **£7,762** (£2,310; £1,154; £577) **Stalls** High

Form RPR

20-3 **1** **Contradict**[12] 2017 3-8-7 **71**.................. SamHitchcott 1 85
(Mick Channon) *hld up in rr: gd hdwy fr 3f out to ld 2f out: pushed clr fnl f: easily* **20/1**

0-51 **2** *6* **Arbaah (USA)**[14] 1955 3-8-10 **74**.................. DaneO'Neill 4 76
(Brian Meehan) *chsd ldrs: slt ld over 2f out: sn hdd: no ch w wnr appr fnl f but kpt on wl for 2nd* **7/1**[2]

1 **3** *1 3/4* **Dream Wild**[17] 1876 3-9-2 **80**.................. JamesDoyle 3 79
(Sir Michael Stoute) *hld up in tch: shkn up over 3f out: rdn over 2f out and fnd only one pce: pushed out to hold wl-hld 3rd clsng stages* **1/2**[1]

13 **4** *nk* **Lady Artiste (IRE)**[13] 1991 3-8-9 **73** ow1.................. NeilCallan 7 71
(Alan Swinbank) *sn chsng ldr: drvn to ld appr fnl 3f: hdd over 2f out: sn no ch w wnr and styd on same pce fr over 1f out* **10/1**[3]

20-0 **5** *7* **Motion Lass**[27] 1671 3-8-3 **67**.................. RichardThomas 6 51
(Ralph Beckett) *plld hrd in rr: hdwy to cl on ldrs 4f out: wknd 2f out* **7/1**[2]

030- **6** *shd* **Polly's Love (IRE)**[211] 7159 3-8-8 **72**.................. JohnFahy 2 56
(Clive Cox) *led and t.k.h: hdd appr fnl 3f: wknd 2f out* **40/1**

2m 10.55s (0.65) **Going Correction** +0.10s/f (Good) 6 Ran SP% **108.0**
Speed ratings (Par 98): **101,96,94,94,88 88**
toteswingers 1&2 £3.00, 1&3 £2.70, 2&3 £1.50 CSF £133.32 TOTE £16.70: £5.90, £2.40; EX 79.30 Trifecta £130.70 Pool: £2831.52 - 16.23 winning units..
Owner Prince A A Faisal **Bred** Nawara Stud Co Ltd **Trained** West Ilsley, Berks

FOCUS
The pace was steady in this 3yo handicap. The winner was a bit of a revelation and the form has been taken literally.

2391 DOUGLAND MAIDEN STKS 5f
2:35 (2:37) (Class 5) 2-Y-0 **£3,234** (£962; £481; £120; £120) **Stalls** Low

Form RPR

22 **1** **Beau Nash (IRE)**[27] 1659 2-9-5 0.................. RichardHughes 7 85
(Richard Hannon) *mde all: qcknd clr wl over 1f out: unchal* **1/3**[1]

0 **2** *3 1/2* **Zain Zone (IRE)**[11] 2048 2-9-5 0.................. EddieAhern 4 71+
(Gerard Butler) *chsd ldrs in 3rd: drvn 2f out: styd on to take 2nd ins fnl f but nvr any ch w wnr* **25/1**

3 *3 1/2* **Mime Dance** 2-9-5 0.................. JimmyFortune 6 59+
(Andrew Balding) *chsd wnr: rdn over 2f out and no imp: wknd into 3rd ins fnl f* **6/1**[2]

4 *4 1/2* **Know Your Name** 2-9-5 0.................. SamHitchcott 5 43
(David Evans) *in rr and sn pushed along: styd on same pce fr over 1f out* **40/1**

4 *dht* **Value (IRE)** 2-9-0 0.................. PatDobbs 3 38
(Richard Hannon) *in rr: hdwy to cl on ldrs over 2f out: nvr nr wnr and wknd fnl f* **12/1**[3]

6 *1* **Tax Enough (USA)** 2-9-5 0.................. DaneO'Neill 8 39
(Brian Meehan) *in rr: hdwy 1/2-way: wknd ins fnl 2f* **14/1**

1m 3.19s (2.19) **Going Correction** +0.10s/f (Good) 6 Ran SP% **109.9**
Speed ratings (Par 93): **86,80,74,67,67 66**
toteswingers 1&2 £2.80, 1&3 £1.10, 2&3 £5.20 CSF £11.02 TOTE £1.10: £1.02, £7.80; EX 9.40 Trifecta £25.20 Pool: £1528.55 - 45.33 winning units..
Owner The Best Turned Out Partnership **Bred** Keatly Overseas Ltd **Trained** East Everleigh, Wilts

FOCUS
Hedy was withdrawn at the start (10/1, deduct 5p in the £ under R4) and the only two runners with experience filled the first two places.

2392 CASTLEPOINT SHOPPING PARK A3060 BOURNEMOUTH MAIDEN FILLIES' STKS (DIV II) 1m 1f 198y
3:05 (3:06) (Class 5) 3-Y-0+ **£3,234** (£962; £481; £240) **Stalls** High

Form RPR

1 **Raushan (IRE)** 3-8-12 0.................. RichardHughes 3 80
(Sir Michael Stoute) *led tl hdd over 4f out: styd chsng ldr: chal 2f out: sn led: rdn ins fnl f: hld on all out* **7/1**

6-0 **2** *shd* **Lemon Pearl**[26] 1684 3-8-12 0..................[1] HarryBentley 10 79
(Ralph Beckett) *chsd ldrs: rdn to go 2nd over 1f out: styd on ins fnl f: gng on cl home: nt quite get up* **4/1**[2]

0- **3** *2 1/2* **Wadaa (USA)**[236] 6489 3-8-12 0.................. NeilCallan 6 74
(James Tate) *in tch: rdn and hdwy over 2f out: styd on to take 3rd ins fnl f: no imp on ldng duo* **6/1**

33- **4** *3 3/4* **Zeyran (IRE)**[197] 7488 4-9-12 0.................. IanMongan 8 67
(Sir Henry Cecil) *t.k.h: chsd wnr tl led over 4f out: jnd 2f out and sn hdd: wknd fnl f* **7/2**[1]

5 1 1/2 **Phiz (GER)** 3-8-12 0 ... RobertHavlin 1 63+
(John Gosden) *chsd ldrs: rdn and one pce over 2f out: styd on again fnl f* **9/2**[3]

0 6 nk **La Rosiere (USA)**[15] 1926 4-9-7 0 ... PhilipPrince(5) 4 63
(Jo Hughes) *in rr: hdwy over 3f out: rdn and hung rt over 2f out: styd on fnl f: nvr a threat* **100/1**

7 2 3/4 **Dukes Delight (IRE)** 3-8-12 0 ... ShaneKelly 2 57+
(David Lanigan) *s.i.s: in rr: pushed along over 2f out: styd on clsng stages* **33/1**

00- 8 1 1/4 **Hermosa Vaquera (IRE)**[247] 6117 3-8-12 0 ... PatCosgrave 5 54
(Peter Chapple-Hyam) *chsd ldrs: rdn 3f out: wknd fr 2f out* **20/1**

9 1 1/2 **Russian Link** 3-8-12 0 ... JamesDoyle 7 51+
(Roger Charlton) *s.i.s: in rr: mod late prog* **9/1**

0 10 8 **Faustinatheyounger (IRE)**[10] 2084 3-8-12 0 ... DaneO'Neill 12 35
(David Elsworth) *s.i.s: a in rr* **40/1**

0-0 11 7 **Crystal Mist**[28] 1636 3-8-12 0 ...[1] JimmyFortune 9 21
(Harry Dunlop) *a in rr* **12/1**

00-0 12 10 **Choisirez (IRE)**[10] 2074 4-9-5 37 ... IanBurns(7) 11
(John Panvert) *a in rr* **250/1**

00- 13 3/4 **Double Star**[211] 7165 3-8-12 0 ... JohnFahy 13
(Jonathan Portman) *bhd fnl 4f* **100/1**

0 14 11 **Map Of Love (IRE)**[27] 1666 3-8-12 0 ... SteveDrowne 14
(Jeremy Gask) *a in rr* **66/1**

2m 12.61s (2.71) **Going Correction** +0.10s/f (Good)
WFA 3 from 4yo 14lb **14 Ran SP% 118.9**
Speed ratings (Par 100): **93,92,90,87,86 86,84,83,82,75 70,62,61,52**
toteswingers 1&2 £6.90, 2&3 £6.60, 1&3 £8.40 CSF £33.62 TOTE £6.40: £2.10, £1.90, £2.50; EX 31.50 Trifecta £294.70 Pool: £3064.03 - 7.79 winning units..
Owner Nurlan Bizakov **Bred** Castlemartin Sky & Skymarc Farm **Trained** Newmarket, Suffolk

FOCUS
The pace was steady in the second division of this fillies' maiden and those ridden prominently were favoured. The weaker division with the third setting the standard.

2393 CASTLEPOINT SUPPORTS ACCESS DORSET CLAIMING STKS 6f 212y
3:40 (3:40) (Class 5) 3-Y-O **£2,749** (£818; £408; £204) **Stalls** Low

Form RPR

2562 1 **Princess Cammie (IRE)**[16] 1903 3-7-7 52 ...(p) JoeyHaynes(7) 5 58
(John Bridger) *led after 1f: pushed along over 2f out: styd on wl fnl f* **12/1**

-501 2 2 3/4 **A Ladies Man (IRE)**[16] 1903 3-9-3 73 ... RichardHughes 4 68
(Richard Hannon) *led 1f: styd chsng wnr: rdn 2f out: no imp fr over 1f out* **6/4**[1]

3-41 3 2 **Majestic Jess (IRE)**[21] 1784 3-8-13 67 ...(b[1]) JimmyFortune 6 58
(Luke Dace) *chsd ldrs: rdn over 2f out: styd on same pce for 3rd fnl f* **3/1**[3]

35-0 4 shd **Don Eduardo**[135] 5 3-8-0 53 ...(v[1]) CharlotteJenner(7) 2 52
(J S Moore) *chsd ldrs: rdn over 2f out: styd on u.p fnl f to chal for wl-hld 4th clsng stages* **50/1**

5312 5 3 **Studfarmer**[31] 1578 3-8-7 69 ...(v) SamHitchcott 8 44
(David Evans) *slowly away: in rr: hdwy u.p on rails over 2f out: sn btn* **11/4**[2]

40-0 6 3 1/2 **Symboline**[10] 2091 3-7-13 60 ... DarrenEgan(3) 7 29
(Mick Channon) *s.i.s: in rr: sme hdwy 3f out: rdn: hung rt and btn 2f out* **16/1**

-006 7 5 **Iwilsayzisonlyonce**[78] 811 3-8-9 62 ...(v[1]) SteveDrowne 3 23
(Joseph Tuite) *bhd most of way* **33/1**

06-0 8 8 **Index Waiter**[8] 2154 3-8-5 54 ...(b) MartinLane 1
(Brian Meehan) *chsd ldrs on rail: rdn: hung rt: hd high over 2f out: wknd qckly* **18/1**

1m 30.61s (2.01) **Going Correction** +0.10s/f (Good) **8 Ran SP% 115.4**
Speed ratings (Par 99): **92,88,86,86,83 79,73,64**
toteswingers 1&2 £3.90, 1&3 £4.10, 2&3 £1.60 CSF £30.85 TOTE £10.00: £1.90, £1.10, £1.80; EX 35.60 Trifecta £153.90 Pool: £3387.01 - 16.49 winning units..
Owner W Wood **Bred** Mrs M Fox **Trained** Liphook, Hants

FOCUS
A modest claimer run at an ordinary pace. Shaky form.

2394 DOUGLAND H'CAP 6f
4:15 (4:16) (Class 5) (0-75,75) 3-Y-O **£2,911** (£866; £432; £216) **Stalls** Low

Form RPR

31-0 1 **Freddy With A Y (IRE)**[31] 1582 3-9-7 75 ... GeorgeBaker 4 92
(Gary Moore) *mde virtually all: pushed along fr 2f out: drvn and hld on wl fnl f* **18/1**

6-42 2 1/2 **Extrasolar**[12] 2010 3-9-6 74 ...(t) PatDobbs 2 89
(Amanda Perrett) *chsd ldrs: wnt 2nd over 1f out: kpt on u.p but a hld by wnr* **7/2**[1]

321- 3 2 3/4 **Gracious George (IRE)**[164] 7965 3-9-5 73 ... PatCosgrave 16 79+
(Jimmy Fox) *s.i.s: in rr: swtchd lft and hdwy over 2f out and sn chsng ldrs: no ex fnl f* **20/1**

241- 4 1/2 **Whipper Snapper (IRE)**[148] 8165 3-9-7 75 ... ShaneKelly 11 80+
(William Knight) *in rr: hdwy u.p fr 2f out: kpt on clsng stages* **11/1**

00-0 5 2 **Kamchatka**[29] 1612 3-9-4 72 ...(t) JimmyFortune 3 70
(Philip Hide) *chsd ldrs: rdn over 2f out: wknd fnl f* **14/1**

20-0 6 3/4 **Rock Up (IRE)**[29] 1618 3-9-5 73 ... DaneO'Neill 7 69
(David Elsworth) *in rr: rdn and styd on fr 2f out: kpt on clsng stages but nvr any ch* **12/1**

0-13 7 nk **Top Trail (USA)**[38] 1433 3-8-13 67 ... JamesDoyle 5 62
(Roger Charlton) *in tch: hdwy on ins to cl on ldrs over 2f out: nvr on terms: wknd fnl f* **11/2**[3]

U3-3 8 1 3/4 **Millers Wharf (IRE)**[29] 1612 3-9-6 74 ... RichardHughes 12 63
(Richard Hannon) *chsd ldrs: rdn 2f out: sn btn* **4/1**[2]

1545 9 2 1/4 **Sand Boy (IRE)**[15] 1935 3-9-4 72 ... SteveDrowne 14 54
(Charles Hills) *chsd ldrs: hung rt u.p 2f out: wknd wl over 1f out* **10/1**

4413 10 3/4 **The Black Jacobin**[104] 468 3-8-10 67 ...(b) DarrenEgan(3) 6 47
(J S Moore) *in rr: rdn and sme hdwy fnl f* **25/1**

42-3 11 12 **Little Choosey**[17] 1875 3-9-2 70 ... JohnFahy 13
(Clive Cox) *chsd ldrs: wknd over 2f out* **16/1**

02-3 12 1 1/4 **Baltic Gin (IRE)**[13] 1978 3-8-8 62 ... SamHitchcott 15
(Malcolm Saunders) *chsd ldrs: rdn and wknd qckly ins fnl 2f* **22/1**

62-4 13 9 **Multitask**[122] 203 3-9-2 70 ... RobertHavlin 17
(Michael Madgwick) *pressed wnr tl over 2f out: sn wknd* **50/1**

-136 14 2 1/2 **Malaysian Boleh**[10] 2098 3-9-0 68 ... NeilCallan 9
(Simon Dow) *chsd ldrs tl wknd qckly 2f out* **12/1**

1m 15.42s (0.62) **Going Correction** +0.10s/f (Good) **14 Ran SP% 123.1**
Speed ratings (Par 99): **99,98,94,94,91 90,89,87,84,83 67,65,53,50**
toteswingers 1&2 £18.70, 1&3 £57.80, 2&3 £19.50 CSF £78.63 CT £1362.73 TOTE £24.10: £5.00, £1.90, £4.20; EX 159.90 Trifecta £1398.10 Pool: £2818.19 - 1.51 winning units..
Owner Mrs M J George **Bred** David McGuinness **Trained** Lower Beeding, W Sussex

FOCUS
A typically wide-open 3yo handicap in which the front two pulled nicely clear. The race lacked depth and progressive runners.

2395 CGA RACING EXCELLENCE APPRENTICE H'CAP (WHIPS SHALL BE CARRIED BUT NOT USED) 6f 212y
4:50 (4:51) (Class 5) (0-70,70) 4-Y-O+ **£2,911** (£866; £432; £216) **Stalls** Low

Form RPR

-051 1 **Intomist (IRE)**[21] 1783 4-8-11 65 ...(p) DanielCremin(5) 2 73
(Jim Boyle) *mde virtually all: pushed along and hld on wl fnl f: all out* **17/2**

2-21 2 shd **Ifan (IRE)**[76] 849 5-9-1 64 ... DanielMuscutt 6 72
(Tim Vaughan) *chsd ldrs: drvn and str run to press wnr fnl 110yds: styd on cl home: jst failed* **13/2**[2]

-022 3 nk **Balmoral Castle**[10] 2089 4-8-2 56 ... DavidCoyle(5) 9 66+
(Jonathan Portman) *chsd ldrs: drvn and styd on wl fnl f: clsng on ldng duo nr fin: nt quite get up* **6/1**[1]

60-6 4 3/4 **The Name Is Frank**[16] 1902 8-8-0 56 oh6 ...(t) OisinMurphy(7) 4 61
(Mark Gillard) *chsd ldrs: drvn and styd on fr over 1f out: kpt on wl clsng stages: nt quite gng pce to chal* **22/1**

-133 5 2 3/4 **South Cape**[24] 1717 10-8-6 62 ... JayneFarwell(7) 7 59
(Gary Moore) *s.i.s: hdwy 4f out: chsd ldrs 3f out: one pce fnl f* **12/1**

40-3 6 shd **Lady Bayside**[14] 1947 5-9-1 67 ... PatMillman(3) 1 64
(Malcolm Saunders) *chsd ldrs: pushed along over 2f out: kpt on fnl f but nvr gng pce to chal* **6/1**[1]

0046 7 3 1/2 **George Benjamin**[14] 1947 6-8-8 62 ...(p) JordanVaughan(5) 10 50
(Christopher Kellett) *in tch: hdwy on outside fr 3f out: styd on same pce fnl f* **16/1**

020- 8 nk **Grand Piano (IRE)**[219] 6967 6-8-4 60 ... JonathanWilletts(7) 3 47
(Andrew Balding) *in rr: pushed along and hung rt 2f out: kpt on clsng stages* **16/1**

000- 9 2 1/4 **Beach Rhythm (USA)**[338] 3012 6-8-2 56 oh3 ... JordanNason(5) 14 37
(Jim Allen) *chsd ldrs: wknd ins fnl 2f* **50/1**

40-5 10 1 **Offbeat Safaris (IRE)**[20] 1800 5-8-8 60 ... ShelleyBirkett(3) 12 38
(Ronald Harris) *slowly away: pushed along 3f out: mod late prog* **11/1**

4500 11 3/4 **Super Duplex**[13] 1985 6-8-7 61 ... SophieRalston(5) 11 37
(Pat Phelan) *s.i.s: in rr: sme late prog* **33/1**

4-03 12 1 1/2 **Shamrocked (IRE)**[19] 1819 4-9-0 68 ... RossWishart(3) 13 40
(Mick Channon) *bhd most of way* **8/1**

1000 13 3 3/4 **Lily Edge**[8] 2155 4-9-4 70 ... JoeyHaynes(3) 15 32
(John Bridger) *bhd most of way* **25/1**

0015 14 4 1/2 **The Mongoose**[5] 2281 5-8-11 63 6ex ...(t) EoinWalsh(3) 5 13
(David Evans) *chsd ldrs: wknd qckly 2f out* **15/2**[3]

66-3 15 7 **Camache Queen (IRE)**[36] 1472 5-9-5 68 ... NoraLooby 16
(Joseph Tuite) *chsd ldrs tl wknd ins fnl 3f* **20/1**

6400 16 28 **Cape Joy (IRE)**[13] 1974 4-8-7 63 ... CameronHardie(7) 8
(Richard Hannon) *early spd* **25/1**

020 17 1 1/2 **Paphos**[23] 1746 6-8-11 65 ...(v) ThomasHemsley(5) 17
(David Evans) *a in rr* **16/1**

1m 30.41s (1.81) **Going Correction** +0.10s/f (Good) **17 Ran SP% 130.7**
Speed ratings (Par 103): **93,92,92,91,88 88,84,84,81,80 79,77,73,68,60 28,26**
toteswingers 1&2 £7.90, 1&3 £14.30, 2&3 £5.50 CSF £61.54 CT £385.52 TOTE £16.10: £3.20, £1.30, £2.50, £4.20; EX 97.70 Trifecta £531.20 Pool: £2799.27 - 3.95 winning units..
Owner The Clueless Syndicate **Bred** P M Guerin **Trained** Epsom, Surrey
■ Stewards' Enquiry : Pat Millman seven-day ban: use of whip (3, 5, 7, 11 -15 June)

FOCUS
An apprentice handicap in which the riders were allowed to carry whips but were not permitted to use them. Modest form with the fourth a slight doubt.
T/Plt: £211.40 to a £1 stake. Pool: £46,952.05 - 162.10 winning tickets. T/Qpdt: £11.20 to a £1 stake. Pool: £3525.55 - 232.00 winning tickets. ST

2365 YORK (L-H)
Thursday, May 16

OFFICIAL GOING: Good changing to good to soft after race 4 (3.15) changing to soft after race 5 (3.50)
Wind: Light half behind Weather: Cloudy with sunny periods

2396 BETFRED MOBILE SPORTS STKS (H'CAP) 5f
1:45 (1:45) (Class 2) (0-105,103) 4-Y-O+ **£16,172** (£4,812; £2,405; £1,202) **Stalls** Centre

Form RPR

2-05 1 **Ancient Cross**[29] 1607 9-8-10 92 ...(t) PaulMulrennan 5 102
(Michael Easterby) *chsd ldrs: rdn along over 2f out: swtchd rt and hdwy to chal over 1f out: led ins fnl f: drvn out* **14/1**

13-0 2 nk **Goldream**[11] 2046 4-8-8 90 ... JimCrowley 15 102+
(Robert Cowell) *lw: in tch: swtchd lft over 2f out: hdwy to chse ldrs wl over 1f out: nt clr run and swtchd rt ent fnl f: sn rdn and styd on wl towards fin* **12/1**

006- 3 3/4 **Judge 'n Jury**[201] 7397 9-8-12 99 ...(t) ThomasBrown(5) 6 105
(Ronald Harris) *cl up: led 1/2-way: rdn jst over 1f out: drvn ins fnl f: sn hdd and no ex last 100yds* **12/1**

0-05 4 hd **Fitz Flyer (IRE)**[8] 2150 7-8-4 86 ...(v) JoeFanning 1 92
(David Nicholls) *chsd ldrs: hdwy 2f out: rdn over 1f out: ev ch: drvn and kpt on fnl f* **10/1**

150- 5 1/2 **Magical Macey (USA)**[298] 4367 6-9-3 99 ...(b) GrahamGibbons 2 103
(David Barron) *sn led: hdd 1/2-way: cl up and pushed along wl over 1f out: ev ch tl one pce ins fnl f* **12/1**

00-0 6 1 **Secret Witness**[1] 2366 7-9-7 103 ...(b) GrahamLee 3 103
(Ronald Harris) *lw: in tch: hdwy 2f out: sn rdn and kpt on fnl f* **16/1**

605- 7 1/2 **Dungannon**[176] 7817 6-8-11 93 ... RyanMoore 10 91+
(Andrew Balding) *sltly hmpd s and in rr: pushed along 1/2-way: styd on fnl 2f: nrst fin* **6/1**[1]

0-41 8 nk **Bedloe's Island (IRE)**[12] 2031 8-8-4 86 ... SilvestreDeSousa 14 83
(David O'Meara) *lw: midfield: rdn along and sltly outpcd 2f out: hdwy over 1f out: kpt on u.p fnl f* **7/1**[2]

32-1 9 1 1/4 **Cheworee**[31] 1581 4-8-4 86 ... PaulHanagan 4 79+
(David Elsworth) *s.i.s and bhd: hdwy and in tch 1/2-way: rdn to chse ldrs on outer 2f out: wknd over 1f out* **7/1**[2]

300- 10 1 **Ponty Acclaim (IRE)**[201] 7397 4-8-12 94 ... DavidAllan 18 83
(Tim Easterby) *in tch: rdn along over 2f out: grad wknd* **14/1**

310- 11 1/2 **Dinkum Diamond (IRE)**[257] 5822 5-9-6 102 ... CathyGannon 8 89
(Henry Candy) *chsd ldrs: rdn along 1/2-way: sn wknd* **12/1**

0-16 12 1 **Mister Manannan (IRE)**[8] 2150 6-8-9 91 ... AdrianNicholls 17 75
(David Nicholls) *dwlt: sn in tch: hdwy to chse ldrs 2f out: sn rdn and wknd ent fnl f* **8/1**[3]

00-0 **13** ¾ **Hazelrigg (IRE)**[12] 2007 8-8-3 **85** JamesSullivan 7 66
(Tim Easterby) *chsd ldrs 2f: sn lost pl and bhd* **33/1**

0-00 **14** *nk* **Cheviot (USA)**[119] 244 7-9-6 **102** PhillipMakin 12 82
(Kevin Ryan) *sltly hmpd s: a in rr* **16/1**

60-0 **15** *3 ¼* **Last Bid**[29] 1607 4-8-2 **84** DuranFentiman 13 52
(Tim Easterby) *towards rr: effrt and sme hdwy 1/2-way: sn rdn and wknd* **33/1**

58.09s (-1.21) **Going Correction** 0.0s/f (Good) **15** Ran SP% **121.2**
Speed ratings (Par 109): **109,108,107,107,106 104,103,103,101,99 98,97,96,95,90**
toteswingers 1&2 £58.10, 1&3 £55.20, 2&3 £51.30 CSF £172.57 CT £2123.16 TOTE £16.90: £4.70, £4.20, £3.20; EX 231.10 Trifecta £2121.80 Part won. Pool: £2829.07 - 0.19 winning units..

Owner Pete Bown,BackUp Technology & Steve Hull **Bred** Darley **Trained** Sheriff Hutton, N Yorks

FOCUS
Course at normal configuration and all distances as advertised. The ground had dried out from the previous day and was described as "good, lovely ground" by Duran Fentiman, while David Allan felt it was "a little loose on top". GoingStick readings were as follows: far side 7.4, middle 7.5 and stands' side 7.3. The rail was on the traditional inside line around the home bend. All the pace was down the centre of the track in a race where it proved tough to make ground. The winner is rated to last year's form but the second is unlucky.

2397 BETFRED MIDDLETON STKS (GROUP 2) (F&M) 1m 2f 88y
2:15 (2:18) (Class 1) 4-Y-0+

£56,710 (£21,500; £10,760; £5,360; £2,690; £1,350) **Stalls** Low

Form RPR

15-4 **1** **Dalkala (USA)**[39] 1420 4-9-0 112 Christophe-PatriceLemaire 3 111
(A De Royer-Dupre, France) *trckd ldrs: smooth hdwy 3f out: led wl over 1f out: rdn and kpt on wl fnl f* **2/1**[1]

150- **2** *1* **Ambivalent (IRE)**[221] 6911 4-8-12 101 RyanMoore 5 107
(Roger Varian) *t.k.h: hld up in tch: hdwy on inner 3f out: effrt wl over 1f out: rdn to chal ent fnl f: sn edgd rt: kpt on same pce* **8/1**

124- **3** *nk* **Ladys First**[230] 6633 4-8-12 103 PaulHanagan 4 106
(Richard Fahey) *trckd ldr: hdwy over 3f out: cl up wl over 2f out: rdn and ev ch wl over 1f out: drvn and kpt on same pce ins fnl f* **8/1**

324- **4** ½ **Starscope**[313] 3879 4-8-12 109 WilliamBuick 8 105
(John Gosden) *hld up towards rr: hdwy 3f out: effrt on outer over 2f out: sn rdn and sltly outpcd: kpt on u.p fnl f: nrst fin* **11/2**[3]

021- **5** *1 ¼* **Cubanita**[187] 7688 4-8-12 102 JimCrowley 2 103
(Ralph Beckett) *trckd ldng pair: hdwy over 3f out: led wl over 2f out: sn rdn and hdd wl over 1f out: grad wknd* **10/3**[2]

205- **6** *nk* **Emirates Queen**[239] 6379 4-8-12 108 KierenFallon 6 103
(Luca Cumani) *dwlt and in rr: hdwy over 3f out: rdn along 2f out: drvn and no imp fnl f* **7/1**

15-0 **7** *5* **Semayyel (IRE)**[11] 2045 4-8-12 105 FrederikTylicki 7 93
(Clive Brittain) *lw: hld up towards rr: sme hdwy over 3f out: rdn along wl over 2f out: sn outpcd* **33/1**

40/5 **8** *1* **Negotiate**[10] 2105 5-8-12 88 PatSmullen 1 91?
(Ms Joanna Morgan, Ire) *lw: led: rdn along over 3f out: hdd wl over 2f out and sn wknd* **66/1**

2m 12.43s (-0.07) **Going Correction** +0.20s/f (Good) **8** Ran SP% **111.0**
Speed ratings (Par 115): **108,107,106,106,105 105,101,100**
toteswingers 1&2 £3.30, 1&3 £3.80, 2&3 £6.40 CSF £17.71 TOTE £2.10: £1.10, £2.70, £2.20; EX 19.50 Trifecta £132.20 Pool: £20,285.43 - 115.04 winning units..

Owner H H Aga Khan **Bred** His Highness The Aga Khan Studs Sc **Trained** Chantilly, France

FOCUS
Some quality fillies have landed this contest in recent seasons including Izzi Top last year, Midday (2011) and Sariska (2010) but, at this stage, it's difficult to know how classy this renewal was considering their overall profile - only the French-trained filly had won at Group level previously. Both Emirates Queen and Starscope were loaded, by design, into the stalls without their jockeys on. The early fractions weren't quick but the tempo lifted on turning in. The form is rated around the winner, who set a good standard.

2398 BETFRED DANTE STKS (GROUP 2) 1m 2f 88y
2:45 (2:46) (Class 1) 3-Y-0

£85,065 (£32,250; £16,140; £8,040; £4,035; £2,025) **Stalls** Low

Form RPR

14 **1** **Libertarian**[20] 1811 3-9-0 94 WilliamBuick 4 114
(Mrs K Burke) *towards rr and sn pushed along: rdn along 3f out: hdwy on outer wl over 1f out: shkn up to chal ent fnl f: sn rdn and led last 100yds: kpt on strly* **33/1**

215- **2** *1 ¼* **Trading Leather (IRE)**[201] 7398 3-9-0 106 KevinManning 1 112
(J S Bolger, Ire) *lw: trckd ldr: hdwy and cl up 3f out: rdn 2f out and sltly outpcd: styd on wl u.p ent fnl f and sn ev ch: no ex towards fin* **5/1**[3]

1 **3** ¾ **Indian Chief (IRE)**[31] 1587 3-9-0 0 JosephO'Brien 2 110+
(A P O'Brien, Ire) *tall: unf: scope: hld up in rr: hdwy wl over 2f out: trckd ldrs over 1f out: sn n.m.r and swtchd lft 1f out: rdn to ld briefly wl ins fnl f: hdd last 100yds: no ex towards fin* **11/4**[1]

51-3 **4** *1 ¼* **Ghurair (USA)**[28] 1636 3-9-0 110 PaulHanagan 5 108
(John Gosden) *trckd ldrs: hdwy over 3f out: slt ld 2f out: rdn over 1f out: edgd rt: hdd ins fnl f: sn drvn and wknd* **9/2**[2]

1-11 **5** *1* **Windhoek**[12] 2023 3-9-0 104 JoeFanning 8 106
(Mark Johnston) *lw: trckd ldng pair: hdwy and cl up 3f out: rdn 2f out and ev ch tl drvn and wknd jst ins fnl f* **11/2**

1-13 **6** *3 ¼* **Secret Number**[47] 1264 3-9-0 109 SilvestreDeSousa 6 100
(Saeed bin Suroor) *hld up in tch: hdwy 3f out: chsd ldrs 2f out: sn rdn and btn over 1f out* **15/2**

31-2 **7** *1 ¾* **Greatwood**[28] 1636 3-9-0 103 KierenFallon 3 97
(Luca Cumani) *s.i.s and niggled along in rr: hdwy 3f out: effrt on wd outside 2f out: sn rdn and btn* **9/2**[2]

31-5 **8** *hd* **Dashing Star**[19] 1847 3-9-0 83 LiamKeniry 7 96
(David Elsworth) *led: qcknd 4f out: rdn 3f out: hdd 2f out and sn wknd* **80/1**

2m 10.59s (-1.91) **Going Correction** +0.20s/f (Good) **8** Ran SP% **111.0**
Speed ratings (Par 111): **115,114,113,112,111 109,107,107**
toteswingers 1&2 £21.60, 1&3 £9.20, 2&3 £3.40 CSF £178.95 TOTE £36.20: £4.60, £1.90, £1.60; EX 200.80 Trifecta £1524.80 Pool: £4268.76 - 2.09 winning units..

Owner Hubert John Strecker **Bred** Serpentine Bloodstock Ltd **Trained** Middleham Moor, N Yorks

FOCUS
The premier British Derby trial of recent times, with North Light (2004), Motivator ('05) and Authorized ('07) having gone on to Epsom glory the following month. This looked the last chance for a legitimate home-trained Derby contender to emerge, but it wasn't to be, as although the shock winner is British-trained, it's a tough race to assess and one can't imagine this form is going to be good enough come the first Saturday in June. Libertarian is just about the pick of the British trial winners this year, though rates a bnThey got racing a fair way out alow-par Dante winner. It turned into a thorough test at the distance, the time not being far off two seconds quicker than the previous Group 2 for older fillies.

2399 BETFRED HAMBLETON STKS (H'CAP) (LISTED RACE) 1m
3:15 (3:17) (Class 1) (0-110,106) 4-Y-0+

£20,982 (£7,955; £3,981; £1,983; £995; £499) **Stalls** Low

Form RPR

400- **1** **Navajo Chief**[201] 7407 6-9-1 **100** MichaelJMMurphy 16 110
(Alan Jarvis) *trckd ldrs: hdwy over 2f out: rdn to ld appr fnl f: drvn and kpt on wl* **12/1**

06-0 **2** *1 ½* **Prince Of Johanne (IRE)**[47] 1235 7-9-1 **100** (p) RobertWinston 14 107
(Tom Tate) *a.p: cl up 1/2-way: rdn and slt ld over 2f out: hdd 1 1/2f out: styd cl up and ev ch: drvn ins fnl f and kpt on same pce towards fin* **16/1**

0-02 **3** *shd* **Anderiego (IRE)**[12] 2029 5-8-10 **95** GrahamGibbons 11 101
(David O'Meara) *lw: midfield: hdwy 3f out: rdn 2f out: n.m.r over 1f out: kpt on wl u.p fnl f* **10/1**

213 **4** *hd* **Two For Two (IRE)**[12] 2029 5-9-1 **100** DanielTudhope 7 106
(David O'Meara) *trckd ldrs on inner: hdwy 3f out: effrt 2f out: sn rdn and ev ch tl drvn and one pce ins fnl f* **7/2**[1]

0-30 **5** *nk* **Brae Hill (IRE)**[26] 1675 7-8-12 **97** JamieSpencer 6 102
(Richard Fahey) *hld up in rr: swtchd rt and hdwy 2f out: sn rdn and styd on strly fnl f: nrest fin* **9/1**[3]

000- **6** *1* **Moran Gra (USA)**[229] 6674 6-8-12 **97** (p) PatSmullen 15 100
(Ms Joanna Morgan, Ire) *trckd ldrs: hdwy and cl up 3f out: rdn to chal 2f out: led briefly 1 1/2f out: sn hdd: drvn and wknd fnl f* **16/1**

1-40 **7** ½ **Justonefortheroad**[26] 1675 7-8-10 **95** PaulHanagan 13 97
(Richard Fahey) *hld up towards rr: hdwy 3f out: rdn to chse ldrs over 1f out: kpt on fnl f: nrst fin* **16/1**

-600 **8** *1 ½* **Dance And Dance (IRE)**[12] 2018 7-8-11 **96** JoeFanning 9 103+
(Ed Vaughan) *lw: dwlt and hld up in rr: hdwy over 2f out: swtchd towards inner and effrt whn nt clr run appr fnl f: no ch after* **20/1**

213- **9** *1* **Sound Hearts (USA)**[222] 6877 4-8-12 **97** WilliamBuick 8 93
(Roger Varian) *trckd ldrs: hdwy 3f out: rdn along 2f out: sn no imp* **9/1**[3]

/11- **10** *4 ½* **Fort Bastion (IRE)**[364] 2198 4-9-7 **106** RyanMoore 1 92
(Ed Dunlop) *lw: a towards rr* **4/1**[2]

0106 **11** *1* **Es Que Love (IRE)**[19] 1830 4-9-1 **100** SilvestreDeSousa 2 83
(Mark Johnston) *in tch on inner: effrt and hdwy over 3f out: rdn along wl over 2f out: sn wknd* **12/1**

10-4 **12** *1 ¼* **Set The Trend**[26] 1691 7-9-5 **104** DavidNolan 4 84
(David O'Meara) *trckd ldr: hdwy and cl up over 3f out: rdn along over 2f out: sn wknd* **25/1**

32-0 **13** *5* **Beacon Lodge (IRE)**[26] 1691 8-9-4 **103** FMBerry 3 72
(David Nicholls) *dwlt: a in rr* **50/1**

0-60 **14** *18* **Marcret (ITY)**[47] 1241 6-9-4 **103** (t) AndreaAtzeni 10
(Marco Botti) *led: rdn along 3f out: hdd over 2f out: sn wknd* **20/1**

0-10 **15** *1* **St Moritz (IRE)**[12] 2029 7-8-10 **95** AdrianNicholls 5
(David Nicholls) *midfield: hdwy on inner 3f out: rdn along to chse ldrs over 2f out: sn wknd* **25/1**

1m 39.64s (0.64) **Going Correction** +0.40s/f (Good) **15** Ran SP% **123.5**
Speed ratings (Par 111): **112,110,110,110,109 108,108,106,105,101 100,99,94,76,75**
totesrifecta £1,263.70 Swingers 1&2 £50.00, 1&3 £14.90, 2&3 £36.10 CSF £180.76 CT £1258.66 TOTE £15.90: £3.70, £4.30, £3.70; EX 144.70 Trifecta £1263.70 Pool: £5992.59 - 3.55 winning units..

Owner Geoffrey Bishop **Bred** Eurostrait Ltd **Trained** Twyford, Bucks

FOCUS
A field worthy of the level but a lot of those who were involved at the end didn't appear particularly well handicapped. The race took place in heavy rain but the gallop appeared good. All of the runners kept towards the inside rail on turning in. Solid form, the winner rated back to last June's win here.

2400 BRITISH STALLION STUDS SUPPORTING BRITISH RACING EBF CONDITIONS STKS 5f
3:50 (3:54) (Class 2) 3-Y-0 **£19,407** (£5,775; £2,886; £1,443) **Stalls** Centre

Form RPR

-123 **1** **Smoothtalkinrascal (IRE)**[11] 2039 3-9-2 99 DanielTudhope 2 101+
(David O'Meara) *lw: hld up: hdwy on outer wl over 1f out: rdn appr fnl f: styd on strly to ld on line* **5/2**[2]

5-32 **2** *nse* **Lucky Beggar (IRE)**[11] 2039 3-9-2 100 RyanMoore 8 101
(Charles Hills) *led: rdn and qcknd over 1f out: drvn ins fnl f: edgd lft and hdd on line* **11/4**[3]

015- **3** *hd* **Cosmic Chatter**[264] 5601 3-9-2 99 GrahamGibbons 3 100
(David Barron) *trckd ldrs: hdwy 2f out: rdn to chse ldr ins fnl f: ev ch tl drvn and no ex nr fin* **16/1**

1-11 **4** *2 ¾* **Polski Max**[11] 2039 3-9-2 97 PaulHanagan 7 90
(Richard Fahey) *trckd ldng pair: hdwy over 2f out and sn pushed along: rdn wl over 1f out: one pce fnl f* **5/4**[1]

25-3 **5** *2* **Mary's Daughter**[47] 1249 3-8-11 95 TonyHamilton 6 78
(Richard Fahey) *cl up: rdn along wl over 1f out: grad wknd appr fnl f* **14/1**

1m 1.84s (2.54) **Going Correction** +0.60s/f (Yiel) **5** Ran SP% **112.2**
Speed ratings (Par 105): **103,102,102,98,95**
CSF £9.94 TOTE £3.30: £1.80, £1.80; EX 11.00 Trifecta £62.20 Pool: £3728.14 - 44.95 winning units..

Owner Middleham Park Racing XXXVIII **Bred** Tony Kilduff **Trained** Nawton, N Yorks

■ Morawij (13/2), Fire Eyes (8/1) & Sound Of Guns (11/4) all w/d - unsuitable ground. Deduct 10p in the £ R4. New market formed.

FOCUS
Following a spell of heavy rain, the ground was changed to good to soft prior to this contest. Arguably the three key players were withdrawn due the softening ground, but this still looked quite a trappy 3yo sprint and there was very little between the first three, who drew a little way on from the favourite, at the line. The runner-up helps set the standard.

2401 STRATFORD PLACE STUD FOR ROYAL ASCOT 2YOS EBF MAIDEN STKS 6f
4:25 (4:28) (Class 3) 2-Y-0 **£9,703** (£2,887; £1,443; £721) **Stalls** Centre

Form RPR

1 **Parbold (IRE)** 2-9-5 0 TonyHamilton 10 81+
(Richard Fahey) *unf: scope: lw: a.p: cl up over 2f out: rdn to ld over 1f out: edgd lft and kpt on wl fnl f* **10/3**[1]

2 3/4 **Art Official (IRE)** 2-9-5 0 JoeFanning 13 79+
(Richard Hannon) *w'like: scope: lw: trckd ldrs: hdwy and cl up 2f out: rdn and ev ch ent fnl f: kpt on same pce towards fin* **20/1**

3 3/4 **Tiger Twenty Two** 2-9-2 0 LeeTopliss(3) 1 77
(Richard Fahey) *w'like: outpcd and rdn along in rr after 2f: edgd rt 1/2-way: rdn and swtchd rt 2f out: styd on wl u.p fnl f: tk 3rd on line* **40/1**

4 shd **Sleeper King (IRE)** 2-9-5 0 PhillipMakin 2 76+
(Kevin Ryan) *unf: cl up: led 1/2-way: rdn and jnd 2f out: hdd and drvn appr fnl f: edgd lft and kpt on same pce fnl f: lost 3rd nr line* **12/1**

3 5 1 **Augusta Ada**[10] 2075 2-9-0 0 PaulMulrennan 8 68
(Ollie Pears) *cmpt: trckd ldrs: hdwy 2f out: rdn to chse ldrs appr fnl f: kpt on same pce* **33/1**

3 6 1 **Bounty Hunter (IRE)**[26] 1680 2-9-5 0 RichardKingscote 4 70
(Tom Dascombe) *w'like: chsd ldrs: rdn along 2f out: one pce appr fnl f* **7/1**[3]

7 hd **Zac Brown (IRE)** 2-9-5 0 GrahamGibbons 5 70
(David Barron) *leggy: t.k.h early: chsd ldrs: rdn along 2f out: grad wknd* **16/1**

2 8 nk **Tanseeb**[13] 1989 2-9-5 0 PaulHanagan 7 69
(Mark Johnston) *w'like: str: led: hdd 1/2-way: cl up tl rdn: edgd rt and wknd over 1f out* **9/2**[2]

9 2 3/4 **Dream And Search (GER)** 2-9-5 0 JamieSpencer 6 60+
(Charles Hills) *w'like: str: in rr: hdwy and in tch 1/2-way: rdn over 2f out: sn wknd* **8/1**

10 2 1/2 **Humour (IRE)** 2-9-5 0 WilliamBuick 14 53
(Roger Varian) *str: chsd ldrs: rdn along wl over 2f out: sn wknd* **7/1**[3]

2 11 3 1/4 **Musical Molly (IRE)**[12] 2005 2-9-0 0 TomEaves 15 38
(Brian Ellison) *leggy: chsd ldrs on wd outside: rdn along over 2f out: sn wknd* **12/1**

12 6 **Exceed And Exceed** 2-9-5 0 RyanMoore 3 25
(Richard Hannon) *lw: a towards rr: bhd fr 1/2-way* **7/1**[3]

13 7 **Two Tykes** 2-9-5 0 JamesSullivan 12 4
(Michael Easterby) *leggy: s.i.s: a bhd* **66/1**

14 2 3/4 **Oscuro** 2-9-5 0 DuranFentiman 9
(Tim Easterby) *w'like: chsd ldrs: rdn along bef 1/2-way: sn wknd* **50/1**

1m 15.87s (3.97) **Going Correction** +0.60s/f (Yiel) **14 Ran SP% 124.7**
Speed ratings (Par 97): **97,96,95,94,93 92,91,91,87,84 80,72,62,59**
toteswingers 1&2 £15.60, 1&3 £23.40, 2&3 £49.00 CSF £79.32 TOTE £4.10: £2.00, £5.80, £6.30; EX 79.20 Trifecta £1464.90 Pool: £5006.49 - 2.56 winning units..
Owner David W Armstrong **Bred** Tony Cosgrave **Trained** Musley Bank, N Yorks

FOCUS
The ground was changed to soft prior to this race. A lot of previous winners of this never went on to land another contest, although the odd decent type emerges, most notably Lord Shanakill in 2008, so this year's winner is one to treat with caution up in Class. The going was changed to soft prior to the off.

2402 INVESTEC SPECIALIST BANK STKS (H'CAP) 2m 88y
5:00 (5:00) (Class 3) (0-90,89) 4-Y-0+ **£9,703** (£2,887; £1,443; £721) **Stalls** Low

Form RPR

006/ 1 **Well Sharp**[168] 6497 5-9-7 **85** FMBerry 9 101
(Jonjo O'Neill) *hld up towards rr: stdy hdwy on outer 5f out: trckd ldrs 3f out: smooth hdwy and cl up 2f out: rdn to ld appr fnl f: sn clr: styd on strly* **16/1**

1-20 2 6 **Moidore**[19] 1841 4-9-9 **89** PatSmullen 13 98
(John Quinn) *trckd ldrs: hdwy on outer 5f out: cl up 3f out: led over 2f out: rdn and hdd appr fnl f: sn drvn and kpt on: no ch w wnr* **14/1**

20-5 3 4 1/2 **Come Here Yew (IRE)**[40] 1390 5-8-6 **73** NeilFarley(3) 8 77
(Declan Carroll) *hld up in rr: hdwy on wd outside 3f out: rdn 2f out: styd on u.p: nrst fin* **16/1**

231- 4 nk **Mashaari (IRE)**[49] 7068 4-9-8 **88** GrahamLee 17 91
(Brian Ellison) *a pominent: trckd ldr 10f out: cl up over 4f out: led over 3f out: rdn and hdd over 2f out: drvn over 1f out and sn one pce* **13/2**[2]

100- 5 2 3/4 **Cloudy Spirit**[28] 4697 8-9-1 **79** PaulMulrennan 14 79
(Andrew Hollinshead) *hld up in rr: hdwy 4f out: rdn along wl over 2f out: styd on appr fnl f: n.d* **14/1**

6463 6 2 1/4 **Mica Mika (IRE)**[11] 2040 5-8-12 **81** GeorgeChaloner(5) 11 78
(Richard Fahey) *in tch: hdwy to trck ldrs 5f out: effrt 3f out: rdn and ev ch 2f out: sn drvn and wknd over 1f out* **14/1**

400- 7 1/2 **Dark Ranger**[195] 7522 7-9-2 **80** AndreaAtzeni 16 77
(Tim Pitt) *hld up towards rr: hdwy 4f out: rdn along 3f out: plugged on u.p fnl 2f: nvr a factor* **12/1**

02-1 8 1 **Hidden Justice (IRE)**[37] 1445 4-9-3 **83** MichaelO'Connell 2 78
(John Quinn) *in tch: hdwy to trck ldrs 5f out: swtchd lft to inner over 2f out: sn rdn and no imp* **7/2**[1]

0-33 9 4 **Flashman**[12] 2009 4-8-11 **77** TonyHamilton 5 68
(Richard Fahey) *trckd ldrs: pushed along and lost pl 5f out: n.d after* **10/1**[3]

1-51 10 12 **Fleur De La Vie (IRE)**[24] 1733 4-8-13 **84** ThomasBrown(5) 1 60
(Ralph Beckett) *nvr bttr than midfield* **16/1**

530- 11 2 1/4 **Harrison's Cave**[207] 7280 5-9-10 **88** JamieSpencer 6 62
(Chris Grant) *hld up and bhd: sme hdwy on wd outside 4f out: rdn along over 3f out: nvr a factor* **33/1**

4-44 12 4 1/2 **The Fun Crusher**[36] 1463 5-9-4 **82** DavidAllan 12 50
(Tim Easterby) *prom: rdn along 4f out: wknd 3f out: bhd and eased fnl 2f* **12/1**

3-64 13 11 **Eagle Rock (IRE)**[20] 1805 5-9-1 **79** MickyFenton 4 34
(Tom Tate) *led 3f: prom tl rdn along 4f out: sn wknd* **12/1**

30-4 14 14 **Dazinski**[19] 1841 7-9-9 **87** RobertWinston 3 25
(Mark H Tompkins) *chsd ldrs on inner: rdn along over 5f out: sn wknd: bhd and eased fnl 2f* **20/1**

2-33 15 9 **Chancery (USA)**[12] 2030 5-8-13 **77** DanielTudhope 15
(David O'Meara) *chsd ldrs: led after 3f: pushed along 5f out: rdn and hdd over 3f out: sn wknd: bhd and eased fnl 2f* **10/1**[3]

3m 44.39s (9.89) **Going Correction** +0.80s/f (Soft)
WFA 4 from 5yo+ 2lb **15 Ran SP% 122.2**
Speed ratings (Par 107): **107,104,101,101,100 99,98,98,96,90 89,86,81,74,69**
toteswingers 1&2 £40.70, 1&3 £77.30, 2&3 £58.10 CSF £225.70 CT £3632.65 TOTE £14.50: £4.50, £6.60, £4.60; EX 511.10 Trifecta £2196.20 Part won. Pool: £2928.37 - 0.21 winning units..
Owner John P McManus **Bred** Equibreed S R L **Trained** Cheltenham, Gloucs

FOCUS
Run in a heavy downpour, they didn't go overly quick, but it was a good test in the conditions and the runners predictably finished quite well strung out. The winner was on a good mark back on the Flat.
T/Jkpt: Not won. T/Plt: £938.30 to a £1 stake. Pool: £203,030.90 - 157.95 winning tickets.
T/Qpdt: £139.60 to a £1 stake. Pool: £12,614.28 - 66.85 winning tickets. JR

LE CROISE-LAROCHE
Thursday, May 16

OFFICIAL GOING: Turf: good to soft

2403a PRIX DE MARQUETTE (CONDITIONS) (3YO) (TURF) 1m 4f 110y
11:30 (12:00) 3-Y-0 **£9,756** (£3,902; £2,926; £1,951; £975)

RPR

1 **Mu Tazz (FR)**[15] 3-9-0 0 ChristopheSoumillon 4 81
(Y Fouin, France) **1/1**[1]

2 3 **Baz (FR)**[12] 2034 3-9-3 0 MarcLerner(3) 2 82
(F-H Graffard, France) **41/10**[3]

3 1/2 **Onkenbayasowaka (FR)**[20] 3-8-11 0 AntoineCoutier(4) 3 76
(S Kobayashi, France) **10/1**

4 2 **Starry Night (FR)**[43] 3-9-3 0 TheoBachelot 6 75
(S Wattel, France) **2/1**[2]

5 1 3/4 **Azabitmour (FR)**[19] 1850 3-8-11 0 Pierre-CharlesBoudot 1 66
(John Best) *broke wl: sn led: under restraint: j. path on first circ: maintained ld into fnlng st: hdd 250yds out: no ex u.p: styd on one pce* **28/1**

6 3 **Salut Gabriel (FR)**[139] 3-8-10 0 MathieuTavaresDaSilva(4) 5 65
(S Jesus, France) **26/1**

2m 44.8s (164.80) **6 Ran SP% 119.2**
WIN (incl. 1 euro stake): 2.00. PLACES: 1.30, 1.90. SF: 6.60.
Owner H H Sheikh Abdulla Bin Khalifa Al Thani **Bred** Sheikh Abdulla Bin Khalifa Al Thani **Trained** France

2217 HAMILTON (R-H)
Friday, May 17

OFFICIAL GOING: Good to soft (7.7)
Wind: Light, half against Weather: Cloudy

2404 BRITISH STALLION STUDS SUPPORTING BRITISH RACING EBF MAIDEN STKS 5f 4y
5:45 (5:45) (Class 5) 2-Y-O **£3,881** (£1,155; £577; £288) **Stalls** High

Form RPR

1 **Good Old Boy Lukey** 2-8-13 0 LeeTopliss(3) 6 79+
(Richard Fahey) *dwlt: sn chsng ldrs: rdn to ld appr fnl f: kpt on strly* **6/4**[1]

2 3 1/4 **Thornaby Nash** 2-9-2 0 DavidNolan 4 68+
(David O'Meara) *in tch: rn green after 2f: effrt and hdwy over 1f out: styd on wl to take 2nd towards fin: no ch w wnr* **4/1**[2]

42 3 1/2 **Robynelle**[20] 1820 2-9-0 0 AdrianNicholls 5 64
(Keith Dalgleish) *led: rdn: hung rt and hdd appr fnl f: kpt on same pce last 150yds* **4/1**[2]

4 5 **Luckys Connoisseur** 2-9-2 0 JoeFanning 1 48
(Mark Johnston) *trckd ldr tl rdn and wknd over 1f out* **7/1**

5 9 **Jimmy Crackle (IRE)** 2-9-2 0 BarryMcHugh 2 15
(Brian Ellison) *s.i.s: bhd and sn struggling: nvr on terms* **18/1**

6 11 **Touch The Clouds** 2-8-13 0 JulieBurke(3) 3
(Kevin Ryan) *sddle slipped sn after s and hung bdly rt: sn lost tch: t.o* **13/2**[3]

1m 2.65s (2.65) **Going Correction** +0.40s/f (Good) **6 Ran SP% 111.1**
Speed ratings (Par 93): **94,88,88,80,65 48**
toteswingers 1&2 £1.30, 1&3 £1.40, 2&3 £2.30 CSF £7.53 TOTE £2.30: £1.30, £2.20; EX 8.20 Trifecta £21.00 Pool: £1374.79 - 49.05 winning units..
Owner Leods Contracts Limited **Bred** Mrs Sarah Hamilton **Trained** Musley Bank, N Yorks
■ Stewards' Enquiry : Julie Burke jockey said saddle slipped leaving stalls.

FOCUS
Races on round course increased in distance by approximately 25yds. A small-field juvenile event. The winner was quite impressive in a race that may not have had much depth.

2405 NAKED GROUSE OPEN MAIDEN STKS 1m 1f 36y
6:15 (6:15) (Class 5) 3-Y-O+ **£3,234** (£962; £481; £240) **Stalls** Low

Form RPR

3-4 1 **Chevalgris**[13] 2027 3-9-0 0 RobertWinston 1 82
(Alan Swinbank) *hld up on ins: effrt and hdwy over 2f out: drvn and kpt on wl fnl f: led nr fin* **9/2**[3]

43-2 2 nk **Pacific Heights (IRE)**[12] 2041 4-9-13 74 BarryMcHugh 2 83
(Brian Ellison) *trckd ldrs: led and qcknd over 2f out: kpt on u.p fnl f: hdd nr fin* **10/3**[2]

-324 3 3 **Eric The Grey (IRE)**[16] 1934 3-8-11 72 LeeTopliss(3) 5 74
(Richard Fahey) *t.k.h early: prom: effrt whn nt clr run but squeezed through over 2f out: sn drvn: kpt on same pce fnl f* **11/8**[1]

65 4 7 **Wadacre Sarko**[31] 1595 3-9-0 0 MichaelStainton 8 59
(Mark Johnston) *hld up: drvn and outpcd over 4f out: styd on fnl 2f: nvr able to chal* **22/1**

40 5 nse **Bonnie Echo**[6] 2279 6-9-1 0 ConnorBeasley(7) 6 56
(Michael Dods) *stdd s: hld up: hdwy and prom over 3f out: wknd over 1f out* **25/1**

2 6 1/2 **Tinctoria**[29] 1648 3-8-6 0 JulieBurke(3) 4 53
(Kevin Ryan) *led at ordinary gallop: rdn and hdd over 2f out: wknd over 1f out* **10/1**

46-0 7 15 **Amelia Jay**[23] 1764 3-8-9 50 DuranFentiman 7 20
(Danielle McCormick) *hld up in tch: stdy hdwy and cl up over 3f out: wknd over 2f out* **66/1**

-002 8 13 **Mojave Desert (IRE)**[16] 1931 3-8-9 68 JoeFanning 3
(Mark Johnston) *cl up: pushed along whn bmpd over 2f out: sn lost pl and struggling* **7/1**

2m 3.32s (3.62) **Going Correction** +0.40s/f (Good)
WFA 3 from 4yo+ 13lb **8 Ran SP% 114.6**
Speed ratings (Par 103): **99,98,96,89,89 87,76,64**
toteswingers 1&2 £4.00, 1&3 £3.00, 2&3 £1.70 CSF £19.57 TOTE £5.50: £1.40, £1.70, £1.10; EX 29.80 Trifecta £73.40 Pool: £1645.21 - 16.79 winning units..
Owner Ms A Findlay **Bred** Castlemartin Sky & Skymarc Farm **Trained** Melsonby, N Yorks
■ Stewards' Enquiry : Lee Topliss two-day ban; careless riding (3rd-4th June).

FOCUS
Fair form from the principals in this maiden. The winner built on his Thirsk reappearance.

2406 SAINTS & SINNERS RACENIGHT IN JUNE H'CAP 1m 65y
6:50 (6:50) (Class 5) (0-75,80) 4-Y-O+ £3,408 (£1,006; £503) Stalls Low

Form RPR
06-1 1 **Coral Sands (IRE)**[12] 2042 5-8-7 **60** 6ex AndrewMullen 2 69
(Alan Swinbank) *t.k.h early: trckd ldr: effrt 2f out: led ent fnl f: rdn and r.o wl* **7/1**
60-1 2 1 1/4 **Never Forever**[9] 2162 4-8-12 **65** 6ex AndrewElliott 9 71+
(George Moore) *hld up: rdn and hdwy 2f out: sn edgd lft: kpt on strly fnl f: tk 2nd towards fin: no ch w wnr* **7/2[1]**
5002 3 1 **Cono Zur (FR)**[6] 2278 6-8-12 **65** JamesSullivan 4 69
(Ruth Carr) *led at modest gallop: rdn over 2f out: hdd ent fnl f: kpt on same pce: lost 2nd towards fin* **4/1[2]**
1004 4 1 1/2 **Dakota Canyon (IRE)**[16] 1932 4-9-2 **72** (b) LeeTopliss(3) 6 72
(Richard Fahey) *in tch: drvn and outpcd wl over 2f out: rallied fnl f: kpt on: nvr able to chal* **13/2**
0-05 5 1/2 **Running Reef (IRE)**[22] 1788 4-8-7 **60** oh3 BarryMcHugh 5 59
(Tracy Waggott) *trckd ldrs: effrt and ev ch over 2f out to over 1f out: outpcd ins fnl f* **13/2**
210- 6 4 **Ingleby Angel (IRE)**[217] 7032 4-9-2 **69** DavidNolan 8 59
(David O'Meara) *t.k.h: hld up: rdn and hung rt over 2f out: sn outpcd: n.d after* **9/2[3]**
0-00 7 2 1/2 **Mick Slates (IRE)**[37] 1462 4-8-9 **69** LukeLeadbitter(7) 3 53
(Declan Carroll) *s.i.s: hld up: drvn along over 3f out: sn outpcd* **16/1**
10-5 8 3 **High Resolution**[7] 2220 6-9-0 **72** GarryWhillans(5) 1 49
(Linda Perratt) *hld up in tch: rdn and struggling over 2f out: sn btn* **9/1**
1m 52.67s (4.27) **Going Correction** +0.40s/f (Good) 8 Ran SP% **115.5**
Speed ratings (Par 103): **94,92,91,90,89 85,83,80**
toteswingers 1&2 £3.90, 1&3 £7.40, 2&3 £3.30 CSF £32.06 CT £113.11 TOTE £6.40: £2.00, £2.20, £1.90; EX 14.80 Trifecta £112.40 Pool: £944.83 - 6.29 winning units..
Owner Mrs J M Penney **Bred** Ger Hayes **Trained** Melsonby, N Yorks

FOCUS
Probably fairly strong form for the level, with the first pair home both ahead of their marks. The winner built on his C&D win.

2407 GINGER GROUSE BRAVEHEART STKS (H'CAP) (LISTED RACE) 1m 4f 17y
7:25 (7:25) (Class 1) (0-110,103) 4-Y-O+ £23,680 (£8,956; £4,476; £2,236) Stalls High

Form RPR
022- 1 **Mijhaar**[200] 7438 5-9-10 **103** AndreaAtzeni 6 113
(Roger Varian) *t.k.h early: mde all: qcknd clr 3f out: rdn over 1f out: kpt on wl fnl f* **6/1**
-113 2 1 1/2 **Beaumont's Party (IRE)**[8] 2185 6-9-1 **94** DaleSwift 3 101
(Brian Ellison) *hld up in midfield: rdn and hdwy to chse (clr) wnr 2f out: kpt on fnl f: nt gng pce to chal* **11/2[3]**
231- 3 3/4 **Rawaki (IRE)**[224] 6848 5-8-12 **91** ShaneKelly 10 97
(Andrew Balding) *hld up towards rr: rdn and hdwy on outside over 2f out: one pce whn hung bdly rt ins fnl f* **8/1**
000- 4 6 **Scrapper Smith (IRE)**[188] 7689 7-8-10 **89** TomEaves 4 85
(Alistair Whillans) *hld up: rdn over 3f out: styd on fnl 2f: nvr able to chal* **40/1**
5-55 5 nk **Allied Powers (IRE)**[9] 2184 8-9-7 **100** MickyFenton 7 96
(Michael Bell) *t.k.h early: in tch: rdn and hdwy to chse wnr briefly over 2f out: sn outpcd* **8/1**
420- 6 4 1/2 **Albamara**[197] 7510 4-9-4 **97** LukeMorris 9 86
(Sir Mark Prescott Bt) *trckd ldrs tl rdn and wknd fr 2f out* **8/1**
10-5 7 5 **Nicholascopernicus (IRE)**[29] 1658 4-9-0 **93** TomMcLaughlin 2 74
(Ed Walker) *hld up towards rr: drvn along over 3f out: sn outpcd: n.d after* **5/1[2]**
0-06 8 2 1/2 **Good Morning Star (IRE)**[9] 2149 4-8-13 **92** JoeFanning 8 69
(Mark Johnston) *cl up tl rdn and wknd over 2f out* **16/1**
43-1 9 nse **Voodoo Prince**[20] 1843 5-9-4 **97** GrahamLee 1 74
(Ed Dunlop) *prom: rdn over 2f out: sn wknd* **3/1[1]**
00-0 10 3 3/4 **Ed De Gas**[27] 1674 4-9-7 **100** ChrisCatlin 5 71
(Rae Guest) *hld up: hdwy to chse ldrs over 3f out: rdn: edgd rt and wknd 2f out* **28/1**
2m 39.86s (1.26) **Going Correction** +0.40s/f (Good) 10 Ran SP% **116.4**
Speed ratings (Par 111): **111,110,109,105,105 102,98,97,97,94**
toteswingers 1&2 £9.30, 1&3 £7.80, 2&3 £4.90 CSF £38.94 CT £267.44 TOTE £6.40: £1.90, £1.60, £3.20; EX 57.00 Trifecta £230.10 Pool: £928.60 - 3.02 winning units..
Owner Sheikh Ahmed Al Maktoum **Bred** Darley **Trained** Newmarket, Suffolk

FOCUS
A good renewal of this Listed handicap and the form is likely to be solid. The winner set what looked a sound gallop and the front three were well clear of the rest. The winner rates a small personal best.

2408 FAMOUS GROUSE H'CAP 6f 5y
8:00 (8:00) (Class 4) (0-85,79) 3-Y-O £6,469 (£1,925; £962; £481) Stalls Centre

Form RPR
1-20 1 **Heaven's Guest (IRE)**[30] 1625 3-9-4 **79** LeeTopliss(3) 7 98+
(Richard Fahey) *hld up bhd main gp: swtchd rt and hdwy to ld over 1f out: edgd lft: drvn out* **9/4[1]**
-351 2 1 1/4 **Antonio Gramsci**[14] 1988 3-8-13 **71** GrahamGibbons 8 86
(David Barron) *cl up: rdn and ev ch over 1f out: carried hd high: kpt on ins fnl f: one pce last 50yds* **5/1[2]**
33-0 3 4 **Sharaarah (IRE)**[18] 1892 3-9-4 **76** DavidNolan 2 78
(David O'Meara) *hld up: hdwy and hung rt over 1f out: kpt on fnl f: nt gng pce to chal* **17/2**
-411 4 2 3/4 **Hit The Lights (IRE)**[16] 1935 3-8-13 **71** ShaneKelly 1 64
(Ollie Pears) *led tl rdn and hdd over 1f out: kpt on same pce fnl f* **10/1**
3-44 5 1 3/4 **Surge Ahead (IRE)**[12] 2056 3-9-7 **79** LukeMorris 9 67
(Ed Walker) *trckd ldrs: rdn over 2f out: no ex over 1f out* **15/2[3]**
21-1 6 1 3/4 **Bogsnog (IRE)**[22] 1791 3-9-7 **79** GrahamLee 6 61
(Kristin Stubbs) *t.k.h: hld up: rdn over 2f out: kpt on fnl f: nvr rchd ldrs* **10/1**
02-0 7 3/4 **Penny Garcia**[21] 1806 3-9-7 **79** DuranFentiman 5 59
(Tim Easterby) *hld up in tch on outside: struggling over 2f out: btn over 1f out* **33/1**
16 8 1/2 **Repetition**[20] 1832 3-8-13 **71** TomEaves 10 49
(Kevin Ryan) *t.k.h: sn prom: rdn over 2f out: wknd wl over 1f out* **5/1[2]**
1-36 9 1 **Dream Ally (IRE)**[16] 1935 3-8-13 **71** MickyFenton 3 46
(Jedd O'Keeffe) *dwlt: bhd and outpcd: no ch fr 1/2-way* **22/1**
22-0 10 23 **Red Joker (IRE)**[29] 1645 3-9-4 **76** RobertWinston 4
(Alan Swinbank) *chsd ldrs: drvn and wknd over 2f out: eased whn no ch over 1f out* **20/1**
1m 14.39s (2.19) **Going Correction** +0.40s/f (Good) 10 Ran SP% **116.6**
Speed ratings (Par 101): **101,99,94,90,88 85,84,84,82,52**
toteswingers 1&2 £4.00, 1&3 £7.60, 2&3 £12.00 CSF £12.79 CT £82.44 TOTE £3.00: £1.90, £1.60, £3.30; EX 15.50 Trifecta £108.70 Pool: £932.87 - 6.43 winning units..
Owner J K Shannon & M A Scaife **Bred** Yeomanstown Stud **Trained** Musley Bank, N Yorks
■ Stewards' Enquiry : David Nolan £280.00 fine: failed to arrive to weigh out.

FOCUS
Another contest which looks a strong race for the level, with the progressive front pair deserving credit for pulling clear.

2409 RACING UK ON SKY CHANNEL 432 H'CAP 6f 5y
8:35 (8:37) (Class 6) (0-65,65) 3-Y-O+ £2,045 (£603; £302) Stalls Centre

Form RPR
4-06 1 **Alexandrakollontai (IRE)**[23] 1759 3-8-9 **58** (b) JulieBurke(3) 4 66
(Alistair Whillans) *dwlt: sn in tch centre: hdwy to ld over 1f out: kpt on strly* **10/1**
0-45 2 1 3/4 **Captain Royale (IRE)**[6] 2276 8-9-8 **59** (p) BarryMcHugh 5 64
(Tracy Waggott) *prom centre: effrt and drvn over 2f out: kpt on fnl f: nt rch wnr* **11/1**
00-5 3 1/2 **Rock Canyon (IRE)**[7] 2217 4-9-2 **53** GrahamLee 9 56
(Linda Perratt) *hld up centre: rdn and hdwy wl over 1f out: kpt on fnl f: nvr able to chal* **16/1**
0-22 4 1/2 **Mandalay King (IRE)**[7] 2217 8-9-13 **64** (p) DaleSwift 3 65
(Marjorie Fife) *hld up centre: hdwy over 1f out: kpt on: nrst fin* **5/1[2]**
3631 5 2 1/2 **Script**[7] 2218 4-9-3 **54** 6ex PaddyAspell 14 47
(Alan Berry) *in tch towards stands' side: smooth hdwy over 2f out: rdn and edgd rt over 1f out: one pce* **10/1**
300- 6 3/4 **Hello Gorgeous**[204] 7357 3-8-4 **50** JamesSullivan 10 39
(Keith Dalgleish) *bhd and drvn along centre: styd on fr over 1f out: nrst fin* **16/1**
2-03 7 1 3/4 **Here Now And Why (IRE)**[12] 2043 6-9-4 **60** (p) JasonHart(5) 16 45
(Iain Jardine) *in tch stands' side: drvn along over 2f out: no imp over 1f out* **8/1**
5322 8 3/4 **Greenhead High**[7] 2222 5-9-12 **63** (v) AdrianNicholls 13 46
(David Nicholls) *led and overall ldr stands' side: hung rt and hdd over 1f: sn outpcd* **9/2[1]**
466- 9 2 **Star Request**[188] 7687 3-9-0 **60** JoeFanning 11 35
(Keith Dalgleish) *bhd towards stands' side: rdn over 2f out: sme late hdwy: nvr on terms* **11/2[3]**
10-4 10 3/4 **Lothair (IRE)**[14] 1994 4-9-1 **52** RobertWinston 2 26
(Alan Swinbank) *cl up far side: rdn and drifted lft over 2f out: wknd wl over 1f out* **20/1**
0605 11 2 1/2 **Ambitious Icarus**[7] 2222 4-9-13 **64** (e) RobbieFitzpatrick 15 30
(Richard Guest) *unruly in stalls: dwlt and rdr lost iron s: bhd: rdn over 2f out: n.d* **14/1**
50-0 12 hd **Tadalavil**[12] 2037 8-9-7 **58** TomEaves 6 24
(Linda Perratt) *racd centre: disp ld tl wknd fr 2f out* **50/1**
50-0 13 3/4 **Lady Del Sol**[27] 1692 5-10-0 **65** DavidNolan 12 28
(Marjorie Fife) *prom towards stands' side: rdn and edgd rt over 2f out: sn btn* **33/1**
00-0 14 3 3/4 **Ballinargh Girl (IRE)**[12] 2043 5-9-3 **54** DuranFentiman 1
(Danielle McCormick) *racd far side: cl up: rdn and hung lft over 2f out: sn wknd* **66/1**
1-00 15 6 **Pivotal Prospect**[34] 1540 5-10-0 **65** RoystonFfrench 8
(Tracy Waggott) *cl up in centre tl rdn and wknd over 2f out* **14/1**
1m 15.19s (2.99) **Going Correction** +0.40s/f (Good)
WFA 3 from 4yo+ 9lb 15 Ran SP% **124.1**
Speed ratings (Par 101): **96,93,93,92,89 88,85,84,82,81 77,77,76,71,63**
toteswingers 1&2 £9.30, 1&3 £55.80, 2&3 £26.90 CSF £115.16 CT £1771.71 TOTE £7.70: £4.20, £4.00, £5.70; EX 122.20 Trifecta £484.10 Part won. Pool: £645.54 - 0.06 winning units..
Owner Chris Spark & William Orr **Bred** Sean O'Sullivan **Trained** Newmill-On-Slitrig, Borders
■ Stewards' Enquiry : David Nolan £140.00: failed to arrive to weigh out.

FOCUS
A modest sprint in which the main action unfolded up the middle of the track. The winner's first real form since a C&D win in September.

2410 DOWNLOAD THE FREE RACING UK APP H'CAP 5f 4y
9:05 (9:05) (Class 5) (0-75,75) 4-Y-O+ £3,234 (£962; £481; £240) Stalls Centre

Form RPR
4601 1 **Tango Sky (IRE)**[18] 1888 4-9-5 **73** AdrianNicholls 5 82
(David Nicholls) *t.k.h: hld up centre: swtchd lft and hdwy over 1f out: str run fnl f: led post* **11/1**
1-35 2 nse **Rothesay Chancer**[13] 2031 5-9-6 **74** GrahamLee 10 83
(Jim Goldie) *hld up in tch: effrt and hdwy over 1f out: led ins fnl f: kpt on wl u.p: hdd post* **7/2[1]**
4-04 3 1 1/4 **Bronze Beau**[10] 2122 6-9-3 **71** (t) JamesSullivan 15 76
(Kristin Stubbs) *chsd ldrs stands' side: led over 1f out to ins fnl f: one pce* **14/1**
0352 4 nk **Phoenix Clubs (IRE)**[6] 2268 4-9-3 **71** (p) BarryMcHugh 3 74+
(Paul Midgley) *hld up in tch: outpcd whn n.m.r briefly wl over 1f out: rallied fnl f: kpt on* **4/1[2]**
5-50 5 1/2 **Lupin Pooter**[13] 2031 4-9-7 **75**[1] GrahamGibbons 4 77
(David Barron) *prom centre: effrt and drvn 2f out: one pce ins fnl f* **4/1[2]**
6653 6 1 **Wicked Wilma (IRE)**[7] 2217 9-7-11 **58** oh2 ow2 JordanHibberd(7) 2 56
(Alan Berry) *hld up on outside: rdn over 2f out: hdwy over 1f out: kpt on same pce ins fnl f* **16/1**
1055 7 nk **Captain Scooby**[6] 2268 7-9-5 **73** RobbieFitzpatrick 1 70
(Richard Guest) *hld up on outside: rdn and hdwy over 1f out: kpt on same pce ins fnl f* **9/1[3]**
0-20 8 nk **Boucher Garcon (IRE)**[37] 1465 5-8-2 **63** LukeLeadbitter(7) 14 59
(Declan Carroll) *led at str pce to over 1f out: sn no ex* **16/1**
301- 9 1 3/4 **Jinky**[202] 7412 5-9-0 **73** GarryWhillans(5) 9 63
(Linda Perratt) *midfield: drvn and outpcd over 2f out: kpt on fnl f: no imp* **14/1**
04-6 10 3/4 **Almond Branches**[10] 2122 4-9-6 **74** PaddyAspell 11 61
(Sharon Watt) *hld up: rdn and effrt over 2f out: outpcd over 1f out* **25/1**
5145 11 1/2 **Avonvalley**[15] 1957 6-8-8 **67** SladeO'Hara(5) 8 52
(Peter Grayson) *bhd and outpcd: sme hdwy over 1f out: nvr rchd ldrs* **28/1**
03-0 12 3 1/2 **The Nifty Fox**[13] 2031 9-9-7 **75** TomEaves 7 47
(Tim Easterby) *hld up: n.m.r briefly over 2f out: sn rdn: wknd fnl f* **20/1**

220- **13** *3* **Sandwith**[198] 7489 10-8-12 71 (p) LMcNiff[(5)] 13 33
(Ian Semple) *chsd ldrs: rdn over 2f out: wknd wl over 1f out* **14/1**

1m 2.11s (2.11) **Going Correction** +0.40s/f (Good) **13** Ran SP% **124.4**
Speed ratings (Par 103): **99,98,96,96,95 94,93,93,90,89 88,82,77**
toteswingers 1&2 £9.40, 1&3 £20.00, 2&3 £4.70 CSF £50.17 CT £583.78 TOTE £16.30: £4.00, £1.80, £2.50; EX 95.70 Trifecta £640.00 Part won. Pool: £853.42 - 0.30 winning units..
Owner Dr Marwan Koukash **Bred** L Mulryan **Trained** Sessay, N Yorks

FOCUS
A fair sprint. With the likes of Bronze Beau and Boucher Garcon in the line-up there was never going to be any hanging about. The winner was closer to his 3yo best.
T/Plt: £90.60 to a £1 stake. Pool: £60,086.27 - 483.83 winning tickets T/Qpdt: £120.40 to a £1 stake.Pool: £6,053.24 - 37.20 winning tickets RY

1673 NEWBURY (L-H)
Friday, May 17

OFFICIAL GOING: Good to firm (good in places; 7.0)
Wind: Moderate behind Weather: Overcast

2411 HILDON MAIDEN STKS — 6f 8y
1:30 (1:31) (Class 4) 2-Y-O **£4,204** (£1,251; £625; £312) **Stalls** High

Form RPR

1 **Championship (IRE)** 2-9-3 0 RichardHughes 8 83+
(Richard Hannon) *s.i.s: in rr: hdwy 2f out: nt clr run appr fnl f and sn swtchd rt to stands' rail: rdn and qcknd fnl 110yds to ld clsng stages: readily* **5/2**[1]

2 *3/4* **Man Amongst Men (IRE)** 2-9-3 0 HayleyTurner 12 80
(Brian Meehan) *in tch: hdwy 2f out: chal fnl 110yds: nt quite pce of wnr clsng stages* **14/1**

3 *nk* **Berkshire (IRE)** 2-9-3 0 JimCrowley 3 79+
(Paul Cole) *racd alone towards centre of crse tl jnd main gp and led jst ins fnl 2f: rdn and kpt on whn jnd fnl 110yds: hdd and outpcd clsng stages* **6/1**[3]

4 *nse* **Gm Hopkins** 2-9-3 0 WilliamBuick 5 80+
(John Gosden) *s.i.s: in rr: stdy hdwy on stands' rail whn nt clr run appr fnl f: shkn up and kpt on strly cl home: promising* **9/1**

5 *shd* **Jallota** 2-9-3 0 MatthewDavies 4 78
(Mick Channon) *in tch: rdn and hdwy over 1f out: chal u.p fnl 50yds: kpt on* **25/1**

6 *1 3/4* **Iftaar (IRE)** 2-9-3 0 PaulHanagan 7 74+
(Charles Hills) *in rr: swtchd lft and hdwy over 1f out: kpt on fnl f: nt rch ldrs* **8/1**

7 *1/2* **Speculative Bid (IRE)** 2-9-3 0 EddieAhern 11 72+
(Gerard Butler) *chsd ldrs: pushed along fnl f: outpcd fnl 110yds* **40/1**

0 **8** *1/2* **Heavens Edge**[15] 1946 2-8-12 0 FergusSweeney 13 65
(Christopher Mason) *led tl hdd ins fnl 2f: styd pressing ldrs tl wknd ins fnl f* **66/1**

9 *1 3/4* **Alaskan (IRE)** 2-9-3 0 PatDobbs 6 65+
(Richard Hannon) *in rr: pushed along and sme hdwy 2f out: wknd over 1f out* **12/1**

0 **10** *3* **Caledonia Laird**[28] 1659 2-9-3 0 CathyGannon 9 56
(Jo Hughes) *chsd ldrs to 2f out: wknd over 1f out* **25/1**

11 *1* **Ambiance (IRE)** 2-9-3 0 MartinHarley 2 53
(Mick Channon) *chsd ldrs: rdn over 2f out: wknd wl over 1f out* **3/1**[2]

12 *15* **Ferngrove (USA)** 2-9-3 0 JohnFahy 1
(Jonathan Portman) *sn bhd* **33/1**

1m 14.63s (1.63) **Going Correction** +0.025s/f (Good) **12** Ran SP% **117.9**
Speed ratings (Par 95): **90,89,88,88,88 86,85,84,82,78 77,57**
toteswingers 1&2 £9.80, 1&3 £8.30, 2&3 £2.50 CSF £36.82 TOTE £2.60: £1.30, £5.20, £2.10; EX 39.90 Trifecta £403.00 Pool: £684.20 - 1.27 winning units..
Owner Mrs J Wood **Bred** Ms Natalie Cleary **Trained** East Everleigh, Wilts

FOCUS
Rail on back straight moved out to give fresh ground increasing races on Round course by 15m. This is often a useful maiden. The pace was not very strong and there was a bunch finish but the favourite cut his way through some traffic problems to provide Richard Hannon with his fifth winning newcomer in this race since 2006. This was probably a lesser renewal of the race but several shaped with bags of promise.

2412 SWETTENHAM STUD FILLIES' TRIAL STKS (LISTED RACE) — 1m 2f 6y
2:00 (2:01) (Class 1) 3-Y-O
£20,982 (£7,955; £3,981; £1,983; £995; £499) **Stalls** Centre

Form RPR

12- **1** **Winsili**[251] 6021 3-8-12 95 [1] WilliamBuick 4 101+
(John Gosden) *trckd ldr: qcknd 2f out to ld wl over 1f out: styd on strly fnl f* **2/1**[1]

-235 **2** *2 1/4* **Cruck Realta**[12] 2049 3-8-12 96 MartinHarley 5 95
(Mick Channon) *chsd ldrs: rdn over 2f out: chsd wnr ins fnl f: kpt on but a wl hld* **6/1**

41- **3** *hd* **The Lark**[203] 7364 3-8-12 76 HayleyTurner 6 95
(Michael Bell) *hld up in last pl: hdwy 3f out: drvn over 2f out: kpt on to cl on 2nd fnl 110yds but no ch w wnr* **9/4**[2]

0-30 **4** *1/2* **Concise**[12] 2049 3-8-12 84 JimCrowley 2 94
(Ed Dunlop) *in rr: rdn over 2f out: styd on u.p ins fnl f to take 4th clsng stages* **33/1**

0-23 **5** *1* **Asgardella (IRE)**[6] 2271 3-8-12 79 PaulHanagan 1 92?
(Richard Fahey) *chsd ldrs in 3rd: pushed along 3f out: styd on but nt qckn fr 2f out: one pce ins fnl f* **9/1**

1 **6** *1 1/4* **Valtina (IRE)**[20] 1828 3-8-12 83 RichardHughes 3 89
(William Haggas) *led: pushed along over 2f out: hdd wl over 1f out: wknd ins fnl f* **4/1**[3]

2m 11.74s (2.94) **Going Correction** +0.025s/f (Good) **6** Ran SP% **111.3**
Speed ratings (Par 104): **89,87,87,86,85 84**
toteswingers 1&2 £4.40, 1&3 £2.50, 2&3 £2.90 CSF £14.09 TOTE £2.60: £1.60, £2.70; EX 9.60 Trifecta £29.50 Pool: £1879.02 - 47.63 winning units..
Owner K Abdullah **Bred** Juddmonte Farms Ltd **Trained** Newmarket, Suffolk

FOCUS
Eswarah won the Oaks after scoring in this race in 2005 and subsequent Oaks heroine Dancing Rain was second in this race in 2011, but this did not look a strong renewal and The Lark was the only runner who was entered at Epsom. This contest became tactical and the winner showed the best turn-of-foot from off the stop-start gallop. The winner can do better still.

2413 SCOPE H'CAP (DIV I) — 1m 2f 6y
2:35 (2:36) (Class 5) (0-70,70) 4-Y-0+ **£2,587** (£770; £384; £192) **Stalls** Centre

Form RPR

6-60 **1** **Emman Bee (IRE)**[32] 1585 4-9-3 66 IanMongan 8 75
(Luke Dace) *chsd ldrs: drvn to ld 1f out: drvn out* **14/1**

2303 **2** *1 3/4* **Brown Pete (IRE)**[7] 2220 5-9-7 70 MartinHarley 13 76
(Violet M Jordan) *chsd ldrs: led 3f out: rdn 2f out: hdd 1f out: styd on same pce fnl f* **5/1**[1]

0-50 **3** *1 3/4* **Choral Festival**[18] 1884 7-9-6 69 RichardHughes 10 71+
(John Bridger) *in rr: hdwy fr 3f out: drvn to chse ldng duo 1f out: kpt on same pce* **11/2**[2]

00-3 **4** *1* **Berwin (IRE)**[14] 1974 4-8-10 66 JoshBaudains[(7)] 11 66
(Sylvester Kirk) *hld up in rr: t.k.h: hdwy 2f out: chsd ldrs over 1f out: rdn and one pce fnl f* **8/1**[3]

1123 **5** *1/2* **Bridge That Gap**[20] 1836 5-9-2 65 (p) AdamKirby 1 65+
(Roger Ingram) *in rr: hdwy fr 3f out: nt seeing much daylight 2f out: swtchd rt and kpt on over 1f out: kpt on but nvr gng pce to rch ldrs* **5/1**[1]

2-04 **6** *4* **Bold Cross (IRE)**[15] 1948 10-8-13 65 MarkCoumbe[(3)] 2 57
(Edward Bevan) *in rr: hdwy 3f out: chsd ldrs over 2f out: wknd over 1f out* **14/1**

6231 **7** *4 1/2* **Matraash (USA)**[14] 1987 7-9-6 69 (be) StephenCraine 6 52
(Daniel Mark Loughnane) *t.k.h: chsd ldrs: rdn over 2f out: btn whn rdr dropped whip over 1f out* **10/1**

21 **8** *1 3/4* **Sinchiroka (FR)**[63] 1015 7-8-4 58 RyanTate[(5)] 14 38
(Ralph Smith) *sn led: hdd 3f out: wknd over 1f out* **14/1**

-306 **9** *3/4* **Fire King**[17] 1901 7-9-0 63 FrankieMcDonald 5 42
(Paul Burgoyne) *in rr: rdn over 3f out: stl last over 1f out: passed btn horses clsng stages* **33/1**

4542 **10** *nk* **Breakheart (IRE)**[105] 477 6-8-7 63 (p) JackGarritty[(7)] 9 41
(Andrew Balding) *in tch: pushed along 3f out: wknd over 2f out* **11/1**

01-0 **11** *hd* **Garrisson (IRE)**[32] 1585 4-9-6 69 WilliamBuick 12 47
(Charles Hills) *t.k.h: chsd ldrs: wnt 2nd 5f out: rdn over 2f out: sn wknd* **12/1**

20-6 **12** *6* **Graylyn Valentino**[15] 1950 4-9-2 65 JimCrowley 4 31
(Robin Dickin) *in tch: chsd ldrs: rdn over 2f out and sn wknd: eased whn no ch* **9/1**

2m 10.76s (1.96) **Going Correction** +0.025s/f (Good) **12** Ran SP% **117.9**
Speed ratings (Par 103): **93,91,90,89,89 85,82,80,80,79 79,75**
toteswingers 1&2 £40.10, 1&3 £25.40, 2&3 £7.40 CSF £82.14 CT £441.90 TOTE £16.70: £5.20, £2.30, £2.00; EX 96.10 Trifecta £663.70 Pool: £1383.31 - 1.56 winning units..
Owner Mark Benton **Bred** O Bourke **Trained** Five Oaks, W Sussex

FOCUS
A minor handicap which was run at a steady pace. The first two were always prominent and the second helps with the level.

2414 RAMSAY HEALTH CARE FILLIES' CONDITIONS STKS — 5f 34y
3:05 (3:07) (Class 3) 2-Y-O **£6,225** (£1,864; £932; £466; £233) **Stalls** High

Form RPR

13 **1** **Alutiq (IRE)**[12] 2053 2-8-10 0 JimCrowley 6 87+
(Eve Johnson Houghton) *in rr but in tch: drvn and qcknd to ld 1f out: pushed out* **4/1**[2]

1 **2** *2 1/4* **Suite (IRE)**[16] 1924 2-8-13 0 PatDobbs 1 82
(Richard Hannon) *trckd ldrs: drvn to chal over 1f out: nt pce of wnr ins fnl f: jst hld on for 2nd* **6/1**[3]

2 **3** *shd* **Oriel**[7] 2204 2-8-10 0 RichardHughes 5 80+
(Richard Hannon) *trckd ldrs: nt clr run 2f out: travelling wl whn nt clr run again and blkd 1f out: swtchd lft ins fnl f and stl green: fin strly to press for 2nd: nt rcvr to get to wnr* **1/2**[1]

241 **4** *4* **Diamond Lady**[11] 2068 2-8-10 0 CathyGannon 2 64
(Jo Hughes) *chsd ldr: led 1/2-way: hdd 1f out: wknd ins fnl f* **25/1**

61 **5** *18* **Hedge End (IRE)**[15] 1946 2-8-13 0 WilliamBuick 4
(Richard Hannon) *led to 1/2-way: wknd qckly wl over 1f out* **20/1**

1m 1.76s (0.36) **Going Correction** +0.025s/f (Good) **5** Ran SP% **109.6**
Speed ratings (Par 94): **98,94,94,87,59**
CSF £25.64 TOTE £5.20: £1.80, £2.40; EX 33.30 Trifecta £60.60 Pool: £1956.65 - 24.17 winning units..
Owner Qatar Racing Limited **Bred** Wardstown Stud Ltd **Trained** Blewbury, Oxon

FOCUS
This fillies conditions event has been won by subsequent Queen Mary/Lowther winners Flashy Wings (2005) and Best Terms (2011) in the last eight years. There were not many runners in this renewal but the hot favourite ran into repetitive traffic problems and couldn't get to the the winner who got first run. The race averages, the time and the fourth help with the level.

2415 BATHWICK TYRES CARNARVON STKS (LISTED RACE) — 6f 8y
3:40 (3:40) (Class 1) 3-Y-O
£20,982 (£7,955; £3,981; £1,983; £995; £499) **Stalls** High

Form RPR

-214 **1** **Zanetto**[16] 1921 3-9-0 100 WilliamBuick 8 111+
(Andrew Balding) *trckd ldr: chal 2f out: sn led: drvn clr fnl f and in n.d after* **10/3**[2]

144- **2** *3 1/4* **City Girl (IRE)**[237] 6467 3-8-9 93 JimCrowley 6 96
(Ralph Beckett) *chsd ldrs: rdn 2f out: chsd wnr ins fnl f but nvr any ch* **14/1**

11-1 **3** *2* **Ninjago**[16] 1921 3-9-3 105 RichardHughes 7 98
(Richard Hannon) *stdd s: hld up in rr: pushed along and hdwy ins fnl 2f: styd on fnl f to take 3rd but no imp on ldng duo* **1/1**[1]

23-0 **4** *1/2* **Sound Of Guns**[30] 1622 3-8-9 105 MartinHarley 2 88
(Ed Walker) *s.i.s: in rr: hdwy 2f out: styd on to dispute one pce 3rd fnl f: nvr any ch w wnr* **9/2**[3]

50-1 **5** *1/2* **Dominate**[32] 1582 3-9-0 90 PatDobbs 9 91
(Richard Hannon) *led: jnd 2f out: sn hdd: no ex fnl 110yds* **25/1**

1-50 **6** *2 1/4* **Glass Office**[92] 658 3-9-5 108 AdamKirby 1 89
(David Simcock) *in rr: sme hdwy over 2f out: sn btn* **12/1**

21-2 **7** *4* **Almalekiah (IRE)**[35] 1515 3-8-9 72 EddieAhern 11 66
(J S Moore) *chsd ldrs: wknd qckly fr 2f out* **66/1**

50-0 **8** *8* **Heavy Metal**[30] 1621 3-9-7 109 FrannyNorton 5 52
(Mark Johnston) *rdn over 2f out: a outpcd* **25/1**

1m 12.01s (-0.99) **Going Correction** +0.025s/f (Good) **8** Ran SP% **114.8**
Speed ratings (Par 107): **107,102,100,99,98 95,90,79**
toteswingers 1&2 £13.10, 1&3 £1.10, 2&3 £5.50 CSF £45.82 TOTE £4.10: £1.40, £2.80, £1.10; EX 50.00 Trifecta £85.20 Pool: £2316.50 - 20.37 winning units..

Owner Mick and Janice Mariscotti **Bred** Aislabie Bloodstock Ltd **Trained** Kingsclere, Hants

FOCUS

A Listed race that has produced some high-class sprinters in recent years, notably Sakhee's Secret who won this in 2007 before taking the July Cup. This did not look a strong renewal and the favourite was a bit laboured but there was a clear-cut winner. He is arguably worth4-5lb more than the bare form. The second was rated to her Lowther form.

2416 SPINAL CORD INJURY AWARENESS DAY H'CAP 1m 3f 5y

4:15 (4:15) (Class 4) (0-85,85) 3-Y-O **£4,690** (£1,395; £697; £348) **Stalls** Centre

Form				RPR
53-2	**1**		**Prairie Ranger**[20] 1826 3-8-8 **77**................................ ThomasBrown(5) 8	94+
			(Andrew Balding) *trckd ldr chal 3f out: sn led: drvn 3 l clr fnl f: jst lasted* **3/1**[2]	
31-3	**2**	*nse*	**Nichols Canyon**[20] 1847 3-9-7 **85**................................ WilliamBuick 5	102+
			(John Gosden) *chsd ldrs: pushed along 3f out: drvn to chse wnr whn veered rt over 1f out: 3 l down and edgd rt again ins fnl f: rallied under hand riding: fin strly: nt quite get up* **2/1**[1]	
01-	**3**	*9*	**Autun (USA)**[219] 6985 3-9-1 **79**................................[1] IanMongan 9	82
			(Sir Henry Cecil) *hld up in rr: hdwy over 2f out: styd on to take wl hld 3rd fnl 110yds* **5/1**[3]	
05-3	**4**	*½*	**Bursledon (IRE)**[45] 1300 3-8-9 **73**................................ RichardHughes 7	75
			(Richard Hannon) *in rr: hdwy 3f out: sn drvn to dispute wl hld 3rd ins fnl f: one pce into 4th fnl 110yds* **12/1**	
4-20	**5**	*3½*	**Royal Skies (IRE)**[20] 1847 3-9-0 **78**................................ FrannyNorton 2	74
			(Mark Johnston) *led: jnd 3f out: sn hdd: wknd appr fnl f* **9/1**	
13-6	**6**	*¾*	**Linguine (FR)**[20] 1847 3-9-6 **84**................................ JohnFahy 1	79
			(Seamus Durack) *chsd ldrs: rdn over 3f out: btn over 2f out* **28/1**	
14	**7**	*½*	**Magical Kingdom (IRE)**[37] 1470 3-8-12 **76**................................ MartinHarley 3	70
			(Marco Botti) *in tch: rdn to chse ldrs over 2f out: hung lft u.p and sn btn* **10/1**	
01-5	**8**	*27*	**Felix Fabulla**[12] 2054 3-8-13 **77**................................ JimCrowley 4	
			(Hughie Morrison) *in rr: sme hdwy 3f out: sn wknd* **12/1**	
3214	**9**	*20*	**Incorporate**[28] 1667 3-9-5 **83**................................ EddieAhern 6	
			(Pat Eddery) *in rr: hdwy to get in tch 3f out: hung lft: wknd and eased over 2f out* **20/1**	

2m 21.74s (0.54) **Going Correction** +0.025s/f (Good) **9** Ran SP% **117.7**

Speed ratings (Par 101): **99,98,92,92,89 88,88,68,54**

toteswingers 1&2 £1.90, 1&3 £6.50, 2&3 £1.80 CSF £9.62 CT £28.60 TOTE £5.40: £1.90, £1.20, £2.20; EX 12.60 Trifecta £66.40 Pool: £2188.81 - 24.71 winning units..

Owner Dr Philip Brown **Bred** Good Breeding **Trained** Kingsclere, Hants

FOCUS

A fascinating handicap. It was won by subsequent multiple Group winner Allied Powers in 2008 and ill-fated Census in 2011, while Arctic Cosmos finished third in this contest in 2010 before winning the St Leger. The pace was solid and there was a very tight finish between the two market leaders who pulled a long way clear. A positive view has been taken of the form.

2417 SCOPE H'CAP (DIV II) 1m 2f 6y

4:50 (4:51) (Class 5) (0-70,70) 4-Y-0+ **£2,587** (£770; £384; £192) **Stalls** Centre

Form				RPR
146-	**1**		**Semeen**[197] 7511 4-9-5 **68**................................ RichardHughes 3	87+
			(Luca Cumani) *chsd ldrs: rdn along 3f out: chsd ldr 2f out: rallied u.p fnl f: hrd rdn to ld last strides* **7/2**[2]	
/3-0	**2**	*hd*	**Cashpoint**[38] 1448 8-9-7 **70**................................ WilliamBuick 11	88
			(Ian Williams) *trckd ldrs: led over 2f out: rdn and eged rt over 1f out: edgd rt again u.p ins fnl f: hdd last strides* **11/1**	
-403	**3**	*6*	**Perfect Cracker**[39] 1422 5-9-6 **69**................................ AdamKirby 5	76
			(Clive Cox) *chsd ldrs: rdn 2f out: outpcd by ldng duo fnl f* **10/3**[1]	
2144	**4**	*4½*	**Ssafa**[2] 2361 5-8-12 **66**................................(p) AmyScott(5) 10	64+
			(Alastair Lidderdale) *in rr: hdwy over 2f out: sn rdn: styd on same pce* **9/1**	
3246	**5**	*hd*	**Spirit Of Xaar (IRE)**[16] 1925 7-8-12 **61**................................(p) EddieAhern 2	59
			(Linda Jewell) *chsd ldrs: rdn 3f out: wknd 2f out* **33/1**	
-056	**6**	*3*	**Monopoli**[25] 1715 4-9-3 **66**................................ RichardThomas 4	58
			(Daniel Kubler) *chsd ldr tl over 2f out: sn btn* **20/1**	
405-	**7**	*½*	**Buster Brown (IRE)**[204] 7359 4-9-6 **69**................................ JimCrowley 14	60+
			(James Given) *s.i.s: in rr: hdwy on ins over 3f out: nvr rchd ldrs and btn 2f out* **6/1**[3]	
32-4	**8**	*1¼*	**Tenessee**[22] 1780 6-9-0 **63**................................(t) PatDobbs 6	52
			(Ben De Haan) *led tl hdd over 2f out: wknd qckly* **9/1**	
4130	**9**	*¾*	**Yourinthewill (USA)**[27] 1699 5-8-12 **61**................................ CathyGannon 13	48+
			(Daniel Mark Loughnane) *in rr: sme hdwy and rdn 3f out: sn wknd* **25/1**	
232-	**10**	*9*	**Laser Blazer**[149] 8175 5-9-6 **69**................................ FergusSweeney 7	39
			(Jeremy Gask) *mid-div: sme hdwy 3f out: sn wknd* **9/1**	
2-24	**11**	*½*	**Grand Theft Equine**[16] 1925 5-8-11 **65**................................ NathanAlison(5) 9	34
			(Jim Boyle) *a in rr* **25/1**	
2030	**12**	*9*	**Jumbo Prado (USA)**[72] 896 4-9-2 **65**................................ StephenCraine 8	17
			(John Stimpson) *bhd most of way* **50/1**	
050-	**13**	*14*	**London Silver**[286] 4797 4-9-1 **64**................................ JohnFahy 1	
			(Ben De Haan) *a in rr* **50/1**	

2m 8.03s (-0.77) **Going Correction** +0.025s/f (Good) **13** Ran SP% **117.2**

Speed ratings (Par 103): **104,103,99,95,95 92,92,91,90,83 83,76,64**

toteswingers 1&2 £6.20, 1&3 £3.30, 2&3 £16.00 CSF £37.13 CT £138.76 TOTE £2.90: £1.40, £4.50, £2.00; EX 44.70 Trifecta £129.70 Pool: £1432.49 - 8.28 winning units..

Owner Sheikh Mohammed Obaid Al Maktoum **Bred** Darley **Trained** Newmarket, Suffolk

■ Stewards' Enquiry : Richard Hughes two-day ban; used whip above permitted level (3rd-4th June).

FOCUS

The first two pulled clear in this handicap. It was run at a decent pace and the field was strung out for most of the way, but not many got involved. The first two came clear and a positive view has been taken of the form.

2418 EVENT BAR MANAGEMENT APPRENTICE H'CAP 1m 4f 5y

5:25 (5:27) (Class 5) (0-75,75) 4-Y-0+ **£2,587** (£770; £384; £192) **Stalls** Centre

Form				RPR
023-	**1**		**Gabrial's King (IRE)**[146] 8235 4-8-13 **70**................................ AliceHaynes(3) 2	80
			(David Simcock) *in rr: hdwy to cl on ldrs towards ins and nt clr run 2f out: swtchd sharply rt sn after then hung rt: rdn and wnt lft ins fnl f: styd on to ld fnl 20yds* **7/2**[1]	
155-	**2**	*½*	**Palus San Marco (IRE)**[77] 6933 4-9-7 **75**................................(t) NedCurtis 9	83
			(Graeme McPherson) *reluctant to load: sn chsng ldrs: led 2f out: drvn fnl f: hdd fnl 20yds* **15/2**	
5220	**3**	*2¼*	**Story Writer**[17] 1899 4-8-2 **63**................................ CameronHardie(7) 8	67
			(William Knight) *s.i.s: in rr: pushed along and hdwy fr 2f out: kpt on fnl f: nt rch ldng duo* **12/1**	
-645	**4**	*¾*	**Bold Duke**[18] 1889 5-8-11 **65**................................ IanBurns 7	68
			(Edward Bevan) *chsd ldrs: wnt 2nd 7f out: rdn over 2f out: wknd fnl 110yds* **16/1**	
106-	**5**	*2½*	**Attraction Ticket**[214] 7117 4-8-9 **66**................................ ShelleyBirkett(3) 11	65
			(David Simcock) *led after 3f: rdn 3f out: hdd 2f out: wknd fnl f* **12/1**	
3532	**6**	*1¼*	**Norfolk Sky**[13] 2004 4-9-2 **70**................................ NoelGarbutt 4	67
			(Laura Mongan) *in tch: chsd ldrs and rdn 3f out: wknd ins fnl 2f* **8/1**	
0-64	**7**	*½*	**Jolly Roger (IRE)**[17] 1899 6-8-6 **67**................................ AidenBlakemore(7) 10	63
			(Tony Carroll) *towards rr: pushed along 3f out: sme late hdwy* **13/2**[3]	
1320	**8**	*8*	**Jacobs Son**[18] 1884 5-9-4 **75**................................ PatMillman(3) 1	59
			(Robert Mills) *chsd ldrs: rdn 4f out: wknd fr 3f out* **12/1**	
310-	**9**	*4½*	**Bouggatti**[255] 5913 5-9-6 **74**................................ RyanWhile 3	50
			(Lady Herries) *rdn 4f out: a in rr* **8/1**	
31/-	**10**	*4*	**Gold Mine**[667] 4209 5-9-6 **74**................................(t) DanielMuscutt 5	44
			(Andrew Balding) *t.k.h: led 3f: wknd 3f out* **4/1**[2]	

2m 41.48s (5.98) **Going Correction** +0.025s/f (Good) **10** Ran SP% **118.5**

Speed ratings (Par 103): **81,80,79,78,77 76,75,70,67,64**

toteswingers 1&2 £8.30, 1&3 £7.60, 2&3 £17.80 CSF £30.62 CT £287.81 TOTE £3.80: £1.30, £2.90, £5.10; EX 34.10 Trifecta £711.70 Pool: £1166.58 - 1.28 winning units..

Owner Dr Marwan Koukash **Bred** Danella Partnership **Trained** Newmarket, Suffolk

FOCUS

They went a steady pace in this handicap and the favourite delivered after finding plenty of trouble in running. Routine form.

T/Plt: £54.50 to a £1 stake. Pool: £49,950.25 - 668.88 winning tickets. T/Qpdt: £15.20 to a £1 stake. Pool: £3400.11 - 164.90 winning tickets. ST

2382 NEWMARKET (R-H)

Friday, May 17

OFFICIAL GOING: Good (8.0)

Wind: medium, across Weather: overcast

2419 CHEMTEST EBF MAIDEN FILLIES' STKS 6f

2:25 (2:26) (Class 4) 2-Y-0 **£4,528** (£1,347; £673; £336) **Stalls** High

Form				RPR
5	**1**		**Corncockle**[7] 2204 2-9-0 0................................ SeanLevey 2	80+
			(Richard Hannon) *mde all: rdn and qcknd clr wl over 1f out: stl 2 l ld fnl 100yds: kpt on and a holding on* **10/3**[2]	
0	**2**	*¾*	**Dutch Courage**[29] 1634 2-9-0 0................................ SebSanders 10	78+
			(Richard Fahey) *in tch in midfield: rdn and effrt to chse ldng trio 2f out: chsd clr wnr 1f out: styd on wl and steadily clsng on wnr fnl 100yds* **15/8**[1]	
	3	*4*	**Aqlaam Vision** 2-9-0 0................................ JamesDoyle 9	66
			(Clive Brittain) *chsd ldrs: chsd wnr over 1f out: 3rd and unable qck whn edgd rt ent fnl f: wknd fnl 150yds* **16/1**	
	4	*1½*	**Prisca** 2-9-0 0................................ KieranO'Neill 6	61+
			(Richard Hannon) *in tch in last trio: rdn and hdwy to chse ldng quartet and edgd rt over 1f out: styd on steadily fnl f: wnt 4th cl home* **10/1**	
	5	*½*	**Alfaayza (IRE)** 2-9-0 0................................ DaneO'Neill 5	60
			(Brian Meehan) *chsd ldrs: wnt 2nd 1/2-way tl rdn and unable qck over 1f out: 4th and btn whn sltly hmpd ent fnl f: wknd fnl 150yds* **6/1**[3]	
	6	*2*	**Gender Agenda** 2-9-0 0................................ TomQueally 4	54
			(Michael Bell) *hld up in tch in last trio: rdn and effrt over 2f out: sn struggling and outpcd 2f out: wknd over 1f out* **7/1**	
	7	*12*	**Baileys Celebrate** 2-9-0 0................................ KierenFallon 1	18
			(Mark Johnston) *chsd wnr tl 1/2-way: sn rdn: lost pl ent fnl 2f: sn wknd: wl btn and eased wl ins fnl f* **8/1**	
	8	*7*	**Tempelfeuer (GER)** 2-9-0 0................................[1] TedDurcan 3	
			(Conrad Allen) *rn green: in tch towards rr: rdn and outpcd over 2f out: wknd 2f out: wl bhd and eased ins fnl f* **40/1**	
	9	*4*	**Ellingham (IRE)** 2-8-11 0................................ DarrenEgan(3) 7	
			(Christine Dunnett) *s.i.s: a in rr: in tch tl over 2f out: sn bhd* **100/1**	

1m 13.19s (0.99) **Going Correction** +0.10s/f (Good) **9** Ran SP% **114.2**

Speed ratings (Par 92): **97,96,90,88,88 85,69,60,54**

toteswingers 1&2 £3.30, 1&3 £9.40, 2&3 £8.30 CSF £9.83 TOTE £4.60: £1.60, £1.10, £5.80; EX 11.70 Trifecta £93.70 Pool: £1519.78 - 12.15 winning units..

Owner Rockcliffe Stud **Bred** Rockcliffe Stud **Trained** East Everleigh, Wilts

FOCUS

Stands' side track used. Stalls far side except 1m4f; centre. A fair fillies' maiden, rated along with the race averages. The winner improved on her Ascot promise.

2420 STREETS CHARTERED ACCOUNTANTS H'CAP 1m

2:55 (2:57) (Class 5) (0-75,76) 3-Y-0 **£3,234** (£962; £481; £240) **Stalls** High

Form				RPR
40-0	**1**		**Llaregyb (IRE)**[27] 1678 3-9-5 **72**................................ DaneO'Neill 7	86+
			(David Elsworth) *stdd s: hld up in tch in rr: smooth hdwy over 1f out: qcknd to ld and edgd rt jst ins fnl f: r.o strly: readily* **5/2**[1]	
-261	**2**	*4*	**Arctic Admiral (IRE)**[7] 2229 3-9-4 **76** 6ex.... WilliamTwiston-Davies(5) 3	78
			(Richard Hannon) *led and set stdy gallop: hrd pressed whn rdn and qcknd gallop wl over 1f out: hdd and edgd lft jst ins fnl f: no ch w wnr after but kpt on* **11/2**[3]	
2120	**3**	*1*	**Red Dragon (IRE)**[25] 1725 3-9-7 **74**................................ SteveDrowne 9	74
			(Charles Hills) *chsd ldr: rdn and ev ch 2f out: cl 3rd but unable qck whn hmpd jst ins fnl f: sn outpcd and btn: kpt on* **10/1**	
0511	**4**	*2¼*	**Echo Brava**[17] 1900 3-9-3 **70**................................ TomQueally 1	65
			(Luke Dace) *hld up in tch in last pair: effrt on far rail wl over 1f out: chsd clr ldng trio 1f out: kpt on ins fnl f: nvr threatened ldrs* **4/1**[2]	
44-0	**5**	*2¾*	**Future Reference (IRE)**[29] 1648 3-9-5 **72**................................ KierenFallon 10	60
			(Saeed bin Suroor) *stdd s: plld hrd: in tch in midfield: hdwy to press ldrs 3f out: rdn and ev ch 2f out: no ex and btn 1f out: fdd ins fnl f* **12/1**	
-665	**6**	*½*	**East Texas Red (IRE)**[11] 2094 3-8-9 **67**................................ RobertTart(5) 8	54
			(Mick Quinn) *chsd ldrs: effrt u.p 3f out: outpcd and btn over 1f out: wknd ins fnl f* **17/2**	
00-0	**7**	*½*	**Bayan Kasirga (IRE)**[22] 1772 3-8-5 **65**................................ SamanthaBell(7) 5	51
			(Richard Fahey) *stdd s: hld up wl in tch towards rr: rdn and outpcd wl over 1f out: wl hld over 1f out: wknd fnl f* **25/1**	
4-1	**8**	*2¼*	**Testa Rossa (IRE)**[133] 59 3-9-0 **67**................................ SebSanders 4	48
			(J W Hills) *in tch in midfield: rdn wl over 2f out: outpcd and btn wl over 1f out: wknd over 1f out* **12/1**	
21-0	**9**	*3*	**Makin (IRE)**[21] 1803 3-9-6 **73**................................(t) JimmyQuinn 6	47
			(Marco Botti) *in tch in midfield: rdn and outpcd over 2f out: lost pl 2f out: wknd over 1f out: bhd fnl f* **16/1**	
46-0	**10**	*5*	**Inaugural**[37] 1471 3-9-5 **72**................................ JamesDoyle 2	34
			(Roger Charlton) *chsd ldrs: rdn and outpcd ent fnl 2f: wknd over 1f out: wl bhd and eased ins fnl f* **12/1**	

1m 38.52s (-0.08) **Going Correction** +0.10s/f (Good) **10** Ran SP% **116.4**

Speed ratings (Par 99): **104,100,99,96,94 93,93,90,87,82**

toteswingers 1&2 £2.10, 1&3 £9.50, 2&3 £8.00 CSF £16.12 CT £119.57 TOTE £3.80: £1.70, £2.20, £2.20; EX 21.70 Trifecta £125.40 Pool: £1590.61 - 9.51 winning units..

Owner Mrs Anne Coughlan **Bred** Corrin Stud **Trained** Newmarket, Suffolk

FOCUS
A competitive 3-y-o handicap with an impressive winner who is potentially a lot better than he's given credit for.

2421 YUTREE INSURANCE NOVICE STKS — 6f
3:30 (3:30) (Class 4) 2-Y-O — **£5,175** (£1,540; £769; £384) **Stalls** High

Form — RPR

12 **1** — **Justice Day (IRE)**[16] 1917 2-9-5 0 — DaneO'Neill 1 — 91+
(David Elsworth) *hld up in tch in rr: swtchd lft 2f out: rdn and hdwy to ld 1f out: styd on wl and in command fnl 100yds: eased towards fin* **4/11**[1]

01 **2** 1 3/4 **Lady Lydia (IRE)**[17] 1910 2-8-11 0 — SebSanders 4 — 75
(Michael Wigham) *led: rdn wl over 1f out: hdd and edgd lft 1f out: outpcd by wnr ins fnl f: kpt on for clr 2nd* **8/1**[3]

13 **3** 4 1/2 **Split Rock**[30] 1619 2-9-5 0 — KierenFallon 2 — 69
(Mark Johnston) *chsd ldr: rdn 2f out: 3rd and struggling whn squeezed for room and hmpd 1f out: wknd ins fnl f* **4/1**[2]

4 2 1/2 **Bens Boy (IRE)** 2-8-7 0 — AdamMcLean(7) 3 — 57
(Derek Shaw) *chsd ldng pair: rdn and dropped to last over 2f out: rn green and hung rt over 1f out: plugged on but wl hld fnl f* **66/1**

1m 13.17s (0.97) **Going Correction** +0.10s/f (Good) — **4** Ran SP% **105.9**
Speed ratings (Par 95): **97,94,88,85**
CSF £3.64 TOTE £1.30; EX 3.70 Trifecta £8.90 Pool: £2833.45 - 237.94 winning units..

Owner Robert Ng **Bred** Gerry Kenny **Trained** Newmarket, Suffolk

FOCUS
A good-quality novice event. The winner looks a decent early 2yo and the second improved on her maiden win.

2422 EDMONDSON HALL SOLICITORS & SPORTS LAWYERS H'CAP — 1m 2f
4:05 (4:06) (Class 3) (0-90,88) 4-Y-0+ — **£7,762** (£2,310; £1,154; £577) **Stalls** High

Form — RPR

61- **1** — **Ehtedaam (USA)**[198] 7488 4-9-1 82 — DaneO'Neill 3 — 91+
(Saeed bin Suroor) *t.k.h: chsd ldrs: rdn to ld and edgd rt over 1f out: styd on wl ins fnl f: rdn out* **8/1**

2-54 **2** 1 **Cayuga**[18] 1883 4-8-9 81 — WilliamTwiston-Davies(5) 6 — 87
(Brett Johnson) *in tch in midfield: stl travelling wl 2f out: rdn and effrt over 1f out: kpt on ins fnl f: wnt 2nd cl home* **10/1**

210- **3** nk **Nabucco**[309] 4009 4-9-7 88 — NickyMackay 5 — 93
(John Gosden) *chsd ldr tl rdn to ld over 2f out: drvn and hdd over 1f out: kpt on same pce ins fnl f: lost 2nd cl home* **5/1**

32-4 **4** 1/2 **Cactus Valley (IRE)**[27] 1673 4-9-4 85 — JamesDoyle 1 — 89
(Roger Charlton) *hld up in tch: rdn and effrt over 1f out: drvn and kpt on same pce ins fnl f* **9/2**[3]

0-32 **5** 1 **Haylaman (IRE)**[8] 2191 5-8-13 83 — DarrenEgan(3) 7 — 86
(David Simcock) *hld up in tch in last pair: rdn and effrt 2f out: chsd ldrs and drvn over 1f out: one pce and no imp ins fnl f* **10/3**[2]

/0-3 **6** 1 3/4 **Status Symbol (IRE)**[20] 1824 8-9-6 87 — (t) WilliamCarson 8 — 86
(Anthony Carson) *stdd s: hld up in tch in rr: rdn and effrt wl over 1f out: styng on but stl plenty to do whn nt clr run and swtchd lft 1f out: kpt on same pce fnl f* **50/1**

356- **7** 1 **Commend**[217] 7017 4-9-2 83 — KierenFallon 9 — 80
(Sir Michael Stoute) *chsd ldrs: rdn and ev ch ent fnl 2f: struggling to qckn whn squeezed for room over 1f out: wknd ins fnl f* **5/2**[1]

260- **8** 7 **Amoya (GER)**[244] 6236 6-9-1 82 — [1] TomQueally 2 — 66
(Philip McBride) *led tl over 2f out: sn struggling and dropped to rr 2f out: wknd over 1f out* **25/1**

2m 7.65s (1.85) **Going Correction** +0.10s/f (Good) — **8** Ran SP% **112.5**
Speed ratings (Par 107): **96,95,94,94,93 92,91,85**
toteswingers 1&2 £6.20, 1&3 £5.60, 2&3 £6.30 CSF £80.50 CT £438.48 TOTE £9.00: £2.90, £2.00, £1.50; EX 78.70 Trifecta £390.40 Pool: £3725.79 - 7.15 winning units..

Owner Godolphin **Bred** Grapestock Llc **Trained** Newmarket, Suffolk

FOCUS
A fair handicap. The winner could have a lot more to offer and the next two give the form some substance.

2423 MCCULLOUGHS MAIDEN FILLIES' STKS — 1m 4f
4:40 (4:43) (Class 5) 3-Y-O — **£3,234** (£962; £481; £240) **Stalls** Centre

Form — RPR

2 **1** — **Riposte**[21] 1813 3-9-0 0 — TomQueally 3 — 88+
(Sir Henry Cecil) *short of room sn after s: hld up in tch: hdwy to ld on bit over 2f out: pushed clr and in command over 1f out: v easily* **10/11**[1]

2-3 **2** 2 **Auld Alliance (IRE)**[21] 1813 3-9-0 0 — KierenFallon 6 — 81
(Sir Michael Stoute) *chsd ldrs: rdn over 2f out: styd on to chse clr wnr over 1f out: kpt on wl for clr 2nd but no threat to wnr* **15/8**[2]

0 **3** 7 **Bossa Nova Baby (IRE)**[29] 1636 3-9-0 0 — SteveDrowne 4 — 69
(Charles Hills) *led for 2f: styd pressing ldr: rdn and ev ch over 2f out: outpcd and btn over 1f out: wknd fnl f* **25/1**

4 3/4 **Silk Train** 3-9-0 0 — MartinLane 2 — 68+
(David Simcock) *hld up in tch towards rr: rdn and outpcd 3f out: wl hld but rallied over 1f out: no threat to wnr but kpt on ins fnl f* **33/1**

3 **5** 1 1/2 **Nellie Forbush**[30] 1611 3-9-0 0 — DavidProbert 7 — 65
(Andrew Balding) *w ldr tl led 10f out: rdn and hdd 2f out: sn drvn and btn: wknd over 1f out* **12/1**

00- **6** 1 3/4 **Skating Over (USA)**[220] 6960 3-9-0 0 — PatCosgrave 8 — 63
(Jane Chapple-Hyam) *chsd ldrs: rdn and lost pl 3f out: bhd 2f out: no ch but plugged on fnl f* **66/1**

7 4 1/2 **Elhathrah (IRE)** 3-9-0 0 — DaneO'Neill 5 — 55
(Ed Dunlop) *s.i.s: rn green in rr: rdn and struggling 4f out: wl btn fnl 2f* **20/1**

20- **8** 1 1/2 **Jadesnumberone (IRE)**[195] 7555 3-9-0 0 — JamesDoyle 1 — 53
(Michael Bell) *t.k.h: hld up in tch in midfield: hdwy to join ldrs 3f out: rdn and fnd nil over 2f out: sn btn: wknd wl over 1f out* **7/1**[3]

2m 34.82s (2.82) **Going Correction** +0.10s/f (Good) — **8** Ran SP% **120.4**
Speed ratings (Par 96): **94,92,88,87,86 85,82,81**
toteswingers 1&2 £1.30, 1&3 £5.10, 2&3 £7.10 CSF £2.88 TOTE £1.60: £1.10, £1.10, £5.40; EX 3.10 Trifecta £33.00 Pool: £5815.45 - 132.00 winning units..

Owner K Abdullah **Bred** Juddmonte Farms Ltd **Trained** Newmarket, Suffolk

FOCUS
An interesting fillies' maiden run at a steady tempo. There was very little between the market principals based on their previous Sandown meeting. They finished clear and the winner can rate a lot better than the bare form.

2424 SIX WHITING STREET H'CAP — 1m
5:15 (5:18) (Class 3) (0-95,95) 4-Y-0+ — **£7,762** (£2,310; £1,154; £577) **Stalls** High

Form — RPR

30-1 **1** — **Directorship**[20] 1848 7-9-4 92 — DaneO'Neill 9 — 105
(Patrick Chamings) *hld up off the pce in midfield: smooth hdwy over 2f out: rdn to ld 1f out: sn clr and r.o wl: readily* **20/1**

0-36 **2** 3 1/2 **Tigers Tale (IRE)**[16] 1922 4-8-4 83 — (v) RobertTart(5) 7 — 88
(Roger Teal) *wnt rt and bmpd s: stdd and bdly jostled sn after s: off the pce in midfield: clsd over 2f out: rdn and ev ch over 1f out: outpcd by wnr but kpt on for 2nd fnl f* **14/1**

00-4 **3** 2 1/4 **Forgotten Hero (IRE)**[20] 1848 4-9-1 89 — SteveDrowne 14 — 89
(Charles Hills) *taken down early: hld up off the pce in rr: hdwy over 2f out: no imp and hung rt over 1f out: kpt on again ins fnl f* **12/1**

025- **4** hd **Stevie Thunder**[197] 6494 8-8-11 88 — RyanPowell(3) 11 — 87
(Ian Williams) *hld up off the pce in rr: rdn and hdwy over 1f out: kpt on wl ins fnl f* **25/1**

046- **5** nk **Vainglory (USA)**[195] 7556 9-8-11 85 — MartinLane 10 — 84
(David Simcock) *off the pce in midfield: rdn and lost pl over 2f out: rallied and styd on u.p ins fnl f* **25/1**

0-62 **6** nk **Ascription (IRE)**[7] 2232 4-8-7 81 oh3 — (t) LiamJones 13 — 79
(Hugo Palmer) *prom in main gp: rdn and effrt over 2f out: unable qck u.p over 1f out: one pce fnl f* **6/1**[3]

1-11 **7** 3/4 **Rockalong (IRE)**[16] 1922 4-9-0 88 — KierenFallon 2 — 84
(Luca Cumani) *prom in main gp: chsd clr ldr 1/2-way: clsd over 2f out: rdn to ld wl over 1f out: hdd 1f out: wknd ins fnl f* **13/8**[1]

32-0 **8** 1 1/4 **Border Legend**[27] 1675 4-8-12 86 — JamesDoyle 12 — 79
(Roger Charlton) *prom in main gp: clsd on ldr over 2f out: rdn and ev ch wl over 1f out: no ex 1f out: wknd ins fnl f* **7/2**[2]

0550 **9** 3 **Spirit Of Sharjah (IRE)**[17] 1913 8-9-0 88 — (p) TedDurcan 5 — 74
(Julia Feilden) *off the pce in midfield: rdn and effrt over 2f out: no imp over 1f out: wknd ins fnl f* **66/1**

04-6 **10** 4 1/2 **Johnno**[22] 1782 4-8-10 84 — SebSanders 1 — 60
(J W Hills) *hld up off the pce in rr: hdwy over 2f out: rdn and no imp wl over 1f out: wl btn and eased ins fnl f* **25/1**

06-0 **11** 2 1/4 **Crius (IRE)**[27] 1675 4-9-7 95 — SeanLevey 6 — 66
(Richard Hannon) *taken down early: wnt lft and bmpd rival s: sn led and wl clr: rdn and hdd wl over 1f out: sn wknd* **25/1**

015- **12** 25 **Starfield**[170] 7904 4-8-13 87 — (p) NickyMackay 16
(John Gosden) *a bhd: rdn and struggling 3f out: wknd over 2f out: t.o and eased ins fnl f* **20/1**

424- **13** 1/2 **Storm King**[155] 8095 4-9-2 90 — PatCosgrave 8
(Jane Chapple-Hyam) *prom in main gp: drvn and lost pl 3f out: t.o and eased ins fnl f* **18/1**

360- **R** **Ducal**[248] 6119 5-8-10 89 — WilliamTwiston-Davies(5) 15
(Mike Murphy) *veered sharply lft leaving stalls and ref to r* **25/1**

1m 37.7s (-0.90) **Going Correction** +0.10s/f (Good) — **14** Ran SP% **124.5**
Speed ratings (Par 107): **108,104,102,102,101 101,100,99,96,91 89,64,64,**
toteswingers 1&2 £49.00, 1&3 £12.90, 2&3 £24.90 CSF £258.21 CT £3583.50 TOTE £21.30: £3.90, £3.70, £3.10; EX 425.70 Trifecta £2993.80 Part won. Pool: £3991.85 - 0.52 winning units..

Owner Mrs R Lyon,Mrs P Hayton,P R Chamings **Bred** Mrs D O Joly **Trained** Baughurst, Hants

FOCUS
A strongly run handicap, rather set up for those held up. A slightly negative view has been taken of the overall form.

2425 SACKERS RECYCLING RACING EXCELLENCE "HANDS N' HEELS" APPRENTICE H'CAP (RACING EXCELLENCE INITIATIVE) — 6f
5:50 (5:50) (Class 5) (0-75,75) 4-Y-0+ — **£3,234** (£962; £481; £240) **Stalls** High

Form — RPR

122- **1** — **See The Storm**[154] 8114 5-8-4 61 — JordanVaughan(3) 10 — 71
(Ian Williams) *hld up in rr: gd hdwy to ld 1f out: pushed along and kpt on wl ins fnl f* **5/1**[1]

43-6 **2** 1 **Flynn's Boy**[15] 1963 5-9-7 75 — MatthewHopkins 8 — 82
(Rae Guest) *hld up in rr: rdn and hdwy over 1f out: chsd wnr ins fnl f: kpt on* **5/1**[1]

-013 **3** 1 1/2 **Two Turtle Doves (IRE)**[6] 2281 7-8-7 61 6ex — JoeyHaynes 14 — 64
(Michael Mullineaux) *in tch in midfield: rdn and n.m.r over 1f out: hdwy ins fnl f: styd on* **9/1**

-400 **4** 1/2 **Afkar (IRE)**[22] 1782 5-9-1 72 — (p) LaurenHaigh(3) 1 — 73+
(Clive Brittain) *chsd ldrs: ev ch and nudged along over 1f out: outpcd and one pce ins fnl f* **5/1**[1]

6250 **5** hd **Welease Bwian (IRE)**[27] 1694 4-8-7 64 — JeanVanOvermeire(3) 12 — 64
(Stuart Williams) *in tch towards rr: hdwy over 1f out: rdn and no ex ins fnl f: wknd towards fin* **16/1**

-036 **6** 1 1/4 **Celtic Sixpence (IRE)**[21] 1802 5-8-12 69 — KevinStott(3) 2 — 66
(Nick Kent) *in tch in midfield: rdn and unable qck over 1f out: kpt on same pce ins fnl f* **7/1**[2]

3623 **7** nse **Alnoomaas (IRE)**[43] 1346 4-9-4 75 — JoshCrane(3) 3 — 72
(Luke Dace) *s.i.s: rcvrd and in midfield after 1f: rdn and pressing ldrs over 1f out: no ex 1f out: wknd ins fnl f* **8/1**[3]

6623 **8** nk **Putin (IRE)**[9] 2171 5-8-4 61 oh1 — (bt) SiobhanMiller(3) 9 — 57
(Phil McEntee) *w ldr: rdn and ev ch over 1f out: led ent fnl f: sn hdd: wknd ins fnl f* **14/1**

226- **9** 1 3/4 **Parisian Pyramid (IRE)**[146] 8232 7-9-0 71 — AdamMcLean(3) 5 — 61
(Patrick Morris) *led tl ent fnl f: wknd fnl 100yds* **9/1**

40-0 **10** 1 3/4 **Dark Ages (IRE)**[73] 963 4-8-13 72 — (t) OisinMurphy(5) 6 — 57
(Paul Burgoyne) *chsd ldrs: shuffled bk and n.m.r over 1f out: wknd fnl f* **16/1**

2060 **11** 1 **Cardinal**[32] 1581 8-9-2 73 — RobJFitzpatrick(3) 15 — 55
(Robert Cowell) *racd alone in centre: midfield overall: rdn and no hdwy over 1f out: wknd fnl f* **14/1**

56-0 **12** 1/2 **Bobbyow**[128] 111 5-8-2 61 oh15 — BradleyBosley(5) 11 — 42
(K F Clutterbuck) *in tch in midfield: rdn and lost pl 2f out: bhd fnl f* **100/1**

1m 12.83s (0.63) **Going Correction** +0.10s/f (Good) — **12** Ran SP% **119.7**
Speed ratings (Par 103): **99,97,95,95,94 93,93,92,90,87 86,85**
toteswingers 1&2 £5.50, 1&3 £6.80, 2&3 £4.70 CSF £28.89 CT £226.62 TOTE £5.10: £2.00, £1.80, £3.30; EX 27.70 Trifecta £110.80 Pool: £1369.94 - 9.27 winning units..

Owner Keating Bradley Fold Ltd **Bred** D R Botterill **Trained** Portway, Worcs

FOCUS
A wide-open sprint handicap and fair form. The winner is quietly progressive.
T/Plt: £132.90 to a £1 stake. Pool: £53,100.96 - 291.66 winning tickets. T/Qpdt: £34.00 to a £1 stake. Pool: £2953.48 - 64.25 winning tickets. SP

2396YORK (L-H)

Friday, May 17

OFFICIAL GOING: Soft (good to soft in places; 6.3)

Wind: fresh 1/2 against Weather: fine and sunny but breezy

2426 LANGLEYS SOLICITORS LLP EBF MARYGATE STKS (LISTED RACE) (FILLIES) 5f

1:45 (1:45) (Class 1) 2-Y-O

£19,848 (£7,525; £3,766; £1,876; £941; £472) **Stalls** Centre

Form RPR

1 **1** **Beldale Memory (IRE)**28 1659 2-8-12 0 JamieSpencer 6 91+
(Clive Cox) *leggy: lengthy: trckd ldrs: swtchd rt over 1f out: led appr fnl f: pushed along and styd on wl: readily* **7/4**1

3 **2** 2 3/4 **Hoku (IRE)**25 1724 2-8-12 0 HarryBentley 8 81
(Olly Stevens) *str: scope: lw: dwlt: hld up towards rr: hdwy over 1f out: styd on wl ins fnl f: tk 2nd post* **15/2**

02 **3** nse **Classy Lassy (IRE)**13 2025 2-8-12 0 DaleSwift 2 81
(Brian Ellison) *w'like: lengthy: in rr: hdwy over 2f out: edgd lft over 1f out: kpt on wl towards fin* **33/1**

31 **4** nk **Lexington Rose**20 1839 2-8-12 0 RoystonFfrench 4 80
(Bryan Smart) *w'like: chsd ldrs: rdn 2f out: kpt on same pce fnl f: lost 2 pls clsng stages* **16/1**

211 **5** 1 1/2 **Quatuor (IRE)**9 2147 2-8-12 0 RichardKingscote 3 75
(Tom Dascombe) *led hdd appr fnl f: wknd last 50yds* **5/1**2

612 **6** 2 **Blithe Spirit**9 2147 2-8-12 0 JasonHart 5 67
(Eric Alston) *swtg: chsd ldr: drvn 2f out: fdd last 150yds* **16/1**

1 **7** 1/2 **Champagne Babe**13 2025 2-8-12 0 JoeFanning 1 66
(Keith Dalgleish) *angular: chsd ldrs: wknd over 1f out* **9/1**

1 **8** 3 3/4 **Majestic Alexander (IRE)**41 1399 2-8-12 0 TomMcLaughlin 7 52
(David Evans) *unf: chsd ldrs: lost pl over 1f out* **13/2**3

310 **9** 3 **Kodafine (IRE)**9 2147 2-8-12 0 NeilCallan 12 41
(David Evans) *leggy: unf: chsd ldrs: drvn over 2f out: lost pl over 1f out: eased clsng stages* **66/1**

3 **10** nk **Heskin (IRE)**25 1718 2-8-12 0 TonyHamilton 11 40
(Richard Fahey) *w'like: str: lw: s.s: nvr on terms: eased towards fin* **9/1**

3 **11** 19 **Abisko (IRE)**9 2161 2-8-12 0 TomEaves 13
(Brian Ellison) *w'like: tall: b.hind: slowly away and wnt rt s: in rr: hung rt and stands' side rail over 2f out: sn bhd: eased ins fnl f: t.o* **50/1**

1m 0.67s (1.37) **Going Correction** +0.425s/f (Yiel) **11** Ran SP% **116.3**
Speed ratings (Par 98): **106,101,101,101,98 95,94,88,83,83 52**
toteswingers 1&2 £4.10, 1&3 £14.60, 2&3 £34.80 CSF £14.91 TOTE £2.50: £1.20, £2.60, £6.30; EX 17.40 Trifecta £320.50 Pool: £4714.30 - 11.02 winning units..

Owner Qatar Racing Limited **Bred** Yeomanstown Stud **Trained** Lambourn, Berks

FOCUS

Rail from 1m1f to entrance to home straight moved out 3m, adding 7yds to races on Round course. The ground had dried a fraction overnight and GoingStick readings were as follows: Far side 6.3, Centre 6.2 and Stands' side 6.0. Richard Kingscote felt it was "dead", while Royston Ffrench described it as "good to soft". They raced centre-to-far side in what was an ordinary race for the grade, and the first two look capable of leaving this form behind in time. Limited form for the grade in behind.

2427 BETFRED JORVIK STKS (H'CAP) 1m 4f

2:15 (2:15) (Class 2) (0-105,103) 4-Y-O+**£29,110** (£8,662; £4,329; £2,164) **Stalls** Centre

Form RPR

04-1 **1** **Sir John Hawkwood (IRE)**8 2185 4-9-12 **103** 6ex RyanMoore 10 113
(Sir Michael Stoute) *trckd ldrs: swtchd lft and hdwy 3f out: led over 2f out: jnd and rdn over 1f out: drvn ins fnl f: kpt on wl* **13/8**1

-210 **2** hd **Hanoverian Baron**48 1242 8-8-6 **88** MichaelJMMurphy(5) 8 98
(Tony Newcombe) *hld up: stdy hdwy 4f out: trckd ldrs over 2f out: effrt to chal wl over 1f out: sn rdn and ev ch tl drvn and no ex towards fin* **14/1**

13-0 **3** 3 **Brockwell**23 1766 4-8-13 **90** RichardKingscote 6 95
(Tom Dascombe) *trckd ldng pair: hdwy 4f out: rdn along wl over 2f out: drvn wl over 1f out: kpt on same pce fnl f* **10/1**3

060- **4** hd **Martin Chuzzlewit (IRE)**224 6832 4-8-10 **87** JamieSpencer 11 92
(David Simcock) *hld up: hdwy wl over 2f out: swtchd rt and rdn wl over 1f out: styd on u.p fnl f: nrst fin* **11/2**2

005/ **5** 1 **Saptapadi (IRE)**229 7-9-1 **95** PaulPickard(3) 4 98
(Brian Ellison) *lw: hld up in rr: gd hdwy over 3f out: rdn to chse ldrs wl over 1f out: kpt on same pce fnl f* **20/1**

4/5 **6** hd **Oriental Fox (GER)**27 1689 5-9-4 **95** JoeFanning 2 98
(Mark Johnston) *trckd ldrs: hdwy to take slt ld 3f out: sn rdn and hdd over 2f out: drvn and wknd fnl f* **16/1**

40-0 **7** 1 3/4 **Rio's Rosanna (IRE)**7 2240 6-8-10 **87** AmyRyan 13 87
(Richard Whitaker) *in tch: effrt 3f out: rdn along 2f out: grad wknd fr wl over 1f out* **12/1**

00-0 **8** 3 1/2 **Crackentorp**20 1841 8-9-3 **94** DavidAllan 12 88
(Tim Easterby) *sn led: pushed clr over 4f out: rdn along and hdd 3f out: sn drvn and wknd* **18/1**

0-40 **9** 1 **Easy Terms**27 1689 6-9-3 **94** JamesSullivan 5 87
(Edwin Tuer) *chsd ldrs: rdn along wl over 2f out: grad wknd* **11/1**

0-60 **10** 1 **Spanish Duke (IRE)**23 1768 6-8-11 **88** DaleSwift 1 79
(Brian Ellison) *dwlt: a in rr* **14/1**

10-4 **11** nk **King's Warrior (FR)**23 1768 6-9-10 **101** RobertHavlin 3 92
(Peter Chapple-Hyam) *lw: hld up: a in rr* **10/1**3

12 3/4 **Pulpitarian (USA)**174 5-9-1 **92** GrahamLee 7 81
(Lucinda Russell) *hld up: a towards rr* **40/1**

2m 35.89s (2.69) **Going Correction** +0.425s/f (Yiel) **12** Ran SP% **119.4**
Speed ratings (Par 109): **108,107,105,105,105 104,103,101,100,100 99,99**
toteswingers 1&2 £6.60, 1&3 £4.50, 2&3 £11.40 CSF £27.20 CT £184.20 TOTE £2.30: £1.10, £4.70, £3.30; EX 28.80 Trifecta £207.50 Pool: £5172.98 - 18.69 winning units..

Owner Ballymacoll Stud **Bred** Ballymacoll Stud Farm Ltd **Trained** Newmarket, Suffolk

FOCUS

A classy handicap. The pace was sound and the field came down the centre of the track up the straight. The race lacked progressive types. Sound form from the principals with further progress from the winner and the second's best run since 2010.

2428 QIPCO YORKSHIRE CUP (BRITISH CHAMPIONS SERIES) (GROUP 2) 1m 6f

2:45 (2:45) (Class 1) 4-Y-O+

£79,394 (£30,100; £15,064; £7,504; £3,766; £1,890) **Stalls** Low

Form RPR

604- **1** **Glen's Diamond**244 6236 5-9-0 104 TonyHamilton 4 114
(Richard Fahey) *led after 1f: jnd jst ins fnl f: styd on gamely: all out* **25/1**

46-6 **2** nse **Top Trip**40 1420 4-9-0 113 MickaelBarzalona 7 114
(F Doumen, France) *sn drvn along in mid-div: hrd drvn and outpcd over 4f out: hdwy to chse ldrs over 2f out: 2nd over 1f out: upsides jst ins fnl f: jst denied* **11/4**1

1-00 **3** 3 1/4 **Royal Diamond (IRE)**48 1268 7-9-4 111 NGMcCullagh 9 113
(Thomas Carmody, Ire) *chsd ldrs: racd wd: 3rd and hung lft over 1f out: kpt on same pce* **11/1**

23-3 **4** 4 1/2 **A Boy Named Suzi**41 1382 5-9-0 98 (v1) JamieSpencer 5 103
(Andrew Balding) *s.v.s: hld up detached in last: smooth hdwy 3f out: sn rdn: one pce over 1f out* **16/1**

10-2 **5** 1 **Quiz Mistress**27 1674 5-8-11 106 JimmyFortune 1 99
(Hughie Morrison) *hld up in rr: hdwy and swtchd lft over 2f out: one pce over 1f out* **5/1**3

310- **6** 2 1/4 **Joshua Tree (IRE)**159 8040 6-9-4 116 RyanMoore 6 103
(Ed Dunlop) *trckd ldrs: drvn to chal over 2f out: wknd appr fnl f* **7/2**2

10-6 **7** 11 **Guarantee**27 1674 4-9-0 105 (v1) PhillipMakin 3 83
(William Haggas) *trckd ldrs: t.k.h: rdn 3f out: sn wknd* **11/2**

1-53 **8** 1 **Sir Graham Wade (IRE)**16 1920 4-9-0 107 JoeFanning 2 82
(Mark Johnston) *lw: led 1f: chsd ldrs: drvn over 4f out: lost pl 3f out* **6/1**

3m 1.39s (1.19) **Going Correction** +0.425s/f (Yiel) **8** Ran SP% **113.3**
Speed ratings (Par 115): **113,112,111,108,107 106,100,99**
toteswingers 1&2 £11.00, 1&3 £12.00, 2&3 £9.70 CSF £91.54 TOTE £28.40: £5.80, £1.20, £4.20; EX 118.10 Trifecta £2013.30 Pool: £6823.76 - 2.54 winning units..

Owner S & G Clayton **Bred** Doverlane Finance Ltd **Trained** Musley Bank, N Yorks

FOCUS

The absence of Cavalryman left this looking quite an average race for the grade and the outcome did little to alter that view, with them going just a steady pace and several of the key players failing to give their running. The form is rated around Glen's Diamond's run in the race last year.

2429 BLADE AMENITY FILLIES' STKS (REGISTERED AS THE MICHAEL SEELY MEMORIAL STAKES) (LISTED RACE) 1m

3:15 (3:17) (Class 1) 3-Y-O

£22,684 (£8,600; £4,304; £2,144; £1,076; £540) **Stalls** Low

Form RPR

1 **1** **Pavlosk (USA)**28 1666 3-8-12 0 RyanMoore 2 103+
(Sir Michael Stoute) *lw: trckd ldrs: qcknd to ld over 2f out: pushed clr over 1f out: v readily* **3/1**2

11-2 **2** 3 1/2 **Senafe**34 1546 3-8-12 86 NeilCallan 4 95
(Marco Botti) *trckd ldrs: t.k.h: effrt 3f out: wnt 2nd over 1f out: kpt on: no imp* **9/1**

50-2 **3** 3/4 **Pearl Sea (IRE)**16 1918 3-8-12 93 JamieSpencer 5 93+
(David Brown) *s.i.s: in rr: hdwy over 2f out: styd on to take 3rd ins fnl f* **8/1**

10- **4** 1 **Orpha**250 6081 3-8-12 91 MickaelBarzalona 7 91
(Mick Channon) *hld up towards rr: effrt over 2f out: kpt on ins fnl f to take 4th nr fin* **11/4**1

20-0 **5** 1 1/4 **Califante**27 1676 3-8-12 97 MartinDwyer 8 88
(William Muir) *mid-div: effrt 3f out: one pce* **25/1**

23-3 **6** 2 1/4 **Hanzada (USA)**17 1908 3-8-12 80 GrahamLee 1 83
(Ed Dunlop) *lengthy : lw: hld up in rr: drvn over 2f out: kpt on: nvr a threat* **22/1**

430- **7** 1 **Annie's Fortune (IRE)**216 7052 3-8-12 98 MichaelJMMurphy 9 81
(Alan Jarvis) *in rr-div: effrt 3f out: sn outpcd: nvr a factor* **7/1**

1-1 **8** 3/4 **How's Life**22 1772 3-8-12 80 AndreaAtzeni 10 79
(Rae Guest) *w'like: trckd ldr: t.k.h: wknd over 1f out* **5/1**3

44-6 **9** 12 **City Image (IRE)**27 1676 3-9-1 99 JimmyFortune 3 54
(Richard Hannon) *led: drvn 3f out: sn hdd lost pl over 1f out: eased ins fnl f: virtually p.u* **14/1**

1m 42.4s (3.40) **Going Correction** +0.425s/f (Yiel) **9** Ran SP% **116.8**
Speed ratings (Par 104): **100,96,95,94,93 91,90,89,77**
toteswingers 1&2 £5.00, 1&3 £5.60, 2&3 £5.90 CSF £30.63 TOTE £3.20: £1.80, £2.70, £2.00; EX 32.00 Trifecta £206.10 Pool: £5122.10 - 18.63 winning units..

Owner K Abdullah **Bred** Juddmonte Farms Inc **Trained** Newmarket, Suffolk

FOCUS

First run in 2006, this Listed race numbers the classy Chachamaidee and Laugh Out Loud among its former winners. This edition looked up to scratch, and was run at a reasonable pace. Again they came down the centre of the straight. The winner looks better than this grade.

2430 RALPH RAPER MEMORIAL STKS (H'CAP) 5f

3:50 (3:53) (Class 3) (0-90,90) 3-Y-O **£9,703** (£2,887; £1,443; £721) **Stalls** Centre

Form RPR

1-01 **1** **Moviesta (USA)**21 1806 3-9-4 **87** PaulMulrennan 17 94
(Bryan Smart) *racd towards stands' rail: prom: effrt to ld wl over 1f out: rdn clr ent fnl f: edgd lft last 100yds and jst hld on* **8/1**3

116- **2** nse **Vincentti (IRE)**223 6865 3-9-3 **86** LukeMorris 18 93
(Ronald Harris) *racd towards stands' rail: chsd ldrs: rdn wl over 1f out: swtchd rt and drvn ent fnl f: styd on strly towards fin: jst failed* **33/1**

160- **3** 1 3/4 **Shrimper Roo**223 6883 3-8-7 **76** oh1 1 SilvestreDeSousa 14 77
(Tim Easterby) *dwlt and outpcd: bhd and rdn along after 2f: swtchd rt to stands' rail wl over 1f out: styd on strly u.p fnl f: tk 3rd nr line* **50/1**

53-5 **4** hd **Secret Look**37 1482 3-9-5 **88** GrahamGibbons 9 88
(Ed McMahon) *in tch centre: hdwy 2f out: sn chsng ldrs: kpt on fnl f* **15/2**2

-165 **5** nk **Top Boy**12 2039 3-9-7 **90** MartinDwyer 2 89
(Derek Shaw) *racd towards far side: trckd ldrs: hdwy 2f out: sn rdn and ev ch tl drvn and one pce fnl f* **16/1**

110- **6** nk **Bachotheque (IRE)**217 7028 3-9-2 **85** GrahamLee 3 83
(Tim Easterby) *lw: racd towards far rail: towards rr: pushed along 1/2-way: sn rdn: styd on appr fnl f: nrst fin* **18/1**

11-5 **7** nk **Dutch Masterpiece**30 1625 3-9-7 **90** RyanMoore 5 87
(Gary Moore) *racd towards far side: cl up: effrt over 2f out: rdn wl over 1f out and ev ch tl wknd ins fnl f* **11/4**1

10-4 **8** 1 1/4 **Lady Ibrox**12 2039 3-9-5 **88** DaleSwift 19 80
(Alan Brown) *racd towards stands' rail: chsd ldrs: rdn along wl over 1f out: one pce appr fnl f* **12/1**

1622 **9** *hd* **Bispham Green**[7] 2213 3-8-13 **82**.................................... TonyHamilton 8 74
(Richard Fahey) *prom towards stands' rail: cl up: hdwy and overall ldr 1/2-way: rdn and hdd wl over 1f out: sn drvn and wknd ent fnl f* **8/1**[3]

115- **10** *1 3/4* **Lastchancelucas**[349] 2702 3-8-13 **87**.................................... JasonHart[(5)] 6 72
(Declan Carroll) *lw: racd towards far side: trckd ldrs: hdwy and cl up 2f out: sn rdn and grad wknd appr fnl f* **16/1**

050- **11** *1/2* **Madam Mojito (USA)**[286] 4820 3-9-3 **86**................ MichaelO'Connell 15 70
(John Quinn) *racd towards stands' rail: prom: rdn along over 2f out: sn wknd* **25/1**

5-34 **12** *1/2* **Chasing Dreams**[9] 2166 3-8-7 **76** oh2.................................. AmyRyan 12 58
(Kevin Ryan) *s.i.s and bhd: styd on fnl 2f: nvr a factor* **20/1**

1-21 **13** *1 1/4* **Space Artist (IRE)**[28] 1661 3-8-11 **80**....................... RoystonFfrench 10 57
(Bryan Smart) *prom in centre: rdn along 2f out: sn wknd* **20/1**

14 **14** *1 1/4* **My Name Is Rio (IRE)**[37] 1482 3-8-7 **76**............................ TomEaves 13 49
(Michael Dods) *chsd ldrs centre: pushed along 1/2-way: sn rdn and wknd* **8/1**[3]

0-63 **15** *1 1/2* **Threes Grand**[21] 1806 3-9-2 **88**... BillyCray[(3)] 1 55
(Scott Dixon) *b.hind: racd on far rail: chsd ldrs: rdn along 2f out: sn wknd* **25/1**

0-11 **16** *1 3/4* **Mayfield Girl (IRE)**[27] 1690 3-9-4 **87**................................ DavidAllan 16 48
(Mel Brittain) *racd towards stands' rail: prom: rdn along over 2f out: sn drvn and wknd* **14/1**

-305 **17** *5* **Satsuma**[7] 2213 3-9-6 **89**.. JamieSpencer 7 32
(David Brown) *racd towards far side: overall ldr: rdn along 1/2-way: sn hdd & wknd* **18/1**

1m 1.05s (1.75) **Going Correction** +0.425s/f (Yiel) **17** Ran SP% **130.5**
Speed ratings (Par 103): **103,102,100,99,99 98,98,96,96,93 92,91,89,87,85 82,74**
toteswingers 1&2 £68.00, 1&3 £110.60, 2&3 £124.30 CSF £272.05 CT £6442.24 TOTE £9.50: £2.60, £7.60, £9.80, £2.40; EX 432.80 Trifecta £3256.00 Part won. Pool: £4341.36 - 0.14 winning units..
Owner Redknapp, Salthouse & Fiddes **Bred** John D Gunther **Trained** Hambleton, N Yorks

FOCUS

They raced centre-to-far side in this wide-open 3yo sprint and both the front pair launched their challenge on the near-side of the main group down the middle. A competitive handicap but the time was 20lb slower than the 2yo opener. The form is rated around the fourth to seventh.

2431 ONE MARKETING COMMUNICATIONS STKS (H'CAP) 1m 2f 88y

4:25 (4:25) (Class 3) (0-90,90) 4-Y-0+ **£9,703** (£2,887; £1,443; £721) **Stalls** Low

Form RPR

412- **1** **Rye House (IRE)**[324] 3509 4-9-5 **88**.................................... RyanMoore 5 101+
(Sir Michael Stoute) *lw: trckd ldrs: pushed along over 2f out: led over 1f out: drvn clr: readily* **15/8**[1]

6-00 **2** *3 1/4* **Maven**[34] 1538 5-8-11 **80**.. DavidAllan 10 87
(Tim Easterby) *stdd s: hld up in rr: hdwy over 2f out: sn chsng ldrs: styd on wl to take 2nd clsng stages* **11/1**

5-11 **3** *hd* **Awake My Soul (IRE)**[7] 2240 4-9-5 **88** 6ex............... DanielTudhope 12 95+
(David O'Meara) *t.k.h: trckd ldrs: drvn on outer over 2f out: edgd rt and chsd wnr over 1f out: kpt on same pce* **5/1**[2]

3430 **4** *2 1/4* **Patriotic (IRE)**[13] 2018 5-8-7 **76**.......................................(p) LukeMorris 3 78
(Chris Dwyer) *hld up in rr: hdwy over 2f out: kpt on same pce fnl f* **12/1**

1004 **5** *1/2* **Suffice (IRE)**[6] 2256 4-8-7 **76** oh4............................ FrederikTylicki 14 77
(Richard Fahey) *in tch: effrt over 2f out: sn outpcd: styd on ins fnl f* **14/1**

-011 **6** *nk* **Take Two**[27] 1673 4-9-1 **84**.. AndreaAtzeni 9 85
(Alex Hales) *chsd ldrs: effrt over 2f out: kpt on one pce* **6/1**[3]

500- **7** *1 1/4* **War Poet**[160] 7689 6-9-0 **88**.. DavidBergin[(5)] 16 86
(David O'Meara) *s.i.s: looked reluctant and drvn early: detached in last: styd on fnl 3f: nvr a factor* **8/1**

05 **8** *1/2* **Moccasin (FR)**[29] 1643 4-9-1 **87**..................................... RaulDaSilva[(3)] 7 85
(Geoffrey Harker) *hld up in rr: effrt and swtchd rt over 2f out: kpt on fnl f* **40/1**

41-0 **9** *1* **Narcissist (IRE)**[12] 2040 4-8-10 **79**................................ PaulMulrennan 19 75
(Michael Easterby) *chsd ldrs: outpcd over 2f out: edgd lft over 1f out: no threat after* **20/1**

21-4 **10** *2 3/4* **Prophesy (IRE)**[48] 1237 4-8-13 **85**................................... NeilFarley[(3)] 11 75
(Declan Carroll) *in tch: effrt over 2f out: sn wknd* **9/1**

0-05 **11** *hd* **Warcrown (IRE)**[11] 2077 4-8-7 **76** oh4........................ PatrickMathers 15 66
(Richard Fahey) *lw: led: hdd over 2f out: lost pl appr fnl f* **33/1**

3-00 **12** *4* **Unex Michelangelo (IRE)**[7] 2240 4-8-13 **87**.......... ShirleyTeasdale[(5)] 1 69
(Michael Easterby) *chsd ldrs: lost pl over 2f out: sn bhd* **33/1**

2m 15.28s (2.78) **Going Correction** +0.425s/f (Yiel) **12** Ran SP% **122.6**
Speed ratings (Par 107): **105,102,102,100,100 99,98,98,97,95 95,92**
toteswingers 1&2 £8.50, 1&3 £3.10, 2&3 £10.50 CSF £24.49 CT £96.11 TOTE £2.60: £2.00, £3.40, £2.20; EX 27.40 Trifecta £208.50 Pool: £3249.09 - 11.68 winning units..
Owner Philip Newton **Bred** Philip Newton **Trained** Newmarket, Suffolk

FOCUS

They went quite steady in this, a race that revolved around the lightly raced winner. He should be capable of better, with the second rated back to form.

2432 GOAL.COM STKS (H'CAP) 1m 4f

5:00 (5:00) (Class 4) (0-80,78) 3-Y-0 **£9,703** (£2,887; £1,443; £721) **Stalls** Low

Form RPR

6-55 **1** **Esteaming**[16] 1934 3-9-1 **72**.. PhillipMakin 13 85
(David Barron) *hld up in rr: smooth hdwy on outside 3f out: led on bit over 1f out: edgd lft and drvn out* **7/1**

01- **2** *1 1/4* **Rundell**[228] 6733 3-9-5 **76**.. RyanMoore 11 87
(Richard Hannon) *b.hind: hld up in rr: hdwy 3f out: chsng ldrs over 1f out: edgd lft: kpt on to chse wnr last 100yds: crowded: no ex* **9/2**[2]

56-1 **3** *1 1/4* **Sioux Chieftain (IRE)**[37] 1487 3-9-3 **74**.................... SilvestreDeSousa 6 83+
(Tim Pitt) *chsd ldrs: upsides 6f out: led 4f out: hdd over 1f out: styd on same pce* **12/1**

4-22 **4** *1 3/4* **Allnecessaryforce (FR)**[37] 1470 3-9-7 **78**................... TonyHamilton 15 84
(Richard Fahey) *chsd ldrs: drvn over 2f out: n.m.r over 1f out: kpt on one pce* **7/1**

002- **5** *1/2* **Chocala (IRE)**[198] 7492 3-8-13 **70**...................................... JimmyFortune 8 75
(Alan King) *lw: hld up in rr: hdwy 3f out: chsng ldrs over 1f out: kpt on one pce* **12/1**

31-3 **6** *2 1/2* **Buckstay (IRE)**[16] 1934 3-9-6 **77**................................... JamieSpencer 12 78+
(Peter Chapple-Hyam) *lw: hld up in rr: hdwy on outer over 2f out: swtchd rt over 1f out: sn drvn and chsng ldrs: wknd fnl 50yds* **6/1**[3]

0-13 **7** *1 1/4* **Pivotal Silence**[18] 1885 3-8-9 **66**...................................... NeilCallan 9 65
(Amanda Perrett) *hld up towards rr: hdwy over 3f out: chsng ldrs 2f out: wknd fnl 100yds* **25/1**

5-13 **8** *6* **Wyldfire (IRE)**[30] 1604 3-8-10 **72**............................. GeorgeChaloner[(5)] 5 62
(Richard Fahey) *in tch: outpcd over 4f out: sme hdwy over 2f out: sn wknd* **12/1**

01-2 **9** *5* **Mombasa**[42] 1365 3-9-7 **78**.. RichardKingscote 10 69+
(Ralph Beckett) *trckd ldrs: t.k.h: drvn over 4f out: wknd 2f out: sn eased* **4/1**[1]

3-30 **10** *shd* **Arthurs Secret**[30] 1604 3-9-6 **77**................................... MichaelO'Connell 7 59
(John Quinn) *in tch: reminders 6f out: lost pl 4f out* **25/1**

2-50 **11** *2 1/2* **Duke Of Yorkshire**[37] 1487 3-8-7 **67**................................... NeilFarley[(3)] 3 45
(Declan Carroll) *mid-div: drvn and lost pl 4f out: sme hdwy over 2f out: sn wknd* **25/1**

5302 **12** *6* **Mad About Harry (IRE)**[9] 2156 3-8-8 **65**....................... FrederikTylicki 2 33
(John Best) *chsd ldrs: lost pl over 2f out: sn bhd* **20/1**

56-0 **13** *25* **Hunting Rights (USA)**[20] 1822 3-9-2 **78**............. MichaelJMMurphy[(5)] 1
(Mark Johnston) *led: hdd 4f out: lost pl over 2f out: eased whn bhd: virtually p.u: t.o* **20/1**

2m 36.6s (3.40) **Going Correction** +0.425s/f (Yiel) **13** Ran SP% **121.6**
Speed ratings (Par 101): **105,104,103,102,101 100,99,95,92,91 90,86,69**
toteswingers 1&2 £11.00, 1&3 £20.10, 2&3 £11.90 CSF £36.03 CT £371.55 TOTE £8.20: £3.00, £2.00, £4.20; EX 56.80 Trifecta £834.80 Pool: £2360.41 - 2.12 winning units..
Owner D E Cook **Bred** Mr & Mrs A E Pakenham & Daniel James **Trained** Maunby, N Yorks
■ Stewards' Enquiry : Phillip Makin caution; careless riding.

FOCUS

A competitive handicap, and good form for the grade. The pace lifted on the entrance to the home straight and the time was just 0.71sec slower than the earlier class 2 handicap.
T/Jkpt: Not won. T/Plt: £117.20 to a £1 stake. Pool: £198,764.44 - 1237.55 winning tickets.
T/Qpdt: £29.40 to a £1 stake. Pool: £9002.90 - 226.47 winning tickets. WG

2355 CHANTILLY (R-H)

Friday, May 17

OFFICIAL GOING: Turf: good; polytrack: standard

2433a PRIX DU MONT DE PO (CONDITIONS) (2YO) (TURF) 5f

12:50 (12:00) 2-Y-0 **£15,040** (£6,016; £4,512; £3,008; £1,504)

RPR

1 **Muharaaj (IRE)**[10] 2-8-11 0.. AntoineHamelin 1 94
(Matthieu Palussiere, France) **23/5**[3]

2 *1/2* **Meritocracy (IRE)**[11] 2082 2-9-0 0.......................... ChristopheSoumillon 7 95
(Paul Cole) *qckly across to nr side rail and led: rdn and qcknd clr over 1f out: 2 l ahd ent fnl f: r.o but clsd down and hdd fnl strides* **9/10**[1]

3 *2* **Atlantic City (FR)**[20] 2-8-8 0.. ThierryJarnet 6 82
(X Nakkachdji, France) **43/10**[2]

4 *4* **Aventure Love (FR)**[18] 1894 2-8-8 0................................ MaximeGuyon 4 68
(M Gentile, France) **5/1**

5 *2 1/2* **Pengabelot (FR)**[18] 2-8-11 0.......................................(p) UmbertoRispoli 5 62
(C Boutin, France) **16/1**

6 *1 1/4* **New Elite (FR)**[18] 1894 2-8-10 0...(p) SylvainRuis 2 56
(C Boutin, France) **34/1**

7 *2 1/2* **Apsis Dream (FR)** 2-8-11 0.. StephanePasquier 3 48
(T Castanheira, France) **28/1**

58.69s (0.39) **7** Ran SP% **118.2**
WIN (incl. 1 euro stake): 5.60. PLACES: 2.10, 1.50. SF: 14.30.
Owner Zalim Bifov **Bred** Mrs E Bifova **Trained** France

2434a PRIX DE PLAILLY (H'CAP) (3YO) (TURF) 1m 4f

1:50 (12:00) 3-Y-0 **£12,195** (£4,878; £3,658; £2,439; £1,219)

RPR

1 **I Thank You (FR)**[56] 3-8-13 **0**..................(b) Christophe-PatriceLemaire 3 78
(Y Barberot, France) **63/10**[3]

2 *snk* **Rodion Raskolnikov (FR)**[20] 1850 3-8-5 **0**............... CesarPasserat[(3)] 7 73
(C Lerner, France) **18/1**

3 *3/4* **Barsam (FR)**[20] 1850 3-8-7 **0**.. StephanePasquier 8 71
(P Bary, France) **18/1**

4 *1 1/4* **Haya Kan (FR)**[24] 1756 3-9-1 **0**...................................(b) ThierryThulliez 1 77
(Mme L Audon, France) **16/1**

5 *2* **Zimbali (FR)**[197] 3-9-5 **0**.. Pierre-CharlesBoudot 13 77
(A Fabre, France) **9/2**[2]

6 *hd* **Destiny Highway (FR)**[13] 2034 3-9-0 **0**.............................. MaximeGuyon 4 72
(Gay Kelleway) *midfield: rdn 3f out: styd on but nt pce to chal* **23/1**

7 *nk* **Sango (IRE)**[25] 3-9-1 **0**...(b) ChristopheSoumillon 2 73
(H-A Pantall, France) **43/10**[1]

8 *1* **Sweni Hill (IRE)**[24] 1756 3-8-8 **0**.................................... AntoineHamelin 16 64
(Y De Nicolay, France) **41/1**

9 *2 1/2* **Churada (IRE)**[20] 3-8-8 **0**.. AnthonyCrastus 15 60
(C Laffon-Parias, France) **34/1**

10 *1 1/4* **Nam June Paik (FR)**[24] 3-9-3 **0**......................................(p) TheoBachelot 5 67
(S Wattel, France) **7/1**

0 **Crackos (FR)**[211] 3-9-1 **0**.. IoritzMendizabal 9
(F Belmont, France) **14/1**

0 **Apollon D'Olivate (FR)**[15] 3-9-4 **0**.................................... RonanThomas 10
(P Van De Poele, France) **14/1**

0 **Instruction (IRE)**[10] 3-8-5 **0**... SylvainRuis 12
(C Boutin, France) **109/1**

0 **Leggy Lass (FR)**[31] 3-8-6 **0**...(b) MarcLerner 14
(S Wattel, France) **43/1**

0 **Ebulli (FR)**[38] 3-9-2 **0**.. MircoDemuro 11
(J Van Handenhove, France) **19/1**

0 **Wingland (FR)**[30] 3-9-2 **0**.. AlexisBadel 6
(Mme M Bollack-Badel, France) **19/1**

2m 32.1s (1.10) **16** Ran SP% **115.6**
WIN (incl. 1 euro stake): 7.30. PLACES: 2.40, 5.70, 6.40. DF: 76.40. SF: 120.50.
Owner G Augustin-Normand & Mme E Vidal **Bred** Mme E Vidal **Trained** France

2306 DONCASTER (L-H)

Saturday, May 18

OFFICIAL GOING: Good to soft (7.8)

Wind: Light half against Weather: Grey cloud

2435 CROWNHOTEL-BAWTRY.COM APPRENTICE H'CAP 1m 4f

5:25 (5:26) (Class 5) (0-70,70) 4-Y-0+ £3,067 (£905; £453) Stalls Low

Form RPR

0-26 **1** **Mr Snoozy**7 2277 4-8-13 **65**........(p) JasonHart(3) 6 74
(Tim Walford) *trckd ldng pair: hdwy 4f out: led 2f out and sn rdn: drvn and edgd lft ins fnl f: kpt on gamely* **11/2**1

3400 **2** 1 1/4 **Rayadour (IRE)**14 2009 4-8-9 **63**........(t) GeorgeChaloner(5) 9 70
(Micky Hammond) *trckd ldrs on inner: hdwy 4f out: rdn along 2f out: kpt on wl u.p fnl f* **12/1**

0-00 **3** 1/2 **Cosmic Moon**23 1790 5-8-2 **56** oh1........ SamanthaBell(5) 18 62
(Richard Fahey) *hld up towards rr: smooth hdwy on wd outside over 3f out: chsd ldrs 2f out: rdn and edgd lft over 1f out: chal and edgd lft again ins fnl f: ev ch tl no ex last 75yds* **16/1**

5006 **4** 1 **Brigadoon**7 2278 6-9-6 **69**........ DeclanCannon 11 74
(Philip Kirby) *hld up towards rr: hdwy wl over 2f out: rdn and kpt on appr fnl f: nrst fin* **15/2**2

4344 **5** 1/2 **Spanish Plume**42 1402 5-8-5 **59**........(p) JackDuern(5) 19 63
(Andrew Hollinshead) *hld up: gd hdwy on outer 4f out: rdn to chse ldrs 2f out: drvn to chal and ev ch ent fnl f: one pce* **20/1**

2544 **6** nk **Brunello**11 2120 5-8-8 **62**........(p) DavidBergin(5) 1 65
(David O'Meara) *hld up towards rr: hdwy 3f out: rdn along 2f out: kpt on appr fnl f: nrst fin* **11/2**1

3301 **7** 3/4 **El Bravo**5 2332 7-8-5 **57** 6ex........ ShirleyTeasdale(3) 8 59
(Shaun Harris) *trckd ldr: hdwy over 3f out: rdn to ld briefly 2 1/2f out: hdd 2f out and cl up tl drvn and wknd appr fnl f* **10/1**

0-02 **8** 1/2 **Silver Tigress**10 2165 5-8-13 **62**........ LeeTopliss 13 63
(George Moore) *hld up towards rr: hdwy into midfield over 4f out: in tch 3f out: rdn 2f out: sn one pce* **8/1**3

-400 **9** 1 1/2 **Amazing Blue Sky**23 1775 7-8-3 **59**........ KevinStott(7) 16 58
(Ruth Carr) *led: rdn along 3f out: sn hdd and grad wknd* **16/1**

014- **10** nk **Phase Shift**24 7602 5-8-4 **60**........(t) RichardOliver(7) 12 58
(Brian Ellison) *hld up: sme hdwy wl over 2f out: sn rdn along and plugged on: nvr a factor* **15/2**2

00-0 **11** 2 **Action Front (USA)**23 1794 5-8-1 **57**........(v1) AdamMcLean(7) 5 52
(Derek Shaw) *hld up towards rr: sme hdwy wl over 2f out: sn rdn along and n.d* **25/1**

/26- **12** 1 3/4 **Kayaan**64 3400 6-9-3 **66**........ BillyCray 17 58
(Pam Sly) *s.i.s: a in rr* **15/2**2

0500 **13** 22 **Munaawib**10 2170 5-8-0 **56** oh11........ CharlotteJenner(7) 2
(Charles Smith) *trckd ldrs on inner: rdn along over 3f out: sn wknd* **100/1**

00-5 **14** 3/4 **Visions Of Johanna (USA)**32 1597 8-8-0 **56** oh8........ AaronJones(7) 4
(Charles Smith) *chsd ldrs: rdn along 4f out: sn wknd* **66/1**

5654 **15** 21 **If What And Maybe**16 1953 5-8-0 **56** oh11........(v) JordonMcMurray(7) 20
(John Ryan) *midfield: rapid hdwy on outer after 2f: sn cl up: wd st: rdn along 4f out: sn wknd* **20/1**

2m 35.77s (0.87) **Going Correction** +0.175s/f (Good) **15** Ran SP% **121.6**
Speed ratings (Par 103): **104,103,102,102,101 101,101,100,99,99 98,97,82,81,67**
toteswingers 1&2 £12.80, 2&3 £34.40, 1&3 £29.10 CSF £68.51 CT £1011.79 TOTE £6.10: £2.00, £4.30, £5.50; EX 75.70 Trifecta £701.90 Part won. Pool: £935.97 - 0.18 winning units..

Owner T W Heseltine **Bred** J W Mursell **Trained** Sheriff Hutton, N Yorks

FOCUS
Round course railed out from 1m1f to where it joins straight adding circa 18yds to races on that course. The opening apprentice handicap appeared competitive on paper, and it turned out that way with a bunch finish. The winner took another step forward.

2436 FREEBETS.CO.UK FREE BETS MAIDEN AUCTION STKS 5f

5:55 (5:55) (Class 5) 2-Y-0 £2,911 (£866; £432; £216) Stalls High

Form RPR

1 **Eccleston** 2-8-11 0........ TonyHamilton 3 85+
(Richard Fahey) *trckd ldrs gng wl: nt clr run 2f out: gd hdwy and swtchd rt to inner over 1f out: led jst ins fnl f: sn qcknd clr: readily* **5/4**1

2 2 1/2 **Tableforten** 2-8-9 0........ LiamJones 7 72
(J S Moore) *in tch: hdwy to chse ldrs 2f out: rdn and ev ch over 1f out: kpt on same pce ins fnl f* **14/1**

3 nk **Fair Ranger** 2-8-13 0........ SeanLevey 5 75
(Richard Hannon) *awkwards s and s.i.s: hdwy on outer 3f out: chsd ldrs 2f out: sn rdn and ev ch appr fnl f: kpt on same pce* **11/4**2

3 **4** 1 **Will To Survive (IRE)**23 1792 2-8-9 0........ RobbieFitzpatrick 4 67
(Richard Guest) *trckd ldrs: hdwy 2f out: sn rdn and kpt on same pce fnl f* **16/1**

5 1 3/4 **Pound Piece (IRE)** 2-8-6 0........ RyanPowell(3) 2 61
(J S Moore) *prom: led over 2f out: sn rdn: hdd jst ins fnl f and wknd* **25/1**

6 3/4 **Mitcd (IRE)** 2-8-6 0........ BarryMcHugh 9 55
(Richard Fahey) *in tch: pushed along and sltly outpcd over 2f out: rdn and kpt on fnl f* **8/1**3

000 **7** 2 1/4 **Doncaster Belle (IRE)**21 1820 2-7-12 0 ow1........(tp) AaronJones(7) 10 46
(Charles Smith) *prom: rdn along 2f out: sn wknd* **66/1**

4 **8** 1/2 **Porsh Herrik**11 2117 2-8-9 0........ MichaelO'Connell 1 48
(John Quinn) *broke wl and led early: cl up: rdn along over 2f out: sn wknd* **10/1**

9 5 **Paint It Red (IRE)** 2-8-4 0........ AndrewMullen 11 25
(Richard Guest) *in tch: rdn along 1/2-way: sn wknd* **25/1**

10 2 **Sands Legends** 2-8-4 0........ LukeMorris 8 18
(James Given) *sn led: rdn along 1/2-way: sn hdd & wknd* **20/1**

11 1 1/2 **It's All A Game** 2-8-6 0........ BillyCray(3) 6 18
(Richard Guest) *s.i.s: a in rr* **33/1**

1m 2.7s (2.20) **Going Correction** +0.175s/f (Good) **11** Ran SP% **120.8**
Speed ratings (Par 93): **89,85,84,82,80 78,75,74,66,63 60**
toteswingers 1&2 £4.20, 2&3 £8.40, 1&3 £2.40 CSF £20.85 TOTE £2.10: £1.20, £5.60, £1.50; EX 27.10 Trifecta £95.40 Pool: £526.54 - 4.13 winning units..

Owner David W Armstrong **Bred** Highfield Farm Llp **Trained** Musley Bank, N Yorks

FOCUS
This maiden auction was won last year by unbeaten Norfolk Stakes and Middle Park winner Reckless Abandon and it could be the starting point for another smart colt here.

2437 BONUS.CO.UK CASINO BONUS MEDIAN AUCTION MAIDEN STKS 6f

6:25 (6:28) (Class 5) 3-4-Y-0 £2,911 (£866; £432; £216) Stalls High

Form RPR

2-32 **1** **Grand Denial (IRE)**14 2016 3-9-3 75........(b1) JohnFahy 9 79
(Clive Cox) *qckly away and sn clr: shkn up wl over 1f out: kpt on strly* **6/4**2

0-4 **2** 4 **Oh So Sassy**25 1750 3-8-12 0........ SebSanders 4 61
(Chris Wall) *t.k.h early: towards rr: hdwy wl over 2f out: sn chsng wnr: tk clsr order wl over 1f out: sn rdn and no imp* **7/1**3

3 7 **Natalia** 4-9-2 0........ JackDuern(5) 6 41
(Andrew Hollinshead) *s.i.s and bhd: swtchd lft to outer and hdwy over 2f out: rdn wl over 1f out: kpt on take modest 3rd ins fnl f* **18/1**

4 2 **Scala Romana (IRE)** 3-8-12 0........ LukeMorris 5 32
(Sir Mark Prescott Bt) *in tch: rdn along and outpcd 1/2-way: kpt on u.p fr over 1f out: n.d* **20/1**

5-2 **5** 2 1/4 **Tomintoul Magic (IRE)**21 1821 3-8-12 0........ IanMongan 3 25
(Sir Henry Cecil) *dwlt: t.k.h and hld up in rr: sme hdwy 1/2-way: rdn over 2f out and n.d* **1/1**1

5 **6** 2 3/4 **Moonvale (IRE)**21 1821 3-8-12 0........ LiamJones 7 16
(Tony Carroll) *t.k.h: chsd ldrs: hdwy 1/2-way: rdn along over 2f out: sn wknd* **50/1**

0 **7** 1/2 **Delicious Patrica**21 1821 4-9-7 0........ MichaelO'Connell 8 17
(Tony Carroll) *chsd wnr: rdn along 1/2-way: sn wknd* **80/1**

1m 15.32s (1.72) **Going Correction** +0.175s/f (Good)
WFA 3 from 4yo 9lb **7** Ran SP% **115.7**
Speed ratings (Par 103): **95,89,80,77,74 71,70**
toteswingers 1&2 £1.60, 2&3 £22.20, 1&3 £6.20 CSF £12.58 TOTE £2.60: £1.30, £2.10; EX 14.10 Trifecta £96.20 Pool: £719.49 - 5.60 winning units..

Owner Alan G Craddock **Bred** A M F Persse **Trained** Lambourn, Berks

FOCUS
A modest median auction maiden which was the scene of a complete blowout by the favourite. The time was slow and it's doubtful the winner needed to improve.

2438 PARK HILL HOSPITAL H'CAP 1m (R)

7:00 (7:00) (Class 3) (0-95,88) 3-Y-0 £8,409 (£2,502; £1,250; £625) Stalls High

Form RPR

3-1 **1** **Cape Peron**28 1678 3-9-6 **87**........ FergusSweeney 8 109+
(Henry Candy) *hld up in rr: smooth hdwy on outer 3f out: led and edgd lft appr fnl f: qcknd impressively and sn clr* **6/4**1

531- **2** 4 1/2 **Gworn**182 7779 3-9-1 **82**........ GrahamLee 7 90
(Ed Dunlop) *t.k.h: trckd ldrs: n.m.r and sltly hmpd wl over 3f out: hdwy 2f out: rdn to chse ldng pair whn n.m.r over 1f out: kpt on u.p: no ch w wnr* **10/1**

33-2 **3** 2 1/2 **Yourartisonfire**18 1912 3-8-12 **82**........ MichaelMetcalfe(3) 6 84
(Mrs K Burke) *hld up towards rr: hdwy on outer and edgd lft over 3f out: rdn to ld 2f out: hdd and drvn appr fnl f: wknd* **9/2**3

1- **4** 1 1/2 **Goodwood Mirage (IRE)**206 7330 3-9-1 **82**........ NeilCallan 2 81
(William Knight) *plld hrd: trckd ldrs: effrt whn n.m.r wl over 2f out: sn rdn and outpcd: sme late hdwy* **7/2**2

210- **5** 1/2 **Simply Shining (IRE)**266 5602 3-8-9 **76**........ TonyHamilton 4 73
(Richard Fahey) *set stdy pce: qcknd over 3f out: rdn and hdd 2f out: grad wknd* **20/1**

10-4 **6** shd **Jalaa (IRE)**22 1812 3-9-6 **87**........ SeanLevey 5 84
(Richard Hannon) *cl up: rdn along wl over 2f out: wknd wl over 1f out* **7/1**

1-0 **7** 4 **Kerbaaj (USA)**31 1623 3-9-1 **82**........(t) SteveDrowne 1 70
(Charles Hills) *trckd ldr on inner: pushed along 3f out: rdn over 2f out: wknd wl over 1f out* **12/1**

1m 42.69s (2.99) **Going Correction** +0.175s/f (Good) **7** Ran SP% **114.4**
Speed ratings (Par 103): **92,87,85,83,83 82,78**
toteswingers 1&2 £3.60, 2&3 £8.80, 1&3 £1.90 CSF £18.02 CT £56.18 TOTE £2.50: £1.40, £4.30; EX 20.20 Trifecta £62.80 Pool: £1102.48 - 13.15 winning units..

Owner The Earl Cadogan **Bred** The Earl Cadogan **Trained** Kingston Warren, Oxon

FOCUS
The 1m 3yo handicap was not only the subject of a performance that lit up the face of the winning trainer Henry Candy but a performance from Cape Peron that lit up the card. The runner-up ran to form but ran into one.

2439 WINNING EXPRESS H'CAP 7f

7:30 (7:37) (Class 4) (0-85,84) 3-Y-0 £5,175 (£1,540; £769; £384) Stalls High

Form RPR

5-1 **1** **Off Art**14 2027 3-9-7 **84**........ DavidAllan 3 91
(Tim Easterby) *cl up on outer: hdwy to ld wl over 2f out: rdn over 1f out: styd on wl fnl f* **6/1**

30-3 **2** 2 1/4 **Entwined (IRE)**21 1832 3-8-8 **71**........ JohnFahy 4 72
(Clive Cox) *trckd ldrs: hdwy on outer 2f out: sn cl up: rdn and ev ch ent fnl f: sn drvn and one pce* **10/1**

560- **3** 3/4 **Elle Woods (IRE)**224 6873 3-9-1 **78**........ PaulMulrennan 2 77
(Michael Dods) *stdd and swtchd rt s: hld up in rr: smooth hdwy to trck ldrs over 2f out: nt clr run over 1f out: swtchd rt and rdn ent fnl f: kpt on same pce* **7/1**

-122 **4** 1 1/2 **Lightning Launch (IRE)**13 2056 3-9-3 **80**........(v1) MartinHarley 1 75
(Mick Channon) *dwlt: trckd ldrs: hdwy 3f out: cl up 2f out: sn rdn and ev ch tl drvn and wknd jst ins fnl f* **4/1**3

530 **5** 2 **Ready (IRE)**16 1958 3-9-0 **77**........ NeilCallan 6 67
(Garry Moss) *trckd ldrs: rdn along 2f out: sn one pce* **14/1**

45-6 **6** 13 **African Oil (FR)**16 1958 3-9-0 **77**........ SteveDrowne 7 33
(Charles Hills) *cl up on inner: rdn along 1/2-way: drvn 3f out and wknd qckly* **11/4**1

3-01 **7** 11 **Intimidate**38 1477 3-9-7 **84**........(p) GrahamLee 5
(Jeremy Noseda) *slt ld: rdn along 3f out: sn hdd & wknd* **3/1**2

1m 28.37s (2.07) **Going Correction** +0.175s/f (Good) **7** Ran SP% **114.2**
Speed ratings (Par 101): **95,92,91,89,87 72,60**
toteswingers 1&2 £6.40, 2&3 £9.90, 1&3 £7.80 CSF £61.32 TOTE £8.00: £4.00, £5.00; EX 49.40 Trifecta £153.40 Pool: £1266.46 - 6.18 winning units..

Owner D B Lamplough **Bred** D B Lamplough **Trained** Great Habton, N Yorks

FOCUS
A strong 7f handicap for 3yo, although the pace, set by the two market leaders (both sons of Royal Applause) collapsed 2f out. The runner-up set the standard.

2440 SAINT GOBAIN WEBER FILLIES' H'CAP — 1m 2f 60y
8:05 (8:05) (Class 3) (0-95,95) 4-Y-0+ **£7,439** (£2,213; £1,106; £553) **Stalls** Low

Form RPR
11- **1** **Albasharah (USA)**[199] 7475 4-9-0 **88** MickaelBarzalona 2 103+
(Saeed bin Suroor) *trckd ldng pair: smooth hdwy 3f out: led jst over 2f out: rdn clr over 1f out: styd on strly* **4/5**[1]
4-00 **2** *8* **No Poppy (IRE)**[14] 2029 5-8-11 **90** DarylByrne(5) 3 88
(Tim Easterby) *dwlt and in rr: pushed along 4f out: rdn over 2f out: hdwy over 1f out: kpt on u.p to take modest 2nd wl ins fnl f: no ch w wnr* **25/1**
2-14 **3** *1 3/4* **Oddysey (IRE)**[21] 1823 4-8-9 **83** TomEaves 5 78
(Michael Dods) *hld up in tch: hdwy over 3f out: chsd ldng pair 2f out: sn rdn and kpt on one pce* **12/1**
24-3 **4** *1 1/4* **Oojooba**[14] 2015 4-9-2 **95** WilliamTwiston-Davies(5) 1 88
(Roger Varian) *led: rdn along and hdd jst over 2f out: sn drvn and one pce appr fnl f* **9/4**[2]
625- **5** *35* **All Annalena (IRE)**[48] 7375 7-8-9 **83** LukeMorris 4
(Lucy Wadham) *trckd ldr: cl up 5f out: rdn along over 3f out: sn wknd* **8/1**[3]

2m 11.52s (2.12) **Going Correction** +0.175s/f (Good) **5** Ran SP% **109.0**
Speed ratings (Par 104): **98,91,90,89,61**
CSF £20.01 TOTE £1.60: £1.10, £3.00; EX 15.60 Trifecta £46.20 Pool: £1013.69 - 16.45 winning units..
Owner Godolphin **Bred** Darley **Trained** Newmarket, Suffolk

FOCUS
As with the first race run on the round course there was a wide-margin winner. She was a big improver, but there are some doubts over what she beat.

2441 EVANS HALSHAW CITROEN DONCASTER H'CAP — 6f
8:35 (8:35) (Class 4) (0-80,80) 4-Y-0+ **£5,175** (£1,540; £769; £384) **Stalls** High

Form RPR
1-40 **1** **Half A Billion (IRE)**[8] 2239 4-8-13 **79** ConnorBeasley(7) 8 87
(Michael Dods) *mde all: rdn wl over 1f out: kpt on gamely ins fnl f* **16/1**
-052 **2** *1/2* **Lenny Bee**[7] 2275 7-9-1 **79** (t) GeorgeChaloner(5) 9 85
(Garry Moss) *a chsng wnr: rdn wl over 1f out: drvn and kpt on fnl f* **7/1**[2]
06-5 **3** *shd* **Mon Brav**[7] 2275 6-9-0 **73** BarryMcHugh 2 79
(Brian Ellison) *in rr: pushed along after 2f: hdwy over 2f out: rdn and n.m.r over 1f out: drvn and styd on wl fnl f* **8/1**[3]
20-0 **4** *hd* **Barney McGrew (IRE)**[23] 1787 10-9-4 **77** PaulMulrennan 4 82+
(Michael Dods) *hld up: hdwy 2f out: chsd ldrs whn n.m.r over 1f out: sn swtchd rt and rdn: styd on wl fnl f: nrst fin* **16/1**
0-15 **5** *1* **Johnny Cavagin**[23] 1787 4-9-7 **80** (t) TomEaves 5 82
(Richard Guest) *dwlt: sn in tch: hdwy to chse ldrs 2f out: effrt whn n.m.r over 1f out: swtchd lft and rdn ent fnl f: kpt on* **9/1**
4-00 **6** *nse* **Dark Castle**[14] 2007 4-9-3 **76** PJMcDonald 18 78
(Micky Hammond) *hld up: hdwy 2f out: rdn to chse ldrs wl over 1f out: drvn and one pce ins fnl f* **14/1**
440- **7** *3* **Bunce (IRE)**[210] 7246 5-8-4 **70** JoshDoyle(7) 7 62
(David O'Meara) *hld up in tch: hdwy to chse ldrs over 2f out: rdn over 1f out and grad wknd* **20/1**
3140 **8** *1 1/2* **Jack My Boy (IRE)**[26] 1726 6-9-7 **80** (b) NeilCallan 10 68
(David Evans) *midfield: effrt and sme hdwy 2f out: sn rdn and no imp* **12/1**
6-00 **9** *1/2* **Italian Tom (IRE)**[7] 2255 6-9-1 **77** DarrenEgan(3) 1 63
(Ronald Harris) *dwlt: a towards rr* **14/1**
620- **10** *2 1/4* **Oh So Spicy**[215] 7113 6-9-0 **73** SebSanders 13 52
(Chris Wall) *awkward s: in rr and sn swtchd lft: nvr a factor* **16/1**
036- **11** *shd* **Bop It**[214] 7145 4-9-2 **80** [1] WilliamTwiston-Davies(5) 14 59
(Bryan Smart) *towards rr: rdn along bef 1/2-way: n.d* **9/1**
42-4 **12** *1* **Dream Catcher (FR)**[11] 2128 5-8-11 **75** AmyScott(5) 6 50
(Henry Candy) *a towards rr* **13/2**[1]
-000 **13** *1 3/4* **Chunky Diamond (IRE)**[14] 2031 4-9-7 **80** JamesSullivan 11 50
(Ruth Carr) *chsd ldrs: rdn along over 2f out: sn wknd* **20/1**
0023 **14** *hd* **Dorback**[7] 2255 6-9-0 **73** MartinHarley 17 42
(Violet M Jordan) *racd alone towards stands' rail: prom: rdn along wl over 2f out: sn wknd* **10/1**
3560 **15** *1/2* **Sulis Minerva (IRE)**[19] 1878 6-8-8 **72** RobertTart(5) 20 40
(Jeremy Gask) *s.i.s: a bhd* **9/1**
0-00 **16** *10* **Noodles Blue Boy**[14] 2031 7-9-2 **75** TonyHamilton 12
(Ollie Pears) *prom: rdn along wl over 2f out: sn wknd* **33/1**

1m 13.86s (0.26) **Going Correction** +0.175s/f (Good) **16** Ran SP% **127.2**
Speed ratings (Par 105): **105,104,104,103,102 102,98,96,95,92 92,91,89,88,88 74**
toteswingers 1&2 £17.10, 2&3 £16.90, 1&3 £36.50 CSF £126.03 CT £993.80 TOTE £22.20: £5.10, £2.40, £2.80, £5.80; EX 220.10 Trifecta £823.20 Part won. £1097.68 - 0.01 winning units..
Owner I Galletley, B Stenson, S Lowthian **Bred** Mount Coote Stud **Trained** Denton, Co Durham
■ Stewards' Enquiry : Barry McHugh two-day ban; used whip above permitted level (3rd-4th June).

FOCUS
The closing sprint handicap was competitive, albeit full of exposed performers. The first two were always at the fore and the form is straightforward.
T/Plt: £173.40 to a £1 stake. Pool of £76493.19 - 321.85 winning tickets. T/Qpdt: £27.70 to a £1 stake. Pool of £6073.55 - 162.20 winning tickets. JR

2411 NEWBURY (L-H)
Saturday, May 18

OFFICIAL GOING: Good to firm (good in places; 7.7)
Wind: Virtually nil Weather: Cloudy

2442 BRITISH STALLION STUDS EBF BETFRED TV MAIDEN STKS — 1m 2f 6y
1:30 (1:32) (Class 4) 3-Y-0 **£6,469** (£1,925; £962; £481) **Stalls** Centre

Form RPR
3 **1** **Remote**[17] 1931 3-9-5 0 MartinDwyer 7 100
(John Gosden) *w'like: scope: in tch: hdwy over 2f out: sn swtchd rt and hdwy: led appr fnl f: pushed clr: readily* **25/1**
6- **2** *3* **Dare To Achieve**[232] 6636 3-9-5 0 JosephO'Brien 16 94
(William Haggas) *b.hind: lw: chsd ldrs: rdn to ld 2f out: hdd appr fnl f: sn outpcd by wnr but styd on wl for clr 2nd* **3/1**[1]
3-0 **3** *4 1/2* **Russian Realm**[10] 2151 3-9-5 0 RyanMoore 3 85
(Sir Michael Stoute) *lw: in tch: hdwy over 3f out: drvn to chse ldrs over 2f out: outpcd by ldng duo over 1f out* **3/1**[1]
0 **4** *3/4* **She's Late**[30] 1635 3-9-5 0 WilliamBuick 10 83
(John Gosden) *in tch: pushed along 4f out: hdwy to chse ldrs ins fnl 3f: one pce fnl 2f* **14/1**
5 *1 3/4* **Bantam (IRE)** 3-9-0 0 JamesDoyle 6 75+
(Ed Dunlop) *lengthy: lw: in rr: pushed along and hdwy fr 2f out: kpt on fnl f but nvr a threat* **50/1**
6 *3 3/4* **Testudo (IRE)** 3-9-5 0 MartinLane 14 72
(Brian Meehan) *str: in rr: pushed along 3f out: styd on ins fnl f* **50/1**
7 *3 1/4* **Asbaab (USA)** 3-9-5 0 PaulHanagan 4 66+
(Brian Meehan) *w'like: scope: lengthy: s.i.s: in rr: pushed along 3f out: styd on fnl f* **28/1**
6 **8** *1 1/2* **Saskatchewan**[30] 1635 3-9-5 0 KierenFallon 2 63
(Luca Cumani) *chsd ldrs: led over 3f out: hdd 2f out: wknd qckly over 1f out* **8/1**[3]
2-6 **9** *3 1/4* **Aficionado**[19] 1882 3-9-5 0 SilvestreDeSousa 13 56
(Ed Dunlop) *in rr: sme hdwy whn bmpd and pushed rt over 2f out: no ch after* **40/1**
10 *1 1/4* **Retirement Plan** 3-9-5 0 TomQueally 8 54+
(Sir Henry Cecil) *unf: scope: s.i.s: rdn 3f out: a bhd* **9/1**
03 **11** *5* **Strawberry Jam**[19] 1882 3-9-5 0 JackMitchell 5 44
(Paul Cole) *led tl over 3f out: sn btn* **40/1**
2 **12** *6* **Gold Medal (IRE)**[46] 1300 3-9-5 0 RichardHughes 11 32
(Richard Hannon) *str: chsd ldrs: pushed along 3f out: wknd qckly 2f out* **6/1**[2]
00- **13** *3 1/4* **Gold Nugget (IRE)**[241] 6371 3-9-5 0 KieranO'Neill 9 25
(Richard Hannon) *bit bkwd: t.k.h: chsd ldrs tl wknd qckly 4f out* **100/1**
14 *3* **Hero's Story** 3-9-5 0 JimCrowley 12 19
(Amanda Perrett) *tall: lengthy: s.i.s: a bhd* **22/1**
15 *3 1/4* **Encapsulated** 3-9-5 0 PatCosgrave 15 13
(Roger Ingram) *lw: s.i.s: plld hrd: in rr and no ch whn hung bdly rt over 2f out: eased* **150/1**

2m 7.35s (-1.45) **Going Correction** 0.0s/f (Good) **15** Ran SP% **114.2**
Speed ratings (Par 101): **105,102,99,98,97 94,91,90,87,86 82,77,75,72,70**
toteswingers 1&2 £17.00, 1&3 £12.20, 2&3 £2.40 CSF £80.69 TOTE £27.60: £6.70, £1.50, £1.40; EX 129.30 Trifecta £554.50 Pool: £2768.90 - 3.74 winning units..
Owner K Abdullah **Bred** Juddmonte Farms Ltd **Trained** Newmarket, Suffolk
■ International Love was withdrawn (8/1, deduct 10p in the £ under R4).

FOCUS
Rail moved out on back straight increasing distances on Round course by 24yds. Potentially a decent 3yo maiden and the form is rated on the positive side. The winner was a big improver from his debut.

2443 JLT ASTON PARK STKS (LISTED RACE) — 1m 5f 61y
2:05 (2:05) (Class 1) 4-Y-0+
£20,982 (£7,955; £3,981; £1,983; £995; £499) **Stalls** Centre

Form RPR
330- **1** **Willing Foe (USA)**[203] 7405 6-8-12 107 SilvestreDeSousa 2 116
(Saeed bin Suroor) *trckd ldrs in 3rd tl wnt 2nd over 3f out: led over 2f out: pushed clr wl over 1f out: easily* **4/1**[3]
203- **2** *6* **Harris Tweed**[171] 7895 6-8-12 110 RichardHughes 5 107
(William Haggas) *led: qcknd 6f out: rdn and hdd over 2f out: outpcd by wnr wl over 1f out but kpt on wl for 2nd* **3/1**[2]
05-2 **3** *1 3/4* **Jehannedarc (IRE)**[14] 2012 5-8-7 102 RyanMoore 4 99
(Ed Dunlop) *s.i.s: sn in tch: hdwy to chse ldrs over 2f out: sn no ch w wnr but styd on wl for clr 3rd over 1f out* **9/2**
141- **4** *4 1/2* **Gallipot**[233] 6598 4-8-10 102 WilliamBuick 6 96
(John Gosden) *trckd ldrs: hdwy to cl 3f out: rdn and no prog 2f out: sn wknd* **9/4**[1]
525- **5** *1/2* **Chiberta King**[98] 6600 7-8-12 105 (p) LiamKeniry 7 97
(Andrew Balding) *chsd ldr tl over 3f out and sn rdn: no ch fr over 2f out but kpt on again clsng stages* **16/1**
510- **6** *nk* **Saint Hilary**[301] 4338 4-8-7 85 MartinDwyer 3 91
(William Muir) *in rr: pushed along over 2f out: styd on clsng stages but nvr any ch* **66/1**
13-0 **7** *7* **Viking Storm**[63] 1034 5-8-12 105 PaulHanagan 1 86
(Harry Dunlop) *lw: sn in tch: hdwy 3f out and sn drvn to chse ldrs: wknd 2f out* **15/2**

2m 50.15s (-1.85) **Going Correction** 0.0s/f (Good) **7** Ran SP% **113.1**
Speed ratings (Par 111): **105,101,100,97,97 96,92**
toteswingers 1&2 £2.40, 1&3 £3.10, 2&3 £3.40 CSF £16.03 TOTE £4.30: £2.20, £2.30; EX 18.20 Trifecta £57.70 Pool: £4049.94 - 52.58 winning units..
Owner Godolphin **Bred** Stonerside Stable **Trained** Newmarket, Suffolk

FOCUS
This was up to scratch and there was a solid pace on. The runners shunned the far rail after straightening for home and the second sets the level. A personal best from Willing Foe.

2444 BETFRED MOBILE LOTTO H'CAP — 6f 8y
2:40 (2:43) (Class 2) (0-100,100) 4-Y-0+
£12,450 (£3,728; £1,864; £932; £466; £234) **Stalls** Centre

Form RPR
30- **1** **Hallelujah**[224] 6878 5-9-2 **95** HayleyTurner 10 107
(James Fanshawe) *chsd ldrs: drvn over 2f out: chal 1f out slt ld fnl 110yds: styd hrd pressed: all out* **16/1**
0-23 **2** *nse* **Poole Harbour (IRE)**[13] 2046 4-8-11 **90** RichardHughes 9 102
(Richard Hannon) *chsd ldrs: led 2f out: jnd 1f out: narrowly hdd fnl 110yds: styd chalng jst failed* **9/2**[2]
4-41 **3** *1 3/4* **Seeking Magic**[21] 1838 5-9-0 **93** (t) AdamKirby 17 99
(Clive Cox) *slt ld after 1f but hrd pressed: narrowly hdd 2f out: styd on same pce to hold 3rd fnl f* **10/1**
4 *shd* **Burn The Boats (IRE)**[17] 1937 4-8-8 **87** GaryCarroll 8 93
(G M Lyons, Ire) *w'like: chsd ldrs: rdn 2f out: styd on same pce to dispute 3rd fnl f: dropped to 4th last strides* **16/1**
3042 **5** *3/4* **Harrison George (IRE)**[7] 2266 8-8-7 **86** oh1 (t) MartinDwyer 12 89
(P J O'Gorman) *chsd ldrs: drvn over 2f out: outpcd fnl f* **20/1**
0-20 **6** *1 1/4* **Khubala (IRE)**[7] 2254 4-9-1 **94** (b) WilliamBuick 15 93+
(Hugo Palmer) *b: outpcd in rr: pushed along and hdwy appr fnl f: kpt on wl clsng stages: nt rch ldrs* **12/1**
00-4 **7** *1/2* **Top Cop**[14] 2014 4-8-9 **88** (v[1]) LiamKeniry 2 86
(Andrew Balding) *led 1f: styd pressing ldr and rdn 2f out: wknd fnl f* **14/1**
214- **8** *3/4* **Signor Sassi**[225] 6835 4-8-7 **86** oh3 SilvestreDeSousa 13 81
(William Knight) *in tch: drvn to chse ldrs 2f out: wknd appr fnl f* **12/1**
600- **9** *1* **Graphic (IRE)**[219] 7010 4-8-7 **86** oh1 PaulHanagan 11 78+
(William Haggas) *in rr: pushed along 1/2-way: kpt on ins fnl f* **20/1**
220- **10** *1/2* **Riot Of Colour**[268] 5520 4-8-8 **87** JimCrowley 5 77
(Ralph Beckett) *in rr: sme hdwy 2f out: sn wknd* **16/1**

001- **11** 1 3/4 **Modern Tutor**[329] 3389 4-8-7 **86** oh1 ...[1] RyanMoore 7 71
(Sir Michael Stoute) *chsd ldrs: rdn 2f out: wknd appr fnl f* **7/1**[3]

1211 **12** nk **Khawatim**[49] 1245 5-8-13 **92** ... BenCurtis 18 76
(Noel Quinlan) *swtg: pushed along 1/2-way: a outpcd towards rr* **10/3**[1]

2-00 **13** 1/2 **Amadeus Wolfe Tone (IRE)**[13] 2046 4-9-2 **95** ...(p) JamesDoyle 16 77
(Jamie Osborne) *rdn 1/2-way and sn outpcd* **25/1**

025- **14** 1 **Joe Packet**[224] 6867 6-9-4 **97** ... TomQueally 3 76
(Jonathan Portman) *bit bkwd: in tch: rdn 1/2-way: sn outpcd* **16/1**

16-5 **15** 1 1/2 **Doctor Parkes**[13] 2046 7-8-8 **87** ... SaleemGolam 6 61
(Stuart Williams) *rrd stalls: t.k.h: towards rr most of way* **25/1**

310- **16** 3 1/2 **Edge Closer**[245] 6244 9-9-1 **94** ... JosephO'Brien 14 57
(Tony Carroll) *chsd ldrs: rdn over 2f out: wknd over 1f out* **25/1**

1m 11.61s (-1.39) **Going Correction** 0.0s/f (Good) **16** Ran SP% **129.5**
Speed ratings (Par 109): **109,108,106,106,105 103,103,102,100,100 97,97,96,95,93 88**
toteswingers 1&2 £22.40, 1&3 £25.10, 2&3 £8.70 CSF £85.22 CT £812.21 TOTE £14.40: £2.90, £1.60, £2.60, £4.30; EX 132.20 Trifecta £1666.20 Pool: £120177.68 - 54.09 winning units..

Owner CLS (Chippenham) Limited **Bred** Chippenham Lodge Stud Ltd **Trained** Newmarket, Suffolk

FOCUS
A highly competitive sprint and solid form, although it was a possible advantage to race prominently.

2445 BETFRED MOBILE SPORTS LONDON GOLD CUP (H'CAP) 1m 2f 6y
3:15 (3:16) (Class 2) (0-105,102) 3-Y-O
£15,562 (£4,660; £2,330; £1,165; £582; £292) **Stalls** Centre

Form RPR

-213 **1** **High Troja (IRE)**[13] 2050 3-8-2 **83** oh2 ... PaulHanagan 2 92
(Ed Dunlop) *chsd ldrs: wnt 2nd 2f out: sn chalng: slt ld appr fnl f: drvn out* **25/1**

41-2 **2** 1/2 **Hillstar**[30] 1641 3-8-11 **92** ... RyanMoore 5 100
(Sir Michael Stoute) *led: jnd fr 3f out: drvn over 2f out: hdd appr fnl f: kpt on but a hld ins fnl f* **10/11**[1]

-111 **3** 2 **Spillway**[21] 1847 3-8-7 **88** ... TomQueally 6 92+
(Eve Johnson Houghton) *lw: in rr: pushed along 3f out: rdn and styd on fr 2f out: tk 3rd last strides: no imp on ldng duo* **11/2**[2]

4 nse **Kitten On The Run (USA)**[160] 3-9-7 **102** ... KierenFallon 7 106+
(Luca Cumani) *w'like: swtg: in rr: hdwy on outer over 2f out: styd on to take narrow 3rd ins fnl f: no imp on ldng duo and dropped to 4th last strides* **9/1**

0-11 **5** 1 1/4 **Ray Ward (IRE)**[8] 2223 3-8-2 **83** oh2 ... MartinLane 4 84
(David Simcock) *chsd ldrs: chal 3f out and sn rdn: dropped to 3rd 2f out: styd on same pce fnl f* **16/1**

16-0 **6** 12 **Azrur (IRE)**[14] 2024 3-8-4 **85** ... HayleyTurner 1 67
(Michael Bell) *t.k.h: chsd ldrs: rdn and btn 3f out* **33/1**

21- **7** 22 **Tarikhi (USA)**[224] 6872 3-8-8 **89** ... SilvestreDeSousa 8
(Saeed bin Suroor) *lw: t.k.h: in tch: hanging rt and wd bnd 7f out and 5f out: wknd 3f out: eased* **6/1**[3]

2m 10.12s (1.32) **Going Correction** 0.0s/f (Good) **7** Ran SP% **104.7**
Speed ratings (Par 105): **94,93,92,91,90 81,63**
toteswingers 1&2 £3.40, 1&3 £8.60, 2&3 £1.90 CSF £40.81 CT £117.30 TOTE £28.80: £7.00, £1.20; EX 46.20 Trifecta £239.60 Pool: £3525.78 - 11.03 winning units..

Owner Robert Ng **Bred** Carrigbeg Stud Co Ltd **Trained** Newmarket, Suffolk

FOCUS
This well established 3-y-o handicap was a classy affair, but it was run at a muddling early pace and the majority proved keen. The first two fought it out from the furlong marker. A surprise winner but the form is given a bit of a chance given the quality of recent renewals.

2446 JLT LOCKINGE STKS (BRITISH CHAMPIONS SERIES) (GROUP 1) 1m (S)
3:50 (3:55) (Class 1) 4-Y-O+
£110,159 (£41,763; £20,901; £10,411; £5,225; £2,622) **Stalls** Centre

Form RPR

222- **1** **Farhh**[244] 6296 5-9-0 124 ... SilvestreDeSousa 5 126
(Saeed bin Suroor) *lw: trckd ldrs: led ins fnl 2f: drvn clr fnl f: readily* **10/3**[2]

5-42 **2** 4 **Sovereign Debt (IRE)**[17] 1919 4-9-0 111 ... AdamKirby 7 117
(Michael Bell) *in rr: hdwy 2f out: rdn and styd on to chse wnr appr fnl f: nvr any ch but hld on wl for 2nd* **80/1**

33-2 **3** nk **Aljamaaheer (IRE)**[21] 1835 4-9-0 110 ... PaulHanagan 6 116
(Roger Varian) *in rr: hdwy 2f out: styd on wl to cl on 2nd ins fnl f but nvr any ch w wnr: no ex clsng stages* **16/1**

10-3 **4** 4 1/2 **Chil The Kite**[22] 1810 4-9-0 108 ...(b[1]) RyanMoore 1 106
(Hughie Morrison) *s.i.s: in rr: drvn 2f out: hdwy over 1f out and kpt on ins fnl f but nvr gng pce to rch ldrs* **25/1**

41-1 **5** 2 1/2 **Declaration Of War (USA)**[34] 1556 4-9-0 112 ... JosephO'Brien 4 100
(A P O'Brien, Ire) *lw: s.i.s: sn rcvrd and in tch: hdwy 3f out: dispued 2nd 2f out: wknd u.p fnl f* **5/4**[1]

04-1 **6** 4 1/2 **Fencing (USA)**[17] 1919 4-9-0 114 ... WilliamBuick 2 90
(John Gosden) *in tch: hdwy 3f out: disp 2nd 2f out and sn rdn: wknd appr fnl f* **10/1**

2-00 **7** 3/4 **Penitent**[13] 2066 7-9-0 115 ... DanielTudhope 8 88
(David O'Meara) *led 2f: styd chsng ldrs: rdn 3f out: wknd 2f out* **33/1**

51-3 **8** 1 3/4 **Amaron**[39] 1456 4-9-0 112 ... AStarke 12 84
(Andreas Lowe, Germany) *chsd ldrs: rdn and btn 3f out* **20/1**

06-0 **9** 5 **Reply (IRE)**[49] 1266 4-9-0 105 ...(v) SeamieHeffernan 9 72
(A P O'Brien, Ire) *led after 2f: hdd & wknd ins fnl 2f* **100/1**

50-1 **10** 42 **Trumpet Major (IRE)**[22] 1810 4-9-0 114 ... RichardHughes 11
(Richard Hannon) *bhd: rdn and btn over 3f out: eased: t.o* **16/1**

00-4 **11** 2 3/4 **Libranno**[22] 1810 5-9-0 112 ... KierenFallon 3
(Richard Hannon) *chsd ldrs tl wknd qckly 3f out: eased: t.o* **50/1**

232- **12** 33 **Cityscape**[210] 7238 7-9-0 124 ... JamesDoyle 13
(Roger Charlton) *in tch whn pushed along and hung lft 1/2-way and sn btn: eased: t.o* **6/1**[3]

1m 35.43s (-4.27) **Going Correction** 0.0s/f (Good) **12** Ran SP% **118.4**
Speed ratings (Par 117): **121,117,116,112,109 105,104,102,97,55 52,19**
toteswingers 1&2 £33.30, 1&3 £33.30, 2&3 £28.50 CSF £271.91 TOTE £3.60: £1.60, £11.60, £3.50; EX 212.70 Trifecta £2038.80 Pool: £9529.33 - 3.50 winning units..

Owner Godolphin **Bred** Darley **Trained** Newmarket, Suffolk

FOCUS
Not the strongest Lockinge, but it was hard not to be impressed with Farhh. It was run at a solid pace, resulting in the field finishing strung out, and the placed horse set the level. The form is sound with Farrh running up to his best.

2447 BETFRED "THE BONUS KING" MAIDEN STKS (DIV I) 7f (S)
4:25 (4:26) (Class 4) 3-Y-O
£5,175 (£1,540; £769; £384) **Stalls** Centre

Form RPR

1 **Prince Of Arabia (IRE)** 3-9-5 0 ... JosephO'Brien 10 80
(Alan Jarvis) *w'like: scope: lw: s.i.s: in rr: hdwy over 2f out: led appr fnl f: drvn and styd on strly ins fnl f* **14/1**

2 3/4 **Plover** 3-9-0 0 ... RyanMoore 3 73+
(Sir Michael Stoute) *s.i.s: hdwy to cl on ldrs 3f out: chal over 1f out: kpt on to chse wnr ins fnl f but no imp* **7/2**[2]

0 **3** 1 1/2 **Tawtheeq (IRE)**[31] 1618 3-9-5 0 ... PaulHanagan 12 74
(Richard Hannon) *in tch: hdwy to press ldrs 2f out: stl chalng 1f out: outpcd fnl 110yds* **9/2**[3]

0-3 **4** 4 **Royal Challis**[13] 2051 3-9-5 0 ... RichardHughes 4 63
(Richard Hannon) *lw: chsd ldrs: rdn 2f out: wknd ins fnl f* **3/1**[1]

5 1 **Bridge Builder** 3-9-0 0 ...(p) RyanTate[(5)] 7 60
(Peter Hedger) *w'like: chsd ldrs: rdn and outpcd in rr 3f out: styd on again u.p fnl f* **66/1**

6 1 1/2 **Gregori (IRE)** 3-9-5 0 ... KierenFallon 2 56
(Brian Meehan) *str: bit bkwd: chsd ldrs: led over 2f out: hdd & wknd over 1f out* **13/2**

4 **7** nse **Baltic Blade (IRE)**[14] 2016 3-9-5 0 ... TomQueally 8 56+
(Gary Moore) *leggy: in rr: pushed along and styd on fnl f: nvr a threat* **16/1**

66- **8** 1 1/2 **Mawson**[185] 7705 3-9-5 0 ... JamesDoyle 1 52+
(Roger Charlton) *lw: in rr: pushed along and sme hdwy over 2f out: nvr rchd ldrs and wknd fnl f: lame after r* **12/1**

9 1 1/4 **Quintet (IRE)** 3-9-0 0 ... JimCrowley 6 44+
(Ralph Beckett) *angular: s.i.s: in rr: sme hdwy over 2f out: sn wknd* **6/1**

10 1 1/4 **Emerald Art (IRE)** 3-9-0 0 ... MartinLane 9 40
(J W Hills) *w'like: bit bkwd: outpcd most of way* **25/1**

0-4 **11** nk **Rectory Lane**[136] 16 3-8-9 0 ... AmyScott[(5)] 11 40
(Eve Johnson Houghton) *w'like: swtg: led tl hdd over 2f out: sn btn* **66/1**

1m 28.09s (2.39) **Going Correction** 0.0s/f (Good) **11** Ran SP% **120.1**
Speed ratings (Par 101): **86,85,83,78,77 76,75,74,72,71 71**
toteswingers 1&2 £12.80, 1&3 £18.30, 2&3 £4.60 CSF £63.53 TOTE £16.00: £5.00, £1.10, £2.10; EX 111.60 Trifecta £2259.90 Pool: £4207.31 - 1.39 winning units..

Owner Cedars Partnership **Bred** Tally-Ho Stud **Trained** Twyford, Bucks

FOCUS
The principals came nicely clear in this fair 3-y-o maiden, with the middle of the track again favoured. It was the slowest of the three C&D times. The form is rated in line with the race averages.

2448 BETFRED "THE BONUS KING" MAIDEN STKS (DIV II) 7f (S)
5:30 (5:31) (Class 4) 3-Y-O
£5,175 (£1,540; £769; £384) **Stalls** Centre

Form RPR

5 **1** **Czech It Out (IRE)**[14] 2016 3-9-5 0 ... JimCrowley 6 79
(Amanda Perrett) *str: chsd ldrs: wnt 2nd ins fnl 2f: sn rdn: styd on u.p to ld fnl 100yds: kpt on strly cl home* **25/1**

40-2 **2** 1 1/4 **Thakana**[15] 1986 3-9-0 72 ... RyanMoore 3 71
(J W Hills) *lw: sn narrow ldr: rdn and kpt on fr over 1f out: hdd fnl 100yds: kpt on same pce* **4/1**[3]

0- **3** 1 **Broadway Duchess (IRE)**[224] 6873 3-9-0 0 ... RichardHughes 2 68+
(Richard Hannon) *lw: t.k.h: in tch: pushed along and hdwy to trck ldrs over 2f out: styd on u.p fnl f: nt pce of ldng duo* **9/4**[1]

4 1/2 **Narmin (IRE)** 3-9-0 0 ... PaulHanagan 9 67+
(John Gosden) *angular: s.i.s: in rr: pushed along and hdwy over 1f out: styd on wl fnl f: gng on clsng stages* **8/1**

0- **5** nse **Patently (IRE)**[238] 6486 3-9-5 0 ... KierenFallon 8 72
(Brian Meehan) *lw: s.i.s: sn pressing ldrs: rdn to chal 2f out: no ex ins fnl f* **9/1**

6 1 1/2 **Glanely (IRE)** 3-9-5 0 ... TomQueally 11 68+
(James Fanshawe) *w'like: scope: s.i.s: in rr: styd on fr 2f out: nvr gng pce to rch ldrs* **20/1**

3-32 **7** 2 1/2 **You're The Boss**[14] 2027 3-9-5 82 ... WilliamBuick 1 61
(Ed Walker) *chsd ldrs: drvn to chal 2f out: wknd over 1f out* **7/2**[2]

8 1 **Shady McCoy (USA)** 3-9-5 0 ... PatCosgrave 7 58
(Peter Chapple-Hyam) *unf: in tch: drvn and effrt to cl on ldrs fr 2f out: wknd fnl f* **25/1**

0- **9** 1 1/4 **My Renaissance**[212] 7191 3-9-5 0 ... MartinDwyer 12 55
(Ben Case) *leggy: in tch to 1/2-way: wknd over 2f out* **100/1**

0- **10** nk **Addictive Nature (IRE)**[291] 4688 3-9-5 0 ... AdamKirby 5 54
(Clive Cox) *in rr: hdwy to cl on ldrs ins fnl 3f: wknd over 2f out* **8/1**

0-20 **11** 5 **Last Hooray**[12] 2084 3-9-0 68 ... LiamKeniry 10 36
(David Elsworth) *pressed ldrs: rdn and wknd ins fnl 2f* **33/1**

1m 27.3s (1.60) **Going Correction** 0.0s/f (Good) **11** Ran SP% **121.6**
Speed ratings (Par 101): **90,88,87,86,86 85,82,81,79,79 73**
toteswingers 1&2 £15.60, 1&3 £18.60, 2&3 £3.00 CSF £121.67 TOTE £19.00: £4.20, £1.60, £1.40; EX 109.10 Trifecta £1694.50 Part won. Pool of £2259.39 - 0.93 winning units..

Owner George Materna **Bred** Paget Bloodstock **Trained** Pulborough, W Sussex

FOCUS
The second division of the fair 7f maiden. It was run at an average pace, with the riders again ignoring both rails, and it was a more muddling affair, but it was the quicker division by 12lb. The form is rated through the runner-up.

2449 COLLECT TOTEPOOL BETS AT ANY BETFRED SHOP FILLIES' H'CAP 7f (S)
6:05 (6:07) (Class 4) (0-85,83) 3-Y-O
£5,175 (£1,540; £769; £384) **Stalls** Centre

Form RPR

41-6 **1** **Annecdote**[9] 2195 3-9-7 **83** ... TomQueally 2 94+
(Jonathan Portman) *swtg: chsd ldrs: led 2f out: rdn and hung rt fnl f: drvn out* **4/1**[2]

102- **2** 1 1/4 **Indignant**[189] 7687 3-9-7 **83** ... RichardHughes 10 91+
(Richard Hannon) *lw: chsd ldrs: wnt 2nd over 1f out: kpt on fnl f but no imp* **7/1**

442- **3** 1 **Martinas Delight (USA)**[239] 6437 3-8-11 **73** ... KierenFallon 1 78
(Alan Jarvis) *lw: sn chsng ldrs: drvn to chse wnr wl over 1f out: styd on same pce into 3rd sn after* **16/1**

21 **4** 6 **Movementneverlies**[89] 706 3-9-1 **77** ... WilliamBuick 9 66
(Charles Hills) *leggy: pushed along in mid-div 1/2-way: styd on ins fnl f: nvr a threat* **12/1**

252- **5** ½ **Serenity Spa**[171] 7894 3-8-11 **73**.. JamesDoyle 7 60
(Roger Charlton) *lw: in rr: drvn and hdwy over 2f out: styd on fnl f: nvr a threat* **11/1**

3116 **6** *hd* **Byroness**[26] 1714 3-8-8 **75**.. RyanTate(5) 4 62
(Heather Main) *chsd ldrs: rdn over 2f out: wknd wl over 1f out* **33/1**

20-2 **7** 3¾ **Bountybeamadam**[19] 1875 3-9-1 **77**.. PatCosgrave 3 54
(George Baker) *sn led: hdd 2f out: wknd qckly* **28/1**

1 **8** *1* **Perfect Haven**[30] 1640 3-9-6 **82**.. JimCrowley 5 56
(Ralph Beckett) *pressed ldr 3f: wknd over 2f out* **13/2**[3]

1-0 **9** *nk* **Amberley Heights (IRE)**[31] 1620 3-9-2 **78**.................... KieranO'Neill 12 51
(Richard Hannon) *wnt rt s: in rr: stl bhd whn rdn and hung lft over 2f out* **20/1**

1 **10** *5* **Azenzar**[43] 1364 3-8-10 **72**.. RyanMoore 8 32
(Roger Varian) *str: swtg: s.i.s: rdn and effrt to cl over 2f out: nvr got beyond mid-div and sn wknd* **7/2**[1]

3-1 **11** 4½ **Milly's Gift**[66] 979 3-9-4 **80**.. AdamKirby 11 28
(Clive Cox) *in tch over 4f* **8/1**

00-1 **12** *8* **Reqaaba**[19] 1875 3-9-6 **82**.. PaulHanagan 6
(John Gosden) *sn chsng ldrs: rdn 3f out: wknd qckly over 2f out* **9/1**

1m 25.49s (-0.21) **Going Correction** 0.0s/f (Good) **12** Ran SP% **122.2**
Speed ratings (Par 98): **101,99,98,91,91 90,86,85,85,79 74,65**
toteswingers 1&2 £6.70, 1&3 £15.30, 2&3 £22.70 CSF £32.63 CT £423.19 TOTE £5.00: £2.20, £2.70, £5.90; EX 36.20 Trifecta £945.20 Pool: £2672.55 - 2.12 winning units..
Owner Tom Edwards & Partners **Bred** The Hon Mrs R Pease **Trained** Upper Lambourn, Berks

FOCUS
A good-quality 3-y-o handicap for fillies. The first three came right away inside the final furlong. A positive view has been taken of the form.
T/Plt: £202.90 to a £1 stake. Pool: £154,790.56 - 556.86 winning tickets T/Qpdt: £46.30 to a £1 stake. Pool: £9066.69 - 144.90 winning tickets ST

2419 NEWMARKET (R-H)
Saturday, May 18

OFFICIAL GOING: Good to firm (8.2)
Wind: Light behind Weather: Overcast

2450 JOIN CORAL.CO.UK AND GET £50 FREE BET H'CAP 7f
1:45 (1:45) (Class 4) (0-80,79) 4-Y-0+ **£5,175** (£1,540; £769; £384) **Stalls** Low

Form RPR

60-6 **1** **Red Seventy**[21] 1849 4-9-3 **75**.. LukeMorris 19 85
(Harry Dunlop) *s.i.s: sn pushed along to chse ldr stands' side: rdn and edgd rt and jnd main gp over 2f out: led over 1f out: drvn out* **14/1**

000 **2** 1¼ **Albaqaa**[7] 2286 8-8-10 **73**.. RobertTart(5) 12 79
(P J O'Gorman) *racd in centre: hld up: hdwy over 1f out: r.o to go 2nd nr fin: nt rch wnr* **14/1**

00-0 **3** *nk* **Poisson D'Or**[17] 1922 4-9-3 **75**.. MickaelBarzalona 10 81
(Rae Guest) *racd in centre: chsd ldrs: rdn: edgd lft and ev ch over 1f out: styd on same pce ins fnl f* **6/1**[1]

0332 **4** *hd* **Mutafaakir (IRE)**[22] 1801 4-8-9 **67**.. FrederikTylicki 2 72
(Ruth Carr) *racd in centre: hld up: hdwy 1/2-way: rdn and ev ch over 1f out: edgd lft ins fnl f: styd on same pce* **15/2**[3]

1002 **5** ¾ **Greyfriarschorista**[8] 2225 6-9-0 **72**..(p) JimmyQuinn 18 75
(Tom Keddy) *overall ldr stands' side: rdn and hung rt over 2f out: hdd over 1f out: styd on same pce ins fnl f* **22/1**

-151 **6** 1½ **Dashwood**[16] 1947 6-8-13 **71**..(t) WilliamCarson 7 70
(Anthony Carson) *racd in centre: hld up in tch: rdn and ev ch over 1f out: no ex ins fnl f* **10/1**

6224 **7** ¾ **Showboating (IRE)**[16] 1963 5-9-5 **77**..(vt) MartinHarley 1 74
(Alan McCabe) *racd in centre: s.i.s: hld up: hdwy over 1f out: r.o: nt rch ldrs* **12/1**

30-4 **8** ½ **Comrade Bond**[18] 1913 5-9-6 **78**.. TedDurcan 11 74
(Mark H Tompkins) *racd in centre: prom: rdn over 1f out: no ex ins fnl f* **16/1**

24-2 **9** ½ **Pashan Garh**[57] 1115 4-9-5 **77**.. JoeFanning 8 71
(Pat Eddery) *racd in centre: chsd ldrs: led that gp over 4f out tl over 2f out: no ex fnl f* **10/1**

00-0 **10** 1¾ **Sea Soldier (IRE)**[25] 1746 5-9-3 **75**..(b[1]) JimmyFortune 4 64
(Andrew Balding) *racd in centre: chsd ldrs: rdn over 2f out: styd on same pce fr over 1f out* **16/1**

5354 **11** *hd* **The Strig**[52] 1198 6-8-7 **65**.. DavidProbert 16 54
(Stuart Williams) *racd in centre: chsd ldrs: rdn over 1f out: no ex fnl f* **25/1**

0-00 **12** *6* **Greensward**[43] 1363 7-9-6 **78**.. EddieAhern 15 51
(Mike Murphy) *racd in centre: dwlt: outpcd: nvr nrr* **33/1**

0000 **13** ¾ **Chiswick Bey (IRE)**[21] 1838 5-9-5 **77**.. ChrisCatlin 3 48
(Noel Quinlan) *racd in centre: in rr and drvn along 1/2-way: n.d* **50/1**

/400 **14** 1¼ **Boom To Bust (IRE)**[35] 889 5-9-7 **79**..(b) SebSanders 13 46
(Sean Curran) *racd in centre: sn pushed along and prom: reminders over 4f out: wknd over 1f out* **25/1**

14-5 **15** 2¾ **Hometown Glory**[128] 133 4-9-7 **79**..(t) DaneO'Neill 9 69+
(Brian Meehan) *hld up: racd in centre: hdwy over 1f out: wknd and eased ins fnl f: b.b.v* **9/1**

220- **16** *1* **Robert The Painter (IRE)**[204] 7370 5-9-2 **74**.............. JamieSpencer 20 31+
(David O'Meara) *swtchd to r in centre and led that gp tl over 4f out: wknd 3f out* **7/1**[2]

35-0 **17** 1¾ **Tevez**[65] 995 8-9-4 **76**.. AndreaAtzeni 5 28
(Des Donovan) *hld up: racd in centre: nvr on terms* **20/1**

050- **18** *7* **Tartan Trip**[385] 1680 6-8-13 **76**.. NicoleNordblad(5) 14 10
(Luke Dace) *chsd ldrs centre tl wknd 2f out* **33/1**

1m 24.28s (-1.12) **Going Correction** -0.025s/f (Good) **18** Ran SP% **124.2**
Speed ratings (Par 105): **105,103,103,103,102 100,99,99,98,96 96,89,88,87,83 82,80,72**
toteswingers 1&2 £61.60, 1&3 £24.70, 2&3 £24.40 CSF £182.39 CT £1359.57 TOTE £15.70: £4.10, £4.30, £1.80, £2.10; EX 283.40 Trifecta £967.60 Part won. Pool: £1290.20 - 0.80 winning units..
Owner Terry Neill **Bred** Sir Eric Parker **Trained** Lambourn, Berks

FOCUS
Stands' side track used. Stalls stands' side except 1m4f &1m6f: centre. Riders in the first thought the ground was a little on the quick side of good. A competitive handicap for the grade, if one lacking in improvers. The winner was a on a good mark on his old form.

2451 DOWNLOAD CORAL APP FROM THE APP STORE H'CAP 1m 6f
2:20 (2:22) (Class 2) (0-105,101) 4-Y-0+
£18,675 (£5,592; £2,796; £1,048; £1,048; £351) **Stalls** Centre

Form RPR

132- **1** **Tiger Cliff (IRE)**[204] 7367 4-8-8 **88**.. EddieAhern 3 101
(Sir Henry Cecil) *hld up: hdwy over 3f out: rdn to ld ins fnl f: styd on wl* **5/1**[3]

-102 **2** 1¼ **De Rigueur**[31] 1615 5-8-4 **84**..(t) AndreaAtzeni 2 95
(Marco Botti) *hdwy to go prom 10f out: chsd ldr over 2f out: rdn to ld over 1f out: edgd rt: hdd and unable qck ins fnl f* **14/1**

1-05 **3** *nk* **Mubaraza (IRE)**[13] 2044 4-8-10 **90**.. DaneO'Neill 4 102
(Ed Dunlop) *hld up: hdwy over 2f out: swtchd lft over 1f out: styd on: wnt 3rd nr fin* **8/1**

121- **4** *nse* **Biographer**[225] 6833 4-9-7 **101**.. TedDurcan 12 112
(David Lanigan) *hld up: hdwy over 3f out: rdn over 1f out: styd on* **9/2**[2]

/15- **4** *dht* **Caravan Rolls On**[246] 6197 5-8-13 **93**.. JamieSpencer 9 104
(Peter Chapple-Hyam) *hld up: hdwy over 2f out: rdn over 1f out: styd on: nt rch ldrs* **4/1**[1]

2-14 **6** *2* **Taglietelle**[36] 1523 4-7-9 **82** oh5.. JoeyHaynes(7) 6 90
(Andrew Balding) *chsd ldr tl rdn over 2f out: styd on same pce fnl f* **25/1**

1-32 **7** 1¼ **Red Orator**[12] 2069 4-8-7 **87**.. JoeFanning 15 93
(Mark Johnston) *led: clr 7f out: rdn and hdd over 1f out: no ex ins fnl f* **16/1**

0-31 **8** *8* **Desert Recluse (IRE)**[35] 1547 6-8-5 **85**.. CathyGannon 16 80
(Pat Eddery) *chsd ldrs: rdn over 4f out: wknd over 1f out* **33/1**

6-12 **9** *9* **Lady Kashaan (IRE)**[21] 1841 4-8-13 **93**.. RobertWinston 8 76
(Alan Swinbank) *mid-div: hdwy over 5f out: rdn over 3f out: wknd over 2f out: eased* **10/1**

65-6 **10** 3½ **Perennial**[24] 1766 4-8-12 **92**.. SteveDrowne 13 70
(Charles Hills) *prom: rdn over 3f out: wknd over 2f out: b.b.v* **9/1**

10-6 **11** *11* **Party Line**[21] 1841 4-8-12 **92**.. JimmyFortune 1 54
(Mark Johnston) *hld up: rdn over 4f out: wknd over 3f out: t.o* **20/1**

650- **12** *35* **Bernie The Bolt (IRE)**[217] 7051 7-8-5 **85**.. DavidProbert 7
(Andrew Balding) *hld up: a in rr: rdn and wknd over 4f out: t.o* **33/1**

205- **13** *13* **Muntasir (IRE)**[199] 7487 4-8-12 **92**.. MickaelBarzalona 14
(Saeed bin Suroor) *s.i.s: hld up: hdwy 8f out: rdn over 4f out: wknd over 3f out: t.o* **14/1**

2m 53.33s (-3.67) **Going Correction** -0.025s/f (Good) **13** Ran SP% **118.8**
Speed ratings (Par 109): **109,108,108,108,108 106,106,101,96,94 88,68,60**
toteswingers 1&2 £16.80, 1&3 £10.00, 2&3 £17.50 CSF £69.07 CT £552.48 TOTE £5.80: £2.30, £5.20, £2.90; EX 82.90 Trifecta £1438.90 Part won. Pool: £11918.63 - 0.69 winning units..
Owner W H Ponsonby **Bred** Mrs Clodagh McStay **Trained** Newmarket, Suffolk

FOCUS
A classy staying handicap which a year ago went to the Group performer Mount Athos. It was well run and should provide winners. Another step forward from the winner.

2452 CORAL.CO.UK SPRINT TROPHY (H'CAP) 6f
2:55 (2:58) (Class 2) (0-105,100) 3-Y-O
£28,012 (£8,388; £4,194; £2,097; £1,048; £526) **Stalls** Low

Form RPR

-533 **1** **Hasopop (IRE)**[17] 1921 3-9-7 **100**.. DaneO'Neill 16 106+
(Marco Botti) *hld up: hdwy over 2f out: nt clr run over 1f out: r.o to ld nr fin* **9/1**

32-1 **2** *nk* **Jubilante**[21] 1821 3-8-0 **79** oh2.. NickyMackay 12 84
(Hughie Morrison) *chsd ldrs: rdn to ld over 1f out: edgd rt ins fnl f: hdd nr fin* **25/1**

55-0 **3** ¾ **Chilworth Icon**[31] 1621 3-9-7 **100**.. MartinHarley 13 103
(Mick Channon) *chsd ldrs: rdn over 1f out: r.o* **50/1**

16-6 **4** *nk* **Victrix Ludorum (IRE)**[31] 1620 3-9-2 **95**.. PatDobbs 5 97
(Richard Hannon) *hld up: hdwy and edgd lft over 1f out: sn rdn: r.o* **16/1**

103- **5** ½ **Burning Blaze**[218] 7028 3-8-7 **86**.. JamieSpencer 8 86+
(Kevin Ryan) *hld up: swtchd rt 2f out: rdn over 1f out: nt clr run ins fnl f: r.o towards fin: nvr nrr* **9/1**

-213 **6** ½ **Purcell (IRE)**[14] 2022 3-8-5 **84**.. DavidProbert 7 85+
(Andrew Balding) *chsd ldrs: rdn and nt clr run over 1f out: styd on same pce ins fnl f* **11/1**

-101 **7** *hd* **Bluegrass Blues (IRE)**[19] 1892 3-8-4 **83**.. ChrisCatlin 1 81
(Paul Cole) *chsd ldrs: rdn over 1f out: styd on same pce ins fnl f* **28/1**

5-05 **8** ¾ **Bapak Sayang (USA)**[14] 2022 3-8-1 **83**.. JulieBurke(3) 15 79
(Kevin Ryan) *led: rdn: edgd lft and hdd over 1f out: no ex towards fin* **28/1**

31-6 **9** *nk* **Vallarta (IRE)**[14] 2022 3-8-3 **82**.. CathyGannon 14 77+
(Mick Channon) *s.i.s: hld up: pushed along 1/2-way: nt clr run over 1f out: n.d* **14/1**

1-1 **10** *nk* **Secretinthepark**[14] 2022 3-8-12 **91**.. SeanLevey 4 85
(Ed McMahon) *chsd ldrs: rdn over 1f out: styd on same pce ins fnl f* **3/1**[1]

1-41 **11** *hd* **Rivellino**[10] 2158 3-8-12 **91**.. LukeMorris 10 84+
(Mrs K Burke) *hld up: rdn and nt clr run over 1f out: nvr able to chal* **13/2**[3]

13-2 **12** *3* **Brazen**[14] 2022 3-8-3 **85**.. DarrenEgan(3) 9 69+
(David Simcock) *hld up: nt clr run over 1f out: nt rcvr* **9/2**[2]

-414 **13** *15* **Shahdaroba (IRE)**[14] 2022 3-9-1 **94**..(p) AndreaAtzeni 6 30+
(Rod Millman) *chsd ldrs: pushed along whn hmpd over 1f out: eased* **12/1**

144- **14** 4½ **Melody Of Love**[193] 7622 3-9-6 **99**.. EddieAhern 3 20
(Ann Duffield) *s.i.s: a in rr: wknd over 2f out* **33/1**

1m 10.9s (-1.30) **Going Correction** -0.025s/f (Good) **14** Ran SP% **120.7**
Speed ratings (Par 105): **107,106,105,105,104 103,103,102,102,101 101,97,77,71**
toteswingers 1&2 £19.00, 1&3 £113.50, 2&3 £126.30 CSF £225.72 CT £5777.53 TOTE £10.00: £3.70, £4.40, £14.20; EX 226.20 Trifecta £1958.80 Pool: £2938.00 - 1.12 winning units..
Owner Giuliano Manfredini **Bred** B Kennedy **Trained** Newmarket, Suffolk

FOCUS
Won by some good sprinters, including Mince 12 months ago, this was a classy and competitive 3yo handicap, but it proved a highly unsatisfactory affair with several hard-luck stories. The bare form should be treated with care, but the winner is the type to do better. The first two raced nearest the stands' rail, with high draws proving advantageous.

2453 CORAL KING CHARLES II STKS (LISTED RACE) 7f
3:30 (3:30) (Class 1) 3-Y-O

£20,982 (£7,955; £3,981; £1,983; £995; £499) **Stalls** Low

Form RPR
24-3 **1** **Dundonnell (USA)**[30] 1638 3-9-7 113 MartinHarley 2 116
(Roger Charlton) *hld up: hdwy over 2f out: rdn to chse ldr over 1f out: r.o u.p to ld wl ins fnl f* **15/8**[1]
4-1 **2** 1 3/4 **Music Master**[31] 1618 3-9-0 84 FergusSweeney 4 104
(Henry Candy) *led: rdn over 1f out: hdd and unable qck wl ins fnl f* **12/1**
21-1 **3** hd **Baltic Knight (IRE)**[29] 1668 3-9-0 103 JimmyFortune 1 103
(Richard Hannon) *a.p: rdn and edgd lft over 1f out: r.o* **11/4**[2]
32-0 **4** 1/2 **Well Acquainted (IRE)**[31] 1621 3-9-0 103 JohnFahy 6 102
(Clive Cox) *edgd lft and bmpd s: sn chsng ldrs: rdn over 1f out: styd on* **10/1**[3]
4-34 **5** 1 3/4 **Exactement (IRE)**[31] 1622 3-8-9 97 RichardKingscote 3 92
(Mrs K Burke) *chsd ldrs: rdn over 1f out: styd on same pce* **14/1**
1-40 **6** 1 3/4 **Correspondent**[14] 2021 3-9-0 92 EddieAhern 9 93
(Brian Meehan) *trckd ldrs: rdn and edgd rt over 1f out: styd on same pce* **22/1**
625- **7** hd **Odooj (IRE)**[203] 7404 3-9-0 100 DaneO'Neill 8 92
(William Haggas) *hld up: rdn over 2f out: n.d* **12/1**
15-5 **8** 1/2 **Tamayuz Star (IRE)**[31] 1620 3-9-0 100 PatDobbs 5 91
(Richard Hannon) *chsd ldr: rdn and edgd rt over 1f out: wknd ins fnl f* **10/1**[3]
006- **9** 3 3/4 **Funk Soul Brother**[217] 7050 3-9-0 86 SteveDrowne 10 81
(Charles Hills) *hld up: rdn over 2f out: wknd over 1f out* **40/1**
014- **10** 4 1/2 **Supernova Heights (IRE)**[231] 6675 3-8-9 89 JamieSpencer 7 63
(Brian Meehan) *hmpd sn after s: hld up: pushed along over 2f out: wknd and eased over 1f out* **16/1**

1m 23.53s (-1.87) **Going Correction** -0.025s/f (Good) **10** Ran SP% **114.4**
Speed ratings (Par 107): **109,107,106,106,104 102,101,101,97,91**
toteswingers 1&2 £6.50, 1&3 £2.10, 2&3 £2.70 CSF £25.61 TOTE £2.50: £1.40, £2.20, £1.40; EX 21.90 Trifecta £49.60 Pool: £2068.93 - 31.24 winning units..
Owner K Abdullah **Bred** Juddmonte Farms Inc **Trained** Beckhampton, Wilts

FOCUS
A good edition of this Listed event. It's a race which has had a considerable bearing in recent years on the Group 3 Jersey Stakes over the same trip at Royal Ascot, with Jeremy and Tariq winning both races, while Fokine and Codemaster won this and were second in the Jersey. Last year's winner Aljamaaheer was third in the Jersey (and in the Lockinge Stakes too). A smart effort from Dundonnell, who was entitled to rate this higher on a best view of this form.

2454 BEST ODDS GUARANTEED ON RACING AT CORAL.CO.UK FAIRWAY STKS (LISTED RACE) 1m 2f
4:05 (4:07) (Class 1) 3-Y-O **£20,982** (£7,955; £3,981; £1,983; £995) **Stalls** Low

Form RPR
3053 **1** **Hoarding (USA)**[14] 2023 3-9-3 96 (p) RobertHavlin 2 101
(John Gosden) *hld up: hdwy to ld over 1f out: sn rdn: edgd rt nr fin: r.o* **11/2**
230- **2** hd **Tha'ir (IRE)**[223] 6910 3-9-7 108 MickaelBarzalona 1 105
(Saeed bin Suroor) *hld up: pushed along over 3f out: hdwy to join wnr over 1f out: sn rdn: r.o* **2/1**[1]
-51 **3** 7 **Jammy Guest (IRE)**[8] 2224 3-9-3 84 SebSanders 3 87
(George Margarson) *s.i.s: rcvrd to ld after 1f: rdn and hdd over 1f out: wknd ins fnl f* **3/1**[3]
-142 **4** nk **Mister Impatience**[9] 2187 3-9-3 97 JoeFanning 5 86+
(Mark Johnston) *led 1f: chsd ldr tl rdn over 2f out: outpcd over 1f out: styd on nr fin* **9/4**[2]
110 **5** 2 1/4 **Holy Warrior (IRE)**[41] 1419 3-9-7 101 RobertWinston 4 86
(Gay Kelleway) *chsd ldrs: rdn and ev ch 2f out: wknd fnl f* **14/1**

2m 2.83s (-2.97) **Going Correction** -0.025s/f (Good) **5** Ran SP% **111.2**
Speed ratings (Par 107): **110,109,104,104,102**
CSF £17.06 TOTE £7.80: £2.60, £1.20; EX 17.70 Trifecta £62.90 Pool: £2592.06 - 30.89 winning units..
Owner HRH Princess Haya Of Jordan **Bred** Sc A R Di Paolo Agostini & Darley **Trained** Newmarket, Suffolk

FOCUS
This Listed event has thrown up a clutch of big-race winners in recent seasons in David Junior (Eclipse), Red Rocks (Breeders' Cup Turf), Lucarno (St Leger) and Green Moon (Melbourne Cup). Last year's winner Thought Worthy was fourth in the Derby next time. This year's renewal looks unlikely to match those heights, however, although the runner-up's effort is up to scratch. The pace was quick and the first two came from the rear to contest a good finish, pulling well clear of the others.

2455 NGK SPARK PLUGS MAIDEN STKS (DIV I) 1m
4:40 (4:43) (Class 5) 3-Y-O **£3,234** (£962; £481; £240) **Stalls** Low

Form RPR
2- **1** **Granell (IRE)**[238] 6481 3-9-5 0 JamieSpencer 11 79+
(Brian Meehan) *chsd ldrs: pushed along over 3f out: led over 2f out: rdn and edgd lft over 1f out: styd on* **8/11**[1]
2 2 3/4 **Dawn Of Empire (USA)** 3-9-0 0 MartinHarley 1 67+
(Roger Charlton) *s.i.s: hld up: hdwy and hung lft over 1f out: wnt 2nd ins fnl f: nt trble wnr* **13/2**[3]
62- **3** 1 3/4 **Mr Fitzroy (IRE)**[234] 6572 3-9-5 0 JimmyFortune 8 68
(Andrew Balding) *w ldrs: pushed along 1/2-way: rdn and ev ch over 1f out: no ex ins fnl f* **4/1**[2]
3- **4** 1 1/4 **Quadriga (IRE)**[157] 8071 3-9-5 82 AndreaAtzeni 12 65
(Robert Eddery) *prom: rdn and edgd rt over 2f out: styd on same pce fr over 1f out* **10/1**
6 **5** 2 1/2 **Bosham**[9] 2192 3-9-5 0 JoeFanning 2 59
(William Jarvis) *unruly in stalls: s.i.s: sn prom: rdn over 2f out: wknd fnl f* **16/1**
0-0 **6** 1 **Penang Power**[22] 1813 3-9-0 0 RobertWinston 5 52+
(Michael Bell) *s.i.s: hld up: hdwy over 1f out: wknd ins fnl f* **40/1**
6- **7** 5 **Sweet Talking Guy (IRE)**[197] 7516 3-9-2 0 (t) SimonPearce(3) 7 45
(Lydia Pearce) *led: hung rt and hdd over 2f out: hmpd and wknd over 1f out* **40/1**
0-0 **8** 1/2 **Sugar Coated (IRE)**[8] 2231 3-8-7 0 ThomasHemsley(7) 10 38
(Michael Bell) *s.i.s: hld up: rdn and wknd over 3f out* **50/1**
0 **9** 1 1/4 **Arjawan**[81] 807 3-9-5 0 FrederikTylicki 9 40
(Clive Brittain) *s.i.s: hdwy over 6f out: wknd over 3f out* **25/1**

1m 38.37s (-0.23) **Going Correction** -0.025s/f (Good) **9** Ran SP% **116.9**
Speed ratings (Par 99): **100,97,95,94,91 90,85,85,84**
CSF £5.96 TOTE £1.60: £1.10, £1.80, £1.30; EX 7.50 Trifecta £19.80 Pool: £3352.56 - 126.58 winning units..
Owner Native Colony Partnership **Bred** Gigginstown House Stud **Trained** Manton, Wilts

FOCUS
A modest maiden for the track. It looked the stronger of the two divisions, but the times were very similar. The form is rated around the third.

2456 NGK SPARK PLUGS MAIDEN STKS (DIV II) 1m
5:15 (5:15) (Class 5) 3-Y-O **£3,234** (£962; £481; £240) **Stalls** Low

Form RPR
53 **1** **Prince's Trust**[9] 2192 3-9-5 0 PatDobbs 8 83
(Richard Hannon) *mde all: clr fr over 1f out: comf* **10/11**[1]
2 2 **Endless Credit (IRE)** 3-9-2 0 PatrickHills(3) 5 78+
(Luca Cumani) *s.i.s: hld up: hdwy over 2f out: shkn up over 1f out: r.o to go 2nd ins fnl f: no ch w wnr* **14/1**
0 **3** 2 1/4 **Persian Patriot**[15] 1986 3-9-0 0 CathyGannon 10 68
(William Jarvis) *chsd wnr: rdn and edgd rt over 1f out: no ex ins fnl f* **40/1**
4 1 1/2 **Song And Dance Man** 3-9-5 0 DavidProbert 11 70+
(William Haggas) *mid-div: rdn over 2f out: hung rt over 1f out: styd on: nt trble ldrs* **9/1**[3]
4 **5** shd **Mutanaweb (IRE)**[17] 1926 3-9-5 0 DaneO'Neill 6 70+
(John Gosden) *prom: rdn over 2f out: styd on same pce fr over 1f out* **2/1**[2]
6 nk **Elusive Band (USA)** 3-9-5 0 JimmyFortune 7 69
(Brian Meehan) *chsd ldrs: rdn over 2f out: wknd fnl f* **25/1**
0 **7** 3 **Investment Expert (IRE)**[26] 1713 3-9-5 0 JamieSpencer 1 62+
(Jeremy Noseda) *wnt rt s: hld up: pushed along over 2f out: nvr on terms* **16/1**
8 2 1/2 **Hispania (IRE)** 3-8-7 0 LouisSteward(7) 2 51
(Michael Bell) *mid-div: pushed along over 2f out: wknd over 1f out* **33/1**
00 **9** 2 3/4 **Kasbhom**[18] 1908 3-9-5 0 WilliamCarson 9 50
(Anthony Carson) *hld up: racd keenly: rdn and hung rt fr over 2f out: wknd over 1f out* **66/1**
10 8 **Olivers Mount** 3-9-5 0 JoeFanning 3 31
(Ed Vaughan) *hld up: sme hdwy over 1f out: sn wknd* **33/1**

1m 38.34s (-0.26) **Going Correction** -0.025s/f (Good) **10** Ran SP% **121.9**
Speed ratings (Par 99): **100,98,95,94,94 93,90,88,85,77**
toteswingers 1&2 £4.50, 1&3 £7.30, 2&3 £13.90 CSF £16.75 TOTE £1.70: £1.10, £2.40, £7.20; EX 14.60 Trifecta £308.00 Pool: £1702.16 - 4.14 winning units..
Owner The Queen **Bred** The Queen **Trained** East Everleigh, Wilts

FOCUS
This was run in an almost identical time to division one. The form is rated around the winner and the race averages.

2457 CORAL MOBILE THREE CLICKS TO BET H'CAP 1m 4f
5:50 (5:51) (Class 3) (0-95,85) 3-Y-O **£7,762** (£2,310; £1,154; £577) **Stalls** Centre

Form RPR
51 **1** **Brass Ring**[21] 1826 3-9-4 82 RobertHavlin 2 100
(John Gosden) *a.p: led over 2f out: rdn: hung lft and flashed tail over 1f out: edgd rt and r.o wl ins fnl f* **2/1**[1]
1 **2** 2 3/4 **Renew (IRE)**[14] 2030 3-9-7 85 AndreaAtzeni 4 99
(Marco Botti) *chsd ldr: rdn over 2f out: styd on* **13/2**
1-2 **3** 2 1/2 **Cafe Society (FR)**[21] 1834 3-8-12 76 DavidProbert 3 86
(David Simcock) *trckd ldrs: racd keenly: rdn over 2f out: styd on same pce fnl f* **9/4**[2]
-121 **4** hd **Love Marmalade (IRE)**[8] 2235 3-8-12 76 JoeFanning 1 86
(Mark Johnston) *led: rdn and hdd over 2f out: styd on same pce fnl f* **6/1**
52-2 **5** 2 1/4 **Persepolis (IRE)**[26] 1727 3-9-4 82 JimmyFortune 5 88
(Sir Michael Stoute) *s.i.s: hld up: racd keenly: swtchd lft over 3f out: hdwy over 2f out: rdn over 1f out: wknd fnl f* **4/1**[3]

2m 32.75s (0.75) **Going Correction** -0.025s/f (Good) **5** Ran SP% **111.7**
Speed ratings (Par 103): **96,94,92,92,90**
CSF £14.94 TOTE £2.20: £2.00, £2.50; EX 12.00 Trifecta £30.80 Pool: £1209.81 - 29.39 winning units..
Owner K Abdullah **Bred** Millsec Limited **Trained** Newmarket, Suffolk

FOCUS
This is often a good little handicap, and the 2011 winner Glencadam Gold went on to Group 1 success when trained in Australia. It was run at a sound pace and all five were more or less in a line heading to the final furlong. It could prove a race to follow, with the winner in particular likely to do better.
T/Jkpt: Not won. T/Plt: £243.10 to a £1 stake. Pool of £138703.35 - 416.44 winning ticket. T/Qpdt: £24.20 to a £1 stake. Pool of £6974.40 - 213.25 winning tickets CR

2274 THIRSK (L-H)
Saturday, May 18

OFFICIAL GOING: Soft
Wind: Breezy, half against Weather: Overcast

2458 IRISH STALLION FARMS EBF MAIDEN FILLIES' STKS 5f
2:15 (2:15) (Class 4) 2-Y-O **£4,204** (£1,251; £625; £312) **Stalls** Low

Form RPR
33 **1** **Ventura Mist**[21] 1839 2-9-0 0 DuranFentiman 6 75
(Tim Easterby) *mde virtually all stands' rail: rdn and edgd lft over 1f out: kpt on wl fnl f: jst hld on* **7/1**[3]
600 **2** nse **Rough Courte (IRE)**[21] 1839 2-8-9 0 CharlesBishop(5) 9 75+
(Mick Channon) *hld up bhd ldng gp: effrt and rdn over 1f out: hdwy whn nt clr run and swtchd lft ent fnl f: kpt on towards fin: jst hld* **9/1**
5 **3** nse **Azagal (IRE)**[30] 1642 2-9-0 0 DavidAllan 3 75+
(Tim Easterby) *in tch: effrt over 2f out: rdn and ev ch fnl f: jst hld* **8/1**
4 nse **Mecca's Angel (IRE)** 2-9-0 0 PaulMulrennan 1 77+
(Michael Dods) *trckd ldrs: effrt and rdn over 1f out: kpt on fnl f: jst hld: improve* **10/1**
3 **5** 1 3/4 **Princess Rose**[12] 2090 2-9-0 0 KellyHarrison 2 70
(William Haggas) *t.k.h: w wnr: rdn over 1f out: no ex last 100yds* **7/2**[1]
6 1 3/4 **Patisserie** 2-9-0 0 PJMcDonald 13 62
(Ann Duffield) *in tch on ins: rdn 2f out: kpt on same pce fnl f* **11/2**[2]
6 **7** 1 **Woodland Girl**[21] 1839 2-9-0 0 TonyHamilton 4 60
(Richard Fahey) *n.m.r and shuffled to rr over 3f out: sn drvn: styd on fnl f: nrst fin* **7/2**[1]

8 nk **Creative Spirit** 2-9-0 0 .... RoystonFfrench 12 59
(David Brown) *in tch: lost pl over 3f out: sn rdn and outpcd: sme late hdwy: n.d* **25/1**

9 1 ½ **Stoney Quine (IRE)** 2-9-0 0 .... ShaneKelly 8 52
(Keith Dalgleish) *sn drvn along in rr: shortlived effrt on outside 2f out: sn no imp* **20/1**

10 1 **Scarborough (IRE)** 2-9-0 0 .... GrahamLee 14 50
(Paul Midgley) *s.i.s: outpcd and bhd: nvr on terms* **20/1**

0 11 ½ **Lady Liz**[26] 1718 2-9-0 0 .... AndrewMullen 5 47
(George Moore) *dwlt: sn rdn in rr: shortlived effrt on outside 2f out: sn btn* **80/1**

1m 2.42s (2.82) **Going Correction** +0.475s/f (Yiel) **11** Ran SP% **117.1**
Speed ratings (Par 92): **96,95,95,95,92 90,88,88,85,84 83**
toteswingers 1&2 £13.90, 1&3 £5.80, 2&3 £17.80 CSF £64.68 TOTE £6.90: £2.70, £2.90, £2.50; EX 79.90 Trifecta £453.10 Pool: £2392.86 - 3.96 winning units..
Owner Middleham Park Racing Xxiv **Bred** Bumble Bloodstock & C Liesack **Trained** Great Habton, N Yorks
■ Kelly Harrison retired after partnering Princess Rose.
■ Stewards' Enquiry : David AllanM two-day ban; used whip above permitted level (3rd-4th June).
Paul MulrennanM two-day ban; used whip above permitted level (3rd-4th June).

FOCUS
Both bends dolled out for fresh ground, adding 20yds to 7f & 1m races and 30yds to 1m4f races. Probably just a modest event and four passed the winning post almost in a line.

2459 JIMMY MCNAUGHT HAPPY 80TH BIRTHDAY H'CAP 5f
2:50 (2:51) (Class 4) (0-85,83) 4-Y-0+ **£4,851** (£1,443; £721; £360) **Stalls** Low

Form RPR

0-60 1 **Towbee**[30] 1646 4-9-1 **77** .... JamesSullivan 10 85
(Michael Easterby) *chsd ldr: rdn 2f out: led ins fnl f: hld on wl u.p* **18/1**

06-0 2 nk **Whozthecat (IRE)**[14] 2031 6-9-2 **83** .... JasonHart(5) 9 90
(Declan Carroll) *chsd ldrs: effrt 2f out: ev ch and rdn ins fnl f: kpt on: hld nr fin* **33/1**

-040 3 1 ¼ **Waseem Faris (IRE)**[2] 2388 4-8-10 **77** .... CharlesBishop(5) 6 79+
(Mick Channon) *stdd s: t.k.h in rr: no room fr 1/2-way tl swtchd lft and hdwy ent fnl f: keeping on strly whn short of room cl home* **5/1**[2]

321- 4 hd **Jack Luey**[236] 6525 6-9-6 **82** .... NeilCallan 5 84
(Lawrence Mullaney) *midfield: effrt and rdn over 1f out: edgd lft: kpt on ins fnl f: nrst fin* **15/2**

-412 5 ¾ **Oldjoesaid**[30] 1649 9-9-5 **81** .... RussKennemore 13 80
(Paul Midgley) *hld up: rdn and hdwy over 1f out: kpt on ins fnl f* **4/1**[1]

3300 6 ¾ **Profile Star (IRE)**[30] 1644 4-9-6 **82** .... GrahamGibbons 11 78
(David Barron) *midfield: rdn and edgd lft over 1f out: kpt on same pce fnl f* **18/1**

00-6 7 shd **Jedward (IRE)**[49] 1253 6-9-5 **81** .... (b[1]) AmyRyan 7 77
(Kevin Ryan) *dwlt: t.k.h in rr: nt clr run and swtchd lft over 1f out: kpt on ins fnl f* **14/1**

240- 8 1 **Master Bond**[141] 8272 4-9-0 **76** .... (t) TomEaves 14 68
(Bryan Smart) *dwlt: hld up against stands' rail: nt clr run over 2f out to over 1f out: kpt on fnl f: nvr rchd ldrs* **11/1**

40-0 9 1 **Kuanyao (IRE)**[14] 2031 7-8-8 **77** .... CarolineKelly(7) 1 66
(David Nicholls) *in tch on wd outside tl rdn and no ex fr over 1f out* **66/1**

0-20 10 1 ½ **Cruise Tothelimit (IRE)**[22] 1814 5-9-2 **81** .... RyanPowell(3) 3 64
(Ian Williams) *midfield: rdn along over 2f out: btn fnl f* **6/1**

-200 11 shd **Come On Dave (IRE)**[14] 2031 4-9-1 **77** .... AdrianNicholls 8 60
(David Nicholls) *led at str pce: rdn and hdd ins fnl f: sn btn* **11/2**[3]

3-06 12 2 ¾ **Lexi's Hero (IRE)**[12] 2097 5-9-2 **83** .... (p) WilliamTwiston-Davies(5) 2 56
(Patrick Morris) *chsd ldrs tl rdn and wknd over 1f out* **11/1**

1m 1.15s (1.55) **Going Correction** +0.475s/f (Yiel) **12** Ran SP% **116.4**
Speed ratings (Par 105): **106,105,103,103,102 100,100,99,97,95 94,90**
toteswingers 1&2 £74.30, 1&3 £26.20, 2&3 £38.30 CSF £493.59 CT £3386.57 TOTE £24.10: £6.30, £7.80, £1.40; EX 861.20 Trifecta £1745.30 Part won. Pool: £2327.06 - 0.45 winning units..
Owner Mrs A Jarvis **Bred** Mrs A Jarvis **Trained** Sheriff Hutton, N Yorks

FOCUS
A fair contest for some seasoned handicappers. The draw seemed to make little difference, although being close to the rail helped. The form is rated around the first two.

2460 MARKET CROSS JEWELLERS H'CAP 6f
3:25 (3:26) (Class 3) (0-90,87) 4-Y-0+ **£7,439** (£2,213; £1,106; £553) **Stalls** Low

Form RPR

0341 1 **Klynch**[8] 2239 7-9-7 **87** .... (b) JamesSullivan 14 97
(Ruth Carr) *cl up stands' rail: rdn to ld appr fnl f: hld on wl fnl f* **11/2**[2]

-003 2 nk **Fast Shot**[8] 2239 5-9-4 **84** .... DavidAllan 6 93
(Tim Easterby) *hld up: rdn and hdwy over 1f out: chsd wnr ins fnl f: kpt on: hld nr fin* **9/1**

2-03 3 2 ¾ **Ashpan Sam**[12] 2097 4-9-1 **81** .... GrahamLee 8 81
(John Spearing) *in tch: effrt and rdn over 1f out: kpt on ins fnl f: nt pce of first two* **8/1**

0450 4 2 **Rusty Rocket (IRE)**[14] 2031 4-8-10 **76** .... TonyHamilton 3 70
(Paul Green) *cl up: rdn over 2f out: kpt on same pce appr fnl f* **25/1**

00-0 5 nk **Roker Park (IRE)**[23] 1787 8-9-0 **80** .... DavidNolan 9 73
(David O'Meara) *bhd and sn drvn along: hdwy on outside over 1f out: kpt on: nt pce to chal* **33/1**

0000 6 nk **Colonel Mak**[8] 2207 6-9-7 **87** .... GrahamGibbons 4 79
(David Barron) *t.k.h: cl up: rdn and sltly outpcd 2f out: kpt on fnl f: no imp* **13/2**[3]

1-04 7 nk **Chooseday (IRE)**[8] 2239 4-9-5 **85** .... (p) AmyRyan 11 76
(Kevin Ryan) *led tl edgd lft and hdd appr fnl f: sn outpcd* **15/2**

1-02 8 1 ¼ **Dick Bos**[8] 2239 4-8-11 **82** .... DavidBergin(5) 5 69
(David O'Meara) *prom: effrt and rdn over 2f out: wknd appr fnl f* **3/1**[1]

1330 9 3 ¼ **Al's Memory (IRE)**[5] 2310 4-9-1 **86** .... DeclanBates(5) 7 63
(David Evans) *in tch: rdn and outpcd over 2f out: n.d after* **20/1**

00-0 10 2 ¼ **Baby Strange**[8] 2214 9-9-1 **81** .... (v) FrannyNorton 13 50
(Derek Shaw) *missed break: bhd and pushed along: sme hdwy fnl f: nvr on terms* **22/1**

-300 11 1 ½ **Head Space (IRE)**[10] 2150 5-9-6 **86** .... (e) PJMcDonald 10 51
(Ruth Carr) *hld up: rdn along over 2f out: sn btn* **8/1**

0-30 12 15 **New Leyf (IRE)**[14] 2007 7-8-13 **79** .... AdrianNicholls 2
(David Nicholls) *in tch on outside: drvn and wknd over 2f out* **22/1**

0-00 13 1 **Bonnie Charlie**[14] 2007 7-8-11 **77** .... PaulQuinn 12
(David Nicholls) *towards rr: drvn along 1/2-way: btn fnl 2f* **25/1**

1m 14.24s (1.54) **Going Correction** +0.475s/f (Yiel) **13** Ran SP% **121.8**
Speed ratings (Par 107): **108,107,103,101,100 100,100,98,94,91 89,69,67**
toteswingers 1&2 £8.70, 1&3 £6.80, 2&3 £9.30 CSF £49.26 CT £415.40 TOTE £5.60: £2.20, £3.60, £1.80; EX 58.20 Trifecta £285.60 Pool: £2566.82 - 6.73 winning units..
Owner Douglas Renton **Bred** J C S Wilson Bloodstock **Trained** Huby, N Yorks

FOCUS
A similar event to the preceding race, but over a furlong further. The winner was close to last year's best.

2461 YORKSHIRE OUTDOORS ADVENTURE EXPERIENCES H'CAP 5f
4:00 (4:00) (Class 2) (0-100,97) 4-Y-0+ **£12,938** (£3,850; £1,924; £962) **Stalls** Low

Form RPR

00-5 1 **Steps (IRE)**[14] 2014 5-8-8 **89** .... (b) ThomasBrown(5) 1 101
(Roger Varian) *hld up in tch: smooth hdwy over 1f out: shkn up to ld ins fnl f: edgd lft: pushed out* **4/1**[2]

0-00 2 1 ¼ **Bosun Breese**[14] 2031 8-8-7 **83** .... GrahamGibbons 6 91
(David Barron) *t.k.h early: trckd ldrs: nt clr run over 2f out to over 1f out: kpt on fnl f: nt rch wnr* **9/1**

00-4 3 1 ½ **Noble Storm (USA)**[10] 2150 7-9-7 **97** .... RoystonFfrench 5 99
(Ed McMahon) *led: rdn along 2f out: hdd ins fnl f: kpt on same pce* **10/1**

20-5 4 1 **First In Command (IRE)**[8] 2227 8-8-7 **83** oh2 .... (t) ShaneKelly 4 82
(Daniel Mark Loughnane) *cl up: rdn and ev ch over 1f out to ins fnl f: kpt on same pce* **11/1**

0-02 5 1 ¾ **Kyleakin Lass**[14] 2014 4-9-6 **96** .... JamesSullivan 7 88
(Paul Fitzsimons) *sn pushed along towards rr: no imp tl styd on fnl f: nvr able to chal* **11/2**[3]

0110 6 nk **Forest Edge (IRE)**[8] 2214 4-8-10 **91** .... (b) DeclanBates(5) 2 82
(David Evans) *chsd ldrs on outside: rdn along 1/2-way: one pce over 1f out* **16/1**

21-0 7 2 ¼ **Naabegha**[14] 2014 6-9-3 **93** .... PhillipMakin 8 76
(Ed de Giles) *dwlt: sn prom: rdn over 2f out: wknd over 1f out* **7/2**[1]

441- 8 ¾ **Pearl Blue (IRE)**[217] 7063 5-9-4 **94** .... NeilCallan 9 74
(Chris Wall) *hld up in tch on ins: drvn over 2f out: btn fnl f* **4/1**[2]

0-00 9 2 **Hazelrigg (IRE)**[2] 2396 8-8-9 **85** .... DavidAllan 3 58
(Tim Easterby) *bhd: pushed along over 2f out: nvr on terms* **22/1**

1m 0.79s (1.19) **Going Correction** +0.475s/f (Yiel) **9** Ran SP% **115.3**
Speed ratings (Par 109): **109,107,104,103,100 99,96,94,91**
toteswingers 1&2 £13.60, 1&3 £5.90, 2&3 £22.20 CSF £39.60 CT £337.28 TOTE £4.50: £2.10, £4.20, £2.40; EX 53.50 Trifecta £531.40 Pool: £1320.97 - 1.86 winning units..
Owner Michael Hill **Bred** Eamon Beston **Trained** Newmarket, Suffolk

FOCUS
Not many runners but a very useful contest for sprinters. The pace seemed good from the outset. The winner is rated back to his best.

2462 DOWNLOAD THE FREE RACING UK APP MAIDEN STKS (DIV I) 1m 4f
4:35 (4:35) (Class 5) 3-Y-0+ **£2,587** (£770; £384; £192) **Stalls** Low

Form RPR

3-20 1 **Fly Solo**[21] 1831 4-10-0 76 .... NeilCallan 6 75
(Alan Swinbank) *mde all at stdy pce: qcknd over 3f out: clr whn edgd rt over 1f out: pushed out: comf* **9/4**[2]

0-5 2 3 **Just Darcy**[21] 1837 3-8-7 0 ow1 .... ShaneKelly 1 66
(Sir Michael Stoute) *trckd ldrs: effrt and wnt 2nd over 3f out: kpt on fr 2f out: nt pce to chal* **5/2**[3]

0 3 5 **Iktiview**[16] 1282 5-10-0 0 .... RussKennemore 9 62
(Philip Kirby) *prom: rdn and outpcd over 3f out: kpt on fr 2f out: nt rch first two* **22/1**

4 1 ½ **Caledonia**[42] 6-9-11 0 .... LucyAlexander(3) 2 60+
(Jim Goldie) *hld up: pushed along whn nt clr run over 4f out: edgd rt and kpt on fr 2f out: n.d* **2/1**[1]

06 5 2 **Enchanted Garden**[21] 1826 5-10-0 0 .... GrahamLee 7 57+
(Malcolm Jefferson) *hld up: rdn over 3f out: edgd lft and no imp fr 2f out* **11/1**

00/- 6 2 ¾ **Princeofthedesert**[1007] 5122 7-10-0 28 .... MickyFenton 8 52
(Garry Woodward) *sn cl up: rdn over 3f out: sn outpcd: btn fnl 2f* **100/1**

00- 7 12 **Rosia Bay**[296] 4507 3-8-6 0 .... RoystonFfrench 5 28
(Tom Dascombe) *prom: drvn over 4f out: struggling fr 3f out* **20/1**

634/ 8 1 **Tourtiere**[628] 5553 5-10-0 63 .... PJMcDonald 3 31
(George Moore) *t.k.h: hld up in tch: struggling over 3f out: sn btn* **18/1**

000- 9 ¾ **Roc Fort**[260] 5803 4-10-0 30 .... PaddyAspell 4 30
(James Moffatt) *hld up in tch: struggling 4f out: sn btn* **80/1**

2m 44.48s (8.28) **Going Correction** +0.75s/f (Yiel)
WFA 3 from 4yo+ 17lb **9** Ran SP% **117.6**
Speed ratings (Par 103): **102,100,96,95,94 92,84,83,83**
toteswingers 1&2 £1.90, 1&3 £6.90, 2&3 £4.60 CSF £8.25 TOTE £3.50: £1.40, £1.10, £5.70; EX 9.80 Trifecta £160.60 Pool: £ 2343.68 - 10.94 winning units..
Owner Exors of The Late Guy Reed **Bred** G Reed **Trained** Melsonby, N Yorks

FOCUS
The first division of a maiden that has produced a few nice types down the years, including Alfie Flits. However, this form looks questionable considering the way things played out. The winner didn't need to run to his best.

2463 MARION GIBSON BROWN MEMORIAL H'CAP 1m
5:10 (5:11) (Class 4) (0-85,85) 4-Y-0+ **£4,851** (£1,443; £721; £360) **Stalls** Low

Form RPR

-330 1 **It's A Mans World**[7] 2278 7-8-6 **73** .... PaulPickard(3) 8 84
(Brian Ellison) *hld up on outside: gd hdwy to ld over 1f out: edgd lft ins fnl f: drvn out* **10/1**

-360 2 1 ¾ **Kingscroft (IRE)**[8] 2214 5-9-5 **83** .... FrannyNorton 14 90
(Mark Johnston) *hld up in midfield on outside: hdwy to chse wnr over 1f out: kpt on ins fnl f* **20/1**

/515 3 ½ **Music In The Rain (IRE)**[21] 1830 5-9-7 **85** .... DavidNolan 13 91
(David O'Meara) *in tch on outside: effrt and pushed along over 2f out: kpt on ins fnl f* **11/2**[2]

-301 4 shd **Invincible Hero (IRE)**[8] 2232 6-9-1 **82** .... NeilFarley(3) 12 88
(Declan Carroll) *t.k.h early: led and sn crossed to ins rail: rdn and hdd over 1f out: rallied: one pce last 100yds* **6/1**[3]

5-00 5 nk **Al Muheer (IRE)**[12] 2078 8-9-4 **82** .... (b) JamesSullivan 6 87
(Ruth Carr) *hld up: hdwy on outside over 2f out: pushed along and kpt on fnl f: nrst fin* **11/1**

5-41 6 1 ¾ **The Osteopath (IRE)**[33] 1569 10-8-5 **76** .... ConnorBeasley(7) 2 77
(John Davies) *hld up: pushed along and hung lft 2f out: kpt on fnl f: nvr able to chal* **8/1**

100- 7 1 **Lady Chaparral**[230] 6710 6-9-4 **82** .... TomEaves 10 81
(Michael Dods) *chsd ldr: drvn over 2f out: outpcd ent fnl f* **20/1**

-003 8 ½ **Our Boy Jack (IRE)**[15] 1992 4-8-8 **79** .... LauraBarry(7) 5 76
(Richard Fahey) *trckd ldrs: effrt and pushed along 2f out: outpcd fnl f* **10/1**

51-6 9 2 ¼ **Self Employed**[8] 2232 6-8-8 **72** oh1 ow1 .... MickyFenton 3 64
(Garry Woodward) *dwlt: t.k.h towards rr: rdn over 3f out: kpt on fnl f: nvr on terms* **20/1**

0600 **10** *1 ¾* **Imperial Djay (IRE)**[14] 2028 8-9-5 **83** .... PJMcDonald 1 71
(Ruth Carr) *hld up: rdn over 2f out: nvr able to chal* **11/1**

15-4 **11** *¾* **Green Howard**[26] 1723 5-9-7 **85** .... NeilCallan 7 77
(Robin Bastiman) *plld hrd early: in tch: rdn over 2f out: wknd over 1f out* **9/2**[1]

030- **12** *¾* **Tiger Reigns**[211] 7210 7-9-4 **82** .... PaulMulrennan 4 67
(Michael Dods) *midfield on ins: struggling 2f out: sn btn* **16/1**

00-0 **13** *2 ¾* **Newnton Lodge**[25] 1745 4-8-13 **77** .... StevieDonohoe 9 55
(Ian Williams) *stdd s: bhd: drvn over 3f out: nvr on terms* **25/1**

0-50 **14** *20* **Queens Revenge**[8] 2214 4-9-2 **80** .... DavidAllan 11 12
(Tim Easterby) *trckd ldr: rdn over 3f out: wknd 2f out: eased whn no ch fnl f* **33/1**

1m 44.77s (4.67) **Going Correction** +0.75s/f (Yiel) **14** Ran SP% **120.8**
Speed ratings (Par 105): **106,104,103,103,103 101,100,100,97,96 95,94,91,71**
toteswingers 1&2 £39.20, 1&3 £11.00, 2&3 £27.30 CSF £202.07 CT £1254.64 TOTE £13.20: £3.80, £6.40, £3.20; EX 260.70 Trifecta £1895.10 Part won. £2526.83 - 0.31 winning units..
Owner David Foster & Brian Ellison **Bred** Cheveley Park Stud Ltd **Trained** Norton, N Yorks

FOCUS
Competitive stuff and the pace was sound from the outset. A step up from the winner on this year's form.

2464 RACING UK YOUR RACING HOME FROM HOME H'CAP 1m
5:45 (5:58) (Class 6) (0-65,67) 3-Y-O **£1,940** (£577; £288; £144) **Stalls** Low

Form RPR

-352 **1** **Krupskaya (FR)**[7] 2274 3-9-4 **67** .... MichaelJMMurphy(5) 6 73
(Mrs K Burke) *trckd ldrs: rdn to ld over 1f out: edgd lft ins fnl f: hld on wl cl home* **10/3**[2]

-340 **2** *hd* **Bitusa (USA)**[16] 1965 3-9-0 **58** .... RussKennemore 16 63
(Alan Swinbank) *hld up: hdwy on outside over 2f out: chsd wnr and hung lft ins fnl f: kpt on wl: jst hld* **28/1**

25-1 **3** *2 ¼* **Mash Potato (IRE)**[42] 1393 3-9-2 **60** .... PaulMulrennan 4 60
(Michael Dods) *t.k.h: prom: effrt and edgd lft 2f out: kpt on fnl f: nt pce to chal* **9/2**[3]

500 **4** *1 ¾* **Zaitsev (IRE)**[30] 1648 3-9-5 **63** .... ShaneKelly 3 59
(Ollie Pears) *led: rdn and hdd over 1f out: kpt on same pce fnl f* **33/1**

-640 **5** *1* **Gold Roll (IRE)**[7] 2274 3-8-13 **57** ....(e[1]) PJMcDonald 10 51
(Ruth Carr) *bhd: rdn over 3f out: hdwy 2f out: kpt on fnl f: nt pce to chal* **10/1**

50-0 **6** *1 ½* **Spivey Cove**[16] 1967 3-8-13 **57** .... FrannyNorton 13 47
(Karen Tutty) *plld hrd in midfield: drvn and outpcd over 2f out: kpt on fnl f: no imp* **66/1**

04-1 **7** *½* **War Lord (IRE)**[7] 2274 3-9-8 **66** .... DavidNolan 8 55
(David O'Meara) *in tch on ins: rdn over 2f out: outpcd over 1f out* **2/1**[1]

-400 **8** *4 ½* **Classy Trick (USA)**[11] 2124 3-8-8 **52** ....(b[1]) TomEaves 14 31
(Richard Fahey) *hld up: effrt and drvn over 2f out: wknd 1f out* **25/1**

003- **9** *1* **Skidby Mill (IRE)**[201] 7441 3-9-6 **64** .... GrahamGibbons 15 40
(Brian Rothwell) *in tch on outside: effrt and rdn over 2f out: wknd over 1f out* **20/1**

0-03 **10** *6* **Fishlake Rebel**[16] 1967 3-8-7 **51** oh1 .... JamesSullivan 2 14
(Ruth Carr) *dwlt: bhd: rdn and c alone to stands' side ent st: sn n.d* **14/1**

43-0 **11** *1 ¼* **Secretori**[26] 1712 3-9-3 **61** .... J-PGuillambert 7 21
(Jo Hughes) *t.k.h: hld up: drvn over 3f out: nvr on terms* **25/1**

604- **12** *¾* **Team Challenge**[238] 6475 3-9-5 **63** .... DuranFentiman 9 21
(Tim Easterby) *prom: rdn over 3f out: wknd fnl 2f* **22/1**

00-0 **13** *6* **Artful Prince**[7] 2274 3-8-9 **53** .... DaleSwift 5
(James Given) *bhd and sn drvn along: no ch fr 1/2-way* **28/1**

00-6 **14** *19* **Mysterious Wonder**[53] 1180 3-9-2 **60** .... PhillipMakin 1
(Noel Quinlan) *prom tl rdn and wknd wl over 2f out* **12/1**

1m 47.38s (7.28) **Going Correction** +0.75s/f (Yiel) **14** Ran SP% **126.2**
Speed ratings (Par 97): **93,92,90,88,87 86,85,81,80,74 73,72,66,47**
toteswingers 1&2 £17.70, 1&3 £4.80, 2&3 £25.50 CSF £104.57 CT £458.95 TOTE £4.30: £2.30, £7.70, £3.00; EX 99.90 Trifecta £716.70 Pool: £1998.03 - 2.09 winning units..
Owner Norton Common Farm & Mrs E Burke **Bred** Peter Webb **Trained** Middleham Moor, N Yorks
■ Stewards' Enquiry : Russ Kennemore two-day ban; used whip excessive force (3rd-4th June).

FOCUS
A modest contest which got delayed when Roland got under his stall and ran loose for quite a while. A small step up from the winner.

2465 DOWNLOAD THE FREE RACING UK APP MAIDEN STKS (DIV II) 1m 4f
6:20 (6:24) (Class 5) 3-Y-O+ **£2,587** (£770; £384; £192) **Stalls** Low

Form RPR

0 **1** **Bold Sniper**[28] 1678 3-8-11 0 ....[1] ShaneKelly 4 89+
(Sir Michael Stoute) *hdwy to press ldr after 3f: shkn up and stdy hdwy to ld over 1f out: qcknd clr fnl f: readily* **5/4**[1]

2 *5* **Stopped Out**[21] 8-10-0 0 ....(p) RussKennemore 8 81
(Philip Kirby) *led: rdn over 3f out: hdd over 1f out: kpt on: nt pce of wnr* **10/3**[2]

3 *3 ¼* **Fair Loch**[42] 5-10-0 0 .... PJMcDonald 9 76
(Mrs K Burke) *t.k.h: in tch: effrt and pushed along over 3f out: no imp fr 2f out* **7/1**

4 *1 ¾* **Mister Pagan**[42] 5-9-11 0 .... LucyAlexander(3) 1 73
(Jim Goldie) *hld up: rdn and hdwy over 2f out: hung lft: kpt on fnl f: nvr able to chal* **28/1**

5 **5** *18* **Attention Seaker**[10] 2164 3-8-6 0 .... DuranFentiman 2 39
(Tim Easterby) *hld up in tch: drvn and outpcd over 3f out: sn n.d* **25/1**

5- **6** *hd* **Equalizer**[233] 6615 4-10-0 0 ....(t) StephenCraine 3 44
(Tom Dascombe) *hld up: rdn over 4f out: sn struggling* **9/1**

34- **7** *4* **The Tiddly Tadpole**[197] 6409 8-10-0 0 .... AndrewElliott 7 37
(Simon West) *pressed ldr 3f: cl up tl rdn and wknd fr 4f out* **20/1**

53 **P** **Tefflah**[13] 2055 3-8-6 0 .... FrannyNorton 5
(Roger Varian) *t.k.h: trckd ldrs: broke down over 4f out: fatally injured* **5/1**[3]

2m 45.64s (9.44) **Going Correction** +0.75s/f (Yiel)
WFA 3 from 4yo+ 17lb **8** Ran SP% **118.7**
Speed ratings (Par 103): **98,94,92,91,79 79,76,**
toteswingers 1&2 £1.90, 1&3 £3.30, 2&3 £7.30 CSF £5.63 TOTE £2.30: £1.20, £1.70, £1.40; EX 7.80 Trifecta £26.60 Pool: £1607.31 - 45.19 winning units..
Owner The Queen **Bred** The Queen **Trained** Newmarket, Suffolk

FOCUS
This had the look of a really interesting maiden, but it was taken easily by Bold Sniper, who should rate higher. It was the slower division.
T/Plt: £1,134.80 to a £1 stake. Pool of £68418.73 - 44.01 winning tickets. T/Qpdt: £44.70 to a £1 stake. Pool of £4778.88 - 79.04 winning tickets. RY

2466 - 2472a (Foreign Racing) - See Raceform Interactive

PIMLICO (L-H)
Saturday, May 18

OFFICIAL GOING: Dirt: fast; tufr: firm

2473a PREAKNESS STKS (GRADE 1) (3YO) (DIRT) 1m 1f 110y(D)
11:20 (12:00) 3-Y-O **£368,098** (£122,699; £67,484; £36,809; £18,404)

RPR

1 **Oxbow (USA)**[14] 2033 3-9-0 0 .... GaryStevens 6 119
(D Wayne Lukas, U.S.A) *broke well; led aftr 200yds; made rest; slowed pace after 2f; qcknd over 3f out; hard rdn 1 1/2f out; r.o.u.p fnl f; a in control* **154/10**

2 *1 ¾* **Itsmyluckyday (USA)**[14] 2033 3-9-0 0 .... JRVelazquez 9 115
(Edward Plesa Jr, U.S.A) *trckd ldrs on outer; 3rd and t.wl over 2 1/2f out; rdn and wnt 2nd under 1 1/2f out; not qckn u.p fnl f; no extra fnl 50yds* **17/2**[2]

3 *½* **Mylute (USA)**[14] 2033 3-9-0 0 .... RosieNapravnik 5 114+
(Thomas Amoss, U.S.A) *last; hdwy 3f out; 5th and rdn on outside 2 1/2f out; styd on to go 3rd ins fnl f; kpt on u.p; not pace to chal* **109/10**

4 *6 ¾* **Orb (USA)**[14] 2033 3-9-0 0 .... JRosario 1 101
(Claude McGaughey III, U.S.A) *midfield; hdwy to chase ldng grp 4 1/2f out; lost place over 3f out; sn rdn and no imp; 6th and styng on appr fnl f; nvr on terms* **7/10**[1]

5 *½* **Goldencents (USA)**[14] 2033 3-9-0 0 .... KKrigger 2 100
(Doug O'Neill, U.S.A) *broke wl; led until hdd after 200yds; trckd ldr; hrd rdn and not qckn over 2f out, wknd appr fnl f* **19/2**

6 *½* **Departing (USA)**[28] 3-9-0 0 .... BHernandezJr 4 99
(Albert M Stall Jr, U.S.A) *midfield; 4th and rdn 2 1/2f out; wknd u.p fr ovr 1f out* **102/10**

7 *6* **Will Take Charge (USA)**[14] 2033 3-9-0 0 ....(b) MESmith 7 86
(D Wayne Lukas, U.S.A) *towards rear; 7th and rdn over 2f out; no imp; nvr in contention* **111/10**

8 *16* **Govenor Charlie (USA)**[55] 3-9-0 0 ....(b) MGarcia 8 53
(Bob Baffert, U.S.A) *towards rear; outpaced and last 2 1/2f out; tailed off* **94/10**[3]

9 *15 ¼* **Titletown Five (USA)**[20] 3-9-0 0 .... JRLeparoux 3 22
(D Wayne Lukas, U.S.A) *chsd ldrs; 4th and pushed along to hold place 3f out; sn wknd; tailed off* **223/10**

1m 57.54s (1.95) **9** Ran SP% **124.5**
PARI-MUTUEL (all including $2 stakes): WIN 32.80; PLACE (1-2) 12.00, 7.80; SHOW (1-2-3) 6.80, 5.00, 5.20; SF 301.40.
Owner Calumet Farm **Bred** Colts Neck Stables Llc **Trained** USA

FOCUS
In contrast to the Kentucky Derby, the second leg of the Triple Crown wasn't run at a breakneck pace and Gary Stevens controlled things from the front on the winner, going the first 6f in 1.13.26.

2237 RIPON (R-H)
Sunday, May 19

OFFICIAL GOING: Good to soft (soft in places; 7.6)
Wind: Virtually Nil Weather: Fine

2474 WOODEN SPOON, CHILDREN'S CHARITY OF RUGBY MAIDEN STKS 6f
2:10 (2:11) (Class 5) 2-Y-O **£3,234** (£962; £481; £240) **Stalls** High

Form RPR

1 **Mr Carbonfootprint** 2-9-5 0 .... TonyHamilton 1 73+
(Richard Fahey) *mde all: swtchd lft to rail after 1f: jnd and rdn over 1f out: drvn ins fnl f: hld on wl towards fin* **5/2**[2]

2 *¾* **Searchlight** 2-9-5 0 .... PhillipMakin 4 71+
(Kevin Ryan) *racd keenly: trckd ldr: moved upsides on bridle over 1f out: rdn 1f out: drvn fnl 100yds: kpt on but hld towards fin* **5/4**[1]

06 **3** *4 ½* **Dancing Sal (IRE)**[17] 1946 2-9-0 0 .... TomMcLaughlin 5 52
(David Evans) *in tch: pushed along 1/2-way: kpt on one pce: no threat to ldng pair* **12/1**

03 **4** *2 ¾* **Earl's Bridge**[13] 2067 2-8-12 0 .... RyanWhile(7) 8 49
(Bill Turner) *dwlt: hld up in tch: pushed along 1/2-way: nvr threatened* **9/2**[3]

5 *½* **Pacarama** 2-8-11 0 .... RaulDaSilva(3) 6 43
(Jason Ward) *cantered loose to post: dwlt and wnt rt s: hld up in tch towards outer: pushed along 1/2-way: nvr threatened* **33/1**

00 **6** *¾* **Jazzy Lady (IRE)**[27] 1718 2-9-0 0 ....(v[1]) LukeMorris 7 40
(David Evans) *chsd ldrs: rdn 1/2-way: wknd over 1f out* **22/1**

7 *3 ½* **Bentons Lad** 2-9-5 0 .... AndrewElliott 2 35
(George Moore) *wnt bdly rt s: sn pushed along towards rr: a bhd* **25/1**

5 **8** *5* **Hebridean Princess (IRE)**[34] 1565 2-9-0 0 .... MickyFenton 3 15
(Paul Midgley) *prom tl wknd qckly 2f out* **20/1**

1m 17.23s (4.23) **Going Correction** +0.325s/f (Good) **8** Ran SP% **114.8**
Speed ratings (Par 93): **84,83,77,73,72 71,67,60**
toteswingers 1&2 £1.80, 1&3 £3.00, 2&3 £4.10 CSF £5.70 TOTE £2.40: £1.10, £1.10, £2.70; EX 8.10 Trifecta £29.60 Pool: £1537.21 - 38.86 winning units..
Owner Mel Roberts and Ms Nicola Meese **Bred** Mel Roberts & Ms Nicola Meese **Trained** Musley Bank, N Yorks

FOCUS
Rail on bend from back straight to home straight moved out 5m, increasing distances on round course by about 12yds. No more than a modest maiden but a couple of newcomers pulled clear of the rest.

2475 AQUASENTRY, STIRRING YORKSHIRE CHILDREN'S SMILES CHARITY (S) STKS 6f
2:40 (2:40) (Class 6) 2-Y-O **£2,911** (£866; £432; £216) **Stalls** High

Form RPR

40 **1** **Ding Ding**[13] 2068 2-8-6 0 ow2 .... CharlesBishop(5) 5 56
(Mick Channon) *in tch: angled towards outer over 2f out: rdn 2f out: rdn to ld fnl 50yds* **9/2**[3]

454 **2** *1 ¼* **Jaga Time**[11] 2161 2-9-0 0 .... TonyHamilton 8 55
(Richard Fahey) *in tch: rdn to chse ldr over 1f out: kpt on: wnt 2nd post* **4/1**[2]

440 **3** *shd* **El Duque**[30] 1659 2-8-9 0 ow2 ....(p) RyanWhile(7) 2 57
(Bill Turner) *led: rdn over 2f out: strly pressed fr 2f out: hdd fnl 50yds: no ex and lost 2nd post* **11/2**

33 **4** *nk* **Sherry For Nanny (IRE)**^{17} [1946] 2-8-9 0 .... LukeMorris 6 49
(David Evans) *prom: rdn 1/2-way: outpcd over 1f out: kpt on ins fnl f* **13/8**^{1}

0 **5** *2 1/2* **Barleycorn**^{13} [2075] 2-9-0 0 .... (b^{1}) DavidAllan 1 47
(Tim Easterby) *wnt rt s: sn trckd ldr: rdn to chal 2f out: wknd ins fnl f* **11/1**

5565 **6** *3/4* **Riley's Missile (IRE)**^{15} [2005] 2-8-9 0 .... (p) DavidBergin$^{(5)}$ 4 44
(Charles Smith) *dwlt: hld up in tch: pushed along over 2f out: minor late hdwy: nvr threatened* **20/1**

46 **7** *4 1/2* **Love's Last Adieu**^{13} [2068] 2-8-9 0 .... TedDurcan 3 26
(J S Moore) *hld up in tch: pushed along over 2f out: wknd fnl f* **14/1**

0 **8** *9* **Elualla (IRE)**^{34} [1574] 2-8-9 0 .... TomEaves 7
(Nigel Tinkler) *prom tl wknd qckly over 1f out* **50/1**

1m 17.73s (4.73) **Going Correction** +0.325s/f (Good) **8** Ran SP% **113.4**
Speed ratings (Par 91): **81,79,79,78,75 74,68,56**
toteswingers 1&2 £3.10, 1&3 £4.30, 2&3 £4.10 CSF £22.43 TOTE £6.60: £2.20, £1.10, £2.20; EX 14.30 Trifecta £126.40 Pool: £1923.95 - 11.41 winning units..There was no bid for winner.

Owner Norman Court Stud I **Bred** Norman Court Stud **Trained** West Ilsley, Berks

■ Stewards' Enquiry : Ryan While seven-day ban; failing to take all reasonable measure to obtain best possible position (3rd-9th June). two-day ban; used whip above permitted level (10th-11th June).

FOCUS
There were no previous winners in this modest seller.

2476 C. B. HUTCHINSON MEMORIAL CHALLENGE CUP (FILLIES' H'CAP) (THE SUNDAY £5K BONUS RACE) 6f
3:10 (3:10) (Class 3) (0-95,95) 3-Y-O- **£8,191** (£2,451; £1,225; £613; £305) **Stalls** High

Form RPR

2-20 **1** **Spinatrix**^{36} [1537] 5-9-5 **93** .... (p) ConnorBeasley$^{(7)}$ 10 102
(Michael Dods) *mde all: rdn over 2f out: strly pressed thrght fnl 2f: hld on wl* **6/1**^{3}

211- **2** *hd* **Athenian (IRE)**^{314} [3912] 4-9-4 **85** .... LukeMorris 4 93
(Sir Mark Prescott Bt) *w ldr: rdn over 2f out: kpt on wl but a jst hld* **13/2**

5-10 **3** *nk* **Love Island**^{15} [2031] 4-8-9 **81** .... GeorgeChaloner$^{(5)}$ 11 88
(Richard Whitaker) *trckd ldng pair: rdn over 2f out: ev ch over 1f out: kpt on* **9/1**

40-6 **4** *3/4* **Misplaced Fortune**^{27} [1720] 8-9-6 **92** .... (v) JasonHart$^{(5)}$ 1 97
(Nigel Tinkler) *midfield on outer: rdn and hdwy to chse ldrs over 1f out: kpt on one pce* **12/1**

131- **5** *1 1/4* **Body And Soul (IRE)**^{225} [6883] 3-9-5 **95** .... DuranFentiman 7 94
(Tim Easterby) *hld up in midfield: rdn over 1f out: one pce and nvr rchd ldrs* **9/2**^{2}

-060 **6** *hd* **Hopes N Dreams (IRE)**^{15} [2007] 5-8-10 **77** .... ^{1} GrahamLee 6 77
(Kevin Ryan) *hld up in midfield: rdn over 2f out: one pce and nvr threatened ldrs* **11/1**

-010 **7** *1* **Gouray Girl (IRE)**^{29} [1675] 6-9-5 **86** .... (t^{1}) DaleSwift 8 83
(Brian Ellison) *dwlt: hld up in rr: rdn over 2f out: minor late hdwy: nvr threatened* **14/1**

00-0 **8** *3 1/2* **Crimson Knot (IRE)**^{50} [1253] 5-8-10 **77** .... TomEaves 9 63
(Alan Berry) *midfield: rdn 2f out: wknd ins fnl f* **50/1**

00-0 **9** *1* **Caranbola**^{32} [1607] 7-8-12 **79** .... PaulMulrennan 5 61
(Mel Brittain) *hld up: pushed along and outpcd 1/2-way: nvr threatened* **25/1**

01-0 **10** *5* **Dutch Rose (IRE)**^{36} [1544] 4-9-10 **91** .... DanielTudhope 3 57
(David O'Meara) *trckd ldng pair: rdn over 2f out: wknd over 1f out* **8/1**

123- **11** *11* **Hoodna (IRE)**^{198} [7518] 3-9-2 **92** .... MickaelBarzalona 2 21
(Saeed bin Suroor) *trckd ldng pair towards outer: rdn over 2f out: sn wknd: eased* **7/2**^{1}

1m 14.36s (1.36) **Going Correction** +0.325s/f (Good)
WFA 3 from 4yo+ 9lb **11** Ran SP% **117.6**
Speed ratings (Par 104): **103,102,102,101,99 99,98,93,92,85 70**
toteswingers 1&2 £8.00, 1&3 £9.80, 2&3 £13.30 CSF £44.83 CT £358.40 TOTE £6.20: £2.30, £1.80, £4.40; EX 47.30 Trifecta £673.20 Pool: £1981.95 - 2.20 winning units..

Owner Mrs J W Hutchinson & Mrs P A Knox **Bred** T K & Mrs P A Knox **Trained** Denton, Co Durham

■ Stewards' Enquiry : Connor Beasley two-day ban; used whip above permitted level (3rd-4th June).

FOCUS
A competitive fillies' sprint and although the gallop was good nothing came from too far off the pace.

2477 RIPON, YORKSHIRE'S GARDEN RACECOURSE H'CAP 1m
3:40 (3:40) (Class 2) (0-105,103) 4-Y-O+
£15,562 (£4,660; £2,330; £1,165; £582; £292) **Stalls** Low

Form RPR

02-0 **1** **Ardmay (IRE)**^{29} [1688] 4-8-6 **88** .... AmyRyan 4 96
(Kevin Ryan) *trckd ldng pair: rdn over 2f out: led over 1f out: kpt on* **16/1**

4-10 **2** *3/4* **Hi There (IRE)**^{22} [1830] 4-8-7 **89** .... FrederikTylicki 2 95
(Richard Fahey) *midfield on inner: in tch over 3f out: angled lft over 2f out: drvn to chse wnr over 1f out: kpt on* **5/2**^{1}

1412 **3** *1/2* **Frontier Fighter**^{16} [1990] 5-8-10 **92** ow1 .... DanielTudhope 5 97
(David O'Meara) *midfield: rdn over 2f out: chsd wnr over 1f out: kpt on one pce* **5/2**^{1}

1406 **4** *nk* **Dubai Dynamo**^{9} [2210] 8-8-8 **90** .... JamesSullivan 8 94
(Ruth Carr) *dwlt: hld up in rr: pushed along and hdwy towards outer over 2f out: chsd wnr over 1f out: kpt on one pce* **10/1**

-006 **5** *1/2* **Osteopathic Remedy (IRE)**^{15} [2029] 9-8-2 **91** .... ConnorBeasley$^{(7)}$ 1 94
(Michael Dods) *trckd ldng pair: wnt prom over 4f out: rdn to ld 3f out: hdd over 1f out: no ex ins fnl f* **9/1**^{3}

2-00 **6** *6* **Beacon Lodge (IRE)**^{3} [2399] 8-9-7 **103** .... PaulMulrennan 7 92
(David Nicholls) *hld up: pushed along over 2f out: nvr threatened* **40/1**

5-00 **7** *7* **Hit The Jackpot (IRE)**^{40} [1446] 4-8-8 **90** .... GrahamGibbons 6 63
(David O'Meara) *sn led: rdn whn hdd 3f out: wknd fnl 2f* **12/1**

0000 **8** *1 1/2* **Memory Cloth**^{15} [2018] 6-8-8 **90** .... DaleSwift 3 60
(Brian Ellison) *prom: rdn over 3f out: wknd over 2f out* **7/2**^{2}

1m 42.18s (0.78) **Going Correction** +0.325s/f (Good) **8** Ran SP% **114.5**
Speed ratings (Par 109): **109,108,107,107,106 100,93,92**
toteswingers 1&2 £10.70, 1&3 £7.00, 2&3 £1.40 CSF £56.27 CT £138.04 TOTE £23.30: £4.80, £1.30, £1.10; EX 99.30 Trifecta £229.90 Pool: £1321.39 - 4.30 winning units..

Owner A C Henson **Bred** Tom Kelly **Trained** Hambleton, N Yorks

FOCUS
A competitive handicap and the pace was honest.

2478 MIDDLEHAM TRAINERS ASSOCIATION H'CAP 1m 1f 170y
4:10 (4:10) (Class 4) (0-85,84) 4-Y-O+ **£5,175** (£1,540; £769; £384) **Stalls** Low

Form RPR

103- **1** **Clon Brulee (IRE)**^{247} [6193] 4-9-4 **81** .... GrahamGibbons 6 95+
(David Barron) *midfield: smooth hdwy over 2f out: led over 1f out: c clr on bit: easily* **7/2**^{2}

25-0 **2** *2 1/2* **Merchant Of Medici**^{40} [1442] 6-8-7 **70** .... TomEaves 2 76
(Micky Hammond) *midfield on inner: rdn and hdwy over 1f out: wnt narrow 2nd ins fnl f: kpt on but no ch w wnr* **50/1**

0-0 **3** *shd* **Demolition**^{22} [1824] 9-9-2 **82** .... RaulDaSilva$^{(3)}$ 1 88
(Noel Wilson) *led: hdd over 7f out: trckd ldrs: rdn over 2f out: ev ch wl over 1f out: sn no ch w wnr: one pce fnl f* **16/1**

-533 **4** *1 3/4* **Gala Casino Star (IRE)**^{16} [1990] 8-8-13 **83** .... (p) JordanNason$^{(7)}$ 7 85
(Geoffrey Harker) *prom towards outer: rdn to ld over 2f out: hdd over 1f out: no ex ins fnl f* **22/1**

04 **5** *1 1/2* **Tetbury (USA)**^{15} [2030] 4-8-13 **76** .... DanielTudhope 3 75
(David O'Meara) *midfield: pushed along over 2f out: briefly n.m.r over 1f out: kpt on: nvr threatened* **10/1**

-630 **6** *1* **Amaze**^{10} [2191] 5-9-7 **84** .... BarryMcHugh 8 81
(Brian Ellison) *hld up: rdn over 2f out: nvr threatened* **6/1**^{3}

014- **7** *3 1/2* **Colinca's Lad (IRE)**^{311} [3995] 11-8-10 **78** .... RosieJessop$^{(5)}$ 5 68
(Peter Charalambous) *hld up: rdn and sme hdwy 3f out: wknd appr fnl f* **25/1**

-054 **8** *nk* **Satanic Beat (IRE)**^{16} [1990] 4-9-2 **79** .... PaulMulrennan 10 68
(Jedd O'Keeffe) *prom on outer: led over 7f out: rdn whn hdd over 2f out: wknd over 1f out* **8/1**

0-00 **9** *24* **Assizes**^{10} [2185] 4-9-5 **82** .... JoeFanning 4 22
(Mark Johnston) *prom: rdn over 3f out: wknd over 2f out: eased* **9/1**

31-2 **10** *1* **Aegaeus**^{41} [1422] 4-9-6 **83** .... GrahamLee 9 21
(Ed Dunlop) *racd keenly: hld up towards outer: rdn over 3f out: sn wknd* **15/8**^{1}

2m 7.75s (2.35) **Going Correction** +0.325s/f (Good) **10** Ran SP% **117.5**
Speed ratings (Par 105): **103,101,100,99,98 97,94,94,75,74**
toteswingers 1&2 £18.10, 1&3 £11.60, 2&3 £27.20 CSF £172.80 CT £2485.51 TOTE £3.60: £1.10, £8.90, £4.20; EX 148.40 Trifecta £1259.80 Pool: £2450.02 - 1.45 winning units..

Owner Ms Colette Twomey **Bred** Collette Twomey **Trained** Maunby, N Yorks

FOCUS
A fair handicap won in some style by a fast-improving 4yo.

2479 BARRY TAYLOR MEMORIAL H'CAP 5f
4:40 (4:40) (Class 5) (0-75,72) 4-Y-O+ **£4,204** (£1,251; £625; £312) **Stalls** High

Form RPR

120- **1** **Avon Breeze**^{183} [7775] 4-9-2 **67** .... AmyRyan 6 82
(Richard Whitaker) *hld up in tch: smooth hdwy on outer 1/2-way: led on bit appr fnl f: pushed clr: easily* **17/2**

-041 **2** *3* **Haajes**^{17} [1961] 9-9-2 **72** .... (v) ShirleyTeasdale$^{(5)}$ 5 76
(Paul Midgley) *chsd ldrs on outer: rdn and ev ch over 1f out: edgd lft appr fnl f: one pce and sn no ch w wnr* **10/3**^{2}

300- **3** *1 1/4* **Needy McCredie**^{241} [6403] 7-8-7 **58** oh2 .... PaddyAspell 8 58
(James Turner) *hld up in tch: rdn over 1f out: kpt on fnl f* **14/1**

03-0 **4** *nk* **Blue Shoes (IRE)**^{29} [1692] 4-9-2 **67** .... DavidAllan 12 65
(Tim Easterby) *led narrowly: rdn whn hdd 2f out: short of room on rail 1f out: no ch after* **11/4**^{1}

3313 **5** *nse* **Dark Lane**^{8} [2268] 7-9-7 **72** .... LukeMorris 11 70
(David Evans) *chsd ldrs: rdn 1/2-way: one pce* **6/1**

-200 **6** *1* **Boucher Garcon (IRE)**^{2} [2410] 5-8-5 **63** .... LukeLeadbitter$^{(7)}$ 9 58
(Declan Carroll) *pushed along leaving stalls: w ldr: rdn to ld narrowly 2f out: hdd appr fnl f: grad wknd* **5/1**^{3}

130- **7** *3 1/4* **Fama Mac**^{190} [7684] 6-8-12 **70** .... EvaMoscrop$^{(7)}$ 7 53
(Neville Bycroft) *prom: lost pl 1/2-way: wknd over 1f out* **5/1**^{3}

1m 1.5s (1.50) **Going Correction** +0.325s/f (Good) **7** Ran SP% **114.6**
Speed ratings (Par 103): **101,96,94,93,93 92,86**
toteswingers 1&2 £4.60, 1&3 £12.70, 2&3 £9.00 CSF £36.96 CT £395.69 TOTE £12.40: £5.20, £1.60; EX 37.20 Trifecta £485.50 Pool: £2140.70 - 3.30 winning units..

Owner Grange Park Racing II & Partner **Bred** Hellwood Stud Farm **Trained** Scarcroft, W Yorks

■ Stewards' Enquiry : David Allan two-day ban; careless riding (3rd-4th June).

FOCUS
A modest sprint handicap run at a good pace.

2480 SIS LIVE MAIDEN STKS 1m 1f
5:10 (5:10) (Class 5) 3-Y-O **£3,234** (£962; £481; £240) **Stalls** Low

Form RPR

2-5 **1** **Tinghir (IRE)**^{32} [1624] 3-9-5 0 .... TedDurcan 2 88
(David Lanigan) *mde all: pushed along over 1f out: rdn ins fnl f: kpt on: a in control* **11/10**^{2}

2-4 **2** *1 1/4* **Thouwra (IRE)**^{29} [1684] 3-9-5 0 .... MickaelBarzalona 5 85
(Saeed bin Suroor) *trckd ldr: rdn over 1f out: kpt on but a hld by wnr* **10/11**^{1}

00 **3** *12* **Big John Cannon (IRE)**^{8} [2279] 3-9-5 0 .... GrahamGibbons 6 59
(David Barron) *in tch: rdn over 2f out: sn no ch w ldng pair: wnt remote 3rd appr fnl f* **28/1**

00 **4** *1 1/4* **Wynyard Boy**^{253} [6042] 3-9-5 0 .... DavidAllan 3 56
(Tim Easterby) *trckd ldr: rdn over 2f out: sn no ch w ldng pair: lost 3rd appr fnl f* **50/1**

5 *9* **Confusing**^{207} 3-9-0 0 .... DanielTudhope 7 31
(David O'Meara) *hld up in tch: brief hdwy on outer 3f out: sn rdn: wknd fnl 2f* **16/1**^{3}

0-6 **6** *3* **Finn Mac**^{8} [2279] 3-9-5 0 .... PaddyAspell 4 30
(John Norton) *racd keenly: in tch: rdn over 3f out: wknd fnl 2f* **66/1**

1m 57.59s (2.89) **Going Correction** +0.325s/f (Good) **6** Ran SP% **112.8**
Speed ratings (Par 99): **100,98,88,87,79 76**
toteswingers 1&2 £1.10, 1&3 £3.30, 2&3 £2.30 CSF £2.40 TOTE £2.40: £1.10, £1.10; EX 2.90 Trifecta £10.90 Pool: £2662.14 - 182.73 winning units..

Owner B E Nielsen **Bred** Bjorn Nielsen **Trained** Upper Lambourn, Berks

FOCUS
What looked a match beforehand proved to be just that as the two principals pulled well clear.
T/Jkpt: Not won. T/Plt: £467.60 to a £1 stake. Pool of £89,977.64 - 140.45 winning tickets
T/Qpdt: £96.30 to a £1 stake. Pool of £5456.64 - 41.90 winning tickets AS

2481 - 2488a (Foreign Racing) - See Raceform Interactive

[2295]CAPANNELLE (R-H)
Sunday, May 19

OFFICIAL GOING: Turf: good

2489a PREMIO CARLO D'ALESSIO (GROUP 3) (3YO+) (TURF) 1m 4f
3:00 (12:00) 4-Y-0+ **£22,764** (£10,016; £5,463; £2,731)

RPR

1 **Romantic Wave (IRE)**[21] 4-8-9 0 .... FabioBranca 2 103
(S Botti, Italy) *led: hdd after 1 1/2f: trckd ldr: swtchd outside and qcknd to ld 2 1/2f out: sn clr: rdn out fnl f: a in control* **17/10**[1]

2 2 ½ **Solomar (ITY)**[893] 5-8-9 0 .... MEsposito 10 99
(S Botti, Italy) *hld up towards rr: hdwy on outside 2f out: styd on to go 2nd ins fnl f: nvr on terms* **63/10**

3 *hd* **Frankenstein**[238] 6554 6-8-9 0 .... GArena 8 99
(B Grizzetti, Italy) *towards rr: hdwy 3f out: wnt 2nd 1 1/2f out: lost 2nd ins fnl f: kpt on u.p* **81/10**

4 1 ½ **Benvenue (IRE)**[203] 4-8-9 0 ....(p) SSulas 6 96
(R Biondi, Italy) *chsd ldrs: 4th and gng wl enough 2 1/2f out: hrd rdn and one pce fnl f* **18/5**[3]

5 ½ **Vola E Va**[7] 2295 4-8-9 0 .... DarioVargiu 11 95
(B Grizzetti, Italy) *chsd ldrs: lost pl 2 1/2f out: kpt on again fnl f: nt pce to chal* **11/5**[2]

6 *1* **Mister Sandro (ITY)**[28] 1709 4-8-9 0 .... AndreaAtzeni 9 94
(S Botti, Italy) *midfield: effrt to chal for 2nd under 2f out: sn rdn: one pce fnl f* **63/10**

7 *2* **Duca Di Mantova**[189] 4-8-9 0 ....(b) PierantonioConvertino 1 91
(R Biondi, Italy) *led after 1 1/2f: hdd 2 1/2f out: sn wknd* **18/5**[3]

8 *2* **Dogma Noir (IRE)**[42] 4-8-9 0 .... CFiocchi 5 87
(F Camici, Italy) *towards rr: bhd fnl 2f: n.d* **217/10**

9 *dist* **Bedetti**[7] 2295 5-8-9 0 .... GBietolini 7
(F Brogi, Italy) *midfield on inner: bhd fr 2f out: nvr in contention* **118/10**

2m 28.22s (1.02) **9** Ran SP% **162.4**
WIN (incl. 1 euro stake): 2.70. PLACES: 1.54, 2.59, 2.67. DF: 15.30.
Owner Effevi **Bred** Razza Del Velino Srl **Trained** Italy

2490a DERBY ITALIANO BETTER (GROUP 2) (3YO COLTS & FILLIES) (TURF) 1m 3f
4:15 (12:00) 3-Y-0 **£284,552** (£125,203; £68,292; £34,146)

RPR

1 **Biz The Nurse (IRE)**[21] 3-9-2 0 .... AndreaAtzeni 7 110
(S Botti, Italy) *midfield: rdn and hdwy 3f out: led appr 2f out: wnt clr over 1f out: drvn out fnl f* **13/4**[3]

2 *4* **Wish Come True (IRE)**[28] 3-9-2 0 .... MEsposito 9 105
(S Botti, Italy) *midfield on outer: hdwy on outside 3f out: wnt 2nd 1 1/2f out: kpt on wl u.p fnl f: no ch w wnr* **48/10**

3 *2* **Ancient King (IRE)**[21] 3-9-2 0 .... CFiocchi 6 100
(S Botti, Italy) *trckd ldng gp: rdn to chse ldr fr over 2 1/2f out: one pce u.p fnl 1 1/2f* **48/10**

4 2 ½ **Lodovico Il Moro (IRE)**[21] 1865 3-9-2 0 .... IoritzMendizabal 2 95
(L Riccardi, Italy) *midfield on inner: rdn and outpcd over 4f out: styd on u.p fnl 1 1/2f: nvr on terms* **15/2**

5 *nk* **Demeteor (ITY)**[28] 3-9-2 0 .... GMarcelli 1 94
(R Menichetti, Italy) *midfield: effrt to chse ldrs 2f out: sn rdn: one pce fnl f* **43/1**

6 3 ½ **Russianduke (IRE)** 3-9-2 0 .... LManiezzi 8 88
(S Botti, Italy) *towards rr: hdwy u.p 2f out: kpt on ins fnl f: nrest at fin* **48/10**

7 2 ½ **Best Tango (ITY)**[21] 1865 3-9-2 0 .... GBietolini 12 84
(Gianluca Bietolini, Italy) *prom: led after 2f: 2 l clr and travelling strly 3f out: rdn and hdd appr 2 out: wknd appr fnl f* **12/5**[1]

8 4 ½ **Boite (IRE)**[18] 1931 3-9-2 0 .... RobertHavlin 10 76
(Peter Chapple-Hyam) *trckd ldr: rdn and nt qckn 2 1/2f out: wknd fnl 1 1/2f* **33/10**

9 *6* **Fairy Nayef**[21] 1865 3-9-2 0 .... DarioVargiu 3 65
(B Grizzetti, Italy) *led tl hdd after 2f: remained prom: wknd u.p fr over 2f out* **13/2**

10 *3* **Notti Magiche (FR)**[28] 3-9-2 0 .... GArena 4 59
(B Grizzetti, Italy) *a towards the rr: nvr a factor* **269/10**

11 *10* **Rottmayer (IRE)**[24] 1799 3-9-2 0 .... MircoDemuro 5 41
(G Botti, France) *a among bkmarkers: nvr in contention* **16/5**[2]

12 *2* **Celticus (IRE)**[28] 3-9-2 0 .... FabioBranca 11 38
(S Botti, Italy) *trckd ldrs on outer: rdn and nt qckn over 2f out: wknd fnl 1 1/2f* **57/10**

2m 17.04s (137.04) **12** Ran SP% **197.6**
WIN (incl. 1 euro stake): 4.27. PLACES: 2.01, 2.54, 5.36. DF: 36.41.
Owner Scuderia Aleali Srl **Bred** Massimo Parri **Trained** Italy

2491a PREMIO TUDINI (GROUP 3) (3YO+) (TURF) 6f
5:25 (12:00) 3-Y-0+ **£22,764** (£10,016; £5,463; £2,731)

RPR

1 **Victory Laurel (IRE)**[30] 3-8-5 0 .... SSulas 1 98
(D Camuffo, Italy) *towards rr on stands' rail: gd hdwy 2 1/2f out: twice denied a clr run and twice swtchd outside: qcknd to ld 100yds out: drvn out* **135/10**

2 ½ **Rosendhal (IRE)**[17] 6-9-4 0 ....(b) MarcoMonteriso 7 102
(G Botti, France) *trckd ldng gp: rdn to ld 1 1/2f out: r.o u.p fnl f: hdd 100yds out: no ex* **31/5**

3 1 ½ **Onlyyouknowme (IRE)**[35] 1563 5-8-10 0 .... MircoDemuro 12 89
(E Botti, Italy) *prom: rdn to ld 2f out: hdd 1 1/2f out: kpt on same pce u.p fnl f* **27/10**[2]

4 *shd* **Bettolle (ITY)**[35] 1563 4-9-1 0 .... MColombi 4 94
(Jessica Lari, Italy) *midfield: rdn to chse ldrs under 2f out: kpt on fnl f: no ex last 100yds* **54/10**[3]

5 *nk* **Traditional Chic (IRE)**[197] 7565 5-9-0 0 .... IoritzMendizabal 14 92
(L Riccardi, Italy) *towards rr: hdwy under 2f out: styd on wl fnl f: nrest at fin* **54/10**[3]

6 ½ **Elettrotreno (IRE)**[22] 3-8-5 0 .... PierantonioConvertino 9 88
(A Giorgi, Italy) *chsd ldrs: rdn and nt qckn 1 1/2f out: one pce fnl f* **115/10**

7 ¾ **Scatt Cirio (ITY)**[79] 4-9-0 0 .... CFiocchi 13 88
(P Riccioni, Italy) *midfield on outer: styd on fnl f: nt pce to chal* **18/1**

8 *nk* **Art Of Dreams (FR)**[22] 4-9-0 0 .... DarioVargiu 8 87
(B Grizzetti, Italy) *towards rr: hdwy over 2f out: one pce fnl f* **54/10**[3]

9 *hd* **Cloud (IRE)**[44] 3-8-5 0 .... AndreaMezzatesta 5 84
(L Riccardi, Italy) *midfield: effrt to chse ldng gp 2f out: carried rt by wnr tl rdn and one pce ins fnl f* **54/10**[3]

10 ½ **Le Vie Infinite (IRE)**[22] 6-9-0 0 .... GMarcelli 11 85
(R Brogi, Italy) *towards rr on outer: rdn and sme hdwy over 1f out: one pce fnl f* **21/1**

11 ½ **Freetown (USA)**[21] 1865 3-8-5 0 .... AndreaAtzeni 10 81
(S Botti, Italy) *midfield: rdn and no imp over 1 1/2f out: one pce fnl f* **12/5**[1]

12 *3* **Mister Vellucci (IRE)**[22] 5-9-0 0 ....(b) GBietolini 6 74
(A Di Dio, Italy) *hld up towards rr: rdn and no imp over 2f out: wknd over 1f out* **42/1**

13 *10* **Chiara Wells (IRE)**[22] 4-8-10 0 .... MEsposito 3 38
(A Floris, Italy) *chsd ldrs: rdn and nt qckn over 2f out: wknd qckly appr fnl f* **131/10**

14 *nse* **Dagda Mor (ITY)**[22] 6-9-0 0 .... FabioBranca 2 41
(S Botti, Italy) *prom on rail: rdn and nt qckn 2f out: wknd qckly 1 1/2f out* **12/5**[1]

15 *hd* **Via Garibaldi (ITY)**[22] 4-9-0 0 ....(p) AFiori 15 41
(L Riccardi, Italy) *broke wl and led: hdd under 2f out: wknd qckly* **187/10**

1m 8.54s (-1.76)
WFA 3 from 4yo+ 9lb **15** Ran SP% **201.4**
WIN (incl. 1 euro stake): 14.53. PLACES: 3.86, 2.12, 1.98. DF: 215.33.
Owner Scuderia Colle Papa **Bred** Mr And Mrs B Firestone **Trained** Italy

HOPPEGARTEN (R-H)
Sunday, May 19

OFFICIAL GOING: Turf: good

2492a OLEANDER-RENNEN (GROUP 3) (4YO+) (TURF) 2m
3:50 (12:00) 4-Y-0+
£26,016 (£8,943; £4,471; £2,439; £1,626; £1,219)

RPR

1 **Altano (GER)**[204] 7427 7-9-2 0 .... JBojko 5 109+
(A Wohler, Germany) *hld up in last trio on inner: swtchd out and rdn to improve on turn into st: styd on to chal wl ins fnl f: led cl home and won gng away* **33/10**[2]

2 ¾ **Supersonic Flight (GER)**[43] 6-8-11 0 .... DPorcu 9 103
(M Rulec, Germany) *midfield on outer: rdn on turn into st: styd on to chal ins fnl f: led briefly ins fnl 100yds: qckly hdd and no ex* **38/1**

3 *1* **Earl Of Tinsdal (GER)**[238] 6523 5-9-6 0 .... EPedroza 3 111
(A Wohler, Germany) *led: skipped clr 3f out: rdn on turn into st: grad diminishing advantage thrght fnl 2f: hdd ins fnl 100yds: no ex and dropped to 3rd* **17/10**[1]

4 ¾ **Lucarelli (GER)**[567] 7-8-11 0 .... LennartHammer-Hansen 10 101+
(Ferdinand J Leve, Germany) *midfield on inner: rdn 2f out: styd on to go 4th ins fnl f: fin strly but nvr able to chal* **115/10**

5 *1* **Leopardin (GER)**[217] 5-8-8 0 .... WPanov 2 97
(H J Groschel, Germany) *hld up in last quartet: rdn on turn into st: styd on steadily but nt pce to chal* **17/2**

6 *2* **Slowfoot (GER)**[204] 7427 5-8-11 0 .... AStarke 8 98
(Markus Klug, Germany) *prom on outer: rdn 3f out: wnt 2nd over 2f out: chsd wnr over 1f out: no ex ins fnl f: steadily fdd and dropped to 6th* **47/10**[3]

7 *9* **Lacateno**[18] 6-8-11 0 ....(b) ADeVries 6 88
(W Hickst, Germany) *hld up in last trio on outer: rdn 3f out: outpcd and btn over 1f out: nvr a factor* **7/1**

8 *nse* **Flamingo Fantasy (GER)**[179] 8-8-11 0 ....(p) EddyHardouin 12 88
(S Smrczek, Germany) *dropped in fr wdst draw and hld up in last: rdn 3f out: outpcd and btn over 1f out: nvr a factor* **25/1**

9 ¾ **Lateran Accord (IRE)**[24] 4-9-0 0 .... APietsch 4 92
(W Hickst, Germany) *settled in midfield on inner: rdn 2f out: outpcd over 1f out and sn btn: fdd and eased* **156/10**

10 *13* **Earlsalsa (GER)**[161] 9-8-11 0 .... FilipMinarik 1 73
(C Von Der Recke, Germany) *prom on inner: rdn on turn into st: lost pl 2f out: no ex and btn: fdd and eased: t.o* **193/10**

11 *2* **Selim (RUS)**[218] 5-8-11 0 ....(b) AndreBest 11 71
(S Arslangirej, Czech Republic) *trckd ldr on outer: rdn over 3f out: lost pl over 2f out: no ex and btn: fdd and dropped to last: eased and t.o* **45/1**

3m 21.3s (201.30)
WFA 4 from 5yo+ 2lb **11** Ran SP% **128.4**
WIN (incl. 10 euro stake): 43. PLACES: 17, 54, 19. SF: 2,349.
Owner Frau Dr I Hornig **Bred** Gestut Hof Ittlingen **Trained** Germany

2493 - (Foreign Racing) - See Raceform Interactive

KRANJI (L-H)
Sunday, May 19

OFFICIAL GOING: Turf: good

2494a SINGAPORE AIRLINES INTERNATIONAL CUP (GROUP 1) (3YO+) (TURF) 1m 2f
1:40 (12:00) 3-Y-0+
£863,636 (£306,818; £155,303; £75,757; £30,303; £15,151)

RPR

1 **Military Attack (IRE)**[21] 1872 5-9-0 0 .... ZacPurton 4 123+
(J Moore, Hong Kong) *prom early: sn settled in midfield in tch on inner: rdn 2f out: qcknd to ld 1 1/2f out: stormed clr ent fnl f: eased ins fnl 100yds and coasted home: v impressive* **12/5**[2]

2 3 ¼ **Dan Excel (IRE)**[14] 2066 5-9-0 0 ....(t) WCMarwing 1 111
(J Moore, Hong Kong) *trckd ldrs on inner: swtchd out and rdn to chal 2f out: wnt 2nd over 1f out: sn outpcd by wnr: hung lft u.p ins fnl f: kpt on* **186/10**

3 *hd* **Mawingo (GER)**[43] 1407 5-9-0 0 ....(t) HughBowman 2 111
(M Freedman, Singapore) *midfield on inner: rdn 2f out: wnt 3rd ins fnl f: styd on wl but no ch w wnr* **26/1**

4 ¾ **Lizarre (SAF)**[21] 7-9-0 0 .... BVorster 9 109
(Patrick Shaw, Singapore) *hld up in last trio on outer: bmpd by rival and forced wd on turn into st: rdn and styd on steadily thrght fnl 1 1/2f: wnt 4th cl home but n.d* **40/1**

5 ½ **Mull Of Killough (IRE)**[31] 1639 7-9-0 0 .... GeorgeBaker 8 108
(Jane Chapple-Hyam) *midfield on outer: rdn and hdwy over 2f out: r.o to chal 1 1/2f out: qckly outpcd by wnr: styd on but dropped to 5th cl home* **18/1**

6 ½ **Hunter's Light (IRE)**[50] 1269 5-9-0 0 .... SilvestreDeSousa 10 107
(Saeed bin Suroor) *midfield: angled out on turn into st: swtchd bk ins and rdn 1 1/2f out: kpt on ins fnl f but nt pce to chal* **54/10**[3]

7 1 **Better Life (AUS)**[23] 5-8-10 0 .... (b) AlanMunro 6 101
(Hideyiki Takaoka, Singapore) *hld up towards rr on inner: swtchd out and rdn over 2f out: angled bk to rail ent fnl f: plugged on but n.d* **9/1**

8 hd **Red Cadeaux**[21] 1868 7-9-0 0 .... GeraldMosse 7 105
(Ed Dunlop) *dwlt sltly and sn towards rr: hld up: hdwy into midfield on outer over 3f out: rdn over 2f out: sn outpcd: plugged on wout threatening* **68/10**

9 1 **Meandre (FR)**[50] 1269 5-9-0 0 .... KUlubaev 12 103
(Doug Watson, UAE) *towards rr early: rapid hdwy on outer 7f out: led over 5f out: rdn over 2f out: hdd 1 1/2f out: sn no ex and btn: fdd* **30/1**

10 2¼ **Deep Pockets (NZ)**[23] 6-9-0 0 .... (t) JohnPowell 13 98
(Cliff Brown, Singapore) *dropped in front wdst draw and hld up in last: rdn over 2f out: hdwy on rail over 1 1/2f out: outpcd by ldrs ent fnl f: sn no ex and btn: fdd* **90/1**

11 7¼ **Ready To Strike (NZ)**[23] 6-9-0 0 .... (p) JoaoMoreira 3 84
(Laurie Laxon, Singapore) *midfield: rdn whn jinked sharply rt and bmpd rival on turn into st: outpcd and btn ent fnl f: fdd and eased* **33/1**

12 ½ **Pastorius (GER)**[21] 1870 4-9-0 0 .... OlivierPeslier 11 83
(Mario Hofer, Germany) *trckd ldrs on outer: rdn and lost pl over 2f out: btn over 1f out: sn eased* **2/1**[1]

13 7¾ **Flax (SAF)**[23] 7-9-0 0 .... MNunes 5 67
(David Hill, Singapore) *led: hdd over 5f out and trckd ldr on inner: rdn over 2f out: sn lost pl and btn: dropped to last over 1f out: eased and t.o* **76/1**

1m 59.58s (119.58) **13** Ran SP% **126.3**
PARI-MUTUEL (including 5 sgd stakes): WIN 17.00; PLACE 8.00, 25.00, 32.00; (including 2 sgd stakes): DF 55.00.
Owner Mr & Mrs Steven Lo Kit Sing **Bred** P E Banahan **Trained** Hong Kong

1832 LEICESTER (R-H)
Monday, May 20

OFFICIAL GOING: Good to firm (good in places; 8.9)
Wind: Light; across Weather: Overcast

2495 WINNING EXPRESS H'CAP — 7f 9y
6:20 (6:20) (Class 4) (0-80,79) 3-Y-O — **£4,690** (£1,395; £697; £348) **Stalls** High

Form				RPR
223-	1		**Pythagorean**[216] 7127 3-9-6 78 .... JamesDoyle 2	96+

(Roger Charlton) *stdd s: hld up: hdwy over 2f out: led over 1f out: r.o strly: eased nr fin* **9/4**[1]

22-0 2 5 **Dance With Dragons (IRE)**[16] 2022 3-9-2 79 .... LauraPike(5) 9 82
(William Stone) *hld up: hdwy and nt clr run over 1f out: wnt 2nd ins fnl f: no ch w wnr* **16/1**

03-3 3 3½ **Evangelist**[28] 1713 3-9-5 77 .... RyanMoore 6 71+
(Sir Michael Stoute) *s.s: hld up: nt clr run over 1f out: styd on to go 3rd nr fin: nvr nrr* **7/2**[2]

1-64 4 nk **Benoni**[23] 1832 3-9-0 72 .... DaneO'Neill 7 65
(Henry Candy) *trckd ldr: racd keenly: rdn and ev ch over 1f out: no ex ins fnl f* **11/1**

1-50 5 nk **Imperial Glance**[20] 1900 3-8-7 65 .... DavidProbert 8 57
(Andrew Balding) *prom: rdn over 2f out: styd on same pce fr over 1f out* **25/1**

-501 6 ½ **Double Your Money (IRE)**[12] 2160 3-9-7 79 .... FrannyNorton 10 73+
(Mark Johnston) *led: rdn: edgd rt and hdd over 1f out: no ex fnl f* **9/1**[3]

40-4 7 1½ **Roanne (USA)**[20] 1900 3-8-9 67 .... JohnFahy 4 54
(Clive Cox) *chsd ldrs: rdn and ev ch over 1f out: wknd ins fnl f* **16/1**

3-50 8 1½ **Winnie Perry**[20] 1900 3-8-9 67 .... AndreaAtzeni 1 49
(Rod Millman) *chsd ldrs: rdn over 2f out: wknd fnl f* **66/1**

1-00 9 6 **Santo Prince (USA)**[23] 1832 3-9-1 73 .... ChrisCatlin 3 39
(Michael Bell) *sn outpcd* **50/1**

1-2 10 5 **Khobaraa**[18] 1958 3-9-6 78 .... PaulHanagan 5 55
(John Gosden) *plld hrd and prom: rdn over 2f out: wknd over 1f out* **7/2**[2]

1m 25.05s (-1.15) **Going Correction** -0.125s/f (Firm) **10** Ran SP% **112.6**
Speed ratings (Par 101): **101,95,91,90,90 90,88,86,79,74**
toteswingers 1&2 £9.10, 1&3 £1.30, 2&3 £11.60 CSF £39.46 CT £125.62 TOTE £2.80: £1.10, £5.10, £1.70; EX 41.90 Trifecta £141.60 Pool: £1,149.88 - 6.08 winning units..
Owner K Abdullah **Bred** Juddmonte Farms Ltd **Trained** Beckhampton, Wilts

FOCUS
False rail from top of hill on back straight all the way to Wining Post added circa 17m to races on Round course. There were some useful but lightly raced 3yos in this line-up, and there should be a number of future winners among them. The first two were both launched from the rear, suggesting there was a decent pace. The fourth helps set the standard.

2496 JAMES WARD (S) STKS — 1m 60y
6:50 (6:50) (Class 6) 3-Y-O+ — **£1,940** (£577; £288; £144) **Stalls** Low

Form RPR

6-30 1 **Prime Exhibit**[25] 1796 8-9-7 76 .... (t) PaulHanagan 2 79
(Daniel Mark Loughnane) *hld up: hdwy to ld over 1f out: shkn up ins fnl f: styd on* **11/4**[2]

-002 2 1½ **Pravda Street**[15] 2042 8-9-7 70 .... DaleSwift 5 76
(Brian Ellison) *chsd ldrs: rdn and ev ch over 1f out: styd on under u.p* **11/4**[2]

0100 3 3¾ **West End Lad**[10] 2234 10-9-9 70 .... (b) MarkCoumbe(3) 1 72
(Roy Bowring) *dwlt: hdwy to chse ldr 5f out: rdn to ld over 2f out: hdd over 1f out: styd on same pce ins fnl f* **13/2**[3]

140 4 2¼ **Azrael**[23] 1819 5-9-12 74 .... (tp) RyanMoore 4 67
(Alan McCabe) *trckd ldrs: racd keenly: rdn and ev ch over 1f out: no ex ins fnl f* **7/4**[1]

060/ 5 6 **Classic Voice (IRE)**[656] 4664 5-9-7 60 .... GrahamLee 3 48
(Roy Brotherton) *prom: rdn over 2f out: wknd over 1f out* **40/1**

40 6 3¼ **Thewestwalian (USA)**[11] 2198 5-9-7 0 .... ChrisCatlin 7 41
(Peter Hiatt) *sn led: rdn and hdd over 2f out: wknd over 1f out* **150/1**

7 37 **Alsaqi (IRE)** 3-8-9 0 .... (e[1]) SamHitchcott 6
(John Butler) *s.s: a in rr: wknd 3f out: t.o* **33/1**

1m 46.85s (1.75) **Going Correction** +0.45s/f (Yiel)
WFA 3 from 5yo+ 12lb **7** Ran SP% **109.1**
Speed ratings (Par 101): **109,107,103,101,95 92,55**
CSF £9.65 TOTE £4.80: £1.60, £2.20; EX 10.20 Trifecta £49.70 Pool: £1,055.07 - 15.90 winning units..There was no bid for the winner.
Owner D Fower & N J Titterton **Bred** Matthews Breeding And Racing Ltd **Trained** Baldwin's Gate, Staffs

FOCUS
This was an above-average seller, with four of the runners rated in the 70s, and the pace was solid. The winner was well-in on his best form, which made it hard for his opponents. He didn't need to match his best.

2497 BRITISH STALLION STUDS SUPPORTING BRITISH RACING E.B.F MAIDEN STKS — 5f 2y
7:20 (7:21) (Class 4) 2-Y-O — **£4,204** (£1,251; £625; £312) **Stalls** High

Form RPR

1 **Andhesontherun (IRE)** 2-9-5 0 .... AndreaAtzeni 1 81+
(Roger Varian) *s.i.s: hld up: hdwy over 1f out: shkn up ins fnl f: r.o to ld nr fin* **8/1**

444 2 ½ **Atlantic Affair (IRE)**[10] 2204 2-9-0 0 .... FrannyNorton 4 71
(Mark Johnston) *led: rdn and hung rt over 1f out: hdd nr fin* **4/1**[2]

3 1½ **Oriental Relation (IRE)** 2-9-5 0 .... GrahamLee 3 71
(James Given) *s.i.s: sn chsng ldr: rdn over 1f out: styd on* **33/1**

4 2¼ **Golden Spear** 2-9-5 0 .... StevieDonohoe 5 63
(Noel Quinlan) *trckd ldrs: racd keenly: rdn over 1f out: styd on same pce* **18/1**

5 1 **Tamayuz Dream (IRE)** 2-9-5 0 .... RyanMoore 2 59
(Mark Johnston) *chsd ldrs: pushed along 3f out: no ex ins fnl f* **11/2**[3]

3 6 5 **Capitulate**[31] 1659 2-9-5 0 .... PaulHanagan 6 41
(Ed McMahon) *chsd ldrs: pushed along 1/2-way: rdn: edgd rt and wknd over 1f out* **4/5**[1]

1m 1.45s (1.45) **Going Correction** -0.125s/f (Firm) **6** Ran SP% **110.3**
Speed ratings (Par 95): **83,82,79,76,74 66**
toteswingers 1&2 £1.80, 1&3 £19.40, 2&3 £13.40 CSF £37.79 TOTE £7.70: £3.60, £1.80; EX 33.30 Trifecta £251.10 Pool: £952.61 - 2.84 winning units..
Owner K J P Gundlach **Bred** John Hutchinson **Trained** Newmarket, Suffolk

FOCUS
Only two of these had previous experience, but they were both beaten despite having run well in those races, and the green-looking winner was clearly the best. He looks sure to better this.

2498 NFU MUTUAL MARKET HARBOROUGH H'CAP — 1m 1f 218y
7:50 (7:51) (Class 4) (0-80,80) 4-Y-O+ — **£4,690** (£1,395; £697; £348) **Stalls** Low

Form RPR

60-0 1 **Dandy (GER)**[30] 1673 4-8-8 67 .... (p) DavidProbert 3 77
(Andrew Balding) *mde virtually all: rdn over 1f out: styd on* **20/1**

5621 2 ½ **Saint Thomas (IRE)**[14] 2077 6-8-9 68 .... FrannyNorton 4 77
(John Mackie) *chsd wnr: chal over 2f out tl rdn over 1f out: r.o* **12/1**

4116 3 1¾ **Goldstorm**[23] 1823 5-9-3 76 .... (p) PaulHanagan 1 82
(Brian Baugh) *chsd ldrs: rdn over 1f out: styd on* **14/1**

1- 4 1¼ **Villoresi (IRE)**[194] 7625 4-9-7 80 .... JamesDoyle 5 83+
(James Fanshawe) *s.i.s: hld up: pushed along and swtchd lft over 2f out: r.o ins fnl f: nvr nrr* **15/8**[1]

3325 5 nk **Brimstone Hill (IRE)**[47] 1327 4-9-7 80 .... GrahamLee 7 82
(Anthony Carson) *chsd ldrs: rdn over 1f out: styd on same pce ins fnl f* **20/1**

1010 6 ½ **Carazam (IRE)**[6] 2339 6-9-2 75 .... DaneO'Neill 8 76+
(William Jarvis) *hld up: racd keenly: swtchd lft and hdwy over 1f out: nt rch ldrs* **13/2**[3]

-263 7 2 **Greylami (IRE)**[21] 1883 8-8-12 76 .... RyanTate(5) 9 73
(Clive Cox) *hld up: hdwy over 2f out: rdn over 1f out: no ex fnl f* **5/2**[2]

00-6 8 nk **May Be Some Time**[10] 2228 5-8-5 69 .... (t) MichaelJMMurphy(5) 10 66
(Stuart Kittow) *s.i.s: hld up: effrt over 1f out: nvr on terms* **11/1**

643/ 9 2¼ **Sagredo (USA)**[191] 5340 9-8-10 69 .... RyanMoore 6 61
(Jonjo O'Neill) *mid-div: hdwy over 4f out: rdn over 2f out: wknd fnl f* **16/1**

341- 10 6 **Kelpie Blitz (IRE)**[173] 7893 4-9-3 76 .... (t) MickyFenton 2 56
(Seamus Durack) *plld hrd and prom: wknd over 1f out* **25/1**

2m 11.02s (3.12) **Going Correction** +0.45s/f (Yiel) **10** Ran SP% **118.6**
Speed ratings (Par 105): **105,104,103,102,101 101,99,99,97,93**
toteswingers 1&2 £72.20, 1&3 £72.20, 2&3 £27.40 CSF £236.95 CT £3457.46 TOTE £33.70: £8.50, £3.70, £3.60; EX 275.20 Trifecta £826.60 Part won. Pool: £1,102.17 - 0.03 winning units..
Owner Robert E Tillett **Bred** Gestut Rottgen **Trained** Kingsclere, Hants

FOCUS
This was a fair handicap, but they were soon stretched out by 10-12 lengths despite the modest pace, and that set it up for those who raced near the front. The form is arted around the runner-up.

2499 SARTORIUS MAIDEN STKS — 5f 218y
8:20 (8:21) (Class 5) 3-Y-O — **£2,726** (£805; £402) **Stalls** High

Form RPR

64-5 1 **Apricot Sky**[15] 2051 3-9-5 72 .... DaneO'Neill 3 78
(Henry Candy) *trckd ldrs: racd keenly: rdn to ld ins fnl f: jst hld on* **10/1**[2]

23- 2 nse **Ian's Dream (USA)**[333] 3291 3-9-5 0 .... RyanMoore 5 78
(Jeremy Noseda) *racd keenly: w ldrs and edgd rt almost thrght: led 1/2-way: rdn and hdd ins fnl f: r.o* **1/8**[1]

0-4 3 7 **Speronella**[21] 1875 3-9-0 0 .... AndreaAtzeni 4 50
(Hughie Morrison) *disp ld to 1/2-way: rdn over 1f out: wknd ins fnl f* **20/1**[3]

0-6 4 hd **Green Monkey**[9] 2267 3-9-5 0 .... (t) JamesDoyle 1 55
(James Fanshawe) *disp ld to 1/2-way: rdn over 1f out: wknd ins fnl f* **40/1**

66 5 8 **Bill Of Rights**[17] 1986 3-9-0 0 .... ChrisCatlin 7 24
(Michael Bell) *sn outpcd* **66/1**

0 6 1½ **Dropping Zone**[9] 2267 3-9-5 0 .... MickyFenton 6 24
(Des Donovan) *s.s: sn chsng ldrs: hung rt over 2f out: wknd over 1f out* **200/1**

1m 13.65s (0.65) **Going Correction** -0.125s/f (Firm) **6** Ran SP% **107.2**
Speed ratings (Par 99): **90,89,80,80,69 67**
toteswingers 1&2 £1.10, 1&3 £2.10, 2&3 £1.60 CSF £11.43 TOTE £12.50: £2.10, £1.02; EX 14.90 Trifecta £44.60 Pool: £1,354.20 - 22.73 winning units..
Owner Simon Broke & Partners III **Bred** Mrs James Bethell **Trained** Kingston Warren, Oxon

The Form Book Flat, Raceform Ltd, Compton, RG20 6NL.

FOCUS
The shape of this race is distorted by the performance of the favourite. The fact that he was only just pipped should not detract from the fact that this was nowhere near the level of his 2yo form. Improvement from the winner.

2500 HENRY ALKEN H'CAP 1m 3f 183y
8:50 (8:52) (Class 5) (0-70,75) 3-Y-O **£2,587** (£770; £384; £192) **Stalls** Low

Form RPR
60-1 **1** **Plutocracy (IRE)**[7] 2325 3-9-12 **75** 5ex................................ TedDurcan 7 89+
(David Lanigan) *a.p: rdn to chse ldr over 1f out: led ins fnl f: r.o wl: readily* **10/11**[1]
6-23 **2** *2* **Town Mouse**[33] 1613 3-9-1 **64**.. RyanMoore 2 73
(Hughie Morrison) *chsd ldrs: led over 8f out: rdn over 1f out: hdd and unable qck ins fnl f* **11/2**[2]
064- **3** *1 ¼* **Deficit (IRE)**[202] 7466 3-9-0 **63**.. JamesDoyle 5 70
(Michael Bell) *s.i.s: hld up: hdwy over 1f out: edgd rt ins fnl f: styd on* **6/1**[3]
0436 **4** *3 ¼* **World Map (IRE)**[18] 1959 3-8-11 **60**................................ FrannyNorton 4 62
(Mark Johnston) *dwlt: hld up: r.o ins fnl f: nvr on terms* **25/1**
600- **5** *hd* **Sunblazer (IRE)**[163] 8032 3-9-6 **69**.................................. MartinDwyer 8 70
(William Muir) *chsd ldr tl led over 10f out: hdd over 8f out: remained handy: rdn over 1f out: wknd ins fnl f* **40/1**
600- **6** *½* **Man From Seville**[264] 5742 3-8-8 **57**.................................. ChrisCatlin 6 58
(Sir Mark Prescott Bt) *chsd ldrs: pushed along over 3f out: wknd ins fnl f* **12/1**
2142 **7** *1 ¾* **El Massivo (IRE)**[28] 1729 3-9-7 **70**.................................... GrahamLee 3 68
(William Jarvis) *sn led: hdd over 10f out: remained handy: rdn over 2f out: wknd over 1f out* **11/2**[2]

2m 38.97s (5.07) **Going Correction** +0.45s/f (Yiel) 7 Ran SP% **111.4**
Speed ratings (Par 99): **101,99,98,96,96 96,95**
toteswingers 1&2 £1.10, 1&3 £2.40, 2&3 £20.00 CSF £5.95 CT £17.75 TOTE £1.50: £1.10, £4.00; EX 5.70 Trifecta £22.90 Pool: £1,182.16 - 38.66 winning units..
Owner B E Nielsen **Bred** Bjorn Nielsen **Trained** Upper Lambourn, Berks

FOCUS
The pace in this middling handicap was ordinary until it quickened 3f out, but the likeable winner wasn't inconvenienced. The race is rated around the runner-up.
T/Plt: £123.30 to a £1 stake. Pool: £59,756.06 - 353.68 winning units T/Qpdt: £26.60 to a £1 stake. Pool: £4,880.80 - 135.30 winning units CR

1960 REDCAR (L-H)
Monday, May 20
OFFICIAL GOING: Good to soft (soft in places; 7.9)
Wind: Light; 1/2 against Weather: Damp & misty; very cool

2501 RACING UK ON CHANNEL 432 H'CAP 7f
2:10 (2:11) (Class 6) (0-60,60) 3-Y-O **£2,045** (£603; £302) **Stalls** Centre

Form RPR
26-2 **1** **Darkside**[18] 1966 3-9-1 **54**.. RoystonFfrench 8 63
(Tracy Waggott) *blind in lft eye: wnt lft s: w ldrs: led and edgd rt 2f out: hung bdly lft over 1f out: styd on wl on stands' rail fnl 100yds: fin strly to ld nr fin* **13/2**[3]
5-05 **2** *¾* **Hot Mustard**[7] 2308 3-9-4 **57**.. LukeMorris 4 64
(Michael Bell) *trckd ldrs: styd on to ld ins fnl f: hdd and no ex nr fin* **8/1**
3434 **3** *1 ½* **Spider House**[14] 2080 3-9-7 **60**...................................... DanielTudhope 2 63
(David O'Meara) *chsd ldrs: led and edgd rt over 1f out: hdd ins fnl f: styd on same pce* **11/2**[2]
-000 **4** *1 ¼* **Look On By**[26] 1762 3-9-2 **55**... JamesSullivan 16 55
(Ruth Carr) *t.k.h in rr: hdwy stands' side over 2f out: n.m.r and swtchd lft over 1f out: kpt on* **50/1**
0-15 **5** *¾* **Loucal**[13] 2129 3-9-7 **60**..(b) StevieDonohoe 10 58
(Noel Quinlan) *mid-div: hdwy stands' side over 2f out: swtchd lft appr fnl f: kpt on* **9/2**[1]
64 **6** *½* **Zainda (IRE)**[16] 2008 3-9-7 **60**.. BarryMcHugh 6 56
(John Wainwright) *in rr: hdwy towards far side over 2f out: kpt on fnl f* **16/1**
0-6 **7** *1* **My Claire**[26] 1760 3-8-13 **52**.. PaulMulrennan 17 46
(Nigel Tinkler) *in rr: hdwy far side over 2f out: one pce over 1f out* **20/1**
4006 **8** *nk* **Panama Cat (USA)**[18] 1966 3-9-0 **53**................................(p) AmyRyan 12 46
(Kevin Ryan) *chsd ldrs: one pce whn hmpd appr fnl f* **14/1**
-643 **9** *5* **Marcus Caesar (IRE)**[9] 2274 3-9-6 **59**........................ GrahamGibbons 19 38
(David Barron) *w ldr: led after 1f: hdd and hmpd 2f out: wknd fnl f* **9/2**[1]
0-00 **10** *nk* **Betty Boo (IRE)**[17] 1988 3-8-0 **46** oh1.................... ConnorBeasley(7) 15 24
(Shaun Harris) *mid-div: sme hdwy over 2f out: wknd over 1f out* **66/1**
00-0 **11** *½* **Erica Starprincess**[16] 2027 3-9-0 **53**............................ AndrewElliott 13 30
(George Moore) *detached in rr after 2f: sme hdwy far side over 2f out: nvr a factor* **33/1**
56-6 **12** *1 ½* **Unassailable**[16] 2010 3-9-5 **58**.. PhillipMakin 3 31
(Kevin Ryan) *chsd ldrs: drvn over 2f out: wknd over 1f out* **10/1**
3240 **13** *1* **Multisure**[14] 2080 3-9-4 **57**.. PJMcDonald 14 27
(Ruth Carr) *led 1f: chsd ldrs: lost pl 2f out* **14/1**
00-5 **14** *¾* **Symphonic Air (IRE)**[13] 2121 3-8-4 **46**........................ RaulDaSilva(3) 18 14
(John Weymes) *reminders after s: a in rr* **50/1**
0-30 **15** *shd* **Pink Cadillac (IRE)**[26] 1764 3-8-8 **47**............................. TomEaves 11 15
(Ben Haslam) *hld up in rr: sme hdwy over 2f out: wknd over 1f out* **20/1**
506- **16** *1* **Alkcama (IRE)**[232] 6708 3-8-13 **52**................................ DuranFentiman 9 17
(John Weymes) *in rr: stmbld after 1f: nvr on terms* **33/1**

1m 27.79s (3.29) **Going Correction** +0.50s/f (Yiel) 16 Ran SP% **125.3**
Speed ratings (Par 97): **101,100,98,97,96 95,94,94,88,88 87,85,84,83,83 82**
toteswingers 1&2 £12.30, 1&3 £7.80, 2&3 £11.00 CSF £55.57 CT £250.32 TOTE £6.90: £2.30, £2.60, £1.80, £7.20; EX 70.80 Trifecta £517.20 Pool: £2,855.26 - 4.13 winning units..
Owner David Tate **Bred** Bearstone Stud **Trained** Spennymoor, Co Durham

FOCUS
After a wet couple of days the official going was good to soft, soft in places. A modest 3yo handicap but sound form.

2502 FOLLOW REDCARRACING ON FACEBOOK AND TWITTER MEDIAN AUCTION MAIDEN STKS 6f
2:40 (2:44) (Class 5) 2-Y-O **£2,587** (£770; £384; £192) **Stalls** Centre

Form RPR
0 **1** **Piazon**[15] 2048 2-9-5 0.. LukeMorris 3 71+
(Michael Bell) *mid-div: hung lft and hdwy to trck ldrs far side over 2f out: sn led: edgd rt and clr over 1f out: drvn out* **7/4**[1]
2 *1* **Supa U** 2-9-0 0.. DavidAllan 2 66+
(Tim Easterby) *s.i.s: hdwy to trck ldrs over 2f out: bdly hmpd over 1f out: swtchd lft and chsd wnr jst ins fnl f: r.o wl* **14/1**
3 *2 ½* **Irondale Express** 2-9-0 0.. BarryMcHugh 5 58+
(Tony Coyle) *difficult to load: s.s: hdwy 3f out: edgd rt and chsng wnr 1f out: kpt on one pce* **9/1**
4 *7* **Twentyfourseven** 2-9-5 0.. PaulMulrennan 9 40
(Ed Dunlop) *wnt rt s: sn chsng ldrs: effrt over 2f out: wknd over 1f out* **7/1**
6 **5** *1 ¾* **Noble Reach**[16] 2025 2-8-7 0.................................... JordanNason(7) 8 29
(Geoffrey Harker) *led: hdd 3f out: edgd lft and wknd over 1f out* **50/1**
0 **6** *1 ¾* **Sirpertan**[19] 1930 2-9-5 0... DuranFentiman 7 29
(Tim Walford) *mid-div: outpcd after 2f: kpt on fnl f: nvr a threat* **33/1**
642 **7** *½* **Dotesy (IRE)**[10] 2238 2-9-0 0.................................. MichaelO'Connell 4 23
(John Quinn) *chsd ldrs: drvn over 2f out: edgd rt: wknd over 1f out* **10/3**[2]
5 **8** *nk* **By The Light (IRE)**[12] 2161 2-9-5 0.................................. JoeFanning 1 27
(Mark Johnston) *chsd ldrs: led 3f out: edgd lft: hdd 2f out: wknd over 1f out* **11/2**[3]
9 *2 ¾* **See Me Sometime** 2-9-5 0... TedDurcan 6 18
(Mark H Tompkins) *s.i.s: sme hdwy over 2f out: hung lft and sn lost pl* **18/1**

1m 15.32s (3.52) **Going Correction** +0.50s/f (Yiel) 9 Ran SP% **114.2**
Speed ratings (Par 93): **96,94,91,82,79 77,76,76,72**
toteswingers 1&2 £5.60, 1&3 £5.40, 2&3 £15.20 CSF £28.80 TOTE £2.40: £1.30, £4.00, £2.80; EX 26.90 Trifecta £237.70 Pool: £2,821.36 - 8.89 winning units..
Owner R P B Michaelson **Bred** Peter Baldwin **Trained** Newmarket, Suffolk

FOCUS
An ordinary maiden, though the first three pulled clear. The winner came from a good Newmarket maiden. This bare form is no more than fair.

2503 WIN A VIP DAY OUT @ REDCARRACING.CO.UK MAIDEN FILLIES' STKS (DIV I) 7f
3:10 (3:13) (Class 5) 3-Y-O+ **£2,726** (£805; £402) **Stalls** Centre

Form RPR
0-0 **1** **Bousatet (FR)**[23] 1828 3-9-0 0.. AmyRyan 3 65+
(Kevin Ryan) *mde all: pushed out: unchal* **3/1**[1]
0- **2** *2* **Thankyou Very Much**[206] 7363 3-9-0 0.............................. TedDurcan 7 59
(James Bethell) *mid-div: drvn over 3f out: hdwy and edgd rt over 1f out: swtchd lft and chsd wnr jst ins fnl f: no imp* **5/1**[3]
004- **3** *5* **Queen's Princess**[261] 5823 5-9-11 42........................ PaulMulrennan 10 46
(John Wainwright) *wnt rt s: mid-div: drvn to chse ldrs 3f out: one pce appr fnl f* **100/1**
4-4 **4** *1* **Mistral Wind (IRE)**[124] 230 3-9-0 0................................... PhillipMakin 4 43
(Ed Dunlop) *chsd ldrs: edgd lft over 1f out: one pce* **4/1**[2]
0-00 **5** *5* **Miss Bossy Boots**[23] 1842 4-9-11 10........................... RoystonFfrench 6 30
(Tracy Waggott) *chsd ldrs: wknd over 1f out* **100/1**
6U0/ **6** *nk* **Bond Artist (IRE)**[577] 6985 4-9-6 0.............. WilliamTwiston-Davies(5) 5 29
(Geoffrey Oldroyd) *mid-div: hdwy far side over 3f out: sn chsng ldrs: wknd over 1f out* **12/1**
5 **7** *1 ¾* **Absolute Diamond**[16] 2027 3-9-0 0........................... MichaelO'Connell 9 24
(John Quinn) *chsd ldrs: wknd over 1f out* **7/1**
060- **8** *¾* **Miss Matiz**[266] 5672 6-9-4 29.................................... ConnorBeasley(7) 11 22
(Alan Kirtley) *carried rt s: in rr: chsd ldrs after 2f: lost pl 3f out* **150/1**
0 **9** *8* **Cannons Hall (IRE)**[18] 1962 4-9-4 0.................... DavidSimmonson(7) 1
(Paul Midgley) *trckd ldrs: t.k.h: lost pl over 2f out: bhd whn eased ins fnl f* **100/1**
10 *17* **Lilyofthevalley** 3-9-0 0.. RussKennemore 8
(John Weymes) *s.s: a detached in last: t.o fnl 3f* **25/1**

1m 28.18s (3.68) **Going Correction** +0.50s/f (Yiel)
WFA 3 from 4yo+ 11lb 10 Ran SP% **89.3**
Speed ratings (Par 100): **98,95,90,88,83 82,80,79,70,51**
toteswingers 1&2 £3.50, 1&3 £20.60, 2&3 £21.40 CSF £10.35 TOTE £3.50: £1.50, £1.30, £6.90; EX 15.40 Trifecta £377.00 Pool: £2,261.63 - 4.49 winning units..
Owner Highbank Stud **Bred** F Bayrou & F A Mc Nulty **Trained** Hambleton, N Yorks

FOCUS
Much of the interest in the first division of this fillies' maiden was lost when expensive purchase Garden Row was withdrawn at the start on veterinary advice. It was the quicker division but still very modest form.

2504 WIN A VIP DAY OUT @ REDCARRACING.CO.UK MAIDEN FILLIES' STKS (DIV II) 7f
3:40 (3:41) (Class 5) 3-Y-O+ **£2,726** (£805; £402) **Stalls** Centre

Form RPR
1 **Drahem** 3-9-0 0.. FrederikTylicki 2 64+
(James Fanshawe) *dwlt: hld up: hdwy to trck ldrs 3f out: styd on to ld last 30yds* **15/8**[1]
2 *nk* **Adiator**[400] 5-9-6 0.. AdamCarter(5) 7 67
(Neville Bycroft) *chsd ldrs: led over 1f out: hdd and no ex towards fin* **7/1**
3 *1 ¾* **Dodina (IRE)** 3-9-0 0.. LukeMorris 9 58
(Peter Chapple-Hyam) *dwlt: hdwy to chse ldrs 3f out: led over 2f out: hdd over 1f out: kpt on same pce ins fnl f* **6/1**[3]
05 **4** *2 ¾* **Lexi's Dancer**[10] 2215 3-9-0 0....................................... PaulMulrennan 1 51
(Ed Dunlop) *w ldrs: one pce over 1f out* **11/4**[2]
63- **5** *¾* **Multilicious**[150] 8207 3-8-7 0.................................. RachelRichardson(7) 6 49
(Tim Easterby) *in rr: hdwy over 2f out: kpt on fnl f* **9/1**
00-0 **6** *9* **Cara's Delight (AUS)**[18] 1962 6-9-11 26..................(tp) DuranFentiman 3 29
(Frederick Watson) *led 2f: chsd ldrs: wknd over 1f out* **100/1**
004- **7** *8* **Endless Applause**[280] 5170 4-9-11 50................................. TomEaves 5
(Richard Whitaker) *trckd ldr: t.k.h: led after 2f: hdd over 2f out: sn lost pl* **15/2**
8 *10* **Forest Philly (IRE)** 3-9-0 0....................................... RussKennemore 8
(John Wainwright) *dwlt: in rr: bhd 3f* **33/1**
000- **9** *18* **Stars Legacy**[244] 6341 4-9-11 0.. PJMcDonald 4
(George Moore) *chsd ldrs: drvn 3f out: sn lost pl and bhd: t.o* **100/1**
10 *¾* **Phoenix Joy** 5-9-11 0.. MichaelStainton 10
(Simon Griffiths) *unruly s: in rr: drvn and lost pl over 3f out: sn bhd: t.o* **50/1**

1m 28.64s (4.14) **Going Correction** +0.50s/f (Yiel)
WFA 3 from 4yo+ 11lb 10 Ran SP% **116.9**
Speed ratings (Par 100): **96,95,93,90,89 79,70,58,38,37**
toteswingers 1&2 £5.00, 1&3 £3.50, 2&3 £8.30 CSF £15.81 TOTE £2.80: £1.40, £2.60, £1.80; EX 22.40 Trifecta £124.60 Pool: £2,845.02 - 17.11 winning units..
Owner Salem Bel Obaida **Bred** Ashbrittle Stud **Trained** Newmarket, Suffolk

FOCUS
The standard set by those with experience was only modest in the second division of the fillies' maiden, which went to a well-backed newcomer. The slower division.

2505 VOLTIGEUR RESTAURANT £10.95 TWO COURSE SPECIAL H'CAP 5f
4:10 (4:10) (Class 3) (0-90,89) 3-Y-0+

£7,158 (£2,143; £1,071; £535; £267; £134) **Stalls** Centre

Form RPR
21-4 **1** **Jack Luey**[2] 2459 6-9-5 **82** .... TomEaves 10 90
(Lawrence Mullaney) *wnt lft after s: sn chsng ldrs: styd on wl ins fnl f: led last stride* **6/1**[3]

-220 **2** *nse* **Last Sovereign**[12] 2150 9-9-5 **89** .... (b) JacobButterfield(7) 5 97
(Ollie Pears) *trckd ldrs: swtchd lft appr fnl f: led last 100yds: hdd post* **7/1**

3352 **3** *1 ½* **Rylee Mooch**[4] 2388 5-8-12 **75** .... (e) RobbieFitzpatrick 6 78
(Richard Guest) *chsd ldr: led briefly jst ins fnl f: kpt on same pce last 75yds* **9/2**[2]

435- **4** *1 ¼* **Cocktail Charlie**[217] 7100 5-8-12 **75** oh1 .... (p) PaulMulrennan 3 73
(Tim Easterby) *hld up in rr: effrt 2f out: n.m.r appr fnl f: styd on ins fnl f* **6/1**[3]

6-00 **5** *shd* **Verinco**[109] 457 7-8-13 **81** .... (vt) WilliamTwiston-Davies(5) 1 79
(Bryan Smart) *wnt rt after s: led: hdd jst ins fnl f: fdd* **10/1**

-410 **6** *½* **Bedloe's Island (IRE)**[4] 2396 8-9-9 **86** .... DanielTudhope 7 82
(David O'Meara) *hld up: bmpd sn after s: effrt 2f out: kpt on ins fnl f: nvr a threat* **15/8**[1]

00-0 **7** *3 ¼* **Medici Time**[24] 1807 8-9-4 **81** .... (v) GrahamGibbons 2 65
(Tim Easterby) *n.m.r sn after s: in rr: effrt 2f out: wknd over 1f out* **20/1**

00-0 **8** *2 ½* **Partner (IRE)**[25] 1787 7-9-2 **79** .... (b) DuranFentiman 9 54
(Noel Wilson) *hmpd sn after s: in rr: drvn over 2f out: lost pl over 1f out* **16/1**

1m 0.16s (1.56) **Going Correction** +0.50s/f (Yiel) **8** Ran SP% **113.8**
Speed ratings (Par 107): **107,106,104,102,102 101,96,92**
toteswingers 1&2 £4.80, 1&3 £3.20, 2&3 £5.20 CSF £46.57 CT £207.40 TOTE £5.50: £1.70, £2.60, £1.80; EX 35.30 Trifecta £145.80 Pool: £2,520.66 - 12.96 winning units..
Owner The Jack Partnership & S Rimmer **Bred** Miss D A Johnson **Trained** Great Habton, N Yorks

FOCUS
A competitive sprint handicap run at a fair pace. Small personal bests from the first two.

2506 WATCH RACING UK ON SKY 432 H'CAP (STRAIGHT-MILE CHAMPIONSHIP QUALIFIER) 1m
4:40 (4:40) (Class 5) 3-Y-0 **£2,587** (£770; £384; £192) **Stalls** Centre

Form RPR
300 **1** **Naaz (IRE)**[15] 2041 3-8-11 **65** .... (b[1]) PhillipMakin 7 77
(Ed Dunlop) *hld up in mid-div: swtchd lft after 1f: drvn over 2f out: edgd lft and led over 1f out: styd on wl* **20/1**

10-5 **2** *2 ¾* **Labienus**[18] 1958 3-9-7 **75** .... TedDurcan 5 81
(David Lanigan) *trckd ldrs: drvn over 2f out: carried hd high: chsd wnr and edgd lft appr fnl f: no imp* **2/1**[1]

4-4 **3** *2* **Rex Whistler (IRE)**[35] 1570 3-8-13 **67** .... PaulMulrennan 2 68
(Julie Camacho) *dwlt: in rr: hdwy over 3f out: outpcd over 2f out: styd on to take 3rd 1f out* **6/1**[3]

5-55 **4** *2 ½* **Curl (IRE)**[18] 1965 3-8-10 **64** .... (b) TomEaves 6 59
(Michael Dods) *sn chsng ldrs: one pce over 1f out* **7/1**

233- **5** *1 ½* **Rust (IRE)**[217] 7096 3-9-2 **70** .... PJMcDonald 1 62
(Ann Duffield) *dwlt: sn chsng ldrs: effrt over 2f out: wknd over 1f out* **4/1**[2]

05-3 **6** *1 ½* **Midnight Warrior**[16] 2027 3-9-2 **70** .... BarryMcHugh 9 58
(Ron Barr) *stmbld bdly s: in rr: effrt over 3f out: hung rt: kpt on stands' side fnl f* **12/1**

25-6 **7** *2 ¼* **Lady Margaeux (IRE)**[16] 2027 3-9-2 **70** .... DanielTudhope 8 53
(David O'Meara) *stmbld s: t.k.h in rr: lost pl over 3f out: bhd tl sme hdwy fnl f* **18/1**

1-3 **8** *2 ¼* **Cinderslipper (IRE)**[25] 1772 3-8-6 **67** .... RowanScott(7) 4 45
(Ann Duffield) *w ldr: led 2f out: hdd over 1f out: sn wknd* **8/1**

42 **9** *9* **Tom's Anna (IRE)**[13] 2121 3-9-3 **71** .... DavidAllan 3 28
(Tim Easterby) *t.k.h: led: hdd 2f out: lost pl appr fnl f: bhd whn eased towards fin* **16/1**

1m 39.71s (3.11) **Going Correction** -0.075s/f (Good) **9** Ran SP% **114.8**
Speed ratings (Par 99): **100,97,95,92,91 89,87,85,76**
toteswingers 1&2 £6.60, 1&3 £18.90, 2&3 £4.30 CSF £60.00 CT £284.60 TOTE £19.00: £3.70, £1.30, £2.80; EX 82.90 Trifecta £596.30 Pool: £2,614.70 - 3.28 winning units..
Owner Robert Ng **Bred** T J Pabst And Newtown Stud **Trained** Newmarket, Suffolk

FOCUS
An open 3yo handicap won by the outsider, who showed big improvement. It was quite strong run.

2507 LADIES' DAY ON SATURDAY 22ND JUNE MEDIAN AUCTION MAIDEN STKS 1m
5:10 (5:11) (Class 6) 3-5-Y-0 **£2,045** (£603; £302) **Stalls** Centre

Form RPR
02-2 **1** **Aneedh**[21] 1891 3-9-1 75 .... GrahamGibbons 4 71+
(William Haggas) *trckd ldrs gng wl: led on bit over 1f out: shkn up ins fnl f: cosily* **10/11**[1]

2 *¾* **Indian Trifone (IRE)** 3-9-1 0 .... LukeMorris 12 69
(Ed Walker) *in rr: hdwy stands' side over 2f out: upsides over 1f out: kpt on same pce clsng stages* **18/1**

5-01 **3** *2 ¾* **Correggio**[13] 2121 3-9-1 76 .... PJMcDonald 2 63
(Micky Hammond) *trckd ldrs: t.k.h: edgd rt and kpt on one pce fnl f* **5/1**[2]

4 *¾* **Gaspard** 3-9-1 0 .... TedDurcan 3 61+
(David Lanigan) *dwlt: mid-div far side: hdwy to trck ldrs 3f out: kpt on one pce fnl f* **10/1**[3]

6-34 **5** *¾* **Exclusive Predator**[111] 434 4-9-8 58 .... WilliamTwiston-Davies(5) 10 63
(Geoffrey Oldroyd) *chsd ldrs: effrt 2f out: sn outpcd: styd on last 150yds* **28/1**

0-00 **6** *6* **Throwing Roses**[26] 1759 3-8-10 49 .... DanielTudhope 11 41
(Lawrence Mullaney) *trckd ldr: led over 2f out: hdd over 1f out: sn wknd* **33/1**

0- **7** *1 ¼* **Rabdaan**[214] 7191 3-9-1 0 .... FrederikTylicki 6 43
(James Fanshawe) *mid-div: hdwy over 3f out: sn drvn and chsng ldrs: lost pl over 1f out* **5/1**[2]

0-4 **8** *5* **Rosie Hall (IRE)**[6] 2340 3-8-10 0 .... RoystonFfrench 1 26
(Bryan Smart) *led: hdd over 2f out: wknd over 1f out* **14/1**

0 **9** *4 ½* **The Troyster**[16] 2027 3-9-1 0 .... JamesSullivan 5 21
(Julie Camacho) *s.i.s: in rr and sn drvn along: nvr on terms* **100/1**

5-0 **10** *7* **Baile Atha Cliath (IRE)**[49] 1282 4-9-10 0 .... NeilFarley(3) 8
(Declan Carroll) *t.k.h towards rr: effrt over 2f out: sn wknd* **50/1**

00- **11** *3* **Billy Redpath**[252] 6102 5-9-13 0 .... DuranFentiman 9
(Frederick Watson) *in rr: drvn over 3f out: lost pl over 2f out: sn bhd* **100/1**

1m 40.7s (4.10) **Going Correction** -0.075s/f (Good)
WFA 3 from 4yo+ 12lb **11** Ran SP% **117.1**
Speed ratings (Par 101): **95,94,91,90,90 84,82,77,73,66 63**
toteswingers 1&2 £5.20, 1&3 £2.20, 2&3 £11.60 CSF £20.57 TOTE £1.70: £1.10, £4.30, £1.40; EX 17.40 Trifecta £64.00 Pool: £2,449.29 - 28.68 winning units..
Owner Mohammed Jaber **Bred** Rabbah Bloodstock Limited **Trained** Newmarket, Suffolk

FOCUS
An uncompetitive 3yo maiden. They finished well strung out and the winner did it nicely. The form is rated a bit cautiously around the fifth.

2508 YORKSHIRE RACING SUMMER FESTIVAL 20TH - 28TH JULY H'CAP 1m 2f
5:40 (5:41) (Class 6) (0-60,60) 3-Y-0 **£2,045** (£603; £302) **Stalls** Low

Form RPR
040- **1** **Alcaeus**[263] 5765 3-9-4 **57** .... LukeMorris 10 71+
(Sir Mark Prescott Bt) *chsd ldrs: cl 2nd over 5f out: drvn to ld over 2f out: kpt on: all out* **3/1**[1]

04-5 **2** *nk* **Topamichi**[27] 1754 3-9-7 **60** .... PhillipMakin 2 73
(Mark H Tompkins) *t.k.h in rr: hdwy 4f out: nt clr run over 2f out: styd on to chal jst ins fnl f: no ex nr fin* **15/2**

405- **3** *4* **Tahaf (IRE)**[227] 6846 3-9-5 **58** .... (t) FrederikTylicki 7 63
(Clive Brittain) *hld up in mid-div: nt clr run over 3f out: chsng ldrs over 2f out: kpt on same pce fnl f* **8/1**

4306 **4** *2 ¼* **Helmsley Flyer (IRE)**[6] 2342 3-9-2 **55** .... DanielTudhope 1 56+
(David O'Meara) *hld up in rr: hdwy and nt clr run over 2f out: kpt on wl fnl f* **9/2**[3]

60-0 **5** *2 ½* **Inovate (IRE)**[25] 1772 3-9-1 **54** .... DavidAllan 5 50
(Tim Easterby) *trckd ldrs: drvn 3f out: one pce* **25/1**

4-36 **6** *5* **Bell'Arte (IRE)**[12] 2175 3-9-6 **59** .... JoeFanning 3 45
(Mark Johnston) *in rr: hdwy ins 4f out: one pce whn hmpd over 1f out: sn wknd* **12/1**

00-6 **7** *¾* **Denton Skyline (IRE)**[40] 1487 3-9-1 **54** .... (p) TomEaves 8 38
(Michael Dods) *trckd ldrs: effrt over 2f out: edgd lft and wknd over 1f out* **20/1**

40-5 **8** *¾* **Perseverent Pete (USA)**[14] 2099 3-8-12 **51** .... RoystonFfrench 12 34
(Christine Dunnett) *mid-div: effrt over 3f out: wknd 2f out* **50/1**

0-40 **9** *¾* **Stagweekend (IRE)**[14] 2080 3-9-6 **59** .... (p) MichaelO'Connell 14 40
(John Quinn) *t.k.h: led 1f: chsd ldrs: weakwning whn dived rt over 1f out* **14/1**

5-00 **10** *1* **Algorithmic (IRE)**[28] 1713 3-9-0 **58** .... WilliamTwiston-Davies(5) 6 37
(Michael Bell) *reluctant and detached sn after s: sme hdwy on outside over 3f out: hung lft and sn wknd* **7/2**[2]

0-46 **11** *2* **Sorcellerie**[18] 1967 3-9-4 **57** .... DuranFentiman 9 32
(Mel Brittain) *sn chsng ldrs: drvn 3f out: sn lost pl* **22/1**

4064 **12** *8* **Abanoas (USA)**[5] 2362 3-8-13 **52** .... RussKennemore 11
(Alan Coogan) *led after 1f: hdd over 2f out: sn wknd: eased whn bhd ins fnl f* **33/1**

2m 9.55s (2.45) **Going Correction** +0.175s/f (Good) **12** Ran SP% **120.5**
Speed ratings (Par 97): **97,96,93,91,89 85,85,84,83,83 81,75**
toteswingers 1&2 £5.80, 1&3 £6.40, 2&3 £9.80 CSF £24.60 CT £168.42 TOTE £3.50: £1.40, £2.50, £2.70; EX 26.20 Trifecta £101.50 Pool: £2,186.40 - 16.14 winning units..
Owner Ne'er Do Wells IV **Bred** Miss K Rausing **Trained** Newmarket, Suffolk

FOCUS
The front two pulled clear in this 3yo handicap, but several others showed promise and the form should hold up. The form is rated loosely around the fourth.
T/Jkpt: £32,452.50 to a £1 stake. Pool: £342,809.13 - 7.50 winning units T/Plt: £26.30 to a £1 stake. Pool: £67,933.39 - 1,878.68 winning units T/Qpdt: £11.30 to a £1 stake. Pool: £3,369.72 - 220.30 winning units WG

2168 SOUTHWELL (L-H)
Monday, May 20

OFFICIAL GOING: Standard
Wind: Moderate; behind Weather: Cloudy

2509 FOLLOW US ON TWITTER @BETVICTORRACING AMATEUR RIDERS' CLASSIFIED CLAIMING STKS 1m 6f (F)
2:30 (2:30) (Class 6) 4-Y-0+ **£1,975** (£607; £303) **Stalls** Low

Form RPR
1242 **1** **Activate**[10] 2221 6-11-0 72 .... (p) MrSWalker 3 79
(Keith Dalgleish) *trckd ldrs: hdwy over 4f out: cl up 3f out: rdn to ld wl over 1f out: drvn and edgd lft ent fnl f: styd on* **7/4**[1]

3115 **2** *1 ¼* **Scribe (IRE)**[14] 2087 5-10-5 69 .... (vt) MrDLevey(5) 7 73
(David Evans) *trckd ldr: cl up 1/2-way: led 4f out: jnd 3f out: rdn over 2f out: hdd wl over 1f out: sn drvn and ev ch tl one pce ins fnl f* **9/4**[2]

/3-3 **3** *11* **Dontpaytheferryman (USA)**[25] 1795 8-9-9 75 .... MrJohnWilley(5) 4 48
(Brian Ellison) *t.k.h: trckd ldrs on outer: effrt 4f out: rdn along over 2f out: sn one pce* **9/4**[2]

350- **4** *12* **Underwritten**[205] 7413 4-9-11 69 .... (b) NickSlatter(3) 6 31
(Donald McCain) *led: pushed along over 5f out: hdd 4f out: sn rdn and outpcd fnl 3f* **8/1**[3]

6005 **5** *13* **Turjuman (USA)**[7] 2332 8-9-7 49 .... (e[1]) MissEmmaBedford(7) 5 13
(Simon West) *dwlt and bhd: hdwy and in tch over 4f out: rdn along wl over 3f out: sn wknd* **33/1**

0000 **6** *7* **Bubbly Braveheart (IRE)**[22] 1752 6-10-7 40 .... (t) MrJAMcEntee(7) 2 17
(Phil McEntee) *trckd ldrs: pushed along over 6f out: sn rdn along and outpcd fr wl over 3f out* **150/1**

000/ **7** *48* **Usquaebach**[838] 391 6-10-1 50 .... MissMBryant(5) 8
(Paddy Butler) *sn outpcd and a bhd* **100/1**

3m 9.0s (0.70) **Going Correction** -0.05s/f (Stan) **7** Ran SP% **113.6**
Speed ratings (Par 101): **96,95,89,82,74 70,43**
toteswingers 1&2 £1.40, 1&3 £1.50, 2&3 £1.80 CSF £5.94 TOTE £2.50: £1.20, £1.30; EX 6.30 Trifecta £11.20 Pool: £2,203.06 - 147.28 winning units..Dontpaytheferryman was claimed by Mr J. K. Price for £5,000
Owner Straightline Construction Ltd **Bred** Card Bloodstock **Trained** Carluke, S Lanarks
■ Stewards' Enquiry : Mr D Levey four-day ban: use of whip (TBA)

FOCUS
The front two pulled well clear in this amateur riders' claimer.

2510 CORRUGATED CASE CO MAIDEN AUCTION STKS 5f (F)
3:00 (3:01) (Class 5) 2-Y-O **£2,587** (£770; £384; £192) **Stalls** High

Form RPR
1 **Loma Mor** 2-8-2 0 ShirleyTeasdale(5) 3 64
(Alan McCabe) *green and chsd ldr: hdwy in centre to ld 2f out: sn rdn and hung lft to far rail: kpt on wl u.p fnl f* **9/2**
2 1 1/2 **Cheeky Peta'S** 2-8-10 0 GrahamLee 5 62+
(James Given) *chsd ldng pair: hdwy 2f out: rdn and ev ch over 1f out: edgd lft and one pce ins fnl f* **2/1**[1]
5 3 1 3/4 **Music Stop**[13] 2117 2-8-7 0 FrannyNorton 6 52
(Mark Johnston) *qckly away: green and hung bdly lft immediately after s: sn racing on far rail and clr: pushed along and hdd 2f out: rallied ins fnl f* **11/4**[3]
4 5 **Maximilianthefirst** 2-9-1 0 TomMcLaughlin 2 42+
(P J O'Gorman) *green: sn outpcd and rdn along: a in rr* **9/4**[2]

1m 2.22s (2.52) **Going Correction** +0.35s/f (Slow) 4 Ran SP% **109.0**
Speed ratings (Par 93): **93,90,87,79**
CSF £13.61 TOTE £7.10; EX 15.50 Trifecta £32.70 Pool: £1,457.27 - 33.41 winning units..
Owner Lucky Heather **Bred** Llety Stud **Trained** Averham Park, Notts
■ Stewards' Enquiry : Shirley Teasdale two-day ban: use of whip (3-4 June)
FOCUS
A very modest juvenile maiden and the time was poor.

2511 £25 FREE BET AT BETVICTOR.COM H'CAP 1m 3f (F)
3:30 (3:30) (Class 6) (0-65,64) 4-Y-0+ **£2,045** (£603; £302) **Stalls** Low

Form RPR
3113 1 **Linroyale Boy (USA)**[34] 1601 5-9-7 **64** RobertWinston 6 79
(Alan Swinbank) *trckd ldrs: pushed along and n.m.r 4f out: gd hdwy 3f out: sn chal: rdn to ld wl over 1f out: styd on wl fnl f* **3/1**[1]
-604 2 2 3/4 **Koo And The Gang (IRE)**[15] 2042 6-8-8 **51** DaleSwift 7 61
(Brian Ellison) *led: pushed along 3f out: sn jnd and rdn: hdd wl over 1f out: sn drvn and kpt on same pce fnl f* **6/1**[2]
5-40 3 4 1/2 **Honoured (IRE)**[117] 338 6-9-4 **61** (t) AndrewMullen 12 63
(Michael Appleby) *trckd ldrs: hdwy and cl up 1/2-way: rdn along 3f out: drvn 2f out: kpt on same pce* **6/1**[2]
4234 4 5 **Solarmaite**[12] 2172 4-9-2 **62** MarkCoumbe(3) 1 55
(Roy Bowring) *a.p: rdn along over 3f out: drvn over 2f out and sn one pce* **33/1**
0-02 5 nk **Akarana (IRE)**[59] 1120 6-8-7 **50** JamieMackay 4 42
(Willie Musson) *hld up in rr: hdwy 3f out: rdn over 2f out: kpt on: nrst fin* **20/1**
0-62 6 1 **Blue Top**[7] 2333 4-8-8 **51** PaddyAspell 8 42
(Tim Walford) *prom: pushed along 4f out: rdn over 3f out: sn drvn and one pce* **12/1**
4004 7 1 1/4 **Follow The Flag (IRE)**[12] 2168 9-8-9 **59** (be) AaronJones(7) 5 47
(Alan McCabe) *in rr: rdn along and hdwy on inner 3f out: kpt on u.p fnl 2f: n.d* **14/1**
0424 8 1 1/2 **Satwa Laird**[18] 1956 7-9-4 **61** CathyGannon 10 47
(Conor Dore) *chsd ldrs: rdn along over 4f out: wknd over 3f out* **16/1**
60-0 8 dht **Shirls Son Sam**[16] 2030 5-8-7 **50** JimmyQuinn 9 36
(Chris Fairhurst) *in rr tl sme late hdwy* **25/1**
2436 10 3/4 **Goldmadchen (GER)**[34] 1600 5-9-4 **61** GrahamLee 13 45
(James Given) *hld up: hdwy on wd outside and in tch 1/2-way: rdn along over 3f out: sn btn* **7/1**[3]
00/0 11 22 **Seven Summits (IRE)**[10] 2234 6-9-6 **63** SaleemGolam 14
(Sophie Leech) *trckd ldrs: hdwy over 4f out: rdn along 3f out: sn drvn and wknd* **100/1**
060- 12 9 **Circle Of Angels**[231] 6734 5-9-3 **60** FrannyNorton 11
(Mark Johnston) *a towards rr* **12/1**
050- 13 1 1/2 **Run Of The Day**[307] 4189 4-8-8 **56** AmyScott(5) 2
(Eve Johnson Houghton) *a in rr* **25/1**
5-04 14 7 **Muzhil (IRE)**[17] 1986 4-9-6 **63** ChrisCatlin 3
(Clive Brittain) *a towards rr: outpcd and wl bhd fr over 3f out* **7/1**[3]

2m 25.79s (-2.21) **Going Correction** -0.05s/f (Stan) 14 Ran SP% **122.9**
Speed ratings (Par 101): **106,104,100,97,96 96,95,94,94,93 77,71,69,64**
toteswingers 1&2 £5.50, 1&3 £6.70, 2&3 £10.20 CSF £19.18 CT £106.18 TOTE £2.90: £1.90, £3.20, £2.30; EX 20.20 Trifecta £182.60 Pool: £1,692.24 - 6.95 winning units..
Owner Spiral Bracken **Bred** Winstar Farm, Llc & Ashford Stud **Trained** Melsonby, N Yorks
■ Stewards' Enquiry : Aaron Jones four-day ban: use of whip (3-6 June)
FOCUS
It paid to be handy in this moderate middle-distance handicap.

2512 DOWNLOAD THE BETVICTOR APP NOW H'CAP 6f (F)
4:00 (4:00) (Class 6) (0-60,59) 3-Y-0 **£2,264** (£673; £336; £168) **Stalls** Low

Form RPR
4-01 1 **Fossa**[20] 1906 3-9-4 **56** FrannyNorton 5 66
(Dean Ivory) *in tch: hdwy 1/2-way: chsd ldng pair wl over 1f out: rdn to ld ent fnl f: kpt on* **9/2**[2]
61-6 2 3/4 **Constant Dream**[27] 1742 3-9-5 **57** GrahamLee 10 65
(James Given) *cl up: pushed along and ev ch whn hmpd wl over 2f out: rdn and styd on to ld briefly over 1f out: hdd ent fnl f: sn drvn and kpt on wl towards fin* **5/1**[3]
005- 3 2 1/4 **Hidden Asset**[202] 7466 3-9-1 **53** AndrewMullen 9 54
(Michael Appleby) *prom: cl up 1/2-way: rdn and edgd lft wl over 2f out: sn led: drvn and hdd over 1f out: kpt on one pce fnl f* **2/1**[1]
623 4 2 1/2 **Una Bella Cosa**[12] 2172 3-9-0 **52** (v) RobertWinston 7 45
(Alan McCabe) *towards rr: hdwy on outer 1/2-way: wd st: rdn 2f out: kpt on fnl f: nrst fin* **9/2**[2]
30-4 5 1 1/4 **Millie N Aire**[14] 2091 3-9-0 **59** MatthewHopkins(7) 8 48
(Danielle McCormick) *chsd ldrs: rdn along wl over 2f out: sn one pce* **20/1**
032- 6 3/4 **Only For You**[181] 7797 3-9-4 **56** DaleSwift 1 42
(Alan Brown) *cl up on inner: rdn along 1/2-way: grad wknd* **14/1**
435 7 1/2 **Viva L'Inghilterra (IRE)**[68] 979 3-9-3 **58** RossAtkinson(3) 2 43
(Robert Cowell) *sn led: rdn along 3f out: hdd wl over 2f out and sn wknd* **16/1**
-452 8 hd **Angels Calling**[20] 1906 3-9-3 **58** MichaelMetcalfe(3) 3 42
(Mrs K Burke) *a towards rr* **7/1**
60-0 9 3 1/4 **Cosmic Dream**[25] 1781 3-8-7 **45** ChrisCatlin 4 19
(Garry Moss) *a towards rr* **20/1**

1m 17.03s (0.53) **Going Correction** -0.05s/f (Stan) 9 Ran SP% **120.9**
Speed ratings (Par 97): **94,93,90,86,85 84,83,83,78**
toteswingers 1&2 £4.00, 1&3 £4.00, 2&3 £4.30 CSF £28.75 CT £58.77 TOTE £5.10: £2.40, £2.10, £1.50; EX 24.00 Trifecta £133.00 Pool: £2,026.64 - 11.42 winning units..
Owner Geoff Copp **Bred** G B Turnbull Ltd **Trained** Radlett, Herts
FOCUS
They went a decent pace in this 3yo sprint handicap and the form should work out.

2513 APPRENTICESHIPS AT SLIC TRAINING FILLIES' H'CAP 6f (F)
4:30 (4:31) (Class 4) (0-80,80) 4-Y-0+ **£4,690** (£1,395; £697; £348) **Stalls** Low

Form RPR
2613 1 **Mata Hari Blue**[12] 2173 7-9-6 **79** (t) AndrewMullen 3 93
(Michael Appleby) *cl up: slt ld 1/2-way: rdn clr wl over 1f out: kpt on strly* **11/4**[2]
6-02 2 2 1/4 **Dancheur (IRE)**[14] 2088 4-9-2 **75** RobertWinston 6 80
(Mrs K Burke) *chsd ldng pair: hdwy on outer 1/2-way: rdn to chse wnr wl over 1f out: drvn and no imp fnl f* **9/4**[1]
3220 3 4 1/2 **Spark Of Genius**[37] 1540 4-8-12 **71** (b[1]) GrahamLee 1 62
(Alan McCabe) *slt ld: rdn along and hdd 1/2-way: drvn 2f out and sn one pce* **7/1**[3]
425- 4 1/2 **Minalisa**[246] 6285 4-9-7 **80** ChrisCatlin 2 69
(Rae Guest) *trckd ldrs: effrt wl over 2f out: sn rdn and one pce* **9/4**[1]
6-30 5 1 1/4 **Camache Queen (IRE)**[4] 2395 5-8-6 **68** DarrenEgan(3) 5 53
(Joseph Tuite) *chsd ldrs: effrt on outer wl over 2f out: sn rdn and n.d* **16/1**
6000 6 8 **Beau Mistral (IRE)**[16] 2028 4-9-2 **75** CathyGannon 4 34
(Paul Green) *s.i.s: a in rr* **14/1**

1m 15.14s (-1.36) **Going Correction** -0.05s/f (Stan) 6 Ran SP% **113.3**
Speed ratings (Par 102): **107,104,98,97,95 85**
toteswingers 1&2 £1.40, 1&3 £2.30, 2&3 £2.00 CSF £9.55 TOTE £4.40: £1.80, £1.10; EX 9.10 Trifecta £22.70 Pool: £2,329.64 - 76.66 winning units..
Owner M J Golding **Bred** R T And Mrs Watson **Trained** Danethorpe, Notts
FOCUS
A fair fillies' handicap.

2514 BETVICTOR CHAMPIONS LEAGUE FINAL MONEY BACK H'CAP 1m (F)
5:00 (5:01) (Class 6) (0-65,64) 4-Y-0+ **£1,940** (£577; £288; £144) **Stalls** Low

Form RPR
4111 1 **Sofias Number One (USA)**[41] 1455 5-9-4 **64** (b) MarkCoumbe(3) 9 77+
(Roy Bowring) *in tch: gd hdwy on wd outside over 3f out: led wl over 2f out and sn clr: rdn over 1f out: kpt on wl* **11/2**[2]
6323 2 2 1/2 **Imaginary World (IRE)**[12] 2155 5-8-13 **61** (e[1]) MichaelJMMurphy(3) 10 67
(John Balding) *hld up: hdwy over 2f out: sn rdn and styd on wl fnl f* **16/1**
533 3 1/2 **Peter's Friend**[25] 1777 4-9-7 **64** GrahamLee 8 69
(Michael Herrington) *chsd ldrs: rdn along over 2f out: styd on u.p ins fnl f* **10/1**
64-2 4 1/2 **Pat's Legacy (USA)**[27] 1752 7-9-7 **64** GeorgeBaker 12 68
(Gary Moore) *sn led: rdn along and hdd wl over 2f out: drvn wl over 1f out: sn one pce* **6/4**[1]
04-0 5 3 3/4 **Men Don't Cry (IRE)**[28] 1710 4-8-7 **53** (b) SimonPearce(3) 1 48+
(Ed de Giles) *chsd ldrs on inner: rdn along over 2f out: drvn wl over 1f out: grad wknd* **20/1**
06-0 6 4 **Catchanova (IRE)**[19] 1925 6-8-13 **61** AmyScott(5) 2 47
(Eve Johnson Houghton) *towards rr: sme hdwy fnl 2f: n.d* **33/1**
0003 7 3/4 **Rockgoat (IRE)**[12] 2168 4-8-7 **50** oh2 NickyMackay 13 34
(Ian McInnes) *dwlt: hdwy to chse ldrs after 2f: cl up 1/2-way: rdn along 3f out: sn drvn and wknd* **50/1**
-006 8 1/2 **Feeling Good**[23] 1842 4-9-3 **60** (t) DaleSwift 7 43
(Brian Ellison) *dwlt: a towards rr* **8/1**[3]
2243 9 1 **Bold Marc (IRE)**[10] 2221 11-9-6 **63** RobertWinston 14 44
(Mrs K Burke) *cl up: rdn along wl over 2f out: sn wknd* **14/1**
-000 10 1 1/2 **Tatting**[38] 1521 4-9-0 **57** SaleemGolam 11 35
(Chris Dwyer) *in tch: hdwy 3f out: rdn along over 2f out: sn wknd* **12/1**
3252 11 1 1/4 **Mcconnell (USA)**[12] 2168 8-8-12 **55** (b) JimmyQuinn 3 30
(Violet M Jordan) *a towards rr* **14/1**
1200 12 1/2 **Mataajir (USA)**[9] 2273 5-9-5 **62** MartinDwyer 6 36
(Derek Shaw) *a in rr* **10/1**
0052 13 5 **On The Cusp (IRE)**[12] 2171 6-8-7 **53** (p) DarrenEgan(3) 4 15
(Violet M Jordan) *chsd ldrs: lost pl bef 1/2-way: sn in rr* **16/1**

1m 43.41s (-0.29) **Going Correction** -0.05s/f (Stan) 13 Ran SP% **127.1**
Speed ratings (Par 101): **99,96,96,95,91 87,87,86,85,84 82,82,77**
toteswingers 1&2 £13.30, 1&3 £16.10, 2&3 £22.80 CSF £94.79 CT £885.87 TOTE £5.90: £2.20, £4.60, £3.90; EX 84.40 Trifecta £1508.10 Part won. Pool: £2,010.87 - 0.58 winning units..
Owner S R Bowring **Bred** Rosecrest Farm Llc **Trained** Edwinstowe, Notts
FOCUS
A competitive low-grade handicap that saw a gamble go astray. The winner took his form to a new high with the second rated to her recent best.

2515 BETVICTOR CASINO ON YOUR MOBILE H'CAP 7f (F)
5:30 (5:30) (Class 5) (0-75,74) 4-Y-0+ **£2,587** (£770; £384; £192) **Stalls** Low

Form RPR
1556 1 **Our Ivor**[28] 1723 4-9-5 **72** AndrewMullen 6 87
(Michael Appleby) *trckd ldrs: hdwy to chal 3f out: sn led: jnd and rdn over 2f out: drvn over 1f out: styd on strly fnl f* **7/2**[2]
-113 2 5 **Eutropius (IRE)**[15] 2042 4-9-7 **74** RobertWinston 8 76
(Alan Swinbank) *trckd ldrs: hdwy on outer 1/2-way: chal over 2f out: sn rdn and ev ch tl drvn: edgd lft and one pce appr fnl f* **1/1**[1]
0-44 3 2 3/4 **Paramour**[23] 1827 6-9-7 **74** DavidNolan 2 69
(David O'Meara) *cl up: ev ch wl over 2f out: sn rdn and grad wknd fr wl over 1f out* **12/1**
3443 4 3 1/4 **Fairy Wing (IRE)**[10] 2222 6-8-10 **66** DarrenEgan(3) 3 52
(Violet M Jordan) *trckd ldrs: pushed along and outpcd 1/2-way: rdn wl over 2f out: kpt on fnl f* **14/1**
3223 5 1 1/4 **Hellbender (IRE)**[34] 1599 7-8-11 **69** (t) DarylByrne(5) 4 52+
(Shaun Harris) *chsd ldrs: rdn along wl over 2f out: n.d* **6/1**[3]
2420 6 7 **Restless Bay (IRE)**[25] 1798 5-9-1 **68** (b) CathyGannon 7 33
(Conor Dore) *in tch on inner whn squeezed out bnd after 3f and bhd after* **25/1**
1405 7 9 **Clubland (IRE)**[6] 2343 4-9-6 **73** JimmyQuinn 1 15
(Roy Bowring) *led: rdn along and hdd 3f out: sn drvn and wknd fnl 2f* **16/1**
1420 8 3/4 **Lieutenant Dan (IRE)**[27] 1746 6-8-11 **69** (v) TobyAtkinson(5) 5
(Michael Appleby) *a in rr: bhd fr 1/2-way* **16/1**

1m 29.36s (-0.94) **Going Correction** -0.05s/f (Stan) 8 Ran SP% **116.5**
Speed ratings (Par 103): **103,97,94,90,89 81,70,69**
toteswingers 1&2 £1.80, 1&3 £5.30, 2&3 £3.10 CSF £7.51 CT £36.28 TOTE £5.40: £1.50, £1.20, £2.90; EX 9.60 Trifecta £56.90 Pool: £1,490.81 - 19.63 winning units..
Owner J&G Bacciochi, A Taylor, Bruce W Wyatt **Bred** B W Wyatt **Trained** Danethorpe, Notts
FOCUS
They went a solid pace in this handicap containing a number of previous course winners.
T/Plt: £614.90 to a £1 stake. Pool: £55,490.81 - 65.87 winning units T/Qpdt: £15.40 to a £1 stake. Pool: £3,904.62 - 187.53 winning units JR

2320 WINDSOR (R-H)

Monday, May 20

OFFICIAL GOING: Good (7.9)

Wind: Almost nil Weather: Overcast, early drizzle

2516 CHRIS LUCAS TRUST CLAIMING STKS 6f

6:10 (6:11) (Class 5) 3-Y-0+ **£2,587** (£770; £384; £192) **Stalls** Low

Form RPR

-551 **1** **North Star Boy (IRE)**[18] 1954 4-9-7 **78** RichardHughes 6 82
(Richard Hannon) *mde all and racd against nr side rail: shkn up and appeared to assert over 1f out: drvn out firmly last 100yds* **7/4**[1]

0400 **2** ½ **Noverre To Go (IRE)**[14] 2097 7-9-5 **82** (p) WilliamCarson 5 78
(Ronald Harris) *t.k.h early: trckd wnr after 2f: rdn and nt qckn 2f out: kpt on to press ins fnl f: a hld* **8/1**

3326 **3** ½ **Commanche**[17] 1985 4-8-11 **65** ThomasBrown(5) 8 73
(Patrick Chamings) *trckd ldrs: rdn 2f out: wnt 3rd over 1f out: styd on fnl f: a hld* **10/1**

-121 **4** ¾ **Tajneed (IRE)**[9] 2276 10-9-3 **72** AdrianNicholls 3 72
(David Nicholls) *trckd ldrs: drvn over 2f out: nt qckn wl over 1f out: kpt on fnl f: nvr able to chal* **9/4**[2]

3100 **5** 1 **Amethyst Dawn (IRE)**[10] 2225 7-8-5 **65** (t) RobertTart(5) 10 62
(Andrew Reid) *prom on outer: chsd ldng pair over 3f out to over 1f out: fdd ins fnl f* **20/1**

1415 **6** 2 **Captain Kendall (IRE)**[30] 1694 4-9-1 **72** TomQueally 1 60
(David Evans) *w ldrs early: lost pl over 4f out on inner: swtchd to wd outside and rdn 2f out: one pce and no imp* **9/2**[3]

0-06 **7** 6 **Kings 'n Dreams**[31] 1665 6-9-3 **50** (b) MartinLane 9 43
(Dean Ivory) *hld up in last trio: shkn up and lft bhd 2f out: no ch after* **66/1**

0 **8** 1 **Rocky Couloir**[7] 2306 3-8-12 **0** SebSanders 7 44
(Michael Easterby) *s.s: jst in tch in rr: lft bhd fr 2f out* **66/1**

0500 **9** 10 **Bird Dog**[49] 1294 7-8-9 **27** (v) DannyBrock(5) 2
(Phil McEntee) *chsd wnr 2f: wknd rapidly 1/2-way: t.o* **200/1**

10 9 **Beltaine (IRE)** 4-8-10 **0** (t) MatthewLawson(5) 11
(Brendan Powell) *s.v.s: a wl bhd in last: t.o* **66/1**

1m 12.85s (-0.15) **Going Correction** 0.0s/f (Good)
WFA 3 from 4yo+ 9lb **10** Ran SP% **115.3**
Speed ratings (Par 103): **101,100,99,98,97 94,86,85,72,60**
toteswingers 1&2 £2.50, 1&3 £3.60, 2&3 £9.00 CSF £16.13 TOTE £2.20: £1.50, £2.40, £2.60; EX 15.50 Trifecta £108.90 Pool: £1,801.16 - 12.40 winning units..North Star Boy was claimed by Amy Weaver for £12,000. Captain Kendall claimed by Mr D Charlesworth for £6,000.
Owner Robert Tyrrell **Bred** Hascombe And Valiant Studs **Trained** East Everleigh, Wilts

FOCUS
Top bend dolled out 8yds from normal configuration adding 29yds to races of 1m and beyond. Inner of straight dolled out 10yds at 6f and 5yds at Winning Post. A fair claimer which was fought out by the two with the highest BHA ratings. It's doubtful the winner had to improve on his winter AW form.

2517 INTERNATIONAL SPORTS MANAGEMENT & EBF MAIDEN FILLIES' STKS 5f 10y

6:40 (6:42) (Class 5) 2-Y-0 **£2,911** (£866; £432; £216) **Stalls** Low

Form RPR

2 **1** **Midnite Angel (IRE)**[9] 2283 2-9-0 **0** RichardHughes 3 79+
(Richard Hannon) *w ldr: led 2f out: sn rdn wl clr: eased last 75yds* **4/6**[1]

34 **2** 7 **Twist And Shout**[19] 1924 2-9-0 **0** NeilCallan 4 54
(Bill Turner) *led: rdn and hdd 2f out: sn no ch w wnr: lost action bdly last strides: dismntd after fin* **9/4**[2]

3 1½ **Yellow Lady (IRE)** 2-9-0 **0** (t) HarryBentley 2 49
(Olly Stevens) *chsd ldng pair but rn green: one pce fr over 1f out* **8/1**[3]

0 **4** ¾ **Wiki Tiki**[15] 2048 2-9-0 **0** AdamBeschizza 6 46
(Stuart Williams) *stdd s: t.k.h and hld up in last pair: pushed along 2f out: nt knocked abt whn no threat fnl f* **33/1**

5 hd **May Whi (IRE)** 2-9-0 **0** RichardKingscote 5 45+
(Tom Dascombe) *t.k.h early: rn green and outpcd in last after 2f: kpt on fnl f* **14/1**

1m 1.05s (0.75) **Going Correction** 0.0s/f (Good) **5** Ran SP% **111.5**
Speed ratings (Par 90): **94,82,80,79,78**
CSF £2.44 TOTE £1.50: £1.10, £1.30; EX 2.20 Trifecta £6.20 Pool: £1,115.81 - 133.96 winning units..
Owner Elaine Chivers & Richard Kidner **Bred** O Bourke **Trained** East Everleigh, Wilts

FOCUS
No Misty Sparkler, so this was left to look a match. The race fell apart making the winner look very good, but this was obviously an improved effort.

2518 WEATHERBYS BANK CONDITIONS STKS 5f 10y

7:10 (7:11) (Class 2) 2-Y-0 **£9,056** (£2,695; £1,346) **Stalls** Low

Form RPR

1 **1** **Thunder Strike**[16] 2005 2-9-0 **0** RichardHughes 3 85+
(Richard Hannon) *disp ld: led 1/2-way: pushed along over 2f out: edgd rt ins fnl f: comf* **4/9**[1]

133 **2** 2¼ **Split Rock**[3] 2421 2-9-0 **0** SilvestreDeSousa 1 77
(Mark Johnston) *dwlt: chsd other pair and pushed along: wnt 2nd 2f out and hanging lft after: drvn to try to chal over 1f out: one pce* **3/1**[2]

0316 **3** 3 **Smugglers Gold (IRE)**[12] 2147 2-8-11 **0** TomQueally 2 63
(David Evans) *disp ld to 1/2-way: sn rdn and dropped to 3rd: steadily fdd* **8/1**[3]

1m 0.45s (0.15) **Going Correction** 0.0s/f (Good) **3** Ran SP% **105.4**
Speed ratings (Par 99): **98,94,89**
CSF £1.97 TOTE £1.40; EX 1.50 Trifecta £1.50 Pool: £943.30 - 467.98 winning units..
Owner Mohamed Saeed Al Shahi **Bred** Southill Stud **Trained** East Everleigh, Wilts

FOCUS
This looked a straightforward task for the favourite, who didn't need much improvement to win easily.

2519 BUGLER DEVELOPMENTS MAIDEN FILLIES' STKS 1m 67y

7:40 (7:42) (Class 5) 3-Y-0+ **£2,587** (£770; £384; £192) **Stalls** Low

Form RPR

23 **1** **Spicy Dal**[17] 1986 3-9-0 **0** JimmyFortune 12 83
(Hughie Morrison) *led 2f: trckd ldr: led again 3f out: rdn and hanging lft fr over 2f out: drvn rt out* **7/2**[1]

56- **2** 1½ **Puligny (IRE)**[200] 7505 3-9-0 **0** WilliamCarson 14 79
(Charles Hills) *chsd ldr 2f: styd prom: shkn up over 3f out: chsd wnr over 2f out: hrd rdn and kpt on: nvr able to chal* **25/1**

3 3 **Aragosta** 3-9-0 **0** HayleyTurner 5 72+
(James Fanshawe) *wl in rr: 9th and a long way off the pce 1/2-way: pushed along and styd on fr over 2f out: tk 3rd nr fin* **5/1**[3]

0 **4** ½ **Beep**[23] 1828 3-9-0 **0** PatDobbs 10 71
(Sir Michael Stoute) *prom: pushed along over 3f out: disp 2nd briefly 2f out: fdd fnl f* **9/2**[2]

4 **5** 1¾ **Gold Chain (IRE)**[31] 1666 3-9-0 **0** IanMongan 11 67
(Clive Cox) *chsd ldrs but nvr on terms: shkn up over 3f out: no imp fnl 2f* **13/2**

0 **6** 3 **Simply Elegant (IRE)**[14] 2084 3-9-0 **0** NeilCallan 3 60
(Amanda Perrett) *dwlt: sn in midfield: pushed along 1/2-way: no imp on ldrs fr 2f out* **8/1**

33 **7** 2¼ **Rubbamaa**[38] 1518 4-9-12 **0** SilvestreDeSousa 4 58
(Clive Brittain) *chsd ldrs: pushed along in 7th bef 1/2-way and struggling: no prog fnl 3f* **10/1**

8 1¾ **Rainbows And Roses** 3-9-0 **0** SebSanders 2 51
(Chris Wall) *v s.i.s: rn green in last: wl bhd 1/2-way: pushed along and mod late prog* **33/1**

0/0 **9** 1½ **Princess Spirit**[21] 1876 4-9-12 **0** MarcHalford 13 50
(Edward Creighton) *t.k.h: led after 2f and awkward arnd bnd sn after: hdd 3f out: wknd qckly u.p* **100/1**

0- **10** ¾ **Chiltern Secret**[238] 6534 3-9-0 **0** MartinLane 9 46
(Martin Bosley) *a in rr: wl bhd bef 1/2-way* **200/1**

60 **11** ¾ **Cherry Princess**[32] 1640 3-9-0 **0** HarryBentley 8 44
(Stuart Williams) *nvr bttr than midfield: pushed along over 3f out: wknd over 2f out* **100/1**

12 7 **Pure Flight (IRE)** 3-8-11 **0** RachaelGreen(3) 6 28
(Anthony Honeyball) *a wl in rr: wl bhd fr 1/2-way* **66/1**

50 **13** 8 **Little Alice**[16] 2016 3-9-0 **0** AdamBeschizza 1
(Stuart Williams) *a wl in rr: wl bhd fr 1/2-way: t.o* **66/1**

1m 45.17s (0.47) **Going Correction** +0.125s/f (Good)
WFA 3 from 4yo 12lb **13** Ran SP% **102.9**
Speed ratings (Par 100): **102,100,97,97,95 92,90,88,86,86 85,78,70**
toteswingers 1&2 £14.00, 1&3 £4.30, 2&3 £18.20 CSF £70.90 TOTE £4.20: £1.30, £6.50, £2.00; EX 69.10 Trifecta £446.50 Pool: £789.05 - 1.32 winning units..
Owner Ben & Sir Martyn Arbib **Bred** Arbib Bloodstock Partnership **Trained** East Ilsley, Berks

FOCUS
A fair fillies' maiden that should produce winners. The early pace was very steady before it quickened at halfway and it paid to race prominently. Probably not as good a renewal as the last two.

2520 CORAL.CO.UK H'CAP 1m 3f 135y

8:10 (8:10) (Class 3) (0-95,95) 4-Y-0+ **£7,439** (£2,213; £1,106; £553) **Stalls** Centre

Form RPR

312- **1** **Ustura (USA)**[256] 5966 4-9-0 **88** (t) SilvestreDeSousa 3 100+
(Saeed bin Suroor) *trckd ldrs: pushed along fr 4f out: nowhere to go on inner fr over 2f out tl swtchd lft 1f out: drvn and r.o to ld post* **7/2**[3]

-441 **2** nse **Duke Of Clarence (IRE)**[21] 1883 4-8-13 **87** RichardHughes 6 96
(Richard Hannon) *pressed ldr: shkn up over 2f out: rdn to ld 1f out: styd on but hdd post* **11/4**[2]

5320 **3** ½ **Mawaakef (IRE)**[26] 1766 5-8-13 **87** IanMongan 8 95
(J R Jenkins) *hld up in tch: prog on wd outside over 2f out: drvn over 1f out: chsd ldr ins fnl f and tried to chal: kpt on but lost 2nd nr fin* **40/1**

2214 **4** 2¼ **Icebuster**[16] 2018 5-8-12 **86** TomQueally 4 91+
(Rod Millman) *hld up in last: two reminders 2f out: sltly hmpd 1f out: shkn up and kpt on: nvr really involved* **5/1**

062- **5** ¾ **Roxy Flyer (IRE)**[173] 7895 6-9-7 **95** PatDobbs 2 98
(Amanda Perrett) *hld up in tch: rdn wl over 2f out: nt qckn and hld jst over 1f out: fdd* **14/1**

10-3 **6** 1 **Proofreader**[11] 2191 4-9-2 **90** RobertHavlin 5 91
(John Gosden) *led: gng bttr than most over 2f out: rdn and hdd 1f out: wknd* **7/4**[1]

30-3 **7** 7 **Sula Two**[21] 1884 6-8-2 **81** oh1 PhilipPrince(5) 7 73
(Ron Hodges) *trckd ldng pair: pushed along over 3f out: rdn and wknd over 1f out: heavily eased last 150yds* **28/1**

2m 28.4s (-1.10) **Going Correction** +0.125s/f (Good) **7** Ran SP% **114.5**
Speed ratings (Par 107): **108,107,107,106,105 104,100**
toteswingers 1&2 £2.40, 1&3 £21.40, 2&3 £19.90 CSF £13.61 CT £319.12 TOTE £4.10: £2.70, £1.10; EX 13.00 Trifecta £86.50 Pool: £1,117.05 - 9.68 winning units..
Owner Godolphin **Bred** Darley **Trained** Newmarket, Suffolk
■ Stewards' Enquiry : Silvestre De Sousa two-day ban: careless riding (3-4 June)

FOCUS
A decent enough handicap, run at a reasonable gallop. The winner can be rated better than the bare form and the second continues to progress.

2521 DOWNLOAD CORAL MOBILE FROM THE APP STORE H'CAP 5f 10y

8:40 (8:41) (Class 4) (0-85,85) 3-Y-0 **£4,851** (£1,443; £721; £360) **Stalls** Low

Form RPR

40-1 **1** **Hoofalong**[16] 2010 3-8-13 **77** (p) RichardHughes 10 88+
(Michael Easterby) *stdd s: hld up in rr: plenty to do whn prog on outer 2f out: chsd ldr jst over 1f out: hrd rdn and r.o to ld post* **9/4**[1]

1121 **2** nse **Riskit Fora Biskit (IRE)**[24] 1808 3-9-7 **85** HayleyTurner 4 96
(Michael Bell) *led and r against nr side rail: gng strly over 1f out: rdn ins fnl f: hdd post* **4/1**[2]

1-33 **3** 2 **Smart Spender (IRE)**[49] 1295 3-9-2 **80** ShaneKelly 2 87+
(Jo Hughes) *hld up towards rr: prog 2f out: chsd ldng pair fnl f but stuck bhd them: eased whn hld nr fin* **5/1**[3]

1-50 **4** 2¼ **Fletcher Christian**[12] 2158 3-8-9 **73** (v[1]) NeilCallan 6 69
(John Gallagher) *mostly chsd ldr tl jst over 1f out: wknd ins fnl f* **25/1**

-050 **5** ¾ **Secret Missile**[16] 2022 3-8-12 **76** SilvestreDeSousa 5 69
(William Muir) *hld up towards rr: rdn 1/2-way: effrt on outer over 1f out: sn no prog* **8/1**

1-51 **6** nk **Exotic Isle**[14] 2098 3-8-12 **76** JimCrowley 3 68
(Ralph Beckett) *chsd ldrs: rdn 2f out: nt qckn over 1f out: wl hld after* **4/1**[2]

3-03 **7** 1¼ **New Fforest**[10] 2213 3-9-5 **83** JimmyFortune 9 70
(Andrew Balding) *hld up in midfield: prog 2f out: disp 2nd briefly over 1f out: wknd fnl f* **11/1**

311- **8** 1 **Saga Lout**[144] 8245 3-8-10 **74** RichardKingscote 1 58
(Tom Dascombe) *restless stalls: dwlt: pushed along in last pair and off the pce: drvn 2f out: racd awkwardly and no real prog* **16/1**

240- **9** hd **Front Page News**[191] 7687 3-8-7 **71** AdamBeschizza 8 54
(Robert Eddery) *dwlt: outpcd in last and urged along: nvr on terms: kpt on ins fnl f* **50/1**

1110 **10** *2 1/4* **Hannahs Turn**[21] 1892 3-8-9 **73**........................ TomQueally 7 48
(Chris Dwyer) *prom tl wknd 2f out* **33/1**

59.93s (-0.37) **Going Correction** 0.0s/f (Good) **10** Ran SP% **121.5**
Speed ratings (Par 101): **102,101,98,95,93 93,91,89,89,85**
toteswingers 1&2 £2.00, 1&3 £5.10, 2&3 £6.70 CSF £11.60 CT £43.15 TOTE £3.70: £2.00, £2.80, £1.90; EX 14.00 Trifecta £47.00 Pool: £1,285.23 - 20.49 winning units..
Owner A Chandler, L Westwood, D & Y Blunt **Bred** D F Spence **Trained** Sheriff Hutton, N Yorks

FOCUS
A good, competitive 3yo sprint, run at a solid gallop, and two progressive types fought out a desperately close finish. Sound form, with more improvement possible from the winner.
T/Plt: £13.70 to a £1 stake. Pool: £73,702.81 - 3,918.62 winning units T/Qpdt: £7.80 to a £1 stake. Pool: £4,737.64 - 444.91 winning units JN

2065 COLOGNE (R-H)
Monday, May 20

OFFICIAL GOING: Turf: soft

2526a MEHL-MULHENS-RENNEN - GERMAN 2000 GUINEAS (GROUP 2) (3YO COLTS & FILLIES) (TURF) 1m
4:55 (4:56) 3-Y-0 £81,300 (£24,390; £10,569; £5,691; £2,439)

RPR

1 **Peace At Last (IRE)**[16] 3-9-2 0........................ FabriceVeron 5 110
(H-A Pantall, France) *hld up towards rr: rdn 3f out: hdwy fr over 2f out: r.o to chal ent fnl f: led ins fnl 150yds: drvn and asserted* **29/1**

2 *1 1/4* **Global Bang (GER)**[29] 1708 3-9-2 0........................ ADeVries 11 107
(Mario Hofer, Germany) *hld up in last and sn detached: stdy hdwy on wd outside fr 3f out: rdn 2f out: drifted rt u.p: r.o to chal ent fnl f: wnt 2nd ins fnl 100yds: kpt on but hld by wnr* **68/10**

3 *1 1/4* **Tawhid**[32] 1638 3-9-2 0........................ MickaelBarzalona 3 104
(Saeed bin Suroor) *midfield: rdn over 3f out: angled out and r.o to ld 1 1/2f out: hung rt u.p: strly pressed ent fnl f: hdd ins fnl 150yds: no ex and dropped to 3rd* **13/5**[2]

4 *10* **String Theory (IRE)**[19] 1926 3-9-2 0........................ AdamKirby 8 81
(Marco Botti) *hld up towards rr on outer: rdn 3f out: outpcd by ldrs over 1f out: styd on to take remote 4th wl ins fnl f* **6/1**[3]

5 *3/4* **Boomshackerlacker (IRE)**[195] 7623 3-9-2 0........................ PatCosgrave 1 80
(George Baker) *midfield on inner: niggled to hold position whn short of room on rail over 3f out: sn rdn and outpcd: last 2f out: rallied u.p and plugged on to take wl hld 5th cl home* **41/5**

6 *1 1/4* **Ayaar (IRE)**[16] 2024 3-9-2 0........................(b) MartinHarley 6 77
(Mick Channon) *led: rdn 2f out: hdd 1 1/2f out: no ex and steadily fdd* **21/1**

7 *2 1/2* **Royal Fox**[36] 3-9-2 0........................ MrDennisSchiergen 4 71
(P Schiergen, Germany) *trckd ldr on outer: rdn 3f out: hdwy to chal and ev ch 2f out: no ex over 1f out: fdd* **113/10**

8 *1* **Limario (GER)**[29] 1708 3-9-2 0........................ APietsch 2 69
(R Dzubasz, Germany) *trckd ldr on inner: rdn 3f out: outpcd and btn over 1f out: fdd* **104/10**

9 *nk* **Law Enforcement (IRE)**[51] 1264 3-9-2 0........................ SeanLevey 9 68
(Richard Hannon) *t.k.h: prom on outer: v awkward and lost pl whn forced wd on bnd over 3f out: sn rdn: dropped to rr and btn ent fnl f: eased cl home* **5/2**[1]

10 *4 1/2* **One Word More (IRE)**[37] 1543 3-9-2 0........................ SteveDrowne 7 58
(Charles Hills) *midfield on outer: rdn over 3f out: outpcd and btn over 1f out: dropped to last ins fnl f: eased* **89/10**

1m 36.08s (-2.31) **10** Ran SP% **129.2**
WIN (incl. 10 euro stake): 302. PLACES: 44, 21, 19. SF: 3,202.
Owner Guy Heald **Bred** G B Partnership **Trained** France

2527 - (Foreign Racing) - See Raceform Interactive

BRIGHTON (L-H)
Tuesday, May 21

OFFICIAL GOING: Good to firm (7.9)
Wind: Fresh, behind Weather: Overcast

2528 HOWLETT CLARKE H'CAP 6f 209y
2:10 (2:10) (Class 6) (0-60,60) 3-Y-0 £1,940 (£577; £288; £144) Stalls Low

Form RPR

400 **1** **Lincolnrose (IRE)**[15] 2084 3-8-11 **50**........................(p[1]) KieranO'Neill 2 54
(Alan McCabe) *mde all: hrd rdn over 1f out: hld on wl* **16/1**

5-50 **2** *nk* **Ishisoba**[29] 1712 3-9-4 **57**........................ GeorgeBaker 7 60
(Alastair Lidderdale) *hld up towards rr: rdn and hdwy in centre over 1f out: r.o fnl f: clsng at fin* **6/1**[3]

6542 **3** *1 1/2* **Handsome Stranger (IRE)**[18] 1982 3-9-3 **56**...............(v) AdamKirby 10 55
(David Evans) *bhd: hrd rdn and hdwy over 1f out: styd on wl fnl f* **10/1**

3506 **4** *1/2* **Katy Spirit (IRE)**[18] 1978 3-9-5 **58**........................ LiamKeniry 3 56
(Michael Blanshard) *dwlt: t.k.h: sn in tch: hrd rdn 2f out: styd on fnl f* **12/1**

5-63 **5** *2* **Red Tulip**[8] 2330 3-9-6 **59**........................ MartinLane 9 52
(James Fanshawe) *cl up: chsd wnr over 4f out tl no ex ins fnl f* **3/1**[1]

-000 **6** *1* **Epic Charm**[8] 2308 3-9-4 **57**........................ MatthewDavies 1 47
(Mick Channon) *prom tl no ex 1f out* **9/2**[2]

5-04 **7** *1* **Don Eduardo**[5] 2393 3-8-7 **53**........................(v) CharlotteJenner[(7)] 6 40
(J S Moore) *in tch: rdn 3f out: n.d after* **10/1**

25-6 **8** *nk* **Kwanto**[39] 1519 3-9-7 **60**........................ TomMcLaughlin 12 46
(Malcolm Saunders) *in tch on outer: rdn and outpcd fnl 2f* **33/1**

000- **9** *nk* **Our Three Graces (IRE)**[151] 8203 3-9-0 **53**........................ WilliamCarson 5 39
(Gary Moore) *t.k.h: towards rr: rdn 3f out: sme hdwy 2f out: wknd and eased ins fnl f* **6/1**[3]

006- **10** *nse* **Sunny Hollow**[178] 7865 3-9-0 **58**........................ RobertTart[(5)] 11 43
(James Toller) *sn stdd to rr: hdwy and n.m.r on inner over 1f out: hung lft: wknd fnl f* **16/1**

0-30 **11** *15* **Serenata (IRE)**[21] 1907 3-9-4 **57**........................[1] ShaneKelly 4
(Paul Cole) *prom: bmpd over 2f out: sn lost pl* **12/1**

1m 22.88s (-0.22) **Going Correction** -0.175s/f (Firm) **11** Ran SP% **120.0**
Speed ratings (Par 97): **94,93,91,91,89 87,86,86,86,86 68**
toteswingers 1&2 £15.30, 1&3 £17.90, 2&3 £7.20 CSF £111.36 CT £1049.39 TOTE £17.50: £4.40, £2.70, £2.50; EX 171.20 Trifecta £1013.00 Part won. Pool: £1350.75 - 0.42 winning units..
Owner Peter Smith P C Coaches Limited **Bred** Irish National Stud **Trained** Averham Park, Notts
■ Stewards' Enquiry : Matthew Davies one-day ban: careless riding (4 June)

FOCUS
Course on inner line and all distances as advertised. This low-grade handicap saw something of upset. Ordinary form, with the first two unexposed on turf.

2529 WEATHERBYS HAMILTON INSURANCE MAIDEN STKS 5f 213y
2:40 (2:40) (Class 5) 3-Y-0+ £2,587 (£770; £384; £192) Stalls Low

Form RPR

-422 **1** **Extrasolar**[5] 2394 3-9-3 74........................(t) AdamKirby 2 86
(Amanda Perrett) *in tch: wnt 2nd 3f out: led over 1f out: drvn clr: readily* **8/13**[1]

5- **2** *3* **Daylight**[294] 4688 3-9-3 0........................ DavidProbert 3 76
(Andrew Balding) *led tl over 1f out: sn outpcd by wnr* **6/4**[2]

0000 **3** *10* **Surrey Dream (IRE)**[16] 2051 4-9-12 40........................(t) KieranO'Neill 5 46
(John Bridger) *hld up in 5th: wnt mod 3rd 2f out: hrd rdn and nt trble first 2* **100/1**

0 **4** *8* **Kaahen (USA)**[50] 1296 3-9-3 0........................ CathyGannon 1 18
(Pat Eddery) *dwlt: in rr: effrt and hrd rdn 2f out: sn wknd* **33/1**[3]

5000 **5** *1* **Back For Tea (IRE)**[33] 1656 5-9-7 42........................(b) DannyBrock[(5)] 6 15
(Phil McEntee) *prom tl wknd 2f out* **100/1**

P **Katie Galore (IRE)**[429] 4-9-2 0........................ DeclanBates[(5)] 4
(David Evans) *prom tl lost action over 2f out: sn p.u: dismntd* **33/1**[3]

1m 8.92s (-1.28) **Going Correction** -0.175s/f (Firm)
WFA 3 from 4yo+ 9lb **6** Ran SP% **109.8**
Speed ratings (Par 103): **101,97,83,73,71**
toteswingers 1&2 £1.10, 1&3 £4.60, 2&3 £4.20 CSF £1.67 TOTE £2.20: £1.02, £1.30; EX 1.90 Trifecta £13.80 Pool: £2829.44 - 153.62 winning units..
Owner Odile Griffith & John Connolly **Bred** Brook Stud Bloodstock Ltd **Trained** Pulborough, W Sussex

FOCUS
Nothing more than a match according to the market and that proved the case in the race itself. The winner has progressed well but the third gives some perspective.

2530 BRASSERIE ITALIAN BRIGHTON MARINA H'CAP 5f 59y
3:10 (3:10) (Class 5) (0-70,71) 4-Y-0+ £2,587 (£770; £384; £192) Stalls Low

Form RPR

6511 **1** **Above The Stars**[6] 2364 5-9-3 **71** 6ex........................ RachealKneller[(5)] 3 78
(Jamie Osborne) *chsd ldng pair: clsd and drvn to go 2nd ins fnl f: r.o to ld nr fin* **7/4**[1]

6230 **2** *1/2* **Putin (IRE)**[4] 2425 5-8-11 **60**........................(bt) DavidProbert 1 65
(Phil McEntee) *led at fast pce: hrd rdn fnl f: ct nr fin* **5/1**[3]

52-6 **3** *1/2* **Rulesn'regulations**[11] 2225 7-8-13 **69**........................ NoraLooby[(7)] 7 72+
(Alastair Lidderdale) *hld up in 5th: shkn up and hdwy over 1f out: r.o wl fnl f: clsng at fin* **7/2**[2]

06-6 **4** *2* **Wooden King (IRE)**[18] 1976 8-9-7 **70**........................(p) TomMcLaughlin 4 66
(Malcolm Saunders) *pressed ldr tl 2f out: styd 2nd tl no ex ins fnl f* **8/1**

0340 **5** *hd* **Gung Ho Jack**[11] 2227 4-9-7 **70**........................ LiamKeniry 6 65
(John Best) *towards rr: rdn and styd on fr over 1f out: nt rch ldrs* **12/1**

00-1 **6** *1 1/4* **Commandingpresence (USA)**[20] 1929 7-9-7 **70**........................ KieranO'Neill 5 61
(John Bridger) *racd in mod 4th: effrt and hrd rdn over 1f out: one pce ins fnl f* **10/1**

0-20 **7** *3* **Stonecrabstomorrow (IRE)**[6] 2364 10-9-0 **66**........................ MarkCoumbe[(3)] 2 46
(Roy Brotherton) *dwlt: a in rr* **8/1**

1m 1.23s (-1.07) **Going Correction** -0.175s/f (Firm) **7** Ran SP% **114.3**
Speed ratings (Par 103): **101,100,99,96,95 93,89**
toteswingers 1&2 £2.50, 1&3 £2.40, 2&3 £3.20 CSF £10.83 TOTE £2.00: £1.90, £2.10; EX 9.70 Trifecta £36.70 Pool: £2580.09 - 52.61 winning units..
Owner Morsethehorse Syndicate **Bred** Manor Farm Stud (rutland) **Trained** Upper Lambourn, Berks

FOCUS
A low-grade sprint handicap, run at a strong pace. The winner is rated just about back to her best.

2531 WEATHERBYS HAMILTON INSURANCE FILLIES' H'CAP 6f 209y
3:40 (3:40) (Class 4) (0-85,85) 4-Y-0+ £4,690 (£1,395; £697; £348) Stalls Low

Form RPR

0-00 **1** **Alice's Dancer (IRE)**[22] 1878 4-9-2 **80**........................ WilliamCarson 1 87
(William Muir) *plld hrd: sn stdd bk to 4th: rdn and hdwy over 1f out: hung lft: r.o to ld fnl 75yds* **3/1**[2]

44-0 **2** *1 3/4* **Fanrouge (IRE)**[10] 2265 4-9-3 **81**........................ TomMcLaughlin 3 83
(Malcolm Saunders) *led 2f: chsd ldr after tl 1f out: kpt on to regain 2nd fnl 75yds* **7/1**

0-10 **3** *1 1/2* **Red Larkspur (IRE)**[14] 2128 4-9-2 **80**........................ GeorgeBaker 4 78
(Roger Teal) *led after 2f: hrd rdn 1f out: hdd and one pce fnl 75yds* **7/2**[3]

11-0 **4** *3 1/4* **Authoritarian**[36] 1583 4-8-12 **76**........................ KieranO'Neill 2 65
(Richard Hannon) *chsd ldrs tl outpcd and btn 2f out* **9/4**[1]

-056 **5** *1 1/2* **Chilli Green**[10] 2270 6-9-7 **85**........................ LiamKeniry 5 70
(Julia Feilden) *t.k.h in 5th: rdn over 2f out: no imp* **4/1**

1m 21.8s (-1.30) **Going Correction** -0.175s/f (Firm) **5** Ran SP% **110.5**
Speed ratings (Par 102): **100,98,96,92,90**
CSF £22.17 TOTE £3.70: £1.80, £2.90; EX 23.40 Trifecta £119.60 Pool: £1780.77 - 11.16 winning units..
Owner Perspicacious Punters Racing Club **Bred** Rathasker Stud **Trained** Lambourn, Berks

FOCUS
A fair fillies' handicap. The winner guides the level.

2532 BRASSERIE ITALIAN H'CAP 1m 1f 209y
4:10 (4:10) (Class 5) (0-75,75) 4-Y-0+ £2,587 (£770; £384; £192) Stalls High

Form RPR

2406 **1** **Presburg (IRE)**[36] 1585 4-9-6 **74**........................ LiamKeniry 1 85
(Joseph Tuite) *hld up in rr: hdwy 3f out: wnt 2nd 2f out: rdn to ld ins fnl f: hld on wl: in control nr fin* **5/1**[2]

04-2 **2** *1/2* **Highland Duke (IRE)**[15] 2101 4-9-7 **75**........................ AdamKirby 4 85
(Clive Cox) *led after 2f: rdn over 2f out: edgd rt and hdd ins fnl f: kpt on wl* **10/11**[1]

3-35 **3** *4 1/2* **Nave (USA)**[113] 420 6-8-13 **67**........................ MartinLane 5 69
(David Simcock) *cl up: chsd ldr 5f out tl 2f out: one pce* **5/1**[2]

1541 **4** *9* **Silver Alliance**[21] 1915 5-8-8 **69**........................(p) ShelleyBirkett[(7)] 6 53
(Julia Feilden) *hld up in tch: outpcd and dropped to last 4f out: n.d fnl 3f* **7/1**[3]

16 **5** *6* **Final Delivery**[14] 2137 4-8-7 **61**........................ WilliamCarson 2 34
(Jim Boyle) *chsd ldrs tl wknd 2f out* **14/1**

0-00 **6** *1 1/2* **Megalala (IRE)**[36] 1586 12-8-11 **65**........................ KieranO'Neill 3 35
(John Bridger) *led 2f: cl up tl wknd 3f out* **20/1**

2m 0.71s (-2.89) **Going Correction** -0.175s/f (Firm) **6** Ran SP% **109.6**
Speed ratings (Par 103): **104,103,100,92,88 86**
toteswingers 1&2 £1.70, 1&3 £2.90, 2&3 £1.50 CSF £9.55 TOTE £5.20: £2.10, £1.20; EX 10.20 Trifecta £29.80 Pool: £1278.37 - 32.06 winning units..
Owner www.isehove.com **Bred** Limestone And Tara Studs **Trained** Great Shefford, Berks

FOCUS
A weak race for the grade, but it served up a thrilling finish. Straightforward form.

2533 BRIGHTON & HOVE INDEPENDENT H'CAP 1m 1f 209y
4:40 (4:41) (Class 6) (0-60,59) 4-Y-O+ **£1,940** (£577; £288; £144) **Stalls** High

Form RPR
-604 **1** **Green Earth (IRE)**[34] 1617 6-8-12 **50**................................ IanMongan 15 60
(Pat Phelan) *hld up in rr: gd hdwy over 1f out: r.o to ld ins fnl f* **8/1**[3]
4102 **2** 1 1/4 **Peace In Our Time**[21] 1909 4-8-13 **56**.....................(p) PhilipPrince(5) 11 64
(Anthony Carson) *chsd ldrs: wnt 2nd over 1f out: chal ins fnl f: kpt on same pce* **8/1**[3]
-400 **3** 3/4 **Whinging Willie (IRE)**[20] 1925 4-9-7 **59**......................... GeorgeBaker 8 65
(Gary Moore) *stdd s: hld up in rr: gd hdwy fr over 1f out: fin wl* **8/1**[3]
0330 **4** 1/2 **Irons On Fire (USA)**[22] 1877 5-8-2 **45**..........................(b) AmyScott(5) 3 50
(Alastair Lidderdale) *chsd ldrs: led after 3f: wnt 7 l clr 5f out: c bk to others over 1f out: hdd and no ex ins fnl f* **25/1**
4250 **5** 1/2 **Having A Ball**[13] 2159 9-8-12 **50**.. ChrisCatlin 4 54
(Geoffrey Deacon) *towards rr: hrd rdn and hdwy fr over 1f out: styd on* **8/1**[3]
5532 **6** 1 1/2 **Redoute Star (AUS)**[14] 2137 7-9-5 **57**.........................(v[1]) SebSanders 9 58
(Paul D'Arcy) *mid-div: effrt 2f out: styd on same pce* **9/2**[1]
6000 **7** 2 1/2 **Menadati (USA)**[10] 2273 5-9-1 **53**........................... WilliamCarson 16 50
(Peter Hiatt) *prom in chsng gp tl wknd and hung lft jst over 1f out* **12/1**
-043 **8** 3/4 **Finlodex**[15] 2072 6-9-3 **55**... ShaneKelly 5 50
(Murty McGrath) *s.s: hld up towards rr: rdn and styd on fnl 2f: nvr nrr* **12/1**
4643 **9** 1 **Dolly Colman (IRE)**[18] 1987 5-8-7 **45**......................(p) CathyGannon 10 38
(Zoe Davison) *chsd ldrs tl wknd jst over 1f out* **20/1**
365- **10** 1/2 **Rhossili Bay**[196] 7619 4-8-7 **50**.. RobertTart(5) 1 42
(Alastair Lidderdale) *mid-div: rdn and no imp fnl 2f* **8/1**[3]
0-00 **11** 1 **Highlife Dancer**[14] 2137 5-9-4 **56**................................ MatthewDavies 6 47
(Mick Channon) *mid-div: hrd rdn 3f out: sn outpcd* **20/1**
4153 **12** 1/2 **Strategic Action (IRE)**[22] 1873 4-9-3 **55**..................(t) SaleemGolam 2 45
(Linda Jewell) *chsd ldrs tl wknd 2f out* **16/1**
42-0 **13** 2 1/4 **Beacon Lady**[19] 1949 4-8-11 **54**............................... RachealKneller(5) 14 39
(William Knight) *a towards rr: bhd fnl 3f* **7/1**[2]
-600 **14** 17 **Bestfootforward**[21] 1916 4-8-7 **45**..................................(p) KierenFox 12
(Olivia Maylam) *led 3f: chsd ldrs tl wknd over 2f out* **50/1**
-66 **P** **Major Buckley (IRE)**[18] 1987 4-8-7 **45**.................................. MartinLane 7
(David Evans) *mid-div tl lost action and p.u 5f out: dismntd* **33/1**

2m 1.34s (-2.26) **Going Correction** -0.175s/f (Firm) **15** Ran SP% **125.8**
Speed ratings (Par 101): **102,101,100,100,99 98,96,95,95,94 93,93,91,78,**
toteswingers 1&2 £19.80, 1&3 £16.10, 2&3 £10.40 CSF £68.73 CT £545.80 TOTE £12.20: £2.50, £3.00, £4.00; EX 81.90 Trifecta £339.40 Pool: £2212.97 - 4.89 winning units..
Owner P Wheatley **Bred** Woodcote Stud Ltd **Trained** Epsom, Surrey
■ Stewards' Enquiry : Philip Prince three-day ban: careless riding (4-6 June)

FOCUS
A competitive contest, run at a stern pace. Obviously limited form.

2534 ATKINSONS CHARTERED ACCOUNTANTS' H'CAP 7f 214y
5:10 (5:10) (Class 6) (0-60,59) 4-Y-O+ **£1,940** (£577; £288; £144) **Stalls** Centre

Form RPR
60-0 **1** **Darnathean**[29] 1717 4-9-5 **57**..(p) SebSanders 13 68
(Paul D'Arcy) *prom: disp ld fr jst over 1f out: jst prevailed* **6/1**[2]
-000 **2** *nse* **Saint Irene**[19] 1950 4-9-7 **59**... DavidProbert 12 70
(Michael Blanshard) *trckd ldrs: disp ld fr jst over 1f out: r.o: jst pipped* **5/1**[1]
3534 **3** 1 3/4 **Fonterutoli (IRE)**[18] 1987 6-8-1 **46**...................(e) TomasHarrigan(7) 14 53
(Roger Ingram) *hld up in rr: hdwy in centre over 2f out: unable qck fnl f* **7/1**[3]
2312 **4** 1 **Hill Of Dreams (IRE)**[34] 1617 4-9-7 **59**..........................(b) EddieAhern 1 64
(Dean Ivory) *chsd ldrs: one pce appr fnl f* **8/1**
36-0 **5** 2 1/4 **Lightning Spirit**[30] 1740 5-9-2 **54**..........................(p) GeorgeBaker 6 53
(Gary Moore) *hld up in rr: gd hdwy on inner over 1f out: no ex fnl f* **5/1**[1]
4052 **6** 1 1/2 **Byrd In Hand (IRE)**[16] 2057 6-9-0 **52**............................ KieranO'Neill 4 48
(John Bridger) *led tl wknd jst over 1f out* **7/1**[3]
20-6 **7** 2 3/4 **Ermyn Flyer**[26] 1781 4-9-0 **52**.. IanMongan 2 42
(Pat Phelan) *in tch: rdn 3f out: sn outpcd* **7/1**[3]
000- **8** 1 1/4 **Devon Diva**[258] 5935 7-8-7 **45**... CathyGannon 15 32
(John Gallagher) *a abt same pl: hrd rdn and no prog fnl 3f* **25/1**
0203 **9** 1 1/2 **Indian Violet (IRE)**[18] 1981 7-9-3 **55**................................ LiamKeniry 16 38
(Zoe Davison) *hld up towards rr: pushed along 2f out: n.d* **20/1**
000- **10** 3 1/4 **Another Squeeze**[207] 7383 5-9-0 **52**............................. WilliamCarson 10 28
(Peter Hiatt) *prom tl wknd 2f out* **12/1**
53-0 **11** 3 **Trust Me Boy**[76] 903 5-8-9 **47**.................................... FrankieMcDonald 9 16
(John E Long) *mid-div: rdn 4f out: wknd over 2f out* **33/1**

1m 34.17s (-1.83) **Going Correction** -0.175s/f (Firm) **11** Ran SP% **115.5**
Speed ratings (Par 101): **102,101,100,99,96 95,92,91,89,86 83**
toteswingers 1&2 £7.10, 1&3 £8.80, 2&3 £9.10 CSF £34.47 CT £215.34 TOTE £9.10: £3.30, £2.40, £3.80; EX 47.20 Trifecta £402.60 Pool: £1734.79 - 3.23 winning units..
Owner K Snell **Bred** K Snell **Trained** Newmarket, Suffolk
■ Stewards' Enquiry : Seb Sanders two-day ban: use of whip (4-5 June)

FOCUS
A weak handicap, but it served up the best finish of the day. Straightforward form, rated around the front pair.
T/Plt: £128.60 to a £1 stake. Pool: £60,302.62 - 342.15 winning units T/Qpdt: £31.20 to a £1 stake. Pool: £4012.26 - 95.10 winning units LM

2161 NEWCASTLE (L-H)
Tuesday, May 21

OFFICIAL GOING: Soft (6.1)
Wind: Light, half behind Weather: Overcast

2535 JOHN SMITH'S / EBF MAIDEN STKS 5f
2:30 (2:30) (Class 5) 3-Y-O **£3,881** (£1,155; £577; £288) **Stalls** Low

Form RPR
0-53 **1** **Ichimoku**[18] 1988 3-9-5 49..(t) TomEaves 3 60
(Bryan Smart) *chsd ldr: rdn over 2f out: hdwy to ld ins fnl f: pushed out* **10/1**[3]
-0 **2** 2 3/4 **Spirit Of Parkes**[39] 1519 3-9-5 0.. RobertWinston 5 50
(Eric Alston) *led at decent gallop: rdn over 2f out: hdd ins fnl f: kpt on same pce* **14/1**
3034 **3** *shd* **Teetotal (IRE)**[15] 2076 3-9-5 61.. PaulMulrennan 1 50
(Nigel Tinkler) *in tch: rdn over 2f out: hdwy over 1f out: kpt on fnl f: nrst fin* **3/1**[2]
0 **4** 1 1/2 **The Nifty Blaze**[31] 1687 3-9-5 0.. DuranFentiman 7 46+
(Tim Easterby) *s.i.s: bhd and sn pushed along: hdwy over 1f out: kpt on: nvr nrr* **12/1**
03 **5** 3 1/4 **Assembly**[7] 2340 3-9-5 0.. GrahamLee 6 33
(William Haggas) *sn niggled along in rr: drvn along 1/2-way: no imp fr 2f out: btn fnl f* **8/13**[1]
50-0 **6** 11 **Sound Affects**[19] 1962 3-9-0 43.. DaleSwift 2
(Alan Brown) *chsd ldrs tl rdn and wknd fr 2f out* **100/1**

1m 4.65s (3.55) **Going Correction** +0.375s/f (Good) **6** Ran SP% **111.4**
Speed ratings (Par 99): **86,81,81,79,73 56**
toteswingers 1&2 £3.10, 1&3 £2.00, 2&3 £2.70 CSF £119.54 TOTE £9.60: £2.40, £4.70; EX 74.10 Trifecta £372.80 Pool: £2275.02 - 4.57 winning units..
Owner Crossfields Racing **Bred** Crossfields Bloodstock Ltd **Trained** Hambleton, N Yorks

FOCUS
Fresh ground after Winning Post and in back straight. Following 8.2mm of rain overnight, the ground had eased and was now soft all over (GoingStick 6.1). A weak maiden and a bit of a turn-up.

2536 JOHN SMITH'S EXTRA SMOOTH H'CAP (DIV I) 1m 3y(S)
3:00 (3:01) (Class 6) (0-60,60) 4-Y-O+ **£1,940** (£577; £288; £144) **Stalls** Low

Form RPR
4621 **1** **Royal Holiday (IRE)**[56] 1184 6-9-5 **58**........................(p) PhillipMakin 15 67
(Marjorie Fife) *in tch: rdn and hdwy to ld over 1f out: rdn and r.o wl fnl f* **6/1**[2]
0-64 **2** 1 1/4 **Dream Walker (FR)**[28] 1752 4-9-3 **56**.................................... DaleSwift 5 62
(Ian McInnes) *in tch: rdn over 3f out: rallied over 1f out: chsd wnr ins fnl f: kpt on* **11/1**
3-00 **3** 3/4 **Lord Franklin**[15] 2089 4-8-9 **53**................................... JasonHart(5) 6 58
(Eric Alston) *trckd ldrs: drvn and effrt over 2f out: kpt on ins fnl f* **11/2**[1]
0-30 **4** 1/2 **Wolf Heart (IRE)**[36] 1572 5-8-7 **49**................................. RaulDaSilva(3) 3 53
(Lucy Normile) *in tch: rdn and outpcd over 3f out: rallied 2f out: kpt on ins fnl f* **40/1**
4-00 **5** 3/4 **Loukoumi**[10] 2280 5-8-6 **52**.. GaryMahon(7) 14 54
(Tim Easterby) *midfield: effrt and rdn over 3f out: hdwy over 1f out: kpt on fnl f: nrst fin* **16/1**
4000 **6** 1 **Nonaynever**[14] 2130 5-8-6 **48**...(b) JulieBurke(3) 7 48
(Ruth Carr) *led in centre: rdn over 2f out: hdd over 1f out: rallied: one pce ins fnl f* **33/1**
0-00 **7** 2 1/4 **Madame Blavatsky (FR)**[8] 2316 5-9-0 **53**........................ GrahamLee 11 48
(Karen McLintock) *hld up: hdwy towards stands' side 2f out: kpt on fnl f: nvr able to chal* **10/1**
06-2 **8** 3/4 **Tectonic (IRE)**[11] 2219 4-9-1 **54**.. JoeFanning 16 47
(Keith Dalgleish) *in tch: effrt and carried hd high over 2f out: fdd over 1f out* **13/2**[3]
0030 **9** *nk* **Pelmanism**[10] 2280 6-9-7 **60**.. BarryMcHugh 8 52
(Brian Ellison) *bhd: rdn over 3f out: styd on fnl f: nvr able to chal* **11/1**
-052 **10** 1 1/2 **Tony Hollis**[18] 1994 5-8-4 **50**.. GemmaTutty(7) 10 39
(Karen Tutty) *prom: drvn and outpcd over 3f out: n.d after* **11/1**
500- **11** 3 1/4 **Galilee Chapel (IRE)**[178] 7869 4-8-11 **55**.................. GarryWhillans(5) 2 37
(Alistair Whillans) *midfield: drvn and outpcd 3f out: n.d after* **16/1**
000- **12** 1 **Ptolomeos**[187] 7731 10-8-1 **47**.. EvaMoscrop(7) 13 27
(Sean Regan) *taken early to post: bhd: rdn whn hung lft over 2f out: nvr on terms* **25/1**
6-05 **13** 1 1/2 **Iceblast**[18] 1994 5-9-4 **57**.. JamesSullivan 1 33
(Michael Easterby) *hld up: rdn 3f out: wknd over 1f out* **8/1**
0-50 **14** 23 **Ma Kellys (IRE)**[10] 2273 4-8-11 **50**................................(p) TomEaves 12
(Micky Hammond) *hld up: rdn and struggling 3f out: sn btn: t.o* **20/1**
34-0 **15** 6 **Blackamoor Harry**[13] 2168 4-8-7 **46** oh1.......................... DuranFentiman 4
(Richard Ford) *racd alone towards far side: in tch to 1/2-way: sn struggling: t.o* **20/1**

1m 45.64s (2.24) **Going Correction** +0.375s/f (Good) **15** Ran SP% **118.7**
Speed ratings (Par 101): **103,101,101,100,99 98,96,95,95,93 90,89,88,65,59**
toteswingers 1&2 £8.00, 1&3 £5.60, 2&3 £15.10 CSF £63.76 CT £396.65 TOTE £4.10: £1.40, £3.40, £3.20; EX 61.30 Trifecta £457.10 Pool: £2021.98 - 3.31 winning units..
Owner Mrs Marion Turner **Bred** E Tynan **Trained** Stillington, N Yorks

FOCUS
A moderate handicap. All bar one raced up the centre and few got into it from off the pace.

2537 JOHN SMITH'S EXTRA SMOOTH H'CAP (DIV II) 1m 3y(S)
3:30 (3:30) (Class 6) (0-60,58) 4-Y-O+ **£1,940** (£577; £216; £216) **Stalls** Low

Form RPR
3-55 **1** **Jupiter Fidius**[18] 1995 6-8-13 **57**............................(b[1]) GemmaTutty(7) 16 65
(Karen Tutty) *hld up in midfield: hdwy to ld over 1f out: edgd lft: kpt on wl fnl f* **7/1**[2]
-550 **2** 1/2 **Rasselas (IRE)**[26] 1788 6-9-4 **55**...............................(p) AdrianNicholls 1 62
(David Nicholls) *hld up: gd hdwy over 2f out: ev ch over 1f out to ins fnl f: one pce last 75yds* **15/2**[3]
0-40 **3** 1 3/4 **Remember Rocky**[26] 1790 4-8-9 **49**..........................(p) RaulDaSilva(3) 6 52
(Lucy Normile) *prom: rdn over 3f out: rallied: kpt on ins fnl f* **8/1**
5503 **3** *dht* **Lil Sophella (IRE)**[11] 2237 4-8-11 **48**.............................. PaddyAspell 15 51
(Patrick Holmes) *midfield: pushed along and hdwy over 2f out: kpt on ins fnl f* **20/1**
402- **5** 4 **Maggie Mey (IRE)**[220] 6105 5-8-13 **50**................................ GrahamLee 8 44
(Lawrence Mullaney) *hld up in tch: edgd to r alone far side fr 1/2-way: drvn and outpcd fr over 1f out* **8/1**
4341 **6** 1 **Monsieur Pontaven**[22] 1893 6-8-4 **48**........................(b) GaryMahon(7) 9 40
(Robin Bastiman) *hld up: gd hdwy to ld over 3f out: rdn and hdd over 1f out: sn btn* **17/2**
500- **7** *nk* **Tenacity**[253] 6102 4-9-1 **52**.. RobertWinston 14 43+
(Karen Tutty) *hld up: outpcd over 3f out: rallied fnl f: nvr rchd ldrs* **16/1**
-003 **8** *nk* **The Blue Banana (IRE)**[10] 2280 4-9-5 **56**.................(b) PaulMulrennan 5 47
(Edwin Tuer) *dwlt: hld up: effrt and hdwy over 2f out: rdn and no imp over 1f out* **11/2**[1]
-161 **9** 6 **Downtown Boy (IRE)**[29] 1730 5-9-2 **58**..............(p) GeorgeChaloner(5) 13 36
(Ray Craggs) *t.k.h: led to over 3f out: rdn and wknd 2f out* **7/1**[2]
400- **10** 4 1/2 **Naafetha (IRE)**[168] 7978 5-8-8 **45**.................................... JoeFanning 11 13
(Ian Semple) *bhd: drvn along 1/2-way: nvr rchd ldrs* **40/1**
4-06 **11** 1 3/4 **Garzoni**[13] 2162 4-9-4 **55**...(bt[1]) GrahamGibbons 3 19
(Tim Easterby) *midfield: outpcd over 3f out: sn n.d* **8/1**
0-00 **12** 1 1/4 **District Attorney (IRE)**[26] 1788 4-9-4 **55**...................... DuranFentiman 2 16
(Chris Fairhurst) *prom tl rdn and wknd over 2f out* **33/1**
4-00 **13** 1 1/2 **Regal Acclaim (IRE)**[29] 1734 4-9-2 **53**............................ DaleSwift 12 11
(Ian McInnes) *cl up: rdn over 3f out: wknd over 2f out* **14/1**

00-0 **14** 2 1/2 **Tukitinyasok (IRE)**[23] 7 6-9-3 **54**..............................(p) TomEaves 10 6
(Clive Mulhall) *w ldr to 1/2-way: wknd over 2f out* **33/1**
1m 45.84s (2.44) **Going Correction** +0.375s/f (Good) **14** Ran SP% **121.6**
Speed ratings (Par 101): **102,101,99,99,95 94,94,94,88,83 81,80,79,76**PL: LS £3.90, RR £1.40; Trifecta: JF/R/LS £375.10, JF/R/RR £375.10; Tricast: JF/R/LS £522.39, JF/R/RR £224.52; Toteswingers: JF/R £13.40, JF/LS £38.00, JF/RR £8.20, R/LS £19.20, R/RR £7.40 CSF £57.16 TOTE £10.90: £2.90, £3.00; EX 82.60 TRIFECTA Pool £1027 Owner.

FOCUS
The whole field raced as one group up the centre early this time. The winning time was 1/5 of a second slower than the first division.

2538 NEWCASTLE BROWN ALE MAIDEN STKS 1m 2f 32y
4:00 (4:02) (Class 5) 3-Y-O **£2,587** (£770; £384; £192) **Stalls** Centre

Form RPR
4-0 **1** **Hasheem**[13] 2151 3-9-5 0.. DaneO'Neill 1 77+
(Roger Varian) *t.k.h: early ldr: trckd ldrs: effrt over 2f out: rdn to ld 1f out: pushed out: comf* **6/5**[1]
2 2 3/4 **Arr' Kid (USA)** 3-9-5 0.. TomEaves 5 71
(Keith Dalgleish) *led at modest gallop: rdn and qcknd over 2f out: hdd 1f out: kpt on same pce* **28/1**
3-03 **3** 1 1/4 **Dark Ocean (IRE)**[16] 2041 3-9-5 69........................... MichaelO'Connell 2 69
(Jedd O'Keeffe) *hld up in tch: effrt and rdn over 2f out: kpt on fnl f: nt pce to chal* **8/1**
4 **4** 1 3/4 **Aramist (IRE)**[24] 1845 3-9-5 0.................................. RobertWinston 6 66
(Alan Swinbank) *t.k.h in rr: rdn along over 3f out: hdwy 2f out: kpt on fnl f: nrst fin* **7/2**[3]
0 **5** 4 **Sacred Square (GER)**[34] 1624 3-9-5 0.........................(v[1]) GrahamLee 4 58
(William Haggas) *t.k.h: in tch: rdn and wandered appr 2f out: sn outpcd* **16/1**
26-2 **6** 14 **Orions Hero (IRE)**[25] 1803 3-9-5 71.............................. TonyHamilton 3 33
(Richard Fahey) *sn chsng ldr: rdn and outpcd over 2f out: sn btn: lost tch fnl f* **3/1**[2]
0 **7** 5 **Missie Snaffles**[70] 972 3-9-0 0.. DaleSwift 7 19
(Ian McInnes) *bhd: rdn along over 4f out: wknd over 2f out: t.o* **150/1**
2m 18.75s (6.85) **Going Correction** +0.75s/f (Yiel) **7** Ran SP% **113.8**
Speed ratings (Par 99): **102,99,98,97,94 83,79**
toteswingers 1&2 £5.80, 1&3 £1.90, 2&3 £26.00 CSF £39.06 TOTE £1.90: £1.40, £2.40; EX 28.60 Trifecta £257.90 Pool: £2051.18 - 5.96 winning units..
Owner Hamdan Al Maktoum **Bred** Shadwell Estate Company Limited **Trained** Newmarket, Suffolk

FOCUS
An uncompetitive maiden.

2539 VERTEM H'CAP 1m 2f 32y
4:30 (4:30) (Class 4) (0-80,78) 4-Y-O+ **£4,690** (£1,395; £697; £348) **Stalls** Centre

Form RPR
/544 **1** **Arc Light (IRE)**[36] 1567 5-8-9 **66**.................................... DuranFentiman 4 73
(Tim Easterby) *t.k.h: hld up in tch: hdwy over 2f out: sn drvn along: led wl ins fnl f: kpt on wl* **6/1**[2]
130- **2** 1/2 **Triple Eight (IRE)**[246] 6313 5-8-12 **69** ow1............(b) MichaelO'Connell 7 75
(Philip Kirby) *t.k.h: trckd ldrs: smooth hdwy to ld over 2f out: sn rdn: hdd wl ins fnl f: kpt on* **33/1**
21-2 **3** 1 1/4 **Mean It (IRE)**[36] 1583 4-9-7 **78**... GrahamLee 6 82
(David Simcock) *plld hrd: hld up in tch: hdwy and cl up after 2f: rdn and outpcd over 2f out: rallied over 1f out: kpt on fnl f* **2/5**[1]
06-3 **4** 3/4 **I'm Super Too (IRE)**[13] 2163 6-9-4 **75**........................... RobertWinston 1 77
(Alan Swinbank) *prom: effrt and drvn over 2f out: one pce ins fnl f* **12/1**[3]
-500 **5** 1/2 **Morocco**[15] 2081 4-8-9 **66**... GrahamGibbons 8 68
(David O'Meara) *hld up in tch: rdn and outpcd over 2f out: rallied fnl f: nvr able to chal* **20/1**
4264 **6** 6 **Blue Maisey**[10] 2278 5-8-7 **64** oh1.................................. RoystonFfrench 3 55
(Edwin Tuer) *cl up: led after 1f and maintained slow pce: rdn and hdd over 2f out: wknd over 1f out* **16/1**
30-0 **7** 2 1/4 **Joshua The First**[16] 2042 4-8-11 **68**.................................... TomEaves 2 55
(Keith Dalgleish) *set slow pce 1f: chsd ldrs: lost pl over 2f out: sn struggling* **33/1**
2m 19.69s (7.79) **Going Correction** +0.75s/f (Yiel) **7** Ran SP% **109.9**
Speed ratings (Par 105): **98,97,96,96,95 90,89**
toteswingers 1&2 £9.50, 1&3 £1.60, 2&3 £4.50 CSF £151.29 CT £231.13 TOTE £6.90: £2.70, £7.00; EX 98.60 Trifecta £117.80 Pool: £2465.17 - 15.69 winning units..
Owner J Beamson **Bred** Monsieurs D Blot & Christian De Asis Trem **Trained** Great Habton, N Yorks

FOCUS
A fair handicap, but spoiled by a pedestrian early pace which caused several to pull hard. The winning time was nearly a second slower than the maiden.

2540 JOHN SMITH'S ESTB 1758 H'CAP 2m 19y
5:00 (5:00) (Class 5) (0-70,69) 4-Y-O+ **£2,587** (£770; £384; £192) **Stalls** Low

Form RPR
/20- **1** **Rock Relief (IRE)**[31] 4590 7-9-4 **63**.............................. PaulMulrennan 5 73
(Chris Grant) *trckd ldrs on ins: rdn over 2f out: effrt whn n.m.r briefly over 1f out: squeezed through on far rail to ld nr fin* **9/2**[2]
-002 **2** hd **Kodicil (IRE)**[14] 2120 5-8-13 **58**................................. GrahamGibbons 15 68
(Tim Walford) *led at stdy pce: pushed along over 3f out: rdn and qcknd over 2f out: edgd lft over 1f out: edgd rt ins fnl f: kpt on: hdd nr fin* **6/1**
-315 **3** 2 3/4 **Naburn**[13] 2165 5-9-5 **64**... RobertWinston 14 70
(Alan Swinbank) *t.k.h: hld up: hdwy and prom over 2f out: sn drvn along: kpt on same pce ins fnl f* **7/2**[1]
02-0 **4** 1 3/4 **Maska Pony (IRE)**[26] 1789 9-8-8 **53** ow1.............................. TomEaves 2 57
(George Moore) *hld up on outside: stdy hdwy 1/2-way: cl up 4f out: rdn and outpcd over 2f out: rallied over 1f out: one pce last 100yds* **10/1**
-611 **5** 3 **Jan Smuts (IRE)**[8] 2313 5-9-1 **60** 6ex...........................(tp) GrahamLee 11 61
(Wilf Storey) *hld up in tch: rdn and outpcd over 2f out: kpt on fnl f: nt pce to chal* **5/1**[3]
-004 **6** 4 **Beat The Shower**[11] 2242 7-9-2 **61**...................................... DaleSwift 17 57
(Peter Niven) *hld up: outpcd over 2f out: kpt on fnl f: n.d* **7/1**
24-0 **7** 1 1/4 **Tropenfeuer (FR)**[36] 1568 6-8-2 **50**................................ JulieBurke(3) 8 44
(James Moffatt) *t.k.h: prom: outpcd over 2f out: sn n.d* **20/1**
-501 **8** 1 1/4 **Mason Hindmarsh**[11] 2242 6-9-8 **67**................................. PhillipMakin 7 60
(Karen McLintock) *cl up tl rdn and wknd fr 2f out* **10/1**
30-6 **9** 5 **Ad Value (IRE)**[52] 1251 5-8-4 **56**...................................... KevinStott(7) 12 43
(Alan Kirtley) *hld up: rdn and struggling over 3f out: nvr on terms* **50/1**
250- **10** 10 **Luctor Emergo (IRE)**[30] 7380 4-9-1 **67**.................(p) GarryWhillans(5) 13 42
(Keith Dalgleish) *hld up on outside: struggling over 3f out: sn btn* **14/1**
54-2 **11** 11 **Destiny Awaits (IRE)**[133] 109 4-8-5 **52**...................(p) DuranFentiman 6 14
(Ian Semple) *hld up on ins: struggling over 3f out: sn btn* **33/1**
3m 49.81s (10.41) **Going Correction** +0.75s/f (Yiel)
WFA 4 from 5yo+ 2lb **11** Ran SP% **118.4**
Speed ratings (Par 103): **103,102,101,100,99 97,96,95,93,88 82**
toteswingers 1&2 £5.40, 1&3 £5.10, 2&3 £5.90 CSF £31.34 CT £106.38 TOTE £7.00: £2.80, £2.40, £2.20; EX 32.90 Trifecta £191.90 Pool: £1364.35 - 5.33 winning units..
Owner David Armstrong **Bred** Max Morris **Trained** Newton Bewley, Co Durham

FOCUS
A staying handicap hit by six non-runners and the pace wasn't strong.

2541 NEWCASTLE BROWN ALE 85TH BIRTHDAY H'CAP 7f
5:30 (5:30) (Class 3) (0-90,90) 4-Y-O+ **£7,439** (£2,213; £1,106; £553) **Stalls** Low

Form RPR
041- **1** **Amazing Amoray (IRE)**[252] 6119 5-8-12 **81**............. GrahamGibbons 7 93
(David Barron) *mde all: rdn 2f out: kpt on wl fnl f* **9/1**
3602 **2** 1 3/4 **Kingscroft (IRE)**[3] 2463 5-9-0 **83**................................ J-PGuillambert 10 90
(Mark Johnston) *sn niggled in rr: hdwy 2f out: chsd wnr ins fnl f: r.o* **6/1**[3]
001- **3** 1 1/2 **Diescentric (USA)**[180] 7826 6-9-6 **89**.......................... PaulMulrennan 12 92
(Julie Camacho) *hld up: smooth hdwy and prom 2f out: sn rdn: one pce fnl f* **9/1**
10-0 **4** 1 1/4 **Sam Nombulist**[8] 2310 5-9-3 **86**.................................(v) RobertWinston 9 86
(Richard Whitaker) *pressed wnr: rdn over 2f out: one pce fnl f* **10/1**
3100 **5** 1 1/2 **Chookie Royale**[11] 2240 5-9-2 **85**....................................(b[1]) TomEaves 8 81
(Keith Dalgleish) *prom: hdwy and ev ch over 1f out: outpcd ins fnl f* **22/1**
00-0 **6** 2 **Well Painted (IRE)**[10] 2254 4-9-7 **90**.................................(t) GrahamLee 4 81
(William Haggas) *prom: effrt and rdn over 2f out: no ex appr fnl f* **7/2**[1]
0100 **7** 1/2 **Gouray Girl (IRE)**[2] 2476 6-9-3 **86**.....................................(t) DaleSwift 11 75
(Brian Ellison) *hld up: hdwy over 2f out: outpcd over 1f out* **5/1**[2]
-020 **8** 19 **Xilerator (IRE)**[24] 1840 6-9-6 **89**..................................... AdrianNicholls 5 29
(David Nicholls) *t.k.h: prom tl wknd over 2f out: t.o* **8/1**
15-0 **9** 9 **Myboyalfie (USA)**[52] 1233 6-9-6 **89**.................................(v) DaneO'Neill 3
(J R Jenkins) *chsd ldrs: rdn 1/2-way: wknd over 2f out: t.o* **5/1**[2]
1m 29.03s (1.23) **Going Correction** +0.375s/f (Good) **9** Ran SP% **114.4**
Speed ratings (Par 107): **107,105,103,101,100 97,97,75,65**
toteswingers 1&2 £4.00, 1&3 £8.60, 2&3 £13.00 CSF £61.34 CT £504.15 TOTE £10.50: £3.70, £2.30, £2.90; EX 72.60 Trifecta £233.90 Pool: £1187.63 - 3.80 winning units..
Owner Raymond Miquel **Bred** Marie & Mossy Fahy **Trained** Maunby, N Yorks

FOCUS
A decent handicap and an all-the-way winner.

2542 SMOOTH AS SILKS FILLIES' H'CAP 5f
6:00 (6:02) (Class 5) (0-70,68) 3-Y-O+ **£2,587** (£770; £384; £192) **Stalls** Low

Form RPR
30-1 **1** **Gowanharry (IRE)**[31] 1681 4-9-11 **67**........................... PaulMulrennan 4 81
(Michael Dods) *mde all: rdn and hrd pressed fr 2f out: edgd lft ins fnl f: hld on wl u.p* **2/1**[1]
4321 **2** nk **Jofranka**[36] 1566 3-8-11 **61**.. GrahamGibbons 2 71
(David Barron) *w wnr: rdn 2f out: kpt on fnl f: hld towards fin* **5/2**[2]
15-6 **3** 2 3/4 **Ingenti**[7] 2338 5-9-4 **60**.. PaddyAspell 10 63
(Christopher Wilson) *hld up: hdwy to chse clr ldng pair over 1f out: kpt on same pce fnl f* **14/1**
3215 **4** 1 1/4 **Sunrise Dance**[13] 2166 4-9-5 **68**....................................... KevinStott(7) 7 67
(Robert Johnson) *chsd ldrs: rdn 2f out: kpt on same pce appr fnl f* **15/2**
-000 **5** 2 **Pivotal Prospect**[4] 2409 5-9-9 **65**................................ RoystonFfrench 5 56
(Tracy Waggott) *prom: effrt and pushed along over 2f out: wknd appr fnl f* **7/1**[3]
06-0 **6** 1 3/4 **Tongalooma**[27] 1758 7-9-4 **60**... GrahamLee 9 45
(James Moffatt) *hld up: rdn and outpcd 1/2-way: sme late hdwy: nvr rchd ldrs* **16/1**
1545 **7** 2 3/4 **Bailadeira**[35] 1596 5-8-12 **54** oh2.. TomEaves 3 29
(Tim Etherington) *taken early to post and unruly bef s: dwlt: sn pushed along in rr: rdn and sme hdwy over 1f out: sn btn* **25/1**
6352 **8** 3/4 **Charlemagne Diva**[14] 2133 3-8-2 **55** oh1 ow1.................... BillyCray(3) 1 24
(Richard Guest) *prom: drvn 1/2-way: wknd wl over 1f out* **16/1**
21-4 **9** 3/4 **Dream Vale (IRE)**[26] 1771 3-9-3 **67**............................... DuranFentiman 6 34
(Tim Easterby) *s.i.s: hld up: rdn 1/2-way: wknd over 1f out* **10/1**
1m 2.23s (1.13) **Going Correction** +0.375s/f (Good)
WFA 3 from 4yo+ 8lb **9** Ran SP% **117.5**
Speed ratings (Par 100): **105,104,100,98,94 92,87,86,85**
toteswingers 1&2 £2.10, 1&3 £7.50, 2&3 £9.30 CSF £7.20 CT £53.81 TOTE £2.90: £1.20, £1.70, £4.00; EX 9.30 Trifecta £74.10 Pool: £1699.06 - 17.17 winning units..
Owner Les Waugh **Bred** L Waugh **Trained** Denton, Co Durham

FOCUS
The two market leaders dominated this modest fillies' handicap throughout.
T/Jkpt: Not won. T/Plt: £619.70 to a £1 stake. Pool: £70,843.02 - 83.45 winning units T/Qpdt: £68.40 to a £1 stake. Pool: £5500.12 - 59.48 winning units RY

2267 NOTTINGHAM (L-H)
Tuesday, May 21

OFFICIAL GOING: Good to soft (good in places; 7.7)
Wind: Virtually nil Weather: Cloudy

2543 BRITISH STALLION STUDS E.B.F MAIDEN STKS 6f 15y
2:20 (2:23) (Class 5) 2-Y-O **£3,234** (£962; £481; £240) **Stalls** High

Form RPR
2 **1** **Windfast (IRE)**[16] 2048 2-9-5 0.. JimmyFortune 3 83+
(Brian Meehan) *mde all: shkn up ent fnl f: pushed out: readily* **1/4**[1]
2 1 1/4 **Mawfoor (IRE)** 2-9-5 0.. PaulHanagan 6 75+
(Brian Meehan) *chsd wnr: pushed along and sltly outpcd wl over 1f out: rdn and kpt on ins fnl f* **33/1**
3 1 3/4 **Brave Boy (IRE)** 2-9-5 0.. SilvestreDeSousa 1 70+
(Saeed bin Suroor) *green and wnt lft s: in rr: hdwy on outer 1/2-way: chsd wnr wl over 1f out: rdn and cl up ent fnl f: kpt on same pce* **12/1**[3]
4 1 1/2 **Cable Bay (IRE)** 2-9-5 0.. SteveDrowne 5 66
(Charles Hills) *trckd ldrs: pushed along over 2f out: rdn wl over 1f out: sn one pce* **25/1**
5 1/2 **Constantine** 2-9-5 0.. RichardHughes 4 64+
(Richard Hannon) *green and sltly hmpd s: t.k.h: hld up in rr: sme hdwy over 1f out: bttr for r* **5/1**[2]

4 **6** 2 ½ **My Little Friend**[14] 2131 2-9-5 0 .... NeilCallan 2 57
(Mark H Tompkins) *chsd wnr: rdn along over 2f out: sn edgd lft and wknd* **200/1**

1m 15.86s (1.16) **Going Correction** -0.075s/f (Good) **6** Ran SP% **111.6**
Speed ratings (Par 93): **89,87,85,83,82 79**
toteswingers 1&2 £3.20, 1&3 £1.40, 2&3 £5.80 CSF £15.00 TOTE £1.20: £1.10, £8.10; EX 9.60 Trifecta £51.60 Pool: £2417.54 - 35.10 winning units..
Owner Trelawny II **Bred** Airlie Stud **Trained** Manton, Wilts

FOCUS
All races on outer course. Only six runners, but this looked a good maiden. They raced up the middle.

2544 EAT IN OUR ROOFTOP RESTAURANT H'CAP (JOCKEY CLUB GRASSROOTS SPRINT SERIES QUALIFIER) 6f 15y
2:50 (2:51) (Class 5) (0-75,75) 3-Y-O **£2,587** (£770; £384; £192) **Stalls** High

Form RPR

1-10 **1** **Hartwright**[20] 1935 3-9-2 **70** .... TomQueally 12 81+
(Michael Bell) *led stands' side gp: cl up: rdn along 2f out: styd on to ld ins fnl f* **10/1**

3-32 **2** 3 **Seven Of Clubs (IRE)**[11] 2229 3-9-7 **75** ....(b) StevieDonohoe 5 77
(Noel Quinlan) *overall ldr far side: rdn 2f out: hung lft ent fnl f: sn hdd and no ex towards fin: 1st of 10 in gp* **14/1**

4232 **3** ½ **Indian Affair**[8] 2329 3-9-2 **70** .... RichardKingscote 15 70
(Milton Bradley) *hld up stands' side: hdwy 2f out: sn rdn and kpt on fnl f: 2nd of 5 in gp* **11/1**

5-00 **4** 1 ¾ **Khefyn (IRE)**[32] 1661 3-9-2 **70** ....(p) LukeMorris 2 65
(Ronald Harris) *chsd ldrs far side: hdwy 2f out: sn rdn and kpt on same pce fnl f: 2nd of 10 in gp* **33/1**

4-44 **5** 1 **Megamunch (IRE)**[8] 2329 3-9-2 **70** .... DavidNolan 16 62
(Kristin Stubbs) *trckd ldrs stands' side: effrt 2f out: sn swtchd lft and rdn: styd on fnl f: 3rd of 5 in gp* **9/1**

245 **6** ¾ **Guishan**[11] 2231 3-8-12 **66** .... AndrewMullen 9 56+
(Michael Appleby) *chsd ldrs far side: rdn along 2f out: no imp fr over 1f out: 3rd of 10 in gp* **22/1**

-015 **7** 3 **Lexington Place**[17] 2010 3-8-11 **65** ....(p) FrederikTylicki 3 46
(Richard Fahey) *prom far side: rdn along over 2f out: sn drvn and wknd wl over 1f out: 4th of 10 in gp* **8/1**[3]

1- **8** hd **Dark Opal (IRE)**[270] 5544 3-9-2 **73** .... MichaelMetcalfe(3) 14 53
(John Weymes) *chsd wnr stands' side: rdn along over 2f out: grad wknd: 4th of 5 in gp* **20/1**

30-0 **9** shd **Balinka**[15] 2076 3-9-0 **68** .... SilvestreDeSousa 11 48
(Mel Brittain) *chsd ldng pair stands' side: rdn along 2f out: sn wknd: last of 5 in gp* **16/1**

2152 **10** ¾ **Boxing Shadows**[15] 2076 3-9-1 **74** .... WilliamTwiston-Davies(5) 1 51
(Bryan Smart) *chsd ldrs far side: rdn along over 2f out: sn wknd: 5th of 10 in gp* **8/1**[3]

401- **11** 2 **Take The Lead**[204] 7433 3-9-0 **68** .... RichardHughes 4 39
(Richard Hannon) *chsd ldrs far side: rdn along over 2f out: sn wknd: 6th of 10 in gp* **6/1**[1]

212- **12** ¾ **Meet Me Halfway**[256] 6016 3-9-4 **72** .... SteveDrowne 8 41
(Chris Wall) *in tch far side: rdn along 2f out: sn wknd: 7th of 10 in gp* **25/1**

4502 **13** ¾ **Laudation**[14] 2135 3-8-13 **67** ....(v[1]) JimmyQuinn 6 34
(William Jarvis) *s.i.s: sme hdwy and in tch far side 1/2-way: rdn along over 2f out: sn wknd: 8th of 10 in gp* **15/2**[2]

-610 **14** 2 ½ **Jontleman (IRE)**[24] 1832 3-9-0 **68** .... MartinHarley 7 27
(Mick Channon) *a towards rr far side: 9th of 10 in gp* **14/1**

43-1 **15** nk **Two In The Pink (IRE)**[132] 114 3-8-11 **65** ....(t[1]) PaulHanagan 10 23
(Hugo Palmer) *a towards rr far side: last of 10 in gp* **14/1**

1m 14.48s (-0.22) **Going Correction** -0.075s/f (Good) **15** Ran SP% **117.5**
Speed ratings (Par 99): **98,94,93,91,89 88,84,84,84,83 80,79,78,75,74**
toteswingers 1&2 £41.90, 1&3 £41.70, 2&3 £9.40 CSF £131.14 CT £1601.77 TOTE £19.50: £5.10, £7.80, £4.30; EX 186.60 Trifecta £458.60 Part won. Pool: £611.55 - 0.60 winning units..
Owner Mrs L J Garton **Bred** New England Stud And Partners **Trained** Newmarket, Suffolk

FOCUS
A modest sprint handicap. They raced in two groups for much of the way but were spread across the track in the closing stages, and the winner raced stands' side while the runner-up was middle to far side.

2545 FIND NOTTINGHAM RACECOURSE ON FACEBOOK H'CAP 2m 9y
3:20 (3:21) (Class 5) (0-75,71) 4-Y-O+ **£2,587** (£770; £384; £192) **Stalls** Low

Form RPR

31-1 **1** **Albonny (IRE)**[20] 1927 4-9-2 **71** .... MichaelJMMurphy(5) 8 78
(Alan Jarvis) *hld up towards rr: gd hdwy 3f out: trckd ldrs over 2f out: rdn to chal over 1f out: led ins fnl f: sn drvn and edgd rt: kpt on gamely* **15/2**

01-1 **2** nk **Zarosa (IRE)**[36] 1572 4-8-4 **61** .... NoelGarbutt(7) 10 68
(John Berry) *in tch: hdwy on outer 4f out: cl up 3f out: rdn to ld wl over 1f out: drvn and hdd ins fnl f: kpt on wl u.p towards fin* **4/1**[1]

0/44 **3** ½ **Chapter Five**[32] 1664 6-8-7 **55** .... AndreaAtzeni 5 61
(Ian Williams) *in tch: hdwy over 3f out: rdn to chal over 1f out: drvn and ev ch ins fnl f: no ex towards fin* **8/1**

0511 **4** nse **Arashi**[15] 2087 7-9-3 **65** ....(v) MartinDwyer 4 72
(Derek Shaw) *hld up and bhd: stdy hdwy on inner 4f out: n.m.r and swtchd rt wl over 1f out: chsd ldrs ent fnl f: nt clr run and swtchd lft last 100yds: drvn and kpt on* **16/1**

1-32 **5** hd **Beyeh (IRE)**[18] 1979 5-9-0 **62** .... AndrewMullen 6 68
(Michael Appleby) *trckd ldrs: hdwy 4f out: sn cl up: led over 2f out and sn rdn: hdd and drvn wl over 1f out: no ex wl ins fnl f* **6/1**[2]

503- **6** ½ **Joe The Coat**[165] 8023 4-9-2 **66** .... NeilCallan 3 71
(Mark H Tompkins) *trckd ldrs: pushed along on inner and sltly outpcd over 2f out: rdn and hdwy over 1f out: sn swtchd rt and styng on whn nt clr run ins fnl f: swtchd rt again and nt clr run: hmpd nr fin* **14/1**

62-2 **7** 1 ¾ **Wily Fox**[42] 1445 6-8-10 **63** .... RyanTate(5) 1 66
(James Eustace) *hld up in rr: hdwy 3f out: rdn along 2f out: kpt on u.p fnl f: nrst fin* **10/1**

22-6 **8** 3 **Queen's Star**[12] 2197 4-8-12 **62** .... JimmyFortune 12 61
(Andrew Balding) *prom: led after 4f: rdn along over 3f out: hdd wl over 2f out: drvn and wknd appr fnl f* **7/1**[3]

211- **9** 3 ¾ **Ministerofinterior**[354] 1952 8-9-7 **69** ....(tp) FrederikTylicki 11 64
(Richard Ford) *trckd ldr: hdwy over 4f out and sn cl up: rdn along 4f out: wknd 3f out* **16/1**

6-46 **10** 17 **Cotton King**[11] 2205 6-9-9 **71** ....(p) PaulHanagan 7 46
(Lady Herries) *sn led: hdd after 4f: cl up on inner: rdn along 3f out: drvn over 2f out: sn wknd* **6/1**[2]

010- **11** 36 **Phantom Ranch**[265] 5744 4-8-4 **54** .... LukeMorris 2
(Alastair Lidderdale) *hld up towards rr: rdn along over 3f out: sn wknd: bhd and eased fnl 2f* **16/1**

3m 35.59s (1.09) **Going Correction** -0.075s/f (Good)
WFA 4 from 5yo+ 2lb **11** Ran SP% **117.4**
Speed ratings (Par 103): **94,93,93,93,93 93,92,90,88,80 62**
toteswingers 1&2 £3.00, 1&3 £5.70, 2&3 £17.60 CSF £37.47 CT £250.76 TOTE £4.90: £2.90, £1.40, £3.10; EX 39.50 Trifecta £395.30 Pool: £933.36 - 1.77 winning units..
Owner M&J Partnership **Bred** J Costello **Trained** Twyford, Bucks

FOCUS
The first six were covered by little more than a length, but the winner, runner-up and fourth had each won their last two starts and this isn't bad form.

2546 PLAN YOUR WEDDING AT NOTTINGHAM RACECOURSE FILLIES' H'CAP 1m 2f 50y
3:50 (3:50) (Class 4) (0-80,78) 3-Y-O **£6,469** (£1,925; £962; £481) **Stalls** Low

Form RPR

031- **1** **Kikonga**[252] 6117 3-9-4 **75** .... KirstyMilczarek 3 86+
(Luca Cumani) *trckd ldr: hdwy 3f out and sn cl up: rdn to ld over 1f out: edgd lft ins fnl f: sn clr: styd on* **5/2**[2]

15-3 **2** 3 **Pompeia**[29] 1725 3-9-7 **78** .... JimCrowley 2 83
(Ralph Beckett) *set stdy pce: hdd 1/2-way: chsd ldr: pushed along to ld wl over 2f out: sn rdn: hdd and drvn over 1f out: sn one pce* **8/11**[1]

0-25 **3** 7 **Lovesome**[31] 1698 3-9-3 **74** .... TomQueally 1 66
(Michael Bell) *dwlt: sn trcking ldng pair: pushed along and outpcd over 3f out: hdwy over 2f out: sn rdn and n.d* **9/1**[3]

0-44 **4** 6 **Dalaway (IRE)**[31] 1697 3-8-7 **64** oh3 .... SamHitchcott 4 44
(Mick Channon) *plld hrd: hld up in rr tl rapid hdwy on outer to ld 1/2-way: rdn along 3f out: sn hdd & wknd* **9/1**[3]

2m 18.14s (3.84) **Going Correction** -0.075s/f (Good) **4** Ran SP% **106.5**
Speed ratings (Par 98): **81,78,73,68**
CSF £4.65 TOTE £3.70; EX 4.10 Trifecta £6.20 Pool: £1301.29 - 157.32 winning units..
Owner Fittocks Stud **Bred** Fittocks Stud Ltd **Trained** Newmarket, Suffolk

FOCUS
This slowly run race rather set up for Kikonga, with Pompeia losing her easy lead to Dalaway.

2547 WATCH RACING UK ON FREEVIEW 231 MAIDEN STKS (DIV I) 1m 75y
4:20 (4:20) (Class 5) 3-Y-O **£3,234** (£962; £481; £240) **Stalls** Centre

Form RPR

0- **1** **Vitruvian Lady**[199] 7552 3-9-0 0 ....(t) StevieDonohoe 2 73+
(Noel Quinlan) *trckd ldrs on inner: hdwy and cl up 4f out: led 3f out: rdn clr appr fnl f: styd on wl* **28/1**

0- **2** 3 ¼ **Herod The Great**[252] 6114 3-9-5 0 .... FergusSweeney 10 71
(Alan King) *hld up towards rr: hdwy on wd outside 3f out: chsd ldrs 2f out: sn rdn to chal and ev ch: drvn and edgd lft ent fnl f: one pce* **50/1**

3 1 ¾ **Ducab (IRE)** 3-9-5 0 .... AndreaAtzeni 1 68+
(Roger Varian) *dwlt and towards rr: hdwy over 3f out: chsd ldrs 2f out: rdn wl over 1f out: kpt on same pce fnl f* **11/2**[3]

4 ½ **Ziekhani** 3-9-5 0 .... RobertHavlin 11 66
(Hughie Morrison) *in tch: hdwy to trck ldrs 1/2-way: cl up over 2f out: sn rdn and ev ch: drvn appr fnl f: sn one pce* **16/1**

5 nk **Red Red Wine** 3-9-5 0 .... JimCrowley 5 66+
(Hugo Palmer) *hld up towards rr: stdy hdwy on wd outside wl over 2f out: rdn to chse ldrs over 1f out: sn no imp* **9/1**

00 **6** 3 **Dalliefour (IRE)**[15] 2093 3-9-0 0 .... TomQueally 3 54+
(Michael Bell) *towards rr: hdwy on inner wl over 2f out: swtchd rt over 1f out: sn rdn and no imp* **25/1**

-2 **7** shd **Mawj Tamy (USA)**[21] 1904 3-9-5 0 .... PaulHanagan 12 59
(Charles Hills) *trckd ldr: cl up 3f out: sn rdn along: wknd fnl 2f* **11/4**[2]

0 **8** 9 **Switch On**[41] 1481 3-9-5 0 .... SteveDrowne 8 39
(Chris Wall) *a towards rr* **66/1**

9 8 **The Power Of One (IRE)** 3-9-5 0 .... FrederikTylicki 6 21
(James Given) *s.i.s: a bhd* **33/1**

06 **10** 3 ½ **Hypnotism**[21] 1896 3-9-5 0 .... LukeMorris 9 14
(Ronald Harris) *a towards rr* **66/1**

2 **11** nk **Reminisce (IRE)**[20] 1926 3-9-5 0 .... NeilCallan 4 13
(Marco Botti) *t.k.h: trckd ldrs: effrt over 3f out: sn rdn along and btn* **6/4**[1]

50 **12** 4 ½ **Misty Pearl**[24] 1828 3-9-0 0 .... SilvestreDeSousa 7
(Michael Appleby) *led: rdn along 4f out: hdd 3f out and sn wknd* **100/1**

1m 49.37s (0.37) **Going Correction** -0.075s/f (Good) **12** Ran SP% **114.1**
Speed ratings (Par 99): **95,91,90,89,89 86,86,77,69,65 65,60**
toteswingers 1&2 £103.40, 2&3 £36.40 CSF £930.06 TOTE £21.10: £4.20, £11.30, £1.60; EX 1394.00 Trifecta £1862.40 Part won. Pool: £2483.28 - 0.11 winning units..
Owner Iain O'Rourke **Bred** Plantation Stud **Trained** Newmarket, Suffolk

FOCUS
No more than a fair maiden.

2548 WATCH RACING UK ON FREEVIEW 231 MAIDEN STKS (DIV II) 1m 75y
4:50 (4:53) (Class 5) 3-Y-O **£3,234** (£962; £481; £240) **Stalls** Centre

Form RPR

3-32 **1** **Secret Art (IRE)**[18] 1977 3-9-5 79 .... JimCrowley 8 85+
(Ralph Beckett) *cl up: led over 3f out: pushed clr over 2f out: rdn over 1f out: kpt on* **8/11**[1]

0 **2** 1 ¾ **Cosseted**[11] 2231 3-9-0 0 .... SilvestreDeSousa 3 76+
(James Fanshawe) *hld up towards rr: pushed along on inner 3f out: nt clr run and swtchd wd to outer 2f out: sn rdn and styd on strly fnl f* **13/2**[3]

0 **3** 1 ¼ **Circus Turn (USA)**[31] 1679 3-9-5 0 .... JimmyFortune 6 78
(Sir Michael Stoute) *in tch: hdwy over 3f out: rdn to chse wnr over 1f out: drvn ent fnl f: sn one pce* **12/1**

6 **4** 3 ¾ **Magic Lando (FR)**[41] 1481 3-9-0 0 .... ThomasBrown(5) 4 70+
(Ismail Mohammed) *hld up towards rr: hdwy over 3f out: rdn to chse wnr wl over 1f out: sn drvn and one pce fnl f* **4/1**[2]

04 **5** 5 **Triple Aitch (USA)**[113] 425 3-9-5 0 .... JimmyQuinn 11 59
(Gay Kelleway) *t.k.h: in tch on outer: hdwy to chse wnr 3f out: rdn 2f out: sn edgd lft and grad wknd* **33/1**

05 **6** 8 **Xclusive**[18] 1975 3-9-5 0 .... LukeMorris 1 41
(Ronald Harris) *trckd ldrs: rdn along over 3f out: sn wknd* **50/1**

0 **7** 1 **Elusive Bleu (IRE)**[22] 1881 3-9-5 0 .... RichardKingscote 5 39
(Tom Dascombe) *dwlt: a towards rr* **66/1**

8 1 ½ **First Peninsular** 3-9-5 0 .... SteveDrowne 7 36
(Chris Wall) *chsd ldrs: rdn along wl over 2f out: sn wknd* **40/1**

9 13 **Speckled Hill** 3-9-5 0 .... AndreaAtzeni 10
(Ed Dunlop) *dwlt: a in rr* **20/1**

5- **10** *11* **Ritaach (IRE)**[342] 3046 3-9-0 0 .... FrederikTylicki 2
(Clive Brittain) *slt ld: rdn along and hdd over 3f out: sn wknd* **25/1**

1m 48.01s (-0.99) **Going Correction** -0.075s/f (Good) **10** Ran SP% **116.4**
Speed ratings (Par 99): **101,99,98,94,89 81,80,78,65,54**
toteswingers 1&2 £2.50, 2&3 £4.00, 1&3 £2.30 CSF £5.36 TOTE £1.80: £1.40, £1.10, £1.70; EX 6.90 Trifecta £29.40 Pool: £2743.34 - 69.79 winning units..
Owner Circuit Racing **Bred** Grange Stud **Trained** Kimpton, Hants

FOCUS
This looked a better race than the first division.

2549 ENJOY AFTERNOON TEA AT FRANKIES BISTRO CLASSIFIED STKS 1m 75y
5:20 (5:24) (Class 5) 3-Y-O **£2,587** (£770; £384; £192) **Stalls** Centre

Form RPR

-430 **1** **Mister Marcasite**[34] 1604 3-9-0 70 .... SilvestreDeSousa 5 76
(Mel Brittain) *cl up: led wl over 2f out: rdn wl over 1f out: drvn ins fnl f: kpt on wl* **7/1**[3]

04-6 **2** *1 ½* **Plenum (GER)**[8] 2324 3-9-0 70 .... MartinDwyer 8 72+
(David Lanigan) *hld up towards rr: hdwy over 3f out: effrt to chse ldrs 2f out: rdn to chse wnr over 1f out: drvn ins fnl f: no imp towards fin* **4/1**[2]

0140 **3** *¾* **Red To Amber (IRE)**[11] 2209 3-9-0 70 .... (b[1]) JohnFahy 4 71
(Clive Cox) *dwlt and towards rr: hdwy 3f out: swtchd rt and rdn over 1f out: styd on wl fnl f* **18/1**

63-3 **4** *¾* **Ersaal**[13] 2167 3-9-0 70 .... (p[1]) PaulHanagan 2 69
(Roger Varian) *led: pushed along 4f out: rdn 3f out: sn hdd and rdn: drvn and one pce appr fnl f* **5/2**[1]

213 **5** *hd* **King Bertie (IRE)**[41] 1476 3-9-0 70 .... RobertHavlin 11 69
(Peter Chapple-Hyam) *t.k.h early: in tch: hdwy on outer 3f out: chsd ldrs over 2f out: sn rdn and kpt on same pce fnl f* **10/1**

1-50 **6** *4* **Mandy's Boy (IRE)**[24] 1829 3-8-11 70 .... DarrenEgan[(3)] 9 60
(Patrick Morris) *dwlt and towards rr: hdwy on outer 5f out: rdn to chse ldrs wl over 2f out: drvn and no imp appr fnl f* **25/1**

42-4 **7** *1 ¼* **Dark Templar**[20] 1928 3-9-0 70 .... (e[1]) JimmyFortune 6 57
(Ed Vaughan) *dwlt and in rr: hdwy on wd outside 3f out: rdn along over 2f out: sn no imp* **18/1**

4-22 **8** *nse* **Poor Duke (IRE)**[8] 2324 3-9-0 70 .... FergusSweeney 7 57
(Jamie Osborne) *trckd ldrs: rdn along over 3f out: sn wknd* **4/1**[2]

6656 **9** *¾* **East Texas Red (IRE)**[4] 2420 3-9-0 66 .... PatCosgrave 1 55
(Mick Quinn) *trckd ldng pair: rdn along 3f out: grad wknd* **33/1**

42-0 **10** *14* **Khelac**[29] 1725 3-9-0 69 .... (t) JimCrowley 3 24
(Philip Hide) *midfield: rdn along on inner over 3f out: sn wknd* **22/1**

16-0 **11** *1* **Red Eight (USA)**[19] 1965 3-9-0 69 .... (p) TomQueally 10 22
(John Butler) *chsd ldng pair: rdn along over 3f out: sn wknd* **66/1**

1m 47.94s (-1.06) **Going Correction** -0.075s/f (Good) **11** Ran SP% **113.3**
Speed ratings (Par 99): **102,100,99,99,98 94,93,93,92,78 77**
toteswingers 1&2 £6.50, 1&3 £13.50, 2&3 £13.00 CSF £32.49 TOTE £8.00: £2.70, £1.90, £3.20; EX 42.20 Trifecta £540.60 Pool: £2035.56 - 2.82 winning units..
Owner Steven J Box **Bred** Aiden Murphy **Trained** Warthill, N Yorks

FOCUS
The time was quicker than both divisions of the maiden and this form looks reasonable for the class.

2550 JOIN US FOR FAMILY FUN DAY H'CAP 5f 13y
5:50 (5:51) (Class 5) (0-75,74) 4-Y-O+ **£2,587** (£770; £384; £192) **Stalls** High

Form RPR

0-65 **1** **Monsieur Jamie**[6] 2364 5-8-13 66 .... (v) JimmyFortune 11 74
(J R Jenkins) *trckd ldng pair stands' rail: hdwy over 1f out: rdn to chal ent fnl f: drvn and led last 100yds:* **8/1**

0-14 **2** *1 ¼* **Monnoyer**[19] 1952 4-9-0 67 .... (be) LukeMorris 2 71
(Scott Dixon) *cl up centre: rdn wl over 1f out: drvn and ev ch ins fnl f: nt qckn last 100yds: 1st of 10 in gp* **9/1**

5200 **3** *nk* **Royal Bajan (USA)**[14] 2122 5-9-2 69 .... (b) FrederikTylicki 13 71
(James Given) *overall ldr stands' rail: rdn along wl over 1f out: drvn ent fnl f: hdd and no ex last 100yds: 2nd of 3 in gp* **14/1**

21-5 **4** *nse* **Passionada**[120] 308 4-9-1 68 .... SeanLevey 5 70
(Ed McMahon) *cl up centre: led that gp over 2f out and ev ch tl rdn and one pce ins fnl f: 2nd of 10 in gp* **7/1**[2]

5220 **5** *1 ½* **Falasteen (IRE)**[19] 1952 6-9-2 69 .... RichardKingscote 4 66
(Milton Bradley) *half-rrd s: sn led centre gp: rdn along 1/2-way and sn hdd: drvn and one pce appr fnl f: 3rd of 10 in gp* **16/1**

-060 **6** *hd* **Sleepy Blue Ocean**[10] 2275 7-8-13 66 .... (p) JimCrowley 12 67+
(John Balding) *trckd ldr stands' rail: cl up 2f out: rdn over 1f out and ev ch tl drvn and wknd jst ins fnl f: last of 3 in gp* **14/1**

004 **7** *¾* **Quality Art (USA)**[10] 2268 5-8-7 60 .... RobbieFitzpatrick 1 53
(Richard Guest) *s.i.s and towards rr centre: hdwy on wd outside over 2f out: rdn to chse ldrs over 1f out: drvn and wknd ent fnl f: 4th of 10 in gp* **16/1**

-116 **8** *nse* **Alpha Delta Whisky**[25] 1814 5-9-0 72 .... MichaelJMMurphy[(5)] 9 65
(John Gallagher) *chsd ldrs centre: rdn along 2f out: drvn and edgd lft ent fnl f: no imp: 5th of 10 in gp* **3/1**[1]

1050 **9** *nk* **Ivestar (IRE)**[88] 760 8-8-6 62 .... (vt) RossAtkinson[(3)] 3 54
(Michael Easterby) *towards rr centre: hdwy 2f out: sn rdn and kpt on fnl f: nt rch ldrs: 6th of 10 in gp* **9/1**

4102 **10** *1 ¼* **Shawkantango**[48] 1331 6-9-3 70 .... (v) SilvestreDeSousa 7 58
(Derek Shaw) *sltly hmpd s: sn outpcd and bhd: rdn and hung rt bef 1/2-way: sme late hdwy: 7th of 10 in gp* **9/1**

-521 **11** *½* **Danzoe (IRE)**[14] 2132 6-9-4 74 .... DarrenEgan[(3)] 10 60
(Christine Dunnett) *racd towards centre: towards rr: rdn 2f out: drvn wl over 1f out: nvr a factor: 8th of 10 in gp* **15/2**[3]

0-00 **12** *2* **El McGlynn (IRE)**[13] 2173 4-8-11 71 .... HannahNunn[(7)] 8 50
(William Kinsey) *cl up centre: rdn 2f out: wknd over 1f out: 9th of 10 in gp* **22/1**

0430 **13** *1 ½* **Charming (IRE)**[19] 1952 4-8-12 65 .... (e) TomQueally 6 38
(Olivia Maylam) *racd in centre: towards rr fr 1/2-way: last of 10 in gp* **25/1**

1m 0.52s (-0.98) **Going Correction** -0.075s/f (Good) **13** Ran SP% **116.6**
Speed ratings (Par 103): **104,102,101,101,99 98,97,97,96,94 94,90,88**
toteswingers 1&2 £10.20, 1&3 £24.70, 2&3 £23.50 CSF £74.42 CT £1025.55 TOTE £10.90: £3.60, £4.00, £5.40; EX 115.30 Trifecta £1038.80 Part won. Pool: £1385.17 - 0.32 winning units..
Owner Mark Goldstein & Stephen Pettman **Bred** Greg Parsons **Trained** Royston, Herts
■ Stewards' Enquiry : Jimmy Fortune two-day ban: (4-5 June)

FOCUS
Much like in the earlier sprint handicap, there were two groups and the winner came from the smaller bunch on the stands' side, but there didn't look a great deal in it.
T/Plt: £432.30 to a £1 stake. Pool: £48,859.89 - 82.50 winning units T/Qpdt: £48.40 to a £1 stake. Pool: £3415.97 - 52.20 winning units JR

1930 PONTEFRACT (L-H)
Tuesday, May 21

OFFICIAL GOING: Good (8.0)
Wind: light 1/2 behind Weather: overcast

2551 REAL RADIO SINGLES NIGHT H'CAP 1m 4y
6:20 (6:20) (Class 5) (0-75,75) 4-Y-O+ **£3,234** (£962; £481; £240) **Stalls** Low

Form RPR

0-06 **1** **Hakuna Matata**[13] 2163 6-8-6 67 .... (b) ConnorBeasley[(7)] 8 79
(Michael Dods) *rr-div: hdwy over 2f out: led jst ins fnl f: edgd lft: forged clr* **14/1**

0556 **2** *2 ½* **Seattle Drive (IRE)**[15] 2078 5-9-6 74 .... RyanMoore 5 81
(Brian Ellison) *mid-div: hdwy over 2f out: led briefly 1f out: styd on same pce* **7/2**[1]

5525 **3** *2 ¼* **Sardanapalus**[10] 2278 4-9-7 75 .... (p) NeilCallan 1 81
(Kevin Ryan) *trckd ldrs: nt clr run on inner over 1f out: swtchd rt and kpt on same pce* **7/2**[1]

242- **4** *½* **Christmas Light**[185] 7530 6-9-2 70 .... RichardHughes 9 70
(Brian Ellison) *in rr: hdwy 2f out: styd on fnl f* **9/2**[2]

0-00 **5** *2 ¼* **Croquembouche (IRE)**[26] 1796 4-9-4 75 .... LeeTopliss[(3)] 7 71
(Ed de Giles) *trckd ldr: led over 2f out: hdd over 1f out: wknd fnl 150yds* **12/1**

-000 **6** *1 ½* **Ellaal**[10] 2278 4-9-1 69 .... JamesSullivan 13 61
(Ruth Carr) *mid-div: hdwy over 2f out: chsng ldrs over 1f out: sn wknd* **40/1**

00-5 **7** *nk* **Sareeah (IRE)**[17] 2026 4-8-7 66 .... DavidBergin[(5)] 12 58
(David O'Meara) *trckd ldrs: led over 1f out: sn hdd: wknd ins fnl f* **20/1**

04-0 **8** *2 ¼* **Save The Bees**[20] 1932 5-8-9 66 .... NeilFarley[(3)] 3 53
(Declan Carroll) *chsd ldrs: wknd over 1f out* **9/1**

2000 **9** *½* **Violent Velocity (IRE)**[31] 1693 10-8-13 67 .... MickyFenton 4 52
(John Quinn) *chsd ldrs: wknd over 1f out* **40/1**

05-0 **10** *5* **Striker Torres (IRE)**[22] 1886 7-8-7 61 oh1 .... (v) AndrewElliott 10 35
(Ian McInnes) *n.m.r after s: in rr: sme hdwy over 2f out: sn wknd* **22/1**

0113 **11** *46* **Thrust Control (IRE)**[15] 2081 6-8-7 61 .... (p) BarryMcHugh 2
(Tracy Waggott) *led: hdd over 2f out: lost pl wl over 1f out: sn bhd and heavily eased: t.o* **11/2**[3]

1m 43.76s (-2.14) **Going Correction** -0.25s/f (Firm) **11** Ran SP% **116.4**
Speed ratings (Par 103): **100,97,95,94,92 91,90,88,87,82 36**
toteswingers 1&2 £10.10, 1&3 £7.60, 2&3 £3.60 CSF £59.62 CT £217.28 TOTE £14.20: £3.00, £1.50, £1.90; EX 84.30 Trifecta £398.80 Pool: £934.71 - 1.75 winning units..
Owner Sekura Group **Bred** Mrs J A Chapman **Trained** Denton, Co Durham

FOCUS
The ground looked in decent nick in the opener. It was run at a solid pace and suited those given waiting rides, which is often not the case at this venue.

2552 TOTEPOOL FAMILY DAY ON 23RD JUNE H'CAP 1m 4f 8y
6:50 (6:50) (Class 4) (0-80,80) 4-Y-O+ **£5,175** (£1,540; £769; £384) **Stalls** Low

Form RPR

3323 **1** **Arizona John (IRE)**[10] 2277 8-9-2 75 .... FrannyNorton 2 85
(John Mackie) *trckd ldrs: effrt over 1f out: led ins last 100yds: styd on* **11/4**[1]

4-00 **2** *1 ¾* **Getabuzz**[31] 1689 5-9-5 78 .... JamesSullivan 1 85
(Tim Easterby) *trckd ldrs: t.k.h: led over 1f out: hdd and no ex ins fnl f* **17/2**[3]

21-0 **3** *5* **Major Domo (FR)**[10] 2277 5-8-9 68 .... RussKennemore 4 67+
(Micky Hammond) *hld up in rr: hdwy on ins over 2f out: kpt on to take 3rd clsng stages* **16/1**

425- **4** *1* **Watts Up Son**[222] 7002 5-9-1 79 .... JasonHart[(5)] 3 76
(Declan Carroll) *led: clr after 2f: hdd over 1f out: one pce* **14/1**

0-40 **5** *1 ¼* **Daring Indian**[29] 1733 5-8-12 71 .... AndreaAtzeni 9 66
(Ian Williams) *chsd ldrs: one pce appr fnl f* **11/4**[1]

00-0 **6** *4* **My Guardian Angel**[28] 1753 4-8-6 68 .... SimonPearce[(3)] 6 57
(Mark H Tompkins) *chsd ldrs: drvn 3f out: sn outpcd: one pce over 1f out* **20/1**

00-0 **7** *1* **Persian Peril**[16] 2040 9-9-7 80 .... NeilCallan 8 67
(Alan Swinbank) *t.k.h in rr: drvn over 4f out: sme hdwy over 1f out: nvr a factor* **20/1**

8 *2* **Kandari (FR)**[66] 9-9-4 77 .... RichardHughes 11 61
(Jonjo O'Neill) *hld up in mid-div: hdwy over 2f out: wknd appr fnl f: eased towards fin* **11/2**[2]

4554 **9** *14* **Sir Boss (IRE)**[15] 2102 8-8-11 75 .... NatashaEaton[(5)] 5 37
(Michael Mullineaux) *mid-div: hdwy on outside to chse ldrs 3f out: wknd over 1f out: eased ins fnl f: b.b.v* **11/1**

410- **10** *59* **Fossgate**[270] 5546 12-9-0 73 .... AmyRyan 7
(James Bethell) *in rr: effrt 3f out: nvr on terms: eased fnl f: virtually p.u: hopelessly t.o* **25/1**

2m 36.3s (-4.50) **Going Correction** -0.25s/f (Firm) **10** Ran SP% **113.5**
Speed ratings (Par 105): **105,103,100,99,99 96,95,94,85,45**
toteswingers 1&2 £6.00, 1&3 £10.30, 2&3 £23.80 CSF £25.59 CT £311.15 TOTE £3.60: £1.60, £2.90, £4.50; EX 22.90 Trifecta £183.50 Pool: £951.80 - 3.88 winning units..
Owner Derbyshire Racing **Bred** Abergwaun Farms **Trained** Church Broughton , Derbys

FOCUS
Few got seriously into modest handicap.

2553 YOUNGSTERS CONDITIONS STKS 6f
7:20 (7:20) (Class 2) 2-Y-O
£9,337 (£2,796; £1,398; £699; £349; £175) **Stalls** Low

Form RPR

13 **1** **Master Carpenter (IRE)**[20] 1917 2-8-12 0 .... AndreaAtzeni 4 84
(Rod Millman) *led tl over 1f out: regained ld jst ins fnl f: won gng away* **11/4**[2]

01 **2** *1 ¾* **Malachim Mist (IRE)**[12] 2194 2-8-12 0 .... RichardHughes 2 79
(Richard Hannon) *dwlt: sn w ldr: narrow ld over 1f out: hdd jst ins fnl f: kpt on same pce* **1/2**[1]

4512 **3** *1 ¼* **Scargill**[15] 2068 2-8-12 0 .... RyanMoore 3 75
(Brian Ellison) *t.k.h: trckd ldrs: hung lft over 2f out: kpt on to take 3rd clsng stages* **16/1**

3163 **4** *½* **Intense Feeling (IRE)**[13] 2147 2-8-7 0 .... FrannyNorton 1 69
(David Evans) *chsd ldrs: kpt on same pce over 1f out* **11/1**[3]

03 **5** *10* **Lendal Bridge**[8] 2314 2-8-12 0 .... BarryMcHugh 8 44
(Tony Coyle) *chsd ldrs: drvn over 2f out: lost pl over 1f out* **100/1**

6 2 1/4 **Fire Fighting (IRE)** 2-8-9 0 .... JoeFanning 5 34
(Mark Johnston) *chsd ldrs on outer: drvn over 2f out: wknd over 1f out* **12/1**

7 1 1/4 **Barbara Elizabeth** 2-8-4 0 .... JamesSullivan 6 25
(Tony Coyle) *sn outpcd in rr: bhd fnl 2f* **100/1**

10 8 3 3/4 **Sleepy Joe (IRE)**[13] 2147 2-8-12 0 .... MartinHarley 7 22
(Mick Channon) *chsd ldrs on outer: t.k.h: drvn over 2f out: lost pl over 1f out* **14/1**

1m 16.18s (-0.72) **Going Correction** -0.075s/f (Good) **8** Ran SP% **123.9**
Speed ratings (Par 99): **101,98,97,96,83 80,78,73**
toteswingers 1&2 £1.30, 2&3 £2.20, 1&3 £2.50 CSF £4.85 TOTE £3.70: £1.10, £1.02, £3.20; EX 6.00 Trifecta £20.40 Pool: £1208.25 - 44.25 winning units..
Owner The Links Partnership **Bred** Naiff Sa & Newtown Stud **Trained** Kentisbeare, Devon

FOCUS
This looked a useful 2yo contest.

2554 TONY LEWIS & OUR BEST PAL H'CAP — 1m 4y
7:50 (7:50) (Class 4) (0-85,82) 3-Y-O — **£5,175** (£1,540; £769; £384) **Stalls** Low

Form — RPR

2-1 1 **Stepping Ahead (FR)**[41] 1481 3-9-2 **77** .... MartinHarley 2 96+
(Mrs K Burke) *trckd ldrs: effrt over 2f out: led jst ins fnl f: wnt clr: v readily* **5/1**[2]

14-6 2 7 **Mystical Man**[60] 1109 3-9-5 **80** .... NeilCallan 3 82
(James Tate) *led: t.k.h: qcknd pce over 2f out: hdd jst ins fnl f: no ch w wnr* **40/1**

1-52 3 1 3/4 **Greeleys Love (USA)**[8] 2322 3-9-3 **78** ....(b[1]) JoeFanning 5 76
(Mark Johnston) *s.i.s: sn trcking ldrs: t.k.h: effrt over 3f out: outpcd over 2f out: kpt on fnl f: tk modest 3rd towards fin* **5/1**[2]

21-1 4 hd **Mission Approved**[19] 1958 3-9-7 **82** .... RyanMoore 1 79
(Sir Michael Stoute) *hld up: t.k.h: effrt over 2f out: sn drvn: wknd fnl f* **8/11**[1]

1-13 5 22 **Melvin The Grate (IRE)**[41] 1477 3-9-7 **82** .... RichardHughes 4 31
(Andrew Balding) *chsd ldrs: effrt over 2f out: hung bdly rt over 1f out: racd stands' side and eased last 100yds: t.o* **11/2**[3]

1m 43.43s (-2.47) **Going Correction** -0.25s/f (Firm) **5** Ran SP% **109.1**
Speed ratings (Par 101): **102,95,93,93,71**
CSF £95.05 TOTE £4.80: £1.60, £9.30; EX 108.90 Trifecta £584.10 Pool: £814.78 - 1.04 winning units..
Owner Mark James & Mrs Elaine Burke **Bred** S C E A Haras De Manneville **Trained** Middleham Moor, N Yorks

FOCUS
A good-quality little 3yo handicap.

2555 RACING UK ON SKY CHANNEL 432 FILLIES' H'CAP — 1m 2f 6y
8:20 (8:22) (Class 5) (0-70,69) 3-Y-O+ — **£3,234** (£962; £481; £240) **Stalls** Low

Form — RPR

01-3 1 **Mad Jazz**[46] 1365 3-8-11 **66** .... BarryMcHugh 4 76+
(Tony Coyle) *led tl over 4f out: led 2f out: wnt clr fnl f: eased towards fin* **5/1**[3]

360- 2 4 **Reset City**[253] 6098 7-9-6 **61** .... JoeFanning 5 65
(Mark Johnston) *trckd ldrs: t.k.h: upsides after 3f: led over 4f out: hdd 2f out: kpt on same pce appr fnl f* **9/1**

41-4 3 1/2 **Magika**[20] 1923 3-8-13 **68** ....(t) AndreaAtzeni 2 70+
(Marco Botti) *swtchd rt after s: sn trcking ldrs: n.m.r over 2f out and appr fnl f: styd on to take 3rd nr fin* **5/2**[1]

-056 4 nk **Croftamie**[26] 1790 4-9-0 **55** oh2 ....(p) RoystonFfrench 3 58
(Tracy Waggott) *edgd lft after s: chsd ldrs: kpt on same pce appr fnl f* **20/1**

055- 5 nk **Nullarbor Sky (IRE)**[201] 7505 3-8-5 **60** .... FrannyNorton 12 61
(Lucy Wadham) *swtchd lft after s: chsd ldrs: drvn over 3f out: one pce over 1f out* **9/2**[2]

115- 6 1 3/4 **Isdaal**[329] 3472 6-9-9 **69** .... GeorgeChaloner(5) 10 68+
(Kevin Morgan) *swtchd lft s: towards rr: styd on fnl f* **25/1**

00-3 7 5 **Ailsa Craig (IRE)**[26] 1775 7-9-3 **58** .... PaulMulrennan 11 48
(Edwin Tuer) *swtchd lft after s: trckd ldrs: wknd fnl 150yds* **8/1**

6024 8 nk **Dutch Delight**[7] 2341 3-8-0 **55** oh6 .... JamesSullivan 8 43
(Tony Coyle) *dwlt: mid-div: outpcd over 2f out: sme hdwy and hung rt 1f out: nvr a threat* **50/1**

235- 9 1 1/4 **Kathlatino**[185] 4683 6-9-2 **57** .... RyanMoore 6 44
(Micky Hammond) *in rr: rdn over 2f out: nvr on terms* **12/1**

3-00 10 3/4 **Elizabeth Coffee (IRE)**[113] 429 5-9-4 **62** .... MichaelMetcalfe(3) 1 48
(John Weymes) *mid-div: effrt on inner 3f out: wknd fnl f* **25/1**

2-00 11 nk **Maybeagrey**[26] 1774 4-9-9 **69** .... DarylByrne(5) 13 54
(Tim Easterby) *mid-div on outer: drvn and sme hdwy over 3f out: lost pl over 1f out* **14/1**

64-0 12 7 **Painted Tail (IRE)**[11] 2220 6-9-13 **68** .... RobertWinston 9 41
(Alan Swinbank) *sn bhd and pushed along: hdwy on outside over 5f out: chsng ldrs over 3f out: lost pl over 1f out* **20/1**

624- 13 2 3/4 **Echo Of Footsteps**[240] 6516 4-9-5 **60** .... TomEaves 7 28
(Michael Herrington) *mid-div: drvn and hdwy on inner 3f out: wknd over 1f out* **33/1**

2m 13.26s (-0.44) **Going Correction** -0.25s/f (Firm)
WFA 3 from 4yo+ 14lb **13** Ran SP% **121.0**
Speed ratings (Par 100): **91,87,87,87,86 85,81,81,80,79 79,73,71**
toteswingers 1&2 £17.00, 1&3 £1.50, 2&3 £9.80 CSF £45.14 CT £141.11 TOTE £5.20: £1.80, £3.00, £1.60; EX 58.00 Trifecta £211.10 Pool: £1031.32 - 3.66 winning units..
Owner Brian Kerr & Chris Green & Tony Coyle **Bred** Usk Valley Stud **Trained** Norton, N Yorks

FOCUS
This moderate fillies' handicap was run at an uneven pace and those held up couldn't land a blow.

2556 PONTEFRACT'S GOT TALENT - FRIDAY EVENING 7TH JUNE MAIDEN STKS — 6f
8:50 (8:51) (Class 5) 3-Y-O — **£3,234** (£962; £481; £240) **Stalls** Low

Form — RPR

2 1 **Duke Cosimo**[10] 2267 3-9-5 0 .... RyanMoore 2 70+
(Sir Michael Stoute) *led: shkn up over 1f out: sn 3 l clr: v readily* **1/5**[1]

6- 2 3 **Timeless Appeal (IRE)**[181] 7813 3-9-0 0 .... RobertHavlin 3 53+
(Peter Chapple-Hyam) *stdd s: t.k.h: nt clr run over 2f out: edgd rt over 1f out: styd on to take 2nd nr fin* **13/2**[2]

0-50 3 3/4 **Another Claret**[24] 1829 3-8-12 60 .... LauraBarry(7) 5 54
(Richard Fahey) *w wnr: kpt on same pce over 1f out* **14/1**[3]

00-3 4 shd **Secret Empress**[49] 1305 3-9-0 50 .... TomEaves 1 48
(Bryan Smart) *dwlt: sn trcking ldrs: t.k.h: kpt on same pce appr fnl f* **25/1**

-00 5 5 **Ground Ginger**[10] 2279 3-9-5 0 .... NeilCallan 6 38
(James Bethell) *chsd ldrs: drvn over 2f out: sn outpcd: wknd over 1f out* **50/1**

0 6 3 1/2 **Cauberg**[11] 2224 3-9-5 0 .... AndreaAtzeni 7 28
(Roger Varian) *swtchd lft and lost pl after 1f: outpcd over 2f out: nvr a factor* **14/1**[3]

1m 17.74s (0.84) **Going Correction** -0.075s/f (Good) **6** Ran SP% **115.8**
Speed ratings (Par 99): **91,87,86,85,79 74**
toteswingers 1&2 £1.10, 1&3 £1.20, 2&3 £1.30 CSF £2.42 TOTE £1.10: £1.02, £2.10; EX 1.70 Trifecta £4.90 Pool: £965.84 - 147.06 winning units..
Owner Cheveley Park Stud **Bred** Cheveley Park Stud Ltd **Trained** Newmarket, Suffolk

FOCUS
Modest form behind the winner.
T/Plt: £58.20 to a £1 stake. Pool: £74,875.33 - 938.93 winning units T/Qpdt: £13.20 to a £1 stake. Pool: £4867.42 - 271.50 winning units WG

2296 LONGCHAMP (R-H)
Tuesday, May 21

OFFICIAL GOING: Turf: very soft

2557a PRIX DES EPINETTES (H'CAP) (3YO) (TURF) — 1m 2f
12:50 (12:50) 3-Y-O
£22,926 (£9,268; £6,829; £4,390; £2,682; £1,707)

RPR

1 **Arthur The King (IRE)**[190] 3-8-9 0 .... JohanVictoire 5 83
(Y Durepaire, France) **101/10**

2 snk **Eurato (FR)**[39] 3-9-4 0 ....(p) OlivierPeslier 9 92
(C Laffon-Parias, France) **73/10**[2]

3 shd **Spirit's Revench (FR)**[28] 3-8-8 0 ....(p) ThierryJarnet 11 82
(P Demercastel, France) **5/2**[1]

4 2 **Niente Paura (IRE)**[12] 2203 3-9-1 0 .... MarcLerner 7 85
(C Lerner, France) **13/1**

5 3/4 **Polo (GER)**[28] 1756 3-9-1 0 .... GregoryBenoist 10 83
(D Smaga, France) **15/2**[3]

6 snk **Chene Boppe (FR)**[28] 1756 3-8-6 0 .... CesarPasserat 6 74
(F-X De Chevigny, France) **19/1**

7 2 **Litian Rocket (FR)**[6] 3-8-8 0 .... AlexandreChampenois 8 72
(M Boutin, France) **23/1**

8 2 **Toni Fortebracci (FR)**[63] 3-8-6 0 .... MircoDemuro 15 66
(G Botti, France) **57/1**

9 snk **Gentle Maine (IRE)** 3-8-13 0 .... ChristopheSoumillon 16 73
(J-M Beguigne, France) **12/1**

10 2 **Aldo Bere (FR)**[8] 3-8-13 0 ....(b) NicolasGauffenic 4 69
(C Boutin, France) **16/1**

11 **Quiet Diplomacy**[19] 1972 3-9-1 0 .... MaximeGuyon 12 71
(A Fabre, France) **9/1**

12 **Turkey Jackson (FR)**[54] 3-8-7 0 .... AlexisBadel 3 63
(F Sanchez, France) **20/1**

13 **Echion (IRE)**[17] 2034 3-8-7 0 .... LudovicProietti 1 63
(C Martinon, France) **66/1**

14 **Habeshia**[26] 1799 3-8-10 0 .... IoritzMendizabal 14 66
(John Best) *worked across fr wd draw and led after 3f: rdn and hdd 2f out: no ex and fdd: eased* **32/1**

15 **Herve (IRE)**[20] 3-8-9 0 .... StephanePasquier 2 65
(T Castanheira, France) **17/2**

2m 19.16s (15.16) **15** Ran SP% **122.8**
WIN (incl. 1 euro stake): 11.10. PLACES: 3.10, 2.60, 1.70. DF: 40.20. SF: 91.30.
Owner Ms Francis Teboul **Bred** Lofts Hall Stud **Trained** France

2558a PRIX DE SAINT-GERMAIN (CLAIMER) (2YO) (TURF) — 5f (S)
1:50 (1:51) 2-Y-O — **£10,975** (£4,390; £3,292; £2,195; £1,097)

RPR

1 **Laia Chope (FR)**[13] 2-8-9 0 ow1 .... JulienAuge 1 73
(A De Watrigant, France) **9/2**[3]

2 4 **Star Chope (FR)**[8] 2-8-6 0 .... JimmyTastayre(5) 2 61
(C Boutin, France) **23/1**

3 3 1/2 **Jolie Demoiselle (FR)** 2-8-8 0 ....(b) JohanVictoire 8 45
(C Boutin, France) **12/1**

4 1 3/4 **Zelia Chope (FR)**[66] 2-8-8 0 .... AntoineHamelin 9 39
(C Boutin, France) **16/1**

5 2 1/2 **Larra Chope (FR)**[24] 2-8-8 0 ....(p) MaximeGuyon 5 30
(C Boutin, France) **5/2**[2]

6 6 **College Succes (FR)** 2-9-4 0 ....(p) SebastienMaillot 4 18
(Robert Collet, France) **7/1**

7 snk **Haswell (SPA)**[14] 2-8-8 0 .... MircoDemuro 3 8
(M Delcher Sanchez, France) **9/1**

8 6 **Princess Pheeny (IRE)**[19] 1960 2-8-10 0 ow2 .... DanielTudhope 7
(Richard Fahey) *midfield in tch: rdn and lost pl 2f out: sn btn and wknd: eased and dropped to last: t.o* **23/10**[1]

1m 1.84s (5.54) **8** Ran SP% **117.3**
WIN (incl. 1 euro stake): 4.50 (Laia Chope coupled with Star Chope). PLACES: 2.00, 6.00, 3.00. DF: 50.50. SF: 78.30.
Owner Alain Chopard **Bred** A Chopard **Trained** France

2559a PRIX DE MONTRETOUT (LISTED RACE) (4YO+) (TURF) — 1m
2:55 (2:55) 4-Y-O+ — **£21,138** (£8,455; £6,341; £4,227; £2,113)

RPR

1 **Spoil The Fun (FR)**[39] 4-8-11 0 .... JulienAuge 7 112
(C Ferland, France) **26/5**[2]

2 3/4 **Pollyana (IRE)**[201] 7515 4-8-13 0 ....(p) IoritzMendizabal 10 112
(D Prod'Homme, France) **11/2**[3]

3 1 3/4 **Mainsail**[47] 1359 4-8-11 0 .... ChristopheSoumillon 4 106
(P Bary, France) **5/2**[1]

4 1 1/2 **Xotic (FR)**[44] 4-8-11 0 .... StephanePasquier 6 103
(D Prod'Homme, France) **6/1**

5 hd **Tagar Bere (FR)**[47] 1359 6-8-11 0 .... MaximeGuyon 2 102
(M Pimbonnet, France) **13/2**

6 2 **Hippolyte (FR)**[63] 1085 4-8-11 0 .... FlavienPrat 9 97
(T Clout, France) **17/2**

7 8 **Moonday Sun (USA)**[44] 4-8-11 0 .... GregoryBenoist 3 79
(D Smaga, France) **13/1**

8 1 3/4 **Stand My Ground (IRE)**[25] 1810 6-8-11 0 .... DanielTudhope 8 75
(David O'Meara) *trckd ldr: rdn to chal over 2f out: sn outpcd and btn: fdd* **12/1**

9 6 **Yes I Do (FR)**[282] 6-8-8 0 ThierryThulliez 1 58
(S Wattel, France) **30/1**
10 dist **Thyan (FR)**[17] 6-8-11 0 ChristianHanotel 11
(P Capelle, France) **99/1**
1m 47.0s (8.60) **10** Ran SP% **117.3**
WIN (incl. 1 euro stake): 6.20. PLACES: 2.00, 2.30, 1.60. DF: 18.60. SF: 54.50.
Owner Prime Equestrian S.A.R.L. **Bred** Snig Elevage **Trained** France

2154 KEMPTON (A.W) (R-H)
Wednesday, May 22

OFFICIAL GOING: Standard
Wind: Moderate ahead Weather: Sunny spells getting darker

2560 £200 FREE BETS AT BETDAQ MEDIAN AUCTION MAIDEN STKS 1m 2f (P)
6:00 (6:05) (Class 5) 3-4-Y-O **£2,587** (£770; £384; £192) **Stalls** Low

Form RPR
6-3 1 **Velvetina (IRE)**[20] 1955 3-8-9 0 TedDurcan 9 75+
(Harry Dunlop) *trckd ldr: led 6f out: drvn over 1f out and kpt on wl* **3/1**[2]
040- 2 ½ **Atlantis City (FR)**[161] 8070 3-9-0 67 SeanLevey 8 79
(Richard Hannon) *in tch: hdwy to chse ldrs 3f out: drvn to take 2nd appr fnl f: kpt on but a hld* **8/1**
4220 3 6 **Solvanna**[18] 2017 3-8-9 62 AndreaAtzeni 3 62
(Heather Main) *chsd ldrs: wnt 2nd 4f out: rdn and hung rt wl over 1f out: wknd into wl hld 3rd fnl f* **20/1**
4 shd **Parker Ridge (FR)** 3-9-0 0 JamieSpencer 6 67+
(Luca Cumani) *in rr: rdn over 4f out: styd on u.p fr over 1f out: kpt on to press for wl-hld 3rd clsng stages* **11/4**[1]
0 5 nk **Violet Dancer**[23] 1881 3-9-0 0 ShaneKelly 5 66+
(Gary Moore) *in tch: outpcd 4f out: pushed along and styd on over 1f out: kpt on clsng stages* **25/1**
6 6 nk **Loved One**[23] 1891 3-8-9 0 MartinLane 14 61
(James Fanshawe) *sn led: hdd 6f out: lost 2nd 4f out: rdn 3f out: styd on same pce fnl 2f* **7/1**
0-0 7 2 ¾ **Jareeda (USA)**[16] 2084 3-8-9 0 PaulHanagan 12 55+
(Sir Michael Stoute) *in rr: pushed along over 3f out: mod late hdwy* **10/3**[3]
50 8 1 **Pursivere**[9] 2321 3-9-0 0 MartinHarley 4 58+
(Hughie Morrison) *in tch: pushed along and bhd 3f out: sme prog fnl f* **20/1**
0 9 3 ¼ **Money Talks**[20] 1955 3-8-11 0 SimonPearce(3) 7 52
(Michael Madgwick) *chsd ldrs: rdn 3f out: wd and wknd 2f out* **100/1**
50 10 6 **Fenton**[14] 2157 3-8-9 0 LiamJones 1 35
(Harry Dunlop) *chsd ldrs: rdn over 3f out: wd and wknd 2f out* **50/1**
0 11 10 **Mrs Mann (USA)**[21] 1926 3-8-9 0 J-PGuillambert 10 15
(Jo Hughes) *a in rr* **66/1**
0 12 7 **We'Re In The Red (IRE)**[22] 1904 3-9-0 0 MarcHalford 2
(Mark Hoad) *chsd ldrs to 1/2-way* **150/1**
2m 7.64s (-0.36) **Going Correction** -0.025s/f (Stan) **12** Ran SP% **116.8**
Speed ratings (Par 103): **100,99,94,94,94 94,92,91,88,83 75,70**
Tote Swingers: 1&2 £4.90, 1&3 £6.60, 2&3 £8.10 CSF £24.99 TOTE £4.20: £1.80, £2.70, £2.90; EX 29.40 Trifecta £90.20 Pool: £2,116.81 - 17.58 winning units..
Owner Windflower Overseas Holdings Inc **Bred** Windflower Overseas **Trained** Lambourn, Berks
FOCUS
This didn't look like it would take much winning and, although the first two finished clear, the third anchors the form.

2561 BETDAQ CUSTOMERS COMMISSION FREE 1ST MONTH H'CAP 5f (P)
6:30 (6:32) (Class 4) (0-85,85) 4-Y-0+ **£4,690** (£1,395; £697; £348) **Stalls** Low

Form RPR
1-00 1 **Church Music (IRE)**[12] 2207 4-8-13 82.(v[1]) WilliamTwiston-Davies(5) 10 94
(Michael Scudamore) *chsd ldrs: drvn to ld fnl 120yds: forged clr: readily* **9/2**[2]
3444 2 3 ¼ **Triple Dream**[34] 1652 8-8-12 81 (tp) MatthewLawson(5) 11 81
(Milton Bradley) *chsd ldrs: rdn 2f out: styd on fnl f to take 2nd last strides: no ch w wnr* **7/1**
0-60 3 hd **West Coast Dream**[28] 1765 6-9-2 83 MarkCoumbe(3) 3 83
(Roy Brotherton) *led: hrd pressed over 1f out: kpt slt ld tl hdd fnl 120yds: lost 2nd last strides* **9/2**[2]
1214 4 2 ¼ **Picansort**[22] 1902 6-9-7 85 (b) ShaneKelly 1 76
(Peter Crate) *s.i.s: in rr: hdwy on inner over 1f out: rdn and no ex ins fnl f* **9/4**[1]
20-0 5 1 ¾ **Powerful Wind (IRE)**[11] 2268 4-8-8 72 LukeMorris 4 57
(Ronald Harris) *chsd ldr: chal u.p over 1f out: wknd fnl 120yds* **8/1**
03-6 6 ¾ **Heartsong (IRE)**[51] 1287 4-9-1 84 MichaelJMMurphy(5) 7 66
(John Gallagher) *s.i.s: in rr: rdn and wd 3f out: a outpcd* **16/1**
016- 7 2 ½ **Cats Eyes**[263] 5815 4-8-12 76 PaulHanagan 8 49
(Robert Cowell) *sn outpcd* **6/1**[3]
59.28s (-1.22) **Going Correction** -0.025s/f (Stan) **7** Ran SP% **110.9**
Speed ratings (Par 105): **108,102,102,98,96 94,90**
Tote Swingers: 1&2 £4.50, 1&3 £4.60, 2&3 £6.40 CSF £32.99 CT £142.07 TOTE £6.00: £3.00, £5.80; EX 24.00 Trifecta £158.10 Pool: £1,219.30 - 5.78 winning units..
Owner JCG Chua & CK Ong **Bred** Mrs Ellen Lyons **Trained** Bromsash, H'fords
FOCUS
There was a strong pace on here.

2562 WINNERS ARE WELCOME AT BETDAQ MAIDEN AUCTION STKS 6f (P)
7:00 (7:01) (Class 5) 2-Y-0 **£2,587** (£770; £384; £192) **Stalls** Low

Form RPR
4 1 **Thewandaofu (IRE)**[11] 2282 2-8-9 0 FergusSweeney 1 70+
(Jamie Osborne) *led: hrd pressed fr 3f out: hdd over 1f out: drvn to ld fnl 110yds: kpt on wl* **11/4**[2]
2 ¾ **Stellarta** 2-8-5 0 JimmyQuinn 3 64
(Michael Blanshard) *s.i.s: in rr: hdwy on ins over 2f out: led over 1f out: sn drvn: hdd and could nt qckn fnl 110yds* **20/1**
3 1 ½ **Top Of The Glas (IRE)** 2-8-8 0 MichaelJMMurphy(5) 6 67+
(Alan Jarvis) *s.i.s: green: drvn and hdwy 2f out: rdn: kpt on and hung rt ins fnl f: nt rch ldng duo* **2/1**[1]
5 4 ¾ **Plucky Dip**[6] 2382 2-8-7 0 RyanPowell(3) 9 61
(John Ryan) *chsd ldrs: rdn over 2f out: styd on same pce fnl f* **8/1**
4 5 ½ **Severnwind (IRE)**[8] 2344 2-8-12 0 LukeMorris 2 62
(Ronald Harris) *chsd ldrs: rdn 2f out: wkng whn bmpd ins fnl f* **11/1**
0 6 ½ **Jana**[11] 2282 2-8-6 0 PaulHanagan 7 54+
(Richard Hannon) *in tch: outpcd ins fnl 3f: pushed along and styd on again fnl f* **14/1**
7 1 ¼ **Valued Opinion (IRE)** 2-8-11 0 ShaneKelly 5 55
(Tim Pitt) *s.i.s: in rr: pushed along and hdwy fr 2f out: kpt on fnl f* **10/1**
5 8 1 ¾ **Red Oasis**[11] 2260 2-8-12 0 AndreaAtzeni 8 51
(Robert Eddery) *in rr: pushed along over 2f out: sme late prog* **6/1**[3]
540 9 nk **Brockholes Flyer (IRE)**[33] 1659 2-8-5 0 MatthewLawson(5) 4 48
(Brendan Powell) *chsd wnr: rdn and wknd ins fnl 2f* **25/1**
66 10 3 ¼ **Bold Max**[11] 2282 2-8-10 0 RichardThomas 10 37
(Zoe Davison) *outpcd* **100/1**
1m 15.24s (2.14) **Going Correction** +0.15s/f (Slow) **10** Ran SP% **119.1**
Speed ratings (Par 93): **91,90,88,87,86 85,84,81,81,76**
Tote Swingers: 1&2 £12.10, 1&3 £1.90, 2&3 £18.10 CSF £59.86 TOTE £5.10: £1.90, £8.50, £1.10; EX 103.30 Trifecta £378.50 Pool: £1,195.38 - 2.36 winning units..
Owner Fromthestables.Com & Partner **Bred** Mrs Eleanor Commins **Trained** Upper Lambourn, Berks
FOCUS
This looked an ordinary maiden. The field finished compressed in a slow time, and it's hard to be overly positive about the form.

2563 CONOR MAYNARD LIVE AT KEMPTON 14.09.13 H'CAP 2m (P)
7:30 (7:30) (Class 6) (0-60,60) 4-Y-0+ **£1,940** (£577; £288; £144) **Stalls** Low

Form RPR
0530 1 **Boston Blue**[37] 1586 6-9-1 54 JimCrowley 9 64
(Tony Carroll) *in rr: hdwy 6f out: led over 2f out: drvn and hld on wl fnl f* **7/2**[1]
0056 2 ½ **Ice Apple**[20] 1953 5-8-7 46 oh1 KirstyMilczarek 6 55
(John E Long) *in rr: hdwy 4f out: styd on u.p over 1f out: edging rt and looking awkward fnl 110yds: tk 2nd last strides* **33/1**
-643 3 hd **Tram Express (FR)**[82] 846 9-8-10 54 (t) WilliamTwiston-Davies(5) 8 63
(Shaun Lycett) *in rr: hdwy 5f out: styd on to chse ldrs 2f out: wnt 2nd over 1f out: styd on same pce: dropped to 3rd last strides* **8/1**
0063 4 7 **Ctappers**[20] 1953 4-9-4 59 (v[1]) MartinHarley 13 60
(Mick Channon) *chsd ldrs: rdn and ev ch over 2f out: wknd over 1f out* **8/1**
0-06 5 ¾ **Blackstone Vegas**[16] 2087 7-9-2 55 (v) SilvestreDeSousa 12 55
(Derek Shaw) *chsd ldrs: led over 4f out: rdn and hdd* **11/2**[2]
600 6 shd **Ernie**[23] 1882 6-9-0 53 ChrisCatlin 4 53
(Geoffrey Deacon) *in rr: hdwy 4f out: drvn to chse ldrs over 2f out: wknd over 1f out* **6/1**[3]
000- 7 2 ¼ **Eanans Bay (IRE)**[152] 8214 4-8-4 48 (b) SimonPearce(3) 11 45
(Mark H Tompkins) *chsd ldrs: rdn 3f out: rdn 3f out: wknd over 2f out* **16/1**
/0-5 8 7 **Celebrian**[9] 2333 6-8-13 52 (t) AndreaAtzeni 5 40
(Alex Hales) *chsd ldrs: rdn 3f out: wknd qckly appr fnl 2f* **25/1**
0-02 9 34 **Fine Kingdom**[14] 2174 4-8-12 53 (b) PaulHanagan 1
(Brian Ellison) *led 2f: chsd ldrs: wknd 5f out: t.o* **6/1**[3]
560- 10 19 **Dream Catcher (SWE)**[248] 6280 10-9-2 55 (p) RichardHughes 10
(Jonjo O'Neill) *sn prom: led 9f out: hdd over 3f out: wknd rapidly over 2f out* **7/1**
00-0 11 27 **Look Left**[19] 1973 5-9-2 60 RobertTart(5) 7
(Nikki Evans) *mid-div: wknd 5f out: t.o* **33/1**
0-01 12 28 **Blue Pencil**[16] 2304 4-8-2 46 oh1 RyanPowell(3) 2
(Roger Curtis) *led after 2f: hdd 9f out: styd pressing ldr: rdn 6f out: sn wknd: t.o* **33/1**
3m 31.47s (1.37) **Going Correction** +0.15s/f (Slow)
WFA 4 from 5yo+ 2lb **12** Ran SP% **119.5**
Speed ratings (Par 101): **102,101,101,98,97 97,96,93,76,66 53,39**
Tote Swingers: 1&2 £24.80, 1&3 £12.40, 2&3 £38.80 CSF £138.20 CT £859.30 TOTE £4.50: £1.60, £6.40, £2.70; EX 150.10 Trifecta £707.10 Part won. Pool: £942.84 - 0.06 winning units..
Owner B J Millen **Bred** Ballykilbride Stud **Trained** Cropthorne, Worcs
FOCUS
An ordinary staying contest that turned into something of a sprint up the straight.

2564 BETDAQ 1ST UK RACE COMMISSION FREE-EVERYDAY H'CAP 1m 4f (P)
8:00 (8:00) (Class 5) (0-75,75) 3-Y-0 **£2,587** (£770; £384; £192) **Stalls** Centre

Form RPR
2-12 1 **Grendisar (IRE)**[35] 1614 3-9-6 74 (p) AdamKirby 1 81+
(Marco Botti) *in rr: hdwy over 2f out: rdn to chse ldrs and edgd rt over 1f out: hrd drvn to ld ins fnl f: rdn out* **5/2**[2]
3-63 2 1 **Portmonarch (IRE)**[20] 1959 3-9-7 75 TedDurcan 6 80
(David Lanigan) *sn led: rdn ins fnl 2f: kpt slt ld tl hdd ins fnl f: hld whn bmpd slowing stages* **2/1**[1]
053- 3 ¾ **Grayswood**[179] 7868 3-8-12 66 SilvestreDeSousa 3 70
(William Muir) *t.k.h: chsd ldrs: drvn 2f out: str chal appr fnl f: one pce fnl 110yds* **9/1**
02-5 4 1 ¾ **Mallory Heights (IRE)**[23] 1885 3-9-2 70 JamieSpencer 2 73+
(Luca Cumani) *chsd ldrs: pushed along over 2f out: stl wl there whn hmpd and swtchd lft over 1f out: kpt edging lft and styd on again clsng stages* **7/2**[3]
1165 5 1 **Flying Tempo**[20] 1959 3-9-6 74 (b) PaulHanagan 4 74
(Ed Dunlop) *in rr: pushed along over 2f out: sme hdwy fnl f* **12/1**
11-3 6 6 **Keep Calm**[9] 2322 3-9-1 69 RichardHughes 5 59
(Richard Hannon) *in tch: chsd ldrs 6f out: drvn over 2f out: wknd over 1f out* **8/1**
2m 37.56s (3.06) **Going Correction** +0.15s/f (Slow) **6** Ran SP% **112.9**
Speed ratings (Par 99): **95,94,93,92,92 88**
Tote Swingers: 1&2 £1.10, 1&3 £7.00, 2&3 £3.90 CSF £8.04 TOTE £4.40: £1.10, £2.50; EX 9.10 Trifecta £43.90 Pool: £816.98 - 13.94 winning units..
Owner Mohamed Albousi Alghufli **Bred** Old Carhue & Graeng Bloodstock **Trained** Newmarket, Suffolk
FOCUS
They didn't go a strong gallop but the second and third started taking each other on from the turn in.

2565 IRISH NIGHT ON 10.07.13 H'CAP 7f (P)
8:30 (8:34) (Class 6) (0-65,65) 4-Y-0+ **£1,940** (£577; £288; £144) **Stalls** Low

Form RPR
0511 1 **Intomist (IRE)**[6] 2395 4-9-2 65 (p) NathanAlison(5) 14 79
(Jim Boyle) *in tch: hdwy over 2f out: drvn to ld wl over 1f out: drvn out* **7/1**[3]
1220 2 1 ¾ **Athletic**[15] 2134 4-8-12 61 (v) RobertTart(5) 13 70
(Andrew Reid) *t.k.h in rr: drvn and hdwy over 1f out: sn chsng wnr but no imp fnl 110yds* **20/1**
4211 3 2 ¼ **Bold Ring**[15] 2125 7-9-5 63 MarcHalford 6 68+
(Edward Creighton) *in tch: hdwy and nt clr run 2f out: drvn and kpt on to take 3rd ins fnl f: no imp on ldng duo* **16/1**

214- 4 nk **Jay Bee Blue**[225] 6968 4-9-5 63....(bt) TomQueally 4 65
(Sean Curran) *t.k.h: in tch: hdwy 2f out: chal over 1f out: outpcd ins fnl f* 10/1
3020 5 ¾ **Warbond**[21] 1925 5-9-2 60....(p) AdamKirby 12 60
(Michael Madgwick) *in rr: hdwy over 2f out: styd on same pce fnl f* 20/1
3605 6 1¼ **West Leake (IRE)**[12] 2228 7-9-5 63.... LiamKeniry 8 60
(Paul Burgoyne) *in rr: hdwy over 2f out: pressed ldrs over 1f out: wknd ins fnl f* 16/1
3620 7 nk **Homeward Strut**[12] 2228 4-9-6 64....(b) JimCrowley 10 60
(Laura Mongan) *chsd ldrs: drvn to chal over 1f out: wknd fnl 110yds* 8/1
4036 8 nk **Unlimited**[23] 1887 11-9-1 59.... JimmyQuinn 11 54
(Tony Carroll) *slowly in stride: in rr: hdwy over 1f out: kpt on clsng stages* 33/1
5-65 9 ½ **Summer Dancer (IRE)**[16] 2081 9-9-7 65.... MickyFenton 5 59+
(Paul Midgley) *in rr: hdwy over 1f out: styd on clsng stages* 8/1
00-2 10 hd **Wise Venture (IRE)**[11] 2286 4-8-11 62.... DavidParkes(7) 1 55
(Alan Jarvis) *w ldr tl led over 2f out: rdn and hdd over 1f out* 11/2[2]
3251 11 1 **Abhaath (USA)**[23] 1886 4-9-4 62.... LukeMorris 9 53
(Ronald Harris) *s.i.s: in rr: styd on fr over 1f out: nvr rchd ldrs* 20/1
0-43 12 ¾ **Mishrif (USA)**[21] 1925 7-9-5 63....(b) RichardHughes 3 51
(J R Jenkins) *chsd ldrs: rdn 2f out: wknd over 1f out* 8/1
2010 13 6 **Bang Tidy (IRE)**[16] 2089 4-9-3 61....(t) SilvestreDeSousa 2 33
(Brian Ellison) *sn slt ld but hrd pressed tl hdd over 2f out: sn btn* 4/1[1]

1m 25.84s (-0.16) **Going Correction** +0.15s/f (Slow) 13 Ran SP% **119.3**
Speed ratings (Par 101): **106,104,101,101,100 98,98,98,97,97 96,95,88**
Tote Swingers: 1&2 £3.10, 2&3 £2.80 CSF £144.24 CT £2225.89 TOTE £6.30: £2.50, £3.20, £4.60; EX 115.10 Trifecta £495.70 Pool: £1,105.02 - 1.67 winning units..
Owner The Clueless Syndicate **Bred** P M Guerin **Trained** Epsom, Surrey

FOCUS
An ordinary handicap. The early pace didn't look that hot, but they got racing on the turn and ultimately the first two came from behind.

2566 LONDON'S RACE TRACKS RACINGANDMUSIC.CO.UK H'CAP 1m (P)
9:00 (9:02) (Class 6) (0-55,56) 3-Y-O **£1,940** (£577; £288; £144) **Stalls** Low

Form RPR
060- 1 **Winslow Arizona (IRE)**[211] 7313 3-8-12 46.... JamieSpencer 12 59+
(Michael Bell) *chsd ldrs: led over 2f out: hung lft u.p ins fnl f: hld on all out* 13/8[1]
660- 2 ¾ **Great Crested (IRE)**[182] 7806 3-9-5 53.... ShaneKelly 9 65+
(Gary Moore) *chsd ldrs: outpcd 2f out: styd on to press wnr whn pushed lft ins fnl f: styd on same pce* 7/2[2]
0-05 3 4 **Rock Diamond (IRE)**[23] 1879 3-9-0 48.... RichardHughes 3 50
(Sylvester Kirk) *chsd ldrs: rdn to go 2nd over 1f out: no imp on wnr and outpcd into 3rd fnl f* 7/1[3]
-440 4 2½ **Booktheband (IRE)**[42] 1469 3-9-7 55.... TedDurcan 11 51
(Clive Brittain) *in tch: rdn 2f out: kpt on fnl f: nt rch ldrs* 16/1
400- 5 nk **Beauchamp Sunset**[167] 8006 3-8-12 51....[1] NicoleNordblad(5) 7 46
(Hans Adielsson) *led tl hdd over 2f out: btn whn nt clr run over 1f out* 10/1
0-01 6 ½ **Noor Al Haya (IRE)**[7] 2362 3-8-10 51 6ex.... DanielMuscutt(7) 4 45+
(Mark Usher) *in rr: hdwy over 1f out: kpt on clsng stages* 12/1
6-50 7 nk **Dancing Chief (IRE)**[35] 1613 3-8-7 46 oh1.... MichaelJMMurphy(5) 6 39+
(Alan Jarvis) *in rr: styd on fr over 1f out: nt rch ldrs* 33/1
64-4 8 1 **Exclusion (USA)**[16] 2095 3-9-7 55....(b) StevieDonohoe 13 46
(Noel Quinlan) *s.i.s: in rr: kpt on fr over 1f out: nt trble ldrs* 14/1
5-64 9 nk **Mastered (IRE)**[118] 350 3-9-5 53.... GeorgeBaker 5 43
(John Best) *in tch: pushed along and one pce fnl 2f* 16/1
04-4 10 3½ **Trymyluck**[22] 1906 3-9-6 54.... AdamKirby 2 36
(Pam Sly) *a towards rr* 20/1
00-0 11 7 **Running Bull (IRE)**[130] 184 3-8-13 47....(p) LiamKeniry 8 12
(Linda Jewell) *towards rr most of way* 66/1
0-00 12 2¼ **I Need A Dollar**[22] 1904 3-9-2 55.... DannyBrock(5) 10 15
(J R Jenkins) *chsd ldr to 3f out: wknd over 2f out* 50/1

1m 41.22s (1.42) **Going Correction** +0.15s/f (Slow) 12 Ran SP% **119.2**
Speed ratings (Par 97): **98,97,93,90,90 89,89,88,88,84 77,75**
Tote Swingers: 1&2 £4.10, 2&3 £8.80 CSF £6.60 CT £32.16 TOTE £2.60: £1.10, £1.50, £2.20; EX 15.70 Trifecta £49.70 Pool: £1,168.26 - 17.61 winning units..
Owner Rathordan Partnership **Bred** Sir E J Loder **Trained** Newmarket, Suffolk
■ Stewards' Enquiry : Jamie Spencer two-day ban: careless riding (5-6 June)

FOCUS
Plenty of these looked open to improvement, the money spoke for two in particular, and they fought out the finish.
T/Jkpt: Not won. T/Plt: £309.60 to a £1 stake. Pool: £68,802.20 - 159.85 winning tickets. T/Qpdt: £22.60 to a £1 stake. Pool: £5,211.50 - 170.60 winning tickets. ST

2260 LINGFIELD (L-H)
Wednesday, May 22

OFFICIAL GOING: Turf course - good (good to firm in places; 8.2); all-weather - standard
Wind: virtually nil Weather: dry, overcast

2567 MAIL PUBLISHER SOLUTIONS H'CAP 1m 3f 106y
2:00 (2:00) (Class 6) (0-60,60) 4-Y-O+ **£2,045** (£603; £302) **Stalls** High

Form RPR
3 1 **Mr Lando**[40] 788 4-8-9 48.... JimmyQuinn 5 56
(Tony Carroll) *stdd after s: t.k.h: hld up in tch towards rr: gd hdwy on outer over 3f out: led over 2f out and sn rdn clr: in command 1f out: eased nr line* 6/1
-620 2 3¾ **Iguacu**[20] 1948 9-8-7 51....(p) CharlesBishop(5) 7 55+
(Richard Price) *hld up in tch in last pair: styng on whn nt clr run and forced to switch rt over 1f out: styd on wl fnl f to go 2nd cl home: no threat to wnr* 12/1
-346 3 ½ **Glens Wobbly**[23] 1877 5-8-7 46 oh1.... HarryBentley 8 47
(Jonathan Geake) *in tch in last quartet: rdn and hdwy over 2f out: chsd clr wnr 1f out: kpt on but no imp: lost 2nd cl home* 7/1
6/0- 4 1½ **Lindsay's Dream**[3] 3968 7-8-10 49....(p) LiamKeniry 3 47
(Zoe Davison) *in tch in midfield: effrt u.p ent fnl 2f: no threat to wnr and kpt on same pce fnl f* 14/1
13-3 5 nk **Uncle Roger (IRE)**[13] 512 4-9-7 60....(v) TomQueally 6 58
(Eve Johnson Houghton) *hld up in tch in last quartet: hdwy whn nt clr run and hmpd over 2f out: rallied u.p to chse wnr over 1f out tl 1f out: one pce after* 9/2[2]
60-0 6 ½ **Mariet**[140] 12 4-9-3 56.... SamHitchcott 2 53
(Suzy Smith) *sn led: hdd and drvn over 2f out: sn outpcd by wnr and btn over 1f out: hld and plugged on same pce fnl f* 20/1
464- 7 1 **Astroscarlet**[162] 8060 4-8-11 53.... SimonPearce(3) 9 48
(Mark H Tompkins) *chsd ldr for 1f: in tch in midfield after: drvn and outpcd 2f out: kpt on again ins fnl f: no threat to wnr* 10/1
6001 8 hd **Minority Interest**[27] 1779 4-9-6 59....(v) GeorgeBaker 14 54
(Brett Johnson) *t.k.h: chsd ldrs: rdn and edgd rt over 2f out: drvn and no imp over 1f out: wknd ins fnl f* 3/1[1]
-060 9 8 **Sassi Sioux**[32] 1700 4-8-2 46 oh1.... DannyBrock(5) 11 27
(Tom Keddy) *chsd ldr after 1f: rdn and ev ch over 2f out: struggling u.p 2f out: sn wknd* 50/1
2303 10 7 **El Libertador (USA)**[23] 1877 7-8-13 52....(b) RichardHughes 1 21
(Eric Wheeler) *chsd ldrs: rdn and lost pl over 2f out: bhd and eased ins fnl f* 5/1[3]
3-40 11 36 **Notabadgirl**[23] 1877 4-9-1 54.... NickyMackay 13
(Simon Dow) *dwlt: sn rdn along and nvr gng wl in last: lost tch 4f out: t.o* 28/1

2m 33.85s (2.35) **Going Correction** +0.25s/f (Good) 11 Ran SP% **120.3**
Speed ratings (Par 101): **101,98,97,96,96 96,95,95,89,84 58**
Tote Swingers: 1&2 £27.70, 1&3 £5.90, 2&3 £13.60 CSF £75.73 CT £523.10 TOTE £8.60: £2.80, £3.40, £3.00; EX 70.80 Trifecta £386.60 Part won. Pool: £515.54 - 0.02 winning units..
Owner Gary Attwood **Bred** Capitana Partnership **Trained** Cropthorne, Worcs

FOCUS
The first of four on the turf, which was just a moderate race with a scarcity of recent winning form. The placed horses all came from the back.

2568 CITIPOST LTD MAIDEN STKS 1m 3f 106y
2:30 (2:30) (Class 5) 3-Y-O+ **£2,726** (£805; £402) **Stalls** High

Form RPR
30-2 1 **Da Do Run Run**[16] 2099 3-8-11 77.... MartinLane 6 80
(Brian Meehan) *chsd ldr tl led over 10f out: mde rest: clr and rdn 3f out: in n.d after: kpt on fnl f* 7/2[2]
3-3 2 2½ **Emperical**[32] 1684 3-8-11 0.... TomQueally 4 76+
(Sir Henry Cecil) *led tl over 10f out: chsd wnr tl rdn and lost pl on downhill run over 4f out: rallied u.p to chse clr wnr 2f out: edgd rt over 1f out: kpt on ins fnl f but nvr gng to rch wnr* 1/3[1]
3 1 **Ataraxis (FR)** 3-8-11 0.... JimmyQuinn 2 74
(Sir Henry Cecil) *awkward leaving stalls: sn chsng ldng trio: effrt to go modest 3rd 2f out: carried sltly rt over 1f out: nudged along and kpt on steadily fnl f: eased towards fin* 5/1[3]
0 4 8 **Sammyman**[26] 1804 6-9-12 0.... LiamKeniry 9 60
(Michael Blanshard) *chsd ldng pair: wnt 2nd over 4f out: rdn and no imp 3f out: 4th and btn 2f out: wknd fnl f* 14/1
00 5 13 **Mr Blue Nose**[29] 1741 3-8-11 0.... JamieMackay 1 38
(Karen George) *bhd: rdn and struggling 7f out: lost tch 4f out: no ch but plugged on past btn horses fnl f* 100/1
30 6 ½ **Rock Of Ages**[26] 1804 4-9-12 0.... LiamJones 10 38
(Michael Murphy) *dwlt: sn rdn along: hdwy into midfield and travelling bttr 8f out: rdn and wknd over 3f out: fdd 2f out* 20/1
0/ 7 7 **Onwards'N'Upwards**[26] 7662 5-9-12 0.... TomMcLaughlin 8 26
(Christine Dunnett) *a in rr: rdn and struggling 6f out: lost tch 4f out* 100/1
60 8 1¼ **Jack Firefly**[14] 2172 4-9-7 0.... TobyAtkinson(5) 7 23
(Michael Murphy) *in tch in midfield: rdn and struggling 5f out: sn lost tch and bhd* 33/1

2m 33.84s (2.34) **Going Correction** +0.25s/f (Good)
WFA 3 from 4yo+ 15lb 8 Ran SP% **130.3**
Speed ratings (Par 103): **101,99,98,92,83 82,77,76**
Tote Swingers: 1&2 £5.60, 1&3 £2.40, 2&3 £8.10 CSF £5.78 TOTE £6.00: £1.20, £1.02, £1.30; EX 7.30 Trifecta £16.20 Pool: £1,823.85 - 84.19 winning units..
Owner W A Harrison-Allan **Bred** W A Harrison-Allan **Trained** Manton, Wilts

FOCUS
An even split between 3yos and older horses, but the market only wanted to know about the youngsters. It was 14-1 bar three and they occupied the first three places, but not in the order the market expected. The time was almost identical to the first, which suggests it was not a great maiden.

2569 CITIBET - THE WEEKEND FOOTBALL MAG H'CAP 1m 3f 106y
3:00 (3:00) (Class 5) (0-70,70) 4-Y-O+ **£2,726** (£805; £402) **Stalls** High

Form RPR
-051 1 **Foxhaven**[30] 1715 11-9-2 70....(v) ThomasBrown(5) 2 78
(Patrick Chamings) *chsd ldng pair: rdn to ld ent fnl 2f: clr over 1f out: rdn out hands and heels ins fnl f: pressed and fnd ex cl home* 9/2
06-0 2 nk **Double Cee**[37] 1586 4-9-7 70.... JimCrowley 3 77
(Warren Greatrex) *in tch in last pair: dropped to rr and rdn 6f out: hdwy u.p over 2f out: chsd clr wnr and swtchd rt over 1f out: edgd lft u.p ins fnl f: clsd to press wnr towards fin: hld cl home* 12/1
2021 3 7 **Highly Likely (IRE)**[23] 1877 4-8-12 61.... RichardHughes 5 56
(Steve Woodman) *hld up in tch in rr: clsd to trck ldrs 4f out: rdn and effrt ent fnl 2f: fnd little and btn over 1f out: wknd* 11/4[2]
5-44 4 1¼ **Hurakan (IRE)**[19] 1973 7-9-2 70....(p) CharlesBishop(5) 7 63
(Richard Price) *w ldr tl led narrowly 7f out: rdn and hdd ent fnl 2f: sn drvn and btn: wknd 1f out* 7/4[1]
30-0 5 39 **Steely**[22] 1899 5-9-4 67.... GeorgeBaker 6
(Gary Moore) *t.k.h and hung rt thrght: led tl 7f out: styd upsides ldr tl rdn and btn over 2f out: sn swtchd rt and virtually p.u fnl f: t.o* 7/2[3]

2m 34.52s (3.02) **Going Correction** +0.25s/f (Good) 5 Ran SP% **111.1**
Speed ratings (Par 103): **99,98,93,92,64**
CSF £46.56 TOTE £7.40: £3.50, £6.60; EX 43.20 Trifecta £422.90 Pool: £725.53 - 1.28 winning units..
Owner The Foxford House Partnership **Bred** Highclere Stud Ltd **Trained** Baughurst, Hants

FOCUS
Only five went to post for this modest race. The time was slower than the first two races run over the same distance and the front two came from off the pace.

2570 MENZIES DISTRIBUTION H'CAP 1m 6f
3:30 (3:30) (Class 5) (0-70,69) 4-Y-O+ **£2,726** (£805; £402) **Stalls** High

Form RPR
1000 1 **Honourable Knight (IRE)**[33] 1670 5-8-12 60.... DavidProbert 7 67
(Mark Usher) *in tch in midfield: effrt u.p over 2f out: led 1f out: kpty on wl: rdn out* 12/1
2455 2 ½ **Bramshill Lass**[13] 2197 4-8-8 56....(b) JimCrowley 4 62
(Amanda Perrett) *hld up in tch: hdwy into midfield 7f out: rdn and styng on whn nt clr run and swtchd rt over 1f out: hdwy u.p and pressing wnr fnl 75yds: hld towards fin* 4/1[3]
6/04 3 1 **Kayef (GER)**[13] 2197 6-9-2 69.... WilliamTwiston-Davies(5) 5 74
(Michael Scudamore) *chsd ldr tl led 10f out: clr 8f out: rdn over 2f out: hdd 1f out and styd on same pce ins fnl f* 3/1[1]

1554 **4** 1 ¾ **Maison Brillet (IRE)**[15] 2136 6-8-13 **61**........................(b[1]) SebSanders 6 63
(Clive Drew) *chsd ldrs: effrt on inner and clsd to chse ldrs whn nt clr run wl over 1f out tl ins fnl f: no imp fnl 150yds* **20/1**

3-54 **5** nk **Ginger Fizz**[21] 1927 6-9-6 **68**..(t) RichardHughes 1 70
(Ben Case) *led tl 10f out: chsd ldr: clsd and rdn over 2f out: no ex 1f out: wknd ins fnl f* **4/1**[3]

0545 **6** 4 **Aviso (GER)**[20] 1949 9-8-5 **53**..(p) AndreaAtzeni 8 49
(David Evans) *hld up in tch in last pair: rdn and effrt ent fnl 2f: no imp* **12/1**

-562 **7** 9 **Vertueux (FR)**[19] 1980 8-8-7 **55**.. HarryBentley 3 39
(Tony Carroll) *in tch in midfield: rdn and no hdwy over 2f out: wknd 2f out* **10/1**

2161 **8** 4 **Honest Strike (USA)**[20] 1953 6-9-0 **62**..............................(b) ShaneKelly 2 40
(Daniel Mark Loughnane) *stdd s: hld up in tch in rr: hdwy 4f out: rdn and no hdwy 3f out: wl btn fnl 2f: eased ins fnl f* **7/2**[2]

3m 16.94s (6.94) **Going Correction** +0.25s/f (Good) **8** Ran SP% **116.5**
Speed ratings (Par 103): **90,89,89,88,87 85,80,78**
Tote Swingers: 1&2 £5.80, 1&3 £10.10, 2&3 £5.10 CSF £60.57 CT £184.98 TOTE £12.80: £3.40, £1.50, £2.30; EX 68.30 Trifecta £533.00 Pool: £837.71 - 1.17 winning units..
Owner Mrs T Channing-Williams **Bred** Mohammed Al Sulaim **Trained** Upper Lambourn, Berks

FOCUS
More modest stuff and with most of these usually seen on the all-weather, it was a question of who could go best on the turf. Yet again, it paid to come from off the pace.

2571 SUN CLAIMING STKS 7f (P)
4:00 (4:01) (Class 6) 3-Y-O+ **£2,045** (£603; £302) **Stalls** Low

Form RPR

1200 **1** **Elusive Hawk (IRE)**[12] 2214 9-9-6 83.................................. AdamKirby 1 76
(David Evans) *mde all: rdn and qcknd 2f out: kpt on wl fnl f: rdn out* **6/1**

3534 **2** 1 ¼ **Moment In The Sun**[14] 2159 4-9-0 60..........................(b) AndreaAtzeni 7 67
(David Flood) *chsd wnr thrght: rdn and effrt 2f out: styd on same pce u.p fnl f* **25/1**

5-05 **3** 1 ¼ **Ertikaan**[119] 340 6-9-7 80..(tp) TomQueally 3 71
(Brendan Powell) *t.k.h: chsd ldrs: rdn and hung lft over 1f out: racd awkwardly and one pce fnl f* **7/1**

200- **4** nk **Mahadee (IRE)**[181] 7823 8-9-5 78....................................(b) LiamKeniry 2 68
(Ed de Giles) *chsd ldrs: rdn and unable qck over 1f out: kpt on same pce fnl f* **16/1**

2616 **5** 1 ¼ **Rakaan (IRE)**[27] 1796 6-9-12 83................................(p) FergusSweeney 4 71
(Jamie Osborne) *dwlt: in tch towards rr: hdwy into midfield and effrt wl over 1f out: no imp fnl f* **3/1**[1]

1111 **6** hd **Saharia (IRE)**[32] 1696 6-9-5 77..(v) ShaneKelly 9 64
(Daniel Mark Loughnane) *stdd s: hld up in last: effrt and hdwy ent fnl f: no imp fnl 150yds: nvr trbld ldrs* **7/2**[2]

043- **7** hd **Rondeau (GR)**[246] 6329 8-9-7 77...................................... GeorgeBaker 6 65
(Patrick Chamings) *taken down early: stdd s: t.k.h: hld up in last pair: rdn and effrt ent fnl f: no imp fnl 150yds: nvr trbld ldrs* **9/2**[3]

6010 **8** ¾ **Flavius Victor (IRE)**[27] 1780 4-9-0 70..................... ThomasBrown(5) 10 61
(Patrick Chamings) *stdd s: t.k.h: hld up towards rr tl hdwy into midfield on outer 4f out: rdn and outpcd wl over 1f out: one pce and n.d after* **8/1**

2500 **9** 2 ¼ **Spin Again (IRE)**[15] 2134 8-8-11 61........................... NatashaEaton(5) 8 52
(John Ryan) *in tch in midfield: rdn and effrt on inner over 1f out: no real prog: wknd ins fnl f* **33/1**

1m 24.14s (-0.66) **Going Correction** -0.05s/f (Stan) **9** Ran SP% **116.0**
Speed ratings (Par 101): **101,99,98,97,96 96,95,95,92**
Tote Swingers: 1&2 £11.80, 1&3 £5.60, 2&3 £13.90 CSF £138.44 TOTE £7.50: £2.70, £5.30, £2.90; EX 94.90 Trifecta £940.20 Pool: £1,409.39 - 1.12 winning units..
Owner Mrs I M Folkes **Bred** J Fike **Trained** Pandy, Monmouths

FOCUS
The first race on the Polytrack was only a claimer, but it featured the highest-rated horses on the card. It was weakened by the morning defection of North Star Boy. There was little pace, the winner led the whole way, and it was hard to get into this from behind.

2572 MAIL PUBLISHER SOLUTIONS FILLIES' H'CAP 6f (P)
4:30 (4:31) (Class 5) (0-70,74) 3-Y-O **£2,726** (£805; £402) **Stalls** Low

Form RPR

141 **1** **Sylvia Pankhurst (IRE)**[9] 2329 3-9-6 **74** 6ex.........(p) ThomasBrown(5) 2 84
(David C Griffiths) *mde all: rdn and qckning clr whn rdr dropped whip over 1f out: styd on wl fnl f: comf* **5/1**[3]

42-1 **2** 1 ¾ **Bright Glow**[15] 2129 3-9-7 **70**... TedDurcan 8 74+
(David Lanigan) *dwlt and pushed along leaving stalls: bhd: effrt and wdst bnd wl over 1f out: styd on wl fnl f: to go 2nd fnl 50yds: no ch w wnr* **4/1**[2]

01- **3** 1 ¼ **Winter Song (IRE)**[201] 7516 3-9-3 **66**.............................. MartinHarley 5 66
(Charles Hills) *chsd wnr: rdn and unable qck over 1f out: styd on same pce and lost 2nd fnl 50yds* **8/1**

0-04 **4** hd **Starlight Angel (IRE)**[16] 2098 3-9-3 **69**........................ DarrenEgan(3) 1 68
(Ronald Harris) *t.k.h: hld up in tch in midfield: swtchd rt and effrt jst over 1f out: styd on same pce u.p fnl f* **25/1**

55-5 **5** ¾ **Spicy (IRE)**[15] 2135 3-8-12 **66**....................................(b[1]) RobertTart(5) 10 63
(Marco Botti) *t.k.h: hld up towards rr: hdwy into midfield over 3f out: rdn and outpcd wl over 1f out: kpt on again ins fnl f* **8/1**

50-1 **6** 1 **Elusive Gold (IRE)**[23] 1874 3-9-6 **69**............................. SebSanders 3 63
(J W Hills) *t.k.h: hld up in last trio: rdn and sme hdwy towards inner ent fnl f: kpt on: nvr trbld ldrs* **14/1**

506- **7** nk **Direct Trade**[167] 8007 3-8-2 **51**.. DavidProbert 9 44
(Mark Usher) *in tch in midfield: unable qck u.p over 1f out: outpcd and btn 1f out: kpt on same pce* **33/1**

5-50 **8** 2 **Bheleyf (IRE)**[16] 2098 3-9-1 **64**.. HarryBentley 11 50
(Joseph Tuite) *hld up in tch in rr: rdn and no imp over 1f out: n.d* **50/1**

150- **9** shd **Grace Hull**[201] 7518 3-9-6 **69**.. RichardHughes 4 55
(J S Moore) *chsd ldrs: rdn and unable qck 2f out: btn over 1f out: wknd ins fnl f* **12/1**

01 **10** 6 **At A Clip**[12] 2226 3-9-7 **70**... JimCrowley 7 37
(Ralph Beckett) *towards rr: rdn over 3f out: no prog u.p 2f out: bhd 1f out and eased wl ins fnl f* **6/4**[1]

1m 11.73s (-0.17) **Going Correction** -0.05s/f (Stan) **10** Ran SP% **122.0**
Speed ratings (Par 96): **99,96,95,94,93 92,92,89,89,81**
Tote Swingers: 1&2 £4.90, 1&3 £6.80, 2&3 £7.50 CSF £26.27 CT £167.85 TOTE £6.00: £1.30, £1.50, £3.00; EX 28.40 Trifecta £156.40 Pool: £2,115.27 - 10.14 winning units..
Owner Norton Common Farm Racing **Bred** T Cahalan & D Cahalan **Trained** Bawtry, S Yorks

FOCUS
Probably a fair race with some unexposed fillies who could prove to be better than this level.

2573 SMITHS NEWS H'CAP (DIV I) 1m (P)
5:00 (5:00) (Class 5) (0-75,75) 4-Y-O+ **£2,726** (£805; £402) **Stalls** High

Form RPR

640- **1** **Emmuska**[258] 5983 4-9-7 **75**... AdamKirby 10 84
(Clive Cox) *chsd ldr tl led after 1f: mde rest: rdn and fnd ex wl over 1f out: kpt on wl u.p fnl f* **7/1**

-216 **2** ¾ **Poetic Lord**[16] 2101 4-9-6 **74**... GeorgeBaker 7 81
(Sylvester Kirk) *in tch in midfield: rdn and effrt on outer wl over 1f out: styng on but hanging lft in bhd wnr ins fnl f: wnt 2nd fnl 100yds: no imp after* **3/1**[2]

6-15 **3** 1 ½ **Kinglami**[23] 1878 4-9-3 **71**.......................................(v[1]) RichardHughes 2 75
(Brian Gubby) *in tch in midfield: rdn and effrt on inner to chse wnr jst over 1f out: no ex and lost 2nd fnl 100yds* **5/2**[1]

U030 **4** ¾ **The Happy Hammer (IRE)**[11] 2286 7-9-0 **68**.............. WilliamCarson 8 70
(Eugene Stanford) *hld up in tch in last trio: swtchd lft and effrt 2f out: drvn and styd on same pce ins fnl f* **20/1**

0320 **5** ¾ **Avertis**[23] 1878 8-9-0 **73**.. AmyScott(5) 1 73
(Alastair Lidderdale) *led for 1f: chsd ldr tl over 4f out: chsd ldrs after tl rdn and lost pl 2f out: no imp u.p fr over 1f out* **14/1**

22-5 **6** 3 ¼ **Derfenna Art (IRE)**[20] 1950 4-8-11 **65**........................(t) JohnFahy 5 58
(Seamus Durack) *dwlt: rdn along and grad rcvrd to chse ldr over 4f out: rdn and unable qck over 1f out: wknd 1f out* **9/2**[3]

7 1 ¾ **Dimitar (USA)**[42] 1491 4-9-4 **72**..................................... LiamKeniry 3 61
(Brendan Powell) *stdd s: t.k.h: hld up in rr: rdn and outpcd over 1f out: n.d after* **12/1**

00-4 **8** 2 ½ **Orpsie Boy (IRE)**[15] 2119 10-9-7 **75**.................... SilvestreDeSousa 4 58
(Ruth Carr) *hld up in tch in last trio: outpcd and rdn over 2f out: n.d after* **7/1**

1m 36.78s (-1.42) **Going Correction** -0.05s/f (Stan) **8** Ran SP% **115.9**
Speed ratings (Par 103): **105,104,102,102,101 98,96,93**
Tote Swingers: 1&2 £5.90, 1&3 £13.60, 2&3 £27.70 CSF £28.74 CT £68.08 TOTE £6.50: £1.50, £1.10, £2.50; EX 29.80 Trifecta £85.00 Pool: £2,093.53 - 18.46 winning units..
Owner Martin A Collins **Bred** Martin A Collins **Trained** Lambourn, Berks

FOCUS
With much C&D form on offer and only 10lb covering these, as the betting suggested it was an open event.

2574 SMITHS NEWS H'CAP (DIV II) 1m (P)
5:30 (5:30) (Class 5) (0-75,75) 4-Y-O+ **£2,726** (£805; £402) **Stalls** High

Form RPR

0-05 **1** **Sir Mike**[13] 2193 4-9-6 **74**.. JimCrowley 9 82
(Amanda Perrett) *chsd ldrs: drvn and effrt to chal over 1f out: led jst ins fnl f: forged ahd fnl 100yds: rdn out* **3/1**[2]

5023 **2** ½ **Prince Of Burma (IRE)**[22] 1901 5-9-7 **75**..............(bt) FergusSweeney 4 82
(Jeremy Gask) *t.k.h: hld up in tch in midfield: effrt to chse ldrs jst over 1f out: hung lft ins fnl f: chsd wnr ins fnl f: a hld* **6/1**

0223 **3** ¾ **Cyflymder (IRE)**[82] 839 7-8-9 **68**........................... ThomasBrown(5) 10 73
(David C Griffiths) *led: rdn 2f out: drvn and hrd pressed over 1f out: hdd jst ins fnl f: no ex and one pce after* **16/1**

56-5 **4** 1 **On My Own (TUR)**[21] 1926 4-9-4 **72**............................... SebSanders 5 75
(J W Hills) *t.k.h: in tch in midfield on outer: wdst and rdn bnd wl over 1f out: kpt on again ins fnl f* **5/1**[3]

2220 **5** ½ **Spring Tonic**[25] 1849 4-9-1 **74**.. RobertTart(5) 3 76
(Simon Dow) *chsd ldrs: rdn and unable qck 2f out: drvn and kpt on same pce fnl f* **11/4**[1]

05 **6** hd **Bankroll**[44] 1430 6-9-3 **71**..(t) GeorgeBaker 6 72
(Jonjo O'Neill) *chsd ldrs: rdn and unable qck wl over 1f out: hld and styd on same pce fnl f* **20/1**

4202 **7** 1 ¼ **Bajan Story**[12] 2228 4-8-7 **61** oh1...................................... DavidProbert 2 59
(Michael Blanshard) *hld up in tch in midfield: rdn and unable qck over 2f out: btn and styd on same pce fr over 1f out* **10/1**

60-0 **8** nk **Batchelors Star (IRE)**[48] 1346 5-9-4 **72**......................(t[1]) TomQueally 1 70
(Seamus Durack) *taken down early: stdd after s: hld up in tch in rr: rdn and effrt over 1f out: kpt on but nvr trbld ldrs* **33/1**

2104 **9** hd **Stormbound (IRE)**[22] 1901 4-8-11 **72**...........................(t) JordanUys(7) 7 69
(Paul Cole) *hld up in tch in last trio: effrt over 1f out: kpt on but nvr trbld ldrs* **10/1**

3460 **10** hd **Standpoint**[25] 1827 7-9-0 **68**... LiamKeniry 8 65
(Conor Dore) *stdd s: hld up in tch in rr: rdn over 1f out: kpt on but nvr trbld ldrs* **40/1**

1m 37.77s (-0.43) **Going Correction** -0.05s/f (Stan) **10** Ran SP% **116.8**
Speed ratings (Par 103): **100,99,98,97,97 97,95,95,95,95**
CSF £21.05 CT £253.51 TOTE £4.20: £1.80, £2.20, £2.40; EX 20.10 Trifecta £83.80 Pool: £1,106.11 - 9.88 winning units..
Owner M H and Mrs G Tourle **Bred** M H And Mrs G Tourle **Trained** Pulborough, W Sussex

FOCUS
This didn't seem as competitive as the first division and the time was a second slower, so just modest form.
T/Plt: £159.90 to a £1 stake. Pool: £63,894.45 - 291.67 winning units. T/Qpdt: £74.70 to a £1 stake. Pool: £3,997.85 - 39.60 winning units. SP

2509 SOUTHWELL (L-H)
Wednesday, May 22

OFFICIAL GOING: Standard
Wind: Fresh behind Weather: Cloudy with sunny periods

2575 £25 FREE BET AT BETVICTOR.COM H'CAP (DIV I) 7f (F)
1:50 (1:50) (Class 6) (0-55,60) 4-Y-O+ **£1,940** (£577; £288; £144) **Stalls** Low

Form RPR

4-11 **1** **Jebel Tara**[9] 2319 8-9-12 **60** 6ex..............................(bt) DaleSwift 13 72
(Alan Brown) *in tch on wd outside: wd st: gd hdwy over 2f out: rdn to chse ldrs over 1f out: led ins fnl f: styd on* **11/4**[1]

2362 **2** 1 ¼ **Mucky Molly**[14] 2170 5-9-5 **53**.....................................(vt) GrahamLee 7 62
(Alison Hutchinson) *slt ld: rdn wl over 1f out: drvn and hdd ins fnl f: kpt on* **4/1**[2]

3-04 **3** 1 ½ **Chez Vrony**[50] 1311 7-8-12 **46** oh1...................................... JoeFanning 2 51
(Dave Morris) *towards rr: wd st: hdwy on outer wl over 2f out: rdn wl over 1f out: styd on wl fnl f* **16/1**

-251 **4** ½ **Just Five (IRE)**[14] 2171 7-9-2 **53**...............................(v) RaulDaSilva(3) 1 57
(John Weymes) *cl up on inner: disp ld 1/2-way: rdn along 2f out: drvn and ch over 1f out: wknd fnl f* **6/1**

0-00 **5** *1 ½* **Master Of Song**[16] 2089 6-9-4 **55**....(t) MarkCoumbe(3) 11 55+
(Roy Bowring) *slowly away and lost several l s: bhd: hdwy on outer 3f out: sn rdn: styd on wl appr fnl f: nrst fin* **5/1**[3]

4-60 **6** *½* **Heidi's Delight (IRE)**[46] 1395 4-8-9 **50**.... RowanScott(7) 8 49
(Ann Duffield) *in tch: hdwy to chse ldrs wl over 2f out: sn rdn: drvn over 1f out and no imp* **33/1**

25-0 **7** *2* **Mistress Shy**[139] 41 6-8-12 **46** oh1....(t) AndrewMullen 10 39
(Michael Appleby) *chsd ldrs: rdn along wl over 2f out: drvn wl over 1f out and grad wknd* **50/1**

0350 **8** *1 ½* **Elusive Warrior (USA)**[71] 965 10-8-9 **50**....(p) NoraLooby(7) 9 39
(Alan McCabe) *chsd ldrs: rdn along 1/2-way: sn wknd* **20/1**

1400 **9** *nk* **Upper Lambourn (IRE)**[20] 1951 5-9-2 **55**....(t1) GeorgeChaloner(5) 6 44
(Christopher Kellett) *a in rr* **12/1**

0-50 **10** *½* **Visions Of Johanna (USA)**[4] 2435 8-8-7 **48**....(bt) AaronJones(7) 5 35
(Charles Smith) *a towards rr* **25/1**

4053 **11** *2 ½* **Jackie Love (IRE)**[20] 1951 5-8-6 **47**....(v) IanBurns(7) 4 28
(Olivia Maylam) *a towards rr* **14/1**

0500 **12** *1 ¾* **Tenancy (IRE)**[17] 2043 9-8-5 **46** oh1.... GaryMahon(7) 3 22
(Shaun Harris) *prom: rdn along bef 1/2-way: sn wknd* **33/1**

-400 **13** *4* **Captain Cavallo**[16] 2074 6-8-12 **46** oh1....(bt) LukeMorris 12 12
(Nicky Vaughan) *chsd ldrs: rdn along 1/2-way: sn wknd* **50/1**

1m 30.5s (0.20) **Going Correction** +0.05s/f (Slow) **13** Ran SP% **116.3**
Speed ratings (Par 101): **100,98,96,96,94 94,91,90,89,89 86,84,79**
Tote Swingers: 1&2 £2.40, 1&3 £9.40, 2&3 £6.20 CSF £11.71 CT £149.41 TOTE £2.60: £1.10, £2.20, £4.30; EX 9.90 Trifecta £97.30 Pool: £1,367.74 - 10.53 winning units..
Owner Miss E Johnston **Bred** Mrs G P Booth And J Porteous **Trained** Yedingham, N Yorks

FOCUS
The pace was sound for this modest handicap.

2576 BETVICTOR CASINO ON YOUR MOBILE MAIDEN STKS 7f (F)
2:20 (2:21) (Class 5) 3-Y-O+ **£2,587** (£770; £384; £192) **Stalls** Low

Form RPR

0333 **1** **Yahilwa (USA)**[15] 2129 3-8-11 65.... NeilCallan 12 81
(James Tate) *cl up: led 3f out: rdn clr over 2f out: kpt on wl fnl f* **5/1**

2 *7* **Celestial Ray** 4-9-13 0.... LukeMorris 5 72+
(Sir Mark Prescott Bt) *dwlt and towards rr: hdwy 3f out: rdn 2f out: styd on to chse wnr ins fnl f: no imp* **6/1**

22 **3** *1 ¾* **Maakirr (IRE)**[40] 1522 4-9-10 0....(t) MarkCoumbe(3) 10 67
(Roy Bowring) *trckd ldng pair: hdwy to chse wnr wl over 2f out and sn rdn: drvn wl over 1f out: sn one pce* **4/1**[2]

4 *nk* **Tee It Up Tommo (IRE)** 4-9-13 0.... FrannyNorton 6 67
(Michael Wigham) *trckd ldrs: hdwy over 2f out: rdn wl over 1f out: sn drvn and one pce* **7/2**[1]

0 **5** *7* **Midaz**[30] 1713 3-9-2 0.... RobertHavlin 1 44
(Hughie Morrison) *towards rr: sme hdwy fnl 2f: nvr a factor* **9/2**[3]

0-35 **6** *3 ¼* **Ebony Express**[17] 2041 4-9-13 66.... RobertWinston 9 40
(Alan Swinbank) *chsd ldrs: rdn along 3f out: sn wknd* **10/1**

-205 **7** *½* **Bougaloo**[20] 1967 3-9-2 67....(b1) SeanLevey 11 35
(Alan McCabe) *dwlt: sn chsng ldrs on outer: rdn along over 3f out: sn wknd* **16/1**

005 **8** *2 ¾* **Stoneacre Oskar**[14] 2172 4-9-8 39.... DaleSwift 8 27
(Peter Grayson) *nvr bttr than midfield* **100/1**

9 *¾* **Threave** 5-9-8 0.... GrahamLee 7 25
(Violet M Jordan) *led: pushed along 1/2-way: sn hdd & wknd over 2f out* **66/1**

10 *¾* **Secret Song** 3-9-2 0.... ChrisCatlin 2 24
(Sir Mark Prescott Bt) *a bhd* **14/1**

11 *2 ¾* **Vital Edition (IRE)** 3-9-2 0.... AndrewMullen 4 17
(David O'Meara) *a in rr* **25/1**

6/0 **12** *19* **Mr Mallo**[14] 2172 4-9-13 0.... StephenCraine 3
(John Stimpson) *chsd ldrs on inner: rdn along 1/2-way: sn wknd* **100/1**

1m 29.51s (-0.79) **Going Correction** +0.05s/f (Slow)
WFA 3 from 4yo+ 11lb **12** Ran SP% **120.3**
Speed ratings (Par 103): **106,98,96,95,87 83,83,80,79,78 75,53**
Tote Swingers: 1&2 £5.60, 1&3 £2.40, 2&3 £8.10 CSF £35.30 TOTE £3.10: £1.20, £3.70, £2.00; EX 31.60 Trifecta £163.50 Pool: £1,425.10 - 6.53 winning units..
Owner Sheikh Juma Dalmook Al Maktoum **Bred** Avalon Farms Inc **Trained** Newmarket, Suffolk

FOCUS
An open if modest maiden, run at a fair pace with the winner scoring impressively.

2577 EBF BETVICTOR.COM MAIDEN STKS 6f (F)
2:50 (2:55) (Class 5) 2-Y-O **£2,911** (£866; £432; £216) **Stalls** Low

Form RPR

1 **Dubawi Fun** 2-9-5 0.... PatCosgrave 6 80+
(Ismail Mohammed) *wnt rt s: sn cl up: led after 2f: rdn and qcknd clr 2f out: styd on strly* **4/1**[3]

54 **2** *4 ½* **Ocean Storm (IRE)**[13] 2194 2-9-5 0.... NeilCallan 1 66
(James Tate) *chsd ldrs on inner: rdn along over 2f out: swtchd rt to chse wnr over 1f out: no imp fnl f* **6/4**[1]

3 **3** *1 ¾* **Tamayuz Magic (IRE)**[8] 2337 2-9-5 0.... JoeFanning 2 61
(Mark Johnston) *trckd ldrs: rdn along over 2f out: edgd lft over 1f out: kpt on same pce* **9/4**[2]

0 **4** *2* **Red Dakota (IRE)**[30] 1718 2-9-0 0.... MartinDwyer 4 50
(David C Griffiths) *led 2f: cl up: rdn along over 2f out: drvn wl over 1f out: wknd* **66/1**

5 *8* **Clarice** 2-9-0 0.... LukeMorris 3 26
(Sir Mark Prescott Bt) *in tch: rdn along bef 1/2-way: sn outpcd* **7/1**

5 **6** *½* **Jimmy Crackle (IRE)**[5] 2404 2-9-5 0.... DaleSwift 5 29
(Brian Ellison) *in tch and sn rdn along: outpcd bef 1/2-way and sn bhd* **14/1**

1m 17.36s (0.86) **Going Correction** +0.05s/f (Slow) **6** Ran SP% **111.4**
Speed ratings (Par 93): **96,90,87,85,74 73**
Tote Swingers: 1&2 £1.80, 1&3 £2.20, 2&3 £1.40 CSF £10.30 TOTE £4.80: £2.40, £1.70; EX 13.80 Trifecta £39.90 Pool: £2,236.73 - 41.94 winning units..
Owner Sultan Ali **Bred** Rabbah Bloodstock Limited **Trained** Newmarket, Suffolk

FOCUS
Not much pace on for this maiden, with the winner scoring impressively.

2578 £25 FREE BET AT BETVICTOR.COM H'CAP (DIV II) 7f (F)
3:20 (3:22) (Class 6) (0-55,55) 4-Y-O+ **£1,940** (£577; £288; £144) **Stalls** Low

Form RPR

5000 **1** **Munaawib**[4] 2435 5-8-12 **46** oh1....(t1) PatCosgrave 8 58
(Charles Smith) *s.i.s and sn swtchd rt to outer: towards rr and rdn along 1/2-way: hdwy and wd st: rdn to ld and hung bdly lft 1 1/2f out: drvn clr: kpt on* **25/1**

6006 **2** *4* **Ishiamiracle**[29] 1748 4-8-7 **46** oh1....(p) RachealKneller(5) 5 48
(Phil McEntee) *led 2f: prom: rdn along 2f out: chsd wnr over 1f out: kpt on same pce fnl f* **20/1**

/05- **3** *1* **Glan Lady (IRE)**[204] 7469 7-8-12 **46** oh1.... AndrewMullen 10 45
(Michael Appleby) *towards rr: hdwy over 2f out: sn rdn: styd on appr fnl f: nrst fin* **12/1**

0520 **4** *hd* **Tony Hollis**[1] 2536 5-8-9 **50**.... GemmaTutty(7) 12 48
(Karen Tutty) *chsd ldrs: rdn along over 2f out: drvn wl over 1f out: kpt on one pce* **7/2**[2]

3500 **5** *¾* **Boy The Bell**[11] 2273 6-8-12 **53**....[1] JacobButterfield(7) 11 50
(Ollie Pears) *s.i.s and reminders s: in rr: hdwy on outer 2f out: drvn along and kpt on appr fnl f: nrst fin* **9/2**[3]

0-60 **6** *½* **Zammy**[14] 2168 4-8-13 **47**....(b) RobertWinston 13 42
(Michael Wigham) *trckd ldrs: hdwy and cl up 3f out: rdn and ev ch over 2f out: sn drvn and one pce* **7/1**

5145 **7** *1 ¾* **Ace Of Spies (IRE)**[14] 2168 8-9-6 **54**.... LukeMorris 9 45
(Conor Dore) *chsd ldrs: rdn along over 2f: sn drvn and btn* **3/1**[1]

2600 **8** *2 ½* **Perfect Ch'I (IRE)**[15] 2134 6-9-7 **55**....(v) DaneO'Neill 7 39
(Paul Fitzsimons) *cl up: led after 2f: rdn along over 2f out: hdd wl over 1f out: sn drvn and wknd* **12/1**

0040 **9** *¾* **Ishetoo**[14] 2170 9-8-12 **46** oh1.... DaleSwift 4 28
(Peter Grayson) *a towards rr* **50/1**

5003 **10** *nse* **Katmai River (IRE)**[15] 2126 6-8-10 **51**....(p) EmilyMelbourn(7) 1 33
(Mark Usher) *a towards rr* **16/1**

035- **11** *26* **Memphis Man**[161] 8077 10-9-0 **48**.... NeilCallan 6
(Milton Bradley) *nvr bttr than midfield:* **16/1**

00-6 **12** *10* **My Stroppy Poppy**[8] 2346 4-9-2 **50**....(tp) MircoMimmocchi 2
(Frank Sheridan) *a in rr* **33/1**

1m 30.88s (0.58) **Going Correction** +0.05s/f (Slow) **12** Ran SP% **118.6**
Speed ratings (Par 101): **98,93,92,92,91 90,88,85,84,84 55,43**
Tote Swingers: 1&2 £117.70, 1&3 £70.90, 2&3 £47.70 CSF £434.18 CT £6255.07 TOTE £62.30: £9.70, £7.30, £3.30; EX 2029.70 Trifecta £1015.00 Part won. Pool: £1,353.40 - 0.01 winning units..
Owner Willie McKay **Bred** Shadwell Estate Company Limited **Trained** Temple Bruer, Lincs

FOCUS
This modest handicap was run at a sound pace, with the winner pulling clear.

2579 TALK TO VICTOR CLAIMING STKS 1m 4f (F)
3:50 (3:50) (Class 5) 3-Y-O+ **£2,726** (£805; £402) **Stalls** Low

Form RPR

00-0 **1** **Reve De Nuit (USA)**[19] 1990 7-9-11 93.... MichaelMetcalfe(3) 2 94
(Mrs K Burke) *trckd ldrs: smooth hdwy 3f out: chal over 2f out: led wl over 1f out: sn rdn clr: readily* **5/1**[3]

4511 **2** *7* **Noguchi (IRE)**[27] 1795 8-9-13 79....(b) NeilCallan 4 82
(Michael Murphy) *trckd ldr: hdwy to ld wl over 2f out: sn jnd and rdn: hdd wl over 1f out: drvn and edgd lft ent fnl f: one pce* **5/2**[2]

1-12 **3** *3* **La Estrella (USA)**[126] 227 10-10-0 88.... DaneO'Neill 5 78
(Don Cantillon) *trckd ldrs: pushed along after 3f: niggled 1/2-way: reminders over 4f out: rdn over 3f out: drvn and edgd lft wl over 1f out: plugged on same pce: tk 3rd towards fin* **10/11**[1]

40-6 **4** *nk* **Ultimate**[17] 2040 7-10-0 80....(b) DaleSwift 3 78
(Brian Ellison) *led and set str pce: rdn along over 3f out: hdd wl over 2f out: sn drvn along and one pce: lost 3rd ins fnl f* **8/1**

0/0- **5** *dist* **Crassula**[354] 2706 5-9-9 80.... RobertWinston 1
(Paul Fitzsimons) *trckd ldng pair on inner: pushed along bef 1/2-way: rdn along over 5f out: sn lost pl and bhd: t.o and eased fnl 3f* **50/1**

2m 37.1s (-3.90) **Going Correction** +0.05s/f (Slow) **5** Ran SP% **110.7**
Speed ratings (Par 103): **115,110,108,108,**
CSF £17.79 TOTE £3.50: £1.70, £1.80; EX 19.20 Trifecta £38.30 Pool: £878.64 - 17.19 winning units..
Owner Mrs Z Wentworth **Bred** Ecurie Du Haras De Meautry **Trained** Middleham Moor, N Yorks

FOCUS
A decent claimer run at a sound pace, with the highest-rated runner in the field scoring impressively.

2580 MIKE MAHONY 65 TODAY H'CAP 1m (F)
4:20 (4:20) (Class 4) (0-80,79) 4-Y-O+ **£4,690** (£1,395; £697; £348) **Stalls** Low

Form RPR

5300 **1** **The Lock Master (IRE)**[25] 1831 6-9-7 **79**.... DaneO'Neill 4 89
(Michael Appleby) *prom: trckd ldr after 3f: hdwy to ld wl over 2f out: sn rdn along: clr ent fnl f: styd on strly* **5/1**[3]

5561 **2** *2 ½* **Our Ivor**[2] 2515 4-9-6 **78** 6ex.... AndrewMullen 6 82
(Michael Appleby) *prom hdwy and cl up 3f out: chal over 2f out: sn rdn and ev ch: drvn edgd lft and one pce ent fnl f* **7/4**[1]

2-21 **3** *¾* **No Dominion (IRE)**[11] 2278 4-9-5 **77**.... GrahamLee 7 80
(James Given) *stdd s and several l adrift in rr: sn pushed along and hdwy after 3f: in tch 3f out: rdn to chse ldrs over 2f out: kpt on u.p appr fnl f: nrst fin* **5/2**[2]

2150 **4** *6* **Alpha Tauri (USA)**[52] 1276 7-8-11 **76**....(t) AaronJones(7) 8 65
(Charles Smith) *sn led and set str pce: rdn along 3f out: sn hdd: drvn on far rail and grad wknd fnl 2f* **25/1**

0036 **5** *3 ½* **Illustrious Prince (IRE)**[11] 2275 6-8-6 **67**.... NeilFarley(3) 1 48
(Declan Carroll) *nvr nr ldrs* **25/1**

0-03 **6** *8* **Halling Dancer**[16] 2085 4-9-1 **73**.... KierenFox 9 35
(Lee Carter) *chsd ldrs: rdn along over 3f out: sn drvn and wknd over 2f out* **14/1**

1333 **7** *12* **Caledonia Prince**[29] 1752 5-9-3 **75**....(b) FrannyNorton 3
(Jo Hughes) *trckd ldrs on inner: rdn along 3f out: sn wknd* **8/1**

14-6 **8** *44* **Sky Crossing**[25] 1827 4-9-1 **73**.... MickyFenton 5
(Tom Tate) *chsd ldrs: rdn along after 2f: sn lost pl and bhd: eased fnl 2f* **14/1**

1m 44.06s (0.36) **Going Correction** +0.05s/f (Slow) **8** Ran SP% **113.7**
Speed ratings (Par 105): **100,97,96,90,87 79,67,23**
Tote Swingers: 1&2 £3.80, 1&3 £3.30, 2&3 £2.40 CSF £14.01 CT £25.88 TOTE £4.60: £2.20, £1.10, £1.10; EX 19.20 Trifecta £47.70 Pool: £1,954.26 - 30.67 winning units..
Owner K G Kitchen **Bred** Patrick F Kelly **Trained** Danethorpe, Notts

The Form Book Flat, Raceform Ltd, Compton, RG20 6NL.

FOCUS
Three non runners took some of the interest out of this fair handicap, which was run at a solid pace.

2581 DOWNLOAD THE BETVICTOR SPINCAST APP NOW CLASSIFIED (S) STKS 7f (F)
4:50 (4:50) (Class 6) 3-Y-O £2,045 (£603; £302) Stalls Low

Form RPR
50-5 **1** **Lexington Blue**[20] 1966 3-8-12 52 GrahamLee 4 58
(David O'Meara) *cl up: rdn to chal 3f out: led 2f out: rdn clr over 1f out: kpt on strly* **11/10**[2]
6-00 **2** 4 ½ **Amelia Jay**[5] 2405 3-8-12 50 DuranFentiman 1 46
(Danielle McCormick) *trckd ldng pair: pushed along 3f out: rdn over 1f out: styd on u.p fnl f* **20/1**[3]
153- **3** 2 ¼ **Done Dreaming (IRE)**[242] 6499 3-8-13 65 GeorgeChaloner(5) 3 46
(Richard Fahey) *slt ld: rdn along and edgd lft over 2f out: sn hdd & wknd appr fnl f* **4/5**[1]
06-0 **4** 42 **Wicked Tara**[12] 2215 3-8-5 13 (t) CharlieBennett(7) 2
(Frank Sheridan) *dwlt and a in rr: outpcd and bhd fr 1/2-way* **100/1**
1m 32.35s (2.05) **Going Correction** +0.05s/f (Slow) 4 Ran SP% 108.9
Speed ratings (Par 97): **90,84,82,34**
CSF £15.77 TOTE £1.80; EX 10.00 Trifecta £16.30 Pool: £1,071.43 - 49.21 winning units..Winner bought in for 9,250gns.
Owner Middleham Park Racing XLIX & Partners **Bred** The National Stud Blakeney Club **Trained** Nawton, N Yorks

FOCUS
This was desperately weak, even for the grade.

2582 DOWNLOAD THE BETVICTOR APP NOW H'CAP 6f (F)
5:20 (5:21) (Class 6) (0-60,60) 4-Y-O+ £1,940 (£577; £288; £144) Stalls Low

Form RPR
6030 **1** **Prince Of Passion (CAN)**[11] 2280 5-9-6 59 JoeFanning 12 70
(Derek Shaw) *chsd ldrs on outer: hdwy over 2f out: rdn to ld appr fnl f: drvn out* **16/1**
0303 **2** ½ **Ridgeway Hawk**[14] 2170 5-8-11 50 (v) RobertHavlin 5 59
(Mark Usher) *towards rr: swtchd to outer and wd st: hdwy 2f out: sn rdn: styd on wl fnl f: nt quite rch wnr* **6/1**[3]
4410 **3** 1 ¼ **Thorpe Bay**[12] 2236 4-9-6 59 AndrewMullen 13 64
(Michael Appleby) *cl up: led wl over 2f out: sn rdn: drvn and hdd appr fnl f: kpt on same pce* **8/1**
4604 **4** 3 **Very First Blade**[14] 2170 4-8-3 49 (p) MatthewHopkins(7) 6 44
(Mark Brisbourne) *towards rr: hdwy 2f out: rdn to chse ldrs and hung rt ent fnl f: drvn and kpt on: nrst fin* **16/1**
0610 **5** 3 ¾ **Loyal Royal (IRE)**[22] 1902 10-9-7 60 (bt) GrahamLee 14 43
(Milton Bradley) *stdd s: hld up: hdwy 1/2-way: rdn to chse ldrs 2f out: sn drvn and no imp* **40/1**
1400 **6** 1 ½ **Whipphound**[77] 898 5-9-2 55 RobertWinston 10 34
(Mark Brisbourne) *trckd ldrs: hdwy 1/2-way: sn cl up: rdn 2f out and sn one pce* **20/1**
000- **7** nk **Layla's King**[193] 7684 5-9-7 60 MartinDwyer 11 38
(David C Griffiths) *sn led: rdn along and hdd wl sn over 2f out: sn drvn and grad wknd* **6/1**[3]
3330 **8** ½ **Flow Chart (IRE)**[15] 2125 6-9-0 53 DaleSwift 3 29
(Peter Grayson) *nvr bttr than midfield* **16/1**
5120 **9** 3 ½ **Mary's Pet**[27] 1783 6-9-4 57 (p) KierenFox 8 22
(Lee Carter) *nvr bttr than midfield* **11/2**[2]
-200 **10** nk **Man Of My Word**[20] 1951 4-9-0 56 (p) BillyCray(3) 1 20
(Scott Dixon) *rdn along on inner after s: chsd ldrs to 1/2-way: sn wknd* **25/1**
-003 **11** ½ **Chester'Slittlegem (IRE)**[16] 2074 4-8-9 48 FrannyNorton 4 10
(Jo Hughes) *a towards rr* **20/1**
-600 **12** 5 **Quan (IRE)**[20] 1951 4-8-10 49 NeilCallan 9
(Milton Bradley) *chsd ldrs: pushed along 1/2-way: rdn wl over 2f out: sn wknd* **9/2**[1]
0/60 **13** 4 **South Kenter (USA)**[30] 1711 4-8-4 48 (v[1]) RyanTate(5) 7
(Heather Main) *a towards rr* **8/1**
3-04 **14** 9 **Windygoul Lad**[17] 2036 4-9-4 57 AdrianNicholls 2
(Michael Smith) *a towards rr: bhd and eased fnl 2f* **20/1**
1m 16.77s (0.27) **Going Correction** +0.05s/f (Slow) 14 Ran SP% 122.6
Speed ratings (Par 101): **100,99,97,93,88 86,86,85,80,80 79,73,67,55**
Tote Swingers: 1&2 £12.80, 1&3 £12.10, 2&3 £5.10 CSF £103.09 CT £872.73 TOTE £14.30: £3.70, £2.20, £2.80; EX 101.40 Trifecta £305.30 Pool: £2,186.95 - 5.37 winning units..
Owner Chris Hamilton **Bred** Majestic Thoroughbred Investments Inc **Trained** Sproxton, Leics
■ Stewards' Enquiry : Robert Havlin four-day ban: use of whip (5-8 June)
Joe Fanning trainer could offer no explanation for the apparent improvment in form
Martin Dwyer two-day ban: careless riding (5-6 June)

FOCUS
An open, if low-grade handicap run at a sound pace with the front three home racing near the stands' rail.
T/Plt: £393.30 to a £1 stake. Pool: £47,073.10 - 87.36 winning tickets. T/Qpdt: £126.30 to a £1 stake. Pool: £2,969.78 - 17.40 winning tickets. JR

2192 GOODWOOD (R-H)
Thursday, May 23
OFFICIAL GOING: Good to firm (8.8) changing to good after race 2 (2.35)
Wind: Moderate, half against Weather: Changeable with showers, cold

2583 BRITISH STALLION STUDS SUPPORTING BRITISH RACING EBF MAIDEN FILLIES' STKS 6f
2:00 (2:01) (Class 5) 2-Y-O £3,881 (£1,155; £577; £288) Stalls High

Form RPR
4 **1** **Kiyoshi**[35] 1634 2-9-0 0 JamieSpencer 8 87+
(Charles Hills) *lw: prom: trckd ldr 1/2-way: pushed into ld over 1f out: edgd lft ins fnl f: styd on wl* **8/11**[1]
2 1 ½ **Ihtimal (IRE)** 2-9-0 0 SilvestreDeSousa 9 82+
(Saeed bin Suroor) *w'like: tall: cl-cpld: led against nr side rail: shkn up and hdd over 1f out: hld whn n.m.r briefly 100yds out: styd on* **9/2**[2]
2622 **3** 7 **Memory Styx**[17] 2090 2-8-9 0 CharlesBishop(5) 2 61
(Mick Channon) *wnt lft s and bdly bmpd rival: chsd ldrs: rdn to go 3rd over 2f out: hanging lft and no imp over 1f out: fdd* **10/1**
4 1 ¾ **Chesturo (IRE)** 2-9-0 0 MartinHarley 5 56
(Mick Channon) *athletic: chsd ldrs: clsd enough over 2f out: shkn up and fdd wl over 1f out* **25/1**
5 1 ½ **Royal Connection** 2-9-0 0 RyanMoore 3 51+
(Richard Hannon) *w'like: bit bkwd: dwlt then bdly hmpd s: struggling in last pair: rdn over 2f out: kpt on one pce over 1f out* **10/1**
6 2 ¾ **Lady Marl** 2-9-0 0 PatDobbs 7 43
(Gary Moore) *str: bit bkwd: chsd ldrs: rdn over 2f out: wknd wl over 1f out* **40/1**
6 **7** 10 **Movie Magic**[12] 2260 2-9-0 0 KierenFox 4 13
(John Bridger) *leggy: wnt rt s and bmpd rival: outpcd in last and rdn after 2f: brief effrt on outer 1/2-way: sn wknd: t.o* **100/1**
8 4 ½ **Mildenhall** 2-9-0 0 RichardHughes 1
(Richard Hannon) *w'like: leggy: racd wd: chsd ldr to 1/2-way: nudged along and sn lost pl: eased fnl f: t.o* **6/1**[3]
1m 12.65s (0.45) **Going Correction** -0.075s/f (Good) 8 Ran SP% 115.8
Speed ratings (Par 90): **94,92,82,80,78 74,61,55**
Tote Swingers 1&2 £1.70, 2&3 £4.40, 1&3 £3.00 CSF £4.34 TOTE £1.50: £1.10, £1.30, £2.40; EX 4.30 Trifecta £18.70 Pool: £3,453.92 - 138.09 winning tickets..
Owner Qatar Racing Limited **Bred** Lowther Racing **Trained** Lambourn, Berks

FOCUS
First 2f of 1m course dolled out 5yds. Lower bend dolled out 6yds from 6f to 2f pole in straight adding 16yds to races using lower bend. The front pair drew clear in what was a fair fillies' maiden, with the third used as a reliable guide to the form.

2584 WINNER PLANT UK STKS (H'CAP) 1m 1f
2:35 (2:35) (Class 4) (0-85,80) 3-Y-O £6,225 (£1,864; £932; £466; £233; £117) Stalls Low

Form RPR
1-21 **1** **King Of The Danes**[13] 2209 3-9-2 77 FrannyNorton 8 96+
(Mark Johnston) *lw: mde all: stretched clr fr 2f out: in n.d after: bolted up* **4/1**[1]
1-43 **2** 6 **Zamoyski**[12] 2259 3-9-5 80 WilliamBuick 5 85
(Jeremy Noseda) *lw: t.k.h: hld up in 4th: rdn over 2f out: styd on to take 2nd over 1f out: no ch w wnr* **9/2**[2]
-133 **3** 2 ¾ **Erodium**[20] 1977 3-9-3 78 (b[1]) RichardHughes 4 77
(Richard Hannon) *lw: hld up in last pair: stdy prog over 2f out: shkn up and fnd nil over 1f out: kpt on to take 3rd nr fin* **12/1**
-126 **4** ½ **Strong Conviction**[20] 1977 3-9-2 77 MartinHarley 6 75
(Mick Channon) *chsd wnr: rdn over 2f out: sn lft bhd: steadily fdd over 1f out* **25/1**
22-4 **5** ½ **Swift Bounty**[13] 2209 3-8-13 79 MichaelJMMurphy(5) 2 76+
(Alan Jarvis) *hld up in 5th: effrt on outer over 2f out: hanging and wandered after: nvr able to make much hdwy* **4/1**[1]
41- **6** 1 **Aussie Lyrics (FR)**[196] 7642 3-9-2 77 JimCrowley 3 72
(George Baker) *dwlt: hld up in last: shkn up and no prog over 2f out: kpt on to press for a pl 1f out: no hdwy after* **6/1**[3]
4-21 **7** 3 ¾ **Mysterial**[52] 1288 3-9-5 80 (b) RyanMoore 7 67
(Richard Hannon) *on toes: chsd ldng pair to over 2f out: sn wknd: eased fnl f* **10/1**
36-1 **8** 7 **Lamusawama**[22] 1923 3-9-5 80 DaneO'Neill 1 51
(Ed Dunlop) *lw: dwlt: t.k.h: hld up in 6th: shkn up over 3f out: sn btn: t.o* **9/2**[2]
1m 55.22s (-1.08) **Going Correction** -0.075s/f (Good) 8 Ran SP% 111.3
Speed ratings (Par 101): **101,95,93,92,92 91,88,81**
Tote Swingers 1&2 £3.40, 2&3 £5.00, 1&3 £5.40 CSF £20.82 CT £190.22 TOTE £3.90: £1.60, £1.70, £2.70; EX 15.80 Trifecta £86.30 Pool: £2,812.60 - 24.42 winning tickets..
Owner Newsells Park Stud **Bred** Newsells Park Stud **Trained** Middleham Moor, N Yorks

FOCUS
Just an ordinary 3yo handicap but the winner is entitled to rate at least this high. The form is taken at something like face value.

2585 WRIGHT JOINERY COMPANY STKS (H'CAP) 7f
3:10 (3:10) (Class 2) (0-100,100) 4-Y-O+ £12,938 (£3,850; £1,924; £962) Stalls Low

Form RPR
1-40 **1** **Head Of Steam (USA)**[19] 2013 6-8-8 87 PatDobbs 7 96
(Amanda Perrett) *trckd ldng quartet: smooth prog over 2f out: led over 1f out gng strly: drvn out and kpt on fnl f* **8/1**
5661 **2** ¾ **George Guru**[19] 2013 6-8-13 92 JamieSpencer 1 99+
(Michael Attwater) *stdd s: hld up in last trio and off the pce: stdy prog 2f out: drvn and styd on fr over 1f out: tk 2nd last strides* **11/4**[1]
00-3 **3** hd **The Confessor**[19] 2013 6-8-11 90 CathyGannon 6 96
(Henry Candy) *lw: w ldr: led 3f out: drvn and hdd over 1f out: kpt on but lost 2nd last strides* **7/2**[2]
-510 **4** 1 **Bronze Prince**[12] 2254 6-8-12 91 RobertHavlin 9 95
(Michael Attwater) *cl up on outer: rdn to chal 2f out: nt qckn over 1f out: one pce after* **14/1**
13-0 **5** 1 ¼ **Silverheels (IRE)**[19] 2013 4-8-9 88 SilvestreDeSousa 2 88
(Paul Cole) *hld up in 7th: effrt on outer over 2f out: drvn and one pce fr over 1f out* **6/1**[3]
20-0 **6** 2 **Noble Citizen (USA)**[23] 1913 8-8-9 88 (b) MartinLane 10 83
(David Simcock) *s.s: hld up in last trio and off the pce: rdn on outer over 2f out: sme prog over 1f out but nvr a threat: fdd fnl f* **20/1**
416- **7** 8 **Common Touch (IRE)**[220] 7097 5-9-1 94 J-PGuillambert 4 67
(Willie Musson) *nvr bttr than midfield: rdn and no prog over 2f out: sn wknd* **20/1**
0556 **8** 2 ½ **Field Of Dream**[68] 1034 6-9-7 100 AdamKirby 3 70
(Jamie Osborne) *lw: dwlt: hld up in last and detached early: jst pushed along fr over 2f out: nvr involved* **8/1**
1/60 **9** 6 **Chandlery (IRE)**[22] 1919 4-9-7 100 RichardHughes 8 61
(Richard Hannon) *pressed ldrs: rdn over 2f out: sn wknd: heavily eased fnl f* **8/1**
05-0 **10** 1 ¼ **Radio Gaga**[40] 1544 4-9-2 95 SeanLevey 5 53
(Ed McMahon) *mde most to 3f out: wknd qckly 2f out: eased ins fnl f* **16/1**
1m 26.39s (-0.61) **Going Correction** +0.15s/f (Good) 10 Ran SP% 118.6
Speed ratings (Par 109): **109,108,107,106,105 103,93,91,84,82**
Tote Swingers 1&2 £5.30, 2&3 £2.70, 1&3 £7.50 CSF £30.81 CT £93.69 TOTE £10.00: £2.90, £1.40, £1.90; EX 49.50 Trifecta £255.10 Pool: £3,291.18 - 9.67 winning tickets..
Owner George Materna **Bred** Juddmonte Farms Inc **Trained** Pulborough, W Sussex

FOCUS
They went a good gallop and the form looks solid with the winner back to his best.

2586 HEIGHT OF FASHION STKS (LISTED RACE) (FILLIES) 1m 1f 192y
3:45 (3:46) (Class 1) 3-Y-O £23,680 (£8,956; £4,476; £2,236) Stalls Low

Form RPR
3-24 **1** **Elik (IRE)**[15] 2148 3-9-0 86 RyanMoore 1 98+
(Sir Michael Stoute) *lw: slowest away and rousted to rch 7th after 1f: gd prog on outer over 2f out: drvn to ld narrowly 1f out: styd on wl to assert last 100yds* **3/1**[2]

1-32 **2** ¾ **Heading North**[22] 1933 3-9-0 85 ... RichardHughes 8 96
(Richard Hannon) *led and sn clr: 5 l ahd 4f out: drvn and hdd 1f out: battled on wl but hld last 100yds* **5/2**[1]

6 **3** 5 **Harmonic Note**[16] 2141 3-9-0 92 ... JamieSpencer 4 86
(G M Lyons, Ire) *hld up in last quartet: hld together tl prog 2f out: rdn over 1f out: tk 3rd fnl f but ldng pair wl away: kpt on one pce* **6/1**

0-31 **4** nse **Contradict**[7] 2390 3-9-0 71 ... SamHitchcott 7 86
(Mick Channon) *hld up in last pair: shkn up over 3f out: effrt on outer u.p over 2f out: styd on to press for 3rd nr fin* **14/1**

0-62 **5** ¾ **Trapeze**[14] 2195 3-9-0 77 ... WilliamBuick 11 84
(John Gosden) *chsd clr ldr: rdn and no imp 2f out: lost 2nd and one pce over 1f out* **7/2**[3]

4-12 **6** 2 **Of Course Darling**[13] 2223 3-9-0 78 ... AndreaAtzeni 6 80
(Ed Dunlop) *sn trckd ldng pair: disp 2nd over 3f out to 2f out: fdd fnl f* **25/1**

16 **7** 2¼ **Valtina (IRE)**[6] 2412 3-9-0 83 ... SilvestreDeSousa 10 76
(William Haggas) *lw: t.k.h: prom: wd bnd 1/2-way: rdn and nt qckn over 2f out: wknd fnl f* **10/1**

0-45 **8** 3 **Starlight Symphony (IRE)**[7] 2387 3-9-0 75 ... TedDurcan 5 70
(Eve Johnson Houghton) *trckd ldrs in 6th: shkn up over 2f out: wknd wl over 1f out* **33/1**

3-23 **9** 1¾ **High Time Too (IRE)**[16] 2127 3-9-0 71 ... AdamKirby 9 66
(Hugo Palmer) *swtg: hld up in last pair: rdn wl over 2f out: no prog and sn btn* **66/1**

-135 **10** 6 **Glenreef**[17] 2079 3-9-0 65 ... FrannyNorton 2 54
(Mark Johnston) *hld up in last quartet: rdn over 3f out: wknd over 2f out* **100/1**

230 **11** nk **Harbinger Lass**[15] 2148 3-9-0 77 ... MartinHarley 3 54
(Mick Channon) *prom tl wknd 3f out* **50/1**

2m 7.34s (-0.76) **Going Correction** +0.15s/f (Good) **11** Ran SP% **117.1**
Speed ratings (Par 104): **109,108,104,104,103 102,100,97,96,91 91**
Tote Swingers 1&2 £2.50, 2&3 £3.60, 1&3 £5.20 CSF £10.53 TOTE £3.50: £1.70, £1.10, £2.30; EX 11.10 Trifecta £48.30 Pool: £3,735.71 - 57.97 winning tickets..
Owner Nurlan Bizakov **Bred** Frau N Bscher **Trained** Newmarket, Suffolk

FOCUS
They were soon quite well strung out, Richard Hughes setting a decent gallop aboard Heading North. It didn't look a strong renewal and has been rated at the low end of the race averages, but several are open to improvement.

2587 HIPPO STKS (H'CAP) 2m
4:20 (4:20) (Class 4) (0-85,83) 4-Y-O+ **£6,469** (£1,925; £962; £481) **Stalls** Low

Form RPR

4-45 **1** **Palazzo Bianco**[12] 2269 5-9-5 **83** ... RobertTart(5) 10 91
(Brian Ellison) *trckd ldrs: pushed along over 3f out: clsd fr 2f out: led 1f out: shkn up and styd on wl* **10/1**

00-6 **2** ¾ **Cosimo de Medici**[31] 1733 6-9-7 **80** ... RobertHavlin 7 87+
(Hughie Morrison) *s.v.s: hld up in last pair: stdy prog fr 4f out: rdn 2f out: sustained effrt to go 2nd ins fnl f: styd on but hld by wnr nr fin* **8/1**[3]

340- **3** 2¼ **Rockfella**[285] 5106 7-9-7 **80** ... ShaneKelly 12 84
(Denis Coakley) *led at gd pce: drvn over 2f out: hdd and one pce 1f out* **16/1**

4250 **4** 2¼ **Tartan Jura**[19] 2009 5-9-0 **73** ...(p) SilvestreDeSousa 11 75
(Mark Johnston) *chsd ldr: urged along 7f out: tried to cl u.str.p 2f out: fdd fnl f* **8/1**[3]

2624 **5** shd **Cool Sky**[31] 1728 4-9-7 **82** ... AdamKirby 9 83
(William Knight) *taken down early: hld up in midfield: prog on outer 3f out: rdn and tried to cl on ldrs 2f out: one pce over 1f out* **16/1**

1224 **6** 6 **Murcar**[56] 1218 8-9-3 **81** ...(b) PhilipPrince(5) 1 75
(Liam Corcoran) *trckd ldrs: rdn over 4f out: wknd over 2f out* **33/1**

20-4 **7** shd **Danvilla**[12] 2269 6-9-8 **81** ... WilliamCarson 3 75
(Paul Webber) *chsd ldrs: rdn over 5f out: lost pl fr 4f out: n.d fnl 3f* **25/1**

6-23 **8** 1¼ **Silver Samba**[13] 2205 4-8-9 **70** ... CathyGannon 2 62
(Andrew Balding) *pushed up fr poor draw to chse ldr: rdn and wknd wl over 2f out* **2/1**[1]

23-3 **9** 3¾ **Sunny Future (IRE)**[23] 1899 7-8-9 **68** ... FrannyNorton 6 56
(Malcolm Saunders) *s.s: hld up wl in rr: bdly hmpd after 6f: nvr really able to rcvr* **20/1**

/664 **10** 5 **Bow To No One (IRE)**[13] 2205 7-8-10 **74** ... MichaelJMMurphy(5) 5 56
(Alan Jarvis) *hld up and sn in last pair: brief effrt over 4f out: sn no prog and wknd* **7/1**[2]

0-50 **11** 39 **Montaff**[13] 2205 7-9-9 **82** ... MartinHarley 4
(Mick Channon) *hld up towards rr: bdly hmpd after 6f: nvr able to rcvr: effrt 4f out: wknd wl over 2f out: eased and t.o* **10/1**

0-00 **12** 50 **Man Of Plenty**[31] 1728 4-9-1 **76** ...(p) DaneO'Neill 8
(Ed Dunlop) *hld up towards rr: virtually b.d after 6f: no ch after and sn t.o* **10/1**

10-4 **F** **Astromagick**[19] 2009 5-9-0 **76** ... SimonPearce(3) 14
(Mark H Tompkins) *settled in midfield: 7th whn stmbld and fell after 6f* **16/1**

3m 31.35s (2.35) **Going Correction** +0.15s/f (Good)
WFA 4 from 5yo+ 2lb **13** Ran SP% **124.5**
Speed ratings (Par 105): **100,99,98,97,97 94,94,93,91,89 69,44,**
Tote Swingers 1&2 £16.30, 2&3 £17.60, 1&3 £17.50 CSF £89.55 CT £1298.67 TOTE £12.30: £3.40, £2.60, £4.50; EX 108.20 Trifecta £1367.80 Pool: £3,240.42 - 1.77 winning tickets..
Owner The Palazzo Bianco Partnership **Bred** Cheveley Park Stud Ltd **Trained** Norton, N Yorks

FOCUS
This appeared to be run at an ordinary gallop. There was a nasty incident on the bend when Astromagick came down, badly hampering both Man Of Plenty and Montaff. The form is rated around the third.

2588 CONSTRUCTION RACEDAY APPRENTICE STKS (H'CAP) 6f
4:55 (4:55) (Class 5) (0-70,70) 4-Y-O+ **£3,234** (£962; £481; £240) **Stalls** High

Form RPR

0000 **1** **Night Trade (IRE)**[21] 1952 6-9-0 **66** ...(p) EDLinehan(3) 13 75
(Ronald Harris) *hld up in last trio: gng bttr than most 2f out: prog towards nr side to ld 1f out: drvn and hld on* **10/1**

0253 **2** nk **Chevise (IRE)**[21] 1957 5-8-4 **56** ...(p) RyanTate(3) 4 64
(Steve Woodman) *chsd ldrs: rdn 2f out: prog to press wnr jst ins fnl f: styd on but jst hld* **5/1**[3]

6053 **3** 1 **Emiratesdotcom**[8] 2364 7-9-3 **66** ... MatthewLawson 3 71
(Milton Bradley) *dwlt and bmpd s: pushed along in last trio: prog u.p over 1f out: styd on wl to take 3rd ins fnl f: nrst fin* **3/1**[1]

0-16 **4** 1½ **Commandingpresence (USA)**[2] 2530 7-9-4 **70** ... IanBurns(3) 5 70
(John Bridger) *chsd ldrs: urged along 2f out: nt qckn over 1f out: one pce fnl f* **14/1**

4602 **5** nk **Gaelic Wizard (IRE)**[28] 1793 5-8-12 **64** ... JoshBaudains(3) 9 63
(Dominic Ffrench Davis) *lw: led: edgd rt fr over 2f out: hdd and fdd u.p 1f out* **8/1**

0003 **6** ¾ **Surrey Dream (IRE)**[2] 2529 4-8-7 **56** oh11 ...(t) MichaelJMMurphy 7 53
(John Bridger) *on toes: outpcd in last: struggling and detached 1/2-way: styd on u.p fnl f: nrst fin* **25/1**

230- **7** ¾ **Ryan Style (IRE)**[180] 7864 7-9-6 **69** ... CharlesBishop 1 63
(Lisa Williamson) *chsd ldrs: prog on wd outside 1/2-way: chal u.p 2f out: fdd fnl f* **6/1**

0/15 **8** 10 **Sister Guru**[43] 1472 4-9-2 **68** ... NedCurtis(3) 2 30
(Peter Hedger) *wnt lft s and bmpd rival: racd freely: prom: chsd ldr 1/2-way to 2f out: wknd rapidly and eased: t.o* **8/1**

0104 **9** 4 **New Decade**[8] 2364 4-9-3 **66** ... ThomasBrown 10 15
(Milton Bradley) *chsd ldr to 1/2-way: wknd rapidly 2f out: t.o* **9/2**[2]

1m 12.37s (0.17) **Going Correction** +0.15s/f (Good) **9** Ran SP% **116.0**
Speed ratings (Par 103): **104,103,102,100,99 98,97,84,79**
Tote Swingers 1&2 £11.90, 2&3 £2.70, 1&3 £7.30 CSF £59.55 CT £189.94 TOTE £11.80: £4.00, £2.10, £2.00; EX 49.80 Trifecta £450.30 Pool: £2,884.41 - 4.80 winning tickets..
Owner Alan & Adam Darlow, A Darlow Productions **Bred** John Foley **Trained** Earlswood, Monmouths
■ Stewards' Enquiry : Ryan Tate four-day ban: use of whip (6-8 June)

FOCUS
The runners were spread middle-to-stands' side in this low-grade sprint handicap, with those coming from just off the pace favoured. The winner is rated to last autumn's form.
T/Jkpt: Not won. T/Plt: £23.80 to a £1 stake. Pool: £98,196.28 - 3,005.56 winning tickets. T/Qpdt: £9.90 to a £1 stake. Pool: £4,277.02 - 318.20 winning tickets. JN

2256 HAYDOCK (L-H)
Thursday, May 23

OFFICIAL GOING: Good (good to firm in places; 8.6)
Wind: Moderate, half against Weather: White cloud and sunny intervals

2589 32RED MAIDEN STKS 1m 3f 200y
2:20 (2:22) (Class 5) 3-Y-O+ **£2,587** (£770; £384; £192) **Stalls** Centre

Form RPR

-2 **1** **Continuum**[26] 1837 4-10-0 0 ... TomQueally 6 85+
(Sir Henry Cecil) *in tch: impr over 2f out: led 1f out: flashed tail u.p ins fnl f: pressed towards fin but jst doing enough* **2/1**[1]

2 ¾ **Bomber Thorn** 3-8-11 0 ... RichardKingscote 4 84+
(Tom Dascombe) *s.s: hld up: rdn over 3f out: sn outpcd: clsd ins fnl f: r.o to press wnr sn after: hld fnl strides: will improve* **13/2**

32 **3** ½ **Royal Signaller**[15] 2157 3-8-11 0 ... PaulMulrennan 5 83
(Amanda Perrett) *chsd ldr: rdn to ld wl over 1f out: hdd 1f out: no ex towards fin* **5/2**[2]

4 **4** 2¼ **Sleeping Giant (GER)**[20] 1975 3-8-11 0 ... KierenFallon 3 79
(Luca Cumani) *chsd ldrs: outpcd over 2f out: swtchd rt over 1f out: one pce ins fnl f* **5/1**[3]

04-6 **5** 2½ **Kelvingrove (IRE)**[30] 1754 3-8-11 72 ... PaulHanagan 1 75
(Ed Vaughan) *led: rdn over 2f out: hdd wl over 1f out: fdd wl ins fnl f* **6/1**

6 17 **Sorn (IRE)** 3-8-11 0 ... JamesDoyle 2 53
(James Fanshawe) *s.v.s: in rr: pushed along and outpcd over 3f out: lft bhd over 1f out* **20/1**

2m 31.9s (-1.90) **Going Correction** -0.175s/f (Firm)
WFA 3 from 4yo 17lb **6** Ran SP% **111.0**
Speed ratings (Par 103): **99,98,98,96,95 83**
Tote Swingers 1&2 £2.30, 2&3 £2.40, 1&3 £1.70 CSF £14.94 TOTE £2.40: £3.00, £2.20; EX 13.20 Trifecta £36.80 Pool: £2,539.50 - 51.66 winning tickets..
Owner K Abdullah **Bred** Juddmonte Farms Ltd **Trained** Newmarket, Suffolk

FOCUS
All races on the day were on the inside home straight, apart from the 6f contest which was run on the stands' side home straight. Precise race distances were 6f, 7f 1y, 1m 1y, 1m2f 96y and 1m3f 201y. Probably a fair maiden and it should produce winners. The form makes a fair bit of sense.

2590 32RED.COM H'CAP 1m 3f 200y
2:55 (2:57) (Class 4) (0-85,85) 4-Y-O+ **£5,175** (£1,540; £769; £384) **Stalls** Centre

Form RPR

3-64 **1** **Swinging Sultan**[27] 1804 6-8-11 **75** ... TomEaves 8 86+
(Keith Reveley) *hld up: nt clr run and swtchd rt over 1f out: prog and shkn up to ld wl ins fnl f: easily* **7/2**[1]

1202 **2** ¾ **Reflect (IRE)**[12] 2277 5-8-13 **77** ...(vt[1]) TomQueally 1 83
(Derek Shaw) *hld up: smooth hdwy over 2f out: led on bit 1f out: shkn up and hdd wl ins fnl f: unable to go w wnr cl home* **4/1**[2]

5-05 **3** ½ **Incendo**[68] 1037 7-9-0 **83** ...(t) WilliamTwiston-Davies(5) 3 88
(Ian Williams) *hld up: hdwy on outer 1f out: chalng wl ins fnl f: styd on same pce cl home* **5/1**

5-40 **4** ¾ **Right Step**[29] 1766 6-9-4 **82** ... KierenFallon 2 86
(Alan Jarvis) *chsd ldrs: chalng on inner 1f out: one pce fnl 75yds* **9/2**[3]

1/60 **5** ¾ **San Cassiano (IRE)**[12] 2277 6-8-13 **77** ... JamesSullivan 6 80
(Ruth Carr) *led: rdn and hdd 1f out: stl ch ins fnl f: no ex fnl 75yds* **8/1**

0-00 **6** 1¼ **Rock A Doodle Doo (IRE)**[18] 2040 6-9-3 **81** ... JimmyFortune 9 82
(Sally Hall) *in tch: rdn to chal 2f out: outpcd ins fnl f* **9/1**

060/ **7** ½ **Ivan Vasilevich (IRE)**[42] 6497 5-9-7 **85** ... MichaelO'Connell 5 85
(John Quinn) *prom: pushed along over 2f out: rdn and ch wl over 1f out: one pce fnl 100yds* **11/2**

2m 35.15s (1.35) **Going Correction** -0.175s/f (Firm) **7** Ran SP% **113.6**
Speed ratings (Par 105): **88,87,87,86,86 85,85**
Tote Swingers 1&2 £2.50, 2&3 £2.70, 1&3 £4.40 CSF £17.39 CT £68.20 TOTE £4.00: £2.00, £2.90; EX 12.30 Trifecta £48.60 Pool: £1,966.03 - 30.33 winning tickets..
Owner Reveley Racing 1 **Bred** Reveley Farms **Trained** Lingdale, Redcar & Cleveland

FOCUS
A few of these had questions to answer for one reason or another. The field finished in a bunch and the form is muddling, but the winner looks a bit better than the bare form.

2591 32RED CASINO MAIDEN STKS 6f
3:30 (3:30) (Class 5) 2-Y-O **£2,587** (£770; £384; £192) **Stalls** Centre

Form RPR

1 **Bunker (IRE)** 2-9-5 0 ... JimmyFortune 1 84+
(Richard Hannon) *a.p: led jst over 1f out: edgd rt wl ins fnl f: r.o wl* **6/1**[3]

3 **2** 2½ **Nathr (USA)**[18] 2048 2-9-5 0 ... PaulHanagan 8 76
(Charles Hills) *in tch: effrt to chal over 1f out: nt qckn wl ins fnl f: one pce cl home* **10/11**[1]

3 shd **Zeshov (IRE)** 2-9-5 0 ... JamesDoyle 2 76+
(Jeremy Noseda) *wnt rt s: hld up: hdwy over 2f out: rdn to chse ldrs over 1f out: styd on towards fin wout troubling wnr* **4/1**[2]

4 3 **Proclamationofwar** 2-9-5 0 TomEaves 7 67+
(Kevin Ryan) *displayed gd spd and led: rdn over 1f out: sn hdd: no ex fnl 100yds* **16/1**
5 7 **Finn Class (IRE)** 2-9-5 0 TomQueally 5 46
(Michael Bell) *dwlt: hld up: pushed along over 2f out: nvr on terms w ldrs* **25/1**
5 6 2 **Bahamian Heights**[36] 1619 2-9-5 0 KierenFallon 3 40
(Clive Brittain) *hmpd s: towards rr: hdwy into midfield 1/2-way: rdn and wknd wl over 1f out* **9/1**
6 7 ¾ **Quincel**[14] 2189 2-9-5 0 RichardKingscote 9 37
(Tom Dascombe) *prom: rdn 2f out: hung lft whn wkng wl over 1f out* **14/1**
8 15 **Triple O Seven (IRE)** 2-9-5 0 RobertWinston 4
(John Best) *chsd ldrs tl rdn and wknd over 2f out* **33/1**
9 13 **Network Perfection** 2-9-5 0 PaulMulrennan 6
(Michael Easterby) *dwlt: a outpcd and bhd* **66/1**

1m 15.62s (1.82) **Going Correction** +0.15s/f (Good) **9 Ran SP% 117.5**
Speed ratings (Par 93): **93,89,89,85,76 73,72,52,35**
Tote Swingers 1&2 £2.30, 2&3 £1.80, 1&3 £2.80 CSF £11.92 TOTE £7.80: £1.90, £1.10, £1.30; EX 12.90 Trifecta £52.00 Pool: £2,517.37 - 36.25 winning tickets..
Owner Morecombe, Anderson, Hughes **Bred** Lynn Lodge Stud **Trained** East Everleigh, Wilts

FOCUS
Four came nicely clear from the 2f marker and look fair prospects. Jimmy Fortune reported the field were running into headwind. The winner can do better and the runner-up is rated to his debut effort.

2592 32RED H'CAP 1m
4:05 (4:07) (Class 3) (0-90,90) 4-Y-O+ **£8,086** (£2,406; £1,202; £601) **Stalls** Low

Form RPR
0-16 1 **Mont Ras (IRE)**[19] 2028 6-9-7 90 DanielTudhope 3 99+
(David O'Meara) *a.p: effrt over 1f out: led ins fnl f: rdn out and r.o* **6/1**[3]
1054 2 ¾ **Dubai Hills**[10] 2310 7-8-13 87 WilliamTwiston-Davies(5) 13 94
(Bryan Smart) *hld up: hdwy over 2f out: led jst over 1f out: hdd ins fnl f: hld towards fin* **20/1**
10- 3 ¾ **Sam Sharp (USA)**[237] 6638 7-9-3 86 RichardKingscote 9 93+
(Ian Williams) *hld up: pushed along over 1f out: swtchd rt ins fnl f to make prog: r.o: fin wl* **12/1**
4064 4 ½ **Dubai Dynamo**[4] 2477 8-9-7 90 JamesSullivan 14 94
(Ruth Carr) *hld up: hdwy over 2f out: hung lft whn chsng ldrs over 1f out: nt qckn ins fnl f: kpt on same pce towards fin* **20/1**
100- 5 hd **Volcanic Wind (USA)**[194] 7691 4-8-13 82 MickaelBarzalona 5 86+
(Saeed bin Suroor) *midfield: effrt 2f out: chsd ldrs over 1f out: kpt on same pce ins fnl f* **11/2**[2]
20-4 6 ¾ **Roserrow**[23] 1905 4-9-2 85 JimmyFortune 12 87
(Andrew Balding) *stdd s: hld up: rdn over 2f out: hdwy over 1f out: kpt on ins fnl f: nt quite able to chal* **20/1**
12-5 7 nse **Basseterre (IRE)**[19] 2018 4-9-3 86 KierenFallon 10 88
(Charles Hills) *hld up: hdwy over 2f out: sn bmpd: chalng fr over 1f out: no ex fnl 75yds* **11/4**[1]
0331 8 ½ **Mia's Boy**[23] 1905 9-8-12 81 SaleemGolam 8 82
(Chris Dwyer) *midfield: u.p whn sltly hmpd over 1f out: one pce ins fnl f* **20/1**
0-42 9 shd **Shavansky**[17] 2085 9-8-12 88 PatMillman(7) 4 88+
(Rod Millman) *s.i.s: hld up in midfield: lost pl 3f out: nt clr run over 1f out: r.o ins fnl f: nt rch ldrs* **33/1**
-600 10 ¾ **Yojimbo (IRE)**[22] 1922 5-8-13 82 MatthewDavies 6 81
(Mick Channon) *chsd ldr: led over 2f out: rdn and hdd over 1f out: no ex fnl 100yds* **50/1**
-002 11 1¾ **Discression**[20] 1992 4-9-2 85 PaulMulrennan 1 80
(Kevin Ryan) *in tch: effrt over 1f out: n.m.r ins fnl f: eased whn no imp fnl 100yds* **10/1**
0-50 12 ½ **Postscript (IRE)**[13] 2210 5-9-6 89 TomQueally 2 83
(David Simcock) *trckd ldrs: rdn and chalng over 1f out: fdd fnl 100yds* **16/1**
610- 13 3¼ **Otto The Great**[50] 1338 4-8-13 82 TonyHamilton 7 68
(Richard Fahey) *led: rdn and hdd over 2f out: wknd over 1f out* **25/1**
0/6 14 5 **Tellovoi (IRE)**[14] 2185 5-9-5 88 RobertWinston 15 63
(Andrew Hollinshead) *racd keenly on outer in tch: struggling to hold pl whn hmpd 2f out: sn wknd* **20/1**
5-04 15 28 **Uppercut**[22] 1922 5-8-13 82 PaulHanagan 11 +
(Stuart Kittow) *trckd ldrs: struggling to hold pl whn hmpd 2f out: sn dropped away and eased* **13/2**

1m 40.77s (-2.93) **Going Correction** -0.175s/f (Firm) **15 Ran SP% 124.9**
Speed ratings (Par 107): **107,106,105,105,104 104,104,103,103,102 100,100,97,92,64**
Tote Swingers 1&2 £27.70, 2&3 £59.60, 1&3 £15.50 CSF £126.44 CT £1454.01 TOTE £6.80: £2.30, £7.60, £4.40; EX 160.90 Trifecta £2248.10 Part won. Pool: £2,997.53 - 0.68 winning tickets..
Owner Colne Valley Racing **Bred** Patrick M Ryan **Trained** Nawton, N Yorks

FOCUS
This appeared competitive, but things got for very tight in the final 2f and plenty looked unlucky to some extent. The improving winner rates better than the bare form.

2593 32RED CASINO H'CAP 7f
4:40 (4:41) (Class 4) (0-80,79) 3-Y-O **£5,175** (£1,540; £769; £384) **Stalls** Low

Form RPR
321- 1 **Homage (IRE)**[217] 7192 3-9-6 78 JamesDoyle 7 90
(Jeremy Noseda) *midfield: hdwy over 1f out: led ins fnl f: sn strly pressed: pushed out to hold on wl cl home* **9/2**[1]
53-2 2 hd **Gravitational (IRE)**[26] 1832 3-9-1 73 SebSanders 10 84
(Chris Wall) *dwlt: hld up: nt clr run 2f out: hdwy over 1f out: str chal wl ins fnl f: r.o: hld fnl strides* **9/2**[1]
3-32 3 2¾ **Caramack**[13] 2224 3-9-1 78 WilliamTwiston-Davies(5) 6 82
(Richard Hannon) *midfield: hdwy over 3f out: led over 1f out: hdd ins fnl f: no ex fnl 75yds* **7/1**
1-66 4 2¼ **Countryman**[13] 2209 3-9-2 74 JimmyFortune 12 72+
(Hughie Morrison) *midfield: hdwy 3f out: led over 2f out: hdd over 1f out: one pce fnl 100yds* **14/1**
10-3 5 2½ **Reconsider Baby (IRE)**[19] 2010 3-8-4 69 JoeyHaynes(7) 5 60
(Mrs K Burke) *hld up: rdn 2f out: hdwy and u.p over 1f out: kpt on: no imp on ldrs ins fnl f* **10/1**
-120 6 ¾ **Archie Stevens**[14] 2190 3-9-6 78 RichardKingscote 11 67
(Tom Dascombe) *hld up: n.m.r over 5f out: hdwy over 2f out: chsd ldrs over 1f out: one pce ins fnl f* **16/1**
3-50 7 ¾ **Delores Rocket**[12] 2285 3-9-0 79 PaulMcGiff(7) 8 66
(Kevin Ryan) *hld up: rdn whn nt clr run over 1f out: kpt on ins fnl f: nvr able to trble ldrs* **50/1**
310- 8 6 **Mitchell**[272] 5563 3-9-3 75 BarryMcHugh 14 46
(David Thompson) *in tch: lost pl over 4f out: u.p over 2f out: no imp after* **50/1**
-303 9 1 **Old Man Clegg**[8] 2371 3-8-13 71 JamesSullivan 1 39+
(Michael Easterby) *led: rdn and hdd over 2f out: wknd over 1f out* **12/1**
26-3 10 ¾ **Bondesire**[22] 1935 3-8-13 71 DanielTudhope 3 37+
(David O'Meara) *w ldr: rdn and chalng over 2f out: n.m.r whn wkng over 1f out* **11/2**[2]
51-0 11 ½ **Shy Bride (IRE)**[36] 1612 3-9-1 73 KirstyMilczarek 2 38
(Alan Jarvis) *chsd ldrs: rdn over 1f out: sn wknd* **33/1**
4-20 12 ½ **Lionheart**[29] 1770 3-8-13 71 KierenFallon 9 35
(Luca Cumani) *chsd ldrs: chalng over 2f out: wknd 1f out* **6/1**[3]
0-06 13 2½ **Dream Scenario**[35] 1647 3-8-12 70 PaulMulrennan 4 27
(Mel Brittain) *chsd ldrs: chalng over 2f out: wknd over 1f out* **40/1**

1m 28.03s (-2.67) **Going Correction** -0.175s/f (Firm) **13 Ran SP% 117.2**
Speed ratings (Par 101): **108,107,104,102,99 98,97,90,89,88 88,87,84**
Tote Swingers 1&2 £4.20, 2&3 £6.90, 1&3 £6.10 CSF £22.80 CT £139.41 TOTE £3.70: £1.30, £2.30, £2.00; EX 26.20 Trifecta £131.30 Pool: £2,053.66 - 11.72 winning tickets..
Owner Highclere Thoroughbred Racing - Dalmeny **Bred** J Hanly **Trained** Newmarket, Suffolk

FOCUS
There was a good pace on early, and two fought out a tight finish. The third helps set the standard.

2594 BETDAQ HAYDOCK PARK APPRENTICE TRAINING SERIES H'CAP (PART OF THE RACING EXCELLENCE INITIATIVE) 1m 2f 95y
5:15 (5:15) (Class 5) (0-75,71) 4-Y-O+ **£2,587** (£770; £384; £192) **Stalls** Centre

Form RPR
6501 1 **Jordaura**[13] 2221 7-8-6 63 JordanHibberd(7) 5 71
(Alan Berry) *hld up: hdwy on inner to ld over 1f out: r.o and in command fnl 100yds* **14/1**
5420 2 2 **Breakheart (IRE)**[6] 2413 6-8-6 63 (v) JackGarritty(7) 2 67
(Andrew Balding) *hld up: hdwy 4f out: chalng over 1f out: hld and no imp on wnr ins fnl 100yds* **14/1**
0-00 3 1¼ **Rosselli (IRE)**[54] 1239 4-8-13 66 JoeyHaynes(3) 4 68
(Mrs K Burke) *led: hdd after 1f: chsd ldr: rdn to chal 2f out: nt qckn 1f out: kpt on same pce towards fin* **4/1**[2]
4-25 4 nse **Zenafire**[17] 2089 4-8-4 58 JackDuern 8 60
(Andrew Hollinshead) *led after 1f: rdn and hdd over 1f out: kpt on same pce fnl 100yds* **9/2**[3]
0546 5 shd **Gran Maestro (USA)**[17] 2077 4-9-2 69 (b) GemmaTutty(3) 7 71
(Ruth Carr) *midfield: rdn and outpcd over 1f out: kpt on towards fin* **13/2**
1344 6 1 **Delightful Sleep**[17] 2302 5-8-9 62 EoinWalsh(3) 1 62
(David Evans) *trckd ldrs: effrt ent fnl f: one pce after* **10/1**
0-26 7 2½ **King Kurt (IRE)**[29] 1763 5-9-2 71 KevinStott(5) 9 66
(Kevin Ryan) *prom: rdn over 2f out: wknd over 1f out* **7/2**[1]
001- 8 ½ **Oetzi**[281] 5239 5-9-1 70 DavidParkes(5) 3 64
(Alan Jarvis) *hld up in rr: rdn over 2f out: no imp* **11/2**

2m 12.82s (-2.68) **Going Correction** -0.175s/f (Firm) **8 Ran SP% 111.5**
Speed ratings (Par 103): **103,101,100,100,100 99,97,97**
Tote Swingers 1&2 £19.20, 2&3 £14.10, 1&3 £12.50 CSF £177.81 CT £916.74 TOTE £14.30: £3.10, £3.90, £1.10; EX 87.10 Trifecta £599.00 Pool: £1,726.11 - 2.16 winning tickets..
Owner Alan Berry **Bred** Pendley Farm **Trained** Cockerham, Lancs
■ Jordan Hibberd's first winner.
■ Stewards' Enquiry : Gemma Tutty three-day ban: careless riding (6-8 June)

FOCUS
The pace was orinary but it paid to be held up. Not form to be confident about.
T/Plt: £115.80 to a £1 stake. Pool: £60,293.99 - 380.07 winning tickets. T/Qpdt: £34.70 to a £1 stake. Pool: £3,388.12 - 72.07 winning tickets. DO

2389 SALISBURY (R-H)
Thursday, May 23

OFFICIAL GOING: Good (8.6)
Wind: quite strong with no real direction Weather: sunny

2595 IRISH STALLION FARMS EBF BATHWICK TYRES MAIDEN STKS 5f
6:10 (6:10) (Class 4) 2-Y-O **£4,204** (£1,251; £625; £312) **Stalls** Centre

Form RPR
1 **Saayerr** 2-9-5 0 LiamJones 5 90+
(William Haggas) *in tch: hdwy 2f out: qcknd up wl whn gap appeared ent fnl f: led fnl 140yds: r.o wl: readily* **7/1**
2 1¼ **Sacha Park (IRE)** 2-9-5 0 RichardHughes 3 87+
(Richard Hannon) *trckd ldrs: nt clr run over 2f out tl gap appeared over 1f out: r.o to have ev ch ins fnl f but nt pce of wnr fnl 75yds* **5/2**[2]
3 nk **Mystique Rider** 2-9-5 0 HarryBentley 8 85
(Olly Stevens) *hld up in last trio in tch: swtchd lft over 2f out: hdwy sn after: rdn and ev ch ins fnl f: no ex fnl 75yds* **25/1**
2 4 2¼ **Finflash (IRE)**[12] 2250 2-9-5 0 SamHitchcott 9 77
(Mick Channon) *trckd ldrs: pushed along to ld narrowly 2f out: sn rdn: hdd fnl 140yds: no ex and fdd into 4th* **2/1**[1]
03 5 3¾ **Seaham**[12] 2283 2-9-5 0 AndreaAtzeni 7 63
(Rod Millman) *towards rr: j. path jst over 3f out: pushed along and hanging rt fr over 2f out: nvr gng pce to get involved* **5/1**[3]
42 6 ¾ **Primitorio (IRE)**[17] 2082 2-9-5 0 JimCrowley 2 60
(Ralph Beckett) *prom: rdn and ev ch over 1f out: wknd ins fnl f* **9/1**
7 shd **Mappa Mundi (USA)** 2-9-5 0 NeilCallan 6 60
(Eve Johnson Houghton) *hmpd after 75yds: sn pushed along in last pair: rdn to chse ldrs 2f out: wknd ent fnl f* **16/1**
8 2 **The Dandy Yank (IRE)** 2-9-5 0 GeorgeBaker 4 53
(Jamie Osborne) *trckd ldrs: rdn 2f out: wknd jst over 1f out* **50/1**
6 9 7 **Denby Dale**[9] 2344 2-8-12 0 JakePayne(7) 1 28
(Bill Turner) *led: rdn whn hdd 2f out: sn wknd* **66/1**

1m 1.43s (0.43) **Going Correction** +0.10s/f (Good) **9 Ran SP% 114.3**
Speed ratings (Par 95): **100,98,97,93,87 86,86,83,72**
Tote Swingers 1&2 £9.50, 2&3 £23.30, 1&3 £51.10 CSF £24.36 TOTE £11.70: £2.70, £1.60, £6.30; EX 28.80 Trifecta £678.50 Part won. Pool: £904.74 - 0.32 winning tickets..
Owner Sheikh Ahmed Al Maktoum **Bred** Cheveley Park Stud Ltd **Trained** Newmarket, Suffolk

FOCUS
Rail dolled out 20ft in home straight. An intriguing juvenile maiden, won 12 months ago by the very useful Bungle Inthejungle and it looks a race worth following again.

2596 BATHWICK TYRES ANDOVER H'CAP 6f
6:40 (6:41) (Class 6) (0-65,65) 4-Y-O+ £2,587 (£770; £384; £192) Stalls Low

Form RPR

331- **1** **Levi Draper**[215] 7253 4-9-3 **61** RichardHughes 7 71+
(James Fanshawe) *mid-div: shkn up to cl on ldrs whn swtchd lft over 1f out: r.o wl whn rdn to ld towards fin: readily* **4/1**[1]

05 **2** ½ **One Last Dream**[18] 2057 4-8-9 **53** (b) DavidProbert 14 61
(Ron Hodges) *led: rdn wl over 1f out: kpt on gamely: hdd towards fin* **16/1**

0604 **3** nk **My Own Way Home**[27] 1802 5-8-10 **54** (v[1]) CathyGannon 2 61
(David Evans) *t.k.h trcking ldrs: stmbld on path jst over 3f out: rdn over 2f out: r.o to nrly mount chal ins fnl f: kpt on but hld towards fin* **4/1**[1]

2000 **4** 1½ **Scommettitrice (IRE)**[17] 2074 5-8-5 **54** (b) PhilipPrince(5) 9 56
(Mark Gillard) *in tch: swtchd lft for effrt jst over 2f out: kpt on same pce ins fnl f* **33/1**

3002 **5** ¾ **Basle**[8] 2364 6-9-0 **58** (t) MartinLane 5 61+
(Michael Blake) *awkwardly away: towards rr: pushed along and hdwy whn nt clr run over 1f out: rdn and r.o whn gap emerged jst ins fnl f: nvr rching ldrs* **7/1**[3]

1-25 **6** ½ **Glastonberry**[124] 271 5-8-13 **57** LiamKeniry 11 55
(Geoffrey Deacon) *s.i.s and bmpd s: t.k.h in rr: rdn and hdwy over 1f out: kpt on same pce fnl f* **10/1**

006- **7** shd **Nubar Boy**[278] 5346 6-9-4 **65** (p) RyanPowell(3) 3 63
(Ian Williams) *awkward leaving stalls: towards rr: swtchd lft and hdwy over 1f out: sn rdn to chse ldrs: kpt on same pce fnl f* **16/1**

0200 **8** 3 **Hatta Stream (IRE)**[30] 1748 7-8-8 **55** SimonPearce(3) 6 43
(Lydia Pearce) *nvr bttr than mid-div* **20/1**

00-0 **9** 1¼ **Bermondsey Bob (IRE)**[14] 2196 7-9-2 **60** ChrisCatlin 8 44
(John Spearing) *chsd ldr: rdn over 2f out: wknd fnl f* **33/1**

5-00 **10** ½ **Ficelle (IRE)**[21] 1952 4-9-1 **59** WilliamCarson 12 42
(Ronald Harris) *slowly away and bmpd s: a towards rr* **25/1**

5303 **11** 3¼ **Dishy Guru**[41] 1516 4-9-5 **63** (b) NeilCallan 4 35
(Michael Blanshard) *chsd ldrs: rdn over 2f out: wknd fnl f* **6/1**[2]

00P- **12** 4 **Samba Night (IRE)**[83] 7297 4-8-13 **57** SteveDrowne 1 17
(Jeremy Gask) *chsd ldrs tl wknd over 1f out* **50/1**

560- **P** **Mr Fickle (IRE)**[225] 6988 4-9-7 **65** GeorgeBaker 13
(Gary Moore) *towards rr: struggling 3f out: eased down fr over 2f out: p.u fnl f* **7/1**[3]

1m 14.99s (0.19) **Going Correction** +0.10s/f (Good) **13 Ran SP% 116.6**
Speed ratings (Par 101): **102,101,100,98,97 97,97,93,91,90 86,81,**
Tote Swingers 1&2 £6.30, 2&3 £4.90, 1&3 £5.40 CSF £66.02 CT £282.61 TOTE £4.10: £1.50, £4.80, £1.40; EX 55.40 Trifecta £174.10 Pool: £645.19 - 2.77 winning tickets..
Owner Andrew & Julia Turner **Bred** Cheveley Park Stud Ltd **Trained** Newmarket, Suffolk

FOCUS
A competitive, if low-grade sprint handicap and a hard-fought success. The winner and third will be of interest in the short term.

2597 BATHWICK TYRES MAIDEN FILLIES' STKS 6f
7:15 (7:15) (Class 5) 3-Y-O+ £3,234 (£962; £481; £240) Stalls Low

Form RPR

5- **1** **Russian Royale**[265] 5785 3-8-12 0 ShaneKelly 2 74+
(Stuart Kittow) *chsd ldrs: pushed along fr over 2f out: swtchd lft over 1f out: r.o wl to chal wl ins fnl f: narrow ld whn edgd lft fnl strides* **20/1**

40-3 **2** nse **It's Taboo**[13] 2226 3-8-12 70 DavidProbert 6 74
(Mark Usher) *mid-div: pushed along over 2f out: weaved way through over 1f out: drvn to ld fnl 120yds: drifted sltly rt: hdd and bmpd fnl strides* **8/1**

3 1½ **Spiraea** 3-8-12 0 PatDobbs 8 71+
(Mark Rimell) *s.i.s: towards rr but travelling wl: smooth hdwy but nvr a clr passage fr jst over 2f out: weaved way through fr over 1f out: fin wl to go 3rd towards fin: nvr able to get on terms: unlucky* **66/1**

- **4** ½ **Celestial Bay** 4-9-7 0 GeorgeBaker 10 69
(Sylvester Kirk) *led: rdn wl over 1f out: kpt on tl hdd fnl 120yds: no ex whn lost 3rd nr fin* **50/1**

62 **5** 1 **Marjong**[18] 2051 3-8-12 0 AndreaAtzeni 9 66+
(Simon Dow) *trckd ldr: rdn and ev ch 2f out: cl 4th but looking hld whn hmpd twice ins fnl f* **2/1**[1]

03-5 **6** 1 **Azelle**[26] 1828 3-8-12 70 RichardHughes 7 61
(Richard Hannon) *in tch: pushed along over 3f out: drvn over 2f out: nt pce to get involved* **4/1**[2]

6 **7** 1½ **Mediska**[18] 2051 3-8-12 0 CathyGannon 13 56
(Henry Candy) *trckd ldr: rdn and ev ch 2f out tl no ex and fdd ins fnl f* **8/1**

65-0 **8** 1½ **Lady Vermeer**[18] 2051 3-8-12 72 JimCrowley 4 51
(Ralph Beckett) *sn mid-div: swtchd lft 2f out: sn rdn to chse ldrs: fdd fnl f* **5/1**[3]

9 4 **Ramata** 3-8-12 0 HarryBentley 5 39
(Harry Dunlop) *s.i.s: sme late prog past btn horses: mainly towards rr* **25/1**

-200 **10** 2¾ **Last Hooray**[5] 2448 3-8-12 68 (b[1]) LiamKeniry 1 30
(David Elsworth) *mid-div tl wknd over 1f out* **10/1**

11 shd **Bustling Darcey** 3-8-7 0 PhilipPrince(5) 3 30
(Mark Gillard) *sn outpcd in rr* **100/1**

02 **12** 2 **Nepalese Pearl**[16] 2123 3-8-12 0 NeilCallan 14 23
(Pat Eddery) *trckd ldr: rdn over 2f out: wknd over 1f out* **28/1**

0-6 **13** 10 **Bella Michelle**[17] 2099 3-8-12 0 LiamJones 11
(Sylvester Kirk) *outpcd in rr whn stmbld v bdly after 1f: looked to lose action: nvr a factor* **66/1**

1m 15.05s (0.25) **Going Correction** +0.10s/f (Good) **13 Ran SP% 119.3**
WFA 3 from 4yo 9lb
Speed ratings (Par 100): **102,101,99,99,97 96,94,92,87,83 83,80,67**
Tote Swingers 1&2 £21.60, 2&3 £92.10, 1&3 £92.10 CSF £165.56 TOTE £26.00: £7.00, £2.70, £23.40; EX 288.20 Trifecta £526.00 Part won. Pool: £701.35 - 0.01 winning tickets..
Owner P A & M J Reditt **Bred** Mrs P A & M J Reditt **Trained** Blackborough, Devon

FOCUS
A modest fillies' maiden but it served up a thrilling finish. The second set the standard.

2598 BATHWICK TYRES SALISBURY H'CAP 1m 6f 21y
7:45 (7:45) (Class 4) (0-85,81) 4-Y-O+ £4,851 (£1,443; £721; £360)

Form RPR

3-00 **1** **Dunhoy (IRE)**[34] 1670 5-8-12 **77** MichaelJMMurphy(5) 4 82
(Tony Newcombe) *hld up but in tch: pushed along to take clsr order 4f out: rdn to chal over 2f out: led narrowly jst over 1f out: styd on u.str.p: drvn rt out* **11/2**

30-0 **2** nk **The Quarterjack**[17] 2102 4-8-12 **72** DavidProbert 8 76
(Ron Hodges) *trckd ldr: rdn to take narrow advantage 2f out: sn str pressed: hdd v narrowly over 1f out: styd on w ev ch fnl f: jst hld nring fin* **6/1**

10-4 **3** ¾ **Porcini**[36] 1615 4-9-2 **76** WilliamCarson 2 79
(Philip McBride) *trckd ldr tl rdn over 3f out: kpt chsng ldrs: styd on ins fnl f: wnt 3rd nring fin* **5/1**[3]

-025 **4** nk **Achalas (IRE)**[17] 2102 5-9-2 **76** AndreaAtzeni 3 79
(Heather Main) *racd in 4th: rdn over 3f out: ch fr 2f out tl styd on same pce fnl f* **5/1**[3]

20-0 **5** ½ **Nordic Quest (IRE)**[18] 2044 4-9-4 **78** NeilCallan 1 80
(Gerard Butler) *hld up: hdwy 3f out: nt best of runs 2f out: sn rdn: disp cl 3rd ins fnl f: styd on same pce* **11/1**

010- **6** 2 **Body Language (IRE)**[243] 6493 5-9-7 **81** (p) RichardHughes 6 81
(Ian Williams) *led: rdn and hdd 2f out: kpt chalng tl no ex ins fnl f* **3/1**[1]

00-0 **7** hd **Spice Fair**[18] 2052 6-9-7 **81** LiamKeniry 7 80
(Mark Usher) *hld up: swtchd out whn rdn over 2f out: sn hung to stands' side rail but nvr pce to threaten* **9/2**[2]

3m 13.86s (6.46) **Going Correction** +0.10s/f (Good) **7 Ran SP% 114.5**
Speed ratings (Par 105): **85,84,84,84,83 82,82**
Tote Swingers 1&2 £5.90, 2&3 £3.60, 1&3 £3.90 CSF £37.82 CT £174.99 TOTE £8.20: £4.40, £2.40; EX 33.40 Trifecta £316.40 Pool: £471.03 - 1.11 winning tickets..
Owner David Gilbert **Bred** Rossenarra Bloodstock Limited **Trained** Yarnscombe, Devon

FOCUS
A tight staying handicap on paper and, with the race developing into nothing more than a mad dash over the final 3f, it remains to be seen how well the form will work out. An ordinary race at best.

2599 BATHWICK TYRES BOURNEMOUTH H'CAP 1m 4f
8:20 (8:21) (Class 6) (0-65,65) 3-Y-O £2,587 (£770; £384; £192) Stalls Low

Form RPR

63-6 **1** **Getaway Car**[24] 1885 3-9-2 **60** (p) NeilCallan 5 69
(Gerard Butler) *trckd ldrs: rdn over 2f out: led over 1f out: styng on strly and asserting whn edgd rt wl ins fnl f: hld on* **8/1**

0423 **2** hd **Alshan Fajer**[15] 2156 3-9-3 **61** AndreaAtzeni 13 69
(Roger Ingram) *mid-div: hdwy on outer over 6f out to sit promly: rdn to ld over 2f out: hdd over 1f out: kpt on gamely but looking hld whn squeezed up towards fin* **7/1**

3224 **3** 3¼ **Knight's Parade (IRE)**[16] 2124 3-9-4 **62** (b) PatDobbs 4 65
(Amanda Perrett) *sn prom: trckd ldrs after 5f: rdn 3f out: styd on fnl f wout threatening ldng pair* **9/2**[1]

060 **4** ½ **Whitefall (USA)**[26] 1837 3-8-7 **51** oh4 WilliamCarson 12 53
(David Evans) *hld up towards rr: hdwy over 5f out on outer: rdn to jst abt chal wl over 2f out: styd on same pce fr over 1f out* **12/1**

00-2 **5** hd **Nateeja (IRE)**[17] 2095 3-9-3 **61** SteveDrowne 1 63
(J W Hills) *s.i.s: trckd ldrs after 2f: lost pl on bnd over 5f out: in tch: rdn over 3f out: styd on same pce fnl 2f* **6/1**[3]

0-63 **6** 1½ **Karl Marx (IRE)**[23] 1897 3-8-0 **51** oh4 OisinMurphy(7) 7 50
(Mark Gillard) *in tch: tk clsr order 5f out: rdn over 3f out: styd on same pce tl no ex ins fnl f* **28/1**

000- **7** ½ **Mr Vendman (IRE)**[171] 7973 3-8-4 **51** oh3 RyanPowell(3) 8 50
(Ian Williams) *s.i.s: towards rr: rdn 4f out: styd on steadily fnl 2f: nvr rchd ldrs* **66/1**

0-54 **8** nk **Star Of Namibia (IRE)**[38] 1584 3-9-6 **64** LiamKeniry 10 62
(J S Moore) *mid-div: rdn 3f out: styd on same pce fnl 2f* **11/1**

000- **9** 1¼ **Rancher (IRE)**[183] 7806 3-8-12 **56** ChrisCatlin 9 52
(Harry Dunlop) *hld up towards rr: rdn 3f out: styd on fnl f: nvr a threat* **11/1**

00-0 **10** 7 **Dusky Lark**[24] 1882 3-9-7 **65** RichardHughes 11 50
(Hughie Morrison) *led: rdn 3f out: hdd over 2f out: wknd over 1f out* **8/1**

5051 **11** ¾ **Brick Rising**[24] 1885 3-9-0 **58** (t) DavidProbert 14 42
(Andrew Balding) *mid-div: hdwy over 3f out: sn rdn: wknd over 1f out* **5/1**[2]

000 **12** 4½ **Fitzwilly**[14] 2192 3-8-7 **51** SamHitchcott 3 28
(Mick Channon) *mid-div: rdn 4f out: wknd over 1f out* **28/1**

060- **13** 1 **North Weald (IRE)**[190] 7708 3-8-13 **57** MartinLane 2 32
(J W Hills) *a towards rr* **50/1**

0-3 **14** 2 **Burma Days (USA)**[17] 2095 3-8-7 **51** oh1 MartinDwyer 6 23
(Sylvester Kirk) *trckd ldrs: rdn over 3f out: wknd 2f out* **14/1**

2m 40.34s (2.34) **Going Correction** +0.10s/f (Good) **14 Ran SP% 125.2**
Speed ratings (Par 97): **96,95,93,93,93 92,91,91,90,86 85,82,82,80**
Tote Swingers 1&2 £28.30, 2&3 £14.30, 1&3 £12.80 CSF £64.23 CT £292.47 TOTE £12.10: £3.30, £3.00, £2.30; EX 95.40 Trifecta £352.40 Pool: £627.57 - 1.33 winning tickets..
Owner A D Spence **Bred** Mascalls Stud **Trained** Newmarket, Suffolk
■ Stewards' Enquiry : Oisin Murphy four-day ban: use of whip (6-9 June)
Andrea Atzeni two-day ban: use of whip (6-7 June)

FOCUS
Plenty of unexposed types in this 3-y-o handicap and a lively market suggested plenty were fancied. Improvement from the first two.

2600 BATHWICK TYRES FERNDOWN CLASSIFIED STKS 1m 1f 198y
8:50 (8:51) (Class 5) 3-Y-O £2,911 (£866; £432; £216) Stalls Low

Form RPR

2303 **1** **Isis Blue**[17] 2094 3-9-0 68 SteveDrowne 4 77
(Rod Millman) *hld up in last: hdwy in centre fr 3f out: led 2f out: drifted rt: clr ent fnl f: pushed out* **8/1**

54-6 **2** 2¾ **Duke Of Perth**[22] 1926 3-9-0 70 KierenFallon 1 72+
(Luca Cumani) *in tch: nt clr run whn chsng ldrs over 2f out: sn rdn: styd on to go 2nd ins fnl f: no ch w wnr* **9/4**[1]

0-31 **3** ¾ **Emulating (IRE)**[10] 2324 3-9-6 66 RichardHughes 8 76
(Richard Hannon) *trckd ldrs: drew upsides ldr travelling wl 3f out: rdn whn nvr hit the front 2f out: nt pce of wnr and sn hld: no ex whn lost 2nd ins fnl f* **11/4**[2]

04-2 **4** 1¾ **Wellingrove (IRE)**[9] 2342 3-8-9 68 MichaelJMMurphy(5) 9 67
(Mark Johnston) *led after 2f: jnd 3f out: sn rdn: hdd 2f out: styd on same pce* **4/1**[3]

3440 **5** nk **Marvelino**[17] 2098 3-9-0 65 NeilCallan 2 66?
(Pat Eddery) *led for 2f: trckd ldr tl rdn 3f out: styd on same pce fnl 2f* **40/1**

6-51 **6** ½ **Jan De Heem**[19] 2017 3-9-0 65 (v) JimCrowley 3 65
(Ralph Beckett) *hld up in last pair: rdn wl over 2f out: no imp: wknd fnl f* **9/2**

35-2 **7** 8 **Snoqualmie Chief**[17] 2071 3-9-0 67 LiamKeniry 5 49
(David Elsworth) *in tch: rdn to chse ldrs whn bmpd over 2f out: fdd fnl f* **14/1**

2m 12.07s (2.17) **Going Correction** +0.10s/f (Good) **7 Ran SP% 115.8**
Speed ratings (Par 99): **95,92,92,90,90 90,83**
Tote Swingers 1&2 £2.70, 2&3 £1.90, 1&3 £6.70 CSF £27.13 TOTE £8.20: £2.30, £1.90; EX 37.10 Trifecta £190.90 Pool: £930.70 - 3.65 winning tickets..
Owner Cantay Racing **Bred** Mette Campbell-Andenaes **Trained** Kentisbeare, Devon

FOCUS
A fair race for the grade and an impressive success, although there are doubts over the form.
T/Plt: £986.50 to a £1 stake. Pool: £74,866.67 - 55.4 winning tickets. T/Qpdt: £129.60 to a £1 stake. Pool: £5,728.84 - 32.7 winning tickets. TM

1846 SANDOWN (R-H)
Thursday, May 23

OFFICIAL GOING: Sprint course - good (good to firm in places); round course - good to firm (good in places; 8.4)
Wind: Moderate across Weather: Sunny spells early

2601 BRITISH STALLION STUDS EBF MAIDEN FILLIES' STKS 5f 6y
6:00 (6:01) (Class 5) 2-Y-O **£3,881** (£1,155; £577; £288) **Stalls** Low

Form RPR
4 **1** **Wind Fire (USA)**^{18} 2048 2-9-0 0 JamieSpencer 8 82+
(David Brown) *trckd ldr: led over 1f out: pushed out fnl f: comf* **9/4**^{1}
2 *1* **Survived** 2-9-0 0 GrahamLee 2 78+
(William Haggas) *chsd ldrs: drvn over 1f out: chsd wnr fnl 110yds: kpt on but comf hld* **7/2**^{3}
3 *1* **Love In The Desert** 2-9-0 0 StevieDonohoe 6 75+
(Noel Quinlan) *chsd ldrs: rdn and kpt on 2f out: n.m.r and green ins fnl f: kpt on* **16/1**
3 **4** *¾* **Caletta Bay**^{13} 2204 2-9-0 0 MartinHarley 7 72
(Mick Channon) *led tl hdd over 1f out: outpcd ins fnl f* **3/1**^{2}
5 *nk* **Miss Lillie** 2-9-0 0 JohnFahy 1 71+
(Roger Teal) *hmpd sn after s: lost momentum and outpcd: hdwy to chse ldrs ins fnl 2f: kpt on clsng stages but nvr gng pce to chal* **11/2**
6 *5* **Cay Dancer** 2-9-0 0 RyanMoore 5 53
(Richard Hannon) *in rr: pushed along 1/2-way: outpcd most of way* **10/1**
7 *4* **Green Run** 2-9-0 0 WilliamBuick 9 39
(Richard Hannon) *early spd: rdn and outpcd after 2f* **16/1**
8 *11* **Dandeena (IRE)** 2-8-11 0 DarrenEgan$^{(3)}$ 3
(Ronald Harris) *slowly away: a wl bhd* **33/1**
1m 0.81s (-0.79) **Going Correction** -0.40s/f (Firm) 8 Ran SP% **117.2**
Speed ratings (Par 90): **90,88,86,85,85 77,70,53**
Tote Swingers 1&2 £2.50, 2&3 £5.00, 1&3 £7.90 CSF £10.68 TOTE £3.10: £1.50, £1.40, £2.30; EX 13.50 Trifecta £123.00 Pool: £1,419.04 - 8.65 winning tickets..
Owner Qatar Racing Limited **Bred** Kinsman Farm **Trained** Averham Park, Notts

FOCUS
Round course home bend at outermost configuration which added 8yds to distances on Round course. A maiden with a history of producing smart fillies headed by 2010 Queen Mary winner Maqaasid.

2602 HAAGEN-DAZS H'CAP 1m 6f
6:30 (6:32) (Class 4) (0-85,82) 3-Y-O **£4,690** (£1,395; £697; £348) **Stalls** Low

Form RPR
1-31 **1** **Lion Beacon**^{17} 2079 3-9-1 **76** RyanMoore 8 86+
(Amanda Perrett) *trckd ldrs: rdn to ld over 2f out: drvn out fnl f* **7/4**^{1}
44-1 **2** *2¾* **Argent Knight**^{13} 2233 3-8-9 **70** GrahamLee 9 76+
(William Jarvis) *in rr: pushed along 5f out: styd on fr over 2f out: kpt on fnl f to take 2nd last strides but no imp on wnr* **7/1**^{2}
00-3 **3** *nk* **Ballinderry Boy**^{23} 1898 3-8-4 **65** FrannyNorton 6 71
(Andrew Balding) *chsd ldrs: rdn over 3f out: chsd wnr over 1f out: no imp: lost 2nd last strides* **12/1**
4111 **4** *3¼* **Poetic Verse**^{31} 1729 3-9-3 **78** JamieSpencer 10 79
(Rod Millman) *hld up in rr: pushed along and hdwy over 2f out: kpt on fnl f but nvr gng pce to rch ldrs* **17/2**
1 **5** *¾* **Deira Phantom (IRE)**^{18} 2055 3-9-7 **82** WilliamBuick 7 82
(David Simcock) *in rr: pushed along over 3f out: stl green over 2f out: swtchd lft to outer: rdn and styd on fnl f but nvr a threat* **12/1**
1-00 **6** *2¾* **Forced Family Fun**^{22} 1923 3-8-8 **69** HayleyTurner 5 65
(Michael Bell) *t.k.h: led: hdd over 2f out: wknd and lost 2nd over 1f out* **20/1**
6-45 **7** *½* **Color Shades**^{16} 2127 3-8-7 **68** JohnFahy 3 63
(Clive Cox) *chsd ldrs: rdn 3f out: wknd 2f out* **25/1**
0131 **8** *3¼* **Dali's Lover (IRE)**^{15} 2153 3-8-10 **71** JimmyQuinn 4 62
(Charles Hills) *in tch: rdn over 3f out: sn btn* **8/1**^{3}
3m 4.93s (0.43) **Going Correction** +0.175s/f (Good) 8 Ran SP% **94.5**
Speed ratings (Par 101): **105,103,103,101,100 99,99,97**
Tote Swingers 1&2 £2.80, 2&3 £16.80, 1&3 £3.00 CSF £9.07 CT £52.44 TOTE £2.10: £1.10, £1.60, £2.90; EX 9.70 Trifecta £76.20 Pool: £1,485.12 - 14.60 winning tickets..
Owner Mrs Alexandra J Chandris **Bred** The Late A M Jenkins & J Chandris **Trained** Pulborough, W Sussex

FOCUS
The 1m6f of Sandown is quite a stamina test for 3-y-os this early in the season and it was a trio of strong stayers who came to the fore. Khotan got upset in the stalls and was withdrawn after the handlers had to open the front. The first three all showed improvement.

2603 WATERLOO H'CAP 1m 14y
7:05 (7:05) (Class 4) (0-85,85) 3-Y-O **£4,690** (£1,395; £697; £348) **Stalls** Low

Form RPR
3-11 **1** **Sea Shanty (USA)**^{17} 2100 3-9-7 **85** RyanMoore 5 96
(Richard Hannon) *sn disputing 2nd: trckd ldr 5f out: drvn to chal 2f out: sn led: styd on u.p: hld on all out* **11/10**^{1}
11-2 **2** *nk* **Jodies Jem**^{131} 188 3-9-4 **82** GrahamLee 1 92
(William Jarvis) *disp 2nd to 5f out: styd cl up tl outpcd in 3rd over 2f out: drvn and styd on to chse wnr ins fnl f: gng on clsng stages: nt quite get up* **12/1**
0-64 **3** *3½* **Saint Jerome (IRE)**^{20} 1977 3-8-12 **76** FergusSweeney 4 78
(Jamie Osborne) *led: rdn and jnd 2f out: sn hdd: wknd into 3rd ins fnl f* **13/2**
14-0 **4** *3½* **Etijaah (USA)**^{13} 2209 3-9-6 **84** DaneO'Neill 6 78
(Brian Meehan) *in rr: hdwy to cl on ldrs over 2f out: sn wknd* **3/1**^{2}
5-46 **5** *4½* **Yul Finegold (IRE)**^{31} 1725 3-8-12 **76** PatCosgrave 2 60
(George Baker) *a in rr* **20/1**
1 **P** **Ogbourne Downs**^{24} 1881 3-9-1 **79** WilliamBuick 3
(Charles Hills) *prom early: btn whn p.u and dismntd over 3f out* **11/2**^{3}
1m 43.17s (-0.13) **Going Correction** +0.175s/f (Good) 6 Ran SP% **113.8**
Speed ratings (Par 101): **107,106,103,99,95**
Tote Swingers 1&2 £1.60, 2&3 £8.30, 1&3 £2.60 CSF £16.21 TOTE £1.60: £1.10, £4.50; EX 10.50 Trifecta £66.50 Pool: £2,253.85 - 25.39 winning tickets..
Owner The Queen **Bred** Her Majesty The Queen **Trained** East Everleigh, Wilts

FOCUS
There were a couple of in-form performers, but this was not the strongest 3-y-o handicap for the track.

2604 XL GROUP WHITSUN H'CAP 1m 2f 7y
7:35 (7:36) (Class 3) (0-90,88) 3-Y-O **£7,439** (£2,213; £1,106; £553) **Stalls** Low

Form RPR
1- **1** **Mutashaded (USA)**^{205} 7468 3-8-12 **79** DaneO'Neill 5 92+
(Roger Varian) *s.i.s: hld up in rr: stdy hdwy fr 2f out: drvn to chse ldr 1f out: qcknd to ld fnl 150yds: styd on strly* **11/4**^{2}
6-20 **2** *2½* **Noble Bull (IRE)**^{15} 2153 3-8-7 **74** (b^{1}) LukeMorris 4 78
(Charles Hills) *led: rdn and kpt on fr over 2f out: hdd and edgd rt into rails fnl 150yds: kpt on to hold 2nd* **33/1**
4-11 **3** *1½* **Theodore Gericault (IRE)**^{22} 1934 3-9-4 **85** RyanMoore 6 86
(Sir Michael Stoute) *t.k.h: towards rr: hdwy to chse ldr ins fnl 2f: no imp and dropped to 3rd fnl f* **4/5**^{1}
1433 **4** *2* **Rouge Nuage (IRE)**^{13} 2223 3-8-2 **74** oh1 RyanTate$^{(5)}$ 2 71
(Conrad Allen) *in rr: in tch fr 5f out: outpcd over 2f out: drvn and styd on again fnl f* **25/1**
63-1 **5** *5* **Dark Emerald (IRE)**^{23} 1912 3-9-7 **88** WilliamBuick 7 75
(Brendan Powell) *in rr early: hdwy to chse ldr 7f out: rdn over 2f out: sn wknd* **7/1**^{3}
12-0 **6** *1½* **Canadian Run (IRE)**^{29} 1767 3-9-0 **81** GrahamLee 3 65
(Robert Mills) *t.k.h: chsd ldrs: rdn 3f out: tk hrd pressed 3rd ins fnl 2f: wknd over 1f out* **20/1**
01-0 **7** *½* **The Gatling Boy (IRE)**^{35} 1636 3-9-1 **82** SeanLevey 1 65
(Richard Hannon) *t.k.h: chsd ldrs: rdn 3f out: sn wknd* **16/1**
2m 11.31s (0.81) **Going Correction** +0.175s/f (Good) 7 Ran SP% **112.2**
Speed ratings (Par 103): **103,101,99,98,94 93,92**
Tote Swingers 1&2 £24.80, 2&3 £9.00, 1&3 £1.10 CSF £81.23 TOTE £3.10: £1.80, £5.40; EX 78.40 Trifecta £293.40 Pool: £2,415.40 - 6.17 winning tickets..
Owner Hamdan Al Maktoum **Bred** Shadwell Farm LLC **Trained** Newmarket, Suffolk

FOCUS
A strong three-year-old handicap even if the seemingly progressive favourite underperformed. It was steadily run and the winner rates better than the bare form.

2605 HAAGEN-DAZS SECRET SENSATIONS MAIDEN STKS 1m 2f 7y
8:10 (8:12) (Class 5) 3-4-Y-O **£3,881** (£1,155; £577; £288) **Stalls** Low

Form RPR
34-0 **1** **Excellent Result (IRE)**^{33} 1679 3-8-12 80 SilvestreDeSousa 7 91+
(Saeed bin Suroor) *sn trcking ldr: drvn to ld 2f out: forged clr appr fnl f: easily* **7/2**^{2}
3-33 **2** *7* **Number One London (IRE)**^{15} 2151 3-8-12 82 HayleyTurner 2 77
(Brian Meehan) *chsd ldrs in 3rd: drvn and kpt on to go 2nd over 1f out: kpt on but nvr any ch w easy wnr* **1/1**^{1}
6-5 **3** *2¼* **Dragon City**^{33} 1679 3-8-12 0 WilliamBuick 6 73
(Harry Dunlop) *chsd ldrs: pushed along and one pce 3f out: kpt on fnl f to take 3rd clsng stages but nvr any ch w ldng duo* **7/1**
4 *nk* **Legends (IRE)** 3-8-12 0 RyanMoore 5 72+
(Sir Michael Stoute) *in tch: drvn to chse ldrs 2f out: styd on same pce* **6/1**^{3}
5 *1¼* **Poyle Thomas** 4-9-12 0 RichardThomas 8 69
(Ralph Beckett) *in tch: pushed along 3f out: kpt on fnl f but nvr any ch* **25/1**
0 **6** *shd* **Halling's Treasure**^{10} 2321 3-8-7 0 ThomasBrown$^{(5)}$ 9 69
(Andrew Balding) *mid-div: pushed along 3f out: kpt on fr over 1f out: nvr any ch* **100/1**
00 **7** *¾* **Maraweh (IRE)**^{15} 2151 3-8-12 0 DaneO'Neill 11 68
(J W Hills) *in rr: pushed along over 2f out: sme hdwy fnl f* **50/1**
8 *hd* **Perfect Spell** 3-8-12 0 JamieSpencer 3 67+
(Andrew Balding) *s.i.s: in rr: pushed along over 2f out: sme late prog* **12/1**
230- **9** *1½* **Claude Monet (BRZ)**^{218} 7174 4-9-8 78 GrahamLee 1 60
(Simon Dow) *led tl hdd 2f out: sn btn* **33/1**
10 *3* **The Green Ogre** 3-8-12 0 FergusSweeney 4 58
(Gary Moore) *s.i.s: bhd most of way* **50/1**
0 **11** *17* **Dalaklear (IRE)**^{33} 1679 3-8-12 0 TedDurcan 10 46
(David Lanigan) *a in rr* **50/1**
2m 12.93s (2.43) **Going Correction** +0.175s/f (Good)
WFA 3 from 4yo 14lb 11 Ran SP% **120.4**
Speed ratings (Par 103): **97,91,89,89,88 88,87,87,86,83 70**
Tote Swingers 1&2 £2.00, 2&3 £1.80, 1&3 £3.90 CSF £7.29 TOTE £4.60: £1.40, £1.10, £2.20; EX 10.20 Trifecta £45.60 Pool: £1,359.83 - 22.33 winning tickets..
Owner Godolphin **Bred** Tom & Geraldine Molan **Trained** Newmarket, Suffolk

FOCUS
A 3yo maiden that has unearthed some smart types in recent years, notably Group 1 winner Sajjhaa and smart handicappers Trade Commissioner and Tanfeeth. It was slowly run and the favourite disappointed, but the winner impressed. The overall form is a little shaky.

2606 FOXWARREN FILLIES' H'CAP 1m 1f
8:40 (8:44) (Class 5) (0-75,74) 3-Y-O+ **£3,234** (£962; £481; £240) **Stalls** Low

Form RPR
443- **1** **Lyric Ballad**^{143} 8302 3-8-3 **62** SilvestreDeSousa 9 70
(Hughie Morrison) *in tch: rdn and hdwy on outer to ld ins fnl 2f: drvn clr fnl f* **10/1**
062- **2** *3¼* **Three Choirs (IRE)**^{241} 6535 3-8-10 **74** RobertTart$^{(5)}$ 4 74
(William Stone) *chsd ldrs: rdn 3f out: outpcd 2f out: rallied u.p and styd on again fnl f to take 2nd clsng stages* **20/1**
632- **3** *½* **Squeeze My Brain (IRE)**^{246} 6355 3-9-1 **74** JamieSpencer 3 75+
(Ralph Beckett) *s.i.s: in rr: rdn and hdwy appr fnl f: fin wl to take 3rd: nt rch ldng duo* **7/2**^{1}
21-4 **4** *shd* **Magique (IRE)**^{16} 2127 3-9-0 **73** ^{1} WilliamBuick 7 72
(Jeremy Noseda) *chsd ldr: drvn to ld over 2f out: sn rdn and hdd: no ch w wnr fnl f and styd on same pce* **5/1**^{3}
60-3 **5** *nse* **Who's That Chick (IRE)**^{133} 140 4-8-4 **55** RyanTate$^{(5)}$ 8 56
(Ralph Smith) *in rr: rdn and hdwy appr fnl f: kpt on wl clsng stages* **33/1**
4-40 **6** *¾* **Jacobella**^{17} 2092 3-8-7 **66** LukeMorris 11 63
(Jonathan Portman) *in rr: pushed along over 1f out: styd on fnl f: gng on clsng stages* **16/1**
002- **7** *nk* **Equitissa (IRE)**^{206} 7432 3-8-8 **67** SeanLevey 12 64
(Richard Hannon) *chsd ldrs: chal 2f out: styd on same pce fnl f* **12/1**
41-6 **8** *1* **Mandy The Nag (USA)**^{16} 2127 3-8-9 **67** ow1 GrahamLee 5 62
(Ed Dunlop) *s.i.s: in rr: hdwy on ins over 2f out: kpt on same pce fnl f* **14/1**
0-50 **9** *1* **Candycakes (IRE)**^{12} 2253 4-9-13 **73** HayleyTurner 1 67
(Michael Bell) *chsd ldrs: rdn over 2f out: sn btn* **14/1**
-004 **10** *nse* **Balady (IRE)**^{15} 2155 4-9-8 **68** (p) DaneO'Neill 2 62
(Dominic Ffrench Davis) *led tl hdd over 2f out: wknd sn after* **25/1**

02-4 **11** *4* **Sweet Martoni**[14] 2192 3-8-11 **70** .... RyanMoore 6 53
(William Knight) *chsd ldrs: rdn over 2f out: sn btn* **4/1**[2]

0-34 **12** *2* **Berwin (IRE)**[6] 2413 4-8-13 **66** .... JoshBaudains(7) 10 47
(Sylvester Kirk) *s.i.s: bhd most of way* **13/2**

1m 57.29s (1.59) **Going Correction** +0.175s/f (Good)
WFA 3 from 4yo 13lb **12** Ran SP% **119.8**
Speed ratings (Par 100): **99,96,95,95,95 94,94,93,92,92 89,87**
Tote Swingers 1&2 £71.00, 2&3 £21.00, 1&3 £13.90 CSF £197.55 CT £858.78 TOTE £5.30: £1.20, £6.80, £1.70; EX 192.20 Trifecta £414.90 Pool: £1,320.81 - 2.38 winning tickets..
Owner T D Rootes & O F Waller **Bred** Shutford Stud And O F Waller **Trained** East Ilsley, Berks

FOCUS
A competitive fillies' handicap won in decisive fashion. A clear personal best from the winner.
T/Plt: £38.90 to a £1 stake. Pool: £77,505.21 - 1452.12 winning tickets. T/Qpdt: £12.50 to a £1 stake. Pool: £5,102.02 - 301.95 winning tickets. ST

2117 CATTERICK (L-H)

Friday, May 24

OFFICIAL GOING: Good to soft (soft in places; 7.6)
Wind: Fresh; half against Weather: Overcast

2611 SUPPORT THE HOUSE THAT JACK BUILT APPRENTICE H'CAP 5f
6:35 (6:35) (Class 6) (0-60,60) 4-Y-O+ **£2,385** (£704; £352) **Stalls** Low

Form RPR

00-4 **1** **Bondi Beach Boy**[14] 2217 4-8-2 **46** oh1 .... JordanNason(5) 6 56
(James Turner) *prom centre: effrt and pushed along over 1f out: styd on wl fnl f to ld nr fin* **14/1**

00-2 **2** *shd* **Choc'A'Moca (IRE)**[44] 1465 6-8-12 **56** ....(v) DavidSimmonson(5) 1 66
(Paul Midgley) *chsd ldrs towards far side: led and rdn over 1f out: kpt on fnl f: hdd nr fin* **9/2**[2]

3040 **3** *1 1/4* **Lord Buffhead**[14] 2217 4-8-10 **56** ....(b) LisaTodd(7) 11 62
(Richard Guest) *hld up centre: hdwy and edgd lft over 1f out: one pce wl ins fnl f* **18/1**

1040 **4** *3/4* **Pull The Pin (IRE)**[11] 2319 4-8-8 **52** ....[1] LukeLeadbitter(5) 7 55
(Declan Carroll) *prom centre: pushed along 1/2-way: kpt on ins fnl f* **10/1**

6032 **5** *shd* **Prigsnov Dancer (IRE)**[14] 2236 8-8-4 **46** ....(p) NoelGarbutt(3) 14 48
(Deborah Sanderson) *midfield on outside: rdn and hdwy over 2f out: kpt on ins fnl f: nt pce to chal* **16/1**

0323 **6** *1 1/4* **Tuibama (IRE)**[17] 2122 4-9-4 **60** ....(p) GeorgeChaloner(3) 3 58
(Tracy Waggott) *led towards far side to over 1f out: sn rdn and outpcd* **2/1**[1]

-000 **7** *2 3/4* **Irish Girls Spirit (IRE)**[18] 2074 4-8-13 **55** .... ShirleyTeasdale(3) 5 43
(Paul Midgley) *prom centre tl rdn and wknd over 1f out* **14/1**

8 *1/2* **Oh Marcius (IRE)**[329] 3597 5-8-6 **48** ....(b[1]) MarcMonaghan(3) 8 34
(Kieran P Cotter, Ire) *hld up centre: pushed along and hung lft 2f out: no imp fnl f* **14/1**

44-5 **9** *1* **Rio Sands**[22] 1961 8-8-2 **48** .... DanielleMooney(7) 13 31
(Richard Whitaker) *hld up on outside: rdn over 1f out: nt pce to chal* **25/1**

63-0 **10** *2 3/4* **Sharp Shoes**[10] 2343 6-8-7 **51** .... ConnorBeasley(5) 4 24
(Christopher Wilson) *cl up centre tl wknd over 1f out* **16/1**

4050 **11** *1 3/4* **Nine Before Ten (IRE)**[32] 1734 5-8-10 **54** ....(t[1]) AaronJones(5) 9 20
(Charles Smith) *midfield centre: outpcd 1/2-way: sn struggling* **18/1**

2000 **12** *4* **Prince James**[30] 1757 6-9-2 **60** .... MatthewHopkins(5) 2 12
(Michael Easterby) *s.i.s: sn wl bhd towards far side: nvr on terms* **9/1**[3]

00-0 **13** *1 1/4* **Tomasini**[17] 2121 4-8-4 **46** oh1 ....(b) JackDuern(3) 12
(John Weymes) *s.i.s: bhd on outside: no ch fr 1/2-way* **66/1**

1m 1.71s (1.91) **Going Correction** +0.35s/f (Good) **13** Ran SP% **118.2**
Speed ratings (Par 101): **98,97,95,94,94 92,88,87,85,81 78,72,70**
toteswingers 1&2 £19.90, 1&3 £40.60, 2&3 £23.10 CSF £75.08 CT £1197.96 TOTE £17.90: £4.10, £2.10, £6.50; EX 136.50 Trifecta £788.70 Part won. Pool: £1,051.60 - 0.17 winning units..
Owner J R Turner **Bred** G R & H Turner **Trained** Norton-le-Clay, N Yorks

FOCUS
A low-grade apprentice handicap and they avoided the stands' side rail, often favoured when conditions are genuine soft. The form makes sense around the placed horses.

2612 BRITISH STALLION STUDS SUPPORTING BRITISH RACING EBF MAIDEN FILLIES' STKS 5f
7:05 (7:06) (Class 5) 2-Y-O **£3,067** (£905; £453) **Stalls** Low

Form RPR

1 **Arabda** 2-9-0 0 .... SilvestreDeSousa 2 70+
(Mark Johnston) *mde all: rdn 2f out: kpt on wl fnl f* **7/4**[1]

2 *1* **Milly's Secret (IRE)** 2-8-7 0 .... RowanScott(7) 1 66
(Ann Duffield) *cl up: effrt and rdn over 1f out: kpt on ins fnl f* **5/1**

3 *1/2* **Sakuramachi** 2-9-0 0 .... SamHitchcott 4 65
(Mick Channon) *chsd ldrs: rdn and sltly outpcd 2f out: rallied appr fnl f: kpt on same pce last 75yds* **7/2**[3]

4 *5* **Tricksome (IRE)** 2-9-0 0 .... PaulMulrennan 5 47
(Ann Duffield) *green in preliminaries: t.k.h: prom: effrt and pushed along wl over 1f out: sn outpcd: eased whn hld wl ins fnl f* **5/2**[2]

5 *6* **Crazy Dancer** 2-9-0 0 .... RobbieFitzpatrick 6 25
(Richard Guest) *s.i.s: bhd and outpcd: no ch fr 1/2-way* **25/1**

1m 2.62s (2.82) **Going Correction** +0.35s/f (Good) **5** Ran SP% **107.7**
Speed ratings (Par 90): **91,89,88,80,71**
CSF £10.20 TOTE £2.30: £1.10, £3.00; EX 13.40 Trifecta £35.30 Pool: £785.91 - 16.66 winning units..
Owner Hamdan Al Maktoum **Bred** Shadwell Estate Company Limited **Trained** Middleham Moor, N Yorks

FOCUS
Five newcomers in this 5f maiden 2yo fillies' race. The time was a fair bit slower than the opening 46-60 handicap. The winner could do better than the bare form.

2613 YORKSHIRE-OUTDOORS.CO.UK (S) STKS 7f
7:35 (7:37) (Class 6) 3-4-Y-O **£2,385** (£704; £352) **Stalls** Centre

Form RPR

4/0-1 **1** **Jessie's Spirit (IRE)**[22] 1963 4-9-0 75 .... PaulMulrennan 2 65
(Ann Duffield) *trckd ldrs on ins: hdwy to ld over 1f out: pushed out: comf* **11/4**[3]

06 **2** *1 3/4* **Trixie Malone**[32] 1722 3-8-0 0 .... RaulDaSilva(3) 7 55
(Mrs K Burke) *trckd ldrs: rdn and outpcd whn m wd bnd ent st: edgd lft 2f out: styd on wl fnl f: tk 2nd nr fin: nt rch wnr* **8/1**

-030 **3** *shd* **Shamrocked (IRE)**[8] 2395 4-9-6 68 .... CharlesBishop(5) 1 70
(Mick Channon) *led: rdn and hdd over 1f out: kpt on same pce fnl f: lost 2nd cl home* **5/2**[2]

14-5 **4** *2 1/4* **Legal Bond**[19] 2036 4-9-11 61 .... SilvestreDeSousa 9 63
(David O'Meara) *sn pushed along in rr: drvn 1/2-way: hdwy on outside and hung lft 2f out: kpt on fnl f: nt pce to chal* **9/4**[1]

0-00 **5** *2 1/2* **Let Me In (IRE)**[30] 1759 3-8-1 44 .... DanielleMooney(7) 4 47
(Nigel Tinkler) *prom: drvn along fr 1/2-way: outpcd fnl 2f* **20/1**

606- **6** *1* **Lady Bentinck (IRE)**[207] 7445 4-9-0 48 .... BarryMcHugh 8 43
(Alan Berry) *missed break: bhd tl styd on fr 2f out: nvr rchd ldrs* **22/1**

-005 **7** *3 1/4* **Miss Bossy Boots**[4] 2503 4-8-9 10 .... GeorgeChaloner(5) 6 34
(Tracy Waggott) *hld up in tch: rdn and outpcd over 3f out: no imp fnl 2f* **50/1**

600 **8** *3 1/2* **Silver Forest (IRE)**[10] 2340 3-8-3 0 .... JamesSullivan 3 21
(John Weymes) *sn in rr: struggling over 3f out: nvr on terms* **100/1**

0135 **9** *40* **Douglas Pasha (IRE)**[29] 1772 3-9-0 56 .... AdrianNicholls 5
(David Nicholls) *trckd ldrs: rdn after 3f: wknd qckly 2f out: eased whn no ch: t.o* **12/1**

1m 29.08s (2.08) **Going Correction** +0.35s/f (Good)
WFA 3 from 4yo 11lb **9** Ran SP% **116.9**
Speed ratings (Par 101): **102,100,99,97,94 93,89,85,39**
toteswingers 1&2 £7.00, 1&3 £3.10, 2&3 £5.40 CSF £24.09 TOTE £4.10: £1.20, £1.90, £2.00; EX 25.70 Trifecta £104.60 Pool: £1,162.12 - 8.32 winning units..There was no bid for the winner. Shamrocked was claimed by Mr Ollie Pears for £5,000.
Owner David & Carole McMahon **Bred** Mountarmstrong Stud **Trained** Constable Burton, N Yorks

FOCUS
Few seriously entered the argument in this weak seller. The winner was the pick on her 2yo form and did not need to match that.

2614 RACINGUK.COM H'CAP 5f
8:05 (8:07) (Class 4) (0-80,80) 3-Y-O+ **£6,469** (£1,925; £962; £481) **Stalls** Low

Form RPR

006- **1** **Lucky Numbers (IRE)**[206] 7452 7-9-11 **79** .... DavidNolan 1 90
(David O'Meara) *cl up: rdn 1/2-way: led over 1f out: hld on wl towards fin* **17/2**

-000 **2** *1/2* **Lost In Paris (IRE)**[20] 2031 7-9-2 **70** ....(p) PaulMulrennan 2 79
(Tim Easterby) *cl up: effrt and edgd rt over 1f out: ev ch ins fnl f: kpt on: hld nr fin* **16/1**

1263 **3** *1 1/2* **Bapak Bangsawan**[18] 2076 3-8-3 **68** ....(b) JulieBurke(3) 4 69
(Kevin Ryan) *prom: effrt and rdn over 1f out: edgd lft ins fnl f: one pce towards fin* **7/1**[3]

0403 **4** *nse* **Waseem Faris (IRE)**[6] 2459 4-9-9 **77** .... SamHitchcott 9 80
(Mick Channon) *sn niggled in rr: rdn and hdwy over 1f out: kpt on fnl f: nt pce to chal* **2/1**[1]

4-01 **5** *1 3/4* **Whitecrest**[13] 2268 5-9-8 **76** .... AdrianNicholls 3 73
(John Spearing) *sn pushed along bhd ldng gp: effrt u.p over 1f out: no imp fnl f* **10/1**

0-12 **6** *nk* **Mr Mo Jo**[17] 2122 5-9-2 **70** ....(b) DuranFentiman 5 66
(Lawrence Mullaney) *led at decent gallop: rdn and hdd over 1f out: outpcd ins fnl f* **13/2**[2]

515- **7** *2* **Pipers Note**[228] 6920 3-8-11 **78** .... GeorgeChaloner(5) 10 67
(Richard Whitaker) *towards rr: drvn along bef 1/2-way: no imp fr over 1f out* **12/1**

-310 **8** *3/4* **Mission Impossible**[13] 2275 8-9-4 **72** ....(p) PatrickMathers 11 58
(Tracy Waggott) *racd on outside: sn outpcd and bhd: sme late hdwy: nvr on terms* **12/1**

60-0 **9** *4 1/2* **Foxy Music**[16] 2150 9-9-10 **78** ....(p) GrahamGibbons 7 48
(Eric Alston) *prom 2f: sn drvn and outpcd on outside: no ch fnl 2f* **14/1**

60-4 **10** *14* **Master Rooney (IRE)**[55] 1253 7-9-9 **80** .... RaulDaSilva(3) 6
(Geoffrey Harker) *sn bhd on outside: struggling 1/2-way: t.o* **10/1**

1m 0.85s (1.05) **Going Correction** +0.35s/f (Good)
WFA 3 from 4yo+ 8lb **10** Ran SP% **115.8**
Speed ratings (Par 105): **105,104,101,101,98 98,95,94,86,64**
toteswingers 1&2 £42.80, 1&3 £12.60, 2&3 £27.00 CSF £133.63 CT £722.88 TOTE £11.00: £2.70, £4.40, £2.00; EX 139.40 Trifecta £676.80 Part won. Pool: £902.45 - 0.24 winning units..
Owner Tom Tuohy & Tony Jafrate **Bred** Rory O'Brien **Trained** Nawton, N Yorks

FOCUS
Plenty of speed in this competitive and quite valuable 5f handicap. The winner's best run since his 2011 debut.

2615 LESLIE PETCH H'CAP (QUALIFIER FOR CATTERICK TWELVE FURLONG SERIES FINAL) 1m 3f 214y
8:35 (8:35) (Class 5) (0-75,78) 3-Y-O+ **£3,881** (£1,155; £577; £288) **Stalls** Low

Form RPR

02-0 **1** **Villa Royale**[13] 2277 4-9-12 **73** .... SilvestreDeSousa 1 87+
(David O'Meara) *chsd ldng pair: rdn over 3f out: hdwy and hung lft to ld over 1f out: rdn clr fnl f* **2/1**[1]

1603 **2** *5* **Royal Sea (IRE)**[11] 2328 4-9-1 **62** oh1 ....(p) BarryMcHugh 2 66
(Barry Leavy) *hld up in tch: effrt and pushed along over 3f out: styd on fnl f to go 2nd nr fin: no ch w wnr* **20/1**

3-54 **3** *nk* **Tinseltown**[13] 2277 7-9-6 **67** ....(p) MickyFenton 8 70
(Brian Rothwell) *t.k.h: pressed ldr: led over 6f out: rdn and hdd over 1f out: one pce fnl f: lost 2nd nr fin* **15/2**

0-11 **4** *2 1/4* **Mohawk Ridge**[11] 2316 7-9-10 **78** 6ex .... ConnorBeasley(7) 4 78
(Michael Dods) *led to over 6f out: rallied: rdn and ev ch over 1f out: sn outpcd* **3/1**[2]

2-03 **5** *5* **Pertuis (IRE)**[23] 1936 7-9-0 **66** .... GeorgeChaloner(5) 5 58
(Micky Hammond) *s.s: bhd and niggled: hdwy over 4f out: rdn and outpcd fr over 2f out* **7/2**[3]

5-00 **6** *1 3/4* **Patavium (IRE)**[16] 2165 10-9-7 **68** .... PaulMulrennan 7 57+
(Edwin Tuer) *in tch: effrt and rdn over 2f out: wknd over 1f out* **12/1**

3-30 **7** *2 1/4* **Graceful Descent (FR)**[21] 1993 8-9-1 **69** .... GemmaTutty(7) 3 54
(Karen Tutty) *s.i.s: bhd: rdn along over 5f out: wknd over 2f out* **12/1**

/00- **8** *nk* **Quite Sparky**[51] 1914 6-9-11 **75** .... LucyAlexander(3) 6 60
(Mike Sowersby) *hld up in tch: pushed along over 4f out: wknd fr 3f out* **100/1**

2m 41.54s (2.64) **Going Correction** +0.35s/f (Good) **8** Ran SP% **113.5**
Speed ratings (Par 103): **105,101,101,99,96 95,93,93**
toteswingers 1&2 £6.40, 1&3 £5.30, 2&3 £7.00 CSF £43.99 CT £250.99 TOTE £2.90: £1.50, £4.20, £1.40; EX 36.20 Trifecta £225.70 Pool: £647.25 - 2.15 winning units..
Owner David Kuss & Tim Pakyurek **Bred** Lawn Stud **Trained** Nawton, N Yorks

FOCUS
The two leaders were keen to take each other one and they rather set it up for the winner. He built on his 3yo progress but the form is modest in behind.

2616 ELLERY HILL RATING RELATED MAIDEN STKS 7f
9:05 (9:06) (Class 6) 3-Y-O+ **£2,385** (£704; £352) **Stalls** Centre

Form RPR
-055 **1** **Running Reef (IRE)**[7] 2406 4-9-11 57 BarryMcHugh 5 65
(Tracy Waggott) *hld up in midfield: rdn and effrt over 2f out: led ins fnl f: r.o wl* **6/1**[2]
4454 **2** ½ **Mishhar (IRE)**[13] 2273 4-9-4 56 (v) DavidSimmonson(7) 6 64
(Tony Coyle) *s.i.s: hld up: rdn and hdwy over 1f out: ev ch ins fnl f: kpt on: hld nr fin* **10/1**
440- **3** 3¼ **My Gigi**[184] 7814 3-9-0 65 SilvestreDeSousa 1 51+
(Gary Moore) *t.k.h: led tl rdn and hdd ins fnl f: kpt on same pce* **5/2**[1]
0-56 **4** nk **Woody Bay**[13] 2272 3-9-0 65 JamesSullivan 11 50+
(James Given) *bhd on outside: rdn and hdwy over 1f out: kpt on fnl f: no imp* **10/1**
30-5 **5** ¾ **Relight My Fire**[36] 1647 3-9-0 64 DuranFentiman 9 48
(Tim Easterby) *prom: effrt and drvn 2f out: kpt on same pce fnl f* **18/1**
-502 **6** 2¼ **Gladsome**[13] 2280 5-9-8 60 RaulDaSilva(3) 10 46
(Jason Ward) *bhd: rdn over 2f out: kpt on fnl f: nvr rchd ldrs* **17/2**
0-55 **7** 1¼ **Red Charmer (IRE)**[10] 2342 3-9-0 65 GrahamGibbons 4 39
(Ann Duffield) *midfield: rdn along over 2f out: sn no imp* **10/1**
-000 **8** ½ **Dolly Diva**[16] 2162 4-9-11 58 MickyFenton 12 41
(Paul Midgley) *cl up tl rdn: hung lft and wknd over 1f out* **80/1**
3-35 **9** 3½ **Eastlands Lad (IRE)**[13] 2280 4-9-6 60 (p) GeorgeChaloner(5) 3 32
(Micky Hammond) *bhd: drvn along 1/2-way: nvr rchd ldrs* **7/1**[3]
3-54 **10** ¾ **Imperial Spirit**[9] 2363 3-9-0 63 (v[1]) SamHitchcott 8 26
(Mick Channon) *cl up: rdn over 3f out: wknd fr 2f out* **25/1**
11 8 **Cluin Aine (IRE)**[21] 1999 4-9-6 62 (b[1]) MarcMonaghan(5) 2
(Kieran P Cotter, Ire) *dwlt: sn pushed along and in tch on ins: wknd 3f out* **25/1**
46-6 **12** 3 **Art Mistress (IRE)**[18] 2080 3-9-0 65 (t) PaulMulrennan 7
(Tim Easterby) *hld up: pushed along on outside over 3f out: rdn and wknd wl over 1f out* **15/2**

1m 28.84s (1.84) **Going Correction** +0.35s/f (Good)
WFA 3 from 4yo+ 11lb **12** Ran SP% **119.1**
Speed ratings (Par 101): **103,102,98,98,97 94,93,92,88,88 78,75**
toteswingers 1&2 £23.80, 1&3 £1.70, 2&3 £13.80 CSF £64.00 TOTE £6.60: £1.90, £4.00, £1.70; EX 95.50 Trifecta £466.10 Part won. Pool: £621.50 - 0.69 winning units..
Owner Elsa Crankshaw Gordon Allan **Bred** C O'Reilly & Co **Trained** Spennymoor, Co Durham

FOCUS
A modest 0-65 ratings related maiden. The gallop was very strong for the grade and the first two home came from off the pace. The winner is rated back to his early maiden form.
T/Plt: £368.90 to a £1 stake. Pool: £67,095.70 - 132.75 winning units T/Qpdt: £49.50 to a £1 stake. Pool: £4,350.06 - 65.00 winning units RY

2583 GOODWOOD (R-H)
Friday, May 24

OFFICIAL GOING: Good (8.2) changing to good to soft on straight course after race 5 (4.20)
Wind: Fresh; against Weather: Overcast with steady rain; cold

2617 GOODWOOD MAIDEN AUCTION STKS 5f
2:00 (2:04) (Class 5) 2-Y-O **£3,234** (£962; £481; £240) **Stalls** High

Form RPR
02 **1** **Our Queenie (IRE)**[8] 2382 2-8-10 0 RichardHughes 8 83
(Richard Hannon) *trckd ldr: pushed along 2f out: led jst over 1f out: edgd rt and shkn up fnl f: a in command* **1/4**[1]
2 ¾ **Ligeia** 2-8-4 0 KieranO'Neill 7 75+
(Richard Hannon) *tall: scope: dwlt: hld up in tch: rn green whn asked for effrt fr 2f out: prog to chse wnr ins fnl f: stl green but styd on: a hld* **7/1**[2]
6 **3** 3¾ **Captain Ryan**[9] 2359 2-8-11 0 SteveDrowne 4 68
(Peter Makin) *w'like: led: hdd jst over 1f out: edgd rt and wknd last 150yds* **50/1**
5 **4** 1½ **Island Kingdom (IRE)**[10] 2344 2-8-9 0 LiamJones 3 61
(J S Moore) *w'like: neat: chsd ldrs: rdn 2f out: outpcd over 1f out: n.d after* **50/1**
4 **5** 2¼ **Talksalot (IRE)**[14] 2238 2-8-9 0 LiamKeniry 2 53
(J S Moore) *tall: lengthy: in tch: effrt on outer and cl enough 2f out: wknd jst over 1f out* **8/1**[3]
6 2¾ **Miracle Of Medinah** 2-8-9 0 LukeMorris 1 43
(Mark Usher) *leggy: s.s: v green and sn t.o: lost no further grnd fr 1/2-way whn racing in more organised manner* **25/1**
5 **7** ½ **Chance Of Romance (IRE)**[14] 2230 2-8-6 0 JohnFahy 5 38
(Clive Cox) *leggy: chsd ldrs: rdn 2f out: wknd qckly over 1f out* **25/1**

59.81s (-0.39) **Going Correction** -0.225s/f (Firm) **7** Ran SP% **115.2**
Speed ratings (Par 93): **94,92,86,84,80 76,75**
toteswingers 1&2 £1.40, 1&3 £5.90, 2&3 £12.00 CSF £2.55 TOTE £1.20: £1.10, £2.60; EX 2.90 Trifecta £39.50 Pool: £5,009.26 - 95.03 winning units..
Owner N A Woodcock **Bred** Liam Brennan **Trained** East Everleigh, Wilts

FOCUS
First 2f of 1m course dolled out 5yds. Lower bend dolled out 6yds from 6f to 2f pole in straight adding 16yds to races using lower bend. An uncompetitive maiden which resulted in a 1-2 for Richard Hannon, but the red-hot favourite was far from convincing and the time was slow. The first two were clear.

2618 REHEAT STKS (H'CAP) 7f
2:35 (2:36) (Class 4) (0-85,85) 4-Y-O+ **£6,469** (£1,925; £962; £481) **Stalls** Low

Form RPR
06-6 **1** **Magic City (IRE)**[49] 1363 4-8-11 80 WilliamTwiston-Davies(5) 6 93
(Richard Hannon) *dwlt: sn in midfield: smooth prog over 2f out: led 1f out and sn rdn 2 l clr: edgd rt but styd on* **16/1**
5-43 **2** 1 **Good Authority (IRE)**[23] 1922 6-9-5 83 WilliamBuick 1 94
(Karen George) *lw: dwlt: hld up in last pair: stl there and looking for room jst over 2f out: gd prog over 1f out: r.o to take 2nd last 100yds: clsd on wnr but nvr able to chal* **5/1**[1]
4360 **3** 1¼ **Bravo Echo**[14] 2207 7-9-4 82 SebSanders 2 89
(Michael Attwater) *lw: mde most: rdn 2f out: rdr dropped whip over 1f out: sn hdd and one pce* **7/1**[3]
0425 **4** nk **Harrison George (IRE)**[6] 2444 8-9-7 85 (t) FrannyNorton 11 91
(P J O'Gorman) *prom: chsd ldr 3f out to over 1f out: kpt on same pce* **8/1**
-661 **5** 1½ **Forceful Appeal (USA)**[25] 1878 5-9-3 81 TomQueally 14 83
(Simon Dow) *dwlt: hld up in last quartet: stdy prog over 2f out: rchd 4th jst over 1f out and rdn: one pce after* **25/1**
5-25 **6** ½ **Flexible Flyer**[18] 2097 4-8-12 76 RichardHughes 9 77
(Hughie Morrison) *lw: awkward s: t.k.h: trckd ldrs: shkn up wl over 1f out: nt qckn and sn btn: one pce* **5/1**[1]
60-1 **7** 1¼ **Royal Reyah**[53] 1286 4-8-13 77 FergusSweeney 7 75
(Stuart Kittow) *lw: hld up towards rr: rdn on outer over 2f out: nvr on terms but kpt on same pce* **10/1**
0-60 **8** shd **Accession (IRE)**[20] 2013 4-9-6 84 (b) AdamKirby 13 87+
(Clive Cox) *lw: hld up in last quartet: stuck on inner over 2f out: eased to outer over 1f out: jst pushed along and kpt on fnl f: nvr involved* **8/1**
04-4 **9** 1¾ **Shamahan**[27] 1838 4-8-13 77 RyanMoore 16 70
(Gary Moore) *dropped in fr wdst draw and hld up in last: rdn over 2f out: nvr a factor but modest late prog* **14/1**
1-00 **10** hd **Rocky Reef**[23] 1922 4-9-2 80 (v) JackMitchell 10 73
(Philip Hide) *nvr bttr than midfield: tried to cl on ldrs 2f out and n.m.r: wknd over 1f out* **33/1**
0-54 **11** ½ **Corporal Maddox**[13] 2265 6-9-6 84 LukeMorris 12 75
(Ronald Harris) *hld up in midfield: looking for room 2f out: rdn over 1f out: sn wknd* **25/1**
00-6 **12** nk **Shifting Star (IRE)**[13] 2266 8-8-5 76 JoeyHaynes(7) 8 67
(John Bridger) *chsd ldr to 3f out: wknd wl over 1f out* **25/1**
1212 **13** 2¼ **Polar Kite (IRE)**[14] 2214 5-9-6 84 JamesDoyle 4 69
(Sean Curran) *in tch in midfield: looking for room 2f out: rdn and wknd over 1f out* **6/1**[2]
416- **14** 5 **Emkanaat**[226] 6979 5-9-6 84 MartinDwyer 15 56
(Amy Weaver) *prom tl lost pl qckly over 2f out: no ch whn impeded over 1f out* **33/1**

1m 27.11s (0.11) **Going Correction** +0.175s/f (Good) **14** Ran SP% **121.4**
Speed ratings (Par 105): **106,104,103,103,101 100,99,99,97,97 96,96,93,87**
toteswingers 1&2 £27.90, 1&3 £31.50, 2&3 £5.60 CSF £89.60 CT £473.10 TOTE £19.50: £4.80, £1.90, £2.40; EX 180.00 Trifecta £743.70 Pool: £3,809.45 - 3.84 winning units..
Owner Barker, Ferguson, Mason, Hassiakos, Done **Bred** Miss Annmarie Burke **Trained** East Everleigh, Wilts

FOCUS
A competitive handicap, and decent form. The winner bounced back to his 2yo best.

2619 AIR BP STKS (FILLIES' H'CAP) 1m 4f
3:10 (3:10) (Class 3) (0-90,88) 3-Y-O+ **£9,703** (£2,887; £1,443; £721) **Stalls** High

Form RPR
216- **1** **Wannabe Loved**[195] 7688 4-10-0 88 WilliamBuick 9 96
(John Gosden) *lw: mde virtually all: shkn up and drew clr fr over 2f out: in n.d over 1f out: rdn out* **9/2**[2]
62-1 **2** 2¾ **Centred (IRE)**[23] 1933 3-8-4 81 FrannyNorton 10 85
(Sir Michael Stoute) *trckd wnr to over 4f out: drvn and nt qckn 3f out: kpt on again fr over 1f out: tk 2nd ins fnl f* **13/8**[1]
621- **3** ½ **Princess Caetani (IRE)**[210] 7375 4-9-11 85 AdamKirby 7 88
(David Simcock) *hld up in 7th: pushed along and no prog 3f out: rdn over 1f out: styd on to take 3rd nr fin* **8/1**[3]
2-21 **4** shd **Hepworth**[116] 429 4-9-7 81 (b) RyanMoore 8 84
(John Gosden) *hld up in 6th: rdn on outer wl over 2f out: no imp tl kpt on fnl f* **9/2**[2]
120 **5** 1 **Dewala**[41] 1538 4-9-1 75 AndrewMullen 11 76
(Michael Appleby) *chsd ldng trio: rdn over 3f out: no imp fr over 2f out* **25/1**
66-6 **6** ¾ **Perfect Delight**[25] 1884 4-9-2 76 JohnFahy 6 76
(Clive Cox) *trckd ldng pair: effrt on inner to chal 4f out: sn btn off: lost grnd on wnr 2f out: lost 2nd and wknd ins fnl f* **14/1**
20-6 **7** ½ **Shades Of Grey**[35] 1663 6-9-1 80 RyanTate(5) 1 79
(Clive Cox) *hld up in 5th: tried to cl on rivals over 2f out: nt qckn u.p over 1f out: no hdwy after* **20/1**
5-21 **8** ½ **Divergence (IRE)**[16] 2164 3-7-11 77 oh2 DarrenEgan(3) 3 76
(Michael Bell) *t.k.h: hld up in last: rdn on outer 3f out: no prog* **8/1**[3]

2m 42.62s (4.22) **Going Correction** +0.275s/f (Good)
WFA 3 from 4yo+ 17lb **8** Ran SP% **112.0**
Speed ratings (Par 104): **96,94,93,93,93 92,92,91**
toteswingers 1&2 £2.30, 1&3 £5.10, 2&3 £3.10 CSF £11.67 CT £54.06 TOTE £5.00: £1.70, £1.10, £2.50; EX 15.50 Trifecta £85.50 Pool: £2,870.13 - 25.15 winning units..
Owner Normandie Stud Ltd **Bred** Normandie Stud Ltd **Trained** Newmarket, Suffolk

FOCUS
A decent fillies' handicap, but they went no pace early and, as is usually the case when that happens, those that raced up front were at a major advantage. Some may be flattered in behind but the form is taken at face value.

2620 CASCO EBF COCKED HAT STKS (LISTED RACE) (C&G) 1m 3f
3:45 (3:45) (Class 1) 3-Y-O **£22,684** (£8,600) **Stalls** High

Form RPR
1-11 **1** **Disclaimer**[18] 2086 3-9-0 94 TomQueally 1 108+
(Sir Henry Cecil) *led at reasonable pce: gng bttr than rival over 2f out: hdd and shkn up wl over 1f out: responded to ld again ins fnl f: sn clr* **13/8**[2]
1-12 **2** 2½ **Contributer (IRE)**[14] 2211 3-9-0 101 RyanMoore 2 104
(Ed Dunlop) *trckd rival: stoked up over 2f out: clsd to ld wl over 1f out but nt decisive move: hdd & wknd ins fnl f* **1/2**[1]

2m 30.47s (3.97) **Going Correction** +0.375s/f (Good) **2** Ran SP% **104.8**
Speed ratings (Par 107): **100,98**
TOTE £1.60.
Owner K Abdullah **Bred** Juddmonte Farms Ltd **Trained** Newmarket, Suffolk

FOCUS
Subsequent Group 1 winners Rewilding and Masked Marvel have taken this race in recent years, but the absence of Fantastic Moon reduced this year's renewal to a match and because of that the form has to be treated some caution. The pace was relatively good and the form is given a token face value rating.

2621 IBA STKS (H'CAP) 6f
4:20 (4:20) (Class 2) (0-105,100) 3-Y-O+
£12,450 (£3,728; £1,864; £932; £466; £234) **Stalls** High

Form RPR
0000 **1** **Piscean (USA)**[13] 2254 8-9-0 86 WilliamBuick 1 93
(Tom Keddy) *hld up in tch: prog on outer fr 2f out: drvn 1f out: clsd to ld nr fin: jst hld on* **25/1**
-103 **2** nse **Prodigality**[9] 2366 5-9-9 100 ThomasBrown(5) 4 107
(Ronald Harris) *b: trckd ldrs: wnt 2nd over 2f out: drvn to chal over 1f out: narrow ld jst ins fnl f: hdd nr fin: styd on: jst failed* **13/8**[1]

611- **3** nk **Wentworth (IRE)**[245] 6447 3-8-11 92 RichardHughes 8 100+
(Richard Hannon) *hld up: gng easily but nightmare run fr 2f out and gaps nvr appeared: r.o to take 3rd nr fin: most unlucky* **5/2**[2]

35/5 **4** 3/4 **Miss Lahar**[16] 2152 4-9-8 94 MatthewDavies 2 97
(Mick Channon) *w ldr: led after 2f: drvn 2f out: hdd jst ins fnl f: styd on* **20/1**

505- **5** 1 1/2 **Tariq Too**[203] 7551 6-9-9 95 MartinDwyer 7 94
(Amy Weaver) *c out of the stalls slowly: detached in last: nudged along over 2f out: sme prog over 1f out: no hdwy fnl f: can do bttr* **10/1**

-010 **6** 1 1/4 **Annunciation**[19] 2039 3-9-4 99 RyanMoore 10 92
(Richard Hannon) *t.k.h: led 2f: u.p and lost 2nd over 2f out: steadily fdd* **4/1**[3]

0-00 **7** hd **Johannes (IRE)**[19] 2046 10-8-10 89 LauraBarry(7) 5 83
(Richard Fahey) *chsd ldrs tl wknd over 1f out* **14/1**

1m 13.09s (0.89) **Going Correction** +0.375s/f (Good)
WFA 3 from 4yo+ 9lb 7 Ran SP% **111.0**
Speed ratings (Par 109): **109,108,108,107,105 103,103**
toteswingers 1&2 £7.30, 1&3 £6.20, 2&3 £1.60 CSF £62.58 CT £139.77 TOTE £17.30: £4.30, £1.60; EX 74.30 Trifecta £252.00 Pool: £5,171.76 - 15.39 winning units..
Owner Andrew Duffield **Bred** Connie And John Iacuone **Trained** Newmarket, Suffolk

FOCUS
A decent sprint handicap run at a good pace, but the post-race analysis centred on the performance of the third horse. The winner is rated close to his turf best.

2622 THAKEHAM HOMES FILLIES' STKS (H'CAP) 1m
4:55 (4:55) (Class 4) (0-80,79) 3-Y-O
£6,225 (£1,864; £932; £466; £233; £117) **Stalls** Low

Form RPR

3-11 **1** **Auction (IRE)**[8] 2387 3-9-11 79 6ex RyanMoore 4 85+
(Ed Dunlop) *hld up bhd ldrs: clsd 2f out: shkn up to ld jst over 1f out: hung rt 100yds out: styd on* **8/11**[1]

40-4 **2** 1 **Strictly Ballroom (IRE)**[16] 2158 3-9-2 75 MichaelJMMurphy(5) 1 78
(Mark Johnston) *lw: led: rdn and hdd 2f out: 3rd 1f out: rallied to take 2nd and nudged by rival 100yds out: hld by wnr after* **16/1**

44-5 **3** 1/2 **Everleigh**[15] 2195 3-9-7 75 RichardHughes 5 77
(Richard Hannon) *hld up in last pair: outpcd 2f out: stl same pl 1f out: rdn and r.o to take 3rd last stride: no ch* **6/1**[3]

6-51 **4** shd **Callmeakhab (IRE)**[14] 2215 3-9-2 70 SteveDrowne 2 72
(Charles Hills) *trckd ldr: shkn up to ld 2f out: hdd jst over 1f out: keeping on but hld whn squeezed for room 100yds out: lost 3rd post* **12/1**

61-0 **5** hd **Iberis**[34] 1683 3-9-6 74 TomQueally 3 75
(Sir Henry Cecil) *lw: hld up bhd ldrs: effrt 2f out: nt clr run over 1f out: sn rdn: styd on same pce fnl f* **9/2**[2]

15 **6** 2 **Whispering Lady (IRE)**[41] 1546 3-9-1 72 DarrenEgan(3) 6 68+
(David Simcock) *veered lft s: reluctant to get gng and virtually t.o after 100yds: then t.k.h and in tch 5f out: rdn over 2f out: wknd fnl f* **14/1**

1m 43.78s (3.88) **Going Correction** +0.475s/f (Yiel) 6 Ran SP% **110.6**
Speed ratings (Par 98): **99,98,97,97,97 95**
toteswingers 1&2 £5.60, 1&3 £1.60, 2&3 £7.30 CSF £13.69 TOTE £1.70: £1.40, £4.70; EX 12.20 Trifecta £53.30 Pool: £3,558.91 - 50.03 winning units..
Owner Highclere Thoroughbred Racing - Coventry **Bred** Edy Srl And Societa Agricola Gem Srl **Trained** Newmarket, Suffolk

FOCUS
A fair fillies' handicap, but the pace was modest and the field finished compressed. It's hard to rate the form any higher.

2623 TURFTV FOR BETTING SHOPS BONUS STKS (H'CAP) 5f
5:30 (5:30) (Class 5) (0-70,68) 3-Y-O **£3,234** (£962; £481; £240) **Stalls** High

Form RPR

-121 **1** **Shirley's Pride**[18] 2091 3-9-0 61 (t) AndrewMullen 5 71+
(Michael Appleby) *trckd overall ldr in centre: shkn up and clsd to ld over 1f out: rdn out* **5/1**

2-43 **2** 1 1/4 **Pixilated**[17] 2135 3-9-7 68 RichardHughes 6 73
(Gay Kelleway) *racd in centre: overall ldr: rdn and hdd over 1f out: one pce* **9/4**[1]

-512 **3** 1 3/4 **Royal Guinevere**[18] 2098 3-9-6 67 [1] PatDobbs 3 66
(Dean Ivory) *last of trio to r in centre: outpcd fr 1/2-way: styd on fr over 1f out to take 3rd last 100yds* **3/1**[2]

-520 **4** 1 1/4 **Harrogate Fair**[17] 2129 3-9-1 62 LiamJones 7 56
(Michael Squance) *mostly racd alone between two mini-gps: 3rd but nt on terms w ldng pair fr 1/2-way: wknd fnl f* **25/1**

1435 **5** 2 1/4 **Silca's Dream**[18] 2098 3-9-0 68 (v) DanielCremin(7) 8 54
(Mick Channon) *led pair that racd nr side but nvr on terms: no ch over 1f out* **7/1**

3113 **6** 10 **Dangerous Age**[79] 894 3-9-2 63 SebSanders 9 13
(J W Hills) *lw: chsd rival on nr side: nvr on terms: wknd over 1f out: t.o* **7/2**[3]

59.16s (-1.04) **Going Correction** -0.225s/f (Firm) 6 Ran SP% **111.0**
Speed ratings (Par 99): **99,97,94,92,88 72**
toteswingers 1&2 £2.40, 1&3 £2.50, 2&3 £1.90 CSF £16.28 CT £36.96 TOTE £4.90: £2.10, £1.50; EX 15.70 Trifecta £55.00 Pool: £2,649.44 - 36.08 winning units..
Owner M Golding & H Singh Birah **Bred** Manor Farm Stud (rutland) **Trained** Danethorpe, Notts

FOCUS
The going was changed to good to soft on the straight course. Despite the field being reduced to six, they still managed to race in three groups for most of the way - three down the centre, two against the stands' rail and one in between. The trio who raced centre-field filled the first three places. The winner's 2yo form guides the level.
T/Plt: £32.60 to a £1 stake. Pool: £65,804.52 - 1,470.29 winning units T/Qpdt: £14.30 to a £1 stake. Pool: £3,491.16 - 179.60 winning units JN

2589 HAYDOCK (L-H)
Friday, May 24

OFFICIAL GOING: Good to firm (8.8)
Wind: Fresh; half behind Weather: Cloudy

2624 PHS WASHROOM SERVICES H'CAP (JOCKEY CLUB GRASSROOTS MIDDLE DISTANCE SERIES QUALIFIER) 1m 2f 95y
2:20 (2:21) (Class 5) (0-75,75) 3-Y-O **£2,587** (£770; £384; £192) **Stalls** Centre

Form RPR

6-52 **1** **Dolphin Village (IRE)**[29] 1776 3-8-12 66 PaulHanagan 2 75
(Richard Fahey) *chsd ldrs: swtchd rt over 2f out: led over 1f out: styd on to draw clr and edgd lft ins fnl f* **5/1**

310- **2** 3 1/2 **Beat The Tide**[270] 5670 3-9-3 71 PaulMulrennan 7 73
(Michael Dods) *hld up: hdwy over 3f out: styd on to take 2nd wl ins fnl f: no imp on wnr* **7/1**

2-40 **3** 1 1/4 **Sabre Rock**[22] 1972 3-9-7 75 JimCrowley 4 75
(John Best) *racd keenly: chsd ldr: led jst over 2f out: rdn and hdd over 1f out: fdd fnl 100yds* **8/1**

6-33 **4** 1/2 **Gabrial The Thug (FR)**[32] 1719 3-9-1 69 JamieSpencer 3 68
(Richard Fahey) *led: hdd jst over 2f out: outpcd by ldrs over 1f out: kpt on same pce ins fnl f: no imp after* **4/1**[2]

000- **5** 8 **Substantivo (IRE)**[252] 6204 3-8-12 66 KierenFallon 10 49
(Alan Jarvis) *hld up: pushed along over 4f out: rdn whn btn over 2f out* **7/2**[1]

460 **6** 3/4 **No Win No Fee**[15] 2198 3-8-6 65 TobyAtkinson(5) 5 47
(Michael Appleby) *chsd ldrs: pushed along and outpcd over 4f out: lost pl and struggling 3f out* **28/1**

06-0 **7** 3 1/2 **Izzy Boy (USA)**[29] 1772 3-8-11 65 SilvestreDeSousa 6 40
(Mark Johnston) *chsd ldrs: pushed along and lost pl over 5f out: bhd after* **11/1**

0-12 **U** **Order Of Service**[18] 2094 3-9-4 72 SeanLevey 8
(David Brown) *rrd and uns rdr s* **9/2**[3]

2m 12.38s (-3.12) **Going Correction** -0.30s/f (Firm) 8 Ran SP% **112.5**
Speed ratings (Par 99): **100,97,96,95,89 88,86,**
toteswingers 1&2 £3.80, 1&3 £3.70, 2&3 £6.90 CSF £38.13 CT £272.28 TOTE £4.40: £1.70, £3.40, £1.80; EX 26.10 Trifecta £1020.90 Pool: £1,612.15 - 1.18 winning units..
Owner Y Nasib **Bred** Gerrardstown House Stud **Trained** Musley Bank, N Yorks

FOCUS
All races on inner home straight except 6f race which was on Stands side home straight. Races on Round course increased in distance by one yard. Only the runner-up managed to make inroads from the rear in what was probably a fair handicap for the level. The winner was back to his 2yo promise.

2625 EBF PHS COMPLIANCE MAIDEN FILLIES' STKS 6f
2:55 (2:56) (Class 5) 2-Y-O **£2,911** (£866; £432; £216) **Stalls** Centre

Form RPR

0 **1** **Red Lady (IRE)**[14] 2204 2-9-0 0 KierenFallon 4 83+
(Brian Meehan) *mde all: drew clr ins fnl f: pushed out and r.o* **25/1**

2 **2** 4 **Stepping Out (IRE)**[14] 2230 2-9-0 0 RichardKingscote 15 71
(Tom Dascombe) *midfield: hdwy 1/2-way: styd on ins fnl f: nosed into 2nd fnl strides: no ch w wnr* **5/1**[3]

3 hd **Sefaat** 2-9-0 0 PaulMulrennan 13 70+
(Brian Meehan) *hld up: hdwy 1/2-way: chsd wnr over 1f out: no imp: lost 2nd fnl strides* **25/1**

4 3 **Herbah** 2-9-0 0 PaulHanagan 9 61
(Roger Varian) *hld up: pushed along 1/2-way: edgd lft whn chsng ldrs over 1f out: nt pce to chal* **4/1**[2]

2 **5** 1 **Rose Gloria (IRE)**[39] 1580 2-9-0 0 MartinHarley 2 58
(Mick Channon) *midfield: hdwy over 1f out: kpt on ins fnl f: nvr able to chal* **6/1**

6 3/4 **Miaplacidus (IRE)** 2-9-0 0 TonyHamilton 12 56+
(Richard Fahey) *bhd: sn outpcd: hung lft and styd on ins fnl f: nt trble ldrs* **20/1**

7 4 1/2 **Fredricka** 2-9-0 0 RobertHavlin 5 43
(Garry Moss) *chsd ldrs tl rdn and wknd over 1f out* **100/1**

0 **8** nk **Madame Mirasol (IRE)**[32] 1718 2-9-0 0 TomEaves 10 42
(Kevin Ryan) *dwlt: prom tl rdn and wknd 2 out* **66/1**

9 nk **Chriselliam (IRE)** 2-9-0 0 JamieSpencer 1 41
(Charles Hills) *in tch tl wknd over 1f out* **8/1**

5 **10** 1 1/2 **Miguela McGuire**[20] 2025 2-8-9 0 JasonHart(5) 7 36
(Eric Alston) *midfield: outpcd 2f out: hung lft over 1f out whn n.d* **150/1**

55 **11** 2 3/4 **Jive**[15] 2189 2-9-0 0 SeanLevey 8 28
(Richard Hannon) *prom: pushed along over 2f out: wknd over 1f out* **14/1**

5 **12** hd **Got To Dance**[19] 2053 2-9-0 0 JimCrowley 3 28
(Ralph Beckett) *in tch: effrt 1/2-way: wknd 1f out* **5/2**[1]

6 **13** nk **Dandy Maid**[18] 2090 2-8-9 0 TobyAtkinson(5) 6 27
(Michael Appleby) *hld up: sn pushed along: nvr on terms* **100/1**

14 13 **Diamond Solitaire (IRE)** 2-9-0 0 KirstyMilczarek 11
(Alan Jarvis) *dwlt: sn pushed along: a bhd* **50/1**

1m 13.23s (-0.57) **Going Correction** -0.225s/f (Firm) 14 Ran SP% **115.9**
Speed ratings (Par 90): **94,88,88,84,83 82,76,75,75,73 69,69,68,51**
toteswingers 1&2 £14.60, 1&3 £55.40, 2&3 £59.20 CSF £136.48 TOTE £19.50: £5.80, £1.90, £8.40; EX 201.90 Trifecta £1113.30 Part won. Pool: £1,484.50 - 0.01 winning units..
Owner D J Burke **Bred** Brook Stud Bloodstock Ltd **Trained** Manton, Wilts

FOCUS
They finished quite strung out in what was probably a decent fillies' maiden. A fairly positive view has been taken of the form, which could easily be worth 5lb more.

2626 PHS WATERLOGIC CLASSIFIED STKS 6f
3:30 (3:32) (Class 4) 3-Y-O **£6,469** (£1,925; £962; £481) **Stalls** Centre

Form RPR

4-1 **1** **Lord Ashley (IRE)**[34] 1687 3-9-0 78 RichardKingscote 1 88+
(Tom Dascombe) *hld up: hdwy 2f out: led wl ins fnl f: r.o* **5/2**[1]

1624 **2** 1 3/4 **Red Refraction (IRE)**[15] 2190 3-9-0 77 SeanLevey 2 82
(Richard Hannon) *w ldr: rdn 2f out: led over 1f out: hdd wl ins fnl f: hld towards fin* **15/2**

-210 **3** 1/2 **Right Touch**[9] 2371 3-9-0 78 PaulHanagan 7 80+
(Richard Fahey) *hld up: hdwy whn hung lft wl ins fnl f: styd on* **9/2**[2]

3-12 **4** 3/4 **Shore Step (IRE)**[13] 2285 3-9-0 78 MartinHarley 6 78
(Mick Channon) *led: rdn and hdd over 1f out: stl ch ins fnl f: kpt on same pce towards fin* **5/1**[3]

-103 **5** 3/4 **Bold Prediction (IRE)**[25] 1892 3-8-11 80 MichaelMetcalfe(3) 4 76
(Mrs K Burke) *hld up: pushed along 1/2-way: trying to keep on whn n.m.r ins fnl f: no imp towards fin* **10/1**

6-1 **6** 4 **Different**[24] 1911 3-9-0 70 TomEaves 8 67
(Bryan Smart) *prom: ev ch ins fnl f: struggling to hold pl whn n.m.r and hmpd wl ins fnl f: sn dropped away* **7/1**

64-4 **7** 16 **Prince Regal**[13] 2285 3-9-0 77 KierenFallon 3 12
(Alan Jarvis) *hld up: pushed along 1/2-way: wl bhd over 1f out* **6/1**

1m 12.3s (-1.50) **Going Correction** -0.225s/f (Firm) 7 Ran SP% **111.1**
Speed ratings (Par 101): **101,98,98,97,96 90,69**
toteswingers 1&2 £3.30, 1&3 £2.20, 2&3 £5.10 CSF £20.41 TOTE £3.00: £1.20, £4.10; EX 18.90 Trifecta £73.90 Pool: £1,803.47 - 18.29 winning units..
Owner D R Passant **Bred** Ms A Lynam **Trained** Malpas, Cheshire

FOCUS
Quite a decent classified sprint, with all bar one of the runners rated 77 plus. The winner can improve again.

2627 PHS DIRECT H'CAP 1m
4:05 (4:06) (Class 4) (0-80,83) 3-Y-O **£6,469** (£1,925; £962; £481) **Stalls** Low

Form RPR
-441 **1** **Kohlaan (IRE)**[18] 2094 3-9-5 **75** .... AndreaAtzeni 3 82
(Roger Varian) *mde all: pressed fr 2f out: rdn over 1f out: styd on ins fnl f* **13/8**[1]
0-35 **2** *1* **Storming (IRE)**[30] 1769 3-9-1 **71** .... KierenFallon 5 76
(Andrew Balding) *hld up: rdn over 1f out: nt qckn: styd on towards fin: nvr able to chal wnr* **3/1**[2]
1615 **3** *½* **Corn Snow (USA)**[13] 2272 3-9-4 **74** .... SilvestreDeSousa 4 78
(Mark Johnston) *chsd ldr: chalng fr 2f out: no ex towards fin* **4/1**[3]
2251 **4** *shd* **Off The Pulse**[25] 1891 3-9-6 **76** .... GrahamGibbons 2 79
(John Mackie) *trckd ldrs: rdn and nt qckn over 1f out: kpt on towards fin* **8/1**
0-21 **5** *hd* **Surround Sound**[22] 1966 3-8-11 **67** .... DuranFentiman 8 70
(Tim Easterby) *racd keenly: hld up in rr: pushed along 3f out: swtchd rt over 2f out: hung lft u.p over 1f out: styd on towards fin: nvr able to chal* **7/1**

1m 40.92s (-2.78) **Going Correction** -0.30s/f (Firm) **5** Ran SP% **106.7**
Speed ratings (Par 101): **101,100,99,99,99**
CSF £6.21 TOTE £2.10: £1.80, £2.30; EX 6.90 Trifecta £17.30 Pool: £2,898.78 - 125.53 winning units..
Owner Sheikh Ahmed Al Maktoum **Bred** Old Carhue Stud **Trained** Newmarket, Suffolk

FOCUS
An ordinary handicap in which the field finished well bunched, despite it being run at a fair gallop. Straightforward bare form.

2628 PHS DATASHRED MAIDEN STKS 1m
4:40 (4:46) (Class 5) 3-Y-O+ **£2,587** (£770; £384; £192) **Stalls** Low

Form RPR
03-2 **1** **Stresa**[18] 2084 3-8-11 87 .... RobertHavlin 10 74
(John Gosden) *chsd ldrs: rdn to ld wl over 1f out: r.o wl to draw clr ins fnl f* **7/4**[1]
2 *2 ¼* **Pressure Point** 3-9-2 0 .... JimCrowley 7 74+
(Sir Michael Stoute) *midfield: hdwy over 2f out: rdn over 1f out: styd on to take 2nd wl ins fnl f: nt rch wnr: promising* **11/2**[3]
0 **3** *2* **Brave Acclaim (IRE)**[34] 1678 3-9-2 0 .... RichardKingscote 4 69
(Tom Dascombe) *chsd ldr: led over 2f out: rdn and hdd wl over 1f out: styd on same pce ins fnl f* **40/1**
0-0 **4** *nk* **Fab Lolly (IRE)**[13] 2279 3-8-11 0 .... SilvestreDeSousa 11 64
(James Bethell) *chsd ldrs: effrt 2f out: styd on same pce ins fnl f* **66/1**
0 **5** *1* **Konzert (ITY)**[16] 2151 3-9-2 0 .... AndreaAtzeni 6 66
(Andrew Hollinshead) *midfield: hdwy over 2f out: rdn over 1f out: one pce fnl 150yds* **66/1**
0-2 **6** *shd* **Manchestar**[29] 1777 3-9-2 0 .... TonyHamilton 1 67+
(Richard Fahey) *chsd ldrs: nt qckn over 1f out: keeping on whn nt clr run briefly ins fnl f: no imp after* **12/1**
00- **7** *2* **Bonne Amie (FR)**[243] 6512 3-8-11 0 .... GrahamGibbons 15 56
(Tom Dascombe) *in tch: rdn over 2f out: outpcd over 1f out: kpt on wout threatening ins fnl f* **50/1**
36- **8** *2 ¼* **Twary (USA)**[198] 7628 3-9-2 0 .... PaulHanagan 5 56
(Roger Varian) *midfield: rdn 2f out: one pce and no imp over 1f out* **3/1**[2]
-05 **9** *8* **Vanvitelli**[15] 2192 3-9-2 0 ....(t) JamieSpencer 13 38
(James Fanshawe) *towards rr: plugged on fnl f wout threatening* **6/1**
00 **10** *¾* **Wesleydale (IRE)**[17] 2118 6-10-0 0 .... AndrewElliott 8 39
(Simon West) *towards rr: sme prog u.p into midfield over 2f out: nvr able to trble ldrs* **150/1**
-0 **11** *2 ¾* **Speedy Utmost Meg**[27] 1828 3-8-11 0 .... AdamBeschizza 14 25
(William Kinsey) *led: rdn and hdd over 2f out: flashed tail whn wkng over 1f out* **100/1**
12 *9* **Teenage Idol (IRE)**[20] 9-9-11 0 .... LucyAlexander(3) 3 15
(Dianne Sayer) *completely missed break: wl bhd and u.p: nvr on terms* **50/1**
13 *¾* **Samoan (IRE)** 4-10-0 0 .... KierenFallon 16 10+
(Brian Meehan) *hld up: outpcd 3f out: nvr on terms* **10/1**
0-0 **14** *1* **Peninsula**[18] 2093 4-9-9 0 .... SeanLevey 2 3
(Tobias B P Coles) *upset bef ent stalls: towards rr: pushed along over 4f out: prog into midfield 3f out: no imp on ldrs: wknd over 1f out* **66/1**
15 *21* **Babushka's Girl** 4-9-6 0 .... MarkCoumbe(3) 9
(Lisa Williamson) *a bhd: nvr on terms* **150/1**

1m 40.74s (-2.96) **Going Correction** -0.30s/f (Firm)
WFA 3 from 4yo+ 12lb **15** Ran SP% **121.0**
Speed ratings (Par 103): **102,99,97,97,96 96,94,92,84,83 80,71,70,69,48**
toteswingers 1&2 £3.70, 1&3 £16.70, 2&3 £35.10 CSF £11.57 TOTE £3.10: £1.30, £2.40, £7.90; EX 15.90 Trifecta £369.40 Pool: £5,531.79 - 11.23 winning units..
Owner Denford Stud **Bred** Denford Stud Ltd **Trained** Newmarket, Suffolk

FOCUS
Little depth to this maiden, which appeared to be run at a fair pace, and it was pleasing to see representatives from two of the major yards come to the fore. The form could easily be rated up to 9lb higher.

2629 PHS TREADSMART H'CAP (FOR LADY AMATEUR RIDERS) 1m 3f 200y
5:15 (5:15) (Class 5) (0-70,69) 4-Y-O+ **£1,634** (£1,634; £386; £193) **Stalls** Centre

Form RPR
601- **1** **Tapis Libre**[216] 7251 5-9-13 **66** ....(p) MissJoannaMason(5) 8 75
(Michael Easterby) *hld up: hdwy over 4f out: chalng over 1f out: disp ld ins fnl f: styd on* **12/1**
51-3 **1** *dht* **Teide Peak (IRE)**[112] 475 4-9-8 **61** .... MrsRWilson(5) 11 70
(Paul D'Arcy) *s.i.s: t.k.h: hld up: handy in chsng gp after 4f: clsd over 4f out: led 3f out: hrd pressed ins fnl f and jnd: styd on* **8/1**
-046 **3** *3* **Tenhoo**[27] 1836 7-10-5 **67** .... MissCWalton 10 71
(Eric Alston) *hld up: hdwy over 3f out: styd on ins fnl f: nt rch ldrs* **4/1**[2]
054- **4** *7* **Cool Hand Luke (IRE)**[204] 5197 4-9-9 **57** ....(p) MissADeniel 6 50
(Ian Williams) *midfield: rdn and lost pl over 5f out: plugged on wout threatening* **14/1**
-010 **5** *1 ½* **Knox Overstreet**[18] 2087 5-10-0 **67** .... MissSMDoolan(5) 5 57
(Mick Channon) *sn chsd clr ldr: ev ch 2f out: rdn over 1f out: wknd ent fnl f:* **14/1**
00-0 **6** *½* **Call Of Duty (IRE)**[11] 2316 8-10-4 **66** .... EmmaSayer 1 56
(Dianne Sayer) *chsd ldrs early: hld up after: rdn over 2f out: no imp on ldrs* **6/1**[3]
50-2 **7** *½* **Al Furat (USA)**[29] 1789 5-9-7 **60** .... MrsVDavies(5) 7 49
(Ron Barr) *sn prom in chsng gp: nt clr runover 2f out: wknd over 1f out* **7/2**[1]
2304 **8** *1 ¾* **Blazing Desert**[16] 2174 9-10-4 **69** .... MissMMullineaux(3) 4 55
(William Kinsey) *midfield: lost pl 5f out: n.d after* **22/1**
6506 **9** *24* **Light The City (IRE)**[16] 2165 6-9-10 **58** .... MissSBrotherton 2 6
(Ruth Carr) *chsd ldrs in main gp: wknd over 3f out* **6/1**[3]
065- **10** *13* **Humungosaur**[166] 8049 4-9-11 **59** .... MissEJJones 3
(Richard Ford) *led: sn clr: hdd 3f out: wknd over 2f out* **22/1**

2m 31.16s (-2.64) **Going Correction** -0.30s/f (Firm) **10** Ran SP% **111.6**
Speed ratings (Par 103): **96,96,94,89,88 88,87,86,70,61**TOTE: WIN: TL £7.60, TP £4.20. PL: TL £4.50, TP £3.70, T 1.70. EX: TL/TP £38.70, TP/TL £38.60. CSF: TL/TP £49.94, TP/TL £47.52. TRICAST: TL/TP/T £223.84, TP/TL/T £216.49 toteswinger: TL&T £14.00, TL&T £13.00, TP&T £7.20 T27 Owner.
Owner Mrs Susan E Mason **Bred** Sedgecroft Stud **Trained** Sheriff Hutton, N Yorks
■ Stewards' Enquiry : Miss Joanna Mason two-day ban; used whip above permitted level (tbd).

FOCUS
The front three drew clear in this truly-run lady amateur riders' handicap, and the first two proved inseparable at the line. The third is a fair guide to the form.
T/Jkpt: Not won. T/Plt: £138.40 to a £1 stake. Pool: £90,688.74 - 478.24 winning units T/Qpdt: £7.00 to a £1 stake. Pool: £5,029.99 - 528.71 winning units DO

2313 MUSSELBURGH (R-H)
Friday, May 24

OFFICIAL GOING: Good to firm (7.6)
Wind: Moderate; across Weather: Cloudy with sunny periods

2630 MCQUAY HIGH EFFICIENCY CLASSIC AMATEURS' H'CAP (£15K BETFAIR SCOTTISH STAYERS' FINAL QUALIFIER) 1m 5f
6:15 (6:15) (Class 6) (0-65,65) 4-Y-O+ **£2,495** (£774; £386; £193) **Stalls** High

Form RPR
60-6 **1** **Goodlukin Lucy**[11] 2313 6-9-6 **46** oh1 ....(t) MrJHamilton(3) 7 54
(Dianne Sayer) *t.k.h early: mde all: sn clr: stdd 1/2-way: pushed along and clr 4f out: rdn 2f out: styd on wl fnl f* **6/1**[3]
605/ **2** *2 ½* **Sergeant Pink (IRE)**[13] 7105 7-9-10 **52** .... MissRobynGray(5) 4 56
(Dianne Sayer) *trckd wnr: pushed along 3f out: rdn 2f out: kpt on u.p appr fnl f* **10/1**
360- **3** *1* **Grand Diamond (IRE)**[28] 6315 9-9-4 **48** .... MrsICGoldie(7) 3 51
(Jim Goldie) *hld up towards rr: hdwy 4f out: chsd ldrs 3f out: rdn wl over 1f out: kpt on same pce appr fnl f* **33/1**
2310 **4** *1 ¼* **Titus Bolt (IRE)**[13] 2277 4-11-0 **65** .... MrsCBartley 6 66
(Jim Goldie) *hld up in tch: hdwy 1/2-way: effrt 3f out: chsd wnr 2f out: sn rdn and one pce appr fnl f* **2/1**[1]
4002 **5** *1* **Rayadour (IRE)**[6] 2435 4-10-7 **63** ....(t) MissBeckySmith(5) 5 62
(Micky Hammond) *trckd ldrs: pushed along 3f out: sn rdn and no imp* **9/4**[2]
-005 **6** *4 ½* **Frosty Berry**[11] 2313 4-10-3 **61** .... MrAFrench(7) 2 54
(John Wainwright) *trckd ldrs: hdwy to chse wnr 7f out: rdn along over 3f out: sn wknd* **10/1**
3024 **7** *3 ¾* **Landesherr (GER)**[17] 2137 6-10-3 **57** .... MissHCuthbert(3) 8 44
(Thomas Cuthbert) *a towards rr* **12/1**
60/0 **8** *11* **Grandad Bill (IRE)**[11] 2313 10-9-10 **54** ....(p) MrsLGoldie(7) 1 25
(Jim Goldie) *hld up: a in rr: bhd fnl 3f* **25/1**

2m 52.86s (0.86) **Going Correction** -0.10s/f (Good) **8** Ran SP% **111.0**
Speed ratings (Par 101): **93,91,90,90,89 86,84,77**
toteswingers 1&2 £11.40, 1&3 £15.30, 2&3 £20.50 CSF £59.44 CT £1742.48 TOTE £6.10: £2.00, £2.90, £8.00; EX 64.10 Trifecta £748.00 Part won. Pool: £997.35 - 0.84 winning units..
Owner Evergreen Racing **Bred** Moretail Ventures **Trained** Hackthorpe, Cumbria

FOCUS
Home bend moved in on to fresher ground. A very modest handicap for amateurs. It wasn't truly run and the form is of limited value. It has been rated around the winner.

2631 CANACCORD GENUITY MAIDEN STKS 5f
6:45 (6:46) (Class 4) 2-Y-O **£4,204** (£1,251; £625; £312) **Stalls** High

Form RPR
2 **1** **Money Team (IRE)**[9] 2358 2-9-5 0 .... JoeFanning 1 80
(Bill Turner) *cl up: rdn and qcknd to ld jst over 1f out: edgd lft ins fnl f: kpt on strly* **11/4**[2]
2 **2** *2 ¼* **Rural Celebration**[11] 2327 2-9-0 0 .... DanielTudhope 3 69
(David O'Meara) *slt ld: pushed along 2f out: rdn and hdd jst over 1f out: n.m.r and hld whn stmbld jst ins fnl f: sn drvn and one pce* **5/6**[1]
3 *3 ½* **Reet Thicknstrong** 2-9-0 0 .... RoystonFfrench 2 54
(Bryan Smart) *t.k.h early: trckd ldng pair: effrt 2f out: sn swtchd rt to outer and rdn over 1f out: one pce fnl f* **11/1**
0 **4** *9* **Native Falls (IRE)**[23] 1930 2-9-5 0 .... RobertWinston 4 27
(Alan Swinbank) *awkward s: t.k.h and chsd ldng pair on inner: rdn along 2f out: sn wknd* **4/1**[3]

59.54s (-0.86) **Going Correction** -0.175s/f (Firm) **4** Ran SP% **109.6**
Speed ratings (Par 95): **99,95,89,75**
CSF £5.60 TOTE £3.00; EX 5.40 Trifecta £8.90 Pool: £664.67 - 55.40 winning units..
Owner A C Elliott **Bred** Mrs Claire Doyle **Trained** Sigwells, Somerset

FOCUS
The winner of this maiden in 2011, Fulbright, went on to win the Woodcote Stakes at Epsom, but this contest looked fairly modest.

2632 FASTER GREENER CENTRAL TAXIS H'CAP (£15K BETFAIR SCOTTISH SPRINT FINAL QUALIFIER) 5f
7:15 (7:16) (Class 6) (0-65,65) 4-Y-O+ **£2,587** (£770; £384; £192) **Stalls** High

Form RPR
-000 **1** **Pavers Star**[10] 2343 4-8-11 **55** .... RobertWinston 8 64
(Noel Wilson) *cl up: rdn along 2f out: led appr fnl f: sn drvn and kpt on wl* **16/1**
-030 **2** *nk* **Here Now And Why (IRE)**[7] 2409 6-9-2 **60** ....(p) DanielTudhope 5 68
(Iain Jardine) *hld up towards rr: hdwy wl over 1f out: effrt and n.m.r appr fnl f: sn swtchd rt and rdn: styd on wl towards fin* **4/1**[2]
40-0 **3** *¾* **Cayman Fox**[19] 2043 8-8-7 **51** .... RoystonFfrench 4 56
(Linda Perratt) *qckly away: led and sn swtchd lft: rdn along 2f out: drvn and hdd jst over 1f out: kpt on wl u.p fnl f* **50/1**
0-00 **4** *hd* **Quaroma**[41] 1540 8-9-4 **65** .... LeeToplis(3) 6 70
(Paul Midgley) *trckd ldrs: hdwy and nt clr run over 1f out: effrt whn hmpd ins fnl f: rdn and kpt on towards fin* **12/1**
400- **5** *hd* **Saxonette**[221] 7099 5-8-6 **50** .... AmyRyan 7 54
(Linda Perratt) *dwlt and in rr: hdwy on inner over 1f out: sn rdn and kpt on fnl f: nrst fin* **25/1**

0032 **6** *nse* **Code Six (IRE)**[19] 2043 4-8-10 **54**..........................(p) RussKennemore 11 58+
(Bryan Smart) *cl up on inner: rdn along 2f out: n.m.r and swtchd rt over 1f out: drvn and n.m.r ins fnl f: kpt on* **5/2**[1]

644 **7** *3/4* **Compton Heights**[14] 2218 4-9-4 **62**.................................. GrahamLee 10 63+
(Jim Goldie) *stdd s and hld up in rr: hdwy wl over 1f out: pushed along: carried hd high and green whn n.m.r over 1f out and jst ins fnl f: kpt on towards fin* **6/1**[3]

6540 **8** *3/4* **Ingleby Star (IRE)**[10] 2338 8-9-4 **65**............................(p) PaulPickard(3) 3 63
(Ian McInnes) *chsd ldrs: rdn along wl over 1f out: kpt on same pce fnl f* **14/1**

6536 **9** *1 1/2* **Wicked Wilma (IRE)**[7] 2410 9-8-8 **52**.............................. PaddyAspell 1 45
(Alan Berry) *trckd ldrs: hdwy on outer 2f out: sn rdn and wknd ent fnl f* **13/2**

0640 **10** *nse* **You'relikemefrank**[11] 2326 7-8-0 **51**..........................(p) VictorSantos(7) 9 44
(Richard Ford) *trckd ldrs on inner: effrt 2f out: sn rdn and n.m.r: no imp fnl f* **20/1**

01-6 **11** *2* **Weetentherty**[14] 2217 6-8-9 **53**.......................................(p) JoeFanning 2 38
(Keith Dalgleish) *a towards rr* **10/1**

59.25s (-1.15) **Going Correction** -0.175s/f (Firm) **11** Ran SP% **116.1**
Speed ratings (Par 101): **102,101,100,100,99 99,98,97,94,94 91**
toteswingers 1&2 £21.90, 1&3 £116.90, 2&3 £30.30 CSF £76.58 CT £3153.34 TOTE £23.30: £4.90, £1.50, £15.30; EX 112.20 Trifecta £670.70 Part won. Pool: £894.26 - 0.02 winning units..
Owner Mrs Michael John Paver **Bred** Mrs C K Paver **Trained** Middleham, N Yorks

FOCUS
A moderate sprint handicap with a blanket finish. It was a bit of a rough race in the latter stages. The winner ran his best race last year over C&D.

2633 PENTLAND LAND ROVER H'CAP — 1m 6f
7:45 (7:45) (Class 4) (0-85,85) 4-Y-0+ **£7,762** (£2,310; £1,154; £577) **Stalls** Low

Form RPR

0542 **1** **Platinum (IRE)**[30] 1464 6-8-8 **72**..............................(p) RussKennemore 8 83
(Philip Kirby) *trckd ldng pair: hdwy 3f out: led 2f out: rdn over 1f out: drvn ins fnl f and kpt on gamely* **7/1**

0-00 **2** *1 1/4* **Merchant Of Dubai**[19] 2040 8-8-5 **69**.................................. JoeFanning 2 78
(Jim Goldie) *trckd ldng pair on inner: hdwy over 3f out: rdn to chse wnr wl over 1f out: drvn ins fnl f: no imp towards fin* **12/1**

-600 **3** *3* **Nanton (USA)**[9] 2369 11-9-4 **82**.. GrahamLee 1 87
(Jim Goldie) *trckd ldrs on inner early: lost pl after 2f and towards rr: hdwy 3f out: rdn to chse ldng pair wl over 1f out: drvn: edgd rt and one pce fnl f* **11/2**

2522 **4** *6* **Northside Prince (IRE)**[9] 2369 7-9-7 **85**..................... RobertWinston 5 81
(Alan Swinbank) *trckd ldrs: effrt over 3f out: sn pushed along: rdn 2f out and no imp* **4/1**[3]

-542 **5** *nk* **Knightly Escapade**[20] 2009 5-8-13 **77**......................... DanielTudhope 3 73
(Brian Ellison) *prom: trckd ldr after 2f: cl up 1/2-way: pushed along to ld 3f out: rdn and hdd 2f out: sn drvn and wknd* **9/4**[1]

-001 **6** *1 3/4* **Rockthérunway (IRE)**[20] 2009 4-9-3 **81**...........................(p) TomEaves 7 75
(Michael Dods) *hld up in rr: effrt 3f out: rdn along over 2f out: n.d* **7/2**[2]

314- **7** *hd* **Houston Dynimo (IRE)**[83] 4766 8-8-10 **74**................ RoystonFfrench 6 67
(Nicky Richards) *led: pushed along over 3f out: sn hdd and rdn: drvn and prom on inner tl wknd wl over 1f out* **22/1**

0-04 **8** *1 1/2* **Raleigh Quay (IRE)**[21] 1993 6-7-13 **66** oh2.............. DeclanCannon(3) 4 57
(Micky Hammond) *in tch on outer: pushed along over 5f out: rdn 4f out: sn wknd* **50/1**

3m 1.68s (-3.62) **Going Correction** -0.10s/f (Good) **8** Ran SP% **114.9**
Speed ratings (Par 105): **106,105,103,100,99 98,98,98**
toteswingers 1&2 £8.00, 1&3 £5.80, 2&3 £6.10 CSF £85.38 CT £495.57 TOTE £8.10: £1.60, £3.10, £2.50; EX 41.30 Trifecta £311.60 Pool: £762.94 - 1.83 winning units..
Owner Mrs Philippa Kirby **Bred** Lodge Park Stud **Trained** Middleham, N Yorks
■ Stewards' Enquiry : Russ Kennemore three-day ban; weighted in light (7th-9th June).

FOCUS
A fair handicap run at a reasonable gallop. The winner is rated in line with his old jumps form.

2634 THOMSON TRAVEL SHOP MAIDEN STKS — 7f 30y
8:15 (8:16) (Class 5) 3-Y-0+ **£2,587** (£770; £384; £192) **Stalls** Low

Form RPR

23 **1** **Size (IRE)**[17] 2121 4-9-11 0.. LeeTopliss(3) 5 67+
(Richard Fahey) *towards rr and pushed along after 2f: hdwy 3f out: rdn to chse ldrs 2f out: green and n.m.r over 1f out: drvn and edgd lft ent fnl f: sn led and rdn clr* **8/13**[1]

45-3 **2** *4 1/2* **Pastoral Prey**[14] 2218 3-9-3 61...(p) TomEaves 7 51
(Ian Semple) *trckd ldng pair: hdwy to ld wl over 2f out: rdn along over 1f out: drvn and hdd jst ins fnl f: wandered and kpt on same pce* **4/1**[2]

3 *shd* **Echo Of Lightning** 3-9-3 0.. GrahamLee 8 50+
(Noel Wilson) *s.i.s and bhd: hdwy 3f out: in tch and rdn 2f out: styng on whn bmpd wl ins fnl f: nrst fin* **6/1**[3]

00- **4** *hd* **Absolute Bearing (IRE)**[211] 7361 4-9-11 42............... BrianToomey(3) 2 54
(Tim Etherington) *sn led: hdd over 3f out: styd prom: rdn along 2f out: keeping on whn hmpd ins fnl f: swtchd lft and kpt on towards fin* **50/1**

30 **5** *1 1/4* **Royal Duchess**[39] 1570 3-8-12 0.. AmyRyan 3 42
(Lucy Normile) *in tch: hdwy 3f out: rdn along 2f out: sn chal and ev ch: drvn ent fnl f: wknd last 100yds* **8/1**

360- **6** *3 1/2* **Benidorm**[211] 7361 5-9-9 48...(v) AdamCarter(5) 4 41
(John Wainwright) *cl up: led over 3f out: rdn along and hdd wl over 2f out: sn drvn and wknd* **20/1**

0 **7** *4* **Bowlands Legacy**[16] 2169 4-9-2 0.............................. VictorSantos(7) 6 26
(Richard Ford) *a towards rr* **50/1**

400- **8** *9* **Dark Marvel (IRE)**[221] 7096 3-8-12 10............................. PaddyAspell 1
(Alan Berry) *in tch: rdn along 3f out: sn wknd* **50/1**

1m 30.59s (1.59) **Going Correction** -0.10s/f (Good)
WFA 3 from 4yo+ 11lb **8** Ran SP% **118.0**
Speed ratings (Par 103): **86,80,80,80,79 75,70,60**
toteswingers 1&2 £1.50, 1&3 £1.90, 2&3 £3.00 CSF £3.46 TOTE £1.50: £1.02, £2.30, £1.60; EX 4.00 Trifecta £8.60 Pool: £1,013.84 - 87.75 winning units..
Owner Sir Robert Ogden **Bred** Manister House Stud **Trained** Musley Bank, N Yorks

FOCUS
A weak maiden which has been rated cautiously. The fourth is the initial guide.

2635 BERNARD HUNTER CRANE HIRE H'CAP (£15K BETFAIR SCOTTISH MILE SERIES FINAL QUALIFIER) — 7f 30y
8:45 (8:45) (Class 5) (0-70,69) 3-Y-0 **£3,234** (£962; £481; £240) **Stalls** Low

Form RPR

051- **1** **Silkelly**[248] 6335 3-9-7 **69**...[1] DanielTudhope 8 78
(David O'Meara) *led: rdn along over 2f out: hdd wl over 1f out and sn drvn: rallied wl to ld again jst ins fnl f: kpt on strly* **3/1**[2]

400- **2** *2* **Lucy Minaj**[223] 7056 3-8-3 **51** ow1................................. RoystonFfrench 4 55
(Bryan Smart) *trckd ldng pair: hdwy to chse wnr 1/2-way: rdn along and sltly outpcd over 2f out: kpt on u.p fnl f: tk 2nd towards fin* **14/1**

4342 **3** *1/2* **Polish Crown**[11] 2331 3-9-2 **64**... JoeFanning 7 66
(Mark Johnston) *trckd ldrs: smooth hdwy 3f out: chal over 2f out: led wl over 1f out and sn rdn: drvn and hdd jst ins fnl f: wknd* **2/1**[1]

00-0 **4** *2 1/4* **Fife Jo**[27] 1829 3-8-9 **57**.. GrahamLee 3 53
(Jim Goldie) *towards rr: hdwy wl over 2f out: rdn and kpt on fnl f: nrst fin* **5/1**[3]

344- **5** *1* **Sakhees Romance**[216] 7244 3-8-4 **55**...................... DeclanCannon(3) 5 48
(Noel Wilson) *s.i.s and bhd: hdwy 3f out: rdn to chse ldrs 2f out: sn drvn and no imp* **15/2**

205- **6** *9* **Spithead**[172] 7973 3-9-1 **63**.. DaleSwift 9 32
(Ian McInnes) *in tch: hdwy over 3f out: rdn along wl over 2f out: sn btn* **10/1**

355- **7** *9* **Princess In Exile**[280] 5313 3-9-0 **62**.................................... TomEaves 6
(Ian Semple) *in tch: sme hdwy to chse ldrs over 3f out: sn rdn along and wknd* **33/1**

6246 **8** *2 1/4* **Irish Dream (IRE)**[25] 1874 3-9-3 **65**............................. RobertWinston 2
(Mark Johnston) *chsd ldng pair whn n.m.r on inner bnd over 3f out: rdn along over 2f out: sn drvn and wknd* **9/1**

1m 30.08s (1.08) **Going Correction** -0.10s/f (Good) **8** Ran SP% **115.5**
Speed ratings (Par 99): **89,86,86,83,82 72,61,59**
toteswingers 1&2 £12.30, 1&3 £1.40, 2&3 £6.00 CSF £43.89 CT £102.91 TOTE £3.50: £1.20, £3.40, £1.30; EX 32.80 Trifecta £235.40 Pool: £686.38 - 2.18 winning units..
Owner Middleham Park Racing XLVIII **Bred** Broughton Bloodstock **Trained** Nawton, N Yorks

FOCUS
A modest handicap but a taking performance from the winner, who is entitled to do better.

2636 CANACCORD GENUITY H'CAP — 1m
9:15 (9:15) (Class 6) (0-65,66) 4-Y-0+ **£2,587** (£770; £384; £192) **Stalls** Low

Form RPR

-111 **1** **Jebel Tara**[2] 2575 8-9-6 **66** 12ex..................................(bt) PaulPickard(3) 4 76
(Alan Brown) *t.k.h early: hld up in rr: stdy hdwy on wd outside wl over 2f out: chal over 1f out: rdn to ld ent fnl f: drvn out* **7/4**[1]

0-00 **2** *3/4* **Flipping**[19] 2037 6-8-10 **53**... RoystonFfrench 3 61
(Nicky Richards) *hld up in tch: n.m.r and hmpd 1/2-way: hdwy over 2f out: rdn over 1f out: styd on wl fnl f* **28/1**

034- **3** *2* **Music Festival (USA)**[189] 7747 6-8-10 **53**......................... JoeFanning 7 57
(Jim Goldie) *hld up in rr: hdwy wl over 2f out: rdn to chse ldrs over 1f out: kpt on u.p fnl f* **11/2**[3]

00-6 **4** *1/2* **Stormont Bridge**[17] 2121 5-8-12 **55**..................................(t) GrahamLee 2 58
(Maurice Barnes) *trckd ldng pair on inner: hdwy over 3f out: led wl over 2f out: rdn along wl over 1f out: drvn and hdd ent fnl f: grad wknd* **20/1**

20-2 **5** *1* **Just The Tonic**[21] 1995 6-9-7 **64**.................................. DanielTudhope 1 64
(Marjorie Fife) *in tch hdwy to trck ldrs 3f out: effrt 2f out: sn rdn: n.m.r over 1f out: sn drvn and one pce* **11/4**[2]

0034 **6** *1 1/4* **Spread Boy (IRE)**[11] 2319 6-8-7 **50** oh2............................ PaddyAspell 5 47
(Alan Berry) *led: rdn along 3f out: sn hdd and grad wknd* **25/1**

43-5 **7** *1* **Edas**[11] 2315 11-8-12 **60**... GarryWhillans(5) 6 55
(Thomas Cuthbert) *trckd ldrs: hdwy over 3f out: chsd ldr over 2f out: sn rdn and wkng whn n.m.r over 1f out* **8/1**

000- **8** *2 1/4* **Military Call**[221] 7095 6-8-10 **53**...................................... TomEaves 8 43
(Alistair Whillans) *trckd ldng pair: hdwy 3f out: chsd ldr 2f out: sn rdn and wknd over 1f out* **7/1**

060- **9** *3/4* **Artillery Train (IRE)**[148] 8257 4-8-7 **50** oh5......................... AmyRyan 9 38
(Tim Etherington) *chsd ldr: hdwy over 3f out: rdn along 2f out: drvn and wknd over 1f out* **50/1**

1m 42.12s (0.92) **Going Correction** -0.10s/f (Good) **9** Ran SP% **116.0**
Speed ratings (Par 101): **91,90,88,87,86 85,84,82,81**
toteswingers 1&2 £10.90, 1&3 £1.90, 2&3 £22.90 CSF £61.07 CT £235.40 TOTE £2.30: £1.60, £7.10, £2.20; EX 50.80 Trifecta £256.20 Pool: £1,778.45 - 5.20 winning units..
Owner Miss E Johnston **Bred** Mrs G P Booth And J Porteous **Trained** Yedingham, N Yorks

FOCUS
A modest handicap run at a sound pace, and the first three came from the rear. The form is rated around the runner-up.
T/Plt: £943.30 to a £1 stake. Pool: £47,423.47 - 36.70 winning units T/Qpdt: £62.90 to a £1 stake. Pool: £4,652.26 - 54.68 winning units JR

2131 YARMOUTH (L-H)
Friday, May 24

OFFICIAL GOING: Good to soft (6.9)
Wind: Fresh; against Weather: Dry after morning rain

2637 NORFOLKTOURISTATTRACTIONS.CO.UK MEDIAN AUCTION MAIDEN STKS — 6f 3y
2:10 (2:12) (Class 6) 3-5-Y-0 **£1,940** (£577; £288; £144) **Stalls** Centre

Form RPR

546- **1** **Rocksilla**[190] 7721 3-8-12 72... TedDurcan 9 75+
(Chris Wall) *in tch in midfield: hdwy 3f out: led wl over 1f out: sn drew clr and in command: easily* **9/4**[2]

-0 **2** *3 3/4* **Crave**[14] 2231 3-8-12 0... HayleyTurner 2 58
(William Jarvis) *chsd ldr tl led 2f out: sn hdd and rdn: btn 1f out but kpt on for clr 2nd* **2/1**[1]

005- **3** *9* **Jamaica Grande**[248] 6345 5-9-12 39............................ WilliamCarson 10 38
(Dave Morris) *bhd and swtchd lft s: hld up in rr: hdwy past btn horses over 1f out: wnt poor 3rd ins fnl f: nvr trbld ldrs* **66/1**

06 **4** *2* **Transluscent (IRE)**[20] 2016 3-8-10 0........................... DanielMuscutt(7) 1 30
(Andrew Balding) *led tl rdn and hdd 2f out: 3rd and wl btn over 1f out: sn wknd* **7/1**[3]

5 *1 1/4* **Immediately** 3-8-12 0.. ShaneKelly 5 21
(Robert Cowell) *in tch towards rr: rdn 4f out: wknd u.p 2f out* **15/2**

6- **6** *1/2* **Sakash**[206] 7466 3-9-3 0.. DavidProbert 3 25
(J R Jenkins) *chsd ldrs: rdn and struggling 3f out: wknd u.p 2f out* **9/1**

4 **7** *1 3/4* **Scala Romana (IRE)**[6] 2437 3-8-12 0............................ ChrisCatlin 7 15
(Sir Mark Prescott Bt) *dwlt: nvr gng wl and pushed along in rr: n.d* **10/1**

0 **8** *2 3/4* **Lily The Dragon (IRE)**[24] 1911 3-8-12 0......................... PatCosgrave 8 6
(Mick Quinn) *in tch in midfield: struggling and rdn 3f out: wknd qckly ent fnl f* **33/1**

00 **9** 3 3/4 **Lady Cavallo**[20] 2016 3-8-12 0 .... FrederikTylicki 4
(J R Jenkins) *chsd ldrs tl 1/2-way: sn lost pl: bhd fnl 2f* **25/1**

1m 16.47s (2.07) **Going Correction** +0.30s/f (Good)
WFA 3 from 5yo 9lb 9 Ran SP% **115.7**
Speed ratings (Par 101): **98,93,81,78,76 76,73,70,65**
toteswingers 1&2 £1.70, 1&3 £25.10, 2&3 £13.90 CSF £7.06 TOTE £2.40: £1.10, £2.00, £7.90; EX 7.20 Trifecta £160.30 Pool: £2,785.75 - 13.02 winning units..
Owner Moyns Park Stud **Bred** Moyns Park Estate And Stud Ltd **Trained** Newmarket, Suffolk

FOCUS
After overnight rain the official going was changed from good to soft, good in places to good to soft. With the short-priced favourite withdrawn in the morning, this looked a weak maiden overall, but the winner is promising.

2638 GUIDE DOGS FOR THE BLIND H'CAP 7f 3y
2:45 (2:46) (Class 5) (0-70,70) 4-Y-0+ **£2,587** (£770; £384; £192) **Stalls** Centre

Form RPR

55-0 **1** **Relentless Harry (IRE)**[28] 1801 4-9-3 **66** .... (t) PatCosgrave 9 78+
(George Baker) *racd in centre: stdd and swtchd lft s: t.k.h: hld up in rr: hdwy on bit over 2f out: rdn to ld ins fnl f: sn wnt clr: comf* **9/2**[2]

00-0 **2** 2 3/4 **Rough Rock (IRE)**[28] 1800 8-9-2 **65** .... HayleyTurner 5 70
(Chris Dwyer) *racd in centre: chsd ldrs: rdn to ld wl over 1f out: hdd ins fnl f: sn brushed aside by wnr but kpt on for clr 2nd* **10/1**

0-42 **3** 3 1/4 **Aaranyow (IRE)**[23] 1929 5-8-7 **56** oh4 .... JimmyQuinn 1 53
(Clifford Lines) *racd in centre: t.k.h: chsd ldrs: rdn and ev ch 2f out: outpcd and btn 1f out: plugged on* **25/1**

22-1 **4** 1/2 **See The Storm**[7] 2425 5-8-12 **61** .... StevieDonohoe 3 56
(Ian Williams) *racd in centre: in tch in midfield overall: effrt to chse ldng trio over 1f out: sn rdn and unable qck: wl hld fnl f* **7/4**[1]

5614 **5** 1 3/4 **Olney Lass**[24] 1914 6-8-10 **64** .... RosieJessop(5) 10 55
(Lydia Pearce) *swtchd rt and racd nr stands' rail: hld up in rr overall: effrt and edging lft to rejoin centre gp over 2f out: plugged on fnl f: nvr trbld ldrs* **8/1**

16-0 **6** 9 **Charity Box**[13] 2255 4-9-7 **70** .... (p) TedDurcan 12 37
(Chris Wall) *swtchd rt and racd nr stands' rail: in tch in midfield overall: rdn and no rspnse over 2f out: edgd lft and wknd 2f out: eased ins fnl f* **20/1**

00-4 **7** 2 3/4 **Saskia's Dream**[24] 1915 5-9-5 **68** .... (p) FrederikTylicki 8 28
(Jane Chapple-Hyam) *swtchd rt and racd nr stands' rail: in tch in midfield overall: rdn and edgd bk lft to rejoin main gp over 2f out: wknd over 1f out: eased ins fnl f* **16/1**

3625 **8** 2 1/4 **Zaheeb**[31] 1752 5-8-8 **57** .... [1] WilliamCarson 7 11
(Dave Morris) *swtchd rt and racd nr stands' rail: rdn along leaving stalls: chsd ldrs overall tl rdn and edgd lft to rejoin centre gp over 2f out: wknd 2f out: eased ins fnl f* **10/1**

4-51 **9** 1 **Shahrazad (IRE)**[32] 1710 4-8-7 **56** .... MickaelBarzalona 4
(Patrick Gilligan) *racd in centre: overall ldr tl rdn and hdd 2f out: sn wknd: bhd and eased ins fnl f* **16/1**

05-0 **10** 4 **First Class**[28] 1801 5-9-0 **63** .... DavidProbert 2
(Rae Guest) *racd in centre: in tch in midfield: rdn and wknd over 2f out: bhd and eased ins fnl f* **6/1**[3]

1m 28.72s (2.12) **Going Correction** +0.30s/f (Good) **10** Ran SP% **118.5**
Speed ratings (Par 103): **99,95,92,91,89 79,76,73,72,67**
toteswingers 1&2 £7.60, 1&3 £22.20, 2&3 £33.80 CSF £49.82 CT £1041.15 TOTE £5.30: £1.70, £2.90, £6.60; EX 56.60 Trifecta £937.00 Pool: £3,882.82 - 3.10 winning units..
Owner PJL Racing **Bred** Corduff Stud Ltd & J Corcoran **Trained** Manton, Wilts

FOCUS
Not much pace on for this handicap with the field splitting into two groups. Those racing up the centre filled the first four places. An impressive, improved performance from the winner.

2639 DENNIS HAROLD BARRETT FILLIES' H'CAP 1m 3y
3:20 (3:26) (Class 4) (0-85,81) 4-Y-0+ **£4,690** (£1,395; £697; £348) **Stalls** Centre

Form RPR

/01- **1** **Bassara (IRE)**[335] 3398 4-9-1 **75** .... TedDurcan 9 84+
(Chris Wall) *stdd s: hld up in tch in last: hdwy 2f out: rdn to chal 1f out: led ins fnl f: sn in command: eased cl home* **9/4**[1]

1045 **2** 1 1/4 **Kickingthelilly**[25] 1883 4-9-4 **78** .... ChrisCatlin 5 82
(Rae Guest) *in tch in last pair: pushed along 1/2-way: hdwy u.p over 1f out: ev ch ins fnl f: outpcd by wnr fnl 75yds* **10/3**[2]

0-23 **3** 1/2 **Tahlia Ree (IRE)**[24] 1914 4-8-4 **71** .... LouisSteward(7) 4 74
(Michael Bell) *t.k.h: chsd ldr tl led 3f out: rdn wl over 1f out: hdd ins fnl f: no ex* **7/1**[3]

11-0 **4** 1 1/4 **Miss Dashwood**[41] 1544 4-9-6 **80** .... HayleyTurner 2 80
(James Fanshawe) *t.k.h: led and set stdy gallop: hdd 3f out: styd pressing ldr: rdn and unable qck over 1f out: btn and one pce fnl f* **9/4**[1]

30-0 **5** 2 **Hurricane Lady (IRE)**[23] 1922 5-9-5 **79** .... NickyMackay 3 75
(Mike Murphy) *dwlt: sn rcvrd and chsd ldng pair: effrt u.p and pressing ldrs 2f out: wknd ent fnl f* **7/1**[3]

1m 44.56s (3.96) **Going Correction** +0.30s/f (Good) 5 Ran SP% **109.6**
Speed ratings (Par 102): **92,90,90,89,87**
CSF £9.87 TOTE £3.30: £1.80, £2.30; EX 9.20 Trifecta £52.50 Pool: £3,278.83 - 46.80 winning units..
Owner Ms Aida Fustoq **Bred** Deerfield Farm **Trained** Newmarket, Suffolk

FOCUS
Plenty of interest was taken out of this fillies' handicap, with four of the nine declared runners withdrawn. It was run at a steady pace, with once again the winner coming from behind. The winner is the type to keep improving.

2640 HOLIDAYS ON THE NORFOLK BROADS H'CAP 1m 3y
3:55 (3:55) (Class 5) (0-70,70) 4-Y-0+ **£2,587** (£770; £384; £192) **Stalls** Centre

Form RPR

25-0 **1** **Qanan**[14] 2232 4-9-7 **70** .... GeorgeBaker 2 78
(Chris Wall) *mde all: rdn over 1f out: hrd pressed and hld on wl ins fnl f* **7/1**

5362 **2** hd **Gift Of Silence**[24] 1914 4-9-2 **65** .... NeilCallan 3 72
(John Berry) *hld up in tch in midfield: effrt u.p 2f out: ev ch fnl f: no ex cl home* **4/1**[3]

3032 **3** 3/4 **Brown Pete (IRE)**[7] 2413 5-9-0 **70** .... EDLinehan(7) 7 76
(Violet M Jordan) *in last pair: hdwy and pushed along 2f out: rdn and chsd ldng pair 1f out: one pce fnl f* **5/2**[1]

306- **4** 2 **Opera Buff**[211] 7359 4-9-3 **66** .... (p) RenatoSouza 5 67
(Alison Batchelor) *chsd ldrs: rdn and unable qck 2f out: styd on same pce u.p ins fnl f* **25/1**

0026 **5** 1 1/4 **Hail Promenader (IRE)**[13] 2273 7-8-8 **62** .... (tp) PhilipPrince(5) 8 60
(Anthony Carson) *chsd wnr: rdn over 2f out: outpcd and lost pl over 1f out: wknd ins fnl f* **3/1**[2]

23/4 **6** 1/2 **Hamble**[17] 2134 4-8-9 **58** .... (t) NickyMackay 1 55
(Marco Botti) *chsd ldrs: rdn and effrt over 2f out: drvn and unable qck over 1f out: wknd ins fnl f* **11/2**

30 **7** 39 **Macdonald Mor (IRE)**[22] 1947 4-9-7 **70** .... MickaelBarzalona 6
(Michael Wigham) *hld up in rr: rdn and no rspnse over 2f out: sn btn: wl bhd and virtually p.u ins fnl f: t.o* **14/1**

1m 42.31s (1.71) **Going Correction** +0.30s/f (Good) 7 Ran SP% **112.0**
Speed ratings (Par 103): **103,102,102,100,98 98,59**
toteswingers 1&2 £3.30, 1&3 £3.20, 2&3 £2.40 CSF £33.39 CT £88.18 TOTE £8.70: £2.80, £1.80; EX 24.50 Trifecta £94.10 Pool: £4,403.88 - 35.07 winning units..
Owner Alan & Jill Smith **Bred** Genesis Green Stud Ltd **Trained** Newmarket, Suffolk
■ Stewards' Enquiry : Renato Souza four-day ban; used whip above permitted level (7th-10th June).

FOCUS
Not the strongest of handicaps, run at a steady pace. The field raced up the centre. Straightforward form, the first pair improvers.

2641 WEDDINGS AT GREAT YARMOUTH RACECOURSE H'CAP 1m 3f 101y
4:30 (4:30) (Class 4) (0-85,85) 3-Y-0 **£4,690** (£1,395; £697; £348) **Stalls** Low

Form RPR

2-41 **1** **Eshtiaal (USA)**[15] 2198 3-9-7 **85** .... DaneO'Neill 1 100+
(Brian Meehan) *chsd ldng pair: swtchd rt and effrt over 2f out: led 2f out: sn clr and r.o wl: easily* **6/4**[1]

-133 **2** 4 1/2 **Debdebdeb**[23] 1923 3-8-7 **71** oh1 .... DavidProbert 5 78+
(Andrew Balding) *led: rdn and hdd 2f out: no threat to wnr but clr 2nd over 1f out: kpt on* **9/2**[3]

0242 **3** 12 **Could Be (IRE)**[24] 1898 3-8-7 **71** .... MartinLane 2 59
(David Simcock) *hld up in tch in last pair: effrt u.p to press ldrs 2f out: sn btn: 3rd and wknd over 1f out* **16/1**

0-21 **4** 9 **Salutation (IRE)**[13] 2271 3-9-7 **85** .... J-PGuillambert 7 66
(Mark Johnston) *chsd ldr: rdn 3f out: pressed ldrs over 2f out tl 2f out: sn btn: 4th and fdd over 1f out* **15/8**[2]

3-10 **5** 25 **Barnaby Brook (CAN)**[19] 2050 3-8-11 **75** .... HayleyTurner 3
(Nick Littmoden) *a last: drvn and struggling over 3f out: lost tch 2f out: virtually p.u fnl f* **12/1**

2m 31.69s (2.99) **Going Correction** +0.30s/f (Good) 5 Ran SP% **106.5**
Speed ratings (Par 101): **101,97,89,82,64**
CSF £7.93 TOTE £2.20: £1.80, £2.20; EX 7.70 Trifecta £40.40 Pool: £2,931.35 - 54.30 winning units..
Owner Hamdan Al Maktoum **Bred** Shadwell Farm LLC **Trained** Manton, Wilts

FOCUS
This was an interesting handicap, despite the small field size, run at an honest pace. There's every chance there's a good bit more to come from the winner.

2642 RACING WELFARE H'CAP 1m 6f 17y
5:05 (5:06) (Class 6) (0-60,60) 4-Y-0+ **£1,940** (£577; £288; £144) **Stalls** High

Form RPR

663/ **1** **Sancho Panza**[576] 7107 6-8-11 **57** .... ShelleyBirkett(7) 6 66
(Julia Feilden) *chsd ldrs: upsides ldr and rdn 2f out: led 1f out: styd on wl* **9/1**

0051 **2** 1 1/4 **Kingarrick**[21] 1993 5-9-1 **57** .... NeilFarley(3) 3 64
(Noel Wilson) *chsd ldrs: lft upsides ldr over 4f out: rdn to ld over 2f out: hdd 1f out and styd on same pce ins fnl f* **9/2**[1]

0P-3 **3** 2 1/4 **Wasabi (IRE)**[24] 1916 4-8-12 **51** .... DaneO'Neill 11 55
(John Berry) *hld up in tch towards rr: swtchd rt and effrt over 2f out: styd on to chse ldng pair ins fnl f: no imp fnl 150yds* **6/1**[3]

000- **4** 1 **Like Clockwork**[208] 6365 4-9-1 **54** .... TedDurcan 12 57
(Mark H Tompkins) *hld up in tch in midfield: hdwy 4f out: rdn to chse ldrs 2f out: no imp and one pce fr over 1f out* **10/1**

00/3 **5** 3/4 **Star Alliance (IRE)**[69] 1040 5-9-7 **60** .... StevieDonohoe 13 62
(Ian Williams) *hld up in tch in midfield: shuffled bk towards rr 4f out: rdn and styng on whn swtchd rt over 1f out: kpt on fnl f: nt rch ldrs* **5/1**[2]

24-5 **6** shd **Gucci D'Oro (USA)**[16] 2159 4-9-2 **55** .... MartinLane 7 57
(David Simcock) *in tch in midfield: rdn and effrt over 2f out: styd on same pce u.p fr over 1f out* **8/1**

2141 **7** 1 1/4 **Corn Maiden**[24] 1916 4-9-6 **59** .... FrederikTylicki 5 59
(Mark Rimmer) *chsd ldr tl 6f out: lft in ld over 4f out: rdn and hdd over 2f out: btn over 1f out: wknd ins fnl f* **7/1**

40-5 **8** nk **Icebreaker Two**[25] 1877 4-9-0 **53** .... FrankieMcDonald 9 53
(John E Long) *dwlt: sn in tch in midfield: rdn 3f out: keeping on same pce whn nt clr run ent fnl f: nvr enough room after and no hdwy* **25/1**

00-6 **9** 1/2 **Absolutely Me (IRE)**[50] 1350 4-8-7 **46** oh1 .... ChrisCatlin 4 45
(Willie Musson) *t.k.h: hld up in tch towards rr: rdn and effrt over 2f out: no real prog and one pce fr over 1f out* **25/1**

0540 **10** 1 1/2 **Torero**[11] 2316 4-9-7 **60** .... NeilCallan 2 57
(Kevin Ryan) *led tl cocked jaw and wnt bdly rt bnd over 4f out: dropped to midfield and sn rdn: btn wl over 1f out: wknd fnl f* **7/1**

450- **11** 1 3/4 **Olimamu (IRE)**[436] 895 6-8-7 **46** oh1 .... [1] NickyMackay 1 41
(Lydia Pearce) *hld up in rr: rdn and no hdwy over 2f out: nvr trbld ldrs* **33/1**

6540 **12** 82 **If What And Maybe**[6] 2435 5-8-4 **46** oh1 .... (v) RyanPowell(3) 10
(John Ryan) *led to s: in tch in midfield: hdwy to chse ldr 6f out tl carried v wd and dropped to rr over 4f out: lost tch 2f and sn eased: t.o* **20/1**

3m 13.9s (6.30) **Going Correction** +0.30s/f (Good) **12** Ran SP% **119.7**
Speed ratings (Par 101): **94,93,92,91,91 90,90,90,89,88 87,41**
toteswingers 1&2 £8.50, 1&3 £15.10, 2&3 £6.80 CSF £47.46 CT £269.51 TOTE £13.20: £4.20, £2.50, £2.80; EX 77.70 Trifecta £1462.30 Pool: £2,587.20 - 1.32 winning units..
Owner Carol Bushnell & Partners **Bred** Harts Farm Stud **Trained** Exning, Suffolk

FOCUS
A moderate yet open contest run at a steady pace, with drama turning for home as front-runner Torero became unsteerable and veered sharply right, hampering If What And Maybe, and badly compromising their chances. A fine training performance from Julia Feilden. The form has a reliable feel.

2643 INJURED JOCKEYS FUND H'CAP 5f 43y
5:40 (5:40) (Class 6) (0-60,60) 3-Y-0+ **£1,940** (£577; £288; £144) **Stalls** Centre

Form RPR

2223 **1** **Speedyfix**[17] 2132 6-9-5 60 .... (t) DanielMuscutt(7) 2 68
(Christine Dunnett) *in tch in midfield: shkn up and hdwy to ld over 1f out: rdn ins fnl f: kpt on wl* **10/3**[1]

4040 **2** nk **Imaginary Diva**[83] 862 7-9-3 54 .... RyanPowell(3) 12 61
(George Margarson) *in tch in midfield: hdwy u.p over 1f out: chsd wnr wl ins fnl f: kpt on but hld towards fin* **8/1**

645- **3** 3/4 **Sarah Berry**[246] 6417 4-9-5 60 .... JoshCrane(7) 7 64
(Chris Dwyer) *dwlt: bhd: rdn and looked to be struggling 1/2-way: swtchd rt wl over 1f out: kpt on wl ins fnl f* **25/1**

60-2 **4** *nse* **Senora Lobo (IRE)**[10] 2347 3-8-13 55 FrederikTylicki 6 56
(Lisa Williamson) *w ldr: ev ch and rdn over 1f out: kpt on same pce wl ins fnl f* **9/2**[3]

-050 **5** *¾* **One Kool Dude**[17] 2132 4-9-9 57 GeorgeBaker 8 58
(Michael Bell) *in tch in midfield: rdn and nt qckn wl over 1f out: kpt on again ins fnl f* **9/2**[3]

5000 **6** *1 ¼* **Bird Dog**[4] 2516 7-8-7 46 oh1 (v) DannyBrock(5) 1 43
(Phil McEntee) *led: rdn wl over 1f out: hdd over 1f out: wknd fnl 100yds* **50/1**

-441 **7** *4 ½* **Cincinnati Kit**[77] 924 4-9-7 60 (t) NicoleNordblad(5) 11 41
(Stuart Williams) *chsd ldrs: rdn and edgd lft over 1f out: sn btn and wknd fnl f* **4/1**[2]

6230 **8** *2 ½* **Magic Ice**[22] 1962 3-8-13 55 DaneO'Neill 10 27
(Brian Ellison) *in tch in midfield: lost pl and rdn over 2f out: wknd u.p over 1f out* **6/1**

00-6 **9** *8* **Marvelous Miss (IRE)**[17] 2133 3-8-4 46 oh1 (p) JimmyQuinn 4
(Christine Dunnett) *s.i.s: in tch in rr: rdn and no hdwy 2f out: wknd over 1f out* **16/1**

1m 4.9s (2.20) **Going Correction** +0.30s/f (Good)
WFA 3 from 4yo+ 8lb **9** Ran SP% **116.5**
Speed ratings (Par 101): **94,93,92,92,91 89,81,77,65**
toteswingers 1&2 £6.30, 1&3 £6.90, 2&3 £15.80 CSF £31.04 CT £576.70 TOTE £3.60: £1.10, £2.80, £5.30; EX 41.20 Trifecta £235.10 Pool: £1,723.54 - 5.49 winning units..
Owner Annwell Inn Syndicate **Bred** Mrs Christine Dunnett **Trained** Hingham, Norfolk

FOCUS
Not a strong sprint handicap but run at a fair pace. The placed horses set the level.
T/Plt: £142.60 to a £1 stake. Pool: £62,770.32 - 321.16 winning units T/Qpdt: £20.30 to a £1 stake. Pool: £4,978.58 - 181.10 winning units SP

2527 SAINT-CLOUD (L-H)
Friday, May 24

OFFICIAL GOING: Turf: very soft

2644a PRIX CORRIDA (GROUP 2) (4YO+ FILLIES & MARES) (TURF) 1m 2f 110y
2:20 (12:00) 4-Y-O+ £52,845 (£21,138; £15,853; £10,569; £5,284)

RPR

1 **Grace Lady (FR)**[25] 1895 4-8-9 0 GeraldMosse 5 115
(Mlle T Puitg, France) *towards rr and t.k.h: c centre trck st and hdwy 2 1/2f out: rdn and edgd lft to join ldr on ins 1 1/2f out: led appr 1f out: rdn clr ins fnl f: comf* **103/10**

2 *3 ½* **Fate (FR)**[22] 4-8-9 0 StephanePasquier 7 108
(A De Royer-Dupre, France) *tk a t.k.h towards rr: c centre trck st: rdn and no imp 2f out: hdwy 1 1/2f out: styd on u.p fnl f: tk 2nd cl home: nvr on terms* **5/1**[3]

3 *snk* **Romantica**[25] 1895 4-9-0 0 MaximeGuyon 6 113
(A Fabre, France) *midfield: c centre trck st: rdn and chsd ldrs appr 2f out: outpcd 1 1/2f out: kpt on u.p fnl f and wnt 2nd 60yds out: ct for 2nd cl home* **14/5**[1]

4 *nse* **Sediciosa (IRE)**[25] 1895 4-8-11 0 ChristopheSoumillon 8 110
(Y Barberot, France) *trckd ldrs: dropped to midfield 1/2-way: c centre trck st: outpcd in rr over 2f out: rdn and styd on u.p fr 1 1/2f out: nt pce to chal* **5/1**[3]

5 *nk* **Yellow And Green**[229] 6912 4-9-0 0 OlivierPeslier 9 112
(N Clement, France) *veered bdly rt leaving stalls: in rr and adrift but sn in tch: hdwy on outside to press ldng pair appr 1/2-way: led centre trck gp over 2f out but bhd ins trio: sn rdn and nt qckn: one pce fnl f* **3/1**[2]

6 *snk* **La Pomme D'Amour**[25] 1895 5-9-0 0 Pierre-CharlesBoudot 10 112
(A Fabre, France) *midfield: towards rr 1/2-way: c centre trck st: sme late prog u.p: nvr in contention* **31/1**

7 *nk* **Pagera (FR)**[47] 1420 5-8-11 0 ThierryJarnet 2 108
(H-A Pantall, France) *trckd ldrs on inner: styd on ins in st and pressed ldr: rdn to ld over 1 1/2f out: hdd appr fnl f: no ex fr 100yds out: lost five pls fnl 60yds* **32/1**

8 *2 ½* **Harem Lady (FR)**[25] 1895 4-8-9 0 GregoryBenoist 4 101
(D Smaga, France) *broke wl and led: set stdy gallop: styd on ins in st: shkn up and qcknd under 2 1/2f out: hdd over 1 1/2f out: wknd appr fnl f* **12/1**

9 *1* **Fairly Fair (FR)**[25] 1895 4-8-9 0 AntoineHamelin 3 99
(A De Royer-Dupre, France) *trckd ldr: c centre trck in st and led that gp tl rdn and wknd over 2f out* **13/1**

10 *8* **Victorinna (FR)**[25] 1895 5-8-9 0 AnthonyCrastus 1 84
(C Laffon-Parias, France) *towards rr: styd on ins in st: hrd rdn and nt qckn over 2f out: wknd appr 1 1/2f out* **37/1**

2m 21.16s (1.56) **10** Ran SP% **117.1**
WIN (incl. 1 euro stake): 11.30. PLACES: 2.50, 2.00, 1.70. DF: 30.50. SF: 40.40.
Owner Ecurie Victoria Dreams **Bred** J P H Dubois **Trained** France

2210 CHESTER (L-H)
Saturday, May 25

OFFICIAL GOING: Good (7.4)
Wind: Fine Weather: Almost nil

2645 APREOL SPRITZ BRITISH STALLION STUDS EBF MAIDEN STKS 6f 18y
2:00 (2:04) (Class 4) 2-Y-O £6,469 (£1,925; £962; £481) Stalls Low

Form RPR

03 **1** **Rosso Corsa**[16] 2194 2-9-5 0 MartinHarley 6 76
(Mick Channon) *sn chsng ldrs: rdn to ld 1f out: edgd lft: r.o* **9/4**[1]

3 **2** *½* **Rizal Park (IRE)**[9] 2382 2-9-5 0 DavidProbert 3 75+
(Andrew Balding) *sn prom: nt clr run over 1f out: sn rdn: r.o to go 2nd towards fin: nt trble wnr* **5/1**[2]

03 **3** *1 ¼* **Party Ruler (IRE)**[21] 2005 2-9-5 0 RichardKingscote 8 71
(Tom Dascombe) *led 5f out: rdn and hdd 1f out: styd on same pce ins fnl f* **9/1**

063 **4** *2 ¼* **Dancing Sal (IRE)**[6] 2474 2-9-0 0 TomMcLaughlin 2 59
(David Evans) *led 1f: chsd ldrs: rdn over 2f out: styd on same pce fnl f* **25/1**

53 **5** *1 ¾* **Azagal (IRE)**[7] 2458 2-9-0 0 PJMcDonald 7 54
(Tim Easterby) *sn pushed along in rr: hdwy over 2f out: rdn over 1f out: no imp ins fnl f* **5/1**[2]

6 *½* **Mandy's Choice** 2-9-0 0 MichaelO'Connell 1 52
(Richard Fahey) *sn outpcd: sme hdwy over 1f out: n.d* **5/1**[2]

7 *2 ½* **Handwoven (IRE)** 2-9-5 0 FrannyNorton 4 50
(Mark Johnston) *chsd ldrs: rdn over 1f out: wknd ins fnl f* **6/1**[3]

0 **8** *9* **Red Forever**[16] 2189 2-9-5 0 DaleSwift 9 23
(Alan Berry) *s.i.s: outpcd* **33/1**

9 *1 ¾* **Letterfromamerica (USA)** 2-9-0 0 TadhgO'Shea 5 13
(John Patrick Shanahan, Ire) *mid-div: pushed along over 3f out: wknd over 2f out* **10/1**

1m 17.66s (3.86) **Going Correction** +0.375s/f (Good) **9** Ran SP% **120.9**
Speed ratings (Par 95): **89,88,86,83,81 80,77,65,63**
toteswingers 1&2 £4.70, 1&3 £4.40, 2&3 £5.40 CSF £14.38 TOTE £3.60: £1.10, £1.20, £3.00; EX 13.30 Trifecta £64.60 Pool: £1113.39 - 12.92 winning units..
Owner Box 41 **Bred** Mervyn Stewkesbury **Trained** West Ilsley, Berks

FOCUS
The entire inside rail had been moved out between 3yds and 9yds. Actual race distances were 6f 55yds, 7f 39yds, 1m2f 116yds, 1m3f 136yds and 1m5f 158yds. Just a fair maiden in which those that had already shown ability dominated. The winner improved a little and the form fits in with the race averages.

2646 REKORDERLIG H'CAP 1m 2f 75y
2:30 (2:30) (Class 4) (0-85,85) 4-Y-O+ £6,469 (£1,925; £962; £481) Stalls High

Form RPR

4-13 **1** **Dolphin Rock**[33] 1723 6-8-12 76 DaleSwift 5 83
(Brian Ellison) *chsd ldrs: pushed along over 2f out: rdn and hmpd 1f out: r.o to ld wl ins fnl f* **7/2**[1]

50-4 **2** *½* **Stellar Express (IRE)**[15] 2232 4-8-11 75 RobertWinston 8 81
(Michael Appleby) *chsd ldrs: rdn over 1f out: ev ch ins fnl f: styd on* **14/1**

1-26 **3** *¾* **Star Lahib (IRE)**[24] 1933 4-9-4 82 FrannyNorton 10 87
(Mark Johnston) *s.i.s: hdwy to chse ldr 8f out: rdn over 2f out: edgd lft 1f out: sn led: hdd and unable qck wl ins fnl f* **4/1**[2]

16-3 **4** *½* **An Cat Dubh (IRE)**[32] 1746 4-9-1 79 MichaelO'Connell 9 83+
(Ian Williams) *hld up: plld hrd: r.o wl ins fnl f: nt rch ldrs* **15/2**

46-5 **5** *hd* **Vainglory (USA)**[8] 2424 9-9-2 85 LauraPike(5) 4 88+
(David Simcock) *prom: stdd and lost pl after 2f: pushed along over 2f out: rdn over 1f out: r.o ins fnl f: nt trble ldrs* **11/2**[3]

3615 **6** *1 ¼* **Lord Of The Dance (IRE)**[15] 2232 7-8-5 76 JoeyHaynes(7) 2 77
(Michael Mullineaux) *hld up: nt clr run over 2f out: rdn over 1f out: r.o: nvr trbld ldrs* **14/1**

6611 **7** *shd* **Honey Of A Kitten (USA)**[9] 1890 5-8-12 76 (v) MartinHarley 3 77
(David Evans) *led: rdn over 1f out: hdd and no ex ins fnl f* **10/1**

310- **8** *½* **Kay Gee Be (IRE)**[150] 8242 9-9-4 82 PJMcDonald 1 82
(Alan Berry) *prom: rdn over 2f out: styd on same pce fr over 1f out* **12/1**

2240 **9** *¾* **Knowe Head (NZ)**[28] 1831 6-8-12 76 (v) DavidProbert 7 74
(James Unett) *dwlt: hld up: rdn over 1f out: n.d* **13/2**

40-0 **10** *19* **Modernism**[16] 2191 4-9-5 83 TonyHamilton 6 45
(Alan McCabe) *hld up: plld hrd: pushed along over 4f out: rdn and wknd over 2f out* **25/1**

2m 13.87s (2.67) **Going Correction** +0.375s/f (Good) **10** Ran SP% **116.7**
Speed ratings (Par 105): **104,103,103,102,102 101,101,100,100,85**
toteswingers 1&2 £20.60, 1&3 £2.50, 2&3 £9.60 CSF £53.55 CT £205.42 TOTE £4.10: £2.00, £3.10, £1.70; EX 57.20 Trifecta £247.70 Pool: £951.26 - 2.87 winning units..
Owner Mia Racing **Bred** Mia Racing **Trained** Norton, N Yorks
■ Stewards' Enquiry : Laura Pike four-day ban; failing to ride out (8th-11th June).

FOCUS
A decent handicap, but several of these had a question mark against them over the trip. However, a steady early pace meant this wasn't the test of stamina it might have been. The first three were always prominent and the winner might not have had to improve on recent form.

2647 KRUSOVICE H'CAP 6f 18y
3:10 (3:12) (Class 3) (0-95,94) 4-Y-O+ £8,409 (£2,502; £1,250; £625) Stalls Low

Form RPR

2023 **1** **Summerinthecity (IRE)**[23] 1963 6-8-12 85 FrannyNorton 3 94
(David Nicholls) *w ldr tl led over 3f out: rdn over 1f out: r.o* **7/2**[1]

-200 **2** *2* **Intransigent**[15] 2207 4-9-5 92 DavidProbert 4 95
(Andrew Balding) *hld up in tch: rdn to chse wnr fnl f: r.o* **4/1**[2]

50-0 **3** *2* **Gatepost (IRE)**[17] 2150 4-9-1 88 TonyHamilton 1 84+
(Richard Fahey) *led: hdd over 3f out: rdn over 2f out: edgd lft ins fnl f: styd on* **9/2**[3]

1106 **4** *¾* **Forest Edge (IRE)**[7] 2461 4-8-12 90 (b) DeclanBates(5) 9 84
(David Evans) *hdwy over 4f out: chsd ldr 1/2-way tl rdn over 1f out: no ex ins fnl f* **20/1**

00-1 **5** *½* **Yair Hill (IRE)**[21] 2028 5-9-4 91 DavidNolan 2 83+
(Kevin Ryan) *prom: rdn over 2f out: hung lft over 1f out: styd on same pce* **7/2**[1]

00-0 **6** *shd* **Pearl Ice**[20] 2046 5-9-5 92 MartinHarley 6 84
(David Barron) *chsd ldrs: rdn over 2f out: styd on same pce fr over 1f out* **13/2**

00-0 **7** *1 ¼* **Graphic (IRE)**[7] 2444 4-8-10 83 RobertWinston 8 75
(William Haggas) *hld up: hdwy over 1f out: nt clr run ins fnl f: eased* **12/1**

1130 **8** *4 ½* **Aubrietia**[18] 2145 4-9-5 92 (b) PJMcDonald 7 65
(Alan McCabe) *s.i.s: hld up: wknd over 2f out* **12/1**

1m 15.07s (1.27) **Going Correction** +0.375s/f (Good) **8** Ran SP% **116.1**
Speed ratings (Par 107): **106,103,100,99,99 98,97,91**
toteswingers 1&2 £3.40, 1&3 £4.80, 2&3 £2.50 CSF £18.00 CT £63.66 TOTE £4.50: £2.20, £1.10, £1.10; EX 20.80 Trifecta £148.50 Pool: £879.56 - 4.44 winning units..
Owner Dr Marwan Koukash **Bred** J Costello **Trained** Sessay, N Yorks

FOCUS
A decent sprint handicap. The winner's best form since he was a 3yo.

2648 BLOOM GIN H'CAP 1m 5f 89y
3:40 (3:41) (Class 3) (0-90,88) 4-Y-O+ £8,409 (£2,502; £1,250; £625) Stalls Low

Form RPR

050- **1** **Swinging Hawk (GER)**[173] 7972 7-8-0 70 RyanPowell(3) 9 78
(Ian Williams) *hld up: hdwy over 1f out: hung lft and led wl ins fnl f: r.o* **25/1**

23-1 **2** *2* **Gabrial's King (IRE)**[8] 2418 4-8-9 76 FrannyNorton 8 81
(David Simcock) *hld up: hdwy over 1f out: sn rdn: r.o* **7/1**[3]

40-2 **3** *hd* **Mysterious Man (IRE)**[20] 2052 4-9-6 87 DavidProbert 3 92
(Andrew Balding) *chsd ldr tl rdn to ld over 1f out: sn hung lft: hdd and unable qck wl ins fnl f* **2/1**[1]

0011 **4** *nk* **Hallstatt (IRE)**[14] 2269 7-7-13 69 oh1 (t) RaulDaSilva(3) 4 74
(John Mackie) *s.i.s: sn prom: rdn over 1f out: styd on* **16/1**

05-0 **5** *1* **Kiama Bay (IRE)**[17] 2149 7-9-6 87 MartinHarley 10 91+
(John Quinn) *chsd ldrs: rdn over 2f out: styng on whn nt clr run wl ins fnl f: eased* **20/1**

The Form Book Flat, Raceform Ltd, Compton, RG20 6NL.

43-6 **6** *hd* **Kiwayu**[9] 2385 4-9-1 **82**........(t) MichaelO'Connell 7 85
(Ian Williams) *s.i.s: hld up: r.o ins fnl f: nt rch ldrs* **16/1**
-440 **7** *½* **The Fun Crusher**[9] 2402 5-8-13 **80**........(b[1]) RobertWinston 5 82
(Tim Easterby) *hld up: nt clr run 2f out: r.o ins fnl f: nvr trbld ldrs* **14/1**
45-3 **8** *1* **Harvard N Yale (USA)**[14] 2251 4-9-5 **86**........(t) SebSanders 2 88+
(Jeremy Noseda) *led: pushed along 3f out: rdn and hdd over 1f out: btn whn hmpd wl ins fnl f* **9/4**[2]
1156 **9** *¾* **Masterful Act (USA)**[42] 1547 6-9-0 **81**........ TadhgO'Shea 6 80
(Alan McCabe) *prom: rdn over 2f out: edgd lft over 1f out: styd on same pce* **25/1**
5-20 **10** *13* **Kuda Huraa (IRE)**[15] 2205 5-9-7 **88**........ TonyHamilton 1 72
(Alan King) *chsd ldrs: rdn over 2f out: wknd over 1f out: eased* **8/1**
2m 57.79s (5.09) **Going Correction** +0.375s/f (Good) **10** Ran SP% **118.6**
Speed ratings (Par 107): **99,97,97,97,96 96,96,95,95,87**
toteswingers 1&2 £19.10, 1&3 £19.10, 2&3 £6.60 CSF £189.52 CT £516.31 TOTE £72.40: £20.00, £1.40, £1.10; EX 438.30 Trifecta £791.30 Part won. Pool: £1055.10 - 0.09 winning units..
Owner Jamie Roberts & Jack Turton **Bred** Gestut Wittekindshof **Trained** Portway, Worcs
FOCUS
A decent handicap, but the pace was steady for the first mile and it developed into something a of a sprint. The third is perhaps the best guide.

2649 MATTHEW CLARK H'CAP 7f 2y
4:15 (4:16) (Class 2) (0-105,95) 4-Y-0+ **£14,231** (£4,235; £2,116; £1,058) **Stalls** Low

Form RPR
6011 **1** **Dr Red Eye**[15] 2214 5-8-13 **90**........(p) BillyCray(3) 3 99
(Scott Dixon) *mde all: rdn clr 2f out: hld on gamely* **9/2**[2]
0-66 **2** *nk* **Clockmaker (IRE)**[15] 2214 7-8-9 **83**........ TadhgO'Shea 12 91
(Tim Easterby) *hld up: pushed along 1/2-way: hdwy over 1f out: rdn to chse wnr fnl f: r.o* **14/1**
-020 **3** *4* **Laffan (IRE)**[35] 1675 4-9-4 **92**........ DavidNolan 8 89
(Kevin Ryan) *sn pushed along to chse wnr: rdn over 2f out: no ex ins fnl f* **7/1**
2600 **4** *1* **Verse Of Love**[14] 2254 4-8-7 **86**........ DeclanBates(5) 1 81
(David Evans) *chsd ldrs: rdn over 2f out: styd on same pce fnl f* **14/1**
-000 **5** *hd* **Mabait**[14] 2254 7-8-12 **91**........ LauraPike(5) 9 85
(David Simcock) *s.i.s: hld up and bhd: nt clr run over 1f out: r.o ins fnl f: nrst fin* **9/1**
3411 **6** *shd* **Klynch**[7] 2460 7-9-4 **92**........(b) JamesSullivan 4 86
(Ruth Carr) *hld up: pushed along over 2f out: r.o ins fnl f: nvr on terms* **6/1**
-002 **7** *shd* **Chosen Character (IRE)**[15] 2210 5-9-7 **95**........(vt) FrannyNorton 6 89
(Tom Dascombe) *sn pushed along to chse ldrs: rdn over 2f out: no ex fnl f* **3/1**[1]
231 **8** *6* **Grey Mirage**[42] 1542 4-9-6 **94**........(p) MartinHarley 10 71
(Marco Botti) *chsd ldrs: rdn over 1f out: wknd fnl f* **5/1**[3]
1m 27.66s (1.16) **Going Correction** +0.375s/f (Good) **8** Ran SP% **110.0**
Speed ratings (Par 109): **108,107,103,101,101 101,101,94**
toteswingers 1&2 £13.60, 1&3 £4.80, 2&3 £13.00 CSF £58.16 CT £375.85 TOTE £4.60: £1.70, £3.20, £1.90; EX 74.50 Trifecta £1019.20 Part won. Pool: £1358.94 - 0.98 winning units..
Owner The Red Eye Partnership **Bred** G E Amey **Trained** Babworth, Notts
■ Stewards' Enquiry : Tadhg O'Shea nine-day ban; used whip above permitted level (8th-16th June).
FOCUS
A decent handicap, though weakened to a degree by three non-runners and another withdrawn. With a few of these effective from the front, a strong pace was always likely. Another personal best from the winner.

2650 STELLA ARTOIS MAIDEN STKS 6f 18y
4:50 (4:51) (Class 4) 3-Y-0 **£6,469** (£1,925; £962; £481) **Stalls** Low

Form RPR
0 **1** **Bethany Bay (IRE)**[19] 2108 3-9-0 80........ TadhgO'Shea 9 69
(John Patrick Shanahan, Ire) *s.i.s: hdwy to ld 5f out: rdn over 1f out: styd on u.p* **5/2**[2]
264- **2** *½* **Martial Art (IRE)**[170] 8006 3-9-5 77........ DavidProbert 7 72
(Andrew Balding) *a.p: rdn to chse wnr over 1f out: styd on u.p* **9/4**[1]
3 *½* **Superboot (IRE)** 3-9-5 0........ RobertWinston 1 71
(Michael Wigham) *chsd ldrs: rdn and hung lft over 1f out: styd on* **6/1**
32-6 **4** *3* **Only For You**[5] 2512 3-9-0 56........ FrannyNorton 5 56
(Alan Brown) *chsd ldr: rdn over 2f out: no ex fnl f* **16/1**
5 **5** *½* **Greek Spirit (IRE)**[22] 1986 3-9-0 0........ SebSanders 6 54+
(Jeremy Noseda) *s.i.s: hld up: rdn over 2f out: r.o ins fnl f: nt trble ldrs* **3/1**[3]
23-6 **6** *nse* **Showtime Girl (IRE)**[15] 2241 3-9-0 65........ JamesSullivan 3 54
(Tim Easterby) *led 1f: chsd ldrs: rdn over 2f out: no ex fnl f* **10/1**
0 **7** *¾* **Serendippidy**[22] 1986 3-9-0 0........ LiamJones 2 52
(James Unett) *s.i.s: hld up: rdn over 1f out: nt trble ldrs* **33/1**
8 *11* **Deva Victrix** 3-9-2 0........ MarkCoumbe(3) 8 22
(Lisa Williamson) *s.s: outpcd* **50/1**
1m 16.95s (3.15) **Going Correction** +0.375s/f (Good) **8** Ran SP% **118.5**
Speed ratings (Par 101): **94,93,92,88,88 87,86,72**
toteswingers 1&2 £2.30, 1&3 £8.60, 2&3 £8.60 CSF £8.96 TOTE £2.60: £1.10, £1.90, £3.00; EX 9.30 Trifecta £61.10 Pool: £2839.36 - 34.83 winning units..
Owner Thistle Bloodstock Limited **Bred** Thistle Bloodstock Ltd **Trained** Danesfort, Co. Kilkenny
FOCUS
An uncompetitive maiden. The form pair finished 1-2 despite wide draws and the fourth is perhaps the key to the form.

2651 RUSSIAN STANDARD VODKA H'CAP 1m 3f 79y
5:20 (5:20) (Class 4) (0-85,83) 3-Y-0 **£6,469** (£1,925; £962; £481) **Stalls** Low

Form RPR
1 **Ralston Road (IRE)**[13] 2293 3-9-7 **83**........ TadhgO'Shea 1 98
(John Patrick Shanahan, Ire) *sn drvn along to ld: reminders over 6f out: rdn over 1f out: styd on gamely* **3/1**[2]
0403 **2** *½* **Snowy Dawn**[17] 2153 3-8-8 **70**........ DavidProbert 2 84
(Andrew Hollinshead) *a.p: pushed along over 3f out: rdn to chse wnr 2f out: ev ch ins fnl f: unable qck towards fin* **17/2**
1-2 **3** *11* **Gioia Di Vita**[24] 1934 3-8-11 **73**........ SebSanders 5 68
(Marco Botti) *hld up: hdwy over 5f out: rdn over 2f out: wknd over 1f out* **9/4**[1]
-114 **4** *nk* **Gabrial's Wawa**[15] 2216 3-9-2 **78**........ TonyHamilton 8 73
(Richard Fahey) *hld up: rdn over 2f out: nvr trbld ldrs* **8/1**
3-04 **5** *3 ½* **Master Ming (IRE)**[14] 2259 3-9-6 **82**........(b[1]) LiamJones 7 71
(Brian Meehan) *prom: chsd ldr over 8f out: rdn over 2f out: wknd wl over 1f out* **10/1**
6-20 **6** *7* **Nice Story (IRE)**[20] 2054 3-9-2 **78**........ MartinHarley 3 55
(Mick Channon) *hld up: pushed along over 4f out: a in rr* **12/1**
-213 **7** *12* **Enzaal (USA)**[16] 2193 3-9-4 **80**........ FrannyNorton 6 37
(Mark Johnston) *chsd wnr 3f: remained handy: rdn over 4f out: wknd 3f out: t.o* **4/1**[3]
2m 27.88s (3.08) **Going Correction** +0.375s/f (Good) **7** Ran SP% **114.2**
Speed ratings (Par 101): **103,102,94,94,91 86,78**
toteswingers 1&2 £4.80, 1&3 £1.30, 2&3 £5.30 CSF £27.94 CT £66.44 TOTE £3.10: £2.10, £2.50; EX 32.20 Trifecta £115.00 Pool: £826.69 - 5.38 winning units..
Owner Thistle Bloodstock Limited **Bred** Thistle Bloodstock Ltd **Trained** Danesfort, Co. Kilkenny
FOCUS
A fair 3yo handicap and, with the pace a good one, they finished spread out all over the Roodeye. The best time on the card with the first pair clear and the form has been given a bit of a chance.
T/Plt: £52.60 to a £1 stake. Pool: £66,465.37 - 921.38 winning units T/Qpdt: £16.60 to a £1 stake. Pool: £3662.92 - 162.40 winning units CR

2617 GOODWOOD (R-H)
Saturday, May 25
OFFICIAL GOING: Good to soft (good in places on round course; 7.5)
Wind: Moderate, across (towards stands) Weather: Fine

2652 32RED FESTIVAL STKS (LISTED RACE) 1m 1f 192y
2:05 (2:08) (Class 1) 4-Y-0+ **£22,684** (£8,600; £4,304; £2,144; £1,076) **Stalls** Low

Form RPR
00-6 **1** **Rewarded**[16] 2186 4-8-12 104........ KirstyMilczarek 5 110
(James Toller) *trckd ldng pair: clsd on inner to ld wl over 1f out: sn in command: styd on fnl f* **25/1**
3-23 **2** *¾* **Stipulate**[24] 1919 4-8-12 110........ IanMongan 6 108
(Sir Henry Cecil) *t.k.h: hld up in 4th: asked for effrt 2f out: rdn and nt qckn over 1f out: styd on to chse wnr fnl f: tended to hang but clsd nr fin* **3/1**[2]
/3-5 **3** *1 ½* **Reckoning (IRE)**[21] 2012 4-8-7 96........(p) HayleyTurner 7 100
(Jeremy Noseda) *dwlt: hld up in last: pushed along and no imp over 2f out: drvn wl over 1f out: styd on fnl f to take 3rd nr fin* **11/1**[3]
114- **4** *½* **Cameron Highland (IRE)**[245] 6482 4-8-12 108........ AndreaAtzeni 4 104
(Roger Varian) *trckd ldr: chal and upsides over 2f out tl wnr wnt by wl over 1f out: nt qckn sn after: wknd fnl f* **11/4**[1]
31- **5** *2 ¼* **Mobaco (FR)**[218] 7234 4-9-4 108........ JimCrowley 1 106
(Luca Cumani) *led: rdn and jnd over 2f out: hdd & wknd wl over 1f out* **11/1**[3]
2m 9.24s (1.14) **Going Correction** +0.025s/f (Good) **5** Ran SP% **72.2**
Speed ratings (Par 111): **96,95,94,93,92**
CSF £39.36 TOTE £18.00: £4.00, £1.50; EX 36.30 Trifecta £135.90 Pool: £370.90 - 2.04 winning units..
Owner P C J Dalby & R D Schuster **Bred** Edward David Kessly **Trained** Newmarket, Suffolk
■ Afsare was withdrawn (11-8F, deduct 40p in the £ under R4).
■ Stewards' Enquiry : Kirsty Milczarek two-day ban; used whip in incorrect placed (8th-9th June).
FOCUS
The first 2f of the 1m course were dolled out five yards, and there was fresh ground from the 6f marker on the lower bend to the 2f marker in the straight. The ground was on the easy side, but drying all the time. This Listed race rather fell apart, not helped by a couple of non-runners, notably Afsare, who refused to enter the stalls. It has to rate a personal best from the surprise winner.

2653 EBF BRIGHTON & HOVE ALBION MAIDEN STKS 6f
2:35 (2:35) (Class 4) 2-Y-0 **£5,175** (£1,540; £769; £384) **Stalls** Low

Form RPR
2 **1** **Lanark (IRE)**[16] 2194 2-9-5 0........ JoeFanning 5 81+
(Mark Johnston) *pressed ldr: rdn over 2f out: lft in ld over 1f out: pushed out and a holding on* **9/4**[1]
2 *½* **Extra Noble** 2-9-5 0........ JimCrowley 10 80+
(Ralph Beckett) *trckd ldrs: shkn up 2f out: lft in 2nd over 1f out: styd on but a hld* **14/1**
3 *1 ½* **Munfallet (IRE)** 2-9-5 0........ KieranO'Neill 2 75+
(Richard Hannon) *trckd ldng pair to 2f out: styd cl up: one pce over 1f out* **7/1**
4 *1 ½* **Ben Hall (IRE)** 2-9-5 0........ NickyMackay 3 71+
(John Gosden) *t.k.h: trckd ldrs: shkn up and no imp over 2f out: wl hld over 1f out: kpt on* **5/1**[3]
5 *½* **Floating Ballerino (IRE)** 2-9-5 0........ HarryBentley 8 69+
(Olly Stevens) *trckd ldrs: shkn up over 2f out: no imp over 1f out: one pce after* **12/1**
6 *1 ¾* **Shimba Hills** 2-9-0 0........ CharlesBishop(5) 11 64
(Mick Channon) *towards rr: rdn over 2f out: nvr on terms but styd on fnl f* **25/1**
7 *1 ¼* **Cape Arrow** 2-9-5 0........ JackMitchell 7 60
(Paul Cole) *s.i.s: a towards rr: shkn up over 2f out: no real imp: kpt on* **33/1**
8 *3 ¾* **Jarlath** 2-9-5 0........ LiamKeniry 9 49
(Seamus Mullins) *s.s: t.k.h and rn green in last: nvr on terms but kpt on fnl f* **100/1**
0 **9** *6* **Deeds Not Words (IRE)**[16] 2194 2-9-5 0........ SamHitchcott 1 31
(Mick Channon) *dwlt: chsd ldrs but sn urged along: wknd over 2f out* **33/1**
10 *1* **Under My Wing (IRE)** 2-9-5 0........ AndreaAtzeni 12 28
(Richard Hannon) *a in rr: struggling fr 1/2-way: sn wknd* **14/1**
3 **U** **Langavat (IRE)**[14] 2250 2-9-5 0........ PatDobbs 4 78+
(Richard Hannon) *mde most: gng best whn veered rt and uns rdr over 1f out* **3/1**[2]
1m 12.45s (0.25) **Going Correction** +0.025s/f (Good) **11** Ran SP% **116.7**
Speed ratings (Par 95): **99,98,96,94,93 91,89,84,76,75**
toteswingers 1&2 £7.60, 1&3 £3.10, 2&3 £27.10 CSF £34.60 TOTE £2.80: £1.30, £3.50, £2.30; EX 34.70 Trifecta £266.00 Pool: £1007.88 - 2.84 winning units..
Owner Sheikh Hamdan Bin Mohammed Al Maktoum **Bred** Norelands Stallions **Trained** Middleham Moor, N Yorks
FOCUS
The runners started off up the middle, but gradually drifted towards the stands' rail. A decent maiden which will produce winners. Lanark should rate a good deal higher.

2654 ALLANS OF PETWORTH H'CAP 1m 6f
3:05 (3:05) (Class 2) (0-105,94) 4-Y-0+ **£16,172** (£4,812; £2,405; £1,202) **Stalls** Low

Form RPR
31-1 **1** **Arch Villain (IRE)**[9] 2385 4-8-12 **85**........ AndreaAtzeni 6 94
(Amanda Perrett) *hld up in midfield: pushed along and prog over 3f out: chsd ldr over 2f out: sustained chal fnl 2f: led nr fin* **7/2**[1]
4/56 **2** *nk* **Oriental Fox (GER)**[8] 2427 5-9-7 **94**........ JoeFanning 5 102
(Mark Johnston) *sn led and set decent pce: rdn over 2f out: hrd pressed fnl 2f: kpt on wl but worn down nr fin* **14/1**

0-21 **3** *3* **Beyond Conceit (IRE)**[31] 1766 4-9-4 **91** LiamKeniry 9 95
(Andrew Balding) *trckd ldr: lost 2nd and rdn over 2f out: steadily outpcd but hld on for 3rd* **6/1**

21-0 **4** *nk* **Lady Rosamunde**[20] 2052 5-8-7 **85** (p) RosieJessop(5) 2 89
(Marcus Tregoning) *chsd ldng pair: rdn 3f out: steadily outpcd fr over 2f out* **12/1**

02- **5** *½* **Sohar**[204] 7522 5-8-12 **85** KirstyMilczarek 3 88
(James Toller) *hld up in 8th: rdn and no prog 3f out: kpt on fr over 1f out: nrst fin* **12/1**

2141 **6** *nk* **Cousin Khee**[10] 2369 6-8-8 **81** MickaelBarzalona 8 83+
(Hughie Morrison) *hld up in tch: plld out wd and effrt over 2f out: hanging lft and nt qckn after* **5/1**[3]

02-0 **7** *4½* **Albert Bridge**[42] 1547 5-9-2 **89** JimCrowley 1 85
(Ralph Beckett) *trckd ldrs: rdn and nt qckn 3f out: no imp and btn 2f out: wknd* **8/1**

6-5 **8** *6* **Moldowney**[31] 1766 4-9-1 **88** KierenFallon 7 78
(Luca Cumani) *t.k.h early: hld up in tch: rdn and no prog 3f out: sn btn: eased fnl f* **4/1**[2]

-252 **9** *1¼* **Porgy**[33] 1733 8-9-0 **87** (b) MartinLane 10 73
(Brian Ellison) *stdd s: hld up in 9th and detached early: in tch 5f out: rdn and no prog 4f out* **16/1**

10-0 **10** *1* **The Betchworth Kid**[20] 2052 8-9-3 **90** HayleyTurner 4 75
(Michael Bell) *stdd s: hld up in detached last early: in tch 5f out: rdn and no prog 4f out* **33/1**

3m 3.56s (-0.04) **Going Correction** +0.025s/f (Good) **10** Ran SP% **115.2**
Speed ratings (Par 109): **101,100,99,98,98 98,95,92,91,91**
toteswingers 1&2 £10.10, 1&3 £3.60, 2&3 £13.80 CSF £52.80 CT £285.37 TOTE £3.80: £1.50, £4.10, £2.90; EX 65.30 Trifecta £495.40 Pool: £1732.57 - 2.62 winning units..

Owner Mr & Mrs F Cotton, Mr & Mrs P Conway **Bred** Summerhill Bloodstock **Trained** Pulborough, W Sussex

FOCUS
A good staying handicap run at a true pace. The form looks solid.

2655 32RED H'CAP 7f
3:35 (3:36) (Class 2) 3-Y-O **£32,345** (£9,625; £4,810; £2,405) **Stalls** Low

Form RPR

-213 **1** **You Da One (IRE)**[16] 2190 3-8-4 **81** HayleyTurner 3 92
(Andrew Balding) *taken down early: mde all: urged along fr 2f out: pressed and drvn 1f out: sn asserted: readily* **8/1**

5-50 **2** *2¼* **Tamayuz Star (IRE)**[7] 2453 3-9-6 **97** KierenFallon 10 102
(Richard Hannon) *sn trckd ldng trio: prog to chse wnr over 1f out and looked dangerous: rdn and one pce fnl f* **15/2**[3]

2453 **3** *1¼* **Flashlight (IRE)**[16] 2188 3-8-8 **85** JoeFanning 5 87
(Mark Johnston) *chsd wnr: rdn and lost 2nd over 1f out: styd on same pce after* **8/1**

02-3 **4** *1½* **Pay Freeze (IRE)**[15] 2208 3-9-6 **97** HarryBentley 6 95
(Mick Channon) *hld up in midfield: shkn up wl over 2f out: prog to go 4th over 1f out but already outpcd: no hdwy after* **7/1**[2]

040- **5** *½* **Ashaadd (IRE)**[231] 6883 3-8-13 **90** AndreaAtzeni 8 87+
(Roger Varian) *dwlt: hld up in last trio: trying to make prog whn squeezed out over 2f out: no ch after: styd on fnl f* **16/1**

10-2 **6** *1* **Flyman**[21] 2008 3-8-13 **95** GeorgeChaloner(5) 7 89
(Richard Fahey) *hld up in midfield: pushed along fr 3f out: nt qckn and no imp on ldrs* **10/1**

11-2 **7** *shd* **Breton Rock (IRE)**[16] 2188 3-9-1 **92** MartinLane 1 86+
(David Simcock) *rrd as stalls opened and completely missed the break: in tch in last after 2f: brought wd: rdn and sme prog 3f out: no hdwy and wl btn 2f out* **15/8**[1]

31-2 **8** *nse* **Gworn**[7] 2438 3-8-6 **83** ChrisCatlin 4 76+
(Ed Dunlop) *dwlt: hld up in last trio: urged along fr 3f out: hanging and no prog tl fnlly styd on fnl f: pressing for 5th whn eased last strides* **7/1**[2]

0006 **9** *nk* **Queen Aggie (IRE)**[16] 2190 3-8-8 **85** AndrewMullen 9 78
(David Evans) *mostly chsd ldng quartet tl steadily wknd fr 2f out* **50/1**

2-04 **10** *nk* **Sorella Bella (IRE)**[16] 2188 3-9-7 **98** SamHitchcott 2 90
(Mick Channon) *trckd ldng pair to over 2f out: sn wknd* **20/1**

1m 26.09s (-0.91) **Going Correction** +0.025s/f (Good) **10** Ran SP% **115.5**
Speed ratings (Par 105): **106,103,102,100,99 98,98,98,98,97**
toteswingers 1&2 £17.40, 1&3 £8.80, 2&3 £12.50 CSF £66.00 CT £509.41 TOTE £7.20: £2.10, £2.70, £2.80; EX 84.40 Trifecta £400.20 Pool: £1264.74 - 2.36 winning units..

Owner Mr & Mrs R M Gorell **Bred** James And Joe Brannigan **Trained** Kingsclere, Hants

FOCUS
It proved hard to make up ground and a few of the beaten runners are better than they showed. The winner built on his Chester run.

2656 TAPSTER STKS (LISTED RACE) 1m 4f
4:05 (4:11) (Class 1) 4-Y-O+ **£23,680** (£8,956; £4,476; £2,236) **Stalls** High

Form RPR

2-34 **1** **Noble Mission**[21] 2020 4-9-0 109 IanMongan 1 111
(Sir Henry Cecil) *stdd s: hld up in 4th: rdn whn pce lifted over 3f out: clsd u.p over 2f out: led over 1f out: drvn clr* **8/13**[1]

42-3 **2** *4* **Genzy (FR)**[56] 1241 5-9-0 103 JimCrowley 5 104
(Ian Williams) *led at mod pce: kicked on over 3f out: drvn and hdd over 1f out: sn outpcd* **12/1**

2-21 **3** *¾* **Moment In Time (IRE)**[21] 2004 4-8-9 93 KierenFallon 3 98
(David Simcock) *trckd ldr 4f: quick move to go 2nd again over 3f out and sn chalng: upsides u.p over 1f out: wnr sn powered past* **4/1**[2]

10-4 **4** *½* **Bana Wu**[20] 2045 4-8-9 99 HayleyTurner 2 97
(Andrew Balding) *stdd s: hld up in last: outpcd over 3f out: shkn up and styd on same pce after: pressed for 3rd nr fin* **7/1**[3]

1116 **5** *23* **Boonga Roogeta**[20] 2045 4-8-9 94 MartinLane 4 60
(Peter Charalambous) *trckd ldng pair: wnt 2nd after 4f tl over 3f out: sn wknd: t.o* **16/1**

2m 40.84s (2.44) **Going Correction** +0.025s/f (Good) **5** Ran SP% **108.0**
Speed ratings (Par 111): **92,89,88,88,73**
CSF £8.50 TOTE £1.40: £1.10, £4.10; EX 7.30 Trifecta £16.40 Pool: £2648.46 - 120.88 winning units..

Owner K Abdullah **Bred** Juddmonte Farms Ltd **Trained** Newmarket, Suffolk

■ Stewards' Enquiry : Ian Mongan four-day ban; used whip above permitted level (8th-11th June).

FOCUS
A weak Listed race but the form makes sense.

2657 JERSEY RACING CLUB H'CAP 6f
4:40 (4:41) (Class 4) (0-80,85) 6-Y-O+ **£6,469** (£1,925; £962; £481) **Stalls** Low

Form RPR

6-53 **1** **Mon Brav**[7] 2441 6-9-2 **74** MartinLane 14 87
(Brian Ellison) *wl in rr: drvn over 2f out: gd prog on outer of gp over 1f out: led ins fnl f: r.o wl* **11/2**[3]

0406 **2** *½* **Docofthebay (IRE)**[12] 2310 9-9-6 **78** (p) IanMongan 5 89
(Scott Dixon) *taken down early: settled in last quartet: drvn over 2f out: gd prog on outer of gp over 1f out: chal ins fnl f: r.o but jst hld* **5/1**[2]

46-1 **3** *2½* **Aye Aye Digby (IRE)**[16] 2196 8-9-5 **77** FergusSweeney 1 80
(Patrick Chamings) *racd on outer of gp: pressed ldr: drvn to ld briefly jst ins fnl f: sn outpcd* **5/1**[2]

6131 **4** *1½* **Mata Hari Blue**[5] 2513 7-9-13 **85** 6ex (t) AndrewMullen 2 83
(Michael Appleby) *racd on outer of gp: led: rdn over 1f out: edgd lft and hdd jst ins fnl f: fdd* **9/2**[1]

3-05 **5** *shd* **Macdillon**[9] 2388 7-9-0 **72** LiamKeniry 3 70
(Stuart Kittow) *trckd ldrs gng wl towards outer of gp: shkn up and nt qckn wl over 1f out: edgd lft and sn lft bhd* **12/1**

0-10 **6** *2* **Tagula Night (IRE)**[14] 2255 7-9-7 **79** (t) JimCrowley 9 70
(Dean Ivory) *racd towards nr side of gp: nvr beyond midfield: rdn over 2f out: no ch over 1f out* **9/1**

6141 **7** *1¼* **Haadeeth**[19] 2303 6-8-9 **67** (t) JoeFanning 6 54
(David Evans) *taken down early: pressed ldng pair: rdn and nt qckn wl over 1f out: wknd fnl f* **16/1**

35-4 **8** *1¼* **Ray Of Joy**[19] 2088 7-9-6 **78** NickyMackay 15 61
(J R Jenkins) *a in rr on nr side of gp: struggling 2f out: no ch after* **12/1**

6-00 **9** *2½* **Interakt**[16] 2196 6-8-11 **69** KirstyMilczarek 7 44
(Joseph Tuite) *trckd ldrs: rdn and nt qckn wl over 1f out: sn wknd* **33/1**

0125 **10** *nk* **Ocean Legend (IRE)**[25] 1901 8-9-0 **72** KierenFallon 11 47
(Tony Carroll) *racd towards nr side of gp: nvr beyond midfield: wl btn fnl 2f* **12/1**

520- **11** *2½* **The Wee Chief (IRE)**[316] 4059 7-8-12 **70** KieranO'Neill 17 37
(Jimmy Fox) *dwlt: racd towards nr side of gp: nvr beyond midfield: wl btn fnl 2f* **33/1**

0-60 **12** *5* **Shifting Star (IRE)**[1] 2618 8-9-4 **76** SamHitchcott 18 27
(John Bridger) *dwlt: racd towards nr side of gp: a struggling* **25/1**

00-2 **13** *17* **We Have A Dream**[18] 2128 8-9-2 **74** HayleyTurner 8
(William Muir) *chsd ldrs: rdn 1/2-way: wknd over 2f out: eased fnl f: t.o* **10/1**

1m 11.37s (-0.83) **Going Correction** +0.025s/f (Good) **13** Ran SP% **124.7**
Speed ratings: **106,105,102,100,99 97,95,93,90,90 86,80,57**
toteswingers 1&2 £10.10, 1&3 £5.80, 2&3 £6.30 CSF £34.11 CT £154.83 TOTE £7.50: £2.60, £2.50, £2.60; EX 56.10 Trifecta £385.40 Pool: £3142.83 - 6.11 winning units..

Owner Koo's Racing Club **Bred** J D Graham **Trained** Norton, N Yorks

■ Stewards' Enquiry : Martin Lane four-day ban; used whip above permitted level (8th-11th June).

FOCUS
A sprint handicap for horses aged six and above. The main action unfolded up the middle of the track. The winner is rated back to something like last year's form.

2658 FEDERATION OF BLOODSTOCK AGENTS MAIDEN FILLIES' STKS 7f
5:15 (5:18) (Class 5) 3-Y-O
£3,112 (£932; £466; £233; £116; £58) **Stalls** Low

Form RPR

0-25 **1** **Saucy Minx (IRE)**[19] 2084 3-9-0 78 JoeFanning 2 80+
(Amanda Perrett) *mde all: rdn over 1f out: hung bdly lft after: hld on last 100yds* **5/2**[1]

4- **2** *¾* **Close At Hand**[302] 4525 3-9-0 0 NickyMackay 10 76+
(John Gosden) *dwlt: hld up in last quartet: prog on outer jst over 2f out: shkn up over 1f out: r.o to take 2nd nr fin* **7/2**[2]

63- **3** *¾* **Icon Dance**[297] 4704 3-9-0 0 JohnFahy 8 74
(Ben De Haan) *trckd ldng trio: prog to chse wnr wl over 1f out: styd on but unable to chal: lost 2nd nr fin* **33/1**

2-4 **4** *½* **Secretly**[20] 2051 3-9-0 0 FergusSweeney 6 73
(Henry Candy) *trckd ldng pair: tried to cl on inner 2f out: styd on same pce fnl f* **6/1**[3]

5 *2½* **Tafaaseel (USA)** 3-9-0 0 KierenFallon 7 66+
(Sir Michael Stoute) *dwlt: sn chsd ldrs: tried to cl on outer over 2f out: no prog over 1f out: fdd* **7/2**[2]

00 **6** *2½* **Dama De La Noche (IRE)**[26] 1876 3-9-0 0 KieranO'Neill 3 59
(Richard Hannon) *chsd ldrs: pushed along 3f out: no prog 2f out: steadily fdd* **25/1**

0 **7** *3½* **Toffee Shot**[15] 2226 3-9-0 0 MartinLane 11 50
(J W Hills) *wnt lft s: hld up in last: shkn up and no prog over 2f out: kpt on nr fin* **50/1**

8 *½* **Marmalady (IRE)** 3-9-0 0 LiamKeniry 5 48
(Gary Moore) *dwlt: hld up in last pair: rn green whn pushed along over 2f out: nvr a threat* **22/1**

0 **9** *nk* **Cape Appeal**[19] 2084 3-9-0 0 HarryBentley 4 47
(Richard Hannon) *chsd wnr to wl over 1f out: wknd qckly* **10/1**

10 *10* **Fonseca (IRE)** 3-9-0 0 HayleyTurner 1 20
(Andrew Balding) *dwlt: a in last quartet: wknd over 2f out: t.o* **10/1**

1m 27.74s (0.74) **Going Correction** +0.025s/f (Good) **10** Ran SP% **118.6**
Speed ratings (Par 96): **96,95,94,93,90 88,84,83,83,71**
toteswingers 1&2 £2.80, 1&3 £11.90, 2&3 £18.00 CSF £11.02 TOTE £3.30: £1.30, £2.20, £6.00; EX 15.30 Trifecta £193.20 Pool: £2836.49 - 11.00 winning units..

Owner Mr & Mrs F Cotton, Mr & Mrs P Conway **Bred** Summerhill & J Osborne **Trained** Pulborough, W Sussex

FOCUS
An ordinary fillies' maiden. The form is rated around the winner, who made all.

T/Plt: £214.50 to a £1 stake. Pool: £79,474.43 - 270.43 winning units T/Qpdt: £26.30 to a £1 stake. Pool: £4882.26 - 137.10 winning units JN

2624 HAYDOCK (L-H)

Saturday, May 25

OFFICIAL GOING: Good to firm (firm in places) changing to firm after race 1 (2.10)

There were no fewer than 25 non-runners on the card, 19 due to the drying ground which had not been watered.

Wind: light half against Weather: Fine and sunny

2659 BETFRED "STILL TREBLE ODDS" H'CAP — 1m

2:10 (2:11) (Class 4) (0-80,82) 4-Y-0+ £5,175 (£1,540; £769; £384) Stalls Low

Form — RPR

002 1 **Albaqaa**[7] 2450 8-8-10 74 RobertTart(5) 6 87
(P J O'Gorman) *in tch: pushed along and hdwy over 2f out: rdn to ld over 1f out: hdd fnl 100yds: sn regained ld after runner-up's jockey eased: jst hld on* 7/2[1]

1023 2 hd **Classic Colori (IRE)**[26] 1890 6-9-0 78 (v) DavidBergin(5) 15 92
(David O'Meara) *dwlt: hld up: hdwy on outer over 2f out: rdn and edgd lft over 1f out: rdr dropped whip ins fnl f: led narrowly 100yds out: rdr sn mistk winning post and eased: sn hdd: rdn again nr fin: jst hld* 10/1

10-3 3 4 1/2 **Restaurateur (IRE)**[28] 1849 4-9-5 78 (p) WilliamBuick 10 81
(Andrew Balding) *midfield: rdn over 2f out: chsd ldng pair over 1f out: one pce fnl f* 9/2[2]

-301 4 1 1/4 **Prime Exhibit**[5] 2496 8-9-6 82 6ex (t) DarrenEgan(3) 16 82
(Daniel Mark Loughnane) *hld up in rr: pushed along and stl plenty to do whn n.m.r 2f out: kpt on fr over 1f out: nrst fin* 16/1

1-22 5 3/4 **Majestic Dream (IRE)**[19] 2081 5-9-0 73 GrahamGibbons 12 71
(Michael Easterby) *midfield: rdn over 2f out: one pce and nvr threatened ldrs* 8/1

46-6 6 1/2 **Barwick**[32] 1751 5-9-5 78 LukeMorris 9 75
(Mark H Tompkins) *s.i.s: hld up: rdn over 2f out: nvr threatened ldrs* 16/1

2600 7 1/2 **One Scoop Or Two**[28] 1827 7-8-13 72 (v[1]) ShaneKelly 13 68
(Andrew Hollinshead) *prom: rdn to ld over 3f out: edgd lft over 1f out and sn hdd: grad wknd* 25/1

-550 8 2 3/4 **Pearl Nation (USA)**[28] 1819 4-9-5 78 FrederikTylicki 5 67
(Brian Baugh) *trckd ldrs: rdn over 3f out: wknd over 1f out* 12/1

2-00 9 4 1/2 **Sword In Hand**[15] 2232 4-8-11 75 MichaelJMMurphy(5) 14 54
(Alan Jarvis) *racd keenly: midfield towards outer: rdn over 2f out: wknd over 1f out* 13/2

5020 10 nk **Silverware (USA)**[23] 1963 5-9-4 77 TomEaves 11 55
(Kristin Stubbs) *racd keenly: trckd ldrs: rdn 3f out: sn wknd* 40/1

0023 11 nk **Cono Zur (FR)**[8] 2406 6-8-10 69 JamesSullivan 1 47
(Ruth Carr) *led: rdn whn hdd over 3f out: sn wknd* 5/1[3]

1m 42.45s (-1.25) **Going Correction** 0.0s/f (Good) 11 Ran SP% 116.3
Speed ratings (Par 105): **106,105,101,100,99 98,98,95,91,90 90**
toteswingers 1&2 £8.30, 1&3 £3.10, 2&3 £10.20 CSF £38.92 CT £163.70 TOTE £4.40: £1.80, £4.00, £1.40; EX 43.00 Trifecta £297.60 Pool: £2240.15 - 5.64 winning units..
Owner Racing To The Max **Bred** C Eddington And Partners **Trained** Newmarket, Suffolk
■ Stewards' Enquiry : David Bergin 28-day ban; failing to ride out (8th june-5th July).

FOCUS
All races on Stands side home straight and races on Round course increased in distance by 50yds. The going had dried out to Good to firm, firm in places, resulting in a host of withdrawals, and the going was changed to Firm all over after this race. The race provided controversy with the rider of the second easing up early. The first pair were clear and are on good marks on their old form.

2660 BETFRED TV H'CAP — 1m 3f 200y

2:40 (2:40) (Class 2) (0-100,92) 3-Y-0 £15,562 (£4,660; £2,330; £1,165; £582) Stalls Centre

Form — RPR

1-42 1 **Van Percy**[15] 2216 3-8-10 81 CathyGannon 4 89+
(Andrew Balding) *racd keenly: led narrowly: hdd 10f out: trckd ldr: pushed along over 2f out: n.m.r on inner over 1f out tl fnl 75yds: r.o strly once clr: led post* 2/1[2]

1135 2 nse **Blue Wave (IRE)**[15] 2216 3-8-8 84 (b[1]) MichaelJMMurphy(5) 7 90
(Mark Johnston) *trckd ldr: led 10f out: rdn 2f out: kpt on: hdd post* 9/1

2126 3 1 1/2 **Naru (IRE)**[20] 2050 3-8-12 83 LukeMorris 5 87
(James Tate) *trckd ldr: rdn 2f out: ev ch tl no ex fnl 100yds* 11/2[3]

-311 4 1 3/4 **Red Runaway**[15] 2216 3-8-10 81 JamesDoyle 1 82
(Ed Dunlop) *hld up: rdn and hdwy over 2f out: briefly chsd ldrs over 1f out: no ex fnl f* 15/8[1]

50-1 5 23 **Flashheart (IRE)**[22] 1975 3-8-11 82 ShaneKelly 6 46
(Marcus Tregoning) *s.i.s: hld up: rdn over 3f out: sn btn: eased* 11/2[3]

2m 31.09s (-2.71) **Going Correction** 0.0s/f (Good) 5 Ran SP% 108.9
Speed ratings (Par 105): **109,108,107,106,91**
CSF £17.90 TOTE £2.80: £1.60, £3.10; EX 21.90 Trifecta £58.10 Pool: £1762.91 - 22.73 winning units..
Owner Mrs L E Ramsden & Richard Morecombe **Bred** Mr & Mrs A E Pakenham **Trained** Kingsclere, Hants

FOCUS
A good 3yo handicap that has been won by such as Opinion Poll and Brown Panther (who were both subsequently placed at Group 1 level) in its short history but this doesn't look up to recent renewals. The race was weakened by two non-runners but produced another dramatic finish. The winner would have won by further with a clear run.

2661 BETFRED.COM SILVER BOWL (H'CAP) — 1m

3:15 (3:15) (Class 2) 3-Y-0

£40,462 (£12,116; £6,058; £3,029; £1,514; £760) Stalls Low

Form — RPR

0-10 1 **Shebebi (USA)**[15] 2208 3-8-2 88 LiamJones 12 94
(Mark Johnston) *mde all: pressed fr over 2f out: hld on gamely u.p ins fnl f* 12/1

-111 2 nk **Newstead Abbey**[56] 1250 3-8-9 95 GrahamGibbons 5 101
(David Barron) *in tch: rdn over 2f out: hdwy over 1f out: edgd lft: drvn to chal jst ins fnl f: kpt on but a jst hld* 9/2[2]

40-5 3 nk **Mocenigo (IRE)**[36] 1667 3-8-13 99 RobertHavlin 2 104
(Peter Chapple-Hyam) *trckd ldrs: rdn over 2f out: briefly n.m.r over 1f out: kpt on fnl f: clsng at fin* 25/1

02-5 4 1 1/4 **Alhebayeb (IRE)**[38] 1621 3-9-7 107 DaneO'Neill 11 109
(Richard Hannon) *midfield: rdn over 2f out: kpt on* 11/2[3]

-114 5 1 **Country Western**[21] 2024 3-8-3 89 WilliamCarson 6 89
(Charles Hills) *racd keenly: trckd ldr: rdn to press ldr over 2f out: wknd ins fnl f* 12/1

0040 6 1/2 **Pure Excellence**[20] 2050 3-7-11 86 DarrenEgan(3) 15 85
(Mark Johnston) *hld up: rdn over 2f out: kpt on fnl f: nvr threatened* 20/1

1-02 7 nse **Red Avenger (USA)**[21] 2024 3-8-7 93 ow1 WilliamBuick 4 92+
(Ed Dunlop) *hld up: pushed along 3f out: sme hdwy over 1f out: kpt on but nvr trbld ldrs* 7/1

5-34 8 2 3/4 **Georgian Bay (IRE)**[15] 2208 3-8-7 93 LukeMorris 7 85
(Mrs K Burke) *midfield: rdn over 3f out: one pce: wknd ins fnl f* 8/1

11-4 9 3 3/4 **Code Of Honor**[42] 1543 3-8-4 90 CathyGannon 1 89+
(Henry Candy) *s.i.s: hld up: pushed along over 3f out: rdn and hdwy 2f out: disputing 4th whn sltly hmpd on inner jst ins fnl f: eased* 7/2[1]

1-35 10 1 1/4 **Gabrial's Kaka (IRE)**[15] 2211 3-8-5 91 BarryMcHugh 13 72
(Richard Fahey) *midfield: rdn over 3f out: sn wknd* 7/1

1m 42.66s (-1.04) **Going Correction** 0.0s/f (Good) 10 Ran SP% 115.9
Speed ratings (Par 105): **105,104,104,103,102 101,101,98,95,93**
toteswingers 1&2 £12.10, 1&3 £35.60, 2&3 £13.80 CSF £64.94 CT £1368.79 TOTE £15.60: £3.90, £1.90, £7.20; EX 72.80 Trifecta £2240.50 Pool: £68,345.95 - 22.87 winning units..
Owner Hamdan Al Maktoum **Bred** Shadwell Farm LLC **Trained** Middleham Moor, N Yorks
■ Stewards' Enquiry : Graham Gibbons two-day ban; careless riding (8th-9th June).
William Buick two-day ban; failing to obtain best possible position (8th-9th June).

FOCUS
One of the most competitive 3-y-o handicaps of the season and this year's renewal looked another strong contest. They appeared to go a good early gallop although the time was 0.21secs slower than the older horse handicap earlier on the card. The form is rated around the winner's Beverley run.

2662 BETFRED TEMPLE STKS (BRITISH CHAMPIONS SERIES) (GROUP 2) — 5f

3:50 (3:53) (Class 1) 3-Y-0+

£51,039 (£19,350; £9,684; £4,824; £2,421; £1,215) Stalls Centre

Form — RPR

00-2 1 **Kingsgate Native (IRE)**[21] 2019 8-9-4 110 ShaneKelly 10 117
(Robert Cowell) *trckd ldrs stands' side: rdn to ld gp jst ins fnl f: r.o strly: edgd lft fnl 100yds: led towards fin* 14/1

10-0 2 nk **Swiss Spirit**[10] 2368 4-9-4 107 WilliamBuick 4 116+
(John Gosden) *hmpd s: swtchd rt to r stands' side: hld up in rr: pushed along 1/2-way: hdwy over 1f out: swtchd lft ins fnl f: r.o strly: edgd lft fnl 75yds: wnt 2nd post: 2nd of 6 in gp* 9/1[3]

111- 3 hd **Reckless Abandon**[224] 7049 3-9-0 117 AdamKirby 5 116+
(Clive Cox) *prom far side: led gp and overall ldr 1/2-way: rdn 2f out: kpt on: hdd towards fin: lost 2nd post: 1st of 4 in gp* 3/1[2]

-241 4 1 1/2 **Sole Power**[21] 2019 6-9-4 113 FMBerry 11 110
(Edward Lynam, Ire) *trckd ldrs stands' side: rdn to ld gp over 1f out: hdd jst ins fnl f: no ex: 3rd of 6 in gp* 11/10[1]

5015 5 1/2 **Spirit Quartz (IRE)**[21] 2019 5-9-4 113 GeorgeBaker 1 108
(Robert Cowell) *w ldr far side: rdn 2f out: wknd fnl 100yds: 2nd of 4 in gp* 11/1

206- 6 3/4 **Morawij**[253] 6196 3-8-10 105 JamesDoyle 2 102
(Roger Varian) *stmbld s: hld up far side: hdwy 1/2-way: rdn and ev ch over 1f out: wknd ins fnl f: 3rd of 4 in gp* 33/1

25-2 7 1 1/4 **Masamah (IRE)**[17] 2152 7-9-4 106 LukeMorris 9 101
(Marco Botti) *racd stands' side: w ldr: rdn 1/2-way: wknd fnl f: 4th of 6 in gp* 33/1

0-40 8 nse **Doc Hay (USA)**[21] 2019 6-9-4 103 GrahamGibbons 8 101
(David O'Meara) *dwlt: in tch stands' side: rdn 1/2-way: sn btn: 5th of 6 in gp* 40/1

0-13 9 nk **Tangerine Trees**[21] 2019 8-9-4 106 (v) TomEaves 12 100
(Bryan Smart) *led stands' side gp: rdn 1/2-way: hdd over 1f out: wknd: last of 6 in gp* 14/1

0201 10 7 **Ballista (IRE)**[17] 2152 5-9-4 111 RichardKingscote 7 74
(Tom Dascombe) *racd far side: overall ldr: hdd 1/2-way: sn wknd* 16/1

59.25s (-1.55) **Going Correction** 0.0s/f (Good)
WFA 3 from 4yo+ 8lb 10 Ran SP% 118.5
Speed ratings (Par 115): **112,111,111,108,108 106,104,104,104,93**
toteswingers 1&2 £8.40, 1&3 £8.90, 2&3 £3.60 CSF £133.20 TOTE £14.40: £2.90, £2.40, £1.40; EX 82.20 Trifecta £527.70 Pool: £6441.66 - 9.15 winning units..
Owner Cheveley Park Stud **Bred** Peter McCutcheon **Trained** Six Mile Bottom, Cambs

FOCUS
This Group 2 sprint is something of a trial for the Group 1 sprints at Royal Ascot, and although there have been no recent winners of both races, the last two winners of this went on to be placed in the King's Stand Stakes. Up-to-scratch form for the grade, but a bit below recent runnings. The winner is rated to his form in this event in 2010 and 2011.

2663 BETFRED MOBILE LOTTO H'CAP (DIV I) — 6f

4:20 (4:21) (Class 4) (0-85,86) 4-Y-0+ £5,175 (£1,540; £769; £384) Stalls Centre

Form — RPR

4-23 1 **Chester Aristocrat**[21] 2028 4-8-10 74 LukeMorris 16 87
(Eric Alston) *trckd ldr against stands' rail: rdn to ld over 1f out: strly pressed ins fnl f: hld on wl* 11/2[3]

12-6 2 1/2 **Saloomy**[14] 2255 4-9-1 79 WilliamBuick 11 90+
(John Butler) *prom towards centre: rdn over 2f out: chal strly ins fnl f: kpt on* 4/1[2]

-200 3 1/2 **Taurus Twins**[31] 1765 7-9-0 78 (b) DaleSwift 13 88
(Richard Price) *led against stands' rail: rdn whn hdd over 1f out: kpt on* 22/1

130 4 4 1/2 **My Son Max**[9] 2388 5-8-13 82 RobertTart(5) 8 77
(P J O'Gorman) *hld up towards centre: rdn 1/2-way: kpt on one pce: nvr threatened ldrs* 8/1

112 5 1 **Polar Venture**[82] 881 4-8-11 75 AdamBeschizza 15 67+
(William Haggas) *stmbld s: hld up in rr towards centre: rdn over 2f out: kpt on one pce: nvr threatened* 9/4[1]

6-02 6 1/2 **Whozthecat (IRE)**[7] 2459 6-9-3 86 JasonHart(5) 1 77
(Declan Carroll) *led trio who racd far side: clrly a bhd ldrs in main gp fr 1/2-way* 16/1

1400 7 1 1/4 **Rio Cobolo (IRE)**[45] 1460 7-8-7 71 oh9 (v) PaulQuinn 6 58
(David Nicholls) *prom towards centre: rdn over 2f out: wknd fnl f* 66/1

0-20 8 nk **Decision By One**[17] 2150 4-9-5 83 (t) RichardKingscote 10 69
(Tom Dascombe) *racd towards centre: w ldr: rdn 1/2-way: wknd fnl f* 8/1

-546 9 1 1/4 **Defence Council (IRE)**[15] 2239 5-9-1 79 TomEaves 9 61
(Mel Brittain) *dwlt: hld up towards centre: nvr threatened* 16/1

10-0 10 2 1/2 **Henry Bee**[15] 2239 4-8-5 76 EireannCagney(7) 14 50
(Richard Fahey) *hld up towards centre: nvr threatened* 33/1

-03 11 3/4 **Sunraider (IRE)**[45] 1460 6-8-9 73 ow1 MickyFenton 12 44
(Paul Midgley) *dwlt: sn in tch towards centre: rdn 1/2-way: sn btn* 25/1

5305 12 3/4 **Holy Angel (IRE)**[15] 2239 4-8-0 71 oh1 (e) RachelRichardson(7) 2 40
(Tim Easterby) *1 of 3 who racd far side: wknd fnl 2f* 33/1

331- **13** *16* **Fathsta (IRE)**[154] 2232 8-9-1 **79** ... AdamKirby 3
(Patrick Morris) *1 of 3 who racd far side: sn struggling: wl bhd 1/2-way: t.o* **14/1**

1m 12.84s (-0.96) **Going Correction** 0.0s/f (Good) **13** Ran SP% **122.4**
Speed ratings (Par 105): **106,105,104,98,97 96,95,94,92,89 88,87,66**
toteswingers 1&2 £4.80, 1&3 £30.90, 2&3 £22.80 CSF £27.00 CT £463.67 TOTE £6.10: £2.00, £1.70, £5.20; EX 40.40 Trifecta £975.10 Pool: £2277.25 - 1.75 winning units..
Owner Paul Buist & John Thompson **Bred** J A E Hobby **Trained** Longton, Lancs

FOCUS
The first division of this fair sprint saw those that raced more towards the stands' side prevailing, with three drawing clear. A similar time to division II and a personal best from the winner.

2664 BETFRED MOBILE LOTTO H'CAP (DIV II) 6f
4:55 (4:55) (Class 4) (0-85,85) 4-Y-O+ **£5,175** (£1,540; £769; £384) **Stalls** Centre

Form RPR

-000 **1** **Bonnie Charlie**[7] 2460 7-8-10 **74** ... PaulQuinn 11 83
(David Nicholls) *hld up in rr: n.m.r 2f out: pushed along and hdwy over 1f out: angled rt into clr appr fnl f: r.o wl to ld post* **33/1**

0-22 **2** *shd* **Meandmyshadow**[17] 2166 5-8-11 **75** ... DaleSwift 9 84
(Alan Brown) *led: rdn over 2f out: strly pressed ins fnl f: kpt on: hdd post* **11/1**

-660 **3** *hd* **Mappin Time (IRE)**[21] 2007 5-9-2 **80** ... (p) FrederikTylicki 8 88
(Tim Easterby) *hld up: hdwy 1/2-way: chsd ldrs whn bmpd over 1f out: rcvrd to chal strly ins fnl f: kpt on: jst failed* **9/2**[2]

6011 **4** *2 ¾* **Tango Sky (IRE)**[8] 2410 4-8-13 **77** ... PatCosgrave 6 76
(David Nicholls) *hld up: stdy hdwy 1/2-way: rdn to chse ldr over 1f out: no ex ins fnl f* **10/1**

1062 **5** *shd* **Waking Warrior**[14] 2255 5-8-5 **76** ... (tp) KevinStott(7) 12 75
(Kevin Ryan) *midfield towards outer: rdn and hdwy to chse ldr 2f out: edgd rt over 1f out: no ex fnl f* **7/1**[3]

3414 **6** *1 ¾* **Beckermet (IRE)**[14] 2275 11-8-8 **72** ... PJMcDonald 13 65
(Ruth Carr) *prom: rdn 1/2-way: wknd over 1f out* **10/1**

5-05 **7** *½* **Pea Shooter**[21] 2031 4-9-0 **78** ... (p) JamesDoyle 4 70
(Kevin Ryan) *chsd ldrs: rdn over 2f out: edgd lft over 1f out: wknd fnl f* **4/1**[1]

60-0 **8** *2 ½* **Springinmystep (IRE)**[32] 1745 4-9-7 **85** ... AdamKirby 14 69
(Ed de Giles) *midfield: rdn 1/2-way: nvr threatened* **9/1**

0-66 **9** *1 ¼* **Oneladyowner**[30] 1787 5-9-1 **79** ... SeanLevey 15 59
(David Brown) *chsd ldrs: rdn 1/2-way: wknd over 1f out* **15/2**

56-0 **10** *¾* **Another Try (IRE)**[24] 1922 8-8-13 **82** ... MichaelJMMurphy(5) 1 59
(Alan Jarvis) *hld up: pushed along 1/2-way: nvr threatened* **10/1**

0-00 **11** *3 ½* **Carambola**[6] 2476 7-9-1 **79** ... TomEaves 7 45+
(Mel Brittain) *trckd ldrs: pushed along and lost pl whn bdly hmpd 2f out: no ch after* **20/1**

61-3 **12** *2 ½* **Going French (IRE)**[35] 1694 6-8-4 **71** oh1 ... RaulDaSilva(3) 5 29
(Dai Burchell) *prom: rdn over 3f out: wknd fnl 2f* **16/1**

1m 12.89s (-0.91) **Going Correction** 0.0s/f (Good) **12** Ran SP% **121.6**
Speed ratings (Par 105): **106,105,105,101,101 99,98,95,93,92 88,84**
toteswingers 1&2 £53.70, 1&3 £37.10, 2&3 £27.10 CSF £369.54 CT £1968.75 TOTE £43.90: £10.60, £3.40, £1.90; EX 170.60 Trifecta £1506.60 Part won. Pool: £2008.83 - 0.80 winning units..
Owner Gaga Syndicate **Bred** C D S Bryce And Mrs M Bryce **Trained** Sessay, N Yorks

FOCUS
The second leg of this sprint handicap was run fractionally slower than the preceding contest. There was a surprise result with the winner bouncing back to form.

2665 BETFRED MOBILE CASINO H'CAP 7f
5:30 (5:31) (Class 3) (0-90,90) 4-Y-O+ **£9,703** (£2,887; £1,443; £721) **Stalls** Low

Form RPR

25-4 **1** **Redvers (IRE)**[14] 2254 5-9-6 **89** ... (b) GeorgeBaker 7 101
(Ed Vaughan) *hld up in midfield: gng wl whn n.m.r over 2f out tl wl over 1f out: angled into clr appr fnl f: pushed along to ld fnl 100yds: kpt on wl* **4/1**[3]

0-63 **2** *2* **Zacynthus (IRE)**[12] 2310 5-9-3 **89** ... PatrickHills(3) 4 96
(Luca Cumani) *midfield: stdy hdwy fr 3f out: rdn to ld appr fnl f: hdd fnl 100yds: sn no ch w wnr* **7/2**[2]

-005 **3** *¾* **Al Muheer (IRE)**[7] 2463 8-8-8 **82** ... (b) JasonHart(5) 12 90+
(Ruth Carr) *swtchd lft s: hld up in rr: n.m.r over 1f out: stl only 8th jst ins fnl f: kpt on wl: nrst fin* **14/1**

60-R **4** *nk* **Ducal**[8] 2424 5-9-6 **89** ... ShaneKelly 13 93
(Mike Murphy) *hld up: rdn and hdwy over 2f out: chsd ldrs over 1f out: one pce fnl f* **28/1**

-211 **5** *1* **Sandy Lane (IRE)**[37] 1646 4-9-1 **84** ... GrahamGibbons 1 85+
(David O'Meara) *led: rdn and one pce whn hdd over 1f out: wknd fnl 100yds* **11/4**[1]

0-54 **6** *¾* **Powerful Presence (IRE)**[22] 1992 7-8-11 **85** ... DavidBergin(5) 3 84
(David O'Meara) *trckd ldrs: rdn over 2f out: one pce: wknd fnl 100yds* **16/1**

00-0 **7** *nk* **Sir Reginald**[33] 1720 5-9-3 **86** ... FrederikTylicki 2 85+
(Richard Fahey) *midfield on inner: pushed along 3f out: persistently n.m.r towards rail fnl 2f* **10/1**

00-0 **8** *nk* **Trade Secret**[56] 1232 6-9-2 **85** ... TomEaves 9 83
(Mel Brittain) *hld up: rdn over 3f out: kpt on fnl f: nvr threatened* **33/1**

6000 **9** *2* **Imperial Djay (IRE)**[7] 2463 8-8-11 **80** ... PJMcDonald 6 72
(Ruth Carr) *prom: rdn to ld over 1f out: hdd appr fnl f: wknd* **20/1**

0-40 **10** *2 ¾* **Comrade Bond**[7] 2450 5-8-8 **77** ... LukeMorris 11 62
(Mark H Tompkins) *chsd ldr: rdn 3f out: wknd appr fnl f* **20/1**

0120 **11** *3* **King Of Eden (IRE)**[14] 2254 7-9-7 **90** ... (b) PatCosgrave 8 67
(Eric Alston) *midfield: rdn over 3f out: sn btn* **16/1**

000- **12** *4* **Johnny Castle**[205] 7508 5-9-5 **88** ... SeanLevey 10 54
(Amanda Perrett) *midfield: rdn over 3f out: wknd over 1f out* **7/1**

1m 29.47s (-1.23) **Going Correction** 0.0s/f (Good) **12** Ran SP% **124.8**
Speed ratings (Par 107): **107,104,103,103,102 101,101,100,98,95 91,87**
toteswingers 1&2 £3.80, 1&3 £12.10, 2&3 £15.50 CSF £18.53 CT £189.58 TOTE £4.40: £1.60, £1.70, £3.10; EX 19.00 Trifecta £184.00 Pool: £2102.36 - 8.56 winning units..
Owner M J C Hawkes and E J C Hawkes **Bred** Peter Jones And G G Jones **Trained** Newmarket, Suffolk

FOCUS
A strong, competitive handicap and a race that could provide pointers for the Buckingham Palace Handicap at Royal Ascot. It was strong run and the winner built on his reappearance for a personal best.

2666 BETFRED "BONUS KING BINGO" H'CAP 7f
6:00 (6:01) (Class 3) (0-95,89) 3-Y-O **£9,703** (£2,887; £1,443; £721) **Stalls** Low

Form RPR

15-0 **1** **So Beloved**[36] 1668 3-9-5 **87** ...[1] JamesDoyle 3 93+
(Roger Charlton) *hld up in tch: rdn to chse ldng pair 2f out: kpt on to ld towards fin* **4/1**[2]

0-01 **2** *½* **Capo Rosso (IRE)**[14] 2285 3-9-6 **88** ... RichardKingscote 7 92
(Tom Dascombe) *led: rdn 2f out: kpt on: edgd rt fnl 100yds: hdd towards fin* **4/1**[2]

0-52 **3** *1 ¼* **Lazarus Bell**[10] 2371 3-9-2 **84** ... DaleSwift 6 85
(Alan Brown) *dwlt: hld up in rr: rdn and hdwy on inner 2f out: kpt on fnl f* **14/1**

11-0 **4** *¾* **George Rooke (IRE)**[10] 2371 3-8-11 **82** ... JulieBurke(3) 1 81
(Kevin Ryan) *pressed ldr: rdn over 2f out: wknd fnl 100yds* **11/2**[3]

3-1 **5** *8* **Enobled**[16] 2192 3-9-7 **89** ... WilliamBuick 4 66
(Sir Michael Stoute) *trckd ldng pair: rdn over 2f out: sn wknd* **6/5**[1]

0-56 **6** *5* **Dream Maker (IRE)**[10] 2371 3-9-7 **89** ... TomEaves 9 53
(Tim Easterby) *hld up in tch: rdn 3f out: sn wknd* **20/1**

1m 30.09s (-0.61) **Going Correction** 0.0s/f (Good) **6** Ran SP% **112.3**
Speed ratings (Par 103): **103,102,101,100,91 85**
toteswingers 1&2 £4.00, 1&3 £2.80, 2&3 £7.80 CSF £20.06 CT £198.26 TOTE £6.20: £2.50, £1.90; EX 26.30 Trifecta £89.80 Pool: £1506.79 - 12.57 winning units..
Owner K Abdullah **Bred** Juddmonte Farms Ltd **Trained** Beckhampton, Wilts

FOCUS
Another good, competitive handicap with only 7lb covering the entire field on official ratings. The time was 0.62.secs slower than the preceding contest for older horses. The bare form is ordinary for the grade.
T/Jkpt: Not won. T/Plt: £830.40 to a £1 stake. Pool: £132,695.78 - 116.65 winning units T/Qpdt: £152.40 to a £1 stake. Pool: £7047.09 - 34.20 winning units AS

2426 YORK (L-H)
Saturday, May 25

OFFICIAL GOING: Good (7.2)
Wind: Light half against Weather: Sunny and warm

2667 32RED CASINO STKS (CONDITIONS RACE) 7f
1:50 (1:50) (Class 3) 3-Y-O+ **£11,320** (£3,368; £1,683; £841) **Stalls** Low

Form RPR

4-06 **1** **Pintura**[14] 2258 6-9-2 **106** ... NeilCallan 5 103
(Kevin Ryan) *in tch: hdwy over 3f out: chsd ldng pair and rdn along over 2f out: led wl over 1f out: sn jnd and drvn: edgd lft ins fnl f: kpt on gamely towards fin* **9/2**[2]

240- **2** *¾* **Morache Music**[245] 6468 5-9-2 **103** ... SteveDrowne 6 101
(Peter Makin) *hld up: hdwy 3f out: trckd ldrs 2f out: rdn to chal over 1f out: ev ch ins fnl f tl drvn and no ex towards fin* **13/2**[3]

00-0 **3** *1 ¾* **Redact (IRE)**[56] 1244 4-9-2 **97** ... RyanMoore 2 96
(Richard Hannon) *hld up in rr: pushed along 3f out: rdn 2f out: styd on wl u.p fnl f: tk 3rd nr fin* **9/2**[2]

0-30 **4** *½* **Our Jonathan**[42] 1537 6-9-2 **104** ... SilvestreDeSousa 1 95
(Tim Pitt) *in tch: hdwy over 3f out: rdn to ld 2 1/2f out: hdd and drvn wl over 1f out: grad wknd* **7/4**[1]

0/5- **5** *8* **Spiritual Star (IRE)**[399] 1509 4-8-11 **109** ... ThomasBrown(5) 3 73
(Andrew Balding) *chsd clr ldr: hdwy over 3f out: cl up 2 1/2f out: sn rdn and wknd wl over 1f out* **9/2**[2]

0-30 **6** *17* **Rodrigo De Torres**[21] 2029 6-9-6 **94** ... (v[1]) PaulMulrennan 4 44
(David Nicholls) *led and sn clr: hdd 2 1/2f out: sn wknd* **14/1**

1m 25.37s (0.07) **Going Correction** +0.125s/f (Good) **6** Ran SP% **110.9**
Speed ratings (Par 107): **104,103,101,100,91 72**
toteswingers 1&2 £4.60, 1&3 £5.70, 2&3 £8.90 CSF £31.50 TOTE £4.80: £2.60, £3.50; EX 35.40 Trifecta £307.20 Pool: £726.48 - 1.77 winning units..
Owner Michael Beaumont **Bred** Dulverton Equine **Trained** Hambleton, N Yorks

FOCUS
Rail from 9f to entrance to home straight moved out 3m adding 7yds to races on Round course. A decent little conditions race, run at a true gallop throughout. The form is rated cautiously, with doubts over the field.

2668 STOWE FAMILY LAW LLP GRAND CUP (LISTED RACE) 1m 6f
2:20 (2:21) (Class 1) 4-Y-O+ **£22,953** (£8,869; £4,573; £2,413) **Stalls** Low

Form RPR

430- **1** **Songcraft (IRE)**[196] 7689 5-9-0 **105** ... SilvestreDeSousa 4 108+
(Saeed bin Suroor) *trckd ldng pair: swtchd rt and rdn to ld 2f out: sn hung lft and clr: idled ins fnl f: sn shkn up and rdn out* **11/10**[1]

46-4 **2** *1 ¼* **Bite Of The Cherry**[21] 2012 4-8-9 **97** ... RyanMoore 6 101
(Michael Bell) *racd wd early: led: qcknd over 4f out: jnd and qcknd again 3f out: rdn and hdd 2f out: sltly hmpd and swtchd rt 1 1/2f out: sn drvn and kpt on wl fnl f* **10/3**[2]

30-1 **3** *6* **Address Unknown**[17] 2149 6-9-0 **101** ... PaulHanagan 2 98
(Richard Fahey) *hld up in tch: effrt on inner 3f out: rdn over 2f out: no imp fnl f* **4/1**[3]

10-0 **4** *¾* **Ile De Re (FR)**[17] 2149 7-9-0 **103** ... GrahamLee 5 97
(Donald McCain) *trckd ldr: hdwy 4f out: cl up 3f out: rdn to chal over 2f out: sn drvn and wknd over 1f out* **12/1**

12 **R** **Mad Moose (IRE)**[15] 2212 9-9-0 **100** ... WilliamTwiston-Davies 3
(Nigel Twiston-Davies) *ref to r: tk no part* **7/1**

3m 1.18s (0.98) **Going Correction** +0.125s/f (Good) **5** Ran SP% **110.9**
Speed ratings (Par 111): **102,101,97,97,**
CSF £5.08 TOTE £2.10: £1.40, £2.10; EX 4.80 Trifecta £13.70 Pool: £1195.59 - 65.08 winning units..
Owner Godolphin **Bred** Darley **Trained** Newmarket, Suffolk

The Form Book Flat, Raceform Ltd, Compton, RG20 6NL.

FOCUS
Not a particularly competitive race for the grade, even before Mad Moose decided to stand still having come out of the stalls, and they went just a steady gallop, resulting in a dash for home. The winner is rated a little off his very best.

2669 32RED.COM SPRINT (HANDICAP STKS) 5f
2:55 (2:56) (Class 2) (0-105,103) 3-Y-O+
£31,125 (£9,320; £4,660; £2,330; £1,165; £585) Stalls Centre

Form RPR
-233 1 **Kingsgate Choice (IRE)**[17] 2150 6-9-4 **100**.................... LeeTopliss(3) 2 111
(Ed de Giles) *chsd ldrs: rdn along 2f out: swtchd lft to outer and gd hdwy over 1f out: led jst ins fnl f: kpt on strly* **9/1**
5614 2 ½ **York Glory (USA)**[10] 2366 5-9-5 **98**..................................(b) NeilCallan 16 110+
(Kevin Ryan) *hld up: hdwy 2f out: effrt and nt clr run over 1f out: rdn and styd on strly fnl f* **13/2**[2]
-066 3 nk **Lady Gibraltar**[15] 2207 4-8-7 **86**... MartinDwyer 5 94
(Alan Jarvis) *prom: hdwy and cl up 2f out: rdn to ld over 1f out: hdd jst ins fnl f: drvn and kpt on* **33/1**
00-6 4 shd **Elusivity (IRE)**[21] 2019 5-9-10 **103**.............................. DanielTudhope 19 111
(David O'Meara) *trckd ldrs: hdwy over 1f out: rdn and ev ch whn hung lft ent fnl f: no ex towards fin* **9/1**
5-01 5 ¾ **Duke Of Firenze**[21] 2014 4-9-4 **97**.................................... RyanMoore 12 102
(Sir Michael Stoute) *hld up: effrt 2f out and sn nt clr run: swtchd lft over 1f out: rdn: n.m.r and swtchd lft again ins fnl f: kpt on: nrst fin* **4/1**[1]
4-00 6 nk **Barnet Fair**[15] 2207 5-8-11 **90**... KierenFox 17 94
(Richard Guest) *stdd s and hld up in rr: gd hdwy wl over 1f out: rdn and styd on wl fnl f: nrst fin* **25/1**
03-1 7 ¾ **Sir Maximilian (IRE)**[9] 2388 4-8-9 **88**......................... StevieDonohoe 20 90
(Ian Williams) *hld up towards rr: hdwy wl over 1f out: rdn and kpt on fnl f: nrst fin* **12/1**
4430 8 nk **Silvanus (IRE)**[17] 2150 8-8-9 **88** ow1.......................... RussKennemore 8 88
(Paul Midgley) *chsd ldrs: rdn along wl over 1f out: kpt on same pce fnl f* **33/1**
10-0 9 shd **Ubetterbegood (ARG)**[17] 2150 5-9-1 **94**........................ SteveDrowne 3 94
(Robert Cowell) *towards rr: pushed along 2f out: sn rdn and edgd lft: kpt on ins fnl f: nrst fin* **33/1**
50-5 10 ½ **Magical Macey (USA)**[9] 2396 6-9-0 **98**............................(b) LMcNiff(5) 6 96
(David Barron) *cl up: rdn along 2f out: sn wknd* **14/1**
-002 11 ¾ **Bosun Breese**[7] 2461 8-8-6 **85**......................... SilvestreDeSousa 10 81
(David Barron) *chsd ldrs: rdn along 2f out: grad wknd* **14/1**
-051 12 nk **Ancient Cross**[9] 2396 9-9-2 **95**................................(t) PaulMulrennan 15 90+
(Michael Easterby) *towards rr: hdwy whn nt clr run over 1f out: sn swtchd rt and rdn: n.m.r ins fnl f: n.d* **14/1**
0-43 13 hd **Noble Storm (USA)**[7] 2461 7-9-3 **96**................................ GrahamLee 13 90
(Ed McMahon) *cl up: rdn along 2f out: sn wknd* **20/1**
00-0 14 nk **Ponty Acclaim (IRE)**[9] 2396 4-8-12 **91**...................... DuranFentiman 14 84
(Tim Easterby) *chsd ldrs: rdn along 2f out: hld whn hmpd 1f out: one pce after* **20/1**
-300 15 ½ **Bogart**[10] 2368 4-9-6 **99**... AmyRyan 9 90
(Kevin Ryan) *cl up: ev ch 2f out: sn rdn and wknd over 1f out* **14/1**
4125 15 dht **Oldjoesaid**[7] 2459 9-7-12 **82** ow1........................... ShirleyTeasdale(5) 18 73
(Paul Midgley) *dwlt: a towards rr* **25/1**
-054 17 nk **Fitz Flyer (IRE)**[9] 2396 7-8-7 **86**................................(v) AdrianNicholls 4 76
(David Nicholls) *dwlt and in rr: hdwy over 2f out: swtchd lft and rdn to chse ldrs wl over 1f out: sn wknd* **14/1**
06-3 18 2½ **Judge 'n Jury**[9] 2396 9-9-1 **99**..................................(t) ThomasBrown(5) 7 80
(Ronald Harris) *slt ld: rdn along 2f out: hdd over 1f out and sn wknd* **8/1**[3]
124- 19 11 **Strange Magic (IRE)**[184] 7828 3-8-8 **95**......................... PaulHanagan 1 36
(Richard Fahey) *racd alone far rail: in tch: rdn along over 2f out: sn wknd* **25/1**

58.58s (-0.72) **Going Correction** +0.125s/f (Good)
WFA 3 from 4yo+ 8lb **19** Ran SP% **135.4**
Speed ratings (Par 109): **110,109,108,108,107 106,105,105,105,104 103,102,102,101,100 100,100,96,78**
CSF £64.91 CT £1953.36 TOTE £13.00: £3.50, £1.80, £6.10, £3.30; EX 83.20 TRIFECTA Not won..
Owner T Gould **Bred** Michael Staunton **Trained** Ledbury, H'fords

FOCUS
A typically wide-open sprint for the track in which they looked to go very quick up front early, with much of the pace coming from the middle-to-low drawn runners. Solid form.

2670 YORKSHIRE REGIMENT EBF MEDIAN AUCTION MAIDEN STKS 6f
3:30 (3:34) (Class 3) 2-Y-O
£7,439 (£2,213; £1,106; £553) Stalls Centre

Form RPR
1 **Astaire (IRE)** 2-9-5 0... NeilCallan 14 89+
(Kevin Ryan) *mde virtually all: rdn over 1f out: kpt on wl towards fin* **14/1**[3]
2 ¾ **Kommander Kirkup** 2-9-5 0... PaulMulrennan 13 87+
(Michael Dods) *chsd ldrs: rdn along 2f out: kpt on wl u.p fnl f* **40/1**
5 3 ½ **Jallota**[8] 2411 2-9-5 0.. MatthewDavies 12 85
(Mick Channon) *a.p: cl up 1/2-way: chsd wnr 2f out: sn rdn: drvn and kpt on same pce ins fnl f* **7/1**[2]
4 3¾ **Munjally** 2-9-5 0.. PaulHanagan 4 74+
(Richard Hannon) *trckd ldrs: effrt 2f out: sn rdn and no imp appr fnl f* **5/1**[1]
6 5 1¼ **New Bidder**[24] 1930 2-9-5 0.. RussKennemore 9 70
(Jedd O'Keeffe) *towards rr: hdwy 2f out: sn rdn and kpt on fnl f: nrst fin* **33/1**
6 1¾ **Tancred (IRE)** 2-9-5 0.. SteveDrowne 5 65+
(Peter Chapple-Hyam) *towards rr: hdwy 2f out: swtchd lft and rdn over 1f out: kpt on fnl f: nrst fin* **33/1**
7 ½ **Sir Jack Layden** 2-9-5 0.. DanielTudhope 1 64
(David Brown) *towards rr: hdwy on wd outside 2f out: rdn along and in tch over 1f out: sn one pce* **25/1**
8 ½ **Imshivalla (IRE)** 2-8-7 0... SamanthaBell(7) 15 57
(Richard Fahey) *towards rr tl sme late hdwy* **40/1**
3 9 1¼ **Tiger Twenty Two**[9] 2401 2-9-2 0.................................... LeeTopliss(3) 16 58
(Richard Fahey) *in tch: rdn along 2f out: drvn and wknd over 1f out* **5/1**[1]
10 3¼ **McCarthy Mor (IRE)** 2-9-5 0.. TedDurcan 11 49
(Richard Fahey) *a towards rr* **7/1**[2]
11 3¾ **Street Boss (IRE)** 2-9-5 0... DuranFentiman 8 37
(Tim Easterby) *s.i.s: a towards rr* **33/1**
12 ¾ **Roman Legend (IRE)** 2-9-5 0... GrahamLee 2 35
(Jeremy Noseda) *a towards rr* **16/1**
13 hd **Who Followed Who** 2-8-12 0.................................. DanielleMooney(7) 18 34
(Nigel Tinkler) *prom: rdn along over 2f out: sn wknd* **50/1**
14 10 **Viva Verglas (IRE)** 2-9-5 0................................... SilvestreDeSousa 7
(David Barron) *t.k.h: hld up: a towards rr* **25/1**
4 P **Bens Boy (IRE)**[8] 2421 2-9-5 0.. MartinDwyer 6
(Derek Shaw) *chsd ldrs whn lost action after 2f and p.u: fatally injured* **25/1**

1m 12.58s (0.68) **Going Correction** +0.125s/f (Good) **15** Ran SP% **98.1**
Speed ratings (Par 97): **100,99,98,93,91 89,88,88,86,82 77,76,75,62,**
toteswingers 1&2 £57.60, 2&3 £57.60, 1&3 £15.30 CSF £271.74 TOTE £14.10: £3.30, £8.70, £2.60; EX 301.00 TRIFECTA Not won..
Owner Mrs Angie Bailey **Bred** John O'Connor **Trained** Hambleton, N Yorks
■ Royal Mezyan was withdrawn (9/4, vet's advice at s). Deduct 30p in the £ under R4.

FOCUS
Little got into this from off the pace, but it was probably a fair maiden, even with the late withdrawal of favourite Royal Mezyan. The winner impressed and will almost certainly do better.

2671 YORK AND RYEDALE DOMESTIC APPLIANCES STKS (H'CAP) 1m 4f
4:00 (4:08) (Class 3) (0-90,90) 4-Y-O+ £9,703 (£2,887; £1,443; £721) Stalls Centre

Form RPR
-040 1 **Sirvino**[10] 2369 8-8-11 **85**.. LMcNiff(5) 11 95
(David Barron) *hld up towards rr: hdwy 3f out: effrt and n.m.r over 1f out: sn swtchd lft and rdn: styd on wl fnl f to ld last 75yds* **8/1**
3-30 2 nk **High Office**[10] 2369 7-8-10 **79**.. PaulHanagan 15 88
(Richard Fahey) *trckd ldrs: hdwy 3f out: effrt 2f out: sn rdn and styd on to ld ins fnl f: sn drvn and edgd lft: hdd and no ex last 75yds* **10/1**
31 3 2¼ **Roman Flight (IRE)**[14] 2277 5-9-5 **88**......................(v) DanielTudhope 9 93
(David O'Meara) *trckd ldng pair: chsd ldr over 5f out: led 3f out: rdn along wl over 1f out: drvn and hdd jst ins fnl f: kpt on same pce* **3/1**[1]
10-0 4 nk **Bridle Belle**[10] 2365 5-9-1 **87**... LeeTopliss(3) 5 92
(Richard Fahey) *trckd ldrs: hdwy 4f out: chsd ldrs over 2f out: sn rdn and kpt on fnl f* **16/1**
5-50 5 shd **Gabrial's Star**[15] 2205 4-8-12 **81**....................................(p) GrahamLee 12 86
(Ed Dunlop) *hld up towards rr: hdwy 3f out: rdn 2f out: kpt on u.p appr fnl f: nrst fin* **25/1**
33-1 6 1½ **Singzak**[26] 1889 5-8-0 **76** oh4.................................. MatthewHopkins(7) 10 78
(Michael Easterby) *led: rdn along and hdd 3f out: cl up tl drvn and wknd over 1f out* **28/1**
01-0 7 nk **Pintrada**[10] 2369 5-8-7 **76** oh1.. TedDurcan 13 78
(James Bethell) *hld up in rr: hdwy 3f out: rdn along 2f out: kpt on appr fnl f: nrst fin* **12/1**
460- 8 hd **Lyric Street (IRE)**[224] 7051 5-9-7 **90**.................................... RyanMoore 14 92
(Jeremy Noseda) *in tch on outer: effrt 3f out: sn rdn along and sltly outpcd: kpt on u.p fnl f* **6/1**[3]
00-0 9 1¾ **Franciscan**[42] 1536 5-9-4 **87**...(b[1]) NeilCallan 7 86
(Luca Cumani) *dwlt: towards rr: hdwy over 3f out: rdn along over 2f out: sn no imp* **14/1**
0004 10 5 **Bollin Greta**[10] 2369 8-8-7 **76** oh1.................................... DuranFentiman 3 67
(Tim Easterby) *hld up towards rr: hdwy on inner 4f out: chsd ldrs wl over 2f out: sn rdn along and wknd* **12/1**
221- 11 1 **Ace Of Valhalla**[292] 4882 4-9-4 **87**.................................... PaulMulrennan 2 76
(Sir Henry Cecil) *trckd ldrs: hdwy 4f out: rdn along wl over 2f out: drvn and wknd wl over 1f out* **7/2**[2]
3120 12 shd **Flying Power**[16] 2185 5-9-2 **85**.. PaddyAspell 1 74
(John Norton) *chsd ldr: rdn along 3f out: grad wknd fnl 2f* **25/1**

2m 32.82s (-0.38) **Going Correction** +0.125s/f (Good) **12** Ran SP% **120.8**
Speed ratings (Par 107): **106,105,104,104,104 103,102,102,101,98 97,97**
toteswingers 1&2 £24.50, 1&3 £7.30, 2&3 £1.90 CSF £85.19 CT £299.09 TOTE £9.40: £2.80, £3.60, £1.60; EX 72.00 Trifecta £208.50 Pool: £1480.06 - 5.32 winning units..
Owner Theo Williams and Charles Mocatta **Bred** Allan Perry **Trained** Maunby, N Yorks

FOCUS
This was run at quite a modest gallop and several were caught out when the tempo quickened early in the straight. Those who raced prominently were generally favoured. The winner is rated in line with last autumn's form.

2672 ICE CO EBF MAIDEN STKS 6f
4:35 (4:36) (Class 4) 3-Y-O £8,086 (£2,406; £1,202; £601) Stalls Centre

Form RPR
3-2 1 **Pearl Bridge**[53] 1299 3-9-5 0.................................. SilvestreDeSousa 8 83
(Ralph Beckett) *prom: pushed along 2f out: rdn over 1f out: drvn and edgd lft ins fnl f: styd on wl to ld nr line* **4/1**[2]
363 2 hd **Nurpur (IRE)**[31] 1760 3-9-0 70...............................[1] DanielTudhope 1 77
(David O'Meara) *wnt lft s: chsd ldrs: hdwy to ld over 2f out: rdn over 1f out: drvn ins fnl f: hdd nr line* **12/1**
4-20 3 1 **Kyllachy Rise**[21] 2021 3-9-5 83.. RyanMoore 4 79
(Richard Hannon) *trckd ldrs: nt clr run 2f out: sn swtchd rt and rdn: drvn and styd on wl fnl f: nrst fin* **8/13**[1]
342- 4 3¼ **Millkwood**[227] 6984 3-9-5 70.. PaulHanagan 2 68
(John Davies) *chsd ldrs: hdwy 1/2-way: cl up 2f out: sn rdn and one pce appr fnl f* **14/1**
0-32 5 3 **Baron Run**[25] 1911 3-9-5 70.. PaulMulrennan 5 59
(Mrs K Burke) *t.k.h: trckd ldrs: rdn along wl over 1f out: no imp* **14/1**
3 6 ½ **Grey Gazelle**[36] 1666 3-8-7 0...................................... DanielCremin(7) 7 52
(Mick Channon) *s.i.s: sn swtchd lft: hdwy to chse ldrs on outer over 2f out: sn rdn and wknd* **8/1**[3]
5-63 7 7 **Wotalad**[12] 2317 3-9-5 59.. AmyRyan 3 35
(Richard Whitaker) *cl up: rdn along 1/2-way: wknd over 2f out* **25/1**
U5- 8 7 **Wishing Bridge**[164] 8068 3-9-5 0.. NeilCallan 6 12
(Pat Eddery) *t.k.h: led: rdn along and hdd over 2f out: sn wknd* **40/1**

1m 12.3s (0.40) **Going Correction** +0.125s/f (Good) **8** Ran SP% **120.3**
Speed ratings (Par 101): **102,101,100,96,92 91,82,72**
toteswingers 1&2 £2.20, 1&3 £2.10, 2&3 £9.40 CSF £52.77 TOTE £4.90: £1.60, £2.30, £1.10; EX 60.00 Trifecta £117.10 Pool: £3707.67 - 23.74 winning units..
Owner Qatar Racing Limited **Bred** Whitsbury Manor Stud & Pigeon House Stud **Trained** Kimpton, Hants

FOCUS
Little depth to what was just an ordinary sprint maiden, with the favourite disappointing. The first two have been given credit, however.

2673 JOHN WRIGHT ELECTRICAL GENTLEMAN AMATEUR RIDERS' H'CAP 1m 2f 88y
5:10 (5:10) (Class 4) (0-80,81) 4-Y-O+ £6,239 (£1,935; £967; £484) Stalls Low

Form RPR
-116 1 **Whispering Warrior (IRE)**[21] 2018 4-11-4 **77**............. MrPCollington 6 94+
(David Simcock) *hld up: stdy hdwy 3f out: trckd ldrs 2f out: swtchd rt and effrt over 1f out: rdn to ld ins fnl f: sn clr* **9/2**[3]
-002 2 2¾ **Maven**[8] 2431 5-11-3 **81**.. MrWEasterby(5) 12 91
(Tim Easterby) *t.k.h early: trckd ldrs on inner: hdwy on bit 3f out: jnd ldr 2f out: led jst over 1f out: rdn and hdd ins fnl f: edgd lft and one pce* **10/3**[1]

5-02 **3** *3¼* **Merchant Of Medici**[6] 2478 6-10-8 **70**.......................... MrFMitchell(3) 8 73
(Micky Hammond) *hld up towards rr: hdwy 4f out: trckd ldrs over 2f out: swtchd lft and rdn over 1f out: one pce fnl f* **12/1**

0-02 **4** *1¼* **Sunnybridge Boy (IRE)**[24] 1936 4-11-1 **74**...................(v[1]) MrSWalker 5 75
(Mrs K Burke) *slt ld at stdy pce: pushed clr over 3f out: jnd 2f out: sn rdn and hdd jst over 1f out: wknd* **7/2**[2]

0022 **5** *5* **Pravda Street**[5] 2496 8-10-6 **70**.................................. MrJohnWilley(5) 2 62
(Brian Ellison) *s.i.s and bhd tl sme late hdwy* **14/1**

6-00 **6** *½* **Capitol Gain (IRE)**[16] 2196 4-10-6 **72**..................... MrORJSangster(7) 1 63
(Brian Meehan) *s.i.s and bhd tl sme late hdwy* **25/1**

0-51 **7** *3* **Meetings Man (IRE)**[15] 2234 6-10-6 **68**..............(p) ConorShoemark(3) 3 53
(Micky Hammond) *chsd ldrs on inner: rdn along 3f out: sn drvn and wknd 2f out* **8/1**

-300 **8** *1½* **Elspeth's Boy (USA)**[46] 1442 6-10-3 **67**.......................... MrDLevey(5) 4 49
(Philip Kirby) *t.k.h: trckd ldrs: hdwy over 3f out: rdn along over 2f out: sn wknd* **10/1**

114- **9** *8* **Jawaab (IRE)**[15] 7293 9-11-1 **74**.............................. MrTomGreenway 11 41
(Philip Kirby) *t.k.h early: a towards rr* **16/1**

6643 **10** *2¼* **Kiwi Bay**[15] 2232 8-11-1 **77**.. MrJHamilton(3) 9 40
(Michael Dods) *t.k.h: trckd ldng pair on outer: pushed along over 3f out: sn rdn and wknd* **17/2**

000- **11** *1* **Bountiful Girl**[159] 8146 4-10-1 **67**.................................... MrAFrench(7) 10 28
(John Wainwright) *plld hrd: cl up tl rdn and wknd qckly over 3f out* **33/1**

2m 15.51s (3.01) **Going Correction** +0.125s/f (Good) **11** Ran SP% **121.2**
Speed ratings (Par 105): **92,89,87,86,82 81,79,78,71,70 69**
toteswingers 1&2 £2.10, 1&3 £23.70, 2&3 £11.80 CSF £20.57 CT £173.63 TOTE £4.50: £1.90, £1.80, £3.70; EX 16.80 Trifecta £264.00 Pool: £1963.90 - 5.57 winning units..
Owner Daniel Pittack **Bred** Epona Bloodstock Ltd **Trained** Newmarket, Suffolk

FOCUS
This was run at little more than a dawdle through the early stages, resulting in a number of the runners racing keenly, and the pace only lifted off the final bend. A fairly positive view has been taken of the form.
T/Plt: £198.60 to a £1 stake. Pool: £120,257.96 - 441.99 winning units T/Qpdt: £26.40 to a £1 stake. Pool: £6530.65 - 182.80 winning units JR

2674 - (Foreign Racing) - See Raceform Interactive

2103 CURRAGH (R-H)

Saturday, May 25

OFFICIAL GOING: Good to firm

2675a COLD MOVE EUROPEAN BREEDERS FUND MARBLE HILL STKS (LISTED RACE) 5f

2:15 (2:15) 2-Y-O **£27,743** (£8,109; £3,841; £1,280)

RPR

1 **Coach House (IRE)**[23] 1968 2-9-3 .... JosephO'Brien 2 101+
(A P O'Brien, Ire) *trckd ldrs in 3rd tl tk clsr order under 2f out: led 1f out: sn pushed clr* **4/6**[1]

2 *1¾* **Club Wexford (IRE)**[10] 2373 2-9-3 .... KevinManning 5 95
(J S Bolger, Ire) *trckd ldr in 2nd: clsd to be on terms appr fnl f: sn hdd by wnr and nt qckn fnl 100yds: kpt on same pce* **7/2**[2]

3 *2¼* **Abbakova (IRE)**[6] 2482 2-8-12 .... PatSmullen 6 82
(W McCreery, Ire) *broke smartly and led tl hdd 1f out: sn no ex* **16/1**[3]

4 *½* **Fast In The Wind (IRE)**[48] 1411 2-9-3 .... ChrisHayes 4 85
(P D Deegan, Ire) *chsd ldrs in 4th tl tk clsr order on outer over 1f out: wandered ent fnl f: sn wknd* **7/2**[2]

5 *4¼* **Thrilled To Bits (IRE)** 2-8-12 ....(t) ShaneFoley 7 65
(A Oliver, Ire) *slowly away and sn in rr: pushed along bef 1/2-way: kpt on same pce for press ins fnl f* **33/1**

6 *nk* **Ain't No Surprise (IRE)**[22] 1996 2-8-12 .... WayneLordan 3 63
(T Stack, Ire) *w.w in 5th: pushed along 1/2-way and sn no imp: dropped to rr ins fnl f* **33/1**

1m 0.44s (-2.46) **Going Correction** -0.275s/f (Firm) **6** Ran SP% **116.2**
Speed ratings: **108,105,101,100,94 93**
CSF £3.63 TOTE £1.40: £1.02, £2.00; DF 3.20.
Owner Mrs John Magnier & Michael Tabor & Derrick Smith **Bred** Lesson In Humility Syndicate **Trained** Ballydoyle, Co Tipperary

FOCUS
The progressive Coach House put up a smart performance and looks Ascot bound. They went a reasonable clip and the form looks up to scratch.

2676a WEATHERBYS IRELAND GREENLANDS STKS (GROUP 3) 6f

2:45 (2:46) 3-Y-O+ **£33,028** (£9,654; £4,573; £1,524)

RPR

1 **Hitchens (IRE)**[20] 2046 8-9-9 .... JohnnyMurtagh 12 113
(David Barron) *chsd ldrs towards stands' side: prog and on terms ent fnl f: led fnl 100yds: styd on wl* **13/2**[3]

2 *nk* **Reply (IRE)**[7] 2446 4-9-9 105.......................................(v) JosephO'Brien 2 112
(A P O'Brien, Ire) *chsd ldrs on far side: prog to ld over 1f out: hdd fnl 100yds: kpt on wl* **11/1**

3 *½* **Slade Power (IRE)**[217] 7236 4-9-9 109......................... WayneLordan 15 110
(Edward Lynam, Ire) *w.w: bit to do 2f out: swtchd rt to outer ent fnl f: styd on wl into 3rd fnl 100yds: nvr quite on terms* **10/3**[1]

4 *½* **Russian Soul (IRE)**[56] 1265 5-9-9 108..........................(p) ShaneFoley 16 109
(M Halford, Ire) *w.w on stands' side: n.m.r over 1f out: styd on wl into 4th fnl 100yds* **14/1**

5 *¾* **Farmleigh House (IRE)**[70] 1032 6-9-9 104.................. NGMcCullagh 13 106+
(W J Martin, Ire) *chsd ldrs on stands' side: 4th 1/2-way: pushed along 2f out and nt qckn 1f out: kpt on again cl home* **33/1**

6 *½* **Arctic (IRE)**[252] 6268 6-9-9 104 .... RonanWhelan 6 105
(Tracey Collins, Ire) *led for nrly 2f: remained cl up and pressed ldr over 1f out: wknd appr fnl 100yds* **33/1**

7 *hd* **Nocturnal Affair (SAF)**[211] 7390 7-9-9 106..................... FergalLynch 8 104
(David Marnane, Ire) *carried rt on leaving stalls: sn towards rr: plenty to do appr fnl f: kpt on wl: nvr nrr* **11/1**

8 *nk* **Leitir Mor (IRE)**[21] 2021 3-9-3 111............................(tp) KevinManning 10 104
(J S Bolger, Ire) *led after nrly 2f tl hdd over 1f out: sn no ex and wknd* **10/1**

9 *½* **Parliament Square (IRE)**[15] 2243 3-9-0 108......(p) SeamieHeffernan 17 100
(A P O'Brien, Ire) *w.w towards rr on stands' side: n.m.r over 1f out: kpt on ins fnl f* **12/1**

10 *¾* **Dandy Boy (ITY)**[77] 954 7-9-9 110.................................. JamieSpencer 7 99
(David Marnane, Ire) *jinked rt on leaving stalls and sn in rr: swtchd rt ent fnl f: kpt on* **7/1**

11 *1* **Infanta Branca (USA)**[19] 2108 3-8-11 92..................... CO'Donoghue 11 91
(A P O'Brien, Ire) *a in rr: no threat appr fnl f* **25/1**

12 *nk* **Tiddliwinks**[10] 2368 7-10-0 .... PatSmullen 9 100
(Kevin Ryan) *jinked rt leaving stalls: chsd ldrs tl nt qckn over 1f out: sltly hmpd ins fnl f: sn no ex* **10/1**

13 *nk* **Antious (ARG)**[315] 6-9-9 110... TomQueally 14 94
(David Marnane, Ire) *nvr bttr than mid-div: no imp appr fnl f* **20/1**

14 *2¼* **Jimmy Styles**[37] 1637 9-9-12 ....(p) RichardHughes 5 90
(Clive Cox) *sn trckd ldr in 2nd tl pushed along 2f out: wknd appr fnl f* **5/1**[2]

15 *4½* **Angel's Pursuit (IRE)**[477] 420 6-9-9 98.......................... SamJames 3 72
(David Marnane, Ire) *chsd ldrs tl wknd over 1f out* **40/1**

16 *15* **Katla (IRE)**[196] 7690 5-9-6 102... WJLee 1 21
(J F Grogan, Ire) *chsd ldrs on far side tl no imp over 1f out and dropped to rr: eased* **33/1**

1m 11.76s (-3.74) **Going Correction** -0.275s/f (Firm)
WFA 3 from 4yo+ 9lb **16** Ran SP% **134.7**
Speed ratings: **113,112,111,111,110 109,109,108,108,107 105,105,105,102,96 76**
CSF £78.71 TOTE £5.90: £1.60, £4.80, £2.60; DF 100.80.
Owner Laurence O'Kane & Paul Murphy **Bred** Curragh Bloodstock Agency Ltd **Trained** Maunby, N Yorks

FOCUS
This was a slightly more competitive contest than the 2011 running but it saw a repeat performance from Hitchens.

2677a TATTERSALLS IRISH 2,000 GUINEAS (GROUP 1) (ENTIRE COLTS & FILLIES) 1m

3:20 (3:20) 3-Y-O

£141,463 (£46,341; £21,951; £7,317; £4,878; £2,439)

RPR

1 **Magician (IRE)**[15] 2211 3-9-0 110.................................. JosephO'Brien 3 123+
(A P O'Brien, Ire) *sn settled in 3rd: travelled wl in 2nd under 3f out: led 1f out and sn qcknd clr: comf* **10/3**[2]

2 *3½* **Gale Force Ten**[13] 2298 3-9-0 115..........................(p) SeamieHeffernan 9 115
(A P O'Brien, Ire) *w.w: prog in 3rd under 2f out: kpt on wl into 2nd fnl 100yds: nt trble wnr* **7/1**

3 *1½* **Trading Leather (IRE)**[9] 2398 3-9-0 109........................ KevinManning 1 112
(J S Bolger, Ire) *led after 1f: extended advantage to 5 l 3f out: sn pushed along and hdd 1f out: one pce and dropped to 3rd fnl 100yds* **6/1**[3]

4 *1½* **Havana Gold (IRE)**[13] 2298 3-9-0 .... JamieSpencer 7 108+
(Richard Hannon) *w.w: kpt on wl fr over 1f out to go 4th ins fnl 100yds: nvr nrr* **7/1**

5 *2½* **First Cornerstone (IRE)**[210] 7398 3-9-0 111.................... ChrisHayes 4 102
(A Oliver, Ire) *chsd ldrs: pushed along in modest 4th 3f out: no imp ent fnl f* **25/1**

6 *2½* **Flying The Flag (IRE)**[13] 2298 3-9-0 109..................... CO'Donoghue 10 97
(A P O'Brien, Ire) *hld up towards rr: pushed along under 3f out: kpt on for press tl no imp ins fnl f* **12/1**

7 *½* **George Vancouver (USA)**[21] 2021 3-9-0 115.................. PatSmullen 8 95
(A P O'Brien, Ire) *hld up in rr: modest late hdwy wout ever threatening* **10/1**

8 *2* **Van Der Neer**[21] 2021 3-9-0 .... RichardHughes 5 91
(Richard Hannon) *racd in mid-div: niggled along after 1/2-way in 5th: no imp whn short of room under 2f out: one pce* **5/2**[1]

9 *3½* **Fort Knox**[41] 1555 3-9-0 107.. JohnnyMurtagh 2 83
(J P Murtagh, Ire) *hld up towards rr: pushed along whn n.m.r under 2f out: nvr a threat* **10/1**

10 *7* **Ask Dad**[10] 2374 3-9-0 96.. NGMcCullagh 6 67
(J P Murtagh, Ire) *led for 1f: racd in clr 2nd tl dropped to 3rd under 3f out: sn wknd* **66/1**

1m 36.81s (-9.19) **Going Correction** -0.75s/f (Hard) **10** Ran SP% **122.1**
Speed ratings: **115,111,110,108,106 103,103,101,97,90**
CSF £28.63 CT £142.62 TOTE £3.10: £1.10, £3.60, £3.30; DF 23.10.
Owner Michael Tabor & Derrick Smith & Mrs John Magnier **Bred** Absolutelyfabulous Syndicate **Trained** Ballydoyle, Co Tipperary

FOCUS
The first two at Newmarket were not here and neither was Cristoforo Colombo. The pre-race billing had this as a pretty average renewal at best but time may reveal it was a bit better than that. Certainly it could prove a key Irish Derby trial. They went what looked a strong gallop - very few got into it. Another step forward from Magician, who rates a better than average winner.

2678a ABU DHABI STKS (GROUP 3) (F&M) 1m

3:55 (3:55) 4-Y-O+ **£31,707** (£9,268; £4,390; £1,463)

RPR

1 **Chigun**[20] 2045 4-9-0 .... TomQueally 2 114+
(Sir Henry Cecil) *w.w: t.k.h early: niggled along 3f out then swtchd lft and travelled wl to press ldrs over 1f out: sn led and qcknd clr fnl 100yds* **11/8**[1]

2 *2¾* **La Collina (IRE)**[10] 2375 4-9-0 106.................................. ChrisHayes 4 108
(Kevin Prendergast, Ire) *w.w tl tk clsr order 3f out: led briefly over 1f out: sn hdd and no match for wnr fnl 100yds* **6/1**

3 *3* **Lily's Angel (IRE)**[14] 2264 4-9-3 106.................................. GaryCarroll 1 104
(G M Lyons, Ire) *chsd ldrs on inner: pushed along over 2f out: nt qckn w principals ins fnl f: kpt on same pce to go 3rd clsng stages* **7/2**[2]

4 *nk* **Was (IRE)**[217] 7237 4-9-5 113......................................(p) JosephO'Brien 3 105
(A P O'Brien, Ire) *disp tl settled in 2nd after 1f: led briefly under 2f out: sn hdd and one pce: dropped to 4th clsng stages* **11/2**[3]

5 *½* **Aloof (IRE)**[27] 1862 4-9-3 106... WayneLordan 8 102
(David Wachman, Ire) *trckd ldrs in 3rd tl pushed along and nt qckn appr fnl f: kpt on one pce* **7/1**

6 *5½* **Precious Stone (IRE)**[52] 1336 4-9-0 95................................(p) WJLee 9 86
(David Wachman, Ire) *led after 1f tl hdd over 1f: sn wknd* **20/1**

7 *3¾* **Sindjara (USA)**[279] 5397 4-9-0 95.............................. DeclanMcDonogh 6 78
(John M Oxx, Ire) *t.k.h and trckd ldrs in 4th: pushed along and nt qckn under 2f out: sn dropped away* **14/1**

8 *41* **Romantic Stroll (IRE)**[47] 1438 4-9-0 87.......................(t) JamieSpencer 5
(T Stack, Ire) *a in rr: detached over 2f out: sn eased: t.o* **40/1**

1m 37.78s (-8.22) **Going Correction** -0.75s/f (Hard) **8** Ran SP% **120.4**
Speed ratings: **111,108,105,104,104 98,95,54**
CSF £11.10 TOTE £2.20: £1.02, £2.00, £2.00; DF 12.30.
Owner V I Araci **Bred** Whatton Manor Stud **Trained** Newmarket, Suffolk

FOCUS
Dermot Weld won this Group 3 for the last two years with Emulous but he was denied a chance to complete the hat-trick as likely favourite Caponata was reported to be in-season. The pace was only moderate, certainly until halfway, and the winner was much the best when it mattered most. Another step up from Chigun.

2674 CURRAGH (R-H)

Sunday, May 26

OFFICIAL GOING: Good to firm

2687a AIRLIE STUD GALLINULE STKS (GROUP 3) 1m 2f

2:45 (2:49) 3-Y-O £31,707 (£9,268; £4,390; £1,463)

RPR

1 **Leading Light (IRE)**[19] 2142 3-9-3 107 (p) JosephO'Brien 8 111+
(A P O'Brien, Ire) *mde virtually all: 2 l clr 1/2-way: reduced advantage and pushed along over 2f out: sn rdn and almost jnd ent fnl f: sn asserted and in command whn edgd lft towards fin: kpt on wl* **4/6**[1]

2 2 1/4 **Little White Cloud (IRE)**[14] 2290 3-9-3 106 DeclanMcDonogh 4 106
(John M Oxx, Ire) *trckd ldr in 2nd: clsd to strly press wnr ent fnl f: sn no ex u.p: kpt on same pce towards fin* **4/1**[2]

3 1 1/4 **Count Of Limonade (IRE)**[46] 1492 3-9-3 100 RyanMoore 5 104
(A P O'Brien, Ire) *chsd ldrs: 4th 1/2-way: clsd into 3rd u.p over 1f out: sn no ex: kpt on same pce* **10/1**

4 1 **Fighter Squadron (USA)**[19] 2142 3-9-3 91 (p) WayneLordan 6 102
(David Wachman, Ire) *chsd ldrs: 3rd 1/2-way: tk clsr order over 3f out: rdn fr 2f out and sn no ex u.p: kpt on same pce in 4th ins fnl f* **16/1**

5 7 1/2 **Sruthan (IRE)**[20] 2107 3-9-3 107 ChrisHayes 2 87
(P D Deegan, Ire) *in tch: t.k.h: 6th 1/2-way: rdn and no imp in 5th fr under 2f out: one pce fnl f* **9/2**[3]

6 3 1/4 **Private Alexander (IRE)**[259] 6081 3-9-0 87 GaryCarroll 7 77
(G M Lyons, Ire) *hld up towards rr: rdn into st and no ex: kpt on one pce fnl f* **25/1**

7 nk **Einsteins Folly (IRE)**[36] 1706 3-9-3 94 KevinManning 1 79
(J S Bolger, Ire) *chsd ldrs: pushed along in 4th 3f out: sn no ex and wknd u.p over 1 1/2f out* **28/1**

8 nk **Live Dangerously** 3-9-3 ShaneFoley 3 79?
(A Oliver, Ire) *w.w in rr: rdn and no imp fr 3f out: kpt on one pce fnl 2f* **50/1**

2m 7.83s (-1.47) **Going Correction** -0.40s/f (Firm) 8 Ran SP% **122.4**
Speed ratings: **109,107,106,105,99 96,96,96**
CSF £4.07 TOTE £1.60: £1.02, £1.50, £2.30; DF 5.20 Trifecta £6.15.
Owner Derrick Smith & Mrs John Magnier & Michael Tabor **Bred** Lynch-Bages Ltd **Trained** Ballydoyle, Co Tipperary

FOCUS
The winner made all at a gradually increasing pace and looks smart.

2688a TATTERSALLS GOLD CUP (GROUP 1) 1m 2f 110y

3:20 (3:22) 4-Y-O+ £105,853 (£32,439; £15,365; £5,121)

RPR

1 **Al Kazeem**[29] 1846 5-9-3 JamesDoyle 1 123+
(Roger Charlton) *hld up in rr of quartet: tk clsr order 3f out and clsd gng best on outer to strly press ldr ent fnl f: rdn to ld over 100yds out and styd on wl* **9/4**[2]

2 1 1/2 **Camelot**[20] 2105 4-9-3 124 JosephO'Brien 3 120
(A P O'Brien, Ire) *w.w in 3rd: gd hdwy to ld 2f out: sn strly pressed and edgd sltly lft u.p ins fnl f: hdd over 100yds out and no ex cl home* **4/11**[1]

3 9 1/2 **Windsor Palace (IRE)**[42] 1556 8-9-3 105 (p) SeamieHeffernan 4 102
(A P O'Brien, Ire) *prom: sn led: over 2 l clr 1/2-way: pushed along into st and hdd 2f out: sn no ex: kpt on same pce to hold mod 3rd ins fnl f* **33/1**[3]

4 2 3/4 **Negotiate**[10] 2397 5-9-0 88 (t) KevinManning 2 93?
(Ms Joanna Morgan, Ire) *led briefly early: sn settled bhd ldr in 2nd: dropped to 4th under 2f out and sn ex u.p: kpt on one pce fnl f* **100/1**

2m 14.48s (-5.52) **Going Correction** -0.40s/f (Firm) 4 Ran SP% **108.0**
Speed ratings: **104,102,96,94**
CSF £3.47 TOTE £4.10; DF 4.60.
Owner D J Deer **Bred** D J And Mrs Deer **Trained** Beckhampton, Wilts

FOCUS
There appeared to be no element of fluke about Al Kazeem's victory as he appeared to beat Camelot fair and square after being held up at the back of the four-runner field. The winner is rated to his best with the second to his mark (excluding his Derby run).

2689a ETIHAD AIRWAYS IRISH 1,000 GUINEAS (FILLIES) (GROUP 1) 1m

3:55 (3:57) 3-Y-O

£141,463 (£46,341; £21,951; £7,317; £4,878; £2,439)

RPR

1 **Just The Judge (IRE)**[21] 2047 3-9-0 JamieSpencer 2 111+
(Charles Hills) *settled bhd ldrs: cl 4th 1/2-way: prog gng best fr 2f out to ld fnl 150yds: pushed out: styd on wl* **2/1**[1]

2 1 1/2 **Rehn's Nest (IRE)**[11] 2375 3-9-0 102 (t) RonanWhelan 13 108+
(J S Bolger, Ire) *in rr of mid-div: rdn over 1 1/2f out and wnt 4th u.p ins fnl f: styd on wl into nvr nrr 2nd fnl strides* **40/1**

3 hd **Just Pretending (USA)**[14] 2289 3-9-0 101 SeamieHeffernan 9 107
(A P O'Brien, Ire) *prom: led narrowly 1/2-way: rdn over 2f out: strly pressed ent fnl f and hdd fnl 150yds: no ex u.p and dropped to 3rd fnl strides* **14/1**

4 nk **Big Break**[211] 7419 3-9-0 106 PatSmullen 16 107
(D K Weld, Ire) *chsd ldrs on outer: cl 5th 1/2-way: rdn in 3rd ent fnl f and sn no ex u.p: kpt on same pce and dropped to 4th cl home* **4/1**[2]

5 2 **Mizzava (IRE)**[14] 2289 3-9-0 95 ShaneFoley 14 102
(M Halford, Ire) *w.w towards rr: rdn on outer fr 2f out and wnt nvr threatening 5th fnl 100yds: kpt on wl* **50/1**

6 1 **Maureen (IRE)**[21] 2047 3-9-0 RichardHughes 3 100
(Richard Hannon) *hld up in rr of mid-div: n.m.r under 2f out and sn swtchd lft: kpt on into nvr nrr 6th nr fin* **11/2**[3]

7 nk **Hanky Panky (IRE)**[11] 2378 3-9-0 93 RyanMoore 7 99
(A P O'Brien, Ire) *hld up towards rr: prog under 3f out: rdn between horses in 7th ins fnl f and kpt on towards fin wout ever threatening principals* **8/1**

8 1 **Bunairgead (IRE)**[20] 2108 3-9-0 100 (b) KevinManning 6 97
(J S Bolger, Ire) *chsd ldrs early: cl 6th after 1/2-way: sn rdn and no ex: kpt on same pce in 8th towards fin* **25/1**

9 1/2 **Exactement (IRE)**[8] 2453 3-9-0 JimCrowley 11 96
(Mrs K Burke) *chsd ldrs early: t.k.h: cl 10th 1/2-way: sn pushed along and no ex fr 2f out: kpt on same pce fnl f* **50/1**

10 nk **Snow Queen (IRE)**[21] 2047 3-9-0 106 (v[1]) JosephO'Brien 15 95
(A P O'Brien, Ire) *dwlt and racd towards rr: sme hdwy fr 1/2-way into 6th: rdn under 2f out and sn no ex: one pce fnl f* **7/1**

11 4 1/4 **Uleavemebreathless**[14] 2289 3-9-0 95 GaryCarroll 4 85
(A Oliver, Ire) *sn led: cl 2nd 1/2-way: rdn and wknd fr 2f out* **66/1**

12 hd **Harasiya (IRE)**[259] 6081 3-9-0 105 DeclanMcDonogh 1 85
(John M Oxx, Ire) *hld up in mid-div: rdn fr 2f out and no imp ent fnl f: eased towards fin* **12/1**

13 4 1/4 **What Style (IRE)**[42] 1557 3-9-0 100 NGMcCullagh 12 75
(John M Oxx, Ire) *chsd ldrs: cl 3rd 1/2-way: rdn and wknd fr over 2f out* **12/1**

14 1/2 **Dubaya**[20] 2108 3-9-0 93 ChrisHayes 8 74
(A Oliver, Ire) *in rr of mid-div thrght: rdn and no imp fr 3f out* **50/1**

15 35 **Masarah (IRE)**[21] 2047 3-9-0 FrederikTylicki 10
(Clive Brittain) *hld up in tch: pushed along in 6th after 1/2-way and sn wknd: detached fnl 2f: t.o* **40/1**

1m 39.37s (-6.63) **Going Correction** -0.575s/f (Hard) 15 Ran SP% **130.5**
Speed ratings: **110,108,108,108,106 105,104,103,103,102 98,98,94,93,58**
CSF £115.19 CT £1008.87 TOTE £2.90: £1.02, £12.40, £5.70; DF 136.10.
Owner Qatar Racing Limited & Sangster Family **Bred** Mrs J Dempsey **Trained** Lambourn, Berks

FOCUS
The Newmarket Guineas form was given a good boost by the authoritative success of Just the Judge. The form is set around the winner, eighth and ninth, and fits the race averages.

2690 - 2692a (Foreign Racing) - See Raceform Interactive

2557 LONGCHAMP (R-H)

Sunday, May 26

OFFICIAL GOING: Turf: soft

2693a POUR MOI COOLMORE PRIX SAINT-ALARY (GROUP 1) (3YO FILLIES) (TURF) 1m 2f

1:30 (12:00) 3-Y-O £116,138 (£46,463; £23,231; £8,709; £8,709)

RPR

1 **Silasol (IRE)**[28] 1869 3-9-0 0 OlivierPeslier 8 111+
(C Laffon-Parias, France) *w.w in rr: shkn up and swtchd outside 2f out: rdn and began styng on fr 1 1/2f out: hrden rdn and r.o wl fnl 125yds: led last stride* **11/4**[1]

2 shd **Alterite (FR)**[14] 2299 3-9-0 0 IoritzMendizabal 4 110
(J-C Rouget, France) *bmpd leaving stalls: settled in midfield: cl 4th and travelling wl 2 1/2f out: rdn and effrt on outside 1 1/2f out: edgd rt u.p and chal ldrs on outside 1f out: led 150yds out: r.o u.p: hdd fnl stride* **9/1**

3 snk **Ferevia (IRE)**[14] 2297 3-9-0 0 ThierryThulliez 7 110+
(C Laffon-Parias, France) *hld up towards rr on inner: pushed along bhd wall of horses 2f out: angled outside 1 1/2f out: rdn and r.o ins fnl f: nrest at fin* **11/1**

4 nk **Artiste Divine**[27] 3-9-0 0 Pierre-CharlesBoudot 2 109+
(A Fabre, France) *trckd ldng gp on inner: in midfield appr 1/2-way: rdn and effrt on ins to chse ldrs under 2f out: swtchd outside three ldrs ent fnl f: r.o u.p: nvr on terms: grabbed share of 4th on line* **14/1**

4 dht **Alumna (USA)**[31] 3-9-0 0 MaximeGuyon 3 109
(A Fabre, France) *wnt lft and bmpd Siyenica leaving stalls: trckd ldr taking t.k.h: rdn to chal on outer 2f out: led 1f out: hdd 150yds out: kpt on same pce u.p: no ex fnl 50yds: jnd for 4th on line* **4/1**[3]

6 2 **Parle Moi (IRE)**[28] 1869 3-9-0 0 ChristopheSoumillon 1 105
(P Bary, France) *led: set stdy gallop: hdd after 2f and trckd ldr on inner: shkn up and short of room 2 1/2f out: nowhere to go tl swtchd outside under 1 1/2f out: sn rdn and nt qckn: one pce ins fnl f* **11/2**

7 1/2 **Siyenica (FR)**[34] 3-9-0 0 Christophe-PatriceLemaire 6 104
(A De Royer-Dupre, France) *bmpd by Alumna leaving stalls: trckd ldrs taking t.k.h: led after 2f and qcknd tempo: shkn up whn chal 2f out: hdd 1f out and grad wknd* **7/2**[2]

8 2 1/2 **Izola**[20] 3-9-0 0 ThierryJarnet 5 99
(F Head, France) *wnt lft and bmpd Alterite leaving stalls: towards rr: rdn and effrt on outside 2f out: sn rdn and no imp: wknd ins fnl f* **20/1**

2m 10.53s (6.53) **Going Correction** +0.575s/f (Yiel) 8 Ran SP% **114.0**
Speed ratings: **96,95,95,95,95 93,93,91**
WIN (incl. 1 euro stake): 4.40. PLACES: 1.70, 3.10, 3.30. DF: 19.60. SF: 30.60.
Owner Wertheimer & Frere **Bred** Wertheimer & Frere **Trained** Chantilly, France

FOCUS
Basically a trial for next month's Prix de Diane, it looked a hot race beforehand, but nobody wanted to send their horse to the front, resulting in a steady early gallop, and although the tempo was gradually increased by Siyenica, it produced the usual bunched French finish.

2694a PRIX D'ISPAHAN (GROUP 1) (4YO+) (TURF) 1m 1f 55y

2:40 (12:00) 4-Y-O+ £116,138 (£46,463; £23,231; £11,605; £5,813)

RPR

1 **Maxios**[28] 1870 5-9-2 0 StephanePasquier 1 120
(J E Pease, France) *settled in midfield on inner: angled off rail and rdn 2f out: styd on to chal wl ins fnl f: led cl home: drvn out* **10/3**[2]

2 1/2 **Planteur (IRE)**[57] 1269 6-9-2 0 ChristopheSoumillon 6 119
(Marco Botti) *led early: trckd ldr whn hdd and keen under restraint: rdn to chal 1 1/2f out: led jst ins fnl f: styd on but worn down and hdd cl home* **9/2**[3]

3 3/4 **Mandour (USA)**[31] 4-9-2 0 Christophe-PatriceLemaire 4 117+
(A De Royer-Dupre, France) *dwlt: hld up in last pair on inner: rdn 2f out: r.o to go 3rd wl ins fnl f: fin strly but nvr able to chal* **6/1**

4 2 **Don Bosco (FR)**[25] 1945 6-9-2 0 GregoryBenoist 3 113
(D Smaga, France) *dwlt: qckly rcvrd and sn led: rdn 2f out: hdd jst ins fnl f: sn no ex: fdd and dropped to 4th* **7/1**

5 hd **Zinabaa (FR)**[25] 1945 8-9-2 0 Francois-XavierBertras 2 113
(Mlle T Puitg, France) *midfield on outer: rdn 2f out: styd on but nt pce to chal* **12/1**

6 1 **Beauty Parlour**[239] 6673 4-8-13 0 TomQueally 7 108
(Sir Henry Cecil) *hld up in last trio on outer: hdwy and stl cruising 2f out: rdn and nt qckn over 1f out: plugged on* **5/2**[1]

7 6 **Sofast (FR)**[25] 1945 4-9-2 0 (b) OlivierPeslier 8 98
(F Head, France) *hld up in last: rdn over 2f out: sn outpcd: plugged on tl eased whn btn ins fnl f* **9/1**

1m 56.55s (1.25) **Going Correction** +0.575s/f (Yiel) 7 Ran SP% **114.3**
Speed ratings: **117,116,115,114,113 113,107**
WIN (incl. 1 euro stake): 3.30. PLACES: 1.30, 1.40, 1.80. DF: 4.50. SF: 12.20.
Owner Niarchos Family **Bred** Niarchos Family **Trained** Chantilly, France

FOCUS
Not a particularly strong Group 1, and with them going just a modest gallop, it paid to race prominently.

2695a PRIX VICOMTESSE VIGIER (GROUP 2) (4YO+) (TURF) 1m 7f 110y
3:10 (12:00) 4-Y-O+ **£60,243** (£23,252; £11,097; £7,398; £3,699)

RPR

1 **Domeside**^{28} [1871] 7-8-11 0 .... ChristopheSoumillon 3 115+
(M Delcher Sanchez, France) *midfield: stdy hdwy fr 3f out: rdn 2f out: styd on to ld ins fnl f: qckly asserted: pushed out* **8/1**

2 *2* **Les Beaufs (FR)**^{28} [1871] 4-9-2 0 .... JulienGuillochon 1 118
(Mme V Seignoux, France) *led and sn clr: 10 l ahd 5f out: reduced advantage but stl gng wl 3f out: rdn 2f out: styd on but clsd down and hdd ins fnl f: no ex* **3/1**^{3}

3 *3* **Last Train**^{28} [1871] 4-8-11 0 .... MaximeGuyon 2 110
(A Fabre, France) *trckd clr ldr: rdn to cl 3f out: 3rd and outpcd by front pair ent fnl f: plugged on* **7/4**^{1}

4 *1 1/4* **Last Born (FR)**^{30} 4-8-8 0 .... FlavienPrat 4 105
(A Fabre, France) *hld up in last trio: rdn over 2f out: 4th and outpcd by ldrs ent fnl f: plugged on* **10/1**

5 *2 1/2* **Verema (FR)**^{28} [1871] 4-8-8 0 .... Christophe-PatriceLemaire 5 102
(A De Royer-Dupre, France) *hld up in last trio on outer: hdwy to be prom in main body of field 6f out: rdn and ev ch 2f out: outpcd over 1f out: fdd* **11/4**^{2}

6 *dist* **Shahwardi (FR)**^{197} [7696] 7-9-0 0 .... AntoineHamelin 7
(A De Royer-Dupre, France) *hld up in last: rdn over 2f out: sn outpcd and btn: eased ins fnl f and t.o: nvr a factor* **12/1**

3m 27.01s (5.51) **Going Correction** +0.575s/f (Yiel)
WFA 4 from 6yo+ 1lb 6 Ran SP% **115.9**
Speed ratings: **109,108,106,105,104**
WIN (incl. 1 euro stake): 5.40. PLACES: 2.80, 2.30. SF: 29.10.
Owner Safsaf Canarias Srl **Bred** Appleby Lodge Stud **Trained** France

1944 MUNICH (L-H)
Sunday, May 26

OFFICIAL GOING: Turf: very soft

2696a ONEXTWO.COM - BAVARIAN CLASSIC 2013 (GROUP 3) (3YO) (TURF) 1m 2f
3:25 (12:00) 3-Y-O
£26,016 (£8,943; £4,471; £2,439; £1,626; £1,219)

RPR

1 **Lucky Speed (IRE)**^{28} [1867] 3-9-2 0 .... AStarke 1 98+
(P Schiergen, Germany) *stdd and hld up in last pair on inner: rdn 3f out: hdwy fr over 1f out: styng on but stl plenty to do ent fnl f: str late run to reel in ldr cl home and won gng away* **63/10**

2 *1/2* **Flamingo Star (GER)**^{28} [1867] 3-9-2 0 .... LennartHammer-Hansen 10 97
(R Dzubasz, Germany) *qckly across fr wd draw and led: rdn clr over 2f out: 3 l ahd and looked in control ent fnl f: rapidly diminishing advantage ins fnl 100yds: hdd cl home* **177/10**

3 *2* **Bermuda Reef (IRE)** 3-9-2 0 .... MrDennisSchiergen 8 93
(P Schiergen, Germany) *prom on inner: 2nd and rdn to chse ldr over 2f out: sn no imp: styd on but dropped to 3rd wl ins fnl f* **239/10**

4 *nk* **Night Wish (GER)** 3-9-2 0 .... FilipMinarik 6 92
(W Figge, Germany) *midfield on inner: rdn and hdwy over 2f out: styd on to go 4th fnl strides: nt pce to chal* **42/10**^{3}

5 *nk* **Saratino (GER)**^{21} 3-9-2 0 .... HarryBentley 2 92
(Mario Hofer, Germany) *midfield on inner: rdn over 2f out: styd on one pce* **15/2**

6 *nk* **Samos (GER)**^{38} 3-9-2 0 .... APietsch 7 91
(W Hickst, Germany) *midfield on outer: rdn over 2f out: styd on one pce* **8/5**^{1}

7 *hd* **Lowenstein (GER)** 3-9-2 0 .... LouisBeuzelin 5 91
(Frau J Mayer, Germany) *slow to stride and pushed along to rcvr: hld up towards rr on outer: rdn and outpcd 3f out: plugged on: fin wl but n.d* **31/1**

8 *4* **Nordvulkan (GER)**^{218} 3-9-2 0 .... BClos 3 83
(R Dzubasz, Germany) *hld up in last and niggled along to keep in tch: hdwy fr over 2f out: outpcd ent fnl f: fdd* **26/1**

9 *18* **Erlkonig (GER)**^{28} [1867] 3-9-2 0 .... DPorcu 9 47
(Markus Klug, Germany) *prom on outer: rdn and lost pl over 3f out: sn in rr and btn: eased and t.o* **148/10**

10 *3/4* **Vif Monsieur (GER)**^{28} [1867] 3-9-2 0 .... KClijmans 11 45
(J Hirschberger, Germany) *qckly across fr wdst draw and trckd ldr: rdn 3f out: sn lost pl and btn: eased and dropped to last: t.o* **4/1**^{2}

2m 15.17s (6.20) 10 Ran SP% **125.7**
WIN (incl. 10 euro stake): 73. PLACES: 25, 54, 51. SF: 928.
Owner Stall Hornoldendorf **Bred** Gestut Hof Ittlingen **Trained** Germany

1709 SAN SIRO (R-H)
Sunday, May 26

OFFICIAL GOING: Turf: heavy

2697a PREMIO OAKS D'ITALIA (GROUP 2) (3YO FILLIES) (TURF) 1m 3f
3:25 (12:00) 3-Y-O **£150,406** (£66,178; £36,097; £18,048)

RPR

1 **Charity Line (IRE)**^{21} 3-8-11 0 .... FabioBranca 4 107+
(S Botti, Italy) *settled towards rr: hdwy 3 1/2f out: pushed along to ld appr 2f out: sn rdn and wnt clr ins fnl f: comf* **7/10**^{1}

2 *4 1/2* **Dancer Destination**^{28} [1866] 3-8-11 0 .... DarioVargiu 12 99
(B Grizzetti, Italy) *t.k.h and trckd ldrs: pressed ldr 3f out: rdn and ev ch 2f out but nt qckn: kpt on at same pce: no ch w wnr fnl f* **42/10**^{3}

3 *nk* **Whippy Cream (IRE)**^{15} [2261] 3-8-11 0 .... NeilCallan 3 98
(Marco Botti) *midfield in tch: 6th and pushed along 3f out: no imp tl styd on u.p fnl f: nvr on terms* **41/10**^{2}

4 *1 1/2* **Licia (ITY)**^{229} 3-8-11 0 .... AndreaAtzeni 1 95
(S Botti, Italy) *midfield: rdn and chsd ldrs fr 2 1/2f out: nt qckn fr 1 1/2f out: plugged on at one pce fnl f* **17/2**

5 *2 1/4* **Mangiapregaama (ITY)**^{28} [1866] 3-8-11 0 .... GArena 6 91
(B Grizzetti, Italy) *hld up towards rr: last 4f out: rdn and hdwy 3f out: no imp u.p fr over 2f out: kpt on ins fnl f: n.d* **42/10**^{3}

6 *1/2* **Claire Song (IRE)** 3-8-11 0 .... LManiezzi 11 90
(S Botti, Italy) *led after 1f: rdn and hdd over 2f out: plugged on u.p tl fdd ins fnl f* **30/1**

7 *1 3/4* **Air Mail (IRE)**^{176} 3-8-11 0 .... PierantonioConvertino 9 87
(A Giorgi, Italy) *trckd ldng gp on outer: hrd rdn and no imp fr 2 1/2f out: kpt on at one pce* **163/10**

8 *1/2* **Collusiva (IRE)**^{28} [1866] 3-8-11 0 .... MircoDemuro 10 86
(G Botti, France) *towards rr: hdwy on outside 3 1/2f out: rdn and no further imp under 2f out: wknd ins fnl f* **49/10**

9 *7* **Road Tosky (IRE)**^{21} 3-8-11 0 .... (b) CColombi 8 74
(A Peraino, Italy) *towards rr: swtchd outside and no imp u.p fr 3f out: wknd fnl f* **44/1**

10 *10* **Fulgetta (ITY)**^{28} [1866] 3-8-11 0 .... GBietolini 2 56
(Gianluca Bietolini, Italy) *midfield on inner: dropped towards rr appr 1/2-way: bhd fr over 2f out* **51/1**

11 *1* **Night Of Light (IRE)**^{28} [1866] 3-8-11 0 .... CFiocchi 7 54
(F Camici, Italy) *t.k.h and led: hdd after 1f: remained prom tl rdn and nt qckn over 3f out: sn wknd* **35/1**

2m 21.8s (3.20) 11 Ran SP% **160.3**
WIN (incl. 1 euro stake): 1.70. PLACES: 1.12, 1.42, 1.44. DF: 6.47.
Owner Effevi **Bred** Razza Del Velino Srl **Trained** Italy

2698a PREMIO CARLO VITTADINI (GROUP 2) (3YO+) (TURF) 1m
4:10 (12:00) 3-Y-O+ **£38,617** (£16,991; £9,268; £4,634)

RPR

1 **Principe Adepto (USA)**^{14} [2295] 5-9-5 0 .... MEsposito 3 102
(E Botti, Italy) *w.w in rr: hdwy 2 1/2f out: chal ldrs on outer ins fnl f: r.o u.p to ld cl home* **183/20**

2 *snk* **Libano (IRE)**^{21} 7-9-5 0 .... DarioVargiu 1 102
(L Polito, Italy) *broke wl and led: rdn over 2f out: kpt on gamely u.p: hdd cl home* **83/10**

3 *snk* **Douce Vie (IRE)**^{14} 7-9-5 0 .... FabioBranca 5 102
(S Botti, Italy) *hld up towards rr: trckd ldng trio into st over 3f out: chal ldr 1f out: kpt on u.p: no ex cl home* **17/10**^{1}

4 *2 1/2* **Malossol (USA)**^{29} 4-9-5 0 .... MircoDemuro 2 96
(G Botti, France) *midfield: styd towards ins as rest of field c into centre of crse in st: rdn to join main gp and ev ch over 1f out: plugged on at same pce fnl f* **49/10**

5 *2 3/4* **Super Test (ITY)**^{35} 4-9-5 0 .... SDiana 4 90
(M Oppo, Italy) *trckd ldr on inner: rdn and chal ldr 2f out: nt qckn over 1f out: fdd u.p ins fnl f* **13/1**

6 *4* **Regarde Moi**^{21} 5-9-5 0 .... GBietolini 6 80
(S Botti, Italy) *towards rr: effrt on outside 2f out: sn rdn and no further imp fr 1 1/2f out* **19/5**^{3}

7 *4* **Lady Jacamira (GER)**^{28} 4-9-2 0 .... AndreaAtzeni 7 68
(R Dzubasz, Germany) *broke wl and trckd ldr on outer: hrd rdn and nt qckn 2 1/2f out: wknd appr fnl f* **27/10**^{2}

1m 40.8s (-1.30) 7 Ran SP% **129.6**
WIN (incl. 1 euro stake): 10.14. PLACES: 5.50, 4.01. DF: 36.26.
Owner Allevamento La Nuova Sbarra **Bred** Allevamento La Nuova Sbarra **Trained** Italy

2699 - 2700a (Foreign Racing) - See Raceform Interactive

CARLISLE (R-H)
Monday, May 27

OFFICIAL GOING: Good to firm (firm in places; 8.6)

2701 32RED EBF MAIDEN STKS 5f
2:10 (2:12) (Class 5) 2-Y-O **£2,911** (£866; £432; £216) **Stalls** High

Form RPR

423 1 **Robynelle**^{10} [2404] 2-9-0 0 .... JoeFanning 10 64
(Keith Dalgleish) *t.k.h early: trckd ldr: led over 1f out: rdn and edgd rt ins fnl f: hld on wl* **3/1**^{2}

2 *nk* **In Focus (IRE)** 2-9-5 0 .... AndrewMullen 2 68
(Alan Swinbank) *chsd ldng gp on ins: rdn and hdwy over 1f out: chsd wnr ins fnl f: kpt on fin* **16/1**

3 *3/4* **Nevada Blue** 2-8-12 0 .... DavidSimmonson$^{(7)}$ 9 65
(Tony Coyle) *coltish and green in paddock: bhd on outside: rdn over 2f out: hdwy over 1f out: kpt on fnl f: improve* **8/1**

4 *3/4* **She Can Jig** 2-9-0 0 .... AmyRyan 3 58+
(Kevin Ryan) *missed break: bhd and detached: hdwy on wd outside 2f out: kpt on fnl f: bttr for r* **7/1**^{3}

2 5 *1 1/2* **Thornaby Nash**^{10} [2404] 2-9-5 0 .... TomEaves 5 57
(David O'Meara) *led tl rdn and hdd over 1f out: outpcd ins fnl f* **6/4**^{1}

0 5 *dht* **Creative Spirit**^{9} [2458] 2-9-0 0 .... RoystonFfrench 7 52
(David Brown) *in tch: edgd rt and outpcd wl over 1f out: kpt on ins fnl f: nvr able to chal* **20/1**

0 7 *1/2* **Scarborough (IRE)**^{9} [2458] 2-9-0 0 .... GrahamLee 1 50
(Paul Midgley) *wnt rt s: sn chsng ldrs: pushed along and edgd rt over 1f out: sn outpcd* **25/1**

0 8 *2 1/2* **Kindanyce (IRE)**^{58} [1240] 2-9-0 0 .... TonyHamilton 4 41
(Richard Fahey) *chsd ldrs: rdn along 1/2-way: wknd wl over 1f out* **8/1**

1m 4.2s (3.40) **Going Correction** +0.425s/f (Yiel) 8 Ran SP% **114.2**
Speed ratings (Par 93): **89,88,87,86,83 83,82,78**
toteswingers 1&2 £6.20, 1&3 £5.90, 2&3 £16.30 CSF £48.41 TOTE £3.30: £1.50, £5.00, £3.30; EX 32.10 Trifecta £184.40 Pool: £1,077.81 - 4.38 winning units..
Owner Mac Asphalt Ltd **Bred** James Ortega Bloodstock **Trained** Carluke, S Lanarks

FOCUS
An ordinary maiden which was won by a fairly exposed type in a bunch finish. The form looks below par for the race but is somewhat fluid.

2702 32RED CASINO H'CAP (DIV I) 5f
2:40 (2:41) (Class 5) (0-70,70) 3-Y-O+ **£2,587** (£770; £384; £192) **Stalls** High

Form RPR

5350 1 **Secret Advice**^{24} [1988] 3-8-4 56 oh1 .... JoeFanning 5 62
(Keith Dalgleish) *trckd ldrs: effrt whn nt clr run and swtchd rt over 1f out: led ins fnl f: edgd lft: kpt on wl* **12/1**

0003 **2** 1 1/4 **Diamond Blue**[13] 2343 5-9-10 **68** AmyRyan 6 72
(Richard Whitaker) *awkward s: bhd on outside: effrt and rdn on outside fr 2f out: styd on fnl f: tk 2nd nr fin* **7/2**[1]

0-31 **3** nse **Black Annis Bower**[13] 2343 5-9-6 **64** PaulMulrennan 9 68
(Michael Easterby) *prom: effrt and drvn 2f out: kpt on ins fnl f* **7/2**[1]

0-00 **4** nk **Commanche Raider (IRE)**[16] 2275 6-9-12 **70** (b) TomEaves 4 73
(Michael Dods) *bhd: rdn over 2f out: no imp tl kpt on wl fnl f: nrst fin* **12/1**

5-63 **5** 1/2 **Ingenti**[6] 2542 5-9-0 **58** PaddyAspell 7 59
(Christopher Wilson) *cl up: rdn to ld over 1f out: hdd ins fnl f: sn no ex* **11/2**[3]

-303 **6** 1 **Art Dzeko**[13] 2338 4-9-10 **68** DuranFentiman 10 66
(Tim Easterby) *chsd ldrs on outside: drvn and effrt 2f out: outpcd last 150yds* **10/1**

0-40 **7** 1 3/4 **Majestic Manannan (IRE)**[16] 2268 4-9-5 **63** AdrianNicholls 3 54
(David Nicholls) *led tl rdn and hdd over 1f out: edgd rt and wknd ins fnl f* **4/1**[2]

6-06 **8** nk **Rio's Girl**[56] 1278 6-8-12 **56** oh3 BarryMcHugh 1 46
(Tony Coyle) *chsd ldrs: drvn and outpcd over 1f out: n.d after* **14/1**

050 **9** 1 **Ambitious Icarus**[10] 2409 4-9-4 **62** (e) RobbieFitzpatrick 2 49+
(Richard Guest) *dwlt: bhd: hdwy against far rail over 1f out: styng on whn hmpd ins fnl f: eased* **16/1**

1m 2.61s (1.81) **Going Correction** +0.425s/f (Yiel)
WFA 3 from 4yo+ 8lb 9 Ran SP% **116.9**
Speed ratings (Par 103): **102,100,99,99,98 97,94,93,92**
toteswingers 1&2 £8.80, 1&3 £16.30, 2&3 £2.80 CSF £54.50 CT £182.86 TOTE £15.30: £4.10, £1.30, £1.90; EX 68.00 Trifecta £601.50 Part won. Pool: £802.05 - 0.23 winning units..
Owner G L S Partnership **Bred** G L S Partnership **Trained** Carluke, S Lanarks

FOCUS
A competitive handicap rated around the placed horses to recent form. The first four all came from off the decent pace.

2703 32RED CASINO H'CAP (DIV II) 5f
3:15 (3:16) (Class 5) (0-70,69) 3-Y-O+ **£2,587** (£770; £384; £192) **Stalls** High

Form RPR

-203 **1** **Spykes Bay (USA)**[16] 2275 4-9-7 **67** (b) MichaelMetcalfe(3) 5 75
(Mrs K Burke) *in tch: effrt over 1f out: led ins fnl f: kpt on wl* **2/1**[1]

-001 **2** nk **Mey Blossom**[13] 2338 8-9-0 **62** (p) GeorgeChaloner(5) 9 69
(Richard Whitaker) *trckd ldrs: effrt and edgd rt over 1f out: kpt on fnl f* **14/1**

20-5 **3** 1/2 **Red Cape (FR)**[16] 2276 10-9-12 **69** PJMcDonald 4 74
(Ruth Carr) *led: rdn over 1f out: edgd lft and hdd ins fnl f: kpt on same pce towards fin* **12/1**

3652 **4** nk **Salvatore Fury (IRE)**[13] 2336 3-8-4 **55** (p) JoeFanning 7 56
(Keith Dalgleish) *hld up: hdwy on outside over 1f out: rdn and kpt on ins fnl f* **9/1**

4-40 **5** 1/2 **Hello Stranger (IRE)**[37] 1692 4-9-9 **66** DuranFentiman 2 68
(Tim Easterby) *hld up: rdn and hdwy over 1f out: kpt on fnl f: nvr able to chal* **9/2**[2]

030- **6** 1 1/4 **Amadeus Denton (IRE)**[149] 8285 4-9-0 **64** ConnorBeasley(7) 6 62
(Michael Dods) *hld up: pushed along 2f out: kpt on ins fnl f: n.d* **12/1**

34-0 **7** 1 **Fidget**[21] 2091 3-8-6 **57** RoystonFfrench 10 48
(David Brown) *prom: rdn and hung rt wl over 1f out: sn outpcd* **33/1**

36-3 **8** nk **Comptonspirit**[24] 1976 9-9-5 **69** MatthewHopkins(7) 1 62
(Brian Baugh) *trckd ldrs: drvn over 1f out: no ex ins fnl f* **14/1**

-602 **9** 7 **Flighty Clarets (IRE)**[26] 1935 3-9-1 **66** TonyHamilton 8 31
(Richard Fahey) *t.k.h: cl up tl rdn and wknd over 1f out* **13/2**[3]

00-3 **10** 24 **Needy McCredie**[8] 2479 7-8-13 **56** PaddyAspell 3
(James Turner) *rdr v slow to remove blindfold: s.v.s and t.o thrght* **7/1**

1m 2.47s (1.67) **Going Correction** +0.425s/f (Yiel)
WFA 3 from 4yo+ 8lb 10 Ran SP% **119.0**
Speed ratings (Par 103): **103,102,101,101,100 98,96,96,85,46**
toteswingers 1&2 £15.50, 1&3 £9.40, 2&3 £4.40 CSF £34.25 CT £287.05 TOTE £2.90: £1.50, £2.10, £4.60; EX 40.30 Trifecta £647.80 Part won. Pool: £863.80 - 0.38 winning units..
Owner Mark T Gittins **Bred** Brylynn Farm Inc **Trained** Middleham Moor, N Yorks
■ Stewards' Enquiry : Michael Metcalfe two-day ban: use of whip (10-11 June)

FOCUS
A gamble was landed in this second division of a sprint handicap. The placed horses are the best guides to the level.

2704 32RED EBF FILLIES' H'CAP 7f 200y
3:50 (3:52) (Class 4) (0-85,80) 3-Y-O+ **£6,469** (£1,925; £962; £481) **Stalls** Low

Form RPR

1-11 **1** **Lilac Lace (IRE)**[23] 2026 3-9-1 **79** DuranFentiman 1 83
(Tim Easterby) *t.k.h early: trckd ldrs: effrt whn nt clr run and swtchd lft over 1f out: led wl ins fnl f: kpt on gamely* **7/2**[2]

41-1 **2** hd **Danat Al Atheer**[30] 1829 3-9-1 **79** GrahamLee 4 83
(William Haggas) *reluctant to enter stalls: t.k.h: prom: rdn and outpcd over 2f out: rallied over 1f out: led briefly ins fnl f: no ex nr fin* **1/1**[1]

00-2 **3** 3/4 **Tussie Mussie**[23] 2026 3-8-12 **76** JoeFanning 7 78
(Mark Johnston) *t.k.h: pressed ldr: led over 3f out to ins fnl f: kpt on same pce* **6/1**[3]

4-06 **4** 3 3/4 **Act Your Shoe Size**[17] 2220 4-9-12 **78** PaulMulrennan 6 74
(Keith Dalgleish) *led at stdy gallop: hdd over 3f out: rallied: no ex over 1f out* **10/1**

00-5 **5** 4 1/2 **Nemushka**[24] 1990 4-9-6 **77** (p) GeorgeChaloner(5) 3 63
(Richard Fahey) *s.i.s: bhd: hdwy on outside over 2f out: wknd appr fnl f* **6/1**[3]

10-0 **6** 3/4 **Supreme Luxury (IRE)**[17] 2220 4-9-6 **72** AmyRyan 5 56
(Kevin Ryan) *in tch: hdwy and cl up 1/2-way: rdn and wknd over 1f out* **20/1**

1m 41.24s (1.24) **Going Correction** +0.075s/f (Good)
WFA 3 from 4yo+ 12lb 6 Ran SP% **114.6**
Speed ratings (Par 102): **96,95,95,91,86 86**
toteswingers 1&2 £1.40, 1&3 £1.20, 2&3 £1.80 CSF £7.67 CT £18.79 TOTE £4.60: £1.70, £1.60; EX 10.10 Trifecta £18.90 Pool: £1,811.79 - 71.63 winning units..
Owner S A Heley **Bred** Robert Ryan, Brendan Quinn & Joan Quinn **Trained** Great Habton, N Yorks

FOCUS
The hot favourite was just denied by a progressive filly in this handicap which was run at a steady pace. The third is rated to form and is the best guide.

2705 32RED CARLISLE BELL TRIAL H'CAP 7f 200y
4:20 (4:20) (Class 4) (0-80,80) 4-Y-O+ **£5,498** (£1,636; £817; £408) **Stalls** Low

Form RPR

3-22 **1** **Pacific Heights (IRE)**[10] 2405 4-8-12 **74** PaulPickard(3) 3 87+
(Brian Ellison) *prom: smooth hdwy on outside 2f out: led 1f out: pushed along: edgd rt and kpt on strly* **7/2**[1]

-233 **2** 3 1/4 **Shadowtime**[13] 2339 8-9-6 **79** BarryMcHugh 12 84
(Tracy Waggott) *hld up on ins: hdwy to chse ldrs over 1f out: drvn and wnt 2nd ins fnl f: nt pce of wnr* **11/1**

-035 **3** 3/4 **Extraterrestrial**[32] 1786 9-9-1 **79** GeorgeChaloner(5) 4 82
(Richard Fahey) *hld up in midfield on ins: shkn up and edgd rt wl over 1f out: kpt on fnl f: nrst fin* **12/1**

0-31 **4** hd **Sound Advice**[19] 2163 4-9-7 **80** JoeFanning 6 83
(Keith Dalgleish) *pressed ldr: ev ch over 2f out to over 1f out: sn drvn: kpt on same pce fnl f* **4/1**[2]

00-1 **5** hd **Staff Sergeant**[14] 2315 6-9-3 **76** GrahamLee 1 79
(Iain Jardine) *led at decent gallop: rdn: edgd lft and hdd 1f out: nt qckn* **5/1**[3]

6324 **6** 1 **Bling King**[13] 2339 4-8-11 **77** (p) JordanNason(7) 2 77
(Geoffrey Harker) *trckd ldrs: rdn whn n.m.r briefly over 1f out: outpcd fnl f* **8/1**

0/0- **7** 4 **Rock Supreme (IRE)**[403] 1468 4-9-2 **75** TomEaves 5 66
(Michael Dods) *s.i.s: bhd: rdn along wl over 2f out: nvr rchd ldrs* **15/2**

6-11 **8** 1 1/2 **Coral Sands (IRE)**[10] 2406 5-8-7 **66** AndrewMullen 11 54
(Alan Swinbank) *hld up towards rr: drvn over 3f out: no imp fr 2f out* **8/1**

4055 **9** 1 1/4 **Solar Spirit (IRE)**[20] 2119 8-9-4 **77** RoystonFfrench 7 62
(Tracy Waggott) *plld hrd: cl up: drvn whn edgd rt and blkd over 1f out: sn wknd* **18/1**

1m 39.56s (-0.44) **Going Correction** +0.075s/f (Good) 9 Ran SP% **114.2**
Speed ratings (Par 105): **105,101,101,100,100 99,95,94,92**
toteswingers 1&2 £8.80, 1&3 £22.40, 2&3 £4.10 CSF £41.91 CT £415.93 TOTE £5.00: £1.70, £3.60, £4.20; EX 64.30 Trifecta £584.30 Pool: £818.27 - 1.05 winning units..
Owner A Barnes **Bred** Smythson **Trained** Norton, N Yorks
■ Stewards' Enquiry : Paul Pickard one-day ban: careless riding (10 June)

FOCUS
They went a good pace in this fair handicap and there was an emphatic winner. The placed horses help to set the standard.

2706 PPM THE PROPERTY MAINTENANCE PEOPLE H'CAP 1m 3f 107y
4:55 (4:55) (Class 4) (0-80,79) 4-Y-O+ **£6,469** (£1,925; £962; £481) **Stalls** High

Form RPR

0-00 **1** **Cosmic Sun**[12] 2369 7-8-13 **71** (tp) TonyHamilton 9 77
(Richard Fahey) *hld up: rdn and hdwy on outside 2f out: kpt on wl fnl f: led nr fin* **9/1**

4-02 **2** nk **Muharrer**[16] 2256 4-9-6 **78** PaulMulrennan 10 83
(Michael Dods) *hld up in tch: smooth hdwy to ld over 1f out: sn rdn: kpt on fnl f: hdd nr fin* **2/1**[1]

4-11 **3** 1 **Bright Applause**[19] 2165 5-9-1 **73** BarryMcHugh 1 76
(Tracy Waggott) *hld up: hdwy and ev ch over 1f out to ins fnl f: kpt on same pce towards fin* **5/1**[2]

111- **4** hd **Forget Me Not Lane (IRE)**[350] 2980 4-9-7 **79** GrahamLee 4 82
(Kevin Ryan) *midfield: effrt and rdn over 2f out: kpt on same pce fnl f* **5/1**[2]

-201 **5** 1 **Fly Solo**[9] 2462 4-9-5 **77** AndrewMullen 2 78
(Alan Swinbank) *t.k.h early: chsd ldrs: nt clr run 2f out: sn rdn: kpt on same pce ins fnl f* **5/1**[2]

0- **6** 2 1/2 **Leroy Parker (IRE)**[26] 1942 5-9-1 **73** TomEaves 5 70
(Barry Murtagh) *trckd ldrs: drvn and outpcd 2f out: rallied ent fnl f: sn no imp* **14/1**

00/0 **7** 1/2 **Party Doctor**[20] 2118 6-9-0 **75** LeeTopliss(3) 7 71
(Martin Todhunter) *bhd: rdn over 3f out: no imp tl sme late hdwy: nvr on terms* **50/1**

422/ **8** 1 1/4 **Mubrook (USA)**[30] 7046 8-8-13 **74** (b) PaulPickard(3) 11 68
(Brian Ellison) *led to over 3f out: rdn and wknd over 1f out* **8/1**[3]

03-0 **9** shd **Choisan (IRE)**[12] 2369 4-9-4 **76** DuranFentiman 6 70
(Tim Easterby) *chsd ldr: led over 3f out to over 1f out: sn wknd* **22/1**

2m 24.08s (0.98) **Going Correction** +0.075s/f (Good) 9 Ran SP% **117.4**
Speed ratings (Par 105): **99,98,98,97,97 95,95,94,94**
toteswingers 1&2 £4.30, 1&3 £15.60, 2&3 £3.20 CSF £27.87 CT £103.87 TOTE £10.30: £2.60, £1.30, £2.00; EX 46.70 Trifecta £383.40 Pool: £827.92 - 1.61 winning units..
Owner The Cosmic Cases **Bred** M Wassall **Trained** Musley Bank, N Yorks

FOCUS
A strongly-run handicap, involving a number of progressive types, but one of the oldest runners in the line-up scored from some way back. The third sets the level backed up by the fourth.

2707 32RED.COM H'CAP 6f 192y
5:25 (5:26) (Class 5) (0-70,68) 4-Y-O+ **£2,587** (£770; £384; £192) **Stalls** Low

Form RPR

4063 **1** **Smalljohn**[20] 2119 7-9-6 **67** (v) TomEaves 2 76
(Bryan Smart) *mde all: rdn 2f out: hld on wl fnl f* **11/2**[2]

210- **2** 2 **Circuitous**[180] 7906 5-9-5 **66** (v) JoeFanning 1 70
(Keith Dalgleish) *trckd ldrs: effrt and wnt 2nd over 2f out: kpt on ins fnl f: nt rch wnr* **9/1**

0/00 **3** 1/2 **Youhavecontrol (IRE)**[31] 1800 5-9-2 **63** (t) PJMcDonald 5 65
(Nicky Vaughan) *midfield on ins: rdn along over 2f out: kpt on fnl f: nrst fin* **16/1**

0-30 **4** 3/4 **Dialogue**[26] 1932 7-9-1 **65** (p) RaulDaSilva(3) 6 65
(Geoffrey Harker) *prom: effrt and drvn over 2f out: kpt on same pce fnl f* **7/1**

40-0 **5** nk **Bunce (IRE)**[9] 2441 5-9-7 **68** AndrewMullen 7 67+
(David O'Meara) *midfield: rdn along whn n.m.r briefly 2f out: kpt on ins fnl f* **13/2**[3]

60-0 **6** 2 1/4 **Little Jimmy Odsox (IRE)**[31] 1801 5-9-2 **63** DuranFentiman 9 56
(Tim Easterby) *sn towards rr: drvn over 3f out: hdwy on outside over 1f out: nvr able to chal* **14/1**

2031 **7** 1 **Ted's Brother (IRE)**[17] 2219 5-9-3 **64** (e) RobbieFitzpatrick 11 55
(Richard Guest) *hld up: drvn along on outside over 2f out: no imp fr over 1f out* **10/3**[1]

210- **8** 1 1/2 **Ferdy (IRE)**[247] 6497 4-9-4 **65** TonyHamilton 8 52
(Paul Green) *in tch tl rdn and wknd over 1f out* **12/1**

050- **9** 1 3/4 **Layla's Hero (IRE)**[198] 7684 6-9-6 **67** (p) PaulMulrennan 10 49
(Patrick Morris) *hld up: pushed along over 2f out: btn over 1f out* **11/1**

46-4 **10** 1 1/4 **Mitchum**[30] 1819 4-9-4 **65** PaddyAspell 4 43
(Ron Barr) *chsd wnr to over 2f out: rdn and wknd over 1f out* **10/1**

1m 27.18s (0.08) **Going Correction** +0.075s/f (Good) 10 Ran SP% **115.4**
Speed ratings (Par 103): **102,99,99,98,97 95,94,92,90,89**
toteswingers 1&2 £5.50, 1&3 £16.80, 2&3 £36.00 CSF £53.56 CT £552.05 TOTE £5.20: £2.30, £3.60, £9.10; EX 33.00 Trifecta £712.70 Part won. Pool: £950.26 - 0.14 winning units..
Owner B Smart **Bred** W H R John And Partners **Trained** Hambleton, N Yorks

FOCUS
There was a decisive front-running winner of this handicap, which was run at a solid pace. The winner is rated back to his old turf form, as is the runner-up.

T/Plt: £57.90 to a £1 stake. Pool: £55,588.15 - 700.36 winning units T/Qpdt: £11.30 to a £1 stake. Pool: £3,389.18 - 221.60 winning units RY

[2495]LEICESTER (R-H)

Monday, May 27

OFFICIAL GOING: Good to firm (good in places; 9.0)

False rail from top of hill on back straight all the way to Winning Post added circa 17m to races on Round course.

Wind: Fresh behind Weather: Fine

2708 BET TOTEJACKPOT TEXT TOTE TO 89660 H'CAP 5f 218y

2:25 (2:25) (Class 4) (0-85,84) 3-Y-O **£6,469** (£1,925; £962; £481) **Stalls** High

Form				RPR
1-2	1		**Equity Risk (USA)**[28] 1892 3-9-0 **77** NeilCallan 2 (Kevin Ryan) *a.p: chsd ldr over 4f out: rdn over 2f out: led ins fnl f: r.o* **9/4**[1]	90+
0-50	2	1 ½	**Sejalaat (IRE)**[16] 2285 3-9-2 **79** PaulHanagan 5 (Ed Dunlop) *led 5f out: rdn over 1f out: hdd and unable qck ins fnl f* **10/1**	87
1-10	3	nk	**Rene Mathis (GER)**[18] 2190 3-9-3 **80** RyanMoore 4 (Richard Fahey) *hld up: hdwy over 2f out: rdn over 1f out: styd on* **13/2**[3]	87
43-1	4	2 ¼	**Secondo (FR)**[22] 2051 3-9-7 **84** GeorgeBaker 1 (Roger Charlton) *dwlt: hld up: swtchd rt and hdwy over 1f out: nt rch ldrs* **10/3**[2]	84+
4-1	5	¾	**Smokethatthunders (IRE)**[35] 1732 3-8-9 **72** RobertHavlin 6 (James Toller) *prom: rdn over 1f out: styd on same pce* **12/1**	69
5-23	6	1 ½	**Angus Og**[21] 2083 3-9-5 **82** CathyGannon 8 (Mrs K Burke) *prom: rdn over 2f out: styd on same pce fr over 1f out* **8/1**	75
100-	7	nse	**Joey's Destiny (IRE)**[213] 7374 3-9-4 **81** PatCosgrave 7 (George Baker) *s.i.s: hld up: styd on fnl f: nvr nrr* **28/1**	73
25-0	8	4	**Badr Al Badoor (IRE)**[40] 1620 3-9-6 **83** FrederikTylicki 3 (James Fanshawe) *hld up: sme hdwy u.p on outer over 2f out: wknd over 1f out* **9/1**	63
246-	9	2 ½	**Secret Rebel**[166] 8070 3-8-9 **72** TedDurcan 9 (Sylvester Kirk) *led 1f: chsd ldrs: rdn 1/2-way: wknd over 1f out* **25/1**	44
-145	10	1 ¼	**Marshland**[22] 2056 3-8-10 **73** FrannyNorton 10 (Mark Johnston) *chsd ldrs: pushed along over 3f out: wknd over 2f out* **20/1**	41

1m 9.62s (-3.38) **Going Correction** -0.525s/f (Hard) **10 Ran SP% 117.1**

Speed ratings (Par 101): **101,99,98,95,94 92,92,87,83,82**

toteswingers 1&2 £6.90, 1&3 £3.50, 2&3 £9.80 CSF £25.41 CT £130.36 TOTE £3.80: £1.30, £3.60, £3.40; EX 30.40 Trifecta £141.80 Pool: £1783.73 - 9.42 winning units..

Owner Clipper Logistics **Bred** Crosshaven Bloodstock Et Al **Trained** Hambleton, N Yorks

FOCUS

A dry weekend and bright and breezy conditions on the day had seen the ground quicken up, with Neil Callan describing it as "beautiful". A competitive handicap that was run at a true gallop and looks decent form for the grade.

2709 PLAY ROULETTE & BLACKJACK AT TOTEPOOL.COM (S) STKS 1m 1f 218y

3:00 (3:00) (Class 6) 3-5-Y-O **£2,045** (£603; £302) **Stalls** Low

Form				RPR
0566	1		**Monopoli**[10] 2417 4-8-13 64 DarrenEgan(3) 1 (Daniel Kubler) *hld up: hdwy over 2f out: sn chsng ldr: rdn over 1f out: styd on u.p to ld wl ins fnl f* **10/11**[1]	58
1300	2	1	**Yourinthewill (USA)**[10] 2417 5-9-12 59 AndreaAtzeni 4 (Daniel Mark Loughnane) *dwlt: hld up: hdwy to ld over 2f out: sn rdn and hung rt: hdd wl ins fnl f* **10/1**	66
0-50	3	4 ½	**Offbeat Safaris (IRE)**[11] 2395 5-9-2 58 EDLinehan(5) 6 (Ronald Harris) *s.i.s: hld up: plld hrd: hdwy over 2f out: rdn and hung rt fr over 1f out: styd on same pce* **5/1**[2]	52
1656	4	2 ½	**Rainford Glory (IRE)**[21] 2095 3-8-12 57 PaulHanagan 3 (David Simcock) *led: rdn and hdd over 2f out: wknd fnl f* **5/1**[2]	51
-601	5	2 ¾	**Sutton Sid**[24] 1982 3-8-12 59 PatCosgrave 5 (George Baker) *plld hrd and prom: hmpd 8f out: sn chsng ldr: rdn over 2f out: wknd over 1f out* **15/2**[3]	46
0-	6	20	**El Camino Real (IRE)**[11] 4410 5-9-7 65 NeilCallan 7 (Barry Leavy) *trckd ldrs: plld hrd: rdn over 2f out: sn wknd: t.o* **22/1**	
0	7	3 ½	**Alsaqi (IRE)**[7] 2496 3-8-7 0 (v[1]) FrankieMcDonald 2 (John Butler) *chsd ldrs: rdn over 3f out: wknd over 2f out: t.o* **66/1**	

2m 8.9s (1.00) **Going Correction** 0.0s/f (Good)

WFA 3 from 4yo+ 14lb **7 Ran SP% 112.4**

Speed ratings (Par 101): **96,95,91,89,87 71,68**

toteswingers 1&2 £2.60, 1&3 £1.70, 2&3 £5.20 CSF £10.95 TOTE £1.70: £2.10, £3.00; EX 10.60 Trifecta £50.40 Pool: £2443.03 - 36.32 winning units..There was no bid for the winner

Owner The Villains **Bred** M H Dixon **Trained** Whitsbury, Hants

FOCUS

A false rail from the top of the hill in the back straight all the way around the bend into the straight added 17m to distances on the round course. A reasonable contest for the grade, but the gallop was steady and many of the runners failed to settle early. The runner-up is rated to his old turf form, while the race could be rated higher at face value.

2710 BET TOTEQUADPOT TEXT TOTE TO 89660 H'CAP 1m 1f 218y

3:35 (3:36) (Class 5) (0-70,73) 4-Y-O+ **£3,881** (£1,155; £577; £288) **Stalls** Low

Form				RPR
4-63	1		**Sehnsucht (IRE)**[26] 1932 4-9-2 **65** (v) RyanMoore 2 (John Quinn) *prom: pushed along and outpcd 4f out: hdwy and hit over hd by rivals whip 2f out: swtchd lft and rdn over 1f out: str run to ld wl ins fnl f* **10/3**[1]	78
-134	2	1 ¾	**Rock Song**[11] 2383 4-9-7 **70** SteveDrowne 8 (John Mackie) *hld up: hdwy over 2f out: led 1f out: rdn and hdd wl ins fnl f* **9/2**[2]	79
6-65	3	1 ¼	**Cravat**[32] 1780 4-9-5 **68** PatCosgrave 12 (Ed de Giles) *plld hrd and prom: rdn over 1f out: styd on same pce wl ins fnl f* **9/1**	75
1003	4	1 ½	**West End Lad**[7] 2496 10-9-4 **70** (b) MarkCoumbe(3) 10 (Roy Bowring) *sn prom: led 8f out: clr 1/2-way: rdn over 2f out: hdd 1f out: no ex ins fnl f* **14/1**	74
60-2	5	1 ¾	**Reset City**[6] 2555 7-8-12 **61** FrannyNorton 1 (Mark Johnston) *s.i.s: sn rcvrd to ld: hdd 8f out: chsd ldr who wnt clr 1/2-way: rdn over 2f out: no ex fnl f* **11/2**[3]	61
624-	6	½	**Chasin' Rainbows**[150] 8265 5-8-7 **56** oh1 DavidProbert 6 (Sylvester Kirk) *hld up: hdwy over 3f out: rdn over 2f out: no ex fnl f* **20/1**	55
25-4	7	1 ¼	**Gaelic Ice**[22] 2057 4-8-9 **58** AndreaAtzeni 11 (Rod Millman) *chsd ldrs: rdn over 4f out: sn outpcd: n.d after* **14/1**	55
0130	8	1 ½	**Scamperdale**[25] 1956 11-8-13 **62** (p) KierenFox 13 (Brian Baugh) *hld up: hdwy 2f out: rdn over 1f out: hung rt and wknd ins fnl f* **22/1**	56
5-40	9	1 ¾	**Toughness Danon**[68] 914 7-8-13 **65** (t) RyanPowell(3) 5 (Ian Williams) *hld up: racd keenly: rdn over 2f out: nvr on terms* **9/1**	55
-046	10	1 ½	**Bold Cross (IRE)**[10] 2413 10-8-6 **62** IanBurns(7) 14 (Edward Bevan) *s.s: bhd: rdn over 2f out: n.d* **16/1**	49
-500	11	4 ½	**Kept**[27] 1901 4-8-10 **64** ow1 EDLinehan(5) 9 (Ronald Harris) *hld up: hdwy on outer 2f out: sn rdn: wknd fnl f* **25/1**	42
3425	12	¾	**Conducting**[63] 1176 5-9-1 **64** JimmyQuinn 7 (Gay Kelleway) *hld up: rdn over 2f out: nvr on terms* **12/1**	41
60-0	13	54	**Beaumont Cooper**[21] 2089 4-8-11 **60** (p) NeilCallan 4 (Anabel K Murphy) *plld hrd and prom: rdn over 4f out: wknd over 3f out: eased* **66/1**	

2m 6.99s (-0.91) **Going Correction** 0.0s/f (Good) **13 Ran SP% 118.0**

Speed ratings (Par 103): **103,101,100,99,98 97,96,95,94,92 89,88,45**

toteswingers 1&2 £3.10, 1&3 £10.00, 2&3 £9.50 CSF £16.32 CT £124.64 TOTE £3.90: £1.90, £1.30, £3.50; EX 18.10 Trifecta £136.90 Pool: £2488.15 - 13.62 winning units..

Owner Charles Wentworth **Bred** Mrs Clodagh McStay **Trained** Settrington, N Yorks

FOCUS

A truly-run contest that was unsurprisingly quicker than the earlier seller, but still just a modest handicap with some old characters in opposition. The fourth sets the level rated to the previous week's selling form.

2711 PLAY DEAL OR NO DEAL AT TOTEPOOL.COM FILLIES' H'CAP 7f 9y

4:05 (4:05) (Class 4) (0-80,80) 4-Y-O+ **£6,301** (£1,886; £943; £472; £235) **Stalls** High

Form				RPR
5510	1		**Available (IRE)**[16] 2255 4-9-3 **76** (p) FrannyNorton 8 (John Mackie) *chsd ldrs: rdn to ld over 1f out: edgd rt: r.o* **9/1**	85
41-5	2	1 ½	**Malekat Jamal (IRE)**[27] 1914 4-8-5 **67** DarrenEgan(3) 3 (David Simcock) *hld up: hdwy over 2f out: rdn to chse wnr ins fnl f: r.o* **11/1**	72
0-05	3	2	**Remix (IRE)**[21] 2092 4-8-2 **61** oh4 (v[1]) DavidProbert 4 (Andrew Hollinshead) *led: rdn and hdd over 1f out: styd on same pce ins fnl f* **20/1**	61
30	4	¾	**Modern Romance (IRE)**[16] 2253 4-8-13 **77** RobertTart(5) 5 (Marco Botti) *a.p: rdn over 1f out: styd on same pce* **7/2**[3]	75
0-31	5	2	**Azzurra Du Caprio (IRE)**[19] 2166 5-9-7 **80** FrederikTylicki 1 (Ben Haslam) *hld up: pushed along 1/2-way: hdwy u.p over 2f out: wknd ins fnl f* **3/1**[2]	73
3-26	6	2 ½	**It's My Time**[16] 2286 4-8-6 **65** PaulHanagan 6 (Richard Fahey) *hld up: rdn over 2f out: nvr on terms* **9/4**[1]	51
00-1	7	7	**Alice Rose (IRE)**[27] 1914 4-8-8 **67** NickyMackay 2 (Rae Guest) *chsd ldr: rdn over 2f out: wknd wl over 1f out* **6/1**	42

1m 23.48s (-2.72) **Going Correction** -0.525s/f (Hard) **7 Ran SP% 115.4**

Speed ratings (Par 102): **94,92,90,89,86 84,76**

toteswingers 1&2 £11.20, 1&3 £16.90, 2&3 £21.00 CSF £99.23 CT £1918.71 TOTE £12.50: £5.90, £4.30; EX 81.70 Trifecta £1002.00 Part won. Pool: £1336.08 - 0.57 winning units..

Owner Derbyshire Racing V **Bred** Carrigbeg Stud & David Powell **Trained** Church Broughton , Derbys

FOCUS

A competitive fillies' handicap, run at a good gallop with the winning time just above standard. The placed horses look the best guides to the level.

2712 BET ON GO WITH TOTEPOOL MOBILE MEDIAN AUCTION MAIDEN STKS 5f 2y

4:40 (4:40) (Class 5) 2-Y-O **£2,587** (£770; £384; £192) **Stalls** High

Form				RPR
	1		**Coulsty (IRE)** 2-9-5 0 RyanMoore 6 (Richard Hannon) *mde virtually all: shkn up over 1f out: rdn and qcknd clr fnl f: impressive* **2/1**[1]	90+
2	2	5	**Disko (IRE)**[12] 2359 2-8-11 0 DarrenEgan(3) 5 (Daniel Kubler) *w wnr tl rdn over 1f out: outpcd ins fnl f* **10/1**	67
	3	shd	**Hay Chewed (IRE)** 2-9-0 0 RobertHavlin 8 (Peter Chapple-Hyam) *s.i.s: hld up: hdwy 2f out: rdn over 1f out: styd on same pce fnl f* **13/2**[3]	67
	4	1 ½	**Umneyati** 2-9-0 0 NeilCallan 2 (James Tate) *chsd ldrs: rdn over 1f out: no ex ins fnl f* **9/1**	61+
4	5	1 ¾	**Luckys Connoisseur**[10] 2404 2-9-5 0 FrannyNorton 9 (Mark Johnston) *chsd ldrs: rdn 1/2-way: wknd fnl f* **7/1**	60
	6	shd	**Andy Dandy (IRE)** 2-9-5 0 SteveDrowne 3 (Tom Dascombe) *hmpd s: sn outpcd: nvr nrr* **16/1**	60+
	7	shd	**Kaab (IRE)** 2-9-5 0 PaulHanagan 1 (Ed Dunlop) *dwlt: in rr and pushed along 1/2-way: hdwy over 1f out: wknd ins fnl f* **5/2**[2]	59
05	8	8	**Baltic Fire (IRE)**[25] 1960 2-9-5 0 CathyGannon 4 (Mrs K Burke) *sn hung rt and outpcd* **25/1**	30
4	9	4	**Pixmiester**[32] 1792 2-9-5 0 DavidProbert 7 (James Unett) *prom: pushed along 1/2-way: wknd over 1f out* **50/1**	16

58.52s (-1.48) **Going Correction** -0.525s/f (Hard) **9 Ran SP% 118.5**

Speed ratings (Par 93): **90,82,81,79,76 76,76,63,57**

toteswingers 1&2 £5.60, 1&3 £6.70, 2&3 £14.50 CSF £24.16 TOTE £3.00: £1.30, £1.90, £3.10; EX 21.40 Trifecta £234.40 Pool: £2906.04 - 9.29 winning units..

Owner Lord Vestey **Bred** Peter & Sarah Fortune **Trained** East Everleigh, Wilts

FOCUS

A modest median auction apart from the winner, who was in a different league. The runner-up is rated a slight improver on her debut form.

2713 PROGRESSIVE CASINO JACKPOTS AT TOTEPOOL.COM EBF MAIDEN FILLIES' STKS 1m 3f 183y

5:10 (5:10) (Class 5) 3-Y-O+ **£4,528** (£1,347; £673; £336) **Stalls** Low

Form				RPR
3	1		**Fersah (USA)**[17] 2206 3-8-10 0 PaulHanagan 9 (William Haggas) *mde virtually all: rdn and edgd rt over 1f out: styd on* **11/10**[1]	77
6	2	½	**Okavango**[17] 2206 3-8-10 0 FrederikTylicki 4 (James Fanshawe) *prom: rdn over 2f out: edgd rt and styd on wl ins fnl f* **20/1**	76
6-2	3	hd	**Playbill**[25] 1955 3-8-10 0 RyanMoore 1 (Sir Michael Stoute) *hld up: hdwy over 2f out: rdn to chsae wnr over 1f out: styd on* **3/1**[2]	76
5-	4	4	**Fatima's Gift**[247] 6489 3-8-10 0 AndreaAtzeni 3 (David Simcock) *hld up: pushed along over 2f out: hdwy over 1f out: nt rch ldrs* **4/1**[3]	70
5	5	hd	**Gertrude Gray (IRE)**[14] 2321 3-8-10 0 PatCosgrave 2 (Sir Henry Cecil) *chsd ldrs: rdn over 2f out: no ex fnl f* **8/1**	69

0 **6** *3 ¾* **Oscilate Wildly (IRE)**[11] 2389 3-8-10 0 RobertHavlin 11 63
(Peter Chapple-Hyam) *chsd wnr tl rdn over 2f out: wknd fnl f* **12/1**
0-5 **7** *1 ¼* **Point Of Control**[28] 1876 3-8-10 0 NeilCallan 7 61
(Michael Bell) *hld up: hdwy over 1f out: wknd ins fnl f* **25/1**
0 **8** *5* **Pure Flight (IRE)**[7] 2519 3-8-10 0 ow3 RachaelGreen(3) 8 56?
(Anthony Honeyball) *hld up: wknd over 2f out* **100/1**
00 **9** *18* **Double Accord**[18] 2198 3-8-10 0 ChrisCatlin 5
(Anthony Honeyball) *prom: pushed along over 5f out: wknd over 2f out: t.o* **100/1**
0 **10** *6* **Dance**[11] 2389 4-9-6 0 PatMillman(7) 6
(Rod Millman) *s.s: a in rr: lost tch fr over 2f out: t.o* **80/1**

2m 32.42s (-1.48) **Going Correction** 0.0s/f (Good)
WFA 3 from 4yo 17lb **10** Ran SP% **123.2**
Speed ratings (Par 100): **104,103,103,100,100 98,97,94,82,78**
toteswingers 1&2 £5.40, 1&3 £1.60, 2&3 £8.40 CSF £32.61 TOTE £2.10: £1.10, £4.10, £1.60; EX 23.70 Trifecta £99.40 Pool: £1179.16 - 8.88 winning units..
Owner Hamdan Al Maktoum **Bred** Shadwell Farm LLC **Trained** Newmarket, Suffolk

FOCUS
Possibly an above-average fillies' maiden and, although the winner is rated below her Ascot form, the form is rated on the positive side.

2714 VIRTUAL RACING EVERY DAY AT TOTEPOOL.COM APPRENTICE H'CAP 1m 3f 183y
5:40 (5:40) (Class 6) (0-60,58) 4-Y-0+ **£2,045** (£603; £302) **Stalls** Low

Form RPR
530- **1** **Iceman George**[179] 7744 9-9-5 **56** (v) PhilipPrince 1 66
(Alison Hutchinson) *a.p: chsd ldr 7f out: pushed along to ld over 2f out: rdn and edgd rt ins fnl f: styd on* **13/2**[3]
3445 **2** *1* **Spanish Plume**[9] 2435 5-9-7 **58** JackDuern 9 66
(Andrew Hollinshead) *hld up: hdwy over 2f out: rdn to chse wnr over 1f out: hung rt ins fnl f: styd on* **3/1**[1]
00-1 **3** *9* **Jewelled Dagger (IRE)**[25] 1949 9-9-5 **56** (t) EDLinehan 8 50
(Sharon Watt) *disp ld tl led 10f out: rdn and hdd over 2f out: wknd fnl f* **3/1**[1]
0402 **4** *¾* **Cane Cat (IRE)**[28] 1893 6-9-0 **54** (t) EoinWalsh(3) 7 46
(Tony Carroll) *hld up: hdwy u.p and hung rt fr over 1f out: nvr nrr* **7/1**
0034 **5** *shd* **Ice Tres**[25] 1949 4-9-1 **55** PatMillman(3) 6 47
(Rod Millman) *s.s and reluctent to r: hdwy over 3f out: rdn over 1f out: wknd fnl f* **5/1**[2]
20-0 **6** *hd* **Naledi**[15] 852 9-8-5 **47** RobJFitzpatrick(5) 10 39
(Richard Price) *hld up: rdn over 2f out: n.d* **20/1**
404- **7** *2* **Captain Oats (IRE)**[208] 7496 10-9-2 **53** GemmaTutty 5 42
(Pam Ford) *hld up: hdwy 1/2-way: rdn over 2f out: wknd over 1f out* **11/1**
0-00 **8** *5* **Maccabees**[25] 1949 4-9-2 **53** NedCurtis 4 34
(Roger Curtis) *chsd ldrs: rdn over 3f out: wknd over 2f out* **16/1**
050- **9** *1 ¼* **Shakespeare Dancer**[194] 7717 4-8-8 **45** RyanTate 2 24
(James Evans) *prom: pushed along and lost pl 1/2-way: rdn and wknd over 2f out* **40/1**
000- **10** *13* **Spanish Trail**[201] 7632 4-8-8 **45** DannyBrock 3
(Christopher Kellett) *disp ld 2f: chsd ldr tl 7f out: remained handy: rdn and wknd over 2f out: t.o* **80/1**

2m 33.96s (0.06) **Going Correction** 0.0s/f (Good) **10** Ran SP% **115.2**
Speed ratings (Par 101): **99,98,92,91,91 91,90,86,86,77**
toteswingers 1&2 £4.40, 1&3 £7.70, 2&3 £5.70 CSF £25.60 CT £70.77 TOTE £6.80: £2.50, £1.10, £1.70; EX 30.60 Trifecta £145.40 Pool: £849.51 - 4.38 winning units..
Owner John Mangan **Bred** T J And J Wells **Trained** Exning, Suffolk

FOCUS
A modest apprentice handicap, and a reasonable gallop saw very few get into the race. The winner is rated to last year's form with the second up slightly on his latest effort.
T/Plt: £84.30 to a £1 stake. Pool: £67,419.88 - 583.74 winning units T/Qpdt: £26.40 to a £1 stake. Pool: £4048.18 - 113.26 winning units CR

2501 REDCAR (L-H)
Monday, May 27

OFFICIAL GOING: Good to firm (good in places; 8.8)
Wind: Moderate; half against Weather: Cloudy with sunny periods

2715 WATCH RACING UK ON SKY 432 MAIDEN AUCTION STKS 5f
2:20 (2:20) (Class 5) 2-Y-0 **£2,726** (£805; £402) **Stalls** Centre

Form RPR
4 **1** **Sandsman's Girl (IRE)**[14] 2327 2-8-8 0 JamesSullivan 5 73
(James Given) *trckd ldrs whn hmpd after 1f: prom on outer whn hmpd 2f out: sn swtchd rt and rdn: styd on wl appr fnl f: led last 100yds* **20/1**
2 *½* **Classical Diva** 2-8-2 0 NeilFarley(3) 8 68
(Declan Carroll) *cl up: effrt wl over 1f out: rdn to ld briefly jst ins fnl f: hdd and no ex last 100yds* **9/2**[3]
432 **3** *½* **Danfazi (IRE)**[19] 2161 2-8-13 0 DavidNolan 1 74
(Kristin Stubbs) *chsd ldrs: hdwy and edgd lft 2f out: sn rdn and hung lft to far rail: ev ch tl drvn and one pce ins fnl f* **6/4**[1]
3 **4** *1* **Ixelles Diamond (IRE)**[16] 2282 2-8-7 0 PatrickMathers 6 64
(Richard Fahey) *chsd ldrs whn hmpd and wnt lft after 1f: rdn along 1/2-way: drvn and kpt on appr fnl f* **3/1**[2]
5 **5** *3 ¾* **Red House**[54] 1328 2-8-9 0 GrahamGibbons 3 53+
(David C Griffiths) *sn led: rdn along wl over 1f out: hdd jst ins fnl f: wknd* **25/1**
34 **6** *1 ¼* **Will To Survive (IRE)**[9] 2436 2-8-9 0 LukeMorris 9 48
(Richard Guest) *towards rr tl sme late hdwy* **10/1**
0 **7** *½* **San Remo Rose (IRE)**[21] 2075 2-8-3 0 DeclanCannon(3) 2 44
(Nigel Tinkler) *a towards rr* **66/1**
6 **8** *¾* **Touch The Clouds**[10] 2404 2-8-12 0 RobertWinston 10 47
(Kevin Ryan) *wnt rt s: sn swtchd lft: a in rr* **16/1**
06 **9** *½* **Highland Princess (IRE)**[13] 2337 2-7-13 0 ShirleyTeasdale(5) 7 37
(Paul Midgley) *chsd ldrs whn stmbld and wnt lft after 1f: rdn along bef 1/2-way: sn wknd* **66/1**
10 *hd* **Dancarina** 2-8-5 0 SilvestreDeSousa 4 37
(Tim Easterby) *s.i.s: a bhd* **10/1**

58.39s (-0.21) **Going Correction** -0.15s/f (Firm) **10** Ran SP% **118.8**
Speed ratings (Par 93): **95,94,93,91,85 83,83,81,81,80**
toteswingers 1&2 £26.70, 1&3 £6.10, 2&3 £3.40 CSF £107.41 TOTE £27.50: £5.80, £2.50, £1.10; EX 236.20 Trifecta £665.10 Part won. Pool: £886.93 - 0.08 winning units..
Owner Peter Swann **Bred** Pat Todd **Trained** Willoughton, Lincs

FOCUS
The ground had dried out a little from that advertised and was now good, good to firm in places. After the opener one rider described the going as "on the quick side". This looked an ordinary maiden and fits in with the averages for the race.

2716 MARKET CROSS JEWELLERS MAIDEN H'CAP 1m 6f 19y
2:50 (2:51) (Class 6) (0-65,63) 3-Y-0 **£2,045** (£603; £302) **Stalls** Low

Form RPR
00-6 **1** **Man From Seville**[7] 2500 3-9-1 **57** LukeMorris 11 66+
(Sir Mark Prescott Bt) *trckd ldrs: hdwy to chse ldng pair 5f out: rdn along and sltly outpcd 3f out: swtchd rt and drvn to chse ldrs 2f out: styd on wl u.p to ld ins fnl f: drvn out* **8/1**
5224 **2** *¾* **Handiwork**[14] 2312 3-9-6 **62** JamieSpencer 2 69
(Michael Bell) *sltly hmpd s: hld up in rr: hdwy 3f out: rdn 2f out: chsd ldrs and swtchd rt over 1f out: drvn and kpt on fnl f* **4/1**[1]
0-03 **3** *1 ¾* **Halfwaytocootehill (IRE)**[13] 2341 3-8-8 **50** (t) DaleSwift 6 55
(Ollie Pears) *trckd ldrs: hdwy 4f out: n.m.r wl over 2f out: sn led and rdn over 1f out: drvn and edgd lft 1f out: hdd ins fnl f: kpt on same pce* **5/1**[3]
3064 **4** *¾* **Helmsley Flyer (IRE)**[7] 2508 3-8-13 **55** DanielTudhope 14 59+
(David O'Meara) *hld up in rr: stdy hdwy on wd outside 3f out: rdn along wl over 1f out: kpt on fnl f: nrst fin* **6/1**
3-42 **5** *nk* **Danehill Flyer (IRE)**[19] 2175 3-9-7 **63** MichaelO'Connell 9 67+
(Philip Kirby) *t.k.h: hld up in rr: hdwy on wd outside over 4f out: rdn to chal and hung lft over 2f out: drvn and edgd lft over 1f out: ev ch tl wknd ins fnl f* **9/2**[2]
04-0 **6** *1* **Spats Colombo**[51] 1393 3-8-6 **48** AndrewElliott 3 50
(Micky Hammond) *in tch: hdwy 3f out: rdn along over 2f out: sn drvn and kpt on one pce* **33/1**
0-00 **7** *3 ¼* **Jomari (IRE)**[17] 2237 3-8-0 **45** NeilFarley(3) 10 43
(Declan Carroll) *sn led: rdn along over 3f out: hdd over 2f out: drvn and grad wknd fr wl over 1f out* **66/1**
0-05 **8** *½* **Inovate (IRE)**[7] 2508 3-8-12 **54** GrahamGibbons 15 51
(Tim Easterby) *chsd ldrs: cl up 4f out: rdn along 3f out: grad wknd fnl 2f* **16/1**
020- **9** *1* **Tobacco**[250] 6356 3-8-7 **54** DarylByrne(5) 4 49
(Tim Easterby) *bhd tl styd on fnl 2f* **20/1**
40-0 **10** *3 ½* **Princess Hollow**[13] 2341 3-8-8 **50** JamesSullivan 7 41
(Tony Coyle) *trckd ldr: cl up 4f out: rdn along over 3f out: drvn and wknd over 2f out* **50/1**
00-6 **11** *5* **Noble Bacchus (IRE)**[20] 2124 3-9-1 **57** (v[1]) StephenCraine 1 41
(Tom Dascombe) *trckd ldrs: effrt 5f out: rdn along over 3f out: wknd over 2f out* **14/1**
0-05 **12** *hd* **French Revolution**[13] 2341 3-8-0 **45** DeclanCannon(3) 8 28
(Jedd O'Keeffe) *trckd ldrs: rdn along 4f out: drvn over 3f out: sn wknd* **40/1**
-060 **13** *12* **Annalova**[13] 2341 3-8-3 **45** PatrickMathers 13
(Richard Fahey) *a towards rr* **66/1**
005- **14** *9* **Fake Or Fortune (IRE)**[239] 6708 3-8-0 **45** JulieBurke(3) 16
(Colin Teague) *a bhd* **25/1**
40-4 **15** *¾* **Angilina**[19] 2175 3-8-10 **52** (b) RobertWinston 5
(Kevin Ryan) *midfield: hdwy to chse ldrs over 5f out: rdn along wl over 3f out: sn wknd* **20/1**
0-52 **16** *2 ¾* **Moaning Butcher**[17] 2233 3-9-3 **59** SilvestreDeSousa 12
(Mark Johnston) *midfield: pushed along bef 1/2-way: sn lost pl: swtchd to outer and rdn along over 3f out: sn bhd* **8/1**

3m 5.27s (0.57) **Going Correction** -0.15s/f (Firm) **16** Ran SP% **127.6**
Speed ratings (Par 97): **92,91,90,90,89 89,87,87,86,84 81,81,74,69,69 67**
toteswingers 1&2 £15.90, 1&3 £7.00, 2&3 £11.10 CSF £38.70 CT £185.34 TOTE £9.30: £2.50, £1.70, £2.40, £1.90; EX 39.20 Trifecta £382.40 Part won. Pool: £509.96 - 0.61 winning units..
Owner Mr & Mrs William Rucker **Bred** Lady Bamford **Trained** Newmarket, Suffolk
■ Stewards' Enquiry : Dale Swift two-day ban: careless riding (10-11 June)

FOCUS
These 3-y-os had raced 82 times between them previously without success. The pace was modest and the third is probably the best guide to the level.

2717 BUY YOUR TICKETS ON-LINE @ REDCARRACING.CO.UK H'CAP 1m 2f
3:25 (3:26) (Class 4) (0-85,82) 3-Y-0 **£6,469** (£1,925; £962; £481) **Stalls** Low

Form RPR
2-1 **1** **Maputo**[22] 2041 3-9-7 **82** SilvestreDeSousa 3 102+
(Mark Johnston) *plld hrd: cl up: led over 7f out: qcknd clr wl over 2f out: styd on strly* **6/5**[1]
1-36 **2** *10* **Buckstay (IRE)**[10] 2432 3-9-2 **77** JamieSpencer 2 78
(Peter Chapple-Hyam) *t.k.h: hld up in rr: hdwy 3f out: swtchd rt and rdn wl over 1f out: kpt on same pce* **4/1**[3]
2-22 **3** *¾* **Legal Waves (IRE)**[14] 2321 3-9-6 **81** KierenFallon 5 81
(Brian Meehan) *t.k.h: trckd ldrs: effrt to chse wnr 3f out: sn rdn and edgd lft: drvn and one pce fr wl over 1f out* **13/8**[2]
-061 **4** *1 ¼* **Marhaba Malayeen (IRE)**[13] 2342 3-8-13 **74** DavidNolan 6 71
(Kevin Ryan) *set stdy pce: hdd over 7 out: chsd wnr: rdn along 3f out: drvn and one pce fnl 2f* **20/1**

2m 5.86s (-1.24) **Going Correction** -0.15s/f (Firm) **4** Ran SP% **108.3**
Speed ratings (Par 101): **98,90,89,88**
CSF £6.20 TOTE £1.50; EX 6.60 Trifecta £11.90 Pool: £742.52 - 46.41 winning units..
Owner Sheikh Hamdan Bin Mohammed Al Maktoum **Bred** Darley **Trained** Middleham Moor, N Yorks

FOCUS
A couple of non-runners reduced this to just the four, but it still produced as impressive a performance as you are likely to see. The winner thrashed two that looked on good marks and could be rated even higher at face value.

2718 ZETLAND GOLD CUP (H'CAP) 1m 2f
4:00 (4:00) (Class 2) (0-105,100) 3-Y-0+**£16,172** (£4,812; £2,405; £1,202) **Stalls** Low

Form RPR
03-1 **1** **Clon Brulee (IRE)**[8] 2478 4-9-1 **87** 6ex GrahamGibbons 5 102
(David Barron) *trckd ldr: hdwy over 3f out: rdn to chal wl over 1f out: led ent fnl f: drvn out* **9/2**[3]
0-02 **2** *½* **Eshtibaak (IRE)**[18] 2185 5-9-9 **95** DaneO'Neill 6 109
(John Gosden) *trckd ldrs: hdwy 3f out: rdn to chal wl over 1f out: ev ch tl drvn ins fnl f and no ex last 50yds* **3/1**[1]
000- **3** *2 ¼* **Gabrial The Great (IRE)**[233] 6875 4-9-1 **87** JamieSpencer 12 96
(Luca Cumani) *sn led: pushed clr 4f out: rdn 3f out: jnd wl over 1f out: drvn and hdd ent fnl f: kpt on same pce* **11/2**
63-5 **4** *3 ½* **Eltheeb**[12] 2369 6-8-11 **83** DanielTudhope 9 85
(David O'Meara) *hld up towards rr: hdwy 3f out: rdn along 2f out: kpt on u.p: nrst fin* **16/1**

2/-5 **5** *2 3/4* **Tahaamah**[16] 2251 5-9-6 **92**......(t) SilvestreDeSousa 7 89
(Saeed bin Suroor) *trckd ldng pair: hdwy over 3f out: rdn 2f out: edgd lft over 1f out and grad wknd* **13/2**

0350 **6** *nk* **Las Verglas Star (IRE)**[18] 2191 5-9-0 **86**...... DavidNolan 1 82
(Richard Fahey) *trckd ldrs on inner: rdn along 4f out: drvn wl over 2f out: grad wknd* **40/1**

03-4 **7** *1 1/2* **Silver Lime (USA)**[22] 2044 4-9-7 **93**...... JamesDoyle 2 86
(Roger Charlton) *hld up in midfield: hdwy over 3f out: rdn along over 2f out: nvr nr ldrs* **7/2**[2]

06-0 **8** *3 3/4* **Warlu Way**[48] 1446 6-9-0 **86**...... JamesSullivan 10 71
(Michael Easterby) *chsd ldrs on outer: rdn along over 3f out: sn wknd* **66/1**

-002 **9** *3 3/4* **No Poppy (IRE)**[9] 2440 5-8-12 **89**...... AdamCarter(5) 4 67
(Tim Easterby) *midfield: effrt and sme hdwy over 4f out: rdn along over 3f out and n.d* **33/1**

030- **10** *3 1/2* **Jo'Burg (USA)**[205] 7556 9-8-12 **89**...... DavidBergin(5) 13 60
(David O'Meara) *hld up: a towards rr* **40/1**

00-0 **11** *11* **War Poet**[10] 2431 6-9-0 **86**...... KierenFallon 3 35
(David O'Meara) *a in rr: bhd fnl 3f* **18/1**

2m 3.5s (-3.60) **Going Correction** -0.15s/f (Firm) **11** Ran SP% **114.6**
Speed ratings (Par 109): **108,107,105,103,100 100,99,96,93,90 81**
toteswingers 1&2 £3.60, 1&3 £9.30, 2&3 £4.20 CSF £17.46 CT £74.95 TOTE £6.50: £2.10, £1.40, £2.40; EX 19.70 Trifecta £125.90 Pool: £1,570.49 - 9.34 winning units..
Owner Ms Colette Twomey **Bred** Collette Twomey **Trained** Maunby, N Yorks

FOCUS
The previous ten winners of the Zetland Gold Cup were officially rated between 91 and 98, but that sequence was broken this time. The pace was solid enough, but it proved very hard to make up ground from behind. This looks good, solid form.

2719 WIN A VIP DAY OUT @ REDCARRACING.CO.UK MEDIAN AUCTION MAIDEN STKS 6f
4:30 (4:31) (Class 5) 3-Y-O **£2,587** (£770; £384; £192) **Stalls** Centre

Form RPR

06- **1** **Jubilee Dancer**[262] 6007 3-9-0 0......[1] RussKennemore 9 65
(Geoffrey Oldroyd) *cl up: effrt 2f out: rdn to ld over 1f out: drvn ins fnl f: kpt on gamely towards fin* **12/1**

00-3 **2** *shd* **Gold Beau (FR)**[55] 1301 3-9-5 63...... DavidNolan 1 70
(Kristin Stubbs) *trckd ldrs: hdwy on outer wl over 1f out: rdn chal 1f out: sddle slipped and ev ch tl drvn: edgd rt and no ex towards fin* **12/1**

24- **3** *2 3/4* **Dream Cast (IRE)**[284] 5260 3-9-5 78...... JamieSpencer 8 61
(David Simcock) *trckd ldrs: effrt whn nt clr run wl over 1f out: sn swtchd rt and rdn: nt clr run and swtchd rt again ent fnl f: sn drvn and one pce* **15/8**[1]

0 **4** *3* **Shady McCoy (USA)**[9] 2448 3-9-5 0...... RobertWinston 7 52
(Peter Chapple-Hyam) *cl up: rdn to chal 2f out: drvn ent fnl f: sn wknd* **7/2**[3]

3-32 **5** *1 1/2* **Nordikhab (IRE)**[19] 2172 3-9-5 76......(b[1]) SilvestreDeSousa 5 47
(Kevin Ryan) *led: rdn along 2f out: drvn and hdd over 1f out: hld whn n.m.r ent fnl f* **5/2**[2]

64-0 **6** *shd* **Knockamany Bends (IRE)**[21] 2076 3-9-5 61...... MickyFenton 6 46
(John Wainwright) *in tch: rdn along and outpcd fr 1/2-way* **50/1**

04 **7** *1 3/4* **The Nifty Blaze**[6] 2535 3-9-5 0...... JamesSullivan 2 41
(Tim Easterby) *in tch: rdn along 1/2-way: sn outpcd* **14/1**

8 *nk* **Vonn (IRE)** 3-9-0 0...... GrahamGibbons 10 35
(Tim Easterby) *dwlt: a in rr* **22/1**

9 *8* **Card High (IRE)** 3-9-2 0...... JulieBurke(3) 4 14
(Wilf Storey) *dwlt: a bhd* **100/1**

1m 10.33s (-1.47) **Going Correction** -0.15s/f (Firm) **9** Ran SP% **114.9**
Speed ratings (Par 99): **103,102,99,95,93 93,90,90,79**
toteswingers 1&2 £8.10, 1&3 £4.60, 2&3 £6.40 CSF £140.51 TOTE £13.30: £2.80, £2.10, £1.30; EX 154.60 Trifecta £506.40 Pool: £2,168.75 - 3.21 winning units..
Owner Moneypenny Racing **Bred** Bond Thoroughbred Corporation **Trained** Brawby, N Yorks
■ Stewards' Enquiry : David Nolan two-day ban: use of whip (10-11 June)

FOCUS
A weak median auction maiden with the two highest-rated horses disappointing. The runner-up looks the best guide for now.

2720 COME RACING AGAIN TOMORROW H'CAP (DIV I) 1m 6f 19y
5:05 (5:05) (Class 6) (0-65,65) 4-Y-O+ **£1,940** (£577; £288; £144) **Stalls** Low

Form RPR

0-03 **1** **Amir Pasha (UAE)**[20] 2120 8-8-6 **50**......(p) SilvestreDeSousa 14 58
(Micky Hammond) *hld up: hdwy on wd outside wl over 2f out: rdn to chse to ld ldrs wl over 1f out: str run to ld jst ins fnl f: drvn out* **10/1**

0422 **2** *1 1/4* **Brasingaman Eric**[14] 2313 6-9-7 **65**...... JamieSpencer 12 71
(George Moore) *led: qcknd over 3f out: rdn over 2f out: drvn and hdd jst ins fnl f: rallied gamely: no ex last 75yds* **7/2**[3]

06-0 **3** *3/4* **Golden Future**[17] 2242 10-8-5 **54**...... DavidBergin(5) 9 59
(Peter Niven) *trckd ldrs: hdwy 4f out: rdn over 2f out: drvn and kpt on fnl f* **16/1**

64-0 **4** *nk* **Ferney Boy**[20] 2120 7-7-13 **46** oh1...... NeilFarley(3) 6 51
(Chris Fairhurst) *trckd ldrs on inner: hdwy over 3f out: rdn over 2f out: drvn and kpt on same pce fnl f* **50/1**

0-03 **5** *1 1/4* **Madrasa (IRE)**[14] 2316 5-9-4 **62**......(t) MickyFenton 3 65
(Keith Reveley) *hld up in rr: hdwy 3f out: rdn along 2f out: styd on wl fnl f: nrst fin* **3/1**[2]

3-53 **6** *hd* **Dr Irv**[17] 2242 4-9-6 **64**...... MichaelO'Connell 11 67
(Philip Kirby) *trckd ldrs: hdwy over 4f out: effrt to chse ldrs over 2f out: sn rdn: drvn over 1f out: wknd ent fnl f* **2/1**[1]

0055 **7** *2 1/4* **Turjuman (USA)**[7] 2509 8-8-6 **50** ow2...... AndrewElliott 8 49
(Simon West) *hld up: hdwy 3f out: rdn over 2f out: styd on fnl f: nrst fin* **66/1**

0-60 **8** *4* **Ad Value (IRE)**[6] 2540 5-8-12 **56**...... JamesSullivan 1 50
(Alan Kirtley) *chsd ldr: rdn along wl over 2f out: sn wknd* **33/1**

0-32 **9** *5* **Politbureau**[14] 2332 6-8-7 **51**...... GrahamGibbons 10 38
(Michael Easterby) *chsd ldrs: hdwy and cl up on outer over 5f out: rdn along 3f out: sn wknd* **14/1**

150- **10** *4* **Bandanaman (IRE)**[135] 6784 7-8-10 **61**...... JoeCosgrove(7) 4 42
(Alan Swinbank) *s.i.s: a bhd* **16/1**

065 **11** *7* **Aura Bora (USA)**[69] 1072 5-7-13 **46** oh1...... DeclanCannon(3) 7 17
(Tim Easterby) *a towards rr* **50/1**

3m 2.76s (-1.94) **Going Correction** -0.15s/f (Firm) **11** Ran SP% **116.4**
Speed ratings (Par 101): **99,98,97,97,96 96,95,93,90,88 84**
toteswingers 1&2 £4.00, 1&3 £16.60, 2&3 £11.20 CSF £43.93 CT £565.89 TOTE £9.50: £2.40, £1.30, £4.70; EX 35.20 Trifecta £335.70 Pool: £1,126.54 - 2.51 winning units..
Owner The Steven Kay Partnership **Bred** Darley **Trained** Middleham Moor, N Yorks

FOCUS
A moderate staying handicap and the pace was ordinary. The form is modest, rated around the first three.

2721 COME RACING AGAIN TOMORROW H'CAP (DIV II) 1m 6f 19y
5:35 (5:35) (Class 6) (0-65,64) 4-Y-O+ **£1,940** (£577; £288; £144) **Stalls** Low

Form RPR

6-03 **1** **Sally Friday (IRE)**[20] 2118 5-8-2 **52**......(p) KevinStott(7) 3 65
(Edwin Tuer) *trckd ldrs: swtchd rt to outer and smooth hdwy 4f out: led 3f out and sn rdn clr: styd on strly* **13/2**[3]

6-43 **2** *6* **Looks Like Rain**[19] 2165 4-9-7 **64**...... DaleSwift 1 69
(Brian Ellison) *hld up in rr: hdwy 3f out: rdn to chse wnr wl over 1f out: sn drvn: edgd lft and no imp* **2/1**[1]

24/ **3** *5* **Miss Mysterious (FR)**[573] 7212 5-8-6 **49**...... SilvestreDeSousa 13 47
(Philip Kirby) *cl up: led after 3f: jnd and rdn along over 4f out: hdd 3f out: sn drvn and kpt on one pce fnl 2f* **8/1**

5400 **4** *1 1/4* **Torero**[3] 2642 4-8-13 **56**......(p) RobertWinston 14 52
(Kevin Ryan) *trckd ldrs: hdwy over 6f out: cl up 4f out: rdn along over 3f out: drvn over 2f out and grad wknd* **7/1**

406- **5** *2 1/4* **Dimashq**[230] 6956 11-8-2 **45**...... JamesSullivan 9 38
(Richard Guest) *hld up and bhd: sme hdwy fnl 2f: n.d* **25/1**

14-3 **6** *4* **Green To Gold (IRE)**[46] 1084 8-9-7 **64**......(b) JamieSpencer 12 54
(Don Cantillon) *trckd ldrs: hdwy on bit and cl up 4f out: rdn over 3f out and sn wknd* **7/2**[2]

00-4 **7** *8* **Kian's Joy**[19] 1700 4-7-9 **45**...... NoelGarbutt(7) 10 21
(Jedd O'Keeffe) *towards rr: effrt and sme hdwy over 4f out: sn rdn along and wknd 3f out* **33/1**

4301 **8** *3/4* **Dubara Reef (IRE)**[14] 2328 6-8-5 **48**......(p) LukeMorris 11 23
(Paul Green) *led 3f: prom: rdn along wl over 3f out and sn wknd* **13/2**[3]

3m 1.99s (-2.71) **Going Correction** -0.15s/f (Firm) **8** Ran SP% **112.6**
Speed ratings (Par 101): **101,97,94,94,92 90,85,85**
toteswingers 1&2 £3.70, 1&3 £3.50, 2&3 £5.40 CSF £19.31 CT £104.52 TOTE £8.90: £2.20, £1.40, £2.00; EX 20.20 Trifecta £252.90 Pool: £722.62 - 2.14 winning units..
Owner E Tuer **Bred** M Stewkesbury **Trained** Birkby, N Yorks

FOCUS
This division was hit with six non-runners, but the winning time was still 0.77 seconds quicker than the first leg. The winner scored easily and used to be capable of better than currently rated.
T/Plt: £60.10 to a £1 stake. Pool: £62,079.01 - 753.34 winning units T/Qpdt: £15.10 to a £1 stake. Pool: £3,454.13 - 169.20 winning units JR

2516 WINDSOR (R-H)

Monday, May 27

OFFICIAL GOING: Good (good to firm in places; 8.7)
Top bend out 8yds from normal configuration adding 34yds to races of 1m and beyond. Inner of straight out 14yds at 6f and 7yds at Winning Post.
Wind: Virtually nil Weather: Sunny

2722 WELCOME TO ROYAL BERKSHIRE FIRE & RESCUE SERVICE MAIDEN STKS 5f 10y
2:15 (2:15) (Class 5) 3-Y-O+ **£2,587** (£770; £384; £192) **Stalls** Low

Form RPR

0-34 **1** **Royal Challis**[9] 2447 3-9-4 75...... RichardHughes 4 79
(Richard Hannon) *sn led: drvn over 1f out: r.o strly* **3/1**[2]

033 **2** *1 1/2* **The Dark Wizard (IRE)**[16] 2267 3-9-4 70...... WilliamBuick 3 74
(Roger Charlton) *trckd ldrs: drvn appr fnl f: sn nt clr run: swtchd lft and rdn to chse wnr fnl 100yds: no imp* **6/4**[1]

0-06 **3** *2 1/4* **Rock Up (IRE)**[11] 2394 3-9-4 70......(b[1]) LiamKeniry 7 66
(David Elsworth) *chsd wnr 3f out: rdn and no imp over 1f out: outpcd into 3rd fnl 100yds* **6/1**

5-30 **4** *3* **Talqaa**[22] 2051 3-8-13 72......(v[1]) MartinHarley 1 50
(Mick Channon) *chsd ldrs: rdn 2f out: wknd appr fnl f* **7/1**

-3 **5** *nse* **Sixty Minutes**[27] 1911 3-9-4 0...... SeanLevey 8 55
(David Brown) *chsd ldrs: rdn 2f out: outpcd fnl f* **5/1**[3]

0450 **6** *11* **Don't Be Scilly**[27] 1896 5-9-0 40...... JoeyHaynes(7) 6 13
(Eric Wheeler) *spd to 1/2-way* **100/1**

500- **7** *2 3/4* **Rupeetoups**[283] 5327 5-9-12 42...... MatthewDavies 5
(Jim Boyle) *outpcd* **100/1**

8 *10* **Xanders Secret** 3-8-13 0...... IanMongan 2
(Brett Johnson) *s.i.s: outpcd* **25/1**

1m 0.56s (0.26) **Going Correction** -0.075s/f (Good)
WFA 3 from 5yo 8lb **8** Ran SP% **114.3**
Speed ratings (Par 103): **94,91,88,83,83 65,61,45**
toteswingers 1&2 £1.70, 1&3 £3.40, 2&3 £3.00 CSF £7.86 TOTE £3.40: £1.30, £1.30, £1.70; EX 5.60 Trifecta £44.80 Pool: £2265.15 - 37.83 winning units..
Owner Longview Stud & Bloodstock Ltd **Bred** Mrs C F Van Straubenzee & Miss A Gibson Fleming **Trained** East Everleigh, Wilts

FOCUS
The watered ground was given as good, good to firm in places (GoingStick 8.7). The inner of the straight was dolled out 14yds at 6f and 7yds at the winning post, while the top bend was dolled out 8yds from its normal inner configuration, adding 34yds to race distances of 1m plus. A fair maiden, although not entirely solid form.

2723 HAPPY BIRTHDAY PAUL MAIDEN AUCTION STKS 6f
2:45 (2:50) (Class 5) 2-Y-O **£2,587** (£770; £384; £192) **Stalls** Low

Form RPR

2 **1** **Tableforten**[9] 2436 2-8-11 0...... LiamJones 3 72
(J S Moore) *led after 1f: drvn over 2f out: hrd pressed ins fnl f: styd on wl u.p* **3/1**[2]

3 **2** *1/2* **Llyrical**[13] 2344 2-8-9 0...... WilliamCarson 2 69
(Derek Haydn Jones) *in rr: hdwy over 2f out: chsd ldrs over 1f out: str chal u.p fnl 100yds: no ex clsng stages* **6/1**

54 **3** *2 1/4* **Left Defender (IRE)**[12] 2359 2-8-9 0...... J-PGuillambert 1 62+
(Jo Hughes) *led 1f: styd pressing ldr: n.m.r on rail over 2f out whn rdn and again whn u.p 1f out: outpcd fnl 110yds* **16/1**

4 *2* **Killing Time (IRE)** 2-9-2 0...... JimCrowley 8 63+
(Ralph Beckett) *chsd ldrs: green and edgd lft 2f out: stl green over 1f out: drvn and kpt on ins fnl f to gain on 3rd but no ch w ldng duo* **9/2**[3]

3 **5** *1 1/4* **Trinity Boy**[30] 1833 2-9-2 0...... AdamKirby 14 59+
(Clive Cox) *trcking ldrs wn bmpd and carried bdly lft over 2f out: stl green and hanging lft again after: rdn over 1f out and kpt on fnl f but nt rcvr* **11/4**[1]

	6	hd	**Rolling Dice** 2-8-11 0 ... LiamKeniry 15	53+
			(Dominic Ffrench Davis) *s.i.s and outpcd: pushed along and hdwy fr 2f out: styd on ins fnl f: nvr a threat* **50/1**	
0	7	2½	**Astral Rose**[38] 1659 2-8-3 0 ... AmyScott(5) 7	43
			(Paul Fitzsimons) *in rr: hdwy 3f out: sn rdn: nvr gng pce to rch ldrs* **33/1**	
	8	2	**Monsieur Blanc (IRE)** 2-8-11 0 ... ShaneKelly 13	40
			(Denis Coakley) *chsd ldrs: rdn over 2f out: btn wl over 1f out* **10/1**	
65	9	nk	**Flying Kyte**[28] 1880 2-8-4 0 ... SophieRalston(7) 11	39
			(Pat Phelan) *chsd ldrs tl over 2f out* **80/1**	
5	10	6	**Oakley Dancer**[16] 2283 2-8-4 0 ... KirstyMilczarek 9	14
			(Tony Carroll) *chsd ldrs: hung bdly lft over 2f out: hung bdly lft again wl over 1f out: sn dropped away* **33/1**	
	11	24	**What A Dandy (IRE)** 2-8-13 0 ... MatthewDavies 12	
			(Jim Boyle) *s.i.s: a wl bhd* **10/1**	

1m 13.92s (0.92) **Going Correction** -0.075s/f (Good) 11 Ran SP% **117.3**
Speed ratings (Par 93): **90,89,86,83,82 81,78,75,75,67 35**
toteswingers 1&2 £4.60, 1&3 £8.80, 2&3 £9.70 CSF £20.93 TOTE £3.80: £1.60, £2.10, £4.00; EX 18.30 Trifecta £112.10 Pool: £2528.62 - 16.91 winning units..

Owner Eventmasters Racing **Bred** Manor Farm Stud (rutland) & Miss S Hoare **Trained** Upper Lambourn, Berks

FOCUS

Perhaps not the strongest of maidens and the form looks ordinary for now.

2724 CONGRATULATIONS MR & MRS BROWN H'CAP (DIV I) 6f

3:20 (3:22) (Class 4) (0-85,85) 4-Y-0+ **£4,851** (£1,443; £721; £360) **Stalls** Low

Form				RPR
13-0	1		**Tropics (USA)**[17] 2207 5-9-6 **84** ...[1] JimCrowley 5	101
			(Dean Ivory) *trckd ldrs: pushed along to ld ins fnl 2f: rdn over 1f out: clr fnl 150yds: easily* **5/2**[1]	
4224	2	3¾	**Peace Seeker**[16] 2286 5-9-1 **79** ... WilliamCarson 4	84
			(Anthony Carson) *led tl over 4f out: rdn and outpcd over 2f out: styd on u.p fnl f to take 2nd cl home but no ch w wnr* **10/1**	
4-40	3	¾	**Arctic Lynx (IRE)**[11] 2388 6-8-13 **82** ... MichaelJMMurphy(5) 12	85
			(Robert Cowell) *chsd ldrs: wnt 2nd ins fnl 2f: no imp on wnr u.p over 1f out: outpcd into 3rd cl home* **20/1**	
00-5	4	1¼	**Orders From Rome (IRE)**[18] 2196 4-8-11 **75** ... JohnFahy 8	74
			(Eve Johnson Houghton) *chsd ldrs: rdn over 2f out: styd on same pce fr over 1f out* **20/1**	
3-10	5	2¼	**The Tichborne (IRE)**[16] 2255 5-8-13 **77** ...(v) JackMitchell 1	68
			(Roger Teal) *towards rr: rdn over 2f out: styd on fnl f but nvr any ch* **16/1**	
40-2	6	3	**Divine Call**[56] 1286 6-8-8 **72** ... ShaneKelly 9	54
			(Milton Bradley) *in rr: hdwy over 2f out: sn rdn and nvr gng pce to chal: wknd fnl f* **20/1**	
50-0	7	2	**Tartan Trip**[9] 2450 6-8-8 **72** ... MarcHalford 10	47
			(Luke Dace) *s.i.s: in rr: rdn 2f out: one pce* **66/1**	
000-	8	½	**Novellen Lad (IRE)**[231] 6938 8-9-5 **83** ... J-PGuillambert 3	57
			(Willie Musson) *a outpcd* **25/1**	
00-0	9	1¼	**Sir Pedro**[16] 2255 4-9-1 **79** ... MartinHarley 6	49
			(Charles Hills) *t.k.h: plld way to ld over 4f out* **8/1**[3]	
102-	10	8	**Jocasta Dawn**[224] 7113 4-9-0 **78** ... FergusSweeney 11	22
			(Henry Candy) *s.i.s: sn in tch* **16/1**	
2-10	11	14	**Cheworee**[11] 2396 4-9-7 **85** ... RichardHughes 2	
			(David Elsworth) *s.i.s: a outpcd* **3/1**[2]	

1m 11.53s (-1.47) **Going Correction** -0.075s/f (Good) 11 Ran SP% **105.2**
Speed ratings (Par 105): **106,101,100,98,95 91,88,88,86,75 57**
toteswingers 1&2 £3.90, 1&3 £12.20, 2&3 £19.70 CSF £20.06 CT £297.22 TOTE £3.10: £1.20, £3.20, £5.90; EX 23.70 Trifecta £373.70 Pool: £2046.30 - 4.10 winning units..

Owner Dean Ivory **Bred** D Konecny, S Branch & A Branch **Trained** Radlett, Herts

FOCUS

There wasn't much pace on early and it paid to race handily. That said, the winner was in a different league to the rest. The winner was quite impressive and the form is taken at face value through the runner-up to his turf form.

2725 CONGRATULATIONS MR & MRS BROWN H'CAP (DIV II) 6f

3:55 (3:58) (Class 4) (0-85,85) 4-Y-0+ **£4,851** (£1,443; £721; £360) **Stalls** Low

Form				RPR
100-	1		**Trojan Rocket (IRE)**[205] 7559 5-9-0 **78** ... MickaelBarzalona 2	87
			(Michael Wigham) *trckd ldr: led ins fnl 2f: rdn appr fnl f: hrd pressed fnl 150yds: hld on: all out* **8/1**	
3035	2	hd	**King Of Jazz (IRE)**[14] 2310 5-9-2 **85** ... WilliamTwiston-Davies(5) 10	93
			(Michael Bell) *chsd ldrs: wnt 2nd over 1f out and sn rdn: str chal fnl 150yds: nt quite get up* **9/2**[1]	
1-54	3	hd	**Lupo D'Oro (IRE)**[11] 2388 4-9-1 **79** ... RichardHughes 12	86
			(John Best) *t.k.h: towards rr: hdwy 2f out: chsd ldrs appr fnl f: rdn to chal fnl 50yds but jst hld clsng stages* **7/1**[3]	
0-15	4	2	**Apollo D'Negro (IRE)**[16] 2255 5-9-3 **81** ...(v) AdamKirby 4	82
			(Clive Cox) *chsd ldrs: rdn appr fnl f: styd on same pce* **11/2**[2]	
0-00	5	hd	**My Kingdom (IRE)**[16] 2255 7-8-11 **75** ...(t) HarryBentley 9	75
			(Stuart Williams) *s.i.s: in rr: hdwy over 1f out: sn rdn: one pce ins fnl f* **28/1**	
5620	6	1¼	**Rocket Rob (IRE)**[16] 2255 7-8-10 **74** ... J-PGuillambert 8	70
			(Willie Musson) *in rr: hdwy over 1f out: pushed along and styd on fnl f but nvr gng pce to rch ldrs* **14/1**	
221-	7	½	**Don Libre**[254] 6256 4-8-7 **74** ow2 ... AshleyMorgan(3) 1	69
			(Paul Cole) *chsd ldrs: rdn 2f out: wknd over 1f out* **15/2**	
00-0	8	nk	**Nasri**[21] 2097 7-9-5 **83** ... SebSanders 5	77
			(Milton Bradley) *led: hdd ins fnl 2f: hung bdly lft and btn fr over 1f out* **25/1**	
40-0	9	1½	**Uprise**[16] 2255 4-8-8 **72** ... JamieMackay 6	61
			(George Margarson) *chsd ldrs: drvn 3f out: wknd over 1f out* **12/1**	
-000	10	1¼	**Perfect Pastime**[16] 2255 5-8-9 **78** ...(p) NathanAlison(5) 11	63
			(Jim Boyle) *a outpcd* **40/1**	
660	11	4	**Oneladyowner**[2] 2664 5-9-1 **79** ... SeanLevey 3	51
			(David Brown) *a outpcd* **10/1**	

1m 12.0s (-1.00) **Going Correction** -0.075s/f (Good) 11 Ran SP% **102.1**
Speed ratings (Par 105): **103,102,102,99,99 97,97,96,94,93 87**
toteswingers 1&2 £5.50, 1&3 £9.70, 2&3 £3.90 CSF £32.24 CT £169.00 TOTE £8.10: £2.90, £1.40, £2.10; EX 37.00 Trifecta £301.20 Pool: £1547.39 - 3.85 winning units..

Owner G D J Linder **Bred** J G F Fox **Trained** Newmarket, Suffolk

■ Stewards' Enquiry : Mickael Barzalona two-day ban: use of whip (10-11 June)

FOCUS

The slower of the two divisions by 0.47sec. The runner-up is rated to this year's form and sets the level.

2726 FIRST CAFE'S POSH FAST FOOD H'CAP 5f 10y

4:25 (4:27) (Class 4) (0-85,82) 3-Y-0 **£4,851** (£1,443; £721; £360) **Stalls** Low

Form				RPR
311-	1		**March**[229] 6984 3-9-6 **82** ... AdamKirby 5	90+
			(Marco Botti) *trckd ldrs: drvn and qcknd over 1f out: sn rdn to chal: led fnl 100yds: kpt on wl* **5/2**[1]	
0-21	2	½	**The Art Of Racing (IRE)**[30] 1844 3-9-6 **82** ...(t) HarryBentley 3	88
			(Olly Stevens) *chsd ldrs: chal fr over 1f out and remained upsides u.p ins fnl f: got tight between horses fnl 110yds: nt pce of wnr clsng stages but kpt on wl to edge 2nd* **11/4**[2]	
-333	3	nse	**Smart Spender (IRE)**[7] 2521 3-9-4 **80** ... ShaneKelly 2	86
			(Jo Hughes) *chsd ldr: chal over 1f out and stl upsides fnl f tl outpcd into 3rd clsng strides* **5/2**[1]	
252-	4	¾	**Dusty Storm (IRE)**[220] 7220 3-9-2 **78** ... SeanLevey 1	81
			(Ed McMahon) *led: hrd pressed fr over 1f out: kpt slt advantage tl hdd and no ex fnl 100yds* **12/1**	
041-	5	¾	**Inka Surprise (IRE)**[262] 6015 3-9-5 **81** ... JimCrowley 4	81+
			(Ralph Beckett) *in tch: pushed along and one pce 2f out: drvn and styd on again fnl f: hld whn no daylight bhd wall of horses fnl 100yds* **9/2**[3]	

59.55s (-0.75) **Going Correction** -0.075s/f (Good) 5 Ran SP% **109.7**
Speed ratings (Par 101): **103,102,102,100,99**
CSF £9.57 TOTE £3.10: £1.20, £1.80; EX 7.90 Trifecta £19.40 Pool: £2026.68 - 78.21 winning units..

Owner Al Asayl Bloodstock Ltd **Bred** T K & Mrs P A Knox **Trained** Newmarket, Suffolk

FOCUS

There was a bunched finish to this handicap. the fourth sets the standard backed up by the third.

2727 HAPPY BIRTHDAY JIM LAFLIN H'CAP 1m 67y

5:00 (5:00) (Class 5) (0-75,73) 3-Y-0 **£1,678** (£1,678; £384; £192) **Stalls** Low

Form				RPR
333-	1		**Freeport**[290] 5060 3-9-7 **73** ... JimmyFortune 4	83
			(Brian Meehan) *chsd ldrs: rdn to ld appr fnl f: styd on u.str.p: ct for dead-heat last stride* **4/1**[2]	
43-6	1	dht	**Aussie Reigns (IRE)**[18] 2193 3-9-5 **71** ...(v) JimCrowley 1	82+
			(William Knight) *in tch: n.m.r over 2f out: drvn and hdwy over 1f out: hanging lft ins fnl f but kpt on clsng stages to force dead-heat last stride* **8/1**[3]	
31-0	3	1½	**Consign**[39] 1636 3-9-7 **73** ...(p) WilliamBuick 8	80
			(Jeremy Noseda) *chsd ldrs: rdn to chal appr fnl f: fnd no ex u.p and one pce fnl 100yds* **4/1**[2]	
5-05	4	3½	**Invincible Cara (IRE)**[17] 2229 3-9-6 **72** ... AdamKirby 2	71
			(Ed Dunlop) *in rr: hdwy and veered bdly lft wl over 2f out: rcvrd and styd on u.p fr over 1f out: no ex and btn ins fnl f* **14/1**	
5214	5	1¾	**Sam Spade (IRE)**[14] 2324 3-9-2 **68** ... RichardHughes 7	62
			(Richard Hannon) *led: jnd over 2f out but kpt slt ld tl hdd appr fnl f: wknd fnl 150yds* **3/1**[1]	
-401	6	1¼	**Tagalaka (IRE)**[19] 2154 3-8-12 **64** ... JohnFahy 5	56
			(Eve Johnson Houghton) *in rr and pushed along 4f out: hdwy u.p over 2f out: nvr rchd ldrs and wknd appr fnl f* **16/1**	
5-36	7	¾	**Carrera**[20] 2129 3-8-10 **62** ... MartinDwyer 11	52
			(J W Hills) *chsd ldr: rdn to chal fr over 2f out: wknd u.p appr fnl f* **20/1**	
1650	8	2¾	**The Scuttler (IRE)**[27] 1900 3-8-11 **63** ...(v[1]) MartinHarley 3	47
			(Mick Channon) *in rr: rdn over 3f out: mod prog over 2f out: sn wknd* **16/1**	
41-0	9	5	**Al Emirati (IRE)**[51] 1400 3-9-7 **73** ... HarryBentley 10	45
			(Marco Botti) *in rr and rn wd bnd after 2f: hdwy 4f out: styng on whn bdly bmpd and pushed lft wl over 2f out: no ch after* **14/1**	
2-40	10	36	**Multitask**[11] 2394 3-9-1 **67** ... IanMongan 6	
			(Michael Madgwick) *in rr and wd bnd after 2f: no ch after: t.o* **50/1**	
252-	11	4	**Anjuna Beach (USA)**[188] 7796 3-9-5 **71** ... ShaneKelly 9	
			(Gary Moore) *chsd ldrs: upsides and hanging lft fr 5f out: hung bdly lft bnd over 3f out: sn t.o and eased* **10/1**	

1m 43.26s (-1.44) **Going Correction** -0.075s/f (Good) 11 Ran SP% **117.0**
Speed ratings (Par 99): **104,104,102,99,97 96,95,92,87,51 47**WIN: AR £3.90, F £2.40; PL: AR £2.30, F £2.00, C £1.70; EX: AR/F £20.40, F/AR £17.90; CSF: AR/F £19.90, F/AR £17.99; Trifecta: AR/F/C £99.80, F/AR/C £100.80; Tricast: AR/F/C £76.03, F/AR/C £69.65; Toteswingers: AR/F £6.70, AR/C £7.00, F/C £2.30 TOTE £27: £Owner, £Raymond Tooth, £Bred, £Theobalds StudTrained Manton, Wilts.

Owner The Old Brokers **Bred** S Connolly **Trained** Patching, W Sussex

FOCUS

The judge couldn't split the first two at the line. The third sets the level of the form.

2728 JOIN THE YOUNG HOOVES KIDS CLUB H'CAP 1m 2f 7y

5:30 (5:31) (Class 4) (0-85,82) 4-Y-0+ **£4,851** (£1,443; £721; £360) **Stalls** Centre

Form				RPR
0-24	1		**Lucky Henry**[18] 2193 4-9-6 **81** ... AdamKirby 5	90
			(Clive Cox) *chsd ldrs: rdn 3f out: chsd ldr over 2f out: sn chalng and styd upsides u.p tl led clsng stages* **4/1**[2]	
-001	2	nk	**Come On Blue Chip (IRE)**[21] 2101 4-9-7 **82** ...(p) RichardHughes 9	90
			(Paul D'Arcy) *led 1f: trckd ldrs: led ins fnl 3f: hrd pressed fr ins fnl 2f: kpt slt advantage tl hdd clsng stages* **5/2**[1]	
0232	3	1¼	**Prince Of Burma (IRE)**[5] 2574 5-8-11 **75** ...(t) RyanClark(3) 1	81
			(Jeremy Gask) *s.i.s: in rr: hdwy over 2f out: styd on to press ldrs jst ins fnl f tl hung bdly lft and btn fnl 100yds* **8/1**	
4460	4	2¼	**Tinshu (IRE)**[16] 2251 7-9-6 **81** ...(p) WilliamCarson 3	82
			(Derek Haydn Jones) *chsd ldrs: rdn over 2f out: wknd ins fnl f* **6/1**	
0050	5	1¾	**Robin Hood (IRE)**[16] 2251 5-9-3 **78** ... JackMitchell 8	76
			(Philip Mitchell) *led after 1f: rdn and hdd ins fnl 3f: wknd wl over 1f out* **11/1**	
-323	6	2½	**Sheila's Buddy**[21] 2101 4-9-3 **78** ... LiamKeniry 6	71
			(J S Moore) *in tch: rdn over 3f out: chsd ldrs 2f out: wknd over 1f out* **10/1**	
0-00	7	½	**Siouxperhero (IRE)**[27] 1901 4-8-7 **68** ... MartinDwyer 10	60
			(William Muir) *rdn 3f out: hrd drvn over 2f out: a bhd* **28/1**	
450-	8	½	**Top Diktat**[332] 3594 5-9-3 **78** ... ShaneKelly 4	69
			(Gary Moore) *pushed along 3f out: a towards rr* **25/1**	
3-5	9	hd	**Break Rank (USA)**[18] 2191 4-9-2 **77** ... JohnFahy 2	68
			(Ed de Giles) *chsd ldrs: rdn over 2f out: sn btn* **9/2**[3]	

2m 7.87s (-0.83) **Going Correction** -0.075s/f (Good) 9 Ran SP% **116.9**
Speed ratings (Par 105): **100,99,98,96,95 93,93,92,92**
toteswingers 1&2 £3.60, 1&3 £5.40, 2&3 £5.10 CSF £14.62 CT £76.27 TOTE £5.30: £2.00, £1.40, £2.70; EX 18.40 Trifecta £111.70 Pool: £1866.95 - 12.53 winning units..

Owner Biddestone Racing Club **Bred** Tim Bostwick **Trained** Lambourn, Berks

FOCUS
A tight little handicap with the winner rated back to near his best and the third to his latest AW mark.

2729 MARK PLAYER 50TH BIRTHDAY FILLIES' H'CAP 1m 3f 135y
6:00 (6:00) (Class 5) (0-75,72) 4-Y-O+ **£2,587** (£770; £384; £192) **Stalls** Centre

Form RPR

241- **1** **Mama Quilla (USA)**[224] 7117 4-9-6 **71** .... RichardHughes 2 81+
(William Haggas) *hld up in rr but in tch: hdwy over 2f out: led appr fnl f: rdn and kpt on wl fnl 150yds* **15/8**[1]

3 **2** *1 1/4* **Danisa**[12] 2360 4-8-11 **62** ....(t) WilliamCarson 5 70
(David Bridgwater) *in rr: rdn over 2f out: hdwy to chse ldrs appr fnl f: chsd wnr u.p fnl 110yds but a hld* **8/1**

/3-5 **3** *1* **Running Deer (IRE)**[38] 1663 4-9-7 **72** .... IanMongan 7 78
(Sir Henry Cecil) *sn led: rdn over 2f out: kpt narrow ld tl hdd appr fnl f: styd on same pce for 3rd* **7/2**[2]

4124 **4** *2 1/4* **The Blue Dog (IRE)**[23] 2004 6-8-13 **64** .... JimCrowley 1 66
(Phil McEntee) *in rr: hdwy fr 3f out to chse ldrs 2f out: disp 2nd u.p over 1f out: wknd fnl 110yds* **8/1**

164- **5** *4 1/2* **Panettone (IRE)**[210] 7444 4-8-10 **66** .... WilliamTwiston-Davies[(5)] 3 61
(Roger Varian) *chsd ldr tl rdn 3f out: wknd fr 2f out* **6/1**

-503 **6** *3/4* **Choral Festival**[10] 2413 7-9-4 **69** .... KieranO'Neill 6 62
(John Bridger) *chsd ldrs: drvn to chal over 2f out: wknd qckly over 1f out* **5/1**[3]

00-0 **7** *14* **Operettist**[25] 1948 4-8-6 **57** ....(v[1]) KirstyMilczarek 4 26
(Tony Carroll) *chsd ldrs tl rdn and btn 3f out* **25/1**

2m 28.15s (-1.35) **Going Correction** -0.075s/f (Good) **7 Ran SP% 114.0**
Speed ratings (Par 100): **101,100,99,98,95 94,85**
toteswingers: 1&2 £3.70, 2&3 £4.80, 1&3 £1.40 CSF £17.69 TOTE £2.30: £1.50, £3.40; EX 15.70 Trifecta £66.60 Pool: £1982.37 - 22.31 winning units..
Owner Mr & Mrs G Middlebrook **Bred** Mr & Mrs Gary Middlebrook **Trained** Newmarket, Suffolk

FOCUS
Not a particularly strong race best rated around the third and fourth.
T/Jkpt: Not won. T/Plt: £29.00 to a £1 stake. Pool: £100,468.54 - 2525.73 winning units T/Qpdt: £12.40 to a £1 stake. Pool: £4587.34 - 272.58 winning units ST

2730 - 2735a (Foreign Racing) - See Raceform Interactive

[2708]LEICESTER (R-H)
Tuesday, May 28

OFFICIAL GOING: Good changing to good (good to soft in places after race 3 (3.00) changing to good to soft after race 6 (4.30)
False rail from top of hill on back straight all the way to Winning Post added circa 17m to races on Round course.
Wind: Light against Weather: Raining

2736 PLAY TOTEPLACEPOT NOW AT TOTEPOOL.COM H'CAP 5f 2y
2:00 (2:00) (Class 5) (0-75,74) 4-Y-O+ **£2,587** (£770; £384; £192) **Stalls** High

Form RPR

-043 **1** **Bronze Beau**[11] 2410 6-9-4 **71** ....(t) JamesSullivan 2 82
(Kristin Stubbs) *mde all: rdn over 1f out: r.o* **11/2**[2]

3304 **2** *2* **Wicked Wench**[20] 2173 4-9-7 **74** .... SteveDrowne 5 78
(Jeremy Gask) *sn chsng ldrs: rdn and ev ch over 1f out: styd on same pce ins fnl f* **15/2**

1020 **3** *hd* **Shawkantango**[7] 2550 6-8-10 **70** ....(v) AdamMcLean[(7)] 10 73
(Derek Shaw) *s.i.s: hld up: hdwy over 1f out: r.o: nrst fin* **20/1**

650- **4** *1* **Indian Tinker**[223] 7177 4-9-1 **68** .... ShaneKelly 4 67
(Robert Cowell) *chsd ldrs: rdn over 1f out: styd on same pce fnl f* **8/1**

4-03 **5** *3/4* **Generalyse**[19] 2196 4-9-4 **71** ....(b) PaulHanagan 1 68
(Ben De Haan) *s.i.s: sn prom: rdn 1/2-way: no ex ins fnl f* **5/2**[1]

4663 **6** *hd* **Swendab (IRE)**[26] 1952 5-8-13 **66** ....(b) MartinHarley 3 62
(John O'Shea) *w wnr tl rdn over 1f out: no ex ins fnl f* **11/2**[2]

513/ **7** *8* **Musical Bridge**[684] 3994 7-9-3 **70** .... GrahamLee 8 37
(Lisa Williamson) *sn pushed along in rr: wknd over 1f out* **25/1**

1203 **8** *1 1/4* **Bussa**[76] 981 5-9-5 **72** ....(t) RichardHughes 7 35
(David Evans) *hld up: hdwy over 1f out: wknd and eased ins fnl f* **7/1**[3]

242- **9** *2 1/4* **Griffin Point (IRE)**[176] 7970 6-8-10 **63** .... JackMitchell 6 18
(William Muir) *sn pushed along and prom: rdn 1/2-way: wknd wl over 1f out* **10/1**

1m 1.44s (1.44) **Going Correction** +0.20s/f (Good) **9 Ran SP% 112.4**
Speed ratings (Par 103): **96,92,92,90,89 89,76,74,70**
Tote Swingers: 1&2 £7.80, 1&3 £16.20, 2&3 £16.80 CSF £44.63 CT £761.34 TOTE £6.70: £1.90, £2.80, £6.40; EX 45.60 Trifecta £557.00 Pool: £2,390.17 - 3.21 winning units..
Owner D Arundale **Bred** Meon Valley Stud **Trained** Norton, N Yorks

FOCUS
The fast ground forecast was eased by overnight and morning rain to Good before this first race. The jockeys described the ground as riding on the slow side of good. An ordinary but quite competitive sprint handicap with the form rated around the placed horses.

2737 TOTEEXACTA ON ALL RACES AT TOTEPOOL.COM CLAIMING STKS 7f 9y
2:30 (2:30) (Class 6) 3-Y-O **£1,940** (£577; £288; £144) **Stalls** High

Form RPR

5362 **1** **Claude Greenwood**[21] 2129 3-8-5 61 ....(b) SilvestreDeSousa 5 63
(David Simcock) *mde all: rdn and hung rt over 1f out: styd on* **6/1**[3]

0-60 **2** *2 1/4* **Avatar Star (IRE)**[26] 1958 3-9-1 70 ....(tp) PaoloSirigu 3 67
(Marco Botti) *hld up: hdwy over 2f out: rdn to chse wnr over 1f out: styd on* **9/1**

2-10 **3** *1/2* **Raging Bear (USA)**[53] 1365 3-9-11 76 .... RichardHughes 4 76
(Richard Hannon) *dwlt: hld up: pushed along 1/2-way: hdwy u.p over 1f out: styd on to take 3rd post* **5/1**[2]

4-00 **4** *shd* **Plunder**[13] 2374 3-8-11 77 ....(p) NeilCallan 6 62
(Kevin Ryan) *chsd wnr tl rdn over 1f out: styd on same pce ins fnl f* **2/1**[1]

0640 **5** *3* **Abanoas (USA)**[8] 2508 3-8-2 50 ....(b[1]) LukeMorris 2 45
(Alan Coogan) *hmpd s: sn prom: rdn over 2f out: no ex ins fnl f* **100/1**

2300 **6** *1 1/4* **Moe's Place (IRE)**[17] 2276 3-8-8 60 .... JulieBurke[(3)] 9 51
(Kevin Ryan) *chsd ldrs: rdn over 2f out: wknd fnl f* **20/1**

5423 **7** *nk* **Handsome Stranger (IRE)**[7] 2528 3-7-12 56 ....(v) NoelGarbutt[(7)] 8 44
(David Evans) *hld up: rdn 1/2-way: nvr on terms* **33/1**

3125 **8** *9* **Studfarmer**[12] 2393 3-8-5 68 ....(v) AndreaAtzeni 7 20
(David Evans) *prom: pushed along 1/2-way: rdn and wknd 2f out* **6/1**[3]

546- **9** *6* **Ingleby Royale**[291] 5041 3-8-10 72 .... PaulHanagan 1 10
(Richard Fahey) *chsd ldrs: rdn 1/2-way: wknd 2f out* **5/1**[2]

1m 28.33s (2.13) **Going Correction** +0.20s/f (Good) **9 Ran SP% 113.9**
Speed ratings (Par 97): **95,92,91,91,88 86,86,76,69**
.The winner was claimed by Mr Roger Curtis for £5,000.\n\x\x
Owner Dr Marwan Koukash **Bred** Mrs J A Rawding **Trained** Newmarket, Suffolk

FOCUS
Not a bad standard for a 3-y-o claimer with four of the runners rated in the 70s. The form looks straightforward rated around the winner and fifth.

2738 PLAY TOTEQUADPOT NOW AT TOTEPOOL.COM H'CAP 7f 9y
3:00 (3:00) (Class 4) (0-80,84) 3-Y-O **£6,301** (£1,886; £943; £472; £235) **Stalls** High

Form RPR

23-1 **1** **Pythagorean**[8] 2495 3-9-12 **84** 6ex .... JamesDoyle 1 92+
(Roger Charlton) *hld up: hdwy over 2f out: rdn to ld and hung lft over 1f out: r.o: hung rt towards fin* **5/6**[1]

40-3 **2** *2* **Majestic Moon (IRE)**[17] 2285 3-9-7 **79** ....(b[1]) PaulHanagan 6 82
(Richard Fahey) *wnt lft s: plld hrd and sn prom: rdn over 1f out: chsd wnr and hung rt ins fnl f: styd on* **9/2**[3]

5-60 **3** *1 3/4* **Ceelo**[41] 1620 3-9-6 **78** .... LiamKeniry 4 77
(Sylvester Kirk) *led: rdn and hdd over 1f out: hmpd sn after: styd on same pce ins fnl f* **50/1**

661- **4** *1 1/2* **Pivotal Movement**[225] 7110 3-9-6 **78** .... RichardHughes 9 73
(Richard Hannon) *chsd ldrs: rdn and ev ch over 1f out: no ex ins fnl f* **4/1**[2]

40-0 **5** *3/4* **Mystical Moment**[19] 2195 3-9-1 **78** .... WilliamTwiston-Davies[(5)] 8 71
(Richard Hannon) *hld up: rdn over 1f out: r.o ins fnl f: nvr nrr* **33/1**

1-55 **6** *1 3/4* **Nenge Mboko**[22] 2303 3-9-3 **75** ....(p) PatCosgrave 5 63
(George Baker) *chsd ldr: rdn over 2f out: ev ch over 1f out: wknd ins fnl f* **33/1**

1341 **7** *3/4* **Skytrain**[15] 2318 3-9-5 **77** .... SilvestreDeSousa 7 63
(Mark Johnston) *hmpd s: sn pushed along in rr: nvr on terms* **11/1**

52-6 **8** *3/4* **Jubilant Queen**[41] 1616 3-8-10 **68** .... JohnFahy 2 52
(Clive Cox) *hld up in tch: racd keenly: rdn over 1f out: sn wknd* **50/1**

20-1 **9** *20* **Testamatta**[20] 2172 3-9-4 **76** .... AndreaAtzeni 3
(Marco Botti) *prom: rdn over 2f out: wknd over 1f out: eased* **14/1**

1m 27.41s (1.21) **Going Correction** +0.20s/f (Good) **9 Ran SP% 117.5**
Speed ratings (Par 101): **101,98,96,95,94 92,91,90,67**
Tote Swingers: 1&2 £1.50, 1&3 £10.70, 2&3 £22.40 CSF £4.89 CT £101.03 TOTE £1.90: £1.50, £1.50, £8.00; EX 5.70 Trifecta £128.40 Pool: £3,556.28 - 20.75 winning units..
Owner K Abdullah **Bred** Juddmonte Farms Ltd **Trained** Beckhampton, Wilts

FOCUS
A tight 3-y-o handicap and the time was 0.92 secs faster than the preceding claimer. The form looks decent and the winner is capable of going on from this.

2739 TOTEPOOL.COM HOME OF KINGSIZE POOLS H'CAP 1m 3f 183y
3:30 (3:30) (Class 5) (0-75,75) 4-Y-O+ **£2,587** (£770; £384; £192) **Stalls** Low

Form RPR

54-2 **1** **Ashdown Lad**[18] 2234 4-9-5 **73** .... PaulHanagan 7 82
(William Jarvis) *prom: racd keenly: lost pl 1/2-way: hdwy over 2f out: rdn to ld post* **11/4**[2]

26-5 **2** *nse* **Burnham**[43] 1586 4-9-6 **74** .... RichardHughes 2 83
(Hughie Morrison) *hld up: hdwy 1/2-way: rdn to ld wl ins fnl f: hdd post* **6/4**[1]

5540 **3** *3/4* **Sir Boss (IRE)**[7] 2552 8-9-0 **75** .... JoeyHaynes[(7)] 4 83
(Michael Mullineaux) *chsd ldrs tl led over 3f out: rdn over 1f out: hdd wl ins fnl f: unable qck nr fin* **20/1**

021- **4** *9* **Abbraccio**[27] 8239 5-8-11 **70** ....(t) WilliamTwiston-Davies[(5)] 6 63
(Fergal O'Brien) *led: hdd over 3f out: rdn over 1f out: wknd fnl f* **16/1**

4224 **5** *6* **Easydoesit (IRE)**[17] 2284 5-8-11 **65** .... GrahamLee 1 49
(Tony Carroll) *hld up: pushed along over 4f out: rdn over 2f out: n.d* **17/2**

2141 **6** *5* **Cape Alex**[20] 2159 4-8-7 **61** .... ChrisCatlin 8 37
(Clive Brittain) *sed stowly: wl bhd tl tk clsr order 7f out: hdwy over 4f out: rdn and wknd over 2f out* **8/1**[3]

34-0 **7** *12* **Tribal Myth (IRE)**[33] 1775 6-8-6 **63** .... JulieBurke[(3)] 5 20
(Kevin Ryan) *chsd ldrs tl rdn and wknd over 2f out: t.o* **12/1**

020- **8** *15* **Bounty Seeker (USA)**[326] 3827 4-9-5 **73** .... SilvestreDeSousa 3
(Mark Johnston) *chsd ldr tl rdn over 3f out: wknd over 2f out: t.o* **12/1**

2m 38.08s (4.18) **Going Correction** +0.45s/f (Yiel) **8 Ran SP% 114.3**
Speed ratings (Par 103): **104,103,103,97,93 90,82,72**
Tote Swingers: 1&2 £1.80, 1&3 £9.80, 2&3 £8.40 CSF £7.24 CT £62.93 TOTE £5.10: £1.90, £1.10, £4.80; EX 6.90 Trifecta £106.90 Pool: £2,733.99 - 19.17 winning units..
Owner The FOPS **Bred** Mr & Mrs A E Pakenham **Trained** Newmarket, Suffolk

FOCUS
A run-of-the-mill handicap, but it produced an exciting finish. The form is straightforward, with the third rated to his best turf form since 2011.

2740 TRY A TOTETRIFECTA AT TOTEPOOL.COM EBF MAIDEN FILLIES' STKS 5f 2y
4:00 (4:00) (Class 5) 2-Y-O **£4,204** (£1,251; £625; £312) **Stalls** High

Form RPR

1 **Kaiulani (IRE)** 2-9-0 0 .... MartinHarley 3 82+
(Mick Channon) *chsd ldrs: shkn up to ld ins fnl f: r.o wl* **2/1**[1]

2 *2* **Excel's Beauty** 2-9-0 0 .... NeilCallan 8 75+
(James Tate) *chsd ldr tl led 1/2-way: shkn up over 1f out: hdd and unable qck ins fnl f* **7/1**

3 *1 3/4* **Brunhilde** 2-9-0 0 .... RichardKingscote 7 68+
(Tom Dascombe) *a.p: rdn over 1f out: styd on same pce ins fnl f* **25/1**

4 *3/4* **Gold Top (IRE)** 2-9-0 0 .... RichardHughes 1 66+
(Richard Hannon) *sn pushed along in rr: swtchd rt and hdwy over 1f out: nt rch ldrs* **11/4**[2]

5 *3/4* **Cockney Belle** 2-9-0 0 .... SilvestreDeSousa 6 63
(Marco Botti) *hld up: hung rt early: swtchd rt and hdwy 1/2-way: rdn over 1f out: edgd lft and no ex fnl f* **12/1**

6 *1* **Bountiful Forest** 2-9-0 0 .... PaulHanagan 4 59
(Richard Fahey) *sn pushed along in rr: nvr on terms* **12/1**

7 *1 3/4* **Sunset Shore** 2-9-0 0 .... LukeMorris 2 53
(Sir Mark Prescott Bt) *sn pushed along to chse ldrs: outpcd over 3f out: rallied over 1f out: wknd ins fnl f* **4/1**[3]

45 **8** *1 3/4* **Anfield**[28] 1910 2-9-0 0 .... PatCosgrave 5 47
(Mick Quinn) *led to 1/2-way: wknd fnl f* **50/1**

1m 2.51s (2.51) **Going Correction** +0.20s/f (Good) **8 Ran SP% 113.7**
Speed ratings (Par 90): **87,83,81,79,78 77,74,71**
Tote Swingers: 1&2 £5.20, 1&3 £17.10, 2&3 £19.60 CSF £16.62 TOTE £3.60: £1.10, £1.50, £8.00; EX 25.80 Trifecta £295.10 Pool: £2,459.87 - 6.24 winning units..
Owner Mrs T P Radford & Tails Partnership **Bred** Summerhill B/S & Lynch Bages **Trained** West Ilsley, Berks

The Form Book Flat, Raceform Ltd, Compton, RG20 6NL.

FOCUS
Traditionally a good fillies' maiden with several of these going on to be Group-class performers, including Cherry Hinton winner Please Sing and Lowther winner Lady Of The Desert. Some major yards were represented and there was a clear-cut winner. The level is rated around averages and time but could under-estimate the winner.

2741 NEW SUPERSCOOP6 BET AT TOTEPOOL.COM EBF MAIDEN STKS 5f 218y
4:30 (4:34) (Class 4) 2-Y-O £4,204 (£1,251; £625; £312) Stalls High

Form RPR
1 **Toormore (IRE)** 2-9-5 0 RichardHughes 1 88+
(Richard Hannon) *chsd ldrs: led over 1f out: r.o wl* **5/2**[1]
2 *nk* **Ertijaal (IRE)** 2-9-5 0 PaulHanagan 6 87+
(William Haggas) *a.p: chsd wnr fnl f: sn rdn: r.o wl* **5/2**[1]
3 *7* **Major Crispies** 2-9-5 0 LukeMorris 10 65
(James Eustace) *hld up: pushed along 1/2-way: hdwy over 1f out: styd on same pce ins fnl f* **66/1**
4 *hd* **Steele Ranger** 2-9-5 0 PatCosgrave 2 64
(Peter Chapple-Hyam) *prom: rdn over 2f out: no ex fnl f* **10/1**
36 5 *hd* **Bounty Hunter (IRE)**[12] 2401 2-9-5 0 RichardKingscote 7 64
(Tom Dascombe) *w ldr tl led over 2f out: rdn and hdd over 1f out: no ex fnl f* **9/1**[3]
4 6 *3* **Know Your Name**[12] 2391 2-9-5 0 JamesDoyle 9 54
(David Evans) *chsd ldrs tl rdn: edgd lft and wknd over 1f out* **100/1**
7 *4 1/2* **Veya (USA)** 2-9-5 0 TomMcLaughlin 8 41+
(Ed Walker) *s.i.s: hdwy over 3f out: hmpd and wknd over 1f out* **20/1**
4 8 *7* **Al Baz**[27] 1930 2-9-5 0 NeilCallan 13 19
(James Tate) *led over 3f: rdn and wknd over 1f out* **4/1**[2]
9 *1/2* **Graphene** 2-9-5 0 GrahamLee 5 17
(Rod Millman) *s.s: a in rr* **66/1**
10 *3/4* **Bold Jack Donahue (IRE)** 2-9-5 0 SilvestreDeSousa 3 15
(Ralph Beckett) *s.i.s: a in rr* **25/1**
11 *2 1/4* **Dylan's Centenary** 2-9-5 0 FergusSweeney 11 8
(Rod Millman) *s.s: a in rr* **50/1**
12 *2 1/4* **Dalaki (IRE)** 2-9-5 0 MickaelBarzalona 12
(Clive Brittain) *sn pushed towards rr and rn green: wknd 1/2-way* **16/1**

1m 14.0s (1.00) **Going Correction** +0.20s/f (Good) 12 Ran SP% **116.7**
Speed ratings (Par 95): **101,100,91,91,90 86,80,71,70,69 66,63**
Tote Swingers: 1&2 £2.40, 1&3 £28.20, 2&3 £40.60 CSF £7.79 TOTE £2.90: £1.30, £1.60, £11.30; EX 10.50 Trifecta £374.60 Pool: £4,809.50 - 9.62 winning units..
Owner Middleham Park Racing IX & James Pak **Bred** BEC Bloodstock **Trained** East Everleigh, Wilts

FOCUS
Roman Soldier, who went on to be runner-up in both the Coventry and July Stakes, was the best recent winner of this maiden. There were plenty of interesting debutants and two of them came clear of the rest. This looks strong form in a race with very decent averages.

2742 YOUR FAVOURITE POOL BETS AT TOTEPOOL.COM H'CAP (DIV I) 1m 1f 218y
5:00 (5:01) (Class 6) (0-65,65) 3-Y-O £1,940 (£577; £288; £144) Stalls Low

Form RPR
36-6 1 **Special Meaning**[125] 332 3-9-4 **62** SilvestreDeSousa 7 73+
(Mark Johnston) *mde all: rdn over 1f out: styd on wl* **5/1**[3]
00-0 2 *4* **Hermosa Vaquera (IRE)**[12] 2392 3-9-4 **62** RichardHughes 6 65
(Peter Chapple-Hyam) *a.p: chsd wnr over 2f out: rdn over 1f out: styd on same pce ins fnl f* **17/2**
600- 3 *1 1/4* **Big Thunder**[258] 6133 3-9-3 **61** LukeMorris 1 62+
(Sir Mark Prescott Bt) *hld up: pushed along 1/2-way: hdwy over 2f out: rdn over 1f out: styd on same pce fnl f* **15/8**[1]
-131 4 *1/2* **Astrum**[22] 2095 3-9-7 **65** GrahamLee 3 66
(Rod Millman) *a.p: nt clr run over 2f out: rdn over 1f out: styd on same pce fnl f* **3/1**[2]
500- 5 *1 3/4* **See And Be Seen**[176] 7973 3-8-7 **51** oh3 LiamKeniry 10 48
(Sylvester Kirk) *hld up: hdwy over 2f out: rdn and edgd rt over 1f out: no ex fnl f* **20/1**
-304 6 *1 1/2* **Our Golden Girl**[21] 2129 3-8-8 **57** ow1 WilliamTwiston-Davies[(5)] 12 51
(Shaun Lycett) *s.i.s: hld up: rdn over 2f out: n.d* **20/1**
006- 7 *6* **Refuse To Mambo**[176] 7971 3-8-7 **51** PaulQuinn 4 34
(Andrew Hollinshead) *hld up: rdn over 2f out: n.d* **22/1**
-030 8 *7* **Fishlake Rebel**[10] 2464 3-8-7 **51** oh1 JamesSullivan 9 20
(Ruth Carr) *chsd ldr tl rdn over 2f out: wknd over 1f out* **16/1**
440- 9 *40* **Beautifulwildthing**[202] 7636 3-9-1 **59** FergusSweeney 5
(William Kinsey) *chsd ldrs tl rdn and wknd over 2f out: t.o* **33/1**

2m 14.58s (6.68) **Going Correction** +0.625s/f (Yiel) 9 Ran SP% **109.7**
Speed ratings (Par 97): **98,94,93,93,92 90,86,80,48**
Tote Swingers: 1&2 £5.50, 1&3 £3.20, 2&3 £4.50 CSF £40.57 CT £98.10 TOTE £5.60: £1.80, £2.60, £1.60; EX 35.90 Trifecta £129.20 Pool: £2,851.72 - 16.54 winning units..
Owner Newsells Park Stud **Bred** Newsells Park Stud **Trained** Middleham Moor, N Yorks

FOCUS
The first division of this modest handicap made interesting by some unexposed sorts from major yards. The winner looks well ahead of her mark and it is worth treating the form positively.

2743 YOUR FAVOURITE POOL BETS AT TOTEPOOL.COM H'CAP (DIV II) 1m 1f 218y
5:35 (5:36) (Class 6) (0-65,65) 3-Y-O £1,940 (£577; £288; £144) Stalls Low

Form RPR
00-0 1 **Rutherglen**[38] 1684 3-9-7 **65** PatCosgrave 1 73+
(George Baker) *hld up: hdwy u.p over 1f out: styd on to ld wl ins fnl f* **5/1**[3]
0 2 *2 1/4* **Aminah**[15] 2308 3-9-2 **60** JamesDoyle 7 64
(Robert Cowell) *plld hrd and prom: rdn over 2f out: led 1f out: hdd and no ex wl ins fnl f* **20/1**
-500 3 *4* **Duke Of Yorkshire**[11] 2432 3-9-1 **62** NeilFarley[(3)] 9 58
(Declan Carroll) *sn pushed along to ld: hdd 3f out: sn rdn: no ex fnl f* **14/1**
3055 4 *1 1/4* **Sweet Alabama**[21] 2124 3-8-7 **51** oh2 (b[1]) FergusSweeney 11 45
(Rod Millman) *prom: racd keenly: trckd ldr over 6f out: led 3f out: rdn: hung lft and hdd 1f out: wknd ins fnl f* **33/1**
05-3 5 *9* **Tahaf (IRE)**[8] 2508 3-9-0 **58** (t) NeilCallan 2 35
(Clive Brittain) *s.i.s: hld up: hdwy over 3f out: rdn and wknd over 1f out* **7/4**[1]
4540 6 *16* **Jd Rockefeller**[20] 2156 3-8-2 **51** oh1 (p) MichaelJMMurphy[(5)] 5
(Paul D'Arcy) *hld up: rdn and wknd over 3f out: t.o* **14/1**
6405 7 *9* **Gold Roll (IRE)**[10] 2464 3-8-10 **54** JamesSullivan 8
(Ruth Carr) *chsd ldrs tl rdn and wknd over 2f out: t.o* **16/1**
30 8 *26* **Burma Days (USA)**[5] 2599 3-8-7 **51** oh1 LiamKeniry 6
(Sylvester Kirk) *hld up: rdn over 4f out: sn lost tch: eased t.o* **25/1**
2140 9 *2 3/4* **Birdy Boy (USA)**[22] 2080 3-9-4 **62** SilvestreDeSousa 4
(Mark Johnston) *chsd ldrs: rdn over 3f out: sn wknd and eased: t.o* **15/2**
33-5 10 *1 1/4* **Super Cookie**[20] 2156 3-9-5 **63** RichardHughes 3
(Philip McBride) *hld up: hdwy 4f out: sn rdn and wknd: eased: t.o* **4/1**[2]

2m 15.04s (7.14) **Going Correction** +0.625s/f (Yiel) 10 Ran SP% **115.6**
Speed ratings (Par 97): **96,94,91,90,82 70,62,42,39,38**
Tote Swingers: 1&2 £3.00, 1&3 £3.00, 2&3 £2.30 CSF £100.27 CT £1309.95 TOTE £5.80: £1.70, £8.70, £2.40; EX 96.60 Trifecta £1183.90 Part won. Pool: £1,578.64 - 0.93 winning units..
Owner Frank Brady **Bred** Frank Brady **Trained** Manton, Wilts

FOCUS
The second leg of this 3-y-o handicap was run 0.46secs slower than the first. The form is rated at face value with the runner-up to her debut form.
T/Plt: £48.00 to a £1 stake. Pool: £55,821.16 - 847.70 winning tickets. T/Qpdt: £4.30 to a £1 stake. Pool: £4,952.27 - 839.71 winning tickets. CR

2567 LINGFIELD (L-H)
Tuesday, May 28

OFFICIAL GOING: Turf course - good to soft changing to good to soft (soft in places) after race 1 (5.50) changing to soft after race 2 (6.20); all-weather - standard
Wind: Light, half behind Weather: Overcast but dry after substantial rain during day

2744 BRITISH STALLION STUDS SUPPORTING BRITISH RACING EBF MAIDEN FILLIES' STKS 6f
5:50 (5:55) (Class 5) 2-Y-O £3,067 (£905; £453) Stalls High

Form RPR
1 **Joyeuse** 2-9-0 0 [1] TomQueally 7 88+
(Sir Henry Cecil) *hld up bhd ldrs: prog over 2f out: pushed into ld over 1f out: readily drew clr* **10/11**[1]
2 *3 1/4* **Dancealot** 2-9-0 0 HayleyTurner 6 71
(Clive Brittain) *trckd ldrs: pushed along wl over 2f out: shkn up and prog to go 2nd jst ins fnl f: styd on but no ch w wnr* **10/1**
3 *1 1/2* **Pieman's Girl** 2-9-0 0 RobertHavlin 5 67
(Anthony Carson) *slowly away: hld up in rr: prog 2f out: shaen up to chse wnr briefly 1f out: one pce after* **50/1**
4 4 *1/2* **Prisca**[11] 2419 2-9-0 0 PatDobbs 4 65
(Richard Hannon) *pressed ldr: led over 2f out: rdn and hdd over 1f out: one pce after* **3/1**[2]
5 *6* **Amontillado (IRE)** 2-9-0 0 SeanLevey 2 47
(Richard Hannon) *pressed ldrs on outer 4f: sn wknd* **12/1**
6 *1* **Atheera (IRE)** 2-9-0 0 DaneO'Neill 3 44
(Mark Johnston) *led against rail to over 2f out: sn wknd* **5/1**[3]
7 *1 3/4* **Anya's Angel** 2-8-11 0 DarrenEgan[(3)] 1 39
(David Simcock) *slowly away: racd wdst of all: a in rr: wknd 2f out* **20/1**
8 *1 1/4* **Who Splashed Me** 2-9-0 0 DavidProbert 9 35
(J R Jenkins) *dwlt: in tch in rr tl wknd 2f out* **100/1**

1m 14.22s (3.02) **Going Correction** +0.35s/f (Good) 8 Ran SP% **118.5**
Speed ratings (Par 90): **93,88,86,86,78 76,74,72**
Tote Swingers: 1&2 £4.60, 1&3 £6.80, 2&3 £28.00 CSF £12.32 TOTE £1.70: £1.02, £4.30, £13.50; EX 15.10 Trifecta £196.10 Pool: £2,261.47 - 8.64 winning units..
Owner K Abdullah **Bred** Juddmonte Farms Ltd **Trained** Newmarket, Suffolk

FOCUS
Unsurprisingly with all the rain around the ground had softened appreciably from the morning description. An interesting fillies' maiden, for no other reason than the presence of Frankel's half-sister, and that filly scored impressive ly. the form is rated around the fourth and race averages.

2745 32RED CASINO FILLIES' H'CAP 6f
6:20 (6:22) (Class 5) (0-75,75) 4-Y-0+ £2,726 (£805; £402) Stalls High

Form RPR
13-1 1 **If So**[26] 1957 4-9-6 **74** HayleyTurner 4 81
(James Fanshawe) *chsd ldr: rdn and no imp 2f out: styd on u.p fnl f to ld last 50yds* **7/4**[1]
1200 2 *1/2* **Mary's Pet**[6] 2582 6-8-4 **61** oh4 (v) DarrenEgan[(3)] 2 66
(Lee Carter) *led and gd spd fr wdst draw to r against nr side rail: 2 l up and gng best over 1f out: tired ins fnl f: hdd last 50yds* **25/1**
5600 3 *3/4* **Sulis Minerva (IRE)**[10] 2441 6-8-13 **70** RyanClark[(3)] 7 73
(Jeremy Gask) *trckd ldrs: urged along and nt qckn 2f out: styd on fnl f alongside wnr: no ex last 75yds* **7/1**
1005 4 *hd* **Amethyst Dawn (IRE)**[8] 2516 7-8-8 **65** (t) BillyCray[(3)] 5 67
(Andrew Reid) *sn pushed along in last trio and off the pce: styd on fr over 1f out: nrst fin* **20/1**
0001 5 *1* **Night Trade (IRE)**[5] 2588 6-8-11 **70** ow4 (p) EDLinehan[(5)] 9 69
(Ronald Harris) *trckd ldrs: urged along over 2f out: kpt on same pce fr over 1f out: nvr able to chal* **3/1**[2]
5402 6 *3 1/2* **Catalinas Diamond (IRE)**[26] 1957 5-8-12 **66** (t) SteveDrowne 6 55
(Pat Murphy) *settled in last trio and off the pce: pushed along over 2f out: couple of reminders over 1f out: nvr involved* **14/1**
1- 7 *1 1/2* **Angel Way (IRE)**[226] 7086 4-9-7 **75** PatDobbs 3 59
(Mike Murphy) *trckd ldrs on outer tl wknd 2f out* **5/1**[3]
220- 8 *6* **Young Dottie**[185] 7858 7-8-7 **66** JemmaMarshall[(5)] 8 32
(Pat Phelan) *dwlt: hld up in last and off the pce: rdn and no prog over 2f out: sn bhd* **12/1**

1m 13.12s (1.92) **Going Correction** +0.35s/f (Good) 8 Ran SP% **113.5**
Speed ratings (Par 100): **101,100,99,99,97 93,91,83**
Tote Swingers: 1&2 £10.50, 1&3 £3.20, 2&3 £24.90 CSF £48.32 CT £251.79 TOTE £2.00: £1.10, £10.00, £2.80; EX 38.10 Trifecta £309.30 Pool: £1,585.40 - 3.84 winning units..
Owner Hopper, Grundy, Handscombe **Bred** Mr & Mrs K W Grundy, Mr & Mrs P Hopper **Trained** Newmarket, Suffolk
■ Stewards' Enquiry : E D Linehan two-day ban; weighted in heavy (11th-12th June).

FOCUS
The ground was changed to soft following this contest. A modest fillies' handicap best rated through the runner-up.

2746 VINES BMW MAIDEN STKS 7f 140y
6:50 (6:57) (Class 5) 3-Y-0+ £2,726 (£805; £402) Stalls Centre

Form RPR
06 1 **Simply Elegant (IRE)**[8] 2519 3-8-10 0 JimCrowley 13 71+
(Amanda Perrett) *trckd ldng pair: rdn over 2f out: prog over 1f out: led ins fnl f: styd on* **5/1**[3]
2 *1 1/4* **Response** 3-9-1 0 LiamJones 12 73+
(William Haggas) *pressed ldr: led over 2f out: shkn up over 1f out: rn green and edgd lft: hdd and one pce ins fnl f* **4/1**[2]

0- **3** 2 ¼ **Meshardal (GER)**[262] 6020 3-9-1 0 DaneO'Neill 18 68+
(Richard Hannon) *dwlt: sn in tch bhd ldrs: shkn up over 2f out: styd on fr over 1f out to take 3rd ins fnl f* **5/2**[1]

0-0 **4** 1 ¼ **Admirable Art (IRE)**[15] 2321 3-9-1 0 PatDobbs 17 65
(Tony Carroll) *trckd ldng pair: shkn up over 2f out: kpt on same pce fr over 1f out* **10/1**

0-5 **5** 1 ¼ **Saxon Soldier**[29] 1881 3-9-1 0 TomQueally 5 62
(Ed Dunlop) *wl in tch: shkn up over 2f out: nt qckn over 1f out: one pce after* **6/1**

0 **6** 3 ¾ **Shikamoo**[23] 2051 3-8-7 0 BillyCray(3) 4 48
(Dr Jeremy Naylor) *in tch: outpcd by ldng gp 3f out: no imp after* **100/1**

7 1 ½ **Sun Valley** 3-8-10 0 MartinLane 7 44+
(Anthony Carson) *nvr bttr than midfield and rn green: pushed along and kpt on one pce fr over 2f out* **66/1**

5- **8** hd **Exempt**[249] 6444 3-8-7 0 [1] DarrenEgan(3) 2 44+
(Jeremy Noseda) *racd on outer in rr: nt on terms fr 1/2-way: kpt on fnl 2f: n.d* **5/1**[3]

0 **9** 2 ¼ **Encapsulated**[10] 2442 3-9-1 0 RobertHavlin 15 43
(Roger Ingram) *led against rail to over 2f out: wknd qckly over 1f out* **33/1**

0 **10** 2 **Sun And Stars**[15] 2321 5-9-8 0 EDLinehan(5) 10 38
(Brendan Powell) *nvr bttr than midfld: shkn up and nt on terms w ldrs fr 3f out: fdd* **50/1**

0 **11** ¾ **Olivers Mount**[10] 2456 3-9-1 0 SteveDrowne 11 37
(Ed Vaughan) *dwlt: nvr beyond midfield: pushed along in 8th over 2f out: slt stumble sn after: fdd* **50/1**

00 **12** 5 **Arjawan**[10] 2455 3-9-1 0 [1] HayleyTurner 8 25
(Clive Brittain) *nvr bttr than midfield: drvn 3f out: no prog and sn btn* **20/1**

0 **13** ½ **Need To Be Bold**[29] 1891 4-9-8 0 CathyGannon 6 18
(Derek Haydn Jones) *uns rdr and bolted to post: dwlt: a wl in rr: no ch over 2f out* **66/1**

14 nk **Shelling Peas** 4-9-8 0 JackMitchell 1 18
(Paul Fitzsimons) *sn struggling in last: nvr a factor* **66/1**

P **15** 10 **Katie Galore (IRE)**[7] 2529 4-9-3 0 DeclanBates(5) 9
(David Evans) *pressed ldrs over 4f: wknd rapidly: t.o* **100/1**

0-0 **16** 2 ¾ **Jessica's Gold**[29] 1876 4-9-1 0 DanielMuscutt(7) 14
(Christine Dunnett) *s.s: a wl in rr: t.o* **100/1**

0-0 **17** 2 ½ **Later In Life**[18] 2224 4-9-8 0 (p[1]) DavidProbert 3
(Christine Dunnett) *early reminder: a struggling in rr: t.o* **100/1**

1m 35.08s (2.78) **Going Correction** +0.475s/f (Yiel)
WFA 3 from 4yo+ 12lb **17** Ran SP% **125.3**
Speed ratings (Par 103): **105,103,101,100,99 95,93,93,91,89 88,83,83,82,72 70,67**
Tote Swingers: 1&2 £5.50, 1&3 £5.30, 2&3 £5.80 CSF £24.76 TOTE £7.50: £2.20, £2.30, £1.40; EX 37.30 Trifecta £126.00 Pool: £1,317.99 - 7.83 winning units..
Owner A D Spence **Bred** J Hanly, A Stroud And T Stewart **Trained** Pulborough, W Sussex

FOCUS
An ordinary maiden in which it paid to race prominently. The form looks fluid and will take time to settle.

2747 32RED.COM H'CAP 7f 140y
7:20 (7:27) (Class 6) (0-55,55) 4-Y-O+ **£2,045** (£603; £302) **Stalls** Centre

Form RPR

00-2 **1** **Pink Lips**[21] 2134 5-9-5 **54** DavidProbert 8 61
(J R Jenkins) *pushed along in midfield 4f out: u.p over 2f out: prog wl over 1f out: styd on fnl f to ld post* **3/1**[1]

1530 **2** nse **Strategic Action (IRE)**[7] 2533 4-9-6 **55** RobertHavlin 6 62
(Linda Jewell) *wl in tch: prog 3f out: pressed ldr over 1f out: drvn ahd last 100yds: hdd post* **20/1**

0526 **3** ½ **Byrd In Hand (IRE)**[7] 2534 6-9-3 **52** (p) SeanLevey 2 58
(John Bridger) *t.k.h: prom on outer: chsd ldr 3f out: rdn to ld over 1f out: hdd last 100yds: kpt on* **12/1**

600 **4** 1 ¾ **Divine Rule (IRE)**[18] 2225 5-8-12 **52** (v) ThomasBrown(5) 16 54
(Laura Mongan) *hld up towards rr: looking for room over 2f out: prog over 1f out: rdn and styd on: nrst fin* **8/1**

3350 **5** ½ **Querido (GER)**[21] 2130 9-8-13 **51** (tp) DarrenEgan(3) 14 52+
(Paddy Butler) *slowly away: wl in rr: rdn over 3f out: prog on outer over 2f out: kpt on but nvr able to threaten* **20/1**

6222 **6** ¾ **Do More Business (IRE)**[22] 2303 6-8-12 **52** (bt) PhilipPrince(5) 13 51
(Liam Corcoran) *racd freely: mde most to over 1f out: wknd fnl f* **12/1**

4325 **7** 3 ½ **Total Obsession**[25] 1981 6-8-10 **52** (v) NoelGarbutt(7) 12 42
(Mark Hoad) *towards rr: rdn 3f out: kpt on fr over 1f out: n.d* **25/1**

0205 **8** 1 ¼ **Warbond**[6] 2565 5-9-2 **51** (v) DaneO'Neill 9 38
(Michael Madgwick) *wl in rr: rdn 3f out: sme prog on outer 2f out: no hdwy over 1f out* **7/1**[3]

4003 **9** 4 ½ **Rapid Water**[21] 2130 7-9-4 **53** (b) PatDobbs 10 30
(Pat Eddery) *hld up wl in rr: nt clr run whn gng bttr than many over 2f out: sme prog over 1f out: wknd fnl f* **12/1**

0246 **10** hd **Teth**[48] 1473 4-8-13 **53** RyanTate(5) 5 29
(Anthony Carson) *chsd ldrs: rdn and wknd wl over 2f out: wl in rr after* **12/1**

0/6- **11** 6 **Annia Galeria (IRE)**[289] 6-9-3 **52** TomQueally 17 14
(John Berry) *trckd ldrs against rail tl wknd rapidly wl over 1f out* **14/1**

0014 **12** 5 **Tooley Woods (IRE)**[22] 2073 4-9-3 **52** CathyGannon 7
(Tony Carroll) *chsd ldr to 3f out: sn wknd qckly* **6/1**[2]

6-05 **13** 2 **Lightning Spirit**[7] 2534 5-9-5 **54** (p) GeorgeBaker 1
(Gary Moore) *prom on outer to 3f out: sn wknd and bhd* **16/1**

1m 36.03s (3.73) **Going Correction** +0.475s/f (Yiel) **13** Ran SP% **119.6**
Speed ratings (Par 101): **100,99,99,97,97 96,92,91,87,87 81,76,74**
Tote Swingers: 1&2 £19.20, 1&3 £10.00, 2&3 £37.70 CSF £72.24 CT £647.03 TOTE £2.50: £1.20, £10.20, £3.30; EX 74.30 Trifecta £736.20 Part won. Pool: £981.72 - 0.27 winning units..
Owner Mr & Mrs J Sales **Bred** Southill Stud **Trained** Royston, Herts

FOCUS
Moderate handicap form with the winner not improving on her best mark to score here.

2748 32RED (S) STKS 1m 4f (P)
7:50 (7:54) (Class 6) 3-Y-O **£2,045** (£603; £302) **Stalls** Low

Form RPR

00-0 **1** **Rancher (IRE)**[5] 2599 3-8-12 56 (b[1]) TomQueally 3 55+
(Harry Dunlop) *dwlt: spent most of r trapped on inner in last pair: gap appeared 2f out and sn shot through to ld: rdn out* **4/6**[1]

00- **2** 1 **Hail To Princess**[159] 8178 3-8-7 0 DavidProbert 5 48+
(Patrick Chamings) *hld up in 4th: rdn over 2f out: chsd wnr over 1f out: styd on but nvr quite able to chal* **5/1**[2]

0-00 **3** 5 **Running Bull (IRE)**[6] 2566 3-8-12 47 RobertHavlin 4 45
(Linda Jewell) *t.k.h: hld up in last pair: effrt 3f out: wdst of all bnd 2f out: sn outpcd: tk modest 3rd fnl f* **33/1**

0-6 **4** ¾ **Camilla De Rossi**[42] 1595 3-8-7 0 ChrisCatlin 1 39
(Rae Guest) *trckd ldr: rdn to chal over 2f out: wknd over 1f out* **10/1**[3]

500 **5** nse **Little Alice**[8] 2519 3-8-8 0 ow1 SeanLevey 2 40
(Stuart Williams) *trckd ldng pair: nt clr run jst over 2f out to wl over 1f out: wknd tamely after* **5/1**[2]

5240 **6** 1 **Ceekay's Girl**[18] 2237 3-8-0 49 (p) JoeyHaynes(7) 6 37
(Mrs K Burke) *led: edgd off rail 2f out: sn hdd & wknd* **12/1**

2m 35.3s (2.30) **Going Correction** -0.125s/f (Stan) **6** Ran SP% **113.0**
Speed ratings (Par 97): **87,86,83,82,82 81**
Tote Swingers: 1&2 £2.50, 1&3 £1.90, 2&3 £8.90 CSF £4.55 TOTE £1.20: £1.02, £4.00; EX 4.60 Trifecta £42.60 Pool: £1,437.06 - 25.27 winning units..The winner was bought by Tony Carroll for 3,600gns.
Owner The Ranchers **Bred** Churchtown House Stud **Trained** Lambourn, Berks

FOCUS
Only a weak seller and not a race to dwell on.

2749 32REDPOKER.COM H'CAP 2m (P)
8:20 (8:20) (Class 5) (0-75,74) 4-Y-O+ **£2,726** (£805; £402) **Stalls** Low

Form RPR

14-6 **1** **Presto Volante (IRE)**[22] 2102 5-9-4 **70** (p) PatDobbs 4 80+
(Amanda Perrett) *hld up in tch: rousted and reminders over 4f out: responded to go 2nd 3f out: led over 2f out: sn drvn clr* **6/4**[1]

1152 **2** 5 **Scribe (IRE)**[8] 2509 5-8-12 **69** (vt) DeclanBates(5) 3 73
(David Evans) *in tch: rdn over 4f out: outpcd over 3f out: kpt on u.p to go 3rd 2f out and 2nd ins fnl f: no ch w wnr* **8/1**

114- **3** nk **Italian Riviera**[176] 7972 4-9-3 **71** LukeMorris 1 75
(Sir Mark Prescott Bt) *dwlt: hld up in last: prog to go 2nd over 5f out and t.k.h: led over 3f out: drvn and hdd over 2f out: fdd and lost 2nd ins fnl f* **2/1**[2]

00-3 **4** 8 **Mohanad (IRE)**[13] 1182 7-9-3 **74** ThomasBrown(5) 2 68
(Philip Hide) *cl up: rdn 4f out: steadily wknd fnl 3f* **16/1**

4542 **5** 3 **Keep Kicking (IRE)**[17] 2284 6-9-2 **68** (p) GeorgeBaker 6 58
(Jonjo O'Neill) *led at decent pce: hdd over 3f out: wknd qckly 2f out* **9/2**[3]

6520 **6** 12 **Where's Susie**[27] 1927 8-9-6 **72** RobertHavlin 5 48
(Michael Madgwick) *mostly chsd ldr to over 5f out: wknd 4f out: t.o* **25/1**

3m 21.83s (-3.87) **Going Correction** -0.125s/f (Stan)
WFA 4 from 5yo+ 2lb **6** Ran SP% **112.4**
Speed ratings (Par 103): **104,101,101,97,95 89**
Tote Swingers: 1&2 £4.00, 2&3 £1.10 CSF £14.18 TOTE £2.30: £2.20, £2.50; EX 15.00 Trifecta £39.10 Pool: £778.18 - 14.91 winning units..
Owner Mrs S Conway Mr & Mrs M Swayne Mr A Brooke Mrs R D **Bred** R A Major **Trained** Pulborough, W Sussex

FOCUS
This was run at little more than a dawdle for much of the race but the winner picked up well. The third is rated close to last year's form.

2750 23REDBET.COM FILLIES' H'CAP 1m 2f (P)
8:50 (8:50) (Class 4) (0-85,85) 4-Y-O+ **£4,690** (£1,395; £697; £348) **Stalls** Low

Form RPR

12-0 **1** **Rhagori**[34] 1768 4-9-7 **85** JimCrowley 5 92+
(Ralph Beckett) *hld up in last: prog 2f out: tk 2nd jst over 1f out: reminders to cl on ldr: led last 100yds: pushed out* **1/1**[1]

2-03 **2** ½ **Four Leaves (IRE)**[31] 1825 4-9-2 **80** MartinHarley 4 86
(Marco Botti) *trckd ldr: led jst over 2f out and kicked on: styd on but hdd and hld last 100yds* **3/1**[2]

331 **3** 1 ½ **Saint Helena (IRE)**[22] 2102 5-8-7 **71** oh1 LukeMorris 2 74
(Harry Dunlop) *trckd ldng pair: rdn and nt qckn over 2f out: sn lost pl: kpt on to take 3rd again fnl f: no imp* **9/2**[3]

32-1 **4** nk **Srinagar Girl**[138] 140 4-8-7 **71** SteveDrowne 3 74
(Clive Cox) *cl up: effrt on outer over 2f out: nt qckn over 1f out: one pce after* **8/1**

4-5 **5** 3 **Adiynara (IRE)**[109] 57 5-8-9 **73** (p) TomQueally 1 70
(Neil Mulholland) *led at reasonable pce: hdd jst over 2f out: wknd over 1f out* **25/1**

2m 4.89s (-1.71) **Going Correction** -0.125s/f (Stan) **5** Ran SP% **108.1**
Speed ratings (Par 102): **101,100,99,99,96**
CSF £4.03 TOTE £1.80: £1.10, £2.70; EX 3.70 Trifecta £15.10 Pool: £949.56 - 47.03 winning units..
Owner Landmark Racing Limited **Bred** P T Tellwright **Trained** Kimpton, Hants

FOCUS
The two with the most potential fought this out. The runner-up is rated to her best with the third to the balance of last year's Polytrack form.
T/Plt: £20.30 to a £1 stake. Pool: £61,428.44 - 2,198.36 winning tickets. T/Qpdt: £7.90 to a £1 stake. Pool: £5,239.32 - 488.50 winning tickets. JN

2715 REDCAR (L-H)
Tuesday, May 28

OFFICIAL GOING: Good to firm (good in places; 9.0)
Wind: light across Weather: cloudy

2751 IRISH STALLION FARMS EBF MEDIAN AUCTION MAIDEN FILLIES' STKS 6f
2:10 (2:13) (Class 5) 2-Y-O **£2,911** (£866; £432; £216) **Stalls** Centre

Form RPR

1 **Sunny Harbor (IRE)** 2-9-0 0 DanielTudhope 1 80+
(David O'Meara) *dwlt: hld up: hdwy 1/2-way: led jst ins fnl f: pushed clr: comf* **16/1**

35 **2** 2 ¾ **Augusta Ada**[12] 2401 2-9-0 0 TomEaves 11 71
(Ollie Pears) *racd keenly: prom: led gng wl over 1f out: sn rdn: hdd jst ins fnl f: one pce* **6/1**[3]

4 **3** 1 **Spiceupyourlife (IRE)**[22] 2075 2-9-0 0 TonyHamilton 5 68
(Richard Fahey) *trckd ldrs: rdn and ev ch over 1f out: kpt on one pce* **7/1**

4 1 **Clever Miss** 2-9-0 0 MartinDwyer 4 65
(Alan McCabe) *hld up in midfield: pushed along and outpcd 1/2-way: hdwy to chse ldrs over 1f out: kpt on one pce* **7/2**[2]

2 **5** 2 ¾ **Kirtling Belle**[26] 1960 2-9-0 0 GrahamGibbons 6 56
(Keith Dalgleish) *led: rdn whn hdd over 1f out: grad wknd* **3/1**[1]

6 1 ¼ **Nelson's Pride** 2-9-0 0 AmyRyan 9 52+
(Kevin Ryan) *s.i.s: sn pushed along towards rr: kpt on fr over 1f out: nrst fin* **10/1**

7 1 **Tautira (IRE)** 2-9-0 0 RobertWinston 3 49
(Michael Bell) *trckd ldrs: rdn over 2f out: wknd ins fnl f* **12/1**

The Form Book Flat, Raceform Ltd, Compton, RG20 6NL.

8 3 1/2 **Another Royal** 2-9-0 0 DuranFentiman 7 38
(Tim Easterby) *dwlt: sn midfield: pushed along to briefly chse ldrs over 1f out: wknd fnl f* 14/1

9 1 1/4 **Midnight Muscida (IRE)** 2-8-9 0 DarylByrne(5) 2 34
(Tim Easterby) *trckd ldrs: rdn over 2f out: sn wknd* 66/1

10 nse **Flora Medici** 2-8-9 0 RosieJessop(5) 12 33
(Sir Mark Prescott Bt) *green and reluctant to post: hld up in midfield: pushed along 4f out: nvr threatened* 25/1

5 11 5 **May Whi (IRE)**[8] 2517 2-9-0 0 StephenCraine 13 17
(Tom Dascombe) *prom: wknd over 2f out* 25/1

12 1 1/2 **Slinky McVelvet** 2-9-0 0 RussKennemore 10 13
(Garry Moss) *sn pushed along in rr: bhd fr 1/2-way* 100/1

1m 11.49s (-0.31) **Going Correction** +0.075s/f (Good) **12** Ran SP% **113.5**
Speed ratings (Par 90): **105,101,100,98,95 93,92,87,85,85 78,76**
Tote Swingers: 1&2 £16.40, 1&3 £18.00, 2&3 £5.00 CSF £102.04 TOTE £23.40: £5.50, £1.50, £2.00; EX 142.70 Trifecta £1176.90 Pool: £1,936.10 - 1.23 winning units..

Owner C Maxsted & Miss S Iggulden **Bred** D Ryan, D S Ryan & R A Williams **Trained** Nawton, N Yorks

FOCUS
Probably just an ordinary fillies' maiden, but a nice performance on her debut from the winner. The runner-up is rated to her York mark.

2752 WATCH RACING UK ON SKY 432 (S) STKS 7f
2:40 (2:42) (Class 6) 3-5-Y-0 **£2,045** (£603; £302) **Stalls** Centre

Form RPR

-000 1 **All Or Nothin (IRE)**[18] 2214 4-9-7 82 MichaelO'Connell 5 63+
(John Quinn) *trckd ldrs: rdn over 2f out: drvn over 1f out: kpt on to ld fnl 50yds* 7/4[1]

0-05 2 nk **Bunce (IRE)**[1] 2707 5-9-2 68 DavidBergin(5) 11 62+
(David O'Meara) *midfield: smooth hdwy 3f out: led 2f out: rdn 2 l clr over 1f out: edgd lft ins fnl f: hdd and no ex fnl 50yds* 11/4[2]

1404 3 nk **Azrael**[8] 2496 5-9-13 74 (vt[1]) MartinDwyer 8 67
(Alan McCabe) *w ldr: led over 4f out: rdn whn hdd 2f out: kpt on* 7/1

3000 5 3/4 **Bachelor Knight (IRE)**[82] 909 5-9-7 47 DaleSwift 1 59
(Suzzanne France) *midfield: rdn over 3f out: kpt on fnl f: nvr threatened: fin 5th: plcd 4th* 100/1

5204 6 7 **Tony Hollis**[6] 2578 5-9-0 50 GemmaTutty(7) 7 40
(Karen Tutty) *trckd ldrs: rdn over 3f out: sn wknd: fin 6th: plcd 5th* 16/1

350- 7 8 **Auto Mac**[189] 7799 5-9-2 59 AdamCarter(5) 2 18
(Neville Bycroft) *hld up in rr: a bhd: fin 7th: plcd 6th* 9/1

6006 8 3 1/2 **Mad For Fun (IRE)**[22] 2073 4-9-2 43 (v) RussKennemore 6
(Paul Midgley) *trckd ldrs: rdn over 3f out: losing pl whn sltly short of room over 2f out: wknd: fin 8th: plcd 7th* 50/1

0 9 16 **Son Of Neptune**[18] 2237 3-8-3 0 DanielleMooney(7) 10
(Nigel Tinkler) *sn pushed along in rr: a bhd: fin 9th: plcd 8th* 100/1

0424 D 2 **Rawaafed (IRE)**[18] 2219 4-9-7 64 GrahamGibbons 4 61
(Keith Dalgleish) *led narrowly: hdd over 4f out: remained prom: rdn over 2f out: one pce: disqualified and plcd last after rdr failed to weigh in* 11/2[3]

1m 24.67s (0.17) **Going Correction** +0.075s/f (Good)
WFA 3 from 4yo+ 11lb **9** Ran SP% **110.7**
Speed ratings (Par 101): **102,101,101,98,90 81,77,58,99**
Tote Swingers: 1&2 £1.50, 1&3 £3.00, 2&3 £3.10 CSF £6.07 TOTE £2.30: £1.40, £1.30, £1.60; EX 7.20 Trifecta £25.80 Pool: £2,522.77 - 73.28 winning units..No bid for the winner.

Owner Ross Harmon **Bred** Ballyhane Stud **Trained** Settrington, N Yorks

■ Stewards' Enquiry : David Bergin one-day ban; careless riding (7th July).
Michael O'Connell two-day; used whip above permitted level (11th-12th June).
Graham Gibbons three-day ban; failed to weigh in (11th-13th June)

FOCUS
A modest seller rated through and limited by the fifth.

2753 YORKSHIRE RACING SUMMER FESTIVAL 20TH - 28TH JULY H'CAP 1m 1f
3:10 (3:11) (Class 5) (0-75,71) 4-Y-0+ **£2,587** (£770; £384; £192) **Stalls** Low

Form RPR

10-6 1 **Ingleby Angel (IRE)**[11] 2406 4-9-5 **69** DanielTudhope 13 85+
(David O'Meara) *hld up: stdy hdwy fr 4f out: angled to outside over 2f out: nudged along to ld over 1f out: pushed clr: easily* 6/1[2]

5-02 2 3 1/2 **Eastward Ho**[15] 2315 5-9-0 **67** RaulDaSilva(3) 9 74
(Jason Ward) *led: rdn over 4f out: hdd over 1f out: kpt on but no ch w wnr* 5/1[1]

05-3 3 3/4 **Rex Romanorum (IRE)**[15] 2315 5-9-1 **65** DuranFentiman 2 70
(Patrick Holmes) *trckd ldr: rdn over 3f out: upsides 2f out: kpt on one pce* 12/1

0044 4 1 1/2 **Dakota Canyon (IRE)**[11] 2406 4-9-7 **71** (v) TonyHamilton 14 73
(Richard Fahey) *trckd ldrs: rdn and ev ch 2f out: one pce* 7/1

-006 5 1 **Hot Rod Mamma (IRE)**[18] 2240 6-9-4 **71** LeeTopliss(3) 5 71
(Dianne Sayer) *dwlt: hld up in rr: pushed along and hdwy on inner over 2f out: one pce ins fnl f* 13/2[3]

0043 6 3 3/4 **Outlaw Torn (IRE)**[17] 2273 4-8-10 **60** (e) RobbieFitzpatrick 7 51
(Richard Guest) *in tch: rdn and ev ch 2f out: wknd fnl f* 15/2

0-00 7 1 1/4 **Jonny Lesters Hair (IRE)**[33] 1775 8-9-1 **65** GrahamGibbons 12 54
(Tim Easterby) *prom: rdn over 3f out: lost pl over 2f out: grad wknd* 15/2

0-06 8 hd **King Of Paradise (IRE)**[23] 2042 4-8-8 **63** JasonHart(5) 11 51
(Eric Alston) *hld up: rdn 4f out: nvr threatened* 12/1

5 9 hd **Hussar Ballad (USA)**[17] 2279 4-9-0 **64** TomEaves 6 52
(Mel Brittain) *dwlt: sn midfield on inner: rdn over 3f out: wknd over 1f out* 20/1

5-00 10 2 1/4 **Striker Torres (IRE)**[7] 2551 7-8-10 **60** (p) FrannyNorton 8 43
(Ian McInnes) *hld up in midfield: rdn over 3f out: wknd over 2f out* 20/1

20-0 11 3 3/4 **Hail Bold Chief (USA)**[48] 1460 6-8-13 **63** RobertWinston 10 37
(Alan Swinbank) *hld up in midfield on outer: pushed along and dropped to rr 4f out: sn btn* 10/1

1m 52.33s (-0.67) **Going Correction** +0.075s/f (Good) **11** Ran SP% **114.3**
Speed ratings (Par 103): **105,101,101,99,99 95,94,94,94,92 88**
Tote Swingers: 1&2 £3.60, 1&3 £13.40, 2&3 £8.70 CSF £34.98 CT £350.36 TOTE £4.50: £2.10, £1.40, £4.80; EX 18.80 Trifecta £200.70 Pool: £2,563.41 - 9.57 winning units..

Owner Dave Scott **Bred** Dave Scott **Trained** Nawton, N Yorks

FOCUS
A modest handicap but the winner scored with something in hand and the others in the frame give the form substance.

2754 BUY YOUR TICKETS ON-LINE @ REDCARRACING.CO.UK MEDIAN AUCTION MAIDEN STKS 1m 2f
3:40 (3:40) (Class 5) 3-5-Y-0 **£2,587** (£770; £384; £192) **Stalls** Low

Form RPR

1 **Cranach**[362] 4-10-0 0 JimmyQuinn 6 74+
(Tom Keddy) *mde all: clr 4f out: rdn over 2f out: kpt on: comf* 10/1

2 5 **Primary Route (IRE)** 3-8-9 0 GrahamGibbons 7 59+
(David Barron) *midfield: pushed along 4f out: hdwy over 2f out: kpt on to take 2nd fnl 100yds: no ch w wnr* 7/1[3]

453- 3 2 **Graceful Act**[200] 7671 5-9-9 53 DaleSwift 2 56
(Ron Barr) *midfield: hdwy to chse clr ldr 4f out: rdn 3f out: one pce: lost 2nd fnl 100yds* 16/1

44 4 1 1/4 **Aramist (IRE)**[7] 2538 3-9-0 0 RobertWinston 5 57
(Alan Swinbank) *trckd ldrs: rdn over 4f out: one pce in 4th fnl 2f* 1/1[1]

20 5 3 1/4 **Royal Style (IRE)**[31] 1828 3-8-9 0 AndrewMullen 15 46
(David Barron) *midfield: pushed along and sltly hmpd over 4f out: nvr threatened ldrs* 14/1

00 6 nse **This Is Me**[15] 2321 5-9-11 0 RaulDaSilva(3) 9 52
(Don Cantillon) *hld up in midfield: rdn over 3f out: nvr threatened* 14/1

0 7 nse **Ardaal**[20] 2157 3-9-0 0 (t) MartinDwyer 4 51
(James Fanshawe) *hld up: pushed along 5f out: nvr threatened* 13/2[2]

8 4 **Van Mildert (IRE)**[26] 4-9-6 0 LucyAlexander(3) 10 39
(Dianne Sayer) *s.i.s: hld up in rr: nvr threatened* 100/1

00- 9 6 **Isle Of Beauty**[222] 7199 3-8-9 0 FrannyNorton 14 27
(Tom Dascombe) *trckd ldrs: rdn over 4f out: grad wknd* 33/1

26 10 19 **Tinctoria**[11] 2405 3-8-9 0 AmyRyan 8
(Kevin Ryan) *hld up: a bhd: t.o* 11/1

00-0 11 22 **Under Ambition**[20] 2164 5-9-4 36 AdamCarter(5) 11
(Frederick Watson) *in tch on outer: rdn over 4f out: sn wknd: t.o* 125/1

2m 6.18s (-0.92) **Going Correction** +0.075s/f (Good)
WFA 3 from 4yo+ 14lb **11** Ran SP% **117.2**
Speed ratings (Par 103): **106,102,100,99,96 96,96,93,88,73 55**
Tote Swingers: 1&2 £12.40, 1&3 £10.50, 2&3 £17.30 CSF £77.74 TOTE £8.90: £4.00, £2.40, £3.70; EX 56.90 Trifecta £634.40 Pool: £2,212.81 - 2.61 winning units..

Owner Andrew Duffield **Bred** Juddmonte Farms Ltd **Trained** Newmarket, Suffolk

FOCUS
A dire maiden with most of these off the bridle before the long straight. The third offers perspective on the weak level of the form.

2755 FOLLOW REDCARRACING ON FACEBOOK & TWITTER H'CAP 5f
4:10 (4:10) (Class 4) (0-85,81) 4-Y-0+ **£6,469** (£1,925; £962; £481) **Stalls** Centre

Form RPR

013- 1 **Above Standard (IRE)**[213] 7411 5-9-5 **79** GrahamGibbons 9 88
(Michael Easterby) *dwlt: sn chsd ldrs: rdn 2f out: led 1f out: edgd lft: kpt on* 7/2[2]

20-1 2 3/4 **Avon Breeze**[9] 2479 4-8-13 **73** 6ex AmyRyan 13 79
(Richard Whitaker) *dwlt: hld up in tch: hdwy 1/2-way: rdn to chal appr fnl f: sn edgd lft: kpt on but a jst hld* 5/1[3]

35-4 3 3/4 **Cocktail Charlie**[8] 2505 5-9-0 **74** DanielTudhope 15 78
(Tim Easterby) *hld up: rdn and hdwy over 1f out: kpt on: wnt 3rd nr fin* 7/1

026- 4 hd **Sunny Side Up (IRE)**[224] 7144 4-8-10 **77** LauraBarry(7) 10 80
(Richard Fahey) *led narrowly: rdn whn hdd 1f out: no ex fnl 100yds* 33/1

00- 5 1/2 **Eland Ally**[305] 4554 5-9-3 **77** MickyFenton 12 78
(Tom Tate) *midfield: pushed along 1/2-way: kpt on fnl f* 66/1

13-2 6 shd **Angelito**[24] 2031 4-9-5 **79** FrannyNorton 1 80
(Ed McMahon) *dwlt: hld up: rdn 2f out: kpt on fnl f* 11/4[1]

3006 7 hd **Profile Star (IRE)**[10] 2459 4-9-1 **80** LMcNiff(5) 8 80
(David Barron) *in tch: pushed along 1/2-way: kpt on fnl f* 18/1

16- 8 2 **Willbeme**[263] 6008 5-9-1 **75** MichaelO'Connell 2 68
(Neville Bycroft) *w ldr: rdn over 1f out: wknd ins fnl f* 7/1

1-00 9 2 1/4 **Elusive Bonus (IRE)**[20] 2173 4-8-10 **75** DavidBergin(5) 11 60
(David O'Meara) *in tch: pushed along 1/2-way: wknd fnl f* 33/1

3614 10 1 1/2 **Lucky Dan (IRE)**[40] 1646 7-9-6 **80** TonyHamilton 14 59
(Paul Green) *hld up: rdn 1/2-way: wknd over 1f out* 20/1

0000 11 6 **Chunky Diamond (IRE)**[10] 2441 4-9-3 **77** PJMcDonald 5 35
(Ruth Carr) *prom: rdn 1/2-way: wknd over 1f out* 33/1

40-0 U **Master Bond**[10] 2459 4-8-11 **74** (t) LeeTopliss(3) 3
(Bryan Smart) *stmbld and uns rdr leaving stalls* 20/1

58.22s (-0.38) **Going Correction** +0.075s/f (Good) **12** Ran SP% **115.7**
Speed ratings (Par 105): **106,104,103,103,102 102,102,98,95,92 83,**
Tote Swingers: 1&2 £5.50, 1&3 £5.90, 2&3 £6.00 CSF £18.86 CT £117.29 TOTE £5.20: £1.40, £2.00, £2.80; EX 26.10 Trifecta £109.80 Pool: £3,157.23 - 21.55 winning units..

Owner A Saha **Bred** Sandro Garavelli **Trained** Sheriff Hutton, N Yorks

■ Stewards' Enquiry : Laura Barry one-day ban; careless riding (11th June).

FOCUS
A fair sprint handicap with the runner-up rated very close to her easy Ripon win.

2756 WIN A VIP DAY OUT @ REDCARRACING.CO.UK H'CAP 6f
4:40 (4:40) (Class 5) (0-70,76) 3-Y-0 **£2,587** (£770; £384; £192) **Stalls** Centre

Form RPR

-542 1 **Someone's Darling**[25] 1988 3-8-9 **58** AndrewElliott 13 69
(Jim Goldie) *chsd ldrs: swtchd rt to chal over 1f out: led ins fnl f: rdn and kpt on* 12/1

5344 2 1/2 **Rangi**[15] 2318 3-9-0 **70** DavidSimmonson(7) 10 79
(Tony Coyle) *hld up in tch: hdwy 2f out: rdn and ev ch 1f out: kpt on* 12/1

-101 3 2 3/4 **Hartwright**[7] 2544 3-9-10 **76** 6ex LucyAlexander(3) 9 76
(Michael Bell) *prom: rdn over 2f out: led narrowly over 1f out: hdd ins fnl f: no ex* 9/4[1]

100- 4 hd **Bond Club**[199] 7687 3-9-4 **70** LeeTopliss(3) 3 70
(Geoffrey Oldroyd) *s.i.s: hld up in rr: rdn and hdwy over 1f out: swtchd rt ins fnl f: kpt on* 11/1

-402 5 2 **A J Cook (IRE)**[18] 2218 3-8-12 **61** GrahamGibbons 6 54
(David Barron) *chsd ldrs: rdn over 2f out: grad wknd over 1f out* 9/1

50-2 6 hd **Annie Gogh**[18] 2241 3-8-13 **62** DuranFentiman 4 55
(Tim Easterby) *hld up: rdn over 2f out: kpt on fnl f: nvr threatened* 20/1

500- 7 3/4 **Abraham Monro**[259] 6121 3-8-7 **56** PJMcDonald 2 46
(Ann Duffield) *hld up: rdn over 2f out: nvr threatened* 66/1

4343 8 1/2 **Spider House**[8] 2501 3-8-11 **60** DanielTudhope 11 49
(David O'Meara) *hld up: rdn 2f out: nvr threatened* 5/1[2]

-413 9 4 **La Luz Del Sol**[15] 2318 3-8-11 **60** TonyHamilton 1 36
(Richard Fahey) *midfield: rdn over 2f out: wknd over 1f out* 13/2[3]

35-0 **10** ½ **Dewi Chinta (IRE)**[27] 1935 3-8-10 **59**..............................(b¹) AmyRyan 7 33
(Kevin Ryan) *w ldr: rdn over 2f out: wknd over 1f out* **50/1**

3-16 **11** *nk* **Edith Anne**[43] 1566 3-8-13 **62**.. MickyFenton 8 35
(Paul Midgley) *led narrowly: rdn over 2f out: hdd over 1f out: wknd:* **25/1**

-531 **12** 3 ¼ **Ichimoku**[7] 2535 3-8-7 **56** 6ex.......................................(t) TomEaves 12 19
(Bryan Smart) *dwlt: racd keenly: sn midfield: rdn over 2f out: wknd over 1f out* **9/1**

0456 **13** *7* **Hawsies Dream**[28] 1906 3-8-7 **56** oh2............................ BarryMcHugh 5
(Tracy Waggott) *chsd ldrs: wknd over 1f out: eased* **40/1**

1m 11.48s (-0.32) **Going Correction** +0.075s/f (Good) **13** Ran SP% **119.0**
Speed ratings (Par 99): **105,104,100,100,97 97,96,95,90,89 89,85,75**
Tote Swingers: 1&2 £33.20, 1&3 £9.30, 2&3 £7.90 CSF £139.96 CT £387.23 TOTE £12.00: £4.10, £3.70, £1.20; EX 197.20 Trifecta £1758.60 Part won. Pool: £2,344.82 - 0.79 winning units..
Owner The McMaster Springford Partnership **Bred** W G H Barrons **Trained** Uplawmoor, E Renfrews

FOCUS
An ordinary sprint handicap in which the winner is rated back to her best pre-race form, backed up by the second.

2757 VOLTIGEUR RESTAURANT 2 COURSES FOR £10.95 AMATEUR RIDERS' MAIDEN H'CAP 6f
5:10 (5:30) (Class 6) (0-65,65) 4-Y-0+ **£1,975** (£607; £303) **Stalls** Centre

Form RPR

0-25 **1** **Adam's Ale**[38] 1687 4-10-12 **63**.. MrSWalker 5 75
(Paul Midgley) *in tch: hdwy to chse ldr 2f out: rdn to ld ent fnl f: kpt on wl* **9/2¹**

-322 **2** 2 ½ **Red Baron (IRE)**[15] 2317 4-10-8 **64**.....................(b) MissSMDoolan(5) 17 68
(Eric Alston) *dwlt: sn led: rdn whn hdd ent fnl f: one pce* **6/1²**

0006 **3** *2* **Nonaynever**[7] 2536 5-10-0 **51** oh3..........................(b) MissSBrotherton 7 49
(Ruth Carr) *sn pushed along in midfield: kpt on fr over 1f out: wnt 3rd nr fin: no threat to ldng pair* **7/1³**

2430 **4** *nk* **Haywain**[32] 1800 4-11-0 **65**......................................(p) MrSCrawford 16 62
(Kevin Ryan) *chsd ldrs: rdn 1/2-way: kpt on one pce* **9/2¹**

0-44 **5** *nse* **Karate Queen**[17] 2276 8-9-10 **52**..............................(p) MrsVDavies(5) 13 48
(Ron Barr) *chsd ldr: rdn 1/2-way: one pce* **10/1**

600- **6** 1 ¼ **Toffee Nose**[231] 6958 6-10-0 **51** oh6.............................. MissADeniel 14 43
(Ron Barr) *midfield: rdn 1/2-way: kpt on: nvr threatened* **50/1**

0-00 **7** ½ **Medecis Mountain**[29] 1893 4-9-7 **51** oh6..................(p) MrAFrench(7) 19 42
(John Wainwright) *hld up: bhd tl late hdwy* **50/1**

40-6 **8** *nk* **Black Douglas**[18] 2222 4-10-3 **54**...................................... MrsCBartley 8 44
(Jim Goldie) *hld up in midfield: pushed along 1/2-way: nvr threatened* **11/1**

550- **9** 1 ¾ **Isle Of Ellis (IRE)**[203] 7604 6-10-0 **51** oh6.................(p) MissCWalton 18 35
(Ron Barr) *hld up: nvr threatened ldrs* **25/1**

0 **10** ¾ **Busy Bimbo (IRE)**[15] 2317 4-9-11 **51** oh6..........(p) MissJRRichards(3) 3 33
(Alan Berry) *chsd ldr: wknd over 2f out* **66/1**

3-04 **11** 2 ½ **My Time**[38] 1681 4-9-12 **52**................................(p) MissMMullineaux(3) 11 26
(Michael Mullineaux) *hld up: rdn 1/2-way: nvr threatened* **6/1²**

000- **12** 3 ¾ **Well Bank (IRE)**[200] 7671 4-9-7 **51** oh6.................... MrDPCostello(7) 12 13
(David Nicholls) *midfield: rdn over 2f out: wknd over 1f out* **7/1³**

-300 **13** 2 ½ **Dr Victoria**[26] 1962 4-9-7 **51** oh6.. MrPHardy(7) 10 5
(John Norton) *chsd ldr: wknd over 2f out* **66/1**

04-3 **14** ½ **Queen's Princess**[8] 2503 5-9-11 **53** oh6 ow2..............(p) MrDLevey(5) 1 5
(John Wainwright) *s.i.s: a towards rr* **25/1**

000- **15** *1* **Zoom In**[211] 7447 5-9-9 **51** oh6...............................(bt) MrAaronJames(5) 9
(Lee James) *v.s.a: a bhd* **50/1**

040- **16** *10* **Face East (USA)**[260] 6100 5-9-9 **51** oh5................ MissKMargarson(5) 4
(Alan Berry) *s.i.s: a bhd* **50/1**

1m 13.11s (1.31) **Going Correction** +0.075s/f (Good) **16** Ran SP% **125.9**
Speed ratings (Par 101): **94,90,88,87,87 85,85,84,82,81 78,73,69,69,67 54**
Tote Swingers: 1&2 £2.50, 1&3 £2.90, 2&3 £3.00 CSF £30.33 CT £201.52 TOTE £5.80: £1.90, £2.00, £2.20, £1.80; EX 33.10 Trifecta £192.90 Pool: £2,952.07 - 11.47 winning units..
Owner Mrs M Hills **Bred** Mrs M J Hills **Trained** Westow, N Yorks

FOCUS
This race was delayed for around 20 minutes for various reasons, notably Dr Victoria losing her weight cloth (later refitted) when fly-leaping on the way to the start, and then Depden running loose before being withdrawn. It was a poor race, full of maidens with only the top-six weighted horses in the handicap proper, and for amateur riders. The winner stepped up on his newcastle form with the third and fourth fitting in but a race rated on the negative side.
T/Jkpt: Not won. T/Plt: £124.50 to a £1 stake. Pool: £59,473.16 - 348.53 winning tickets. T/Qpdt: £30.50 to a £1 stake. Pool: £3,488.94 - 84.52 winning tickets. AS

2637 YARMOUTH (L-H)
Tuesday, May 28

OFFICIAL GOING: Good to firm (7.5)
Wind: fresh, across Weather: overcast, dry

2758 IRISH STALLION FARMS EBF NOVICE STKS 6f 3y
5:40 (5:43) (Class 5) 2-Y-O **£3,234** (£962; £481; £240) **Stalls** Centre

Form RPR

1 **1** **Lucky Kristale**[12] 2382 2-8-11 0.. RyanMoore 2 83+
(George Margarson) *chsd ldr: rdn and effrt to ld over 1f out: clr and r.o wl fnl f: comf* **4/9¹**

2 *4* **Vigor (IRE)** 2-9-0 0.. WilliamBuick 7 73+
(David Simcock) *hld up in tch in last trio: effrt and edgd lft over 1f out: no ch w wnr but kpt on to go 2nd cl home* **8/1³**

1 **3** *nk* **Loma Mor**[8] 2510 2-8-6 0.. ShirleyTeasdale(5) 5 69
(Alan McCabe) *t.k.h: chsd ldrs: effrt and hung lft over 1f out: stl gng lft and chsd wnr ins fnl f: no imp: lost 2nd cl home* **33/1**

3163 **4** 2 ¼ **Smugglers Gold (IRE)**[8] 2518 2-9-2 0..............................(t) AdamKirby 4 67
(David Evans) *led tl rdn and hdd over 1f out: btn 1f out: wknd ins fnl f* **10/1**

5 1 ½ **Surety (IRE)** 2-9-0 0.. FrederikTylicki 1 60+
(Clive Brittain) *in tch in midfield: rdn and outpcd wl over 1f out: wl hld and plugged on same pce fnl f* **16/1**

6 ¾ **Song Of Rowland (IRE)** 2-9-0 0.. JamieSpencer 3 58+
(Peter Chapple-Hyam) *stdd s: hld up in tch in last pair: swtchd lft and effrt wl over 1f out: sn no imp: kpt on same pce fnl f* **7/1²**

7 *6* **Basil Berry** 2-9-0 0.. SaleemGolam 6 38
(Chris Dwyer) *s.i.s: rn green: in tch in rr: lost tch wl over 1f out* **33/1**

1m 14.92s (0.52) **Going Correction** -0.05s/f (Good) **7** Ran SP% **113.7**
Speed ratings (Par 93): **94,88,88,85,82 83,74**
Tote Swingers: 1&2 £2.30, 1&3 £2.80, 2&3 £22.90 CSF £4.77 TOTE £1.30: £1.10, £4.10; EX 4.20 Trifecta £51.70 Pool: £2,192.22 - 31.75 winning units..
Owner Graham Lodge Partnership **Bred** Lilac Bloodstock & Redmyre Bloodstock **Trained** Newmarket, Suffolk

FOCUS
Following a dry night the ground was changed to Good to firm and the straight course was watered in the morning. Jamie Spencer and William Buick both stated the ground to be "fast but with no jar in it". A race that has thrown up some smart sorts in the last decade, notably subsequent Breeders' Cup Juvenile Dirt winner Wilko in 2004 and Nunthorpe winner Margot Did in 2010. The field tacked to the stands' rail soon after the start and the gallop was an ordinary one. The winner is rated towards the higher end of recent race averages, with the fourth close to his best turf form.

2759 CONFERENCES AT GREAT YARMOUTH (S) STKS 6f 3y
6:10 (6:12) (Class 6) 2-Y-O **£1,940** (£577; £288; £144) **Stalls** Centre

Form RPR

4403 **1** **El Duque**[9] 2475 2-8-4 0..............................(p) JakePayne(7) 4 52
(Bill Turner) *t.k.h early: led for 1f: chsd ldr after tl rdn to ld over 1f out: kpt on edging lft u.p but kpt on wl fnl f* **6/4¹**

0 **2** *1* **See Me Sometime**[8] 2502 2-8-11 0.. TedDurcan 3 49
(Mark H Tompkins) *dwlt: t.k.h early: hdwy to ld after 1f out: rdn 2f out: hdd over 1f out: carried lft and kpt on same pce fnl f* **11/4³**

006 **3** *nk* **Nomathemba (IRE)**[31] 1833 2-8-6 0.. SaleemGolam 5 43
(David Evans) *in tch in rr: rdn 2f out: no imp tl kpt on u.p ins fnl f* **14/1**

401 **4** 1 ½ **Ding Ding**[9] 2475 2-8-5 0.. DanielCremin(7) 2 44
(Mick Channon) *chsd ldrs: rdn over 2f out: unable qck over 1f out: wl hld and one pce fnl f* **2/1²**

1m 17.41s (3.01) **Going Correction** -0.05s/f (Good) **4** Ran SP% **106.7**
Speed ratings (Par 91): **77,75,75,73**
CSF £5.72 TOTE £2.40; EX 5.10 Trifecta £17.60 Pool: £908.33 - 38.58 winning units..There was no bid for the winner.
Owner Ansells Of Watford **Bred** John James **Trained** Sigwells, Somerset
■ Stewards' Enquiry : Jake Payne caution; careless riding.

FOCUS
Not much to dwell on in a moderate seller. The gallop was an ordinary one and the quartet stayed in the centre this time. The winner is rated to his mark.

2760 TRAFALGAR RESTAURANT AT GREAT YARMOUTH RACECOURSE MAIDEN STKS 1m 3y
6:40 (6:42) (Class 5) 3-Y-O+ **£2,587** (£770; £384; £192) **Stalls** Centre

Form RPR

2 **1** **Stableford**[15] 2306 3-9-2 0.. JimmyFortune 11 87
(Brian Meehan) *mde all: travelling best 2f out: rdn and drew clr over 1f out: pushed out fnl f: easily* **5/4¹**

4-3 **2** *3* **Clear Pearl (USA)**[29] 1876 3-8-11 0.. JamieSpencer 9 75
(Ed Vaughan) *t.k.h: hld up wl in tch: rdn and effrt to chse clr wnr wl over 1f out: no imp but kpt on* **14/1**

3 ¾ **Don't Stare** 3-9-2 0..¹ FrederikTylicki 6 78
(James Fanshawe) *hld up towards rr: hdwy over 1f out: rdn and styd on strly ins fnl f: wnt 3rd fnl 100yds: gng on wl at fin* **33/1**

4 **4** 3 ½ **Short Shrift (IRE)**[123] 377 3-8-11 0.. KirstyMilczarek 4 65
(James Toller) *wl in tch in midfield: effrt u.p and chsd clr ldng pair over 1f out: no imp fnl f* **50/1**

5 **5** *hd* **Spirit Rider (USA)**[15] 2306 3-9-2 0.. WilliamBuick 2 69
(John Gosden) *chsd ldrs: rdn and unable qck over 1f out: no threat to ldrs and kpt on same pce fnl f* **5/2²**

6 *hd* **Ravensburg** 3-8-11 0.. TedDurcan 7 66+
(Chris Wall) *stdd s: hld up in last: stl last and nt clr run 2f out: swtchd lft and hdwy over 1f out: styng on and swtchd rt ins fnl f: no threat to ldrs but gng on wl at fin* **33/1**

7 ½ **Stomachion (IRE)** 3-9-2 0.. RyanMoore 1 67+
(Sir Michael Stoute) *hld up in last trio: rdn 2f out: hdwy over 1f out: no threat to ldrs but kpt on ins fnl f* **9/1³**

0- **8** 1 ½ **Kensington Gardens**[217] 7312 3-8-11 0.. KierenFallon 16 59
(Michael Bell) *s.i.s: sn rcvrd and in tch in midfield: rdn and unable qck whn edgd lft wl over 1f out: wknd 1f out* **20/1**

9 *nk* **Top Set (IRE)** 3-9-2 0.. AdamKirby 12 63
(Marco Botti) *hld up in tch in last quartet: swtchd rt and rdn over 2f out: no hdwy tl kpt on ins fnl f: nvr trbld ldrs* **20/1**

10 *hd* **West Of The Moon** 3-8-11 0.. SebSanders 15 58
(Sir Michael Stoute) *t.k.h: hld up in tch in last quartet: rdn and no hdwy 2f out: no threat to ldrs but plugged on fnl f* **25/1**

0 **11** 1 ¾ **Keene**[29] 1891 3-9-2 0.. WilliamCarson 8 58
(Philip McBride) *hld up in tch in midfield: rdn and no hdwy over 2f out: wknd over 1f out* **100/1**

12 *1* **You Look So Good** 3-8-11 0.. StevieDonohoe 3 51
(Roger Varian) *t.k.h: chsd wnr tl 1/2-way: rdn and no ex over 2f out: btn over 1f out and sn wknd* **20/1**

13 1 ¼ **Petrify** 3-8-9 0.. SAJackson(7) 14 53
(Luca Cumani) *t.k.h: chsd ldrs: wnt 2nd 1/2-way tl wl over 1f out: sn struggling: fdd fnl f* **50/1**

5- **14** *21* **Grapes Hill**[392] 1738 3-8-11 0..(b¹) JoeFanning 5
(Mark Rimmer) *in tch in midfield: rdn and wknd over 2f out: virtually p.u ins fnl f: t.o* **100/1**

1m 41.05s (0.45) **Going Correction** -0.05s/f (Good) **14** Ran SP% **119.6**
Speed ratings (Par 103): **95,92,91,87,87 87,86,85,85,84 83,82,80,59**
Tote Swingers: 1&2 £4.60, 1&3 £19.30, 2&3 £40.60 CSF £18.66 TOTE £2.10: £1.10, £2.40, £8.50; EX 17.60 Trifecta £411.90 Pool: £1,481.20 - 2.69 winning units..
Owner Sangster Family **Bred** Ben Sangster & Swettenham Stud **Trained** Manton, Wilts

FOCUS
A maiden that has thrown up several smart sorts since its first running in 2007, the pick being dual Group 3 winner (and Group/Grade 1-placed) Tazeez in 2008 and, although the market suggested not too many of these were fancied, this year's winner looks sure to hold his own in stronger company. The form is rated around the first two and looks reasonable.

2761 BBC RADIO NORFOLK H'CAP 1m 3y
7:10 (7:13) (Class 4) (0-80,80) 4-Y-0+ **£4,690** (£1,395; £697; £348) **Stalls** Centre

Form RPR

33-4 **1** **Zeyran (IRE)**[12] 2392 4-8-12 **71**.. RyanMoore 7 81+
(Sir Henry Cecil) *t.k.h: chsd ldrs: rdn to ld over 1f out: hung rt 1f out: clr and r.o wl fnl f* **3/1¹**

4304 **2** 2 ¼ **Patriotic (IRE)**[11] 2431 5-9-2 **75**..............................(p) AdamKirby 4 80
(Chris Dwyer) *in tch in midfield: rdn and effrt over 2f out: kpt on u.p to go 2nd wl ins fnl f: no threat to wnr* **7/2²**

-220 **3** ½ **Cruiser**[17] 2278 5-8-13 **72**.. JamieSpencer 1 75
(William Muir) *in tch in midfield: rdn and effrt to chal over 1f out: styd on same pce ins fnl f* **6/1**

35-5 **4** ½ **My Single Malt (IRE)**[26] 1963 5-8-12 **71** PaulMulrennan 5 73
(Julie Camacho) *t.k.h: hld up in tch in last pair: rdn and effrt over 1f out: kpt on same pce ins fnl f* **10/1**

3/61 **5** 1¼ **Nimiety**[13] 2361 4-8-11 **70** JoeFanning 2 69
(Mark Johnston) *chsd ldrs: rdn and ev ch over 1f out: no ex 1f out: wknd ins fnl f* **9/2**

2-41 **6** 1 **Great Expectations**[17] 2266 5-9-3 **76** JimmyFortune 6 73
(J R Jenkins) *stdd s: hld up in tch in rr: shkn up over 2f out: rdn and no imp over 1f out: wknd ins fnl f* **4/1**[3]

60-0 **7** nk **Amoya (GER)**[11] 2422 6-9-4 **77** WilliamCarson 8 73
(Philip McBride) *led and set stdy gallop: rdn and qcknd ent fnl 2f: hdd over 1f out: wknd ins fnl f* **20/1**

1m 39.35s (-1.25) **Going Correction** -0.05s/f (Good) 7 Ran SP% **113.5**
Speed ratings (Par 105): **104,101,101,100,99 98,98**
Tote Swingers: 1&2 £3.90, 1&3 £4.00, 2&3 £4.70 CSF £13.51 CT £57.38 TOTE £2.60: £1.70, £2.30; EX 12.10 Trifecta £67.40 Pool: £1,351.51 - 15.02 winning units..
Owner Miss Zeynep Araci **Bred** Mrs E J O'Grady **Trained** Newmarket, Suffolk

FOCUS
A fair handicap in which the gallop was on the steady side. The progressive winner drifted towards the stands' rail in the closing stages. The form is rated around those in the frame behind the winner.

2762 NORFOLK & SUFFOLK ANIMAL TRUST H'CAP 1m 3y
7:40 (7:40) (Class 6) (0-60,60) 3-Y-O **£1,940** (£577; £288; £144) **Stalls** Centre

Form RPR

006- **1** **Blackball (USA)**[159] 8185 3-9-6 **59** (b[1]) TedDurcan 8 72+
(David Lanigan) *hld up in rr: hdwy 3f out: drvn and edgd lft over 1f out: led jst ins fnl f: styd on wl: rdn out* **8/1**[3]

000- **2** 1¾ **Aloha**[165] 8102 3-9-5 **58** StevieDonohoe 6 67
(Roger Varian) *t.k.h: chsd ldrs: rdn and ev ch over 1f out: edgd lft and kpt on same pce ins fnl f* **6/1**[2]

-052 **3** nse **Hot Mustard**[8] 2501 3-9-3 **56** JamieSpencer 5 65
(Michael Bell) *hld up in midfield: rdn and hdwy over 2f out: drvn and chsd ldrs over 1f out: kpt on same pce ins fnl f* **2/1**[1]

3063 **4** 3¼ **Napinda**[33] 1781 3-9-1 **54** (v) WilliamCarson 2 55
(Philip McBride) *t.k.h: w ldrs: chsd clr ldr over 4f out tl rdn to ld wl over 1f out: hdd jst ins fnl f: wknd fnl 100yds* **20/1**

460 **5** 2 **Maughami**[29] 1876 3-9-2 **60** RobertTart[(5)] 9 56
(Marco Botti) *hld up in tch in rr: hdwy nrest stands' rail over 2f out: rdn and chsd ldrs wl over 1f out: btn 1f out: wknd ins fnl f* **9/1**

0-60 **6** 1¾ **My Claire**[8] 2501 3-8-13 **52** PaulMulrennan 12 44
(Nigel Tinkler) *t.k.h: hld up in midfield: effrt u.p over 2f out: no imp u.p over 1f out* **25/1**

-505 **7** 3½ **Bullseye Babe**[20] 2154 3-9-0 **53** [1] HarryBentley 16 37
(Mark Usher) *in tch in midfield: rdn and effrt over 2f out: wknd u.p over 1f out* **25/1**

46-5 **8** 6 **Barbsiz (IRE)**[83] 904 3-9-2 **55** KierenFallon 13 24
(Mark H Tompkins) *hld up towards rr: hdwy 1/2-way: rdn and no prog 2f out: wknd over 1f out* **22/1**

0-50 **9** 1¾ **Perseverent Pete (USA)**[8] 2508 3-8-12 **51** (p) IanMongan 10 16
(Christine Dunnett) *hld up in midfield: rdn 1/2-way: wknd wl over 1f out* **16/1**

5-05 **10** 2¼ **Cara Gina**[17] 2267 3-8-7 **46** oh1 (b[1]) FrederikTylicki 1 6
(William Haggas) *stdd s: t.k.h: hld up in tch: hdwy to ld 5f out and sn clr: rdn and hdd wl over 1f out: sn hung lft and wknd: eased ins fnl f* **8/1**[3]

4630 **11** nk **Daisie Cutter**[21] 2133 3-8-5 **47** SimonPearce[(3)] 4 6
(Lydia Pearce) *t.k.h: hld up in midfield: dropped to rr and struggling 3f out: bhd fnl 2f* **25/1**

000- **12** 2¾ **Good As New**[180] 7926 3-8-13 **52** SebSanders 11 4
(Chris Wall) *a towards rr: drvn and no rspnse over 3f out: bhd fnl 2f* **14/1**

065- **13** 2¼ **Planchette**[210] 7468 3-8-13 **52** WilliamBuick 7
(Jane Chapple-Hyam) *led tl 5f out: lost pl and bhd over 2f out: wl bhd fnl f* **16/1**

666 **14** 11 **Satwa's Sister**[61] 1215 3-8-4 **46** oh1 RossAtkinson[(3)] 15
(Robert Cowell) *in tch in midfield: rdn and lost pl over 3f out: wl bhd fnl f: t.o* **50/1**

1m 41.51s (0.91) **Going Correction** -0.05s/f (Good) 14 Ran SP% **120.9**
Speed ratings (Par 97): **93,91,91,87,85 84,80,74,72,70 70,67,65,54**
Tote Swingers: 1&2 £12.40, 1&3 £5.10, 2&3 £2.20 CSF £50.40 CT £135.51 TOTE £13.30: £3.70, £3.60, £1.10; EX 105.70 Trifecta £234.50 Pool: £584.74 - 1.84 winning units..
Owner B E Nielsen **Bred** Turner Breeders LLC **Trained** Upper Lambourn, Berks

FOCUS
Several unexposed sorts in a moderate handicap. An ordinary gallop increased after 3f but the first three finished clear and this looks a race to be positive about.

2763 NORFOLKBROADS.COM H'CAP 7f 3y
8:10 (8:11) (Class 5) (0-75,75) 3-Y-O **£2,587** (£770; £384; £192) **Stalls** Centre

Form RPR

21-3 **1** **Maid A Million**[18] 2229 3-9-3 **71** SebSanders 6 86
(David Elsworth) *mde all: rdn and wnt clr over 1f out: in command fnl f: eased towards fin* **8/1**[3]

3441 **2** 7 **Black Rider (IRE)**[15] 2308 3-8-13 **67** PaulMulrennan 7 63
(Julie Camacho) *stdd s: hld up in rr: rdn and hdwy over 2f out: chsd clr wnr over 1f out: no imp but kpt on for 2nd* **8/1**[3]

-061 **3** 1 **Declamation (IRE)**[14] 2340 3-9-7 **75** JoeFanning 10 68
(Mark Johnston) *chsd ldr: rdn and unable qck 2f out: outpcd and btn 1f out: wl hld but plugged on fnl f* **15/8**[1]

05-5 **4** hd **Emerald Sea**[24] 2006 3-9-2 **70** TedDurcan 4 63
(Chris Wall) *hld up in midfield: rdn and hdwy over 2f out: outpcd and no ch w wnr ent fnl f: plugged on* **10/1**

05-6 **5** 1¼ **Raven's Rock (IRE)**[27] 1928 3-8-10 **64** [1] AndreaAtzeni 1 53
(Roger Varian) *t.k.h: chsd ldrs: rdn and lost pl 1/2-way: rdn and sme hdwy over 2f out: wknd over 1f out* **5/1**[2]

3-4 **6** 1 **Quadriga (IRE)**[10] 2455 3-9-5 **73** FrederikTylicki 5 60
(Robert Eddery) *chsd ldrs: rdn and no rspnse over 2f out: wknd over 1f out* **10/1**

32-0 **7** 19 **Bellitudo (IRE)**[29] 1892 3-9-1 **69** AdamKirby 3
(Marco Botti) *in tch in midfield: rdn and no hdwy jst over 2f out: wknd over 1f out: virtually p.u ins fnl f* **20/1**

4625 **8** 4 **Gabrial The Boss (USA)**[80] 949 3-9-7 **75** (t) WilliamBuick 9
(David Simcock) *stdd s: in rr: rdn 5f out: sme hdwy u.p over 2f out: wknd over 1f out: virtually p.u ins fnl f* **14/1**

4-50 **9** ½ **Marsh Dragon**[12] 2387 3-8-9 **63** KierenFallon 8
(Mark H Tompkins) *chsd ldrs: rdn and struggling over 2f out: wknd over 1f out: virtually p.u ins fnl f* **12/1**

4-44 **10** 3¾ **Princess Patsky (USA)**[28] 1907 3-8-8 **62** (v) JamieSpencer 2
(Michael Bell) *stdd s: hld up in rr: rdn and no hdwy over 2f out: bhd over 1f out: virtually p.u ins fnl f* **16/1**

1m 26.03s (-0.57) **Going Correction** -0.05s/f (Good) 10 Ran SP% **116.9**
Speed ratings (Par 99): **101,93,91,91,90 89,67,62,62,57**
Tote Swingers: 1&2 £14.30, 1&3 £4.40, 2&3 £1.90 CSF £70.55 CT £170.57 TOTE £7.50: £2.20, £2.80, £1.10; EX 43.40 Trifecta £60.60 Pool: £649.00 - 8.02 winning units..
Owner Khalifa Dasmal **Bred** Barton Bloodstock **Trained** Newmarket, Suffolk

FOCUS
A fair handicap in which the pace was just an ordinary one. The winner edged towards the stands' side in the last quarter mile. This form could be rated up to 6lb higher, with the runner-up rated below his previous Doncaster mark.

2764 GREAT YARMOUTH TOURIST AUTHORITY H'CAP 1m 2f 21y
8:40 (8:40) (Class 6) (0-55,55) 4-Y-O+ **£1,940** (£577; £288; £144) **Stalls** Low

Form RPR

0006 **1** **Cufflink**[18] 2219 4-9-4 **52** (v[1]) AdamKirby 1 60
(Iain Jardine) *chsd ldrs: rdn and effrt 2f out: led and edgd lft over 1f out: flashed tail u.p but kpt on wl fnl f* **7/1**[3]

0131 **2** 1 **I'm Harry**[22] 2302 4-9-2 **50** (tp) WilliamBuick 2 56
(George Baker) *in tch in midfield: rdn and effrt wl over 1f out: styd on u.p to chse wnr ins fnl f: no imp fnl 50yds* **4/1**[2]

040- **3** 2½ **Opus (IRE)**[45] 6395 4-9-1 **49** PaulMulrennan 9 50
(Lucy Wadham) *chsd ldrs: rdn and effrt over 2f out: unable qck over 1f out: kpt on u.p ins fnl f to go 3rd cl home* **22/1**

00/ **4** ½ **Global Recovery (IRE)**[21] 2833 6-8-12 **46** oh1 (p) AndreaAtzeni 5 46
(Des Donovan) *led: rdn and hdd over 2f out: no ex u.p over 1f out: plugged on same pce fnl f* **25/1**

0-00 **5** shd **Capriska**[28] 1909 4-8-12 **46** J-PGuillambert 8 46
(Willie Musson) *hld up in last trio: hdwy towards inner over 2f out: swtchd 1f out: kpt on wl ins fnl f: nvr trbld ldrs* **25/1**

000- **6** 1 **Land Hawk (IRE)**[275] 5638 7-9-4 **55** SimonPearce[(3)] 6 53
(Lydia Pearce) *hld up in midfield: effrt and n.m.r towards inner 2f out: drvn and hdwy ent fnl f: one pce fnl 150yds* **33/1**

6042 **7** nk **Koo And The Gang (IRE)**[8] 2511 6-8-12 **51** RobertTart[(5)] 14 49
(Brian Ellison) *chsd ldr tl rdn to ld over 2f out: hdd and no ex u.p over 1f out: wknd ins fnl f* **7/4**[1]

3530 **8** 3 **Frosty Friday**[63] 1183 5-8-13 **52** (p) DannyBrock[(5)] 11 44
(J R Jenkins) *hld up in rr: hdwy towards centre over 2f out: rdn and no hdwy over 1f out: wknd fnl f* **40/1**

5500 **9** ½ **Miss Chardonay**[36] 1730 6-8-12 **46** oh1 (t) SaleemGolam 4 40
(Mandy Rowland) *in tch in midfield: n.m.r over 2f out: rdn and no hdwy 2f out: wknd 1f out* **66/1**

00-0 **10** 3¼ **Frosty Secret**[25] 1987 4-8-12 **53** (p) IanBurns[(7)] 13 38
(Jane Chapple-Hyam) *wl in tch in midfield: rdn and unable qck over 2f out: wknd 1f out* **25/1**

0-66 **11** ½ **Norse Song**[21] 2134 4-8-12 **46** oh1 WilliamCarson 12 30
(David Elsworth) *hld up towards rr: hdwy on inner 3f out: rdn and no ex 2f out: wknd over 1f out* **10/1**

0060 **12** ¾ **Feeling Good**[8] 2514 4-9-1 **52** (t) PaulPickard[(3)] 7 34
(Brian Ellison) *hld up in rr: short-lived effrt towards centre 3f out: wknd wl over 1f out* **14/1**

-026 **13** 2 **Firefly**[22] 2072 4-9-3 **51** JamieSpencer 10 30
(John Weymes) *hld up in midfield: rdn and no hdwy over 2f out: wknd over 1f out: eased wl ins fnl f* **20/1**

06-0 **14** 37 **Autumnus (IRE)**[123] 381 4-9-0 **48** (b[1]) JoeFanning 3
(Ismail Mohammed) *t.k.h: hld up in midfield: lost pl 3f out: t.o and eased fnl f* **8/1**

2m 9.44s (-1.06) **Going Correction** -0.05s/f (Good) 14 Ran SP% **123.3**
Speed ratings (Par 101): **102,101,99,98,98 97,97,95,94,92 91,91,89,60**
Tote Swingers: 1&2 £9.30, 1&3 £40.30, 2&3 £13.50 CSF £32.37 CT £607.11 TOTE £9.20: £2.20, £1.90, £7.70; EX 39.00 Trifecta £811.10 Part won. Pool: £1,081.54 - 0.72 winning units..
Owner Mr Greedy & Little Miss Stubborn **Bred** C J Murfitt **Trained** Bonchester Bridge, Borders

FOCUS
A low-grade handicap in which the gallop was just an ordinary one but the first two pulled clear. The third helps set the level.
T/Plt: £11.50 to a £1 stake. Pool: £57,312.80 - 3,614.79 winning tickets. T/Qpdt: £6.10 to a £1 stake. Pool: £5,285.30 - 636.90 winning tickets. SP

2336 BEVERLEY (R-H)
Wednesday, May 29

OFFICIAL GOING: Good changing to good (good to soft in places) after race 1 (6.35)
Rail around bottom bend moved out increasing distances on Round course by 18yds.
Wind: Light across Weather: Heavy cloud and rain showers

2765 IT'S LUCKY IN LOVE NIGHT TONIGHT MAIDEN STKS 7f 100y
6:35 (6:36) (Class 5) 3-Y-O+ **£3,234** (£962; £481; £240) **Stalls** Low

Form RPR

43 **1** **Defendant**[16] 2306 3-9-3 0 RyanMoore 3 84+
(Sir Michael Stoute) *trckd ldr: cl up 2f out: rdn to ld appr fnl f: sn clr and styd on strly* **4/7**[1]

0-22 **2** 4½ **Dairam (USA)**[15] 2346 3-9-3 75 PaulHanagan 4 73
(Charles Hills) *led: pushed along over 2f out: jnd wl over 1f out: sn rdn and hdd appr fnl f: kpt on same pce* **10/3**[2]

0 **3** 1½ **Gone Dutch**[19] 2224 3-9-3 0 KierenFallon 9 69+
(James Fanshawe) *trckd ldrs: pushed along 3f out: rdn 2f out: kpt on fnl f* **20/1**

2 **4** 1¾ **Adiator**[9] 2504 5-9-4 0 AdamCarter[(5)] 2 64
(Neville Bycroft) *trckd ldrs: effrt wl over 2f out: sn rdn and kpt on same pce* **12/1**

0-0 **5** hd **Three Glasses (IRE)**[18] 2279 3-9-3 0 DavidAllan 8 64+
(Tim Easterby) *towards rr: pushed along over 3f out: rdn along 2f out: kpt on fnl f* **66/1**

60 **6** 3 **Orbison (IRE)**[16] 2306 3-9-3 0 NeilCallan 6 57+
(Roger Varian) *t.k.h: trckd ldrs: effrt to chse ldng pair 2f out: sn rdn and wknd appr fnl f* **6/1**[3]

50 **7** 1¼ **Absolute Diamond**[9] 2503 3-8-12 0 MichaelO'Connell 12 49
(John Quinn) *in tch: rdn along 3f out: sn wknd* **80/1**

646 **8** ¾ **Zainda (IRE)**[9] 2501 3-8-12 60 BarryMcHugh 1 47
(John Wainwright) *trckd ldng pair on inner: rdn along wl over 2f out: sn wknd* **50/1**

9 *15* **Sanderiana** 3-8-12 0 .... PaulMulrennan 7
(Mel Brittain) *a towards rr* **80/1**

0 **10** *10* **Forest Philly (IRE)**[9] 2504 3-8-12 0 .... RussKennemore 11
(John Wainwright) *sn outpcd and bhd fr 1/2-way* **200/1**

1m 33.85s (0.05) **Going Correction** -0.10s/f (Good)
WFA 3 from 5yo+ 11lb **10** Ran SP% **119.9**
Speed ratings (Par 103): **95,89,88,86,85 82,81,80,63,51**
toteswingers 1&2 £1.10, 2&3 £7.80, 1&3 £3.50 CSF £2.77 TOTE £1.50: £1.10, £1.40, £4.10; EX 2.90 Trifecta £25.80 Pool: £2404.83 - 69.89 winning units..
Owner K Abdullah **Bred** Juddmonte Farms Ltd **Trained** Newmarket, Suffolk

FOCUS
A dry night but 5mm of rain from midday saw conditions ease to good. Jockeys reported the ground to be on the soft side of good and the ground was changed accordingly after the opener. An uncompetitive maiden in which the gallop was on the steady side and both market leaders were in the first two positions throughout. More to come from the winner with the runner-up rated to his latest Chepstow form.

2766 COLLECT YOUR KEY AND PADLOCK H'CAP 1m 1f 207y
7:05 (7:07) (Class 4) (0-85,85) 4-Y-0+ **£4,690** (£1,395; £697; £348) **Stalls** Low

Form RPR

/0-0 **1** **Garde Cotiere (USA)**[60] 1233 5-9-7 **85** .... PaulHanagan 9 93
(Richard Fahey) *set stdy pce: qcknd wl over 2f out: rdn over 1f out: jnd and drvn ins fnl f: hld on wl: bled fr the nose* **12/1**

3001 **2** *shd* **The Lock Master (IRE)**[7] 2580 6-9-0 **78** 6ex .... KierenFallon 2 86
(Michael Appleby) *trckd ldng pair: effrt to chse wnr wl over 1f out: sn rdn: chal ent fnl f and ev ch: sn drvn and no ex nr line* **5/1**

050 **3** *3* **Moccasin (FR)**[12] 2431 4-8-13 **84** .... JordanNason[(7)] 1 86+
(Geoffrey Harker) *trckd ldrs on inner: swtchd lft and effrt whn n.m.r 2f out: sn rdn and kpt on fnl f* **20/1**

2150 **4** *3* **Carragold**[14] 2369 7-8-9 **73** .... PaulMulrennan 5 69
(Mel Brittain) *in tch: hdwy 3f out: chsd ldng pair and rdn along wl over 1f out: sn wknd* **11/4**[1]

0-03 **5** *1 3/4* **Demolition**[10] 2478 9-9-1 **82** ....(p) RaulDaSilva[(3)] 7 74
(Noel Wilson) *dwlt: hld up in rr: hdwy on outer over 2f out: rdn to chse ldrs wl over 1f out: sn drvn and no imp* **9/2**[3]

0-63 **6** *hd* **Tartan Gigha (IRE)**[23] 2077 8-8-10 **74** .... JoeFanning 6 66
(Geoffrey Harker) *hld up: a towards rr* **6/1**

66-1 **7** *15* **Classic Punch (IRE)**[23] 2077 10-9-4 **82** .... DanielTudhope 8 51
(Tim Etherington) *trckd wnr: cl up 1/2-way: rdn along over 2f out: sn wknd and eased over 1f out* **3/1**[2]

2m 4.4s (-2.60) **Going Correction** -0.10s/f (Good) **7** Ran SP% **113.3**
Speed ratings (Par 105): **106,105,103,101,99 99,87**
toteswingers 1&2 £4.20, 2&3 £12.00, 1&3 £7.90 CSF £68.45 CT £1192.36 TOTE £13.50: £5.20, £3.10; EX 56.30 Trifecta £215.80 Pool: £1307.87 - 4.54 winning units..
Owner Sir Robert Ogden **Bred** Haras Du Mezeray & Ships Commodities Int **Trained** Musley Bank, N Yorks

FOCUS
Mainly exposed performers in a useful handicap. The gallop was only fair but the first two pulled clear. The winner can do better while the second recorded a slight personal-best on turf.

2767 HILARY NEEDLER TROPHY (CONDITIONS STKS) (FILLIES) 5f
7:35 (7:35) (Class 2) 2-Y-0
£15,562 (£4,660; £2,330; £1,165; £582; £292) **Stalls** Low

Form RPR

331 **1** **Ventura Mist**[11] 2458 2-8-12 0 ....(p) DuranFentiman 9 78
(Tim Easterby) *dwlt and swtchd rt s: in rr: hdwy whn n.m.r over 1f out: sn swtchd lft and rdn: str run on outer ins fnl f to ld nr fin* **14/1**

314 **2** *nk* **Lexington Rose**[12] 2426 2-8-12 0 .... TomEaves 1 77
(Bryan Smart) *led: pushed along and edgd lft over 1f out: rdn and hung lft ins fnl f: hdd and no ex nr line* **6/4**[1]

351 **3** *3/4* **Lorimer's Lot (IRE)**[22] 2117 2-8-12 0 .... PaulMulrennan 3 75
(Tim Walford) *prom: cl up 2f out: sn rdn and ev ch tl drvn and nt qckn wl ins fnl f* **33/1**

041 **4** *3/4* **Iseemist (IRE)**[25] 2011 2-8-12 0 .... MichaelJMMurphy 6 72
(John Gallagher) *dwlt and in rr: hdwy 2f out: sn rdn: styng on whn n.m.r ins fnl f: nrst fin* **20/1**

031 **5** *1/2* **Blockade (IRE)**[16] 2327 2-8-12 0 .... NeilCallan 8 70
(James Tate) *t.k.h: trckd ldrs: hdwy 2f out: rdn over 1f out: kpt on same pce fnl f* **14/1**

01 **6** *1/2* **Rosebay Coral (IRE)**[19] 2238 2-8-12 0 .... BarryMcHugh 5 68
(Tony Coyle) *hld up: hdwy 2f out: rdn to chse ldrs over 1f out: kpt on same pce fnl f* **33/1**

124 **7** *nk* **Limegrove**[21] 2147 2-8-12 0 .... JimmyFortune 7 67
(David Evans) *chsd ldrs: rdn along 2f out: drvn and one pce ent fnl f* **11/2**[3]

0 **8** *1 3/4* **Fredricka**[5] 2625 2-8-12 0 .... DanielTudhope 4 61
(Garry Moss) *dwlt and in rr: sme hdwy on inner 2f out: sn rdn and no imp* **50/1**

10 **9** *3/4* **Champagne Babe**[12] 2426 2-8-12 0 .... GrahamGibbons 2 58
(Keith Dalgleish) *in tch: hdwy 2f out: rdn to chse ldrs over 1f out: wknd fnl f* **4/1**[2]

41 **10** *1/2* **Mops Angel**[37] 1718 2-8-12 0 .... AndrewMullen 10 56+
(Michael Appleby) *sn chsng ldng pair: rdn along wl over 1f out and grad wknd* **13/2**

1634 **11** *1/2* **Intense Feeling (IRE)**[8] 2553 2-8-12 0 .... DavidAllan 11 55
(David Evans) *chsd ldrs on outer: rdn along 2f out: wknd over 1f out* **14/1**

1m 3.05s (-0.45) **Going Correction** -0.15s/f (Firm) **11** Ran SP% **121.3**
Speed ratings (Par 96): **97,96,95,94,93 92,92,89,88,87 86**
toteswingers 1&2 £9.30, 2&3 £16.30, 1&3 £0.00 CSF £35.51 TOTE £11.90: £3.10, £1.20, £6.00; EX 53.90 Trifecta £524.90 Pool: £959.61 - 1.37 winning units..
Owner Middleham Park Racing Xxiv **Bred** Bumble Bloodstock & C Liesack **Trained** Great Habton, N Yorks

FOCUS
A valuable race, despite being downgraded from Listed status in 2011 but, although only one of the field hadn't previously won a race, this form looks no more than useful and it is hard to think that any of these is up to group company in the short-term. The gallop was sound and the field fanned across the track in the last quarter mile.

2768 WEATHERBYS HAMILTON INSURANCE CONDITIONS STKS 5f
8:05 (8:05) (Class 3) 3-Y-0+
£7,158 (£2,143; £1,071; £535; £267; £134) **Stalls** Low

Form RPR

6-41 **1** **Hamza (IRE)**[24] 2046 4-8-12 108 ....(b) NeilCallan 4 112
(Kevin Ryan) *qckly away and wnt lft s: mde all: rdn and edgd lft ent fnl f: kpt on strly* **2/1**[2]

5-14 **2** *1 1/4* **Heeraat (IRE)**[25] 2019 4-8-12 108 .... PaulHanagan 6 108
(William Haggas) *trckd ldrs: hdwy over 2f out: rdn to chal ent fnl f: sn drvn: hung lft and one pce* **1/1**[1]

5520 **3** *1 1/4* **Justineo**[25] 2013 4-8-12 97 .... JimmyFortune 7 103
(Roger Varian) *trckd ldrs: hdwy 2f out: rdn to chse ldng pair ins fnl f: kpt on* **16/1**

-025 **4** *1 1/2* **Kyleakin Lass**[11] 2461 4-8-7 96 .... JamesSullivan 5 93
(Paul Fitzsimons) *towards rr: hdwy wl over 1f out: sn rdn and kpt on fnl f* **22/1**

3465 **5** *1/2* **Bear Behind (IRE)**[17] 2300 4-8-12 103 ....[1] RichardKingscote 3 96
(Tom Dascombe) *cl up: rdn along wl over 1f out: wknd ent fnl f* **10/1**

5-40 **6** *1 1/2* **Face The Problem (IRE)**[14] 2368 5-8-12 105 .... KierenFallon 1 90
(Jamie Osborne) *chsd ldrs: rdn along 2f out: sn wknd* **7/1**[3]

3460 **7** *5* **Inxile (IRE)**[60] 1255 8-9-9 105 ....(p) AdrianNicholls 8 83
(David Nicholls) *in tch on outer: rdn along 2f out: sn wknd* **33/1**

400- **8** *1/2* **Burning Thread (IRE)**[196] 7704 6-8-12 82 .... DaleSwift 2 71
(Tim Etherington) *chsd ldrs: rdn 2f out: sn wknd* **50/1**

1m 1.26s (-2.24) **Going Correction** -0.15s/f (Firm) **8** Ran SP% **120.1**
Speed ratings (Par 107): **111,109,107,104,103 101,93,92**
toteswingers 1&2 £2.40, 2&3 £4.30, 1&3 £8.60 CSF £4.53 TOTE £4.20: £1.10, £1.10, £3.90; EX 6.60 Trifecta £39.80 Pool: £1674.35 - 31.51 winning units..
Owner Mubarak Al Naemi **Bred** Castlemartin Stud And Skymarc Farm **Trained** Hambleton, N Yorks

FOCUS
Several smart sorts in a good-quality conditions event. The pace was sound and the field raced centre to stands side in the last half of the contest. The third sets the standard with the winner pretty much to form, but these races are rarely too solid.

2769 BEVERLEY MIDDLE DISTANCE SERIES H'CAP 1m 4f 16y
8:35 (8:36) (Class 5) (0-70,72) 3-Y-0 **£3,234** (£962; £481; £240) **Stalls** Low

Form RPR

2-60 **1** **Aficionado**[11] 2442 3-9-5 **66** ....(p) NeilCallan 7 73
(Ed Dunlop) *t.k.h: trckd ldrs: hdwy 3f out: rdn along and sltly outpcd wl over 1f out: drvn appr fnl f and styd on wl to ld nr fin* **3/1**[2]

5261 **2** *1/2* **Flamingo Beat**[15] 2341 3-9-4 **65** .... StevieDonohoe 2 71
(Rae Guest) *a.p: cl up after 4f: led over 2f out: rdn clr jst over 1f out: drvn ins fnl f: hdd and no ex nr fin* **3/1**[2]

2-44 **3** *nk* **Chant (IRE)**[27] 1965 3-9-3 **64** .... PJMcDonald 3 70
(Ann Duffield) *hld up in tch: effrt over 2f out and sn pushed along: swtchd to outer and rdn over 1f out: styd on wl fnl f* **12/1**

1-31 **4** *3* **Mad Jazz**[8] 2555 3-9-4 **72** 6ex .... DavidSimmonson[(7)] 1 73
(Tony Coyle) *led 3f: trckd ldrs: effrt over 2f out: rdn to chal wl over 1f out: drvn and edgd lft appr fnl f: sn wknd* **2/1**[1]

40-6 **5** *1 1/2* **Attansky (IRE)**[53] 1393 3-8-11 **58** .... DavidAllan 5 56
(Tim Easterby) *hld up in rr: hdwy 3f out: rdn along 2f out: sn drvn and no imp* **10/1**

2264 **6** *6* **Mirth**[42] 1613 3-8-13 **60** .... JoeFanning 8 49
(Mark Johnston) *cl up on outer: led after 3f: rdn along and hdd over 2f out: sn drvn and wknd 1 1/2f out* **5/1**[3]

2m 39.39s (-0.41) **Going Correction** -0.10s/f (Good) **6** Ran SP% **116.8**
Speed ratings (Par 99): **97,96,96,94,93 89**
toteswingers 1&2 £4.10, 2&3 £4.20, 1&3 £4.10 CSF £13.08 CT £93.46 TOTE £3.40: £1.60, £1.90; EX 15.00 Trifecta £75.90 Pool: £973.30 - 9.61 winning units..
Owner Red Book Partnership **Bred** Bloomsbury Stud **Trained** Newmarket, Suffolk

FOCUS
A modest handicap run at a no more than a fair gallop. The winner came down the centre in the last 2f. The third looks the best guide to the level.

2770 KC LIGHTSTREAM H'CAP 1m 100y
9:05 (9:05) (Class 5) (0-70,69) 3-Y-0 **£3,234** (£962; £481; £240) **Stalls** Low

Form RPR

2222 **1** **Clock On Tom**[23] 2080 3-8-12 **60** .... GrahamGibbons 8 67
(Michael Easterby) *mde all: rdn and qcknd 2f out: drvn ins fnl f and kpt on strly* **5/1**[2]

11-3 **2** *1 3/4* **Mushaakis (IRE)**[37] 1712 3-9-6 **68** .... PaulHanagan 7 71
(Mark Johnston) *in tch: hdwy over 2f out: rdn over 1f out: drvn to chse wnr ins fnl f: no imp* **9/4**[1]

3-32 **3** *shd* **Knight Owl**[16] 2308 3-9-5 **67** .... KierenFallon 4 70+
(James Fanshawe) *hld up in rr: hdwy 2f out: rdn over 1f out: styd on wl fnl f: nrst fin* **9/4**[1]

6-04 **4** *1 3/4* **Medici Dancer**[16] 2308 3-9-7 **69** .... DavidAllan 1 68
(Tim Easterby) *hld up towards rr: hdwy over 3f out: chsd ldrs 2f out: sn rdn and kpt on same pce appr fnl f* **11/2**[3]

314- **5** *3/4* **Lucy Bee**[166] 8101 3-9-0 **62** .... JoeFanning 3 59
(Keith Dalgleish) *trckd ldrs on inner: hdwy 3f out: rdn to chse wnr 2f out: drvn appr fnl f: sn wknd* **20/1**

-330 **6** *1* **Rocket Ronnie (IRE)**[23] 2080 3-8-9 **57** .... AdrianNicholls 2 52
(David Nicholls) *hld up in rr: hdwy on wd outside wl over 2f out: rdn wl over 1f out: sn no imp* **10/1**

46-6 **7** *9* **Annie Besant**[15] 2345 3-8-7 **55** oh3 .... JimmyQuinn 6 29
(Michael Mullineaux) *plld hrd: in tch: pushed along over 3f out: sn wknd* **50/1**

1124 **8** *shd* **Taxiformissbyron**[107] 615 3-9-5 **67** .... TomEaves 10 41
(Michael Herrington) *t.k.h early: chsd ldrs: rdn along wl over 2f out: sn wknd* **25/1**

00 **9** *3/4* **Inigo Montoya**[49] 1481 3-8-2 **55** oh2 .... ShirleyTeasdale[(5)] 5 27
(Alan McCabe) *chsd ldrs: rdn along 3f out: wknd over 2f out* **40/1**

5-05 **10** *19* **Miss Mocca**[16] 2324 3-9-1 **63** .... PaulMulrennan 9
(Paul Fitzsimons) *sn chsng wnr: rdn along 3f out: sn wknd* **20/1**

1m 47.44s (-0.16) **Going Correction** -0.10s/f (Good) **10** Ran SP% **120.5**
Speed ratings (Par 99): **96,94,94,92,91 90,81,81,80,61**
toteswingers 1&2 £2.50, 2&3 £2.50, 1&3 £3.50 CSF £16.25 CT £33.10 TOTE £7.40: £2.30, £1.20, £1.50; EX 22.00 Trifecta £77.00 Pool: £908.80 - 8.84 winning units..
Owner A Simpson & J Rooney **Bred** Kingwood Bloodstock **Trained** Sheriff Hutton, N Yorks

FOCUS
A modest handicap in which an ordinary gallop only increased turning for home. The field stayed against the far rail in the home straight. The fifth, to last year's AW form, sets the standard.

T/Plt: £54.60 to a £1 stake. Pool of £65464.71 - 874.81 winning tickets. T/Qpdt: £5.40 to a £1 stake. Pool of £5605.92 - 758.80 winning tickets. JR

The Form Book Flat, Raceform Ltd, Compton, RG20 6NL.

[2560]KEMPTON (A.W) (R-H)
Wednesday, May 29

OFFICIAL GOING: Standard
Wind: Light, against Weather: Murky, drizzly

2771 CONOR MAYNARD LIVE AT KEMPTON 14.09.13 MEDIAN AUCTION MAIDEN STKS 5f (P)
5:55 (5:56) (Class 6) 2-Y-O **£1,940** (£577; £288; £144) **Stalls** Low

Form RPR
5 **1** **A Childs Dream (IRE)**[23] 2090 2-9-0 0 RichardHughes 5 69
(Richard Hannon) *mde virtually all: edgd lft fr 2f out: rdn fnl f: hld on* **7/4**[2]
5 **2** *nk* **Costa Filey**[18] 2250 2-9-5 0 GeorgeBaker 3 73
(Ed Vaughan) *chsd ldng pair: wd bnd over 3f out: chal on outer of ldng trio fr 1/2-way: upsides over 1f out: hanging lft fnl f: nt qckn nr fin* **4/6**[1]
3 *½* **Flying Bear (IRE)** 2-9-5 0 SteveDrowne 2 71
(Jeremy Gask) *chsd ldng trio: shkn up on inner over 1f out: chal fnl f: no ex last 50yds* **20/1**
4 *3* **Jalebi** 2-9-0 0 MatthewDavies 4 55
(Jim Boyle) *chsd wnr: lost 2nd wl over 1f out and sltly intimidated: wknd fnl f* **33/1**
5 *8* **Hostile Takeover (IRE)** 2-9-0 0 (t) CharlesBishop(5) 1 32
(Olly Stevens) *v s.i.s: a detached in last* **14/1**[3]
1m 1.61s (1.11) **Going Correction** -0.10s/f (Stan) **5** Ran SP% **110.7**
Speed ratings (Par 91): **87,86,85,80,68**
CSF £3.26 TOTE £1.70: £1.30, £1.10; EX 3.50 Trifecta £9.80 Pool: £1718.39 - 130.75 winning units..
Owner Michael Cohen & Adam Victor **Bred** Messrs Mark Hanly & James Hanly **Trained** East Everleigh, Wilts
FOCUS
A fair contest with the market principals having shown promise on their debuts. A guessy opening level and the form might need time to settle.

2772 BETDAQ 1ST UK COMMISSION FREE-EVERYDAY H'CAP 5f (P)
6:25 (6:25) (Class 5) (0-70,70) 3-Y-O+ **£2,587** (£770; £384; £192) **Stalls** Low

Form RPR
2313 **1** **Desert Strike**[26] 1985 7-9-12 **70** (p) LiamKeniry 5 77
(Conor Dore) *mde all: drvn fnl f: hld on nr fin* **5/1**[3]
4460 **2** *nk* **Steelcut**[18] 2268 9-9-1 **59** (p) SteveDrowne 1 65
(Mark Buckley) *trckd ldng pair: plld out jst over 1f out: shkn up and r.o to take 2nd last 75yds: clsd on wnr but too late* **8/1**
432 **3** *1 ¼* **Love You Louis**[22] 2132 7-9-11 **69** (v) RichardHughes 6 70
(J R Jenkins) *pressed wnr: rdn over 1f out: nt qckn fnl f and lost 2nd last 75yds* **9/4**[2]
3232 **4** *4* **Where's Reiley (USA)**[20] 2196 7-9-11 **69** (v) SebSanders 4 56
(Michael Attwater) *sn outpcd and drvn: nvr gng wl and no imp on ldrs* **13/8**[1]
224 **5** *½* **Clock Opera (IRE)**[29] 1911 3-8-5 **62** RobertTart(5) 7 47
(William Stone) *dwlt: settled in last and sn wl outpcd: urged along over 1f out: no imp* **8/1**
59.82s (-0.68) **Going Correction** -0.10s/f (Stan)
WFA 3 from 4yo+ 8lb **5** Ran SP% **107.8**
Speed ratings (Par 103): **101,100,98,92,91**
CSF £37.36 TOTE £7.50: £4.10, £3.40; EX 26.30 Trifecta £127.40 Pool: £ 1047.92 - 6.16 winning units..
Owner Andrew Page **Bred** Mrs Mary Rowlands **Trained** Hubbert's Bridge, Lincs
FOCUS
Two non-runners weakened this already modest sprint handicap, in which it was vital to be up with the pace.

2773 IRISH NIGHT ON 10.07.13 H'CAP 7f (P)
6:55 (6:55) (Class 6) (0-65,65) 4-Y-O+ **£1,940** (£577; £288; £144) **Stalls** Low

Form RPR
510 **1** **Shahrazad (IRE)**[5] 2638 4-8-12 **56** (t) SilvestreDeSousa 4 65
(Patrick Gilligan) *mde all: drvn at least 2 l clr 2f out: kpt on fnl f: nvr really chal* **12/1**
3-24 **2** *1 ½* **Duke Of Destiny (IRE)**[23] 2089 4-9-7 **65** GeorgeBaker 5 70+
(Ed Walker) *hld up towards rr: shkn up and prog 2f out: drvn to chse wnr jst over 1f out: styd on but nvr really clsd* **1/1**[1]
0130 **3** *nk* **Penbryn (USA)**[34] 1797 6-9-1 **59** SebSanders 14 63
(Nick Littmoden) *trckd ldrs on outer: rdn and nt qckn 2f out: renewed effrt over 1f out: disp 2nd fnl f: styd on* **25/1**
14-4 **4** *½* **Jay Bee Blue**[7] 2565 4-9-5 **63** (bt) AdamKirby 1 66
(Sean Curran) *trckd ldrs: prog 2f out to dispute 2nd over 1f out and looked a threat: sn rdn and one pce* **8/1**[3]
6446 **5** *¾* **Floralys (USA)**[19] 2236 4-8-8 **57** DannyBrock(5) 9 58
(Amy Weaver) *t.k.h: hld up towards rr: prog 2f out: urged along and kpt on same pce fnl f on inner* **50/1**
2202 **6** *nse* **Athletic**[7] 2565 4-8-12 **61** (v) RobertTart(5) 11 61+
(Andrew Reid) *dwlt: hld up in last trio: trying to mount an effrt whn rn into wall of horses over 1f out: plld wd and r.o fnl f: no ch* **6/1**[2]
2200 **7** *3 ¾* **Rose Garnet (IRE)**[18] 2281 5-8-9 **58** RyanTate(5) 10 48
(Tony Carroll) *trckd ldrs: rdn and prog to dispute 2nd over 1f out: wknd fnl f* **33/1**
6200 **8** *nk* **Homeward Strut**[7] 2565 4-9-6 **64** (v[1]) IanMongan 13 54
(Laura Mongan) *trckd ldrs: rdn to dispute 2nd briefly over 1f out: sn wknd* **16/1**
0055 **9** *½* **Kindia (IRE)**[21] 2155 5-9-4 **62** (p) RobertHavlin 6 50
(Michael Attwater) *dwlt: drvn in rr early: nvr a factor: fnlly styd on last 150yds* **33/1**
3602 **10** *1 ½* **Tenbridge**[15] 2345 4-8-13 **57** (b) WilliamCarson 2 41
(Derek Haydn Jones) *mostly in last trio: drvn over 2f out: no great prog* **16/1**
6-22 **11** *½* **High On The Hog (IRE)**[22] 2130 5-9-1 **59** TomMcLaughlin 3 42
(Mark Brisbourne) *t.k.h early: chsd wnr 2f: styd prom: wnt 2nd again jst over 2f out to over 1f out: wknd qckly* **8/1**[3]
00-0 **12** *1 ¼* **Cocohatchee**[23] 2096 5-8-12 **63** (p) JakePayne(7) 7 42
(Pat Phelan) *t.k.h: trckd wnr after 2f tl jst over 2f out: wkng whn hmpd jst over 1f out* **33/1**
20-0 **13** *2* **Grand Piano (IRE)**[13] 2395 6-8-7 **58** (v) RobHornby(7) 8 32
(Andrew Balding) *mostly in last: detached fr 1/2-way* **33/1**
1m 26.24s (0.24) **Going Correction** +0.075s/f (Slow) **13** Ran SP% **123.5**
Speed ratings (Par 101): **101,99,98,98,97 97,93,92,92,90 89,88,86**
toteswingers 1&2 £6.50, 2&3 £11.30, 1&3 £46.60 CSF £23.89 CT £346.76 TOTE £11.30: £4.20, £1.40, £9.90; EX 32.60 Trifecta £725.90 Pool: £1277.38 - 1.31 winning units..
Owner Linton Doolan **Bred** Shadwell Estate Company Limited **Trained** Newmarket, Suffolk
FOCUS
A low-grade handicap.

2774 £200 FREE BETS AT BETDAQ/BRITISH STALLION STUDS EBF MAIDEN FILLIES' STKS 6f (P)
7:25 (7:27) (Class 5) 2-Y-O **£2,911** (£866; £432; £216) **Stalls** Low

Form RPR
1 **Princess Noor (IRE)** 2-9-0 0 WilliamBuick 5 73+
(Roger Varian) *slowest away: hld up in last: prog on outer 2f out: nudged along over 1f out: clsd to ld 150yds out: cosily* **7/2**[2]
2 *¾* **Bewitchment** 2-9-0 0 LukeMorris 7 71+
(Sir Mark Prescott Bt) *chsd ldrs in 4th: rn green and pushed along: clsd fr 2f out: rdn and styd on fnl f but no real ch w wnr* **14/1**
3 **3** *shd* **Misty Sparkler**[19] 2230 2-9-0 0 HayleyTurner 2 70
(Brian Meehan) *t.k.h early: trckd ldng pair: wnt 2nd jst over 2f out: clsd on ldr 1f out: styd on same pce after* **9/2**[3]
4 *¾* **Manderley (IRE)** 2-9-0 0 RichardHughes 1 69
(Richard Hannon) *dwlt: hld up in 5th: effrt on inner 2f out: shkn up briefly over 1f out: kpt on same pce: a hld* **11/8**[1]
6223 **5** *shd* **Memory Styx**[6] 2583 2-9-0 0 MartinHarley 6 68
(Mick Channon) *led at mod pce: tried to kick on 2f out: hdd and btn last 150yds* **6/1**
6 *10* **Swale Star** 2-9-0 0 LiamKeniry 9 38
(Seamus Mullins) *chsd ldr to jst over 2f out: wknd qckly* **66/1**
1m 14.79s (1.69) **Going Correction** +0.075s/f (Slow) **6** Ran SP% **105.0**
Speed ratings (Par 90): **91,90,89,88,88 75**
toteswingers 1&2 £6.10, 2&3 £4.40, 1&3 £3.00 CSF £39.42 TOTE £3.70: £1.60, £4.10; EX 25.00 Trifecta £139.20 Pool: £842.49 - 4.53 winning units..
Owner Saleh Al Homaizi & Imad Al Sagar **Bred** Lynch Bages Ltd & Camas Park Stud **Trained** Newmarket, Suffolk
FOCUS
A fillies' maiden that has produced some smart performers in recent years, notably Listed winner Lily Again and champion 2-y-o filly Hooray. The form is limited by the fifth but the winner can go on to rate higher.

2775 BETDAQ CUSTOMERS COMMISSION FREE 1ST MONTH H'CAP (LONDON MIDDLE DISTANCE SERIES QUALIFIER) 1m 3f (P)
7:55 (7:55) (Class 3) (0-95,95) 4-Y-O+
£7,158 (£2,143; £1,071; £535; £267; £134) **Stalls** Low

Form RPR
104- **1** **Expert Fighter (USA)**[253] 6348 4-9-0 **88** SilvestreDeSousa 2 99+
(Saeed bin Suroor) *t.k.h early: trckd ldr at mod pce: clsd to ld 2f out and sn drvn clr: in n.d fnl f though ld dwindled* **5/2**[1]
1245 **2** *1* **Spifer (IRE)**[35] 1768 5-9-3 **91** (p) AndreaAtzeni 6 100+
(Marco Botti) *hld up in 6th in modly run event: prog wl over 1f out: rdn to chse wnr last 150yds: r.o to cl gap but no ch to chal* **7/2**[2]
4104 **3** *3* **Fennell Bay (IRE)**[14] 2365 4-8-9 **83** FrannyNorton 4 87
(Mark Johnston) *led: set mod: pce: kicked on wl over 2f out: hdd 2f out and sn outpcd: lost 2nd last 150yds* **4/1**[3]
1- **4** *½* **Bishop Roko**[375] 2266 4-9-7 **95** GeorgeBaker 3 98+
(Roger Charlton) *trckd ldng trio: jst pushed along whn wnr wnt for home 2f out: outpcd after: nt disgracd* **7/2**[2]
31S- **5** *½* **Romeo Montague**[301] 4697 5-9-5 **93** GrahamLee 7 95
(Ed Dunlop) *s.s: hld up in last in modly run event: effrt on inner 2f out: one pce and no ch* **14/1**
-000 **6** *nk* **Layline (IRE)**[13] 2383 6-8-7 **81** oh1 LukeMorris 1 82
(Gay Kelleway) *trckd ldng pair: rdn 2f out: sn outpcd* **50/1**
124 **7** *1 ¾* **English Summer**[13] 2385 6-8-10 **84** (t) HayleyTurner 5 82
(David Simcock) *hld up in 5th: shkn up once pce lifted over 2f out: no prog and sn btn* **7/1**
2m 24.39s (2.49) **Going Correction** +0.075s/f (Slow) **7** Ran SP% **114.1**
Speed ratings (Par 107): **93,92,90,89,89 89,87**
toteswingers 1&2 £3.00, 2&3 £4.60, 1&3 £2.30 CSF £11.46 TOTE £3.00: £2.30, £2.40; EX 11.90 Trifecta £49.80 Pool: £786.17 - 11.83 winning units..
Owner Godolphin **Bred** Darley **Trained** Newmarket, Suffolk
FOCUS
A strong handicap for older horses.

2776 WINNERS ARE WELCOME AT BETDAQ H'CAP (LONDON MILE SERIES QUALIFIER) 1m (P)
8:25 (8:25) (Class 4) (0-85,85) 3-Y-O **£4,690** (£1,395; £697; £348) **Stalls** Low

Form RPR
1-11 **1** **Prophets Pride**[60] 1246 3-9-7 **85** SebSanders 1 91+
(Jeremy Noseda) *trckd ldng pair: sltly outpcd 2f out: hrd rdn fr over 1f out: styd on fnl f to ld post* **6/4**[1]
2-42 **2** *nse* **George Cinq**[19] 2209 3-9-4 **82** HayleyTurner 4 88
(Michael Bell) *trckd ldr: rdn 2f out: clsd to take narrow ld 1f out: styd on but hdd post* **11/4**[2]
-105 **3** *½* **Mumeyez**[35] 1770 3-8-12 **76** WilliamBuick 2 81
(John Gosden) *led: kicked on jst over 2f out: narrowly hdd 1f out: styd on but lost 2nd nr fin* **12/1**
30-4 **4** *1 ½* **Living Desert**[29] 1908 3-9-1 **79** RobertHavlin 7 80
(James Toller) *restrained into last sn after s: stl there as ldrs kicked on jst over 2f out: prog over 1f out: styd on fnl f: clsng grad at fin* **25/1**
00-1 **5** *½* **Derwent (USA)**[16] 2309 3-9-5 **83** GeorgeBaker 3 83
(Roger Charlton) *hld up in 5th: outpcd and pushed along 2f out: shkn up over 1f out: styd on but nvr nr enough to threaten* **9/2**[3]
4110 **6** *5* **Camachoice (IRE)**[39] 1683 3-9-1 **79** (p) AdamKirby 6 68
(Marco Botti) *s.i.s: mostly in last pair: rdn over 2f out: wknd over 1f out* **10/1**
0035 **7** *3 ¼* **Fraserburgh (IRE)**[16] 2309 3-8-13 **77** FrannyNorton 5 58
(Mark Johnston) *chsd ldng pair: rdn over 2f out bef main kick had sed: wknd over 1f out* **20/1**
1m 39.93s (0.13) **Going Correction** +0.075s/f (Slow) **7** Ran SP% **110.2**
Speed ratings (Par 101): **102,101,101,99,99 94,91**
toteswingers 1&2 £1.70, 2&3 £6.40, 1&3 £4.30 CSF £5.24 TOTE £2.10: £1.40, £1.90; EX 5.70 Trifecta £32.60 Pool: £813.05 - 18.65 winning units..
Owner Saeed Suhail **Bred** Rabbah Bloodstock Limited **Trained** Newmarket, Suffolk

FOCUS
An excellent three-year-old handicap with a thrilling finish fought out between two progressive horses.

2777 LONDON'S TRACKS RACINGANDMUSIC.CO.UK APPRENTICE H'CAP 1m 4f (P)
8:55 (8:55) (Class 6) (0-65,67) 4-Y-O+ **£1,940** (£577; £288; £144) **Stalls** Centre

Form RPR
06-5 **1** **Attraction Ticket**[12] 2418 4-9-2 **65** SiobhanMiller(5) 7 75+
(David Simcock) *t.k.h: hld up disputing 5th: quick move to ld jst over 2f out and sn 3 l clr: urged along and styd on* **11/4**[1]
0-21 **2** 1 1/4 **Gladstone (IRE)**[16] 2333 5-8-9 **53** WilliamTwiston-Davies 4 58
(Polly Gundry) *hld up in 7th: pushed along over 3f out: prog u.p 2f out: styd on to take 2nd ins fnl f: unable to chal* **5/1**
0/60 **3** 1 **Between The Lines (IRE)**[10] 1882 4-8-12 **59** (t) EDLinehan(3) 11 62
(Anthony Middleton) *hld up in last pair: prog on inner over 2f out: styd on same pce fr over 1f out to take 3rd last stride* **25/1**
/2-0 **4** shd **Now What**[79] 131 6-8-12 **61** DavidCoyle(5) 6 64
(Jonathan Portman) *pressed ldr to over 2f out: chsd wnr sn after: no imp: lost 2nd ins fnl f: one pce* **16/1**
0-44 **5** 3 1/4 **Barnacle**[36] 1744 4-8-4 **51** oh6 (v) PhilipPrince(3) 3 49
(Pat Eddery) *trckd ldng pair: pushed along and nt qckn over 2f out: sn lost pl and btn* **25/1**
-34 **6** 3 3/4 **The Yank**[37] 1730 4-8-11 **55** RobertTart 1 47
(Tony Carroll) *hld up disputing 5th: rdn and no prog over 2f out: sn btn* **7/2**[2]
0213 **7** 2 1/2 **Highly Likely (IRE)**[7] 2569 4-9-0 **61** (t) RyanTate(3) 5 49
(Steve Woodman) *led to jst over 2f out: wknd sn after* **4/1**[3]
0124 **8** 2 1/4 **Shirataki (IRE)**[26] 1983 5-9-2 **65** PatMillman(5) 2 49
(Peter Hiatt) *s.i.s: plld hrd early: chsd ldng pair tl wknd over 2f out* **13/2**
00-0 **9** 1 1/2 **Suhailah**[21] 2159 7-8-7 **51** oh6 NicoleNordblad 8 33
(Michael Attwater) *a in last pair: struggling sn after 1/2-way: bhd over 2f out* **50/1**

2m 35.47s (0.97) **Going Correction** +0.075s/f (Slow) 9 Ran SP% **114.4**
Speed ratings (Par 101): **99,98,97,97,95 92,91,89,88**
toteswingers 1&2 £5.00, 2&3 £27.30, 1&3 £12.00 CSF £16.30 CT £278.49 TOTE £3.70: £1.60, £1.90, £7.90; EX 14.20 Trifecta £285.80 Pool: £938.45 - 2.46 winning units..
Owner Oliver Brendon **Bred** The Kathryn Stud Ltd **Trained** Newmarket, Suffolk

FOCUS
The card closed with an apprentice handicap, in which they came home slowly.
T/Plt: £69.30 to a £1 stake. Pool of £47571.31 - 500.48 winning tickets. T/Qpdt: £24.50 to a £1 stake. Pool of £3633.02 - 109.60 winning tickets. JN

2543 NOTTINGHAM (L-H)
Wednesday, May 29

OFFICIAL GOING: Good to soft (soft in places) changing to soft after race 2 (2.00)
All races on outer course and home bend moved out 2m.
Wind: Light behind Weather: Raining

2778 BET TOTEPLACEPOT AT TOTEPOOL.COM EBF MAIDEN STKS 5f 13y
1:30 (1:32) (Class 5) 2-Y-O **£3,234** (£962; £481; £240) **Stalls** High

Form RPR
2 **1** **Legend Rising (IRE)**[16] 2307 2-9-5 0 SeanLevey 9 80
(Richard Hannon) *mde all: shkn up over 1f out: pushed out* **15/8**[2]
6 **2** 1 **Iftaar (IRE)**[12] 2411 2-9-5 0 PaulHanagan 2 76
(Charles Hills) *a.p: chsd wnr 3f out: shkn up over 1f out: styd on* **8/11**[1]
3 6 **Meaning Of Life (IRE)** 2-9-5 0 AdamKirby 3 55+
(Marco Botti) *sn prom: pushed along 1/2-way: outpcd fr over 1f out* **11/1**[3]
4 2 1/2 **Global Explorer (USA)** 2-9-5 0 DavidProbert 8 46+
(Stuart Williams) *s.i.s: sn chsng ldrs: rdn 1/2-way: wknd over 1f out* **50/1**
5 2 1/2 **John Lea (IRE)** 2-9-5 0 MartinDwyer 10 37
(Derek Shaw) *dwlt: sn pushed along in rr: rdn and hung lft over 1f out: n.d* **50/1**
0 **6** 3 1/2 **Faye Belle**[37] 1724 2-8-7 0 AdamMcLean(7) 6 19
(Derek Shaw) *chsd wnr 2f: sn rdn: wknd 2f out* **100/1**
4 **7** 3 3/4 **Redlorryellowlorry (IRE)**[25] 2011 2-9-5 0 PatCosgrave 7 11
(George Baker) *s.s: outpcd* **28/1**

1m 2.51s (1.01) **Going Correction** +0.10s/f (Good) 7 Ran SP% **109.4**
Speed ratings (Par 93): **95,93,83,79,75 70,64**
toteswingers 1&2 £1.10, 2&3 £1.90, 1&3 £2.30 CSF £3.21 TOTE £2.60: £1.70, £1.10; EX 4.00 Trifecta £11.20 Pool: £2902.20 - 193.92 winning units..
Owner Mohamed Saeed Al Shahi **Bred** Gus Roche **Trained** East Everleigh, Wilts

FOCUS
Following significant rain the going had eased to good to soft, soft in places and there were several non-runners throughout the afternoon. Despite heavy rain and the time of the opener being 3.91 seconds outside standard, the winning rider felt that the rain had not yet got into the ground. This maiden was dominated by the two market principals. They both showed improved form and are rated close to the race average.

2779 TOTEEXACTA ON ALL RACES AT TOTEPOOL.COM H'CAP 5f 13y
2:00 (2:01) (Class 5) (0-75,75) 3-Y-O **£2,587** (£770; £384; £192) **Stalls** High

Form RPR
3212 **1** **Jofranka**[8] 2542 3-8-7 **61** GrahamGibbons 1 71
(David Barron) *mde all: rdn over 1f out: r.o* **5/6**[1]
-322 **2** 2 **Seven Of Clubs (IRE)**[8] 2544 3-9-7 **75** (b) StevieDonohoe 3 78
(Noel Quinlan) *chsd ldrs: rdn over 1f out: edgd lft ins fnl f: styd on same pce* **2/1**[2]
5204 **3** 1 **Harrogate Fair**[5] 2623 3-8-8 **62** JimmyQuinn 8 61
(Michael Squance) *s.i.s: hdwy 2f out: rdn over 1f out: hung lft ins fnl f: styd on same pce* **16/1**
-540 **4** 4 **Deepest Blue**[23] 2098 3-8-5 **66** LukeLeadbitter(7) 5 51
(Declan Carroll) *chsd ldrs: rdn and hung rt over 1f out: sn wknd* **10/1**[3]
4121 **5** 8 **La Sylphe**[34] 1771 3-8-8 **62** MartinDwyer 4 18
(Derek Shaw) *chsd wnr to 3f: wknd over 1f out* **16/1**
15-5 **6** 29 **Mossgo (IRE)**[112] 531 3-9-0 **68** LukeMorris 2
(John Best) *s.s: sn in tch: hung lft and wknd 1/2-way: t.o* **40/1**

1m 2.06s (0.56) **Going Correction** +0.25s/f (Good) 6 Ran SP% **111.2**
Speed ratings (Par 99): **105,101,100,93,81 34**
toteswingers 1&2 £1.10, 2&3 £3.40, 1&3 £3.40 CSF £2.61 CT £9.76 TOTE £2.00: £1.40, £1.30; EX 3.00 Trifecta £13.80 Pool: £3578.16 - 193.12 winning units..
Owner M Dalby **Bred** Harrowgate Bloodstock Ltd **Trained** Maunby, N Yorks

FOCUS
The market only wanted to know about a couple of these and they filled the first two places. The third sets the level rated close to his AW mark.

2780 NEW SUPERSCOOP6 BET AT TOTEPOOL.COM H'CAP (DIV I) 6f 15y
2:30 (2:31) (Class 5) (0-70,70) 4-Y-O+ **£3,234** (£962; £481; £240) **Stalls** High

Form RPR
4015 **1** **Point North (IRE)**[34] 1798 6-9-2 **65** (b) DanielTudhope 6 81+
(John Balding) *trckd ldrs: led on bit over 1f out: shkn up ins fnl f: easily* **11/4**[1]
0366 **2** 1 3/4 **Celtic Sixpence (IRE)**[12] 2425 5-9-4 **67** MichaelStainton 8 72
(Nick Kent) *sn led: rdn and hdd over 1f out: styd on same pce ins fnl f* **13/2**[3]
0133 **3** 1/2 **Two Turtle Doves (IRE)**[12] 2425 7-8-4 **60** JoeyHaynes(7) 4 63
(Michael Mullineaux) *chsd ldrs: rdn and ev ch over 1f out: styd on same pce ins fnl f* **11/2**[2]
500 **4** hd **Ambitious Icarus**[2] 2702 4-8-13 **62** (e) RobbieFitzpatrick 7 65
(Richard Guest) *dwlt: hld up: hdwy over 1f out: r.o: nt rch ldrs* **10/1**
2205 **5** 1 1/2 **Falasteen (IRE)**[8] 2550 6-9-1 **69** MatthewLawson(5) 1 67
(Milton Bradley) *chsd ldrs: pushed along 1/2-way: rdn over 1f out: styd on same pce* **14/1**
3-04 **6** 4 1/2 **Dancing Maite**[19] 2236 8-8-2 **56** oh4 (b) PhilipPrince(5) 10 40
(Roy Bowring) *s.i.s: hdwy over 3f out: rdn and wknd over 1f out* **14/1**
-116 **7** 5 **Whisky Bravo**[24] 2036 4-8-12 **68** ClaireMurray(7) 13 36
(David Brown) *chsd ldrs: ev ch over 2f out: wknd over 1f out* **22/1**
6-10 **8** 3/4 **Common Cents**[55] 1351 4-9-7 **70** LukeMorris 9 35
(Ronald Harris) *mid-div: drvn along over 3f out: wknd over 1f out* **13/2**[3]
00-0 **9** nk **Hamis Al Bin (IRE)**[27] 1950 4-8-11 **60** RichardKingscote 5 24
(Milton Bradley) *chsd ldrs: rdn over 2f out: wknd over 1f out* **40/1**
11-0 **10** 11 **Dana's Present**[34] 1780 4-9-7 **70** PatCosgrave 12
(George Baker) *s.i.s: a in rr: wknd 2f out* **13/2**[3]

1m 16.96s (2.26) **Going Correction** +0.40s/f (Good) 10 Ran SP% **111.3**
Speed ratings (Par 103): **100,97,97,96,94 88,82,81,80,66**
toteswingers 1&2 £3.60, 2&3 £7.40, 1&3 £3.40 CSF £19.23 CT £87.26 TOTE £3.50: £1.40, £2.00, £1.40; EX 18.70 Trifecta £95.00 Pool: £2127.51 - 16.78 winning units..
Owner Billy Herring **Bred** Barronstown Stud **Trained** Scrooby, Notts

FOCUS
The going was changed to soft all over before this race. A modest handicap but sound enough with the placed horses close to their marks.

2781 NEW SUPERSCOOP6 BET AT TOTEPOOL.COM H'CAP (DIV II) 6f 15y
3:00 (3:03) (Class 5) (0-70,70) 4-Y-O+ **£3,234** (£962; £481; £240) **Stalls** High

Form RPR
4050 **1** **Clubland (IRE)**[9] 2515 4-8-13 **62** JimmyQuinn 9 76
(Roy Bowring) *racd centre: chsd ldrs: rdn to ld overall over 1f out: r.o: 1st of 4 in gp* **9/1**
-060 **2** 2 1/2 **Kings 'n Dreams**[9] 2516 6-8-7 **56** oh6 (b) MartinLane 8 62
(Dean Ivory) *racd far side: bhd: hdwy over 2f out: r.o to go 2nd nr fin: no ch w wnr: 1st of 8 in gp* **20/1**
4456 **3** 1/2 **Key Ambition**[74] 1038 4-9-2 **65** (vt) AdamKirby 12 69
(Garry Moss) *racd centre: chsd ldr: rdn and ev ch over 1f out: styd on same pce ins fnl f: 2nd of 4 in gp* **6/1**[2]
0-00 **4** 1/2 **Indego Blues**[19] 2239 4-9-7 **70** AdrianNicholls 10 73
(David Nicholls) *led centre gp: rdn and hdd over 1f out: no ex ins fnl f: 3rd of 4 in gp* **9/2**[1]
26-0 **5** 2 1/4 **Parisian Pyramid (IRE)**[12] 2425 7-9-7 **70** (v[1]) JamieSpencer 3 66
(Patrick Morris) *overall ldr far side: rdn and hdd over 1f out: no ex ins fnl f: 2nd of 8 in gp* **7/1**[3]
4560 **6** 1 3/4 **Reginald Claude**[23] 2096 5-8-6 **60** ow1 RachealKneller(5) 14 50
(Mark Usher) *racd centre: s.i.s: bhd: r.o ins fnl f: nvr nrr: last of 4 in gp* **8/1**
0614 **7** 3 3/4 **Divertimenti (IRE)**[15] 2338 9-8-12 **64** (b) MarkCoumbe(3) 6 42
(Roy Bowring) *racd far side: chsd ldrs: rdn and hung rt over 2f out: wknd over 1f out: 3rd of 8 in gp* **10/1**
06-0 **8** nk **Loyal N Trusted**[27] 1950 5-8-8 **57** LukeMorris 1 34
(Richard Price) *racd far side: s.i.s: hdwy over 4f out: rdn and wknd over 1f out: 4th of 8 in gp* **12/1**
34-0 **9** 1 1/2 **Half A Crown (IRE)**[18] 2275 8-8-11 **67** KevinStott(7) 7 39
(Nick Kent) *racd far side: a in rr: bhd fr 1/2-way: 5th of 8 in gp* **16/1**
0-35 **10** 1/2 **Big Wave (IRE)**[15] 2338 5-9-4 **67** (t) TomEaves 2 38
(Alison Hutchinson) *racd far side: chsd ldrs: rdn over 2f out: sn wknd: 6th of 8 in gp* **9/1**
4144 **11** 1/2 **Colourbearer (IRE)**[40] 1665 6-8-4 **56** (t) DarrenEgan(3) 5 25
(Milton Bradley) *racd far side: s.i.s: rdn over 2f out: a in rr: 7th of 8 in gp* **9/1**
000 **12** 1 1/2 **Quasi Congaree (GER)**[20] 2196 7-9-1 **64** (t[1]) SeanLevey 4 28
(Paul Fitzsimons) *racd far side: chsd ldrs: lost pl 4f out: wknd 1/2-way: last of 8 in gp* **20/1**

1m 17.59s (2.89) **Going Correction** +0.55s/f (Yiel) 12 Ran SP% **118.3**
Speed ratings (Par 103): **102,98,98,97,94 92,87,86,84,83 83,81**
toteswingers 1&2 £36.90, 2&3 £28.70, 1&3 £10.30 CSF £174.67 CT £1160.44 TOTE £9.30: £3.60, £6.80, £3.10; EX 236.40 Trifecta £1226.20 Part won. Pool: £1635.02 - 0.47 winning units..
Owner S R Bowring **Bred** Mrs Sharon Slattery **Trained** Edwinstowe, Notts

FOCUS
The winning time was 0.63 seconds slower than the first division, but the ground was easing all the time. The field split into three groups early, but it was the centre-to-nearside group which provided the winner, third and fourth. The winner is rated to his AW form.

2782 TOTEPOOL.COM CONDITIONS STKS 1m 75y
3:30 (3:32) (Class 2) 3-Y-O+ **£13,072** (£3,914; £1,957; £978) **Stalls** Centre

Form RPR
10-3 **1** **Moonstone Magic**[23] 2108 4-8-11 106 JimCrowley 5 104
(Ralph Beckett) *hld up: hdwy over 2f out: rdn ins fnl f: r.o to ld nr fin* **11/10**[1]
262 **2** hd **Don't Call Me (IRE)**[16] 2323 6-9-2 105 (t) AdrianNicholls 3 109
(David Nicholls) *led 1f: chsd ldr tl led again over 2f out: rdn over 1f out: hdd nr fin* **5/1**[3]
054- **3** hd **Questioning (IRE)**[245] 6575 5-9-2 110 (p) WilliamBuick 2 109
(John Gosden) *chsd ldrs: rdn over 2f out: ev ch fr over 1f out: styd on* **11/8**[2]
/00- **4** 15 **Cocozza (USA)**[417] 1212 5-9-2 95 JimmyQuinn 1 74
(K F Clutterbuck) *led over 7f out tl rdn and hdd over 2f out: wknd over 1f out* **125/1**

1m 52.21s (3.21) **Going Correction** +0.30s/f (Good) 4 Ran SP% **107.2**
Speed ratings (Par 109): **95,94,94,79**
CSF £6.64 TOTE £2.20; EX 5.40 Trifecta £6.30 Pool: £1426.85 - 167.26 winning units..

Owner Tullpark Limited **Bred** Lady Marchwood **Trained** Kimpton, Hants

FOCUS

The Godolphin trio of Dubai Destination, Librettist and Rio De La Plata were amongst the better winners of this race in the previous ten years. A fascinating conditions event and quite tactical, so the form is muddling. The runner-up looks the best guide.

2783 KING SIZE POOLS AT TOTEPOOL.COM EBF FILLIES' H'CAP 1m 75y

4:05 (4:06) (Class 4) (0-85,85) 3-Y-O **£6,469** (£1,925; £962; £481) **Stalls** Centre

Form RPR

0-34 **1** **Sharqawiyah**[19] 2206 3-9-3 **81**.. KirstyMilczarek 6 87+
(Luca Cumani) *hld up: racd keenly: hdwy over 2f out: rdn to ld over 1f out: r.o: comf* **5/4**[1]

10-0 **2** *1* **Tosca (GER)**[55] 1358 3-9-2 **80**.................................... MickaelBarzalona 1 83
(Mrs Ilka Gansera-Leveque) *chsd ldrs: pushed along over 3f out: rdn over 1f out: styd on to go 2nd wl ins fnl f* **18/1**

0-54 **3** *1 ½* **Lady Of The House (IRE)**[25] 2026 3-9-5 **83**.................... PhillipMakin 2 83
(Kevin Ryan) *led: rdn and hdd over 1f out: edgd lft ins fnl f: styd on same pce* **5/1**[3]

-161 **4** *½* **Zero Game (IRE)**[16] 2331 3-8-7 **71**...............................(e) HayleyTurner 5 70
(Michael Bell) *chsd ldr: rdn over 2f out: styd on same pce ins fnl f* **8/1**

060- **5** *25* **All On Red (IRE)**[243] 6632 3-9-5 **83**..............................(p) PatCosgrave 8 24
(George Baker) *in rr: pushed along over 3f out: wknd over 2f out* **12/1**

212- **6** *4 ½* **Give Way Nelson (IRE)**[206] 7588 3-9-7 **85**...................... KierenFallon 4 16
(Brian Meehan) *plld hrd and prom: effrt over 3f out: wknd over 2f out* **10/3**[2]

1m 51.18s (2.18) **Going Correction** +0.35s/f (Good) **6** Ran SP% **108.3**

Speed ratings (Par 98): **103,102,100,100,75 70**

toteswingers 1&2 £5.30, 2&3 £7.10, 1&3 £1.90 CSF £23.03 CT £73.83 TOTE £2.20: £1.20, £7.10; EX 28.90 Trifecta £96.60 Pool: £2845.35 - 22.08 winning units..

Owner Sheikh Mohammed Obaid Al Maktoum **Bred** Mrs Fiona Denniff **Trained** Newmarket, Suffolk

FOCUS

The early pace didn't look that strong for this fillies' handicap, but the time was still over a second quicker than the older horses in the preceding conditions event, which shows how steadily run that race was. The fourth to her latest AW form sets the standard.

2784 KAY'S BIRTHDAY BASH H'CAP 1m 6f 15y

4:40 (4:41) (Class 5) (0-70,70) 3-Y-O **£2,587** (£770; £384; £192) **Stalls** Low

Form RPR

02-5 **1** **Chocala (IRE)**[12] 2432 3-9-7 **70**.................................... FergusSweeney 8 81+
(Alan King) *a.p: reminders over 3f out: chsd ldr over 2f out: rdn to ld over 1f out: hung lft ins fnl f: styd on wl* **3/1**[1]

64-3 **2** *3 ½* **Deficit (IRE)**[9] 2500 3-9-0 **63**... JamieSpencer 6 69
(Michael Bell) *hld up: hdwy over 3f out: rdn and hung lft over 1f out: styd on* **3/1**[1]

-232 **3** *¾* **Town Mouse**[9] 2500 3-9-1 **64**.. JimmyFortune 9 69+
(Hughie Morrison) *led: hung rt and hdd over 8f out: chsd ldr tl led again over 3f out: rdn and hdd over 1f out: styd on same pce* **10/1**[3]

4123 **4** *shd* **Good Evans**[19] 2216 3-9-5 **68**.................................... RichardKingscote 11 73
(Tom Dascombe) *wnt rt s: sn chsng ldr: lft in ld over 8f out: rdn and hdd over 3f out: styd on same pce fnl f* **4/1**[2]

0023 **5** *4* **Bold Assertion**[19] 2233 3-9-6 **69**.............................. MickaelBarzalona 10 68
(John Best) *s.i.s: hld up: hdwy over 2f out: sn rdn: wknd and eased ins fnl f* **40/1**

1631 **6** *5* **Darakti (IRE)**[16] 2312 3-8-4 **58**...............................(v) ShirleyTeasdale(5) 1 50
(Alan McCabe) *prom: rdn over 3f out: hung lft and wknd over 2f out* **25/1**

1221 **7** *2 ½* **Gabrial The Duke (IRE)**[64] 1177 3-9-4 **67**...................... StevieDonohoe 7 56
(David Simcock) *hld up: hdwy over 6f out: rdn over 3f out: wknd wl over 1f out* **10/1**[3]

4-32 **8** *34* **Hello Sailor**[30] 1885 3-8-12 **61**.. JimCrowley 3
(Ralph Beckett) *chsd ldrs: rdn 6f out: wknd over 4f out: t.o* **4/1**[2]

3m 13.93s (6.93) **Going Correction** +0.40s/f (Good) **8** Ran SP% **114.5**

Speed ratings (Par 99): **96,94,93,93,91 88,86,67**

toteswingers 1&2 £3.10, 2&3 £6.40, 1&3 £4.90 CSF £12.05 CT £77.46 TOTE £4.60: £1.80, £1.40, £1.70; EX 13.00 Trifecta £61.90 Pool: £2601.41 - 31.62 winning units..

Owner High 5 **Bred** Peter Harris **Trained** Barbury Castle, Wilts

FOCUS

A few of these had the potential to improve for the longer trip including the winner. The fourth and fifth are the best guides to the level.

2785 FOLLOW TOTEPOOL ON TWITTER AND FACEBOOK "HANDS AND HEELS" APPRENTICE SERIES H'CAP 1m 2f 50y

5:15 (5:16) (Class 6) (0-65,65) 4-Y-O+ **£1,940** (£577; £288; £144) **Stalls** Low

Form RPR

203 **1** **Tyrur Ted**[15] 2348 8-8-11 **58**................................(t) DanaZamecnikova(3) 2 66
(Frank Sheridan) *s.i.s: hld up: hdwy over 3f out: styd on to ld nr fin* **8/1**

050- **2** *nk* **Hydrant**[161] 8162 7-9-7 **65**.. ConnorBeasley 6 72
(Richard Guest) *hld up in tch: chsd ldr over 3f out: led over 2f out: hdd towards fin* **11/4**[2]

6454 **3** *hd* **Bold Duke**[12] 2418 5-9-6 **64**... EoinWalsh 8 71
(Edward Bevan) *chsd ldrs: ev ch fr over 2f out: styd on* **5/2**[1]

4000 **4** *2 ¼* **Amazing Blue Sky**[11] 2435 7-8-12 **56**.............................. KevinStott 10 59
(Ruth Carr) *led: pushed along and hdd over 2f out: styd on same pce fnl f* **15/2**[3]

4103 **5** *3 ¾* **The Ducking Stool**[22] 2137 6-9-2 **63**.......................... ShelleyBirkett(3) 7 59
(Julia Feilden) *prom: pushed along and hung lft over 2f out: styd on same pce appr fnl f* **10/1**

46-0 **6** *2 ¼* **Harare**[44] 1572 12-8-6 **53**...(v) GemmaTutty(3) 3 44
(Karen Tutty) *s.i.s: hld up: pushed along 1/2-way: r.o ins fnl f: nvr nrr* **16/1**

0-00 **7** *1 ½* **Action Front (USA)**[11] 2435 5-8-7 **54**......................(v) AdamMcLean(3) 12 42
(Derek Shaw) *hld up: sme hdwy over 3f out: wknd over 2f out* **12/1**

4-00 **8** *2 ¼* **Penderyn**[42] 1603 6-8-7 **51** oh6.................................... CharlotteJenner 13 35
(Charles Smith) *chsd ldrs tl wknd 2f out* **66/1**

0040 **9** *2 ¾* **Follow The Flag (IRE)**[9] 2511 9-8-8 **55**........................(p) AaronJones(3) 9 34
(Alan McCabe) *chsd ldrs: pushed along over 3f out: wknd over 2f out* **12/1**

3326 **10** *6* **Xpres Maite**[21] 2174 10-9-3 **61**..(b) JoshCrane 1 29
(Roy Bowring) *s.i.s: a in rr* **18/1**

00-0 **11** *76* **Primo Blanca**[32] 1826 4-8-7 **51** oh6.............................(v) DanielCremin 15
(Michael Mullineaux) *s.i.s: pushed along 6f out: bhd fr 1/2-way: t.o* **50/1**

2m 17.99s (3.69) **Going Correction** +0.45s/f (Yiel) **11** Ran SP% **117.2**

Speed ratings (Par 101): **103,102,102,100,97 96,94,93,90,86 25**

toteswingers 1&2 £5.70, 2&3 £2.70, 1&3 £5.20 CSF £30.08 CT £72.44 TOTE £10.30: £2.70, £1.10, £1.40; EX 29.70 Trifecta £84.10 Pool: £1978.89 - 17.64 winning units..

Owner Frank Sheridan **Bred** A G Greenwood **Trained** Wolverhampton, W Midlands

FOCUS

A moderate "hands and heels" apprentice handicap in which the riders of the winner and third were both dumped in the mud after crossing the line. The placed horses have both run well hee before and give the form a sound look.

T/Jkpt: £11,943.30 to £1 stake. Pool of £33643.21 - 2.00 winning tickets. T/Plt: £143.80 to a £1 stake. Pool of £50230.44 - 254.97 winning tickets. T/Qpdt: £146.90 to £1 stake. Pool of £3457.94 - 17.41 winning tickets. CR

2528 BRIGHTON (L-H)

Thursday, May 30

OFFICIAL GOING: Good to soft (7.3)

All races on inner line and distances as advertised.

Wind: fairly light, across Weather: overcast, dry

2786 RYANVEHICLES.COM DFSK H'CAP 1m 1f 209y

2:30 (2:30) (Class 5) (0-75,72) 3-Y-O **£2,587** (£770; £384; £192) **Stalls** High

Form RPR

33-3 **1** **Duroble Man**[17] 2325 3-9-7 **72**... NeilCallan 6 82+
(Roger Varian) *t.k.h: sn chsng ldr: led over 2f out and sn rdn clr: drvn and a holding runner-up ins fnl f* **6/4**[1]

4-34 **2** *1 ¼* **Couloir Extreme (IRE)**[26] 2017 3-9-1 **66**......................... LiamKeniry 5 73
(Gary Moore) *t.k.h early: hld up in tch: rdn and effrt 3f out: chsd clr wnr jst over 1f out: grad clsd tl no imp and hld fnl 75yds* **8/1**

46-0 **3** *4 ½* **Janie Runaway (IRE)**[20] 2206 3-9-2 **67**.......................... MartinLane 4 65
(Brian Meehan) *led: rdn and hdd over 2f out: sn drvn and outpcd by wnr: wknd ins fnl f* **14/1**

025- **4** *10* **Spanish Art**[233] 6945 3-9-5 **70**.. RobertWinston 1 48
(Gay Kelleway) *stdd and dropped in bhd after s: hld up in tch in rr: rdn and effrt over 3f out: struggling over 2f out: wknd wl over 1f out* **33/1**

40-2 **5** *7* **Atlantis City (FR)**[8] 2560 3-9-2 **67**..................................... SeanLevey 3 31
(Richard Hannon) *chsd ldrs: rdn and no rspnse wl over 2f out: sn wknd: wl bhd and eased ins fnl f* **7/4**[2]

3514 **6** *33* **Ofcoursewecan (USA)**[24] 2079 3-9-6 **71**..........(b[1]) SilvestreDeSousa 2
(Mark Johnston) *nvr travelling and sn rdn along: chsd ldrs early: reminders and lost pl 6f out: dropped to last 5f out: lost tch 3f out: t.o and eased ins fnl f* **7/1**[3]

2m 3.99s (0.39) **Going Correction** +0.025s/f (Good) **6** Ran SP% **109.6**

Speed ratings (Par 101): **98,98,94,86,80 54**

toteswingers 1&2 £1.80, 1&3 £3.90, 2&3 £10.10 CSF £13.25 CT £107.07 TOTE £2.30: £1.10, £3.70; EX 11.60 Trifecta £49.10 Pool: £1742.50 - 26.59 winning units..

Owner Dennis Yardy **Bred** D A Yardy **Trained** Newmarket, Suffolk

FOCUS

The jockeys reported that the ground was on the soft side of good. The softening of the ground led to the withdrawal of a couple of runners and there's no doubt that this handicap took less winning than would otherwise have been the case, with the fifth and sixth below par.

2787 NEVA CONSULTANTS CONTRACT HIRE H'CAP 7f 214y

3:00 (3:00) (Class 6) (0-60,59) 4-Y-O+ **£1,940** (£577; £288; £144) **Stalls** Centre

Form RPR

3124 **1** **Hill Of Dreams (IRE)**[9] 2534 4-9-7 **59**............................(b) JimCrowley 1 72
(Dean Ivory) *t.k.h: trckd ldrs: effrt to ld over 1f out: drew clr 1f out: sn in command: eased towards fin* **11/4**[1]

5343 **2** *4* **Fonterutoli (IRE)**[9] 2534 6-8-8 **46**...............................(e) RobertHavlin 6 50
(Roger Ingram) *dwlt and rdn along leaving stalls: hdwy to press ldrs after 2f: led over 2f out: sn rdn: hdd and unable qck over 1f out: wl hld but hld on for 2nd cl home* **4/1**[3]

4003 **3** *nk* **Whinging Willie (IRE)**[9] 2533 4-9-0 **59**............................ NedCurtis(7) 4 62
(Gary Moore) *t.k.h: stdd bk into last pair after 1f: rdn and effrt 2f out: kpt on u.p fnl f and pressing for 2nd cl home: no ch w wnr* **6/1**

200 **4** *1 ¾* **Bloodsweatandtears**[35] 1779 5-9-6 **58**.............................. NeilCallan 2 57
(William Knight) *led: hdd and rdn over 2f out: no ex and btn ent fnl f: plugged on same pce* **3/1**[2]

4400 **5** *1* **The Which Doctor**[28] 1951 8-8-7 **45**...............................(b) KieranO'Neill 8 42
(Violet M Jordan) *s.i.s: hld up in last pair: rdn and swtchd rt 2f out: no imp over 1f out: plugged on same pce after* **25/1**

4503 **6** *nk* **Rooknrasbryripple**[23] 2133 4-8-4 **47**................................ RyanTate(5) 7 43
(Ralph Smith) *plld hrd: hld up in midfield: swtchd lft and effrt on inner 2f out: drvn and no imp over 1f out: wl hld fnl f* **20/1**

0000 **7** *1 ½* **Menadati (USA)**[9] 2533 5-9-1 **53**...................................[1] WilliamCarson 5 46
(Peter Hiatt) *t.k.h: chsd ldr: drvn and no ex over 2f out: edgd rt and wknd wl over 1f out* **6/1**

1m 36.43s (0.43) **Going Correction** +0.025s/f (Good) **7** Ran SP% **108.8**

Speed ratings (Par 101): **99,94,93,91,90 90,89**

toteswingers 1&2 £1.40, 1&3 £2.50, 2&3 £5.10 CSF £12.61 CT £51.95 TOTE £3.80: £1.60, £3.70; EX 12.90 Trifecta £43.00 Pool: £1682.95 - 29.31 winning units..

Owner I Gethin & R Gethin **Bred** Miss Breda Wright **Trained** Radlett, Herts

FOCUS

A devilishly tricky handicap, despite the small field, and with very little in the way of early pace it remains to be seen how well this form works out. Weak form, taken at face value.

2788 RYAN VEHICLES SUPPORTS CRAWLEYTOWNFC.COM MAIDEN STKS 6f 209y

3:30 (3:30) (Class 5) 3-Y-O+ **£2,587** (£770; £384; £192) **Stalls** Low

Form RPR

653- **1** **This Is Nice (IRE)**[178] 7965 3-8-10 69.................................. JimCrowley 2 73
(Tom Dascombe) *mde all: rdn and fnd ex over 1f out: in command fnl f: kpt on wl* **7/4**[2]

3 **2** *1 ½* **Dodina (IRE)**[10] 2504 3-8-10 0.. RobertHavlin 1 69
(Peter Chapple-Hyam) *t.k.h: chsd wnr for 2f: effrt and wnt between horses to chse wnr again 2f out: rdn and effrt over 1f out: one pce fnl f* **9/2**[3]

323- **3** *3 ¾* **Watcheroftheskies**[190] 7807 3-9-1 77.................................. SebSanders 5 64
(J W Hills) *dwlt: hdwy to chse wnr after 2f: rdn and unable qck over 2f out: 3rd and btn 1f out: wknd ins fnl f* **11/10**[1]

0-0 **4** *2 ¾* **Secret Success**[41] 1660 3-9-1 0.. NeilCallan 3 56
(Paul Cole) *plld hrd: hld up in tch: rdn and no prog over 2f out: wknd over 1f out* **16/1**

5-63 **5** *12* **Give Us A Belle (IRE)**[23] 2134 4-9-9 46.......................(t) DarrenEgan(3) 4 28
(Christine Dunnett) *hld up in rr: rdn and struggling 1/2-way: bhd fnl 2f* **33/1**

1m 24.96s (1.86) **Going Correction** +0.025s/f (Good)

WFA 3 from 4yo 11lb **5** Ran SP% **111.0**

Speed ratings (Par 103): **90,88,84,80,67**

CSF £9.92 TOTE £2.50: £1.10, £2.30; EX 9.10 Trifecta £11.40 Pool: £2290.27 - 150.38 winning units..

Owner Laurence A Bellman **Bred** D Boocock **Trained** Malpas, Cheshire
FOCUS
Only a couple could be seriously considered for this and, with the strongly supported favourite appearing to run well below the form he'd shown as a juvenile, perhaps it didn't take much winning. The form is rated around the winner.

2789 DFSK MINI VANS AT RYANVEHICLES.COM CLAIMING STKS 5f 59y
4:00 (4:00) (Class 6) 3-Y-O+ **£1,940** (£577; £288; £144) **Stalls** Low

Form RPR
00-0 1 **Racy**36 1765 6-9-7 91 SeanLevey 3 94
(Ed McMahon) *mde all: rdn and readily asserted over 1f out: easily* **6/4**1
4002 2 3 1/4 **Noverre To Go (IRE)**10 2516 7-9-7 82 (p) WilliamCarson 1 83
(Ronald Harris) *t.k.h: chsd wnr thrght: rdn and outpcd by wnr over 1f out: one pce fnl f* **5/2**2
5111 3 2 1/4 **Above The Stars**9 2530 5-8-9 70 RachealKneller(5) 5 68
(Jamie Osborne) *chsd ldng pair: rdn and effrt whn rdr dropped whip ent fnl f: no imp* **6/4**1
-050 4 18 **Batchworth Firefly**16 2345 5-8-12 45 (v1) RobertWinston 2
(Dean Ivory) *dwlt: a outpcd in rr: rdn and c centre over 3f out: wl bhd 1f out: no ch and virtually p.u ins fnl f* **66/1**3
1m 1.42s (-0.88) **Going Correction** +0.025s/f (Good) 4 Ran SP% **110.1**
Speed ratings (Par 101): **108,102,99,70**
CSF £5.70 TOTE £2.40; EX 6.20 Trifecta £6.70 Pool: £1500.01 - 166.66 winning units..Racy was claimed by Mr Brian Ellison for £10000
Owner The C H F Partnership **Bred** Cheveley Park Stud Ltd **Trained** Lichfield, Staffs
FOCUS
This had looked an outstanding opportunity for the winner on paper and he made no mistake. The race is rated around the winner's form last year.

2790 RYAN VEHICLES CAR & VAN HIRE H'CAP 5f 59y
4:30 (4:30) (Class 4) (0-80,78) 4-Y-O+ **£4,690** (£1,395; £697; £348) **Stalls** Low

Form RPR
-015 1 **Whitecrest**6 2614 5-9-5 76 ChrisCatlin 9 85
(John Spearing) *chsd ldrs: c towards centre over 3f out: hdwy u.p 1f out: led fnl 75yds: styd on wl* **5/1**3
0230 2 1 **Dorback**12 2441 6-9-2 73 KieranO'Neill 8 78
(Violet M Jordan) *sn rdn along to ld: rdn over 1f out: hdd and no ex fnl 75yds* **7/1**
14-1 3 shd **Langley Vale**27 1985 4-9-0 71 SebSanders 6 76
(Roger Teal) *chsd ldrs: rdn over 2f out: kpt on u.p ins fnl f* **7/4**1
2302 4 2 **Putin (IRE)**9 2530 5-8-7 64 oh4 (bt) SilvestreDeSousa 1 62
(Phil McEntee) *chsd ldr: rdn and stl pressing wnr over 1f out: no ex jst ins fnl f: wknd towards fin* **9/2**2
6-64 5 3/4 **Wooden King (IRE)**9 2530 8-8-13 70 (p) TomMcLaughlin 5 65
(Malcolm Saunders) *s.i.s: racd off the pce in last trio: edgd out rt and drvn 2f out: styd on ins fnl f: nvr threatened ldrs* **16/1**
5210 6 6 **Danzoe (IRE)**9 2550 6-9-0 74 DarrenEgan(3) 4 48
(Christine Dunnett) *outpcd in last trio: drvn over 2f out: no imp: nvr trbld ldrs* **10/1**
5-10 7 hd **Magical Speedfit (IRE)**20 2225 8-8-6 70 JordanVaughan(7) 7 43
(George Margarson) *sn outpcd in rr: n.d* **7/1**
1m 1.87s (-0.43) **Going Correction** +0.025s/f (Good) 7 Ran SP% **111.2**
Speed ratings (Par 105): **104,102,102,99,97 88,87**
toteswingers 1&2 £4.90, 1&3 £2.90, 2&3 £3.20 CSF £36.69 CT £80.97 TOTE £6.50: £4.50, £3.60; EX 44.10 Trifecta £86.70 Pool: £1760.19 - 15.21 winning units..
Owner G M Eales **Bred** J Spearing And Kate Ive **Trained** Kinnersley, Worcs
FOCUS
An ordinary sprint, with a personal best from the winner.

2791 RYAN VEHICLES ANY MAKE NEW CAR SALES H'CAP 5f 213y
5:00 (5:00) (Class 6) (0-60,60) 3-Y-O **£1,940** (£577; £288; £144) **Stalls** Low

Form RPR
14-3 1 **My Sweet Lord**16 2347 3-9-2 55 HarryBentley 6 59
(Mark Usher) *trckd ldrs: effrt to ld over 1f out: rdn ent fnl f: kpt on and a holding runner-up fnl f* **1/1**1
0-00 2 3/4 **Foie Gras**16 2345 3-8-10 49 (b1) JackMitchell 2 51
(William Muir) *jostled leaving stalls: hld up in tch in rr: rdn and hdwy 2f out: chsd wnr jst over 1f out: kpt on wl but a hld by wnr* **20/1**
0-06 3 5 **Symboline**14 2393 3-8-13 52 MatthewDavies 9 38
(Mick Channon) *dwlt and pushed along early: chsd ldr 4f out tl over 1f out: outpcd and btn 1f out: plugged on to hold 3rd ins fnl f* **8/1**3
00-5 4 1/2 **Majestic Red (IRE)**15 2363 3-9-7 60 TomMcLaughlin 5 44
(Malcolm Saunders) *chsd ldrs: rdn and effrt 2f out: outpcd and btn whn hung lft 1f out: wl hld and plugged on same pce fnl f* **8/1**3
40-0 5 1/2 **Persian Marvel (IRE)**136 207 3-8-9 48 (v1) WilliamCarson 7 31
(Jim Boyle) *t.k.h: stdd s: hld up in tch in rr: rdn and effrt ent fnl 2f: no imp and btn 1f out* **4/1**2
-6U0 6 3/4 **Forceful Flame**17 2324 3-9-7 60 (v1) MartinLane 4 40
(Robert Eddery) *jostled leaving stalls: in tch towards rr: rdn wl over 1f out: n.m.r over 1f out: sn rdn, edgd lft and btn* **10/1**
0060 7 2 1/4 **Iwilsayzisonlyonce**14 2393 3-9-6 59 (b1) LiamKeniry 1 32
(Joseph Tuite) *led tl rdn and hdd over 1f out: sn btn: wknd fnl f* **14/1**
1m 11.6s (1.40) **Going Correction** +0.025s/f (Good) 7 Ran SP% **112.7**
Speed ratings (Par 97): **91,90,83,82,82 81,78**
toteswingers 1&2 £4.60, 1&3 £2.70, 2&3 £12.40 CSF £23.45 CT £108.15 TOTE £1.50: £1.50, £9.10; EX 18.30 Trifecta £87.20 Pool: £2205.27 - 18.95 winning units..
Owner The Ridgeway Alchemist's **Bred** Ridgeway Bloodstock **Trained** Upper Lambourn, Berks
FOCUS
A desperately weak handicap, run in deteriorating conditions, which prompted the jockeys to head more towards the centre of the track in the home straight. The first two were clear but it's hard to enthuse about this form.

2792 DFSK CUTIE CAMPERVAN FILLIES' H'CAP 7f 214y
5:30 (5:30) (Class 5) (0-75,67) 4-Y-O+ **£2,587** (£770; £384; £192) **Stalls** Centre

Form RPR
1231 1 **Yojojo (IRE)**22 2155 4-9-7 67 RobertWinston 2 76
(Gay Kelleway) *chsd ldrs: rdn and led over 1f out: kpt on wl u.p fnl f* **7/2**3
0-36 2 1/2 **Lady Bayside**14 2395 5-9-5 65 TomMcLaughlin 4 73
(Malcolm Saunders) *in tch in last pair: hdwy 3f out: rdn and pressed wnr over 1f out: kpt on same pce ins fnl f* **9/4**1
0-35 3 2 1/2 **Who's That Chick (IRE)**7 2606 4-8-4 55 RobertTart(5) 5 57
(Ralph Smith) *chsd ldr tl led 3f out: rdn and hdd over 1f out: no ex and wknd ins fnl f* **3/1**2
2113 4 4 1/2 **Bold Ring**8 2565 7-9-3 63 MarcHalford 3 55
(Edward Creighton) *hld up in tch in rr: rdn and effrt 2f out: sn no imp: wknd ins fnl f* **9/2**
300- 5 17 **Polar Annie**242 6709 8-9-1 66 RachealKneller(5) 7 19
(Tim Vaughan) *led tl 3f out: sn dropped to rr: wl bhd over 1f out* **7/1**
1m 35.65s (-0.35) **Going Correction** +0.025s/f (Good) 5 Ran SP% **108.7**
Speed ratings (Par 100): **102,101,99,94,77**
CSF £11.42 TOTE £2.70: £1.10, £1.50; EX 7.90 Trifecta £18.30 Pool: £1805.76 - 73.95 winning units..
Owner Winterbeck Manor Stud **Bred** Rossenarra Bloodstock Limited **Trained** Exning, Suffolk
FOCUS
Just fillies' form, but the time was relatively good. The winner has improved this year.
T/Plt: £179.80 to a £1 stake. Pool of £59,360.04 - 240.91 winning tickets. T/Qpdt: £41.20 to a £1 stake. Pool of £3588.08 - 64.30 winning tickets. SP

2404 HAMILTON (R-H)
Thursday, May 30

OFFICIAL GOING: Good (good to firm in places; 8.7)
Races on round course increased in distance by about 25yds due to rail realignment around the loop.
Wind: Almost nil Weather: Overcast, sunny from Race 3 (3.10) onwards

2793 BOOK YOUR PARTY AT THE PARK MAIDEN AUCTION STKS 6f 5y
2:10 (2:11) (Class 6) 2-Y-O **£2,264** (£673; £336; £168) **Stalls** High

Form RPR
1 **Angel Rosa** 2-8-4 0 LukeMorris 2 63
(Keith Dalgleish) *trckd ldrs on outside: effrt and rdn over 1f out: led ins fnl f: kpt on strly* **12/1**
6 2 1 3/4 **Mitcd (IRE)**12 2436 2-8-8 0 FrederikTylicki 5 62
(Richard Fahey) *cl up: drvn over 2f out: effrt and ev ch ins fnl f: kpt on: hld nr fin* **9/4**1
46 3 hd **Princess Tamay (IRE)**42 1642 2-8-8 0 FrannyNorton 3 61
(Mark Johnston) *led and sn tacked over to stands' rail: rdn over 1f out: hdd ins fnl f: kpt on same pce* **3/1**2
0000 4 1 1/2 **Doncaster Belle (IRE)**12 2436 2-8-6 0 (p) AdrianNicholls 6 55
(Charles Smith) *chsd ldrs: effrt and rdn over 2f out: edgd rt and one pce over 1f out* **40/1**
5 nk **Crakehall Lad (IRE)** 2-9-1 0 AndrewMullen 4 63+
(Alan Swinbank) *chsd ldng gp: effrt and rn green over 2f out: styd on steadily fnl f: nt pce to chal* **8/1**
6 5 **Please Let Me Go** 2-8-8 0 TomEaves 7 41+
(Kevin Ryan) *missed break: bhd and green: hdwy over 1f out: styd on but no imp: bttr for r* **9/2**3
5 7 5 **Pacarama**11 2474 2-8-1 0 RaulDaSilva(3) 8 22
(Jason Ward) *in tch: sn pushed along: struggling over 2f out: sn btn* **40/1**
8 14 **Frost In May (IRE)** 2-8-11 0 ow1 DanielTudhope 9
(David O'Meara) *sn bhd: outpcd whn hung bdly rt fr 2f out: sn btn* **11/2**
1m 14.24s (2.04) **Going Correction** +0.15s/f (Good) 8 Ran SP% **113.0**
Speed ratings (Par 91): **92,89,89,87,87 80,73,55**
toteswingers 1&2 £7.80, 1&3 £6.30, 2&3 £2.10 CSF £38.45 TOTE £24.40: £6.80, £1.10, £1.50; EX 52.50 Trifecta £317.50 Pool: £1418.08 - 3.34 winning units..
Owner Lamont Racing **Bred** Richard Kent **Trained** Carluke, S Lanarks
FOCUS
All races beyond 6f were run over 25yds further than advertised due to the positioning of the rail on the loop. Few got into what was quite a modest maiden (fourth holds the form down), and the runners raced near to the stands' rail. The form is rated through the third.

2794 DOWNLOAD THE FREE RACING UK APP CLAIMING STKS 1m 1f 36y
2:40 (2:40) (Class 6) 3-5-Y-O **£2,045** (£603; £302) **Stalls** Low

Form RPR
4244 1 **Rawaafed (IRE)**2 2752 4-9-10 64 GrahamGibbons 5 69
(Keith Dalgleish) *t.k.h early: hld up: smooth hdwy to ld over 1f out: sn rdn: edgd lft wl ins fnl f: pushed out* **3/1**2
050- 2 3/4 **Chloe's Image**277 5619 3-8-2 50 DeclanCannon(3) 7 59
(Philip Kirby) *hld up in tch: hdwy to ld over 2f out: sn rdn and hung rt: hdd over 1f out: rallied: one pce whn carried lft wl ins fnl f* **33/1**
6102 3 9 **Royal Opera**4 2118 5-9-6 71 (b) PaulPickard(3) 1 47
(Brian Ellison) *rrd and lost grnd s: hld up: smooth hdwy to ld over 3f out: rdn and hdd over 2f out: outpcd over 1f out* **4/9**1
0240 4 1/2 **Dutch Delight**9 2555 3-8-5 48 ow1 BarryMcHugh 3 38
(Tony Coyle) *t.k.h: prom: effrt and rdn over 2f out: wknd over 1f out* **20/1**3
6600 5 9 **Imtithal (IRE)**22 2155 4-9-2 54 LukeMorris 6 19
(John Weymes) *led 3f: cl up: pushed along whn n.m.r over 3f out: sn wknd* **50/1**
304 6 1 1/2 **Irons On Fire (USA)**9 2533 5-9-8 43 (b) TomEaves 4 21
(Alastair Lidderdale) *early reminders in rr: hdwy on outside to ld after 3f: rdn and hdd over 3f out: sn wknd* **22/1**
036 7 4 1/2 **Bix (IRE)**20 2237 3-8-3 50 JordanHibberd(7) 2
(Alan Berry) *prom tl rdn and wknd fr 3f out* **25/1**
1m 59.27s (-0.43) **Going Correction** +0.15s/f (Good)
WFA 3 from 4yo+ 13lb 7 Ran SP% **112.1**
Speed ratings (Par 101): **107,106,98,97,89 88,84**
toteswingers 1&2 £10.40, 1&3 £1.02, 2&3 £6.50 CSF £72.37 TOTE £6.00: £1.40, £12.40; EX 47.60 Trifecta £127.00 Pool: £2126.44 - 12.55 winning units..
Owner Straightline Construction Ltd **Bred** Brian Walsh **Trained** Carluke, S Lanarks
■ Stewards' Enquiry : Graham Gibbons caution; careless riding.
FOCUS
Rather weak claiming form, with the favourite performing below par. The form is rated around the winner.

2795 OGILVIE COMMUNICATIONS H'CAP 5f 4y
3:10 (3:10) (Class 6) (0-65,60) 3-Y-O+ **£2,045** (£603; £302) **Stalls** Centre

Form RPR
6524 1 **Salvatore Fury (IRE)**3 2703 3-9-1 55 (p) GrahamGibbons 4 60
(Keith Dalgleish) *chsd ldrs: smooth hdwy over 1f out: rdn to ld ins fnl f: hung lft: hld on fin* **3/1**1
-333 2 3/4 **Chloe's Dream (IRE)**16 2336 3-9-6 60 (p) PJMcDonald 10 61
(Ann Duffield) *in tch: effrt and rdn 2f out: chsd wnr ins fnl f: kpt on fin* **9/1**
-060 3 nk **Rio's Girl**3 2702 6-9-0 53 DavidSimmonson(7) 5 56
(Tony Coyle) *chsd ldrs: drvn and outpcd 1/2-way: rallied over 1f out: edgd lft ins fnl f: kpt on* **16/1**
30-6 4 1 1/4 **Sugar Blaze**33 1821 3-8-11 51 AndrewElliott 11 46
(Jim Goldie) *s.i.s: bhd: rdn and hung rt over 2f out: styd on wl fnl f: nrst fin* **22/1**

0051 **5** 1/2 **Auntie Mildred (IRE)**16 2336 3-8-13 **53** DanielTudhope 7 47
(David O'Meara) *racd alone towards stands' side: in tch: rdn and hdwy over 1f out: one pce ins fnl f* **7/2**2

150- **6** *shd* **Distant Sun (USA)**213 7447 9-9-13 **59** (p) PhillipMakin 3 55
(Linda Perratt) *led at decent gallop: rdn 2f out: hdd ins fnl f: sn btn* **33/1**

0-40 **7** 1/2 **Bridge Valley**19 2276 6-8-13 **48** RaulDaSilva(3) 1 42
(Jason Ward) *s.i.s: sn drvn along towards rr: hdwy over 1f out: kpt on ins fnl f* **13/2**

5360 **8** 3/4 **Wicked Wilma (IRE)**6 2632 9-9-7 **53** PaddyAspell 6 45
(Alan Berry) *midfield: rdn over 2f out: hdwy 1f out: kpt on: nt pce to chal* **11/1**

0-53 **9** *3* **Rock Canyon (IRE)**13 2409 4-9-6 **52** PaulMulrennan 12 33
(Linda Perratt) *hld up: rdn over 2f out: no imp fr over 1f out* **6/1**3

0-03 **10** *hd* **Cayman Fox**6 2632 8-9-5 **51** RoystonFfrench 2 31
(Linda Perratt) *chsd ldr tl rdn and wknd over 1f out* **11/1**

0-00 **11** *12* **Tomasini**6 2611 4-8-13 **45** LukeMorris 9
(John Weymes) *sn outpcd: hung rt 1/2-way: btn and eased over 1f out* **100/1**

1m 0.88s (0.88) **Going Correction** +0.15s/f (Good)
WFA 3 from 4yo+ 8lb **11** Ran SP% **115.7**
Speed ratings (Par 101): **98,96,96,94,93 93,92,91,86,86 67**
toteswingers 1&2 £4.00, 1&3 £8.90, 2&3 £19.50 CSF £29.65 CT £378.18 TOTE £4.00: £2.10, £2.00, £4.40; EX 29.80 Trifecta £233.30 Pool: £847.57 - 2.72 winning units..
Owner Prestige Thoroughbred Racing **Bred** Ken Harris & Dr Brid Corkery **Trained** Carluke, S Lanarks

FOCUS
The main action took place centre field in this low-grade sprint, with a pair of the 3yos coming to the fore. They went fast up front. The winner stepped up on his recent form.

2796 PRESTIGE SCOTLAND FILLIES' H'CAP — 1m 65y
3:40 (3:40) (Class 5) (0-70,67) 3-Y-O+ **£3,234** (£962; £481; £240) **Stalls** Low

Form RPR

34-4 **1** **Al Thumama**17 2331 3-8-9 **60** FrannyNorton 4 65
(Kevin Ryan) *led at modest gallop: hrd pressed fr 3f out: hld on gamely u.p fnl f* **8/1**

1444 **2** 3/4 **Ssafa**13 2417 5-9-12 **65** (p) TomEaves 8 71
(Alastair Lidderdale) *hld up in tch: hdwy to chse ldrs 2f out: sn rdn: wnt 2nd ins fnl f: kpt on: hld nr fin* **5/1**2

00-6 **3** 3/4 **Hello Gorgeous**13 2409 3-8-0 **51** oh1 JamesSullivan 6 52+
(Keith Dalgleish) *prom: rdn and outpcd over 2f out: rallied fnl f: kpt on: nvr able to chal* **7/1**

-653 **4** 1 1/2 **Adorable Choice (IRE)**43 1610 5-9-4 **57** (vt) StephenCraine 5 58
(Tom Dascombe) *pressed wnr: disp ld 3f out to ent fnl f: sn outpcd* **7/1**

0-50 **5** *hd* **Sareeah (IRE)**9 2551 4-9-13 **66** DanielTudhope 7 66
(David O'Meara) *hld up: pushed along over 2f out: hdwy on outside over 1f out: no imp fnl f* **11/2**3

-000 **6** 1 3/4 **Madame Blavatsky (FR)**9 2536 5-8-13 **52** (v1) PhillipMakin 1 48
(Karen McLintock) *chsd ldrs: rdn over 2f out: no ex over 1f out* **11/1**

0330 **7** *hd* **Cheers For Thea (IRE)**17 2311 8-9-12 **65** (bt) DuranFentiman 3 61
(Tim Easterby) *t.k.h early: stdd in tch: rdn over 2f out: no ex over 1f out* **14/1**

05-1 **8** 3/4 **Spavento (IRE)**35 1788 7-10-0 **67** DavidAllan 2 61
(Eric Alston) *hld up: rdn over 2f out: hdwy over 1f out: wknd ins fnl f* **9/4**1

1m 50.0s (1.60) **Going Correction** +0.15s/f (Good)
WFA 3 from 4yo+ 12lb **8** Ran SP% **113.9**
Speed ratings (Par 100): **98,97,96,95,94 93,92,92**
toteswingers 1&2 £1.30, 1&3 £9.50, 2&3 £11.00 CSF £47.14 CT £296.37 TOTE £9.90: £2.60, £1.30, £3.00; EX 34.80 Trifecta £219.60 Pool: £1468.34 - 5.01 winning units..
Owner Mubarak Al Naemi **Bred** John James **Trained** Hambleton, N Yorks

FOCUS
This was run at just a steady gallop and it paid to race prominently. No surprise to see it go to one of the unexposed 3yos, who showed improvement.

2797 EQUI'S "EQUINE GOLDEN STIRRUP" FLAVOUR H'CAP (£15,000 BETFAIR SCOTTISH SPRINT FINAL QUALIFIER) — 6f 5y
4:10 (4:10) (Class 5) (0-75,80) 4-Y-O+ **£3,234** (£962; £481; £240) **Stalls** Centre

Form RPR

-231 **1** **Chester Aristocrat**5 2663 4-9-7 **80** 6ex JasonHart(5) 4 90
(Eric Alston) *mde all: rdn over 1f out: kpt on wl fnl f* **6/5**1

0300 **2** 1/2 **Pelmanism**9 2536 6-8-6 **60** (b) PJMcDonald 9 68
(Brian Ellison) *hld up: hdwy and edgd rt over 1f out: chsd wnr ins fnl f: kpt on fin* **9/1**

0446 **3** 2 1/4 **Bassett Road (IRE)**25 2037 5-8-9 **63** (p) PaulMulrennan 7 64
(Keith Dalgleish) *in tch: effrt and rdn over 1f out: kpt on same pce ins fnl f* **11/1**

2-63 **4** *1* **Rulesn'regulations**9 2530 7-9-1 **69** TomEaves 3 67
(Alastair Lidderdale) *cl up: rdn and outpcd 2f out: rallied fnl f: kpt on* **5/1**3

3-00 **5** *shd* **The Nifty Fox**13 2410 9-9-6 **74** (p) DavidAllan 1 71
(Tim Easterby) *in tch: effrt and rdn over 1f out: one pce fnl f* **18/1**

6-40 **6** 1 1/4 **Dutch Heritage**33 1838 4-9-1 **72** (b) LeeTopliss(3) 6 65
(Richard Fahey) *unruly in preliminaries: s.i.s: bhd and outpcd: hdwy stands' rail fnl f: nrst fin* **9/2**2

0314 **7** 3/4 **Economic Crisis (IRE)**20 2222 4-9-7 **75** PaddyAspell 5 66
(Alan Berry) *t.k.h: cl up tl rdn and wknd appr fnl f* **16/1**

01-0 **8** 3 1/2 **Jinky**13 2410 5-9-4 **72** PhillipMakin 2 52
(Linda Perratt) *cl up tl rdn and wknd over 1f out* **16/1**

1m 12.22s (0.02) **Going Correction** +0.15s/f (Good) **8** Ran SP% **115.7**
Speed ratings (Par 103): **105,104,101,100,99 98,97,92**
toteswingers 1&2 £3.10, 1&3 £3.70, 2&3 £10.90 CSF £13.43 CT £84.40 TOTE £2.00: £1.30, £2.20, £2.90; EX 13.70 Trifecta £100.90 Pool: £3516.21 - 26.11 winning units..
Owner Paul Buist & John Thompson **Bred** J A E Hobby **Trained** Longton, Lancs

FOCUS
A straightforward success. for the winner, with the third the best guide to the form.

2798 HAMILTON-PARK.CO.UK H'CAP (£15,000 BETFAIR SCOTTISH STAYERS' FLAT SERIES FINAL QUALIFIER) — 1m 4f 17y
4:40 (4:40) (Class 5) (0-70,70) 4-Y-O+ **£3,234** (£962; £481; £240) **Stalls** High

Form RPR

10-0 **1** **A Southside Boy (GER)**45 1572 5-8-5 **54** ow2 AndrewElliott 8 64
(Jim Goldie) *t.k.h: chsd ldrs: pushed along and hdwy to ld over 1f out: edgd rt: rdn out fnl f* **8/1**

16-5 **2** 1 3/4 **Schmooze (IRE)**17 2316 4-8-8 **57** DaleSwift 2 64
(Linda Perratt) *hld up: effrt over 2f out: hdwy to chse wnr ins fnl f: one pce towards fin* **7/1**

204- **3** *3* **Potentiale (IRE)**255 6304 9-8-4 **60** 1 NoraLooby(7) 4 62
(Alastair Lidderdale) *hld up: stdy hdwy on outside over 3f out: pushed along over 2f out: kpt on fnl f: nt pce to chal* **16/1**

51-0 **4** 1/2 **Aleksandar**25 2040 4-9-4 **70** LucyAlexander(3) 7 71
(Jim Goldie) *hld up towards rr: stdy hdwy over 3f out: sn rdn: kpt on same pce fr over 1f out* **6/1**3

00-0 **5** *2* **Geanie Mac (IRE)**17 2316 4-8-6 **55** (b) RoystonFfrench 9 53
(Linda Perratt) *rrd s: bhd: hdwy and cl up after 2f: led over 2f out to over 1f out: wknd fnl f* **40/1**

0-00 **6** 3 1/2 **Alsahil (USA)**17 2316 7-9-6 **69** PJMcDonald 6 62
(Micky Hammond) *hld up in tch: rdn and edgd rt 3f out: wknd wl over 1f out* **6/1**3

6104 **7** 1/2 **Yeomanoftheguard**22 2165 4-9-1 **64** (p) BarryMcHugh 1 56
(Richard Fahey) *t.k.h mde most to over 2f out: wknd over 1f out* **7/2**2

5005 **8** 2 1/2 **Morocco**9 2539 4-9-3 **66** DanielTudhope 5 54
(David O'Meara) *trckd ldrs tl rdn and wknd fr 2f out* **10/3**1

405 **9** 2 1/4 **Bonnie Echo**13 2405 6-8-7 **56** TomEaves 3 40
(Michael Dods) *t.k.h: hld up in tch: rdn over 2f out: sn wknd* **9/1**

2m 39.65s (1.05) **Going Correction** +0.15s/f (Good) **9** Ran SP% **115.8**
Speed ratings (Par 103): **102,100,98,98,97 94,94,92,91**
toteswingers 1&2 £9.90, 1&3 £19.40, 2&3 £17.90 CSF £62.85 CT £877.61 TOTE £8.50: £2.20, £2.70, £5.80; EX 57.10 Trifecta £886.10 Pool: £2161.71 - 1.82 winning units..
Owner Connor & Dunne **Bred** Gestut Karlshof **Trained** Uplawmoor, E Renfrews

FOCUS
Modest handicap form, with the pace steady. The runnerordinary.-up sets the standard.

2799 RACING UK LIVE ON SKY CHANNEL 432 H'CAP — 1m 3f 16y
5:10 (5:11) (Class 6) (0-65,64) 3-Y-O **£2,045** (£603; £302) **Stalls** High

Form RPR

40-1 **1** **Alcaeus**10 2508 3-9-6 **63** 6ex LukeMorris 6 73+
(Sir Mark Prescott Bt) *trckd ldrs: effrt whn n.m.r over 2f out: rdn to ld over 1f out: styd on wl fnl f* **1/2**1

-413 **2** *1* **Niknad**23 2124 3-8-8 **51** (p) TomEaves 7 59
(Brian Ellison) *t.k.h early: cl up: led over 2f out to over 1f out: rallied: kpt on same pce ins fnl f* **10/1**

654 **3** *1* **Wadacre Sarko**13 2405 3-9-7 **64** FrannyNorton 8 70
(Mark Johnston) *prom on outside: hdwy over 4f out: rdn and rn green over 2f out: kpt on same pce fnl f* **7/1**3

00-4 **4** *8* **Vision Of Judgment**28 1967 3-8-4 **47** RoystonFfrench 5 39
(Ollie Pears) *t.k.h: led to over 2f out: wknd over 1f out* **20/1**

000- **5** 3/4 **Oh Boy Oh Boy**261 6121 3-8-1 **47** NeilFarley(3) 1 37
(James Moffatt) *hld up: rdn over 3f out: no imp fnl 2f* **33/1**

21-4 **6** *nse* **Corton Lad**22 2167 3-9-6 **63** (p) GrahamGibbons 3 53
(Keith Dalgleish) *t.k.h: in tch: rdn and outpcd over 2f out: sn btn* **13/2**2

00-0 **7** 1 1/2 **Rosia Bay**12 2462 3-8-5 **48** BarryMcHugh 9 35
(Tom Dascombe) *hld up in tch: struggling wl over 2f out: sn wknd* **33/1**

56-5 **8** *10* **Hayley**60 1274 3-8-5 **48** ow3 AndrewElliott 2 17
(Jim Goldie) *tk keek hold early: prom tl rdn and wknd over 3f out* **33/1**

2m 28.49s (2.89) **Going Correction** +0.15s/f (Good) **8** Ran SP% **115.2**
Speed ratings (Par 97): **95,94,93,87,87 87,86,78**
toteswingers 1&2 £2.90, 1&3 £2.00, 2&3 £4.30 CSF £6.12 CT £17.29 TOTE £1.40: £1.10, £1.80, £1.90; EX 7.10 Trifecta £18.90 Pool: £3300.40 - 130.83 winning units..
Owner Ne'er Do Wells IV **Bred** Miss K Rausing **Trained** Newmarket, Suffolk

FOCUS
Three progressive types pulled clear despite the steady pace. There could be a fair bit more to come from the winner.

T/Plt: £296.00 to a £1 stake. Pool of £122.33 - 49,617.55 winning tickets. T/Qpdt: £47.50 to a £1 stake. Pool of £4224.28 - 65.80 winning tickets. RY

2744 LINGFIELD (L-H)
Thursday, May 30

OFFICIAL GOING: Turf course - soft changing to heavy after race 3 (3.20); all-weather - standard
Wind: Light against Weather: Overcast

2800 BETVICTOR JENIFER FLORENCE THOMAS H'CAP — 1m 3f 106y
2:20 (2:20) (Class 6) (0-60,60) 3-Y-O **£2,045** (£603; £302) **Stalls** High

Form RPR

553- **1** **Afro**223 7205 3-9-7 **60** 1 AdamKirby 6 68
(Peter Hedger) *a.p: chsd ldr over 3f out: rdn over 1f out: styd on u.p to ld post* **7/1**

0604 **2** *shd* **Whitefall (USA)**7 2599 3-8-8 **47** CathyGannon 4 55
(David Evans) *hld up in tch: pushed along over 3f out: rdn to ld over 1f out: hdd post* **4/1**2

056- **3** *5* **Vandross (IRE)**225 7172 3-9-7 **60** (b) GeorgeBaker 9 60
(Chris Wall) *hld up: rdn over 3f out: hung lft and r.o to go 3rd ins fnl f: nvr nrr* **9/2**3

4404 **4** 4 1/2 **Booktheband (IRE)**8 2566 3-9-2 **55** TedDurcan 3 48
(Clive Brittain) *chsd ldr tl pushed along over 3f out: nt clr run over 2f out: wknd over 1f out* **12/1**

00-0 **5** 1/2 **Halling's Wish**26 2017 3-9-5 **58** SteveDrowne 8 50
(John Best) *chsd ldrs: rdn over 3f out: wknd over 1f out* **16/1**

0-60 **6** 1 1/2 **Al Zein**15 2362 3-8-12 **56** WilliamTwiston-Davies(5) 13 46
(Richard Hannon) *led: rdn and hdd over 1f out: wknd fnl f* **7/1**

006- **7** *5* **Helamis**237 6846 3-9-1 **54** AndreaAtzeni 5 36
(Stuart Williams) *hld up: rdn over 3f out: wknd over 2f out* **3/1**1

043- **8** 3 1/2 **Unidexter (IRE)**167 8112 3-8-12 **51** SamHitchcott 2 27
(Mick Channon) *hld up: a in rr: rdn and wknd 3f out* **8/1**

000- **9** 1 1/4 **Terpsichore**194 7779 3-8-8 **47** DavidProbert 1 21
(Sylvester Kirk) *hld up: a in rr: rdn and wknd 3f out* **33/1**

0-50 **10** *25* **Rapid Rabbit Foot**20 2231 3-8-7 **46** oh1 JimmyQuinn 7
(John Holt) *prom: rdn over 4f out: wknd over 3f out: t.o* **50/1**

2m 44.33s (12.83) **Going Correction** +1.025s/f (Soft) **10** Ran SP% **117.8**
Speed ratings (Par 97): **94,93,90,87,86 85,81,79,78,60**
toteswingers 1&2 £5.50, 2&3 £4.60, 1&3 £5.30 CSF £35.53 CT £142.31 TOTE £9.00: £2.90, £1.90, £1.90; EX 50.00 Trifecta £240.80 Pool: £2792.78 - 8.69 winning units..
Owner P C F Racing Ltd **Bred** The Lavington Stud **Trained** Dogmersfield, Hampshire

FOCUS
Times showed the ground was testing. This was a weak 3yo handicap.

2801 BEATTHEBOOKIE.TV H'CAP — 1m 3f 106y
2:50 (2:52) (Class 6) (0-55,55) 4-Y-0+ — **£2,045** (£603; £302) **Stalls** High

Form — RPR

31 **1** **Mr Lando**[8] 2567 4-9-6 **54** 6ex .... JimmyQuinn 9 — 65+
(Tony Carroll) *plld hrd and prom: led over 2f out: rdn out* — **6/4**[1]

6-30 **2** 2 3/4 **Royal Defence (IRE)**[17] 1601 7-8-12 **46** .... AndreaAtzeni 4 — 53
(Mick Quinn) *chsd ldr tl led over 3f out: rdn and hdd over 2f out: styd on same pce fr over 1f out* — **25/1**

30-0 **3** 4 **King's Road**[39] 120 8-9-6 **54** .... (t) AdamKirby 10 — 55
(Anabel K Murphy) *hld up: rdn over 4f out: hdwy over 2f out: styd on to go 3rd ins fnl f: nt trble ldrs* — **10/1**

00-3 **4** 3/4 **Minstrel Lad**[16] 1949 5-9-7 **55** .... GeorgeBaker 13 — 54
(Jonjo O'Neill) *broke wl: sn stdd and lost pl: hdwy over 5f out: rdn and ev ch over 2f out: wknd ins fnl f* — **8/1**[3]

600/ **5** 3/4 **Lady Bridget**[16] 4337 5-9-0 **53** .... (bt) PhilipPrince(5) 12 — 51
(Mark Gillard) *hld up: rdn over 3f out: r.o ins fnl f: nvr nrr* — **20/1**

-502 **6** 3 1/4 **Princess Willow**[22] 2159 5-9-5 **53** .... KirstyMilczarek 8 — 46
(John E Long) *prom: rdn over 3f out: wknd over 1f out* — **10/1**

00-3 **7** 4 1/2 **Penang Pegasus**[30] 1909 4-8-13 **52** ....[1] MichaelJMMurphy(5) 3 — 38
(Roger Teal) *s.i.s: sn prom: rdn over 3f out: wknd over 2f out* — **5/1**[2]

-000 **8** 1/2 **Maccabees**[3] 2714 4-9-5 **53** .... DaneO'Neill 6 — 38
(Roger Curtis) *s.i.s: hld up: rdn over 3f out: n.d* — **25/1**

65-0 **9** 1 1/4 **Rhossili Bay**[9] 2533 4-9-2 **50** .... RichardKingscote 5 — 33
(Alastair Lidderdale) *hld up: rdn over 3f out: a in rr* — **14/1**

-001 **10** 1 **Kingscombe (USA)**[22] 2168 4-9-6 **54** .... SteveDrowne 1 — 35
(Linda Jewell) *chsd ldrs tl rdn and wknd 3f out* — **14/1**

/0-4 **11** nk **Lindsay's Dream**[8] 2567 7-9-1 **49** .... (p) CathyGannon 2 — 30
(Zoe Davison) *sn led: hdd over 3f out: wknd over 2f out* — **16/1**

2m 44.59s (13.09) **Going Correction** +1.025s/f (Soft) — **11** Ran SP% **117.6**
Speed ratings (Par 101): **93,91,88,87,87 84,81,81,80,79 79**
toteswingers 1&2 £8.10, 1&3 £5.60, 2&3 £29.80 CSF £51.00 CT £284.73 TOTE £2.30: £1.40, £4.50, £2.90; EX 49.60 Trifecta £486.40 Pool: £3149.78 - 4.85 winning units..
Owner Gary Attwood **Bred** Capitana Partnership **Trained** Cropthorne, Worcs
FOCUS
It was raining heavily during this race and the ground was already quite demanding. The form is only moderate but the winner built on his recent C&D win.

2802 BRIT GLOBAL SPECIALTY H'CAP — 1m 1f
3:20 (3:21) (Class 6) (0-60,60) 3-Y-O — **£2,045** (£603; £302) **Stalls** Low

Form — RPR

4-52 **1** **Topamichi**[10] 2508 3-9-7 **60** .... TomQueally 3 — 73+
(Mark H Tompkins) *hld up: hdwy over 3f out: led over 1f out: shkn up and styd on wl: comf* — **6/4**[1]

000- **2** 1 3/4 **Lady Of Yue**[167] 8112 3-9-0 **53** .... WilliamBuick 13 — 59
(Ed Dunlop) *hld up: rdn over 3f out: hdwy over 2f out: hung lft fr over 1f out: styd on to go 2nd wl ins fnl f: no ch w wnr* — **14/1**

-254 **3** 3 1/2 **Suspension**[17] 2330 3-9-1 **54** .... JimmyFortune 7 — 53
(Hughie Morrison) *a.p: rdn and ev ch wl over 1f out: no ex ins fnl f* — **12/1**

000- **4** 1 1/2 **Ebony Roc (IRE)**[204] 7627 3-9-0 **53** .... PatDobbs 9 — 49
(Amanda Perrett) *chsd ldr tl led 7f out: rdn and hdd 2f out: wknd ins fnl f* — **9/4**[2]

3310 **5** 2 **Entrapping**[22] 2154 3-9-5 **58** .... KirstyMilczarek 10 — 50
(John E Long) *hld up: hdwy u.p fr over 1f out: n.d* — **20/1**

-502 **6** 1 1/4 **Ishisoba**[9] 2528 3-9-4 **57** .... GeorgeBaker 12 — 47
(Alastair Lidderdale) *prom: chsd ldr over 4f out: led 2f out: sn rdn and hdd: wknd fnl f* — **10/1**[3]

-410 **7** 3 3/4 **Little Indian**[29] 1928 3-9-3 **56** .... DavidProbert 1 — 38
(J R Jenkins) *chsd ldrs: rdn over 3f out: hung lft and wknd over 1f out* — **20/1**

5400 **8** nk **Early One Morning**[16] 2341 3-9-0 **53** .... (b[1]) SteveDrowne 2 — 34
(Hugo Palmer) *hld up: hdwy over 4f out: rdn over 2f out: wknd over 1f out* — **33/1**

0-06 **9** 12 **Sonnetation (IRE)**[20] 2224 3-8-11 **50** .... PatCosgrave 4 — 9
(Jim Boyle) *led 2f: chsd ldr tl over 4f out: rdn and wknd over 2f out* — **16/1**

5130 **10** 14 **Brynford**[17] 2330 3-9-3 **56** .... SaleemGolam 6
(Chris Dwyer) *plld hrd and prom: wknd over 3f out* — **33/1**

2m 6.46s (9.86) **Going Correction** +1.025s/f (Soft) — **10** Ran SP% **115.5**
Speed ratings (Par 97): **97,95,92,91,89 88,84,84,73,61**
toteswingers 1&2 £6.30, 1&3 £4.80, 2&3 £12.00 CSF £22.85 CT £187.31 TOTE £2.40: £1.70, £4.00, £2.10; EX 27.90 Trifecta £127.10 Pool: £3226.32 - 19.03 winning units..
Owner Roalco Limited **Bred** Dullingham Park Stud & M P Bowring **Trained** Newmarket, Suffolk
FOCUS
Another moderate contest. The winner was value for extra and looks capable of better again.

2803 BETVICTOR DAVE DEE MEMORIAL MAIDEN FILLIES' STKS (DIV I) — 1m 2f
3:50 (3:52) (Class 5) 3-Y-0+ — **£2,726** (£805; £402) **Stalls** Low

Form — RPR

2-2 **1** **Butterfly McQueen (USA)**[22] 2151 3-8-10 0 .... DavidProbert 12 — 83
(Andrew Balding) *trckd ldr: led over 2f out: hung lft and pushed clr fnl f* — **4/7**[1]

0 **2** 9 **Kenny's Girl (IRE)**[20] 2231 3-8-10 0 .... MartinDwyer 2 — 68
(William Muir) *edgd lft s: hld up: hdwy over 4f out: led 3f out: sn hdd: outpcd fr over 1f out* — **20/1**

3 1 **Astorgs Galaxy** 3-8-10 0 .... RyanMoore 11 — 65+
(Sir Michael Stoute) *in rr and pushed along: styd on fr over 1f out: nvr nrr* — **9/2**[2]

0- **4** 1 **Wild Anthem**[215] 7403 3-8-10 0 .... JimmyFortune 10 — 63
(Hughie Morrison) *hld up: hdwy over 3f out: no ex fr over 1f out* — **14/1**

23 **5** 6 **Huffoof (IRE)**[22] 2164 3-8-10 0 .... (b[1]) AndreaAtzeni 5 — 52
(Roger Varian) *sn led: hdd after 1f: chsd ldrs: rdn and wknd over 2f out* — **5/1**[3]

6 12 **Youmaysee** 3-8-10 0 .... SamHitchcott 4 — 31
(Mick Channon) *s.i.s and hmpd s: hld up: plld hrd: rdn and wknd over 3f out* — **33/1**

0 **7** 4 **Sureness (IRE)**[14] 2389 3-8-10 0 .... WilliamBuick 1 — 24
(Marco Botti) *w ldrs: led over 7f out: rdn and hdd 3f out: wknd over 1f out* — **16/1**

00 **8** 20 **Indy Spirit (IRE)**[49] 1499 3-8-10 0 .... FergusSweeney 9
(Laura Mongan) *led after 1f tl hdd over 7f out: chsd ldrs: rdn and wknd over 3f out: t.o* — **66/1**

2m 21.35s (10.85) **Going Correction** +1.025s/f (Soft) — **8** Ran SP% **120.2**
Speed ratings (Par 100): **97,89,89,88,83 73,70,54**
toteswingers 1&2 £4.70, 1&3 £2.00, 2&3 £6.20 CSF £19.00 TOTE £1.50: £1.10, £3.50, £1.40; EX 12.60 Trifecta £54.70 Pool: £3270.72 - 44.76 winning units..
Owner Sir A Ferguson, G Mason & P Done **Bred** Pollock Farms **Trained** Kingsclere, Hants
FOCUS
The ground was changed to heavy ahead of this maiden. It was an uncompetitive contest and a few of these looked ill at ease on the ground. The easy winner was entitled to improve but may not have had to. The time was slower than division II.

2804 BETVICTOR DAVE DEE MEMORIAL MAIDEN FILLIES' STKS (DIV II) — 1m 2f
4:20 (4:21) (Class 5) 3-Y-0+ — **£2,726** (£805; £402) **Stalls** Low

Form — RPR

62- **1** **Audacia (IRE)**[219] 7306 3-8-10 0 .... JimmyFortune 9 — 80
(Hugo Palmer) *mde all: clr fr over 3f out: shkn up over 1f out: easily* — **9/2**[3]

5 **2** 4 1/2 **Bantam (IRE)**[12] 2442 3-8-10 0 .... WilliamBuick 10 — 72
(Ed Dunlop) *prom: chsd wnr 4f out: rdn over 2f out: styd on same pce* — **2/1**[2]

3 3/4 **Maypole Lass** 3-8-10 0 .... RyanMoore 4 — 71+
(Sir Michael Stoute) *chsd wnr 6f: sn outpcd: styd on again fr over 1f out* — **6/1**

4 9 **Tamaletta (IRE)** 3-8-10 0 .... RichardKingscote 5 — 54
(Tom Dascombe) *chsd ldrs tl rdn and hung lft over 3f out: sn wknd* — **33/1**

5 4 **Phaenomena (IRE)** 3-8-10 0 .... TomQueally 1 — 47
(Sir Henry Cecil) *awkward leaving stalls: rn green and pushed along almost thrght: nvr on terms* — **7/4**[1]

0 **6** 9 **Dukes Delight (IRE)**[14] 2392 3-8-10 0 .... TedDurcan 8 — 31
(David Lanigan) *s.i.s: hld up: rdn and wknd 3f out* — **14/1**

2m 20.94s (10.44) **Going Correction** +1.025s/f (Soft) — **6** Ran SP% **111.8**
Speed ratings (Par 100): **99,95,94,87,84 77**
toteswingers 1&2 £2.10, 1&3 £3.80, 2&3 £3.20 CSF £13.83 TOTE £5.40: £2.80, £1.50; EX 15.00 Trifecta £66.40 Pool: £3211.93 - 36.24 winning units..
Owner Carmichael Simmons Humber **Bred** Rathasker Stud **Trained** Newmarket, Suffolk
FOCUS
Much like the first division, uncompetitive stuff with several non-runners, and they came home strung out behind the front-running winner. It was the quicker division and the form is taken at face value.

2805 BETVICTOR "E" IS FOR ELEPHANT MEDIAN AUCTION MAIDEN STKS — 6f (P)
4:50 (4:51) (Class 6) 2-Y-O — **£2,045** (£603; £302) **Stalls** Low

Form — RPR

550 **1** **Jive**[6] 2625 2-9-0 0 .... DaneO'Neill 6 — 66
(Richard Hannon) *led 5f out: rdn and edgd lft ins fnl f: styd on* — **7/1**

5 **2** 3/4 **Pound Piece (IRE)**[12] 2436 2-9-5 0 .... LiamJones 7 — 69+
(J S Moore) *a.p: chsd wnr over 1f out: nt clr run and swtchd rt ins fnl f: r.o* — **8/1**

4 **3** 3 **Twentyfourseven**[10] 2502 2-9-5 0 .... WilliamBuick 1 — 60
(Ed Dunlop) *chsd ldrs: outpcd over 2f out: r.o ins fnl f* — **5/2**[2]

25 **4** nse **Rose Gloria (IRE)**[6] 2625 2-9-0 0 .... SamHitchcott 5 — 55
(Mick Channon) *led 1f: chsd ldr: pushed along over 3f out: lost 2nd over 1f out: styd on same pce fnl f* — **6/4**[1]

5 1 1/4 **Oxlip** 2-9-0 0 ....[1] PatDobbs 3 — 51+
(Richard Hannon) *chsd ldrs: pushed along over 2f out: no ex fnl f* — **6/1**[3]

6 2 3/4 **Speed Society** 2-9-5 0 .... PatCosgrave 2 — 48
(Jim Boyle) *s.i.s: outpcd* — **25/1**

7 8 **Crazy Brenda (IRE)** 2-9-0 0 .... JimmyFortune 9 — 19
(Sylvester Kirk) *s.i.s: a in rr* — **33/1**

8 4 1/2 **My My My Diliza** 2-9-0 0 .... AndreaAtzeni 8 — 6
(J S Moore) *dwlt: outpcd* — **25/1**

1m 12.92s (1.02) **Going Correction** -0.05s/f (Stan) — **8** Ran SP% **117.1**
Speed ratings (Par 91): **91,90,86,85,84 80,69,63**
toteswingers 1&2 £5.60, 1&3 £2.60, 2&3 £3.70 CSF £60.17 TOTE £5.50: £1.60, £1.60, £1.40; EX 48.60 Trifecta £170.20 Pool: £2903.52 - 12.79 winning units..
Owner T G & Mrs M E Holdcroft **Bred** Bearstone Stud **Trained** East Everleigh, Wilts
FOCUS
An ordinary-looking juvenile maiden. Improvement from the first two.

2806 BETVICTOR BEWICK FILLIES' H'CAP — 7f (P)
5:20 (5:21) (Class 5) (0-75,75) 3-Y-O — **£3,408** (£1,006; £503) **Stalls** Low

Form — RPR

21- **1** **Miss Avonbridge (IRE)**[194] 7778 3-8-11 **65** .... RichardKingscote 1 — 70
(Tom Dascombe) *mde all: rdn and edgd lft ins fnl f: r.o* — **4/1**[3]

4-50 **2** 1 1/4 **Summer Dream (IRE)**[26] 2010 3-9-5 **73** .... (b[1]) AdamKirby 9 — 75
(Marco Botti) *hld up: hdwy and nt clr run over 1f out: rdn and r.o ins fnl f: nt rch wnr* — **6/1**

000- **3** nk **Olympic Jule**[250] 6489 3-9-2 **70** .... CathyGannon 6 — 71
(Harry Dunlop) *chsd ldrs: rdn over 1f out: styd on* — **25/1**

3061 **4** hd **Moma Lee**[17] 2330 3-8-13 **67** .... WilliamBuick 3 — 67
(John Gosden) *prom: pushed along over 2f out: rdn and r.o ins fnl f* — **3/1**[2]

6000 **5** nk **Lucky Di**[14] 2387 3-9-7 **75** .... DaneO'Neill 2 — 75
(Peter Hedger) *a.p: rdn over 1f out: r.o* — **20/1**

21-0 **6** hd **Glossy Posse**[17] 2308 3-8-7 **66** .... WilliamTwiston-Davies(5) 5 — 65
(Richard Hannon) *chsd wnr: rdn over 1f out: no ex ins fnl f* — **12/1**

2-12 **7** 1 **Bright Glow**[8] 2572 3-9-2 **70** .... TedDurcan 8 — 66
(David Lanigan) *hld up: nt clr run over 1f out: r.o ins fnl f: nvr nrr* — **5/2**[1]

-345 **8** 3/4 **Puteri Nur Laila (IRE)**[22] 2169 3-8-8 **62** .... DavidProbert 4 — 56
(Paul Cole) *hld up: rdn over 1f out: styd on same pce fnl f* — **50/1**

1-43 **9** 3 **Gift Of Music (IRE)**[17] 2329 3-9-0 **68** .... TomQueally 7 — 54
(James Eustace) *hld up: hdwy over 3f out: rdn and edgd rt over 1f out: wknd ins fnl f* — **8/1**

1m 24.66s (-0.14) **Going Correction** -0.05s/f (Stan) — **9** Ran SP% **117.2**
Speed ratings (Par 96): **98,96,96,96,95 95,94,93,90**
toteswingers 1&2 £6.10, 1&3 £7.90, 2&3 £10.80 CSF £27.98 CT £534.06 TOTE £5.10: £2.00, £1.50, £4.20; EX 29.30 Trifecta £847.50 Pool: £2020.81 - 1.78 winning units..
Owner Deva Racing Avonbridge Partnership **Bred** T Whitehead **Trained** Malpas, Cheshire
FOCUS
It proved hard to make up ground with the winner and third sitting more or less one-two for much of the way. The third helps to set an ordinary standard.

2807 BETVICTOR KATE FIRTH MEMORIAL H'CAP — 1m (P)
5:55 (5:56) (Class 5) (0-70,70) 4-Y-0+ — **£2,726** (£805; £402) **Stalls** High

Form — RPR

0024 **1** **Copperwood**[17] 2315 8-9-2 **65** .... AdamKirby 10 — 72
(Mark Johnston) *chsd ldr: pushed along over 2f out: hrd rdn to ld ins fnl f: styd on u.p* — **5/1**[3]

3240 **2** 1 1/4 **Vastly (USA)**[20] 2234 4-9-7 **70** .... DaneO'Neill 1 — 74
(Julia Feilden) *chsd ldrs: rdn over 1f out: r.o* — **8/1**

5540 **3** 3/4 **Titan Triumph**[48] 1514 9-9-3 **66**......(t) JimmyQuinn 9 68
(Michael Attwater) *hld up: hdwy over 1f out: r.o: nt rch ldrs* **20/1**
00-2 **4** *shd* **Kakapuka**[29] 1925 6-9-6 **69**...... GeorgeBaker 7 71
(Anabel K Murphy) *led: rdn: hdd and no ex ins fnl f* **15/2**
/36- **5** *1* **Menelik (IRE)**[194] 7776 4-8-12 **61**......(v1) RichardKingscote 2 61
(Tom Dascombe) *hld up: rdn over 1f out: r.o: nt rch ldrs* **5/2**[1]
5033 **6** 3/4 **Mafi (IRE)**[20] 2228 5-9-3 **66**......(t) RobertHavlin 6 64
(Mark Hoad) *chsd ldrs: rdn over 1f out: styd on same pce fnl f* **10/1**
2-56 **7** *shd* **Derfenna Art (IRE)**[8] 2573 4-9-2 **65**......(t) MickyFenton 8 63
(Seamus Durack) *prom: rdn over 2f out: styd on same pce fnl f* **12/1**
3311 **8** 1/2 **Midnight Feast**[20] 2228 5-9-6 **69**......(v) KierenFox 4 66
(Lee Carter) *hld up: hdwy over 1f out: sn rdn: styd on same pce fnl f* **3/1**[2]
355- **9** *shd* **Yajber (USA)**[456] 737 4-9-3 **66**...... CathyGannon 5 63
(Jamie Poulton) *s.i.s: hld up: rdn over 2f out: n.d* **33/1**

1m 37.13s (-1.07) **Going Correction** -0.05s/f (Stan) **9** Ran SP% **117.6**
Speed ratings (Par 103): **103,101,101,100,99 99,99,98,98**
toteswingers 1&2 £9.40, 1&3 £14.30, 2&3 £15.80 CSF £45.37 CT £744.15 TOTE £5.10: £1.70, £2.70, £4.00; EX 36.90 Trifecta £536.00 Pool: £2045.00 - 2.86 winning units..
Owner Ready To Run Partnership **Bred** Hertford Offset Press **Trained** Middleham Moor, N Yorks

FOCUS
A modest contest in which the winner did not need to match his winter best.
T/Jkpt: £5,071.40 to a £1 stake. Pool of £25,000.00 - 3.50 winning tickets. T/Plt: £42.30 to a £1 stake. Pool of £68,008.12 - 1171.97 winning tickets. T/Qpdt: £18.70 to a £1 stake. Pool of £4361.62 - 172.31 winning tickets. CR

2601 SANDOWN (R-H)
Thursday, May 30

OFFICIAL GOING: Good to soft (6.9)
Sprint track at full width, rail on Round course at innermost configuration and all distances as advertised.
Wind: Moderate, across (towards stands) Weather: Overcast, drizzly

2808 CANTOR CAPITAL H'CAP (JOCKEY CLUB GRASSROOTS MIDDLE DISTANCE SERIES QUALIFIER) 1m 2f 7y
6:10 (6:10) (Class 5) (0-75,75) 4-Y-0+ **£3,234** (£962; £481; £240) **Stalls** Low

Form RPR
6203 **1** **Tight Lipped (IRE)**[14] 2383 4-9-2 **75**...... RyanTate(5) 8 83
(James Eustace) *mde all: untrbld in front: kicked on 3f out: edgd rt u.p 1f out: styd on* **13/2**[3]
5036 **2** 3/4 **Choral Festival**[3] 2729 7-9-1 **69**...... SeanLevey 9 76
(John Bridger) *trckd ldrs in 5th: rdn and prog to chse wnr over 1f out: trying to chal on inner whn no room ins fnl f and swtchd lft: styd on and clsng nr fin* **10/1**
0000 **3** 1 1/2 **Mountain Range (IRE)**[45] 1585 5-8-10 **64**...... J-PGuillambert 4 68
(Willie Musson) *hld up disputing 6th: rdn over 2f out: prog over 1f out: styd on fnl f to take 3rd nr fin* **8/1**
4622 **4** *hd* **Syncopate**[28] 1956 4-9-4 **72**...... FergusSweeney 5 75
(Pam Sly) *awkward s: quick rcvry to trck ldng pair: rdn over 2f out: one pce and no imp on wnr fr over 1f out* **12/1**
000- **5** 1/2 **My Lord**[75] 8174 5-9-3 **71**...... RichardHughes 7 73
(Luke Dace) *stdd s: hld up in last pair: prog 2f out: rdn over 1f out: kpt on same pce* **10/1**
3-10 **6** *hd* **Tafawuk (USA)**[27] 1973 4-9-5 **73**...... RyanMoore 10 75
(Roger Varian) *trckd wnr: rdn over 2f out: no imp and lost 2nd over 1f out: fdd nr fin* **4/1**[2]
000- **7** 1 1/4 **Bobbyscot (IRE)**[176] 7986 6-9-7 **75**...... SamHitchcott 2 74
(Gary Moore) *hld up in last pair: stl last 2f out: urged along and styd on fr over 1f out: nvr rchd ldrs* **25/1**
4-13 **8** *8* **Significant Move**[19] 2256 6-9-5 **73**...... NeilCallan 6 56
(Stuart Kittow) *trckd ldrs: drvn and no rspnse 2f out: sn wknd qckly: t.o* **2/1**[1]
0112 **9** 3 1/2 **Rezwaan**[35] 1780 6-8-13 **74**......(be) NedCurtis(7) 3 50
(Murty McGrath) *hld up disputing 6th: pushed along over 2f out: wknd qckly wl over 1f out: t.o* **25/1**

2m 16.08s (5.58) **Going Correction** +0.40s/f (Good) **9** Ran SP% **111.3**
Speed ratings (Par 103): **93,92,91,91,90 90,89,83,80**
toteswingers 1&2 £10.40, 1&3 £11.20, 2&3 £20.80 CSF £65.53 CT £511.81 TOTE £8.00: £2.50, £3.10, £3.40; EX 62.10 Trifecta £1153.60 Pool: £1951.54 - 1.26 winning units..
Owner Blue Peter Racing 11 **Bred** P F Headon **Trained** Newmarket, Suffolk
■ Stewards' Enquiry : Ryan Tate two-day ban; used whip above permitted level (13th-14th June).

FOCUS
The rail was at the innermost configuration and after 5mm of rain overnight the going was good to soft. This was slowly run and the winner made all off an easy lead. He rates a small personal best.

2809 CANTOR FITZGERALD EQUITIES NATIONAL STKS (LISTED RACE) 5f 6y
6:40 (6:40) (Class 1) 2-Y-0 **£14,461** (£5,482; £2,743; £1,366; £685) **Stalls** Low

Form RPR
51 **1** **Rizeena (IRE)**[20] 2204 2-8-9 0...... RyanMoore 2 97+
(Clive Brittain) *mde all and racd against rail: drvn clr jst over 1f out: styd on wl and in n.d fnl f* **9/4**[2]
1 **2** *3* **Andhesontherun (IRE)**[10] 2497 2-9-0 0...... AndreaAtzeni 5 91
(Roger Varian) *hld up: shkn up over 1f out: styd on fnl f to take 2nd last stride: no ch w wnr* **5/1**[3]
1 **3** *nse* **Eastern Impact (IRE)**[35] 1785 2-9-0 0...... TonyHamilton 6 91
(Richard Fahey) *pressed wnr: rdn wl over 1f out: sn outpcd: lost 2nd last stride* **15/2**
211 **4** 1 3/4 **Steventon Star**[15] 2370 2-9-0 0...... RichardHughes 8 85
(Richard Hannon) *racd wdst of all: hld up in tch gng wl: shkn up over 1f out: immediately floundering and btn* **11/10**[1]
022 **5** 2 1/2 **Urban Dreamer (IRE)**[19] 2260 2-9-0 0...... SteveDrowne 4 76
(Rod Millman) *racd against rail: trckd ldrs: pushed along and wknd 1f out* **25/1**

1m 3.57s (1.97) **Going Correction** +0.40s/f (Good) **5** Ran SP% **110.7**
Speed ratings (Par 101): **100,95,95,92,88**
CSF £13.42 TOTE £2.30: £1.80, £3.40; EX 11.60 Trifecta £28.80 Pool: £1778.13 - 46.18 winning units..
Owner Sheikh Rashid Dalmook Al Maktoum **Bred** Round Hill Stud **Trained** Newmarket, Suffolk

FOCUS
The last winner of the National Stakes to follow up at Royal Ascot was Russian Valour in the Norfolk Stakes in 2003 but last year's winner Sir Prancealot ran well behind Dawn Approach in the Coventry before ending last season with a win in the Group 2 Flying Childers. There were not many runners for this renewal and the favourite found a limited response off the steady pace but the winner was impressive under a positive ride. She tallies with the race averages.

2810 SEYMOUR PIERCE HENRY II STKS (GROUP 3) 2m 78y
7:15 (7:15) (Class 1) 4-Y-0+
£34,026 (£12,900; £6,456; £3,216; £1,614; £810) **Stalls** Centre

Form RPR
030- **1** **Gloomy Sunday (FR)**[51] 1457 4-8-11 98...... OlivierPeslier 7 110
(C Ferland, France) *prog to trck ldng pair after 6f: shkn up to ld over 2f out: sn wl in command: drvn and styd on stoutly fnl f* **20/1**
30-4 **2** *4* **Number Theory**[19] 2252 5-9-2 98...... SebSanders 1 108
(John Holt) *settled in midfield: rdn 3f out: prog to chse wnr 2f out: no imp 1f out: tired after but hld on wl for 2nd* **40/1**
3-14 **3** 1 3/4 **Model Pupil**[40] 1674 4-9-0 104...... RichardHughes 8 106
(Charles Hills) *hld up in midfield: rdn and nt qckn wl over 2f out: styd on again fr over 1f out to take 3rd ins fnl f* **8/1**[3]
222- **4** 1/2 **High Jinx (IRE)**[235] 6914 5-9-2 113...... GrahamLee 4 105
(James Fanshawe) *hld up in 7th: rdn 4f out: no real prog and hanging 2f out: fnlly styd on over 1f out: continued to hang but tk 4th nr fin* **3/1**[1]
0-31 **5** *2* **Cavalryman**[61] 1263 7-9-4 115...... MickaelBarzalona 6 105
(Saeed bin Suroor) *hld up in last pair: rdn and prog on outer wl over 2f out: chsd ldng pair wl over 1f out: no imp: wknd ins fnl f* **3/1**[1]
011- **6** *2* **Times Up**[258] 6198 7-9-6 115...... RyanMoore 2 105
(Ed Dunlop) *hld up in 8th: rdn 3f out: no prog and btn over 2f out: plugged on* **8/1**[3]
030- **7** 1 1/2 **Colour Vision (FR)**[222] 7235 5-9-2 116...... SilvestreDeSousa 5 99
(Saeed bin Suroor) *settled in last pair: nt gng wl fr 1/2-way: bhd and no ch 3f out: passed a couple of stragglers late on* **4/1**[2]
-530 **8** *1* **Sir Graham Wade (IRE)**[13] 2428 4-9-0 107...... JoeFanning 3 98
(Mark Johnston) *trckd ldng pair: rdn 3f out: wknd jst over 2f out* **12/1**
63-0 **9** *10* **Askar Tau (FR)**[29] 1920 8-9-2 110......(v) HayleyTurner 9 86
(Marcus Tregoning) *swift move fr wdst draw to ld after 1f: upped the pce after 5f: drvn and hdd over 2f out: wknd steadily then rapidly fnl f* **25/1**
3/0- **10** *16* **Ley Hunter (USA)**[364] 2639 6-9-2 110...... KierenFallon 10 66
(Saeed bin Suroor) *t.k.h: led 1f: pressed ldr: rdn to chal over 3f out: wknd rapidly wl over 2f out: t.o* **25/1**

3m 44.57s (5.87) **Going Correction** +0.40s/f (Good)
WFA 4 from 5yo+ 2lb **10** Ran SP% **114.8**
Speed ratings (Par 113): **101,99,98,97,96 95,95,94,89,81**
toteswingers 1&2 £8.90, 1&3 £28.70, 2&3 £43.40 CSF £605.20 TOTE £12.50: £2.00, £6.90, £2.80; EX 389.80 Trifecta £2280.00 Part won. Pool: £3040.12 - 0.67 winning units..
Owner Simon Springer **Bred** M Parrish **Trained** France

FOCUS
The last horse to complete the Henry II Stakes/Ascot Gold Cup double was Papineau in 2004. However, Opinion Poll went close at Ascot after winning this race last year and this looked a strong renewal, with six of the runners rated 110 or higher. However the first three were the three lowest rated pre-race, and the form horses were clearly not at their best. A couple of the market leaders were a bit disappointing but the pace was fair and a big-priced French raider scored in good style.

2811 CANTOR FITZGERALD BRIGADIER GERARD STKS (GROUP 3) 1m 2f 7y
7:50 (7:51) (Class 1) 4-Y-0+ **£34,026** (£12,900; £6,456; £3,216; £1,614) **Stalls** Low

Form RPR
425- **1** **Mukhadram**[243] 6674 4-9-0 101...... PaulHanagan 6 112
(William Haggas) *mde all at decent pce: pushed along and maintained 3 l ld fr 3f out tl tired and drvn jst over 1f out: hld on wl* **3/1**[3]
25-3 **2** 1/2 **Main Sequence (USA)**[19] 2252 4-9-0 112...... TedDurcan 5 111
(David Lanigan) *trckd wnr: pushed along 3f out: no imp and flashed tail whn rdn wl over 1f out: nvr looked wholehearted but clsd fnl f: gaining fin* **15/8**[1]
-214 **3** 2 1/4 **Miblish**[21] 2186 4-9-0 105......(t) RyanMoore 2 106
(Clive Brittain) *chsd ldng pair: rdn wl over 2f out: no imp tl grad clsd fnl f* **5/1**
4-53 **4** *9* **Proud Chieftain**[26] 2018 5-9-0 98...... RichardHughes 4 88
(Clifford Lines) *hld up in last: shkn up and lft bhd fr 3f out: modest 4th fnl 2f* **20/1**
01-1 **5** 4 1/2 **Danadana (IRE)**[21] 2186 5-9-3 111...... KierenFallon 3 82
(Luca Cumani) *hld up in 4th: struggling 3f out: sn no ch and dropped to last 2f out* **9/4**[2]

2m 11.78s (1.28) **Going Correction** +0.40s/f (Good) **5** Ran SP% **112.0**
Speed ratings (Par 113): **110,109,107,100,97**
CSF £9.24 TOTE £4.90: £2.50, £1.30; EX 15.60 Trifecta £54.80 Pool: £8078.45 - 110.55 winning units..
Owner Hamdan Al Maktoum **Bred** Wardall Bloodstock **Trained** Newmarket, Suffolk

FOCUS
There was a small field for a Group 3 event which was won by former Derby hero Workforce in 2011. The race was tactical but a progressive 4yo dominated and just held off the favourite. Probably a weak renewal, with the form taken at face value.

2812 CANTOR FITZGERALD CORPORATE FINANCE HERON STKS (LISTED RACE) 1m 14y
8:20 (8:21) (Class 1) 3-Y-0 **£20,982** (£7,955; £3,981; £1,983) **Stalls** Low

Form RPR
12-3 **1** **Montiridge (IRE)**[17] 2323 3-8-12 104...... RichardHughes 5 116
(Richard Hannon) *mde all: upped the pce over 2f out and had rest in trble: stretched clr over 1f out: styd on wl* **13/8**[1]
2-1 **2** 3 3/4 **Mango Diva**[24] 2084 3-8-7 92...... RyanMoore 2 102+
(Sir Michael Stoute) *hld up in last pair: rdn over 2f out: chsd wnr over 1f out: kpt on but nvr any imp* **7/2**[3]
44-1 **3** *6* **Ebn Arab (USA)**[26] 2008 3-8-12 103...... PaulHanagan 4 94
(Charles Hills) *chsd wnr: rdn over 2f out: lost 2nd and wl btn over 1f out: wknd fnl f* **7/2**[3]
23-6 **4** *1* **Al Waab (IRE)**[34] 1811 3-8-12 101...... TomQueally 3 91
(Sir Henry Cecil) *t.k.h: hld up in last pair: rdn over 2f out: sn struggling and bhd* **11/4**[2]

1m 44.84s (1.54) **Going Correction** +0.40s/f (Good) **4** Ran SP% **109.2**
Speed ratings (Par 107): **108,104,98,97**
CSF £7.45 TOTE £1.50; EX 6.00 Trifecta £14.90 Pool: £7938.63 - 398.65 winning units..
Owner M Clarke,J Jeffries,R Ambrose,B Reilly **Bred** Century Bloodstock **Trained** East Everleigh, Wilts

FOCUS
There were not many runners but this was an interesting Listed event. The pace was steady but the leading contender scored in smooth style and could go on to better things.

2813 CANTOR FITZGERALD WHITSUN CUP H'CAP — 1m 14y
8:50 (8:51) (Class 3) (0-95,95) 4-Y-0+

£7,781 (£2,330; £1,165; £582; £291; £146) **Stalls** Low

Form — RPR

60-2 **1** **Spa's Dancer (IRE)**[33] 1848 6-9-4 **92** ... RyanMoore 13 — 103
(James Eustace) *prog to press ldr after 2f: led wl over 1f out but hrd pressed: drvn and asserted fnl f* **2/1**[1]

-455 **2** 2 ¼ **Shamaal Nibras (USA)**[26] 2013 4-9-2 **95** ... ThomasBrown(5) 7 — 101
(Ismail Mohammed) *hld up towards rr: rdn and prog to chal 2f out: chsd wnr over 1f out: kpt on but readily hld fnl f* **5/1**[3]

-056 **3** shd **Gaul Wood (IRE)**[21] 2191 4-8-13 **87** ... RichardKingscote 4 — 93
(Tom Dascombe) *trckd ldrs: rdn to chal 2f out: disp 2nd bhd wnr fr over 1f out: kpt on but readily hld* **9/2**[2]

-214 **4** 1 ½ **Swing Alone (IRE)**[21] 2191 4-9-0 **88** ... GrahamLee 3 — 90
(Gay Kelleway) *hld up towards rr: rdn over 2f out: no prog tl kpt on fr over 1f out to take 4th nr fin* **11/1**

220- **5** ½ **Trader Jack**[243] 6677 4-9-1 **89** ... SteveDrowne 2 — 90+
(Roger Charlton) *dwlt: tried to rcvr but no room on inner and hld up in last pair: prog over 2f out: kpt on one pce over 1f out* **5/1**[3]

03-5 **6** nk **Shamdarley (IRE)**[37] 1751 5-8-7 **81** oh3 ... AndreaAtzeni 11 — 81
(Marco Botti) *led after 2f but pressed: hdd wl over 1f out: wknd fnl f* **10/1**

000- **7** 5 **Hadaj**[285] 5334 4-8-8 **82** ... HayleyTurner 8 — 71
(Clive Brittain) *led 2f: chsd ldng pair to over 2f out: steadily wknd* **20/1**

00-0 **8** 10 **Forest Row**[29] 1922 4-8-2 **81** oh5 ... (b1) RyanTate(5) 9 — 47
(Clive Cox) *chsd ldrs tl wknd over 2f out: sn bhd* **16/1**

4/0- **9** 13 **Commissar**[406] 1477 4-8-9 **83** ... PaulHanagan 14
(Ian Williams) *dwlt: hld up in last pair: shkn up and no prog 3f out: sn t.o* **25/1**

1m 44.76s (1.46) **Going Correction** +0.40s/f (Good) — **9 Ran SP% 116.8**
Speed ratings (Par 107): **108,105,105,104,103 103,98,88,75**
toteswingers 1&2 £3.20, 1&3 £3.40, 2&3 £5.90 CSF £12.18 CT £40.61 TOTE £2.60: £1.20, £1.90, £2.10; EX 13.70 Trifecta £54.80 Pool: £1492.16 - 20.40 winning units..
Owner The MacDougall Two **Bred** Giacinto Gugliemi **Trained** Newmarket, Suffolk

FOCUS
There were a number of withdrawals but the favourite delivered in good style in this decent handicap and the form looks solid. The winner rates a small personal best, with the third setting the standard.
T/Plt: £505.60 to a £1 stake. Pool of £91,716.61 - 132.41 winning tickets. T/Qpdt: £63.70 to a £1 stake. Pool of £8718.07 - 101.14 winning tickets. JN

2814 - 2821a (Foreign Racing) - See Raceform Interactive

2526 COLOGNE (R-H)
Thursday, May 30

OFFICIAL GOING: Turf: soft

2822a GERLING-PREIS (GROUP 2) (4YO+) (TURF) — 1m 4f
4:15 (12:00) 4-Y-0+

£32,520 (£12,601; £5,284; £3,252; £2,032; £1,219)

RPR

1 **Girolamo (GER)**[18] 2294 4-9-6 0 ... AStarke 4 — 114+
(P Schiergen, Germany) *midfield: rdn 3f out: styd on to ld ent fnl f: forged clr: v readily* **9/5**[1]

2 3 **Runaway (GER)**[34] 6-9-0 0 ... AHelfenbein 7 — 103
(A Trybuhl, Germany) *trckd ldr: rdn to chal 3f out: jnd ldr over 2f out: hdd ent fnl f and outpcd by wnr: styd on and jst prevailed for 2nd* **79/10**

3 hd **Wilddrossel (GER)**[22] 4-8-10 0 ... SHellyn 5 — 99
(Markus Klug, Germany) *sltly slow to stride: qckly rcvrd and sn led: rdn 3f out: jnd over 2f out: hdd ent fnl f and outpcd by wnr: styd on but jst denied for 2nd* **149/10**

4 4 **Silvaner (GER)**[18] 2294 5-9-0 0 ... FilipMinarik 2 — 96
(P Schiergen, Germany) *hld up in last pair on outer: rdn 3f out: plugged on but nt pce to chal* **44/5**

5 1 ¼ **Quidamo**[20] 2249 6-9-0 0 ... ADeVries 3 — 94
(Frau J Mayer, Germany) *midfield on inner: rdn to chal 3f out: kpt on and ev ch tl outpcd by ldrs ent fnl f: fdd* **23/5**[3]

6 ½ **Technokrat (IRE)**[18] 2294 5-9-0 0 ... (b) APietsch 6 — 93
(W Hickst, Germany) *midfield on outer: rdn 3f out: kpt on and ev ch tl outpcd by ldrs ent fnl f: fdd* **21/10**[2]

7 3 ½ **Andolini (GER)**[39] 4-9-0 0 ... EPedroza 1 — 88
(A Wohler, Germany) *hld up in last pair on inner: rdn and hdwy 3f out: ev ch 2f out: no ex over 1f out: fdd and dropped to last: eased* **51/10**

2m 32.71s (-0.19) — **7 Ran SP% 130.0**
WIN (incl. 10 euro stake): 28. PLACES: 19, 23. SF: 340.
Owner Gestut Ebbesloh **Bred** Gestut Ebbesloh **Trained** Germany

2358 BATH (L-H)
Friday, May 31

OFFICIAL GOING: Good (good to soft in places; 8.0)
Far bend positioned 3-4m off inside line adding about 10yds to races of 1m and beyond as has been the case at all previous meetings this season.
Wind: Moderate across Weather: Sunny spells early

2823 BATH ALES HOP POLE MAIDEN STKS — 5f 11y
5:50 (5:51) (Class 5) 2-Y-0 — **£2,587** (£770; £384; £192) **Stalls** Centre

Form — RPR

1 **Emirates Flyer** 2-9-5 0 ... MickaelBarzalona 4 — 78+
(Saeed bin Suroor) *trckd ldrs: n.m.r and edgd rt 2f out: pushed along to ld 1f out: drvn and edgd rt fnl 75yds: kpt on wl* **5/4**[1]

0 **2** nse **Biography**[42] 1669 2-9-0 0 ... WilliamTwiston-Davies(5) 5 — 65+
(Richard Hannon) *in rr: hdwy on outer fr 2f out: styng on wl to cl on ldr whn hmpd and stmbld fnl 30yds: dropped to 3rd: rallied: nt rcvr: fin 3rd: plcd 2nd* **15/8**[2]

3 1 ¼ **Thrtypointstothree (IRE)** 2-9-0 0 ... RyanTate(5) 8 — 65
(Nikki Evans) *chsd ldrs: rdn over 2f out: wknd fnl f: fin 4th: plcd 3rd* **66/1**

256 **4** hd **Mr Dandy Man (IRE)**[16] 2358 2-9-5 0 ... WilliamCarson 2 — 65
(Ronald Harris) *t.k.h: trckd ldr tl led 3f out: rdn 2f out: hdd 1f out and sn wknd: fin 5th: plcd 4th* **12/1**

5 4 **Black Geronimo** 2-9-0 0 ... DeclanBates(5) 3 — 51
(David Evans) *chsd ldrs: rdn over 2f out: wknd wl over 1f out: fin sixth: plcd 5th* **14/1**

4 **6** 8 **Paradise Child**[18] 2320 2-8-7 0 ... RyanWhile(7) 1 — 17
(Bill Turner) *t.k.h: led to 3f out: sn btn: fin seventh: plcd sixth* **50/1**

7 9 **Go Charlie** 2-9-0 0 ... EDLinehan(5) 6
(Ronald Harris) *taken down early: wnt rt s: a outpcd in rr: lost tch fnl 2f: fin eighth: plcd seventh* **14/1**

D 2 ¼ **Speed The Plough** 2-9-5 0 ... SeanLevey 7 — 61+
(Richard Hannon) *chsd ldrs: chal fr 2f out whn bmpd: styd upsides tl outpcd fnl f: fin 2nd, 2 ¼l: disqualified and plcd last* **9/2**[3]

1m 3.34s (0.84) **Going Correction** +0.125s/f (Good) — **8 Ran SP% 121.9**
Speed ratings (Par 93): **98,94,92,92,85 72,58,94**
Tote Swingers 1&2 £1.50, 2&3 £20.70, 1&3 £25.20 CSF £4.14 TOTE £2.00: £1.20, £8.10, £8.10; EX 5.00 Trifecta £130.20 Pool: £1,703.70 - 9.80 winning tickets..
Owner Godolphin **Bred** Carmel Stud **Trained** Newmarket, Suffolk
■ Stewards' Enquiry : Sean Levey three-day ban; improper riding (14th-16th June).
Mickael Barzalona three-day ban; careless riding (14th-16th June).

FOCUS
The pace was not strong in this maiden and it was a messy race but a well-backed Godolphin newcomer scored with something in hand, value for extra. The weights carried by the Hannon pair were reportedly transposed.

2824 BATH ALES SPECIAL PALE ALE MAIDEN FILLIES' STKS — 5f 161y
6:20 (6:20) (Class 5) 3-Y-0+ — **£2,587** (£770; £384; £192) **Stalls** Centre

Form — RPR

2 **1** **Dilgura**[42] 1660 3-9-0 0 ... ShaneKelly 8 — 71+
(Stuart Kittow) *hld up in tch: hdwy over 2f out: trckd ldr appr fnl f: qcknd under hand riding to ld fnl 25yds: cosily* **6/4**[1]

-4 **2** nk **Celestial Bay**[8] 2597 4-9-9 0 ... MartinDwyer 1 — 72
(Sylvester Kirk) *s.i.s: sn rcvrd to ld: hrd rdn to keep narrow advantage ins fnl f: readily outpcd fnl 25yds* **4/1**[3]

223- **3** 3 ½ **Sky Garden**[211] 7498 3-9-0 74 ... LiamJones 3 — 58
(William Haggas) *sn chsng ldr: drvn wl over 1f out: easily outpcd fnl f* **5/2**[2]

0-40 **4** nk **Roanne (USA)**[11] 2495 3-9-0 67 ... JohnFahy 7 — 57
(Clive Cox) *chsd ldrs: drvn to dispute 2nd wl over 1f out: easily outpcd fnl f* **9/2**

06- **5** 2 ¾ **Indigo Moon**[170] 8068 3-9-0 0 ... CathyGannon 9 — 48
(Denis Coakley) *in rr: rdn and sme hdwy 2f out: nvr rchd ldrs and wknd over 1f out* **33/1**

04 **6** 1 **Calm Attitude (IRE)**[21] 2241 3-9-0 0 ... ChrisCatlin 2 — 44
(Rae Guest) *outpcd tl shkn up and styd on fr over 1f out: nvr a threat* **16/1**

3 **7** 1 ½ **Natalia**[13] 2437 4-9-4 0 ... JackDuern(5) 5 — 41
(Andrew Hollinshead) *chsd ldrs: rdn over 3f out: sn btn* **33/1**

00 **8** 1 ½ **Delicious Patrica**[13] 2437 4-9-4 0 ... WilliamTwiston-Davies(5) 6 — 36
(Tony Carroll) *s.i.s: a outpcd* **100/1**

1m 11.2s **Going Correction** +0.125s/f (Good)
WFA 3 from 4yo 9lb — **8 Ran SP% 119.5**
Speed ratings (Par 100): **105,104,99,99,95 94,92,90**
Tote Swingers 1&2 £2.60, 2&3 £2.00, 1&3 £1.10 CSF £8.42 TOTE £3.20: £1.20, £1.30, £1.20; EX 9.60 Trifecta £22.40 Pool: £1,476.10 - 49.26 winning tickets..
Owner S Kittow, R Perry, B Hopkins **Bred** Hopkins, Kittow & Mrs Perry **Trained** Blackborough, Devon

FOCUS
The went a fair pace in this fillies' maiden. There was a tight finish and the four market leaders filled the first four places. The first two built on their respective recent debuts.

2825 BATH ALES SUMMER'S HARE H'CAP — 5f 161y
6:50 (6:50) (Class 4) (0-80,80) 3-Y-0+ — **£4,690** (£1,395; £697; £348) **Stalls** Centre

Form — RPR

360- **1** **Bilash**[263] 6094 6-8-7 **66** oh2 ... JackDuern(5) 1 — 73
(Andrew Hollinshead) *disp ld tl over 2f out: styd chalng and led again over 1f out: hld on wl clsng stages* **16/1**

-000 **2** nk **Italian Tom (IRE)**[13] 2441 6-9-2 **75** ... EDLinehan(5) 4 — 81
(Ronald Harris) *chsd ldrs: rdn over 1f out: kpt on ins fnl f to press wnr clsng stages but a jst hld* **8/1**

10-0 **3** hd **Ginzan**[20] 2266 5-9-0 **75** ... RyanWhile(7) 11 — 80
(Malcolm Saunders) *disp ld tl slt advantage fr over 2f out: hdd over 1f out but styd chalng: no ex cl home* **8/1**

-666 **4** ½ **Street Power (USA)**[24] 2128 8-9-7 **75** ... SteveDrowne 8 — 79
(Jeremy Gask) *in tch: hdwy fr 2f out: pressed ldrs ins fnl f: no ex clsng stages* **5/1**[3]

3135 **5** shd **Dark Lane**[12] 2479 7-8-13 **72** ... DeclanBates(5) 6 — 75
(David Evans) *chsd ldrs: drvn over 2f out: styd on u.p fnl f: no ex clsng stages* **20/1**

3550 **6** 1 **Sole Danser (IRE)**[22] 2196 5-9-0 **68** ... RichardKingscote 5 — 68
(Milton Bradley) *s.i.s: in rr: hdwy to cl on ldrs fr 2f out: nt qckn ins fnl f* **10/1**

0-26 **7** ¾ **Divine Call**[4] 2724 6-8-13 **72** ... RobertTart(5) 2 — 69
(Milton Bradley) *chsd ldrs: rdn 2f out: wknd ins fnl f* **7/2**[1]

-500 **8** 4 ½ **Barons Spy (IRE)**[21] 2214 12-9-12 **80** ... ShaneKelly 7 — 62
(Richard Price) *s.i.s: outpcd: mod prog fnl f* **12/1**

1050 **9** 3 ¾ **Pick A Little**[20] 2255 5-9-7 **75** ... ChrisCatlin 3 — 44
(Michael Blake) *a outpcd* **22/1**

2-24 **10** 6 **Small Fury (IRE)**[25] 2083 3-9-0 **77** ... J-PGuillambert 9 — 26
(Jo Hughes) *disp ld 3f: wknd over 2f out* **4/1**[2]

4442 **11** nk **Triple Dream**[9] 2561 8-9-6 **79** ... (tp) MatthewLawson(5) 10 — 27
(Milton Bradley) *chsd ldrs: rdn 3f out: wknd over 2f out* **12/1**

1m 11.07s (-0.13) **Going Correction** +0.125s/f (Good)
WFA 3 from 5yo+ 9lb — **11 Ran SP% 120.6**
Speed ratings (Par 105): **105,104,104,103,103 102,101,95,90,82 81**
Tote Swingers 1&2 £42.70, 2&3 £14.60, 1&3 £22.20 CSF £141.76 CT £1135.23 TOTE £22.90: £6.60, £4.00, £2.60; EX 230.40 Trifecta £795.80 Part won. Pool: £1,061.16 - 0.01 winning tickets..
Owner Pyle & Hollinshead **Bred** M Pyle & Mrs T Pyle **Trained** Upper Longdon, Staffs
■ Stewards' Enquiry : Jack Duern two-day ban; used whip above permitted level.

FOCUS
There was a bunch finish in this sprint handicap, which was run at a good pace. They finished in a heap but the form makes sense.

2826 BATH ALES SALAMANDER H'CAP — 1m 2f 46y
7:25 (7:31) (Class 5) (0-70,68) 4-Y-O+ — **£2,587** (£770; £384; £192) **Stalls** Low

Form — RPR

4033 **1** **Perfect Cracker**[14] 2417 5-9-2 **68** RyanTate(5) 7 — 80
(Clive Cox) *in tch: outpcd 4f out: hdwy over 2f out: led over 1f out: drvn clr* **7/4**[1]

0342 **2** 3 ½ **Pandorica**[17] 2349 5-8-13 **67** (p) DanielMuscutt(7) 5 — 72
(Bernard Llewellyn) *chsd ldr: rdn to chal wl over 1f out: nt pce of wnr ins fnl f but kpt on to hold 2nd* **5/1**[3]

1425 **3** ¾ **Mazij**[21] 2234 5-9-1 **62** WilliamCarson 4 — 66
(Peter Hiatt) *led: rdn over 2f out: hdd over 1f out: kpt on same pce for 3rd ins fnl f* **8/1**

-012 **4** nk **April Ciel**[17] 2348 4-9-1 **67** EDLinehan(5) 1 — 70
(Ronald Harris) *disp 2nd tl n.m.r on rails and t.k.h over 5f out: rdn and one pce wl over 2f out: styd on same pce* **5/2**[2]

0460 **5** 1 ¼ **Bold Cross (IRE)**[4] 2710 10-8-12 **62** MarkCoumbe(3) 6 — 63
(Edward Bevan) *in rr: hdwy 5f out to cl on ldrs 4f out: rdn 3f out: outpcd u.p fnl 2f* **14/1**

2m 11.04s (0.04) **Going Correction** +0.125s/f (Good) **5** Ran SP% **99.4**
Speed ratings (Par 103): **104,101,100,100,99**
CSF £8.34 TOTE £2.00: £1.90, £1.40; EX 8.70 Trifecta £60.50 Pool: £570.35 - 7.05 winning tickets..
Owner Mildmay Racing **Bred** Mildmay Bloodstock Ltd **Trained** Lambourn, Berks
■ Drummond was withdrawn (9-2, broke out of stalls). Deduct 15p in the £ under R4.
■ Stewards' Enquiry : Daniel Muscutt four-day ban; used whip above permitted level (14th-17th June).

FOCUS
The went a steady pace in this minor handicap but the winner score in good style under a waiting ride. He's rated back towards his better turf form.

2827 BATH ALES BREWERY CLASSIFIED STKS — 1m 2f 46y
8:00 (8:00) (Class 6) 3-Y-O — **£2,045** (£603; £302) **Stalls** Low

Form — RPR

02-0 **1** **Northern Star (IRE)**[20] 2261 3-9-0 75 RichardKingscote 2 — 85+
(Tom Dascombe) *mde all: drvn and hrd pressed ins fnl f: hld on all out* **2/1**[1]

43-3 **2** hd **Interior Minister**[38] 1754 3-9-0 74 CathyGannon 4 — 84+
(Jo Hughes) *chsd ldrs: wnt 2nd 2f out: styd on wl u.p fnl f to chal fnl 100yds: nt quite get up* **7/2**[3]

40-4 **3** 6 **Arlecchino (IRE)**[20] 2271 3-9-0 74 RoystonFfrench 6 — 73
(Ed McMahon) *chsd wnr: rdn over 2f out: sn dropped to 3rd: wknd u.p over 1f out* **8/1**

2210 **4** 1 ¼ **Excellent Puck (IRE)**[23] 2153 3-9-0 75 FergusSweeney 1 — 71
(Jamie Osborne) *sn chsng ldrs: rdn over 2f out: sn btn* **9/4**[2]

530- **5** 3 ¼ **Mick Duggan**[170] 8072 3-9-0 72 WilliamCarson 3 — 64
(Simon Hodgson) *s.i.s: in rr: rdn over 3f out: no prog and wknd 2f out* **25/1**

213 **6** 6 **Back On The Trail**[31] 1903 3-9-0 75 SteveDrowne 5 — 53
(Michael Blake) *in rr but in tch: rdn over 3f out: sn btn* **7/1**

2m 12.44s (1.44) **Going Correction** +0.125s/f (Good) **6** Ran SP% **113.8**
Speed ratings (Par 97): **99,98,94,93,90 85**
Tote Swingers 1&2 £1.80, 2&3 £13.20, 1&3 £4.00 CSF £9.63 TOTE £3.10: £1.80, £2.50; EX 12.50 Trifecta £95.60 Pool: £761.98 - 5.97 winning tickets..
Owner D Ward **Bred** Slow Sand Syndicate **Trained** Malpas, Cheshire

FOCUS
There was a tight finish in this classified event and the first two pulled clear. A slightly positive view has been taken of the form.

2828 BATH ALES GRAZE BAR AND CHOP HOUSE H'CAP — 1m 5f 22y
8:30 (8:30) (Class 6) (0-60,59) 4-Y-O+ — **£1,940** (£577; £288; £144) **Stalls** High

Form — RPR

26-6 **1** **Kashgar**[17] 2350 4-9-0 **59** SiobhanMiller(7) 13 — 71
(Bernard Llewellyn) *in rr: hdwy on outside 3f out: rdn and hung lft over 2f out: kpt on over 1f out and sn pressing ldr: led fnl 120yds: styd on strly* **16/1**

1205 **2** 2 **Party Palace**[3] 1040 9-8-5 **48** NatashaEaton(5) 5 — 57
(Stuart Howe) *chsd ldrs: chal 2f out tl led appr fnl f: hdd and outpcd fnl 120yds* **9/2**[2]

60-4 **3** 1 ½ **Golden Jubilee (USA)**[17] 2350 4-8-12 **55**(b) WilliamTwiston-Davies(5) 3 — 62
(Nigel Twiston-Davies) *narrow ldr but sn jnd: rdn and narrow advantage over 2f out: hdd u.p over 1f out: styd on same pce* **8/1**

0114 **4** shd **Midnight Sequel**[38] 1342 4-9-1 **53** SteveDrowne 11 — 59
(Michael Blake) *in rr and drvn along fr 6f out: hdwy fr 2f out: kpt on u.p to take one pce 3rd fnl 110yds* **14/1**

033- **5** 1 ¾ **Arch Event**[83] 7377 8-8-7 **52** (p) DanielMuscutt(7) 10 — 56
(Bernard Llewellyn) *in tch: chsd ldrs 6f out: chal over 2f out tl over 1f out: wknd ins fnl f* **12/1**

404 **6** 1 ¼ **Hell Hath No Fury**[34] 1826 4-8-12 **50** (v[1]) AndrewMullen 2 — 53
(Michael Appleby) *chsd ldrs: rdn over 3f out: styd on same pce fnl 2f* **11/4**[1]

2065 **7** nk **Dream Prospector**[18] 2328 4-9-0 **52** FergusSweeney 1 — 53
(James Evans) *in rr: drvn over 3f out: sme hdwy fr 2f out: nvr rchd ldrs* **8/1**

2133 **8** 2 ¼ **Thane Of Cawdor (IRE)**[39] 1715 4-9-6 **58** LiamKeniry 6 — 56
(Joseph Tuite) *chsd ldrs: rdn 3f out: wknd ins fnl 2f* **7/1**[3]

100 **9** 7 **Sir Dylan**[29] 789 4-9-0 **57** EDLinehan(5) 7 — 43
(Ronald Harris) *t.k.h in rr: hdwy to cl on ldrs 3f out: wknd 2f out* **20/1**

030- **10** 12 **Kozmina Bay**[55] 7196 4-8-7 **52** (p) JoeyHaynes(7) 4 — 19
(Bernard Llewellyn) *bhd most of way* **25/1**

0-60 **11** ½ **Madam Tessa (IRE)**[29] 1949 5-8-7 **45** DavidProbert 9 — 11
(Tim Vaughan) *pressed ldr to 3f out: sn wknd* **20/1**

/0-0 **12** 2 ¼ **Balaton**[29] 1953 4-8-7 **45** (b[1]) MartinDwyer 12
(William Muir) *chsd ldrs tl wknd and hmpd 4f out* **33/1**

00-3 **13** 4 **Transfer**[19] 1297 8-9-4 **56** WilliamCarson 8
(Richard Price) *t.k.h: chsd ldrs: wknd over 3f out* **10/1**

2m 54.19s (2.19) **Going Correction** +0.125s/f (Good) **13** Ran SP% **125.2**
Speed ratings (Par 101): **98,96,95,95,94 93,93,92,88,80 80,78,76**
Tote Swingers 1&2 £13.10, 2&3 £14.60, 1&3 £31.10 CSF £86.70 CT £645.96 TOTE £20.30: £7.40, £2.00, £2.30; EX 143.70 Trifecta £294.30 Part won. Pool: £392.49 - 0.13 winning tickets..
Owner Alex James & B J Llewellyn **Bred** J L C Pearce **Trained** Fochriw, Caerphilly

FOCUS
They went a good pace in this handicap and the big-priced winner forged clear. He was entitled to win this ordinary race on the pick of his form.

2829 BATH ALES GEM FILLIES' H'CAP — 5f 11y
9:00 (9:00) (Class 5) (0-70,69) 3-Y-O — **£2,587** (£770; £384; £192) **Stalls** Centre

Form — RPR

120- **1** **Spray Tan**[235] 6929 3-8-12 **60** SeanLevey 7 — 65
(Tony Carroll) *t.k.h: trckd ldrs: drvn to ld fnl 50yds: kpt on wl* **20/1**

3-22 **2** nk **Silverrica (IRE)**[16] 2363 3-9-4 **66** TomMcLaughlin 9 — 70
(Malcolm Saunders) *t.k.h: trckd ldrs: rdn to ld 1f out: hdd and hung rt fnl 50yds* **6/1**

2-30 **3** 1 **Little Choosey**[15] 2394 3-9-1 **68** RyanTate(5) 3 — 68
(Clive Cox) *in rr: pushed along over 2f out: hdwy over 1f out: briefly nt clr run fnl 110yds: fin wl* **20/1**

-044 **4** ¾ **Starlight Angel (IRE)**[9] 2572 3-9-2 **69** EDLinehan(5) 6 — 67
(Ronald Harris) *chsd ldrs: rdn over 2f out: one pce fnl f* **8/1**

4121 **5** hd **Batchworth Lady**[17] 2347 3-9-2 **64** JimmyQuinn 11 — 61
(Dean Ivory) *in rr: rdn over 2f out: hdwy over 1f out: styd on wl fnl f: nvr gng pce to rch ldrs* **9/2**[2]

1211 **6** ¾ **Shirley's Pride**[7] 2623 3-9-5 **67** 6ex (t) AndrewMullen 4 — 61
(Michael Appleby) *pressed ldr: led appr fnl 2f: hdd 1f out: sn btn* **2/1**[1]

-420 **7** 4 ½ **Sibaya**[26] 2051 3-8-8 **61** RobertTart(5) 2 — 39
(Roger Charlton) *sn narrow ld: rdn hdd and edgd lft appr fnl 2f: sn btn* **5/1**[3]

540- **8** hd **Koharu**[177] 7989 3-8-7 **55** oh1 (t) JohnFahy 10 — 32
(Peter Makin) *pressed ldrs: rdn over 2f out: wknd wl over 1f out* **25/1**

0-01 **9** hd **Edged Out**[28] 1978 3-9-7 **69** DavidProbert 12 — 46
(Christopher Mason) *pressed ldrs: rdn over 2f out: wknd wl over 1f out* **8/1**

50-0 **10** 3 **Grace Hull**[9] 2572 3-9-7 **69** LiamKeniry 8 — 35
(J S Moore) *spd 3f* **33/1**

1m 3.54s (1.04) **Going Correction** +0.125s/f (Good) **10** Ran SP% **121.0**
Speed ratings (Par 96): **96,95,93,92,92 91,84,83,83,78**
Tote Swingers 1&2 £23.30, 2&3 £12.30, 1&3 £73.60 CSF £134.43 CT £2507.93 TOTE £21.70: £4.50, £2.00, £2.50; EX 117.00 Trifecta £393.40 Pool: £1,118.90 - 2.13 winning tickets..
Owner Lady Whent **Bred** Lady Whent **Trained** Cropthorne, Worcs

FOCUS
The leaders went off fast in this fillies' sprint handicap and the first three all came from off the pace. The form amongst the principals makes sense.
T/Plt: £60.00 to a £1 stake. Pool of £64,074.99 - 779.06 winning tickets. T/Qpdt: £70.80 to a £1 stake. Pool of £4,980.17 - 51.99 winning tickets. ST

2611 CATTERICK (L-H)
Friday, May 31

OFFICIAL GOING: Good to soft (good in places; 8.1)
Wind: Virtually nil Weather: Cloudy with sunny periods

2830 IRISH STALLION FARMS EBF MAIDEN STKS — 5f
1:45 (1:45) (Class 5) 2-Y-O — **£2,911** (£866; £432; £216) **Stalls** Low

Form — RPR

1 **Race Hunter (USA)** 2-9-0 0 HarryBentley 5 — 80+
(David Barron) *trckd ldng pair: cl up 1/2-way: chal over 1f out: pushed ahd last 100yds: kpt on strly: readily* **13/8**[2]

3 **2** 2 ¼ **Lord Clyde**[70] 1108 2-9-5 0 TonyHamilton 1 — 74+
(Richard Fahey) *led: pushed along and jnd wl over 1f out: rdn ent fnl f: hdd and kpt on same pce last 100yds* **6/5**[1]

20 **3** 2 ¾ **Hello Beautiful (IRE)**[34] 1839 2-9-0 0 PJMcDonald 3 — 59
(Ann Duffield) *trckd ldr: cl up 1/2-way: rdn along wl over 1f out: sn one pce* **5/1**[3]

4 5 **Think Again** 2-9-0 0 PhillipMakin 4 — 41+
(Kevin Ryan) *s.i.s and bhd: hdwy over 2f out: kpt on appr fnl f: bttr for r* **14/1**

0 **5** 14 **Gerdani**[17] 2337 2-9-0 0 PaulMulrennan 6
(Michael Easterby) *chsd ldrs: sn pushed along and outpcd: bhd fr 1/2-way* **66/1**

1m 0.67s (0.87) **Going Correction** -0.025s/f (Good) **5** Ran SP% **108.4**
Speed ratings (Par 93): **92,88,84,76,53**
CSF £3.78 TOTE £1.80: £1.20, £1.20; EX 3.80 Trifecta £7.60 Pool: £1290.61 - 127.19 winning units..
Owner Qatar Racing Limited **Bred** Bruce Berenson & Laurie Berenson **Trained** Maunby, N Yorks

FOCUS
Paul Mulrennan described the ground as just on the soft side of good after the first. The winner posted quite useful form and the runner-up built on his Brocklesby debut.

2831 YORKSHIRE-OUTDOORS.CO.UK (S) STKS — 1m 5f 175y
2:20 (2:20) (Class 6) 4-Y-O+ — **£2,385** (£704; £352) **Stalls** Low

Form — RPR

50-4 **1** **Underwritten**[11] 2509 4-8-12 69 (v) GrahamLee 4 — 63
(Donald McCain) *mde all: set sound pce: pushed along and qcknd wl over 2f out: jnd and rdn wl over 1f out: drvn ins fnl f: n.m.r and kpt on wl towards fin* **7/2**[3]

00/5 **2** nk **Spiekeroog**[28] 1993 7-8-12 65 (v) DavidNolan 2 — 63
(David O'Meara) *hld up in rr: hdwy on outer after 3f to trck ldng pair: tk clsr order over 4f out: cl up 3f out: rdn to chal wl over 1f out: ev ch tl drvn ins fnl f: edgd lft and no ex nr fin* **2/1**[1]

2/4 **3** 2 ¼ **Summerlea (IRE)**[18] 2313 7-8-12 55 DuranFentiman 1 — 60
(Patrick Holmes) *trckd ldrs on inner: n.m.r and lost pl bnd 4f out: swtchd to outer and rdn wl over 2f out: styd on fr over 1f out: drvn and one pce ins fnl f* **8/1**

0-25 **4** 4 **Eijaaz (IRE)**[24] 2118 12-8-9 58 (p) RaulDaSilva(3) 5 — 54
(Geoffrey Harker) *trckd ldrs: hdwy 3f out: effrt 2f out: rdn over 1f out: wknd ent fnl f* **3/1**[2]

34 **5** 9 **Munro Bagger (IRE)**[21] 2237 4-8-5 0 (p) JoeDoyle(7) 3 — 40
(John Quinn) *t.k.h: trckd wnr: pushed along over 4f out: rdn 3f out: drvn 2f out: sn wknd* **11/2**

3m 5.44s (1.84) **Going Correction** -0.025s/f (Good) **5** Ran SP% **107.1**
Speed ratings (Par 101): **93,92,91,89,84**
CSF £10.27 TOTE £5.00: £2.40, £1.20; EX 12.10 Trifecta £45.50 Pool: £1687.57 - 27.80 winning units..There was no bid for the winner
Owner D McCain Jnr **Bred** W And R Barnett Ltd **Trained** Cholmondeley, Cheshire

FOCUS
An ordinary seller run at a modest pace in which the winner made all. He's rated close to his best Flat form for McCain.

2832 LIONWELD KENNEDY H'CAP — 5f
2:55 (2:56) (Class 5) (0-70,70) 3-Y-0+ — **£2,911** (£866; £432; £216) **Stalls** Low

Form — RPR

0002 **1** — **Lost In Paris (IRE)**[7] 2614 7-9-12 **70**.....(p) DavidAllan 5 — 80
(Tim Easterby) *trckd ldng pair: hdwy to ld wl over 1f out: rdn and edgd lft jst ins fnl f: kpt on wl* **3/1**[1]

6-50 **2** 1 **Mercers Row**[20] 2275 6-9-4 **69**..... GemmaTutty(7) 7 — 75
(Karen Tutty) *trckd ldrs: n.m.r and swtchd lft wl over 1f out: sn rdn to chal and ev ch ins fnl f: kpt on same pce* **10/1**

135- **3** 1 **Ypres**[258] 6264 4-9-4 **65**..... RaulDaSilva(3) 10 — 68+
(Jason Ward) *towards rr: hdwy 2f out: swtchd rt and rdn over 1f out: styd on wl fnl f* **12/1**

1110 **4** 2 ¼ **Chosen One (IRE)**[17] 2343 8-9-9 **67**..... PJMcDonald 8 — 62
(Ruth Carr) *chsd ldrs: rdn along wl over 1f out: drvn and one pce fnl f* **15/2**[3]

40-0 **5** ¾ **Rat Catcher (IRE)**[43] 1647 3-8-10 **65**.....(b) DeclanCannon(3) 4 — 57
(Andrew Crook) *towards rr: rdn along on inner over 2f out: styd on u.p fnl f: nrst fin* **66/1**

0000 **6** 1 ½ **Amenable (IRE)**[23] 2170 6-9-2 **60**..... GrahamLee 15 — 47
(Violet M Jordan) *in rr: hdwy on wd outside wl over 1f out: sn rdn and kpt on fnl f: nrst fin* **25/1**

232 **7** nse **Modern Lady**[58] 1315 3-8-7 **66**..... LisaTodd(7) 1 — 52
(Richard Guest) *slt ld: rdn along and edgd rt 2f out: hdd wl over 1f out and grad wknd* **16/1**

0606 **8** ¾ **Sleepy Blue Ocean**[10] 2550 7-9-8 **66**.....(p) PaulMulrennan 13 — 50
(John Balding) *chsd ldrs: rdn along wl over 1f out: grad wknd* **16/1**

-142 **9** 1 ½ **Monnoyer**[10] 2550 4-9-6 **67**.....(be) BillyCray(3) 2 — 45
(Scott Dixon) *cl up: rdn along over 2f out: sn drvn and wknd* **10/3**[2]

110- **10** ½ **Lizzy's Dream**[257] 6288 5-9-6 **64**..... RobertWinston 6 — 45
(Robin Bastiman) *s.i.s: a in rr* **12/1**

0-04 **11** hd **Tom Sawyer**[24] 2132 5-9-9 **67**.....(b) TomEaves 11 — 43
(Julie Camacho) *dwlt and towards rr: rapid hdwy to chse ldrs after 1 1/2f: rdn wl over 1f out: sn wknd* **11/1**

400- **12** shd **Koolgreycat (IRE)**[256] 6314 4-8-12 **56**..... DuranFentiman 9 — 34
(Noel Wilson) *a towards rr* **40/1**

2006 **13** hd **Boucher Garcon (IRE)**[12] 2479 5-9-0 **61**..... NeilFarley(3) 12 — 36
(Declan Carroll) *midfield: rdn along 2f out: sn wknd* **18/1**

1m 1.19s (1.39) **Going Correction** -0.025s/f (Good)
WFA 3 from 4yo+ 8lb — **13** Ran SP% **117.5**
Speed ratings (Par 103): **87,85,83,80,79 76,76,75,72,72 71,71,71**
toteswingers 1&2 £12.50, 1&3 £13.50, 2&3 £55.00 CSF £32.50 CT £319.18 TOTE £4.40: £2.10, £4.20, £3.30; EX 38.30 Trifecta £915.70 Part won. Pool: £1220.96 - 0.24 winning units..
Owner W H Ponsonby **Bred** Yeomanstown Stud **Trained** Great Habton, N Yorks

FOCUS
A modest sprint handicap. The gallop was sound but not many challenged from off the pace. Straightforward form, with the winner looking as good as ever.

2833 RACINGUK.COM MAIDEN STKS — 1m 3f 214y
3:30 (3:35) (Class 5) 3-Y-0+ — **£2,911** (£866; £432; £216) **Stalls** Low

Form — RPR

452- **1** — **Hawk High (IRE)**[206] 7598 3-8-11 68..... DavidAllan 2 — 72+
(Tim Easterby) *trckd ldrs: hdwy to chse ldr 4f out: rdn 2f out: drvn to chal ent fnl f: styd on u.p to ld nr line* **5/2**[2]

3-54 **2** hd **Dalgig**[23] 2151 3-8-11 81..... GrahamLee 11 — 72
(Jamie Osborne) *sn led: pushed along 2f out: rdn ent fnl f: sn drvn: hdd and no ex nr line* **10/11**[1]

55 **3** 4 **Attention Seaker**[13] 2465 3-8-6 0..... DuranFentiman 1 — 60+
(Tim Easterby) *in tch: hdwy to trck ldrs over 4f out: chsd ldng pair 3f out: rdn wl over 1f out: kpt on same pce* **50/1**

4 3 **Down Time (USA)** 3-8-11 0..... HarryBentley 4 — 60+
(Jamie Osborne) *hld up: hdwy over 4f out: chsd ldrs 3f out: rdn over 2f out and sn no imp* **14/1**

0 **5** 14 **Teenage Idol (IRE)**[7] 2628 9-9-11 0..... LucyAlexander(3) 3 — 39
(Dianne Sayer) *s.i.s and in rr tl styd on fnl 3f: n.d* **25/1**

0-6 **6** nk **King's Request (IRE)**[39] 1727 3-8-11 0..... TomEaves 8 — 38
(Sir Michael Stoute) *sn chsng ldr: rdn along over 4f out: wknd 3f out* **11/2**[3]

00-0 **7** 12 **Roc Fort**[13] 2462 4-10-0 34..... PaddyAspell 6 — 19
(James Moffatt) *midfield: rdn along over 4f out: sn outpcd* **100/1**

0 **8** 1 ½ **Whistle We Go (GER)**[20] 2279 5-9-9 0..... MichaelStainton 5 — 11
(Nick Kent) *chsd ldrs: rdn along 4f out: sn wknd* **100/1**

9 21 **Fridaynight Girl (IRE)** 4-9-9 0..... RobertWinston 7
(Alan Swinbank) *midfield: rdn along 1/2-way: sn outpcd and bhd* **25/1**

10 49 **Sunny Reagh** 8-9-9 0..... JamesSullivan 9
(Tim Etherington) *s.i.s: green and flashed tail: a bhd: t.o fnl 3f* **100/1**

11 34 **The Red Arctic** 3-8-11 0..... AmyRyan 10
(Lisa Williamson) *sn outpcd and a bhd: t.o fnl 3f* **50/1**

2m 38.76s (-0.14) **Going Correction** -0.025s/f (Good)
WFA 3 from 4yo+ 17lb — **11** Ran SP% **117.6**
Speed ratings (Par 103): **99,98,96,94,84 84,76,75,61,29 6**
toteswingers 1&2 £1.10, 1&3 £19.70, 2&3 £11.60 CSF £4.91 TOTE £3.50: £1.50, £1.10, £9.20; EX 6.00 Trifecta £103.50 Pool: £4236.59 - 30.68 winning units..
Owner Trevor Hemmings **Bred** Gleadhill House Stud Ltd **Trained** Great Habton, N Yorks
■ Stewards' Enquiry : James Sullivan caution; entered wrong stall.

FOCUS
Little depth to this maiden which was dominated by the 3yos. The time and the first three guide the level of the form.

2834 PIN POINT RECRUITMENT H'CAP — 5f 212y
4:10 (4:11) (Class 4) (0-85,85) 4-Y-0+ — **£6,469** (£1,925; £962; £481) **Stalls** Low

Form — RPR

-222 **1** — **Meandmyshadow**[6] 2664 5-8-12 **75**..... DaleSwift 6 — 85
(Alan Brown) *mde all: rdn over 1f out: drvn and edgd lft ins fnl f: hld on gamely* **4/1**[1]

2250 **2** ¾ **Free Spin (IRE)**[48] 1542 4-9-0 **82**..... LMcNiff(5) 1 — 90
(David Barron) *trckd ldrs: effrt 2f out: rdn over 1f out: drvn and ev ch ins fnl f: no ex towards fin* **9/2**[2]

0550 **3** ½ **Solar Spirit (IRE)**[4] 2705 8-9-0 **77**..... BarryMcHugh 3 — 85
(Tracy Waggott) *dwlt: sn in tch on inner: hdwy 2f out: chsd ldrs over 1f out: effrt whn nt clr run and hmpd ins fnl f: swtchd rt and kpt on wl towards fin* **8/1**

6603 **4** nse **Mappin Time (IRE)**[6] 2664 5-9-3 **80**.....(p) DavidAllan 2 — 86
(Tim Easterby) *trckd ldrs: effrt 2f out: rdn over 1f out: drvn and kpt on fnl f tl eased sltly and lost 3rd on line* **9/2**[2]

06-1 **5** 1 ½ **Lucky Numbers (IRE)**[7] 2614 7-9-8 **85** 6ex..... DavidNolan 8 — 86
(David O'Meara) *cl up: rdn wl over 1f out: drvn and wknd ent fnl f* **8/1**

3000 **6** hd **Head Space (IRE)**[13] 2460 5-9-7 **84**..... JamesSullivan 10 — 84+
(Ruth Carr) *hld up towards rr: hdwy on wd outside wl over 1f out: sn rdn and kpt on fnl f: nrst fin* **16/1**

-050 **7** ½ **Green Park (IRE)**[21] 2239 10-8-9 **77**.....(b) JasonHart(5) 11 — 76
(Declan Carroll) *towards rr: hdwy 2f out: sn rdn and kpt on fnl f: nrst fin* **25/1**

0550 **8** 1 **Captain Scooby**[14] 2410 7-8-8 **71**..... RobbieFitzpatrick 7 — 67
(Richard Guest) *midfield: pushed along 2f out: rdn wl over 1f out: kpt on fnl f* **40/1**

-006 **9** ¾ **Dark Castle**[13] 2441 4-8-12 **75**..... PJMcDonald 9 — 68
(Micky Hammond) *chsd ldrs on outer: rdn along over 2f out: sn wknd* **15/2**[3]

0-00 **10** ½ **Breezolini**[27] 2031 5-8-6 **72**..... RaulDaSilva(3) 5 — 64
(Geoffrey Harker) *in rr: hdwy wl over 1f out: sn rdn and kpt on fnl f: n.d* **20/1**

104 **11** ¾ **Al Khan (IRE)**[21] 2214 4-9-4 **81**.....(p) GrahamLee 4 — 70
(Violet M Jordan) *chsd ldrs: rdn along 2f out: sn drvn and wknd over 1f out* **11/1**

-300 **12** 19 **New Leyf (IRE)**[13] 2460 7-9-0 **77**.....(b) AdrianNicholls 12
(David Nicholls) *wnt rt s: racd wd: towards rr: effrt 2f out: sn rdn: bhd and eased fnl f* **33/1**

1m 13.45s (-0.15) **Going Correction** -0.025s/f (Good) — **12** Ran SP% **118.6**
Speed ratings (Par 105): **100,99,98,98,96 96,95,94,93,92 91,66**
toteswingers 1&2 £2.70, 1&3 £10.70, 2&3 £10.50 CSF £20.71 CT £141.28 TOTE £3.10: £1.70, £1.80, £4.10; EX 18.50 Trifecta £209.50 Pool: £2935.00 - 10.50 winning units..
Owner G Morrill **Bred** M J Dawson **Trained** Yedingham, N Yorks
■ Stewards' Enquiry : David Allan 10-day ban; failing to ride out (14th-23rd June).

FOCUS
A decent sprint handicap. The winner registered a career-best in making all and the form is straightforward.

2835 GO RACING IN YORKSHIRE H'CAP — 5f 212y
4:35 (4:35) (Class 6) (0-65,65) 3-Y-0+ — **£2,385** (£704; £352) **Stalls** Low

Form — RPR

0-30 **1** — **Needy McCredie**[4] 2703 7-9-3 **56**..... GrahamLee 8 — 66
(James Turner) *trckd ldrs: hdwy 2f out: rdn ent fnl f: styd on to ld last 75yds* **8/1**[3]

040- **2** ¾ **Lady Kildare (IRE)**[177] 7990 5-9-1 **54**..... TomEaves 10 — 62
(Jedd O'Keeffe) *led: rdn along wl over 2f out: drvn ins fnl f: hdd and no ex last 75yds* **16/1**

40-3 **3** 1 **Mcmonagle (USA)**[23] 2162 5-9-9 **62**.....(bt) DaleSwift 6 — 66
(Alan Brown) *chsd ldr: cl up wl over 1f out: sn rdn and ev ch tl drvn and one pce ins fnl f* **7/2**[2]

0-04 **4** nse **Baltic Bomber (IRE)**[17] 2343 4-9-9 **62**.....(v) MichaelO'Connell 3 — 66
(John Quinn) *trckd ldrs on inner: hdwy 2f out: rdn over 1f out: drvn and ch ins fnl f: wknd last 75yds* **17/2**

-003 **5** 1 **Celestial Dawn**[26] 2037 4-9-5 **58**..... JamesSullivan 1 — 59+
(John Weymes) *in rr: hdwy on outer wl over 1f out: sn rdn and styd on wl fnl f: nrst fin* **17/2**

000- **6** 1 ¾ **Sinai (IRE)**[280] 5538 4-9-0 **60**..... JordanNason(7) 2 — 55
(Geoffrey Harker) *dwlt: sn in tch: rdn to chse ldrs: edgd rt and one pce appr fnl f* **10/1**

141 **7** ½ **Dartrix**[21] 2217 4-9-5 **65**..... ConnorBeasley(7) 4 — 59
(Michael Dods) *a towards rr* **9/4**[1]

0403 **8** ½ **Lord Buffhead**[7] 2611 4-8-10 **56**.....(b) LisaTodd(7) 9 — 48
(Richard Guest) *a towards rr* **14/1**

01-0 **9** 1 ¼ **Ryedane (IRE)**[20] 2276 11-9-4 **64**.....(b) RachelRichardson(7) 11 — 52
(Tim Easterby) *chsd ldrs: rdn along 2f out: sn wknd* **22/1**

0500 **10** 6 **Ivestar (IRE)**[10] 2550 8-9-2 **62**.....(vt) MatthewHopkins(7) 5 — 31
(Michael Easterby) *a towards rr* **16/1**

1m 13.8s (0.20) **Going Correction** -0.025s/f (Good) — **10** Ran SP% **117.0**
Speed ratings (Par 101): **97,96,94,94,93 90,90,89,87,79**
toteswingers 1&2 £19.30, 1&3 £3.60, 2&3 £8.70 CSF £127.46 CT £531.54 TOTE £7.70: £3.00, £6.80, £2.00; EX 134.30 Trifecta £791.60 Pool: £3692.45 - 3.45 winning units..
Owner J R Turner **Bred** Mrs C M Brown **Trained** Norton-le-Clay, N Yorks

FOCUS
A modest handicap but the pace was sound. The winner is rated to her level from this time last year.

2836 RACING AGAIN SATURDAY 8TH JUNE H'CAP (DIV I) — 7f
5:10 (5:10) (Class 5) (0-70,70) 3-Y-0+ — **£3,067** (£905; £453) **Stalls** Centre

Form — RPR

-010 **1** — **Macaabra (IRE)**[18] 2329 3-8-10 **63**..... PaulMulrennan 6 — 73+
(James Tate) *mde all at solid pce: rdn clr wl over 1f out: eased towards fin* **11/2**[3]

-030 **2** 1 ¼ **West Leake Hare (IRE)**[20] 2278 4-9-4 **60**..... AdrianNicholls 2 — 70
(David Nicholls) *chsd wnr: rdn wl over 1f out: drvn and no imp fnl f* **4/1**[2]

3442 **3** nk **Rangi**[3] 2756 3-8-10 **70**.....(b[1]) DavidSimmonson(7) 1 — 75
(Tony Coyle) *hld up in tch: hdwy wl over 2f out: rdn wl over 1f out: drvn and one pce fnl f* **11/8**[1]

0401 **4** 3 ½ **Powerful Pierre**[55] 1397 6-9-7 **63**.....(b) DavidNolan 8 — 63
(Ian McInnes) *towards rr: hdwy wl over 1f out: sn rdn: kpt on fnl f: nrst fin* **16/1**

-000 **5** ½ **Mick Slates (IRE)**[14] 2406 4-9-8 **67**..... NeilFarley(3) 4 — 66
(Declan Carroll) *in rr: hdwy 2f out: sn rdn and kpt on fnl f: nrst fin* **7/1**

00-4 **6** 3 **Don't Tell**[24] 2121 3-8-3 **56** oh10..... JamesSullivan 5 — 43
(George Moore) *chsd wnr: rdn along over 2f out: drvn and wknd over 1f out* **50/1**

06-0 **7** nk **Last Supper**[21] 2219 4-9-1 **62**.....(p) GeorgeChaloner(5) 3 — 52
(James Bethell) *chsd ldrs: rdn along 2f out: sn drvn and wknd: bled fr nose* **25/1**

000- **8** nk **Rub Of The Relic (IRE)**[263] 6103 8-9-5 **61**.....(v) BarryMcHugh 7 — 50
(Paul Midgley) *a towards rr* **33/1**

0603 **9** 3 ¼ **Glenridding**[32] 1887 9-9-6 **62**.....(p) GrahamLee 10 — 43
(James Given) *chsd ldrs: rdn along 1/2-way: sn wknd* **17/2**

1m 26.6s (-0.40) **Going Correction** -0.025s/f (Good)
WFA 3 from 4yo+ 11lb — **9** Ran SP% **115.1**
Speed ratings (Par 103): **101,99,99,95,94 91,90,90,86**
toteswingers 1&2 £3.70, 1&3 £2.20, 2&3 £2.50 CSF £27.24 CT £46.57 TOTE £6.00: £2.20, £1.60, £1.20; EX 37.00 Trifecta £72.30 Pool: £3499.81 - 36.27 winning units..
Owner Saif Ali **Bred** Rabbah Bloodstock Limited **Trained** Newmarket, Suffolk

FOCUS
A modest handicap and another race on the card when the winner made all. The second and third are the key to the form.

2837 RACING AGAIN SATURDAY 8TH JUNE H'CAP (DIV II) 7f
5:40 (5:41) (Class 5) (0-70,71) 3-Y-O+ **£3,067** (£905; £453) **Stalls** Centre

Form RPR
5-50 **1** **Just Paul (IRE)**[29] 1966 3-8-2 **56**.......... DeclanCannon(3) 6 66
(Philip Kirby) *trckd ldrs: hdwy over 2f out: rdn over 1f out: chsd ldr appr fnl f: sn drvn and styd on wl to ld last 40yds* **14/1**
3331 **2** *½* **Yahilwa (USA)**[9] 2576 3-9-6 **71** 6ex.......... PaulMulrennan 3 79
(James Tate) *led: rdn and clr over 1f out: drvn ins fnl f: hdd and no ex last 40yds* **11/2**
6001 **3** *3* **No Quarter (IRE)**[20] 2280 6-9-8 **62**.......... BarryMcHugh 8 66
(Tracy Waggott) *chsd ldrs: rdn along 2f out: drvn to chse ldng pair ent fnl f: sn no imp* **12/1**
06 **4** *4* **Decent Fella (IRE)**[29] 1952 7-9-13 **67**..........(tp) RobertWinston 1 60+
(Violet M Jordan) *hld up towards rr: hdwy wl over 2f out: sn rdn and no imp appr fnl f* **11/4**[1]
-565 **5** *1 ¼* **Viking Warrior (IRE)**[20] 2273 6-9-1 **62**.......... ConnorBeasley(7) 4 52
(Michael Dods) *cl up: rdn along over 2f out: drvn wl over 1f out and sn wknd* **4/1**[3]
2233 **6** *hd* **Cyflymder (IRE)**[9] 2574 7-9-9 **68**.......... ThomasBrown(5) 2 57
(David C Griffiths) *chsd ldng pair: rdn along over 2f out: drvn wl over 1f out and sn wknd* **8/1**
4542 **7** *2 ¼* **Mishhar (IRE)**[7] 2616 4-8-10 **57** ow1..........(v) DavidSimmonson(7) 7 40
(Tony Coyle) *hld up: hdwy over 2f out: rdn to chse ldrs on outer wl over 1f out: sn drvn and wknd* **10/3**[2]
00-6 **8** *nse* **Vale Of Clara (IRE)**[39] 1736 5-9-5 **59**.......... TomEaves 9 42
(Peter Niven) *a in rr* **50/1**
0-00 **9** *7* **Lady Del Sol**[14] 2409 5-9-9 **63**..........(b) PhillipMakin 5 27
(Marjorie Fife) *dwlt: a in rr* **50/1**

1m 26.27s (-0.73) **Going Correction** -0.025s/f (Good)
WFA 3 from 4yo+ 11lb 9 Ran SP% **114.5**
Speed ratings (Par 103): **103,102,99,94,93 92,90,90,82**
toteswingers 1&2 £9.00, 1&3 £10.80, 2&3 £7.10 CSF £88.16 CT £959.44 TOTE £8.60: £1.90, £2.60, £4.00; EX 69.10 Trifecta £838.90 Pool: £1673.69 - 1.49 winning units..
Owner Mr and Mrs Paul Chapman **Bred** Oghill House Stud **Trained** Middleham, N Yorks

FOCUS
They appeared to go a decent gallop, with the runner-up forcing the pace, but it still proved difficult to make ground. Only two 3yos were represented and they fought out the finish. The form could be rated 4lb higher through the third.
T/Plt: £35.30 to a £1 stake. Pool of £42,432.01 - 876.44 winning tickets. T/Qpdt: £19.20 to a £1 stake. Pool of £3671.79 - 141.25 winning tickets. JR

1765 EPSOM (L-H)
Friday, May 31

OFFICIAL GOING: Good to soft (6.7)
Rail dolled out up to 5yds from 1m to Winning Post adding 10yds to advertised distances.
Wind: light, across Weather: sunny

2838 PRINCESS ELIZABETH STKS (SPONSORED BY INVESTEC) (GROUP 3) (F&M) 1m 114y
1:35 (1:35) (Class 1) 3-Y-O+
£34,026 (£12,900; £6,456; £3,216; £1,614; £810) **Stalls** Low

Form RPR
12-3 **1** **Thistle Bird**[26] 2045 5-9-6 107.......... JamesDoyle 1 112
(Roger Charlton) *taken down early: chsd clr ldr: rdn 3f out: grad clsd and led over 1f out: kpt on wl and a holding rivals ins fnl f: rdn out* **3/1**[1]
61-1 **2** *¾* **Gifted Girl (IRE)**[20] 2253 4-9-6 104.......... TomQueally 9 110
(Paul Cole) *t.k.h: hld up in last quartet: rdn and effrt over 2f out: hdwy over 1f out: chsd wnr ins fnl f: r.o but a hld* **13/2**[3]
24-3 **3** *1* **Ladys First**[15] 2397 4-9-6 105.......... PaulHanagan 2 108
(Richard Fahey) *chsd ldng pair: effrt and rdn 3f out: grad clsd on ldr and chsd wnr over 1f out tl ins fnl f: one pce after* **9/1**
0-05 **4** *1 ¼* **Ighraa (IRE)**[33] 1869 3-8-7 105.......... MickaelBarzalona 8 107
(F-H Graffard, France) *t.k.h: hld up in last pair: swtchd rt and effrt ent fnl 2f: kpt on ins fnl f: nvr gng to rch ldrs* **17/2**
22-4 **5** *1 ¼* **Ultrasonic (USA)**[20] 2264 4-9-6 102.......... RyanMoore 6 102+
(Sir Michael Stoute) *hld up in last quartet: effrt on inner whn bdly hmpd 2f out: stl trying for inner run tl forced to switch rt arnd field 1f out: styd on: no threat to ldrs* **15/2**
24-4 **6** *1 ¼* **Starscope**[15] 2397 4-9-6 105.......... WilliamBuick 7 99+
(John Gosden) *stdd and awkward leaving stalls: t.k.h: hld up in rr: swtchd rt and effrt jst over 2f out: no imp tl kpt on ins fnl f: nvr trbld ldrs: sddle slipped* **7/1**
31-2 **7** *nk* **Sentaril**[27] 2015 4-9-6 103.......... JohnnyMurtagh 5 99
(William Haggas) *hld up in midfield: rdn and no imp over 2f out: styd on same pce and no threat to ldrs fnl 2f* **5/1**[2]
00-0 **8** *2* **Making Eyes (IRE)**[27] 2015 5-9-6 96.......... RichardHughes 3 94
(Hugo Palmer) *led and sn clr: qcknd gallop and wnt further clr on downhill run 5f out: rdn over 2f out: hdd over 1f out: sn btn: wknd ins fnl f* **33/1**
622- **9** *5* **Beatrice Aurore (IRE)**[250] 6518 5-9-6 105.......... FrankieDettori 4 90
(Ed Dunlop) *hld up in midfield: rdn and unable qck over 2f out: hanging lft down camber and struggling 2f out: bhd and eased ins fnl f* **17/2**

1m 46.9s (0.80) **Going Correction** +0.375s/f (Good)
WFA 3 from 4yo+ 13lb 9 Ran SP% **113.3**
Speed ratings (Par 113): **111,110,109,108,107 106,105,104,99**
toteswingers 1&2 £3.10, 1&3 £6.10, 2&3 £10.10 CSF £22.08 TOTE £3.60: £1.40, £2.30, £2.80; EX 19.60 Trifecta £87.30 Pool: £4224.50 - 36.26 winning units..
Owner Lady Rothschild **Bred** The Rt Hon Lord Rothschild **Trained** Beckhampton, Wilts

FOCUS
Following a dry night the going was given as good to soft, a view that appeared to be confirmed by the hand-timed first race. There was only one previous Group race winner in the line-up, but this was a competitive heat on paper, and it was run at a sound gallop thanks to Making Eyes. Pretty straightforward form. The third helps with the standard.

2839 INVESTEC WEALTH & INVESTMENT H'CAP 1m 2f 18y
2:10 (2:10) (Class 2) 4-Y-O+
£31,125 (£9,320; £4,660; £2,330; £1,165; £585) **Stalls** Low

Form RPR
022- **1** **Resurge (IRE)**[243] 6702 8-9-0 **94**..........(t) NeilCallan 12 102
(Stuart Kittow) *t.k.h: hld up in tch in last trio: hdwy 3f out: rdn to ld wl over 1f out: edgd lft on to rail 1f out: styd on wl fnl f: rdn out* **6/1**
0-14 **2** *1 ¼* **Area Fifty One**[22] 2185 5-9-7 **101**.......... JamieSpencer 4 107
(Richard Fahey) *in tch in midfield: shuffled bk to rr 4f out: hdwy u.p over 1f out: chsd wnr ins fnl f: kpt on but no imp towards fin* **4/1**[2]
4221 **3** *nk* **Tres Coronas (IRE)**[22] 2191 6-8-9 **89**.......... GrahamGibbons 5 94
(David Barron) *stdd s: t.k.h: hld up in tch in rr: hdwy and carried lft over 1f out: styng on wl whn nt clr run and swtchd rt ins fnl f: wnt 3rd cl home* **5/1**[3]
310- **4** *½* **Blue Surf**[202] 7689 4-9-4 **98**.......... PatDobbs 11 102
(Amanda Perrett) *chsd ldr for 2f: styd chsng ldrs: rdn and ev ch whn squeezed for room 2f out: chsd wnr and no ex over 1f out: one pce and lost 2 pls ins fnl f* **3/1**[1]
-020 **5** *½* **Fattsota**[41] 1674 5-9-10 **104**.......... FrankieDettori 7 107
(Marco Botti) *hld up in tch in last trio: effrt and trying to switch rt 2f out: hanging lft down camber and no imp over 1f out: rallied and kpt on ins fnl f* **9/1**
230- **6** *11* **Circumvent**[178] 7985 6-9-2 **96**.......... TomQueally 9 77
(Paul Cole) *wnt sltly lft s: led tl over 7f out: chsd ldr tl led again 3f out: sn drvn and hdd wl over 1f out: sn btn and fdd fnl f* **12/1**
1165 **7** *10* **Boonga Roogeta**[6] 2656 4-8-9 **94**.......... RosieJessop(5) 8 55
(Peter Charalambous) *dwlt and hmpd s: towards rr: grad rcvrd and led over 7f out: rdn and hdd 3f out: sn btn: wl bhd and eased ins fnl f* **16/1**
2-02 **8** *1* **Pilgrims Rest (IRE)**[22] 2193 4-8-9 **89** ow1.......... RichardHughes 2 55
(Richard Hannon) *in tch in midfield: effrt but struggling to qckn whn short of room and hmpd 2f out: sn btn: wl bhd and eased ins fnl f* **15/2**

2m 10.78s (1.08) **Going Correction** +0.375s/f (Good) 8 Ran SP% **111.3**
Speed ratings (Par 109): **110,109,108,108,107 99,91,90**
toteswingers 1&2 £5.50, 1&3 £4.90, 2&3 £4.90 CSF £28.52 TOTE £6.60: £2.00, £1.70, £2.00; EX 23.50 Trifecta £72.10 Pool: £3917.91 - 40.71 winning units..
Owner Chris & David Stam **Bred** Sweetmans Bloodstock **Trained** Blackborough, Devon

FOCUS
A race hit by five non-runners. The pace was solid enough and a reminder that previous course form counts for plenty here. Resurge is rated in line with last year's form.

2840 INVESTEC DIOMED STKS (GROUP 3) 1m 114y
2:45 (2:47) (Class 1) 3-Y-O+
£34,026 (£12,900; £6,456; £3,216; £1,614; £810) **Stalls** Low

Form RPR
12-2 **1** **Gregorian (IRE)**[20] 2258 4-9-5 111.......... WilliamBuick 7 115
(John Gosden) *chsd ldr tl 4f out: styd chsng ldrs: rdn and effrt to ld over 1f out: edging lft down camber ent fnl f: in command after and r.o wl* **3/1**[1]
-000 **2** *1 ½* **Penitent**[13] 2446 7-9-10 113.......... DanielTudhope 6 117
(David O'Meara) *chsd ldng trio tl 4f out: outpcd and swtchd rt 2f out: rallied and hdwy over 1f out: kpt on ins fnl f to go 2nd cl home* **15/2**[3]
3-13 **3** *hd* **Gabrial (IRE)**[22] 2186 4-9-5 111..........(v[1]) JamieSpencer 1 111+
(Richard Fahey) *s.i.s and pushed along early: travelling on bit in rr after 2f out: hdwy over 1f out: chsd wnr ins fnl f: kpt on but no imp fnl 100yds: lost 2nd cl home* **11/2**[2]
-201 **4** *2 ¾* **Producer**[34] 1835 4-9-5 111.......... RichardHughes 4 105
(Richard Hannon) *chsd ldrs tl quick move to join ldr 4f out: rdn and led over 2f out: hdd over 1f out: sn short of room and swtchd rt: no ex and lost 2 pls ins fnl f: eased cl home* **3/1**[1]
504- **5** *2 ¼* **Tales Of Grimm (USA)**[279] 5594 4-9-5 106.......... RyanMoore 3 100
(Sir Michael Stoute) *t.k.h: hld up in tch in last trio: effrt on inner 2f out: no imp and swtchd rt jst over 1f out: plugged on but no threat to ldrs* **8/1**
-012 **6** *¾* **Custom Cut (IRE)**[19] 2288 4-9-8 109.......... JohnnyMurtagh 2 101
(George J Kent, Ire) *led: jnd 4f out: rdn and hdd over 2f out: no ex and btn 1f out: eased wl ins fnl f* **8/1**
160- **7** *8* **Sri Putra**[187] 7872 7-9-5 115.......... FrankieDettori 8 91
(Roger Varian) *t.k.h: hld up in tch in last trio: effrt but no imp whn edgd lft 2f out: bhd and eased ins fnl f* **11/2**[2]

1m 48.68s (2.58) **Going Correction** +0.375s/f (Good)
WFA 3 from 4yo+ 13lb 7 Ran SP% **114.8**
Speed ratings (Par 113): **103,101,101,99,97 96,89**
toteswingers 1&2 £4.80, 1&3 £2.70, 2&3 £7.10 CSF £26.37 TOTE £3.10: £2.00, £4.70; EX 24.40 Trifecta £125.20 Pool: £11,206.09 - 67.11 winning units..
Owner HRH Princess Haya Of Jordan **Bred** Rathasker Stud **Trained** Newmarket, Suffolk

FOCUS
Not a big field, but a competitive heat and an up-to-scratch renewal. The early pace didn't look as strong as in the Group 3 for fillies earlier on the card and the final time was also slower. The form has been taken at face value.

2841 INVESTEC MILE (H'CAP) 1m 114y
3:20 (3:21) (Class 2) (0-105,97) 4-Y-O+
£18,675 (£5,592; £2,796; £1,398; £699; £351) **Stalls** Low

Form RPR
6-55 **1** **Vainglory (USA)**[6] 2646 9-8-9 **85**.......... MartinLane 11 95
(David Simcock) *hld up in rr: last and rdn 4f out: str run on outer 2f out: led ins fnl f: sn clr: idling towards fin but a doing enough* **12/1**
-042 **2** *½* **Lord Ofthe Shadows (IRE)**[58] 1327 4-8-7 **83**..........(b) JoeFanning 6 92+
(Richard Hannon) *hld up in tch in last quartet: effrt whn nt clr run over 2f out: swtchd rt and stmbld wl over 1f out: str run 1f out: chsd wnr fnl 100yds: nvr quite getting to wnr* **16/1**
1-50 **3** *1 ¾* **Ocean Tempest**[27] 2018 4-8-7 **83**..........(p) KirstyMilczarek 13 88
(John Ryan) *chsd ldrs tl rdn to ld and immediately hung lft down camber on to rail 2f out: hdd and no ex ins fnl f* **10/1**
0-10 **4** *nse* **Levitate**[41] 1675 5-9-3 **93**..........(v) RyanMoore 5 98
(John Quinn) *chsd ldrs: rdn and effrt whn short of room and hmpd 2f out: swtchd rt over 1f out: kpt on u.p ins fnl f* **8/1**[3]
1505 **5** *1 ½* **Benzanno (IRE)**[22] 2185 4-8-13 **89**.......... DavidProbert 7 90
(Andrew Balding) *taken down early: chsd ldrs: rdn and effrt over 2f out: lft chsng wnr wl over 1f out: unable qck and lost 2nd ent fnl f: wknd wl ins fnl f* **15/2**[2]

00-3 **6** 3 ¼ **Hefner (IRE)**[21] 2210 4-8-13 **89** AndreaAtzeni 4 83+
(Marco Botti) *in tch in midfield: n.m.r and effrt ent fnl 2f: short of room and hmpd wl over 1f out: edging lft down camber and rallied 1f out: no imp fnl f* **17/2**

-305 **7** 1 ¼ **Brae Hill (IRE)**[15] 2399 7-9-7 **97** JamieSpencer 9 88
(Richard Fahey) *taken down early: dwlt and hmpd s: sn swtchd rt and hdwy into midfield: rdn and struggling to qckn whn short of room and hmpd 2f out: plugged on but n.d after* **12/1**

-102 **8** shd **Hi There (IRE)**[12] 2477 4-8-13 **89** PaulHanagan 12 80+
(Richard Fahey) *hld up in tch in midfield: travelling wl but trapped on inner whn shuffled bk jst over 2f out: swtchd rt and trying to rally whn hmpd over 1f out: lost all ch and nt given hrd time after* **8/1**[3]

60/6 **9** 1 ¾ **Karam Albaari (IRE)**[31] 1913 5-9-0 **90** FrederikTylicki 10 77+
(J R Jenkins) *hld up in tch towards rr: effrt whn nt clr run and hmpd 2f out: kpt on but nvr threatened ldrs* **20/1**

2013 **10** 1 **Maverik**[34] 1848 5-9-2 **92** JimCrowley 1 76
(William Knight) *led tl rdn and hdd over 2f out: struggling whn squeezed for room and bdly hmpd 2f out: sn btn and n.d after* **11/2**[1]

-011 **11** 2 **Toto Skyllachy**[17] 2339 8-9-7 **97** DanielTudhope 3 77
(David O'Meara) *hld up in tch in last quartet: rdn and effrt 2f out: no imp: swtchd rt over 1f out: nvr trbld ldrs* **14/1**

4506 **12** ½ **Takeitfromalady (IRE)**[32] 1883 4-8-6 **82** (v[1]) KierenFox 14 61
(Lee Carter) *chsd ldrs: struggling u.p 3f out: dropping towards rr whn sltly hmpd wl over 1f out: bhd after* **33/1**

360- **13** ½ **Asatir (USA)**[235] 6921 4-9-3 **93** SilvestreDeSousa 8 70+
(Saeed bin Suroor) *chsd ldr: rdn and ev ch 3f out: struggling to qckn whn squeezed for room and bdly hmpd 2f out: nt rcvr and wknd over 1f out* **12/1**

0-50 **14** 1 ½ **Mister Music**[34] 1848 4-9-6 **96** RichardHughes 2 70
(Richard Hannon) *hld up in tch towards rr: effrt towards inner over 2f out: no prog and sn btn: bhd over 1f out* **17/2**

1m 47.44s (1.34) **Going Correction** +0.375s/f (Good) **14** Ran SP% **122.8**
Speed ratings (Par 109): **109,108,107,106,105 102,101,101,99,99 97,96,96,95**
toteswingers 1&2 £40.00, 1&3 £24.20, 2&3 £32.30 CSF £194.77 CT £2055.84 TOTE £19.00: £4.00, £6.60, £4.40; EX 320.40 Trifecta £4977.30 Part won. Pool: £6636.43 - 0.86 winning units..

Owner D M I Simcock **Bred** Darley **Trained** Newmarket, Suffolk

■ Stewards' Enquiry : Kirsty Milczarek four-day ban; careless riding (14th-17th June).

FOCUS
A competitive handicap, run at a true pace, and there was some trouble. The front pair came from right at the back of the field. The winner is rated back to something like last year's form.

2842 INVESTEC OAKS (GROUP 1) (FILLIES) 1m 4f 10y
4:00 (4:04) (Class 1) 3-Y-O

£241,726 (£91,643; £45,864; £22,847; £11,466; £5,754) **Stalls** Centre

Form RPR

31-1 **1** **Talent**[26] 2049 3-9-0 96 RichardHughes 3 115
(Ralph Beckett) *hld up in tch in rr: switching out rt over 4f out: 9th st: nt clr run over 2f out: drvn and str run over 1f out: led ins fnl f: sn stormed clr and r.o strly* **20/1**

21-1 **2** 3 ¾ **Secret Gesture**[20] 2261 3-9-0 111 JimCrowley 1 109
(Ralph Beckett) *chsd ldrs: 4th st: rdn and effrt to ld 2f out: edging lft down camber over 1f out: hdd ins fnl f: immediately outpcd by wnr and btn: tiring but hld on for 2nd* **3/1**[2]

41-3 **3** ¾ **The Lark**[14] 2412 3-9-0 93 JamieSpencer 6 108
(Michael Bell) *hld up in tch in last quartet: hdwy on inner over 2f out: chsng ldrs whn swtchd rt 2f out: wnt bk lft and hdwy to chse ldr briefly over 1f out: switching rt and kpt on same pce u.p fnl f* **16/1**

3 **4** hd **Moth (IRE)**[26] 2047 3-9-0 107 JosephO'Brien 2 107
(A P O'Brien, Ire) *hld up in tch in midfield: 7th st: switching out rt over 2f out: hdwy u.p to chse ldrs wl over 1f out: unable qck 1f out: plugged on same pce after* **5/2**[1]

1-1 **5** 3 ½ **Liber Nauticus (IRE)**[16] 2367 3-9-0 99 RyanMoore 7 102+
(Sir Michael Stoute) *hld up wl in tch in midfield: 5th st: effrt u.p to chal and edging lft 2f out: no ex over 1f out: wknd fnl f* **4/1**[3]

23-2 **6** 3 ¾ **Miss You Too**[20] 2261 3-9-0 93 IanMongan 8 96
(David Simcock) *taken down early: racd keenly: led: hung lft: rdn and hdd 2f out: btn whn squeezed for room and hmpd over 1f out: wl hld after* **40/1**

11 **7** 2 ¼ **Banoffee (IRE)**[23] 2148 3-9-0 93 KierenFallon 5 92
(Hughie Morrison) *hld up in tch in last quartet: niggled along at times: hdwy on downhill run and 6th st: outpcd u.p and btn 2f out: sn wknd and edgd lft over 1f out* **7/1**

-212 **8** 1 ½ **Gertrude Versed**[23] 2148 3-9-0 89 WilliamBuick 10 90
(John Gosden) *chsd ldrs: 3rd st: rdn and unable qck whn sltly hmpd jst over 2f out: sn outpcd and btn: wknd over 1f out* **25/1**

12-0 **9** ¾ **Roz**[26] 2047 3-9-0 104 JohnnyMurtagh 9 89
(Harry Dunlop) *t.k.h early: chsd ldrs tl stdd bk into midfield after 2f: 8th st: rdn and lost pl 3f out: wl btn fnl 2f* **40/1**

10 1 ¼ **Say (IRE)**[21] 2248 3-9-0 92 SeamieHeffernan 4 87
(A P O'Brien, Ire) *chsd ldr: 2nd st: drvn and losing pl whn short of room over 2f out: sn wknd* **12/1**

1-3 **11** 9 **Madame Defarge (IRE)**[26] 2049 3-9-0 90 TomQueally 11 72
(Michael Bell) *wnt rt s and pushed along early: hld up in last quartet: 10th and wdst bnd into st: sn outpcd: lost tch 2f out* **16/1**

2m 42.0s (3.10) **Going Correction** +0.375s/f (Good) **11** Ran SP% **119.0**
Speed ratings (Par 110): **104,101,101,100,98 96,94,93,93,92 86**
toteswingers 1&2 £9.50, 1&3 £14.00, 2&3 £8.20 CSF £78.17 CT £1015.80 TOTE £25.00: £4.70, £1.10, £4.90; EX 71.90 Trifecta £1012.40 Pool: £19,167.68 - 14.19 winning units..

Owner J L Rowsell & M H Dixon **Bred** Ashbrittle Stud & M H Dixon **Trained** Kimpton, Hants
■ A 1-2 for Ralph Beckett, and a firest Oaks for Richard Hughes.

■ Stewards' Enquiry : Ian Mongan one-day ban; arrived late to start (17th June). three-day ban; improper conduct towards an official (14th-16th June).

FOCUS
Most of the trial winners were here and the Guineas was represented by the third from Newmarket. The winner overcame one or two difficulties to score quite easily in the end, but the early pace had been strong and that had set things up for something closing from behind. The overall form is rated a little below the race standard but Talent is rated an up-to-scratch winner. Secret Gesture ran close to her Lingfueld mark, with the form is set around the third and fourth.

2843 INVESTEC SURREY STKS (LISTED RACE) 7f
4:45 (4:45) (Class 1) 3-Y-O

£22,684 (£8,600; £4,304; £2,144; £1,076; £540) **Stalls** Low

Form RPR

2-04 **1** **Well Acquainted (IRE)**[13] 2453 3-8-13 102 RyanMoore 1 107
(Clive Cox) *chsd ldr: drvn to chal 2f out: drew clr w rival over 1f out: led narrowly 1f out: kpt on gamely u.p and forged ahd fnl 75yds* **4/1**[3]

-225 **2** 1 **Emell**[20] 2258 3-8-13 102 (p) RichardHughes 5 104
(Richard Hannon) *led: jnd and rdn over 2f out: drvn and drew clr w wnr over 1f out: hdd 1f out: battled on gamely tl no ex fnl 75yds* **6/1**

5331 **3** 2 ½ **Hasopop (IRE)**[13] 2452 3-8-13 105 DaneO'Neill 7 98+
(Marco Botti) *stdd and dropped in bhd s: hld up in last pair: clsng but bhd a wall of horses whn swtchd rt 2f out: edging lft and hdwy over 1f out: chsd ldng pair ins fnl f: r.o but no threat to ldrs* **11/4**[2]

4-21 **4** 3 ¾ **Here Comes When (IRE)**[22] 2188 3-8-13 97 DavidProbert 4 87+
(Andrew Balding) *in tch in midfield: rdn and effrt over 2f out: outpcd by ldng pair and btn over 1f out: wknd ins fnl f* **5/2**[1]

0-63 **5** hd **Birdman (IRE)**[27] 2008 3-8-13 103 MartinLane 2 87
(David Simcock) *in tch in midfield: effrt u.p and chsd ldng pair 2f out: outpcd and btn over 1f out: wknd ins fnl f* **12/1**

33-5 **6** 3 ½ **Boomshackerlacker (IRE)**[11] 2526 3-9-3 108 PatCosgrave 3 89+
(George Baker) *chsd ldng pair tl unable qck ent fnl 2f: sn outpcd: wl hld whn short of room and snatched up 1f out: eased wl ins fnl f* **8/1**

0-35 **7** 1 ¾ **Graphic Guest**[30] 1921 3-8-8 96 SamHitchcott 6 68
(Mick Channon) *taken down early: stdd s: hld up in last pair: rdn and no hdwy over 3f out: wl bhd over 1f out* **20/1**

1m 25.33s (2.03) **Going Correction** +0.375s/f (Good) **7** Ran SP% **113.1**
Speed ratings (Par 107): **103,101,99,94,94 90,88**
toteswingers 1&2 £3.10, 1&3 £2.40, 2&3 £3.40 CSF £27.15 TOTE £4.60: £2.50, £2.80; EX 24.50 Trifecta £104.70 Pool: £7151.76 - 51.21 winning units..

Owner The Orienteers **Bred** Stunning Rose Syndicate **Trained** Lambourn, Berks

FOCUS
The front pair dominated throughout in this Listed race. The winner is rated to a best view of his 2yo form.

2844 INVESTEC ASSET MANAGEMENT H'CAP 7f
5:20 (5:20) (Class 2) (0-100,100) 3-Y-O

£15,562 (£4,660; £2,330; £1,165; £582; £292) **Stalls** Low

Form RPR

-201 **1** **Heaven's Guest (IRE)**[14] 2408 3-8-7 **86** FrederikTylicki 6 98+
(Richard Fahey) *wl in tch in midfield: rdn and hdwy to ld 2f out: sn clr and edging lft: drvn fnl f: pressed and edgd rt cl home: hld on* **9/2**[2]

1210 **2** nk **Intrigo**[21] 2209 3-8-3 **82** KieranO'Neill 8 93+
(Richard Hannon) *t.k.h: in tch in midfield: hmpd and lost pl after 2f: nt clr run and switching rt 2f out: hdwy u.p 1f out: wnt 2nd ins fnl f: pressing wnr and clsng whn veered rt and hld cl home* **10/1**

2131 **3** 2 ¼ **You Da One (IRE)**[6] 2655 3-8-8 **87** 6ex HayleyTurner 14 92
(Andrew Balding) *taken down early: chsd ldr: rdn and ev ch 2f out: sn outpcd by wnr: lost 2nd and styd on same pce ins fnl f* **9/2**[2]

2221 **4** 5 **Firmdecisions (IRE)**[27] 2016 3-8-2 **81** oh5 (p) JimmyQuinn 15 73
(Brett Johnson) *towards rr: rdn and struggling 1/2-way: styd on u.p past btn horses ent fnl f: kpt on but no threat to ldrs* **33/1**

1-2 **5** shd **Love Magic**[34] 1822 3-8-5 **84** DavidProbert 13 75+
(Sir Michael Stoute) *stdd and dropped in s: towards rr: rdn over 3f out: no imp tl hdwy and edging lft over 1f out: kpt on fnl f: nvr trbld ldrs* **7/1**[3]

-142 **6** 1 ¼ **Keene's Pointe**[23] 2160 3-8-2 **81** oh3 MartinLane 4 69
(J W Hills) *wl in tch in midfield: drvn and outpcd 2f out: no threat to ldrs and one pce after* **33/1**

3-03 **7** nk **Kimberella**[39] 1714 3-8-4 **83** NickyMackay 2 70
(Michael Attwater) *hld up wl in tch: nt clr run 3f out: outpcd and swtchd rt 2f out: sn rdn and kpt on same pce* **22/1**

4533 **8** hd **Flashlight (IRE)**[6] 2655 3-8-6 **85** JoeFanning 5 72
(Mark Johnston) *led tl 2f out: sn drvn and outpcd: wknd fnl f* **10/1**

22-1 **9** 2 ¼ **Lancelot Du Lac (ITY)**[16] 2371 3-8-9 **88** RyanMoore 9 68+
(Dean Ivory) *stdd and short of room sn after s: hld up in last pair: effrt but nvr much room over 2f out: sme hdwy but stl little room 1f out: switching lft and nt given a hrd time after: n.d* **7/2**[1]

1-00 **10** 1 ¾ **Gigawatt**[20] 2285 3-7-11 **81** oh5 NathanAlison(5) 1 57
(Jim Boyle) *hld up in rr: effrt on inner 3f out: no real hdwy: n.d* **50/1**

3-13 **11** 3 ¾ **Hipster**[25] 2100 3-8-6 **85** (v) AndreaAtzeni 12 51
(Ralph Beckett) *chsd ldrs: drvn and outpcd 2f out: sn btn and wknd over 1f out* **10/1**

-036 **12** 15 **Discernable**[16] 2367 3-9-1 **94** SilvestreDeSousa 3
(Mark Johnston) *pressed ldr on inner tl rdn and lost pl 4f out: bhd and hmpd 2f out: sn lost tch and eased over 1f out* **20/1**

1105 **13** 1 ½ **Ashamaly**[48] 1543 3-8-10 **89** NeilCallan 10
(James Tate) *sn bustled along in midfield: struggling 3f out: bhd fnl 2f: eased ins fnl f* **25/1**

1m 25.58s (2.28) **Going Correction** +0.375s/f (Good) **13** Ran SP% **119.2**
Speed ratings (Par 105): **101,100,98,92,92 90,90,90,87,85 81,64,62**
toteswingers 1&2 £14.00, 1&3 £8.80, 2&3 £14.40 CSF £44.12 CT £225.59 TOTE £4.80: £2.10, £3.20, £2.20; EX 58.40 Trifecta £365.30 Pool: £4880.19 - 10.01 winning units..

Owner J K Shannon & M A Scaife **Bred** Yeomanstown Stud **Trained** Musley Bank, N Yorks

■ Stewards' Enquiry : Frederik Tylicki two-day ban; used whip above permitted level (14th-115th June)

FOCUS
Fast and furious stuff in this handicap, with a four-way battle for the early lead. Those held up just off the pace were favoured. Another personalo best from the winner.

T/Jkpt: Not won. T/Plt: £881.00 to a £1 stake. Pool of £238,010.69 - 197.21 winning tickets. T/Qpdt: £193.50 to a £1 stake. Pool of £13,326.95 - 50.95 winning tickets. SP

[2652] GOODWOOD (R-H)

Friday, May 31

OFFICIAL GOING: Good (good to soft in places; 7.7)

First 2f of 1m course dolled out 5yds.

Wind: virtually nil Weather: sunny

2845 GORDON'S AMATEUR RIDERS' STKS (H'CAP) 1m 1f

6:05 (6:06) (Class 5) (0-70,70) 4-Y-O+ **£3,119** (£967; £483; £242) **Stalls** Low

Form RPR

0223 **1** **Balmoral Castle**[15] 2395 4-9-12 **59**.................. MrJHarding(5) 16 73+
(Jonathan Portman) *racd v wd fr outside draw: in tch tl lost pl on bnd 5f out: c wd into st: stdy prog fr 3f out: led ent fnl f: kpt on wl: pushed out* **4/1**[1]

4353 **2** ½ **Time Square (FR)**[23] 2159 6-9-11 **56** oh2..............(t) MrChrisMartin(3) 15 68
(Tony Carroll) *hld up towards rr: swtchd lft and hdwy 3f out: rdn to ld over 1f out: hdd ent fnl f: kpt on w ev ch tl no ex fnl 50yds* **16/1**

5-30 **3** 5 **Lady Sylvia**[98] 749 4-10-7 **66**.................. MissHayleyMoore(3) 2 67
(Joseph Tuite) *mid-div: rdn over 2f out to chse ldrs: kpt on to go 3rd towards fin: no ch w ldng pair* **14/1**

60-5 **4** ½ **Attain**[32] 1893 4-10-0 **56** oh2..................(p) MrRossBirkett 7 56
(Julia Feilden) *trckd ldrs: rdn and ch over 2f out: kpt on same pce ins fnl f: no ex whn lost 3rd towards fin* **20/1**

/224 **5** ½ **Piccolo Mondo**[21] 2228 7-9-13 **62**.................. MissChelseyBanks(7) 4 61
(Philip Hide) *led: rdn over 2f out: hdd over 1f out: no ex fnl f* **10/1**

0040 **6** 1 ½ **Balady (IRE)**[8] 2606 4-10-7 **68**.................. MrBenFfrenchDavis(5) 14 64
(Dominic Ffrench Davis) *hld up towards rr: hdwy to trck ldrs after 3f: effrt wl over 2f out: kpt on same pce fnl f* **8/1**

3522 **7** 1 **Chrissycross (IRE)**[67] 1176 4-9-12 **59**..................(v) MrGeorgeCrate(5) 10 52
(Roger Teal) *s.i.s: towards rr: rdn and sme hdwy into midfield 3f out: no further imp fnl 2f* **8/1**

00-0 **8** hd **Bountiful Girl**[6] 2673 4-10-4 **67**.................. MrAFrench(7) 5 60
(John Wainwright) *nvr bttr than mid-div* **40/1**

0651 **9** 1 ¾ **Space War**[21] 2225 6-10-9 **70**..................(t) AnnaHesketh(5) 6 59
(Michael Easterby) *hld up towards rr: hdwy 3f out: nt clr run whn rdn and swtchd rt 2f out: no further imp* **6/1**[2]

-006 **10** 2 ¼ **Megalala (IRE)**[10] 2532 12-10-9 **65**.................. MissSBrotherton 11 49
(John Bridger) *fly-leapt leaving stalls: sn rcvrd to be in tch: effrt wl over 2f out: wknd over 1f out* **12/1**

-000 **11** ½ **King Of Windsor (IRE)**[85] 921 6-10-5 **68**.................. MrKWood(7) 3 51
(John Wainwright) *hld up towards rr: rdn and stdy prog on far rails whn bdly hmpd 2f out: no ch after* **33/1**

5263 **12** shd **Byrd In Hand (IRE)**[3] 2747 6-10-0 **56** oh4..................(p) MissADeniel 13 39
(John Bridger) *racd keenly in mid-div: rdn 3f out: sn btn* **8/1**

2400 **13** 1 ½ **Benandonner (USA)**[26] 2057 10-9-9 **56** oh2.................. MissMBryant(5) 12 35
(Paddy Butler) *trckd ldrs tl c wd ent st: sn btn* **33/1**

05-0 **14** ¾ **Wordismybond**[146] 80 4-10-7 **63**.................. MrSWalker 8 41
(Peter Makin) *prom: rdn 3f out: wkng whn hung lft over 1f out* **7/1**[3]

1m 58.33s (2.03) **Going Correction** +0.175s/f (Good) **14** Ran SP% **122.5**
Speed ratings (Par 103): **97,96,92,91,91 89,89,88,87,85 84,84,83,82**
Tote Swingers 1&2 £19.70, 2&3 £44.40, 1&3 £8.90 CSF £70.42 TOTE £5.60: £2.60, £3.60, £3.10; EX 103.30 Trifecta £717.30 Part won. Pool: £956.52 - 0.89 winning tickets..
Owner J G B Portman **Bred** Springcombe Park Stud **Trained** Upper Lambourn, Berks
■ Stewards' Enquiry : Anna Hesketh two-day ban; careless riding (14th-15th June).

FOCUS
Following a dry night and warm day the ground was changed to good, good to soft in places. Mainly exposed performers in a modest handicap. The early gallop was on the steady side and the first two did well to pull clear. The winner looks capable of better.

2846 LEVY RESTAURANTS CLASSIFIED STKS 1m 3f

6:35 (6:36) (Class 5) 3-Y-O **£3,408** (£1,006; £503) **Stalls** High

Form RPR

-400 **1** **Kuantan One (IRE)**[18] 2322 3-9-0 73.................. LukeMorris 6 79
(Paul Cole) *hld up in last pair: hdwy whn swtchd to centre over 6f out: trckd ldr: rdn 3f out: chalng whn bmpd jst over 1f out: led jst ins fnl f: kpt on wl to assert nring fin: drvn out* **20/1**

-512 **2** ½ **Arbaah (USA)**[15] 2390 3-9-0 74.................. PaulHanagan 5 78
(Brian Meehan) *trckd ldr: rdn over 2f out: chal over 1f out: led v briefly ent fnl f: kpt pressing wnr: hld fnl 50yds* **4/1**[3]

5-34 **3** 2 ¾ **Bursledon (IRE)**[14] 2416 3-9-0 72.................. RichardHughes 7 73
(Richard Hannon) *hld up: tk clsr order fr over 6f out whn swtchd to centre: rdn 3f out: nt pce to chal: styd on ins fnl f: wnt 3rd towards fin* **6/1**

33-2 **4** ½ **Neamour**[24] 2127 3-8-11 72.................. DarrenEgan(3) 2 72
(David Simcock) *t.k.h: cl up tl dropped to last pair over 6f out: rdn 3f out: nt pce to chal: styd on ins fnl f: wnt 4th nring fin* **15/2**

2-52 **5** ¾ **Short Squeeze (IRE)**[21] 2235 3-9-0 75.................. JamesDoyle 1 71+
(Hugo Palmer) *racd keenly: led: kpt wdst bef bnd over 5f out: stl 2 l advantage over 2f out: rdn over 1f out: sn edgd lft and hdd: no ex and lost 2 pls towards fin* **11/4**[1]

2-43 **6** 1 **Jebril (FR)**[39] 1729 3-9-0 74.................. TomQueally 4 69
(Jonathan Portman) *cl up tl shuffled bk to last pair over 6f out: rdn to chse ldrs 3f out: nt pce to chal: no ex fnl f* **3/1**[2]

4-65 **7** 50 **Chief Executive (IRE)**[27] 2030 3-9-0 75.................. WilliamBuick 3
(Jo Hughes) *racd keenly: trckd ldrs: rdn 5f out: wknd over 3f out: virtually p.u* **8/1**

2m 28.46s (1.96) **Going Correction** +0.175s/f (Good) **7** Ran SP% **113.6**
Speed ratings (Par 99): **99,98,96,96,95 95,58**
Tote Swingers 1&2 £7.10, 2&3 £2.30, 1&3 £18.60 CSF £96.01 TOTE £30.30: £8.80, £2.60; EX 164.00 Trifecta £903.80 Part won. Pool: £1,205.11 - 0.94 winning tickets..
Owner H R H Sultan Ahmad Shah **Bred** Manister House Stud **Trained** Whatcombe, Oxon
■ Stewards' Enquiry : Darren Egan two-day ban; used whip above permitted level (14th-15th June).

FOCUS
A fair but tight classified event and a race run at a steady gallop to the home straight. The jockeys described the ground as "good, lovely ground". The winner is rated back to form, with a personal best from the second too.

2847 BRITISH STALLION STUDS EBF MAIDEN STKS 6f

7:10 (7:12) (Class 5) 2-Y-O **£3,234** (£962; £481; £240) **Stalls** High

Form RPR

1 **Wahaab (IRE)** 2-9-5 0.................. PaulHanagan 4 79+
(Richard Hannon) *broke wl: trckd ldr: shkn up and hanging rt whn led over 1f out: r.o strly fnl f: readily* **8/15**[1]

56 **2** 2 ¾ **Jazz (IRE)**[20] 2250 2-9-5 0.................. WilliamBuick 5 71
(Charles Hills) *racd freely: led: rdn whn hdd wl over 1f out: kpt on but nt pce of wnr fnl f* **7/1**[3]

3 ½ **Downturn** 2-9-5 0.................. RichardHughes 1 69+
(Richard Hannon) *slowly away and wnt rt s: last: hdwy over 2f out: shkn up wl over 1f out: nt pce to get on terms but kpt on fnl 75yds* **4/1**[2]

4 ½ **Double Point (IRE)** 2-9-5 0.................. TomQueally 2 68
(Paul Cole) *trckd ldrs: pushed along 3f out: rdn 2f out: nt pce to mount chal: kpt on ins fnl f* **33/1**

5 1 **Double Czech (IRE)** 2-9-5 0.................. PatDobbs 6 65+
(Amanda Perrett) *s.i.s: sn cl up 4th: effrt wl over 1f out: nt pce to get on terms* **12/1**

1m 13.09s (0.89) **Going Correction** -0.05s/f (Good) **5** Ran SP% **108.4**
Speed ratings (Par 93): **92,88,87,87,85**
Tote Swinger 1&2 £3.80 CSF £4.67 TOTE £1.40: £1.10, £2.90; EX 4.20 Trifecta £6.70 Pool: £955.83 - 106.87 winning tickets..
Owner Hamdan Al Maktoum **Bred** Shadwell Estate Company Limited **Trained** East Everleigh, Wilts

FOCUS
This is a race that often throws up a decent sort and subsequent French Group 1 winner Olympic Dream took this on his debut last year. The gallop was reasonable and the winner has the obvious scope to rate a good deal higher than the bare form.

2848 BRITISH STALLION STUDS SUPPORTING BRITISH RACING EBF FILLIES' STKS (H'CAP) 6f

7:45 (7:45) (Class 3) (0-95,94) 3-Y-O+ **£9,056** (£2,695; £1,346; £673) **Stalls** High

Form RPR

5-00 **1** **Links Drive Lady**[25] 2097 5-9-1 **81**.................. KierenFallon 10 89
(Dean Ivory) *mid-div: hdwy over 1f out: shkn up and r.o strly to ld fnl 120yds: on top at fin* **14/1**

10-5 **2** ¾ **Picabo (IRE)**[20] 2270 5-9-12 **92**.................. DaneO'Neill 6 98
(Henry Candy) *hld up bhd: swtchd lft 2f out: sn rdn and hdwy: r.o strly fnl f: snatched 2nd fnl stride* **12/1**

0-61 **3** hd **Charlotte Rosina**[25] 2088 4-9-9 **89**.................. SebSanders 13 94
(Roger Teal) *led: rdn over 1f out: kpt on gamely whn hdd fnl 120yds: lost 2nd fnl stride* **10/1**

0-06 **4** nk **Tassel**[20] 2264 3-9-0 **89**.................. RichardHughes 8 91
(Richard Hannon) *hld up: pushed along over 1f out: r.o but nvr rchd ldrs: wnt 4th nr fin* **8/1**

11-2 **5** ¾ **Athenian (IRE)**[12] 2476 4-9-5 **85**.................. LukeMorris 11 87
(Sir Mark Prescott Bt) *trckd ldr: rdn 2f out: kpt on same pce ins fnl f* **11/4**[1]

22-1 **6** 1 **Silken Express (IRE)**[23] 2173 4-9-5 **85**.................. NeilCallan 3 84
(Robert Cowell) *trckd ldrs: rdn to chal over 1f out tl fdd fnl 120yds* **5/1**[2]

04-3 **7** nk **Tantshi (IRE)**[26] 2056 3-8-13 **88**.................. AndreaAtzeni 7 84
(Roger Varian) *trckd ldr: rdn 2f out: nt pce to chal: fdd fnl 120yds* **11/2**[3]

220- **8** 3 ¼ **Rebel Magic**[300] 4820 3-8-13 **88**.................. PatDobbs 12 73
(Richard Hannon) *trckd ldrs: rdn over 2f out: wknd over 1f out* **16/1**

3-66 **9** hd **Heartsong (IRE)**[9] 2561 4-8-13 **84**.................. MichaelJMMurphy(5) 4 71
(John Gallagher) *sn pushed along in midfield: wknd jst over 1f out* **40/1**

-001 **10** 1 ¾ **Effie B**[22] 2190 3-9-4 **93**.................. WilliamBuick 5 72
(Mick Channon) *mid-div: rdn to chse ldrs 2f out: wknd jst over 1f out* **10/1**

41-0 **11** nk **Pearl Blue (IRE)**[13] 2461 5-10-0 **94**.................. GeorgeBaker 1 74
(Chris Wall) *hld up: effrt to cl 2f out: sn hung rt: wknd over 1f out* **10/1**

1m 11.12s (-1.08) **Going Correction** -0.05s/f (Good)
WFA 3 from 4yo+ 9lb **11** Ran SP% **119.8**
Speed ratings (Par 104): **105,104,103,103,102 101,100,96,96,93 93**
Tote Swingers 1&2 £47.60, 2&3 £29.10, 1&3 £38.50 CSF £174.10 CT £1798.12 TOTE £19.70: £5.20, £3.10, £2.90; EX 165.20 Trifecta £808.40 Part won. Pool: £1,077.94 - 0.01 winning tickets..
Owner It's Your Lucky Day **Bred** Peter Webb **Trained** Radlett, Herts

FOCUS
A very useful fillies' handicap in which the gallop was sound throughout. Sound form with the third setting the standard.

2849 RUDIMENTAL STKS (H'CAP) 1m 4f

8:15 (8:15) (Class 4) (0-85,79) 4-Y-O+ **£5,175** (£1,540; £769; £384) **Stalls** High

Form RPR

62-3 **1** **Stock Hill Fair**[20] 2269 5-9-7 **79**.................. KierenFallon 1 89
(Brendan Powell) *mde all: nudged into ld sn after s: qcknd pce 4f out and sn had evthing struggling: styd on gamely fr over 1f out: drifted lft ins fnl f: rdn out* **13/8**[1]

0-15 **2** 3 ¼ **Paloma's Prince (IRE)**[32] 1884 4-9-5 **77**.................. PatCosgrave 2 82
(Jim Boyle) *broke wl ldng briefly: chsd wnr thrght: rdn over 3f out: nvr got on terms w wnr but hld on gamely for 2nd fr over 1f out* **11/2**

365 **3** ½ **Luggers Hall (IRE)**[15] 2385 5-9-1 **73**.................. TomQueally 4 77
(Tony Carroll) *trckd ldrs: rdn to chal for 2nd fr 2f out but nvr on terms w wnr: kpt on same pce fnl f* **3/1**[2]

25-5 **4** 7 **All Annalena (IRE)**[13] 2440 7-9-6 **78**.................. DaneO'Neill 5 71
(Lucy Wadham) *hood got ct and s.i.s: last but sn in tch: rdn over 4f out: wnt 4th over 2f out: nvr threatened ldrs: wknd fnl f* **9/1**

624/ **5** 4 **Paintball (IRE)**[22] 6813 6-9-3 **75**.................. SamHitchcott 3 61
(Charlie Longsdon) *chsd ldrs: rdn over 4f out: btn over 3f out: wknd over 1f out* **12/1**

0254 **6** 1 **Achalas (IRE)**[8] 2598 5-9-4 **76**.................. RichardHughes 6 61
(Heather Main) *hld up in tch: rdn over 3f out: wknd over 1f out* **9/2**[3]

2m 41.75s (3.35) **Going Correction** +0.175s/f (Good) **6** Ran SP% **114.4**
Speed ratings (Par 105): **95,92,92,87,85 84**
Tote Swingers 1&2 £1.40, 2&3 £3.40, 1&3 £1.70 CSF £11.42 TOTE £2.80: £1.70, £2.20; EX 13.10 Trifecta £39.60 Pool: £705.40 - 13.35 winning tickets..
Owner Mrs M Fairbairn, E Gadsden & P Dean **Bred** Mrs M Fairbairn And E Gadsden **Trained** Upper Lambourn, Berks

FOCUS
A fair handicap in which a steady gallop picked up around 4f out and this bare form doesn't look entirely reliable. The winner is on the upgrade, though.

2850 YACHT WEEK MAIDEN FILLIES' STKS 1m

8:45 (8:48) (Class 5) 3-Y-O+ **£3,234** (£962; £481; £240) **Stalls** Low

Form RPR

1 **Integral** 3-9-0 0.................. RyanMoore 5 89+
(Sir Michael Stoute) *trckd ldrs: shkn up to ld 2f out: r.o wl to draw clr fnl f: readily* **4/1**[3]

64 **2** 2 ¾ **Magic Of Reality (FR)**[26] 2049 3-9-0 0.................. TomQueally 9 83
(Sir Henry Cecil) *trckd ldrs: rdn over 2f out: styd on to chse wnr over 1f out but nvr any ch* **11/10**[1]

0-6 **3** 6 **Mesmerized (IRE)**[34] 1828 3-9-0 0.................. MircoMimmocchi 3 69
(Marco Botti) *led after 1f: rdn and hdd 2f out: sn hld: lost 2nd over 1f out: fdd fnl 120yds but a holding 3rd* **33/1**

4 1 **Ardingly (IRE)** 3-9-0 0 AndreaAtzeni 12 67+
(Roger Varian) *mid-div: rdn over 2f out: styd on same pce: wnt 4th fnl strides* **14/1**

60 5 nk **Lybica (IRE)**[22] 2192 3-9-0 0 DaneO'Neill 4 66
(Gary Moore) *t.k.h early: trckd ldrs: reigned bk into midfield after 1f: rdn over 2f out: styd on same pce: wnt 5th fnl strides* **40/1**

6 hd **Stockhill Diva** 3-9-0 0 PatDobbs 8 66+
(Brendan Powell) *s.i.s: towards rr: styd on fr over 1f out wout ever threatening to get on terms w ldrs* **66/1**

7 nk **Chocolate Caviar (IRE)** 3-8-7 0 NedCurtis(7) 10 65
(Gary Moore) *hld up towards rr: rdn over 2f out: styd on fnl f: nvr a threat* **33/1**

3-36 8 ¾ **Hanzada (USA)**[14] 2429 3-9-0 83 WilliamBuick 2 63
(Ed Dunlop) *led for 1f: trckd ldr: rdn and ev ch 2f out: wknd fnl f* **3/1**[2]

9 1 **Mint Crisp** 3-9-0 0[1] JimmyFortune 7 61
(Hughie Morrison) *a towards rr* **25/1**

36 10 ½ **Grey Gazelle**[6] 2672 3-8-9 0 CharlesBishop(5) 1 60
(Mick Channon) *mid-div: rdn over 2f out: wknd fnl f* **20/1**

6 11 hd **Rail Star**[25] 2084 3-9-0 0 JamesDoyle 6 59
(Roger Charlton) *mid-div: rdn over 2f out: sn btn* **9/1**

1m 40.93s (1.03) **Going Correction** +0.175s/f (Good) 11 Ran SP% **127.7**
Speed ratings (Par 100): **101,98,92,91,90 90,90,89,88,88 88**
Tote Swingers 1&2 £1.40, 2&3 £21.90, 1&3 £40.50 CSF £9.09 TOTE £5.30: £1.70, £1.10, £6.50; EX 9.40 Trifecta £154.90 Pool: £1,611.25 - 7.79 winning tickets..
Owner Cheveley Park Stud **Bred** Cheveley Park Stud Ltd **Trained** Newmarket, Suffolk

FOCUS
The seventh running of a maiden that has been won in the past by very useful pair Red Dune (2008) and Cosmopolitan (2009) but there was little depth to this race. The gallop was a steady one but the two market leaders pulled clear. The winner looks useful.
T/Plt: £175.20 to a £1 stake. Pool: £71,623.38 - 298.37 winning tickets. T/Qpdt: £29.70 to a £1 stake. Pool: £5,902.26 - 147.05 winning tickets. TM

2851 - 2854a (Foreign Racing) - See Raceform Interactive

2435 DONCASTER (L-H)
Saturday, June 1

OFFICIAL GOING: Good (8.8)
Rail realignment on Round course added about 18yds to advertised distances on that track.
Wind: light 1/2 behind Weather: fine and sunny, becoming overcast

2855 LADBROKES BET ON YOUR MOBILE H'CAP 1m 4f
2:00 (2:00) (Class 4) (0-85,84) 4-Y-O+ **£5,175** (£1,540; £769; £384) **Stalls** Low

Form RPR

-641 1 **Swinging Sultan**[9] 2590 6-9-5 82 PaulHanagan 9 94+
(Keith Reveley) *swtchd lft after s: t.k.h in rr: effrt and c wd over 3f out: chsng ldrs and edgd lft over 1f out: led last 100yds: styd on strly* **5/2**[2]

4-33 2 1¼ **Novirak (IRE)**[17] 2369 5-9-4 81 KierenFallon 2 91
(James Fanshawe) *s.i.s: hld up in rr: effrt over 3f out: chsng ldrs and swtchd lft over 1f out: upsides ins fnl f: no ex* **15/8**[1]

103- 3 ¾ **Between Us**[254] 6416 4-9-6 83 LukeMorris 4 92
(Sir Mark Prescott Bt) *led 2f: chsd ldrs: led 2f out: hdd ins fnl f: styd on same pce* **8/1**[3]

045 4 2 **Tetbury (USA)**[13] 2478 4-8-11 74[1] GrahamGibbons 1 80
(David O'Meara) *chsd ldrs: drvn over 4f out: outpcd over 2f out: styd on fnl f* **14/1**

0-00 5 nk **Rio's Rosanna (IRE)**[15] 2427 6-9-7 84 AmyRyan 5 91+
(Richard Whitaker) *dwlt: t.k.h in rr: hdwy 3f out: chsng ldrs whn hmpd over 1f out: styd on ins fnl f* **10/1**

020- 6 7 **Livia's Dream (IRE)**[178] 7999 4-8-13 76 TomMcLaughlin 6 73
(Ed Walker) *t.k.h: trckd ldrs: led over 2f out: sn hdd: one pce whn hmpd over 1f out: eased towards fin* **16/1**

/605 7 2¼ **San Cassiano (IRE)**[9] 2590 6-8-13 76 PJMcDonald 8 66
(Ruth Carr) *chsd ldr: led after 2f: increased pce 5f out: hdd over 2f out: sn btn* **25/1**

30-0 8 2¼ **Harrison's Cave**[16] 2402 5-9-7 84 TomQueally 10 71
(Chris Grant) *t.k.h in rr: effrt 3f out: sn wknd* **20/1**

-002 9 4 **Getabuzz**[11] 2552 5-9-5 82 DuranFentiman 3 62
(Tim Easterby) *hld up in mid-div: hdwy 4f out: rdn and wknd over 1f out* **8/1**[3]

34-0 10 1¾ **The Tiddly Tadpole**[14] 2465 8-8-8 71 ow1 RussKennemore 7 49
(Simon West) *hld up: hdwy to chse ldrs after 3f: drvn over 4f out: lost pl over 2f out* **40/1**

2m 31.59s (-3.31) **Going Correction** -0.175s/f (Firm) 10 Ran SP% **118.3**
Speed ratings (Par 105): **104,103,102,101,101 96,94,93,90,89**
toteswingers 1&2 £1.10, 2&3 £3.00, 1&3 £6.10 CSF £7.51 CT £31.89 TOTE £3.80: £1.40, £1.20, £2.90; EX 10.10 Trifecta £46.90 Pool: £692.38 - 11.05 winning units..
Owner Reveley Racing 1 **Bred** Reveley Farms **Trained** Lingdale, Redcar & Cleveland

FOCUS
Rail realignment on Round course added about 18yds to advertised distances on that track. The early gallop looked pretty steady but they wound things up quite a long way out here and the first two home were the last to make their challenges. The winner progressed again.

2856 LOCATE SUPPLIES LTD 25TH ANNIVERSARY EBF MAIDEN FILLIES STKS 6f
2:35 (2:39) (Class 5) 2-Y-O **£2,911** (£866; £432; £216) **Stalls** High

Form RPR

1 **Rasheeda** 2-9-0 0 LukeMorris 6 78+
(Marco Botti) *chsd ldrs: n.m.r over 1f out: swtchd lft: fin strly to ld towards fin* **3/1**[2]

2 ¾ **Genuine Quality (USA)** 2-9-0 0 JimmyFortune 5 76+
(Ed Vaughan) *t.k.h: w ldrs: led over 2f out: hdd and no ex in clsng stages* **8/1**

3 nk **Tinga (IRE)** 2-9-0 0 MartinHarley 11 75+
(Mick Channon) *s.i.s: hdwy over 2f out: styd on strly ins fnl f* **11/2**[3]

30 4 nk **Heskin (IRE)**[15] 2426 2-9-0 0 PaulHanagan 8 74
(Richard Fahey) *mde most: hdd over 2f out: kpt on same pce last 100yds* **3/1**[2]

5 ½ **Musicora** 2-9-0 0 PatDobbs 1 73+
(Richard Hannon) *dwlt: swtchd rt after s: hdwy over 2f out: chsng ldrs over 1f out: styd on same pce last 100yds* **11/4**[1]

6 6 7 **Hustle Bustle (IRE)**[22] 2230 2-9-0 0 SeanLevey 12 52
(David Brown) *w ldrs: wknd over 1f out* **33/1**

0 7 2½ **Queenie's Home**[40] 1718 2-9-0 0 JamesSullivan 14 44
(James Given) *hld up in mid-div: effrt over 2f out: wknd over 1f out* **20/1**

8 2 **Volodina (IRE)** 2-9-0 0 MartinDwyer 9 38
(Alan McCabe) *dwlt: sn outpcd in rr* **16/1**

9 4 **Emily Davison (IRE)** 2-9-0 0 GrahamGibbons 13 26
(David C Griffiths) *dwlt: sn chsng ldrs: effrt over 2f out: lost pl over 1f out* **25/1**

0 10 13 **Packet Station**[31] 1924 2-8-7 0 AaronJones(7) 2
(Alan McCabe) *swvd lft s: sn w ldrs: hung bdly lft over 3f out: lost pl over 2f out* **66/1**

11 7 **Princess Florentia** 2-9-0 0 TomQueally 7
(John Gallagher) *s.s: sn detached in last* **28/1**

1m 13.12s (-0.48) **Going Correction** -0.175s/f (Firm) 11 Ran SP% **125.5**
Speed ratings (Par 93): **96,95,94,94,93 84,80,78,72,55 46**
toteswingers 1&2 £4.10, 2&8 £19.70, 1&8 £9.20 CSF £27.60 TOTE £6.40: £1.80, £2.90, £2.80; EX 46.40 Trifecta £272.50 Pool: £970.86 - 2.67 winning units..
Owner Mubarak Al Naemi **Bred** Limestone Stud **Trained** Newmarket, Suffolk

FOCUS
Plenty to take out of what might turn out to be a useful maiden, and form that has been rated on the positive side with the front five clear.

2857 LADBROKES DOWNLOAD THE APP H'CAP 1m (S)
3:10 (3:12) (Class 2) (0-105,103) 3-Y-O **£12,938** (£3,850; £1,924; £962) **Stalls** High

Form RPR

31 1 **Remote**[14] 2442 3-8-7 89 MartinDwyer 1 113
(John Gosden) *trckd ldrs: led over 2f out: drvn clr over 1f out: styd on strly* **10/3**[2]

1-13 2 6 **Baltic Knight (IRE)**[14] 2453 3-9-2 103 WilliamTwiston-Davies(5) 3 113
(Richard Hannon) *w ldrs: chal over 2f out: kpt on: no ch w wnr* **9/2**[3]

41 3 2¼ **Matrooh (USA)**[19] 2306 3-8-5 87 PaulHanagan 2 92
(William Haggas) *dwlt: in rr on wd outside: hdwy 4f out: chsng ldrs and drvn over 2f out: wknd towards fin* **11/4**[1]

-261 4 2¼ **Hay Dude**[21] 2259 3-8-10 95 MichaelMetcalfe(3) 10 95
(Mrs K Burke) *swtchd lft after s: hld up in rr: hdwy over 3f out: chsng ldrs over 2f out: kpt on one pce* **8/1**

61-5 5 1 **Steelriver (IRE)**[17] 2371 3-8-6 88 TedDurcan 4 86
(James Bethell) *hld up in rr: effrt over 2f out: one pce* **16/1**

13-3 6 nk **Ajmany (IRE)**[22] 2209 3-8-5 87 (b) KirstyMilczarek 5 84
(Luca Cumani) *chsd ldrs: drvn over 3f out: outpcd over 2f out: hung lft and kpt on fnl f* **7/1**

62-0 7 8 **Dashing David (IRE)**[23] 2188 3-8-9 91 ow1 PatDobbs 8 69
(Richard Hannon) *sn trcking ldrs: drvn over 3f out: lost pl over 2f out* **33/1**

3525 8 nse **Luhaif**[45] 1623 3-9-6 102 (v) MartinHarley 6 80
(Mick Channon) *led: hdd over 2f out: lost pl over 1f out* **50/1**

1 9 2¼ **Autspread**[61] 1291 3-8-3 85 AndreaAtzeni 7 58
(Marco Botti) *chsd ldrs: drvn over 4f out: lost pl over 2f out* **9/1**

3-66 10 3¾ **Operation Chariot (IRE)**[38] 1767 3-8-10 92 JimmyFortune 9 57
(Andrew Balding) *t.k.h: racd along stands' side: sn w ldrs: edgd lft and lost pl over 2f out* **33/1**

1m 35.8s (-3.50) **Going Correction** -0.175s/f (Firm) 10 Ran SP% **115.3**
Speed ratings (Par 105): **110,104,101,99,98 98,90,90,87,84**
toteswingers 1&2 £5.00, 2&3 £4.20, 1&3 £2.70 CSF £18.28 CT £45.89 TOTE £4.80: £1.80, £2.10, £1.50; EX 20.90 Trifecta £35.20 Pool: £1347.00 - 28.65 winning units..
Owner K Abdullah **Bred** Juddmonte Farms Ltd **Trained** Newmarket, Suffolk

FOCUS
This looked a warm 3yo handicap on paper and winners of the race in recent years have generally gone on to be smart performers. Remote impressed in a fast time, and the form is sound.

2858 LADBROKES H'CAP 7f
3:45 (3:47) (Class 2) (0-105,98) 4-Y-O+ **£12,938** (£3,850; £1,924; £962) **Stalls** High

Form RPR

01-3 1 **Diescentric (USA)**[11] 2541 6-8-12 89 PaulHanagan 13 102
(Julie Camacho) *hld up in rr: hdwy and nt clr run 2f out: str run over 1f out: r.o wl to ld in clsng stages* **16/1**

0-0 2 1¼ **Rex Imperator**[128] 367 4-9-7 98 PatCosgrave 16 108+
(William Haggas) *hld up in rr: smooth hdwy over 2f out: led 1f out: hdd and no ex last 50yds* **28/1**

0-66 3 1¼ **Lutine Bell**[21] 2265 6-8-5 82 (b) MartinDwyer 3 88
(Mike Murphy) *s.s: swtchd rt after s: gd hdwy and nt clr run over 1f out: swtchd lft: fin strly* **12/1**

0-20 4 1¼ **Glen Moss (IRE)**[21] 2254 4-8-11 88 JamesMcDonald 2 91
(Charles Hills) *w ldrs: led over 3f out: hdd 1f out: kpt on same pce* **12/1**

1-16 5 1¼ **Tartiflette**[21] 2254 4-9-3 94 SeanLevey 8 94
(Ed McMahon) *hld up in mid-div: effrt 2f out: kpt on ins fnl f* **4/1**[1]

10-0 6 2¼ **Born To Surprise**[21] 2254 4-9-4 95 TomQueally 11 89
(Michael Bell) *hld up towards rr: hdwy over 2f out: n.m.r and edgd lft over 1f out: wknd last 150yds* **13/2**[2]

3-30 7 nk **Lightning Cloud (IRE)**[21] 2254 5-9-3 94 (t) AmyRyan 15 87
(Kevin Ryan) *hld up in rr: hdwy over 2f out: hung lft over 1f out: nvr trbld ldrs* **15/2**[3]

55-2 8 hd **Poetic Dancer**[19] 2310 4-8-7 89 RyanTate(5) 10 81
(Clive Cox) *trckd ldrs: effrt over 2f out: one pce over 1f out* **12/1**

1060 9 1 **Es Que Love (IRE)**[16] 2399 4-9-7 98 KierenFallon 6 88
(Mark Johnston) *mid-div: hdwy over 2f out: chsng ldrs over 1f out: wkng whn hmpd jst ins fnl f* **14/1**

25-4 10 ¾ **Stevie Thunder**[15] 2424 8-8-8 88 RyanPowell(3) 9 75
(Ian Williams) *s.i.s: in rr and sn drvn along: sme hdwy 2f out: nvr a factor* **22/1**

5-01 11 1¾ **Mezzotint (IRE)**[19] 2310 4-9-1 92 AndreaAtzeni 7 75
(Marco Botti) *mid-div: drvn to chse ldrs over 3f out: wknd 2f out* **8/1**

6-00 12 nse **Crius (IRE)**[15] 2424 4-8-13 90 PatDobbs 12 73
(Richard Hannon) *in tch: effrt over 2f out: lost pl 2f out* **16/1**

0-00 13 3 **I'm So Glad**[28] 2013 4-9-1 92 MartinHarley 1 67
(Mick Channon) *racd wd far side: w ldrs: wknd over 1f out* **50/1**

41-1 14 3½ **Amazing Amoray (IRE)**[11] 2541 5-8-9 86 GrahamGibbons 5 51+
(David Barron) *led tl over 3f out: wknd and heavily eased over 1f out* **9/1**

0-61 15 22 **Red Seventy**[14] 2450 4-8-2 79 LukeMorris 4
(Harry Dunlop) *chsd ldrs: lost pl over 2f out: bhd whn heavily eased over 1f out: t.o* **11/1**

1m 23.37s (-2.93) **Going Correction** -0.175s/f (Firm) 15 Ran SP% **125.8**
Speed ratings (Par 109): **109,107,106,104,103 100,100,100,99,98 96,96,92,88,63**
toteswingers 1&2 £74.60, 2&3 £41.60, CSF £422.32 CT £5605.76 TOTE £24.00: £6.10, £8.40, £3.00; EX 486.10 Trifecta £1602.50 Part won. Pool: £2136.66 - 0.01 winning units..
Owner Axom (XVIII) **Bred** Morgan's Ford Farm **Trained** Norton, N Yorks
■ Stewards' Enquiry : Martin Dwyer one-day ban; careless riding (15th June).

 The Form Book Flat, Raceform Ltd, Compton, RG20 6NL.

FOCUS
An ultra-competitive handicap and the pace was sound, allowing those coming from off the pace to play their cards late. A clear personal best from the winner.

2859 LADBROKES CONDITIONS STKS 1m 2f 60y
4:45 (4:45) (Class 2) 3-Y-O £12,938 (£3,850; £1,924) Stalls Low

Form RPR
42-1 1 **Elkaayed (USA)**16 2384 3-8-12 83 PaulHanagan 3 111
(Roger Varian) *mde all: t.k.h: qcknd pce over 3f out: clr over 1f out: unchal* 6/4[1]
1 2 2 3/4 **Sea Meets Sky (FR)**22 2206 3-8-7 87 TomQueally 4 100
(Sir Henry Cecil) *sltly hmpd s: hld up: effrt over 3f out: styd on to chse wnr 1f out: no imp* 7/4[2]
11 3 5 **Queensberry Rules (IRE)**36 1812 3-8-12 97 KierenFallon 5 98
(William Haggas) *swtchd lft after s: trckd wnr: t.k.h: effrt over 3f out: edgd lft over 1f out: wknd last 150yds: eased towards fin* 9/4[3]
2m 8.23s (-1.17) **Going Correction** -0.175s/f (Firm) **3 Ran SP% 107.1**
Speed ratings (Par 105): **97,94,90**
CSF £4.27 TOTE £2.60; EX 4.90 Trifecta £3.90 Pool: £1222.40 - 230.69 winning units..
Owner Hamdan Al Maktoum **Bred** Shadwell Farm LLC **Trained** Newmarket, Suffolk

FOCUS
Three promising 3yos on show in a hot little contest. A positive view has been taken of the form.

2860 LADBROKES MOBILE H'CAP 1m 6f 132y
5:20 (5:21) (Class 5) (0-70,70) 4-Y-O+ £2,911 (£866; £432; £216) Stalls Low

Form RPR
261 1 **Mr Snoozy**14 2435 4-9-1 69 (p) JasonHart(5) 5 76
(Tim Walford) *trckd ldrs: led 3f out: kpt on wl fnl f: drvn rt out* 4/1[2]
300/ 2 1 1/4 **Rumble Of Thunder (IRE)**21 5593 7-9-7 70 RussKennemore 4 75
(Philip Kirby) *trckd ldrs: effrt 3f out: styd on to take 2nd nr fin* 9/2[3]
-035 3 hd **Madrasa (IRE)**5 2720 5-8-13 62 (bt) PaulHanagan 11 67+
(Keith Reveley) *swtchd lft s: hld up in rr: hdwy and n.m.r 2f out: edgd rt ins fnl f: styd on wl to take 3rd fnl strides* 7/2[1]
0105 4 1/2 **Knox Overstreet**8 2629 5-9-3 66 MartinHarley 7 70
(Mick Channon) *hld up in rr: hdwy over 2f out: chsd wnr over 1f out: kpt on same pce last 150yds* 28/1
43/0 5 3/4 **Sagredo (USA)**12 2498 9-9-2 65 (p) TomQueally 8 70+
(Jonjo O'Neill) *hld up in rr: hdwy on ins over 3f out: repeatedly denied clr run: kpt on towards fin* 20/1
062- 6 nk **My Destination (IRE)**215 7444 4-9-0 66 NeilFarley(3) 2 69
(Declan Carroll) *mid-div: hdwy over 1f out: styng on at fin* 25/1
0/-6 7 4 **Princeofthedesert**14 2462 7-8-6 55 KirstyMilczarek 10 53
(Garry Woodward) *trckd ldrs: t.k.h: drvn 4f out: wknd appr fnl f* 66/1
630- 8 1/2 **Eastern Magic**194 7791 6-8-3 57 (p) JackDuern(5) 3 54
(Andrew Hollinshead) *chsd ldrs: drvn over 3f out: wknd over 1f out* 16/1
3400 9 2 1/4 **Kingaroo (IRE)**24 2174 7-7-13 51 oh3 RyanPowell(3) 9 45
(Garry Woodward) *mid-div: hdwy 4f out: lost pl over 2f out* 50/1
0-11 10 1 1/4 **Full Speed (GER)**22 1251 8-9-0 68 WilliamTwiston-Davies(5) 12 60
(Philip Kirby) *swtchd lft s: led hdd 3f out: wknd over 1f out* 9/2[3]
64-0 11 17 **Key Gold**74 1083 4-9-7 70 AndreaAtzeni 1 40
(Ian McInnes) *chsd ldrs: lost pl 3f out: bhd whn eased fnl f* 25/1
6-63 12 hd **La Bacouetteuse (FR)**29 1993 8-9-6 69 (v) KierenFallon 6 39
(Iain Jardine) *s.i.s: sn drvn along: bhd fnl 3f: eased ins fnl f* 13/2
3m 9.44s (2.04) **Going Correction** -0.175s/f (Firm) **12 Ran SP% 117.2**
Speed ratings (Par 103): **87,86,86,85,85 85,83,83,81,81 72,71**
toteswingers 1&2 £5.50, 2&3 £5.50, 1&3 £1.20 CSF £20.21 CT £69.17 TOTE £4.60: £1.90, £1.50, £1.20; EX 31.10 Trifecta £98.90 Pool: £1360.57 - 10.31 winning units..
Owner T W Heseltine **Bred** J W Mursell **Trained** Sheriff Hutton, N Yorks

FOCUS
Competitive enough for the grade, but the pace was ordinary with a pretty congested finish. The winner can probably do a bit better.

2861 PARK HILL HOSPITAL MAIDEN STKS 5f
5:50 (5:52) (Class 5) 3-Y-O+ £2,911 (£866; £432; £216) Stalls High

Form RPR
5-03 1 **Little Eli**26 2091 3-9-0 52 JasonHart(5) 3 61
(Eric Alston) *t.k.h: led 1f: hung lft over 1f out: kpt on fnl f: led nr fin* 18/1
2 nk **Idle Warrior** 3-9-5 0 PaulHanagan 2 60
(Richard Fahey) *sn trcking ldng pair: effrt on outer 2f out: edgd lft and led 1f out: hdd and no ex nr fin* 4/1[2]
23-2 3 3/4 **Ian's Dream (USA)**12 2499 3-9-5 105 JimmyFortune 5 57
(Jeremy Noseda) *ponied to s and wore rug for stalls entry: stmbld s: pushed along over 3f out: hdwy over 1f out: kpt on last 75yds* 2/7[1]
-400 4 5 **Queen Flush (IRE)**19 2317 3-9-0 63 PaulQuinn 1 34
(David Nicholls) *wnt lft s and racd wd: led after 1f: edgd rt over 1f out: sn hdd: wknd fnl 150yds* 11/1[3]
235- 5 7 **Red Highlites (IRE)**313 4395 3-9-0 62 TomQueally 6 9
(Ann Duffield) *sn trcking ldrs: effrt 2f out: sn wknd: eased clsng stages* 16/1
1m 1.04s (0.54) **Going Correction** -0.175s/f (Firm) **5 Ran SP% 117.2**
Speed ratings (Par 103): **88,87,86,78,67**
CSF £88.12 TOTE £14.00: £5.80, £2.00; EX 129.30 Trifecta £76.50 Pool: £1478.55 - 14.48 winning units..
Owner Whittle Racing Partnership **Bred** J E Jackson **Trained** Longton, Lancs

FOCUS
A modest sprint maiden, and it's hard to know what to make of this form.
T/Plt: £141.30 to a £1 stake. Pool of £83359.29 - 430.54 winning tickets. T/Qpdt: £57.00 to a £1 stake. Pool of £4529.40 - 58.75 winning tickets. WG

2838 EPSOM (L-H)
Saturday, June 1

OFFICIAL GOING: Good (good to soft in places; derby course 7.1; 5f course 7.3)
Course at normal configuration and all distances as advertised.
Wind: very light, against Weather: dry, bright spells

2862 INVESTEC OUT OF THE ORDINARY H'CAP 1m 2f 18y
1:35 (1:37) (Class 2) (0-105,93) 3-Y-O £31,125 (£9,320; £4,660; £2,330; £1,165; £585) Stalls Low

Form RPR
0-43 1 **Pasaka Boy**21 2262 3-8-12 84 RichardKingscote 7 93
(Jonathan Portman) *chsd ldng pair: clr in ldng trio over 4f out: switching rt and effrt over 3f out: chsd ldr 2f out: led 1f out: r.o wl u.p* 25/1
-523 2 1 1/2 **Greeleys Love (USA)**11 2554 3-8-11 83 (v1) SilvestreDeSousa 6 89+
(Mark Johnston) *dwlt: t.k.h: hdwy into midfield after 2f out: hdwy u.p and edging lft jst over 2f out: chsd ldng pair over 1f out: kpt on to go 2nd last strides* 9/1
3-10 3 nk **King Muro**24 2153 3-8-2 74 [1] HayleyTurner 1 79
(Andrew Balding) *t.k.h: led: clr w 2 rivals over 4f out: drvn over 2f out: hdd 1f out: styd on same pce fnl f: lost 2nd last strides* 33/1
2131 4 1 1/2 **High Troja (IRE)**14 2445 3-9-1 87 RyanMoore 3 89+
(Ed Dunlop) *hld up in midfield: rdn and effrt 3f out: edging out rt 2f out: chsd ldng trio over 1f out: kpt on but no imp fnl f* 7/2[1]
2-34 5 2 **London Citizen (USA)**29 1991 3-9-2 88 JimCrowley 5 88+
(Mrs K Burke) *lw: chsd ldng trio: rdn and effrt over 2f out: squeezed for room and hmpd 2f out: rallied and kpt on ins fnl f: no threat to ldrs* 12/1
-221 6 1 1/4 **Space Ship**24 2151 3-9-7 93 WilliamBuick 11 89+
(John Gosden) *hld up in last pair: hdwy into midfield but stl plenty to do 2f out: nvr gng to rch ldrs and nt given too hrd a time after: kpt on ins fnl f* 9/2[2]
-214 7 1 1/2 **Salutation (IRE)**8 2641 3-8-13 85 FMBerry 12 78
(Mark Johnston) *chsd ldr: clr in ldng trio over 4f out: rdn and effrt to chal 3f out tl ent fnl 2f: sn btn: wknd over 1f out* 10/1
50-4 8 1 3/4 **Makafeh**27 2050 3-9-3 89 JamieSpencer 2 78
(Luca Cumani) *taken down early and ponied to s: hld up in last quartet: effrt but no hdwy on inner over 2f out: plugged on but wl hld after* 9/2[2]
01-0 9 nse **St Paul De Vence (IRE)**40 1725 3-8-9 81 ow1 NeilCallan 8 70
(Paul Cole) *lw: hld up in last quartet: effrt but edging down camber 3f out: sn struggling and outpcd: no ch but plugged on ins fnl f* 8/1[3]
00-1 10 3 3/4 **Forging The Path (USA)**21 2279 3-8-7 79 FrederikTylicki 9 60
(Richard Fahey) *b: hld up in midfield: rdn and lost pl wl over 2f out: bhd fnl 2f* 14/1
21-0 11 43 **Mundahesh (IRE)**17 2371 3-8-10 82 RichardHughes 10
(William Haggas) *b.hind: stdd s: a in rr: struggling and losing tch on downhill run over 4f out: t.o and eased fnl f* 11/1
2m 8.79s (-0.91) **Going Correction** +0.25s/f (Good) **11 Ran SP% 118.3**
Speed ratings (Par 105): **113,111,111,110,108 107,106,105,105,102 67**
toteswingers 1&2 £42.20, 2&3 £53.60, 1&3 £57.40 CSF £235.86 CT £7272.58 TOTE £34.70: £8.10, £3.20, £7.40; EX 390.00 Trifecta £6035.20 Pool: £9659.86 - 1.20 winning units..
Owner RWH Partnership **Bred** G Wickens And J Homan **Trained** Upper Lambourn, Berks

FOCUS
The ground had dried out a little since the previous day, officially being described as good, good to soft in places. There was a fresh strip of ground about 8 yards wide from a mile out. A 3yo handicap that's been won by some really smart sorts over the years, notably subsequent Group 1 winners Lailani (2002) and Conduit (2008), but this looked just an ordinary edition. The third helps with the standard. Three horses, including the winner and the front-running third, got a bit of a break on the field and the visual impression was they had saved plenty early before catching the others out when upping the tempo running downhill into the straight.

2863 INVESTEC WOODCOTE STKS (LISTED RACE) 6f
2:05 (2:06) (Class 1) 2-Y-O £17,013 (£6,450; £3,228; £1,608; £807; £405) Stalls High

Form RPR
11 1 **Thunder Strike**12 2518 2-9-0 0 RichardHughes 1 101+
(Richard Hannon) *str: lw: w ldng pair on inner: travelling best over 2f out: pushed into ld and qcknd clr over 1f out: in command whn looking at crowd and edging rt ins fnl f: easily: quite impressive* 3/1[1]
1 2 3 1/2 **Riverboat Springs (IRE)**17 2358 2-9-0 0 WilliamBuick 6 90+
(Mick Channon) *leggy: sn outpcd in last trio and nt handling trck: wl off the pce in 11th and hanging lft down camber fr over 3f out: stl 11th whn plld out rt 1f out: str run fnl f to go 2nd towards fin: no threat wnr* 5/1[2]
13 3 1 **Haikbidiac (IRE)**17 2370 2-9-0 0 RyanMoore 4 87
(William Haggas) *w ldr: rdn and ev ch over 2f out: outpcd and drvn 2f out: no ch w wnr and kpt on same pce fnl f* 3/1[1]
51 4 nk **Ifwecan**21 2250 2-9-0 0 SilvestreDeSousa 11 86
(Mark Johnston) *lw: led narrowly on outer: rdn wl over 2f out: hdd 2f out and sn outpcd by wnr: kpt on same pce fnl f: lost 2 pls towards fin* 13/2[3]
1 5 1/2 **Cool Bahamian (IRE)**21 2260 2-9-0 0 JohnFahy 7 85
(Eve Johnson Houghton) *w'like: tall: swtg: in tch in rr of main gp: outpcd and struggling 4f out: rallied and styd on past btn horses over 1f out: kpt on fnl f: no ch w wnr* 11/1
21 6 1 3/4 **Money Team (IRE)**8 2631 2-9-0 0 JimCrowley 5 79
(Bill Turner) *lw: in tch in midfield: hdwy and swtchd rt 4f out: chsd ldng trio jst over 2f out: no imp: wknd ins fnl f* 12/1
7 nk **Soul Of Motion** 2-9-0 0 Pierre-CharlesBoudot 10 78+
(Gay Kelleway) *w'like: sn outpcd in last trio: rdn 3f out: hdwy and swtchd rt jst over 1f out: kpt on steadily ins fnl f: nvr trbld ldrs* 40/1
3215 8 4 **Far Gaze (IRE)**31 1917 2-9-0 0 LiamJones 2 66
(J S Moore) *lw: in tch in midfield: rdn and struggling 4f out: sn outpcd: n.d fnl 2f* 25/1
01 9 shd **Neighbother**21 2283 2-9-0 0 FrederikTylicki 9 66
(Richard Fahey) *str: chsd ldrs early: losing pl whn pushed rt 4f out: sn rdn and struggling: n.d after* 11/1
61 10 4 1/2 **Zalzilah**26 2075 2-9-0 0 NeilCallan 8 53
(James Tate) *chsd ldrs: 4th and outpcd u.p over 2f out: wknd over 1f out* 14/1
06 11 10 **Flying Author (IRE)**16 2382 2-9-0 0 [1] AdamKirby 3 23
(Phil McEntee) *s.i.s: a wl outpcd in rr* 66/1
1m 11.26s (1.86) **Going Correction** +0.25s/f (Good) **11 Ran SP% 118.8**
Speed ratings (Par 101): **97,92,91,90,89 87,87,81,81,75 62**
toteswingers 1&2 £3.10, 2&3 £4.80, 1&3 £2.60 CSF £17.80 TOTE £3.50: £1.40, £2.10, £1.40; EX 15.20 Trifecta £47.10 Pool: £7576.06 - 120.48 winning units..
Owner Mohamed Saeed Al Shahi **Bred** Southill Stud **Trained** East Everleigh, Wilts

FOCUS
Declaration of War and Fulbright were the best recent winners of this Listed juvenile contest and this year's winner has the potential to rank near the same level as both of those. The form looks solid with the third to sixth all close to pre-race marks.

2864 INVESTEC CORONATION CUP (GROUP 1) 1m 4f 10y
2:40 (2:42) (Class 1) 4-Y-O+ £198,485 (£75,250; £37,660; £18,760; £9,415) Stalls Centre

Form RPR
03-1 1 **St Nicholas Abbey (IRE)**63 1268 6-9-0 124 JosephO'Brien 3 126
(A P O'Brien, Ire) *swtg: hld up in last pair: wnt 3rd and clsd on ldrs over 3f out: led jst over 2f out and sn rdn clr: in command and r.o wl fnl f* 30/100[1]
5-43 2 3 3/4 **Dunaden (FR)**34 1870 7-9-0 117 JamieSpencer 5 121
(M Delzangles, France) *stdd and dropped in bhd after s: hld up in last: trcking wnr and clsd on ldrs 3f out: rdn and chsd clr wnr 2f out: no imp: hld and eased wl ins fnl f* 4/1[2]

10-6 **3** *7* **Joshua Tree (IRE)**[15] 2428 6-9-0 115................................ RyanMoore 2 109
(Ed Dunlop) *lw: chsd clr ldng pair: clsd over 3f out: drvn and outpcd 2f out: wnt modest 3rd over 1f out: no imp* **10/1**[3]

6-63 **4** *5* **Chapter Seven**[42] 1675 4-9-0 100................................ HarryBentley 4 101
(Stuart Williams) *lw: led tl 9f out: styd upsides ldr and steadily drew clr: led again 4f out: rdn 3f out: hdd jst over 2f out: sn wknd* **50/1**

5 *18* **Chamonix (IRE)**[230] 7088 4-9-0 110........................ SeamieHeffernan 1 87
(A P O'Brien, Ire) *w'like: scope: dwlt: sn rcvrd to press ldr: led 9f out tl 4f out: sn rdn and struggling: bhd fnl 2f: eased ins fnl f* **16/1**

2m 37.76s (-1.14) **Going Correction** +0.25s/f (Good) **5** Ran SP% **113.9**
Speed ratings (Par 117): **113,110,105,102,90**
CSF £2.07 TOTE £1.30: £1.02, £1.80; EX 1.90 Trifecta £2.80 Pool: £27682.54 - 7194.89 winning units..
Owner Derrick Smith & Mrs John Magnier & Michael Tabor **Bred** Barton Bloodstock & Villiers Synd **Trained** Ballydoyle, Co Tipperary

FOCUS
Essentially a two-horse race, which was disappointing, but this was still another high-class performance from the winner. The final time was over a second quicker than the Derby, but hand-timed sectionals showed the pace was much faster through the middle section thanks to the pacemakers. St Nicholas Abbey is rated to the same figure as when winning this last year.

2865 INVESTEC SPECIALIST BANK "DASH" (HERITAGE H'CAP) 5f
3:15 (3:16) (Class 2) 3-Y-O+

£62,250 (£18,640; £9,320; £4,660; £2,330; £1,170) **Stalls** Low

Form RPR

-015 **1** **Duke Of Firenze**[7] 2669 4-9-0 **97**................................ RyanMoore 19 105+
(Sir Michael Stoute) *racd off the pce in last quartet: nt clr run and switching lft over 1f out: hdwy 1f out: stl switching lft and str run ins fnl f: burst between horse to ld nr fin* **5/1**[1]

1231 **2** *nk* **Smoothtalkinrascal (IRE)**[16] 2400 3-8-13 **103** 4ex..... DanielTudhope 1 107+
(David O'Meara) *stdd and pushed lft s: sn swtchd rt but wl off the pce in last quartet: stl plenty to do whn hdwy 1f out: str run fnl 150yds: wnt 2nd last strides* **7/1**[3]

10-0 **3** *nk* **Dinkum Diamond (IRE)**[16] 2396 5-9-5 **102**.................. CathyGannon 5 108
(Henry Candy) *racd in midfield: effrt and pushed lft ent fnl f: r.o wl u.p fnl 150yds: snatched 3rd last stride* **25/1**

00-3 **4** *shd* **Fair Value (IRE)**[28] 2014 5-8-7 **90**................................ HayleyTurner 13 96
(Simon Dow) *chsd ldr: rdn to ld 1f out: drvn and looked wnr ins fnl f: hdd and lost 3 pls last strides* **12/1**

3/0- **5** *nk* **Jiroft (ITY)**[273] 6-9-5 **102**.. ShaneKelly 2 106
(Robert Cowell) *trckd ldrs: rdn and effrt 1f out: chsd ldr briefly ins fnl f: no ex and lost 3 pls towards fin* **33/1**

56-2 **6** *½* **La Fortunata**[38] 1765 6-8-2 **90**............................ MichaelJMMurphy(5) 6 93
(Mike Murphy) *chsd ldrs: effrt over 1f out: styd on u.p tl no ex towards fin* **14/1**

20-2 **7** *½* **Captain Dunne (IRE)**[24] 2150 8-8-12 **95**.....................(p) DavidAllan 18 96
(Tim Easterby) *broke v fast and led at fast gallop against stand's rail: rdn over 1f out: hdd 1f out: no ex and wknd towards fin* **7/1**[3]

6-50 **8** *½* **Doctor Parkes**[14] 2444 7-8-5 **88**................................ HarryBentley 10 87
(Stuart Williams) *in tch in midfield: effrt u.p over 1f out: styd on same pce u.p ins fnl f* **25/1**

0546 **9** *nk* **Confessional**[24] 2152 6-9-5 **102**........................(be) SilvestreDeSousa 11 100
(Tim Easterby) *in tch in midfield: rdn and effrt over 1f out: kpt on same pce ins fnl f* **14/1**

0-05 **10** *nk* **Taajub (IRE)**[43] 1672 6-9-1 **98**.. IanMongan 4 95
(Peter Crate) *hld up in midfield: swtchd lft and effrt u.p over 1f out: kpt on ins fnl f same pce* **20/1**

53-1 **11** *hd* **Ajjaadd (USA)**[38] 1765 7-9-2 **99**................................ KieranO'Neill 9 95+
(Ted Powell) *hld up in midfield: swtchd lft and effrt whn short of room 1f out: kpt on same pce ins fnl f* **12/1**

132- **12** *shd* **Long Awaited (IRE)**[245] 6666 5-8-12 **95**................(b) RichardHughes 16 94+
(David Barron) *lw: racd off the pce towards rr: effrt and clsd over 1f out: keeping on whn nt clr wl ins fnl f: nvr able to chal* **11/2**[2]

-001 **13** *1* **Church Music (IRE)**[10] 2561 4-8-1 **87** 4ex...............(v) DarrenEgan(3) 17 79
(Michael Scudamore) *off the pce towards rr: effrt u.p and edging lft over 1f out: kpt on but no threat to ldrs* **20/1**

6-30 **14** *nk* **Judge 'n Jury**[7] 2669 9-8-11 **99**............................(t) ThomasBrown(5) 3 90
(Ronald Harris) *chsd ldrs: rdn and edgd rt ent fnl f: wknd ins fnl f* **20/1**

0-40 **15** *hd* **Top Cop**[14] 2444 4-7-12 **88**.......................................(b[1]) JoeyHaynes(7) 20 78
(Andrew Balding) *dwlt: sn bustled in rr: kpt on ins fnl f: nvr trbld ldrs* **14/1**

-160 **16** *2 ¾* **Mister Manannan (IRE)**[16] 2396 6-8-8 **91**...............(p) FrederikTylicki 7 72
(David Nicholls) *racd in centre: in tch: effrt u.p to chse ldrs 2f out: wknd ins fnl f* **20/1**

40- **17** *½* **Ballesteros**[207] 7624 4-9-10 **107**.................................... WilliamBuick 14 86
(Brian Meehan) *swtg: s.i.s: a outpcd in rr* **16/1**

55.22s (-0.48) **Going Correction** +0.175s/f (Good)
WFA 3 from 4yo+ 7lb **17** Ran SP% **128.0**
Speed ratings (Par 109): **110,109,109,108,108 107,106,106,105,105 104,104,102,102,102 97,96**
toteswingers 1&2 £7.00, 2&3 £73.50, 1&3 £45.20 CSF £36.14 CT £859.85 TOTE £4.80: £1.50, £2.40, £5.60, £3.20; EX 46.50 Trifecta £1550.70 Pool: £ 58633.46 - 41.60 winning units..
Owner Cheveley Park Stud **Bred** Cheveley Park Stud Ltd **Trained** Newmarket, Suffolk

FOCUS
A typically competitive renewal of this hot sprint handicap, and a fantastic finish, with the first two home cutting through the field in the closing stages from seemingly impossible positions. The level is set around the fourth.

2866 INVESTEC DERBY (GROUP 1) (ENTIRE COLTS & FILLIES) 1m 4f 10y
4:00 (4:00) (Class 1) 3-Y-O

£782,314 (£296,592; £148,434; £73,941; £37,108; £18,623) **Stalls** Centre

Form RPR

1 **1** **Ruler Of The World (IRE)**[23] 2187 3-9-0 109.............(p) RyanMoore 10 121
(A P O'Brien, Ire) *swtg: in tch in last quartet: 7th st: rdn and hdwy whn edging lft over 2f out: chsd ldr 2f out: led over 1f out: styd on wl and forged clr 1f out: drvn out* **7/1**[3]

141 **2** *1 ½* **Libertarian**[16] 2398 3-9-0 112.. WilliamBuick 5 118
(Mrs K Burke) *lw: dwlt and pushed along leaving stalls: in tch in last pair: 10th and rdn st: no imp and edging lft tl hdwy u.p over 1f out: styd on strly ins fnl f to snatch 2nd last stride* **14/1**

5-3 **3** *shd* **Galileo Rock (IRE)**[36] 1811 3-9-0 108......................... WayneLordan 11 118
(David Wachman, Ire) *t.k.h: chsd ldrs: 3rd st: drvn and chsd ldr 3f out tl 2f out: kpt on wl but one pce ins fnl f* **25/1**

1-11 **4** *shd* **Battle Of Marengo (IRE)**[20] 2290 3-9-0 117.............(p) JosephO'Brien 9 118
(A P O'Brien, Ire) *w'like: chsd ldrs tl led over 9f out: hdd 6f out: 2nd st: rdn to ld again 3f out: hdd over 1f out: kpt on same pce u.p fnl f: lost 2 pls last strides* **11/2**[2]

1 **5** *½* **Ocovango**[28] 2035 3-9-0 114................................ Pierre-CharlesBoudot 1 117+
(A Fabre, France) *w'like: t.k.h: in tch in midfield: 6th st: switching rt and hmpd over 2f out: clsng on ldrs and short of room again 2f out: rdn and hdwy over 1f out: n.m.r 1f out: kpt on but nvr quite gng pce to threaten wnr* **8/1**

1-6 **6** *1 ½* **Mars (IRE)**[28] 2021 3-9-0 108..................................... RichardHughes 12 116+
(A P O'Brien, Ire) *lw: stdd s: hld up in tch in rr: 11th st: nt clr run and swtchd lft over 2f out: swtchd rt and barging match wl over 1f out: hdwy 1f out: styd on wl fnl 100yds: nvr trbld ldrs* **12/1**

1 **7** *nse* **Chopin (GER)**[41] 1708 3-9-0 115..................................... JamieSpencer 4 116+
(A Wohler, Germany) *str: lw: hld up in tch in last quartet: 9th st: rdn and hdwy over 2f out: chsd ldrs over 1f out: no ex and styng on same pce whn squeezed for room wl ins fnl f* **12/1**

0-06 **8** *2 ¼* **Flying The Flag (IRE)**[7] 2677 3-9-2 108 ow2.......... CO'Donoghue 8 111
(A P O'Brien, Ire) *lengthy: led for 2f: chsd ldr tl 6f out: 4th st: rdn and unable qck over 2f out: outpcd and btn over 1f out: plugged on same pce after* **66/1**

30-1 **9** *1 ¼* **Mirsaale**[38] 1767 3-9-0 96.. NeilCallan 6 109
(James Tate) *t.k.h: hld up wl in tch in midfield: 5th st: rdn and struggling to qckn whn short of room 2f out: kpt on same pce and no threat to ldrs after* **50/1**

3 **10** *4 ½* **Festive Cheer (FR)**[20] 2297 3-9-0 111..................... SeamieHeffernan 2 102
(A P O'Brien, Ire) *str: chsd ldr for 2f: styd chsng ldrs: lost pl and 8th st: drvn and struggling whn barging match wl over 1f out: sn wknd* **25/1**

-000 **11** *21* **Ocean Applause**[38] 1767 3-9-0 74.....................(p) DaraghO'Donohoe 3 68
(John Ryan) *chsd ldrs: rdn and lost pl over 4f out: 12th and wkng st: sn lost tch: t.o fnl 2f* **200/1**

11-1 **12** *½* **Dawn Approach (IRE)**[28] 2021 3-9-0 125..................... KevinManning 7 88
(J S Bolger, Ire) *stdd s: plld hrd and ref to settle in midfield: allowed his hd and hdwy to ld 6f out: hdd 3f out and sn rdn and btn: eased fnl 2f: t.o* **5/4**[1]

2m 39.06s (0.16) **Going Correction** +0.25s/f (Good) **12** Ran SP% **117.1**
Speed ratings (Par 113): **109,108,107,107,107 106,106,105,104,101 87,86**
toteswingers 1&2 £8.10, 2&3 £32.80, 1&3 £18.20 CSF £94.54 CT £2305.71 TOTE £9.10: £2.50, £3.40, £7.10; EX 65.40 Trifecta £744.70 Pool: £43975.33 - 44.24 winning units..
Owner Mrs John Magnier & Michael Tabor & Derrick Smith **Bred** Southern Bloodstock **Trained** Ballydoyle, Co Tipperary

■ A fourth Derby for Aidan O'Brien and a second for Ryan Moore. Just 3 GB-trained runners, the lowest ever domestic challenge.

■ Stewards' Enquiry : Wayne Lordan two-day ban; used whip above permitted level (15th-16 June).

FOCUS
This year's Derby was a messy affair and, with Dawn Approach, who had upwards of 9lb in hand on RPRs, failing to run his race, and a rather compressed finish, it's hard to consider the form particularly strong. Ruler Of The World rates an ordinary winner at this stage. However, a number of these look capable of progressing and it might just pay to take a positive view of the race, especially bearing in mind last season's Classic generation are/were a below-par bunch. The time was over a second off the Coronation Cup, and only fractionally quicker than the following Class 2 handicap, and that can be explained by the pace, or more specifically the lack of it. Indeed, hand-timed sectionals showed, while the gallop was fair enough for the first couple of furlongs or so, the middle section was much slower than the other two races at the trip. Considering the way the race unfolded, the front three, who are strong-staying types, deserve extra credit.

2867 INVESTEC ZEBRA H'CAP 1m 4f 10y
4:50 (4:52) (Class 2) (0-100,92) 4-Y-O+

£15,562 (£4,660; £2,330; £1,165; £582; £292) **Stalls** Centre

Form RPR

5-12 **1** **Sheikhzayedroad**[21] 2263 4-9-7 **92**................................ MartinLane 11 107+
(David Simcock) *stdd s: hld up wl off the pce in rr: hdwy on outer 3f out: hanging lft down camber but gd hdwy to chse ldr over 1f out: stl hanging but led ins fnl f: sn in command and r.o wl* **5/1**[2]

4412 **2** *3 ¼* **Duke Of Clarence (IRE)**[12] 2520 4-9-3 **88**................. RichardHughes 12 95+
(Richard Hannon) *hld up off the pce in midfield: rdn and hdwy over 2f out: chsd ldng pair over 1f out: kpt on to go 2nd towards fin: no threat to wnr* **11/4**[1]

14-0 **3** *1 ½* **Colinca's Lad (IRE)**[13] 2478 11-8-0 **76**...................... RosieJessop(5) 10 81
(Peter Charalambous) *led and steadily drew clr: stl 8 l clr and rdn over 3f out: kpt on tl hdd ins fnl f: no ex and lost 2nd towards fin* **33/1**

0P05 **4** *½* **John Biscuit (IRE)**[17] 2365 5-9-0 **85**................................ HayleyTurner 8 89+
(Andrew Balding) *taken down early: hld up off the pce in last quartet: effrt whn squeezed for room and hmpd 3f out: rallied and hdwy over 1f out: styd on fnl f: no threat to wnr* **6/1**[3]

3-04 **5** *1 ¼* **First Avenue**[78] 739 8-8-4 **82**................................ CharlotteJenner(7) 5 84
(Laura Mongan) *hld up off the pce in midfield: effrt on inner 3f out: squeezed through on rail and chsd ldng trio over 1f out: no imp* **16/1**

3323 **6** *3 ¾* **Tepmokea (IRE)**[21] 2263 7-9-7 **92**.. ShaneKelly 1 88
(Mrs K Burke) *hld up off the pce in midfield: rdn and effrt to chse ldrs 3f out: struggling to qckn whn short of room and swtchd rt 2f out: no prog: wknd 1f out* **25/1**

542 **7** *shd* **Cayuga**[15] 2422 4-8-5 **81**.. RobertTart(5) 2 77
(Brett Johnson) *lw: stdd s: hld up in rr: rdn and effrt 3f out: no real imp: no ch but styd on past btn horses fnl f* **14/1**

3240 **8** *3* **Aquilonius (IRE)**[21] 2251 4-8-11 **82**...........................(t) JamieSpencer 9 73
(Stuart Williams) *chsd ldr: rdn 3f out: lost 2nd and struggling whn pushed rt over 1f out: sn wknd* **25/1**

0401 **9** *2 ½* **Sirvino**[7] 2671 8-9-5 **90**.. RyanMoore 4 77
(David Barron) *hld up wl off pce in last quartet: struggling on downhill run 5f out: n.d after* **5/1**[2]

-404 **10** *4 ½* **Right Step**[9] 2590 6-8-5 **81**................................ MichaelJMMurphy(5) 7 61
(Alan Jarvis) *hld up off the pce in midfield: rdn and effrt 3f out: no prog 2f out: wknd over 1f out* **14/1**

-430 **11** *4 ½* **Scatter Dice (IRE)**[21] 2251 4-9-7 **92**.. FMBerry 6 65
(Mark Johnston) *chsd ldrs but off the pce: rdn and struggling over 3f out: wknd over 2f out: bhd fnl f* **10/1**

0-60 **12** *6* **Party Line**[14] 2451 4-9-5 **90**................................ SilvestreDeSousa 3 53
(Mark Johnston) *chsd ldrs but off the pce: rdn and losing pl over 3f out: sn wknd: bhd over 1f out* **14/1**

2m 39.12s (0.22) **Going Correction** +0.25s/f (Good) **12** Ran SP% **119.9**
Speed ratings (Par 109): **109,106,105,105,104 102,102,100,98,95 92,88**
toteswingers 1&2 £3.60, 2&3 £27.00, 1&3 £38.00 CSF £18.88 CT £419.94 TOTE £4.80: £1.80, £1.80, £8.90; EX 21.40 Trifecta £588.50 Pool: £10068.61 - 12.83 winning units..
Owner Mohammed Jaber **Bred** Rabbah Bloodstock Limited **Trained** Newmarket, Suffolk

FOCUS
A good handicap over the same trip as the preceding Coronation Cup and Investec Derby but run only fractionally slower than the latter race due to the gallop here being more even. 4-y-os have the best record in this race and that was enhanced with the first two home both in that age group. The form is rated around the third, with the value value for a bit extra.

2868 VOYAGE BY INVESTEC H'CAP 6f
5:25 (5:26) (Class 2) (0-100,100) 4-Y-0+

£15,562 (£4,660; £2,330; £1,165; £582; £292) Stalls High

Form RPR
-040 1 **Arctic Feeling (IRE)**[17] 2366 5-8-2 81 JimmyQuinn 10 92
(Richard Fahey) *hld up wl in tch: effrt towards inner to chal over 1f out: led 1f out: kpt on and a gng to hold on: drvn out* 25/1
-042 2 ½ **Titus Gent**[22] 2227 8-8-5 84 ow2 JohnFahy 3 93
(Jeremy Gask) *hld up in last quartet: hdwy on inner over 1f out: str run 1f out: chsd wnr wl ins fnl f: r.o but nvr quite gng to rch wnr* 20/1
-413 3 1¼ **Seeking Magic**[14] 2444 5-9-0 93 (t) AdamKirby 1 98
(Clive Cox) *lw: chsd ldrs: rdn to ld 2f out: hdd over 1f out and no ex ent fnl f: styd on same pce and lost 2nd wl ins fnl f* 4/1[1]
0-00 4 1 **Baby Strange**[14] 2460 9-7-13 81 oh2 DarrenEgan(3) 5 83
(Derek Shaw) *s.i.s: bhd: stl last and no imp u.p over 1f out: str run ins fnl f: wnt 4th towards fin: nvr trbld ldrs* 25/1
0111 5 ¾ **Dr Red Eye**[7] 2649 5-8-13 95 (p) BillyCray(3) 13 95
(Scott Dixon) *chsd ldr tl led after 1f: edgd rt u.p and hdd 2f out: no ex u.p and wknd ins fnl f* 7/1
4026 6 shd **Blue Jack**[16] 2388 8-8-3 82 (t) NickyMackay 6 81
(Stuart Williams) *in tch in midfield: effrt u.p on inner 2f out: chsd ldrs 1f out: styd on same pce after* 20/1
4-60 7 ½ **Compton**[17] 2366 4-8-9 93 ThomasBrown(5) 2 91+
(Robert Cowell) *in tch: rdn and effrt 2f out: no imp over 1f out: styd on same pce fnl f* 6/1[2]
3300 8 ¾ **Al's Memory (IRE)**[14] 2460 4-8-6 85 CathyGannon 14 80
(David Evans) *racd in midfield: rdn 4f out: outpcd over 2f out: styng on u.p but stl plenty to do whn nt clr run jst ins fnl f: kpt on* 33/1
0100 9 hd **Thunderball**[40] 1720 7-9-1 94 (p) IanMongan 4 89
(Scott Dixon) *b: wl in tch: rdn and effrt 2f out: no imp and styd on same pce fr over 1f out* 20/1
5011 10 1 **Gabbiano**[21] 2255 4-8-0 84 ow2 RobertTart(5) 8 76
(Jeremy Gask) *lw: hld up in rr: rdn 2f out: rdn and hdwy whn nt clr run over 1f out tl swtchd lft 1f out: no real imp fnl f* 15/2
1064 11 ½ **Forest Edge (IRE)**[7] 2647 4-8-10 89 (b) JFEgan 15 79
(David Evans) *pressed ldrs: wnt 2nd 5f out tl ent fnl 2f: btn ent fnl f: wknd fnl 150yds* 33/1
6-00 12 1 **Another Try (IRE)**[7] 2664 8-8-2 81 oh1 MartinLane 11 68
(Alan Jarvis) *in tch in midfield: rdn and lost pl 3f out: outpcd and bhd whn nt clr run and swtchd rt 1f out: sme hdwy ins fnl f but no threat to ldrs* 33/1
2110 13 1 **Khawatim**[14] 2444 5-8-8 92 MichaelJMMurphy(5) 16 76
(Noel Quinlan) *a towards rr and stuck wd: rdn and no hdwy over 2f out: wl hld whn hung lft 1f out* 9/1
1023 14 1¼ **Crew Cut (IRE)**[22] 2207 5-8-7 86 (b) SilvestreDeSousa 12 74
(Jeremy Gask) *a towards rr: rdn and no hdwy 2f out: wl hld whn allowed to drift lft and eased ins fnl f* 8/1
-000 15 ¾ **Pabusar**[100] 746 5-9-7 100 HayleyTurner 7 77
(Jamie Osborne) *chsd ldrs: rdn and unable qck 2f out: btn over 1f out: wknd fnl f* 25/1
3114 16 ¾ **Gandalak (FR)**[22] 2210 4-9-2 95 DanielTudhope 17 70
(David O'Meara) *broke fast: led for 1f: chsd ldr after tl carried rt ent fnl 2f: sn struggling u.p: wknd jst over 1f out* 13/2[3]

1m 9.81s (0.41) **Going Correction** +0.25s/f (Good) 16 Ran SP% 127.6
Speed ratings (Par 109): **107,106,104,103,102 102,101,100,100,98 98,96,95,93,92 91**
toteswingers 1&2 £66.00, 2&3 £15.10, 1&3 £29.20 CSF £439.74 CT £2514.67 TOTE £46.80: £6.10, £4.50, £1.50, £4.30; EX 1308.30 Trifecta £5404.20 Part won. Pool: £7205.67 - 0.28 winning units..
Owner Percy / Green Racing 2 **Bred** John McEnery **Trained** Musley Bank, N Yorks
■ Stewards' Enquiry : John Fahy four-day ban; used whip above permitted level (15th-17th, 23rd June).
Silvestre De Sousa caution; failling to obtain best possible postion.

FOCUS
Another good sprint handicap in which the pace was good and the time was 1.45secs faster the the earlier juvenile Listed race. A surprise winner, but no fluke with Arctic Feeling rated back to last year's best.
T/Jkpt: Not won. T/Plt: £1,135.00 to a £1 stake. Pool of £338600.80 - 217.76 winning tickets. T/Qpdt: £44.20 to a £1 stake. Pool of £22277.38 - 372.64 winning tickets. SP

2800 LINGFIELD (L-H)
Saturday, June 1

OFFICIAL GOING: Turf course - good to soft (good in places; 7.4); all-weather - standard
Wind: nil to very light, head on Weather: sunny

2869 PREMIER 10 YEARS ANNIVERSARY MAIDEN FILLIES' STKS 5f
5:55 (5:56) (Class 5) 2-Y-O £2,726 (£805; £402) Stalls High

Form RPR
0 1 **Green Run**[9] 2601 2-9-0 0 HarryBentley 3 73+
(Richard Hannon) *racd w hd to one side: trckd ldr: rdn to chal 2f out: led jst over 1f out: r.o: hld on gamely whn strly pressed fnl 120yds* 7/1[3]
3 2 hd **Aqlaam Vision**[15] 2419 2-9-0 0 JamesDoyle 6 72
(Clive Brittain) *trckd ldr tl outpcd 2f out: r.o wl ent fnl f: str chal fnl 120yds: jst hld* 4/1[2]
3 3 1¾ **Senorita Guest (IRE)**[19] 2320 2-9-0 0 MatthewDavies 7 66+
(Mick Channon) *j. leaving stalls: sn nudged along bhd ldrs: rdn over 2f out: r.o fnl f: nt gng pce to get on terms w front 2* 12/1
2 4 ¾ **Blhadawa (IRE)**[44] 1634 2-9-0 0 NeilCallan 8 63
(James Tate) *led: pushed along over 2f out: hdd wl over 1f out: sn hld: kpt on same pce* 2/5[1]
5 2 **Hopefilly (IRE)** 2-9-0 0 TomMcLaughlin 2 56
(Ed Walker) *little slowly away: sn trcking ldr: rdn to ld wl over 1f out: hdd jst bef fnl f: fdd fnl 120yds* 25/1
6 1 **Our Sherona** 2-9-0 0 J-PGuillambert 5 53
(Gary Harrison) *pushed along bhd ldrs after 1f: swtchd out for effrt 2f out: fdd fnl 120yds* 25/1

1m 0.52s (2.32) **Going Correction** +0.325s/f (Good) 6 Ran SP% **119.3**
Speed ratings (Par 90): **94,93,90,89,86 84**
toteswingers 1&2 £2.10, 2&3 £1.90, 1&3 £3.70 CSF £36.85 TOTE £7.70: £3.10, £2.90; EX 30.80 Trifecta £174.90 Pool: £1694.21 - 7.26 winning units..
Owner Qatar Racing Limited **Bred** Plantation Stud **Trained** East Everleigh, Wilts

FOCUS
After a dry night and warm weather during the day, the ground had dried out to good to soft, good in places. A fair-looking fillies' maiden with the favourite having finished runner-up in a Newmarket maiden that had produced nine subsequent winners. The front three all improved but the race was weakened by the fourth being below her debut level.

2870 CAVELL NURSES' TRUST FILLIES' H'CAP 5f
6:25 (6:25) (Class 5) (0-70,70) 3-Y-0+ £2,726 (£805; £402) Stalls High

Form RPR
561- 1 **Rock On Candy**[214] 7457 4-9-8 64 ChrisCatlin 3 72+
(John Spearing) *racd keenly: trckd ldrs: shkn up to ld jst over 1f out: r.o wl: rdn out* 7/2[2]
0402 2 1 **Imaginary Diva**[8] 2643 7-8-7 56 JordanVaughan(7) 2 60
(George Margarson) *hld up: hdwy over 2f out: rdn whn nt clrest of runs on heels of ldrs over 1f out: swtchd lft ent fnl f: r.o wl to snatch 2nd fnl strides* 5/1[3]
0050 3 shd **Little China**[26] 2074 4-8-10 52 (p) WilliamCarson 6 56
(William Muir) *led: rdn 2f out: hdd jst over 1f out: sn hld by wnr: kpt on: lost 2nd fnl strides* 6/1
5621 4 hd **Princess Cammie (IRE)**[16] 2393 3-8-1 57 (p) JoeyHaynes(7) 5 57
(John Bridger) *chsd ldrs: rdn and ev ch 2f out tl jst over 1f out: kpt on but no ex* 5/1[3]
1030 5 2½ **Danziger (IRE)**[36] 1807 4-10-0 70 RichardHughes 1 64
(David Evans) *nudged along bhd ldrs after 2f out: rdn over 2f out: nvr gng pce to get on terms* 9/4[1]
34- 6 1 **Marmalade Moon**[320] 4144 4-8-13 58 RossAtkinson(3) 4 49
(Robert Cowell) *prom: rdn and ev ch over 1f out: fdd ins fnl f* 20/1
4300 7 3¼ **Charming (IRE)**[11] 2550 4-9-7 63 (e) NeilCallan 7 42
(Olivia Maylam) *s.i.s: sn rcvrd: trckd ldrs tl outpcd over 2f out: wknd fnl f* 10/1

1m 0.31s (2.11) **Going Correction** +0.325s/f (Good)
WFA 3 from 4yo+ 7lb 7 Ran SP% **114.5**
Speed ratings (Par 100): **96,94,94,93,89 88,83**
toteswingers 1&2 £4.20, 2&3 £66.50, 1&3 £7.30 CSF £21.25 TOTE £4.40: £2.40, £2.30; EX 13.40 Trifecta £87.80 Pool: £1049.54 - 8.96 winning units..
Owner Tom Hayes **Bred** T M Hayes **Trained** Kinnersley, Worcs

FOCUS
A very modest fillies' handicap run just 0.21sec faster than the preceding juvenile contest. The third and fourth set the standard.

2871 PREMIER ADMINISTRATION H'CAP 6f
6:55 (6:56) (Class 4) (0-80,82) 4-Y-0+ £4,690 (£1,395; £697; £348) Stalls High

Form RPR
500- 1 **Tidentime (USA)**[194] 7790 4-9-2 75 MatthewDavies 11 84
(Mick Channon) *trckd ldrs: pushed along over 2f out: rdn over 1f out: str run to ld jst ins fnl f: kpt on wl* 8/1
00-0 2 1 **Picture Dealer**[21] 2255 4-9-5 78 GeorgeBaker 10 84
(Gary Moore) *s.i.s: in rr: travelling wl but nt clr run on rails fr 2f out tl jst over 1f out: shkn up and r.o strly: snatched 2nd fnl strides* 9/2[2]
2-62 3 nk **Saloomy**[7] 2663 4-9-9 82 WilliamBuick 2 87
(John Butler) *sweating: trckd ldrs: rdn to chal over 1f out: ev ch jst ins fnl f: kpt on but nt gng pce of wnr: lost 2nd fnl strides* 5/4[1]
3024 4 hd **Putin (IRE)**[2] 2790 5-8-3 62 (bt) LiamJones 8 66
(Phil McEntee) *led: wandered u.p over 1f out: hdd jst ins fnl f: kpt on but no ex: lost 3rd fnl strides* 14/1
1136 5 1¾ **Mambo Spirit (IRE)**[21] 2281 9-8-5 64 ow1 ChrisCatlin 6 62
(Tony Newcombe) *racd keenly: hld up: gd hdwy over 1f out: rdn to chse ldrs ent fnl f: no ex fnl 100yds* 20/1
0100 6 ½ **Clear Praise (USA)**[21] 2255 6-9-3 76 SebSanders 7 73
(Simon Dow) *hld up: rdn 2f out: sme late prog: nt gng pce to get on terms* 16/1
-303 7 1¼ **Kellys Eye (IRE)**[25] 2128 6-8-11 73 DarrenEgan(3) 1 66
(Zoe Davison) *in tch: rdn 2f out: sn chsng ldrs: fdd ins fnl f* 16/1
1400 8 nse **Jack My Boy (IRE)**[14] 2441 6-9-5 78 (b) RichardHughes 12 71
(David Evans) *mid-div: effrt 2f out: wknd ins fnl f* 5/1[3]
0-20 9 10 **We Have A Dream**[7] 2657 8-9-1 74 WilliamCarson 3 35
(William Muir) *trckd ldr tl rdn 2f out: wknd fnl f* 33/1

1m 12.29s (1.09) **Going Correction** +0.325s/f (Good) 9 Ran SP% **116.5**
Speed ratings (Par 105): **105,103,103,103,100 100,98,98,84**
toteswingers: 1&2 £8.30, 2&3 £1.70, 1&3 £3.30 CSF £44.30 CT £75.63 TOTE £9.60: £2.90, £2.10, £1.10; EX 57.80 Trifecta £193.50 Pool: £1369.38 - 5.30 winning units..
Owner Jon and Julia Aisbitt **Bred** Big C Farms **Trained** West Ilsley, Berks

FOCUS
A quite competitive sprint handicap. The winners's best form since early last year. The fourth helps to limit the form.

2872 PREMIER ACTUARIAL MAIDEN STKS 7f
7:25 (7:26) (Class 5) 3-Y-O £2,726 (£805; £402) Stalls High

Form RPR
00 1 **Evident (IRE)**[19] 2306 3-9-5 0 WilliamBuick 6 78
(Jeremy Noseda) *s.i.s and hmpd s: sn mid-div: hdwy 2f out: chal over 1f out: led ent fnl f: kpt on wl: rdn out* 14/1
30-4 2 nk **Arbeel**[22] 2215 3-9-0 80 RichardHughes 4 72
(Peter Chapple-Hyam) *travelled wl: trckd ldrs: swtchd lft over 1f out: rdn and ev ch ent fnl f: kpt on but hld fnl 120yds* 5/2[2]
3 1¼ **Paradise Watch** 3-9-2 0 PatrickHills(3) 8 74
(Luca Cumani) *mid-div: hdwy 2f out: sn rdn to chse ldrs: kpt on ins fnl f* 5/1[3]
45 4 nk **Call Ahead**[33] 1891 3-9-0 0 RyanMoore 3 68
(Sir Michael Stoute) *sn prom: led over 3f out: rdn 2f out: hdd ent fnl f: kpt on same pce* 15/8[1]
0-64 5 1¾ **Mrs Warren**[22] 2226 3-9-0 63 WilliamCarson 7 63
(Charles Hills) *wnt lft s: sn swtchd to stands' side rails: mid-div: hdwy over 1f out: sn rdn: kpt on same pce* 14/1
65 6 3¾ **Bosham**[14] 2455 3-9-0 0 MichaelJMMurphy(5) 11 58
(William Jarvis) *led tl over 3f out: rdn over 2f out: wknd ent fnl f* 8/1
0 7 3 **First Peninsular**[11] 2548 3-9-5 0 SebSanders 1 50
(Chris Wall) *towards rr: rdn over 2f out: nvr any imp* 33/1

40 8 ½ **Baltic Blade (IRE)**[14] 2447 3-9-5 0 GeorgeBaker 12 48
(Gary Moore) *chsd ldrs: struggling over 2f out: wknd over 1f out* **16/1**
00 9 2 **Welsh Moonlight**[32] 1904 3-9-0 0 SaleemGolam 2 38
(Stuart Williams) *s.i.s: a towards rr* **50/1**
10 8 **Tannhauser Gate (IRE)** 3-9-5 0 FergusSweeney 9 21
(Jamie Osborne) *a towards rr* **33/1**
5 11 19 **Bridge Builder**[14] 2447 3-9-5 0 (p) ChrisCatlin 5
(Peter Hedger) *sn outpcd: a bhd: t.o* **25/1**
1m 25.89s (2.59) **Going Correction** +0.325s/f (Good) 11 Ran SP% **122.0**
Speed ratings (Par 99): **98,97,96,95,93 89,86,85,83,74 52**
toteswingers 1&2 £5.70, 2&3 £3.30, 1&3 £3.90 CSF £49.77 TOTE £12.10: £4.40, £1.70, £1.80; EX 52.10 Trifecta £478.40 Pool: £1149.11 - 1.80 winning units..
Owner Miss Yvonne Jacques **Bred** M C Grassick **Trained** Newmarket, Suffolk
FOCUS
An ordinary maiden, the form set around the fifth.

2873 PREMIER WEALTH (S) STKS 5f (P)
7:55 (7:55) (Class 6) 3-Y-O+ £2,045 (£603; £302) Stalls High

Form RPR
5141 1 **Nafa (IRE)**[19] 2326 5-9-7 56 ShaneKelly 7 62
(Daniel Mark Loughnane) *trckd ldrs: chal gng best 2f out: qckd to ld ins fnl f: readily* **5/2**[2]
1410 2 1½ **Haadeeth**[7] 2657 6-9-12 72 (t) RichardHughes 6 61
(David Evans) *chsd ldrs: rdn and ev ch ent fnl f: nt gng pce of ready wnr fnl 100yds* **1/1**[1]
3350 3 1½ **Annaley My Darling (IRE)**[25] 2135 3-8-9 56 NickyMackay 4 43
(Mark Rimmer) *in tch: swtchd rt over 1f out: sn rdn and hdwy: r.o to go 3rd ins fnl f: nt gng pce to rch ldng pair* **20/1**
105- 4 ¾ **Coconut Kisses**[219] 7355 3-8-7 65 RyanWhile(7) 1 48
(Bill Turner) *squeezed up on rails sn after s: trckd ldr tl rdn 2f out: kpt on same pce fnl f* **7/1**
600 5 ¾ **Fairy Mist (IRE)**[27] 2057 6-9-12 41 KieranO'Neill 5 51
(John Bridger) *outpcd in rr: hdwy over 1f out: r.o ins fnl f: wnt 5th on line* **50/1**
0253 6 nse **Spic 'n Span**[19] 2326 8-9-12 60 (be) LukeMorris 2 50
(Ronald Harris) *led: rdn over 1f out: hdd jst ins fnl f: fdd* **6/1**[3]
59.02s (0.22) **Going Correction** +0.075s/f (Slow)
WFA 3 from 5yo+ 7lb 6 Ran SP% **112.1**
Speed ratings (Par 101): **101,98,96,95,93 93**
toteswingers 1&2 £1.10, 2&3 £2.70, 1&3 £4.70 CSF £5.35 TOTE £3.40: £1.60, £1.50; EX 5.20 Trifecta £30.20 Pool: £989.33 - 24.50 winning units..There was no bid for the winner.
Owner Ian O'Connor **Bred** Basil Brindley **Trained** Baldwin's Gate, Staffs
FOCUS
A poor seller. The winner could be in trouble if the handicapper takes this too literally.

2874 PREMIER CONSULTING H'CAP 1m 2f (P)
8:25 (8:25) (Class 5) (0-70,72) 3-Y-O £2,726 (£805; £402) Stalls Low

Form RPR
00-4 1 **Soul Intent (IRE)**[56] 1387 3-9-6 69 GeorgeBaker 2 76
(J W Hills) *trckd ldrs: rdn to ld jst ins fnl f: kpt on wl: enough in hand whn veered rt nr fin* **10/1**
4-62 2 1 **Plenum (GER)**[11] 2549 3-9-9 72 TedDurcan 3 77
(David Lanigan) *mid-div: hdwy over 2f out: pushed along whn nt clr run sn after: swtchd rt and lost pl: styd on again ent fnl f: wnt 2nd towards fin* **6/4**[1]
02-0 3 shd **Equitissa (IRE)**[9] 2606 3-9-4 67 RichardHughes 6 72+
(Richard Hannon) *hld up bhd: swtchd to outer over 2f out: c wd into st: r.o strly ins fnl f: snatched 3rd nring fin* **7/1**[3]
000- 4 nk **Duchess Of Gazeley (IRE)**[246] 6644 3-8-7 56 ShaneKelly 4 60
(Gary Harrison) *s.i.s: towards rr: hdwy on outer over 2f out: c wd ent st: styd on wl ent fnl f: wnt 4th nring fin* **50/1**
000- 5 ¾ **Inherited**[267] 6014 3-8-12 61 LukeMorris 10 64+
(Sir Mark Prescott Bt) *s.i.s: sn rousted along to chse ldrs: pushed along fr over 4f out: drvn fr 2f out: ev ch jst ins fnl f: no ex whn lost 3 pls fnl 50yds* **8/1**
2123 6 1¼ **Mizyen (IRE)**[22] 2235 3-9-6 69 NeilCallan 11 69
(James Tate) *led for over 1f: trckd ldr: led 2f out: sn rdn: hdd jst ins fnl f: no ex* **4/1**[2]
56-0 7 4 **Something Magic**[32] 1907 3-9-0 63 ChrisCatlin 12 55
(Sylvester Kirk) *wnt rt s: hld up towards rr of midfield: rdn 2f out: nvr any imp* **50/1**
006- 8 nk **Marguerite St Just**[180] 7973 3-8-6 55 JimmyQuinn 8 47
(Olivia Maylam) *hld up towards rr: rdn 3f out: nvr a threat* **66/1**
35-6 9 2 **Hazzaat (IRE)**[35] 1829 3-9-7 70 (b[1]) StevieDonohoe 13 58
(Roger Varian) *s.i.s: sn rousted along: led after 1f: drvn and hdd 2f out: wknd ent fnl f* **8/1**
04-0 10 nk **Platinum Proof (USA)**[28] 2017 3-8-12 61 SebSanders 7 48
(John Berry) *mid-div: pushed along 3f out: nt clr run ent st: wknd fnl f* **16/1**
2-64 11 17 **Prospera (IRE)**[30] 1959 3-8-10 66 JaneElliott(7) 1 19
(Ralph Beckett) *mid-div tl 3f out: sn bhd: t.o* **16/1**
2m 4.36s (-2.24) **Going Correction** +0.075s/f (Slow) 11 Ran SP% **121.0**
Speed ratings (Par 99): **111,110,110,109,109 108,105,104,103,103 89**
toteswingers 1&2 £5.50, 2&3 £1.40, 1&3 £7.70 CSF £26.00 CT £120.87 TOTE £15.20: £3.70, £1.10, £2.40; EX 47.40 Trifecta £441.70 Pool: £770.07 - 1.30 winning units..
Owner Andy Weller & Gary Styles **Bred** Flamingo Guitar Syndicate **Trained** Upper Lambourn, Berks
FOCUS
An ordinary 3yo handicap, but not without interest and a success for a handicap debutant. The winner should do better again.

2875 PREMIER SEE CHANGE AMATEUR RIDERS' H'CAP 1m 2f (P)
8:55 (8:56) (Class 6) (0-65,63) 4-Y-O+ £1,975 (£607; £303) Stalls Low

Form RPR
000- 1 **City Ground (USA)**[224] 7245 6-11-7 63 MissSBrotherton 8 70
(Michael Easterby) *trckd ldrs: chal ent fnl f: r.o strly to ld fnl 50yds: pushed out* **9/4**[1]
4056 2 nk **Automotive**[32] 1909 5-10-7 49 MrRossBirkett 4 56
(Julia Feilden) *trckd ldrs: str chal jst over 1f out: led fnl 120yds: kpt on but no ex whn hdd fnl 50yds* **16/1**
1022 3 nk **Peace In Our Time**[11] 2533 4-10-11 58 (p) MrGrahamCarson(5) 7 64
(Anthony Carson) *trckd ldrs: rdn 2f out: styd on wl fnl f: fin strly to snatch 3rd fnl stride* **5/1**[2]
0164 4 ½ **Flag Of Glory**[72] 1107 6-11-1 62 MissMEdden(5) 1 67
(Peter Hiatt) *led: rdn whn jnd jst over 1f out: hdd fnl 100yds: kpt on but no ex* **12/1**
230- 5 1¾ **Hernando Torres**[213] 7496 5-10-13 60 AnnaHesketh(5) 5 62
(Michael Easterby) *mid-div: hdwy to chse ldrs over 2f out: sn rdn: no ex fnl 75yds* **7/1**
3446 6 1½ **Delightful Sleep**[9] 2594 5-11-0 61 MissHDoyle(5) 11 60
(David Evans) *hld up towards rr: rdn and hdwy wl over 1f out: kpt on same pce fnl f* **8/1**
4253 7 1¾ **Young Jackie**[19] 2333 5-10-6 53 (b) MissKMargarson(5) 10 48
(George Margarson) *hld up towards rr: styd on fr over 1f out: nvr a danger* **6/1**[3]
0-04 8 ¾ **Heading To First**[19] 2332 6-9-12 45 (p) MissMBryant(5) 9 39
(Paddy Butler) *hld up towards rr: styd on fr over 1f out: nvr a factor* **50/1**
024 9 ¾ **Signora Frasi (IRE)**[51] 1497 8-10-5 52 MrMatthewStanley(5) 3 44
(Tony Newcombe) *hld up towards rr: sme late prog: nvr a factor* **20/1**
4240 10 2¾ **Satwa Laird**[12] 2511 7-11-3 59 MrSWalker 13 46
(Conor Dore) *trckd ldrs: bmpd 3f out: sn u.p: wknd over 1f out* **6/1**[3]
5/ 11 2¼ **Franklino (FR)**[94] 6-10-11 60 MissMTrainor(7) 2 42
(Chris Gordon) *chsd ldrs tl 2f out: sn wknd* **33/1**
0/ 12 7 **Owner Occupier**[6] 7753 8-9-12 45 MrGeorgeCrate(5) 14 13
(Chris Gordon) *struggling 4f out: a towards rr* **50/1**
00-5 13 hd **King Of Wing (IRE)**[32] 1915 4-10-6 55 (p) MrJAMcEntee(7) 12 23
(Phil McEntee) *mid-div tl over 3f out* **50/1**
2m 8.28s (1.68) **Going Correction** +0.075s/f (Slow) 13 Ran SP% **126.8**
Speed ratings (Par 101): **96,95,95,95,93 92,91,90,89,87 85,80,80**
toteswingers 1&2 £19.70, 2&3 £17.80, 1&3 £5.10 CSF £45.64 CT £174.24 TOTE £3.30: £1.50, £6.30, £1.90; EX 75.10 Trifecta £603.20 Part won. Pool: £804.30 - 0.59 winning units..
Owner Steve Hull **Bred** Mrs E Scott Jr & Mrs L Macelree **Trained** Sheriff Hutton, N Yorks
■ Stewards' Enquiry : Mr Graham Carson three-day ban; careless riding (17th,24th,26th June).
FOCUS
A moderate amateur riders' handicap run 3.92sec slower than the preceding 3-y-o handicap. A rather messy race. The winner had been given a chance by the handicapper.
T/Plt: £53.10 to a £1 stake. Pool of £66862.30 - 917.50 winning tickets. T/Qpdt: £4.90 to a £1 stake. Pool of £6184.43 - 922.30 winning tickets. TM

[2630] MUSSELBURGH (R-H)
Saturday, June 1

OFFICIAL GOING: Good to firm (good in places; 8.4)
Back straight and home bend dropped in on to fresh ground.
Wind: moderate half against Weather: Cloudy with sunny periods

2876 BET TOTEPLACEPOT NOW AT TOTEPOOL.COM H'CAP 1m
1:50 (1:50) (Class 4) (0-85,84) 3-Y-O £7,762 (£2,310; £1,154; £577) Stalls Low

Form RPR
0-01 1 **Llaregyb (IRE)**[15] 2420 3-9-5 82 DaneO'Neill 7 94+
(David Elsworth) *hld up towards rr: smooth hdwy over 2f out: swtchd rt wl over 1f out and sn cl up: chal 1f out: shkn up to ld ins fnl f: readily* **11/10**[1]
6153 2 2 **Corn Snow (USA)**[8] 2627 3-8-11 74 FrannyNorton 6 81
(Mark Johnston) *led 1f: cl up: led again wl over 2f out: jnd and rdn over 1f out: drvn and hdd ins fnl f: kpt on* **9/1**
00-2 3 2¼ **Grey Street**[24] 2167 3-8-8 71 BarryMcHugh 3 73+
(Richard Fahey) *hld up in rr: hdwy over 2f out: sn rdn and styd on wl fnl f: nrst fin* **11/2**[2]
-622 4 3¾ **Mowhoob**[19] 2318 3-8-12 75 GrahamLee 4 68
(Jim Goldie) *hld up in tch on inner: hdwy 3f out: chsd ldrs 2f out: sn rdn and one pce appr fnl f* **14/1**
023- 5 1 **Party Royal**[178] 7994 3-9-4 81 JoeFanning 5 72
(Mark Johnston) *t.k.h early: trckd ldrs: hdwy 3f out: rdn along to chse ldrs 2f out: sn one pce* **12/1**
100- 6 1¼ **Winged Icarus (USA)**[241] 6775 3-8-7 70 ow2 TomEaves 1 58
(Brian Ellison) *dwlt: pushed along on inner and hdwy to ld after 1f: rdn along over 3f out: hdd wl over 2f out and sn wknd* **8/1**[3]
-523 7 1½ **Lazarus Bell**[7] 2666 3-9-7 84 DaleSwift 9 69
(Alan Brown) *chsd ldrs on outer: rdn along over 2f out: sn wknd* **8/1**[3]
-216 8 7 **Brooke's Bounty**[21] 2259 3-8-12 75 TonyHamilton 8 44
(Richard Fahey) *chsd ldng pair on outer: pushed along 3f out: rdn 2f out: sn wknd and bhd* **20/1**
1m 38.76s (-2.44) **Going Correction** -0.05s/f (Good) 8 Ran SP% **114.3**
Speed ratings (Par 101): **110,108,105,102,101 99,98,91**
toteswingers 1&2 £3.00, 2&3 £7.80, 1&3 £3.20 CSF £11.98 CT £39.74 TOTE £2.20: £1.10, £2.70, £2.10; EX 12.90 Trifecta £70.20 Pool: £3259.61 - 34.78 winning units..
Owner Lee Man Bun **Bred** Corrin Stud **Trained** Newmarket, Suffolk
FOCUS
The going was given as good to firm, good in places (GoingStick 8.4) and riders returning after the first described it as "good, fast ground" and "nice, but on the quick side". The early pace was nothing special but the time broke the standard. The first two are progressing.

2877 TOTESCOOP6 EDINBURGH CASTLE STKS (CONDITIONS RACE) 5f
2:20 (2:23) (Class 2) 2-Y-O
£12,450 (£3,728; £1,864; £932; £466; £234) Stalls High

Form RPR
4 1 **Sleeper King (IRE)**[16] 2401 2-8-12 0 ow1 PhillipMakin 2 85+
(Kevin Ryan) *cl up: rdn over 1f out: drvn ins fnl f: kpt on wl to ld last 50yds* **9/4**[2]
121 2 hd **Justice Day (IRE)**[15] 2421 2-9-3 0 DaneO'Neill 5 89
(David Elsworth) *slt ld: rdn along 2f out: drvn ins fnl f: hdd and no ex last 50yds* **1/1**[1]
2 3 ¾ **Jacquotte Delahaye**[18] 2337 2-8-7 0 ow1 TomEaves 6 76
(Bryan Smart) *towards rr: hdwy 1/2-way: rdn over 1f out: styd on to chal ins fnl f: no ex last 100yds* **16/1**
1 4 1 **Suzi's Connoisseur**[19] 2314 2-8-11 0 FrannyNorton 1 77
(Mark Johnston) *hld up in rr: hdwy 1/2-way: rdn to chse ldng pair over 1f out: drvn and one pce ins fnl f* **9/1**
514 5 ½ **Vine De Nada**[37] 1785 2-8-11 0 GrahamLee 4 75
(Mark Johnston) *hld up: hdwy over 2f out: rdn wl over 1f out: kpt on fnl f: nrst fin* **33/1**
41 6 6 **Withernsea (IRE)**[29] 1989 2-9-0 0 TonyHamilton 7 56
(Richard Fahey) *chsd ldrs: rdn along 1/2-way: sn wknd* **7/1**[3]
1 7 3¾ **Pigeon Pie**[47] 1565 2-8-9 0 JoeFanning 3 38
(Mark Johnston) *chsd ldrs: rdn along over 2f out: sn wknd* **14/1**
59.48s (-0.92) **Going Correction** -0.05s/f (Good) 7 Ran SP% **118.8**
Speed ratings (Par 99): **105,104,103,101,101 91,85**
toteswingers 1&2 £1.70, 2&3 £4.50, 1&3 £7.90 CSF £5.15 TOTE £3.30: £2.00, £1.20; EX 7.60 Trifecta £62.50 Pool: £4355.49 - 52.18 winning units..
Owner Mrs June Bownes **Bred** Brighton Farm Ltd **Trained** Hambleton, N Yorks
■ Stewards' Enquiry : Phillip Makin £650 fine; modifing safety jacket.

The Form Book Flat, Raceform Ltd, Compton, RG20 6NL.

FOCUS
The market made this a two-horse race and that's how it turned out. Useful form from the first two, the time backing it up.

2878 TOTEPOOL.COM TRADESMAN'S DERBY (H'CAP) 1m 4f 100y
2:55 (2:56) (Class 4) (0-80,78) 3-Y-O £12,938 (£3,850; £1,924; £962) Stalls Low

Form RPR
-134 1 **Emerging**27 2054 3-9-4 75....(p) LiamKeniry 8 82
(David Elsworth) *trckd ldr: cl up over 3f out: led wl over 2f out and sn pushed along: rdn and hdd jst over 1f out: drvn and rallied gamely to ld again ins fnl f: styd on wl towards fin* **11/1**
-205 2 3/4 **Royal Skies (IRE)**15 2416 3-9-6 77.... JoeFanning 7 83
(Mark Johnston) *hld up towards rr: hdwy 3f out: trckd ldrs over 2f out: sn cl up: rdn to ld jst over 1f out: drvn and hdd ins fnl f: no ex* **4/1**2
4-01 3 1/2 **Hasheem**11 2538 3-9-7 78.... DaneO'Neill 1 83+
(Roger Varian) *hld up in tch: hdwy 3f out: chsd ldng pair over 1f out: sn rdn and kpt on fnl f: nrst fin* **11/4**1
-521 4 1 1/2 **Dolphin Village (IRE)**8 2624 3-9-2 73.... TonyHamilton 2 76+
(Richard Fahey) *trckd ldrs on inner: effrt whn nt clr run and swtchd lft over 2f out: hdwy whn hmpd wl over 1f out: sn rdn and styd on fnl f: nrst fin* **11/2**3
-212 5 1/2 **Good Speech (IRE)**26 2079 3-9-0 71.... MickyFenton 6 73
(Tom Tate) *led: rdn along 3f out: sn hdd and drvn: hld whn edgd lft wl over 1f out: one pce after* **6/1**
32-2 6 nk **Bin Singspiel**61 1296 3-9-1 72.... PaulMulrennan 5 73
(James Tate) *chsd ldrs: pushed along and sltly outpcd wl over 2f out: kpt on u.p fnl f* **4/1**2
-560 7 nk **Open Letter (IRE)**25 2127 3-8-5 62.... FrannyNorton 4 63
(Mark Johnston) *half-rrd s and s.i.s: bhd tl styd on fnl 2f: nrst fin* **20/1**
3-61 8 4 **Getaway Car**9 2599 3-8-8 65....(p) TomEaves 3 60
(Gerard Butler) *a towards rr* **16/1**
2m 42.28s (0.28) **Going Correction** -0.05s/f (Good) 8 Ran SP% **115.3**
Speed ratings (Par 101): **97,96,96,95,94 94,94,91**
toteswingers 1&2 £8.50, 2&3 £2.60, 1&3 £6.10 CSF £55.07 CT £157.38 TOTE £13.70: £2.80, £1.50, £1.60; EX 72.70 Trifecta £291.40 Pool: £4355.19 - 11.20 winning units..
Owner Ben CM Wong **Bred** D R Tucker **Trained** Newmarket, Suffolk
FOCUS
An ordinary pace after an early dash to the first bend. A 5lb best from the winner.

2879 TOTEPOOL EDINBURGH CUP (H'CAP) 1m 4f 100y
3:30 (3:31) (Class 2) (0-105,86) 3-Y-O
£37,350 (£11,184; £5,592; £2,796; £1,398; £702) Stalls Low

Form RPR
1-50 1 **Dashing Star**16 2398 3-9-4 83.... LiamKeniry 10 91+
(David Elsworth) *stdd s and hld up in rr: sme hdwy 3f out: sn pushed along: swtchd rt to inner 2f out and sn rdn: styd on wl u.p appr fnl f: led last 100yds: kpt on strly* **9/1**3
1263 2 2 **Naru (IRE)**7 2660 3-9-4 83.... PaulMulrennan 2 88
(James Tate) *set str pce: pushed along 3f out: rdn 2f out: edgd lft and drvn ent fnl f: hdd and one pce last 100yds* **18/1**
-421 3 1 1/4 **Van Percy**7 2660 3-9-7 86.... DavidProbert 8 89
(Andrew Balding) *hld up: hdwy over 4f out: effrt to chse ldrs over 2f out: rdn over 1f out: drvn and kpt on same pce fnl f* **9/4**1
-551 4 shd **Esteaming**15 2432 3-8-13 78.... PhillipMakin 5 81+
(David Barron) *hld up towards rr: gd hdwy over 3f out: chsd ldrs 2f out: rdn over 1f out: drvn and no imp fnl f* **7/2**2
1352 5 1/2 **Blue Wave (IRE)**7 2660 3-9-7 86....(b) GrahamLee 1 88
(Mark Johnston) *trckd ldrs: hdwy over 3f out: rdn to chse ldr 2f out: sn drvn and wknd ins fnl f* **14/1**
1214 6 8 **Love Marmalade (IRE)**14 2457 3-8-11 76.... JoeFanning 9 66
(Mark Johnston) *in tch: hdwy 3f out: rdn along over 2f out: sn drvn and wknd* **14/1**
-414 7 nk **Alta Lilea (IRE)**21 2261 3-9-5 84.... FrannyNorton 3 73
(Mark Johnston) *trckd ldr: cl up 4f out: rdn along 3f out: wknd fnl 2f* **14/1**
-224 8 1 **Allnecessaryforce (FR)**15 2432 3-8-13 78....(v1) TonyHamilton 4 66
(Richard Fahey) *chsd ldrs on outer: rdn along whn hung bdly lft and rn wd home bnd: sn bhd* **16/1**
2-13 9 18 **Grandorio (IRE)**19 2309 3-9-2 81.... DavidNolan 6 41
(David O'Meara) *t.k.h: trckd ldrs: hdwy to chse ldng trio 3f out: sn rdn and wknd* **14/1**
2m 39.97s (-2.03) **Going Correction** -0.05s/f (Good) 9 Ran SP% **100.8**
Speed ratings (Par 105): **104,102,101,101,101 96,95,95,83**
toteswingers 1&2 £20.00, 2&3 £7.00, 1&3 £4.00 CSF £108.26 CT £268.44 TOTE £10.80: £2.80, £5.40, £1.10; EX 126.40 Trifecta £733.00 Pool: £2126.92 - 2.17 winning units..
Owner J C Smith **Bred** Littleton Stud **Trained** Newmarket, Suffolk
■ Stewards' Enquiry : David Probert one-day ban; careless riding (15th June).
FOCUS
Nothing like as classy a race as the conditions would suggest, with the top weights rated 19lb below the ceiling for the race. The form is solid, however.

2880 TOTEPOOL MOBILE H'CAP 5f
4:30 (4:30) (Class 4) (0-85,85) 4-Y-O+ £6,469 (£1,925; £962; £481) Stalls High

Form RPR
-352 1 **Rothesay Chancer**15 2410 5-8-13 77.... GrahamLee 1 85
(Jim Goldie) *steadied and swtchd lft s: hld up in rr: hdwy and pushed along over 1f out: nt clr run and swtchd lft ent fnl f: sn rdn and str run on stands' rail to ld nr line* **9/4**1
00-0 2 nk **Flash City (ITY)**63 1253 5-8-11 80....(vt) JustinNewman(5) 8 87
(Bryan Smart) *slt ld: rdn along 1/2-way: hdd 2f out and sn drvn: rallied gamely u.p fnl f: ev ch tl nt qckn nr line* **6/1**
0020 3 hd **Bosun Breese**7 2669 8-9-2 85.... LMcNiff(5) 7 91
(David Barron) *cl up: led 2f out: rdn ins fnl f: hdd and nt qckn nr line* **5/2**2
-000 4 3/4 **Tax Free (IRE)**17 2366 11-9-7 85.... AdrianNicholls 4 89
(David Nicholls) *swtchd lft s: trckd ldrs: effrt and n.m.r over 1f out: sn swtchd rt and rdn to chal ent fnl f: sn drvn and ev ch tl edgd rt and one pce towards fin* **7/2**3
013- 5 9 **Liberty Island (IRE)**245 6688 8-8-11 80....(p) GeorgeChaloner(5) 3 51
(Ian Semple) *chsd ldrs: rdn along 2f out: sn outpcd* **15/2**
20-0 6 2 1/2 **Sandwith**15 2410 10-8-0 71 ow1....(p) KevinStott(7) 6 33
(Ian Semple) *chsd ldrs: rdn along 2f out: sn wknd* **25/1**
59.82s (-0.58) **Going Correction** -0.05s/f (Good) 6 Ran SP% **111.5**
Speed ratings (Par 105): **102,101,101,100,85 81**
toteswingers 1&2 £2.40, 2&3 £0.90, 1&3 £2.20 CSF £15.74 CT £33.85 TOTE £2.70: £1.70, £3.10; EX 16.70 Trifecta £45.40 Pool: £3085.28 - 50.88 winning units..
Owner Discovery Racing Club 2 **Bred** Mrs S R Kennedy **Trained** Uplawmoor, E Renfrews

FOCUS
The picture changed inside the last here as the leaders began to paddle. The winner is rated in line with his Hamilton third.

2881 TOTEEXACTA AVAILABLE ON ALL RACES H'CAP 1m 1f
5:05 (5:05) (Class 4) (0-85,85) 4-Y-O+ £6,469 (£1,925; £962; £481) Stalls Low

Form RPR
0232 1 **Classic Colori (IRE)**7 2659 6-9-7 85....(v) DavidNolan 4 93
(David O'Meara) *trckd ldrs: hdwy 2f out: swtchd lft and rdn over 1f out: led jst ins fnl f: drvn and hld on wl towards fin* **10/3**3
-121 2 nk **Karaka Jack**22 2220 6-9-4 82.... AdrianNicholls 3 90+
(David Nicholls) *hld up in rr: hdwy 2f out: nt clr run over 1f out: squeezed through and rdn ins fnl f: styd on: jst hld* **11/4**1
-000 3 hd **Assizes**13 2478 4-9-1 79.... JoeFanning 5 86
(Mark Johnston) *trckd ldrs: cl up 3f out: led 2f out: rdn over 1f out: drvn and hdd jst ins fnl f: kpt on wl u.p towards fin* **9/2**
360- 4 3 1/2 **Ventura Spirit**337 3558 4-8-2 66 oh1.... PatrickMathers 6 65
(Richard Fahey) *dwlt: hdwy on outer to trck ldrs after 2f: hdwy 3f out: rdn to chse ldrs 2f out: drvn and edgd rt jst over 1f out: sn wknd* **14/1**
3301 5 2 1/2 **It's A Mans World**14 2463 7-8-11 78.... PaulPickard(3) 2 71
(Brian Ellison) *hld up in rr: hdwy 3f out: rdn along 2f out: drvn and no imp over 1f out* **6/1**
01/2 6 3/4 **Spes Nostra**22 2220 5-8-7 71.... TomEaves 1 63
(David Barron) *led: rdn along 3f out: hdd 2f out: sn drvn and n.m.r wl over 1f out: sn wknd* **3/1**2
1m 52.21s (-1.69) **Going Correction** -0.05s/f (Good) 6 Ran SP% **113.9**
Speed ratings (Par 105): **105,104,104,101,99 98**
toteswingers 1&2 £1.10, 2&3 £3.50, 1&3 £3.00 CSF £13.21 TOTE £3.30: £2.00, £1.60; EX 9.10 Trifecta £38.90 Pool: £2592.60 - 49.88 winning units..
Owner The Classic Strollers Partnership **Bred** Frank Dunne **Trained** Nawton, N Yorks
FOCUS
Three came clear here. The winner back up his Haydock latest.

2882 TRY A TOTETRIFECTA AT TOTEPOOL.COM H'CAP 7f 30y
5:35 (5:35) (Class 4) (0-85,84) 4-Y-O+ £6,469 (£1,925; £962; £481) Stalls Low

Form RPR
-546 1 **Powerful Presence (IRE)**7 2665 7-9-6 83.... DavidNolan 2 94
(David O'Meara) *trckd ldrs: hdwy over 2f out: swtchd lft and rdn to ld over 1f out: drvn ins fnl f: kpt on wl towards fin* **6/1**3
0000 2 hd **Alejandro (IRE)**19 2310 4-9-2 79.... TonyHamilton 5 89
(Richard Fahey) *hld up towards rr: gd hdwy over 2f out: rdn over 1f out: str run ent fnl f: ev ch tl no ex towards fin* **13/2**
-000 3 3/4 **Kalk Bay (IRE)**19 2310 6-8-9 79....(t) MatthewHopkins(7) 11 87+
(Michael Easterby) *stdd s and hld up in rr: hdwy on wd outside 2f out: rdn wl over 1f out: styd on strly fnl f* **33/1**
1005 4 1 3/4 **Chookie Royale**11 2541 5-9-5 82....(b) JoeFanning 3 85
(Keith Dalgleish) *hld up and bhd: hdwy on inner wl over 2f out: effrt and n.m.r over 1f out: sn swtchd lft and rdn ent fnl f: kpt on same pce* **5/1**2
6140 5 2 1/2 **Roninski (IRE)**19 2310 5-9-2 84.... JustinNewman(5) 4 81
(Garry Moss) *in tch: hdwy wl over 2f out: rdn along wl over 1f out: sn no imp* **8/1**
0-0 6 3/4 **Reposer (IRE)**20 2291 5-9-7 84.... DavidProbert 10 78+
(Muredach Kelly, Ire) *cl up: rdn to ld 2f out: hdd and drvn over 1f out: wknd fnl f* **4/1**1
-212 7 2 **Snow Bay**25 2119 7-9-1 83.... ShirleyTeasdale(5) 6 72+
(Paul Midgley) *set str pce: rdn along and hdd 2f out: grad wknd* **4/1**1
110- 8 nse **Midnight Dynamo**229 7100 6-8-11 74.... AndrewElliott 7 63
(Jim Goldie) *chsd ldrs: hdwy 3f out: rdn wl over 1f out: sn wknd* **20/1**
0-06 9 3/4 **Viva Ronaldo (IRE)**42 1693 7-8-10 73.... PatrickMathers 8 60
(Richard Fahey) *a in rr* **14/1**
24-0 10 1/2 **Dubious Escapade (IRE)**35 1823 4-8-5 68....(p) FrannyNorton 9 54
(Ann Duffield) *chsd ldng pair: rdn along 3f out: drvn and wknd 2f out* **20/1**
2030 11 2 1/4 **Sans Loi (IRE)**28 2007 4-9-3 80.... TomEaves 1 59
(Brian Ellison) *midfield: pushed along wl over 2f out: sn rdn and wknd wl over 1f out* **14/1**
1m 27.58s (-1.42) **Going Correction** -0.05s/f (Good) 11 Ran SP% **121.2**
Speed ratings (Par 105): **106,105,104,102,100 99,96,96,96,95 92**
toteswingers 1&2 £9.70, 2&3 £63.30, 1&3 £70.30 CSF £45.03 CT £1230.67 TOTE £8.50: £2.20, £2.00, £15.00; EX 58.40 Trifecta £1091.70 Part won. Pool: £1455.65 - 0.26 winning units..
Owner The Lawton Bamforth Partnership **Bred** Corduff Stud **Trained** Nawton, N Yorks
FOCUS
There was a strong pace on here as joint-favourites Snow Bay and Reposer ruined each other's chances by taking each other on up front. The winenr is rated close to last year's form.
T/Plt: £11.00 to a £1 stake. Pool of £61207.68 - 4040.45 winning tickets T/Qpdt: £6.70 to a £1 stake. Pool of £2770.52 - 302.58 winning tickets. JR

2535 NEWCASTLE (L-H)
Saturday, June 1

OFFICIAL GOING: Good (good to soft in places) changing to good after race 1 (6.10)
Rails as at last meeting on May 21st.
Wind: Breezy, half against Weather: Cloudy

2883 BETFRED TV MAIDEN AUCTION STKS 6f
6:10 (6:10) (Class 5) 2-Y-O £2,587 (£770; £384; £192) Stalls Centre

Form RPR
3 1 **Secret Applause**28 2025 2-8-9 0 ow3.... PaulMulrennan 3 65
(Michael Dods) *mde all: rdn over 1f out: edgd rt ins fnl f: kpt on strly* **5/1**2
2 1 3/4 **Henke (IRE)** 2-8-6 0.... DanielleMooney(7) 15 63+
(Nigel Tinkler) *dwlt: in rr: rdn 1/2-way: hdwy nr side over 1f out: chsd wnr ins fnl f: r.o* **66/1**
3 nk **Darling Boyz** 2-8-11 0.... MichaelO'Connell 7 60+
(John Quinn) *dwlt: towards rr: hdwy over 3f out: rdn and outpcd 2f out: kpt on fnl f: bttr for r* **11/2**3
4 nk **Yorkshire Relish (IRE)** 2-8-13 0.... PhillipMakin 11 61
(Kevin Ryan) *in tch: effrt and rdn 2f out: kpt on ins fnl f* **14/1**
4 5 nse **Uncle Bobby**18 2337 2-8-11 0.... JamesSullivan 5 59
(Michael Easterby) *hld up in tch: effrt and pushed along 2f out: kpt on same pce ins fnl f* **20/1**
023 6 1 **Classy Lassy (IRE)**15 2426 2-8-8 0.... DaleSwift 9 53
(Brian Ellison) *t.k.h early: chsd ldrs: wnt 2nd and pushed along over 2f out: outpcd whn hung bdly lft ins fnl f* **8/11**1

0 **7** 1 ¾ **It's All A Game**[14] 2436 2-8-11 0 .... RobbieFitzpatrick 13 50
(Richard Guest) *hld up: rdn over 2f out: kpt on fnl f: nvr able to chal* **66/1**

8 ½ **Bar Shy** 2-8-11 0 .... DuranFentiman 6 49
(Tim Easterby) *t.k.h in rr: rdn and rn green over 2f out: kpt on fnl f: no imp* **40/1**

0 **9** *nk* **Paint It Red (IRE)**[14] 2436 2-8-6 0 .... AndrewMullen 2 43
(Richard Guest) *cl up: rdn over 2f out: wknd ins fnl f* **100/1**

10 *2* **Maupiti Express (FR)** 2-9-1 0 .... GrahamGibbons 4 45
(David O'Meara) *hld up in tch: rdn and rn green over 2f out: btn fnl f* **20/1**

04 **11** 1 ¼ **Blades Boy**[28] 2025 2-8-11 0 .... BarryMcHugh 12 37
(Richard Fahey) *midfield: pushed along whn n.m.r briefly over 2f out: no imp fr over 1f out* **12/1**

12 *6* **Astral Pursuits** 2-8-5 0 .... DeclanCannon(3) 8 15
(Nigel Tinkler) *bhd: rdn and struggling 1/2-way: nvr on terms* **50/1**

13 1 ¼ **Petergate** 2-8-13 0 .... MickyFenton 10 16
(Brian Rothwell) *prom: rdn over 2f out: wknd over 1f out* **80/1**

14 3 ¼ **Greenbury (IRE)** 2-9-1 0 .... PJMcDonald 1 8
(Ann Duffield) *hld up in tch: rdn and rn green over 2f out: sn wknd* **50/1**

1m 17.22s (2.62) **Going Correction** +0.025s/f (Good) **14** Ran SP% **125.4**
Speed ratings (Par 93): **83,80,80,79,79 78,76,75,75,72 70,62,61,56**
toteswingers 1&2 £27.20, 2&3 £78.70, 1&3 £5.60 CSF £317.62 TOTE £6.50: £1.80, £18.90, £1.90; EX 557.20 Trifecta £1615.60 Part won. Pool: £2154.20 - 0.42 winning units..
Owner K Knox & M Hutchinson **Bred** T K & Mrs P A Knox **Trained** Denton, Co Durham

FOCUS
They changed the official going to good after this event. While Maze backed up his debut victory here in 2007 with another in the Chesham Stakes at Royal Ascot, this race rarely throws up many classy individuals. This again looked a weak renewal and they came up the middle of the track. A compressed finish and ordinary form.

2884 BETFRED "DON'T MISS FRED'S PUSHES" H'CAP 7f
6:40 (6:41) (Class 5) (0-70,73) 4-Y-0+ **£2,587** (£770; £384; £192) **Stalls** Centre

Form RPR

3-05 **1** **Day Of The Eagle (IRE)**[47] 1569 7-9-6 **69** .... GrahamGibbons 5 81
(Michael Easterby) *prom centre: hdwy to ld over 1f out: rdn and veered both ways last 110yds: kpt on strly* **5/1**[2]

3002 **2** *2* **Pelmanism**[2] 2797 6-8-10 **59** .... (b) DaleSwift 6 66
(Brian Ellison) *hld up centre: hdwy over 1f out: rdn to chse wnr ins fnl f: kpt on but nt gng pce to chal* **12/1**

6-40 **3** *2* **Mitchum**[5] 2707 4-9-2 **65** .... PhillipMakin 9 67
(Ron Barr) *hld up centre: rdn and hdwy over 1f out: kpt on ins fnl f: nrst fin* **50/1**

2155 **4** *nk* **Keep It Dark**[27] 2037 4-8-10 **66** .... DavidSimmonson(7) 4 67
(Tony Coyle) *hld up in tch: hdwy to chse wnr over 1f out to ins fnl f: kpt on same pce* **14/1**

3324 **5** 2 ¼ **Mutafaakir (IRE)**[14] 2450 4-9-4 **67** .... PJMcDonald 8 62
(Ruth Carr) *led centre tl hdd over 1f out: sn outpcd* **5/1**[2]

1212 **6** 2 ½ **Maggie Pink**[26] 2092 4-9-6 **69** .... AndrewMullen 14 57
(Michael Appleby) *led stands' side and overall ldr to over 1f out: sn outpcd* **7/1**[3]

0-46 **7** *nk* **Rutterkin (USA)**[30] 1951 5-7-12 **54** oh1 ow3 .... VictorSantos(7) 1 41
(Richard Ford) *trckd centre ldrs: rdn over 2f out: wknd fnl f* **66/1**

2235 **8** ½ **Hellbender (IRE)**[12] 2515 7-8-8 **57** .... (t) DuranFentiman 2 43
(Shaun Harris) *disp ld centre to 2f out: wknd fnl f* **33/1**

-614 **9** 2 ½ **King Pin**[24] 2163 8-9-5 **68** .... BarryMcHugh 12 47
(Tracy Waggott) *dwlt: hld up in tch stands' side: hdwy and hung lft 2f out: nvr rchd ldrs* **11/1**

060- **10** 2 ¾ **Monel**[229] 7099 5-7-13 **51** oh2 .... [1] RaulDaSilva(3) 13 23
(Jim Goldie) *chsd stands' side ldr: rdn and hung lft fr over 2f out: wknd over 1f out* **33/1**

120- **11** *4* **Clumber Place**[203] 7685 7-9-2 **65** .... GrahamLee 7 26
(James Given) *chsd centre ldrs tl rdn and wknd 2f out* **20/1**

5-01 **12** *19* **Relentless Harry (IRE)**[8] 2638 4-9-10 **73** .... (t) PatCosgrave 10
(George Baker) *hld up on outside of stands' side gp: rdn over 2f out: fnd little and sn btn* **11/4**[1]

0063 **13** *shd* **Nonaynever**[4] 2757 5-8-2 **51** oh5 .... (b) JamesSullivan 15
(Ruth Carr) *chsd stands' side ldrs: hung lft thrght: wknd wl over 2f out* **28/1**

0310 **14** 2 ½ **Ted's Brother (IRE)**[5] 2707 5-9-1 **64** .... (e) RobbieFitzpatrick 11
(Richard Guest) *hld up in tch: rdn and carried lft wl over 2f out: sn btn* **12/1**

1m 29.39s (1.59) **Going Correction** +0.025s/f (Good) **14** Ran SP% **120.4**
Speed ratings (Par 103): **91,88,86,86,83 80,80,79,76,73 69,47,47,44**
toteswingers 1&2 £17.70, 2&3 £33.00, 1&3 £45.80 CSF £59.17 CT £2699.48 TOTE £5.70: £2.30, £3.30, £10.80; EX 85.40 Trifecta £824.30 Part won. Pool: £1099.10- 0.65 winning units..
Owner Steve Hull & Steve Hollings **Bred** Swersky & Associates **Trained** Sheriff Hutton, N Yorks

FOCUS
An ordinary handicap run at a fair pace and they split into two groups, with eight coming up the centre of the track. The first five came from this group. The winner's best form since he was a 4yo.

2885 BETFRED MOBILE LOTTO MAIDEN STKS 1m 2f 32y
7:10 (7:12) (Class 5) 3-Y-0+ **£2,587** (£770; £384; £192) **Stalls** Low

Form RPR

0-4 **1** **Carthaginian (IRE)**[27] 2041 4-9-13 0 .... BarryMcHugh 4 81
(Richard Fahey) *prom: smooth hdwy 3f out: shkn up to ld over 1f out: pushed out fnl f: comf* **14/1**

4 **2** 1 ¼ **Song And Dance Man**[14] 2456 3-9-0 0 .... GrahamLee 6 78
(William Haggas) *hld up: hdwy on outside over 2f out: shkn up to chse wnr over 1f out: kpt on fnl f: hld towards fin* **4/1**[3]

0- **3** *4* **Inaad (IRE)**[336] 3634 3-9-0 0 .... [1] MickaelBarzalona 7 70
(Saeed bin Suroor) *plld hrd in rr: rdn and hdwy over 2f out: edgd lft over 1f out: kpt on fnl f: nt rch first two* **2/1**[2]

54- **4** 1 ¼ **Qawaafy (USA)**[218] 7364 3-8-9 0 .... DaneO'Neill 10 62
(Roger Varian) *t.k.h: hld up in tch: hdwy over 2f out: chsng ldrs whn edgd lft over 1f out: no ex ins fnl f* **6/5**[1]

3 **5** *3* **Samoset**[44] 1648 3-9-0 0 .... RobertWinston 2 61
(Alan Swinbank) *led at modest gallop: rdn and hdd over 1f out: wknd ins fnl f* **16/1**

0 **6** *10* **Jimmy Sewell (IRE)**[26] 2093 4-9-13 0 .... AndrewMullen 8 42
(Michael Appleby) *in tch: rdn and edgd lft over 2f out: sn outpcd: n.d after* **50/1**

06- **7** *10* **Distant Sunrise**[215] 7442 3-8-9 0 .... PJMcDonald 3 16
(Ann Duffield) *hld up on ins: struggling over 2f out: sn btn* **100/1**

0 **8** *hd* **The Power Of One (IRE)**[11] 2547 3-9-0 0 .... JamesSullivan 9 21
(James Given) *dwlt: t.k.h and sn cl up: struggling over 2f out: sn btn* **66/1**

00/- **9** ½ **Freddie Bolt**[586] 7061 7-9-13 40 .... DuranFentiman 5 21
(Frederick Watson) *cl up tl rdn and wknd fr 2f out* **100/1**

2m 15.15s (3.25) **Going Correction** +0.025s/f (Good)
WFA 3 from 4yo+ 13lb **9** Ran SP% **116.8**
Speed ratings (Par 103): **88,87,83,82,80 72,64,64,63**
CSF £69.75 TOTE £12.20: £2.30, £1.80, £1.20; EX 70.80 Trifecta £156.60 Pool: £1737.16 - 8.31 winning units..
Owner Sir Robert Ogden **Bred** Patrick M Ryan **Trained** Musley Bank, N Yorks

FOCUS
A decent maiden for 3yos and upwards with some big yards represented, but the pace was merely adequate early on and it proved a messy affair. One or two doubts over the form, but a step up from the winner.

2886 BETFRED "THE BONUS KING" H'CAP 1m 2f 32y
7:40 (7:40) (Class 5) (0-75,72) 4-Y-0+ **£2,587** (£770; £384; £192) **Stalls** Low

Form RPR

5441 **1** **Arc Light (IRE)**[11] 2539 5-9-5 **70** .... DuranFentiman 13 76
(Tim Easterby) *taken early to post: t.k.h early: hld up on outside: smooth hdwy over 2f out: drvn over 1f out: led wl ins fnl f: styd on* **5/1**[2]

5465 **2** ¾ **Gran Maestro (USA)**[9] 2594 4-9-4 **69** .... (b) MickyFenton 6 73+
(Ruth Carr) *hld up: rdn and hdwy over 2f out: rdn over 1f out: kpt on fnl f: tk 2nd cl home* **8/1**

2241 **3** *hd* **Day Of Destiny (IRE)**[46] 1600 8-9-4 **69** .... GrahamLee 9 73
(James Given) *hld up in midfield on outside: hdwy to chse ldrs over 2f out: sn drvn along: kpt on u.p fnl f* **7/1**

0-65 **4** *nse* **Border Bandit (USA)**[37] 1790 5-8-2 **53** oh3 .... AndrewMullen 2 57
(Tracy Waggott) *t.k.h early: cl up: rdn over 2f out: led over 1f out: edgd lft ins fnl f: hdd and no ex last 75yds* **12/1**

-356 **5** *nse* **Ebony Express**[10] 2576 4-8-11 **62** .... RobertWinston 14 65
(Alan Swinbank) *hld up: rdn over 2f out: gd hdwy over 1f out: r.o ins fnl f* **12/1**

00-4 **6** 3 ¼ **Sinatramania**[25] 2118 6-8-4 **55** oh1 ow2 .... RoystonFfrench 4 58+
(Tracy Waggott) *hld up in midfield on ins: effrt over 2f out: cl 3rd and styng on whn hmpd ins fnl f: nt rcvr* **16/1**

05-0 **7** *nk* **Buster Brown (IRE)**[15] 2417 4-9-4 **69** .... DaleSwift 7 65
(James Given) *plld hrd in midfield: effrt and pushed along over 2f out: kpt on same pce ins fnl f* **11/2**[3]

140- **8** 2 ¾ **Spin Cast**[197] 7409 5-9-7 **72** .... MichaelO'Connell 8 63
(Philip Kirby) *hld up: pushed along and hdwy over 2f out: no imp over 1f out* **18/1**

0004 **9** 1 ½ **Amazing Blue Sky**[3] 2785 7-8-5 **56** .... JamesSullivan 11 44+
(Ruth Carr) *led 2f: chsd ldr: led over 2f out to over 1f out: sn wknd* **7/2**[1]

631- **10** 3 ¼ **Adili (IRE)**[245] 4188 4-9-3 **71** .... PaulPickard(3) 3 52
(Brian Ellison) *t.k.h: prom tl rdn and wknd over 2f out* **33/1**

000- **11** ½ **Comical**[298] 4914 4-8-11 **62** .... PJMcDonald 1 42
(George Moore) *in tch on ins: strruggling over 2f out: sn btn* **9/1**

610- **12** 4 ½ **Monthly Medal**[206] 7640 10-9-0 **65** .... (t) AmyRyan 12 36
(Wilf Storey) *hld up: rdn over 2f out: sn wknd* **28/1**

1/0- **13** *32* **Destination Aim**[218] 7369 6-9-5 **70** .... PaulMulrennan 10
(Frederick Watson) *led after 2f: hdd over 2f out: sn n.m.r and wknd: eased whn no ch* **100/1**

2m 13.33s (1.43) **Going Correction** +0.025s/f (Good) **13** Ran SP% **121.8**
Speed ratings (Par 103): **95,94,94,94,94 91,91,89,87,85 84,81,55**
toteswingers 1&2 £18.90, 2&3 £12.20, 1&3 £4.30 CSF £45.29 CT £287.50 TOTE £5.90: £1.90, £3.80, £1.80; EX 49.50 Trifecta £381.00 Pool: £743.03 - 1.46 winning units..
Owner J Beamson **Bred** Monsieurs D Blot & Christian De Asis Trem **Trained** Great Habton, N Yorks

■ Stewards' Enquiry : Andrew Mullen three-day ban; careless riding (15th-17th June).

FOCUS
A modest, if competitive, handicap run at an inconsistent gallop. There were a couple of hard-luck stories as they finished in a heap and the form may not prove solid. The winner continues in good form.

2887 BETFRED MOBILE SPORTS H'CAP 2m 19y
8:10 (8:10) (Class 6) (0-65,65) 4-Y-0+ **£1,940** (£577; £288; £144) **Stalls** Low

Form RPR

065 **1** **Enchanted Garden**[14] 2462 5-9-5 **60** .... FrederikTylicki 2 70+
(Malcolm Jefferson) *in tch: n.m.r over 4f out: hdwy over 2f out: led appr fnl f: drvn and kpt on strly* **3/1**[1]

2-04 **2** 3 ¾ **Maska Pony (IRE)**[11] 2540 9-8-11 **52** .... TomEaves 5 57
(George Moore) *cl up: led over 2f out: rdn and hdd appr fnl f: kpt on same pce ins fnl f* **9/2**[3]

6115 **3** *nk* **Jan Smuts (IRE)**[11] 2540 5-9-7 **62** .... (tp) GrahamLee 3 68
(Wilf Storey) *hld up: hdwy and in tch over 2f out: sn rdn: kpt on ins fnl f* **4/1**[2]

0-00 **4** 1 ½ **Shirls Son Sam**[12] 2511 5-8-6 **47** .... DuranFentiman 9 50
(Chris Fairhurst) *t.k.h: hld up: hdwy on outside and cl up over 2f out: rdn and one pce fnl f* **16/1**

006/ **5** *6* **Wee Giant (USA)**[359] 5069 7-9-6 **61** .... BarryMcHugh 7 57
(Tony Coyle) *hld up: effrt whn n.m.r briefly over 2f out: hdwy over 1f out: no imp fnl f* **25/1**

00-5 **6** 1 ½ **Jeu De Roseau (IRE)**[40] 1721 9-9-7 **62** .... TonyHamilton 11 56
(Chris Grant) *hld up in tch on outside: stdy hdwy over 3f out: rdn and wknd fr 2f out* **9/2**[3]

26-0 **7** *6* **Hi Dancer**[25] 2120 10-8-9 **50** .... PJMcDonald 10 37
(Ben Haslam) *chsd ldrs: rdn over 3f out: edgd lft and wknd 2f out* **8/1**

-020 **8** 3 ½ **Fine Kingdom**[10] 2563 4-8-6 **53** .... (b) PhilipPrince(5) 4 35
(Brian Ellison) *t.k.h early: cl up: drvn over 6f out: rallied: rdn over 2f out: wknd wl over 1f out* **11/1**

06-6 **9** 3 ½ **Miss Mohawk (IRE)**[24] 2164 4-8-1 **46** oh1 .... RaulDaSilva(3) 8 24
(Alan Brown) *led to over 2f out: rdn and wknd wl over 1f out* **16/1**

3m 39.28s (-0.12) **Going Correction** +0.025s/f (Good)
WFA 4 from 5yo+ 1lb **9** Ran SP% **116.4**
Speed ratings (Par 101): **101,99,98,98,95 94,91,89,87**
toteswingers 1&2 £3.10, 2&3 £5.00, 1&3 £4.80 CSF £16.70 TOTE £4.00: £1.70, £1.80, £2.00; EX 16.40 Trifecta £48.40 Pool: £615.47 - 9.53 winning units..
Owner Mrs D W Davenport **Bred** Mrs S Camacho **Trained** Norton, N Yorks

FOCUS
An ordinary staying handicap but the pace was solid enough. The second and third set the standard.

2888 BETFRED MOBILE CASINO H'CAP — 5f
8:40 (8:40) (Class 5) (0-75,74) 3-Y-O — **£2,587** (£770; £384; £192) **Stalls** Centre

Form — RPR

100 **1** **Aetna**[17] 2371 3-9-7 **74** .... PaulMulrennan 7 — 84
(Michael Easterby) *in tch: effrt and pushed along 2f out: led last 75yds: r.o strly* **5/1**[3]

4114 **2** 1 1/2 **Hit The Lights (IRE)**[15] 2408 3-9-3 **70** .... FrederikTylicki 3 — 75
(Ollie Pears) *led tl rdn and hdd over 1f out: kpt on fnl f to take 2nd cl home: nt rch wnr* **5/1**[3]

2633 **3** nk **Bapak Bangsawan**[8] 2614 3-8-8 **68** ....(p) KevinStott(7) 5 — 72
(Kevin Ryan) *cl up: rdn to ld over 1f out: edgd lft and hdd last 75yds: sn no ex: lost 2nd nr fin* **10/1**

1 **4** 3 **Algar Lad**[19] 2317 3-9-7 **74** .... GrahamLee 6 — 67
(Jim Goldie) *t.k.h: hld up: stdy hdwy 1/2-way: rdn over 1f out: kpt on fnl f: no imp* **4/1**[2]

1-0 **5** shd **Dark Opal (IRE)**[11] 2544 3-9-5 **72** .... PhillipMakin 10 — 65
(John Weymes) *hld up: rdn 1/2-way: hdwy over 1f out: kpt on fnl f: nvr able to chal* **20/1**

0150 **6** 2 **Lexington Place**[11] 2544 3-8-10 **63** ....(v[1]) TonyHamilton 9 — 49
(Richard Fahey) *chsd ldrs: hung lft and outpcd 2f out: no imp fnl f* **15/2**

6-16 **7** 1/2 **Different**[8] 2626 3-9-3 **70** .... TomEaves 4 — 54
(Bryan Smart) *cl up: rdn and effrt wl over 1f out: wknd ins fnl f* **3/1**[1]

4-45 **8** 7 **Our Diane (IRE)**[26] 2076 3-8-10 **63** .... GrahamGibbons 8 — 22
(David O'Meara) *chsd ldrs tl rdn and wknd over 1f out* **13/2**

656- **9** nk **Lothian Countess**[240] 6809 3-8-7 **60** .... DuranFentiman 1 — 18
(Ian Semple) *hld up in tch: effrt 1/2-way: wknd over 1f out* **66/1**

1m 0.77s (-0.33) **Going Correction** +0.025s/f (Good) **9** Ran SP% **118.8**
Speed ratings (Par 99): **103,100,100,95,95 91,91,79,79**
toteswingers 1&2 £9.10, 2&3 £6.70, 1&3 £9.10 CSF £31.17 TOTE £6.90: £2.20, £1.90, £3.00; EX 19.90 Trifecta £174.80 Pool: £767.27 - 3.29 winning units..
Owner B Padgett **Bred** Bearstone Stud **Trained** Sheriff Hutton, N Yorks

FOCUS
Very few got into this competitive sprint handicap and there was plenty of daylight between the first three and the remainder. The form should hold true, with the second the best guide.

2889 BETFRED "BONUS KING BINGO" H'CAP — 1m 3y(S)
9:10 (9:10) (Class 5) (0-70,73) 4-Y-O+ — **£2,587** (£770; £384; £192) **Stalls** Centre

Form — RPR

0-12 **1** **Never Forever**[15] 2406 4-9-5 **68** .... PJMcDonald 3 — 77+
(George Moore) *in tch: effrt and rdn 2f out: led wl ins fnl f: edgd rt: jst hld on* **9/2**[2]

34-3 **2** shd **Music Festival (USA)**[8] 2636 6-8-4 **53** .... JoeFanning 2 — 62+
(Jim Goldie) *hld up: n.m.r over 2f out: hdwy over 1f out: effrt and styd on wl fnl f: jst failed* **25/1**

10-3 **3** 1/2 **Dandarrell**[37] 1788 6-8-12 **61** .... FrederikTylicki 8 — 69
(Julie Camacho) *trckd ldr: rdn to ld over 1f out: hdd wl ins fnl f: kpt on same pce* **11/2**[3]

3-50 **4** 1 3/4 **Falcon's Reign (FR)**[30] 1950 4-9-4 **67** .... AndrewMullen 14 — 71
(Michael Appleby) *trckd ldrs: effrt and rdn 2f out: kpt on same pce wl ins fnl f* **16/1**

-061 **5** 1/2 **Hakuna Matata**[11] 2551 6-9-3 **73** ....(b) ConnorBeasley(7) 13 — 75
(Michael Dods) *stdd s: hld up: rdn and hung lft 2f out: styd on wl fnl f: nrst fin* **7/1**

1-60 **6** 1/2 **Kuwait Star**[21] 2278 4-9-7 **70** .... TonyHamilton 9 — 71
(Jason Ward) *hld up midfield: effrt and pushed along over 2f out: edgd lft and one pce ins fnl f* **33/1**

6000 **7** hd **Moheebb (IRE)**[24] 2163 9-9-0 **63** .... KirstyMilczarek 1 — 64
(Robert Johnson) *midfield: drvn and outpcd over 2f out: rallied over 1f out: kpt on ins fnl f: no imp* **20/1**

-642 **8** hd **Dream Walker (FR)**[11] 2536 4-8-8 **57** .... DaleSwift 16 — 57
(Ian McInnes) *led: rdn over 2f out: hdd over 1f out: outpcd ins fnl f* **16/1**

46-5 **9** 3/4 **Liliargh (IRE)**[47] 1578 4-9-5 **68** .... GrahamLee 4 — 68+
(Ben Haslam) *hld up: rdn and hdwy over 1f out: no imp wl ins fnl f* **40/1**

5-22 **10** 1 1/4 **Skyfire**[21] 2273 6-8-11 **67** .... KevinStott(7) 6 — 63
(Nick Kent) *trckd ldrs: rdn over 2f out: wknd ins fnl f* **15/2**

50-2 **11** 1 **Cross The Boss (IRE)**[37] 1788 6-8-9 **58** .... GrahamGibbons 7 — 51
(David O'Meara) *missed break: racd keenly towards rr: rdn and hdwy wl over 1f out: btn fnl f* **11/4**[1]

0436 **12** 2 1/4 **Outlaw Torn (IRE)**[4] 2753 4-8-11 **60** ....(e) RobbieFitzpatrick 12 — 48
(Richard Guest) *t.k.h early: hld up: rdn along and hdwy 2f out: wknd fnl f* **20/1**

0006 **13** 8 **Ellaal**[11] 2551 4-9-2 **65** .... JamesSullivan 11 — 35
(Ruth Carr) *hld up: pushed along over 2f out: wknd over 1f out* **40/1**

5502 **14** 9 **Rasselas (IRE)**[11] 2537 6-8-9 **58** ....(p) AdrianNicholls 15
(David Nicholls) *hld up in tch: struggling over 2f out: sn wknd* **14/1**

1m 43.72s (0.32) **Going Correction** +0.025s/f (Good) **14** Ran SP% **124.1**
Speed ratings (Par 103): **99,98,98,96,96 95,95,95,94,93 92,90,82,73**
toteswingers 1&2 £44.70, 2&3 £47.30, 1&3 £5.60 CSF £124.61 CT £645.72 TOTE £6.00: £2.40, £5.40, £1.80; EX 152.60 Trifecta £331.80 Pool: £1019.45 - 2.30 winning units..
Owner Northern Premier Partnership **Bred** Millsec Limited **Trained** Middleham Moor, N Yorks

FOCUS
A modest, if competitive handicap, run at a true pace. They came up the centre of the track and it provided a tight finish. The winner is entitled to improve on this.
T/Plt: £306.40 to £1 stake. Pool of £71490.44 - 170.32 winning tickets. T/Qpdt: £14.20 to a £1 stake. Pool of £7713.32 - 401.23 winning tickets. RY

2890 - 2896a (Foreign Racing) - See Raceform Interactive

2692 LONGCHAMP (R-H)
Saturday, June 1

OFFICIAL GOING: Turf: soft

2897a PRIX DU PALAIS-ROYAL (GROUP 3) (3YO+) (TURF) — 7f
1:00 (12:00) 3-Y-O+ — **£32,520** (£13,008; £9,756; £6,504; £3,252)

RPR

1 **Pearl Flute (IRE)**[20] 2298 3-8-9 0 .... UmbertoRispoli 8 — 111
(F-H Graffard, France) *midfield on outer: 6th and travelling wl 2 1/2f out: short of room 1 1/2f out: gap appeared: rdn and qcknd appr fnl f to ld last 75yds: drvn out* **27/1**

2 3/4 **Tulips (IRE)**[20] 2300 4-9-0 0 .... MaximeGuyon 6 — 108
(A Fabre, France) *disp 4th on outside: 4th and rdn over 2f out: r.o u.p to ld ent fnl f: hdd 75yds out: no ex* **6/1**[3]

3 3/4 **Pollyana (IRE)**[11] 2559 4-9-0 0 ....(p) ChristopheSoumillon 11 — 106
(D Prod'Homme, France) *towards rr: rdn and hdwy on outside under 2f out: styd on u.p ins fnl f: nt pce to chal* **43/10**[2]

4 snk **Spinacre (IRE)**[20] 2299 3-8-4 0 .... GregoryBenoist 12 — 102
(P Bary, France) *towards rr: hdwy on outside over 1 1/2f out: r.o u.p ins fnl f: nrest at fin* **12/1**

5 snk **Silas Marner (FR)**[53] 1456 6-9-5 0 .... Jean-BernardEyquem 9 — 110
(J-C Rouget, France) *midfield: dropped towards rr 2 1/2f out: swtchd ins and hdwy 1 1/2f out: r.o to go 3rd 75yds out: nvr on terms* **2/1**[1]

6 1/2 **American Devil (FR)**[39] 1755 4-9-3 0 .... RonanThomas 2 — 107
(J Van Handenhove, France) *trckd ldrs in 3rd: rdn 1 1/2f out and r.o to chse ldr ins fnl f: wknd last 75yds* **12/1**

7 3/4 **Kendam (FR)**[21] 2264 4-9-0 0 .... ThierryJarnet 10 — 102
(H-A Pantall, France) *towards rr: hdwy on outside over 2f out: chsd ldng gp tl one pce u.p ins fnl f* **13/2**

8 3 1/2 **Takar (IRE)**[53] 1456 4-9-5 0 .... IoritzMendizabal 5 — 97
(Rod Collet, France) *dwlt: towards rr: short of room 2f out: sme late prog: nvr plcd to chal* **43/1**

9 1 1/2 **Foreign Tune**[31] 1945 4-9-0 0 .... OlivierPeslier 4 — 88
(C Laffon-Parias, France) *towards rr on inner: sme mod late hdwy: nvr in contention* **32/1**

10 1 **King Air (FR)**[31] 1945 6-9-7 0 .... StephanePasquier 1 — 93
(R Pritchard-Gordon, France) *disp 4th on inner: lost pl over 2f out: sn rdn: fdd fr over 1f out* **41/1**

11 1 **Coup De Theatre (FR)**[31] 1945 4-9-3 0 .... Christophe-PatriceLemaire 7 — 86
(P Van De Poele, France) *led: hdd after 1f: chsd ldr: rdn and no imp over 1 1/2f out: wknd fnl f* **19/1**

12 snk **Blue Soave (FR)**[31] 1945 5-9-5 0 .... ThierryThulliez 13 — 87
(F Chappet, France) *slow to stride: led after 1f: clr by 1/2-way: 5 l ld over 1 1/2f out: rdn and hdd ent fnl f: wknd qckly* **37/1**

13 snk **Mil Azul (SPA)**[27] 5-9-3 0 .... J-LMartinez 3 — 85
(E Leon Penate, Spain) *midfield: rdn and btn fr over 1 1/2f out* **40/1**

1m 24.36s (3.66)
WFA 3 from 4yo+ 10lb **13** Ran SP% **116.5**
WIN (incl. 1 euro stake): 28.20. PLACES: 6.10, 2.70, 2.30. DF: 108.20. SF: 333.30.
Owner Qatar Racing Limited **Bred** Petra Bloodstock Agency Ltd **Trained** France

2898 - 2904a (Foreign Racing) - See Raceform Interactive

2433 CHANTILLY (R-H)
Sunday, June 2

OFFICIAL GOING: Turf: good to soft

2905a PRIX DE ROYAUMONT (GROUP 3) (3YO FILLIES) (TURF) — 1m 4f
1:20 (12:00) 3-Y-O — **£32,520** (£13,008; £9,756; £6,504; £3,252)

RPR

1 **Eleuthera (FR)**[18] 2381 3-9-0 0 .... EddyHardouin 7 — 106
(P Demercastel, France) *stdd and hld up in last pair: angled out and rdn to improve 2f out: styd on to chal ent fnl f: led ins fnl 120yds: drvn clr* **14/1**

2 1 1/2 **Orion Love**[21] 2296 3-9-0 0 ....(p) FabriceVeron 9 — 104
(H-A Pantall, France) *t.k.h: trckd ldr: chal gng wl 2f out: rdn to ld over 1 1/2f out: strly pressed ent fnl f: styd on but hdd ins fnl 120yds and no ex* **9/1**[3]

3 2 **Dance In The Park (FR)**[37] 1816 3-9-0 0 .... Jean-BaptisteHamel 6 — 101
(D Guillemin, France) *hld up in last: rdn 2f out: drifted rt u.p but styd on steadily: wnt 3rd ins fnl 100yds: nvr able to chal* **9/1**[3]

4 2 1/2 **Planete Bleue (IRE)**[32] 3-9-0 0 .... AntoineHamelin 3 — 97
(F-H Graffard, France) *t.k.h: led: rdn and strly pressed 2f out: hdd over 1 1/2f out: no ex ent fnl f: fdd and dropped to 4th* **7/2**[2]

5 1 3/4 **Hey Little Gorl (GER)**[28] 3-9-0 0 .... ThierryThulliez 5 — 94
(Markus Klug, Germany) *settled in midfield on inner: rdn 2f out: outpcd by ldrs over 1f out: swtchd to outer and styd on to go 5th wl ins fnl f: n.d* **16/1**

6 1 3/4 **Shahad (IRE)**[18] 2381 3-9-0 0 .... OlivierPeslier 4 — 91
(F Head, France) *dwlt: qckly rcvrd and racd in midfield on outer: rdn 2f out: outpcd by ldrs over 1f out: plugged on* **14/1**

7 2 1/2 **Lava Flow (IRE)**[21] 2296 3-9-0 0 .... MaximeGuyon 8 — 87
(A Fabre, France) *midfield in tch on outer: clsd 3f out: rdn over 2f out: awkward u.p and btn ent fnl f: fdd* **1/1**[1]

8 15 **Sole Reign (FR)**[26] 3-9-0 0 ....(b[1]) AlexisBadel 2 — 63
(Mme M Bollack-Badel, France) *prom on inner: rdn over 2f out: sn no ex and btn: dropped to last and eased over 1f out: t.o* **25/1**

2m 31.8s (0.80) **Going Correction** +0.25s/f (Good) **8** Ran SP% **115.3**
Speed ratings: **107,106,104,103,101 100,99,89**
WIN (incl. 1 euro stake): 19.00. PLACES: 3.70, 2.50, 2.20. DF: 41.60. SF: 92.70.
Owner Mme Philippe Demercastel **Bred** P Demercastel **Trained** France

2906a PRIX DE SANDRINGHAM (GROUP 2) (3YO FILLIES) (TURF) — 1m
2:30 (12:00) 3-Y-O — **£60,243** (£23,252; £11,097; £7,398; £3,699)

RPR

1 **Peace Burg (FR)**[59] 1358 3-8-11 0 .... ChristopheSoumillon 3 — 111
(J-C Rouget, France) *a.p: rdn to chal 1 1/2f out: led ent fnl f: r.o: drvn out and a holding fast fining runner-up* **11/2**[3]

2 nk **Topaze Blanche (IRE)**[21] 2299 3-8-11 0 .... OlivierPeslier 5 — 110+
(C Laffon-Parias, France) *t.k.h: hld up in last: rdn and hdwy over 1f out: r.o to go 2nd ins fnl 100yds: fin wl and pressed wnr cl home but nvr getting there* **9/2**[2]

3 1 1/2 **Kenhope (FR)**[21] 2299 3-8-11 0 .... ThierryJarnet 1 — 107+
(H-A Pantall, France) *t.k.h: prom early: sn restrained and hld up in last pair on inner: angled out and rdn over 1f out: r.o to go 3rd post: nvr able to chal* **7/1**

4 shd **Dauphine Russe (FR)**[21] 2299 3-8-11 0 .... IoritzMendizabal 4 — 106
(F Doumen, France) *midfield on outer: rdn 1 1/2f out: r.o: wnt 3rd ins fnl 100yds: dropped to 4th post* **9/1**

5 1/2 **White Waves (USA)**[25] 2183 3-8-11 0 .... MaximeGuyon 7 — 105
(A Fabre, France) *sn led: hdd after 2f and trckd ldr: rdn 1 1/2f out: r.o but nt pce to chal* **11/1**

6 *snk* **What A Name (IRE)**[28] 2047 3-9-2 0.......... Christophe-PatriceLemaire 6 110
(M Delzangles, France) *t.k.h early: hld up tl allowed to stride on and ld after 2f: rdn and strly pressed 1 1/2f out: hdd ent fnl f: sn no ex and btn: fdd* **11/10**[1]

7 *1/2* **Sparkling Beam (IRE)**[22] 3-8-11 0.............................. RonanThomas 2 104
(J E Pease, France) *prom early: sn settled in midfield on inner: looking for room 1 1/2f out: rdn and ev ch whn nt clr run and hmpd ent fnl f: nt rcvr and dropped to last: keeping on again cl home* **18/1**

1m 40.57s (2.57) **Going Correction** +0.25s/f (Good) 7 Ran SP% **117.3**
Speed ratings: **97,96,95,95,94 94,93**
WIN (incl. 1 euro stake): 4.80. PLACES: 2.70, 2.70. SF: 30.00.
Owner Cuadra Montalban & Ecurie D Primes **Bred** Ecurie D **Trained** Pau, France

2907a PRIX DU JOCKEY CLUB (GROUP 1) (3YO COLTS & FILLIES) (TURF) 1m 2f 110y
3:15 (12:00) 3-Y-O **£696,829** (£278,780; £139,390; £69,634; £34,878)

RPR

1 **Intello (GER)**[21] 2298 3-9-2 0.. OlivierPeslier 10 121+
(A Fabre, France) *a.p: rdn to chal 2f out: led 1 1/2f out: qcknd clr ent fnl f: styd on strly: drvn out* **15/8**[1]

2 *2* **Morandi (FR)**[21] 2298 3-9-2 0.............................. ChristopheSoumillon 3 117
(J-C Rouget, France) *prom in midfield: hdwy 2f out: rdn to chal 1 1/2f out: outpcd by wnr ent fnl f: styd on to go 2nd cl home* **13/2**[2]

3 *snk* **Sky Hunter**[20] 3-9-2 0.. MaximeGuyon 9 117
(A Fabre, France) *a.p: rdn to chal 2f out: wnt 2nd 1 1/2f out: outpcd by wnr ent fnl f: styd on but dropped to 3rd cl home* **7/1**[3]

4 *2 1/2* **Mshawish (USA)**[19] 2355 3-9-2 0................................ GregoryBenoist 1 112
(M Delzangles, France) *a.p: rdn and ev ch 1 1/2f out: wnt 4th over 1f out: outpcd by ldng trio ins fnl f: styd on and jst hld on for 4th* **20/1**

5 *hd* **Shikarpour (IRE)**[21] 3-9-2 0... ThierryJarnet 6 112
(A De Royer-Dupre, France) *dwlt: sn rcvrd and racd in midfield: rdn over 2f out: styd on steadily: wnt 5th ent fnl f: no threat to ldng trio but almost snatched 4th post* **16/1**

6 *1 1/4* **Willie The Whipper**[23] 2211 3-9-2 0............................ JamieSpencer 15 109+
(Ann Duffield) *dwlt: dropped in and hld up in last: rdn and hdwy on wd outside fr 2f out: hung rt u.p but styd on to take nvr nrr 6th fnl strides* **40/1**

7 *hd* **Bravodino (USA)**[29] 2035 3-9-2 0.......................... StephanePasquier 14 109
(J E Pease, France) *settled in midfield: rdn and hdwy over 2f out: wnt 6th jst ins fnl f: styd on but dropped to 7th fnl strides* **7/1**[3]

8 *1* **Max Dynamite (FR)**[21] 2297 3-9-2 0......................... AntoineHamelin 17 107
(J Van Handenhove, France) *hld up towards rr on outer: rdn over 2f out: styd on but n.d* **66/1**

9 *2* **Dalwari (USA)**[19] 2355 3-9-2 0.................. Christophe-PatriceLemaire 16 103
(J-C Rouget, France) *reluctant to load: midfield on outer: rdn 2f out: edgd rt u.p: plugged on wout threatening* **10/1**

10 *2* **Loch Garman (IRE)**[21] 2290 3-9-2 0........................... KevinManning 5 99
(J S Bolger, Ire) *sltly slow to stride and drvn to hold position: sn settled in midfield on inner: rdn over 2f out: styd on one pce: n.d* **10/1**

11 *3/4* **Superplex (FR)**[29] 2035 3-9-2 0................................ IoritzMendizabal 8 98
(M Figge, Germany) *trckd ldr: smooth hdwy to chal 2f out: rdn and ev ch 1 1/2f out: sn outpcd by ldrs: no ex ent fnl f: steadily fdd* **40/1**

12 *hd* **Ares D'Emra (FR)**[37] 1818 3-9-2 0................... Francois-XavierBertras 4 97
(C Delcher-Sanchez, Spain) *dwlt and bmpd s: qckly rcvrd and settled in midfield on inner: rdn over 2f out: outpcd over 1f out: plugged on* **33/1**

13 *shd* **Glacial Age (IRE)**[23] 2211 3-9-2 0.............................. HayleyTurner 19 97
(Jo Hughes) *dropped in fr wdst draw and hld up in last pair on inner: rdn in last 3f out: styd on ins fnl 2f but nvr remotely dangerous* **66/1**

14 *9* **Beyond Thankful (IRE)**[49] 1558 3-9-2 0....................(p) RonanWhelan 7 79
(J S Bolger, Ire) *drvn to go forward and sn led: 3 l advantage 4f out: rdn over 2f out: hdd 1 1/2f out: sn btn and fdd: eased ins fnl f* **66/1**

15 *2 1/2* **First Cornerstone (IRE)**[8] 2677 3-9-2 0...................... FrankieDettori 13 75
(A Oliver, Ire) *hld up towards rr on inner: ct on heels and sltly hmpd 5f out: rdn over 2f out: outpcd and btn ent fnl f* **20/1**

16 *3/4* **Lion D'Anvers (FR)**[21] 2298 3-9-2 0............................ RonanThomas 12 73
(J Van Handenhove, France) *prom early: drifted bk through field and hld up towards rr: rdn 3f out: no ex and btn over 1f out: eased ins fnl f* **50/1**

17 *shd* **Milano Blues (FR)**[25] 3-9-2 0.. JimmyMartin 18 73
(B De Montzey, France) *trapped wd in midfield: rdn over 2f out: hanging rt u.p and btn ent fnl f: sn eased* **200/1**

18 *12* **Haya Kan (FR)**[16] 2434 3-9-2 0....................................(b) FranckBlondel 2 50
(Mme L Audon, France) *hld up towards rr on inner: rdn 3f out: sn bhd and btn: eased ent fnl f: t.o* **200/1**

19 *nk* **Dastarhon (IRE)**[21] 2298 3-9-2 0.............................. UmbertoRispoli 11 49
(Mme Pia Brandt, France) *hld up towards rr: rdn over 2f out: sn no ex and btn: eased over 1f out: t.o and dropped to last cl home* **11/1**

2m 7.89s (-0.91) **Going Correction** +0.25s/f (Good) 19 Ran SP% **130.3**
Speed ratings: **113,111,111,109,109 108,108,107,106,104 104,104,104,97,95 95,95,86,86**
WIN (incl. 1 euro stake): 3.30. PLACES: 1.50, 2.40, 2.30. DF: 13.40. SF: 23.60.
Owner Wertheimer & Frere **Bred** Wertheimer Et Frere **Trained** Chantilly, France

FOCUS
This can often be a messy race with trouble in running playing a large part, especially in big fields, but few could have excuses this time in a race run at a fair gallop from the start. The form looks solid rated around the runner-up and eighth to their best.

2908a GRAND PRIX DE CHANTILLY (GROUP 2) (4YO+) (TURF) 1m 4f
4:00 (12:00) 4-Y-O+ **£60,243** (£23,252; £11,097; £7,398; £3,699)

RPR

1 **Now We Can**[45] 1658 4-8-11 0... ThierryThulliez 8 112
(N Clement, France) *trckd ldr on outer: virtually jnd ldr 2 1/2f out: rdn and nt qckn immediately over 1 1/2f out: r.o u.p fnl f: led last 50yds: drvn out* **5/2**[1]

2 *hd* **Haya Landa (FR)**[25] 2184 5-8-8 0................................. FranckBlondel 7 109
(Mme L Audon, France) *settled in 4th: rdn to chse ldrs 1 1/2f out: styd on u.p fnl f: a hld by wnr cl home* **14/1**

3 *snk* **Remus De La Tour (FR)**[25] 2184 4-8-11 0...................... NicolasPerret 9 112
(K Borgel, France) *led: virtually jnd on outer 2 1/2f out: shkn up and qcknd tempo under 2f out: 1 l clr and rdn 1f out: kpt on u.p tl hdd 50yds out: no ex* **16/1**

4 *nse* **Pirika (IRE)**[25] 2184 5-8-8 0................................. Pierre-CharlesBoudot 6 109
(A Fabre, France) *w.w in rr: last and shkn up 1 1/2f out: stl last and styd on u.p 1f out: r.o to be nrest at fin* **7/2**[2]

5 *nk* **Dance Moves**[37] 1817 5-8-11 0...................................... MaximeGuyon 4 111
(A Fabre, France) *towards rr: angled out and rdn 2f out: styd on u.p fr over 1f out: nt pce to chal* **10/1**

6 *1 1/2* **I'm Your Man (FR)**[23] 2249 4-8-11 0........................ StephanePasquier 1 109
(A De Royer-Dupre, France) *trckd ldr on inner: rdn and nt qckn 1 1/2f out: kpt on at same pce fnl f* **12/1**

7 *3/4* **Only A Pleasure (IRE)**[239] 6896 4-8-11 0................ MickaelBarzalona 2 108
(A Fabre, France) *midfield on inner: rdn and no imp 2f out: one pce fnl f* **18/1**

8 *shd* **Saonois (FR)**[35] 1870 4-9-2 0...................................... AntoineHamelin 3 112
(J-P Gauvin, France) *towards rr: hemmed in and nowhere to go fr 2f out: hrd rdn and nt qckn whn gap appeared 1 1/2f out: no imp u.p fnl f* **9/2**[3]

9 *1/2* **Saga Dream (FR)**[56] 1420 7-9-2 0................................. ThierryJarnet 5 112
(F Lemercier, France) *midfield on outer: shkn up and no imp 1 1/2f out: rdn and wknd appr fnl f* **6/1**

2m 33.16s (2.16) **Going Correction** +0.25s/f (Good) 9 Ran SP% **117.9**
Speed ratings: **102,101,101,101,101 100,100,99,99**
Win (incl. 1 euro stake): 3.00. PLACES: 1.60, 3.40, 3.90. DF: 18.90. SF: 27.80.
Owner Winfried Engelbrecht-Bresges **Bred** Gestut Zoppenbroich **Trained** Chantilly, France

2909a PRIX DU GROS-CHENE (GROUP 2) (3YO+) (TURF) 5f
4:35 (12:00) 3-Y-O+ **£60,243** (£23,252; £11,097; £7,398; £3,699)

RPR

1 **Spirit Quartz (IRE)**[8] 2662 5-9-2 0.............................(p) JamieSpencer 9 114
(Robert Cowell) *trckd ldr: led gng wl over 2f out: rdn over 1f out: qcknd clr ent fnl f: drvn and diminishing advantage cl home but a holding on* **7/2**[1]

2 *1/2* **Catcall (FR)**[21] 2300 4-9-2 0............................... Francois-XavierBertras 7 112
(P Sogorb, France) *dwlt: hld up towards rr on outer but wl in tch: rdn 2f out: r.o: wnt 2nd ins fnl f: clsng on wnr at fin but nvr getting there* **7/2**[1]

3 *3/4* **Gammarth (FR)**[21] 2300 5-9-2 0...................................... FabriceVeron 6 109
(H-A Pantall, France) *midfield on outer: bmpd after 1f: rdn 2f out: r.o but nt pce to chal* **12/1**

4 *2 1/2* **Elusivity (IRE)**[8] 2669 5-9-2 0.................................... DanielTudhope 2 100
(David O'Meara) *hld up in tch: hmpd whn short of room after 1f: gng wl enough but had to wait for run 2f out: in the clr and rdn over 1f out: r.o but nvr able to chal* **6/1**[3]

5 *1* **Stepper Point**[21] 2300 4-9-2 0............................. ChristopheSoumillon 4 97
(William Muir) *midfield: bmpd after 1f: rdn and ev ch 2f out: outpcd by wnr ent fnl f: fdd* **8/1**

6 *1* **Myasun (FR)**[40] 1755 6-9-2 0... MaximeGuyon 3 84
(C Baillet, France) *midfield: stmbld whn squeezed for room after 1f: rdn over 2f out: outpcd and btn ent fnl f: fdd: fin 7th: plcd 6th* **7/1**

7 *1 1/4* **Mirza**[44] 1672 6-9-2 0...(p) OlivierPeslier 1 81
(Rae Guest) *prom on inner: drifted rt and hmpd rivals whn short of room as ldr cut across after 1f: gng wl enough but nt clr run on rail fr over 3f out tl ins fnl f: rdn whn clr but ch gone: fin 8th: plcd 7th* **25/1**

8 *2 1/2* **Mazameer (IRE)**[20] 2334 3-8-9 0...............................(b) ThierryJarnet 5 73
(F Head, France) *prom: bmpd after 1f: outpcd 2f out and qckly lost pl: last and btn ent fnl f: eased: fin 9th: plcd 8th* **9/1**

D *1* **Hamish McGonagall**[64] 1249 8-9-2 0................................. DavidAllan 8 88
(Tim Easterby) *broke wl and led: cut across field whn swtchd to rail after 1f and hmpd rivals: rdn and hdd over 2f out: no ex and btn ent fnl f: fdd: fin 6th: disqualified* **5/1**[2]

57.63s (-0.67) **Going Correction** +0.15s/f (Good)
WFA 3 from 4yo+ 7lb 9 Ran SP% **120.5**
Speed ratings: **111,110,109,105,103 100,98,94,101**
WIN (incl. 1 euro stake): 5.10. PLACES: 1.90, 1.50, 3.00. DF: 10.50. SF: 19.50.
Owner Qatar Racing Limited **Bred** Ballygallon Stud Limited **Trained** Six Mile Bottom, Cambs

1564 DUSSELDORF (R-H)
Sunday, June 2

OFFICIAL GOING: Turf: soft

2910a RACEBETS.COM 1000 GUINEAS 2013 (GROUP 2) (3YO FILLIES) (TURF) 1m
4:25 (12:00) 3-Y-O

£56,910 (£22,764; £11,382; £5,691; £2,845; £2,032)

RPR

1 **Akua'da (GER)**[28] 2065 3-9-2 0... EPedroza 4 106
(A Wohler, Germany) *broke wl and mde all: rdn and qcknd 2f out: 2 l clr ent fnl f: r.o gamely u.p: jst hld on* **12/1**

2 *shd* **Calyxa**[28] 2065 3-9-2 0.................................. LennartHammer-Hansen 5 106
(Ferdinand J Leve, Germany) *chsd ldrs on inner: rdn and outpcd 2 1/2f out: 6th and u.p over 1 1/2f out: hrd rdn and styd on strly fnl f: jst failed* **7/1**

3 *3 1/2* **Senafe**[16] 2429 3-9-2 0.. NeilCallan 8 98
(Marco Botti) *trckd ldr: 2nd and ev ch over 2f out: sn rdn and nt qckn: one pce u.p fnl f* **5/1**[2]

4 *shd* **Beatrice**[28] 2065 3-9-2 0.. AlexandreRoussel 7 98
(H-A Pantall, France) *midfield: rdn to chse ldng gp 2 1/2f out: short or room 2f out: swtchd outside and in clr under 1 1/2f out: styd on u.p fnl f: nvr on terms* **4/1**[1]

5 *2 1/2* **Dancing Shuffle (GER)**[28] 3-9-2 0................................ AHelfenbein 11 92
(S Smrczek, Germany) *midfield: hdwy on inner to chse ldng gp 3f out: 4th and rdn 1 1/2f out: fdd u.p ins fnl f* **40/1**

6 *nk* **Molly Mara (GER)**[28] 2065 3-9-2 0.............................. AndreaAtzeni 13 91
(J Hirschberger, Germany) *broke wl fr wd draw: racd promly: rdn and nt qckn 1 1/2f out: one pce fnl f* **16/1**

7 *1 1/4* **Red Lips (GER)**[28] 2065 3-9-2 0.. DPorcu 6 88
(Andreas Lowe, Germany) *plld hrd: prom: rdn to hold pl on heels of ldng gp 2 1/2f out: hrd rdn and no imp fnl 2f* **6/1**[3]

8 *hd* **Penelopa**[277] 5755 3-9-2 0... ADeVries 2 88
(M G Mintchev, Germany) *midfield: rdn and outpcd over 2f out: n.d* **12/1**

9 *nk* **Melbourne Memories**[21] 2299 3-9-2 0.............................. AdamKirby 10 87
(Clive Cox) *midfield: towards rr 3f out: rdn and no real imp fnl 2f: nvr in contention* **4/1**[1]

10 *shd* **Ratana (GER)**[28] 3-9-2 0... APietsch 5 87
(Andreas Lowe, Germany) *midfield on outer: hrd rdn and nt qckn over 2f out: one pce u.p: n.d* **16/1**

11 *1* **Agama (GER)**[43] 3-9-2 0... WPanov 1 85
(C Sprengel, Germany) *towards rr: rdn 2 1/2f out and no imp: nvr a factor* **33/1**

12 *hd* **Kathinka (GER)**[32] 3-9-2 0 .... MartinHarley 14 84
(M Munch, Germany) *towards rr: bhd fr 2 1/2f out* **22/1**
13 *1* **Diaccia (GER)**[35] 3-9-2 0 .... (b) AStarke 12 82
(P Schiergen, Germany) *towards rr on outer: nvr threatened* **16/1**
14 *3/4* **Isioma**[28] 2065 3-9-2 0 .... MircoDemuro 3 80
(Mario Hofer, Germany) *a towards rr on outer: rdn and no imp fnl 2f* **33/1**
15 *8* **Legenda Aurea (GER)**[28] 2065 3-9-2 0 .... FilipMinarik 9 62
(P Schiergen, Germany) *a bhd: wl btn fr over 3f out* **50/1**

1m 38.95s (-2.21) **15** Ran SP% **131.1**
WIN (incl. 10 euro stake): 140. PLACES: 41, 23, 30. SF: 803.
Owner Gestut Brummerhof **Bred** Gestut Brummerhof **Trained** Germany

2701 CARLISLE (R-H)

Monday, June 3

OFFICIAL GOING: Good to firm (8.4)
Wind: Light, half behind Weather: Cloudy, warm

2911 32REDPOKER.COM APPRENTICE H'CAP 7f 200y

6:15 (6:15) (Class 5) (0-75,73) 4-Y-0+ **£2,587** (£770; £384; £192) **Stalls** Low

Form RPR
0-60 **1** **Talent Scout (IRE)**[33] 1932 7-9-1 **70** .... (p) GemmaTutty(3) 6 81
(Karen Tutty) *mde all: rdn over 1f out: hld on wl towards fin* **9/2**[3]
00-0 **2** *nk* **Icy Blue**[39] 1788 5-7-13 **54** oh1 .... (p) NoelGarbutt(3) 7 64
(Richard Whitaker) *hld up: effrt whn n.m.r briefly over 2f out: hdwy over 1f out: kpt on wl fnl f: jst hld* **25/1**
40-0 **3** *5* **Last Destination (IRE)**[38] 1801 5-8-3 **55** .... DeclanCannon 5 54
(Nigel Tinkler) *hld up in tch: rdn 3f out: hdwy 2f out: kpt on same pce fnl f* **11/1**
430/ **4** *nk* **Dazeen**[611] 6520 6-9-7 **73** .... LucyAlexander 1 71
(Richard Ford) *t.k.h early: hld up on ins: effrt whn n.m.r briefly wl over 1f out: no imp fnl f* **14/1**
-443 **5** *1 1/2* **Paramour**[14] 2515 6-9-4 **73** .... DavidBergin(3) 4 68
(David O'Meara) *chsd ldrs: wnt 2nd and rdn over 2f out: rdn and wknd ins fnl f* **6/4**[1]
052 **6** *1 1/4* **True Prince (USA)**[27] 2125 4-8-3 **55** .... (b) NeilFarley 8 47
(Brian Ellison) *hld up in tch: rdn along 3f out: no imp fr 2f out: btn fnl f* **4/1**[2]
0346 **7** *7* **Spread Boy (IRE)**[10] 2636 6-7-11 **54** oh8 .... JordanHibberd(5) 2 30
(Alan Berry) *prom tl rdn and wknd over 2f out* **28/1**
1130 **8** *4 1/2* **Thrust Control (IRE)**[13] 2551 6-8-6 **61** .... (p) GeorgeChaloner(3) 3 26
(Tracy Waggott) *t.k.h: chsd wnr to over 2f out: sn rdn and wknd* **10/1**

1m 39.89s (-0.11) **Going Correction** +0.10s/f (Good) **8** Ran SP% **109.6**
Speed ratings (Par 103): **104,103,98,98,96 95,88,84**
toteswingers 1&2 £9.50, 1&3 £12.60, 2&3 £17.40 CSF £93.45 CT £1065.97 TOTE £4.90: £1.70, £4.00, £1.60; EX 149.60 Trifecta £730.90 Part won. Pool: £974.62 - 0.21 winning units..
Owner Thoroughbred Homes Ltd **Bred** Johnston King **Trained** Osmotherley, N Yorks

FOCUS
An ordinary apprentice handicap and the winner made all.

2912 MATTHEW ELLIOTT 30TH BIRTHDAY CELEBRATION CLAIMING STKS 7f 200y

6:45 (6:45) (Class 5) 3-Y-0+ **£2,587** (£770; £384; £192) **Stalls** Low

Form RPR
00-6 **1** **Springheel Jake**[48] 1599 4-9-10 73 .... PJMcDonald 6 84
(Ann Duffield) *mde all: rdn over 1f out: hld on wl fnl f* **5/1**[3]
0353 **2** *1 1/4* **Extraterrestrial**[7] 2705 9-9-1 79 .... GeorgeChaloner(5) 4 77
(Richard Fahey) *in tch: rdn and hdwy to chse wnr over 2f out: hung rt over 1f out: one pce ins fnl f* **1/1**[1]
1116 **3** *5* **Saharia (IRE)**[12] 2571 6-9-6 72 .... (be) GrahamLee 8 66
(Daniel Mark Loughnane) *hld up: rdn and hdwy to chse (clr) ldrs appr fnl f: sn no imp* **5/2**[2]
-440 **4** *7* **River Ardeche**[58] 1394 8-9-3 57 .... (p) RoystonFfrench 5 47
(Tracy Waggott) *pressed wnr: rdn over 2f out: wknd over 1f out* **14/1**
2046 **5** *2* **Tony Hollis**[6] 2752 5-8-10 48 .... GemmaTutty(7) 7 42
(Karen Tutty) *prom on outside: rdn over 2f out: sn wknd* **20/1**
050- **6** *8* **Eilean Mor**[220] 7385 5-8-10 48 .... NoelGarbutt(7) 3 24
(R Mike Smith) *prom: drvn and outpcd over 2f out: sn btn* **80/1**
06-6 **7** *3* **Lady Bentinck (IRE)**[10] 2613 4-8-13 48 .... PaddyAspell 1 13
(Alan Berry) *missed break: bhd: struggling 3f out: sn btn* **100/1**

1m 39.96s (-0.04) **Going Correction** +0.10s/f (Good) **7** Ran SP% **108.9**
Speed ratings (Par 103): **104,102,97,90,88 80,77**
toteswingers 1&2 £1.10, 1&3 £2.20, 2&3 £1.10 CSF £9.45 TOTE £3.40: £1.70, £1.10; EX 11.00 Trifecta £26.70 Pool: £1255.31 - 35.14 winning units..
Owner Jimmy Kay **Bred** Mrs T Brudenell **Trained** Constable Burton, N Yorks

FOCUS
The usual mixed levels of ability in this claimer, although three stood out on the ratings. The time was fractionally slower that the opening apprentice handicap.

2913 32REDBINGO MEDIAN AUCTION MAIDEN STKS 5f

7:15 (7:18) (Class 5) 2-Y-0 **£2,587** (£770; £384; £192) **Stalls** High

Form RPR
25 **1** **Muspelheim**[31] 1989 2-9-5 0 .... PJMcDonald 3 76
(Ann Duffield) *in tch: gd hdwy and edgd lft over 1f out: led ins fnl f: edgd rt: pushed out* **9/2**[2]
4 **2** *2 1/2* **Proclamationofwar**[11] 2591 2-9-5 0 .... PhillipMakin 6 67+
(Kevin Ryan) *pressed clr ldr and clr of remainder: rdn to ld over 1f out: hdd and no ex ins fnl f* **8/13**[1]
3 *1 1/4* **Too Elusive** 2-9-5 0 .... DavidNolan 8 63+
(Kristin Stubbs) *bhd and sn outpcd: drvn and plenty to do 1/2-way: gd hdwy over 1f out: r.o fnl f* **22/1**
45 **4** *3* **Luckys Connoisseur**[7] 2712 2-9-5 0 .... FrannyNorton 7 52
(Mark Johnston) *chsd clr ldng pair: drvn and effrt 2f out: wknd ins fnl f* **14/1**
3 **5** *3/4* **Reet Thicknstrong**[10] 2631 2-9-0 0 .... RoystonFfrench 4 44+
(Bryan Smart) *reluctant to enter stalls: led at str pce: hdd over 1f out: sn wknd* **9/1**
6 *9* **Latenightrequest** 2-8-9 0 .... GeorgeChaloner(5) 5 12
(Richard Fahey) *s.v.s and wl bhd: no imp whn hung bdly lft fr over 1f out* **6/1**[3]

1m 2.04s (1.24) **Going Correction** +0.10s/f (Good) **6** Ran SP% **115.4**
Speed ratings (Par 93): **94,90,88,83,82 67**
toteswingers 1&2 £1.10, 1&3 £4.10, 2&3 £5.90 CSF £8.01 TOTE £3.80: £1.50, £1.30; EX 8.60 Trifecta £197.90 Pool: £1237.72 - 4.69 winning units..
Owner Grange Park Racing & Partner **Bred** Longdon Stud Ltd **Trained** Constable Burton, N Yorks

FOCUS
This has proven a very decent juvenile maiden in recent years. The leaders appeared to go overly quick early and set it up for the late closer.

2914 32RED.COM H'CAP (JOCKEY CLUB GRASSROOTS SPRINT SERIES QUALIFIER) 5f

7:45 (7:46) (Class 4) (0-80,80) 4-Y-0+ **£6,469** (£1,925; £962; £481) **Stalls** High

Form RPR
62-5 **1** **Just Like Heaven (IRE)**[27] 2122 4-8-4 **63** .... DuranFentiman 6 72
(Tim Easterby) *mde all at decent gallop: rdn over 1f out: r.o strly fnl f: unchal* **25/1**
3222 **2** *1 1/2* **Red Baron (IRE)**[6] 2757 4-8-2 **64** .... (p) NeilFarley(3) 10 68
(Eric Alston) *in tch on outside: hdwy to chse wnr 2f out: sn rdn and edgd rt: kpt on fnl f: nt rch wnr* **11/2**[3]
0606 **3** *1/2* **Hopes N Dreams (IRE)**[15] 2476 5-9-2 **75** .... PhillipMakin 8 77
(Kevin Ryan) *hld up in midfield: effrt and rdn over 1f out: kpt on ins fnl f: nrst fin* **3/1**[1]
0-53 **4** *nse* **Red Cape (FR)**[7] 2703 10-8-10 **69** .... JamesSullivan 11 71
(Ruth Carr) *chsd ldrs: rdn and chsd wnr briefly over 2f out: kpt on same pce ins fnl f* **14/1**
2-66 **5** *hd* **Rasaman (IRE)**[37] 1819 9-9-2 **75** .... GrahamLee 9 76+
(Jim Goldie) *hld up: shkn up and hdwy over 1f out: n.m.r ins fnl f: kpt on fin* **10/1**
0032 **6** *1 3/4* **Diamond Blue**[7] 2702 5-8-9 **68** .... (p) AmyRyan 1 63
(Richard Whitaker) *rrd s: bhd: rdn and hdwy on outside over 1f out: no imp fnl f* **7/1**
4114 **7** *3/4* **Hamoody (USA)**[32] 1964 9-9-7 **80** .... AdrianNicholls 7 72
(David Nicholls) *taken early to post: dwlt: hld up bhd ldng gp: effrt and rdn over 1f out: no ex ins fnl f* **20/1**
0522 **8** *1 1/4* **Lenny Bee**[16] 2441 7-9-2 **80** .... (t) GeorgeChaloner(5) 2 67
(Garry Moss) *prom: drvn over 2f out: wknd appr fnl f* **5/1**[2]
0-00 **9** *3/4* **Partner (IRE)**[14] 2505 7-9-0 **76** .... (p) DeclanCannon(3) 3 61
(Noel Wilson) *prom: drvn and lost pl 1/2-way: n.d after* **28/1**
6140 **10** *1 1/2* **Lucky Dan (IRE)**[6] 2755 7-9-7 **80** .... FrannyNorton 5 59
(Paul Green) *chsd wnr to over 2f out: sn rdn and wknd* **16/1**
0-04 **11** *1/2* **Barney McGrew (IRE)**[16] 2441 10-9-5 **78** .... TomEaves 4 56
(Michael Dods) *taken early to post: dwlt: bhd: rdn along over 2f out: btn over 1f out* **8/1**

1m 0.77s (-0.03) **Going Correction** +0.10s/f (Good) **11** Ran SP% **114.4**
Speed ratings (Par 105): **104,101,100,100,100 97,96,94,93,90 90**
toteswingers 1&2 £41.20, 1&3 £26.70, 2&3 £1.60 CSF £150.17 CT £542.38 TOTE £29.10: £8.00, £2.90, £1.50; EX 209.00 Trifecta £432.40 Pool: £966.78 - 1.67 winning units..
Owner D B Lamplough **Bred** Derek Veitch And Mark Tong **Trained** Great Habton, N Yorks

FOCUS
A competitive sprint handicap run 1.27sec faster than the preceding juvenile maiden.

2915 32RED WESTMORLAND FILLIES' H'CAP (JOCKEY CLUB GRASSROOTS MIDDLE DISTANCE SERIES QUALIFIER) 1m 1f 61y

8:15 (8:15) (Class 4) (0-80,78) 3-Y-0+ **£4,690** (£1,395; £697; £348) **Stalls** Low

Form RPR
1-1 **1** **Regal Hawk**[67] 1219 3-9-0 **76** .... GrahamLee 7 83+
(James Tate) *prom: effrt and chsd wnr over 1f out: sn drvn and edgd lft: styd on wl fnl f to ld nr fin* **5/4**[1]
-064 **2** *shd* **Act Your Shoe Size**[7] 2704 4-10-0 **78** .... TomEaves 3 87
(Keith Dalgleish) *led: rdn and edgd lft 2f out: kpt on wl u.p fnl f: hdd nr fin* **14/1**
0065 **3** *1 1/4* **Hot Rod Mamma (IRE)**[6] 2753 6-9-4 **71** .... LucyAlexander(3) 4 77+
(Dianne Sayer) *hld up: squeezed through over 4f out: effrt and rdn whn hung rt over 1f out: kpt on ins fnl f* **12/1**
0-00 **4** *8* **Bayan Kasirga (IRE)**[17] 2420 3-7-11 **62** .... NeilFarley(3) 1 49
(Richard Fahey) *hld up on ins: rdn whn carried rt wl over 1f out: n.d after* **20/1**
2646 **5** *shd* **Blue Maisey**[13] 2539 5-8-11 **61** .... JamesSullivan 5 49
(Edwin Tuer) *chsd ldrs: drvn along over 2f out: wknd appr fnl f* **10/1**
2-10 **6** *7* **Reggae Star**[18] 2387 3-9-0 **76** .... FrannyNorton 2 47
(Mark Johnston) *t.k.h: chsd ldr tl edgd rt and wknd wl over 1f out* **3/1**[2]
220- **7** *17* **Vicky Valentine**[220] 7364 3-8-3 **65** .... RoystonFfrench 8
(Alistair Whillans) *hld up in tch: hmpd and outpcd over 4f out: sn struggling: t.o* **13/2**[3]

1m 57.9s (0.30) **Going Correction** +0.10s/f (Good)
WFA 3 from 4yo+ 12lb **7** Ran SP% **111.0**
Speed ratings (Par 102): **102,101,100,93,93 87,72**
toteswingers 1&2 £6.50, 1&3 £2.80, 2&3 £4.90 CSF £19.43 CT £138.06 TOTE £1.90: £1.20, £5.30; EX 8.20 Trifecta £46.10 Pool: £934.49 - 15.19 winning units..
Owner Saeed Manana **Bred** Hesmonds Stud Ltd **Trained** Newmarket, Suffolk

FOCUS
A fair fillies' handicap.

2916 32RED CASINO H'CAP 6f 192y

8:45 (8:46) (Class 5) (0-70,70) 3-Y-0 **£2,587** (£770; £384; £192) **Stalls** Low

Form RPR
5015 **1** **Baltic Prince (IRE)**[21] 2330 3-8-7 **59** .... RaulDaSilva(3) 6 67
(Paul Green) *mde all: rdn over 1f out: kpt on wl fnl f: unchal* **16/1**
0-32 **2** *1 1/4* **Gold Beau (FR)**[7] 2719 3-9-0 **63** .... (p) DavidNolan 5 68
(Kristin Stubbs) *chsd ldrs: effrt and drvn 2f out: kpt on fnl f: tk 2nd nr fin* **7/1**
3423 **3** *nk* **Polish Crown**[10] 2635 3-9-1 **64** .... FrannyNorton 7 68
(Mark Johnston) *chsd ldrs: drvn and wnt 2nd 2f out: sn edgd rt: kpt on fnl f: lost 2nd nr fin* **9/2**[3]
4520 **4** *2 1/2* **Angels Calling**[14] 2512 3-8-9 **58** .... MichaelO'Connell 10 55
(Mrs K Burke) *t.k.h: hld up in tch: effrt and drvn on outside over 2f out: one pce fnl f* **33/1**
6-13 **5** *nse* **Red Paladin (IRE)**[21] 2308 3-9-7 **70** .... AmyRyan 2 67+
(Kevin Ryan) *bhd: sn rdn along: hdwy u.p on outside over 1f out: kpt on fnl f: nt pce to chal* **7/2**[2]
5 **6** *nk* **Confusing**[15] 2480 3-9-2 **65** .... GrahamGibbons 11 64+
(David O'Meara) *hld up: shkn up and hdwy whn nt clr run over 1f out: swtiched rt and kpt on fnl f: no imp* **14/1**
4050 **7** *1/2* **Gold Roll (IRE)**[6] 2743 3-8-5 **54** .... JamesSullivan 9 49
(Ruth Carr) *pressed wnr: rdn over 2f out: no ex fr over 1f out* **40/1**
0-20 **8** *1 1/4* **Nelson Quay (IRE)**[21] 2306 3-9-2 **65** .... GrahamLee 1 62+
(Jeremy Gask) *hld up in tch: pushed along over 2f out: no imp fr over 1f out* **10/3**[1]
-554 **9** *nk* **Curl (IRE)**[14] 2506 3-8-13 **62** .... (b) TomEaves 3 53
(Michael Dods) *bhd: drvn along 1/2-way: sme late hdwy: nvr on terms* **8/1**

042 **10** *1¾* **Burren View Lady (IRE)**^{32} 1962 3-8-9 **58**.............(v^{1}) DuranFentiman 4 44
(Tim Easterby) *t.k.h: chsd ldrs tl rdn and wknd over 1f out* **7/1**

1m 28.6s (1.50) **Going Correction** +0.10s/f (Good) **10** Ran SP% **117.5**
Speed ratings (Par 99): **95,93,93,90,90 89,89,87,87,85**
toteswingers 1&2 £15.70, 1&3 £9.60, 2&3 £3.00 CSF £124.50 CT £597.97 TOTE £11.80: £4.60, £1.70, £1.60; EX 131.80 Trifecta £364.90 Pool: £1286.42 - 2.64 winning units..
Owner A Mills **Bred** William Pilkington **Trained** Lydiate, Merseyside
■ Stewards' Enquiry : David Nolan two-day ban; used whip above permitted level (17th,23rd June).
Graham Gibbons one-day ban; careless riding (17th June).

FOCUS
A modest 3yo handicap, but the fourth all-the-way winner of the evening.
T/Plt: £164.80 to a £1 stake. Pool of £58,708.25 - 260.05 winning tickets. T/Qpdt: £10.00 to a £1 stake. Pool of £6910.32 - 509.30 winning tickets. RY

2344 CHEPSTOW (L-H)
Monday, June 3

OFFICIAL GOING: Good to firm (good in places; 8.0)
Wind: Virtually nil Weather: Sunny spells

2917 BATHWICK TYRES MAIDEN AUCTION STKS 5f 16y
2:30 (2:32) (Class 5) 2-Y-O **£2,587** (£770; £384; £192) **Stalls** Centre

Form RPR
2565 **1** **Mr Dandy Man (IRE)**^{3} 2823 2-8-12 0.............................. LukeMorris 4 73
(Ronald Harris) *mde all: rdn wl over 1f out: styd on strly* **6/1^{3}**
3 **2** *¾* **Bonjour Steve**^{19} 2359 2-8-10 0.............................. AndreaAtzeni 3 68
(J S Moore) *chsd ldrs: wnt 2nd and rdn over 2f out: edgd lft 1f out: styng on whn edgd rt clsng stages and no imp on wnr* **5/2^{2}**
3 *6* **Taquka (IRE)** 2-8-12 0.............................. JimCrowley 5 48
(Ralph Beckett) *in tch: pushed along over 2f out: outpcd by ldng duo appr fnl f* **8/11^{1}**
4 *nk* **Sartorialist (IRE)** 2-8-11 0.............................. JohnFahy 8 46
(J S Moore) *s.i.s: sn in tch and clsd on ldrs 1/2-way: outpcd wl over 1f out* **25/1**
05 **5** *12* **Zac's Princess**^{21} 2327 2-8-5 0.............................. CathyGannon 6
(Milton Bradley) *chsd ldr to 1/2-way: sn hung lft and btn* **25/1**
6 *2½* **Notnow Penny** 2-8-2 0.............................. DarrenEgan$^{(3)}$ 1
(Milton Bradley) *disp 2nd tl wknd 1/2-way* **100/1**
7 *4½* **My Secret Dream (FR)** 2-8-6 0.............................. DavidProbert 2
(Ron Hodges) *sn wl bhd* **33/1**

59.32s (0.02) **Going Correction** -0.275s/f (Firm) **7** Ran SP% **112.4**
Speed ratings (Par 93): **88,86,77,76,57 53,46**
toteswingers 1&2 £1.30, 1&3 £1.90, 2&3 £2.00 CSF £20.34 TOTE £5.30: £2.00, £1.60; EX 14.20 Trifecta £33.60 Pool: £2439.01 - 54.37 winning units..
Owner S & A Mares **Bred** Oliver Donlon **Trained** Earlswood, Monmouths

FOCUS
An ordinary juvenile contest and it's unlikely this took much winning. The first two pulled clear.

2918 BATHWICK TYRES CARDIFF H'CAP 6f 16y
3:00 (3:01) (Class 5) (0-70,68) 4-Y-O+ **£2,587** (£770; £384; £192) **Stalls** Centre

Form RPR
14-3 **1** **Gabrial's Gift (IRE)**^{148} 86 4-9-4 **65**.............................. JimCrowley 15 77+
(David Simcock) *trckd ldrs: led over 2f out: rdn and styd on wl fnl f* **4/1^{1}**
4200 **2** *2* **Belle Bayardo (IRE)**^{83} 971 5-9-5 **66**.............................. LukeMorris 12 72
(Ronald Harris) *chsd ldrs: rdn to go 2nd over 1f out: kpt on but no imp on wnr* **16/1**
0533 **3** *1½* **Emiratesdotcom**^{11} 2588 7-9-0 **66**.............................. MatthewLawson$^{(5)}$ 13 67+
(Milton Bradley) *s.i.s: in rr: hdwy fr 2f out: styd on wl fnl f to take 3rd clsng stages but no imp on ldng duo* **10/1**
-563 **4** *¾* **Ghostwing**^{24} 2225 6-9-5 **66**..............................(vt) IanMongan 17 65
(Luke Dace) *in rr: hdwy fr 3f out: rdn wl over 1f out: hd high: nt keen and styd on same pce ins fnl f* **6/1^{2}**
0150 **5** *nk* **The Mongoose**^{18} 2395 5-8-9 **61**..............................(t) DeclanBates$^{(5)}$ 5 59
(David Evans) *chsd ldrs: rdn over 1f out: styd on same pce* **40/1**
052 **6** *nk* **One Last Dream**^{11} 2596 4-8-9 **56**..............................(b) DavidProbert 7 53
(Ron Hodges) *chsd ldr: rdn 2f out: outpcd ins fnl f* **6/1^{2}**
14-0 **7** *1* **Cristaliyev**^{20} 2345 5-7-10 **50**..............................(b) OisinMurphy$^{(7)}$ 10 44
(John Flint) *s.i.s: in rr: rdn and hdwy 2f out: styd on same pce ins fnl f* **25/1**
41-0 **8** *1¾* **Pettochside**^{23} 2255 4-9-5 **66**..............................(t) SaleemGolam 8 54
(Stuart Williams) *in rr: hdwy over 1f out: rdn fnl f and kpt on same pce* **7/1^{3}**
06-0 **9** *¾* **Nubar Boy**^{11} 2596 6-9-0 **64**..............................(v) RyanPowell$^{(3)}$ 9 50
(Ian Williams) *in rr: hdwy over 1f out: styd on same pce ins fnl f* **12/1**
4462 **10** *½* **Master Of Disguise**^{23} 2281 7-9-4 **65**.............................. J-PGuillambert 2 52
(Brian Baugh) *in tch: rdn 2f out: wknd appr fnl f* **16/1**
6600 **11** *nk* **Dancing Welcome**^{28} 2096 7-8-6 **58**..............................(bt) RyanTate$^{(5)}$ 16 41
(Milton Bradley) *in rr: rdn over 2f out: sme late prog* **33/1**
2-20 **12** *1½* **Superior Edge**^{19} 2364 6-9-3 **64**..............................(p) CathyGannon 6 42
(Christopher Mason) *led tl hdd over 2f out: wknd over 1f out* **16/1**
2055 **13** *1* **Falasteen (IRE)**^{5} 2780 6-9-4 **68**..............................^{1} DarrenEgan$^{(3)}$ 11 43
(Milton Bradley) *chsd ldrs over 4f out* **16/1**
50-0 **14** *shd* **Gracie's Games**^{26} 2170 7-8-6 **53**..............................(p) ChrisCatlin 14 28
(John Spearing) *chsd ldrs: rdn over 2f out: sn wknd* **25/1**
000 **15** *½* **Ficelle (IRE)**^{11} 2596 4-8-3 **57**..............................(p) JoeyHaynes$^{(7)}$ 4 30
(Ronald Harris) *s.i.s: chsd ldrs 1/2-way: sn wknd* **33/1**
/003 **16** *6* **Youhavecontrol (IRE)**^{7} 2707 5-9-2 **63**..............................(t) MartinHarley 1 17
(Nicky Vaughan) *sn chsng ldrs: wknd qckly over 2f out* **10/1**

1m 9.79s (-2.21) **Going Correction** -0.275s/f (Firm) **16** Ran SP% **126.5**
Speed ratings (Par 103): **103,100,98,97,96 96,95,92,91,91 90,88,87,87,86 78**
toteswingers 1&2 £13.50, 1&3 £5.90, 2&3 £46.00 CSF £70.20 CT £464.93 TOTE £2.70: £1.50, £3.80, £2.20, £1.30; EX 97.30 Trifecta £863.20 Pool: £1642.76 - 1.42 winning units..
Owner Dr Marwan Koukash **Bred** Skymarc Farm **Trained** Newmarket, Suffolk

FOCUS
A highly competitive, if only modest sprint handicap in which the high-drawn horses held the advantage.

2919 BATHWICK TYRES CLASSIFIED STKS 6f 16y
3:30 (3:30) (Class 6) 3-Y-O **£1,940** (£577; £288; £144) **Stalls** Centre

Form RPR
4130 **1** **The Black Jacobin**^{18} 2394 3-9-0 65..............................(b) AndreaAtzeni 7 69
(J S Moore) *chsd ldrs: drvn over 2f out: led 1f out: kpt on wl clsng stages* **5/1**
3-10 **2** *1* **Girl Of Cadiz**^{18} 2387 3-8-9 65.............................. WilliamTwiston-Davies$^{(5)}$ 4 66
(Richard Hannon) *in rr: hdwy over 1f out: sn swtchd lft: kpt on to take 2nd last strides but no imp on wnr* **7/2^{2}**
1-60 **3** *shd* **Barbs Princess**^{37} 1832 3-9-0 65.............................. SteveDrowne 8 66
(Charles Hills) *chsd ldrs: chal over 2f out: led sn after: hdd 1f out: styd on same pce: lost 2nd last strides* **9/2^{3}**
4040 **4** *2¾* **Half Turn**^{27} 2129 3-9-0 60..............................(t) IanMongan 3 57
(Luke Dace) *in rr: hdwy over 2f out: clsd on ldrs wl over 1f out: wknd ins fnl f* **20/1**
034- **5** *3¾* **New Rich**^{278} 5727 3-9-0 65.............................. LukeMorris 2 45
(Sylvester Kirk) *chsd ldrs: rdn over 2f out: wknd over 1f out* **3/1^{1}**
0050 **6** *7* **Nellie Bly**^{21} 2329 3-9-0 65.............................. J-PGuillambert 6 22
(Mark Johnston) *led: jnd over 2f out: hdd sn after: wknd qckly over 1f out* **16/1**
-520 **7** *1¼* **Duke Of Orange (IRE)**^{27} 2135 3-9-0 63..............................(v^{1}) MartinHarley 5 18
(Mick Channon) *chsd ldrs tl wknd qckly over 2f out* **7/2^{2}**
3500 **8** *10* **Exit Clause**^{28} 2095 3-8-7 50..............................(tp) OisinMurphy$^{(7)}$ 1
(Mark Gillard) *chsd ldrs: rdn and btn 1/2-way* **100/1**

1m 10.69s (-1.31) **Going Correction** -0.275s/f (Firm) **8** Ran SP% **115.9**
Speed ratings (Par 97): **97,95,95,91,86 77,75,62**
toteswingers 1&2 £4.50, 1&3 £4.50, 2&3 £4.50 CSF £23.22 TOTE £7.80: £2.30, £2.10, £1.70; EX 26.20 Trifecta £108.50 Pool: £1598.23 - 11.04 winning units..
Owner Norton Common Farm Racing **Bred** T R Watson & Miss D S Peasley **Trained** Upper Lambourn, Berks

FOCUS
There were doubts surrounding the majority of these coming into this and it's debatable as to what the form is worth. The time was modest compared to the previous handicap.

2920 BATHWICK TYRES H'CAP 1m 14y
4:00 (4:00) (Class 5) (0-75,75) 4-Y-O+ **£2,587** (£770; £384; £192) **Stalls** Centre

Form RPR
0641 **1** **Peak Storm**^{20} 2345 4-8-5 **59**.............................. LukeMorris 4 71
(John O'Shea) *in rr: hdwy 2f out: nt clr run and swtchd lft to ld 1f out: drvn clr ins fnl f: comf* **5/1^{3}**
-212 **2** *3¾* **Ifan (IRE)**^{18} 2395 5-8-5 **66**.............................. DanielMuscutt$^{(7)}$ 5 69
(Tim Vaughan) *chsd ldrs: drvn along 3f out: led ins fnl 2f: hdd 1f out: sn outpcd by wnr but hld on wl for 2nd* **7/2^{1}**
0 **3** *hd* **Dimitar (USA)**^{12} 2573 4-8-13 **70**.............................. BrendanPowell$^{(3)}$ 8 73
(Brendan Powell) *in rr: rdn and hdwy 2f out: styd on to press for 2nd ins fnl f but nvr any ch w wnr* **25/1**
0-00 **4** *1¾* **Batchelors Star (IRE)**^{12} 2574 5-9-2 **70**..............................(t) JohnFahy 3 69
(Seamus Durack) *s.i.s: in rr: hdwy over 1f out: styd on fnl f: nt rch ldrs* **33/1**
40-3 **5** *2¼* **George Baker (IRE)**^{23} 2286 6-9-2 **75**........ WilliamTwiston-Davies$^{(5)}$ 10 69
(George Baker) *chsd ldrs: wnt 2nd over 3f out: rdn and ev ch 2f out: wknd fnl f* **5/1^{3}**
111- **6** *nk* **Croeso Mawr**^{269} 5998 7-9-2 **70**.............................. CathyGannon 2 63
(John Spearing) *chsd ldr tl over 3f out: styd wl there but sn rdn: wknd over 1f out* **9/2^{2}**
00-4 **7** *nk* **Mahadee (IRE)**^{12} 2571 8-9-0 **71**..............................(b) MarkCoumbe$^{(3)}$ 9 63
(Ed de Giles) *in rr but in tch: hdwy to cl on ldrs 2f out: wknd fnl f* **10/1**
0-00 **8** *2¾* **Sea Soldier (IRE)**^{16} 2450 5-9-4 **72**..............................(p) DavidProbert 1 58
(Andrew Balding) *chsd ldrs: rdn over 3f out: sn btn* **9/2^{2}**
0-30 **9** *1* **Uncle Dermot (IRE)**^{24} 2232 5-9-7 **75**.............................. ChrisCatlin 6 59
(Brendan Powell) *rdn 1/2-way: a outpcd* **14/1**
5000 **10** *½* **Kept**^{7} 2710 4-8-9 **63**..............................(p) AndreaAtzeni 7 46
(Ronald Harris) *led tl hdd ins fnl 2f: wknd qckly over 1f out* **25/1**

1m 33.66s (-2.54) **Going Correction** -0.275s/f (Firm) **10** Ran SP% **118.3**
Speed ratings (Par 103): **101,97,97,95,93 92,92,89,88,88**
toteswingers 1&2 £4.40, 1&3 £22.50, 2&3 £19.20 CSF £22.75 CT £404.25 TOTE £5.90: £1.90, £1.30, £7.60; EX 26.40 Trifecta £658.20 Pool: £2870.93 - 3.27 winning units..
Owner The Cross Racing Club **Bred** Redhill Bloodstock Limited **Trained** Elton, Gloucs

FOCUS
A devilishly tricky race on paper.

2921 BATHWICK TYRES BRIDGEND H'CAP (DIV I) 2m 49y
4:30 (4:31) (Class 6) (0-60,65) 4-Y-O+ **£1,940** (£577; £288; £144) **Stalls** Low

Form RPR
6-61 **1** **Kashgar**^{3} 2828 4-9-7 **65** 6ex.............................. RobertWilliams$^{(5)}$ 6 74
(Bernard Llewellyn) *hld up in mid-div: hdwy over 4f out: led ins fnl 3f: rdn over 1f out: hld on wl clsng stages* **9/4^{1}**
4552 **2** *3* **Bramshill Lass**^{12} 2570 4-9-5 **58**..............................(b) JimCrowley 10 63
(Amanda Perrett) *chsd ldrs tl led 1/2-way: rdn and hdd ins fnl 3f: rallied fr over 1f out: no ex and btn fnl 110yds* **3/1^{2}**
5620 **3** *¾* **Vertueux (FR)**^{12} 2570 8-9-2 **54**.............................. LukeMorris 3 58
(Tony Carroll) *chsd ldr tl over 4f out: rdn fr 3f out: styd on same pce for 3rd ins fnl f* **8/1**
0634 **4** *½* **Ctappers**^{12} 2563 4-9-5 **58**..............................(v) MartinHarley 5 61
(Mick Channon) *in rr: rdn over 3f out: styd on appr fnl f: kpt on to take 4th clsng stages* **5/1^{3}**
-001 **5** *½* **Pass The Time**^{17} 2301 4-8-10 **49**..............................(p) ChrisCatlin 1 52
(Neil Mulholland) *chsd ldrs: drvn and outpcd 6f out: rdn and hdwy fr 2f out: kpt on clsng stages* **12/1**
33-5 **6** *½* **Arch Event**^{3} 2828 8-8-7 **52**..............................(p) DanielMuscutt$^{(7)}$ 7 54
(Bernard Llewellyn) *chsd ldrs: rdn over 3f out: kpt on ins fnl f* **6/1**
0-05 **7** *2½* **Lucky Diva**^{31} 1980 6-9-2 **59**..............................(p) JakePayne$^{(5)}$ 4 58
(Bill Turner) *s.i.s: in rr: rdn along fr 4f out: styd on same pce fnl 2f* **12/1**
0-00 **8** *20* **Choisirez (IRE)**^{18} 2392 4-8-6 **45**.............................. CathyGannon 2 20
(John Panvert) *sn led: hdd 1/2-way: wknd over 3f out* **66/1**
0562 **P** **Ice Apple**^{12} 2563 5-8-10 **48**.............................. KirstyMilczarek 9
(John E Long) *a in rr: t.o fnl 4f: p.u and dismntd fnl f* **14/1**

3m 43.86s (4.96) **Going Correction** -0.20s/f (Firm)
WFA 4 from 5yo+ 1lb **9** Ran SP% **121.4**
Speed ratings (Par 101): **79,77,77,76,76 76,75,65,**
toteswingers 1&2 £1.90, 1&3 £5.40, 2&3 £5.30 CSF £9.62 CT £47.20 TOTE £4.00: £1.40, £1.50, £2.50; EX 12.40 Trifecta £52.30 Pool: £3316.06 - 47.53 winning units..
Owner Alex James & B J Llewellyn **Bred** J L C Pearce **Trained** Fochriw, Caerphilly
■ Stewards' Enquiry : Chris Catlin caution; careless riding.

FOCUS
A moderate, steadily run staying handicap, and the slower division.

2922 BATHWICK TYRES BRIDGEND H'CAP (DIV II) 2m 49y
5:00 (5:00) (Class 6) (0-60,60) 4-Y-O+ £1,940 (£577; £288; £144) Stalls Low

Form				RPR
2-60	1		**Queen's Star**[13] 2545 4-9-6 60 DavidProbert 9 (Andrew Balding) *in rr: hdwy to chse ldrs 4f out: chsd ldr over 2f out: rdn and styd on fnl f: led last strides: hmpd and uns rdr after line* **7/2**[2]	68
6-24	2	*hd*	**Fuzzy Logic (IRE)**[9] 1980 4-8-7 47 MartinLane 8 (Bernard Llewellyn) *in tch: hdwy 6f out: led over 3f out: wnt lft to rail sn after: rdn 2f out: kpt on u.p* **9/2**[3]	55
2231	3	*1 ½*	**Neighbourhood (USA)**[26] 2174 5-8-13 57 (b) RyanTate(5) 2 (James Evans) *chsd ldrs: rdn and styd on fnl 2f: no imp on ldng duo fnl f* **7/2**[2]	63
234-	4	*3*	**Annaluna (IRE)**[106] 7862 4-8-8 53 DeclanBates(5) 3 (David Evans) *led 4f: styd chsng ldr: rdn and wl there whn hmpd and lost position ins fnl 3f: rdn and rallied over 1f out: edgd rt but kpt on cl home* **7/1**	58+
/443	5	*hd*	**Chapter Five**[13] 2545 6-8-13 55 RyanPowell(3) 1 (Ian Williams) *t.k.h: trckd ldrs: travelling ok whn hmpd and lost pl ins fnl 3f: rallied over 1f out: kpt on fnl f: nt rch ldrs* **3/1**[1]	59+
0/00	6	*3 ¼*	**William Hogarth**[21] 2328 8-8-11 50 (p) CathyGannon 4 (Keith Goldsworthy) *led after 4f: rdn 4f out: hdd over 3f out: wknd 2f out* **20/1**	48
00-0	7	*16*	**Falcun**[26] 2165 6-8-13 52 (v) FrankieMcDonald 6 (Nikki Evans) *a in rr* **50/1**	31
405/	8	*4*	**Golden Games (IRE)**[38] 1446 7-9-5 58 IanMongan 5 (Daniel O'Brien) *rdn 4f out: a in rr* **10/1**	32

3m 40.39s (1.49) **Going Correction** -0.20s/f (Firm)
WFA 4 from 5yo+ 1lb 8 Ran SP% **115.9**
Speed ratings (Par 101): **88,87,87,85,85 83,75,73**
toteswingers 1&2 £4.00, 1&3 £2.30, 2&3 £4.10 CSF £19.98 CT £58.64 TOTE £4.40: £2.70, £1.10, £1.50; EX 16.20 Trifecta £43.40 Pool: £2503.68 - 43.24 winning units..
Owner Sir Gordon Brunton **Bred** Sir Gordon Brunton **Trained** Kingsclere, Hants
■ Stewards' Enquiry : Declan Bates two-day ban; careless riding (17th,23rd June).

FOCUS
This didn't look as strong as the first division, but the time was a bit quicker and it served up a tremendous finish.

2923 BATHWICK TYRES NEWPORT H'CAP 1m 2f 36y
5:35 (5:35) (Class 5) (0-75,75) 4-Y-O+ £2,587 (£770; £384; £192) Stalls Low

Form				RPR
0-01	1		**Dandy (GER)**[14] 2498 4-9-4 72 (p) CathyGannon 2 (Andrew Balding) *chsd ldr: led 6f out: hrd pressed fr over 3f out: kpt slt ld u.p fnl f: hld on all out* **11/4**[1]	79
0124	2	*nk*	**April Ciel**[3] 2826 4-8-13 67 LukeMorris 6 (Ronald Harris) *sn led: hdd 6f out: styd pressing wnr fr over 3f out: hrd rdn to chal fnl f: no ex cl home* **7/2**[3]	73
2-01	3	*1 ½*	**Tawseef (IRE)**[20] 2348 5-8-13 70 MarkCoumbe(3) 3 (Roy Brotherton) *in rr: hdwy 4f out: chal over 3f out tl over 1f out: no ex ins fnl f* **5/1**	73+
32-1	4	*nk*	**Astra Hall**[20] 2349 4-9-3 71 JimCrowley 1 (Ralph Beckett) *chsd ldrs: rdn 2f out: sn outpcd: kpt on fnl f: gng on again cl home* **3/1**[2]	73
004	5	*hd*	**Drummond**[20] 2348 4-8-3 57 MartinLane 5 (Bernard Llewellyn) *chsd ldrs: rdn 3f out: outpcd 2f out: kpt on again fnl f: gng on clsng stages* **8/1**	59
60-0	6	*nk*	**Handsome Ransom**[41] 1753 4-9-7 75 (p) SteveDrowne 8 (David Lanigan) *plld hrd in rr: pushed along over 2f out: styd on fnl f: gng on clsng stages* **16/1**	76
6110	7	*hd*	**Honey Of A Kitten (USA)**[9] 2646 5-8-12 73 (v) EoinWalsh(7) 7 (David Evans) *in tch whn rn wd into st over 4f out: sn rdn and outpcd: styd on fnl f over 1f out: kpt on clsng stages* **14/1**	74

2m 10.31s (-0.29) **Going Correction** -0.20s/f (Firm) 7 Ran SP% **114.2**
Speed ratings (Par 103): **93,92,91,91,91 90,90**
toteswingers 1&2 £3.00, 1&3 £4.00, 2&3 £3.60 CSF £12.67 CT £44.39 TOTE £4.70: £4.50, £1.02; EX 13.80 Trifecta £101.70 Pool: £1491.40 - 10.98 winning units..
Owner Robert E Tillett **Bred** Gestut Rottgen **Trained** Kingsclere, Hants

FOCUS
A fascinating handicap, littered with potential improvers, but the pace was muddling and the front pair always dominated.

2924 BATHWICK TYRES BRISTOL H'CAP 1m 4f 23y
6:05 (6:06) (Class 6) (0-65,65) 3-Y-O £1,940 (£577; £288; £144) Stalls Low

Form				RPR
2243	1		**Knight's Parade (IRE)**[11] 2599 3-9-3 61 JimCrowley 7 (Amanda Perrett) *chsd ldrs: led 3f out: rdn out fnl f* **3/1**[1]	71
-540	2	*1 ½*	**Star Of Namibia (IRE)**[11] 2599 3-9-3 61 (b[1]) JDSmith 1 (J S Moore) *sn chsng ldrs: rdn to go 2nd 2f out: kpt on u.p fnl f but a hld* **12/1**	68
-636	3	*11*	**Karl Marx (IRE)**[11] 2599 3-7-10 47 OisinMurphy(7) 9 (Mark Gillard) *s.i.s: in rr: hdwy 5f out: rdn 4f out: styd on fr over 1f out to take wl hld 3rd clsng stages* **16/1**	36
50-0	4	*½*	**Boogie De Bispo**[19] 2362 3-8-2 46 oh1 CathyGannon 4 (Stuart Kittow) *in tch: rdn over 4f out and no prog: styd on u.p fr over 1f out to take wl hld 4th clsng stages* **20/1**	35
2523	5	*½*	**Bain's Pass (IRE)**[28] 2079 3-8-13 60 (p) JulieBurke(3) 6 (Kevin Ryan) *chsd ldr: led 7f out: rdn and hdd 3f out: dropped to 3rd and no ch fnl 2f: dropped two pls clsng stages* **4/1**[2]	48
-022	6	*8*	**Winter Music (IRE)**[34] 1897 3-8-9 60 (v) DanielMuscutt(7) 10 (Andrew Balding) *rdn over 3f out: a towards rr* **7/1**[3]	35+
-421	7	*¾*	**Miss Tiger Lily**[27] 2124 3-9-7 65 SteveDrowne 8 (Harry Dunlop) *s.i.s: pushed along over 3f out: a in rr* **3/1**[1]	39+
4465	8	*6*	**Jawinski (IRE)**[21] 2312 3-8-9 53 AndreaAtzeni 5 (David Evans) *led tl hdd7f out: wknd over 3f out* **8/1**	17
00-0	9	*2*	**Mr Vendman (IRE)**[11] 2599 3-8-0 47 RyanPowell(3) 3 (Ian Williams) *s.i.s: a in rr* **16/1**	
000-	10	*4*	**Rio Cato**[265] 6115 3-8-2 46 oh1 (t[1]) LukeMorris 2 (Alex Hales) *a in rr* **33/1**	

2m 35.93s (-3.07) **Going Correction** -0.20s/f (Firm) 10 Ran SP% **120.8**
Speed ratings (Par 97): **102,101,93,93,93 87,87,83,81,79**
toteswingers 1&2 £13.90, 1&3 £13.70, 2&3 £29.50 CSF £42.88 CT £510.18 TOTE £3.50: £1.10, £5.30, £4.10; EX 39.40 Trifecta £311.20 Pool: £1039.67 - 2.50 winning units..
Owner The Recitation Partnership **Bred** E Heary **Trained** Pulborough, W Sussex

FOCUS
A modest handicap in which there was no let up in pace and very few got involved. The first three came from Getaway Car's race at Salisbury.
T/Jkpt: Not won. T/Plt: £21.10 to a £1 stake. Pool of £68,975.43 - 2378.92 winning tickets.
T/Qpdt: £6.10 to a £1 stake. Pool of £4983.32 - 596.07 winning tickets. ST

2736 LEICESTER (R-H)
Monday, June 3

OFFICIAL GOING: Good (good to firm in places; 8.3)
False rail from top of hill on back straight all the way to Wining Post added circa 17m to races on Round course.
Wind: Almost nil Weather: Fine

2925 PYTCHLEY MAIDEN STKS 5f 218y
2:15 (2:15) (Class 4) 2-Y-O £3,881 (£1,155; £577; £288) Stalls High

Form				RPR
4	1		**Cable Bay (IRE)**[13] 2543 2-9-5 0 JamesMcDonald 5 (Charles Hills) *trckd ldrs: racd keenly: shkn up over 1f out: r.o to ld and hung rt nr fin* **7/1**	82+
	2	*¾*	**Whaleweigh Station** 2-9-5 0 RichardKingscote 1 (Tom Dascombe) *chsd ldrs: rdn and ev ch ins fnl f: r.o* **3/1**[2]	80
6	3	*nse*	**Hatha Hooh**[25] 2194 2-9-5 0 JimmyFortune 6 (Richard Hannon) *led 1f: chsd ldr: shkn up to ld again wl over 1f out: sn rdn and edgd rt: hdd nr fin* **7/4**[1]	80
0	4	*4*	**Handwoven (IRE)**[9] 2645 2-9-5 0 JoeFanning 2 (Mark Johnston) *led 5f out: shkn up and hdd wl over 1f out: no ex ins fnl f* **10/1**	68
	5	*1 ¾*	**Khee Society** 2-9-5 0 TomQueally 8 (David Evans) *chsd ldrs: rdn over 2f out: sn outpcd: styd on towards fin* **50/1**	62
	6	*1 ¼*	**Juvenile Lead (IRE)** 2-9-5 0 RyanMoore 3 (Sir Michael Stoute) *s.i.s: sn pushed along and prom: rdn over 2f out: sn outpcd* **5/1**[3]	59
	7	*1 ½*	**Nova Champ (IRE)** 2-9-5 0 JamieSpencer 7 (Stuart Williams) *s.s: hld up: nvr on terms* **11/1**	54
	8	*7*	**St Vincent (IRE)** 2-9-5 0 TedDurcan 4 (David Lanigan) *s.s: hld up: wknd over 2f out* **40/1**	33

1m 13.47s (0.47) **Going Correction** -0.075s/f (Good) 8 Ran SP% **112.4**
Speed ratings (Par 95): **93,92,91,86,84 82,80,71**
toteswingers 1&2 £3.90, 1&3 £3.70, 2&3 £2.70 CSF £27.30 TOTE £7.10: £2.30, £1.60, £1.02; EX 29.70 Trifecta £87.80 Pool: £3474.92 - 29.66 winning units..
Owner Julie Martin & David R Martin & Partner **Bred** Irish National Stud **Trained** Lambourn, Berks
■ The first winner in Britain for Australian rider James McDonald.

FOCUS
False rail from the top of the hill on the back straight all the way around the bend, increasing all the round course distances by 17 metres. A fair juvenile maiden in which they went a decent gallop.

2926 HICKLING (S) STKS 5f 218y
2:45 (2:45) (Class 6) 3-5-Y-O £2,045 (£603; £302) Stalls High

Form				RPR
1113	1		**Above The Stars**[4] 2789 5-9-0 75 RachealKneller(5) 5 (Jamie Osborne) *s.i.s: sn hung rt and outpcd: hdwy over 2f out: chsd ldr over 1f out: styd on to ld wl ins fnl f* **1/4**[1]	61
0500	2	*1 ¾*	**Nine Before Ten (IRE)**[10] 2611 5-9-0 52 (t) PatCosgrave 3 (Charles Smith) *led: rdn over 2f out: hdd and unable qck wl ins fnl f* **6/1**[2]	50
00	3	*hd*	**Coastal Passage**[26] 2170 5-9-5 52 PhilipPrince(5) 4 (Charles Smith) *trckd ldrs: stdd and lost pl wl over 4f out: sn bhd: pushed along 1/2-way: hdwy over 1f out: running on whn eased nr fin: nvr nr to chal* **12/1**	59+
6-00	4	*7*	**Index Waiter**[18] 2393 3-8-11 49 (b) JoeFanning 1 (Brian Meehan) *chsd ldr: rdn over 2f out: wknd over 1f out* **10/1**[3]	32
	5	*6*	**Lenderking (IRE)**[9] 5-8-12 0 DanielleMooney(7) 2 (Michael Chapman) *s.i.s: sn racd keenly and prom: rdn and wknd over 2f out* **100/1**	13

1m 13.71s (0.71) **Going Correction** -0.075s/f (Good)
WFA 3 from 5yo 8lb 5 Ran SP% **112.1**
Speed ratings (Par 101): **92,89,89,80,72**
CSF £2.44 TOTE £1.20: £1.10, £2.00; EX 2.80 Trifecta £6.50 Pool: £2685.11 - 306.99 winning units..The winner was bought in for 5,500 guineas
Owner Morsethehorse Syndicate **Bred** Manor Farm Stud (rutland) **Trained** Upper Lambourn, Berks
■ Stewards' Enquiry : Philip Prince twelve-day ban; failing to take all reasonable measures to obtain best possible position (17th-28th June).

FOCUS
An ordinary seller and a modest time.

2927 NORMAN LOVE H'CAP 1m 1f 218y
3:15 (3:15) (Class 4) (0-85,83) 3-Y-O £4,690 (£1,395; £697; £348) Stalls Low

Form				RPR
01	1		**Bold Sniper**[16] 2465 3-9-5 81 RyanMoore 3 (Sir Michael Stoute) *chsd ldrs: led over 2f out: pushed clr fr over 1f out* **11/4**[2]	99+
01-2	2	*3 ¼*	**Rundell**[17] 2432 3-9-4 80 SeanLevey 4 (Richard Hannon) *hld up in tch: rdn over 3f out: styd on to go 2nd and edgd rt ins fnl f: nt rch wnr* **3/1**[3]	90
-432	3	*2 ¾*	**Zamoyski**[11] 2584 3-9-5 81 WilliamBuick 7 (Jeremy Noseda) *plld hrd and prom: hung lft almost thrght: rdn over 2f out: styd on same pce fnl f* **9/2**	86
2-51	4	*hd*	**Tinghir (IRE)**[15] 2480 3-9-7 83 TedDurcan 6 (David Lanigan) *chsd ldr: rdn and ev ch over 2f out: hung rt and wknd ins fnl f* **5/2**[1]	87
54-1	5	*7*	**Unmoothaj**[37] 1837 3-9-4 80 PaulHanagan 2 (Charles Hills) *led: rdn and hdd over 2f out: wknd over 1f out* **16/1**	70
515-	6	*1*	**Nile Knight**[261] 6247 3-9-0 76 HayleyTurner 5 (Marcus Tregoning) *hld up: pushed along over 4f out: wknd over 2f out* **14/1**	64

2m 5.82s (-2.08) **Going Correction** -0.075s/f (Good) 6 Ran SP% **111.0**
Speed ratings (Par 101): **105,102,100,100,94 93**
toteswingers 1&2 £1.60, 1&3 £2.20, 2&3 £2.60 CSF £11.12 CT £32.57 TOTE £2.70: £1.10, £2.20; EX 11.00 Trifecta £28.80 Pool: £2337.56 - 60.85 winning units..
Owner The Queen **Bred** The Queen **Trained** Newmarket, Suffolk

FOCUS
A decent and interesting 3yo handicap.

2928 CHARNWOOD FOREST FILLIES' CONDITIONS STKS 7f 9y
3:45 (3:46) (Class 3) 3-Y-0+ **£7,781** (£2,330; £1,165; £582; £291) **Stalls** High

Form RPR

-13 **1** **Woodland Aria**[19] 2367 3-8-7 93 .... WilliamBuick 5 92+
(John Gosden) *hld up: wnt centre over 4f out: hdwy to chse ldr over 2f out: shkn up to ld ins fnl f: pushed out* **5/4**[1]

14-0 **2** *½* **Supernova Heights (IRE)**[16] 2453 3-8-7 89 .... KierenFallon 1 90
(Brian Meehan) *chsd ldrs: wnt centre and overall ldr over 4f out: rdn over 1f out: hdd ins fnl f: kpt on: 2nd of three in gp* **7/2**[2]

140- **3** *½* **Sweetnessandlight**[257] 6379 4-8-13 100 .... TedDurcan 3 89
(Jason Ward) *plld hrd: led stands' side 6f out: rdn and hung rt fr over 2f out: styd on: 1st of 2 that side* **10/1**

1-06 **4** *½* **Hairy Rocket**[29] 2039 3-8-7 94 .... PaulHanagan 4 87
(William Haggas) *led stands' side 1f: trckd ldr: plld hrd: rdn and hung rt fr over 2f out: styd on same pce ins fnl f: last of 2 that side* **7/2**[2]

221- **5** *19* **Rivas Rhapsody (IRE)**[299] 4968 5-8-13 83 .... TomQueally 2 49
(Rae Guest) *hld up: wnt centre and lft 2nd over 4f out: rdn over 2f out: wknd over 1f out: last of 3 in gp* **6/1**[3]

1m 26.06s (-0.14) **Going Correction** -0.075s/f (Good)
WFA 3 from 4yo+ 10lb 5 Ran SP% **112.3**
Speed ratings (Par 104): **97,96,95,95,73**
CSF £6.07 TOTE £2.00: £1.80, £2.00; EX 4.90 Trifecta £16.30 Pool: £2224.83 - 102.12 winning units..
Owner R J H Geffen **Bred** Wardall Bloodstock **Trained** Newmarket, Suffolk

FOCUS
A good quality, small-field fillies' conditions' contest in which they went a steady gallop. The race developed in two separate groups of two runners on the near rail and three towards the centre of the track.

2929 PETER ANDRE HERE ON AUGUST 11TH H'CAP 7f 9y
4:15 (4:16) (Class 5) (0-75,75) 4-Y-0+ **£2,587** (£770; £384; £192) **Stalls** High

Form RPR

6010 **1** **Creek Falcon (IRE)**[23] 2255 4-9-5 73 .... DanielTudhope 4 87+
(David O'Meara) *chsd ldrs: led over 1f out: rdn out* **3/1**[1]

1043 **2** *2¾* **Exceedexpectations (IRE)**[23] 2278 4-9-1 69 .... JamieSpencer 5 75
(Conor Dore) *led: hdd over 5f out: chsd ldrs: rdn and ev ch over 1f out: styd on same pce ins fnl f* **7/1**[3]

500- **3** *nk* **Bajan Bear**[192] 7843 5-9-0 68 .... KierenFallon 9 73
(Michael Blanshard) *s.i.s: hld up: hdwy over 1f out: sn rdn: styd on same pce ins fnl f* **8/1**

52-0 **4** *1¼* **Excellent Jem**[23] 2286 4-8-12 66 .... TedDurcan 11 68
(Jane Chapple-Hyam) *prom: rdn over 2f out: sn outpcd: rallied and hung rt u.p over 1f out: r.o* **20/1**

6620 **5** *hd* **Fred Willetts (IRE)**[24] 2225 5-9-1 69 .... TomQueally 6 70
(David Evans) *mid-div: pushed along 1/2-way: hdwy u.p over 1f out: styd on same pce ins fnl f* **16/1**

1516 **6** *nk* **Dashwood**[16] 2450 6-9-2 70 ....(t) WilliamCarson 8 70
(Anthony Carson) *hld up: hdwy over 2f out: rdn over 1f out: styd on same pce ins fnl f* **6/1**[2]

0-40 **7** *½* **Diamondhead (IRE)**[23] 2286 4-9-3 71 .... LiamKeniry 2 70
(Ed de Giles) *stmbld s: sn chsng ldrs: led over 5f out: rdn and hdd over 1f out: no ex ins fnl f* **8/1**

1111 **8** *3* **Sofias Number One (USA)**[14] 2514 5-8-3 62 ....(b) PhilipPrince[(5)] 3 53
(Roy Bowring) *chsd ldrs: pushed along 1/2-way: rdn over 2f out: wknd fnl f* **10/1**

0-00 **9** *3½* **Easy Over (IRE)**[23] 2286 5-8-8 62 .... SeanLevey 13 43
(Ed McMahon) *hld up: rdn over 1f out: n.d* **14/1**

0-00 **10** *½* **Oratory (IRE)**[44] 1699 7-9-0 68 .... DaneO'Neill 1 48
(Noel Quinlan) *s.i.s: hld up: rdn over 2f out: nvr on terms* **28/1**

0-00 **11** *3¾* **Newnton Lodge**[16] 2463 4-9-4 72 ....(t) StevieDonohoe 7 42
(Ian Williams) *hld up: effrt over 2f out: sn wknd* **25/1**

4350 **12** *1¼* **The Guru Of Gloom (IRE)**[23] 2286 5-8-13 67 .... WilliamBuick 12 34
(William Muir) *trckd ldrs: plld hrd: rdn over 2f out: wknd over 1f out* **11/1**

1m 24.84s (-1.36) **Going Correction** -0.075s/f (Good) 12 Ran SP% **116.0**
Speed ratings (Par 103): **104,100,100,99,98 98,97,94,90,89 85,84**
toteswingers 1&2 £4.50, 1&3 £7.00, 2&3 £6.80 CSF £21.97 CT £154.92 TOTE £2.90: £1.40, £1.80, £3.10; EX 18.80 Trifecta £132.80 Pool: £3556.11 - 20.07 winning units..
Owner Direct Racing Partnership **Bred** Shadwell Estate Company Limited **Trained** Nawton, N Yorks

FOCUS
A fair handicap for older horses in which they went an honest gallop up the centre of the track. Few managed to get involved.

2930 BRITISH STALLION STUDS COPLOW E.B.F MAIDEN STKS (DIV I) 1m 60y
4:45 (4:47) (Class 5) 3-Y-0 **£4,528** (£1,347; £673; £336) **Stalls** Low

Form RPR

5 **1** **Velox**[28] 2093 3-9-5 0 .... KierenFallon 9 90+
(Luca Cumani) *s.i.s: hld up: hdwy over 2f out: rdn to ld over 1f out: r.o* **3/1**[2]

56-2 **2** *1¼* **Puligny (IRE)**[14] 2519 3-9-0 78 .... JamesMcDonald 10 81
(Charles Hills) *chsd ldrs: rdn over 1f out: r.o* **9/4**[1]

0- **3** *½* **Rosaceous**[182] 7962 3-9-0 0 .... MickaelBarzalona 5 80
(Daniel Kubler) *sn led: hdd over 7f out: chsd ldr tl led again over 2f out: rdn edgd rt and hdd over 1f out: rdr dropped whip ins fnl f: styd on same pce* **12/1**

4 **4** *hd* **Ziekhani**[13] 2547 3-9-5 0 .... RobertHavlin 8 84
(Hughie Morrison) *trckd ldrs: racd keenly: rdn and ev ch over 1f out: no ex wl ins fnl f* **4/1**[3]

4 **5** *12* **Viennese Verse**[28] 2099 3-9-5 0 .... DaneO'Neill 7 57
(Henry Candy) *hld up: rdn over 3f out: wknd 2f out* **25/1**

60 **6** *1* **Atlantic Isle (GER)**[28] 2084 3-8-7 0 .... AmeliaGreen[(7)] 2 49
(Sir Henry Cecil) *s.i.s: hld up: hdwy 1/2-way: wknd 2f out* **25/1**

3- **7** *1¼* **Berkeley Street (USA)**[236] 6985 3-9-5 0 .... JimmyFortune 1 52
(Sir Michael Stoute) *led over 7f out: rdn and hdd over 2f out: wknd over 1f out* **4/1**[3]

1m 45.5s (0.40) **Going Correction** -0.075s/f (Good) 7 Ran SP% **111.2**
Speed ratings (Par 99): **95,93,93,93,81 80,78**
toteswingers 1&2 £2.30, 1&3 £7.40, 2&3 £6.50 CSF £9.58 TOTE £5.10: £1.90, £1.50; EX 9.10 Trifecta £116.90 Pool: £3274.65 - 20.99 winning units..
Owner S Stuckey **Bred** Stuart Stuckey **Trained** Newmarket, Suffolk

FOCUS
The first division of a decent 3yo maiden, but the time was slower than the second leg.

2931 BRITISH STALLION STUDS COPLOW E.B.F MAIDEN STKS (DIV II) 1m 60y
5:15 (5:15) (Class 5) 3-Y-0 **£4,528** (£1,347; £673; £336) **Stalls** Low

Form RPR

02 **1** **Yeager (USA)**[35] 1881 3-9-5 0 .... WilliamBuick 6 88+
(Jeremy Noseda) *hld up: hdwy over 2f out: rdn and edgd lft over 1f out: sn led: drvn out* **15/8**[1]

2 *nk* **Archive** 3-9-0 0 ....[1] TomQueally 5 82+
(Sir Henry Cecil) *hld up: hdwy over 2f out: edgd rt fr over 1f out: r.o wl* **8/1**[3]

5-5 **3** *1* **Dance King**[18] 2384 3-9-5 0 .... TedDurcan 2 85+
(David Lanigan) *hld up: hdwy over 3f out: led over 2f out: rdn and hdd 1f out: styd on same pce* **15/8**[1]

0 **4** *8* **Canon Law (IRE)**[21] 2306 3-9-5 0 .... KierenFallon 1 71+
(Luca Cumani) *trckd ldrs: racd keenly: rdn whn hmpd over 1f out: wknd ins fnl f* **11/2**[2]

0-5 **5** *nk* **Patently (IRE)**[16] 2448 3-9-5 0 ....(t) JamieMackay 9 66
(Brian Meehan) *chsd ldrs: rn wd bnd over 4f out: chsd ldr over 3f out: sn rdn: wknd over 1f out* **14/1**

0- **6** *nk* **Estibdaad (IRE)**[222] 7330 3-9-5 0 .... PaulHanagan 3 65
(Charles Hills) *prom: racd keenly: nt clr run over 2f out: sn rdn and hung rt: wknd over 1f out* **9/1**

000 **7** *10* **Sakhee's Alround**[18] 2384 3-9-0 0 .... SeanLevey 7 44
(K F Clutterbuck) *led: racd keenly: rdn and hdd over 2f out: wknd over 1f out: eased* **250/1**

6-0 **8** *6* **Sweet Talking Guy (IRE)**[16] 2455 3-9-2 0 ....(t) SimonPearce[(3)] 4 29
(Lydia Pearce) *hld up: rdn over 2f out: sn wknd* **100/1**

0 **9** *24* **Deva Victrix**[9] 2650 3-9-5 0 .... DaleSwift 8
(Lisa Williamson) *plld hrd: trckd ldr: rdn over 3f out: sn wknd* **150/1**

1m 45.26s (0.16) **Going Correction** -0.075s/f (Good) 9 Ran SP% **114.8**
Speed ratings (Par 99): **96,95,94,86,86 86,76,70,46**
toteswingers 1&2 £2.50, 1&3 £1.80, 2&3 £3.40 CSF £19.07 TOTE £2.20: £1.10, £2.20, £1.90; EX 12.70 Trifecta £31.70 Pool: £3505.56 - 82.80 winning units..
Owner C Fox & B Wilson **Bred** Cloverleaf Farms II Llc **Trained** Newmarket, Suffolk

FOCUS
The second division of a decent 3yo maiden. The time was faster than the first leg and it looked the better race.

2932 SWANNINGTON H'CAP 7f 9y
5:45 (5:45) (Class 6) (0-60,60) 4-Y-0+ **£1,940** (£577; £288; £144) **Stalls** High

Form RPR

-046 **1** **Dancing Maite**[5] 2780 8-8-13 52 ....(b) MickaelBarzalona 16 67
(Roy Bowring) *hld up: hdwy over 2f out: led over 1f out: r.o wl* **8/1**[3]

5005 **2** *4½* **Boy The Bell**[12] 2578 6-8-12 51 ....(be) PaulHanagan 9 54
(Ollie Pears) *chsd ldrs: rdn and ev ch over 1f out: styd on same pce fnl f* **12/1**

0460 **3** *4½* **George Benjamin**[18] 2395 6-9-2 60 ....(tp) RachealKneller[(5)] 1 51
(Christopher Kellett) *s.i.s: bhd: rdn over 1f out: r.o ins fnl f: nvr nrr* **12/1**

0030 **4** *¾* **Katmai River (IRE)**[12] 2578 6-8-3 49 ....(v) EmilyMelbourn[(7)] 4 38
(Mark Usher) *hld up: hdwy over 1f out: no ex ins fnl f* **16/1**

-422 **5** *½* **Moss Hill**[35] 1887 4-9-0 53 .... JamesMcDonald 10 40
(Charles Hills) *chsd ldrs: rdn over 2f out: ev ch over 1f out: wknd ins fnl f* **7/1**[2]

/-06 **6** *¾* **Tweedle Dee**[34] 1914 4-9-1 54 .... StevieDonohoe 13 39
(Noel Quinlan) *hld up: rdn over 1f out: r.o towards fin: nvr nrr* **16/1**

2115 **7** *1¾* **Ace Master**[24] 2236 5-9-2 58 ....(b) BillyCray[(3)] 6 39
(Roy Bowring) *led: clr 5f out: rdn and hdd over 1f out: wknd fnl f* **10/1**

2020 **8** *¾* **Bajan Story**[12] 2574 4-9-7 60 .... FergusSweeney 5 39
(Michael Blanshard) *s.i.s: hld up: hdwy 1/2-way: rdn over 1f out: hung lft and wknd fnl f* **12/1**

0301 **9** *¾* **Prince Of Passion (CAN)**[12] 2582 5-9-0 60 .... AdamMcLean[(7)] 11 37
(Derek Shaw) *s.i.s: hld up: hdwy over 2f out: rdn over 1f out: wknd fnl f* **14/1**

064- **10** *¾* **Opus Maximus (IRE)**[251] 6569 8-8-11 50 ....(p) SamHitchcott 18 25
(Jennie Candlish) *hld up: rdn over 2f out: n.d* **6/1**[1]

1534 **11** *½* **Amis Reunis**[39] 1783 4-9-1 59 ....(p) PhilipPrince[(5)] 15 32
(Anthony Carson) *mid-div: rdn over 2f out: sn edgd rt: wknd over 1f out* **8/1**[3]

1-04 **12** *1* **Whitstable Native**[27] 2130 5-9-5 58 .... LiamKeniry 14 28
(Joseph Tuite) *hld up: rdn over 2f out: wknd over 1f out* **12/1**

3250 **13** *1¼* **Spartic**[44] 1681 5-8-11 50 .... SeanLevey 7 17
(Alan McCabe) *chsd clr ldr: rdn 1/2-way: wknd over 1f out* **16/1**

302- **14** *3¾* **Aussie Blue (IRE)**[293] 5203 9-9-7 60 .... MichaelStainton 2 17
(Charles Pogson) *chsd ldrs: rdn and ev ch wl over 1f out: sn wknd* **28/1**

00- **15** *41* **Ellies Image**[238] 6941 6-8-10 49 .... WilliamCarson 12
(Brian Baugh) *s.i.s: outpcd* **33/1**

/360 **16** *6* **Lhotse Sherpa**[58] 1394 4-8-13 52 .... MircoMimmocchi 3
(John Holt) *s.i.s: outpcd* **50/1**

1m 24.95s (-1.25) **Going Correction** -0.075s/f (Good) 16 Ran SP% **121.5**
Speed ratings (Par 101): **104,98,93,92,92 91,89,88,87,86 86,85,83,79,32 25**
toteswingers 1&2 £17.40, 1&3 £21.10, 2&3 £47.60 CSF £98.75 CT £1207.62 TOTE £7.90: £2.30, £2.60, £3.50, £4.90; EX 48.50 Trifecta £683.60 Part won. Pool: £911.56 - 0.15 winning units..
Owner S R Bowring **Bred** S R Bowring **Trained** Edwinstowe, Notts

FOCUS
A moderate handicap for older horses in which they went a decent gallop.
T/Plt: £7.30 to a £1 stake. Pool of £56,716.05 - 5604.73 winning tickets. T/Qpdt: £4.90 to a £1 stake. Pool of £3632.00 - 544.75 winning tickets. CR

2722 WINDSOR (R-H)

Monday, June 3

OFFICIAL GOING: Good to firm (8.3)

Top bend out 8yds adding 34yds to races of 1m and beyond. Inner of straight out 14yds at 6f and 7yds at Winning Post.

Wind: Light, against Weather: Fine, warm

2933 AT THE RACES SKY 415/EBF NOVICE STKS 5f 10y

5:30 (5:30) (Class 5) 2-Y-O £2,911 (£866; £432; £216) Stalls Low

Form RPR

1 **1** **Saayerr**[11] 2595 2-9-5 0 LiamJones 1 95+
(William Haggas) *trckd ldng pair: pushed along over 1f out: gap appeared against rail sn after: drvn fnl f: r.o to ld post* **1/2**[1]

1 **2** *shd* **Lilbourne Lass**[19] 2359 2-8-11 0 RyanMoore 4 87+
(Richard Hannon) *pressed ldr: shkn up 1/2-way: carried sltly lft over 1f out: drvn to ld ins fnl f: r.o but hdd post* **5/2**[2]

01 **3** *2 3/4* **Peterkin (IRE)**[51] 1534 2-9-5 0 NeilCallan 3 85
(Mark Johnston) *led: kicked on 1/2-way: hung lft over 1f out away fr rail: hdd and fdd ins fnl f* **9/1**[3]

1230 **4** *26* **M'Selle (IRE)**[26] 2147 2-9-0 0 JamesDoyle 5
(Ronald Harris) *s.s: in tch to 1/2-way: sn wknd: t.o* **50/1**

1m 0.4s (0.10) **Going Correction** -0.05s/f (Good) 4 Ran SP% **107.2**

Speed ratings (Par 93): **97,96,92,50**

CSF £1.96 TOTE £1.20; EX 1.90 Trifecta £4.10 Pool: £2344.78 - 428.79 winning units..

Owner Sheikh Ahmed Al Maktoum **Bred** Cheveley Park Stud Ltd **Trained** Newmarket, Suffolk

FOCUS

Just the four runners, but three of them had the potential to be useful and there was very little between the front pair in the market at the finish. It developed into a real dash for the line, with the early pace a steady one for the distance.

2934 GET YOUR ATR TRACKER READY MAIDEN STKS 6f

6:00 (6:01) (Class 5) 3-Y-O+ £2,726 (£805; £402) Stalls Low

Form RPR

346- **1** **Noble Deed**[229] 7167 3-9-4 73 LiamJones 10 79
(William Haggas) *prom: shkn up over 2f out: rdn and flashed tail over 1f out: drvn ahd sn after: hld on* **11/4**[1]

33 **2** *nk* **Realize**[24] 2224 3-9-4 0 HayleyTurner 4 78
(Hughie Morrison) *trckd ldr against rail: gap appeared over 1f out: rdn to chal sn after but hanging: pressed wnr ins fnl f: nt qckn* **10/3**[2]

5-2 **3** *2 1/4* **Aglaophonos**[42] 1732 3-9-4 0 NeilCallan 2 71
(Roger Varian) *dwlt: t.k.h early: hld up tl trckd ldr after 2f: rdn and nt qckn 2f out: wandering over 1f out: one pce* **11/2**

6 **4** *2* **Glanely (IRE)**[16] 2448 3-9-4 0 JamesDoyle 8 65
(James Fanshawe) *dwlt: hld up in last pair: prog on wd outside over 2f out: rdn and kpt on wout enthusiasm fr over 1f out* **7/2**[3]

3-22 **5** *3/4* **Hornboy**[58] 1384 3-9-4 70 (p) RyanMoore 7 62
(Jeremy Noseda) *in tch: rdn over 2f out: one pce and no threat over 1f out* **6/1**

6-0 **6** *3/4* **Dee Aitch Dove**[24] 2226 3-8-13 0 KieranO'Neill 6 55
(George Baker) *led: hld hd high and hanging whn rdn 2f out: hdd & wknd jst over 1f out* **66/1**

200- **7** *1 1/2* **Herbalist**[232] 7078 3-8-13 75 (b[1]) AmyScott(5) 1 55
(Alastair Lidderdale) *t.k.h: hld up in rr: shkn up to try to cl on ldrs 2f out: sn nt qckn and btn* **12/1**

04 **8** *16* **Kaahen (USA)**[13] 2529 3-9-4 0 AdamKirby 5
(Pat Eddery) *hld up in tch: pushed along over 2f out: wknd qckly over 1f out: t.o* **100/1**

1m 14.26s (1.26) **Going Correction** -0.05s/f (Good)

WFA 3 from 4yo 8lb 8 Ran SP% **111.8**

Speed ratings (Par 103): **89,88,85,82,81 80,78,57**

toteswingers 1&2 £3.00, 1&3 £4.50, 2&3 £3.50 CSF £11.53 TOTE £3.30: £1.50, £1.60, £1.60; EX 13.40 Trifecta £39.10 Pool: £2299.90 - 44.06 winning units..

Owner Cheveley Park Stud **Bred** Cheveley Park Stud Ltd **Trained** Newmarket, Suffolk

FOCUS

They went a relatively modest gallop in the early stages and it paid to race prominently. This is ordinary maiden form.

2935 JOIN AT THE RACES ON FACEBOOK H'CAP 1m 67y

6:30 (6:30) (Class 5) (0-75,77) 3-Y-O £2,587 (£770; £384; £192) Stalls Low

Form RPR

-053 **1** **Harry Bosch**[21] 2324 3-9-2 **70** (b) HayleyTurner 2 75
(Brian Meehan) *mde all: clr whn wd bnd 6f out: c bk to field 1/2-way: drew clr again 3f out w rivals impeding each other bhd: drvn out fnl f* **4/1**[1]

-331 **2** *1 1/2* **On With The Dance (IRE)**[68] 1213 3-9-1 **69** SebSanders 12 71
(Ed Vaughan) *hld up in midfield: rdn wl over 2f out: prog on outer over 1f out: styd on to take 2nd ins fnl f: unable to chal* **14/1**

6 **3** *nk* **Breccbennach**[28] 2093 3-9-7 **75** MickyFenton 10 76
(Seamus Durack) *pushed along in midfield after3f: rdn wl over 2f out: styd on fr wl over 1f out to take 3rd ins fnl f* **33/1**

214 **4** *3/4* **Movementneverlies**[16] 2449 3-9-7 **75** FrankieDettori 3 74
(Charles Hills) *s.i.s: sn rcvrd to chse ldng trio: rdn and edgd rt over 2f out: chsd wnr over 1f out to ins fnl f: no ex* **9/2**[2]

4-63 **5** *1* **Mojo Bear**[21] 2331 3-8-11 **65** LiamJones 5 62+
(Sylvester Kirk) *hld up in 5th: rdn over 2f out: lost pl sltly wl over 1f out and n.m.r: kpt on* **28/1**

004- **6** *nk* **Admirals Walk (IRE)**[210] 7592 3-8-5 **66** JoshBaudains(7) 7 62+
(Sylvester Kirk) *hld up in midfield: effrt whn sltly hmpd and stmbld over 2f out: nvr really able to rcvr* **66/1**

320- **7** *nk* **Lambert Pen (USA)**[173] 8072 3-8-2 **63** DanielCremin(7) 13 59
(Mick Channon) *hld up towards rr: shkn up on outer over 2f out: one pce and no threat* **40/1**

-106 **8** *1* **Woodstock (IRE)**[21] 2325 3-9-2 **70** RyanMoore 6 63+
(Richard Hannon) *hld up towards rr: rdn whn nt clr run over 2f out: n.m.r over 1f out: nvr a threat* **15/2**[3]

30-6 **9** *1/2* **Polly's Love (IRE)**[18] 2390 3-9-1 **69** AdamKirby 4 61
(Clive Cox) *mostly chsd wnr: drvn over 3f out: lost 2nd over 2f out: losing pl whn hmpd sn after* **10/1**

52-0 **10** *3/4* **Anjuna Beach (USA)**[7] 2727 3-9-3 **71** GeorgeBaker 8 61
(Gary Moore) *stdd s: hld up in last: taken to outer and shkn up 2f out: nvr remotely involved* **33/1**

3-61 **11** *1 1/4* **Aussie Reigns (IRE)**[7] 2727 3-9-4 **77** 6ex (v) ThomasBrown(5) 14 65+
(William Knight) *hld up in rr: trying to make prog whn repeatedly hmpd fr over 2f out: no ch over 1f out and eased* **9/2**[2]

46-0 **12** *nse* **Choral Prince (IRE)**[42] 1725 3-9-1 **69** (b[1]) NeilCallan 9 56
(Mike Murphy) *t.k.h: chsd ldng pair: drvn to chse wnr over 2f out and hung rt: lost 2nd over 1f out: wandered and wknd qckly* **28/1**

055- **13** *1 1/4* **Bold And Free**[194] 7806 3-8-8 **67** RobertTart(5) 1 52+
(David Elsworth) *dwlt: hld up in last pair: rdn and no prog over 2f out: fnlly sing to stay on whn rn into the bk of rival ins fnl f: eased* **9/2**[2]

1m 44.62s (-0.08) **Going Correction** -0.15s/f (Firm) 13 Ran SP% **118.8**

Speed ratings (Par 99): **94,92,92,91,90 90,89,88,88,87 86,86,85**

toteswingers 1&2 £10.80, 1&3 £34.70, 2&3 £144.00 CSF £56.67 CT £1679.30 TOTE £4.90: £1.70, £3.40, £8.70; EX 72.70 Trifecta £1213.10 Part won. Pool: £1617.47 - 0.15 winning units..

Owner Michael Buckley **Bred** C J Murfitt **Trained** Manton, Wilts

FOCUS

Quite a modest 3yo handicap and the winner was soon clear.

2936 CORAL.CO.UK LEISURE STKS (LISTED RACE) 6f

7:00 (7:00) (Class 1) 3-Y-O+

£20,982 (£7,955; £3,981; £1,983; £995; £499) Stalls Low

Form RPR

33-3 **1** **Boomerang Bob (IRE)**[23] 2257 4-9-0 104 SebSanders 1 105
(J W Hills) *trckd ldng pair gng wl: waiting for a gap tl squeezed through over 1f out: drvn and r.o to ld wl ins fnl f* **12/1**

6-64 **2** *nk* **Victrix Ludorum (IRE)**[16] 2452 3-8-1 95 KieranO'Neill 7 97
(Richard Hannon) *chsd ldrs: pushed along sn after 1/2-way: drvn to chal over 1f out: led briefly ins fnl f: styd on* **17/2**[3]

11-0 **3** *shd* **Mince**[19] 2368 4-9-2 113 JamesDoyle 5 106
(Roger Charlton) *trckd ldr: moved upsides gng wl 1/2-way: led 2f out: rdn over 1f out and hrd pressed: hdd ins fnl f: styd on* **8/13**[1]

43-0 **4** *nk* **Sirius Prospect (USA)**[19] 2368 5-9-0 105 RobertWinston 4 103
(Dean Ivory) *hld up in last trio: drvn on outer wl over 1f out: styd on fnl f: nvr quite able to chal* **9/2**[2]

000- **5** *1* **Palace Moon**[235] 7010 8-9-0 101 JimmyQuinn 3 100
(William Knight) *hld up in last trio: shkn up over 2f out: hanging and nt qckn wl over 1f out: styd on ins fnl f* **20/1**

0661 **6** *3* **Regal Parade**[23] 2257 9-9-0 103 (t) MatthewLawson 2 90
(Milton Bradley) *hld up in last: shkn up over 2f out and no prog: no imp on ldrs over 1f out* **33/1**

0-54 **7** *1/2* **Pandar**[23] 2257 4-9-0 101 NeilCallan 6 88
(Robert Cowell) *led: jnd 1/2-way: hdd 2f out: wknd over 1f out* **20/1**

1m 11.66s (-1.34) **Going Correction** -0.05s/f (Good)

WFA 3 from 4yo+ 8lb 7 Ran SP% **110.8**

Speed ratings (Par 111): **106,105,105,105,103 99,99**

toteswingers 1&2 £2.60, 1&3 £2.50, 2&3 £1.90 CSF £95.19 TOTE £8.90: £2.90, £2.20; EX 78.70 Trifecta £125.00 Pool: £4182.70 - 25.09 winning units..

Owner R J Tufft **Bred** Dr Dean Harron & Ederidge Ltd **Trained** Upper Lambourn, Berks

■ Stewards' Enquiry : Kieran O'Neill two-day ban; used whip above permitted level (17th-23rd June).

FOCUS

Hard to know what to make of this, with red-hot favourite Mince clearly not running to her mark of 113, and the first four were separated by under a length at the line. The time was relatively slow and the form is rated around the winner.

2937 DOWNLOAD CORAL MOBILE FROM THE APP STORE H'CAP 6f

7:30 (7:31) (Class 3) (0-95,95) 4-Y-O+ £7,439 (£2,213; £1,106; £553) Stalls Low

Form RPR

-206 **1** **Khubala (IRE)**[16] 2444 4-9-5 **93** (b) GeorgeBaker 9 105
(Hugo Palmer) *t.k.h: hld up bhd ldrs: rdn over 1f out: r.o against rail fnl f to ld last strides* **12/1**

3-01 **2** *nk* **Tropics (USA)**[7] 2724 5-9-2 **90** 6ex KierenFallon 12 101+
(Dean Ivory) *hld up in rr: stdy prog on outer fr 1/2-way: rdn to ld over 1f out: c across towards rail: styd on but hdd last strides* **5/2**[1]

-232 **3** *1* **Poole Harbour (IRE)**[16] 2444 4-9-7 **95** RyanMoore 5 103
(Richard Hannon) *taken down early: led against rail: rdn and hdd over 1f out: styd on wl but lost 2nd nr fin* **7/2**[2]

0-51 **4** *4 1/2* **Steps (IRE)**[16] 2461 5-9-2 **95** (b) ThomasBrown(5) 1 89
(Roger Varian) *t.k.h: hld up bhd ldrs: cl up but nt qckn over 1f out: wknd ins fnl f* **14/1**

00-0 **5** *1* **B Fifty Two (IRE)**[24] 2207 4-9-3 **91** SebSanders 11 81
(J W Hills) *settled towards rr: prog on outer fr 1/2-way: nvr pce to threaten ldrs: hld in 5th over 1f out: fdd fnl f* **16/1**

4254 **6** *hd* **Harrison George (IRE)**[10] 2618 8-8-5 **84** (t) RobertTart(5) 10 74
(P J O'Gorman) *w ldrs on outer: urged along sn after 1/2-way: steadily outpcd fr over 2f out* **14/1**

0001 **7** *hd* **Piscean (USA)**[10] 2621 8-9-0 **88** JimmyQuinn 7 77
(Tom Keddy) *hld up towards rr: shkn up and no prog 2f out: kpt on one pce fnl f* **40/1**

25-0 **8** *3/4* **L'Ami Louis (IRE)**[24] 2207 5-9-0 **88** DaneO'Neill 6 75
(Henry Candy) *w ldr to jst over 2f out: sn wknd* **10/1**

25-0 **9** *6* **Joe Packet**[16] 2444 6-9-7 **95** NeilCallan 4 63+
(Jonathan Portman) *chsd ldrs: stmbld and snatched up over 3f out: no ch to rcvr* **20/1**

05-0 **10** *1/2* **Dungannon**[18] 2396 6-9-3 **91** JimmyFortune 2 57
(Andrew Balding) *hld up in rr: shkn up 2f out: nt on terms after and no prog* **8/1**[3]

5500 **11** *7* **Spirit Of Sharjah (IRE)**[17] 2424 8-8-12 **86** (p) RobertWinston 8 30
(Julia Feilden) *w ldrs on outer to over 2f out: sn wknd: t.o* **66/1**

00-0 **12** *1 1/4* **Tioman Legend**[24] 2207 4-9-4 **92** JamesDoyle 3 32
(Roger Charlton) *trckd ldrs: nt qckn over 2f out: wknd tamely over 1f out: t.o* **12/1**

510- **13** *4* **Esprit De Midas**[247] 6676 7-8-9 **90** [1] PaulBooth(7) 13 17
(Dean Ivory) *sn struggling in last: t.o* **66/1**

1m 11.41s (-1.59) **Going Correction** -0.05s/f (Good) 13 Ran SP% **115.8**

Speed ratings (Par 107): **108,107,106,100,98 98,98,97,89,88 79,77,72**

toteswingers 1&2 £12.70, 1&3 £10.00, 2&3 £2.70 CSF £39.74 CT £134.05 TOTE £16.40: £5.70, £1.50, £1.10; EX 62.40 Trifecta £287.90 Pool: £3176.80 - 8.27 winning units..

Owner Mrs Pinar Araci Bas **Bred** James F Hanly **Trained** Newmarket, Suffolk

FOCUS
Solid sprint form with the first three pulling a little way clear and the placed runners coming into this in good form. The time was the fastest of the three races over the trip.

2938 AT THE RACES VIRGIN 534 MEDIAN AUCTION MAIDEN STKS 1m 2f 7y
8:00 (8:03) (Class 5) 3-Y-O £2,587 (£770; £384; £192) **Stalls Centre**

Form RPR

1 **Court Pastoral** 3-9-0 0 .... TomQueally 8 75
(Sir Henry Cecil) *w ldrs: pressed ldr 4f out: upsides 2f out: rdn to take narrow ld ins fnl f: leant on rival: hld on* **5/2**[2]

06- 2 *nk* **Forward March**[230] 7143 3-9-5 0 .... ShaneKelly 10 79
(Gary Harrison) *t.k.h early: w ldrs: led 4f out: drvn and jnd 2f out: narrowly hdd ins fnl f: intimidated by wnr and jst hld* **50/1**

3- 3 *4* **Omnipresent**[269] 6014 3-9-5 0 .... RyanMoore 1 71
(Sir Michael Stoute) *mde most: hdd and hanging 4f out: nt qckn u.p 3f out: steadily lft bhd by front pair* **6/4**[1]

4 4 *½* **Sultanah Heyam**[35] 1876 3-9-0 0 .... LiamJones 3 65
(William Haggas) *pressed ldrs: rdn over 3f out: nt qckn over 2f out: steadily lft bhd* **6/1**[3]

00 5 *1* **Bombardier**[21] 2321 3-9-5 0 .... MartinLane 4 68+
(James Fanshawe) *shoved along vigorously in midfield after 3f and stl looked green: nvr on terms but styd on fnl 2f: nrst fin* **25/1**

0 6 *½* **Russian Link**[18] 2392 3-9-0 0 .... [1] JamesDoyle 9 62
(Roger Charlton) *chsd ldrs: urged along wl over 3f out: no imp after but kpt on fnl 2f* **20/1**

7 *hd* **Markttag** 3-9-5 0 .... KierenFallon 5 67+
(Luca Cumani) *in tch: shkn up in 7th over 3f out: one pce and no imp on ldrs after* **10/1**

8 *1 ¾* **Le Tigre De Bronze** 3-9-5 0 .... HayleyTurner 14 65+
(Hughie Morrison) *slowly away: wl off the pce in last quartet: green and hanging fr 4f out but kpt on fnl 2f: nrst fin* **33/1**

4 9 *2 ½* **Miss Mitigate**[20] 2346 3-9-0 0 .... JimmyFortune 6 53
(Andrew Balding) *nvr bttr than midfield: drvn 4f out: struggling after* **16/1**

0 10 *1 ½* **The Green Ogre**[11] 2605 3-9-5 0 .... GeorgeBaker 16 55
(Gary Moore) *chsd ldrs: cl up and rdn over 3f out: wknd over 2f out* **50/1**

65- 11 *2* **Exclusive Waters (IRE)**[175] 8052 3-9-5 0 .... AdamKirby 13 51
(William Knight) *rn green in rr and reminder after 3f: nvr a factor* **25/1**

12 *2 ¾* **Hallingham** 3-9-0 0 .... MatthewLawson(5) 15 46
(Jonathan Portman) *slowly away: rn green and a struggling in rr* **66/1**

0 13 *1 ¾* **Pure Mischief (IRE)**[18] 2389 3-9-0 0 .... TedDurcan 7 37+
(David Lanigan) *a towards rr: shkn up and no prog over 4f out: wknd over 2f out* **50/1**

0- 14 *3 ¾* **Nandura**[243] 6795 3-9-0 0 .... DaneO'Neill 11 30
(Harry Dunlop) *hld up towards rr: gng bttr than sme 4f out: wknd qckly over 2f out* **100/1**

15 *82* **Indian Billionaire (IRE)** 3-9-5 0 .... JackMitchell 2
(Paul Fitzsimons) *v green and wl in rr: t.o fr 1/2-way: virtually p.u* **100/1**

2m 9.2s (0.50) **Going Correction** -0.15s/f (Firm) **15 Ran SP% 122.6**
Speed ratings (Par 99): **92,91,88,88,87 86,86,85,83,82 80,78,77,74,8**
toteswingers 1&2 £39.90, 1&3 £2.10, 2&3 £64.60 CSF £137.96 TOTE £3.80: £1.90, £15.90, £1.20; EX 154.00 Trifecta £1305.70 Pool: £3041.55 - 1.74 winning units..
Owner J Shack **Bred** Newsells Park Stud **Trained** Newmarket, Suffolk
■ Stewards' Enquiry : Tom Queally one-day day ban; careless riding (17th June).

FOCUS
Ordinary maiden form and they didn't go much of a gallop, but as expected it went to one of the front two in the market. The front pair came close, but it couldn't be said for certain the result was affected.

2939 ATTHERACES.COM EXCLUSIVE WILLIAM BUICK BLOG H'CAP 1m 3f 135y
8:30 (8:35) (Class 4) (0-80,80) 4-Y-O+ £4,851 (£1,443; £721; £360) **Stalls Centre**

Form RPR

03-1 1 **Jupiter Storm**[31] 1973 4-9-3 **76** .... RyanMoore 5 88
(Gary Moore) *mde all: clr after 3f: nvr threatened after: drvn and maintain advantage fnl 2f* **7/2**[1]

313 2 *8* **Saint Helena (IRE)**[6] 2750 5-9-6 **79** .... JamesDoyle 1 77
(Harry Dunlop) *awkward on way to post: hld up in last pair and wl bhd: rdn and prog over 3f out: styd on to take 2nd ins fnl f: no ch w wnr* **9/2**[3]

0313 3 *1* **If I Were A Boy (IRE)**[32] 1956 6-8-7 **66** .... (b) MartinLane 12 62
(Dominic Ffrench Davis) *hld up in 10th and wl off the pce: prog wl over 2f out: styd on to take 3rd ins fnl f: no ch* **25/1**

5110 4 *¾* **Linkable**[55] 1445 4-8-11 **70** ow1 .... (t) SebSanders 10 65
(Brendan Powell) *hld up off the pce towards rr: prog 3f out: styd on fnl f: n.d* **25/1**

0-05 5 *¾* **Nordic Quest (IRE)**[11] 2598 4-9-3 **76** .... NeilCallan 7 70
(Gerard Butler) *prom: rdn to chse clr wnr 3f out: nvr any imp: fdd fnl f* **11/1**

0440 6 *3* **Thecornishcowboy**[18] 2383 4-8-9 **68** .... (tp) KirstyMilczarek 2 57
(John Ryan) *chsd wnr: no imp and lost 2nd 3f out: wknd over 1f out* **33/1**

2 7 *½* **Duaiseoir (IRE)**[28] 2102 7-9-1 **74** .... HayleyTurner 4 62
(Venetia Williams) *chsd ldrs: rdn over 4f out: no prog u.p 3f out: fdd* **8/1**

0-30 8 *12* **Sula Two**[14] 2520 6-9-2 **80** .... PhilipPrince(5) 6 47
(Ron Hodges) *s.s: wl bhd in last and rdn after 5f: nvr a factor* **25/1**

132/ 9 *12* **Waahej**[559] 7506 7-8-12 **71** .... ChrisCatlin 11 18
(Peter Hiatt) *nvr beyond midfield and nvr remotely on terms: no prog over 3f out: t.o* **40/1**

05-0 10 *1 ¼* **Scarlet Whispers**[23] 2277 4-9-3 **76** .... MickyFenton 9 21
(Pam Sly) *prom: rdn 1/2-way: wknd over 3f out: t.o* **8/1**

211- 11 *1 ¼* **Miss Blakeney**[155] 8297 4-9-7 **80** .... GeorgeBaker 3 23
(Marcus Tregoning) *chsd ldrs: shkn up 3f out: rchd 4th but no ch over 2f out: wknd rapidly over 1f out and virtually p.u* **14/1**

6 12 *7* **Mexicali (IRE)**[23] 2251 5-9-7 **80** .... TedDurcan 8 11
(Dean Ivory) *chsd ldrs: rdn and wknd 4f out: virtually p.u over 1f out* **4/1**[2]

2m 25.91s (-3.59) **Going Correction** -0.15s/f (Firm) **12 Ran SP% 114.5**
Speed ratings (Par 105): **105,99,99,98,98 96,95,87,79,78 78,73**
toteswingers 1&2 £3.50, 1&3 £20.20, 2&3 £31.10 CSF £17.02 CT £335.31 TOTE £3.90: £1.80, £1.70, £3.80; EX 19.90 Trifecta £281.00 Pool: £1730.01 - 4.61 winning units..
Owner Heart Of The South Racing **Bred** Breeding Capital, Watership Down, Farish **Trained** Lower Beeding, W Sussex

FOCUS
A second winner on the night to have opened up a clear early advantage and maintained it.
T/Plt: £140.70 to a £1 stake. Pool of £75,715.78 - 392.63 winning tickets. T/Qpdt: £47.90 to a £1 stake. Pool of £7097.84 - 109.45 winning tickets. JN

2940 - 2942a (Foreign Racing) - See Raceform Interactive

2372 NAAS (L-H)
Monday, June 3

OFFICIAL GOING: Good to firm (good in places)

2943a ALFRED NOBEL ROCHESTOWN STKS (LISTED RACE) (C&G) 6f
4:05 (4:07) 2-Y-O £31,707 (£9,268; £4,390; £1,463)

RPR

1 **Stubbs (IRE)**[15] 2482 2-9-3 .... JosephO'Brien 2 101+
(A P O'Brien, Ire) *w.w in rr: clsr in 3rd bef 1/2-way: smooth hdwy on outer to ld narrowly fr under 2f out: rdn clr and edgd lft ent fnl f: kpt on wl towards fin: comf* **8/13**[1]

2 *1 ¾* **Sacha Park (IRE)**[11] 2595 2-9-3 .... PatDobbs 4 95
(Richard Hannon) *sn led: jnd 1/2-way: hdd narrowly fr under 2f out: no imp on wnr ent fnl f: kpt on wl towards fin* **11/4**[2]

3 *2* **Club Wexford (IRE)**[9] 2675 2-9-3 .... KevinManning 3 89
(J S Bolger, Ire) *trckd ldr in 2nd: t.k.h: rdn and no imp in 3rd over 1f out: kpt on same pce* **4/1**[3]

4 *6 ½* **All Set To Go (IRE)**[8] 2685 2-9-3 .... ChrisHayes 1 70
(A Oliver, Ire) *settled bhd ldrs in 3rd: lost pl bef 1/2-way: rdn and no imp fr 2f out: one pce fnl f* **25/1**

1m 11.9s (-1.30) **4 Ran SP% 112.4**
CSF £2.81 TOTE £1.80; DF 3.50.
Owner Derrick Smith & Mrs John Magnier & Michael Tabor **Bred** Orpendale, Chelston & Wynatt **Trained** Ballydoyle, Co Tipperary

FOCUS
This has tended to be a strong race but this was an unsatisfactory contest run at a sluggish speed. This did not help Club Wexford, who was quite keen.

2944a COOLMORE STUD EUROPEAN BREEDERS FUND FILLIES' SPRINT STKS (LISTED RACE) 6f
4:35 (4:36) 2-Y-O £30,386 (£8,882; £4,207; £1,402)

RPR

1 **Sandiva (IRE)**[24] 2230 2-9-0 .... PatSmullen 8 105+
(Richard Fahey) *wnt sltly rt s: settled bhd ldrs: wnt 2nd gng best over 2f out: sn drew clr w rival and led over 1f out: styd on wl towards fin* **7/4**[1]

2 *2* **Heart Focus (IRE)**[19] 2372 2-9-0 .... KevinManning 3 99
(J S Bolger, Ire) *trckd ldr: cl 2nd bef 1/2-way: rdn to ld narrowly over 2f out: sn strly pressed by wnr clr of remainder: hdd over 1f out and sn no ex u.p: kpt on wl towards fin* **8/1**

3 *4 ½* **Fig Roll**[29] 2053 2-9-0 .... PatDobbs 5 85
(Richard Hannon) *chsd ldrs: pushed along in 3rd 1 1/2f out: sn outpcd by ldng pair: kpt on same pce ins fnl f* **9/2**[2]

4 *hd* **Glassatura (IRE)**[9] 2674 2-9-0 .... ShaneFoley 6 84
(M Halford, Ire) *chsd ldrs: rdn in 6th 2f out: sn no imp on principals: wnt mod 4th fnl 100yds: kpt on* **5/1**[3]

5 *nk* **Adeste Fideles (USA)** 2-9-0 .... SeamieHeffernan 9 84+
(A P O'Brien, Ire) *in tch: pushed along in 5th over 2f out: sn outpcd: kpt on same pce ins fnl f* **20/1**

6 *1 ¼* **Corncockle**[17] 2419 2-9-0 .... WayneLordan 4 80
(Richard Hannon) *awkward s: t.k.h: settled bhd ldrs: rdn and no imp on principals fr 2f out: kpt on same pce in 6th ins fnl f* **8/1**

7 *nk* **Dimity (IRE)**[19] 2372 2-9-0 .... BenCurtis 7 79
(John Joseph Murphy, Ire) *hld up: short of room and checked briefly early: rdn fr 1/2-way and no imp: kpt on same pce in 7th ins fnl f* **33/1**

8 *1 ¾* **Bracelet (IRE)** 2-9-0 .... JosephO'Brien 11 80+
(A P O'Brien, Ire) *sltly hmpd s: sn chsd ldrs on outer: pushed along fr 2f out and no imp in 8th ent fnl f: kpt on* **6/1**

9 *½* **Thrilled To Bits (IRE)**[9] 2675 2-9-0 .... (t) ChrisHayes 10 72
(A Oliver, Ire) *wnt rt s: racd towards rr: pushed along fr 1/2-way and no imp fr 2f out: one pce fnl f* **33/1**

10 *4 ¼* **Homeric Hymn (FR)**[19] 2372 2-9-0 .... FMBerry 2 59
(Mrs John Harrington, Ire) *sn led: pushed along fr 1/2-way and hdd over 2f out: wknd* **16/1**

1m 10.26s (-2.94) **10 Ran SP% 124.2**
CSF £17.99 TOTE £2.30: £1.02, £2.30, £1.90; DF 16.10.
Owner Middleham Park Racing XXX **Bred** Denis McDonnell **Trained** Musley Bank, N Yorks

FOCUS
Usually a hot race and this looked no exception.

2945 - 2946a (Foreign Racing) - See Raceform Interactive

2869 LINGFIELD (L-H)
Tuesday, June 4

OFFICIAL GOING: Standard
Wind: Moderate; half against Weather: Sunny; warm

2947 BHEST MEDIAN AUCTION MAIDEN STKS 5f (P)
2:15 (2:20) (Class 6) 2-Y-O £2,045 (£603; £302) **Stalls High**

Form RPR

1 **Baytown Kestrel** 2-9-0 0 .... AdamKirby 1 75
(Phil McEntee) *mde all: shkn up 2f out: drew rt away over 1f out: unchal* **50/1**

24 2 *4 ½* **Finflash (IRE)**[12] 2595 2-9-5 0 .... MartinHarley 4 63
(Mick Channon) *trckd ldng pair: wnt 2nd 2f out: shkn up and lft bhd by wnr over 1f out: no ch after* **1/4**[1]

0 3 *¾* **Flora Medici**[7] 2751 2-9-0 0 .... LukeMorris 6 56
(Sir Mark Prescott Bt) *chsd wnr to 2f out: rdn and one pce after* **33/1**

23 4 *3 ½* **Weisse Girl**[28] 2117 2-9-0 0 .... (b) StevieDonohoe 3 43
(Noel Quinlan) *awkward s: racd awkwardly: in tch to 2f out: sn btn* **8/1**[2]

5 *1 ¾* **Vallila** 2-9-0 0 .... [1] JamesDoyle 2 37
(Roger Charlton) *dwlt: rn green at bk of main gp: outpcd over 2f out* **10/1**[3]

5656 6 *2* **Riley's Missile (IRE)**[16] 2475 2-9-5 0 .... PatCosgrave 5 35
(Charles Smith) *dwlt: in tch: rdn 1/2-way: outpcd fr 2f out* **100/1**

7 *76* **Ivan B** 2-9-5 0 .... MatthewDavies 7
(Mick Channon) *s.v.s: hopelessly green and immediately wl t.o* **20/1**

1m 0.67s (1.87) **Going Correction** +0.05s/f (Slow) **7 Ran SP% 110.9**
Speed ratings (Par 91): **87,79,78,73,70 67,**
toteswingers 1&2 £6.80, 1&3 £27.70, 2&3 £3.10 CSF £61.95 TOTE £66.00: £15.70, £1.10; EX 100.50 Trifecta £1735.40 Pool: £1735.40 - 2.15 winning units..
Owner Mrs Rebecca McEntee **Bred** R F And S D Knipe **Trained** Newmarket, Suffolk

The Form Book Flat, Raceform Ltd, Compton, RG20 6NL.

FOCUS
An uncompetitive maiden and the sort of result that would have had most punters on their knees.

2948 LINGFIELD PARK RACING SHIRES JUNE 15TH (S) STKS 1m (P)
2:45 (2:46) (Class 6) 3-5-Y-0 £2,045 (£603; £302) Stalls High

Form RPR
2510 1 **Abhaath (USA)**[13] 2565 4-9-10 62 LukeMorris 5 69
(Ronald Harris) *w ldr at stdy pce: led wl over 1f out and sn urged along: kpt on fnl f: hld on nr fin* **7/2**[3]
5342 2 *nk* **Moment In The Sun**[13] 2571 4-9-0 61 (b) MickaelBarzalona 6 58
(David Flood) *t.k.h: trckd ldng pair: urged along and nt qckn over 1f out: chsd wnr ins fnl f: clsd but a hld* **1/1**[1]
/ 3 *1 ¼* **Madeira Girl (IRE)**[16] 7340 4-9-0 74 TomQueally 1 55
(Jonjo O'Neill) *led at mod pce: rdn and hdd 2f out: one pce after* **11/4**[2]
5000 4 *1 ¾* **Blue Deer (IRE)**[69] 1194 5-9-2 60 (v) DarrenEgan(3) 8 56
(Lee Carter) *t.k.h: hld up in last pair: gng wl 2f out but sn outpcd: drvn and styd on fnl f: no ch* **8/1**
5 *5* **Father Fred** 3-8-8 0 SaleemGolam 4 41
(Chris Dwyer) *s.s: t.k.h in last pair: wknd over 1f out* **33/1**
40 6 *2 ¼* **Sextons House (IRE)**[25] 2236 5-9-5 45 (v[1]) KieranO'Neill 2 38
(Alan McCabe) *t.k.h: trckd ldng pair to 2f out: sn wknd* **50/1**

1m 41.3s (3.10) **Going Correction** +0.05s/f (Slow)
WFA 3 from 4yo+ 11lb 6 Ran SP% **114.9**
Speed ratings (Par 101): **86,85,84,82,77 75**
toteswingers 1&2 £1.10, 1&3 £1.70, 2&3 £1.10 CSF £7.69 TOTE £3.40: £2.20, £1.10; EX 7.20 Trifecta £20.40 Pool: £2,155.12 - 79.23 winning units..There was no bid for the winner.
Owner Ridge House Stables Ltd **Bred** Santa Rosa Partners **Trained** Earlswood, Monmouths

FOCUS
A moderate seller and they didn't go much of a pace, causing several to take a grip.

2949 VINES BMW CLASSIFIED CLAIMING STKS 7f (P)
3:15 (3:16) (Class 6) 3-Y-0+ £2,726 (£805; £402) Stalls Low

Form RPR
3263 1 **Commanche**[15] 2516 4-9-3 66 JimCrowley 5 77
(Patrick Chamings) *trckd clr ldrs: wnt 3rd 1/2-way: clsd to chal 2f out: drvn to ld jst over 1f out: styd on u.p* **6/4**[1]
2203 2 *1 ¼* **Spark Of Genius**[15] 2513 4-9-1 70 (v) WilliamTwiston-Davies(5) 4 77
(Alan McCabe) *chsd clr ldr: clsd to ld 2f out: drvn and hdd jst over 1f out: kpt on but hld fnl f* **6/1**[3]
-602 3 *3 ½* **Avatar Star (IRE)**[7] 2737 3-8-10 70 (tp) PaoloSirigu 7 64
(Marco Botti) *sn outpcd in last and scrubbed along: wl bhd 3f out: styd on fnl 2f to take 3rd ins fnl f: nrst fin* **9/2**[2]
4304 4 *1 ¼* **Haywain**[7] 2757 4-9-4 65 (p) JamieSpencer 8 62
(Kevin Ryan) *sn pushed along in 5th and outpcd: tried to cl over 2f out: tk modest 3rd briefly 1f out* **9/2**[2]
1002 5 *1* **Homeboy (IRE)**[33] 1954 5-9-3 62 GeorgeBaker 6 59
(Marcus Tregoning) *hld up in 6th and sn wl off the pce: coaxed along to try to cl 2f out: no imp over 1f out* **12/1**
0600 6 *2 ¾* **Lucky Mark (IRE)**[24] 2280 4-9-1 62 (p) AdamKirby 9 50
(Garry Moss) *clr ldr and sn spreadeagled field: hdd & wknd 2f out* **14/1**
6-00 7 *3 ¾* **Red Eight (USA)**[14] 2549 3-8-12 65 (p) TomQueally 3 43
(John Butler) *chsd ldng pair to 1/2-way: wknd u.p* **25/1**
32/4 R **Desert Icon (IRE)**[36] 1888 7-8-6 67 NoraLooby(7) 2
(Alastair Lidderdale) *turned arnd leaving stalls and stopped* **25/1**

1m 25.29s (0.49) **Going Correction** +0.05s/f (Slow)
WFA 3 from 4yo+ 10lb 8 Ran SP% **112.7**
Speed ratings (Par 101): **99,97,93,92,91 87,83,**
toteswingers 1&2 £3.10, 1&3 £2.70, 2&3 £4.10 CSF £10.57 TOTE £2.10: £1.50, £1.70, £1.40; EX 11.60 Trifecta £31.00 Pool: £4,170.56 - 100.85 winning units..Commanche was claimed by Mr C. A. Dwyer for £7,000
Owner K W Tyrrell **Bred** Paramount Bloodstock **Trained** Baughurst, Hants

FOCUS
A moderate claimer and they were soon spread out.

2950 WILLIAM PEARS H'CAP 7f (P)
3:45 (3:47) (Class 6) (0-55,55) 3-Y-0 £2,045 (£603; £302) Stalls Low

Form RPR
1225 1 **Black Truffle (FR)**[32] 1978 3-9-7 55 (v) GeorgeBaker 6 63
(Mark Usher) *hld up in midfield: gd prog over 1f out: rdn and r.o fnl f to ld nr fin* **12/1**
00-0 2 *nk* **Our Three Graces (IRE)**[14] 2528 3-9-4 52 RyanMoore 4 59
(Gary Moore) *pressed ldr: drvn to ld wl over 1f out: styd on but hdd nr fin* **16/1**
05-3 3 *1 ½* **Reggie Bond**[29] 2080 3-9-1 54 WilliamTwiston-Davies(5) 8 57
(Geoffrey Oldroyd) *trckd ldrs: rdn to chal wl over 1f out: hanging and nt qckn: kpt on ins fnl f* **5/2**[2]
6-60 4 *shd* **Unassailable**[15] 2501 3-9-3 54 (b[1]) JulieBurke(3) 5 57
(Kevin Ryan) *trckd ldrs: rdn on inner wl over 1f out: kpt on to press for a pl ins fnl f* **33/1**
60-1 5 *½* **Winslow Arizona (IRE)**[13] 2566 3-9-7 55 JamieSpencer 1 57
(Michael Bell) *led: rdn and hdd wl over 1f out: one pce fnl f* **5/4**[1]
5404 6 *1* **Spreading**[79] 1055 3-9-5 53 LiamKeniry 9 52
(Michael Blanshard) *wl in tch in midfield on outer: shkn up and nt qckn wl over 1f out: one pce after* **25/1**
-053 7 *¾* **Rock Diamond (IRE)**[13] 2566 3-9-0 48 JamesDoyle 12 45
(Sylvester Kirk) *pushed along towards rr over 4f out: effrt and sme prog over 1f out: nvr on terms* **20/1**
3430 8 *1 ¼* **Otto The First**[28] 2129 3-9-0 53 RyanTate(5) 2 47
(John Best) *trckd ldrs: effrt on inner and n.m.r 2f out: styd against rail over 1f out: fdd fnl f* **50/1**
0-04 9 *nk* **Carneades (IRE)**[24] 2267 3-9-1 49 LukeMorris 3 42
(Ed Walker) *pressed ldrs: drvn over 2f out: wknd over 1f out* **25/1**
000- 10 *5* **Chandelle Celeste**[181] 7987 3-9-5 53 TomQueally 13 33
(James Toller) *slowest away: hld up in last quartet: pushed along 2f out: no prog and btn over 1f out* **33/1**
060- 11 *2 ½* **Elvin**[173] 8094 3-9-2 50 [1] JimCrowley 14 23
(Amanda Perrett) *hld up in last pair and racd wd: urged along wl over 1f out: no rspnse* **10/1**[3]
0-55 12 *½* **So Lyrical**[40] 1781 3-8-12 46 oh1 (p) CathyGannon 7 18+
(Jo Hughes) *mostly in last quartet: rdn whn nt clr run 3f out: no prog after* **50/1**
-040 13 *1 ½* **Don Eduardo**[14] 2528 3-9-3 51 (v) LiamJones 11 19
(J S Moore) *sn rdn and nvr gng wl: a in last quartet* **33/1**
50-0 14 *nse* **Cool And Clear (IRE)**[64] 1289 3-8-13 52 CharlesBishop(5) 10 20
(Pat Eddery) *racd wd: rdn over 4f out and struggling towards rr: nvr a factor* **50/1**

1m 25.82s (1.02) **Going Correction** +0.05s/f (Slow) 14 Ran SP% **122.8**
Speed ratings (Par 97): **96,95,93,93,93 92,91,89,89,83 80,80,78,78**
toteswingers 1&2 £11.10, 1&3 £5.00, 2&3 £9.50 CSF £167.83 CT £639.31 TOTE £9.10: £2.20, £3.70, £1.50; EX 103.20 Trifecta £422.00 Pool: £5,101.78 - 9.06 winning units..
Owner Ushers Court **Bred** Peter Harris **Trained** Upper Lambourn, Berks

FOCUS
A moderate handicap in which only two of these had hit the target and that remains the case. It resulted in another Lingfield master-class from replacement rider George Baker.

2951 AURORA FIREWORKS H'CAP 7f (P)
4:15 (4:18) (Class 5) (0-75,75) 3-Y-0 £3,234 (£962; £481; £240) Stalls Low

Form RPR
-201 1 **Clement (IRE)**[34] 1928 3-9-2 70 JohnFahy 3 77
(Eve Johnson Houghton) *hld up in 6th: prog on inner wl over 1f out: clsd to ld last 120yds: styd on wl* **12/1**[3]
160 2 *1* **Repetition**[18] 2408 3-9-3 71 TomQueally 2 76
(Kevin Ryan) *trckd clr ldr: clsd to chal jst ins fnl f: styd on but nt pce of wnr* **5/1**[2]
305 3 *1* **Ready (IRE)**[17] 2439 3-9-7 75 (p) AdamKirby 5 77+
(Garry Moss) *hld up in 7th: nt clr run briefly over 1f out: rdn and r.o fnl f to take 3rd last strides* **5/1**[2]
02-0 4 *nse* **Danz Choice (IRE)**[24] 2272 3-9-5 73 RyanMoore 1 76
(Richard Hannon) *chsd ldng trio: drvn to dispute 2nd over 1f out: styd on same pce after* **5/1**[2]
123 5 *1* **Kabbaas (IRE)**[27] 2160 3-9-7 75 AndreaAtzeni 4 74
(Roger Varian) *chsd ldrs in 5th: urged along fr 3f out: nvr rchd ldrs but styd on same pce fr over 1f out* **3/1**[1]
03-0 6 *2* **Poitin**[30] 2049 3-9-0 68 (v[1]) JamesDoyle 7 62
(Harry Dunlop) *led: drew clr after 3f: 5 l ahd whn hanging rt bnd 2f out: wknd and hdd last 120yds* **20/1**
-514 7 *1* **Callmeakhab (IRE)**[11] 2622 3-9-2 70 JamieSpencer 9 61
(Charles Hills) *racd wd: chsd ldng pair: rdn 2f out: lost pl and struggling over 1f out* **3/1**[1]
5064 8 *½* **Katy Spirit (IRE)**[14] 2528 3-8-8 62 LiamKeniry 8 52
(Michael Blanshard) *hld up in last pair: pushed along 2f out: reminders and no prog fnl f* **66/1**
0-54 9 *3* **Whitford (IRE)**[112] 623 3-8-6 60 ow2 SaleemGolam 6 42
(Chris Dwyer) *hld up in last pair: rdn and no prog over 2f out* **66/1**

1m 25.21s (0.41) **Going Correction** +0.05s/f (Slow) 9 Ran SP% **115.4**
Speed ratings (Par 99): **99,97,96,96,95 93,92,91,88**
toteswingers 1&2 £10.30, 1&3 £8.60, 2&3 £5.80 CSF £69.85 CT £342.68 TOTE £13.30: £2.80, £2.10, £2.20; EX 78.30 Trifecta £846.10 Pool: £4,332.23 - 3.84 winning units..
Owner Mrs R F Johnson Houghton **Bred** P Kelly **Trained** Blewbury, Oxon

FOCUS
An ordinary 3yo handicap run at a furious pace.

2952 FOLLOW US ON TWITTER @LINGFIELDPARK MAIDEN STKS (DIV I) 1m 2f (P)
4:45 (4:46) (Class 5) 3-Y-0 £2,726 (£805; £402) Stalls Low

Form RPR
1 **Air Of Glory (IRE)** 3-9-5 0 MickaelBarzalona 10 84+
(Saeed bin Suroor) *rn green at various times in rr: prog on wd outside fr 4f out: led jst over 2f out: drvn to assert over 1f out: hld on nr fin* **7/4**[1]
03 2 *¾* **Circus Turn (USA)**[14] 2548 3-9-5 0 RyanMoore 4 83
(Sir Michael Stoute) *trckd ldrs: pushed along 3f out: outpcd 2f out: drvn and rallied over 1f out: chsd wnr ins fnl f: clsng at fin* **11/4**[2]
-225 3 *2* **Khudoua**[39] 1804 3-9-5 77 (b) RobertHavlin 5 79
(John Gosden) *trckd ldr after 2f: upsides 3f out: nt qckn sn after and lost pl: tried to rally over 1f out: one pce* **4/1**[3]
3325 4 *2 ½* **Punditry**[33] 1955 3-9-5 72 (b) NickyMackay 9 74
(John Gosden) *trckd ldrs: prog on outer to ld briefly over 2f out: nt qckn w wnr over 1f out: fdd ins fnl f* **14/1**
5 *½* **Pernica** 3-9-0 0 LukeMorris 2 68+
(Lucy Wadham) *settled in last pair: pumped along and sme prog on outer over 2f out: styd on fr over 1f out: nrst fin* **16/1**
05 6 *2 ¼* **Delicious Poison**[21] 2340 3-9-5 0 (t) JamesDoyle 8 68
(James Fanshawe) *settled in midfield: outpcd fr 3f out: urged along and kpt on one pce fnl 2f* **16/1**
3-4 7 *3 ¼* **Zeva**[27] 2164 3-9-0 0 AdamKirby 7 57
(David Simcock) *mde most to over 2f out: wknd qckly over 1f out* **8/1**
0 8 *7* **Emerald Art (IRE)**[17] 2447 3-9-0 0 SteveDrowne 3 43
(J W Hills) *a towards rr: rdn and struggling wl over 2f out* **50/1**
00 9 *1 ¾* **Alsaqi (IRE)**[8] 2709 3-9-5 0 (b[1]) FrankieMcDonald 11 45
(John Butler) *hld up in last pair: outpcd fr 3f out: nvr a factor* **100/1**
00 10 *2 ¼* **Switch On**[14] 2547 3-9-5 0 GeorgeBaker 6 41
(Chris Wall) *chsd ldr 2f: prom tl wknd 3f out: eased* **50/1**

2m 5.56s (-1.04) **Going Correction** +0.05s/f (Slow) 10 Ran SP% **117.5**
Speed ratings (Par 99): **106,105,103,101,101 99,97,91,90,88**
toteswingers 1&2 £2.50, 1&3 £2.50, 2&3 £2.30 CSF £6.58 TOTE £1.90: £1.20, £1.60, £1.40; EX 8.50 Trifecta £17.00 Pool: £4,152.33 - 182.91 winning units..
Owner Godolphin **Bred** Mark & Pippa Hackett **Trained** Newmarket, Suffolk

FOCUS
An interesting maiden in which they went a fair pace.

2953 FOLLOW US ON TWITTER @LINGFIELDPARK MAIDEN STKS (DIV II) 1m 2f (P)
5:15 (5:17) (Class 5) 3-Y-0 £2,726 (£805; £402) Stalls Low

Form RPR
0-2 1 **Bedouin Invader (IRE)**[36] 1882 3-9-5 0 RyanMoore 7 87
(Sir Michael Stoute) *mde virtually all: drvn and hrd pressed fr over 1f out: hld on wl* **8/1**[3]
2-42 2 *nk* **Thouwra (IRE)**[16] 2480 3-9-5 79 MickaelBarzalona 5 86
(Saeed bin Suroor) *trckd wnr after 2f: rdn to chal over 1f out: edgd lft sn after: failed to go past* **4/5**[1]
24-4 3 *3 ¾* **Estifzaaz (IRE)**[48] 1618 3-9-5 77 SteveDrowne 3 79
(Charles Hills) *t.k.h: trckd wnr 2f: styd cl up: rdn to try to chal on inner over 1f out: fdd fnl f* **14/1**
04 4 *nk* **She's Late**[17] 2442 3-9-5 0 RobertHavlin 10 78+
(John Gosden) *t.k.h: hld up bhd ldrs: outpcd and shkn up briefly 2f out: kpt on one pce after* **7/2**[2]
0 5 *1 ½* **Bravestar (IRE)**[34] 1926 3-9-5 0 TedDurcan 4 75
(David Lanigan) *hld up in midfield: gng bttr than many 3f out: outpcd and shkn up 2f out: kpt on* **100/1**

6 nk **Hunting Ground (USA)** 3-9-5 0 KierenFallon 9 74
(Saeed bin Suroor) *sn wl there on outer: lost pl and grnd whn wd bnd 2f out: one pce after* **8/1**[3]

0- 7 1 1/4 **Missed Call (IRE)**[284] 5551 3-9-0 0 TomQueally 8 67
(Sir Henry Cecil) *hld up in midfield: outpcd over 2f out: shkn up over 1f out: hanging and rn green: no prog* **25/1**

8 2 3/4 **Elas Law** 3-9-0 0 JamesDoyle 11 61
(Jeremy Noseda) *hld up in rr: outpcd over 2f out: no ch after* **33/1**

0 9 12 **Secret Song**[13] 2576 3-9-5 0 LukeMorris 6 42
(Sir Mark Prescott Bt) *a in rr: lost tch w main gp over 3f out: bhd after* **100/1**

10 25 **Violet Plum** 3-9-0 0 IanMongan 2
(Laura Mongan) *slowly away: a last: t.o 4f out* **100/1**

-0 P **Salford Excel**[29] 2084 3-9-0 0 AdamKirby 1
(Marco Botti) *chsd ldrs tl lost action and p.u 4f out: dismntd* **33/1**

2m 6.48s (-0.12) **Going Correction** +0.05s/f (Slow) 11 Ran SP% **119.4**
Speed ratings (Par 99): **102,101,98,98,97 97,96,93,84,64**
toteswingers 1&2 £1.90, 1&3 £7.60, 2&3 £4.30 CSF £14.77 TOTE £6.50: £2.40, £1.10, £4.20; EX 15.90 Trifecta £83.90 Pool: £4,433.41 - 39.58 winning units..
Owner Saeed Suhail **Bred** L Mulryan **Trained** Newmarket, Suffolk

FOCUS
They didn't seem to go as quick early in this division and the winning time was nearly a second slower then the first leg.

2954 LINGFIELD PARK SUPPORTS YOUNG EPILEPSY H'CAP 1m (P)
5:45 (5:55) (Class 6) (0-60,60) 4-Y-0+ **£2,045** (£603; £302) **Stalls** High

Form RPR

5000 1 **Super Duplex**[19] 2395 6-9-5 **58** IanMongan 10 66
(Pat Phelan) *chsd ldr: rdn wl over 2f out and stl 3 l down: clsd over 1f out: led jst ins fnl f: drvn out* **8/1**[3]

5511 2 3/4 **Teen Ager (FR)**[57] 1426 9-9-7 **60** (p) TomMcLaughlin 8 66
(Paul Burgoyne) *hld up in midfield: prog on outer over 2f out: chsd ldng pair over 1f out: styd on to take 2nd ins fnl f: nt rch wnr* **8/1**[3]

004 3 hd **Divine Rule (IRE)**[7] 2747 5-9-7 **60** (p) JimCrowley 4 66
(Laura Mongan) *hld up in rr: prog jst over 2f out: rdn and styd on to take 3rd wl ins fnl f: gaining at fin* **8/1**[3]

2030 4 1 1/4 **Indian Violet (IRE)**[14] 2534 7-8-12 **54** DarrenEgan(3) 11 57
(Zoe Davison) *dwlt: hld up in last pair: prog wl over 1f out: styd on wl fnl f: nrst fin* **33/1**

0001 5 1/2 **Munaawib**[13] 2578 5-8-13 **52** (t) PatCosgrave 7 54
(Charles Smith) *racd wd: shoved along in midfield and struggling fr 1/2-way: styd on fr over 1f out: nrst fin* **14/1**

00-1 6 hd **Poetry Writer**[40] 1781 4-9-3 **56** LiamKeniry 3 57
(Michael Blanshard) *chsd ldrs: rdn 3f out: tried to cl fr 2f out: kpt on same pce* **6/1**[2]

4-05 7 nk **Men Don't Cry (IRE)**[15] 2514 4-8-12 **51** TomQueally 12 51
(Ed de Giles) *racd wd: prom: rdn wl over 2f out: tried to cl over 1f out: one pce* **8/1**[3]

2465 8 3/4 **Spirit Of Xaar (IRE)**[13] 2417 7-9-7 **60** (p) RobertHavlin 6 59
(Linda Jewell) *hld up in last pair: rdn and prog wl over 1f out: styd on same pce fnl f* **6/1**[2]

0502 9 hd **Karate (IRE)**[32] 1981 5-9-0 **58** (vt) NicoleNordblad(5) 9 56
(Hans Adielsson) *led at str pce: 3 l clr 2f out: hdd & wknd rapidly jst ins fnl f* **5/1**[1]

300- 10 3 3/4 **Mitch Rapp (USA)**[286] 5479 4-9-4 **57** JamieSpencer 2 47
(Jamie Osborne) *chsd ldng pair: str reminders 1/2-way and racd awkwardly: wknd over 2f out* **5/1**[1]

5061 11 18 **Spinning Ridge (IRE)**[29] 2072 8-9-5 **58** (b) LukeMorris 1 6
(Ronald Harris) *dwlt: rcvrd into midfield: wknd rapidly over 2f out: t.o* **16/1**

00-0 12 23 **Fault**[40] 1783 7-8-13 **52** FrankieMcDonald 5
(Zoe Davison) *chsd ldrs tl wknd rapidly over 2f out: wl t.o* **66/1**

1m 38.22s (0.02) **Going Correction** +0.05s/f (Slow) 12 Ran SP% **123.3**
Speed ratings (Par 101): **101,100,100,98,98 98,97,97,96,93 75,52**
toteswingers 1&2 £19.10, 1&3 £16.10, 2&3 £18.10 CSF £73.64 CT £548.87 TOTE £9.60: £3.50, £2.90, £2.70; EX 116.10 Trifecta £2241.00 Pool: £3,596.41 - 1.20 winning units..
Owner Special Piping Materials Ltd **Bred** Ermyn Lodge Stud Limited **Trained** Epsom, Surrey

FOCUS
A moderate if competitive handicap, run at a true pace.
T/Plt: £32.10 to a £1 stake. Pool: £60,965.41 - 1,383.18 winning units T/Qpdt: £15.20 to a £1 stake. Pool: £4,294.70 - 209.03 winning units JN

2474 RIPON (R-H)
Tuesday, June 4

OFFICIAL GOING: Good (good to firm in places; 8.5)
Wind: Light; half against Weather: Warm sunshine

2955 BRITISH STALLION STUDS SUPPORTING BRITISH RACING EBF MAIDEN STKS 5f
2:00 (2:01) (Class 5) 2-Y-0 **£3,881** (£1,155; £577; £288) **Stalls** High

Form RPR

0 1 **Ambiance (IRE)**[18] 2411 2-9-5 SamHitchcott 3 77+
(Mick Channon) *pushed rt s: cl up on outer: led wl over 1f out: sn rdn and edgd lft ent fnl f: kpt on strly* **10/3**[3]

2 2 1 3/4 **Searchlight**[16] 2474 2-9-5 PhillipMakin 11 71
(Kevin Ryan) *slt ld on stands' rail: rdn along 2f out: sn hdd: swtchd rt and drvn ent fnl f: kpt on same pce* **5/2**[2]

3 1/2 **Bounty Girl (IRE)** 2-9-0 DuranFentiman 4 64+
(Tim Easterby) *in tch on outer: pushed along and hdwy wl over 1f out: rdn ent fnl f: styd on wl to take 3rd nr fin* **33/1**

0 4 shd **Zac Brown (IRE)**[19] 2401 2-9-5 GrahamGibbons 5 69
(David Barron) *wnt rt s: cl up: pushed along 2f out: sn rdn and one pce* **9/4**[1]

5 3/4 **Offshore Bond** 2-9-5 MichaelO'Connell 6 66
(Jedd O'Keeffe) *chsd ldrs: pushed along over 2f out: rdn wl over 1f out: no imp fnl f* **12/1**

6 2 1/4 **Minley** 2-9-5 GrahamLee 7 58+
(Rae Guest) *midfield: pushed along 1/2-way: styd on appr fnl f: nrst fin* **20/1**

00 7 1 1/2 **Lady Liz**[17] 2458 2-9-0 AndrewMullen 8 50+
(George Moore) *in rr: pushed along bef 1/2-way: swtchd rt and rdn over 2f out: n.d* **200/1**

44 8 1/2 **Bandolier**[31] 2005 2-9-0 GeorgeChaloner(5) 2 51
(Richard Fahey) *s.i.s: a towards rr* **40/1**

33 9 8 **Captain Midnight (IRE)**[32] 1989 2-9-5 RobertWinston 9 22
(David Brown) *chsd ldrs: stmbld and lost action over 1f out: hvly eased* **9/1**

10 1 **Under Approval** 2-9-5 DanielTudhope 1 18
(David O'Meara) *a towards rr* **28/1**

11 1 1/4 **Beltor** 2-9-5 TomEaves 10 14
(Michael Dods) *stdd s: a bhd* **33/1**

1m 0.18s (0.18) **Going Correction** -0.05s/f (Good) 11 Ran SP% **117.1**
Speed ratings (Par 93): **96,93,92,92,91 87,85,84,71,69 67**
toteswingers 1&2 £3.00, 1&3 £30.80, 2&3 £15.80 CSF £11.26 TOTE £5.10: £1.70, £1.40, £9.20; EX 14.30 Trifecta £394.80 Pool: £3,434.13 - 6.52 winning units..
Owner Prince A A Faisal **Bred** John McEnery **Trained** West Ilsley, Berks

FOCUS
Some leading stables were represented in this maiden which was run at a fair pace, with the prominent runners dominating. The form looks decent.

2956 FOLLOW @RIPONRACES ON TWITTER FILLIES' H'CAP 1m 1f 170y
2:30 (2:31) (Class 5) (0-70,65) 4-Y-0+ **£3,234** (£962; £481; £240) **Stalls** Low

Form RPR

363- 1 **Maybeme**[216] 7495 7-8-8 **52** ow1 (p) AndrewElliott 13 64
(Neville Bycroft) *midfield: hdwy on outer 4f out: trckd ldrs 3f out: sn cl up: rdn to ld wl over 1f out: drvn and edgd rt ent fnl f: styd on wl towards fin* **14/1**

0-25 2 1 **Reset City**[8] 2710 7-9-3 **61** FrannyNorton 11 71
(Mark Johnston) *hld up in rr: hdwy on outer over 3f out: trckd ldrs 2f out: effrt over 1f out: sn swtchd rt and rdn to chal ent fnl f: ev ch tl drvn and no ex last 100yds* **13/2**[2]

5-52 3 3 3/4 **Cabal**[81] 1015 6-8-9 **56** (b) NeilFarley(3) 7 58
(Andrew Crook) *hld up: hdwy over 4f out: chsd ldrs wl over 2f out: sn rdn and ev ch tl drvn and one pce ent fnl f* **22/1**

0-30 4 1 1/4 **Ailsa Craig (IRE)**[14] 2555 7-9-0 **58** JamesSullivan 12 58
(Edwin Tuer) *trckd ldr: cl up 4f out: led 3f out: rdn and hdd 2f out: sn drvn and grad wknd* **7/1**[3]

3-23 5 3/4 **Bobs Her Uncle**[22] 2311 4-9-7 **65** GrahamLee 2 63
(James Bethell) *trckd ldrs: effrt over 2f out: sn rdn and no imp* **2/1**[1]

36-0 6 1 **Miss Ella Jade**[22] 2316 4-8-7 **51** PaulQuinn 1 47
(Richard Whitaker) *trckd ldrs: pushed along 3f out: rdn over 2f out: sn one pce* **17/2**

3232 7 3 1/2 **Imaginary World (IRE)**[15] 2514 5-9-4 **62** RobertWinston 3 51
(John Balding) *hld up in rr: hdwy 3f out: nt clr run and sltly hmpd over 2f out: sn swtchd lft to outer and rdn: nvr nr ldrs* **8/1**

-005 8 4 1/2 **Loukoumi**[14] 2536 5-8-7 **51** DuranFentiman 10 31
(Tim Easterby) *trckd ldrs: hdwy 4f out: effrt 3f out: rdn over 2f out and sn wknd* **16/1**

650- 9 17 **Margo Channing**[239] 6924 4-8-8 **52** TomEaves 5
(Micky Hammond) *a in rr: bhd whn hmpd wl over 1f out* **40/1**

01- 10 23 **Silly Gilly (IRE)**[252] 6562 9-9-3 **61** DaleSwift 9
(Ron Barr) *led: rdn along 4f out: hdd 3f out and sn wknd: in rr whn hmpd wl over 1f out* **16/1**

30-2 P **Her Nibbs**[25] 2237 4-8-13 **57** PJMcDonald 8
(Micky Hammond) *chsd ldrs on inner: rdn along wl over 2f out: lost action and p.u wl over 1f out: fatally injured* **9/1**

2m 2.09s (-3.31) **Going Correction** -0.275s/f (Firm) 11 Ran SP% **116.0**
Speed ratings (Par 100): **102,101,98,97,96 95,93,89,75,57**
toteswingers 1&2 £11.60, 1&3 £13.50, 2&3 £14.60 CSF £100.91 CT £1999.91 TOTE £18.70: £5.60, £2.10, £4.00; EX 136.90 Trifecta £2355.20 Part won. Pool: £3,140.39 - 0.58 winning units..
Owner Mrs J Dickinson **Bred** Harts Farm And Stud **Trained** Brandsby, N Yorks

FOCUS
An open handicap run at a steady pace.

2957 WEATHERBYS BANK H'CAP 1m 1f 170y
3:00 (3:00) (Class 4) (0-80,77) 3-Y-0 **£4,851** (£1,443; £721; £360) **Stalls** Low

Form RPR

5004 1 **Zaitsev (IRE)**[17] 2464 3-8-5 **61** JoeFanning 5 76+
(Ollie Pears) *led: qcknd clr 2f out: rdn and kpt on wl fnl f* **25/1**

6-61 2 3 1/4 **Special Meaning**[7] 2742 3-8-12 **68** 6ex FrannyNorton 6 79+
(Mark Johnston) *towards rr: pushed along over 4f out: rdn 3f out: hdwy over 2f out: swtchd rt and drvn ent fnl f: keeping on same pce whn n.m.r on inner wl ins fnl f: tk 2nd last 75yds* **11/4**[1]

000- 3 1/2 **Tuscan Fun**[224] 7304 3-8-12 **68** DaneO'Neill 2 75+
(Roger Varian) *trckd ldrs: hdwy 3f out: chsd wnr over 2f out: rdn wl over 1f out: drvn and edgd rt ins fnl f: one pce* **5/1**

240 4 6 **Cavalieri (IRE)**[22] 2306 3-9-1 **71** GrahamLee 7 66
(William Jarvis) *dwlt and pushed along s: in rr: stdy hdwy 4f out: rdn to chse ldrs 2f out: kpt on u.p fnl f* **7/2**[2]

-202 5 2 1/2 **Noble Bull (IRE)**[12] 2604 3-9-6 **76** (b) JamesMcDonald 4 66
(Charles Hills) *hld up towards rr: hdwy 1/2-way: trckd ldrs 3f out: rdn to chse ldng pair wl over 1f out: sn drvn and wknd fnl f* **4/1**[3]

5214 6 5 **Shearian**[21] 2342 3-8-10 **66** RoystonFfrench 1 46
(Tracy Waggott) *chsd ldrs on inner: rdn along over 3f out: wknd over 2f out* **12/1**

-12U 7 2 1/4 **Order Of Service**[11] 2624 3-9-2 **72** SeanLevey 9 47
(David Brown) *t.k.h: trckd ldr: pushed along over 3f out: rdn wl over 2f out: sn edgd rt and wknd* **9/1**

05-6 8 10 **Spithead**[11] 2635 3-8-6 **62** ow1 PJMcDonald 3 17
(Ian McInnes) *chsd ldrs: rdn along wl over 3f out: sn wknd* **20/1**

6-50 9 4 1/2 **Jackaddock**[22] 2306 3-8-8 **64** TomEaves 10
(James Bethell) *chsd ldrs: rdn along 4f out: sn wknd* **50/1**

2m 1.26s (-4.14) **Going Correction** -0.275s/f (Firm) 9 Ran SP% **113.8**
Speed ratings (Par 101): **105,102,102,97,95 91,89,81,77**
toteswingers 1&2 £7.20, 1&3 £17.70, 2&3 £3.80 CSF £90.44 CT £413.13 TOTE £34.30: £6.60, £1.70, £2.50; EX 109.30 Trifecta £1265.90 Pool: £3,661.46 - 2.16 winning units..
Owner Mrs Z Wentworth **Bred** J F Tuthill **Trained** Norton, N Yorks

FOCUS
Plenty of unexposed types in this interesting handicap. The pace was honest with the winner making all.

2958 WILMOT-SMITH MEMORIAL H'CAP 1m
3:30 (3:31) (Class 3) (0-95,93) 4-Y-0 **£7,561** (£2,263; £1,131; £566; £282) **Stalls** Low

Form RPR

350- 1 **Suits Me**[235] 7030 10-9-1 **87** PhillipMakin 9 99
(David Barron) *mde virtually all: rdn and qcknd clr wl over 1f out: r.o strly* **16/1**

The Form Book Flat, Raceform Ltd, Compton, RG20 6NL.

3-25 **2** 2¾ **Lord Aeryn (IRE)**^{31} 2029 6-9-3 **89**.................................... DavidNolan 4 95
(Richard Fahey) *trckd ldrs: hdwy 3f out: rdn wl over 1f out: drvn and kpt on fnl f* **11/2**^{2}

0644 **3** *nk* **Dubai Dynamo**^{12} 2592 8-9-3 **89**.................................... PJMcDonald 2 95
(Ruth Carr) *dwlt and in rr: hdwy wl over 2f out: rdn over 1f out: drvn and kpt on fnl f: nrst fin* **7/2**^{1}

0065 **4** *hd* **Osteopathic Remedy (IRE)**^{16} 2477 9-9-4 **90**.................. TomEaves 1 95
(Michael Dods) *trckd ldrs on inner: hdwy 3f out: rdn along wl over 1f out: n.m.r on inner and kpt on fnl f* **14/1**

4123 **5** *shd* **Frontier Fighter**^{16} 2477 5-9-5 **91**............................. DanielTudhope 11 95
(David O'Meara) *t.k.h: trckd wnr: effrt 3f out: rdn along 2f out: drvn and one pce fnl f* **7/2**^{1}

-100 **6** ½ **St Moritz (IRE)**^{19} 2399 7-9-7 **93**.................................. AdrianNicholls 3 96
(David Nicholls) *hld up in rr: swtchd to outer and hdwy 3f out: rdn to chse ldrs wl over 1f out: drvn and one pce fnl f* **16/1**

5-40 **7** *nk* **Green Howard**^{17} 2463 5-8-11 **83**.................................. RobertWinston 5 85
(Robin Bastiman) *dwlt and in rr: hdwy on wd outside wl over 2f out: rdn wl over 1f out: drvn and one pce fnl f* **13/2**^{3}

0-04 **8** 6 **Sam Nombulist**^{14} 2541 5-8-13 **85**..............................(p) FrannyNorton 6 74
(Richard Whitaker) *trckd ldrs on inner: rdn along over 2f out: grad wknd* **12/1**

400- **9** 8 **Venutius**^{235} 7030 6-8-13 **85**...................................... MichaelO'Connell 10 55
(Philip Kirby) *dwlt and in rr: hdwy 1/2-way: rdn to chse ldrs over 2f out: wknd wl over 1f out* **28/1**

2-01 **10** *hd* **Ardmay (IRE)**^{16} 2477 4-9-4 **90**.. AmyRyan 7 60
(Kevin Ryan) *trckd ldrs: hdwy on outer over 3f out: rdn along wl over 2f out: sn wknd* **7/1**

1m 37.51s (-3.89) **Going Correction** -0.275s/f (Firm) **10** Ran SP% **115.2**
Speed ratings (Par 107): **108,105,104,104,104 104,103,97,89,89**
toteswingers 1&2 £22.20, 1&3 £18.60, 2&3 £5.80 CSF £100.43 CT £392.78 TOTE £24.30: £5.30, £1.80, £1.60; EX 176.50 Trifecta £649.50 Pool: £3,304.18 - 3.81 winning units..
Owner D E Cook **Bred** R S A Urquhart **Trained** Maunby, N Yorks

FOCUS
An honest pace for this decent handicap, with the winner once again making all.

2959 WEATHERBYS HAMILTON INSURANCE H'CAP 6f
4:00 (4:03) (Class 5) (0-70,70) 3-Y-O **£3,234** (£962; £481; £240) **Stalls** High

Form RPR

6-30 **1** **Bondesire**^{12} 2593 3-9-7 **70**.. DanielTudhope 11 77+
(David O'Meara) *mde all: rdn 2f out and sn edgd rt: drvn and hung rt ins fnl f: kpt on wl towards fin* **9/4**^{1}

5450 **2** 1 **Sand Boy (IRE)**^{19} 2394 3-9-7 **70**.............................. JamesMcDonald 2 74
(Charles Hills) *wnt rt s: trckd ldrs on outer: effrt 2f out: rdn to chal and edgd lft ins fnl f: kpt on* **10/1**

5404 **3** ½ **Deepest Blue**^{6} 2779 3-8-10 **66**................................ LukeLeadbitter$^{(7)}$ 12 69
(Declan Carroll) *t.k.h: trckd wnr on rail: hdwy 2f out: rdn to chal ent fnl f and ev ch tl edgd rt and one pce last 100yds* **14/1**

1-40 **4** 2 **Dream Vale (IRE)**^{14} 2542 3-8-12 **66**.............................. DarylByrne$^{(5)}$ 6 63
(Tim Easterby) *dwlt and hmpd s: in rr and sn swtchd lft to stands' rail: hdwy 2f out: sn rdn and kpt on fnl f: nrst fin* **40/1**

-360 **5** 3½ **Dream Ally (IRE)**^{18} 2408 3-9-7 **70**..............................(p) PhillipMakin 10 56
(Jedd O'Keeffe) *cl up: rdn along over 2f out: sn drvn and grad wknd* **5/1**^{2}

13-0 **6** *hd* **Gallena**^{29} 2098 3-9-6 **69**.. GrahamLee 8 54
(William Haggas) *cl up: rdn along 2f out: sn drvn and grad wknd* **7/1**^{3}

6333 **7** 2¼ **Bapak Bangsawan**^{3} 2888 3-8-12 **68**.........................(p) KevinStott$^{(7)}$ 4 47
(Kevin Ryan) *cl up: rdn to chal 2f out: sn drvn and wknd appr fnl f* **5/1**^{2}

420 **8** 2 **Tom's Anna (IRE)**^{15} 2506 3-9-5 **68**............................. DuranFentiman 3 41
(Tim Easterby) *hld up in tch: effrt on outer wl over 2f out: sn rdn along and n.d* **25/1**

030- **9** ½ **Masai King (IRE)**^{238} 6953 3-8-7 **56**............................ AndrewMullen 9 27
(Robin Bastiman) *trckd ldrs: rdn along over 2f out: sn wknd* **50/1**

0340 **10** 3½ **Ayasha**^{29} 2076 3-9-3 **66**.. TomEaves 7 27
(Bryan Smart) *dwlt: hdwy 1/2-way: rdn to chse ldrs over 2f out: sn wknd* **18/1**

4355 **11** 8 **Silca's Dream**^{11} 2623 3-9-3 **66**..............................(v) SamHitchcott 5 3
(Mick Channon) *wnt lft s: a towards rr* **14/1**

1m 12.81s (-0.19) **Going Correction** -0.05s/f (Good) **11** Ran SP% **112.5**
Speed ratings (Par 99): **99,97,97,94,89 89,86,83,83,78 67**
toteswingers 1&2 £9.30, 1&3 £10.50, 2&3 £25.60 CSF £24.30 CT £255.36 TOTE £2.30: £1.50, £3.70, £4.40; EX 39.10 Trifecta £490.00 Pool: £2,547.86 - 3.89 winning units..
Owner Geoff & Sandra Turnbull **Bred** A C M Spalding **Trained** Nawton, N Yorks

FOCUS
An open handicap run at a fair pace with the winner again making all.

2960 SIS LIVE MAIDEN STKS 1m
4:30 (4:31) (Class 5) 3-Y-O **£3,234** (£962; £481; £240) **Stalls** Low

Form RPR

-242 **1** **Sublimation (IRE)**^{45} 1684 3-9-5 80........................... RobertWinston 11 89+
(David Barron) *trckd ldr: cl up over 4f out: led 3f out: rdn clr wl over 1f out: kpt on strly* **5/2**^{2}

54 **2** 2¼ **Mutajally**^{22} 2306 3-9-5 0.. DaneO'Neill 6 84
(Sir Michael Stoute) *trckd ldrs: hdwy 3f out: chsd wnr 2f out and sn rdn: drvn and no imp fnl f* **4/6**^{1}

0 **3** ½ **Rock Choir**^{46} 1666 3-9-0 0..^{1} GrahamLee 10 78+
(William Haggas) *trckd ldrs: hdwy on outer over 3f out: rdn to chse ldng pair wl over 1f out: drvn and one pce fnl f* **7/1**^{3}

0- **4** 8 **Arch Ebony (USA)**^{304} 4792 3-9-5 0........................... DanielTudhope 3 64+
(David O'Meara) *trckd ldrs: hdwy 3f out: rdn along over 2f out: sn one pce* **25/1**

-013 **5** 2 **Correggio**^{15} 2507 3-9-5 73.. PJMcDonald 1 60
(Micky Hammond) *chsd ldng pair on inner: rdn along over 3f out: one pce fnl 2f* **12/1**

0 **6** 4 **West Beat**^{22} 2306 3-9-0 0... DavidNolan 2 45
(David O'Meara) *in tch: effrt over 3f out: sn rdn along and no imp* **66/1**

04 **7** 2½ **Woodley Wonder (IRE)**^{63} 1305 3-9-5 0.............................. PhillipMakin 4 45
(Ben Haslam) *led: rdn along 4f out: hdd 3f out and sn wknd* **66/1**

06 **8** 8 **Bannockburn Boy**^{21} 2340 3-9-5 0.............................. DuranFentiman 9 26
(Tim Easterby) *a towards rr* **66/1**

0 **9** 3¼ **Sanderiana**^{6} 2765 3-9-0 0... TomEaves 8 14
(Mel Brittain) *a in rr: bhd fnl 3f* **100/1**

00- **10** 1 **Haarmonic**^{206} 7686 3-9-5 0.. AmyRyan 7 17
(Richard Whitaker) *a in rr: bhd fnl 3f* **100/1**

11 *28* **Lucky Rebel** 3-9-2 0.. MarkCoumbe$^{(3)}$ 5
(Lisa Williamson) *s.i.s: a bhd* **100/1**

1m 38.34s (-3.06) **Going Correction** -0.275s/f (Firm) **11** Ran SP% **120.0**
Speed ratings (Par 99): **104,101,101,93,91 87,84,76,73,72 44**
toteswingers 1&2 £1.30, 1&3 £2.60, 2&3 £1.80 CSF £4.52 TOTE £4.00: £1.30, £1.10, £1.50; EX 6.90 Trifecta £18.30 Pool: £5,001.52 - 204.33 winning units..
Owner The Dream Team **Bred** Pier House Stud **Trained** Maunby, N Yorks

FOCUS
The pace was steady for this uncompetitive maiden, with the market principals dominating.

2961 LADIES DAY 20TH JUNE BOOK NOW H'CAP 1m 4f 10y
5:00 (5:04) (Class 5) (0-70,64) 4-Y-O+ **£3,234** (£962; £481; £240) **Stalls** Low

Form RPR

50-0 **1** **Valantino Oyster (IRE)**^{40} 1789 6-8-12 **55**.....................(p) JoeFanning 5 63
(Tracy Waggott) *trckd ldr: cl up 4f out: led over 2f out: rdn over 1f out: drvn fnl f: kpt on wl towards fin* **9/2**^{3}

-403 **2** 1 **Honoured (IRE)**^{15} 2511 6-9-4 **61**..............................(t) AndrewMullen 4 68
(Michael Appleby) *trckd ldrs: hdwy 4f out: swtchd lft and rdn wl over 1f out: chsd wnr ent fnl f: sn drvn and ev ch tl no ex last 75yds* **4/1**^{2}

5060 **3** 1¾ **Light The City (IRE)**^{11} 2629 6-8-11 **54**.......................... JamesSullivan 3 58
(Ruth Carr) *led: jnd 4f out: rdn along over 3f out: drvn and hdd over 2f out: kpt on u.p fnl f* **16/1**

-122 **4** 1¼ **Amtired**^{83} 989 7-9-3 **60**.. DaleSwift 1 64
(Brian Ellison) *trckd ldrs on inner: effrt 3f out: rdn along to chse ldng trio wl over 1f out: drvn and kpt on same pce fnl f* **11/4**^{1}

066- **5** 1¼ **Swift Encounter (IRE)**^{252} 6559 4-9-5 **62**........................ PJMcDonald 2 62+
(Ann Duffield) *hld up towards rr: hdwy on inner wl over 2f out: rdn along wl over 1f out: kpt on fnl f: nrst fin* **9/1**

500- **6** 1¼ **The Lodge Road (IRE)**^{262} 6258 5-9-5 **62**.......................... GrahamLee 12 60+
(Martin Todhunter) *hld up towards rr: stdy hdwy on outer over 4f out: rdn to chse ldrs wl over 2f out: drvn and wknd over 1f out* **25/1**

350- **7** 1¼ **Bavarian Nordic (USA)**^{238} 6957 8-9-2 **59**.....................(v) AmyRyan 11 55
(Richard Whitaker) *hld up and bhd: stdy hdwy on wd outside 3f out: chsd ldrs 2f out: sn rdn and no imp* **25/1**

420- **8** ¾ **Celtic Step**^{227} 7251 9-8-12 **55**................................... RoystonFfrench 13 50
(Peter Niven) *in tch: hdwy to chse ldrs 3f out: rdn along 2f out: drvn and wknd over 1f out* **11/1**

-040 **9** 1¼ **Raleigh Quay (IRE)**^{11} 2633 6-9-5 **62**............................... PhillipMakin 7 55+
(Micky Hammond) *hld up: a in rr* **10/1**

35-0 **10** ½ **Kathlatino**^{14} 2555 6-8-13 **56**.. DuranFentiman 9 49
(Micky Hammond) *a towards rr* **28/1**

34/0 **11** 1 **Tourtiere**^{17} 2462 5-9-0 **57**.. AndrewElliott 6 48
(George Moore) *a towards rr* **16/1**

50 **12** 1½ **Hussar Ballad (USA)**^{7} 2753 4-9-7 **64**................................ TomEaves 8 53
(Mel Brittain) *trckd ldrs on outer: hdwy to chse ldng pair 1/2-way: rdn along over 3f out: drvn over 2f out and sn wknd* **50/1**

2m 34.25s (-2.45) **Going Correction** -0.275s/f (Firm) **12** Ran SP% **117.1**
Speed ratings (Par 103): **97,96,95,94,93 92,91,91,90,90 89,88**
toteswingers 1&2 £5.10, 1&3 £16.40, 2&3 £15.70 CSF £21.61 CT £265.95 TOTE £4.50: £1.80, £1.70, £5.60; EX 20.80 Trifecta £267.70 Pool: £3,198.35 - 8.95 winning units..
Owner Steve Sawley **Bred** Des Vere Hunt Farm Co And Jack Ronan **Trained** Spennymoor, Co Durham

FOCUS
A moderate handicap run at a steady pace with the prominent racers again at an advantage.
T/Jkpt: Not won. T/Plt: £127.10 to a £1 stake. Pool: £71,474.20 - 410.40 winning units T/Qpdt: £17.70 to a £1 stake. Pool £6,695.13 - 279.35 winning units JR

2758 YARMOUTH (L-H)
Tuesday, June 4

OFFICIAL GOING: Good to firm (7.5)
Wind: Fresh; behind Weather: Dry and bright

2962 SEALIFE CENTRE H'CAP 6f 3y
5:55 (5:59) (Class 6) (0-65,65) 3-Y-O **£1,940** (£577; £288; £144) **Stalls** Centre

Form RPR

2-20 **1** **Alhaarth Beauty (IRE)**^{41} 1762 3-9-0 **63**................^{1} ThomasBrown$^{(5)}$ 2 74
(Ismail Mohammed) *mde all: rdn and hrd pressed over 1f out: hld hd high but forged ahd ins fnl f: styd on* **8/1**^{3}

002- **2** 1¾ **Blessing Box**^{216} 7481 3-9-6 **64**.. ChrisCatlin 8 70+
(Chris Wall) *plld hrd: chsd ldng pair: rdn and effrt wl over 1f out: styd on same pce fnl f: snatched 2nd on post* **4/1**^{1}

3340 **3** *shd* **Free Island**^{34} 1935 3-9-3 **61**.......................................(b^{1}) NeilCallan 6 66
(James Tate) *chsd wnr: rdn and effrt to chal over 1f out: nt qckn 1f out: btn ins fnl f: wknd towards fin and lost 2nd on post* **9/1**

20-6 **4** 3 **Shamiana**^{25} 2215 3-9-3 **61**..(p) MartinDwyer 7 57
(Gerard Butler) *in tch in midfield: rdn and outpcd by ldng trio 2f out: no threat to ldrs but plugged on ins fnl f* **14/1**

3501 **5** 2½ **Secret Advice**^{8} 2702 3-9-3 **61** 6ex.................................... FrederikTylicki 11 50+
(Keith Dalgleish) *taken down early: towards rr and sn niggled along: rdn 1/2-way: outpcd and btn 2f out: plugged on but wl hld after* **9/2**^{2}

-540 **6** *hd* **Imperial Spirit**^{11} 2616 3-8-11 **55**..................................(v) HarryBentley 9 43
(Mick Channon) *in tch in midfield: rdn and outpcd 2f out: plugged on same pce and wl hld fr over 1f out* **16/1**

-534 **7** 2¾ **The Manx Missile**^{42} 1742 3-9-1 **59**................................ HayleyTurner 14 39
(Michael Bell) *in rr: rdn and effrt 1/2-way: no real imp tl plugged on past btn horses fnl f: nvr trbld ldrs* **14/1**

050- **8** ½ **Our Sweet Art**^{165} 8203 3-8-11 **55**................................... PaulHanagan 3 34
(John Best) *in tch in midfield: rdn and struggling over 2f out: sn outpcd and btn 2f out* **20/1**

6200 **9** ¾ **Megaleka**^{33} 1962 3-8-2 **53**.. TimClark$^{(7)}$ 10 29
(Alan Bailey) *in tch in midfield: rdn and struggling over 2f out: wknd 2f out* **33/1**

0-64 **10** 1¾ **Green Monkey**^{15} 2499 3-9-1 **59**..................................(t) FrankieDettori 13 30
(James Fanshawe) *bhd: rdn 1/2-way: no imp: n.d* **8/1**^{3}

3465 **11** *nk* **Al Gharrafa**^{53} 1524 3-9-2 **65**......................................(b) RobertTart$^{(5)}$ 1 35
(Marco Botti) *in tch in midfield: rdn and outpcd jst over 2f out: sn btn: wknd over 1f out* **14/1**

3-00 **12** *nk* **Hats Off**^{141} 207 3-8-2 **46** oh1... JimmyQuinn 5 15
(John Best) *in tch towards rr: rdn and struggling 1/2-way: wl btn fnl 2f* **50/1**

262- **13** ¾ **Pearl Noir**^{202} 7711 3-9-2 **63**..(p) BillyCray$^{(3)}$ 12 30
(Scott Dixon) *stdd s: t.k.h: hld up in rr: rdn and no hdwy 2f out: n.d* **11/1**

6U06 14 3¾ **Forceful Flame**[5] 2791 3-9-2 **60**........(v) MartinLane 4 16
(Robert Eddery) *s.i.s: hdwy into midfield after 1f out: lost pl u.p 1/2-way: sn bhd* **40/1**

1m 12.24s (-2.16) **Going Correction** -0.30s/f (Firm) **14** Ran SP% **116.7**
Speed ratings (Par 97): **102,99,99,95,92 91,88,87,86,84 83,83,82,77**
toteswingers 1&2 £8.80, 1&3 £11.60, 2&3 £10.20 CSF £37.28 CT £306.66 TOTE £8.80: £3.50, £1.80, £2.70; EX 63.80 Trifecta £261.40 Pool: £819.97 - 2.35 winning units..
Owner Abdulla Al Mansoori **Bred** T Boylan **Trained** Newmarket, Suffolk

FOCUS
A modest 3yo sprint handicap in which they went a decent gallop. The first three came clear.

2963 NORFOLKATTRACTIONS.CO.UK FILLIES' H'CAP 1m 3y
6:25 (6:28) (Class 5) (0-70,70) 3-Y-0+ **£2,587** (£770; £384; £192) **Stalls** Centre

Form RPR

020- **1** **Estiqaama (USA)**[220] 7403 3-9-3 **70**........[1] PaulHanagan 6 90+
(William Haggas) *mde all: readily drew wl clr over 2f out: in n.d fnl 2f: eased wl ins fnl f* **11/8**[1]

4442 **2** 6 **Ssafa**[5] 2796 5-9-9 **65**........[1] FrankieDettori 3 71
(Alastair Lidderdale) *hld up in last pair: rdn and effrt 3f out: 3rd and wl btn 2f out: wnt 2nd 1f out: plugged on but wl hld* **2/1**[2]

3622 **3** 3¾ **Gift Of Silence**[11] 2640 4-9-11 **67**........ NeilCallan 8 64
(John Berry) *stmbld leaving stalls: sn rcvrd and chsd ldng pair: wnt 2nd 1/2-way: rdn and outpcd over 2f out: wl btn after and lost 2nd 1f out* **3/1**[3]

34-0 **4** 11 **Atmanna**[36] 1882 4-8-6 **51** oh1........ SimonPearce(3) 7 22
(Zoe Davison) *reluctant to go to post: bhd and nvr gng wl: lost tch 3f out: poor 4th fnl 2f* **50/1**

4-60 **5** 11 **Boleyn**[45] 1697 3-8-6 **59**........ HarryBentley 5 3
(Olly Stevens) *in tch in midfield: rdn and wknd over 3f out: wl bhd fnl 2f* **20/1**

0-60 **6** 16 **Eton Miss (IRE)**[35] 1906 3-8-0 **53** oh8........ JimmyQuinn 2
(Mike Murphy) *taken down early: dwlt: t.k.h and sn rcvrd to chse wnr: lost 2nd over 3f out: sn bhd: t.o fnl 2f* **50/1**

1m 37.86s (-2.74) **Going Correction** -0.30s/f (Firm)
WFA 3 from 4yo+ 11lb **6** Ran SP% **109.1**
Speed ratings (Par 100): **101,95,91,80,69 53**
toteswingers 1&2 £1.10, 1&3 £1.60, 2&3 £1.30 CSF £4.09 CT £5.00 TOTE £2.60: £1.20, £1.60; EX 4.10 Trifecta £5.40 Pool: £2,483.05 - 339.87 winning units..
Owner Hamdan Al Maktoum **Bred** Shadwell Farm LLC **Trained** Newmarket, Suffolk

FOCUS
A modest fillies' handicap for 3yos and up in which they went a decent gallop. The winner looks an improved performer.

2964 MOULTON NURSERIES H'CAP 7f 3y
6:55 (6:55) (Class 4) (0-80,80) 4-Y-0+ **£4,690** (£1,395; £697; £348) **Stalls** Centre

Form RPR

4043 **1** **Azrael**[7] 2752 5-9-0 **73**........ MartinDwyer 9 81
(Alan McCabe) *chsd ldr: rdn and ev ch 2f out: led over 1f out: kpt on u.p fnl f: rdn out* **20/1**

5-00 **2** ½ **First Class**[11] 2638 5-8-2 **61**........ MartinLane 5 68
(Rae Guest) *chsd ldrs: rdn and ev ch 2f out: kpt on u.p but hld fnl 100yds* **16/1**

3-62 **3** ¾ **Flynn's Boy**[18] 2425 5-9-5 **78**........ NeilCallan 6 83
(Rae Guest) *in tch towards rr: swtchd rt and effrt u.p over 1f out: chsd ldng pair ins fnl f: kpt on* **4/1**[2]

0025 **4** 1 **Greyfriarschorista**[17] 2450 6-8-13 **72**........(p) JimmyQuinn 2 74
(Tom Keddy) *racd towards far side tl 1/2-way: in tch: effrt and chsd ldrs 2f out: styd on same pce ins fnl f* **10/1**

-634 **5** nk **Rulesn'regulations**[5] 2797 7-8-8 **70**........ SimonPearce(3) 8 72+
(Alastair Lidderdale) *awkward leaving stalls: hld up in rr: rdn and hdwy over 1f out: kpt on ins fnl f* **16/1**

0-02 **6** ½ **Rough Rock (IRE)**[11] 2638 8-8-7 **66**........ HayleyTurner 7 66+
(Chris Dwyer) *in tch in midfield: rdn 2f out: unable qck over 1f out: kpt on again ins fnl f* **13/2**[3]

-314 **7** ½ **Sound Advice**[8] 2705 4-9-7 **80**........ FrankieDettori 3 80
(Keith Dalgleish) *racd towards far side tl 1/2-way: overall ldr: rdn over 2f out: hdd over 1f out: no ex and btn ins fnl f: eased cl home* **3/1**[1]

1414 **8** 1½ **Valdaw**[32] 1985 5-8-9 **73**........ MichaelJMMurphy(5) 1 68+
(Mike Murphy) *racd towards far side: in tch towards rr: rdn and effrt 2f out: no imp and styd on same pce fnl f* **12/1**

0320 **9** 1 **Savanna Days (IRE)**[24] 2266 4-9-4 **77**........ MartinHarley 4 70
(Mick Channon) *in tch in midfield: hdwy to chse ldrs 1/2-way: rdn and fnd little over 2f out: wknd ins fnl f* **9/1**

2-00 **10** ½ **Lunar Deity**[24] 2255 4-9-6 **79**........(b[1]) ShaneKelly 11 70
(Eve Johnson Houghton) *hld up in tch in last pair: rdn and no hdwy 2f out: nvr trbld ldrs* **10/1**

060- **11** 1¾ **Sheikh The Reins (IRE)**[238] 6973 4-8-9 **68**........ PaulHanagan 10 55
(John Best) *in tch in midfield: rdn and struggling over 2f out: bhd 1f out* **20/1**

1m 23.52s (-3.08) **Going Correction** -0.30s/f (Firm) **11** Ran SP% **115.5**
Speed ratings (Par 105): **105,104,103,102,102 101,100,99,98,97 95**
toteswingers 1&2 £64.70, 1&3 £4.70, 2&3 £14.60 CSF £300.10 CT £1537.01 TOTE £21.80: £6.30, £4.20, £1.60; EX 323.80 Trifecta £960.20 Part won. Pool: £1,280.32 - 0.20 winning units..

Owner Mrs M J McCabe **Bred** Ian Neville Marks **Trained** Averham Park, Notts

FOCUS
A fair handicap for older horses in which they went a strong gallop.

2965 INJURED JOCKEYS FUND H'CAP 5f 43y
7:25 (7:25) (Class 5) (0-70,70) 3-Y-0 **£2,587** (£770; £384; £192) **Stalls** Centre

Form RPR

-432 **1** **Pixilated**[11] 2623 3-9-2 **70**........ RobertTart(5) 2 79+
(Gay Kelleway) *mde all: pushed along and readily wnt clr over 1f out: easily* **5/6**[1]

2-10 **2** 5 **Hand In Glove**[106] 710 3-9-2 **65**........ ShaneKelly 6 56
(Robert Cowell) *chsd wnr: rdn and effrt wl over 1f out: outpcd and btn 1f out: wl but plugged on fnl f* **4/1**[3]

2315 **3** 2½ **Balatina**[29] 2091 3-8-9 **58**........ HayleyTurner 3 40
(Chris Dwyer) *trckd ldrs: effrt and drvn to chse wnr 1f out: sn outpcd and btn: lost 2nd fnl 100yds* **11/4**[2]

000- **4** 12 **Simply Dreaming**[293] 5242 3-8-5 **54**........ JimmyQuinn 4
(Michael Squance) *a outpcd in last* **18/1**

1m 1.47s (-1.23) **Going Correction** -0.30s/f (Firm) **4** Ran SP% **106.5**
Speed ratings (Par 99): **97,89,85,65**
CSF £4.32 TOTE £1.60; EX 4.60 Trifecta £7.80 Pool: £778.27 - 74.63 winning units..
Owner Patricia Crook & Francis Aspin **Bred** A Christou **Trained** Exning, Suffolk

FOCUS
A fair 3yo sprint handicap.

2966 NORFOLKBROADS.COM H'CAP 1m 1f
7:55 (7:55) (Class 5) (0-70,65) 4-Y-0+ **£2,587** (£770; £384; £192) **Stalls** Low

Form RPR

0-06 **1** **My Guardian Angel**[14] 2552 4-9-7 **65**........ NeilCallan 5 72
(Mark H Tompkins) *sn led and mde rest: kpt on u.p fr over 2f out: a holding rivals fnl f: rdn out* **9/2**[3]

30-6 **2** 1¼ **Essell**[147] 105 4-8-6 **50**........ MartinLane 1 55
(Mick Channon) *chsd wnr: rdn and effrt over 2f out: kpt on same pce u.p ins fnl f* **8/1**

6364 **3** shd **Standing Strong (IRE)**[33] 1950 5-9-4 **62**........(b) PaulHanagan 4 66
(Zoe Davison) *t.k.h: hld up in tch in midfield: swtchd rt and effrt over 1f out: chsd ldng pair and drvn ins fnl f: kpt on and pressing for 2nd cl home* **11/4**[2]

03-0 **4** 3½ **Flash Crash**[19] 2383 4-9-2 **63**........ RossAtkinson(3) 6 60
(Robert Cowell) *chsd ldrs: rdn and effrt to press ldrs 2f out: unable qck over 1f out: wknd ins fnl f* **20/1**

110- **5** 3 **Enriching (USA)**[243] 6819 5-9-5 **63**........ ShaneKelly 8 54
(Gary Harrison) *in tch in midfield: rdn and effrt over 2f out: fnd little for press and no imp: wknd ent fnl f* **6/4**[1]

5000 **6** 3¼ **Dubai Emerald (USA)**[88] 927 4-7-9 **46** oh1........ NoelGarbutt(7) 2 31
(Chris Dwyer) *a off the pce in last pair: rdn and no hdwy 4f out: n.d* **33/1**

0400 **7** ¾ **Follow The Flag (IRE)**[6] 2785 9-8-9 **53**........(v) MartinDwyer 9 36
(Alan McCabe) *a bhd: rdn and no hdwy 4f out: n.d* **11/1**

1m 54.97s (-0.83) **Going Correction** -0.025s/f (Good) **7** Ran SP% **112.0**
Speed ratings (Par 103): **102,100,100,97,95 92,91**
toteswingers 1&2 £8.90, 1&3 £3.30, 2&3 £1.30 CSF £37.47 CT £114.77 TOTE £5.70: £3.30, £2.50; EX 31.50 Trifecta £206.80 Pool: £638.68 - 2.31 winning units..
Owner Sarabex **Bred** Dullingham Park **Trained** Newmarket, Suffolk

FOCUS
A modest handicap for older horses.

2967 RACING WELFARE MAIDEN STKS 1m 6f 17y
8:25 (8:25) (Class 5) 3-Y-0 **£2,587** (£770; £384) **Stalls** High

Form RPR

2 **1** **Baihas**[30] 2055 3-9-5 0........ PaulHanagan 2 86+
(Sir Michael Stoute) *chsd rivals: rdn 4f out: hdwy to ld 2f out: wnt clr ent fnl f: rn green but styd on: comf* **8/13**[1]

-035 **2** 2½ **Enaitch (IRE)**[24] 2261 3-9-0 78........ MartinHarley 1 76
(Mick Channon) *t.k.h: chsd ldr tl led 7f out: rdn over 3f out: hdd 2f out: no ex and btn 1f out: plugged on* **9/4**[2]

0-64 **3** 27 **Astrosapphire**[19] 2386 3-9-0 71........ NeilCallan 3 47
(Mark H Tompkins) *racd keenly: led tl 7f out: rdn 3f out: dropped to last over 2f out: wknd 2f out: eased fnl f* **6/1**[3]

3m 7.08s (-0.52) **Going Correction** -0.025s/f (Good) **3** Ran SP% **107.0**
Speed ratings (Par 99): **100,98,83**
CSF £2.25 TOTE £1.50; EX 2.20 Trifecta £1.40 Pool: £754.23 - 389.45 winning units..
Owner Hamdan Al Maktoum **Bred** Cheveley Park Stud Ltd **Trained** Newmarket, Suffolk

FOCUS
A fair small-field staying 3yo maiden in which they went a steady gallop until reaching the back straight. The first two are of interest.

2968 SCROBY SANDS WINDFARM H'CAP 1m 6f 17y
8:55 (8:55) (Class 5) (0-70,70) 4-Y-0+ **£2,587** (£770; £384; £192) **Stalls** High

Form RPR

0240 **1** **Dr Finley (IRE)**[26] 2197 6-8-11 **63**........(v[1]) SimonPearce(3) 3 70
(Lydia Pearce) *led tl rdn ent fnl 2f: hdd and drvn over 1f out: battled on u.p ins fnl f to ld again on post* **16/1**

1054 **2** nse **Knox Overstreet**[3] 2860 5-9-3 **66**........ MartinHarley 1 73
(Mick Channon) *t.k.h: chsd ldng pair: wnt 2nd and stl gng wl over 2f out: led narrowly over 1f out: drvn and fnd little ins fnl f: hdd on post* **11/4**[2]

343 **3** 2½ **Smalib Monterg (FR)**[15] 1837 7-9-7 **70**........(t) HayleyTurner 2 73
(Dr Richard Newland) *hld up in 3rd: hdwy over 3f out: rdn and effrt over 2f out: styd on same pce u.p ins fnl f* **6/4**[1]

1410 **4** 1 **Corn Maiden**[11] 2642 4-8-10 **59**........ FrederikTylicki 4 61
(Mark Rimmer) *racd in 4th: rdn 4f out: rdn and clsd over 3f out: chsd ldrs and styd on same pce u.p fr over 1f out* **7/1**

/603 **5** 15 **Between The Lines (IRE)**[6] 2777 4-8-10 **59**........(t) ChrisCatlin 7 40
(Anthony Middleton) *chsd ldr tl over 2f out: lost pl 2f out: 5th and wl btn over 1f out* **14/1**

04-3 **6** 7 **Potentiale (IRE)**[5] 2798 9-8-11 **60**........ PaulHanagan 5 31
(Alastair Lidderdale) *stdd s: hld up in rr: lost tch over 2f out: eased ins fnl f* **5/1**[3]

3m 10.66s (3.06) **Going Correction** -0.025s/f (Good) **6** Ran SP% **108.4**
Speed ratings (Par 103): **90,89,88,87,79 75**
toteswingers 1&2 £6.10, 1&3 £7.60, 2&3 £1.10 CSF £55.48 TOTE £11.10: £4.90, £1.40; EX 45.70 Trifecta £186.00 Pool: £741.86 - 2.99 winning units..
Owner Killarney Glen **Bred** Darley **Trained** Newmarket, Suffolk
■ Stewards' Enquiry : Hayley Turner two-day ban; used whip down shoulder (23rd-24th June).

FOCUS
A fair staying handicap for older horses on quick ground, but the time was slow.
T/Plt: £86.90 to a £1 stake. Pool: £71,067.17 - 596.45 winning units T/Qpdt: £36.10 to a £1 stake. Pool £5,913.96 - 120.95 winning units SP

2897 LONGCHAMP (R-H)
Tuesday, June 4

OFFICIAL GOING: Turf: good to soft

2970a PRIX DES LILAS (LISTED RACE) (3YO FILLIES) (TURF) 1m
2:20 (2:20) 3-Y-0 **£22,357** (£8,943; £6,707; £4,471; £2,235)

RPR

1 **Snow Bell (FR)**[31] 3-8-11 0........ GregoryBenoist 1 106
(N Clement, France) **9/5**[1]

2 2½ **Meri Shika (FR)**[23] 2299 3-8-11 0........ ThierryJarnet 6 100
(J Bertran De Balanda, France) **58/10**

3 nk **Holy Dazzle**[21] 2356 3-9-2 0........ RonanThomas 8 104
(J E Pease, France) **7/1**

4 ¾ **Balashkova (FR)**[39] 1816 3-8-11 0........ ChristopheSoumillon 3 98
(J-C Rouget, France) **5/1**[3]

The Form Book Flat, Raceform Ltd, Compton, RG20 6NL.

5 shd **Flawless Beauty**[59] 1383 3-8-11 0.........(b[1]) Christophe-PatriceLemaire 4 97
(Hugo Palmer) *broke wl and settled in 4th on outer: shkn up and and nt qckn under 2f out: kpt on at same pce u.p fnl f* **34/1**

6 hd **Single (FR)**[31] 3-8-11 0.. OlivierPeslier 7 97
(C Laffon-Parias, France) **3/1**[2]

7 ½ **Her Star (USA)**[43] 3-8-11 0.. StephanePasquier 2 96
(P Bary, France) **20/1**

8 ¾ **Linarda (DEN)**[34] 3-8-11 0.. UmbertoRispoli 5 94
(M Rulec, Germany) **19/1**

1m 42.5s (4.10) **8** Ran SP% **117.2**
WIN (incl. 1 euro stake): 2.80. PLACES: 1.40, 1.70, 2.00. DF: 8.70. SF: 14.10.
Owner L Haegel & G Augustin-Normand **Bred** Mme J Hulin & Mme P Lemonnier **Trained** Chantilly, France

AYR (L-H)

Wednesday, June 5

OFFICIAL GOING: Good changing to good (good to firm in places) after race 1 (2.10)

All races on hurdles track. No speed figures are possible for this meeting.
Wind: Slight, half against Weather: Cloudy

2971 EMPLOYMENT ENTERPRISE 10 YEARS IN BUSINESS MAIDEN STKS 1m 6f

2:10 (2:11) (Class 4) 3-Y-O+ **£4,204** (£1,251; £625; £312) **Stalls** Low

Form RPR

4 **1** **Mister Pagan**[18] 2465 5-10-0 0.. GrahamLee 4 69+
(Jim Goldie) *in tch: rdn and sltly outpcd over 3f out: rallied to ld over 1f out: rdn out* **8/1**[3]

05 **2** 2½ **Teenage Idol (IRE)**[5] 2833 9-10-0 0............................... AndrewElliott 6 66+
(Dianne Sayer) *hld up: rdn over 2f out: edgd lft and hdwy to chse wnr over 1f out: kpt on ins fnl f* **25/1**

4 **3** ½ **Caledonia**[18] 2462 6-9-11 0.. LucyAlexander(3) 1 65+
(Jim Goldie) *hld up: pushed along 5f out: hdwy and swtchd rt over 1f out: kpt on wl fnl f* **2/1**[2]

52-2 **4** 3½ **Khotan**[23] 2312 3-8-9 71.. LukeMorris 3 60
(Sir Mark Prescott Bt) *chsd ldrs: pushed along 3f out: edgd lft and led briefly 2f out: sn one pce* **1/1**[1]

5-00 **5** 3¾ **Altnaharra**[33] 1993 4-10-0 44..(v[1]) JoeFanning 7 55?
(Jim Goldie) *led: rdn and hdd 2f out: sn outpcd* **80/1**

6 1½ **Yourholidayisover (IRE)**[355] 6-10-0 0.................... RussKennemore 8 53?
(Patrick Holmes) *missed break: bhd: rdn over 3f out: hdwy and drifted rt over 1f out: kpt on: n.d* **40/1**

-530 **7** 4 **Argaki (IRE)**[22] 2342 3-8-9 66... TomEaves 2 47
(Keith Dalgleish) *in tch: hdwy over 2f out: rdn and one pce whn hmpd over 1f out: sn btn* **14/1**

3- **8** 12 **Camelopardalis**[302] 4908 4-9-9 0.................................. RobertWinston 5 25
(Tobias B P Coles) *chsd ldr: ev ch over 3f out: outpcd whn n.m.r over 1f out: sn btn* **11/1**

3m 6.37s (186.37)
WFA 3 from 4yo+ 19lb **8** Ran SP% **117.0**
toteswingers 1&2 £12.90, 2&3 £9.80, 1&3 £3.30 CSF £165.28 TOTE £7.40: £1.60, £4.60, £1.80; EX 363.50 Trifecta £305.90 Pool: £3190.04 - 7.82 winning units..
Owner Richard Murray **Bred** Richard Murray & Archie Turner **Trained** Uplawmoor, E Renfrews

FOCUS
This was a moderate staying maiden, but it was run at a decent pace.

2972 GEOFFREY AND LILY HELLINGS MEMORIAL H'CAP 1m 2f

2:40 (2:40) (Class 6) (0-60,58) 4-Y-O+ **£1,940** (£577; £288; £144) **Stalls** High

Form RPR

30-4 **1** **Barton Bounty**[41] 1790 6-9-4 52.. TomEaves 6 61
(Peter Niven) *dwlt: sn in midfield: effrt and hdwy to ld 2f out: sn hrd pressed: drvn out fnl f* **13/2**

6-20 **2** nk **Tectonic (IRE)**[15] 2536 4-9-6 54.. JoeFanning 8 63
(Keith Dalgleish) *hld up: hdwy on outside over 2f out: rdn and ev ch over 1f out: kpt on fnl f: hld nr fin* **5/1**[3]

-003 **3** 1¼ **Lord Franklin**[15] 2536 4-9-0 53.......................................(p) JasonHart(5) 5 59
(Eric Alston) *t.k.h: cl up: effrt whn n.m.r briefly 3f out: rallied 2f out: kpt on ins fnl f* **9/2**[2]

0-53 **4** ½ **Cherry Tree Hill (IRE)**[23] 2332 5-9-6 54...................... RobertWinston 2 59
(Alan Swinbank) *hld up: stdy hdwy over 2f out: rdn over 1f out: kpt on ins fnl f* **9/1**

5033 **5** 8 **Lil Sophella (IRE)**[15] 2537 4-9-0 48...................... RussKennemore 11 37
(Patrick Holmes) *t.k.h: cl up: led briefly over 2f out: wknd over 1f out* **8/1**

60-3 **6** 2¼ **Grand Diamond (IRE)**[12] 2630 9-9-0 48.......................(p) GrahamLee 1 33
(Jim Goldie) *hld up: rdn over 3f out: sme late hdwy: nvr able to chal* **10/1**

0061 **7** ½ **Cufflink**[8] 2764 4-9-10 58 6ex.......................................(v) PaulMulrennan 4 42
(Iain Jardine) *dwlt: sn prom: effrt over 2f out: wknd over 1f out* **4/1**[1]

500- **8** 3 **Oddsmaker (IRE)**[261] 6315 12-9-2 50.......................(t) MichaelO'Connell 10 28
(Maurice Barnes) *led to over 2f out: rdn and wknd over 1f out* **40/1**

00-0 **9** 1¼ **Galilee Chapel (IRE)**[15] 2536 4-8-13 52................... GarryWhillans(5) 3 27
(Alistair Whillans) *hld up in midfield on ins: outpcd 4f out: n.d after* **22/1**

00-0 **10** 15 **Naafetha (IRE)**[15] 2537 5-8-11 45..............................(b) DanielTudhope 9
(Ian Semple) *towards rr: drvn along over 3f out: sn struggling: t.o* **80/1**

65-0 **11** 14 **Humungosaur**[12] 2629 4-9-7 55...................................... FrederikTylicki 7
(Richard Ford) *prom tl rdn and wknd over 2f out: sn btn: t.o* **12/1**

2m 4.03s (-7.97) **11** Ran SP% **114.1**
CSF £37.22 CT £161.02 TOTE £6.20: £2.10, £2.40, £2.00; EX 45.60 Trifecta £301.30 Pool: £1781.74 - 4.43 winning units..
Owner Francis Green Racing Ltd **Bred** Mrs M L Parry **Trained** Barton-le-Street, N Yorks

FOCUS
This was competitive for the class and, with a sound pace set, the first four came clear in a tight finish.

2973 EMPLOYMENT ENTERPRISE SCOTLAND: NATION OF ENTERPRISE H'CAP 1m 6f

3:10 (3:10) (Class 4) (0-85,83) 4-Y-O+ **£5,175** (£1,540; £769; £384) **Stalls** Low

Form RPR

334- **1** **Jonny Delta**[20] 7367 6-8-9 71 ow1.. GrahamLee 5 86
(Jim Goldie) *hld up in last pl: gd hdwy over 2f out: led over 1f out: pushed clr fnl f* **13/2**

111- **2** 6 **Mutual Regard (IRE)**[194] 7839 4-9-7 83............................. LukeMorris 6 90
(Sir Mark Prescott Bt) *t.k.h early: in tch: pushed along briefly 5f out: hdwy to ld over 2f out: drvn and hdd over 1f out: kpt on same pce* **15/8**[1]

2421 **3** 2¼ **Activate**[16] 2509 6-8-12 74..(p) JoeFanning 8 77
(Keith Dalgleish) *t.k.h early: chsd ldrs: rdn along over 2f out: rallied over 1f out: kpt on fnl f: no imp* **7/1**

-330 **4** 1 **Flashman**[20] 2402 4-8-11 76.. LeeTopliss(3) 2 79
(Richard Fahey) *in tch: pushed along fr 1/2-way: effrt over 2f out: no imp whn n.m.r ins fnl f* **3/1**[2]

2-01 **5** 1¼ **Villa Royale**[12] 2615 4-9-4 80.. DanielTudhope 3 80
(David O'Meara) *w ldr: led 1/2-way to over 2f out: sn rdn: wknd 1f out* **9/2**[3]

4-52 **6** 8 **Hawdyerwheesht**[23] 2316 5-8-5 67................................. AndrewElliott 7 56
(Jim Goldie) *led to 1/2-way: w ldr tl rdn and wknd over 2f out* **16/1**

3m 3.73s (183.73) **6** Ran SP% **109.7**
toteswingers 1&2 £2.60, 2&3 £1.80, 1&3 £4.40 CSF £18.28 CT £79.86 TOTE £5.50: £2.80, £1.90; EX 23.50 Trifecta £105.40 Pool: £2163.62 - 15.38 winning units..
Owner Johnnie Delta Racing **Bred** Miss Gill Quincey **Trained** Uplawmoor, E Renfrews

FOCUS
This fair staying handicap was a strongly run affair and that teed things up ideally for the winner.

2974 JIM AND MARGARET SMITH MEMORIAL FILLIES' H'CAP (QUALIFIER FOR £15000 BETFAIR SCOTTISH MILE FINAL) 1m 1f

3:40 (3:40) (Class 5) (0-70,68) 4-Y-O+ **£3,881** (£1,155; £577; £288) **Stalls** Low

Form RPR

5-10 **1** **Spavento (IRE)**[6] 2796 7-9-1 67.. JasonHart(5) 4 76
(Eric Alston) *trckd ldrs: wnt 2nd over 3f out: rdn to ld over 1f out: styd on strly fnl f* **2/1**[1]

6005 **2** 3¼ **Imtithal (IRE)**[6] 2794 4-8-7 54...(b) JoeFanning 3 56
(John Weymes) *led: rdn over 2f out: hdd over 1f out: kpt on same pce fnl f* **20/1**

4-00 **3** ¾ **Painted Tail (IRE)**[15] 2555 6-9-5 66............................... RobertWinston 2 66
(Alan Swinbank) *t.k.h: in tch: rdn and outpcd over 2f out: rallied fnl f: nt gng pce to chal* **3/1**[2]

4/00 **4** 1¼ **Lady Tycoon**[30] 2073 4-8-2 49 oh2... LukeMorris 7 46
(Mark Brisbourne) *in tch: rdn over 2f out: styd on fnl f: no imp* **20/1**

-000 **5** 3 **Elizabeth Coffee (IRE)**[15] 2555 5-8-13 60............................ TomEaves 1 51
(John Weymes) *t.k.h: in tch: drvn and effrt over 2f out: wknd over 1f out* **12/1**

6-50 **6** 2 **Liliargh (IRE)**[4] 2889 4-9-7 68... GrahamLee 8 54
(Ben Haslam) *hld up: pushed along over 2f out: no imp fr over 1f out* **10/3**[3]

2-00 **7** shd **Social Rhythm**[26] 2220 9-9-4 65...................................... PaulMulrennan 5 51
(Alistair Whillans) *hld up towards rr: rdn over 2f out: sn n.d* **7/1**

/00- **8** 10 **Grethel (IRE)**[7] 4869 9-7-9 49 oh4.............................. JordanHibberd(7) 6
(Alan Berry) *missed break: bhd: struggling 3f out: sn btn: t.o* **25/1**

1m 55.73s (115.73) **8** Ran SP% **115.0**
toteswingers 1&2 £6.30, 2&3 £8.30, 1&3 £2.30 CSF £46.50 CT £119.61 TOTE £2.80: £1.40, £3.30, £1.60; EX 43.20 Trifecta £198.30 Pool: £2606.79 - 9.85 winning units..
Owner Whitehills Racing Syndicate **Bred** E Prosser, J Singh, & N & E Kent **Trained** Longton, Lancs

FOCUS
A very weak fillies' handicap, run at a strong early pace.

2975 JOHN AND BETTY DOWSE MEMORIAL H'CAP (QUALIFIER FOR £15000 BETFAIR SCOTTISH STAYERS' FINAL) 1m 7f

4:10 (4:10) (Class 6) (0-60,60) 4-Y-O+ **£1,940** (£577; £288; £144) **Stalls** Low

Form RPR

00-4 **1** **Forrest Flyer (IRE)**[67] 1251 9-9-7 **60**................................ GrahamLee 9 70
(Jim Goldie) *cl up: led over 5f out: qcknd over 3f out: kpt on strly: unchal* **10/3**[1]

0-61 **2** 4 **Goodlukin Lucy**[12] 2630 6-8-12 **51**..............................(t) AndrewElliott 5 56
(Dianne Sayer) *hld up: hdwy on outside to chse (clr) wnr over 2f out: sn rdn and drifted lft: kpt on same pce fnl f* **4/1**[2]

-600 **3** 9 **Ad Value (IRE)**[9] 2720 5-8-8 **52**.. JasonHart(5) 4 45
(Alan Kirtley) *in tch on ins: rdn over 3f out: no imp fr 2f out* **14/1**

00-5 **4** ½ **Uncut Stone (IRE)**[28] 755 5-9-1 **54**............................(b) PaulMulrennan 8 46
(Peter Niven) *led: rdn and hdd over 5f out: sn nt keen and lost pl: styd on fr over 1f out: n.d* **8/1**

0-05 **5** 3 **Geanie Mac (IRE)**[6] 2798 4-9-2 **55**.............................(b) FrederikTylicki 6 44
(Linda Perratt) *cl up: rdn over 3f out: edgd lft and outpcd fr 2f out* **17/2**

55-6 **6** 7 **Vittachi**[23] 2316 6-9-2 **55**... MichaelO'Connell 10 34
(Alistair Whillans) *hld up in tch: stdy hdwy over 4f out: rdn over 3f out: wknd over 2f out* **5/1**

4-20 **7** ¾ **Destiny Awaits (IRE)**[15] 2540 4-8-11 **50**...........................(p) TomEaves 7 28
(Ian Semple) *t.k.h: in tch on outside: effrt over 4f out: wknd over 2f out* **20/1**

-003 **8** 8 **Cosmic Moon**[18] 2435 5-8-11 **57**..................................... SamanthaBell(7) 3 25
(Richard Fahey) *missed break: bhd: hdwy over 3f out: rdn and wknd over 2f out* **9/2**[3]

3m 19.75s (-0.65) **8** Ran SP% **111.0**
toteswingers 1&2 £3.60, 2&3 £9.90, 1&3 £9.80 CSF £15.65 CT £153.23 TOTE £4.80: £1.90, £1.20, £3.20; EX 14.70 Trifecta £122.60 Pool: £2308.86 - 14.12 winning units..
Owner Mrs Camille Macdonald **Bred** Philip Lau **Trained** Uplawmoor, E Renfrews

FOCUS
A moderate staying handicap which proved a decent test.

2976 EMPLOYMENT ENTERPRISE 10 YEARS IN BUSINESS H'CAP 1m 2f

4:40 (4:48) (Class 3) (0-90,90) 4-Y-O+ **£7,762** (£2,310; £1,154; £577) **Stalls** High

Form RPR

-113 **1** **Awake My Soul (IRE)**[19] 2431 4-9-6 89........................ DanielTudhope 1 94+
(David O'Meara) *sddle slipped leaving stalls: t.k.h: trckd ldrs: effrt 2f out: kpt on wl fnl f to ld cl home* **7/4**[1]

0-00 **2** nse **Another For Joe**[26] 2220 5-8-6 75.................................. AndrewElliott 9 80
(Jim Goldie) *w ldr: rdn 2f out: kpt on wl fnl f: jst hld* **17/2**

02 **3** nk **Fort Belvedere**[22] 2339 5-9-7 90... LukeMorris 6 94
(Keith Dalgleish) *led: rdn 2f out: kpt on wl fnl f: hdd cl home* **5/1**[2]

22-6 **4** 1¾ **Red Inca**[25] 239 5-8-8 77... TomEaves 4 78
(Brian Ellison) *prom: effrt and rdn 2f out: kpt on same pce fnl f* **11/2**[3]

5/0- **5** shd **Cockney Class (USA)**[383] 2250 6-9-7 90..................... FrederikTylicki 8 90
(Dave Roberts) *s.i.s: hld up: effrt and swtchd rt over 1f out: kpt on ins fnl f: nrst fin* **28/1**

5334 **6** ¾ **Gala Casino Star (IRE)**[17] 2478 8-8-6 82...............(v) JordanNason(7) 7 81
(Geoffrey Harker) *in tch on outside: rdn and hung lft 2f out: sn one pce* **8/1**

5011 **7** 1½ **Jordaura**[13] 2594 7-7-9 71 oh4...................................... JordanHibberd(7) 3 67
(Alan Berry) *hld up in tch: pushed along over 2f out: nvr able to chal* **20/1**

3-21 **8** 9 **Cosmic Halo**[23] 2311 4-8-4 73 .... PatrickMathers 5 51
(Richard Fahey) *hld up: rdn and edgd lft over 2f out: sn struggling* **6/1**

2m 3.62s (-8.38) course record **8** Ran SP% **112.5**
toteswingers 1&2 £4.60, 2&3 £6.80, 1&3 £2.60 CSF £17.05 CT £61.89 TOTE £2.30: £1.20, £2.30, £2.20; EX 18.20 Trifecta £89.00 Pool: £3771.65 - 31.75 winning units..
Owner K Nicholson **Bred** Grundy Bloodstock Srl **Trained** Nawton, N Yorks

FOCUS
This looked competitive, but it was run at an uneven pace and it proved a big advantage to race handily.

2977 ENTERPRISE SCREEN VIDEO PRODUCTION SCOTLAND APPRENTICE H'CAP — 1m 1f
5:10 (5:12) (Class 6) (0-60,58) 4-Y-0+ **£1,940** (£577; £288; £144) **Stalls** Low

Form RPR
512- **1** **Mac Tiernan (IRE)**[296] 5175 6-9-4 **58** .... EvaMoscrop(3) 10 72
(Philip Kirby) *mde all: pushed along whn edgd rt fr over 1f out: hld on wl fnl f* **4/1**[2]
566/ **2** 3/4 **Scoglio**[21] 7247 5-8-10 **50** .... SamanthaBell(3) 11 62
(Dave Roberts) *hld up in midfield: hdwy on outside over 2f out: chsd wnr over 1f out: kpt on ins fnl f: hld towards fin* **4/1**[2]
4-32 **3** 2 **Music Festival (USA)**[4] 2889 6-8-9 **53** .... SophieRobertson(7) 7 61+
(Jim Goldie) *hld up: stdy hdwy over 2f out: chsd ldrs over 1f out: kpt on same pce ins fnl f* **7/2**[1]
00-5 **4** 5 **Heart Beat Song**[37] 1887 5-8-8 **45** .... JoshBaudains 3 42
(Richard Ford) *prom: effrt and rdn over 2f out: outpcd over 1f out* **20/1**
00-0 **5** 2 3/4 **Military Call**[12] 2636 6-9-0 **51** ....(p) DavidSimmonson 9 42
(Alistair Whillans) *trckd ldrs: rdn and edgd lft over 2f out: btn fnl f* **12/1**
35-5 **6** shd **Amno Dancer (IRE)**[23] 2319 6-8-10 **47** .... LauraBarry 5 37
(Keith Dalgleish) *in tch: rdn and outpcd over 2f out: n.d after* **11/1**
2545 **7** 3/4 **Availed Speaker (IRE)**[39] 1842 4-8-10 **54** .... JoshQuinn(7) 12 43
(Richard Fahey) *chsd ldrs: rdn over 3f out: one pce fr 2f out* **6/1**[3]
-030 **8** 1 **Goninodaethat**[23] 2319 5-8-9 **51** .... KevinStott(5) 2 37
(Jim Goldie) *j.w but sn faltered and hung bdly rt: t.k.h towards rr: effrt over 2f out: n.d* **12/1**
6-06 **9** nk **Harare**[7] 2785 12-9-2 **53** ....(v) GemmaTutty 4 39
(Karen Tutty) *hld up: rdn and hung lft over 2f out: nvr rchd ldrs* **9/1**
0-64 **10** shd **Stormont Bridge**[12] 2636 5-8-12 **54** ....(t) JordanVaughan(5) 1 40
(Maurice Barnes) *midfield: rdn and outpcd over 2f out: btn over 1f out* **25/1**
3460 **11** 2 1/2 **Spread Boy (IRE)**[2] 2911 6-8-2 **46** .... NicolaGrundy(7) 6 26
(Alan Berry) *prom tl rdn and wknd over 2f out* **33/1**

1m 55.46s (115.46) **11** Ran SP% **121.8**
toteswingers 1&2 £5.00, 2&3 £5.70, 1&3 £3.10 CSF £20.73 CT £63.13 TOTE £4.90: £1.40, £2.00, £2.20; EX 27.20 Trifecta £87.20 Pool: £2319.48 - 19.94 winning units..
Owner The Philip Kirby Racing Partnership **Bred** Paul Kiernan **Trained** Middleham, N Yorks

FOCUS
An ordinary handicap, confined to apprentice riders. Fair form for the class.
T/Plt: £31.10 to a £1 stake. Pool of £57577.97 - 1350.76 winning tickets. T/Qpdt: £3.40 to a £1 stake. Pool of £4311.03 - 927.14 winning tickets. RY

2771 KEMPTON (A.W) (R-H)
Wednesday, June 5

OFFICIAL GOING: Standard
Wind: Light, across (towards stands) Weather: Fine, warm

2978 CONOR MAYNARD LIVE AT KEMPTON 14.09.13 MAIDEN AUCTION STKS — 6f (P)
6:00 (6:00) (Class 5) 2-Y-0 **£2,587** (£770; £384; £192) **Stalls** Low

Form RPR
4 **1** **Razor Quest**[20] 2382 2-8-9 0 .... WilliamCarson 6 73+
(Philip McBride) *in tch: rdn to chse ldng pair 2f out: clsd u.p to ld last 100yds* **11/4**[2]
54 **2** 1 **Island Kingdom (IRE)**[12] 2617 2-8-9 0 .... LiamKeniry 4 70
(J S Moore) *led at mod pce: edgd lft and narrowly hdd 2f out: continued to edge lft but led again 1f out: hdd and outpcd last 100yds* **10/1**
2 **3** 3/4 **Stellarta**[14] 2562 2-8-5 0 .... JimmyQuinn 5 64
(Michael Blanshard) *pressed ldr: carried lft but led narrowly 2f out: hdd and one pce 1f out* **5/1**[3]
4 nse **Emperor's Hope (IRE)** 2-8-10 0 .... RyanMoore 9 69+
(Richard Hannon) *s.s: in tch on outer: shkn up over 2f out: hanging and green after: tk 4th over 1f out: styd on but nvr able to chal* **6/4**[1]
660 **5** 8 **Bold Max**[14] 2562 2-8-10 0 .... RichardThomas 7 45
(Zoe Davison) *racd wd: chsd ldng pair to 2f out: wknd* **100/1**
6 1 1/4 **Dark Phantom (IRE)** 2-8-12 0 .... SteveDrowne 1 43
(Peter Makin) *dwlt: in tch in rr: brief effrt on inner over 2f out: sn wknd* **10/1**
7 3/4 **Tidal Beauty** 2-8-6 0 .... MartinLane 8 35
(Tony Carroll) *s.s: in tch in rr tl over 2f out* **20/1**
8 5 **Society Diva (IRE)** 2-8-7 0 .... KieranO'Neill 3 21
(George Baker) *in tch: pushed along bef 1/2-way: wknd 2f out* **14/1**

1m 15.58s (2.48) **Going Correction** +0.075s/f (Slow) **8** Ran SP% **113.9**
Speed ratings (Par 93): **86,84,83,83,72 71,70,63**
toteswingers 1&2 £5.30, 2&3 £5.50, 1&3 £2.90 CSF £29.87 TOTE £3.40: £1.20, £1.90, £2.40; EX 30.70 Trifecta £104.60 Pool: £1400.69 - 10.04 winning units..
Owner P J McBride **Bred** Mrs J A Cornwell **Trained** Newmarket, Suffolk

FOCUS
The went a steady pace in this maiden There was not much separating the first four who finished a long way clear.

2979 IRISH NIGHT ON 10.07.13 MAIDEN FILLIES' STKS — 7f (P)
6:30 (6:40) (Class 5) 3-Y-0+ **£2,587** (£770; £384; £192) **Stalls** Low

Form RPR
2 **1** **Plover**[18] 2447 3-9-0 0 .... RyanMoore 4 89+
(Sir Michael Stoute) *wore net-muzzle: hld up bhd ldrs: prog to ld wl over 1f out: sn clr: easily* **10/11**[1]
2 6 **Ethel** 3-9-0 0 .... WilliamBuick 3 73+
(John Gosden) *trckd ldrs: shkn up and outpcd over 2f out: prog over 1f out: jst won gd battle for 2nd ins fnl f: shaped w promise* **6/1**[3]
3 hd **Ghasabah** 3-9-0 0 .... PaulHanagan 13 73+
(William Haggas) *restrained fr wdst draw: hld up in last pair and t.k.h early: gd prog 2f out: disp 2nd fnl f: promising debut* **12/1**
6- **4** 2 1/2 **Soryah (IRE)**[180] 8017 3-9-0 0 .... KierenFallon 9 66+
(Luca Cumani) *racd wd and stdd in rr: pushed along and styd on steadily fnl 2f: nrst fin* **9/2**[2]
40 **5** 1 1/4 **Scala Romana (IRE)**[12] 2637 3-8-9 0 .... RosieJessop(5) 7 63
(Sir Mark Prescott Bt) *pressed ldr after 1f: led v briefly 2f out: sn lft bhd by wnr: wknd fnl f* **66/1**
4-3 **6** 5 **Perfect Calm (USA)**[44] 1711 3-9-0 0 .... PatDobbs 6 49
(Richard Hannon) *chsd ldrs tl easily lft bhd fr 2f out* **10/1**
0 **7** 3/4 **Fonseca (IRE)**[11] 2658 3-9-0 0 .... LiamKeniry 14 47
(Andrew Balding) *stdd fr wd draw: sn in midfield: shkn up and lft bhd fr over 2f out* **40/1**
3 **8** 1 1/4 **Timeless**[32] 2006 3-9-0 0 .... MartinLane 11 44
(Tobias B P Coles) *s.s: a in rr: rdn and no prog over 2f out* **16/1**
00 **9** hd **Serendippidy**[11] 2650 3-9-0 0 .... AdamBeschizza 5 43
(James Unett) *towards rr: pushed along and sme prog 2f out: sn wknd* **66/1**
10 hd **Trisara** 3-9-0 0 .... JamesDoyle 8 43
(Harry Dunlop) *pressed ldrs on outer: wknd qckly 2f out* **33/1**
11 2 1/2 **Jameela's Dream**[251] 6619 3-9-0 0 .... FrankieDettori 12 36
(Robert Cowell) *led after 1f to 2f out: wknd rapidly* **25/1**
12 hd **Pingit** 3-9-0 0 .... KieranO'Neill 1 35
(Alan McCabe) *a struggling in last pair* **50/1**
0 **13** 11 **Xanders Secret**[9] 2722 3-9-0 0 .... WilliamCarson 2 6
(Brett Johnson) *led 1f: prom tl wknd rapidly over 2f out: t.o* **100/1**

1m 26.94s (0.94) **Going Correction** +0.075s/f (Slow) **13** Ran SP% **122.7**
Speed ratings (Par 100): **97,90,89,87,85 79,79,77,77,77 74,74,61**
toteswingers 1&2 £1.90, 2&3 £7.30, 1&3 £4.10 CSF £6.60 TOTE £1.90: £1.10, £2.10, £2.00; EX 6.70 Trifecta £38.30 Pool: £2177.54 - 42.57 winning units..
Owner K Abdullah **Bred** Juddmonte Farms Ltd **Trained** Newmarket, Suffolk

FOCUS
The hot favourite was an impressive winner of this fillies maiden, but there was also promise from the next three home. There was a nasty incident before the race when Arabian Dawn crashed through the rails.

2980 LONDON'S RACE TRACKS RACINGANDMUSIC.CO.UK H'CAP — 2m (P)
7:00 (7:06) (Class 5) (0-70,69) 4-Y-0+ **£2,587** (£770; £384; £192) **Stalls** Low

Form RPR
0-11 **1** **Almost Gemini (IRE)**[43] 1744 4-9-6 **66** ....(p) RyanMoore 3 72+
(Don Cantillon) *trckd ldr: first one rdn over 3f out: u.p and looked to be fighting losing battle over 2f out: kpt on and lifted ahd last 100yds* **11/8**[1]
3106 **2** 1/2 **Fulgora**[21] 2360 5-9-10 **69** .... KierenFallon 5 74
(Brendan Powell) *led: wound it up fr slow early pce: rdn over 2f out and pressed: kpt on but hdd last 100yds* **10/1**
5301 **3** 1 1/4 **Boston Blue**[14] 2563 6-8-12 **57** .... JimCrowley 7 61
(Tony Carroll) *hld up in 4th: rdn over 2f out: clsd to press ldng pair over 1f out: nt qckn ins fnl f* **11/2**[3]
5114 **4** 3/4 **Arashi**[15] 2545 7-9-6 **65** ....(v) NeilCallan 6 68
(Derek Shaw) *hld up in last: quick move to press ldng pair 3f out and gng wl: rdn and nt qckn over 2f out: one pce after* **7/2**[2]
1241 **5** 3 3/4 **Bold Adventure**[62] 1348 9-9-0 **59** .... JamieMackay 1 57
(Willie Musson) *hld up in 5th: pushed along and outpcd over 2f out: plugged on same pce fnl 2f* **9/1**
1632 **6** 14 **Llamadas**[35] 1927 11-9-8 **67** .... GeorgeBaker 4 54
(Olivia Maylam) *trckd ldng pair to 3f out: rdn and nt qckn over 2f out: wknd and eased over 1f out: t.o* **9/1**

3m 35.19s (5.09) **Going Correction** +0.075s/f (Slow)
WFA 4 from 5yo+ 1lb **6** Ran SP% **108.8**
Speed ratings (Par 103): **90,89,89,88,86 79**
toteswingers 1&2 £2.70, 2&3 £11.90, 1&3 £1.20 CSF £14.88 TOTE £2.20: £1.40, £3.80; EX 11.80 Trifecta £103.40 Pool: £941.15 - 6.82 winning units..
Owner Don Cantillon **Bred** Rockhart Trading Ltd **Trained** Newmarket, Suffolk

FOCUS
A staying handicap, involving three last-time-out winners. There was a tight finish and the favourite just prevailed under a powerful ride from Ryan Moore.

2981 BETDAQ 1ST UK RACE COMMISSION FREE-EVERYDAY H'CAP — 1m (P)
7:30 (7:32) (Class 5) (0-75,75) 4-Y-0+ **£2,587** (£770; £384; £192) **Stalls** Low

Form RPR
00-0 **1** **Legendary**[26] 2232 4-9-7 **75** ....(p) KierenFallon 4 90
(Ed Vaughan) *t.k.h early: trckd ldrs: rdn and clsd to ld over 1f out: sn clr: drvn out* **9/2**[2]
0-46 **2** 6 **Wilfred Pickles (IRE)**[37] 1878 7-9-7 **75** .... IanMongan 3 76
(Jo Crowley) *sn in last trio: rdn and prog over 2f out: drvn to chse clr wnr 1f out: all out to hold on for 2nd* **10/1**
4-30 **3** 3/4 **Xinbama (IRE)**[39] 1827 4-9-5 **73** ....(t) FrankieDettori 5 72
(J W Hills) *hld up towards rr: rdn over 2f out: kpt on fr over 1f out: tk 3rd ins fnl f and pressed runner-up* **6/1**[3]
0-46 **4** 1/2 **Kalily**[20] 2383 4-8-11 **68** .... PatrickHills(3) 9 66
(Rae Guest) *dwlt: hld up in last trio: rdn over 2f out: styd on same pce fr over 1f out: nrst fin* **8/1**
2205 **5** 3/4 **Spring Tonic**[14] 2574 4-9-5 **73** .... NeilCallan 1 69
(Simon Dow) *led at fair pce but hdd after 1f: rdn to ld again jst over 2f out to over 1f out: wknd fnl f* **9/2**[2]
0106 **6** 3/4 **Carazam (IRE)**[16] 2498 6-9-7 **75** .... DaneO'Neill 6 70
(William Jarvis) *settled in last trio: rdn over 2f out: plugged on same pce fr over 1f out: n.d* **3/1**[1]
-036 **7** 8 **Halling Dancer**[14] 2580 4-9-5 **73** ....(v[1]) KierenFox 10 49
(Lee Carter) *led after 1f: hdd & wknd qckly jst over 2f out* **14/1**
00/4 **8** 1 3/4 **Kilburn**[26] 2225 9-9-5 **73** ....(b) GeorgeBaker 8 45
(Alastair Lidderdale) *trckd ldng pair tl wknd qckly over 2f out: sn bhd* **12/1**
5-00 **9** 12 **Mr Spiggott (IRE)**[46] 1673 4-9-7 **75** ....(v) TedDurcan 11 20
(Joseph Tuite) *stdd s: hld up in last pair: shkn up over 2f out: sn wknd: t.o* **25/1**

1m 38.54s (-1.26) **Going Correction** +0.075s/f (Slow) **9** Ran SP% **114.1**
Speed ratings (Par 103): **109,103,102,101,101 100,92,90,78**
toteswingers 1&2 £10.80, 2&3 £17.00, 1&3 £2.30 CSF £47.90 CT £270.60 TOTE £5.10: £1.90, £3.70, £1.30; EX 62.40 Trifecta £177.70 Pool: £791.75 - 3.34 winning units..
Owner Mrs Doreen M Swinburn **Bred** Genesis Green Stud Ltd **Trained** Newmarket, Suffolk

FOCUS
There was an emphatic winner of this minor handicap, which was run at a fair pace.

2982 £200 FREE BETS AT BETDAQ H'CAP (LONDON MIDDLE DISTANCE SERIES QUALIFIER) — 1m 3f (P)
8:00 (8:03) (Class 5) (0-70,70) 4-Y-0+ **£2,587** (£770; £384; £192) **Stalls** Low

Form RPR
0003 **1** **Mountain Range (IRE)**[6] 2808 5-9-1 **64** .... WilliamBuick 3 78
(Willie Musson) *trckd ldrs: prog to press ldr over 1f out: drvn to ld on inner ins fnl f: asserted last 75yds* **11/4**[1]

1/-0 **2** 1 1/4 **Gold Mine**[19] 2418 5-9-7 **70**.....(t) LiamKeniry 1 82
(Andrew Balding) *trckd ldr: led over 2f out: drvn over 1f out: hdd ins fnl f: no ex last 100yds* **14/1**
000- **3** 3 1/4 **Hector's Chance**[168] 7655 4-9-2 **65**..... NeilCallan 6 71
(Heather Main) *trckd ldrs on outer: rdn to dispute 2nd 2f out: chsd ldng pair after: no imp but clr in 3rd fr over 1f out* **10/1**
00-0 **4** 2 1/4 **Star Date (IRE)**[37] 1884 4-9-4 **67**..... KierenFallon 7 69
(Michael Attwater) *hld up in midfield: cl enough over 2f out: sn rdn and nt qckn: kpt on to take 4th fnl f* **7/1**
1 **5** *hd* **Arabela (IRE)**[90] 921 4-8-9 **58**.....(e[1]) AdamBeschizza 10 60+
(James Unett) *reluctant to enter stalls: hld up in last: urged along over 2f out: kpt on fr over 1f out to press for 4th nr fin* **12/1**
4015 **6** 1 **Shalambar (IRE)**[25] 2284 7-9-7 **70**.....(v) JimCrowley 9 70+
(Tony Carroll) *dwlt: hld up in last trio: shkn up over 2f out: kpt on one pce fr over 1f out: no ch* **12/1**
1235 **7** *hd* **Bridge That Gap**[19] 2413 5-9-1 **64**..... AdamKirby 2 64
(Roger Ingram) *hld up in midfield: sme prog on inner 2f out: wknd over 1f out* **6/1**[3]
6-51 **8** 4 1/2 **Attraction Ticket**[7] 2777 4-8-9 **65**..... SiobhanMiller(7) 11 56
(David Simcock) *racd wd in midfield: pushed along over 2f out: no prog and sn btn* **4/1**[2]
0-0 **9** 2 1/2 **Addikt (IRE)**[64] 1303 8-8-10 **64**..... WilliamTwiston-Davies(5) 4 51
(Michael Scudamore) *dwlt: hld up in last trio: shkn up and no real prog over 2f out* **25/1**
000 **10** *shd* **Six Silver Lane**[22] 2348 5-8-8 **57**.....(t) MartinLane 8 44
(Derek Shaw) *led: tried to kick on over 3f out: hdd over 2f out: sn wknd* **25/1**
40-3 **11** 5 **Miss Fortywinks**[22] 2349 4-9-4 **67**..... GeorgeBaker 5 45
(Joseph Tuite) *pressed ldrs tl wknd qckly over 2f out* **25/1**

2m 21.0s (-0.90) **Going Correction** +0.075s/f (Slow) **11** Ran SP% **116.1**
Speed ratings (Par 103): **106,105,102,101,100 100,100,96,94,94 91**
toteswingers 1&2 £13.90, 2&3 £10.50, 1&3 £8.30 CSF £41.81 CT £330.74 TOTE £3.50: £1.70, £2.50, £2.50; EX 44.80 Trifecta £879.50 Part won. Pool: £1172.78 - 0.22 winning units..
Owner W J Musson **Bred** Holborn Trust Co **Trained** Newmarket, Suffolk

FOCUS
The favourite delivered and the first two pulled clear in this handicap.

2983 NEW CUSTOMERS COMMISSION FREE 1ST MONTH H'CAP 6f (P)
8:30 (8:32) (Class 4) (0-80,79) 3-Y-O **£4,690** (£1,395; £697; £348) **Stalls** Low

Form RPR
3-10 **1** **Milly's Gift**[18] 2449 3-9-6 **78**..... AdamKirby 3 91
(Clive Cox) *trckd ldng trio: prog to chse ldr over 1f out: hrd rdn and styd on wl to ld last strides* **6/1**[2]
4221 **2** *hd* **Extrasolar**[15] 2529 3-9-7 **79**.....(t) PatDobbs 4 91
(Amanda Perrett) *trckd ldr: clsd to ld wl over 1f out: drifted lft after: styd on wl but hdd last strides* **5/1**[1]
1-20 **3** 4 1/2 **Almalekiah (IRE)**[19] 2415 3-9-0 **72**..... LiamKeniry 6 70
(J S Moore) *in tch in midfield: rdn 2f out: styd on fr over 1f out to take 3rd last 75yds* **12/1**[3]
1-20 **4** 3/4 **Khobaraa**[16] 2495 3-9-6 **78**..... PaulHanagan 1 73
(John Gosden) *hld up in midfield: prog towards inner wl over 1f out: one pce and no imp fnl f* **5/1**[1]
4210 **5** *hd* **Hard Walnut (IRE)**[25] 2264 3-9-4 **76**..... HarryBentley 9 71
(Olly Stevens) *led: 2 l clr over 2f out: hdd wl over 1f out: steadily wknd* **12/1**[3]
-016 **6** *shd* **Jimmy Elder**[62] 1345 3-8-11 **69**..... RyanMoore 11 63
(Richard Hannon) *hld up towards rr: rdn over 2f out: hd high and nt qckn: pushed along and kpt on fnl f* **20/1**
2605 **7** 2 **Midnight Dream (FR)**[37] 1892 3-9-6 **78**..... DaneO'Neill 5 66
(Kristin Stubbs) *trckd ldng pair to 2f out: steadily wknd* **16/1**
1-03 **8** 1 1/2 **Tartary (IRE)**[28] 2158 3-9-5 **77**.....(t) JamesDoyle 10 60
(Roger Charlton) *hld up in rr: shkn up and no prog 2f out: wl btn after* **6/1**[2]
4-10 **9** *nk* **El Mirage (IRE)**[32] 2010 3-9-3 **75**..... KierenFallon 8 57
(Dean Ivory) *racd wd in midfield: no prog 2f out: sn wknd* **14/1**
411- **10** 20 **Pira Palace (IRE)**[231] 7164 3-9-7 **79**..... JimCrowley 2
(William Knight) *s.v.s: detached in last most of way: t.o* **14/1**
10- **11** 6 **Red Turban**[249] 6675 3-9-4 **76**..... WilliamBuick 7
(Jeremy Noseda) *chsd ldrs: wknd qckly over 2f out: eased whn no ch: t.o* **5/1**[1]

1m 12.71s (-0.39) **Going Correction** +0.075s/f (Slow) **11** Ran SP% **117.9**
Speed ratings (Par 101): **105,104,98,97,97 97,94,92,92,65 57**
toteswingers 1&2 £6.70, 2&3 £6.70, 1&3 £17.10 CSF £36.20 CT £353.42 TOTE £8.30: £3.10, £1.60, £3.20; EX 42.80 Trifecta £386.00 Part won. Pool: £514.70- 0.99 winning units..
Owner Ken Lock Racing **Bred** Ken Lock Racing **Trained** Lambourn, Berks

FOCUS
A fair handicap, which was run at a strong pace. There was a tight finish and the first two pulled clear.

2984 WINNERS ARE WELCOME AT BETDAQ H'CAP 7f (P)
9:00 (9:00) (Class 4) (0-80,80) 3-Y-O **£4,690** (£1,395; £697; £348) **Stalls** Low

Form RPR
0-52 **1** **Labienus**[16] 2506 3-9-5 **78**..... TedDurcan 3 90
(David Lanigan) *wnt lft s: hld up in last trio: prog on outer 2f out: shkn up to ld jst over 1f out: sn clr: decisively* **3/1**[1]
4-05 **2** 2 **Future Reference (IRE)**[19] 2420 3-8-11 **70**.....(t) SilvestreDeSousa 10 77
(Saeed bin Suroor) *trckd ldng trio on outer: rdn 2f out: trying to cl whn wnr swept by over 1f out: styd on to take 2nd ins fnl f* **4/1**[2]
001- **3** 1 1/4 **Intrepid (IRE)**[167] 8185 3-9-5 **78**..... WilliamBuick 5 81
(Jeremy Noseda) *chsd ldr: shkn up over 2f out: clsd to chal jst over 1f out but wnr sn swept by* **9/2**[3]
2100 **4** *shd* **Limit Up**[32] 2022 3-9-2 **80**..... MichaelJMMurphy(5) 6 83
(Mark Johnston) *led at brisk pce: kicked on over 2f out: hdd and outpcd jst over 1f out* **20/1**
1-00 **5** 1 **The Gatling Boy (IRE)**[13] 2604 3-9-7 **80**..... RyanMoore 2 80
(Richard Hannon) *chsd ldrs in 5th: rdn over 2f out: tried to cl over 1f out: no hdwy fnl f* **5/1**
1166 **6** 1 3/4 **Byroness**[18] 2449 3-8-10 **74**..... RyanTate(5) 8 70
(Heather Main) *hld up in last: stl last and pushed along 2f out: shkn up and plugged on one pce fnl f* **25/1**
0135 **7** *hd* **Grilletto (USA)**[25] 2285 3-9-7 **80**.....(b) NeilCallan 7 75
(James Tate) *chsd ldng pair: drvn on inner over 2f out: steadily wknd over 1f out* **7/1**
-000 **8** 6 **Gigawatt**[5] 2844 3-9-3 **76**..... MatthewDavies 4 55
(Jim Boyle) *dwlt and hmpd s: hld up in last trio: tried to make prog 2f out: wknd qckly fnl f* **33/1**

214- **9** 7 **Aye Aye Skipper (IRE)**[201] 7737 3-9-6 **79**..... KierenFallon 9 39
(Dean Ivory) *racd wd: nvr bttr than midfield: shkn up over 2f out: wknd and eased* **20/1**

1m 25.45s (-0.55) **Going Correction** +0.075s/f (Slow) **9** Ran SP% **116.4**
Speed ratings (Par 101): **106,103,102,102,101 99,98,91,83**
toteswingers 1&2 £4.50, 2&3 £5.50, 1&3 £1.30 CSF £14.77 CT £53.31 TOTE £3.90: £1.30, £1.80, £1.90; EX 23.20 Trifecta £113.20 Pool: £632.44 - 4.18 inning units..
Owner B E Nielsen **Bred** Mrs S L Gibson Fleming **Trained** Upper Lambourn, Berks

FOCUS
The two unexposed market leaders filled the first two positions in this handicap and the form looks solid.
T/Plt: £110.70 to £1 stake. Pool of £55609.41 - 366.54 winning tickets. T/Qpdt: £62.50 to £1 stake. Pool of £4665.37 - 55.15 winning tickets. JN

2955 RIPON (R-H)
Wednesday, June 5

OFFICIAL GOING: Good (good to firm in places; 8.6)
Wind: light 1/2 against Weather: fine and sunny

2985 BRITISH STALLION STUDS SUPPORTING BRITISH RACING EBF MAIDEN STKS 6f
6:45 (6:46) (Class 5) 2-Y-O **£3,881** (£1,155; £577; £288) **Stalls** High

Form RPR
3 **1** **Howz The Family (IRE)**[23] 2307 2-9-5 0..... RichardKingscote 9 71
(Tom Dascombe) *mde all: jnd 1f out: kpt on wl towards fin* **4/1**[1]
634 **2** 3/4 **Queen Of The Tarts**[30] 2090 2-9-0 0..... MickaelBarzalona 4 64
(Olly Stevens) *w ldrs: upsides 1f out: no ex in clsng stages* **13/2**
3 1 1/4 **Kirkstall Abbey (IRE)** 2-9-0 0..... BarryMcHugh 8 60
(Tony Coyle) *s.i.s: hdwy to chse ldrs 3f out: n.m.r on inner over 1f out: styd on to take 3rd nr fin* **6/1**[3]
4 1/2 **Ahoy There (IRE)** 2-9-5 0..... MickyFenton 6 64
(Tom Tate) *chsd ldrs: kpt on same pce fnl f* **16/1**
6 **5** *nk* **Shimba Hills**[11] 2653 2-9-5 0..... MartinHarley 3 63
(Mick Channon) *chsd ldrs: edgd rt over 1f out: kpt on same pce* **9/2**[2]
6 4 **Tohono** 2-9-5 0..... AmyRyan 11 54+
(Kevin Ryan) *hld up in rr: effrt and n.m.r over 2f out: nt clr run and hung rt over 1f out: nvr trbld ldrs* **9/1**
33 **7** 1/2 **Tamayuz Magic (IRE)**[14] 2577 2-9-5 0..... FrannyNorton 2 49
(Mark Johnston) *chsd ldrs on outer: wknd over 1f out* **7/1**
8 1 1/2 **Mfiftythreedotcom (IRE)** 2-9-5 0..... TonyHamilton 10 45
(Richard Fahey) *dwlt: sme hdwy over 2f out: nvr a factor* **7/1**
0 **9** 3/4 **Bentons Lad**[17] 2474 2-9-5 0..... PJMcDonald 1 43
(George Moore) *swvd rt s: swtchd lft after s: a in rr* **100/1**
6 **10** 8 **Wolfwood**[28] 2161 2-9-5 0..... PhillipMakin 5 19
(John Davies) *t.k.h in rr: lost pl over 2f out: sn bhd* **66/1**
11 1/2 **Blue Talisman (IRE)** 2-9-5 0..... DavidAllan 7 17
(Tim Easterby) *in rr: hdwy over 3f out: lost pl over 2f out: sn bhd* **14/1**

1m 14.4s (1.40) **Going Correction** +0.075s/f (Good) **11** Ran SP% **115.8**
Speed ratings (Par 93): **93,92,90,89,89 83,83,81,80,69 68**
toteswingers 1&2 £3.80, 2&3 £9.50, 1&3 £10.00 CSF £29.54 TOTE £5.40: £2.10, £2.00, £2.70; EX 38.20 Trifecta £262.80 Pool: £940.27 - 2.68 winning units..
Owner Ham N Eggers **Bred** S F Bloodstock LLC **Trained** Malpas, Cheshire

FOCUS
An open race according to the market and something of a blanket finish with only a little over two lengths covering the first five home. The runner-up sets the level.

2986 EURA AUDIT UK (S) H'CAP 1m 4f 10y
7:15 (7:16) (Class 6) (0-60,57) 4-5-Y-O **£2,587** (£770; £384; £192) **Stalls** Low

Form RPR
00-0 **1** **Chankillo**[36] 1916 4-9-2 **52**..... TomQueally 1 58+
(Mark H Tompkins) *trckd ldrs: nt clr run and lost pl 4 f out: hdwy to chse ldrs over 2f out: chsd ldrs 1f out: led nr fin* **7/1**
0624 **2** *nk* **Petrol**[41] 1789 4-9-7 **57**..... DavidNolan 4 66+
(David O'Meara) *mid-div: effrt over 3f out: hung rt and led 2f out: 2 l clr ins fnl f: eased and hdd fnl strides* **7/2**[1]
-626 **3** 1 **Blue Top**[16] 2511 4-9-2 **52**..... GrahamGibbons 3 56
(Tim Walford) *trckd ldr: led briefly over 1f out: styd on same pce appr fnl f* **7/2**[1]
-530 **4** *nk* **Operateur (IRE)**[29] 2120 5-9-5 **55**..... PhillipMakin 5 59+
(Ben Haslam) *chsd ldrs: nt clr run over 1f out: siwtched lft: kpt on same pce* **4/1**[2]
4004 **5** 6 **Torero**[9] 2721 4-9-6 **56**.....(p) FrannyNorton 11 50
(Kevin Ryan) *s.i.s: sn chsng ldrs on outside: hung lft over 1f out: sn wknd* **6/1**[3]
000 **6** *hd* **Rolen Sly**[32] 2030 4-8-9 **45**..... MickyFenton 10 39
(Brian Rothwell) *s.s: bhd: drvn and sme hdwy 4f out: lost pl over 2f out* **80/1**
40-0 **7** *nk* **Nippy Nikki**[70] 1207 5-8-9 **45**..... PaddyAspell 2 38
(John Norton) *led 4f: chsd ldrs: drvn over 3f out: lost pl over 1f out* **66/1**
3000 **8** 1 **Quintain (IRE)**[25] 2273 5-9-2 **52**..... DavidAllan 8 44
(Tim Easterby) *in rr: drvn 7f out: sme hdwy and nt clr run over 2f out: nvr a factor* **7/1**
04-6 **9** 1 1/2 **One Million**[34] 1270 4-8-9 **45**.....(t) JamesSullivan 7 34
(Rose Dobbin) *in rr: drvn 6f out: hdwy 4f out: lost pl over 1f out* **66/1**
0030 **10** 1 1/4 **Rockgoat (IRE)**[16] 2514 4-8-12 **48**..... AndreaAtzeni 6 35
(Ian McInnes) *chsd ldrs: led 8f out: hdd over 2f out: lost pl over 1f out* **14/1**
635- **11** 24 **Valentine's Gift**[228] 7248 5-9-2 **52**..... DuranFentiman 9
(Neville Bycroft) *in rr: hdwy over 5f out: lost pl over 2f out: t.o whn eased 1f out: virtually p.u* **20/1**

2m 36.34s (-0.36) **Going Correction** -0.15s/f (Firm) **11** Ran SP% **119.4**
Speed ratings: **95,94,94,93,89 89,89,88,87,87 71**
toteswingers 1&2 £6.80, 2&3 £3.40, 1&3 £7.60 CSF £31.70 CT £102.82 TOTE £12.40: £2.80, £1.10, £2.30; EX 43.30 Trifecta £337.90 Pool: £996.74 - 2.21 winning units..The winner was bought in £7,500.
Owner H-Squared Electronics Ltd **Bred** Dullingham Park **Trained** Newmarket, Suffolk
■ Stewards' Enquiry : David Nolan ten-day ban: failed to ride out a horse that could have finished first (19, 20, 21, 22, 24 - 29 June)

FOCUS
A weak race, even for the grade but it provided the most dramatic of finishes with David Nolan appearing to drop his hands aboard the runner-up. The third helps set the level.

2987 RIPON FARM SERVICES H'CAP 6f
7:45 (7:45) (Class 4) (0-85,78) 3-Y-O £4,851 (£1,443; £721; £360) Stalls High

Form RPR
3512 1 **Antonio Gramsci**[19] 2408 3-9-4 **75** GrahamGibbons 7 83+
(David Barron) *led stands' side tl over 3f out: led 1f out: hung rt: kpty on wl towards fin* **11/8**[1]
60-3 2 ¾ **Shrimper Roo**[19] 2430 3-9-5 **76** DuranFentiman 3 81
(Tim Easterby) *mid-div: hdwy on outer over 2f out: sn chsng ldrs: styd on to take 2nd in clsng stages* **9/1**
-231 3 ¾ **Tumblewind**[30] 2076 3-9-2 **78** GeorgeChaloner(5) 2 81
(Richard Whitaker) *chsd ldrs on outer: rdn to chal over 2f out: kpt on same pce last 75yds* **6/1**[3]
5016 4 shd **Double Your Money (IRE)**[16] 2495 3-9-4 **75** FrannyNorton 1 78
(Mark Johnston) *wnt rt s: sn w ldrs on outer: led over 3f out: hung rt: hdd 1f out: styd on same pce last 75yds* **6/1**[3]
2010 5 ¾ **Khelman (IRE)**[21] 2371 3-9-4 **75** TonyHamilton 4 75
(Richard Fahey) *chsd ldrs: rdn over 2f out: kpt on same pce fnl f* **4/1**[2]
5-20 6 ½ **Tatlisu (IRE)**[27] 2190 3-9-2 **73** BarryMcHugh 6 76+
(Richard Fahey) *in rr: hdwy over 2f out: styng on whn nt clr run appr fnl f and ins fnl f: styd on in clsng stages* **22/1**
040- 7 ¾ **Cumbrian Craic**[266] 6130 3-9-0 **71** DavidAllan 8 67
(Tim Easterby) *sn in rr: rdn over 2f out: kpt on: nvr a factor* **20/1**
040- 8 3 ½ **Scentpastparadise**[238] 6984 3-9-7 **78** PJMcDonald 5 63
(Ann Duffield) *chsd ldrs: lost pl over 1f out* **20/1**
1m 13.44s (0.44) **Going Correction** +0.075s/f (Good) 8 Ran SP% **114.5**
Speed ratings (Par 101): **100,99,98,97,96 96,95,90**
toteswingers 1&2 £4.10, 2&3 £2.90, 1&3 £2.00 CSF £14.37 CT £57.68 TOTE £1.70: £1.02, £2.60, £2.80; EX 7.50 Trifecta £25.60 Pool: £1456.49 - 42.52 winning units..
Owner Norton Common Farm Racing **Bred** A C M Spalding **Trained** Maunby, N Yorks

FOCUS
A highly competitive 3yo sprint handicap, despite the relatively small field. It's doubtful the winner had to match his Hamilton form.

2988 DIRECTORS CUP (HANDICAP STKS) 6f
8:15 (8:16) (Class 3) (0-95,94) 4-Y-O **£7,561** (£2,263; £1,131; £566; £282) Stalls High

Form RPR
-020 1 **Dick Bos**[18] 2460 4-8-9 **82** GrahamLee 10 97+
(David O'Meara) *mde all stands' side: drvn over 1f out: styd on wl* **9/2**[2]
0032 2 2 **Fast Shot**[18] 2460 5-9-1 **88** DavidAllan 9 95+
(Tim Easterby) *hld up in rr: nt clr run and swtchd rt 2f out: styd on wl to chse wnr last 75yds: no real imp* **13/2**[3]
-103 3 nk **Love Island**[17] 2476 4-8-4 **82** GeorgeChaloner(5) 6 88
(Richard Whitaker) *w ldrs: styd on same pce last 100yds* **8/1**
0-64 4 1 ¾ **Misplaced Fortune**[17] 2476 8-9-5 **92** (v) DaleSwift 4 92
(Nigel Tinkler) *w ldrs on outer: styd on same pce fnl f* **12/1**
0001 5 hd **Bonnie Charlie**[11] 2664 7-8-4 **77** PaulQuinn 1 77+
(David Nicholls) *wnt rt s: swtchd lft after 150yds: swtchd outside 2f out: sn chsng ldrs: kpt on same pce fnl f* **20/1**
25-4 6 1 **Minalisa**[16] 2513 4-8-5 **78** ChrisCatlin 7 75
(Rae Guest) *chsd ldrs: drvn and outpcd over 2f out: one pce* **10/1**
4062 7 ½ **Docofthebay (IRE)**[11] 2657 9-8-9 **82** (p) TomQueally 3 77
(Scott Dixon) *swtcted lft after s: sn chsng ldrs: one pce over 1f out* **10/1**
4116 8 nk **Klynch**[11] 2649 7-9-5 **92** (b) JamesSullivan 2 86
(Ruth Carr) *chsd ldrs on outer: kpt on same pce over 1f out* **16/1**
-601 9 1 ½ **Towbee**[18] 2459 4-8-2 **82** ow1 MatthewHopkins(7) 5 71
(Michael Easterby) *chsd ldrs: lost pl over 1f out* **40/1**
-500 10 shd **Queens Revenge**[18] 2463 4-8-2 **75** DuranFentiman 13 64
(Tim Easterby) *chsd ldrs: wknd over 1f out* **16/1**
1251 11 nk **Yeeoow (IRE)**[26] 2207 4-9-7 **94** MartinHarley 11 82+
(Mrs K Burke) *in rr stands' side: effrt and nt clr run over 2f out: n.m.r and stumled over 1f out: nvr a factor* **5/2**[1]
1m 12.11s (-0.89) **Going Correction** +0.075s/f (Good) 11 Ran SP% **116.0**
Speed ratings (Par 107): **108,105,104,102,102 101,100,99,97,97 97**
toteswingers 1&2 £4.50, 2&3 £6.60, 1&3 £6.70 CSF £33.44 CT £227.86 TOTE £4.00: £2.20, £1.40, £3.90; EX 25.80 Trifecta £280.70 Pool: £956.49 - 2.55 winning units..
Owner Middleham Park Racing III & Partners **Bred** Gracelands Stud **Trained** Nawton, N Yorks

FOCUS
An excellent turnout for the feature. The winner made all up stands' rail, as with the other two sprints, and looks on the upgrade.

2989 SIS LIVE MAIDEN STKS 1m 1f 170y
8:45 (8:48) (Class 5) 3-Y-O+ £3,234 (£962; £481; £240) Stalls Low

Form RPR
50- 1 **Broughton (GER)**[258] 6412 3-8-11 0 FrannyNorton 8 81+
(Mark Johnston) *hld up in mid-div: effrt over 3f out: swtchd lft over 1f out: r.o to ld towards fin* **17/2**
0-3 2 ½ **Paris Rose**[30] 2093 3-8-6 0 [1] LiamJones 4 75+
(William Haggas) *trckd ldrs: led 2f out: hdd and no ex nr fin* **11/8**[1]
3 1 ½ **I'm Fraam Govan**[84] 5-9-10 0 (t) GrahamLee 3 78+
(George Baker) *sn trcking ldrs: t.k.h: nt clr run on inner over 2f out: chsng ldrs 1f out: styd on same pce* **8/1**
5- 4 2 ½ **Famlllarity**[180] 8018 3-8-6 0 AndreaAtzeni 9 67
(Roger Varian) *mid-div: hdwy to trck ldrs 4f out: edgd rt and led over 2f out: sn hdd: wknd last 75yds* **9/2**[3]
-06 5 4 ½ **Woodacre**[32] 2030 6-9-10 0 (p) AmyRyan 6 64+
(Richard Whitaker) *t.k.h in rr: hdwy over 3f out: sn chsng ldrs: hung rt and sltly hmpd appr fnl f: fdd* **22/1**
30- 6 1 ¾ **Uncle Bernie (IRE)**[263] 6237 3-8-11 0 TomQueally 10 59
(Andrew Hollinshead) *hld up in rr: hdwy over 2f out: sn chsng ldrs: edgd rt and wknd over 1f out* **22/1**
7 3 ½ **Eium Mac** 4-9-5 0 AdamCarter(5) 1 53
(Neville Bycroft) *chsd ldrs: drvn over 4f out: lost pl over 3f out* **100/1**
00 8 1 **Rocky Couloir**[16] 2516 3-8-11 0 GrahamGibbons 5 50
(Michael Easterby) *led: hdd over 2f out: wknd over 1f out* **80/1**
6 9 ½ **Elusive Band (USA)**[18] 2456 3-8-11 0 RichardKingscote 11 49
(Brian Meehan) *t.k.h: trckd ldrs: rdn whn hmpd over 2f out: sn wknd* **10/3**[2]
0 10 20 **Miss Chuckles**[23] 2306 3-8-6 0 DuranFentiman 7
(Tim Easterby) *s.i.s: in rr: rdn 4f out: sn bhd: t.o* **80/1**
2m 2.87s (-2.53) **Going Correction** -0.15s/f (Firm)
WFA 3 from 4yo+ 13lb 10 Ran SP% **117.2**
Speed ratings (Par 103): **104,103,102,100,96 95,92,91,91,75**
toteswingers 1&2 £4.20, 2&3 £2.90, 1&3 £9.30 CSF £20.28 TOTE £6.40: £3.00, £1.10, £4.50; EX 28.30 Trifecta £212.80 Pool: £1434.16 - 5.05 winning units..
Owner Sheikh Hamdan Bin Mohammed Al Maktoum **Bred** Gestut Westerberg **Trained** Middleham Moor, N Yorks

FOCUS
The form of these was nothing to write home about but there were some potential improvers in the line-up and the first two could prove better than the bare form.

2990 LADIES DAY 20TH JUNE BOOK NOW H'CAP 2m
9:15 (9:15) (Class 5) (0-75,73) 4-Y-O+ £3,234 (£962; £481; £240) Stalls Low

Form RPR
40-0 1 **Big Time Billy (IRE)**[29] 12 7-8-6 **57** (v) MickaelBarzalona 3 67+
(Peter Bowen) *mid-div: hdwy 7f out: drvn 4f out: upsides over 1f out: led last 100yds: drvn out* **7/4**[1]
0022 2 nk **Kodicil (IRE)**[15] 2540 5-8-11 **62** GrahamGibbons 8 71
(Tim Walford) *w ldr: led after 2f: edgd rt over 1f out: hdd last 100yds: kpt on wl* **11/1**
2504 3 4 **Tartan Jura**[13] 2587 5-9-7 **72** (p) FrannyNorton 1 77
(Mark Johnston) *chsd ldrs: effrt over 2f out: kpt on same pce appr fnl f* **10/1**
0046 4 ½ **Beat The Shower**[15] 2540 7-8-9 **60** GrahamLee 13 64
(Peter Niven) *in tch: effrt over 5f out: upsides 2f out: one pce appr fnl f* **25/1**
6-06 5 ¾ **Petella**[26] 2242 7-8-5 **56** oh1 (p) JamesSullivan 11 59
(George Moore) *in rr: hdwy on inner over 3f out: chsng ldrs over 1f out: one pce* **16/1**
15-1 6 nk **Filatore (IRE)**[33] 1979 4-8-11 **70** (p) DanielMuscutt(7) 4 73
(Bernard Llewellyn) *mid-div: hdwy to trck ldrs 7f out: one pce fnl 2f* **13/2**[3]
1100 7 ½ **Foster's Road**[31] 2052 4-9-7 **73** MartinHarley 7 75
(Mick Channon) *hld up in mid-div: hdwy over 3f out: kpt on same pce fnl 2f* **25/1**
5010 8 1 ¾ **Mason Hindmarsh**[15] 2540 6-9-2 **67** PhillipMakin 5 67
(Karen McLintock) *led 2f: chsd ldr: upsides 3f out: wknd appr fnl f* **20/1**
0-10 9 nk **Rapid Heat Lad (IRE)**[117] 563 4-9-2 **68** AndreaAtzeni 9 68
(Andrew Hollinshead) *chsd ldrs: drvn over 3f out: lost pl 2f out* **20/1**
5446 10 nse **Brunello**[18] 2435 5-8-10 **61** (p) MichaelO'Connell 12 61
(Philip Kirby) *in rr: drvn and sme hdwy 4f out: edgd rt and lost pl 2f out* **20/1**
-140 11 shd **Sohcahtoa (IRE)**[26] 2242 7-9-0 **70** LMcNiff(5) 6 70
(Andrew Crook) *in rr: effrt over 4f out: hdwy on inner 3f out: lost pl 2f out* **66/1**
35-0 12 hd **Toptempo**[26] 2205 4-9-4 **70** TomQueally 2 69
(Mark H Tompkins) *mid-div: effrt over 3f out: wknd 2f out* **11/2**[2]
1-03 13 2 ¾ **Major Domo (FR)**[15] 2552 5-9-3 **68** PJMcDonald 10 64
(Micky Hammond) *s.v.s: a detached in last* **11/1**
3m 29.81s (-1.99) **Going Correction** -0.15s/f (Firm)
WFA 4 from 5yo+ 1lb 13 Ran SP% **120.2**
Speed ratings (Par 103): **98,97,95,95,95 95,94,93,93,93 93,93,92**
toteswingers 1&2 £3.70, 2&3 £8.40, 1&3 £6.10 CSF £19.72 CT £158.94 TOTE £2.70: £1.40, £4.50, £1.90; EX 20.80 Trifecta £132.10 Pool: £714.66 - 4.05 winning units..
Owner Miss R L Bryan **Bred** A And C Enterprises **Trained** Little Newcastle, Pembrokes

FOCUS
A fair staying handicap. The winner was on a good mark compared with last year's Flat form, let along her recent jumps improvement.
T/Jkpt: £10,592.10 to a £1 stake. Pool of £37296.26 - 2.50 winning units. T/Plt: £26.00 to a £1 stake. Pool of £84388.76 - 2363.28 winning units. T/Qpdt: £9.00 to a £1 stake. Pool of £6,610.06 - 537.94 winning units. WG

2575 SOUTHWELL (L-H)
Wednesday, June 5

OFFICIAL GOING: Standard
Wind: Moderate across Weather: Grey cloud

2991 DOWNLOAD THE BETVICTOR APP NOW H'CAP 1m 6f (F)
2:00 (2:00) (Class 6) (0-60,60) 4-Y-O+ £1,940 (£577; £288; £144) Stalls High

Form RPR
-445 1 **Barnacle**[7] 2777 4-8-7 **46** oh1 (vt) CathyGannon 11 56
(Pat Eddery) *trckd ldrs: hdwy and cl up 6f out: chal 3f out: led 2f out and sn rdn: drvn clr fnl f: kpt on wl towards fin* **25/1**
306 2 ½ **Rock Of Ages**[14] 2568 4-9-0 **53** (b[1]) LiamJones 6 62
(Michael Murphy) *dwlt: swtchd to outer and sn pushed along: hdwy and cl up after 4f: led 1/2-way: rdn along 3f out: hdd 2f out: cl up and drvn over 1f out: ev ch tl edgd rt and no ex wl ins fnl f* **14/1**
301- 3 7 **Tobrata**[197] 7800 7-9-7 **60** SilvestreDeSousa 3 59
(Mel Brittain) *hld up in tch: swtchd to outer and hdwy over 4f out: rdn to chse ldng pair wl over 1f out: drvn and no imp appr fnl f* **15/2**
4-56 4 3 ¼ **Gucci D'Oro (USA)**[12] 2642 4-9-1 **54** (b[1]) MartinLane 10 49
(David Simcock) *trckd ldrs: hdwy 6f out: chsd ldng trio 3f out: sn rdn along: drvn 2f out: sn one pce* **3/1**[1]
-025 5 8 **Akarana (IRE)**[16] 2511 6-8-11 **50** J-PGuillambert 7 37
(Willie Musson) *trckd ldrs: hdwy to chse ldng pair 1/2-way: rdn along 3f out: wknd over 2f out* **15/2**
33-5 6 2 ¼ **Dancing Paddy (IRE)**[50] 1600 5-8-7 **46** PaddyAspell 1 26
(Alan Swinbank) *a towards rr* **12/1**
0420 7 1 ¾ **Koo And The Gang (IRE)**[8] 2764 6-8-12 **54** PaulPickard(3) 5 32
(Brian Ellison) *t.k.h early: hld up in rr: hdwy 1/2-way: chsd ldrs 4f out: swtchd to inner and rdn wl over 2f out: sn wknd* **11/2**[3]
0-36 8 14 **Omid**[92] 887 5-9-4 **57** (vt) AndreaAtzeni 8 15
(Nicky Vaughan) *sn outpcd and a bhd* **10/1**
6-42 9 4 ½ **Medieval Bishop (IRE)**[23] 2328 4-8-12 **51** (v[1]) DuranFentiman 9
(Tim Walford) *led and sn clr: pushed along and hdd 1/2-way: sn rdn and wknd over 4f out* **7/2**[2]
0-00 10 41 **Peninsula**[12] 2628 4-9-7 **60** SeanLevey 4
(Tobias B P Coles) *prom: rdn along and lost pl after 6f: bhd fr 1/2-way: t.o fnl 3f* **40/1**
3m 9.93s (1.63) **Going Correction** +0.175s/f (Slow) 10 Ran SP% **115.9**
Speed ratings (Par 101): **102,101,97,95,91 90,89,81,78,55**
toteswingers 1&2 £34.40, 2&3 £13.40, 1&3 £22.30 CSF £331.95 CT £2874.98 TOTE £19.20: £4.00, £4.70, £2.00; EX 186.00 Trifecta £1137.50 Part won. Pool: £1516.77 - 0.44 winning units..

Owner P J J Eddery **Bred** Shortgrove Manor Stud **Trained** Nether Winchendon, Bucks
FOCUS
The track was watered both before and during racing to ensure it did not slow up too much. A moderate staying race, but it appeared to be reasonably competitive on paper. However, they ultimately finished well strung out.

2992 £25 FREE BET AT BETVICTOR.COM RATING RELATED MAIDEN STKS 6f (F)
2:30 (2:31) (Class 6) 3-Y-0+ **£1,940** (£577; £288; £144) **Stalls** Low

Form RPR
2522 **1** **Gebayl**[71] 1190 3-9-0 62....(p) AndreaAtzeni 5 60
(James Tate) *chsd ldng pair: hdwy on outer over 2f out: rdn to ld wl over 1f out: rdn out* **6/5**[1]
5-00 **2** *2 1/4* **Mistress Shy**[14] 2575 6-9-8 43....(t) AndrewMullen 4 55
(Michael Appleby) *cl up: rdn to ld over 2f out: drvn and hdd wl over 1f out: kpt on u.p fnl f* **50/1**
50-0 **3** *5* **Stand N Applaude**[23] 2308 3-9-0 54.... FrannyNorton 6 37
(David Nicholls) *s.i.s and bhd: rdn along 1/2-way: hdwy wl over 1f out: kpt on fnl f: nrst fin* **10/1**
64-0 **4** *2* **Speed Date**[26] 2226 3-9-0 65....(bt[1]) MartinLane 1 30
(Tobias B P Coles) *slt ld: rdn along 1/2-way: sn hdd & wknd wl over 1f out* **12/1**
340- **5** *6* **Sandy's Row (USA)**[300] 5009 3-9-0 65.... SilvestreDeSousa 3 18
(Mark Johnston) *sltly hmpd s: sn swtchd to inner and chsd ldrs: rdn wl over 2f out: sn outpcd* **3/1**[2]
2344 **U** **Solarmaite**[16] 2511 4-9-5 60....(b[1]) MarkCoumbe[(3)] 2
(Roy Bowring) *wnt rt and stmbld s: uns rdr* **9/2**[3]
1m 17.37s (0.87) **Going Correction** +0.175s/f (Slow)
WFA 3 from 4yo+ 8lb 6 Ran SP% **107.4**
Speed ratings (Par 101): **101,98,91,88,80**
toteswingers 1&2 £5.60, 2&3 £18.20, 1&3 £3.30 CSF £48.72 TOTE £1.80: £1.10, £15.40; EX 29.80 Trifecta £112.30 Pool: £1703.20 - 11.36 winning units..
Owner Saeed Manana **Bred** Wickfield Farm Partnership **Trained** Newmarket, Suffolk
FOCUS
These six had run up 50 appearances between them on the racecourse without winning coming into this rating related maiden.

2993 BETVICTOR.COM NOVICE AUCTION STKS 6f (F)
3:00 (3:02) (Class 5) 2-Y-0 **£2,587** (£770; £384; £192) **Stalls** Low

Form RPR
543 **1** **Left Defender (IRE)**[9] 2723 2-8-9 0.... CathyGannon 5 73
(Jo Hughes) *trckd ldng pair: hdwy on outer 1/2-way: effrt and edgd lft wl over 1f out: rdn to chal and hung lft ent fnl f: styd on to ld last 100yds* **11/4**[2]
41 **2** *3/4* **Thewandaofu (IRE)**[14] 2562 2-8-8 0.... FergusSweeney 1 70
(Jamie Osborne) *trckd ldr: cl up 1/2-way: led 2f out and sn shkn up: rdn over 1f out: drvn and sltly hmpd jst ins fnl f: sn hdd and one pce* **9/4**[1]
13 **3** *13* **Loma Mor**[8] 2758 2-8-6 0.... AndrewMullen 2 29
(Alan McCabe) *led: rdn along and hdd 2f out: sn drvn and wknd over 1f out* **3/1**[3]
2 **4** *4 1/2* **Cheeky Peta'S**[16] 2510 2-8-6 0.... JamesSullivan 4 16
(James Given) *chsd ldng pair: rdn along wl over 2f out: sn outpcd* **3/1**[3]
5 *11* **Mystic Angellina** 2-7-11 0.... DanielleMooney[(7)] 3
(Michael Chapman) *s.i.s: green: outpcd and a bhd* **25/1**
1m 18.73s (2.23) **Going Correction** +0.175s/f (Slow) 5 Ran SP% **111.3**
Speed ratings (Par 93): **92,91,73,67,53**
CSF £9.45 TOTE £3.00: £1.80, £1.10; EX 9.00 Trifecta £29.50 Pool: £1244.11 - 31.53 winning units..
Owner East Wind Racing, J Hearne, H Downs **Bred** Meadowlands Stud **Trained** Lambourn, Berks
FOCUS
A poorly competed novice, but a chance could be given to four of the five. The front two pulled well clear, but the time was nearly a second and half slower than the preceding maiden.

2994 SHANE W DARBY MEMORIAL H'CAP 5f (F)
3:30 (3:30) (Class 4) (0-80,76) 3-Y-0 **£4,690** (£1,395; £697; £348) **Stalls** High

Form RPR
3-03 **1** **Sharaarah (IRE)**[19] 2408 3-9-7 **76**.... SilvestreDeSousa 1 88+
(David O'Meara) *wnt sltly lft s: sn prom and led after 1f: rdn clr over 1f out: sn edgd rt and kpt on strly* **6/4**[1]
-340 **2** *2* **Chasing Dreams**[19] 2430 3-9-5 **74**.... PhillipMakin 5 78
(Kevin Ryan) *trckd ldrs: hdwy 1/2-way: swtchd lft and rdn to chse wnr over 1f out: sn drvn and kpt on same pce* **6/1**
2-31 **3** *3/4* **Flirtinaskirt**[28] 2169 3-9-6 **75**.... SeanLevey 3 76
(Ed McMahon) *hld up in tch: hdwy 2f out: rdn wl over 1f out: kpt on same pce fnl f* **4/1**[3]
6133 **4** *7* **Miako (USA)**[70] 1204 3-9-3 **72**....(v[1]) AndrewMullen 6 48
(Michael Appleby) *trckd ldrs: effrt 2f out: sn rdn and edgd lft wl over 1f out: sn btn* **11/1**
0331 **5** *1/2* **Harbour Captain (IRE)**[21] 2363 3-9-0 **69**.... CathyGannon 4 43
(Jo Hughes) *led 1f: cl up: rdn along 1/2-way: sn drvn and wknd wl over 1f out* **11/4**[2]
1m 0.08s (0.38) **Going Correction** +0.225s/f (Slow) 5 Ran SP% **109.3**
Speed ratings (Par 101): **105,101,100,89,88**
CSF £10.59 TOTE £2.00: £1.10, £3.80; EX 8.80 Trifecta £36.10 Pool: £799.45 - 16.57 winning units..
Owner Middleham Park Racing XXXVII & C Tasker **Bred** Shadwell Estate Company Limited **Trained** Nawton, N Yorks
FOCUS
The best race on the card and it was a fair sprint handicap where all of them could be given a chance.

2995 BETVICTOR CASINO ON YOUR MOBILE MAIDEN STKS 1m 4f (F)
4:00 (4:01) (Class 5) 3-Y-0+ **£2,587** (£770; £384; £192) **Stalls** Low

Form RPR
06 **1** **Jimmy Sewell (IRE)**[4] 2885 4-9-12 0.... AndrewMullen 3 75
(Michael Appleby) *a.p: pushed along and sltly outpcd over 4f out: hdwy over 3f out: rdn to chse ldng pair and edging lft wl over 1f out: drvn and hung lft ent fnl f: styd on u.p to ld last 50yds* **20/1**
22 **2** *1 1/2* **Street Artist (IRE)**[32] 2030 3-8-11 0.... SilvestreDeSousa 9 73
(Mark Johnston) *trckd ldrs: hdwy on outer and cl up after 4f: led 7f out: rdn along 3f out: slt ld and drvn wl over 1f out: hdd and no ex last 50yds* **10/11**[1]
3 *1/2* **Gwael (USA)** 3-8-6 0.... AndreaAtzeni 10 67
(James Tate) *in tch: hdwy 1/2-way and sn trcking ldr: cl up 4f out: chal 3f out: rdn over 2f out: sn drvn and ev ch tl no ex wl ins fnl f* **4/1**[2]
23 **4** *6* **Fantasy In Blue**[48] 1653 3-8-6 0....(v[1]) HayleyTurner 4 58
(Sir Michael Stoute) *chsd ldrs: rdn along wl over 3f out: drvn 2f out and sn one pce* **4/1**[2]
0-06 **5** *27* **Marina Ballerina**[28] 2168 5-9-4 42....(b) MarkCoumbe[(3)] 6 14
(Roy Bowring) *in rr: rdn along 1/2-way: nvr a factor* **40/1**
00 **6** *11* **Celtic Legacy**[40] 1804 6-9-4 0.... RaulDaSilva[(3)] 2
(Michael Murphy) *a in rr: bhd fnl 4f* **50/1**
7 *40* **Sam Run**[55] 4-9-12 0.... ChrisCatlin 5
(Christopher Kellett) *sn outpcd and alwys bhd: t.o fnl 4f* **100/1**
5-6 **8** *7* **Equalizer**[18] 2465 4-9-12 0....(t) RichardKingscote 11
(Tom Dascombe) *prom: rdn along over 5f out: sn wknd* **6/1**[3]
05-0 **9** *12* **Fake Or Fortune (IRE)**[9] 2716 3-8-11 45....(b[1]) DuranFentiman 8
(Colin Teague) *led: hdd 7f out: sn rdn along: wknd 5f out: sn bhd: t.o* **66/1**
2m 42.33s (1.33) **Going Correction** +0.175s/f (Slow)
WFA 3 from 4yo+ 15lb 9 Ran SP% **118.3**
Speed ratings (Par 103): **102,101,100,96,78 71,44,40,32**
toteswingers 1&2 £4.70, 2&3 £1.80, 1&3 £7.60 CSF £39.53 TOTE £25.10: £4.00, £1.10, £1.10; EX 62.90 Trifecta £234.40 Pool: £3782.01 - 12.09 winning units..
Owner W Sewell **Bred** Noel And Michael Buckley **Trained** Danethorpe, Notts
FOCUS
Typically little depth to this 3yo+ maiden and a bit of a turn-up, but it may not necessarily be poor form. They went off a strong gallop which contributed to the first four finishing in another parish to the rest and a slow-motion finish. The well-bred types from big stables occupied the places.

2996 PLAY GOLF AT SOUTHWELL GOLF CLUB H'CAP 5f (F)
4:30 (4:30) (Class 6) (0-65,60) 3-Y-0 **£1,940** (£577; £288; £144) **Stalls** High

Form RPR
-234 **1** **Confidential Creek**[22] 2336 3-9-0 **60**....(p) JacobButterfield[(7)] 9 67
(Ollie Pears) *mde virtually all: rdn wl over 1f out: edgd lft and kpt on wl fnl f* **3/1**[2]
36-0 **2** *1/2* **Laughing Rock (IRE)**[30] 2095 3-9-3 **56**.... AndrewMullen 3 61
(Michael Appleby) *cl up: rdn and ev ch over 1f out: sn drvn and kpt on same pce fnl f* **4/1**[3]
-150 **3** *hd* **Outbid**[110] 669 3-9-7 **60**.... FergusSweeney 5 64
(Jamie Osborne) *dwlt and in rr: hdwy on outer 2f out: sn rdn and kpt on fnl f: nrst fin* **12/1**
6531 **4** *1/2* **Whiteflats**[48] 1651 3-8-12 **51**....(v) HarryBentley 4 53
(Derek Shaw) *prom: hdwy over 2f out: rdn to chal over 1f out and ev ch tl drvn and one pce ins fnl f* **4/1**[3]
-335 **5** *4 1/2* **Red Star Lady (IRE)**[61] 1367 3-8-6 **45**.... DuranFentiman 2 31
(Shaun Harris) *chsd ldrs on outer: rdn along over 2f out: grad wknd* **25/1**
1-62 **6** *shd* **Constant Dream**[16] 2512 3-9-7 **60**.... JamesSullivan 6 46
(James Given) *in tch: rdn along 2f out: sn one pce* **9/4**[1]
4350 **7** *1 1/4* **Viva L'Inghilterra (IRE)**[16] 2512 3-8-13 **55**.... RossAtkinson[(3)] 7 36
(Robert Cowell) *chsd ldrs: rdn along and outpcd fr 1/2-way* **14/1**
0-06 **8** *7* **Sound Affects**[15] 2535 3-8-3 **45**.... RaulDaSilva[(3)] 8
(Alan Brown) *chsd ldrs: rdn along 1/2-way: sn wknd* **50/1**
1m 1.6s (1.90) **Going Correction** +0.225s/f (Slow) 8 Ran SP% **115.9**
Speed ratings (Par 97): **93,92,91,91,83 83,81,70**
toteswingers 1&2 £3.30, 2&3 £8.70, 1&3 £5.60 CSF £15.75 CT £125.87 TOTE £4.70: £2.20, £1.50, £3.00; EX 18.60 Trifecta £147.30 Pool: £2900.42 - 14.76winning units..
Owner John H Sissons **Bred** Kirtlington Stud Ltd **Trained** Norton, N Yorks
FOCUS
Moderate form.

2997 TALK TO VICTOR APPRENTICE H'CAP (DIV I) 6f (F)
5:00 (5:01) (Class 6) (0-55,54) 3-Y-0+ **£1,940** (£577; £288; £144) **Stalls** Low

Form RPR
06-0 **1** **Insolenceofoffice (IRE)**[25] 2281 5-9-7 **54**....(p) ConnorBeasley[(3)] 2 66
(Richard Ford) *prom: hdwy over 2f out: led wl over 1f out: rdn and kpt on wl fnl f* **13/2**
526 **2** *2 1/4* **Doctor Hilary**[28] 2170 11-9-4 **48**....(v) NoelGarbutt 8 53
(Mark Hoad) *towards rr: hdwy over 2f out: rdn wl over 1f out: edgd lft and styd on fnl f* **6/1**[3]
420- **3** *nk* **Depden (IRE)**[263] 6233 5-9-2 **46**.... JacobButterfield 11 50
(Richard Price) *chsd ldng pair: hdwy on outer whn carried sltly rt 2f out: sn rdn to chse wnr wl over 1f out: drvn and one pce fnl f* **16/1**
005- **4** *2 1/2* **Queen Hermione (IRE)**[276] 5852 5-8-10 **45**....(v[1]) AdamMcLean[(5)] 10 39
(Derek Shaw) *in tch: hdwy to chse ldrs wl over 2f out: sn rdn: drvn and one pce fr over 1f out* **25/1**
0006 **5** *4* **Amenable (IRE)**[5] 2832 6-8-13 **50**.... OisinMurphy[(7)] 5 33
(Violet M Jordan) *hld up in midfield: sme hdwy 2f out: sn rdn and n.d* **4/1**[2]
4055 **6** *2 3/4* **Nors The Panic**[22] 2336 3-8-3 **48** ow2....(e) LisaTodd[(7)] 9 20
(Richard Guest) *dwlt: sn chsng ldrs: rdn along wl over 2f out: sn wknd* **16/1**
655 **7** *1* **Rose Of May (IRE)**[26] 2241 3-9-1 **53**.... DavidBergin 6 22
(David O'Meara) *a towards rr* **3/1**[1]
0-00 **8** *1/2* **Verus Delicia (IRE)**[31] 2043 4-9-4 **51**....[1] EoinWalsh[(3)] 7 20
(Daniel Mark Loughnane) *dwlt: a in rr* **10/1**
5350 **9** *nk* **Sophie's Beau (USA)**[42] 1758 6-8-8 **45**....(b) DanielleMooney[(7)] 3
(Michael Chapman) *led: clr after 1f: rdn and hung rt 2f out: sn hdd & wknd* **20/1**
4006 **10** *2* **Whipphound**[14] 2582 5-9-9 **53**.... JackDuern 4
(Mark Brisbourne) *chsd ldrs on inner: rdn along 1/2-way: sn wknd* **6/1**[3]
1m 16.8s (0.30) **Going Correction** +0.175s/f (Slow)
WFA 3 from 4yo+ 8lb 10 Ran SP% **116.4**
Speed ratings (Par 101): **105,102,101,98,92 89,87,87,86,84**
toteswingers 1&2 £6.90, 2&3 £7.00, 1&3 £24.70 CSF £45.18 CT £616.95 TOTE £6.30: £1.80, £2.10, £3.90; EX 73.40 Trifecta £458.20 Pool: £2010.48 - 3.29 winning units..
Owner CCCNLP **Bred** Gerard Kennedy **Trained** Garstang, Lancs
FOCUS
An apprentice handicap which was little better than most plating-class races.

2998 TALK TO VICTOR APPRENTICE H'CAP (DIV II) 6f (F)
5:30 (5:30) (Class 6) (0-55,53) 3-Y-0+ **£1,940** (£577; £288; £144) **Stalls** Low

Form RPR
6044 **1** **Very First Blade**[14] 2582 4-9-3 **49**....(p) MatthewHopkins[(3)] 7 58
(Mark Brisbourne) *trckd ldrs: hdwy 2f out: rdn wl over 1f out: drvn to chal ent fnl f: sn led: kpt on wl towards fin* **5/2**[1]
4000 **2** *nk* **Upper Lambourn (IRE)**[14] 2575 5-9-10 **53**....(t) JackDuern 6 61
(Christopher Kellett) *in tch: hdwy on wd outside over 2f out: rdn to chse ldrs over 1f out: styd on and ev ch ins fnl f: no ex towards fin* **4/1**[2]
0062 **3** *1 1/4* **Ishiamiracle**[14] 2578 4-9-2 **45**....(p) DannyBrock 9 49
(Phil McEntee) *cl up: led wl over 1f out and sn rdn: drvn ent fnl f: sn hdd and kpt on same pce* **9/2**[3]

00-0 **4** *3* **Beach Rhythm (USA)**[20] 2395 6-9-2 **50**........................ LewisWalsh(5) 1 44
(Jim Allen) *chsd ldrs on inner: rdn along 2f out: drvn over 1f out: kpt on one pce* **9/1**

-002 **5** *1/2* **Amelia Jay**[14] 2581 3-8-7 **47**........................ JoeyHaynes(3) 5 38
(Danielle McCormick) *slt ld: rdn along wl over 2f out: hdd and drvn wl over 1f out: wknd appr fnl f* **11/2**

0-05 **6** *3 3/4* **Farmers Dream (IRE)**[29] 2125 6-8-11 **45**................(t) AdamMcLean(5) 2 26
(Derek Shaw) *a towards rr* **12/1**

0-06 **7** *1 1/2* **Fathey (IRE)**[103] 754 7-9-2 **45**........................ IanBurns 10 21
(Charles Smith) *cl up on outer: rdn along 1/2-way: wknd over 2f out* **33/1**

4030 **8** *3/4* **Lord Buffhead**[5] 2835 4-9-3 **53**........................(be) LisaTodd(7) 3 27
(Richard Guest) *s.i.s: a in rr* **8/1**

1m 17.71s (1.21) **Going Correction** +0.175s/f (Slow)
WFA 3 from 4yo+ 8lb **8** Ran SP% **113.9**
Speed ratings (Par 101): **98,97,95,91,91 86,84,83**
toteswingers 1&2 £4.50, 2&3 £4.50, 1&3 £3.90 CSF £12.39 CT £41.35 TOTE £3.40: £1.60, £1.40, £2.00; EX 12.00 Trifecta £36.80 Pool: £1253.92 - 25.53 winning units..
Owner L R Owen **Bred** L R Owen **Trained** Great Ness, Shropshire
■ Stewards' Enquiry : Jack Duern two-day ban: use of whip (23-24 June)

FOCUS
The card was rounded off with the second division of the apprentice handicap which was similarly weak. It lost a realistic contender when John Coffey was withdrawn as his trainer deemed the surface had been riding too deep throughout the afternoon.
T/Plt: £266.30 to a £1 stake. Pool of £50731.87 - 139.03 winning tickets. T/Qpdt: £22.40 to a £1 stake. Pool of £4514.71 - 149.10 winning tickets JR

2999 - 3006a (Foreign Racing) - See Raceform Interactive

[2334]MAISONS-LAFFITTE (R-H)
Wednesday, June 5

OFFICIAL GOING: Turf: good

3007a PRIX MATCHEM (LISTED RACE) (3YO COLTS & GELDINGS) (TURF) 1m 1f
4:10 (12:00) 3-Y-O £22,357 (£8,943; £6,707; £4,471; £2,235)

RPR

1 **Pilote (IRE)**[21] 3-8-11 0........................ OlivierPeslier 5 104
(A Fabre, France) **7/10**[1]

2 *3* **Onedargent (FR)**[16] 2527 3-8-11 0........................(p) ThierryJarnet 1 98
(J-P Gallorini, France) **43/10**[2]

3 *1/2* **Kapstadt (FR)**[16] 2527 3-8-11 0........................(p) IoritzMendizabal 4 97
(F Doumen, France) **11/2**[3]

4 *2 1/2* **Herve (IRE)**[15] 2557 3-8-11 0........................ StephanePasquier 2 92?
(T Castanheira, France) **8/1**

5 *20* **Holy Warrior (IRE)**[18] 2454 3-9-2 0..............(b[1]) Pierre-CharlesBoudot 3 55
(Gay Kelleway) *led: hdd over 2f out and immediately btn: wknd and dropped to last: eased and t.o* **68/10**

1m 52.9s (-1.80) **5** Ran SP% **117.0**
WIN (incl.1 euro stake): 1.70. PLACES: 1.10, 1.40. SF: 4.00.
Owner Wertheimer & Frere **Bred** Wertheimer Et Frere **Trained** Chantilly, France

3008 - (Foreign Racing) - See Raceform Interactive

[2786]BRIGHTON (L-H)
Thursday, June 6

OFFICIAL GOING: Firm (8.7)
Rail dolled out 2.5yds from 4.5f to 2.5f adding 8yds to advertised distances.
Wind: fresh, behind Weather: sunny and breezy

3009 JAMES ROSS JEWELLERS MAIDEN AUCTION STKS 5f 59y
2:00 (2:00) (Class 5) 2-Y-O £2,587 (£770; £384; £192) Stalls Low

Form RPR

52 **1** **Pound Piece (IRE)**[7] 2805 2-9-5 0........................ LiamJones 2 71
(J S Moore) *mde all: rdn and asserted over 1f out: styd on wl fnl f* **8/13**[1]

0 **2** *1 1/2* **Zafraaj**[22] 2359 2-9-5 0........................ LukeMorris 4 66+
(Ronald Harris) *chsd wnr: drvn ent fnl 2f: unable qck over 1f out: hld by wnr but kpt on for clr 2nd fnl f* **16/1**

3 *3 3/4* **Goadby** 2-8-9 0........................ MichaelJMMurphy(5) 6 47
(John Holt) *s.i.s: sn pushed along and in tch in last pair: chsd ldrs and rdn 2f out: rn green: hung lft and btn over 1f out: plugged on fnl f* **20/1**

50 **4** *1 3/4* **Bonnie Wee Lassie**[45] 1724 2-8-7 0........................ CameronHardie(7) 1 41
(Richard Hannon) *t.k.h: chsd ldrs: rdn and effrt ent fnl 2f: outpcd and btn over 1f out: wknd ins fnl f* **10/1**[3]

5 *12* **Dawnfromthepast (IRE)** 2-9-5 0........................ FergusSweeney 5
(Jamie Osborne) *s.i.s: hld up in tch: clsd to press ldrs 1/2-way: rdn and effrt 2f out: sn btn: hung lft and wknd over 1f out* **11/4**[2]

1m 2.02s (-0.28) **Going Correction** -0.40s/f (Firm) **5** Ran SP% **108.3**
Speed ratings (Par 93): **86,83,77,74,55**
Tote Swinger 1&2 £5.80 CSF £11.28 TOTE £1.40: £1.10, £4.40; EX 7.70 Trifecta £30.40 Pool: £2,239.88 - 55.22 winning tickets..
Owner G B Watts & J S Moore **Bred** Grangemore Stud **Trained** Upper Lambourn, Berks

FOCUS
The ground was described as firm and there was a strong wind blowing them home up the straight. A modest juvenile maiden in which they went a decent gallop. The winner may prove better than the bare form.

3010 GEOFF PYGALL H'CAP 5f 213y
2:30 (2:31) (Class 5) (0-75,75) 4-Y-O+ £2,587 (£770; £384; £192) Stalls Low

Form RPR

4-13 **1** **Langley Vale**[7] 2790 4-9-3 **71**........................ SebSanders 2 85+
(Roger Teal) *mde all: clr w runner-up and rdn 2f out: forged ahd ins fnl f: styd on: rdn out* **15/8**[1]

30-4 **2** *1/2* **Maria Montez**[31] 2096 4-7-10 **57**........................ ShelleyBirkett(7) 8 69
(J W Hills) *t.k.h: chsd wnr: clr w wnr and rdn wl over 1f out: kpt on wl but one pce fnl 100yds* **16/1**

3-00 **3** *1/2* **Clear Spring (IRE)**[26] 2255 5-9-7 **75**........................ NickyMackay 6 85
(John Spearing) *s.i.s: in last pair early: stdy hdwy 4f out: rdn and hdwy over 1f out: chsd clr ldng pair 1f out: styd on wl: nt rch ldrs* **4/1**[2]

1-05 **4** *2 1/4* **Dear Maurice**[34] 1976 9-9-0 **68**........................(t) MartinLane 11 71
(Tobias B P Coles) *in tch in midfield: rdn 1/2-way: outpcd u.p 2f out: no threat to ldrs but kpt on again ins fnl f* **12/1**

1160 **5** *nk* **Alpha Delta Whisky**[16] 2550 5-8-13 **72**.............. MichaelJMMurphy(5) 9 74
(John Gallagher) *hld up in tch in midfield: rdn and outpcd over 2f out: no threat to ldrs but styd on again ins fnl f* **7/1**

1355 **6** *nk* **Dark Lane**[6] 2825 7-9-3 **71**........................ AdamKirby 10 72
(David Evans) *racd in last trio: rdn and hdwy over 1f out: swtchd lft 1f out: kpt on: nvr trbld ldrs* **5/1**[3]

0026 **7** *1 1/4* **Diamond Vine (IRE)**[92] 898 5-8-6 **60**........................(p) LukeMorris 5 57
(Ronald Harris) *chsd ldrs: outpcd and drvn over 2f out: wknd 1f out* **14/1**

60-P **8** *3 1/4* **Mr Fickle (IRE)**[14] 2596 4-8-11 **65**........................ FergusSweeney 3 52
(Gary Moore) *s.i.s: a outpcd in rr* **33/1**

-000 **9** *3/4* **Interakt**[12] 2657 6-8-12 **66**........................ HarryBentley 1 50
(Joseph Tuite) *in tch in midfield: rdn and struggling over 2f out: wknd 2f out* **14/1**

1m 8.34s (-1.86) **Going Correction** -0.40s/f (Firm) **9** Ran SP% **113.8**
Speed ratings (Par 103): **96,95,94,91,91 90,89,84,83**
Tote Swingers 1&2 £7.40, 2&3 £11.50, 1&3 £2.40 CSF £34.98 CT £109.59 TOTE £2.50: £1.30, £4.30, £1.10; EX 27.80 Trifecta £125.00 Pool: £3,227.21 - 19.35 winning tickets..
Owner Dr G F Forward & F C Taylor **Bred** Miss Brooke Sanders **Trained** Ashtead, Surrey

FOCUS
A fair sprint handicap for older horses in which they went a good clip from the outset. The first two were 102 throughout and the winner continues on the upgrade.

3011 HARRINGTONS LETTINGS MAIDEN STKS 7f 214y
3:05 (3:06) (Class 5) 3-Y-O+ £2,587 (£770; £384; £192) Stalls Centre

Form RPR

3-22 **1** **Bartack (IRE)**[24] 2309 3-9-3 80........................(b[1]) KierenFallon 1 83
(Luca Cumani) *chsd ldrs: wnt 2nd 1/2-way: chalng and followed ldr across to stands' rail over 1f out: led ins fnl f: sn clr: comf* **6/4**[1]

-323 **2** *3 3/4* **Caramack**[14] 2593 3-8-12 78........................ WilliamTwiston-Davies(5) 7 74
(Richard Hannon) *chsd ldr tl 1/2-way: cl 3rd whn carried rt wl over 1f out: swtchd lft over 1f out: chsd clr wnr ins fnl f: no imp* **15/8**[2]

2-40 **3** *3/4* **Dark Templar**[16] 2549 3-9-3 67........................ MartinLane 8 73
(Ed Vaughan) *led: rdn and edgd rt to stands' rail over 1f out: hdd ins fnl f: sn outpcd and btn* **10/1**

00-2 **4** *3 1/4* **Mazaaher**[31] 2093 3-9-3 70........................ PaulHanagan 2 65
(J W Hills) *in tch in midfield: rdn and effrt over 1f out: no imp 1f out: sn wknd and eased wl ins fnl f* **4/1**[3]

0-6 **5** *18* **Cherry Tiger**[37] 1904 3-9-3 0........................ KirstyMilczarek 4 24
(James Toller) *t.k.h: hld up in tch in midfield: rdn 1/2-way: wknd 3f out: wl bhd over 1f out* **16/1**

00 **6** *1 3/4* **Sun And Stars**[9] 2746 5-9-9 0........................ EDLinehan(5) 5 23
(Brendan Powell) *a bhd in last pair: lost tch 3f out* **66/1**

0 **7** *18* **Beltaine (IRE)**[17] 2516 4-9-9 0........................(t) JemmaMarshall(5) 6
(Brendan Powell) *s.i.s: t.k.h and sn in tch in midfield: rdn and struggling over 3f out: sn btn and wknd: t.o* **66/1**

0 **8** *3* **Tannhauser Gate (IRE)**[5] 2872 3-9-3 0........................ FergusSweeney 3
(Jamie Osborne) *sn bhd: lost tch 1/2-way: t.o* **66/1**

1m 31.8s (-4.20) **Going Correction** -0.40s/f (Firm)
WFA 3 from 4yo+ 11lb **8** Ran SP% **114.2**
Speed ratings (Par 103): **105,101,100,97,79 77,59,56**
Tote Swingers 1&2 £1.10, 2&3 £3.00, 1&3 £3.00 CSF £4.51 TOTE £1.80: £1.10, £1.10, £1.80; EX 4.30 Trifecta £17.80 Pool: £4,580.78 - 192.36 winning tickets..
Owner Bruce Corman **Bred** Alberto Panetta **Trained** Newmarket, Suffolk

FOCUS
A fair maiden in which they went an honest gallop. The level of the form revolves around the third.

3012 SE TYRES H'CAP 1m 3f 196y
3:40 (3:40) (Class 5) (0-75,71) 4-Y-O+ £2,587 (£770; £384; £192) Stalls High

Form RPR

0-43 **1** **The Holyman (IRE)**[34] 1973 5-9-7 **71**........................ IanMongan 3 80
(Jo Crowley) *chsd ldr tl led 6f out: rdn and wnt clr over 2f out: hld on wl u.p fnl 100yds* **5/4**[1]

32-0 **2** *nk* **Laser Blazer**[20] 2417 5-9-5 **69**........................(p) FergusSweeney 2 77
(Jeremy Gask) *stdd s: hld up in last: hdwy to chse ldng pair over 3f out: chsd wnr over 2f out: drvn and clsd over 1f out: ev ch ins fnl f: kpt on but a hld* **5/2**[2]

/00- **3** *13* **Eseej (USA)**[246] 6802 8-9-1 **65**........................ LiamKeniry 1 53
(Geoffrey Deacon) *taken down early: led tl 6f out: pressed wnr tl rdn and outpcd over 2f out: 3rd and btn 2f out: sn wknd* **12/1**

000- **4** *6* **Dubai Glory**[11] 5772 5-8-13 **70**........................ NedCurtis(7) 6 48
(Sheena West) *chsd ldng trio: wnt 3rd 5f out tl over 3f out: sn struggling: bhd fnl 2f* **5/1**[3]

0336 **5** *1/2* **Sommersturm (GER)**[15] 2328 9-9-1 **65**........................(t) AdamKirby 4 42
(David Evans) *chsd ldng pair tl dropped to rr 5f out: lost tch 3f out* **7/1**

2m 31.27s (-1.43) **Going Correction** -0.40s/f (Firm) **5** Ran SP% **109.9**
Speed ratings (Par 103): **88,87,79,75,74**
Tote Swinger 1&2 £3.70 CSF £4.57 TOTE £1.90: £1.70, £1.10; EX 4.20 Trifecta £23.00 Pool: £1,869.51 - 60.78 winning tickets..
Owner Kilstone Limited **Bred** Old Carhue Stud **Trained** Whitcombe, Dorset

FOCUS
A fair middle-distance handicap for older horses in which they went an even gallop. Only the front two showed their form.

3013 FROSTS4CARS.CO.UK H'CAP (DIV I) 1m 1f 209y
4:15 (4:15) (Class 6) (0-65,65) 3-Y-O £1,940 (£577; £288; £144) Stalls High

Form RPR

6-60 **1** **London Bridge (USA)**[31] 2093 3-9-6 **64**........................ MartinLane 3 77
(Jo Hughes) *chsd ldrs: rdn over 3f out: c centre and hdwy u.p to ld ent fnl f: styd on wl: readily* **3/1**[1]

556- **2** *1 3/4* **Spieta (IRE)**[224] 7357 3-9-5 **63**........................ KierenFallon 7 72
(Luca Cumani) *t.k.h: led for 1f: chsd ldrs tl lost pl 5f out: hdwy u.p over 1f out: chsd wnr ins fnl f: no imp and eased towards fin* **7/2**[2]

006 **3** *4 1/2* **Dalliefour (IRE)**[16] 2547 3-8-10 **54**........................ HayleyTurner 8 54
(Michael Bell) *dwlt: t.k.h: chsd ldr after 1f: led 6f out tl rdn and hdd over 2f out: ev ch after tl unable qck ent fnl f: wknd ins fnl f* **3/1**[1]

03-0 **4** *1 3/4* **Eton Rambler (USA)**[33] 2017 3-9-7 **65**........................(b) PatCosgrave 9 62
(George Baker) *dwlt: t.k.h: hdwy to ld after 1f: hdd 6f out but styd upsides ldr: rdn to ld again over 2f out: hdd ent fnl f: no ex: wknd ins fnl f* **8/1**

-444 **5** *3 1/4* **Dalaway (IRE)**[16] 2546 3-9-2 **60**........................[1] SamHitchcott 2 50
(Mick Channon) *v.s.a: sn rcvrd and hld up in tch: rdn and effrt over 2f out: wknd u.p over 1f out* **20/1**

0-45 **6** *2 3/4* **Thomasina**[22] 2362 3-8-7 **51**........................ JimmyQuinn 4 36
(Denis Coakley) *in tch in midfield: rdn and effrt over 2f out: sn struggling: wknd wl over 1f out* **20/1**

604- **7** *3 ¾* **Believe In Me**[238] 7008 3-8-2 **46** AnnelieHollstenius 1 23
(Julia Feilden) *chsd ldrs: rdn and effrt on inner over 1f out: sn struggling: wknd qckly ent fnl f* **66/1**

01-4 **8** *¾* **Pink Mischief**[37] 1897 3-8-9 **53** (p) CathyGannon 5 29
(Harry Dunlop) *hld up in tch towards rr: hdwy to chse ldrs on outer over 2f out: wknd u.p over 1f out* **6/1**[3]

05-0 **9** *68* **Doctor's Gift**[29] 2151 3-8-13 **62** MichaelJMMurphy(5) 6
(Pat Eddery) *in tch towards rr: dropped to last and rdn along 6f out: lost tch 4f out: t.o and eased fnl 2f* **20/1**

2m 0.37s (-3.23) **Going Correction** -0.40s/f (Firm) **9** Ran SP% **113.4**
Speed ratings (Par 97): **96,94,91,89,87 84,81,81,26**
Tote Swingers 1&2 £3.50, 2&3 £3.20, 1&3 £3.50 CSF £12.61 CT £32.75 TOTE £4.30: £1.50, £1.40, £1.70; EX 15.40 Trifecta £39.20 Pool: £3,770.16 - 72.04 winning tickets..
Owner Eastwind Racing Ltd And Martha Trussell **Bred** Patricia S Purdy **Trained** Lambourn. Berks

FOCUS
The first division of a modest 3yo handicap, and slightly the quicker. The first three all had unexposed profiles.

3014 FROSTS4CARS.CO.UK H'CAP (DIV II) 1m 1f 209y
4:50 (4:52) (Class 6) (0-65,65) 3-Y-0 **£1,940** (£577; £288; £144) **Stalls** High

Form RPR

00-3 **1** **Big Thunder**[9] 2742 3-9-3 **61** LukeMorris 3 79+
(Sir Mark Prescott Bt) *mde all: rdn and readily drew clr 2f out: in n.d over 1f out: heavily eased fnl 75yds* **3/1**[2]

006 **2** *8* **Dama De La Noche (IRE)**[12] 2658 3-9-5 **63** KieranO'Neill 1 59
(Richard Hannon) *in tch in midfield: lost pl 6f out: rdn and outpcd 3f out: no ch w wnr but rallied u.p 1f out: wnt modest 2nd fnl 75yds* **7/1**

0-02 **3** *¾* **Hermosa Vaquera (IRE)**[9] 2742 3-9-4 **62** IanMongan 8 57
(Peter Chapple-Hyam) *chsd wnr: rdn and outpcd 2f out: wl btn 2nd over 1f out: plugged on but lost 2nd fnl 75yds* **7/2**[3]

1-4 **4** *nk* **Streak**[29] 2156 3-9-7 **65** TedDurcan 7 59
(David Lanigan) *stdd s: hld up in midfield: rdn and effrt to chse ldrs 3f out: outpcd and btn 2f out: wl hld but plugged on fnl f* **2/1**[1]

4230 **5** *¾* **Handsome Stranger (IRE)**[9] 2737 3-9-0 **58** ow2 (v) AdamKirby 2 50
(David Evans) *in tch in midfield: drvn and unable qck over 2f out: sn outpcd and wl hld over 1f out: plugged on fnl f* **12/1**

P6-0 **6** *1 ¼* **Smart Alice**[37] 1904 3-8-8 **52** HarryBentley 9 42
(Chris Wall) *hld up in tch in last trio: rdn and struggling 4f out: n.d fnl 3f: plugged on* **14/1**

2-66 **7** *22* **Ruff Luck**[77] 1095 3-8-10 **54** LiamKeniry 6
(Seamus Mullins) *t.k.h: chsd ldrs tl 3f out: wknd u.p over 2f out: wl bhd and virtually p.u ins fnl f* **33/1**

-500 **8** *31* **Tilly T (IRE)**[37] 1897 3-8-2 **46** oh1 (p) CathyGannon 4
(J S Moore) *hld up in tch in rr: rdn 1/2-way: lost tch 3f out: t.o and virtually p.u fnl f* **33/1**

2m 0.93s (-2.67) **Going Correction** -0.40s/f (Firm) **8** Ran SP% **113.3**
Speed ratings (Par 97): **94,87,87,86,86 85,67,42**
Tote Swingers 1&2 £4.30, 2&3 £4.40, 1&3 £2.30 CSF £23.76 CT £74.39 TOTE £3.20: £1.10, £3.60, £1.50; EX 21.70 Trifecta £106.10 Pool: £4,872.72 - 34.41 winning tickets..
Owner John Brown & Megan Dennis **Bred** Stanley House Stud **Trained** Newmarket, Suffolk

FOCUS
The second division of a modest 3yo handicap, and slightly the slower. The easy winner reversed Leciester form with the third.

3015 BRIGHTONBOATSALES.CO.UK H'CAP 7f 214y
5:20 (5:20) (Class 6) (0-60,60) 4-Y-0+ **£1,940** (£577; £288; £144) **Stalls** Centre

Form RPR

-300 **1** **Aqua Ardens (GER)**[47] 1681 5-9-6 **59** (t) PatCosgrave 2 70
(George Baker) *chsd ldrs: swtchd lft and rdn to ld 2f out: hrd drvn fnl f: hld on towards fin* **11/4**[1]

0200 **2** *hd* **Paphos**[21] 2395 6-9-7 **60** AdamKirby 5 71
(David Evans) *led: rdn and hdd 2f out: kpt on u.p and ev ch ins fnl f: hld cl home* **8/1**

4-10 **3** *2 ¼* **Ermyntrude**[113] 630 6-9-2 **55** (v) IanMongan 1 61
(Pat Phelan) *chsd ldr: ev ch 2f out: unable qck over 1f out: styd on same pce ins fnl f* **5/1**

5530 **4** *2 ¾* **Khajaaly (IRE)**[30] 2134 6-8-8 **54** (p) ShelleyBirkett(7) 10 54
(Julia Feilden) *in tch in midfield: rdn and nt qckn over 1f out: btn 1f out: wknd ins fnl f* **8/1**

-033 **5** *¾* **Renoir's Lady**[92] 903 5-9-0 **53** HayleyTurner 6 51
(Simon Dow) *in tch in last trio: rdn and no hdwy 2f out: btn and edgd lft ins fnl f* **4/1**[3]

0/0- **6** *3* **Princess Palmer**[373] 2582 4-8-6 **50** RosieJessop(5) 12 41
(Lydia Pearce) *s.i.s: in tch in rr: pushed along and outpcd 3f out: n.d after* **33/1**

0-03 **7** *½* **Fushicho**[31] 2073 4-8-9 **48** SteveDrowne 11 38
(Brendan Powell) *stdd s: t.k.h: hld up in last pair: rdn and struggling 3f out: n.d fnl 2f* **3/1**[2]

1m 33.78s (-2.22) **Going Correction** -0.40s/f (Firm) **7** Ran SP% **113.5**
Speed ratings (Par 101): **95,94,92,89,89 86,85**
Tote Swingers 1&2 £3.40, 2&3 £3.70, 1&3 £3.40 CSF £24.56 CT £103.32 TOTE £4.20: £2.40, £3.90; EX 24.80 Trifecta £146.00 Pool: £2,323.96 - 11.93 winning tickets..
Owner M Khan X2 **Bred** Gestut Karlshof **Trained** Manton, Wilts

FOCUS
A moderate handicap for older horses in which they went a good gallop. The winner was a length of his AW winter best.

3016 BRIGHTON STREAMLINE TAXIS H'CAP 6f 209y
5:50 (5:50) (Class 6) (0-65,69) 3-Y-0 **£1,940** (£577; £288; £144) **Stalls** Centre

Form RPR

0101 **1** **Macaabra (IRE)**[6] 2836 3-9-12 **69** 6ex NeilCallan 4 83
(James Tate) *mde all: rdn and readily wnt clr 2f out: in n.d after: eased towards fin: easily* **5/4**[1]

-306 **2** *7* **Pippy**[24] 2308 3-9-6 **63** SteveDrowne 2 58
(Tom Dascombe) *bustled along leaving stalls: chsd ldrs 5f out: rdn and outpcd by wnr 2f out: chsd clr wnr wl over 1f out: kpt on for 2nd but no ch w wnr* **7/2**[2]

06-0 **3** *1 ¼* **Sunny Hollow**[16] 2528 3-8-13 **56** KirstyMilczarek 5 48
(James Toller) *in tch in midfield: rdn over 2f out: outpcd and btn 2f out: wnt 3rd 1f out: edgd lft but kpt on: no threat to wnr* **20/1**

026 **4** *1 ¾* **Is This Love (IRE)**[27] 2226 3-9-4 **61** AdamKirby 1 48
(Jamie Osborne) *dwlt: hld up in tch: rdn and effrt towards inner 2f out: no ch w wnr and one pce fnl f* **8/1**

0-34 **5** *shd* **Assertive Agent**[37] 1896 3-9-7 **64** (p) HayleyTurner 8 51
(Ben De Haan) *in tch in rr of main gp: rdn and effrt over 2f out: sn struggling and no ch w wnr over 1f out: kpt on ins fnl f* **5/1**[3]

6405 **6** *2 ¼* **Abanoas (USA)**[9] 2737 3-8-4 **47** (b) MartinLane 6 28
(Alan Coogan) *sn outpcd and rdn in detached last: modest hdwy over 1f out: n.d* **20/1**

01 **7** *¾* **Lincolnrose (IRE)**[16] 2528 3-8-11 **54** (p) KieranO'Neill 7 33
(Alan McCabe) *chsd wnr tl wl over 1f out: sn btn: wknd fnl f* **7/1**

00-0 **8** *13* **Atilia**[23] 2346 3-8-2 **45** (b[1]) CathyGannon 9
(Harry Dunlop) *chsd ldrs for 2f: rdn and lost pl 1/2-way: bhd over 1f out* **33/1**

1m 20.23s (-2.87) **Going Correction** -0.40s/f (Firm) **8** Ran SP% **119.4**
Speed ratings (Par 97): **100,92,90,88,88 85,85,70**
Tote Swingers 1&2 £2.30, 2&3 £12.60, 1&3 £7.10 CSF £5.90 CT £58.95 TOTE £2.00: £1.10, £2.30, £7.50; EX 5.40 Trifecta £71.40 Pool: £1,885.75 - 19.80 winning tickets..
Owner Saif Ali **Bred** Rabbah Bloodstock Limited **Trained** Newmarket, Suffolk

FOCUS
A modest 3yo handicap in which they went a decent gallop. The winner is getting her act together now.
T/Plt: £5.30 to a £1 stake. Pool: £56,391.15 - 7730.85 winning tickets. T/Qpdt: £3.60 to a £1 stake. Pool: £3,912.47 - 800.63 winning tickets. SP

2808 SANDOWN (R-H)
Thursday, June 6

OFFICIAL GOING: Good to firm (good in places on sprint course; 8.7)
Sprint track at full width, rail on Round course out 2yds from innermost configuration in back straight and bottom bend then out 5yds up home straight.
Wind: Light, behind Weather: Sunny, warm

3017 WEST END MAIDEN AUCTION STKS 5f 6y
6:15 (6:18) (Class 5) 2-Y-0 **£3,234** (£962; £481; £240) **Stalls** Low

Form RPR

54 **1** **Honey Meadow**[45] 1724 2-8-5 0 ow1 AdamBeschizza 7 67
(Robert Eddery) *chsd ldr 1f: swtchd to rail sn after: rdn 1/2-way: prog to go 2nd jst over 1f out: drvn and styd on to ld last strides* **20/1**

04 **2** *½* **Wiki Tiki**[17] 2517 2-8-6 0 SilvestreDeSousa 2 66
(Stuart Williams) *led: clr 1/2-way: 4 l clr 1f out: tired ins fnl f: collared last strides* **33/1**

0225 **3** *hd* **Urban Dreamer (IRE)**[7] 2809 2-8-13 0 JamesDoyle 9 72
(Rod Millman) *chsd ldrs and racd off rail: rdn 1/2-way: clsd w wnr on flagging ldr fnl f: jst hld* **7/2**[2]

6 **4** *1* **Miracle Of Medinah**[13] 2617 2-8-9 0 JohnFahy 1 65
(Mark Usher) *dwlt: settled in rr: taken out wd and prog 2f out: hanging bdly lft after: styd on fnl f: nt quite rch ldrs* **50/1**

22 **5** *5* **Inciting Incident (IRE)**[28] 2189 2-8-11 0 SeanLevey 6 49
(Ed McMahon) *chsd ldr after 1f to jst over 1f out: wknd qckly* **9/2**[3]

6 *1 ½* **Blurred Vision** 2-8-13 0 FrankieDettori 10 45+
(William Jarvis) *athletic: slowest away: racd wd and wl in rr: no prog 2f out: hanging and green fnl f* **9/2**[3]

623 **7** *hd* **Sartori**[26] 2260 2-8-13 0 MartinHarley 5 45
(Mick Channon) *chsd ldrs against rail to 1/2-way: wknd wl over 1f out* **9/2**[3]

8 *1 ¼* **Dont Have It Then** 2-8-11 0 J-PGuillambert 8 38
(Willie Musson) *w'like: bit bkwd: dwlt: nvr bttr than midfield: wknd wl over 1f out* **100/1**

9 *nk* **Rising Dawn (IRE)** 2-9-2 0 RichardHughes 3 42
(Richard Hannon) *w'like: dwlt: outpcd in last pair: nvr a factor* **3/1**[1]

0 **10** *4 ½* **The Dandy Yank (IRE)**[14] 2595 2-8-13 0 FergusSweeney 4 23
(Jamie Osborne) *s.i.s: a outpcd in last* **20/1**

1m 0.26s (-1.34) **Going Correction** -0.20s/f (Firm) **10** Ran SP% **117.2**
Speed ratings (Par 93): **102,101,100,99,91 88,88,86,86,78**
Tote Swingers 1&2 £21.30, 2&3 £25.00, 1&3 £15.30 CSF £508.09 TOTE £32.50: £7.50, £5.60, £2.10; EX 594.20 Trifecta £1106.40 Part won. Pool: £1,475.20 - 0.89 winning tickets..
Owner G & L Knight, J Mitchell & N Donaldson **Bred** R J Budge **Trained** Newmarket, Suffolk

FOCUS
This looked a modest maiden with the winner and runner-up lightly weighted fillies who had only previously run to an ordinary level. They both improved, with the third giving perspective.

3018 LAMMAS LANE H'CAP 5f 6y
6:50 (6:51) (Class 4) (0-85,84) 3-Y-0+ **£4,690** (£1,395; £697; £348) **Stalls** Low

Form RPR

22-1 **1** **Asian Trader**[37] 1896 4-9-5 **75** (t) FrankieDettori 2 84+
(William Haggas) *lw: awkward s: sn in midfield against rail: prog 2f out: gap appeared and drvn to chse ldr fnl f: styd on to ld last 50yds* **5/2**[1]

6230 **2** *½* **Alnoomaas (IRE)**[20] 2425 4-9-5 **75** JimmyFortune 1 82
(Luke Dace) *racd against rail: pressed ldr: led 2f out: drvn fnl f: hdd last 50yds* **10/1**

-103 **3** *hd* **Gladiatrix**[31] 2088 4-9-6 **81** (b[1]) MichaelJMMurphy(5) 13 87+
(Rod Millman) *racd wd thrght: chsd ldrs: rdn to chal 2f out: stl upsides ins fnl f: styd on* **14/1**

4034 **4** *1* **Waseem Faris (IRE)**[13] 2614 4-9-8 **78** MartinHarley 10 81
(Mick Channon) *slowest away: swtchd to inner and hld up in last trio: prog but nt clr run briefly over 1f out: drvn and styd on fnl f: nvr pce to threaten* **8/1**[3]

346 **5** *shd* **Rowe Park**[34] 1984 10-9-13 **83** (p) FergusSweeney 9 85
(Linda Jewell) *pressed ldrs but racd away fr rail: upsides 2f out: nt qckn over 1f out and lost pl: kpt on fnl f* **33/1**

3-32 **6** *¾* **Rebecca Romero**[21] 2388 6-9-6 **76** RichardHughes 6 76
(Denis Coakley) *hld up towards rr: shkn up over 1f out: styd on same pce: nt pce to threaten* **3/1**[2]

0-03 **7** *½* **Ginzan**[6] 2825 5-9-5 **75** TomMcLaughlin 7 73
(Malcolm Saunders) *chsd ldrs: u.p bef 1/2-way: lost pl 2f out: kpt on u.p* **11/1**

00-0 **8** *2* **Best Be Careful (IRE)**[27] 2227 5-8-9 **70** RachealKneller(5) 3 61
(Mark Usher) *hld up in midfield: nt clr run briefly 2f out: sn dropped to last trio and btn* **14/1**

1104 **9** *1 ¾* **Diamond Charlie (IRE)**[27] 2227 5-10-0 **84** TomQueally 8 68
(Simon Dow) *led but unable to grab far rail: hdd 2f out: wknd over 1f out* **12/1**

00-0 **10** *¾* **Solemn**[52] 1581 8-9-4 **79** (b) MatthewLawson(5) 11 61
(Milton Bradley) *racd on outer: prom: rdn bef 1/2-way whn upsides: steadily wknd fnl 2f* **25/1**

0151 **11** *hd* **Whitecrest**[7] 2790 5-9-11 **81** 6ex ChrisCatlin 15 62
(John Spearing) *racd v wd thrght: a wl in rr* **25/1**

11-0 **12** *shd* **Muhdiq (USA)**[26] 2255 4-9-8 **78** .... PatDobbs 14 59
(Mike Murphy) *hld up in last quartet and racd towards outer: shkn up and no prog 2f out: nvr a factor* **12/1**

59.83s (-1.77) **Going Correction** -0.20s/f (Firm) **12** Ran SP% **121.5**
Speed ratings (Par 105): **106,105,104,103,103 101,101,97,95,93 93,93**
Tote Swingers 1&2 £7.90, 2&3 £24.50, 1&3 £11.30 CSF £28.72 CT £307.90 TOTE £3.50: £1.80, £3.40, £3.10; EX 33.30 Trifecta £548.10 Pool: £1,430.54 - 1.95 winning tickets..

Owner Somerville Lodge Limited **Bred** Mike Smith **Trained** Newmarket, Suffolk

■ Frankie Dettori's first winner since returning from a six-month drugs ban.

FOCUS
Just an ordinary-looking sprint handicap for the class and the front two were favourably drawn. Not many were involved and the form is rated around the runner-up.

3019 TELLISFORD H'CAP — 1m 14y
7:25 (7:26) (Class 4) (0-85,85) 4-Y-0+ **£4,690** (£1,395; £697; £348) **Stalls** Low

Form — RPR

0-46 **1** **Roserrow**[14] 2592 4-9-7 **85** .... JimmyFortune 8 98
(Andrew Balding) *lw: led 1f: trckd ldng pair after: n.m.r over 2f out but sn wnt 2nd: drvn to take narrow ld jst over 1f out: asserted nr fin* **8/1**

-362 **2** *½* **Tigers Tale (IRE)**[20] 2424 4-9-5 **83** .... (v) FrankieDettori 11 95
(Roger Teal) *led after 1f and maintained mod pce: kicked on over 3f out: drvn and narrowly hdd jst over 1f out: battled on wl but hld last 75yds* **6/1**[3]

6-66 **3** *3 ¼* **Barwick**[12] 2659 5-8-12 **76** .... TomQueally 2 81
(Mark H Tompkins) *slowly away: hld up towards rr in steadily run event: prog but nt clr run 2f out: styd on fr over 1f out to take 3rd last stride* **15/2**

00-5 **4** *shd* **Volcanic Wind (USA)**[14] 2592 4-9-4 **82** .... SilvestreDeSousa 4 86
(Saeed bin Suroor) *lw: hld up in midfield: nt clr run over 2f out: prog to chse clr ldng pair over 1f out: no imp: lost 3rd last stride* **7/2**[1]

00-0 **5** *hd* **Mingun Bell (USA)**[23] 1878 6-8-13 **77** .... (b) LiamKeniry 1 81
(Ed de Giles) *trckd ldrs on inner: looking for room over 2f out: prog to dispute 3rd over 1f out: styd on same pce after* **50/1**

56-0 **6** *1 ¼* **Commend**[20] 2422 4-9-3 **81** .... (v[1]) RyanMoore 12 82+
(Sir Michael Stoute) *stdd s: hld up in last in steadily run event: trying to make prog but no ch whn squeezed for room wl over 1f out: styd on: nrst fin* **4/1**[2]

-051 **7** *nk* **Sir Mike**[15] 2574 4-9-0 **78** .... JimCrowley 5 78+
(Amanda Perrett) *hld up towards rr in steadily run event: gng wl whn plld out wd 2f out but plenty to do: styd on same pce after but n.d* **10/1**

6165 **8** *nk* **Rakaan (IRE)**[15] 2571 6-9-4 **82** .... (p) FergusSweeney 7 82
(Jamie Osborne) *hld up in last quartet in steadily run r: nt clr run over 2f out: styd on fr over 1f out: no ch* **33/1**

-540 **9** *4* **Corporal Maddox**[13] 2618 6-9-3 **81** .... (p) LukeMorris 13 71
(Ronald Harris) *hld up towards rr in steadily run event: trying to raise an effrt whn hmpd wl over 1f out: no prog after* **33/1**

0-00 **10** *3* **First Post (IRE)**[36] 1922 6-9-1 **79** .... DaneO'Neill 14 62
(Derek Haydn Jones) *wl in tch on outer: rdn over 2f out: nt qckn and wknd over 1f out* **14/1**

0030 **11** *½* **Cawett Cove (IRE)**[28] 2191 5-8-12 **76** .... MickaelBarzalona 3 58
(Jane Chapple-Hyam) *plld hrd: trckd ldrs: rdn over 2f out: wknd wl over 1f out* **25/1**

2162 **12** *2 ¾* **Poetic Lord**[15] 2573 4-8-13 **77** .... RichardHughes 9 53
(Sylvester Kirk) *hld up in last pair: brief effrt over 2f out: sn no prog* **20/1**

4/0- **13** *5* **Sergeant Ablett (IRE)**[404] 1654 5-9-7 **85** .... IanMongan 6 50
(Luke Dace) *prom: rdn wl over 2f out: wknd wl over 1f out* **50/1**

0-20 **14** *nse* **Charitable Act (FR)**[28] 2193 4-9-1 **79** ow1 .... WilliamBuick 10 43
(Gary Moore) *chsd ldr after 1f to over 2f out: wknd rapidly* **14/1**

1m 40.57s (-2.73) **Going Correction** -0.20s/f (Firm) **14** Ran SP% **120.2**
Speed ratings (Par 105): **105,104,101,101,100 99,99,99,95,92 91,88,83,83**
Tote Swingers 1&2 £14.90, 2&3 £13.70, 1&3 £12.80 CSF £51.53 CT £388.92 TOTE £11.80: £2.60, £2.30, £2.50; EX 60.70 Trifecta £1022.10 Part won. Pool: £1,362.83 - 0.47 winning tickets..

Owner Sir Roger Buckley, Gerald Oury **Bred** Sir R J Buckley & G Oury **Trained** Kingsclere, Hants

FOCUS
It paid to be handy off an ordinary pace. The winner built on his previous form.

3020 BRIDGET STACK MEMORIAL SUPPORTING GRACE H'CAP — 7f 16y
7:55 (7:56) (Class 3) (0-90,90) 3-Y-0 **£7,439** (£2,213; £1,106; £553) **Stalls** Low

Form — RPR

40-5 **1** **Ashaadd (IRE)**[12] 2655 3-9-7 **90** .... RyanMoore 10 101+
(Roger Varian) *dwlt: hld up in last: trying to make prog whn short of room over 1f out and plld out wd: r.o strly under firm hands and heels to ld last 50yds: impressive* **8/1**

21-1 **2** *½* **Homage (IRE)**[14] 2593 3-9-2 **85** .... WilliamBuick 5 92+
(Jeremy Noseda) *lw: trckd ldrs: shkn up over 2f out: prog over 1f out to ld jst ins fnl f: edgd rt but r.o: hdd and outpcd last 50yds* **7/4**[1]

51 **3** *1 ¾* **Czech It Out (IRE)**[19] 2448 3-8-11 **80** .... JimCrowley 3 84
(Amanda Perrett) *lw: trckd ldng pair: shkn up over 2f out: clsd to chal jst ins fnl f: styng on but hld in 3rd whn hmpd nr fin* **12/1**

321- **4** *1* **Altharoos (IRE)**[254] 6558 3-8-11 **80** .... PaulHanagan 1 84+
(Sir Michael Stoute) *hld up in midfield: tried to make grnd 2f out: nt clr run 1f out: rdn and styd on fnl f to take 4th nr fin* **9/4**[2]

10-6 **5** *nk* **Banovallum**[26] 2285 3-8-13 **82** .... LiamKeniry 9 81
(Sylvester Kirk) *trckd ldr: chal 2f out: led over 1f out to jst ins fnl f: fading whn sltly short of room last 50yds* **25/1**

12-0 **6** *4 ½* **Mutazamen**[48] 1668 3-9-6 **89** .... RichardHughes 6 83
(Richard Hannon) *led: rdn and pressed 2f out: hdd over 1f out: no ex and wl hld whn squeezed for room last 75yds and eased* **16/1**

51-0 **7** *2 ¼* **Tommy's Secret**[41] 1806 3-8-11 **87** .... IanBurns(7) 2 68
(Jane Chapple-Hyam) *hld up towards rr: urged along and no prog 2f out: wl btn after* **33/1**

000- **8** *hd* **Rayaheen**[251] 6632 3-9-3 **86** .... DaneO'Neill 7 66
(Richard Hannon) *hld up in last pair: rdn and no prog 2f out: wl btn after* **33/1**

1-60 **9** *½* **Vallarta (IRE)**[19] 2452 3-8-12 **81** .... MartinHarley 4 60
(Mick Channon) *hld up in rr: rdn and no prog 2f out: wl btn after* **6/1**[3]

1m 27.45s (-2.05) **Going Correction** -0.20s/f (Firm) **9** Ran SP% **115.8**
Speed ratings (Par 103): **103,102,100,99,98 93,91,91,90**
Tote Swingers 1&2 £4.30, 2&3 £2.90, 1&3 £12.00 CSF £22.15 CT £169.39 TOTE £9.70: £2.70, £1.40, £2.10; EX 17.30 Trifecta £165.60 Pool: £1,109.73 - 5.02 winning tickets..

Owner Sheikh Ahmed Al Maktoum **Bred** Socrates Partnership **Trained** Newmarket, Suffolk

FOCUS
A good 3yo handicap run at what appeared a fair pace, and a number of these look capable of rating higher.

3021 BRITISH STALLION STUDS EBF MAIDEN STKS — 1m 2f 7y
8:30 (8:30) (Class 5) 3-Y-0 **£3,881** (£1,155; £577; £288) **Stalls** Low

Form — RPR

6 **1** **Testudo (IRE)**[19] 2442 3-9-5 0 .... KierenFallon 6 89+
(Brian Meehan) *racd frely and led 2f: restrained bhd ldrs after: shkn up and clsd to ld over 1f out: rdn and pressed ins fnl f: pushed out and in command nr fin* **5/1**[1]

3 **2** *nk* **Ducab (IRE)**[16] 2547 3-9-5 0 .... RichardHughes 4 88+
(Roger Varian) *str: dwlt: hld up in rr: stdy prog gng strly over 2f out: rdn to chal ins fnl f: styd on but hld nr fin* **10/1**

6-02 **3** *2 ½* **Lemon Pearl**[21] 2392 3-9-0 76 .... HarryBentley 2 78
(Ralph Beckett) *unf: scope: lengthy: trckd ldrs: rdn over 2f out: styd on same pce to take 3rd ins fnl f* **7/1**[2]

0 **4** *shd* **Respect Me**[49] 1635 3-9-5 0 .... SilvestreDeSousa 3 83+
(Saeed bin Suroor) *hld up in rr: rdn and prog fr over 2f out: styd on fnl f: nrly snatched 3rd* **9/1**[3]

6 **5** *½* **Near Time**[41] 1813 3-9-0 0 .... JimmyFortune 11 77
(Andrew Balding) *trckd ldr over 7f out: led wl over 2f out: rdn and hdd over 1f out: one pce* **10/1**

6 *3 ¼* **Dambuster (IRE)** 3-9-5 0 .... RyanMoore 17 75+
(Sir Michael Stoute) *w'like: scope: pressed ldrs on outer: pushed along 3f out: cl enough to chal 2f out: fdd* **10/1**

06 **7** *2 ¼* **Halling's Treasure**[14] 2605 3-9-0 0 .... ThomasBrown(5) 1 71
(Andrew Balding) *athletic: str: dwlt but rcvrd qckly to trck ldrs: pushed along over 2f out: short of room briefly sn after: fdd: nt knocked abt* **66/1**

4-3 **8** *4* **Thomas Hobson**[45] 1727 3-9-5 0 .... WilliamBuick 5 63+
(John Gosden) *hld up in rr: shkn up and no prog 3f out: n.d after: sme prog past btn rivals 1f out* **5/1**[1]

00 **9** *1 ¼* **Brave Helios**[24] 2321 3-9-0 0 .... MatthewLawson(5) 12 60
(Jonathan Portman) *w'like: sn in last: shkn up 3f out: nvr any ch: passed a few stragglers late on* **100/1**

10 *nse* **Qibtee (FR)** 3-9-5 0 .... MartinHarley 13 60
(Mick Channon) *w'like: a wl in rr: rdn and no prog 3f out: no ch after* **33/1**

0 **11** *nk* **Hero's Story**[19] 2442 3-9-5 0 .... PatDobbs 10 60
(Amanda Perrett) *a towards rr: rdn and no prog over 2f out: wl btn after* **50/1**

12 *1* **Achtung** 3-9-5 0 .... FrankieDettori 9 58
(Jeremy Noseda) *w'like: s.i.s: sn wl in tch on outer: shkn up wl over 2f out: sn wknd* **5/1**[1]

00 **12** *dht* **Kazak**[24] 2306 3-9-5 0 .... JamesDoyle 15 58
(Roger Charlton) *lw: wl in rr: shkn up and no prog 3f out: hld together after* **10/1**

0-3 **14** *12* **Meshardal (GER)**[9] 2746 3-9-5 0 .... PaulHanagan 7
(Richard Hannon) *led after 2f tl wl over 2f out: wknd qckly and eased* **20/1**

2m 9.22s (-1.28) **Going Correction** -0.20s/f (Firm) **14** Ran SP% **121.0**
Speed ratings (Par 99): **97,96,94,94,94 91,89,86,85,85 85,84,84,75**
Tote Swingers 1&2 £13.50, 2&3 £9.00, 1&3 £11.30 CSF £54.27 TOTE £5.50: £2.40, £3.00, £2.30; EX 60.80 Trifecta £268.80 Pool: £1,152.80 - 3.21 winning tickets..

Owner Sangster Family **Bred** Aylesfield Farms Stud **Trained** Manton, Wilts

FOCUS
Plenty of decent connections represented and this maiden ought to produce a few winners. The form is rated above the race averages, the level set around the third and the seventh.

3022 LILY FOUNDATION H'CAP (JOCKEY CLUB GRASSROOTS MIDDLE DISTANCE SERIES QUALIFIER) — 1m 2f 7y
9:00 (9:00) (Class 4) (0-80,80) 4-Y-0+ **£4,690** (£1,395; £697; £348) **Stalls** Low

Form — RPR

3-02 **1** **Cashpoint**[20] 2417 8-9-2 **75** .... WilliamBuick 9 83+
(Ian Williams) *lw: hld up in 7th: shkn up 2f out: prog on outer over 1f out: r.o to ld 150yds out: in command after* **11/4**[1]

41-0 **2** *1* **Kelpie Blitz (IRE)**[17] 2498 4-9-3 **76** .... (t) GeorgeBaker 4 82
(Seamus Durack) *awkward and stdd s: hld up in last: stl there and shkn up wl over 1f out: prog on outer fnl f: r.o to take 2nd nr fin* **25/1**

4061 **3** *½* **Presburg (IRE)**[16] 2532 4-9-5 **78** .... LiamKeniry 10 83+
(Joseph Tuite) *hld up in last trio: tried to make prog on inner fr over 2f out but repeatedly denied: r.o whn in the clr fnl f: tk 3rd post* **12/1**

1400 **4** *nk* **Scottish Star**[36] 1922 5-9-6 **79** .... LukeMorris 7 83
(James Eustace) *chsd ldr: rdn wl over 2f out: kpt on same pce after but outpcd fnl f by those coming fr bhd* **7/1**

4-22 **5** *shd* **Highland Duke (IRE)**[16] 2532 4-9-5 **78** .... AdamKirby 6 82
(Clive Cox) *led: set gd pce to 1/2-way then stdd: kicked on 3f out: hdd 150yds out: lost pls nr fin* **3/1**[2]

-531 **6** *½* **Frozen Over**[21] 2383 5-8-13 **72** .... MickaelBarzalona 2 75
(Stuart Kittow) *lw: chsd ldrs in 5th: rdn over 2f out: nt qckn over 1f out: one pce fnl f* **7/2**[3]

01-0 **7** *1 ¼* **Oetzi**[14] 2594 5-8-6 **70** .... MichaelJMMurphy(5) 8 71
(Alan Jarvis) *in tch in 6th: rdn over 2f out: nt qckn whn n.m.r briefly over 1f out: fdd ins fnl f* **16/1**

0323 **8** *1 ½* **Brown Pete (IRE)**[13] 2640 5-9-0 **73** .... MartinHarley 1 71
(Violet M Jordan) *chsd ldng pair: rdn over 2f out: no imp over 1f out: fdd fnl f* **16/1**

-134 **9** *1 ¾* **Destiny Of Dreams**[48] 1663 5-9-4 **77** .... DaneO'Neill 3 71
(Jo Crowley) *chsd ldng pair: rdn over 2f out: no imp over 1f out: wknd ins fnl f* **16/1**

2m 8.33s (-2.17) **Going Correction** -0.20s/f (Firm) **9** Ran SP% **115.6**
Speed ratings (Par 105): **100,99,98,98,98 98,97,95,94**
Tote Swingers 1&2 £14.50, 2&3 £75.10, 1&3 £4.70 CSF £70.89 CT £715.64 TOTE £3.30: £1.70, £5.90, £3.40; EX 57.60 Trifecta £838.00 Part won. Pool: £1,117.41 - 0.67 winning tickets..

Owner Macable Partnership **Bred** Stowell Park Stud **Trained** Portway, Worcs

FOCUS
A fair handicap run at a decent pace. The winner did not need to match his Newbury latest.

T/Jkpt: Not won. T/Plt: £233.00 to a £1 stake. Pool: £86,341.56 - 270.50 winning tickets. T/Qpdt: £19.40 to a £1 stake. Pool: £9,102.03 - 346.89 winning tickets. JN

[2458] THIRSK (L-H)

Thursday, June 6

OFFICIAL GOING: Good to firm (9.9)

Both bends dolled out circa 3-4 yds adding 20yds to races on Round course.
Wind: light against Weather: sunny

3023 EBF/BET & WATCH WITH RACING UK'S APP MAIDEN STKS 5f

2:10 (2:12) (Class 4) 2-Y-O **£4,528** (£1,347; £673; £336) **Stalls** High

Form RPR

3 **1** **Love In The Desert**[14] 2601 2-9-0 0 StevieDonohoe 10 75
(Noel Quinlan) *trckd ldrs: rdn over 1f out: kpt on to ld fnl 100yds* **15/8**[1]

20 **2** *1* **Tanseeb**[21] 2401 2-9-5 0 JoeFanning 12 76+
(Mark Johnston) *hld up in tch on inner: n.m.r 2f out: rdn and hdwy appr fnl f: r.o wl: wnt 2nd towards fin* **3/1**[3]

2 **3** *nk* **Weisse Socken (IRE)**[24] 2320 2-9-0 0 RichardKingscote 11 71
(Ralph Beckett) *trckd ldrs: swtchd lft and hmpd appr fnl f: sn rdn: kpt on wl: wnt 3rd towards fin* **11/4**[2]

0 **4** *¾* **Viva Verglas (IRE)**[12] 2670 2-9-5 0 GrahamGibbons 9 73
(David Barron) *led: rdn and hung lft over 1f out: hdd fnl 100yds: no ex and lost 2 more pls towards fin* **10/1**

5 *2 ¼* **Heroique (IRE)** 2-9-0 0 DavidAllan 3 60+
(Tim Easterby) *hld up: pushed along 1/2-way: kpt on fnl f: nrst fin* **40/1**

6 *nk* **Soul Instinct** 2-9-5 0 PhillipMakin 1 66+
(Kevin Ryan) *wnt lft s: hld up in rr: kpt on fnl f: nrst fin* **18/1**

0 **7** *1 ¼* **Pavers Bounty**[40] 1820 2-9-5 0 DuranFentiman 8 59
(Noel Wilson) *w ldr: rdn 2f out: wknd fnl f* **100/1**

04 **8** *3* **Red Dakota (IRE)**[15] 2577 2-9-0 0 PaulMulrennan 7 44
(David C Griffiths) *chsd ldrs: wknd over 1f out* **100/1**

6 **9** *2* **Patisserie**[19] 2458 2-9-0 0 PJMcDonald 2 36
(Ann Duffield) *in tch towards outer: pushed along 1/2-way: wknd fnl f* **18/1**

10 *1 ¾* **Laraaj (IRE)** 2-9-0 0 AndrewMullen 4 30
(David Barron) *dwlt: midfield: pushed along whn hmpd appr fnl f: no ch after* **25/1**

11 *2 ½* **Miss Tallulah (IRE)** 2-9-0 0 TomEaves 5 21
(Mel Brittain) *dwlt: hld up: nvr threatened* **80/1**

1m 0.36s (0.76) **Going Correction** +0.125s/f (Good) **11 Ran SP% 115.6**
Speed ratings (Par 95): **98,96,95,94,91 90,88,83,80,77 73**
Tote Swingers 1&2 £2.00, 2&3 £2.30, 1&3 £2.20 CSF £7.25 TOTE £2.90: £1.30, £1.50, £1.30; EX 7.60 Trifecta £24.60 Pool: £3,317.02 - 101.07 winning tickets..
Owner Ibrahim Rachid **Bred** Shawahed Thoroughbred Corporation **Trained** Newmarket, Suffolk

FOCUS
Probably a decent 2yo maiden but the winner probably didn't need to improve.

3024 DOWNLOAD THE FREE RACING UK APP H'CAP 5f

2:40 (2:40) (Class 6) (0-60,60) 4-Y-O+ **£1,940** (£577; £288; £144) **Stalls** High

Form RPR

0-41 **1** **Bondi Beach Boy**[13] 2611 4-8-11 50 PJMcDonald 2 59
(James Turner) *cl up: led narrowly after 1f: rdn whn hdd wl over 1f out: drvn and carried hd high ins fnl f: kpt on to ld again nr fin* **13/2**[3]

001- **2** *shd* **Ballarina**[202] 7746 7-8-13 57 JasonHart(5) 1 66
(Eric Alston) *cl up: rdn to ld narrowly wl over 1f out: kpt on: hdd nr fin* **9/1**

1504 **3** *1 ¾* **Alpha Tauri (USA)**[15] 2580 7-8-8 47 (t) GrahamGibbons 12 50
(Charles Smith) *hld up: rdn 2f out: styd on ins fnl f: wnt 3rd post: nvr threatened ldng pair* **6/1**[2]

40-0 **4** *nse* **See Vermont**[45] 1731 5-8-0 46 GaryMahon(7) 8 49
(Robin Bastiman) *chsd ldrs: rdn 1/2-way: kpt on one pce* **14/1**

40 **5** *shd* **Quality Art (USA)**[16] 2550 5-9-6 59 RobbieFitzpatrick 3 61
(Richard Guest) *led for 1f: remained cl up: rdn 2f out: no ex ins fnl f: lost 2 pls post* **7/1**

54-6 **6** *1 ½* **Lees Anthem**[32] 2043 6-8-10 49 GrahamLee 5 46
(Michael Smith) *hld up: rdn 1/2-way: kpt on fnl f: nvr threatened ldrs* **13/2**[3]

0-60 **7** *1* **Arch Walker (IRE)**[23] 2338 6-9-4 57 (b) JamesSullivan 9 50
(John Weymes) *sn rdn along to chse ldrs: wknd fnl f* **11/1**

0603 **8** *¾* **Rio's Girl**[7] 2795 6-9-0 53 BarryMcHugh 7 43
(Tony Coyle) *hld up: rdn 1/2-way: nvr threatened* **7/1**

-600 **9** *4* **Cheyenne Red (IRE)**[85] 991 7-8-7 46 oh1 TomEaves 6 22
(Michael Herrington) *hld up: a towards rr* **50/1**

4602 **10** *nse* **Steelcut**[8] 2772 9-9-6 59 (p) ShaneKelly 10 35
(Mark Buckley) *chsd ldrs: wknd over 1f out* **9/2**[1]

600- **11** *8* **Myjestic Melody (IRE)**[202] 7748 5-8-7 46 DuranFentiman 4
(Noel Wilson) *dwlt: sn pushed along in rr: a bhd* **20/1**

1m 0.67s (1.07) **Going Correction** +0.125s/f (Good) **11 Ran SP% 115.9**
Speed ratings (Par 101): **96,95,93,92,92 90,88,87,81,81 68**
Tote Swingers 1&2 £10.90, 2&3 £12.20, 1&3 £6.40 CSF £62.84 CT £376.66 TOTE £8.70: £3.40, £2.50, £2.30; EX 65.50 Trifecta £701.20 Pool: £2,321.58 - 2.48 winning tickets..
Owner J R Turner **Bred** G R & H Turner **Trained** Norton-le-Clay, N Yorks

FOCUS
Plenty of pace here, but it was away from the normally favoured stands' side rail. The first two were one-two throughout and the winner built on his Catterick win.

3025 WATCH RACING UK ON SKY 432 H'CAP (QUALIFIER FOR £15,000 BETFAIR SCOTTISH SPRINT SERIES FINAL) 6f

3:15 (3:16) (Class 5) (0-70,70) 3-Y-O **£2,587** (£770; £384; £192) **Stalls** High

Form RPR

3520 **1** **Charlemagne Diva**[16] 2542 3-8-2 53 ow1 BillyCray(3) 10 60
(Richard Guest) *mde all towards stands' rail: rdn over 2f out: kpt on wl* **20/1**

-060 **2** *1 ¼* **Dream Scenario**[14] 2593 3-9-4 67 PaulMulrennan 8 69
(Mel Brittain) *chsd wnr towards stands' rail: rdn over 2f out: kpt on but a jst hld* **17/2**[3]

5-66 **3** *2* **Perfect Words (IRE)**[31] 2076 3-8-11 60 DanielTudhope 9 56
(Marjorie Fife) *hld up in tch: rdn and hdwy over 1f out: kpt on* **10/1**

011- **4** *1* **Hardy Blue (IRE)**[224] 7355 3-9-6 69 JoeFanning 12 61
(Danielle McCormick) *chsd wnr towards stands' rail: rdn over 2f out: no ex ins fnl f* **12/1**

51-0 **5** *1* **Monsieur Royale**[31] 2076 3-9-5 68 (b) RussKennemore 1 57+
(Geoffrey Oldroyd) *hld up towards centre: rdn over 2f out: kpt on fnl f: nvr threatened ldrs* **17/2**[3]

21-0 **6** *1 ½* **Red Cobra (IRE)**[49] 1647 3-9-5 68 DuranFentiman 7 52
(Tim Easterby) *hld up towards stands' rail: rdn over 2f out: nvr threatened* **18/1**

4-21 **7** *1 ½* **Rapscallion Deep (IRE)**[27] 2241 3-9-7 70 AmyRyan 5 50+
(Kevin Ryan) *dwlt: hld up towards centre: rdn and sme hdwy over 1f out: wknd fnl f* **11/4**[1]

42-4 **8** *1* **Millkwood**[12] 2672 3-9-7 70 PJMcDonald 2 46
(John Davies) *chsd ldrs towards centre: wknd fnl f* **9/2**[2]

-503 **9** *1* **Another Claret**[16] 2556 3-8-11 60 TonyHamilton 3 33
(Richard Fahey) *chsd ldrs towards centre: wknd over 1f out* **9/1**

-160 **10** *3 ¾* **Edith Anne**[9] 2756 3-8-13 62 MickyFenton 14 23
(Paul Midgley) *hld up towards stands' rail: nvr threatened* **16/1**

03-0 **11** *5* **Bernardino**[43] 1759 3-8-7 56 TomEaves 6
(David Barron) *chsd wnr towards stands' rail: rdn 1/2-way: wknd fnl 2f* **12/1**

64-0 **12** *11* **Shatin Secret**[49] 1647 3-9-2 65 RobertWinston 4
(Noel Wilson) *hld up towards centre: a bhd* **20/1**

1m 12.96s (0.26) **Going Correction** +0.125s/f (Good) **12 Ran SP% 121.0**
Speed ratings (Par 99): **103,101,98,97,96 94,92,90,89,84 77,63**
Tote Swingers 1&2 £42.70, 2&3 £17.00, 1&3 £39.70 CSF £184.64 CT £1812.70 TOTE £30.10: £7.80, £3.90, £3.10; EX 383.70 Trifecta £2143.60 Part won. Pool: £2,858.19 - 0.24 winning tickets..
Owner Chris Penney **Bred** Marston Stud And Fleming Thoroughbreds **Trained** Wetherby, W Yorks
■ Richard Guest's first winner from his new yard in Yorkshire.

FOCUS
The five lowest drawn runners raced wide towards the centre, but the first four home raced stands' side. Modest and suspect form.

3026 RACING UK YOUR RACING HOME FROM HOME H'CAP 6f

3:50 (3:52) (Class 6) (0-60,59) 4-Y-O+ **£1,940** (£577; £288; £144) **Stalls** High

Form RPR

50-0 **1** **Feel The Heat**[66] 1280 6-9-0 57 (v) JustinNewman(5) 18 68
(Bryan Smart) *mde all towards stands' rail: rdn over 2f out: kpt on wl* **8/1**[3]

-000 **2** *2* **Verus Delicia (IRE)**[1] 2997 4-9-2 54 [1] ShaneKelly 17 59
(Daniel Mark Loughnane) *chsd wnr stands' side: rdn over 2f out: kpt on but a hld: 2nd of 9 in gp* **16/1**

0404 **3** *nk* **Pull The Pin (IRE)**[13] 2611 4-8-6 51 LukeLeadbitter(7) 11 55
(Declan Carroll) *chsd wnr stands' side: rdn over 2f out: kpt on: 3rd of 9 in gp* **8/1**[3]

-632 **4** *¾* **Headstight (IRE)**[26] 2276 4-9-1 53 (p) MickyFenton 4 54+
(Paul Midgley) *dwlt: sn chsd ldrs far side: led gp 2f out: kpt on: 1st of 8 in gp* **14/1**

0043 **5** *1 ¾* **Hab Reeh**[24] 2319 5-9-0 52 (t) AmyRyan 7 48+
(Ruth Carr) *in tch far side: rdn over 2f out: kpt on: 2nd of 8 in gp* **9/1**

00-4 **6** *hd* **Absolute Bearing (IRE)**[13] 2634 4-8-10 48 [1] JamesSullivan 5 43+
(Tim Etherington) *hld up far side: rdn over 3f out: kpt on wl ins fnl f: nrst fin: 3rd of 8 in gp* **28/1**

60-0 **7** *½* **Slewtoo**[65] 1311 4-8-11 49 GrahamLee 8 42+
(James Given) *midfield far side: rdn over 2f out: kpt on one pce: 4th of 8 in gp* **33/1**

0325 **8** *1* **Prigsnov Dancer (IRE)**[13] 2611 8-8-5 46 (p) BillyCray(3) 3 36+
(Deborah Sanderson) *chsd ldrs far side: wknd ins fnl f: 5th of 8 in gp* **22/1**

30-5 **9** *1 ¼* **Novalist**[43] 1758 5-9-7 59 (b) RobertWinston 9 45+
(Robin Bastiman) *prom far side: rdn over 2f out: wknd ins fnl f: 6th of 8 in gp* **11/1**

-400 **10** *hd* **Bridge Valley**[7] 2795 6-8-10 48 TonyHamilton 16 34
(Jason Ward) *midfield: rdn over 2f out: sn no imp on ldrs: 4th of 9 in gp* **9/1**

526 **11** *nk* **True Prince (USA)**[3] 2911 4-9-3 55 (tp) DanielTudhope 6 40+
(Brian Ellison) *sn pushed along in rr far side: nvr threatened: 7th of 8 in gp* **5/1**[1]

/6-0 **12** *¾* **Annia Galeria (IRE)**[9] 2747 6-9-0 52 FrannyNorton 13 34
(John Berry) *midfield stands' side: rdn 1/2-way: sn no imp: 5th of 9 in gp* **22/1**

00-0 **13** *2* **Koolgreycat (IRE)**[6] 2832 4-9-4 56 DuranFentiman 15 32
(Noel Wilson) *hld up stands' side: nvr threatened: 6th of 9 in gp* **25/1**

4000 **14** *3 ¼* **Sally's Swansong**[32] 2043 7-8-6 49 (b) JasonHart(5) 10 14
(Eric Alston) *hld up stands' side: nvr threatened: 7th of 9 in gp* **33/1**

40-2 **15** *2* **Lady Kildare (IRE)**[6] 2835 5-9-2 54 TomEaves 14 13
(Jedd O'Keeffe) *prom stands' side: wknd over 2f out: 8th of 9 in gp* **11/2**[2]

000- **16** *shd* **Majestic Angel (IRE)**[284] 5621 4-8-7 45 BarryMcHugh 12
(Brian Rothwell) *hld up stands'side: nvr threatened: last of 9 in gp* **50/1**

5002 **17** *4* **Nine Before Ten (IRE)**[3] 2926 5-9-0 52 (t) GrahamGibbons 2 +
(Charles Smith) *led far side: hdd 2f out: wknd and eased* **16/1**

1m 13.09s (0.39) **Going Correction** +0.125s/f (Good) **17 Ran SP% 124.9**
Speed ratings (Par 101): **102,99,98,97,95 95,94,93,91,91 91,90,87,83,80 80,74**
Tote Swingers 1&2 £33.30, 2&3 £27.90, 1&3 £16.00 CSF £121.35 CT £1110.36 TOTE £10.50: £2.50, £1.90, £2.60, £3.30; EX 214.10 Trifecta £2714.10 Pool: £3,836.02 - 1.06 winning tickets..
Owner B Smart **Bred** Bearstone Stud **Trained** Hambleton, N Yorks
■ Justin Newman's first winner since a lengthy injury lay-off.

FOCUS
The eight lowest drawn horses went to the far side, but the first three home raced against the normally favoured stands' side. Another sprint winner to make all on the day. The form makes a fair bit of sense at face value.

3027 WATCH RACING UK ON FREEVIEW 231 H'CAP (QUALIFIER TO £15,000 BETFAIR SCOTTISH MILE SERIES FINAL) 1m

4:25 (4:26) (Class 5) (0-70,75) 4-Y-O+ **£2,587** (£770; £384; £192) **Stalls** Low

Form RPR

0-61 **1** **Ingleby Angel (IRE)**[9] 2753 4-9-12 75 6ex DanielTudhope 4 91+
(David O'Meara) *midfield: smooth hdwy fr over 2f out: pushed along to ld appr fnl f: rdn out fnl 100yds* **6/5**[1]

5612 **2** *1 ¼* **Our Ivor**[15] 2580 4-9-7 70 AndrewMullen 9 81
(Michael Appleby) *trckd ldrs: rdn over 2f out: kpt on wl but a hld by wnr* **9/2**[2]

0230 **3** *5* **Cono Zur (FR)**[12] 2659 6-9-4 67 JamesSullivan 6 67
(Ruth Carr) *led: rdn whn hdd appr fnl f: grad wknd* **15/2**[3]

005- **4** *nk* **Thatcherite (IRE)**[119] 7415 5-9-1 64 (t) StephenCraine 1 63
(Tony Coyle) *hld up in rr: hdwy over 2f out: rdn over 1f out: kpt on ins fnl f: nrst fin* **12/1**

0030 **5** *½* **The Blue Banana (IRE)**[16] 2537 4-8-5 54 (b) PJMcDonald 2 52
(Edwin Tuer) *hld up: rdn and hdwy 2f out: kpt on one pce: nvr threatened* **16/1**

-0 **6** *1* **Dance For Georgie**[42] 1788 4-9-1 64 PhillipMakin 10 59
(Ben Haslam) *hld up: rdn over 2f out: nvr threatened ldrs* **9/1**

0260 **7** *2 ½* **Firefly**[9] 2764 4-8-2 51 (b[1]) DuranFentiman 3 41
(John Weymes) *trckd ldr: pressed ldr 1/2-way: rdn 3f out: wknd fnl f* **66/1**

4416 **8** 1 3/4 **Mujaadel (USA)**23 2339 8-9-7 70 ....(p) PaulMulrennan 8 56
(David Nicholls) *hld up: nvr threatened* **10/1**
0-25 **9** 1/2 **Just The Tonic**13 2636 6-8-12 64 .... PaulPickard(3) 5 48
(Marjorie Fife) *dwlt: sn midfield: rdn over 2f out: wknd over 1f out* **20/1**
600- **10** nk **First Class Favour (IRE)**229 7246 5-9-5 68 .... DavidAllan 7 52
(Tim Easterby) *trckd ldrs: rdn 3f out: wknd over 1f out* **33/1**

1m 40.27s (0.17) **Going Correction** +0.125s/f (Good) 10 Ran SP% **117.3**
Speed ratings (Par 103): **104,102,97,97,96 95,93,91,91,90**
Tote Swingers 1&2 £2.00, 2&3 £3.80, 1&3 £3.40 CSF £6.39 CT £29.38 TOTE £1.90: £1.10, £1.90, £2.70; EX 5.70 Trifecta £20.80 Pool: £3,320.32 - 119.48 winning tickets..
Owner Dave Scott **Bred** Dave Scott **Trained** Nawton, N Yorks

FOCUS
A truly run handicap and the first two pulled clear in the end. The winner may be able to cope with a higher grade.

3028 GBI RACING WELCOMES NICOSIA RACE CLUB H'CAP 7f
5:00 (5:00) (Class 3) (0-95,90) 3-Y-O **£7,762** (£2,310; £1,154; £577) **Stalls** Low

Form RPR
1 **1** **Ajraam (USA)**49 1635 3-9-7 90 .... GrahamLee 2 97+
(Charles Hills) *sn trckd ldr: rdn to ld wl over 1f out: drvn ins fnl f: hld on wl* **4/1**3
12 **2** 3/4 **Henry The Aviator (USA)**111 666 3-8-7 76 .... FrannyNorton 6 81+
(Mark Johnston) *hld up: pushed along over 3f out: r.o wl fnl f: nrst fin* **4/1**3
1-04 **3** hd **George Rooke (IRE)**12 2666 3-8-12 81 .... AmyRyan 5 85
(Kevin Ryan) *hld up: rdn over 2f out: kpt on ins fnl f* **11/4**1
3-23 **4** 1 1/4 **Yourartisonfire**19 2438 3-8-10 82 .... MichaelMetcalfe(3) 3 83
(Mrs K Burke) *hld up in tch: rdn over 2f out: hdwy to chse wnr over 1f out: one pce ins fnl f* **7/2**2
015- **5** 1 1/2 **Steer By The Stars (IRE)**222 7406 3-9-7 90 .... JoeFanning 4 87
(Mark Johnston) *in tch: rdn and hdwy over 2f out: stl ev ch jst ins fnl f: wknd* **9/2**
42-1 **6** 4 **Le Deluge (FR)**57 1495 3-9-7 90 .... FrederikTylicki 1 76
(John Best) *led: rdn whn hdd wl over 1f out: wknd* **20/1**

1m 27.56s (0.36) **Going Correction** +0.125s/f (Good) 6 Ran SP% **111.8**
Speed ratings (Par 103): **102,101,100,99,97 93**
Tote Swingers 1&2 £2.70, 2&3 £4.30, 1&3 £3.00 CSF £19.90 TOTE £2.70: £1.40, £2.30; EX 13.50 Trifecta £43.30 Pool: £2,187.46 - 37.88 winning tickets..
Owner Hamdan Al Maktoum **Bred** Shadwell Estate Co Ltd **Trained** Lambourn, Berks

FOCUS
An interesting and good-class 3yo handicap. Improvement from the winer, whose Wood Ditton form has received some boosts.

3029 READ HAYLEY TURNER EVERY FRIDAY RACINGUK.COM H'CAP (DIV I) 7f
5:30 (5:32) (Class 6) (0-60,59) 4-Y-O+ **£1,940** (£577; £288; £144) **Stalls** Low

Form RPR
0-02 **1** **Ptolemy**24 2319 4-9-6 58 .... GrahamGibbons 4 66
(David Barron) *dwlt: sn midfield towards outer: smooth hdwy 2f out: rdn to ld fnl 75yds: kpt on: edgd lft nr fin* **7/2**1
02-5 **2** nk **Maggie Mey (IRE)**16 2537 5-8-12 50 .... DanielTudhope 11 57
(Lawrence Mullaney) *led at stdy pce: rdn over 2f out: drvn fnl f: hdd fnl 75yds: kpt on* **11/2**3
05-3 **3** 1/2 **Glan Lady (IRE)**15 2578 7-8-7 45 .... AndrewMullen 8 51
(Michael Appleby) *in tch: rdn over 2f out: kpt on* **16/1**
-006 **4** 3/4 **Hoppy's Flyer (FR)**26 2280 5-9-7 59 ....(v) MickyFenton 12 64
(Paul Midgley) *prom: rdn and ev ch 2f out: kpt on one pce: short of room nr fin* **12/1**
3416 **5** 3/4 **Monsieur Pontaven**16 2537 6-8-10 48 ....(b) RobertWinston 2 50
(Robin Bastiman) *hld up: sme hdwy on outer over 2f out: kpt on: nvr threatened ldrs* **6/1**
003 **6** 1 1/4 **Coastal Passage**3 2926 5-9-0 52 .... PhillipMakin 7 50
(Charles Smith) *hld up: pushed along over 2f out: kpt on fnl f: nvr threatened* **4/1**2
0005 **7** nk **Bachelor Knight (IRE)**9 2752 5-8-9 47 .... DaleSwift 3 45
(Suzzanne France) *midfield: pushed along whn n.m.r over 1f out: one pce fnl f: nvr threatened ldrs* **9/1**
-000 **8** 5 **Regal Acclaim (IRE)**16 2537 4-9-1 53 ....(v1) DavidNolan 6 37
(Ian McInnes) *trckd ldrs: rdn over 2f out: wknd over 1f out* **25/1**
3066 **9** 4 1/2 **North Central (USA)**24 2319 6-8-12 50 ....(e) JamesSullivan 9 22
(Ruth Carr) *trckd ldrs on inner: n.m.r over 2f out: wknd over 1f out* **25/1**
230- **10** 2 1/4 **Pendle Lady (IRE)**342 3555 4-9-6 58 .... FrannyNorton 1 24
(Mark Brisbourne) *hld up: a towards rr* **8/1**

1m 29.74s (2.54) **Going Correction** +0.125s/f (Good) 10 Ran SP% **114.3**
Speed ratings (Par 101): **90,89,89,88,87 85,85,79,74,72**
Tote Swingers 1&2 £3.00, 2&3 £10.70, 1&3 £10.60 CSF £22.26 CT £270.72 TOTE £3.70: £2.20, £3.60, £3.60; EX 16.20 Trifecta £186.00 Pool: £2,433.52 - 9.81 winning tickets..
Owner Reg Gifford **Bred** R S E Gifford (wordsworth Hotel Ltd) **Trained** Maunby, N Yorks
■ Stewards' Enquiry : Graham Gibbons three-day ban: careless riding (23-25 June)

FOCUS
The pace seemed to slacken around the halfway mark in this modest but open-looking handicap.

3030 READ HAYLEY TURNER EVERY FRIDAY RACINGUK.COM H'CAP (DIV II) 7f
6:00 (6:04) (Class 6) (0-60,59) 4-Y-O+ **£1,940** (£577; £288; £144) **Stalls** Low

Form RPR
0000 **1** **Dhhamaan (IRE)**30 2125 8-8-12 50 ....(b) JamesSullivan 6 59
(Ruth Carr) *mde all: rdn over 2f out: drvn ins fnl f: hld on all out* **16/1**
064- **2** hd **Crossley**212 7600 4-9-7 59 .... BarryMcHugh 10 67+
(Geoffrey Oldroyd) *hld up: rdn and hdwy over 2f out: squeezed through gap to chse wnr jst ins fnl f: kpt on: jst hld* **12/1**
0-20 **3** 2 1/4 **Cross The Boss (IRE)**5 2889 6-9-6 58 .... DanielTudhope 4 60
(David O'Meara) *s.i.s: hld up: pushed along 3f out: swtchd to outer 2f out and sn mde hdwy: rdn and edgd lft appr fnl f: kpt on one pce* **5/4**1
000- **4** 1 **Deliberation (IRE)**315 4495 5-9-6 58 .... MichaelO'Connell 9 58
(John Quinn) *trckd ldrs: rdn over 2f out: kpt on one pce* **5/1**3
6400 **5** 2 3/4 **You'relikemefrank**13 2632 7-8-11 49 .... FrederikTylicki 1 41
(Richard Ford) *trckd ldrs: rdn over 2f out: grad wknd fnl f* **22/1**
300/ **6** 1/2 **Inca Chief**733 1749 5-9-0 52 .... PJMcDonald 5 43
(Ann Duffield) *midfield: rdn over 2f out: one pce and nvr threatened ldrs* **50/1**
2401 **7** 1 3/4 **For Shia And Lula (IRE)**31 2073 4-9-5 57 .... ShaneKelly 2 43
(Daniel Mark Loughnane) *midfield: rdn over 2f out: wknd ins fnl f* **7/2**2
00-0 **8** 1 **Triskaidekaphobia**35 1961 10-8-7 45 ....(t) AmyRyan 3 28
(Wilf Storey) *dwlt: hld up: nvr threatened* **66/1**
00-0 **9** 1 1/4 **Jay Kay**31 2089 4-8-10 48 .... DuranFentiman 12 28
(Danielle McCormick) *prom: rdn 3f out: wknd over 1f out* **33/1**

0000 **10** 2 3/4 **Dolly Diva**13 2616 4-9-3 55 .... MickyFenton 8 35
(Paul Midgley) *hld up in midfield: rdn over 2f out: hld whn short of room on rail jst ins fnl f* **25/1**
60-0 **11** 34 **Artillery Train (IRE)**13 2636 4-8-7 45 .... TomEaves 11
(Tim Etherington) *midfield towards outer: dropped to rr over 3f out: eased* **33/1**

1m 28.69s (1.49) **Going Correction** +0.125s/f (Good) 11 Ran SP% **114.4**
Speed ratings (Par 101): **96,95,93,92,88 88,86,85,83,80 41**
Tote Swingers 1&2 £9.50, 2&3 £2.80, 1&3 £5.00 CSF £168.53 CT £421.38 TOTE £29.10: £4.80, £2.50, £1.10; EX 190.90 Trifecta £775.50 Pool: £1,480.94 - 1.43 winning tickets..
Owner S B Clark **Bred** D Veitch And Musagd Abo Salim **Trained** Huby, N Yorks

FOCUS
The faster division. The winner made all and is rated to last year's form.
T/Plt: £556.20 to a £1 stake. Pool: £54,896.77 - 72.05 winning tickets. T/Qpdt: £47.20 to a £1 stake. Pool: £3,932.60 - 61.6 winning tickets. AS

2823 BATH (L-H)
Friday, June 7

OFFICIAL GOING: Firm (9.8)
Far bend positioned 3-4m off inside line adding about 10yds to races of 1m and beyond as has been the case at all previous meetings this season.
Wind: Moderate behind Weather: White cloud

3035 BRITISH STALLION STUDS EBF MAIDEN STKS 5f 11y
2:00 (2:00) (Class 4) 2-Y-O **£4,075** (£1,212; £606; £303) **Stalls** Centre

Form RPR
63 **1** **Hatha Hooh**4 2925 2-9-5 0 .... PatDobbs 4 81+
(Richard Hannon) *mde all: qcknd readily clr fnl f: easily* **10/11**1
2253 **2** 4 1/2 **Urban Dreamer (IRE)**1 3017 2-9-5 0 .... FergusSweeney 7 65
(Rod Millman) *chsd wnr thrght: rdn over 1f out and sn outpcd but hld on wl for 2nd clsng stages* **4/1**2
3 nse **Fiftyshadesofgrey (IRE)** 2-9-5 0 .... PatCosgrave 3 65+
(George Baker) *s.i.s: in rr: hdwy fr 2f out: drvn and styd on wl fnl f to press for 2nd last strides but nvr any ch w wnr* **15/2**
4 1 **Dodger Marley (IRE)** 2-9-5 0 .... HarryBentley 1 61
(Stuart Williams) *chsd ldrs: rdn over 1f out: kpt on same pce ins fnl f* **11/2**3
5 3 3/4 **State Anthem** 2-9-0 0 .... SamHitchcott 8 43
(Mick Channon) *in tch: drvn along 3f out: wknd over 1f out* **20/1**
54 **6** 7 **Fantasy Justifier (IRE)**27 2260 2-9-5 0 .... SteveDrowne 5 22
(Ronald Harris) *chsd ldrs: rdn 2f out: wknd over 1f out* **14/1**

1m 0.71s (-1.79) **Going Correction** -0.275s/f (Firm) 6 Ran SP% **111.0**
Speed ratings (Par 95): **103,95,95,94,88 76**
toteswingers 1&2 £1.10, 1&3 £3.40, 2&3 £9.50 CSF £4.66 TOTE £2.00: £1.20, £2.40; EX 4.00 Trifecta £19.90 Pool: £1589.68 - 59.65 winning tickets..
Owner Saeed H Altayer **Bred** Mill House Stud **Trained** East Everleigh, Wilts
■ Stewards' Enquiry : Pat Cosgrave caution; careless riding.

FOCUS
Far bend positioned 3-4yds off inside, adding about 10yds to races of 1m and further. The jockeys confirmed the ground to be riding firm after the opener. Front-runners generally did well on the card so the winner has been rated to the bare form only.

3036 BREEDERS BACKING RACING EBF MAIDEN STKS 5f 11y
2:30 (2:30) (Class 5) 3-Y-O **£3,881** (£1,155; £577; £288) **Stalls** Centre

Form RPR
5-2 **1** **Daylight**17 2529 3-9-5 0 .... LiamKeniry 1 81
(Andrew Balding) *mde all: pushed clr fnl f: unchal* **4/5**1
-222 **2** 4 **Silverrica (IRE)**7 2829 3-9-0 66 .... TomMcLaughlin 2 61
(Malcolm Saunders) *edgd rt s: chsd ldrs in 3rd tl wnt 2nd over 1f out: kpt on but nvr any ch w wnr* **7/4**2
00 **3** 1 3/4 **Cape Appeal**13 2658 3-9-0 0 .... PatDobbs 4 55
(Richard Hannon) *chsd wnr: rdn and no imp over 2f out: lost 2nd over 1f out: no ch after* **8/1**3
0-40 **4** 10 **Rectory Lane**20 2447 3-8-9 50 ....(b1) AmyScott(5) 5 19
(Eve Johnson Houghton) *pushed rt s: rdn 1/2-way: a wl outpcd* **40/1**
-500 **5** 3 1/2 **Woodland Fleur**128 442 3-9-0 48 .... CathyGannon 3
(Tony Carroll) *pushed rt s: rdn 1/2-way and a wl outpcd* **100/1**

1m 1.27s (-1.23) **Going Correction** -0.275s/f (Firm) 5 Ran SP% **106.5**
Speed ratings (Par 99): **98,91,88,72,67**
CSF £2.20 TOTE £2.30: £1.10, £1.30; EX 2.10 Trifecta £4.70 Pool: £1932.81 - 302.05 winning tickets..
Owner Kennet Valley Thoroughbreds V **Bred** Bearstone Stud And T Herbert Jackson **Trained** Kingsclere, Hants

FOCUS
Little depth to this maiden in which the winner made all. He's the safest guide to the form.

3037 BETVICTOR.COM H'CAP 1m 3f 144y
3:00 (3:01) (Class 6) (0-60,58) 4-Y-O+ **£1,940** (£577; £288; £144) **Stalls** Low

Form RPR
-000 **1** **Highlife Dancer**17 2533 5-8-11 53 ....(v) CharlesBishop(5) 1 63
(Mick Channon) *mde all: pushed along 2f out: jnd over 1f out: hrd pressed ins fnl f: staged on gamely clsng stages* **9/1**
4452 **2** nk **Spanish Plume**11 2714 5-9-2 58 ....(b1) JackDuern(5) 7 68
(Andrew Hollinshead) *in tch: hdwy to chse wnr over 2f out: chal fr over 1f out and stl upsides fnl 110yds: fnd no ex clsng stages* **7/2**2
3463 **3** 4 **Glens Wobbly**16 2567 5-8-9 46 .... HarryBentley 8 49
(Jonathan Geake) *chsd ldrs: rdn 3f out: styd on same pce for wl-hld over 1f out* **5/1**3
30-1 **4** 1 **Iceman George**11 2714 9-9-0 56 ....(v) PhilipPrince(5) 2 58
(Alison Hutchinson) *chsd ldrs: rdn 3f out: outpcd over 1f out* **11/4**1
0345 **5** 7 **Ice Tres**11 2714 4-9-4 55 .... SteveDrowne 5 45
(Rod Millman) *slowly away and bhd: sme hdwy over 2f out: nvr rchd ldrs and sn wknd* **10/1**
-020 **6** 1 1/2 **Youm Jamil (USA)**29 653 6-9-3 54 ....(b) PatDobbs 6 42
(Tony Carroll) *in rr but in tch: hdwy 3f out: wknd ins fnl 2f* **20/1**
60-2 **7** 1 3/4 **Perfect Outlook**32 2073 5-8-10 47 .... SamHitchcott 4 32
(Charlie Longsdon) *in rr: rdn and sme hdwy whn hanging lft fr 3f out: stl hanging whn wknd ins fnl 2f* **9/1**
-212 **8** 8 **Gladstone (IRE)**9 2777 5-9-2 53 .... LiamKeniry 3 32
(Polly Gundry) *chsd ldr tl over 2f out: sn btn* **5/1**3

2m 31.67s (1.07) **Going Correction** -0.025s/f (Good) 8 Ran SP% **116.1**
Speed ratings (Par 101): **95,94,92,91,86 85,84,79**
toteswingers 1&2 £17.40, 1&3 £9.90, 2&3 £13.10 CSF £41.21 CT £178.14 TOTE £7.00: £2.50, £1.90, £1.50; EX 55.50 Trifecta £264.80 Pool: £1765.36 - 4.99 winning tickets..

Owner The Highlife Racing Club **Bred** Imperial & Mike Channon Bloodstock Ltd **Trained** West Ilsley, Berks

FOCUS
A moderate handicap. They went steady early until the pace quickened on the turn into the straight. Straightforward form, with the front pair clear.

3038 BARONS SPY CLASSIFIED STKS 5f 161y
3:35 (3:35) (Class 3) 4-Y-O+ **£7,439** (£2,213; £1,106; £553) **Stalls** Centre

Form RPR
0640 **1** **Forest Edge (IRE)**[6] 2868 4-8-12 89..........................(b) DeclanBates(5) 6 99+
(David Evans) *trckd ldrs: wnt 2nd over 3f out: led ins fnl 2f: pushed clr fnl f: easily* **6/1**[3]
-400 **2** *8* **Top Cop**[6] 2865 4-9-3 87..(v) LiamKeniry 3 73
(Andrew Balding) *trckd ldrs: rdn over 2f out: styd on fnl f to take wl hld 2nd clsng stages* **11/4**[2]
0-34 **3** *1 ¼* **Fair Value (IRE)**[6] 2865 5-9-0 90...................................... HayleyTurner 4 65
(Simon Dow) *led: rdn and hdd ins fnl 2f: no ch w wnr fnl f and lost 2nd clsng stages* **5/6**[1]
0-00 **4** *2* **Nasri**[11] 2725 7-8-12 83.. MatthewLawson(5) 1 62
(Milton Bradley) *chsd ldr tl over 3f out: sn rdn: outpcd and no ch fnl 2f* **16/1**
5000 **5** *7* **Barons Spy (IRE)**[7] 2825 12-8-10 80......................... DanielMuscutt(7) 2 39
(Richard Price) *s.i.s: a outpcd in rr* **33/1**
00-0 **6** *15* **Burning Thread (IRE)**[9] 2768 6-9-3 82...................... AdamBeschizza 7
(Tim Etherington) *s.i.s: sn rdn: lost tch fnl 2f* **20/1**

1m 8.48s (-2.72) **Going Correction** -0.275s/f (Firm) **6 Ran SP% 109.1**
Speed ratings (Par 107): **107,96,94,92,82 62**
toteswingers 1&2 £1.10, 1&3 £1.20, 2&3 £1.10 CSF £21.44 TOTE £8.00: £2.40, £1.50; EX 21.00 Trifecta £34.20 Pool: £2837.71 - 62.07 winning tickets..
Owner P & K Swinnerton **Bred** Alberto Panetta **Trained** Pandy, Monmouths

FOCUS
A fair classified event which was turned into a procession by the winner. The form can't be taken literally but could be rated 7lb+ better.

3039 £25 FREE BET AT BETVICTOR.COM FILLIES' H'CAP 1m 5y
4:10 (4:10) (Class 5) (0-75,77) 3-Y-O **£2,587** (£770; £384; £192) **Stalls** Low

Form RPR
04-4 **1** **Waverunner**[48] 1698 3-9-6 73.. HarryBentley 3 80+
(Saeed bin Suroor) *trckd ldrs: led appr fnl f: drvn and styd on fnl 110yds* **4/1**[2]
10-0 **2** *1 ¼* **New Falcon (IRE)**[34] 2026 3-9-7 74............................(b[1]) PatCosgrave 8 76
(James Tate) *edgd rt s and sn drvn to ld: jnd ins fnl 2f: hdd appr fnl f: kpt on same pce* **12/1**
053 **3** *1 ½* **Bee Jay Kay**[34] 2016 3-8-3 63...................................... DanielCremin(7) 1 61
(Mick Channon) *in rr: rdn 3f out: hdwy 2f out: kpt on to take one pce 3rd ins fnl f* **16/1**
3-56 **4** *1 ½* **Azelle**[15] 2597 3-9-1 68.. CathyGannon 2 63
(Richard Hannon) *loose to s: in rr: rdn along 3f out: styd on fr over 1f out: nvr rchd ldrs* **14/1**
0-52 **5** *hd* **Fair Comment**[23] 2362 3-8-8 61.................................. FergusSweeney 4 55
(Michael Blanshard) *rrrdn over 2f out: kpt on fr over 1f out: nt trble ldrs* **10/1**[3]
1666 **6** *nse* **Byroness**[2] 2984 3-9-3 70.. TomMcLaughlin 7 64
(Heather Main) *in tch: hdwy 2f out: chsd ldrs over 1f out: wknd ins fnl f* **20/1**
1-31 **7** *1 ¼* **Maid A Million**[10] 2763 3-9-10 77 6ex.................................. LiamKeniry 5 68
(David Elsworth) *chsd ldr: drvn and effrt ins fnl 2f: fnd no ex over 1f out: wknd fnl f* **8/11**[1]
5-43 **8** *24* **Followeveryrainbow**[32] 2071 3-8-10 63.............................. PatDobbs 6
(Richard Hannon) *chsd ldrs: rdn 4f out: wknd qckly over 2f out* **20/1**

1m 40.61s (-0.19) **Going Correction** -0.025s/f (Good) **8 Ran SP% 116.8**
Speed ratings (Par 96): **99,97,96,94,94 94,93,69**
toteswingers 1&2 £8.50, 1&3 £4.80, 2&3 £18.70 CSF £51.08 CT £691.72 TOTE £4.40: £1.10, £4.20, £4.50; EX 70.50 Trifecta £556.70 Pool: £4569.50 - 6.15 winning tickets..
Owner Godolphin **Bred** Darley **Trained** Newmarket, Suffolk

FOCUS
The pace was honest in this 3yo fillies' handicap. The runner-up limits the bare form but the winner should go in again.

3040 DOWNLAOD THE BETVICTOR APP NOW H'CAP (DIV I) 1m 5y
4:45 (4:45) (Class 6) (0-60,60) 3-Y-O **£1,940** (£577; £288; £144) **Stalls** Low

Form RPR
00-0 **1** **Double Star**[22] 2392 3-8-5 47 oh1 ow3.................. MatthewLawson(5) 3 56+
(Jonathan Portman) *in rr: rdn over 3f out: hdwy over 2f out: styd on wl fnl f to ld fnl 75yds: pushed out* **33/1**
4303 **2** *1 ¼* **Eyeline**[23] 2362 3-8-4 48 ow1..(v) JackDuern(5) 10 54
(Andrew Hollinshead) *sn led: jnd fr over 2f out but kpt advanatge u.p tl hdd and outpcd fnl 75yds* **13/2**
050 **3** *3* **Just Isla**[32] 2093 3-8-0 46...(p) CameronHardie(7) 8 45
(Peter Makin) *t.k.h: sn trcking ldr: chal fr over 2f out: rdn and no ex fnl f: wknd fnl 110yds* **25/1**
6015 **4** *1 ¾* **Sutton Sid**[11] 2709 3-9-6 59... PatCosgrave 7 54
(George Baker) *in rr: hdwy over 2f out: styd on same pce u.p fnl 2f* **5/1**[2]
-016 **5** *¾* **Noor Al Haya (IRE)**[16] 2566 3-8-5 51.......................... DanielMuscutt(7) 1 44
(Mark Usher) *chsd ldrs: outpcd and rdn 3f out: effrt 2f out: styd on same pce* **7/2**[1]
-645 **6** *3* **Loraine**[32] 2095 3-9-5 58.. FergusSweeney 4 44
(Jamie Osborne) *chsd ldrs: rdn over 2f out: wknd over 1f out* **7/2**[1]
300 **7** *12* **Burma Days (USA)**[10] 2743 3-8-10 49................................ LiamKeniry 9 6
(Sylvester Kirk) *s.i.s: sn chsng ldrs: rdn 3f out: wknd ins fnl 2f* **20/1**
2203 **8** *2 ¾* **Solvanna**[16] 2560 3-9-7 60.. TomMcLaughlin 5 10
(Heather Main) *rdn 3f out: a towards rr* **7/1**
3-00 **9** *4* **Secretori**[20] 2464 3-9-5 58..(p) CathyGannon 2
(Jo Hughes) *a in rr* **6/1**[3]
5140 **10** *1 ½* **Schottische**[107] 732 3-9-2 55.......................................(p) HarryBentley 6
(Derek Haydn Jones) *rn wd bnd 4f out: a towards rr* **16/1**

1m 41.14s (0.34) **Going Correction** -0.025s/f (Good) **10 Ran SP% 118.7**
Speed ratings (Par 97): **97,95,92,91,90 87,75,72,68,67**
toteswingers 1&2 £29.00, 1&3 £35.30, 2&3 £29.70 CSF £234.23 CT £5539.09 TOTE £34.50: £8.00, £2.30, £7.50; EX 288.70 Trifecta £1389.20 Pool: £4385.13 - 2.36 winning tickets..
Owner Mrs D Joly **Bred** Mrs D O Joly **Trained** Upper Lambourn, Berks
■ Stewards' Enquiry : Matthew Lawson three-day ban; weighted in heavy (23rd-25th June).

FOCUS
The winning time of the first division of this handicap was marginally quicker than the second. Very few got into it from off the pace. A weak race, but the winner was much improved.

3041 DOWNLAOD THE BETVICTOR APP NOW H'CAP (DIV II) 1m 5y
5:15 (5:17) (Class 6) (0-60,60) 3-Y-O **£1,940** (£577; £288; £144) **Stalls** Low

Form RPR
20-0 **1** **Just A Pound (IRE)**[39] 1885 3-8-13 57.......................... PhilipPrince(5) 2 63
(Jo Hughes) *trckd ldr: led over 2f out: pushed out fnl f: comf* **20/1**
-155 **2** *2 ¼* **Loucal**[18] 2501 3-9-6 59.. StevieDonohoe 7 60
(Noel Quinlan) *in rr but in tch: drvn and hdwy over 1f out: styd on wl to take 2nd clsng stages but no ch w wnr* **7/4**[1]
0530 **3** *nk* **Rock Diamond (IRE)**[3] 2950 3-8-9 48.................................. PatDobbs 9 48
(Sylvester Kirk) *sn led: rdn and hdd over 2f out: sn one pce: rallied to chse wnr fnl 110yds: dropped to 3rd clsng stages* **9/2**[3]
00-6 **4** *¾* **Choral Rhythm (IRE)**[23] 2362 3-8-7 46 oh1..................... HarryBentley 1 44
(Tony Carroll) *chsd ldrs: rdn to go 2nd 2f out but no imp: one pce fnl f* **16/1**
06-3 **5** *1* **Sovereign Power**[30] 2154 3-9-7 60.................................... LiamKeniry 3 56
(Paul Cole) *chsd ldrs: rdn over 2f out: kpt on same pce* **7/2**[2]
06-0 **6** *2 ½* **Dawn Rock**[44] 1769 3-8-5 49 ow2...................................... JackDuern(5) 8 39
(Simon Dow) *in tch and rdn 3f out: n.m.r but no ch over 1f out: mod late prog* **14/1**
-650 **7** *1* **Beautiful Story (IRE)**[25] 2324 3-9-5 58............................ PatCosgrave 4 45
(Mick Channon) *s.i.s: in rr: rdn over 3f out: mod late prog* **16/1**
004 **8** *½* **Culture Trip**[98] 841 3-8-13 52... SamHitchcott 5 38
(Gary Moore) *rdn over 3f out: a in rr* **20/1**
0554 **9** *2* **Sweet Alabama**[10] 2743 3-8-10 49..............................(b) FergusSweeney 6 30
(Rod Millman) *chsd ldrs: rdn over 2f out: wknd qckly appr fnl f* **7/1**

1m 42.04s (1.24) **Going Correction** -0.025s/f (Good) **9 Ran SP% 117.2**
Speed ratings (Par 97): **92,89,89,88,87 85,84,83,81**
toteswingers 1&2 £11.80, 1&3 £11.50, 2&3 £2.80 CSF £56.31 CT £193.55 TOTE £24.90: £5.70, £1.20, £2.30; EX 115.70 Trifecta £574.00 Pool: £2740.02 - 3.57 winning tickets..
Owner Joseph Smith **Bred** Mrs J F Hughes **Trained** Lambourn, Berks

FOCUS
A modest handicap and those ridden prominently were favoured. The winner is rated back to his 2yo Polytrack form.

3042 BETVICTOR CASINO ON YOUR MOBILE H'CAP 5f 11y
5:45 (5:46) (Class 5) (0-70,70) 4-Y-O+ **£2,587** (£770; £384; £192) **Stalls** Centre

Form RPR
0-05 **1** **Powerful Wind (IRE)**[16] 2561 4-9-1 69.......................... PhilipPrince(5) 5 81
(Ronald Harris) *mde all: clr 1/2-way: rdn over 1f out: unchal* **8/1**
000- **2** *3* **Baby Queen (IRE)**[367] 2789 7-9-2 70......................... MatthewLawson(5) 4 71
(Brian Baugh) *chsd ldr: rdn and no ch fnl 2f but kpt on wl for 2nd fnl f* **33/1**
-645 **3** *½* **Wooden King (IRE)**[8] 2790 8-9-6 69........................(p) TomMcLaughlin 1 68
(Malcolm Saunders) *chsd ldrs: rdn over 2f out: one pce fnl f* **8/1**
6432 **4** *1 ¼* **Molly Jones**[32] 2074 4-7-12 52 oh1 ow1....................(p) RosieJessop(5) 7 47+
(Derek Haydn Jones) *in rr: hdwy over 1f out: styd on clsng stages* **6/1**[3]
6636 **5** *¾* **Swendab (IRE)**[10] 2736 5-8-10 66...........................(b) DanielMuscutt(7) 10 58
(John O'Shea) *chsd ldrs: rdn over 2f out: kpt on same pce fnl f* **6/1**[3]
0030 **6** *1 ¾* **Chester'Slittlegem (IRE)**[16] 2582 4-7-9 51 oh4...... CameronHardie(7) 9 37+
(Jo Hughes) *in rr: pushed along over 1f out: kpt on ins fnl f: nvr a threat* **10/1**
0-14 **7** *shd* **Amber Heights**[36] 1957 5-8-10 64...................................... AmyScott(5) 2 50+
(Henry Candy) *slowly away and wl off the pce: stl last ins fnl f: styd on wl clsng stages but nt rcvr* **9/2**[1]
6025 **8** *hd* **Gaelic Wizard (IRE)**[15] 2588 5-8-7 63....................... JoshBaudains(7) 8 48
(Dominic Ffrench Davis) *early spd: sn outpcd: rdn over 2f out: sme late prog* **8/1**
55-6 **9** *½* **Fathom Five (IRE)**[149] 124 9-9-2 65........................... FergusSweeney 11 48
(Gary Moore) *chsd ldrs: rdn over 2f out: styd on same pce* **20/1**
0305 **10** *1 ¼* **Danziger (IRE)**[6] 2870 4-9-2 70...................................... DeclanBates(5) 6 49
(David Evans) *in rr: sme hdwy over 1f out: wknd ins fnl f* **10/1**
-423 **11** *4* **Novabridge**[91] 924 5-9-6 69...(b) LiamKeniry 3 43
(Neil Mulholland) *chsd ldrs to 1/2-way* **11/2**[2]

1m 1.12s (-1.38) **Going Correction** -0.275s/f (Firm) **11 Ran SP% 121.4**
Speed ratings (Par 103): **100,95,94,92,91 88,88,87,87,85 78**
toteswingers 1&2 £33.90, 1&3 £8.70, 2&3 £16.20 CSF £244.06 CT £2188.86 TOTE £9.70: £4.10, £4.20, £2.90; EX 133.10 Trifecta £812.60 Pool: £2416.11 - 2.22 winning tickets..
Owner Anthony Cooke **Bred** Miss Ciara Doyle **Trained** Earlswood, Monmouths

FOCUS
A competitive sprint handicap which featured several front-runners, but the winner still made all under a positive ride. Front runners were favoured on the card.
T/Plt: £120.20 to a £1 stake. Pool: £50,984.85 - 309.52 winning tickets T/Qpdt: £87.20 to a £1 stake. Pool: £3,040.95 - 25.80 winning tickets ST

2659 HAYDOCK (L-H)
Friday, June 7

OFFICIAL GOING: Good to firm (8.0)
All races on Inner home straight except 6f race on Stands side home straight. Races on Round course reduced in distance by 5yds.
Wind: Light, behind Weather: Hot and Sunny

3043 BETDAQ HAYDOCK PARK APPRENTICE TRAINING SERIES H'CAP (PART OF THE RACING EXCELLENCE INITIATIVE) 1m 2f 95y
6:45 (6:46) (Class 5) (0-70,70) 4-Y-O+ **£2,587** (£770; £384; £192) **Stalls** Centre

Form RPR
4652 **1** **Gran Maestro (USA)**[6] 2886 4-9-11 69.............................(b) LMcNiff 5 82
(Ruth Carr) *chsd ldrs: rdn to ld wl over 1f out: styd on to draw clr ins fnl 150yds* **4/1**[2]
-000 **2** *5* **Market Puzzle (IRE)**[46] 1730 6-8-7 51 oh6....................(p) NoelGarbutt 4 54
(Mark Brisbourne) *midfield: hdwy 2f out: wnt 2nd and chalng over 1f out: unable to go w wnr ins fnl 150yds: no ex cl home* **40/1**
4202 **3** *½* **Breakheart (IRE)**[15] 2594 6-8-12 63........................(v) JackGarritty(7) 9 65
(Andrew Balding) *dwlt: hld up: rdn and hdwy over 1f out: sn lugged lft and rdr briefly dropped reins: kpt on ins fnl f* **5/1**[3]
500- **4** *1* **Badea**[169] 8182 4-9-11 69...(v) GeorgeChaloner 7 69
(Richard Fahey) *chsd ldr: rdn to chal wl over 1f out: no ex ins fnl f* **6/1**
20-1 **5** *¾* **Special Mix**[37] 1936 5-9-9 70...................................... MatthewHopkins(3) 3 69
(Michael Easterby) *hld up: rdn over 2f out: kpt on ins fnl f: nvr able to chal* **7/2**[1]

0-06 6 1 1/4 **Call Of Duty (IRE)**[14] 2629 8-8-13 **62** ...... JoshCrane(5) 2 58
(Dianne Sayer) *in rr: rdn over 2f out: kpt on one pce ins fnl f* **5/1**[3]

626- 7 3 3/4 **Taro Tywod (IRE)**[168] 8213 4-8-9 **58** ...... GaryMahon(5) 6 47
(Mark Brisbourne) *chsd ldrs: effrt over 2f out: wknd fnl f* **10/1**

2310 8 10 **Matraash (USA)**[21] 2413 7-9-3 **68** ......(p) AaronFallon(7) 8 38
(Daniel Mark Loughnane) *racd keenly: led: rdn and hdd wl over 1f out: sn wknd* **14/1**

5246 9 2 1/2 **Kyle Of Bute**[32] 2089 7-8-9 **53** ...... DarylByrne 1 18
(Brian Baugh) *hld up: rdn over 3f out: struggling over 2f out: nvr a threat* **14/1**

2m 10.26s (-5.24) **Going Correction** -0.425s/f (Firm) **9** Ran SP% **114.7**
Speed ratings (Par 103): **103,99,98,97,97 96,93,85,83**
toteswingers 1&2 £32.80, 1&3 £5.80, 2&3 £69.40 CSF £137.63 CT £814.36 TOTE £3.60: £1.70, £8.60, £2.00; EX 189.80 Trifecta £354.20 Pool: £1009.62 - 2.13 winning tickets..
Owner Paul Saxton & The Bottom Liners **Bred** Darley **Trained** Huby, N Yorks

FOCUS
A dry and warm run up to a meeting that saw in excess of 30mm of water applied to the track in the last week. All races (apart from the 6f maiden) were run on the inner home straight. The distances of races beyond sprint distances were 5 yards less than advertised. A modest handicap and, although the gallop was a reasonable one, not many figured. A personal best from the winner.

3044 EBF TAYLORMADE TELEBETTING ON 08456008006 MAIDEN STKS 6f
7:15 (7:18) (Class 5) 2-Y-O **£2,911** (£866; £432; £216) **Stalls** Centre

Form RPR

2 1 **Mawfoor (IRE)**[17] 2543 2-9-5 0 ...... PaulHanagan 3 89+
(Brian Meehan) *w ldr: led over 2f out: rdn and hdd over 1f out: regained ld fnl 100yds: r.o and in command towards fin* **11/8**[1]

2 2 1/4 **Safety Check (IRE)** 2-9-5 0 ...... MickaelBarzalona 12 83+
(Saeed bin Suroor) *hld up: hdwy 2f out: rdn to ld over 1f out: edgd lft ins fnl f: hdd fnl 100yds: no ex towards fin* **6/1**[3]

3 3 2 1/4 **Fair Ranger**[20] 2436 2-9-5 0 ...... RyanMoore 10 75+
(Richard Hannon) *hld up: pushed along over 2f out: hdwy over 1f out: styd on ins fnl f: nt trble ldrs* **11/2**[2]

0 4 nk **Dream And Search (GER)**[22] 2401 2-9-5 0 ...... JamieSpencer 11 74+
(Charles Hills) *hld up: swtchd rt over 2f out: rdn over 1f out: styd on ins fnl f: nt trble ldrs* **6/1**[3]

5 4 **Haayil** 2-9-5 0 ...... WilliamBuick 6 61
(John Gosden) *dwlt: hld up: hdwy over 2f out: green and outpcd over 1f out: n.d after* **16/1**

6 1 **De Repente (IRE)** 2-9-0 0 ...... ShaneKelly 8 53
(Paul Green) *in rr: pushed along over 3f out: outpcd 2f out: kpt on ins fnl f: nvr able to trble ldrs* **100/1**

0 7 hd **Exceed And Exceed**[22] 2401 2-9-5 0 ...... JimmyFortune 2 57
(Richard Hannon) *prom: rdn 2f out: sn hung lft: btn over 1f out* **25/1**

634 8 1 3/4 **Donny Rover (IRE)**[41] 1820 2-9-5 0 ...... DanielTudhope 1 51
(David C Griffiths) *chsd ldrs: rdn 2f out: wknd over 1f out* **33/1**

9 1 **Ticking Katie (IRE)** 2-9-0 0 ...... MartinHarley 4 43
(Mrs K Burke) *midfield: rdn 2f out: wknd over 1f out* **33/1**

10 2 1/4 **The Boss Of Me** 2-9-5 0 ...... TomEaves 9 41+
(Kevin Ryan) *dwlt: hld up and racd keenly: hdwy to ld over 3f out: hdd over 2f out: wknd over 1f out* **25/1**

11 1 1/2 **Thataboy (IRE)** 2-9-5 0 ...... RichardKingscote 7 36
(Tom Dascombe) *midfield: rdn over 1f out: sn wknd* **8/1**

0 12 1 3/4 **Kopkap**[27] 2282 2-9-5 0 ...... SeanLevey 5 31
(Ed McMahon) *led: hdd over 3f out: stl ev ch 2f out: rdn and wknd over 1f out* **66/1**

1m 12.52s (-1.28) **Going Correction** -0.275s/f (Firm) **12** Ran SP% **119.1**
Speed ratings (Par 93): **97,94,91,90,85 83,83,81,80,77 75,72**
toteswingers 1&2 £4.40, 1&3 £2.10, 2&3 £8.90 CSF £9.16 TOTE £2.10: £1.30, £2.10, £1.70; EX 15.50 Trifecta £51.70 Pool: £1403.38 - 20.33 winning tickets..
Owner Hamdan Al Maktoum **Bred** E Tynan **Trained** Manton, Wilts

FOCUS
The winning rider described the ground as "good to firm but safe".Several smart sorts have won this in the last decade, including Group 1 Sun Chariot winner Spinning Queen in 2005 and Group 2 Hungerford Stakes winner Shakespearean in 2009 and this year's winner looks another decent prospect. The gallop was reasonable and this race should throw up winners. The form could rate a bit higher.

3045 EBF PIPER HEIDSIECK CHAMPAGNE MAIDEN STKS 5f
7:45 (7:50) (Class 5) 2-Y-O **£2,911** (£866; £432; £216) **Stalls** Centre

Form RPR

4 1 **Ben Hall (IRE)**[13] 2653 2-9-5 0 ...... WilliamBuick 3 84+
(John Gosden) *mde all: shkn up over 1f out: pushed out ins fnl f: comf* **8/13**[1]

66 2 2 3/4 **The Smart One (IRE)**[33] 2048 2-9-5 0 ...... MartinHarley 1 70
(Mick Channon) *a.p: rdn and tried to chal over 1f out: nt qckn ins fnl f* **4/1**[2]

3 1 **Captain Whoosh (IRE)** 2-9-5 0 ...... RichardKingscote 6 66
(Tom Dascombe) *coltish bef r: racd keenly: hld up: rdn and edgd lft over 1f out: kpt on same pce ins fnl f: nvr able to chal* **7/1**[3]

36 4 1/2 **Capitulate**[18] 2497 2-9-5 0 ......(b[1]) SeanLevey 4 65
(Ed McMahon) *prom: pushed along over 2f out: rdn wl over 1f out: one pce fnl f* **16/1**

5 dist **Evie Jay (IRE)** 2-9-0 0 ...... ShaneKelly 5
(Paul Green) *in rr: sn wl bhd and lost tch: virtually p.u 3f out* **50/1**

59.75s (-1.05) **Going Correction** -0.275s/f (Firm) **5** Ran SP% **102.3**
Speed ratings (Par 93): **97,92,91,90,**
CSF £2.72 TOTE £1.50: £1.10, £1.50; EX 3.10 Trifecta £7.60 Pool: £1040.33 - 101.81 winning tickets..
Owner Saeed Manana **Bred** Ringfort Stud Ltd **Trained** Newmarket, Suffolk

FOCUS
A race won in the past by smart sprinting trio Cosmic Chatter (last year), Shumoos in 2011 and Ballista in 2010 but, although this looked an uncompetitive event, the winner looks a very useful prospect. He rates value for extra. The gallop was no more than fair.

3046 MERE GOLF RESORT & SPA ACHILLES STKS (LISTED RACE) 5f
8:15 (8:18) (Class 1) 3-Y-O+
£20,982 (£7,955; £3,981; £1,983; £995; £499) **Stalls** Centre

Form RPR

1360 1 **Medicean Man**[69] 1265 7-9-3 110 ......(p) SteveDrowne 10 113
(Jeremy Gask) *hld up in rr: hdwy over 1f out: r.o ins fnl f to ld fnl 75yds* **10/1**

2-50 2 1 **Jwala**[30] 2152 4-8-12 101 ...... JamieSpencer 9 104
(Robert Cowell) *w ldr: led over 1f out: hdd fnl 75yds: outpcd by wnr cl home* **10/1**

1-20 3 1 **My Propeller (IRE)**[34] 2019 4-8-12 100 ...... RyanMoore 3 101
(Peter Chapple-Hyam) *hld up: hdwy 2f out: chalng over 1f out: styd on same pce fnl 100yds* **9/2**[2]

5/54 4 1 1/4 **Miss Lahar**[14] 2621 4-8-12 93 ...... MartinHarley 5 96
(Mick Channon) *midfield: effrt to chse ldrs over 1f out: kpt on ins fnl f: nt quite gng pce to chal* **22/1**

/0-5 5 3/4 **Jiroft (ITY)**[6] 2865 6-9-3 102 ...... ShaneKelly 1 99
(Robert Cowell) *led: rdn and hdd over 1f out: no ex fnl 100yds* **9/1**

52-0 6 1 1/2 **Free Zone**[34] 2019 4-9-3 104 ...... TomEaves 8 93
(Bryan Smart) *chsd ldrs: rdn over 1f out: one pce ins fnl f* **20/1**

34-4 7 3/4 **Excelette (IRE)**[49] 1662 4-8-12 104 ...... RoystonFfrench 7 86
(Bryan Smart) *w ldr: rdn over 1f out: wknd ins fnl f* **6/1**[3]

-400 8 3/4 **Doc Hay (USA)**[13] 2662 6-9-7 102 ...... DanielTudhope 2 92
(David O'Meara) *dwlt: hld up: pushed along over 1f out: nvr nr to chal* **9/1**

22-0 9 1/2 **Nocturnal Affair (SAF)**[13] 2676 7-9-3 105 ...... WilliamBuick 11 86
(David Marnane, Ire) *hld up: pushed along over 2f out: lugged lft over 1f out: nvr able to trble ldrs* **3/1**[1]

-003 10 1 3/4 **Secret Asset (IRE)**[30] 2152 8-9-3 100 ...... GeorgeBaker 4 80
(Jane Chapple-Hyam) *broke wl: sn dropped bhd ldrs in tch: rdn over 1f out: sn wknd* **20/1**

3-60 11 3 1/4 **Swan Song**[34] 2019 4-8-12 94 ...... JimmyFortune 6 63
(Andrew Balding) *trckd ldrs: rdn 2f out: wknd over 1f out: eased whn wl btn fnl 100yds* **8/1**

58.0s (-2.80) **Going Correction** -0.275s/f (Firm) **11** Ran SP% **120.6**
Speed ratings (Par 111): **111,109,107,105,104 102,101,99,99,96 91**
toteswingers 1&2 £13.30, 1&3 £13.40, 2&3 £9.40 CSF £105.13 TOTE £10.80: £3.70, £3.70, £2.00; EX 128.00 Trifecta £449.80 Pool: £1575.42 - 2.62 winning tickets..
Owner Stuart Dobb & Miss Kate Dobb **Bred** Barry Taylor **Trained** Sutton Veny, Wilts

FOCUS
A competitive Listed event in which the gallop was sound throughout. The winner is rated to his best with the second and fourth pretty much to form.

3047 WHITE EVENTS MAIDEN STKS 1m
8:50 (8:50) (Class 5) 3-Y-O+ **£2,587** (£770; £384; £192) **Stalls** Low

Form RPR

03 1 **Brave Acclaim (IRE)**[14] 2628 3-9-3 0 ......(p) RichardKingscote 7 81
(Tom Dascombe) *mde all: rdn 2f out: pressed fr over 1f out: kpt on gamely* **6/1**[3]

2 2 3/4 **Pressure Point**[14] 2628 3-9-3 0 ...... RyanMoore 2 79
(Sir Michael Stoute) *chsd wnr: pushed along over 3f out: rdn 2f out: chalng fr over 1f out: nt qckn wl ins fnl f* **1/3**[1]

6-6 3 1 **Visit Copenhagen (USA)**[55] 1546 3-8-12 0 ......[1] MartinHarley 6 72
(Mrs K Burke) *trckd ldrs: effrt to try and chal over 1f out: styd on same pce towards fin* **7/1**

5 4 4 1/2 **Red Red Wine**[17] 2547 3-9-3 0 ...... WilliamBuick 3 66
(Hugo Palmer) *chsd ldrs: pushed along over 3f out: one pce over 1f out: no imp fnl f* **9/2**[2]

05 5 1/2 **Konzert (ITY)**[14] 2628 3-9-3 0 ...... ShaneKelly 4 65
(Andrew Hollinshead) *racd keenly: hld up: rdn over 2f out: one pce fr over 1f out* **20/1**

-00 6 7 **Speedy Utmost Meg**[14] 2628 3-8-12 0 ...... AdamBeschizza 8 43
(William Kinsey) *racd keenly: hld up: pushed along and outpcd 3f out: nvr a threat* **66/1**

7 6 **Captain Rhyric**[47] 4-9-11 0 ...... LucyAlexander(3) 5 37
(James Moffatt) *racd keenly: hld up: struggling 3f out: nvr a threat* **50/1**

00- 8 11 **Buds Bruvver**[399] 1824 4-10-0 0 ...... TomEaves 1
(Brian Baugh) *s.i.s: in rr: struggling 3f out: nvr on terms* **100/1**

1m 42.05s (-1.65) **Going Correction** -0.425s/f (Firm)
WFA 3 from 4yo 11lb **8** Ran SP% **129.2**
Speed ratings (Par 103): **91,90,89,84,84 77,71,60**
toteswingers 1&2 £2.30, 1&3 £3.7, 2&3 £1.90 CSF £9.61 TOTE £7.60: £1.60, £1.02, £1.90; EX 20.00 Trifecta £71.70 Pool: £1425.26 - 14.90 winning tickets..
Owner G Lowe & Mrs A Whiteside **Bred** Jaykayenn Syndicate **Trained** Malpas, Cheshire

FOCUS
Not a competitive maiden and a race run at just an ordinary gallop. The winner reversed C&D form with the runner-up, and the form is taken at something like face value.

3048 BIANCHI, DENNING, JONES, HORNSBY, MATHIAS, ROWLEY H'CAP 1m 3f 200y
9:20 (9:22) (Class 4) (0-85,83) 3-Y-O **£4,690** (£1,395; £697; £348) **Stalls** Centre

Form RPR

612- 1 **Ennistown**[241] 6963 3-9-7 **83** ......[1] MickaelBarzalona 3 97+
(Saeed bin Suroor) *racd keenly: hld up: outpcd 2f out: prog over 1f out: r.o to ld fnl 150yds: comf* **3/1**[2]

-115 2 1 3/4 **Ray Ward (IRE)**[20] 2445 3-9-5 **81** ...... MartinLane 5 90
(David Simcock) *hld up in rr: impr over 3f out: led over 2f out: hdd fnl 150yds: one pce cl home* **2/1**[1]

2215 3 3 **Ambleside**[30] 2153 3-8-11 **73** ......(b) JoeFanning 7 77
(Mark Johnston) *led: pushed along and hdd over 2f out: outpcd over 1f out: kpt on towards fin but no ch* **2/1**[1]

31-5 4 nk **Mystery Bet (IRE)**[50] 1641 3-9-3 **82** ...... LeeTopliss(3) 6 86
(Richard Fahey) *racd keenly: chsd ldr: chalng over 2f out: nt qckn over 1f out: no ex wl ins fnl f* **9/2**[3]

2m 35.58s (1.78) **Going Correction** -0.425s/f (Firm) **4** Ran SP% **109.8**
Speed ratings (Par 101): **77,75,73,73**
CSF £9.36 TOTE £4.30; EX 8.90 Trifecta £13.50 Pool: £1007.45 - 55.81 winning tickets..
Owner Godolphin **Bred** Darley **Trained** Newmarket, Suffolk

FOCUS
A depleted field and a farcical race that turned into a two-furlong sprint. The winner is rated better than the bare form.
T/Plt: £52.40 to a £1 stake. Pool £56,901.72 - 792.14 winning tickets. T/Qpdt: £16.80 to a £1 stake. Pool £3672.21 - 161.00 winning tickets. DO

2947 LINGFIELD (L-H)

Friday, June 7

OFFICIAL GOING: Turf course - good to firm (8.5); all-weather - standard

Wind: Light, half against Weather: Cloudy but soon becoming fine, warm

3049 ST CATHERINE'S HOSPICE MAIDEN FILLIES' STKS 5f

2:20 (2:22) (Class 5) 2-Y-O £2,726 (£805; £402) Stalls High

Form RPR

2 **1** **Survived**15 2601 2-9-0 0 GrahamLee 6 83+
(William Haggas) *w ldr: led 1/2-way: c across to nr side rail over 1f out: pushed out: comf* 4/5[1]

5 **2** 2 1/4 **Miss Lillie**15 2601 2-9-0 0 JohnFahy 4 71
(Roger Teal) *chsd ldrs: rdn over 1f out: styd on to take 2nd ins fnl f: no threat* 7/2[2]

0 **3** 1 **Sunset Shore**10 2740 2-9-0 0 LukeMorris 8 67
(Sir Mark Prescott Bt) *led against nr side rail: hdd and shkn up 1/2-way: no ch w wnr over 1f out: one pce and lost 2nd ins fnl f* 16/1

4 1 1/4 **Talent Spotter** 2-9-0 0 AdamKirby 3 63+
(Saeed bin Suroor) *sn off the pce in rr: pushed along towards outer 2f out: styd on fnl f: nrst fin* 6/1[3]

5 shd **Inspiriter** 2-9-0 0 IanMongan 2 62+
(Saeed bin Suroor) *s.i.s: wl off the pce in last pair: pushed along on outer 2f out: styd on fnl f: nrst fin* 12/1

6 3/4 **Mahlah (IRE)** 2-9-0 0 KieranO'Neill 7 60
(Richard Hannon) *chsd ldrs but sn pushed along: no imp over 1f out: fdd ins fnl f* 20/1

4 **7** 4 1/2 **Think Again**7 2830 2-9-0 0 FrederikTylicki 5 48
(Kevin Ryan) *s.i.s: a off the pce in rr: no prog fnl 2f* 33/1

8 3/4 **Porteous** 2-9-0 0 SaleemGolam 9 41
(Mick Channon) *a in rr and off the pce: no prog fnl 2f* 50/1

9 8 **Streethowlingmama (USA)** 2-9-0 0 JimCrowley 10 12
(George Baker) *chsd ldrs to 1/2-way: wknd qckly: t.o* 33/1

58.42s (0.22) **Going Correction** 0.0s/f (Good) 9 Ran SP% 118.2

Speed ratings (Par 90): **98,94,92,90,90 89,82,81,68**

toteswingers 1&2 £1.10, 1&3 £9.80, 2&3 £6.40 CSF £3.67 TOTE £1.70: £1.10, £1.30, £3.40; EX 4.20 Trifecta £21.70 Pool: £1945.97 - 67.04 winning tickets..

Owner Cheveley Park Stud **Bred** Cheveley Park Stud Ltd **Trained** Newmarket, Suffolk

FOCUS

There was 2mm of rain before racing, but the watered ground (5mm Wednesday, and again Thursday) on the turf course remained good to firm (GoingStick 8.7). The concensus from the jockeys was that that was a fair description, although it was apparently a bit loose on top. The winner had a good bit in hand and the form could be rated higher.

3050 JIM BEAN BOURBON H'CAP 6f

2:50 (2:50) (Class 5) (0-75,75) 3-Y-O £2,726 (£805; £402) Stalls High

Form RPR

2323 **1** **Indian Affair**17 2544 3-9-2 70 JimmyQuinn 5 75
(Milton Bradley) *w ldr and one off the pce: narrow ld fr 2f out: drvn out fnl f* 3/1[2]

1563 **2** nk **Buy Art**32 2098 3-8-13 67 LukeMorris 6 71
(Gary Moore) *mde most and racd against rail: narrowly hdd 2f out: hrd rdn and kpt on wl: jst hld* 11/4[1]

5600 **3** 1 1/4 **Black Dave (IRE)**25 2308 3-8-8 62 SaleemGolam 4 62
(David Evans) *hld up in tch: drvn over 1f out: styd on to chse ldng pair ins fnl f: no imp* 20/1

60-5 **4** 3/4 **Ishi Honest**25 2329 3-8-7 66 RachealKneller(5) 7 64
(Mark Usher) *unable to hold pl against rail and sn in rr: wl in tch 2f out: shuffled along and styd on same pce* 6/1

-504 **5** 1/2 **Fletcher Christian**18 2521 3-9-3 71 (p) IanMongan 3 68
(John Gallagher) *racd quite wd: chsd ldng pair: drvn over 2f out: no imp over 1f out: wknd ins fnl f* 4/1[3]

-160 **6** 2 **Blazing Knight (IRE)**39 1892 3-9-7 75 JimCrowley 1 66
(Ralph Beckett) *hld up: gng strly 2f out: plld out and shkn up over 1f out: fnd nil* 8/1

6-05 **7** 3 3/4 **Knight Charm**30 2158 3-9-3 71 JohnFahy 2 50
(Eve Johnson Houghton) *racd wdst of all: chsd ldrs: rdn over 2f out: wknd over 1f out* 10/1

1m 12.07s (0.87) **Going Correction** 0.0s/f (Good) 7 Ran SP% 110.9

Speed ratings (Par 99): **94,93,91,90,90 87,82**

toteswingers 1&2 £1.10, 1&3 £20.30, 2&3 £13.50 CSF £10.94 TOTE £3.80: £2.10, £2.20; EX 10.20 Trifecta £107.80 Pool: £1939.87 - 13.49 winning tickets..

Owner J M Bradley **Bred** Mette Campbell-Andenaes **Trained** Sedbury, Gloucs

FOCUS

The early pace was ordinary in this handicap and the first two filled those positions throughout. Modest form.

3051 ANTHONY HAYWARD RETIREMENT H'CAP (DIV I) 7f

3:20 (3:20) (Class 6) (0-65,65) 4-Y-O+ £2,045 (£603; £302) Stalls High

Form RPR

0-50 **1** **Wishformore (IRE)**57 1497 6-8-4 48 ow2 (p) RichardThomas 9 57
(Zoe Davison) *awkward s: t.k.h: hld up in 6th: rdn and prog towards nr side 2f out: styd on to ld last 100yds* 25/1

0100 **2** 1/2 **Flavius Victor (IRE)**16 2571 4-9-5 63 JimCrowley 4 70
(Patrick Chamings) *stdd s: hld up in last trio: rdn and prog on wd outside 2f out: styd on to chal ins fnl f: jst hld* 7/2[2]

1505 **3** 2 **The Mongoose**4 2918 5-9-3 61 (t) AdamKirby 5 63
(David Evans) *led against nr side rail but pressed: tried to assert 2f out: wknd and hdd last 100yds* 11/4[1]

0036 **4** hd **Surrey Dream (IRE)**15 2588 4-8-4 48 (t) KieranO'Neill 3 49
(John Bridger) *slowly away: detached in last: sed to stay on 2f out and swtchd out wd: drvn and styd on fnl f: nrly snatched 3rd* 16/1

4 **5** 2 3/4 **Bint Alzain (IRE)**58 1479 4-9-4 62 IanMongan 7 56
(Pat Phelan) *in tch: prog to chse ldr over 2f out tl wknd fnl f* 10/1

3-60 **6** 1 1/2 **Comadoir (IRE)**43 1783 7-8-13 57 [1] LiamJones 2 47
(Jo Crowley) *chsd ldrs: drvn over 2f out: no imp: wknd over 1f out* 8/1

1530 **7** shd **Johnny Splash (IRE)**56 1516 4-8-4 53 (b) NathanAlison(5) 6 43
(Roger Teal) *t.k.h: w ldr to 1/2-way: lost pl over 2f out: wknd fnl f* 10/1

2000 **8** 1 1/2 **Homeward Strut**9 2773 4-8-12 59 (p) SimonPearce(3) 10 45
(Laura Mongan) *hld up in last trio: urged along and no prog over 2f out: fdd* 6/1[3]

646- **9** 1/2 **Compton Prince**232 7203 4-9-7 65 LukeMorris 8 49
(Milton Bradley) *chsd ldrs: rdn 1/2-way: sn struggling: wknd 2f out* 7/1

1m 24.39s (1.09) **Going Correction** 0.0s/f (Good) 9 Ran SP% 114.7

Speed ratings (Par 101): **93,92,90,89,86 85,84,83,82**

toteswingers 1&2 £16.80, 1&3 £19.90, 2&3 £2.90 CSF £110.23 CT £329.55 TOTE £41.30: £6.30, £2.00, £1.10; EX 159.00 Trifecta £865.50 Pool: £1595.72 - 1.38 winning tickets..

Owner Paul Mannion **Bred** Tally-Ho Stud **Trained** Hammerwood, E Sussex

FOCUS

The leaders went for home too soon here and the first two came from behind. The winner is rated back to his 2012 form.

3052 ANTHONY HAYWARD RETIREMENT H'CAP (DIV II) 7f

3:55 (3:55) (Class 6) (0-65,64) 4-Y-O+ £2,045 (£603; £302) Stalls High

Form RPR

0-01 **1** **Darnathean**17 2534 4-9-5 62 (p) JimCrowley 4 76
(Paul D'Arcy) *taken down early: sn w ldr: led 2f out gng strly: shkn up and clr fnl f* 5/2[1]

60-3 **2** 3 1/2 **Takitwo**33 2057 10-9-1 58 JohnFahy 6 62
(Geoffrey Deacon) *hld up in last trio: rdn and prog on outer over 2f out: kpt on to take 2nd ins fnl f: no ch w wnr* 8/1

5036 **3** 1 3/4 **Rooknrasbryripple**8 2787 4-8-4 47 KieranO'Neill 3 46
(Ralph Smith) *stdd s: t.k.h and hld up in last: prog and swtchd sharply to outer wl over 1f out: styd on u.p to take 3rd nr fin* 25/1

6511 **4** 1/2 **Jonnie Skull (IRE)**31 2134 7-9-7 64 (vt) AdamKirby 8 62
(Phil McEntee) *led against nr side rail: drvn and hdd 2f out: wknd fnl f* 5/2[1]

0240 **5** 5 **Pharoh Jake**58 1467 5-8-7 57 JoeyHaynes(7) 1 42
(John Bridger) *prom on outer: rdn over 2f out: nt qckn wl over 1f out: wknd fnl f* 20/1

35-0 **6** nk **Leadenhall Lass (IRE)**29 2196 7-9-3 60 IanMongan 7 44
(Pat Phelan) *taken down early: hld up in rr: rdn over 2f out: sn no prog and btn* 6/1[2]

0003 **7** 1 **Dvinsky (USA)**31 2125 12-8-2 45 (b) JimmyQuinn 10 26
(Roger Ingram) *rousted early but unable to capitalise on gd draw against rail: lost pl 1/2-way: struggling after* 7/1[3]

5-40 **8** 4 1/2 **Hawk Moth (IRE)**19 1303 5-9-4 61 (p) LukeMorris 5 30
(John Spearing) *chsd ldrs tl wknd u.p 2f out* 14/1

025- **9** 4 1/2 **Waspy**232 7201 4-9-2 59 RichardThomas 2 16
(Dr Jeremy Naylor) *t.k.h: hld up in midfield: wknd wl over 2f out* 25/1

35-0 **10** 3/4 **Memphis Man**16 2578 10-8-11 54 FrederikTylicki 9 9
(Milton Bradley) *a in last trio: shkn up 3f out: sn toiling* 33/1

1m 22.82s (-0.48) **Going Correction** 0.0s/f (Good) 10 Ran SP% 117.1

Speed ratings (Par 101): **102,98,96,95,89 89,88,83,77,77**

toteswingers 1&2 £4.90, 1&3 £17.80, 2&3 £26.40 CSF £22.90 CT £408.74 TOTE £3.30: £1.20, £3.20, £7.30; EX 27.20 Trifecta £421.70 Pool: £4106.65 - 7.30 winning tickets..

Owner K Snell **Bred** K Snell **Trained** Newmarket, Suffolk

■ Stewards' Enquiry : Ian Mongan one-day ban; careless riding (23rd June).

FOCUS

Just a modest handicap. The winner is rated to his best Polytrack form.

3053 BREWERS FOR DECORATING MATERIALS CLASSIFIED STKS 7f

4:30 (4:30) (Class 5) 3-Y-O £2,726 (£805; £402) Stalls High

Form RPR

41-4 **1** **Whipper Snapper (IRE)**22 2394 3-9-0 75 JimCrowley 3 82
(William Knight) *hld up in last: prog to chse ldr over 1f out: drvn and sustained chal to ld last strides* 6/4[1]

5-40 **2** shd **Al Udeid (IRE)**29 2190 3-9-0 75 FrederikTylicki 2 82
(Kevin Ryan) *led against nr side rail: rdn 2f out: kpt on wl fnl f: hdd last strides* 9/2

0-42 **3** 6 **Strictly Ballroom (IRE)**14 2622 3-9-0 75 AdamKirby 1 66
(Mark Johnston) *chsd ldr after 2f: rdn wl over 2f out: lost 2nd and wknd qckly over 1f out* 5/2[2]

2301 **4** 1/2 **Star Of Rohm**27 2267 3-8-7 75 LouisSteward(7) 4 64
(Michael Bell) *chsd ldr 2f: pushed along 1/2-way: wknd qckly over 1f out* 3/1[3]

1m 23.06s (-0.24) **Going Correction** 0.0s/f (Good) 4 Ran SP% 111.8

Speed ratings (Par 99): **101,100,94,93**

CSF £8.49 TOTE £2.30; EX 8.10 Trifecta £20.40 Pool: £1826.03 - 66.83 winning tickets..

Owner The Oil Merchants **Bred** Michael Mullins **Trained** Patching, W Sussex

FOCUS

A level-weights contest with each of the runners rated 75. The winner has the scope to do better again.

3054 ST CATHERINE'S HOSPICE LOTTERY H'CAP 1m (P)

5:05 (5:07) (Class 6) (0-65,65) 4-Y-O+ £2,045 (£603; £302) Stalls High

Form RPR

6600 **1** **Shared Moment (IRE)**32 2089 7-8-2 49 ow1 SimonPearce(3) 9 56
(Luke Dace) *uns rdr and cantered off bef gng to post: pressed ldr: rdn to ld wl over 1f out: hrd pressed fnl f: jst hld on* 14/1

6056 **2** hd **West Leake (IRE)**16 2565 7-8-11 62 EoinWalsh(7) 2 68
(Paul Burgoyne) *awkward s: t.k.h: hld up in last: taken wd 3f out: rdn over 2f out: styd on wl over 1f out: tk 2nd nr fin: jst failed* 5/1[3]

5000 **3** hd **Spin Again (IRE)**16 2571 8-9-2 60 AdamKirby 3 66
(John Ryan) *hld up in midfield: drvn and prog to go 2nd jst ins fnl f: sn pressed wnr: nt qckn and lost 2nd nr fin* 12/1

0300 **4** 1/2 **Jumbo Prado (USA)**21 2417 4-9-5 63 LukeMorris 5 68
(John Stimpson) *hld up in last trio: rdn wl over 1f out: prog on outer sn after: r.o fnl f: nrst fin* 6/1

-430 **5** 2 **Mishrif (USA)**16 2565 7-9-4 62 (v) IanMongan 6 62
(J R Jenkins) *led to wl over 1f out: styd on inner and wknd fnl f* 14/1

6301 **6** nse **Cuthbert (IRE)**35 1981 6-8-6 50 (b) JimmyQuinn 4 50
(Michael Attwater) *t.k.h: trckd ldrs: rdn and nt qckn wl over 1f out: wl hld fnl f* 8/1

0616 **7** 3/4 **Beauchamp Xerxes**66 1311 7-9-2 65 (t) NicoleNordblad(5) 8 63
(Hans Adielsson) *chsd ldng pair: tried to chal on inner over 1f out: wknd fnl f* 9/2[2]

0530 **8** hd **Jackie Love (IRE)**16 2575 5-7-11 46 (v) NathanAlison(5) 1 44
(Olivia Maylam) *t.k.h: hld up in last trio: styd on inner and pushed along over 1f out: nvr involved* 7/1

1303 **9** 2 1/4 **Penbryn (USA)**9 2773 6-9-1 59 JimCrowley 7 53
(Nick Littmoden) *s.i.s: racd on outer in midfield: rdn 2f out: wknd jst over 1f out* 7/2[1]

1m 37.98s (-0.22) **Going Correction** 0.0s/f (Stan) 9 Ran SP% 116.0

Speed ratings (Par 101): **101,100,100,100,98 98,97,97,94**

toteswingers 1&2 £22.40, 1&3 £12.50, 2&3 £11.60 CSF £82.79 CT £881.92 TOTE £18.10: £4.60, £2.90, £4.70; EX 150.60 Trifecta £734.60 Pool: £2964.71 - 3.02 winning tickets..

Owner Mark Benton **Bred** Mrs E R Cantillon **Trained** Five Oaks, W Sussex

FOCUS
A competitive handicap and a bunched finish. Limited form, rated around the second.

3055 STAR SPORTS SUPPORTS ST CATHERINE'S HOSPICE RACEDAY H'CAP 1m 4f (P)
5:35 (5:36) (Class 5) (0-75,72) 3-Y-O £2,726 (£805; £402) **Stalls Low**

Form RPR

0-11 **1** **Alcaeus**[8] 2799 3-9-4 **69** 6ex LukeMorris 9 82+
(Sir Mark Prescott Bt) *trckd ldr: led 3f out: shkn up 2f out: pressed and drvn over 1f out: drifted lft but styd on wl* **7/4**[1]

00-4 **2** 1 ½ **Kastini**[39] 1879 3-8-3 **54** JimmyQuinn 5 65
(Denis Coakley) *hld up in midfield: prog gng wl fr 3f out: drvn to go 3rd over 1f out: styd on to chse wnr last 100yds: no imp* **25/1**

5-02 **3** 1 ¾ **White Month**[36] 1959 3-9-5 **70** JimCrowley 4 78
(Andrew Balding) *trckd ldng pair: gng wl 3f out: chsd wnr 2f out: drvn and tried to chal on inner over 1f out: nt qckn fnl f and lost 2nd last 100yds* **5/2**[2]

1-43 **4** 7 **Magika**[17] 2555 3-9-3 **68** (t) AdamKirby 7 65
(Marco Botti) *hld up in midfield: effrt over 2f out: drvn wl over 1f out: wl outpcd but tk 4th fnl f* **7/1**

00-5 **5** 5 **Sunblazer (IRE)**[18] 2500 3-9-0 **65** FrederikTylicki 6 54
(William Muir) *chsd ldrs: rdn 4f out: stl in tch 2f out: wknd qckly* **25/1**

600- **6** ¾ **Star Of Missouri**[260] 6414 3-8-9 **63** SimonPearce(3) 1 51
(Mark H Tompkins) *hld up in last pair: pushed along over 4f out: no prog over 2f out: sn no ch* **33/1**

4314 **7** 2 ¼ **Strategic Strike (IRE)**[25] 2325 3-9-7 **72** IanMongan 3 56
(Paul Cole) *t.k.h: hld up bhd ldrs: rdn 4f out: wknd over 2f out* **5/1**[3]

1420 **8** 1 ½ **El Massivo (IRE)**[18] 2500 3-9-4 **69** KieranO'Neill 8 51
(William Jarvis) *led at decent pce: drvn and hdd 3f out: sn wknd* **17/2**

364 **9** ¾ **World Map (IRE)**[18] 2500 3-8-6 **57** LiamJones 2 38
(Mark Johnston) *dwlt: a in last pair: rdn 5f out: struggling 3f out* **20/1**

2m 29.38s (-3.62) **Going Correction** 0.0s/f (Stan) 9 Ran SP% **120.0**
Speed ratings (Par 99): **112,111,109,105,101 101,99,98,98**
toteswingers 1&2 £8.40, 1&3 £1.60, 2&3 £10.60 CSF £55.70 CT £115.96 TOTE £2.60: £1.10, £3.90, £2.30; EX 45.50 Trifecta £201.90 Pool: £1715.12 - 6.36 winning tickets..
Owner Ne'er Do Wells IV **Bred** Miss K Rausing **Trained** Newmarket, Suffolk
■ Stewards' Enquiry : Kieran O'Neill two-day ban; careless riding (24th-25th June).

FOCUS
They went a sound gallop here. A decent handicap for the grade and the winner should do better again after this.

3056 RACING EXCELLENCE "HANDS AND HEELS" APPRENTICE SERIES H'CAP 1m 2f (P)
6:05 (6:05) (Class 6) (0-60,59) 4-Y-O+ £2,045 (£603; £302) **Stalls Low**

Form RPR

000- **1** **Entrance**[191] 7898 5-8-6 **47** ShelleyBirkett(3) 3 55
(Julia Feilden) *hld up in 5th: smooth prog to trck ldr over 1f out: led 150yds out but immediately jnd: styd on wl to assert nr fin* **9/2**

2530 **2** nk **Young Jackie**[6] 2875 5-8-12 **53** (b) JordanVaughan(3) 4 60
(George Margarson) *hld up in last pair: prog over 1f out: jnd wnr ins fnl f: r.o but jst hld* **9/4**[1]

3-35 **3** 1 ¾ **Uncle Roger (IRE)**[16] 2567 4-9-7 **59** (v) CharlieBennett 7 63
(Eve Johnson Houghton) *trckd ldr: nt qckn and lost 2nd over 1f out: styd on but nvr able to chal after* **11/4**[2]

650- **4** 2 ¼ **Anginola (IRE)**[263] 6323 4-8-11 **57** CarolineKelly(8) 5 56
(John Ryan) *led at mod pce: tried to qckn over 2f out: hdd & wknd last 150yds* **20/1**

0425 **5** 2 ¾ **Queenie's Star (IRE)**[35] 1987 6-8-2 **48** PaigeBolton(8) 6 42
(Michael Attwater) *t.k.h: trckd ldng pair: nt qckn wl over 1f out: outpcd after* **10/1**

0600 **6** 2 ¼ **Sassi Sioux**[16] 2567 4-8-7 **45** PaulBooth 2 35
(Tom Keddy) *t.k.h: trckd ldng pair: outpcd wl over 1f out: fdd* **33/1**

210 **P** **Sinchiroka (FR)**[21] 2413 7-9-6 **58** EoinWalsh 1
(Ralph Smith) *t.k.h: hld up in last pair: lost tch 1/2-way: nt moving wl after: p.u over 1f out: dismntd* **3/1**[3]

2m 9.44s (2.84) **Going Correction** 0.0s/f (Stan) 7 Ran SP% **117.4**
Speed ratings (Par 101): **88,87,86,84,82 80,**
toteswingers 1&2 £4.20, 1&3 £4.50, 2&3 £2.50 CSF £15.74 CT £33.03 TOTE £6.70: £3.40, £1.20; EX 12.40 Trifecta £83.40 Pool: £1653.32 - 14.86 winning tickets..
Owner Miss J Feilden **Bred** Cheveley Park Stud Ltd **Trained** Exning, Suffolk

FOCUS
An ordinary race. The winner was well treated on old course form and the third gives perspective.
T/Plt: £125.20 to a £1 stake. Pool: £54,227.86 - 315.96 winning tickets T/Qpdt: £73.60 to a £1 stake. Pool: £2,668.18 - 26.80 winning tickets JN

2450 NEWMARKET (R-H)
Friday, June 7

OFFICIAL GOING: Good to firm (good in places; 7.8)
Far side track with stalls on far side except 10f &12f: Centre. Bend into home straight repositioned, increasing distance of 10f & 12f races by 18m.
Wind: moderate, across Weather: sunny

3057 COUNTRYSIDE ALLIANCE FOUNDATION EBF MAIDEN FILLIES' STKS 6f
2:10 (2:11) (Class 4) 2-Y-O £4,528 (£1,347; £673; £336) **Stalls High**

Form RPR

1 **Wedding Ring (IRE)** 2-9-0 0 MickaelBarzalona 9 86+
(Saeed bin Suroor) *hld up in tch in last trio: hdwy over 2f out: rdn to chal over 1f out: led ins fnl f: hld on wl towards fin* **8/1**[3]

2 **2** nk **Ihtimal (IRE)**[15] 2583 2-9-0 0 SilvestreDeSousa 1 85
(Saeed bin Suroor) *led and set stdy gallop: qcknd ent fnl 2f: rdn and hdd over 1f out: rallied ins fnl f: kpt on wl but hld towards fin* **6/4**[1]

3 1 ¾ **Queen Catrine (IRE)** 2-9-0 0 JamesMcDonald 4 79
(Charles Hills) *wnt lft s: t.k.h: hld up in tch in midfield: rdn and sltly outpcd 2f out: rallied ent fnl f: kpt on* **11/1**

4 hd **Sunrise Star** 2-9-0 0 TomQueally 10 79
(Sir Henry Cecil) *s.i.s: hld up in tch in rr: hdwy and swtchd rt 2f out: n.m.r jst over 1f out: rdn and kpt on ins fnl f* **10/1**

5 1 ¾ **Lamar (IRE)** 2-9-0 0 NeilCallan 5 73+
(James Tate) *hmpd leaving stalls: hmpd again and pushed rt after 100yds: t.k.h: hld up in tch: rdn and effrt to chse ldrs over 1f out: no ex 1f out: wknd fnl 100yds* **50/1**

3 **6** ½ **Sefaat**[14] 2625 2-9-0 0 PaulHanagan 6 72
(Brian Meehan) *chsd ldr: rdn and unable qck over 1f out: wknd ins fnl f* **8/1**[3]

34 **7** ½ **Caletta Bay**[15] 2601 2-9-0 0 MartinHarley 8 70
(Mick Channon) *hld up wl in tch in midfield: rdn and unable qck 2f out: wknd 1f out* **12/1**

8 ½ **Sleepy Sioux** 2-9-0 0 RyanMoore 3 68
(David Elsworth) *t.k.h: chsd ldrs tl lost pl after 2f out: rdn and outpcd 2f out: rallied and kpt on steadily ins fnl f* **22/1**

9 ¾ **Chutney (IRE)** 2-9-0 0 RichardHughes 2 66
(Richard Hannon) *chsd ldrs: rdn over 2f out: unable qck and outpcd over 1f out: wknd over 1f out* **16/1**

10 1 **Swiss Kiss** 2-9-0 0 WilliamBuick 7 63
(John Gosden) *plld hrd: chsd ldrs tl rn green and lost pl ent fnl 2f: wknd over 1f out* **13/2**[2]

11 4 ½ **Adhwaa** 2-9-0 0 DaneO'Neill 11 48
(J W Hills) *s.i.s: rn green and a outpcd in rr: hung rt 2f out* **66/1**

1m 13.14s (0.64) **Going Correction** -0.025s/f (Good) 11 Ran SP% **114.4**
Speed ratings (Par 92): **94,93,91,91,88 88,87,86,85,84 78**
toteswingers 1&2 £4.70, 1&3 £16.50, 2&3 £5.80 CSF £19.46 TOTE £9.20: £3.20, £1.10, £3.30; EX 27.90 Trifecta £302.10 Pool: £3899.36 - 9.68 winning tickets..
Owner Godolphin **Bred** Swettenham Stud **Trained** Newmarket, Suffolk

FOCUS
General opinion amongst those who rode in the opener was that the ground was as officially described. Probably quite a decent fillies' maiden, won last year by the smart but ill-fated Newfangled, and the two Godolphin runners had it to themselves late on. They raced centre-field and the runner-up, sixth and seventh help with the form.

3058 CHEFFINS EBF FILLIES' H'CAP 6f
2:40 (2:40) (Class 4) (0-85,85) 3-Y-O £6,469 (£1,925; £962; £481) **Stalls High**

Form RPR

21-5 **1** **Midnight Flower (IRE)**[30] 2160 3-8-8 **75** DarrenEgan(3) 7 90+
(David Simcock) *travelled strly: trckd ldrs: jnd ldrs and gng wl 2f out: led over 1f out: sn rdn and readily asserted: in command and rdn out hands and heels ins fnl f* **25/1**

421- **2** 1 **Nardin**[259] 6453 3-9-0 **78** PaulHanagan 10 90
(Ed Dunlop) *t.k.h: hld up in tch in midfield: hdwy wl over 1f out: drvn to chse wnr 1f out: kpt on u.p but a hld* **16/1**

2-12 **3** hd **Jubilante**[20] 2452 3-9-4 **82** RyanMoore 2 93
(Hughie Morrison) *hld up in tch towards rr: rdn and hdwy towards stands' rail over 1f out: drvn 1f out: kpt on wl and pressing for 2nd cl home: no real threat to wnr* **2/1**[1]

143- **4** 1 ½ **Exceptionelle**[282] 5743 3-9-7 **85** RichardHughes 3 92
(Roger Varian) *stdd s: t.k.h: hld up in tch in rr: hdwy against stands' rail over 1f out: kpt on ins fnl f: nvr gng pce to threaten wnr* **6/1**[3]

40-0 **5** 1 ½ **Front Page News**[18] 2521 3-8-5 **69** SilvestreDeSousa 5 71
(Robert Eddery) *hld up in tch towards rr: rdn over 2f out: no imp whn nt clr run over 1f out: rallied and styd on wl ins fnl f: nvr trbld ldrs* **33/1**

-423 **6** 1 ½ **Hot Secret**[23] 2363 3-8-7 **71** JoeFanning 1 69
(Andrew Balding) *in tch in midfield: hdwy over 2f out: rdn and ev ch over 1f out: sn outpcd by wnr and btn 1f out: wknd ins fnl f* **20/1**

44-1 **7** hd **Burning Dawn (USA)**[31] 2135 3-8-9 **73** JamieSpencer 4 70
(David Brown) *chsd ldrs: rdn and unable qck 2f out: lost pl over 1f out: wknd ins fnl f* **3/1**[2]

50-0 **8** 1 **Madam Mojito (USA)**[21] 2430 3-9-1 **84** EDLinehan(5) 6 78
(John Quinn) *in tch in midfield: rdn over 2f out: lost pl and struggling over 1f out: wknd fnl f* **16/1**

1411 **9** ¾ **Sylvia Pankhurst (IRE)**[16] 2572 3-8-11 **80** (p) ThomasBrown(5) 9 72
(David C Griffiths) *led: rdn and hdd 1f out: sn struggling u.p: wknd 1f out* **14/1**

4-00 **10** shd **Miss Diva**[27] 2270 3-9-1 **84** WilliamTwiston-Davies(5) 8 76
(Richard Hannon) *chsd ldr tl 2f out: sn rdn and unable qck: wknd 1f out* **33/1**

0000 **11** 16 **Fantacise**[23] 2371 3-8-9 **73** (v[1]) KierenFallon 11
(Richard Fahey) *wnt lft s: nvr gng wl and a towards rr: rdn struggling 1/2-way: lost tch 2f out: virtually p.u ins fnl f* **11/1**

1m 11.74s (-0.76) **Going Correction** -0.025s/f (Good) 11 Ran SP% **113.9**
Speed ratings (Par 98): **104,102,102,100,98 96,96,94,93,93 72**
toteswingers 1&2 £32.30, 1&3 £9.40, 2&3 £7.80 CSF £350.49 CT £1181.84 TOTE £36.90: £6.60, £4.50, £1.10; EX 640.10 Trifecta £1091.90 Pool: £4483.60 - 3.07 winning tickets..
Owner Saeed Suhail **Bred** Rabbah Bloodstock Limited **Trained** Newmarket, Suffolk

FOCUS
A decent fillies' handicap, run at a reasonable pace, and the action unfolded centre-to-stands' side, with the front two coming up the middle. The form has been rated positively.

3059 LLOYDS TSB FOR THE JOURNEY MAIDEN STKS 1m 4f
3:10 (3:12) (Class 5) 3-Y-O £3,234 (£962; £481; £240) **Stalls Centre**

Form RPR

0-6 **1** **Great Hall**[22] 2384 3-9-5 0 RichardHughes 1 90+
(Brian Meehan) *hld up wl in tch in midfield: drew clr in ldng quartet 2f out: drvn and effrt over 1f out: led and veered lft 1f out: keeping on whn wnt lft again whn hit w whip fnl 100yds: pushed out and holding runner-up cl home* **11/4**[1]

-0 **2** ½ **Fledged**[22] 2384 3-9-5 0 WilliamBuick 4 89
(John Gosden) *hld up wl in tch in midfield: drew clr in ldng quartet 2f out: drvn and styd on to chse ldng pair ins fnl f: kpt on to go 2nd and pressing wnr towards fin: hld cl home* **7/2**[2]

-432 **3** nk **Seamless**[29] 2198 3-9-5 84 JamesMcDonald 2 89
(Charles Hills) *led tl 4f out: styd pressing ldr: rdn and led again over 1f out: hdd and bmpd 1f out: kpt on same pce and lost 2nd towards fin* **7/2**[2]

0 **4** 2 ½ **Asbaab (USA)**[20] 2442 3-9-5 0 PaulHanagan 7 85
(Brian Meehan) *chsd ldr tl led 4f out: rdn and hdd over 1f out: unable qck and edgd lft 1f out: styng on same pce whn n.m.r fnl 150yds: wknd towards fin* **12/1**

43 **5** 12 **Jazz Master**[25] 2321 3-9-5 0 KierenFallon 3 66
(Luca Cumani) *wl in tch in midfield: rdn over 3f out: outpcd u.p over 2f out: wknd and wl btn over 1f out* **9/1**[3]

00 **6** ½ **Faustinatheyounger (IRE)**[22] 2392 3-9-0 0 SebSanders 6 60
(David Elsworth) *wl in tch towards rr: rdn and unable qck 3f out: outpcd over 2f out: wknd and wl btn over 1f out* **100/1**

60 **7** 9 **Kattaf (IRE)**[22] 2384 3-9-5 0 NeilCallan 5 51
(Marco Botti) *wl in tch towards rr: rdn 3f out: sn struggling and btn: bhd fnl 2f* **100/1**

0 **8** 6 **Fanny Squeers**[22] 2384 3-9-0 0 JamieSpencer 8 36
(Michael Bell) *s.i.s: hld up wl in tch in rr: rdn 4f out: lost tch over 2f out: eased ins fnl f: t.o* **40/1**

The Form Book Flat, Raceform Ltd, Compton, RG20 6NL.

4 9 4 1/2 **Legends (IRE)**[15] 2605 3-9-5 0 RyanMoore 9 42
(Sir Michael Stoute) *chsd ldrs: rdn and fnd nil jst over 2f out: sn btn and nt given a hrd time: wl bhd and eased ins fnl f: t.o* **7/2**[2]

2m 33.88s (0.98) **Going Correction** -0.025s/f (Good) **9** Ran SP% **115.4**
Speed ratings (Par 99): **95,94,94,92,84 84,78,74,71**
toteswingers 1&2 £3.40, 1&3 £3.30, 2&3 £3.10 CSF £12.58 TOTE £3.60: £1.30, £1.80, £1.70; EX 13.90 Trifecta £67.10 Pool: £4178.56 - 46.65 winning tickets..

Owner Raymond Tooth **Bred** Aston House Stud **Trained** Manton, Wilts

FOCUS
A useful maiden, with the first four clear and the third carrying a BHA rating of 84. The winner is progressing with racing. They went just a steady pace.

3060 LLOYDS TSB CARDNET H'CAP 7f
3:45 (3:46) (Class 3) (0-95,95) 4-Y-0+ **£7,762** (£2,310; £1,154; £577) **Stalls** High

Form RPR

0-40 **1** **Highland Colori (IRE)**[27] 2254 5-9-4 **92** WilliamBuick 7 106+
(Andrew Balding) *chsd ldng trio: rdn over 2f out: chsd ldr over 1f out: led ent fnl f and sn clr: r.o wl: rdn out* **4/1**[1]

634 **2** 3 1/4 **Kakatosi**[34] 2013 6-8-10 **84** TomQueally 14 90
(Mike Murphy) *stdd s: hld up wl off the pce in midfield: rdn and effrt over 2f out: styd on u.p to chse clr wnr ins fnl f: kpt on but no ch w wnr* **25/1**

6615 **3** 1 1/4 **Forceful Appeal (USA)**[14] 2618 5-8-7 **81** PaulHanagan 12 83
(Simon Dow) *hld up wl off the pce in rr: rdn 2f out: effrt whn n.m.r and swtchd lft 1f out: r.o strly ins fnl f: no threat to wnr* **25/1**

2610 **4** 1 **Fast Finian (IRE)**[27] 2254 4-9-0 **88** (b) KierenFallon 6 88+
(Paul D'Arcy) *led and set fast gallop: rdn over 1f out: hdd ent fnl f: no ex and sn btn: lost 2 pls ins fnl f* **10/1**

0021 **5** 2 1/2 **Albaqaa**[13] 2659 8-8-3 **80** DarrenEgan(3) 10 73
(P J O'Gorman) *hld up wl off the pce in rr: rdn and effrt over 1f out: styd on wl fnl f: nvr trbld ldrs* **16/1**

064- **6** nk **Axiom**[176] 8098 9-8-12 **86** (b) JamieSpencer 9 78
(Ed Walker) *racd off the pce in midfield: no imp whn edgd lft u.p over 1f out: plugged on but n.d* **20/1**

0-06 **7** 1/2 **Born To Surprise**[6] 2858 4-9-2 **95** WilliamTwiston-Davies(5) 5 86
(Michael Bell) *chsd ldng pair: wnt 2nd 2f out tl over 1f out: sn rdn and fnd little: wknd ins fnl f* **10/1**

2-00 **8** 1 **Elusive Flame**[27] 2254 4-9-1 **89** RyanMoore 8 78
(David Elsworth) *racd wl off the pce in midfield: rdn and no real imp over 1f out: plugged on but n.d* **5/1**[2]

2240 **9** 3/4 **Showboating (IRE)**[20] 2450 5-8-2 **76** (vt) SilvestreDeSousa 11 63
(Alan McCabe) *stdd s: hld up wl off the pce in rr: rdn and sme hdwy over 1f out: kpt on but n.d* **16/1**

00-0 **10** 2 **Johnny Castle**[13] 2665 5-8-12 **86** RichardHughes 2 67
(Amanda Perrett) *hld up wl off the pce in rr: sme hdwy over 1f out: rdn and no imp 1f out: n.d* **16/1**

/00- **11** 1/2 **Top Offer**[372] 2641 4-9-7 **95** JamesDoyle 13 75
(Roger Charlton) *stdd s: hld up wl off the pce in rr: swtchd lft and rdn 2f out: no real imp: n.d* **6/1**[3]

16-0 **12** shd **Emkanaat**[14] 2618 5-8-9 **83** JoeFanning 1 63
(Amy Weaver) *hld up wl off the pce in rr: n.d* **66/1**

16-0 **13** nk **Common Touch (IRE)**[15] 2585 5-9-5 **93** J-PGuillambert 15 72
(Willie Musson) *prom in main gp but stl wl off the pce: rdn and struggling over 2f out: wknd over 1f out* **50/1**

0-03 **14** 2 **Princess Of Orange**[27] 2253 4-9-2 **90** TedDurcan 4 64
(Rae Guest) *racd off the pce in midfield: rdn and struggling over 2f out: wkng and dropping towards rr whn hmpd over 1f out* **11/1**

0203 **15** hd **Laffan (IRE)**[13] 2649 4-9-3 **91** (p) NeilCallan 3 69
(Kevin Ryan) *chsd ldr: rdn over 2f out: lost 2nd 2f out and sn struggling: fdd fnl f* **10/1**

1m 23.99s (-1.71) **Going Correction** -0.025s/f (Good) **15** Ran SP% **120.1**
Speed ratings (Par 107): **108,104,102,101,98 98,97,96,95,93 93,92,92,90,90**
toteswingers 1&2 £28.50, 1&3 £21.70, 2&3 £61.50 CSF £114.87 CT £2287.55 TOTE £3.90: £1.80, £8.80, £7.00; EX 125.90 Trifecta £1926.40 Pool: £3343.12 - 1.30 winning tickets..

Owner Evan M Sutherland **Bred** Rathbarry Stud **Trained** Kingsclere, Hants

FOCUS
The field were soon quite strung out, with them appearing to go fast early, but little actually got into the race. The winner impressed and the form is rated positively.

3061 LLOYDS TSB COMMERCIAL H'CAP 1m 2f
4:20 (4:21) (Class 3) (0-95,92) 3-Y-0 **£7,762** (£2,310; £1,154; £577) **Stalls** Centre

Form RPR

2-11 **1** **Maputo**[11] 2717 3-9-3 **88** 6ex JoeFanning 2 101+
(Mark Johnston) *racd keenly: mde all: gng best 3f out: rdn 2f out: in command after: rdn and edging lft but kpt on ins fnl f* **4/5**[1]

-332 **2** 2 **Number One London (IRE)**[15] 2605 3-8-11 **82** KierenFallon 5 91
(Brian Meehan) *chsd ldrs: rdn 3f out: 4th and no imp over 1f out: kpt on u.p ins fnl f to go 2nd towards fin* **16/1**

1- **3** 1/2 **Chesterfield (IRE)**[349] 3397 3-8-12 **83** MickaelBarzalona 4 91
(Saeed bin Suroor) *hld up in last pair: rdn over 3f out: hdwy u.p to chse ldrs 2f out: kpt on and chsd wnr ins fnl f: no imp and lost 2nd towards fin* **7/2**[2]

411- **4** 2 **Cat O'Mountain (USA)**[226] 7325 3-9-3 **88** SilvestreDeSousa 1 92
(Saeed bin Suroor) *chsd wnr: rdn over 3f out: edgd lft and no imp over 1f out: lost 2nd ins fnl f: wknd towards fin* **10/1**

14 **5** 2 1/4 **Feel Like Dancing**[29] 2187 3-9-7 **92** WilliamBuick 6 92+
(John Gosden) *s.i.s: hld up in tch in last pair: rdn and swtchd lft 3f out: struggling 2f out: 5th and plugged on same pce fr over 1f out* **11/2**[3]

62-3 **6** 19 **Mr Fitzroy (IRE)**[20] 2455 3-8-6 **77** PaulHanagan 3 41
(Andrew Balding) *chsd ldrs: rdn over 3f out: lost pl and dropped to rr over 2f out: sn wknd* **33/1**

2m 5.7s (0.20) **Going Correction** -0.025s/f (Good) **6** Ran SP% **111.1**
Speed ratings (Par 103): **98,96,96,94,92 77**
toteswingers 1&2 £3.90, 1&3 £1.40, 2&3 £5.70 CSF £15.24 TOTE £2.00: £1.40, £5.50; EX 14.30 Trifecta £53.60 Pool: £4513.29 - 63.14 winning tickets..

Owner Sheikh Hamdan Bin Mohammed Al Maktoum **Bred** Darley **Trained** Middleham Moor, N Yorks

FOCUS
Quite a strong 3yo handicap, won last year by subsequent Group 2 King Edward scorer Thomas Chippendale. Maputo more than confirmed the merit of his Redcar win and the form could be a bit higher than rated.

3062 LLOYDS TSB CARDNET CLASSIFIED STKS 1m
4:55 (4:55) (Class 5) 3-Y-0 **£3,234** (£962; £360; £360) **Stalls** High

Form RPR

1-03 **1** **Consign**[11] 2727 3-9-0 73 (v[1]) WilliamBuick 7 81
(Jeremy Noseda) *hld up wl in tch in midfield: clsng whn nt clr run 2f out: swtchd rt and effrt over 1f out: chsng ldrs and edgd lft u.p ins fnl f: r.o under mainy hands and heels to ld towards fin* **9/2**[1]

10- **2** 1/2 **Footstepsintherain (IRE)**[218] 7501 3-9-0 75 TedDurcan 3 80+
(David Lanigan) *hld up in tch in rr: swtchd rt and effrt wl over 1f out: hdwy u.p 1f out: r.o wl fnl 100yds: snatched 2nd last strides* **20/1**

3-30 **3** nk **Millers Wharf (IRE)**[22] 2394 3-9-0 74 (b[1]) RichardHughes 12 79
(Richard Hannon) *t.k.h: trckd ldrs: rdn and effrt over 1f out: led 1f out: kpt on u.p tl hdd and lost 2 pls towards fin* **17/2**

632- **3** dht **Trucanini**[275] 5947 3-9-0 75 SebSanders 1 79
(Chris Wall) *stdd and dropped in bhd after s: t.k.h: hld up in tch in rr: swtchd lft and hdwy 2f out: chsd ldrs and drvn 1f out: kpt on* **6/1**[3]

2-21 **5** 1 3/4 **Aneedh**[18] 2507 3-9-0 75 JamesMcDonald 5 75
(William Haggas) *v keen to post: chsd ldrs: wnt 2nd 2f out tl over 1f out: unable qck u.p 1f out: styd on same pce fnl f* **9/2**[1]

0613 **6** 2 **Declamation (IRE)**[10] 2763 3-9-0 75 JoeFanning 9 71
(Mark Johnston) *racd keenly: led: rdn 2f out: hdd 1f out: no ex and wknd ins fnl f* **5/1**[2]

646 **7** nse **Sedenoo**[25] 2306 3-9-0 74 NeilCallan 4 70
(Marco Botti) *t.k.h: hld up wl in tch in midfield: effrt u.p 2f out: styd on same pce ins fnl f* **7/1**

100- **8** 9 **Rich Forever (IRE)**[219] 7478 3-9-0 74 JamieSpencer 11 50
(James Bethell) *in tch in last quartet: rdn over 3f out: lost pl and bhd 2f out* **33/1**

02-0 **9** 1/2 **Harwoods Star (IRE)**[29] 2192 3-9-0 73 RyanMoore 10 49
(Amanda Perrett) *wl in tch in midfield: swtchd lft and effrt u.p ent fnl 2f: no ex and btn over 1f out: sn wknd* **10/1**

1-05 **10** 1 1/2 **Iberis**[14] 2622 3-9-0 74 TomQueally 2 45
(Sir Henry Cecil) *wl in tch in midfield: rdn and effrt over 2f out: wknd u.p over 1f out* **12/1**

4230 **11** 2 3/4 **Beau Select (IRE)**[25] 2324 3-9-0 67 (b) MickaelBarzalona 8 39
(Robert Eddery) *t.k.h: chsd ldr tl 2f out: sn wknd* **40/1**

1m 38.74s (-1.26) **Going Correction** -0.025s/f (Good) **11** Ran SP% **117.3**
Speed ratings (Par 99): **105,104,104,104,102 100,100,91,90,89 86**
PLACE: Millers Wharf £1.80. Truscanini £1.20. toteswingers 1&2 £22.10, 1&MW £4.30, 1&T £4.30, 2&MW £15.20, 2&T £7.30 CSF £95.75 TOTE £4.70: £1.70, £5.60; EX 107.30 Trifecta £1427.90 Part won. Pool: £3807.89 - 0.64 winning tickets..

Owner Miss Yvonne Jacques **Bred** Natton House Thoroughbreds & Mark Woodall **Trained** Newmarket, Suffolk

FOCUS
Probably relatively ordinary form for the level with a compressed finish. They went an even pace.

3063 LLOYDS TSB COMMERCIAL SUPPORTING YOUR BUSINESS H'CAP 1m 2f
5:30 (5:30) (Class 5) (0-75,74) 4-Y-0+ **£3,408** (£1,006; £503) **Stalls** Centre

Form RPR

055- **1** **Mankini (IRE)**[349] 3399 4-8-7 **60** KirstyMilczarek 2 73+
(Luca Cumani) *in tch in midfield: jnd ldrs 3f out: sn rdn to ld: sustained duel w rival fr 2f out: forged ahd fnl 100yds: styd on wl* **3/1**[1]

3-24 **2** 1 **Curly Come Home**[25] 2311 4-9-2 **69** (t) TedDurcan 3 78
(Chris Wall) *chsd ldng pair: effrt against stands' rail to chal 2f out: sustained duel w wnr tl no ex and one pce fnl 100yds* **7/1**

1553 **3** 4 **Mcbirney (USA)**[22] 2385 6-9-2 **74** RobertTart(5) 5 75
(Paul D'Arcy) *stdd s: hld up in last pair: effrt to chse ldrs 2f out: drvn and no ex ent fnl f: wknd fnl 100yds* **6/1**

6-54 **4** 2 **On My Own (TUR)**[16] 2574 4-9-5 **72** SebSanders 4 70
(J W Hills) *t.k.h: hld up in tch in last pair: rdn and effrt over 2f out: 4th and no imp over 1f out: wknd ins fnl f* **4/1**[2]

-601 **5** 12 **Emman Bee (IRE)**[21] 2413 4-9-5 **72** RichardHughes 7 47
(Luke Dace) *chsd ldr tl led after 1f: hdd wl over 2f out: sn struggling and wkng whn short of room 2f out: wl btn and eased ins fnl f* **4/1**[2]

11-0 **6** 1/2 **Grand Liaison**[41] 1849 4-9-4 **71** TomQueally 6 45
(John Berry) *hld up wl in tch in last trio: hdwy 3f out: rdn and btn over 2f out: sn bhd: eased ins fnl f* **5/1**[3]

615- **7** 3 1/4 **Warden Bond**[259] 6458 5-8-2 **55** oh5 (p) SilvestreDeSousa 1 23
(William Stone) *t.k.h: led for 1f: chsd ldr after: rdn and ev ch 3f: losing pl whn hmpd 2f out: sn wknd: bhd and eased ins fnl f* **33/1**

2m 8.68s (3.18) **Going Correction** -0.025s/f (Good) **7** Ran SP% **111.4**
Speed ratings (Par 103): **86,85,82,80,70 70,67**
CSF £23.03 CT £113.34 TOTE £3.80: £1.70, £3.40; EX 25.50 Trifecta £134.40 Pool: £2734.25 - 15.25 winning tickets..

Owner Leonidas Marinopoulos **Bred** Oak Hill Stud **Trained** Newmarket, Suffolk

■ Stewards' Enquiry : Kirsty Milczarek four-day ban; used whip above permitted level (23rd-26th June).

FOCUS
They raced against the stands' rail in the straight and the front pair came clear late on, despite the steady pace. Modest handicap form for the track, but there could be a fair bit more to come from the winner.

T/Plt: £44.50 to a £1 stake. Pool: £76,775.06 - 1,257.35 winning tickets T/Qpdt: £17.90 to a £1 stake. Pool: £4,242.22 - 174.58 winning tickets SP

[2551]PONTEFRACT (L-H)

Friday, June 7

OFFICIAL GOING: Good to firm (8.1)

Rail moved out from 6f to Winning Post adding circa 16yds to advertised distances.

Wind: Light across Weather: Sunny and dry

3064 CHRIS SHAW 50TH BIRTHDAY CELEBRATION MAIDEN AUCTION FILLIES' STKS 6f

6:35 (6:38) (Class 5) 2-Y-O **£3,234** (£962; £481; £240) **Stalls** Low

Form RPR

2 **1** **Milly's Secret (IRE)**[14] [2612] 2-8-6 0................................ PJMcDonald 16 77
(Ann Duffield) *towards rr: pushed along 1/2-way: hdwy on wd outside 2f out: rdn to chal over 1f out: led ent fnl f: sn edgd lft and clr: rdn out* **6/1**

2 2 ½ **Khalice** 2-8-8 0................................ TonyHamilton 6 72
(Richard Fahey) *trckd ldrs: hdwy 2f out: effrt whn nt clr run over 1f out: sn swtchd rt and rdn: styd on wl towards fin* **7/1**

2 **3** 6 **Supa U**[18] [2502] 2-8-4 0................................ DuranFentiman 5 50
(Tim Easterby) *trckd ldrs: hdwy 1/2-way: sn cl up: rdn to ld wl over 1f out: hdd ent fnl f and sn one pce* **4/1**[2]

22 **4** 3 ¼ **Rural Celebration**[14] [2631] 2-8-8 0 ow2................................ GrahamGibbons 8 44+
(David O'Meara) *cl up: led wl over 2f out: rdn along and hdd wl over 1f out: sn wknd* **5/1**[3]

0 **5** ¾ **Strictly Glitz (IRE)**[51] [1605] 2-8-8 0................................ MichaelO'Connell 13 42
(John Quinn) *midfield: rdn along and sme hdwy 2f out: n.d* **66/1**

6 1 ½ **Francisca** 2-8-4 0................................ JamesSullivan 2 33
(James Given) *towards rr: rdn along on inner and nt clr run over 2f out: swtchd to wd outside wl over 1f out: styd on fnl f* **25/1**

7 ½ **Bertha Burnett (IRE)** 2-8-3 0 ow2................................ MichaelJMMurphy(5) 7 36
(Brian Rothwell) *towards rr tl rdn along and sme hdwy fnl 2f: n.d* **40/1**

8 4 **Tweety Pie (IRE)** 2-8-2 0 ow1................................ JasonHart(5) 15 24
(Declan Carroll) *a towards rr* **40/1**

0 **9** 2 ¼ **Barbara Elizabeth**[17] [2553] 2-8-5 0 ow1................................ BarryMcHugh 9 14
(Tony Coyle) *a towards rr* **50/1**

10 1 ½ **Notts So Blue** 2-8-2 0 ow1................................ DeclanCannon(3) 10 9
(Shaun Harris) *a towards rr* **66/1**

11 6 **Pyjama Day** 2-8-6 0................................ FrannyNorton 4
(Hugo Palmer) *s.i.s: a bhd* **14/1**

4 **12** shd **Clever Miss**[10] [2751] 2-8-6 0................................ AndrewMullen 1 +
(Alan McCabe) *led: rdn along wl over 2f out: sn hdd & wknd wl over 1f out* **10/3**[1]

0 **13** 7 **Shamouti (IRE)**[41] [1839] 2-8-8 0................................ AmyRyan 3
(Kevin Ryan) *dwlt: t.k.h and sn chsng ldrs on inner: rdn along over 2f out: sn wknd* **7/1**

1m 18.67s (1.77) **Going Correction** +0.225s/f (Good) **13** Ran SP% **119.4**
Speed ratings (Par 90): **97,93,85,81,80 78,77,72,69,67 59,59,49**
toteswingers 1&2 £5.40, 1&3 £8.80, 2&3 £4.50 CSF £45.52 TOTE £8.00: £2.90, £3.40, £1.20; EX 49.60 Trifecta £765.10 Part won. Pool: £1020.19 - 0.95 winning tickets..
Owner Jimmy Kay **Bred** John B Hughes **Trained** Constable Burton, N Yorks

FOCUS
A biggish field for this 2yo maiden auction fillies' race with previous form thin on the ground. The two leaders took each other on from the start and neither got home. With the first two clear the form could have been rated higher.

3065 TONY BETHELL MEMORIAL H'CAP 2m 1f 22y

7:05 (7:06) (Class 4) (0-80,79) 4-Y-O+ **£6,469** (£1,925; £962; £481) **Stalls** Low

Form RPR

0-30 **1** **Riptide**[28] [2205] 7-9-1 70................................(v) PaulMulrennan 5 80
(Michael Scudamore) *trckd ldng pair: hdwy and cl up over 3f out: rdn to ld wl over 1f out: styd on strly fnl f* **12/1**

2-11 **2** 4 **Our Folly**[29] [2197] 5-8-12 72................................(t) MichaelJMMurphy(5) 8 78
(Stuart Kittow) *hld up in midfield: hdwy 5f out: pushed along to chse ldrs 3f out: rdn 2f out: ev ch appr fnl f: sn drvn and kpt on same pce* **9/2**[1]

0-40 **3** ½ **Danvilla**[15] [2587] 6-9-10 79................................ WilliamCarson 13 84
(Paul Webber) *trckd ldr: cl up 1/2-way: effrt 3f out: rdn along over 2f out: drvn and one pce appr fnl f* **12/1**

0-53 **4** nk **Come Here Yew (IRE)**[22] [2402] 5-9-0 72................................ NeilFarley(3) 7 77
(Declan Carroll) *midfield: pushed along 5f out: rdn and outpcd over 3f out: styd on u.p fnl 2f: nrst fin* **9/2**[1]

243- **5** 2 **Mojolika**[59] [5256] 5-9-5 74................................ GrahamGibbons 9 77
(Tim Easterby) *t.k.h early: trckd ldrs: hdwy over 4f out: chsd ldrs 2f out: sn rdn and no imp appr fnl f* **9/2**[1]

4222 **6** 3 **Brasingaman Eric**[11] [2720] 6-8-10 65................................ PJMcDonald 11 64
(George Moore) *led: pushed along 3f out: rdn over 2f out: drvn and hdd wl over 1f out: sn wknd* **6/1**[2]

1522 **7** 2 ½ **Scribe (IRE)**[10] [2749] 5-9-0 69................................(vt) DaneO'Neill 1 65
(David Evans) *hld up in rr: rapid hdwy on outer 4f out: cl up over 2f out: sn rdn and ev ch: drvn and wknd wl over 1f out* **16/1**

0005 **8** 1 ¾ **Maid Of Meft**[31] [2120] 6-8-0 60 oh1................................ ShirleyTeasdale(5) 10 55
(Paul Midgley) *trckd ldrs on inner: rdn along over 3f out: sn drvn and grad wknd fnl 2f* **8/1**[3]

0-00 **9** 28 **Mr Crystal (FR)**[28] [2242] 9-8-10 65................................ MichaelO'Connell 6 29
(Micky Hammond) *chsd ldrs: rdn along 5f out: wknd 4f out: sn bhd* **33/1**

-002 **10** 29 **Vimiero (USA)**[32] [2087] 6-9-4 73................................ PhillipMakin 3
(Jonjo O'Neill) *hld up in rr: smooth hdwy on outer 5f out: chsd ldrs over 3f out: sn rdn and wknd qckly over 2f out* **8/1**[3]

3m 47.13s (2.53) **Going Correction** -0.275s/f (Firm) **10** Ran SP% **115.3**
Speed ratings (Par 105): **83,81,80,80,79 78,77,76,63,49**
toteswingers 1&2 £14.70, 1&3 £52.30, 2&3 £7.60 CSF £64.58 CT £670.89 TOTE £15.00: £2.90, £2.10, £3.20; EX 95.00 Trifecta £399.30 Part won. Pool: £532.48 - 0.19 winning tickets..
Owner Middletons **Bred** D Robb **Trained** Bromsash, H'fords

FOCUS
The gallop was unrelenting and this proved a real test of stamina. The winner is rated back to something like last year's form.

3066 MR WOLF SPRINT H'CAP 6f

7:35 (7:37) (Class 3) (0-90,85) 3-Y-O
£9,337 (£2,796; £1,398; £699; £349; £175) **Stalls** Low

Form RPR

2120 **1** **Line Of Reason (IRE)**[23] [2371] 3-9-7 85................................ KierenFallon 5 92
(Paul Midgley) *trckd ldrs: hdwy over 2f out: rdn to ld ins fnl f: kpt on wl* **9/1**

15-0 **2** ½ **Pipers Note**[14] [2614] 3-8-12 76................................ AmyRyan 2 83+
(Richard Whitaker) *trckd ldrs on inner: nt clr run wl over 1f out and again 1f out: sn swtchd rt: squeezed through wl ins fnl f: sn rdn and styd on wl towards fin* **33/1**

-103 **3** hd **Rene Mathis (GER)**[11] [2708] 3-9-2 80................................ TonyHamilton 1 85+
(Richard Fahey) *hld up in tch: hdwy 2f out: swtchd rt and rdn over 1f out: squeezed through ent fnl f: drvn and kpt on wl towards fin* **8/1**[3]

1010 **4** nk **Bluegrass Blues (IRE)**[20] [2452] 3-9-5 83................................ RobertWinston 8 87
(Paul Cole) *prom: hdwy over 2f out: rdn to ld jst over 1f out: hdd and drvn ins fnl f: no ex last 75yds* **8/1**[3]

0-11 **5** 1 ½ **Hoofalong**[18] [2521] 3-9-6 84................................ GrahamGibbons 7 83
(Michael Easterby) *cl up: rdn and ev ch wl over 1f out: drvn ins fnl f: wknd last 100yds* **2/1**[1]

15-0 **6** nk **Lastchancelucas**[21] [2430] 3-9-2 85................................ JasonHart(5) 10 83
(Declan Carroll) *hld up towards rr: hdwy on outer over 2f out: rdn to chse ldrs wl over 1f out: sltly hmpd ent fnl f: one pce* **25/1**

241 **7** ½ **Can You Conga**[34] [2006] 3-9-4 82................................ PhillipMakin 6 78+
(Kevin Ryan) *dwlt and in rr: hdwy wl over 1f out: sn rdn and kpt on: nrst fin* **18/1**

324- **8** ¾ **Funding Deficit (IRE)**[250] [6708] 3-8-11 75................................ FrannyNorton 9 69
(David Barron) *sn led: rdn along 2f out: drvn over 1f out: hdd appr fnl f: sn wknd* **16/1**

4-12 **9** hd **Mayaasem**[29] [2190] 3-9-5 83................................ DaneO'Neill 4 76
(Charles Hills) *chsd ldrs: rdn along over 2f out: drvn wl over 1f out: sn wknd* **4/1**[2]

10-6 **10** 2 ½ **Bachotheque (IRE)**[21] [2430] 3-9-6 84................................ DavidAllan 3 69
(Tim Easterby) *towards rr and sn pushed along: sme hdwy on inner wl over 1f out: sn rdn along and n.d* **12/1**

60-3 **11** 1 ¼ **Elle Woods (IRE)**[20] [2439] 3-9-0 78................................ PaulMulrennan 11 59
(Michael Dods) *a towards rr* **12/1**

1m 18.14s (1.24) **Going Correction** +0.225s/f (Good) **11** Ran SP% **118.9**
Speed ratings (Par 103): **100,99,99,98,96 96,95,94,94,91 89**
toteswingers 1&2 £29.00, 1&3 £9.70, 2&3 £53.80 CSF £266.71 CT £2468.25 TOTE £6.90: £1.80, £10.60, £2.50; EX 267.20 Trifecta £970.10 Part won. Pool: £1293.52 - 0.09 winning tickets..
Owner Taylor's Bloodstock Ltd **Bred** Corduff Stud Ltd, J Corcoran & J Judd **Trained** Westow, N Yorks

FOCUS
A highly competitive 3yo sprint handicap and it paid to come from off the pace. The bare form is ordinary for the grade.

3067 CONSTANT SECURITY SERVING YORKSHIRE RACECOURSES H'CAP 1m 2f 6y

8:05 (8:07) (Class 4) (0-80,80) 3-Y-O **£6,469** (£1,925; £962; £481) **Stalls** Low

Form RPR

2052 **1** **Royal Skies (IRE)**[6] [2878] 3-9-4 77................................ FrannyNorton 5 104
(Mark Johnston) *chsd clr ldr: tk clsr order 3f out: led wl over 1f out: sn clr: readily* **3/1**[2]

4-62 **2** 9 **Duke Of Perth**[15] [2600] 3-8-12 71................................ KierenFallon 2 80
(Luca Cumani) *in tch: hdwy 3f out: rdn to chse wnr appr fnl f: sn drvn and no imp* **2/1**[1]

4-62 **3** 5 **Mystical Man**[17] [2554] 3-9-7 80................................ PaulMulrennan 9 79
(James Tate) *led and sn clr at str pce: rdn along over 2f out: hdd wl over 1f out: sn drvn and plugged on one pce* **16/1**

3-41 **4** 1 **Chevalgris**[21] [2405] 3-9-2 75................................ RobertWinston 3 72
(Alan Swinbank) *hld up in rr: hdwy over 2f out: rdn wl over 1f out: kpt on u.p fnl f: n.d* **4/1**[3]

-314 **5** 1 ½ **Mad Jazz**[9] [2769] 3-9-0 73................................ BarryMcHugh 8 67
(Tony Coyle) *trckd ldrs: effrt 4f out: rdn wl over 2f out: sn no imp* **10/1**

0614 **6** 2 **Marhaba Malayeen (IRE)**[11] [2717] 3-9-1 74................................(p) PhillipMakin 6 64
(Kevin Ryan) *chsd ldrs: rdn along over 2f out: drvn wl over 1f out: sn wknd* **20/1**

-215 **7** ½ **Surround Sound**[14] [2627] 3-8-8 67................................ DavidAllan 1 56
(Tim Easterby) *dwlt: a in rr* **12/1**

030 **8** 5 **Strawberry Jam**[20] [2442] 3-8-5 71................................ JordanUys(7) 7 50
(Paul Cole) *hld up: a towards rr* **16/1**

6-26 **9** 1 ¾ **Orions Hero (IRE)**[17] [2538] 3-8-12 71................................ TonyHamilton 4 47
(Richard Fahey) *chsd ldrs: rdn along over 3f out: sn wknd* **18/1**

2m 10.7s (-3.00) **Going Correction** -0.275s/f (Firm) **9** Ran SP% **116.9**
Speed ratings (Par 101): **101,93,89,89,87 86,85,81,80**
toteswingers 1&2 £1.90, 1&3 £5.00, 2&3 £3.90 CSF £9.54 CT £80.34 TOTE £3.70: £1.10, £1.40, £5.30; EX 9.00 Trifecta £142.20 Pool: £1014.76 - 5.35 winning tickets..
Owner Sheikh Hamdan Bin Mohammed Al Maktoum **Bred** P Moen **Trained** Middleham Moor, N Yorks

FOCUS
An interesting contest for the grade with the winner and fourth well in. A decent pace and the standout time on the card.

3068 CONSTANT SECURITY SERVICES H'CAP 6f

8:40 (8:41) (Class 5) (0-70,70) 3-Y-O+ **£3,234** (£962; £481; £240) **Stalls** Low

Form RPR

54-0 **1** **Who's Shirl**[27] [2278] 7-9-9 65................................ PaulMulrennan 2 77
(Chris Fairhurst) *towards rr: hdwy on inner 2f out: rdn over 1f out: str run to ld ins fnl f: kpt on* **10/1**

-052 **2** 1 ½ **Bunce (IRE)**[10] [2752] 5-9-12 68................................ KierenFallon 4 75
(David O'Meara) *trckd ldrs: hdwy 2f out: swtchd rt and rdn over 1f out: drvn and kpt on fnl f* **10/3**[1]

0365 **3** nk **Illustrious Prince (IRE)**[16] [2580] 6-9-2 65................................ LukeLeadbitter(7) 7 71
(Declan Carroll) *cl up: led over 2f out: rdn over 1f out and sn edgd rt: hdd ins fnl f: kpt on same pce* **20/1**

33-5 **4** 1 ¼ **Rust (IRE)**[18] [2506] 3-9-4 68................................ PJMcDonald 1 68
(Ann Duffield) *trckd ldrs on inner: hdwy 2f out: rdn over 1f out: drvn and kpt on same pce fnl f* **5/1**[2]

030 **5** hd **Sunraider (IRE)**[13] [2663] 6-10-0 70................................ MickyFenton 13 71+
(Paul Midgley) *stdd and swtchd lft s: hld up in rr: swtchd rt to outer and hdwy wl over 1f out: sn rdn and styd on fnl f: nrst fin* **33/1**

4/0 **6** nk **Mr Man In The Moon (IRE)**[48] [1681] 5-9-0 61................................ DavidBergin(5) 16 61
(Mandy Rowland) *stdd and swtchd lft s: hdwy on outer 1/2-way: cl up 2f out: rdn to chal over 1f out: sn drvn and wknd fnl f* **50/1**

410 **7** ½ **Dartrix**[7] [2835] 4-9-2 65................................ ConnorBeasley(7) 3 64+
(Michael Dods) *towards rr: swtchd rt and hdwy wl over 1f out: rdn and kpt on fnl f: nrst fin* **17/2**

-224 **8** 1 ¼ **Mandalay King (IRE)**[21] [2409] 8-9-4 65................................(p) ShirleyTeasdale(5) 9 60
(Marjorie Fife) *chsd ldrs: rdn along wl over 1f out: sn one pce* **14/1**

-230 **9** 3 1/2 **Strong Man**[127] 453 5-9-9 **65** GrahamGibbons 8 49
(Michael Easterby) *cl up: rdn along wl over 2f out: drvn wl over 1f out and grad wknd* **14/1**

0-33 **10** *nk* **Mcmonagle (USA)**[7] 2835 5-9-6 **62** (bt) DaleSwift 15 45
(Alan Brown) *chsd ldrs: rdn along 1/2-way: sn wknd* **12/1**

0-00 **11** 1 1/4 **Consistant**[56] 1525 5-9-2 **58** WilliamCarson 11 37
(Brian Baugh) *slt ld: pushed along and hdd over 2f out: sn rdn and wknd* **25/1**

4146 **12** 1 1/2 **Beckermet (IRE)**[13] 2664 11-10-0 **70** JamesSullivan 6 44
(Ruth Carr) *chsd ldrs: rdn along wl over 2f out: sn wknd* **11/1**

-405 **13** 1/2 **Hello Stranger (IRE)**[11] 2703 4-9-10 **66** DuranFentiman 5 38
(Tim Easterby) *a towards rr* **7/1**[3]

4014 **14** *nk* **Powerful Pierre**[7] 2836 6-9-7 **63** (b) DavidNolan 14 34
(Ian McInnes) *a towards rr* **25/1**

4000 **15** 3 **Rio Cobolo (IRE)**[13] 2663 7-9-6 **62** (v) AdrianNicholls 10 24
(David Nicholls) *in tch: reminders after 2f: hdwy to chse ldrs 2f out: rdn and wknd over 1f out: eased* **28/1**

410- **16** 19 **Albert Tatlock (IRE)**[223] 7395 4-10-0 **70** RobertWinston 12
(John Butler) *cl up on outer: rdn along wl over 2f out: sn wknd* **20/1**

1m 17.69s (0.79) **Going Correction** +0.225s/f (Good)
WFA 3 from 4yo+ 8lb **16** Ran SP% **126.8**
Speed ratings (Par 103): **103,101,100,98,98 98,97,95,91,90 89,87,86,86,82 56**
toteswingers 1&2 £8.70, 1&3 £40.50, 2&3 £13.00 CSF £41.16 CT £691.31 TOTE £13.90: £3.60, £1.20, £4.80, £1.80; EX 69.70 Trifecta £411.70 Pool: £696.60 - 1.26 winning tickets..
Owner Mrs Shirley France **Bred** Mrs S France **Trained** Middleham Moor, N Yorks

FOCUS
A maximum field of mainly fully exposed modest sprinters. Low draws proved best and the level is set around the third.

3069 LOGIC LETTINGS PONTEFRACT H'CAP 5f
9:10 (9:10) (Class 5) (0-75,77) 4-Y-0+ **£3,234** (£962; £481; £240) **Stalls** Low

Form RPR

0412 **1** **Haajes**[19] 2479 9-9-6 **72** (v) MickyFenton 2 81
(Paul Midgley) *trckd ldrs on inner: hdwy wl over 1f out: swtchd rt and rdn ent fnl f: styd on u.p to ld last 50yds* **7/1**

0431 **2** 1/2 **Bronze Beau**[10] 2736 6-9-11 **77** 6ex (t) JamesSullivan 6 84
(Kristin Stubbs) *led: rdn over 1f out: drvn ins fnl f: hdd and no ex last 50yds* **11/2**[3]

2031 **3** 1 1/2 **Spykes Bay (USA)**[11] 2703 4-9-7 **73** 6ex (bt) RobertWinston 9 75
(Mrs K Burke) *hld up: hdwy on inner wl over 1f out: sn rdn and styd on fnl f: nrst fin* **3/1**[1]

3524 **4** 1 **Phoenix Clubs (IRE)**[21] 2410 4-9-7 **73** (p) BarryMcHugh 8 71
(Paul Midgley) *trckd ldrs: hdwy on outer 2f out: rdn and ch over 1f out: drvn and one pce ins fnl f* **9/1**

-534 **5** *shd* **Red Cape (FR)**[4] 2914 10-9-3 **69** PJMcDonald 5 67
(Ruth Carr) *prom: rdn along 2f out: drvn over 1f out and sn one pce* **9/2**[2]

06-0 **6** 3 **Imperial Legend (IRE)**[31] 2122 4-9-2 **73** (p) ShirleyTeasdale(5) 4 60
(David Nicholls) *trckd ldr: hdwy 2f out: rdn over 1f out: wknd ent fnl f* **14/1**

0012 **7** 2 1/4 **Mey Blossom**[11] 2703 8-8-5 **62** (p) GeorgeChaloner(5) 7 41
(Richard Whitaker) *chsd ldrs: rdn along 2f out: sn wknd* **8/1**

-004 **8** 1 1/2 **Commanche Raider (IRE)**[11] 2702 6-9-4 **70** (b) PaulMulrennan 3 44
(Michael Dods) *dwlt: a in rr* **9/2**[2]

1m 4.46s (1.16) **Going Correction** +0.225s/f (Good) **8** Ran SP% **117.0**
Speed ratings (Par 103): **99,98,95,94,94 89,85,83**
toteswingers 1&2 £8.70, 1&3 £9.10, 2&3 £6.00 CSF £46.10 CT £142.56 TOTE £6.50: £3.50, £1.90, £1.30; EX 56.70 Trifecta £180.80 Pool: £545.27 - 2.26 winning tickets..
Owner Sandfield Racing **Bred** Irish National Stud **Trained** Westow, N Yorks

FOCUS
A fair handicap and routine form.
T/Jkpt: Not won. T/Plt: £372.00 to a £1 stake. Pool £68,363.81 - 134.14 winning tickets. T/Qpdt: £39.30 to a £1 stake. Pool £4641.52 - 87.20 winning tickets. JR

3070 - 3072a (Foreign Racing) - See Raceform Interactive

2287 LEOPARDSTOWN (L-H)
Friday, June 7

OFFICIAL GOING: Good to firm

3073a SEAMUS & ROSEMARY MCGRATH MEMORIAL SAVAL BEG STKS (LISTED RACE) 1m 6f
7:20 (7:20) 4-Y-0+ **£25,101** (£7,337; £3,475; £1,158)

RPR

1 **Pale Mimosa (IRE)**[244] 6896 4-9-3 **104** PatSmullen 2 110+
(D K Weld, Ire) *chsd ldrs: mod 3rd 1/2-way: hdwy to cl on ldrs over 3f out: prog on outer to chal 1 1/2f out: led narrowly ent fnl f and styd on wl towards fin* **5/4**[1]

2 2 1/2 **Missunited (IRE)**[19] 2485 6-9-0 **100** SeamieHeffernan 6 103
(Michael Winters, Ire) *chsd ldr in 2nd: 3 l bhd at 1/2-way and clr of remainder: rdn into st and got on terms briefly over 1f out: sn hdd narrowly and no ex u.p ins fnl f: kpt on same pce* **4/1**[3]

3 1 3/4 **El Salvador (IRE)**[19] 2485 4-9-5 **105** (p) JosephO'Brien 4 106
(A P O'Brien, Ire) *attempted to make all: 3 l clr 1/2-way: reduced advantage fr over 3f out: rdn into st and sn strly pressed: hdd ent fnl f and dropped to 3rd: kpt on same pce* **5/2**[2]

4 22 **Zafarqand (IRE)**[12] 2691 5-9-5 **82** FMBerry 1 75
(Patrick O Brady, Ire) *hld up: mod 6th 1/2-way: pushed along fr over 3f out and no imp on clr ldrs into st: wnt mod 4th ins fnl f: kpt on* **33/1**

5 3 **Fleur De Nuit (IRE)**[5] 2903 8-9-0 **88** DeclanMcDonogh 7 66
(John Bleahen, Ire) *hld up: mod 4th 1/2-way: rdn over 3f out and no imp: dropped to 5th ins fnl f: one pce towards fin* **8/1**

6 5 1/2 **Fully Funded (USA)**[41] 6580 8-9-5 **93** EmmetMcNamara 3 63
(Noel Meade, Ire) *hld up: dropped to rr after 1/2-way: rdn and no imp fr over 3f out: trailing into st: nvr a factor* **33/1**

7 26 **Chicago (IRE)**[33] 2062 4-9-5 **96** TadhgO'Shea 5 26
(John Patrick Shanahan, Ire) *hld up towards rr: mod 5th 1/2-way: rdn over 3f out and no imp: wknd: t.o* **16/1**

2m 54.81s (-6.19) **Going Correction** -0.15s/f (Firm) **7** Ran SP% **115.9**
Speed ratings: **111,109,108,96,94 91,76**
CSF £6.94 TOTE £1.70: £1.20, £1.70; DF 6.60.
Owner Dr R Lambe **Bred** Irish National Stud **Trained** The Curragh, Co Kildare

FOCUS
Run at strong gallop, this was a proper test of stamina. The form is rated around the first three.

3074 - 3076a (Foreign Racing) - See Raceform Interactive

2765 BEVERLEY (R-H)
Saturday, June 8

OFFICIAL GOING: Good to firm (9.0)
Rail around bottom bend moved out adding 18yds to races on Round course.
Wind: Virtually nil Weather: Cloudy

3077 HAPPY BIRTHDAY GRAHAM HALLETT MEDIAN AUCTION MAIDEN STKS (DIV I) 5f
2:00 (2:01) (Class 5) 2-Y-0 **£3,234** (£962; £481; £240) **Stalls** Low

Form RPR

0 **1** **Anjaal**[34] 2048 2-9-5 0 DaneO'Neill 5 85+
(Richard Hannon) *sn trcking ldr: cl up 2f out: shkn up to ld ent fnl f: sn rdn clr: styd on strly* **1/1**[1]

2 4 **Alpine Flower (IRE)** 2-9-0 0 DuranFentiman 6 66+
(Tim Easterby) *trckd ldrs: hdwy on outer to chse ldng pair 2f out: rdn over 1f out: kpt on fnl f* **33/1**

32 **3** 1 1/2 **Lord Clyde**[8] 2830 2-9-5 0 TonyHamilton 2 65
(Richard Fahey) *led: jnd 2f out and sn rdn along: hdd ent fnl f: kpt on same pce* **2/1**[2]

5 **4** 6 **Tamayuz Dream (IRE)**[19] 2497 2-9-5 0 LiamJones 4 44
(Mark Johnston) *chsd ldrs: rdn along 2f out: sn one pce* **15/2**[3]

5 2 **Centre Haafhd** 2-9-5 0 HarryBentley 9 36
(David Barron) *a towards rr* **25/1**

6 1/2 **Sakhalin Star (IRE)** 2-9-5 0 MickyFenton 3 35
(John Quinn) *chsd ldrs on inner: rdn along over 2f out: sn wknd* **40/1**

7 4 **Sukari Gold (IRE)** 2-9-0 0 PhillipMakin 1 15
(Kevin Ryan) *in tch on inner: rdn along 1/2-way: sn outpcd* **10/1**

1m 1.4s (-2.10) **Going Correction** -0.375s/f (Firm) **7** Ran SP% **113.4**
Speed ratings (Par 93): **101,94,92,82,79 78,72**
Tote Swingers: 1&2 £3.40, 2&3 £40.70, 1&3 £6.20 CSF £40.77 TOTE £1.70: £1.20, £6.80; EX 27.30 Trifecta £140.40 Pool: £1,363.79 - 7.28 winning tickets..
Owner Hamdan Al Maktoum **Bred** Carmel Stud **Trained** East Everleigh, Wilts

FOCUS
Not much depth to this maiden but the winner looks a nice type. The third is the key to the level.

3078 STRAWBERRY FILLIES' H'CAP 5f
2:35 (2:35) (Class 5) (0-75,75) 4-Y-0+ **£3,234** (£962; £481; £240) **Stalls** Low

Form RPR

-313 **1** **Black Annis Bower**[12] 2702 5-8-10 **64** JamesSullivan 6 72
(Michael Easterby) *trckd ldr: cl up 2f out: rdn over 1f out: kpt on u.p to ld ins fnl f: sn drvn and hld on wl* **7/1**

0-0 **2** *hd* **Dreaming Of Rubies**[61] 1431 4-9-4 **72** (t[1]) DaneO'Neill 9 79
(Ben Haslam) *sn trcking ldrs: hdwy on outer wl over 1f out: rdn appr fnl f: styd on strly towards fin* **20/1**

16-0 **3** 1/2 **Cats Eyes**[17] 2561 4-9-4 **75** RossAtkinson(3) 2 80
(Robert Cowell) *trckd ldrs on inner: effrt and nt clr run wl over 1f out: sn rdn: squeezed through ent fnl f: kpt on* **12/1**

0326 **4** 1 1/2 **Diamond Blue**[5] 2914 5-9-0 **68** (e[1]) PhillipMakin 8 68
(Richard Whitaker) *rrd and hmpd s: bhd: swtchd to outer and rdn over 1f out: styd on strly fnl f: nrst fin* **10/3**[2]

0-11 **5** 1/2 **Gowanharry (IRE)**[18] 2542 4-9-6 **74** PaulMulrennan 3 72
(Michael Dods) *led: pushed along and jnd wl over 1f out: rdn ent fnl f: sn edgd lft and hdd: wknd last 100yds* **9/4**[1]

-000 **6** 1/2 **Elusive Bonus (IRE)**[11] 2755 4-8-12 **73** KevinStott(7) 4 69
(David O'Meara) *in tch: rdn along 2f out: drvn and no imp appr fnl f* **14/1**

1-54 **7** 1 **Passionada**[18] 2550 4-9-0 **68** RoystonFfrench 7 61
(Ed McMahon) *wnt lft s: in tch: hdwy over 2f out: rdn along wl over 1f out: sn no imp* **11/2**[3]

6-30 **8** *nk* **Comptonspirit**[12] 2703 9-8-13 **67** DuranFentiman 1 59
(Brian Baugh) *chsd ldrs: hdwy 2f out: rdn wl over 1f out: grad wknd* **14/1**

-301 **9** 2 1/4 **Needy McCredie**[8] 2835 7-8-3 **60** JulieBurke(3) 5 43
(James Turner) *s.i.s: a in rr* **11/1**

1m 1.38s (-2.12) **Going Correction** -0.375s/f (Firm) **9** Ran SP% **115.9**
Speed ratings (Par 100): **101,100,99,97,96 95,94,93,90**
Tote Swingers: 1&2 £16.40, 2&3 £17.80, 1&3 £30.30 CSF £133.03 CT £1652.70 TOTE £6.60: £2.40, £6.20, £3.80; EX 111.00 Trifecta £504.40 Pool: £1,112.13 - 1.65 winning tickets..
Owner Mrs A Jarvis **Bred** Mrs A Jarvis **Trained** Sheriff Hutton, N Yorks
■ Stewards' Enquiry : Ross Atkinson two-day ban; used whip above permitted level (23rd-24th June).

FOCUS
Quite competitive for the grade featuring a few in-form sprinters, but the time was modest. The winner's best run since she was a 3yo.

3079 BRIAN YEARDLEY CONTINENTAL TWO YEAR OLD TROPHY CONDITIONS STKS (C&G) 5f
3:10 (3:10) (Class 2) 2-Y-0
£9,337 (£2,796; £1,398; £699; £349; £175) **Stalls** Low

Form RPR

3U **1** **Langavat (IRE)**[14] 2653 2-8-12 0 DaneO'Neill 1 85
(Richard Hannon) *mde all: rdn over 1f out: drvn ins fnl f: hld on gamely towards fin* **5/4**[1]

2 *nk* **My Catch (IRE)** 2-8-9 0 HarryBentley 5 81+
(David Brown) *dwlt: sn trcking ldrs on inner: nt clr run and swtchd lft 2f out: hdwy to chal over 1f out: sn rdn and ev ch tl no ex nr fin* **10/1**

1 **3** *nk* **Supplicant**[25] 2337 2-9-2 0 TonyHamilton 7 87
(Richard Fahey) *chsd ldng pair on outer: hdwy over 2f out: rdn along and sltly outpcd wl over 1f out: styd on strly fnl f* **4/1**[2]

610 **4** 4 **Zalzilah**[7] 2863 2-8-12 0 PaulMulrennan 2 69
(James Tate) *cl up: chal 2f out: sn rdn and wknd appr fnl f* **4/1**[2]

14 **5** 4 1/2 **Suzi's Connoisseur**[7] 2877 2-9-0 0 LiamJones 3 54
(Mark Johnston) *chsd ldrs: rdn along wl over 1f out: sn wknd* **9/2**[3]

3 **6** 6 **Nevada Blue**[12] 2701 2-8-12 0 BarryMcHugh 6 31
(Tony Coyle) *a in rr: rdn along and outpcd fnl 2f* **20/1**

1m 0.89s (-2.61) **Going Correction** -0.375s/f (Firm) 2y crse rec **6** Ran SP% **116.5**
Speed ratings (Par 99): **105,104,104,97,90 80**
Tote Swingers: 1&2 £3.20, 2&3 £4.80, 1&3 £1.10 CSF £15.97 TOTE £2.60: £1.30, £5.70; EX 16.50 Trifecta £65.30 Pool: £1,689.78 - 19.40 winning tickets..
Owner Kennet Valley Thoroughbreds II **Bred** Tally-Ho Stud **Trained** East Everleigh, Wilts

FOCUS
A good quality juvenile conditions race in which the first three were clear. The form could be worth 5lb more.

3080 BRITISH STALLION STUDS BRANTINGHAM E B F CONDITIONS STKS 1m 100y
3:45 (3:46) (Class 4) 3-Y-O **£6,225** (£1,864; £932; £466) **Stalls** Low

Form RPR
0-46 **1** **Jalaa (IRE)**[21] 2438 3-9-1 84 DaneO'Neill 4 97
(Richard Hannon) *set stdy pce: qckng 3f out: rdn and qcknd again wl over 1f out: styd on strly fnl f* **9/4**[2]
-646 **2** 2 ¼ **Maxentius (IRE)**[35] 2023 3-9-1 99 LukeMorris 1 92
(Peter Chapple-Hyam) *trckd ldng pair: effrt on inner 3f out: swtchd lft and rdn over 2f out: drvn to chse wnr over 1f out: no imp* **7/4**[1]
-235 **3** 2 ¾ **Asgardella (IRE)**[22] 2412 3-8-10 90 TonyHamilton 3 81
(Richard Fahey) *sn trcking wnr: effrt 3f out: rdn along over 2f out: drvn over 1f out and sn one pce* **7/2**[3]
-465 **4** ½ **Top Notch Tonto (IRE)**[28] 2259 3-8-12 89 NeilFarley(3) 2 85
(Ian McInnes) *t.k.h: hld up in rr: pushed along and hdwy on outer 3f out: rdn over 2f out: drvn wl over 1f out and sn one pce* **4/1**
1m 44.64s (-2.96) **Going Correction** -0.275s/f (Firm) **4** Ran SP% **109.4**
Speed ratings (Par 101): **103,100,98,97**
CSF £6.61 TOTE £3.00; EX 6.40 Trifecta £12.80 Pool: £1,195.43 - 69.72 winning tickets..
Owner Hamdan Al Maktoum **Bred** Airlie Stud And R N Clay **Trained** East Everleigh, Wilts
FOCUS
Much hinged on who would lead this small-field event, and in the end the winner got an easy lead. A tricky race to assess, rated loosely around the third.

3081 EMPRESS HULL 25 YEAR CELEBRATION H'CAP 1m 100y
4:20 (4:20) (Class 5) (0-70,70) 4-Y-O+ **£3,234** (£962; £481; £240) **Stalls** Low

Form RPR
/00- **1** **Joyful Sound (IRE)**[277] 5917 5-8-5 54 BarryMcHugh 2 62
(Brian Ellison) *mde all: rdn clr wl over 1f out: drvn fnl f and kpt on gamely* **11/1**
-000 **2** ¾ **District Attorney (IRE)**[18] 2537 4-8-2 51 oh1 DuranFentiman 1 57
(Chris Fairhurst) *hld up towards rr: hdwy wl over 2f out: rdn to chse ldrs over 1f out: drvn and styd on wl fnl f* **40/1**
0034 **3** 1 **Rockweiller**[44] 1775 6-8-7 56 (v) LukeMorris 6 60
(Steve Gollings) *trckd ldrs: pushed along over 3f out: rdn over 2f out: drvn to chse wnr over 1f out: kpt on u.p fnl f* **7/2**[1]
0-03 **4** 4 **Last Destination (IRE)**[5] 2911 5-8-3 55 DeclanCannon(3) 9 50
(Nigel Tinkler) *hld up in rr: hdwy over 2f out: rdn over 1f out: kpt on fnl f: nrst fin* **8/1**
-022 **5** nse **Eastward Ho**[11] 2753 5-9-4 67 TonyHamilton 8 62
(Jason Ward) *trckd wnr: effrt 3f out: rdn along over 2f out: drvn and wknd over 1f out* **4/1**[2]
60-0 **6** ¾ **Pivotman**[60] 1442 5-9-7 70 JamesSullivan 3 63
(Michael Easterby) *trckd ldrs: hdwy 3f out: chsd ldrs 2f out: rdn over 1f out: wknd ent fnl f* **9/2**[3]
2600 **7** 2 ½ **Firefly**[2] 3027 4-8-2 51 oh3 (b) PatrickMathers 5 38
(John Weymes) *a towards rr* **33/1**
4-00 **8** 1 ¼ **Save The Bees**[18] 2551 5-8-11 63 NeilFarley(3) 4 47
(Declan Carroll) *in tch: hdwy over 3f out: rdn to chse ldrs 2f out: sn drvn and wknd* **6/1**
4056 **9** ¾ **Sir George (IRE)**[52] 1603 8-8-0 52 ow1 (p) SimonPearce(3) 10 35
(Suzzanne France) *hld up: a towards rr* **20/1**
0241 **10** 4 ½ **Copperwood**[9] 2807 8-9-7 70 LiamJones 7 42
(Mark Johnston) *prom: hdwy and cl up 3f out: sn rdn and wknd* **11/2**
1m 44.68s (-2.92) **Going Correction** -0.275s/f (Firm) **10** Ran SP% **119.7**
Speed ratings (Par 103): **103,102,101,97,97 96,93,92,91,87**
Tote Swingers: 1&2 £40.50, 2&3 £50.60, 1&3 £13.70 CSF £387.15 CT £1900.38 TOTE £14.90: £3.50, £15.70, £1.60; EX 506.50 Trifecta £1216.00 Part won. Pool: £1,621.41 - 0.06 winning units..
Owner Mr & Mrs E J Dolan-Abrahams **Bred** Rathbarry Stud **Trained** Norton, N Yorks
FOCUS
Just ordinary handicap form. The winner made all and is rated back to his previous best.

3082 BERYL AND JOE TURNER MEMORIAL STKS (H'CAP) 7f 100y
4:55 (4:58) (Class 5) (0-70,66) 3-Y-O **£3,234** (£962; £481; £240) **Stalls** Low

Form RPR
0-51 **1** **Lexington Blue**[17] 2581 3-8-9 54 TonyHamilton 12 60+
(David O'Meara) *in tch: hdwy wl over 2f out: rdn wl over 1f out: drvn and styd on wl fnl f to ld nr fin* **8/1**[3]
4233 **2** nk **Polish Crown**[5] 2916 3-9-5 64 LiamJones 1 69
(Mark Johnston) *trckd ldrs: hdwy 1/2-way: led wl over 2f out: rdn clr over 1f out: drvn ins fnl f: hdd and no ex nr fin* **5/2**[2]
606 **3** 1 ¼ **My Claire**[11] 2762 3-8-4 49 HarryBentley 3 51+
(Nigel Tinkler) *hld up in rr whn n.m.r on inner after 1 1/2f: swtchd rt to outer and gd hdwy 2f out: sn rdn and str run to chse ldrs whn hung rt ins fnl f: kpt on: nrst fin* **18/1**
0-55 **4** 1 **Relight My Fire**[15] 2616 3-9-3 62 MickyFenton 4 61+
(Tim Easterby) *hld up towards rr: hdwy 2f out: nt clr run over 1f out: swtchd lft and rdn ent fnl f: fin wl* **16/1**
2221 **5** nk **Clock On Tom**[10] 2770 3-9-7 66 PaulMulrennan 9 65
(Michael Easterby) *trckd ldrs: hdwy wl over 2f out: rdn wl over 1f out: sn drvn and one pce ent fnl f* **9/4**[1]
-000 **6** ½ **Blue Clumber**[44] 1786 3-8-5 53 (t) DeclanCannon(3) 2 50
(Shaun Harris) *chsd ldrs on inner: nt clr run and swtchd lft over 1f out: sn rdn and kpt on same pce* **33/1**
0004 **7** 1 **Look On By**[19] 2501 3-8-3 55 KevinStott(7) 7 50
(Ruth Carr) *dwlt and in rr: hdwy 2f out: rdn and n.m.r over 1f out: kpt on fnl f: nrst fin* **16/1**
0-26 **8** ¾ **Annie Gogh**[11] 2756 3-9-2 61 DuranFentiman 11 54
(Tim Easterby) *hld up towards rr: hdwy wl over 2f out: rdn over 1f out: no imp fnl f* **16/1**
-656 **9** ½ **Out Of The Blocks**[26] 2318 3-8-7 52 PatrickMathers 14 44
(Ruth Carr) *hld up in rr: sme hdwy on outer over 2f out: rdn wl over 1f out: n.d* **25/1**
5-00 **10** 3 ¼ **Dewi Chinta (IRE)**[11] 2756 3-8-8 56 (b) JulieBurke(3) 6 40
(Kevin Ryan) *cl up: led 1/2-way: rdn along and hdd wl over 2f out: sn wknd* **33/1**
0300 **11** 1 ½ **Fishlake Rebel**[11] 2742 3-8-3 48 JamesSullivan 10 28
(Ruth Carr) *nvr bttr than midfield* **12/1**
00-2 **12** 2 **Lucy Minaj**[15] 2635 3-8-7 52 RoystonFfrench 13 27
(Bryan Smart) *prom: effrt on outer wl over 2f out: rdn along wl over 1f out: sn wknd* **10/1**
5152 **13** 44 **Roland**[101] 811 3-9-5 64 PhillipMakin 8
(Kevin Ryan) *sn led: hdd 1/2-way: rdn along wl over 2f out: sn wknd: bhd and eased fnl f* **20/1**
1m 32.59s (-1.21) **Going Correction** -0.275s/f (Firm) **13** Ran SP% **124.6**
Speed ratings (Par 99): **95,94,93,92,91 91,90,89,88,84 83,80,30**
Tote Swingers: 1&2 £5.70, 2&3 £52.40, 1&3 £52.40 CSF £28.28 CT £378.56 TOTE £7.30: £1.90, £1.90, £5.90; EX 30.20 Trifecta £1312.10 Part won. Pool: £1,749.47 - 0.28 winning units..
Owner Middleham Park Racing XLIX & Partners **Bred** The National Stud Blakeney Club **Trained** Nawton, N Yorks
FOCUS
Very modest fare, but evenly run. The winner built on his Southwell success.

3083 VERY BRITISH SING SONG AFTER RACING H'CAP 1m 1f 207y
5:30 (5:30) (Class 5) (0-75,75) 4-Y-O+ **£3,408** (£1,006; £503) **Stalls** Low

Form RPR
42-4 **1** **Christmas Light**[18] 2551 6-9-2 70 DaneO'Neill 7 81
(Brian Ellison) *hld up: stdy hdwy over 4f out: chsd ldrs 2f out: rdn to ld appr fnl f: styd on strly* **4/1**[2]
1112 **2** 1 ¾ **Apache Glory (USA)**[26] 2311 5-9-7 75 (p) LukeMorris 8 83
(John Stimpson) *hld up in rr: stdy hdwy over 3f out: effrt to chse ldrs over 1f out: rdn to chal ent fnl f: sn drvn and kpt on same pce* **4/1**[2]
6212 **3** 1 ¼ **Saint Thomas (IRE)**[19] 2498 6-9-3 71 PaulMulrennan 9 76
(John Mackie) *trckd ldrs: hdwy to chse ldr 2f out: led briefly wl over 1f out: hdd and drvn jst over 1f out: kpt on same pce* **3/1**[1]
4-00 **4** 8 **Tribal Myth (IRE)**[11] 2739 6-8-3 60 (b) JulieBurke(3) 4 49
(Kevin Ryan) *hld up towards rr: hdwy wl over 2f out: rdn to chse ldrs and edgd rt wl over 1f out: sn no imp* **7/1**
30-2 **5** 2 **Triple Eight (IRE)**[18] 2539 5-8-10 71 (b) EvaMoscrop(7) 1 56
(Philip Kirby) *sn led and clr: rdn along over 2f out: hdd & wknd wl over 1f out* **11/2**[3]
0045 **6** 9 **Lady Macduff (IRE)**[25] 2339 4-9-6 74 LiamJones 3 41
(Mark Johnston) *hld up: hdwy to chse ldrs whn n.m.r over 2f out: sn rdn and wknd* **8/1**
6420 **7** ¾ **Dream Walker (FR)**[7] 2889 4-8-0 57 NeilFarley(3) 6 23
(Ian McInnes) *chsd ldr: rdn along wl over 2f out: sn wknd* **16/1**
4510 **8** 113 **Going Grey (IRE)**[42] 1836 4-8-5 59 (p) BarryMcHugh 2
(Richard Fahey) *chsd ldrs on inner: lost pl over 4f out: sn bhd and heavily eased* **17/2**
2m 4.07s (-2.93) **Going Correction** -0.275s/f (Firm) **8** Ran SP% **120.4**
Speed ratings (Par 103): **100,98,97,91,89 82,81,**
Tote Swingers: 1&2 £4.30, 2&3 £1.40, 1&3 £1.60 CSF £21.65 CT £55.68 TOTE £5.00: £1.80, £1.70, £1.40; EX 22.60 Trifecta £75.30 Pool: £1,448.85 - 14.42 winning tickets..
Owner Mrs Lynne Lumley **Bred** Rabbah Bloodstock Limited **Trained** Norton, N Yorks
■ Stewards' Enquiry : Luke Morris two-day ban; careless riding (23rd-24th June).
FOCUS
This was teed up perfectly for the hold-up horses. The winner is rated to his best, with the third helping with the standard.

3084 HAPPY BIRTHDAY GRAHAM HALLETT MEDIAN AUCTION MAIDEN STKS (DIV II) 5f
6:00 (6:04) (Class 5) 2-Y-O **£3,234** (£962; £481; £240) **Stalls** Low

Form RPR
20 **1** **Musical Molly (IRE)**[23] 2401 2-9-0 0 DaneO'Neill 6 65
(Brian Ellison) *cl up: rdn to ld jst over 1f out: drvn ins fnl f: hld on wl towards fin* **5/4**[1]
0 **2** nk **Midnight Muscida (IRE)**[11] 2751 2-9-0 0 DuranFentiman 8 64
(Tim Easterby) *trckd ldrs: hdwy 2f out: rdn over 1f out: styd on to chal ins fnl f: ev ch tl no ex nr fin* **25/1**
346 **3** 1 ¼ **Will To Survive (IRE)**[12] 2715 2-9-5 0 RobbieFitzpatrick 5 64
(Richard Guest) *slt ld: rdn along 2f out: hdd jst over 1f out: kpt on same pce ins fnl f* **20/1**
463 **4** ¾ **Princess Tamay (IRE)**[9] 2793 2-9-0 0 LiamJones 3 57
(Mark Johnston) *trckd ldrs: effrt 2f out: sn rdn and kpt on same pce fnl f* **11/4**[2]
5 1 **Baileys Forever** 2-9-0 0 JamesSullivan 1 53
(James Given) *chsd ldrs on inner: rdn along 2f out: no imp appr fnl f* **11/1**
6 2 ½ **Local Flier** 2-8-11 0 NeilFarley(3) 2 44+
(Ian McInnes) *dwlt and in rr: swtchd wd and hdwy 1/2-way: rdn to chse ldrs 2f out: sn no imp* **28/1**
7 1 **Mornin Mr Norris** 2-9-5 0 MickyFenton 7 46+
(John Quinn) *s.i.s: a bhd* **8/1**
0 **8** ½ **Who Followed Who**[14] 2670 2-9-5 0 PaulMulrennan 9 44
(Nigel Tinkler) *a towards rr* **4/1**[3]
1m 4.42s (0.92) **Going Correction** -0.375s/f (Firm) **8** Ran SP% **122.6**
Speed ratings (Par 93): **77,76,74,73,71 67,66,65**
Tote Swingers: 1&2 £25.70, 2&3 £14.50, 1&3 £5.80 CSF £44.08 TOTE £2.30: £1.80, £5.20, £4.60; EX 48.80 Trifecta £320.40 Pool: £2,190.92 - 5.12 winning tickets..
Owner Mrs J A Martin **Bred** W Maxwell Ervine **Trained** Norton, N Yorks
FOCUS
Probably just ordinary maiden form with only a couple of lengths covering the first four home.
T/Plt: £2,136.80 to a £1 stake. Pool: £46,835.00 - 16.00 winning units. T/Qpdt: £247.10 to a £1 stake. Pool: £2,805.00 - 8.40 winning units. JR

2830 CATTERICK (L-H)
Saturday, June 8

OFFICIAL GOING: Good to firm (9.2)

3085 WIN BIG WITH TOTEJACKPOT AT TOTEPOOL.COM CLASSIFIED CLAIMING STKS 1m 3f 214y
2:25 (2:25) (Class 6) 4-Y-O+ **£2,726** (£805; £402) **Stalls** Low

Form RPR
4213 **1** **Activate**[3] 2973 6-8-11 75 (p) DanielTudhope 3 78
(Keith Dalgleish) *mde all: qcknd clr over 2f out: kpt on wl fnl f: unchal* **13/8**[1]
0-01 **2** 2 ¾ **Reve De Nuit (USA)**[17] 2579 7-9-4 73 MichaelMetcalfe(3) 8 83
(Mrs K Burke) *in tch: hdwy to chse wnr over 4f out: effrt over 2f out: one pce fr over 1f out* **4/1**[3]
-510 **3** 1 ½ **Meetings Man (IRE)**[14] 2673 6-8-5 68 (p) AndrewElliott 2 65
(Micky Hammond) *in tch: drvn and outpcd over 3f out: rallied over 1f out: kpt on fnl f: nt pce to chal* **9/1**
2115 **4** 4 **Gabrial's Hope (FR)**[32] 2136 4-7-12 64 (t) DarrenEgan(3) 1 55
(David Simcock) *t.k.h: cl up: drvn and outpcd over 2f out: btn over 1f out* **8/1**

The Form Book Flat, Raceform Ltd, Compton, RG20 6NL.

4-21 **5** 1/2 **Just Lille (IRE)**[32] 2118 10-8-11 75....(p) PJMcDonald 7 64
(Ann Duffield) *prom: drvn and lost pl 1/2-way: effrt u.p 3f out: sn no imp* **5/2**[2]
00-0 **6** 14 **Hawk Mountain (UAE)**[32] 2118 8-9-7 75.... MichaelO'Connell 6 51
(John Quinn) *hld up: drvn and outpcd over 4f out: n.d after* **16/1**
040- **7** 10 **Escape Artist**[37] 4209 6-7-12 40....(p) RaulDaSilva(3) 4 15
(David Thompson) *chsd wnr to over 4f out: drvn and wknd over 3f out* **100/1**
045 **8** 1/2 **Revolving World (IRE)**[109] 714 10-7-8 44....(t) NoelGarbutt(7) 5 15
(Lee James) *s.i.s: bhd: rdn over 4f out: nvr on terms* **100/1**

2m 33.66s (-5.24) **Going Correction** -0.225s/f (Firm) **8** Ran SP% **115.6**
Speed ratings (Par 101): **108,106,105,102,102 92,86,85**
Tote Swingers: 1&2 £1.10, 2&3 £11.70, 1&3 £4.70 CSF £8.69 TOTE £2.40: £1.20, £1.10, £3.80; EX 8.40 Trifecta £33.40 Pool: £514.65 - 11.54 winning tickets..Meetings Man claimed by Miss Ali Brewer £7,000.
Owner Straightline Construction Ltd **Bred** Card Bloodstock **Trained** Carluke, S Lanarks

FOCUS
A decent contest for the grade, run at a sound pace. The form is rated around the winner to his recent form.

3086 YOUR FAVOURITE POOL BETS AT TOTEPOOL.COM MEDIAN AUCTION MAIDEN STKS 5f
3:00 (3:00) (Class 6) 3-Y-O **£2,726** (£805; £402) **Stalls** Low

Form RPR
24-3 **1** **Dream Cast (IRE)**[12] 2719 3-9-2 75.... DarrenEgan(3) 1 77
(David Simcock) *t.k.h: prom: effrt and rdn over 1f out: squeezed through to ld ins fnl f: kpt on strly* **7/4**[2]
-35 **2** 1 3/4 **Sixty Minutes**[12] 2722 3-9-5 0....(t) SeanLevey 5 70
(David Brown) *pressed ldr: rdn 1/2-way: ev ch and edgd lft over 1f out: kpt on ins fnl f: nt pce of wnr* **6/1**[3]
4004 **3** 3 **Queen Flush (IRE)**[7] 2861 3-9-0 59....(p) AdrianNicholls 6 54
(David Nicholls) *led: rdn 2f out: hdd ins fnl f: sn outpcd* **12/1**
5-25 **4** 3 **Tomintoul Magic (IRE)**[21] 2437 3-9-0 72.... DanielTudhope 2 43
(Sir Henry Cecil) *dwlt: sn in tch: hdwy on outside 1/2-way: hung lft and wknd wl over 1f out* **6/5**[1]
0 **5** 1 3/4 **Vonn (IRE)**[12] 2719 3-9-0 0.... DavidAllan 4 37
(Tim Easterby) *chsd ldrs: rdn along 1/2-way: wknd wl over 1f out* **16/1**
0- **6** 9 **Partner's Gold (IRE)**[293] 5382 3-9-5 0.... PaddyAspell 3
(Alan Berry) *sn bhd: struggling over 3f out: sn lost tch* **100/1**

59.59s (-0.21) **Going Correction** -0.025s/f (Good) **6** Ran SP% **110.7**
Speed ratings (Par 97): **100,97,92,87,84 70**
Tote Swingers: 1&2 £3.00, 2&3 £12.30, 1&3 £4.00 CSF £12.16 TOTE £2.70: £1.20, £2.00; EX 11.10 Trifecta £52.50 Pool: £775.65 - 11.06 winning tickets..
Owner Khalifa Dasmal **Bred** Limetree Stud **Trained** Newmarket, Suffolk

FOCUS
A moderate maiden run at a fair pace. With the favourite below par, it proved easy enough for the winner and he's been rated to form.

3087 TOTEQUADPOT FOUR PLACES IN FOUR RACES H'CAP 7f
3:35 (3:35) (Class 4) (0-80,80) 4-Y-O+ **£6,476** (£1,912; £956) **Stalls** Centre

Form RPR
0302 **1** **West Leake Hare (IRE)**[8] 2836 4-8-3 62.... PaulQuinn 11 72
(David Nicholls) *t.k.h: hld up in midfield on outside: hdwy to ld over 1f out: edgd lft: kpt on wl fnl f* **7/1**
20-0 **2** 1/2 **Robert The Painter (IRE)**[21] 2450 5-8-13 72....(v) DanielTudhope 6 80
(David O'Meara) *prom: effrt and ev ch over 1f out: sn chsng wnr: kpt on fnl f* **9/2**[1]
64 **3** hd **Decent Fella (IRE)**[8] 2837 7-8-6 65....(t) JimmyQuinn 5 72
(Violet M Jordan) *hld up in midfield: effrt and pushed along 2f out: kpt on ins fnl f: nrst fin* **9/1**
3050 **4** 1 1/2 **Holy Angel (IRE)**[14] 2663 4-8-9 68....(e) FrederikTylicki 3 71
(Tim Easterby) *hld up in midfield on ins: effrt over 2f out: n.m.r briefly over 1f out: kpt on: nt pce to chal* **18/1**
3425 **5** shd **Hierarch (IRE)**[31] 2163 6-8-4 66.... DarrenEgan(3) 2 69
(David Simcock) *hld up: rdn over 2f out: gd hdwy fnl f: nrst fin* **13/2**[3]
000- **6** hd **Ewell Place (IRE)**[203] 7769 4-9-7 80.... AdrianNicholls 1 82
(David Nicholls) *in tch on ins: rdn over 2f out: effrt over 1f out: outpcd ins fnl f* **25/1**
13-0 **7** 1 **Fayr Fall (IRE)**[33] 2081 4-9-0 73....(p) DavidAllan 8 72
(Tim Easterby) *cl up tl rdn and no ex over 1f out* **16/1**
-225 **8** 1 1/2 **Majestic Dream (IRE)**[14] 2659 5-8-7 73....(v) MatthewHopkins(7) 4 68
(Michael Easterby) *led: rdn over 2f out: hdd over 1f out: sn outpcd* **5/1**[2]
0-40 **9** 3/4 **Orpsie Boy (IRE)**[17] 2573 10-8-13 72.... PJMcDonald 7 65
(Ruth Carr) *hld up in midfield: drvn and outpcd over 2f out: sn btn* **16/1**
0631 **10** 1 **Smalljohn**[12] 2707 7-8-8 72....(v) JustinNewman(5) 10 63
(Bryan Smart) *cl up on outside: rdn over 2f out: wknd wl over 1f out* **9/2**[1]
03-0 **11** 1/2 **Orbit The Moon (IRE)**[35] 2028 5-8-11 77....(t) ConnorBeasley(7) 9 66
(Michael Dods) *hld up: rdn and outpcd over 2f out: sn btn* **10/1**

1m 25.08s (-1.92) **Going Correction** -0.225s/f (Firm) **11** Ran SP% **118.8**
Speed ratings (Par 105): **101,100,100,98,98 98,97,95,94,93 92**
Tote Swingers: 1&2 £12.70, 2&3 £11.30, 1&3 £22.60 CSF £38.96 CT £296.81 TOTE £8.00: £2.40, £1.80, £3.70; EX 56.90 Trifecta £305.40 Part won. Pool: £407.25 - 0.68 winning units..
Owner Neil Yeoman & Mrs Alex Nicholls **Bred** Churchtown House Stud **Trained** Sessay, N Yorks

FOCUS
Plenty of pace on for this open handicap. The winner is rated back to last year's form.

3088 TOTEPOOL.COM H'CAP 7f
4:10 (4:10) (Class 3) (0-90,90) 4-Y-O+ **£9,703** (£2,887; £1,443; £721) **Stalls** Centre

Form RPR
5461 **1** **Powerful Presence (IRE)**[7] 2882 7-9-4 87.... MichaelO'Connell 1 97
(David O'Meara) *trckd ldrs: rdn 2f out: edgd lft and led 1f out: hld on wl* **11/4**[2]
26-0 **2** 1 3/4 **Able Master (IRE)**[26] 2310 7-9-7 90.... DanielTudhope 2 95
(David O'Meara) *w ldr: rdn and led over 2f out: hdd 1f out: kpt on same pce last 100yds* **9/4**[1]
-500 **3** nk **Postscript (IRE)**[16] 2592 5-9-0 86.... DarrenEgan(3) 6 90
(David Simcock) *in tch on outside: effrt and hdwy over 2f out: hung lft: over 1f out: kpt on ins fnl f* **9/2**[3]
5503 **4** 3/4 **Solar Spirit (IRE)**[8] 2834 8-8-8 77.... PJMcDonald 5 82+
(Tracy Waggott) *missed break: hld up in tch: stdy hdwy on ins whn nt clr run and swtchd rt over 1f out: kpt on fnl f: no imp* **12/1**
-662 **5** 1 **Clockmaker (IRE)**[14] 2649 7-9-4 87.... DavidAllan 3 87
(Tim Easterby) *t.k.h: slt ld to over 2f out: rdn and outpcd whn n.m.r 1f out: no imp* **11/4**[2]
0500 **6** 3 **Green Park (IRE)**[8] 2834 10-8-6 75....(b) JimmyQuinn 4 67
(Declan Carroll) *hld up in tch: drvn over 2f out: btn appr fnl f* **28/1**

1m 24.45s (-2.55) **Going Correction** -0.225s/f (Firm) **6** Ran SP% **113.4**
Speed ratings (Par 107): **105,103,102,101,100 97**
Tote Swingers: 1&2 £1.10, 2&3 £5.30, 1&3 £3.80 CSF £9.57 CT £25.31 TOTE £3.80: £3.00, £3.70; EX 8.90 Trifecta £34.80 Pool: £597.11 - 12.86 winning tickets..
Owner The Lawton Bamforth Partnership **Bred** Corduff Stud **Trained** Nawton, N Yorks
■ Stewards' Enquiry : David Allan two-day ban; careless riding (23rd-24th June).

FOCUS
Two David O'Meara runners at the head of the market and they filled the first two places in this decent handicap. The winner is rated back to last year's best.

3089 PLAY TOTESUPERSCOOP6 AT ROYAL ASCOT H'CAP 1m 7f 177y
4:45 (4:45) (Class 5) (0-70,69) 4-Y-O+ **£3,234** (£962; £481; £240) **Stalls** Low

Form RPR
1 **Miss Macnamara (IRE)**[28] 8027 4-8-13 60.... FrederikTylicki 4 67
(Martin Todhunter) *prom: wnt 2nd over 4f out: effrt and ev ch over 1f out: led ins fnl f: styd on wl* **25/1**
1462 **2** 1 1/2 **Zaplamation (IRE)**[29] 2242 8-9-9 69.... MichaelO'Connell 13 74
(John Quinn) *t.k.h: hld up: hdwy on outside over 3f out: led over 1f out to ins fnl f: kpt on same pce* **5/1**[2]
-630 **3** 1 **La Bacouetteuse (FR)**[7] 2860 8-9-8 68....(p) DavidAllan 9 72
(Iain Jardine) *hld up: rdn and hdwy over 2f out: kpt on fnl f: nrst fin* **11/1**
31-0 **4** 5 **Nashville (IRE)**[28] 2277 4-9-5 69.... LucyAlexander(3) 5 67
(Richard Fahey) *hld up on outside: effrt over 4f out: rdn and kpt on same pce fr over 1f out* **6/1**
0/52 **5** hd **Spiekeroog**[8] 2831 7-9-3 63....(v) DanielTudhope 10 61
(David O'Meara) *t.k.h: prom on outside: hdwy to chal after 6f: led over 5f out: qcknd clr 4f out: rdn and hdd over 1f out: sn btn* **7/2**[1]
435- **6** 1 1/2 **Sheila's Castle**[196] 7862 9-8-2 55.... DanielleMooney(7) 12 51
(Sean Regan) *bhd: struggling 1/2-way: styd on wl fnl 2f: nvr able to chal* **12/1**
-031 **7** 3 **Amir Pasha (UAE)**[12] 2720 8-8-7 53....(p) AndrewElliott 3 45
(Micky Hammond) *stmbld s: sn rcvrd and led after 1f: hdd over 5f out: outpcd over 3f out: n.d after* **11/2**[3]
05- **8** 2 1/2 **Strikemaster (IRE)**[242] 6956 7-8-7 53....(t) PaddyAspell 2 42
(Lee James) *midfield: drvn along over 3f out: outpcd fr 2f out* **17/2**
0-56 **9** 1/2 **Jeu De Roseau (IRE)**[7] 2887 9-9-0 60.... JimmyQuinn 11 49
(Chris Grant) *prom: drvn and outpcd over 3f out: btn fnl 2f* **10/1**
0-06 **10** 1 1/4 **Bijou Dan**[32] 2120 12-8-6 52 oh2 ow1.... PJMcDonald 8 39
(George Moore) *s.i.s: bhd: struggling over 4f out: sn btn* **16/1**
000- **11** 1 1/2 **Cowslip**[243] 6930 4-8-1 51 oh6.... RaulDaSilva(3) 1 36
(George Moore) *bhd: struggling over 5f out: nvr on terms* **40/1**
3010 **12** 15 **Dubara Reef (IRE)**[12] 2721 6-8-2 51 oh3....(p) DarrenEgan(3) 6 18
(Paul Green) *led 1f: cl up tl rdn and wknd qckly wl over 3f out: t.o* **16/1**

3m 28.52s (-3.48) **Going Correction** -0.225s/f (Firm)
WFA 4 from 6yo+ 1lb **12** Ran SP% **122.3**
Speed ratings (Par 103): **99,98,97,95,95 94,92,91,91,90 90,82**
Tote Swingers: 1&2 £22.40, 2&3 £9.00, 1&3 £33.20 CSF £150.45 CT £1498.32 TOTE £37.70: £8.30, £1.80, £4.50; EX 123.80 Trifecta £870.60 Part won. Pool: £1,160.93 - 0.12 winning units..
Owner Javas Charvers **Bred** Airlie Stud **Trained** Orton, Cumbria

FOCUS
Not the strongest of staying handicaps, run at a steady pace with the complexion of the race changing in the straight. A clear best from the winner.

3090 LUCKY 15 BONUS AT TOTEPOOL.COM H'CAP 5f 212y
5:20 (5:20) (Class 5) (0-75,75) 4-Y-O+ **£3,234** (£962; £481; £240) **Stalls** Low

Form RPR
3245 **1** **Mutafaakir (IRE)**[7] 2884 4-8-12 66.... PJMcDonald 5 78
(Ruth Carr) *midfield: rdn over 2f out: gd hdwy over 1f out: led wl ins fnl f: r.o* **7/4**[1]
3523 **2** 3/4 **Rylee Mooch**[19] 2505 5-9-0 75....(e) ConnorBeasley(7) 2 84
(Richard Guest) *led: rdn over 2f out: hdd and no ex wl ins fnl f* **6/1**[2]
-540 **3** 3/4 **See Clearly**[43] 1802 4-8-11 65.... DavidAllan 1 72
(Tim Easterby) *in tch: rdn over 2f out: kpt on ins fnl f: nvr able to chal* **8/1**
2154 **4** 1 **Sunrise Dance**[18] 2542 4-8-9 66.... MarkCoumbe(3) 3 70
(Robert Johnson) *chsd ldng pair: rdn over 2f out: hdwy wl over 1f out: one pce ins fnl f* **16/1**
3-04 **5** 3/4 **Blue Shoes (IRE)**[20] 2479 4-8-7 66.... DarylByrne(5) 9 67
(Tim Easterby) *in tch: effrt and rdn over 2f out: kpt on fnl f: nt pce to chal* **14/1**
0000 **6** nk **Rio Cobolo (IRE)**[1] 3068 7-8-8 62....(v) PaulQuinn 10 62
(David Nicholls) *hld up: rdn and outpcd wl over 2f out: styd on wl fnl f: nrst fin* **22/1**
3405 **7** hd **Gung Ho Jack**[18] 2530 4-9-1 69.... FrederikTylicki 4 69
(John Best) *hld up on ins: drvn along over 2f out: styd on fnl f: nvr able to chal* **14/1**
302 **8** 1 3/4 **Dorback**[9] 2790 6-9-5 73.... JimmyQuinn 6 67
(Violet M Jordan) *t.k.h: w ldr: rdn over 2f out: wknd ent fnl f* **7/1**[3]
0-00 **9** 2 1/4 **Kuanyao (IRE)**[21] 2459 7-9-7 75.... PatCosgrave 11 62
(David Nicholls) *hld up: rdn and hung lft fr over 2f out: no imp whn nt clr run over 1f out* **14/1**
-044 **10** hd **Baltic Bomber (IRE)**[8] 2835 4-8-8 62....(p) MichaelO'Connell 12 48
(John Quinn) *in tch on outside: rdn and hung lft over 2f out: sn wknd* **16/1**
50-0 **11** 3 1/2 **Layla's Hero (IRE)**[12] 2707 6-8-10 64....(p) AdrianNicholls 8 39
(David Nicholls) *sn wl bhd: struggling 1/2-way: nvr on terms* **20/1**
0-00 **12** 1/2 **Henry Bee**[14] 2663 4-8-13 74.... EireannCagney(7) 7 48
(Richard Fahey) *sn wl bhd: no ch fr 1/2-way* **28/1**

1m 11.59s (-2.01) **Going Correction** -0.225s/f (Firm) **12** Ran SP% **118.6**
Speed ratings (Par 103): **104,103,102,100,99 99,99,96,93,93 88,88**
Tote Swingers: 1&2 £4.30, 2&3 £10.30, 1&3 £5.30 CSF £11.21 CT £68.80 TOTE £2.50: £1.40, £1.80, £2.50; EX 15.80 Trifecta £116.90 Pool: £1,156.86 - 7.41 winning tickets..
Owner Michael Hill **Bred** Shadwell Estate Company Limited **Trained** Huby, N Yorks
■ Stewards' Enquiry : Daryl Byrne three-day ban: careless riding (23-25 June)

FOCUS
The pace was sound for this open handicap with the heavily backed favourite pouncing late. His best form since early last year.

3091 MORE FOOTBALL THAN EVER AT TOTEPOOL.COM MEDIAN AUCTION MAIDEN FILLIES' STKS 5f 212y
5:50 (5:50) (Class 6) 3-4-Y-O **£2,726** (£805; £402) **Stalls** Low

Form RPR
3632 **1** **Nurpur (IRE)**[14] 2672 3-9-0 74.... DanielTudhope 5 75+
(David O'Meara) *in tch: smooth hdwy over 2f out: led ent fnl f: c clr on bit* **4/7**[1]

2-64 **2** 6 **Only For You**14 2650 3-8-11 56 RaulDaSilva(3) 2 56
(Alan Brown) *chsd ldrs: rdn over 2f out: led over 1f out: hdd ent fnl f: sn no ch w wnr* **20/1**

6-5 **3** 1 3/4 **Birdie Queen**29 2226 3-9-0 0 FrederikTylicki 8 50
(John Best) *dwlt: hld up in tch: tk clsr order 1/2-way: rdn over 2f out: kpt on one pce* **6/1**3

0-20 **4** 2 1/4 **Bountybeamadam**21 2449 3-9-0 75 PatCosgrave 7 43
(George Baker) *prom: rdn over 2f out: wknd ins fnl f* **7/2**2

35-5 **5** 3/4 **Red Highlites (IRE)**7 2861 3-9-0 59 (v1) PJMcDonald 1 41
(Ann Duffield) *led narrowly: rdn over 2f out: hdd over 1f out: wknd fnl f* **33/1**

60 **6** 2 1/2 **Lasaraleen (IRE)**125 509 3-8-7 0 LauraBarry(7) 4 33
(Richard Fahey) *hld up: pushed along over 3f out: nvr threatened* **25/1**

00 **7** hd **Busy Bimbo (IRE)**11 2757 4-9-1 40 (p) JordanHibberd(7) 6 32
(Alan Berry) *a in rr* **100/1**

1m 12.51s (-1.09) **Going Correction** -0.225s/f (Firm)
WFA 3 from 4yo 8lb **7 Ran SP% 112.7**
Speed ratings (Par 98): **98,90,87,84,83 80,80**
Tote Swingers: 1&2 £1.80, 2&3 £4.30, 1&3 £2.20 CSF £17.03 TOTE £1.80: £1.10, £8.90; EX 10.00 Trifecta £38.20 Pool: £1,491.07 - 29.21 winning tickets..
Owner Middleham Park Racing XXIX & Partners **Bred** B P Hayes **Trained** Nawton, N Yorks

FOCUS
A weak contest run at an honest pace. The winner didn't need to improve but could be capable of better.
T/Plt: £63.40 to a £1 stake. Pool: £46,001.00 - 529.05 winning units. T/Qpdt: £23.80 to a £1 stake. Pool: £2,990.00 - 92.70 winning units. RY

2645 CHESTER (L-H)
Saturday, June 8

OFFICIAL GOING: Good (good to firm in places; 7.4)
Wind: Light, variable Weather: Sunny

3092 HALEWOOD INTERNATIONAL MAIDEN STKS 5f 16y
2:10 (2:14) (Class 4) 2-Y-O **£6,469** (£1,925; £962; £481) **Stalls Low**

Form RPR

3 **1** **Salford Red Devil**30 2189 2-9-5 0 FrannyNorton 9 85+
(Richard Fahey) *displayed plenty of spd to go prom: led jst over 2f out: drew clr over 1f out: r.o wl: eased cl home* **4/1**2

2235 **2** 2 **Memory Styx**10 2774 2-9-0 0 TomEaves 1 71
(Mick Channon) *midfield: n.m.r on rail early on: plld out whn hdwy over 1f out: sn wnt 2nd: kpt on but nt trble wnr ins fnl f* **11/2**3

3 nk **Edge (IRE)** 2-9-5 0 JimmyFortune 8 77+
(Richard Hannon) *outpcd and bhd: hdwy 1f out: swtchd lft whn running on ins fnl f: gng on at fin* **7/1**

4 2 3/4 **Quantum Dot (IRE)** 2-9-5 0 StephenCraine 5 66+
(Tom Dascombe) *dwlt: pushed along towards rr: effrt whn nt clr run and checked ins fnl f: sn swtchd rt: styd on towards fin: nt rch ldrs* **15/2**

02 **5** nk **Zain Zone (IRE)**23 2391 2-9-5 0 MartinDwyer 7 64
(Gerard Butler) *unruly bef r and uns rdr at s: hmpd at s: sn pushed along towards rr: styd on u.p ins fnl f: nt gng pce to trble ldrs* **14/1**

4442 **6** 2 1/4 **Atlantic Affair (IRE)**19 2497 2-9-0 0 JoeFanning 4 51
(Mark Johnston) *led: hdd jst over 2f out: outpcd by wnr over 1f out: wknd ins fnl f* **7/4**1

4535 **7** 1/2 **Marilyn Marquessa**31 2147 2-9-0 0 CathyGannon 2 52
(Jo Hughes) *prom: n.m.r and squeezed out jst over 3f out: pushed along over 2f out: forced wd over 1f out: wknd ins fnl f: eased whn btn fnl 75yds* **11/1**

00 **8** 1/2 **Red Forever**14 2645 2-9-0 0 SladeO'Hara(5) 3 52
(Alan Berry) *dwlt: sn chsd ldrs: outpcd 2f out: wknd over 1f out* **50/1**

1m 1.56s (0.56) **Going Correction** +0.05s/f (Good) **8 Ran SP% 113.0**
Speed ratings (Par 95): **97,93,93,88,88 84,84,83**
toteswingers 1&2 £6.50, 1&3 £7.70, 2&3 £11.20 CSF £25.52 TOTE £5.20: £2.00, £1.10, £2.00; EX 33.80 Trifecta £162.20 Pool: £1,432.50 - 6.62 winning tickets..
Owner Dr Marwan Koukash **Bred** Wickfield Stud & Roan Rocket Partnership **Trained** Musley Bank, N Yorks

FOCUS
The early pace was decent. The winner was well on top and the consistent runner-up helps with the level of the form.

3093 TSINGTAO CHINESE BEER H'CAP 6f 18y
2:45 (2:46) (Class 4) (0-85,85) 4-Y-O+ **£6,469** (£1,925; £962; £481) **Stalls Low**

Form RPR

6-15 **1** **Lucky Numbers (IRE)**8 2834 7-9-7 85 DavidNolan 1 94
(David O'Meara) *a.p: rdn to ld jst over 1f out: edgd rt and r.o ins fnl f: hld on wl cl home* **8/1**3

040 **2** 3/4 **Chooseday (IRE)**21 2460 4-9-6 84 (p) AmyRyan 14 91+
(Kevin Ryan) *dwlt: hld up in rr: swtchd rt and hdwy over 1f out: str run wl ins fnl f: clsng at fin* **12/1**

0-02 **3** 1/2 **Picture Dealer**7 2871 4-9-1 79 JimmyFortune 4 84+
(Gary Moore) *hld up: hdwy on outer into midfield over 2f out: chsd ldrs over 1f out: styd on ins fnl f: gng on at fin* **11/2**2

2311 **4** nk **Chester Aristocrat**9 2797 4-9-2 85 JasonHart(5) 6 89
(Eric Alston) *in tch: effrt on outer to chse ldrs over 1f out: styd on ins fnl f: nt quite pce to chal* **7/2**1

0-05 **5** nk **Roker Park (IRE)**21 2460 8-9-1 79 TomEaves 2 82
(David O'Meara) *midfield: hdwy on inner over 1f out: styd on ins fnl f: nt quite pce of ldrs* **8/1**3

0022 **6** 1/2 **Noverre To Go (IRE)**9 2789 7-9-0 78 (p) SteveDrowne 3 79
(Ronald Harris) *prom: led 2f out: rdn and hdd jst over 1f out: carried sltly rt ins fnl f: no ex fnl 50yds* **14/1**

0114 **7** 2 1/4 **Tango Sky (IRE)**14 2664 4-8-13 77 FrannyNorton 5 71
(David Nicholls) *towards rr: hdwy over 2f out: chsng ldrs whn nt clr run ins fnl f: one pce fnl 75yds* **8/1**3

2001 **8** 4 1/2 **Elusive Hawk (IRE)**17 2571 9-8-11 80 (v) DeclanBates(5) 9 60
(David Evans) *chsd ldrs: effrt 3 wd 2f out: rdn over 1f out: fdd fnl 150yds* **33/1**

-060 **9** 2 1/2 **Lexi's Hero (IRE)**21 2459 5-9-2 80 (p) ShaneKelly 12 52
(David Nicholls) *dwlt: hld up: hdwy wl over 1f out: no imp on ldrs fnl f* **16/1**

2320 **10** 1 1/4 **Tyfos**23 2388 8-9-3 81 MartinDwyer 15 49
(Brian Baugh) *sn led: pushed along and hdd 2f out: rdn and wknd over 1f out* **50/1**

024- **11** 1 1/4 **Mount Hollow**175 8143 8-8-10 79 (p) JackDuern(5) 7 43
(Andrew Hollinshead) *hld up: pushed along over 1f out: nvr a threat* **25/1**

1006 **12** 3/4 **Bubbly Ballerina**57 1517 4-8-7 76 NatashaEaton(5) 8 37
(Alan Bailey) *midfield: pushed along and outpcd over 1f out: nvr a threat* **16/1**

1400 **13** 5 **Lucky Dan (IRE)**5 2914 7-8-13 77 JoeFanning 10 22
(Paul Green) *chsd ldrs: forced wd and lost pl over 2f out: n.d after* **20/1**

2221 **14** 3 1/2 **Meandmyshadow**8 2834 5-9-0 78 DaleSwift 13 12
(Alan Brown) *sn pushed along in tch: wknd over 2f out* **10/1**

3000 **15** 5 **Al's Memory (IRE)**7 2868 4-9-6 84 CathyGannon 11
(David Evans) *sddle slipped early: a bhd: nvr on terms* **16/1**

1m 14.21s (0.41) **Going Correction** +0.05s/f (Good) **15 Ran SP% 125.5**
Speed ratings (Par 105): **99,98,97,96,96 95,92,86,83,81 80,79,72,67,61**
Tote Swingers: 1&2 £11.20, 2&3 £39.70, 1&3 £22.90 CSF £100.34 CT £599.46 TOTE £12.90: £5.20, £4.80, £1.90; EX 146.10 Trifecta £341.00 Part won. Pool: £454.73 - 0.02 winning units..
Owner Tom Tuohy & Tony Jafrate **Bred** Rory O'Brien **Trained** Nawton, N Yorks

FOCUS
A lot of runners but it looked a clean race. The winning time appeared quite good. The well-drawn winner and the fourth set the standard.

3094 CRABBIE'S STRAWBERRY AND LIME H'CAP 1m 2f 75y
3:20 (3:20) (Class 2) (0-105,102) 3-Y-O+**£32,345** (£9,625; £4,810; £2,405) **Stalls High**

Form RPR

-142 **1** **Area Fifty One**8 2839 5-9-9 102 GeorgeChaloner(5) 4 108
(Richard Fahey) *mde all: rdn over 1f out: kpt on gamely ins fnl f* **11/4**1

0-43 **2** 3/4 **Forgotten Hero (IRE)**22 2424 4-9-1 89 SteveDrowne 3 93
(Charles Hills) *in tch: clsd to chse ldrs over 3f out: rdn over 1f out: tk 2nd fnl 110yds: styd on towards fin* **7/1**

-325 **3** 3/4 **Haylaman (IRE)**22 2422 5-8-13 87 FrannyNorton 6 90
(David Simcock) *hld up in midfield: hdwy 2f out: chsd ldrs over 1f out: styd on u.p ins fnl f wout threatening wnr* **6/1**3

4-03 **4** 3/4 **Calaf**85 329 5-8-7 84 oh1 ow1 PaulPickard(3) 2 86
(Brian Ellison) *w wnr: rdn and unable qck over 1f out: lost 2nd ins fnl f: kpt on same pce* **20/1**

0110 **5** 1 **Toto Skyllachy**8 2841 8-9-9 97 DavidNolan 1 97
(David O'Meara) *chsd ldrs: rdn over 1f out: kpt on same pce fnl 150yds* **16/1**

5232 **6** hd **Greeleys Love (USA)**7 2862 3-8-0 87 oh2 (v) JoeFanning 11 86
(Mark Johnston) *s.i.s: hld up: hdwy over 3f out: hung lft and kpt on ins fnl f: nvr able to chal* **9/2**2

03/0 **7** 1 3/4 **Prompter**24 2365 6-9-4 92 JimmyFortune 13 88
(Jonjo O'Neill) *hld up: effrt over 1f out: kpt on ins fnl f wout threatening: eased fnl 50yds* **20/1**

2452 **8** 3/4 **Spifer (IRE)**10 2775 5-9-6 94 (p) MircoMimmocchi 5 89
(Marco Botti) *s.s: hld up: hdwy over 1f out: one pce and no imp on ldrs ins fnl f* **8/1**

1043 **9** 1 **Fennell Bay (IRE)**10 2775 4-8-13 87 AmyRyan 7 80
(Mark Johnston) *in rr: u.p over 2f out: plugged on at one pce fnl f: nvr able to trble ldrs* **9/1**

6-34 **10** 27 **An Cat Dubh (IRE)**14 2646 4-8-6 83 oh4 RyanPowell(3) 9 24
(Ian Williams) *in tch: effrt to chse ldrs over 3f out: wknd over 2f out* **10/1**

10-0 **11** 2 3/4 **Kay Gee Be (IRE)**14 2646 9-8-9 83 oh2 TomEaves 8 19
(Alan Berry) *chsd ldrs tl pushed along and wknd 4f out* **50/1**

12 12 **Mespone (FR)**49 4-8-11 85 MartinDwyer 12
(Paul Midgley) *midfield: hdwy on outer 7f out: pushed along and wknd qckly over 3f out* **40/1**

2m 9.21s (-1.99) **Going Correction** +0.05s/f (Good)
WFA 3 from 4yo+ 13lb **12 Ran SP% 121.6**
Speed ratings (Par 109): **109,108,107,107,106 106,104,104,103,81 79,70**
Tote Swingers: 1&2 £11.20, 2&3 £15.60, 1&3 £6.00 CSF £21.84 CT £111.13 TOTE £3.10: £2.00, £1.50, £2.40; EX 31.70 Trifecta £140.50 Pool: £922.77 - 4.92 winning tickets..
Owner Dr Marwan Koukash **Bred** Carmel Stud **Trained** Musley Bank, N Yorks

FOCUS
Quite a range of abilities on show here (four of the field were running from out of the handicap), and it produced a fine performance from the top weight. The overall form is not as strong as might be expected for the grade.

3095 LAMB'S NAVY RUM FILLIES' H'CAP 1m 4f 66y
3:55 (3:55) (Class 4) (0-85,85) 4-Y-O+ **£6,469** (£1,925; £962; £481) **Stalls Low**

Form RPR

-263 **1** **Star Lahib (IRE)**14 2646 4-9-4 82 FrannyNorton 2 93
(Mark Johnston) *chsd ldng trio: clsd 4f out: rdn to ld 1f out: r.o wl and in command wl ins fnl f* **2/1**1

3422 **2** 3 1/4 **Pandorica**8 2826 5-7-11 68 (p) JoeyHaynes(7) 5 74
(Bernard Llewellyn) *a.p: rdn and ev ch 1f out: sn unable to go w wnr: one pce wl ins fnl f* **11/1**

21-3 **3** nk **Princess Caetani (IRE)**15 2619 4-9-7 85 ShaneKelly 4 90
(David Simcock) *dwlt: hld up in rr: hdwy over 1f out: styd on towards fin* **11/4**2

0-00 **4** 3/4 **Amoya (GER)**11 2761 6-8-11 75 AdamBeschizza 6 79
(Philip McBride) *led: rdn 2f out: hdd 1f out: no ex fnl 75yds* **20/1**

05-1 **5** 7 **Our Phylli Vera (IRE)**36 1974 4-8-11 75 FergusSweeney 7 68
(Alan King) *hld up: hdwy to chse ldrs 3f out: rdn wl over 1f out: sn wknd* **4/1**3

0-55 **6** 7 **Dancing Primo**35 2004 7-8-9 78 JackDuern(5) 3 60
(Mark Brisbourne) *racd keenly: prom: rdn 2f out: wknd over 1f out* **7/1**

15-6 **7** 14 **Isdaal**18 2555 6-8-4 68 JoeFanning 8 27
(Kevin Morgan) *hld up: u.p and outpcd over 2f out: eased whn wl btn fnl f* **10/1**

2m 37.12s (-1.38) **Going Correction** +0.05s/f (Good) **7 Ran SP% 114.7**
Speed ratings (Par 102): **106,103,103,103,98 93,84**
Tote Swingers: 1&2 £5.00, 2&3 £5.70, 1&3 £1.90 CSF £25.09 CT £60.96 TOTE £3.00: £2.50, £4.70; EX 16.80 Trifecta £88.90 Pool: £1,257.31 - 10.59 winning tickets..
Owner Jaber Abdullah **Bred** Piercetown Stud **Trained** Middleham Moor, N Yorks

FOCUS
A muddling contest as two groups soon developed, with Amoya leading a couple of rivals with a gap back to the remainder. Improvement from the unexposed winner.

3096 CRABBIE'S SCOTTISH RASPBERRY H'CAP 7f 122y
4:30 (4:31) (Class 4) (0-85,85) 3-Y-O£18,903 (£5,658; £2,829; £1,416; £705) **Stalls Low**

Form RPR

0053 **1** **Al Muheer (IRE)**14 2665 8-8-13 82 (b) JasonHart(5) 4 91
(Ruth Carr) *racd on inner: trckd ldrs: rdn and edgd rt ins fnl f: r.o to ld towards fin* **8/1**3

0-00 **2** nk **Springinmystep (IRE)**14 2664 4-9-2 83 LeeTopliss(3) 3 91
(Ed de Giles) *midfield: rdn and hdwy over 1f out: r.o ins fnl f: pressed wnr cl home* **20/1**

The Form Book Flat, Raceform Ltd, Compton, RG20 6NL.

1040 **3** ½ **Al Khan (IRE)**[8] 2834 4-9-2 **80**.......... SteveDrowne 5 87
(Violet M Jordan) *broke loose bef r: prom: rdn over 1f out: chalng ins fnl f: r.o u.p: hld towards fin* **25/1**

0-01 **4** nse **Best Trip (IRE)**[32] 2119 6-9-2 **83**.......... PaulPickard(3) 2 90
(Brian Ellison) *led: rdn over 1f out: hdd and hld towards fin* **5/1**[1]

6022 **5** 1¼ **Kingscroft (IRE)**[18] 2541 5-9-6 **84**.......... FrannyNorton 14 90+
(Mark Johnston) *midfield: rdn and hdwy over 1f out: styng on whn nt clr run and checked ins fnl f: sn swtchd lft: one pce fnl strides* **10/1**

0050 **6** shd **Frog Hollow**[38] 1922 4-9-2 **80**.......... DavidNolan 1 84+
(David O'Meara) *hld up: hdwy whn nt clr run ins fnl f: sn swtchd lft: gng on at fin* **5/1**[1]

2502 **7** ¾ **Free Spin (IRE)**[8] 2834 4-9-5 **83**.......... JoeFanning 7 85
(David Barron) *chsd ldrs: rdn over 1f out: one pce wl ins fnl f* **6/1**[2]

01-0 **8** ½ **Modern Tutor**[21] 2444 4-9-6 **84**.......... ShaneKelly 6 84+
(Sir Michael Stoute) *dwlt: midfield: rdn over 1f out: prog whn hung lft ins fnl f: styd on towards fin: nt pce to rch ldrs* **12/1**

6004 **9** 1¼ **Verse Of Love**[14] 2649 4-9-6 **84**.......... JimmyFortune 10 81
(David Evans) *prom: rdn over 1f out: fdd fnl 110yds* **16/1**

0002 **10** hd **Alejandro (IRE)**[7] 2882 4-8-13 **82**.......... GeorgeChaloner(5) 9 79
(Richard Fahey) *chsd ldrs: rdn over 1f out: no ex ins fnl f* **8/1**[3]

2546 **11** ½ **Harrison George (IRE)**[5] 2937 8-9-6 **84**..........(t) MartinDwyer 15 80
(P J O'Gorman) *hld up in rr: rdn over 1f out: kpt on ins fnl f: no imp on ldrs* **12/1**

0620 **12** 1 **Docofthebay (IRE)**[3] 2988 9-9-1 **82**..........(p) BillyCray(3) 8 75
(Scott Dixon) *s.i.s: hld up in rr: rdn over 1f out: one pce ins fnl f* **16/1**

-040 **13** ½ **Sam Nombulist**[4] 2958 5-9-7 **85**..........(v) AmyRyan 11 77
(Richard Whitaker) *bhd: rdn over 1f out: nvr a threat* **20/1**

0/60 **14** 10 **Tellovoi (IRE)**[16] 2592 5-9-7 **85**.......... AndrewMullen 12 52
(Andrew Hollinshead) *hld up: pushed along over 2f out: nvr a threat* **33/1**

1600 **15** 8 **Light From Mars**[56] 1542 8-9-2 **85**.......... EDLinehan(5) 16 32
(Ronald Harris) *midfield: rdn and wknd over 1f out* **40/1**

1m 33.08s (-0.72) **Going Correction** +0.05s/f (Good) **15** Ran SP% **124.8**
Speed ratings (Par 105): **105,104,104,104,102 102,102,101,100,100 99,98,98,88,80**
Tote Swingers: 1&2 £71.00, 2&3 £64.30, 1&3 £46.20 CSF £168.77 CT £2286.50 TOTE £9.70: £3.40, £12.20, £13.30; EX 263.70 Trifecta £952.50 Part won. Pool: £1,270.02 - 0.18 winning units..
Owner Antigua Cavaliers & Mrs R Carr **Bred** Foursome Thoroughbreds **Trained** Huby, N Yorks

FOCUS
A hugely competitive handicap. The draw played its part with stall four beating three, five and two. The winner didn't need to find much on his Haydock latest.

3097 CRABBIE'S ORIGINAL H'CAP 5f 16y
5:05 (5:11) (Class 3) (0-95,93) 3-Y-0 **£7,762** (£2,310; £1,154; £577) **Stalls** Low

Form RPR

1-50 **1** **Dutch Masterpiece**[22] 2430 3-9-3 **89**.......... JimmyFortune 2 101
(Gary Moore) *chsd ldrs: rdn to ld 1f out: r.o ins fnl f: stretched clrer fnl 100yds* **9/4**[1]

-050 **2** 3¼ **Bapak Sayang (USA)**[21] 2452 3-8-10 **82**.......... AmyRyan 5 82
(Kevin Ryan) *led: rdn over 1f out: sn hdd: outpcd by wnr fnl 100yds* **9/2**[2]

210- **3** nk **Smart Daisy K**[204] 7745 3-7-11 **74** oh2.......... ShirleyTeasdale(5) 10 73
(Andrew Hollinshead) *broke loose bef r: chsd ldr: rdn and chalng 1f out: nt qckn ins fnl f* **33/1**

0060 **4** ¾ **Queen Aggie (IRE)**[14] 2655 3-8-5 **82**.......... DeclanBates(5) 8 78+
(David Evans) *hmpd s: towards rr: hdwy wl over 1f out: styd on ins fnl f: nt quite rch ldrs* **33/1**

1655 **5** 1½ **Top Boy**[22] 2430 3-9-3 **89**.......... MartinDwyer 13 80+
(Derek Shaw) *swtchd lft s: bhd: rdn over 1f out: styd on ins fnl f: nvr nrr* **14/1**

24-0 **6** hd **Strange Magic (IRE)**[14] 2669 3-9-2 **93**.......... GeorgeChaloner(5) 1 83
(Richard Fahey) *midfield and pushed along: effrt on inner 2f out: one pce ins fnl f* **20/1**

3006 **7** hd **Jillnextdoor (IRE)**[29] 2213 3-9-1 **87**.......... ShaneKelly 4 76+
(Mick Channon) *midfield: styd on for press on outer ins fnl f: nt pce to trble ldrs* **8/1**

3-54 **8** 2 **Secret Look**[22] 2430 3-9-2 **88**.......... FrannyNorton 9 70+
(Ed McMahon) *hmpd s: bhd: rdn whn nt clr run over 1f out: allowed to coast home wl ins fnl f* **11/2**[3]

-030 **9** hd **New Fforest**[19] 2521 3-8-9 **81**.......... SteveDrowne 6 62
(Andrew Balding) *chsd ldrs: rdn over 1f out: wknd ins fnl f* **10/1**

-210 **10** 1¼ **Space Artist (IRE)**[22] 2430 3-8-8 **80**.......... TomEaves 7 57
(Bryan Smart) *in tch: rdn and wknd wl over 1f out* **16/1**

-630 **11** 2 **Threes Grand**[22] 2430 3-8-12 **87**.......... BillyCray(3) 3 57
(Scott Dixon) *restless in stalls: midfield: rdn over 1f out: no imp on ldrs: wl btn wl ins fnl f* **8/1**

44-2 **12** 7 **Layla's Oasis**[154] 75 3-8-2 **74** oh1.......... JoeFanning 11 19
(Richard Fahey) *in tch: lost pl wl over 2f out: bhd over 1f out* **16/1**

1m 0.9s (-0.10) **Going Correction** +0.05s/f (Good) **12** Ran SP% **124.7**
Speed ratings (Par 103): **102,96,96,95,92 92,92,88,88,86 83,72**
Tote Swingers: 1&2 £3.90, 2&3 £34.70, 1&3 £19.90 CSF £12.20 CT £274.63 TOTE £2.20: £1.40, £2.10, £10.70; EX 17.50 Trifecta £354.20 Pool: £2,301.68 - 4.87 winning tickets..
Owner R A Green **Bred** Bumble Bloodstock Ltd **Trained** Lower Beeding, W Sussex

FOCUS
A well-contested sprint, in which none of the runners wore any kind of headgear. The winner was well drawn and the form is rated around the runner-up.

3098 LAMBRINI CIDER FILLIES' H'CAP 7f 122y
5:40 (5:42) (Class 4) (0-80,77) 4-Y-0+ **£6,469** (£1,925; £962; £481) **Stalls** Low

Form RPR

-266 **1** **It's My Time**[12] 2711 4-8-7 **63**..........(p) FrannyNorton 8 72
(Richard Fahey) *towards rr: hdwy on inner over 2f out: rdn and r.o ins fnl f: led fnl strides* **11/2**

3-13 **2** shd **Dutch Mistress**[33] 2092 4-8-8 **64**.......... AdamBeschizza 1 73
(James Unett) *chsd ldrs: rdn to ld jst over 1f out: hdd fnl strides* **4/1**[2]

0064 **3** 1¼ **Hoppy's Flyer (FR)**[2] 3029 5-7-12 **59**.......... ShirleyTeasdale(5) 9 65
(Paul Midgley) *midfield: hdwy over 1f out: rdn and chalng ins fnl f: nt qckn towards fin* **8/1**

0-42 **4** 1 **Stellar Express (IRE)**[14] 2646 4-9-6 **76**.......... AndrewMullen 10 79
(Michael Appleby) *chsd ldrs: rdn over 3f out: ev ch ins fnl f: no ex towards fin* **5/1**[3]

000- **5** 1 **Lolita Lebron (IRE)**[225] 7370 4-9-2 **77**..........(t[1]) JasonHart(5) 5 78
(Lawrence Mullaney) *in rr: struggling 3f out: styd on u.p ins fnl f: nt trble ldrs* **14/1**

30-4 **6** nk **Silvas Romana (IRE)**[33] 2070 4-9-4 **74**.......... ShaneKelly 4 74
(Mark Brisbourne) *midfield: pushed along over 4f out: sn lost pl and outpcd: styd on u.p ins fnl f* **33/1**

200- **7** 4½ **Portrush Storm**[230] 7275 8-7-9 **58** oh1.......... JoeyHaynes(7) 6 47
(Ray Peacock) *led: rdn and hdd 2f out: wknd ins fnl f* **66/1**

1-31 **8** 3¾ **Finesse**[28] 2286 4-9-6 **76**.......... JimmyFortune 2 63
(Ralph Beckett) *w ldr: led 2f out: rdn and hdd jst over 1f out: wknd and eased ins fnl f* **7/4**[1]

-053 **9** 3¼ **Remix (IRE)**[12] 2711 4-8-2 **58** oh1..........(v) JoeFanning 7 29
(Andrew Hollinshead) *chsd ldrs tl wknd over 2f out* **12/1**

1m 35.12s (1.32) **Going Correction** +0.05s/f (Good) **9** Ran SP% **118.3**
Speed ratings (Par 102): **95,94,93,92,91 91,86,83,79**
Tote Swingers: 1&2 £3.60, 2&3 £10.90, 1&3 £10.40 CSF £28.54 CT £178.67 TOTE £6.80: £1.80, £1.90, £2.90; EX 31.40 Trifecta £167.30 Pool: £1,340.57 - 6.00 winning tickets..
Owner Mrs Doreen M Swinburn **Bred** Genesis Green Stud Ltd And Thurso Ltd **Trained** Musley Bank, N Yorks

FOCUS
Nothing more than a fair event for fillies and the winning time was ordinary. Reasonable form for the grade with the first two not fully exposed.
T/Plt: £370.90 to a £1 stake. Pool: £71,117.00 - 139.94 winning units. T/Qpdt: £49.90 to a £1 stake. Pool: £4,371.00 - 64.80 winning units. DO

3043 HAYDOCK (L-H)
Saturday, June 8

OFFICIAL GOING: Good to firm (8.4)
All races on Stands side home straight and rail realignment on Round course added about 57yds to advertised distances on that track.
Wind: light 1/2 behind Weather: fine and sunny

3099 BETVICTOR ROYAL ASCOT NO LOSE HUGHES STKS (H'CAP) 2m 45y
2:05 (2:05) (Class 2) (0-100,97) 4-Y-0+ **£16,172** (£4,812; £2,405; £1,202) **Stalls** Low

Form RPR

1022 **1** **De Rigueur**[21] 2451 5-8-13 **86**..........(tp) AdamKirby 9 100
(Marco Botti) *hld up towards rr: stdy hdwy over 4f out: wnt 3rd 2f out: led 1f out: drvn out* **11/2**[2]

10-1 **2** 1½ **Sun Central (IRE)**[34] 2052 4-9-8 **96**.......... SebSanders 1 108
(William Haggas) *trckd ldrs: drvn over 3f out: chsd ldr over 2f out: hung lft and upsides 1f out: styd on same pce* **4/1**[1]

-213 **3** 4½ **Beyond Conceit (IRE)**[14] 2654 4-9-3 **91**.......... JamieSpencer 12 98
(Andrew Balding) *swtchd lft after s: led: drvn over 3f out: hdd 1f out: one pce* **9/1**

3-03 **4** 2¼ **Brockwell**[22] 2427 4-9-2 **90**.......... RichardKingscote 3 94
(Tom Dascombe) *trckd ldrs: drvn 3f out: one pce* **7/1**

3/60 **5** ½ **Apache (IRE)**[34] 2044 5-9-2 **89**..........[1] GeorgeBaker 14 93
(Jane Chapple-Hyam) *hld up and bhd: hdwy 0ver 2f out: swtchd rt over 1f out: styd on same pce ins fnl f* **20/1**

01-5 **6** 3¼ **Castilo Del Diablo (IRE)**[34] 2052 4-8-11 **85**.......... JimCrowley 10 85
(David Simcock) *hld up in rr: drvn 6f out: hdwy over 3f out: wknd fnl 150yds* **6/1**[3]

3335 **7** 2¼ **Tappanappa (IRE)**[29] 2205 6-8-10 **83**..........(b) KierenFallon 5 80
(Brian Ellison) *dwlt: hdwy 3f out: wknd over 1f out* **16/1**

10-6 **8** ½ **Body Language (IRE)**[16] 2598 5-8-6 **79**.......... AndreaAtzeni 4 76
(Ian Williams) *mid-div: drvn over 6f out: wknd 2f out* **40/1**

0/50 **9** nk **Theology**[31] 2149 6-9-3 **90**.......... GrahamLee 7 86
(Steve Gollings) *dwlt: hld up in rr: effrt over 3f out: nvr a factor* **33/1**

-451 **10** 1½ **Palazzo Bianco**[16] 2587 5-8-8 **86**.......... RobertTart(5) 15 80
(Brian Ellison) *sn bhd: t.o 3f out: kpt on over 1f out* **11/1**

/562 **11** ½ **Oriental Fox (GER)**[14] 2654 5-9-5 **97**.......... MichaelJMMurphy(5) 11 91
(Mark Johnston) *chsd ldr after 2f: drvn 4f out: lost pl wl over 1f out* **11/1**

0-40 **12** 3¾ **Dazinski**[23] 2402 7-8-12 **85**.......... NeilCallan 8 74
(Mark H Tompkins) *chsd ldrs: lost pl over 2f out* **16/1**

5-05 **13** 8 **Kiama Bay (IRE)**[14] 2648 7-9-0 **87**.......... MartinHarley 2 67
(John Quinn) *mid-div: hdwy on ins over 4f out: wknd 2f out* **25/1**

05-0 **14** 59 **Muntasir (IRE)**[21] 2451 4-9-1 **89**..........(p) MickaelBarzalona 6
(Saeed bin Suroor) *mid-div: hdwy to chse ldrs 7f out: drvn over 4f out: bhd and eased over 2f out: virtually p.u: hopelessly t.o* **20/1**

3m 26.98s (-7.32) **Going Correction** -0.25s/f (Firm)
WFA 4 from 5yo+ 1lb **14** Ran SP% **119.4**
Speed ratings (Par 109): **108,107,105,103,103 102,100,100,100,99 99,97,93,64**
toteswingers 1&2 £4.80, 1&3 £5.50, 2&3 £7.40 CSF £25.40 CT £199.03 TOTE £6.20: £2.20, £1.90, £3.20; EX 30.30 Trifecta £144.20 Pool: £2048.25 - 10.65 winning tickets..
Owner K J P Gundlach **Bred** Cheveley Park Stud Ltd **Trained** Newmarket, Suffolk

FOCUS
A decent staying handicap and a true test of stamina with the third horse setting a solid pace. Despite covering an extra 63yds, they took 0.11sec off the 2m course record which had stood for 29 years. Solid form, rated around the third and fourth.

3100 BETVICTOR ROYAL ASCOT MONEY BACK PINNACLE STKS (GROUP 3) (F&M) 1m 3f 200y
2:40 (2:42) (Class 1) 4-Y-0+
£34,026 (£12,900; £6,456; £3,216; £1,614; £810) **Stalls** Centre

Form RPR

-213 **1** **Moment In Time (IRE)**[14] 2656 4-8-12 97.......... JimCrowley 3 109
(David Simcock) *hld up in mid-div: hdwy over 3f out: styd on wl appr fnl f: led last 50yds: kpt on* **8/1**

324- **2** hd **Nymphea (IRE)**[31] 4-8-12 106.......... AStarke 4 108
(P Schiergen, Germany) *set stdy pce: increased gallop over 3f out: hdd wl ins fnl f: r.o* **6/1**[3]

50-2 **3** 2¼ **Ambivalent (IRE)**[23] 2397 4-8-12 106.......... AndreaAtzeni 1 105
(Roger Varian) *t.k.h in rr: effrt over 2f out: rdn and hung lft over 1f out: styd on ins fnl f: tk 3rd nr fin* **3/1**[2]

3 **4** nk **Souviens Toi**[35] 2012 4-8-12 102.......... NeilCallan 6 104
(Marco Botti) *trckd ldrs: effrt over 3f out: kpt on fnl f: tk 4th nr fin* **8/1**

32-2 **5** nk **Prussian**[107] 743 4-8-12 107.......... MickaelBarzalona 2 104
(Saeed bin Suroor) *trckd ldrs: t.k.h: effrt over 3f out: upsides 2f out: wknd and lost 2 pls towards fin* **2/1**[1]

0-25 **6** 1¾ **Quiz Mistress**[22] 2428 5-8-12 106.......... PatDobbs 5 101
(Hughie Morrison) *hld up in rr: effrt over 3f out: edgd lft over 1f out: nvr a threat* **7/1**

5-23 **7** 10 **Jehannedarc (IRE)**[21] 2443 5-8-12 100.......... GrahamLee 8 85
(Ed Dunlop) *trckd ldrs: chal 3f out: lost pl over 1f out: bhd whn eased towards fin* **12/1**

2m 30.87s (-2.93) **Going Correction** -0.25s/f (Firm) **7** Ran SP% **115.0**
Speed ratings (Par 113): **99,98,97,97,96 95,89**
toteswingers 1&2 £4.80, 1&3 £5.10, 2&3 £5.20 CSF £54.79 TOTE £10.30: £3.90, £1.90; EX 49.00 Trifecta £261.50 Pool: £2054.50 - 5.89 winning tickets..
Owner Mrs Julia Annable **Bred** L K I Bloodstock Ltd **Trained** Newmarket, Suffolk

FOCUS
The 11th running of the Pinnacle Stakes and the second time as a Group 3. Five previous winners of this have gone on to contest next month's Lancashire Oaks, but only Pongee in 2004 has so far managed to complete the double. The runner-up set a reasonable pace and all seven runners were within a length or so of each other passing the 2f pole. A personal best from the winner but the form is rated a bit cautiously.

3101 TIMEFORM JURY STKS (REGISTERED AS THE JOHN OF GAUNT STAKES) (GROUP 3) 7f
3:15 (3:15) (Class 1) 4-Y-O+
£34,026 (£12,900; £6,456; £3,216; £1,614; £810) **Stalls** Low

Form — RPR

2-04 **1** **Amarillo (IRE)**30 2202 4-9-0 109 .... AStarke 2 114
(P Schiergen, Germany) *trckd ldrs: led over 1f out: jst hld on* **10/1**

2-04 **2** *shd* **Pastoral Player**28 2258 6-9-0 111 .... GrahamLee 4 114+
(Hughie Morrison) *t.k.h in rr: stdy hdwy over 2f out: nt clr run and edgd rt over 1f out: styd on wl to chse wnr fnl 100yds: jst failed* **5/2**[1]

-003 **3** *2* **Red Jazz (USA)**28 2258 6-9-0 110 .... RobertWinston 8 108
(Charles Hills) *swtchd lft after s: led tl over 4f out: rdn over 2f out: hung lft over 1f out: kpt on to take 3rd nr fin* **6/1**[3]

0-40 **4** *hd* **Libranno**21 2446 5-9-5 110 .... PatDobbs 7 113
(Richard Hannon) *dwlt: sn chsng ldr: led over 4f out: hdd over 1f out: styd on same pce* **7/1**

01-1 **5** *2 3/4* **Eton Forever (IRE)**28 2258 6-9-0 112 .... NeilCallan 3 100
(Roger Varian) *mid-div: effrt over 3f out: chsng ldrs and drvn over 2f out: wknd clsng stages* **3/1**[2]

4145 **6** *2 1/2* **Monsieur Chevalier (IRE)**26 2323 6-9-0 104 .... KierenFallon 1 94
(P J O'Gorman) *chsd ldrs: drvn and outpcd over 5f out: kpt on fnl 2f* **12/1**

3-56 **7** *1 1/4* **Premio Loco (USA)**51 1639 9-9-0 109 .... GeorgeBaker 5 90
(Chris Wall) *hld up in rr: effrt over 3f out: drvn and outpcd over 2f out* **9/1**

6306 **8** *hd* **Red Duke (USA)**26 2323 4-9-0 100 .... (p) JimCrowley 6 90
(David Simcock) *trckd ldrs: 2nd over 3f out: wknd fnl f* **18/1**

1m 27.99s (-2.71) **Going Correction** -0.25s/f (Firm) **8 Ran SP% 112.4**
Speed ratings (Par 113): **105,104,102,102,99 96,94,94**
toteswingers 1&2 £5.70, 1&3 £7.20, 2&3 £2.10 CSF £34.12 TOTE £8.70: £2.20, £1.60, £1.70; EX 44.20 Trifecta £212.80 Pool: £2340.90 - 8.24 winning tickets..
Owner Stall Nizza **Bred** Juergen Imm **Trained** Germany

FOCUS
The early pace didn't look that strong for this Group 3. The winner is rated in line with a positive view of his German form.

3102 BETVICTOR.COM EBF CECIL FRAIL STKS (LISTED RACE) (FILLIES) 6f
3:50 (3:50) (Class 1) 3-Y-O+
£26,653 (£10,105; £5,057; £2,519; £1,264; £634) **Stalls** Centre

Form — RPR

326- **1** **Artistic Jewel (IRE)**203 7772 4-9-2 98 .... GrahamLee 2 108
(Ed McMahon) *trckd ldrs: n.m.r 2f out: r.o to ld last 50yds* **8/1**

00-2 **2** *1 1/4* **Gracia Directa (GER)**38 1944 5-9-2 99 .... OliverWilson 7 104
(D Moser, Germany) *trckd ldrs: led over 1f out: hdd and no ex wl ins fnl f* **4/1**[1]

0-02 **3** *1* **Hoyam**28 2270 3-8-8 102 .... HayleyTurner 6 99
(Michael Bell) *t.k.h: hdwy on outside over 2f out: chsng ldrs over 1f out: kpt on same pce fnl 150yds* **4/1**[1]

-000 **4** *hd* **Angels Will Fall (IRE)**24 2368 4-9-2 98 .... RobertWinston 9 100
(Charles Hills) *stdd s: hld up in rr: effrt over 2f out: hung lft 1f out: kpt on same pce* **7/1**[3]

-110 **5** *2 1/2* **Ladies Are Forever**24 2368 5-9-6 108 .... WilliamTwiston-Davies 4 96
(Geoffrey Oldroyd) *w ldr: drvn over 2f out: wknd fnl 100yds* **9/2**[2]

-000 **6** *nk* **I'm So Glad**7 2858 4-9-2 90 .... MartinHarley 1 91
(Mick Channon) *led: hdd over 1f out: wknd last 100yds* **28/1**

44-2 **7** *2 3/4* **City Girl (IRE)**22 2415 3-8-8 95 .... JimCrowley 5 98+
(Ralph Beckett) *trckd ldrs: effrt over 2f out: one pce whn hmpd 1f out: sn wknd* **4/1**[1]

0-5 **8** *4 1/2* **Pleine Forme (USA)**28 2264 5-9-2 100 .... AdamKirby 8 68
(Marco Botti) *hld up in rr: effrt 2f out: sn wknd* **11/1**

1m 11.6s (-2.20) **Going Correction** -0.25s/f (Firm)
WFA 3 from 4yo+ 8lb **8 Ran SP% 113.6**
Speed ratings (Par 108): **104,102,101,100,97 97,93,87**
toteswingers 1&2 £9.20, 1&3 £5.40, 2&3 £3.90 CSF £39.40 TOTE £10.70: £2.40, £1.90, £1.70; EX 52.40 Trifecta £176.40 Pool: £8230.31 - 12.02 winning tickets..
Owner Exors of the Late R L Bedding **Bred** Jim McDonald **Trained** Lichfield, Staffs
■ Stewards' Enquiry : Robert Winston three-day ban; careless riding (23rd-25th June).

FOCUS
The Classic generation had won four of the last six runnings of this race, but this was one for the older brigade. The field ended up racing centre-to-far side. Not form to be too positive or liberal about.

3103 BETVICTOR NO LOSE HUGHES MONEY BACK SANDY LANE STKS (LISTED RACE) 6f
4:25 (4:27) (Class 1) 3-Y-O
£20,982 (£7,955; £3,981; £1,983; £995; £499) **Stalls** Centre

Form — RPR

1-41 **1** **Professor**29 2208 3-9-0 105 .... PatDobbs 8 112+
(Richard Hannon) *trckd ldrs: n.m.r and edgd rt 2f out: r.o to ld last 50yds: readily* **11/8**[1]

-506 **2** *1 3/4* **Glass Office**22 2415 3-9-5 103 .... JimCrowley 7 110
(David Simcock) *hld up in rr: hdwy 2f out: kpt on fnl f: tk 2nd nr line* **11/1**

-446 **3** *3/4* **Mar Mar (IRE)**100 837 3-8-9 97 .... (b) MickaelBarzalona 5 98
(Saeed bin Suroor) *trckd ldrs: led appr fnl f: hung bdly lft: hdd last 50yds: lost 2nd nr fin* **7/1**

-322 **4** *2 3/4* **Lucky Beggar (IRE)**23 2400 3-9-0 100 .... RobertWinston 4 94
(Charles Hills) *dwlt: led after 100yds: hdd over 3f out: led briefly over 1f out: wknd last 75yds* **13/2**[3]

55-0 **5** *5* **Pearl Acclaim (IRE)**38 1921 3-9-0 100 .... JamieSpencer 2 78
(Robert Cowell) *hld up in rr: hdwy over 2f out: drvn and wknd over 1f out* **17/2**

-600 **6** *hd* **Jadanna (IRE)**38 1921 3-8-9 95 .... GrahamLee 3 73
(James Given) *chsd ldrs: outpcd over 3f out: sme hdwy 2f out: sn wknd* **25/1**

16-5 **7** *1 1/2* **Valais Girl**49 1676 3-8-9 94 .... (v[1]) HayleyTurner 6 68
(Marcus Tregoning) *t.k.h: led 100yds: led over 3f out: hdd & wknd over 1f out* **16/1**

6-2 **8** *2* **Clancy Avenue (USA)**52 1620 3-9-0 98 .... WayneLordan 1 66
(T Stack, Ire) *trckd ldrs: effrt over 2f out: hung lft and lost pl over 1f out* **9/2**[2]

1m 11.09s (-2.71) **Going Correction** -0.25s/f (Firm) **8 Ran SP% 114.7**
Speed ratings (Par 107): **108,105,104,101,94 94,92,89**
toteswingers 1&2 £24.90, 1&3 £2.20, 2&3 £27.60 CSF £18.35 TOTE £2.10: £1.20, £3.10, £2.40; EX 16.10 Trifecta £106.30 Pool: £3949.50 - 27.85 winning tickets..
Owner Mrs P Good **Bred** Exors Of The Late J R Good **Trained** East Everleigh, Wilts

FOCUS
They raced up the centre for most of this contest and the pace looked solid. The winning time was around half a second faster than the older fillies and mares in the Cecil Frail. Another step forward from the progressive winner.

3104 DONWLOAD THE BETVICTOR APP NOW H'CAP 6f
5:00 (5:01) (Class 4) (0-85,85) 3-Y-O
£6,469 (£1,925; £962; £481) **Stalls** Centre

Form — RPR

-124 **1** **Shore Step (IRE)**15 2626 3-9-0 78 .... MartinHarley 9 92
(Mick Channon) *chsd ldrs: led over 1f out: edgd lft: drvn out* **10/1**

-100 **2** *1 1/2* **Robot Boy (IRE)**24 2371 3-9-4 82 .... JamieSpencer 4 91
(David Barron) *hld up in rr: effrt over 2f out: chsng ldrs over 1f out: kpt on to take 2nd nr fin* **6/1**[2]

3-20 **3** *1/2* **Brazen**21 2452 3-9-7 85 .... AdamKirby 3 92
(David Simcock) *hld up in rr: effrt over 2f out: chsng wnr over 1f out: styd on same pce ins fnl f* **7/4**[1]

140 **4** *5* **My Name Is Rio (IRE)**22 2430 3-8-10 74 .... NeilCallan 1 65
(Michael Dods) *chsd ldrs on outer: one pce fnl 2f* **12/1**

2-00 **5** *1/2* **Penny Garcia**22 2408 3-8-13 77 .... RobertWinston 7 67
(Tim Easterby) *hamperded s: in rr: effrt over 2f out: kpt on fnl f* **40/1**

3050 **6** *1 1/4* **Satsuma**22 2430 3-9-7 85 .... KierenFallon 10 71
(David Brown) *hld up: hdwy over 3f out: sn trcking ldrs: edgd lft over 2f out: one pce* **20/1**

1-16 **7** *2 1/4* **Bogsnog (IRE)**22 2408 3-9-1 79 .... GrahamLee 8 58
(Kristin Stubbs) *chsd ldrs: outpcd over 2f out: wknd over 1f out* **8/1**[3]

21-6 **8** *3/4* **Huntsmans Close**29 2208 3-9-7 85 .... HayleyTurner 2 61
(Michael Bell) *led: hdd over 1f out: sn wknd: eased towards fin* **6/1**[2]

1206 **9** *2 1/4* **Archie Stevens**16 2593 3-8-11 75 .... (p) RichardKingscote 5 44
(Tom Dascombe) *stdd s: t.k.h: sn trcking ldrs: lost pl over 1f out* **10/1**

-162 **10** *14* **Foxtrot Jubilee (IRE)**31 2158 3-9-5 83 .... JimCrowley 6
(Ralph Beckett) *wnt rt s: chsd ldrs: lost pl 2f out: bhd and eased fnl f* **12/1**

1m 11.54s (-2.26) **Going Correction** -0.25s/f (Firm) **10 Ran SP% 116.8**
Speed ratings (Par 101): **105,103,102,95,95 93,90,89,86,67**
toteswingers 1&2 £55.40, 1&3 £27.70, 2&3 £23.20 CSF £68.99 CT £159.37 TOTE £10.20: £2.90, £1.80, £1.40; EX 68.30 Trifecta £301.60 Pool: £2288.31 - 5.68 winning tickets..
Owner Jon and Julia Aisbitt **Bred** Lynn Lodge Stud **Trained** West Ilsley, Berks

FOCUS
A fair 3yo sprint handicap and the front three pulled well clear. The form is rated on the positive side.

3105 ROYAL ASCOT MONEY BACK AT BETVICTOR.COM CLASSIFIED STKS 1m 2f 95y
5:35 (5:36) (Class 4) 3-Y-O
£7,115 (£2,117; £1,058; £529) **Stalls** Centre

Form — RPR

3-46 **1** **Double Discount (IRE)**31 2151 3-9-0 79 .... RichardKingscote 3 88+
(Tom Dascombe) *trckd ldr: effrt 4f out: upsides 3f out: led over 1f out: edgd lft ins fnl f: hld on wl* **13/8**[1]

02-2 **2** *3/4* **Elhaame (IRE)**59 1481 3-9-0 77 .... KierenFallon 1 86+
(Luca Cumani) *trckd ldng pair: effrt 4f out: rdn over 2f out: styd on to chse wnr last 75yds: no real imp* **9/4**[2]

2130 **3** *2 3/4* **Enzaal (USA)**14 2651 3-9-0 80 .... NeilCallan 2 83
(Mark Johnston) *set stdy pce: increased gallop over 4f out: rdn 2f out: sn hdd: one pce whn hmpd ins fnl f* **11/2**

2-01 **4** *9* **Song Light**23 2386 3-9-0 78 .... JamieSpencer 4 69
(David Elsworth) *dwlt: hld up in last: effrt over 3f out: wknd over 1f out: eased towards fin* **11/4**[3]

2m 14.57s (-0.93) **Going Correction** -0.25s/f (Firm) **4 Ran SP% 110.9**
Speed ratings (Par 101): **93,92,90,83**
toteswingers 1&2 £5.10, 1&3 £3.50, 2&3 £10.40 CSF £5.71 TOTE £2.80; EX 6.90 Trifecta £7.20 Pool: £949.59 - 98.28 winning tickets..
Owner Laurence A Bellman **Bred** Bernard Cooke **Trained** Malpas, Cheshire

FOCUS
Just 3lb covered the quartet on these terms and, with the pace an ordinary one, they raced in Indian file until the home bend. Steps up from the first two.
T/Jkpt: Not won. T/Plt: £100.60 to a £1 stake. Pool: £127,271.18 - 923.31 winning tickets T/Qpdt: £5.30 to a £1 stake. Pool: £7,775.80 - 1078.4 winning tickets WG

2442 NEWBURY (L-H)
Saturday, June 8

OFFICIAL GOING: Good to firm (7.4)
Rail on Round course moved between 8f and 5f increasing distances by 9m. Straight course far rail moved out 4m with a cut-off at 2.5f.
Wind: Moderate behind Weather: Sunny

3106 FREDDIE MILO AMATEUR RIDERS' H'CAP 1m 2f 6y
6:30 (6:31) (Class 5) (0-70,69) 4-Y-O+
£2,807 (£870; £435; £217) **Stalls** Centre

Form — RPR

2231 **1** **Balmoral Castle**8 2845 4-10-3 63 .... MrJHarding(5) 1 73+
(Jonathan Portman) *trckd ldrs: pushed along to ld appr fnl f: styd on strly clsng stages* **2/1**[1]

0033 **2** *1* **Whinging Willie (IRE)**9 2787 4-10-2 60 .... MissHayleyMoore(3) 12 68
(Gary Moore) *t.k.h: stdd towards rr: gd hdwy fr 2f out: rdn and styd on wl fnl f to take 2nd fnl 50yds: no imp on wnr* **6/1**[2]

0021 **3** *1 1/4* **Edgware Road**32 2130 5-10-1 63 .... MissBHampson(7) 6 69
(Sean Curran) *chsd ldrs: led 2f out: sn jnd: hdd appr fnl f: no ex and dropped to 3rd fnl 50yds* **22/1**

63-5 **4** *1/2* **Laconicos (IRE)**23 2383 11-9-13 59 .... (t) MissCScott(5) 8 64
(William Stone) *in rr: hdwy fr 2f out: styd on to go 4th ins fnl f: nt rch ldrs* **11/1**

0000 **5** *1/2* **Lily Edge**23 2395 4-10-10 65 .... MissSBrotherton 4 69
(John Bridger) *chsd ldrs: rdn over 2f out: styd on same pce fnl f* **20/1**

00-0 **6** *nse* **Rub Of The Relic (IRE)**8 2836 8-10-0 60 .... (v) MissHDukes(5) 5 63
(Paul Midgley) *led: hdd 4f out: styd chsng ldrs: one pce fnl 2f* **25/1**

1-00 **7** ½ **Garrisson (IRE)**[22] 2413 4-10-9 **64**........................ MrSWalker 2 66
(Charles Hills) *in rr: pushed along over 2f out: hdwy fnl f: kpt on clsng stages but nvr a threat* **14/1**

3/0- **8** hd **Piers Gaveston (IRE)**[409] 1607 4-10-9 **67**.................. MrFMitchell(3) 13 69
(George Baker) *chsd ldrs: pushed along and outpcd over 2f out: swtchd rt 2f out: styd on again u.p fnl f* **20/1**

-006 **9** ¾ **Capitol Gain (IRE)**[14] 2673 4-10-7 **69**.................(p) MrORJSangster(7) 14 70
(Brian Meehan) *chsd ldrs: pushed along and c centre fr 3f out: hung rt and wknd fnl f* **10/1**[3]

2555 **10** 1¼ **Merrjanah**[110] 703 5-9-2 **50** oh2........................ MrAFrench(7) 11 48
(Neville Bycroft) *in rr: hdwy 3f out: wknd ins fnl 2f* **25/1**

1644 **11** 4½ **Flag Of Glory**[7] 2875 6-10-2 **62**........................ MissMEdden(5) 10 51
(Peter Hiatt) *chsd ldr: led 4f out: hdd 2f out: wknd over 1f out* **20/1**

2-14 **12** 2 **Srinagar Girl**[11] 2750 4-10-12 **67**........................ MissRachelKing 3 52
(Clive Cox) *chsd ldrs: wknd over 2f out* **6/1**[2]

1060 **13** 2¼ **Strike Force**[23] 2383 9-10-11 **69**.......................(t) MissALHutchinson(3) 7 50
(Alison Hutchinson) *racd wd towards centre: a in rr* **25/1**

-340 **14** 11 **Berwin (IRE)**[16] 2606 4-10-6 **64**........................ MissCBoxall(3) 9 23
(Sylvester Kirk) *slowly away: in rr: sme hdwy over 3f out: nvr any ch and sn wknd* **14/1**

2m 8.17s (-0.63) **Going Correction** -0.025s/f (Good) **14** Ran SP% **122.8**
Speed ratings (Par 103): **101,100,99,98,98 98,97,97,97,96 92,91,89,80**
Tote Swingers: 1&2 £3.40, 2&3 £40.70, 1&3 £6.20 CSF £11.55 CT £201.12 TOTE £3.00: £1.70, £2.20, £4.20; EX 16.60 Trifecta £189.30 Pool: £1,913.38 - 7.57 winning units..
Owner J G B Portman **Bred** Springcombe Park Stud **Trained** Upper Lambourn, Berks
■ Stewards' Enquiry : Miss Hayley Moore seven-day ban: use of whip (24, 27 June, 1, 6, 7, 11 & 12 July)

FOCUS
This was an amateur riders' race of reasonable quality, run at a good pace, with the lightly raced winner looking progressive enough to make his mark in open handicaps from now on. Straightforward form.

3107 RELYON CLEANING NEWBURY MAIDEN AUCTION FILLIES' STKS 6f 8y
7:00 (7:01) (Class 5) 2-Y-O **£2,911** (£866; £432; £216) **Stalls** High

Form RPR

2 **1** **Ligeia**[15] 2617 2-8-4 0........................ KieranO'Neill 14 75
(Richard Hannon) *mde virtually all but sn jnd then hrd pressed fr 2f out and rdn: hrd drvn to assert ins fnl f: kpt on wl* **5/4**[1]

2 2 **Gown (IRE)** 2-8-6 0........................ SamHitchcott 4 71
(Charles Hills) *chsd ldrs: drvn to chal and hung lft fr over 1f out: nt pce of wnr ins fnl furlong* **20/1**

3 1¼ **Kendal Mint** 2-8-8 0........................ JohnFahy 9 69+
(Clive Cox) *s.i.s: and outpcd: pushed along and hdwy fr 3f out to chse ldrs 2f out: kpt on wl for 3rd fnl f but nt pce of ldng duo* **7/2**[3]

40 **4** 1 **Sweet Alibi (IRE)**[23] 2382 2-8-4 0........................ ChrisCatlin 10 62
(J S Moore) *pressed wnr: rdn and stl ev wl over 1f out: one pce ins fnl f* **40/1**

5 3 **Sleeping Venus (IRE)** 2-8-6 0........................ NickyMackay 8 55+
(George Baker) *in rr: pushed along over 2f out: kpt on fnl f: nvr a threat* **33/1**

06 **6** hd **Jana**[17] 2562 2-7-13 0........................ CameronHardie(7) 13 55
(Sylvester Kirk) *chsd ldrs: rdn and styd on same pce fnl 2f* **40/1**

0 **7** 4½ **My My My Diliza**[9] 2805 2-8-1 0........................ RyanPowell(3) 6 39
(J S Moore) *chsd ldrs: rdn and hung lft ins fnl 2f: sn wknd* **66/1**

8 2¾ **Sakhee'Ssquirrel** 2-8-6 0........................ CathyGannon 5 33
(David Evans) *pressed ldrs tl appr fnl 2f: sn wknd* **40/1**

9 ½ **Cueca (FR)** 2-8-3 0 ow2........................ MatthewLawson(5) 2 33
(Jonathan Portman) *towards rr: sme hdwy 2f out: one pce whn pushed lft and wknd sn after* **14/1**

10 ½ **Sheacheval (IRE)** 2-8-1 0........................ MichaelJMMurphy(5) 3 30
(J S Moore) *s.i.s: in rr: rdn over 2f out: mod prog clsng stages* **33/1**

11 2¼ **Assoluta (IRE)** 2-8-8 0........................ JackMitchell 12 25
(Sylvester Kirk) *outpcd* **40/1**

5 **12** 37 **Amontillado (IRE)**[11] 2744 2-8-11 0........................ RichardHughes 7
(Richard Hannon) *early spped: sn bhd: eased fnl 2f* **3/1**[2]

1m 13.6s (0.60) **Going Correction** +0.125s/f (Good) **12** Ran SP% **120.2**
Speed ratings (Par 90): **101,98,96,95,91 91,85,81,80,80 77,27**
Tote Swingers: 1&2 £5.90, 2&3 £10.50, 1&3 £1.40 CSF £34.66 TOTE £2.10: £1.10, £4.10, £1.60; EX 26.40 Trifecta £99.00 Pool: £1,775.79 - 13.44 winning units..
Owner Pineapple Stud **Bred** Plantation Stud **Trained** East Everleigh, Wilts

FOCUS
Although this is unlikely to be a classic Newbury maiden, there will be future winners in the line-up and the winner looked potentially useful. Avertage form for the grade, the winner to her Goodwood level.

3108 BATHWICK TYRES H'CAP 1m 7y(R)
7:30 (7:31) (Class 4) (0-85,86) 4-Y-O+ **£4,851** (£1,443; £721; £360) **Stalls** Centre

Form RPR

-134 **1** **Ree's Rascal (IRE)**[33] 2085 5-8-13 **82**........................ NathanAlison(5) 7 89
(Jim Boyle) *in tch: hdwy to chse ldrs fr 3f out: led ins fnl 2f: hrd drvn fnl f: kpt on wl* **6/1**[3]

-500 **2** 1 **Starwatch**[30] 2193 6-8-11 **80**........................ MichaelJMMurphy(5) 2 85
(John Bridger) *chsd ldrs: led 2f out: sn hdd: styd pressing wnr tl one pce ins fnl f* **28/1**

-053 **3** nk **Ertikaan**[17] 2571 6-9-2 **80**........................(tp) SebSanders 9 84
(Brendan Powell) *in rr: hdwy on inner fr 2f out: keeping on whn nt much daylight ins fnl f: styd on clsng stages* **40/1**

0422 **4** 1¾ **Lord Ofthe Shadows (IRE)**[8] 2841 4-9-8 **86**.........(b) RichardHughes 10 92+
(Richard Hannon) *in rr: hdwy to cl on ldrs whn nt clr run ins fnl f: kpt on again fnl f: no ex clsng stages* **11/4**[2]

6000 **5** 2¼ **Yojimbo (IRE)**[16] 2592 5-9-2 **80**........................ MatthewDavies 6 75
(Mick Channon) *chsd ldrs: rdn over 2f out: sn hung lft: styd on same pce fnl f* **12/1**

0-54 **6** 1 **Orders From Rome (IRE)**[12] 2724 4-8-4 **73**.................. AmyScott(5) 5 66
(Eve Johnson Houghton) *in rr but in tch: hdwy 3f out: chsd ldrs fr over 2f out: wknd appr fnl f* **20/1**

15-4 **7** ½ **Net Whizz (USA)**[40] 1878 4-9-6 **84**........................ FrankieDettori 1 75
(Jeremy Noseda) *led after 1f: pushed along fr 3f out: hdd 2f out: wknd over 1f out* **7/4**[1]

51-5 **8** 2 **Scottish Glen**[28] 2286 7-8-8 **72**........................ JohnFahy 4 59
(Patrick Chamings) *in tch on rails: rdn and outpcd over 2f out: swtchd rt to outside and sn wl bhd: sme late prog* **10/1**

0250 **9** 7 **Nazreef**[56] 1545 6-8-12 **76**........................ ChrisCatlin 8 47
(Hughie Morrison) *in tch chsd ldrs 3f out: wknd over 2f out* **16/1**

0030 **10** 2½ **Ortac Rock (IRE)**[28] 2266 4-9-6 **84**........................(t) KieranO'Neill 3 49
(Richard Hannon) *led 1f: styd pressing ldrs: wkng whn hmpd ins fnl 2f: eased clsng stages* **16/1**

1m 37.12s (-1.58) **Going Correction** -0.025s/f (Good) **10** Ran SP% **116.5**
Speed ratings (Par 105): **106,105,104,102,100 99,99,97,90,87**
Tote Swingers: 1&2 £19.20, 2&3 £80.90, 1&3 £41.20 CSF £161.53 CT £6125.25 TOTE £7.70: £2.20, £7.00, £7.90; EX 162.60 Trifecta £1159.70 Part won. Pool: £1,546.34 - 0.48 winning units..
Owner Walter Hayford **Bred** Pier House Stud **Trained** Epsom, Surrey

FOCUS
This was an above-average handicap in which the winner is generally more reliable than some of his opponents. He posted a small personal best.

3109 BATHWICK TYRES MAIDEN STKS 6f 8y
8:00 (8:00) (Class 5) 3-Y-O **£2,587** (£770; £384; £192) **Stalls** High

Form RPR

42-2 **1** **Floating Along (IRE)**[35] 2006 3-9-0 75........................ RichardHughes 5 79+
(William Haggas) *mde all: drvn and qcknd appr fnl f: easily* **4/6**[1]

2 3 **Hi Filwah (USA)** 3-9-5 0........................ SebSanders 3 73+
(Jeremy Noseda) *in tch: pushed along and hdwy fr 2f out: edging lft but kpt on wl fnl f to take 2nd fnl 110yds but nvr any ch w wnr* **8/1**[3]

3 **3** ¾ **Superboot (IRE)**[14] 2650 3-9-5 0........................ FrankieDettori 2 71
(Michael Wigham) *in tch: hdwy 2f out: trckd wnr and rdn over 1f out but no imp: one pce and lost 2nd fnl 110yds* **3/1**[2]

00- **4** 3¼ **Blue Twister**[236] 7110 3-9-5 0........................ LiamKeniry 4 61
(Andrew Balding) *chsd ldrs and sn disputing 2nd: rdn over 2f out: wknd ins fnl f* **16/1**

5 ¾ **Coire Gabhail** 3-9-0 0........................ NickyMackay 1 53
(Hughie Morrison) *chsd ldrs and sn disputing 2nd: rdn over 2f out: wknd over 1f out* **14/1**

-304 **6** nse **Talqaa**[12] 2722 3-9-0 69........................ MatthewDavies 6 53
(Mick Channon) *sn disputing 2nd: rdn over 2f out: wknd u.p over 1f out* **20/1**

7 26 **Chilworth Diva** 3-9-0 0........................ SamHitchcott 7
(Mick Channon) *s.i.s: in rr: managed to get in tch over 3f out: sn wknd* **25/1**

8 ¾ **Telamon (IRE)** 3-9-0 0........................ MatthewLawson(5) 8
(Milton Bradley) *s.i.s: in rr: sme prog to get in tch over 3f out: sn wknd* **66/1**

1m 13.01s (0.01) **Going Correction** +0.125s/f (Good) **8** Ran SP% **118.7**
Speed ratings (Par 99): **104,100,99,94,93 93,58,57**
Tote Swingers: 1&2 £3.20, 2&3 £3.20, 1&3 £1.02 CSF £7.40 TOTE £1.70: £1.10, £1.80, £1.50; EX 8.50 Trifecta £23.80 Pool: £1,434.87 - 45.03 winning units..
Owner Lael Stable **Bred** Wentworth Racing **Trained** Newmarket, Suffolk

FOCUS
There were some interesting late-developers in this 3yo maiden, with the winner being worthy of particular note. This bare form could easily underrate her.

3110 GP MASONRY H'CAP 1m 5f 61y
8:30 (8:30) (Class 5) (0-75,75) 4-Y-O+ **£2,587** (£770; £384; £192) **Stalls** Centre

Form RPR

1442 **1** **Admirable Duque (IRE)**[37] 1949 7-8-9 **63**..................(b) HayleyTurner 5 75
(Dominic Ffrench Davis) *in tch: stdy hdwy over 3f out: to chal 2f out and sn led: pushed clr appr fnl f: comf* **15/2**[3]

51-2 **2** 4 **Passion Play**[24] 2360 5-9-2 **70**........................ JimCrowley 10 76
(William Knight) *trckd ldrs: wnt 2nd 6f out: drvn to chal appr fnl 2f: sn rdn to chse wnr but no imp and one pce fr over 1f out* **5/4**[1]

6-02 **3** 2½ **Double Cee**[17] 2569 4-9-5 **73**........................ RichardHughes 8 75
(Warren Greatrex) *in rr: hdwy fr 4f out: drvn to chse ldrs over 2f out: kpt on same pce for 3rd fnl f* **8/1**

4/0- **4** 1 **Venir Rouge**[30] 28 9-7-12 **57**........................ RosieJessop(5) 9 58
(Harry Whittington) *chsd ldrs: rdn wl over 2f out: styd on same pce for wl-hld 4th fnl f* **50/1**

0010 **5** 2 **Minority Interest**[17] 2567 4-8-3 **57**........................(v) KieranO'Neill 7 55
(Brett Johnson) *led: rdn and hdd 2f out: wknd over 1f out* **16/1**

0/56 **6** 1¾ **Eshtyaaq**[28] 2269 6-9-2 **70**........................ FrankieDettori 3 65
(David Evans) *in rr: hdwy to cl on ldrs over 2f out: sn rdn and btn* **7/2**[2]

-545 **7** 9 **Ginger Fizz**[17] 2570 6-8-13 **67**........................(t[1]) ChrisCatlin 4 49
(Ben Case) *sn chsng ldr: lost 2nd 6f out: rdn over 4f out: wknd over 2f out* **12/1**

0001 **8** 8 **Honourable Knight (IRE)**[17] 2570 5-8-9 **63**........................ LiamKeniry 1 33
(Mark Usher) *in tch early: bhd fnl 5f* **16/1**

334/ **9** 6 **Grams And Ounces**[56] 3399 6-9-2 **75**..................(t) ThomasBrown(5) 2 36
(John Flint) *rdn 3f out: a in rr* **14/1**

2m 52.25s (0.25) **Going Correction** -0.025s/f (Good) **9** Ran SP% **117.6**
Speed ratings (Par 103): **98,95,94,93,92 91,85,80,76**
Tote Swingers: 1&2 £2.50, 2&3 £1.40, 1&3 £8.20 CSF £17.61 CT £80.87 TOTE £6.40: £2.30, £1.10, £3.10; EX 14.90 Trifecta £80.50 Pool: £1,294.72 - 12.05 winning units..
Owner Mrs J E Taylor **Bred** Airlie Stud And R N Clay **Trained** Lambourn, Berks

FOCUS
This was a middling handicap, won easily by a horse whose turf rating needs adjusting upwards. The second is a solid guide.

3111 GT EXHIBITIONS FILLIES' H'CAP 7f (S)
9:00 (9:01) (Class 5) (0-75,73) 3-Y-O+ **£2,587** (£770; £384; £192) **Stalls** High

Form RPR

15P1 **1** **Amosite**[33] 2092 7-9-9 **68**........................(p) FrankieDettori 1 76
(J R Jenkins) *mde all: pushed along 2f out: drvn and qcknd thrght fnl f: hld on all out* **5/1**[2]

0-32 **2** hd **It's Taboo**[16] 2597 3-9-1 **70**........................ RichardHughes 5 73+
(Mark Usher) *hld up in rr but in tch: hdwy and nt clr run 2f out: swtchd lft wl over 1f out: drvn and styd on strly to cl on wnr fnl 110yds: jst failed* **2/1**[1]

6043 **3** ¾ **My Own Way Home**[16] 2596 5-8-11 **56**........................ CathyGannon 3 61
(David Evans) *chsd ldr: rdn 2f out: chal over 1f out: kpt on same pce into 3rd fnl 110yds* **6/1**[3]

320 **4** ½ **Ellie In The Pink (IRE)**[112] 689 5-9-1 **65**.............. JemmaMarshall(5) 2 69
(Pat Phelan) *chsd ldrs: rdn to chal appr fnl f: outpcd fnl 110yds* **8/1**

24-0 **5** ¾ **Macchiara**[46] 1751 4-10-0 **73**........................ ChrisCatlin 6 75
(Rae Guest) *in rr: hdwy to cl on ldrs 1/2-way: rdn 2f out: wknd ins fnl f* **7/1**

0-16 **6** ¾ **Elusive Gold (IRE)**[17] 2572 3-8-12 **67**........................ JamesMcDonald 7 63
(J W Hills) *chsd ldrs: rdn over 1f out: wknd fnl 110yds* **12/1**

0002 **7** 2 **Saint Irene**[18] 2534 4-9-4 **63**........................ LiamKeniry 4 58
(Michael Blanshard) *chsd ldrs: rdn and one pce whn hmpd ins fnl 2f: no ch after* **7/1**

62-5 **P** **Spiritual Girl**[85] 1019 3-9-3 **72** HayleyTurner 8
(Michael Bell) *p.u and dismntd after 1f* **14/1**

1m 26.38s (0.68) **Going Correction** +0.125s/f (Good)
WFA 3 from 4yo+ 10lb **8** Ran SP% **114.8**
Speed ratings (Par 100): **101,100,99,99,98 97,95,**
Tote Swingers: 1&2 £1.10, 2&3 £4.90, 1&3 £6.80 CSF £15.50 CT £62.00 TOTE £4.60: £2.40, £1.40, £2.30; EX 17.60 Trifecta £99.60 Pool: £1,418.36 - 10.67 winning units..
Owner Mrs Claire Goddard **Bred** Richard Kent **Trained** Royston, Herts

FOCUS
This was competitive despite the smallish field. The winner is in the form of her life and the runner-up was arguably unlucky.
T/Plt: £34.10 to a £1 stake. Pool: £73,500.00 - 1,571.28 winning tickets. T/Qpdt: £20.90 to a £1 stake. Pool: £4,567.00 - 161.30 winning tickets. ST

3057 NEWMARKET (R-H)

Saturday, June 8

OFFICIAL GOING: Good to firm (good in places; 7.8)
Far side course used and stalls on far side except 10f, 12f & 15f: Centre. Bend into home straight repositioned, adding 18m to races of 10f, 12f and 15f.
Wind: moderate, across Weather: overcast

3112 ANIMAL HEALTH TRUST EBF MAIDEN STKS 6f
1:45 (1:46) (Class 4) 2-Y-O **£4,528** (£1,347; £673; £336) **Stalls** High

Form RPR

53 **1** **Jallota**[14] 2670 2-9-5 0 SamHitchcott 1 85
(Mick Channon) *wnt rt s: sn rcvrd and chsng ldr: rdn to ld wl over 1f out: forged clr 1f out: styd on wl: rdn out* **12/1**

2 1 ¼ **Brown Sugar (IRE)** 2-9-5 0 JamesDoyle 15 81+
(Richard Hannon) *dwlt: hld up towards rr of main gp: stl towards rr and forced to switch arnd many horses over 1f out: rdn along mainly hands and heels and str run fnl f: wnt 2nd towards fin: no threat to wnr* **40/1**

4 **3** ¾ **Munjally**[14] 2670 2-9-5 0 FrankieDettori 11 79
(Richard Hannon) *led: rdn and hdd wl over 1f out: styd on same pce ins fnl f: lost 2nd towards fin* **6/1**[2]

4 2 **Zarwaan** 2-9-5 0 PaulHanagan 12 73
(Ed Dunlop) *wl in tch in midfield: rdn and effrt 2f out: chsd ldrs and unable qck ent fnl f: plugged on same pce after* **16/1**

0 **5** nse **Speculative Bid (IRE)**[22] 2411 2-9-5 0 TomQueally 13 73
(Gerard Butler) *in tch in midfield: rdn 1/2-way: hdwy and chsd ldrs over 1f out: unable qck ent fnl f: plugged on same pce after* **16/1**

6 nk **L'Importante** 2-9-5 0 RyanMoore 2 73+
(Marco Botti) *rn green: in tch in rr of main gp: rdn and hdwy jst over 1f out: styd on wl fnl f: nvr trbld ldrs* **12/1**

7 ¾ **Speedfiend** 2-9-5 0 StevieDonohoe 8 70
(Noel Quinlan) *hld up in tch in midfield: rdn and effrt 2f out: unable qck and outpcd over 1f out: no threat to wnr but kpt on again ins fnl f* **13/2**[3]

8 5 **Musical Comedy** 2-9-5 0 RichardHughes 6 56
(Richard Hannon) *chsd ldrs: rdn and unable qck over 2f out: btn over 1f out: wknd fnl f: eased towards fin* **12/1**

9 1 ¾ **Bow Creek (IRE)** 2-9-5 0 TedDurcan 9 50
(Mark Johnston) *restless in stalls: chsd ldrs: rdn and struggling ent fnl 2f: wknd over 1f out: eased wl ins fnl f* **25/1**

10 4 ½ **Stalactite (IRE)** 2-9-5 0 SilvestreDeSousa 3 39
(Saeed bin Suroor) *towards rr of main gp: rdn and outpcd 1/2-way: n.d after: eased ins fnl f* **8/1**

50 **11** 6 **Red Oasis**[17] 2562 2-9-5 0 NickyMackay 5 22
(Robert Eddery) *in tch in midfield: rdn and struggling jst over 2f out: wkng whn carried rt over 1f out: sn bhd: eased ins fnl f* **150/1**

4 **12** 6 **Gm Hopkins**[22] 2411 2-9-5 0 WilliamBuick 14
(John Gosden) *wl in tch: moving poorly and lost pl 2f out: sn eased* **7/4**[1]

13 7 **Chainsaw** 2-9-5 0 JamesMcDonald 4
(Stuart Williams) *plld hrd: hld up in tch in midfield: wknd ent fnl 2f: wl bhd and eased ins fnl f: eased ins fnl f: t.o* **40/1**

14 3 ½ **Aspenbreeze** 2-9-5 0 LiamKeniry 10
(Alan Bailey) *a outpcd in rr: rdn after 2f out: lost tch over 2f out: t.o and eased fnl f* **150/1**

15 2 ½ **Primrose Posy** 2-8-7 0 [1] ShelleyBirkett(7) 7
(Julia Feilden) *sn outpcd in rr and rdn: lost tch 1/2-way: t.o over 2f out* **150/1**

1m 12.96s (0.46) **Going Correction** +0.125s/f (Good) **15** Ran SP% **120.6**
Speed ratings (Par 95): **101,99,98,95,95 95,94,87,85,79 71,63,53,49,45**
toteswingers 1&2 £31.40, 1&3 £13.30, 2&3 £40.10 CSF £441.42 TOTE £15.70: £3.80, £5.80, £3.20; EX 293.00 Trifecta £1239.50 Part won. Pool: £1652.73 - 0.01 winning tickets..
Owner Nick & Olga Dhandsa & John & Zoe Webster **Bred** Barry Walters **Trained** West Ilsley, Berks
■ Stewards' Enquiry : James Doyle one-day ban; careless riding (23rd June).

FOCUS
Richard Hughes described conditions as good to firm, with Ted Durcan calling it "lovely ground". An interesting maiden, run in a time just under three seconds outside standard. The race was weakened by the favourite's no-show, but winners should come out of it. Jallota is rated to his York level.

3113 LADBROKES CHARITABLE TRUST H'CAP 1m 2f
2:20 (2:21) (Class 3) (0-95,89) 4-Y-O+ **£9,703** (£2,887; £1,443; £721) **Stalls** Centre

Form RPR

42-1 **1** **Niceofyoutotellme**[58] 1501 4-9-5 **87** JamesDoyle 2 97+
(Ralph Beckett) *stdd s: hld up in tch in rr: hdwy 2f out: drvn and chal jst ins fnl f: led wl ins fnl f: r.o wl* **9/2**[2]

10-3 **2** 1 **Nabucco**[22] 2422 4-9-6 **88** WilliamBuick 3 96
(John Gosden) *chsd ldrs: drvn and ev ch over 1f out: led jst ins fnl f: hdd and no ex wl ins fnl f* **5/1**[3]

630- **3** 1 ¾ **Beaufort Twelve**[252] 6677 4-9-7 **89** RichardHughes 1 94
(William Jarvis) *hld up in tch towards rr: clsd on ldrs over 2f out: effrt and nt clr run over 1f out tl jst ins fnl f: drvn and kpt on to go 3rd towards fin* **14/1**

2-50 **4** ¾ **Basseterre (IRE)**[16] 2592 4-9-4 **86** JamesMcDonald 8 89
(Charles Hills) *hld up in tch towards rr: hdwy 3f out: rdn to ld over 1f out: hdd and drvn jst ins fnl f: no ex and one pce fnl 100yds* **8/1**

61-1 **5** 2 ¼ **Ehtedaam (USA)**[22] 2422 4-9-4 **86** PaulHanagan 6 85
(Saeed bin Suroor) *t.k.h: chsd ldrs: rdn and ev ch over 1f out: no ex jst ins fnl f: wknd fnl 100yds* **2/1**[1]

0003 **6** 2 **Assizes**[7] 2881 4-8-11 **79** TedDurcan 9 74
(Mark Johnston) *chsd ldrs: rdn 3f out: no ex u.p and outpcd over 1f out: wknd 1f out* **9/1**

00-0 **7** 2 ½ **Invisible Hunter (USA)**[49] 1675 4-9-7 **89** (t[1]) SilvestreDeSousa 5 79
(Saeed bin Suroor) *rrd as stalls opened: t.k.h: hld up in tch in midfield: lost pl and rdn 3f out: wknd u.p over 1f out: wl btn whn hung lft ins fnl f* **9/1**

50-0 **8** 3 **Halfsin (IRE)**[30] 2185 5-9-7 **89** (t) FrankieDettori 7 73
(Marco Botti) *led: rdn 2f out: hdd over 1f out and sn btn: wknd 1f out* **16/1**

0-36 **9** 8 **Status Symbol (IRE)**[22] 2422 8-9-2 **84** (t) WilliamCarson 4 52
(Anthony Carson) *in tch in last pair: hdwy into midfield 1/2-way: lost pl u.p over 2f out: wknd and bhd over 1f out* **25/1**

2m 5.98s (0.48) **Going Correction** +0.125s/f (Good) **9** Ran SP% **115.7**
Speed ratings (Par 107): **103,102,100,100,98 96,94,92,86**
toteswingers 1&2 £3.00, 1&3 £16.40, 2&3 £20.00 CSF £27.34 CT £291.22 TOTE £5.00: £1.50, £1.80, £4.70; EX 20.00 Trifecta £455.40 Pool: £1914.03 - 3.15 winning tickets..
Owner R Roberts **Bred** Minster Stud **Trained** Kimpton, Hants

FOCUS
A decent handicap. Once into the long straight they gradually tacked over to the far rail. The winner looks capable of better.

3114 BETFAIR SUPPORTING THE ANIMAL HEALTH TRUST H'CAP 6f
2:55 (2:56) (Class 2) (0-105,104) 3-Y-O+**£19,407** (£5,775; £2,886; £1,443) **Stalls** High

Form RPR

2112 **1** **Nocturn**[24] 2366 4-9-4 **94** (p) WilliamBuick 3 105+
(Jeremy Noseda) *chsd ldrs: rdn and effrt over 1f out: drvn to ld ins fnl f: jst hld on* **3/1**[2]

11-1 **2** nse **Enrol**[35] 2007 4-9-0 **90** RyanMoore 7 100+
(Sir Michael Stoute) *hld up towards rr: rdn and hdwy wl over 1f out: str run u.p ins fnl f: chsd wnr wl ins fnl f: jst failed* **2/1**[1]

-010 **3** ¾ **Mezzotint (IRE)**[7] 2858 4-9-2 **92** PaoloSirigu 12 100+
(Marco Botti) *stdd s: hld up in rr: rdn and effrt over 1f out: hdwy and swtchd rt jst ins fnl f: r.o wl fnl 100yds: wnt 3rd last strides* **25/1**

-026 **4** nk **Whozthecat (IRE)**[14] 2663 6-8-3 **86** (v) LukeLeadbitter(7) 6 93
(Declan Carroll) *led: rdn and hdd over 1f out: styd pressing ldrs: kpt on same pce ins fnl f* **40/1**

-500 **5** hd **Doctor Parkes**[7] 2865 7-8-9 **85** SaleemGolam 15 91
(Stuart Williams) *taken down early: chsd ldrs: rdn and ev ch over 1f out: led and edgd lft 1f out: hdd ins fnl f: lost 2nd wl ins fnl f and wknd cl home* **25/1**

2002 **6** ½ **Intransigent**[14] 2647 4-8-11 **92** ThomasBrown(5) 10 97
(Andrew Balding) *hld up in tch in midfield: rdn and effrt over 1f out: no imp 1f out: swtchd rt ins fnl f and styd on fnl 100yds* **9/1**[3]

-000 **7** ½ **Johannes (IRE)**[15] 2621 10-8-3 **86** SamanthaBell(7) 14 89
(Richard Fahey) *taken down early: hld up towards rr: rdn and effrt over 1f out: styd on ins fnl f: nt rch ldrs* **40/1**

600- **8** nk **Zero Money (IRE)**[273] 6028 7-9-8 **98** (b) JamesDoyle 5 100
(Hugo Palmer) *chsd ldr tl rdn to ld over 1f out: hdd 1f out: no ex and wknd ins fnl f* **16/1**

0-00 **9** ¾ **Heavy Metal**[22] 2415 3-9-6 **104** (b[1]) SilvestreDeSousa 9 104
(Mark Johnston) *sn pushed along in midfield: rdn 2f out: kpt on u.p but nvr gng pce to chal* **20/1**

0-03 **10** nk **Gatepost (IRE)**[14] 2647 4-8-11 **87** PaulHanagan 11 88
(Richard Fahey) *hld up towards rr: hdwy over 1f out: nt clr run ent fnl f: swtchd rt and stl nowhere to go ins fnl f: nvr able to chal* **11/1**

002- **11** ½ **Gramercy (IRE)**[315] 4611 6-9-4 **94** StevieDonohoe 4 91
(David Simcock) *bhd: rdn 2f out: styd on ins fnl f: nvr trbld ldrs* **16/1**

0231 **12** 1 ¼ **Summerinthecity (IRE)**[14] 2647 6-9-1 **91** TomQueally 13 84
(David Nicholls) *in tch in midfield: rdn 2f out: unable qck over 1f out: wknd ins fnl f* **11/1**

-100 **13** 1 **Cheworee**[12] 2724 4-8-9 **85** (t[1]) LiamKeniry 1 75
(David Elsworth) *hld up in midfield: rdn and effrt over 1f out: no prog and no threat to ldrs fnl f* **20/1**

0-06 **14** 1 ¾ **Secret Witness**[23] 2396 7-9-11 **101** (b) RichardHughes 2 85
(Ronald Harris) *stdd and dropped in bhd after s: rdn and effrt over 1f out: no prog: eased towards fin* **18/1**

1m 11.86s (-0.64) **Going Correction** +0.125s/f (Good)
WFA 3 from 4yo+ 8lb **14** Ran SP% **124.1**
Speed ratings (Par 109): **109,108,107,107,107 106,105,105,104,104 103,101,100,98**
toteswingers 1&2 £2.90, 1&3 £135.00, 2&3 £58.10 CSF £8.71 CT £132.64 TOTE £3.40: £1.80, £1.30, £8.60; EX 8.00 Trifecta £270.40 Pool: £88549.11 - 245.59 winning tickets..
Owner Miss Yvonne Jacques **Bred** J Ellis **Trained** Newmarket, Suffolk

FOCUS
A good sprint handicap, and solid form with the fourth and fifth the key to the level. The first two are progressive.

3115 JOHN SUNLEY MEMORIAL LEVY BOARD H'CAP 1m 4f
3:30 (3:31) (Class 2) (0-105,99) 4-Y-O+ **£32,345** (£9,625; £4,810; £2,405) **Stalls** Centre

Form RPR

2/45 **1** **Highland Castle**[28] 2252 5-9-0 **89** LiamKeniry 6 99+
(David Elsworth) *taken down early: stdd s: t.k.h: hld up in rr: hdwy u.p over 1f out: kpt on wl ins fnl f: led last strides* **12/1**

61-2 **2** nk **Handsome Man (IRE)**[49] 1689 4-9-6 **95** SilvestreDeSousa 2 104
(Saeed bin Suroor) *t.k.h: hld up wl in tch: rdn and effrt 3f out: styd on u.p and chal jst ins fnl f: sn led: kpt on tl hdd and no ex last strides* **6/1**

13-1 **3** nk **No Heretic**[34] 2044 5-9-4 **93** WilliamBuick 1 102
(David Simcock) *t.k.h: chsd ldr: rdn wl over 2f out: styd on and grad clsd over 1f out: ev ch ins fnl f: kpt on wl: no ex nr fin* **7/2**[1]

00-3 **4** 2 ¼ **Gabrial The Great (IRE)**[12] 2718 4-8-13 **88** RyanMoore 8 93
(Luca Cumani) *chsd ldrs: rdn and effrt wl over 2f out: styd on and grad clsd over 1f out: ev ch jst ins fnl f tl wknd fnl 75yds* **4/1**[2]

0-03 **5** ¾ **Vasily**[45] 1768 5-9-1 **90** PaulHanagan 3 94
(Robert Eddery) *led and sn clr: stl 3 l clr and rdn over 2f out: hdd ins fnl f: sn btn and wknd fnl 100yds* **16/1**

2/0- **6** ½ **Parlour Games**[423] 1318 5-9-10 **99** JamesDoyle 7 102
(Saeed bin Suroor) *hld up in midfield: effrt u.p 3f out: awkward hd carriage but sme hdwy over 1f out: no ex 1f out: wknd ins fnl f* **25/1**

-620 **7** 2 ¼ **Solaras Exhibition (IRE)**[52] 1273 5-8-1 **83** DanielMuscutt(7) 10 83
(Tim Vaughan) *hld up in midfield: rdn and unable qck 2f out: drvn and wknd over 1f out* **50/1**

1-42 **8** 3 ¼ **Suegioo (FR)**[34] 2044 4-9-0 **89** (p) FrankieDettori 5 84
(Marco Botti) *hld up in midfield: rdn and unable qck over 2f out: wknd over 1f out* **5/1**[3]

31-3 **9** 1 **Rawaki (IRE)**[22] 2407 5-8-11 **91** ThomasBrown(5) 11 84
(Andrew Balding) *stdd s: t.k.h: hld up towards rr: dropped to last 8f out: rdn and effrt over 2f out: awkward hd carriage and no imp: wknd over 1f out* **8/1**

The Form Book Flat, Raceform Ltd, Compton, RG20 6NL.

-021 **10** *15* **Angel Gabrial (IRE)**[28] 2251 4-9-2 **91** RichardHughes 9 71
(Ian Williams) *t.k.h: hld up in midfield: rdn and effrt 3f out: wknd wl over 1f out: bhd and eased ins fnl f* **8/1**

2m 32.43s (-0.47) **Going Correction** +0.125s/f (Good) **10** Ran SP% **114.8**
Speed ratings (Par 109): **106,105,105,104,103 103,101,99,98,88**
toteswingers 1&2 £27.20, 1&3 £13.30, 2&3 £2.60 CSF £80.98 CT £308.56 TOTE £17.40: £4.40, £2.50, £1.50; EX 139.90 Trifecta £408.40 Pool: £3463.57 - 6.36 winning tickets..
Owner J Wotherspoon & W Harrison-Allan **Bred** John Wotherspoon **Trained** Newmarket, Suffolk

FOCUS
A valuable handicap that was won last year by High Jinx, who developed into a high-class stayer. It was run at an ordinary gallop and there was a tight finish. The form is perhaps not as solid as it might have been.

3116 OFQUEST OFFICE FURNITURE SUPPORTING AHT MAIDEN FILLIES' STKS 7f
4:05 (4:08) (Class 5) 3-Y-O **£3,881** (£1,155; £577; £288) **Stalls** High

Form RPR

0-3 **1** **Broadway Duchess (IRE)**[21] 2448 3-9-0 0 RichardHughes 6 80+
(Richard Hannon) *chsd ldr tl led over 2f out: rdn and qcknd clr jst ins fnl f: r.o wl: comf* **5/2**[1]

2 *2 ¾* **Fashion Line (IRE)** 3-9-0 0 JamesMcDonald 9 71+
(Michael Bell) *dwlt: hld up towards rr: rdn 2f out: stl plenty to do whn hdwy over 1f out: str run ins fnl f to go 2nd towards fin: no threat to wnr* **33/1**

4 **3** *½* **Narmin (IRE)**[21] 2448 3-9-0 0 PaulHanagan 8 69
(John Gosden) *chsd ldrs: rdn and effrt over 1f out: drvn and unable qck 1f out: kpt on same pce after* **7/2**[2]

4 *hd* **Ruffled** 3-9-0 0 [1] WilliamBuick 7 69+
(John Gosden) *s.i.s: rn green in rr: stl only 14th whn swtchd rt over 1f out: stl green but r.o strly ins fnl f: no threat to wnr* **9/2**[3]

45-4 **5** *nk* **Cloudwalker (USA)**[29] 2224 3-9-0 79 TomQueally 3 68
(Ed Vaughan) *chsd ldrs: drvn and unable qck over 1f out: no threat to wnr and kpt on same pce fnl f* **8/1**

03 **5** *dht* **Persian Patriot**[21] 2456 3-9-0 0 FrankieDettori 13 68
(William Jarvis) *racd against far rail thrght: led tl over 2f out: drvn and outpcd by wnr 1f out: kpt on same pce: lost 3 pls cl home* **14/1**

26-4 **7** *1 ¼* **Hidden Belief (IRE)**[33] 2084 3-9-0 80 SilvestreDeSousa 2 65
(Ralph Beckett) *t.k.h: hld up in tch in midfield: rdn and effrt to chse ldrs over 1f out: no ex and btn 1f out: wknd ins fnl f* **5/1**

8 *hd* **Sharareh** 3-8-11 0 PatrickHills(3) 12 64+
(Luca Cumani) *in tch in midfield: shkn up over 1f out: pushed along and kpt on same pce ins fnl f* **16/1**

4-0 **9** *1 ½* **Ningbo Express (IRE)**[47] 1711 3-9-0 0 J-PGuillambert 4 60
(Rae Guest) *chsd ldrs: rdn and unable qck over 1f out: no ex and btn 1f out: wkng whn short of room ins fnl f* **50/1**

44 **10** *3* **Short Shrift (IRE)**[11] 2760 3-9-0 0 WilliamCarson 5 52
(James Toller) *hld up in midfield: rdn and effrt 2f out: no imp and swtchd rt over 1f out: no prog 1f out* **33/1**

5-0 **11** *shd* **Grapes Hill**[11] 2760 3-9-0 0 (b) NickyMackay 1 52?
(Mark Rimmer) *dwlt: hdwy into midfield after 2f: rdn and unable qck 2f out: wknd over 1f out* **150/1**

5-0 **12** *hd* **Exempt**[11] 2746 3-9-0 0 JamesDoyle 10 51
(Jeremy Noseda) *taken down early: hld up in tch in midfield: rdn and effrt over 1f out: fnd little and sn edgd lft: wknd ins fnl f* **25/1**

0- **13** *nse* **Mill I Am (USA)**[311] 4701 3-9-0 0 SaleemGolam 15 51
(Stuart Williams) *dwlt: hld up towards rr: rdn and outpcd 2f out: swtchd rt and wandered ent fnl f: no prog* **50/1**

14 *8* **Erin's Grace (IRE)**[66] 1341 3-9-0 0 StevieDonohoe 14 29
(Gay Kelleway) *racd against far rail thrght: in tch in midfield: rdn and lost pl over 2f out: bhd over 1f out* **50/1**

05- **15** *9* **Sporting Club Girl**[236] 7104 3-8-9 0 ThomasBrown(5) 11
(William Knight) *in tch in midfield: rdn and lost pl 3f out: bhd over 1f out* **66/1**

1m 26.19s (0.49) **Going Correction** +0.125s/f (Good) **15** Ran SP% **127.1**
Speed ratings (Par 96): **102,98,98,98,97 97,96,96,94,90 90,90,90,81,71**
toteswingers 1&2 £24.90, 1&3 £2.20, 2&3 £27.60 CSF £105.21 TOTE £3.70: £1.50, £9.30, £2.30; EX 111.40 Trifecta £1580.10 Part won. Pool: £2106.81 - 0.89 winning tickets..
Owner Michael Pescod **Bred** Ceka Ireland Limited **Trained** East Everleigh, Wilts

FOCUS
A fair fillies' maiden. The bulk of the field raced down the centre until edging over in the second half of the race to join the pair who had been on the far rail from the start. The winner built on her Newbury form, with Persian Patriot among those who help with the level.

3117 TRINIDAD AND TOBAGO TOURISM H'CAP 1m
4:40 (4:40) (Class 3) (0-90,88) 3-Y-O **£9,703** (£2,887; £1,443; £721) **Stalls** High

Form RPR

03-4 **1** **Monsieur Rieussec**[26] 2322 3-8-10 **77** TedDurcan 5 84
(Jonathan Portman) *stdd s: hld up in last trio: hdwy and swtchd lft 2f out: rdn to ld over 1f out: hrd pressed and drvn ins fnl f: hld on gamely towards fin* **7/1**

4-10 **2** *nk* **Royal Prize**[34] 2054 3-9-0 **81** JamesDoyle 4 87
(Ralph Beckett) *stdd s: hld up in tch in rr: rdn ent fnl 2f: drvn and hdwy over 1f out: pressing wnr ins fnl f: wnt 2nd fnl 100yds: kpt on wl* **22/1**

1145 **3** *½* **Country Western**[14] 2661 3-9-7 **88** JamesMcDonald 6 93
(Charles Hills) *t.k.h: chsd ldrs: rdn ent fnl 2f: styd on u.p to press wnr 1f out: kpt on same pce fnl 100yds* **10/1**

2-1 **4** *4 ½* **Granell (IRE)**[21] 2455 3-9-6 **87** FrankieDettori 3 82
(Brian Meehan) *hld up in midfield: effrt over 2f out: drvn wl over 1f out: 4th and no ex 1f out: wknd ins fnl f* **9/4**[1]

0-44 **5** *2 ¼* **Living Desert**[10] 2776 3-8-12 **79** RichardHughes 7 68
(James Toller) *t.k.h: hld up in midfield: hdwy and hung lft u.p over 1f out: no imp 1f out: wknd ins fnl f* **12/1**

06-0 **6** *4* **Funk Soul Brother**[21] 2453 3-9-5 **86** WilliamBuick 8 66
(Charles Hills) *in tch in midfield: rdn and no hdwy 2f out: wknd over 1f out* **12/1**

3-46 **7** *2* **Quadriga (IRE)**[11] 2763 3-8-3 **70** PaulHanagan 10 46
(Robert Eddery) *hld up in last pair: rdn and no hdwy 2f out: wknd over 1f out* **33/1**

0-31 **8** *2 ¾* **Ghost Runner (IRE)**[33] 2099 3-8-13 **80** TomQueally 9 49
(Sir Henry Cecil) *t.k.h: chsd ldr: rdn 2f out: lost pl qckly over 1f out: sn wknd* **9/2**[3]

1532 **9** *¾* **Corn Snow (USA)**[7] 2876 3-8-8 **75** (b[1]) SilvestreDeSousa 1 43
(Mark Johnston) *racd freely: sn led and clr: rdn 2f out: hdd over 1f out: sn btn: fdd fnl f* **7/2**[2]

1m 38.76s (-1.24) **Going Correction** +0.125s/f (Good) **9** Ran SP% **115.4**
Speed ratings (Par 103): **111,110,110,105,103 99,97,94,93**
toteswingers 1&2 £55.40, 1&3 £27.70, 2&3 £23.20 CSF £143.38 CT £1530.86 TOTE £8.30: £2.60, £5.80, £2.90; EX 213.40 Trifecta £1637.31 Part won. Pool: £1637.31 - 0.51 winning tickets..
Owner J T Habershon-Butcher **Bred** Mrs James Wigan **Trained** Upper Lambourn, Berks

FOCUS
This event was won a year ago by Fast Or Free, who went on to take the Britannia Handicap at Royal Ascot. The runners in this decent handicap quickly congregated towards the far side. The first three finished clear with the 1-2 coming from the back. The form is perhaps as strong as it might have been.

3118 ANIMAL HEALTH TRUST ROYAL CHARTER ANNIVERSARY H'CAP 1m 6f 175y
5:15 (5:15) (Class 4) (0-85,85) 4-Y-O+ **£7,762** (£2,310; £1,154; £577) **Stalls** Centre

Form RPR

-146 **1** **Taglietelle**[21] 2451 4-8-11 **80** ThomasBrown(5) 8 88
(Andrew Balding) *led: hdd over 2f out but styd pressing ldr: rdn to ld again over 1f out: kpt on wl u.p fnl f* **11/4**[2]

00-0 **2** *¾* **Dark Ranger**[23] 2402 7-8-13 **77** TomQueally 1 84
(Tim Pitt) *hld up in tch in midfield: hdwy u.p and swtchd lft ent fnl f: styd on wl to press wnr fnl 50yds: hld towards fin* **8/1**

3-12 **3** *½* **Gabrial's King (IRE)**[14] 2648 4-8-13 **77** WilliamBuick 5 83
(David Simcock) *in tch in midfield: effrt u.p over 2f out: awkward had carriage but styd on to press wnr jst ins fnl f: nt qckn and lost 2nd fnl 50yds* **11/2**[3]

15- **4** *¾* **Teak (IRE)**[204] 6066 6-8-11 **75** JamesDoyle 2 80
(Ian Williams) *in tch in midfield: rdn and effrt over 2f out: unable qck and outpcd over 1f out: rallied and styd on u.p ins fnl f* **10/1**

0-43 **5** *2 ¼* **Porcini**[16] 2598 4-8-12 **76** (p) WilliamCarson 4 78
(Philip McBride) *chsd ldrs: rdn and effrt over 2f out: keeping on same pce whn sltly hmpd jst over 1f out: wknd ins fnl f* **16/1**

4636 **6** *2 ¼* **Mica Mika (IRE)**[23] 2402 5-9-3 **81** PaulHanagan 3 81
(Richard Fahey) *t.k.h: chsd ldr tl led over 2f out: drvn and hdd over 1f out: btn 1f out: wknd ins fnl f* **11/1**

000- **7** *1 ½* **Kangaroo Court (IRE)**[295] 5306 9-9-0 **78** LiamKeniry 9 76
(Emma Lavelle) *stdd and dropped in bhd s: hld up in rr: effrt u.p 3f out: no imp: wknd over 1f out* **20/1**

64-4 **8** *½* **Maria's Choice (IRE)**[28] 2251 4-9-4 **82** RyanMoore 7 79
(Sir Michael Stoute) *hld up in last pair: rdn and effrt wl over 2f out: no prog and btn over 1f out: wknd fnl f* **2/1**[1]

3m 18.31s (9.91) **Going Correction** +0.125s/f (Good) **8** Ran SP% **114.6**
Speed ratings (Par 105): **78,77,77,76,75 74,73,73**
toteswingers 1&2 £5.10, 1&3 £3.50, 2&3 £10.40 CSF £25.03 CT £112.77 TOTE £3.50: £1.30, £2.30, £1.80; EX 29.20 Trifecta £182.10 Pool: £2604.29 - 10.72 winning tickets..
Owner Kingsclere Racing CLub **Bred** Kingsclere Stud **Trained** Kingsclere, Hants

FOCUS
They went a steady pace in this fair staying handicap, which developed into a sprint. The runners came down the centre in the long straight. The winner is rated to his latest form, with the third and fourth fitting in.
T/Plt: £601.80 to a £1 stake. Pool: £111,613.30 - 135.37 winning tickets T/Qpdt: £36.50 to a £1 stake. Pool: £8,105.41 - 164.15 winning tickets SP

3119 - 3126a (Foreign Racing) - See Raceform Interactive

2733 BELMONT PARK (L-H)
Saturday, June 8

OFFICIAL GOING: Dirt: muddy (races 1-5), standard (6-7), fast (9-11), turf: yielding

3127a BELMONT STKS (GRADE 1) (3YO) (DIRT) 1m 4f (D)
11:36 (11:38) 3-Y-O **£368,098** (£122,699; £67,484; £36,809; £18,404)

RPR

1 **Palace Malice (USA)**[35] 2033 3-9-0 0 MESmith 12 122
(Todd Pletcher, U.S.A) **138/10**

2 *3 ¼* **Oxbow (USA)**[21] 2473 3-9-0 0 GaryStevens 7 116
(D Wayne Lukas, U.S.A) **101/10**

3 *1 ¾* **Orb (USA)**[21] 2473 3-9-0 0 JRosario 5 114+
(Claude McGaughey III, U.S.A) **11/5**[1]

4 *1* **Incognito (USA)**[28] 3-9-0 0 (b) IOrtizJr 6 112
(Kiaran McLaughlin, U.S.A) **182/10**

5 *½* **Revolutionary (USA)**[35] 2033 3-9-0 0 JJCastellano 9 111
(Todd Pletcher, U.S.A) **53/10**[2]

6 *2* **Unlimited Budget (USA)**[36] 2003 3-8-9 0 RosieNapravnik 13 103
(Todd Pletcher, U.S.A) **143/10**

7 *nse* **Overanalyze (USA)**[35] 2033 3-9-0 0 JRVelazquez 3 108
(Todd Pletcher, U.S.A) **103/10**

8 *1 ½* **Vyjack (USA)**[35] 2033 3-9-0 0 JRLeparoux 11 106
(Rudy Rodriguez, U.S.A) **243/10**

9 *¾* **Golden Soul (USA)**[35] 2033 3-9-0 0 RAlbarado 14 104
(Dallas Stewart, U.S.A) **119/10**

10 *6 ¼* **Will Take Charge (USA)**[21] 2473 3-9-0 0 (b) JKCourt 10 94
(D Wayne Lukas, U.S.A) **221/10**

11 *18 ¼* **Giant Finish (USA)**[35] 2033 3-9-0 0 EPrado 4 65
(Anthony Dutrow, U.S.A) **32/1**

12 *14* **Midnight Taboo (USA)**[31] 3-9-0 0 GKGomez 8 43
(Todd Pletcher, U.S.A) **30/1**

13 *9 ¼* **Freedom Child (USA)**[28] 3-9-0 0 LSaez 2 28
(Thomas Albertrani, U.S.A) **81/10**[3]

14 *5 ¼* **Frac Daddy (USA)**[35] 2033 3-9-0 0 AGarcia 1 20
(Kenneth McPeek, U.S.A) **31/1**

2m 30.7s (1.74) **14** Ran SP% **119.9**
PARI-MUTUEL (all including $2 stakes): WIN 29.60; PLACE (1-2) 11.20, 9.90; SHOW (1-2-3) 6.70, 6.10, 3.90; SF 323.50.
Owner Dogwood Stable **Bred** W S Farish **Trained** USA

FOCUS
The concluding race for the Triple Crown saw both the Kentucky Derby and Preakness winners try and secure the third and final leg. Early fractions were strong before the tempo slowed down in the back stretch for a while. However, plenty finished tired, suggesting it was a decent test of stamina.

[2905]CHANTILLY (R-H)
Saturday, June 8

OFFICIAL GOING: Turf: good ; polytrack: standard

3128a PRIX PAUL DE MOUSSAC (GROUP 3) (3YO COLTS & GELDINGS) (TURF) 1m
5:40 (12:00) 3-Y-0 **£32,520** (£13,008; £9,756; £6,504; £3,252)

RPR

1 **Anodin (IRE)**[27] 2298 3-8-10 0 OlivierPeslier 1 109
(F Head, France) *mde all: shkn up 2f out: strly pressed over 1f out: rdn and asserted ins fnl 100yds: shade cosily* **23/10**[1]

2 1 **San Marino Grey (FR)**[19] 2527 3-8-10 0 MaximeGuyon 4 107
(A Fabre, France) *midfield in tch: rdn 2f out: angled lft for clr run and bmpd rival ent fnl f: r.o to go 2nd fnl strides* **6/1**

3 hd **Gengis (FR)**[27] 2298 3-8-13 0 StephanePasquier 5 109
(G Doleuze, France) *t.k.h: trckd ldr: rdn to chal over 1f out: r.o and ev ch tl hld by wnr ins fnl 100yds: dropped to 3rd fnl strides* **14/5**[2]

4 snk **Saint Thomas (FR)**[35] 3-8-10 0 ThierryJarnet 2 106
(P Bary, France) *prom on inner: rdn over 1f out: r.o but nt pce to chal* **63/10**

5 1 **Guajaraz (FR)**[31] 2183 3-8-10 0 ChristopheSoumillon 6 104
(J-C Rouget, France) *midfield in tch on outer: rdn 2f out: sltly outpcd by ldrs but stl ev ch whn bmpd by rival and lost momentum ent fnl f: kpt on wout threatening after* **9/2**[3]

6 1 1/2 **Pont Neuilly (FR)**[17] 3-8-10 0 Pierre-CharlesBoudot 7 100
(Y De Nicolay, France) *hld up in last pair on outer: rdn 2f out: hung rt u.p ins fnl f: kpt on but n.d* **19/1**

7 1/2 **Wire To Wire (FR)**[35] 2035 3-8-10 0 IoritzMendizabal 3 99
(J-C Rouget, France) *hld up in last pair on inner: rdn over 1f out: sn outpcd: kpt on but nvr a factor* **9/1**

1m 39.09s (1.09) **7 Ran SP% 117.8**
WIN (incl. 1 euro stake): 3.30. PLACES: 2.00, 2.90. SF: 20.40.
Owner Wertheimer & Frere **Bred** Wertheimer Et Frere **Trained** France

3129a PRIX DE L'ETANG CHAPON (H'CAP) (3YO) (POLYTRACK) 1m 6f
6:10 (12:00) 3-Y-0 **£12,195** (£4,878; £3,658; £2,439; £1,219)

RPR

1 **Ball Lightning (FR)**[32] 3-9-4 0 (p) MaximeGuyon 10 80
(E Libaud, France) **28/1**

2 2 1/2 **Noble Inn (FR)**[34] 3-9-2 0 UmbertoRispoli 7 75
(M Delzangles, France) **22/1**

3 nse **Zimbali (FR)**[22] 2434 3-9-6 0 Pierre-CharlesBoudot 5 79
(A Fabre, France) **9/5**[1]

4 1 1/4 **Yeoman (USA)**[131] 445 3-9-5 0 JulienAuge 13 76
(C Ferland, France) **11/2**[2]

5 1 1/4 **Montesquieu (FR)**[32] 3-9-4 0 ThierryThulliez 12 73
(S Wattel, France) **11/2**[2]

6 1 1/4 **Markami (FR)**[264] 3-9-2 0 Christophe-PatriceLemaire 14 70
(A De Royer-Dupre, France) **17/1**

7 snk **Baz (FR)**[23] 2403 3-9-3 0 RaphaelDesanti(3) 1 73
(F-H Graffard, France) **13/1**

8 1 1/2 **Andi'Amu (FR)**[27] 3-9-5 0 OlivierPeslier 9 70
(C Ferland, France) **12/1**

9 nk **Forty Winks** 3-9-0 0 (b[1]) FabriceVeron 15 65
(H-A Pantall, France) **11/1**[3]

10 1/2 **Boissey (FR)** 3-9-5 0 GregoryBenoist 3 69
(Mme Pia Brandt, France) **19/1**

11 **Destiny Highway (FR)**[22] 2434 3-9-2 0 (p) SylvainRuis 4 66
(Gay Kelleway) *midfield on inner: rdn 2f out: sn outpcd: eased whn btn ins fnl f* **21/1**

12 **River Prince (FR)**[26] 3-9-4 0 AntoineHamelin 11 68
(P Adda, France) **54/1**

13 **Porte Dauphine (IRE)**[19] 3-7-11 0 (p) JimmyTastayre(3) 6 50
(C Boutin, France) **110/1**

14 **Leggy Lass (FR)**[22] 2434 3-8-5 0 (b) EddyHardouin 8 55
(S Wattel, France) **74/1**

15 **Azabitmour (FR)**[23] 2403 3-8-11 0 IoritzMendizabal 2 61
(John Best) *led: rdn and hdd 2f out: no ex and btn: fdd: eased ins fnl f and dropped to last cl home* **50/1**

3m 4.73s (184.73) **15 Ran SP% 118.6**
WIN (incl. 1 euro stake): 29.30. PLACES: 5.60, 6.00, 1.50. DF: 162.60. SF: 404.60.
Owner John Fairley **Bred** Trainers House Enterprises Ltd **Trained** France

3130 - 3131a (Foreign Racing) - See Raceform Interactive

[2778]NOTTINGHAM (L-H)
Sunday, June 9

OFFICIAL GOING: Good to firm (good in places; 9.0)
Outer track used. All rails moved and races on Round course increased in distance by about 12yds.
Wind: moderate 1/2 behind Weather: fine and sunny

3132 IRISH E B F YOUR EXPERT GUIDE NOTTINGHAMRACECOURSETIPS.CO.UK MAIDEN STKS 5f 13y
2:15 (2:15) (Class 5) 2-Y-0 **£3,881** (£1,155; £577; £288) **Stalls High**

Form RPR

2 1 **Excel's Beauty**[12] 2740 2-9-0 0 NeilCallan 1 73+
(James Tate) *fly-jmpd sn after s: chsd ldr: led over 2f out: edgd rt 1f out: drvn out* **2/1**[1]

2 2 1 1/4 **Speed The Plough**[9] 2823 2-9-5 0 SeanLevey 4 74
(Richard Hannon) *led: hdd over 2f out: swtchd lft and styd on same pce fnl f* **2/1**[1]

3 1 **Pensax Lad (IRE)** 2-9-5 0 LukeMorris 5 70
(Ronald Harris) *s.i.s: swtchd lft and chsd ldrs over 3f out: drvn over 2f out: kpt on same pce fnl f* **66/1**

4 1 1/4 **Relation Alexander (IRE)** 2-9-0 0 FrannyNorton 7 60+
(Paul D'Arcy) *s.i.s: outpcd over 2f out: kpt on fnl f* **9/2**[3]

5 3 1/4 **Grandad Chunk (IRE)** 2-9-5 0 AdamKirby 3 54+
(Noel Quinlan) *chsd ldrs: drvn over 2f out: wknd fnl f* **3/1**[2]

6 17 **Celtic Ice (IRE)** 2-9-5 0 MartinDwyer 2
(Alan McCabe) *swvd bdly lft s: detached in last: t.o 2f out* **28/1**

1m 0.67s (-0.83) **Going Correction** -0.475s/f (Firm) **6 Ran SP% 114.8**
Speed ratings (Par 93): **87,85,83,81,76 49**
Tote Swingers: 1&2 £1.20, 1&3 £11.10, 2&3 £8.90 CSF £6.48 TOTE £3.40: £1.70, £1.20; EX 6.20 Trifecta £55.30 Pool: £2,576.05 - 34.93 winning units..
Owner Sheikh Juma Dalmook Al Maktoum **Bred** Glebe Stud, J F Dean & Lady Trenchard **Trained** Newmarket, Suffolk

FOCUS
Sean Levey described the ground as being "genuinely quick, good to firm". All rails were moved out onto fresh lines, increasing round course distances by 12yds. They raced stands' side in this ordinary juvenile contest, which was dominated by the front pair in the market. The form is rated to the mid-point of the race averages.

3133 ALAN BIRD MEMORIAL H'CAP (THE SUNDAY £5K BONUS RACE) 1m 6f 15y
2:45 (2:45) (Class 5) (0-70,69) 4-Y-0+ **£3,234** (£962; £481; £240) **Stalls Low**

Form RPR

60/- 1 **Street Entertainer (IRE)**[29] 6781 6-9-3 65 (bt) NeilCallan 3 78+
(David Pipe) *hld up towards rr: hdwy over 4f out: wnt lft over 3f out: led over 1f out: edgd lft: easily* **11/8**[1]

2-05 2 dht **Taste The Wine (IRE)**[15] 1973 7-8-11 66 DanielMuscutt(7) 4 70
(Bernard Llewellyn) *mid-div: trckd ldrs 7f out: bmpd over 3f out: outpcd over 2f out: styd on appr fnl f: fin dead-heat 2nd: plcd 2nd outright* **6/1**[3]

0114 3 hd **Hallstatt (IRE)**[15] 2648 7-9-4 69 (t) RaulDaSilva(3) 11 73
(John Mackie) *chsd ldrs: drvn 4f out: one pce whn sltly hmpd over 1f out: fin 4th: plcd 3rd* **5/2**[2]

3040 4 3 3/4 **Blazing Desert**[16] 2629 9-9-3 65 AdamBeschizza 13 69
(William Kinsey) *dwlt: led after 1f: hdd and edgd lft over 1f out: kpt on same pce: fin dead-heat 2nd: disq & plcd 4th* **20/1**

000- 5 8 **Excellent News (IRE)**[293] 5408 4-7-11 50 ShirleyTeasdale(5) 1 43
(Tony Forbes) *led 1f: t.k.h: trckd ldrs: lost pl over 2f out* **33/1**

033- 6 hd **Sedgwick**[188] 7968 11-9-2 64 DuranFentiman 2 57
(Shaun Harris) *hld up in last: drvn over 3f out: sn lost pl* **16/1**

6202 7 2 **Iguacu**[18] 2567 9-8-4 52 (p) LukeMorris 8 42
(Richard Price) *sn chsng ldrs: drvn over 3f out: lost pl wl over 1f out* **10/1**

-300 8 1 **Graceful Descent (FR)**[16] 2615 8-8-13 68 (p) GemmaTutty(7) 7 57
(Karen Tutty) *in rr: drvn over 5f out: bhd fnl 3f* **20/1**

3m 4.2s (-2.80) **Going Correction** -0.275s/f (Firm) **8 Ran SP% 112.4**
Speed ratings (Par 103): **97,94,94,94,90 90,88,88**
Tote Swingers: 1&2 £2.20, 1&3 £1.60, 2&3 £4.60 CSF £9.64 CT £18.13 TOTE £2.20: £1.90, £1.90, £1.90; EX 9.10 Trifecta £17.60 Pool: £2,487.06 - 105.93 winning units..
Owner Barnett, Manasseh & Partners **Bred** Marston Stud And Fleming Thoroughbreds **Trained** Nicholashayne, Devon

FOCUS
A moderate handicap, run at a steady gallop early, and the market got it right.

3134 IAN POLES TAXI TO RETIREMENT H'CAP 5f 13y
3:15 (3:16) (Class 6) (0-65,64) 3-Y-0 **£2,587** (£770; £384; £192) **Stalls High**

Form RPR

5-00 1 **Clean Blow (USA)**[34] 2098 3-9-7 64 SeanLevey 2 76
(David Brown) *mde all: edgd rt fnl 2f: styd on strly* **12/1**

3332 2 3 3/4 **Chloe's Dream (IRE)**[10] 2795 3-9-3 60 (p) PJMcDonald 11 58
(Ann Duffield) *chsd ldrs: wnt 2nd over 1f out: styd on same pce* **7/2**[1]

0-00 3 1/2 **Lucky Lodge**[43] 1844 3-9-5 62 PaulMulrennan 3 58
(Mel Brittain) *chsd ldrs on outer: kpt on same pce appr fnl f* **12/1**

-604 4 3/4 **Beacon Tarn**[27] 2317 3-8-11 54 (b) LukeMorris 8 48
(Eric Alston) *dwlt: in rr: hdwy 2f out: styd on fnl f* **4/1**[2]

4-05 5 1 **Borough Boy (IRE)**[26] 2347 3-8-11 54 (v) MartinDwyer 13 44
(Derek Shaw) *hld up in rr: hdwy stands' side over 1f out: gng on at fin* **16/1**

0000 6 shd **Moss The Boss (IRE)**[37] 1988 3-7-11 45 ShirleyTeasdale(5) 4 35
(Paul Midgley) *chsd ldrs on outer: one pce fnl 2f* **50/1**

0-05 7 nk **Rat Catcher (IRE)**[9] 2832 3-9-3 63 (b) DeclanCannon(3) 9 51
(Andrew Crook) *wnt rt after s: mid-div: styd on fnl f* **18/1**

-356 8 1 1/2 **Tregereth (IRE)**[34] 2091 3-8-10 58 MatthewLawson(5) 6 41
(Jonathan Portman) *sn outpcd and bhd on outer: kpt on fnl 2f: nvr a factor* **4/1**[2]

1215 9 3 1/2 **La Sylphe**[11] 2779 3-9-3 60 FrannyNorton 12 30
(Derek Shaw) *chsd wnr: wknd over 1f out* **8/1**[3]

1136 10 nk **Dangerous Age**[16] 2623 3-9-5 62 AdamKirby 7 31
(J W Hills) *mid-div: sme hdwy over 2f out: wknd fnl f* **10/1**

3503 11 4 1/2 **Annaley My Darling (IRE)**[8] 2873 3-8-10 53 NickyMackay 1
(Mark Rimmer) *chsd ldrs on outer: lost pl over 1f out* **25/1**

000- 12 4 1/2 **Jackpot**[227] 7355 3-7-13 45 NeilFarley(3) 5
(Brendan Powell) *in rr: bhd fnl 2f* **66/1**

2625 13 6 **Lexi's Beauty (IRE)**[52] 1651 3-8-4 47 (b) SilvestreDeSousa 10
(Patrick Morris) *hmpd sn after s: in rr: bhd whn eased over 1f out* **20/1**

59.6s (-1.90) **Going Correction** -0.475s/f (Firm) **13 Ran SP% 121.0**
Speed ratings (Par 97): **96,90,89,88,86 86,85,83,77,77 70,62,53**
Tote Swingers: 1&2 £8.50, 1&3 £28.90, 2&3 £9.00 CSF £52.82 CT £555.05 TOTE £18.40: £5.50, £1.80, £4.70; EX 87.40 Trifecta £702.90 Pool: £3,194.90 - 3.40 winning units..
Owner J C Fretwell **Bred** Map Mare Partnership No 3 **Trained** Averham Park, Notts

FOCUS
What had looked an open 3yo sprint was ultimately won with a bit in hand by the top weight.

3135 EAT IN OUR ROOFTOP RESTAURANT H'CAP 5f 13y
3:45 (3:45) (Class 3) (0-95,94) 4-Y-0+ **£9,703** (£2,887; £1,443; £721) **Stalls High**

Form RPR

11-2 1 **Demora**[32] 2173 4-8-11 84 AndrewMullen 8 97
(Michael Appleby) *mde all: hung lft thrght: styd on wl fnl f* **4/1**[2]

0004 2 1 1/4 **Tax Free (IRE)**[8] 2880 11-8-10 83 AdrianNicholls 6 92
(David Nicholls) *wnt lft s: hld up in mid-div: effrt and swtchd lft over 2f out: chsd wnr 1f out: no imp* **16/1**

1-61 3 1 1/4 **Blanc De Chine (IRE)**[30] 2227 4-8-12 85 JimmyFortune 7 89
(Peter Makin) *chsd ldrs stands' side: kpt on same pce fnl f* **8/1**

3-10 4 3/4 **Sir Maximilian (IRE)**[15] 2669 4-9-0 87 StevieDonohoe 5 88
(Ian Williams) *hmpd s: in rr: effrt over 2f out: hdwy over 1f out: styd on same pce* **5/2**[1]

2202 5 nk **Last Sovereign**[20] 2505 9-8-12 92 (b) JacobButterfield(7) 2 92
(Ollie Pears) *chsd ldrs on outer: drvn over 2f out: one pce over 1f out* **10/1**

1-00 6 nse **Naabegha**[22] 2461 6-9-4 91 LiamKeniry 1 91
(Ed de Giles) *dwlt: t.k.h in rr: hdwy over 1f out: kpt on same pce* **7/1**[3]

003 7 1 1/4 **Taurus Twins**[15] 2663 7-8-7 80 (b) LukeMorris 4 76
(Richard Price) *wnt rt s: chsd ldrs: fdd jst ins fnl f* **7/1**[3]

0-54 **8** *3 ¼* **First In Command (IRE)**[22] 2461 8-8-8 **81**........................ ShaneKelly 9 65
(Daniel Mark Loughnane) *in rr: outpcd over 3f out: nvr on terms* **18/1**

2U00 **9** *9* **Whaileyy (IRE)**[35] 2046 5-9-7 **94**..(b) AdamKirby 3 56
(Marco Botti) *trckd ldrs: drvn 2f out: sn wknd: eased whn bhd clsng stages* **17/2**

58.09s (-3.41) **Going Correction** -0.475s/f (Firm) course record **9** Ran SP% **115.4**
Speed ratings (Par 107): **108,106,104,102,102 102,100,95,80**
Tote Swingers: 1&2 £14.30, 1&3 £5.40, 2&3 £13.10 CSF £64.88 CT £489.73 TOTE £5.40: £1.50, £2.50, £2.40; EX 41.40 Trifecta £161.00 Pool: £1,862.44 - 8.67 winning units..
Owner Goldform Racing **Bred** A M Wragg **Trained** Danethorpe, Notts

FOCUS
Fair sprinting form.

3136 SPONSOR A RACE AT NOTTINGHAM RACECOURSE MAIDEN FILLIES' STKS 1m 75y
4:15 (4:20) (Class 5) 3-Y-O **£3,881** (£1,155; £577; £288) **Stalls** Centre

Form RPR

4 **1** **Odeliz (IRE)**[43] 1828 3-9-0 0........................ DanielTudhope 5 82+
(Mrs K Burke) *hld up towards rr: hdwy whn edgd rt over 2f out: styd on wl fnl f: led nr fin* **10/3**[2]

6- **2** *nk* **Star Pearl (USA)**[289] 5550 3-9-0 0........................ JimmyFortune 6 81
(Roger Varian) *led: drvn 3 l clr over 1f out: hdd and no ex nr fin* **20/1**

4-2 **3** *¾* **Close At Hand**[15] 2658 3-9-0 0........................ WilliamBuick 12 80+
(John Gosden) *mid-div: lost pl bnd over 5f out: hdwy on outer whn edgd lft over 2f out: styd on fnl f* **3/1**[1]

66 **4** *¾* **Loved One**[18] 2560 3-9-0 0........................ LukeMorris 1 78
(James Fanshawe) *chsd ldrs: drvn to chse ldr over 2f out: one pce fnl f* **50/1**

2 **5** *6* **Dawn Of Empire (USA)**[22] 2455 3-9-0 0........................ JamesDoyle 2 64
(Roger Charlton) *mid-div: effrt 3f out: wknd over 1f out* **7/1**

6 *3 ¾* **Controversy** 3-9-0 0........................ MickaelBarzalona 3 56
(Saeed bin Suroor) *mid-div: rdn and outpcd 3f out: wknd appr fnl f* **7/2**[3]

5 **7** *4 ½* **Tafaaseel (USA)**[15] 2658 3-9-0 0........................ PaulHanagan 4 45
(Sir Michael Stoute) *trckd ldrs: t.k.h: effrt over 3f out: hung lft and wknd over 1f out* **16/1**

8 *2 ¾* **Cherokee Princess (IRE)** 3-9-0 0........................[1] ShaneKelly 13 39
(Tim Pitt) *s.i.s: racd keen early and racd wd: sn in rr: nvr a factor* **100/1**

0- **9** *5* **Travel (USA)**[377] 2541 3-9-0 0........................ SilvestreDeSousa 8 27
(Saeed bin Suroor) *chsd ldr: drvn over 3f out: wknd over 2f out* **16/1**

0-0 **10** *nk* **Kensington Gardens**[12] 2760 3-9-0 0........................ HayleyTurner 9 27
(Michael Bell) *s.i.s: in rr: drvn 4f out: sn bhd* **66/1**

11 *20* **Ismaali** 3-9-0 0........................ GrahamLee 7
(James Given) *in rr and sn drvn along: bhd fnl 4f: t.o 2f out* **100/1**

42-3 **U** **Martinas Delight (USA)**[22] 2449 3-8-9 75........ MichaelJMMurphy(5) 11
(Alan Jarvis) *sn chsng ldrs: wkng whn n.m.r: stmbld and uns rdr jst over 2f out* **6/1**

1m 44.48s (-4.52) **Going Correction** -0.275s/f (Firm) **12** Ran SP% **119.0**
Speed ratings (Par 96): **111,110,109,109,103 99,94,92,87,86 66,**
Tote Swingers: 1&2 £13.00, 1&3 £3.60, 2&3 £11.90 CSF £74.13 TOTE £4.70: £1.40, £6.00, £1.50; EX 81.10 Trifecta £436.20 Pool: £5,229.32 - 8.99 winning units..
Owner McMahon Thoroughbreds Ltd & Mrs E Burke **Bred** Aleyrion Bloodstock Ltd **Trained** Middleham Moor, N Yorks

FOCUS
A fair fillies' maiden.

3137 HAPPY RETIREMENT JOHN BARNETT H'CAP 1m 75y
4:45 (5:00) (Class 5) (0-70,70) 3-Y-O **£3,234** (£962; £481; £240) **Stalls** Centre

Form RPR

-564 **1** **Woody Bay**[16] 2616 3-9-0 **63**........................ GrahamLee 3 69
(James Given) *trckd ldrs on inner: t.k.h: led ins fnl f: drvn out* **7/2**[2]

43-3 **2** *1 ¼* **Not Rigg (USA)**[137] 341 3-9-4 **67**........................(t[1]) ShaneKelly 4 70
(Gary Harrison) *led after 1f: hdd and no ex ins fnl f* **20/1**

0-46 **3** *2* **Star Of Mayfair (USA)**[36] 2017 3-9-2 **65**........................ JimmyFortune 14 64+
(Alan Jarvis) *hld up in rr: outpcd over 3f out: swtchd outside and styd on over 1f out: kpt on wl to take 3rd nr line* **10/3**[1]

1-60 **4** *¾* **Mandy The Nag (USA)**[17] 2606 3-9-3 **66**........................ PaulHanagan 5 63
(Ed Dunlop) *mid-div: effrt over 3f out: kpt on one pce fnl 2f* **6/1**

3446 **5** *1* **Impeccability**[50] 1685 3-7-13 **51** oh1........................ RaulDaSilva(3) 7 46
(John Mackie) *chsd ldrs: chal over 2f out: one pce over 1f out* **12/1**

045 **6** *1* **Triple Aitch (USA)**[19] 2548 3-9-1 **64**........................ JimmyQuinn 12 56
(Gay Kelleway) *trckd ldrs: effrt over 3f out: one pce fnl 2f* **12/1**

1025 **7** *3* **Mixed Message (IRE)**[30] 2235 3-9-7 **70**........................ DanielTudhope 8 57
(John Mackie) *trckd ldrs on outer: effrt over 3f out: eased whn wl hld clsng stages* **5/1**[3]

04-6 **8** *½* **The Ginger Berry**[48] 1711 3-8-8 **57**........................ WilliamCarson 2 41
(Dr Jon Scargill) *hld up in rr: hdwy into mid-div: drvn over 3f out: lost pl over 1f out* **25/1**

03-0 **9** *1 ¼* **Skidby Mill (IRE)**[22] 2464 3-9-0 **63**........................ MichaelO'Connell 11 44
(Brian Rothwell) *in rr: effrt over 3f out: edgd lft over 1f out: nvr a factor* **33/1**

056 **10** *7* **Xclusive**[19] 2548 3-8-13 **62**........................ LukeMorris 13 27
(Ronald Harris) *in tch: drvn over 4f out: lost pl over 3f out* **14/1**

60-5 **11** *7* **Lucky Prize**[64] 1389 3-8-2 **51** oh6........................ SilvestreDeSousa 6
(Mel Brittain) *mid-div: lost pl over 4f out: bhd whn eased over 1f out* **25/1**

-545 **12** *31* **Sweet Vintage (IRE)**[29] 2274 3-8-7 **56**........................ MartinDwyer 10
(Mark Brisbourne) *led 1f: lost pl over 3f out: sn bhd: eased over 1f out: t.o: virtually p.u* **16/1**

1m 46.78s (-2.22) **Going Correction** -0.275s/f (Firm) **12** Ran SP% **119.6**
Speed ratings (Par 99): **100,98,96,96,95 94,91,90,89,82 75,44**
Tote Swingers: 1&2 £11.80, 1&3 £3.10, 2&3 £13.10 CSF £77.82 CT £261.16 TOTE £4.60: £1.50, £3.10, £1.80; EX 74.90 Trifecta £341.90 Pool: £2,731.37 - 5.98 winning units..
Owner J Barson **Bred** Cheveley Park Stud Ltd **Trained** Willoughton, Lincs

FOCUS
Little got into this from off the pace.

3138 SEE YOU ALL ON 13TH JUNE H'CAP 1m 2f 50y
5:15 (5:21) (Class 6) (0-65,65) 4-Y-O+ **£2,587** (£770; £384; £192) **Stalls** Low

Form RPR

4032 **1** **Honoured (IRE)**[5] 2961 6-9-3 **61**........................(t) AndrewMullen 4 72
(Michael Appleby) *mid-div: sn pushed along: hdwy 3f out: led 1f out: all out* **9/4**[1]

4024 **2** *nk* **Cane Cat (IRE)**[13] 2714 6-8-10 **54**........................(t) SeanLevey 2 64
(Tony Carroll) *hld up in rr: smooth hdwy and swtchd rt over 2f out: chal jst ins fnl f: no ex nr fin* **10/1**

3010 **3** *7* **El Bravo**[22] 2435 7-8-12 **56**........................ DuranFentiman 10 53
(Shaun Harris) *led tl 7f out: led over 2f out: hdd 1f out: one pce* **10/1**

00-0 **4** *½* **Greyemkay**[51] 1665 5-7-13 **50** ow1........................ DanielMuscutt(7) 8 46
(Richard Price) *mid-div: effrt 3f out: styd on fnl f: tk modest 4th nr fin* **33/1**

40-3 **5** *1 ¾* **Seldom (IRE)**[55] 1568 7-9-0 **58**........................ SilvestreDeSousa 6 51
(Mel Brittain) *chsd ldrs: led 7f out: hdd over 2f out: fdd over 1f out* **4/1**[2]

6205 **6** *9* **Ogaritmo**[25] 2360 4-9-7 **65**........................ FrannyNorton 7 41
(Alastair Lidderdale) *chsd ldrs: drvn over 5f out: wknd fnl 2f* **12/1**

0660 **7** *nk* **Hawaiian Freeze**[38] 1951 4-7-11 **48** oh1 ow2........................ AaronFallon(7) 3 23
(John Stimpson) *rrd s and reluctant: detached in last: rdn 4f out: nvr on terms* **80/1**

500- **8** *1 ¼* **Arkaim**[21] 8051 5-9-0 **58**........................(v) MickyFenton 9 31
(Pam Sly) *chsd ldrs: t.k.h and h8ung rt: drvn over 4f out: lost pl 2f out* **20/1**

0-00 **9** *2 ½* **Mullins Way (USA)**[68] 1303 5-9-3 **61**........................(p) J-PGuillambert 5 29
(Jo Hughes) *detached in rr: bhd and drvn over 4f out: nvr on terms* **11/2**[3]

3002 **10** *15* **Yourinthewill (USA)**[13] 2709 5-9-4 **62**........................ ShaneKelly 1
(Daniel Mark Loughnane) *dwlt: hdwy on outer over 7f out: wknd 2f out: sn heavily eased* **13/2**

2m 10.95s (-3.35) **Going Correction** -0.275s/f (Firm) **10** Ran SP% **114.3**
Speed ratings (Par 101): **102,101,96,95,94 87,86,85,83,71**
Tote Swingers: 1&2 £6.30, 1&3 £7.00, 2&3 £9.90 CSF £25.12 CT £187.05 TOTE £2.90: £1.60, £2.20, £2.60; EX 18.20 Trifecta £273.90 Pool: £2,562.89 - 7.01 winning units..
Owner Dallas Racing **Bred** Kilfrush Stud **Trained** Danethorpe, Notts

FOCUS
They appeared to go a reasonable gallop in this low-grade handicap, and the front pair drew right away.
T/Jkpt: £14,513.40 to a £1 stake. Pool: £51,104.00 - 2.50 winning tickets. T/Plt: £20.90 to a £1 stake. Pool: £95,674.00 - 3,341.53 winning tickets. T/Qpdt: £16.90 to a £1 stake. Pool: £5,998.00 - 261.80 winning tickets. WG

3139 - 3141a (Foreign Racing) - See Raceform Interactive

2685 CURRAGH (R-H)
Sunday, June 9

OFFICIAL GOING: Good to firm

3142a TRM SILVER STKS (LISTED RACE) 1m 2f
3:50 (3:52) 3-Y-O+ **£22,195** (£6,487; £3,073; £1,024)

RPR

1 **Trading Leather (IRE)**[15] 2677 3-8-13 111........................ KevinManning 10 115
(J S Bolger, Ire) *chsd ldr in 3rd tl wnt 2nd 1/2-way: pushed along over 2f out and sn led: styd on wl and in command ins fnl f* **5/4**[1]

2 *3 ½* **Lines Of Battle (USA)**[36] 2033 3-9-1 109........................(p) JosephO'Brien 6 110
(A P O'Brien, Ire) *chsd ldrs in 4th: prog in 3rd 3f out: pushed along appr fnl 2f: chsd ldr in 2nd ent fnl f: no imp fnl 100yds* **3/1**[2]

3 *1* **Kingston Jamaica (IRE)**[287] 5642 3-8-10 100........ SeamieHeffernan 4 103
(A P O'Brien, Ire) *w.w tl gd prog on inner 2f out into 3rd: sn no imp on wnr: kpt on same pce fnl f* **20/1**

4 *3 ½* **Aloof (IRE)**[15] 2678 4-9-7 105........................ WayneLordan 5 95
(David Wachman, Ire) *chsd ldrs in 5th: pushed along to cl under 2f out: sn no imp: kpt on one pce fnl f* **14/1**

5 *1 ½* **Captain Joy (IRE)**[15] 2679 4-9-9 106........................ PatSmullen 1 94
(Tracey Collins, Ire) *chsd ldr in 2nd: dropped to 4th 3f out: no ex appr fnl f: kpt on one pce* **11/1**[3]

6 *2 ¼* **Zand (IRE)**[225] 7421 3-8-10 99........................ DeclanMcDonogh 7 89
(John M Oxx, Ire) *w.w: 6th 3f out and sn pushed along: no imp under 2f out: nt hrd-rdn ins fnl f* **3/1**[2]

7 *2 ¼* **Salam Alaykum (IRE)**[28] 2292 5-9-9 87........................ JFEgan 8 85
(John Francis Egan, Ire) *w.w towards rr: no imp fr 2f out* **50/1**

8 *1* **Ansgar (IRE)**[15] 2679 5-9-9 96........................(t) RoryCleary 2 83
(Sabrina J Harty, Ire) *led and clr tl advantage reduced under 3f out: hdd under 2f out: sn wknd* **33/1**

9 *4 ¾* **Foxtrot Romeo (IRE)**[6] 2941 4-9-9 102........................ JohnnyMurtagh 9 74
(J P Murtagh, Ire) *a in rr: no threat under 3f out* **25/1**

10 *16* **Macbeth (IRE)**[21] 2485 4-9-9 98........................(v) ShaneFoley 3 42
(K J Condon, Ire) *hld up towards rr: no imp over 2f out: eased* **33/1**

2m 5.34s (-3.96) **Going Correction** -0.60s/f (Hard)
WFA 3 from 4yo+ 13lb **10** Ran SP% **125.9**
Speed ratings: **111,108,107,104,103 101,99,99,95,82**
CSF £5.37 TOTE £2.00: £1.02, £1.40, £4.00; DF 6.80.
Owner Mrs J S Bolger **Bred** J S Bolger **Trained** Coolcullen, Co Carlow

FOCUS
A high-quality event for the grade and a fascinating race with a view to the Irish Derby.

3143 - 3145a (Foreign Racing) - See Raceform Interactive

2492 HOPPEGARTEN (R-H)
Sunday, June 9

OFFICIAL GOING: Turf: good

3146a DIANA-TRIAL (GROUP 2) (3YO FILLIES) (TURF) 1m 2f
3:40 (12:00) 3-Y-O
£32,520 (£12,601; £5,284; £3,252; £2,032; £1,219)

RPR

1 **Ars Nova (GER)**[35] 2065 3-9-2 0........................ AndreaAtzeni 4 100+
(W Figge, Germany) *led on inner: hdd 3 1/2f out: remained prom: short of room on rail and swtchd outside 2f out: rdn to chal ins fnl f: led 50yds fr home: drvn out* **73/10**

2 *1 ½* **Oriental Lady (GER)**[231] 7281 3-9-2 0........................ MircoDemuro 5 97
(J Hirschberger, Germany) *settled in rr: rapid hdwy on outside to ld 3 1/2f out: rdn 2f out and r.o: hdd 50yds out: no ex* **125/10**

3 *2* **Artemisia (IRE)**[35] 2065 3-9-2 0........................ FilipMinarik 10 93
(P Schiergen, Germany) *a.p: cl 2nd and ev ch 2f out: sn rdn and nt qckn: kpt on at same pce fnl f* **159/10**

4 *¾* **Adoya (GER)** 3-9-2 0........................ FabienLefebvre 2 92
(Andreas Lowe, Germany) *towards rr: prog on inner 3f out: 5th and rdn fr 2f out: kpt on u.p fnl f: nvr on terms* **12/1**

5 *hd* **Daksha (FR)**[29] 3-9-2 0........................ JohanVictoire 8 91
(W Hickst, Germany) *towards rr: last and scrubbed along 2 1/2f out: briefly short of room 1 1/2f out: hung and no imp 1f out: styd on ins fnl f: nvr in contention* **27/10**[1]

6 *hd* **Quilita (GER)**[29] 3-9-2 0 AStarke 1 91
(P Schiergen, Germany) *broke fr stalls bef off: trckd ldrs on inner: 4th and styng on 2 1/2f out: hrd rdn and nt qckn fr 1 1/2f out: kpt on at one pce: dropped two pls cl home* **14/5**[2]

7 *2* **Princess Kaiulani (GER)** 3-9-2 0 HarryBentley 3 87
(A Wohler, Germany) *midfield: dropped to last over 3f out: rdn and shortlived effrt on inner 2 1/2f out: no further imp over 1 1/2f out: wknd fnl f* **96/10**

8 *3/4* **Waletta (GER)** 3-9-2 0 NRichter 7 85
(H J Groschel, Germany) *prom on outer early: settled in midfield 1/2-way: dropped towards rr over 2 1/2f out: sn rdn and no imp* **35/1**

9 *1/2* **Giulietta (GER)**[29] 3-9-2 0 LennartHammer-Hansen 6 84
(W Hickst, Germany) *plld hrd on heels of ldr: restrained bhd ldrs bef 1/2-way: rdn and lost pl 3f out: towards rr fr 1 1/2f out* **118/10**

10 *nse* **Swordhalf**[231] 7281 3-9-2 0 EPedroza 9 84
(A Wohler, Germany) *midfield: rdn appr 2 out: no imp and dropped away* **7/2**[3]

2m 4.9s (-1.80) **10** Ran SP% **128.7**
WIN (incl. 10 euro stake): 83. PLACES: 27, 48, 47. SF: 1006.
Owner Stall Salzburg **Bred** Gestut Karlshof **Trained** Germany

[2697] SAN SIRO (R-H)
Sunday, June 9

OFFICIAL GOING: Turf: good

3147a GRAN PREMIO DI MILANO (GROUP 1) (3YO+) (TURF) 1m 4f
3:50 (12:00) 3-Y-0+ **£77,235** (£33,983; £18,536; £9,268)

RPR

1 **Biz The Nurse (IRE)**[21] 2490 3-8-6 0 CristianDemuro 4 111+
(S Botti, Italy) *w.w in 5th: niggled along 3f out: swtchd outside and rdn 2f out: r.o wl appr fnl f: led ins fnl f: pushed clr: won a shade cosily* **1/2**[1]

2 *2 1/4* **Wild Wolf (IRE)**[224] 4-9-7 0 (b) CColombi 1 107
(S Botti, Italy) *led: 3 l clr 4f out: hdd narrowly 1 1/2f out: rallied u.p: jst getting bttr of ldr whn passed by eventual wnr ins fnl f: kpt on wl u.p* **17/10**[2]

3 *1 1/2* **Romantic Wave (IRE)**[21] 2489 4-9-7 0 FabioBranca 6 105
(S Botti, Italy) *trckd ldr taking a t.k.h: rdn to chal ldr 2 1/2f out: led narrowly 1 1/2f out: hdd ins fnl f: no ex* **17/10**[2]

4 *1* **Vola E Va**[21] 2489 4-9-7 0 DarioVargiu 7 103
(B Grizzetti, Italy) *chsd ldrs: rdn and nt qckn over 1 1/2f out: one pce fnl f* **122/10**

5 *1/2* **Frankenstein**[21] 2489 6-9-7 0 GArena 3 103
(B Grizzetti, Italy) *towards rr: hdwy over 2f out: rdn and no further imp appr fnl f: one pce* **187/10**

6 *3 1/2* **Duca Di Mantova**[21] 2489 4-9-7 0 PierantonioConvertino 2 97
(R Biondi, Italy) *midfield: 4th and scrubbed along 3f out: squeezed out and sn btn ins fnl 2f* **227/10**

P **Solomar (ITY)**[21] 2489 5-9-7 0 MEsposito 5
(S Botti, Italy) *towards rr: last and rdn over 2 1/2f out: lost action and p.u sn after* **44/5**[3]

2m 27.4s (-4.10)
WFA 3 from 4yo+ 15lb **7** Ran SP% **167.8**
WIN (incl. 1 euro stake): 1.50. PLACES: 1.31, 3.56. DF: 11.73.
Owner Scuderia Aleali Srl **Bred** Massimo Parri **Trained** Italy

[3009] BRIGHTON (L-H)
Monday, June 10

OFFICIAL GOING: Firm (8.7)
Wind: Fresh, half against Weather: Cloudy

3148 IT FIRST MEDIAN AUCTION MAIDEN STKS 5f 213y
2:15 (2:15) (Class 5) 2-Y-0 **£2,587** (£770; £384; £192) **Stalls** Centre

Form RPR

22 1 **Stepping Out (IRE)**[17] 2625 2-9-0 0 RichardKingscote 3 80
(Tom Dascombe) *mde all: pushed along fnl 2f: comf* **4/7**[1]

40 2 *3 1/2* **Al Baz**[13] 2741 2-9-5 0 NeilCallan 2 74
(James Tate) *chsd wnr: rdn 2f out: one pce* **5/1**[3]

33 3 *2 1/4* **Senorita Guest (IRE)**[9] 2869 2-9-0 0 MartinHarley 1 62
(Mick Channon) *a 3rd: outpcd fnl 2f* **7/2**[2]

4 *1 1/4* **G Man (IRE)** 2-9-5 0 HarryBentley 4 63+
(Olly Stevens) *a in last: wl hld fnl 2f* **25/1**

1m 9.6s (-0.60) **Going Correction** -0.075s/f (Good) **4** Ran SP% **106.4**
Speed ratings (Par 93): **101,96,93,91**
CSF £3.65 TOTE £1.30; EX 3.50 Trifecta £4.70 Pool: £1763.73 - 276.87 winning units..
Owner Attenborough Bellman Ingram Lowe **Bred** Glending Bloodstock **Trained** Malpas, Cheshire

FOCUS
The ground was officially firm and the rail was dolled out slightly at the top of the straight, adding 8yds to race distances. A modest maiden, but the three with experience has all previously shown some level of ability. The second was back to, or stepped up on, his debut form.

3149 ITFIRST.CO.UK SUPPORT SERVICES MEDIAN AUCTION MAIDEN STKS 6f 209y
2:45 (2:45) (Class 5) 3-4-Y-0 **£2,587** (£770; £384; £192) **Stalls** Centre

Form RPR

03- 1 **Al Manaal**[237] 7143 3-8-12 0 SilvestreDeSousa 3 82+
(Saeed bin Suroor) *mde all: shkn up 2f out: sn clr: easily* **1/1**[1]

-02 2 *8* **Crave**[17] 2637 3-8-12 0 HayleyTurner 5 63
(William Jarvis) *hld up in 3rd: chsd wnr 4f out: easily outpcd fnl 2f* **9/4**[2]

360 3 *8* **Grey Gazelle**[10] 2850 3-8-12 73 MartinHarley 1 38
(Mick Channon) *hld up in 4th: rdn over 2f out: sn wknd* **3/1**[3]

00 4 *18* **Keene**[13] 2760 3-9-3 0 WilliamCarson 2
(Philip McBride) *chsd wnr 3f: rdn and btn over 2f out: 4th and wl hld whn virtually p.u over 1f out* **33/1**

1m 21.86s (-1.24) **Going Correction** -0.075s/f (Good) **4** Ran SP% **108.7**
Speed ratings (Par 103): **104,94,85,65**
CSF £3.56 TOTE £2.00; EX 3.30 Trifecta £4.70 Pool: £1900.75 - 298.53 winning units..
Owner Godolphin **Bred** Darley **Trained** Newmarket, Suffolk

FOCUS
Not the strongest of maidens, but it was won in good style.

3150 CHARLIE QUANTICK MEMORIAL H'CAP 1m 3f 196y
3:15 (3:15) (Class 5) (0-75,78) 4-Y-0+ **£2,587** (£770; £384; £192) **Stalls** High

Form RPR

4406 1 **Thecornishcowboy**[7] 2939 4-9-0 68 (tp) AdamKirby 4 75
(John Ryan) *hld up in 4th: hdwy over 2f out: hung lft and led over 1f out: drvn clr* **9/2**[3]

011 2 *3 1/4* **Dandy (GER)**[7] 2923 4-9-5 78 6ex (p) ThomasBrown[(5)] 2 81
(Andrew Balding) *led: set modest pce: qcknd over 2f out: rdr dropped whip and hdd over 1f out: n.m.r on rail: no ex fnl f* **5/4**[1]

10-5 3 *1 1/2* **No Such Number**[37] 2009 5-9-5 73 GeorgeBaker 1 73
(Julia Feilden) *t.k.h in 3rd: rdn and hld whn squeezed for room wl over 1f out: one pce* **6/4**[2]

00-4 4 *14* **Dubai Glory**[4] 3012 5-9-2 70 ChrisCatlin 5 47
(Sheena West) *chsd ldr tl wknd 2f out* **20/1**

2m 32.49s (-0.21) **Going Correction** -0.075s/f (Good) **4** Ran SP% **107.4**
Speed ratings (Par 103): **97,94,93,84**
CSF £10.52 TOTE £6.90; EX 10.30 Trifecta £12.30 Pool: £1836.22 - 111.32 winning units..
Owner C Letcher & J Ryan **Bred** Hadi Al Tajir **Trained** Newmarket, Suffolk

FOCUS
With only four runners and a moderate pace this might not be the strongest bit of form going forward.

3151 CHARLIE Q "DID IT LARGE" H'CAP 1m 3f 196y
3:45 (3:45) (Class 6) (0-55,59) 4-Y-0+ **£1,940** (£577; £288; £144) **Stalls** High

Form RPR

0001 1 **Highlife Dancer**[3] 3037 5-9-6 59 6ex (v) CharlesBishop[(5)] 2 71
(Mick Channon) *chsd ldr: led 3f out: drvn clr fnl f* **6/4**[1]

2-00 2 *2 1/4* **Beacon Lady**[20] 2533 4-8-12 51 NicoleNordblad[(5)] 1 59+
(William Knight) *dwlt: hld up in rr: hdwy in centre over 2f out: styd on to take 2nd ins fnl f* **11/4**[2]

0-00 3 *1* **Frosty Secret**[13] 2764 4-8-8 49 (b[1]) IanBurns[(7)] 4 56
(Jane Chapple-Hyam) *hld up in 4th: chsd wnr 2f out tl ins fnl f: one pce* **8/1**

-302 4 *4 1/2* **Royal Defence (IRE)**[11] 2801 7-9-0 48 AndreaAtzeni 3 48
(Mick Quinn) *led tl 3f out: wknd over 1f out* **7/2**[3]

-040 5 *1/2* **Heading To First**[9] 2875 6-8-5 46 oh1 (p) JoeyHaynes[(7)] 6 45
(Paddy Butler) *s.s: hld up in 5th: effrt over 2f out: wknd over 1f out* **20/1**

605 6 *8* **Revert (USA)**[82] 1089 4-8-13 47 (b[1]) ChrisCatlin 7 33
(Gerry Enright) *chsd ldrs tl wknd 2f out* **20/1**

2m 35.4s (2.70) **Going Correction** -0.075s/f (Good) **6** Ran SP% **109.5**
Speed ratings (Par 101): **88,86,85,82,82 77**
toteswingers 1&2 £1.30, 2&3 £3.10, 1&3 £2.00 CSF £5.49 TOTE £2.80: £1.20, £1.40; EX 6.50 Trifecta £33.10 Pool: £2909.58 - 65.77 winning units..
Owner The Highlife Racing Club **Bred** Imperial & Mike Channon Bloodstock Ltd **Trained** West Ilsley, Berks

FOCUS
A modest middle-distance handicap, but they went an honest pace and the form looks straightforward.

3152 ROBERT EATON MEMORIAL FUND H'CAP 1m 1f 209y
4:15 (4:15) (Class 5) (0-70,63) 4-Y-0+ **£2,587** (£770; £384; £192) **Stalls** High

Form RPR

6041 1 **Green Earth (IRE)**[20] 2533 6-8-7 54 JemmaMarshall[(5)] 1 66
(Pat Phelan) *trckd ldrs: led wl over 1f out: drvn clr ent fnl f: comf* **11/10**[1]

165 2 *6* **Final Delivery**[20] 2532 4-9-3 59 PatCosgrave 5 60
(Jim Boyle) *led: set stdy pce: rdn 3f out: hdd wl over 1f out: no ex fnl f* **6/1**[3]

0-00 3 *7* **Uncle Fred**[31] 2228 8-9-7 63 JimCrowley 4 49
(Patrick Chamings) *blindfold removed late and missed break: stdd in 4th: clsd on ldrs 4f out: btn wl over 1f out* **13/8**[2]

0/0- 4 *20* **Unbreak My Heart (IRE)**[501] 306 8-8-6 48 (p) JimmyQuinn 2
(Violet M Jordan) *plld hrd: pressed ldr tl wknd qckly 2f out* **12/1**

2m 6.19s (2.59) **Going Correction** -0.075s/f (Good) **4** Ran SP% **107.7**
Speed ratings (Par 103): **86,81,75,59**
CSF £7.59 TOTE £1.70; EX 4.60 Trifecta £6.30 Pool: £1884.99 - 221.53 winning units..
Owner P Wheatley **Bred** Woodcote Stud Ltd **Trained** Epsom, Surrey

FOCUS
A slow early pace for this modest handicap and several were keen early.

3153 ANDY CLIFFORD H'CAP 6f 209y
4:45 (4:45) (Class 4) (0-85,81) 3-Y-0+ **£4,690** (£1,395; £697; £348) **Stalls** Centre

Form RPR

1-54 1 **Good Luck Charm**[30] 2266 4-9-9 76 GeorgeBaker 5 85
(Gary Moore) *hld up in 5th: hdwy over 2f out: led ins fnl f: hld on nr fin* **7/1**

-050 2 *hd* **Mr David (USA)**[31] 2214 6-10-0 81 (b) FergusSweeney 4 89
(Jamie Osborne) *hld up in rr: rdn and hdwy over 1f out: wnt 2nd and clsd on wnr fnl f: jst hld* **16/1**

112- 3 *3* **Take A Note**[265] 6331 4-9-10 77 JimCrowley 1 77
(Patrick Chamings) *towards rr: last and rdn over 2f out: styd on wl fnl f* **5/1**[3]

1011 4 *1/2* **Macaabra (IRE)**[4] 3016 3-8-12 75 6ex NeilCallan 7 70
(James Tate) *led: hrd rdn over 1f out: hdd & wknd ins fnl f* **13/8**[1]

1-42 5 *3/4* **Excuse To Linger**[35] 2100 3-9-3 80 WilliamBuick 6 73
(Jeremy Noseda) *prom tl outpcd and hung lft 2f out* **9/4**[2]

5114 6 *1 1/4* **Jonnie Skull (IRE)**[3] 3052 7-8-13 66 (vt) SilvestreDeSousa 3 59
(Phil McEntee) *t.k.h: prom tl wknd over 1f out* **14/1**

6-50 7 *2 3/4* **Bayleyf (IRE)**[41] 1913 4-9-13 80 (t) AdamKirby 2 66
(John Best) *in tch: n.m.r over 4f out: wknd 2f out* **25/1**

1m 21.4s (-1.70) **Going Correction** -0.075s/f (Good)
WFA 3 from 4yo+ 10lb **7** Ran SP% **114.4**
Speed ratings (Par 105): **106,105,102,101,100 99,96**
toteswingers 1&2 £7.50, 2&3 £7.00, 1&3 £4.50 CSF £102.83 TOTE £8.40: £2.70, £4.30; EX 81.30 Trifecta £397.80 Pool: £3249.63 - 6.12 winning units..
Owner Heart Of The South Racing **Bred** John And Caroline Penny **Trained** Lower Beeding, W Sussex

FOCUS
A fair handicap featuring a couple of improving 3yos taking on their elders. They went a solid pace and the older brigade were on top at the finish.

3154 HARRINGTONS LETTINGS H'CAP 5f 59y
5:15 (5:15) (Class 6) (0-55,55) 4-Y-0+ **£1,940** (£577; £288; £144) **Stalls** Centre

Form RPR
4-00 **1** **Even Bolder**[41] 1902 10-9-0 **55** .... JoeyHaynes(7) 10 61
(Eric Wheeler) *towards rr: hung lft and hdwy over 1f out: str run to ld nr fin* **20/1**
2242 **2** *nk* **Slatey Hen (IRE)**[28] 2326 5-9-4 **52** .... (p) JimmyQuinn 4 57
(Violet M Jordan) *chsd ldr: led ins fnl f: hdd and unable qck nr fin* **5/1**[3]
3604 **3** *1 ½* **Russian Bullet**[28] 2326 4-8-12 **46** oh1 .... (b) FergusSweeney 8 46
(Jamie Osborne) *in tch on outer: rdn to chse ldrs 2f out: n.m.r ins fnl f: kpt on same pce* **8/1**
0055 **4** *shd* **Volcanic Dust (IRE)**[41] 1902 5-9-6 **54** .... (t) SilvestreDeSousa 2 53
(Milton Bradley) *led tl ins fnl f: one pce* **9/2**[2]
5/00 **5** *nk* **Mousie**[95] 917 4-8-12 **46** oh1 .... KieranO'Neill 7 44
(Alan McCabe) *towards rr: rdn 3f out: styd on fnl f* **25/1**
0P-0 **6** *nse* **Samba Night (IRE)**[18] 2596 4-9-6 **54** .... (t) SteveDrowne 6 52
(Jeremy Gask) *in tch: hung lft and lost pl over 2f out: styd on again fnl f* **20/1**
0004 **7** *½* **Scommettitrice (IRE)**[18] 2596 5-9-5 **53** .... (b) GeorgeBaker 5 49
(Mark Gillard) *outpcd in rr tl r.o fnl f* **4/1**[1]
0306 **8** *hd* **Whiskey Junction**[34] 2132 9-9-5 **53** .... AndreaAtzeni 3 49
(Mick Quinn) *chsd ldrs: rdn over 2f out: no ex fnl f* **10/1**
0503 **9** *½* **Little China**[9] 2870 4-9-4 **52** .... (p) WilliamCarson 9 46
(William Muir) *prom tl wknd over 1f out* **4/1**[1]
0 **10** *½* **Ferocious Fran (IRE)**[35] 2074 5-8-7 **46** oh1 .... (t) DeclanBates(5) 1 38
(R McGlinchey, Ire) *s.i.s: in rr: hdwy on inner over 2f out: lost pl fnl f* **12/1**

1m 2.82s (0.52) **Going Correction** -0.075s/f (Good) **10** Ran SP% **116.1**
Speed ratings (Par 101): **92,91,89,88,88 88,87,87,86,85**
toteswingers 1&2 £20.00, 2&3 £4.50, 1&3 £21.00 CSF £113.94 CT £903.99 TOTE £18.90: £4.00, £1.70, £2.60; EX 112.00 Trifecta £749.20 Pool: £3141.84 - 3.14 winning units..
Owner E A Wheeler **Bred** Raffin Bloodstock **Trained** Lambourn, Berks

FOCUS
A competitive, low-grade sprint handicap, but plenty of these came here on lengthy losing runs.
T/Plt: £759.90 to a £1 stake. Pool of £59378.83 - 57.04 winning tickets. T/Qpdt: £122.90 to a £1 stake. Pool of £3689.21 - 22.20 winning tickets. LM

2933 WINDSOR (R-H)
Monday, June 10

OFFICIAL GOING: Good to firm (8.8)
Wind: Almost nil Weather: Cloudy

3155 BETVICTOR ROYAL ASCOT MONEY BACK SPECIAL/EBF MAIDEN STKS 6f
6:30 (6:31) (Class 5) 2-Y-0 **£2,911** (£866; £432; £216) **Stalls** Low

Form RPR
1 **Homestretch** 2-9-5 0 .... MartinHarley 7 75+
(Mick Channon) *outpcd in 6th after 2f and pushed along: rdn and clsd fr 2f out: led ins fnl f: edgd lft and pushed out* **8/1**[3]
2 *½* **Rock Of Dreams (IRE)** 2-9-5 0 .... JamesMcDonald 4 73+
(Charles Hills) *dwlt: chsd ldrs: pushed along fr 1/2-way: effrt on wd outside 2f out: styd on to press wnr last 100yds: a hld* **10/1**
3 *¾* **Ice Slice (IRE)** 2-9-5 0 .... PatDobbs 2 71
(Richard Hannon) *slowly away: led after 1f to 1/2-way: led again jst over 2f out: hung bdly lft over 1f out: hdd and nt qckn ins fnl f* **8/1**[3]
5 **4** *1* **Constantine**[20] 2543 2-9-5 0 .... RichardHughes 6 69
(Richard Hannon) *stdd s: t.k.h and w ldr after 1f: led 1/2-way to jst over 2f out: nt qckn sn after: hmpd over 1f out: kpt on same pce* **5/6**[1]
5 *4* **Silver Starlet (IRE)** 2-9-0 0 .... FrankieDettori 3 50
(Alastair Lidderdale) *chsd ldrs: pushed along 1/2-way: no imp over 1f out: fdd* **33/1**
6 *2* **Aspirant** 2-9-5 0 .... JamesDoyle 1 49
(Roger Charlton) *led 1f: chsd ldng pair after and rn green: hung lft 2f out: wknd fnl f* **7/2**[2]
7 *3 ¾* **Loving Your Work** 2-9-5 0 .... PatCosgrave 5 37
(George Baker) *completely missed the break: a trailing in last* **33/1**

1m 14.43s (1.43) **Going Correction** +0.025s/f (Good) **7** Ran SP% **114.0**
Speed ratings (Par 93): **91,90,89,88,82 80,75**
toteswingers 1&2 £9.20, 2&3 £8.60, 1&3 £6.20 CSF £80.37 TOTE £10.40: £2.70, £3.70; EX 81.60 Trifecta £434.20 Pool: £2311.02 - 3.99 winning units..
Owner Prince A A Faisal **Bred** Nawara Stud Co Ltd **Trained** West Ilsley, Berks

FOCUS
Top bend dolled out 8yds from normal configuration, adding 34yds to races of 1m and beyond. Inner of straight dolled out 14yds at 6f and 7yds at winning post. No rain had fallen after the previous meeting here a week earlier and officials selectively put on 20-23mm of water over the past five days. Although a little messy, this could work out to be an above-average 2yo maiden.

3156 BETVICTOR ROYAL ASCOT NO LOSE HUGHES CLAIMING STKS 1m 2f 7y
7:00 (7:00) (Class 5) 3-Y-0+ **£2,587** (£770; £384; £192) **Stalls** Centre

Form RPR
4-46 **1** **Breaking The Bank**[31] 2234 4-9-9 67 .... MartinDwyer 6 73
(William Muir) *hld up in 4th: shkn up over 3f out: prog to chse ldr wl over 1f out: sustained chal after tl led nr fin* **5/2**[2]
1100 **2** *hd* **Honey Of A Kitten (USA)**[7] 2923 5-9-9 73 .... (v) AdamKirby 5 72
(David Evans) *trckd ldr: led 3f out: hrd rdn and pressed over 1f out: hdd nr fin* **2/1**[1]
0-24 **3** *4* **Royal Etiquette (IRE)**[89] 747 6-9-5 62 .... (v) DaneO'Neill 1 60
(Lawney Hill) *t.k.h: hld up in 5th: prog to chse ldng pair over 1f out and cl enough: sn rdn and nt qckn: eased whn hld last 50yds* **8/1**
21-4 **4** *6* **Abbraccio**[13] 2739 5-9-2 68 .... (t) WilliamTwiston-Davies(5) 3 50
(Fergal O'Brien) *led to 3f out: wknd qckly over 1f out* **3/1**[3]
3422 **5** *11* **Moment In The Sun**[6] 2948 4-9-2 61 .... (b) FrankieDettori 4 23
(David Flood) *t.k.h: trckd ldng pair: pushed along over 3f out: wknd qckly 2f out: sn bhd* **6/1**
0 **6** *1 ½* **Shameless Man (IRE)**[35] 2093 6-9-1 0 .... (t) SimonPearce(3) 2 22
(Anthony Middleton) *s.v.s and shoved along to get gng: immediately 10 l bhd rest: nvr able to catch up* **100/1**

2m 8.8s (0.10) **Going Correction** +0.025s/f (Good) **6** Ran SP% **113.3**
Speed ratings (Par 103): **100,99,96,91,83 81**
toteswingers 1&2 £1.40, 2&3 £3.60, 1&3 £2.00 CSF £8.09 TOTE £3.80: £1.90, £1.60; EX 9.30 Trifecta £38.80 Pool: £1528.26 - 29.49 winning units..
Owner R W Devlin **Bred** Cheveley Park Stud Ltd **Trained** Lambourn, Berks

FOCUS
A modest claimer.

3157 TRINITY MAXWELL H'CAP 1m 2f 7y
7:30 (7:30) (Class 4) (0-85,85) 4-Y-0+ **£4,851** (£1,443; £721; £360) **Stalls** Centre

Form RPR
2-44 **1** **Cactus Valley (IRE)**[24] 2422 4-9-6 **84** .... JamesDoyle 7 94
(Roger Charlton) *s.i.s: hld up: stl last of main gp 2f out: prog on outer over 1f out: led jst ins fnl f: edgd lft but r.o wl* **11/4**[2]
0012 **2** *¾* **Come On Blue Chip (IRE)**[14] 2728 4-9-7 **85** .... (p) RichardHughes 9 94
(Paul D'Arcy) *stdd s: hld up in rr: stl in last pair of main gp 2f out: prog on wd outside over 1f out: rdn to chal ins fnl f: r.o but a hld* **5/2**[1]
-500 **3** *2 ½* **Daghash**[47] 1766 4-8-13 **77** .... NeilCallan 8 81
(Clive Brittain) *prom: chsd ldr over 4f out: rdn over 3f out: chal and upsides jst over 1f out: first pair swept by fnl f* **6/1**[3]
-005 **4** *2 ¾* **Croquembouche (IRE)**[20] 2551 4-8-8 **72** .... LiamKeniry 1 70
(Ed de Giles) *mde most: drvn 2f out: jnd jst over 1f out: hdd & wknd jst ins fnl f* **10/1**
2630 **5** *1* **Greylami (IRE)**[21] 2498 8-8-12 **76** .... FrankieDettori 10 72
(Clive Cox) *hld up in tch: shkn up 3f out: nt qckn 2f out: outpcd fnl f* **7/1**
444 **6** *4* **Hurakan (IRE)**[19] 2569 7-8-5 **69** .... (p) HarryBentley 6 57
(Richard Price) *trckd ldrs: rdn 3f out: no prog 2f out: wknd over 1f out* **20/1**
15-0 **7** *8* **Starfield**[24] 2424 4-9-7 **85** .... WilliamBuick 3 57
(John Gosden) *trckd ldrs: wnt 2nd briefly 1/2-way: shkn up 3f out: wknd over 1f out* **12/1**
2323 **8** *shd* **Prince Of Burma (IRE)**[14] 2728 5-8-10 **77** .... (tp) RyanClark(3) 2 49
(Jeremy Gask) *dwlt: hld up in tch: rdn 3f out: no imp on ldrs 2f out: sn wknd* **9/1**
30-0 **9** *dist* **Claude Monet (BRZ)**[18] 2605 4-8-8 **75** .... ChrisCatlin 4
(Simon Dow) *t.k.h: chsd ldr to 1/2-way: wknd v rapidly and sn t.o: virtually p.u 2f out* **50/1**

2m 7.33s (-1.37) **Going Correction** +0.025s/f (Good) **9** Ran SP% **115.5**
Speed ratings (Par 105): **106,105,103,101,100 97,90,90,**
toteswingers 1&2 £2.50, 2&3 £4.60, 1&3 £5.30 CSF £10.07 CT £36.88 TOTE £3.90: £1.50, £1.40, £2.30; EX 10.80 Trifecta £48.10 Pool: £1726.68 - 26.88 winning units..
Owner H R H Sultan Ahmad Shah **Bred** Gerrardstown House Stud **Trained** Beckhampton, Wilts

FOCUS
A fair handicap, run at a solid pace and the first pair came clear having charted a wide course off the home turn.

3158 MAGGIE COSTELLO WILL YOU MARRY ME FILLIES' H'CAP 1m 67y
8:00 (8:00) (Class 4) (0-85,84) 4-Y-0+ **£4,851** (£1,443; £721; £360) **Stalls** Low

Form RPR
1-52 **1** **Malekat Jamal (IRE)**[14] 2711 4-8-1 **67** .... DarrenEgan(3) 1 75
(David Simcock) *t.k.h: hld up in last: bustled along and prog on outer 2f out: pushed into narrow but decisive ld fnl f: rdn out nr fin to maintain advantage* **6/1**
316- **2** *nk* **Miss Cap Estel**[254] 6661 4-9-2 **79** .... JimmyFortune 4 86
(Andrew Balding) *t.k.h: trckd ldr: rdn to chal over 2f out: led over 1f out w hd quite high: hdd fnl f: styd on u.p* **9/4**[1]
-001 **3** *3 ½* **Alice's Dancer (IRE)**[20] 2531 4-9-7 **84** .... WilliamCarson 6 82
(William Muir) *plld hrd: hld up and sn in 4th: chsd ldng pair 3f out: nt qckn 2f out: outpcd fnl f* **12/1**
12-0 **4** *1 ¾* **Fulney**[30] 2253 4-9-4 **81** .... DaneO'Neill 3 74
(James Eustace) *led at gd pce: rdn 3f out: hdd over 1f out: fdd* **4/1**[3]
1-04 **5** *4* **Authoritarian**[20] 2531 4-8-12 **75** .... RichardHughes 2 57
(Richard Hannon) *hld up and sn in 5th: pushed along over 2f out: swtchd fr rail to outer over 1f out and reminders: sn wknd* **7/1**
-032 **6** *2* **Four Leaves (IRE)**[13] 2750 4-9-3 **80** .... AdamKirby 5 57
(Marco Botti) *trckd ldng pair to 3f out: rdn and wknd 2f out* **3/1**[2]

1m 44.46s (-0.24) **Going Correction** +0.025s/f (Good) **6** Ran SP% **110.2**
Speed ratings (Par 102): **102,101,98,96,92 90**
toteswingers 1&2 £3.10, 2&3 £6.20, 1&3 £8.30 CSF £19.18 TOTE £7.40: £3.30, £1.70; EX 19.70 Trifecta £147.90 Pool: £1212.35 - 6.14 winning units..
Owner Saeed Manana **Bred** Adrian Purvis & Luke Barry **Trained** Newmarket, Suffolk

FOCUS
A modest fillies' handicap. It was run at a brisk early pace before slowing up nearing the home straight and again it saw a winner that challenged wide.

3159 BETVICTOR NO LOSE HUGHES MONEY BACK CLASSIFIED STKS 6f
8:30 (8:30) (Class 5) 3-Y-0 **£2,587** (£770; £384; £192) **Stalls** Low

Form RPR
-321 **1** **Grand Denial (IRE)**[23] 2437 3-9-0 75 .... (b) AdamKirby 2 82+
(Clive Cox) *scratchy to post: led after 1f: pushed along and looked wl in command 2f out: edgd rt and hrd rdn fnl f: hld on* **1/1**[1]
22-3 **2** *½* **Charter (IRE)**[33] 2169 3-9-0 75 .... FrankieDettori 3 80
(Michael Wigham) *hld up: prog 1/2-way: chsd wnr over 1f out: trying to cl whn nt clr run and swtchd lft 150yds out: styd on: nvr quite able to chal* **7/1**[3]
-341 **3** *1 ¾* **Royal Challis**[14] 2722 3-9-0 75 .... RichardHughes 6 75
(Richard Hannon) *racd wd: mostly chsd wnr over 4f out to over 1f out: nt qckn after* **2/1**[2]
0005 **4** *2* **Lucky Di**[11] 2806 3-9-0 71 .... DaneO'Neill 4 68
(Peter Hedger) *rrd s: mostly in last pair: no prog over 2f out: drvn into 4th over 1f out: no imp* **20/1**
51-0 **5** *3* **Keep The Dream**[46] 1784 3-9-0 70 .... (t) WilliamBuick 1 59
(Paul Cole) *led 1f: sn outpcd by ldrs: no imp 2f out: hanging lft fnl f* **20/1**
5045 **6** *10* **Fletcher Christian**[3] 3050 3-9-0 71 .... (v) NeilCallan 5 36
(John Gallagher) *bmpd s: veered lft sn after and str reminder: then t.k.h and pressed ldng pair after 2f: wknd 2f out: eased fnl f* **20/1**

1m 12.6s (-0.40) **Going Correction** +0.025s/f (Good) **6** Ran SP% **110.1**
Speed ratings (Par 99): **103,102,100,97,93 80**
CSF £8.05 TOTE £1.90: £1.20, £3.50; EX 8.50 Trifecta £19.70 Pool: £1136.95 - 43.18 winning units..
Owner Alan G Craddock **Bred** A M F Persse **Trained** Lambourn, Berks

FOCUS
This wasn't as tight as it looked on paper and the market leaders dominated.

3160 ROYAL ASCOT MONEY BACK AT BETVICTOR.COM H'CAP 5f 10y
9:00 (9:00) (Class 4) (0-85,78) 3-Y-0 **£4,851** (£1,443; £721; £360) **Stalls** Low

Form RPR
-516 **1** **Exotic Isle**[21] 2521 3-9-5 76 .... JamieSpencer 1 85
(Ralph Beckett) *w.w in last: prog over 1f out: chsd ldr fnl f: drvn and r.o to ld last 75yds* **1/1**[1]

52-4 **2** ¾ **Dusty Storm (IRE)**[14] 2726 3-9-7 78 .... SeanLevey 2 84
(Ed McMahon) *fast away: led against nr side rail: drvn over 1f out: edgd lft and hdd last 75yds* **5/2**[2]

-010 **3** 2½ **Edged Out**[10] 2829 3-8-12 69 .... CathyGannon 3 66
(Christopher Mason) *dwlt: chsd ldr after 1f: rdn sn after 1/2-way: lost 2nd and one pce fnl f* **14/1**

21-0 **4** 4½ **Star Up In The Sky (USA)**[51] 1690 3-9-5 76 .... NeilCallan 4 60
(Kevin Ryan) *chsd ldr 1f: rdn after 2f: struggling 2f out: wknd fnl f* **7/2**[3]

1m 0.18s (-0.12) **Going Correction** +0.025s/f (Good) **4** Ran SP% **107.5**
Speed ratings (Par 101): **101,99,95,88**
CSF £3.71 TOTE £1.80; EX 4.20 Trifecta £19.50 Pool: £740.87 - 28.40 winning units..
Owner Pearl Bloodstock Ltd & N H Wrigley **Bred** T R G Vestey **Trained** Kimpton, Hants
FOCUS
There was no hanging about in this tight little sprint handicap.
T/Plt: £290.20 to a £1 stake. Pool of £84746.39 - 213.11 winning units. T/Qpdt: £9.80 to a £1 stake. Pool of £7762.35 - 583.65 winning units. JN

3161 - 3164a (Foreign Racing) - See Raceform Interactive

2970 LONGCHAMP (R-H)
Monday, June 10

OFFICIAL GOING: Turf: good to soft

3165a LA COUPE (GROUP 3) (4YO+) (TURF) 1m 2f
2:20 (12:00) 4-Y-O+ **£32,520** (£13,008; £9,756; £6,504; £3,252)

RPR

1 **Slow Pace (USA)**[33] 2184 5-8-11 0 .... OlivierPeslier 8 111
(F Head, France) *got across fr wd draw and mde virtually all: set slow pce: shkn up whn jnd 2f out: rdn and qcknd clr ent fnl f: kpt on: rapidly diminishing advantage cl home but a holding on: gd ride* **7/2**[2]

2 snk **Smoking Sun (USA)**[267] 6294 4-8-11 0 .... StephanePasquier 6 111
(P Bary, France) *hld up in last pair on inner: stl gng wl enough but last and looking for clr run 2f out: rdn over 1f out: swtchd rt and styd on strly ins fnl f: wnt 2nd fnl strides and clsng rapidly on wnr: unlucky* **8/1**

3 snk **Harem Lady (FR)**[17] 2644 4-8-8 0 .... GregoryBenoist 1 108
(D Smaga, France) *trckd ldr on inner: rdn 2f out: styd on and wnt 2nd wl ins fnl f: clsng on wnr but dropped to 3rd fnl strides* **12/1**

4 snk **Galvaun (IRE)**[212] 7694 4-8-8 0 .... Pierre-CharlesBoudot 3 107
(A Fabre, France) *midfield on inner: angled out gng best 2f out: rdn over 1f out: nt qckn but styd on to go 4th post* **5/1**

5 shd **Saga Dream (FR)**[8] 2908 7-9-4 0 .... ThierryJarnet 2 117
(F Lemercier, France) *midfield in tch on outer: rdn to chal 2f out: nt qckn and outpcd by ldr over 1f out: kpt on but dropped to 5th post* **3/1**[1]

6 1 **Pagera (FR)**[17] 2644 5-8-13 0 .... (p) FabriceVeron 4 110
(H-A Pantall, France) *t.k.h early: trckd ldr on outer: rdn and jnd ldr 2f out: outpcd by ldr over 1f out: kpt on tl no ex and fdd wl ins fnl f* **17/2**

7 2½ **Albion**[26] 4-8-11 0 .... MaximeGuyon 5 103
(A Fabre, France) *hld up in midfield: rdn 3f out: outpcd by ldrs over 1f out: kpt on but n.d* **4/1**[3]

8 nk **Samba Brazil (GER)**[32] 2202 4-8-8 0 .... MircoDemuro 7 100
(A Wohler, Germany) *hld up in last pair on outer: hdwy 3f out: rdn over 2f out: sn outpcd: fdd and dropped to last* **16/1**

2m 9.24s (5.24) **8** Ran SP% **119.1**
WIN (incl. 1 euro stake): 3.80. PLACES: 1.80, 3.00, 2.80. DF: 13.60. SF: 25.00.
Owner Wertheimer & Frere **Bred** Wertheimer & Frere **Trained** France

3166a PRIX DE CLICHY (CONDITIONS) (3YO) (TURF) 1m 4f
3:55 (12:00) 3-Y-O **£9,756** (£3,902; £2,926; £1,951; £975)

RPR

1 **Solow**[53] 3-9-4 0 .... OlivierPeslier 5 85
(F Head, France) **13/10**[1]

2 ½ **Grey Hawk (FR)**[34] 3-9-4 0 .... (p) MaximeGuyon 7 84
(X Thomas-Demeaulte, France) **4/1**[3]

3 2 **Golden Buck (FR)**[164] 3-9-4 0 .... RonanThomas 8 81
(P Van De Poele, France) **58/10**

4 1¼ **Horse No Name (FR)**[68] 3-9-4 0 .... FabriceVeron 4 79
(H-A Pantall, France) **7/2**[2]

5 1¼ **Sweni Hill (IRE)**[24] 2434 3-8-10 0 .... Pierre-CharlesBoudot 1 69
(Y De Nicolay, France) **23/1**

6 nse **Purple American (FR)**[19] 3-8-8 0 .... ThibaultSpeicher(6) 3 73
(E Lellouche, France) **12/1**

7 6 **Habeshia**[20] 2557 3-8-11 0 .... JohanVictoire 2 60
(John Best) *prom on inner: rdn over 2f out: outpcd over 1f out: fdd: eased whn btn ins fnl f* **23/1**

8 nse **Inchelle (IRE)** 3-8-8 0 .... (b[1]) AnthonyCrastus 6 57
(E Lellouche, France) **50/1**

2m 35.63s (5.23) **8** Ran SP% **118.4**
WIN (incl. 1 euro stake): 2.30. Places: 1.10, 1.30, 1.60. DF: 5.00. SF: 8.00..
Owner Wertheimer & Frere **Bred** Wertheimer Et Frere **Trained** France

3049 LINGFIELD (L-H)
Tuesday, June 11

OFFICIAL GOING: Standard
Wind: Light, behind Weather: Overcast, drizzly

3167 THREE BRIDGES MEDIAN AUCTION MAIDEN STKS 5f (P)
6:00 (6:01) (Class 5) 2-Y-O **£2,726** (£805; £402) **Stalls** High

Form RPR

4 **1** **Umneyati**[15] 2712 2-9-0 0 .... NeilCallan 4 64+
(James Tate) *mde all: a in command: shkn up over 1f out: unchal* **1/3**[1]

55 **2** 3½ **Red House**[15] 2715 2-9-5 0 .... MartinDwyer 2 56
(David C Griffiths) *a 2nd and nvr win 2 l of wnr: rdn over 2f out: no imp after* **10/1**[3]

50 **3** 4½ **Oakley Dancer**[15] 2723 2-9-0 0 .... JimmyQuinn 1 35
(Tony Carroll) *stdd s: chsd ldng pair but nt on terms: shkn up and stl green over 1f out: no prog* **16/1**

06 **4** nk **Faye Belle**[13] 2778 2-8-7 0 .... AdamMcLean(7) 5 34
(Derek Shaw) *slowly away: outpcd in 4th and hanging: kpt on fnl f and nrly snatched 3rd* **25/1**

5 **5** 4 **Vanvidd (FR)** 2-9-0 0 .... NicoleNordblad(5) 6 25
(Hans Adielsson) *slowly away: outpcd and a last* **5/1**[2]

59.71s (0.91) **Going Correction** -0.05s/f (Stan) **5** Ran SP% **110.5**
Speed ratings (Par 93): **90,84,77,76,70**
CSF £4.67 TOTE £1.10: £1.10, £3.20; EX 3.00 Trifecta £12.10 Pool: £720.09 - 44.47 winning units..
Owner Sheikh Rashid Dalmook Al Maktoum **Bred** Mrs Hugh Maitland-Jones **Trained** Newmarket, Suffolk
FOCUS
The going was standard. Plenty of interest was taken out of this weak maiden, with the two paper favourites withdrawn. It was run at a fair pace, with the order unchanged throughout. The winner can't start too high in nurseries after this.

3168 LINGFIELD PARK SUPPORTS BHEST H'CAP 1m 4f (P)
6:30 (6:30) (Class 6) (0-65,62) 4-Y-O+ **£2,045** (£603; £302) **Stalls** Low

Form RPR

004/ **1** **Cornish Beau (IRE)**[366] 6303 6-9-0 55 .... LukeMorris 1 65+
(Dr Richard Newland) *hld up in 5th: prog over 2f out: clsd over 1f out: hrd rdn to ld last 150yds: styd on* **14/1**

1416 **2** 2 **Cape Alex**[14] 2739 4-9-6 61 .... NeilCallan 4 68
(Clive Brittain) *awkward s: t.k.h and pressed ldr after 2f: led 4f out: drvn 3f out: hdd and one pce last 150yds* **7/4**[1]

2130 **3** 3¼ **Highly Likely (IRE)**[13] 2777 4-9-5 60 .... (t) AdamKirby 6 61
(Steve Woodman) *hld up in 4th: cl up 3f out: shkn up over 2f out: nt qckn over 1f out and btn after: kpt on* **8/1**

0-05 **4** nk **Steely**[20] 2569 5-9-7 62 .... RyanMoore 8 63
(Gary Moore) *led after 1f to 4f out: shkn up 3f out: chsd ldr to over 1f out: wknd fnl f* **9/2**

64-0 **5** 1¼ **Astroscarlet**[20] 2567 4-8-9 53 .... SimonPearce(3) 7 52
(Mark H Tompkins) *led 1f: trckd ldrs after: rdn and nt qckn over 2f out: fdd* **4/1**[3]

5304 **6** 6 **Mayan Flight (IRE)**[29] 2333 5-8-4 45 .... (b) JimmyQuinn 2 34
(Tony Carroll) *hld up in last pair: pushed along 4f out: no imp on ldrs 2f out: wknd* **20/1**

1330 **7** 20 **Thane Of Cawdor (IRE)**[11] 2828 4-9-2 57 .... GeorgeBaker 5 14
(Joseph Tuite) *hld up in last pair: dropped away tamely fr 3f out: sn eased: t.o* **7/2**[2]

2m 30.22s (-2.78) **Going Correction** -0.05s/f (Stan) **7** Ran SP% **119.3**
Speed ratings (Par 101): **107,105,103,103,102 98,85**
toteswingers 1&2 £6.20, 1&3 £12.50, 2&3 £2.80 CSF £41.32 CT £223.93 TOTE £22.40: £3.60, £1.70; EX 60.30 Trifecta £480.40 Pool: £1462.21 - 2.28 winning units..
Owner The London Foot & Ankle Centre **Bred** Thomas Heatrick **Trained** Claines, Worcs
FOCUS
This moderate handicap was run at a steady pace.

3169 LINGFIELD PARK OWNERS GROUP H'CAP 1m 2f (P)
7:00 (7:01) (Class 6) (0-55,55) 4-Y-O+ **£2,045** (£603; £302) **Stalls** Low

Form RPR

5302 **1** **Young Jackie**[4] 3056 5-9-5 53 .... (b) TomQueally 5 60
(George Margarson) *pushed along early to rch position to trck ldrs: rdn and prog over 2f out: chsd ldr 1f out: sustained chal last 150yds: led post* **2/1**[1]

00-0 **2** nse **Lady Barastar (IRE)**[97] 579 5-9-2 50 .... (b) GeorgeBaker 12 57
(Amanda Perrett) *t.k.h: hld up in last trio: prog on wd outside 2f out: drvn and r.o wl fnl f: jst failed* **14/1**

0611 **3** nse **Salient**[42] 1909 9-9-5 53 .... NeilCallan 6 60
(Michael Attwater) *led: shkn up over 2f out: drvn and wnt for home wl over 1f out: kpt on wl whn pressed: hdd by two rivals post* **6/1**[3]

-050 **4** 1¼ **Men Don't Cry (IRE)**[7] 2954 4-9-0 51 .... (b) MarkCoumbe(3) 2 55
(Ed de Giles) *cl up bhd ldrs: rdn 3f out: responded to press and disp 2nd briefly over 1f out on inner: one pce after* **8/1**

5300 **5** ½ **Frosty Friday**[14] 2764 5-9-1 49 .... (p) FergusSweeney 14 52
(J R Jenkins) *hld up in last trio: prog on outer wl over 2f out: tried to cl on ldrs over 1f out: kpt on same pce fnl f* **33/1**

-050 **6** 1¼ **Lightning Spirit**[14] 2747 5-9-1 49 .... (p) RyanMoore 1 50
(Gary Moore) *hld up in midfield on inner: gng wl enough 3f out but outpcd sn after: tried to cl on ldrs over 1f out: one pce* **14/1**

0430 **7** 1¼ **Finlodex**[21] 2533 6-9-2 55 .... RyanTate(5) 9 54
(Murty McGrath) *trckd ldrs on outer: prog to go 2nd 3f out: rdn over 2f out: wknd 1f out* **8/1**

3250 **8** nse **Total Obsession**[14] 2747 6-8-10 51 .... (v) NoelGarbutt(7) 10 50
(Mark Hoad) *towards rr: rdn and no prog over 2f out: styd on fnl f: nrst fin* **25/1**

24-6 **9** ½ **Chasin' Rainbows**[15] 2710 5-9-6 54 .... AdamKirby 8 54
(Sylvester Kirk) *slowest away: hld up in last trio: stl there on inner over 2f out: shuffled along and kpt on same pce fr over 1f out: nvr involved* **5/1**[2]

3004 **10** 1¼ **Missionaire (USA)**[47] 1779 6-9-4 52 ....[1] JimmyQuinn 11 47
(Tony Carroll) *a towards rr: rdn over 2f out: dropped to last wl over 1f out: kpt on last 150yds* **14/1**

0/00 **11** 1 **Princess Spirit**[22] 2519 4-9-4 52 .... MarcHalford 13 45
(Edward Creighton) *racd wd thrght: trckd ldrs: prog to dispute 2nd over 2f out: wknd over 1f out* **33/1**

0-00 **12** ¾ **Operettist**[15] 2729 4-9-5 53 .... (p) HarryBentley 4 45
(Tony Carroll) *trckd ldr 2f: prom tl wknd 3f out* **20/1**

0/30 **13** 2½ **Walter De La Mare (IRE)**[33] 921 6-9-0 48 .... LukeMorris 7 35
(Anabel K Murphy) *chsd ldr after 2f to 3f out: sn wknd* **33/1**

2m 7.2s (0.60) **Going Correction** -0.05s/f (Stan) **13** Ran SP% **123.9**
Speed ratings (Par 101): **95,94,94,93,93 92,91,91,91,90 89,88,86**
toteswingers 1&2 £7.30, 1&3 £2.60, 2&3 £18.90 CSF £32.97 CT £149.40 TOTE £2.90: £1.80, £2.30, £2.10; EX 41.50 Trifecta £384.20 Pool: £1361.26 - 2.65 winning units..
Owner Miss J Kentish **Bred** M F Kentish **Trained** Newmarket, Suffolk
FOCUS
A modest yet open contest which saw a thrilling finish. The front three home raced up the centre.

3170 LINGFIELDPARK.CO.UK MAIDEN STKS 6f (P)
7:30 (7:35) (Class 5) 3-Y-O+ **£2,726** (£805; £402) **Stalls** Low

Form RPR

3-23 **1** **Ian's Dream (USA)**[10] 2861 3-9-4 95 .... RyanMoore 5 74
(Jeremy Noseda) *trckd ldr: shkn up to chal over 2f out: drvn ahd over 1f out: sn hrd pressed: hld on u.p* **4/5**[1]

0- **2** shd **Meridius (IRE)**[367] 2929 3-9-4 0 .... ShaneKelly 3 74
(Gary Harrison) *trckd ldng trio: prog to go 2nd jst over 1f out: sn chalng and looked likely to win: drvn and nt qckn nr fin* **5/1**[3]

2 **3** 4½ **Celestial Ray**[20] 2576 4-9-12 0 .... LukeMorris 7 64
(Sir Mark Prescott Bt) *racd on outer: trckd ldng pair: shkn up over 2f out: hanging and readily lft bhd over 1f out* **11/4**[2]

4 ¾ **Josefa Goya** 3-8-13 0 HayleyTurner 2 53
(Hughie Morrison) *led: shkn up and hdd over 1f out: wknd* **12/1**
00-0 5 10 **Rupeetoups**[15] 2722 5-9-7 39 NathanAlison(5) 6 30
(Jim Boyle) *t.k.h in last: pushed along and lost tch sn after 1/2-way* **100/1**
1m 11.04s (-0.86) **Going Correction** -0.05s/f (Stan)
WFA 3 from 4yo+ 8lb **5** Ran SP% **107.6**
Speed ratings (Par 103): **103,102,96,95,82**
CSF £4.99 TOTE £1.30: £1.10, £1.90; EX 5.70 Trifecta £9.20 Pool: £1065.26 - 86.22 winning units..
Owner Nigel O'Sullivan **Bred** M L Burleson, Hart Farm & A Lakin & Sons **Trained** Newmarket, Suffolk
■ Lebresem was withdrawn (14/1, deduct 5p in the £ under R4).
FOCUS
Plenty of pace on for this uncompetitive maiden, with the front two pulling clear.

3171 VINES BMW H'CAP 5f (P)
8:00 (8:02) (Class 5) (0-75,70) 3-Y-O+ **£2,726** (£805; £402) **Stalls** Low

Form RPR
3131 1 **Desert Strike**[13] 2772 7-9-12 73 (p) HayleyTurner 5 83
(Conor Dore) *mde all and travelled wl: 2 l clr 2f out: drvn fnl f: styd on: unchal* **6/1**[3]
-063 2 2 ¼ **Rock Up (IRE)**[15] 2722 3-8-12 66 (b) RyanMoore 7 65+
(David Elsworth) *slowest away: pushed along in last 1/2-way: prog on inner over 1f out: drvn and styd on to take 2nd last strides* **5/4**[1]
-141 3 hd **Monumental Man**[39] 1984 4-10-0 75 (p) AdamKirby 1 76
(James Unett) *chsd wnr: rdn and no imp wl over 1f out: kpt on but lost 2nd last strides* **5/2**[2]
2035 4 ½ **Song Of Parkes**[34] 2173 6-9-8 74 SladeO'Hara(5) 4 73
(Peter Grayson) *chsd ldng quartet: urged along 2f out: kpt on same pce fr over 1f out* **14/1**
2106 5 ½ **Danzoe (IRE)**[12] 2790 6-9-12 73 TomMcLaughlin 3 71
(Christine Dunnett) *settled in last trio: prog on inner 2f out: chal for 2nd 1f out: fdd* **20/1**
160- 6 1 **Pucon**[175] 8157 4-9-0 61 NeilCallan 8 55
(Roger Teal) *racd on outer of trio chsng wnr: lost grnd wl over 1f out: sn btn* **25/1**
4206 7 ½ **Restless Bay (IRE)**[22] 2515 5-9-4 65 (b) GeorgeBaker 2 57
(Conor Dore) *taken down early and walked to post: rrd bef stalls opened: disp 2nd tl wl over 1f out: sn lost pl and btn* **12/1**
1120 8 7 **Billy Red**[39] 1985 9-10-0 75 (b) FergusSweeney 6 42
(J R Jenkins) *a in last trio: wknd 2f out: t.o* **16/1**
58.1s (-0.70) **Going Correction** -0.05s/f (Stan)
WFA 3 from 4yo+ 7lb **8** Ran SP% **116.2**
Speed ratings (Par 103): **103,99,99,98,97 95,95,83**
toteswingers 1&2 £3.50, 1&3 £3.80, 2&3 £2.40 CSF £14.17 CT £24.03 TOTE £4.90: £2.90, £1.10, £1.30; EX 23.60 Trifecta £39.80 Pool: £1157.21 - 21.77 winning units..
Owner Andrew Page **Bred** Mrs Mary Rowlands **Trained** Hubbert's Bridge, Lincs
FOCUS
This sprint handicap was run at a sound pace.

3172 YOUNG EPILEPSY H'CAP 7f (P)
8:30 (8:30) (Class 5) (0-75,73) 4-Y-O+ **£2,897** (£855; £427) **Stalls** Low

Form RPR
-220 1 **Pategonia**[97] 906 4-9-4 70 WilliamBuick 1 83+
(John Gosden) *mde all: dashed for home over 2f out: abt 3 l clr after: rdn out: unchal* **4/1**[2]
4004 2 3 ¼ **Afkar (IRE)**[25] 2425 5-9-5 71 HayleyTurner 7 75
(Clive Brittain) *chsd wnr: lft bhd fr over 2f out: kpt on but no imp after* **5/1**[3]
-005 3 ½ **My Kingdom (IRE)**[15] 2725 7-9-7 73 (t) NeilCallan 5 76
(Stuart Williams) *dwlt: sn in midfield: rdn over 2f out: prog over 1f out: chal for pls fnl f: tk 3rd nr fin* **7/2**[1]
-005 4 nk **Rigolleto (IRE)**[32] 2225 5-9-2 68 LukeMorris 6 70
(Anabel K Murphy) *chsd ldng trio: rdn over 2f out: pressed for pls fnl f: kpt on* **33/1**
2336 5 1 **Cyflymder (IRE)**[11] 2837 7-8-11 68 NicoleNordblad(5) 3 67
(David C Griffiths) *chsd ldng pair: rdn over 2f out: chal for 2nd on inner over 1f out: one pce* **14/1**
0000 6 ½ **Perfect Pastime**[15] 2725 5-9-5 71 (p) SebSanders 9 69
(Jim Boyle) *towards rr: urged along over 2f out: sn outpcd: kpt on again fnl f* **20/1**
5403 7 hd **Titan Triumph**[12] 2807 9-9-0 66 (t) JimmyQuinn 2 63
(Michael Attwater) *wl in tch: rdn over 2f out: tried to cl on plcd horses over 1f out: one pce* **20/1**
201- 8 ½ **Eager To Bow (IRE)**[201] 7827 7-9-7 73 GeorgeBaker 8 69
(Patrick Chamings) *hld up in rr: rdn wl over 2f out and sn outpcd: kpt on fnl f: no ch* **8/1**
0400 9 4 **Dutch Old Master**[32] 2225 4-9-6 72 RyanMoore 4 57
(Gary Moore) *dwlt: a towards rr: shkn up and no prog over 2f out: wl btn after* **7/2**[1]
2000 10 ¾ **Hatta Stream (IRE)**[19] 2596 7-8-12 67 SimonPearce(3) 11 50
(Lydia Pearce) *racd wd: in tch: rdn 3f out: wknd 2f out* **33/1**
5-00 11 nk **Tevez**[24] 2450 8-9-7 73 TomQueally 10 55
(Des Donovan) *slowly away: mostly in last: shoved along 3f out: no ch over 2f out* **16/1**
1m 24.65s (-0.15) **Going Correction** -0.05s/f (Stan) **11** Ran SP% **120.2**
Speed ratings (Par 103): **98,94,93,93,92 91,91,90,86,85 85**
toteswingers 1&2 £3.80, 1&3 £3.00, 2&3 £7.10 CSF £23.70 CT £78.39 TOTE £4.60: £2.10, £2.00, £1.30; EX 26.30 Trifecta £81.50 Pool: £813.40 - 7.47 winning units..
Owner A E Oppenheimer **Bred** Hascombe & Valiant Studs **Trained** Newmarket, Suffolk
FOCUS
Few came into this in any sort of form. It was run at a steady pace, which suited the prominent runners.

3173 RACING SHIRES HERE NEXT SATURDAY H'CAP 1m 2f (P)
9:00 (9:00) (Class 5) (0-75,73) 3-Y-O **£2,726** (£805; £402) **Stalls** Low

Form RPR
41- 1 **Press Room (USA)**[206] 7780 3-9-7 73 SilvestreDeSousa 8 87+
(Saeed bin Suroor) *t.k.h: prom: rdn over 2f out: chsd ldr wl over 1f out: styd on wl fnl f to ld last 50yds* **6/4**[2]
0-31 2 ½ **Big Thunder**[5] 3014 3-9-1 67 6ex LukeMorris 9 80+
(Sir Mark Prescott Bt) *slowly away and rousted to get competitive: prog arnd field to go 2nd after 4f: led wl over 2f out: drvn for home wl over 1f out: collared last 50yds* **5/4**[1]
3001 3 4 ½ **Naaz (IRE)**[22] 2506 3-9-7 73 (b) RyanMoore 6 77
(Ed Dunlop) *mostly racd in 6th: rdn to go 4th over 2f out: styd on to take 3rd fnl f: no ch w ldng pair* **6/1**[3]
0-60 4 nk **Muskat Link**[29] 2324 3-8-6 63 AmyScott(5) 1 66
(Henry Candy) *chsd ldr 3f: dropped bk to 5th sn after: outpcd and rdn over 2f out: kpt on to press for 3rd fnl f* **50/1**
3-16 5 1 ¼ **Aint Got A Scooby (IRE)**[29] 2322 3-9-7 73 JohnFahy 4 74
(Clive Cox) *settled in last trio: rdn and wl outpcd whn n.m.r on inner 2f out: plugged on after: no ch* **16/1**
30-5 6 ½ **Mick Duggan**[11] 2827 3-9-4 70 GeorgeBaker 2 70
(Simon Hodgson) *settled in last trio: wl outpcd fr 3f out: drvn over 1f out: styd on fnl f* **33/1**
0-15 7 7 **Al Enbess (IRE)**[110] 738 3-9-3 69 AdamKirby 3 55
(David Simcock) *hld up in last: rdn and wl outpcd over 2f out: no real prog after* **25/1**
36-0 8 1 **Twary (USA)**[18] 2628 3-9-7 73 PaulHanagan 5 57
(Roger Varian) *led at str pce: hdd wl over 2f out: wknd rapidly wl over 1f out* **25/1**
1-44 9 8 **Magique (IRE)**[19] 2606 3-9-7 73 WilliamBuick 7 41
(Jeremy Noseda) *t.k.h: prom on outer tl lost pl fr 3f out: wl bhd over 1f out: t.o* **12/1**
2m 3.6s (-3.00) **Going Correction** -0.05s/f (Stan) **9** Ran SP% **124.9**
Speed ratings (Par 99): **110,109,106,105,104 104,98,97,91**
toteswingers 1&2 £2.00, 1&3 £4.70, 2&3 £1.30 CSF £3.98 CT £8.67 TOTE £1.90: £1.02, £1.10, £1.90; EX 6.30 Trifecta £17.90 Pool: £1031.73 - 43.04 winning units..
Owner Godolphin **Bred** Darley **Trained** Newmarket, Suffolk
FOCUS
Runners from some powerful stables in oppostion for this handicap, which was run at a fair pace. The form looks strong.
T/Plt: £5.80 to a £1 stake. Pool of £59,949.14 - 7492.31 winning tickets. T/Qpdt: £3.30 to a £1 stake. Pool of £5848.81 - 1297.21 winning tickets. JN

2595 SALISBURY (R-H)
Tuesday, June 11

OFFICIAL GOING: Good (8.6)
Wind: mild breeze Weather: overcast with light rain

3174 GLEBE FARM STUD MAIDEN AUCTION STKS (DIV I) 6f
2:00 (2:04) (Class 5) 2-Y-O **£2,911** (£866; £432; £216) **Stalls** Low

Form RPR
4 1 **Emperor's Hope (IRE)**[6] 2978 2-8-11 0 RichardHughes 5 79+
(Richard Hannon) *prom: led 3f out: in command ent fnl f: pushed out* **5/2**[1]
4 2 1 ½ **Double Point (IRE)**[11] 2847 2-9-2 0 RyanMoore 8 78
(Paul Cole) *trckd ldrs: rdn to chse ldng pair over 2f out: kpt on ins fnl f: wnt 2nd towards fin* **9/2**[3]
035 3 ¾ **Seaham**[19] 2595 2-9-2 0 AndreaAtzeni 2 75
(Rod Millman) *led tl 3f out: sn rdn to chse wnr: styd on same pce fnl 2f: no ex whn lost 2nd towards fin* **3/1**[2]
4 4 6 **Killing Time (IRE)**[15] 2723 2-9-2 0 JimCrowley 7 57
(Ralph Beckett) *chsd ldrs tl outpcd 3f out: styd on again fr over 1f out but no ch w ldrs* **5/2**[1]
0 5 2 ¾ **Connaught Water (IRE)**[27] 2359 2-8-4 0 MatthewLawson(5) 4 42+
(Jonathan Portman) *hmpd s: towards rr: hdwy wl over 2f out: sn rdn: wnt wl hld 4th over 1f out tl no ex ins fnl f* **66/1**
6 1 ¼ **Choral Clan (IRE)** 2-8-9 0 JackMitchell 6 38
(Philip Mitchell) *towards rr: sme prog 3f out: rdn and no further imp fnl 2f* **50/1**
7 1 ½ **Solo Hunter** 2-9-2 0 TomQueally 10 41
(David Evans) *dwlt: a towards rr* **20/1**
8 7 **Rural Affair** 2-8-4 0 CathyGannon 3 8
(Harry Dunlop) *wnt lft s: sn pushed along in tch: wknd wl over 1f out* **25/1**
0 9 1 ¼ **Mr Childrey (IRE)**[57] 1580 2-8-12 0 LiamKeniry 9 12
(J S Moore) *in tch: pushed along over 2f out: sn wknd* **66/1**
00 10 2 ¾ **Astral Rose**[15] 2723 2-8-4 0 DarrenEgan(3) 1
(Paul Fitzsimons) *chsd ldrs tl wknd 2f out* **100/1**
1m 15.17s (0.37) **Going Correction** 0.0s/f (Good) **10** Ran SP% **114.9**
Speed ratings (Par 93): **97,95,94,86,82 80,78,69,67,64**
toteswingers 1&2 £2.60, 1&3 £2.40, 2&3 £3.20 CSF £13.26 TOTE £3.00: £1.10, £1.90, £1.50; EX 14.80 Trifecta £33.80 Pool: £3029.42 - 67.15 winning units..
Owner P A Byrne **Bred** Lynch Bages Ltd & Camas Park Stud **Trained** East Everleigh, Wilts
FOCUS
A modest maiden auction and nothing could get into it from off the pace. The first three pulled well clear.

3175 GLEBE FARM STUD MAIDEN AUCTION STKS (DIV II) 6f
2:30 (2:32) (Class 5) 2-Y-O **£2,911** (£866; £432; £216) **Stalls** Low

Form RPR
1 **Lone Warrior (IRE)** 2-9-2 0 TomQueally 4 75
(David Evans) *little slowly away and wnt lft: sn pushed along in tch: outpcd 3f out: swtchd lft 2f out: str run ent fnl f: led nring fin* **12/1**
2 ½ **Starlight Serenade** 2-8-4 0 RichardThomas 1 62
(Ralph Beckett) *green to s: in tch: swtchd lft over 1f out: pushed into ld fnl 120yds: drifted rt: kpt on but outpcd by wnr nring fin* **6/1**
35 3 3 ½ **Trinity Boy**[15] 2723 2-9-2 0 AdamKirby 8 63
(Clive Cox) *hmpd s: sn prom: rdn 2f out: led 1f out: hdd fnl 120yds: nt pce of front pair* **9/4**[1]
32 4 ½ **Bonjour Steve**[8] 2917 2-8-9 0 LiamKeniry 10 55
(J S Moore) *wnt rt s: racd freely: prom: rdn and ev ch 2f out tl jst ins fnl f: kpt on same pce* **5/2**[2]
5 2 **Baker Man (IRE)** 2-9-2 0 JamesDoyle 3 56+
(Sylvester Kirk) *trckd ldrs: nt clrest of runs whn rdn 2f out: stmbld whn mounting chal fnl 120yds: hld after* **11/2**[3]
6 1 ¼ **Cornish Path** 2-8-4 0 CathyGannon 9 40
(Henry Candy) *hld up in last trio: pushed along whn snatched up over 2f out: kpt on but nt pce to get involved* **12/1**
6 7 2 **Dark Phantom (IRE)**[6] 2978 2-8-12 0 SteveDrowne 6 42
(Peter Makin) *led: rdn 2f out: hdd ent fnl f: wknd* **16/1**
8 9 **Jazri** 2-8-4 0 MatthewLawson(5) 5 12
(Milton Bradley) *s.i.s: a bhd* **80/1**
9 shd **Bright Society (IRE)** 2-8-9 0 LiamJones 7 11
(J S Moore) *wnt rt s: chsd ldrs: rdn 3f out: wknd 2f out* **25/1**
1m 16.43s (1.63) **Going Correction** 0.0s/f (Good) **9** Ran SP% **115.4**
Speed ratings (Par 93): **89,88,83,83,80 78,76,64,63**
toteswingers 1&2 £5.50, 1&3 £6.10, 2&3 £4.00 CSF £81.91 TOTE £11.10: £3.20, £1.40, £1.50; EX 68.00 Trifecta £289.40 Pool: £2403.32 - 6.22 winning units..
Owner Wayne Clifford **Bred** Grangemore Stud **Trained** Pandy, Monmouths

FOCUS
The winning time was 1.26 seconds slower than the first division.

3176 BATHWICK TYRES MAIDEN STKS 6f 212y
3:00 (3:02) (Class 5) 3-Y-O+ £3,234 (£962; £481; £240) Stalls Low

Form RPR

-203 1 **Kyllachy Rise**[17] 2672 3-9-3 83 RichardHughes 8 84+
(Richard Hannon) *trckd ldrs: cruised up to join ldrs over 2f out: shkn up to ld ent fnl f: r.o wl to draw clr: readily* **4/5**[1]

2 3½ **Saigon City** 3-9-0 0 (b[1]) PatrickHills(3) 3 73
(Luca Cumani) *mid-div: rdn 2f out: hdwy ent fnl f: r.o wl to snatch 2nd nr fin: no ch w wnr* **50/1**

6 3 nk **Meddling**[32] 2231 3-8-12 0 RyanMoore 11 67
(Sir Michael Stoute) *prom: rdn 2f out: led over 1f out tl ent fnl f: sn outpcd by wnr: lost 2nd fnl strides* **13/2**[3]

4 nk **Muthmir (IRE)** 3-9-3 0 PaulHanagan 13 71+
(William Haggas) *hld up towards rr: pushed along for stdy prog fr 3f out: styd on ins fnl f: snatched 4th fnl stride* **11/4**[2]

0 5 hd **Quintet (IRE)**[24] 2447 3-8-12 0 JimCrowley 5 66+
(Ralph Beckett) *mid-div: hdwy 3f out: sn rdn to chse ldrs: wnt 3rd briefly ins fnl f: no ex whn lost 2 pls nring fin* **33/1**

00 6 5 **Encapsulated**[14] 2746 3-9-3 0 RobertHavlin 4 57
(Roger Ingram) *led: rdn 2f out: hdd over 1f out: hld whn hmpd on rails ent fnl f: wknd fnl 120yds* **100/1**

03 7 1¼ **Gone Dutch**[13] 2765 3-9-3 0 TomQueally 9 54
(James Fanshawe) *mid-div: rdn over 2f out: nvr any real imp* **8/1**

8 8 **Get Going** 3-9-3 0 GeorgeBaker 1 32
(Hughie Morrison) *stdd s: styd on past btn horses fnl f: nvr a factor* **40/1**

06 9 ¾ **Cauberg**[21] 2556 3-9-3 0 AndreaAtzeni 12 30
(Roger Varian) *mid-div: hdwy 3f out: sn rdn: wknd over 1f out* **50/1**

0 10 ¾ **Bustling Darcey**[19] 2597 3-8-7 0 PhilipPrince(5) 6 23
(Mark Gillard) *trckd ldrs: rdn over 2f out: wknd over 1f out* **100/1**

11 ½ **Polish Rider** 3-9-3 0 SeanLevey 14 27
(Richard Hannon) *rdn over 3f out: a towards rr* **40/1**

12 5 **K Lightning (IRE)** 3-9-3 0 SebSanders 10 13
(J W Hills) *a towards rr* **66/1**

13 3¾ **Cadeaux Royale** 5-9-1 0 JoshBaudains(7) 7
(Dominic Ffrench Davis) *trckd ldrs: rdn 3f out: sn wknd* **100/1**

00 14 shd **Tannhauser Gate (IRE)**[5] 3011 3-9-3 0 FergusSweeney 2
(Jamie Osborne) *struggling over 3f out: a towards rr* **150/1**

1m 28.2s (-0.40) **Going Correction** 0.0s/f (Good)
WFA 3 from 5yo 10lb **14 Ran SP% 123.5**
Speed ratings (Par 103): **102,98,97,97,97 91,89,80,79,79 78,72,68,68**
toteswingers 1&2 £16.00, 1&3 £2.00, 2&3 £35.50 CSF £74.50 TOTE £1.50: £1.10, £12.40, £1.60; EX 53.30 Trifecta £270.00 Pool: £4074.18 - 11.31 winning units..
Owner Arjun Waney **Bred** Whatton Manor Stud **Trained** East Everleigh, Wilts

FOCUS
They bet 33-1 bar four in this uncompetitive maiden.

3177 BRITISH STALLION STUDS EBF MARGADALE FILLIES' H'CAP 1m 1f 198y
3:30 (3:30) (Class 4) (0-85,82) 3-Y-O+ £6,469 (£1,925; £962; £481) Stalls Low

Form RPR

43-1 1 **Lyric Ballad**[19] 2606 3-8-2 69 SilvestreDeSousa 5 80+
(Hughie Morrison) *trckd ldrs: shkn up to ld ent fnl f: edgd rt: styd on strly: readily* **11/2**

1 2 2 **Raushan (IRE)**[26] 2392 3-8-10 77 RyanMoore 2 84+
(Sir Michael Stoute) *trckd ldr: led 3f out: sn drvn: hdd ent fnl f: styd on but nt pce of wnr* **9/4**[2]

1-04 3 1¼ **Miss Dashwood**[18] 2639 4-9-10 78 [1] TomQueally 1 85
(James Fanshawe) *t.k.h early: in tch: hdwy over 2f out: sn rdn: ev ch ent fnl f: no ex fnl 120yds* **14/1**

5-21 4 2½ **Iffraaj Pink (IRE)**[32] 2231 3-9-1 82 JamieSpencer 4 82
(Roger Varian) *trckd ldrs: rdn over 2f out: kpt on same pce fnl f* **2/1**[1]

5-32 5 ½ **Pompeia**[21] 2546 3-8-11 78 (p) JimCrowley 3 77
(Ralph Beckett) *hld up in last pair: rdn over 2f out: kpt on but nt pce to get on terms* **9/2**[3]

0-62 6 nk **Musikhani**[39] 1975 3-8-8 75 LiamKeniry 6 74
(Andrew Balding) *led tl 3f out: sn rdn: kpt chsng ldrs tl no ex ent fnl f* **16/1**

2-03 7 1 **Equitissa (IRE)**[10] 2874 3-8-1 68 KieranO'Neill 7 65
(Richard Hannon) *hld up last but in tch: rdn over 2f out: sn hung rt: nt pce to get on terms* **20/1**

2m 10.53s (0.63) **Going Correction** -0.10s/f (Good)
WFA 3 from 4yo 13lb **7 Ran SP% 115.0**
Speed ratings (Par 102): **93,91,90,88,88 87,86**
toteswingers 1&2 £2.10, 1&3 £10.40, 2&3 £5.10 CSF £18.53 TOTE £6.20: £2.60, £1.40; EX 16.80 Trifecta £141.90 Pool: £3162.87 - 16.70 winning units..
Owner T D Rootes & O F Waller **Bred** Shutford Stud And O F Waller **Trained** East Ilsley, Berks

FOCUS
This fillies' handicap contained some unexposed types, but the pace was far from generous and all seven runners were within a couple of lengths of each other coming to the last furlong. The field angled for the centre of the track inside the last half-mile.

3178 MOLSON COORS H'CAP 6f 212y
4:05 (4:06) (Class 6) (0-65,65) 3-Y-O £2,587 (£770; £384; £192) Stalls Low

Form RPR

0-24 1 **Tight Fit**[26] 2387 3-9-4 62 DaneO'Neill 9 74+
(Henry Candy) *in tch: rdn 2f out: stdy run fr jst over 1f out: led fnl 140yds: r.o wl: won gng away* **5/2**[1]

-102 2 3¼ **Girl Of Cadiz**[8] 2919 3-9-2 65 WilliamTwiston-Davies(5) 6 68
(Richard Hannon) *mid-div: hdwy over 2f out: sn rdn: styd on to go 2nd fnl 120yds: a being hld by wnr* **7/1**

00-0 3 nk **Maisie's Moon (USA)**[49] 1747 3-8-12 56 SilvestreDeSousa 1 58
(Hughie Morrison) *trckd ldr: rdn over 3f out: ch ent fnl f: styd on gamely but no ex fnl 120yds* **20/1**

6214 4 1¾ **Princess Cammie (IRE)**[10] 2870 3-8-6 57 (p) JoeyHaynes(7) 12 54
(John Bridger) *led: rdn fr over 2f out: hdd fnl 140yds: no ex* **7/1**

-360 5 nk **Carrera**[15] 2727 3-9-0 58 SebSanders 13 55
(J W Hills) *hld up towards rr: rdn into midfield 2f out: chsd ldrs jst over 1f out: styd on same pce ins fnl f* **15/2**

40-3 6 nk **My Gigi**[18] 2616 3-9-5 63 RyanMoore 8 59
(Gary Moore) *mid-div: rdn wl over 2f out: styd on wout ever threatening to rch ldrs fnl f* **6/1**[3]

3062 7 1 **Pippy**[5] 3016 3-9-5 63 RichardKingscote 10 56
(Tom Dascombe) *hld up towards rr: stdy prog whn rdn fr 2f out: styd on fnl f but nvr rching ldrs* **9/2**[2]

064 8 5 **Transluscent (IRE)**[18] 2637 3-8-10 61 (t[1]) DanielMuscutt(7) 2 41
(Andrew Balding) *t.k.h: mid-div: rdn over 2f out: wknd fnl f* **25/1**

-500 9 shd **Winnie Perry**[22] 2495 3-9-7 65 AndreaAtzeni 4 44
(Rod Millman) *trckd ldr: rdn over 2f out: wknd over 1f out* **20/1**

4000 10 2¾ **Club House (IRE)**[32] 2209 3-9-2 65 RobertTart(5) 5 37
(Robert Mills) *hld up towards rr: effrt to cl u.p 2f out: wknd fnl f* **12/1**

0-54 11 6 **Majestic Red (IRE)**[12] 2791 3-8-8 57 MatthewLawson(5) 3 13
(Malcolm Saunders) *s.i.s and wnt lft: towards rr: hdwy over 3f out: rdn to chse ldrs over 2f out: wknd over 1f out* **40/1**

0-05 12 15 **Persian Marvel (IRE)**[12] 2791 3-8-4 48 (v) WilliamCarson 11
(Jim Boyle) *unsettled in stalls: slowly away: a towards rr* **40/1**

06-0 13 17 **Direct Trade**[20] 2572 3-8-4 48 CathyGannon 14
(Mark Usher) *rrd leaving stalls: plld hrd early: a towards rr: wknd over 2f out* **40/1**

1m 28.96s (0.36) **Going Correction** 0.0s/f (Good) **13 Ran SP% 126.2**
Speed ratings (Par 97): **97,93,92,90,90 90,89,83,83,80 73,56,36**
toteswingers 1&2 £4.70, 1&3 £11.90, 2&3 £23.90 CSF £19.86 CT £308.25 TOTE £3.90: £1.20, £2.70, £6.20; EX 19.90 Trifecta £281.00 Pool: £3260.22 - 8.69 winning units..
Owner W M Lidsey & H Candy **Bred** W M Lidsey **Trained** Kingston Warren, Oxon

FOCUS
A moderate handicap in which it paid to race handily.

3179 SHARP'S DOOM BAR FILLIES' H'CAP 6f 212y
4:35 (4:36) (Class 4) (0-85,80) 3-Y-O £4,851 (£1,443; £721; £360) Stalls Low

Form RPR

213- 1 **Ghanaian (FR)**[255] 6675 3-9-4 77 SilvestreDeSousa 2 91
(Saeed bin Suroor) *trckd ldrs: pushed along to hold pl over 3f out: hdwy to ld narrowly over 2f out: sn rdn: styd on wl ins fnl f: wl on top at fin* **5/6**[1]

31- 2 2¾ **Elnadwa (USA)**[242] 7020 3-9-4 77 PaulHanagan 1 84
(Saeed bin Suroor) *trckd ldrs: rdn and ev ch fr over 2f out tl no ex fnl 120yds* **11/2**[2]

53-1 3 1¾ **This Is Nice (IRE)**[12] 2788 3-8-11 70 RichardKingscote 4 72
(Tom Dascombe) *led: rdn and hdd over 2f out: styd on same pce fr over 1f out* **11/1**

10 4 1¾ **Perfect Haven**[24] 2449 3-9-7 80 [1] JimCrowley 6 77
(Ralph Beckett) *stdd sn after s: sltly outpcd over 3f out: hdwy into 4th over 2f out: no further imp on ldrs fr over 1f out* **8/1**[3]

2456 5 2 **Guishan**[21] 2544 3-8-6 65 AndrewMullen 5 57
(Michael Appleby) *racd keenly: sn trcking ldrs: rdn over 2f out: sn one pce* **20/1**

5-1 6 1¾ **Russian Royale**[19] 2597 3-8-12 71 ShaneKelly 7 58
(Stuart Kittow) *sn trcking ldrs: rdn wl over 2f out: sn outpcd by ldrs: fdd fnl 120yds* **8/1**[3]

2-44 7 3 **Secretly**[17] 2658 3-9-3 76 DaneO'Neill 3 55
(Henry Candy) *s.i.s: sn cl up: rdn over 2f out: wknd ent fnl f* **12/1**

1m 27.53s (-1.07) **Going Correction** 0.0s/f (Good) **7 Ran SP% 112.9**
Speed ratings (Par 98): **106,102,100,98,96 94,91**
toteswingers 1&2 £2.10, 1&3 £2.90, 2&3 £4.40 CSF £5.61 TOTE £1.70: £1.20, £2.20; EX 5.60 Trifecta £24.70 Pool: £4041.22 - 122.27 winning units..
Owner Godolphin **Bred** M Daguzan-Garros & Rolling Hills Farm **Trained** Newmarket, Suffolk

FOCUS
An interesting fillies' handicap and a 1-2 for Godolphin.

3180 BATHWICK TYRES H'CAP 1m 4f
5:05 (5:05) (Class 5) (0-70,70) 4-Y-O+ £2,911 (£866; £432; £216) Stalls Low

Form RPR

3-30 1 **Sunny Future (IRE)**[19] 2587 7-8-13 67 MatthewLawson(5) 7 78
(Malcolm Saunders) *hld up: hdwy 3f out: sn rdn: led over 1f out: styd on wl to assert fnl 120yds* **8/1**

-353 2 ¾ **Nave (USA)**[21] 2532 6-8-13 65 DarrenEgan(3) 2 75
(David Simcock) *trckd ldrs: rdn wl over 2f out: sn chalng: ev ch ent fnl f: styd on but hld fnl 120yds* **7/2**[2]

6-20 3 2¾ **Sherman McCoy**[138] 351 7-9-0 68 WilliamTwiston-Davies(5) 4 74
(Daniel Kubler) *led: rdn wl over 2f out: hdd over 1f out: no ex fnl f* **13/2**

10-3 4 9 **Into The Wind**[57] 1586 6-9-3 66 AndreaAtzeni 6 59
(Rod Millman) *hld up: hdwy over 4f out: rdn 3f out: wknd ent fnl f* **9/2**[3]

466/ 5 2½ **Faith Jicaro (IRE)**[16] 444 6-8-2 51 oh1 CathyGannon 8 40
(Andy Hobbs) *trckd ldrs: rdn over 3f out: wknd jst over 1f out* **14/1**

3030 6 3 **El Libertador (USA)**[20] 2567 7-7-9 51 oh2 (b) JoeyHaynes(7) 1 35
(Eric Wheeler) *trckd ldrs: rdn wl over 2f out: wknd jst over 1f out* **33/1**

/-02 7 8 **Gold Mine**[6] 2982 5-9-7 70 (t) LiamKeniry 3 45
(Andrew Balding) *trckd ldr: rdn wl over 2f out: nt pce to mount chal: wknd wl over 1f out* **13/8**[1]

/0-0 8 39 **Grace And Beauty (IRE)**[33] 1466 5-8-2 51 oh1 FrankieMcDonald 5
(Paul Henderson) *in tch tl dropped to rr u.p 5f out: lost tch fnl 3f* **80/1**

2m 35.8s (-2.20) **Going Correction** -0.10s/f (Good) **8 Ran SP% 113.8**
Speed ratings (Par 103): **103,102,100,94,93 91,85,59**
toteswingers 1&2 £4.10, 1&3 £5.70, 2&3 £3.50 CSF £35.77 CT £193.67 TOTE £8.70: £1.80, £1.30, £2.20; EX 33.90 Trifecta £237.30 Pool: £3285.90 - 10.38 winning units..
Owner M S Saunders **Bred** Mrs G Stanga **Trained** Green Ore, Somerset

FOCUS
An ordinary handicap, but a good pace set by the third horse.

3181 CGA RACING EXCELLENCE APPRENTICE H'CAP (WHIPS SHALL BE CARRIED BUT NOT USED) 6f
5:35 (5:37) (Class 5) (0-75,75) 4-Y-O+ £2,911 (£866; £432; £216) Stalls Low

Form RPR

0-42 1 **Maria Montez**[5] 3010 4-8-5 57 ShelleyBirkett(3) 5 70
(J W Hills) *mde all: pushed along whn strly pressed fr over 2f out: r.o wl to assert fnl 120yds* **5/2**[1]

5111 2 2¼ **Intomist (IRE)**[20] 2565 4-9-4 72 (p) DanielCremin(5) 4 78
(Jim Boyle) *trckd wnr most of way: pushed along and ev ch fr over 2f out tl no ex fnl 120yds* **5/2**[1]

0-64 3 shd **The Name Is Frank**[26] 2395 8-8-0 56 oh1 (t) OisinMurphy(7) 7 61
(Mark Gillard) *chsd ldrs: sn pushed along: nvr gng pce to chal but styd on ins fnl f: jst failed to snatch 2nd* **9/2**[2]

400- 4 2½ **Judd Street**[201] 7827 11-9-4 72 CharlieBennett(5) 1 69
(Eve Johnson Houghton) *awkward and wnt rt leaving stalls: trckd ldrs: pushed along fr over 2f out: kpt on same pce* **14/1**

4102 5 ½ **Haadeeth**[10] 2873 6-8-12 64 (t) EoinWalsh(3) 8 60
(David Evans) *hld up in tch: pushed along 3f out: kpt on ins fnl f but nvr gng pce to threaten* **8/1**[3]

0516 6 ¾ **Sweet Ovation**[62] 1472 4-8-8 57 DanielMuscutt 10 50
(Mark Usher) *rrd leaving stalls: hld up but in tch: pushed along over 2f out: swtchd rt over 1f out: nvr any real imp* **16/1**

-164 7 ½ **Commandingpresence (USA)**[19] 2588 7-9-2 68........ JoeyHaynes(3) 9 60
(John Bridger) *chsd ldrs: pushed along fr over 2f out: fdd ins fnl f* **10/1**

500- 8 2¼ **My Learned Friend (IRE)**[350] 3471 9-9-2 72................ RobHornby(7) 2 57
(Andrew Balding) *hld up in tch: swtchd rt to chse ldrs and pushed along fr 2f out: nt pce to get on terms: wknd fnl 140yds* **20/1**

1m 15.15s (0.35) **Going Correction** 0.0s/f (Good) 8 Ran SP% **112.8**
Speed ratings (Par 103): **97,94,93,90,89 88,88,85**
toteswingers 1&2 £2.30, 1&3 £2.60, 2&3 £3.10 CSF £8.22 CT £24.83 TOTE £3.00: £1.60, £1.10, £1.80; EX 12.20 Trifecta £32.90 Pool: £2644.56 - 60.18 winning units..
Owner John M Cole & Abbott Racing Partners **Bred** D R Tucker **Trained** Upper Lambourn, Berks

FOCUS
A modest apprentice handicap in which the riders could carry whips, but not use them. It was another race where nothing got into it from off the pace.
T/Plt: £17.50 to a £1 stake. Pool of £63,093.92 - 2623.91 winning tickets. T/Qpdt: £3.60 to a £1 stake. Pool of £4266.88 - 855.53 winning tickets. IM

3182 - 3186a (Foreign Racing) - See Raceform Interactive

3007 MAISONS-LAFFITTE (R-H)
Tuesday, June 11

OFFICIAL GOING: Turf: good

3187a PRIX HAMPTON (LISTED RACE) (3YO+) (TURF) 5f
1:35 (1:39) 3-Y-O+ £21,138 (£8,455; £6,341; £4,227; £2,113)

RPR

1 **Lover Man (IRE)**[12] 4-9-2 0.. MaximeGuyon 4 104
(Mme Pia Brandt, France) **113/10**

2 shd **Mister Ryan (FR)**[12] 4-9-2 0.. FabriceVeron 5 104
(H-A Pantall, France) **11/1**

3 2 **Ghor (FR)**[12] 5-9-2 0..(b) StephanePasquier 1 97
(M Boutin, France) **17/2**

4 ½ **Humidor (IRE)**[30] 2300 6-9-2 0.................................. IoritzMendizabal 6 95
(George Baker) *twice bmpd leaving the stalls: in rr: shkn up and hdwy on outside under 2f out: 4th and ev ch 1f out: one pce u.p fnl f* **4/1**[2]

5 ½ **Prohibit**[332] 4113 8-9-2 0..(p) JosephO'Brien 8 93
(Robert Cowell) *bmpd leaving stalls: trckd ldrs: 3rd and short of room under 2f out: ev ch whn rdn 1f out: nt qckn and one pce u.p ins fnl f* **9/2**

6 ¾ **Mariol (FR)**[6] 10-9-2 0.. UmbertoRispoli 3 91
(Robert Collet, France) **18/1**

7 snk **Monsieur Joe (IRE)**[30] 2300 6-9-8 0.............................. OlivierPeslier 9 96
(Robert Cowell) *wnt lft s and bmpd horse on ins: w ldrs on outer: shkn up and nt qckn over 1 1/2f out: wknd ins fnl f* **43/10**[3]

8 hd **Ghost Army (IRE)**[36] 4-9-2 0.............................. Pierre-CharlesBoudot 2 89
(A Fabre, France) *towards rr on inner: swtchd outside and rdn fr 2f out: no imp* **5/2**[1]

58.4s (58.40) 8 Ran SP% **117.9**
WIN (incl. 1 euro stake): 12.30. PLACES: 3.30, 3.20, 3.00. DF: 51.60. SF: 104.60.
Owner Salinity Stables **Bred** N P Bloodstock Ltd **Trained** France

TABY (R-H)
Tuesday, June 11

OFFICIAL GOING: Turf: good

3188a IKC FONDER STOCKHOLMS STORA PRIS (GROUP 3) (4YO+) (TURF) 1m 1f 165y
8:13 (12:00) 4-Y-O+ £47,303 (£23,651; £11,352; £7,568; £4,730)

RPR

1 **Without Fear (FR)**[101] 873 5-9-2 0............................(b) ElioneChaves 8 101
(Niels Petersen, Norway) *trckd ldr on outer: rdn to cl 3f out: styd on chal ins fnl f: sn led: drvn clr* **26/5**

2 1½ **Berling (IRE)**[257] 6600 6-9-2 0..................................(b) ManuelMartinez 2 98
(Jessica Long, Sweden) *led: clr 4f out: reduced advantage fr 3f out: rdn 2f out: styd on but strly pressed and hdd ins fnl f: no ex* **15/1**

3 1 **Bank Of Burden (USA)**[45] 6-9-2 0....................(b) Per-AndersGraberg 1 96
(Niels Petersen, Norway) *midfield on inner: swtchd out and smooth hdwy fr 3f out: rdn 2f out: ev ch ent fnl f: styd on but nt pce of wnr* **12/5**[1]

4 1 **Bomar (IRE)**[71] 4-9-2 0.. ManuelSantos 4 94
(Wido Neuroth, Norway) *hld up towards rr on inner: rdn over 3f out: styd on steadily: wnt 4th ent fnl f: no imp on ldrs* **62/1**

5 1½ **Lindenthaler (GER)**[35] 2146 5-9-2 0.................................... AStarke 12 91
(Fredrik Reuterskiold, Sweden) *midfield: rdn and hdwy over 2f out: styd on but nt pce to chal* **73/10**

6 1¼ **Sir Lando**[30] 2294 6-9-2 0..........................(p) LennartHammer-Hansen 6 88
(Wido Neuroth, Norway) *hld up towards rr on outer: hdwy into midfield 4f out: rdn 3f out: styd on but n.d* **47/10**[3]

7 2 **Street Band (IRE)**[45] 5-9-2 0.. OliverWilson 3 84
(Johan Reuterskiold, Sweden) *hld up towards rr: rdn over 3f out: plugged on but nvr a factor* **29/1**

8 3 **Touch Of Hawk (FR)**[257] 7-9-2 0...................................... EspenSki 11 78
(Wido Neuroth, Norway) *midfield: rdn and outpcd in rr 2f out: plugged on in st but n.d* **119/10**

9 5 **Plantagenet (SPA)**[35] 2146 6-9-2 0.............................. RafaelSchistl 10 68
(Niels Petersen, Norway) *hld up towards rr: hdwy into midfield 4f out: rdn 3f out: kpt on tl outpcd and btn ins fnl f: eased and fdd* **29/10**[2]

10 7 **East Meets West (IRE)**[35] 2146 4-9-2 0..................(b) JacobJohansen 7 53
(Bent Olsen, Denmark) *trckd ldr on inner: rdn and outpcd over 2f out: sn no ex and btn: fdd and eased* **79/1**

11 1¾ **Jimmy Mack (SWE)**[240] 4-9-2 0...................................... CarlosLopez 5 50
(Patrick Wahl, Sweden) *midfield on inner: dropped to rr 5f out: rdn in last 2f out: sn btn and eased: nvr a factor* **189/10**

2m 2.5s (3.20) 11 Ran SP% **126.0**
DIVIDENDS (all including 1sek stake): WIN 6.21; PLACE 1.92, 6.42, 1.56; SF 143.38.
Owner Stall Bonne Nuit **Bred** Zamim Ralphy Meahjohn **Trained** Norway

3077 BEVERLEY (R-H)
Wednesday, June 12

OFFICIAL GOING: Good to firm (9.3)
Wind: Moderate; half against Weather: Cloudy with sunny periods

3189 HORSE TRADER CLAIMING STKS 5f
2:00 (2:02) (Class 6) 2-Y-O £2,264 (£673; £336; £168) Stalls Low

Form RPR

0 1 **Lady Montenegro**[46] 1839 2-7-9 0 ow2...................... RowanScott(7) 10 50
(Ann Duffield) *trckd ldng pair: hdwy 1/2-way: rdn to ld over 1f out: edgd lft ins fnl f: kpt on wl u.p towards fin* **40/1**

6 2 ½ **Bountiful Forest**[15] 2740 2-9-0 0.. DavidNolan 5 60
(Richard Fahey) *trckd ldrs: effrt whn nt clr run on inner over 1f out: swtchd lft and rdn to chal ent fnl f: ev ch tl drvn and no ex towards fin* **6/1**[1]

66 3 1½ **Lady Captain (IRE)**[41] 1960 2-8-6 0...................................... AmyRyan 6 47
(Kevin Ryan) *towards rr: hdwy on outer 2f out: rdn over 1f out: ev ch ins fnl f: one pce towards fin* **14/1**[3]

0004 4 hd **Doncaster Belle (IRE)**[13] 2793 2-9-0 0............................ DaneO'Neill 2 54
(Charles Smith) *hld up in rr: hdwy wl over 1f out: chsd ldrs whn nt clr run ins fnl f: sn rdn and kpt on* **25/1**

40 5 hd **Porsh Herrik**[25] 2436 2-8-13 0...................................... MickyFenton 8 52
(John Quinn) *cl up: effrt and ev ch over 1f out and sn rdn: drvn ins fnl f: wknd towards fin* **12/1**[2]

6 3 **Chanceuse** 2-7-11 0..(p) NatashaEaton(5) 4 30
(Gay Kelleway) *chsd ldrs: rdn along over 2f out: wknd wl over 1f out* **20/1**

4031 7 6 **El Duque**[15] 2759 2-8-6 0...(p) JakePayne(5) 1 18
(Bill Turner) *slt ld: rdn along and edgd rt over 1f out: sn hdd & wknd* **6/1**[1]

1m 5.65s (2.15) **Going Correction** -0.15s/f (Firm) 7 Ran SP% **54.0**
Speed ratings (Par 91): **76,75,72,72,72 67,57**
toteswingers 1&2 £11.80, 1&3 £16.30, 2&3 £2.10 CSF £40.88 TOTE £29.60: £10.50, £1.10; EX 85.10 Trifecta £445.80 Part won. Pool: £594.45 - 0.75 winning units..
Owner Mrs Ann Duffield **Bred** Bambi Bloodstock **Trained** Constable Burton, N Yorks
■ Rowan Scott's first winner. Limegrove (4-11F) was withdrawn after proving unruly in the stalls. Deduct 70p in the £ under R4.

FOCUS
Rail around bottom bend moved out on to better ground adding 18yds to races on Round course.
A poor claimer for mainly unexposed juveniles, weakened severely when the heavily odds-on Limegrove got upset in the stalls and was withdrawn. The runner-up helps with the form.

3190 FOLLOW US ON TWITTER @RACEHORSETRADER H'CAP (DIV I) 5f
2:30 (2:30) (Class 6) (0-65,65) 3-Y-O+ £2,264 (£673; £336; £168) Stalls Low

Form RPR

3500 1 **Sophie's Beau (USA)**[7] 2997 6-8-5 49................(b) DanielleMooney(7) 8 56
(Michael Chapman) *trckd ldrs: hdwy and cl up 1/2-way: rdn to chal over 1f out and sn ev ch: kpt on u.p ins fnl f to ld nr line* **25/1**

0-22 2 nse **Choc'A'Moca (IRE)**[19] 2611 6-9-8 59............................(v) MickyFenton 5 66
(Paul Midgley) *sn led: rdn wl over 1f out: drvn ins fnl f: hdd and no ex nr line* **7/2**[2]

4043 3 hd **Pull The Pin (IRE)**[6] 3026 4-8-7 51.......................... LukeLeadbitter(7) 4 58+
(Declan Carroll) *cl up: pushed along over 1f out: effrt and nt clr run ins fnl f: swtchd lft and styd on wl towards fin* **7/2**[2]

30-6 4 nk **Amadeus Denton (IRE)**[16] 2703 4-9-5 63............... ConnorBeasley(7) 3 68
(Michael Dods) *trckd ldrs: pushed along 2f out: sn rdn: kpt on u.p fnl f: nrst fin* **10/3**[1]

0600 5 shd **Lady Royale**[47] 1802 5-10-0 65.................................(b) RussKennemore 9 70
(Geoffrey Oldroyd) *wnt lft s: in tch: hdwy on outer 2f out: rdn over 1f out: drvn and kpt on fnl f: nrst fin* **8/1**

3-66 6 ½ **Showtime Girl (IRE)**[18] 2650 3-9-4 62.......................... DuranFentiman 2 62
(Tim Easterby) *dwlt and in rr: swtchd lft and hdwy over 1f out: sn rdn and kpt on wl fnl f: nrst fin* **14/1**

0065 7 ¾ **Amenable (IRE)**[7] 2997 6-9-2 58........................... CharlesBishop(5) 1 58
(Violet M Jordan) *hld up in tch: hdwy on inner wl over 1f out: effrt and nt clr run ins fnl f: nt rcvr* **9/1**

0440 8 1 **Baltic Bomber (IRE)**[4] 3090 4-9-6 62........................(p) DeclanBates(5) 7 59
(John Quinn) *a towards rr* **11/2**[3]

-060 9 1 **Fathey (IRE)**[7] 2998 7-8-9 46 oh1............................. RobbieFitzpatrick 6 39
(Charles Smith) *prom: rdn along over 2f out: sn drvn and wknd over 1f out* **50/1**

1m 3.83s (0.33) **Going Correction** -0.15s/f (Firm)
WFA 3 from 4yo+ 7lb 9 Ran SP% **116.5**
Speed ratings (Par 101): **91,90,90,90,89 89,87,86,84**
toteswingers 1&2 £9.00, 1&3 £13.80, 2&3 £2.30 CSF £111.91 CT £397.32 TOTE £35.10: £5.90, £1.40, £1.70; EX 108.00 Trifecta £333.30 Pool: £2,375.06 - 5.34 winning units..
Owner Mrs M Chapman **Bred** Steve C Snowden & Doug Wilson **Trained** Market Rasen, Lincs

FOCUS
There wasn't much distance between the first and last, so this is unreliable form.

3191 SYNDICATE YOUR HORSE AT RACEHORSETRADER.COM MAIDEN STKS 7f 100y
3:00 (3:00) (Class 5) 3-Y-O+ £2,098 (£2,098; £481; £240) Stalls Low

Form RPR

0-2 1 **Thankyou Very Much**[23] 2503 3-8-9 0................................. AmyRyan 2 61
(James Bethell) *chsd ldng pair: pushed along wl over 2f out: rdn to chse ldr over 1f out: drvn and styd on to ld wl ins fnl f: jnd on line* **5/2**[2]

1 dht **Nonotnow** 3-9-0 0.. DavidAllan 5 66+
(Tim Easterby) *s.i.s and bhd: hdwy whn n.m.r over 2f out: sn swtchd rt: str run towards inner ent fnl f: jnd ldr nr line* **14/1**

3 ½ **Dual Mac**[61] 6-9-10 0... DaleSwift 4 68
(Neville Bycroft) *towards rr: hdwy over 2f out: swtchd lft and rdn over 1f out: styd on strly* **40/1**

4-04 4 ¾ **Mujarrad (USA)**[32] 2279 3-9-0 70.................................... DaneO'Neill 1 63
(J W Hills) *led: clr 1/2-way: rdn over 1f out: hdd wl ins fnl f* **8/11**[1]

5 3½ **Lulu The Zulu (IRE)**[423] 5-9-0 0................................ TobyAtkinson(5) 7 52
(Michael Appleby) *towards rr: hdwy on outer 2f out: rdn wl over 1f out: no imp* **10/1**

000 6 5 **Arjawan**[15] 2746 3-9-0 58.. FrederikTylicki 8 42
(Clive Brittain) *chsd ldrs: hdwy to chse ldr over 2f out: sn rdn: wknd over 1f out* **7/1**[3]

-000 **7** 1 1/4 **Penderyn**[14] 2785 6-9-5 34 .... RobbieFitzpatrick 3 37
(Charles Smith) *chsd ldr: rdn wl over 2f out: wknd wl over 1f out* **100/1**

1m 32.7s (-1.10) **Going Correction** -0.30s/f (Firm)
WFA 3 from 5yo+ 10lb 7 Ran SP% **118.2**
Speed ratings (Par 103): **94,94,93,92,88 82,81**TOTES: Win: N £9.50; TVM £1.20 PL: N £4.60; TVM £1.30 Tote Exacta: N, TVM £21.60; TVM, N £12.60 CSF: N, TVM £25.72; TVM, N £18.70 toteswingers N&TVM £2.90, TVM&3 £23.30, N&3 £6.90 TRIFECTA 7-8-1 £252.00; 8-7-1 £142.10 - Pool27 Owner.
Owner Robert Gibbons **Bred** Robert Gibbons **Trained** Middleham Moor, N Yorks

FOCUS
A weak contest that ended in a dead-heat. The winning time was slower than the 0-70 handicap that followed it.

3192 SELL RACE HORSES ONLINE AT RACEHORSETRADER.COM H'CAP 7f 100y
3:30 (3:30) (Class 5) (0-70,70) 4-Y-O+ **£3,234** (£962; £481; £240) **Stalls** Low

Form RPR
-601 **1** **Talent Scout (IRE)**[9] 2911 7-9-0 **70** .... (p) GemmaTutty(7) 11 79
(Karen Tutty) *in tch: rdn over 3f out: hdwy over 2f out: kpt on to ld fnl 100yds: hld on all out* **5/1**[3]

0013 **2** *nse* **Muftarres (IRE)**[37] 2089 8-9-5 **68** .... (t) PhillipMakin 3 77
(Frank Sheridan) *hld up in midfield: hdwy over 1f out: rdn fnl f: r.o strly: jst failed* **9/2**[2]

0432 **3** 1/2 **Exceedexpectations (IRE)**[9] 2929 4-9-6 **69** .... DaneO'Neill 6 77
(Conor Dore) *chsd ldrs: rdn to ld 2f out: hdd fnl 100yds: one pce* **3/1**[1]

00-1 **4** 1 1/2 **Whispered Times (USA)**[53] 1693 6-9-0 **63** .... (p) FrannyNorton 7 67
(Tracy Waggott) *chsd ldrs: rdn to chal 2f out: ev ch tl no ex fnl 100yds* **8/1**

0140 **5** *nk* **Powerful Pierre**[5] 3068 6-9-0 **63** .... (b) DavidNolan 8 67
(Ian McInnes) *midfield: rdn over 2f out: kpt on one pce* **16/1**

5-34 **6** 4 1/2 **Eeny Mac (IRE)**[37] 2081 6-8-6 **60** .... AdamCarter(5) 12 52
(Neville Bycroft) *midfield towards outer: rdn over 2f out: sn no imp* **15/2**

430 **7** 1 1/2 **Moral Issue**[67] 1401 5-8-11 **60** ow1 .... (b) DaleSwift 2 49
(Ian McInnes) *dwlt: hld up: rdn over 2f out: nvr threatened* **20/1**

-650 **8** 3/4 **Summer Dancer (IRE)**[21] 2565 9-9-0 **63** .... MickyFenton 9 50
(Paul Midgley) *hld up: rdn over 2f out: nvr threatened* **6/1**

4-60 **9** 2 **Sky Crossing**[21] 2580 4-9-0 **63** .... RoystonFfrench 4 45
(Tom Tate) *led: rdn whn hdd 2f out: wknd* **14/1**

1300 **10** 1 1/2 **Thrust Control (IRE)**[9] 2911 6-8-12 **61** .... (p) FrederikTylicki 1 39
(Tracy Waggott) *racd keenly: prom: rdn over 2f out: wknd over 1f out* **12/1**

0000 **11** 1/2 **Regal Acclaim (IRE)**[6] 3029 4-8-1 **53** .... (v) DeclanCannon(3) 10 30
(Ian McInnes) *s.i.s: hld up: rdn over 2f out: nvr threatened* **28/1**

00/0 **12** 41 **Fred Archer (IRE)**[32] 2278 5-9-5 **68** .... RussKennemore 14
(Sue Smith) *hld up: dropped to rr over 3f out: sn wl bhd: eased* **33/1**

1m 31.1s (-2.70) **Going Correction** -0.30s/f (Firm) 12 Ran SP% **128.4**
Speed ratings (Par 103): **103,102,102,100,100 95,93,92,90,88 88,41**
toteswingers 1&2 £7.70, 1&3 £6.80, 2&3 £6.90 CSF £29.72 CT £84.90 TOTE £8.50: £2.70, £2.30, £1.90; EX 40.00 Trifecta £86.80 Pool: £805.17 - 6.95 winning units..
Owner Thoroughbred Homes Ltd **Bred** Johnston King **Trained** Osmotherley, N Yorks

FOCUS
The leaders went off at a decent gallop, which resulted in a close finish.

3193 RACE HORSE TRADER "COMMISSION FREE" H'CAP 1m 100y
4:00 (4:00) (Class 4) (0-80,80) 4-Y-O+ **£6,817** (£2,013; £1,007) **Stalls** Low

Form RPR
2410 **1** **Copperwood**[4] 3081 8-8-11 **70** .... FrannyNorton 3 80
(Mark Johnston) *mde all: set stdy pce: rdn 2f out: sn qcknd clr: kpt on* **12/1**

0506 **2** 1 3/4 **Frog Hollow**[4] 3096 4-9-7 **80** .... DavidNolan 7 86
(David O'Meara) *hld up in tch: rdn over 2f out: stl plenty to do ent fnl f: r.o wl: wnt 2nd fnl 100yds: gaining at fin but nvr gng to rch wnr* **10/11**[1]

-213 **3** 3 **No Dominion (IRE)**[21] 2580 4-9-4 **77** .... JamesSullivan 6 76
(James Given) *racd keenly: trckd ldr: rdn over 2f out: sn one pce: lost 2nd fnl 100yds* **11/2**[3]

2332 **4** 1/2 **Shadowtime**[16] 2705 8-9-6 **79** .... BarryMcHugh 1 77
(Tracy Waggott) *hld up in tch: rdn over 2f out: one pce* **6/1**

5420 **5** 3/4 **Mishhar (IRE)**[12] 2837 4-7-13 **61** oh1 .... (v) NeilFarley(3) 4 57
(Tony Coyle) *hld up: pushed along over 2f out: kpt on fnl f: nvr threatened* **20/1**

5253 **6** 1 **Sardanapalus**[22] 2551 4-9-2 **75** .... (p) PhillipMakin 5 69
(Kevin Ryan) *racd keenly in tch: pushed along over 2f out: rdn over 1f out: sn no imp* **5/1**[2]

-000 **7** 2 1/2 **Hayek**[37] 2081 6-8-9 **68** .... (b) DuranFentiman 2 56
(Tim Easterby) *trckd ldr: rdn over 2f out: wknd ins fnl f* **20/1**

1m 45.18s (-2.42) **Going Correction** -0.30s/f (Firm) 7 Ran SP% **115.9**
Speed ratings (Par 105): **100,98,95,94,94 93,90**
toteswingers 1&2 £3.40, 1&3 £3.50, 2&3 £2.30 CSF £24.25 TOTE £5.70: £9.00, £1.10; EX 16.50 Trifecta £57.60 Pool: £2,813.96 - 36.59 winning units..
Owner Ready To Run Partnership **Bred** Hertford Offset Press **Trained** Middleham Moor, N Yorks

FOCUS
Quite an easy race to sum up, as the majority of these like to be held up, while the winner can get on with things in front.

3194 PROMOTE YOUR HORSE PRE-AUCTION AT RACEHORSETRADER.COM H'CAP (BEVERLEY MIDDLE DISTANCE SERIES) 1m 4f 16y
4:30 (4:31) (Class 6) (0-60,60) 3-Y-O **£2,587** (£770; £384; £192) **Stalls** Low

Form RPR
5235 **1** **Bain's Pass (IRE)**[9] 2924 3-9-4 **60** .... (p) JulieBurke(3) 4 65
(Kevin Ryan) *hld up in rr: hdwy over 2f out: rdn over 1f out: swtchd lft and drvn to last 100yds: hld on gamely* **8/1**[3]

0-65 **2** *shd* **Attansky (IRE)**[14] 2769 3-9-2 **55** .... DavidAllan 7 60
(Tim Easterby) *trckd ldr: reminders 1/2-way: effrt and cl up 3f out: led over 2f out: rdn wl over 1f out: hdd ent fnl f: sn drvn and edgd lft: rallied wl u.p towards fin* **12/1**

2646 **3** *hd* **Mirth**[14] 2769 3-9-5 **58** .... FrannyNorton 11 63
(Mark Johnston) *midfield: hdwy and in tch on outer 1/2-way: hdwy to chse ldrs over 2f out: rdn to ld ent fnl f: drvn and hdd last 100yds: no ex towards fin* **14/1**

5003 **4** 1/2 **Duke Of Yorkshire**[15] 2743 3-9-4 **60** .... NeilFarley(3) 9 65+
(Declan Carroll) *hld up in rr: hdwy over 2f out: pushed along over 1f out: sn rdn and styng on whn n.m.r and swtchd lft ins fnl f: nt clr run again towards fin* **9/1**

0-00 **5** 1 **Sugar Coated (IRE)**[25] 2455 3-9-1 **54** .... BarryMcHugh 8 56+
(Michael Bell) *hld up in rr: pushed along 3f out: hdwy 2f out: rdn over 1f out: styng on whn n.m.r and swtchd lft and then rt ins fnl f: kpt on: nrst fin* **16/1**

4132 **6** 1 1/4 **Niknad**[13] 2799 3-9-0 **53** .... DaneO'Neill 12 53+
(Brian Ellison) *hld up in rr: hdwy on outer over 5f out: rdn to chse ldrs over 2f out: drvn over 1f out: kpt on same pce fnl f* **7/2**[1]

054 **7** 2 1/2 **Lexi's Dancer**[23] 2504 3-9-5 **58** .... RoystonFfrench 10 54
(Ed Dunlop) *trckd ldrs: hdwy 3f out: rdn along wl over 1f out: sn drvn and one pce* **16/1**

00-0 **8** 3/4 **Noosa Sound**[32] 2274 3-9-1 **54** .... PhillipMakin 1 49
(John Davies) *led: rdn along 3f out: hdd over 2f out and grad wknd* **80/1**

003 **9** 1/2 **Big John Cannon (IRE)**[24] 2480 3-9-2 **60** .... LMcNiff(5) 2 54
(David Barron) *trckd ldrs on inner: effrt 3f out: rdn along 2f out: sn drvn and one pce* **7/2**[1]

60-6 **10** 4 1/2 **Master Hamilton**[149] 211 3-9-7 **60** .... MickyFenton 5 47
(Tobias B P Coles) *dwlt: a in rr: n.m.r on inner over 5f out: sn rdn along and nvr a factor* **9/1**

5-35 **11** 1/2 **Tahaf (IRE)**[15] 2743 3-9-4 **57** .... (t) FrederikTylicki 6 49
(Clive Brittain) *midfield: hdwy and in tch over 5f out: chsd ldrs 3f out: rdn over 2f out: sn wknd* **4/1**[2]

2m 39.31s (-0.49) **Going Correction** -0.30s/f (Firm) 11 Ran SP% **122.9**
Speed ratings (Par 97): **89,88,88,88,87 86,85,84,84,81 81**
toteswingers 1&2 £13.90, 1&3 £12.80, 2&3 £15.20 CSF £104.56 CT £1343.29 TOTE £9.70: £3.00, £3.30, £4.40; EX 80.80 Trifecta £715.40 Pool: £2,317.37 - 2.42 winning units..
Owner Mrs Margaret Forsyth **Bred** Ballyreddin Stud **Trained** Hambleton, N Yorks
■ Stewards' Enquiry : Franny Norton two-day ban: use of whip (26-27 June)

FOCUS
This had the look of an interesting handicap before the off, but it developed into a somewhat messy affair.

3195 BUY HORSES ONLINE AT RACEHORSETRADER.COM H'CAP 1m 1f 207y
5:00 (5:03) (Class 5) (0-70,70) 4-Y-O+ **£3,234** (£962; £481; £240) **Stalls** Low

Form RPR
-252 **1** **Reset City**[8] 2956 7-8-11 **60** .... FrannyNorton 9 70
(Mark Johnston) *hld up towards rr: gd hdwy over 2f out: rdn to chse ldng pair over 1f out: styd on strly fnl f to ld last 50yds* **7/2**[1]

6-06 **2** 3/4 **Miss Ella Jade**[8] 2956 4-8-2 **51** .... PaulQuinn 11 59
(Richard Whitaker) *trckd ldr: cl up 3f out: slt ld 2f out: rdn over 1f out: drvn ins fnl f: hdd and no ex last 50yds* **20/1**

0040 **3** *nk* **Amazing Blue Sky**[11] 2886 7-8-4 **53** .... JamesSullivan 10 60
(Ruth Carr) *led: rdn along and hdd 2f out: cl up and drvn over 1f out: rallied and ev ch ins fnl f tl no ex last 50yds* **9/1**

4600 **4** 1 1/4 **Standpoint**[21] 2574 7-9-3 **66** .... DaneO'Neill 8 71
(Conor Dore) *hld up in rr: hdwy 2f out: swtchd to inner and rdn over 1f out: styd on fnl f: nrst fin* **16/1**

-260 **5** 2 1/4 **King Kurt (IRE)**[20] 2594 5-9-7 **70** .... PhillipMakin 12 70
(Kevin Ryan) *trckd ldng pair: effrt over 2f out: sn rdn and no imp appr fnl f* **14/1**

-035 **6** *shd* **Pertuis (IRE)**[19] 2615 7-9-2 **65** .... RussKennemore 2 65
(Micky Hammond) *trckd ldrs on inner: pushed along 3f out: rdn 2f out: sn one pce* **12/1**

63-1 **7** 2 1/2 **Maybeme**[8] 2956 7-8-1 **57** 6ex .... (p) EvaMoscrop(7) 3 52
(Neville Bycroft) *towards rr: hdwy on outer 2f out: sn rdn and kpt on fnl f: nrst fin* **11/2**[3]

0-46 **8** 3/4 **Sinatramania**[11] 2886 6-8-3 **52** .... RoystonFfrench 15 46
(Tracy Waggott) *hld up towards rr: hdwy over 3f out: rdn to chse ldrs over 2f out: sn drvn and no imp* **11/1**

006- **9** 2 1/2 **Korngold**[218] 7602 5-8-9 **58** .... FrederikTylicki 13 47
(Ollie Pears) *nvr bttr then midfield* **20/1**

0343 **10** 2 1/4 **Rockweiller**[4] 3081 6-8-7 **56** .... DavidAllan 16 40
(Steve Gollings) *chsd ldrs: rdn along over 2f out: sn drvn and wknd* **4/1**[2]

0500 **11** 1 3/4 **General Tufto**[56] 1603 8-7-13 **51** oh6 .... (b) NeilFarley(3) 5 32
(Charles Smith) *chsd ldrs: rdn along 3f out: sn wknd* **66/1**

0-01 **12** 1/2 **Valantino Oyster (IRE)**[8] 2961 6-8-12 **61** 6ex .... (p) BarryMcHugh 7 41
(Tracy Waggott) *t.k.h early: hld up in midfield: pushed along over 5f out: rdn over 3f out: sn wknd* **17/2**

6460 **13** 8 **Monzino (USA)**[24] 2081 5-7-13 **55** .... DanielleMooney(7) 6 19
(Michael Chapman) *s.i.s: a in rr* **50/1**

000- **14** 5 **Fairlie Dinkum**[194] 7935 5-8-7 **59** .... DeclanCannon(3) 1 13
(Andrew Crook) *in tch on inner: rdn along 3f out: sn wknd* **50/1**

-400 **15** 9 **Oneofapear (IRE)**[48] 1790 7-8-11 **59** ow1 .... DaleSwift 17
(Ian McInnes) *in tch on outer: rdn along 1/2-way: sn lost pl and bhd* **40/1**

2m 3.99s (-3.01) **Going Correction** -0.30s/f (Firm) 15 Ran SP% **124.1**
Speed ratings (Par 103): **100,99,99,98,96 96,94,93,91,89 88,88,81,77,70**
toteswingers 1&2 £19.90, 1&3 £9.30, 2&3 £42.50 CSF £83.05 CT £605.46 TOTE £4.70: £2.60, £7.80, £4.00; EX 100.10 Trifecta £1460.20 Part won. Pool: £1,946.98 - 0.33 winning units..
Owner R S Brookhouse **Bred** R S Brookhouse **Trained** Middleham Moor, N Yorks

FOCUS
A modest contest.

3196 FOLLOW US ON TWITTER @RACEHORSETRADER H'CAP (DIV II) 5f
5:30 (5:31) (Class 6) (0-65,65) 3-Y-O+ **£2,264** (£673; £336; £168) **Stalls** Low

Form RPR
000- **1** **China Excels**[263] 6479 6-9-4 55 .... RussKennemore 9 68
(Sue Smith) *qckly away and mde all: edgd rt towards inner rail after 1f: sn clr: rdn and styd on strly fnl f* **20/1**

0302 **2** 3 1/2 **Here Now And Why (IRE)**[19] 2632 6-9-11 62 .... (p) DavidAllan 4 62
(Iain Jardine) *chsd ldrs: hdwy 2f out: sn rdn: styd on to take 2nd ins fnl f: no ch w wnr* **7/2**[2]

1150 **3** *hd* **Ace Master**[9] 2932 5-9-4 58 .... (b) MarkCoumbe(3) 1 57
(Roy Bowring) *wnt rt s: sn chsng ldr: n.m.r on inner and sltly hmpd after 1f: rdn 2f out: drvn over 1f out: one pce and lost 2nd ins fnl f* **3/1**[1]

-630 **4** 4 1/2 **Wotalad**[18] 2672 3-9-1 59 .... AmyRyan 5 39
(Richard Whitaker) *dwlt and towards rr: hdwy on inner wl over 1f out: sn rdn and kpt on fnl f: nrst fin* **13/2**

4103 **5** 2 **Thorpe Bay**[21] 2582 4-9-3 59 .... TobyAtkinson(5) 6 35
(Michael Appleby) *chsd wnr whn n.m.r and sltly hmpd after 1f: rdn along 2f out: drvn appr fnl f: sn wknd* **9/2**[3]

3250 **6** 3/4 **Prigsnov Dancer (IRE)**[6] 3026 8-8-6 46 .... (p) BillyCray(3) 7 19
(Deborah Sanderson) *chsd ldrs on outer: rdn along over 2f out: sn drvn and wknd* **9/2**[3]

0-02 **7** 1 1/4 **Irish Boy (IRE)**[29] 2338 5-10-0 65 .... (t) RoystonFfrench 2 34
(Christine Dunnett) *sltly hmpd s: a towards rr* **11/2**

00/0 **8** 1/2 **Storey Hill (USA)**[32] 2280 8-8-13 50 .... RobbieFitzpatrick 3 17
(Charles Smith) *wnt rt s: a in rr* **66/1**

00-0 **9** *7* **Majestic Angel (IRE)**^{6} 3026 4-8-9 46 oh1 MickyFenton 8
(Brian Rothwell) *a in rr: outpcd and bhd fnl 2f* **50/1**
1m 2.49s (-1.01) **Going Correction** -0.15s/f (Firm)
WFA 3 from 4yo+ 7lb **9** Ran SP% **120.5**
Speed ratings (Par 101): **102,96,96,88,85 84,82,81,70**
toteswingers 1&2 £9.70, 1&3 £16.30, 2&3 £3.50 CSF £91.94 CT £283.53 TOTE £25.50: £6.30, £2.10, £1.60; EX 85.00 Trifecta £1162.50 Pool: £2,539.07 - 1.63 winning units..
Owner Mrs S Smith **Bred** Brook Stud Bloodstock Ltd **Trained** High Eldwick, W Yorks
■ Stewards' Enquiry : Russ Kennemore three-day ban: careless riding (26, 27, 28 June)

FOCUS
A modest sprint run at a generous pace.
T/Jkpt: Not won. T/Plt: £152.80 to a £1 stake. Pool: £60,360.69 - 288.27 winning units T/Qpdt: £132.20 to a £1 stake. Pool: £3,670.51 - 20.54 winning units JR

2793 HAMILTON (R-H)
Wednesday, June 12

OFFICIAL GOING: Good to firm (9.7)
Wind: Light; half behind Weather: Cloudy

3197 JOIN JOHNNIE DELTA RACING ON-LINE AMATEUR RIDERS' H'CAP 6f 5y
6:20 (6:23) (Class 6) (0-60,63) 4-Y-0+ **£1,975** (£607; £303) **Stalls** Centre

Form RPR
0435 **1** **Hab Reeh**^{6} 3026 5-9-13 **52** (t) MrRColley$^{(7)}$ 13 63
(Ruth Carr) *dwlt: bhd stands' side: gd hdwy over 1f out: styd on to ld towards fin* **11/2**
1-60 **2** *nk* **Weetentherty**^{19} 2632 6-9-13 **52** (b) MrRyanClark$^{(7)}$ 6 62
(Keith Dalgleish) *prom centre: effrt and hung rt fr over 1f out: led ins fnl f: hdd towards fin* **22/1**
0-01 **3** *½* **Feel The Heat**^{6} 3026 6-10-10 **63** 6ex (v) MrLABeardsley$^{(7)}$ 8 71
(Bryan Smart) *s.i.s: bhd centre: hdwy over 2f out: kpt on ins fnl f* **7/2**^{1}
-103 **4** *1 ½* **Foreign Rhythm (IRE)**^{35} 2166 8-10-9 **60** MrsVDavies$^{(5)}$ 10 64
(Ron Barr) *cl up centre: led 1/2-way to ins fnl f: sn one pce* **17/2**
6315 **5** *6* **Script**^{26} 2409 4-10-6 **55** MissJRRichards$^{(3)}$ 16 39
(Alan Berry) *spd stands' side: led that gp over 2f out to over 1f out: sn outpcd* **16/1**
1333 **6** *nk* **Two Turtle Doves (IRE)**^{14} 2780 7-10-11 **60** MissMMullineaux$^{(3)}$ 12 43
(Michael Mullineaux) *prom centre: rdn and outpcd over 2f out: n.d after* **9/2**^{2}
-530 **7** *2 ¼* **Rock Canyon (IRE)**^{13} 2795 4-10-3 **52** (p) MrJHamilton$^{(3)}$ 3 28
(Linda Perratt) *prom tl rdn and outpcd over 2f out: btn over 1f out* **12/1**
5000 **8** *1* **Ivestar (IRE)**^{12} 2835 8-11-0 **60** (vt) MissJCoward 15 33
(Michael Easterby) *led stands' side gp to over 2f out: sn n.d* **16/1**
50-6 **9** *1* **Eilean Mor**^{9} 2912 5-9-11 **48** CallumBewley$^{(5)}$ 11 18
(R Mike Smith) *prom on outside of stands' side gp: struggling over 2f out: sn btn* **33/1**
4005 **10** *1 ¼* **You'relikemefrank**^{6} 3030 7-9-10 **49** (b) MrTGreenwood$^{(7)}$ 2 15
(Richard Ford) *dwlt: sn chsng ldrs centre: rdn and wknd 2f out* **16/1**
4210 **11** *nk* **Almaty Express**^{51} 1731 11-9-7 **46** MissAChadwick$^{(7)}$ 9 11
(John Weymes) *led centre to 1/2-way: rdn and wknd 2f out* **25/1**
5043 **12** *6* **Alpha Tauri (USA)**^{6} 3024 7-10-1 **47** (e^{1}) MissSBrotherton 1
(Charles Smith) *cl up centre tl wknd over 2f out* **5/1**^{3}
050- **13** *29* **Just For Mary**^{282} 5876 9-10-5 **58** (b) MrSClarke$^{(7)}$ 7
(Daniel Mark Loughnane) *upset in stalls: missed break: sn hung rt: t.o thrght* **33/1**
1m 12.24s (0.04) **Going Correction** -0.125s/f (Firm) **13** Ran SP% **122.4**
Speed ratings (Par 101): **94,93,92,90,82 82,79,78,76,75 74,66,28**
toteswingers 1&2 £37.70, 1&3 £8.30, 2&3 £20.10 CSF £128.92 CT £504.75 TOTE £8.00: £2.40, £5.50, £1.60; EX 264.80 Trifecta £802.90 Part won. Pool: £1,070.56 - 0.70 winning units..
Owner Mrs B Taylor, A Dickman, Mrs R Carr **Bred** The Anglo Irish Choral Society **Trained** Huby, N Yorks
■ Stewards' Enquiry : Mr Ryan Clark nine-day ban: use of whip (26 June, 7, 11, 17, 24, 27, 31 July, 2&4 August(

FOCUS
Rails realignment around the loop reduced distances on Round course by about 25yds. A low-grade handicap for amateurs, which was run at a fast pace. Pretty straightforward form.

3198 MCGHEE'S TEAZ RACEDAY NEXT WEDNESDAY H'CAP 5f 4y
6:50 (6:51) (Class 6) (0-65,64) 3-Y-O **£2,045** (£603; £302) **Stalls** Centre

Form RPR
5015 **1** **Secret Advice**^{8} 2962 3-9-3 **60** AdrianNicholls 10 66
(Keith Dalgleish) *hld up: effrt and hdwy wl over 1f out: edgd lft: kpt on fnl f: led nr fin* **5/1**^{2}
5241 **2** *nse* **Salvatore Fury (IRE)**^{13} 2795 3-9-1 **58** (p) PaddyAspell 7 64
(Keith Dalgleish) *t.k.h: cl up: led ins fnl f: hung lft: kpt on: hdd nr fin* **11/2**^{3}
-663 **3** *½* **Perfect Words (IRE)**^{6} 3025 3-8-12 **60** (p) ShirleyTeasdale$^{(5)}$ 6 64
(Marjorie Fife) *chsd ldrs: effrt and squeezed through over 1f out: ev ch ins fnl f: kpt on towards fin* **7/1**
0-64 **4** *1 ½* **Sugar Blaze**^{13} 2795 3-8-8 **51** AndrewElliott 4 50+
(Jim Goldie) *chsd ldng gp: effrt and hung rt 2f out: kpt on ins fnl f: nrst fin* **7/1**
5-32 **5** *nk* **Pastoral Prey**^{19} 2634 3-9-1 **58** (p) RobertWinston 11 57
(Ian Semple) *hld up: rdn and hdwy over 1f out: one pce whn n.m.r briefly wl ins fnl f* **12/1**
2246 **6** *½* **Cracking Choice (IRE)**^{30} 2317 3-9-7 **64** (p) PaulMulrennan 3 60
(Michael Dods) *slt ld tl rdn and hdd ins fnl f: sn outpcd* **6/1**
-031 **7** *2 ¼* **Little Eli**^{11} 2861 3-8-9 **57** JasonHart$^{(5)}$ 2 45
(Eric Alston) *prom: effrt and rdn 2f out: outpcd ins fnl f* **7/2**^{1}
-546 **8** *4* **Wildcrafting**^{36} 2135 3-8-9 **52** HayleyTurner 9 25
(Michael Bell) *t.k.h: disp ld to 2f out: sn rdn and wknd* **8/1**
0556 **9** *nk* **Nors The Panic**^{7} 2997 3-8-3 **46** (e) AndrewMullen 5 25
(Richard Guest) *t.k.h: cl up: rdn over 2f out: one pce whn hmpd over 1f out: sn btn* **33/1**
59.55s (-0.45) **Going Correction** -0.125s/f (Firm) **9** Ran SP% **115.3**
Speed ratings (Par 97): **98,97,97,94,94 93,89,83,82**
toteswingers 1&2 £5.80, 1&3 £8.20, 2&3 £5.80 CSF £32.56 CT £192.58 TOTE £7.40: £2.00, £2.40, £1.50; EX 40.70 Trifecta £188.10 Pool: £1,356.39 - 5.40 winning units..
Owner G L S Partnership **Bred** G L S Partnership **Trained** Carluke, S Lanarks
■ Stewards' Enquiry : Paddy Aspell one-day ban: careless riding (26 June)

FOCUS
A modest sprint, and something of a rough race. The form is rated around the third.

3199 LANARKSHIRE CHAMBER OF COMMERCE H'CAP 1m 3f 16y
7:20 (7:20) (Class 6) (0-65,62) 4-Y-0+ **£2,045** (£603; £302) **Stalls** Low

Form RPR
-060 **1** **King Of Paradise (IRE)**^{15} 2753 4-9-0 **60** JasonHart$^{(5)}$ 10 77
(Eric Alston) *mde all: qckn: kicked clr 1/2-way: rdn and styd on wl fnl 2f: unchal* **10/1**
13-5 **2** *5* **Red Tyke (IRE)**^{82} 1111 4-9-6 **61** (p) HayleyTurner 6 69
(John Quinn) *chsd (clr) wnr: effrt and rdn wl over 2f out: kpt on fnl f: nt pce to chal* **3/1**^{2}
3565 **3** *½* **Ebony Express**^{11} 2886 4-9-7 **62** RobertWinston 9 69
(Alan Swinbank) *hld up: rdn and hdwy 3f out: swtchd rt over 1f out: kpt on: nrst fin* **11/4**^{1}
6-52 **4** *2 ½* **Schmooze (IRE)**^{13} 2798 4-8-13 **59** GarryWhillans$^{(5)}$ 3 62
(Linda Perratt) *bhd: rdn and outpcd over 3f out: rallied over 1f out: nvr able to chal* **8/1**
000/ **5** *½* **Lochiel**^{595} 7102 9-8-13 **54** PaulMulrennan 7 56
(Ian Semple) *hld up in tch: stdy hdwy and rdn over 3f out: one pce over 1f out* **18/1**
0-01 **6** *1* **A Southside Boy (GER)**^{13} 2798 5-9-4 **59** AndrewElliott 8 59
(Jim Goldie) *prom: effrt and drvn 3f out: kpt on same pce over 1f out* **9/2**^{3}
00-0 **7** *6* **Comical**^{11} 2886 4-9-1 **56** PJMcDonald 2 45
(George Moore) *prom: drvn and outpcd wl over 2f out: sn wknd* **8/1**
0-05 **8** *9* **Euston Square**^{33} 2219 7-9-7 **62** (p) PaddyAspell 4 35
(Alistair Whillans) *hld up: rdn over 3f out: nvr on terms* **20/1**
-005 **9** *8* **Altnaharra**^{7} 2971 4-8-4 **45** (v) AdrianNicholls 1
(Jim Goldie) *chsd ldrs tl lost pl qckly 1/2-way: n.d after* **20/1**
0000 **10** *20* **Orpen Bid (IRE)**^{30} 2333 8-8-0 **46** ow1 (v^{1}) ShirleyTeasdale$^{(5)}$ 5
(Michael Mullineaux) *hld up in tch: struggling over 3f out: sn btn: t.o* **100/1**
2m 20.9s (-4.70) **Going Correction** -0.40s/f (Firm) **10** Ran SP% **116.9**
Speed ratings (Par 101): **101,97,97,95,94 94,89,83,77,62**
toteswingers 1&2 £7.10, 1&3 £6.70, 2&3 £3.10 CSF £39.52 CT £107.78 TOTE £8.50: £2.30, £1.60, £1.10; EX 47.70 Trifecta £208.70 Pool: £952.24 - 3.42 winning units..
Owner P G Buist **Bred** Sandro Garavelli **Trained** Longton, Lancs

FOCUS
A moderate handicap dominated by the winner. There is some doubt about how literally to take the form but the winner was on a good mark on his 3yo best.

3200 BOOK NOW FOR SAINTS & SINNERS H'CAP 6f 5y
7:50 (7:50) (Class 4) (0-80,79) 4-Y-0+ **£6,469** (£1,925; £962; £481) **Stalls** Centre

Form RPR
6063 **1** **Hopes N Dreams (IRE)**^{9} 2914 5-9-3 **75** PaulMulrennan 7 85
(Kevin Ryan) *mde all: shkn up over 1f out: rdn and r.o wl fnl f* **11/4**^{1}
-636 **2** *¾* **Barkston Ash**^{46} 1838 5-9-1 **78** (p) JasonHart$^{(5)}$ 8 86
(Eric Alston) *chsd wnr: drvn over 2f out: rallied appr fnl f: kpt on towards fin* **7/2**^{3}
-665 **3** *nk* **Rasaman (IRE)**^{9} 2914 9-9-3 **75** GrahamLee 2 82
(Jim Goldie) *hld up in tch: stdy hdwy and shkn up over 1f out: rdn and r.o fnl f: nrst fin* **5/1**
362 **4** *1 ½* **Chookie Avon**^{104} 822 6-8-11 **76** (p) GeorginaBaxter$^{(7)}$ 6 78+
(Keith Dalgleish) *t.k.h: in tch: nt clr run and swtchd both ways over 1f out: kpt on fnl f: nvr able to chal* **20/1**
5004 **5** *shd* **Ambitious Icarus**^{14} 2780 4-8-4 **62** (e) AndrewMullen 5 64
(Richard Guest) *cl up: rdn 2f out: kpt on same pce fnl f* **20/1**
-055 **6** *3* **Roker Park (IRE)**^{4} 3093 8-9-7 **79** DanielTudhope 1 71
(David O'Meara) *bhd: outpcd and lost tch after 2f: rdn and rapid hdwy fnl f: nvr rchd ldrs* **3/1**^{2}
40-6 **7** *nk* **Jeannie Galloway (IRE)**^{35} 2166 6-9-3 **75** TomEaves 4 66
(Keith Dalgleish) *trckd ldrs tl rdn and no ex over 1f out* **20/1**
36-0 **8** *1 ¼* **Bop It**^{25} 2441 4-9-2 **79** JustinNewman$^{(5)}$ 3 66
(Bryan Smart) *in tch on outside: rdn and hung rt over 2f out: wknd wl over 1f out* **8/1**
1m 10.64s (-1.56) **Going Correction** -0.125s/f (Firm) **8** Ran SP% **116.0**
Speed ratings (Par 105): **105,104,103,101,101 97,97,95**
toteswingers 1&2 £3.40, 1&3 £5.80, 2&3 £4.10 CSF £12.44 CT £43.59 TOTE £3.20: £2.00, £2.20, £2.00; EX 14.30 Trifecta £52.10 Pool: £665.00 - 9.56 winning units..
Owner JCG Chua & CK Ong **Bred** J & Mrs Brennan & Edward & Mrs O'Regan **Trained** Hambleton, N Yorks

FOCUS
A fair sprint handicap, won in 2010 by subsequent Prix de l'Abbaye winner Tangerine Trees. As in the two earlier races on the straight course, the stands' side proved the place to be. The winner rates back to her best.

3201 RACING UK MAIDEN STKS 1m 1f 36y
8:20 (8:20) (Class 5) 3-Y-0+ **£3,234** (£962; £481; £240) **Stalls** Low

Form RPR
2-03 **1** **A Star In My Eye (IRE)**^{33} 2231 3-8-9 79 GrahamLee 7 81
(Kevin Ryan) *in tch on outside: rn wd bnd over 5f out: led 3f out: drvn and edgd lft ins fnl f: kpt on strly* **1/1**^{1}
20-0 **2** *3 ¾* **Jadesnumberone (IRE)**^{26} 2423 3-8-9 76 HayleyTurner 5 73
(Michael Bell) *in tch: smooth hdwy to press wnr over 2f out: rdn over 1f out: one pce ins fnl f* **3/1**^{3}
2 **3** *6* **Arr' Kid (USA)**^{22} 2538 3-9-0 0 TomEaves 4 65
(Keith Dalgleish) *t.k.h: chsd ldrs: outpcd over 3f out: rallied over 1f out: nt pce of first two* **5/2**^{2}
35 **4** *7* **Samoset**^{11} 2885 3-9-0 0 RobertWinston 1 49
(Alan Swinbank) *t.k.h: led at stdy pce to 3f out: hung rt and wknd fnl 2f* **12/1**
0/-0 **5** *3 ½* **Freddie Bolt**^{11} 2885 7-9-7 40 JasonHart$^{(5)}$ 2 43
(Frederick Watson) *pressed ldr: rdn and ev ch over 3f out: wknd over 2f out* **100/1**
0 **6** *20* **Vital Edition (IRE)**^{21} 2576 3-9-0 0 AndrewMullen 3
(David O'Meara) *in tch: struggling over 4f out: no ch after: t.o* **33/1**
7 *2* **Eaton Oak** 3-9-0 0 PJMcDonald 6
(Lisa Williamson) *dwlt: bhd: rdn and struggling over 5f out: t.o* **66/1**
1m 56.34s (-3.36) **Going Correction** -0.40s/f (Firm)
WFA 3 from 7yo 12lb **7** Ran SP% **116.7**
Speed ratings (Par 103): **98,94,89,83,80 62,60**
toteswingers 1&2 £1.80, 1&3 £1.10, 2&3 £3.30 CSF £4.47 TOTE £1.80: £1.10, £3.30; EX 4.20 Trifecta £10.70 Pool: £583.05 - 40.72 winning units..
Owner Sultan Ali **Bred** Mrs Joan Murphy **Trained** Hambleton, N Yorks

FOCUS
A maiden lacking depth but the first two, both daughters of Authorized, showed fair form. The winner should do better. The early pace soon slowed and they stacked up going into the final turn.

3202 TURFTV CLASSIFIED STKS — 1m 1f 36y
8:50 (8:50) (Class 5) 3-4-Y-O — £3,408 (£1,006; £503) Stalls Low

Form — RPR
1-46 1 **Corton Lad**[13] 2799 3-8-9 60..........(bt[1]) TomEaves 4 — 74
(Keith Dalgleish) *mde all at stdy pce: rdn and edgd lft 2f out: kpt on wl fnl f* — 18/1
5300 2 2 1/2 **Argaki (IRE)**[7] 2971 3-8-9 66.......... JoeFanning 3 — 68
(Keith Dalgleish) *trckd ldrs: effrt and wnt 2nd over 1f out: edgd lft ins fnl f: kpt on: nt rch wnr* — 11/2[3]
134 3 2 3/4 **Lady Artiste (IRE)**[27] 2390 3-8-9 70.......... RobertWinston 5 — 62
(Alan Swinbank) *t.k.h: hld up in tch: stdy hdwy over 3f out: edgd lft and pushed along fr 2f out: sn one pce* — 13/8[2]
1-20 4 3 3/4 **Oilinda**[27] 2387 3-8-9 70.......... HayleyTurner 1 — 54
(Michael Bell) *taken early to post: trckd wnr tl rdn: edgd lft and wknd over 1f out* — 6/4[1]
5-60 5 6 **Lady Margaeux (IRE)**[23] 2506 3-8-11 67 ow2.......... DanielTudhope 2 — 43
(David O'Meara) *chsd ldrs: rdn over 3f out: wknd over 2f out* — 8/1
1m 55.98s (-3.72) **Going Correction** -0.40s/f (Firm) — 5 Ran SP% **109.9**
Speed ratings (Par 103): **100,97,95,92,86**
CSF £102.63 TOTE £14.00: £9.30, £1.20; EX 58.00 Trifecta £189.80 Pool: £499.29 - 1.97 winning units..
Owner J Hutton **Bred** Frank Brady And Brian Scanlon **Trained** Carluke, S Lanarks
FOCUS
A very modest classified stakes in which Keith Dalgleish sent out his second 1-2 of the evening. The form is rated around the first two but there are doubts.

3203 FOLLOW @HAMILTONPARKRC ON TWITTER H'CAP — 1m 65y
9:20 (9:22) (Class 6) (0-60,60) 3-Y-O+ — £1,940 (£577; £288; £144) Stalls Low

Form — RPR
0033 1 **Lord Franklin**[7] 2972 4-9-2 53.......... JasonHart(5) 11 — 67
(Eric Alston) *chsd clr ldr: led over 2f out: rdn and hdd ins fnl f: rallied gamely to ld towards fin* — 9/2[2]
-202 2 hd **Tectonic (IRE)**[7] 2972 4-9-7 53.......... JoeFanning 3 — 66
(Keith Dalgleish) *hld up in midfield: stdy hdwy over 2f out: rdn to ld ins fnl f: hdd towards fin* — 85/40[1]
0015 3 1 1/4 **Munaawib**[8] 2954 5-9-6 52..........(b) DanielTudhope 2 — 62
(Charles Smith) *hld up: rdn and hdwy over 2f out: kpt on ins fnl f* — 28/1
00-0 4 2 **Bonne Amie (FR)**[19] 2628 3-9-3 60.......... RichardKingscote 8 — 62
(Tom Dascombe) *prom: hdwy and ev ch over 2f out: kpt on same pce fnl f* — 9/2[2]
0-23 5 9 **Meglio Ancora**[34] 312 6-9-7 53.......... GrahamLee 5 — 38
(Richard Ford) *bhd: rdn over 3f out: styd on fr 2f out: nvr rchd ldrs* — 18/1
000 6 4 **Wesleydale (IRE)**[19] 2628 6-9-0 46 oh1.......... AndrewElliott 1 — 22
(Simon West) *t.k.h: hld up: rdn and hung lft 3f out: nvr rchd ldrs* — 40/1
/0-0 7 2 3/4 **Conjuror's Bluff**[35] 2163 5-9-6 52.......... PaddyAspell 6 — 21
(Frederick Watson) *hld up: pushed along over 3f out: sme hdwy 2f out: nvr able to chal* — 100/1
-002 8 1/2 **Flipping**[19] 2636 6-9-9 55.......... PJMcDonald 14 — 23
(Nicky Richards) *midfield: drvn and outpcd wl over 2f out: nvr able to chal* — 10/1
0-63 9 6 **Hello Gorgeous**[13] 2796 3-8-8 51.......... TomEaves 12
(Keith Dalgleish) *reluctant to enter stalls: midfield on outside: struggling over 3f out: sn btn* — 7/1[3]
0052 10 1 1/4 **Imtithal (IRE)**[7] 2974 4-9-0 51..........(b) JustinNewman(5) 10
(John Weymes) *led at gd pce: rdn and hdd over 2f out: wknd wl over 1f out* — 25/1
6-50 11 5 **Carla Allegra**[40] 1994 4-9-0 46 oh1.......... AdrianNicholls 9
(Jim Goldie) *s.i.s: bhd and sn pushed along: nvr on terms* — 66/1
504 12 1/2 **Chrisnickdave (FR)**[55] 1648 3-9-2 59.......... PaulMulrennan 13
(Michael Easterby) *midfield: rdn over 3f out: wknd fr 2f out* — 9/1
-534 13 14 **Cherry Tree Hill (IRE)**[7] 2972 5-9-8 54.......... RobertWinston 7
(Alan Swinbank) *chsd ldrs tl rdn and wknd fr 3f out: t.o* — 9/1
1m 45.34s (-3.06) **Going Correction** -0.40s/f (Firm)
WFA 3 from 4yo+ 11lb — 13 Ran SP% **127.4**
Speed ratings (Par 101): **99,98,97,95,86 82,79,79,73,72 67,66,52**
toteswingers 1&2 £3.30, 1&3 £33.50, 2&3 £19.20 CSF £15.02 CT £266.58 TOTE £5.10: £2.10, £1.60, £9.20; EX 18.20 Trifecta £173.60 Pool: £927.13 - 4.00 winning units..
Owner Liam & Tony Ferguson **Bred** Tony Ferguson & Liam Ferguson **Trained** Longton, Lancs
FOCUS
A modest handicap run at a brisk pace. The winner reversed Ayr latest with the runner-up.
T/Plt: £134.90 to a £1 stake. Pool: £59,889.68 - 324.02 winning units T/Qpdt: £27.60 to a £1 stake. Pool: £4,681.75 - 125.10 winning units RY

3099 HAYDOCK (L-H)
Wednesday, June 12
OFFICIAL GOING: Good to firm (good in places; 8.0) changing to good after race 2 (2.50)
Wind: Fresh; half-against Weather: Overcast; rain during race 6

3204 FAMILY FUN DAY HERE 8TH AUGUST H'CAP — 1m 2f 95y
2:20 (2:21) (Class 4) (0-85,83) 4-Y-O+ — £5,175 (£1,540; £769; £384) Stalls Centre

Form — RPR
-035 1 **Now My Sun**[32] 2256 4-8-12 74.......... DanielTudhope 4 — 83
(Mrs K Burke) *s.i.s: hld up in rr: hdwy and swtchd ins 3f out: nt clr run 2f out: chsng ldrs over 1f out: styd on to ld nr fin* — 6/1[2]
3506 2 nk **Las Verglas Star (IRE)**[16] 2718 5-9-1 82.......... GeorgeChaloner(5) 10 — 91
(Richard Fahey) *chsd ldrs on outer: 2nd over 4f out: led jst ins fnl f: no ex and hdd nr fin* — 14/1
6521 3 1/2 **Gran Maestro (USA)**[5] 3043 4-8-7 69..........(b) PJMcDonald 9 — 77
(Ruth Carr) *trckd ldrs on outer: drvn over 3f out: kpt on same pce fnl f* — 15/8[1]
6050 4 1 1/2 **San Cassiano (IRE)**[11] 2855 6-8-12 74.......... TomEaves 8 — 79
(Ruth Carr) *led: hdd jst ins fnl f: kpt on same pce* — 25/1
0503 5 hd **Moccasin (FR)**[14] 2766 4-9-7 83.......... SilvestreDeSousa 12 — 88
(Geoffrey Harker) *s.i.s: hld up in rr: drvn 3f out: hdwy over 1f out: styd on towards fin* — 14/1
-002 6 3 **Another For Joe**[7] 2976 5-8-13 75.......... GrahamLee 2 — 74
(Jim Goldie) *trckd ldrs: drvn over 2f out: fdd fnl f* — 13/2[3]
0005 7 nk **Super Say (IRE)**[51] 1728 7-9-7 83.......... AndrewMullen 5 — 81
(Michael Appleby) *rrd s: sn mid-div: effrt over 3f out: wknd over 1f out* — 8/1
1342 8 2 1/2 **Rock Song**[16] 2710 4-8-10 72.......... SteveDrowne 7 — 66
(John Mackie) *hld up in rr: drvn 3f out: kpt on fnl f: nvr a factor* — 12/1
0540 9 1 1/2 **Satanic Beat (IRE)**[24] 2478 4-9-1 77.......... TomQueally 11 — 68
(Jedd O'Keeffe) *hld up in rr: effrt 3f out: nvr a factor* — 16/1
5005 10 3 3/4 **Dubawi Phantom**[46] 1831 6-9-1 77..........(be) JamesDoyle 6 — 61
(David C Griffiths) *chsd ldrs: drvn over 3f out: wknd 2f out* — 33/1
1122 11 2 1/4 **Apache Glory (USA)**[4] 3083 5-8-13 75..........(p) AndreaAtzeni 3 — 54
(John Stimpson) *mid-div: outpcd over 3f out: hung lft and sn lost pl* — 11/1
360- 12 5 **Queen's Estate (GER)**[215] 7672 4-8-12 74.......... JoeFanning 1 — 44
(Mark Johnston) *chsd ldrs: drvn over 3f out: lost pl over 2f out* — 40/1
2m 11.67s (-3.83) **Going Correction** -0.225s/f (Firm) — 12 Ran SP% **118.0**
Speed ratings (Par 105): **106,105,105,104,104 101,101,99,98,95 93,89**
toteswingers 1&2 £13.20, 1&3 £2.40, 2&3 £6.40 CSF £84.84 CT £218.06 TOTE £9.30: £2.80, £4.80, £1.10; EX 101.40 Trifecta £275.00 Pool: £1,398.80 - 3.81 winning units..
Owner Ray Bailey **Bred** Ray Bailey **Trained** Middleham Moor, N Yorks
FOCUS
All races on Inner home straight and races on Round course increased in distance by 1yd. All races were run on the inner home straight. The ground, given as good to firm, good in places (GoingStick 8.0) had been watered, and there was 2mm of rain overnight. Tom Eaves called it "good", and James Doyle said it was "a little bit loose" after the first.

3205 IRISH STALLION FARMS EBF MAIDEN FILLIES' STKS — 6f
2:50 (2:51) (Class 5) 2-Y-O — £2,911 (£866; £432; £216) Stalls Centre

Form — RPR
1 **Autumn Lily (USA)** 2-9-0 0.......... MickaelBarzalona 1 — 79+
(Saeed bin Suroor) *w ldrs on wd outside: led over 2f out: qcknd clr fnl f: v readily* — 5/6[1]
2 2 1/4 **Lady Red Oak** 2-9-0 0.......... SteveDrowne 8 — 71+
(Tom Dascombe) *s.i.s: hld up in rr: t.k.h: hdwy and swtchd stands' side 2f out: r.o to take 2nd nr fin* — 66/1
6 3 3/4 **Miaplacidus (IRE)**[19] 2625 2-9-0 0.......... TonyHamilton 9 — 68
(Richard Fahey) *wnt rt s: w ldrs: wnt 2nd last 100yds: lost 2nd nr line* — 12/1
6 4 1 **Atheera (IRE)**[15] 2744 2-9-0 0.......... JoeFanning 10 — 65
(Mark Johnston) *wnt rt s: hdwy stands' side 3f out: kpt on same pce fnl f* — 20/1
3 5 1/2 **Brunhilde**[15] 2740 2-9-0 0.......... RichardKingscote 4 — 64
(Tom Dascombe) *led tl over 2f out: fdd last 100yds* — 6/1[3]
60 6 1 **Woodland Girl**[25] 2458 2-9-0 0.......... PatrickMathers 3 — 60
(Richard Fahey) *chsd ldrs: outpcd over 1f out* — 25/1
7 1/2 **Taleteller (USA)** 2-9-0 0.......... SilvestreDeSousa 2 — 59
(Saeed bin Suroor) *chsd ldrs on outer: fdd over 1f out* — 5/1[2]
8 shd **Where The Boys Are (IRE)** 2-9-0 0.......... SeanLevey 6 — 58
(Ed McMahon) *chsd ldrs: kpt on same pce fnl 2f* — 22/1
9 1 **Rayoumti (IRE)** 2-9-0 0.......... FrankieDettori 5 — 55
(Marco Botti) *s.i.s: drvn and sme hdwy over 2f out: lost pl over 1f out* — 12/1
1m 14.5s (0.70) **Going Correction** -0.125s/f (Firm) — 9 Ran SP% **115.3**
Speed ratings (Par 90): **90,87,86,84,84 82,82,81,80**
toteswingers 1&2 £14.50, 1&3 £6.60, 2&3 £27.10 CSF £96.64 TOTE £1.80: £1.10, £8.10, £2.60; EX 77.90 Trifecta £996.20 Pool: £1,526.24 - 1.14 winning units..
Owner Godolphin **Bred** Darley **Trained** Newmarket, Suffolk
FOCUS
The winner did this well and looks a surefire improver. The field finished rather in a heap behind her.

3206 80'S LEGENDS MUSIC HERE 22ND JUNE H'CAP — 1m 6f
3:20 (3:22) (Class 4) (0-85,82) 3-Y-O — £5,175 (£1,540; £769; £384) Stalls Low

Form — RPR
1234 1 **Good Evans**[14] 2784 3-8-7 68.......... RichardKingscote 4 — 78
(Tom Dascombe) *led: drvn over 3f out: styd on gamely to forge away fnl f* — 3/1[2]
4-12 2 2 1/4 **Argent Knight**[20] 2602 3-8-12 73..........(p) GrahamLee 5 — 80
(William Jarvis) *s.i.s: hdwy to trck ldr after 2f: chal travelling bttr over 2f out: rdn appr fnl f: kpt on same pce* — 15/8[1]
0-14 3 4 1/2 **Sizzler**[37] 2086 3-9-7 82.......... JamesDoyle 6 — 83
(Ralph Beckett) *upset in stalls: rrd s: hld up in detached last: effrt and 3rd 4f out: sn rdn: hung bdly rt over 1f out: nvr able to chal* — 15/2
-121 4 64 **Grendisar (IRE)**[21] 2564 3-9-3 78..........(p) AndreaAtzeni 1
(Marco Botti) *chsd wnr 2f: outpcd and shkn up 7f out: rdn and outpcd over 3f out: sn bhd: eased 2f out: virtually p.u: eventually fin* — 6/1[3]
3m 0.86s (-1.14) **Going Correction** -0.225s/f (Firm) — 4 Ran SP% **85.8**
Speed ratings (Par 101): **94,92,90,53**
CSF £5.56 TOTE £3.20; EX 5.50 Trifecta £14.00 Pool: £652.99 - 34.91 winning units..
Owner Rawhide Racing **Bred** Newsells Park Stud **Trained** Malpas, Cheshire
■ Ambleside was withdrawn (3-1, ref to ent stalls). Deduct 25p in the £ under R4.
FOCUS
The going was changed to good before this race. With Ambleside refusing to go in the stalls, Grendisar failing to run his race, and Argent Knight looking less than enthusiastic in the finish, the winner probably didn't achieve a great deal in victory.

3207 RITA ORA HERE 9TH AUGUST H'CAP — 1m
3:50 (3:53) (Class 3) (0-90,90) 3-Y-O+ — £8,086 (£2,406; £1,202; £601) Stalls Centre

Form — RPR
6156 1 **Lord Of The Dance (IRE)**[18] 2646 7-8-7 76.......... JoeyHaynes(7) 10 — 86
(Michael Mullineaux) *gave problems gng to s: hld up in rr: hdwy 3f out: r.o to ld ins fnl f* — 16/1
23-5 2 nk **Party Royal**[11] 2876 3-8-7 80.......... JoeFanning 9 — 86
(Mark Johnston) *set stdy pce: qcknd gallop over 2f out: hdd last 100yds: no ex* — 12/1
0542 3 3/4 **Dubai Hills**[20] 2592 7-9-7 88.......... JustinNewman(5) 4 — 96
(Bryan Smart) *trckd ldrs: effrt over 2f out: nt clr run: edgd rt appr fnl f: r.o* — 9/2[1]
505- 4 3/4 **The Rectifier (USA)**[202] 7826 6-9-12 88..........(t) TomQueally 2 — 96+
(Seamus Durack) *trckd ldr: nt clr run over 2f out tl ins fnl f: r.o at fin* — 12/1
0-44 5 hd **Wannabe King**[39] 2029 7-10-0 90..........(v) SilvestreDeSousa 8 — 95
(Geoffrey Harker) *trckd ldrs: cl 2nd over 4f out: kpt on same pce fnl f* — 15/2[3]
6443 6 1 1/4 **Dubai Dynamo**[8] 2958 8-9-13 89.......... PJMcDonald 3 — 92
(Ruth Carr) *mid-div: effrt on ins and n.m.r over 2f out: kpt on same pce over 1f out* — 5/1[2]
0020 7 1 1/4 **Discression**[20] 2592 4-9-8 84.......... GrahamLee 5 — 84
(Kevin Ryan) *hld up in rr: hdwy over 2f out: kpt on same pce appr fnl f* — 9/2[1]
-000 8 nk **Hit The Jackpot (IRE)**[24] 2477 4-9-10 86.......... DanielTudhope 6 — 85
(David O'Meara) *trckd ldrs: effrt over 2f out: one pce* — 9/2[1]

The Form Book Flat, Raceform Ltd, Compton, RG20 6NL.

522- **9** 1 3/4 **Jubilee Games**[246] [6955] 3-8-5 **78**.................................. PatrickMathers 7 70
(Richard Fahey) *blind removed late and rrd s: detached in last: t.k.h: drvn 3f out: nvr a factot* **10/1**

1m 41.86s (-1.84) **Going Correction** -0.225s/f (Firm)
WFA 3 from 4yo+ 11lb **9** Ran SP% **113.3**
Speed ratings (Par 107): **100,99,98,98,98 96,95,95,93**
toteswingers 1&2 £28.10, 1&3 £12.50, 2&3 £6.90 CSF £187.49 CT £1017.33 TOTE £14.60: £4.50, £4.00, £2.20; EX 190.50 Trifecta £2088.80 Pool: £3,073.28 - 1.10 winning units..
Owner H Clewlow **Bred** Bridgewater Equine Ltd **Trained** Alpraham, Cheshire

FOCUS
This looked pretty competitive, but luck in running played a part.

3208 JAMES HOWARD H'CAP 1m 3f 200y
4:20 (4:21) (Class 3) (0-95,90) 4-Y-0+ **£8,086** (£2,406; £1,202; £601) **Stalls** Centre

Form RPR
41-0 **1** **Al Saham**[38] [2052] 4-9-4 **87**.............................. SilvestreDeSousa 7 97+
(Saeed bin Suroor) *hld up in rr: t.k.h: hdwy 3f out: nt clr runover 1f out: swtchd lft and qcknd to ld last 75yds: readily* **3/1**[1]

2144 **2** 1 **Icebuster**[23] [2520] 5-9-3 **86**.............................. AndreaAtzeni 5 92
(Rod Millman) *dwlt: hld up in rr: t.k.h: effrt on outer 3f out: edgd rt over 1f out: led briefly 100yds out: edgd lft and no ex* **9/2**[3]

4300 **3** nk **Scatter Dice (IRE)**[11] [2867] 4-9-7 **90**.............................. JoeFanning 3 96
(Mark Johnston) *led at stdy pce: qcknd gallop over 3f out: hdd ins fnl f: no ex* **7/1**

6411 **4** shd **Swinging Sultan**[11] [2855] 6-9-6 **89**.............................. TomEaves 2 94
(Keith Reveley) *dwlt: hld up: hdwy on ins 3f out: chal over 1f out: sn rdn and kpt on same pce last 150yds* **7/2**[2]

3-66 **5** 2 1/4 **Kiwayu**[18] [2648] 4-8-12 **81**.............................. StevieDonohoe 6 83
(Ian Williams) *t.k.h in mid-div: drvn 3f out: wknd jst ins fnl f* **8/1**

0116 **6** 4 **Take Two**[26] [2431] 4-8-13 **82**.............................. GrahamLee 1 77
(Alex Hales) *trckd ldr: stmbld 8f out: rdn over 2f out: wkng whn hmpd ins fnl f* **11/1**

6-50 **7** 1 3/4 **Moldowney**[18] [2654] 4-9-3 **86**.............................. FrankieDettori 4 79
(Luca Cumani) *chsd ldrs: rdn over 2f out: wknd over 1f out* **5/1**

2m 31.13s (-2.67) **Going Correction** -0.225s/f (Firm) **7** Ran SP% **114.0**
Speed ratings (Par 107): **99,98,98,98,96 93,92**
toteswingers 1&2 £3.40, 1&3 £4.20, 2&3 £4.20 CSF £16.64 TOTE £4.40: £2.40, £2.40; EX 17.20 Trifecta £83.10 Pool: £2,688.93 - 24.24 winning units..
Owner Godolphin **Bred** Darley **Trained** Newmarket, Suffolk

FOCUS
They didn't go that quick early and it turned into something of a sprint.

3209 MADNESS MUSIC NIGHT HERE 20TH JULY MAIDEN STKS 1m 3f 200y
4:50 (4:51) (Class 5) 3-Y-0+ **£2,587** (£770; £384; £192) **Stalls** Centre

Form RPR
6 **1** **Federal Blue (USA)**[140] [333] 3-8-13 0.............................. JoeFanning 9 85
(Mark Johnston) *trckd ldr: drvn over 4f out: styd on to ld appr fnl f: edgd lft: hld on towards fin* **25/1**

2 **2** nk **Bomber Thorn**[20] [2589] 3-8-13 0.............................. RichardKingscote 8 84
(Tom Dascombe) *in rr: drvn and 3rd over 3f out: rdn over 2f out: chsd wnr 1f out: edgd lft: kpt on: no ex clsng stages* **4/9**[1]

44 **3** 10 **Sleeping Giant (GER)**[20] [2589] 3-8-13 0.............................. FrankieDettori 3 68
(Luca Cumani) *led: qcknd pce over 4f out: hdd appr fnl f: sn wknd* **4/1**[2]

4 2 3/4 **Massena (IRE)**[31] 6-10-0 **78**.............................. TonyHamilton 2 64
(Venetia Williams) *trckd ldrs: lost pl 3f out: tk poor 4th towards fin* **50/1**

3 **5** 2 1/4 **Fair Loch**[25] [2465] 5-10-0 0.............................. TomQueally 7 60+
(Mrs K Burke) *hld up in rr: hdwy and modest 4th over 3f out: hung lft and wknd over 1f out* **13/2**[3]

6 1/2 **Yes Daddy (IRE)**[24] 5-9-11 0.............................. BrianToomey(3) 4 59
(Kevin Ryan) *hld up in rr: effrt over 3f out: sn btn: swtchd rt ins fnl f* **33/1**

04 **7** 2 3/4 **Sammyman**[21] [2568] 6-10-0 0.............................. StevieDonohoe 5 55
(Michael Blanshard) *chsd ldrs: drvn over 4f out: lost pl over 3f out* **50/1**

2m 30.92s (-2.88) **Going Correction** -0.225s/f (Firm)
WFA 3 from 5yo+ 15lb **7** Ran SP% **113.3**
Speed ratings (Par 103): **100,99,93,91,89 89,87**
toteswingers 1&2 £3.30, 1&3 £6.30, 2&3 £2.30 CSF £37.13 TOTE £18.70: £7.00, £1.20; EX 45.20 Trifecta £126.00 Pool: £3,174.26 - 18.89 winning units..
Owner Sheikh Hamdan Bin Mohammed Al Maktoum **Bred** Darley **Trained** Middleham Moor, N Yorks

FOCUS
The market saw this as a fine opportunity for Bomber Thorn to get off the mark, but the odds-on favourite was turned over.
T/Plt: £435.70 to a £1 stake. Pool: £66,508.49 - 111.41 winning units T/Qpdt: £80.00 to a £1 stake. Pool: £3,975.13 - 36.75 winning units WG

[2978] KEMPTON (A.W) (R-H)
Wednesday, June 12

OFFICIAL GOING: Standard
Wind: Brisk; half behind Weather: Overcast; heavy rain race 3

3210 IRISH NIGHT ON 10.07.13 APPRENTICE H'CAP 1m (P)
6:10 (6:10) (Class 5) (0-75,71) 4-Y-0+ **£2,587** (£770; £384; £192) **Stalls** Low

Form RPR
3110 **1** **Midnight Feast**[13] [2807] 5-9-10 **69**.............................. (v) ThomasBrown 2 74
(Lee Carter) *t.k.h: trckd ldr: led over 1f out: rdn and idled in front: fnd enough whn pressed last 100yds* **2/1**[1]

341 **2** 1/2 **Jake The Snake (IRE)**[48] [1793] 12-9-9 **71**.............................. RyanTate(3) 6 75
(Tony Carroll) *hld up in last: prog 2f out: rdn over 1f out: wnt 2nd last 100yds on inner and chal: nt qckn nr fin* **4/1**[2]

020- **3** 1/2 **Edgewater (IRE)**[279] [5983] 6-9-6 **65**.............................. NathanAlison 4 68
(Lee Carter) *led: set v stdy pce to 1/2-way: tried to kick on 3f out: hdd over 1f out: cl up after but lost 2nd fnl 100yds* **8/1**

0-00 **4** 3/4 **Tartan Trip**[16] [2724] 6-9-11 **70**.............................. MatthewLawson 5 71
(Luke Dace) *hld up in 6th: rdn and nt qckn over 2f out: kpt on fr over 1f out: nvr quite able to chal* **5/1**[3]

-220 **5** 2 1/4 **High On The Hog (IRE)**[14] [2773] 5-8-9 **59**.............................. MatthewHopkins(5) 7 55
(Mark Brisbourne) *racd wd: pressed ldrs: rdn over 2f out: fdd over 1f out* **8/1**

1-46 **6** 2 **Spitfire**[77] [1205] 8-9-7 **66**.............................. (t) WilliamTwiston-Davies 1 57
(J R Jenkins) *stdd s: t.k.h: hld up bhd ldrs: rdn over 2f out: wknd over 1f out* **11/2**

2000 **7** 2 3/4 **Mataajir (USA)**[23] [2514] 5-8-10 **60**.............................. (t) AdamMcLean(5) 3 45
(Derek Shaw) *t.k.h: trckd ldr to over 2f out: wknd qckly* **16/1**

1m 42.06s (2.26) **Going Correction** +0.075s/f (Slow) **7** Ran SP% **113.5**
Speed ratings (Par 103): **91,90,90,89,87 85,82**
toteswingers 1&2 £1.10, 1&3 £3.90, 2&3 £5.30 CSF £9.93 TOTE £3.30: £2.00, £1.70; EX 10.20 Trifecta £51.70 Pool: £1,265.41 - 18.33 winning units..
Owner One More Bid Partnership **Bred** Whitsbury Manor Stud **Trained** Epsom, Surrey

FOCUS
A modest apprentice handicap and the early pace was steady.

3211 ABY SMITH 30TH BIRTHDAY MAIDEN STKS 6f (P)
6:40 (6:40) (Class 5) 2-Y-0 **£2,587** (£770; £384; £192) **Stalls** Low

Form RPR
1 **Grecian (IRE)** 2-9-5 0.............................. JimCrowley 3 76+
(Paul Cole) *trckd ldng pair: wnt 2nd 2f out: led over 1f out: reminder and asserted jst ins fnl f: pushed out* **10/1**

3 **2** 3/4 **Munfallet (IRE)**[18] [2653] 2-9-5 0.............................. PaulHanagan 1 74
(Richard Hannon) *led: hung lft bnd after 1f: rdn over 2f out: hdd over 1f out: kpt on but readily hld* **1/3**[1]

3 **3** 1 1/4 **Meaning Of Life (IRE)**[14] [2778] 2-9-5 0.............................. AdamKirby 8 70
(Marco Botti) *in tch: rdn over 2f out: prog wl over 1f out: styd on fnl f to take 3rd last stride* **5/1**[2]

0 **4** shd **Roman Legend (IRE)**[18] [2670] 2-9-5 0.............................. RyanMoore 2 70
(Jeremy Noseda) *dwlt: in tch: pushed along firmly on inner to chal over 1f out: reminder and one pce fnl f: lost 3rd last stride* **8/1**[3]

5 **5** 5 **Clarice**[21] [2577] 2-9-0 0.............................. LukeMorris 6 49+
(Sir Mark Prescott Bt) *in tch: pushed along jst over 2f out: wknd over 1f out* **25/1**

45 **6** nk **Severnwind (IRE)**[21] [2562] 2-9-5 0.............................. GeorgeBaker 5 53
(Ronald Harris) *pressed ldr to 2f out: sn wknd* **20/1**

7 3/4 **Hija** 2-8-7 0.............................. RyanWhile(7) 7 45
(Bill Turner) *dwlt: mostly in last pair: urged along over 2f out: nvr on terms w ldrs* **20/1**

8 8 **Buckland Beau** 2-9-0 0.............................. NicoleNordblad(5) 4 25
(Hans Adielsson) *dwlt: hld up in last: nvr on terms: bhd fnl 2f* **33/1**

5 **9** 5 **John Lea (IRE)**[14] [2778] 2-8-12 0.............................. AdamMcLean(7) 9 9
(Derek Shaw) *dwlt: t.k.h: racd wd and looked awkward: in tch to 1/2-way: sn wknd and bhd* **50/1**

1m 14.17s (1.07) **Going Correction** +0.075s/f (Slow) **9** Ran SP% **130.2**
Speed ratings (Par 93): **95,94,92,92,85 85,84,73,66**
toteswingers 1&2 £4.00, 1&3 £7.60, 2&3 £2.30 CSF £15.14 TOTE £11.90: £3.10, £1.10, £1.10; EX 20.80 Trifecta £188.10 Pool: £1,356.39 - 5.40 winning units..
Owner Mrs Fitri Hay **Bred** Mrs Anne Marie Burns **Trained** Whatcombe, Oxon

FOCUS
Limited experience amongst the runners in this maiden. The first four finished clear. The runner-up is only rated to his debut form.

3212 £200 FREE BETS AT BETDAQ H'CAP 6f (P)
7:10 (7:10) (Class 5) (0-75,75) 3-Y-0 **£2,587** (£770; £384; £192) **Stalls** Low

Form RPR
21 **1** **Duke Cosimo**[22] [2556] 3-9-6 **74**.............................. RyanMoore 5 89+
(Sir Michael Stoute) *trckd ldng trio tl chsd ldr 2f out: clsd to ld 1f out: drvn and grad asserted* **10/11**[1]

4-15 **2** 1 1/4 **Smokethatthunders (IRE)**[16] [2708] 3-9-2 **70**.............................. RichardHughes 3 80
(James Toller) *led: shkn up 2f out: edgd lft and hdd 1f out: tried to rally but hld last 100yds* **11/4**[2]

-100 **3** 1 1/2 **El Mirage (IRE)**[7] [2983] 3-9-7 **75**.............................. AdamKirby 1 80
(Dean Ivory) *hld up in tch: prog to chse ldng pair over 1f out: sn drvn: styd on but nvr able to chal* **16/1**

5-36 **4** 2 1/4 **Clearing**[50] [1750] 3-8-1 **60**.............................. NathanAlison(5) 9 58
(Jim Boyle) *stdd s: plld hrd and sn racd wd: wd bnd 3f out: hung across to nr side rail fr 2f out: kpt on* **33/1**

-325 **5** 1 3/4 **Baron Run**[18] [2672] 3-9-0 **68**.............................. JimmyFortune 4 60
(Mrs K Burke) *plld hrd: hld up in rr: shuffled along and no real prog fr 2f out* **7/1**[3]

11-0 **6** hd **Saga Lout**[23] [2521] 3-9-5 **73**.............................. StephenCraine 6 65
(Tom Dascombe) *t.k.h: hld up in tch: shkn up and hanging lft 2f out: sn btn* **16/1**

1606 **7** 3/4 **Blazing Knight (IRE)**[5] [3050] 3-9-7 **75**.............................. JimCrowley 2 64
(Ralph Beckett) *hld up in last: pushed along fr 2f out: nt qckn and v limited prog* **12/1**

160- **8** 2 1/4 **Time For Lambrini (IRE)**[225] [7462] 3-9-4 **72**.............................. GeorgeBaker 7 54
(Lisa Williamson) *chsd ldr to 2f out: sn wknd* **50/1**

302- **9** 19 **Kodatish (IRE)**[187] [8016] 3-9-0 **68**.............................. LukeMorris 8
(Ronald Harris) *free to post: plld hrd: prom on outer: wknd rapidly over 2f out: t.o* **33/1**

1m 13.48s (0.38) **Going Correction** +0.075s/f (Slow) **9** Ran SP% **118.9**
Speed ratings (Par 99): **100,98,96,93,91 90,89,86,61**
toteswingers 1&2 £1.20, 1&3 £5.20, 2&3 £9.10 CSF £3.52 CT £23.01 TOTE £2.00: £1.10, £1.60, £3.20; EX 4.80 Trifecta £26.20 Pool: £948.11 - 27.07 winning units..
Owner Cheveley Park Stud **Bred** Cheveley Park Stud Ltd **Trained** Newmarket, Suffolk

FOCUS
A tightly knit 3yo sprint handicap that has fallen to unexposed types on several occasions, and that was the case again. The time was 0.69secs faster than the preceding maiden.

3213 LONDON'S TRACKS RACINGANDMUSIC.CO.UK H'CAP 1m 3f (P)
7:40 (7:40) (Class 6) (0-55,55) 4-Y-0+ **£1,940** (£577; £288; £144) **Stalls** Low

Form RPR
0-43 **1** **Golden Jubilee (USA)**[12] [2828] 4-9-2 **55**..(b) WilliamTwiston-Davies(5) 7 65
(Nigel Twiston-Davies) *trckd ldng quartet: nt clr run briefly wl over 2f out: drvn and prog after: wnt 2nd over 1f out: led jst ins fnl f: won gng away* **11/2**[2]

5026 **2** 2 1/4 **Princess Willow**[13] [2801] 5-9-7 **55**.............................. KirstyMilczarek 3 61
(John E Long) *trckd ldng pair: quick move to ld over 2f out and set sail for home: drvn and hdd jst ins fnl f: one pce* **4/1**[1]

4200 **3** 3 1/2 **Lytham (IRE)**[40] [1987] 12-9-6 **54**.............................. AdamKirby 2 54
(Tony Carroll) *hld up in last trio: urged along and prog over 2f out: drvn over 1f out: styd on to take 3rd ins fnl f* **15/2**

6430 **4** 3 **Dolly Colman (IRE)**[22] [2533] 5-8-12 **46** oh1.............................. (p) CathyGannon 5 40
(Zoe Davison) *hld up in last: gd prog fr over 3f out to chse ldr over 2f out: lost 2nd and wknd over 1f out* **20/1**

3300 **5** 2 **Petersboden**[44] [1877] 4-8-12 **46** oh1.............................. JimmyQuinn 4 37
(Michael Blanshard) *settled in midfield: pushed along 1/2-way: prog u.p to press for 2nd over 2f out: sn lft bhd* **10/1**

-005 **6** 2 ½ **Capriska**[15] 2764 4-8-12 **46**............ RichardHughes 9 32
(Willie Musson) *hld up in 10th: shkn up and no prog over 2f out: n.d after* **6/1**[3]

0/0- **7** 2 **Boogie Dancer**[21] 4994 9-8-12 **46** oh1............ HarryBentley 13 29
(Jim Best) *racd wd in midfield: shkn up 3f out: nvr on terms* **33/1**

0-03 **8** 2 ½ **King's Road**[13] 2801 8-9-6 **54**............(tp) GeorgeBaker 10 32
(Anabel K Murphy) *hld up in midfield: rdn and dropped to rr 3f out: tried to rally on inner 2f out: no hdwy sn after* **7/1**

-660 **9** 6 **Norse Song**[15] 2764 4-8-12 **46** oh1............ LiamKeniry 1 13
(David Elsworth) *trckd ldrs disputing 5th: drvn and brief effrt over 2f out: sn wknd: eased ins fnl f* **14/1**

4000 **10** 3 ¼ **Cape Joy (IRE)**[27] 2395 4-9-7 **55**............ LukeMorris 12 16
(Sylvester Kirk) *hld up in last trio: shoved along fr 1/2-way: no prog and struggling 3f out* **25/1**

600 **11** 1 ¾ **Jack Firefly**[21] 2568 4-8-7 **46** oh1............ RyanTate(5) 8
(Michael Murphy) *led at gd pce but hdd 7f out: led again over 3f out to over 2f out: wknd qckly* **25/1**

600 **12** 9 **Numen (IRE)**[19] 2333 9-9-3 **51**............(v¹) JimCrowley 11
(Barry Brennan) *trckd ldng pair tl wknd qckly over 3f out: eased 2f out and sn wl bhd* **20/1**

0-30 **13** 15 **Penang Pegasus**[13] 2801 4-9-4 **52**............ JackMitchell 14
(Roger Teal) *prom: prog to ld 7f out: hdd over 3f out: wknd rapidly: t.o* **8/1**

2m 21.58s (-0.32) **Going Correction** +0.075s/f (Slow) **13 Ran SP% 121.0**
Speed ratings (Par 101): **104,102,99,97,96 94,92,91,86,84 83,76,65**
toteswingers 1&2 £3.20, 1&3 £8.50, 2&3 £7.40 CSF £25.87 CT £170.47 TOTE £6.40: £2.80, £3.00, £1.40; EX 32.10 Trifecta £85.10 Pool: £400.73 - 3.52 winning units..
Owner Mrs J K Powell **Bred** Dixiana Farms Llc **Trained** Naunton, Gloucs

FOCUS
A very moderate middle-distance handicap. in which they appeared to go a decent gallop and they finished well strung out.

3214 COMMISSION FREE 1ST MONTH AT BETDAQ H'CAP (LONDON MIDDLE DISTANCE SERIES QUALIFIER) 1m 3f (P)
8:10 (8:10) (Class 4) (0-85,83) 3-Y-O **£4,690** (£1,395; £697; £348) **Stalls** Low

Form RPR

3-32 **1** **Interior Minister**[12] 2827 3-9-3 **79**............ RyanMoore 7 86
(Jo Hughes) *mde all: dictated mod pce: wound it up over 3f out: kicked on over 2f out: hrd pressed fnl f: drvn and hld on wl* **12/1**

01 **2** ½ **Masquerading (IRE)**[35] 2157 3-9-6 **82**............ TedDurcan 8 88
(David Lanigan) *trckd wnr 5f: styd cl up: wnt 2nd again 2f out: str chal on inner fr 1f out: nt qckn last 50yds* **4/1**[2]

6-41 **3** 2 ¼ **Glorious Protector (IRE)**[30] 2321 3-9-7 **83**............ JamieSpencer 1 85+
(Ed Walker) *trckd ldng pair 5f: lost pl sltly: plenty to do once wnr kicked on over 2f out: styd on to take 3rd over 1f out: nvr able to threaten* **6/4**[1]

451- **4** 1 ½ **Alwilda**[230] 7349 3-8-11 **73**............ LukeMorris 5 72+
(Sir Mark Prescott Bt) *hld up in 7th in modly run event: outpcd and drvn over 2f out: styd on to take 4th ins fnl f: effrt petered out nr fin* **12/1**

6-10 **5** ¾ **Lamusawama**[20] 2584 3-9-4 **80**............ PaulHanagan 6 78
(Ed Dunlop) *stdd s: hld up in last in modly run event: ldrs already gone whn sme prog 2f out: no ch* **7/1**[3]

1-00 **6** shd **St Paul De Vence (IRE)**[11] 2862 3-9-1 **77**............ RichardHughes 4 75
(Paul Cole) *hld up in 6th: quick move to press wnr 6f out: drvn and fnd nil wl over 2f out: sn lost 2nd and btn* **7/1**[3]

26-0 **7** 1 **Rock God (IRE)**[53] 1678 3-9-3 **79**............ JimCrowley 2 75?
(Eve Johnson Houghton) *hld up in 5th/6th: outpcd whn wnr kicked on over 2f out: n.d after* **16/1**

53-3 **8** ½ **Grayswood**[21] 2564 3-8-5 **67**............ HarryBentley 3 62
(William Muir) *trckd ldrs: outpcd over 2f out: no imp after: fdd* **12/1**

2m 21.96s (0.06) **Going Correction** +0.075s/f (Slow) **8 Ran SP% 114.0**
Speed ratings (Par 101): **102,101,100,98,98 98,97,97**
toteswingers 1&2 £14.90, 1&3 £1.10, 2&3 £2.80 CSF £59.03 CT £114.68 TOTE £7.60: £3.60, £2.20, £1.30; EX 65.30 Trifecta £123.90 Pool: £567.40 - 3.43 winning units..
Owner Eastwind Racing Ltd And Martha Trussell **Bred** Cliveden Stud Ltd **Trained** Lambourn, Berks

FOCUS
Plenty of interest in this feature race, with several recent winners in opposition. The pace was steadied down the back evidenced by the fact that the time was 0.36secs slower than the preceding handicap.

3215 BETDAQ 1ST UK COMMISSION FREE-EVERYDAY H'CAP 7f (P)
8:40 (8:40) (Class 4) (0-80,79) 4-Y-0+ **£4,690** (£1,395; £697; £348) **Stalls** Low

Form RPR

0-33 **1** **Restaurateur (IRE)**[18] 2659 4-9-6 **78**............(v) JimmyFortune 12 87+
(Andrew Balding) *hld up in last trio: gd prog over 2f out: tk 2nd 1f out: drvn to cl on ldr: led last strides and eased* **5/1**[3]

1250 **2** nse **Ocean Legend (IRE)**[18] 2657 8-8-13 **76**............ RyanTate(5) 6 85
(Tony Carroll) *pressed ldr: led over 2f out: over a l clr 1f out: styd on but hdd last strides* **16/1**

331- **3** 2 ¼ **Anya**[229] 7376 4-9-5 **77**............ RyanMoore 8 80
(Ed Walker) *trckd ldng pair on outer: drvn over 2f out: styd on fr over 1f out to take 3rd ins fnl f* **9/2**[2]

-256 **4** 2 ¾ **Flexible Flyer**[19] 2618 4-9-6 **78**............ RichardHughes 2 73
(Hughie Morrison) *t.k.h: trckd ldng pair: shkn up and nt qckn 2f out: one pce and no imp after* **11/8**[1]

43-0 **5** 1 **Rondeau (GR)**[21] 2571 8-9-5 **77**............ GeorgeBaker 4 70
(Patrick Chamings) *dwlt: t.k.h: hld up towards rr: encouraged along and prog over 1f out: tk 5th nr fin: nvr on terms w ldrs* **20/1**

2-03 **6** 1 **Jungle Bay**[32] 2266 6-9-5 **77**............(p) AdamKirby 5 67
(Jane Chapple-Hyam) *racd freely: led to over 2f out: lost 2nd and wknd 1f out* **6/1**

-600 **7** 1 ¼ **Shifting Star (IRE)**[18] 2657 8-8-10 **73**........(v) WilliamTwiston-Davies(5) 1 60
(John Bridger) *hld up in midfield: rdn and no imp 2f out: wl btn whn nowhere to go ins fnl f* **33/1**

0 **8** ½ **Storm Lightning**[32] 2275 4-9-3 **75**............ TomMcLaughlin 3 62
(Mark Brisbourne) *plld hrd early: trckd ldng pair tl wknd over 1f out: eased ins fnl f* **66/1**

2100 **9** 1 ¾ **Brocklebank (IRE)**[37] 2101 4-9-4 **76**............ JimCrowley 9 57
(Simon Dow) *hld up in last: rdn and no prog over 2f out* **25/1**

210- **10** 3 ¼ **Majestic Zafeen**[277] 6023 4-9-7 **79**............ LukeMorris 10 51
(Alastair Lidderdale) *t.k.h: hld up in midfield: no prog 2f out: sn wknd* **20/1**

000 **11** 3 **Lastkingofscotland (IRE)**[36] 2128 7-9-6 **78**............(b) LiamKeniry 7 42
(Conor Dore) *hld up in last trio: jinked lft wl over 2f out: sn rdn and btn* **50/1**

1m 26.55s (0.55) **Going Correction** +0.075s/f (Slow) **11 Ran SP% 116.9**
Speed ratings (Par 105): **99,98,96,93,92 90,89,88,86,83 79**
toteswingers 1&2 £7.70, 1&3 £3.80, 2&3 £17.60 CSF £69.51 CT £393.51 TOTE £6.40: £1.90, £4.30, £2.40; EX 32.10 Trifecta £102.90 Pool: £893.59 - 6.51 winning units..
Owner Brook Farm Bloodstock **Bred** Glashare House Stud **Trained** Kingsclere, Hants

FOCUS
A very competitive handicap with only 6lb covering the entire field on the ratings but they finished well strung out.

3216 WINNERS ARE WELCOME AT BETDAQ FILLIES' H'CAP 7f (P)
9:10 (9:10) (Class 5) (0-70,70) 3-Y-O **£2,587** (£770; £384; £192) **Stalls** Low

Form RPR

3-54 **1** **Fiducia**[43] 1903 3-8-13 **62**............ RichardHughes 1 69
(Simon Dow) *hld up in midfield: prog 2f out: chsd ldr ins fnl f: hrd rdn and upsides nr fin: led post* **6/1**[2]

21-1 **2** nse **Miss Avonbridge (IRE)**[13] 2806 3-9-6 **69**............ StephenCraine 9 76
(Tom Dascombe) *trckd ldr after 1f: led 2f out: drvn and hrd pressed ins fnl f: hdd post* **15/8**[1]

532 **3** 3 **Clary (IRE)**[33] 2215 3-9-3 **66**............ AdamKirby 3 65
(James Unett) *t.k.h early: hld up in 5th: prog 2f out: drvn to chse ldr briefly 1f out: one pce after* **6/1**[2]

00-3 **4** 1 ¾ **Olympic Jule**[13] 2806 3-9-7 **70**............ CathyGannon 5 64
(Harry Dunlop) *trckd ldng trio: moved up to try to chal over 1f out: fdd fnl f* **8/1**[3]

5-55 **5** nk **Spicy (IRE)**[21] 2572 3-8-10 **64**............(b) RobertTart(5) 10 57
(Marco Botti) *dwlt: hld up in last trio: pushed along and prog on inner 2f out: rdn and kpt on same pce fnl f: nvr nrr* **20/1**

5204 **6** 2 **Angels Calling**[9] 2916 3-8-4 **58**............ NicoleNordblad(5) 8 46
(Mrs K Burke) *racd freely: led after 1f: hdd 2f out: wknd fnl f* **25/1**

5-00 **7** 1 ½ **Lady Vermeer**[20] 2597 3-9-4 **67**............¹ JimCrowley 4 51
(Ralph Beckett) *hld up in midfield: shkn up briefly and no prog 2f out: no ch after* **8/1**[3]

2-00 **8** 1 ¼ **Bellitudo (IRE)**[15] 2763 3-9-3 **66**............(p) RyanMoore 11 47
(Marco Botti) *sn in last: detached and rdn 3f out: rdr persisted and passed a few stragglers late on* **10/1**

0444 **9** 2 **Starlight Angel (IRE)**[12] 2829 3-9-5 **68**............ LukeMorris 7 43
(Ronald Harris) *awkward s: t.k.h: hld up in last trio: pushed along 2f out: no prog* **14/1**

-415 **10** 3 ½ **Idle Curiosity (IRE)**[51] 1710 3-8-1 **55**............ NathanAlison(5) 6 21
(Jim Boyle) *nvr bttr than midfield: drvn over 2f out: sn btn* **16/1**

306- **11** 1 **Cio Cio San (IRE)**[292] 5532 3-9-2 **65**............ JimmyQuinn 2 28
(Bill Turner) *led 1f: prom tl wknd qckly over 2f out* **33/1**

1m 26.8s (0.80) **Going Correction** +0.075s/f (Slow) **11 Ran SP% 118.8**
Speed ratings (Par 96): **98,97,94,92,92 89,88,86,84,80 79**
toteswingers 1&2 £1.90, 1&3 £4.90, 2&3 £3.50 CSF £17.34 CT £73.81 TOTE £6.00: £2.20, £1.50, £2.70; EX 17.60 Trifecta £75.10 Pool: £778.10 - 7.76 winning units..
Owner Paul G Jacobs **Bred** Aldridge Racing Partnership **Trained** Epsom, Surrey

FOCUS
This modest 3yo fillies' handicap was run a quarter of a second slower than the previous contest but it produced a really close finish.
T/Plt: £5.90 to a £1 stake. Pool: £57,658.55 - 7,084.09 winning units T/Qpdt: £4.40 to a £1 stake. Pool: £4,480.10 - 740.35 winning units JN

2962 YARMOUTH (L-H)
Wednesday, June 12

OFFICIAL GOING: Good to firm (7.5)
Wind: Fresh; across Weather: Cloudy with sunny spells

3217 BETVICTOR ROYAL ASCOT MONEY BACK MAIDEN AUCTION STKS 5f 43y
2:10 (2:10) (Class 5) 2-Y-O **£2,587** (£770; £384; £192) **Stalls** Centre

Form RPR

1 **Peter Mac (IRE)** 2-8-11 0............ LeeTopliss(3) 3 85+
(Richard Fahey) *chsd ldrs: rdn over 1f out: r.o to ld wl ins fnl f* **10/3**[2]

3 **2** ¾ **Hay Chewed (IRE)**[16] 2712 2-8-8 0............ RobertHavlin 6 76
(Peter Chapple-Hyam) *trckd ldr: plld hrd: led over 1f out: sn edgd rt: rdn and hdd wl ins fnl f* **8/13**[1]

3 5 **Hatti (IRE)** 2-8-1 0............ RyanPowell(3) 5 54+
(John Ryan) *dwlt: hdwy over 3f out: rdn over 1f out: styd on same pce fnl f* **33/1**

450 **4** 6 **Anfield**[15] 2740 2-8-5 0............ LiamJones 1 33
(Mick Quinn) *led: rdn and hdd over 1f out: wknd fnl f* **50/1**

5 ½ **Witchy Woman** 2-8-2 0............ DarrenEgan(3) 4 32
(Mrs K Burke) *sn pushed along towards rr: rdn and wknd over 1f out* **7/1**[3]

0 **6** 3 ½ **Anya's Angel**[15] 2744 2-8-8 0............ MartinLane 2 22
(David Simcock) *s.i.s: hld up: rdn 1/2-way: wknd wl over 1f out* **14/1**

1m 3.36s (0.66) **Going Correction** +0.05s/f (Good) **6 Ran SP% 109.1**
Speed ratings (Par 93): **96,94,86,77,76 70**
toteswingers 1&2 £1.30, 1&3 £7.20, 2&3 £4.10 CSF £5.40 TOTE £4.30: £1.70, £1.10; EX 5.60 Trifecta £55.40 Pool: £1,774.24 - 24.00 winning units..
Owner Middleham Park Racing LXX **Bred** Tally-Ho Stud **Trained** Musley Bank, N Yorks

FOCUS
Only a couple could be seriously considered for this juvenile contest. Ordinary form, but a nice start from the winner.

3218 BETVICTOR NO LOSE HUGHES MONEY BACK H'CAP 1m 1f
2:40 (2:40) (Class 5) (0-75,78) 4-Y-0+ **£2,587** (£770; £384; £192) **Stalls** Low

Form RPR

5414 **1** **Silver Alliance**[22] 2532 5-8-10 **69**............(p) ShelleyBirkett(7) 2 81
(Julia Feilden) *hld up: hdwy over 3f out: nt clr run over 2f out: sn swtchd rt: led over 1f out: r.o wl* **10/1**

0-01 **2** 3 ¾ **Legendary**[7] 2981 4-9-12 **78** 6ex............(p) WilliamBuick 1 82
(Ed Vaughan) *chsd ldr over 3f: remained handy: rdn and ev ch over 1f out: styd on same pce ins fnl f* **5/6**[1]

-061 **3** 5 **My Guardian Angel**[8] 2966 4-9-5 **71** 6ex............ NeilCallan 4 64
(Mark H Tompkins) *prom: chsd ldr over 5f out: rdn and ev ch fr over 2f tl over 1f out: wknd ins fnl f* **6/1**[3]

6224 **4** 1 **Syncopate**[13] 2808 4-9-6 **72**............ FergusSweeney 6 63
(Pam Sly) *led: rdn over 2f out: hdd over 1f out: wknd fnl f* **11/2**[2]

3643 **5** ¾ **Standing Strong (IRE)**[8] 2966 5-8-10 **62**............(b) RobertHavlin 3 51
(Zoe Davison) *hld up: rdn over 2f out: wknd over 1f out* **12/1**

3230 **6** 5 **Brown Pete (IRE)**[6] 3022 5-9-7 **73**............ MartinHarley 7 51
(Violet M Jordan) *prom: pushed along over 3f out: wknd over 1f out* **10/1**

1m 53.32s (-2.48) **Going Correction** -0.175s/f (Firm) **6 Ran SP% 110.1**
Speed ratings (Par 103): **104,100,96,95,94 90**
toteswingers 1&2 £3.00, 1&3 £6.60, 2&3 £1.70 CSF £18.34 TOTE £6.30: £3.40, £2.00; EX 28.70 Trifecta £104.80 Pool: £2,071.77 - 14.81 winning units..
Owner In It To Win Partnership **Bred** Peter Harris **Trained** Exning, Suffolk

3219 DOWNLOAD THE BETVICTOR APP APPRENTICE (S) STKS 1m 1f
3:10 (3:10) (Class 6) 3-Y-O £1,940 (£577; £288; £144) Stalls Low

Form RPR
2305 1 **Handsome Stranger (IRE)**[6] 3014 3-8-7 56.............(v) NoelGarbutt(5) 1 64
(David Evans) *a.p: chsd ldr over 2f out: led over 1f out: sn clr: easily* **3/1**[2]
3621 2 10 **Claude Greenwood**[15] 2737 3-8-13 61..........................(b) NedCurtis(5) 2 48
(Roger Curtis) *chsd ldrs: lft in ld 5f out: rdn and hung rt over 2f out: hdd over 1f out: wknd fnl f* **7/2**[3]
65-0 3 nk **Planchette**[15] 2762 3-8-2 49.. IanBurns(5) 6 36
(Jane Chapple-Hyam) *s.i.s: hld up: styd on fr over 1f out: nvr on terms* **12/1**
43-0 4 3 **Unidexter (IRE)**[13] 2800 3-8-5 50.................................. DanielCremin(7) 8 35
(Mick Channon) *s.s: hdwy over 5f out: chsd ldr 4f out: rdn over 2f out: wknd over 1f out* **7/1**
25-4 5 16 **Spanish Art**[13] 2786 3-8-9 64.......................................(b[1]) RobertTart(3) 7
(Gay Kelleway) *led 1f: chsd ldrs: rdn over 3f out: sn wknd* **2/1**[1]
00-0 6 1 3/4 **Windsor Rose (IRE)**[46] 1842 3-8-13 44.............................. RyanClark 4
(Mark Brisbourne) *plld hrd: led after 1f: hung rt over 5f out: sn hdd: rdn and wknd 3f out* **33/1**
6-04 7 13 **Paige Flyer**[132] 447 3-8-7 50.. RossAtkinson 9
(Mick Quinn) *prom tl rdn and wknd over 3f out: t.o* **33/1**
4056 8 3/4 **Abanoas (USA)**[6] 3016 3-8-2 47.......................................(b) ShelleyBirkett(5) 3
(Alan Coogan) *s.i.s: a in rr: wknd 4f out: t.o* **11/1**

1m 55.1s (-0.70) **Going Correction** -0.175s/f (Firm) **8 Ran SP% 115.0**
Speed ratings (Par 97): **96,87,86,84,69 68,56,56**
toteswingers 1&2 £3.00, 1&3 £8.10, 2&3 £5.50 CSF £14.07 TOTE £4.30: £1.20, £2.10, £2.60; EX 14.30 Trifecta £163.70 Pool: £1,711.53 - 7.83 winning units..The winner was bought in for 5,000 guineas. There were no claims.
Owner P D Evans **Bred** Gerrardstown House Stud **Trained** Pandy, Monmouths
■ Stewards' Enquiry : Ian Burns two-day ban: use of whip (26-27 June)

FOCUS
A desperately weak race even accounting for the grade, but it was run at a fair pace throughout.

3220 BETVICTOR.COM H'CAP 6f 3y
3:40 (3:41) (Class 3) (0-90,90) 3-Y-O+ £7,246 (£2,168; £1,084; £542; £270) Stalls Centre

Form RPR
361- 1 **Out Do**[231] 7322 4-9-5 81.. WilliamBuick 6 95+
(Luca Cumani) *trckd ldrs: led over 1f out: shkn up ins fnl f: r.o wl: readily* **5/2**[1]
4-50 2 3 **Piazza San Pietro**[37] 2097 7-9-6 82..................................(p) NeilCallan 5 86
(Zoe Davison) *hld up: hdwy over 1f out: sn rdn: styd on* **16/1**
0-00 3 shd **Balty Boys (IRE)**[33] 2210 4-9-9 85..........................(b[1]) FergusSweeney 7 89
(Jamie Osborne) *sn led: rdn and hdd over 1f out: edgd lft: styd on same pce fnl f* **11/1**
0422 4 hd **Titus Gent**[11] 2868 8-9-8 87.. RyanClark(3) 3 90
(Jeremy Gask) *chsd ldrs: rdn and ev ch over 1f out: no ex ins fnl f* **8/1**
-403 5 1 1/2 **Arctic Lynx (IRE)**[16] 2724 6-9-5 81..................................(p) LiamJones 10 80
(Robert Cowell) *chsd ldrs: rdn and ev ch over 1f out: no ex fnl f* **7/1**[3]
2505 6 3/4 **Frognal (IRE)**[40] 1985 7-8-9 71......................................(bt) MartinHarley 2 69
(Violet M Jordan) *hld up: hdwy and hmpd over 1f out: nt trble ldrs* **25/1**
1113 7 1 **Tarooq (USA)**[88] 1032 7-10-0 90......................................(t) SebSanders 8 83
(Stuart Williams) *hld up: swtchd rt over 2f out: rdn over 1f out: no ex fnl f* **7/2**[2]
0006 8 2 1/4 **Woolfall Sovereign (IRE)**[33] 2227 7-8-6 71 oh1.......... RyanPowell(3) 1 57
(George Margarson) *chsd ldrs: rdn over 2f out: wknd fnl f* **14/1**
0304 9 1 1/4 **Equitania**[33] 2213 3-8-13 88... RobertTart(5) 4 70
(Alan Bailey) *plld hrd and prom: rdn over 2f out: wknd over 1f out* **17/2**
0260 10 31 **Red Aggressor (IRE)**[51] 1720 4-9-6 82.............................. MartinLane 9
(Clive Brittain) *hld up: rdn over 2f out: wknd wl over 1f out: t.o* **33/1**

1m 13.62s (-0.78) **Going Correction** +0.05s/f (Good)
WFA 3 from 4yo+ 8lb **10 Ran SP% 112.6**
Speed ratings (Par 107): **107,103,102,102,100 99,98,95,93,52**
toteswingers 1&2 £9.30, 1&3 £5.60, 2&3 £23.60 CSF £43.34 CT £369.32 TOTE £2.70: £1.60, £4.20, £4.50; EX 48.20 Trifecta £301.80 Pool: £2,994.34 - 7.44 winning units..
Owner Leonidas Marinopoulos **Bred** Equibreed S R L **Trained** Newmarket, Suffolk

FOCUS
A decent turnout for the feature sprint handicap.

3221 BETVICTOR ROYAL ASCOT NO LOSE HUGHES H'CAP 6f 3y
4:10 (4:11) (Class 6) (0-65,65) 3-Y-O £1,940 (£577; £288; £144) Stalls Centre

Form RPR
6003 1 **Black Dave (IRE)**[5] 3050 3-9-4 62.................................... MartinHarley 2 69
(David Evans) *hld up: hdwy over 2f out: rdn to ld ins fnl f: edgd rt: r.o* **4/1**[2]
656 2 1 1/4 **Bosham**[11] 2872 3-9-2 65... RobertTart(5) 5 68
(William Jarvis) *led: rdn and hdd over 1f out: ev ch ins fnl f: styd on same pce* **4/1**[2]
0-42 3 1/2 **Oh So Sassy**[25] 2437 3-9-2 60... SebSanders 3 61
(Chris Wall) *trckd ldrs: rdn and ev ch fr over 1f out tl no ex wl ins fnl f* **11/10**[1]
-640 4 3/4 **Green Monkey**[8] 2962 3-9-1 59... MartinLane 4 58
(James Fanshawe) *chsd ldr tl led over 1f out: rdn and hdd ins fnl f: no ex* **20/1**
-500 5 6 **Lively Little Lady**[36] 2129 3-8-3 50.............................. DarrenEgan(3) 6 30
(Tim Pitt) *chsd ldrs: rdn over 2f out: wknd over 1f out* **50/1**
4-40 6 3/4 **Trymyluck**[21] 2566 3-8-3 50.......................................(b[1]) SimonPearce(3) 9 27
(Pam Sly) *s.i.s: sn pushed along in rr: bhd and drvn along wl over 3f out: nvr nrr* **18/1**
53-3 7 1/2 **Done Dreaming (IRE)**[21] 2581 3-9-3 64......................... LeeToplis(3) 1 40
(Richard Fahey) *prom: rdn over 2f out: edgd lft and wknd over 1f out* **12/1**[3]
40-5 8 1 1/4 **Speedfit Boy (IRE)**[50] 1750 3-9-4 65........................... RyanPowell(3) 8 37
(George Margarson) *hld up: rdn over 2f out: wknd over 1f out* **16/1**

1m 14.78s (0.38) **Going Correction** +0.05s/f (Good) **8 Ran SP% 113.2**
Speed ratings (Par 97): **99,97,96,95,87 86,86,84**
toteswingers 1&2 £2.20, 1&3 £2.20, 2&3 £2.10 CSF £19.94 CT £27.95 TOTE £5.00: £1.90, £1.50, £1.02; EX 16.60 Trifecta £44.70 Pool: £3,403.74 - 57.01 winning units..
Owner Mrs E Evans & J Smith **Bred** Richard Frayne **Trained** Pandy, Monmouths

FOCUS
Only a modest handicap.

3222 BETVICTOR CASINO ON YOUR MOBILE MAIDEN H'CAP 1m 3y
4:40 (4:42) (Class 6) (0-65,65) 4-Y-O+ £1,940 (£577; £288; £144) Stalls Centre

Form RPR
05-3 1 **Jamaica Grande**[19] 2637 5-8-4 48................................ WilliamCarson 7 57
(Dave Morris) *hld up: hdwy over 3f out: led over 2f out: rdn out* **25/1**
-040 2 2 3/4 **Muzhil (IRE)**[23] 2511 4-9-2 60.. NeilCallan 3 63
(Clive Brittain) *a.p: chsd ldr 5f out: rdn and ev ch over 2f out: styd on same pce fnl f* **4/1**[3]
2402 3 6 **Vastly (USA)**[13] 2807 4-9-0 65.................................... ShelleyBirkett(7) 2 54
(Julia Feilden) *chsd ldr 3f: remained handy: rdn and ev ch over 2f out: wknd fnl f* **15/8**[1]
0-62 4 1 **Essell**[8] 2966 4-8-6 50.. MartinLane 6 37
(Mick Channon) *chsd ldrs: rdn over 3f out: styd on same pce fr over 2f out* **7/2**[2]
5643 5 8 **Bit Windy**[61] 1520 4-8-4 48.. SaleemGolam 4 17
(Chris Dwyer) *led over 5f: wknd over 1f out* **6/1**
006 6 16 **This Is Me**[15] 2754 5-9-5 63.. SebSanders 8
(Don Cantillon) *s.s: a in rr: lost tch fr 1/2-way: t.o* **4/1**[3]

1m 42.7s (2.10) **Going Correction** +0.05s/f (Good) **6 Ran SP% 115.1**
Speed ratings (Par 101): **91,88,82,81,73 57**
toteswingers 1&2 £5.80, 1&3 £4.40, 2&3 £2.10 CSF £122.73 CT £286.21 TOTE £20.20: £4.80, £2.60; EX 103.70 Trifecta £440.60 Pool: £2,541.91 - 4.32 winning units..
Owner Stuart Wood **Bred** Mrs J A Gawthorpe **Trained** Baxter's Green, Suffolk

FOCUS
A weak handicap and a big upset.

3223 ROYAL ASCOT MONEY BACK AT BETVICTOR.COM FILLIES' H'CAP 6f 3y
5:10 (5:11) (Class 5) (0-75,75) 4-Y-O+ £2,587 (£770; £384; £192) Stalls Centre

Form RPR
-022 1 **Dancheur (IRE)**[23] 2513 4-9-7 75...................................... MartinHarley 5 83
(Mrs K Burke) *mde all: rdn over 1f out: styd on* **11/8**[1]
-350 2 3/4 **Big Wave (IRE)**[14] 2781 5-8-12 66.................................. RobertHavlin 8 72
(Alison Hutchinson) *rrd s: hld up: hdwy over 1f out: sn rdn: styd on* **14/1**
0433 3 nk **My Own Way Home**[4] 3111 5-8-2 56..................................(v) MartinLane 2 61
(David Evans) *hld up: hdwy 1/2-way: rdn over 1f out: styd on* **9/2**[2]
20-0 4 hd **Oh So Spicy**[25] 2441 6-9-4 72.. SebSanders 6 76
(Chris Wall) *trckd ldrs: rdn and hung lft over 1f out: styd on* **9/2**[2]
630- 5 1/2 **Isola Verde**[209] 7725 4-8-12 66...[1] WilliamBuick 4 68
(James Fanshawe) *chsd wnr: rdn over 1f out: unable qck wl ins fnl f* **13/2**[3]
45-3 6 9 **Sarah Berry**[19] 2643 4-8-6 60.. SaleemGolam 1 34
(Chris Dwyer) *prom: rdn over 2f out: wknd fnl f* **16/1**
0/0- 7 13 **Electrickery**[307] 5000 4-8-2 56 oh4.......................................[1] LiamJones 3
(Mark Buckley) *chsd ldrs tl wknd over 2f out* **50/1**
2431 8 nk **Artful Lady (IRE)**[32] 2281 4-8-1 58.............................. RyanPowell(3) 9
(George Margarson) *hld up: wknd 1/2-way* **11/1**

1m 14.22s (-0.18) **Going Correction** +0.05s/f (Good) **8 Ran SP% 114.6**
Speed ratings (Par 100): **103,102,101,101,100 88,71,70**
toteswingers 1&2 £4.90, 1&3 £2.70, 2&3 £9.50 CSF £23.68 CT £72.15 TOTE £2.60: £1.10, £3.90, £1.20; EX 24.20 Trifecta £186.60 Pool: £2,431.85 - 9.77 winning units..
Owner Mark James & Mrs Elaine Burke **Bred** A F O'Callaghan **Trained** Middleham Moor, N Yorks

FOCUS
There was no shortage of pace on in this fillies' handicap.
T/Plt: No Placepot; technical issues with the Tote. T/Qpdt: No Quadpot; technical issues with the Tote. CR

3224 - 3230a (Foreign Racing) - See Raceform Interactive

3204 HAYDOCK (L-H)
Thursday, June 13

OFFICIAL GOING: Good to soft (7.9)
Wind: Fresh, against Weather: Cloudy

3231 BETDAQ HAYDOCK PARK APPRENTICE TRAINING SERIES H'CAP (PART OF THE RACING EXCELLENCE INITIATIVE) 1m 3f 200y
6:20 (6:20) (Class 5) (0-70,67) 4-Y-O+ £2,587 (£770; £384; £192) Stalls Centre

Form RPR
0463 1 **Tenhoo**[20] 2629 7-9-11 66.. JasonHart 7 75
(Eric Alston) *hld up: hdwy 3f out: smoothly moved upsides to chal 2f out: pushed along over 1f out: r.o to nose ahd cl home* **11/4**[1]
-254 2 hd **Zenafire**[21] 2594 4-8-13 57.. JackDuern(3) 9 66
(Andrew Hollinshead) *in tch: impr to ld 2f out: rdn whn strly pressed over 1f out: r.o for press: hdd narrowly cl home* **13/2**[3]
0-30 3 4 1/2 **Transfer**[13] 2828 8-8-8 52.. JacobButterfield(3) 6 54
(Richard Price) *in rr: niggled along 6f out: u.p after: rdn over 2f out: hung lft and stdy hdwy over 1f out: kpt on to take 3rd wl ins fnl f: nt trble front pair* **16/1**
-020 4 4 1/2 **Silver Tigress**[26] 2435 5-9-1 61.................................. ConnorBeasley(5) 3 56
(George Moore) *midfield: hdwy 3f out: ev ch over 2f out: rdn and outpcd by front pair over 1f out: no ex and lost 3rd wl ins fnl f* **11/4**[1]
0110 5 1 3/4 **Jordaura**[8] 2976 7-9-7 67.. JordanHibberd(5) 8 59
(Alan Berry) *hld up in rr: pushed along over 1f out: no imp* **9/1**
00-5 6 3 **Excellent News (IRE)**[4] 3133 4-8-9 50......................... ShirleyTeasdale 1 37
(Tony Forbes) *led: hdd 9f out: trckd ldrs after: effrt over 2f out: wknd over 1f out* **40/1**
0402 7 1 3/4 **Blazing Desert**[4] 3133 9-9-7 65................................ ThomasGarner(3) 10 49
(William Kinsey) *prom: led over 3f out: hdd 2f out: rdn and wknd over 1f out* **14/1**
0603 8 18 **Light The City (IRE)**[9] 2961 6-8-10 54...................... GeorgeChaloner(3) 2 9
(Ruth Carr) *prom tl rdn and wknd over 3f out* **5/1**[2]
0005 9 31 **Elizabeth Coffee (IRE)**[8] 2974 5-9-5 60........................ JustinNewman 5
(John Weymes) *prom: led 9f out: rdn and hdd over 3f out: wknd over 2f out: t.o* **33/1**

2m 35.16s (1.36) **Going Correction** -0.05s/f (Good) **9 Ran SP% 111.3**
Speed ratings (Par 103): **93,92,89,86,85 83,82,70,49**
Tote Swingers: 1&2 £1.30, 1&3 £18.60, 2&3 £19.60 CSF £19.99 CT £228.10 TOTE £3.90: £1.40, £2.50, £4.80; EX 19.70 Trifecta £186.70 Pool: £1,044.58 - 4.19 winning units..
Owner Edges Farm Racing Stables Ltd **Bred** A G Antoniades **Trained** Longton, Lancs

FOCUS
All races were run on the inner home straight and the action began with a modest apprentice handicap, with a slightly reduced distance of 1m 3f 200y.

3232 SILK MILL RIPPONDEN WELCOMES YOU H'CAP 1m 2f 95y
6:50 (6:51) (Class 5) (0-70,70) 3-Y-O £2,587 (£770; £384; £192) Stalls Centre

Form RPR
03-1 **1** **Tajheez (IRE)**[36] 2156 3-9-7 **69**.. PaulHanagan 14 76+
(Roger Varian) *hld up in midfield: hdwy over 3f out: rdn to ld over 1f out: edgd lft ins fnl f: kpt on towards fin* **15/8**[1]
1314 **2** *1* **Astrum**[16] 2742 3-9-2 **64**.. PJMcDonald 12 69
(Rod Millman) *in tch: impr over 3f out: led 2f out: rdn and hdd over 1f out: intimidated by wnr ins fnl f whn stl chalng: hld towards fin* **8/1**
4-43 **3** *3/4* **Rex Whistler (IRE)**[24] 2506 3-9-3 **65**.. PaulMulrennan 3 69
(Julie Camacho) *hld up: rdn and hdwy over 2 out: lugged lft and wnt 3rd over 1f out: styd on towards fin: nt quite get to front two* **11/2**[3]
60-0 **4** *2* **Marlborough House**[43] 1926 3-9-0 **62**.. RichardKingscote 4 62
(James Given) *midfield: rdn and hdwy over 1f out: styd on ins fnl f: nt rch ldrs* **10/1**
0-05 **5** *5* **Three Glasses (IRE)**[15] 2765 3-9-6 **68**.. DavidAllan 2 59
(Tim Easterby) *in tch: effrt and ch over 2f out: wknd over 1f out* **16/1**
0-60 **6** *shd* **Noble Bacchus (IRE)**[17] 2716 3-8-4 **52**..(b[1]) RoystonFfrench 5 42
(Tom Dascombe) *s.i.s: bhd: u.p over 3f out: styd on fnl f: nvr able to trble ldrs* **16/1**
34-6 **7** *7* **Bahamamay**[62] 1522 3-9-2 **67**.. LeeTopliss(3) 10 44
(Richard Fahey) *hld up: pushed along 5f out: rdn and hung lft over 2f out: midfield and no imp over 1f out* **16/1**
0151 **8** *1* **Baltic Prince (IRE)**[10] 2916 3-8-12 **65** 6ex.. JasonHart(5) 8 40
(Paul Green) *racd keenly: chsd ldrs: rdn over 3f out: ev ch over 2f out: wknd over 1f out* **25/1**
0041 **9** *1 1/2* **Zaitsev (IRE)**[9] 2957 3-9-5 **67** 6ex.. ShaneKelly 11 39
(Ollie Pears) *led: kicked on over 3f out: rdn and hdd 2f out: wknd over 1f out* **9/2**[2]
1350 **10** *1/2* **Glenreef**[21] 2586 3-9-3 **65**.. JoeFanning 6 36
(Mark Johnston) *bhd: u.p over 2f out: nvr on terms* **22/1**
0-00 **11** *3 1/2* **Erica Starprincess**[24] 2501 3-8-2 **50**.. AndrewMullen 1 15
(George Moore) *hld up: struggling 4f out: nvr on terms* **100/1**
00-0 **12** *1 1/2* **Ella Motiva (IRE)**[33] 2274 3-8-7 **55**.. DuranFentiman 7 17
(Mark Brisbourne) *prom: rdn over 4f out: wknd over 3f out* **66/1**
410 **13** *10* **Hot Right Now**[36] 2156 3-8-10 **63**..(v[1]) JackDuern(5) 9 6
(Mrs K Burke) *chsd ldr tl rdn over 3f out: wknd over 2f out* **25/1**

2m 15.55s (0.05) **Going Correction** -0.05s/f (Good) 13 Ran SP% **120.7**
Speed ratings (Par 99): **97,96,95,94,90 89,84,83,82,81 79,77,69**
Tote Swingers: 1&2 £4.80, 1&3 £4.00, 2&3 £4.40 CSF £16.66 CT £74.20 TOTE £2.50: £1.30, £3.20, £2.40; EX 19.30 Trifecta £125.10 Pool: £693.97 - 4.15 winning units..
Owner Hamdan Al Maktoum **Bred** Shadwell Estate Company Limited **Trained** Newmarket, Suffolk
FOCUS
No stars here, but on paper a competitive event nonetheless. They raced centre-track in the home straight.

3233 SILK MILL BAR RIPPONDEN MAIDEN STKS (C&G) 7f
7:20 (7:20) (Class 5) 2-Y-O £2,587 (£770; £384; £192) Stalls Low

Form RPR
1 **Washaar (IRE)** 2-9-0 0.. PaulHanagan 6 87+
(Richard Hannon) *chsd ldrs: led 2f out: rdn and edgd lft over 1f out: r.o and drew away fnl 150yds* **5/2**[2]
0 **2** *2 1/4* **Sir Jack Layden**[19] 2670 2-9-0 0.. PJMcDonald 1 81
(David Brown) *chsd ldrs: rdn and ev ch over 2f out: wnt 2nd over 1f out and trying to chal: sn intimidated by wnr: no imp fnl 150yds* **9/4**[1]
30 **3** *6* **Tiger Twenty Two**[19] 2670 2-8-11 0.. LeeTopliss(3) 5 65
(Richard Fahey) *chsd ldr: rdn and ev ch over 2f out: one pce over 1f out* **5/1**[3]
6 **4** *1/2* **Fire Fighting (IRE)**[23] 2553 2-9-0 0.. JoeFanning 3 64
(Mark Johnston) *led: hdd 2f out: u.p and no ex over 1f out* **11/1**
5 *nk* **The Kid** 2-9-0 0.. RichardKingscote 2 63
(Tom Dascombe) *midfield: pushed along over 1f out: kpt on ins fnl f: no imp* **6/1**
0 **6** *5* **Network Perfection**[21] 2591 2-9-0 0.. PaulMulrennan 4 50+
(Michael Easterby) *in rr: u.p over 1f out: no imp on ldrs: wl ins fnl f* **100/1**
7 *2* **Broadcaster (IRE)** 2-9-0 0.. SeanLevey 8 45
(Ed McMahon) *hld up: pushed along over 1f out: no impression: wl ins fnl f* **14/1**
8 *7* **Chinese Jade** 2-9-0 0.. ChrisCatlin 7 27
(Sir Mark Prescott Bt) *s.i.s: v green: in rr: u.p over 3f out: wl outpcd over 1f out* **16/1**

1m 30.39s (-0.31) **Going Correction** -0.05s/f (Good) 8 Ran SP% **112.2**
Speed ratings (Par 93): **99,96,89,89,88 82,80,72**
Tote Swingers: 1&2 £2.80, 1&3 £4.40, 2&3 £1.10 CSF £8.18 TOTE £3.80: £1.70, £1.80, £1.10; EX 9.00 Trifecta £21.40 Pool: £733.82 - 25.63 winning units..
Owner Hamdan Al Maktoum **Bred** Gerard Corry & Cristian Healy **Trained** East Everleigh, Wilts
FOCUS
An interesting juvenile maiden featuring a clutch of runners from high-profile stables.

3234 STEPHANIE RUNS RIPPONDEN'S SILK MILL H'CAP 7f
7:50 (7:51) (Class 4) (0-85,84) 3-Y-O £5,175 (£1,540; £769; £384) Stalls Low

Form RPR
1-21 **1** **Equity Risk (USA)**[17] 2708 3-9-7 **84**.. NeilCallan 1 95
(Kevin Ryan) *chsd ldrs: rdn over 2f out: sn chalng: r.o for press ins fnl f: nosed ahd cl home* **9/4**[2]
0-20 **2** *hd* **Beach Club**[33] 2285 3-9-7 **84**.. SeanLevey 4 94
(David Brown) *led: rdn over 2f out: sn hrd pressed: hdd narrowly cl home* **20/1**
0-32 **3** *1 1/4* **Majestic Moon (IRE)**[16] 2738 3-9-3 **80**..(b) PaulHanagan 3 87
(Richard Fahey) *s.i.s: t.k.h: hld up: hdwy over 2f out: prog to take 3rd fnl 100yds: styd on towards fin: nvr able to chal front pair* **3/1**[3]
4-11 **4** *1 1/2* **Lord Ashley (IRE)**[20] 2626 3-9-7 **84**.. RichardKingscote 5 87
(Tom Dascombe) *chsd ldr: rdn and ev ch 2f out: stl ch over 1f out: one pce fnl 100yds* **15/8**[1]
10-0 **5** *7* **Mitchell**[21] 2593 3-8-7 **73**.. RaulDaSilva(3) 9 57
(David Thompson) *chsd ldrs: u.p over 4f out: wknd over 2f out* **40/1**
-360 **6** *1 1/2* **Opt Out**[35] 2190 3-8-13 **76**.. PJMcDonald 8 56
(Alistair Whillans) *hld up: outpcd over 1f out: nvr a threat* **50/1**
-500 **7** *1 1/4* **Delores Rocket**[21] 2593 3-8-7 **77**.. PaulMcGiff(7) 7 53
(Kevin Ryan) *hld up in rr: pushed along 3f out: no imp on ldrs: wl btn fnl f* **25/1**
1224 **8** *3 1/2* **Lightning Launch (IRE)**[26] 2439 3-9-3 **80**..(v) MartinHarley 2 47
(Mick Channon) *midfield: hdwy over 3f out: chalng fr 2f out: wknd fnl 150yds* **9/1**

1m 29.9s (-0.80) **Going Correction** -0.05s/f (Good) 8 Ran SP% **113.6**
Speed ratings (Par 101): **102,101,100,98,90 88,87,83**
Tote Swingers: 1&2 £6.60, 1&3 £1.10, 2&3 £7.10 CSF £45.91 CT £136.71 TOTE £3.20: £1.10, £3.90, £1.20; EX 38.20 Trifecta £166.90 Pool: £1,056.64 - 4.74 winning units..
Owner Clipper Logistics **Bred** Crosshaven Bloodstock Et Al **Trained** Hambleton, N Yorks
FOCUS
A fair handicap, with a top weight rated 84, and it looked more open than the market suggested.

3235 JOHN AND JOHANNA ARE GETTING MARRIED H'CAP 1m
8:20 (8:20) (Class 3) (0-95,95) 3-Y-O £8,086 (£2,406; £1,202; £601) Stalls Low

Form RPR
122 **1** **Henry The Aviator (USA)**[7] 3028 3-8-2 **76**.. JoeFanning 4 90+
(Mark Johnston) *dwlt: hld up in rr: hdwy 3f out: led wl over 1f out: drew clr and edgd lft ins fnl f: comf* **13/8**[1]
3-33 **2** *3 1/2* **Evangelist**[24] 2495 3-8-2 **76**.. AndreaAtzeni 6 82+
(Sir Michael Stoute) *a.p: led over 2f out: sn hung lft: hdd wl over 1f out: unable to go w wnr and one pce ins fnl f* **5/2**[2]
5250 **3** *2 1/4* **Luhaif**[12] 2857 3-9-7 **95**..(v) MartinHarley 7 96?
(Mick Channon) *led: hdd over 2f out: outpcd over 1f out: kpt on ins fnl f wout troubling front two* **14/1**
-310 **4** *1 1/4* **World Record (IRE)**[31] 2322 3-8-4 **78**.. JamesSullivan 5 76
(Paul Green) *chsd ldrs: rdn and outpcd over 2f out: n.d after* **25/1**
4-04 **5** *5* **Etijaah (USA)**[21] 2603 3-8-6 **80**.. PaulHanagan 2 66
(Brian Meehan) *chsd ldr to 4f out: rdn and outpcd over 2f out: hung lft over 1f out whn no imp on ldrs: wknd ins fnl f* **3/1**[3]
-543 **6** *2 1/2* **Lady Of The House (IRE)**[15] 2783 3-8-9 **83**.. NeilCallan 3 64
(Kevin Ryan) *hld up: impr 4f out: effrt to chal over 2f out: wknd over 1f out* **10/1**

1m 44.09s (0.39) **Going Correction** -0.05s/f (Good) 6 Ran SP% **111.3**
Speed ratings (Par 103): **96,92,90,89,84 81**
Tote Swingers: 1&2 £1.70, 1&3 £5.80, 2&3 £4.10 CSF £5.81 TOTE £2.40: £1.20, £2.70; EX 5.50 Trifecta £24.80 Pool: £847.96 - 4.74 winning units..
Owner Crone Stud Farms Ltd **Bred** Summer Wind Farm **Trained** Middleham Moor, N Yorks
FOCUS
A decent handicap with a top weight rated 95.

3236 RIPPONDEN'S SILK MILL FOR GREAT COMPANY H'CAP 5f
8:50 (8:50) (Class 4) (0-80,80) 3-Y-O+ £5,175 (£1,540; £769; £384) Stalls Centre

Form RPR
4504 **1** **Rusty Rocket (IRE)**[26] 2460 4-9-9 **75**.. PaulMulrennan 14 84
(Paul Green) *racd stands' side: a.p: pushed along to ld overall over 1f out: rdn whn pressed ins fnl f: hld on wl cl home: 1st of 5 in gp* **11/2**[2]
6003 **2** *nk* **Sulis Minerva (IRE)**[16] 2745 6-9-1 **70**.. RyanClark(3) 10 78
(Jeremy Gask) *racd stands' side: hld up in rr: effrt over 1f out: prog ins fnl f: r.o cl home: 2nd of 5 in gp* **8/1**
3042 **3** *hd* **Wicked Wench**[16] 2736 4-9-8 **74**..(p) NeilCallan 13 81
(Jeremy Gask) *racd stands' side: chsd ldrs: effrt over 1f out: chalng ins fnl f: no ex fnl strides: 3rd of 5 in gp* **11/2**[2]
-200 **4** *3 3/4* **Cruise Tothelimit (IRE)**[26] 2459 5-10-0 **80**.. PaulHanagan 11 74
(Ian Williams) *racd stands' side: a.p: rdn over 1f out: no ex fnl 100yds: 4th of 5 in gp* **4/1**[1]
51-0 **5** *1* **Diman Waters (IRE)**[42] 1963 6-9-2 **73**.. JasonHart(5) 4 63
(Eric Alston) *racd far side and t.k.h: chsd ldrs: led gp over 1f out: no imp on ldrs ins fnl f: one pce fnl 110yds: 1st of 8 in gp* **11/1**
4312 **6** *3/4* **Bronze Beau**[6] 3069 6-9-11 **77**..(t) JamesSullivan 12 64+
(Kristin Stubbs) *racd stands' side: led overall: pushed along and hdd over 1f out: wknd fnl 150yds: 5th of 5 in gp* **6/1**[3]
0006 **7** *1 1/2* **Beau Mistral (IRE)**[24] 2513 4-9-6 **72**..(v[1]) JoeFanning 2 54
(Paul Green) *racd far-side: chsd ldrs: rdn and ch in gp over 1f out: no ex fnl 75yds: eased whn btn towards fin: 2nd of 8 in gp* **14/1**
0354 **8** *3 1/4* **Song Of Parkes**[2] 3171 6-8-11 **68**.. SladeO'Hara(5) 6 38
(Peter Grayson) *racd far-side: hld up: impr into midfield over 1f out: one pce fnl f: nvr able to chal: 3rd of 8 in gp* **14/1**
1104 **9** *1 1/2* **Chosen One (IRE)**[13] 2832 8-9-0 **66**.. PJMcDonald 1 31
(Ruth Carr) *racd far-side: prom: led gp over 2f out tl hdd over 1f out: wknd ins fnl f: 4th of 8 in gp* **18/1**
-460 **10** *3/4* **Rutterkin (USA)**[12] 2884 5-8-2 **61** oh11.. VictorSantos(7) 9 23
(Richard Ford) *racd far-side: hld up: rdn over 1f out: no imp: 5th of 8 in gp* **66/1**
2-51 **11** *1/2* **Just Like Heaven (IRE)**[10] 2914 4-9-3 **69** 6ex.. DuranFentiman 5 29
(Tim Easterby) *racd far-side: led gp tl hdd over 2f out: rdn and wknd over 1f out: 6th of 8 in gp* **12/1**
13/0 **12** *1 1/4* **Musical Bridge**[16] 2736 7-9-1 **67**.. TomEaves 3 23
(Lisa Williamson) *racd far-side: hld up: rdn over 1f out: no imp: 7th of 8 in gp* **40/1**
3140 **13** *3/4* **Economic Crisis (IRE)**[14] 2797 4-9-8 **74**.. PaddyAspell 7 27
(Alan Berry) *racd far side: hld up: rdn over 1f out: no imp: 8th of 8 in gp* **25/1**

1m 2.3s (1.50) **Going Correction** +0.425s/f (Yiel) 13 Ran SP% **118.6**
Speed ratings (Par 105): **105,104,104,98,96 95,93,87,85,84 83,81,80**
Tote Swingers: 1&2 £14.50, 1&3 £7.60, 2&3 £17.00 CSF £48.10 CT £212.06 TOTE £8.50: £2.90, £3.20, £2.30; EX 58.60 Trifecta £327.00 Pool: £701.90 - 1.60 winning units..
Owner Seven Stars Racing **Bred** Mike Hyde **Trained** Lydiate, Merseyside
FOCUS
A competitive finale in which all but a handful had feasible claims. The field split into two groups on leaving the stalls, with the stands' side contingent taking the first four places.
T/Plt: £18.20 to a £1 stake. Pool: £66,849.28 - 2,674.18 winning tickets T/Qpdt: £6.60 to a £1 stake. Pool: £4,941.85 - 551.40 winning tickets DO

3106 NEWBURY (L-H)
Thursday, June 13

OFFICIAL GOING: Good to firm (good in places; 7.3) changing to good after race 1 (1.50)
Wind: Strong, ahead Weather: Overcast, showers

3237 CROSSLAND MAIDEN FILLIES' STKS (DIV I) 1m 2f 6y
1:50 (1:51) (Class 4) 3-Y-O £4,690 (£1,395; £697; £348) Stalls Low

Form RPR
0-3 **1** **Rosaceous**[10] 2930 3-9-0 0.. SilvestreDeSousa 7 84
(Daniel Kubler) *chsd ldrs: pushed along over 3f out: chsd ldr appr fnl 2f: kpt on u.p to ld last strides* **33/1**

The Form Book Flat, Raceform Ltd, Compton, RG20 6NL.

32-4 **2** *nk* **Muthmera (USA)**[48] 1813 3-9-0 78 DaneO'Neill 3 83
(Roger Varian) *led: pushed along and styd on over 2f out: kpt on fnl f: hdd last strides* **3/1**[2]

00 **3** *½* **Bohemian Dance (IRE)**[34] 2206 3-9-0 0 [1] RyanMoore 13 82
(Sir Michael Stoute) *in rr: pushed along over 2f out: hdwy over 1f out: styd on wl to take 3rd clsng stages: nt quite rch ldng duo* **16/1**

4 *1½* **Bonanza Creek (IRE)** 3-9-0 0 (b[1]) KierenFallon 5 79+
(Luca Cumani) *in rr: pushed along over 3f out: hdwy over 1f out: kpt on fnl f: nt rch ldrs* **8/1**

350- **5** *3¼* **Alnawiyah**[253] 6790 3-9-0 71 FrankieDettori 12 73
(Charles Hills) *in rr: pushed along and hdwy over 2f out: kpt on same pce fnl f* **12/1**

4- **6** *2* **Pearl Street (USA)**[262] 6535 3-9-0 0 JamieSpencer 4 69
(Henry Candy) *chsd ldrs: drvn over 2f out: wknd ins fnl f* **6/1**[3]

02 **7** *¾* **Kenny's Girl (IRE)**[14] 2803 3-9-0 0 MartinDwyer 11 67
(William Muir) *s.i.s: in rr: hdwy fr 2f out: nt rch ldrs* **66/1**

5 **8** *2½* **Phaenomena (IRE)**[14] 2804 3-9-0 0 PatCosgrave 2 62
(Lady Cecil) *in rr: sme hdwy over 2f out: no ex fnl f* **22/1**

02 **9** *7* **Toast Of The Town (IRE)**[34] 2206 3-9-0 0 WilliamBuick 1 48
(John Gosden) *chsd ldrs: pushed along over 3f out: rdn over 2f out and sn btn* **11/8**[1]

6- **10** *1½* **Happy Families**[167] 8262 3-9-0 0 JimCrowley 9 45
(Heather Main) *chsd ldrs tl wknd 2f out* **150/1**

0 **11** *2¼* **A Good Year (IRE)**[45] 1876 3-9-0 0 JamesMcDonald 6 41
(J W Hills) *prom early: bhd fr 1/2-way* **100/1**

12 *5* **Calling** 3-9-0 0 JimmyFortune 10 31
(Brian Meehan) *towards rr most of way* **66/1**

13 *1¼* **Lady Montjeu (IRE)** 3-9-0 0 MartinHarley 8 28
(Alan Jarvis) *s.i.s: a in rr* **80/1**

2m 10.62s (1.82) **Going Correction** +0.20s/f (Good) **13** Ran SP% **119.2**
Speed ratings (Par 98): **100,99,99,98,95 93,93,91,85,84 82,78,77**
toteswingers 1&2 £19.80, 1&3 £31.40, 2&3 £8.00 CSF £129.15 TOTE £50.90: £7.60, £1.30, £4.20; EX 234.00 Trifecta £2585.50 Pool: £3,796.33 - 1.10 winning units..
Owner Mr & Mrs G Middlebrook **Bred** Mr & Mrs G Middlebrook **Trained** Whitsbury, Hants

FOCUS
Rail on Round course moved between 1m and 5f, increasing distances on Round course by 12m. To rest ground for later in the year the Straight course far rail was out 4m with a cut-off at 2.5f. There was a heavy downpour before racing and the ground appeared to be riding slower than the official description, with Jimmy Fortune describing it as "good to soft". The first division of what was quite an ordinary fillies' maiden by track standards. The winner didn't need to improve greatly on her latest form. They appeared to go a reasonable gallop and as a result the time was 0.33secs quicker than division two.

3238 THURLOE THOROUGHBREDS BILL BARLOW MEMORIAL MAIDEN STKS 6f 110y
2:20 (2:24) (Class 4) 2-Y-O **£3,881** (£1,155; £577; £288) **Stalls** High

Form RPR

1 **Recanted (USA)** 2-9-5 0 FrankieDettori 7 81+
(Brian Meehan) *s.i.s: hld up towards rr: gd hdwy over 2f out: pushed along to ld ins fnl f: readily* **14/1**

2 *¾* **Pearl Spectre (USA)** 2-9-5 0 JamieSpencer 10 79+
(Andrew Balding) *in rr: hdwy over 2f out: led over 1f out: hdd ins fnl f: kpt on but nt pce of wnr* **9/1**

3 *1½* **Showpiece** 2-9-5 0 RichardHughes 11 76+
(Richard Hannon) *chsd ldrs: rdn and outpcd over 2f out: pushed along and styd on again fnl f to take 3rd clsng stages* **13/8**[1]

4 *¾* **Sebs Sensei (IRE)** 2-9-5 0 RyanMoore 9 73
(Richard Hannon) *chsd ldrs: pushed along 2f out: kpt on same pce fnl f* **6/1**[2]

5 **5** *hd* **Floating Ballerino (IRE)**[19] 2653 2-9-5 0 HarryBentley 8 72
(Olly Stevens) *trckd ldr: led ins fnl 3f: rdn 2f out: hdd over 1f out: no ex ins fnl f* **6/1**[2]

6 *nk* **Speedy Approach** 2-9-5 0 JamesMcDonald 6 72+
(Michael Bell) *chsd ldrs: rdn over 1f out: styd on same pce ins fnl f* **6/1**[2]

6 **7** *1¾* **Mister Mayday (IRE)**[38] 2067 2-9-5 0 PatCosgrave 5 67
(George Baker) *s.i.s: in rr: rdn over 2f out: kpt on ins fnl f but nvr a threat* **40/1**

5 **8** *½* **Double Czech (IRE)**[13] 2847 2-9-5 0 PatDobbs 2 65
(Amanda Perrett) *chsd ldrs: rdn over 2f out: wknd appr fnl f* **8/1**[3]

0 **9** *11* **Cape Arrow**[19] 2653 2-9-5 0 JackMitchell 3 34
(Paul Cole) *led tl hdd ins fnl 3f: wknd ins fnl 2f* **20/1**

10 *shd* **Laughing Musketeer (IRE)** 2-8-12 0 JordanUys(7) 1 34
(Paul Cole) *outpcd* **40/1**

1m 23.58s (4.28) **Going Correction** +0.625s/f (Yiel) **10** Ran SP% **118.4**
Speed ratings (Par 95): **100,99,97,96,96 96,94,93,80,80**
toteswingers 1&2 £12.60, 1&3 £6.20, 2&3 £3.60 CSF £132.57 TOTE £13.60: £3.60, £3.20, £1.10; EX 60.90 Trifecta £139.80 Pool: £2,801.35 - 15.01 winning units..
Owner Reddam Racing Llc **Bred** Betz, Kidder, Nines Enough & Graves **Trained** Manton, Wilts

FOCUS
Often a good maiden, with the last six winners all going on to be rated at least 100, among them Sri Putra and Toronado. They raced a little away from the stands' rail for much of the race. There was lots of promise on show but it's hard tpo rate the form much higher wuth the field finishing compressed.

3239 CROSSLAND MAIDEN FILLIES' STKS (DIV II) 1m 2f 6y
2:50 (2:51) (Class 4) 3-Y-O **£4,690** (£1,395; £697; £348) **Stalls** High

Form RPR

2-52 **1** **Cushion**[28] 2389 3-9-0 78 WilliamBuick 7 86
(John Gosden) *hld up in tch: stdy hdwy over 2f out to ld appr fnl f: pushed clr: readily* **9/2**[3]

52 **2** *3* **Bantam (IRE)**[14] 2804 3-9-0 0 FrankieDettori 4 80
(Ed Dunlop) *in tch: hdwy and swtchd rt 2f out: rdn and styd on to take 2nd fnl 110yds but nvr any ch w wnr* **8/1**

6- **3** *1¼* **Astonishing (IRE)**[280] 5978 3-9-0 0 RyanMoore 5 78
(Sir Michael Stoute) *hld up in tch: hdwy fr 3f out: slt ld ins fnl 2f: hdd appr fnl f: no ex and dropped to 3rd fnl 110yds* **2/1**[1]

46-4 **4** *1¼* **Society Pearl (IRE)**[28] 2389 3-9-0 72 JamieSpencer 11 75
(Charles Hills) *in rr: hdwy 3f out: chsd ldrs and pushed along 2f out: styd on same pce fr over 1f out* **12/1**

3 **5** *3½* **International Love (IRE)**[38] 2084 3-9-0 0 JimmyFortune 12 68
(Andrew Balding) *sn led: hdd ins fnl 2f: wknd fnl f* **11/4**[2]

6 *8* **Silk Route** 3-9-0 0 FergusSweeney 3 52
(Henry Candy) *in rr: pushed along and 3f out: sn green and wnt lft over 2f out: nvr nr ldrs* **33/1**

7 *1* **Obaha (USA)** 3-9-0 0 DaneO'Neill 10 50
(J W Hills) *in tch: rdn 3f out: wknd over 2f out* **33/1**

0 **8** *5* **Caperina (IRE)**[28] 2384 3-9-0 0 JimCrowley 9 40
(Ralph Beckett) *chsd ldrs: rdn 3f out: sn btn* **20/1**

9 *1½* **Mystery Drama** 3-9-0 0 LiamKeniry 1 37
(Alan King) *s.i.s: in rr: mod prog over 2f out: nvr a threat* **66/1**

6 **10** *¾* **Youmaysee**[14] 2803 3-9-0 0 MartinHarley 13 36
(Mick Channon) *chsd ldr tl wknd over 2f out* **50/1**

11 *9* **Rajaratna (IRE)** 3-9-0 0 PatCosgrave 2 18
(Lady Cecil) *in rr: sme hdwy 4f out: sn wknd* **14/1**

0- **12** *3½* **Secret Woman (IRE)**[239] 7165 3-9-0 0 KirstyMilczarek 6 11
(Alan Jarvis) *chsd ldrs tl ins fnl 3f* **66/1**

13 *11* **Tammis** 3-9-0 0 MatthewDavies 8
(Ron Hodges) *a bhd* **100/1**

2m 10.95s (2.15) **Going Correction** +0.20s/f (Good) **13** Ran SP% **120.2**
Speed ratings (Par 98): **99,96,95,94,91 85,84,80,79,78 71,68,60**
toteswingers 1&2 £4.70, 1&3 £3.10, 2&3 £6.70 CSF £38.68 TOTE £4.40: £1.40, £2.70, £1.30; EX 24.70 Trifecta £87.40 Pool: £2,988.45 - 25.63 winning units..
Owner The Duke Of Roxburghe & Mrs Sue Magnier **Bred** Floors Farming **Trained** Newmarket, Suffolk

FOCUS
This looked stronger than the first division, despite the time being 0.33secs slower. The form is rated slightly on the positive side.

3240 LORD WEINSTOCK MEMORIAL STKS (REGISTERED AS THE BALLYMACOLL STUD STAKES) (LISTED RACE) (FILLIES) 1m 2f 6y
3:25 (3:25) (Class 1) 3-Y-O
£20,982 (£7,955; £3,981; £1,983; £995; £499) **Stalls** Low

Form RPR

2352 **1** **Cruck Realta**[27] 2412 3-8-12 94 MartinHarley 4 97
(Mick Channon) *in tch: drvn and hdwy over 2f out: led appr fnl f: drvn out* **16/1**

231 **2** *2¾* **Spicy Dal**[24] 2519 3-8-12 82 JimmyFortune 3 92
(Hughie Morrison) *in rr: hdwy fr 3f out: rdn and styd on u.p appr fnl f: tk 2nd fnl 110yds: no imp on wnr* **22/1**

1-02 **3** *1¼* **Lady Nouf**[39] 2049 3-8-12 94 WilliamBuick 1 89
(William Haggas) *led: rdn 2f out: hdd appr fnl f: no ex and dropped to 3rd fnl 110yds* **2/1**[1]

3143 **4** *hd* **Jathabah (IRE)**[36] 2148 3-8-12 89 KierenFallon 6 89
(Clive Brittain) *chsd ldrs: rdn over 2f out: styd on to dispute 2nd over 1f out: sn one pce* **16/1**

1-12 **5** *1¾* **Romantic Settings**[29] 2367 3-8-12 95 JamieSpencer 8 86
(Richard Fahey) *chsd ldrs: rdn over 2f out: kpt on same pce* **4/1**[2]

-133 **6** *¾* **Music Chart (USA)**[105] 837 3-8-12 102 SilvestreDeSousa 9 84
(Saeed bin Suroor) *in rr: t.k.h: rdn and hung lft over 1f out: mod late prog* **11/2**

0 **7** *nk* **Soho Dancer**[28] 2384 3-8-12 0 KirstyMilczarek 2 83
(James Toller) *s.i.s: t.k.h: in rr: rdn over 2f out: styd on clsng stages nvr a threat* **80/1**

-322 **8** *½* **Heading North**[21] 2586 3-8-12 95 RichardHughes 5 82
(Richard Hannon) *in tch: hdwy on outside to cl on ldrs ins fnl 3f: wknd ins fnl 2f* **5/1**[3]

2-21 **9** *¾* **Butterfly McQueen (USA)**[14] 2803 3-8-12 87 RyanMoore 7 81
(Andrew Balding) *chsd ldr: rdn over 2f out: wknd wl over 1f out* **6/1**

2m 11.53s (2.73) **Going Correction** +0.20s/f (Good) **9** Ran SP% **117.0**
Speed ratings (Par 104): **97,94,93,93,92 91,91,91,90**
toteswingers 1&2 £18.00, 1&3 £9.80, 2&3 £8.10 CSF £313.25 TOTE £23.00: £3.30, £5.10, £1.10; EX 148.70 Trifecta £2175.40 Part won. Pool: £2,900.59 - 0.87 winning units..
Owner Anne & Steve Fisher **Bred** Wansdyke Farms Limited **Trained** West Ilsley, Berks

FOCUS
A rather muddling fillies' Listed race, with them going just a steady gallop, and it doesn't look particularly strong form. This has to rate a personal best for the winner, but with reservations.

3241 OUTWARD BOUND TRUST H'CAP 1m (S)
4:00 (4:00) (Class 5) (0-75,75) 3-Y-O **£2,587** (£770; £384; £192) **Stalls** High

Form RPR

0-1 **1** **Pleasure Bent**[38] 2093 3-9-4 72 KierenFallon 9 78+
(Luca Cumani) *hld up in rr: hdwy and swtchd lft appr fnl 2f: drvn and styd on over 1f out: kpt on wl to ld last strides* **7/4**[1]

-132 **2** *shd* **Tilstarr (IRE)**[28] 2387 3-8-13 67 FrankieDettori 2 73
(Roger Teal) *in rr: hdwy on outside over 2f out: sn drvn and hung rt wl over 1f out: sn chalng and led jst ins fnl f: ct last strides* **12/1**[3]

-506 **3** *nk* **Mandy's Boy (IRE)**[23] 2549 3-8-13 67 JimCrowley 11 73+
(Ian Williams) *trckd ldrs: nt clr run fr over 1f out tl wl ins fnl f whn drvn and qcknd fnl 75yds: nt quite rch ldng duo* **16/1**

32-4 **4** *1½* **Banreenahreenkah (IRE)**[44] 1904 3-8-13 67 JimmyFortune 10 69
(Denis Coakley) *t.k.h towards rr: hdwy 2f out: nt much daylight sn after tl pushed along and hdwy ins fnl f: nt qckn nr fin* **16/1**

00-0 **5** *¾* **Haatefina**[31] 2324 3-8-12 66 (v[1]) DaneO'Neill 8 66
(Mark Usher) *in rr: hdwy on outer over 2f out and sn bmpd: rdn and kpt on ins fnl f: nt rch ldrs* **33/1**

1403 **6** *nk* **Red To Amber (IRE)**[23] 2549 3-9-2 70 (b) JohnFahy 5 69
(Clive Cox) *chsd ldrs: rdn and styng on whn hmpd over 1f out: kpt on ins fnl f: nt pce to rch ldrs* **14/1**

4-10 **7** *nk* **Testa Rossa (IRE)**[27] 2420 3-8-10 64 WilliamBuick 3 63
(J W Hills) *in rr: hdwy over 2f out: chsd ldrs over 1f out: styd on same pce* **33/1**

-313 **8** *½* **Emulating (IRE)**[21] 2600 3-9-7 75 RichardHughes 1 73
(Richard Hannon) *chsd ldrs: led 2f out: hdd jst ins fnl f: wknd clsng stages* **7/1**[2]

012- **9** *nk* **Seaside Rock (IRE)**[174] 8203 3-9-2 70 RyanMoore 15 67+
(Richard Hannon) *in rr and wlel off pce: hdwy over 1f out: nt much daylight ins fnl f but kpt on wl* **16/1**

-643 **10** *2¼* **Saint Jerome (IRE)**[21] 2603 3-9-7 75 FergusSweeney 14 67
(Jamie Osborne) *chsd ldrs: outpcd over 2f out: sme hdwy and nt much daylight over 1f out: sn btn* **7/1**[2]

000- **11** *½* **Downhill Dancer (IRE)**[253] 6790 3-8-6 60 HarryBentley 16 51
(Brian Meehan) *towards rr: pushed along 2f out: sme late hdwy* **20/1**

00-5 **12** *3¼* **Substantivo (IRE)**[20] 2624 3-8-9 63 MartinDwyer 7 46
(Alan Jarvis) *chsd ldrs: chal 2f out: wknd 1f out* **25/1**

1203 **13** *1* **Red Dragon (IRE)**[27] 2420 3-9-6 74 JamesMcDonald 4 55
(Charles Hills) *chsd ldrs over 5f* **12/1**[3]

63 **P** **Breccbennach**[10] 2935 3-9-7 75 MickyFenton 12
(Seamus Durack) *led tl hdd & wknd jst ins fnl 2f: eased and p.u ins fnl f* **25/1**

1m 44.6s (4.90) **Going Correction** +0.625s/f (Yiel) **14** Ran SP% **119.4**
Speed ratings (Par 99): **100,99,99,98,97 97,96,96,95,93 93,89,88,**
toteswingers 1&2 £5.50, 1&3 £8.00, 2&3 £22.40 CSF £21.52 CT £267.13 TOTE £2.30: £1.50, £2.80, £4.60; EX 18.20 Trifecta £295.90 Pool: £2,864.81 - 7.26 winning units..

Owner Craig Bennett **Bred** Whitley Stud **Trained** Newmarket, Suffolk
■ Stewards' Enquiry : Kieren Fallon three-day ban; careless riding (27th-29th June).\n\x\x two-day ban; excessive use of whip (30th June - 1st July
John Fahy one-day ban; careless riding (27th June).

FOCUS
They raced against the stands' rail in this competitive handicap, which was run at a reasonable gallop, and there was a compressed finish. The winner should rate a lot higher in time.

3242 BE WISER INSURANCE H'CAP 7f (S)
4:30 (4:32) (Class 5) (0-75,75) 3-Y-O **£2,587** (£770; £384; £192) **Stalls** High

Form RPR
3-04 **1** **Swift Cedar (IRE)**[50] 1770 3-9-5 **73** KierenFallon 6 82
(Alan Jarvis) *trckd ldrs: chal fr 3f out and stl upsides u.p ins fnl f tl led clsng stages* **5/1**[2]
46-0 **2** *hd* **Secret Rebel**[17] 2708 3-9-1 **69** RyanMoore 10 77
(Sylvester Kirk) *pressed ldrs tl led appr fnl 3f: sn jnd by wnr and hrd pressed: kpt slt advantage tl hdd and no ex clsng stages* **12/1**
0-04 **3** *nk* **Admirable Art (IRE)**[16] 2746 3-8-11 **65** JimmyFortune 7 72
(Tony Carroll) *towards rr: hdwy u.p over 1f out: styd on wl clsng stages but a jst hld by ldng duo* **22/1**
21-3 **4** *¾* **Gracious George (IRE)**[28] 2394 3-9-5 **73** PatDobbs 5 78+
(Jimmy Fox) *s.i.s: in rr: pushed along and edgd lft over 2f out: kpt on fr over 1f out: styd on wl clsng stages: nt quite rch ldrs* **5/1**[2]
0-32 **5** *1* **Entwined (IRE)**[26] 2439 3-9-4 **72** JohnFahy 9 74
(Clive Cox) *in tch: hdwy fr 2f out to chse ldrs appr fnl f: outpcd fnl 110yds* **17/2**
0-05 **6** *1 ½* **Mystical Moment**[16] 2738 3-9-2 **75** WilliamTwiston-Davies(5) 8 73
(Richard Hannon) *in tch: hdwy fr 2f out to chse ldrs over 1f out: wknd ins fnl f* **12/1**
-200 **7** *shd* **Sinaadi (IRE)**[34] 2231 3-9-1 **69** JamesMcDonald 2 67
(Clive Brittain) *pressed ldrs: rdn over 2f out: wknd fnl f* **25/1**
-303 **8** *7* **Millers Wharf (IRE)**[6] 3062 3-9-6 **74** (b) RichardHughes 1 53
(Richard Hannon) *wnt lft s: sn in tch: chsd ldrs 3f out: rdn over 2f out: sn btn* **9/4**[1]
-634 **9** *13* **Jullundar (IRE)**[44] 1898 3-8-10 **69** CharlesBishop(5) 3
(Mick Channon) *slt ld tl over 3f out: wknd 2f out* **33/1**
0-22 **10** *22* **Thakana**[26] 2448 3-9-4 **72** DaneO'Neill 4
(J W Hills) *chsd ldrs tl wknd rapidly over 2f out* **13/2**[3]

1m 30.07s (4.37) **Going Correction** +0.625s/f (Yiel) **10 Ran SP% 114.5**
Speed ratings (Par 99): **100,99,99,98,97 95,95,87,72,47**
toteswingers 1&2 £11.30, 1&3 £20.70, 2&3 £16.20 CSF £60.07 CT £1200.46 TOTE £5.40: £1.90, £3.30, £5.60; EX 79.00 Trifecta £988.90 Pool: £3,436.08 - 2.60 winning units..
Owner Cedars Partnership **Bred** Carlingford Breeding Syndicate **Trained** Twyford, Bucks

FOCUS
Those who raced nearest to the stands' rail were favoured in this modest handicap. Ordinary form which may not prove reliable.

3243 INSURE WISER H'CAP 1m 4f 5y
5:05 (5:08) (Class 5) (0-70,70) 3-Y-O **£2,587** (£770; £384; £192) **Stalls** Low

Form RPR
1332 **1** *nse* **Debdebdeb**[20] 2641 3-9-2 **70** ThomasBrown(5) 8 82
(Andrew Balding) *in rr: hdwy and edgd lft over 2f out: str run fnl f to cl on wnr whn bmpd fnl strides: jst failed: fin 2nd: plcd 1st* **5/1**[1]
-130 **2** **Pivotal Silence**[27] 2432 3-9-2 **65** JimCrowley 5 76
(Amanda Perrett) *chsd ldrs: rdn 2f out: styd on to ld fnl 110yds: hung rt cl home: jst lasted: fin 1st: plcd 2nd* **14/1**
0-42 **3** *3 ½* **Kastini**[6] 3055 3-8-5 **54** JimmyQuinn 10 59
(Denis Coakley) *chsd ldrs: chal 3f out: led wl over 2f out: hrd rdn over 1f out: hdd & wknd fnl 110yds* **8/1**
5-02 **4** *nk* **Ivanhoe**[31] 2325 3-9-5 **68** LiamKeniry 6 73
(Michael Blanshard) *in tch: hdwy to chse ldrs over 2f out: styd on same pce u.p fnl f* **9/1**
0-52 **5** *2* **Just Darcy**[26] 2462 3-9-5 **68** RyanMoore 11 69
(Sir Michael Stoute) *led: jnd 3f out: hdd over 2f out: wknd fnl f* **8/1**
55-5 **6** *1 ¼* **Nullarbor Sky (IRE)**[23] 2555 3-8-10 **59** WilliamBuick 12 58
(Lucy Wadham) *chsd ldr: rdn 3f out: wknd over 1f out* **9/1**
2612 **7** *1 ½* **Flamingo Beat**[15] 2769 3-9-4 **67** SilvestreDeSousa 13 64
(Rae Guest) *s.i.s: in rr: hdwy 3f out: drvn to chse ldrs 2f out: wknd fnl f* **7/1**[3]
0-00 **8** *1 ¼* **Crystal Mist**[28] 2392 3-9-1 **64** (b[1]) JimmyFortune 3 59
(Harry Dunlop) *mid-div: hrd rdn over 2f out and no prog* **40/1**
-601 **9** *8* **Aficionado**[15] 2769 3-9-6 **69** (p) FrankieDettori 7 51
(Ed Dunlop) *pushed along and hung lft over 2f out: a towards rr* **8/1**
2-54 **10** *½* **Mallory Heights (IRE)**[22] 2564 3-9-7 **70** KierenFallon 1 56
(Luca Cumani) *in rr: drvn and sme hdwy fr 3f out: in tch over 2f out: sn wknd* **13/2**[2]
4405 **11** *3 ½* **Marvelino**[21] 2600 3-8-11 **65** PhilipPrince(5) 15 41
(Pat Eddery) *chsd ldrs: wknd 3f out* **50/1**
00-0 **12** *1 ¾* **Terpsichore**[14] 2800 3-7-9 **51** oh6 CameronHardie(7) 16 24
(Sylvester Kirk) *wd bnd over 5f out: a in rr* **100/1**
3020 **13** *1 ½* **Mad About Harry (IRE)**[27] 2432 3-9-2 **65** RichardHughes 14 36
(John Best) *chsd ldrs: rdn 4f out: wknd over 2f out* **20/1**
00-5 **14** *10* **See And Be Seen**[16] 2742 3-8-2 **51** oh3 KieranO'Neill 4 6
(Sylvester Kirk) *a in rr* **50/1**
6-03 **15** *2 ¾* **Janie Runaway (IRE)**[14] 2786 3-9-2 **65** DaneO'Neill 2 15
(Brian Meehan) *chsd ldrs: wknd ins fnl 3f* **16/1**

2m 38.03s (2.53) **Going Correction** +0.20s/f (Good) **15 Ran SP% 120.5**
Speed ratings (Par 99): **98,99,96,96,95 94,93,92,87,86 84,83,82,75,73**
toteswingers 1&2 £15.10, 1&3 £8.00, 2&3 £21.40 CSF £79.56 CT £615.38 TOTE £5.90: £2.30, £5.40, £2.90; EX 77.10 Trifecta £545.80 Pool: £3,703.54 - 5.08 winning units..
Owner C C Buckley **Bred** C C And Mrs D J Buckley **Trained** Kingsclere, Hants
■ Stewards' Enquiry : Jim Crowley one-day ban; careless riding (27th June).

FOCUS
This proved a decent test at the distance, with the front pair pulling away late on. There's little doubt the interference the first past the post, Pivotal Silence, caused to Debdebdeb cost the latter the race, and the result was rightly amended. The time was good and Debdebdeb has been rated the narrow winner.

3244 BE WISER INSURANCE GENTLEMAN AMATEUR RIDERS' H'CAP 1m 2f 6y
5:35 (5:35) (Class 5) (0-70,70) 4-Y-O+ **£2,495** (£774; £386; £193) **Stalls** Low

Form RPR
0562 **1** **Automotive**[12] 2875 5-10-2 **51** oh1 MrRossBirkett 4 63
(Julia Feilden) *hld up in rr: stdy hdwy fr 2f out to ld 1f out: pushed clr fnl 110yds* **20/1**
0060 **2** *4 ½* **Capitol Gain (IRE)**[5] 3106 4-10-13 **69** MrORJSangster(7) 3 72
(Brian Meehan) *chsd ldrs in main gp bhd clr ldr: hdwy over 2f out: ev ch 1f out: sn outpcd by wnr but hld on wl for 2nd* **14/1**
6320 **3** *1 ½* **Supa Seeker (USA)**[85] 1093 7-10-2 **51** oh4 NicodeBoinville 9 51
(Tony Carroll) *in rr: hdwy fr 2f out: rdn over 1f out: styd on to take 3rd fnl 100yds but no ch w ldng duo* **40/1**
4253 **4** *1 ½* **Mazij**[13] 2826 5-10-13 **62** MrPCollington 1 59
(Peter Hiatt) *led 1f: styd chsng clr ldr tl led ins fnl 3f: hdd 1f out: sn btn* **9/1**
0362 **5** *1* **Choral Festival**[14] 2808 7-11-4 **70** MrChrisMartin(3) 5 65
(John Bridger) *towards rr of main gp: hdwy 2f out: styd on same pce fr over 1f out* **6/1**[3]
5550 **6** *4* **Merrjanah**[5] 3106 5-9-9 **51** oh3 MrAFrench(7) 8 38
(Neville Bycroft) *chsd ldrs in main gp bhd clr ldr: rdn over 2f out: wknd over 1f out* **25/1**
000 **7** *6* **Garrisson (IRE)**[5] 3106 4-11-1 **64** [1] MrSWalker 2 39
(Charles Hills) *rdn over 2f out: a towards rr* **4/1**[2]
2311 **8** *7* **Balmoral Castle**[5] 3106 4-11-1 **69** 6ex MrJHarding(5) 7 30
(Jonathan Portman) *chsd ldrs in maiden gp bhd clr ldr: ev ch 2f out: wknd over 1f out* **13/8**[1]
3133 **9** *3 ¾* **If I Were A Boy (IRE)**[10] 2939 6-10-12 **66** (b) MrBenFfrenchDavis(5) 6 20
(Dominic Ffrench Davis) *t.k.h: led after 1f and sn clr: hdd ins fnl 3f: sn wknd* **7/1**

2m 13.07s (4.27) **Going Correction** +0.20s/f (Good) **9 Ran SP% 112.6**
Speed ratings (Par 103): **90,86,85,84,83 80,75,69,66**
toteeswingers 1&2 £15.70, 1&3 £9.60, 2&3 £48.50 CSF £256.50 CT £10535.37 TOTE £18.70: £3.00, £5.00, £4.90; EX 143.20 Trifecta £1350.30 Part won. Pool: £1,800.51 - 0.57 winning units..
Owner Stowstowquickquickstow Partnership **Bred** Juddmonte Farms Ltd **Trained** Exning, Suffolk

FOCUS
Quite weak form, with the market leaders failing to give their running. The pace was overstrong and the winner and third came from the rear.
T/Jkpt: Not won. T/Plt: £173.50 to a £1 stake. Pool: £70,145.46. 295.00 winning tickets. T/Qpdt: £26.90 to a £1 stake. Pool: £5,510.64. 151.20 winning tickets. ST

3132 NOTTINGHAM (L-H)
Thursday, June 13

OFFICIAL GOING: Good to firm (good in places; 8.7) changing to good after race 1 (2.00) changing to soft after race 3 (3.00)
Wind: Light, half against Weather: Heavy thundershowers

3245 EBF 1ST SECURITY SOLUTIONS LTD MAIDEN STKS 6f 15y
2:00 (2:01) (Class 5) 2-Y-O **£3,234** (£962; £481; £240) **Stalls** High

Form RPR
46 **1** **Know Your Name**[16] 2741 2-9-5 0 WilliamCarson 11 72+
(David Evans) *in rr and pushed along 1/2-way: hdwy 2f out: swtchd rt and rdn over 1f out: str run fnl f: led nr fin* **40/1**
2 *½* **Exceeder** 2-9-5 0 AndreaAtzeni 10 71
(Marco Botti) *hmpd s: trckd ldrs: hdwy 2f out: chal over 1f out: rdn to ld ins fnl f: sn edgd lft and hdd nr fin* **8/1**[3]
5 **3** *1* **Khee Society**[10] 2925 2-9-0 0 DeclanBates(5) 14 68
(David Evans) *in tch: pushed along and lost pl bef 1/2-way: sn in rr: rdn and hdwy on wd outside over 1f out: styd on wl fnl f: nrst fin* **20/1**
365 **4** *nk* **Bounty Hunter (IRE)**[16] 2741 2-9-5 0 RichardKingscote 9 67
(Tom Dascombe) *wnt rt s: sn slt ld: rdn along 2f out: hdd 1 1/2f out: kpt on same pce* **3/1**[2]
5 *2 ¼* **Chord Chart (IRE)** 2-9-5 0 MickaelBarzalona 6 60+
(Saeed bin Suroor) *in tch: hdwy to trck ldrs 1/2-way: effrt to ld 1 1/2f out: sn rdn: hdd & wknd ins fnl f* **13/8**[1]
43 **6** *½* **Twentyfourseven**[14] 2805 2-9-5 0 GrahamLee 7 58
(Ed Dunlop) *towards rr: stdy hdwy 2f out: kpt on appr fnl f: nrst fin* **14/1**
5 **7** *shd* **Finn Class (IRE)**[21] 2591 2-9-5 0 HayleyTurner 2 58
(Michael Bell) *chsd ldrs: rdn along 2f out: no imp appr fnl f* **16/1**
8 *4* **Scottish Strand** 2-9-5 0 GeorgeBaker 8 46
(Ed Walker) *in rr: hdwy over 2f out: kpt on appr fnl f: nrst fin* **20/1**
0 **9** *2 ½* **Volodina (IRE)**[12] 2856 2-8-9 0 ShirleyTeasdale(5) 15 34
(Alan McCabe) *chsd ldrs: rdn along over 2f out: sn wknd* **100/1**
0 **10** *2* **Slinky McVelvet**[16] 2751 2-8-9 0 JustinNewman(5) 1 28
(Garry Moss) *in tch: rdn along 1/2-way: sn wknd* **200/1**
0 **11** *½* **St Vincent (IRE)**[10] 2925 2-9-5 0 JamesDoyle 3 31
(David Lanigan) *a towards rr* **33/1**
66 **12** *3* **Hustle Bustle (IRE)**[12] 2856 2-9-0 0 SeanLevey 13 17
(David Brown) *cl up: rdn along over 2f out: grad wknd* **40/1**
13 *2* **Village Cricket** 2-9-5 0 PaulMulrennan 4 16
(Pam Sly) *a towards rr* **66/1**
0 **14** *3 ½* **Dylan's Centenary**[16] 2741 2-9-5 0 ChrisCatlin 5 6
(Rod Millman) *a towards rr: bhd fnl 2f* **66/1**
15 *¾* **Overstep (IRE)** 2-9-5 0 JoeFanning 12 3
(Mark Johnston) *hmpd s and bhd: hdwy and in tch 1/2-way: rdn and edgd lft 2f out: sn wknd* **17/2**

1m 15.72s (1.02) **Going Correction** +0.125s/f (Good) **15 Ran SP% 119.1**
Speed ratings (Par 93): **98,97,96,95,92 91,91,86,83,80 79,75,73,68,67**
toteswingers 1&2 £33.70, 1&3 £33.70, 2&3 £33.70 CSF £314.48 TOTE £66.40: £10.00, £2.50, £5.10; EX 702.70 Trifecta £475.70 Part won. Pool: £634.32 - 0.02 winning units..
Owner David Lockwood & Fred Lockwood **Bred** Mill Farm Stud **Trained** Pandy, Monmouths

FOCUS
Races on Outer track. The meeting started on ground given as good to firm, good in places after 5mm of water had been applied the previous day, but rain fell during the afternoon and the last five contests were run on soft. Not a race that has produced any big stars in the past, so it's probably best to presume this is only fair form at best until proven otherwise. It is limited by a few down the field.

3246 CORONA H'CAP (DIV I) 6f 15y
2:30 (2:32) (Class 6) (0-65,65) 3-Y-O+ **£2,587** (£770; £384; £192) **Stalls** High

Form RPR
2-60 **1** **Jubilant Queen**[16] 2738 3-9-6 **65** JamesDoyle 15 74+
(Clive Cox) *hld up: pushed along and hdwy over 1f out: r.o to ld fnl 100yds* **3/1**[1]
-423 **2** *1 ½* **Aaranyow (IRE)**[20] 2638 5-8-10 **52** RobertTart(5) 4 59
(Clifford Lines) *prom: rdn over 2f out: kpt on* **13/2**[2]
0-60 **3** *½* **Graylyn Valentino**[27] 2413 4-9-12 **63** AndreaAtzeni 3 68+
(Robert Eddery) *hld up in rr: rdn and hdwy over 1f out: kpt on fnl f* **14/1**

The Form Book Flat, Raceform Ltd, Compton, RG20 6NL.

02-0 **4** *hd* **Aussie Blue (IRE)**[10] 2932 9-9-9 **60**........................(p) MichaelStainton 13 64
(Charles Pogson) *w ldr: rdn over 2f out: led over 1f out: hdd fnl 100yds: no ex and lost 2 more pls towards fin* **25/1**

1040 **5** *shd* **New Decade**[21] 2588 4-10-0 **65**........................ GrahamLee 17 69
(Milton Bradley) *in tch: rdn 2f out: kpt on* **16/1**

400 **6** *2 1/2* **Mr Snooks**[34] 2241 3-8-8 **53**........................(v[1]) AdrianNicholls 14 47
(David Nicholls) *s.i.s: hld up in rr: rdn over 2f out: kpt on ins fnl f: nrst fin* **16/1**

20-3 **7** *3/4* **Depden (IRE)**[8] 2997 5-8-9 **46**........................ WilliamCarson 9 40
(Richard Price) *chsd ldrs: rdn and outpcd over 1f out: kpt on fnl f* **14/1**

03-0 **8** *hd* **Errigal Lad**[54] 1681 8-8-7 **51**........................ GemmaTutty(7) 5 44
(Garry Woodward) *midfield towards outer: rdn over 2f out: nvr threatened ldrs* **13/2**[2]

6140 **9** *1* **Divertimenti (IRE)**[15] 2781 9-9-9 **63**........................(b) MarkCoumbe(3) 7 53
(Roy Bowring) *led narrowly: rdn whn hdd over 1f out: wknd* **14/1**

4-00 **10** *nk* **Cristaliyev**[10] 2918 5-8-6 **50**........................(b) OisinMurphy(7) 8 39
(John Flint) *midfield: rdn over 2f out: nvr threatened* **20/1**

0-00 **11** *3/4* **Hamis Al Bin (IRE)**[15] 2780 4-9-6 **57**........................ JoeFanning 12 43
(Milton Bradley) *midfield: rdn over 2f out: nvr threatened* **33/1**

05 **12** *1* **Quality Art (USA)**[7] 3024 5-9-8 **59**........................ RobbieFitzpatrick 1 42
(Richard Guest) *chsd ldrs towards outer: rdn over 2f out: wknd fnl f* **14/1**

5000 **13** *8* **Sairaam (IRE)**[37] 2134 7-9-4 **55**........................ AndrewElliott 10 32
(Charles Smith) *in tch: rdn over 2f out: already btn whn stmbld bdly jst ins fnl f: eased* **25/1**

06-5 **14** *2 1/2* **Compton Albion (IRE)**[151] 197 3-8-9 **54**........................ ChrisCatlin 6
(Jeremy Gask) *hld up: a in rr* **11/1**

0326 **15** *3 1/2* **Code Six (IRE)**[20] 2632 4-9-3 **54**........................(p) TomEaves 16
(Bryan Smart) *prom tl wknd over 2f out* **8/1**[3]

1m 15.94s (1.24) **Going Correction** +0.125s/f (Good)
WFA 3 from 4yo+ 8lb **15 Ran SP% 124.9**
Speed ratings (Par 101): **96,94,93,93,92 89,88,88,87,86 85,84,73,70,65**
toteswingers 1&2 £4.50, 1&3 £43.20, 2&3 £27.90 CSF £20.36 CT £253.60 TOTE £3.90: £1.80, £2.70, £2.60; EX 29.10 Trifecta £285.30 Part won. Pool: £380.46 - 0.99 winning units..
Owner Doreen Swinburn & Pierpont Scott **Bred** Genesis Green Stud & P Scott **Trained** Lambourn, Berks
■ Stewards' Enquiry : Mark Coumbe three-day ban; careless riding (27th-29th June).

FOCUS
The going was changed to good prior to this race, and it was run in driving rain. Being close to the stands' rail was beneficial

3247 CORONA H'CAP (DIV II) 6f 15y
3:00 (3:01) (Class 6) (0-65,64) 3-Y-0+ **£2,587** (£770; £384; £192) **Stalls** High

Form RPR

4563 **1** **Key Ambition**[15] 2781 4-9-9 **64**........................(vt) JustinNewman(5) 14 72
(Garry Moss) *sn cl up: chal 1/2-way: led 2f out: rdn clr over 1f out: edgd lft and drvn ins fnl f: kpt on* **10/3**[1]

0060 **2** *nk* **Whipphound**[8] 2997 5-9-3 **53**........................ GeorgeBaker 1 60
(Mark Brisbourne) *dwlt: hld up towards rr: hdwy on outer wl over 2f out: rdn to chse ldrs over 1f out: drvn to chse wnr ins fnl f: sn edgd rt: kpt on* **16/1**

344U **3** *3/4* **Solarmaite**[8] 2992 4-9-7 **60**........................(b) MarkCoumbe(3) 12 65
(Roy Bowring) *chsd ldrs: pushed along 1/2-way: rdn wl over 1f out: edgd lft ins fnl f: hld whn n.m.r nr fin* **10/1**

3010 **4** *hd* **Prince Of Passion (CAN)**[10] 2932 5-9-10 **60**........................ JoeFanning 16 64
(Derek Shaw) *chsd ldng pair on wd outside: rdn 2f out: styng on whn edgd lft ins fnl f: no ex towards fin* **6/1**[2]

0-00 **5** *1 1/4* **Bermondsey Bob (IRE)**[21] 2596 7-9-7 **57**........................ ChrisCatlin 4 57
(John Spearing) *prom on outer: effrt 2f out and sn rdn: drvn and one pce whn n.m.r wl ins fnl f* **10/1**

5606 **6** *1 1/4* **Reginald Claude**[15] 2781 5-9-3 **58**........................ RachealKneller(5) 13 54
(Mark Usher) *hld up towards rr: hdwy 2f out: chsd ldrs and n.m.r ins fnl f: sn swtchd rt and rdn: kpt on: nrst fin* **7/1**[3]

400- **7** *1/2* **Niceonemyson**[264] 6477 4-9-0 **50**........................ PaddyAspell 5 44
(Christopher Wilson) *prom: cl up 1/2-way: rdn along 2f out: drvn over 1f out: grad wknd* **40/1**

1440 **8** *nk* **Colourbearer (IRE)**[15] 2781 6-9-5 **55**........................(t) GrahamLee 2 48
(Milton Bradley) *hld up towards rr: hdwy 2f out: rdn to chse ldrs over 1f out: no imp fnl f* **10/1**

643- **9** *3 1/2* **Therapeutic**[314] 4767 3-9-0 **61**........................ BillyCray(3) 9 43
(Scott Dixon) *led: rdn along and hdd 2f out: sn drvn and wknd jst over 1f out* **12/1**

4-00 **10** *8* **Fidget**[17] 2703 3-8-10 **54**........................ PaulMulrennan 11 11
(David Brown) *chsd ldrs: rdn along 1/2-way: sn wknd* **10/1**

650- **11** *3/4* **Ridgeway Sapphire**[281] 5937 6-8-2 **45**........................(v) DanielMuscutt(7) 8
(Mark Usher) *dwlt: a in rr* **14/1**

6-00 **12** *nk* **Bobbyow**[27] 2425 5-8-10 **46**........................ SeanLevey 10
(K F Clutterbuck) *chsd ldrs: rdn along 1/2-way: sn wknd* **25/1**

-050 **13** *10* **We Are City**[59] 1566 3-8-11 **55**........................ RoystonFfrench 17
(Bryan Smart) *a in rr* **25/1**

4-66 **14** *7* **Copper Leyf**[30] 2347 3-8-7 **54**........................ RyanClark(3) 7
(Jeremy Gask) *chsd ldrs: rdn along 1/2-way: sn wknd: bhd and eased over 1f out* **33/1**

1m 16.81s (2.11) **Going Correction** +0.125s/f (Good)
WFA 3 from 4yo+ 8lb **14 Ran SP% 119.5**
Speed ratings (Par 101): **90,89,88,88,86 85,84,83,79,68 67,67,53,44**
toteswingers 1&2 £7.70, 1&3 £7.20, 2&3 £18.30 CSF £57.76 CT £506.36 TOTE £3.10: £1.10, £5.90, £3.20; EX 51.50 Trifecta £490.40 Part won. Pool: £653.89 - 0.59 winning units..
Owner Ron Hull **Bred** Giles W Pritchard-Gordon (farming) Ltd **Trained** Tickhill, S Yorks

FOCUS
Despite the main body of runners heading down the stands' rail in the first division, where it seemed to be an advantage, the field ran down the middle this time.

3248 COORS LIGHT H'CAP 1m 6f 15y
3:35 (3:35) (Class 5) (0-75,74) 4-Y-0+ **£2,587** (£770; £384; £192) **Stalls** Low

Form RPR

-000 **1** **Man Of Plenty**[21] 2587 4-9-7 **74**........................(p) JamesDoyle 1 83
(Ed Dunlop) *hld up and bhd: stdy hdwy 3f out: chsd ldng pair ent fnl f: sn rdn and styd on strly to ld last 50yds* **3/1**[2]

0400 **2** *1* **Rowlestone Lad**[37] 2130 6-7-13 **55**........................ RaulDaSilva(3) 4 62
(John Flint) *cl up: led 1/2-way: pushed along 4f out: jnd 3f out: rdn and hdd 2f out: cl and drvn: rallied gamely to ld again ins fnl f: hdd and no ex last 50yds* **7/1**[3]

3433 **3** *hd* **Smalib Monterg (FR)**[9] 2968 7-9-3 **70**........................(t) GrahamLee 3 77
(Dr Richard Newland) *t.k.h early: trckd ldng pair: hdwy to trck ldr over 4f out: cl up 3f out: slt ld 2f out: sn rdn: drvn and hdd ins fnl f: one pce towards fin* **6/4**[1]

6032 **4** *6* **Royal Sea (IRE)**[20] 2615 4-8-9 **62**........................(p) BarryMcHugh 8 61
(Barry Leavy) *hld up in tch: hdwy on outer to chse ldrs 4f out: rdn along 3f out: wknd fnl 2f* **8/1**

010/ **5** *6* **King's Realm (IRE)**[453] 7067 6-8-5 **58**........................(e[1]) JamesSullivan 7 48
(Tina Jackson) *led to 1/2-way: rdn along over 4f out: sn wknd* **25/1**

1040 **6** *2 1/2* **Yeomanoftheguard**[14] 2798 4-8-10 **63**........................(p) TonyHamilton 2 50
(Richard Fahey) *hld up in tch: effrt 4f out: rdn along 3f out: sn btn* **15/2**

6433 **7** *32* **Tram Express (FR)**[22] 2563 9-8-3 **56**........................(t) HayleyTurner 5
(Shaun Lycett) *trckd ldrs: pushed along 5f out: rdn over 3f out: sn outpcd and bhd* **11/1**

3m 12.34s (5.34) **Going Correction** +0.30s/f (Good) **7 Ran SP% 112.6**
Speed ratings (Par 103): **96,95,95,91,88 87,68**
toteswingers 1&2 £11.70, 1&3 £2.20, 2&3 £3.10 CSF £23.14 CT £41.49 TOTE £4.80: £2.00, £4.00; EX 27.80 Trifecta £89.30 Pool: £1,547.51 - 12.99 winning units..
Owner Bluehills Racing Limited **Bred** Hesmonds Stud Ltd **Trained** Newmarket, Suffolk

FOCUS
There was a second change to the going before this handicap, the ground now being described as soft, having originally been good to firm, good in places.

3249 ENJOY AFTERNOON TEA IN FRANKIES BISTRO H'CAP 6f 15y
4:10 (4:11) (Class 2) (0-105,95) 4-Y-0+
£12,450 (£3,728; £1,864; £932; £466; £234) **Stalls** High

Form RPR

5460 **1** **Harrison George (IRE)**[5] 3096 8-8-5 **84**........................(bt[1]) NatashaEaton(5) 5 99
(P J O'Gorman) *prom: rdn to ld ent fnl f: kpt on* **11/1**

0201 **2** *1 1/2* **Dick Bos**[8] 2988 4-9-0 **88** 6ex........................ DanielTudhope 1 98
(David O'Meara) *led: rdn whn hdd ent fnl f: kpt on but a hld* **11/4**[1]

5-00 **3** *2 1/2* **Joe Packet**[10] 2937 6-9-7 **95**........................ GrahamLee 2 97
(Jonathan Portman) *midfield: pushed along over 2f out: rdn to go 3rd ent fnl f: one pce and no threat to ldng pair* **15/2**

0006 **4** *1* **Head Space (IRE)**[13] 2834 5-8-9 **83**........................ JamesSullivan 8 82
(Ruth Carr) *hld up: pushed along 2f out: kpt on fnl f: nrst fin* **13/2**

6401 **5** *3/4* **Forest Edge (IRE)**[6] 3038 4-9-1 **94** 6ex........................(b) DeclanBates(5) 3 91
(David Evans) *chsd ldng pair: rdn over 2f out: grad wknd fnl f* **12/1**

02-5 **6** *nse* **Nassau Storm**[34] 2207 4-9-4 **92**........................ MickaelBarzalona 6 88
(William Knight) *midfield on outer: pushed along 1/2-way: rdn over 1f out: no ex ins fnl f* **9/2**[2]

-644 **7** *hd* **Misplaced Fortune**[8] 2988 8-8-11 **92**........................ DanielleMooney(7) 9 88
(Nigel Tinkler) *hld up: pushed along 1/2-way: nvr threatened* **16/1**

-600 **8** *1 3/4* **Compton**[12] 2868 4-9-4 **92**........................ GeorgeBaker 12 82
(Robert Cowell) *hld up: pushed along over 2f out: nvr threatened* **11/2**[3]

0010 **9** *2* **Church Music (IRE)**[12] 2865 4-8-10 **87**........................(v) DarrenEgan(3) 10 71
(Michael Scudamore) *in tch: rdn over 2f out: wknd over 1f out* **20/1**

10-0 **10** *2* **Cheveton**[29] 2366 9-8-13 **87**........................ WilliamCarson 7 64
(Richard Price) *half-rrd s: hld up: nvr threatened* **20/1**

1m 14.21s (-0.49) **Going Correction** +0.125s/f (Good) **10 Ran SP% 116.8**
Speed ratings (Par 109): **108,106,102,101,100 100,100,97,95,92**
toteswingers 1&2 £7.70, 1&3 £18.70, 2&3 £5.20 CSF £41.46 CT £214.24 TOTE £19.40: £5.20, £2.80, £2.30; EX 67.50 Trifecta £778.70 Pool: £3,152.68 - 3.03 winning units..
Owner Racing To The Max **Bred** R P Ryan **Trained** Newmarket, Suffolk

FOCUS
It's difficult to know what to make of this form as the field soon diverted towards the stands' side after leaving the stalls, which had looked an advantage in an earlier contest, despite the jockeys choosing to avoid it in the third race.

3250 ABG LAW CLASSIC MAIDEN STKS 1m 75y
4:45 (4:47) (Class 5) 3-Y-0+ **£3,234** (£962; £481; £240) **Stalls** Centre

Form RPR

0-62 **1** **Morpheus**[35] 2192 3-9-0 82........................ JamesDoyle 12 87
(Lady Cecil) *t.k.h early: trckd ldrs: smooth hdwy 3f out: led 2f out: sn rdn and hung bdly lft over 1f out: sn clr: styd on strly* **4/5**[1]

2 *4 1/2* **Elsiniaar** 3-9-0 0........................ AndreAtzeni 5 77
(Roger Varian) *t.k.h: trckd ldrs: hdwy 4f out: cl up over 2f out: sn rdn: n.m.r appr fnl f: sn drvn and one pce* **7/2**[2]

3 *hd* **Magistral** 3-9-0 0........................ NickyMackay 7 76+
(John Gosden) *s.i.s and in rr: gd hdwy over 4f out: swtchd to inner 3f out and sn cl up: rdn and ev ch 2f out: drvn whn n.m.r jst over 1f out: kpt on same pce* **16/1**

05 **4** *5* **Sacred Square (GER)**[23] 2538 3-9-0 0........................ PhillipMakin 8 65
(William Haggas) *trckd ldrs: hdwy on outer over 3f out: pushed along whn sltly hmpd 2f out: sn rdn and one pce* **33/1**

0 **5** *nk* **Royal Marskell**[31] 2321 4-9-6 0........................ LauraPike(5) 4 67
(K F Clutterbuck) *chsd ldng pair: cl up 1/2-way: rdn and hld whn hmpd 2f out: sn swtchd rt and wknd* **150/1**

55 **6** *hd* **Spirit Rider (USA)**[16] 2760 3-9-0 0........................ MarcHalford 11 64
(John Gosden) *s.i.s: hdwy 3f out: rdn along over 2f out: kpt on fnl f: nrst fin* **12/1**

64 **7** *1/2* **Magic Lando (FR)**[23] 2548 3-9-0 0........................ MickaelBarzalona 6 62+
(Ismail Mohammed) *led 1 1/2f: cl up: led again 1/2-way: rdn and hdd 2f out: sn drvn and wknd* **14/1**

0-6 **8** *2 3/4* **Shades Of Silver**[54] 1684 3-9-0 0........................ GrahamLee 10 56
(Sir Michael Stoute) *towards rr: sme hdwy fnl 2f: n.d* **7/1**[3]

9 *9* **Able Dash** 3-9-0 0........................(p) HayleyTurner 13 35
(Ed Walker) *a towards rr* **40/1**

10 *shd* **Roxy Lane** 4-9-6 0........................ WilliamCarson 3 33
(Peter Hiatt) *s.i.s: a in rr* **100/1**

00 **11** *3 1/4* **Olivers Mount**[16] 2746 3-9-0 0........................ TonyHamilton 2 28
(Ed Vaughan) *midfield: rdn along 1/2-way: sn outpcd* **80/1**

60 **12** *2 1/4* **Elusive Band (USA)**[8] 2989 3-9-0 0........................ SamHitchcott 14 22
(Brian Meehan) *midfield: rdn along over 3f out: sn wknd* **40/1**

00 **13** *10* **Whistle We Go (GER)**[13] 2833 5-9-6 0........................ MichaelStainton 1
(Nick Kent) *t.k.h: cl up: led after 1 1/2f: hdd 1/2-way: sn wknd* **150/1**

00 **14** *3 3/4* **The Power Of One (IRE)**[12] 2885 3-9-0 0........................ JamesSullivan 9
(James Given) *s.i.s: a bhd* **80/1**

1m 49.66s (0.66) **Going Correction** +0.30s/f (Good)
WFA 3 from 4yo+ 11lb **14 Ran SP% 123.1**
Speed ratings (Par 103): **108,103,103,98,98 97,97,94,85,85 82,79,69,66**
toteswingers 1&2 £2.00, 1&3 £6.30, 2&3 £8.00 CSF £3.57 TOTE £2.20: £1.40, £1.20, £4.50; EX 4.90 Trifecta £41.70 Pool: £4,086.01 - 73.34 winning units..
Owner K Abdullah **Bred** Juddmonte Farms Ltd **Trained** Newmarket, Suffolk

FOCUS
It was fitting that a half-brother to Sir Henry Cecil's greatest racehorse provided Lady Cecil with her first winner on her opening day with a trainer's licence following the death of her husband.

3251 1ST SECURITY SOLUTIONS LTD FILLIES' H'CAP (JOCKEY CLUB GRASSROOTS MIDDLE DIST SERIES QUALIFIER) 1m 2f 50y
5:15 (5:21) (Class 5) (0-75,75) 3-Y-O £3,881 (£1,155; £577; £288) Stalls Low

Form RPR
54-6 1 **Fast Pace**[28] 2389 3-9-2 70 GrahamLee 2 77+
(Amanda Perrett) *w ldr: led 4f out: pushed along to assert over 1f out: rdn out fnl 100yds: a jst holding clsng runner-up* 9/4[1]
-210 2 nk **Divergence (IRE)**[20] 2619 3-9-7 75 HayleyTurner 10 81+
(Michael Bell) *hld up: swtchd rt to outer over 2f out: sn rdn: r.o wl fr over 1f out: jst hld* 11/2
2-40 3 2 **Sweet Martoni**[21] 2606 3-9-1 69 MickaelBarzalona 6 71
(William Knight) *trckd ldrs on inner: rdn over 2f out: kpt on* 5/1[3]
4-44 4 ½ **Mistral Wind (IRE)**[24] 2503 3-8-8 62 AndreaAtzeni 5 63
(Ed Dunlop) *led narrowly: hdd 4f out: rdn over 2f out: outpcd over 1f out: kpt on again fnl 100yds* 12/1
-230 5 1½ **High Time Too (IRE)**[21] 2586 3-9-3 71 JamesDoyle 8 69
(Hugo Palmer) *prom towards outer: rdn 2f out: wknd ins fnl f* 9/1
50-2 6 5 **Chloe's Image**[14] 2794 3-7-13 56 DeclanCannon(3) 7 45
(Philip Kirby) *in tch: pushed along over 3f out: wknd over 1f out* 8/1
4-53 7 2¾ **Everleigh**[20] 2622 3-9-7 75 SeanLevey 12 59
(Richard Hannon) *in tch: rdn over 3f out: wknd over 1f out* 9/2[2]
41-5 8 3¼ **Mandeville (IRE)**[36] 2167 3-9-4 72 TomEaves 9 50
(Michael Dods) *hld up in rr: pushed along over 4f out: a bhd* 16/1

2m 18.54s (4.24) **Going Correction** +0.30s/f (Good) 8 Ran SP% 115.7
Speed ratings (Par 96): **95,94,93,92,91 87,85,82**
toteswingers 1&2 £2.90, 1&3 £4.30, 2&3 £5.40 CSF £15.08 CT £55.91 TOTE £2.30: £1.10, £2.20, £2.20; EX 15.70 Trifecta £67.90 Pool: £2,736.52 - 30.21 winning units..
Owner K Abdullah **Bred** Juddmonte Farms Ltd **Trained** Pulborough, W Sussex
FOCUS
The early gallop didn't look strong (the winning time was slower than the weak 0-60 contest that followed it).

3252 DOOM BAR H'CAP 1m 2f 50y
5:45 (5:46) (Class 6) (0-60,60) 4-Y-O+ £1,940 (£577; £288; £144) Stalls Low

Form RPR
12-1 1 **Mac Tiernan (IRE)**[8] 2977 6-9-5 58 RussKennemore 7 72
(Philip Kirby) *t.k.h: trckd ldr: cl up 1/2-way: led 4f out: rdn clr wl over 2f out: kpt on* 11/10[1]
00-0 2 4½ **Ptolomeos**[23] 2536 10-8-2 46 AmyScott(5) 10 51
(Sean Regan) *dwlt and hld up in rr: hdwy on inner 3f out: rdn over 1f out: styd on to take 2nd ins fnl f: no ch w wnr* 12/1
-030 3 ½ **Fushicho**[7] 3015 4-8-9 48 WilliamCarson 3 53
(Brendan Powell) *hld up towards rr: hdwy 3f out: rdn along 2f out: styd on fnl f* 16/1
0300 4 1¼ **Rockgoat (IRE)**[8] 2986 4-8-9 48 NickyMackay 11 50
(Ian McInnes) *chsd ldrs: rdn along 3f out: drvn wl over 1f out: kpt on same pce* 33/1
24-0 5 ½ **Echo Of Footsteps**[23] 2555 4-9-6 59 TomEaves 15 60
(Michael Herrington) *in rr: hdwy wl over 2f out: sn rdn and kpt on fnl f: nrst fin* 20/1
060- 6 4 **Cometography (IRE)**[268] 6334 4-9-7 60 TonyHamilton 14 54
(Ismail Mohammed) *midfield: hdwy on outer to chse ldrs 4f out: rdn along wl over 2f out: sn one pce* 14/1
00-5 7 1 **Present Day**[42] 1948 4-8-12 51 (b) JamesDoyle 2 43
(Clive Cox) *t.k.h: trckd ldng pair on inner: effrt to chse wnr wl over 2f out: sn rdn and wknd over 1f out* 5/1[2]
5000 8 13 **Miss Chardonay**[16] 2764 6-8-7 46 oh1 (t) RenatoSouza 8 13
(Mandy Rowland) *t.k.h: led: pushed along and hdd 4f out: rdn over 3f out: drvn and wknd 2f out* 50/1
60/5 9 6 **Classic Voice (IRE)**[24] 2496 5-9-4 57 (p) GrahamLee 4 13
(Roy Brotherton) *in tch: rdn along over 4f out: sn wknd* 20/1
2/0- 10 nse **Crystal High**[230] 5-9-2 55 (t[1]) MickaelBarzalona 13 10
(Mrs Ilka Gansera-Leveque) *a in rr* 13/2[3]
500- 11 shd **Speedy Star (IRE)**[239] 7174 4-8-7 46 oh1 JamesSullivan 9
(Tina Jackson) *plld hrd early: chsd ldrs: rdn along 1/2-way: sn wknd* 66/1

2m 16.83s (2.53) **Going Correction** +0.30s/f (Good) 11 Ran SP% 113.8
Speed ratings (Par 101): **101,97,97,96,95 92,91,81,76,76 76**
toteswingers 1&2 £8.30, 1&3 £6.20, 2&3 £25.00 CSF £13.89 CT £138.62 TOTE £1.50: £1.02, £4.30, £4.40; EX 21.40 Trifecta £267.90 Pool: £1,898.81 - 5.31 winning units..
Owner The Philip Kirby Racing Partnership **Bred** Paul Kiernan **Trained** Middleham, N Yorks
FOCUS
A moderate handicap.
T/Plt: £452.20 to a £1 stake. Pool: £49,204.73. 79.42 winning tickets. T/Qpdt: £15.70 to a £1 stake. Pool: £4,943.52. 232.64 winning tickets. JR

3217 YARMOUTH (L-H)
Thursday, June 13

OFFICIAL GOING: Good to firm (7.7)
Wind: Fresh, across Weather: Overcast

3253 BETVICTOR ROYAL ASCOT MONEY BACK MAIDEN STKS 6f 3y
2:10 (2:15) (Class 5) 3-Y-O+ £2,587 (£770; £384; £192) Stalls Centre

Form RPR
1 **Maria Lombardi** 3-9-0 0 SebSanders 7 68+
(Jeremy Noseda) *mid-div: hdwy over 1f out: shkn up ins fnl f: r.o to ld post* 9/2[3]
044- 2 nse **Cape Of Hope (IRE)**[233] 7311 3-9-5 72 RobertHavlin 2 73
(Peter Chapple-Hyam) *led: hdd over 2f out: rdn over 1f out: rallied to ld wl ins fnl f: hdd post* 11/8[1]
2420 3 ½ **Go Far**[31] 2308 3-8-12 67 (b[1]) TimClark(7) 4 71
(Alan Bailey) *chsd ldr tl led over 2f out: rdn over 1f out: edgd lft and hdd wl ins fnl f* 11/2
4- 4 6 **Honeymoon Express (IRE)**[265] 6431 3-9-0 0 AnnelieHollstenius 1 47
(Julia Feilden) *s.i.s: sn chsng ldrs: rdn over 1f out: wknd fnl f* 100/1
6-6 5 ¾ **Sakash**[20] 2637 3-9-5 0 FrederikTylicki 8 49
(J R Jenkins) *prom: rdn over 2f out: wknd over 1f out* 33/1
20 6 4 **Reminisce (IRE)**[23] 2547 3-9-5 0 LukeMorris 9 37
(Marco Botti) *s.i.s: pushed along towards rr thrght: wknd over 2f out* 3/1[2]
7 14 **Tumbleweed Finale** 3-9-0 0 SteveDrowne 10
(Rae Guest) *s.i.s and wnt rt s: outpcd* 16/1
0- 8 7 **Grey Poppett**[222] 7553 3-9-0 0 SaleemGolam 3
(Chris Dwyer) *hld up: bhd fr 1/2-way: t.o* 50/1

1m 15.69s (1.29) **Going Correction** +0.175s/f (Good) 8 Ran SP% 112.4
Speed ratings (Par 103): **98,97,97,89,88 82,64,54**
toteswingers 1&2 £2.20, 1&3 £4.10, 2&3 £2.80 CSF £10.72 TOTE £5.60: £1.50, £1.40, £1.40; EX 10.80 Trifecta £38.00 Pool: £3,97.72 - 76.77 winning units..
Owner Cheveley Park Stud **Bred** Newsells Park Stud **Trained** Newmarket, Suffolk
FOCUS
Not the strongest of maidens, but it was run at a fair pace and the first three pulled clear.

3254 BETVICTOR NO LOSE HUGHES MONEY BACK CLASSIFIED STKS 1m 3y
2:40 (2:41) (Class 6) 3-Y-O £1,940 (£577; £288; £144) Stalls Centre

Form RPR
1 1 **Drahem**[24] 2504 3-9-0 65 FrederikTylicki 1 74+
(James Fanshawe) *s.i.s: hld up: hdwy 1/2-way: rdn to ld 1f out: edgd rt: styd on* 2/1[2]
6500 2 3½ **The Scuttler (IRE)**[17] 2727 3-8-7 60 DanielCremin(7) 3 66
(Mick Channon) *chsd ldrs: led over 2f out: rdn over 1f out: sn edgd rt and hdd: styd on same pce ins fnl f* 16/1
0-43 3 1¼ **Zhuba (IRE)**[104] 845 3-9-0 65 SteveDrowne 8 63
(John Best) *hld up: hdwy over 4f out: rdn over 2f out: styd on same pce fnl f* 10/1
40-5 4 hd **Sandy's Row (USA)**[8] 2992 3-9-0 65 FrannyNorton 4 62
(Mark Johnston) *s.i.s: hdwy over 4f out: rdn over 1f out: styd on same pce fnl f* 16/1
000- 5 1¼ **Marju's Quest (IRE)**[226] 7458 3-9-0 65 IanMongan 5 59
(David Simcock) *hld up: plld hrd: hdwy u.p over 1f out: nt rch ldrs* 8/1[3]
6560 6 2¼ **East Texas Red (IRE)**[23] 2549 3-8-11 62 RossAtkinson(3) 9 54
(Mick Quinn) *chsd ldr tl led over 5f: sn rdn: wknd fnl f* 16/1
63-4 7 3½ **Posh Boy (IRE)**[38] 2094 3-9-0 64 TedDurcan 2 46
(Chris Wall) *chsd ldrs: lost pl 1/2-way: rdn over 2f out: wknd fnl f* 15/8[1]
04-0 8 12 **Tuffan (USA)**[73] 1293 3-9-0 65 RobertWinston 7 17
(Clive Brittain) *plld hrd and prom: rdn over 3f out: wknd over 2f out* 33/1
4-30 9 2¾ **Dutch Gal**[31] 2308 3-9-0 60 SebSanders 6 10
(John Holt) *led: hdd over 5f out: rdn and wknd over 2f out* 18/1

1m 42.35s (1.75) **Going Correction** +0.175s/f (Good) 9 Ran SP% 114.2
Speed ratings (Par 97): **98,94,93,93,91 89,86,74,71**
toteswingers 1&2 £9.50, 1&3 £3.70, 2&3 £13.70 CSF £33.65 TOTE £3.80: £1.30, £3.50, £2.20; EX 44.20 Trifecta £245.10 Pool: £2,581.20 - 7.89 winning units..
Owner Salem Bel Obaida **Bred** Ashbrittle Stud **Trained** Newmarket, Suffolk
FOCUS
This looked an interesting race with only 5lb covering the nine runners. It was run at a steady pace with the winner scoring easily.

3255 WELL BALANCED LEDGER AT J & H SIMPSON (S) STKS 7f 3y
3:15 (3:18) (Class 6) 2-Y-O £1,940 (£577; £288; £144) Stalls Centre

Form
1 **One Penny Piece** 2-8-6 0 FrannyNorton 6 67+
(Philip McBride) *mde all: shkn and qcknd clr over 1f out: idled wl ins fnl f* 11/4[1]
55 2 ½ **Shot In The Sun (IRE)**[33] 2282 2-8-6 0 LukeMorris 4 66+
(David Evans) *a.p: rdn to chse wnr over 1f out: edgd rt: styd on u.p* 4/1[2]
02 3 19 **See Me Sometime**[16] 2759 2-8-11 0 TedDurcan 5 20
(Mark H Tompkins) *hld up: hdwy 1/2-way: rdn and wknd over 1f out* 13/2
0044 4 1½ **Doncaster Belle (IRE)**[1] 3189 2-8-3 0 SimonPearce(3) 1
(Charles Smith) *chsd ldrs: rdn over 2f out: wknd wl over 1f out* 7/1
5 4 **Arthur's Melody** 2-8-4 0 RyanWhile(7) 8
(Bill Turner) *s.s: green: outpcd and racd alone on stands' side rail: sme hdwy 1/2-way: wknd over 2f out* 7/1
460 6 1 **Love's Last Adieu**[25] 2475 2-8-6 0 (b[1]) LiamJones 2
(J S Moore) *chsd ldrs: rdn over 2f out: sn wknd* 20/1
0 7 5 **Primrose Posy**[5] 3112 2-7-13 0 ShelleyBirkett(7) 9
(Julia Feilden) *chsd ldrs tl rdn and wknd over 2f out: t.o* 10/1
0 8 4½ **Mannerist**[30] 2344 2-8-11 0 FrederikTylicki 7
(Daniel Mark Loughnane) *prom: lost pl over 4f out: wknd 1/2-way: t.o* 5/1[3]

1m 30.46s (3.86) **Going Correction** +0.175s/f (Good) 8 Ran SP% 115.5
Speed ratings (Par 91): **84,83,61,60,55 54,48,43**
toteswingers 1&2 £2.10, 1&3 £2.90, 2&3 £2.00 CSF £13.92 TOTE £2.70: £1.10, £1.80, £2.00; EX 12.40 Trifecta £44.90 Pool: £2,581.51 - 43.11 winning units..There was no bid for the winner. Shot In The Sun was claimed by Mr R. A. Fahey for £5,000.
Owner P J McBride **Bred** Mrs Sarah Hamilton **Trained** Newmarket, Suffolk
FOCUS
A weak contest lacking depth, and the time was poor, but the first two pulled 19l clear, the equivalent of 50lb.

3256 BETVICTOR.COM H'CAP 2m
3:50 (3:51) (Class 6) (0-60,58) 4-Y-O+ £1,940 (£577; £288; £144) Stalls High

Form RPR
2545 1 **Baan (USA)**[42] 1953 10-8-9 51 RosieJessop(5) 5 60
(James Eustace) *hld up: hdwy over 3f out: rdn over 2f out: chsd ldr over 1f out: styd on to ld nr fin* 9/2[2]
-322 2 ½ **If I Had Him (IRE)**[38] 2301 9-9-7 58 (v) LukeMorris 2 66
(George Baker) *led 2f: chsd ldr tl led again over 3f out: sn drvn along: clr over 1f out: hdd nr fin* 7/4[1]
00-0 3 9 **Eanans Bay (IRE)**[22] 2563 4-8-8 46 (b) TedDurcan 4 43
(Mark H Tompkins) *chsd ldrs: led after 2f: rdn and hdd over 3f out: wknd fnl f* 5/1[3]
0-60 4 6 **Absolutely Me (IRE)**[20] 2642 4-8-7 45 FrederikTylicki 9 35
(Willie Musson) *sn chsng ldrs: rdn over 3f out: wknd over 2f out* 13/2
50-0 5 7 **Olimamu (IRE)**[20] 2642 6-8-5 45 SimonPearce(3) 1 27
(Lydia Pearce) *prom: rdn over 4f out: wknd over 3f out* 16/1
5450 6 13 **Soweto Star (IRE)**[71] 1325 5-9-4 55 SteveDrowne 6 21
(John Best) *prom tl rdn and wknd over 2f out: eased over 1f out: t.o* 7/1
0006 7 5 **Dubai Emerald (USA)**[9] 2966 4-8-0 45 NoelGarbutt(7) 7
(Chris Dwyer) *hld up: bhd fnl 7f: t.o* 20/1
2/0- 8 10 **Cape Schanck**[11] 1014 9-8-1 45 ShelleyBirkett(7) 8
(Alan Coogan) *chsd ldrs: lost pl after 3f: bhd fr 1/2-way: t.o* 33/1

3m 32.84s (0.44) **Going Correction** -0.175s/f (Firm)
WFA 4 from 5yo+ 1lb 8 Ran SP% 110.6
Speed ratings (Par 101): **91,90,86,83,79 73,70,65**
toteswingers 1&2 £2.70, 1&3 £4.10, 2&3 £2.80 CSF £11.91 CT £37.05 TOTE £7.40: £2.30, £1.10, £1.40; EX 12.60 Trifecta £49.90 Pool: £2,952.56 - 44.29 winning units..
Owner Mrs James Eustace **Bred** Shadwell Farm Inc **Trained** Newmarket, Suffolk

The Form Book Flat, Raceform Ltd, Compton, RG20 6NL.

FOCUS
A modest staying handicap run at a steady pace. It was slow motion stuff late on.

3257 BETVICTOR ROYAL ASCOT NO LOSE HUGHES H'CAP 1m 6f 17y
4:20 (4:20) (Class 5) (0-70,75) 3-Y-0 **£2,587** (£770; £384; £192) **Stalls** High

Form RPR
-111 **1** **Alcaeus**[6] 3055 3-9-13 **75** 6ex LukeMorris 6 92+
(Sir Mark Prescott Bt) *chsd ldrs: led over 1f out: sn rdn: edgd lft ins fnl f: styd on* **4/7**[1]
0-25 **2** *hd* **Nateeja (IRE)**[21] 2599 3-8-12 **60** SebSanders 1 76
(J W Hills) *chsd ldr tl led 4f out: rdn and hdd over 1f out: n.m.r ins fnl f: styd on* **6/1**[3]
4-32 **3** *2 1/2* **Deficit (IRE)**[15] 2784 3-9-2 **64** RobertWinston 3 76
(Michael Bell) *hld up: hdwy over 3f out: rdn and hung lft fr over 2f out: no imp fnl f* **9/2**[2]
06-0 **4** *15* **Helamis**[14] 2800 3-8-4 **52** LiamJones 5 43
(Stuart Williams) *sn led: pushed along and hdd 4f out: rdn and wknd 2f out* **28/1**
0235 **5** *12* **Bold Assertion**[15] 2784 3-9-5 **67** SteveDrowne 2 41
(John Best) *prom tl rdn and wknd over 3f out* **28/1**
56-3 **6** *2 1/4* **Vandross (IRE)**[14] 2800 3-8-12 **60** (b) TedDurcan 4 31
(Chris Wall) *sn pushed along in rr: last and drvn along over 9f out: wknd over 4f out* **16/1**

3m 4.97s (-2.63) **Going Correction** -0.175s/f (Firm) **6** Ran SP% **108.9**
Speed ratings (Par 99): **100,99,98,89,83 81**
toteswingers 1&2 £1.80, 1&3 £1.20, 2&3 £2.40 CSF £4.15 CT £6.57 TOTE £1.30: £1.10, £2.80; EX 5.10 Trifecta £11.10 Pool: £3,281.72 - 220.63 winning units..
Owner Ne'er Do Wells IV **Bred** Miss K Rausing **Trained** Newmarket, Suffolk

FOCUS
An uncompetitive handicap run at an honest pace.

3258 ROYAL ASCOT MONEY BACK AT BETVICTOR.COM FILLIES' H'CAP 1m 3f 101y
4:55 (4:55) (Class 4) (0-85,88) 4-Y-0+ **£4,690** (£1,395; £697) **Stalls** Low

Form RPR
1 **1** **Songbird (IRE)**[28] 2389 4-9-7 **85** IanMongan 3 103
(Lady Cecil) *trckd ldr tl led over 2f out: clr over 1f out: easily* **2/5**[1]
-214 **2** *11* **Hepworth**[20] 2619 4-9-3 **81** (b) RobertHavlin 4 81
(John Gosden) *hld up in tch: rdn over 2f out: outpcd fr over 1f out* **3/1**[2]
4625 **3** *nk* **Dazzling Valentine**[31] 2311 5-7-13 **70** TimClark(7) 1 69
(Alan Bailey) *led: rdn and hdd over 2f out: outpcd fr over 1f out* **10/1**[3]

2m 27.64s (-1.06) **Going Correction** -0.175s/f (Firm) **3** Ran SP% **105.5**
Speed ratings (Par 102): **96,88,87**
CSF £1.81 TOTE £1.30; EX 1.50 Trifecta £1.90 Pool: £1,505.64 - 587.76 winning units..
Owner Sir Robert Ogden **Bred** Mine Excavation Syndicate **Trained** Newmarket, Suffolk

FOCUS
Two non-runners took plenty of interest out of this handicap, but the crowd were treated to an impressive display by the beautifully bred winner.

3259 SIS LIVE FILLIES' H'CAP 7f 3y
5:25 (5:25) (Class 4) (0-85,78) 4-Y-0+ **£4,690** (£1,395; £697) **Stalls** Centre

Form RPR
0-03 **1** **Poisson D'Or**[26] 2450 4-9-2 **75** TedDurcan 3 80+
(Rae Guest) *mde all: shkn up and edgd lft over 1f out: r.o: eased nr fin* **8/15**[1]
-060 **2** *2* **Shesastar**[31] 2310 5-9-5 **78** FrannyNorton 2 76
(David Barron) *chsd wnr: shkn up over 2f out: styd on same pce fnl f* **3/1**[2]
5-40 **3** *4* **Ray Of Joy**[19] 2657 7-9-3 **76** IanMongan 1 66
(J R Jenkins) *chsd ldrs: rdn over 2f out: no ex fnl f* **5/1**[3]

1m 28.4s (1.80) **Going Correction** +0.175s/f (Good) **3** Ran SP% **106.9**
Speed ratings (Par 102): **96,93,89**
CSF £2.38 TOTE £1.30; EX 2.30 Trifecta £3.10 Pool: £513.40 - 122.99 winning units..
Owner The Family Fish **Bred** New England, Stanley House & Mount Coote Studs **Trained** Newmarket, Suffolk

FOCUS
A poor turnout for the money. The pace was honest, with the winner making all.
T/Plt: £6.90 to a £1 stake. Pool: £57,710.21. 6,082.62 winning tickets. T/Qpdt: £1.90 to a £1 stake. Pool: £4,011.16. 1,552.54 winning tickets. CR

3260 - 3261a (Foreign Racing) - See Raceform Interactive

3070 LEOPARDSTOWN (L-H)
Thursday, June 13

OFFICIAL GOING: Good to yielding

3262a BALLYCORUS STKS (GROUP 3) 7f
6:55 (6:56) 3-Y-0+ **£31,707** (£9,268; £4,390; £1,463)

RPR
1 **Leitir Mor (IRE)**[19] 2676 3-9-2 107 (tp) KevinManning 6 109
(J S Bolger, Ire) *trckd ldr: cl 2nd 1/2-way: outpcd briefly and rdn in 3rd ins fnl f where hung rt: sn clsd u.p nr fin to ld fnl strides: jst* **13/2**
2 *nk* **Lily's Angel (IRE)**[19] 2678 4-9-9 106 GaryCarroll 1 109
(G M Lyons, Ire) *led: 1 l clr 1/2-way: rdn fr 2f out and stl in front ins fnl f: strly pressed nr fin and hdd fnl strides: jst denied* **7/2**[2]
3 *shd* **Yellow Rosebud (IRE)**[67] 1413 4-9-9 105 (b) PatSmullen 5 109
(D K Weld, Ire) *trckd ldrs: cl 3rd 1/2-way: tk clsr order in 2nd 2f out: rdn and kpt on wl towards fin: jst failed and denied 2nd fnl strides* **10/1**
4 *1/2* **Bold Thady Quill (IRE)**[32] 2288 6-9-9 103 (v[1]) ShaneFoley 4 108+
(K J Condon, Ire) *s.i.s and racd in rr: tk clsr order fr 2f out where sn n.m.r bhd horses: swtchd and kpt on wl u.p ins fnl f: nrst fin* **16/1**
5 *1 1/4* **Reply (IRE)**[10] 2941 4-9-9 107 (v) JosephO'Brien 2 104
(A P O'Brien, Ire) *in tch: 4th 1/2-way: rdn fr 2f out and no imp in 5th fnl 100yds: kpt on same pce* **11/10**[1]
6 *2 1/2* **Sruthan (IRE)**[18] 2687 3-8-13 107 ChrisHayes 3 93
(P D Deegan, Ire) *dwlt and racd towards rr: 5th 1/2-way: pushed along into st and sn no imp: dropped to rr ins fnl f: eased nr fin* **5/1**[3]

1m 31.68s (2.98) **Going Correction** +0.725s/f (Yiel)
WFA 3 from 4yo+ 10lb **6** Ran SP% **114.8**
Speed ratings: **111,110,110,109,108 105**
CSF £29.99 TOTE £9.50: £4.20, £1.90; DF 27.40.
Owner Mrs J S Bolger **Bred** J S Bolger **Trained** Coolcullen, Co Carlow

FOCUS
Solid Group 3 form and the winner looks set to be a pacemaker for Dawn Approach at Royal Ascot. The winner has been rated to his best, his Dewhurst figure aside.

3263a BALLYOGAN STKS (GROUP 3) 6f
7:30 (7:32) 3-Y-0+ **£31,707** (£9,268; £4,390; £1,463)

RPR
1 **Fiesolana (IRE)**[19] 2679 4-9-8 101 CO'Donoghue 4 108
(W McCreery, Ire) *hld up in mid-div: prog on inner into st and wnt 3rd over 1 1/2f out: sn chal and led ins fnl f: kpt on wl towards fin* **10/1**
2 *1 1/4* **Boston Rocker (IRE)**[29] 2374 3-9-0 99 DeclanMcDonogh 6 102
(Edward Lynam, Ire) *trckd ldr: cl up in 2nd appr st: effrt over 1 1/2f out: kpt on wl towards fin wout matching wnr* **14/1**
3 *3/4* **Hanky Panky (IRE)**[18] 2689 3-9-0 100 JosephO'Brien 8 100+
(A P O'Brien, Ire) *w.w towards rr: pushed along in 11th into st: sn rdn and hdwy on outer fr over 1f out into nvr threatening 3rd nr fin: nvr nrr* **8/1**[3]
4 *1/2* **Place In My Heart**[32] 2300 4-9-8 AdamKirby 3 100
(Clive Cox) *hld up in tch: pushed along in 6th fr 2f out: sn rdn and no imp on principals 1f out: kpt on into nvr nrr 4th cl home* **5/1**[2]
5 *nk* **Tickled Pink (IRE)**[29] 2368 4-9-11 TomQueally 1 102
(Lady Cecil) *led on inner: narrow advantage 1/2-way: strly pressed fr 1 1/2f out and hdd ins fnl f: sn no ex and dropped to 3rd: wknd cl home* **6/4**[1]
6 *1/2* **True Verdict (IRE)**[25] 2481 3-9-0 95 WJLee 12 95
(David Wachman, Ire) *w.w in rr: plenty to do appr st: rdn fr 2f out and clsd u.p into nvr threatening 6th fnl 50yds: kpt on* **20/1**
7 *1/2* **Tobann (IRE)**[10] 2941 3-9-0 95 (t) KevinManning 2 94
(J S Bolger, Ire) *hld up in rr of mid-div: t.k.h: rdn in 8th fr 2f out and wnt 5th briefly ins fnl f: sn no ex: wknd cl home* **11/1**
8 *1 1/2* **Liberating**[43] 1921 3-9-0 93 (p) FMBerry 7 89
(Mrs John Harrington, Ire) *chsd ldrs: 5th 1/2-way: rdn and no imp fr over 2f out* **20/1**
9 *nk* **Coolnagree (IRE)**[10] 2941 4-9-8 94 (b) PatSmullen 11 90
(W McCreery, Ire) *in rr of mid-div for most: pushed along fr 2f out and sn n.m.r bhd horses: sn swtchd rt and rdn: kpt on u.p towards fin* **33/1**
10 *1/2* **Scream Blue Murder (IRE)**[33] 2270 3-9-0 103 WayneLordan 9 86
(T Stack, Ire) *chsd ldrs: cl 3rd 1/2-way: rdn and no imp fr 2f out: wknd ins fnl f* **5/1**[2]
11 *3 1/4* **Katla (IRE)**[19] 2676 5-9-8 101 SeamieHeffernan 5 78
(J F Grogan, Ire) *trckd ldrs: cl 4th 1/2-way: pushed along in 3rd into st: sn rdn and no imp: wknd* **25/1**
12 *1 3/4* **Core Element (IRE)**[10] 2941 6-9-8 89 ChrisHayes 10 72
(P J Prendergast, Ire) *mid-div: 6th 1/2-way: rdn and wknd fr over 2f out* **50/1**

1m 13.93s (-0.17) **Going Correction** +0.20s/f (Good)
WFA 3 from 4yo+ 8lb **12** Ran SP% **126.8**
Speed ratings: **109,107,106,105,105 104,103,101,101,100 96,94**
CSF £139.66 TOTE £11.70: £3.40, £3.20, £2.20; DF 155.40.
Owner K Leavy/L Cribben/Mrs A McCreery **Bred** Robert De Vere Hunt **Trained** The Curragh, Co.Kildare

FOCUS
Form which is rated around the placed horses. The winner appreciated the slower ground.

3264 - 3266a (Foreign Racing) - See Raceform Interactive

2917 CHEPSTOW (L-H)
Friday, June 14

OFFICIAL GOING: Good to soft
Wind: Brisk, across Weather: Bright early

3267 FREEBETS.CO.UK FREE BETS EBF NOVICE STKS 6f 16y
5:30 (5:30) (Class 4) 2-Y-0 **£4,075** (£1,212; £606; £303) **Stalls** Centre

Form RPR
21 **1** **Legend Rising (IRE)**[16] 2778 2-9-5 0 RichardHughes 7 91+
(Richard Hannon) *in tch: stdy hdwy to ld jst ins fnl 2f: pushed clr fnl f: easily* **2/5**[1]
01 **2** *4 1/2* **Piazon**[25] 2502 2-9-2 0 HayleyTurner 1 74
(Michael Bell) *t.k.h: in tch: hdwy to ld 3f out: drvn and hdd jst ins fnl 2f: no ch w wnr appr fnl f but styd on for clr 2nd* **5/1**[2]
3100 **3** *5* **Kodafine (IRE)**[28] 2426 2-8-11 0 TomQueally 2 54
(David Evans) *led to 3f out: rdn over 2f out: wknd over 1f out* **25/1**
5431 **4** *1 3/4* **Left Defender (IRE)**[9] 2993 2-9-2 0 CathyGannon 4 54
(Jo Hughes) *chsd ldr to 1/2-way: rdn: hung lft and wknd fr 2f out* **12/1**[3]
100 **5** *2 1/4* **Sleepy Joe (IRE)**[24] 2553 2-8-9 0 DanielCremin(7) 5 47
(Mick Channon) *chsd ldrs over 3f* **14/1**
6 *1 1/2* **Big Kenny** 2-8-9 0 DeclanBates(5) 3 41
(David Evans) *s.i.s: outpcd thrght* **50/1**

1m 13.03s (1.03) **Going Correction** +0.15s/f (Good) **6** Ran SP% **108.3**
Speed ratings (Par 95): **99,93,86,84,81 79**
toteswingers: 1&2 £1.50, 1&3 £3.60, 2&3 £6.90 CSF £2.46 TOTE £1.10: £1.10, £2.10; EX 2.30 Trifecta £17.20 Pool: £2,588.32 - 112.78 winning units..
Owner Mohamed Saeed Al Shahi **Bred** Gus Roche **Trained** East Everleigh, Wilts

FOCUS
After 7.5mm of rain during the day the going was changed to good to soft. They went a fair pace in this novice event and the hot favourite powered clear from his main market rival. He looks progressive and this form could rate higher.

3268 CWMTILLERY GLASS CENTRE MAIDEN H'CAP 6f 16y
6:05 (6:05) (Class 5) (0-70,68) 3-Y-0+ **£2,587** (£770; £384; £192) **Stalls** Centre

Form RPR
05-4 **1** **Queen Hermione (IRE)**[9] 2997 5-8-2 **49** oh4 (vt) AdamMcLean(7) 6 59
(Derek Shaw) *trckd ldrs: bmpd wl over 2f out: drvn to ld jst ins fnl f: shkn up and sn c clr* **18/1**
-056 **2** *2 3/4* **Farmers Dream (IRE)**[9] 2998 6-8-9 **49** oh4 (t) MartinDwyer 10 50
(Derek Shaw) *in rr and off pce tl hdwy over 2f out: drvn to ld jst over 1f out: hdd jst ins fnl f and sn outpcd by wnr but kpt on wl for clr 2nd* **20/1**
46-0 **3** *2 3/4* **Compton Prince**[7] 3051 4-9-6 **65** (b) MatthewLawson(5) 3 57
(Milton Bradley) *chsd ldrs: led appr fnl 3f: sn rdn: hdd jst over 1f out: sn outpcd into 3rd* **16/1**
0064 **4** *3/4* **Vergality Ridge (IRE)**[31] 2347 3-8-3 **51** ow1 (be) WilliamCarson 4 39
(Ronald Harris) *led tl appr fnl 3f: wknd fnl f* **10/1**
0-43 **5** *3/4* **Speronella**[25] 2499 3-9-3 **65** RichardHughes 1 50
(Hughie Morrison) *in tch: hdwy to cl on ldrs whn bmpd wl over 2f out: wknd over 1f out* **7/2**[2]
-303 **6** *6* **Little Choosey**[14] 2829 3-9-6 **68** AdamKirby 9 37
(Clive Cox) *in rr: hdwy to cl on ldrs 2f out: sn rdn and btn* **15/8**[1]

0053 **7** *hd* **Minty Jones**[35] 2236 4-8-10 **50** oh4 ow1........................(v) TomQueally 7 18
(Michael Mullineaux) *chsd ldrs: rdn and wknd appr fnl 2f* **16/1**
44-0 **8** *1* **Jawim**[56] 1665 4-8-9 **49** oh1.. CathyGannon 8 13
(Malcolm Saunders) *chsd ldrs: rdn over 2f out: wknd qckly wl over 1f out* **12/1**
3350 **R** **Brown Volcano (IRE)**[31] 2345 4-8-12 **52**.................... FergusSweeney 5
(John O'Shea) *hdwy to cl on ldrs over 3f out: veered lft: crashed through rails and collapsed wl over 2f out: b.b.v* **4/1**[3]
1m 12.99s (0.99) **Going Correction** +0.15s/f (Good)
WFA 3 from 4yo+ 8lb **9** Ran SP% **115.6**
Speed ratings (Par 103): **99,95,91,90,89 81,81,80,**
toteswingers: 1&2 £28.40, 1&3 £27.40, 2&3 £43.50 CSF £320.87 CT £5770.99 TOTE £26.90: £5.40, £7.00, £5.20; EX 310.20 Trifecta £1100.20 Part won. Pool: £1,467.00 - 0.04 winning units..
Owner Dr David Chapman-Jones **Bred** Knocklong House Stud **Trained** Sproxton, Leics
FOCUS
They went a good pace in this maiden handicap and Derek Shaw trained the first two home. Poor form, with only a couple racing off their correct marks.

3269 BATHWICK TYRES FILLIES' H'CAP 1m 14y
6:40 (6:40) (Class 5) (0-75,74) 4-Y-0+ **£2,587** (£770; £384; £192) **Stalls** Centre

Form RPR
-362 **1** **Lady Bayside**[15] 2792 5-9-1 **68**..................................... RichardHughes 5 76
(Malcolm Saunders) *trckd ldrs: drvn to ld jst over 1f out: sn rdn: styd on strly clsng stages* **15/8**[1]
40-1 **2** *1 3/4* **Emmuska**[23] 2573 4-9-1 **68**.. AdamKirby 7 72
(Clive Cox) *slt ld on rails but sn hrd pressed: kpt slt ld u.p tl hdd jst over 1f out: outpcd by wnr but styd on wl to keep 2nd* **2/1**[2]
0-46 **3** *3/4* **Silvas Romana (IRE)**[6] 3098 4-9-7 **74**.............................. ShaneKelly 3 76
(Mark Brisbourne) *sn pressing ldr: rdn and upsides whn edgd lft 2f out: styd on same pce u.p fnl f* **8/1**
303 **4** *1 1/4* **Lady Sylvia**[14] 2845 4-8-12 **65**.. TomQueally 1 64
(Joseph Tuite) *s.i.s: t.k.h in rr: hdwy to cl on ldrs over 2f out: sn rdn: btn appr fnl f* **7/1**
6000 **5** *1 1/4* **Dancing Welcome**[11] 2918 7-8-5 **58**.............................(bt) JimmyQuinn 6 55
(Milton Bradley) *in rr: pushed along over 2f out: nvr gng pce to be competitive* **25/1**
11-6 **6** *shd* **Croeso Mawr**[11] 2920 7-9-3 **70**.. CathyGannon 2 66
(John Spearing) *chsd ldrs: rdn over 2f out: btn wl over 1f out* **9/2**[3]
1m 36.45s (0.25) **Going Correction** +0.15s/f (Good) **6** Ran SP% **113.8**
Speed ratings (Par 100): **104,102,101,100,99 98**
toteswingers: 1&2 £1.40, 1&3 £4.10, 2&3 £2.70 CSF £6.11 TOTE £3.10: £1.50, £1.40; EX 6.10 Trifecta £31.40 Pool: £1,222.80 - 29.13 winning units..
Owner Tim Bostwick **Bred** M Saunders & T Bostwick **Trained** Green Ore, Somerset
FOCUS
A competitive fillies' handicap. The pace was not very strong but the winner can be marked up for running down the two front-runners. Sound form, rated around the winner.

3270 BET YOUR BOXERCHIPS ON IT H'CAP 7f 16y
7:15 (7:16) (Class 5) (0-70,71) 4-Y-0+ **£2,587** (£770; £384; £192) **Stalls** Centre

Form RPR
-523 **1** **Sarangoo**[30] 2361 5-9-7 **68**.. CathyGannon 9 78
(Malcolm Saunders) *chsd ldrs: wnt 2nd 2f out: hung lft u.p and led 1f out: drvn out* **11/2**[3]
5333 **2** *2* **Emiratesdotcom**[11] 2918 7-9-0 **66**...................... MatthewLawson(5) 10 71
(Milton Bradley) *in rr: drvn and hdwy over 1f out: edging lft but styd on wl fnl f to take 2nd fnl 110yds: no imp on wnr* **5/1**[2]
-503 **3** *3/4* **Offbeat Safaris (IRE)**[18] 2709 5-8-7 **54**........................... WilliamCarson 7 57
(Ronald Harris) *in rr: rdn and hdwy fr 2f out: styd on u.p fnl f to take 3rd clsng stages: no imp on wnr* **9/1**
0025 **4** *shd* **Basle**[22] 2596 6-8-12 **59**..(t) RichardHughes 13 61
(Michael Blake) *t.k.h and stdd in rr: drvn and hdwy over 1f out: kpt on fnl f to press for 3rd clsng stages: no imp on wnr* **9/2**[1]
6365 **5** *1 3/4* **Swendab (IRE)**[7] 3042 5-9-3 **64**..............................(b) FergusSweeney 12 62
(John O'Shea) *led after 1f: rdn 2f out: hung lft and hdd 1f out: wknd fnl 110yds* **12/1**
40-2 **6** *2 1/2* **Cheers Big Ears (IRE)**[43] 1951 7-7-13 **51** oh2 ow2...... PhilipPrince(5) 6 42
(Richard Price) *in rr: hdwy and nt clr run ins fnl 2f: kpt on fnl f: nvr a threat* **7/1**
0000 **7** *6* **Courageous (IRE)**[30] 2364 7-8-12 **59**................................ JimmyQuinn 4 34
(Milton Bradley) *chsd ldrs: rdn over 2f out: wknd wl over 1f out* **20/1**
2500 **8** *1 3/4* **Olynard (IRE)**[40] 2037 7-7-9 **49** oh3..............................(p) NoraLooby(7) 8 19
(Michael Mullineaux) *chsd ldrs: rdn over 2f out: sn btn* **33/1**
5-00 **9** *3/4* **Memphis Man**[7] 3052 10-8-7 **54**.. SamHitchcott 1 22
(Milton Bradley) *rdn over 3f out: a in rr* **33/1**
0-35 **10** *1/2* **Shomberg**[31] 2345 4-8-2 **54**...(p) AmyScott(5) 2 21
(Dai Burchell) *led 1f: wknd u.p over 1f out* **8/1**
5053 **11** *2* **The Mongoose**[7] 3051 5-8-9 **61**....................................(t) DeclanBates(5) 5 22
(David Evans) *chsd ldrs tl wknd qckly ins fnl 2f* **6/1**
300- **12** *nk* **Euroquip Boy (IRE)**[284] 5874 6-8-10 **57**........................... HayleyTurner 11 17
(Michael Scudamore) *chsd ldrs to 1/2-way* **16/1**
1m 24.63s (1.43) **Going Correction** +0.15s/f (Good) **12** Ran SP% **122.3**
Speed ratings (Par 103): **97,94,93,93,91 88,82,80,79,78 76,75**
toteswingers: 1&2 £5.50, 1&3 £11.40, 2&3 £11.10 CSF £33.61 CT £248.32 TOTE £8.20: £2.40, £2.00, £3.70; EX 30.90 Trifecta £372.70 Pool: £1,107.63 - 2.22 winning units..
Owner Lockstone Business Services Ltd **Bred** M S Saunders And Chris Scott **Trained** Green Ore, Somerset
FOCUS
They went a decent pace in this handicap and the first five finished clear. A personal best from the winner.

3271 BATHWICK TYRES H'CAP 2m 49y
7:50 (7:51) (Class 6) (0-65,65) 4-Y-0+ **£1,940** (£577; £288; £144) **Stalls** Low

Form RPR
1-03 **1** **Tijori (IRE)**[31] 2350 5-9-7 **62**...(p) NeilCallan 1 70
(Bernard Llewellyn) *impr into mid-div 1/2-way: hdwy to cl on ldrs over 3f out: styd on u.p fnl f to ld cl home: hld on all out* **8/1**
1233 **2** *hd* **Jezza**[17] 1744 7-9-9 **64**...(bt[1]) AdamKirby 7 72
(Karen George) *in rr: rdn over 3f out: hdwy fr 2f out: str run u.p to cl ldrs fnl 110yds: tk 2nd last stride: nt quite rch wnr* **14/1**
0015 **3** *shd* **Pass The Time**[11] 2921 4-8-7 **49**..................................(p) HayleyTurner 5 57
(Neil Mulholland) *led: narrowly hdd 3f out: styd pressing ldrs and regained ld 1f out: kpt on wl: hdd and lost two pls last strides* **12/1**
32 **4** *3* **Danisa**[18] 2729 4-9-8 **64**...(t) WilliamCarson 3 68+
(David Bridgwater) *towards rr: hdwy fr 5f out: slt ld 3f out: sn rdn: hdd 1f out: wknd fnl 110yds* **6/1**[3]
-242 **5** *4* **Fuzzy Logic (IRE)**[11] 2922 4-8-5 **47**.................................... MartinLane 8 46
(Bernard Llewellyn) *in tch: chsd ldrs 6f out: drvn to chal over 3f out: wknd fnl f* **5/1**[2]
/006 **6** *2 1/2* **William Hogarth**[8] 2922 8-8-9 **50**..................................... CathyGannon 11 46
(Keith Goldsworthy) *chsd ldr tl over 3f out: sn btn* **33/1**
3/05 **7** *1/2* **Sagredo (USA)**[13] 2860 9-9-10 **65**..........................(p) RichardHughes 13 61
(Jonjo O'Neill) *mid-div: hdwy to trck ldrs 7f out: chal over 3f out: sn rdn: wknd fr 2f out* **3/1**[1]
6344 **8** *3 3/4* **Ctappers**[11] 2921 4-8-9 **58**... DanielCremin(7) 6 49
(Mick Channon) *in rr: pushed along 4f out: mod prog clsng stages* **14/1**
5-36 **9** *1/2* **Captain Sharpe**[4] 1980 5-9-1 **63**...............................(tp) SiobhanMiller(7) 4 53
(Bernard Llewellyn) *s.i.s: in rr: mod late prog* **20/1**
00/5 **10** *1 1/2* **Lady Bridget**[15] 2801 5-8-5 **51**....................................(bt) PhilipPrince(5) 2 40
(Mark Gillard) *in tch: rdn and wknd 4f out* **25/1**
13/ **11** *2 1/2* **Rock Peak (IRE)**[575] 7264 8-8-0 **48**.................................. TimClark(7) 12 34
(Bernard Llewellyn) *sn bhd* **14/1**
50-3 **12** *1 1/4* **Spinning Waters**[21] 1980 7-8-0 **46** oh1...........................(p) AmyScott(5) 9 30
(Dai Burchell) *chsd ldrs: wknd over 4f out* **12/1**
6203 **13** *3* **Vertueux (FR)**[11] 2921 8-8-13 **54**..................................... JimmyQuinn 14 35
(Tony Carroll) *chsd ldrs: rdn 4f out: sn wknd* **16/1**
3m 40.41s (1.51) **Going Correction** +0.15s/f (Good)
WFA 4 from 5yo+ 1lb **13** Ran SP% **119.9**
Speed ratings (Par 101): **102,101,101,100,98 97,96,94,94,93 92,92,90**
toteswingers: 1&2 £15.60, 1&3 £31.20, 2&3 £12.20 CSF £112.48 CT £1347.57 TOTE £9.00: £2.80, £4.00, £4.20; EX 133.60 Trifecta £879.50 Part won. Pool: £1,172.79 - 0.62 winning units..
Owner G Robinson **Bred** Polish Belle Partnership **Trained** Fochriw, Caerphilly
■ Stewards' Enquiry : Hayley Turner two-day ban; used whip above permitted level.
FOCUS
There was a tight three-way finish in this minor staying handicap after a muddling gallop. The winner was not far off his 3yo level.

3272 ROBERTS & CO ESTATE AGENTS EBF MAIDEN FILLIES' STKS 1m 4f 23y
8:25 (8:30) (Class 5) 3-Y-0+ **£3,881** (£1,155; £577; £288) **Stalls** Low

Form RPR
2-32 **1** **Auld Alliance (IRE)**[28] 2423 3-8-12 83....................(v[1]) RichardHughes 13 80
(Sir Michael Stoute) *mde all: drvn and styd on strly whn pressed fr over 1f out* **5/6**[1]
55 **2** *1* **Gertrude Gray (IRE)**[18] 2713 3-8-12 0............................ TomQueally 11 78
(Lady Cecil) *chsd ldrs: wnt 2nd ins fnl 3f: effrt to press wnr over 1f out: no imp and styd on same pce ins fnl f* **7/1**[3]
0-3 **3** *1 1/2* **Wadaa (USA)**[29] 2392 3-8-12 0... NeilCallan 3 76
(James Tate) *chsd ldrs: rdn to take 3rd over 2f out: kpt on same pce fnl f* **4/1**[2]
0352 **4** *1/2* **Enaitch (IRE)**[10] 2967 3-8-12 78...................................... SamHitchcott 4 75
(Mick Channon) *chsd ldrs: rdn over 2f out: kpt on same pce u.p fnl f* **8/1**
5 *12* **Sunday Meadow (IRE)**[367] 4-9-13 0............................. HayleyTurner 10 56
(William Knight) *chsd ldrs: rdn and wknd 3f out* **33/1**
46 **6** *5* **Dawn Beat**[37] 2157 3-8-7 0................................. MatthewLawson(5) 5 48
(Jonathan Portman) *s.i.s: in rr: rdn 4f out: mod prog fnl 2f* **25/1**
6- **7** *8* **Primacy (IRE)**[31] 4188 4-9-8 0.............................. RobertWilliams(5) 16 35
(Neil Mulholland) *towards rr most of way* **100/1**
0-0 **8** *2 1/2* **Endura**[53] 1727 3-8-12 0.. CathyGannon 9 31
(Harry Dunlop) *in tch: rdn over 4f out: sn btn* **66/1**
9 *1* **Bella's Charm** 3-8-12 0.. MartinLane 12 29
(James Tate) *s.i.s: a in rr* **20/1**
00 **10** *2 3/4* **Dance**[18] 2713 4-9-13 0.. FergusSweeney 15 25
(Rod Millman) *bhd most of way* **100/1**
11 *3* **Lulu's Gift (IRE)**[27] 7-9-6 0.. DanielCremin(7) 7 20
(Michael Mullineaux) *in tch: rdn and wknd 5f out* **80/1**
0/6 **12** *1/2* **Narla**[146] 275 4-9-13 0.. AdamKirby 14 19
(Clive Cox) *chsd wnr tl wknd qckly ins fnl 3f* **20/1**
00 **13** *6* **Pure Flight (IRE)**[18] 2713 3-8-12 0...................................... JohnFahy 1 10
(Anthony Honeyball) *bdly hmpd after 1f and no ch after* **66/1**
0 **P** **Heavenly Prospect**[29] 2389 3-8-12 0.............................. MartinDwyer 2
(William Muir) *fatally injured and p.u after 1f* **50/1**
2m 39.81s (0.81) **Going Correction** +0.15s/f (Good)
WFA 3 from 4yo+ 15lb **14** Ran SP% **122.6**
Speed ratings (Par 100): **103,102,101,101,93 89,84,82,82,80 78,77,73,**
toteswingers: 1&2 £1.80, 1&3 £2.00, 2&3 £2.80 CSF £6.58 TOTE £1.70: £1.10, £1.90, £1.50; EX 8.10 Trifecta £17.60 Pool: £1,318/73 - 56.12 winning units..
Owner Ballymacoll Stud **Bred** Ballymacoll Stud Farm Ltd **Trained** Newmarket, Suffolk
FOCUS
The hot favourite showed a good attitude to deliver in this decent maiden for the track and the four market leaders pulled a long way clear. The winner did not need to match her previous form.

3273 BONUS.CO.UK CASINO BONUS H'CAP 1m 2f 36y
8:55 (8:56) (Class 5) (0-75,74) 4-Y-0+ **£2,587** (£770; £384; £192) **Stalls** Low

Form RPR
-024 **1** **Play Street**[31] 2349 4-9-0 **72**..................................... MatthewLawson(5) 6 82+
(Jonathan Portman) *chsd ldrs: wnt 2nd over 3f out: led over 2f out: clr ins fnl f: eased and idled clsng stages* **7/1**
0-60 **2** *nk* **May Be Some Time**[25] 2498 5-9-0 **67**................................(t) NeilCallan 5 74
(Stuart Kittow) *in tch: hdwy 2f out: wnt 2nd over 1f out: drvn and kpt on to cl on idling wnr clsng stages* **9/1**
3 *2* **Tempuran**[286] 4-9-1 **68**.. WilliamCarson 7 71
(David Bridgwater) *slowly away: in rr: drvn over 3f out: styd on over 1f out to take 3rd fnl 75yds: no imp on ldng duo* **14/1**
0505 **4** *1* **Robin Hood (IRE)**[18] 2728 5-9-7 **74**...............................(b) JackMitchell 4 75
(Philip Mitchell) *chsd ldr: rdn over 4f out: lost pl 3f out: sme prog again fnl f* **11/2**
1242 **5** *1 1/2* **April Ciel**[11] 2923 4-9-0 **67**... SteveDrowne 1 65
(Ronald Harris) *led tl hdd over 2f out: wknd ins fnl f* **3/1**[2]
-013 **6** *1 1/2* **Tawseef (IRE)**[11] 2923 5-9-0 **70**.................................... MarkCoumbe(3) 2 65
(Roy Brotherton) *in rr: drvn and hdwy over 3f out: nvr rchd ldrs and sn wknd* **5/1**[3]
51 **7** *1 3/4* **He's No Angel (IRE)**[116] 708 4-9-4 **71**............................... AdamKirby 3 63
(Clive Cox) *in rr: hdwy and rdn to cl on ldrs 3f out: hung lft and wknd 2f out* **2/1**[1]
2m 12.05s (1.45) **Going Correction** +0.15s/f (Good) **7** Ran SP% **119.6**
Speed ratings (Par 103): **100,99,98,97,96 94,93**
toteswingers: 1&2 £33.60, 1&3 £28.10, 2&3 £49.80 CSF £69.33 TOTE £10.60: £4.70, £2.70; EX 44.80 Trifecta £575.50 Part won. Pool: £767.39 - 0.88 winning units..
Owner Anthony Boswood **Bred** The Hon Mrs R Pease **Trained** Upper Lambourn, Berks
FOCUS
A competitive handicap, which was run at a fair pace. The winner is rated a bit better than the bare form.

The Form Book Flat, Raceform Ltd, Compton, RG20 6NL.

T/Plt: £717.50 to a £1 stake. Pool: £60,960.59 - 62.02 winning tickets T/Qpdt: £18.20 to a £1 stake. Pool: £6,283.14 - 255.12 winning tickets ST

2845 GOODWOOD (R-H)

Friday, June 14

OFFICIAL GOING: Good (7.8)

Wind: Fairly light, across Weather: Dry

3274 GORDON'S APPRENTICE STKS (H'CAP) 7f

6:20 (6:20) (Class 4) (0-85,85) 4-Y-0+ **£5,175** (£1,540; £769; £384) **Stalls** Low

Form RPR

-432 **1** **Good Authority (IRE)**[21] 2618 6-9-9 **85**.................. ThomasBrown(3) 7 95+
(Karen George) *stdd s: hld up in last pair: clsng and gng wl whn nt clr run wl over 1f out tl ins fnl f: rdn and str run ins fnl f: led fnl 50yds* **7/2**[1]

3603 **2** ½ **Bravo Echo**[21] 2618 7-9-6 **82**.................................... NicoleNordblad(3) 1 88
(Michael Attwater) *led: rdn ent fnl f: battled on wl u.p tl hdd and no ex fnl 50yds* **4/1**[2]

00-1 **3** hd **Tidentime (USA)**[13] 2871 4-9-3 **79**............................ CharlesBishop(3) 9 85
(Mick Channon) *chsd ldr: rdn over 2f out: ev ch fnl f: kpt on but unable qck towards fin* **12/1**

-000 **4** ½ **Rocky Reef**[21] 2618 4-9-4 **77**..(v) PatrickHills 5 81
(Philip Hide) *hld up in tch in last quartet: rdn and effrt whn edgd rt wl over 1f out: drvn ent fnl f: styd on fnl 100yds* **20/1**

3-10 **5** ¾ **Golden Desert (IRE)**[120] 650 9-8-11 **75**.......................... IanBurns(5) 8 77
(Simon Dow) *stdd s: hld up in last pair: hdwy on inner over 2f out: chsd ldrs and rdn over 1f out: no ex and one pce fnl 100yds* **50/1**

-223 **6** 1 **Jack Of Diamonds (IRE)**[34] 2265 4-9-6 **82**............... NathanAlison(3) 2 82
(Roger Teal) *dwlt and pushed along early: sn in tch in midfield: rdn and effrt over 1f out: n.m.r ins fnl f: no imp ins fnl f* **4/1**[2]

0510 **7** 1 **Sir Mike**[8] 3019 4-9-5 **78**... RyanClark 3 75
(Amanda Perrett) *wl in tch in midfield: rdn and effrt over 1f out: unable qck whn short of room jst ins fnl f: no threat to ldrs but kpt on fnl 100yds* **13/2**

0300 **8** ¾ **Ortac Rock (IRE)**[6] 3108 4-9-4 **84**..........................(t) CameronHardie(7) 4 79
(Richard Hannon) *hld up in tch in midfield: rdn and effrt 2f out: no imp tl kpt on ins fnl f: no threat to ldrs* **28/1**

5002 **9** 7 **Starwatch**[6] 3108 6-9-4 **80**.............................. WilliamTwiston-Davies(3) 6 56
(John Bridger) *wl in tch in midfield: lost pl and drvn over 2f out: wknd over 1f out* **6/1**[3]

21-0 **10** 17 **Don Libre**[18] 2725 4-8-11 **70**.......................................(t) AshleyMorgan 10
(Paul Cole) *t.k.h: chsd ldrs: losing pl whn hmpd wl over 1f out: bhd and heavily eased fnl f* **18/1**

1m 27.83s (0.83) **Going Correction** +0.025s/f (Good) **10** Ran SP% **113.0**
Speed ratings (Par 105): **96,95,95,94,93 92,91,90,82,63**
toteswingers: 1&2 £3.70, 1&3 £8.70, 2&3 £9.70 CSF £16.45 CT £150.36 TOTE £4.10: £1.80, £2.00, £3.50; EX 13.50 Trifecta £174.90 Pool: £1,415.96 - 6.06 winning units..
Owner Kilcash Bloodstock & Karen George **Bred** Mountarmstrong Stud **Trained** Higher Eastington, Devon

FOCUS
A dry night and day. The first two furlongs of the 1 mile course were dolled out 5yds. The top bend was dolled out 3yds, increasing distances by 10yds and the lower also by 3yds, increasing distances by 10yds. Mainly exposed performers in a useful handicap. The gallop was no more than fair and the runner-up sets the standard.

3275 ADVANCE RESOURCE MANAGERS MAIDEN AUCTION STKS 6f

6:50 (6:51) (Class 4) 2-Y-0 **£3,881** (£1,155; £577; £288) **Stalls** High

Form RPR

0 **1** **Stormy Paradise (IRE)**[34] 2250 2-9-1 0......................... FrankieDettori 8 76+
(Brian Meehan) *chsd ldrs: rdn and effrt over 1f out: drvn 1f out: r.o wl to ld fnl 50yds* **11/4**[1]

2 ½ **Salford Secret (IRE)** 2-9-1 0... DaneO'Neill 2 75+
(Marco Botti) *rn green early: racd in midfield: rdn and hdwy to chse ldrs 2f out: chal 1f out: ro u.p to ld ins fnl f: hdd and no ex fnl 50yds* **13/2**

5 **3** 1¼ **Royal Connection**[22] 2583 2-8-8 0.............. WilliamTwiston-Davies(5) 6 69
(Richard Hannon) *sn led: rdn over 1f out: hdd and no ex fnl 100yds: edgd rt towards fin* **7/2**[2]

6 **4** 2½ **Lady Marl**[22] 2583 2-8-9 0... ChrisCatlin 5 57+
(Gary Moore) *rn green towards rr: pushed along and hdwy on stands' rail over 2f out: stl green but styng on whn nt clr run jst over 1f out: no threat to ldrs but kpt on and edgd rt fnl 100yds* **33/1**

6342 **5** ½ **Queen Of The Tarts**[9] 2985 2-8-13 0................................ JimCrowley 3 60
(Olly Stevens) *chsd ldr: rdn and unable qck over 1f out: wknd ins fnl f* **4/1**[3]

6 **6** 2 **Speed Society**[15] 2805 2-9-2 0... PatCosgrave 4 59
(Jim Boyle) *wnt lft s: pushed along early: hdwy to chse ldrs 4f out: rdn and unable qck 2f out: wknd ins fnl f* **40/1**

7 3¾ **Ultimate Warrior (IRE)** 2-9-1 0... PatDobbs 7 45
(Richard Hannon) *sn rdn along in rr: n.d* **5/1**

8 10 **No Easy Day** 2-9-3 0... HarryBentley 1 17
(David Simcock) *rn green: in tch towards rr: struggling whn wnt bdly rt u.p 2f out: sn bhd* **8/1**

1m 13.21s (1.01) **Going Correction** -0.10s/f (Good) **8** Ran SP% **115.4**
Speed ratings (Par 95): **89,88,86,83,82 80,75,61**
toteswingers: 1&2 £4.50, 1&3 £2.20, 2&3 £7.40 CSF £21.49 TOTE £2.70: £1.60, £2.00, £1.40; EX 19.90 Trifecta £101.00 Pool: £1,413.11 - 10.48 winning units..
Owner Decadent Racing **Bred** Rodger O'Dwyer **Trained** Manton, Wilts

FOCUS
No more than a fair maiden, rated around the race averages. The gallop was sound and the first three pulled a couple of lengths clear late on.

3276 BIBENDUM STKS (H'CAP) 1m 1f 192y

7:25 (7:25) (Class 3) (0-90,88) 3-Y-0 **£7,762** (£2,310; £1,154; £577) **Stalls** Low

Form RPR

1-4 **1** **Goodwood Mirage (IRE)**[27] 2438 3-9-1 **82**.................. FrankieDettori 5 95
(William Knight) *hld up in last trio: smooth hdwy over 2f out: rdn to ld over 1f out: edgd rt and hdd 1f out: led again fnl 100yds: r.o wl and gng away at fin* **5/1**[3]

2-25 **2** 1¼ **Persepolis (IRE)**[27] 2457 3-9-0 **81**....................................... RyanMoore 7 91
(Sir Michael Stoute) *stdd s: t.k.h: hld up in rr: smooth hdwy on outer over 2f out: rdn to chal and edgd rt over 1f out: wnt clr w wnr and led 1f out: hdd fnl 100yds: no ex* **6/4**[1]

2-21 **3** 3 **Rosie Rebel**[31] 2346 3-8-6 **73**... ChrisCatlin 4 78
(Rae Guest) *hld up in last trio: effrt on inner 2f out: stl midfield and gap clsng ent fnl f: swtchd lft jst ins fnl f: styd on wl to go 3rd wl ins fnl f: no threat to ldng pair* **16/1**

2221 **4** 1¼ **Sennockian Star**[42] 1977 3-8-10 **77**...........................(b) FrannyNorton 8 79
(Mark Johnston) *t.k.h: led for 1f: chsd ldr tl over 6f out: styd chsng ldrs: rdn and led 2f out: sn hdd: edgd rt and outpcd: wl hld and plugged on same pce fnl f* **9/2**[2]

3-15 **5** 5 **Dark Emerald (IRE)**[22] 2604 3-9-7 **88**.............................. GeorgeBaker 2 80
(Brendan Powell) *chsd ldrs: chsd ldr over 6f out tl rdn to ld jst over 2f out: sn hdd and drvn: btn over 1f out: wknd fnl f* **8/1**

-103 **6** 1 **King Muro**[13] 2862 3-8-9 **76**.. LiamKeniry 6 66
(Andrew Balding) *led: wnt clr 5f out tl rdn and hdd jst over 2f out: losing pl whn short of room and swtchd lft over 1f out: wknd 1f out* **7/1**

041- **7** nk **Empiricist (IRE)**[243] 7079 3-8-13 **80**..................................... PatDobbs 3 69
(Amanda Perrett) *in tch in midfield: lost pl and rdn over 2f out: bhd over 1f out* **14/1**

1-55 **8** 4½ **Ronaldinho (IRE)**[39] 2086 3-9-1 **87**............. WilliamTwiston-Davies(5) 1 67
(Richard Hannon) *in tch in midfield: rdn and unable qck over 2f out: sn struggling: bhd over 1f out* **25/1**

2m 7.54s (-0.56) **Going Correction** +0.025s/f (Good) **8** Ran SP% **114.9**
Speed ratings (Par 103): **103,102,99,98,94 93,93,89**
toteswingers: 1&2 £2.30, 1&3 £7.60, 2&3 £11.00 CSF £12.98 CT £110.41 TOTE £4.20: £1.50, £1.10, £3.20; EX 10.10 Trifecta £297.20 Pool: £1,243.31 - 3.13 winning units..
Owner Goodwood Racehorse Owners Group (19) Ltd **Bred** Mrs Chris Harrington **Trained** Patching, W Sussex

FOCUS
A race that has been won by several smart types, notably subsequent Group 2 Park Hill winner Eastern Aria in 2009 and multiple UAE dirt winner Treble Jig the following year. The first two, who pulled clear off an ordinary gallop, are unexposed sorts who should be able to rate higher.

3277 CRIMBOURNE STUD STKS (H'CAP) 1m 4f

8:00 (8:00) (Class 4) (0-85,83) 3-Y-0 **£6,469** (£1,925; £962; £481) **Stalls** High

Form RPR

323 **1** **Royal Signaller**[22] 2589 3-9-0 **76**...(p) PatDobbs 2 82
(Amanda Perrett) *in tch in midfield: hdwy to join ldr 8f out: rdn and led 2f out: sustained duel w rival after: forged ahd ins fnl f: styd on wl* **8/1**

3-66 **2** ¾ **Linguine (FR)**[28] 2416 3-9-6 **82**.. GeorgeBaker 5 87
(Seamus Durack) *led: jnd 8f out: rdn and hdd 2f out: battled on wl u.p and sustained duel w wnr after tl no ex ins fnl f* **12/1**

6-14 **3** 2¾ **Majeed**[37] 2153 3-9-3 **79**... RyanMoore 4 84+
(David Simcock) *t.k.h: hld up in tch in last pair: swtchd lft and rdn 4f out: hdwy u.p to chse ldng pair 2f out: no ex and btn 1f out: wknd fnl 100yds* **9/4**[2]

6-53 **4** ½ **Dragon City**[22] 2605 3-9-2 **78**.. JamesDoyle 6 78
(Harry Dunlop) *chsd ldr tl 8f out: chsd ldrs after tl drvn and unable qck 2f out: no threat to ldng pair but kpt on ins fnl f* **20/1**

21-3 **5** nk **Lady Pimpernel**[40] 2054 3-8-13 **75**..................................... DaneO'Neill 8 75+
(Henry Candy) *t.k.h: hld up in tch in midfield: rdn and effrt over 2f out: drvn and outpcd wl over 1f out: no threat to ldrs but plugged on ins fnl f* **15/8**[1]

1-20 **6** 8 **Mombasa**[28] 2432 3-9-2 **78**... JimCrowley 3 65
(Ralph Beckett) *hld up in last pair: rdn and struggling 3f out: wknd over 2f out* **6/1**[3]

62-2 **7** 3 **Three Choirs (IRE)**[22] 2606 3-8-13 **75**............................ FrankieDettori 1 65
(William Stone) *chsd ldng pair: rdn and unable qck wl over 2f out: wknd 2f out: bhd and eased wl ins fnl f* **10/1**

2m 41.83s (3.43) **Going Correction** +0.025s/f (Good) **7** Ran SP% **112.5**
Speed ratings (Par 101): **89,88,86,86,86 80,78**
toteswingers: 1&2 £13.30, 1&3 £4.60, 2&3 £8.00 CSF £90.44 CT £285.16 TOTE £11.20: £3.90, £6.10; EX 94.90 Trifecta £373.90 Pool: £1,141.38 - 2.28 winning units..
Owner Woodcote Stud Ltd **Bred** Woodcote Stud Ltd **Trained** Pulborough, W Sussex

FOCUS
A useful handicap featuring several unexposed types. The gallop was on the steady side and it paid to race close to the pace. It's hard to get behind this form.

3278 FRANKIE'S 26TH ANNIVERSARY MAIDEN STKS 1m

8:35 (8:35) (Class 5) 3-Y-0 **£3,234** (£962; £481; £240) **Stalls** Low

Form RPR

42-0 **1** **Anna's Pearl**[58] 1621 3-9-5 113.................................(b) JamieSpencer 3 88
(Ralph Beckett) *chsd ldr: jnd ldr and gng best over 2f out: led over 1f out: rdn and qcknd clr 1f out: easily* **6/4**[1]

-222 **2** 4½ **Dairam (USA)**[16] 2765 3-9-5 75... DaneO'Neill 1 78
(Charles Hills) *led: rdn ent fnl 2f: hdd over 1f out: unable qck w wnr and btn 1f out: kpt on same pce on for clr 2nd* **5/1**[3]

0 **3** 2¾ **Stomachion (IRE)**[17] 2760 3-9-5 0...................................... RyanMoore 2 72
(Sir Michael Stoute) *chsd ldrs: rdn and effrt ent fnl 2f: outpcd and btn over 1f out: plugged on fnl f* **5/2**[2]

0- **4** 1¼ **First Secretary**[225] 7505 3-9-0 0... JamesDoyle 4 64
(Roger Charlton) *t.k.h: hld up in tch in midfield: rdn and effrt jst over 2f out: outpcd and btn over 1f out: wl hld but kpt on fnl f* **12/1**

5 1 **Majesty (IRE)** 3-9-5 0.. PatDobbs 6 67+
(Richard Hannon) *wnt sharply lft s: in tch in midfield: rdn and effrt over 2f out: outpcd and btn whn nt clr run over 1f out: wl hld and one pce fnl f* **7/1**

6 hd **Hattie Jacques** 3-9-0 0.. MatthewDavies 5 61
(Mick Channon) *in tch in midfield: hdwy to chse ldrs 1/2-way: rdn and unable qck over 2f out: wknd over 1f out* **14/1**

7 21 **Medburn Singer** 3-9-5 0.. PatCosgrave 7 25
(George Baker) *pushed bdly lft s: a in last pair: lost tch 2f out: wl bhd and eased ins fnl f* **50/1**

8 11 **Feather Dancer** 3-9-0 0.. HarryBentley 8
(Jamie Poulton) *pushed bdly lft s: rn green and a bhd: lost tch 3f out: t.o fnl 2f* **40/1**

1m 41.87s (1.97) **Going Correction** +0.025s/f (Good) **8** Ran SP% **116.5**
Speed ratings (Par 99): **91,86,83,82,81 81,60,49**
toteswingers: 1&2 £1.80, 1&3 £2.20, 2&3 £3.10 CSF £9.82 TOTE £2.30: £1.10, £1.80, £1.50; EX 9.80 Trifecta £17.70 Pool: £795.96 - 33.61 winning units..
Owner Qatar Racing Limited **Bred** Aston House Stud **Trained** Kimpton, Hants

FOCUS
A maiden that threw up several smart types in the early 2000's - the pick being subsequent Hardwicke winner Indian Creek in 2001 - and also unearthed a very useful winner in Galiando in 2011. This year's winner - already a smart sort - didn't have to improve to win an uncompetitive event run at just an ordinary gallop. The second sets the standard.

3279 TFN STKS (H'CAP) 6f
9:05 (9:05) (Class 4) (0-85,84) 3-Y-O **£5,175** (£1,540; £769; £384) **Stalls** High

Form RPR

2212 **1** **Extrasolar**[9] 2983 3-9-2 **79**........(t) PatDobbs 5 90
(Amanda Perrett) *racd towards centre: in tch in midfield: hdwy 2f out: rdn to chal ent fnl f: led fnl 100yds: r.o wl* **4/1**[1]

1-01 **2** ½ **Freddy With A Y (IRE)**[29] 2394 3-9-5 **82**........ GeorgeBaker 2 91
(Gary Moore) *racd towards centre: chsd ldrs: rdn and ev ch wl over 1f out: led ent fnl f: hdd fnl 100yds: kpt on but a hld after* **8/1**

-000 **3** 2 **Miss Diva**[7] 3058 3-9-2 **84**........ WilliamTwiston-Davies(5) 10 87
(Richard Hannon) *chsd ldr: rdn and ev ch over 1f out: no ex and outpcd by ldng pair ins fnl f: hld on for 3rd cl home* **33/1**

-030 **4** hd **Kimberella**[14] 2844 3-9-0 **82**........ ThomasBrown(5) 1 84+
(Michael Attwater) *racd off the pce in last quartet: edging lft and clsng over 2f out: nt clr run over 1f out tl wnt between horses and hdwy ins fnl f: r.o wl fnl 100yds: no threat to ldrs* **14/1**

-664 **5** shd **Countryman**[22] 2593 3-8-9 **72**........ JimCrowley 7 74
(Hughie Morrison) *in tch in midfield: rdn and unable qck over 1f out: rallied and styd on again ins fnl f: no threat to ldrs* **6/1**[2]

00-0 **6** 1½ **Joey's Destiny (IRE)**[18] 2708 3-9-2 **79**........ PatCosgrave 9 76
(George Baker) *chsd ldrs: rdn and pressed ldrs over 1f out: no ex 1f out: wknd ins fnl f* **25/1**

14-5 **6** dht **Claim (IRE)**[45] 1912 3-9-0 **77**........ RyanMoore 6 74
(Sir Michael Stoute) *s.i.s: bhd: rdn over 2f out: sme hdwy and edging rt 2f out: styd on fnl f: nvr trbld ldrs* **8/1**

-502 **8** hd **Sejalaat (IRE)**[18] 2708 3-9-5 **82**........ DaneO'Neill 8 79
(Ed Dunlop) *led: rdn and hdd jst over 1f out: wknd ins fnl f* **6/1**[2]

0104 **9** 1¼ **Bluegrass Blues (IRE)**[7] 3066 3-9-6 **83**........ JamesDoyle 11 76
(Paul Cole) *racd in midfield: rdn and effrt ent fnl 2f: no imp over 1f out: wl hld whn n.m.r ins fnl f* **7/1**[3]

2332 **10** 2½ **Polish Crown**[6] 3082 3-8-2 **65** oh1........ FrannyNorton 12 50
(Mark Johnston) *in tch in midfield: rdn and unable qck ent fnl 2f: wknd over 1f out* **9/1**

6100 **11** 2 **Jontleman (IRE)**[24] 2544 3-8-4 **67** ow1........ ChrisCatlin 4 45
(Mick Channon) *racd towards centre: a outpcd in last quartet: n.d* **33/1**

125- **12** nse **Rio's Pearl**[251] 6883 3-9-5 **82**........ JamieSpencer 3 60
(Ralph Beckett) *sn outpcd in rr: n.d* **9/1**

1m 11.27s (-0.93) **Going Correction** -0.10s/f (Good) **12 Ran SP% 119.7**
Speed ratings (Par 101): **102,101,98,98,98 96,96,96,94,91 88,88**
toteswingers: 1&2 £4.80, 1&3 £21.90, 2&3 £43.60 CSF £35.64 TOTE £4.40: £2.00, £2.40, £5.80; EX 13.90 Trifecta £366.30 Pool: £1,271.75 - 2.60 winning units..
Owner Odile Griffith & John Connolly **Bred** Brook Stud Bloodstock Ltd **Trained** Pulborough, W Sussex

FOCUS
A couple of potential improvers in a useful handicap. The first two, who pulled a couple of lengths clear, raced on the outside of the group in a truly run race. The form is rated around the 1-2.
T/Plt: £288.90 to a £1 stake. Pool: £71,444.85 - 180.46 winning tickets T/Qpdt: £93.40 to a £1 stake. Pool: £4,697.02 - 37.20 winning tickets SP

2876 MUSSELBURGH (R-H)
Friday, June 14

OFFICIAL GOING: Good to firm (8.3)
Wind: Moderate across Weather: Cloudy

3280 GAYNOR WINYARD MAIDEN AUCTION STKS 5f
1:50 (1:51) (Class 6) 2-Y-O **£2,587** (£770; £384; £192) **Stalls** High

Form RPR

2 **1** **Classical Diva**[18] 2715 2-8-2 0........ NeilFarley(3) 8 71
(Declan Carroll) *cl up: rdn to ld jst over 1f out: drvn ins fnl f: kpt on wl towards fin* **9/2**[3]

2352 **2** ½ **Memory Styx**[6] 3092 2-8-7 0........ TomEaves 9 71
(Mick Channon) *cl up on inner: slt ld after 2f out: rdn 2f out: hdd jst over 1f out: drvn ins fnl f and kpt on wl towards fin* **5/1**

2 **3** 2¾ **Alpine Flower (IRE)**[6] 3077 2-8-4 0........ JamesSullivan 11 58
(Tim Easterby) *trckd ldrs on inner: swtchd rt and hdwy 2f out: rdn to chal over 1f out and ev ch tl drvn: edgd lft and one pce ins fnl f* **11/4**[1]

4 ¾ **Simply Black (IRE)** 2-8-7 0........ RoystonFfrench 7 59
(Bryan Smart) *trckd ldrs on outer: cl up 1/2-way: rdn and ev ch wl over 1f out: wknd ent fnl f* **7/2**[2]

5 2 **The Dukkerer (IRE)** 2-8-9 0 ow2........ GrahamLee 4 53
(David O'Meara) *towards rr: hdwy 2f out: sn rdn and kpt on fnl f* **22/1**

6 1¾ **Oasis Town** 2-8-3 0........ JulieBurke(3) 2 44+
(Kevin Ryan) *s.i.s and in rr tl styd on fnl f* **28/1**

7 shd **Lomond Lassie** 2-8-5 0........ JoeFanning 3 43
(Keith Dalgleish) *qckly away and slt ld for 2f: cl up tl rdn 2f out and sn wknd* **17/2**

4 **8** ½ **Tricksome (IRE)**[21] 2612 2-8-7 0........ PJMcDonald 1 43
(Ann Duffield) *a towards rr* **16/1**

25 **9** 2¾ **Kirtling Belle**[17] 2751 2-8-4 0........ LukeMorris 10 30
(Keith Dalgleish) *chsd ldrs: rdn along 2f out: sn wknd* **8/1**

59.95s (-0.45) **Going Correction** -0.125s/f (Firm) **9 Ran SP% 119.1**
Speed ratings (Par 91): **98,97,92,91,88 85,85,84,80**
toteswingers 1&2 £7.60, 1&3 £2.50, 2&3 £2.30 CSF £28.24 TOTE £6.40: £2.40, £1.70, £1.50; EX 25.00 Trifecta £56.20 Pool: £799.37 - 10.65 winning units..
Owner Classical Partnership **Bred** D Carroll **Trained** Sledmere, E Yorks

FOCUS
An informative, if probably only ordinary, juvenile contest and it was won in decisive.

3281 MADELEINE CUP (H'CAP) 1m
2:20 (2:21) (Class 5) (0-70,70) 3-Y-O **£5,175** (£1,540; £769; £384) **Stalls** Low

Form RPR

1-32 **1** **Mushaakis (IRE)**[16] 2770 3-9-7 **70**........ JoeFanning 11 88+
(Mark Johnston) *cl up: led wl over 2f out and sn qcknd clr: unchal* **11/4**[1]

2146 **2** 8 **Shearian**[10] 2957 3-9-3 **66**........ RoystonFfrench 1 65
(Tracy Waggott) *trckd ldrs: hdwy 3f out: swtchd lft and rdn 2f out: styd on u.p fnl f: no ch w wnr* **18/1**

4-10 **3** ¾ **War Lord (IRE)**[27] 2464 3-9-3 **66**........ DavidNolan 9 63
(David O'Meara) *led: pushed along and jnd 3f out: sn hdd and rdn: drvn wl over 1f out: sn one pce* **10/3**[2]

0-26 **4** hd **Manchestar**[21] 2628 3-9-4 **70**........ LeeTopliss(3) 7 67+
(Richard Fahey) *hld up towards rr: hdwy 3f out: swtchd lft wl over 1f out: sn rdn and kpt on fnl f* **7/2**[3]

14-5 **5** 1¼ **Lucy Bee**[16] 2770 3-8-13 **62**........ TomEaves 13 56
(Keith Dalgleish) *chsd ldrs: effrt 3f out: rdn along 2f out: sn drvn and grad wknd* **14/1**

20-0 **6** 1¼ **Lambert Pen (USA)**[11] 2935 3-9-0 **63**........ GrahamLee 4 54
(Mick Channon) *chsd ldng pair on inner: rdn along 3f out: wknd 2f out* **11/1**

-260 **7** ½ **Annie Gogh**[6] 3082 3-8-12 **61**........ PaulMulrennan 2 51
(Tim Easterby) *hld up in rr: hdwy on inner wl over 2f out: rdn wl over 1f out: sn no imp* **7/1**

0500 **8** 4½ **Gold Roll (IRE)**[11] 2916 3-8-0 **52**........ JulieBurke(3) 6 32
(Ruth Carr) *midfield: rdn along over 3f out: sn outpcd* **25/1**

3000 **9** 1¼ **Fishlake Rebel**[6] 3082 3-8-2 **51** oh3........ JamesSullivan 5 28
(Ruth Carr) *a in rr* **33/1**

000- **10** 5 **Starbotton**[294] 5544 3-9-2 **65**........ AndrewElliott 8 30
(James Bethell) *a towards rr* **25/1**

6-50 **11** 13 **Hayley**[15] 2799 3-8-2 **51** oh6........ NickyMackay 10
(Jim Goldie) *chsd ldrs on outer: rdn along 1/2-way: sn wknd* **66/1**

1m 39.58s (-1.62) **Going Correction** -0.225s/f (Firm) **11 Ran SP% 116.9**
Speed ratings (Par 99): **99,91,90,90,88 87,87,82,81,76 63**
toteswingers 1&2 £9.80, 1&3 £2.20, 2&3 £15.50 CSF £52.12 CT £176.02 TOTE £2.90: £1.10, £5.60, £1.70; EX 45.30 Trifecta £121.90 Pool: £808.08 - 4.96 winning units..
Owner Hamdan Al Maktoum **Bred** Shadwell Estate Company Limited **Trained** Middleham Moor, N Yorks

FOCUS
A fair race for the grade and a great deal to like about the performance of the winner.

3282 HBJ CLAIM SOLUTIONS EBF MAIDEN STKS 7f 30y
2:50 (2:50) (Class 5) 2-Y-O **£4,204** (£1,251; £625; £312) **Stalls** Low

Form RPR

1 **Somewhat (USA)** 2-9-5 0........ JoeFanning 1 88+
(Mark Johnston) *green early: sn led: jnd: rn green and edgd lft 2f out: sn pushed along and wnt clr wl over 1f out: styd on strly* **5/6**[1]

2 7 **New Street (IRE)** 2-9-2 0........ LeeTopliss(3) 5 70+
(Richard Fahey) *hld up: hdwy to chse wnr 3f out: chal over 2f out: sn rdn and kpt on: no ch w wnr* **7/2**[2]

65 **3** 2¾ **Shimba Hills**[9] 2985 2-9-5 0........ GrahamLee 4 63
(Mick Channon) *chsd ldng pair on inner: rdn along 3f out: kpt on one pce fnl 2f* **5/1**[3]

03 **4** 6 **Flora Medici**[10] 2947 2-9-0 0........ LukeMorris 2 42
(Sir Mark Prescott Bt) *hld up: sme hdwy over 2f out: n.d* **10/1**

5 2¼ **Paddy's Bay** 2-9-5 0........ PaulMulrennan 6 42
(Kevin Ryan) *trckd wnr: rdn along 3f out: sn wknd* **9/1**

6 4½ **Porthos Du Vallon** 2-9-5 0........ TomEaves 3 30
(Keith Dalgleish) *a in rr* **16/1**

1m 28.72s (-0.28) **Going Correction** -0.225s/f (Firm) **6 Ran SP% 118.4**
Speed ratings (Par 93): **92,84,80,74,71 66**
toteswingers 1&2 £1.10, 1&3 £1.10, 2&3 £1.90 CSF £4.46 TOTE £2.00: £1.50, £1.90; EX 6.30 Trifecta £12.90 Pool: £1155.23 - 66.88 winning units..
Owner Sheikh Majid Bin Mohammed al Maktoum **Bred** B P Walden Jr, P W Madden Et Al **Trained** Middleham Moor, N Yorks

FOCUS
An impressive winner.

3283 M AND F FUNERAL SERVICES H'CAP (QUALIFIER FOR THE £15,000 BETFAIR SCOTTISH SPRINT SERIES FINAL) 5f
3:25 (3:26) (Class 5) (0-75,73) 3-Y-O+ **£5,175** (£1,540; £769; £192; £192) **Stalls** High

Form RPR

2222 **1** **Red Baron (IRE)**[11] 2914 4-9-2 **64**........ NeilFarley(3) 9 77
(Eric Alston) *cl up: rdn over 1f out: drvn and styd on ins fnl f to ld last 50yds* **10/3**[1]

6-06 **2** 1¼ **Imperial Legend (IRE)**[7] 3069 4-10-0 **73**........(v[1]) PaulQuinn 12 82
(David Nicholls) *led: rdn clr over 1f out: drvn ins fnl f: hdd and no ex last 50yds* **12/1**

13-0 **3** nk **Findog**[32] 2318 3-9-4 **70**........ PaulMulrennan 7 74
(Linda Perratt) *midfield: hdwy 2f out: n.m.r and swtchd lft ent fnl f: sn rdn and kpt on: nrst fin* **20/1**

-005 **4** 2¼ **The Nifty Fox**[15] 2797 9-10-0 **73**........(p) JamesSullivan 13 72
(Tim Easterby) *trckd ldrs on inner: n.m.r and swtchd rt 1/2-way: hdwy wl over 1f out: rdn to chse ldrs ent fnl f: sn drvn and one pce* **12/1**

-502 **4** dht **Mercers Row**[14] 2832 6-9-5 **71**........ GemmaTutty(7) 11 70
(Karen Tutty) *trckd ldrs: effrt wl over 1f out and sn rdn: kpt on fnl f* **4/1**[2]

3022 **6** ¾ **Here Now And Why (IRE)**[2] 3196 6-8-12 **62**........(p) GarryWhillans(5) 1 59
(Iain Jardine) *in tch on wd outside: pushed along and outpcd 1/2-way: swtchd lft and rdn wl over 1f out: kpt on fnl f: nrst fin* **9/2**[3]

6440 **7** 1½ **Compton Heights**[21] 2632 4-9-3 **62**........ GrahamLee 4 53
(Jim Goldie) *hld up: hdwy and in tch 2f out: sn rdn and no imp* **10/1**

013- **8** 2¼ **Mandy Layla (IRE)**[232] 7355 3-9-1 **72**........ JustinNewman(5) 5 52
(Bryan Smart) *cl up: rdn along 2f out: sn wknd* **9/1**

50-6 **9** 1¼ **Distant Sun (USA)**[15] 2795 9-8-13 **58**........(p) TomEaves 8 37
(Linda Perratt) *cl up: rdn 2f out: wknd over 1f out* **20/1**

-452 **10** nk **Captain Royale (IRE)**[28] 2409 8-9-0 **59**........(p) JoeFanning 2 37
(Tracy Waggott) *in tch on outer: rdn along over 2f out: sn wknd* **7/1**

3150 **11** 6 **Windforpower (IRE)**[39] 2076 3-8-8 **60**........(be) RoystonFfrench 6 13
(Tracy Waggott) *dwlt and plld hrd: a in rr* **25/1**

060- **12** nse **Baker's Pursuit**[275] 6130 3-8-3 **55**........ NickyMackay 14 8
(Jim Goldie) *a in rr* **40/1**

59.25s (-1.15) **Going Correction** -0.125s/f (Firm)
WFA 3 from 4yo+ 7lb **12 Ran SP% 124.0**
Speed ratings (Par 103): **104,102,101,97,97 96,94,90,88,88 78,78**
toteswingers 1&2 £9.20, 1&3 £6.30, 2&3 £30.20 CSF £44.70 CT £721.75 TOTE £3.60: £1.60, £3.50, £6.20; EX 52.00 Trifecta £485.10 Pool: £1122.33 - 1.73 winning units..
Owner J Stephenson **Bred** Mrs C A Moore **Trained** Longton, Lancs

The Form Book Flat, Raceform Ltd, Compton, RG20 6NL.

FOCUS
A competitive sprint handicap, run at a fierce early pace.

3284 STOBO CASTLE LADIES DAY CUP (H'CAP) 1m 6f
4:00 (4:00) (Class 4) (0-85,83) 4-Y-0+ £12,938 (£3,850; £1,924; £962) Stalls Centre

Form RPR
-002 1 **Merchant Of Dubai**21 2633 8-8-12 71 GrahamLee 9 80
(Jim Goldie) *trckd ldr: cl up over 4f out: led over 2f out: sn rdn: drvn ins fnl f: jst hld on* 10/1

1-04 2 shd **Aleksandar**15 2798 4-8-10 69 AndrewElliott 3 78
(Jim Goldie) *led: stdd pce after 5f: pushed along and qcknd over 4f out: rdn 3f out: hdd over 2f out: cl up: drvn and rallied gamely ins fnl f: jst failed* 22/1

11-2 3 2 3/4 **Mutual Regard (IRE)**9 2973 4-9-10 83 LukeMorris 7 88
(Sir Mark Prescott Bt) *trckd ldrs: effrt 3f out: rdn to chal 2f out: sn drvn and ev ch tl one pce fnl f* 2/1[2]

0/-1 4 shd **Street Entertainer (IRE)**5 3133 6-8-12 71 6ex (bt) PaulMulrennan 4 76
(David Pipe) *hld up in rr: hdwy 4f out: chsd ldrs on outer 3f out: rdn over 2f out: cl up and drvn over 1f out: edgd lft and one pce fnl f* 6/5[1]

5421 5 7 **Platinum (IRE)**21 2633 6-9-5 78 (p) RussKennemore 8 73
(Philip Kirby) *trckd ldrs: hdwy to chse ldng pair 1/2-way: rdn along 3f out: drvn 2f out: sn wknd* 5/1[3]

0040 6 10 **Bollin Greta**20 2671 8-9-2 75 JamesSullivan 1 56
(Tim Easterby) *hld up: a in rr* 25/1

0542 7 49 **Knox Overstreet**10 2968 5-8-7 66 RoystonFfrench 5
(Mick Channon) *chsd ldng pair on inner: rdn along over 4f out: sn wknd and bhd* 28/1

2m 59.79s (-5.51) **Going Correction** -0.225s/f (Firm) 7 Ran SP% 116.2
Speed ratings (Par 105): **106,105,104,104,100 94,66**
toteswingers 1&2 £8.10, 1&3 £5.20, 2&3 £7.90 CSF £179.43 CT £617.37 TOTE £8.00: £3.30, £5.20; EX 65.10 Trifecta £191.70 Pool: £2287.35 - 8.94 winning units..
Owner Highland Racing 2 **Bred** A Smith **Trained** Uplawmoor, E Renfrews

FOCUS
The absence of proven front-runner Outrageous Request always threatened to impact heavily on this staying handicap and, with the race developing into nothing more than a sprint down the home straight, it remains to be seen how well the form works out.

3285 HBJ EMPLOYMENT SOLUTIONS H'CAP (DIV I) 7f 30y
4:30 (4:30) (Class 6) (0-65,65) 4-Y-0+ £3,234 (£962; £481; £240) Stalls Low

Form RPR
0465 1 **Tony Hollis**11 2912 5-8-1 48 NeilFarley(3) 5 57
(Karen Tutty) *mde all: rdn 2f out: clr appr fnl f: kpt on strly* 3/1[3]

6-01 2 3 1/4 **Insolenceofoffice (IRE)**9 2997 5-8-10 54 (p) PJMcDonald 4 55
(Richard Ford) *sn trcking wnr: hdwy 3f out: rdn to chal 2f out: drvn over 1f out: kpt on same pce fnl f* 9/4[1]

0-00 3 1 1/2 **Joshua The First**24 2539 4-9-7 65 (t) JoeFanning 6 62
(Keith Dalgleish) *hld up in tch: hdwy 3f out: chsd ldrs 2f out: swtchd lft and rdn wl over 1f out: kpt on fnl f* 11/4[2]

050- 4 1/2 **Captain Baldwin**218 5589 4-8-2 46 oh1 (v) NickyMackay 2 41
(Jim Goldie) *in tch: pushed along to chse ldrs 3f out: rdn over 2f out: sn one pce* 20/1

0-56 5 shd **Silver Rime (FR)**32 2315 8-9-7 65 GrahamLee 7 60
(Linda Perratt) *hld up: hdwy to trck ldrs 5f out: effrt 3f out: rdn over 2f out and ev ch tl drvn and wknd appr fnl f* 8/1

60-0 6 1 3/4 **Tropical Duke (IRE)**50 1786 7-8-4 48 ow1 RoystonFfrench 3 39
(Ron Barr) *hld up in rr: hdwy 3f out: rdn 2f out: sn drvn and no imp* 11/1

0660 7 31 **North Central (USA)**8 3029 6-8-6 50 (e) JamesSullivan 9
(Ruth Carr) *chsd ldng pair: rdn along 3f out: sn wknd and bhd whn eased appr fnl f* 12/1

1m 28.08s (-0.92) **Going Correction** -0.225s/f (Firm) 7 Ran SP% 114.3
Speed ratings (Par 101): **96,92,90,90,89 87,52**
toteswingers 1&2 £1.90, 1&3 £6.10, 2&3 £1.40 CSF £10.20 CT £19.51 TOTE £4.20: £2.00, £1.90; EX 12.50 Trifecta £41.40 Pool: £914.48 - 16.53 winning units..
Owner Thoroughbred Homes Ltd **Bred** Seasons Holidays **Trained** Osmotherley, N Yorks

FOCUS
A modest handicap but no let up in pace.

3286 HBJ EMPLOYMENT SOLUTIONS H'CAP (DIV II) 7f 30y
5:05 (5:05) (Class 6) (0-65,65) 4-Y-0+ £3,234 (£962; £481; £240) Stalls Low

Form RPR
0551 1 **Running Reef (IRE)**21 2616 4-9-7 65 JoeFanning 9 73
(Tracy Waggott) *hld up in tch: hdwy 3f out: swtchd lft to outer and rdn over 1f out: led jst ins fnl f: sn drvn and hld on wl towards fin* 11/4[1]

4-66 2 hd **Lees Anthem**8 3024 6-8-5 49 RoystonFfrench 2 57
(Michael Smith) *towards rr: hdwy on inner 2f out: sn rdn: drvn and styd on to chal ins fnl f: ev ch tl nt qckn nr fin* 11/1

5-56 3 nk **Amno Dancer (IRE)**9 2977 6-8-3 47 (p) JamesSullivan 1 54
(Keith Dalgleish) *hld up in rr: hdwy 3f out: swtchd lft and rdn wl over 1f out: styd on to chal ins fnl f: ev ch tl drvn and no ex towards fin* 7/1

0300 4 1 1/2 **Goninodaethat**9 2977 5-8-7 51 AndrewElliott 5 54
(Jim Goldie) *led and sn clr at str pce: rdn 2f out: drvn over 1f out: hdd jst ins fnl f: no ex last 100yds* 6/1

0630 5 3/4 **Nonaynever**13 2884 5-7-13 46 (b) JulieBurke(3) 3 47
(Ruth Carr) *chsd ldrs: rdn along on inner 2f out: cl up whn drvn and hung lft jst ins fnl f: keeping on whn n.m.r towards fin* 12/1

00-0 6 7 **Myjestic Melody (IRE)**8 3024 5-7-13 46 NeilFarley(3) 8 28
(Noel Wilson) *chsd clr ldr: rdn along wl over 2f out: drvn wl over 1f out: grad wknd* 25/1

5655 7 1 3/4 **Viking Warrior (IRE)**14 2837 6-9-2 60 (p) TomEaves 6 37
(Michael Dods) *chsd ldng pair: hdwy over 2f out: sn rdn: sn drvn and wknd wl over 1f out* 11/2[3]

-551 8 4 1/2 **Jupiter Fidius**24 2537 6-8-10 61 (b) GemmaTutty(7) 4 26
(Karen Tutty) *hld up: a bhd* 7/2[2]

/53- 9 23 **Logans Legend (IRE)**345 3751 5-8-13 57 DavidNolan 7
(Lawrence Mullaney) *chsd ldrs: rdn along 3f out: sn wknd* 12/1

1m 29.25s (0.25) **Going Correction** -0.225s/f (Firm) 9 Ran SP% 118.6
Speed ratings (Par 101): **89,88,88,86,85 77,75,70,44**
toteswingers 1&2 £5.30, 1&3 £3.20, 2&3 £11.20 CSF £35.36 CT £198.01 TOTE £3.30: £1.60, £5.80, £3.10; EX 35.00 Trifecta £681.00 Pool: £1283.41 - 1.41 winning units..
Owner Elsa Crankshaw Gordon Allan **Bred** C O'Reilly & Co **Trained** Spennymoor, Co Durham

FOCUS
This looked marginally stronger than the first division.

3287 SPRINGFIELD PROPERTIES PLC H'CAP (LADY AMATEURS) (QUALIFIER FOR £15,000 BETFAIR STAYER' SERIES) 1m 4f 100y
5:35 (5:35) (Class 5) (0-70,70) 4-Y-0+ £3,743 (£1,161; £580; £290) Stalls Low

Form RPR
0-36 1 **Grand Diamond (IRE)**9 2972 9-9-2 51 oh3 (p) MissCWalton 9 58
(Jim Goldie) *hld up towards rr: hdwy 5f out: chsd ldrs 3f out: rdn to chal over 1f out: led ent fnl f: drvn and edgd rt last 100yds: styd on wl towards fin* 16/1

-526 2 3/4 **Hawdyerwheesht**9 2973 5-10-4 67 (v) MrsCBartley 10 73
(Jim Goldie) *a.p: trckd ldr after 2f: cl up 1/2-way: chal 3f out: rdn to ld over 1f out: edgd lft and hdd ent fnl f: sn edgd rt and no ex last 75yds* 4/1[1]

0-20 3 1 3/4 **Al Furat (USA)**21 2629 5-9-6 60 MrsVDavies(5) 3 63
(Ron Barr) *cl up: led after 2f: jnd and rdn 3f out: hdd over 1f out: grad wknd fnl f* 4/1[1]

0/4- 4 nk **Endeavor**19 3307 8-8-11 51 oh6 MissRobynGray(5) 2 54
(Dianne Sayer) *trckd ldrs on inner: pushed along 5f out: rdn along and outpcd over 3f out: kpt on u.p fnl 2f* 4/1[1]

-060 5 4 **Harare**9 2977 12-8-13 53 (v) MissJoannaMason(5) 1 49
(Karen Tutty) *in rr tl styd on fnl 3f: nt rch ldrs* 20/1

1400 6 1 3/4 **Sohcahtoa (IRE)**9 2990 7-10-2 70 MissRMcDonald(5) 7 63
(Andrew Crook) *hld up and bhd tl styd on fnl 3f: nvr a factor* 20/1

-006 7 5 **Patavium (IRE)**21 2615 10-10-2 65 MissSBrotherton 6 50
(Edwin Tuer) *trckd ldrs: hdwy to chse ldng pair 5f out: rdn along 3f out: drvn over 2f out: grad wknd* 11/2[2]

0240 8 16 **Landesherr (GER)**21 2630 6-9-2 54 (p) MissHCuthbert(3) 4 14
(Thomas Cuthbert) *in tch: pushed along 4f out: rdn over 3f out and sn wknd* 14/1

00-3 9 2 1/4 **Talk Of Saafend (IRE)**32 2313 8-9-8 57 MissADeniel 8 13
(Dianne Sayer) *dwlt and veered bdly rt s: a bhd* 7/1[3]

0-41 10 nse **Underwritten**14 2831 4-9-8 64 (v) MissKYoung(7) 5 20
(Donald McCain) *led tl rn wd bnd after 2f and sn hdd: chsd ldrs on outer: rdn along over 5f out: sn wknd* 15/2

2m 42.99s (0.99) **Going Correction** -0.225s/f (Firm) 10 Ran SP% 121.7
Speed ratings (Par 103): **87,86,85,85,82 81,77,67,65,65**
toteswingers 1&2 £6.70, 1&3 £24.60, 2&3 £8.00 CSF £82.59 CT £313.96 TOTE £17.80: £5.40, £2.40, £1.90; EX 69.20 Trifecta £869.70 Part won. Pool: £1159.60 - 0.03 winning units..
Owner Caledonia Racing **Bred** Newberry Stud Company **Trained** Uplawmoor, E Renfrews

FOCUS
A moderate lady riders' handicap, the finish of which was dominated by a pair of Jim Goldie-trained runners.
T/Plt: £162.20 to a £1 stake. Pool: £44,404.22 - 199.76 winning tickets T/Qpdt: £46.50 to a £1 stake. Pool: £2726.57 - 43.35 winning tickets JR

3017 SANDOWN (R-H)
Friday, June 14

OFFICIAL GOING: Good (good to firm in places; sprint course 8.4, round course 8.1)
Wind: Moderate, across Weather: Fine

3288 BRITISH STALLION STUDS EBF SPRINT MAIDEN STKS 5f 6y
1:40 (1:44) (Class 5) 2-Y-0 £3,881 (£1,155; £577; £288) Stalls Low

Form RPR
03 1 **Biography**14 2823 2-9-5 0 RichardHughes 6 81+
(Richard Hannon) *mde all and crossed to rail after 1f: stretched on 2f out: in command after: pushed out* 3/1[1]

2 1 1/2 **Meeting Waters** 2-9-0 0 RyanMoore 5 71+
(William Haggas) *racd against rail: trckd wnr to 1/2-way: sltly outpcd and pushed along 2f out: wnt 2nd over 1f out: styd on but no imp fnl f* 4/1[2]

3 1 3/4 **Bushcraft (IRE)** 2-9-5 0 WilliamBuick 8 69+
(Ed Walker) *prom: shkn up to chse wnr 1/2-way to over 1f out: styd on same pce after* 10/1

52 4 6 **Costa Filey**16 2771 2-9-5 0 GeorgeBaker 1 48
(Ed Vaughan) *s.v.s: t.k.h and disp 4th but racd on outer: pushed along 2f out: hanging rt and wknd jst over 1f out* 9/2[3]

0 5 1 3/4 **Soul Of Motion**13 2863 2-9-5 0 NeilCallan 4 41
(Gay Kelleway) *t.k.h: hld up disputing 4th: shkn up 2f out: sn wknd* 3/1[1]

6 nk **Le Laitier (FR)** 2-9-5 0 AndreaAtzeni 3 40
(Scott Dixon) *last whn stmbld over 3f out: struggling after* 40/1

7 1/2 **Fine Art Fair (IRE)** 2-9-5 0 JimmyFortune 2 39
(Gary Moore) *racd against rail: trckd ldrs disputing 4th: pushed along 2f out: wknd wl over 1f out* 20/1

8 2 1/2 **Joybringer (IRE)** 2-9-0 0 PatDobbs 7 25
(Richard Hannon) *dwlt: a in last pair: pushed along 1/2-way: no prog* 14/1

1m 2.65s (1.05) **Going Correction** +0.075s/f (Good) 8 Ran SP% 111.1
Speed ratings (Par 93): **94,91,88,79,76 75,75,71**
toteswingers 1&2 £2.40, 1&3 £2.40, 2&3 £5.30 CSF £14.22 TOTE £3.70: £1.10, £1.90, £3.70; EX 11.90 Trifecta £90.50 Pool: £1720.48 - 14.24 winning units..
Owner Mrs V Hubbard & Mrs J K Powell **Bred** P Balding & W Clifford **Trained** East Everleigh, Wilts

FOCUS
Sprint track at full width. Home bend at mid-configuration, rail out 5yds up home straight, adding 5yds to races on Round Course. An ordinary juvenile maiden in which the pace was not that strong early and the prominent racers dominated. There's a good chance the winner can do better from here.

3289 ALEX MOILLIETT NORTHERN HAMMER H'CAP 7f 16y
2:10 (2:15) (Class 5) (0-75,75) 3-Y-0 £3,881 (£1,155; £577; £288) Stalls Low

Form RPR
-644 1 **Benoni**25 2495 3-9-2 70 DaneO'Neill 5 75
(Henry Candy) *hld up in last trio: rdn over 2f out: prog wl over 1f out: clsd to ld ins fnl f: styd on wl* 7/2[1]

-506 2 1/2 **Magical Rose (IRE)**35 2223 3-9-4 72 (p) NeilCallan 6 75
(Paul D'Arcy) *trckd ldrs: clsd fr 2f out: rdn to ld briefly jst ins fnl f: r.o but hld nr fin* 10/1

0-65 3 1 3/4 **Dividend Dan (IRE)**50 1784 3-8-2 56 [1] KieranO'Neill 2 55
(Mike Murphy) *trckd ldrs: effrt and smuggled through on inner to chal 1f out: styd on but nt qckn w ldng pair* 50/1

235 4 2 1/2 **Kabbaas (IRE)**10 2951 3-9-7 75 (b[1]) AndreaAtzeni 4 68
(Roger Varian) *hld up in last trio: tried to cl on ldrs 2f out: swtchd lft jst over 1f out: kpt on same pce after: no ch* 6/1[3]

4-40 **5** 1 **Prince Regal**[21] 2626 3-9-7 **75** KierenFallon 1 65
(Alan Jarvis) *pressed ldr: rdn 2f out: led briefly 1f out: wknd ins fnl f* **8/1**
2145 **6** nk **Sam Spade (IRE)**[18] 2727 3-8-12 **66** RichardHughes 3 55
(Richard Hannon) *led: rdn 2f out: hdd & wknd 1f out* **9/2**[2]
2135 **7** 6 **King Bertie (IRE)**[24] 2549 3-9-1 **69** WilliamBuick 9 42
(Peter Chapple-Hyam) *chsd ldng pair to 2f out: wknd qckly over 1f out* **7/2**[1]
14-0 **8** 12 **King Of Kudos (IRE)**[43] 1958 3-9-0 **68** (p) PaulHanagan 7 10
(Scott Dixon) *wl in tch tl wknd rapidly 2f out: t.o* **25/1**
1450 **9** 1 **Marshland**[18] 2708 3-9-2 **70** SilvestreDeSousa 8 10
(Mark Johnston) *dwlt: a in last trio: pushed along on outer over 2f out: sn wknd qckly: t.o* **12/1**

1m 30.72s (1.22) **Going Correction** +0.075s/f (Good) **9** Ran SP% **110.6**
Speed ratings (Par 99): **96,95,93,90,89 89,82,68,67**
toteswingers 1&2 £7.60, 1&3 £19.90, 2&3 £17.60 CSF £36.78 CT £1395.95 TOTE £4.90: £1.30, £1.80, £9.70; EX 42.90 Trifecta £858.20 Pool: £1438.00 - 1.25 winning units..
Owner Clayton, Frost, Kebell & Candy **Bred** New Hall Farms Estate **Trained** Kingston Warren, Oxon

FOCUS
A quite competitive handicap with several trying headgear for the first time, and it did lack progressive types. Ordinary form.

3290 BRITISH STALLION STUDS EBF MAIDEN STKS (DIV I) 7f 16y
2:40 (2:45) (Class 5) 2-Y-O **£3,881** (£1,155; £577; £288) **Stalls** Low

Form RPR
3 **1** **Zeshov (IRE)**[22] 2591 2-9-5 0 WilliamBuick 7 79
(Jeremy Noseda) *trckd ldng pair: moved up gng strly to ld 1f out: edgd both lft and rt after: firmly rdn to assert narrowly nr fin* **10/11**[1]
2 nk **Bureau (IRE)** 2-9-0 0 LiamJones 2 73
(Mark Johnston) *led: rdn 2f out: hdd 1f out: fought on wl but hld nr fin* **8/1**
542 **3** 1 1/4 **Ocean Storm (IRE)**[23] 2577 2-9-5 0 NeilCallan 6 76
(James Tate) *trckd ldng pair: shkn up to dispute 2nd 2f out: cl up but hld whn hmpd 1f out: styd on* **12/1**
4 hd **Street Force (USA)** 2-9-5 0 JamesDoyle 4 74+
(Clive Brittain) *v green in preliminaries: wl in rr: shkn up over 2f out: prog on inner over 1f out: sltly checked jst ins fnl f: styd on* **25/1**
5 1 1/2 **The Alamo (IRE)** 2-9-5 0 RichardHughes 10 71+
(Richard Hannon) *dwlt: hld up in rr: nudged along and no prog over 2f out: reminder and hdwy over 1f out: tk 5th fnl f: no imp after* **16/1**
6 1 **Mabdhool (IRE)** 2-9-5 0 PaulHanagan 1 68+
(Marcus Tregoning) *slowly away: hld up in last pair: pushed along over 2f out: stl in last pair jst over 1f out: styd on fnl f* **20/1**
7 2 1/2 **Dullingham** 2-9-5 0 SilvestreDeSousa 5 61
(Saeed bin Suroor) *wl in tch in 6th but rn green and often pushed along: effrt over 2f out: wknd over 1f out* **5/1**[2]
32 **8** 1 1/2 **Llyrical**[18] 2723 2-9-5 0 DaneO'Neill 8 58
(Derek Haydn Jones) *chsd ldr to wl over 1f out: wknd* **12/1**
9 1 **Collaboration** 2-9-5 0 JimmyFortune 3 55
(Andrew Balding) *trckd ldrs in 5th: nudged along over 2f out: steadily wknd wl over 1f out* **7/1**[3]
10 7 **Haines** 2-9-5 0 KieranO'Neill 9 37
(Brett Johnson) *dwlt: a in last pair: t.o* **100/1**

1m 31.78s (2.28) **Going Correction** +0.075s/f (Good) **10** Ran SP% **123.5**
Speed ratings (Par 93): **89,88,87,87,85 84,81,79,78,70**
toteswingers 1&2 £5.50, 1&3 £3.40, 2&3 £23.20 CSF £9.72 TOTE £2.20: £1.20, £2.70, £2.80; EX 16.20 Trifecta £170.60 Pool: £2551.16 - 11.21 winning units..
Owner Richard Keen & Paul Smith **Bred** Rathbarry Stud **Trained** Newmarket, Suffolk

FOCUS
The first division of this 7f juvenile maiden that has thrown up several 100-rated performers. Winners should come from it.

3291 BRITISH STALLION STUDS EBF MAIDEN STKS (DIV II) 7f 16y
3:15 (3:17) (Class 5) 2-Y-O **£3,881** (£1,155; £577; £288) **Stalls** Low

Form RPR
3 **1** **Downturn**[14] 2847 2-9-5 0 RichardHughes 3 79+
(Richard Hannon) *mde all: dictated mod pce: shkn up over 1f out: asserted jst ins fnl f: pushed out: comf* **5/4**[1]
2 1 1/2 **Diapenko** 2-9-5 0 KierenFallon 9 76+
(Brian Meehan) *bmpd by rival after 1f: racd on outer in 6th after: nudged by same rival jst over 3f out: prog 2f out: styd on wl fnl f to take 2nd last strides* **12/1**
56 **3** hd **Bahamian Heights**[22] 2591 2-9-5 0 JamesDoyle 8 75
(Clive Brittain) *pressed wnr: shkn up and stl rt on terms over 1f out: hld fnl f: lost 2nd last strides* **25/1**
4 1 **Sbraase** 2-9-5 0 NeilCallan 7 72+
(James Tate) *chsd ldrs: shkn up to take 3rd 2f out tl ins fnl f: styd on same pce* **16/1**
5 3 **The Wallace Line (IRE)** 2-9-5 0 MatthewDavies 2 64+
(Mick Channon) *slowly away: rn green in last trio: no prog over 2f out: pushed along and kpt on fr over 1f out* **25/1**
6 nk **Il Paparazzi** 2-9-5 0 JimmyFortune 5 63+
(Daniel Kubler) *chsd ldng pair to 2f out: wknd jst over 1f out* **25/1**
7 6 **Solidarity** 2-9-5 0 SilvestreDeSousa 1 48+
(Saeed bin Suroor) *slowest away: mostly in last: no prog and wl btn over 2f out* **13/8**[2]
8 1 1/4 **Leaderene** 2-9-0 0 LiamJones 6 40
(Mark Johnston) *chsd ldrs but wandering and bmpd rival after 1f and jst over 3f out: wknd 2f out* **9/1**[3]
9 15 **Storm Of Choice** 2-9-5 0 J-PGuillambert 4 6
(Michael Attwater) *slowly away: rn green and a in last pair: wknd over 2f out: t.o* **50/1**

1m 32.72s (3.22) **Going Correction** +0.075s/f (Good) **9** Ran SP% **119.6**
Speed ratings (Par 93): **84,82,82,80,77 77,70,68,51**
toteswingers 1&2 £4.90, 1&3 £9.30, 2&3 £21.50 CSF £17.83 TOTE £2.20: £1.30, £2.80, £6.30; EX 12.50 Trifecta £131.40 Pool: £1762.09 - 10.05 winning units..
Owner Mrs J Wood **Bred** New England Stud, Myriad And N Wright **Trained** East Everleigh, Wilts

FOCUS
The second leg of this maiden was run 0.94secs slower than the first division. The winner progressed from his debut and a number can build on this bare form.

3292 WESTON GREEN FILLIES' H'CAP 1m 14y
3:50 (3:50) (Class 4) (0-85,85) 3-Y-O **£5,175** (£1,540; £769; £384) **Stalls** Low

Form RPR
20-1 **1** **Estiqaama (USA)**[10] 2963 3-8-12 **76** 6ex PaulHanagan 2 93
(William Haggas) *mde all at gd pce: pressed on and decisive ld 3f out: drvn over 1f out: tired fnl f: jst lasted* **9/2**[3]
41- **2** nk **Great Timing (USA)**[265] 6489 3-9-7 **85** SilvestreDeSousa 5 101+
(Saeed bin Suroor) *sn restrained into midfield: prog over 2f out: rdn to chse wnr over 1f out: clsd fnl f: nvr quite got there* **5/4**[1]
10 **3** 8 **Azenzar**[27] 2449 3-8-6 **70** AndreaAtzeni 10 68
(Roger Varian) *chsd wnr: rdn and no imp over 2f out: lost 2nd over 1f out: wknd but clung on for 3rd* **16/1**
62-6 **4** 1 **Vanity Rules**[40] 2049 3-9-6 **84** [1] WilliamBuick 9 80
(John Gosden) *chsd ldng pair: rdn over 2f out: no imp and wl hld over 1f out: wknd* **4/1**[2]
061 **5** 2 **Simply Elegant (IRE)**[17] 2746 3-8-8 **72** NeilCallan 1 63
(Amanda Perrett) *chsd ldng pair: rdn 3f out: no imp 2f out: wknd over 1f out* **20/1**
4463 **6** 1 1/2 **Azma (USA)**[29] 2387 3-8-5 **69** MartinLane 4 57
(Conrad Allen) *nvr bttr than midfield: rdn jst over 3f out: struggling over 2f out: wknd over 1f out* **14/1**
302- **7** 1 1/4 **Signature Dish (IRE)**[272] 6253 3-8-5 **69** FrannyNorton 7 54
(Andrew Balding) *hld up in 8th: pushed along over 2f out: no prog and nt persevered w over 1f out* **20/1**
10-4 **8** 4 1/2 **Miss Marjurie (IRE)**[36] 2195 3-8-13 **77** KierenFallon 3 51
(Denis Coakley) *hld up in midfield: rdn and no prog wl over 2f out: wknd over 1f out* **11/1**
20-0 **9** 7 **Rebel Magic**[14] 2848 3-9-7 **85** RichardHughes 6 43
(Richard Hannon) *stdd s: hld up in last: rdn and no prog over 2f out: eased whn no ch fnl f* **20/1**

1m 42.81s (-0.49) **Going Correction** +0.075s/f (Good) **9** Ran SP% **117.8**
Speed ratings (Par 98): **105,104,96,95,93 92,90,86,79**
toteswingers 1&2 £1.70, 1&3 £14.30, 2&3 £5.80 CSF £10.39 CT £78.28 TOTE £4.90: £1.20, £1.10, £6.10; EX 10.80 Trifecta £105.00 Pool: £2059.17 - 14.70 winning units..
Owner Hamdan Al Maktoum **Bred** Shadwell Farm LLC **Trained** Newmarket, Suffolk
■ Stewards' Enquiry : Silvestre De Sousa two-day ban; excessive use of whip (28th-29th June).

FOCUS
A fair fillies' handicap but the time was good, very few got involved and the first two came well clear. The winner is rated to last week's Yarmouth form, and the race could be worth 5lb higher.

3293 SUMMER H'CAP 1m 2f 7y
4:20 (4:26) (Class 3) (0-90,88) 4-Y-O+ **£8,086** (£2,406; £1,202; £601) **Stalls** Low

Form RPR
1- **1** **Clowance Estate (IRE)**[387] 2393 4-9-4 **85** JamesDoyle 4 97+
(Roger Charlton) *trckd ldr 2f and fr 1/2-way: drvn to cl and led jst over 1f out: steadily asserted last 150yds* **11/4**[1]
2031 **2** 1 1/2 **Tight Lipped (IRE)**[15] 2808 4-8-5 **77** RosieJessop(5) 1 85
(James Eustace) *bowled along in ld and at least 2 l clr mostly: drvn over 2f out: hdd jst over 1f out: kpt on wl* **8/1**
4604 **3** 1 3/4 **Tinshu (IRE)**[18] 2728 7-8-12 **79** (p) DaneO'Neill 2 84
(Derek Haydn Jones) *trckd ldrs disputing 4th: wnt 3rd wl over 2f out: rdn and kpt on same pce: nvr able to chal* **14/1**
1-20 **4** 1 **Aegaeus**[26] 2478 4-8-13 **80** RyanMoore 3 83
(Ed Dunlop) *hld up disputing 6th: shkn up 2f out: kpt on fr over 1f out: no hope of threatening* **5/1**[2]
5420 **5** shd **Cayuga**[13] 2867 4-9-0 **81** JimmyFortune 5 84
(Brett Johnson) *hld up disputing 8th: shkn up 2f out: kpt on fr over 1f out: no hope of threatening* **7/1**
0613 **6** nk **Presburg (IRE)**[8] 3022 4-8-11 **78** LiamKeniry 10 80
(Joseph Tuite) *slowly away: hld up in last: stl there whn swtchd sharply lft 2f out: drvn over 1f out: kpt on but no ch* **7/1**
-420 **7** hd **Shavansky**[22] 2592 9-9-7 **88** AndreaAtzeni 9 90
(Rod Millman) *hld up disputing 8th: shkn up over 2f out: kpt on one pce fr over 1f out: no hope of threatening* **11/1**
4-60 **8** 5 **Johnno**[28] 2424 4-9-1 **82** MartinLane 6 74
(J W Hills) *hld up disputing 6th: rdn 3f out: no prog over 2f out: wknd fnl f* **16/1**
0012 **9** 3 **The Lock Master (IRE)**[16] 2766 6-9-1 **82** KierenFallon 8 68
(Michael Appleby) *t.k.h: hld up disputing 4th: rdn over 3f out: wknd wl over 1f out* **6/1**[3]
105- **10** 3 **Dellbuoy**[338] 3963 4-8-8 **80** JemmaMarshall(5) 7 61
(Pat Phelan) *t.k.h: chsd ldr after 2f to 1/2-way: lost pl qckly 3f out: last wl over 1f out* **16/1**

2m 9.34s (-1.16) **Going Correction** +0.075s/f (Good) **10** Ran SP% **120.5**
Speed ratings (Par 107): **107,105,104,103,103 103,103,99,96,94**
toteswingers 1&2 £4.50, 1&3 £10.20, 2&3 £19.80 CSF £26.39 CT £270.34 TOTE £3.40: £1.70, £2.80, £4.20; EX 31.60 Trifecta £282.90 Pool: £3666.00 - 9.71 winning units..
Owner Seasons Holidays **Bred** Woodcote Stud Ltd **Trained** Beckhampton, Wilts

FOCUS
A good handicap and it again paid to race close to the pace. The winner looks capable of more improvement.

3294 BECK H'CAP 1m 2f 7y
4:55 (4:58) (Class 4) (0-80,80) 3-Y-O **£5,175** (£1,540; £769; £384) **Stalls** Low

Form RPR
601 **1** **London Bridge (USA)**[8] 3013 3-8-11 **70** 6ex MartinLane 3 87+
(Jo Hughes) *trckd ldrs: rdn 4f out: kpt on u.p fr over 2f out to take 2nd 1f out: styd on wl to collar ldr last strides* **7/2**[1]
3-31 **2** 3/4 **Duroble Man**[15] 2786 3-9-3 **76** NeilCallan 2 92
(Roger Varian) *mde most: skipped clr fr 3f out: 4 l up 2f out: drvn over 1f out: kpt on but collared last strides* **5/1**[3]
1341 **3** 5 **Emerging**[13] 2878 3-9-7 **80** (p) LiamKeniry 10 87
(David Elsworth) *t.k.h: trckd ldrs: drvn to chse clr ldr 2f out: no imp and lost 2nd 1f out: fdd* **6/1**
5114 **4** 1 3/4 **Echo Brava**[28] 2420 3-8-11 **70** JimmyFortune 8 73+
(Luke Dace) *hld up in midfield: prog 3f out: rdn to press for 2nd 2f out: fdd jst over 1f out* **16/1**
3031 **5** 2 3/4 **Isis Blue**[12] 2600 3-9-2 **75** SteveDrowne 11 73+
(Rod Millman) *hld up in last pair: wl bhd over 3f out: shuffled along and styd on steadily fr over 2f out: nrst fin* **10/1**
2025 **6** 1 1/2 **Noble Bull (IRE)**[10] 2957 3-9-3 **76** (b) JamesMcDonald 5 71
(Charles Hills) *pressed ldr: outpcd fr 3f out: lost 2nd 2f out and sn wknd* **20/1**
4-22 **7** 2 1/4 **Cash Is King**[34] 2272 3-9-0 **73** RyanMoore 1 64
(Jonjo O'Neill) *awkward s: hld up in last pair: lost tch and wl bhd over 3f out: drvn and passed wkng rivals last 2f* **7/1**
-352 **8** 9 **Storming (IRE)**[21] 2627 3-8-12 **71** KierenFallon 6 45
(Andrew Balding) *t.k.h: trckd ldrs: rdn 3f out: wknd jst over 2f out* **9/2**[2]
0-41 **9** 3 3/4 **Soul Intent (IRE)**[13] 2874 3-9-0 **73** JimCrowley 9 40
(J W Hills) *hld up in midfield: rdn 1/2-way: wknd wl over 2f out* **9/1**

 The Form Book Flat, Raceform Ltd, Compton, RG20 6NL.

-403 **10** *5* **Sabre Rock**[21] 2624 3-9-2 **75**.. JamesDoyle 4 32
(John Best) *hld up in last quartet: lost tch w main gp and wl bhd over 3f out* **25/1**

0-25 **11** *31* **Atlantis City (FR)**[15] 2786 3-8-12 **71**.. WilliamBuick 7
(Richard Hannon) *hld up in last quartet: lost tch and wl bhd over 3f out: wknd over 2f out: eased and t.o* **33/1**

2m 9.53s (-0.97) **Going Correction** +0.075s/f (Good) **11** Ran SP% **120.4**
Speed ratings (Par 101): **106,105,101,100,97 96,94,87,84,80 55**
toteswingers 1&2 £5.40, 1&3 £3.40, 2&3 £4.90 CSF £20.80 CT £104.29 TOTE £3.70: £1.10, £2.30, £2.40; EX 28.90 Trifecta £133.10 Pool: £3916.19 - 22.06 winning units..
Owner Eastwind Racing Ltd And Martha Trussell **Bred** Patricia S Purdy **Trained** Lambourn, Berks

FOCUS
This 3-y-o contest was run just 0.19secs slower than the preceding Class 3 for older horses, and again very few got involved. A likeable effort from the winner.
T/Plt: £18.30 to a £1 stake. Pool: £61,505.42 - 2453.05 winning tickets T/Qpdt: £5.70 to a £1 stake. Pool: £4377.94 - 565.40 winning tickets JN

2667 YORK (L-H)
Friday, June 14

OFFICIAL GOING: Good to firm (far side 7.8; centre 7.9; stands' side 7.8)
Wind: Fresh; half behind Weather: Overcast and breezy; occasional light showers

3295 MCARTHURGLEN YORK DESIGNER OUTLET EBF MAIDEN STKS 5f
2:00 (2:01) (Class 3) 2-Y-O **£6,792** (£2,021; £1,010; £505) **Stalls** Centre

Form RPR

1 **Reroute (IRE)** 2-9-0 0.. RobertWinston 5 91+
(Ed Walker) *chsd ldr stands' side: led that gp over 1f out: r.o to ld overall last 75yds* **16/1**

4 **2** *1 1/4* **Royal Mezyan (IRE)**[34] 2250 2-9-5 0.. SebSanders 3 91
(William Haggas) *led three others far side: hdd and no ex ins fnl f* **15/8**[1]

3 *3 1/2* **Morning Post** 2-9-5 0.. PhillipMakin 6 78+
(Kevin Ryan) *sn chsng ldrs: styd on same pce fnl f* **10/1**

4 *nk* **Fast Track** 2-9-5 0.. GrahamGibbons 2 77
(David Barron) *w ldr far side: styd on same pce fnl f* **22/1**

5 *1 1/4* **Inyordreams** 2-9-0 0.. DaleSwift 10 68+
(James Given) *in rr: kpt on wl fnl f* **50/1**

5 **6** *1/2* **Crowdmania**[40] 2048 2-9-5 0.. AdrianNicholls 4 71
(Mark Johnston) *dwlt: sn chsng ldrs far side: drvn over 2f out: one pce* **7/2**[2]

7 *nse* **Lincoln (IRE)** 2-9-5 0.. MartinHarley 1 71
(Mick Channon) *s.i.s: sn chsng ldrs far side: drvn over 2f out: one pce* **9/1**

8 *1* **Soul Brother (IRE)** 2-9-5 0.. DuranFentiman 7 67+
(Tim Easterby) *outpcd and in rr over 3f out: kpt on fnl f* **11/2**[3]

9 *3* **Grande Mago (IRE)** 2-9-2 0.. RossAtkinson(3) 9 56
(Robert Cowell) *s.i.s: a bhd* **14/1**

042 **10** *2 1/2* **Wiki Tiki**[8] 3017 2-9-0 0.. JamieSpencer 8 42
(Stuart Williams) *upset in stalls: led stands' side gp: hdd wl over 1f out: edgd lft and wknd* **10/1**

57.39s (-1.91) **Going Correction** -0.175s/f (Firm) **10** Ran SP% **119.4**
Speed ratings (Par 97): **108,106,100,99,97 97,97,95,90,86**
toteswingers 1&2 £8.80, 1&3 £22.20, 2&3 £4.10 CSF £47.45 TOTE £20.00: £4.50, £1.30, £4.20; EX 74.20 Trifecta £615.30 Pool: £2759.01 - 3.36 winning units..
Owner Sheikh Rashid Dalmook Al Maktoum **Bred** Carrigbeg Stud & David Powell **Trained** Newmarket, Suffolk

FOCUS
Rail moved out 3m from 1m1f to entrance to home straight, adding 7yds to distances of 1m and over. The winning time for this maiden was only 6/100ths of a second outside the 2yo course record, which shows how quick the conditions were. The field split into two groups early, with six racing close to the stands' rail and four racing up the centre. The winner looks a nice recruit.

3296 NEPTUNE INVESTMENT MANAGEMENT STKS (H'CAP) 1m 2f 88y
2:30 (2:30) (Class 2) (0-100,91) 3-Y-O **£16,172** (£4,812; £2,405; £1,202) **Stalls** Low

Form RPR

-130 **1** **Grandorio (IRE)**[13] 2879 3-8-11 **81**.. DanielTudhope 7 97+
(David O'Meara) *stdd s: hld up detached in last: shkn up 6f out: hdwy 4f out: led wl over 2f out: pushed clr appr fnl f: heavily eased clsng stages* **5/1**[3]

-111 **2** *8* **Lilac Lace (IRE)**[18] 2704 3-8-13 **83**.. DuranFentiman 4 82
(Tim Easterby) *hld up in rr: hdwy over 4f out: n.m.r 3f out: chsd wnr over 1f out: styd on same pce* **8/1**

4654 **3** *shd* **Top Notch Tonto (IRE)**[6] 3080 3-9-5 **89**.. DaleSwift 3 88
(Ian McInnes) *trckd ldr: led and edgd lft 3f out: sn hdd: kpt on same pce* **14/1**

2-11 **4** *6* **Stepping Ahead (FR)**[24] 2554 3-9-7 **91**.. MartinHarley 1 79
(Mrs K Burke) *trckd ldrs: t.k.h: effrt over 4f out: lost pl over 1f out* **1/1**[1]

2326 **5** *28* **Greeleys Love (USA)**[6] 3094 3-9-1 **85**..........................(v) AdrianNicholls 6 23
(Mark Johnston) *t.k.h: led: hdd 3f out: sn wknd: bhd and eased over 1f out: t.o* **10/3**[2]

2m 10.08s (-2.42) **Going Correction** -0.175s/f (Firm) **5** Ran SP% **107.5**
Speed ratings (Par 105): **102,95,95,90,68**
CSF £37.20 TOTE £5.50: £2.40, £1.90; EX 32.40 Trifecta £183.90 Pool: £2776.00 - 11.31 winning units..
Owner Hambleton Racing Ltd - Three In One **Bred** The Grand Splendour Partnership **Trained** Nawton, N Yorks

FOCUS
Just the five runners and something of a strange race, as a few pulled hard early and they finished spread out all over the Knavesmire. It lacked depth, and has been rated lower than it could have been, but the winner was value for extra.

3297 JIGSAW SPONSORSHIP SERVICES STKS (H'CAP) 1m 6f
3:05 (3:07) (Class 2) (0-105,96) 4-Y-O+ **£16,172** (£4,812; £2,405; £1,202) **Stalls** Low

Form RPR

120- **1** **Montaser (IRE)**[244] 7051 4-9-7 **96**.. JamieSpencer 8 103+
(David Simcock) *hld up in last: effrt over 3f out: r.o to ld over 1f out: pushed out* **9/4**[1]

-542 **2** *1* **Quixote**[35] 2205 4-9-1 **90**..(t) TedDurcan 1 95
(Clive Brittain) *trckd ldr: led over 2f out: hdd over 1f out: styd on same pce* **9/1**

0-10 **3** *nk* **Itlaaq**[30] 2365 7-9-3 **92**..(t) GrahamGibbons 3 97
(Michael Easterby) *trckd ldrs: smooth hdwy and nt clr run over 2f out: swtchd lft: styd on same pce fnl f* **15/2**

406- **4** *1/2* **Blue Bajan (IRE)**[208] 7051 11-9-6 **95**.. DanielTudhope 5 99
(David O'Meara) *trckd ldrs: upsides over 1f out: kpt on same pce* **13/2**[3]

03/0 **5** *hd* **All The Aces (IRE)**[40] 2044 8-9-0 **89**.. PhillipMakin 2 93
(Nicky Henderson) *led: qckna pce over 4f out: hdd over 2f out: one pce over 1f out* **16/1**

60-4 **6** *1 1/4* **Martin Chuzzlewit (IRE)**[28] 2427 4-8-12 **87**.. MartinHarley 6 89
(David Simcock) *trckd ldrs: drvn over 4f out: fdd fnl 150yds* **11/4**[2]

-302 **7** *1 1/4* **High Office**[20] 2671 7-8-7 **82**.. BarryMcHugh 4 83
(Richard Fahey) *hld up: hdwy over 3f out: sn drvn and hung lft: wknd appr fnl f* **13/2**[3]

3m 2.82s (2.62) **Going Correction** -0.175s/f (Firm) **7** Ran SP% **111.7**
Speed ratings (Par 109): **85,84,84,83,83 83,82**
toteswingers 1&2 £2.90, 1&3 £4.30, 2&3 £5.60 CSF £21.84 CT £126.26 TOTE £3.10: £2.00, £2.90; EX 23.80 Trifecta £82.30 Pool: £3925.35 - 35.73 winning units..
Owner Dr Marwan Koukash **Bred** Airlie Stud **Trained** Newmarket, Suffolk

FOCUS
They went only a steady early gallop in this decent staying handicap and all seven runners were still within a length or so of each other coming to the last furlong.

3298 SKF ROUS (S) STKS 6f
3:40 (3:42) (Class 3) 2-Y-O **£7,762** (£2,310; £1,154; £577) **Stalls** Centre

Form RPR

4 **1** **Yorkshire Relish (IRE)**[13] 2883 2-9-0 0.. PhillipMakin 4 71
(Kevin Ryan) *trckd ldrs: effrt over 1f out: led jst ins fnl f: edgd lft: r.o* **4/1**[2]

6 **2** *2 3/4* **Song Of Rowland (IRE)**[17] 2758 2-9-0 0.. JamieSpencer 2 63
(Peter Chapple-Hyam) *trckd ldrs: nt clr run and edgd rt over 1f out: upsides jst ins fnl f: no ex* **7/2**[1]

016 **3** *nk* **Rosebay Coral (IRE)**[16] 2767 2-8-9 0.. BarryMcHugh 3 57
(Tony Coyle) *led: hdd jst ins fnl f: kpt on same pce* **4/1**[2]

6 **4** *3/4* **Latenightrequest**[11] 2913 2-8-9 0.. PatrickMathers 11 55+
(Richard Fahey) *in rr: hdwy over 2f out: styd on fnl f* **40/1**

5 **5** *1 1/4* **Lady Mai (IRE)**[60] 1573 2-8-9 0.. AdamBeschizza 8 51
(William Kinsey) *mid-div: hdwy over 2f out: kpt on one pce over 1f out* **16/1**

00 **6** *3/4* **Kindanyce (IRE)**[18] 2701 2-8-4 0.. GeorgeChaloner(5) 13 49
(Richard Fahey) *chsd ldrs: drvn over 2f out: one pce over 1f out* **33/1**

0 **7** *hd* **Porteous**[7] 3049 2-8-9 0.. MartinHarley 7 48
(Mick Channon) *prom: rdn over 2f out: kpt on: nvr able to chal* **11/2**[3]

4542 **8** *8* **Jaga Time**[26] 2475 2-9-0 0.. TonyHamilton 6 35
(Richard Fahey) *chsd ldrs: drvn over 2f out: wknd fnl f: eased towards fin* **10/1**

00 **9** *2 3/4* **It's All A Game**[13] 2883 2-9-0 0.. RobbieFitzpatrick 10 21
(Richard Guest) *mid-div: hdwy u.p over 2f out: wknd fnl f* **25/1**

60 **10** *1* **Touch The Clouds**[18] 2715 2-9-0 0.. RobertWinston 1 36
(Kevin Ryan) *w ldrs: wandered over 1f out: sn wknd and heavily eased* **50/1**

0 **11** *2 1/4* **Maupiti Express (FR)**[13] 2883 2-9-0 0.. DanielTudhope 15 11
(David O'Meara) *sn outpcd and in rr* **12/1**

46 **12** *3 1/2* **My Little Friend**[24] 2543 2-9-0 0.. TedDurcan 14
(Mark H Tompkins) *in rr: reminders after s: sn bhd* **20/1**

13 *1* **Angus Mac Og (IRE)** 2-8-7 0.. DanielleMooney(7) 9
(Nigel Tinkler) *sn wl outpcd and bhd* **25/1**

14 *6* **Sicilian Bay (IRE)** 2-8-9 0.. MickyFenton 12
(Paul Midgley) *missed break and wnt lft s: sn detached in last and hung bdly lft* **66/1**

1m 11.25s (-0.65) **Going Correction** -0.175s/f (Firm) **14** Ran SP% **121.6**
Speed ratings (Par 97): **97,93,92,91,90 89,89,78,74,73 70,65,64,56**
toteswingers 1&2 £4.70, 1&3 £4.50, 2&3 £4.60 CSF £17.22 TOTE £5.10: £1.60, £1.90, £2.00; EX 22.30 Trifecta £115.10 Pool: £5418.83 - 35.28 winning units..Song Of Rowland was claimed by Mr D O'Meara for £12,000.
Owner Mr & Mrs J Berry I **Bred** C Marnane **Trained** Hambleton, N Yorks

FOCUS
A traditionally valuable 2yo seller, and the betting got it right with this year's renewal as the market leaders filled the first three places. The trio were up with the pace throughout and they all came from low draws. Better than the usual form for the grade.

3299 BELL TRAILERS 25TH ANNIVERSARY STKS (H'CAP) 5f
4:10 (4:13) (Class 3) (0-95,95) 3-Y-O+ **£7,439** (£2,213; £1,106; £553) **Stalls** Centre

Form RPR

13-1 **1** **Above Standard (IRE)**[17] 2755 5-9-3 **84**..........................(t) GrahamGibbons 19 93+
(Michael Easterby) *chsd ldrs: led last 100yds: hld on wl* **11/2**[1]

0-00 **2** *nk* **Ponty Acclaim (IRE)**[20] 2669 4-9-7 **88**..........................(t[1]) RobertWinston 9 96
(Tim Easterby) *half-rrd s: sn mid-div: upsides 1f out: no ex clsng stages* **10/1**

0000 **3** *1/2* **Pabusar**[13] 2868 5-10-0 **95**.. JamieSpencer 18 101+
(Jamie Osborne) *stdd s: s.i.s: hdwy stands' side 2f out: r.o ins fnl f* **20/1**

4106 **4** *hd* **Bedloe's Island (IRE)**[25] 2505 8-9-4 **85**.. DanielTudhope 1 90
(David O'Meara) *awkward to load: chsd ldrs: upsides 1f out: no ex last 50yds* **8/1**[3]

6220 **5** *hd* **Bispham Green**[28] 2430 3-8-9 **83**.. TonyHamilton 7 86
(Richard Fahey) *w ldr: led over 1f out: hdd ins fnl f: no ex* **12/1**

0344 **6** *3/4* **Waseem Faris (IRE)**[8] 3018 4-8-11 **78**.. MartinHarley 11 81
(Mick Channon) *hld up in mid-div: hdwy and nt clr run over 1f out: styd on ins fnl f* **15/2**[2]

402 **7** *nk* **Chooseday (IRE)**[6] 3093 4-9-3 **84**..........................(p) AmyRyan 8 86
(Kevin Ryan) *hood removed late: s.i.s: in rr: hdwy: nt clr run and swtchd lft over 1f out: kpt on same pce last 100yds* **11/2**[1]

-663 **8** *nk* **Another Wise Kid (IRE)**[41] 2007 5-9-4 **85**.. MickyFenton 3 85
(Paul Midgley) *mid-div: nt clr run over 1f out: styd on ins fnl f* **8/1**[3]

26-4 **9** *nk* **Sunny Side Up (IRE)**[17] 2755 4-8-4 **78** ow1.. LauraBarry(7) 13 77
(Richard Fahey) *led: hdd over 1f out: one pce* **16/1**

1314 **10** *nk* **Mata Hari Blue**[20] 2657 7-9-4 **85**..........................(t) AndrewMullen 2 83
(Michael Appleby) *chsd ldrs: one pce fnl 150yds* **16/1**

120- **11** *1* **Mayoman (IRE)**[265] 6466 8-9-7 **88**.. MichaelO'Connell 17 85+
(David O'Meara) *hood removed v late: s.i.s: in rr: hdwy whn nt clr run and swtchd rt over 1f out: nvr a factor* **33/1**

4300 **12** *1 1/2* **Silvanus (IRE)**[20] 2669 8-9-0 **86**.. ShirleyTeasdale(5) 16 75
(Paul Midgley) *chsd ldrs: wknd fnl f* **20/1**

0-05 **13** *3/4* **B Fifty Two (IRE)**[11] 2937 4-9-10 **91**..........................(t) SebSanders 15 77
(J W Hills) *w ldrs: wknd fnl f* **12/1**

0-00 **14** *3 3/4* **Last Bid**[29] 2396 4-9-0 **81**.. DuranFentiman 5 53
(Tim Easterby) *chsd ldrs: wknd over 1f out* **33/1**

0060 **15** *1/2* **Profile Star (IRE)**[17] 2755 4-8-12 **79**.. PhillipMakin 12 50
(David Barron) *mid-div: drvn over 2f out: lost pl over 1f out* **25/1**

30-6 **16** *3 ¾* **Lady Poppy**[55] 1690 3-8-3 **77** .... AdrianNicholls 14 32
(George Moore) *sn outpcd and in rr* **25/1**

57.81s (-1.49) **Going Correction** -0.175s/f (Firm)
WFA 3 from 4yo+ 7lb **16** Ran SP% **124.1**
Speed ratings (Par 107): **104,103,102,102,102 100,100,99,99,98 97,94,93,87,86 80**
CSF £54.81 CT £1080.90 TOTE £4.90: £1.80, £3.10, £4.50, £2.70; EX 63.80 Trifecta £633.50 Pool: £4299.34 - 5.08 winning units..
Owner A Saha **Bred** Sandro Garavelli **Trained** Sheriff Hutton, N Yorks

FOCUS
Fast and furious stuff in this competitive sprint handicap, and a compressed finish. The fifth and the time offer perspective but the winner is looking progressive.

3300 GARBUTT & ELLIOTT STKS (H'CAP) 7f
4:45 (4:46) (Class 3) (0-95,95) 4-Y-0+ **£7,439** (£2,213; £1,106; £553) **Stalls** Low

Form RPR
0-00 **1** **Smarty Socks (IRE)**[34] 2254 9-9-1 **89** .... DanielTudhope 1 103+
(David O'Meara) *dwlt: hld up in rr: nt clr run over 2f out tl swtchd rt over 1f out: led and edgd lft last 100yds: styd on* **11/2**
1-00 **2** *1 ¾* **Nameitwhatyoulike**[55] 1688 4-8-13 **87** .... GrahamGibbons 11 96
(Michael Easterby) *trckd ldrs: led over 1f out: hdd: edgd rt and crowded ins fnl f: no ex* **8/1**
02-5 **3** *1 ¼* **Lisiere (IRE)**[48] 1823 4-8-5 **79** ....(p) BarryMcHugh 8 85
(Mrs K Burke) *chsd ldrs: led over 2f out: hdd over 1f out: styd on same pce* **12/1**
-051 **4** *hd* **Day Of The Eagle (IRE)**[13] 2884 7-7-11 **76** oh1...... ShirleyTeasdale(5) 7 81
(Michael Easterby) *trckd ldrs: edgd rt over 1f out: rdn and hung lft ins fnl f: kpt on* **4/1**[2]
0005 **5** *2 ¼* **Mabait**[20] 2649 7-9-1 **89** .... JamieSpencer 13 89
(David Simcock) *hld up in rr: hdwy whn nt clr run over 1f out: styng on whn hmpd ins fnl f* **7/2**[1]
-306 **6** *1 ½* **Rodrigo De Torres**[20] 2667 6-9-6 **94** ....[1] AndrewMullen 10 89
(David Nicholls) *swtchd lft after s: t.k.h: chsd ldrs: one pce over 1f out* **25/1**
6034 **7** *2* **Mappin Time (IRE)**[14] 2834 5-8-7 **81** ....(p) RobertHavlin 3 71
(Tim Easterby) *in tch: effrt over 2f out: fdd fnl f* **14/1**
0400 **8** *3 ¼* **Sam Nombulist**[6] 3096 5-8-11 **85** ....(v) RobertWinston 2 67
(Richard Whitaker) *led: hdd over 2f out: hung rt and wknd over 1f out* **12/1**
3-15 **9** *3 ¾* **Personal Touch**[35] 2214 4-8-8 **82** .... TonyHamilton 4 54
(Richard Fahey) *chsd ldrs: edgd lft and wknd 1f out* **9/2**[3]
-000 **10** *7* **Capaill Liath (IRE)**[55] 1675 5-9-0 **88** ....(p) AmyRyan 5 42
(Kevin Ryan) *s.s: sn detached in last: nvr on terms* **16/1**
0-00 **11** *4 ½* **Trade Secret**[20] 2665 6-8-9 **83** .... DuranFentiman 6 25
(Mel Brittain) *s.i.s: hdwy on wd outside to chse ldrs over 3f out: wknd and eased over 1f out* **28/1**

1m 22.6s (-2.70) **Going Correction** -0.175s/f (Firm) **11** Ran SP% **122.1**
Speed ratings (Par 107): **108,106,104,104,101 100,97,94,89,81 76**
toteswingers 1&2 £9.20, 1&3 £18.20, 2&3 £22.20 CSF £51.20 CT £527.40 TOTE £4.20: £1.60, £4.10, £4.30; EX 51.60 Trifecta £503.80 Pool: £3099.59 - 4.61 winning units..
Owner Direct Racing Partnership **Bred** Mick McGinn **Trained** Nawton, N Yorks

FOCUS
A decent handicap run at a good pace. Straightforward form.

3301 FUTURE CLEANING SERVICES APPRENTICE STKS (H'CAP) 1m 4f
5:15 (5:17) (Class 4) (0-80,79) 4-Y-0+ **£6,469** (£1,925; £962; £481) **Stalls** Centre

Form RPR
-432 **1** **Looks Like Rain**[18] 2721 4-8-5 **65** .... KevinStott(7) 14 74+
(Brian Ellison) *swtchd lft after s: detached in last: hdwy on wd outside over 2f out: r.o to ld last 100yds* **6/1**[2]
3-16 **2** *1 ¾* **Singzak**[20] 2671 5-9-2 **74** .... MatthewHopkins(5) 13 80
(Michael Easterby) *trckd ldrs: led over 2f out: hdd and no ex ins fnl f* **10/1**
41-1 **3** *½* **Mama Quilla (USA)**[18] 2729 4-9-6 **76** .... RobertTart(3) 16 82+
(William Haggas) *in rr: rdn over 2f out: edgd lft and styd on over 1f out: tk 3rd last 50yds* **7/2**[1]
-536 **4** *1* **Dr Irv**[18] 2720 4-8-5 **63** .... EvaMoscrop(5) 1 67
(Philip Kirby) *half-rrd at s: in rr: swtchd outside over 2f out: styd on over 1f out* **9/1**
0045 **5** *1 ½* **Suffice (IRE)**[28] 2431 4-9-1 **73** .... GeorgeChaloner(5) 15 75
(Richard Fahey) *chsd ldrs: led over 3f out: hdd over 2f out: one pce over 1f out* **8/1**
1224 **6** *2 ¾* **Amtired**[10] 2961 7-8-7 **60** ....(p) RossAtkinson 7 58
(Brian Ellison) *mid-div: hdwy whn hmpd 3f out: edgd lft over 1f out: nvr nr to chal* **16/1**
5213 **7** *nse* **Gran Maestro (USA)**[2] 3204 4-9-5 **75** 6ex........(b) LMcNiff(3) 6 74
(Ruth Carr) *mid-div: hmpd 3f out: edgd rt over 1f out: styd on* **6/1**[2]
-050 **8** *½* **Warcrown (IRE)**[28] 2431 4-8-10 **68** ....(t) LauraBarry(5) 9 65
(Richard Fahey) *mid-div: chsd ldrs over 3f out: edgd lft and one pce over 1f out* **20/1**
120- **9** *¾* **Song Of The Siren**[294] 5546 5-8-13 **73** .... JoshDoyle(7) 18 69
(David O'Meara) *swtchd lft after s: in rr: hdwy over 3f out: one pce and edgd lft fnl f* **22/1**
4411 **10** *1 ½* **Arc Light (IRE)**[13] 2886 5-9-2 **72** .... DarylByrne(3) 11 66
(Tim Easterby) *in rr: hdwy and swtchd to inner over 2f out: chsng ldrs over 1f out: fdd last 100yds* **7/1**[3]
31-0 **11** *6* **Adili (IRE)**[13] 2886 4-8-5 **65** .... RichardOliver(7) 12 50
(Brian Ellison) *chsd ldrs: drvn whn hmpd 3f out: sn lost pl* **50/1**
1244 **12** *3 ¼* **The Blue Dog (IRE)**[18] 2729 6-8-9 **62** .... BillyCray 3 42
(Phil McEntee) *in tch: hdwy to chse ldrs over 3f out: lost pl over 1f out* **25/1**
-110 **13** *25* **Full Speed (GER)**[13] 2860 8-9-0 **67** .... DeclanCannon 5 9
(Philip Kirby) *chsd ldrs: lost pl over 2f out: eased whn bhd: t.o* **20/1**
0-00 **14** *38* **Modernism**[20] 2646 4-9-9 **79** ....(p) ShirleyTeasdale(3) 8
(Alan McCabe) *led: hdd over 3f out: sn lost pl and bhd: eased whn t.o: virtually p.u* **33/1**

2m 31.47s (-1.73) **Going Correction** -0.175s/f (Firm) **14** Ran SP% **122.0**
Speed ratings (Par 105): **98,96,96,95,94 93,92,92,92,91 87,84,68,42**
toteswingers 1&2 £13.10, 1&3 £5.90, 2&3 £7.10 CSF £59.17 TOTE £7.50: £2.50, £4.00, £1.30; EX 99.80 Trifecta £975.90 Pool: £1903.36 - 1.46 winning units..
Owner Peter Alderson & Brian Ellison **Bred** Whitley Stud **Trained** Norton, N Yorks
■ Stewards' Enquiry : Richard Oliver five-day ban; used whip when out of contention (28th June - 2nd July).

FOCUS
An ordinary apprentice handicap, but they went a decent pace and that suited the hold-up horses. The winner looks better than ever.
T/Jkpt: Not won. T/Plt: £486.80 to a £1 stake. Pool: £89,292.04 - 133.87 winning tickets T/Qpdt: £26.00 to a £1 stake. Pool: £7261.65 - 206.28 winning tickets WG

3302 - 3309a (Foreign Racing) - See Raceform Interactive

3035 BATH (L-H)
Saturday, June 15

OFFICIAL GOING: Firm (9.7)
Wind: Strong ahead

3310 PROFAB WINDOWS MAIDEN AUCTION STKS 5f 11y
2:30 (2:32) (Class 6) 2-Y-O **£1,940** (£577; £288; £144) **Stalls** Centre

Form RPR
4323 **1** **Danfazi (IRE)**[19] 2715 2-8-13 0........ AmyRyan 8 74
(Kristin Stubbs) *pressed ldr: led 2f out: drvn and styd on strly fnl f* **5/2**[2]
4 **2** *1 ¼* **Sartorialist (IRE)**[12] 2917 2-8-11 0........ LiamJones 3 67
(J S Moore) *in rr: pushed along 3f out: hdwy and edgd rt over 1f out: styd on to take 2nd clsng stages but no ch w wnr* **9/1**
63 **3** *2* **Captain Ryan**[22] 2617 2-8-13 0 ow2........ SebSanders 2 62
(Peter Makin) *sn led: rdn and hdd 2f out: sn no ch w wnr: wknd and dropped to 3rd clsng stages* **9/4**[1]
4 *2 ¾* **Douneedahand** 2-8-4 0........ KieranO'Neill 4 43
(Seamus Mullins) *chsd ldrs: rdn 1/2-way: sn one pce* **33/1**
5 *4 ½* **The Doyle Machine (IRE)** 2-8-12 0 ow1........ StevieDonohoe 7 34
(Noel Quinlan) *chsd ldrs: rdn and btn whn pushed rt over 1f out* **12/1**
0 **6** *shd* **Scooping (IRE)**[30] 2382 2-8-9 0 ow1........ PatDobbs 6 31
(Richard Hannon) *early spd: sn outpcd* **5/1**[3]
5 **7** *2 ¼* **Dawnfromthepast (IRE)**[9] 3009 2-8-11 0........ FergusSweeney 5 24
(Jamie Osborne) *in tch: sme hdwy whn pushed rt and wknd over 1f out* **20/1**
0 **8** *8* **Monsieur Blanc (IRE)**[19] 2723 2-8-11 0........ MartinDwyer 1
(Denis Coakley) *a outpcd* **7/1**

1m 3.75s (1.25) **Going Correction** -0.025s/f (Good) **8** Ran SP% **113.9**
Speed ratings (Par 91): **89,87,83,79,72 72,68,55**
toteswingers 1&2 £4.40, 1&3 £1.10, 2&3 £3.40 CSF £24.98 TOTE £2.60: £1.10, £3.40, £1.70; EX 18.60 Trifecta £43.80 Pool: £987.05 - 16.89 winning units..
Owner Facts & Figures **Bred** Kiltown Bloodstock Ltd **Trained** Norton, N Yorks

FOCUS
As at all meetings this year the far bend was positioned 3-4 yds off the inside line, adding 10yds to races of 1m and beyond. The going remained firm despite 3.5mm of rain before racing. This was a routine maiden but it was run at a furious tempo. A fair effort by the winner in the circumstances.

3311 FESTIVAL RACING BRITISH STALLION STUDS/EBF NOVICE STKS 5f 11y
3:05 (3:06) (Class 4) 2-Y-O **£4,075** (£1,212; £606; £303) **Stalls** Centre

Form RPR
12 **1** **Lilbourne Lass**[12] 2933 2-8-11 0........ PatDobbs 1 93+
(Richard Hannon) *t.k.h: trckd ldr: slt ld 2f out: pushed clr fnl f: easily* **4/11**[1]
10 **2** *3 ¾* **Majestic Alexander (IRE)**[29] 2426 2-8-9 0........ DeclanBates(5) 5 82
(David Evans) *trckd ldrs: chal 2f out: chsd wnr over 1f out but nvr any ch* **4/1**[2]
662 **3** *3 ¼* **The Smart One (IRE)**[8] 3045 2-8-9 0........ CharlesBishop(5) 2 70
(Mick Channon) *chsd ldrs: chal 2f out: sn rdn: wknd appr fnl f* **7/1**[3]
5651 **4** *8* **Mr Dandy Man (IRE)**[12] 2917 2-9-2 0........ WilliamCarson 3 42
(Ronald Harris) *sn led: hdd 2f out: sn wknd* **16/1**
0 **5** *3 ½* **Ivan B**[11] 2947 2-9-0 0........ SamHitchcott 4 27
(Mick Channon) *slowly away: a outpcd* **66/1**

1m 2.65s (0.15) **Going Correction** -0.025s/f (Good) **5** Ran SP% **113.2**
Speed ratings (Par 95): **97,91,85,73,67**
toteswingers 1&2 £2.20, 1&3 £5.40, 2&3 £1.50 CSF £2.37 TOTE £1.30: £1.02, £2.50; EX 1.60 Trifecta £4.10 Pool: £872.97 - 156.17 winning units..
Owner Hon Mrs Sarah Ensor **Bred** Alvediston Stud **Trained** East Everleigh, Wilts

FOCUS
Both the winner and the runner-up set a good standard in this novice event. The winner continues on the upgrade and is ready for Listed races.

3312 MODERN GLASS BRISTOL H'CAP 1m 3f 144y
3:40 (3:40) (Class 6) (0-60,64) 4-Y-0+ **£1,940** (£577; £288; £144) **Stalls** Low

Form RPR
0011 **1** **Highlife Dancer**[5] 3151 5-9-7 **64** 6ex........(v) CharlesBishop(5) 7 74
(Mick Channon) *mde all: pushed along over 2f out: styd on strly fr over 1f out: unchal* **6/4**[1]
4605 **2** *3 ¼* **Bold Cross (IRE)**[15] 2826 10-9-2 **59**........ PhilipPrince(5) 3 63
(Edward Bevan) *in rr: rdn over 4f out: hdwy on outer fr 2f out: rdn to go 2nd jst ins fnl f but no imp on wnr* **14/1**
3-56 **3** *1* **Arch Event**[12] 2921 8-8-5 **50**........(p) OisinMurphy(7) 1 53
(Bernard Llewellyn) *trckd ldrs: rdn to chse wnr 2f out: no imp and styd on same pce into 3rd fnl f* **12/1**
4633 **4** *1 ¾* **Glens Wobbly**[8] 3037 5-8-3 **46**........ RyanTate(5) 5 46
(Jonathan Geake) *in tch: drvn along 5f out: chsd ldrs 2f out: wknd ins fnl f* **3/1**[2]
02-0 **5** *1 ¼* **Josie's Dream (IRE)**[57] 1664 5-8-6 **51**........ JosephineGordon(7) 9 49
(Jo Hughes) *trckd wnr 7f out: rdn 3f out: lost 2nd 2f out: wknd over 1f out* **10/1**
1144 **6** *½* **Midnight Sequel**[15] 2828 4-9-1 **53**........ LiamJones 8 50
(Michael Blake) *in tch: drvn over 4f out: chsd ldrs u.p and disp 2nd wl over 1f out: wknd fnl f* **6/1**[3]
045 **7** *9* **Drummond**[12] 2923 4-9-4 **56**........ WilliamCarson 4 41
(Bernard Llewellyn) *rdn 4f out: sme prog 3f out: sn wknd* **6/1**[3]

2m 31.47s (0.87) **Going Correction** +0.10s/f (Good) **7** Ran SP% **117.0**
Speed ratings (Par 101): **101,98,98,97,96 95,89**
toteswingers 1&2 £17.70, 1&3 £1.10, 2&3 £17.70 CSF £25.57 CT £192.79 TOTE £2.10: £1.60, £7.10; EX 14.10 Trifecta £61.90 Pool: £644.58 - 7.80 winning units..
Owner The Highlife Racing Club **Bred** Imperial & Mike Channon Bloodstock Ltd **Trained** West Ilsley, Berks

FOCUS
The winner, who had already demonstrated that he is happy to make the running, was allowed to set a modest pace, which suited him but hardly any of the others. The form is taken at face value for now.

3313 DISTINCTION PROPERTY SERVICES H'CAP 1m 3f 144y
4:15 (4:15) (Class 5) (0-75,71) 3-Y-O **£2,587** (£770; £384; £192) **Stalls** Low

Form RPR
2431 **1** **Knight's Parade (IRE)**[12] 2924 3-9-2 **66**........ PatDobbs 2 74+
(Amanda Perrett) *mde all: jnd over 2f out: pushed along over 1f out: sn asserted: readily* **10/11**[1]
1310 **2** *1 ¼* **Dali's Lover (IRE)**[23] 2602 3-9-7 **71**........ WilliamCarson 3 76
(Charles Hills) *chsd ldrs: rdn and one pce 3f out: rallied to chse wnr 1f out but a readily hld* **4/1**[3]

The Form Book Flat, Raceform Ltd, Compton, RG20 6NL.

0-01 **3** *6* **Just A Pound (IRE)**[8] 3041 3-8-7 **62** PhilipPrince(5) 4 57
(Jo Hughes) *chsd ldrs: rdn and outpcd 5f out: rallied to press wnr 4f out: rdn and stl ev ch 2f out: wknd ins fnl f* **6/1**

-202 **4** *11* **Hamla**[81] 1177 3-8-12 **62** LiamJones 1 38
(Mark Johnston) *s.i.s: sn t.k.h and chsng ldrs: rdn and wknd over 3f out* **10/3[2]**

2m 31.04s (0.44) **Going Correction** +0.10s/f (Good) 4 Ran SP% **109.7**
Speed ratings (Par 99): **102,101,97,89**
CSF £4.91 TOTE £1.40; EX 4.70 Trifecta £9.40 Pool: £837.76 - 66.69 winning units..
Owner The Recitation Partnership **Bred** E Heary **Trained** Pulborough, W Sussex

FOCUS
The four runners had all been in decent form but this was a tactical race and, though the best horse won, the form doesn't mean much. The first 2f were run at a crawl until the winner was sent on to make it at a better, though not strong, gallop. The winner is rated to his Chepstow mark.

3314 BRIGHTVIEW WINDOWS H'CAP 1m 2f 46y
4:45 (4:46) (Class 6) (0-55,55) 4-Y-0+ **£2,045** (£603; £302) **Stalls** Low

Form RPR

6600 **1** **Hawaiian Freeze**[6] 3138 4-8-12 **46** oh1 StevieDonohoe 8 51
(John Stimpson) *in rr: rdn: hdwy and swtchd lft jst ins fnl 2f: str run fnl f: kpt on u.p to ld cl home* **66/1**

00-0 **2** *hd* **Devon Diva**[25] 2534 7-8-12 **46** oh1 AmyRyan 13 51
(John Gallagher) *led tl hdd 6f out: styd chsng ldr: rdn 2f out: styd on wl clsng stages to press wnr: no ex last strides* **50/1**

-600 **3** *nse* **Madam Tessa (IRE)**[15] 2828 5-8-5 **46** oh1 ChloeIngram(7) 3 51
(Tim Vaughan) *chsd ldrs: styd on towards outside appr fnl f: chal clsng stages: nt quite get up* **66/1**

0-20 **4** *nk* **Perfect Outlook**[8] 3037 5-8-12 **46** (p) SamHitchcott 4 50
(Charlie Longsdon) *chsd ldr: led 7f out: rdn over 2f out: kpt slt ld ins fnl f tl outpcd into 4th clsng stages* **10/1**

0242 **5** *1* **Cane Cat (IRE)**[6] 3138 6-9-6 **54** (t) PatDobbs 1 56+
(Tony Carroll) *in rr: hdwy on inner whn hmpd jst ins fnl 2f: riddn and styd on fnl f: n.m.r on ins appr fnl f: kpt on clsng stages* **2/1[1]**

5-40 **6** *1 ½* **Gaelic Ice**[19] 2710 4-9-7 **55** [1] FergusSweeney 11 54
(Rod Millman) *in rr: hdwy whn n.m.r jst ins fnl 2f: hdwy over 1f out: styd on clsng stages* **17/2**

200- **7** *nk* **Lisselan Pleasure (USA)**[118] 6794 6-8-12 **53** (t) SiobhanMiller(7) 5 52
(Bernard Llewellyn) *in tch: rdn 3f out: styd on fr over if out: nt rch ldrs* **20/1**

1420 **8** *½* **Stag Hill (IRE)**[32] 2348 4-9-7 **55** WilliamCarson 6 53
(Bernard Llewellyn) *chsd ldrs: rdn 4f out: wknd fnl 110yds* **4/1[2]**

0-6 **9** *¾* **Belle Park**[54] 1730 6-8-10 **51** RyanWhile(7) 2 47
(Karen George) *in rr: c wd into st: hdwy u.p over 1f out: nt rch ldrs* **15/2[3]**

60-2 **10** *3 ½* **Mr Udagawa**[40] 2072 7-8-7 **48** (p) OisinMurphy(7) 10 37
(Bernard Llewellyn) *chsd ldrs: rdn over 2f out: wknd over 1f out* **16/1**

460/ **11** *1* **Mr Dream Maker (IRE)**[694] 4281 5-9-4 **55** DeclanCannon(3) 12 42
(Noel Wilson) *chsd ldrs: rdn 4f out: wknd 2f out* **8/1**

0002 **12** *4* **Market Puzzle (IRE)**[8] 3043 6-8-10 **51** (p) NoelGarbutt(7) 9 30
(Mark Brisbourne) *c wd bnd over 3f out: a in rr* **10/1**

4060 **13** *24* **Titan Diamond (IRE)**[40] 2073 5-8-9 **48** oh1 ow2 [1] RachealKneller(5) 7
(Mark Usher) *chsd ldrs: rdn over 3f out: wknd whn bdly hmpd ins fnl 2f* **25/1**

2m 11.85s (0.85) **Going Correction** +0.10s/f (Good) 13 Ran SP% **124.4**
Speed ratings (Par 101): **100,99,99,99,98 97,97,96,96,93 92,89,70**
toteswingers 1&2 not won, 1&3 £33.60, 2&3 £33.60 CSF £1918.22 CT £95077.79 TOTE £73.10: £11.10, £2.60, £15.10; EX 759.70 Trifecta £713.60 Part won. Pool: £951.49 - 0.01 winning units..
Owner J T S (International) Ltd **Bred** Mrs D O Joly **Trained** Butterton, Staffs
■ Stewards' Enquiry : Stevie Donohoe two-day ban; careless riding (29th-30th June).\n\x\x two-day ban; careless riding (1st-2nd July)

FOCUS
This low-grade race threw up a bizarre result, the first three being returned at 66-1, 50-1 and 66-1 and fillies or mares filling the first seven places. The early pace was nothing special, but it was decent enough from halfway and the long-time leader eventually succumbed near the finish. Hard form to fathom.

3315 P.K. BUILDING H'CAP 5f 161y
5:15 (5:17) (Class 4) (0-80,79) 3-Y-0+ **£4,690** (£1,395; £697; £348) **Stalls** Centre

Form RPR

-003 **1** **Clear Spring (IRE)**[9] 3010 5-9-10 **75** LiamJones 7 91+
(John Spearing) *chsd ldrs: drvn to ld 1f out: drvn clr: kpt on wl* **9/2[2]**

1365 **2** *2 ¾* **Mambo Spirit (IRE)**[14] 2871 9-8-11 **62** WilliamCarson 10 69
(Tony Newcombe) *chsd ldrs: over 2f out: wnt 2nd ins fnl f but no ch w wnr* **14/1**

1006 **3** *¾* **Clear Praise (USA)**[14] 2871 6-9-9 **74** SebSanders 5 79
(Simon Dow) *in tch: rdn over 2f out: styd on to take 3rd fnl 110yds: nt rch ldng duo* **17/2**

51-0 **4** *1* **Annes Rocket (IRE)**[35] 2255 8-9-8 **73** (p) PatDobbs 2 74
(Jimmy Fox) *s.i.s: in rr: hdwy over 1f out: kpt on wl clsng stages* **6/1[3]**

4420 **5** *¾* **Triple Dream**[15] 2825 8-9-10 **75** (tp) AmyRyan 11 74
(Milton Bradley) *pressed ldr: led 2f out: hdd over 1f out: no ex ins fnl f* **25/1**

4026 **6** *¾* **Catalinas Diamond (IRE)**[18] 2745 5-8-12 **63** (t) SamHitchcott 14 59
(Pat Murphy) *chsd ldrs: rdn to chal appr fnl f: fdd fnl 110yds* **25/1**

3556 **7** *½* **Dark Lane**[9] 3010 7-9-0 **70** DeclanBates(5) 8 65
(David Evans) *sn led: hdd 2f out: wknd fnl f* **14/1**

-164 **8** *hd* **Drawnfromthepast (IRE)**[115] 727 8-10-0 **79** FergusSweeney 4 73
(Jamie Osborne) *chsd ldrs: led over 1f out: sn hdd wknd fnl f* **16/1**

360- **9** *½* **Valmina**[254] 6820 6-9-6 **76** (t) CharlesBishop(5) 6 68
(Tony Carroll) *s.i.s: in rr: hdwy over 1f out: styd on same pce ins fnl f* **10/1**

0500 **10** *¾* **Pick A Little**[15] 2825 5-9-8 **73** JackMitchell 12 63
(Michael Blake) *rdn 1/2-way: a outpcd* **33/1**

6453 **11** *2 ¼* **Wooden King (IRE)**[8] 3042 8-8-9 **67** RyanWhile(7) 9 49
(Malcolm Saunders) *chsd ldrs: rdn over 2f out: wknd wl over 1f out* **8/1**

5250 **12** *2 ¾* **Tidal's Baby**[103] 878 4-9-1 **66** StevieDonohoe 15 39
(Tony Carroll) *outpcd* **12/1**

0002 **13** *3* **Italian Tom (IRE)**[15] 2825 6-9-6 **76** EDLinehan(5) 1 39
(Ronald Harris) *chsd ldrs to 1/2-way: sn btn* **3/1[1]**

1m 11.75s (0.55) **Going Correction** +0.225s/f (Good) 13 Ran SP% **125.7**
Speed ratings (Par 105): **105,101,100,99,98 97,96,96,95,94 91,87,83**
toteswingers 1&2 £23.80, 1&3 £23.80, 2&3 £23.80 CSF £68.65 CT £536.62 TOTE £8.30: £2.30, £5.30, £3.30; EX 91.90 Trifecta £356.80 Part won. Pool: £475.78 - 0.31 winning units..
Owner H James **Bred** Rocal Bloodstock **Trained** Kinnersley, Worcs

FOCUS
This looked to be a typically competitive Bath sprint, but the winner scored with a bit in hand. A slightly positive view has been taken of the form.

3316 EXPRESS GLAZING H'CAP 5f 161y
5:45 (5:49) (Class 6) (0-55,54) 3-Y-0 **£2,045** (£603; £302) **Stalls** Centre

Form RPR

-050 **1** **Cara Gina**[18] 2762 3-8-12 **45** (b) LiamJones 8 61
(William Haggas) *s.i.s: sn trcking ldrs: led 2f out: drvn clr fnl f: easily* **7/2[2]**

-002 **2** *5* **Foie Gras**[16] 2791 3-9-5 **52** (b) JackMitchell 6 51
(William Muir) *towards rr: pushed along and hdwy 2f out: styd on to chse wnr fnl 110yds: nvr any ch* **3/1[1]**

40-0 **3** *2 ½* **Koharu**[15] 2829 3-9-0 **52** (t) DeclanBates(5) 5 43
(Peter Makin) *in rr: pushed along over 2f out: styd on fnl f to take wl-hld 3rd clsng stages* **14/1**

5406 **4** *hd* **Imperial Spirit**[11] 2962 3-9-1 **53** (v) CharlesBishop(5) 3 43
(Mick Channon) *pressed ldr: led over 3f out: hdd 2f out: wknd fnl f* **4/1[3]**

5006 **5** *4* **Twinwood Star (IRE)**[32] 2336 3-8-12 **45** SamHitchcott 7 22
(John Weymes) *chsd ldrs: rdn over 2f out: wknd appr fnl f* **25/1**

10 **6** *1 ¼* **Lincolnrose (IRE)**[9] 3016 3-8-13 **53** (p) NoelGarbutt(7) 4 26
(Alan McCabe) *chsd ldrs: rdn over 2f and ev ch wknd over 1f out* **6/1**

060- **7** *½* **Delphica (IRE)**[241] 7156 3-9-0 **54** (p) NedCurtis(7) 10 25
(Gary Moore) *outpcd most of way* **8/1**

606- **8** *21* **Lucky Suit (IRE)**[193] 7977 3-8-10 **48** EDLinehan(5) 1
(Ronald Harris) *led tl hdd over 3f out: wknd qckly over 2f out* **8/1**

1m 13.03s (1.83) **Going Correction** +0.225s/f (Good) 8 Ran SP% **114.2**
Speed ratings (Par 97): **96,89,86,85,80 78,78,50**
toteswingers 1&2 £4.10, 1&3 £6.70, 2&3 £23.30 CSF £14.42 CT £127.54 TOTE £4.40: £1.60, £1.50, £3.70; EX 16.00 Trifecta £151.30 Pool: £1,326.45 - 6.57 winning units..
Owner Mrs Deborah June James **Bred** Old Mill Stud & S Williams & J Parry **Trained** Newmarket, Suffolk

FOCUS
Most of the runners here were moderate, and the unexposed winner bolted up. The form could have been rated higher.
T/Plt: £3,723.60 to a £1 stake. Pool: £59,936.22 - 11.75 winning tickets T/Qpdt: Part won. £1,646.10 to a £1 stake. Pool: £2,224.50 - 0.40 winning tickets. ST

2925 LEICESTER (R-H)
Saturday, June 15

OFFICIAL GOING: Good (8.7)
Wind: Fresh, Half behind Weather: Breezy, showers

3317 BULMERS CIDER H'CAP 5f 2y
6:05 (6:05) (Class 5) (0-70,68) 3-Y-0+ **£3,234** (£962; £481; £240) **Stalls** High

Form RPR

4110 **1** **Cincinnati Kit**[22] 2643 4-9-3 **60** (t) AdamBeschizza 3 72
(Stuart Williams) *a.p: rdn to ld over 1f out: r.o ins fnl f: in command towards fin* **16/1**

50-4 **2** *1 ½* **Indian Tinker**[18] 2736 4-9-7 **67** RossAtkinson(3) 7 73
(Robert Cowell) *a.p: rdn to chal over 1f out: nt qckn ins fnl f* **11/4[1]**

0061 **3** *3* **Methaaly (IRE)**[40] 2096 10-8-11 **59** (be) NatashaEaton(5) 8 54
(Michael Mullineaux) *hld up in rr: hdwy over 1f out: styd on ins fnl f: no imp on ldrs* **8/1**

3-0 **4** *½* **Trending (IRE)**[46] 1902 4-9-4 **61** (b) TomQueally 6 55
(Jeremy Gask) *racd keenly in midfield: rdn and nt qckn over 1f out: prog ins fnl f: styd on towards fin: nt gng pce to chal* **9/2[2]**

4323 **5** *1* **Love You Louis**[17] 2772 7-9-11 **68** (v) PatCosgrave 9 58
(J R Jenkins) *led: rdn and hdd over 1f out: no ex fnl 100yds* **5/1[3]**

4/06 **6** *1 ½* **Mr Man In The Moon (IRE)**[8] 3068 5-9-3 **60** SaleemGolam 2 45
(Mandy Rowland) *hld up: rdn over 1f out: one pce fnl f: nvr able to chal* **9/2[2]**

3150 **7** *hd* **Liberty Ship**[39] 2132 8-9-4 **61** MartinHarley 1 45
(Mark Buckley) *chsd ldrs: rdn 2f out: fdd fnl f* **25/1**

-200 **8** *2 ¼* **Stonecrabstomorrow (IRE)**[25] 2530 10-9-5 **65** MarkCoumbe(3) 10 41
(Roy Brotherton) *s.i.s: towards rr: u.p and no imp over 1f out* **25/1**

42-0 **9** *4* **Griffin Point (IRE)**[18] 2736 6-9-4 **61** MartinDwyer 5 22
(William Muir) *bustled along to r in midfield: wknd over 1f out* **12/1**

1m 0.04s (0.04) **Going Correction** -0.225s/f (Firm) 9 Ran SP% **112.1**
Speed ratings (Par 103): **90,87,82,82,80 78,77,74,67**
toteswingers 1&2 £10.20, 1&3 £12.80, 2&3 £5.40 CSF £57.75 CT £388.28 TOTE £18.60: £4.60, £1.50, £3.10; EX 88.40 Trifecta £206.60 Pool: £827.41 - 3.00 winning units..
Owner J W Parry **Bred** Old Mill Stud & S Williams & J Parry **Trained** Newmarket, Suffolk

FOCUS
A modest handicap.

3318 FOSTER'S RADLER MAIDEN FILLIES' STKS 5f 218y
6:35 (6:37) (Class 5) 2-Y-0 **£3,234** (£962; £481; £240) **Stalls** High

Form RPR

1 **Majeyda (USA)** 2-9-0 0 SilvestreDeSousa 9 83+
(Saeed bin Suroor) *chsd ldrs: pushed along over 1f out: qcknd up to ld ins fnl f: stretched clr ins fnl 100yds: looks useful* **9/2[3]**

2 **2** *4 ½* **Genuine Quality (USA)**[14] 2856 2-9-0 0 JamieSpencer 6 69+
(Ed Vaughan) *racd keenly: prom: led 4f out: rdn and hdd ins fnl f: no ch w wnr ins fnl 100yds* **4/5[1]**

44 **3** *½* **Prisca**[18] 2744 2-9-0 0 KieranO'Neill 2 67
(Richard Hannon) *a.p: rdn 2f out: ev ch 1f out: kpt on same pce fnl 100yds* **16/1**

4 *2 ¼* **Shamardyh (IRE)** 2-9-0 0 TomQueally 7 60
(James Tate) *missed break: racd keenly: sn prom: rdn and ev ch over 1f out: no ex fnl 100yds* **20/1**

5 *1 ¾* **Mimbleberry** 2-9-0 0 RichardKingscote 8 54+
(Tom Dascombe) *hld up in rr: rdn over 2f out: kpt on fnl f but nvr a threat* **14/1**

4 **6** *½* **Herbah**[22] 2625 2-9-0 0 PaulHanagan 4 53
(Roger Varian) *upset at s: missed break: hld up: pushed along 3f out: sme hdwy over 1f out: nvr able to trble ldrs* **11/4[2]**

7 *3 ½* **Slanderous** 2-9-0 0 MartinDwyer 3 41
(Scott Dixon) *missed break: racd keenly in tch: rdn over 2f out: wknd over 1f out* **50/1**

05 **8** *13* **Creative Spirit**[19] 2701 2-9-0 0 .... FrannyNorton 5
(David Brown) *edgy and t.k.h to post: sddle slipped: led: hdd 4f out: wknd qckly over 2f out* **33/1**

1m 12.73s (-0.27) **Going Correction** -0.225s/f (Firm) **8** Ran SP% **122.6**
Speed ratings (Par 90): **92,86,85,82,80 79,74,57**
toteswingers 1&2 £1.60, 1&3 £5.20, 2&3 £3.10 CSF £9.06 TOTE £5.00: £2.50, £1.02, £4.80; EX 10.90 Trifecta £71.20 Pool: £1773.68 - 18.66 winning units..
Owner Godolphin **Bred** Darley **Trained** Newmarket, Suffolk

FOCUS
Probably not a particularly strong maiden overall, but the winner will make her mark up in grade.

3319 FOSTER'S SUPER CHILLED CLAIMING STKS 1m 1f 218y
7:05 (7:05) (Class 6) 3-4-Y-0 **£1,940** (£577; £288; £144) **Stalls** Low

Form RPR

2323 **1** **Town Mouse**[17] 2784 3-9-1 65 .... SilvestreDeSousa 1 73
(Hughie Morrison) *unruly in preliminaries: missed break: racd keenly: racd off the pce: hdwy 6f out: led wl over 2f out: edgd rt ent fnl 2f: drew clr over 1f out: styd on wl* **4/7**[1]

-000 **2** *15* **Newnton Lodge**[12] 2929 4-9-12 68 .... JamieSpencer 3 46
(Ian Williams) *racd keenly: hld up in rr: hdwy over 3f out: chsd wnr 2f out: sn hung rt whn no imp: eased whn wl btn fnl 100yds* **9/2**[2]

264 **3** *6* **Priestley's Reward (IRE)**[92] 1010 4-9-8 62 ....(p) MartinHarley 4 25
(Mrs K Burke) *disp ld: rdn whn def advantage over 3f out: hdd wl over 2f out: wl btn over 1f out* **11/2**[3]

5005 **4** *1 3/4* **Little Alice**[18] 2748 3-8-4 45 .... AdamBeschizza 2 17
(Stuart Williams) *chsd ldrs: rdn and outpcd 4f out: n.d after* **16/1**

6000 **5** *2* **Special Report (IRE)**[33] 2330 3-8-4 48 .... GeorgeChaloner(5) 7 18
(Peter Hiatt) *disp ld tl rdn over 3f out: wknd wl under 2f out* **50/1**

6 *16* **Mr Lover Lover (IRE)**[13] 4-9-7 0 ....(b[1]) TomQueally 5
(John Butler) *chsd ldrs tl pushed along and outpcd over 4f out: n.d after: hung rt whn bhd over 2f out* **14/1**

0 **7** *97* **Idolise (IRE)**[94] 990 4-9-8 0 .... PatCosgrave 6
(John Spearing) *chsd ldrs: wknd over 5f out: sn lost tch: t.o* **40/1**

2m 6.91s (-0.99) **Going Correction** 0.0s/f (Good)
WFA 3 from 4yo 13lb **7** Ran SP% **114.2**
Speed ratings (Par 101): **103,91,86,84,83 70,**
toteswingers 1&2 £1.10, 1&3 £1.60, 2&3 £7.30 CSF £3.54 TOTE £1.50: £1.10, £2.30; EX 3.70 Trifecta £9.80 Pool: £1162.82 - 88.60 winning units..Town Mouse was claimed by Mr Neil King for £12,000.
Owner Justin Dowley & Mouse Hamilton-Fairley **Bred** Bishop Wilton Stud **Trained** East Ilsley, Berks

FOCUS
They went off very hard in this claimer courtesy of Priestley's Reward and Special Report and they ended up finishing strung out like jumpers.

3320 STRONGBOW H'CAP 5f 218y
7:35 (7:35) (Class 4) (0-80,83) 3-Y-O **£6,469** (£1,925; £962; £481) **Stalls** High

Form RPR

-206 **1** **Tatlisu (IRE)**[10] 2987 3-8-9 73 .... GeorgeChaloner(5) 1 81
(Richard Fahey) *towards rr: hdwy over 2f out: rdn to ld narrowly ins fnl f: jst hld on* **9/1**

5250 **2** *shd* **Fortinbrass (IRE)**[66] 1477 3-9-5 78 .... MartinDwyer 6 86
(Ralph Beckett) *a.p: led over 2f out: rdn over 1f out: hdd narrowly ins fnl f: rallied fnl strides* **14/1**

1520 **3** *3 1/2* **Boxing Shadows**[25] 2544 3-9-1 74 .... PaulHanagan 4 71
(Bryan Smart) *chsd ldrs: rdn over 1f out: kpt on ins fnl f but unable to chal front pair* **12/1**

6242 **4** *1* **Red Refraction (IRE)**[22] 2626 3-9-6 79 .... KieranO'Neill 5 73
(Richard Hannon) *hld up: effrt whn nt clr run and snatched up over 1f out: sn swtchd rt: styd on ins fnl f: nt trble ldrs* **9/2**[3]

5121 **5** *2 1/4* **Antonio Gramsci**[10] 2987 3-9-7 80 .... GrahamGibbons 8 66
(David Barron) *prom: rdn and hung rt fr over 2f out: wknd fnl 150yds* **9/4**[1]

320- **6** *3 3/4* **Trinityelitedotcom (IRE)**[361] 3242 3-9-4 77 .... RichardKingscote 7 51
(Tom Dascombe) *led: hdd over 2f out: wknd over 1f out* **16/1**

1004 **7** *31* **Limit Up**[10] 2984 3-9-4 77 .... SilvestreDeSousa 3
(Mark Johnston) *dwlt: in rr: effrt and hdwy over 2f out whn hung rt: wknd over 1f out: sn eased* **17/2**

-031 **8** *13* **Sharaarah (IRE)**[10] 2994 3-9-10 83 .... DanielTudhope 2
(David O'Meara) *hld up: swtchd lft after 1f: rdn over 2f out: no imp: eased whn wl btn ins fnl f* **7/2**[2]

1m 11.71s (-1.29) **Going Correction** -0.225s/f (Firm) **8** Ran SP% **111.9**
Speed ratings (Par 101): **99,98,94,92,89 84,43,26**
toteswingers 1&2 £26.20, 1&3 £23.10, 2&3 £35.10 CSF £117.48 CT £1510.04 TOTE £11.90: £3.50, £5.90, £4.00; EX 112.70 Trifecta £649.20 Part won. Pool: £865.64 - 0.86 winning units..
Owner Middleham Park Racing LIV **Bred** J C And Rocal Bloodstock **Trained** Musley Bank, N Yorks

FOCUS
A couple ran below expectations here but the leading pair still deserve some credit for pulling nicely clear in what was a fairly useful 3yo sprint.

3321 FOSTER'S GOLD H'CAP 1m 3f 183y
8:05 (8:06) (Class 5) (0-75,77) 4-Y-O+ **£3,234** (£962; £481; £240) **Stalls** Low

Form RPR

46-1 **1** **Semeen**[29] 2417 4-9-9 77 .... JamieSpencer 6 89+
(Luca Cumani) *trckd ldrs: shkn up to cl over 3f out: led 2f out: a travelling wl and in control: readily* **10/11**[1]

3-53 **2** *1 3/4* **Running Deer (IRE)**[19] 2729 4-9-4 72 .... TomQueally 5 79
(Lady Cecil) *led after 1f: hdd 2f out: rdn after: kpt on but a fighting losing battle w wnr fnl f* **9/1**[3]

4-21 **3** *nk* **Ashdown Lad**[18] 2739 4-9-7 75 .... PaulHanagan 1 82
(William Jarvis) *racd keenly: hld up: rdn and hdwy over 1f out: kpt on towards fin but hld* **2/1**[2]

1-50 **4** *2 3/4* **Kittens**[31] 2360 4-8-9 63 .... MartinDwyer 3 65
(William Muir) *in rr: hdwy over 2f out: one pce fnl f* **18/1**

0-60 **5** *9* **Sondeduro**[47] 1884 4-9-5 73 .... FergusSweeney 4 61
(Jamie Osborne) *led for 1f: remained prom: rdn over 2f out: wknd over 1f out* **33/1**

1-6 **6** *6* **Estemaala (IRE)**[49] 1825 4-9-5 73 .... DanielTudhope 2 51
(David O'Meara) *hld up: pushed along over 2f out: sn outpcd* **14/1**

2m 35.51s (1.61) **Going Correction** 0.0s/f (Good) **6** Ran SP% **110.6**
Speed ratings (Par 103): **94,92,92,90,84 80**
toteswingers 1&2 £2.10, 1&3 £1.30, 2&3 £1.40 CSF £9.89 TOTE £1.90: £1.10, £2.50; EX 10.10 Trifecta £28.40 Pool: £1144.92 - 30.14 winning units..
Owner Sheikh Mohammed Obaid Al Maktoum **Bred** Darley **Trained** Newmarket, Suffolk

FOCUS
Not the most competitive of handicaps, but still hard not to be taken with the performance of the winner.

3322 JOHN SMITH'S EXTRA SMOOTH H'CAP 7f 9y
8:35 (8:35) (Class 4) (0-80,79) 3-Y-O+ **£6,301** (£1,886; £943; £472; £235) **Stalls** High

Form RPR

5050 **1** **Askaud (IRE)**[49] 1823 5-9-8 73 ....(p) TomQueally 1 87
(Scott Dixon) *a.p: led over 3f out: rdn over 1f out: r.o to draw clr ins fnl f: comf* **11/1**

10-0 **2** *3 1/2* **Otto The Great**[23] 2592 4-9-9 79 .... GeorgeChaloner(5) 3 84
(Richard Fahey) *a.p: led over 4f out: hdd over 3f out: continued to chse wnr: rdn and nt qckn over 1f out: no imp ins fnl f* **12/1**

4-31 **3** *1* **Gabrial's Gift (IRE)**[12] 2918 4-9-7 72 .... JamieSpencer 6 74
(David Simcock) *hld up: hdwy over 2f out: kpt on u.p ins fnl f: no imp on wnr* **11/4**[1]

3232 **4** *2 3/4* **Caramack**[9] 3011 3-9-3 78 .... SteveDrowne 12 54
(Richard Hannon) *hld up: outpcd over 4f out: plugged on fnl f: nvr a threat: fin 5th: plcd 4th* **6/1**[3]

00-6 **5** *4 1/2* **Ewell Place (IRE)**[7] 3087 4-9-13 78 .... PatCosgrave 11 45
(David Nicholls) *hld up in midfield: pushed along 3f out: hung rt 2f out: no imp and btn over 1f out: fin 6th: plcd 5th* **20/1**

4-40 **6** *1 1/4* **Shamahan**[22] 2618 4-9-11 76 .... PaulHanagan 2 40
(Gary Moore) *in tch: lost pl and outpcd over 3f out: n.d after: fin 7th: plcd 6th* **5/1**[2]

-106 **7** *2* **Reggae Star**[12] 2915 3-8-12 73 .... SilvestreDeSousa 8 29
(Mark Johnston) *led: hdd over 4f out: pushed along over 3f out: rdn and wknd under 2f out: fin 8th: plcd 7th* **8/1**

31-0 **8** *5* **Fathsta (IRE)**[21] 2663 8-10-0 79 .... DanielTudhope 9 25
(Patrick Morris) *midfield: pushed along and wknd over 2f out: fin 9th: plcd 8th* **25/1**

5101 **9** *1* **Available (IRE)**[19] 2711 4-10-0 79 ....(p) FrannyNorton 5 22
(John Mackie) *racd keenly: prom tl rdn and wknd over 2f out: fin 10th: plcd 9th* **8/1**

00 **10** *22* **Greensward**[28] 2450 7-9-10 75 .... MartinDwyer 4
(Mike Murphy) *missed break: a wl bhd: eased wl over 1f out: fin 11th: plcd 10th* **40/1**

00-3 **D** *6* **Bajan Bear**[12] 2929 5-9-3 68 .... MartinHarley 10 54
(Michael Blanshard) *hld up in midfield: hdwy over 2f out: chsd ldrs over 1f out: one pce ins fnl f: disqualified and plcd last after rdr failed to weigh in* **8/1**

1m 23.56s (-2.64) **Going Correction** -0.25s/f (Firm)
WFA 3 from 4yo+ 10lb **11** Ran SP% **118.0**
Speed ratings (Par 105): **105,101,99,89,84 83,81,75,74,49 93**
toteswingers 1&2 £31.90, 1&3 £19.30, 2&3 £6.70 CSF £132.60 TOTE £14.00: £4.20, £3.70, £1.10; EX 162.50 Trifecta £418.10 Part won. Pool: £557.53 - 0.01 winning units..
Owner Paul J Dixon **Bred** John P Jones **Trained** Babworth, Notts
■ Stewards' Enquiry : Martin Harley three-day ban; rider failed to weigh-in (29th June - 1st July).

FOCUS
A fair handicap. They were well strung out from an early stage and not many threatened to get in a serious blow, the leading pair both in front rank throughout.

3323 KRONENBOURG H'CAP 5f 2y
9:05 (9:06) (Class 6) (0-60,60) 3-Y-O **£1,940** (£577; £288; £144) **Stalls** High

Form RPR

0343 **1** **Teetotal (IRE)**[25] 2535 3-9-6 59 .... SilvestreDeSousa 3 66
(Nigel Tinkler) *in tch: impr to ld wl over 1f out: edgd lft ins fnl f: r.o and in command after* **9/4**[1]

-055 **2** *1 1/4* **Borough Boy (IRE)**[6] 3134 3-9-1 54 ....(v) MartinDwyer 7 57
(Derek Shaw) *hld up in rr: hdwy over 1f out: styd on to take 2nd wl ins fnl f: no imp on wnr* **11/2**[3]

5314 **3** *1* **Whiteflats**[10] 2996 3-8-12 51 ....(v) HarryBentley 2 50
(Derek Shaw) *chsd ldrs: rdn to ld 2f out: sn hdd: no ex fnl 100yds* **6/1**

3500 **4** *2 1/4* **Viva L'Inghilterra (IRE)**[10] 2996 3-8-10 52 ....(p) RossAtkinson(3) 8 43
(Robert Cowell) *prom: led 3f out: rdn and hanging rt whn hdd 2f out: no ex fnl f* **20/1**

640- **5** *1 1/2* **Cymeriad**[183] 8108 3-8-8 54 .... MatthewHopkins(7) 6 39
(Michael Easterby) *hld up: rdn over 1f out: no imp and one pce fnl f* **9/1**

1503 **6** *1 1/2* **Outbid**[10] 2996 3-9-7 60 .... FergusSweeney 4 40
(Jamie Osborne) *prom: pushed along 3f out: rdn and wknd over 2f out* **6/1**

0-24 **7** *nk* **Senora Lobo (IRE)**[22] 2643 3-9-3 56 .... GrahamGibbons 1 37
(Lisa Williamson) *led: hdd 3f out: lost pl u.p over 2f out: sn wknd* **3/1**[2]

1m 1.2s (1.20) **Going Correction** -0.225s/f (Firm) **7** Ran SP% **114.5**
Speed ratings (Par 97): **81,79,77,73,71 69,68**
toteswingers 1&2 £1.30, 1&3 £2.80, 2&3 £2.00 CSF £15.13 TOTE £2.70: £1.90, £2.60; EX 16.70 TRIFECTA Pool: £906.41 - 10.34 winning units..
Owner Raybould & Scott **Bred** T Jones **Trained** Langton, N Yorks

FOCUS
A low-grade three-year-old sprint.
T/Plt: £78.50 to a £1 stake. Pool: £71212.57 - 661.53 winning tickets T/Qpdt: £61.30 to a £1 stake. Pool: £4618.50 - 55.70 winning tickets DO

3167 LINGFIELD (L-H)
Saturday, June 15

OFFICIAL GOING: Turf course - good to firm (8.8); all-weather - standard
Wind: strong, half behind Weather: windy, bright spells

3324 COMPLETE PLUMBING MEDIAN AUCTION MAIDEN FILLIES' STKS 5f
5:55 (6:04) (Class 6) 2-Y-O **£2,045** (£603; £302) **Stalls** High

Form RPR

22 **1** **Disko (IRE)**[19] 2712 2-9-0 0 .... JamesMcDonald 1 70
(Daniel Kubler) *broke fast and crossed to r against stands' rail: mde all: rdn jst over 1f out: styd on wl fnl f: rdn out* **7/4**[1]

0 **2** *1* **Tautira (IRE)**[18] 2751 2-9-0 0 .... HayleyTurner 6 66
(Michael Bell) *chsd ldrs: rdn and effrt to chse wnr 1f out: styd on same pce fnl 100yds* **10/1**

5 **3** *1* **Cockney Belle**[18] 2740 2-8-9 0 .... RobertTart(5) 5 63
(Marco Botti) *chsd ldrs: rdn and effrt over 1f out: chsd ldrs and styd on same pce ins fnl f* **4/1**[3]

4 *2 1/4* **Boston Alex (IRE)** 2-8-11 0 .... SimonPearce(3) 2 55
(Conor Dore) *chsd wnr tl rn green and hung lft 1f out: wknd fnl 100yds* **50/1**

3 **5** 1 ½ **Hatti (IRE)**[3] 3217 2-9-0 0 BrettDoyle 4 49
(John Ryan) *s.i.s: sn bustled and rcvrd to chse ldrs after 2f: rdn and unable qck over 1f out: wknd ins fnl f* **20/1**

333 **6** 1 **Senorita Guest (IRE)**[5] 3148 2-9-0 0 MatthewDavies 8 46
(Mick Channon) *hld up in rr of main gp: rdn and effrt wl over 1f out: no imp: nvr trbld ldrs* **7/2**[2]

7 3 ¾ **Green Music** 2-9-0 0 LukeMorris 3 32
(James Eustace) *in tch in midfield: rdn and no ex wl over 1f out: sn wknd* **7/1**

5 **8** nk **Oxlip**[16] 2805 2-9-0 0 ChrisCatlin 10 31
(Richard Hannon) *chsd ldrs early: steadily lost pl and bhd whn rdn 2f out: sn btn* **8/1**

6 **9** 4 **Local Flier**[7] 3084 2-9-0 0 RobertHavlin 9 17
(Ian McInnes) *sn outpcd in rr* **50/1**

57.17s (-1.03) **Going Correction** -0.20s/f (Firm) **9** Ran SP% **120.0**
Speed ratings (Par 88): **100,98,96,93,90 89,83,82,76**
toteswingers 1&2 £5.60, 1&3 £2.60, 2&3 £8.50 CSF £21.88 TOTE £2.30: £1.10, £2.90, £2.10; EX 24.20 Trifecta £90.90 Pool: £1606.74 - 13.25 winning units..
Owner Diskovery Partnership **Bred** Patrick A Cassidy **Trained** Whitsbury, Hants

FOCUS
Just ordinary maiden form but the winner has bumped into a couple of 90+ performers and could do a good bit better than this. The time and pre-race form set the opening level.

3325 COUNTRYSIDE ALLIANCE FOUNDATION H'CAP 6f
6:25 (6:31) (Class 6) (0-60,60) 3-Y-0+ **£2,045** (£603; £302) **Stalls** High

Form RPR

421 **1** **Maria Montez**[4] 3181 4-9-3 **58** ShelleyBirkett(7) 6 73
(J W Hills) *chsd ldrs tl led over 4f out: mde rest and clr whn rdn over 1f out: styd on wl: comf* **5/4**[1]

5262 **2** 3 ¼ **Doctor Hilary**[10] 2997 11-8-12 **46** oh1 (v) RobertHavlin 11 51
(Mark Hoad) *racd in midfield: swtchd lft over 4f out: rdn and effrt wl over 1f out: styd on fnl f to go 2nd fnl 50yds: no ch w wnr* **7/1**[3]

0050 **3** 1 ¾ **You'relikemefrank**[3] 3197 7-8-13 **47** (p) CathyGannon 13 46
(Richard Ford) *led tl over 4f out: chsd wnr after: 3 l down and drvn over 1f out: no imp: lost 2nd fnl 50yds* **8/1**

-000 **4** 1 **Hamis Al Bin (IRE)**[2] 3246 4-9-9 **57** LukeMorris 12 53
(Milton Bradley) *hld up in midfield: rdn and effrt 2f out: styd on ins fnl f: no ch w wnr* **5/1**[2]

2405 **5** 1 ¾ **Pharoh Jake**[8] 3052 5-9-1 **54** WilliamTwiston-Davies(5) 3 45
(John Bridger) *hld up in rr: clsng whn nt clr run 2f out tl 1f out: swtchd rt and styd on wl ins fnl f: nvr trbld ldrs* **20/1**

0040 **6** nk **Scommettitrice (IRE)**[5] 3154 5-9-5 **53** (b) MartinLane 5 43
(Mark Gillard) *racd in midfield: rdn and no prog ent fnl 2f: no ch w wnr but styd on ins fnl f* **16/1**

6403 **7** 1 ½ **Brandywell Boy (IRE)**[105] 862 10-8-7 **48** JoshBaudains(7) 8 33
(Dominic Ffrench Davis) *in tch in midfield: rdn and struggling over 2f out: wl hld and plugged on same pce fnl f* **20/1**

3355 **8** 2 ½ **Red Star Lady (IRE)**[10] 2996 3-8-2 **47** oh1 ow1 BillyCray(3) 9 24
(Shaun Harris) *chsd ldrs tl over 2f out: sn lost pl u.p: wknd over 1f out* **50/1**

-434 **9** 1 ½ **Microlight**[44] 1954 5-8-12 **46** oh1 (b) RichardThomas 1 18
(John E Long) *wnt lft s: towards rr of main gp: sme hdwy 1/2-way: rdn and no prog wl over 1f out: wknd ins fnl f* **20/1**

0/6- **10** nk **Seraphiel**[396] 2147 4-9-11 **59** BrettDoyle 10 30
(Chris Down) *t.k.h: chsd ldrs: rdn and struggling over 2f out: sn btn: wknd over 1f out* **50/1**

-435 **11** 2 ½ **Guru Baby**[39] 2123 3-8-3 **50** JemmaMarshall(5) 15 13
(John E Long) *a in rr of main gp: rdn and no hdwy over 2f out: wl btn and hung lft over 1f out* **33/1**

4-00 **12** 3 ½ **Running Mate (IRE)**[115] 728 6-9-12 **60** [1] ChrisCatlin 2 12
(Jo Crowley) *taken down early: a towards rr of main gp: rdn and struggling 1/2-way: bhd over 1f out* **20/1**

5550 **13** 2 **Sherjawy (IRE)**[38] 2170 9-8-10 **47** SimonPearce(3) 14
(Laura Mongan) *towards rr of main gp: rdn and struggling over 2f out: sn wknd* **16/1**

0000 **14** 5 **Sakhee's Alround**[12] 2931 3-8-4 **46** oh1 JamieMackay 7
(K F Clutterbuck) *v.s.a: a detached in last* **40/1**

1m 9.83s (-1.37) **Going Correction** -0.20s/f (Firm)
WFA 3 from 4yo+ 8lb **14** Ran SP% **124.8**
Speed ratings (Par 101): **101,96,94,93,90 90,88,84,82,82 79,74,71,65**
toteswingers 1&2 £3.50, 1&3 £3.90, 2&3 £14.10 CSF £9.12 CT £56.54 TOTE £1.90: £1.10, £2.10, £3.30; EX 12.20 Trifecta £77.60 Pool: £1421.20 - 13.72 winning units..
Owner John M Cole & Abbott Racing Partners **Bred** D R Tucker **Trained** Upper Lambourn, Berks
■ Stewards' Enquiry : Shelley Birkett one-day ban; arrived late at start (one-day ban).

FOCUS
Weak handicap form and this was over as a contest well over a furlong out.

3326 STEPHEN THOMAS MAGEE MEMORIAL H'CAP 7f
6:55 (7:02) (Class 6) (0-55,55) 3-Y-0+ **£2,045** (£603; £302) **Stalls** High

Form RPR

51-1 **1** **Resonare**[39] 2133 4-9-10 **55** ChrisCatlin 15 64+
(Stuart Williams) *chsd ldr tl led 2f out: edging lft but kpt on wl ins fnl f: rdn out* **4/1**[1]

-501 **2** ½ **Wishformore (IRE)**[8] 3051 6-9-7 **52** (p) RichardThomas 14 60
(Zoe Davison) *trckd ldrs: rdn and effrt to chal over 1f out: carried sltly lft ins fnl f: unable qck and hld towards fin* **7/1**[2]

4225 **3** hd **Moss Hill**[12] 2932 4-9-3 **51** PatrickHills(3) 6 58+
(Charles Hills) *in tch: rdn and effrt to chse ldrs over 1f out: drvn 1f out: kpt on but no imp fnl 50yds* **4/1**[1]

4465 **4** shd **Floralys (USA)**[17] 2773 4-9-10 **55** LukeMorris 2 62
(Amy Weaver) *in tch in last quartet: rdn 1/2-way: stl plenty to do 1f out: weaving through and str run fnl 100yds: nt quite rch ldrs* **20/1**

506- **5** ¾ **Saint Boniface**[234] 7326 4-9-7 **52** (e[1]) JimmyFortune 11 57
(Peter Makin) *in tch in midfield: rdn and effrt over 1f out: styd on same pce ins fnl f* **20/1**

0010 **6** 1 **Kingscombe (USA)**[16] 2801 4-9-7 **52** (p) RobertHavlin 9 54
(Linda Jewell) *dwlt and rdn along: steadily rcvrd and in midfield 1/2-way: switching lft over 1f out: kpt on fnl f: nvr quite pce to rch ldrs* **16/1**

60-0 **7** 1 ¼ **Coach Montana (IRE)**[39] 2134 4-9-2 **47** JamesMcDonald 10 46
(Jane Chapple-Hyam) *chsd ldrs: rdn and ev ch 2f out tl ent fnl f: wknd ins fnl f* **20/1**

-643 **8** 2 **The Name Is Frank**[4] 3181 8-9-10 **55** (t) MartinLane 1 48
(Mark Gillard) *taken down early: chsd ldrs: rdn and ev ch 2f out tl no ex over 1f out: wknd ins fnl f* **7/1**[2]

-000 **9** 1 ¾ **Vermeyen**[135] 456 4-9-2 **47** HayleyTurner 8 36
(Geoffrey Deacon) *in tch in midfield: rdn and lost pl 3f out: styd on same pce fr over 1f out* **25/1**

0364 **10** nse **Surrey Dream (IRE)**[8] 3051 4-8-11 **47** (tp) WilliamTwiston-Davies(5) 5 35
(John Bridger) *dwlt: sn rdn along towards rr: sme hdwy over 1f out: no imp fnl f* **12/1**

6000 **11** hd **Quan (IRE)**[24] 2582 4-8-12 **48** MatthewLawson(5) 13 36
(Milton Bradley) *led tl 2f out: sn rdn and no ex: wknd fnl f* **16/1**

/0-6 **12** ½ **Princess Palmer**[9] 3015 4-8-13 **47** SimonPearce(3) 7 33
(Lydia Pearce) *in tch in last trio: rdn over 2f out: no prog: nvr trbld ldrs* **50/1**

000- **13** 7 **Rio Royale (IRE)**[226] 7512 7-9-3 **48** CathyGannon 12 16
(Amanda Perrett) *s.i.s: a bhd: rdn and no hdwy over 2f out: wknd over 1f out* **10/1**

-000 **14** 9 **Green Mitas (ITY)**[58] 1657 4-9-7 **52** GeorgeBaker 3
(Frank Sheridan) *hld up in tch in midfield: rdn and wknd ent fnl 2f: bhd and eased ins fnl f* **8/1**[3]

1m 23.2s (-0.10) **Going Correction** -0.20s/f (Firm) **14** Ran SP% **124.8**
Speed ratings (Par 101): **92,91,91,91,90 89,87,85,83,83 83,82,74,64**
toteswingers 1&2 £8.30, 1&3 £3.80, 2&3 £3.70 CSF £30.00 CT £126.67 TOTE £4.50: £1.80, £3.20, £2.00; EX 27.00 Trifecta £107.70 Pool: £834.75 - 5.80 winning units..
Owner G D Thompson **Bred** Old Mill Stud **Trained** Newmarket, Suffolk

FOCUS
More low grade fare although this looked slightly more competitive than the previous contest. Once again the the winner came up the stands' rail.

3327 DEEP BLUE RESTAURANTS MEDIAN AUCTION MAIDEN STKS 7f
7:25 (7:29) (Class 6) 3-4-Y-0 **£2,045** (£603; £302) **Stalls** High

Form RPR

-225 **1** **Hornboy**[12] 2934 3-9-2 67 (p) JimmyFortune 6 74+
(Jeremy Noseda) *mde all: pushed along and readily asserted 2f out: wl clr and in n.d 1f out: eased towards fin: unchal* **2/1**[2]

3324 **2** 5 **Tanawar (IRE)**[108] 814 3-9-2 69 CathyGannon 7 58
(William Haggas) *sn pushed along: chsd ldrs: rdn 4f out: drvn and chsd wnr jst over 2f out: clr 2nd but no ch w wnr over 1f out* **4/7**[1]

6220 **3** 5 **Loulou Vuitton**[99] 923 3-8-11 60 (p) LukeMorris 1 40
(Frank Sheridan) *t.k.h: hld up in tch: hdwy 1/2-way: rdn and wknd over 1f out: wnt modest 3rd 1f out: plugged on* **12/1**[3]

4 shd **Ghetto Diva** 3-8-11 0 JamesMcDonald 4 40
(Daniel Kubler) *in tch in rr: rdn and outpcd 2f out: no ch w wnr but plugged on and battled for modest 3rd ins fnl f* **20/1**

00 **5** 2 ¾ **We'Re In The Red (IRE)**[24] 2560 3-9-2 0 (t) RobertHavlin 2 38
(Mark Hoad) *chsd ldrs tl jst over 2f out: sn rdn and struggling: wknd over 1f out* **66/1**

00 **6** 19 **Deva Victrix**[12] 2931 3-9-2 0 ChrisCatlin 5
(Lisa Williamson) *t.k.h: hld up wl in tch: wknd qckly ent fnl 2f: eased ins fnl f* **100/1**

1m 23.23s (-0.07) **Going Correction** -0.20s/f (Firm)
WFA 3 from 4yo 10lb **6** Ran SP% **111.9**
Speed ratings (Par 101): **92,86,80,80,77 55**
toteswingers 1&2 £1.10, 1&3 £2.40, 2&3 £1.50 CSF £3.45 TOTE £3.40: £1.20, £1.10; EX 4.50 Trifecta £7.60 Pool: £1066.96 - 104.39 winning units..
Owner Nigel O'Sullivan **Bred** Cheveley Park Stud Ltd **Trained** Newmarket, Suffolk

FOCUS
A weak race but a fair performance from the winner.

3328 OLD HOUSE INN H'CAP 2m (P)
7:55 (7:55) (Class 5) (0-75,72) 4-Y-0+ **£3,234** (£962; £481; £240) **Stalls** Low

Form RPR

14-3 **1** **Italian Riviera**[18] 2749 4-9-7 **72** LukeMorris 2 86+
(Sir Mark Prescott Bt) *a gng wl: trckd ldrs: swtchd rt and chsd ldr over 5f out: led over 2f out and sn pushed clr: drvn over 1f out: rdr looking arnd and eased fr 1f out: virtually p.u fnl 50yds* **6/4**[1]

2203 **2** ¾ **Story Writer**[29] 2418 4-9-2 **67** HayleyTurner 1 71
(William Knight) *in tch in midfield: rdn and no rspnse over 2f out: hdwy u.p on inner over 1f out: chsd clr wnr jst ins fnl f: r.o but v flattered to fin so cl* **4/1**[2]

03-6 **3** 2 ¾ **Joe The Coat**[25] 2545 4-9-1 **66** JimmyFortune 3 67
(Mark H Tompkins) *in tch in last pair: rdn and no imp 3f out: 4th and looked wl hld over 1f out: kpt on u.p but no ch w wnr* **4/1**[2]

/043 **4** shd **Kayef (GER)**[24] 2570 6-9-1 **70** WilliamTwiston-Davies(5) 8 71
(Michael Scudamore) *chsd ldr for 2f: chsd ldrs after: drvn and outpcd wl over 2f out: kpt on u.p fnl f: no ch w wnr* **10/1**

5522 **5** 7 **Bramshill Lass**[12] 2921 4-9-0 **65** (v) MartinLane 5 57
(Amanda Perrett) *chsd ldrs tl wnt 2nd after 2f: led 8f out tl rdn and hdd over 2f out: sn brushed aside by wnr: lost 2nd jst ins fnl f: fdd* **12/1**

000- **6** 2 **Epsom Salts**[225] 7522 8-9-3 **72** JemmaMarshall(5) 7 62
(Pat Phelan) *stdd and dropped in bhd after s: hld up in tch in rr: rdn 7f out: lost tch u.p 3f out* **33/1**

5544 **7** 13 **Maison Brillet (IRE)**[24] 2570 6-9-0 **64** (b) RobertHavlin 6 38
(Clive Drew) *in tch in midfield: lost pl and rdn over 4f out: lost tch 3f out* **33/1**

1062 **8** 22 **Fulgora**[10] 2980 5-9-6 **70** SebSanders 4 18
(Brendan Powell) *led tl 8f out: lost pl and bhd 4f out: sn lost tch: t.o over 1f out* **8/1**[3]

3m 21.86s (-3.84) **Going Correction** -0.15s/f (Stan)
WFA 4 from 5yo+ 1lb **8** Ran SP% **113.8**
Speed ratings (Par 103): **103,102,101,101,97 96,90,79**
toteswingers 1&2 £1.30, 1&3 £2.50, 2&3 £5.10 CSF £7.45 CT £18.65 TOTE £1.80: £1.10, £2.10, £1.80; EX 8.00 Trifecta £19.70 Pool: £768.46 - 29.12 winning units..
Owner J L C Pearce **Bred** J L C Pearce **Trained** Newmarket, Suffolk

FOCUS
This was over as a contest by the turn for home.

3329 ITC CONCEPTS H'CAP 1m (P)
8:25 (8:30) (Class 6) (0-60,61) 4-Y-0+ **£2,045** (£603; £302) **Stalls** High

Form RPR

6001 **1** **Shared Moment (IRE)**[8] 3054 7-8-9 **51** SimonPearce(3) 5 59
(Luke Dace) *chsd ldng pair on inner: rdn and effrt to ld over 1f out: clr jst ins fnl f: drvn fnl 100yds: hung rt and flashed tail nr fin: a holding on* **5/1**[2]

0003 **2** ½ **Spin Again (IRE)**[8] 3054 8-9-8 **61** (p) BrettDoyle 8 68
(John Ryan) *wl in tch in midfield: rdn and effrt over 1f out: chsd clr wnr jst ins fnl f: r.o and pressing wnr towards fin* **5/1**[2]

0304 **3** 1 ¼ **Indian Violet (IRE)**[11] 2954 7-8-10 **54** (p) WilliamTwiston-Davies(5) 9 58
(Zoe Davison) *hld up in tch in last trio: rdn and hdwy on outer bnd 2f out: kpt on u.p ins fnl f* **8/1**[3]

3016 **4** *nk* **Cuthbert (IRE)**[8] 3054 6-8-11 **50**........(b) RobertHavlin 4 53
(Michael Attwater) *stdd after s: hld up in tch in last trio: nt clr run bnd 2f out: lost pl and swtchd rt over 1f out: styd on u.p ins fnl f* **12/1**

5300 **5** *nk* **Spirit Of Gondree (IRE)**[44] 1950 5-9-6 **59**........(b) LukeMorris 7 62
(Milton Bradley) *s.i.s: in tch in rr: swtchd rt and effrt bnd 2f out: hdwy u.p 1f out: kpt on ins fnl f* **5/1**[2]

4200 **6** *2* **Dream Walker (FR)**[7] 3083 4-9-3 **56**........ SebSanders 3 54
(Ian McInnes) *led tl rdn and hdd over 2f out: no ex u.p over 1f out: wknd ins fnl f* **5/1**[2]

1235 **7** *hd* **Seamster**[74] 1310 6-9-1 **59**........(vt) RachealKneller(5) 10 57
(Richard Ford) *t.k.h: hld up wl in tch in midfield but stuck wd: hdwy to ld over 2f out: hdd over 1f out and sn drvn: wknd ins fnl f* **16/1**

2400 **8** *2 ¾* **Satwa Laird**[14] 2875 7-9-6 **59**........(b[1]) HayleyTurner 11 50
(Conor Dore) *t.k.h: hld up wl in tch in midfield: rdn and unable qck 2f out: wknd over 1f out* **12/1**

6250 **9** *11* **Zaheeb**[22] 2638 5-9-2 **60**........(b) RobertTart(5) 6 26
(Dave Morris) *pressed ldr: rdn and lost pl over 2f out: bhd over 1f out* **4/1**[1]

1m 38.24s (0.04) **Going Correction** -0.15s/f (Stan) 9 Ran SP% **119.0**
Speed ratings (Par 101): **93,92,91,90,90 88,88,85,74**
toteswingers 1&2 £3.70, 1&3 £13.50, 2&3 £5.90 CSF £31.25 CT £201.94 TOTE £6.10: £1.80, £1.80, £1.90; EX 20.80 Trifecta £136.20 Pool: £941.00 - 5.18 winning units..
Owner Mark Benton **Bred** Mrs E R Cantillon **Trained** Five Oaks, W Sussex
■ Stewards' Enquiry : Brett Doyle three-day ban; used whip without giving mount time to respond (29th June-1st July).
Simon Pearce one-day ban; careless riding (29th June).
Robert Havlin ome-day ban; careless riding (29th June).

FOCUS
A poor bunch.

3330 HURST GREEN SHIRES H'CAP — 1m 2f (P)
8:55 (8:57) (Class 5) (0-70,70) 4-Y-O+ **£3,234** (£962; £481; £240) **Stalls** Low

Form RPR

6004 **1** **Standpoint**[3] 3195 7-9-3 **66**........ HayleyTurner 3 73
(Conor Dore) *in tch in midfield: rdn and qcknd between horses to ld ins fnl f: r.o wl* **3/1**[1]

1-00 **2** *1 ¼* **Langham Lily (USA)**[120] 668 4-8-12 **61**........ SebSanders 5 65
(Chris Wall) *hld up in tch in last trio: rdn and hdwy on inner over 1f out: chsd wnr fnl 100yds: r.o but no imp* **3/1**[1]

5220 **3** *hd* **Chrissycross (IRE)**[15] 2845 4-9-4 **67**........(v) JimmyFortune 8 71
(Roger Teal) *dwlt and pushed along leaving stalls: in tch in rr: hdwy to chse ldrs 2f out: drvn ent fnl f: carried sltly rt and kpt on same pce ins fnl f* **7/1**[3]

1561 **4** *shd* **Understory (USA)**[44] 1956 6-9-7 **70**........ GeorgeBaker 2 73
(Tim McCarthy) *chsd ldr: rdn and unable qck over 1f out: edgd rt and styd on same pce ins fnl f* **9/2**[2]

0060 **5** *1* **Megalala (IRE)**[15] 2845 12-8-8 **62** ow2........ WilliamTwiston-Davies(5) 1 63
(John Bridger) *led: rdn ent fnl 2f: edgd rt over 1f out: hdd and no ex ins fnl f* **25/1**

0043 **6** *¾* **Divine Rule (IRE)**[11] 2954 5-8-9 **61**........ SimonPearce(3) 6 61
(Laura Mongan) *hld up in tch in last trio: hdwy on outer 3f out: rdn and chsd ldrs jst over 2f out: outpcd and lost pl over 1f out: one pce after* **8/1**

123- **7** *1 ½* **Russian Storm**[393] 2233 5-8-8 **62**........ JemmaMarshall(5) 7 59
(Pat Phelan) *chsd ldrs: rdn and effrt on inner over 1f out: unable qck and outpcd 1f out: wknd ins fnl f* **9/2**[2]

2m 6.01s (-0.59) **Going Correction** -0.15s/f (Stan) 7 Ran SP% **113.8**
Speed ratings (Par 103): **96,95,94,94,93 93,92**
toteswingers 1&2 £1.60, 1&3 £5.50, 2&3 £4.60 CSF £11.89 CT £56.00 TOTE £3.40: £1.70, £2.30; EX 14.50 Trifecta £65.70 Pool: £1169.69 - 11.41 winning units..
Owner Mrs Jennifer Marsh **Bred** Juddmonte Farms Ltd **Trained** Hubbert's Bridge, Lincs
■ Stewards' Enquiry : Jimmy Fortune caution; careless riding.

FOCUS
This seemed to be run at quite a steady pace and they were well bunched early in the straight.
T/Plt: £4.60 to a £1 stake. Pool: £75,139.68 - 11916.81 winning tickets T/Qpdt: £2.20 to a £1 stake. Pool: £4481.24 - 1488.42 winning tickets SP

3280 MUSSELBURGH (R-H)
Saturday, June 15

OFFICIAL GOING: Good to firm (firm in places; 8.6)
Wind: Moderate; half against Weather: Cloudy and blustery with sunny periods

3331 WILLIAM HILL - DOWNLOAD THE APP H'CAP — 5f
1:55 (1:55) (Class 4) (0-80,80) 4-Y-O+ **£6,469** (£1,925; £962; £481) **Stalls** High

Form RPR

0054 **1** **The Nifty Fox**[1] 3283 9-9-0 **73**........(p) JamesSullivan 5 85
(Tim Easterby) *hmpd s and towards rr: gd hdwy to trck ldrs 2f out: n.m.r and swtchd lft to inner over 1f out: sn rdn and styd on strly to ld nr line* **14/1**

0 **2** *hd* **Jedward (IRE)**[28] 2459 6-9-6 **79**........(b) PhillipMakin 14 90
(Kevin Ryan) *trckd ldrs: hdwy 2f out: n.m.r and swtchd rt over 1f out: rdn to ld ent fnl f: drvn and edgd rt last 100yds: hdd and no ex nr line* **6/1**[3]

10-0 **3** *1 ½* **Midnight Dynamo**[14] 2882 6-9-0 **73**........ GrahamLee 6 79
(Jim Goldie) *hmpd s and towards rr: hdwy wl over 1f out: rdn and styd on wl fnl f: nrst fin* **10/1**

0021 **4** *nk* **Lost In Paris (IRE)**[15] 2832 7-9-2 **75**........(p) MickyFenton 4 80
(Tim Easterby) *chsd ldrs: effrt on outer 2f out: rdn over 1f out: kpt on same pce fnl f* **8/1**

/521 **5** *hd* **Go Nani Go**[43] 1976 7-9-5 **78**........ LiamKeniry 3 82
(Ed de Giles) *chsd ldrs on wd outside: hdwy 2f out and sn rdn: drvn and one pce fnl f* **13/2**

1-00 **6** *shd* **Jinky**[16] 2797 5-8-11 **70**........ RoystonFfrench 15 73
(Linda Perratt) *chsd ldrs: n.m.r and rdn over 1f out: kpt on same pce ins fnl f* **25/1**

13-5 **7** *1 ½* **Liberty Island (IRE)**[14] 2880 8-9-0 **78**........(p) JasonHart(5) 13 76
(Ian Semple) *trckd ldrs: hdwy and cl up 2f out: rdn and ev ch over 1f out: wknd fnl f: lame* **14/1**

2000 **8** *1* **Come On Dave (IRE)**[28] 2459 4-9-4 **77**........ AdrianNicholls 11 73
(David Nicholls) *hmpd s: led after 1f: rdn wl over 1f out: drvn and hdd ent fnl f: wknd* **7/1**

0-00 **9** *nk* **Crimson Knot (IRE)**[27] 2476 5-9-2 **75**........ TomEaves 2 68
(Alan Berry) *nvr bttr than midfield* **20/1**

-505 **10** *1* **Lupin Pooter**[29] 2410 4-8-10 **74**........ LMcNiff(5) 7 64
(David Barron) *rrd and wnt rt s: a towards rr* **3/1**[1]

-005 **11** *13* **Verinco**[26] 2505 7-9-1 **79**........(vt) JustinNewman(5) 16 22
(Bryan Smart) *wnt bdly rt s: led 1f: cl up: rdn along wl over 1f out: sn wknd* **5/1**[2]

59.59s (-0.81) **Going Correction** -0.05s/f (Good) 11 Ran SP% **123.9**
Speed ratings (Par 105): **104,103,101,100,100 100,97,96,95,94 73**
toteswingers 1&2 £26.10, 1&3 £26.10, 2&3 £14.70 CSF £100.92 CT £921.58 TOTE £17.20: £4.20, £2.30, £2.70; EX 168.70 Trifecta £204.10 Part won. Pool: £272.18 - 0.01 winning units..
Owner Roy Peebles **Bred** Mrs Norma Peebles **Trained** Great Habton, N Yorks

FOCUS
With a drying wind the going was changed to Good to firm, firm in places before this first race. A fair but competitive sprint handicap which was a story of changing fortunes in the latter stages. The runner-up is the best guide.

3332 WILLIAMHILL.COM EBF STALLIONS CONDITIONS STKS — 5f
2:25 (2:27) (Class 3) 2-Y-O **£8,086** (£2,406; £1,202; £601) **Stalls** High

Form RPR

3142 **1** **Lexington Rose**[17] 2767 2-8-6 0........ RoystonFfrench 4 80+
(Bryan Smart) *mde all: rdn clr over 1f out: edgd rt ins fnl f: kpt on wl* **11/8**[1]

42 **2** *2 ½* **Proclamationofwar**[12] 2913 2-8-11 0........ PhillipMakin 6 76+
(Kevin Ryan) *trckd ldrs: hdwy 2f out: rdn to chse wnr over 1f out: sn drvn and no imp ins fnl f* **7/2**[3]

1332 **3** *nk* **Split Rock**[26] 2518 2-9-0 0........ JoeFanning 2 78
(Mark Johnston) *chsd wnr: rdn along wl over 1f out: one pce fnl f* **3/1**[2]

144 **4** *1* **Orton Park (IRE)**[47] 1894 2-8-9 0........ GrahamLee 3 69
(Tobias B P Coles) *hld up in tch: hdwy 2f out: effrt over 1f out: sn rdn and no imp whn n.m.r wl ins fnl f* **10/1**

4231 **5** *nk* **Robynelle**[19] 2701 2-8-9 0........ TomEaves 5 68
(Keith Dalgleish) *in tch: rdn along 2f out: n.d* **12/1**

100 **6** *23* **Champagne Babe**[17] 2767 2-8-6 0........ AdrianNicholls 1
(Keith Dalgleish) *wnt rt and reminders s: prom on outer: rdn along over 2f out: sn wknd* **10/1**

59.83s (-0.57) **Going Correction** -0.05s/f (Good) 6 Ran SP% **115.2**
Speed ratings (Par 97): **102,98,97,95,95 58**
toteswingers 1&2 £1.40, 1&3 £2.10, 2&3 £1.20 CSF £6.78 TOTE £1.90: £1.20, £2.50; EX 6.70 Trifecta £20.80 Pool: £837.97 - 30.18 winning units..
Owner Middleham Park Racing VIII & Partners **Bred** Mickley Stud & Richard Kent **Trained** Hambleton, N Yorks

FOCUS
Probably just ordinary form for the level.

3333 WILLIAM HILL - IPHONE, IPAD, IPAD MINI H'CAP — 2m
3:00 (3:01) (Class 2) (0-100,93) 4-Y-O+ **£16,172** (£4,812; £2,405; £1,202) **Stalls** High

Form RPR

2244 **1** **Capellanus (IRE)**[33] 2316 7-8-5 **74** oh2........ JamesSullivan 4 81
(Brian Ellison) *hld up towards rr: hdwy wl over 2f out: rdn to chse ldrs and swtchd lft over 1f out: sn chal: led last 150yds and kpt on strly* **20/1**

31-2 **2** *1 ¾* **Twelve Strings (IRE)**[35] 2269 4-8-12 **82**........ TomEaves 3 87
(Brian Ellison) *trckd ldng pair: hdwy 3f out: rdn over 1f out: led briefly ent fnl f: sn drvn and hdd last 150yds: one pce* **5/1**[3]

34-1 **3** *nk* **Jonny Delta**[10] 2973 6-8-11 **80**........ GrahamLee 10 86+
(Jim Goldie) *hld up in rr: hdwy over 2f out: effrt whn nt clr run jst over 1f out: sn rdn and kpt on towards fin* **3/1**[2]

-500 **4** *nk* **Montaff**[23] 2587 7-8-11 **80**........ NickyMackay 9 84
(Mick Channon) *hld up towards rr: hdwy 3f out: rdn to chse ldrs 2f out: drvn and one pce fnl f* **10/1**

-060 **5** *¾* **Good Morning Star (IRE)**[29] 2407 4-9-9 **93**........ JoeFanning 6 96
(Mark Johnston) *trckd ldr: cl up 1/2-way: led over 2f out: sn rdn: drvn and hdd ent fnl f: grad wknd* **6/1**

120 **6** *3 ¼* **Lady Kashaan (IRE)**[28] 2451 4-9-8 **92**........ LiamKeniry 8 91
(Alan Swinbank) *trckd ldng pair: hdwy 3f out: pushed along over 2f out: sn rdn and btn over 1f out* **5/2**[1]

2131 **7** *1 ¾* **Activate**[7] 3085 6-8-6 **75**........(p) RoystonFfrench 2 72
(Keith Dalgleish) *led: rdn along 3f out: hdd over 2f out: sn drvn and grad wknd* **11/2**

3m 29.11s (-4.39) **Going Correction** -0.05s/f (Good)
WFA 4 from 5yo+ 1lb 7 Ran SP% **113.8**
Speed ratings (Par 109): **108,107,106,106,106 104,103**
toteswingers 1&2 £2.20, 1&3 £5.40, 2&3 £1.50 CSF £113.66 CT £391.42 TOTE £28.80: £13.20, £3.10; EX 83.70 Trifecta £323.60 Pool: £939.11 - 2.17 winning units..
Owner Mrs Claire Ellison **Bred** C H Wacker Iii **Trained** Norton, N Yorks
■ Stewards' Enquiry : Graham Lee one-day ban; careless riding (29th June).

FOCUS
A decent prize for this stayers' handicap and a one-two for the Brian Ellison yard, although not in the order the betting indicated. Not the easiest race to assess but the winner is rated to his spring AW form.

3334 WILLIAM HILL SCOTTISH SPRINT CUP (H'CAP) — 5f
3:35 (3:38) (Class 2) 4-Y-O+
£43,575 (£13,048; £6,524; £3,262; £1,631; £819) **Stalls** High

Form RPR

2331 **1** **Kingsgate Choice (IRE)**[21] 2669 6-9-7 **104**........ LiamKeniry 1 113
(Ed de Giles) *chsd ldrs on outer: hdwy 2f out: rdn to chal and edgd lft ent fnl f: drvn and kpt on to ld last 50yds* **6/1**[1]

0-01 **2** *hd* **Racy**[16] 2789 6-8-1 **91**........ ConnorBeasley(7) 8 99
(Brian Ellison) *hld up towards rr: swtchd rt to outer and gd hdwy 2f out: rdn to ld jst ins fnl f: sn drvn and edgd lft: hdd and nt qckn last 50yds* **12/1**

-006 **3** *1 ¼* **Barnet Fair**[21] 2669 5-8-7 **90**........ KierenFox 13 94+
(Richard Guest) *towards rr: hdwy whn nt clr run over 1f out: sn rdn and styd on strly fnl f: nrst fin* **9/1**[2]

32-0 **4** *nk* **Long Awaited (IRE)**[14] 2865 5-8-6 **94**........(b) JasonHart(5) 3 97+
(David Barron) *towards rr: hdwy towards outer wl over 1f out: rdn and styd on wl fnl f: nrst fin* **6/1**[1]

60-5 **5** *½* **Bajan Tryst (USA)**[144] 319 7-8-9 **92** ow1........(p) GrahamLee 2 93
(Kevin Ryan) *chsd ldrs towards outer: rdn and hdwy over 1f out: drvn and kpt on fnl f* **16/1**

052- **6** *hd* **Stone Of Folca**[269] 6382 5-8-13 **96**........ DavidNolan 16 96
(John Best) *sn led: rdn along 2f out: drvn and hdd jst ins fnl f: sn edgd rt and kpt on same pce* **10/1**[3]

-406 **7** *1* **Face The Problem (IRE)**[17] 2768 5-9-6 **103**........ JoeFanning 18 100+
(Jamie Osborne) *in tch whn n.m.r and lost pl after 1 1/2f: towards rr: hdwy and nt clr run over 1f out: rdn and kpt on fnl f: nrst fin* **12/1**

3521 **8** *nk* **Rothesay Chancer**[14] 2880 5-8-0 **83** oh4........ NickyMackay 14 79
(Jim Goldie) *trckd ldrs: hdwy 2f out: rdn over 1f out: sn drvn and one pce* **11/1**

5460 **9** *nk* **Confessional**[14] 2865 6-9-3 **100**....(e[1]) TomEaves 11 94+
(Tim Easterby) *blind removed late and s.i.s: in rr: hdwy towards outer wl over 1f out: sn rdn and kpt on: nrst fin* **14/1**

0-00 **10** *1* **Ubetterbegood (ARG)**[21] 2669 5-8-9 **92**.... PaddyAspell 20 83+
(Robert Cowell) *hld up on inner: effrt and nt clr run 2f out: sn swtchd rt and rdn: kpt on fnl f* **25/1**

-000 **11** *1* **Cheviot (USA)**[30] 2396 7-9-3 **100**....(p) PhillipMakin 15 87
(Kevin Ryan) *prom: rdn along 2f out: sn wknd* **18/1**

0203 **12** *½* **Bosun Breese**[14] 2880 8-7-13 **85**.... NeilFarley(3) 17 70
(David Barron) *in tch whn n.m.r after 1 1/2f: swtchd rt towards outer and hdwy 2f out: rdn wl over 1f out: sn btn* **16/1**

0-02 **13** *½* **Flash City (ITY)**[14] 2880 5-8-0 **83** oh2....(vt) JamesSullivan 7 67
(Bryan Smart) *a towards rr* **28/1**

1600 **14** *¾* **Mister Manannan (IRE)**[14] 2865 6-8-6 **89**....(p) AdrianNicholls 19 70+
(David Nicholls) *stmbld shortly after s and towards rr: effrt and nt clr run on inner 1/2-way: n.d* **22/1**

3-56 **15** *shd* **Hamish McGonagall**[13] 2909 8-9-9 **111**.... DarylByrne(5) 10 92
(Tim Easterby) *chsd ldrs: rdn along wl over 1f out: hld whn hmpd ins fnl f* **16/1**

0-20 **16** *2¾* **Captain Dunne (IRE)**[14] 2865 8-8-11 **94**....(p) MickyFenton 5 65+
(Tim Easterby) *prom: rdn along wl over 1f out: hld whn hmpd and wknd ent fnl f* **18/1**

/0-0 **17** *2* **Nero Emperor (IRE)**[44] 1970 4-8-6 **94**.... ShaneGray(5) 12 57
(T Stack, Ire) *cl up: rdn along 2f out: wknd qckly over 1f out: eased* **10/1**[3]

59.6s (-0.80) **Going Correction** -0.05s/f (Good) **17** Ran SP% **127.0**
Speed ratings (Par 109): **104,103,101,101,100 100,98,98,97,95 94,93,92,91,91 86,83**
toteswingers 1&2 £16.00, 1&3 £11.70, 2&3 £73.50 CSF £77.28 CT £687.08 TOTE £5.60: £1.90, £4.70, £2.60, £1.80; EX 115.40 Trifecta £443.00 Pool: £1,965.33 - 3.32 winning units..
Owner T Gould **Bred** Michael Staunton **Trained** Ledbury, H'fords
■ Stewards' Enquiry : Connor Beasley three-day ban; careless riding (29th June-1st July).

FOCUS
A strong renewal of one of the highlights of Musselburgh's season, with two previous winners bidding to score again. Unsurprisingly with such a big field it was rough race in which several did not get the clearest of runs, but the winner overcame the worst draw of all. That said, he and the second avoided the trouble on the outside. A small personal best from the winner.

3335 WILLIAM HILL - NEW IPAD H'CAP 7f 30y
4:10 (4:10) (Class 2) (0-100,100) 4-Y-0+ **£12,938** (£3,850; £1,924; £962) **Stalls** Low

Form RPR

6625 **1** **Clockmaker (IRE)**[7] 3088 7-8-8 **87**.... TomEaves 8 97
(Tim Easterby) *trckd ldr: hdwy and cl up 2f out: rdn to ld 1/2f out: drvn and hld on gamely towards fin* **12/1**

0600 **2** *½* **Es Que Love (IRE)**[14] 2858 4-9-3 **96**.... GrahamLee 1 104
(Mark Johnston) *dwlt: sn pushed along on inner to trck ldrs: effrt over 2f out: rdn over 1f out: styd on to chal ins fnl f: ev ch tl drvn and one pce towards fin* **9/2**[3]

0054 **3** *2½* **Chookie Royale**[14] 2882 5-8-2 **81**....(b) JamesSullivan 7 82
(Keith Dalgleish) *hld up in rr: hdwy wl over 2f out: chsd ldrs whn n.m.r and swtchd lft over 1f out: styd on wl fnl f: nrst fin* **14/1**

0-40 **4** *½* **Set The Trend**[30] 2399 7-9-7 **100**.... DavidNolan 3 100
(David O'Meara) *trckd ldrs: hdwy 3f out: rdn 2f out: drvn and one pce fnl f* **8/1**

-006 **5** *¾* **Beacon Lodge (IRE)**[27] 2477 8-9-4 **97**....[1] PaddyAspell 4 95
(David Nicholls) *chsd ldrs: rdn over 2f out: sn drvn and one pce appr fnl f* **33/1**

0225 **6** *3* **Kingscroft (IRE)**[7] 3096 5-8-5 **84**.... JoeFanning 9 74
(Mark Johnston) *hld up towards rr: stdy hdwy on outer over 3f out: chsd ldrs 2f out: sn rdn and wknd appr fnl f* **5/2**[1]

1140 **7** *1¼* **Gandalak (FR)**[14] 2868 4-8-11 **93**.... LeeTopliss(3) 2 83
(David O'Meara) *led: pushed along wl over 2f out: rdn wl over 1f out: sn hdd & wknd* **10/3**[2]

-210 **8** *nk* **Fieldgunner Kirkup (GER)**[42] 2029 5-8-1 **87**.... ConnorBeasley(7) 5 73
(David Barron) *hld up in rr: hdwy 3f out: rdn 2f out: sn btn* **11/1**

-600 **9** *1¼* **Marcret (ITY)**[30] 2399 6-9-5 **98**.... LiamKeniry 10 80
(David Nicholls) *in tch: rdn along 3f out: sn wknd* **40/1**

0200 **10** *10* **Xilerator (IRE)**[25] 2541 6-8-9 **88**.... AdrianNicholls 11 59
(David Nicholls) *chsd ldng pair: rdn along over 2f out: wkng whn n.m.r wl over 1f out: sn bhd* **16/1**

1m 26.94s (-2.06) **Going Correction** -0.05s/f (Good) **10** Ran SP% **114.9**
Speed ratings (Par 109): **109,108,105,105,104 100,99,98,97,86**
toteswingers 1&2 £8.50, 1&3 £6.50, 2&3 £11.40 CSF £64.37 CT £788.55 TOTE £9.40: £3.00, £2.20, £2.80; EX 66.70 Trifecta £641.70 Pool: £1,626.12 - 1.90 winning units..
Owner Middleham Park Racing XI & Partners **Bred** Lemongrove Stud & Brendan Arthur **Trained** Great Habton, N Yorks

FOCUS
Another good handicap and a competitive affair but it paid to race close to the pace. Straightforward form.

3336 WILLIAM HILL - IN THE APP STORE H'CAP 1m 4f 100y
4:40 (4:43) (Class 4) (0-85,90) 3-Y-0 **£9,035** (£3,127) **Stalls** Low

Form RPR

0521 **1** **Royal Skies (IRE)**[8] 3067 3-9-12 **90**.... JoeFanning 1 101+
(Mark Johnston) *set stdy pce: qcknd 5f out: qcknd again over 3f out: sn pushed clr: easily* **1/2**[1]

3243 **2** *6* **Eric The Grey (IRE)**[29] 2405 3-8-7 **71**.... TomEaves 3 73
(Richard Fahey) *trckd wnr: effrt 3f out: rdn along 2f out: sn drvn and one pce* **9/4**[2]

1U4 **U** **Dorfman**[49] 1834 3-8-8 **72**....(b) AdrianNicholls 2
(Mark Johnston) *trckd ldng pair tl veered violently lft and uns rdr jst over 3f out* **10/1**[3]

2m 44.04s (2.04) **Going Correction** -0.05s/f (Good) **3** Ran SP% **106.5**
Speed ratings (Par 101): **91,87,**
CSF £1.87 TOTE £1.50; EX 1.50 Trifecta £1.40 Pool: £900.46 - 457.54 winning units..
Owner Sheikh Hamdan Bin Mohammed Al Maktoum **Bred** P Moen **Trained** Middleham Moor, N Yorks

FOCUS
A disappointing turnout for this 3-y-o handicap, which was slowly run. The winner's Pontefract form is the best guide.

3337 WILLIAM HILL - DOWNLOAD THE APP APPRENTICE H'CAP 1m
5:10 (5:14) (Class 6) (0-65,65) 4-Y-0+ **£3,234** (£962; £481; £240) **Stalls** Low

Form RPR

231 **1** **Size (IRE)**[22] 2634 4-9-5 **63**.... LeeTopliss 5 76+
(Richard Fahey) *mde all: set stdy pce: rdn and qcknd 2f out: sn clr: readily* **1/1**[1]

0335 **2** *3* **Lil Sophella (IRE)**[10] 2972 4-7-11 **48**.... JackGarritty(7) 7 54
(Patrick Holmes) *t.k.h: chsd wnr: rdn along wl over 2f out: kpt on u.p fnl f: no ch w wnr* **20/1**

2441 **3** *1* **Rawaafed (IRE)**[16] 2794 4-9-3 **64**.... JasonHart(3) 6 68
(Keith Dalgleish) *trckd ldrs: pushed along 3f out: rdn wl over 1f out: drvn and edgd lft fnl f: kpt on one pce* **8/1**[3]

-523 **4** *1* **Cabal**[11] 2956 6-8-11 **55**....(b) NeilFarley 4 57
(Andrew Crook) *hld up: hdwy 3f out: rdn along 2f out: drvn and no imp fnl f* **16/1**

3021 **5** *½* **West Leake Hare (IRE)**[7] 3087 4-9-2 **65**.... JordanNason(5) 8 66
(David Nicholls) *hld up: hdwy over 3f out: rdn along and outpcd over 2f out: styd on fnl f* **11/4**[2]

-323 **6** *1* **Music Festival (USA)**[10] 2977 6-8-5 **56**.... SophieRobertson(7) 11 54
(Jim Goldie) *stdd s and hld up in rr: hdwy on wd outside wl over 2f out: sn chsng ldrs: rdn wl over 1f out and one pce* **9/1**

05-4 **7** *hd* **Thatcherite (IRE)**[9] 3027 5-9-0 **63**....(t) DavidSimmonson(5) 1 61
(Tony Coyle) *dwlt: hld up: a in rr* **11/1**

-021 **8** *1½* **Ptolemy**[9] 3029 4-9-0 **61**.... LMcNiff(3) 2 55
(David Barron) *trckd ldng pair on inner: pushed along 3f out: rdn 2f out: sn wknd* **12/1**

1m 42.48s (1.28) **Going Correction** -0.05s/f (Good) **8** Ran SP% **124.4**
Speed ratings (Par 101): **91,88,87,86,85 84,84,82**
toteswingers 1&2 £12.40, 1&3 £4.40, 2&3 £7.10 CSF £29.12 CT £126.58 TOTE £1.60: £1.10, £6.20, £2.30; EX 37.00 Trifecta £491.30 Pool: £1,303.17 - 1.98 winning units..
Owner Sir Robert Ogden **Bred** Manister House Stud **Trained** Musley Bank, N Yorks

FOCUS
A modest but quite competitive apprentice handicap that fell to the least exposed runner in the race. The winner is probably capable of better again.
T/Plt: £617.20 to a £1 stake. Pool: £59,815.51 - 70.74 winning units T/Qpdt: £62.70 to a £1 stake. Pool: £4,124.17 - 48.60 winning units JR

3288 SANDOWN (R-H)
Saturday, June 15

OFFICIAL GOING: Round course - good (good to firm in places) changing to good (good to soft in places) after race 1 (1.50) changing to good to soft after race 6 (4.35); sprint course - good (good to firm in places)
Moderate; against**Overcast with showers**

3338 CASH OUT MULTIPLES ONLY ON BETFAIR H'CAP 1m 1f
1:50 (1:52) (Class 3) (0-90,87) 3-Y-0
£12,450 (£3,728; £1,864; £932; £466; £234) **Stalls** Low

Form RPR

1-25 **1** **Ningara**[120] 666 3-8-8 **74**.... CathyGannon 3 81+
(Andrew Balding) *hld up in rr: rdn and prog fr 2f out: nt clr run over 1f out: gap appeared fnl f: drvn to ld last 75yds* **14/1**

2140 **2** *½* **Salutation (IRE)**[14] 2862 3-9-4 **84**.... FrannyNorton 8 90
(Mark Johnston) *led: drvn and hdd 2f out: kpt on wl to press ldr after: edgd lft but upsides 100yds out: outpcd nr fin* **9/1**

4334 **3** *nk* **Rouge Nuage (IRE)**[23] 2604 3-8-6 **72**.... AndreaAtzeni 2 77
(Conrad Allen) *mostly trckd ldng pair: first one to be rdn 3f out: kpt on wl for press: upsides ins fnl f: jst outpcd* **16/1**

21 **4** *hd* **Stableford**[18] 2760 3-9-3 **83**.... JimmyFortune 10 88
(Brian Meehan) *trckd ldr: rdn to ld 2f out but only narrowly: hdd and no ex last 75yds* **15/8**[1]

-045 **5** *½* **Master Ming (IRE)**[21] 2651 3-9-1 **81**....(b) KierenFallon 1 84
(Brian Meehan) *trckd ldrs: rdn on inner 2f out: cl enough 1f out: styd on same pce after* **12/1**

01-1 **6** *nk* **Noble Gift**[35] 2272 3-8-13 **79**.... JimCrowley 6 82+
(William Knight) *t.k.h: hld up in rr: rdn and nt qckn over 2f out: no hdwy after tl styd on ins fnl f* **11/2**[3]

-113 **7** *½* **Theodore Gericault (IRE)**[23] 2604 3-9-5 **85**.... RyanMoore 9 87
(Sir Michael Stoute) *trckd ldrs in 5th: tried to mount an effrt fr 2f out but nvr enough room to make prog: no hdwy fnl f* **3/1**[2]

1-00 **8** *nk* **Mundahesh (IRE)**[14] 2862 3-9-2 **82**.... DaneO'Neill 7 83
(William Haggas) *s.v.s: ct up at bk after 2f: rdn and no prog over 2f out: kpt on ins fnl f* **25/1**

15-6 **9** *8* **Nile Knight**[12] 2927 3-8-6 **72**.... HayleyTurner 4 55
(Marcus Tregoning) *hld up in rr: rdn and no prog over 2f out: wknd over 1f out* **16/1**

1m 57.86s (2.16) **Going Correction** +0.25s/f (Good) **9** Ran SP% **115.1**
Speed ratings (Par 103): **100,99,99,99,98 98,97,97,90**
toteswingers 1&2 £44.00, 1&3 £44.00, 2&3 £14.00 CSF £132.20 CT £2046.19 TOTE £17.60: £4.80, £2.80, £5.10; EX 75.40 Trifecta £1305.10 Pool: £1,950.76 - 1.12 winning units..
Owner G B Russell **Bred** S R Hope **Trained** Kingsclere, Hants

FOCUS
Sprint track at full width. Home bend at mid-configuration, rail out 5yds up home straight, adding 5yds to races on Round Course. A decent 3yo handicap, but they went no pace and the front eight finished in a heap. The form may therefore not be reliable.

3339 NOVAE INSURANCE H'CAP 1m 14y
2:20 (2:23) (Class 2) (0-100,99) 3-Y-0+
£31,125 (£9,320; £4,660; £2,330; £1,165; £585) **Stalls** Low

Form RPR

-461 **1** **Roserrow**[9] 3019 4-9-5 **90**.... JimmyFortune 9 103
(Andrew Balding) *led after 1f: mde most after: 2 l up and rdn 2f out: drvn and hld on wl fnl f* **11/1**

15-2 **2** *1* **Danchai**[42] 2018 4-9-4 **89**.... FrankieDettori 11 100
(William Haggas) *t.k.h: hld up towards rr on outer: prog over 2f out: drvn to chse wnr jst over 1f out: kpt on but a hld* **4/1**[2]

0563 **3** *1¼* **Gaul Wood (IRE)**[16] 2813 4-9-2 **87**....(p) FrannyNorton 12 95
(Tom Dascombe) *trckd ldng pair: chsd wnr 3f out to 2f out: kpt on u.p* **11/1**

6612 **4** *nse* **George Guru**[23] 2585 6-9-8 **93**.... KierenFallon 17 101
(Michael Attwater) *racd wd: hld up in last quartet: prog on outer 2f out: drvn and styd on fnl f: nvr able to chal* **14/1**

20-5 **5** *nk* **Trader Jack**[16] 2813 4-9-3 **88**.... JamesDoyle 15 95
(Roger Charlton) *racd wd early: trckd ldrs: prog to chse wnr 2f out: no imp and lost 2nd jst over 1f out: one pce* **10/1**

0-51 **6** *1* **Ashaadd (IRE)**[9] 3020 3-8-13 **95**.... RyanMoore 6 97
(Roger Varian) *hld up in last quartet: rdn and prog on outer 2f out: tried to cl on ldrs 1f out: effrt flattened out fnl f* **7/2**[1]

13-5 **7** *1 1/4* **Fire Ship**[49] 1848 4-10-0 **99** JimCrowley 5 101
(William Knight) *hld up in midfield: 8th 1/2-way: rdn over 2f out: tried to make prog over 1f out: one pce* **16/1**

0-06 **8** *2 1/4* **Noble Citizen (USA)**[23] 2585 8-9-1 **86** HayleyTurner 2 83
(David Simcock) *a in midfield: 7th 1/2-way: rdn over 2f out: no real imp on ldrs over 1f out: fdd fnl f* **33/1**

-061 **9** *1 1/2* **Bancnuanaheireann (IRE)**[37] 2193 6-9-6 **91** GeorgeBaker 3 89
(Michael Appleby) *hld up in last: stl in last pair whn sed to make prog on inner 2f out: stuck bhd rivals over 1f out: rchd 9th fnl f: nvr involved* **12/1**

4-25 **10** *3 3/4* **Weapon Of Choice (IRE)**[36] 2210 5-9-5 **90** ShaneKelly 1 75
(Stuart Kittow) *trckd ldrs: cl up and rdn over 2f out: wknd over 1f out* **22/1**

-551 **11** *3 1/4* **Vainglory (USA)**[15] 2841 9-9-5 **90** MartinLane 4 67
(David Simcock) *a wl in rr: rdn and struggling over 2f out* **18/1**

4135 **12** *2 1/4* **Lowther**[35] 2265 8-9-2 **87** (v) LukeMorris 7 59
(Lee Carter) *fast away: led 1f: stdd: rdn over 2f out: sn wknd* **50/1**

5-01 **13** *nk* **Norse Blues**[42] 2029 5-9-8 **93** JamieSpencer 14 64
(David Barron) *racd wd early: chsd wnr after 1f to 3f out: sn wknd* **6/1**[3]

110- **14** *nk* **Forgive**[226] 7509 4-9-0 **90** WilliamTwiston-Davies(5) 8 61
(Richard Hannon) *hld up in midfield: 8th 1/2-way: rdn wl over 2f out: sn wknd* **16/1**

405/ **15** *6* **Zafisio (IRE)**[516] 6149 7-9-5 **90** CathyGannon 10 47
(Jo Hughes) *hld up in midfield: 10th 1/2-way: rdn and no prog over 2f out: sn wknd* **66/1**

1m 43.4s (0.10) **Going Correction** +0.25s/f (Good) **15** Ran SP% **124.4**
WFA 3 from 4yo+ 11lb
Speed ratings (Par 109): **109,108,106,106,106 105,104,101,100,96 93,91,90,90,84**
toteswingers 1&2 £4.70, 1&3 £90.60, 2&3 £10.40 CSF £54.61 CT £517.58 TOTE £14.40: £4.40, £2.00, £5.00; EX 71.60 Trifecta £1675.00 Part won. Pool: £2,233.41 - 0.41 winning units..
Owner Sir Roger Buckley, Gerald Oury **Bred** Sir R J Buckley & G Oury **Trained** Kingsclere, Hants
FOCUS
A hot and competitive handicap run at a good pace and those that raced near the front seemed to hold an advantage. Good, solid form.

3340 NOVAE BLOODSTOCK INSURANCE SCURRY STKS (LISTED RACE) 5f 6y
2:55 (2:56) (Class 1) 3-Y-O
£20,982 (£7,955; £3,981; £1,983; £995; £499) **Stalls** Low

Form RPR

06-6 **1** **Morawij**[21] 2662 3-9-2 **105** RyanMoore 1 111
(Roger Varian) *mde all: racd against rail and travelled easily: shkn up and drew at least 2 l clr 1f out: drvn fnl f: jst hld on* **10/11**[1]

11-1 **2** *nk* **March**[19] 2726 3-8-8 **86** AndreaAtzeni 8 102+
(Marco Botti) *hld up in last trio against rail: prog and nt clr run over 1f out: hdwy to chse wnr last 100yds: r.o wl nr fin: jst failed* **8/1**[3]

61-0 **3** *3 3/4* **Sandreamer (IRE)**[45] 1921 3-8-11 **100** (v[1]) MartinHarley 3 91
(Mick Channon) *cl up against rail: rdn to chse wnr over 1f out: edgd lft: nt qckn and sn hld: lost 2nd and fdd last 110yds* **12/1**

3-04 **4** *1 1/4* **Sound Of Guns**[29] 2415 3-8-8 **103** LukeMorris 7 84
(Ed Walker) *racd wd in midfield: u.p over 2f out: kpt on to take 4th fnl f: no ch* **8/1**[3]

0-15 **5** *hd* **Dominate**[29] 2415 3-8-13 **90** DaneO'Neill 6 88
(Richard Hannon) *chsd ldrs: rdn 2f out: sn outpcd: kpt on one pce fnl f* **14/1**

0-41 **6** *1 1/4* **Normal Equilibrium**[36] 2213 3-8-13 **93** JamieSpencer 4 84
(Robert Cowell) *dwlt: hld up in last pair: swtchd to outer and drvn wl over 1f out: no real prog* **5/1**[2]

0-40 **7** *1* **Lady Ibrox**[29] 2430 3-8-8 **90** RobertHavlin 10 75
(Alan Brown) *fast away fr wd draw: chsd wnr to 1/2-way: wknd over 1f out* **25/1**

6-00 **8** *1/2* **Lady Phill**[45] 1921 3-8-8 **87** ShaneKelly 2 73
(Bill Turner) *dwlt: mostly in last and nvr on terms: no ch over 1f out* **33/1**

0-04 **9** *1 1/4* **Lasilia (IRE)**[35] 2270 3-8-8 **87** FrannyNorton 9 69
(Kevin Ryan) *prom: chsd wnr 1/2-way to over 1f out: wknd qckly* **50/1**

1m 1.54s (-0.06) **Going Correction** +0.15s/f (Good) **9** Ran SP% **114.4**
Speed ratings (Par 107): **106,105,99,97,97 95,93,92,90**
toteswingers 1&2 £1.30, 1&3 £4.70, 2&3 £7.40 CSF £8.59 TOTE £1.60: £1.10, £2.50, £3.70; EX 11.50 Trifecta £59.80 Pool: £2,000.15 - 25.07 winning units..
Owner Sheikh Ahmed Al Maktoum **Bred** Dunchurch Lodge Stud Co **Trained** Newmarket, Suffolk
FOCUS
An interesting Listed sprint for 3yos and we should be hearing a lot more about at least one of these, if not necessarily the winner. He rates a personal best.

3341 PRITCH LONDON H'CAP 5f 6y
3:30 (3:34) (Class 4) (0-80,80) 4-Y-0+ **£5,822** (£1,732; £865; £432) **Stalls** Low

Form RPR

-543 **1** **Lupo D'Oro (IRE)**[19] 2725 4-9-7 **80** JamesDoyle 9 89
(John Best) *hld up in last trio: prog and swtchd towards outer wl over 1f out: str run to ld last 150yds: drvn out* **5/1**[2]

6206 **2** *3/4* **Rocket Rob (IRE)**[19] 2725 7-9-0 **73** JamieMackay 2 79
(Willie Musson) *slowly away: t.k.h and hld up: hemmed in by rival over 3f out and dropped to last: prog on wd outside over 1f out: r.o to take 2nd last 75yds: nt rch wnr* **10/3**[1]

-106 **3** *1 1/4* **Tagula Night (IRE)**[21] 2657 7-9-5 **78** (bt) KierenFallon 6 80
(Dean Ivory) *trckd ldng pair: prog to ld over 1f out: hdd and outpcd last 150yds* **11/2**[3]

-651 **4** *nk* **Monsieur Jamie**[25] 2550 5-8-12 **71** (v) JimmyFortune 3 71
(J R Jenkins) *appeared to anticipate s: led against rail at mod pce: hdd and nt qckn over 1f out: one pce* **8/1**

-610 **5** *1 1/2* **Dreams Of Glory**[40] 2074 5-8-6 **65** LukeMorris 5 60
(Ron Hodges) *w ldr to over 1f out: nt qckn* **16/1**

0004 **6** *1/2* **Jarrow (IRE)**[43] 1976 6-9-2 **75** RyanMoore 10 68
(Milton Bradley) *chsd ldrs on outer: drvn 2f out: one pce over 1f out: fdd ins fnl f* **10/1**

2505 **7** *nse* **Welease Bwian (IRE)**[29] 2425 4-8-4 **63** AndreaAtzeni 11 56
(Stuart Williams) *t.k.h: hld up in last pair: taken to outer and drvn over 1f out: no real prog* **20/1**

5232 **8** *1* **Rylee Mooch**[7] 3090 5-9-4 **77** (e) RobbieFitzpatrick 4 66+
(Richard Guest) *slowly away and awkward s: rcvrd to trck ldng pair against rail: nt clr run over 1f out: rdn whn trapped against rail fnl f: no ch* **7/1**

4153 **9** *nk* **Sandfrankskipsgo**[36] 2227 4-9-6 **79** ShaneKelly 8 67+
(Peter Crate) *t.k.h: hld up in midfield: nowhere to go fr 2f out: eased whn no ch nr fin* **7/1**

1m 4.0s (2.40) **Going Correction** +0.15s/f (Good) **9** Ran SP% **111.0**
Speed ratings (Par 105): **86,84,82,82,79 79,79,77,76**
toteswingers 1&2 £5.20, 1&3 £6.40, 2&3 £4.00 CSF £20.70 CT £90.17 TOTE £4.20: £1.10, £2.10, £2.30; EX 20.80 Trifecta £52.80 Pool: £1,655.27 - 23.48 winning units..
Owner S Malcolm M Winwright P Tindall **Bred** Mrs E Fitzsimons **Trained** Hucking, Kent
FOCUS
They didn't seem to go that fast early in this fair sprint handicap and the time was 2.46 seconds slower than the 3yo Listed event. Rather muddling form but a personal best from the winner.

3342 THWAITES WAINWRIGHT H'CAP 7f 16y
4:05 (4:08) (Class 3) (0-95,93) 3-Y-O
£12,450 (£3,728; £1,864; £932; £466; £234) **Stalls** Low

Form RPR

-321 **1** **Secret Art (IRE)**[25] 2548 3-8-8 **80** ow1 JimCrowley 8 93+
(Ralph Beckett) *trckd ldrs in 6th: nt clr run over 2f out: prog over 1f out: drvn and r.o wl fnl f to ld nr fin* **12/1**

02-2 **2** *3/4* **Indignant**[28] 2449 3-8-10 **87** WilliamTwiston-Davies(5) 7 98
(Richard Hannon) *prom: trckd clr ldr wl over 2f out: steadily clsd to ld jst over 1f out: sn drvn and pressed: hdd nr fin* **13/2**[3]

03-5 **3** *nse* **Burning Blaze**[28] 2452 3-9-0 **86** JamieSpencer 1 96+
(Kevin Ryan) *hld up towards rr: stdy prog over 2f out: wnt 2nd 1f out and sn chal ldr: outpcd nr fin* **6/1**[2]

3-11 **4** *1 1/4* **Pythagorean**[18] 2738 3-9-3 **89** JamesDoyle 9 96+
(Roger Charlton) *stdd s: hld up in last trio: prog on wd outside over 2f out: drvn to cl on ldrs 1f out: one pce fnl f* **9/4**[1]

4140 **5** *1* **Shahdaroba (IRE)**[28] 2452 3-9-7 **93** FrankieDettori 6 97
(Rod Millman) *trckd ldrs: rdn to go 3rd 2f out to 1f out: one pce after* **28/1**

431 **6** *2* **Defendant**[17] 2765 3-8-13 **85** RyanMoore 5 84+
(Sir Michael Stoute) *hld up towards rr: rdn and no great prog whn hmpd wl over 1f out: plugged on fnl f* **13/2**[3]

-603 **7** *1* **Ceelo**[18] 2738 3-8-5 **77** ChrisCatlin 4 73
(Sylvester Kirk) *racd freely: led: clr after 2f: wknd and hdd jst over 1f out* **33/1**

21- **8** *4 1/2* **Beautiful View**[224] 7553 3-9-2 **88** DaneO'Neill 14 72+
(Richard Hannon) *stdd s: hld up in last: shuffled along over 2f out: stl last 1f out: passed 6 rivals last 100yds* **12/1**

3410 **9** *hd* **Skytrain**[18] 2738 3-8-4 **76** FrannyNorton 3 60
(Mark Johnston) *chsd clr ldr to wl over 2f out: steadily wknd* **20/1**

1- **10** *nse* **Chelwood Gate (IRE)**[379] 2667 3-9-7 **93** AndreaAtzeni 15 76
(Roger Varian) *t.k.h: hld up towards rr: rdn and no prog over 2f out* **20/1**

-010 **11** *1 1/4* **Intimidate**[28] 2439 3-8-12 **84** (p) JimmyFortune 2 64
(Jeremy Noseda) *plld hrd in midfield: rdn and no rspnse over 2f out: sn wknd* **33/1**

2-10 **12** *1/2* **Lancelot Du Lac (ITY)**[15] 2844 3-9-2 **88** [1] GeorgeBaker 11 67+
(Dean Ivory) *stdd s: t.k.h and hld up in rr: shkn up and no prog over 2f out* **16/1**

41-4 **13** *2 1/4* **Unknown Villain (IRE)**[31] 2371 3-8-4 **76** CathyGannon 13 49
(Tom Dascombe) *racd wd: chsd ldrs: rdn wl over 2f out: sn wknd* **16/1**

4-6 **14** *3/4* **Baddilini**[37] 2188 3-9-5 **91** KierenFallon 10 62
(Alan Bailey) *a in last trio: struggling over 2f out* **50/1**

1m 30.87s (1.37) **Going Correction** +0.25s/f (Good) **14** Ran SP% **119.7**
Speed ratings (Par 103): **102,101,101,99,98 96,95,89,89,89 88,87,85,84**
toteswingers 1&2 £19.00, 1&3 £35.20, 2&3 £15.00 CSF £80.40 CT £541.14 TOTE £13.90: £3.60, £2.60, £1.40; EX 110.90 Trifecta £1730.40 Part won. Pool: £2,307.20 - 0.12 winning units..
Owner Circuit Racing **Bred** Grange Stud **Trained** Kimpton, Hants
FOCUS
A competitive handicap run at a true pace once the seventh went clear. Not rock-sold form, the runner-up the best guide.

3343 AGELOU HORSE RACING & PRUDENCE PRODUCTION EBF MAIDEN STKS 1m 2f 7y
4:35 (4:40) (Class 5) 3-Y-O **£3,881** (£1,155; £577; £288) **Stalls** Low

Form RPR

0- **1** **Vital Evidence (USA)**[260] 6636 3-9-5 **0** RyanMoore 8 88
(Sir Michael Stoute) *trckd ldr: shkn up 3f out: clsd to ld over 2f out: drvn and pressed over 1f out: styd on* **5/6**[1]

2 *1* **Vermont (IRE)** 3-9-5 **0** KierenFallon 5 86
(Luca Cumani) *trckd ldng pair: shkn up to chse wnr 2f out: tried to chal over 1f out: one pce fnl f* **6/1**[3]

4- **3** *2 1/4* **Sadiq**[248] 6985 3-9-5 **0** DaneO'Neill 4 82
(Saeed bin Suroor) *dwlt: hld up in last: prog on outer over 2f out: tk cl 3rd wl over 1f out: nt qckn and wl hld fnl f* **4/1**[2]

4 *shd* **Sagua La Grande (IRE)** 3-9-5 **0** GeorgeBaker 3 81
(Lady Cecil) *hld up in 5th: shkn up over 2f out: nvr on terms but kpt on to press for 3rd nr fin* **12/1**

00 **5** *8* **Hero's Story**[9] 3021 3-9-5 **0** JimCrowley 1 65
(Amanda Perrett) *led: hdd and shkn up over 2f out: wknd over 1f out: eased* **28/1**

0-2 **6** *14* **Herod The Great**[25] 2547 3-9-5 **0** JimmyFortune 7 51
(Alan King) *t.k.h: hld up in 4th: rdn over 2f out: wknd rapidly wl over 1f out: t.o* **13/2**

2m 12.96s (2.46) **Going Correction** +0.25s/f (Good) **6** Ran SP% **113.3**
Speed ratings (Par 99): **100,99,97,97,90 79**
toteswingers 1&2 £2.00, 1&3 £1.60, 2&3 £3.30 CSF £6.61 TOTE £1.50: £1.10, £3.10; EX 7.40 Trifecta £19.50 Pool: £4,032.28 - 154.91 winning units..
Owner K Abdullah **Bred** Juddmonte Farms Inc **Trained** Newmarket, Suffolk
FOCUS
Not a very competitive maiden, but a couple of these should make their mark. The form is rated around the race averages.

3344 AQUARIVA TEQUILA H'CAP 1m 6f
5:05 (5:10) (Class 4) (0-85,85) 4-Y-0+ **£5,822** (£1,732; £865; £432) **Stalls** Low

Form RPR

6245 **1** **Cool Sky**[23] 2587 4-9-3 **81** GeorgeBaker 8 89
(William Knight) *trckd ldng pair: moved up smoothly to ld wl over 1f out: drvn and kpt on wl fnl f* **16/1**

0-00 **2** *1* **Spice Fair**[23] 2598 6-9-1 **79** JimmyFortune 3 86+
(Mark Usher) *s.s: hld up in detached last: prog on inner over 2f out: rdn to chse wnr 1f out: styd on but nt qckn* **12/1**

110- **3** *3/4* **Saborido (USA)**[266] 6493 7-9-5 **83** DaneO'Neill 4 89
(Amanda Perrett) *trckd ldng trio: rdn to dispute 2nd over 1f out: styd on fnl f: a hld* **25/1**

0-32 **4** *1/2* **Abundantly**[43] 1973 4-8-11 **75** RyanMoore 12 80+
(Hughie Morrison) *hld up and sn in last trio: pushed along whn nt clr run over 2f out to over 1f out: styd on fnl f: nrst fin* **9/4**[1]

6465 **5** *1* **The Bull Hayes (IRE)**[41] 2040 7-9-5 **83** KierenFallon 10 86
(Michael Appleby) *led 1f: t.k.h and led again after 4f: shkn up and hdd wl over 1f out: steadily fdd* **14/1**

The Form Book Flat, Raceform Ltd, Compton, RG20 6NL.

-505 **6** *shd* **Gabrial's Star**[21] 2671 4-9-3 **81**....(p) FrankieDettori 6 84
(Ed Dunlop) *dwlt: hld up in last pair: shkn up and limited prog on outer 2f out: drvn and kpt on fnl f: n.d* **9/2**[2]

1-04 **7** *3 ¾* **Lady Rosamunde**[21] 2654 5-9-2 **85**....(p) RosieJessop(5) 7 83
(Marcus Tregoning) *hld up in 6th: rdn whn n.m.r over 2f out: nt qckn over 1f out: wl hld after* **7/1**[3]

0-02 **8** *1* **The Quarterjack**[23] 2598 4-8-8 **72**.... AndreaAtzeni 13 69
(Ron Hodges) *trckd ldrs: pushed along 4f out: wknd 2f out* **14/1**

40-3 **9** *nk* **Rockfella**[23] 2587 7-9-2 **80**.... ShaneKelly 5 76
(Denis Coakley) *led after 1f tl after 4f: chsd ldr tl wknd over 2f out* **15/2**

-510 **10** *½* **Fleur De La Vie (IRE)**[30] 2402 4-9-2 **80**.... JimCrowley 14 76
(Ralph Beckett) *hld up towards rr: shkn up over 2f out: steadily wknd wl over 1f out* **8/1**

3m 8.64s (4.14) **Going Correction** +0.45s/f (Yiel) **10** Ran SP% **115.1**
Speed ratings (Par 105): **106,105,105,104,104 104,101,101,101,100**
toteswingers 1&2 £20.70, 1&3 £47.70, 2&3 £45.20 CSF £190.67 CT £4698.81 TOTE £21.80: £5.50, £3.80, £7.80; EX 224.40 Trifecta £2428.30 Part won. Pool: £3,237.85 - 0.33 winning units..
Owner No Quarter Partnership **Bred** Miss K J Keir **Trained** Patching, W Sussex

FOCUS
A fair staying handicap and a solid pace thanks to a disputed lead. The third helps with the standard.
T/Plt: £306.30 to a £1 stake. Pool: £131,879.74 - 314.21 winning units T/Qpdt: £12.70 to a £1 stake. Pool: £8,192.97 - 475.75 winning units JN

3295 YORK (L-H)
Saturday, June 15

OFFICIAL GOING: Good to firm (good in places; 7.7)
Wind: Strong; half behind Weather: Changeable, blustery; heavy showers

3345 QUEEN MOTHER'S CUP (LADY AMATEUR RIDERS) (H'CAP) 1m 4f
2:05 (2:05) (Class 3) (0-95,93) 3-Y-0+ **£12,478** (£3,870; £1,934; £968) **Stalls** Centre

Form RPR

6003 **1** **Nanton (USA)**[22] 2633 11-10-1 **80**.... MrsCBartley 13 90
(Jim Goldie) *hld up in rr: hdwy on outside over 2f out: styd on wl fnl f: edgd lft and led last stride* **9/1**

6-00 **2** *nse* **Warlu Way**[19] 2718 6-9-13 **81**.... MissJoannaMason(3) 3 91
(Michael Easterby) *mid-div: hdwy on inner to chse ldrs over 3f out: led last 50yds: hdd post* **22/1**

-012 **3** *½* **Reve De Nuit (USA)**[7] 3085 7-9-12 **77**.... MissHayleyMoore 4 86
(Mrs K Burke) *trckd ldrs: led 8f out: clr over 5f out: hdd wl ins fnl f: no ex* **9/1**

-005 **4** *1 ¾* **Rio's Rosanna (IRE)**[14] 2855 6-10-4 **83**.... MissJRRichards 15 91+
(Richard Whitaker) *chsd ldrs: keeping on same pce whn hmpd nr fin* **10/1**

-600 **5** *1 ½* **Party Line**[14] 2867 4-10-9 **88**.... MissCWalton 8 92
(Mark Johnston) *mid-div: effrt on inner over 3f out: chsng ldrs 2f out: one pce* **20/1**

-640 **6** *2* **Eagle Rock (IRE)**[30] 2402 5-9-6 **77**.... MissEmilyBullock(6) 1 78
(Tom Tate) *drvn early to chse ldrs: kpt on one pce fnl 2f* **14/1**

4010 **7** *hd* **Sirvino**[14] 2867 8-10-11 **90**.... MissSBrotherton 6 90
(David Barron) *in rr: hdwy over 2f out: chsng ldrs over 1f out: kpt on same pce* **8/1**[3]

5425 **8** *3 ½* **Knightly Escapade**[22] 2633 5-9-5 **76**.... MissNHayes(6) 2 71
(Brian Ellison) *in rr: swtchd outside and hdwy over 2f out: lost pl over 1f out* **14/1**

-001 **9** *hd* **Cosmic Sun**[19] 2706 7-9-10 **75**....(t) MissADeniel 12 70
(Richard Fahey) *mid-div: hdwy to chse ldrs over 3f out: fdd fnl f* **12/1**

-400 **10** *shd* **Easy Terms**[29] 2427 6-10-13 **92**.... MissBAndrews 10 86
(Edwin Tuer) *hld up in rr: hdwy over 2f out: wknd fnl f* **20/1**

0 **11** *2 ¼* **Pulpitarian (USA)**[29] 2427 5-10-5 **87**.... MissRMcDonald(3) 14 78
(Lucinda Russell) *chsd ldrs: wknd over 1f out* **50/1**

0-00 **12** *1 ¼* **Crackentorp**[29] 2427 8-11-0 **93**.... MissJCoward 9 82
(Tim Easterby) *led tl 8f out: wknd 2f out* **7/1**[2]

-556 **13** *1* **Dancing Primo**[7] 3095 7-9-11 **76**.... MissBeckyBrisbourne 7 63
(Mark Brisbourne) *s.i.s: t.k.h in rr: nvr a factor* **25/1**

0-13 **14** *1* **Next Edition (IRE)**[36] 2240 5-10-4 **83**.... MissHBethell 11 69
(Philip Kirby) *mid-div: edgd lft and lost pl 2f out* **16/1**

-000 **15** *2 ¾* **Unex Michelangelo (IRE)**[29] 2431 4-10-0 **82**.... MissPhillipaTutty(3) 17 63
(Michael Easterby) *in rr: lost pl over 2f out* **50/1**

5403 **16** *9* **Sir Boss (IRE)**[18] 2739 8-9-10 **75**.... MissMMullineaux 5 42
(Michael Mullineaux) *chsd ldrs: lost pl over 2f out* **25/1**

304- **17** *¾* **War Singer (USA)**[224] 6010 6-10-7 **86**....(t) MissJMMangan 16 52
(David Pipe) *mid-div: slipped on bnd over 4f out: hdwy on outside over 3f out: lost pl 2f out* **7/2**[1]

2m 32.62s (-0.58) **Going Correction** -0.075s/f (Good) **17** Ran SP% **127.3**
Speed ratings (Par 107): **98,97,97,96,95 94,94,91,91,91 89,89,88,87,85 79,79**
toteswingers 1&2 £43.20, 1&3 £20.40, 2&3 £44.90 CSF £203.25 CT £1856.70 TOTE £10.40: £2.50, £5.50, £2.70, £2.70; EX 223.50 Trifecta £1488.90 Pool: £2,881.76 - 1.45 winning units..
Owner J S Morrison **Bred** Samuel H And Mrs Rogers, Jr **Trained** Uplawmoor, E Renfrews

FOCUS
Rail moved out 3m from 1m1f to entrance to home straight, adding 7yds to distances of 1m and over. They were on the stretch a fair way out in what is traditionally a competitive lady riders' event, with them racing middle-to-far side in the straight. The winner was not far off last summer's form.

3346 LADBROKES.COM STKS (H'CAP) 1m 208y
2:40 (2:42) (Class 2) (0-105,96) 3-Y-0+ **£17,466** (£5,197; £2,597; £1,298) **Stalls** Low

Form RPR

10-3 **1** **Sam Sharp (USA)**[23] 2592 7-9-4 **86**.... RichardKingscote 3 99
(Ian Williams) *hld up in rr: effrt and swtchd lft 2f out: sn chsng ldrs: led jst ins fnl f: drvn out* **15/2**[3]

0-00 **2** *2 ¼* **Silvery Moon (IRE)**[31] 2365 6-9-3 **85**.... RobertWinston 1 93
(Tim Easterby) *hld up in rr: hdwy to chse ldrs over 2f out: kpt on to take 2nd last 50yds* **20/1**

0022 **3** *hd* **Maven**[21] 2673 5-9-0 **82**.... DuranFentiman 8 90
(Tim Easterby) *led early: chsd ldrs: 2nd over 3f out: styd on same pce last 100yds* **8/1**

41-5 **4** *nk* **Ginger Jack**[49] 1840 6-9-4 **86**.... PJMcDonald 11 93
(Geoffrey Harker) *chsd ldrs: kpt on same pce fnl 150yds* **9/1**

-252 **5** *1 ¾* **Lord Aeryn (IRE)**[11] 2958 6-9-7 **89**.... PaulHanagan 14 92
(Richard Fahey) *in rr: hdwy on wd outside over 2f out: styd on fnl f* **14/1**

50-1 **6** *1 ½* **Suits Me**[11] 2958 10-9-11 **93**.... GrahamGibbons 7 93
(David Barron) *drvn to sn ld: hdd jst ins fnl f: kpt on one pce* **14/1**

4-12 **7** *nse* **Westwiththenight (IRE)**[35] 2253 4-9-10 **92**.... RichardHughes 13 92
(William Haggas) *dwlt and wnt rt s: hld up in rr: effrt whn nt clr run and hmpd 2f out: kpt on: nvr nr to chal* **4/1**[1]

00-0 **8** *2 ½* **Swiftly Done (IRE)**[77] 1235 6-9-10 **92**.... DaleSwift 2 86
(Declan Carroll) *mid-div: hmpd over 4f out: one pce fnl 2f* **20/1**

2321 **9** *1 ¼* **Classic Colori (IRE)**[14] 2881 6-9-5 **87**....(v) DanielTudhope 9 78
(David O'Meara) *mid-div: effrt on outside over 2f out: wknd fnl f* **12/1**

3050 **10** *1* **Brae Hill (IRE)**[15] 2841 7-9-9 **96**.... GeorgeChaloner(5) 12 85
(Richard Fahey) *t.k.h in rr: effrt 3f out: wknd over 1f out* **16/1**

-060 **11** *9* **Mr Red Clubs (IRE)**[91] 1036 4-9-5 **87**....(v[1]) AdamKirby 5 56
(Tim Pitt) *drvn to chse ldrs: lost pl over 1f out: sn bhd* **20/1**

00 **12** *½* **Fluidity**[31] 2365 4-9-12 **94**.... PaulMulrennan 6 62
(Nigel Tinkler) *uns rdr and rn loose bef ss: trckd ldrs: t.k.h: drvn over 3f out: lost pl over 1f out* **50/1**

0-26 **13** *23* **Clayton**[31] 2365 4-9-11 **93**.... NeilCallan 10
(Kevin Ryan) *chsd ldrs: slipped on bnd and heavily eased over 4f out: bhd fnl 2f: t.o* **11/2**[2]

023 **14** *17* **Fort Belvedere**[10] 2976 5-9-8 **90**.... WilliamBuick 4
(Keith Dalgleish) *chsd ldrs: slipped bdly on bnd over 4f out: sn heavily eased and bhd: t.o fnl 2f* **9/1**

1m 50.76s (-1.24) **Going Correction** -0.075s/f (Good) **14** Ran SP% **121.4**
Speed ratings (Par 109): **102,100,99,99,98 96,96,94,93,92 84,83,63,48**
toteswingers 1&2 £43.70, 1&3 £10.60, 2&3 £40.70 CSF £155.58 CT £1275.45 TOTE £9.20: £2.90, £8.90, £2.30; EX 217.90 Trifecta £2944.30 Pool: £5,819.59 - 1.48 winning units..
Owner N Martin **Bred** Michael Cahan Thoroughbreds **Trained** Portway, Worcs

FOCUS
They appeared to go a fairly steady pace in this, but the closers still emerged on top. They raced centre-field down the straight. The winner confirmed that he is better than ever.

3347 IAN AND KATE HALL MACMILLAN GANTON STKS (LISTED RACE) 1m
3:15 (3:15) (Class 1) 3-Y-0+
£20,982 (£7,955; £3,981; £1,983; £995; £499) **Stalls** Low

Form RPR

-132 **1** **Baltic Knight (IRE)**[14] 2857 3-8-10 105.... RichardHughes 2 111
(Richard Hannon) *trckd ldrs: swtchd lft over 1f out: r.o to ld last 100yds: drvn out* **2/1**[1]

-601 **2** *1* **Quick Wit**[105] 873 6-9-7 109....(p) SilvestreDeSousa 6 112
(Saeed bin Suroor) *trckd ldr: led over 1f out: hdd and no ex last 100yds* **10/1**

-232 **3** *1 ½* **Stipulate**[21] 2652 4-9-7 109....(b[1]) TomQueally 5 109
(Lady Cecil) *hld up in tch: effrt 2f out: sn rdn: kpt on same pce* **9/2**[3]

66-2 **4** *1 ¼* **Sir Patrick Moore (FR)**[56] 1677 3-8-10 110.... RichardKingscote 4 103
(Harry Dunlop) *led: hdd over 1f out: kpt on same pce* **7/1**

24-0 **5** *¾* **Storm King**[29] 2424 4-9-7 87....(p) PatCosgrave 7 104
(Jane Chapple-Hyam) *in rr: drvn over 3f out: kpt on fnl f: nvr a factor* **50/1**

4-33 **6** *1 ½* **Ladys First**[15] 2838 4-9-2 105....[1] PaulHanagan 3 96
(Richard Fahey) *in rr: drvn and outpcd over 3f out: kpt on same pce fnl 2f* **7/2**[2]

54-3 **7** *2* **Questioning (IRE)**[17] 2782 5-9-7 110....(p) WilliamBuick 8 96
(John Gosden) *trckd ldrs: drvn and outpcd over 3f out: kpt on fnl f* **9/1**

-061 **8** *14* **Pintura**[21] 2667 6-9-7 106.... NeilCallan 1 75
(Kevin Ryan) *trckd ldrs: drvn and outpcd over 3f out: wknd fnl f* **16/1**

1m 37.48s (-1.52) **Going Correction** -0.075s/f (Good)
WFA 3 from 4yo+ 11lb **8** Ran SP% **113.2**
Speed ratings (Par 111): **104,103,101,100,99 98,96,82**
toteswingers 1&2 £5.30, 1&3 £2.40, 2&3 £5.70 CSF £22.92 TOTE £2.60: £1.10, £2.50, £1.70; EX 24.60 Trifecta £85.80 Pool: £4,494.69 - 39.27 winning units..
Owner Thurloe Thoroughbreds XXX **Bred** Henry O'Callaghan **Trained** East Everleigh, Wilts

FOCUS
Sand was put down on the bend into the straight before this race in order to sure-up footing, with two runners in the previous race having stumbled there. They appeared to go an even tempo, although it's likely the form is just fair for the grade judged around the second and third.

3348 MACMILLAN CHARITY SPRINT TROPHY (H'CAP) 6f
3:50 (3:50) (Class 2) (0-105,105) 3-Y-0
£62,250 (£18,640; £9,320; £4,660; £2,330; £1,170) **Stalls** Centre

Form RPR

31-5 **1** **Body And Soul (IRE)**[27] 2476 3-8-11 **95**.... DuranFentiman 14 107
(Tim Easterby) *trckd ldrs stands' side: r.o to ld last 50yds* **7/1**[1]

-011 **2** *nk* **Moviesta (USA)**[29] 2430 3-8-9 **93**.... PaulMulrennan 9 104
(Bryan Smart) *t.k.h: trckd ldrs: led appr fnl f: hdd and no ex wl ins fnl f* **8/1**[3]

10-3 **3** *½* **Barracuda Boy (IRE)**[50] 1808 3-8-6 **90**.... RichardKingscote 16 99+
(Tom Dascombe) *swtchd lft after 1f: mid-div: hdwy over 2f out: styd on wl ins fnl f: tk 3rd nr fin* **12/1**

2011 **4** *¾* **Heaven's Guest (IRE)**[15] 2844 3-8-9 **93**.... TonyHamilton 3 100
(Richard Fahey) *chsd ldrs on outer: styd on same pce last 100yds* **9/1**

-410 **5** *¾* **Rivellino**[28] 2452 3-8-7 **91**.... RobertWinston 18 96
(Mrs K Burke) *t.k.h in mid-div stands' side: hdwy over 2f out: kpt on fnl f* **15/2**[2]

3313 **6** *¾* **Hasopop (IRE)**[15] 2843 3-9-7 **105**.... AdamKirby 6 107+
(Marco Botti) *dwlt: hmpd after 100yds: in rr: hdwy far side 2f out: styd on fnl f* **8/1**[3]

-010 **7** *1 ¼* **Storm Moon (USA)**[36] 2213 3-8-6 **90**.... SilvestreDeSousa 13 88
(Mark Johnston) *led: hdd appr fnl f: wknd last 75yds* **33/1**

25-0 **8** *1* **Odooj (IRE)**[28] 2453 3-9-1 **99**....(b[1]) PaulHanagan 1 94
(William Haggas) *hld up in mid-div: hdwy on outer over 2f out: kpt on same pce appr fnl f* **12/1**

3224 **9** *¾* **Lucky Beggar (IRE)**[7] 3103 3-9-2 **100**.... WilliamBuick 12 93
(Charles Hills) *in rr: effrt over 2f out: kpt on fnl f* **16/1**

30-0 **10** *hd* **Ahern**[45] 1921 3-9-4 **102**....(b[1]) HarryBentley 7 94
(David Barron) *hld up in rr: hmpd after 100yds: t.k.h: hdwy 2f out: swtchd lft ins fnl f: kpt on* **33/1**

-064 **11** *½* **Hairy Rocket**[12] 2928 3-8-6 **90**.... JimmyQuinn 4 80
(William Haggas) *w ldrs on outer: wknd appr fnl f* **25/1**

15-3 **12** *1 ¾* **Cosmic Chatter**[30] 2400 3-9-2 **100**.... GrahamGibbons 2 85
(David Barron) *chsd ldrs on outer: fdd fnl f* **10/1**

5-03 **13** *hd* **Chilworth Icon**[28] 2452 3-9-3 **101**.... RichardHughes 5 85
(Mick Channon) *hmpd after 100yds: mid-div: effrt over 2f out: fdd fnl f* **16/1**

16-2 **14** *½* **Vincentti (IRE)**[29] 2430 3-8-7 **91**.... SteveDrowne 19 74
(Ronald Harris) *mid-div stands' side: drvn over 2f out: nvr a factor* **16/1**

0-21 **15** *shd* **Lewisham**[39] 2123 3-8-8 **92**.... NeilCallan 15 74
(Ralph Beckett) *mid-div: drvn over 2f out: nvr a factor* **20/1**

-114 **16** *2 ½* **Polski Max**[30] 2400 3-8-13 **102**............................ GeorgeChaloner(5) 10 76
(Richard Fahey) *mid-div: drvn and stmbld over 2f out: sn lost pl* **16/1**

5-35 **17** *nk* **Mary's Daughter**[30] 2400 3-8-8 **92**............................ BarryMcHugh 20 65
(Richard Fahey) *a towards rr stands' side* **33/1**

20-0 **18** *3 ¾* **No Jet Lag (USA)**[57] 1668 3-9-0 **98**............................[1] TedDurcan 17 59
(David Lanigan) *s.s: a bhd* **25/1**

-000 **19** *10* **Heavy Metal**[7] 3114 3-9-4 **102**............................(b) J-PGuillambert 11 31
(Mark Johnston) *sn bhd: eased ins fnl f* **33/1**

1m 9.84s (-2.06) **Going Correction** -0.075s/f (Good) **19** Ran SP% **128.7**
Speed ratings (Par 105): **110,109,108,107,106 105,104,102,101,101 101,98,98,97,97 94,93,88,75**
toteswingers 1&2 £9.20, 1&3 £19.30, 2&3 £21.30 CSF £57.83 CT £685.96 TOTE £7.00: £2.20, £2.30, £3.50, £2.40; EX 63.90 Trifecta £1128.90 Pool: £72,541.72 - 48.19 winning units..
Owner C H Stevens **Bred** Michael Downey & Roalso Ltd **Trained** Great Habton, N Yorks

FOCUS
Traditionally a hot 3yo sprint, it again looked wide-open, and the main action unfolded up the middle-to-stands' side. The time was very respectable and the form looks strong, although not many got involved.

3349 ICE CO SUPPORTING MACMILLAN STKS (H'CAP) 1m 208y
4:20 (4:23) (Class 4) (0-80,82) 4-Y-0+ **£7,762** (£2,310; £1,154; £577) **Stalls** Low

Form RPR

2-41 **1** **Christmas Light**[7] 3083 6-9-2 **75**............................ HarryBentley 4 86
(Brian Ellison) *s.i.s: hdwy over 3f out: edgd rt and hmpd 2f out: led over 1f out: kpt on wl* **8/1**[3]

0-02 **2** *1 ½* **Robert The Painter (IRE)**[7] 3087 5-9-0 **73**............................(v) DanielTudhope 2 80
(David O'Meara) *trckd ldrs: styd on same pce last 100yds* **11/1**

0225 **3** *shd* **Pravda Street**[21] 2673 8-8-4 **70**............................ KevinStott(7) 1 77
(Brian Ellison) *hld up in rr: gd hdwy on outer over 2f out: chsng ldrs jst ins fnl f: styd on same pce last 100yds* **25/1**

0003 **4** *1 ¼* **Kalk Bay (IRE)**[14] 2882 6-9-7 **80**............................(t) GrahamGibbons 7 84
(Michael Easterby) *mid-div: hdwy to trck ldrs whn edgd lft over 2f out: keeping on same pce whn intimidated nr fin* **5/1**[2]

00-0 **5** *hd* **Barren Brook**[61] 1576 6-9-6 **79**............................[1] TedDurcan 5 84
(Michael Easterby) *s.s: hdwy into mid-div 6f out: chsng ldrs over 2f out: hung lft and eased fnl strides* **8/1**[3]

0036 **6** *1 ½* **Assizes**[7] 3113 4-9-6 **79**............................ J-PGuillambert 20 81
(Mark Johnston) *in rr: hdwy 3f out: chsng ldrs whn n.m.r jst ins fnl f: kpt on same pce* **28/1**

-023 **7** *2 ¾* **Merchant Of Medici**[21] 2673 6-8-11 **70**............................ WilliamBuick 11 64
(Micky Hammond) *swtchd rt after s: in rr: hdwy over 2f out: kpt on: nvr trbld ldrs* **14/1**

1163 **8** *nk* **Goldstorm**[26] 2498 5-9-3 **76**............................(p) JimmyQuinn 18 70
(Brian Baugh) *mid-div: hdwy over 3f out: one pce fnl 2f* **25/1**

425- **9** *1 ½* **Daddy Warbucks (IRE)**[246] 7032 4-9-2 **75**............................ BarryMcHugh 6 66
(David Nicholls) *led: styd alone far side and clr over 3f out: edgd rt 2f out: sn hdd & wknd* **14/1**

1561 **10** *¾* **Lord Of The Dance (IRE)**[3] 3207 7-9-6 **82** 6ex............ RyanClark(3) 8 79
(Michael Mullineaux) *mid-div: hdwy 3f out: styng on whn hmpd wl over 1f out: wknd fnl f* **20/1**

3014 **11** *½* **Prime Exhibit**[21] 2659 8-9-3 **76**............................(t) AdamKirby 15 64
(Daniel Mark Loughnane) *in rr: kpt on fnl 2f: nvr a factor* **20/1**

2400 **12** *shd* **Knowe Head (NZ)**[21] 2646 6-9-0 **73**............................(v) SteveDrowne 14 61
(James Unett) *in rr: nvr a factor* **50/1**

206- **13** *1 ¼* **Central**[304] 5224 5-9-0 **76**............................ PaulPickard(3) 13 61
(Mel Brittain) *in rr whn hmpd and stmbld after 100yds: kpt on fnl 2f: nvr on terms* **40/1**

11-4 **14** *1 ¼* **Forget Me Not Lane (IRE)**[19] 2706 4-9-6 **79**............................ NeilCallan 3 61
(Kevin Ryan) *chsd ldrs: lost pl over 2f out* **9/2**[1]

6-34 **15** *9* **I'm Super Too (IRE)**[25] 2539 6-9-0 **73**............................ RobertWinston 10 35
(Alan Swinbank) *chsd ldrs: lost pl over 2f out* **33/1**

0642 **16** *2 ¾* **Act Your Shoe Size**[12] 2915 4-9-7 **80**............................ RichardHughes 17 36
(Keith Dalgleish) *mid-div: effrt over 2f out: sn wknd: bhd whn eased clsng stages* **12/1**

0444 **17** *3 ¾* **Dakota Canyon (IRE)**[18] 2753 4-8-11 **70**............................(v) TonyHamilton 19 18
(Richard Fahey) *in rr: effrt on outside over 2f out: sn btn: eased clsng stages* **25/1**

014- **18** *15* **My Mate Jake (IRE)**[15] 7529 5-9-4 **77**............................(b) DaleSwift 12
(James Given) *chsd ldrs: drvn 6f out: lost pl over 3f out: bhd whn eased fnl f* **25/1**

-024 **19** *53* **Sunnybridge Boy (IRE)**[21] 2673 4-9-0 **73**............(v) MichaelO'Connell 16
(Mrs K Burke) *chsd ldrs: lost pl over 3f out: sn bhd: t.o whn virtually p.u over 1f out: eventually completed: b.b.v* **20/1**

1m 50.01s (-1.99) **Going Correction** -0.075s/f (Good) **19** Ran SP% **126.9**
Speed ratings (Par 105): **105,103,103,102,102 100,98,98,96,96 95,95,94,93,85 83,79,66,19**
toteswingers 1&2 £15.30, 1&3 £57.60, 2&3 £55.20 CSF £79.85 CT £1310.58 TOTE £8.40: £2.40, £2.90, £6.70, £1.90; EX 115.60 Trifecta £3613.50 Part won. Pool: £4,818.03 - 0.77 winning units..
Owner Mrs Lynne Lumley **Bred** Rabbah Bloodstock Limited **Trained** Norton, N Yorks
■ Stewards' Enquiry : Barry McHugh three-day ban; careless riding (29th June - 1st July).
William Buick three-day ban; careless riding (29th June - 1st July).

FOCUS
They didn't appeared to go overly fast in this, but they got racing early in the straight and the winner came from well back. The overall time was quicker than the earlier 0-105 and the winner took her form to a new high.

3350 REG GRIFFIN APPRECIATION EBF MAIDEN STKS 6f
4:50 (4:54) (Class 3) 2-Y-0 **£7,439** (£2,213; £1,106; £553) **Stalls** Centre

Form RPR

1 **Rufford (IRE)** 2-9-5 0............................ TonyHamilton 8 83+
(Richard Fahey) *trckd ldrs travelling strly: led appr fnl f: shkn up and styd on towards fin* **7/1**[3]

2 *¾* **Bahamian C** 2-9-5 0............................ PatrickMathers 2 81
(Richard Fahey) *dwlt: hdwy on outer to chse ldrs over 4f out: led over 2f out: hdd 1f out: kpt on wl* **33/1**

3 **3** *½* **Edge (IRE)**[7] 3092 2-9-5 0............................ RichardHughes 15 79
(Richard Hannon) *mid-div: outpcd and lost pl over 3f out: hdwy 2f out: chsng ldng pair 1f out: kpt on same pce* **6/4**[1]

5 **4** *4* **Wickhambrook (IRE)**[56] 1680 2-9-5 0............................ WilliamBuick 11 67
(Saeed bin Suroor) *trckd ldrs: effrt over 2f out: one pce appr fnl f* **4/1**[2]

5 *2* **Instant Attraction (IRE)** 2-9-5 0............................ NeilCallan 12 61
(Kevin Ryan) *chsd ldrs: wknd fnl f* **12/1**

2 **6** *1* **Bajan Rebel**[39] 2117 2-9-0 0............................ GrahamGibbons 10 53
(Michael Easterby) *narrow ld: hdd over 4f out: fdd over 1f out* **20/1**

7 *nk* **Right Of Appeal** 2-9-5 0............................ PJMcDonald 7 57
(Mark Johnston) *chsd ldrs: wknd appr fnl f* **20/1**

8 *½* **Greed Is Good** 2-9-5 0............................ MichaelO'Connell 9 56
(Mrs K Burke) *dwlt: hdwy over 2f out: sn chsng ldrs: wknd jst ins fnl f* **16/1**

0 **9** *1 ¾* **Petergate**[14] 2883 2-9-5 0............................ DaleSwift 3 51
(Brian Rothwell) *outpcd and in rr: kpt on over 1f out: nvr a factor* **80/1**

10 *½* **Danzig In The Dark (IRE)** 2-9-0 0............................ DuranFentiman 1 44
(Tim Easterby) *mid-div: effrt over 2f out: wknd over 1f out* **33/1**

2 **11** *2 ¾* **In Focus (IRE)**[19] 2701 2-9-5 0............................ RobertWinston 6 41
(Alan Swinbank) *chsd ldrs: drvn over 2f out: hung lft and wknd over 1f out* **12/1**

00 **12** *2 ½* **Scarborough (IRE)**[19] 2701 2-9-0 0............................ JimmyQuinn 14 28
(Paul Midgley) *mid-div: effrt over 2f out: wknd over 1f out* **66/1**

45 **13** *4* **Uncle Bobby**[14] 2883 2-9-5 0............................ TedDurcan 5 21
(Michael Easterby) *dwlt: a in rr: hung lft and bhd fnl 2f* **28/1**

14 *2 ¾* **My Boy Bob** 2-9-5 0............................ BarryMcHugh 13 13
(Richard Fahey) *in rr: hung lft over 2f out: sn bhd* **10/1**

15 *4* **How Rude** 2-9-0 0............................ PaulMulrennan 4
(Mel Brittain) *s.i.s: bhd fnl 2f* **28/1**

1m 11.49s (-0.41) **Going Correction** -0.075s/f (Good) **15** Ran SP% **127.9**
Speed ratings (Par 97): **99,98,97,92,89 88,87,86,84,83 80,76,71,67,62**
toteswingers 1&2 £79.40, 1&3 £4.40, 2&3 £27.10 CSF £234.09 TOTE £8.60: £3.00, £14.50, £1.20; EX 317.90 Trifecta £988.90 Pool: £3,714.38 - 2.81 winning units..
Owner David W Armstrong **Bred** Old Carhue Stud **Trained** Musley Bank, N Yorks

FOCUS
The front three pulled clear in this decent maiden and the form is sound.

3351 CHARLES HENRY MEMORIAL STKS (H'CAP) 6f
5:20 (5:22) (Class 4) (0-80,80) 3-Y-0+ **£7,115** (£2,117; £1,058; £529) **Stalls** Centre

Form RPR

0226 **1** **Noverre To Go (IRE)**[7] 3093 7-9-6 **77**............................(p) SteveDrowne 18 85
(Ronald Harris) *mid-div stands' side: hdwy over 1f out: str run ins fnl f: led last strides* **16/1**

0-00 **2** *nk* **Sir Pedro**[19] 2724 4-9-6 **77**............................[1] TonyHamilton 15 84
(Charles Hills) *rrd s: in rr: hdwy over 1f out: styd on wl ins fnl f: tk 2nd post* **20/1**

-531 **3** *nse* **Mon Brav**[21] 2657 6-9-9 **80**............................ MichaelO'Connell 7 87
(Brian Ellison) *mid-div: drvn over 2f out: styd on wl ins fnl f: tk 3rd post* **10/1**[2]

0015 **4** *hd* **Bonnie Charlie**[10] 2988 7-9-6 **77**............................ PaulQuinn 10 83+
(David Nicholls) *hld up: hdwy over 2f out: chsng ldrs whn n.m.r ins fnl f: stuck on to take 4th post* **10/1**[2]

5460 **5** *shd* **Defence Council (IRE)**[21] 2663 5-9-6 **77**............................ DaleSwift 12 83
(Mel Brittain) *s.i.s: sn chsng ldrs: led last 50yds: hdd nr fin* **33/1**

0403 **6** *¾* **Al Khan (IRE)**[7] 3096 4-9-9 **80**............................ RobertWinston 2 84
(Violet M Jordan) *chsd ldrs on outside: edgd rt over 1f out: kpt on same pce last 50yds* **16/1**

0625 **7** *hd* **Waking Warrior**[21] 2664 5-8-12 **76**............................(tp) KevinStott(7) 5 79
(Kevin Ryan) *chsd ldrs: narrow ld over 1f out: hdd last 50yds: no ex* **20/1**

-050 **8** *nse* **Pea Shooter**[21] 2664 4-9-6 **77**............................(p) NeilCallan 16 80
(Kevin Ryan) *mid-div: hdwy over 1f out: kpt on wl last 50yds* **10/1**[2]

2400 **9** *hd* **Showboating (IRE)**[8] 3060 5-9-4 **75**............................(tp) HarryBentley 20 77
(Alan McCabe) *in rr stands' side: hdwy over 1f out: styd on ins fnl f* **11/1**[3]

-040 **10** *1 ½* **Barney McGrew (IRE)**[12] 2914 10-9-7 **78**............................ PaulMulrennan 9 75
(Michael Dods) *dwlt: hld up in rr: hdwy over 1f out: kpt on: nvr a threat* **20/1**

0060 **11** *hd* **Dark Castle**[15] 2834 4-9-3 **74**............................ WilliamBuick 14 78+
(Micky Hammond) *in rr: hdwy and edgd lft over 1f out: styng on whn nt clr run and eased nr fin* **20/1**

-155 **12** *¾* **Johnny Cavagin**[28] 2441 4-9-9 **80**............................(t) PatrickMathers 3 74
(Richard Guest) *mid-div: hdwy on outside over 1f out: kpt on same pce last 100yds* **16/1**

5-43 **13** *1* **Cocktail Charlie**[18] 2755 5-9-3 **74**............................(p) DuranFentiman 17 65
(Tim Easterby) *trckd ldrs: wknd jst ins fnl f* **12/1**

-000 **14** *nk* **Caranbola**[21] 2664 7-9-6 **77**............................ JimmyQuinn 1 67
(Mel Brittain) *w ldrs: led wl over 1f out: sn hdd: wknd last 50yds* **40/1**

1125 **15** *2 ½* **Polar Venture**[21] 2663 4-9-4 **75**............................ RichardHughes 11 57
(William Haggas) *chsd ldrs: wknd last 150yds* **2/1**[1]

0-40 **16** *4* **Master Rooney (IRE)**[22] 2614 7-9-7 **78**............................(p) PJMcDonald 4 47
(Geoffrey Harker) *led: hdd wl over 1f out: sn wknd* **40/1**

0-00 **17** *¾* **Medici Time**[26] 2505 8-9-8 **79**............................(v) TedDurcan 8 46
(Tim Easterby) *hld up in mid-div: effrt over 2f out: rdn and wknd over 1f out* **25/1**

-315 **18** *6* **Azzurra Du Caprio (IRE)**[19] 2711 5-9-9 **80**............................(b[1]) AdamKirby 13 28
(Ben Haslam) *w ldrs stands' side: lost pl over 1f out: sn bhd* **20/1**

1m 11.11s (-0.79) **Going Correction** -0.075s/f (Good) **18** Ran SP% **129.8**
Speed ratings (Par 105): **102,101,101,101,101 100,99,99,99,97 97,96,94,94,91 85,84,76**
toteswingers 1&2 £114.60, 1&3 £17.90, 2&3 £68.20 CSF £314.63 CT £3468.18 TOTE £23.40: £4.10, £7.20, £2.70, £2.80; EX 542.00 Trifecta £1657.90 Part won. Pool: £2,210.61 - 0.16 winning units..
Owner Robert & Nina Bailey **Bred** Gestut Gorlsdorf **Trained** Earlswood, Monmouths

FOCUS
The runners were spread across the track in this competitive sprint, in which any number held their chance in the final furlong. Those who raced nearer the stands' side came through late on, with those towards the far side appearing to tire. The time was relatively ordinary and the winner is rated only to this year's form.
T/Jkpt: Not won. T/Plt: £223.30 to a £1 stake. Pool: £208,673.55 - 681.92 winning units T/Qpdt: £10.00 to a £1 stake. Pool: £11,274.30 - 833.80 winning units WG

3352 - 3359a (Foreign Racing) - See Raceform Interactive

3126

BELMONT PARK (L-H)
Saturday, June 15

OFFICIAL GOING: Turf: good; dirt: fast

3360a HILL PRINCE STKS (GRADE 3) (3YO) (TURF) 1m (T)
9:45 (12:00) 3-Y-0
£55,214 (£18,404; £9,202; £4,601; £2,760; £263)

RPR

1 **Notacatbutallama (USA)**[28] 3-8-6 0............................ JRVelazquez 12 99
(Todd Pletcher, U.S.A) **49/10**[3]

2 *nk* **Play It Loud (USA)** 3-8-4 0............................ CVelasquez 3 96
(Michelle Nihei, U.S.A) **37/1**

3 *1 ½* **Chamois (USA)** 3-8-4 0............................ JAlvarado 5 93
(Christophe Clement, U.S.A) **123/10**

4 1 **Red Rifle (USA)** 3-8-4 0 .... JJCastellano 9 91
(Todd Pletcher, U.S.A) **49/20**[1]
5 ¾ **Sayaad (USA)**[310] 3-8-4 0 .... JLEspinoza 1 89
(Kiaran McLaughlin, U.S.A) **132/10**
6 ¾ **Infinite Magic (USA)**[35] 3-8-4 0 .... EPrado 2 87
(Richard C Mettee, U.S.A) **47/10**[2]
7 ½ **Shining Copper (USA)**[28] 3-8-5 0 ow1 .... (b) ASolis 11 87
(Oussama Aboughazale, U.S.A) **107/10**
8 hd **Michael With Us (USA)**[70] 3-8-4 0 .... GSaez 7 86
(Stephen DiMauro, U.S.A) **44/5**
9 3 ¾ **Special Skills (USA)**[250] 3-8-4 0 .... RMaragh 4 77
(Alan E Goldberg, U.S.A) **35/1**
10 nk **Joha (USA)**[203] 3-8-4 0 .... LSaez 6 76
(Thomas Albertrani, U.S.A) **115/10**
11 5 ¼ **Bernie The Jet (USA)**[289] 3-8-4 0 .... JLOrtiz 10 64
(Gary Contessa, U.S.A) **37/1**
12 15 ½ **Red Rocker (IRE)**[59] 1618 3-8-6 0 ow2 .... (b[1]) DCohen 8 30
(Brian Meehan) **132/10**

1m 34.82s (0.22) **12** Ran SP% **119.9**
PARI-MUTUEL (all including $2 stakes): WIN 11.80; PLACE (1-2) 6.50, 30.40; SHOW (1-2-3) 4.20, 17.20, 6.30; SF 451.00.
Owner Repole Stable **Bred** Happy Hill Farm **Trained** USA

3361a STARTER OPTIONAL CLAIMING RACE (CLAIMER) (3YO+) (TURF) 1m 110y

10:17 (12:00) 3-Y-O+

£20,613 (£6,871; £3,435; £1,717; £1,030; £343)

RPR
1 **Money In Motion (USA)**[22] 4-8-10 0 .... IOrtizJr 9 86
(Philip M Serpe, U.S.A) **23/5**[3]
2 hd **North Star Boy (IRE)**[26] 2516 4-8-10 0 .... XPerez 5 86
(Amy Weaver) **106/10**
3 1 ½ **Street Fight (CAN)**[314] 4-8-10 0 .... JAlvarado 3 83
(Gary Contessa, U.S.A) **27/10**[2]
4 ½ **Situational Ethics (USA)** 4-8-10 0 .... (b) ASolis 8 82
(Mark Hennig, U.S.A) **47/20**[1]
5 ½ **Bold Forest (USA)** 4-8-10 0 .... JLEspinoza 7 81
(Patrick J Quick, U.S.A) **13/2**
6 hd **Shotinthefog (USA)** 4-8-10 0 .... (b) LSaez 2 80
(Danny Gargan, U.S.A) **48/10**
7 8 ½ **Wild Perfection (USA)** 3-8-5 0 .... JJCastellano 11 66
(Jena M Antonucci, U.S.A) **147/10**

1m 44.82s (104.82)
WFA 3 from 4yo+ 11lb **7** Ran SP% **120.3**
PARI-MUTUEL (all including $2 stakes): WIN 11.20; PLACE (1-2) 6.00, 11.20; SHOW (1-2-3) 3.20, 5.50, 3.20; SF 69.50.
Owner Brian & Kerry Novak **Bred** Jeanne H Cutrona & Jerry M Cutrona Sr **Trained** North America

LYON PARILLY (R-H)

Saturday, June 15

OFFICIAL GOING: Turf: good

3362a GRAND PRIX DE LYON (5EME ETAPE DU DEFI DU GALOP) (LISTED RACE) 1m 4f

5:45 (5:45) 4-Y-O+ **£24,390** (£9,756; £7,317; £4,878; £2,439)

RPR
1 **Zack Hall (FR)**[21] 2683 6-8-11 .... Francois-XavierBertras 3 107
(F Rohaut, France) **27/10**[1]
2 1 **Quidamo**[16] 2822 6-9-2 .... MircoDemuro 6 110
(Frau J Mayer, Germany) **12/1**
3 nk **Temple Bar (FR)**[36] 2249 4-8-11 .... FranckBlondel 2 105
(F Rossi, France) **5/1**[3]
4 1 ¼ **Griraz (FR)**[36] 2249 8-9-2 .... MaximeGuyon 8 108
(P Sogorb, France) **9/2**[2]
5 nk **Pump Pump Boy (FR)**[42] 5-8-11 .... Pierre-CharlesBoudot 5 102
(M Pimbonnet, France) **11/1**
6 1 **Last Born (FR)**[20] 2695 4-8-8 .... FlavienPrat 7 97
(A Fabre, France) **68/10**
7 nk **Propulsion (IRE)**[72] 1359 4-8-11 .... OlivierPeslier 9 100
(F Head, France) **78/10**
8 2 ½ **Silver Valny (FR)**[48] 1871 7-9-2 .... ThomasMessina 10 101
(Mlle M-L Mortier, France) **17/2**
9 10 **Kindergarden Kid (USA)**[182] 6-9-6 .... FredericSpanu 1 89
(M Nigge, France) **19/1**

2m 37.09s (3.58) **9** Ran SP% **117.6**
WIN (incl. 1 euro stake): 3.70. PLACES: 1.40, 2.80, 1.90. DF: 25.50. SF: 31.30.
Owner Mathieu Offenstadt **Bred** Kilboy Estate Inc **Trained** Sauvagnon, France

2855 DONCASTER (L-H)

Sunday, June 16

OFFICIAL GOING: Good to firm (9.3)
Wind: light 1/2 behind Weather: fine

3363 FSB HEALTH & WELLBEING APPRENTICE H'CAP 1m 6f 132y

2:30 (2:30) (Class 5) (0-70,70) 4-Y-O+ **£2,911** (£866; £432; £216) **Stalls** Low

Form RPR
-065 1 **Petella**[11] 2990 7-8-6 **55** .... (p) ConnorBeasley[(5)] 2 63
(George Moore) *in rr: hdwy 4f out: 4th over 2f out: led over 1f out: drvn out* **11/2**
20-0 2 1 **Bounty Seeker (USA)**[19] 2739 4-9-9 **70** .... RobertTart[(3)] 9 77
(Mark Johnston) *chsd ldrs: drvn and lost pl 10f out: rallied 2f out: 3rd 1f out: styd on to take 2nd nr fin* **12/1**
0222 3 ¾ **Kodicil (IRE)**[11] 2990 5-9-4 **65** .... JasonHart[(3)] 5 71
(Tim Walford) *led: drvn 3f out: hdd over 1f out: kpt on same pce* **7/4**[1]
4622 4 3 ½ **Zaplamation (IRE)**[8] 3089 8-9-9 **70** .... WilliamTwiston-Davies[(3)] 4 71
(John Quinn) *hld up: trckd ldrs 9f out: wnt 2nd over 5f out: wknd over 1f out* **11/4**[2]
/6-0 5 ½ **Heart Of Dubai (USA)**[40] 2120 8-8-0 **51** oh3 .... (p) KevinStott[(7)] 8 52
(Micky Hammond) *hld up in rr: hdwy to trck ldrs 8f out: 3rd over 4f out: wknd over 1f out* **14/1**
4-04 6 16 **Ferney Boy**[20] 2720 7-8-7 **51** oh6 .... DeclanCannon 7 31
(Chris Fairhurst) *chsd ldrs: rdn 3f out: sn lost pl and bhd* **33/1**
62-6 7 15 **My Destination (IRE)**[15] 2860 4-9-7 **65** .... NeilFarley 1 25
(Declan Carroll) *s.i.s: drvn to sn r upsides: drvn over 5f out: lost pl over 3f out: sn bhd: t.o* **5/1**[3]

3m 8.69s (1.29) **Going Correction** -0.225s/f (Firm) **7** Ran SP% **112.4**
Speed ratings (Par 103): **87,86,86,84,83 75,67**
Tote Swingers: 1&2 £8.60, 1&3 £2.70, 2&3 £5.60 CSF £63.19 CT £159.31 TOTE £7.10: £3.00, £5.10; EX 89.40 Trifecta £406.30 £2,051.39 - 3.78 winning units..
Owner A Crute & Partners **Bred** C And Mrs Wilson **Trained** Middleham Moor, N Yorks

FOCUS
Rail on Round course moved out 3yds from 1m2f to where it joins Straight course to provide fresh ground. The pace looked ordinary for this modest staying apprentice handicap, but the first two home held the last two positions turning in.

3364 FSB PENSION SCHEME FOR MEMBERS MAIDEN STKS 1m 4f

3:00 (3:01) (Class 4) 3-Y-O+ **£5,175** (£1,540; £769; £384) **Stalls** Low

Form RPR
0 1 **Retirement Plan**[29] 2442 3-8-13 0 .... RyanMoore 6 96+
(Lady Cecil) *led 1f: chsd ldr: led over 2f out: drvn and styd on wl* **11/2**[2]
6-33 2 2 **Shwaiman (IRE)**[38] 2198 3-8-13 83 .... FrederikTylicki 4 92
(James Fanshawe) *chsd ldrs: drvn over 5f out: chsd wnr over 1f out: no imp* **4/5**[1]
42- 3 4 **Spiritoftomintoul**[291] 5753 4-9-13 0 .... PatCosgrave 2 86
(Lady Cecil) *dwlt: sn chsng ldrs: n.m.r 2f out: kpt on one pce* **12/1**
4 4 1 ¾ **Parker Ridge (FR)**[25] 2560 3-8-13 0 .... KierenFallon 5 83+
(Luca Cumani) *upset in stalls: shkn up 9f out: sn chsng ldrs: rdn and outpcd 3f out: kpt on to take 4th ins fnl f* **6/1**[3]
6 5 3 ¾ **Hunting Ground (USA)**[12] 2953 3-8-13 0 .... HarryBentley 7 77
(Saeed bin Suroor) *trckd ldrs: effrt 3f out: wknd over 1f out* **10/1**
03 6 10 **Bossa Nova Baby (IRE)**[30] 2423 3-8-8 0 .... JamieSpencer 3 56
(Charles Hills) *led after 1f: hdd over 2f out: wkng whn hmpd over 1f out* **11/1**
7 4 ½ **Flaming Arrow (IRE)**[31] 5-9-10 0 .... BrianToomey[(3)] 11 54
(Kevin Ryan) *s.i.s: in rr: sme hdwy on inner over 3f out: sn lost pl* **33/1**
6 8 1 ½ **Yourholidayisover (IRE)**[11] 2971 6-9-10 0 .... NeilFarley[(3)] 9 51
(Patrick Holmes) *hld up in rr: hdwy 7f out: hung rt and lost pl over 2f out* **66/1**
9 5 **Snow Train** 3-8-8 0 .... JamesSullivan 1 38
(James Given) *dwlt: in rr: lost pl over 2f out: sn bhd* **50/1**

2m 31.44s (-3.46) **Going Correction** -0.225s/f (Firm)
WFA 3 from 4yo+ 14lb **9** Ran SP% **116.7**
Speed ratings (Par 105): **102,100,98,96,94 87,84,83,80**
Tote Swingers: 1&2 £2.60, 1&3 £6.30, 2&3 £2.80 CSF £10.32 TOTE £5.80: £1.90, £1.10, £2.70; EX 13.40 Trifecta £80.30 £2,557.95 - 23.86 winning units..
Owner K Abdullah **Bred** Juddmonte Farms Ltd **Trained** Newmarket, Suffolk

FOCUS
Some interesting types lined up for this middle-distance maiden.

3365 FSB 24/7 LEGAL ADVICE LINE CLASSIFIED STKS (THE SUNDAY £5K BONUS RACE) 1m 2f 60y

3:35 (3:36) (Class 5) 3-Y-O **£2,911** (£866; £432; £216) **Stalls** Low

Form RPR
6-30 1 **Typhon (USA)**[46] 1923 3-9-0 68 .... TedDurcan 7 76
(David Lanigan) *hld up in rr: hdwy on outside 2f out: styd on to ld nr fin* **20/1**
-054 2 nk **Invincible Cara (IRE)**[20] 2727 3-9-0 70 .... GrahamLee 6 75
(Ed Dunlop) *hld up in rr: effrt 2f out: r.o to ld last 100yds: no ex and hdd nr fin* **11/2**[3]
-323 3 2 **Knight Owl**[18] 2770 3-9-0 69 .... KierenFallon 2 72
(James Fanshawe) *trckd ldrs: led over 1f out: hdd ins fnl f: styd on same pce* **5/4**[1]
0-01 4 2 ¼ **Rutherglen**[19] 2743 3-9-0 70 .... PatCosgrave 3 67
(George Baker) *trckd ldrs: upsides over 3f out: led over 2f out: hdd over 1f out: one pce* **9/2**[2]
1060 5 hd **Woodstock (IRE)**[13] 2935 3-9-0 69 .... RyanMoore 4 67
(Richard Hannon) *mid-div: effrt 4f out: rdn to chse ldrs over 2f out: one pce* **7/1**
-044 6 6 **Medici Dancer**[18] 2770 3-8-9 68 .... DarylByrne[(5)] 5 56
(Tim Easterby) *hld up in mid-div: hdwy 4f out: lost pl over 1f out* **14/1**
5146 7 ¾ **Ofcoursewecan (USA)**[17] 2786 3-9-0 70 .... JoeFanning 1 54
(Mark Johnston) *led: drvn over 4f out: hdd over 2f out: lost pl over 1f out* **14/1**

2m 13.33s (3.93) **Going Correction** -0.225s/f (Firm) **7** Ran SP% **108.6**
Speed ratings (Par 99): **75,74,73,71,71 66,65**
Tote Swingers: 1&2 £19.60, 1&3 £5.50, 2&3 £2.20 CSF £111.73 TOTE £24.90: £9.90, £2.50; EX 93.20 Trifecta £330.60 £2,283.10 - 5.17 winning units..
Owner Niarchos Family **Bred** Flaxman Holdings Limited **Trained** Upper Lambourn, Berks

FOCUS
A tight classified event with a few of these stepping up to this trip for the first time. The pace looked ordinary and, as in the opener, the first two came from last and last-but-one.

3366 FSB INSURANCE SERVICE EBF MEDIAN AUCTION MAIDEN STKS 6f

4:10 (4:10) (Class 5) 2-Y-O **£3,234** (£962; £481; £240) **Stalls** High

Form RPR
33 1 **Fair Ranger**[9] 3044 2-9-5 0 .... RyanMoore 6 83
(Richard Hannon) *chsd ldrs: drvn over 3f out: 3rd over 2f out: styd on to ld last 50yds* **5/4**[1]
535 2 nk **Azagal (IRE)**[22] 2645 2-9-0 0 .... DuranFentiman 4 77
(Tim Easterby) *led: 2 l clr stands' side rail over 1f out: hdd and no ex clsng stages* **14/1**
3 1 ¼ **Mitchelton (FR)** 2-9-0 0 .... JoeFanning 5 73+
(Mark Johnston) *mid-div: hdwy to chse ldrs on outer over 3f out: 2nd over 2f out: styd on same pce last 50yds* **16/1**
4 4 ½ **Red Tide (IRE)** 2-9-5 0 .... MartinDwyer 7 64+
(Alan McCabe) *mid-div: outpcd over 2f out: kpt on fnl f* **20/1**
5 3 **Regiment** 2-9-5 0 .... TonyHamilton 2 54
(Richard Fahey) *w ldrs: t.k.h: wknd over 1f out* **5/2**[2]
3 6 ½ **Darling Boyz**[15] 2883 2-9-5 0 .... MichaelO'Connell 3 52
(John Quinn) *chsd ldrs: drvn 3f out: wknd 2f out* **9/1**[3]
7 1 **Rockwood** 2-9-5 0 .... GrahamLee 1 49
(Jane Chapple-Hyam) *dwlt: in rr: drvn over 2f out: kpt on fnl f* **25/1**

8 1 1/4 **Barbary (IRE)** 2-9-5 0 FrederikTylicki 9 45
(James Fanshawe) *mid-div: outpcd and lost pl over 3f out* **16/1**
9 2 1/2 **Seven Lucky Seven** 2-9-5 0 ShaneKelly 10 37
(Gary Harrison) *dwlt: in rr: bhd whn edgd lft over 1f out* **12/1**
10 10 **Biscuiteer** 2-9-0 0 PaulMulrennan 8
(Scott Dixon) *s.i.s: sn chsng ldrs: lost pl over 2f out: sn bhd* **33/1**

1m 12.29s (-1.31) **Going Correction** -0.225s/f (Firm) **10** Ran SP% **120.7**
Speed ratings (Par 93): **99,98,96,90,86 86,84,83,79,66**
Tote Swingers: 1&2 £5.10, 1&3 £7.20, 2&3 £8.40 CSF £22.13 TOTE £2.20: £1.10, £3.80, £4.30; EX 16.00 Trifecta £160.10 £3,986.32 - 18.66 winning units..
Owner D W Barker **Bred** D R Botterill **Trained** East Everleigh, Wilts

FOCUS
The first three pulled well clear of the others and the form tallies with the race averages.

3367 FSB CARE H'CAP 6f
4:40 (4:42) (Class 3) (0-95,93) 3-Y-O+ **£8,409** (£2,502; £1,250; £625) **Stalls** High

Form RPR
0264 1 **Whozthecat (IRE)**[8] 3114 6-9-2 **86** JasonHart(5) 11 96
(Declan Carroll) *sn led: kpt on fnl f: jst hld on* **14/1**
6-02 2 *nse* **Mississippi**[43] 2007 4-9-5 **84** GrahamGibbons 10 94+
(David Barron) *hld up in mid-div: smooth hdwy 2f out: chsd wnr jst ins fnl f: edgd lft: jst failed* **15/8**[1]
0-52 3 2 1/4 **Picabo (IRE)**[16] 2848 5-10-0 **93** DaneO'Neill 3 96+
(Henry Candy) *s.i.s: hdwy on outside to chse ldrs over 2f out: styd on same pce fnl f* **13/2**[3]
1201 4 *nk* **Line Of Reason (IRE)**[9] 3066 3-9-2 **88** KierenFallon 6 90+
(Paul Midgley) *hld up towards rr: n.m.r and swtchd stands' side over 2f out: styd on over 1f out: keeping on at fin* **6/1**[2]
000/ 5 *nk* **Enderby Spirit (GR)**[604] 6987 7-9-8 **87** (t) TomEaves 8 88
(Bryan Smart) *s.i.s: sn chsng ldrs: one pce over 1f out* **40/1**
0010 6 1 3/4 **Piscean (USA)**[13] 2937 8-9-9 **88** JimmyQuinn 5 83
(Tom Keddy) *t.k.h in rr: rdn and outpcd over 2f out: styd on fnl f* **25/1**
6653 7 *hd* **Rasaman (IRE)**[4] 3200 9-8-10 **75** GrahamLee 7 70
(Jim Goldie) *hld up in rr: drvn over 2f out: styd on fnl f* **6/1**[2]
6300 8 1 1/4 **Threes Grand**[8] 3097 3-8-13 **85** FrederikTylicki 2 76
(Scott Dixon) *racd wd: w wnr: wknd fnl 150yds* **20/1**
1160 9 2 1/2 **Klynch**[11] 2988 7-9-12 **91** (b) JamesSullivan 13 74
(Ruth Carr) *chsd ldrs: rdn over 2f out: wknd fnl f* **22/1**
-060 10 1 3/4 **Escape To Glory (USA)**[34] 2310 5-9-5 **84** (p) PaulMulrennan 4 61
(Michael Dods) *led early: chsd ldrs: wknd over 1f out* **20/1**
-000 11 1 1/4 **Amadeus Wolfe Tone (IRE)**[29] 2444 4-9-13 **92** (p) JamieSpencer 12 65
(Jamie Osborne) *towards rr: effrt over 2f out: wknd appr fnl f* **10/1**
1033 12 2 1/4 **Love Island**[11] 2988 4-9-3 **82** PaulQuinn 1 48
(Richard Whitaker) *chsd ldrs: wknd appr fnl f* **12/1**

1m 10.91s (-2.69) **Going Correction** -0.225s/f (Firm)
WFA 3 from 4yo+ 7lb **12** Ran SP% **120.3**
Speed ratings (Par 107): **108,107,104,104,104 101,101,99,96,94 92,89**
Tote Swingers: 1&2 £7.50, 1&3 £12.20, 2&3 £4.40 CSF £38.29 CT £202.62 TOTE £14.40: £3.50, £1.50, £2.10; EX 59.50 Trifecta £358.40 £3,490.42 - 7.30 winning units..
Owner Simon Bean **Bred** Liam Queally **Trained** Sledmere, E Yorks

FOCUS
A competitive sprint handicap, but agony for those who plunged on the well-backed favourite.

3368 FSB LOBBYING FOR SMALL BUSINESSES H'CAP 1m (R)
5:15 (5:16) (Class 4) (0-85,84) 4-Y-O+ **£5,175** (£1,540; £769; £384) **Stalls** High

Form RPR
01-1 1 **Bassara (IRE)**[23] 2639 4-9-4 **81** TedDurcan 1 89+
(Chris Wall) *hld up in rr: stdy hdwy over 2f out: swtchd rt over 1f out: edgd lft 1f out: styd on wl to ld post* **7/4**[1]
6430 2 *nse* **Kiwi Bay**[22] 2673 8-8-12 **75** TomEaves 4 83
(Michael Dods) *led early: trckd ldrs: upsides on inner over 2f out: sn led: hdd fnl stride* **16/1**
255- 3 1 **Bank On Me**[178] 8181 4-8-13 **76** WilliamCarson 2 82
(Philip McBride) *hld up in rr: effrt over 2f out: chsd wnr jst ins fnl f: kpt on same pce* **12/1**
3340 4 2 1/4 **Chapter And Verse (IRE)**[46] 1922 7-9-1 **78** RyanMoore 3 79
(Mike Murphy) *dwlt: hld up: hdwy over 3f out: swtchd lft appr fnl f: kpt on one pce* **9/2**[3]
3014 5 1 **Invincible Hero (IRE)**[29] 2463 6-9-2 **82** NeilFarley(3) 6 80
(Declan Carroll) *drvn to ld sn after s: edgd rt 3f out: hdd 2f out: one pce* **4/1**[2]
0431 6 2 1/4 **Azrael**[12] 2964 5-9-0 **77** MartinDwyer 5 70
(Alan McCabe) *chsd ldrs: effrt and hung lft over 2f out: one pce whn sltly hmpd 1f out* **16/1**
0531 7 3 **Al Muheer (IRE)**[8] 3096 8-9-2 **84** (b) JasonHart(5) 7 70
(Ruth Carr) *hld up in rr: effrt over 2f out: hung rt: nvr a factor* **5/1**
30-0 8 89 **Nelson's Bay**[25] 759 4-8-13 **76** (t) KierenFallon 8
(Noel Quinlan) *trckd ldrs: rdn and lost pl over 3f out: sn bhd: virtually p.u: hopelessly t.o* **16/1**

1m 37.31s (-2.39) **Going Correction** -0.225s/f (Firm) **8** Ran SP% **116.6**
Speed ratings (Par 105): **102,101,100,98,97 95,92,3**
Tote Swingers: 1&2 £7.70, 1&3 £5.50, 2&3 £17.50 CSF £34.14 CT £266.34 TOTE £2.90: £1.20, £4.50, £3.10; EX 37.70 Trifecta £296.10 £2,931.84 - 7.42 winning units..
Owner Ms Aida Fustoq **Bred** Deerfield Farm **Trained** Newmarket, Suffolk

FOCUS
A decent handicap, run at a fair gallop.

3369 FSB MOBILE CARD PAYMENT TERMINALS H'CAP 1m (R)
5:45 (5:46) (Class 4) (0-85,78) 3-Y-O **£5,175** (£1,540; £769; £384) **Stalls** High

Form RPR
4411 1 **Kohlaan (IRE)**[23] 2627 3-9-7 **78** DaneO'Neill 2 84
(Roger Varian) *mde all: 5 l clr over 4f out: kpt on u.p fnl f: hld on gamely nr fin* **9/2**[3]
33-1 2 *nk* **Freeport**[20] 2727 3-9-5 **76** KierenFallon 6 81
(Brian Meehan) *trckd ldrs: 2nd 4f out: drvn 3f out: chalng over 1f out: styd on same pce and edgd lft clsng stages* **5/2**[2]
31-4 3 *nse* **Leitrim Pass (USA)**[60] 1612 3-9-4 **75** ShaneKelly 8 80+
(William Haggas) *hld up: effrt over 2f out: chsng ldrs 1f out: kpt on towards fin* **15/8**[1]
10-5 4 1/2 **Simply Shining (IRE)**[29] 2438 3-9-3 **74** TonyHamilton 5 78
(Richard Fahey) *hld up: hdwy over 2f out: chsng ldrs last 100yds: over 1f out: styd on same pce lclsng stages* **16/1**
0-12 5 *shd* **Endorsing (IRE)**[50] 1829 3-9-7 **78** RyanMoore 1 82
(Richard Hannon) *trckd ldrs: drvn over 2f out: keeping on same pce whn n.m.r and nr fin* **9/2**[3]

2514 6 2 **Off The Pulse**[23] 2627 3-9-5 **76** GrahamGibbons 4 76
(John Mackie) *trckd ldrs: nt clr run over 2f out and over 1f out: one pce last 100yds* **20/1**
-325 7 2 1/2 **Nordikhab (IRE)**[20] 2719 3-9-1 **72** AmyRyan 7 65
(Kevin Ryan) *dwlt: detached in last: drvn over 3f out: nvr a factor* **33/1**

1m 37.61s (-2.09) **Going Correction** -0.225s/f (Firm) **7** Ran SP% **113.3**
Speed ratings (Par 101): **101,100,100,100,100 98,95**
Tote Swingers: 1&2 £2.90, 1&3 £2.70, 2&3 £1.90 CSF £15.87 CT £27.29 TOTE £5.90: £2.30, £2.50; EX 15.10 Trifecta £44.10 £2,819.45 - 47.91 winning units..
Owner Sheikh Ahmed Al Maktoum **Bred** Old Carhue Stud **Trained** Newmarket, Suffolk

FOCUS
A thrilling finish to this decent 3yo handicap with barely a length covering the first five.
T/Plt: £343.30 to a £1 stake. Pool: £117,526.00 - 249.90 winning tickets. T/Qpdt: £44.80 to a £1 stake. Pool: £9,676.00 - 159.70 winning tickets. WG

3174 SALISBURY (R-H)
Sunday, June 16

OFFICIAL GOING: Good to firm (good between 6.5f & 4.5f; 8.8)
Wind: virtually nil Weather: overcast, humid

3370 PETER SYMONDS CATERING H'CAP 1m 4f
2:20 (2:20) (Class 4) (0-85,84) 4-Y-O+ **£5,175** (£1,540; £769; £384) **Stalls** High

Form RPR
-21 1 **Continuum**[24] 2589 4-9-3 **80** TomQueally 2 91+
(Lady Cecil) *little slowly away: sn trcking ldrs: rdn over 2f out: led over 1f out: styd on: drvn out* **6/4**[1]
-001 2 *nk* **Dunhoy (IRE)**[24] 2598 5-9-1 **78** RichardHughes 4 86
(Tony Newcombe) *trckd ldrs: rdn over 3f out: styd on ent fnl f: pressed wnr fnl 120yds: kpt on but hld nring fin* **12/1**
1-4 3 *nk* **Villoresi (IRE)**[27] 2498 4-9-3 **80** HayleyTurner 7 88
(James Fanshawe) *hld up in last pair but in tch: pushed along fr 5f out: nt clr run whn making hdwy 3f out: sn swtchd lft and rdn: styd on ent fnl f: wnt 3rd towards fin: a being hld* **15/8**[2]
2256 4 2 **Tingo In The Tale (IRE)**[81] 1200 4-8-8 **71** LiamKeniry 1 76
(David Arbuthnot) *trckd ldr: led 3f out: sn rdn: hdd over 1f out: kpt pressing wnr tl no ex and lost 2 pls fnl 120yds* **50/1**
P054 5 4 **John Biscuit (IRE)**[15] 2867 5-9-7 **84** JimmyFortune 5 82
(Andrew Balding) *slowly away: sn in tch: rdn to chse ldrs wl over 2f out: kpt on same pce* **9/2**[3]
1120 6 5 **Wordiness**[55] 1733 5-9-5 **82** PatDobbs 8 72
(Brendan Powell) *hld up in last pair but in tch: rdn 3f out: nvr any real imp: wknd jst over 1f out* **25/1**
5112 7 15 **Noguchi (IRE)**[25] 2579 8-9-0 **77** (b) JamesDoyle 3 54
(Michael Murphy) *led: kpt wdst after 2f tl over 6f out: rdn and hdd 3f out: wknd 2f out* **16/1**

2m 36.64s (-1.36) **Going Correction** -0.025s/f (Good) **7** Ran SP% **112.3**
Speed ratings (Par 105): **103,102,102,101,98 95,85**
Tote Swingers: 1&2 £4.80, 1&3 £1.50, 2&3 £5.10 CSF £19.89 CT £34.63 TOTE £2.60: £1.50, £3.20; EX 13.20 Trifecta £31.10 £1,175.09 - 28.33 winning units..
Owner K Abdullah **Bred** Juddmonte Farms Ltd **Trained** Newmarket, Suffolk
■ Stewards' Enquiry : Hayley Turner two-day ban; used whip above the permitted level (30th june - 1st July).

FOCUS
Fresh ground was provided with there being a temporary rail in place around 20ft from the permanent one. Both Tom Queally and Liam Keniry felt the ground was "good". A fair handicap, run at just a steady pace.

3371 WESTOVER GROUP H'CAP (THE SUNDAY £5K BONUS RACE) 5f
2:50 (2:51) (Class 4) (0-85,85) 3-Y-O+ **£5,175** (£1,540; £769; £384) **Stalls** Low

Form RPR
-326 1 **Rebecca Romero**[10] 3018 6-9-4 **75** JamesDoyle 11 87
(Denis Coakley) *towards rr: swtchd lft and hdwy over 1f out: str run ins fnl f: led towards fin: rdn out* **9/1**
2-11 2 1/2 **Asian Trader**[10] 3018 4-9-8 **79** (t) GeorgeBaker 7 89+
(William Haggas) *travelled wl in mid-div: smooth hdwy to ld ent fnl f: sn rdn: no ex whn hdd towards fin* **9/4**[1]
-603 3 4 1/2 **West Coast Dream**[25] 2561 6-9-8 **82** MarkCoumbe(3) 13 76
(Roy Brotherton) *chsd ldrs: rdn over 2f out: ev ch ent fnl f: drifted rt ins fnl f: kpt on but nt pce of front pair* **40/1**
020 4 *shd* **Dorback**[8] 3090 6-9-2 **73** (t) MartinHarley 6 66
(Violet M Jordan) *fly-leapt leaving stalls: sn chsng ldrs: rdn over 2f out: led briefly over 1f out: drifted rt ins fnl f: kpt on but no ch* **18/1**
-055 5 1 1/2 **Macdillon**[22] 2657 7-8-13 **70** LiamKeniry 4 58
(Stuart Kittow) *mid-div: rdn wl over 2f out: nvr any real imp* **9/1**
1510 6 1 **Whitecrest**[10] 3018 5-9-8 **79** ChrisCatlin 12 63
(John Spearing) *sn struggling towards rr: styd on fnl f: nvr a threat* **33/1**
5560 7 *shd* **Dark Lane**[1] 3315 7-8-8 **70** DeclanBates(5) 9 54
(David Evans) *sn drvn towards rr: styd on fnl f: nvr a danger* **33/1**
-200 8 *nse* **Decision By One**[22] 2663 4-9-11 **82** (tp) RichardKingscote 5 66
(Tom Dascombe) *prom: rdn over 2f out: ev ch jst over 1f out: fdd ins fnl f* **16/1**
1033 9 1 **Gladiatrix**[10] 3018 4-9-11 **82** (b) RichardHughes 8 88+
(Rod Millman) *little outpcd towards rr early: rdn and nt best of runs fr over 2f out: gd hdwy over 1f out: abt to mount str chal whn completely squeezed out: no ch after* **10/3**[2]
4002 10 2 1/2 **Top Cop**[9] 3038 4-10-0 **85** (v) JimmyFortune 3 65
(Andrew Balding) *trckd ldrs: rdn over 2f out: wkng whn squeezed up ent fnl f* **11/2**[3]
-051 11 1 1/2 **Powerful Wind (IRE)**[9] 3042 4-9-1 **77** PhilipPrince(5) 1 43
(Ronald Harris) *led: rdn over 2f out: hdd over 1f out: wknd fnl f* **14/1**
-660 12 7 **Heartsong (IRE)**[16] 2848 4-9-9 **80** NeilCallan 2 21
(John Gallagher) *s.i.s: sn mid-div: rdn 3f out: wknd over 1f out* **50/1**

1m 0.11s (-0.89) **Going Correction** -0.025s/f (Good) **12** Ran SP% **117.3**
Speed ratings (Par 105): **106,105,98,97,95 93,93,93,92,88 85,74**
Tote Swingers: 1&2 £3.00, 1&3 £32.00, 2&3 £19.60 CSF £28.49 CT £807.36 TOTE £9.40: £3.40, £1.40, £4.90; EX 38.50 Trifecta £844.70 £1,763.70 - 1.56 winning units..
Owner Keepers Racing Ii **Bred** D W Armstrong **Trained** West Ilsley, Berks

The Form Book Flat, Raceform Ltd, Compton, RG20 6NL.

FOCUS
No hanging around here and the race predictably set up for the closers, with the main action unfolding centre-track and the front pair pulling right away.

3372 WATERAID MILDREN CONSTRUCTION MAIDEN FILLIES' STKS 1m
3:25 (3:25) (Class 5) 3-Y-O **£4,204** (£1,251; £625; £312) **Stalls** Low

Form RPR
642 **1** **Magic Of Reality (FR)**[16] 2850 3-9-0 87 TomQueally 3 82+
(Lady Cecil) *mde all: kpt on wl: pushed out: unchal* **1/3**[1]
2 2 1/4 **Noble Protector** 3-9-0 0 NeilCallan 1 77
(Stuart Kittow) *trckd ldrs: rdn over 2f out: hung lft fr over 1f out: wnt 2nd ent fnl f where bmpd: kpt on but a being readily hld* **25/1**
5 **3** 2 1/2 **Rufoof**[58] 1666 3-9-0 0 PaulHanagan 2 71
(Charles Hills) *in tch: rdn over 2f out: styd on to go 3rd ins fnl f: nt pce to threaten* **3/1**[2]
06- **4** nk **Candoluminescence**[225] 7552 3-9-0 0 JamesDoyle 4 71
(Roger Charlton) *trckd wnr: rdn over 2f out: lost 2nd whn bmpd ent fnl f: no ex* **8/1**[3]
6 **5** 9 **Stockhill Diva**[16] 2850 3-9-0 0 PatDobbs 8 49
(Brendan Powell) *mid-div: rdn over 2f out: wknd over 1f out* **14/1**
00 **6** hd **Toffee Shot**[22] 2658 3-8-11 0 PatrickHills(3) 7 48
(J W Hills) *mid-div tl outpcd over 2f out: wknd over 1f out* **33/1**
0 **7** 2 **Marmalady (IRE)**[22] 2658 3-9-0 0 LiamKeniry 5 43
(Gary Moore) *hld up last: rdn over 2f out: nvr any imp: wknd over 1f out* **25/1**
0 **8** 6 **Mint Crisp**[16] 2850 3-9-0 0 JimmyFortune 6 29
(Hughie Morrison) *trckd ldrs: rdn over 2f out: sn wknd* **20/1**

1m 43.22s (-0.28) **Going Correction** -0.025s/f (Good) 8 Ran SP% **133.2**
Speed ratings (Par 96): **100,97,95,94,85 85,83,77**
Tote Swingers: 1&2 £13.20, 1&3 £1.20, 2&3 £6.40 CSF £22.73 TOTE £1.20: £1.02, £8.00, £1.20; EX 24.30 Trifecta £95.30 £2,132.29 - 16.76 winning units..
Owner Niarchos Family **Bred** Suc S Niarchos **Trained** Newmarket, Suffolk
■ Stewards' Enquiry : Neil Callan caution; careless riding.

FOCUS
An uncompetitive maiden, run at a steady gallop.

3373 EUROPEAN BREEDERS' FUND CATHEDRAL STKS (LISTED RACE) 6f
4:00 (4:00) (Class 1) 3-Y-O+
£23,818 (£9,030; £4,519; £2,251; £1,129; £567) **Stalls** Low

Form RPR
-411 **1** **Professor**[8] 3103 3-9-1 109 RichardHughes 5 114+
(Richard Hannon) *trckd ldr: nudged along fr over 3f out: chal over 1f out: led fnl 140yds: r.o wl: pushed out* **5/6**[1]
5203 **2** 1 3/4 **Justineo**[18] 2768 4-9-4 101 WilliamBuick 10 104
(Roger Varian) *led: rdn whn jnd over 1f out: hdd fnl 140yds: kpt on gamely but nt pce of wnr* **12/1**
/544 **3** 1 **Miss Lahar**[9] 3046 4-8-13 95 MartinHarley 9 96
(Mick Channon) *in tch: tk clsr order over 2f out: rdn over 1f out: kpt on but nt pce to chal* **20/1**
0-1 **4** 1/2 **Hallelujah**[29] 2444 5-8-13 101 HayleyTurner 6 94+
(James Fanshawe) *mid-div: drvn along fr over 3f out: stdy prog fr over 1f out: styd on ins fnl f: clsng at fin* **5/2**[2]
6616 **5** 2 1/2 **Regal Parade**[13] 2936 9-9-4 103 (t) MatthewLawson 8 91
(Milton Bradley) *dwlt: towards rr: rdn over 2f out: nvr gng pce to get involved* **33/1**
40-2 **6** 1/2 **Morache Music**[22] 2667 5-9-4 103 SteveDrowne 2 90
(Peter Makin) *mid-div tl stmbld after 1f and lost pl: rdn over 2f out: kpt on but nt pce to threaten ldrs* **8/1**[3]
/5-5 **7** 3 **Spiritual Star (IRE)**[22] 2667 4-9-4 105 JimmyFortune 1 80
(Andrew Balding) *trckd ldr tl rdn 2f out: wknd ent fnl f* **20/1**
-540 **8** 7 **Pandar**[13] 2936 4-9-4 100 (p) NeilCallan 11 71
(Robert Cowell) *virtually fell leaving stalls: t.k.h towards rr: effrt over 2f out: nvr threatened: wknd ent fnl f* **33/1**

1m 13.19s (-1.61) **Going Correction** -0.025s/f (Good)
WFA 3 from 4yo+ 7lb 8 Ran SP% **117.3**
Speed ratings (Par 111): **109,106,105,104,101 100,96,87**
Tote Swingers: 1&2 £2.80, 1&3 £5.50, 2&3 £7.60 CSF £12.34 TOTE £1.80: £1.10, £2.80, £3.70; EX 11.80 Trifecta £113.40 £4,555.21 - 30.10 winning units..
Owner Mrs P Good **Bred** Exors Of The Late J R Good **Trained** East Everleigh, Wilts

FOCUS
An ordinary Listed contest.

3374 BRIDGET SWIRE MEMORIAL MAIDEN STKS 6f
4:30 (4:31) (Class 2) 2-Y-O **£9,056** (£2,695; £1,346; £673) **Stalls** Low

Form RPR
1 **Intermath (IRE)** 2-9-5 0 TomQueally 12 76
(David Evans) *mid-div: rdn over 2f out: hdwy over 1f out: str run ins fnl f: led wl ins fnl f* **33/1**
25 **2** nk **Culdaff (IRE)**[38] 2194 2-9-5 0 JamesMcDonald 15 76
(Charles Hills) *trckd ldr: rdn 2f out: 1 l down whn hmpd over 1f out: rcvrd to hold ev ch ins fnl f: kpt on* **10/1**[3]
3 **3** hd **Major Crispies**[19] 2741 2-9-5 0 SteveDrowne 16 74
(James Eustace) *prom: hung lft whn rdn over 2f out: chsng ldrs whn hmpd over 1f out: ev ch ins fnl f: kpt on* **12/1**
2 **4** hd **Art Official (IRE)**[31] 2401 2-9-5 0 RichardHughes 1 74+
(Richard Hannon) *led: rdn and allowed to drift to nrside rails over 1f out: hdd wl ins fnl f: kpt on* **4/6**[1]
5 1 3/4 **Charlie Wells (IRE)** 2-9-5 0 NeilCallan 10 68+
(Eve Johnson Houghton) *s.i.s: towards rr: pushed along and hdwy over 2f out: kpt on fnl f: nt rch ldrs* **50/1**
6 1 **Truth Or Dare** 2-9-5 0 KieranO'Neill 7 65+
(Richard Hannon) *s.i.s: towards rr: last w plenty to do over 1f out: n.d but styd on nicely fnl f* **25/1**
7 1 1/2 **Treaty Of Paris (IRE)** 2-9-5 0 FergusSweeney 5 60
(Henry Candy) *prom tl 3f out: sn rdn to chse ldrs: one pce fnl f* **9/1**[2]
8 1 3/4 **Cabaan (IRE)** 2-9-5 0 MartinLane 6 55+
(Brian Meehan) *a in mid-div* **25/1**
9 shd **Bowsers Bold** 2-9-5 0 HayleyTurner 13 54
(Marcus Tregoning) *towards rr: sme late prog: nvr a factor* **40/1**
0 **10** 1 1/4 **Bold Jack Donahue (IRE)**[19] 2741 2-9-5 0 RichardThomas 4 50
(Ralph Beckett) *nvr bttr than mid-div* **50/1**
11 1/2 **Major Jack** 2-9-5 0 JamesDoyle 14 49+
(Roger Charlton) *s.i.s: towards rr: sme late minor prog: nvr a threat* **14/1**
12 1 1/4 **Trading Profit** 2-9-5 0 JimmyFortune 3 45+
(Andrew Balding) *trckd ldrs: rdn over 2f out: wknd ent fnl f* **12/1**
0 **13** 1 1/2 **Ghasaq (IRE)**[38] 2194 2-9-5 0 (b[1]) PaulHanagan 8 40
(Brian Meehan) *mid-div: rdn over 2f out: no imp: wknd fnl f* **25/1**
0 **14** 1 **Mildenhall**[24] 2583 2-9-0 0 PatDobbs 9 32
(Richard Hannon) *mid-div: rdn over 2f out: no imp: wknd fnl f* **40/1**
15 4 **Fiftyshadesfreed (IRE)** 2-9-5 0 LiamKeniry 2 24
(George Baker) *s.i.s: mid-div tl over 2f out* **33/1**

1m 14.83s (0.03) **Going Correction** -0.025s/f (Good) 15 Ran SP% **127.4**
Speed ratings (Par 99): **98,97,97,97,94 93,91,89,88,87 86,84,82,81,76**
Tote Swingers: 1&2 £38.40, 1&3 £51.30, 2&3 £7.30 CSF £327.08 TOTE £43.90: £5.70, £2.70, £3.30; EX 424.60 Trifecta £1065.00 £3,120.02 - 2.19 winning units..
Owner Wayne Clifford **Bred** Mr And Mrs P McEnery **Trained** Pandy, Monmouths
■ Stewards' Enquiry : James McDonald four-day ban; excessive use of whip (30th June - 3rd July).

FOCUS
They were soon quite well strung out in what was an average juvenile maiden, and it produced a rather messy finish. The runner-up helps with the level.

3375 RAY "RASHER" AMES MEMORIAL FILLIES' H'CAP 6f 212y
5:05 (5:05) (Class 5) (0-75,74) 3-Y-O+ **£3,234** (£962; £481; £240) **Stalls** Centre

Form RPR
1-06 **1** **Glossy Posse**[17] 2806 3-8-10 65 RichardHughes 10 72
(Richard Hannon) *racd centre: chsd ldrs: rdn 2f out: led ent fnl f: kpt on: rdn out* **6/1**[3]
52-5 **2** 1 1/4 **Serenity Spa**[29] 2449 3-9-2 71 [1] JamesDoyle 8 75
(Roger Charlton) *racd centre: hld up: swtchd rt 2f out: sn rdn and hdwy: styd on fnl f: wnt 2nd towards fin: nvr rching wnr* **5/2**[2]
625 **3** 1 **Marjong**[24] 2597 3-9-5 74 TomQueally 1 75
(Simon Dow) *racd centre: hld up: hdwy 2f out: sn rdn: ev ch jst over 1f out: kpt on same pce ins fnl f: lost 2nd nring fin* **15/2**
63-3 **4** 1 1/4 **Icon Dance**[22] 2658 3-9-5 74 PatDobbs 7 72
(Ben De Haan) *racd centre: in tch: rdn over 2f out: swtchd rt ent fnl f: kpt on same pce* **8/1**
/3 **5** 1 1/4 **Madeira Girl (IRE)**[12] 2948 4-9-10 70 JimmyFortune 5 67
(Jonjo O'Neill) *racd centre: chsd ldrs tl lost pl after 2f: rdn wl over 2f out: chsd ldrs over 1f out: kpt on same pce fnl f* **20/1**
3312 **6** 1/2 **Yahilwa (USA)**[16] 2837 3-9-5 74 NeilCallan 4 67
(James Tate) *led centre gp: rdn into overall ld 2f out: hdd ent fnl f: no ex* **9/4**[1]
0-64 **7** 8 **Uncomplicated**[41] 2092 3-8-13 68 (b) MatthewDavies 9 39
(Jim Boyle) *racd centre: chsd ldrs: rdn over 2f out: wknd over 1f out* **16/1**
150- **8** 2 1/4 **Shes Rosie**[286] 5877 5-9-7 70 [1] MarkCoumbe(3) 2 38
(Ed de Giles) *racd between gps: s.i.s: chsd ldr after 2f: edgd lft u.p over 2f out: wknd over 1f out* **14/1**
60-0 **9** 10 **Madame Kintyre**[41] 2096 5-8-9 55 oh1 (b) RichardKingscote 3
(Rod Millman) *stmbld leaving stalls: racd alone on far side rails: sn led: rdn over 2f out: sn hdd: wknd* **33/1**

1m 27.83s (-0.77) **Going Correction** -0.025s/f (Good)
WFA 3 from 4yo+ 9lb 9 Ran SP% **116.8**
Speed ratings (Par 100): **103,101,100,99,97 97,87,85,73**
Tote Swingers: 1&2 £3.60, 1&3 £5.90, 2&3 £4.10 CSF £21.64 CT £116.42 TOTE £6.90: £1.90, £1.30, £2.10; EX 27.40 Trifecta £160.50 £2,260.65 - 10.55 winning units..
Owner J G Davis **Bred** J G Davis & Star Pointe Ltd **Trained** East Everleigh, Wilts

FOCUS
A modest fillies' handicap. There was a difference of opinion, with the majority of runners racing centre-field early and ending up under the stands' rail.

3376 GOLDRING SECURITY SERVICES "HANDS AND HEELS" APPRENTICE SERIES H'CAP (RACING EXCELLENCE INITIATIVE) 1m
5:35 (5:35) (Class 6) (0-65,65) 3-Y-O **£2,587** (£770; £384; £192) **Stalls** Low

Form RPR
-505 **1** **Imperial Glance**[27] 2495 3-9-0 63 OisinMurphy(8) 12 71
(Andrew Balding) *led after 1f: edgd lft but in command fr over 1f out: pushed out* **3/1**[1]
-013 **2** 3 1/2 **Just A Pound (IRE)**[1] 3313 3-8-13 62 JosephineGordon(8) 9 62
(Jo Hughes) *mid-div: hdwy over 2f out: sn chsng wnr: edgd to stands' side rails over 1f out: kpt on but a being readily hld* **13/2**
046 **3** 5 **Calm Attitude (IRE)**[16] 2824 3-9-0 55 MatthewHopkins 6 44+
(Rae Guest) *s.i.s: t.k.h: towards rr: hdwy fr 2f out: styd on to go 3rd ins fnl f* **6/1**[3]
3605 **4** 2 3/4 **Carrera**[5] 3178 3-9-3 58 ShelleyBirkett 8 40
(J W Hills) *mid-div: wnt 3rd 2f out tl no ex ins fnl f* **5/1**[2]
0533 **5** 1/2 **Bee Jay Kay**[9] 3039 3-9-5 63 DanielCremin(3) 11 44
(Mick Channon) *hld up towards rr: nudged along 1/2-way: styd on fr over 1f out: nvr trbld ldrs* **8/1**
2543 **6** nk **Suspension**[17] 2802 3-8-9 53 CharlieBennett(3) 2 33
(Hughie Morrison) *chsd ldrs: effrt over 2f out: sn one pce* **12/1**
5540 **7** 1 **Sweet Alabama**[9] 3041 3-8-3 49 (b) JackGarritty(5) 7 27
(Rod Millman) *mid-div: hdwy over 2f out: wknd fnl f* **20/1**
-635 **8** 8 **Mojo Bear**[13] 2935 3-9-4 64 CameronHardie(5) 1 24
(Sylvester Kirk) *mid-div: effrt 2f out: wknd ent fnl f* **20/1**
3-04 **9** 3 **Eton Rambler (USA)**[10] 3013 3-9-8 63 (b) AdamMcLean 4 16
(George Baker) *mid-div: rdn over 2f out: wknd ent fnl f* **9/1**
5000 **10** 3/4 **Winnie Perry**[5] 3178 3-9-7 65 PatMillman(3) 5 16
(Rod Millman) *led for 1f: prom tl wknd wl over 1f out* **25/1**
2-40 **11** 1 1/2 **Day In Day Out**[55] 1712 3-9-0 63 JaneElliott(8) 3 11
(Ralph Beckett) *mid-div: effrt 2f out: sn wknd* **20/1**
0-00 **12** 1/2 **Ropehanger**[67] 1476 3-8-11 52 JordanVaughan 10
(Lee Carter) *a towards rr* **66/1**

1m 42.99s (-0.51) **Going Correction** -0.025s/f (Good) 12 Ran SP% **117.7**
Speed ratings (Par 97): **101,97,92,89,89 88,87,79,76,76 74,74**
Tote Swingers: 1&2 £5.70, 1&3 £5.10, 2&3 £7.00 CSF £20.23 CT £113.03 TOTE £4.20: £1.40, £2.40, £2.60; EX 25.30 Trifecta £189.20 £1,362.04 - 5.39 winning units..
Owner Mrs Sandie Newton **Bred** Mrs J S Newton **Trained** Kingsclere, Hants

FOCUS
A moderate handicap, although it may throw up winners at a similar level. That went just an ordinary gallop.

T/Jkpt: £56,786.30 to a £1 stake. Pool: £159,962.00 - 2.00 winning tickets. T/Plt: £137.20 to a £1 stake. Pool: £96,145.00 - 511.49 winning tickets. T/Qpdt: £35.80 to a £1 stake. Pool: £7,263.00 - 150.10 winning tickets. TM

3377 - 3380a (Foreign Racing) - See Raceform Interactive

2243 CORK (R-H)

Sunday, June 16

OFFICIAL GOING: Sprint course - soft (soft to heavy in places); round course - soft (yielding in places)

3381a CORK RACECOURSE MALLOW NOBLESSE STKS (GROUP 3) (F&M) 1m 4f

4:20 (4:22) 3-Y-O+ **£39,634** (£11,585; £5,487; £1,829)

RPR

1 **Midnight Soprano (IRE)**[230] 7449 6-9-9 106........... MarcMonaghan 10 103+
(P D Deegan, Ire) *w.w: prog to press ldrs in 4th 2f out: styd on wl for press ins fnl f to ld clsng strides* **5/1**[3]

2 *hd* **Magical Dream (IRE)**[40] 2141 3-8-12 102................ SeamieHeffernan 7 106+
(A P O'Brien, Ire) *hld up towards rr: pushed along in 6th 2f out: styd on wl between rivals to dispute ins fnl f: led fnl 100yds tl hdd clsng strides* **8/1**

3 *shd* **Cubanita**[31] 2397 4-9-9 .... JimCrowley 4 103
(Ralph Beckett) *chsd ldrs tl tk clsr order 3f out: led over 1f out: hdd fnl 100yds: kpt on same pce* **9/4**[1]

4 *2 1/4* **Silky (IRE)**[24] 2607 3-8-9 .... WJLee 1 99
(David Wachman, Ire) *w.w towards rr: pushed along in 6th 2f out: kpt on fnl f: nt rch ldrs* **18/1**

5 *1 3/4* **Say (IRE)**[16] 2842 3-8-9 90.. CO'Donoghue 2 96
(A P O'Brien, Ire) *trckd ldr in 2nd: edgd out over 2f out to chal and sn led: hdd over 1f out: sn no ex* **9/2**[2]

6 *3/4* **We'll Go Walking (IRE)**[35] 2289 3-8-9 106.................. RonanWhelan 5 95
(J S Bolger, Ire) *t.k.h and sn led: hung lft off bnd over 3f out: hdd 2f out: wknd ent fnl f* **6/1**

7 *2* **Testosterone (IRE)**[39] 2184 5-9-9 .... KevinManning 9 92
(Ed Dunlop) *chsd ldrs in 3rd: pushed along 3f out: no ex ent fnl 2f* **5/1**[3]

8 *37* **Beach Of Falesa (IRE)**[7] 3143 4-9-9 89........................ JosephO'Brien 3 33
(A P O'Brien, Ire) *a in rr: detached fnl 2f and sn eased: t.o* **20/1**

2m 40.81s (-7.09)
WFA 3 from 4yo+ 14lb **8** Ran SP% **117.7**
CSF £45.47 TOTE £7.40: £1.80, £2.50, £1.50; DF 51.90.
Owner J Monaghan **Bred** J Monaghan **Trained** The Curragh, Co Kildare

FOCUS
The likely favourite's withdrawal was disappointing but expected on the ground. This was run at a strong pace and produced a gripping finish. The runner-up and fifth have been rated as running fair personal bests, with the winner and third not quite at their best.

3382 - 3384a (Foreign Racing) - See Raceform Interactive

3128 CHANTILLY (R-H)

Sunday, June 16

OFFICIAL GOING: Turf: good

3385a PRIX DE DIANE LONGINES (GROUP 1) (3YO FILLIES) (TURF) 1m 2f 110y

2:45 (12:00) 3-Y-O **£464,552** (£185,853; £92,926; £46,422; £23,252)

RPR

1 **Treve (FR)**[32] 3-9-0 0.. ThierryJarnet 2 120+
(Mme C Head-Maarek, France) *dwlt sltly: hld up towards rr on inner: smooth hdwy fr 3f out: qcknd sharply to ld over 1 1/2f: rdn and styd on strly: forged clr: v impressive* **11/1**

2 *4* **Chicquita (IRE)**[23] 3-9-0 0.. AntoineHamelin 10 112+
(A De Royer-Dupre, France) *hld up in last: stl last but gng wl enough 2f out: sn rdn: hung lft and awkward u.p but styd on down wd outside to go 2nd fnl strides: no ch w v impressive wnr* **25/1**

3 *snk* **Silasol (IRE)**[21] 2693 3-9-0 0.. OlivierPeslier 3 111
(C Laffon-Parias, France) *t.k.h: midfield in tch on inner: swtchd out and rdn to chal 2f out: wnt 2nd 1 1/2f out: chsd wnr but readily outpcd: styd on but dropped to 3rd fnl strides* **7/2**[3]

4 *1 1/4* **Tasaday (USA)**[35] 2299 3-9-0 0............................... MickaelBarzalona 11 109
(A Fabre, France) *hld up towards rr on outer: rdn and hdwy 2f out: wnt 3rd over 1f out: styd on but dropped to 4th ins fnl 100yds* **12/1**

5 *3* **Pearlside (FR)**[49] 1869 3-9-0 0................................ StephanePasquier 7 103
(M Delcher Sanchez, France) *dwlt: hld up towards rr: hdwy into midfield 5f out: rdn and ev ch 2f out: sn outpcd by ldrs: styd on* **22/1**

6 *2 1/2* **Alterite (FR)**[21] 2693 3-9-0 0....................................... IoritzMendizabal 8 98
(J-C Rouget, France) *t.k.h: midfield: rdn and ev ch 2f out: outpcd by ldrs over 1f out: styd on* **12/1**

7 *1 1/2* **Esoterique (IRE)**[35] 2299 3-9-0 0.................................. MaximeGuyon 4 95
(A Fabre, France) *t.k.h: midfield on outer: rdn 2f out: outpcd by ldrs over 1f out: styd on* **5/2**[2]

8 *3/4* **Flotilla (FR)**[35] 2299 3-9-0 0........................ Christophe-PatriceLemaire 9 94
(M Delzangles, France) *t.k.h: trckd ldr on outer: shkn up to chal 2f out: rdn and no ex over 1f out: fdd* **9/4**[1]

9 *4* **Endio (FR)**[34] 3-9-0 0... FranckBlondel 6 86
(Mme L Audon, France) *hld up in last trio: rdn over 2f out: outpcd and btn ent fnl f: eased 100yds out* **150/1**

10 *1 1/2* **Baltic Baroness (GER)**[32] 2381 3-9-0 0........... Pierre-CharlesBoudot 1 83
(A Fabre, France) *led 2f then trckd ldr on inner: rdn to chal 2f out: no ex and btn over 1f out: fdd and eased* **16/1**

11 *12* **Sage Melody (FR)**[35] 2299 3-9-0 0................................. UmbertoRispoli 5 60
(M Delzangles, France) *pressed ldr tl led after 2f: rdn 3f out: hdd over 1 1/2f out: immediately btn and wknd: eased and dropped to last over 1f out: t.o* **150/1**

2m 3.77s (-5.03) **Going Correction** -0.10s/f (Good) **11** Ran SP% **120.7**
Speed ratings: **114,111,110,110,107 106,104,104,101,100 91**
WIN (incl. 1 euro stake): 9.30. PLACES: 3.50, 4.50, 2.10. DF: 55.40. SF: 144.70.
Owner Haras Du Quesnay **Bred** Haras Du Quesnay **Trained** Chantilly, France

FOCUS
A strong renewal on paper of the premier fillies' classic in France, with the first three from the Pouliches reopposing plus the first two from the principal trial, the Prix Saint-Alary; although there were no challengers from Britain or Ireland. As it was they were all well beaten by a filly having her first try at this level. The course record was broken.

3386a PRIX DU LYS LONGINES (GROUP 3) (3YO COLTS & GELDINGS) (TURF) 1m 4f

4:05 (12:00) 3-Y-O **£32,520** (£13,008; £9,756; £6,504; £3,252)

RPR

1 **Flintshire**[15] 3-8-11 0.. MaximeGuyon 6 115+
(A Fabre, France) **7/2**[2]

2 *3* **Park Reel (FR)**[35] 2297 3-8-11 0.................................. GregoryBenoist 1 110
(E Lellouche, France) **15/8**[1]

3 *nk* **Tres Blue (IRE)**[38] 2203 3-8-11 0.................................. FabriceVeron 2 110
(H-A Pantall, France) **14/1**

4 *1/2* **Manndawi (FR)**[25] 3-8-11 0........................ Christophe-PatriceLemaire 9 109
(A De Royer-Dupre, France) **9/2**[3]

5 *2* **Garrogorille (FR)**[38] 2203 3-8-11 0................................... OlivierPeslier 5 106
(Y Durepaire, France) **11/1**

6 *nse* **Green Byron (FR)**[21] 2692 3-8-11 0.......................... IoritzMendizabal 8 106
(J-M Lefebvre, France) **11/1**

7 *snk* **Golden Bowl (FR)**[35] 2297 3-8-11 0................................ ThierryJarnet 7 105
(J Bertran De Balanda, France) **10/1**

8 *1/2* **Himalaya Dream (FR)**[48] 3-8-11 0..................... ChristopheSoumillon 3 105
(E Libaud, France) **11/1**

9 *2* **Artibai**[29] 3-8-11 0.. UmbertoRispoli 4 101
(M Delzangles, France) **14/1**

2m 28.03s (-2.97) **Going Correction** -0.10s/f (Good) **9** Ran SP% **122.6**
Speed ratings: **105,103,102,102,101 101,101,100,99**
WIN (incl. 1 euro stake): 3.70. PLACES: 1.50, 1.30, 2.90. DF: 5.30. SF: 12.00.
Owner K Abdullah **Bred** Juddmonte Farms Ltd **Trained** Chantilly, France

3387a PRIX BERTRAND DU BREUIL LONGINES (EX.PRIX DU CHEMIN DE FER DU NORD) (GROUP 3) (4YO+) (TURF) 1m

5:15 (12:00) 4-Y-O+ **£32,520** (£13,008; £9,756; £6,504; £3,252)

RPR

1 **Mainsail**[26] 2559 4-8-11 0.................................... ChristopheSoumillon 5 110
(P Bary, France) **2/1**[2]

2 *1 3/4* **Laygirl (FR)**[33] 5-8-8 0.. UmbertoRispoli 3 103
(J-M Capitte, France) **14/1**

3 *nse* **Poupee Flash (USA)**[261] 6656 4-8-8 0..................... StephanePasquier 6 103
(P Bary, France) **10/1**

4 *shd* **Foreign Tune**[15] 2897 4-8-8 0.. OlivierPeslier 2 103
(C Laffon-Parias, France) **8/1**

5 *1* **Caserta**[27] 4-8-8 0.. MaximeGuyon 4 100
(A Fabre, France) **11/2**[3]

6 *2* **Spoil The Fun (FR)**[26] 2559 4-8-11 0................................. JulienAuge 1 99
(C Ferland, France) **13/8**[1]

1m 41.94s (3.94) **Going Correction** -0.10s/f (Good) **6** Ran SP% **113.7**
Speed ratings: **76,74,74,74,73 71**
WIN (incl. 1 euro stake): 2.20 (Mainsail coupled with Caserta). PLACES: 2.40, 4.30. SF: 26.10.
Owner K Abdullah **Bred** Juddmonte Farms **Trained** Chantilly, France

3388 - (Foreign Racing) - See Raceform Interactive

2822 COLOGNE (R-H)

Sunday, June 16

OFFICIAL GOING: Turf: good

3389a OPPENHEIM-UNION-RENNEN (GROUP 2) (3YO) (TURF) 1m 3f

3:55 (12:00) 3-Y-O

£32,520 (£12,601; £5,284; £3,252; £2,032; £1,219)

RPR

1 **Ivanhowe (GER)**[252] 3-9-2 0.. ADeVries 4 103
(W Giedt, Germany) **9/5**[1]

2 *2 1/2* **Empoli (GER)**[36] 3-9-2 0.. AStarke 1 99
(P Schiergen, Germany) **44/5**

3 *1 1/2* **Orsello (GER)**[49] 1867 3-9-2 0............................ MrDennisSchiergen 7 96
(N Sauer, Germany) **30/1**

4 *1/2* **Schulz (GER)**[36] 3-9-2 0... DPorcu 9 95
(Markus Klug, Germany) **37/10**[3]

5 *1 3/4* **Quinzieme Monarque (USA)**[71] 1404 3-9-2 0............ MircoDemuro 8 92
(J Hirschberger, Germany) **121/10**

6 *2 1/2* **Nuntius (GER)** 3-9-2 0.. EPedroza 3 87
(A Wohler, Germany) **12/5**[2]

7 *4* **Noble Galileo (GER)**[27] 3-9-2 0...................................(b) AndreaAtzeni 2 80
(Mario Hofer, Germany) **204/10**

8 *nk* **Saint And Sinner (GER)**[36] 3-9-2 0.. SHellyn 6 80
(A Wohler, Germany) **39/1**

9 *23* **Night Wish (GER)**[21] 2696 3-9-2 0.................................. FrankieDettori 5 38
(W Figge, Germany) **54/10**

2m 14.01s (-6.79) **9** Ran SP% **130.3**
WIN (incl. 10 euro stake): 28. PLACES: 15, 27, 42. SF: 331.
Owner Gestut Schlenderhan **Bred** Gestut Schlenderhan **Trained** Germany

2911 CARLISLE (R-H)

Monday, June 17

OFFICIAL GOING: Good to firm (good in places; 7.8)

Old stable bend and home straight moved out 2yds, adding 2yds to distances.

Wind: Breezy; half behind Weather: Overcast

3391 BOOK YOUR CONFERENCE AT CARLISLE RACECOURSE MAIDEN AUCTION STKS 5f 193y

2:15 (2:18) (Class 5) 2-Y-O **£2,587** (£770; £384; £192) **Stalls** Low

Form RPR

2 1 **Mr Matthews (IRE)**[37] 2282 2-8-9 0.......................... MichaelO'Connell 10 79
(Mrs K Burke) *t.k.h early: cl up: led 2f out: drvn and styd on strly to go clr fnl f* **11/4**[2]

6 **2** 2 3/4 **Disclosure**[45] 1989 2-8-11 0 ....(p) TomEaves 11 73
(Bryan Smart) *prom on outside: hdwy to chse wnr appr fnl f: kpt on: no imp* **14/1**

34 **3** 3/4 **Ixelles Diamond (IRE)**[21] 2715 2-8-8 0 .... TonyHamilton 2 68
(Richard Fahey) *led to 2f out: sn drvn and rallied: kpt on same pce fnl f* **9/4**[1]

62 **4** 2 **Mitcd (IRE)**[18] 2793 2-8-1 0 .... SamanthaBell(7) 7 62
(Richard Fahey) *chsd ldng gp on ins: effrt and hdwy over 1f out: kpt on same pce fnl f* **12/1**

3 **5** 3 3/4 **Kirkstall Abbey (IRE)**[12] 2985 2-8-11 0 .... BarryMcHugh 5 53
(Tony Coyle) *prom: effrt and pushed along 2f out: btn ins fnl f* **7/2**[3]

6 3 1/2 **Meconopsis** 2-8-11 0 .... DuranFentiman 4 43+
(Tim Easterby) *hld up towards rr: rdn over 2f out: no imp fr over 1f out* **40/1**

7 2 1/4 **Trinity Star (IRE)** 2-9-2 0 .... PaulMulrennan 8 42
(Michael Dods) *prom: lost pl whn n.m.r over 2f out: wknd over 1f out* **20/1**

8 1 3/4 **Autumn Tide (IRE)** 2-8-6 0 .... JoeFanning 1 26+
(John Quinn) *hld up: rdn and outpcd 2f out: sn btn* **16/1**

6 **9** 1/2 **Please Let Me Go**[18] 2793 2-8-8 0 .... FrannyNorton 9 26+
(Kevin Ryan) *missed break and wnt bdly lft s: nvr on terms* **16/1**

040 **10** 2 **Countess Lupus (IRE)**[39] 2189 2-8-6 0 .... AmyRyan 12 18
(Lisa Williamson) *hld up in midfield on outside: rdn over 2f out: edgd rt and wknd over 1f out* **200/1**

0 **11** 2 1/2 **Sarlat**[42] 2067 2-8-9 0 ow1 .... GrahamGibbons 6 14
(Mark Brisbourne) *cl up: outpcd over 2f out: hung rt and wknd over 1f out* **66/1**

1m 14.89s (1.19) **Going Correction** +0.125s/f (Good) **11** Ran SP% **115.0**
Speed ratings (Par 93): **97,93,92,89,84 80,77,74,74,71 68**
toteswingers 1&2 £6.30, 1&3 £2.10, 2&3 £2.10 CSF £15.05 TOTE £4.10: £1.60, £4.20, £1.10; EX 47.40 Trifecta £165.00 Pool: £4,614.19 - 20.96 winning units..
Owner Living The Dream Partnership & Mrs Burke **Bred** Liam Wright **Trained** Middleham Moor, N Yorks

FOCUS
Not much pace on for this maiden, which suited those up with the pace.

3392 WATCH RACING UK ON SKY 432 H'CAP (JOCKEY CLUB GRASSROOTS SPRINT SERIES QUALIFIER) (DIV I) 5f 193y
2:45 (2:46) (Class 5) (0-70,70) 3-Y-0+ **£2,587** (£770; £384; £192) **Stalls** Low

Form RPR

2412 **1** **Salvatore Fury (IRE)**[5] 3198 3-8-9 **58** ....(p) JoeFanning 5 65+
(Keith Dalgleish) *took keen hold: hld up: not clear run well over 1f out: shkn up to ld wl ins fnl f: edgd lft: kpt on wl* **9/2**[3]

-000 **2** 3/4 **Consistant**[10] 3068 5-9-0 **56** .... DuranFentiman 1 63
(Brian Baugh) *led: rdn over 2f out: edgd lft 1f out: hdd wl ins fnl f: kpt on same pce* **25/1**

10-0 **3** 1/2 **Ferdy (IRE)**[21] 2707 4-9-3 **64** .... JasonHart(5) 6 69
(Paul Green) *sn rdn along towards rr: hdwy on outside over 1f out: kpt on ins fnl f: nrst fin* **22/1**

-045 **4** 1 **Blue Shoes (IRE)**[9] 3090 4-9-9 **65** .... RobertWinston 8 67
(Tim Easterby) *prom: effrt and ch appr fnl f: one pce last 100yds* **8/1**

0522 **5** 3 1/4 **Bunce (IRE)**[10] 3068 5-9-13 **69** ....(v[1]) DanielTudhope 4 61
(David O'Meara) *trckd ldrs: effrt and rdn 2f out: edgd rt and one pce appr fnl f* **11/4**[2]

6-05 **6** 2 **Parisian Pyramid (IRE)**[19] 2781 7-9-7 **68** ....(v) GeorgeChaloner(5) 10 53
(Patrick Morris) *wnt sltly lft s: bhd: rdn 1/2-way: hdwy fnl f: n.d* **14/1**

503- **7** 1/2 **Oil Strike**[245] 7100 6-9-13 **69** .... GrahamGibbons 7 53
(Michael Easterby) *t.k.h: w ldr tl rdn and wknd appr fnl f* **9/4**[1]

6030 **8** 3 1/2 **Rio's Girl**[11] 3024 6-8-11 **53** .... BarryMcHugh 3 26
(Tony Coyle) *chsd ldrs: drvn and outpcd over 2f out: sn wknd* **40/1**

0-04 **9** nk **Fife Jo**[24] 2635 3-8-6 **55** .... AndrewElliott 9 25
(Jim Goldie) *sn bhd and outpcd: no ch fr 1/2-way* **16/1**

0030 **10** 1 **Youhavecontrol (IRE)**[14] 2918 5-9-6 **62** ....(t) TomEaves 2 30
(Nicky Vaughan) *in tch on ins: rdn over 2f out: outpcd whn hmpd over 1f out* **50/1**

1m 14.42s (0.72) **Going Correction** +0.125s/f (Good)
WFA 3 from 4yo+ 7lb **10** Ran SP% **111.9**
Speed ratings (Par 103): **100,99,98,97,92 90,89,84,84,82**
toteswingers 1&2 £16.00, 1&3 £8.90, 2&3 £24.30 CSF £110.47 CT £2235.97 TOTE £4.70: £1.70, £7.80, £5.70; EX 118.10 Trifecta £1562.00 Pool: £3,841.09 - 1.84 winning units..
Owner Prestige Thoroughbred Racing **Bred** Ken Harris & Dr Brid Corkery **Trained** Carluke, S Lanarks

FOCUS
Not many came here in much form. It was run at a fair pace but was the slower division, with the winner scoring impressively. There could be a bit more to come from him at a modest level.

3393 WATCH RACING UK ON SKY 432 H'CAP (JOCKEY CLUB GRASSROOTS SPRINT SERIES QUALIFIER) (DIV II) 5f 193y
3:15 (3:15) (Class 5) (0-70,70) 3-Y-0+ **£2,587** (£770; £384; £192) **Stalls** Low

Form RPR

-004 **1** **Indego Blues**[19] 2781 4-9-13 **69** .... FrannyNorton 6 79
(David Nicholls) *trckd ldrs: effrt and swtchd lft over 1f out: edgd rt and led ins fnl f: hld on wl* **9/2**[2]

-400 **2** nk **Diamondhead (IRE)**[14] 2929 4-9-10 **69** .... LeeTopliss(3) 5 78
(Ed de Giles) *w ldr: rdn to ld over 1f out: hdd ins fnl f: rallied: hld cl home* **2/1**[1]

10-2 **3** 1/2 **Circuitous**[21] 2707 5-9-11 **67** ....(v) JoeFanning 2 74
(Keith Dalgleish) *led: rdn and hdd over 1f out: rallied and ev ch ins fnl f: kpt on: hld nr fin* **9/2**[2]

4-01 **4** hd **Who's Shirl**[10] 3068 7-10-0 **70** .... PaulMulrennan 1 76
(Chris Fairhurst) *hld up on ins: rdn and hdwy over 1f out: r.o ins fnl f* **9/2**[2]

0-06 **5** 2 3/4 **Little Jimmy Odsox (IRE)**[21] 2707 5-9-5 **61** ....(b) GrahamGibbons 9 59
(Tim Easterby) *prom: effrt and carried sltly lft over 1f out: sn rdn: one pce fnl f* **10/1**[3]

4600 **6** 2 3/4 **Rutterkin (USA)**[4] 3236 5-8-2 **51** oh1 .... VictorSantos(7) 10 40
(Richard Ford) *chsd ldng gp: drvn over 2f out: no imp over 1f out* **50/1**

0035 **7** 1 3/4 **Celestial Dawn**[17] 2835 4-9-1 **57** .... JamesSullivan 4 40
(John Weymes) *dwlt: bhd: hdwy on outside over 2f out: edgd rt over 1f out: no imp* **12/1**

3010 **8** hd **Needy McCredie**[9] 3078 7-9-4 **60** .... PJMcDonald 8 43
(James Turner) *bhd: rdn over 2f out: edgd rt over 1f out: n.d* **22/1**

-445 **9** 5 **Karate Queen**[20] 2757 8-8-11 **53** oh1 ow2 ....(p) DaleSwift 7 20
(Ron Barr) *chsd ldng gp: outpcd over 2f out: sn btn* **33/1**

1m 14.24s (0.54) **Going Correction** +0.125s/f (Good) **9** Ran SP% **113.9**
Speed ratings (Par 103): **101,100,99,99,96 92,90,89,83**
toteswingers 1&2 £3.90, 1&3 £4.20, 2&3 £2.80 CSF £13.46 CT £41.77 TOTE £7.90: £2.20, £1.10, £1.30; EX 20.80 Trifecta £79.10 Pool: £3,258.53 - 30.89 winning units..
Owner Pinnacle Indesatchel Partnership **Bred** Bearstone Stud **Trained** Sessay, N Yorks

FOCUS
A open handicap run at a fair pace, with little covering the front four at the line. It suited those racing prominently and was the quicker division. The winner was a length off his previous form.

3394 ULTIMATE LADIES NIGHT ON 5TH AUGUST H'CAP 1m 3f 107y
3:45 (3:46) (Class 5) (0-70,68) 3-Y-0 **£1,678** (£1,678; £384; £192) **Stalls** High

Form RPR

-443 **1** **Chant (IRE)**[19] 2769 3-9-4 **65** .... PJMcDonald 3 75
(Ann Duffield) *chsd ldr: chal over 2f out: sn rdn: led ins fnl f: kpt on: jnd on line* **4/1**[3]

4-06 **1** dht **Spats Colombo**[21] 2716 3-8-2 **49** oh2 .... FrannyNorton 5 59
(Micky Hammond) *hld up towards rr: drvn and plenty to do over 3f out: gd hdwy and hung rt fr 2f out: kpt on wl fnl f to dead-heat on line* **10/1**

6543 **3** 3/4 **Wadacre Sarko**[18] 2799 3-9-3 **64** .... JoeFanning 1 73
(Mark Johnston) *chsd ldrs: hdwy to ld over 2f out: rdn and hung lft over 1f out: hdd ins fnl f: kpt on same pce nr fin* **9/4**[1]

553 **4** 7 **Attention Seaker**[17] 2833 3-9-3 **64** .... DuranFentiman 7 61
(Tim Easterby) *prom: drvn and outpcd over 2f out: edgd rt and no imp over 1f out* **7/1**

-006 **5** 3 3/4 **Forced Family Fun**[25] 2602 3-9-5 **66** ....[1] PhillipMakin 2 57
(Michael Bell) *hld up: drvn and outpcd over 3f out: sme late hdwy: nvr on terms* **7/2**[2]

55-0 **6** 3 1/4 **Rocky Two (IRE)**[51] 1829 3-9-7 **68** .... PaulMulrennan 4 53
(Michael Dods) *hld up in tch: drvn and outpcd over 2f out: btn over 1f out* **7/1**

00-5 **7** 6 **Oh Boy Oh Boy**[18] 2799 3-7-13 **49** oh4 ....(p) NeilFarley(3) 6 24
(James Moffatt) *s.i.s: bhd and sn pushed along: nvr on terms* **66/1**

34-6 **8** 14 **Baraboy (IRE)**[37] 2274 3-8-11 **58** .... JamesSullivan 8
(Barry Murtagh) *led to over 2f out: sn rdn and wknd* **22/1**

2m 27.86s (4.76) **Going Correction** +0.125s/f (Good) **8** Ran SP% **112.9**
27 Trifecta £Owner M H O G Bred.
Owner Mrs Ann Starkie & Mrs I Starkie **Bred** Roger K Lee **Trained** Constable Burton, N Yorks

FOCUS
Plenty of unexposed types in this handicap, which was run at an honest pace and saw a thrilling finish. The form makes sense rated around dead-heater Chant and the third.

3395 BELL & PLATE DAY NEXT WEDNESDAY H'CAP 7f 200y
4:15 (4:15) (Class 5) (0-70,69) 4-Y-0+ **£2,587** (£770; £384; £192) **Stalls** Low

Form RPR

4-00 **1** **Dubious Escapade (IRE)**[16] 2882 4-9-3 **65** ....(p) PJMcDonald 13 74
(Ann Duffield) *prom: hdwy on outside over 2f out: rdn and led ins fnl f: kpt on wl* **15/2**[3]

3120 **2** 1 3/4 **Alluring Star**[40] 2162 5-9-2 **64** .... GrahamGibbons 12 69
(Michael Easterby) *led: rdn 2f out: hdd ins fnl f: kpt on same pce towards fin* **5/4**[1]

6211 **3** 2 **Royal Holiday (IRE)**[27] 2536 6-9-0 **62** ....(p) DanielTudhope 8 62
(Marjorie Fife) *pressed ldr: rdn and ev ch over 2f out: nt qckn appr fnl f* **9/4**[2]

0-00 **4** 1 1/4 **Conjuror's Bluff**[5] 3203 5-8-1 **52** .... NeilFarley(3) 4 49
(Frederick Watson) *trckd ldrs: drvn over 2f out: one pce over 1f out* **100/1**

-600 **5** 5 **Aquarian Spirit**[37] 2278 6-8-9 **57** ....(b) TonyHamilton 9 43
(Richard Fahey) *s.i.s: sn niggled in rr: drvn 4f out: hdwy and edgd rt over 1f out: nvr rchd ldrs* **10/1**

30-0 **6** 3 1/2 **Pendle Lady (IRE)**[11] 3029 4-8-7 **55** .... JamesSullivan 2 33
(Mark Brisbourne) *hld up in tch: drvn and outpcd wl over 3f out: n.d after* **25/1**

4404 **7** 14 **River Ardeche**[14] 2912 8-8-7 **55** ....(p) FrannyNorton 5
(Tracy Waggott) *chsd ldrs tl hung rt and wknd fr 2f out* **17/2**

1m 41.63s (1.63) **Going Correction** +0.125s/f (Good) **7** Ran SP% **111.4**
Speed ratings (Par 103): **96,94,92,91,86 82,68**
toteswingers 1&2 £2.80, 1&3 £3.80, 2&3 £1.20 CSF £16.49 CT £27.13 TOTE £7.10: £3.50, £1.40; EX 25.90 Trifecta £60.40 Pool: £1,725.29 - 21.38 winning units..
Owner Les Stirling **Bred** Ballygallon Stud Limited **Trained** Constable Burton, N Yorks

FOCUS
Six non-runners in this handicap, which was run at a sound pace. Little depth to the race, in which the winner is rated back to her old form.

3396 JOIN NOW AT REWARDS4RACING.COM FILLIES' H'CAP 6f 192y
4:45 (4:45) (Class 4) (0-80,77) 3-Y-0 **£6,469** (£1,925; £962; £481) **Stalls** Low

Form RPR

-005 **1** **Penny Garcia**[9] 3104 3-9-5 **75** .... DuranFentiman 2 85
(Tim Easterby) *midfield: rdn over 2f out: hdwy to ld over 1f out: edgd rt: hld on wl* **16/1**

0-30 **2** hd **Elle Woods (IRE)**[10] 3066 3-9-7 **77** ....(p) PaulMulrennan 1 86
(Michael Dods) *hld up in tch: n.m.r over 2f out: swtchd lft and hdwy over 1f out: chsd wnr fnl f: r.o: jst hld* **8/1**

0-01 **3** 5 **Bousatet (FR)**[28] 2503 3-8-9 **65** .... AmyRyan 3 68+
(Kevin Ryan) *trckd ldrs: effrt whn no room fr 2f out: swtchd lft and hdwy appr fnl f: kpt on to go 3rd cl home: no ch w first two* **10/1**

0-23 **4** nk **Tussie Mussie**[21] 2704 3-9-6 **76** .... JoeFanning 7 71
(Mark Johnston) *prom: disp ld over 2f out to over 1f out: outpcd fnl f* **7/2**[2]

51-1 **5** shd **Silkelly**[24] 2635 3-9-5 **75** .... DanielTudhope 8 69
(David O'Meara) *led: jnd over 2f out: hdd over 1f out: sn rdn: outpcd fnl f* **9/4**[1]

6020 **6** 1/2 **Flighty Clarets (IRE)**[21] 2703 3-8-9 **65** .... TonyHamilton 5 58
(Richard Fahey) *dwlt: bhd: rdn over 2f out: hdwy over 1f out: kpt on fnl f: nrst fin* **25/1**

0-04 **7** 1 1/4 **Fab Lolly (IRE)**[24] 2628 3-8-10 **66** .... AndrewElliott 6 56
(James Bethell) *prom: effrt on outside over 2f out: wknd fnl f* **20/1**

1-5S **8** nk **Elle Rebelle**[42] 2071 3-8-10 **66** .... PaulQuinn 11 55
(Mark Brisbourne) *taken early to post: dwlt: bhd: swtchd lft and hdwy over 1f out: nvr rchd ldrs* **25/1**

0-35 **9** 1/2 **Reconsider Baby (IRE)**[25] 2593 3-8-12 **68** ....(v[1]) BarryMcHugh 4 56
(Mrs K Burke) *towards rr: drvn over 3f out: wknd 2f out* **6/1**[3]

1-30 **10** nk **Cinderslipper (IRE)**[28] 2506 3-8-9 **65** .... PJMcDonald 9 52
(Ann Duffield) *hld up: shortlived effrt 3f out: sn btn* **12/1**

4200 **11** 13 **Tom's Anna (IRE)**[13] 2959 3-8-9 **65** .... GrahamGibbons 10 17
(Tim Easterby) *wnt lft s: chsd ldrs tl rdn and wknd 2f out* **33/1**

1m 28.6s (1.50) **Going Correction** +0.125s/f (Good) **11** Ran SP% **116.4**
Speed ratings (Par 98): **96,95,90,89,89 89,87,87,86,86 71**
toteswingers 1&2 £11.90, 1&3 £24.80, 2&3 £13.40 CSF £129.97 CT £933.19 TOTE £26.90: £7.00, £3.20, £3.10; EX 92.60 Trifecta £1538.30 Pool: £2,989.76 - 1.45 winning units..
Owner Jim & Helen Bowers **Bred** J Bowers **Trained** Great Habton, N Yorks

FOCUS
Plenty of unexposed types in this fillies' handicap, which was run at a sound pace. The first two finished clear and this is sound form.

3397 CUMWHINTON H'CAP (JOCKEY CLUB GRASSROOTS MIDDLE DISTANCE SERIES QUALIFIER) 1m 1f 61y
5:15 (5:15) (Class 5) (0-70,70) 4-Y-0+ £2,587 (£770; £384; £192) Stalls Low

Form RPR
50-2 1 **Hydrant**[19] 2785 7-8-9 **65** ConnorBeasley(7) 11 73
(Richard Guest) *mde all: rdn 2f out: edgd lft ins fnl f: sn hrd pressed: hld on wl cl home* **11/4**[1]
4413 2 *hd* **Rawaafed (IRE)**[2] 3337 4-9-1 **64** JoeFanning 10 72
(Keith Dalgleish) *hld up: hdwy on outside wl over 1f out: chsd wnr ins fnl f: kpt on: jst hld* **3/1**[2]
-066 3 *3/4* **Call Of Duty (IRE)**[10] 3043 8-8-10 **59** PJMcDonald 5 65
(Dianne Sayer) *hld up: rdn and hdwy over 1f out: edgd rt ins fnl f: r.o* **5/1**
-654 4 *2 1/4* **Border Bandit (USA)**[16] 2886 5-8-4 **53** BarryMcHugh 3 54
(Tracy Waggott) *in tch: effrt and rdn 2f out: one pce fnl f* **4/1**[3]
/0-0 5 *1* **Destination Aim**[16] 2886 6-9-7 **70** PaddyAspell 9 69
(Frederick Watson) *dwlt: bhd tl hdwy on outside over 1f out: kpt on: n.d* **100/1**
3-50 6 *1 3/4* **Edas**[24] 2636 11-8-5 **59** JasonHart(5) 4 54
(Thomas Cuthbert) *in tch: hdwy to chse wnr over 2f out: sn hung rt: wknd ins fnl f* **16/1**
5450 7 *3 1/4* **Availed Speaker (IRE)**[12] 2977 4-7-10 **52** SamanthaBell(7) 7 40
(Richard Fahey) *t.k.h: hld up in tch: hdwy to chse wnr after 3f to over 2f out: wknd over 1f out* **16/1**
515- 8 *10* **Gadobout Dancer**[265] 6561 6-8-4 **53** JamesSullivan 6 19
(Julie Camacho) *prom: drvn over 3f out: wknd over 2f out* **14/1**
53-3 9 *9* **Graceful Act**[20] 2754 5-8-8 **57** ow2 TomEaves 8
(Ron Barr) *chsd wnr 3f: cl up tl rdn and wknd over 2f out* **14/1**

1m 57.98s (0.38) **Going Correction** +0.125s/f (Good) **9 Ran SP% 114.4**
Speed ratings (Par 103): **103,102,102,100,99 97,94,85,77**
toteswingers 1&2 £2.70, 1&3 £4.40, 2&3 £3.70 CSF £11.05 CT £37.85 TOTE £3.60: £1.10, £1.90, £2.50; EX 14.10 Trifecta £47.60 Pool: £2,175.89 - 34.24 winning units..
Owner C Hatch **Bred** Lord Halifax **Trained** Wetherby, W Yorks

FOCUS
This handicap was run at a fair pace with the winner making all. Modest, sound form.

3398 WETHERAL MAIDEN STKS 1m 1f 61y
5:45 (5:45) (Class 5) 3-Y-0+ £2,587 (£770; £384; £192) Stalls Low

Form RPR
050- 1 **Returntobrecongill**[284] 5962 3-9-3 60 JamesSullivan 1 72
(Sally Hall) *t.k.h early: mde all: hrd pressed fr over 1f out: hld on gamely nr fin* **40/1**
2 2 *hd* **Fashion Line (IRE)**[9] 3116 3-8-12 0 PaulMulrennan 10 67
(Michael Bell) *in tch: hdwy over 2f out: disp ld fr over 1f out: kpt on fnl f: jst hld: fin lame* **1/3**[1]
40- 3 *5* **Perfect Pose (IRE)**[279] 6117 3-8-12 0 TomEaves 2 56
(Michael Dods) *trckd ldrs: effrt and rdn 3f out: outpcd by first two over 1f out* **20/1**[3]
0- 4 *1 1/2* **Obboorr**[396] 2197 4-10-0 0 MickyFenton 3 57
(Brian Rothwell) *dwlt: bhd: shkn up over 4f out: styd on fr 2f out: nvr nr to chal* **25/1**
3- 5 *2 3/4* **My Mum Mo**[182] 8151 5-9-9 0 PaddyAspell 8 46
(Simon West) *hld up in midfield: effrt and pushed along over 3f out: wknd over 1f out* **20/1**[3]
32-0 6 *shd* **Loch Moy**[58] 1683 3-9-3 73 TonyHamilton 11 51
(Richard Fahey) *prom on outside: rdn 3f out: wknd over 1f out* **3/1**[2]
60-0 7 *2* **Miss Matiz**[28] 2503 6-9-2 29 ConnorBeasley(7) 6 42
(Alan Kirtley) *hld up: rdn and hdwy on outside wl over 2f out: wknd over 1f out* **100/1**
8 *7* **Bollin Bob**[46] 4-9-9 0 AdamCarter(5) 9 31
(Tim Easterby) *bhd: rdn and outpcd over 4f out: n.d after* **33/1**
00-0 9 *5* **Billy Redpath**[28] 2507 5-10-0 28 (p) DuranFentiman 7 20
(Frederick Watson) *hld up in midfield: drvn and outpcd over 3f out: sn btn* **100/1**
0 10 *26* **Captain Rhyric**[10] 3047 4-9-11 0 LucyAlexander(3) 5
(James Moffatt) *t.k.h: prom tl rdn and wknd over 3f out: t.o* **66/1**
06-0 11 *32* **Online**[16] 1282 3-9-3 0 (t) BarryMcHugh 4
(Tracy Waggott) *cl up tl wknd over 3f out: eased whn no ch fnl 2f: t.o* **100/1**

1m 59.79s (2.19) **Going Correction** +0.125s/f (Good)
WFA 3 from 4yo+ 11lb **11 Ran SP% 123.2**
Speed ratings (Par 103): **95,94,90,89,86 86,84,78,74,50 22**
toteswingers 1&2 £6.90, 1&3 £25.80, 2&3 £3.70 CSF £56.38 TOTE £66.00: £8.60, £1.02, £4.80; EX 123.50 Trifecta £743.80 Pool: £3,265.08 - 3.29 winning units..
Owner Mrs Joan Hodgson **Bred** Miss S E Hall **Trained** Middleham Moor, N Yorks
■ Stewards' Enquiry : Paul Mulrennan two-day ban; used whip above permitted level (1st-2nd July).

FOCUS
A modest and uncompetitive maiden run in a relatively slow time. The first two finished clear, with the shock winner too strong for the disappointing favourite.
T/Plt: £83.60 to a £1 stake. Pool: £82,461.36 - 719.99 winning units T/Qpdt: £19.50 to a £1 stake. Pool: £5,389.17 - 204.10 winning units RY

3210 KEMPTON (A.W) (R-H)
Monday, June 17

OFFICIAL GOING: Standard
Wind: Light; across Weather: Light cloud; dry

3399 CONOR MAYNARD LIVE AT KEMPTON 14.09.13 H'CAP 1m 2f (P)
2:30 (2:30) (Class 6) (0-60,60) 4-Y-0+ £1,940 (£577; £288; £144) Stalls Low

Form RPR
3532 1 **Time Square (FR)**[17] 2845 6-9-5 **58** AdamKirby 3 68
(Tony Carroll) *sn bustled along to ld and mde rest: rdn clr 2f out: styd on u.p fnl f* **6/4**[1]
0-34 2 *2* **Minstrel Lad**[18] 2801 5-9-1 **54** HayleyTurner 1 60
(Jonjo O'Neill) *chsd ldrs: chsd wnr 6f out: rdn and effrt 2f out: kpt on fnl f but nvr gng pce to threaten wnr* **6/1**[2]
0/00 3 *1* **True Pleasure (IRE)**[21] 921 6-8-10 **49** TedDurcan 2 53
(James Bethell) *t.k.h: broke wl: sn stdd bk to chse ldrs: rdn and wnt 3rd jst over 2f out: kpt on wl ins fnl f: nvr gng to chal wnr* **25/1**
6-06 4 *3/4* **Catchanova (IRE)**[28] 2514 6-9-6 **59** NeilCallan 5 62+
(Eve Johnson Houghton) *hld up in midfield: nt clr run and shuffled bk 3f out: plenty to do whn swtchd lft and hdwy over 1f out: r.o strly fnl f: nt rch ldrs* **8/1**
2505 5 *3 3/4* **Having A Ball**[27] 2533 9-9-5 **58** ChrisCatlin 8 53
(Geoffrey Deacon) *racd in last quartet: plenty to do and hdwy over 1f out: styd on fnl f: nvr trbld ldrs* **8/1**
0-25 6 *3/4* **Buaiteoir (FR)**[49] 1890 7-9-2 **60** RobertTart(5) 10 54
(Nikki Evans) *stdd s: t.k.h: hld up in last pair: stl bhd whn swtchd lft and forced v wd bnd 2f out: hdwy over 1f out: r.o fnl f: nvr trbld ldrs* **13/2**[3]
0-16 7 *4 1/2* **Poetry Writer**[13] 2954 4-9-2 **55** LiamKeniry 7 40
(Michael Blanshard) *chsd wnr tl 6f out: 4th and btn u.p 2f out: wknd over 1f out* **12/1**
600- 8 *2 1/4* **Bull Five**[11] 1299 6-9-4 **57** SebSanders 4 37
(Nick Littmoden) *dwlt: sn rdn along and rcvrd to r in midfield after 2f: rdn and struggling 3f out: wknd 2f out* **33/1**
00-0 9 *1/2* **Compton Bird**[103] 903 4-8-10 **54** (t) NicoleNordblad(5) 9 33
(Hans Adielsson) *stdd s: bhd: niggled along 6f out: n.d* **16/1**
-600 10 *1* **Rasteau (IRE)**[39] 703 5-8-7 **46** oh1 LukeMorris 6 23
(Tom Keddy) *dwlt: bustled along early: a towards rr: n.d* **66/1**
415- 11 *7* **Barathea Dancer (IRE)**[77] 7599 5-9-1 **54** (tp) IanMongan 12 17
(Christine Dunnett) *in tch in midfield: rdn and struggling 3f out: wknd over 2f out: bhd and eased wl ins fnl f* **33/1**
4255 12 *17* **Queenie's Star (IRE)**[10] 3056 6-8-8 **47** JimmyQuinn 13
(Michael Attwater) *in tch in midfield: rdn and lost pl 3f out: wl bhd and eased ins fnl f: t.o* **25/1**

2m 7.47s (-0.53) **Going Correction** 0.0s/f (Stan) **12 Ran SP% 118.5**
Speed ratings (Par 101): **102,100,99,99,96 95,91,90,89,88 83,69**
toteswingers 1&2 £2.40, 1&3 £15.30, 2&3 £25.60 CSF £9.65 CT £163.22 TOTE £2.50: £1.70, £2.10, £8.10; EX 8.60 Trifecta £232.10 Pool: £2,369.41 - 7.65 winning units..
Owner M S Cooke **Bred** Mme Therese Bouche & Isabelle Roussel **Trained** Cropthorne, Worcs

FOCUS
A moderate handicap in which the low draws dominated and it paid to race close to the pace. The winner is rated in line with his turf latest.

3400 BETVICTOR ROYAL ASCOT NO LOSE HUGHES H'CAP 5f (P)
3:00 (3:02) (Class 4) (0-80,80) 3-Y-O £4,690 (£1,395; £697; £348) Stalls Low

Form RPR
41-0 1 **Royal Acquisition**[51] 1844 3-8-11 **70** ShaneKelly 1 74
(Robert Cowell) *mde all: rdn and qcknd 2 l clr ent fnl f: drvn ins fnl f: being ct towards fin but a gng to hold on* **7/2**[3]
3413 2 *nk* **Royal Challis**[7] 3159 3-8-11 **75** WilliamTwiston-Davies(5) 4 78+
(Richard Hannon) *racd in midfield: sltly outpcd over 1f out: rallied and hdwy u.p 1f out: sn swtchd rt: chsd wnr fnl 75yds: r.o wl: nvr quite getting to wnr* **3/1**[2]
3550 3 *1* **Silca's Dream**[13] 2959 3-7-12 **64** DanielCremin(7) 5 63
(Mick Channon) *chsd wnr: rdn and pressed wnr over 1f out: unable qck ent fnl f: styd on same pce after* **14/1**
336- 4 *1* **Pal Of The Cat**[213] 7738 3-9-0 **73** AdamBeschizza 2 69
(Brian Gubby) *racd in midfield: rdn and clsd on ldrs wl over 1f out: styd on same pce ins fnl f* **33/1**
266- 5 *1* **Max The Machine**[256] 6808 3-8-8 **67** MartinDwyer 3 59
(Derek Shaw) *racd in last pair: rdn and effrt wl over 1f out: no imp tl styd on ins fnl f: nvr trbld ldrs* **25/1**
3-21 6 *1* **Pearl Bridge**[23] 2672 3-9-7 **80** JamieSpencer 6 69
(Ralph Beckett) *stdd leaving stalls: sn dropped to last and racing awkwardly: last and hanging bnd 4f out tl 2f out: swtchd lft 1f out: styd on fnl f: n.d* **1/1**[1]

1m 0.33s (-0.17) **Going Correction** 0.0s/f (Stan) **6 Ran SP% 110.7**
Speed ratings (Par 101): **101,100,98,97,95 94**
toteswingers 1&2 £1.60, 1&3 £4.80, 2&3 £4.40 CSF £13.93 TOTE £5.10: £2.40, £2.40; EX 16.30 Trifecta £80.70 Pool: £3,574.47 - 33.21 winning units..
Owner J Sargeant **Bred** Dunchurch Lodge Stud Co **Trained** Six Mile Bottom, Cambs

FOCUS
More than half the field in this 3-y-o sprint handicap were returning from breaks. The winner, with the best draw, made all the running. Modest form, with the favourite disappointing.

3401 BETVICTOR ROYAL ASCOT MONEY BACK SPECIAL MAIDEN STKS 6f (P)
3:30 (3:35) (Class 5) 3-Y-O+ £2,587 (£770; £384; £192) Stalls Low

Form RPR
3-40 1 **Zhiggy's Stardust**[45] 1985 4-9-12 69 DaneO'Neill 9 86
(Henry Candy) *sn led: drew clr w rival 2f out: hdd over 1f out: battled on u.p to ld again ins fnl f: styd on wl* **7/2**[2]
0332 2 *1 1/2* **The Dark Wizard (IRE)**[21] 2722 3-9-5 70 JamesDoyle 12 79
(Roger Charlton) *chsd ldrs: wnt 2nd after 2f: rdn and drew clr w wnr 2f out: drvn to ld over 1f out: hdd ins fnl f: no ex and wknd towards fin* **7/4**[1]
23 3 *2 3/4* **Celestial Ray**[6] 3170 4-9-12 0 LukeMorris 8 72+
(Sir Mark Prescott Bt) *hld up in midfield: effrt and swtchd lft over 1f out: hdwy to chse ldng pair 1f out: kpt on u.p but nvr a threat* **4/1**[3]
0- 4 *2* **Oasis Spirit**[234] 7372 3-9-0 0 LiamKeniry 11 59+
(Andrew Balding) *slowly away: sn swtchd lft and racd in last trio: plenty to do and effrt on inner 2f out: wnt 4th jst ins fnl f: kpt on but no threat to ldrs* **12/1**
55 5 *1* **Greek Spirit (IRE)**[23] 2650 3-9-0 0 SebSanders 4 56+
(Jeremy Noseda) *hld up in last trio: plenty to do and effrt 2f out: sme hdwy whn swtchd lft jst ins fnl f: styd on: nvr trbld ldrs* **9/1**
0-0 6 *1* **Addictive Nature (IRE)**[30] 2448 3-9-5 0 AdamKirby 3 58
(Clive Cox) *in tch in midfield: rdn and unable qck ent fnl 2f: outpcd and wl hld over 1f out: plugged on* **10/1**
5 7 *2 1/4* **Immediately**[24] 2637 3-9-0 0 ShaneKelly 2 45
(Robert Cowell) *chsd ldng trio: rdn and unable qck ent fnl 2f: wknd over 1f out* **50/1**
U5-0 8 *1 3/4* **Wishing Bridge**[23] 2672 3-9-5 0 CathyGannon 7 45
(Pat Eddery) *chsd ldr for 2f: rdn and struggling jst over 2f out: wknd over 1f out* **33/1**
06 9 *8* **Shikamoo**[20] 2746 3-9-0 0 RichardThomas 1
(Dr Jeremy Naylor) *in tch in midfield: rdn and lost pl over 2f out: bhd over 1f out* **100/1**
10 *nk* **Lady Tabitha (IRE)** 3-9-0 0 IanMongan 5
(Jo Crowley) *a bhd* **25/1**

6- **11** *28* **Lebresem**[273] 6320 3-9-5 0 NeilCallan 10
(James Tate) *dwlt: sn rdn along and rcvrd to r in midfield: lost pl and bhd 1/2-way: t.o fnl 2f* **20/1**

1m 12.27s (-0.83) **Going Correction** 0.0s/f (Stan)
WFA 3 from 4yo 7lb **11** Ran SP% **119.9**
Speed ratings (Par 103): **105,103,99,96,95 94,91,88,78,77 40**
toteswingers 1&2 £2.40, 1&3 £3.00, 2&3 £2.30 CSF £9.75 TOTE £4.50: £1.50, £1.10, £1.40; EX 11.60 Trifecta £40.90 Pool: £4,822.37 - 88.27 winning units..
Owner Henry Candy **Bred** Mr And Mrs L Baker **Trained** Kingston Warren, Oxon

FOCUS
The experienced runners set a modest standard in this older-horse maiden and they had the race between them throughout. A personal best from the winner.

3402 BETVICTOR.COM MEDIAN AUCTION MAIDEN STKS 1m 4f (P)
4:00 (4:03) (Class 5) 3-5-Y-O **£2,587** (£770; £384; £192) **Stalls** Centre

Form RPR
5 **1** **Poyle Thomas**[25] 2605 4-9-13 0 SebSanders 5 81+
(Ralph Beckett) *t.k.h: hld up in tch: clsd on ldrs 5f out: rdn and effrt over 2f out: led over 1f out: hld on wl fnl f* **3/1**[2]

05 **2** *nk* **Violet Dancer**[26] 2560 3-8-13 0 ShaneKelly 7 80+
(Gary Moore) *hld up in tch in last pair: hdwy to trck ldrs 4f out: ev ch u.p wl over 1f out: hrd drvn and kpt on wl fnl f: a jst hld* **10/1**[3]

2423 **3** *3 3/4* **Could Be (IRE)**[24] 2641 3-8-13 70 MartinLane 3 74
(David Simcock) *in tch in midfield: hdwy to chse ldr 4f out tl led over 3f out: veered rt u.p ent fnl 2f: wnt rt again and hdd over 1f out: wknd ins fnl f* **3/1**[2]

0 **4** *10* **Qibtee (FR)**[11] 3021 3-8-13 0 SamHitchcott 4 58
(Mick Channon) *hld up in tch in rr: hdwy on inner to chse ldrs 4f out: rdn and outpcd over 2f out: wknd 2f out* **33/1**

35 **5** *nk* **Nellie Forbush**[31] 2423 3-8-8 0 LiamKeniry 2 53
(Andrew Balding) *chsd ldr tl 4f out: sn rdn and racing awkwardly: lost pl and no rspnse whn rdn over 3f out: wl btn 2f out* **6/4**[1]

06 **6** *22* **Russian Link**[14] 2938 3-8-8 0 JamesDoyle 6 32
(Roger Charlton) *rrd as stalls opened and slowly away: rcvrd to chse ldrs after 2f: lost pl 4f out: t.o over 2f out* **10/1**[3]

000- **7** *37* **Play Tiger (FR)**[385] 2560 4-9-13 58 WilliamCarson 1
(Peter Hiatt) *led tl over 3f out: sn dropped out: t.o fnl 2f* **100/1**

00 **8** *103* **Ardaal**[20] 2754 3-8-13 0 (vt[1]) FrederikTylicki 8
(James Fanshawe) *sn niggled along in midfield: dropped to rr and rdn 7f out: lost tch and eased fr over 4f out* **20/1**

2m 33.53s (-0.97) **Going Correction** 0.0s/f (Stan)
WFA 3 from 4yo 14lb **8** Ran SP% **116.9**
Speed ratings (Par 103): **103,102,100,93,93 78,54,**
toteswingers 1&2 £4.80, 1&3 £2.30, 2&3 £5.80 CSF £32.34 TOTE £3.40: £1.10, £3.50, £1.30; EX 32.00 Trifecta £115.20 Pool: £3,837.05 - 24.96 winning units..
Owner Cecil And Miss Alison Wiggins **Bred** Miss Alison Wiggins **Trained** Kimpton, Hants

FOCUS
A modest maiden with a disappointing favourite. The form makes sense amongst the front three, who were clear.

3403 BETVICTOR NO LOSE HUGHES MONEY BACK H'CAP 1m 4f (P)
4:30 (4:31) (Class 6) (0-60,60) 3-Y-O **£1,940** (£577; £288; £144) **Stalls** Centre

Form RPR
6-00 **1** **Choral Prince (IRE)**[14] 2935 3-9-5 58 ShaneKelly 3 66+
(Mike Murphy) *hld up in rr: clsd over 2f out: swtchd rt and qcknd to chse ldrs over 1f out: chal and nudged along jst ins fnl f: led fnl 75yds: tenderly handled and a doing enough after* **8/1**

00-4 **2** *nk* **Ebony Roc (IRE)**[18] 2802 3-8-13 52 PatDobbs 1 59
(Amanda Perrett) *chsd ldrs: rdn to ld over 1f out: pressed and hrd drvn ins fnl f: hdd fnl 75yds: kpt on but a hld* **11/8**[1]

00-5 **3** *1 1/2* **Frederick Alfred**[122] 663 3-8-10 49 TedDurcan 8 54
(Mark H Tompkins) *t.k.h: hld up in last pair early: hdwy into midfield 6f out: effrt u.p 2f out: swtchd lft over 1f out: edging rt and kpt on ins fnl f* **7/1**

00-6 **4** *1* **Skating Over (USA)**[31] 2423 3-9-7 60 PatCosgrave 10 63
(Jane Chapple-Hyam) *chsd ldr: rdn and ev ch over 1f out tl unable qck 1f out: carried rt and styd on same pce ins fnl f* **7/2**[2]

00-1 **5** *7* **Instinctual**[48] 1897 3-8-12 51 CathyGannon 4 43
(Brendan Powell) *in tch in midfield: lost pl 1/2-way: pushed along 4f out: rdn and no hdwy wl over 2f out: wknd 2f out* **6/1**[3]

600 **6** *1* **Cherry Princess**[28] 2519 3-8-7 46 ChrisCatlin 5 37
(Stuart Williams) *t.k.h early: in tch in midfield: rdn and unable qck over 2f out: wknd 2f out* **16/1**

-003 **7** *5* **Running Bull (IRE)**[20] 2748 3-8-0 46 oh1 NoelGarbutt[(7)] 2 31
(Linda Jewell) *led: clr 7f out tl rdn over 2f out: hdd over 1f out: sn btn: fdd fnl f* **25/1**

000- **8** *3/4* **Modern Society**[235] 7357 3-8-0 46 oh1 (b[1]) GemmaTutty[(7)] 6 27
(Andrew Reid) *in tch in midfield: rdn and unable qck over 2f out: wknd 2f out* **33/1**

000 **9** *99* **Indy Spirit (IRE)**[18] 2803 3-9-0 53 (p) IanMongan 9
(Laura Mongan) *hld up in tch in rr: rdn and struggling 3f out: sn lost tch: t.o fnl 2f* **33/1**

2m 37.0s (2.50) **Going Correction** 0.0s/f (Stan) **9** Ran SP% **117.8**
Speed ratings (Par 97): **91,90,89,89,84 83,80,79,13**
toteswingers 1&2 £2.90, 1&3 £10.20, 2&3 £3.50 CSF £19.56 CT £82.90 TOTE £8.50: £2.00, £1.40, £1.70; EX 24.40 Trifecta £220.40 Pool: £3,420.11 - 11.63 winning units..
Owner The Oratorios **Bred** Stonethorn Stud Farms Ltd **Trained** Westoning, Beds

FOCUS
Another moderate handicap and the time was 3.47secs slower than the preceding maiden. However the first four were clear and the form is interesting for the level.

3404 ROYAL ASCOT MONEY BACK AT BETVICTOR.COM H'CAP 7f (P)
5:00 (5:00) (Class 5) (0-75,74) 3-Y-O+ **£2,587** (£770; £384; £192) **Stalls** Low

Form RPR
31-1 **1** **Levi Draper**[25] 2596 4-9-9 69 HayleyTurner 4 80+
(James Fanshawe) *wl in tch in midfield: rdn and effrt 2f out: hdwy to ld jst ins fnl f: in command and idling towards fin* **9/4**[1]

1112 **2** *1* **Intomist (IRE)**[6] 3181 4-9-7 72 (p) NathanAlison[(5)] 6 78+
(Jim Boyle) *hld up in tch in midfield: rdn and effrt 2f out: styd on wl ins fnl f: wnt 2nd towards fin* **7/2**[2]

5112 **3** *nk* **Teen Ager (FR)**[13] 2954 9-9-2 62 (p) JimmyQuinn 5 67
(Paul Burgoyne) *hld up in tch in midfield: rdn 2f out: swtchd rt and effrt 2f out: hdwy u.p to chse wnr ins fnl f: kpt on but a hld: lost 2nd towards fin* **12/1**

0006 **4** *1 3/4* **Perfect Pastime**[6] 3172 5-9-11 71 (p) SebSanders 1 71
(Jim Boyle) *sn led: rdn ent fnl 2f: hdd jst ins fnl f: no ex and wknd fnl 75yds* **16/1**

1125 **5** *nk* **Admiralofthesea (USA)**[51] 1832 3-9-1 70 AdamBeschizza 8 67
(Robert Eddery) *hld up in tch towards rr: edgd rt 5f out: rdn ent fnl 2f: sltly outpcd over 1f out: rallied and styd on ins fnl f* **4/1**[3]

101 **6** *3/4* **Shahrazad (IRE)**[19] 2773 4-9-0 60 (t) LukeMorris 10 58
(Patrick Gilligan) *w ldr: ev ch and rdn ent fnl 2f: no ex jst over 1f out: wknd ins fnl f* **12/1**

0562 **7** *1/2* **West Leake (IRE)**[10] 3054 7-8-10 63 OisinMurphy[(7)] 2 59
(Paul Burgoyne) *chsd ldrs: effrt u.p on inner 2f out: no imp and struggling over 1f out: wknd fnl f* **14/1**

0-00 **8** *1* **Cocohatchee**[19] 2773 5-9-0 60 (p) IanMongan 3 54
(Pat Phelan) *in tch towards rr: hmpd and lost pl 5f out: sme hdwy u.p over 1f out: no imp fnl f* **50/1**

0300 **9** *1 1/4* **Cawett Cove (IRE)**[11] 3019 5-9-7 74 IanBurns[(7)] 11 64
(Jane Chapple-Hyam) *chsd ldrs tl lost pl u.p jst over 2f out: wknd over 1f out* **25/1**

-546 **10** *nse* **Orders From Rome (IRE)**[9] 3108 4-9-5 70 AmyScott[(5)] 7 60
(Eve Johnson Houghton) *stdd s: hld up in rr: shkn up and effrt ent fnl 2f: rdn and no prog over 1f out* **6/1**

00-3 **11** *11* **Al Aqabah (IRE)**[46] 1954 8-9-7 67 (b) GeorgeBaker 9 35
(Brian Gubby) *in tch towards rr: c wd off bnd over 2f out: sn struggling u.p: wknd wl over 1f out* **33/1**

1m 25.79s (-0.21) **Going Correction** 0.0s/f (Stan)
WFA 3 from 4yo+ 9lb **11** Ran SP% **124.0**
Speed ratings (Par 103): **101,99,99,97,97 96,95,94,93,93 80**
toteswingers 1&2 £3.80, 1&3 £6.10, 2&3 £7.00 CSF £10.42 CT £81.81 TOTE £3.40: £1.10, £1.40, £2.60; EX 15.10 Trifecta £61.70 Pool: £3,606.56 - 43.78 winning units..
Owner Andrew & Julia Turner **Bred** Cheveley Park Stud Ltd **Trained** Newmarket, Suffolk

FOCUS
Quite a competitive contest, and straightforward form.

3405 LADIES DAY WITH TOBY ANSTIS 07.09.13 H'CAP 7f (P)
5:30 (5:31) (Class 6) (0-60,60) 3-Y-O **£1,940** (£577; £216; £216) **Stalls** Low

Form RPR
60-2 **1** **Great Crested (IRE)**[26] 2566 3-9-7 60 (b[1]) ShaneKelly 11 75+
(Gary Moore) *hld up in tch in midfield: rdn and effrt over 1f out: drvn and qcknd to ld ins fnl f: r.o strly* **11/4**[1]

000- **2** *3 3/4* **Silvala Dance**[219] 7686 3-8-9 48 TedDurcan 4 53+
(Chris Wall) *bmpd s: hld up wl in tch: travelling wl and switching out lft ent fnl 2f: drvn and chsd ldrs over 1f out: outpcd by wnr but styd on to go 2nd wl ins fnl f* **4/1**[2]

4150 **3** *3/4* **Idle Curiosity (IRE)**[5] 3216 3-9-2 55 PatCosgrave 10 58
(Jim Boyle) *t.k.h: chsd ldrs tl led 2f out: drvn and hrd pressed over 1f out: hdd and immediately outpcd ins fnl f: kpt on* **20/1**

1300 **3** *dht* **Brynford**[18] 2802 3-9-3 56 SaleemGolam 2 59
(Chris Dwyer) *chsd ldrs: drvn and ev ch on inner over 1f out: outpcd by wnr but kpt on fnl f* **20/1**

2251 **5** *2* **Black Truffle (FR)**[13] 2950 3-9-6 59 (v) GeorgeBaker 12 57+
(Mark Usher) *t.k.h: hld up wl off the pce in last quartet: rdn and hdwy over 1f out: kpt on: nvr trbld ldrs* **5/1**[3]

06-5 **6** *6* **Indigo Moon**[17] 2824 3-9-3 56 JamesMcDonald 7 37
(Denis Coakley) *led: rdn and hdd 2f out: sn struggling: fdd fnl f* **6/1**

0-06 **7** *nse* **Royal Caper**[38] 2229 3-9-6 59 (p) AdamKirby 14 40
(John Ryan) *swtchd sharply rt leaving stalls: wl off the pce in last quartet: rdn and sme hdwy but wandering over 1f out: nvr trbld ldrs* **7/1**

066- **8** *1/2* **Iffley Fields**[347] 3789 3-9-4 57 JimmyQuinn 5 37
(Michael Squance) *wnt rt s: hld up in midfield: rdn and struggling over 2f out: wknd over 1f out* **33/1**

-005 **9** *3/4* **Ground Ginger**[27] 2556 3-8-12 51 MartinDwyer 6 29
(James Bethell) *racd in midfield: pushed along 4f out: rdn and no hdwy over 2f out: wknd 2f out* **20/1**

4000 **10** *1/2* **Early One Morning**[18] 2802 3-8-11 50 (b) LukeMorris 9 27
(Hugo Palmer) *chsd ldrs: rdn and unable qck over 2f out: wknd u.p over 1f out* **16/1**

5-46 **11** *9* **Man In The Arena**[140] 414 3-9-2 55 SebSanders 8
(Dr Jon Scargill) *racd wl off the pce in last quartet: rdn and no hdwy over 2f out: n.d* **25/1**

020 **12** *1 1/4* **Nepalese Pearl**[25] 2597 3-9-5 58 CathyGannon 1
(Pat Eddery) *wl off the pce in last quartet: n.d* **16/1**

0-4 **13** *12* **Simply Dreaming**[13] 2965 3-8-13 52 (p) AdamBeschizza 3
(Michael Squance) *in tch in midfield: rdn and wknd over 2f out: fdd bdly over 1f out: t.o* **50/1**

050 **14** *61* **Persian Marvel (IRE)**[6] 3178 3-8-4 48 (b) NathanAlison[(5)] 13
(Jim Boyle) *rrd as stalls opened and walked out of stalls: wl t.o thrght* **25/1**

1m 26.51s (0.51) **Going Correction** 0.0s/f (Stan) **14** Ran SP% **128.8**
CSF £12.89 CT £101.67 TOTE £3.10: £1.40, £2.00, £3.10; EX 17.60 Trifecta £242.00 1-13-7 £204.60, 1-13-9 £242.00. Pool: £2,349.20 - 4.30 & 3.627 Owner.

FOCUS
This moderate 3-y-o handicap was run 0.71 secs slower than the preceding, slightly higher-grade contest. The dead-heaters for third help set the standard.
T/Plt: £22.90 to a £1 stake. Pool: £69,354.02 - 2,205.63 winning units T/Qpdt: £6.50 to a £1 stake. Pool: £4,680.63 - 527.42 winning units SP

2281 WARWICK (L-H)
Monday, June 17

OFFICIAL GOING: Good (good to firm in places; 8.1)
Wind: Light; behind Weather: Cloudy with sunny spells

3406 BRIDGWATER PR AMATEUR RIDERS' H'CAP 1m 4f 134y
6:20 (6:20) (Class 6) (0-60,59) 4-Y-O+ **£1,871** (£580; £290; £145) **Stalls** Low

Form RPR
2-05 **1** **Josie's Dream (IRE)**[2] 3312 5-9-13 51 MrJamesHughes[(7)] 4 60
(Jo Hughes) *trckd ldr: racd keenly: led 9f out: clr 6f out: shkn up over 1f out: styd on* **4/1**[2]

0-13 **2** *2 1/2* **Jewelled Dagger (IRE)**[21] 2714 9-10-11 56 (t) MrSWalker 7 61
(Sharon Watt) *led: hdd 9f out: chsd wnr: rdn over 1f out: styd on* **5/1**[3]

05-5 **3** *1 3/4* **Cuckoo Rock (IRE)**[34] 2350 6-10-9 59 (p) MrJHarding[(5)] 6 61
(Jonathan Portman) *a.p: rdn over 1f out: styd on* **9/1**

2020 **4** *hd* **Iguacu**[8] 3133 9-10-7 52 (p) MissSBrotherton 1 54
(Richard Price) *hld up: hdwy over 2f out: rdn over 1f out: nt rch ldrs* **10/1**

4002 **5** *1* **Rowlestone Lad**[4] 3248 6-10-10 55 NicodeBoinville 12 56
(John Flint) *mid-div: hdwy 2f out: rdn and hung lft over 1f out: nvr nrr* **7/4**[1]

/44- **6** 3/4 **Picalily**[518] 195 4-10-10 **58** ConorShoemark(3) 5 57
(Brendan Powell) *fly-jmpd leaving stalls: chsd ldrs: rdn over 2f out: no ex fnl f* **14/1**

/60- **7** 3 1/4 **Star Hill**[36] 5936 6-10-2 **52** MrJoshuaNewman(5) 9 46
(Alan King) *hld up: rdn over 3f out: nvr on terms* **22/1**

0-50 **8** nk **King Of Wing (IRE)**[16] 2875 4-10-3 **55** (p) MrJAMcEntee(7) 10 49
(Phil McEntee) *hld up: sme hdwy over 2f out: rdn over 1f out: wknd fnl f* **66/1**

04-0 **9** 2 1/4 **Captain Oats (IRE)**[21] 2714 10-9-13 **51** MissSLBowen(7) 11 41
(Pam Ford) *hld up: hdwy over 6f out: wknd over 2f out* **40/1**

10 1/2 **Blewit (IRE)**[32] 7705 5-10-10 **58** MissBAndrews(3) 3 48
(William Kinsey) *chsd ldrs: n.m.r and stmbld over 10f out: lost pl over 5f out: n.d after* **28/1**

2120 **11** 7 **Gladstone (IRE)**[10] 3037 5-10-8 **53** MissRachelKing 2 32
(Polly Gundry) *mid-div: rdn over 3f out: sn wknd* **10/1**

4000 **12** 1/2 **Benandonner (USA)**[17] 2845 10-10-3 **53** MissMBryant(5) 13 31
(Paddy Butler) *s.i.s: hld up: a in rr: wknd 3f out* **66/1**

2m 47.31s (2.71) **Going Correction** -0.025s/f (Good) **12** Ran SP% **121.1**
Speed ratings (Par 101): **90,88,87,87,86 86,84,84,82,82 78,77**
toteswingers 1&2 £5.90, 1&3 £10.20, 2&3 £12.00 CSF £23.93 CT £173.14 TOTE £6.50: £1.90, £1.70, £2.70; EX 36.80 Trifecta £605.80 Pool: £1,029.27 - 1.27 winning units..
Owner Joseph Smith **Bred** Mrs J F Hughes **Trained** Lambourn, Berks
■ The first winner for 16-y-o James Hughes, son of the winning trainer trainer Jo Hughes.

FOCUS
A typically moderate amateur riders' handicap that was run at a steady early gallop. Doubts over the form given the way this panned out.

3407 ASSET FINANCE SOLUTIONS FUNDING UK BUSINESSES' FILLIES' H'CAP 6f
6:50 (6:53) (Class 4) (0-85,83) 3-Y-O+ **£4,690** (£1,395; £697; £348) **Stalls** Low

Form RPR

4-02 **1** **Fanrouge (IRE)**[27] 2531 4-9-12 **81** AndreaAtzeni 3 89
(Rod Millman) *hld up: hdwy over 2f out: rdn to ld ins fnl f: r.o* **15/2**

21-5 **2** 3/4 **Rivas Rhapsody (IRE)**[14] 2928 5-10-0 **83** SilvestreDeSousa 1 89
(Rae Guest) *s.i.s: sn chsng ldrs: rdn to ld over 1f out: edgd rt and hdd ins fnl f: styd on* **8/1**

0423 **3** 3/4 **Wicked Wench**[4] 3236 4-9-5 **74** (p) NeilCallan 4 78
(Jeremy Gask) *hld up: hmpd 2f out: hdwy over 1f out: edgd rt: r.o* **7/2**[3]

5403 **4** 3 **See Clearly**[9] 3090 4-8-10 **65** (p) KierenFallon 2 59
(Tim Easterby) *prom: rdn over 1f out: styd on same pce ins fnl f* **5/2**[1]

/0-0 **5** 2 1/4 **Royal Award**[40] 2173 4-9-2 **76** MatthewLawson(5) 5 63
(Jonathan Portman) *led: rdn and hdd over 1f out: wknd ins fnl f* **25/1**

-240 **6** 1/2 **Small Fury (IRE)**[17] 2825 3-9-0 **76** (p) J-PGuillambert 6 59
(Jo Hughes) *chsd ldr tl rdn over 1f out: wknd fnl f* **25/1**

0-54 **7** 1/2 **Ishi Honest**[10] 3050 3-8-3 **65** HarryBentley 7 57
(Mark Usher) *chsd ldrs: rdn and nt clr run over 1f out: wknd fnl f* **20/1**

0221 **8** 1 1/4 **Dancheur (IRE)**[5] 3223 4-9-7 **81** 6ex WilliamTwiston-Davies(5) 8 61
(Mrs K Burke) *s.i.s: hdwy over 3f out: edgd rt over 2f out: wknd over 1f out* **3/1**[2]

1m 12.66s (0.86) **Going Correction** +0.225s/f (Good)
WFA 3 from 4yo+ 7lb **8** Ran SP% **111.1**
Speed ratings (Par 102): **103,102,101,97,94 93,92,91**
toteswingers 1&2 £10.70, 1&3 £4.70, 2&3 £3.60 CSF £60.18 CT £238.56 TOTE £8.00: £3.30, £2.30, £2.10; EX 31.60 Trifecta £251.50 Pool: £1,012.14 - 3.01 winning units..
Owner Chris Scott **Bred** Silk Fan Syndicate **Trained** Kentisbeare, Devon

FOCUS
Reasonable form for the grade. The winner is rated back to form with the next two close to their marks.

3408 TURFTV MEDIAN AUCTION MAIDEN STKS 5f
7:20 (7:23) (Class 5) 2-Y-O **£2,587** (£770; £384; £192) **Stalls** Low

Form RPR

1 **Scruffy Tramp (IRE)** 2-9-5 0 SeanLevey 5 77+
(Michael Wigham) *s.i.s: sn trcking ldrs: shkn up to ld over 1f out: pushed out* **12/1**

3 **2** 1 1/2 **Taquka (IRE)**[14] 2917 2-9-5 0 JimCrowley 2 72
(Ralph Beckett) *chsd ldrs: nt clr run and swtchd rt over 1f out: rdn to chse wnr ins fnl f: r.o* **11/4**[3]

3 **3** 5 **Yellow Lady (IRE)**[28] 2517 2-9-0 0 (t) HarryBentley 3 49
(Olly Stevens) *led 1f: led again 3f out: rdn: edgd rt and hdd over 1f out: wknd ins fnl f* **15/8**[1]

4 4 1/2 **Saxony** 2-9-0 0 RenatoSouza 1 32
(Mark Usher) *chsd ldrs: outpcd over 3f out: sn bhd* **33/1**

5 1 **Pusey Street Vale** 2-9-0 0 NeilCallan 4 29
(John Gallagher) *racd keenly: led 4f out: hdd 3f out: hmpd over 1f out: sn wknd* **16/1**

6 27 **Dancing Juice** 2-9-5 0 KierenFallon 6
(Alan Jarvis) *wnt rt s and v slow to get gng: a t.o* **9/4**[2]

1m 1.53s (1.93) **Going Correction** +0.225s/f (Good) **6** Ran SP% **108.7**
Speed ratings (Par 93): **93,90,82,75,73 30**
toteswingers 1&2 £3.30, 1&3 £4.00, 2&3 £1.20 CSF £42.06 TOTE £10.00: £6.10, £1.10; EX 38.20 Trifecta £78.90 Pool: £1,005.64 - 9.54 winning units..
Owner D Hassan & B Green **Bred** Edmond Kent **Trained** Newmarket, Suffolk

FOCUS
A weak juvenile contest but the form could possibly be rated a few lengths better.

3409 VOUTE SALES WARWICKSHIRE OAKS STKS (LISTED RACE) (F&M) 1m 2f 188y
7:50 (7:51) (Class 1) 4-Y-O+
£22,684 (£8,600; £4,304; £2,144; £1,076; £540) **Stalls** Low

Form RPR

2- **1** **La Arenosa (IRE)**[241] 7234 4-8-12 **104** HarryBentley 7 95+
(Saeed bin Suroor) *hld up: hdwy over 2f out: nt clr run over 1f out: rdn to ld ins fnl f: r.o* **7/1**

13-0 **2** 3/4 **Sound Hearts (USA)**[32] 2399 4-8-12 **97** AndreaAtzeni 3 94
(Roger Varian) *plld hrd and sn prom: rdn and ev ch over 1f out: styd on* **4/1**[2]

4-56 **3** 1 1/2 **Dark Orchid (USA)**[116] 743 4-8-12 **105** SilvestreDeSousa 8 91
(Saeed bin Suroor) *trckd ldrs: plld hrd: led over 1f out: sn rdn: hdd and unable qck ins fnl f* **9/2**[3]

10-6 **4** 1/2 **Saint Hilary**[30] 2443 4-8-12 **88** NeilCallan 2 90
(William Muir) *trckd ldr: rdn over 2f out: sn ev ch: edgd rt and styd on same pce ins fnl f* **50/1**

41-4 **5** hd **Gallipot**[30] 2443 4-9-1 **102** WilliamBuick 5 93+
(John Gosden) *stmbld s: hld up: pushed along over 3f out: r.o ins fnl f: nvr nrr* **5/4**[1]

0240 **6** 3/4 **Signora Frasi (IRE)**[16] 2875 8-8-12 **50** SeanLevey 9 88?
(Tony Newcombe) *hld up: hdwy over 4f out: rdn over 1f out: styd on same pce ins fnl f: edgd rt nr fin* **200/1**

0-04 **7** 1/2 **Bridle Belle**[23] 2671 5-8-12 **87** JamieSpencer 1 87
(Richard Fahey) *led at stdy pce tl qcknd over 2f out: rdn and hdd over 1f out: no ex ins fnl f: hmpd nr fin* **18/1**

2-01 **8** 3 **Rhagori**[20] 2750 4-8-12 **88** JimCrowley 4 82
(Ralph Beckett) *plld hrd and prom: stdd and lost pl 6f out: hdwy over 3f out: rdn and ev ch 2f out: wknd ins fnl f* **11/1**

2m 21.22s (0.12) **Going Correction** -0.025s/f (Good) **8** Ran SP% **111.2**
Speed ratings (Par 111): **98,97,96,96,95 95,94,92**
toteswingers 1&2 £4.00, 1&3 £2.50, 2&3 £2.30 CSF £33.09 TOTE £8.70: £2.00, £1.70, £1.40; EX 33.60 Trifecta £114.00 Pool: £941.26 - 6.18 winning units..
Owner Godolphin **Bred** Darley **Trained** Newmarket, Suffolk

FOCUS
There was little depth to this Listed contest, especially following the absence of Shirocco Star, and it turned into a very muddling affair, with them going just a steady gallop and the field finishing in a bunch, with the 50-rated Signora Frasi being beaten under 3l. There are big doubts over the form given the lack of pace.

3410 MONTAGUE STORAGE H'CAP 1m 2f 188y
8:20 (8:22) (Class 6) (0-65,64) 4-Y-O+ **£1,940** (£577; £288; £144) **Stalls** Low

Form RPR

4250 **1** **Conducting**[21] 2710 5-9-2 **59** KierenFallon 3 67
(Gay Kelleway) *chsd ldrs: led over 8f out: rdn over 1f out: styd on* **10/1**[3]

311 **2** hd **Mr Lando**[18] 2801 4-9-4 **61** JimmyQuinn 5 69
(Tony Carroll) *a.p: racd keenly: rdn to chse wnr over 1f out: r.o* **7/4**[1]

4522 **3** 2 **Spanish Plume**[10] 3037 5-9-0 **62** (b) JackDuern(5) 2 66
(Andrew Hollinshead) *s.i.s: hld up: hdwy over 1f out: rdn ins fnl f: r.o* **7/2**[2]

3-04 **4** hd **Flash Crash**[13] 2966 4-9-4 **61** JimCrowley 4 64
(Robert Cowell) *led: hdd over 8f out: chsd wnr tl rdn over 1f out: styd on same pce ins fnl f* **10/1**[3]

4-0 **5** hd **Certavi (IRE)**[56] 1711 4-8-7 **55** MatthewLawson(5) 10 58
(Brendan Powell) *mid-div: rdn over 2f out: r.o ins fnl f: nt trble ldrs* **14/1**

536 **6** 1 1/4 **Lacey**[101] 925 4-8-12 **55** SeanLevey 9 56
(Andrew Hollinshead) *hld up: rdn over 1f out: styd on: nt rch ldrs* **22/1**

046- **7** 3/4 **Edgeworth (IRE)**[208] 7819 7-9-0 **62** (p) WilliamTwiston-Davies(5) 11 61+
(David Bridgwater) *hld up: rdn over 1f out: nt trble ldrs* **14/1**

4430 **8** 1 **The Great Gabrial**[77] 1297 4-9-0 **57** JamieSpencer 7 54
(Ian Williams) *chsd ldrs: rdn over 1f out: no ex fnl f* **16/1**

66-3 **9** 10 **King Fingal (IRE)**[27] 1 8-9-7 **64** (p) MichaelO'Connell 6 42
(John Quinn) *sn pushed along towards rr: hdwy u.p 1/2-way: rdn over 3f out: wknd 2f out* **22/1**

2m 20.11s (-0.99) **Going Correction** -0.025s/f (Good) **9** Ran SP% **104.7**
Speed ratings (Par 101): **102,101,100,100,100 99,98,97,90**
toteswingers 1&2 £2.80, 1&3 £6.60, 2&3 £1.20 CSF £23.20 CT £54.88 TOTE £8.90: £2.30, £1.30, £1.30; EX 21.10 Trifecta £141.50 Pool: £424.66 - 2.25 winning units..
Owner J Farley, M Brunner & M Whatley **Bred** David J Brown **Trained** Exning, Suffolk

FOCUS
Little got into this, which wasn't strong run. The winner looked potentially well treated.

3411 RACINGUK.COM H'CAP 7f 26y
8:50 (8:51) (Class 4) (0-85,85) 4-Y-O+ **£4,690** (£1,395; £697; £348) **Stalls** Low

Form RPR

-201 **1** **Boots And Spurs**[37] 2265 4-9-7 **85** (v) JimCrowley 1 97
(Mrs K Burke) *a.p: shkn up over 2f out: rdn to ld 1f out: r.o wl* **10/3**[2]

0030 **2** 2 1/4 **Our Boy Jack (IRE)**[30] 2463 4-8-13 **77** SilvestreDeSousa 2 83
(Richard Fahey) *sn led: hdd 6f out: chsd ldrs: rdn to chse wnr ins fnl f: styd on* **8/1**

5003 **3** nk **Postscript (IRE)**[9] 3088 5-9-7 **85** JamieSpencer 7 90
(David Simcock) *chsd ldrs: nt clr run and swtchd rt over 1f out: r.o* **8/1**

3-05 **4** 3/4 **Silverheels (IRE)**[25] 2585 4-9-2 **85** WilliamTwiston-Davies(5) 3 88
(Paul Cole) *s.i.s: hld up: pushed along over 2f out: r.o ins fnl f: nvr nrr* **6/1**[3]

-145 **5** nk **Light Burst (USA)**[37] 2266 4-9-0 **83** ThomasBrown(5) 8 85
(Ismail Mohammed) *prom: rdn over 1f out: styd on same pce fnl f* **14/1**

000- **6** 1 1/4 **Red Art (IRE)**[228] 7508 4-9-6 **84** HarryBentley 5 84
(Charles Hills) *hld up: effrt over 1f out: nvr on terms* **25/1**

300- **7** 3/4 **Rustic Deacon**[196] 7966 6-9-5 **83** KierenFallon 6 80
(Willie Musson) *sn prom: led over 5f out: rdn and hdd 1f out: no ex* **12/1**

0-10 **8** hd **Royal Reyah**[24] 2618 4-8-12 **76** SeanLevey 10 72
(Stuart Kittow) *s.i.s: hld up: hdwy 1/2-way: rdn over 2f out: styd on same pce fr over 1f out* **10/1**

-600 **9** nk **Accession (IRE)**[24] 2618 4-9-5 **83** (b) WilliamBuick 9 79
(Clive Cox) *chsd ldrs: led 6f out: sn hdd: remained handy: rdn and edgd lft over 1f out: no ex* **11/4**[1]

0005 **10** 3 1/2 **Barons Spy (IRE)**[10] 3038 12-8-9 **73** AndreaAtzeni 4 59
(Richard Price) *hld up: effrt over 1f out: wknd fnl f* **40/1**

1m 23.21s (-1.39) **Going Correction** -0.025s/f (Good) **10** Ran SP% **116.0**
Speed ratings (Par 105): **106,103,103,102,101 100,99,99,99,95**
toteswingers 1&2 £4.80, 1&3 £4.00, 2&3 £9.00 CSF £30.16 CT £201.86 TOTE £4.50: £1.70, £1.90, £2.20; EX 30.30 Trifecta £158.80 Pool: £1,086.80 - 5.13 winning units..
Owner Colin Bryce **Bred** Miss G Abbey **Trained** Middleham Moor, N Yorks

FOCUS
They went a decent gallop and this is probably reasonable form for the grade with some depth to the race.
T/Plt: £141.20 to a £1 stake. Pool: £72,760.82 - 375.94 winning units T/Qpdt: £20.80 to a £1 stake. Pool: £5,406.36 - 191.70 winning units CR

3155 WINDSOR (R-H)

Monday, June 17

OFFICIAL GOING: Good (8.1)

Top bend dolled out 11yds from normal configuration adding 45yds to races of 1m plus. Inner of straight dolled out 17yds at 6f and 8yds at Winning Post.
Wind: Moderate; half against Weather: Fair; warm

3412 MGJV APPRENTICE H'CAP — 1m 3f 135y

6:05 (6:05) (Class 5) (0-70,70) 4-Y-0+ **£2,587** (£770; £384; £192) **Stalls** Centre

Form RPR

0411 **1** **Green Earth (IRE)**[7] 3152 6-8-12 **60** 6ex ... SophieRalston(5) 3 64
(Pat Phelan) *hld up in 5th: lost pl and trapped bhd rivals 2f out: swtchd lft towards far side over 1f out: prog after: r.o to ld last 100yds: pushed out* **7/1**

0406 **2** ½ **Balady (IRE)**[17] 2845 4-9-8 **65** ... JoshBaudains 6 68
(Dominic Ffrench Davis) *t.k.h: trckd ldng pair: pushed up on inner to ld wl over 2f out: hung lft fr over 1f out: hdd u.p last 100yds* **10/1**

3-33 **3** 1¼ **Thundering Home**[37] 2284 6-8-13 **56** ... NoelGarbutt 4 57
(Richard Mitchell) *dwlt: hld up in 8th: prog on wd outside over 2f out and ended nr to far rail: rdn to chal ins fnl f: nt qckn* **6/1[3]**

0-06 **4** 1 **Mariet**[26] 2567 4-8-10 **53** ... RyanWhile 8 52
(Suzy Smith) *t.k.h early: trckd ldng trio: rdn over 2f out: chsd ldr u.p over 1f out: nt qckn after* **10/1**

1104 **5** ¾ **Linkable**[14] 2939 4-9-7 **69** ... (t) SiobhanMiller(5) 9 67
(Brendan Powell) *hld up in 8th: effrt on outer over 2f out: rdn to chse ldrs over 1f out: no ex* **3/1[1]**

3-00 **6** ½ **Bondi Mist (IRE)**[33] 2360 4-9-1 **58** ... (v[1]) RyanTate 1 55
(Jonathan Geake) *led 2f: chsd ldr to 3f out: u.p and hld whn squeezed out over 1f out* **16/1**

4061 **7** hd **Thecornishcowboy**[7] 3150 4-9-6 **70** 6ex ... (tp) JordonMcMurray(7) 7 67
(John Ryan) *hld up in 6th: in tch and looked be gng wl 2f out: nudged along and wknd over 1f out* **9/2[2]**

0111 **8** 1¼ **Highlife Dancer**[2] 3312 5-9-8 **70** 12ex ... (v) DanielCremin(5) 5 65
(Mick Channon) *led after 2f out: hdd and shkn up wl over 2f out: nt qckn over 1f out: fdd ins fnl f* **9/2[2]**

4600 **9** 12 **Monzino (USA)**[5] 3195 5-8-7 **55** ... (p) DanielleMooney(5) 2 29
(Michael Chapman) *dwlt: a last: lost tch bef 1/2-way: wl bhd after* **50/1**

2m 31.85s (2.35) **Going Correction** +0.125s/f (Good) **9** Ran SP% **114.2**
Speed ratings (Par 103): **97,96,95,95,94 94,94,93,85**
toteswingers 1&2 £10.70, 1&3 £3.30, 2&3 £8.20 CSF £73.30 CT £444.05 TOTE £7.40: £2.10, £2.80, £1.50; EX 71.50 Trifecta £191.50 Pool: £2,110.85 - 8.26 winning units..
Owner P Wheatley **Bred** Woodcote Stud Ltd **Trained** Epsom, Surrey

FOCUS
The ground was described as good after a dry day. The opening apprentice handicap featured three last-time-out winners who'd all been successful at Brighton seven days previously. Only Monzino wasn't in with a chance 2f out and the field finished fanned out across the track.

3413 THIRD HORIZON/EBF MAIDEN STKS — 5f 10y

6:35 (6:35) (Class 5) 2-Y-0 **£2,911** (£866; £432; £216) **Stalls** Low

Form RPR

54 **1** **Constantine**[7] 3155 2-9-5 0 ... RyanMoore 10 73+
(Richard Hannon) *racd on outer: pressed ldr: hrd rdn over 1f out: led ins fnl f: drvn out* **3/1[2]**

22 **2** ¾ **Speed The Plough**[8] 3132 2-9-5 0 ... RichardHughes 11 70
(Richard Hannon) *led and sn crossed fr wd draw to nr side rail: shkn up over 1f out: hdd and nt qckn ins fnl f* **5/6[1]**

00 **3** ½ **The Dandy Yank (IRE)**[11] 3017 2-9-5 0 ... FergusSweeney 4 69
(Jamie Osborne) *trckd ldrs: gng wl 2f out: shkn up over 1f out: styd on but nvr really chal* **33/1**

6 **4** ½ **Minley**[13] 2955 2-9-5 0 ... GrahamLee 9 67
(Rae Guest) *pressed ldrs: rdn and outpcd 2f out: kpt on again fnl f: unable to chal* **8/1[3]**

3 **5** 3¾ **Narborough**[74] 1344 2-9-5 0 ... MartinHarley 1 53
(Mick Channon) *chsd ldrs: hanging and nt qckn u.p over 1f out: fdd* **10/1**

0 **6** ½ **Sakhee'Ssquirrel**[9] 3107 2-9-0 0 ... WilliamCarson 5 46+
(David Evans) *wl in rr: shkn up 1/2-way: modest late prog* **33/1**

3 **7** 1 **Pensax Lad (IRE)**[8] 3132 2-9-5 0 ... SteveDrowne 6 48
(Ronald Harris) *free to post: pressed ldrs: rdn 2f out: wknd over 1f out* **10/1**

8 1¾ **Debt Settler (IRE)** 2-9-2 0 ... SimonPearce(3) 2 42
(Luke Dace) *dwlt: wl in rr: shkn up and sme prog 2f out: wknd over 1f out* **100/1**

0 **9** 1 **Sands Legends**[30] 2436 2-9-0 0 ... JimmyFortune 8 33
(James Given) *slowly away: hld up in last and detached early: nvr a factor* **66/1**

0 **10** 6 **Ellingham (IRE)**[31] 2419 2-9-0 0 ... TomMcLaughlin 7 11
(Christine Dunnett) *a towards rr: struggling 2f out: t.o* **100/1**

1m 1.56s (1.26) **Going Correction** +0.125s/f (Good) **10** Ran SP% **118.2**
Speed ratings (Par 93): **94,92,92,91,85 84,82,80,78,68**
toteswingers 1&2 £1.10, 1&3 £20.60, 2&3 £10.40 CSF £5.84 TOTE £4.20: £1.10, £1.10, £12.10; EX 6.40 Trifecta £121.00 Pool: £1,716.90 - 10.63 winning units..
Owner The Royal Ascot Racing Club **Bred** D J & Mrs Brown **Trained** East Everleigh, Wilts

FOCUS
Richard Hannon dominated the market for this 5f 2yo maiden but stable jockey Richard Hughes picked the wrong one. As in the first the winner came down the middle of the track and the form's nothing to get carried away with for the track. The winner is progressing with racing.

3414 LANES GROUP (S) STKS — 6f

7:05 (7:06) (Class 5) 2-Y-0 **£2,587** (£770; £384; £192) **Stalls** Low

Form RPR

1634 **1** **Smugglers Gold (IRE)**[20] 2758 2-9-2 0 ... (t) AdamKirby 6 71
(David Evans) *mde virtually all: def advantage 2f out: drvn over 1f out: jinked rt briefly ins fnl f: styd on* **5/4[1]**

00 **2** 1¼ **Porteous**[3] 3298 2-8-6 0 ... SamHitchcott 2 57
(Mick Channon) *wl in tch: shkn up and prog 2f out: chsd wnr jst over 1f out and looked a threat: one pce ins fnl f* **4/1[2]**

43 **3** 1½ **Marti's Girl**[35] 2327 2-7-13 0 ... CharlotteJenner(7) 1 53
(J S Moore) *w wnr 1f: styd prom: rdn to go 2nd again 2f out to jst over 1f out: one pce* **16/1**

5 **4** 1½ **Vallila**[13] 2947 2-7-13 0 ... JoeyHaynes(7) 14 48
(Roger Charlton) *racd on outer: nudged by rival after 1f: towards rr: rdn and sme prog over 2f out: kpt on to take n.d 4th fnl f* **14/1**

50 **5** ¾ **Oxlip**[2] 3324 2-8-6 0 ... FrankieMcDonald 8 49+
(Richard Hannon) *hld up in tch: nt clr run over 2f out: hanging and nt clr run over 1f out: kpt on fnl f* **8/1**

066 **6** 2½ **Jana**[9] 3107 2-8-6 0 ... ChrisCatlin 11 39
(Sylvester Kirk) *pressed ldrs: rdn wl over 2f out: wknd wl over 1f out* **16/1**

7 ½ **Tunnel Tiger (IRE)** 2-8-6 0 ... LiamJones 7 37
(J S Moore) *wl in rr: pushed along 1/2-way: nvr a factor but modest late prog* **16/1**

02 **8** 1½ **Kitty Brown (IRE)**[69] 1449 2-8-6 0 ... SaleemGolam 12 33
(David Evans) *trckd ldrs: rdn over 2f out: wknd over 1f out* **7/1[3]**

005 **9** ½ **Chilly In Rio (IRE)**[42] 2068 2-8-6 0 ... NickyMackay 10 31
(William Muir) *mostly chsd wnr after 1f to 2f out: wknd u.p* **66/1**

650 **10** 4½ **Flying Kyte**[21] 2723 2-8-6 0 ... JemmaMarshall(5) 4 23
(Pat Phelan) *wl in rr: shkn up 1/2-way: no ch whn rn into trble 1f out* **40/1**

504 **11** 7 **Bonnie Wee Lassie**[11] 3009 2-7-13 0 ... CameronHardie(7) 15
(Richard Hannon) *t.k.h: racd on outer: nudged rival after 1f: prom: wknd rapidly 2f out* **33/1**

12 21 **Courtezan** 2-8-6 0 ... MartinDwyer 9
(Jamie Osborne) *s.s: a bhd: t.o* **20/1**

0 **13** 7 **She's A Lucky Lady**[56] 1718 2-8-3 0 ... DarrenEgan(3) 5
(Bill Turner) *sn bhd: t.o fr 1/2-way* **16/1**

1m 15.09s (2.09) **Going Correction** +0.125s/f (Good) **13** Ran SP% **129.9**
Speed ratings (Par 93): **91,89,87,85,84 81,80,78,77,71 62,34,25**
toteswingers 1&2 £2.60, 1&3 £7.90, 2&3 £17.40 CSF £6.34 TOTE £2.40: £1.10, £2.00, £5.80; EX 8.80 Trifecta £62.60 Pool: £1,097.05 - 13.13 winning units..The winner sold for £8,000 to Sheikh Ahfma Al-Sabah
Owner T Earle, Graham Evans, P D Evans **Bred** John Graham **Trained** Pandy, Monmouths
■ Stewards' Enquiry : Nicky Mackay two-day ban; careless riding (1st-2nd July).

FOCUS
Little worthwhile form on offer in this seller which went the way of the one runner to have won previously. He is better than the grade.

3415 CORAL.CO.UK H'CAP — 6f

7:35 (7:36) (Class 4) (0-85,85) 4-Y-0+ **£4,851** (£1,443; £721; £360) **Stalls** Low

Form RPR

234 **1** **O'Gorman**[42] 2097 4-9-2 **80** ... RichardHughes 8 90
(Gary Brown) *fractious bef ent stalls: hld up in last quartet: stdy prog on outer 2f out: rdn to ld jst ins fnl f: readily* **3/1[1]**

0266 **2** 1 **Blue Jack**[16] 2868 8-9-3 **81** ... (t) GrahamLee 7 88
(Stuart Williams) *in tch in midfield: prog 2f out: rdn to chal and upsides 1f out: chsd wnr after: styd on* **7/2[2]**

2302 **3** nk **Alnoomaas (IRE)**[11] 3018 4-8-12 **76** ... JimmyFortune 6 82
(Luke Dace) *hld up in last quartet: prog wl over 1f out: rdn and styd on fnl f: nt pce to chal* **15/2**

003 **4** 1 **Balty Boys (IRE)**[5] 3220 4-9-7 **85** ... (b) FergusSweeney 5 89+
(Jamie Osborne) *chsd ldrs in 5th: pushed along bef 1/2-way: nt pce to hold pl and shuffled bk to last pair jst over 1f out: styd on again fnl f to take 4th nr fin* **7/1**

6-13 **5** shd **Aye Aye Digby (IRE)**[23] 2657 8-8-13 **77** ... LiamJones 13 79
(Patrick Chamings) *chsd ldr: wnt 2nd 2f out: drvn upsides 1f out: one pce ins fnl f* **9/1**

030 **6** shd **Taurus Twins**[8] 3135 7-9-2 **80** ... (b) ShaneKelly 12 82
(Richard Price) *led at str pce: hdd and one pce jst ins fnl f* **16/1**

3030 **7** ¾ **Kellys Eye (IRE)**[16] 2871 6-8-5 **72** ... DarrenEgan(3) 3 72
(Zoe Davison) *slowly away: mostly in last pair: taken to outer and drvn over 1f out: kpt on but no ch* **33/1**

-154 **8** 1 **Apollo D'Negro (IRE)**[21] 2725 5-9-3 **81** ... (v) AdamKirby 1 77+
(Clive Cox) *hld up in midfield: nvr any clr run fr 2f out: kpt on late but no ch* **5/1[3]**

-200 **9** ¾ **We Have A Dream**[16] 2871 8-8-8 **72** ... MartinDwyer 2 66
(William Muir) *chsd ldng pair but drvn bef 1/2-way: lost pl and btn wl over 1f out* **25/1**

-004 **10** 1½ **Nasri**[10] 3038 7-9-1 **79** ... (b) MartinHarley 9 68
(Milton Bradley) *chsd ldr to 2f out: wknd* **33/1**

00-0 **11** 2½ **Novellen Lad (IRE)**[21] 2724 8-9-3 **81** ... TedDurcan 11 62
(Willie Musson) *hld up in last: pushed along 2f out: nvr involved* **25/1**

1m 12.81s (-0.19) **Going Correction** +0.125s/f (Good) **11** Ran SP% **117.6**
Speed ratings (Par 105): **106,104,104,102,102 102,101,100,99,97 94**
toteswingers 1&2 £3.80, 1&3 £3.80, 2&3 £7.30 CSF £12.80 CT £70.36 TOTE £3.50: £1.40, £2.00, £2.30; EX 12.90 Trifecta £139.00 Pool: £1,476.99 - 7.96 winning units..
Owner We Haven't Told The Wives Syndicate **Bred** Whitsbury Manor Stud **Trained** Lambourn, Berks

FOCUS
A fair sprint handicap in which the market told.

3416 HSBC H'CAP — 1m 67y

8:05 (8:05) (Class 4) (0-80,80) 4-Y-0+ **£4,851** (£1,443; £721; £360) **Stalls** Low

Form RPR

2203 **1** **Cruiser**[20] 2761 5-8-12 **71** ... (p) MartinDwyer 13 83
(William Muir) *w ldr: led 3f out: drvn and hrd pressed over 1f out: hld on wl* **5/1[2]**

3-56 **2** ½ **Shamdarley (IRE)**[18] 2813 5-9-5 **78** ... (p) AdamKirby 2 89
(Marco Botti) *trckd ldrs: wnt 2nd wl over 1f out: persistent chal sn after: jst hld last 75yds* **5/4[1]**

1650 **3** 3 **Rakaan (IRE)**[11] 3019 6-9-7 **80** ... (p) FergusSweeney 4 84
(Jamie Osborne) *s.i.s: hld up in rr: prog 2f out: rdn to take 3rd fnl f: edgd lft and no imp on ldng pair* **10/1**

-000 **4** ½ **First Post (IRE)**[11] 3019 6-9-2 **75** ... WilliamCarson 1 78
(Derek Haydn Jones) *hld up in midfield: shkn up 2f out: kpt on same pce fr over 1f out: n.d* **12/1**

4000 **5** ½ **Boom To Bust (IRE)**[30] 2450 5-9-3 **76** ... (b) TedDurcan 7 78
(Sean Curran) *mostly in 7th: rdn wl over 2f out: no prog and struggling wl over 1f out: nt looking wholly enthusiastic but kpt on again fnl f* **33/1**

-045 **6** 2 **Authoritarian**[7] 3158 4-9-2 **75** ... RichardHughes 10 72
(Richard Hannon) *trckd ldrs: shkn up 2f out: steadily wknd over 1f out* **8/1[3]**

-300 **7** ½ **Uncle Dermot (IRE)**[14] 2920 5-9-0 **73** ... JackMitchell 8 69
(Brendan Powell) *settled towards rr: taken wd 3f out: rdn and no great prog* **20/1**

1-50 **8** 1 **Scottish Glen**[9] 3108 7-8-13 **72** ... JimmyFortune 5 66
(Patrick Chamings) *mde most to 3f out: steadily wknd wl over 1f out* **10/1**

50-0 **9** ¾ **Top Diktat**[21] 2728 5-9-2 **75** ... ShaneKelly 11 67
(Gary Moore) *mostly in last pair: pushed along 1/2-way: nvr any real prog* **16/1**

0340 **10** 10 **Kung Hei Fat Choy (USA)**[58] 1692 4-9-2 **75** ... (b) GrahamLee 12 44
(James Given) *trckd ldrs to 3f out: sn wknd qckly* **12/1**

0-P0 11 38 **Mr Fickle (IRE)**[11] 3010 4-8-4 63 ow1..............................(p) ChrisCatlin 3
(Gary Moore) *s.i.s: sn detached in last: wl t.o* 66/1

1m 44.76s (0.06) **Going Correction** +0.125s/f (Good) 11 Ran SP% 120.9
Speed ratings (Par 105): **104,103,100,100,99 97,97,96,95,85 47**
toteswingers 1&2 £2.50, 1&3 £11.50, 2&3 £2.40 CSF £11.72 CT £64.11 TOTE £5.60: £1.80, £1.10, £3.40; EX 19.00 Trifecta £134.50 Pool: £865.15 - 4.82 winning units..
Owner C L A Edginton **Bred** The Hill Stud **Trained** Lambourn, Berks

FOCUS
A run-of-the-mill handicap in which a plunge was narrowly denied.

3417 MWH MAIDEN STKS 1m 2f 7y
8:35 (8:37) (Class 5) 3-Y-O+ **£2,587** (£770; £384; £192) **Stalls** Centre

Form RPR

1 **Pomology (USA)** 3-8-10 0.............................. NickyMackay 5 80
(John Gosden) *hld up towards rr: prog over 3f out: swtchd to rail 2f out: pushed along and clsd to ld last 75yds: won gng away* 16/1

33-0 2 1 ½ **Zipp (IRE)**[59] 1671 3-8-10 70.............................. JamesMcDonald 11 77
(Charles Hills) *w ldr: led 4f out: drvn and pressed over 1f out: kpt on wl but hdd and outpcd last 75yds* 33/1

32 3 ½ **Ducab (IRE)**[11] 3021 3-9-1 0.............................. RichardHughes 3 81
(Roger Varian) *trckd ldrs: coaxed along over 2f out: wnt 2nd over 1f out: chalng whn wnr dashed past last 75yds* 5/6[1]

2- 4 3 ¾ **Hassle (IRE)**[229] 7494 4-9-13 0.............................. AdamKirby 14 74
(Clive Cox) *w ldrs: shkn up over 2f out: rdn to press ldr 2f out to over 1f out: fdd* 4/1[2]

0 5 ½ **Chocolate Caviar (IRE)**[17] 2850 3-8-10 0.............................. ShaneKelly 8 68
(Gary Moore) *hld up in midfield: lost pl 4f out: gng bttr than most sn after: sme prog 3f out: shuffled along and no real imp on ldrs fnl 2f: nt disgracd* 50/1

0 6 8 **Markttag**[14] 2938 3-8-12 0.............................. PatrickHills(3) 7 57
(Luca Cumani) *hld up towards rr: prog on outer 4f out: shkn up and no hdwy over 2f out: wknd* 14/1[3]

6 7 hd **Dambuster (IRE)**[11] 3021 3-9-1 0.............................. RyanMoore 15 56
(Sir Michael Stoute) *mde most to 4f out: sn shkn up: lost 2nd and wknd 2f out* 4/1[2]

0 8 2 **Samoan (IRE)**[24] 2628 4-9-13 0.............................. JimmyFortune 10 52
(Brian Meehan) *hld up in midfield: lost pl 4f out: pushed along in rr 3f out: nvr on terms after* 50/1

05 9 ¾ **Bravestar (IRE)**[13] 2953 3-9-1 0.............................. TedDurcan 4 51
(David Lanigan) *wl in rr: taken to outer and shkn up over 3f out: wknd over 2f out* 33/1

10 nse **Mme Sans Gene** 3-8-10 0.............................. RichardThomas 6 46
(Ralph Beckett) *mostly in last: pushed along over 3f out: passed a few stragglers fnl 2f* 40/1

11 1 ¼ **Never Too Much (IRE)** 3-8-12 0.............................. AshleyMorgan(3) 12 48
(Chris Wall) *a towards rr: shkn up on outer over 3f out: sn btn* 66/1

06 12 1 ¼ **Shameless Man (IRE)**[7] 3156 6-9-8 0..............(t) ThomasGarner(5) 2 46
(Anthony Middleton) *s.i.s: sn in midfield: shkn up over 3f out: wknd over 2f out* 150/1

13 6 **Hilden**[23] 4-9-8 0.............................. MartinDwyer 13 29
(William Muir) *stdd s: hld up in last trio: rdn 4f out: sn bhd* 100/1

14 4 ½ **Nifty Kier** 4-9-10 0.............................. BrendanPowell(3) 9 25
(Martin Bosley) *prom tl wknd qckly wl over 2f out* 150/1

0-0 15 ¾ **Chiltern Secret**[28] 2519 3-8-10 0.............................. SteveDrowne 1 18
(Martin Bosley) *chsd ldrs to over 3f out: wknd qckly* 100/1

2m 8.49s (-0.21) **Going Correction** +0.125s/f (Good)
WFA 3 from 4yo+ 12lb 15 Ran SP% 124.1
Speed ratings (Par 103): **105,103,103,100,100 93,93,91,91,91 90,89,84,80,80**
toteswingers 1&2 £8.70, 1&3 £7.40, 2&3 £13.70 CSF £455.44 TOTE £12.10: £3.50, £5.20, £1.20; EX 143.30 Trifecta £1614.50 Part won. Pool: £2,152.72 - 0.79 winning units..
Owner HRH Princess Haya Of Jordan **Bred** Dr John A Chandler **Trained** Newmarket, Suffolk

FOCUS
A fair maiden and the first three pulled well clear.

3418 CH2M HILL H'CAP 1m 2f 7y
9:05 (9:07) (Class 5) (0-70,70) 3-Y-O **£2,587** (£770; £384; £192) **Stalls** Centre

Form RPR

-342 1 **Couloir Extreme (IRE)**[18] 2786 3-9-4 67.............................. RyanMoore 8 83+
(Gary Moore) *trckd ldng pair: led 3f out: sn dashed wl clr: in n.d after: eased nr fin* 7/4[1]

01-0 2 8 **Teolagi (IRE)**[68] 1486 3-9-4 67.............................. LiamJones 5 67
(J S Moore) *hld up in midfield: rdn 3f out: wandered u.p but kpt on fr over 1f out to take 2nd nr fin* 33/1

5-13 3 nk **Mash Potato (IRE)**[30] 2464 3-8-12 61..............(p) RichardHughes 4 60
(Michael Dods) *trckd ldng pair: shkn up over 3f out: drvn to chse clr wnr 1f out: no imp: lost 2nd nr fin* 9/2[3]

0165 4 1 ¾ **Noor Al Haya (IRE)**[10] 3040 3-7-9 51 oh1.............................. JoeyHaynes(7) 2 47
(Mark Usher) *hld up towards rr: rdn over 2f out: impeded over 1f out: kpt on fnl f to take 4th nr fin* 33/1

0-33 5 nk **First Sargeant**[154] 209 3-9-1 69..............(p) RobertTart(5) 9 64
(Marco Botti) *settled in midfield: lost pl and struggling in last pair 3f out: kpt on fr over 1f out* 10/1

1614 6 ¾ **Zero Game (IRE)**[19] 2783 3-9-7 70..............(e) JamesMcDonald 10 64
(Michael Bell) *w ldr: led briefly over 3f out: chsd clr wnr to 1f out: wknd* 16/1

55-0 7 1 ¼ **Bold And Free**[14] 2935 3-9-4 67.............................. JimmyFortune 11 58
(David Elsworth) *in tch on outer: drvn and struggling 3f out: sn wl btn* 20/1

6063 8 nk **My Claire**[9] 3082 3-7-13 51 oh2.............................. DarrenEgan(3) 3 42
(Nigel Tinkler) *hld up in last: pair: shkn up 3f out: nvr any great prog* 20/1

02 9 nk **Aminah**[20] 2743 3-8-11 60.............................. ShaneKelly 1 50
(Robert Cowell) *hld up towards rr: jst pushed along fr 3f out: nt clr run briefly 2f out: nvr involved* 12/1

3-35 10 6 **Guilded Spirit**[45] 1977 3-9-7 70..............................[1] FergusSweeney 7 49
(Stuart Kittow) *hld up in last: taken out wd and rdn 3f out: sn no prog: wknd 2f out* 3/1[2]

535- 11 2 ¼ **Lucky Black Star (IRE)**[224] 7592 3-9-2 65.............................. PatCosgrave 6 39
(George Baker) *t.k.h: led to over 3f out: sn wknd* 66/1

2m 9.01s (0.31) **Going Correction** +0.125s/f (Good) 11 Ran SP% 119.1
Speed ratings (Par 99): **103,96,96,94,94 94,93,92,92,87 86**
toteswingers 1&2 £25.10, 1&3 £2.90, 2&3 £47.10 CSF £79.50 CT £239.19 TOTE £2.70: £1.30, £10.90, £2.10; EX 92.50 Trifecta £268.20 Pool: £1,695.52 - 4.74 winning units..
Owner C E Stedman **Bred** Irish National Stud **Trained** Lower Beeding, W Sussex

FOCUS
The closing 1m2f handicap was the scene of a rout.
T/Jkpt: Not won. T/Plt: £10.10 to a £1 stake. Pool £98,999.30 - 7,122.25 winning units T/Qpdt: £3.20 to a £1 stake. Pool £7,520.21 - 1,729.70 winning units JN

2250 ASCOT (R-H)
Tuesday, June 18

OFFICIAL GOING: Good (stands' side 8.9, centre 9.0, far side 9.1, round 8.3)
Rail on Round course approximately 3yds out from 9f to home straight adding 6yds to Old Mile, 9yds to 10f and 12yds to races of 12f plus.

3419 QUEEN ANNE STKS (BRITISH CHAMPIONS SERIES) (GROUP 1) 1m (S)
2:30 (2:36) (Class 1) 4-Y-O+
£198,485 (£75,250; £37,660; £18,760; £9,415; £4,725) **Stalls** Centre

Form RPR

1-15 1 **Declaration Of War (USA)**[31] 2446 4-9-0 112.............. JosephO'Brien 6 122+
(A P O'Brien, Ire) *lw: hld up wl in tch in midfield: clsd to trck ldrs and gng wl whn nt clr run jst over 1f out: swtchd lft and forced way through jst ins fnl f: rdn and qcknd to ld wl ins fnl f: sn in command* 15/2[2]

3-23 2 ¾ **Aljamaaheer (IRE)**[31] 2446 4-9-0 111.............................. PaulHanagan 7 119
(Roger Varian) *t.k.h: stl travelling on bit over 2f out: effrt and hdwy 2f out: rdn and ev ch ent fnl f: led fnl 100yds: hdd and no ex wl ins fnl f* 8/1[3]

2-21 3 ½ **Gregorian (IRE)**[18] 2840 4-9-0 113.............................. TomQueally 1 118
(John Gosden) *hld up wl in tch in midfield: hdwy ent fnl 2f: rdn and ev ch over 1f out: led 1f out tl hdd and one pce fnl 100yds* 16/1

323- 4 2 **Elusive Kate (USA)**[241] 7238 4-8-11 116.............................. WilliamBuick 3 110
(John Gosden) *t.k.h: chsd ldrs: jnd ldr 3f out tl rdn to ld 2f out: hdd and drvn 1f out: wknd wl ins fnl f* 15/2[2]

0114 5 hd **Trade Storm**[80] 1267 5-9-0 113.............................. JamieSpencer 12 113
(David Simcock) *lw: s.i.s and swtchd rt after s: hld up wl in tch in rr: hdwy and swtchd lft over 1f out: chsng ldrs and styng on whn pushed lft jst ins fnl f: kpt on same pce fnl 100yds* 12/1

-404 6 1 ¼ **Libranno**[10] 3101 5-9-0 111.............................. PatCosgrave 4 110
(Richard Hannon) *led and set stdy gallop for 2f: jnd and rdn 3f out: hdd and drvn 2f out: no ex whn pushed lft jst ins fnl f: wknd ins fnl f* 100/1

0-34 7 hd **Chil The Kite**[31] 2446 4-9-0 108..............................(p) RyanMoore 5 109
(Hughie Morrison) *dwlt: hld up in tch in rr: effrt u.p and hdwy 2f out: drvn and styd on same pce fnl f* 16/1

0002 8 hd **Penitent**[18] 2840 7-9-0 115.............................. DanielTudhope 2 109
(David O'Meara) *chsd ldrs: hdwy to join ldrs and rdn 3f out: no ex u.p jst over 1f out: wknd ins fnl f* 33/1

-422 9 1 ½ **Sovereign Debt (IRE)**[31] 2446 4-9-0 112.............................. AdamKirby 10 106
(Michael Bell) *t.k.h: hld up in tch in midfield: rdn and effrt 2f out: outpcd u.p over 1f out: no threat but plugged on ins fnl f* 16/1

0-10 10 2 ¾ **Trumpet Major (IRE)**[31] 2446 4-9-0 114.............................. RichardHughes 9 99
(Richard Hannon) *hld up in tch in midfield: effrt but struggling to qckn whn short of room and sltly hmpd over 1f out: sn outpcd: wknd ent fnl f* 25/1

/2-1 11 2 **Animal Kingdom (USA)**[80] 1269 5-9-0 126..............(bt) JRVelazquez 13 95
(H Graham Motion, U.S.A) *tall: str: lw: ponied to s: plld hrd: hld up wl in tch in midfield: rdn and lost pl wl over 2f out: wl btn whn hung rt u.p over 1f out* 5/4[1]

1456 12 nse **Monsieur Chevalier (IRE)**[10] 3101 6-9-0 100........(b[1]) DarryllHolland 11 95
(P J O'Gorman) *t.k.h: chsd ldrs: rdn ent fnl 2f: struggling whn short of room and hmpd wl over 1f out: sn wknd* 100/1

-133 13 9 **Gabrial (IRE)**[18] 2840 4-9-0 111..............................(p) KierenFallon 8 74
(Richard Fahey) *v awkward leaving stalls and v.s.a: rcvrd and in tch in rr over 6f out: rdn and no hdwy wl over 2f out: wknd wl over 1f out* 33/1

1m 38.48s (-2.32) **Going Correction** +0.075s/f (Good) 13 Ran SP% 116.1
Speed ratings (Par 117): **114,113,112,110,110 109,109,108,107,104 102,102,93**
Tote Swingers: 1&2 £8.80, 1&3 £17.20, 2&3 £16.60 CSF £62.12 CT £961.92 TOTE £9.70: £2.90, £2.80, £3.10; EX 65.10 Trifecta £657.90 Pool: £37,111.05 - 42.30 winning units..
Owner Mrs J Magnier & Michael Tabor & Derrick Smith & Jo **Bred** Joseph Allen **Trained** Ballydoyle, Co Tipperary
■ Stewards' Enquiry : Joseph O'Brien caution: careless riding

FOCUS
Due to just 9mm of rainfall at the track this month, officials selectively watered throughout the past week and it was dry overnight into the opening day. The ground was considered consistent around the course, thanks to grass growth coming good, and compliments were plentiful about its state from those that walked it before racing. Plaudits also continued from riders after the first. This year's Queen Anne was below the level of the last three vintage years and centred around Animal Kingdom. However, with him failing to fire it left a wide-open contest and there were plenty in with a chance nearing the final furlong. Runner-up Aljamaaheer placed behind Farhh at Newbury last month on his debut in this grade and ran close to that level, rating the best guide as to the strength of the form. It rates an ordinary renewal, with the winner towards the lower end of the race standard.

3420 KING'S STAND STKS (BRITISH CHAMPIONS SERIES & GLOBAL SPRINT CHALLENGE) (GROUP 1) 5f
3:05 (3:10) (Class 1) 3-Y-O+
£198,485 (£75,250; £37,660; £18,760; £9,415; £4,725) **Stalls** Centre

Form RPR

2414 1 **Sole Power**[24] 2662 6-9-4 113.............................. JohnnyMurtagh 14 120
(Edward Lynam, Ire) *hld up: swtchd lft w plenty to do over 1f out: hdwy sn after: str run ins fnl f to ld towards fin* 8/1

011 2 nk **Shea Shea (SAF)**[80] 1265 6-9-4 120.............................. ChristopheSoumillon 5 119
(M F De Kock, South Africa) *str: good-bodied: ponied to s: in tch: effrt over 1f out: led ent fnl f: r.o gamely: hdd towards fin* 11/4[1]

110- 3 1 ¼ **Pearl Secret**[298] 5561 4-9-4 109.............................. JamieSpencer 10 114
(David Barron) *lw: stdd s and sn swtchd lft: hld up: hdwy wl over 1f out: r.o ins fnl f: gng on at fin: nt quite get to ldrs* 10/1

-106 4 nk **Jack Dexter**[34] 2368 4-9-4 109.............................. GrahamLee 6 113
(Jim Goldie) *hld up: nt clr run 2f out: rdn and hdwy over 1f out: r.o ins fnl f: nt quite get to ldrs* 33/1

11-3 5 ½ **Reckless Abandon**[24] 2662 3-8-12 117.............................. AdamKirby 13 110
(Clive Cox) *taken down early: w ldrs: led over 2f out: rdn and hung lft over 1f out: hdd ent fnl f: kpt on against stands' rail tl no ex fnl 50yds* 4/1[2]

-142 6 1 **Heeraat (IRE)**[20] 2768 4-9-4 107.............................. PaulHanagan 15 108
(William Haggas) *lw:w ldrs: rdn and nt qckn over 1f out: styd on same pce fnl 110yds* 25/1

1132 7 nk **Move In Time**[37] 2300 5-9-4 109.............................. DanielTudhope 4 107
(David O'Meara) *chsd ldrs: rdn and virtually upsides over 1f out: no ex fnl 100yds* 33/1

0-02 8 ¾ **Swiss Spirit**[24] 2662 4-9-4 111.............................. WilliamBuick 17 104
(John Gosden) *lw: hld up: rdn and hdwy over 1f out: one pce and no imp on ldrs ins fnl f* 13/2[3]

9 *hd* **Shamexpress (NZ)**[101] 951 4-9-4 115............................(t) CraigNewitt 3 103
(Danny O'Brien, Australia) *lengthy: well-made: lw: midfield: hdwy 2f out: sn chsd ldrs: ev ch 1f out: no ex fnl 75yds* **12/1**

1-40 **10** *nk* **Bungle Inthejungle**[45] 2019 3-8-12 107.......................... MartinHarley 8 100
(Mick Channon) *taken down early: w ldr: rdn 2f out: stl ev ch over 1f out: fdd fnl 75yds* **66/1**

3601 **11** *nk* **Medicean Man**[11] 3046 7-9-4 110..................................(p) SteveDrowne 9 101
(Jeremy Gask) *towards rr: u.p to go pce over 2f out: proged ins fnl f: styd on: nvr able to trble ldrs* **25/1**

5045 **12** *¾* **Stepper Point**[16] 2909 4-9-4 104..................................... MartinDwyer 11 99
(William Muir) *displayed gd spd: led: hdd over 2f out: rdn and stl there under 2f out: wknd ins fnl f* **100/1**

-023 **13** *hd* **Hoyam**[10] 3102 3-8-9 102.. HarryBentley 16 93
(Michael Bell) *taken down early: hld up: outpcd over 1f out: nvr a threat* **100/1**

4000 **14** *½* **Doc Hay (USA)**[11] 3046 6-9-4 102.......................... KierenFallon 18 101
(David O'Meara) *taken down early: racd keenly: hung rt thrght: sn chsd ldrs: wknd over 1f out: eased whn wl btn fnl 150yds* **100/1**

04-5 **15** *½* **Prohibit**[7] 3187 8-9-4 108..(p) JimCrowley 2 94
(Robert Cowell) *in tch: effrt 2f out: sn chsd ldrs: wknd ins fnl f* **66/1**

0-21 **16** *shd* **Kingsgate Native (IRE)**[24] 2662 8-9-4 112...................... ShaneKelly 7 94
(Robert Cowell) *midfield: rdn and outpcd 2f out: wknd fnl f* **16/1**

0004 **17** *1½* **Angels Will Fall (IRE)**[10] 3102 4-9-1 98.................. JamesMcDonald 1 86
(Charles Hills) *hld up: outpcd 2f out: no imp whn n.m.r ins fnl f: nvr on terms w ldrs* **100/1**

1551 **18** *shd* **Spirit Quartz (IRE)**[16] 2909 5-9-4 111.......................(p) JosephO'Brien 19 88
(Robert Cowell) *swtchd lft to r alone stands' side: racd off the pce: rdn over 2f out: no imp: wl btn ins fnl f* **16/1**

40-0 **19** *6* **Ballesteros**[17] 2865 4-9-4 105..[1] TomQueally 12 67
(Brian Meehan) *racd keenly in midfield: pushed along 1/2-way: wknd over 1f out: bhd fnl f* **100/1**

58.88s (-1.62) **Going Correction** +0.075s/f (Good)
WFA 3 from 4yo+ 6lb **19** Ran SP% **121.2**
Speed ratings (Par 117): **115,114,112,112,111 109,109,107,107,107 106,105,105,104,103 103,101,100,91**
Tote Swingers: 1&2 £5.80, 1&3 £16.20, 2&3 £5.40 CSF £27.64 CT £232.71 TOTE £10.30: £3.20, £1.30, £3.30; EX 36.70 Trifecta £423.30 Pool: £24,152.04 - 42.79 winning units..
Owner Mrs S Power **Bred** G Russell **Trained** Dunshaughlin, Co Meath

FOCUS
The King's Stand is normally marked for export, with the home team only managing to win the race five times since 2000, and the International flavour was maintained this year with one challenger each from Ireland, Australia and South Africa. All bar Spirit Quartz came up the centre of the track and overseas raiders took the first two places. The time was only 0.94sec faster than the Windsor Castle. The form is rated around Sole Power to his best, with She Shea not quite at his best.

3421 ST JAMES'S PALACE STKS (BRITISH CHAMPIONS SERIES) (GROUP 1) (ENTIRE COLTS) 1m (R)

3:45 (3:46) (Class 1) 3-Y-O

£198,485 (£75,250; £37,660; £18,760; £9,415; £4,725) **Stalls** Low

Form RPR

1-10 **1** **Dawn Approach (IRE)**[17] 2866 3-9-0 125...................... KevinManning 5 126+
(J S Bolger, Ire) *lw: t.k.h: hld up in midfield: effrt whn bmpd and pushed lft 2f out: rallied over 1f out: edging rt but qcknd to ld ent fnl f: sustained duel w rival fnl f: r.o strly and jst prevailed* **5/4**[1]

1-14 **2** *shd* **Toronado (IRE)**[45] 2021 3-9-0 118.............................. RichardHughes 9 126+
(Richard Hannon) *lw: stdd s: hld up in rr: hdwy on outer whn hmpd and pushed lft 2f out: rallied over 1f out: edging rt but qcknd to chal ent fnl f: sustained duel w wnr fnl f: r.o strly: jst hld* **5/1**[3]

1-66 **3** *2¾* **Mars (IRE)**[17] 2866 3-9-0 114...................................... RyanMoore 4 121+
(A P O'Brien, Ire) *swtg: chsd ldng trio: effrt whn short of room: hmpd and swtchd rt 2f out: rallying whn n.m.r again jst ins fnl f: r.o to go 3rd wl ins fnl f: no threat to ldrs but gng on at fin* **10/1**

24 **4** *1¼* **Mshawish (USA)**[16] 2907 3-9-0 114.............................. FrankieDettori 1 117
(M Delzangles, France) *tall: athletic: swtg: t.k.h: hld up in tch in last quartet: rdn and hdwy towards inner ent fnl 2f: drvn to ld over 1f out: hdd ent fnl f and outpcd by ldng pair: one pce and lost 3rd wl ins fnl f* **25/1**

4-32 **5** *1¾* **Glory Awaits (IRE)**[45] 2021 3-9-0 114..........................(b) JamieSpencer 6 113
(Kevin Ryan) *led for 1f: chsd ldr after: rdn over 2f out: wnt lft u.p and bmpd rival 2f out: unable qck and btn over 1f out: one pce and wl hld fnl f* **25/1**

4-31 **6** *½* **Dundonnell (USA)**[31] 2453 3-9-0 113.............................. JamesDoyle 3 112
(Roger Charlton) *ponied to s: stdd after s: plld hrd and hld up in tch towards rr: clsng but running into a wall of horses and swtchd rt 2f out: rallying and swtchd lft 1f out: styd on ins fnl f but no threat to ldrs* **12/1**

1-00 **7** *3½* **George Vancouver (USA)**[24] 2677 3-9-0 110......... SeamieHeffernan 8 104
(A P O'Brien, Ire) *hld up in tch in last quartet: rdn and effrt ent fnl 2f: no prog: wknd over 1f out* **50/1**

6001 **8** *2½* **Leitir Mor (IRE)**[5] 3262 3-9-0 107...............................(tp) RonanWhelan 2 98
(J S Bolger, Ire) *lw: slipped leaving stalls and rdr briefly lost iron: rcvrd and hdwy to ld after 1f: rdn and hdd over 1f out: sn wknd: eased ins fnl f* **66/1**

0-11 **9** *shd* **Magician (IRE)**[24] 2677 3-9-0 122.................................. JosephO'Brien 7 101
(A P O'Brien, Ire) *chsd ldng pair: rdn and effrt whn hmpd and pushed lft 2f out: unable to rcvr and no prog u.p over 1f out: wl btn and eased ins fnl f* **5/2**[2]

1m 39.23s (-1.47) **Going Correction** +0.15s/f (Good) **9** Ran SP% **117.6**
Speed ratings (Par 113): **113,112,110,108,107 106,103,100,100**
Tote Swingers: 1&2 £2.40, 1&3 £3.50, 2&3 £5.40 CSF £7.97 CT £44.74 TOTE £2.10: £1.10, £1.50, £2.60; EX 8.30 Trifecta £53.80 Pool: £32,323.23 - 449.99 winning units..
Owner Godolphin **Bred** J S Bolger **Trained** Coolcullen, Co Carlow

FOCUS
The defining event for 3yo milers and it was an absorbing race with both the domestic and Irish Guineas winners lining up. It proved a rough and muddling race with the winner's pacemaker Leitir Mor, who himself landed a Group 3 at Leopardstown only the previous week, setting an uneven tempo up front. The field bunched up after straightening for home and Glory Awaits hung left when under maximum pressure and caused something of a concertina effect. That changed the complexion of the race and caused a lengthy stewards' enquiry, but the result was unaltered. Pretty straightforward form, Dawn Approach back to his Guineas level with Toronado improving in line with his Craven form.

3422 COVENTRY STKS (GROUP 2) 6f

4:25 (4:26) (Class 1) 2-Y-O

£68,052 (£25,800; £12,912; £6,432; £3,228; £1,620) **Stalls** Centre

Form RPR

1 **War Command (USA)**[11] 3070 2-9-1 0.................. SeamieHeffernan 15 115+
(A P O'Brien, Ire) *str: well-made: gd sort: lw: hld up in rr: hdwy 2f out: r.o to ld wl over 1f out: edgd rt and qcknd clr ins fnl f: impressive* **20/1**

1 **2** *6* **Parbold (IRE)**[33] 2401 2-9-1 0.................................. TonyHamilton 13 98+
(Richard Fahey) *hld up: hdwy over 2f out: pushed rt wl over 1f out: r.o ins fnl f: tk 2nd towards fin: no ch w wnr* **16/1**

3 *¾* **Sir John Hawkins (USA)**[23] 2685 2-9-1 0...................... RyanMoore 10 95
(A P O'Brien, Ire) *w'like: scope: lw: a.p: rdn and ev ch over 1f out: outpcd by wnr and edgd rt ins fnl f: no ex and lost 2nd towards fin* **6/1**[3]

111 **4** *½* **Thunder Strike**[17] 2863 2-9-1 0.................................. FrankieDettori 7 93
(Richard Hannon) *a.p: pushed along and chal 2f out: stl ev ch over 1f out: nt qckn and edgd lft ins fnl f: styd on same pce clsng stages* **11/2**[2]

531 **5** *1¼* **Jallota**[10] 3112 2-9-1 0.. MartinHarley 16 90
(Mick Channon) *racd keenly: hld up: hdwy over 2f out: sn hung rt: sltly outpcd over 1f out: continued to hang rt but kpt on ins fnl f wout threatening* **20/1**

1 **6** *nk* **Stubbs (IRE)**[15] 2943 2-9-1 0.. JosephO'Brien 1 89
(A P O'Brien, Ire) *w'like: str: racd keenly: hld up: hdwy over 2f out: rdn and chal over 1f out: nt qckn: no ex fnl 100yds* **5/2**[1]

1 **7** *1* **Wahaab (IRE)**[18] 2847 2-9-1 0.. DaneO'Neill 9 86
(Richard Hannon) *racd keenly: in tch: effrt and ev ch 2f out: nt qckn over 1f out: one pce ins fnl f* **16/1**

21 **8** *nse* **Mawfoor (IRE)**[11] 3044 2-9-1 0...................................... PaulHanagan 14 85
(Brian Meehan) *athletic: lw: in tch: effrt whn hmpd and shuffled bk ent fnl 2f: styd on ins fnl f but unable to trble ldrs* **12/1**

031 **9** *hd* **Rosso Corsa**[24] 2645 2-9-1 0.................................... JamesMcDonald 2 85
(Mick Channon) *lw: in tch: effrt to chse ldrs 2f out: wknd ins fnl f* **100/1**

10 *¾* **Rogue Wave (IRE)** 2-9-1 0.. JimCrowley 5 83
(Alan Jarvis) *str: hld up: pushed along over 2f out: kpt on and sme prog ins fnl f wout threatening* **66/1**

1 **11** *1½* **Dubawi Fun**[27] 2577 2-9-1 0.. PatCosgrave 8 78
(Ismail Mohammed) *w'like: lengthy: attractive: led: rdn over 2f out: hdd wl over 1f out: stl there tl wknd ins fnl f* **66/1**

21 **12** *shd* **Lanark (IRE)**[24] 2653 2-9-1 0... JoeFanning 11 78
(Mark Johnston) *chsd ldrs: u.p and struggling to hold pl whn hmpd ent fnl 2f: sn wknd* **25/1**

12 **13** *hd* **Riverboat Springs (IRE)**[17] 2863 2-9-1 0...................... WilliamBuick 6 77
(Mick Channon) *hld up: outpcd over 2f out: nvr a threat* **8/1**

1 **14** *1¼* **Championship (IRE)**[32] 2411 2-9-1 0.......................... RichardHughes 3 73
(Richard Hannon) *w'like: midfield: pushed along over 2f out: bmpd wl over 1f out: sn lost pl: bhd fnl f* **6/1**[3]

4 **15** *8* **Thrtypointstothree (IRE)**[18] 2823 2-9-1 0...................... RyanTate 12 49
(Nikki Evans) *leggy: hld up: struggling fr 1/2-way: wl btn* **200/1**

1m 12.86s (-1.64) **Going Correction** +0.075s/f (Good) **15** Ran SP% **120.9**
Speed ratings (Par 105): **113,105,104,103,101 101,99,99,99,98 96,96,96,94,83**
Tote Swingers: 1&2 £51.20, 1&3 £20.90, 2&3 £17.30 CSF £297.45 CT £2166.55 TOTE £21.00: £5.00, £4.00, £2.10; EX 403.10 Trifecta £2865.50 Pool: £20,635.11 - 5.40 winning units..
Owner J Allen/Mrs J Magnier/M Tabor/D Smith **Bred** Joseph Allen **Trained** Ballydoyle, Co Tipperary

FOCUS
The Coventry has been won by some top-class performers in recent years with the likes of Henrythenavigator, Canford Cliffs and Dawn Approach each proving successful since 2007, but the performance of this year's winner was as impressive as any. The first two horses home occupied the last two places early on, suggesting the leaders went quick enough. War Command rates towards the top of the race averages.

3423 ASCOT STKS (H'CAP) 2m 4f

5:00 (5:01) (Class 2) (0-95,95) 4-Y-O+

£37,350 (£11,184; £5,592; £2,796; £1,398; £702) **Stalls** Centre

Form RPR

06/1 **1** **Well Sharp**[33] 2402 5-9-10 **95**.. FMBerry 16 107+
(Jonjo O'Neill) *swtg: hld up in tch in midfield and a travellling wl: clsd to chse ldrs over 2f out: rdn and effrt to ld ent fnl f: sn in command and r.o strly* **9/1**

32-1 **2** *2½* **Tiger Cliff (IRE)**[31] 2451 4-9-7 **94**.. TomQueally 8 103+
(Lady Cecil) *lw: hld up towards rr of midfield: effrt and hdwy u.p on outer over 2f out: styd on wl u.p fnl f to go 2nd fnl 50yds: no threat to wnr* **4/1**[1]

3-21 **3** *1* **Lieutenant Miller**[53] 1805 7-9-1 **86**.. GrahamLee 17 94
(Nicky Henderson) *t.k.h: chsd ldrs: rdn and effrt wl over 2f out: chsd clr wnr jst ins fnl f: styd on same pce and lost 2nd fnl 50yds* **8/1**[3]

-053 **4** *1* **Mubaraza (IRE)**[31] 2451 4-9-5 **92**.. PaulHanagan 7 99
(Ed Dunlop) *hld up in tch in midfield: effrt u.p over 2f out: edging rt over 1f out: styd on u.p fnl f but no threat to wnr* **10/1**

0-23 **5** *1¼* **Mysterious Man (IRE)**[24] 2648 4-9-1 **88**...................... JimmyFortune 11 94
(Andrew Balding) *t.k.h: chsd ldrs tl led after 3f: rdn ent fnl 2f: hdd ent fnl f: no ex and sn btn: plugged on same pce and lost 3 pls ins fnl f* **14/1**

06-4 **6** *¾* **Blue Bajan (IRE)**[4] 3297 11-9-10 **95**.............................. DanielTudhope 3 100+
(David O'Meara) *hld up in last trio: hdwy on inner whn nt clr run over 2f out: styng on and switching lft over 1f out: kpt on wl fnl f: no threat to wnr* **33/1**

1-51 **7** *hd* **Homeric (IRE)**[39] 2205 4-9-3 **90**.. FrankieDettori 4 95
(Ed Dunlop) *lw: hld up towards rr: stdy hdwy on inner 6f out: nt clr run and swtchd lft over 2f out: sn rdn and no imp tl kpt on steadily ins fnl f: no threat to wnr* **12/1**

8 *1¼* **Big Easy (GER)**[61] 6-9-1 **91**.......................... WilliamTwiston-Davies(5) 10 95
(Philip Hobbs) *hld up in midfield: lost pl and dropped towards rr 8f out: hdwy 5 out: switching rt and hdwy towards inner 2f out: kpt on steadily but no threat to wnr* **11/1**

9 *1¾* **Marchese Marconi (IRE)**[16] 2903 4-9-2 **89**...................(p) RyanMoore 9 91
(A P O'Brien, Ire) *chsd ldr tl led after 2f tl after 3f: chsd ldr tl 5f out: rdn to chse ldr again 3f out tl over 1f out: wknd fnl f* **16/1**

625/ **10** 4 **Midnight Oil**[36] 6497 5-9-8 **93** RichardHughes 15 93
(W P Mullins, Ire) *hld up towards rr: hdwy on outer 3f out: styaing on same pce and no imp whn carried rt over 1f out: wl hld and eased ins fnl f* **10/1**

63-0 **11** 2 **Suraj**[41] 2149 4-9-8 **95** JamieSpencer 2 93
(Michael Bell) *dwlt: t.k.h: hld up in midfield: hdwy to chse ldr 5f out tl 3f out: sn drvn and unable qck: wknd over 1f out: eased ins fnl f* **20/1**

33/0 **12** 1 **Investissement**[41] 2149 7-9-9 **94** (t) WilliamBuick 13 89
(David Pipe) *t.k.h: chsd ldrs early: grad stdd bk into midfield: rdn and effrt over 2f out: no imp: wknd over 1f out* **33/1**

0 **13** 1 1/2 **Justification**[41] 2149 5-9-6 **91** JosephO'Brien 14 85
(A P O'Brien, Ire) *hld up in last quartet: stl plenty to do whn rdn and effrt jst over 2f out: no imp: nvr trbld ldrs* **15/2**[2]

/605 **14** 1/2 **Apache (IRE)**[10] 3099 5-9-3 **88** GeorgeBaker 18 81
(Jane Chapple-Hyam) *swtg: stdd and dropped in bhd after s: t.k.h and hld up in rr: rdn and effrt over 2f out: no hdwy: n.d* **25/1**

24-6 **15** 1 1/4 **Mawaqeet (USA)**[44] 2052 4-9-3 **90** (b[1]) DaneO'Neill 12 82
(Sir Michael Stoute) *dwlt: a towards rr: rdn and struggling 4f out: no ch over 2f out* **25/1**

313 **16** 7 **Roman Flight (IRE)**[24] 2671 5-9-3 **88** (v) KierenFallon 1 78
(David O'Meara) *t.k.h: chsd ldrs: rdn and btn over 2f out: eased fnl f* **25/1**

0- **17** 7 **Tantalising (IRE)**[30] 2485 5-8-12 **86** RonanWhelan(3) 6 64
(P J Prendergast, Ire) *lw: t.k.h: chsd ldrs: rdn and struggling wl over 3f out: wkng whn hmpd over 2f out: sn bhd* **50/1**

-123 **18** 7 **La Estrella (USA)**[27] 2579 10-9-2 **87** (p) ShaneKelly 19 58
(Don Cantillon) *t.k.h: hld up in rr: hdwy on outer into midfield 5f out: btn 3f out: bhd and eased ins fnl f: t.o* **80/1**

/0-0 **19** 156 **Softsong (FR)**[41] 2149 5-9-10 **95** AdamKirby 5
(Philip Hobbs) *led for 2f: chsd ldrs tl rdn and lost pl qckly wl 2f out: t.o and virtually plld fr over 1f out* **33/1**

4m 28.41s (3.61) **Going Correction** +0.15s/f (Good)
WFA 4 from 5yo+ 2lb **19** Ran SP% **128.0**
Speed ratings (Par 109): **98,97,96,96,95 95,95,94,94,92 91,91,90,90,90 87,84,81,**
Tote Swingers: 1&2 £9.10, 1&3 £13.40, 2&3 £4.60 CSF £41.21 CT £317.13 TOTE £10.80: £2.80, £1.90, £2.10, £3.00; EX 52.20 Trifecta £195.20 Pool: £17,743.74 - 68.14 winning units..
Owner John P McManus **Bred** Equibreed S R L **Trained** Cheltenham, Gloucs

FOCUS
A typically well-contested running of this staying handicap. Those held up under restraint found it tough to make a serious impression due to the routine gallop, but the form still looks strong. It was the eighth time in the last 11 years the race has gone to a trainer more known for handing jumpers. The form looks more solid than some renewals.

3424 WINDSOR CASTLE STKS (LISTED RACE) 5f
5:35 (5:39) (Class 1) 2-Y-O

£34,026 (£12,900; £6,456; £3,216; £1,614; £810) **Stalls** Centre

Form RPR

14 **1** **Extortionist (IRE)**[34] 2370 2-9-3 0 JohnnyMurtagh 28 100
(Olly Stevens) *str: racd stands' side: hld up: rdn over 1f out: nt pick-up immediately: hdwy ins fnl f: r.o to ld towards fin: 1st of 11 in gp* **16/1**

13 **2** nk **Supplicant**[10] 3079 2-9-3 0 TonyHamilton 27 99
(Richard Fahey) *racd stands' side: a.p: rdn over 1f out: r.o ins fnl f: no answer to wnr fnl strides: 2nd of 11 in gp* **20/1**

11 **3** shd **Anticipated (IRE)**[48] 1917 2-9-3 0 RichardHughes 20 99
(Richard Hannon) *lengthy: athletic: lw: racd stands' side: chsd gp ldr: r.o to ld overall fnl 110yds: hdd and hld towards fin: 3rd of 11 in gp* **4/1**[1]

4 nk **Fountain Of Youth (IRE)**[12] 3031 2-9-3 0 RyanMoore 12 97+
(A P O'Brien, Ire) *str: lengthy: racd far side: chsd ldrs: effrt over 2f out: edgd lft over 1f out: r.o to chal ins fnl f: hld fnl strides: 1st of 13 in gp* **7/1**[2]

2 **5** nk **My Catch (IRE)**[10] 3079 2-9-3 0 JamieSpencer 18 96+
(David Brown) *w'like: scope: lengthy: lw: racd stands' side: hld up: swtchd lft over 1f out: sn rdn: hdwy ins fnl f: r.o and lugged rt towards fin: 4th of 11 in gp* **12/1**

22 **6** 1 1/4 **Sacha Park (IRE)**[15] 2943 2-9-3 0 PatDobbs 4 92+
(Richard Hannon) *racd far side: in tch: rdn over 1f out: r.o ins fnl f: sn chal: styd on same pce towards fin: 2nd of 13 in gp* **12/1**

41 **7** shd **Ben Hall (IRE)**[11] 3045 2-9-3 0 WilliamBuick 22 92
(John Gosden) *lw: racd stands' side: chsd ldrs: rdn over 1f out: styd on towards fin: 5th of 11 in gp* **7/1**[2]

41 **8** hd **Sleeper King (IRE)**[17] 2877 2-9-3 0 PhillipMakin 24 91
(Kevin Ryan) *racd stands' side: led gp: rdn over 1f out: hdd ins fnl f: styd on same pce fnl 110yds: 6th of 11 in gp* **14/1**

1212 **9** 1/2 **Justice Day (IRE)**[17] 2877 2-9-3 0 DaneO'Neill 6 89
(David Elsworth) *racd far side: chsd ldrs: rdn 2f out: led overall over 1f out: hdd fnl 110yds: no ex towards fin: 3rd of 13 in gp* **16/1**

10 nk **Wilshire Boulevard (IRE)**[4] 3304 2-9-3 0 JosephO'Brien 8 88
(A P O'Brien, Ire) *racd far side: hld up: hdwy over 1f out: styd on ins fnl f: nt quite pce of ldrs: 4th of 13 in gp* **12/1**

133 **11** 3/4 **Haikbidiac (IRE)**[17] 2863 2-9-3 0 KierenFallon 25 85
(William Haggas) *racd stands' side: midfield: rdn over 1f out: kpt on ins fnl f: nvr able to chal: 7th of 11 in gp* **20/1**

12 **12** hd **Andhesontherun (IRE)**[19] 2809 2-9-3 0 AndreaAtzeni 11 85+
(Roger Varian) *w'like: racd far side: hld up: rdn and hdwy whn nt clr run and swtchd rt over 1f out: sn chsd ldrs: one pce fnl 50yds: 5th of 13 in gp* **25/1**

3 **13** nse **Fiftyshadesofgrey (IRE)**[11] 3035 2-9-3 0 PatCosgrave 23 84
(George Baker) *w'like: racd stands' side: dwlt: hld up: hdwy over 2f out: one pce and no imp ins fnl f: 8th of 11 in gp* **66/1**

221 **14** 1/2 **Beau Nash (IRE)**[33] 2391 2-9-3 0 SeanLevey 21 83
(Richard Hannon) *athletic: racd stands' side: midfield: rdn 2f out: kpt on and lugged rt towards fin: nt trble ldrs: 9th of 11 in gp* **40/1**

15 shd **Ogermeister (USA)**[33] 2-9-3 0 (bt[1]) JRosario 3 82
(Wesley A Ward, U.S.A) *strong: well-made: racd far side: chsd ldr: rdn 2f out: lost 2nd over 1f out: one pce fnl 100yds: 6th of 13 in gp* **8/1**[3]

562 **16** 1 1/2 **Jazz (IRE)**[18] 2847 2-9-3 0 [1] JamesMcDonald 16 77
(Charles Hills) *racd far side: midfield: rdn and hdwy over 1f out: one pce and no imp ins fnl f: 7th of 13 in gp* **66/1**

21 **17** 1/2 **Tableforten**[22] 2723 2-9-3 0 LiamJones 14 75
(J S Moore) *w'like: racd far side: bhd: sn outpcd: styd on ins fnl f: nt pce to trble ldrs: 8th of 13 in gp* **100/1**

36 **18** shd **Sefaat**[11] 3057 2-8-12 0 PaulHanagan 2 70
(Brian Meehan) *racd far side: chsd ldrs: rdn over 1f out: wknd fnl 110yds: 9th of 13 in gp* **66/1**

242 **19** 1 1/2 **Finflash (IRE)**[14] 2947 2-9-3 0 MartinHarley 10 69
(Mick Channon) *racd far side: bhd: outpcd over 2f out: nvr a threat: 10th of 13 in gp* **66/1**

6104 **20** 1/2 **Zalzilah**[10] 3079 2-9-3 0 NeilCallan 17 67
(James Tate) *racd stands' side: chsd ldrs tl rdn and wknd over 1f out: 10th of 11 in gp* **100/1**

6340 **21** shd **Intense Feeling (IRE)**[20] 2767 2-8-12 0 StevieDonohoe 26 62
(David Evans) *racd stands' side: a bhd: wl outpcd over 2f out: 11th of 11 in gp* **100/1**

013 **22** 3 3/4 **Peterkin (IRE)**[15] 2933 2-9-3 0 JoeFanning 1 54
(Mark Johnston) *w'like: tall: racd far side: led overall tl over 1f out: wknd ins fnl f: 11th of 13 in gp* **66/1**

2114 **23** 5 **Steventon Star**[19] 2809 2-9-3 0 FrankieDettori 13 36
(Richard Hannon) *swtg: racd far side: bhd: outpcd over 2f out: eased whn wl btn ins fnl f: 12th of 13 in gp* **16/1**

1 **24** 6 **Der Blaue Reiter (IRE)**[56] 1749 2-9-3 0 JamesDoyle 7 14
(George Baker) *cmpt: racd far side: midfield tl rdn and wknd 2f out: 13th of 13 in gp* **66/1**

59.82s (-0.68) **Going Correction** +0.075s/f (Good) **24** Ran SP% **131.2**
Speed ratings (Par 101): **108,107,107,106,106 104,104,103,103,102 101,101,101,100,100 97,96,96,94,93 93,87,79,69**
Tote Swingers: 1&2 £75.70, 1&3 £21.50, 2&3 £3.70 CSF £322.75 CT £1569.17 TOTE £23.50: £7.30, £8.00, £2.60; EX 492.60 Trifecta £7804.00 Pool: £10,571.42 - 1.01 winning units..
Owner Qatar Racing Limited **Bred** Mrs Louise Lyons **Trained** Chiddingfold, Surrey
■ Stewards' Enquiry : Johnny Murtagh two-day ban: used whip with above the permitted level (Jul 2-3)

FOCUS
Predictably this big field soon split into two and the far-side group were well ahead at halfway, but perhaps the leader on that flank, Peterkin, went off too quickly, as by the time they reached the line the nearside group were well on top. The time was fast but there was a very congested finish and this has to rate an average renewal.
T/Jkpt: Not won. T/Plt: £564.20 to a £1 stake. Pool: £663,102.00 - 857.87 winning units T/Qpdt: £38.10 to a £1 stake. Pool: £30,816.00 - 597.38 winning units

3148 BRIGHTON (L-H)
Tuesday, June 18

OFFICIAL GOING: Good to firm (8.3)
Wind: Moderate, half against Weather: Sunny spells

3425 CASHOUT MULTIPLES ONLY ON BETFAIR H'CAP 5f 59y
6:00 (6:01) (Class 6) (0-60,61) 3-Y-O+ **£1,940** (£577; £288; £144) **Stalls** Low

Form RPR

6043 **1** **Russian Bullet**[8] 3154 4-9-0 **45** (b) FergusSweeney 6 53
(Jamie Osborne) *mde all: hrd rdn 1f out: jst hld on* **5/1**[3]

0406 **2** nk **Scommettitrice (IRE)**[3] 3325 5-9-1 **53** (b) OisinMurphy(7) 7 60
(Mark Gillard) *disp 2nd: rdn 3f out: r.o fnl f: jst failed* **3/1**[2]

4022 **3** 1 3/4 **Imaginary Diva**[17] 2870 7-9-9 **57** RyanPowell(3) 1 58
(George Margarson) *chsd ldrs: rdn over 2f out: kpt on same pce* **2/1**[1]

5300 **4** shd **Johnny Splash (IRE)**[11] 3051 4-9-1 **51** (b) NathanAlison(5) 3 52
(Roger Teal) *in tch: rdn over 2f out: styd on fnl f* **6/1**

4-00 **5** 4 1/2 **Jawim**[4] 3268 4-9-3 **48** TomMcLaughlin 5 33
(Malcolm Saunders) *disp 2nd tl wknd jst over 1f out* **10/1**

5-41 **6** 3 3/4 **Burnt Cream**[132] 529 6-9-5 **50** (t) MartinLane 4 22
(Martin Bosley) *s.s: bhd: mod effrt 2f out: sn wknd* **8/1**

1m 2.77s (0.47) **Going Correction** -0.15s/f (Firm) **6** Ran SP% **109.5**
Speed ratings (Par 101): **90,89,86,86,79 73**
Tote Swingers: 1&2 £2.70, 1&3 £2.40, 2&3 £1.70 CSF £19.21 TOTE £5.80: £3.30, £3.00; EX 16.90 Trifecta £72.80 Pool: £2,355.99 - 24.26 winning units..
Owner Steve Jakes **Bred** Cranford Bloodstock Uk Ltd **Trained** Upper Lambourn, Berks
■ Stewards' Enquiry : Fergus Sweeney two-day ban: careless riding (Jul 2-3)

FOCUS
Following a dry and warm spell the ground was changed to good to firm all over. The winning rider said: "It's very quick ground, typical of Brighton at this time of year." A moderate handicap run at a reasonable gallop.

3426 IRISH EBF/BETFAIR MULTIPLES CASHOUT MAIDEN STKS 5f 213y
6:30 (6:30) (Class 5) 2-Y-O **£2,911** (£866; £432; £216) **Stalls** Low

Form RPR

2 **1** **Vigor (IRE)**[21] 2758 2-9-5 MartinLane 1 89+
(David Simcock) *chsd ldr: led over 4f out: clr fnl f: comf* **5/2**[2]

2 **2** 6 **Bewitchment**[20] 2774 2-9-0 LukeMorris 2 65
(Sir Mark Prescott Bt) *trckd ldrs: wnt 2nd over 2f out: one pce appr fnl f* **4/5**[1]

0 **3** 2 1/2 **Faintly (USA)**[40] 2194 2-9-5 IanMongan 5 62
(Amanda Perrett) *t.k.h in 4th: rdn over 2f out: one pce* **9/2**[3]

50 **4** 1/2 **By The Light (IRE)**[29] 2502 2-9-5 MartinDwyer 3 60
(Mark Johnston) *led over 1f: wknd and hung lft fr 2f out* **33/1**

5 2 1/2 **Resist** 2-9-0 FergusSweeney 4 47
(Tobias B P Coles) *hld up in 5th: rdn and btn 2f out: hng lft* **25/1**

1m 9.35s (-0.85) **Going Correction** -0.15s/f (Firm) **5** Ran SP% **109.1**
Speed ratings (Par 93): **99,91,87,87,83**
CSF £4.80 TOTE £2.40: £1.10, £1.40; EX 6.50 Trifecta £13.80 Pool: £1,718.05 - 92.98 winning units..
Owner Al Asayl Bloodstock Ltd **Bred** Peter & Hugh McCutcheon **Trained** Newmarket, Suffolk

FOCUS
A couple of fair sorts in an uncompetitive maiden but an improved effort from the winner, and this could underplay him. The gallop was just an ordinary one to the home turn.

3427 BETFAIR MULTIPLES CASHOUT "DO YOU? DON'T YOU?" FILLIES' H'CAP 1m 1f 209y
7:00 (7:00) (Class 4) (0-80,78) 4-Y-O+ **£4,690** (£1,395; £697; £348) **Stalls** High

Form RPR

311 **1** **Yojojo (IRE)**[19] 2792 4-9-1 **72** LukeMorris 2 79
(Gay Kelleway) *chsd ldr 5f: rdn and outpcd 3f out: rallied fnl f: r.o to ld fnl stride* **5/1**

2521 **2** shd **Reset City**[6] 3195 7-8-12 **69** 6ex MartinDwyer 1 76
(Mark Johnston) *hld up in 4th: hdwy 3f out: drvn to ld wl ins fnl f: jst ct* **5/4**[1]

4-22 **3** 1 3/4 **Waveguide (IRE)**[34] 2361 4-8-13 **70** MartinLane 3 73
(David Simcock) *cl up: wnt 2nd 5f out: led 2f out tl no ex wl ins fnl f* **11/4**[2]

6-66 **4** 2 1/4 **Perfect Delight**[25] 2619 4-9-3 **74** JohnFahy 5 73
(Clive Cox) *sn led: hdd 2f out: wknd jst over 1f out* **7/2**[3]

2m 3.05s (-0.55) **Going Correction** -0.15s/f (Firm) **4** Ran SP% **110.0**
Speed ratings (Par 102): **96,95,94,92**
CSF £11.94 TOTE £3.10; EX 10.70 Trifecta £35.20 Pool: £950.13 - 20.23 winning units..
Owner Winterbeck Manor Stud **Bred** Rossenarra Bloodstock Limited **Trained** Exning, Suffolk

The Form Book Flat, Raceform Ltd, Compton, RG20 6NL.

FOCUS
A fair fillies' handicap but a steady side to the home straight means this bare form isn't entirely reliable.

3428 WHEN DO YOU? CASHOUT ONLY ON BETFAIR H'CAP 1m 1f 209y
7:30 (7:31) (Class 6) (0-60,66) 3-Y-O £1,940 (£577; £288; £144) Stalls High

Form RPR

6-35 **1** **Sovereign Power**[11] 3041 3-9-4 **57** MartinLane 6 65
(Paul Cole) *led after 1f: rdn and styd on wl fnl 2f* **7/1**[3]

4-40 **2** 2 3/4 **Uganda Glory (USA)**[59] 1698 3-9-2 **55** PatCosgrave 5 58
(George Baker) *t.k.h: prom: chsd wnr fnl 2f: no imp* **9/2**[2]

5303 **3** 3 **Rock Diamond (IRE)**[11] 3041 3-8-8 **47** FergusSweeney 3 44
(Sylvester Kirk) *led 1f: chsd ldrs tl outpcd and lost pl 4f out: styd on again fr over 1f out* **7/1**[3]

-060 **4** 1 1/4 **Sonnetation (IRE)**[19] 2802 3-8-11 **50** SamHitchcott 7 44
(Jim Boyle) *t.k.h: prom tl no ex over 1f out* **25/1**

6-06 **5** 1 **Smart Alice**[12] 3014 3-8-8 **50** AshleyMorgan(3) 1 42
(Chris Wall) *hld up: effrt over 2f out: no imp* **14/1**

4-40 **6** 1 **Exclusion (USA)**[27] 2566 3-9-1 **54** TomMcLaughlin 4 44
(Noel Quinlan) *in tch tl rdn and outpcd fnl 3f* **8/1**

60-0 **7** 2 1/4 **Elvin**[14] 2950 3-8-6 **48** SimonPearce(3) 11 34
(Amanda Perrett) *towards rr: rdn over 2f out: n.d* **20/1**

0-06 **8** 6 **Penang Power**[31] 2455 3-9-4 **57** AdamKirby 2 31
(Michael Bell) *in tch: plld out 3f out: rdn and wknd 2f out* **6/4**[1]

6-00 **9** 32 **Something Magic**[17] 2874 3-9-7 **60** IanMongan 10
(Sylvester Kirk) *hit gate and s.i.s: towards rr: sme hdwy and rdn 4f out: wknd over 2f out: bhd whn eased over 1f out* **14/1**

2m 3.78s (0.18) **Going Correction** -0.15s/f (Firm) 9 Ran SP% **116.2**
Speed ratings (Par 97): **93,90,88,87,86 85,84,79,53**
Tote Swingers: 1&2 £6.50, 1&3 £4.50, 2&3 £3.40 CSF £38.78 CT £231.03 TOTE £9.90: £3.30, £2.70, £1.50; EX 42.90 Trifecta £154.00 Pool: £926.23 - 4.50 winning units..
Owner Jill Haines,Josephine Green,PFI Cole Ltd **Bred** Tafiya Syndicate **Trained** Whatcombe, Oxon

FOCUS
A moderate handicap in which the well-backed market leader disappointed. The gallop was just an ordinary one to the 3f marker and this suited the prominent-racers.

3429 WHEN DON'T YOU? CASHOUT ONLY ON BETFAIR H'CAP 7f 214y
8:00 (8:01) (Class 6) (0-65,65) 4-Y-O+ £1,940 (£577; £288; £144) Stalls Low

Form RPR

002 **1** **Paphos**[12] 3015 6-9-7 **65** (v) AdamKirby 5 76
(David Evans) *led tl 4f out: rdn to ld again 2f out: drvn clr ins fnl f* **5/2**[2]

-242 **2** 3 **Duke Of Destiny (IRE)**[20] 2773 4-9-7 **65** TomMcLaughlin 11 69+
(Ed Walker) *trckd ldrs: effrt and hung bdly lft over 1f out: unable qck* **5/4**[1]

1040 **3** 5 **Stormbound (IRE)**[27] 2574 4-8-12 **63** (p) JordanUys(7) 2 56
(Paul Cole) *prom: led 4f out tl 2f out: wknd 1f out* **4/1**[3]

-400 **4** shd **Hawk Moth (IRE)**[11] 3052 5-9-1 **59** (p) SamHitchcott 7 51
(John Spearing) *hld up in 5th: hmpd bnd over 4f out: rdn and hdwy 2f out: styd on same pce* **25/1**

-006 **5** 6 **Sangrail**[123] 662 4-8-2 **46** oh1 NickyMackay 8 25
(William Muir) *twrds rr: rdn 3f out: nvr trbld ldrs* **20/1**

3-50 **6** 4 1/2 **Aciano (IRE)**[44] 2057 5-9-5 **63** (tp) StevieDonohoe 10 31
(Brendan Powell) *rdn along in rr: sme hdwy 2f out: sn wknd* **10/1**

00-0 **7** 31 **Plus Fours (USA)**[10] 2171 4-7-9 **46** oh1 (b[1]) NoraLooby(7) 4
(Michael Appleby) *t.k.h: prom over 4f* **33/1**

1m 34.35s (-1.65) **Going Correction** -0.15s/f (Firm) 7 Ran SP% **113.7**
Speed ratings (Par 101): **102,99,94,93,87 83,52**
Tote Swingers: 1&2 £1.02, 1&3 £2.70, 2&3 £3.10 CSF £5.90 CT £10.54 TOTE £2.90: £1.40, £1.10; EX 6.30 Trifecta £16.10 Pool: £1,690.44 - 78.74 winning units..
Owner Mrs E Evans **Bred** L Ellinas And Old Mill Stud Ltd **Trained** Pandy, Monmouths
■ Stewards' Enquiry : Sam Hitchcott three-day ban: careless riding (Jul 2-4)
Jordan Uys four-day ban: used whip above the permitted level (Jul 2-5)

FOCUS
Mainly exposed performers in a modest handicap. The gallop was reasonable throughout.

3430 BETFAIR MULTIPLES CASHOUT YOU DECIDE WHEN H'CAP 6f 209y
8:30 (8:30) (Class 6) (0-65,65) 4-Y-O+ £1,940 (£577; £288; £144) Stalls Low

Form RPR

0530 **1** **The Mongoose**[4] 3270 5-9-2 **60** (t) AdamKirby 4 65
(David Evans) *chsd ldrs: effrt in centre over 2f out: led over 1f out: drvn out* **7/4**[1]

6005 **2** 1 1/4 **Fairy Mist (IRE)**[17] 2873 6-8-2 **46** KieranO'Neill 5 48
(John Bridger) *in tch in 5th: hdwy on rail 2f out: ev ch over 1f out: unable qck* **14/1**

146 **3** 1/2 **Jonnie Skull (IRE)**[8] 3153 7-9-6 **64** (vt) TomMcLaughlin 9 65
(Phil McEntee) *led tl over 1f out: styd on same pce* **7/2**[3]

5300 **4** 3/4 **Jackie Love (IRE)**[11] 3054 5-8-2 **51** (v) NathanAlison(5) 3 50
(Olivia Maylam) *t.k.h: cl up: rdn and one pce fnl 2f* **5/1**

3500 **5** 3/4 **The Guru Of Gloom (IRE)**[15] 2929 5-9-7 **65** MartinDwyer 6 62
(William Muir) *t.k.h: trckd ldr: rdn 2f out: sn outpcd* **5/2**[2]

1m 22.29s (-0.81) **Going Correction** -0.15s/f (Firm) 5 Ran SP% **110.5**
Speed ratings (Par 101): **98,96,96,95,94**
Tote Swingers: 1&2 £26.50 CSF £23.63 TOTE £2.40: £1.10, £7.10; EX 26.00 Trifecta £82.60 Pool: £915.23 - 8.30 winning units..
Owner G Evans & P D Evans **Bred** Kincorth Investments Inc **Trained** Pandy, Monmouths

FOCUS
Not many in-form sorts in a modest handicap. The pace was an ordinary one.

3431 NO MORE #IFONLY CASHOUT ONLY AT BETFAIR H'CAP 5f 213y
9:00 (9:00) (Class 5) (0-70,70) 3-Y-O+ £2,587 (£770; £384; £192) Stalls Low

Form RPR

2631 **1** **Commanche**[14] 2949 4-9-7 **70** JoshCrane(7) 3 82
(Chris Dwyer) *chsd ldrs: hung lft and led 1f out: rdn out* **8/1**[3]

-005 **2** 2 1/2 **Bermondsey Bob (IRE)**[5] 3247 7-9-1 **57** SamHitchcott 2 61
(John Spearing) *led 2f: led again over 2f out tl 1f out: unable qck* **5/1**[2]

1025 **3** 3/4 **Haadeeth**[7] 3181 6-9-8 **64** (t) AdamKirby 7 66
(David Evans) *outpcd in rr: gd hdwy over 1f out: styd on* **12/1**

5-33 **4** 1 3/4 **Glan Lady (IRE)**[12] 3029 7-8-5 **52** oh5 ow1 TobyAtkinson(5) 1 48
(Michael Appleby) *sn pshd along in 5th: effrt over 2f out: one pce* **33/1**

0244 **5** 1 3/4 **Putin (IRE)**[17] 2871 5-9-1 **62** (bt) RachealKneller(5) 8 52
(Phil McEntee) *prom tl hrd rdn and wknd over 1f out* **12/1**

3540 **6** 4 1/2 **The Strig**[31] 2450 6-9-7 **63** (v) PatCosgrave 6 39
(Stuart Williams) *s.s: bhd: wd st: n.d* **8/1**[3]

211 **7** 1 1/4 **Maria Montez**[3] 3325 4-9-1 **64** 6ex ShelleyBirkett(7) 4 36
(J W Hills) *prom: led 4f out tl over 2f out: wknd over 1f out* **4/5**[1]

1m 9.19s (-1.01) **Going Correction** -0.15s/f (Firm) 7 Ran SP% **112.8**
Speed ratings (Par 103): **100,96,95,93,91 85,83**
Tote Swingers: 1&2 £2.30, 1&3 £4.70, 2&3 £5.40 CSF £45.71 CT £476.07 TOTE £8.80: £2.40, £2.30; EX 41.80 Trifecta £252.00 Pool: £1,451.84 - 4.32 winning units..
Owner M M Foulger **Bred** Paramount Bloodstock **Trained** Newmarket, Suffolk

FOCUS
A modest finale which took less winning than had seemed likely with the market leader disappointing. The gallop was sound.
T/Plt: £77.50 to a £1 stake. Pool: £56,525.00 - 531.77 winning units T/Qpdt: £21.70 to a £1 stake. Pool: £4,970.00 - 168.88 winning units LM

3399 KEMPTON (A.W) (R-H)
Tuesday, June 18

OFFICIAL GOING: Standard
Wind: Almost nil Weather: Cloudy, quite humid

3432 LADIES DAY AT KEMPTON 07.09.2013 APPRENTICE H'CAP 1m 3f (P)
6:10 (6:10) (Class 6) (0-60,60) 3-Y-O £1,940 (£577; £288; £144) Stalls Low

Form RPR

2-23 **1** **Alpine Mysteries (IRE)**[50] 1879 3-9-7 **60** ThomasBrown 8 71
(Harry Dunlop) *trckd ldr: led over 2f out: rdn wl clr fr over 1f out* **9/4**[2]

5240 **2** 6 **Aphrodite Spirit (IRE)**[49] 1897 3-8-7 **46** CharlesBishop 9 46
(Pat Eddery) *led and dictated mostly modest gallop: rdn and hdd over 2f out: no ch w wnr sn after but kpt on for 2nd* **16/1**

0-50 **3** 3/4 **See And Be Seen**[5] 3243 3-8-6 **48** DanielMuscutt(3) 3 47
(Sylvester Kirk) *trckd ldng pair: rdn over 2f out: pressed runner-up fnl f but no ch* **16/1**

0-00 **4** 1/2 **Mr Vendman (IRE)**[15] 2924 3-8-7 **46** oh1 (p) DeclanBates 6 44
(Ian Williams) *pushed along early to rch 4th: drvn and outpcd over 2f out: kpt on u.p to press for a pl nr fin* **33/1**

560- **5** 1 **Slip Of The Tongue**[245] 7127 3-9-6 **59** RosieJessop 7 55
(Sir Mark Prescott Bt) *fractious gng to post: t.k.h: hld up in last trio: outpcd and rdn over 2f out: no ch after: plugged on* **10/11**[1]

345- **6** 5 **Dude Alert (IRE)**[209] 7812 3-9-4 **60** JoshBaudains(3) 5 47
(Peter Chapple-Hyam) *hld up in last pair: rdn wl over 2f out: sn lft bhd* **10/1**[3]

-640 **7** 1/2 **Mastered (IRE)**[27] 2566 3-8-11 **50** MatthewLawson 1 36
(John Best) *hld up in last trio: rdn wl over 2f out: sn lft wl bhd* **20/1**

2m 23.86s (1.96) **Going Correction** 0.0s/f (Stan) 7 Ran SP% **111.7**
Speed ratings (Par 97): **92,87,87,86,86 82,82**
Tote Swingers: 1&2 £2.80, 1&3 £9.10, 2&3 £20.00 CSF £34.24 CT £452.99 TOTE £2.00: £3.10, £5.20; EX 17.00 Trifecta £169.50 Pool: £1,510.47 - 6.68 winning units..
Owner Windflower Overseas Holdings Inc **Bred** Windflower Overseas Holdings Inc **Trained** Lambourn, Berks

FOCUS
Little strength in depth in this apprentice handicap and with the favourite bombing out the winner had nothing to beat.

3433 BETVICTOR NO LOSE HUGHES MONEY BACK H'CAP 1m (P)
6:40 (6:42) (Class 6) (0-58,58) 4-Y-O+ £1,940 (£577; £288; £144) Stalls Low

Form RPR

00/ **1** **Two Minds (FR)**[1142] 1766 6-9-4 **55** WilliamCarson 14 66
(Eugene Stanford) *hld up in 6th: rdn over 2f out: prog over 1f out: led and edgd rt last 150yds: drvn out* **12/1**

3-11 **2** 1 1/2 **Victorian Number (FR)**[42] 2126 5-9-7 **58** GeorgeBaker 12 66
(Geoffrey Deacon) *trckd ldr: rdn to ld over 1f out: hdd and one pce last 150yds* **4/1**[2]

5302 **3** 1 3/4 **Strategic Action (IRE)**[21] 2747 4-9-7 **58** RobertHavlin 10 62
(Linda Jewell) *trckd ldrs: gng strly over 2f out: rdn and trying to mount a chal whn squeezed out 1f out: kpt on to take 3rd nr fin* **8/1**

30-0 **4** nk **Wyndham Wave**[47] 1948 4-9-4 **55** (p) SteveDrowne 4 58
(Rod Millman) *trckd ldrs on inner: rdn over 2f out: nvr able to threaten but kpt on fnl f* **7/1**[3]

/000 **5** shd **Princess Spirit**[7] 3169 4-8-8 **52** (p) JenniferFerguson(7) 8 55
(Edward Creighton) *t.k.h: hld up towards rr: tried to weave through fr 2f out: urged along and styd on fnl f: nrst fin* **33/1**

/600 **6** 1/2 **South Kenter (USA)**[27] 2582 4-8-11 **48** (p) CathyGannon 3 50
(Heather Main) *led: rdn and hdd over 1f out: wknd fnl f* **33/1**

1035 **7** 1 1/4 **Rigid**[23] 2072 6-8-4 **46** RobertTart(5) 9 45
(Tony Carroll) *disp 2nd pl to over 2f out: steadily wknd over 1f out* **12/1**

0030 **8** 2 **Rapid Water**[21] 2747 7-9-2 **53** (b) LiamKeniry 5 47
(Pat Eddery) *hld up in midfield: gng strly 2f out: hld together tl rdn and wknd ins fnl f* **20/1**

0004 **9** 1 3/4 **Blue Deer (IRE)**[14] 2948 5-9-4 **58** (p) DarrenEgan(3) 1 48
(Lee Carter) *hld up towards rr on inner: drvn and no prog 2f out* **20/1**

-306 **10** 2 **Guardi (IRE)**[44] 2057 4-9-4 **55** [1] TedDurcan 13 41
(Dean Ivory) *t.k.h: racd on outer: rdn and wknd over 2f out* **14/1**

000 **11** 1/2 **Delicious Patrica**[18] 2824 4-8-6 **48** CharlesBishop(5) 2 33
(Tony Carroll) *a in rr: rdn and no prog over 2f out* **50/1**

5020 **12** 1/2 **Karate (IRE)**[14] 2954 5-9-2 **58** (t) NicoleNordblad(5) 11 42
(Hans Adielsson) *restrained into last trio sn after s: t.k.h on outer: rdn over 2f out: sn btn* **7/1**[3]

/0-0 **13** 1/2 **Ebony Song (USA)**[49] 1901 5-9-6 **57** ChrisCatlin 7 39
(Jo Crowley) *hld up: a wl in rr: rdn and struggling over 2f out* **33/1**

1240 **14** 6 **Spellmaker**[60] 1665 4-9-0 **51** SebSanders 6 20+
(Tony Newcombe) *plld hrd: hld up in midfield: wknd rapidly 2f out* **7/2**[1]

1m 39.63s (-0.17) **Going Correction** 0.0s/f (Stan) 14 Ran SP% **120.7**
Speed ratings (Par 101): **100,98,96,96,96 95,94,92,90,88 88,87,87,81**
Tote Swingers: 1&2 £13.90, 1&3 £16.20, 2&3 £5.00 CSF £55.19 CT £333.80 TOTE £23.20: £5.60, £1.40, £3.10; EX 132.20 Trifecta £988.00 Pool: £1,512.63 - 1.14 winning units..
Owner Lemberg Stables **Bred** John Stevens & John Morgan **Trained** Newmarket, Suffolk
■ Stewards' Enquiry : William Carson two-day ban: careless riding (Jul 2-3)

FOCUS
A tactical handicap, which was noteworthy for a terrific training performance from Eugene Stanford.

3434 BETVICTOR ROYAL ASCOT NO LOSE HUGHES H'CAP (LONDON MILE SERIES QUALIFIER) 1m (P)
7:10 (7:15) (Class 5) (0-75,75) 3-Y-0+ **£2,587** (£770; £384; £192) **Stalls** Low

Form RPR

1241 **1** **Hill Of Dreams (IRE)**[19] 2787 4-9-7 **68**.........................(b) JimCrowley 8 83
(Dean Ivory) *hld up towards rr: rdn and prog fr 2f out to ld over 1f out: sn clr: pushed out* **14/1**

-052 **2** *5* **Future Reference (IRE)**[13] 2984 3-9-1 **72**............(t) SilvestreDeSousa 9 74
(Saeed bin Suroor) *trckd ldng trio: wnt 2nd jst over 2f out: trying to chal whn wnr swept by over 1f out: kpt on same pce fnl f* **11/10**[1]

3-50 **3** *nse* **Break Rank (USA)**[22] 2728 4-10-0 **75**................................ LiamKeniry 3 78
(Ed de Giles) *trckd ldng pair: rdn 2f out: kpt on fnl f to press for 2nd nr fin* **6/1**[3]

6160 **4** *½* **Beauchamp Xerxes**[11] 3054 7-8-11 **63**..................(t) NicoleNordblad(5) 2 65
(Hans Adielsson) *led at decent pce: hdd over 1f out: no ch w wnr but kpt battling for a pl* **20/1**

2026 **5** *shd* **Athletic**[20] 2773 4-8-12 **64**...(v) RobertTart(5) 12 66
(Andrew Reid) *t.k.h: hld up in midfield: clsd on ldrs over 2f out: rdn and nt qckn wl over 1f out: kpt on to press for a pl nr fin* **20/1**

0-55 **6** *1 ¼* **Saxon Soldier**[21] 2746 3-8-13 **70**.. TomQueally 4 67
(Ed Dunlop) *trckd ldrs: pushed along 2f out: nt qckn over 1f out: rdn and fdd last 100yds* **8/1**

223- **7** *2 ¼* **Be My Rock**[234] 7395 4-10-0 **75**.. ChrisCatlin 11 69
(Rae Guest) *broke on terms but sn heavily restrained into last: shuffled along on outer over 2f out: reminder over 1f out: kpt on but nvr remotely involved* **20/1**

-460 **8** *5* **Quadriga (IRE)**[10] 3117 3-8-10 **67**...................................... AndreaAtzeni 5 47
(Robert Eddery) *trckd ldr to jst over 2f out: sn lost pl: wknd qckly fnl f* **5/1**[2]

205 **9** *10* **Diplomatic (IRE)**[78] 1292 8-9-7 **68**.................................(p) KierenFallon 6 27
(Michael Squance) *trckd ldrs: pushed along over 3f out: wknd 2f out: eased whn no ch fnl f: t.o* **14/1**

0350 **10** *3 ¼* **Fraserburgh (IRE)**[20] 2776 3-9-1 **75**........................ DarrenEgan(3) 10 25
(Mark Johnston) *a in rr: rdn sn after 1/2-way: t.o* **25/1**

2-00 **11** *3 ¼* **Khelac**[28] 2549 3-8-8 **65**.. SteveDrowne 7
(Philip Hide) *s.i.s: a wl in rr: t.o* **66/1**

0200 **12** *7* **Bajan Story**[15] 2932 4-8-13 **60**.. TedDurcan 13
(Michael Blanshard) *dwlt: a in last pair: u.p bef 1/2-way: t.o* **33/1**

1m 38.38s (-1.42) **Going Correction** 0.0s/f (Stan)
WFA 3 from 4yo+ 10lb **12** Ran SP% **125.6**
Speed ratings (Par 103): **107,102,101,101,101 100,97,92,82,79 76,69**
Tote Swingers: 1&2 £3.20, 1&3 £15.00, 2&3 £3.80 CSF £29.30 CT £120.42 TOTE £11.60: £4.10, £1.10, £1.80; EX 31.80 Trifecta £261.60 Pool: £1,811.32 - 5.19 winning units..
Owner I Gethin & R Gethin **Bred** Miss Breda Wright **Trained** Radlett, Herts
FOCUS
A ready winner of this modest handicap.

3435 BETVICTOR ROYAL ASCOT MONEY BACK SPECIAL MEDIAN AUCTION MAIDEN STKS 1m (P)
7:40 (7:45) (Class 5) 3-4-Y-0 **£2,749** (£818; £408; £204) **Stalls** Low

Form RPR

0 **1** **Laura Secord (CAN)**[68] 1499 3-8-12 0.............................. AndreaAtzeni 2 74
(Heather Main) *trckd ldr after 100yds: clsd to ld jst over 2f out: sn rdn: kpt on to draw steadily away over 1f out* **50/1**

2 *3* **Blighty (IRE)** 3-9-3 0.. TomQueally 11 72+
(Lady Cecil) *in tch: trckd ldng pair over 3f out: pushed along and nt on terms over 2f out: rdn and kpt on same pce fr over 1f out to take 2nd nr fin* **11/4**[2]

44 **3** *nk* **Conquestadim**[41] 2157 3-9-3 0............................ SilvestreDeSousa 1 71
(Hughie Morrison) *pushed up to ld after 100yds: rdn and hdd jst over 2f out: nt qckn and hld after: lost 2nd nr fin* **7/4**[1]

4 *3 ¾* **Tiger Jim** 3-9-3 0.. TedDurcan 7 62+
(Chris Wall) *hld up in rr: sme prog to take 4th over 2f out but nt on terms: kpt on* **20/1**

00 **5** *3 ¾* **Secret Song**[14] 2953 3-8-12 0...................................... RosieJessop(5) 6 54
(Sir Mark Prescott Bt) *reluctant to enter stalls: fast away: led 100yds then restrained on outer and sn taking t.k.h in midfield: bmpd along over 2f out: n.d after* **66/1**

6 *11* **Glassenbury Lass** 3-8-12 0.. RobertHavlin 5 23
(Mark Hoad) *difficult to load into stalls: a in rr: bhd over 2f out* **66/1**

0 **7** *6* **Echoes Of War**[39] 2224 4-9-13 0.. SebSanders 3 17
(Michael Attwater) *in tch to 3f out: sn wknd* **66/1**

00 **8** *1* **Fonseca (IRE)**[13] 2979 3-8-12 0.. LiamKeniry 10 7
(Andrew Balding) *chsd ldng pair after 1f to over 3f out: sn wknd* **12/1**[3]

9 *1* **Sweet Marwell (IRE)** 3-8-12 0.. ChrisCatlin 8 5
(Jo Crowley) *a bhd: lost tch 3f out* **20/1**

1m 40.15s (0.35) **Going Correction** 0.0s/f (Stan)
WFA 3 from 4yo 10lb **9** Ran SP% **86.7**
Speed ratings (Par 103): **98,95,94,90,87 76,70,69,68**
Tote Swingers: 1&2 £1.10, 1&3 £7.60, 2&3 £6.00 CSF £93.82 TOTE £25.40: £7.20, £1.10, £1.02; EX 57.30 Trifecta £230.50 Pool: £594.02 - 1.93 winning units..
Owner Les Chevaliers **Bred** William D Graham **Trained** Kingston Lisle, Oxon
FOCUS
With Master Wizard having to be withdrawn after getting upset in the stalls this was a weak maiden.

3436 BETVICTOR.COM MAIDEN AUCTION STKS 6f (P)
8:10 (8:13) (Class 5) 2-Y-O **£2,587** (£770; £384; £192) **Stalls** Low

Form RPR

45 **1** **Talksalot (IRE)**[25] 2617 2-8-10 0...................................... LiamJones 6 73
(J S Moore) *racd keenly: mde all: rdn 2f out: kpt on fnl f* **16/1**

4223 **2** *1* **Cockney Bob**[34] 2358 2-8-9 0.. CathyGannon 8 69
(J S Moore) *chsd ldrs: rdn over 2f out: kpt on one pce to take 2nd ins fnl f: unable to chal* **6/4**[1]

43 **3** *nk* **Lucky Visione**[54] 1778 2-8-11 0....................................(p) JackMitchell 2 70
(Gay Kelleway) *chsd ldrs: rdn bef 1/2-way and struggling: rallied on inner over 2f out: chsd wnr over 1f out tl ins fnl f: kpt on* **10/1**

4634 **4** *2 ¾* **Princess Tamay (IRE)**[10] 3084 2-8-8 0.................. SilvestreDeSousa 5 59
(Mark Johnston) *chsd wnr to over 1f out: fdd* **6/1**[3]

36 **5** *½* **Evacusafe Lady**[57] 1724 2-8-2 0...................................... RyanPowell(3) 3 54
(John Ryan) *chsd ldrs: wd in st: rdn over 2f out: fdd over 1f out* **8/1**

0 **6** *13* **Mount Cheiron (USA)**[33] 2382 2-9-1 0.............................. KierenFallon 9 25
(Brian Meehan) *chsd ldrs but sn pushed along: lost tch and rdn over 2f out: sn wl bhd* **9/4**[2]

7 *6* **Monashka Bay (IRE)** 2-8-10 0.. LiamKeniry 10 2
(Michael Blanshard) *s.s: a bhd: edgd lft fr 3f out tl jinked lft to nr side rail over 1f out: t.o* **20/1**

8 *2 ¼* **Redy To Rumble** 2-8-10 0.. RobertHavlin 1
(Michael Attwater) *v s.i.s: v green and a bhd: t.o* **25/1**

9 *10* **Phoenix Angel** 2-8-7 0.. AdamMcLean(7) 7
(Derek Shaw) *v awkward s and immediately t.o: hung violently lft bnd 3f out and virtually unrideable* **33/1**

1m 13.59s (0.49) **Going Correction** 0.0s/f (Stan) **9** Ran SP% **122.7**
Speed ratings (Par 93): **96,94,94,90,89 72,64,61,48**
Tote Swingers: 1&2 £4.60, 1&3 £9.50, 2&3 £3.80 CSF £42.37 TOTE £32.20: £9.10, £1.10, £2.70; EX 50.50 Trifecta £714.40 Pool: £1,400.00 - 1.46 winning units..
Owner J Bond-Smith & J S Moore **Bred** C Kelly **Trained** Upper Lambourn, Berks
FOCUS
A very modest maiden auction which saw a one-two for Stan Moore. The fourth gives perspective.

3437 SILVER BLAZE WESSEX CUP FILLIES' H'CAP 1m 4f (P)
8:40 (8:41) (Class 5) (0-70,70) 3-Y-0+ **£2,587** (£770; £384; £192) **Stalls** Centre

Form RPR

3-21 **1** **Thwart**[42] 2127 3-8-12 **68**.. JimCrowley 5 78+
(Ralph Beckett) *t.k.h: hld up disputing 4th: prog to chse ldr 2f out: rdn over 1f out: clsd fnl f: led last 50yds: shade in hand* **7/4**[1]

56-2 **2** *½* **Spieta (IRE)**[12] 3013 3-8-11 **67**.. KierenFallon 9 76
(Luca Cumani) *led: allowed to dictate modest pce tl past 1/2-way: kicked on over 2f out: styd on fnl f but hdd last 50yds* **5/2**[2]

03-1 **3** *1* **Brigh (IRE)**[115] 774 3-8-11 **70**.. DarrenEgan(3) 1 77+
(David Simcock) *hld up disputing 4th: rdn and prog to chse ldng pair over 1f out: styd on wl but unable to chal* **4/1**[3]

-406 **4** *4* **Jacobella**[26] 2606 3-8-4 **65**......................................[1] MatthewLawson(5) 2 66
(Jonathan Portman) *hld up in 6th: shkn up and outpcd over 2f out: kpt on to take modest 4th ins fnl f* **14/1**

3151 **5** *1 ½* **Irene Kennet**[34] 2360 6-9-13 **69**.. JimmyQuinn 3 68
(Paul Burgoyne) *t.k.h ar various stages: trckd ldr: nt qckn over 2f out: sn lost pl and btn* **7/1**

4-04 **6** *1* **Atmanna**[14] 2963 4-8-9 **51** oh6.. RichardThomas 8 48
(Zoe Davison) *hld up in last: pushed along and outpcd over 2f out: reminder over 1f out: nvr in it* **100/1**

1336 **7** *hd* **Asia Minor (IRE)**[61] 1654 4-9-5 **61**.................................... TomQueally 7 58
(Dr Jon Scargill) *sn trckd ldr: nt qckn over 2f out: sn lost pl and btn* **12/1**

2m 36.92s (2.42) **Going Correction** 0.0s/f (Stan)
WFA 3 from 4yo+ 14lb **7** Ran SP% **112.8**
Speed ratings (Par 100): **91,90,90,87,86 85,85**
Tote Swingers: 1&2 £1.70, 1&3 £2.10, 2&3 £3.60 CSF £6.12 CT £13.83 TOTE £3.70: £3.00, £2.30; EX 8.30 Trifecta £23.00 Pool: £1,028.51 - 33.47 winning units..
Owner M H Dixon **Bred** M H Dixon **Trained** Kimpton, Hants
FOCUS
A cracking finish to this 0-70 fillies' handicap.

3438 ROYAL ASCOT MONEY BACK AT BETVICTOR.COM H'CAP 7f (P)
9:10 (9:11) (Class 5) (0-75,75) 3-Y-O **£2,587** (£770; £384; £192) **Stalls** Low

Form RPR

12U0 **1** **Order Of Service**[14] 2957 3-9-4 **72**.. SeanLevey 8 82
(David Brown) *wnt sltly rt s: mde all at decent pce: rdn wl over 1f out: styd on stoutly and firmly in command fnl f* **12/1**

14-0 **2** *2 ¾* **Exzachary**[57] 1725 3-9-5 **73**.. CathyGannon 1 76
(Jo Hughes) *t.k.h: trckd ldng pair: rdn to chse wnr over 2f out: nt qckn and no imp fr over 1f out* **14/1**

530- **3** *1* **North Pole**[224] 7609 3-8-13 **67**.. LukeMorris 9 67
(Sir Mark Prescott Bt) *chsd wnr: rdn and lost 2nd over 2f out: one pce after* **5/1**[3]

-403 **4** *2* **Dark Templar**[12] 3011 3-9-2 **70**.. TedDurcan 4 65
(Ed Vaughan) *dwlt: in tch: rdn and effrt on inner over 2f out: no imp on ldrs over 1f out* **3/1**[1]

2011 **5** *2 ¼* **Clement (IRE)**[14] 2951 3-9-6 **74**.. JohnFahy 7 63
(Eve Johnson Houghton) *sltly impeded s: plld hrd early: hld up in last pair: rdn over 2f out: no real prog* **7/2**[2]

1426 **6** *nk* **Keene's Pointe**[18] 2844 3-9-7 **75**...................................... SebSanders 10 63
(J W Hills) *chsd ldrs on outer: rdn over 2f out: wknd wl over 1f out* **7/2**[2]

5-65 **7** *14* **Raven's Rock (IRE)**[21] 2763 3-8-6 **63**............................ DarrenEgan(3) 5 13
(Roger Varian) *plld hrd early: hld up in last pair: wknd 2f out: t.o* **5/1**[3]

056- **8** *6* **Birdie King**[202] 7894 3-8-8 **62**.. SteveDrowne 6
(John Best) *plld hrd early: hld up in tch: wknd over 2f out: t.o* **25/1**

1m 25.35s (-0.65) **Going Correction** 0.0s/f (Stan) **8** Ran SP% **121.0**
Speed ratings (Par 99): **103,99,98,96,93 93,77,70**
Tote Swingers: 1&2 £18.00, 1&3 £13.10, 2&3 £26.60 CSF £169.39 CT £966.59 TOTE £17.70: £3.60, £4.90, £2.40; EX 145.70 Trifecta £795.70 Part won. Pool: £1,061.05 - 0.85 winning units..

Owner J C Fretwell **Bred** Cheveley Park Stud Ltd **Trained** Averham Park, Notts
FOCUS
Modest form.
T/Plt: £8.90 to a £1 stake. Pool: £61,670.00 - 5,033.83 winning units T/Qpdt: £2.50 to a £1 stake. Pool: £5,688.00 - 1,671.98 winning units JN

[3023]THIRSK (L-H)
Tuesday, June 18

OFFICIAL GOING: Good to firm (8.8)
Wind: light 1/2 behind Weather: fine and sunny, very warm

3439 IRISH STALLION FARMS EBF NOVICE STKS 5f
2:20 (2:24) (Class 4) 2-Y-O **£4,204** (£1,251; £625; £312) **Stalls** High

Form RPR

12 **1** **Peniaphobia (IRE)**[34] 2370 2-9-2 0...................................... LeeTopliss(3) 6 90
(Richard Fahey) *chsd ldr: swtchd lft over 3f out: sn led: rdn and wandered fnl f: hld on towards fin* **1/5**[1]

0315 **2** *½* **Blockade (IRE)**[20] 2767 2-8-11 0................................ PaulMulrennan 2 80
(James Tate) *trckd ldrs: effrt: nt clr run and swtchd lft jst ins fnl f: sn almost upsides: no ex clsng stages* **6/1**[2]

16 **3** *10* **Innocently (IRE)**[34] 2370 2-9-2 0.. DavidNolan 4 49
(David O'Meara) *led 2f: wknd qckly fnl f* **11/1**[3]

0 **4** *1 ½* **Beltor**[14] 2955 2-9-0 0.. TomEaves 3 42
(Michael Dods) *dwlt: outpcd and detached in last: kpt on fnl f* **80/1**

The Form Book Flat, Raceform Ltd, Compton, RG20 6NL.

133 5 10 **Loma Mor**[13] 2993 2-8-6 0 ShirleyTeasdale(5) 1
(Alan McCabe) *chsd ldrs on outside: hmpd over 3f out: hung lft 2f out: sn lost pl and bhd: eased clsng stages* **25/1**

58.94s (-0.66) **Going Correction** -0.025s/f (Good) 5 Ran SP% **111.0**
Speed ratings (Par 95): **104,103,87,84,68**
CSF £2.00 TOTE £1.10: £1.02, £2.00; EX 2.00 Trifecta £3.00 Pool: £2,365.83 - 577.81 winning units..
Owner P Timmins & A Rhodes Haulage **Bred** Aidan Fogarty **Trained** Musley Bank, N Yorks

FOCUS
A race won 12 months ago by the very useful Body And Soul and, whilst it would be foolish to believe this was as strong, the form looks fairly solid with the principals pulling a long way clear of the remainder.

3440 GBI RACING WELCOMES NICOSIA RACE CLUB (S) STKS 6f
2:55 (2:55) (Class 5) 2-Y-O **£2,587** (£770; £384; £192) **Stalls** High

Form RPR
1 **Cascadia (IRE)** 2-8-9 0 PJMcDonald 4 57
(Mrs K Burke) *s.i.s: detached in last: hdwy and swtchd ins appr fnl f: r.o to ld last 30yds* **9/4**[1]

334 2 2 **Sherry For Nanny (IRE)**[30] 2475 2-8-4 0 ShirleyTeasdale(5) 2 51
(Marjorie Fife) *trckd ldrs: effrt on inner 2f out: led last 75yds: hdd and no ex* **7/2**[2]

663 3 ½ **Lady Captain (IRE)**[6] 3189 2-8-9 0 [1] RobertWinston 5 49
(Kevin Ryan) *led: rdn and hung lft 2f out: hdd wl ins fnl f: kpt on same pce* **5/1**[3]

6420 4 1¼ **Dotesy (IRE)**[29] 2502 2-8-9 0 MichaelO'Connell 3 45
(John Quinn) *w ldrs: rdn and edgd lft over 1f out: wknd towards fin* **9/4**[1]

040 5 ½ **Blades Boy**[17] 2883 2-8-11 0 (b[1]) LeeTopliss(3) 1 49
(Richard Fahey) *w ldrs on outside: intimidated over 1f out: wknd towards fin* **8/1**

1m 14.0s (1.30) **Going Correction** -0.025s/f (Good) 5 Ran SP% **111.5**
Speed ratings (Par 93): **90,87,86,85,84**
CSF £10.51 TOTE £2.80: £1.40, £1.60; EX 9.50 Trifecta £40.40 Pool: £1,747.65 - 32.39 winning units..No bid for the winner.
Owner Mrs Elaine M Burke **Bred** John Wholey **Trained** Middleham Moor, N Yorks
■ Stewards' Enquiry : Shirley Teasdale two-day ban: used whip above the permitted level (Jul 2-3)

FOCUS
A weak juvenile seller but it was won in taking fashion by Cascadia, who should get a fair nursery mark.

3441 MARKET CROSS JEWELLERS H'CAP 6f
3:30 (3:31) (Class 4) (0-85,83) 3-Y-O+ **£4,851** (£1,443; £721; £360) **Stalls** High

Form RPR
2210 1 **Meandmyshadow**[10] 3093 5-9-9 78 DaleSwift 11 88
(Alan Brown) *mde all: edgd lft fnl f: hld on nr fin* **6/1**[2]

-020 2 nk **Baldemar**[39] 2239 8-9-1 73 LeeTopliss(3) 9 82
(Richard Fahey) *swtchd rt after s: in rr: effrt on inner whn nt clr run 2f out: hdwy over 1f out: styd on wl to take 2nd nr fin* **25/1**

0501 3 hd **Clubland (IRE)**[20] 2781 4-8-13 68 JimmyQuinn 4 77+
(Roy Bowring) *chsd ldrs: 2nd jst ins fnl f: carried lft and kpt on same pce last 50yds* **16/1**

0-21 4 1¾ **Secret City (IRE)**[38] 2275 7-9-3 72 (b) RobertWinston 3 77+
(Robin Bastiman) *in rr and sn drvn along: nt clr run and swtchd ins over 1f out: styd on to take 4th nr fin* **11/1**

036- 5 1¼ **Imperator Augustus (IRE)**[200] 7935 5-9-4 73 DuranFentiman 12 72
(Patrick Holmes) *hld up in mid-div: effrt on inner over 1f out: kpt on ins fnl f* **25/1**

6-0 6 1¼ **Willbeme**[21] 2755 5-9-4 73 AndrewElliott 7 68
(Neville Bycroft) *w ldrs: edgd lft over 1f out: wknd jst ins fnl f* **7/2**[1]

-401 7 ½ **Half A Billion (IRE)**[31] 2441 4-9-6 82 ConnorBeasley(7) 5 75
(Michael Dods) *w ldrs: t.k.h: one pce appr fnl f* **8/1**

0045 8 ½ **Victoire De Lyphar (IRE)**[45] 2007 6-9-9 78 PJMcDonald 2 70+
(Ruth Carr) *chsd ldrs on outer: outpcd and lost pl over 2f out: kpt on ins fnl f* **7/1**[3]

0313 9 ½ **Spykes Bay (USA)**[11] 3069 4-9-2 71 (bt) TomEaves 8 61
(Mrs K Burke) *mid-div: effrt 2f out: no imp whn hung rt ins fnl f* **7/1**[3]

-000 10 ½ **Trade Secret**[4] 3300 6-10-0 83 PaulMulrennan 6 72
(Mel Brittain) *chsd ldrs: drvn over 2f out: lost pl over 1f out* **10/1**

6010 11 ½ **Towbee**[13] 2988 4-9-12 81 JamesSullivan 1 68
(Michael Easterby) *in rr: sme hdwy whn nt clr run 2f out: sn wknd* **28/1**

5220 12 1½ **Lenny Bee**[15] 2914 7-9-6 80 (t) JustinNewman(5) 10 62
(Garry Moss) *chsd ldrs: lost pl over 1f out* **8/1**

1m 11.65s (-1.05) **Going Correction** -0.025s/f (Good) 12 Ran SP% **118.2**
Speed ratings (Par 105): **106,105,105,103,101 99,99,98,97,97 96,94**
Tote Swingers: 1&2 £31.10, 1&3 £26.60, 2&3 £32.80 CSF £150.17 CT £2314.96 TOTE £7.50: £1.90, £8.60, £5.40; EX 174.20 Trifecta £1952.40 Part won. Pool: £2,603.31 - 0.41 winning units..
Owner G Morrill **Bred** M J Dawson **Trained** Yedingham, N Yorks
■ Stewards' Enquiry : Dale Swift caution: careless riding

FOCUS
No hanging around in this feature sprint handicap.

3442 THEAKSTON BEST BITTER H'CAP 1m 4f
4:05 (4:05) (Class 3) (0-90,86) 4-Y-O+ **£7,762** (£2,310; £1,154; £577) **Stalls** High

Form RPR
0430 1 **Fennell Bay (IRE)**[10] 3094 4-9-7 86 FrannyNorton 2 94
(Mark Johnston) *mde virtually all: edgd rt fnl f: hld on wl towards fin* **4/1**[3]

1-00 2 ½ **Pintrada**[24] 2671 5-8-9 74 MickaelBarzalona 7 81
(James Bethell) *hld up detached in last: effrt over 3f out: swtchd outside over 2f out: chsng wnr 1f out: sn upsides: no ex nr fin* **10/3**[2]

0-00 3 nk **War Poet**[22] 2718 6-9-3 82 (v) DavidNolan 8 89
(David O'Meara) *hld up towards rr: stdy hdwy 3f out: swtchd rt over 1f out: sn cl 3rd: no ex last 30yds* **15/2**

-306 4 1½ **Royal Peculiar**[68] 1501 5-9-1 80 AndrewMullen 5 84
(Michael Appleby) *chsd ldrs: drvn over 3f out: one pce appr fnl f* **6/1**

-022 5 2¼ **Muharrer**[22] 2706 4-9-1 80 PaulMulrennan 1 81
(Michael Dods) *trckd ldrs: effrt on ins over 2f out: wknd last 50yds* **3/1**[1]

1200 6 1¼ **Flying Power**[24] 2671 5-9-0 79 PaddyAspell 3 78
(John Norton) *w wnr: drvn 3f out: wknd clsng stages* **20/1**

650/ 7 9 **Keep It Cool (IRE)**[16] 1629 9-8-6 78 JoshDoyle(7) 4 62
(David O'Meara) *mid-div: sme hdwy over 3f out: lost pl over 2f out: sn bhd* **33/1**

20-0 8 1¾ **Dark Dune (IRE)**[38] 2277 5-8-9 74 DuranFentiman 6 56
(Tim Easterby) *hld up in rr: hdwy after 3f: sn chsng ldrs: wknd 2f out* **18/1**

9 1¼ **Patterning**[836] 6-8-10 75 PJMcDonald 9 55
(Chris Grant) *in rr: sn drvn along: lost pl over 3f out: sn bhd* **40/1**

052 10 2¾ **Teenage Idol (IRE)**[13] 2971 9-8-8 73 ow1 TomEaves 10 48
(Dianne Sayer) *sn chsng ldrs: drvn over 4f out: lost pl over 2f out: sn bhd* **28/1**

2m 33.58s (-2.62) **Going Correction** -0.15s/f (Firm) 10 Ran SP% **113.0**
Speed ratings (Par 107): **102,101,101,100,98 98,92,90,90,88**
Tote Swingers: 1&2 £4.80, 1&3 £7.80, 2&3 £9.90 CSF £16.34 CT £93.75 TOTE £5.70: £2.10, £2.00, £2.10; EX 22.50 Trifecta £110.90 Pool: £2,146.62 - 14.51 winning units..
Owner Sheikh Hamdan Bin Mohammed Al Maktoum **Bred** J R Wills **Trained** Middleham Moor, N Yorks

FOCUS
Not the strongest of races for the grade.

3443 BRITISH STALLION STUDS SUPPORTING BRITISH RACING EBF FILLIES' H'CAP 1m
4:45 (4:45) (Class 3) (0-90,89) 3-Y-O+ **£8,733** (£2,598; £1,298; £649) **Stalls** Low

Form RPR
-143 1 **Oddysey (IRE)**[31] 2440 4-9-3 81 LeeTopliss(3) 1 91
(Michael Dods) *stmbld s: sn trcking ldrs: effrt 3f out: r.o to ld jst ins fnl f: hld on wl* **5/1**[3]

0653 2 nk **Hot Rod Mamma (IRE)**[15] 2915 6-8-10 71 PJMcDonald 5 80
(Dianne Sayer) *mid-div: hdwy on ins over 2f out: sn swtchd rt: styd on and upsides jst ins fnl f: no ex nr fin* **9/1**

1-00 3 2½ **Dutch Rose (IRE)**[30] 2476 4-10-0 89 DavidNolan 3 92
(David O'Meara) *led 1f: chsd ldr: led over 1f out: hdd jst ins fnl f: kpt on same pce* **16/1**

0-55 4 ½ **Nemushka**[22] 2704 4-9-0 75 (p) BarryMcHugh 6 77
(Richard Fahey) *in rr: effrt 3f out: swtchd ins 2f out: nt clr run and swtchd rt 1f out: styd on towards fin* **25/1**

1112 5 4 **Lilac Lace (IRE)**[4] 3296 3-8-12 83 DuranFentiman 2 76
(Tim Easterby) *led after 1f: qcknd pce over 3f out: hdd over 1f out: sn wknd* **4/1**[2]

15-5 6 3½ **Steer By The Stars (IRE)**[12] 3028 3-9-3 88 FrannyNorton 7 73
(Mark Johnston) *trckd ldrs: drvn over 4f out: wknd over 1f out* **6/1**

4-41 7 4 **Waverunner**[11] 3039 3-8-7 78 MickaelBarzalona 4 54
(Saeed bin Suroor) *hld up in last: drvn 3f out: fnd nthing: nvr on terms* **6/4**[1]

1m 38.0s (-2.10) **Going Correction** -0.15s/f (Firm)
WFA 3 from 4yo+ 10lb 7 Ran SP% **110.7**
Speed ratings (Par 104): **104,103,101,100,96 93,89**
Tote Swingers: 1&2 £8.40, 1&3 £10.00, 2&3 £11.90 CSF £44.46 TOTE £6.30: £2.10, £4.60; EX 50.50 Trifecta £541.40 Pool: £2,989.33 - 4.14 winning units..
Owner Pearson & Lowthian **Bred** Darling Smile Syndicate **Trained** Denton, Co Durham

FOCUS
Some likeable fillies in the line-up for this handicap but, with the strongly fancied favourite running no sort of race, it took less than winning had previously looked the case.

3444 REMEMBER JOHN HUBBARD H'CAP (DIV I) 7f
5:20 (5:21) (Class 5) (0-70,70) 3-Y-O+ **£2,587** (£770; £384; £192) **Stalls** Low

Form RPR
0215 1 **West Leake Hare (IRE)**[3] 3337 4-9-9 65 PaulQuinn 5 76+
(David Nicholls) *in rr: drvn over 4f out: swtchd outer and hdwy over 2f out: styd on to ld nr fin* **9/4**[1]

3100 2 nk **Ted's Brother (IRE)**[17] 2884 5-9-7 63 (e) RobbieFitzpatrick 10 73
(Richard Guest) *swtchd lft after s: hld up in rr: hdwy over 2f out: chsng ldrs over 1f out: styd on to take cl 2nd fnl strides* **18/1**

0001 3 hd **Dhhamaan (IRE)**[12] 3030 8-8-12 54 (b) JamesSullivan 2 63
(Ruth Carr) *best away: 3 l clr 3f out: hdd and no ex clsng stages* **9/1**

0504 4 6 **Holy Angel (IRE)**[10] 3087 4-9-11 67 (e) DuranFentiman 4 60
(Tim Easterby) *s.i.s: sn mid-div: hdwy over 2f out: tk modest 4th 1f out: one pce* **6/1**[3]

2-52 5 1 **Maggie Mey (IRE)**[12] 3029 5-8-10 52 AndrewMullen 3 43
(Lawrence Mullaney) *sn chsng ldrs: drvn over 4f out: one pce fnl 2f* **12/1**

0052 6 3¾ **Boy The Bell**[15] 2932 6-8-9 51 (be) GrahamGibbons 9 31
(Ollie Pears) *drvn to sn chse ldr: wknd over 1f out* **5/1**[2]

-251 7 3 **Adam's Ale**[21] 2757 4-10-0 70 MickyFenton 8 42
(Paul Midgley) *t.k.h: stdd into mid-div after 1f: effrt on outer and hung lft 2f out: sn wknd* **10/1**

-403 8 nk **Mitchum**[17] 2884 4-9-8 64 RussKennemore 7 36
(Ron Barr) *hld up in rr: drvn over 2f out: nvr on terms* **10/1**

0100 9 2½ **Bang Tidy (IRE)**[27] 2565 4-9-4 60 (t) TomEaves 6 25
(Brian Ellison) *t.k.h: trckd ldrs: effrt over 1f out: sn lost pl* **15/2**

1m 25.46s (-1.74) **Going Correction** -0.15s/f (Firm) 9 Ran SP% **114.6**
Speed ratings (Par 103): **103,102,102,95,94 90,86,86,83**
Tote Swingers: 1&2 £10.10, 1&3 £7.20, 2&3 £36.10 CSF £46.91 CT £311.79 TOTE £2.80: £1.10, £8.10, £3.70; EX 51.40 Trifecta £1065.40 Pool: £2,467.88 - 1.73 winning units..
Owner Neil Yeoman & Mrs Alex Nicholls **Bred** Churchtown House Stud **Trained** Sessay, N Yorks

FOCUS
Favourite backers were richly rewarded in the first division of this handicap. The first three were clear.

3445 REMEMBER JOHN HUBBARD H'CAP (DIV II) 7f
5:50 (5:51) (Class 5) (0-70,69) 3-Y-O+ **£2,587** (£770; £384; £192) **Stalls** Low

Form RPR
-501 1 **Just Paul (IRE)**[18] 2837 3-8-7 60 DeclanCannon(3) 9 64
(Philip Kirby) *t.k.h: hld up sn towards rr: hdwy over 2f out: led narrowly 1f out: all out* **9/2**[2]

0643 2 nse **Hoppy's Flyer (FR)**[10] 3098 5-9-4 59 (v) MickyFenton 6 66
(Paul Midgley) *mid-div: effrt and n.m.r over 2f out: chsng ldrs over 1f out: styd on towards fin: jst failed* **12/1**

56 3 nse **Confusing**[15] 2916 3-9-1 65 DavidNolan 7 69
(David O'Meara) *hld up in rr: hdwy and swtchd outside over 1f out: styd on towards fin: jst failed* **14/1**

0-14 4 nk **Whispered Times (USA)**[6] 3192 6-9-8 63 (p) FrannyNorton 8 69
(Tracy Waggott) *trckd ldrs: led briefly over 1f out: styd on same pce last 50yds* **4/1**[1]

6305 5 ½ **Nonayneve**r[4] 3286 5-8-9 50 oh4 (b) JamesSullivan 5 55?
(Ruth Carr) *w ldrs: kpt on same pce last 100yds* **28/1**

1554 6 1 **Keep It Dark**[17] 2884 4-9-3 65 (p) DavidSimmonson(7) 3 67
(Tony Coyle) *wnt rt s: hld up in rr: hdwy 2f out: one pce appr fnl f* **5/1**[3]

0602 7 ½ **Dream Scenario**[12] 3025 3-9-5 69 PaulMulrennan 1 70+
(Mel Brittain) *trckd ldrs: t.k.h: nt clr run fr over 1f out: nt rcvr* **7/1**

3653 8 nk **Illustrious Prince (IRE)**[11] 3068 6-9-3 65 (v) LukeLeadbitter(7) 4 65
(Declan Carroll) *bmpd s: t.k.h: sn trcking ldrs: rdn and hung lft over 2f out: fdd fnl f* **6/1**

00-4 9 ½ **Deliberation (IRE)**[12] 3030 5-9-2 57 MichaelO'Connell 2 55
(John Quinn) *led: hdd over 1f out: fdd last 50yds* **12/1**

4160 **10** *1 ¼* **Mujaadel (USA)**[12] 3027 8-10-0 **69**............................(v) AndrewMullen 11 64
(David Nicholls) *s.v.s and swtchd lft s: sme hdwy on ins whn nt clr run 1f out: nvr a factor* **14/1**

20-0 **11** *1 ¼* **Clumber Place**[17] 2884 7-9-8 **63**.. DaleSwift 10 55
(James Given) *t.k.h in rr: nvr on terms* **28/1**

1m 26.91s (-0.29) **Going Correction** -0.15s/f (Firm)
WFA 3 from 4yo+ 9lb **11** Ran SP% **117.2**
Speed ratings (Par 103): **95,94,94,94,93 92,92,91,91,89 88**
Tote Swingers: 1&2 £15.30, 1&3 £15.50, 2&3 £14.30 CSF £57.43 CT £694.29 TOTE £5.40: £2.00, £5.70, £4.60; EX 81.20 Trifecta £1072.00 Pool: £1,436.56 - 1.00 winning units..
Owner Mr and Mrs Paul Chapman **Bred** Oghill House Stud **Trained** Middleham, N Yorks

FOCUS
A thrilling finish to the second division of this handicap with the first four home covered by a little over a neck.

3446 READ HAYLEY TURNER EVERY FRIDAY RACINGUK.COM H'CAP 5f
6:20 (6:20) (Class 6) (0-65,70) 3-Y-O+ **£2,726** (£805; £402) **Stalls** High

Form RPR

1544 **1** **Sunrise Dance**[10] 3090 4-9-7 **65**................................ ConnorBeasley(7) 7 76
(Robert Johnson) *mde all: kpt on wl fnl f* **9/2**[2]

364 **2** *1 ¼* **John Coffey (IRE)**[138] 449 4-9-0 **51**............................ RobertWinston 9 57+
(Michael Appleby) *hld up towards rr: t.k.h: swtchd rt over 3f out: effrt and nt clr run over 1f out: swtchd ins: r.o to take 2nd last 100yds: no real imp* **8/1**[3]

4520 **3** *2* **Captain Royale (IRE)**[4] 3283 8-9-8 **59**.........................(p) BarryMcHugh 6 58
(Tracy Waggott) *chsd wnr: t.k.h: kpt on same pce appr fnl f* **14/1**

1503 **4** *nk* **Ace Master**[6] 3196 5-9-2 **56**..............................(b) MarkCoumbe(3) 10 54
(Roy Bowring) *hld up: chsd ldrs over 3f out: drvn over 2f out: kpt on fnl f* **9/2**[2]

1-00 **5** *1 ¾* **Ryedane (IRE)**[18] 2835 11-9-4 **62**.....................(b) RachelRichardson(7) 1 53
(Tim Easterby) *in rr: kpt on fnl f: nvr a factor* **33/1**

050 **6** *nk* **Quality Art (USA)**[5] 3246 5-9-8 **59**............................ RobbieFitzpatrick 5 49
(Richard Guest) *mid-div: hdwy to chse ldrs over 1f out: wknd fnl 50yds* **16/1**

-003 **7** *nse* **Lucky Lodge**[9] 3134 3-9-5 **62**....................................... PaulMulrennan 13 50
(Mel Brittain) *chsd ldrs: drvn over 2f out: sn outpcd: one pce over 1f out* **9/1**

0000 **8** *nk* **Ivestar (IRE)**[6] 3197 8-9-9 **60**...................................(t) GrahamGibbons 3 49
(Michael Easterby) *in rr: rdn over 2f out: nvr a factor* **25/1**

-001 **9** *2 ½* **Clean Blow (USA)**[9] 3134 3-9-8 **70** 6ex......................... JasonHart(5) 11 48
(David Brown) *s.s: swtchd lft over 3f out: sn chsd ldrs: swtchd lft over 1f out: sn wknd* **7/4**[1]

5-45 **10** *4 ½* **Whatwehavewehold**[69] 1461 3-9-1 **58**................................ TomEaves 4 20
(Alan McCabe) *awkward leaving stalls: sn w ldrs on outside: lost pl over 1f out: sn bhd* **28/1**

58.9s (-0.70) **Going Correction** -0.025s/f (Good)
WFA 3 from 4yo+ 6lb **10** Ran SP% **116.6**
Speed ratings (Par 101): **104,102,98,98,95 95,94,94,90,83**
Tote Swingers: 1&2 £7.30, 1&3 £14.60, 2&3 £11.30 CSF £39.39 CT £468.43 TOTE £6.00: £1.80, £3.80, £4.20; EX 53.60 Trifecta £463.80 Pool: £1,607.54 - 2.59 winning units..
Owner M Saunders **Bred** Mrs Ann Jarvis **Trained** Newburn, Tyne & Wear

FOCUS
A modest finale.
T/Plt: £139.20 to a £1 stake. Pool: £45,053.00 - 236.15 winning units T/Qpdt: £64.20 to a £1 stake. Pool: £2,757.00 - 31.77 winning units WG

3447 - 3453a (Foreign Racing) - See Raceform Interactive

DIEPPE (R-H)
Tuesday, June 18
OFFICIAL GOING: Turf: good to soft

3454a PRIX DE LA VILLE DE HAUTOT SUR MER (MAIDEN) (3YO COLTS & GELDINGS) (TURF) 7f
1:20 (12:00) 3-Y-O **£8,130** (£3,252; £2,439; £1,626; £813)

RPR

1 **Finaz**[12] 3-8-10 0... StephaneLaurent(6) 3 77
(Braem Horse Racing Sprl, Belgium) **172/10**

2 *hd* **Maximum Velocity (FR)**[218] 3-8-11 0.......................... FabienLefebvre 4 72
(J E Hammond, France) **53/10**[3]

3 *2 ½* **Omy**[28] 3-9-2 0.. GregoryBenoist 9 70
(D Smaga, France) **5/2**[1]

4 *hd* **Preempt**[28] 3-9-2 0... ThierryThulliez 7 69
(P Bary, France) **4/1**[2]

5 *2* **Majestic Mount**[41] 3-9-2 0.................................. Pierre-CharlesBoudot 2 64
(R Pritchard-Gordon, France) **5/2**[1]

6 *snk* **Mack The Knife (FR)** 3-8-8 0.................................... CesarPasserat(3) 5 59
(C Lerner, France) **38/1**

7 *7* **Lewamy (IRE)**[36] 2335 3-9-2 0..................................... AntoineHamelin 1 45
(John Best) *t.k.h: prom on inner: trckd ldr after 2f: shkn up and nt qckn ent fnl 2f: hrd rdn and no imp 1 1/2f out: wknd ins fnl f* **8/1**

8 *3* **The Body (USA)**[10] 3-8-11 0......................................(b) MircoDemuro 6 32
(Mlle S Sine, France) **44/1**

9 *3* **Fin Bon (FR)** 3-8-8 0.. AntoineCoutier(3) 8 24
(R Chotard, France) **54/1**

1m 25.29s (85.29) **9** Ran SP% **116.2**
PARI-MUTUEL (all including 1 euro stakes): WIN 18.20; PLACE 3.20, 2.20, 1.60; DF 43.00; SF 117.10.
Owner Stal Martensberg **Bred** P Docherty **Trained** Belgium

3419 **ASCOT** (R-H)
Wednesday, June 19
OFFICIAL GOING: Good to firm (good in places; stands' side 9.2, centre 9.4, far side 9.3, round 8.4)
Rail on Round course approximately 3yds out from 9f to home straight adding 6yds to Old Mile, 9yds to 10f and 12yds to races of 12f plus.
Wind: nil Weather: hot & sunny

3455 JERSEY STKS (GROUP 3) 7f
2:30 (2:32) (Class 1) 3-Y-O
£42,532 (£16,125; £8,070; £4,020; £2,017; £1,012) **Stalls** Centre

Form RPR

3-42 **1** **Gale Force Ten**[25] 2677 3-9-1 114...............................(p) JosephO'Brien 4 115
(A P O'Brien, Ire) *cmpt: str: chsd ldr: led over 2f out: rdn over 1f out: hdd narrowly 150yds out: rallied gamely to regain ld fnl stride* **9/2**[1]

2-31 **2** *hd* **Montiridge (IRE)**[20] 2812 3-9-1 109.......................... RichardHughes 11 114
(Richard Hannon) *lw: hld up: hmpd and snatched up over 2f out: swtchd lft and hdwy ent fnl 2f: sn rdn: r.o to ld narrowly 150yds: hdd and no ex fnl stride* **15/2**[3]

1-43 **3** *1 ½* **Tawhid**[30] 2526 3-9-4 109.. SilvestreDeSousa 21 113
(Saeed bin Suroor) *lw: hld up in midfield: hdwy 2f out: rdn to chal towards nr side 1f out: hung lft fnl 150yds: styd on cl home but hld* **25/1**

2-10 **4** *1* **Garswood**[46] 2021 3-9-1 113.. PatSmullen 3 108
(Richard Fahey) *lw: in tch: effrt 2f out: rdn over 1f out: tried to chal ins fnl f: styd on same pce fnl 110yds* **5/1**[2]

4-12 **5** *2* **Music Master**[32] 2453 3-9-1 103.. DaneO'Neill 16 102
(Henry Candy) *handy nr side: rdn 2f out: chal 1f out: carried lft whn stl ch fnl 150yds: kpt on same pce towards fin* **14/1**

6-01 **6** *1 ¼* **Pearl Flute (IRE)**[18] 2897 3-9-4 113................................ JamieSpencer 17 102
(F-H Graffard, France) *w'like: hld up: rdn and hdwy 2f out: styng on whn edgd rt ins fnl f: no further prog towards fin* **16/1**

-204 **7** *hd* **Dont Bother Me (IRE)**[38] 2290 3-9-1 105........................ MartinHarley 6 98
(Niall Moran, Ire) *led: rdn and hdd over 2f out: one pce wl ins fnl f* **66/1**

1-13 **8** *1* **Ninjago**[33] 2415 3-9-1 105... JimmyFortune 13 96
(Richard Hannon) *hld up: hdwy 2f out: chsng ldrs whn carried rt over 1f out: kpt on ins fnl f: nvr able to mount serious chal* **16/1**

-513 **9** *½* **Jammy Guest (IRE)**[32] 2454 3-9-1 84................................ TomQueally 2 94
(George Margarson) *hld up: hdwy over 2f out: rdn to chse ldrs over 1f out: no imp ins fnl f* **66/1**

-502 **10** *shd* **Tamayuz Star (IRE)**[25] 2655 3-9-1 99................................ PatDobbs 20 94
(Richard Hannon) *lw: chsd ldrs: pushed along over 2f out: outpcd over 1f out: edgd rt and one pce ins fnl f* **50/1**

3-3 **11** *1 ¾* **The Brothers War (USA)**[63] 1633 3-9-1 106................. OlivierPeslier 18 89
(J-C Rouget, France) *w'like: midfield: effrt over 1f out: keeping on u.p whn faltered ins fnl f: one pce and no imp after* **11/1**

-214 **12** *½* **Here Comes When (IRE)**[19] 2843 3-9-1 97..................... JimCrowley 19 88
(Andrew Balding) *on toes: missed break: bhd: rdn over 2f out: nvr able to get into contention* **33/1**

-041 **13** *1* **Well Acquainted (IRE)**[19] 2843 3-9-1 107........................ AdamKirby 12 85
(Clive Cox) *in tch: effrt to chse ldrs over 2f out: carried lft ent fnl 2f: edgd rt whn no impresssion over 1f out: n.d after* **20/1**

10-0 **14** *½* **Blaine**[37] 2334 3-9-6 107.. NeilCallan 15 89
(Kevin Ryan) *prom towards nr side: rdn and hung bdly rt fr 2f out: wknd fnl f* **66/1**

41-2 **15** *3* **Complimentor (IRE)**[42] 2183 3-9-1 102........................ FrankieDettori 14 76
(X Thomas-Demeaulte, France) *w'like: in rr: sme hdwy into midfield 2f out but no imp on ldrs: sn hmpd and lost pl: struggling over 1f out: eased whn wl btn ins fnl f* **25/1**

55-0 **16** *nk* **Parliament Square (IRE)**[16] 2941 3-9-1 103...................(p) RyanMoore 8 75
(A P O'Brien, Ire) *w'like: hld up: pushed along over 3f out: struggling after: nvr a threat* **20/1**

0-23 **17** *¾* **Pearl Sea (IRE)**[33] 2429 3-8-13 93 ow1........................ JohnnyMurtagh 10 71
(David Brown) *on toes: hld up: rdn 2f out: eased whn n.d ins fnl f* **50/1**

18 *4* **Mutin (FR)**[30] 2527 3-9-1 101..................................... ChristopheSoumillon 9 62
(J-C Rouget, France) *tall: str: hld up in rr: pushed along whn n.m.r and squeezed out 2f out: n.d after* **15/2**[3]

-231 **19** *¾* **Ian's Dream (USA)**[8] 3170 3-9-1 95..............................(p) KierenFallon 7 60
(Jeremy Noseda) *midfield tl rdn and wknd over 2f out* **66/1**

6-10 **20** *1 ½* **One Word More (IRE)**[30] 2526 3-9-1 100......................... WilliamBuick 1 56
(Charles Hills) *chsd ldrs tl rdn and wknd over 2f out* **100/1**

11 **21** *2* **Ajraam (USA)**[13] 3028 3-9-1 93.. PaulHanagan 5 51
(Charles Hills) *chsd ldrs: pushed along and lost pl over 2f out: eased whn wl btn and bhd fnl f* **20/1**

1m 25.32s (-2.28) **Going Correction** -0.125s/f (Firm) **21** Ran SP% **120.9**
Speed ratings (Par 109): **108,107,106,104,102 101,100,99,99,99 97,96,95,94,91 91,90,85,84,83 80**
toteswingers 1&2 £3.80, 2&3 £48.90, 1&3 £37.50 CSF £30.62 CT £787.05 TOTE £5.50: £2.20, £3.70, £10.70; EX 32.90 Trifecta £725.30 Pool: £10596.03 - 10.95 winning units..
Owner Michael Tabor & Derrick Smith & Mrs John Magnier **Bred** S Tindall, D Ludlow & Stowell Hill Ltd **Trained** Ballydoyle, Co Tipperary
■ Stewards' Enquiry : Richard Hughes one-day ban: careless riding (3 July)

FOCUS
The rail on the Round course was positioned approximately 3yds out from the 9f marker to the home straight, adding roughly 6yds to the old mile, 9yds to the 1m2f, and 12yds to the races of 1m4f and further. It was dry overnight and on what was a hot, sunny day it was no surprise to see the ground changed to good to firm, good in places before racing, with the general opinion amongst jockeys being that it was 'quick'. GoingStick readings were as follows: Stands' side 9.2; Centre 9.4; Far side 9.3; Round course 8.4. Staged over a specialist trip, this is often an open contest and it attracted a huge field for the second consecutive year. The front pair fought out the finish centre-field (where the pace had been), and with the right horses coming to the fore, the form looks up to scratch for the grade. The first two are rated to their marks. The time was under the RP Standard and not far off a course record.

3456 DUKE OF CAMBRIDGE STKS (FORMERLY THE WINDSOR FOREST STAKES) (GROUP 2) (F&M) 1m (S)
3:05 (3:05) (Class 1) 4-Y-O+

£77,375 (£29,334; £14,680; £7,313; £3,670; £1,841) **Stalls** Centre

Form RPR
11-1 **1** **Duntle (IRE)**[38] 2288 4-8-12 113 WayneLordan 1 111
(David Wachman, Ire) *hld up wl in tch in midfield: hdwy to chse ldr wl over 2f out: rdn and ev ch over 1f out: led 1f out: forged ahd ins fnl f: r.o wl: rdn out* **10/3**[2]

-336 **2** ½ **Ladys First**[4] 3347 4-8-12 105 PaulHanagan 3 110
(Richard Fahey) *led and set stdy gallop: pushed along and qcknd 3f out: hrd pressed and drvn over 1f out: hdd 1f out: battled on gamely but hld towards fin* **25/1**

15-1 **3** *hd* **Dank**[45] 2045 4-8-12 109 RyanMoore 2 110
(Sir Michael Stoute) *t.k.h: clsd to press ldrs over 1f out: drvn over 1f out: kpt on wl but unable qck fnl 75yds* **7/2**[3]

22-0 **4** *hd* **Beatrice Aurore (IRE)**[19] 2838 5-8-12 105 FrankieDettori 5 109
(Ed Dunlop) *on toes: stdd s: hld up wl in tch in rr: rdn and hdwy over 2f out: pressing ldrs and drvn over 1f out: kpt on wl but unable qck fnl 75yds* **33/1**

3-42 **5** 2¾ **Sarkiyla (FR)**[49] 1945 4-8-12 108 (t) Christophe-PatriceLemaire 8 103
(A De Royer-Dupre, France) *w'like: t.k.h: hld up wl in tch in midfield: rdn and lost pl 1/2-way: drvn and rallying whn hmpd and swtchd lft over 1f out: kpt on fnl f: no threat to ldrs* **6/1**

1-21 **6** 3 **Chigun**[25] 2678 4-8-12 114 TomQueally 9 96
(Lady Cecil) *lw: t.k.h: hld up wl in tch in midfield: clsd to press ldrs 3f out: rdn and unable qck 2f out: wknd over 1f out* **11/4**[1]

40-3 **7** 1¼ **Sweetnessandlight**[16] 2928 4-8-12 95 KierenFallon 11 93
(Jason Ward) *stdd s: t.k.h: hld up in tch towards rr: hdwy into midfield 1/2-way: rdn and wknd ent fnl 2f: n.d and swtchd rt over 1f out: plugged on fnl f* **66/1**

8 *hd* **Dancewiththedevil (SAF)**[417] 7-8-12 112 RichardHughes 6 92
(Roger Varian) *str: on toes: stdd s: hld up wl in tch in rr: rdn and effrt over 2f out: drvn and no imp 2f out: wknd over 1f out* **20/1**

2-31 **9** 11 **Thistle Bird**[19] 2838 5-8-12 108 JamesDoyle 4 67
(Roger Charlton) *lw: chsd ldr tl wl over 2f out: sn struggling u.p: bhd over 1f out: eased ins fnl f* **7/1**

1m 39.47s (-1.33) **Going Correction** -0.125s/f (Firm) **9 Ran SP% 111.8**
Speed ratings (Par 115): **101,100,100,100,97 94,93,92,81**
toteswingers 1&2 £9.00, 2&3 £12.60, 1&3 £1.60 CSF £82.46 CT £274.48 TOTE £4.20: £1.60, £6.00, £1.90; EX 86.90 Trifecta £441.10 Pool: £16312.18 - 27.73 winning units..
Owner Flaxman Stables Ireland Ltd **Bred** Airlie Stud **Trained** Goolds Cross, Co Tipperary
■ This event was previously run as the Windsor Forest Stakes.

FOCUS
This fillies and mares' Group 2, run under a new title this year, had been dominated by Sir Michael Stoute in its nine-year history, with three winners and three placings. All but one of the previous winners had either previously or subsequently scored at Group 1 level, or were placed in the highest grade. They went steady until the pace picked up from around halfway, and the time was 18lb lower than the Sandringham. The form is a bit below par and the winner didn't have to be at her best.

3457 PRINCE OF WALES'S STKS (BRITISH CHAMPIONS SERIES) (GROUP 1) 1m 2f
3:45 (3:45) (Class 1) 4-Y-O+

£283,550 (£107,500; £53,800; £26,800; £13,450; £6,750) **Stalls** Low

Form RPR
1-11 **1** **Al Kazeem**[24] 2688 5-9-0 119 JamesDoyle 9 124
(Roger Charlton) *lw: racd keenly: trckd ldrs: effrt to chse wnr over 2f out but abt 3 l down: rdn to cl over 1f out: r.o ins fnl f: led towards fin* **11/4**[2]

25-1 **2** *nk* **Mukhadram**[20] 2811 4-9-0 111 PaulHanagan 7 123
(William Haggas) *lw: led: kicked abt 3 l clr over 2f out: rdn over 1f out: hrd pressed wl ins fnl f: collared towards fin* **14/1**

123- **3** 3¼ **The Fugue**[229] 7549 4-8-11 116 WilliamBuick 8 114+
(John Gosden) *dull in coat: hld up off the pce: pushed along over 2f out: hdwy and edgd rt over 1f out: styd on to take 3rd wl ins fnl f: nt trble front pair* **13/2**[3]

0-12 **4** ½ **Camelot**[24] 2688 4-9-0 120 JosephO'Brien 6 116
(A P O'Brien, Ire) *lw: midfield: pushed along over 2f out: sme hdwy but nt gng pce to chal ldrs whn edgd rt over 1f out: kpt on but no imp ins fnl f* **5/2**[1]

2143 **5** 1¼ **Miblish**[20] 2811 4-9-0 105 (t) RyanMoore 1 113
(Clive Brittain) *chsd ldrs: pushed along over 2f out: outpcd over 1f out: plugged on u.p but hld ins fnl f* **66/1**

-121 **6** ¾ **Maxios**[24] 2694 5-9-0 120 StephanePasquier 5 112
(J E Pease, France) *w'like: swtg: edgy: hld up: pushed along over 2f out: rdn and no imp over 1f out: kpt on ins fnl f but nvr able to chal* **13/2**[3]

6-44 **7** 1 **Side Glance**[81] 1269 6-9-0 115 JamieSpencer 10 110
(Andrew Balding) *sn chsd ldr: rdn and lost 2nd over 2f out: no imp over 1f out: wknd ins fnl f* **33/1**

122- **8** 2 **Afsare**[305] 5377 6-9-0 116 RichardHughes 4 106
(Luca Cumani) *midfield: pushed along over 2f out: effrt but no imp on ldrs whn n.m.r over 1f out: wknd and wl btn fnl f* **25/1**

-230 **9** 6 **Red Cadeaux**[31] 2494 7-9-0 121 FrankieDettori 3 94
(Ed Dunlop) *hld up towards rr: u.p and outpcd over 2f out: nvr a threat: wl btn* **12/1**

31-4 **10** ¾ **Saint Baudolino (IRE)**[132] 556 4-9-0 115 MickaelBarzalona 11 92
(Saeed bin Suroor) *w'like: attr: stdd s: hld up in rr: u.p and outpcd over 2f out: nvr a threat: wl btn* **12/1**

0-33 **11** 29 **Windsor Palace (IRE)**[24] 2688 8-9-0 103 (p) SeamieHeffernan 2
(A P O'Brien, Ire) *missed break: bustled along early: hld up after: niggled along over 3f out: wl btn and eased 2f out: sn lost tch* **100/1**

2m 3.06s (-4.34) **Going Correction** -0.05s/f (Good) **11 Ran SP% 113.2**
Speed ratings (Par 117): **115,114,112,111,110 110,109,107,102,102 79**
toteswingers 1&2 £9.70, 2&3 £15.70, 1&3 £3.50 CSF £37.97 CT £227.40 TOTE £3.00: £1.40, £4.50, £2.30; EX 49.20 Trifecta £485.70 Pool: £29503.09 - 45.55 winning units..
Owner D J Deer **Bred** D J And Mrs Deer **Trained** Beckhampton, Wilts

FOCUS
This looked an average edition of the race, despite it featuring five Group 1 scorers, including last year's Epsom Derby winner, and it was missing a couple of big names, with Farhh (also had the Queen Anne as an option) and Snow Fairy being absent due to injury. Despite Ballydoyle pacemaker Windsor Palace blowing the start and being unable to fulfil his role, they still went a really good gallop early courtesy of the runner-up and most of them were beaten off the final bend, with little getting involved from off the pace. The front pair drew clear and this rates towards the lower end of the race averages, but another improved effort from Al Kazeem. Camelot was 10lb off his best mark.

3458 ROYAL HUNT CUP (HERITAGE H'CAP) 1m (S)
4:25 (4:25) (Class 2) 3-Y-O+

£93,375 (£27,960; £13,980; £6,990; £3,495; £1,755) **Stalls** Centre

Form RPR
0020 **1** **Belgian Bill**[60] 1675 5-8-11 **97** (tp) JamesDoyle 6 107
(George Baker) *racd far side: hld up towards rr overall: clsd 2f out: rdn and effrt over 1f out: hdwy to ld jst ins fnl f: r.o wl: rdn out: 1st of 7 in gp* **33/1**

-560 **2** ¾ **Premio Loco (USA)**[11] 3101 9-9-9 **109** GeorgeBaker 2 117
(Chris Wall) *racd far side: hld up in midfield overall: rdn and effrt over 2f out: hdwy u.p and ev ch jst ins fnl f: wnt 2nd and kpt on same pce wl ins fnl f: 2nd of 7 in gp* **40/1**

3-00 **3** ½ **Arsaadi (IRE)**[39] 2253 4-8-12 **98** (b) LiamJones 10 105
(William Haggas) *racd far side: racd keenly: overall ldr and sn clr: rdn 2f out: drvn 2f out: hdd 1f out: kpt on wl but no ex wl ins fnl f: 3rd of 7 in gp* **50/1**

622 **4** ½ **Don't Call Me (IRE)**[21] 2782 6-9-5 **105** (t) PatDobbs 7 111
(David Nicholls) *racd far side: chsd overall ldr: rdn and effrt 2f out: drvn and led 1f out: sn hdd: no ex and one pce fnl 100yds: 4th of 7 in gp* **25/1**

43-0 **5** *shd* **David Livingston (IRE)**[111] 838 4-9-2 **102** PatCosgrave 12 107
(M F De Kock, South Africa) *racd stands' side: hld up in midfield overall: rdn and effrt 2f out: hdwy over 1f out: r.o u.p fnl f: 1st of 21 in gp* **12/1**[2]

5560 **6** *shd* **Field Of Dream**[27] 2585 6-8-12 **98** (b) AdamKirby 19 103
(Jamie Osborne) *racd stands' side: stdd s: hld up towards rr overall: rdn and effrt over 2f out: styd on wl u.p fnl f: nt pce of far side ldrs: 2nd of 21 in gp* **12/1**[2]

046- **7** *hd* **Trade Commissioner (IRE)**[228] 7558 5-9-4 **104** WilliamBuick 4 109
(John Gosden) *swtg: racd far side: hld up in midfield overall: rdn and hdwy 2f out: drvn and chsd ldrs ent fnl f: no ex and one pce ins fnl f: 5th of 7 in gp* **14/1**[3]

2-41 **8** ½ **Burke's Rock**[46] 2015 4-8-11 **97** (p) FrankieDettori 21 101
(Jeremy Noseda) *racd stands' side: hld up in midfield overall: rdn and hdwy to ld gp over 1f out: kpt on same pce u.p ins fnl f: 3rd of 21 in gp* **12/1**[2]

00-1 **9** ½ **Excellent Guest**[39] 2254 6-8-12 **98** TomQueally 1 100
(George Margarson) *lw: racd far side: hld up in midfield overall: rdn and hdwy 2f out: drvn and chsd ldrs ent fnl f: no ex and hld fnl 100yds: 6th of 7 in gp* **16/1**

/26- **10** ½ **Winter's Night (IRE)**[389] 2515 5-8-6 **97** RyanTate[(5)] 9 98
(Clive Cox) *racd far side: racd in midfield overall: drvn and clsd ent fnl 2f: no ex ent fnl f: kpt on same pce after: 7th of 7 in gp* **33/1**

6002 **11** ½ **Es Que Love (IRE)**[4] 3335 4-8-12 **98** GrahamLee 17 98
(Mark Johnston) *racd stands' side: t.k.h: chsd ldrs: rdn and effrt over 1f out: swtchd lft 1f out: styd on same pce ins fnl f: 4th of 21 in gp* **33/1**

2134 **12** ¾ **Two For Two (IRE)**[34] 2399 5-9-0 **100** DanielTudhope 27 98+
(David O'Meara) *racd stands' side: hld up wl in tch in midfield overall: n.m.r over 1f out: styd on u.p ins fnl f: no threat to ldrs: 5th of 21 in gp* **10/1**[1]

6-02 **13** *shd* **Prince Of Johanne (IRE)**[34] 2399 7-9-0 **100** (p) JohnFahy 8 98
(Tom Tate) *lw: racd stands' side: swtchd lft to join gp after 1f: in tch in midfield overall: drvn and hdwy over 2f out: no ex 1f out: wknd ins fnl f: 6th of 21 in gp* **12/1**[2]

6030 **14** *nk* **Santefisio**[46] 2029 7-9-0 **100** (b) JimmyFortune 20 98+
(Keith Dalgleish) *racd stands' side: stdd s: hld up in rr overall: pushed lft 2f out: switching rt and hdwy over 1f out: r.o ins fnl f: no threat to ldrs: 7th of 21 in gp* **66/1**

-101 **15** *hd* **Educate**[39] 2263 4-8-12 **98** JamieSpencer 13 95+
(Ismail Mohammed) *racd stands' side: swtchd lft after s: hld up in rr overall: stl in rr whn bdly hmpd 2f out: swtchd rt arnd many horses but hdwy over 1f out: r.o but nvr able to rcvr: eased towards fin: 8th of 21 in gp* **12/1**[2]

0-11 **16** *shd* **Directorship**[33] 2424 7-8-13 **99** DaneO'Neill 26 96+
(Patrick Chamings) *racd stands' side: hld up towards rr overall: nt clr run and edgd lft 2f out: switching rt and hdwy over 1f out: r.o ins fnl f: no threat to ldrs: 9th of 21 in gp* **14/1**[3]

3020 **17** ½ **Sandagiyr (FR)**[111] 836 5-9-3 **103** SilvestreDeSousa 32 99+
(Saeed bin Suroor) *lw: racd stands' side: hld up wl in tch in midfield overall: nt clr run wl over 1f out tl ins fnl f: r.o wl fnl 100yds: no threat to ldrs: 10th of 21 in gp* **33/1**

50-4 **18** ¼ **Fury**[37] 2323 5-9-0 **100** (b[1]) JosephO'Brien 22 95
(William Haggas) *racd stands' side: dwlt: sn rcvrd and in tch in midfield overall: rdn and no hdwy over 2f out: plugged on same pce fr over 1f out: 11th of 21 in gp* **10/1**[1]

00-6 **19** *nse* **Moran Gra (USA)**[25] 2679 6-8-10 **96** (p) PatSmullen 33 91
(Ms Joanna Morgan, Ire) *racd stands' side: led gp and chsd ldrs overall: rdn over 2f out: lost pl over 1f out: wknd ins fnl f: 12th of 21 in gp* **16/1**

-143 **20** 1 **Sweet Lightning**[38] 2288 8-9-3 **110** (t) LukeDempsey[(7)] 29 103
(J P Murtagh, Ire) *racd stands' side: wl in tch overall: rdn and effrt to chse ldrs over 2f out: no ex over 1f out: wknd ins fnl f: 13th of 21 in gp* **25/1**

-001 **21** *nk* **Captain Bertie (IRE)**[40] 2210 5-8-10 **96** JamesMcDonald 23 88
(Charles Hills) *racd stands' side: chsd gp ldrs and handy overall: rdn and unable qck over 2f out: lost pl over 1f out: wknd fnl f: 14th of 21 in gp* **28/1**

-324 **22** *shd* **Stirring Ballad**[46] 2015 4-8-11 **97** RichardHughes 3 89+
(Andrew Balding) *racd stands' side: swtchd lft to join gp after 1f: t.k.h: in rr overall: hdwy 2f out: nt clr run: hmpd and swtchd rt over 1f out: sme hdwy but no threat whn nt pushed ins fnl f: 15th of 21 in gp* **10/1**[1]

0-21 **23** ½ **Spa's Dancer (IRE)**[20] 2813 6-8-11 **97** 5ex........................ RyanMoore 30 88
(James Eustace) *racd stands' side: chsd ldrs and handy overall: rdn and unable qck over 2f out: wknd over 1f out: 16th of 21 in gp* **16/1**

1105 **24** 4½ **Toto Skyllachy**[11] 3094 8-8-6 **97**.............................. ThomasBrown(5) 14 77
(David O'Meara) *swtg: racd stands' side: chsd gp ldrs and in tch overall: rdn and struggling wl over 2f out: wknd wl over 1f out: 17th of 21 in gp* **66/1**

0-03 **25** 6 **Redact (IRE)**[25] 2667 4-8-11 **97**.. JimCrowley 24 63
(Richard Hannon) *racd stands' side: hld up in rr overall: stl plenty to do and pushed lft 2f out: no hdwy and sn btn: bhd fnl f: 18th of 21 in gp* **40/1**

4-36 **26** 3¼ **Burwaaz**[39] 2257 4-9-0 **100**..............................(p) PaulHanagan 16 59
(Ed Dunlop) *lw: racd stands' side: t.k.h: hld up in rr overall: rdn and wknd 2f out: bhd fnl f: 19th of 21 in gp* **66/1**

00-1 **27** 5 **Navajo Chief**[34] 2399 6-9-4 **104**................................ KierenFallon 28 52
(Alan Jarvis) *racd stands' side: chsd gp ldr and handy overall tl over 2f out: sn wknd u.p: bhd fnl f: 20th of 21 in gp* **25/1**

5/ **28** nse **Elusive Time (IRE)**[283] 5-9-6 **106**......................... MasamiMatsuoka 18 53
(Takashi Kodama, Ire) *racd stands' side: t.k.h: chsd gp ldrs and handy overall: rdn and lost pl 3f out: bhd fnl f: 21st of 21 in gp* **50/1**

1m 38.68s (-2.12) **Going Correction** -0.125s/f (Firm) **28** Ran SP% **136.7**
Speed ratings (Par 109): **105,104,103,103,103 103,102,102,101,101 100,100,100,99,99 99,98,98,98,97 97,97,96,92,86 82,77**
toteswingers 1&2 £423.60, 2&3 £601.40, 1&3 £601.40 CSF £1046.01 CT £47237.78 TOTE £43.90: £9.00, £14.50, £17.60, £5.90; EX 6082.30 TRIFECTA Not won..
Owner PJL, Byrne & Baker **Bred** Wickfield Stud And Hartshill Stud **Trained** Manton, Wilts
■ George Baker's first Royal Ascot winner.

FOCUS
Probably the hottest mile handicap of the year. The draw had been a factor, with seven of the last ten winners drawn in the six highest stalls (allowing for withdrawals) but, despite the majority racing towards the stands' side, including some who switched from low draws, it was the group of seven racing centre to far side that dominated throughout. Belgian Bill is rated close to his sand form, with Premio Loco in line with his best form of the past year.

3459 QUEEN MARY STKS (GROUP 2) (FILLIES) 5f
5:00 (5:03) (Class 1) 2-Y-O

£56,710 (£21,500; £10,760; £5,360; £2,690; £1,350) **Stalls** Centre

Form RPR

511 **1** **Rizeena (IRE)**[20] 2809 2-8-12 0.. JamesDoyle 16 107+
(Clive Brittain) *swtg: on toes: racd in midfield in gp towards nr side: hdwy over 2f out: edgd rt over 1f out: r.o ins fnl f: led fnl 100yds: wl in command cl home* **6/1**[3]

2 2 **Sweet Emma Rose (USA)**[32] 2-8-12 0..........................(bt) JRosario 1 100
(Wesley A Ward, U.S.A) *lengthy: str: displayed gd pce: led: rdn over 1f out: hdd fnl 100yds: unable to go w wnr cl home* **16/1**

61 **3** 1 **One Chance (IRE)**[44] 2090 2-8-12 0.............................. AndreaAtzeni 6 96
(Tim Pitt) *lw: chsd ldrs: rdn and no imp on ldr over 1f out: kpt on ins fnl f but hld* **66/1**

213 **4** ½ **Fig Roll**[16] 2944 2-8-12 0.. PatDobbs 4 94
(Richard Hannon) *midfield: rdn 2f out: sn impr to chse ldrs: styd on towards fin: nt quite gng pce to get there* **33/1**

1 **5** hd **Reroute (IRE)**[5] 3295 2-8-12 0...................................... RobertWinston 11 94
(Ed Walker) *w'like: b.hind: midfield: rdn 2f out: hdwy to chse ldrs over 1f out: styd on ins fnl f tl one pce fnl 75yds* **8/1**

21 **6** ¾ **Survived**[12] 3049 2-8-12 0.. GrahamLee 5 91+
(William Haggas) *midfield: effrt to chse ldrs over 1f out: one pce fnl 50yds* **16/1**

131 **7** nse **Alutiq (IRE)**[33] 2414 2-8-12 0... JimCrowley 22 91
(Eve Johnson Houghton) *lengthy: lw racd in gp towards nr side: hld up: hdwy under 2f out: sn rdn: r.o and edgd rt ins fnl f: nt rch ldrs* **14/1**

3311 **8** 1 **Ventura Mist**[21] 2767 2-8-12 0..................................(p) DuranFentiman 3 87
(Tim Easterby) *tall: lengthy: chsd ldrs: rdn over 1f out: no ex fnl 75yds* **40/1**

1 **9** nk **Kaiulani (IRE)**[22] 2740 2-8-12 0...................................... MartinHarley 17 86
(Mick Channon) *w'like: attr: lw: hld up in gp towards nr side: hdwy 2f out: rn green over 1f out: kpt on ins fnl f: nt trble ldrs* **20/1**

1 **10** 1 **Fast (IRE)**[36] 2344 2-8-12 0... DaneO'Neill 19 83
(Richard Hannon) *leggy: scope: hmpd s: racd in gp towards nr side: rdn 2f out: prog ins fnl f: styd on: nt trble ldrs* **12/1**

1 **11** hd **Fire Blaze (IRE)**[62] 1634 2-8-12 0............................ MickaelBarzalona 2 82
(Saeed bin Suroor) *chsd ldrs: effrt over 1f out: no ex wl fnl 75yds and allowed to coast home* **10/1**

12 2 **Bye Bye Birdie (IRE)**[3] 3379 2-8-12 0.........................(p) RyanMoore 20 75
(A P O'Brien, Ire) *racd in gp towards nr side: chsd ldrs: rdn over 2f out: outpcd over 1f out: hung rt ins fnl f whn no imp* **12/1**

6126 **13** shd **Blithe Spirit**[33] 2426 2-8-12 0.. PatSmullen 9 74
(Eric Alston) *on toes: in rr: pushed along to go pce over 2f out: impr into midfield 1f out: no imp on ldrs* **100/1**

11 **14** ¾ **Beldale Memory (IRE)**[33] 2426 2-8-12 0...................... JamieSpencer 8 72
(Clive Cox) *in rr: pushed along wl over 2f out: nvr bttr than midfield over 1f out: no imp* **4/1**[1]

2315 **15** nk **Robynelle**[4] 3332 2-8-12 0... SilvestreDeSousa 24 70
(Keith Dalgleish) *chsd ldrs in gp towards nr side: rdn 2f out: wknd over 1f out* **150/1**

3513 **16** ½ **Lorimer's Lot (IRE)**[21] 2767 2-8-12 0............................ DanielTudhope 7 69
(Tim Walford) *chsd ldrs: rdn 2f out: wknd fnl f* **100/1**

23 **17** 1 **Oriel**[33] 2414 2-8-12 0... RichardHughes 18 65
(Richard Hannon) *on toes: unruly at s: racd in midfield in gp towards nr side: rdn over 1f out: no imp on ldrs* **11/2**[2]

2414 **18** ¾ **Diamond Lady**[33] 2414 2-8-12 0..................................... CathyGannon 15 62
(Jo Hughes) *racd in gp towards nr side and in rr-div: rdn and gng nowhere over 2f out: nvr a threat* **100/1**

2115 **19** hd **Quatuor (IRE)**[33] 2426 2-8-12 0............................... RichardKingscote 12 62
(Tom Dascombe) *in tch: rdn over 1f out: sn wknd* **25/1**

41 **20** ½ **Sandsman's Girl (IRE)**[23] 2715 2-8-12 0.......................... TomQueally 13 60
(James Given) *a bhd: nvr able to get on terms* **100/1**

1 **21** 1 **Baytown Kestrel**[15] 2947 2-8-12 0....................................... AdamKirby 21 56
(Phil McEntee) *racd in gp towards nr side and led gp tl merged over 2f out: wknd u.p over 1f out* **25/1**

516 **22** nk **Corncockle**[16] 2944 2-8-12 0.. SeanLevey 10 55
(Richard Hannon) *chsd ldrs: rdn over 2f out: wknd over 1f out* **80/1**

222 **23** ½ **Go Glamorous (IRE)**[49] 1924 2-8-12 0............................ SteveDrowne 14 53
(Ronald Harris) *lengthy: bhd in gp towards nr side: rdn and outpcd over 1f out: nvr a threat* **100/1**

59.29s (-1.21) **Going Correction** -0.125s/f (Firm) **23** Ran SP% **129.9**
Speed ratings (Par 102): **104,100,99,98,98 96,96,95,94,93 92,89,89,88,87 86,85,84,83,83 81,80,80**
toteswingers 1&2 £55.40, 2&3 £225.50, 1&3 £275.00 CSF £94.19 CT £5875.70 TOTE £7.60: £3.00, £4.90, £24.00; EX 129.70 Trifecta £7203.00 Pool: £12293.20 - 1.28 winning units..
Owner Sheikh Rashid Dalmook Al Maktoum **Bred** Round Hill Stud **Trained** Newmarket, Suffolk
■ An 891-1 treble for James Doyle, his first winners at Royal Ascot.

FOCUS
The top 5f juvenile fillies' race of the season but, although in the past it has produced the subsequent 1000 Guineas winner Attraction, in recent seasons it has fallen to sharper, precocious types who have been unable to carry their form into their 3yo season (Maqaasid excepted). Those racing far side mostly dominated again, although the winner came up the centre. Rizeena is rated up to the standard of recent winners. This form can't be rated any higher but the winner can progress again.

3460 SANDRINGHAM H'CAP (LISTED RACE) (FILLIES) 1m (S)
5:35 (5:39) (Class 1) (0-110,105) 3-Y-O

£34,026 (£12,900; £6,456; £3,216; £1,614; £810) **Stalls** Centre

Form RPR

1-61 **1** **Annecdote**[32] 2449 3-8-7 **91** oh1............................ RichardKingscote 3 101
(Jonathan Portman) *racd far side: in tch in midfield: rdn and hdwy whn gps merged 2f out: ev ch and drvn over 1f out: r.o gamely to ld wl ins fnl f: hld on gamely towards fin* **11/1**

-111 **2** nk **Auction (IRE)**[26] 2622 3-8-7 **91** oh8.......................... SilvestreDeSousa 5 100
(Ed Dunlop) *racd far side: chsd ldrs overall: rdn to ld whn gps merged 2f out: drvn and hrd pressed over 1f out: hdd ins fnl f: battled on gamely but hld cl home* **16/1**

-131 **3** nk **Woodland Aria**[16] 2928 3-8-9 **93**.. WilliamBuick 2 101
(John Gosden) *racd far side: hld up towards rr: hdwy as gps merged 2f out: rdn and effrt to chal over 1f out: drvn and led ins fnl f: hdd wl ins fnl f: r.o but lost 2nd cl home* **7/1**[2]

22-0 **4** ½ **Nargys (IRE)**[63] 1622 3-9-5 **103**.................................. JamieSpencer 22 110+
(Luca Cumani) *racd in centre: stdd s: hld up in rr: gd hdwy on bit as gps merged 2f out: rdn and produced to chal jst ins fnl f: ev ch but nt qckn u.p fnl 100yds* **20/1**

02 **5** 2¼ **Hint Of A Tint (IRE)**[38] 2289 3-9-2 **100**..............................[1] FMBerry 14 102
(David Wachman, Ire) *racd in centre: hld up in midfield overall: rdn and hdwy as gps merged 2f out: chsd ldrs and styd on same pce ins fnl f* **7/1**[2]

32-0 **6** ¾ **Light Up My Life (IRE)**[63] 1622 3-9-2 **100**......................... PatDobbs 26 100+
(Richard Hannon) *racd stands' side: hld up in rr: rdn and hdwy as gps merged 2f out: hung rt but styd on wl fnl f: no threat to ldrs* **40/1**

-040 **7** ½ **Sorella Bella (IRE)**[25] 2655 3-8-11 **95**........................... MartinHarley 16 94
(Mick Channon) *racd in centre: chsd ldrs: drvn and stl pressing ldrs as gps merged 2f out: no ex 1f out: wknd ins fnl f* **40/1**

8 1¾ **Bracing Breeze**[40] 2243 3-8-12 **96**...................................... PatSmullen 9 91
(D K Weld, Ire) *w'like: cl cpld: racd far side: t.k.h: hld up in midfield: rdn and effrt as gps merged 2f out: chsd ldrs but no ex u.p over 1f out: wknd ins fnl f* **8/1**[3]

2-12 **9** ½ **Mango Diva**[20] 2812 3-8-10 **94**.. RyanMoore 15 88
(Sir Michael Stoute) *racd in centre: stl bhd as gps merged 2f out: hdwy over 1f out: styd on u.p fnl f: nvr trbld ldrs* **6/1**[1]

3-40 **10** hd **Uleavemebreathless**[24] 2689 3-8-10 **94**.......................... ChrisHayes 18 87
(A Oliver, Ire) *lw: racd in centre: hld up towards rr: sme hdwy and rdn as gps merged 2f out: styd on fnl f: nvr threatened ldrs* **50/1**

63 **11** 1 **Harmonic Note**[27] 2586 3-8-7 **91** oh1................................ HarryBentley 11 82
(G M Lyons, Ire) *lw: racd far side: chsd ldrs: rdn and unable qck as gps merged 2f out: btn jst over 1f out: wknd ins fnl f* **66/1**

4 **12** nk **Typhoon Lily (USA)**[49] 1918 3-8-8 **92**..................(t) StephanePasquier 4 82
(M D O'Callaghan, Ire) *racd far side: hld up in rr: rdn as gps merged 2f out: hdwy over 1f out: no imp fnl f: nvr trbld ldrs* **25/1**

02-1 **13** ¾ **Fleeting Smile (USA)**[45] 2056 3-8-11 **95**........................ PaulHanagan 20 84
(Richard Hannon) *racd in centre: chsd ldrs: rdn and pressing ldrs as gps merged 2f out: btn over 1f out: wknd fnl f* **16/1**

160 **14** ½ **Valtina (IRE)**[27] 2586 3-8-7 **91** oh3.................................... WayneLordan 1 79
(William Haggas) *racd far side: t.k.h: hld up in midfield overall: effrt as gps merged 2f out: sn no imp: nvr trbld ldrs* **50/1**

35-0 **15** ¾ **The Gold Cheongsam (IRE)**[60] 1676 3-9-7 **105**......(t) FrankieDettori 24 91
(Jeremy Noseda) *racd stands' side: chsd ldrs overall: rdn and handy as gps merged 2f out: stl chsng ldrs and hung rt over 1f out: sn btn and wknd fnl f* **33/1**

3-21 **16** hd **Stresa**[26] 2628 3-8-7 **91** oh4.. RobertHavlin 17 76
(John Gosden) *racd in centre: racd keenly: prom: rdn and pressing ldrs as gps merged 2f out: btn over 1f out: wknd fnl f* **25/1**

0-05 **17** 9 **Califante**[33] 2429 3-8-9 **93**.. MartinDwyer 12 58
(William Muir) *racd far side: chsd ldrs: rdn and ev ch as gps merged 2f out: sn struggling and btn over 1f out: fdd fnl f* **40/1**

12-4 **18** 2¼ **Lizzie Tudor**[39] 2253 3-8-7 **91** oh4................................ CathyGannon 21 51
(Andrew Balding) *racd stands' side: in tch in midfield overall: rdn and struggling over 2f out: losing pl as gps merged 2f out: bhd fnl f* **33/1**

-505 **19** 3¾ **Flawless Beauty**[15] 2970 3-8-8 **92**................................(b) HayleyTurner 23 43
(Hugo Palmer) *swtg: racd stands' side: in tch in midfield: rdn and btn as gps merged 2f out: sn wknd and bhd fnl f* **50/1**

-223 **20** hd **Senafe**[17] 2910 3-9-2 **100**.. NeilCallan 6 50
(Marco Botti) *racd far side: overall ldr tl rdn and hdd as gps merged 2f out: sn btn: wknd over 1f out* **40/1**

6-56 **21** 1½ **Waterway Run (USA)**[38] 2299 3-9-5 **103**........................... JimCrowley 7 50
(Ralph Beckett) *lw: racd far side: chsd ldrs: rdn and struggling over 2f out: losing pl as gps merged 2f out: bhd fnl f* **20/1**

0-00 **22** 1¾ **Go Angellica (IRE)**[111] 837 3-8-8 **92**................................ MartinLane 19 35
(David Simcock) *racd in centre: chsd ldrs: rdn and lost pl over 2f out: wkng as gps merged 2f out: bhd fnl f* **66/1**

12-0 **23** 14 **Desert Image**[60] 1676 3-9-0 **98**...................................... JamesMcDonald 25
(Charles Hills) *racd stands' side: in tch in midfield overall: rdn and struggling whn sltly hmpd as gps merged 2f out: sn bhd: t.o and eased fnl f* **40/1**

6-14 **24** 12 **Zurigha (IRE)**[38] 2299 3-9-7 **105**.................................. RichardHughes 8
(Richard Hannon) *racd far side: t.k.h: hld up in midfield: wknd over 2f out and bhd as gps merged 2f out: wl bhd and eased over 1f out: t.o* **12/1**

30-0 **25** 1¾ **Annie's Fortune (IRE)**[33] 2429 3-8-11 **95**........................ KierenFallon 13
(Alan Jarvis) *racd in centre: stdd s: t.k.h: and hld up towards rr: sme hdwy 1/2-way: wknd qckly over 2f out and wl btn as gps merged 2f out: bhd and eased over 1f out: t.o* **33/1**

-625 **26** *6* **Trapeze**[27] 2586 3-8-7 **91** oh5 NickyMackay 10
(John Gosden) *racd far side: in tch overall: rdn and struggling over 3f out: bhd as gps merged 2f out: t.o and eased fnl f* **33/1**

1m 38.34s (-2.46) **Going Correction** -0.125s/f (Firm) **26** Ran SP% **128.2**
Speed ratings (Par 104): **107,106,106,105,103 102,102,100,100,99 98,98,97,97,96 96,87,85,81,81 79,78,64,52,50 44**
toteswingers 1&2 £60.00, 2&3 £3.80, 1&3 £46.50 CSF £142.90 CT £870.19 TOTE £16.00: £3.60, £2.90, £2.30, £5.10; EX 234.20 Trifecta £2005.30 Pool: £8221.34 - 3.00 winning units..
Owner Tom Edwards & Partners **Bred** The Hon Mrs R Pease **Trained** Upper Lambourn, Berks

FOCUS
Often a strong fillies' handicap, it was hard to comfortably rule out any more than a couple of the runners, despite no less than seven of them having to run from out of the handicap. More or less racing in two groups, it was another clean sweep for the low-drawn runners, following on from the Queen Mary, which was in complete contrast from the previous day where the stands' side appeared to hold sway. The fancied runners came to the fore and the form looks solid, with the time being especially notable (quicker than both the Duke Of Cambridge and Hunt Cup). Improvement from the first two.
T/Jkpt: Not won. T/Plt: £5,559.90 to a £1 stake. Pool of £665820.82 - 87.42 winning tickets T/Qpdt: £1,884.60 to a £1 stake. Pool of £24449.93 - 9.60 winning tickets. SP

3197 HAMILTON (R-H)

Wednesday, June 19

OFFICIAL GOING: Good to firm (9.1)
Rails realignment around the loop reduced distances on Round course by about 25yds.
Wind: Breezy, across Weather: Cloudy, warm

3461 BRITISH STALLION STUDS SUPPORTING BRITISH RACING EBF MAIDEN STKS 6f 5y
2:20 (2:20) (Class 5) 2-Y-0 **£3,234** (£962; £481; £240) **Stalls** High

Form				RPR
5	**1**		**Centre Haafhd**[11] 3077 2-9-3 0 GrahamGibbons 5 (David Barron) *led 2f: cl up: led ent fnl f: kpt on strly* **14/1**	73
0	**2**	*2 ¼*	**Stoney Quine (IRE)**[32] 2458 2-8-12 0 TomEaves 1 (Keith Dalgleish) *wnt rt s: sn cl up: led after 2f to ent fnl f: kpt on same pce last 100yds* **16/1**	61
6	**3**	*¾*	**Nelson's Pride**[22] 2751 2-8-12 0 PhillipMakin 6 (Kevin Ryan) *chsd ldrs: rdn and edgd rt over 1f out: kpt on same pce ins fnl f* **5/2**[2]	61
	4	*1 ½*	**Brownsville (USA)** 2-9-0 0 FrannyNorton 4 (Mark Johnston) *green in preliminaries: prom: outpcd over 2f out: rallied over 1f out: no imp fnl f* **12/1**	57
	5	*nk*	**Our Gabrial (IRE)** 2-9-0 0 TonyHamilton 3 (Richard Fahey) *green in preliminaries: hld up in tch: effrt over 2f out: rdn and hung rt over 1f out: sn outpcd* **13/8**[1]	56+
	6	*3 ¼*	**Emaad (USA)** 2-9-0 0 JoeFanning 2 (Mark Johnston) *chsd ldrs: rdn over 2f out: wknd over 1f out* **9/2**[3]	46+
0	**7**	*4*	**Greenbury (IRE)**[18] 2883 2-9-3 0 PaulMulrennan 8 (Ann Duffield) *t.k.h: sn bhd: hdwy over 2f out: nvr able to chal* **66/1**	39
	8	*2 ¼*	**Fair Flutter (IRE)** 2-8-11 0 LeeTopliss(3) 9 (Richard Fahey) *s.i.s: bhd: hdwy on outside wl over 2f out: btn over 1f out* **14/1**	27
060	**9**	*3 ¼*	**Highland Princess (IRE)**[23] 2715 2-8-12 0 MickyFenton 7 (Paul Midgley) *t.k.h: in tch to 1/2-way: sn wknd* **100/1**	15

1m 12.87s (0.67) **Going Correction** +0.10s/f (Good) **9** Ran SP% **114.2**
Speed ratings (Par 93): **99,96,95,93,92 88,82,79,75**
toteswingers 1&2 £10.40, 2&3 £6.20, 1&3 £7.50 CSF £210.33 TOTE £16.70: £4.00, £3.30, £1.10; EX 82.80 Trifecta £918.20 Pool: £2512.13 - 2.05 winning units..
Owner D G Pryde, Jim Beaumont & James Callow **Bred** Shadwell Estate Company Limited **Trained** Maunby, N Yorks

FOCUS
The rail had been moved on the loop to provide fresh ground for the meeting. The by-product of this was that all races over a mile or further were approximately 25yds shorter than the official distances given. Kevin Ryan and Mark Johnston had taken this opening maiden twice each in the last four years. Both stables had representatives here, but could not continue their domination of the race. Experience told with the first three home all having their second starts. The winner left her debut behind and this was no fluke.

3462 SAM COLLINGWOOD-CAMERON H'CAP 6f 5y
2:55 (2:55) (Class 5) (0-75,72) 3-Y-0+ **£3,234** (£962; £481; £240) **Stalls** High

Form				RPR
305	**1**		**Sunraider (IRE)**[12] 3068 6-9-11 **69** MickyFenton 2 (Paul Midgley) *hld up in tch: pushed along over 2f out: hdwy and swtchd lft over 1f out: led wl ins fnl f: r.o* **7/2**[3]	79
2250	**2**	*1*	**Majestic Dream (IRE)**[11] 3087 5-10-0 **72** (v) GrahamGibbons 5 (Michael Easterby) *led: rdn over 2f out: hdd wl ins fnl f: kpt on same pce* **11/4**[1]	78
00	**3**	*¾*	**Captain Scooby**[19] 2834 7-9-7 **70** JasonHart(5) 3 (Richard Guest) *chsd ldrs: rdn and ev ch over 1f out to ins fnl f: kpt on same pce towards fin* **15/2**	74
3155	**4**	*1 ¼*	**Script**[7] 3197 4-8-11 **55** PaddyAspell 1 (Alan Berry) *chsd ldrs on outside: effrt and rdn 2f out: kpt on same pce fnl f* **20/1**	55
3-03	**5**	*nk*	**Findog**[5] 3283 3-9-5 **70** PaulMulrennan 6 (Linda Perratt) *t.k.h: in tch: nt clr run over 2f out to over 1f out: effrt whn blkd appr fnl f: no room ins fnl f: nt rcvr* **3/1**[2]	73+
0-64	**6**	*1 ¾*	**Amadeus Denton (IRE)**[7] 3190 4-8-12 **63** ConnorBeasley(7) 4 (Michael Dods) *prom: effrt and pushed along whn hmpd and lost pl over 1f out: n.d after* **6/1**	59+
140-	**7**	*2 ¾*	**Prince Of Vasa (IRE)**[424] 1526 6-9-7 **65** AndrewMullen 7 (Michael Smith) *t.k.h: cl up tl rdn and wknd fr 2f out* **16/1**	50

1m 12.17s (-0.03) **Going Correction** +0.10s/f (Good)
WFA 3 from 4yo+ 7lb **7** Ran SP% **110.6**
Speed ratings (Par 103): **104,102,101,100,99 97,93**
toteswingers 1&2 £1.70, 2&3 £3.70, 1&3 £6.40 CSF £12.61 TOTE £5.30: £4.70, £1.50; EX 15.70 Trifecta £86.20 Pool: £2247.29 - 19.53 winning units..
Owner R Wardlaw **Bred** Lodge Park Stud **Trained** Westow, N Yorks
■ Stewards' Enquiry : Paul Mulrennan two-day ban: carelress riding (3-4 July)

FOCUS
A modest affair with not much in the way of convincing form. It was scrappy and, despite just the seven runners, there was trouble in running.

3463 D M HALL H'CAP 1m 65y
3:30 (3:33) (Class 6) (0-60,60) 3-Y-0 **£1,940** (£577; £288; £144) **Stalls** Low

Form				RPR
3306	**1**		**Rocket Ronnie (IRE)**[21] 2770 3-9-2 **55** BarryMcHugh 12 (David Nicholls) *in tch: effrt whn nt clr run over 2f out and over 1f out: styd on wl u.p fnl f to ld cl home* **4/1**[2]	61+
00-0	**2**	*hd*	**Isle Of Beauty**[22] 2754 3-8-7 **46** FrannyNorton 2 (Tom Dascombe) *chsd ldr: rdn over 2f out: led ins fnl f: kpt on: hdd cl home* **12/1**	51
63-5	**3**	*¾*	**Multilicious**[30] 2504 3-9-1 **54** MickyFenton 3 (Tim Easterby) *trckd ldrs: rdn over 2f out: rallied whn hung rt ins fnl f: kpt on: hld nr fin* **12/1**	57
0040	**4**	*nk*	**Look On By**[11] 3082 3-9-0 **53** JamesSullivan 8 (Ruth Carr) *t.k.h: hld up: rdn over 2f out: swtchd lft and hdwy over 1f out: kpt on: nrst fin* **6/1**[3]	56+
006-	**5**	*½*	**El Molino Blanco**[296] 5668 3-9-3 **56** GrahamGibbons 7 (Michael Easterby) *hld up: effrt over 2f out: nt clr run over 1f out: swtchd lft and r.o fnl f* **33/1**	57
44-5	**6**	*2*	**Sakhees Romance**[26] 2635 3-8-11 **53** DeclanCannon(3) 10 (Noel Wilson) *missed break: bhd: hdwy on outside over 2f out: no imp fnl f* **16/1**	49
1400	**7**	*1*	**Birdy Boy (USA)**[22] 2743 3-9-5 **58** JoeFanning 14 (Mark Johnston) *midfield on outside: hdwy to ld over 2f out: edgd rt and hdd ins fnl f: sn btn* **15/2**	52
-511	**8**	*½*	**Lexington Blue**[11] 3082 3-9-6 **59** TonyHamilton 11 (David O'Meara) *prom: effrt over 2f out: outpcd fnl f* **11/4**[1]	52
1430	**9**	*nk*	**Silver Fawn (IRE)**[42] 2156 3-8-10 **52** ow1 (be) LeeTopliss(3) 4 (John Weymes) *missed break: t.k.h in rr: rdn 3f out: styd on fnl f: nrst fin* **25/1**	44
0-60	**10**	*1*	**Denton Skyline (IRE)**[30] 2508 3-8-12 **51** (p) TomEaves 9 (Michael Dods) *hld up in midfield on ins: effrt over 2f out: n.m.r over 1f out: sn outpcd* **25/1**	41
-400	**11**	*hd*	**Riponian**[48] 1967 3-9-0 **53** PaddyAspell 1 (Susan Corbett) *led: rdn and hdd over 2f out: rallied: one pce whn hmpd ins fnl f* **50/1**	42
260	**12**	*1*	**Tinctoria**[22] 2754 3-9-7 **60** PhillipMakin 15 (Kevin Ryan) *trckd ldrs on outside tl rdn and wknd over 1f out* **25/1**	47
-000	**13**	*½*	**Betty Boo (IRE)**[30] 2501 3-8-4 **46** oh1 NeilFarley(3) 13 (Shaun Harris) *missed break: bhd: struggling 3f out: nvr on terms* **66/1**	32
66-0	**14**	*nse*	**Star Request**[33] 2409 3-9-6 **59** PaulMulrennan 6 (Keith Dalgleish) *t.k.h: hld up: drvn 3f out: nvr on terms* **12/1**	45

1m 48.31s (-0.09) **Going Correction** -0.30s/f (Firm) **14** Ran SP% **119.6**
Speed ratings (Par 97): **88,87,87,86,86 84,83,82,82,81 81,80,79,79**
toteswingers 1&2 £11.80, 2&3 £8.80, 1&3 £6.30 CSF £47.13 CT £552.45 TOTE £4.90: £1.60, £5.40, £3.50; EX 83.60 Trifecta £561.70 Pool: £3148.39 - 4.20 winning units..
Owner Mills, Fallon, Purchase & Love **Bred** Sandra Russell **Trained** Sessay, N Yorks
■ Stewards' Enquiry : Barry McHugh two-day ban: careless riding (3-4 July)
Franny Norton two-day ban: use of whip (3-4 July)

FOCUS
A big field for this 3yo handicap, but most of these had shown little on the racecourse. There was no great pace bias, but luck in-running once again played a part.

3464 MCGHEE'S TEAZ H'CAP 1m 65y
4:10 (4:10) (Class 4) (0-80,80) 3-Y-0+ **£5,822** (£1,732; £865; £432) **Stalls** Low

Form				RPR
0-61	**1**		**Springheel Jake**[16] 2912 4-9-4 **77** RowanScott(7) 1 (Ann Duffield) *t.k.h: mde all: rdn and edgd lft 2f out: kpt on wl fnl f* **7/2**[3]	89
3-52	**2**	*2*	**Party Royal**[7] 3207 3-9-4 **80** JoeFanning 3 (Mark Johnston) *trckd ldrs: effrt and wnt 2nd 2f out: kpt on same pce ins fnl f* **11/4**[2]	85
6136	**3**	*2 ½*	**Declamation (IRE)**[12] 3062 3-8-11 **73** FrannyNorton 6 (Mark Johnston) *pressed wnr: rdn and edgd lft over 2f out: one pce wl over 1f out* **5/2**[1]	73
0026	**4**	*1 ¼*	**Another For Joe**[7] 3204 5-9-10 **76** AndrewElliott 4 (Jim Goldie) *prom: effrt and hung rt over 2f out: sn no imp* **7/2**[3]	75
-060	**5**	*10*	**Viva Ronaldo (IRE)**[18] 2882 7-9-4 **70** TonyHamilton 2 (Richard Fahey) *hld up in tch: drvn and outpcd 3f out: n.d after* **8/1**	46

1m 44.9s (-3.50) **Going Correction** -0.30s/f (Firm)
WFA 3 from 4yo+ 10lb **5** Ran SP% **110.8**
Speed ratings (Par 105): **105,103,100,99,89**
CSF £13.45 TOTE £5.10: £1.90, £1.20; EX 11.50 Trifecta £35.50 Pool: £2092.67 - 44.14 winning units..
Owner Jimmy Kay **Bred** Mrs T Brudenell **Trained** Constable Burton, N Yorks

FOCUS
Nominally the best race on the card, but it was a poor turnout. A few of these had shown a liking in the past for dominating races and that contributed to a strong pace and a time over three seconds quicker than the preceding 3yo handicap. There was nothing between the front four in the betting and they all had their chance.

3465 SCOT INDUSTRIAL PRODUCTS MEDIAN AUCTION MAIDEN STKS 1m 1f 36y
4:45 (4:45) (Class 6) 3-5-Y-0 **£2,726** (£805; £402) **Stalls** Low

Form				RPR
32	**1**		**Wall Of Sound**[40] 2231 3-8-9 0 JoeFanning 3 (Tom Dascombe) *mde all: shkn up and qcknd 2f out: edgd lft ins fnl f: easily* **1/4**[1]	82+
3002	**2**	*6*	**Argaki (IRE)**[7] 3202 3-9-0 65 TomEaves 1 (Keith Dalgleish) *trckd ldrs: effrt and chse wnr over 2f out: kpt on same pce fr over 1f out* **12/1**[3]	74
2	**3**	*13*	**Primary Route (IRE)**[22] 2754 3-8-9 0 GrahamGibbons 5 (David Barron) *chsd wnr to over 2f out: sn rdn and wknd* **4/1**[2]	51
	4	*11*	**Amisfield Lad**[24] 4-9-11 0 AndrewMullen 4 (Michael Smith) *slowly away: hld up in tch: rdn over 3f out: wknd over 2f out* **50/1**	21
	5	*47*	**Redwood Blade** 4-9-6 0 AndrewElliott 2 (Jim Goldie) *bhd: lost tch after 3f: t.o* **33/1**	

1m 56.44s (-3.26) **Going Correction** -0.30s/f (Firm)
WFA 3 from 4yo 11lb **5** Ran SP% **112.6**
Speed ratings (Par 101): **102,96,85,75,33**
CSF £4.91 TOTE £1.10: £1.02, £3.10; EX 4.10 Trifecta £6.00 Pool: £3174.84 - 392.63 winning units..
Owner A Black **Bred** A Black **Trained** Malpas, Cheshire

FOCUS
An uncompetitive maiden, but the winner could be decent.

3466 RACING UK FREE TRIAL ON SKY H'CAP 1m 1f 36y
5:20 (5:21) (Class 5) (0-70,70) 3-Y-O+ £3,234 (£962; £481; £240) Stalls Low

Form RPR
2022 1 **Tectonic (IRE)**[7] 3203 4-9-0 **56**.....(p) TomEaves 7 62
(Keith Dalgleish) *hld up in tch: stdy hdwy over 2f out: effrt and edgd rt over 1f out: led ins fnl f: edgd lft: jst hld on* 11/4[3]
0-00 2 *shd* **Royal Straight**[37] 2315 8-9-11 **67**.....(t) PhillipMakin 3 73
(Linda Perratt) *hld up in tch: rdn and hdwy 2f out: kpt on u.p fnl f: jst hld* 22/1
4-24 3 1 ½ **Wellingrove (IRE)**[27] 2600 3-9-3 **70**..... JoeFanning 4 71
(Mark Johnston) *led: rdn over 2f out: hdd ins fnl f: kpt on same pce* 5/2[2]
-003 4 ½ **Joshua The First**[5] 3285 4-9-4 **65**.....(t) JasonHart(5) 2 66
(Keith Dalgleish) *prom: effrt whn nt clr run over 2f out: rallied over 1f out: one pce ins fnl f* 8/1
0663 5 ½ **Call Of Duty (IRE)**[2] 3397 8-9-0 **59**..... LucyAlexander(3) 6 59
(Dianne Sayer) *sn chsng ldr: ev ch and rdn over 2f out: kpt on same pce ins fnl f* 2/1[1]
0000 6 2 ½ **Moheebb (IRE)**[18] 2889 9-9-2 **61**..... MarkCoumbe(3) 5 56
(Robert Johnson) *chsd ldrs: drvn along over 2f out: edgd rt and wknd over 1f out* 11/1
00/6 7 13 **Inca Chief**[13] 3030 5-8-4 **53** oh3..... RowanScott(7) 8 19
(Ann Duffield) *plld hrd: prom on outside: rdn over 2f out: wknd wl over 1f out* 50/1

1m 57.23s (-2.47) **Going Correction** -0.30s/f (Firm)
WFA 3 from 4yo+ 11lb **7 Ran SP% 114.3**
Speed ratings (Par 103): **98,97,96,96,95 93,81**
toteswingers 1&2 £9.00, 2&3 £6.90, 1&3 £1.80 CSF £55.46 CT £168.59 TOTE £5.10: £3.10, £11.20; EX 52.90 Trifecta £221.30 Pool: £1613.60 - 5.46 winning units..
Owner Mrs L A Ogilvie **Bred** W Maxwell Ervine **Trained** Carluke, S Lanarks

FOCUS
A good finish to this competitive, if modest handicap where they went a decent gallop.

3467 TURFTV IN YOUR BETTING SHOP APPRENTICE H'CAP (ROUND TWO OF THE HAMILTON PARK APPRENTICE SERIES) 1m 4f 17y
5:55 (5:55) (Class 6) (0-60,60) 4-Y-O+ £2,045 (£603; £302) Stalls High

Form RPR
-524 1 **Schmooze (IRE)**[7] 3199 4-9-6 **59**..... LeeTopliss 2 70
(Linda Perratt) *hld up in last pl: hdwy over 2f out: rdn to ld wl ins fnl f: kpt on wl* 7/2[2]
0103 2 *hd* **El Bravo**[10] 3138 7-9-0 **56**..... JasonHart(3) 3 67
(Shaun Harris) *led 2f: cl up: led and rdn 3f out: hdd wl ins fnl f: kpt on: hld nr fin* 9/2[3]
-055 3 5 **Geanie Mac (IRE)**[14] 2975 4-8-8 **50**.....(b) GeorgeChaloner(3) 1 53
(Linda Perratt) *led after 2f tl rdn and hdd 3f out: one pce fnl 2f* 12/1
-612 4 *nk* **Goodlukin Lucy**[14] 2975 6-8-13 **52**.....(t) LucyAlexander 5 55
(Dianne Sayer) *dwlt: t.k.h and sn cl up: ev ch over 3f out: rdn and wknd 2f out* 7/2[2]
-200 5 7 **Destiny Awaits (IRE)**[14] 2975 4-8-0 **46** oh1.....(b[1]) KevinStott(7) 6 37
(Ian Semple) *hld up in tch: rdn and outpcd over 3f out: n.d after* 20/1
000- 6 1 ¼ **Slide Show**[226] 7594 5-8-2 **46** oh1..... GemmaTutty(5) 7 35
(David Nicholls) *plld hrd: prom tl rdn and wknd 2f out* 6/1
0- 7 ½ **Mystified (IRE)**[21] 4959 10-8-0 **46** oh1..... JordanHibberd(7) 8 35
(Alan Berry) *trckd ldrs tl rdn and wknd over 2f out* 50/1
0512 8 23 **Kingarrick**[26] 2642 5-9-7 **60**..... NeilFarley 4
(Noel Wilson) *t.k.h: hld up in tch: struggling over 3f out: lost tch fnl 2f* 3/1[1]

2m 34.55s (-4.05) **Going Correction** -0.30s/f (Firm) **8 Ran SP% 116.3**
Speed ratings (Par 101): **101,100,97,97,92 91,91,76**
toteswingers 1&2 £3.40, 2&3 £5.20, 1&3 £4.50 CSF £20.06 CT £169.78 TOTE £5.50: £1.80, £1.50, £2.10; EX 21.60 Trifecta £111.30 Pool: £1392.38 - 9.37 winning units..
Owner Jackton Racing Club **Bred** Chris McHale And Oghill House Stud **Trained** East Kilbride, S Lanarks

FOCUS
Moderate fare, but a number of these came into the race with some recent form to their name.
T/Plt: £245.10 to a £1 stake. Pool of £48683.57 - 144.95 winning tickets. T/Qpdt: £16.20 to a £1 stake. Pool of £2605.18 - 118.60 winning tickets. RY

3432 KEMPTON (A.W) (R-H)
Wednesday, June 19

OFFICIAL GOING: Standard
Wind: Light, across Weather: Cloudy, humid

3468 £200 FREE BETS AT BETDAQ APPRENTICE H'CAP 1m 2f (P)
6:10 (6:10) (Class 4) (0-80,78) 4-Y-O+ £4,690 (£1,395; £697; £348) Stalls Low

Form RPR
1114 1 **Mubtadi**[40] 2234 5-9-7 **77**..... ThomasBrown 1 86+
(Ismail Mohammed) *hld up in 6th: prog to chse ldng trio over 2f out: sn chalng as they drifted wd bnd sn after: led over 1f out: rdn and kpt on* 11/4[1]
6212 2 1 ¼ **King Olav (UAE)**[47] 1983 8-9-4 **74**..... CharlesBishop 6 80
(Tony Carroll) *led to 1/2-way: rdn and stl chalng whn carried lft and squeezed out 2f out: swtchd to inner and kpt on fnl f to take 2nd nr fin* 3/1[2]
0456 3 *shd* **Lady Macduff (IRE)**[11] 3083 4-9-2 **72**..... RobertTart 8 78
(Mark Johnston) *w ldr: led 1/2-way: hung lft bnd 2f out: hdd and nt qckn over 1f out* 12/1
-303 4 *hd* **Xinbama (IRE)**[14] 2981 4-8-13 **72**.....(t) ShelleyBirkett(3) 2 77
(J W Hills) *trckd ldrs: moving up to chal whn carried lft bnd 2f out: stl trying over 1f out: one pce* 7/1
20-5 5 11 **Checkpoint**[28] 1898 4-8-9 **72**..... HectorCrouch(7) 4 55
(Gary Moore) *trckd ldrs on outer tl steadily wknd fr 3f out* 33/1
1210 6 *nse* **Ishikawa (IRE)**[51] 1883 5-9-5 **78**..... ThomasGarner(3) 5 61
(Alan King) *blindfold off late and s.s: hld up in last: rdn 3f out: rchd 5th 2f out but no ch: wknd fnl f* 5/1
-132 7 18 **Purple 'n Gold (IRE)**[140] 439 4-9-7 **77**.....(v) NathanAlison 3 24
(David Pipe) *chsd ldrs tl wknd 3f out: t.o* 7/2[3]

2m 6.78s (-1.22) **Going Correction** +0.075s/f (Slow) **7 Ran SP% 113.7**
Speed ratings (Par 105): **107,106,105,105,96 96,82**
toteswingers 1&2 £2.70, 2&3 £5.60, 1&3 £4.80 CSF £11.16 CT £81.41 TOTE £3.60: £2.20, £2.80; EX 14.10 Trifecta £132.50 Pool: £2288.73 - 12.94 winning units..
Owner Abdulla Al Mansoori **Bred** Whitsbury Manor Stud **Trained** Newmarket, Suffolk

FOCUS
An apprentice handicap run at a sound pace thanks to the two leaders taking each other on.

3469 RACINGANDMUSIC.CO.UK MAIDEN FILLIES' STKS 1m 2f (P)
6:40 (6:42) (Class 5) 3-Y-O+ £1,678 (£1,678; £384; £192) Stalls Low

Form RPR
4 1 **Ardingly (IRE)**[19] 2850 3-9-0 0..... AndreaAtzeni 2 77
(Roger Varian) *led: shkn up over 1f out: hrd pressed fnl f: jnd last strides* 5/2[1]
6 1 *dht* **Controversy**[10] 3136 3-9-0 0..... MickaelBarzalona 11 77
(Saeed bin Suroor) *trckd ldr: rdn to chal over 1f out: sustained battle fnl f: forced dead-heat last strides* 3/1[2]
0- 3 1 ¾ **Are You Mine (IRE)**[259] 6796 3-9-0 0..... JamesDoyle 10 74
(Ralph Beckett) *trckd ldrs: rdn to chse ldng pair over 1f out: styd on but nvr able to chal* 6/1[3]
4 ¾ **Rancho Montoya (IRE)** 3-9-0 0..... LiamKeniry 4 72
(Andrew Balding) *chsd ldng pair: shkn up over 2f out: lost 3rd over 1f out: kpt on wl: pleasing debut* 20/1
2/ 5 *hd* **Fragonard**[705] 4061 4-9-12 0..... TomQueally 5 72+
(Lady Cecil) *chsd ldrs: pushed along 4f out: outpcd over 2f out: styd on fr over 1f out: nrst fin* 3/1[2]
6 1 ¾ **Aiyana** 3-9-0 0..... JimmyFortune 1 68
(Hughie Morrison) *chsd ldrs: shkn up over 2f out: outpcd in 5th wl over 1f out: one pce after* 33/1
7 ½ **Silk Sari** 3-9-0 0..... KirstyMilczarek 6 67+
(Luca Cumani) *s.i.s: hld up in last quartet: pushed along and styd on steadily fnl 2f: nrst fin: likely improver* 33/1
00 8 6 **Pure Mischief (IRE)**[16] 2938 3-9-0 0..... TedDurcan 14 55
(David Lanigan) *towards rr: rdn in 11th over 2f out: nvr a threat: passed a few stragglers late on* 100/1
9 ½ **Mignonne** 3-8-9 0..... NicoleNordblad(5) 9 54+
(Hans Adielsson) *fractious preliminaries: slowly away: hld up in last quartet: prog arnd outside bnd 3f out: chsd ldrs 2f out: wknd qckly over 1f out* 66/1
0 10 2 **Wolfs Breath (TUR)**[40] 2206 3-9-0 0..... SteveDrowne 12 50
(Charles Hills) *racd on outer: chsd ldng pair and flicked tail several times: wknd qckly over 2f out* 16/1
11 4 ½ **Ninja Lady** 3-9-0 0..... FrederikTylicki 7 41
(James Fanshawe) *dwlt: a in last quartet: lost tch over 2f out: bhd after* 25/1
0 12 *nk* **West Of The Moon**[22] 2760 3-8-9 0..... WilliamTwiston-Davies(5) 8 41
(Sir Michael Stoute) *wl in tch in midfield tl wknd wl over 2f out* 25/1
0 13 6 **Elhathrah (IRE)**[33] 2423 3-9-0 0..... AdamKirby 13 29
(Ed Dunlop) *sn in last: shoved along fr 1/2-way: bhd 3f out: t.o* 25/1
00 14 3 ¾ **Need To Be Bold**[22] 2746 4-9-7 0..... RobertTart(5) 3 21
(Derek Haydn Jones) *s.i.s: a towards rr: wknd 3f out: t.o* 200/1

2m 8.84s (0.84) **Going Correction** +0.075s/f (Slow)
WFA 3 from 4yo 12lb **14 Ran SP% 123.9**
Speed ratings (Par 100): **99,99,97,97,96 95,95,90,89,88 84,84,79,76**WIN: Ardingly £1.40, Controversy £2.00 PL: A £1.10, C £1.30 EX: A/C £5.60, C/A £7.60 CSF: A/C £4.69 C/A £5.10 toteswingers 1&1 £2.00, 1&3 £2.40, 1&3 £5.10 CSF £5.10 TOTE £2.00: £1.30, £3.70; EX 7.60 Trifecta £30.90 A/C/Are You Mine: £22.80, C/A/AYM £30.90. Pool of £1430.68 -27 Owner.
Owner Mrs Fitri Hay **Bred** Ben Sangster **Trained** Newmarket, Suffolk

FOCUS
Previous form was thin on the ground in this fillies' maiden race which was run at just a steady pace to past halfway. The two dead-heaters were one-two throughout.

3470 WINNERS ARE WELCOME AT BETDAQ H'CAP (LONDON MIDDLE DISTANCE SERIES QUALIFIER) 1m 3f (P)
7:10 (7:10) (Class 4) (0-85,84) 3-Y-O £4,690 (£1,395; £697; £348) Stalls Low

Form RPR
1-22 1 **Rundell**[16] 2927 3-9-3 **80**..... RichardHughes 7 92
(Richard Hannon) *hld up in last pair: prog fr 5f out to trck ldrs 3f out: shkn up over 2f out: led over 1f out: edgd rt and lft but styd on wl* 5/2[2]
01-3 2 1 ¾ **Autun (USA)**[33] 2416 3-9-1 **78**..... TomQueally 8 87
(Lady Cecil) *hld up in last pair: rdn jst over 2f out: prog over 1f out: clsng whn hung rt jst ins fnl f: styd on to take 2nd nr fin* 8/1
012 3 ¾ **Masquerading (IRE)**[7] 3214 3-9-5 **82**..... TedDurcan 5 90
(David Lanigan) *s.i.s: hld up in tch: trckd ldrs over 2f out: rdn over 1f out: kpt on but nvr gng pce to chal* 4/1[3]
044 4 ½ **She's Late**[15] 2953 3-8-13 **76**..... WilliamBuick 3 83
(John Gosden) *trckd ldr: led over 7f out: rdn and pressed over 2f out: hdd and one pce over 1f out* 10/1
1-23 5 2 ¼ **Gioia Di Vita**[25] 2651 3-8-10 **73**..... MartinHarley 6 76
(Marco Botti) *trckd ldrs: briefly moved up to chal 8f out: wnt 2nd 4f out: rdn to chal over 2f out: upsides over 1f out: wknd ins fnl f* 14/1
1-53 6 ¾ **Zeus Magic**[44] 2086 3-8-13 **76**..... LiamKeniry 4 77
(David Elsworth) *trckd ldrs: lost pl over 4f out: in last and struggling over 2f out: plugged on fnl f* 10/1
1 7 2 ¾ **Air Of Glory (IRE)**[15] 2952 3-9-7 **84**..... MickaelBarzalona 2 80
(Saeed bin Suroor) *led: tried to stdy pce after 3f but sn hdd: lost pl fr 4f out: wl btn over 1f out* 9/4[1]

2m 19.68s (-2.22) **Going Correction** +0.075s/f (Slow) **7 Ran SP% 115.3**
Speed ratings (Par 101): **111,109,109,108,107 106,104**
toteswingers 1&2 £2.80, 2&3 £4.00, 1&3 £1.20 CSF £22.92 CT £77.68 TOTE £4.00: £3.40, £5.30; EX 20.70 Trifecta £49.60 Pool: £1264.55 - 19.10 winning units..
Owner Mrs James Wigan **Bred** Mrs James Wigan **Trained** East Everleigh, Wilts

FOCUS
Rather a stop-start pace before they sprinted off the home turn. The eventual one-two both came from the back of the field.

3471 BRITISH STALLION STUDS SUPPORTING BRITISH RACING EBF MAIDEN FILLIES' STKS 7f (P)
7:40 (7:40) (Class 5) 2-Y-O £2,911 (£866; £432; £216) Stalls Low

Form RPR
1 **Feedyah (USA)** 2-9-0 0..... MickaelBarzalona 3 83+
(Saeed bin Suroor) *t.k.h: hld up: smooth prog over 2f out: pushed into ld jst ins fnl f: readily drew away* 5/4[1]
2 2 1 ¾ **Dancealot**[22] 2744 2-9-0 0..... HayleyTurner 6 76
(Clive Brittain) *pressed ldr: led 1/2-way: shkn up over 2f out: styd on but hdd and brushed aside jst ins fnl f* 5/1[3]
6 3 1 **Gender Agenda**[33] 2419 2-9-0 0..... TomQueally 8 73
(Michael Bell) *trckd ldrs: wnt 2nd over 2f out: tried to chal over 1f out: kpt on same pce* 16/1

4 1 1/4 **Joohaina (IRE)** 2-9-0 0 ... AdamKirby 5 70
(Marco Botti) *trckd ldrs: shkn up to go 3rd 2f out: tried to cl over 1f out: one pce after* **10/1**

5 2 **Mawzoona** 2-9-0 0 ... MartinHarley 1 65
(Mick Channon) *hld up in last pair: pushed along over 2f out: no imp but nt disgracd* **33/1**

6 nk **Enraptured (IRE)** 2-9-0 0 ... WilliamBuick 2 64
(John Gosden) *chsd ldrs: hanging bdly lft bnd over 4f out to 3f out and dropped to last pair: no ch after: kpt on again fr over 1f out* **9/4²**

7 3 3/4 **Soiree D'Ete** 2-9-0 0 ... LukeMorris 7 54
(Sir Mark Prescott Bt) *rn green in last pair and pushed along over 5f out: outpcd over 2f out: no ch after* **50/1**

8 2 **Acquaint (IRE)** 2-9-0 0 ... RichardHughes 4 49
(Richard Hannon) *led at sedate pce to 1/2-way: lost 2nd and wknd over 2f out* **16/1**

1m 29.34s (3.34) **Going Correction** +0.075s/f (Slow) 8 Ran SP% **117.6**
Speed ratings (Par 90): **83,81,79,78,76 75,71,69**
toteswingers 1&2 £2.50, 2&3 £10.60, 1&3 £7.90 CSF £8.48 TOTE £1.80: £1.20, £1.60, £3.10; EX 6.20 Trifecta £52.20 Pool: £1129.78 - 16.21 winning units..
Owner Godolphin **Bred** Darley **Trained** Newmarket, Suffolk

FOCUS
Only two of these had previous experience and they finished second and third behind an impressive newcomer. The form has been given a chance but may overplay the third.

3472 COMMISSION FREE 1ST MONTH AT BETDAQ H'CAP 7f (P)
8:10 (8:12) (Class 4) (0-85,85) 3-Y-0+ **£4,690** (£1,395; £697; £348) **Stalls** Low

Form RPR

-521 1 **Labienus**[14] 2984 3-9-5 **85** ... TedDurcan 7 97
(David Lanigan) *hld up towards rr: prog on inner jst over 2f out: chsd ldr over 1f out: drvn and r.o wl to ld last 100yds* **3/1²**

1-00 2 1/2 **Don Libre**[5] 3274 4-9-9 **80** ... TomQueally 3 93
(Paul Cole) *led: rdn 2f out: edgd rt over 1f out: hdd last 100yds: styd on but hld* **8/1**

3-11 3 2 **If So**[22] 2745 4-9-7 **78** ... HayleyTurner 2 86
(James Fanshawe) *trckd ldrs in 5th: prog 2f out to chse ldng pair over 1f out: styd on and sn clr of rest but no imp last 150yds* **8/1**

0502 4 4 1/2 **Mr David (USA)**[9] 3153 6-9-10 **81** ... (b) FergusSweeney 6 77
(Jamie Osborne) *hld up in rr: pushed along in last 3f out: rdn and stl last over 1f out: passed 7 rivals fnl f to take modest 4th nr fin* **14/1**

2502 5 1 **Ocean Legend (IRE)**[7] 3215 8-9-5 **76** ... AdamKirby 9 69
(Tony Carroll) *hld up towards rr on outer: shkn up over 2f out: sme prog to take modest 4th 1f out tl nr fin: n.d* **14/1**

51- 6 1/2 **Utterance**[379] 2799 4-9-11 **82** ... WilliamBuick 1 74
(John Gosden) *t.k.h: trckd ldng pair: rdn to dispute 2nd wl over 1f out: wknd qckly sn after: b.b.v* **9/4¹**

1050 7 2 **Ashamaly**[19] 2844 3-9-5 **85** ... NeilCallan 10 68
(James Tate) *s.i.s: hld up in rr: brief effrt on inner 2f out: sn no prog and wl btn* **16/1**

4323 8 3/4 **Exceedexpectations (IRE)**[7] 3192 4-9-7 **78** ... LiamKeniry 11 62
(Conor Dore) *chsd ldr to wl over 1f out: wknd qckly* **25/1**

61-4 9 nk **Pivotal Movement**[22] 2738 3-8-11 **77** ... RichardHughes 8 58
(Richard Hannon) *wl in tch in midfield: rdn over 2f out: wknd wl over 1f out* **6/1³**

-445 10 1/2 **Surge Ahead (IRE)**[33] 2408 3-8-10 **76** ... LukeMorris 5 55
(Ed Walker) *a towards rr: rdn and struggling over 2f out* **25/1**

0565 11 3 **Chilli Green**[29] 2531 6-9-4 **82** ... (p) ShelleyBirkett(7) 4 56
(Julia Feilden) *trckd ldng pair tl wknd over 2f out* **50/1**

1m 24.8s (-1.20) **Going Correction** +0.075s/f (Slow)
WFA 3 from 4yo+ 9lb 11 Ran SP% **121.1**
Speed ratings (Par 105): **109,108,106,101,99 99,97,96,95,95 91**
toteswingers 1&2 £4.80, 2&3 £7.40, 1&3 £7.40 CSF £27.90 CT £183.48 TOTE £3.90: £1.90, £2.40, £2.40; EX 37.90 Trifecta £323.10 Pool: £850.00 - 1.97 winning units..
Owner B E Nielsen **Bred** Mrs S L Gibson Fleming **Trained** Upper Lambourn, Berks

FOCUS
A handicap for useful types.

3473 EDWARD KIDGER H'CAP 2m (P)
8:40 (8:42) (Class 6) (0-65,65) 4-Y-0+ **£1,940** (£577; £288; £144) **Stalls** Low

Form RPR

1144 1 **Arashi**[14] 2980 7-9-7 **65** ... (v) NeilCallan 2 74+
(Derek Shaw) *hld up in last: gd prog fr 3f out to ld over 1f out: drvn and styd on wl* **3/1¹**

-400 2 1 3/4 **Toughness Danon**[23] 2710 7-9-2 **60** ... (t) StevieDonohoe 5 67
(Ian Williams) *hld up in midfield: prog on outer 5f out to press ldrs over 3f out: rdn to ld over 2f out: hung lft and hdd over 1f out: ended against nr side rail and kpt on to take 2nd again nr fin* **7/2²**

3365 3 1/2 **Sommersturm (GER)**[13] 3012 9-9-4 **62** ... (t) AdamKirby 4 68
(David Evans) *hld up in midfield: rdn and prog over 2f out but wnr had already gone past: styd on u.p fnl f* **7/1³**

3013 4 1/2 **Boston Blue**[14] 2980 6-8-13 **57** ... JimCrowley 14 63
(Tony Carroll) *trckd ldr 6f: styd prom: rdn to chal and upsides over 1f out: edgd lft and one pce* **3/1¹**

/66- 5 1 3/4 **Lombok**[28] 3961 7-8-13 **64** ... (v) JayneFarwell(7) 12 68
(Gary Moore) *t.k.h in midfield: prog on outer over 3f out: str reminder 2f out and then unbalanced: one pce after* **50/1**

0/55 6 1/2 **Fair Breeze**[21] 1080 6-7-13 **46** oh1 ... SimonPearce(3) 6 49
(Richard Phillips) *prom: rdn over 2f out: tried to chal wl over 1f out: fdd fnl f* **20/1**

5400 7 6 **If What And Maybe**[26] 2642 5-7-13 **46** oh1 ... (p) RyanPowell(3) 11 42
(John Ryan) *dwlt: hld up tl quick move after 4f to press ldr after 6f: rdn to ld 4f out: hdd over 2f out: wknd over 1f out* **50/1**

0-00 8 2 **Suhailah**[21] 2777 7-8-2 **46** oh1 ... LukeMorris 10 39
(Michael Attwater) *a in mdifield: wknd over 2f out* **66/1**

3005 9 3/4 **Petersboden**[7] 3213 4-7-11 **46** oh1 ... NathanAlison(5) 1 39
(Michael Blanshard) *hld up in last trio: pushed along and lft bhd fr over 2f out* **20/1**

0650 10 5 **Dream Prospector**[19] 2828 4-9-4 **62** ... (b¹) FergusSweeney 9 49
(James Evans) *t.k.h: hld up in last trio: pushed along and lft bhd fr over 2f out* **7/1³**

10-0 11 5 **Phantom Ranch**[29] 2545 4-8-7 **51** ... HayleyTurner 8 32
(Alastair Lidderdale) *trckd ldrs tl shkn up and wknd wl over 2f out* **25/1**

00-0 12 20 **Gilded Age**[21] 1670 7-9-7 **65** ... (tp) IanMongan 13 22
(Chris Gordon) *led at mostly pedestrian pce: rdn and hdd 4f out: wknd qckly: t.o* **20/1**

3m 36.8s (6.70) **Going Correction** +0.075s/f (Slow) 12 Ran SP% **120.8**
Speed ratings (Par 101): **86,85,84,84,83 83,80,79,79,76 74,64**
toteswingers 1&2 £7.50, 2&3 £9.30, 1&3 £6.30 CSF £12.66 CT £69.53 TOTE £2.40: £1.70, £1.30, £2.10; EX 22.30 Trifecta £102.80 Pool: £689.55 - 5.03 winning units..
Owner Philip Derbyshire **Bred** Wyck Hall Stud Ltd **Trained** Sproxton, Leics

FOCUS
A modest stayers' handicap. Despite the very steady pace until the final half-mile the winner still managed to come from last to first.

3474 BETDAQ 1ST UK RACE COMMISSION FREE-EVERYDAY H'CAP 6f (P)
9:10 (9:11) (Class 4) (0-85,85) 3-Y-0 **£4,690** (£1,395; £697; £348) **Stalls** Low

Form RPR

-203 1 **Brazen**[11] 3104 3-9-7 **85** ... NeilCallan 1 93
(David Simcock) *racd freely: mde all: rdn and hung bdly lft 2f out: ended against nr side rail: drvn out fnl f: hld on* **7/2³**

2136 2 nk **Purcell (IRE)**[32] 2452 3-9-6 **84** ... JimmyFortune 3 91
(Andrew Balding) *cl up: chsd wnr wl over 2f out: hung bdly lft wl over 1f out and ended towards nr side rail: drvn and clsd fnl f: jst hld* **3/1²**

12-0 3 3/4 **Agerzam**[46] 2022 3-9-7 **85** ... WilliamBuick 5 92+
(Roger Varian) *t.k.h: in tch on outer: shkn up over 2f out: trying to cl whn hmpd twice over 1f out: swtchd rt and styd on fnl f: nvr able to chal* **6/1**

221- 4 2 1/4 **Red Explorer (USA)**[330] 4419 3-9-0 **78** ... SteveDrowne 4 75
(Charles Hills) *chsd wnr: pushed along 1/2-way: sn lost 2nd: nt qckn 2f out: one pce after* **12/1**

41-5 5 5 **Inka Surprise (IRE)**[23] 2726 3-9-3 **81** ... JimCrowley 6 62
(Ralph Beckett) *hld up in last: rdn and no rspnse over 2f out: sn wl btn* **5/4¹**

1m 12.46s (-0.64) **Going Correction** +0.075s/f (Slow) 5 Ran SP% **113.6**
Speed ratings (Par 101): **107,106,105,102,95**
CSF £14.65 TOTE £3.40: £1.50, £2.00; EX 9.70 Trifecta £39.90 Pool: £687.66 - 12.91 winning units..
Owner Al Asayl Bloodstock Ltd **Bred** Lostford Manor Stud Ltd **Trained** Newmarket, Suffolk

FOCUS
The majority of these had something to prove and in the end it was an unsatisfactory contest.
T/Plt: £44.00 to a £1 stake. Pool of £55311.76 - 915.67 winning tickets T/Qpdt: £13.90 to a £1 stake. Pool of £3628.26 - 191.90 winning tickets. JN

2985 RIPON (R-H)
Wednesday, June 19

OFFICIAL GOING: Good to firm (good in places; 8.6)
Wind: Light haflf behind Weather: Fine & dry

3475 ELAINE WILES LIFETIME IN RACING APPRENTICE CLASSIFIED (S) STKS 6f
6:50 (6:50) (Class 6) 3-4-Y-0 **£2,587** (£770; £384; £192) **Stalls** High

Form RPR

0-00 1 **Planetex (IRE)**[40] 2239 4-9-7 70 ... [1] OisinMurphy 2 66
(John Quinn) *sn trcking ldr: cl up 1/2-way: rdn to ld appr fnl f: kpt on* **11/4¹**

4-54 2 3/4 **Legal Bond**[26] 2613 4-9-7 61 ... (p) JoshDoyle 4 64
(David O'Meara) *led: pushed along 1/2-way: rdn 2f out: hdd appr fnl f: kpt on same pce towards fin* **3/1²**

-404 3 2 1/4 **Dream Vale (IRE)**[15] 2959 3-9-0 65 ... CameronHardie 3 54
(Tim Easterby) *trckd ldrs: hdwy on outer over 2f out: rdn wl over 1f out: one pce fnl f* **11/4¹**

0303 4 3 **Shamrocked (IRE)**[26] 2613 4-9-7 66 ... EireannCagney 6 47
(Ollie Pears) *trckd ldrs: pushed along and outpcd wl over 2f out: sn rdn and no imp* **3/1²**

-005 5 1/2 **Let Me In (IRE)**[26] 2613 3-9-0 44 ... JackGarritty 7 43
(Nigel Tinkler) *dwlt and in rr: hdwy and pushed along on inner over 2f out: sn rdn and kpt on fnl f: nrst fin* **18/1³**

000 6 2 1/2 **Busy Bimbo (IRE)**[11] 3091 4-9-7 40 ... NicolaGrundy 5 37
(Alan Berry) *towards rr: rdn along 2f out: sn no imp* **100/1**

5560 7 7 **Nors The Panic**[7] 3198 3-9-0 45 ... (e) LisaTodd 1 13
(Richard Guest) *chsd ldrs on outer: rdn along 1/2-way: sn edgd lft and wknd* **66/1**

1m 11.96s (-1.04) **Going Correction** -0.225s/f (Firm)
WFA 3 from 4yo 7lb 7 Ran SP% **111.1**
Speed ratings (Par 101): **97,96,93,89,88 85,75**
toteswingers 1&2 £1.80, 2&3 £6.00, 1&3 £1.20 CSF £10.68 TOTE £3.40: £1.10, £1.60; EX 19.00 Trifecta £37.00 Pool: £1133.62 - 22.96 winning units..There was no bid for the winner.
Owner Ross Harmon **Bred** Mrs Diane Williams **Trained** Settrington, N Yorks

FOCUS
Fast ground as advertised, Micky Fenton calling it "quick but safe" after riding in the second. This was a weak race, confined to apprentices who had not ridden a winner prior to Sunday. The form is rated negatively.

3476 BONDGATE MAIDEN AUCTION STKS 5f
7:20 (7:21) (Class 5) 2-Y-0 **£3,234** (£962; £481; £240) **Stalls** High

Form RPR

203 1 **Hello Beautiful (IRE)**[19] 2830 2-9-0 0 ... PJMcDonald 4 67
(Ann Duffield) *cl up: chal 2f out: rdn ent fnl f: sn led: drvn out* **5/2¹**

2 1 **Margrets Gift** 2-9-0 0 ... MickyFenton 1 63
(Tim Easterby) *hdwy on outer 1/2-way: sn chsng ldng pair: rdn over 1f out: kpt on ins fnl f: tk 2nd nr line* **7/2²**

0 3 hd **Emily Davison (IRE)**[18] 2856 2-9-0 0 ... RoystonFfrench 8 63
(David C Griffiths) *led: rdn along 1 1/2f out: drvn and hdd ins fnl f: one pce towards fin* **20/1**

65 4 3 3/4 **Noble Reach**[30] 2502 2-8-7 0 ... JordanNason(7) 2 50
(Geoffrey Harker) *wnt rt s and towards rr: hdwy on outer whn hmpd 2f out: sn rdn and styd on wl fnl f: nrst fin* **33/1**

3 5 1/2 **Goadby**[13] 3009 2-9-0 0 ... PaulQuinn 6 48+
(John Holt) *dwlt and towards rr: hdwy 1/2-way: rdn along wl over 1f out: sn one pce* **14/1**

463 6 1/2 **Will To Survive (IRE)**[11] 3084 2-9-5 0 ... (e¹) RobbieFitzpatrick 7 51
(Richard Guest) *prom: pushed along bef 1/2-way: sn rdn and wknd wl over 1f out* **10/1**

7 2 1/2 **Lady Alaska (IRE)** 2-9-0 0 ... MichaelO'Connell 9 37
(John Quinn) *trckd ldrs on inner: rdn along 2f out: sn wknd* **15/2³**

8 3/4 **Camatini (IRE)** 2-9-0 0 ... PaulMulrennan 3 34
(Michael Dods) *a in rr* **7/2²**

24 **F** **Cheeky Peta'S**[14] 2993 2-9-0 0 .... JamesSullivan 5
(James Given) *dwlt: sn trcking ldrs: edgd rt, clipped heels and fell 2f out* **18/1**

1m 0.47s (0.47) **Going Correction** -0.225s/f (Firm) **9** Ran SP% **113.5**
Speed ratings (Par 93): **87,85,85,79,78 77,73,72,**
toteswingers 1&2 £3.70, 2&3 £16.70, 1&3 £13.10 CSF £10.95 TOTE £2.20: £1.02, £3.40, £9.20; EX 16.40 Trifecta £195.30 Pool: £1015.69 - 3.89 winning units..
Owner Nick Allenby **Bred** Peter Molony **Trained** Constable Burton, N Yorks

FOCUS
A very ordinary maiden which went to the form pick, whose debut effort sets the level.

3477 RIPON-RACES.CO.UK H'CAP 1m 1f 170y
7:50 (7:50) (Class 4) (0-85,83) 4-Y-O+ **£4,851** (£1,443; £721; £360) **Stalls** Low

Form RPR
0504 **1** **San Cassiano (IRE)**[7] 3204 6-8-12 **74** .... JamesSullivan 9 87
(Ruth Carr) *mde all: rdn clr wl over 1f out: readily* **9/2**[2]
-000 **2** 4 ½ **Maybeagrey**[29] 2555 4-8-5 **67** .... PaulQuinn 6 71
(Tim Easterby) *hld up and bhd: pushed along over 3f out: rdn 2f out: hdwy on inner over 1f out: squeezed through and drvn ent fnl f: kpt on: no ch w wnr* **25/1**
-035 **3** nk **Demolition**[21] 2766 9-9-6 **82** .... BarryMcHugh 1 85
(Noel Wilson) *hld up towards rr: pushed along 4f out: hdwy on inner 3f out: rdn 2f out: chsd wnr over 1f out: drvn and edgd lft ent fnl f: sn no imp: lost 2nd towards fin* **8/1**
0452 **4** 4 ½ **Kickingthelilly**[26] 2639 4-9-2 **78** .... ChrisCatlin 7 72
(Rae Guest) *hld up in rr: hdwy on outer over 3f out: rdn to chse ldrs 2f out: sn drvn and one pce* **7/1**
5035 **5** ¾ **Moccasin (FR)**[7] 3204 4-9-0 **83** .... JordanNason(7) 8 75
(Geoffrey Harker) *sn trcking wnr: cl up on outer 1/2-way: rdn along over 2f out: drvn wl over 1f out: sn one pce* **6/1**[3]
-121 **6** 2 ½ **Never Forever**[18] 2889 4-8-10 **72** .... PJMcDonald 2 71+
(George Moore) *trckd ldrs: effrt 3f out and sn pushed along: effrt 2f out: nt clr run and swtchd rt over 1f out: sn rdn: n.m.r and wknd* **7/2**[1]
-140 **7** 1 **Gold Show**[39] 2277 4-8-9 **71** .... PaulMulrennan 5 56
(Edwin Tuer) *trckd ldrs: pushed along 3f out: rdn whn n.m.r wl over 1f out: sn wknd* **9/1**
1132 **8** ½ **Eutropius (IRE)**[30] 2515 4-8-12 **74** .... RussKennemore 4 58
(Alan Swinbank) *trckd ldrs: hdwy to trck wnr 1/2-way: pushed along 3f out: rdn 2f out: sn drvn and wknd over 1f out* **9/2**[2]

2m 0.87s (-4.53) **Going Correction** -0.30s/f (Firm) **8** Ran SP% **110.3**
Speed ratings (Par 105): **106,102,102,98,97 95,95,94**
toteswingers 1&2 £23.80, 2&3 £35.10, 1&3 £3.20 CSF £94.74 CT £819.71 TOTE £4.60: £2.30, £3.40, £2.10; EX 20.40 Trifecta £223.80 Pool: £741.65 - 2.48 winning units..
Owner Mitchell,Jackson,Shaw,Joseph & Martin **Bred** Peter Savill **Trained** Huby, N Yorks

FOCUS
A fair handicap run in a time inside the standard. The form is rated around the winner, who enjoyed an uncontested lead.

3478 WELLS MEMORIAL CHALLENGE TROPHY H'CAP 6f
8:20 (8:20) (Class 3) (0-95,87) 3-Y-O **£7,561** (£2,263; £1,131; £566; £282) **Stalls** High

Form RPR
5-02 **1** **Pipers Note**[12] 3066 3-8-12 **78** .... AmyRyan 6 91
(Richard Whitaker) *hld up: smooth hdwy to trck ldrs 2f out: effrt and squeezed through over 1f out: led ent fnl f: rdn clr and kpt on strly* **7/2**[2]
6321 **2** 3 **Nurpur (IRE)**[11] 3091 3-8-8 **74** .... GrahamGibbons 5 77
(David O'Meara) *trckd ldrs: hdwy and cl up 1/2-way: rdn and hung lft wl over 1f out: drvn to chse wnr and edgd lft fnl f: sn no imp* **2/1**[1]
1-40 **3** 2 **Rhagori Aur**[45] 2039 3-8-9 **80** .... JustinNewman(5) 2 79+
(Bryan Smart) *dwlt sltly: plld hrd and hdwy to ld after 1f: rdn along and hdd whn hmpd 1 1/2f out: kpt on one pce* **9/1**
0-60 **4** ½ **Bachotheque (IRE)**[12] 3066 3-9-3 **83** .... MickyFenton 8 78
(Tim Easterby) *trckd ldrs whn n.m.r on inner and lost pl after 1f: in rr: rdn along and sltly outpcd 2f out: styd on fnl f: nrst fin* **10/1**
-110 **5** nk **Mayfield Girl (IRE)**[33] 2430 3-9-7 **87** .... PaulMulrennan 4 83+
(Mel Brittain) *cl up: rdn along 2f out: grad wknd* **12/1**
0060 **6** ½ **Jillnextdoor (IRE)**[11] 3097 3-9-4 **84** .... SamHitchcott 7 77
(Mick Channon) *led 1f: cl up on tl rdn to ld again 1 1/2f out: drvn and hdd ent fnl f: sn wknd* **8/1**
0-32 **7** shd **Shrimper Roo**[14] 2987 3-8-12 **78** .... JamesSullivan 3 71
(Tim Easterby) *trckd ldrs: hdwy on outer and cl up 1/2-way: rdn 2f out and sn wknd* **4/1**[3]

1m 11.32s (-1.68) **Going Correction** -0.225s/f (Firm) **7** Ran SP% **113.4**
Speed ratings (Par 103): **102,98,95,94,94 93,93**
toteswingers 1&2 £1.10, 2&3 £28.50, 1&3 £13.10 CSF £10.76 CT £55.39 TOTE £3.50: £1.40, £1.90; EX 12.60 Trifecta £100.20 Pool: £803.44 - 6.01 winning units..
Owner Six Iron Partnership & Partner **Bred** Wadacre Stud **Trained** Scarcroft, W Yorks

FOCUS
A decent little sprint, but quite a messy race and the time was modest. The winner confirmed his Pontefract impression.

3479 SIS LIVE MAIDEN STKS 6f
8:50 (8:51) (Class 5) 3-Y-O **£3,234** (£962; £481; £240) **Stalls** High

Form RPR
46-2 **1** **Strictly Silca**[81] 1243 3-9-0 76 .... (v) SamHitchcott 11 81
(Mick Channon) *trckd ldr: effrt to chal wl over 1f out: sn led and rdn clr: readily* **13/8**[1]
24-0 **2** 6 **Funding Deficit (IRE)**[12] 3066 3-9-5 73 .... GrahamGibbons 5 70
(David Barron) *led: rdn along 2f out: hdd over 1f out: sn one pce* **7/4**[2]
3 11 **Helterskelter Girl** 3-9-0 0 .... PJMcDonald 1 27
(Ann Duffield) *chsd ldrs: rdn along over 2f out: kpt on u.p to take remote 3rd fnl f: n.d* **6/1**[3]
0 **4** ½ **Card High (IRE)**[23] 2719 3-9-5 0 .... AmyRyan 3 30
(Wilf Storey) *towards rr: pushed along 1/2-way: sme hdwy fnl 2f: n.d* **100/1**
5 shd **Duke Of Grazeon (IRE)** 3-9-5 0 .... RoystonFfrench 4 30
(Mrs Ilka Gansera-Leveque) *s.i.s and bhd: pushed along 1/2-way: rdn and sme hdwy fnl 2f: n.d* **18/1**
6 shd **True That (IRE)** 3-9-5 0 .... PhillipMakin 6 29
(David Nicholls) *chsd ldng pair: rdn along over 2f out: drvn wl over 1f out: sn wknd* **12/1**
7 1 ¼ **Manatee Bay** 3-9-5 0 .... PaulMulrennan 8 25
(David Nicholls) *dwlt: a in rr* **9/1**
60- **8** 11 **Indastar**[376] 2873 3-9-5 0 .... ChrisCatlin 7
(John Weymes) *a in rr: bhd fr 1/2-way* **50/1**

0-6 **9** 4 **Partner's Gold (IRE)**[11] 3086 3-9-5 0 .... TomEaves 10
(Alan Berry) *in tch: rdn along bef 1/2-way: sn wknd* **125/1**

1m 11.19s (-1.81) **Going Correction** -0.225s/f (Firm) **9** Ran SP% **115.4**
Speed ratings (Par 99): **103,95,80,79,79 79,77,63,57**
toteswingers 1&2 £2.40, 2&3 £4.90, 1&3 £3.90 CSF £4.70 TOTE £1.80: £1.10, £1.50, £1.50; EX 2.80 Trifecta £10.00 Pool: £545.11 - 40.63 winning units..
Owner Aldridge Racing Partnership **Bred** Aldridge Racing Partnership **Trained** West Ilsley, Berks

FOCUS
A maiden lacking depth and the first two dominated both the market and the race. Straightforward form. It was the quickest of the three C&D times.

3480 FOSSGATE H'CAP 1m 4f 10y
9:20 (9:20) (Class 5) (0-75,74) 4-Y-O+ **£3,234** (£962; £481; £240) **Stalls** Low

Form RPR
0454 **1** **Tetbury (USA)**[18] 2855 4-9-6 **73** .... GrahamGibbons 5 82
(David O'Meara) *madle virtually all: jnd and pushed along 3f out: rdn 2f out: drvn ent fnl f and styd on strly* **9/4**[2]
3-00 **2** 1 ¾ **Choisan (IRE)**[23] 2706 4-9-7 **74** .... MickyFenton 7 80
(Tim Easterby) *a trcking wnr: hdwy 3f out: cl up over 2f out: sn rdn and ev ch tl drvn and one pce ins fnl f* **11/1**
-113 **3** ¾ **Bright Applause**[23] 2706 5-9-6 **73** .... BarryMcHugh 1 78
(Tracy Waggott) *trckd ldrs on inner: hdwy 3f out: swtchd lft and rdn wl over 1f out: drvn ent fnl f: kpt on same pce* **7/4**[1]
-006 **4** 1 **Alsahil (USA)**[20] 2798 7-9-0 **67** .... (p) AndrewMullen 2 70
(Micky Hammond) *in tch on inner: hdwy over 3f out: rdn along wl over 2f out: drvn over 1f out: kpt on fnl f* **33/1**
006 **5** nk **Layline (IRE)**[21] 2775 6-9-3 **70** .... PhillipMakin 6 73
(Gay Kelleway) *dwlt and in rr: hdwy over 3f out: rdn to chse ldrs 2f out: sn drvn and one pce* **11/1**
260- **6** 1 ¾ **Authentication**[236] 7380 4-8-12 **65** .... (t) PaulMulrennan 8 65
(Mel Brittain) *t.k.h early: trckd ldng pair: pushed along 3f out: rdn over 2f out: grad wknd* **16/1**
10-0 **7** 1 **Fossgate**[29] 2552 12-9-1 **68** .... AmyRyan 3 66
(James Bethell) *s.i.s and bhd: hdwy 3f out: rdn along 2f out: n.d* **14/1**
23-6 **8** 10 **Up Ten Down Two (IRE)**[46] 2009 4-8-11 **71** .... MatthewHopkins(7) 4 53
(Michael Easterby) *trckd ldrs: pushed along 3f out: rdn over 2f out and sn wknd* **13/2**[3]

2m 36.95s (0.25) **Going Correction** -0.30s/f (Firm) **8** Ran SP% **112.6**
Speed ratings (Par 103): **87,85,85,84,84 83,82,75**
toteswingers 1&2 £22.10, 2&3 £5.50, 1&3 £2.00 CSF £26.17 CT £50.88 TOTE £3.30: £2.20, £1.90, £1.10; EX 33.40 Trifecta £49.30 Pool: £595.90 - 9.05 winning units..
Owner Ebor Racing Club II **Bred** Juddmonte Farms Inc **Trained** Nawton, N Yorks
■ Stewards' Enquiry : Graham Gibbons two-day ban: use of whip (3-4 July)

FOCUS
They went a moderate pace in this ordinary handicap and the first three filled the same positions virtually throughout. The winner is getting his act together for O'Meara and will still be on a good mark after this.

T/Plt: £16.40 to a £1 stake. Pool of £76509.93 - 3390.94 winning tickets T/Qpdt: £5.60 to a £1 stake. Pool of £5340.36 - 699.70 winning tickets JR

3455 ASCOT (R-H)
Thursday, June 20

OFFICIAL GOING: Good to firm (stands' side 9.8, centre 10.1, far side 10.1, round 9.3)
Rail on Round course approximately 3yds out from 9f to home straight adding 6yds to Old Mile, 9yds to 10f and 12yds to races of 12f plus.
Wind: Light, half behind Weather: Overcast

3481 NORFOLK STKS (GROUP 2) 5f
2:30 (2:32) (Class 1) 2-Y-O
£45,368 (£17,200; £8,608; £4,288; £2,152; £1,080) **Stalls** Centre

Form RPR
1 **No Nay Never (USA)**[55] 2-9-1 0 .... (b) JRosario 8 109+
(Wesley A Ward, U.S.A) *str: powerful: lw: awkward leaving stalls: racd keenly and sn rcvrd to ld: restrained and hdd 1/2-way but styd w ldrs: rdn and effrt whn hung rt over 1f out: led ins fnl f: r.o strly: impressive* **4/1**[2]
1 **2** 1 **Coach House (IRE)**[26] 2675 2-9-1 0 .... JosephO'Brien 4 104
(A P O'Brien, Ire) *lengthy: str: hld up in tch in midfield: hdwy and chsd ldrs 2f out: rdn and ev ch over 1f out: drvn and nt quite pce of wnr fnl 100yds: kpt on to hold 2nd* **9/4**[1]
41 **3** hd **Wind Fire (USA)**[28] 2601 2-8-12 0 .... JamieSpencer 1 100
(David Brown) *hld up in tch towards rr: hdwy travelling wl 2f out: rdn and effrt to chse ldrs ent fnl f: kpt on same pce u.p fnl 100yds* **16/1**
01 **4** 1 ¼ **Ambiance (IRE)**[16] 2955 2-9-1 0 .... MartinHarley 3 99
(Mick Channon) *leggy: chsd ldrs: hdwy to ld 1/2-way: drvn over 1f out: hdd ins fnl f: no ex fnl 100yds: wknd towards fin* **40/1**
1 **5** hd **Emirates Flyer**[20] 2823 2-9-1 0 .... SilvestreDeSousa 2 98
(Saeed bin Suroor) *athletic: str: hld up towards rr: rdn and effrt 2f out: hdwy u.p over 1f out: kpt on ins fnl f: no threat to wnr* **16/1**
42 **6** 3 **Royal Mezyan (IRE)**[6] 3295 2-9-1 0 .... SebSanders 5 87
(William Haggas) *lw: wl in tch in midfield: clsd to chse ldrs and drvn 2f out: no ex ent fnl f: wknd fnl 150yds* **28/1**
41 **7** 1 ¼ **Green Door (IRE)**[46] 2048 2-9-1 0 .... JimCrowley 12 83
(Olly Stevens) *in tch in midfield: rdn and effrt over 2f out: unable qck over 1f out: wknd fnl f* **9/1**
11 **8** nk **Saayerr**[17] 2933 2-9-1 0 .... LiamJones 9 82
(William Haggas) *str: in tch in midfield: rdn and outpcd 2f out: swtchd rt over 1f out: no threat to ldrs and continued edging rt fnl f* **9/1**
3 **9** ½ **Oriental Relation (IRE)**[31] 2497 2-9-1 0 .... GrahamLee 14 80
(James Given) *unf: s.i.s: a towards rr: rdn 1/2-way: styd on past btn horses ent fnl f: nvr trbld ldrs* **100/1**
211 **10** nk **Legend Rising (IRE)**[6] 3267 2-9-1 0 .... RyanMoore 10 79
(Richard Hannon) *leggy: sn niggled along: dropped towards rr after 1f: drvn and no imp jst over 2f out: nvr trbld ldrs* **10/1**
1 **11** 1 ½ **Coulsty (IRE)**[24] 2712 2-9-1 0 .... RichardHughes 6 73
(Richard Hannon) *w'like: chsd ldr tl 1/2-way: sn rdn and struggling: wknd over 1f out: fdd fnl f* **7/1**[3]
12 1 ¼ **Extreme Supreme** 2-9-1 0 .... HarryBentley 13 69
(Derek Shaw) *w'like: broke wl enough: sn pushed along and dropped to rr: n.d but kpt on ins fnl f* **150/1**
514 **13** 1 ½ **Ifwecan**[19] 2863 2-9-1 0 .... JoeFanning 7 64
(Mark Johnston) *chsd ldrs: rdn and struggling 1/2-way: wknd wl over 1f out* **28/1**

1 **14** ¾ **Eccleston**[33] 2436 2-9-1 0 TonyHamilton 11 61
(Richard Fahey) *leggy: sn niggled along in midfield: rdn and struggling over 2f out: wknd over 1f out* **16/1**

58.8s (-1.70) **Going Correction** -0.10s/f (Good) 2y crse rec **14** Ran SP% **121.0**
Speed ratings (Par 105): **109,107,107,105,104 99,97,97,96,96 93,91,89,88**
toteswingers 1&2 £2.70, 2&3 £9.00, 1&3 £16.40 CSF £13.01 CT £137.50 TOTE £4.60: £1.90, £1.40, £5.40; EX 12.10 Trifecta £168.70 Pool: £20459.64 - 90.93 winning units..
Owner Mrs Paul Shanahan & Ice Wine Stable **Bred** Jayne Doi Johnson & David Sparrow **Trained** North America

FOCUS
The rail on the round course was positioned approximately 3yds out from 1m1f to the home straight, adding approximately the following: Old Mile 6yds, 1m2f 9yds and races of 1m4f-plus 12yds. There had been no rain by the time racing got going and, with the track drying all the time, the juvenile course record was lowered in this opening contest. They raced up the middle of the track. The winner rates a little above the solid average figure for the race, but could well rate a good bit higher. The runner-up brought solid pre-race form.

3482 RIBBLESDALE STKS (GROUP 2) (FILLIES) 1m 4f
3:05 (3:05) (Class 1) 3-Y-O

£85,065 (£32,250; £16,140; £8,040; £4,035; £2,025) Stalls Low

Form RPR
21 **1** **Riposte**[34] 2423 3-8-12 89 TomQueally 5 111
(Lady Cecil) *lw: s.s: racd keenly: hld up: hdwy wl over 2f out: qcknd to ld ent fnl 2f: edgd rt whn in command wl ins fnl f: r.o wl* **9/2**[2]

13 **2** 2¼ **Just Pretending (USA)**[25] 2689 3-8-12 107 SeamieHeffernan 10 107
(A P O'Brien, Ire) *w'like: scope: gd-bodied: racd keenly: hld up: hdwy 2f out but unable to go w wnr: rdn to take 2nd over 1f out: edgd rt ins fnl f: kpt on but no imp* **9/2**[2]

-241 **3** 1½ **Elik (IRE)**[28] 2586 3-8-12 97 RyanMoore 3 105
(Sir Michael Stoute) *lw: chsd ldrs: effrt over 2f out: sn ev ch: outpcd by wnr over 1f out: kpt on ins fnl f but hld* **9/2**[2]

12-1 **4** 1 **Winsili**[34] 2412 3-8-12 100 WilliamBuick 12 103
(John Gosden) *lw: hld up in rr: hdwy on outer 2f out: chalng for pls over 1f out: styd on same pce fnl 100yds* **3/1**[1]

0-1 **5** 1 **Waila**[55] 1813 3-8-12 86 KierenFallon 2 102
(Sir Michael Stoute) *lw: racd keenly: hld up: pushed along whn nt clr run and nt qckn over 2f out: keeping on u.p whn hung rt over 1f out: one pce ins fnl f* **7/1**[3]

2120 **6** 7 **Gertrude Versed**[20] 2842 3-8-12 90 FrankieDettori 1 91
(John Gosden) *racd keenly on inner: trckd ldrs: pushed along and nt qckn over 2f out: wkng whn carried rt jst over 1f out: wl btn fnl f* **12/1**

13-4 **7** 5 **Indigo Lady**[36] 2367 3-8-12 98 SilvestreDeSousa 8 83
(Peter Chapple-Hyam) *racd keenly w ldr tl rdn over 2f out: sn wknd* **16/1**

31 **8** 4 **Fersah (USA)**[24] 2713 3-8-12 83 PaulHanagan 4 76
(William Haggas) *lengthy: str: led: pushed along over 2f out: hdd ent fnl 2f: sn wknd* **20/1**

4-55 **9** 1 **Hollowina**[36] 2367 3-8-12 85 GrahamLee 9 75
(David Brown) *racd on outer: chsd ldrs: rdn 4f out: wknd ent fnl 3f: lft bhd 2f out* **33/1**

2m 29.41s (-3.09) **Going Correction** -0.025s/f (Good) **9** Ran SP% **113.3**
Speed ratings (Par 108): **109,107,106,105,105 100,97,94,93**
toteswingers 1&2 £4.10, 1&3 £4.30, 2&3 £5.20 CSF £24.55 CT £94.83 TOTE £5.50: £1.80, £1.40, £1.80; EX 22.90 Trifecta £127.90 Pool: £14714.53 - 86.22 winning units..
Owner K Abdullah **Bred** Juddmonte Farms Ltd **Trained** Newmarket, Suffolk
■ The first Royal Ascot success for Lady Cecil.
■ Stewards' Enquiry : Seamie Heffernan two-day ban: careless riding (4-5 July)

FOCUS
Not a strong race on paper, with the first two in the betting (Alive Alive Oh and The Lark) being withdrawn on account of the fast ground, leaving only two runners in the line-up rated in three figures. They were taken on by some lightly raced and well-bred maiden rivals though, among whom was Riposte, who ranks as an average winner of this race. The level of the form is pretty straightforward.

3483 GOLD CUP (BRITISH CHAMPIONS SERIES) (GROUP 1) 2m 4f
3:45 (3:45) (Class 1) 4-Y-O+

£198,485 (£75,250; £37,660; £18,760; £9,415; £4,725) Stalls Low

Form RPR
33-1 **1** **Estimate (IRE)**[50] 1920 4-8-11 108 RyanMoore 5 113
(Sir Michael Stoute) *lw: in tch: rdn and effrt over 2f out: chsd ldr 2f out: drvn to ld 1f out but hrd pressed: edgd lft u.p: battled on v gamely and holding runner-up towards fin* **7/2**[1]

55-4 **2** nk **Simenon (IRE)**[43] 2149 6-9-2 108 JohnnyMurtagh 16 115
(W P Mullins, Ire) *t.k.h: hld up in tch in midfield swtchd out lft and effrt over 2f out: hweadway whn pushed lft 2f out: drvn and str chal 1f out: carried sltly lft fnl 100yds: r.o wl but hld towards fin* **5/1**[3]

6-62 **3** 1 **Top Trip**[34] 2428 4-9-0 113 MickaelBarzalona 15 114
(F Doumen, France) *wl in tch in midfield: swtchd out lft and effrt 2f out: hdwy to press ldrs 1f out: keeping on same pce whn carried lft fnl 100yds: hld whn short of room towards fin* **7/1**

30-0 **4** 2 **Colour Vision (FR)**[21] 2810 5-9-2 114 (v[1]) SilvestreDeSousa 3 112
(Saeed bin Suroor) *s.i.s: t.k.h: hdwy to chse ldr after 2f tl 16f out: wnt 2nd again 9f out tl rdn to ld jst over 2f out: drvn and hdd 1f out: no ex and wknd fnl 100yds* **12/1**

12-1 **5** ½ **Altano (GER)**[32] 2492 7-9-2 112 (t) EPedroza 7 112
(A Wohler, Germany) *lw: hld up in tch in last trio: 13th and effrt on outer ent fnl 2f: stl only 12th but hdwy and hanging rt over 1f out: r.o strly ins fnl f: nt rch ldrs* **16/1**

3 **6** 2¼ **El Salvador (IRE)**[13] 3073 4-9-0 105 JosephO'Brien 18 109
(A P O'Brien, Ire) *swtg: hld up in tch towards rr: hdwy into midfield 16f out: rdn and effrt 3f out: drvn and pushed lft 2f out: styd on same pce and no imp after* **16/1**

-143 **7** hd **Model Pupil**[21] 2810 4-9-0 106 JamesMcDonald 4 109
(Charles Hills) *swtg: hld up wl in tch in midfield: rdn and effrt over 2f out: no imp u.p: plugged on but no threat to ldrs fnl f* **33/1**

6-50 **8** 1½ **Saddler's Rock (IRE)**[82] 1263 5-9-2 112 (t) DeclanMcDonogh 6 108
(John M Oxx, Ire) *lw: led for 4f: chsd ldr tl 9f out: cl 3rd and effrt u.p 3f out: outpcd and btn over 1f out: wknd fnl f* **9/2**[2]

0-42 **9** 1 **Number Theory**[21] 2810 5-9-2 108 SebSanders 13 107
(John Holt) *hld up wl in tch towards rr: rdn and hdwy ent fnl 2f: kpt on but no imp fr over 1f out: nvr threatened ldrs* **50/1**

446- **10** 2¼ **Repeater**[273] 6415 4-9-0 106 LukeMorris 17 104
(Sir Mark Prescott Bt) *stdd s: hld up wl in tch in rr: swtchd lft and effrt u.p over 2f out: no imp and btn over 1f out* **50/1**

3-13 **11** nse **Last Train**[25] 2695 4-9-0 113 MaximeGuyon 2 104
(A Fabre, France) *trckd ldrs: rdn and effrt wl over 2f out: drvn and outpcd 2f out: wknd over 1f out* **14/1**

35-3 **12** 2½ **Earl Of Tinsdal (GER)**[32] 2492 5-9-2 116 WilliamBuick 8 102
(A Wohler, Germany) *swtg: t.k.h: hld up in midfield but ref to settle: hdwy to ld after 4f but stl t.k.h: rdn and qcknd 3f out: sn hdd and btn: wknd over 1f out* **20/1**

11-6 **13** 21 **Times Up**[21] 2810 7-9-2 115 FrankieDettori 10 89
(Ed Dunlop) *hld up in tch in last trio: effrt on outer 3f out: drvn and outpcd over 2f out: wl btn and hung rt over 1f out: eased ins fnl f: t.o* **11/1**

450- **14** 14 **Vadamar (FR)**[22] 5-9-2 115 JamieSpencer 14 75
(M Delzangles, France) *stdd s: t.k.h and nvr settled: hld up in tch towards rr: rdn and no rspnse over 2f out: sn wknd: wl bhd and eased ins fnl f: t.o* **16/1**

4m 20.51s (-4.29) **Going Correction** -0.025s/f (Good)
WFA 4 from 5yo+ 2lb **14** Ran SP% **121.5**
Speed ratings (Par 117): **107,106,106,105,105 104,104,103,103,102 102,101,93,87**
toteswingers 1&2 £4.70, 1&3 £5.80, 2&3 £8.30 CSF £19.75 CT £118.62 TOTE £3.80: £1.60, £1.90, £2.40; EX 15.50 Trifecta £204.60 Pool: £20408.90 - 74.79 winning units..
Owner The Queen **Bred** His Highness The Aga Khan's Studs S C **Trained** Newmarket, Suffolk
■ A hugely popular result. Aaim To Prosper and Biographer were withdrawn. Deduct 5p in the £ under R4. New market formed.
■ Stewards' Enquiry : Johnny Murtagh four-day ban: use of whip (4, 5, 7, 8 July)
Mickael Barzalona three-day ban: careless riding (4, 6, 7 July)

FOCUS
The staying division currently lacks a real top notcher and, while last year's winner Colour Vision was back for more, 2010 hero Rite Of Passage was withdrawn on account of the ground, joining three other non-runners. The early pace was slow, leaving the field still quite well bunched on the turn into the straight and, all things considered, the form is ordinary for the grade. Estimate continues to progress.

3484 BRITANNIA STKS (HERITAGE H'CAP) 1m (S)
4:25 (4:26) (Class 2) (0-105,105) 3-Y-O

£74,700 (£22,368; £11,184; £5,592; £2,796; £1,404) Stalls Centre

Form RPR
1 **Roca Tumu (IRE)**[26] 2680 3-8-12 **96** WJLee 15 107
(Ms Joanna Morgan, Ire) *tall: lengthy: a.p: led ent fnl 2f: rdn over 1f out: r.o ins fnl f: kpt on wl and doing enough cl home* **20/1**

21-0 **2** nk **Tarikhi (USA)**[33] 2445 3-8-5 **89** SilvestreDeSousa 12 99
(Saeed bin Suroor) *trckd ldrs: rdn and ev ch 2f out: str chal and r.o ins fnl f: hld fnl strides* **33/1**

113 **3** ½ **Queensberry Rules (IRE)**[19] 2859 3-8-11 **95** RyanMoore 24 104
(William Haggas) *hld up: hdwy over 2f out: sn rdn: plld out whn chsng ldrs over 1f out: r.o wl and clsd fnl 100yds: hld fnl strides* **16/1**

11-3 **4** 1 **Wentworth (IRE)**[27] 2621 3-8-10 **94** RichardHughes 30 101+
(Richard Hannon) *hld up: rdn 2f out: stdy hdwy over 1f out: r.o ins fnl f: gng on at fin* **7/2**[1]

3-11 **5** 1 **Cape Peron**[33] 2438 3-9-2 **100** FergusSweeney 20 105+
(Henry Candy) *lw: hld up: hdwy over 2f out: chal over 1f out: nt qckn whn edgd rt fnl 100yds: no ex cl home* **6/1**[2]

6 nk **Machete Mark (IRE)**[26] 2680 3-8-1 **88** IJBrennan[(3)] 16 92
(G M Lyons, Ire) *str: hld up in midfield: chsd ldrs 1/2-way: rdn 2f out: edgd rt ins fnl f: no ex fnl 50yds* **33/1**

-155 **7** ½ **Fehaydi**[55] 1809 3-8-8 **92** JamieSpencer 33 99+
(William Haggas) *lw: towards rr: rdn 2f out: hdwy whn nt clr run and snatched up over 1f out: r.o ins fnl f: fin full of running* **22/1**

3-12 **8** 1¼ **Market Town (USA)**[55] 1809 3-8-5 **89** Christophe-PatriceLemaire 25 92+
(Charles Hills) *lw: hld up: pushed along whn nt clr run over 1f out: styd on ins fnl f: eased fnl 50yds* **20/1**

-101 **9** nk **Shebebi (USA)**[26] 2661 3-8-8 **92** PaulHanagan 10 91
(Mark Johnston) *led: rdn and hdd ent fnl 2f: stl chsng ldrs over 1f out: one pce fnl 150yds* **33/1**

-466 **10** 1¼ **Ayaar (IRE)**[31] 2526 3-9-2 **100** MartinHarley 14 96
(Mick Channon) *hld up: hdwy 3f out: rdn over 2f out: styd on and clsd ins fnl f: one pce fnl 100yds* **66/1**

-111 **11** nk **Sea Shanty (USA)**[28] 2603 3-8-7 **91** PatDobbs 28 87
(Richard Hannon) *towards rr: rdn 2f out: styd on and clsd under hand ride ins fnl f: nt rch ldrs* **20/1**

5-01 **12** ½ **So Beloved**[26] 2666 3-8-7 **91** JamesDoyle 18 85
(Roger Charlton) *hld up: hdwy 1/2-way: rdn to chse ldrs over 2f out: hung rt over 1f out: one pce ins fnl f: wl btn fnl 100yds* **16/1**

-020 **13** hd **Red Avenger (USA)**[26] 2661 3-8-8 **92** JRosario 31 86
(Ed Dunlop) *racd towards nr side and sltly isolated fr others: wl bhd and struggling to keep up 3f out tl styd on fnl f: fin wl: nt rch ldrs* **40/1**

1313 **14** nk **You Da One (IRE)**[20] 2844 3-8-4 **88** HayleyTurner 17 81
(Andrew Balding) *midfield: rdn 1/2-way: outpcd over 1f out: one pce and no imp fnl f* **33/1**

2031 **15** ¾ **Kyllachy Rise**[9] 3176 3-8-4 **88** 5ex JimmyQuinn 13 80
(Richard Hannon) *in tch: prom 3f out: rdn 2f out: stl wl there over 1f out: no ex fnl 110yds* **33/1**

2-16 **16** 1 **Le Deluge (FR)**[14] 3028 3-8-3 **87** WilliamCarson 29 76
(John Best) *towards rr: rdn and hdwy 2f out: kpt on wout threatening ins fnl f* **100/1**

1-50 **17** ¾ **Law Enforcement (IRE)**[31] 2526 3-9-2 **105** WilliamTwiston-Davies[(5)] 22 93
(Richard Hannon) *midfield: rdn over 2f out: no imp on ldrs: plugged on at one pce fnl f* **50/1**

-011 **18** ½ **Llaregyb (IRE)**[19] 2876 3-8-5 **89** HarryBentley 26 75
(David Elsworth) *racd keenly in tch: pushed along 3f out: ch over 2f out: wknd ins fnl f* **10/1**

19 1 **Won Diamond**[12] 3122 3-8-11 **95** ShaneFoley 23 79
(M Halford, Ire) *tall: str: towards rr: u.p over 2f out: plugged on fnl f wout troubling ldrs* **33/1**

4-13 **20** ½ **Ebn Arab (USA)**[21] 2812 3-9-2 **100** DaneO'Neill 11 83
(Charles Hills) *s.i.s: in tch: rdn to chse ldrs over 2f out: wknd ins fnl f* **50/1**

-111 **21** 3¼ **Prophets Pride**[22] 2776 3-8-4 **88** (p) ChrisCatlin 4 63
(Jeremy Noseda) *hld up: pushed along after 2f: n.m.r whn outpcd 2f out: nvr a threat* **25/1**

1112 **22** nk **Newstead Abbey**[26] 2661 3-9-0 **98** GrahamGibbons 7 73
(David Barron) *chsd ldrs tl rdn and wknd over 2f out* **28/1**

-111 **23** 1¾ **Maputo**[13] 3061 3-8-11 **95** JoeFanning 3 66
(Mark Johnston) *lw: prom: rdn over 2f out: sn wknd* **7/1**[3]

-012 **24** 3 **Capo Rosso (IRE)**[26] 2666 3-8-6 **90** RichardKingscote 8 54
(Tom Dascombe) *trckd ldrs: pushed along over 3f out: wknd over 2f out: wl btn whn n.m.r over 1f out* **40/1**

-461 **25** ¾ **Jalaa (IRE)**[12] 3080 3-8-11 **95** FrankieDettori 5 62
(Richard Hannon) *in tch: pushed along over 2f out: no imp over 1f out: sn eased whn btn* **50/1**

2-12 **26** 7 **Secret Talent**[41] 2208 3-8-6 **90** JimCrowley 2 45
(Hughie Morrison) *midfield: rdn after 3f: wknd over 2f out: sn bhd: eased wl over 1f out* **16/1**

314 **27** 59 **String Theory (IRE)**[31] 2526 3-8-11 **95** (t) WilliamBuick 21
(Marco Botti) *hld up: u.p over 2f out: eased and dropped away tamely over 1f out: virtually p.u nr fin* **40/1**

1m 37.52s (-3.28) **Going Correction** -0.10s/f (Good) course record **27** Ran SP% **135.0**
Speed ratings (Par 105): **112,111,111,110,109 108,108,107,106,105 105,104,104,104,103 102,101,101,100,99 96,96,94,91,90**
toteswingers 1&2 £285.60, 1&3 £317.10, 2&3 £373.00 CSF £563.01 CT £10418.39 TOTE £32.80: £5.60, £14.80, £4.30, £1.80; EX 2591.70 Trifecta £7722.50 Part won. Pool: £10296.75 - 0.03 winning units..
Owner Roca Tumu Syndicate **Bred** Tommy Murphy **Trained** Ballivor, Co Meath
■ Joanna Morgan and Billy Lee's first winners at Royal Ascot.

FOCUS
With the far side having been the place to be in the Hunt Cup the previous day, the whole field headed over to race centre to far side. A typical Britannia with lots of improvers, and the form makes sense.

3485 TERCENTENARY STKS (FORMERLY THE HAMPTON COURT STAKES) (GROUP 3) 1m 2f
5:00 (5:01) (Class 1) 3-Y-O
£42,532 (£16,125; £8,070; £4,020; £2,017; £1,012) **Stalls** Low

Form RPR

311 **1** **Remote**[19] 2857 3-9-0 103 WilliamBuick 5 116+
(John Gosden) *lw: hld up in tch in midfield: rdn and effrt to chse ldng trio ent fnl 2f: drvn and styd on strly to ld fnl 75yds: r.o wl* **9/4**[1]

5 **2** ¾ **Shikarpour (IRE)**[18] 2907 3-9-0 114 Christophe-PatriceLemaire 6 114
(A De Royer-Dupre, France) *str: lw: hld up in tch in last quartet: rdn and hdwy ent fnl 2f: styng on whn swtchd lft ent fnl f: r.o wl to go 2nd last strides* **7/1**[3]

-130 **3** nk **Van Der Neer**[26] 2677 3-9-0 113 RichardHughes 9 113
(Richard Hannon) *chsd ldr: rdn and effrt wl over 2f out: ev ch wl over 1f out: drvn and led 1f out: hdd and no ex fnl 75yds: lost 2nd last strides* **14/1**

-136 **4** 1 **Secret Number**[35] 2398 3-9-0 103 SilvestreDeSousa 11 111
(Saeed bin Suroor) *hld up wl in tch in midfield: rdn and effrt over 2f out: no imp u.p over 1f out tl styd on wl fnl 100yds: nt pce to threaten ldrs* **20/1**

2-11 **5** nse **Elkaayed (USA)**[19] 2859 3-9-0 100 PaulHanagan 1 111
(Roger Varian) *lw: led: rdn jst over 2f out: hdd over 1f out: no ex jst ins fnl f: styd on same pce fnl 150yds* **8/1**

-115 **6** 1 **Windhoek**[35] 2398 3-9-0 104 JoeFanning 10 109
(Mark Johnston) *lw: t.k.h early: chsd ldrs: rdn to chal 2f out: led narrowly over 1f out: hdd 1f out: no ex ins fnl f: wknd fnl 100yds* **9/1**

10 **7** 1 ¼ **Chopin (GER)**[19] 2866 3-9-4 116 JamieSpencer 7 110
(A Wohler, Germany) *lw: hld up in tch in midfield: rdn and effrt 2f out: edgd rt and no imp over 1f out: plugged on same pce fnl f* **15/2**

4 **8** 2 ½ **Kitten On The Run (USA)**[33] 2445 3-9-0 102 KierenFallon 12 101
(Luca Cumani) *in tch in midfield: rdn and effrt towards inner over 1f out: no imp and btn 1f out: wknd ins fnl f* **14/1**

13 **9** hd **Indian Chief (IRE)**[35] 2398 3-9-0 110 [1] JosephO'Brien 2 101
(A P O'Brien, Ire) *hld up in last pair: rdn and effrt but plenty to do 2f out: no imp: nvr trbld ldrs* **5/1**[2]

0531 **10** 7 **Hoarding (USA)**[33] 2454 3-9-0 96 (p) RyanMoore 3 87
(John Gosden) *hld up in last quartet: rdn and no prog over 2f out: wl hld and edgd rt over 1f out: wknd* **40/1**

3 **11** 6 **Ideal (GER)**[46] 3-9-0 101 AStarke 8 75
(Ferdinand J Leve, Germany) *w'like: chsd ldng trio: rdn 3f out: sn struggling: wknd 2f out: bhd fnl f* **66/1**

12 **12** nk **Centurius**[47] 2023 3-9-0 97 AdamKirby 4 74
(Marco Botti) *hld up in last pair: rdn and no hdwy over 2f out: lost tch 2f out* **40/1**

2m 4.46s (-2.94) **Going Correction** -0.025s/f (Good) **12** Ran SP% **117.3**
Speed ratings (Par 109): **110,109,109,108,108 107,106,104,104,98 93,93**
toteswingers 1&2 £4.00, 1&3 £8.70, 2&3 £14.70 CSF £17.11 CT £181.43 TOTE £2.90: £1.50, £2.10, £4.30; EX 16.40 Trifecta £219.80 Pool: £19671.04 - 67.10 winning units..
Owner K Abdullah **Bred** Juddmonte Farms Ltd **Trained** Newmarket, Suffolk

FOCUS
Only the third running of this race as a Group 3 and it looked quite a strong contest, well up to scratch. The pace did not seem overly quick and, while the winner and runner-up stayed on from a fair way back, they may be worthy of extra credit.

3486 KING GEORGE V STKS (H'CAP) 1m 4f
5:35 (5:35) (Class 2) (0-105,95) 3-Y-O
£46,687 (£13,980; £6,990; £3,495; £1,747; £877) **Stalls** Low

Form RPR

-322 **1** **Elidor**[40] 2262 3-9-0 **88** MartinHarley 10 97
(Mick Channon) *broke wl: led early: t.k.h in tch: dropped to midfield over 3f out: hdwy 2f out: r.o to ld ins fnl f: drvn out and kpt on wl towards fin* **20/1**

2216 **2** 1 **Space Ship**[19] 2862 3-9-3 **91** WilliamBuick 15 98
(John Gosden) *swtg: midfield: rdn and outpcd 3f out: lost pl: hdwy on outer over 1f out: r.o ins fnl f: gng on at fin* **16/1**

011 **3** shd **Bold Sniper**[17] 2927 3-9-2 **90** RyanMoore 16 97+
(Sir Michael Stoute) *swtg: t.k.h: hld up: rdn and hdwy on outer 2f out: r.o ins fnl f: nt rch wnr: lost 2nd fnl stride* **7/2**[1]

62-3 **4** ¾ **Cap O'Rushes**[62] 1667 3-9-7 **95** MickaelBarzalona 21 101
(Saeed bin Suroor) *lw: hld up in rr: rdn over 2f out: hdwy and styd on ins fnl f: clsd on outer towards fin: nt quite get to ldrs* **20/1**

-124 **5** ½ **Another Cocktail**[40] 2262 3-9-5 **93** JimmyFortune 2 98
(Hughie Morrison) *trckd ldrs: rdn over 2f out: wnt rt and nt qckn over 1f out: styd on same pce cl home* **16/1**

1402 **6** shd **Salutation (IRE)**[5] 3338 3-8-7 **84** DarrenEgan(3) 19 89
(Mark Johnston) *plld hrd on outer: in tch: rdn and nt qckn over 2f out: styd on to chse ldrs ins fnl f: edgd rt: one pce cl home* **28/1**

4-01 **7** ½ **Excellent Result (IRE)**[28] 2605 3-9-6 **94** SilvestreDeSousa 7 98
(Saeed bin Suroor) *lw: racd keenly: prom: led over 2f out: sn rdn: hdd ins fnl f: no ex and lost several pls ins fnl 75yds* **12/1**

1-11 **8** ½ **Soviet Rock (IRE)**[46] 2050 3-9-1 **94** ThomasBrown(5) 11 97+
(Andrew Balding) *midfield: rdn and outpcd over 2f out: no imp over 1f out: prog ins fnl f: styd on towards fin* **13/2**[3]

3114 **9** nk **Red Runaway**[26] 2660 3-8-7 **81** JamesDoyle 17 84
(Ed Dunlop) *hld up in midfield: hdwy on outer over 4f out: chal over 2f out: stl ev ch over 1f out: no exrra fnl 75yds* **20/1**

1113 **10** ½ **Spillway**[33] 2445 3-9-0 **88** TomQueally 13 92+
(Eve Johnson Houghton) *midfield: pushed along over 2f out: nt clr run and swtchd rt over 1f out: styd on ins fnl f: one pce towards fin* **14/1**

2-12 **11** ½ **Pether's Moon (IRE)**[46] 2054 3-9-2 **90** RichardHughes 9 98+
(Richard Hannon) *t.k.h: hld up in midfield: pushed along over 2f out: trying to make hdwy on inner whn nt clr run over 1f out and snatched up twice: unable to rcvr: fin full of running* **6/1**[2]

-411 **12** ½ **Eshtiaal (USA)**[27] 2641 3-9-6 **94** PaulHanagan 1 95
(Brian Meehan) *hld up in midfield: rdn 4f out: effrt over 3f out: chsd ldrs over 2f out: one pce ins fnl f: eased fnl 50yds* **8/1**

2225 **13** 1 ¼ **Carry On Sydney**[46] 2050 3-8-12 **86** PatDobbs 14 85
(Richard Hannon) *lw: hld up: u.p over 2f out: kpt on ins fnl f: nt trble ldrs* **25/1**

-431 **14** hd **Pasaka Boy**[19] 2862 3-9-1 **89** RichardKingscote 18 87
(Jonathan Portman) *swtg: prom: rdn over 3f out: nt qckn over 1f out: fdd ins fnl f* **20/1**

3265 **15** 2 **Greeleys Love (USA)**[6] 3296 3-8-11 **85** JamieSpencer 3 88+
(Mark Johnston) *hmpd s: in rr: u.p over 2f out: effrt whn nt clr run and hmpd jst over 1f out: eased whn no imp fnl 110yds* **20/1**

3322 **16** 2 **Number One London (IRE)**[13] 3061 3-8-8 **82** KierenFallon 6 80+
(Brian Meehan) *swtg: racd keenly: trckd ldrs: rdn over 3f out: hmpd whn strugging to hold pl over 1f out: sn lost grnd: eased whn wl btn ins fnl f* **10/1**

161- **17** ½ **Shrewd**[239] 7335 3-9-3 **91** JamesMcDonald 12 82
(Michael Bell) *sn led: rdn and hdd over 2f out: wknd over 1f out* **33/1**

3525 **18** 1 **Blue Wave (IRE)**[19] 2879 3-8-12 **86** (b) FMBerry 4 75
(Mark Johnston) *lw: hmpd s: hld up: u.p over 2f out: no imp fnl f* **28/1**

2m 30.81s (-1.69) **Going Correction** -0.025s/f (Good) **18** Ran SP% **133.7**
Speed ratings (Par 105): **104,103,103,102,102 102,102,101,101,101 100,100,99,99,98 96,96,95**
toteswingers 1&2 £73.20, 1&3 £21.60, 2&3 £12.50 CSF £296.86 CT £1415.71 TOTE £27.60: £4.90, £4.80, £1.50, £5.50; EX 608.40 Trifecta £7827.90 Pool: £15676.53 - 1.50 winning units..
Owner Jon and Julia Aisbitt **Bred** Ashley House Stud **Trained** West Ilsley, Berks
■ Martin Harley's first winner at Royal Ascot.

FOCUS
There was a lack of early pace, some trouble in running and the final time was 1.4sec slower than the Ribblesdale earlier on the card. The top weight was rated 10lb below the ceiling for the race, so not as classy a contest as billed, but there were still a few interesting lightly raced types in the line-up. It was a bit of a messy race too but the form makes a good bit of sense.
T/Jkpt: Not won. T/Plt: £63.00 to a £1 stake. Pool of £743,013.99 - 8601.46 winning tickets. T/Qpdt: £10.60 to a £1 stake. Pool of £37,056.20 - 2586.58 winning tickets. SP

3317 LEICESTER (R-H)
Thursday, June 20

OFFICIAL GOING: Good to firm changing to good after race 2 (6.55)
Wind: almost nil Weather: raining

3487 IBSTOCK H'CAP 5f 2y
6:20 (6:20) (Class 4) (0-85,80) 3-Y-O+ **£4,851** (£1,443; £721; £360) **Stalls** High

Form RPR

204 **1** **Dorback**[4] 3371 6-9-5 **73** (t) SeanLevey 4 81
(Violet M Jordan) *mde virtually all: rdn over 12f out: styd on* **5/2**[2]

-033 **2** 1 ½ **Ashpan Sam**[33] 2460 4-9-12 **80** LiamJones 3 83
(John Spearing) *dwlt: sn chsng ldrs: drvn over 2f out: kpt on fnl f: tk 2nd nr fin* **5/4**[1]

6-03 **3** 1 ¼ **Cats Eyes**[12] 3078 4-9-9 **77** ShaneKelly 6 75
(Robert Cowell) *chsd wnr: swtchd rt over 3f out: chal over 1f out: edgd rt ins fnl f: wknd nr fin* **5/1**

00-5 **4** 7 **Eland Ally**[23] 2755 5-9-8 **76** MickyFenton 1 52
(Tom Tate) *trckd ldrs: t.k.h: drvn over 2f out: wknd over 1f out: eased* **7/2**[3]

1m 0.16s (0.16) **Going Correction** +0.15s/f (Good)
WFA 3 from 4yo+ 6lb **4** Ran SP% **111.9**
Speed ratings (Par 105): **104,101,99,88**
CSF £6.30 TOTE £2.70; EX 7.40 Trifecta £8.00 Pool: £529.50 - 49.28 winning units..
Owner Rakebackmypoker.com **Bred** Winterbeck Manor Stud **Trained** Moreton Morrell, Warwicks

FOCUS
A weak handicap with the first two not at their best recently. The time was reasonable.

3488 TOWN HALL (S) STKS 1m 1f 218y
6:55 (6:56) (Class 6) 3-Y-O **£1,940** (£577; £288; £144) **Stalls** Low

Form RPR

1 **Pixie Cut (IRE)** 3-8-12 **0** LiamJones 1 64
(J S Moore) *trckd ldrs: drvn 4f out: styd on to ld over 1f out: styd on wl* **16/1**

5540 **2** 2 ¼ **Curl (IRE)**[17] 2916 3-8-12 **60** (v[1]) TomEaves 4 59
(Michael Dods) *hld up: t.k.h: hdwy whn nt clr run over 2f out: chsd wnr 1f out: kpt on: no imp* **5/4**[1]

5-45 **3** 8 **Spanish Art**[8] 3219 3-9-3 **64** MickyFenton 2 48
(Gay Kelleway) *led 1f: chsd ldr: effrt over 3f out: led briefly 2f out: one pce* **7/1**

0226 **4** hd **Winter Music (IRE)**[17] 2924 3-8-10 **59** (v) DanielMuscutt(7) 5 48
(Andrew Balding) *trckd ldrs: t.k.h: hung lft 2f out: one pce whn rdr dropped whip over 1f out* **7/2**[3]

06-0 **5** 12 **Refuse To Mambo**[7] 2742 3-9-3 **48** (p) ShaneKelly 6 24
(Andrew Hollinshead) *led after 1f: hdd 2f out: sn lost pl* **20/1**

3603 **6** 2 **Grey Gazelle**[10] 3149 3-8-5 **73** DanielCremin(7) 3 15
(Mick Channon) *dwlt: hld up in last: hdwy on ins over 3f out: rdn: lost pl and edgd lft over 1f out* **11/4**[2]

2m 9.28s (1.38) **Going Correction** +0.15s/f (Good) **6** Ran SP% **116.5**
Speed ratings (Par 97): **100,98,91,91,82 80**
CSF £38.58 TOTE £31.60: £13.20, £1.30; EX 89.20 Trifecta £592.30 Pool: £982.39 - 1.24 winning units..There was no bid for the winner
Owner G V March & J S Moore **Bred** Rocal Bloodstock **Trained** Upper Lambourn, Berks
■ Stewards' Enquiry : Daniel Muscutt seven-day ban: failed to ride out for best possible placing (4, 5, 6, 7 ,8, 9 July)

FOCUS
A weak seller which has been rated cautiously.

3489 JEANETTE'S 25 YEAR CELEBRATION FILLIES' H'CAP 5f 218y
7:30 (7:30) (Class 5) (0-75,75) 3-Y-O+ £3,234 (£962; £481; £240) Stalls High

Form RPR
3502 1 **Big Wave (IRE)**[8] 3223 5-9-5 66 RobertHavlin 5 74
(Alison Hutchinson) *mde all: drvn 2 l clr 1f out: edgd rt ins fnl f: jst hld on* 3/1[2]
06-0 2 *nse* **Fenella Fudge**[169] 27 5-8-7 61 (v) AdamMcLean(7) 1 69
(Derek Shaw) *swtchd lft after s: hld up in last: hdwy on ins to chse wnr 1f out: styd on towards fin: jst failed* 5/1[3]
410- 3 *4 ½* **Sakhee's Rose**[195] 8016 3-8-13 67 RoystonFfrench 6 58
(Ed McMahon) *trckd ldrs: t.k.h: drvn over 2f out: one pce appr fnl f* 5/1[3]
46-1 4 *nk* **Rocksilla**[27] 2637 3-9-4 75 AshleyMorgan(3) 2 67
(Chris Wall) *trckd wnr: drvn over 2f out: one pce appr fnl f* 4/5[1]
1m 13.8s (0.80) **Going Correction** +0.15s/f (Good)
WFA 3 from 5yo+ 7lb 4 Ran SP% **113.9**
Speed ratings (Par 100): **100,99,93,93**
CSF £16.61 TOTE £2.50; EX 13.10 Trifecta £37.10 Pool: £601.63 - 12.14 winning units..
Owner Miss A L Hutchinson **Bred** P De Vere Hunt **Trained** Exning, Suffolk

FOCUS
A moderate little fillies' sprint handicap in which the favourite disappointed. The form is rated around the winner.

3490 DINGLEY MAIDEN STKS 7f 9y
8:05 (8:05) (Class 4) 2-Y-O £3,881 (£1,155; £577; £288) Stalls High

Form RPR
1 **Noble Metal** 2-9-5 0 ShaneKelly 2 76+
(Peter Chapple-Hyam) *dwlt: hld up: hdwy to trck ldrs over 3f out: led over 1f out: sn jnd: hld on wl nr fin* 16/1
2 *nk* **Banaadeer (IRE)** 2-9-5 0 DaneO'Neill 4 75+
(Richard Hannon) *s.s: hld up: stdy hdwy to join ldr 1f out: upsides ins fnl f: no ex nr fin* 4/5[1]
3 *nk* **Istimraar (IRE)** 2-9-5 0 RobertHavlin 5 75+
(Saeed bin Suroor) *led: hdd over 1f out: kpt on wl ins fnl f* 10/1
4 *1 ¾* **Stars Over The Sea (USA)** 2-9-5 0 FrannyNorton 6 70+
(Mark Johnston) *s.i.s: sn chsng ldrs: drvn over 3f out: kpt on fnl f* 3/1[2]
5 *shd* **Diplomatic Force (USA)** 2-9-5 0 GrahamLee 7 70+
(Saeed bin Suroor) *dwlt: sn chsng ldrs: outpcd and edgd rt over 1f out: kpt on ins fnl f* 6/1[3]
6 *5* **Newmarket Warrior (IRE)** 2-9-5 0 StevieDonohoe 8 57
(Michael Bell) *chsd ldrs: drvn over 2f out: sn outpcd and lost pl* 33/1
6 7 *2 ¼* **Tax Enough (USA)**[35] 2391 2-9-5 0 PaulMulrennan 1 51
(Brian Meehan) *w ldrs: lost pl over 1f out* 20/1
1m 28.4s (2.20) **Going Correction** +0.15s/f (Good) 7 Ran SP% **117.5**
Speed ratings (Par 95): **93,92,92,90,90 84,81**
toteswingers 1&2 £5.70, 1&3 £10.30, 2&3 £2.10 CSF £30.88 TOTE £24.60: £12.00, £1.40; EX 61.70 Trifecta £252.10 Pool: £760.27 - 2.26 winning units..
Owner The HPT Partnership **Bred** Miss K Rausing **Trained** Newmarket, Suffolk

FOCUS
Not a bad 2-y-o maiden with some nice types on show. The bare form is rated in line with the race average, but the first five should do better.

3491 GLEBE MAIDEN STKS 1m 3f 183y
8:35 (8:35) (Class 5) 3-Y-O+ £3,234 (£962; £481; £240) Stalls Low

Form RPR
0 1 **Madame Vestris (IRE)**[35] 2389 3-8-5 0 JimmyQuinn 5 79+
(Sir Michael Stoute) *trckd ldng pair: effrt 3f out: rdn to chse ldrs 1f out: r.o to ld clsng stages* 11/4[2]
5 2 *nk* **Battalion (IRE)**[43] 2151 3-8-10 0 GrahamLee 4 83
(William Haggas) *trckd ldr: chal 3f out: sn led: drvn fnl f: no ex and hdd nr fin* 4/5[1]
2-26 3 *1 ¼* **Bin Singspiel**[19] 2878 3-8-10 71 PaulMulrennan 1 81
(James Tate) *led: qcknd pce over 3f out: sn jnd: hdd over 2f out: rallied over 1f out: one pce last 50yds* 7/2[3]
0 4 *9* **Perfect Spell**[28] 2605 3-8-10 0 FrannyNorton 6 67
(Andrew Balding) *in last: t.k.h early: pushed along over 6f out: outpcd and lost pl over 4f out* 9/1
2m 34.26s (0.36) **Going Correction** +0.15s/f (Good)
WFA 3 from 4yo 14lb 4 Ran SP% **114.4**
Speed ratings (Par 103): **104,103,102,96**
CSF £5.80 TOTE £5.30; EX 7.00 Trifecta £20.50 Pool: £363.08 - 13.25 winning units..
Owner Cheveley Park Stud **Bred** Derry Meeting, Mrs A Wigan & Lts Ltd **Trained** Newmarket, Suffolk

FOCUS
A modest 3-y-o maiden, run at a steady pace and rated around the front-running third. The winner can better this.

3492 FOSTON H'CAP 1m 60y
9:10 (9:11) (Class 4) (0-85,83) 3-Y-O+ £4,851 (£1,443; £721; £360) Stalls Low

Form RPR
1-20 1 **Gworn**[26] 2655 3-9-2 83 GrahamLee 2 93
(Ed Dunlop) *hld up: t.k.h: hdwy over 2f out: 2nd over 1f out: sn led: drvn out* 4/1[2]
2031 2 *1 ¾* **Cruiser**[3] 3416 5-8-13 77 6ex (p) DanielMuscutt(7) 3 85
(William Muir) *led: t.k.h: qcknd pce over 2f out: hdd 1f out: kpt on same pce* 5/1[3]
1221 3 *2 ¼* **Henry The Aviator (USA)**[7] 3235 3-9-2 83 6ex FrannyNorton 4 84
(Mark Johnston) *trckd ldr: t.k.h: drvn over 2f out: rdn over 1f out: edgd lft and kpt on one pce* 4/7[1]
0331 4 *1 ¾* **Perfect Cracker**[20] 2826 5-8-13 75 RyanTate(5) 1 74
(Clive Cox) *trckd ldrs: t.k.h: drvn over 2f out: one pce* 7/1
1m 44.91s (-0.19) **Going Correction** +0.15s/f (Good)
WFA 3 from 5yo 10lb 4 Ran SP% **112.8**
Speed ratings (Par 105): **106,104,102,100**
CSF £21.34 TOTE £4.90; EX 23.90 Trifecta £36.60 Pool: £695.62 - 14.22 winning units..
Owner N Martin **Bred** Azienda Agricola F Lli Nencini **Trained** Newmarket, Suffolk

FOCUS
A tight little handicap, rated around the runner-up with the favourite a little disappointing.
T/Plt: £1388.70 to a £1 stake. Pool of £47,599.44 - 25.02 winning tickets. T/Qpdt: £229.90 to a £1 stake. Pool of £3884.56 - 12.50 winning tickets. WG

3324 LINGFIELD (L-H)
Thursday, June 20

OFFICIAL GOING: Standard
Wind: Moderate, half behind Weather: Cloudy

3493 EDEN BROOK MAIDEN STKS 6f (P)
5:40 (5:40) (Class 5) 2-Y-O £2,726 (£805; £402) Stalls Low

Form RPR
64 1 **Miracle Of Medinah**[14] 3017 2-9-5 0 LiamKeniry 6 79
(Mark Usher) *mde all: rdn over 2f out: drew clr ins fnl f: readily* 3/1[2]
2 *3 ½* **Blue Bounty** 2-9-5 0 TedDurcan 2 68+
(Mark H Tompkins) *prom: rdn to chse wnr 2f out: outpcd ins fnl f* 25/1
3 *½* **Classified Weapon (USA)** 2-9-5 0 MartinLane 4 66+
(David Simcock) *hld up in 4th: rdn over 2f out: no imp tl styd on fnl f* 4/5[1]
55 4 *5* **Clarice**[8] 3211 2-9-0 0 LukeMorris 3 45
(Sir Mark Prescott Bt) *chsd wnr 4f: wknd over 1f out* 16/1
5 *½* **Holystones (IRE)** 2-9-5 0 PaoloSirigu 7 49
(Marco Botti) *dwlt: bhd: rdn over 2f out: n.d* 7/1[3]
6 *nk* **Mersad (IRE)** 2-9-5 0 AndreaAtzeni 1 48
(James Tate) *towards rr: green and rdn on bnd after 1f: nvr trbld ldrs* 7/1[3]
0 7 *2 ¾* **Triple O Seven (IRE)**[28] 2591 2-9-0 0 RobertTart(5) 5 39
(John Best) *chsd ldrs on outer tl wknd 2f out* 33/1
1m 12.72s (0.82) **Going Correction** -0.075s/f (Stan) 7 Ran SP% **118.2**
Speed ratings (Par 93): **91,86,85,79,78 77,74**
toteswingers 1&2 £13.30, 1&3 £2.20, 2&3 £6.00 CSF £69.20 TOTE £5.50: £2.20, £13.80; EX 141.50 Trifecta £221.20 Pool: £937.37 - 3.17 winning units..
Owner The High Jinks Partnership **Bred** A C M Spalding **Trained** Upper Lambourn, Berks

FOCUS
They went a fair pace and one with previous experience held sway. Difficult form to pin down.

3494 LINGFIELD PARK SUPPORTS YOUNG EPILEPSY (S) STKS 6f (P)
6:10 (6:12) (Class 6) 3-Y-O £2,045 (£603; £302) Stalls Low

Form RPR
1000 1 **Jontleman (IRE)**[6] 3279 3-8-12 66 CharlesBishop(5) 1 67
(Mick Channon) *broke wl: stdd to chse ldrs: rdn 2f out: led ins fnl f: drvn out* 9/4[2]
-413 2 *2 ¼* **Majestic Jess (IRE)**[35] 2393 3-9-3 73 (v[1]) TomMcLaughlin 6 60
(Luke Dace) *led: hrd rdn over 1f out: hdd and one pce ins fnl f* 1/1[1]
05-4 3 *1 ¾* **Coconut Kisses**[19] 2873 3-8-7 62 KieranO'Neill 2 44
(Bill Turner) *plld hrd in 5th: effrt 2f out: styd on same pce* 10/1
6-63 4 *1* **Poetic Belle**[51] 1906 3-8-7 55 (v) LukeMorris 5 41
(Alan Jarvis) *chsd wnr tl no ex over 1f out* 5/1[3]
5 5 *1 ½* **Father Fred**[16] 2948 3-8-12 0 SaleemGolam 7 41
(Chris Dwyer) *s.s: bhd tl rdn and sme hdwy fnl 2f* 33/1
00 6 *15* **Lily The Dragon (IRE)**[27] 2637 3-8-7 0 AndreaAtzeni 8
(Mick Quinn) *outpcd towards rr: no ch fnl 2f* 33/1
00 7 *3 ¼* **Xanders Secret**[15] 2979 3-8-7 0 WilliamCarson 9
(Brett Johnson) *prom on outer 3f: no ch fnl 2f* 33/1
1m 11.24s (-0.66) **Going Correction** -0.075s/f (Stan) 7 Ran SP% **115.4**
Speed ratings (Par 97): **101,98,95,94,92 72,68**
.There was no bid for the winner.\n\x\x Majestic Jess was bought by Amy Weaver for £6,000.
Owner Paul Corbett **Bred** Old Carhue & Graeng Bloodstock **Trained** West Ilsley, Berks

FOCUS
A weak race and it paid to race up with the pace. The favourite was again below form and the winner could be rated higher at face value.

3495 VINES BMW H'CAP 1m (P)
6:40 (6:41) (Class 6) (0-60,66) 3-Y-O £2,045 (£603; £302) Stalls High

Form RPR
0-42 1 **Bertie Moon**[43] 2154 3-9-6 59 SteveDrowne 9 64
(Geoffrey Deacon) *led 1f: prom in chsng gp: wnt 2nd 3f out: led again over 1f out: rdn out* 12/1
0-21 2 *¾* **Great Crested (IRE)**[3] 3405 3-9-13 66 6ex (b) AndreaAtzeni 4 69
(Gary Moore) *hld up in tch and gng wl: effrt 2f out: r.o to press wnr ins fnl f: a jst hld* 4/6[1]
-635 3 *1* **Red Tulip**[30] 2528 3-9-3 56 [1] FrederikTylicki 11 57
(James Fanshawe) *dwlt: t.k.h towards rr: rdn and hdwy 2f out: styd on fnl f* 8/1[3]
5050 4 *nk* **Bullseye Babe**[23] 2762 3-8-12 51 TedDurcan 1 51
(Mark Usher) *mid-div: hrd rdn 3f out: hdwy on inner over 1f out: one pce ins fnl f* 40/1
6615 5 *1 ½* **Compton Silver**[77] 1349 3-9-2 60 (b) NicoleNordblad(5) 10 57
(Hans Adielsson) *led after 1f and c across fr wd stall: wnt 4 l clr 4f out: hdd & wknd over 1f out* 7/1[2]
-040 6 *3 ½* **Carneades (IRE)**[16] 2950 3-8-8 47 (t) LukeMorris 6 36
(Ed Walker) *prom in chsng gp tl outpcd fnl 2f* 16/1
-540 7 *¾* **Whitford (IRE)**[16] 2951 3-9-4 57 SaleemGolam 2 44
(Chris Dwyer) *dwlt: hld up in rr: hdwy wl over 1f out: shkn up and no imp* 50/1
06-0 8 *hd* **Marguerite St Just**[19] 2874 3-8-12 51 SebSanders 5 38
(Olivia Maylam) *mid-div: rdn and no hdwy fnl 3f* 16/1
0154 9 *1 ½* **Sutton Sid**[13] 3040 3-9-5 58 LiamKeniry 7 41
(Chris Gordon) *a towards rr: drvn along and struggling 3f out* 14/1
404 10 *1 ¾* **Half Turn**[17] 2919 3-9-6 59 [1] TomMcLaughlin 3 38
(Luke Dace) *dwlt: a towards rr: rdn 3f out: n.d whn rn wd into st* 20/1
-000 11 *1* **Hats Off**[16] 2962 3-8-7 46 oh1 WilliamCarson 12 23
(John Best) *chsd ldr tl wknd 3f out* 33/1
-000 12 *30* **I Need A Dollar**[29] 2566 3-8-11 50 NickyMackay 8
(J R Jenkins) *in tch on outer in chsng gp: rdn over 4f out: wknd 3f out: bhd and eased 2f out* 66/1
1m 38.11s (-0.09) **Going Correction** -0.075s/f (Stan) 12 Ran SP% **123.3**
Speed ratings (Par 97): **97,96,95,94,93 89,89,89,87,85 84,54**
toteswingers 1&2 £2.30, 1&3 £5.30, 2&3 £3.30 CSF £20.55 CT £83.34 TOTE £7.40: £1.40, £1.10, £1.90; EX 24.70 Trifecta £83.40 Pool: £1454.34 - 13.07 winning units..
Owner Jim Kelly **Bred** M E Wates **Trained** Compton, Berks

FOCUS
They went a sensible pace for this modest handicap. A personal best from the winner with the favourite a little below his Kempton win.

3496 LINGFIELD PARK OWNERS GROUP FILLIES' H'CAP 1m (P)
7:15 (7:15) (Class 5) (0-70,67) 4-Y-O+ **£2,726** (£805; £402) **Stalls High**

Form RPR
3-41 1 **Absent Amy (IRE)**97 1013 4-9-4 64.....(t) JamieMackay 1 75+
(Alastair Lidderdale) *hld up in rr: gd hdwy to ld 1f out: rdn clr: comf* **2/1**1
4225 2 2 3/4 **Moment In The Sun**10 3156 4-8-10 61.....(b) JemmaMarshall(5) 9 65
(David Flood) *w ldr: led and qcknd over 2f out: hdd 1f out: one pce* **12/1**
0054 3 6 **Amethyst Dawn (IRE)**23 2745 7-9-2 67.....(t) RobertTart(5) 3 57
(Andrew Reid) *hld up in rr: rdn and styd on fnl 2f: nvr nrr* **6/1**
0623 4 1/2 **Ishiamiracle**15 2998 4-7-11 48 oh3.....(p) NathanAlison(5) 2 37
(Phil McEntee) *slt ld and restrained in front: hdd over 2f out: sn outpcd* **20/1**
40-3 5 3/4 **Raamz (IRE)**41 2219 6-9-1 66..... ThomasBrown(5) 7 53
(Kevin Morgan) *t.k.h: in tch: rdn and outpcd over 2f out: tried to rally on inner over 1f out: no imp* **11/4**2
-353 6 1 1/4 **Who's That Chick (IRE)**21 2792 4-8-8 54..... WilliamCarson 5 38
(Ralph Smith) *t.k.h: prom: rdn 3f out: wknd 2f out* **9/2**3
000 7 6 **Ela Goog La Mou**64 1611 4-8-2 48 oh3.....1 LukeMorris 8 19
(Peter Charalambous) *plld hrd: sn in tch on outer: rdn over 3f out: wknd over 2f out* **14/1**
1m 36.79s (-1.41) **Going Correction** -0.075s/f (Stan) **7 Ran SP% 111.6**
Speed ratings (Par 100): **104,101,95,94,94 92,86**
toteswingers 1&2 £7.00, 1&3 £2.20, 2&3 £6.10 CSF £25.44 CT £119.69 TOTE £2.20: £1.10, £5.20; EX 24.50 Trifecta £54.40 Pool: £948.71 - 13.07 winning units..
Owner The Strawberries To A Donkey Partnership **Bred** Tally-Ho Stud **Trained** Lambourn, Berks

FOCUS
A modest handicap, run at a true pace and it produced a clear-cut winner. The front two drew clear and the form is rated around the winner.

3497 BREATHE SPA AT LINGFIELD MARRIOTT H'CAP 1m 4f (P)
7:50 (7:51) (Class 5) (0-70,68) 3-Y-O **£3,408** (£1,006; £503) **Stalls Low**

Form RPR
1301 1 **Pivotal Silence**7 3243 3-9-4 65..... AndreaAtzeni 10 78
(Amanda Perrett) *sn disputing ld: rdn along over 2f out: slt ld 1f out: hld on gamely* **11/4**2
2210 2 1 **Gabrial The Duke (IRE)**22 2784 3-9-6 67..... MartinLane 1 78
(David Simcock) *disp ld most of way tl 1f out: kpt on gamely u.p: jst hld* **5/1**3
0-05 3 8 **Halling's Wish**21 2800 3-8-8 55..... WilliamCarson 6 54
(John Best) *towards rr: rdn and styd on fnl 3f: nt trble first 2* **25/1**
00-5 4 1/2 **Inherited**19 2874 3-9-0 61..... LukeMorris 9 59
(Sir Mark Prescott Bt) *chsd ldrs: rdn 4f out: outpcd fnl 2f* **6/1**
06-0 5 1 **Furibondo**59 1727 3-9-7 68..... TedDurcan 8 64
(David Lanigan) *sn prom on outer: drvn along 4f out: one pce* **8/1**
50-1 6 nse **Chocolate Block (IRE)**52 1879 3-8-4 56..... RobertTart(5) 5 52
(William Haggas) *mid-div: dropped to rr and rdn 3f out: n.d after* **2/1**1
3051 7 hd **Handsome Stranger (IRE)**8 3219 3-8-1 55.....(v) TimClark(7) 4 51
(Alan Bailey) *hld up in rr: rdn and sme hdwy over 2f out: nvr able to chal* **25/1**
6463 8 6 **Mirth**8 3194 3-8-11 58..... JoeFanning 2 44
(Mark Johnston) *prom tl wknd 3f out* **16/1**
4-05 9 2 1/2 **Himalayan Peak**43 2157 3-9-3 64..... SteveDrowne 3 46
(James Eustace) *a in rr: struggling fnl 3f* **20/1**
2m 29.33s (-3.67) **Going Correction** -0.075s/f (Stan) **9 Ran SP% 120.4**
Speed ratings (Par 99): **109,108,103,102,102 101,101,97,96**
toteswingers 1&2 £3.80, 1&3 £18.90, 2&3 £36.00 CSF £17.36 CT £283.14 TOTE £4.20: £2.20, £1.50, £8.70; EX 18.20 Trifecta £579.60 Part won. Pool: £772.83 - 0.42 winning units..
Owner M H and Mrs G Tourle **Bred** M H And Mrs G Tourle **Trained** Pulborough, W Sussex

FOCUS
It paid to be up with the pace in this competitive handicap and the front pair drew well clear after having it to themselves from a long way out. The form looks solid, the winner similar to her Newbury mark.

3498 LINGFIELD PARK OWNERS GROUP H'CAP 5f (P)
8:25 (8:25) (Class 6) (0-65,63) 4-Y-O+ **£1,324** (£1,324; £302) **Stalls High**

Form RPR
60-6 1 **Pucon**9 3171 4-9-5 61..... LiamKeniry 3 68
(Roger Teal) *led: hrd rdn over 1f out: kpt on u.p: jnd on line* **10/1**
1411 1 dht **Nafa (IRE)**19 2873 5-9-4 60..... AndreaAtzeni 7 67
(Daniel Mark Loughnane) *travelled wl in 4th: wnt 2nd 1f out: rdn to cl fnl f: jnd ldr on line* **5/4**1
0554 3 1 **Volcanic Dust (IRE)**10 3154 5-8-12 54.....(t) LukeMorris 2 57
(Milton Bradley) *chsd ldr tl 1f out: kpt on u.p* **10/1**
1640 4 3/4 **Commandingpresence (USA)**9 3181 7-9-4 60..... KieranO'Neill 6 61
(John Bridger) *bhd: rdn and r.o fnl 2f: nvr nrr* **14/1**
6354 5 shd **Catflap (IRE)**71 1467 4-8-9 56..... RosieJessop(5) 8 56
(Derek Haydn Jones) *racd wd: towards rr: hdwy over 2f out: styd on same pce* **6/1**2
3000 6 1/2 **Charming (IRE)**19 2870 4-9-5 61.....(e) SebSanders 9 60
(Olivia Maylam) *prom: hrd rdn over 1f out: no ex fnl f* **8/1**3
5-36 7 shd **Sarah Berry**8 3223 4-8-13 60..... RobertTart(5) 4 58
(Chris Dwyer) *mid-div: rdn over 2f out: no imp* **20/1**
6105 8 1/2 **Loyal Royal (IRE)**29 2582 10-9-4 60.....(bt) JoeFanning 5 56
(Milton Bradley) *plld hrd: sn stdd in rr: rdn 2f out: nvr able to chal* **25/1**
2231 9 shd **Speedyfix**27 2643 6-9-7 63.....(t) TomMcLaughlin 1 59
(Christine Dunnett) *bhd: effrt on inner ent st: hld fnl f* **6/1**2
58.82s (0.02) **Going Correction** -0.075s/f (Stan) **9 Ran SP% 117.6**
: £027, £Owner, £lan O'Connor, £BredBasil Brindley Trained Trifecta £Baldwin's Gate, Staffs.
Owner J A Redmond **Bred** J Redmond **Trained** Ashtead, Surrey

FOCUS
The pace was true for this competitive but modest sprint handicap and they finished in close proximity to one another. There were few hard-luck stories and it resulted a dead-heat.

3499 BHEST H'CAP 6f (P)
8:55 (8:55) (Class 6) (0-65,65) 3-Y-O+ **£2,045** (£603; £302) **Stalls Low**

Form RPR
-364 1 **Clearing**8 3212 3-9-2 60..... JoeFanning 8 67
(Jim Boyle) *mde all: wnt clr over 1f out: hrd rdn fnl f: hld on nr fin* **2/1**1
-011 2 3/4 **Fossa**31 2512 3-9-3 61..... SebSanders 12 71+
(Dean Ivory) *dwlt: bhd: hdwy on inner ent st: r.o wl fnl f: nt rch wnr* **7/2**2
000- 3 1/2 **Ghost Train (IRE)**194 8036 4-9-6 62.....(p) RobertTart(5) 10 67
(Tim McCarthy) *chsd wnr tl ins fnl f: kpt on u.p* **25/1**
6-03 4 1/2 **Compton Prince**6 3268 4-9-12 63.....(b) LukeMorris 5 66
(Milton Bradley) *prom: rdn over 2f out: kpt on fnl f* **8/1**3
2060 5 1/2 **Restless Bay (IRE)**9 3171 5-10-0 65.....(v) LiamKeniry 4 67
(Conor Dore) *trckd ldrs in 5th: effrt and hrd rdn over 1f out: styd on same pce* **10/1**
6066 6 hd **Reginald Claude**7 3247 5-9-2 58..... RachealKneller(5) 6 59
(Mark Usher) *sn outpcd and bhd: rapid hdwy fnl f: fin wl* **7/2**2
5166 7 3 1/2 **Sweet Ovation**9 3181 4-9-6 57..... TedDurcan 1 47
(Mark Usher) *a towards rr: n.d fnl 2f* **20/1**
210- 8 2 1/2 **The Wonga Coup (IRE)**29 8175 6-9-4 60..... JemmaMarshall(5) 2 42
(Pat Phelan) *outpcd: a bhd* **20/1**
P-06 9 1/2 **Samba Night (IRE)**10 3154 4-9-3 54.....(t) SteveDrowne 7 34
(Jeremy Gask) *chsd ldrs over 4f* **25/1**
0203 10 12 **Waterloo Dock**56 1793 8-9-4 55.....(v) WilliamCarson 9
(Mick Quinn) *in tch: rdn 3f out: sn lost pl: bhd and eased over 1f out* **20/1**
1m 11.91s (0.01) **Going Correction** -0.075s/f (Stan)
WFA 3 from 4yo+ 7lb **10 Ran SP% 120.0**
Speed ratings (Par 101): **96,95,94,93,93 92,88,84,84,68**
toteswingers 1&2 £3.60, 1&3 £19.80, 2&3 £16.40 CSF £8.36 CT £129.76 TOTE £4.70: £1.80, £1.80, £4.90; EX 15.30 Trifecta £347.10 Pool: £961.37 - 2.07 winning units..
Owner The Paddock Space Partnership **Bred** Paddock Space **Trained** Epsom, Surrey

FOCUS
Very few got into this modest sprint handicap, the pace holding up well.
T/Plt: £29.70 to a £1 stake. Pool of £43,367.21 - 1062.88 winning tickets. T/Qpdt: £8.40 to a £1 stake. Pool of £4719.68 - 412.39 winning tickets. LM

3475 RIPON (R-H)
Thursday, June 20

OFFICIAL GOING: Good to firm (good in places; 8.6)
Wind: Virtually nil Weather: Cloudy

3500 BRITISH STALLION STUDS SUPPORTING BRITISH RACING EBF MAIDEN STKS 6f
2:10 (2:12) (Class 5) 2-Y-O **£3,881** (£1,155; £577; £288) **Stalls High**

Form RPR
43 1 **Spiceupyourlife (IRE)**23 2751 2-8-11 0..... LeeTopliss(3) 2 73
(Richard Fahey) *prom: cl up 1/2-way: rdn to ld wl over 1f out: edgd lft ent fnl f: kpt on wl* **5/2**2
4 2 3 **Ahoy There (IRE)**15 2985 2-9-5 0..... MickyFenton 1 68
(Tom Tate) *trckd ldrs on outer: hdwy 2f out: rdn and kpt on fnl f* **8/1**
3 3 2 **Bounty Girl (IRE)**16 2955 2-9-0 0..... DuranFentiman 3 57
(Tim Easterby) *cl up: led after 1f: rdn and green 2f out: sn edgd rt and hdd: one pce after* **3/1**3
6 4 2 1/4 **Sakhalin Star (IRE)**12 3077 2-9-5 0..... MichaelO'Connell 5 54
(John Quinn) *in tch: rdn along over 2f out: sn one pce* **40/1**
6 5 hd **Soul Instinct**14 3023 2-9-5 0..... PhillipMakin 8 54+
(Kevin Ryan) *led 1f: cl up: rdn along over 2f out: sn wknd* **2/1**1
6 1 **Omanome (IRE)** 2-9-0 0..... DanielTudhope 4 46
(David O'Meara) *a towards rr* **17/2**
7 37 **Irish Star (IRE)** 2-9-0 0..... PJMcDonald 6
(Paul Midgley) *dwlt: green and sn outpcd in rr: bhd fnl 2f* **66/1**
1m 13.12s (0.12) **Going Correction** -0.125s/f (Firm) **7 Ran SP% 112.5**
Speed ratings (Par 93): **94,90,87,84,84 82,33**
toteswingers 1&2 £1.60, 1&3 £1.50, 2&3 £2.50 CSF £21.69 TOTE £3.10: £1.10, £4.60; EX 21.60 Trifecta £47.40 Pool: £2502.80 - 39.58 winning units..
Owner Diamond Racing Ltd **Bred** Kildaragh Stud **Trained** Musley Bank, N Yorks

FOCUS
An ordinary juvenile maiden in which they went a contested gallop on ground officially described as good to firm, good in places. The winner progressed a little.

3501 NATASHA CAVEN WILL YOU MARRY ME CLAIMING STKS 6f
2:45 (2:45) (Class 5) 3-Y-O+ **£2,911** (£866; £432; £216) **Stalls High**

Form RPR
2025 1 **Last Sovereign**11 3135 9-9-0 92.....(b) JacobButterfield(7) 6 89
(Ollie Pears) *trckd ldrs: swtchd rt 2f out: sn cl up: rdn to ld appr fnl f: sn clr* **11/8**1
1214 2 3 3/4 **Tajneed (IRE)**31 2516 10-8-13 71..... PaulMulrennan 3 69
(David Nicholls) *trckd ldr: hdwy on bit and cl up over 2f out: led wl over 1f out: sn jnd and shkn up: hdd appr fnl f: kpt on same pce* **9/4**2
1460 3 1 1/4 **Beckermet (IRE)**13 3068 11-8-12 68..... JamesSullivan 1 64
(Ruth Carr) *trckd ldrs: hdwy on outer 1/2-way: cl up over 2f out: sn rdn and edgd lft: one pce appr fnl f* **12/1**
-01 4 1 1/2 **Jessie's Spirit (IRE)**27 2613 4-8-9 75..... PJMcDonald 7 56
(Ann Duffield) *hld up towards rr: pushed along over 2f out: rdn wl over 1f out: swtchd rt ent fnl f: no imp* **7/2**3
5345 5 3/4 **Red Cape (FR)**13 3069 10-8-12 68.....(b) DaleSwift 5 57
(Ruth Carr) *led: pushed along 1/2-way: rdn 2f out: sn hdd & wknd* **14/1**
0306 6 1 1/4 **Chester'Slittlegem (IRE)**13 3042 4-8-7 47..... FrannyNorton 2 48
(Jo Hughes) *cl up: rdn along when sltly hmpd wl over 1f out: sn wknd* **50/1**
-600 7 2 3/4 **Vogarth**43 2168 9-8-5 36.....(b) DanielleMooney(7) 4 44
(Michael Chapman) *dwlt: a in rr* **200/1**
1m 11.11s (-1.89) **Going Correction** -0.125s/f (Firm) **7 Ran SP% 111.9**
Speed ratings (Par 103): **107,102,100,98,97 95,92**
toteswingers 1&2 £1.70, 1&3 £4.90, 2&3 £2.70 CSF £4.44 TOTE £2.20: £1.70, £1.30; EX 4.70 Trifecta £22.90 Pool: £2424.97 - 79.40 winning units..
Owner Richard Walker **Bred** Gestut Hof Ittlingen & Cheveley Park Stud Ltd **Trained** Norton, N Yorks

FOCUS
Other than the winner this was no more than a fair claimer, but his BHA rating of 92 upholds the strength of this contest from the previous five seasons, with three of those rated 85 plus. The winner didn't need to match his best this year.

3502 CURVY BRIDAL BOROUGHBRIDGE H'CAP 1m 4f 10y
3:20 (3:20) (Class 4) (0-80,79) 3-Y-O **£4,851** (£1,443; £721; £360) **Stalls Low**

Form RPR
011 1 **London Bridge (USA)**6 3294 3-9-5 77 6ex..... DanielTudhope 2 98+
(Jo Hughes) *mde all: jnd and pushed along over 3f out: rdn wl over 1f out: styd on strly fnl f* **5/4**1
50-1 2 2 3/4 **Broughton (GER)**15 2989 3-9-7 79..... FrannyNorton 6 94
(Mark Johnston) *trckd ldr: cl up 5f out: chal 3f out: rdn 2f out and ev ch tl drvn and one pce appr fnl f* **5/2**2

2102 **3** *4* **Divergence (IRE)**[7] 3251 3-9-0 **75**.............................. LucyAlexander(3) 5 84
(Michael Bell) *trckd ldrs: hdwy to chse ldng pair over 4f out: rdn along 3f out: drvn fnl 2f: no imp* **7/1**[3]

52-1 **4** *2* **Hawk High (IRE)**[20] 2833 3-9-3 **75**.............................. DuranFentiman 4 81
(Tim Easterby) *t.k.h early: trckd ldrs: effrt over 3f out: rdn and edgd rt 2f out: drvn: hung rt and one pce fr over 1f out* **9/1**

6146 **5** *6* **Marhaba Malayeen (IRE)**[13] 3067 3-9-1 **73**.................... PhillipMakin 3 69
(Kevin Ryan) *hld up: effrt 4f out: rdn along 3f out: drvn over 2f out and n.d* **28/1**

0-43 **6** *4 ½* **Arlecchino (IRE)**[20] 2827 3-9-1 **73**.............................. RoystonFfrench 8 62
(Ed McMahon) *chsd ldrs: rdn along 4f out: wknd wl over 2f out* **22/1**

-300 **7** *16* **Arthurs Secret**[34] 2432 3-9-1 **73**..........................(v[1]) MichaelO'Connell 1 36
(John Quinn) *s.i.s and rdn along in rr: hdwy on inner and in tch after 2f: chsd ldrs and rdn along 1/2-way: drvn over 3f out: sn wknd* **16/1**

2m 32.06s (-4.64) **Going Correction** -0.35s/f (Firm) 7 Ran SP% **109.2**
Speed ratings (Par 101): **101,99,96,95,91 88,77**
toteswingers 1&2 £1.50, 1&3 £3.60, 2&3 £3.60 CSF £3.97 CT £11.47 TOTE £1.70: £3.60, £1.10; EX 4.90 Trifecta £13.30 Pool: £2700.02 - 151.48 winning units..

Owner Eastwind Racing Ltd And Martha Trussell **Bred** Patricia S Purdy **Trained** Lambourn, Berks

FOCUS
A fair middle-distance 3yo handicap in which the winner made all on a good track. The form is taken at face value.

3503 LADIES DAY H'CAP 1m 1f
4:00 (4:00) (Class 3) (0-90,90) 4-Y-0-**£7,561** (£2,263; £1,131; £566; £282) **Stalls** Low

Form RPR

1-54 **1** **Ginger Jack**[5] 3346 6-9-3 **86**.............................. PJMcDonald 5 95
(Geoffrey Harker) *hld up towards rr: hdwy over 3f out: rdn to chse ldr over 1f out: styd on to ld ins fnl f: sn drvn and hld on wl towards fin* **13/8**[1]

2144 **2** *½* **Swing Alone (IRE)**[21] 2813 4-9-5 **88**.............................. RobertWinston 7 96
(Gay Kelleway) *trckd ldng pair: chsd ldr after 2f: cl up over 4f out: led 2f out: sn rdn: drvn and hdd ins fnl f: rallied gamely last 100yds: no ex nr fin* **9/2**[3]

5062 **3** *4 ½* **Las Verglas Star (IRE)**[8] 3204 5-8-8 **82**................ GeorgeChaloner(5) 3 80
(Richard Fahey) *trckd ldrs: hdwy 3f out: rdn to chse ldrs 2f out: drvn and kpt on one pce fnl f* **2/1**[2]

0-00 **4** *1 ½* **Invisible Hunter (USA)**[12] 3113 4-9-3 **86**......................(t) RobertHavlin 8 81
(Saeed bin Suroor) *led after 1f: pushed along over 3f out: sn rdn and hdd 2f out: sn drvn and wknd* **5/1**

0 **5** *4 ½* **Mespone (FR)**[12] 3094 4-8-10 **82**.............................. LeeTopliss(3) 6 67
(Paul Midgley) *led 1f: trckd ldrs: rdn along 4f out: wknd over 2f out* **66/1**

0020 **6** *hd* **No Poppy (IRE)**[24] 2718 5-8-13 **87**.............................. AdamCarter(5) 2 71
(Tim Easterby) *hld up in rr: rdn along and outpcd over 3f out: swtchd lft to outer over 2f out: sn drvn and no imp* **16/1**

1m 49.97s (-4.73) **Going Correction** -0.35s/f (Firm) course record 6 Ran SP% **113.7**
Speed ratings (Par 107): **107,106,102,101,97 97**
toteswingers 1&2 £1.60, 2&3 £3.40, 1&3 £1.40 CSF £9.69 CT £14.54 TOTE £2.40: £1.20, £3.50; EX 14.40 Trifecta £27.60 Pool: £2095.67 - 56.87 winning units..

Owner C H McGhie **Bred** Darley **Trained** Thirkleby, N Yorks

FOCUS
A decent handicap for older horses in which they went a good clip from the outset. The first pair were clear, and the winner showed his best form since he was a 3yo.

3504 BEAUMONT ROBINSON LADIES' DERBY H'CAP (LADY AMATEUR RIDERS) 1m 4f 10y
4:35 (4:36) (Class 6) (0-65,65) 4-Y-0+ **£3,119** (£967; £483; £242) **Stalls** Low

Form RPR

0356 **1** **Pertuis (IRE)**[8] 3195 7-10-7 **65**.............................. MissSBrotherton 11 72
(Micky Hammond) *hld up in tch: trckd ldrs 1/2-way: hdwy 3f out: effrt 2f out: rdn to ld jst ins fnl f: kpt on wl* **13/2**[2]

-320 **2** *¾* **Politbureau**[24] 2720 6-9-0 **49**.............................. MissJoannaMason(5) 5 55
(Michael Easterby) *cl up on inner: effrt over 2f out: rdn and ev ch over 1f out tl drvn and no ex wl ins fnl f* **9/1**

3-10 **3** *hd* **Maybeme**[8] 3195 7-9-13 **57**..(p) MissCWalton 4 62+
(Neville Bycroft) *hld up and bhd: stdy hdwy 3f out: swtchd lft and chsd ldrs over 1f out: rdn and styng on whn n.m.r and stmbld sltly wl ins fnl f: kpt on wl towards fin* **8/1**

0-06 **4** *½* **Rub Of The Relic (IRE)**[12] 3106 8-9-10 **59**............(v) MissHDukes(5) 14 64
(Paul Midgley) *led: rdn along and hdd 2f out: rallied u.p and ev ch ent fnl f: sn drvn and no ex* **14/1**

30-5 **5** *hd* **Hernando Torres**[19] 2875 5-9-10 **59**.............................. AnnaHesketh(5) 6 63
(Michael Easterby) *hld up: hdwy on inner over 2f out: rdn to chse ldrs over 1f out: drvn and kpt on fnl f: nrst fin* **8/1**

1153 **6** *1* **Jan Smuts (IRE)**[19] 2887 5-10-0 **63**......................(tp) MissSMDoolan(5) 1 66
(Wilf Storey) *hld up in rr: swtchd lft to outer and hdwy 3f out: rdn to chse ldrs on wd outside 2f out: drvn and one pce fnl f* **11/1**

-203 **7** *shd* **Al Furat (USA)**[6] 3287 5-9-11 **60**.............................. MrsVDavies(5) 13 63
(Ron Barr) *t.k.h: prom: cl up over 4f out: led 2f out: rdn and hdd jst ins fnl f: grad wknd* **7/1**[3]

0025 **8** *6* **Rayadour (IRE)**[27] 2630 4-10-7 **65**..............................(t) MrsCBartley 10 58
(Micky Hammond) *hld up in rr: hdwy on wd outside 4f out: rdn along to chse ldrs wl over 2f out: wknd over 1f out* **16/1**

0060 **9** *½* **Patavium (IRE)**[6] 3287 10-10-7 **65**..............................(p) MissADeniel 9 57
(Edwin Tuer) *hld up in midfield: hdwy over 3f out: chsd ldrs over 2f out: sn rdn and wknd over 1f out* **20/1**

000/ **10** *2 ¼* **Suprise Vendor (IRE)**[25] 2636 7-9-7 **54**.............. MissJRRichards(3) 12 43
(Stuart Coltherd) *prom: rdn along over 3f out: wknd over 2f out* **33/1**

1-31 **11** *1* **Teide Peak (IRE)**[27] 2629 4-10-2 **65**.............................. MrsRWilson(5) 7 52
(Paul D'Arcy) *t.k.h: trckd ldrs on inner: effrt over 3f out: sn rdn along and wknd over 2f out* **5/2**[1]

3-54 **12** *1 ½* **Laconicos (IRE)**[12] 3106 11-9-10 **59**..............................(t) MissCScott(5) 8 44
(William Stone) *chsd ldrs on outer: rdn along wl over 2f out: sn wknd* **25/1**

2m 36.72s (0.02) **Going Correction** -0.35s/f (Firm) 12 Ran SP% **119.1**
Speed ratings (Par 101): **85,84,84,84,83 83,83,79,78,77 76,75**
toteswingers 1&2 £7.40, 1&3 £14.90, 2&3 £15.60 CSF £62.58 CT £480.95 TOTE £5.00: £1.80, £3.10, £2.20; EX 58.10 Trifecta £300.90 Pool: £2952.41 - 7.35 winning units..

Owner M H O G **Bred** Killeen Castle Stud **Trained** Middleham Moor, N Yorks

FOCUS
Judging by how a few of these were pulling and struggling to settle in the formative stages, the lady amateur riders set a sedate gallop on these modest middle-distance handicappers. Modest form, taken at face value.

3505 SUPPORT THE YORKSHIRE AIR AMBULANCE TODAY H'CAP 5f
5:10 (5:10) (Class 5) (0-75,75) 3-Y-0+ **£3,234** (£962; £481; £240) **Stalls** High

Form RPR

35-3 **1** **Ypres**[20] 2832 4-9-4 **65**.............................. PJMcDonald 2 75
(Jason Ward) *hld up: hdwy on outer 2f out: rdn ent fnl f: styd on wl to ld last 50yds* **9/2**[2]

3106 **2** *nk* **Another Citizen (IRE)**[40] 2268 5-9-5 **73**......................(b) GaryMahon(7) 5 82
(Tim Easterby) *chsd ldrs: hdwy over 2f out: rdn over 1f out: led ins fnl f: edgd rt: hdd and nt qckn last 50yds* **5/1**[3]

5244 **3** *1 ½* **Phoenix Clubs (IRE)**[13] 3069 4-9-11 **72**......................(p) BarryMcHugh 7 76
(Paul Midgley) *hmpd s: in tch: hdwy over 1f out: rdn ent fnl f: sn swtchd rt and kpt on: nrst fin* **6/1**

25-0 **4** *hd* **Fol Hollow (IRE)**[49] 1971 8-9-3 **64**.............................. MichaelO'Connell 1 67
(Stuart Coltherd) *chsd ldrs: hdwy 2f out: rdn over 1f out: styng on whn n.m.r and sltly hmpd ent fnl f: one pce after* **25/1**

-062 **5** *1* **Imperial Legend (IRE)**[6] 3283 4-9-5 **71**..............(v) ShirleyTeasdale(5) 9 70+
(David Nicholls) *sltly hmpd and wnt bdly rt s: plld hrd and led after 1f: sn clr: rdn over 1f out: hdd & wknd ins fnl f* **11/4**[1]

3264 **6** *1 ½* **Diamond Blue**[12] 3078 5-9-7 **68**.............................. PhillipMakin 4 62
(Richard Whitaker) *hmpd s: in rr tl styd on appr fnl f: nrst fin* **6/1**

10-0 **7** *½* **Lizzy's Dream**[20] 2832 5-9-2 **63**.............................. RobertWinston 10 55
(Robin Bastiman) *hmpd s: a in rr* **14/1**

0006 **8** *nse* **Elusive Bonus (IRE)**[12] 3078 4-9-3 **71**.............................. JoshDoyle(7) 6 63
(David O'Meara) *hmpd s: in tch: rdn along over 2f out: sn no imp* **16/1**

0000 **9** *3 ½* **Chunky Diamond (IRE)**[23] 2755 4-9-13 **74**................ JamesSullivan 11 53
(Ruth Carr) *wnt bdly rt s: led 1f: sn hdd and chsd ldr: rdn along wl over 1f out: wknd ent fnl f* **9/1**

59.12s (-0.88) **Going Correction** -0.125s/f (Firm) 9 Ran SP% **116.5**
Speed ratings (Par 103): **102,101,99,98,97 94,94,93,88**
toteswingers 1&2 £7.20, 1&3 £4.40, 2&3 £5.80 CSF £27.55 CT £137.30 TOTE £5.50: £1.80, £2.30, £3.10; EX 25.10 Trifecta £160.80 Pool: £2057.79 - 9.59 winning units..

Owner Pear Tree, Brian Harker, Panther Racing **Bred** Philip Graham Harvey **Trained** Middleham, N Yorks

■ Stewards' Enquiry : Barry McHugh two-day ban: careless riding (4-5 July)

FOCUS
There was plenty of scrimmaging for a position in the early stages of this fair sprint handicap. The race was set up perfectly for closers. The winner is generally progressive.

3506 RACING AGAIN ON MONDAY 8TH JULY H'CAP 1m
5:45 (5:46) (Class 5) (0-75,75) 4-Y-0+ **£3,234** (£962; £481; £240) **Stalls** Low

Form RPR

0615 **1** **Hakuna Matata**[19] 2889 6-8-12 **73**..........................(b) ConnorBeasley(7) 1 83
(Michael Dods) *hld up towards rr: hdwy on inner 3f out: swtchd lft over 2f out: rdn to chal on outer over 1f out: led ent fnl f: drvn out* **4/1**[2]

2303 **2** *2* **Cono Zur (FR)**[14] 3027 6-8-12 **66**.............................. JamesSullivan 7 71
(Ruth Carr) *hld up in rr: swtchd lft to outer and hdwy over 2f out: rdn over 1f out: styd on fnl f: nt rch wnr* **8/1**[3]

/615 **3** *½* **Nimiety**[23] 2761 4-9-2 **70**.............................. J-PGuillambert 8 74
(Mark Johnston) *in tch: hdwy 3f out: chsd ldrs 2f out: rdn and edgd rt over 1f out: drvn and ev ch ent fnl f: kpt on same pce* **16/1**

3-35 **4** *1 ¾* **Fame Again**[141] 443 5-9-4 **72**.............................. PhillipMakin 9 73+
(Michael Easterby) *trckd ldrs: hdwy whn nt clr run wl over 1f out: sn swtchd lft and n.m.r ent fnl f: rdn and kpt on same pce after* **14/1**

2311 **5** *hd* **Size (IRE)**[5] 3337 4-8-8 **65** ow2.............................. LeeTopliss(3) 2 64+
(Richard Fahey) *hld up in tch on inner: effrt and nt clr run over 2f out: swtchd lft and nt clr run wl over 1f out: swtchd rt and rdn ent fnl f: squeezed through and styd on: nrst fin* **4/5**[1]

0225 **6** *¾* **Eastward Ho**[12] 3081 5-8-13 **67**.............................. PJMcDonald 5 65
(Jason Ward) *trckd ldrs: hdwy 2f out: nt clr run and swtchd rt to inner appr fnl f: sn drvn and one pce* **9/1**

1250 **7** *1 ¼* **Berlusca (IRE)**[112] 832 4-9-5 **73**.............................. DanielTudhope 10 68
(David O'Meara) *prom: hdwy on outer 3f out: led 2f out: sn rdn: hdd and drvn ent fnl f: sn wknd* **16/1**

00-0 **8** *4* **First Class Favour (IRE)**[14] 3027 5-8-12 **66**.............. DuranFentiman 6 52
(Tim Easterby) *trckd ldr: hdwy and cl up 3f out: rdn over 2f out: wknd over 1f out* **40/1**

0000 **9** *8* **Violent Velocity (IRE)**[30] 2551 10-8-9 **63**................ MichaelO'Connell 4 30
(John Quinn) *sn led: rdn along 3f out: hdd 2f out and sn wknd* **40/1**

000- **10** *7* **Ongoodform (IRE)**[204] 7901 6-9-6 **74**..........................(v) PaddyAspell 3 25
(David Nicholls) *a towards rr* **28/1**

1m 37.66s (-3.74) **Going Correction** -0.35s/f (Firm) 10 Ran SP% **123.4**
Speed ratings (Par 103): **104,102,101,99,99 98,97,93,85,78**
toteswingers 1&2 £7.60, 1&3 £9.10, 2&3 £9.80 CSF £37.81 CT £483.28 TOTE £5.40: £1.20, £4.60, £4.10; EX 46.00 Trifecta £265.50 Pool: £1362.19 - 3.84 winning units..

Owner Sekura Group **Bred** Mrs J A Chapman **Trained** Denton, Co Durham

FOCUS
There was never any likelihood of any hanging about from this field of fair, older handicappers, and so it proved. There wasn't much depth and the favourite got no run.
T/Plt: £88.00 to a £1 stake. Pool of £55,917.47 - 463.60 winning tickets. T/Qpdt: £15.80 to a £1 stake. Pool of £3782.60 - 176.07 winning tickets. JR

3406 WARWICK (L-H)
Thursday, June 20

OFFICIAL GOING: Good to firm (good in places; 8.2)
Wind: Light half-against Weather: Hazy sunshine

3507 TURFTV CLAIMING STKS 1m 22y
2:20 (2:20) (Class 5) 3-Y-0+ **£2,587** (£770; £384; £192) **Stalls** Low

Form RPR

-210 **1** **Mysterial**[28] 2584 3-9-3 79..(b) SeanLevey 3 68+
(Richard Hannon) *mde all: shkn up over 2f out: sn clr: comf* **1/1**[1]

0002 **2** *2 ½* **Newnton Lodge**[5] 3319 4-9-11 68.............................. StevieDonohoe 6 62
(Ian Williams) *s.i.s: hld up: racd keenly: hdwy over 1f out: r.o to go 2nd ins fnl f: nvr nr to chal* **12/1**

6000 **3** *6* **Light From Mars**[12] 3096 8-9-9 83.............................. GeorgeBaker 1 46
(Ronald Harris) *chsd wnr over 2f: remained handy: wnt 2nd again over 2f out: rdn over 1f out: wknd ins fnl f* **7/2**[3]

642/ **4** *4* **Four Winds**[1402] 5141 7-9-10 88 .... RossAtkinson(3) 7 41
(Robert Cowell) *racd keenly: prom: trckd wnr over 5f out tl pushed along over 2f out: wknd wl over 1f out* **11/4**[2]

6 **5** *4 1/2* **Sextons House (IRE)**[16] 2948 5-8-11 45 ....(p) AaronJones(7) 2 22
(Alan McCabe) *s.i.s: hld up: wknd 2f out* **125/1**

1m 39.23s (-1.77) **Going Correction** -0.125s/f (Firm)
WFA 3 from 4yo+ 10lb **5** Ran SP% **107.4**
Speed ratings (Par 103): **103,100,94,90,86**
CSF £12.95 TOTE £1.60: £1.20, £3.10; EX 6.80 Trifecta £21.50 Pool: £1099.12 - 38.19 winning units..Mysterial was claimed by Mr Steve Barker for £12,000
Owner Highclere Thoroughbred Racing - Sloan **Bred** Ladyswood, Canning Down & D Farrington **Trained** East Everleigh, Wilts
FOCUS
Little depth to this fair claimer, which has been rated cautiously.

3508 REWARDS4RACING.COM MAIDEN FILLIES' STKS 6f
2:55 (2:55) (Class 5) 3-Y-O+ **£2,587** (£770; £384; £192) **Stalls** Low

Form RPR
-42 **1** **Celestial Bay**[20] 2824 4-9-7 0 ....[1] GeorgeBaker 5 72
(Sylvester Kirk) *chsd ldrs: outpcd over 3f out: hdwy 2f out: sn rdn to chse ldr: r.o to ld wl ins fnl f* **8/11**[1]

2 *3/4* **Hand Grenade (IRE)** 3-9-0 0 .... JohnFahy 2 67
(Eve Johnson Houghton) *led 2f: led again 3f out: edgd rt over 2f out: rdn over 1f out: hdd wl ins fnl f* **12/1**

04- **3** *3 1/2* **Tammuz (IRE)**[174] 8262 3-9-0 0 .... StevieDonohoe 1 56
(Tony Carroll) *s.i.s: outpcd: r.o ins fnl f: nvr nrr* **17/2**[3]

0-42 **4** *10* **Hasbah (IRE)**[41] 2226 3-9-0 67 .... NeilCallan 4 35
(Peter Chapple-Hyam) *chsd ldr tl led 4f out: hdd 3f out: sn pushed along: wknd over 1f out: eased ins fnl f* **9/4**[2]

1m 12.34s (0.54) **Going Correction** +0.05s/f (Good)
WFA 3 from 4yo 7lb **4** Ran SP% **106.9**
Speed ratings (Par 100): **98,97,92,79**
CSF £9.08 TOTE £1.50; EX 5.10 TRIFECTA Pool: £1592.41 - 51.18 winning units..
Owner Homebred Racing **Bred** Chris Wall **Trained** Upper Lambourn, Berks
FOCUS
They went fast in this modest maiden, with Hasbah and Hand Grenade taking each other on, and the race set up nicely for the favourite. Modest form.

3509 EVANS DERRY SOLICITORS THOROUGHBRED LEGAL ADVICE H'CAP 6f
3:30 (3:30) (Class 6) (0-65,65) 3-Y-O **£1,940** (£577; £288; £144) **Stalls** Low

Form RPR
1520 **1** **Roland**[12] 3082 3-9-6 64 ....(b) NeilCallan 9 74
(Kevin Ryan) *mde all: rdn and hung rt over 1f out: r.o* **22/1**

6562 **2** *2 3/4* **Bosham**[8] 3221 3-9-4 62 .... CathyGannon 2 63
(William Jarvis) *chsd ldrs: rdn over 1f out: styd on same pce ins fnl f* **15/8**[2]

02-2 **3** *3/4* **Blessing Box**[16] 2962 3-9-7 65 .... GeorgeBaker 10 64
(Chris Wall) *plld hrd and prom: trckd ldr 4f out: rdn and hung lft over 1f out: no ex ins fnl f* **7/4**[1]

405- **4** *1* **Ladweb**[216] 7738 3-9-4 62 .... JohnFahy 4 58
(John Gallagher) *chsd ldrs: rdn over 1f out: styd on same pce fnl f* **28/1**

0U6- **5** *shd* **Fantasy Invader (IRE)**[272] 6438 3-9-0 58 ....[1] TomEaves 8 53
(John Quinn) *prom: rdn over 1f out: styd on same pce ins fnl f* **25/1**

400- **6** *1/2* **Somethingboutmary**[244] 7206 3-9-7 65 .... ShaneKelly 6 59
(Tim Pitt) *s.i.s: hld up: pushed along over 2f out: rdn over 1f out: nt trble ldrs* **22/1**

00-4 **7** *hd* **Blue Twister**[12] 3109 3-8-10 61 ....(v[1]) DanielMuscutt(7) 3 54
(Andrew Balding) *prom: rdn over 2f out: no ex ins fnl f* **10/3**[3]

6-60 **8** *3 1/2* **Annie Besant**[22] 2770 3-8-1 52 ....(t) JoeyHaynes(7) 12 34
(Michael Mullineaux) *s.i.s: sn pushed along and a in rr* **33/1**

1m 12.3s (0.50) **Going Correction** +0.05s/f (Good) **8** Ran SP% **113.2**
Speed ratings (Par 97): **98,94,93,92,91 91,90,86**
toteswingers 1&2 £4.80, 1&3 £2.20, 2&3 £1.30 CSF £60.19 CT £114.77 TOTE £19.40: £4.40, £1.10, £1.30; EX 65.00 Trifecta £278.50 Pool: £2096.12 - 5.64 winning units..
Owner Mrs Angie Bailey **Bred** Minster Stud And Bickerton Racing **Trained** Hambleton, N Yorks
FOCUS
A low-grade handicap where it paid to race prominently. The three market leaders were all a little disappointing.

3510 BRITISH STALLION STUDS SUPPORTING BRITISH RACING EBF MAIDEN FILLIES' STKS 5f
4:10 (4:11) (Class 5) 2-Y-O **£2,911** (£866; £432; £216) **Stalls** Low

Form RPR
1 **Lady Chantilly (IRE)** 2-9-0 0 .... CathyGannon 1 74+
(Jo Hughes) *s.i.s: outpcd: hdwy over 1f out: led ins fnl f: r.o* **20/1**

03 **2** *nk* **Sunset Shore**[13] 3049 2-8-11 0 .... RyanPowell(3) 4 73
(Sir Mark Prescott Bt) *chsd ldrs: outpcd 1/2-way: rallied to ld and hung rt over 1f out: rdn and hdd ins fnl f: r.o* **7/2**[2]

0 **3** *5* **Anytimeatall (IRE)**[42] 2189 2-9-0 0 .... SamHitchcott 7 55
(Alan Bailey) *led: rdn and hdd over 1f out: wknd ins fnl f* **6/1**

5 **4** *1 3/4* **Inspiriter**[13] 3049 2-9-0 0 .... NeilCallan 6 49+
(Saeed bin Suroor) *swvd rt s and s.i.s: plld hrd and hung rt thrght: hdwy over 3f out: rdn over 1f out: nt run on* **5/4**[1]

4 **5** *3/4* **She Can Jig**[24] 2701 2-9-0 0 .... TomEaves 5 46
(Kevin Ryan) *chsd ldrs: rdn over 1f out: wknd fnl f* **11/2**[3]

6 *5* **Charlie's Wish (FR)** 2-9-0 0 .... StevieDonohoe 2 28
(Conrad Allen) *s.i.s: outpcd* **10/1**

59.86s (0.26) **Going Correction** +0.05s/f (Good) **6** Ran SP% **110.2**
Speed ratings (Par 90): **99,98,90,87,86 78**
toteswingers 1&2 £8.50, 1&3 £14.10, 2&3 £3.70 CSF £84.18 TOTE £30.30: £8.60, £1.40; EX 108.10 Trifecta £506.00 Pool: £3545.80 - 5.25 winning units..
Owner D Mossop, J Henderson, J Hughes **Bred** Tally-Ho Stud **Trained** Lambourn, Berks
FOCUS
Ordinary maiden form. They went hard enough up front early on perhaps making the first two, who finished clear, look good on the day.

3511 DINE IN THE 1707 RESTAURANT H'CAP 7f 26y
4:45 (4:45) (Class 5) (0-70,69) 3-Y-O+ **£2,587** (£770; £384; £192) **Stalls** Low

Form RPR
2-14 **1** **See The Storm**[27] 2638 5-9-12 67 .... StevieDonohoe 6 76
(Ian Williams) *hld up: hdwy 1/2-way: rdn over 1f out: r.o u.p to ld nr fin* **11/4**[1]

0-24 **2** *nk* **Kakapuka**[21] 2807 6-10-0 69 .... GeorgeBaker 11 77
(Anabel K Murphy) *w ldr tl led over 1f out: sn rdn: hdd nr fin* **17/2**

60-0 **3** *1/2* **Sheikh The Reins (IRE)**[16] 2964 4-9-10 65 ....(v[1]) JohnFahy 4 72
(John Best) *trckd ldrs: racd keenly: rdn over 1f out: unable qck nr fin* **12/1**

0360 **4** *2 1/4* **Unlimited**[29] 2565 11-8-6 50 .... AmyBaker(3) 8 51
(Tony Carroll) *hld up: pushed along over 2f out: rdn and r.o ins fnl f: nt rch ldrs* **12/1**

5-00 **5** *1* **Wordismybond**[20] 2845 4-9-5 60 .... NeilCallan 7 58
(Peter Makin) *chsd ldrs: rdn over 2f out: no ex ins fnl f* **5/1**[2]

0250 **6** *1/2* **Gaelic Wizard (IRE)**[13] 3042 5-8-12 60 .... JoshBaudains(7) 9 57
(Dominic Ffrench Davis) *prom: rdn over 1f out: styd on same pce* **18/1**

0054 **7** *shd* **Rigolleto (IRE)**[9] 3172 5-9-13 68 .... SamHitchcott 10 64
(Anabel K Murphy) *led: rdn and hdd over 1f out: no ex ins fnl f* **16/1**

4603 **8** *4* **George Benjamin**[17] 2932 6-8-12 58 .... RachealKneller(5) 5 43
(Christopher Kellett) *s.i.s: sn prom: lost pl 1/2-way: n.d after* **5/1**[2]

3332 **9** *2 1/4* **Emiratesdotcom**[6] 3270 7-9-6 66 ....(p) MatthewLawson(5) 13 45
(Milton Bradley) *s.i.s: hld up: hdwy 1/2-way: rdn over 2f out: sn wknd* **11/2**[3]

00-0 **10** *5* **Ellies Image**[17] 2932 6-8-9 50 oh3 ....(p) CathyGannon 12 16
(Brian Baugh) *s.i.s: outpcd* **40/1**

1m 23.29s (-1.31) **Going Correction** -0.125s/f (Firm) **10** Ran SP% **114.9**
Speed ratings (Par 103): **102,101,101,98,97 96,96,92,89,83**
toteswingers 1&2 £4.00, 1&3 £5.60, 2&3 £14.10 CSF £26.49 CT £244.99 TOTE £3.70: £1.70, £4.10, £4.10; EX 28.60 Trifecta £188.20 Pool: £1685.06 - 6.71 winning units..
Owner Ecking Bradley Fold Ltd **Bred** D R Botterill **Trained** Portway, Worcs
■ Stewards' Enquiry : Matthew Lawson five-day ban: use of whip (4, 5, 6, 7 8 July)
John Fahy two-day ban: use of whip (4-5 July)
FOCUS
Moderate handicap form. The first three finished a little clear, with the winner posting another personal best.

3512 FOLLOW US ON TWITTER @WARWICKRACES H'CAP 1m 6f 213y
5:20 (5:21) (Class 5) (0-75,78) 4-Y-O+ **£2,587** (£770; £384; £192) **Stalls** Low

Form RPR
-305 **1** **Wild Desert (FR)**[132] 562 8-9-2 69 .... CathyGannon 2 83
(Tony Carroll) *mde all: set stdy pce tl qcknd clr over 2f out: easily* **6/1**[3]

4-31 **2** *19* **Italian Riviera**[5] 3328 4-9-8 78 6ex .... SimonPearce(3) 4 67
(Sir Mark Prescott Bt) *unruly in stalls: wnt rt s and s.i.s: hld up: stmbld bnd and rdr lost iron 11f out: nt clr run over 3f out: rdn to go 2nd over 1f out: nvr nr to chal* **4/5**[1]

1-43 **3** *2* **Hi Note**[36] 1158 5-8-8 61 .... JohnFahy 3 48
(Sheena West) *chsd wnr 3f: remained handy: wnt 2nd again 4f out: rdn over 2f out: wknd over 1f out* **3/1**[2]

24/5 **4** *3 1/2* **Paintball (IRE)**[20] 2849 6-9-2 69 .... SamHitchcott 7 51
(Charlie Longsdon) *s.v.s and sn wl bhd: pushed along over 6f out: hdwy over 4f out: rdn and wknd 2f out* **16/1**

00/ **5** *19* **Mister Carter (IRE)**[324] 4691 6-9-7 74 .... StevieDonohoe 1 31
(Ian Williams) *chsd ldrs tl rdn and wknd over 2f out: t.o* **16/1**

333- **6** *34* **Finch Flyer (IRE)**[9] 6278 6-7-11 55 oh3 ....(b) NatashaEaton(5) 5
(Aytach Sadik) *plld hrd and prom: trckd wnr after 3f: hung rt 8f out: lost 2nd 4f out: hung rt and wknd over 3f out: t.o* **40/1**

3m 15.2s (-3.80) **Going Correction** -0.125s/f (Firm) **6** Ran SP% **109.0**
Speed ratings (Par 103): **105,94,93,91,81 63**
toteswingers 1&2 £1.60, 1&3 £2.30, 2&3 £1.40 CSF £10.67 TOTE £9.70: £3.50, £1.20; EX 17.90 Trifecta £50.60 Pool: £3438.35 - 50.87 winning units..
Owner Whites Of Coventry & Stephen Dunn **Bred** Wertheimer Et Frere **Trained** Cropthorne, Worcs
FOCUS
A messy race, with Paintball walking out of the stalls, red-hot favourite Italian Riviera rearing and getting a bump, ending up out of his ground, and them going a stop-start gallop. The winner got an easy lead and this form is tricky to assess.

3513 RACINGUK.COM APPRENTICE TRAINING SERIES H'CAP (PART OF THE RACING EXCELLENCE INITIATIVE) 1m 22y
5:50 (5:54) (Class 6) (0-60,58) 4-Y-O+ **£1,940** (£577; £288; £144) **Stalls** Low

Form RPR
3203 **1** **Supa Seeker (USA)**[7] 3244 7-8-4 48 ow1 .... AidenBlakemore(7) 8 56
(Tony Carroll) *a.p: shkn up over 1f out: r.o to ld wl ins fnl f* **15/2**

0153 **2** *1/2* **Munaawib**[8] 3203 5-9-1 52 ....(bt) RyanWhile 9 59
(Charles Smith) *a.p: chsd ldr 5f out: led over 1f out: rdn and hdd wl ins fnl f* **5/1**[2]

0-04 **3** *1 1/4* **Greyemkay**[11] 3138 5-8-12 49 .... JoshBaudains 12 53
(Richard Price) *hld up: hdwy over 1f out: r.o: nt rch ldrs* **12/1**

0-26 **4** *hd* **Cheers Big Ears (IRE)**[6] 3270 7-8-7 47 .... EoinWalsh(3) 13 51
(Richard Price) *hld up: rdn over 1f out: hung lft and r.o ins fnl f: nrst fin* **7/1**[3]

100- **5** *1 1/4* **Tanforan**[259] 6829 11-9-0 54 .... MatthewHopkins(3) 5 55
(Brian Baugh) *led: rdn and hdd over 1f out: no ex ins fnl f* **18/1**

0-54 **6** *nk* **Attain**[20] 2845 4-9-3 54 ....(p) ShelleyBirkett 4 54
(Julia Feilden) *chsd ldr 3f: remained handy: rdn over 1f out: styd on same pce* **9/4**[1]

0610 **7** *1* **Spinning Ridge (IRE)**[16] 2954 8-9-7 58 ....(b) EDLinehan 10 56
(Ronald Harris) *s.i.s: hld up: hdwy over 1f out: styd on same pce ins fnl f* **16/1**

4010 **8** *1 1/2* **For Shia And Lula (IRE)**[14] 3030 4-8-12 56 .... AaronFallon(7) 11 50
(Daniel Mark Loughnane) *s.i.s: hld up: rdn over 1f out: nvr trbld ldrs* **14/1**

240 **9** *1/2* **Daniel Thomas (IRE)**[64] 1617 11-9-2 58 ....(tp) OisinMurphy(5) 14 51
(Violet M Jordan) *s.i.s: hld up: rdn over 1f out: n.d* **20/1**

-400 **10** *2 3/4* **Orla (IRE)**[37] 2345 5-8-10 47 .... NoelGarbutt 6 34
(John Gallagher) *prom: rdn over 2f out: wknd fnl f* **33/1**

5000 **11** *nk* **Olynard (IRE)**[6] 3270 7-8-9 46 ....(p) NoraLooby 7 32
(Michael Mullineaux) *hld up: plld hrd: hdwy over 3f out: rdn and wknd over 1f out* **28/1**

0453 **12** *6* **Hittin'The Skids (IRE)**[37] 2345 5-8-7 49 ....(p) AaronJones(5) 3 21
(Mandy Rowland) *s.i.s: plld hrd and sn prom: rdn and wknd over 1f out* **8/1**

000- **13** *10* **Komreyev Star**[370] 3099 11-8-5 45 .... JoeyHaynes(3) 1
(Ray Peacock) *prom tl rdn and wknd over 2f out* **50/1**

1m 40.39s (-0.61) **Going Correction** -0.125s/f (Firm) **13** Ran SP% **121.4**
Speed ratings (Par 101): **98,97,96,96,94 94,93,92,91,88 88,82,72**
toteswingers 1&2 £8.50, 1&3 £14.50, 2&3 £13.60 CSF £43.92 CT £457.67 TOTE £6.90: £3.50, £1.40, £5.00; EX 58.40 Trifecta £544.50 Pool: £1562.34 - 2.15 winning units..
Owner A W Carroll **Bred** Arbib Bloodstock Partnership **Trained** Cropthorne, Worcs
FOCUS
They appeared to go a steady gallop and this time they raced centre-to-far side. Straightforward low-grade form.
T/Plt: £13.00 to a £1 stake. Pool of £40,884.48 - 2284.28 winning tickets. T/Qpdt: £5.90 to a £1 stake. Pool of £2271.43 - 282.34 winning tickets. CR

3514 - 3521a (Foreign Racing) - See Raceform Interactive

3481 ASCOT (R-H)

Friday, June 21

OFFICIAL GOING: Good to firm (stands' side 9.0, centre 9.1, far side 9.3, round 8.1)

False rail on Round course removed, track at full width and distances as advertised.

Wind: Virtually nil Weather: White cloud

3522 ALBANY STKS (GROUP 3) (FILLIES) 6f

2:30 (2:32) (Class 1) 2-Y-O

£39,697 (£15,050; £7,532; £3,752; £1,883; £945) **Stalls** Centre

Form RPR

41 **1** **Kiyoshi**[29] 2583 2-8-12 0........ JamieSpencer 20 111+
(Charles Hills) *lw: dwlt: hld up in rr: hdwy over 2f out: qcknd to ld over 1f out: hung rt whn running on and drawing clr ins fnl f: readily* **8/1**[3]

11 **2** *3 1/4* **Sandiva (IRE)**[18] 2944 2-8-12 0........ FrankieDettori 15 101
(Richard Fahey) *athletic: lw: hld up: hdwy over 2f out: rdn and chalng over 1f out: nt qckn ent fnl f: unable to go w wnr after: kpt on* **7/4**[1]

1 **3** *nk* **Joyeuse**[24] 2744 2-8-12 0........ TomQueally 7 100
(Lady Cecil) *str: lw: hld up in midfield: hdwy over 2f out: nt clr run briefly over 1f out: sn chsd ldrs: r.o ins fnl f: gng on at fin* **6/1**[2]

2 **4** *1/2* **Heart Focus (IRE)**[18] 2944 2-8-12 0........ KevinManning 17 99
(J S Bolger, Ire) *tall: lengthy: lw: hld up: hdwy over 2f out: rdn over 1f out and chalng: nt qckn ent fnl f: sn hung rt: kpt on but hld* **14/1**

1 **5** *2* **Wedding Ring (IRE)**[14] 3057 2-8-12 0........ MickaelBarzalona 18 93
(Saeed bin Suroor) *athletic: in tch: effrt over 2f out: chal over 1f out: nt qckn ent fnl f: one pce fnl 100yds* **9/1**

11 **6** *nk* **Lucky Kristale**[24] 2758 2-8-12 0........ GrahamLee 16 92
(George Margarson) *w'like: a.p: rdn and ev ch over 1f out: nt qckn ins fnl f: styd on same pce fnl 150yds* **20/1**

7 *1* **Wonderfully (IRE)**[16] 2999 2-8-12 0........ RyanMoore 5 89
(A P O'Brien, Ire) *w'like: scope: gd-bodied: chsd ldrs: niggled along and outpcd after 2f: styd on u.p fr 2f out: gng on at fin but nt pce to chal* **8/1**[3]

8 *3/4* **Lady Lara (IRE)** 2-8-12 0........ JimCrowley 4 86
(Alan Jarvis) *w'like: scope: wl-made: hld up in midfield: effrt to chse ldrs over 1f out: kpt on ins fnl f: one pce fnl 100yds: nt pce to trble ldrs* **80/1**

1 **9** *1/2* **Princess Noor (IRE)**[23] 2774 2-8-12 0........ WilliamBuick 11 85
(Roger Varian) *str: midfield: lost pl and outpcd over 2f out: styd on steadily and edgd rt ins fnl f: nt trble ldrs* **33/1**

21 **10** *2 1/4* **Midnite Angel (IRE)**[32] 2517 2-8-12 0........ RichardHughes 6 78
(Richard Hannon) *w'like: scope: tall: hld up: hdwy u.p 2f out: chsd ldng bunch over 1f out: one pce and no imp ins fnl f* **16/1**

01 **11** *shd* **Red Lady (IRE)**[28] 2625 2-8-12 0........ KierenFallon 19 78
(Brian Meehan) *w'like: sturdy: ponied to s: dipslayed gd pce and led: rdn and hdd over 1f out: wknd ins fnl f* **20/1**

12 *1 1/4* **Sacred Aspect (IRE)**[40] 2287 2-8-12 0........ ShaneFoley 1 74
(K J Condon, Ire) *unf: prom: rdn and ev ch ent fnl 2f: nt qckn over 1f out: wknd ins fnl f* **50/1**

0 **13** *2 3/4* **Sleepy Sioux**[14] 3057 2-8-12 0........ DaneO'Neill 3 66
(David Elsworth) *w'like: chsd ldrs: rdn and ch over 2f out: wknd over 1f out* **100/1**

1 **14** *1 1/2* **Rasheeda**[20] 2856 2-8-12 0........ NeilCallan 13 61
(Marco Botti) *w'like: hld up: impr to chse ldrs after 2f: rdn and wknd over 1f out* **33/1**

12 **15** *1 1/2* **Suite (IRE)**[35] 2414 2-8-12 0........ PatDobbs 8 57
(Richard Hannon) *w'like: hld up: pushed along over 3f out: rdn over 2f out: nvr on terms* **66/1**

0414 **16** *9* **Iseemist (IRE)**[23] 2767 2-8-12 0........ PatSmullen 14 30
(John Gallagher) *w'like: swtg: chsd ldrs: pushed along over 2f out: wknd over 1f out* **150/1**

3241 **17** *1 1/4* **Kidmenot (IRE)**[41] 2282 2-8-12 0........ LiamJones 2 26
(J S Moore) *w'like: prom: u.p over 3f out: wknd over 2f out* **150/1**

1 **18** *3/4* **Race Hunter (USA)**[21] 2830 2-8-12 0........ JohnnyMurtagh 12 24
(David Barron) *str: swtg: b.hind: displayed gd spd: prom: pushed along over 2f out: wknd wl over 1f out: sn eased whn btn* **16/1**

1 **19** *3 1/4* **Arabda**[28] 2612 2-8-12 0........ PaulHanagan 10 14
(Mark Johnston) *str: in tch: rdn 3f out: sn wknd: eased whn btn fnl f* **50/1**

1m 13.82s (-0.68) **Going Correction** +0.075s/f (Good) **19** Ran SP% **125.7**

Speed ratings (Par 100): **107,102,102,101,98 98,97,96,95,92 92,90,87,85,83 71,69,68,64**

Tote Swingers 1&2 £4.70, 2&3 £3.10, 1&3 £10.60 CSF £20.88 CT £99.86 TOTE £10.30: £3.00, £1.40, £2.30; EX 31.80 Trifecta £91.10 Pool: £17,589.07 - 144.69 winning tickets..

Owner Qatar Racing Limited **Bred** Lowther Racing **Trained** Lambourn, Berks

FOCUS

Another overcast morning leading up to racing on day four of the meeting and there was drizzle which fell on top of the watered (4mm) good to firm ground. GoingStick readings suggested it was marginally quickest up the far side in the straight. The false rail on the round course was down, providing fresh ground between the 9f pole and the straight, leaving the course at full width and distances as advertised.A cracking renewal of the Albany Stakes. In keeping with the previous day riders shunned the stands' rail and they went a solid pace, with the main action developing down the centre. The form looks rock solid rated around the placed horses. Solid form, with a cracking effort from the wayward winner.

3523 KING EDWARD VII STKS (GROUP 2) (C&G) 1m 4f

3:05 (3:05) (Class 1) 3-Y-O

£99,242 (£37,625; £18,830; £9,380; £4,707; £2,362) **Stalls** Low

Form RPR

1-22 **1** **Hillstar**[34] 2445 3-8-12 95........ RyanMoore 8 116+
(Sir Michael Stoute) *t.k.h: stdd s: hld up in rr: effrt but stl plenty to do over 2f out: gd hdwy to chse clr ldr and edging rt jst over 1f out: styd on strly to ld fnl 75yds: gng away at fin* **15/2**[3]

-114 **2** *1* **Battle Of Marengo (IRE)**[20] 2866 3-9-1 117........(p) JosephO'Brien 5 117
(A P O'Brien, Ire) *chsd ldr tl led 6f out: grad increased gallop fr 4f out: rdn and wnt clr ent fnl 2f: drvn ent fnl f: hdd and no ex fnl 75yds* **10/11**[1]

1-1 **3** *2 1/4* **Mutashaded (USA)**[29] 2604 3-8-12 88........ PaulHanagan 4 110
(Roger Varian) *lw: hld up in tch in last pair: rdn and effrt into midfield wl over 2f out: 5th and slty outpcd 2f out: styd on again 1f out: wnt 3rd ins fnl f: kpt on but no threat to ldrs* **11/2**[2]

-122 **4** *2* **Contributer (IRE)**[28] 2620 3-8-12 101........ FrankieDettori 6 107
(Ed Dunlop) *stmbld after 100yds: chsd ldng trio: effrt u.p to chse clr ldr 2f out: no imp over 1f out: plugged on same pce after* **11/1**

1-43 **5** *3 3/4* **Havana Beat (IRE)**[43] 2187 3-8-12 100........ WilliamBuick 3 101
(Andrew Balding) *hld up in tch in last trio: dropped to rr over 3f out: rdn and outpcd over 2f out: no threat to ldrs but plugged on past btn horses fnl f* **20/1**

50-5 **6** *nse* **Fantastic Moon**[56] 1811 3-8-12 102........ KierenFallon 7 101
(Jeremy Noseda) *t.k.h: hld up in midfield: hdwy to chse ldrs 8f out tl wnt 2nd 4f: sn rdn: struggling u.p and lost 2nd 2f out: wknd over 1f out* **16/1**

1-20 **7** *6* **Greatwood**[36] 2398 3-8-12 103........ RichardHughes 2 94
(Luca Cumani) *led tl 6f out: chsd ldr tl 4f out: rdn over 3f out: outpcd and btn 2f out: wknd over 1f out: bhd and eased wl ins fnl f* **10/1**

30-2 **8** *1 1/2* **Tha'ir (IRE)**[34] 2454 3-8-12 100........(p) SilvestreDeSousa 1 92
(Saeed bin Suroor) *plld hrd and nt settle: chsd ldrs tl 3f out: lost pl and btn ent fnl 2f: bhd and eased wl ins fnl f* **12/1**

2m 30.09s (-2.41) **Going Correction** +0.15s/f (Good) **8** Ran SP% **115.3**

Speed ratings (Par 111): **114,113,111,110,108 107,103,102**

Tote Swingers 1&2 £2.40, 2&3 £2.40, 1&3 £5.30 CSF £14.89 CT £42.01 TOTE £8.80: £2.20, £1.10, £1.60; EX 18.20 Trifecta £40.50 Pool: £18,310.37 - 338.56 winning tickets..

Owner Sir Evelyn De Rothschild **Bred** Southcourt Stud **Trained** Newmarket, Suffolk

FOCUS

A fair renewal of this historic Group 2, the best recent winners of which have been Monterosso and Nathaniel. It was run at a steady early pace until Battle Of Marengo went on at halfway. Solid form which fits the race standard. Big improvement from the winner and third.

3524 CORONATION STKS (BRITISH CHAMPIONS SERIES) (GROUP 1) (FILLIES) 1m (R)

3:45 (3:47) (Class 1) 3-Y-O

£216,348 (£82,022; £41,049; £20,448; £10,262; £5,150) **Stalls** Low

Form RPR

0-21 **1** **Sky Lantern (IRE)**[47] 2047 3-9-0 111........ RichardHughes 16 120+
(Richard Hannon) *lw: stdd s: hld up in rr: smooth hdwy on outer 2f out: qcknd to ld 1f out: sn dashed clr: impressive* **9/2**[1]

-103 **2** *4* **Kenhope (FR)**[19] 2906 3-9-0 110........ ThierryJarnet 6 110+
(H-A Pantall, France) *str: racd keenly: hld up towards rr: nt clr run wl over 2f out: swtchd lft and hdwy wl over 1f out: styd on and hung rt ins fnl f: tk 2nd towards fin: no ch w wnr* **33/1**

1-21 **3** *nk* **Just The Judge (IRE)**[26] 2689 3-9-0 110........ JamieSpencer 17 110
(Charles Hills) *in tch on outer: effrt 2f out: led over 1f out: sn hdd: unable to go w wnr and edgd rt ins fnl f: lost 2nd towards fin* **5/1**[2]

-166 **4** *1 1/2* **Maureen (IRE)**[26] 2689 3-9-0 106........ FrankieDettori 11 106
(Richard Hannon) *in tch: impr to chse ldrs over 2f out: tried to chal over 1f out: edgd rt ins fnl f: nt qckn: styd on same pce fnl 100yds* **10/1**

35 **5** *3/4* **Mizzava (IRE)**[26] 2689 3-9-0 102........ ShaneFoley 15 104
(M Halford, Ire) *unf: midfield: pushed along whn nt clr run briefly and snatched up over 2f out: hdwy sn after: rdn whn chsng ldrs over 1f out: styd on ins fnl f: unable to chal* **50/1**

2-1 **6** *hd* **Viztoria (IRE)**[46] 2108 3-9-0 110........ JohnnyMurtagh 7 104
(Edward Lynam, Ire) *midfield: hdwy on inner 3f out: rdn to chal wl over 1f out: nt qckn ent fnl f: no ex fnl 150yds* **8/1**

1-4 **7** *1 1/2* **Big Break**[26] 2689 3-9-0 106........ PatSmullen 1 100
(D K Weld, Ire) *lengthy: racd on inner and trckd ldrs: wnt 2nd over 2f out: led under 2f out: hdd over 1f out: no ex fnl 100yds* **9/2**[1]

120- **8** *1 1/2* **Purr Along**[257] 6909 3-9-0 111........ MartinDwyer 9 97+
(William Muir) *racd keenly: hld up: hmpd whn n.m.r after 2f: rdn and hdwy on outer over 1f out: sn hung rt: kpt on ins fnl f but nvr a danger* **25/1**

11 **9** *1 1/4* **Pavlosk (USA)**[35] 2429 3-9-0 103........ RyanMoore 12 94+
(Sir Michael Stoute) *lw: trckd ldrs: effrt 2f out: tried to chal wl over 1f out: one pce ins fnl f: fdd fnl 100yds* **7/1**[3]

6-0 **10** *2 1/4* **Ollie Olga (USA)**[47] 2047 3-9-0 104........ MartinHarley 13 88
(Mick Channon) *hld up: rdn and hdwy over 2f out: nt trble ldrs: no imp fnl f* **50/1**

0 **11** *5* **Siyenica (FR)**[26] 2693 3-9-0 0........ Christophe-PatriceLemaire 4 76+
(A De Royer-Dupre, France) *tall: athletic: racd keenly: trckd ldrs: rdn over 2f out: wknd over 1f out* **12/1**

5100 **12** *1 1/4* **Masarah (IRE)**[26] 2689 3-9-0 100........ JamesDoyle 2 73
(Clive Brittain) *hld up: pushed along over 2f out: nvr able to trble ldrs: wl btn fnl f* **100/1**

0-20 **13** *hd* **Agent Allison**[47] 2047 3-9-0 103........ JimCrowley 10 73+
(Peter Chapple-Hyam) *hld up: nt clr run and hmpd over 2f out: nvr able to get competitive: no imp fnl f* **66/1**

1-12 **14** *1 1/4* **Lovely Pass (IRE)**[113] 837 3-9-0 105........(p) MickaelBarzalona 3 70
(Saeed bin Suroor) *racd on inner w ldr: led 4f out: rdn over 2f out: hdd under 2f out: sn wknd* **25/1**

142 **15** *13* **Rehn's Nest (IRE)**[26] 2689 3-9-0 107........(t) KevinManning 14 39
(J S Bolger, Ire) *w'like: lw: prom tl rdn and wknd qckly over 2f out: eased whn wl btn ins fnl f* **16/1**

2-00 **16** *3 1/4* **Roz**[21] 2842 3-9-0 100........ KierenFallon 5 31
(Harry Dunlop) *led narrowly: hdd 4f out: u.p over 2f out: sn wknd: eased whn wl btn ins fnl f* **66/1**

-350 **17** *40* **Snow Queen (IRE)**[26] 2689 3-9-0 106........(p) JosephO'Brien 8
(A P O'Brien, Ire) *awkward s: hld up: pushed along whn hmpd and lost pl over 2f out: wl bhd over 1f out: sn eased: t.o* **20/1**

1m 39.75s (-0.95) **Going Correction** +0.15s/f (Good) **17** Ran SP% **122.6**

Speed ratings (Par 110): **110,106,105,104,103 103,101,100,99,96 91,90,90,89,76 72,32**

Tote Swingers 1&2 £34.90, 2&3 £35.80, 1&3 £3.60 CSF £165.19 CT £812.78 TOTE £5.70: £2.30, £11.50, £1.80; EX 192.10 Trifecta £1404.80 Pool: £27,738.13 - 14.80 winning tickets..

Owner B Keswick **Bred** Tally-Ho Stud **Trained** East Everleigh, Wilts

FOCUS

A huge field of 17 fillies lined up for this year's Coronation Stakes and both the domestic and Irish Guineas winners were in attendance. The draw played a part in the race, but there was a solid pace on and the right horses fought out the finish. Sky Lantern impressed and the form is taken at near face value with Just The Judge a bit off her best.

3525 WOLFERTON H'CAP (LISTED RACE) 1m 2f

4:25 (4:26) (Class 1) (0-110,110) 4-Y-O+

£34,026 (£12,900; £6,456; £3,216; £1,614; £810) **Stalls** Low

Form RPR

050/ **1** **Forgotten Voice (IRE)**[77] 4457 8-9-2 **105**........ JohnnyMurtagh 7 114+
(Nicky Henderson) *hld up wl in tch in midfield: n.m.r 2f out: swtchd lft and effrt over 1f out: chsng ldrs whn pushed rt and then swtchd rt ent fnl f: r.o u.p to ld fnl 75yds: rdn out* **12/1**

-121 **2** *1/2* **Sheikhzayedroad**[20] 2867 4-8-12 **101**........ MartinLane 14 108
(David Simcock) *stdd and dropped in bhd after s: hld up in rr: clsd and nt clr run whn swtchd lft 2f out: str run over 1f out: drvn and ev ch jst ins fnl f: r.o but hld cl home* **8/1**[3]

0-44 **3** *shd* **Bana Wu**[27] 2656 4-8-10 **99** .... RichardHughes 15 106
(Andrew Balding) *stdd and dropped in bhd after s: hld up in rr: swtchd lft and hdwy over 2f out: gd hdwy u.p over 1f out: ev ch jst ins fnl f: r.o but no ex and hld cl home* **16/1**

-051 **4** *1* **Ottoman Empire (FR)**[134] 552 7-8-13 **102** .... HarryBentley 8 107
(John Butler) *lw: hld up in tch in midfield: clsd on ldrs over 2f out: rdn to ld over 1f out: hrd pressed jst ins fnl f: hdd fnl 75yds: no ex and wknd towards fin* **33/1**

11-1 **5** *¾* **Albasharah (USA)**[34] 2440 4-9-1 **104** .... SilvestreDeSousa 2 114+
(Saeed bin Suroor) *lw: hld up in last quartet: clsng whn short of room and bdly hmpd and dropped to last 2f out: swtchd lft and rallied over 1f out: styd on wl ins fnl f: nt rcvr and unable to rch ldrs* **3/1**[1]

1340 **6** *hd* **Two For Two (IRE)**[2] 3458 5-8-11 **100** .... DanielTudhope 12 103
(David O'Meara) *lw: stdd s: hld up in last pair: effrt and swtchd lft over 1f out: hdwy u.p ent fnl f: kpt on wl but no threat to ldrs* **10/1**

-634 **7** *hd* **Chapter Seven**[20] 2864 4-8-11 **100** .... JamieSpencer 6 103+
(Stuart Williams) *hld up in tch in midfield: rdn 3f out: short of room and hmpd wl over 1f out: switching rt and rallied 1f out: styd on wl ins fnl f: unable to threaten ldrs* **14/1**

110/ **8** *½* **Ocean War**[748] 2715 5-9-2 **105** .... MickaelBarzalona 10 108+
(Saeed bin Suroor) *hld up towards rr: hdwy but edging rt 2f out: rdn and chse ldr and edging rt over 1f out tl jst ins fnl f: stl pressing ldrs but styng on same pce whn short of room and eased wl ins fnl f* **16/1**

0205 **9** *4 ½* **Fattsota**[21] 2839 5-9-0 **103** .... MartinHarley 5 96
(Marco Botti) *t.k.h: chsd ldr tl led 3f out: rdn over 2f out: drvn and hdd over 1f out: btn 1f out: wknd ins fnl f* **9/1**

0-61 **10** *nk* **Rewarded**[27] 2652 4-9-5 **108** .... KirstyMilczarek 4 100
(James Toller) *hld up in tch in midfield: swtchd lft and effrt 2f out: no imp u.p over 1f out: wknd fnl f* **25/1**

31-5 **11** *1* **Mobaco (FR)**[27] 2652 4-9-2 **105** .... JamesMcDonald 3 95
(Luca Cumani) *t.k.h: chsd ldrs: effrt wl over 1f out: no imp and btn over 1f out: wknd fnl f* **16/1**

010- **12** *1 ½* **Labarinto**[251] 7054 5-8-13 **102** .... RyanMoore 9 89
(Sir Michael Stoute) *chsd ldrs: effrt u.p over 2f out: unable qck over 1f out: wknd 1f out* **7/1**[2]

42 **13** *hd* **Inis Meain (USA)**[47] 2062 6-9-7 **110** .... DannyMullins 13 97
(Denis Gerard Hogan, Ire) *led tl hdd 3f out: drvn ent fnl 2f: no ex over 1f out: btn and hung rt 1f out: wknd* **25/1**

1-55 **14** *1 ½* **Dick Doughtywylie**[43] 2186 5-9-1 **104** .... WilliamBuick 1 88
(John Gosden) *lw: racd in midfield: effrt on inner 2f out: no hdwy and btn over 1f out: wknd fnl f* **8/1**[3]

2-32 **15** *7* **Genzy (FR)**[27] 2656 5-9-0 **103** .... JimCrowley 11 78
(Ian Williams) *lw: chsd ldrs: rdn and outpcd 2f out: wknd and bhd over 1f out* **20/1**

2m 6.06s (-1.34) **Going Correction** +0.15s/f (Good) **15** Ran SP% **126.2**
Speed ratings (Par 111): **111,110,110,109,109 108,108,108,104,104 103,102,102,101,95**
Tote Swingers 1&2 £28.10, 2&3 £29.30, 1&3 £60.30 CSF £104.44 CT £1576.79 TOTE £14.80: £3.40, £3.40, £7.10; EX 201.20 Trifecta £2953.10 Pool: £20,492.77 - 5.20 winning tickets..
Owner Mrs Susan Roy **Bred** Swettenham Stud And Ben Sangster **Trained** Upper Lambourn, Berks

FOCUS
They went a decent pace in this high-class handicap, which is in its twelfth year, and there was a very tight finish. Not a great renewal, few having scope for being ahead of their marks, but the winner was close to his best.

3526 QUEEN'S VASE (IN MEMORY OF SIR HENRY CECIL) (GROUP 3) 2m
5:00 (5:02) (Class 1) 3-Y-O

£42,532 (£16,125; £8,070; £4,020; £2,017; £1,012) **Stalls** Low

Form RPR

1 **1** **Leading Light (IRE)**[26] 2687 3-9-4 110 .... (p) JosephO'Brien 5 103+
(A P O'Brien, Ire) *lengthy: trckd ldrs: effrt on outer over 3f out: led over 2f out: hrd pressed and jnd wl over 1f out: styd on gamely and fnd more towards fin* **5/4**[1]

145 **2** *1 ½* **Feel Like Dancing**[14] 3061 3-9-1 89 .... (p) RyanMoore 6 98
(John Gosden) *swtg: sweating: hld up towards rr: hdwy over 2f out: str chal fr wl over 1f out: upsides sn after: no ex towards fin* **20/1**

-210 **3** *1 ½* **Boite (IRE)**[33] 2490 3-9-1 87 .... RobertHavlin 13 96
(Peter Chapple-Hyam) *hld up: hdwy over 2f out: rdn and chal wl over 1f out: nt qckn ins fnl f: styd on u.p: no imp on ldrs fnl 100yds* **66/1**

1424 **4** *nse* **Mister Impatience**[34] 2454 3-9-1 97 .... JoeFanning 11 96
(Mark Johnston) *midfield: hdwy over 3f out: chal wl over 1f out: nt qckn ins fnl f: styd on u.p: no imp on ldrs fnl 100yds* **14/1**

1152 **5** *hd* **Ray Ward (IRE)**[14] 3048 3-9-1 81 .... JamieSpencer 12 96
(David Simcock) *stdd s: hld up: hdwy fr 2f out: styd on ins fnl f: gng on at fin but nt trble ldrs* **40/1**

1-32 **6** *2 ¼* **Nichols Canyon**[35] 2416 3-9-1 97 .... WilliamBuick 3 96+
(John Gosden) *lw: midfield: hmpd after 3f: pushed along and outpcd over 2f out: stdy hdwy over 1f out: kpt on towards fin: nvr able to chal* **7/1**[3]

-013 **7** *½* **Hasheem**[20] 2878 3-9-1 80 .... PaulHanagan 17 93
(Roger Varian) *lw: hld up: rdn and hdwy over 2f out: chsd ldrs over 1f out: hung rt ins fnl f: kpt on but no imp* **33/1**

1 **8** *1 ½* **Ralston Road (IRE)**[27] 2651 3-9-1 88 .... TadhgO'Shea 7 92
(John Patrick Shanahan, Ire) *sn led: hdd over 6f out: rdn 5f out: outpcd over 2f out: trying to keep on whn nt clr run and hmpd ins fnl f: no imp after* **25/1**

21 **9** *¾* **Baihas**[17] 2967 3-9-1 85 .... (p) DaneO'Neill 18 90
(Sir Michael Stoute) *lw: trckd ldrs: rdn over 4f out: wknd over 1f out* **25/1**

5211 **10** *6* **Royal Skies (IRE)**[6] 3336 3-9-1 90 .... SilvestreDeSousa 16 87
(Mark Johnston) *midfield: hdwy over 3f out: chal 2f out: nt qckn ins fnl f: wknd fnl 150yds: eased* **9/1**

-501 **11** *½* **Dashing Star**[20] 2879 3-9-1 90 .... LiamKeniry 9 82
(David Elsworth) *racd keenly: hld up in midfield: pushed along 4f out: outpcd over 3f out: nvr able to get on terms w ldrs: eased whn btn ins fnl f* **14/1**

-111 **12** *6* **Disclaimer**[28] 2620 3-9-1 102 .... TomQueally 15 79
(Lady Cecil) *racd keenly in tch: clsd to take 2nd over 4f out: led 3f out: rdn and hdd over 2f out: wknd wl over 1f out: eased whn btn ins fnl f* **4/1**[2]

61 **13** *50* **Federal Blue (USA)**[9] 3209 3-9-1 0 .... JohnnyMurtagh 2
(Mark Johnston) *in tch: n.m.r and hmpd after 3f: in midfield after: reminder 7f out: rdn and wknd over 2f out: eased whn wl btn fnl f: t.o* **25/1**

0-21 **14** *18* **Da Do Run Run**[30] 2568 3-9-1 80 .... MartinLane 4
(Brian Meehan) *ponied to s: prom tl rdn and wknd over 5f out: eased whn wl btn fnl f: t.o* **66/1**

2632 **15** *4* **Naru (IRE)**[20] 2879 3-9-1 85 .... NeilCallan 14
(James Tate) *led early: chsd ldr after tl regained ld over 6f out: hdd 3f out: rdn and wknd over 2f out: eased whn wl btn fnl f: t.o* **66/1**

3m 25.26s (-3.74) **Going Correction** +0.15s/f (Good) **15** Ran SP% **126.4**
Speed ratings (Par 109): **115,114,113,113,113 112,112,111,110,107 107,104,79,70,68**
Tote Swingers 1&2 £7.90, 2&3 £107.00, 1&3 £42.70 CSF £37.07 CT £1213.09 TOTE £2.50: £1.10, £4.30, £22.90; EX 28.90 Trifecta £2188.80 Pool: £19,996.77 - 6.85 winning tickets..
Owner Derrick Smith & Mrs John Magnier & Michael Tabor **Bred** Lynch-Bages Ltd **Trained** Ballydoyle, Co Tipperary
■ This race was run in memory of Sir Henry Cecil, who died ten days earlier.

FOCUS
Another intriguing Queen's Vase and the race got a huge boost when last year's winner Estimate landed the Gold Cup earlier in the week. They went a decent pace. The form is rated at the lower end of the race averages and Leading Light is rated 8lb off his form in better races over shorter.

3527 BUCKINGHAM PALACE STKS (H'CAP) 7f
5:35 (5:41) (Class 2) (0-105,104) 3-Y-O+

£46,687 (£13,980; £6,990; £3,495; £1,747; £877) **Stalls** Centre

Form RPR

-300 **1** **Lightning Cloud (IRE)**[20] 2858 5-8-13 **93** .... NeilCallan 32 106
(Kevin Ryan) *racd in stands' side gp: hld up in midfield and a travelling wl: trckd ldrs over 1f out: rdn and qcknd to chal 1f out: led ins fnl f: r.o strly and sn in command: rdn out: 1st of 12 in gp* **25/1**

5-55 **2** *1 ¼* **Dream Tune**[41] 2254 4-8-11 **91** .... JamesDoyle 30 101
(Clive Cox) *racd in stands' side gp: overall ldr tl drvn and hdd 1f out: kpt on same pce u.p fnl 100yds: snatched 2nd on post: no threat to wnr: 2nd of 12 in gp* **7/1**[2]

4552 **3** *nse* **Shamaal Nibras (USA)**[22] 2813 4-8-10 **95** .... ThomasBrown(5) 24 104
(Ismail Mohammed) *swtg: racd in centre tl jnd stands' side gp 1/2-way: chsd ldrs overall: rdn to ld 1f out: hdd and no ex ins fnl f: wknd cl home and lost 2nd on post: 3rd of 12 in gp* **33/1**

0300 **4** *nse* **Santefisio**[2] 3458 7-9-6 **100** .... (b) JoeFanning 15 109
(Keith Dalgleish) *racd in far side gp: dwlt: t.k.h: hld up towards rr overall: hdwy 2f out: nt clr run and swtchd lft over 1f out: str run to ld gp 1f out: r.o but no threat to wnr: 1st of 15 in gp* **40/1**

0020 **5** *¾* **Es Que Love (IRE)**[2] 3458 4-9-2 **96** .... GrahamLee 26 103
(Mark Johnston) *racd in stands' side gp: t.k.h: hld up in midfield overall: clsd 2f out: effrt and rdn to chse ldrs 1f out: styd on same pce fnl 100yds: 4th of 12 in gp* **25/1**

2-20 **6** *¾* **Loving Spirit**[41] 2254 5-9-0 **94** .... SilvestreDeSousa 25 99
(James Toller) *racd in stands' side gp: in tch in midfield overall: rdn and effrt 2f out: edgd out rt over 1f out: styd on same pce ins fnl f: 5th of 12 in gp* **12/1**

5-41 **7** *½* **Redvers (IRE)**[27] 2665 5-9-1 **95** .... (b) GeorgeBaker 14 102+
(Ed Vaughan) *racd in far side gp: hld up towards rr: hdwy and gng wl whn nt clr run over 1f out: hdwy and edgd rt 1f out: drvn and kpt on but no threat to wnr: 2nd of 15 in gp* **20/1**

02-5 **8** *nk* **Jack's Revenge (IRE)**[83] 1235 5-8-11 **91** .... (bt) PatCosgrave 23 94
(George Baker) *racd in stands' side gp: stdd and swtchd lft s: hld up towards rr: hdwy over 2f out: keeping on u.p whn pushed rt over 1f out: styd on same pce ins fnl f: 6th of 12 in gp* **20/1**

10-1 **9** *1* **Baccarat (IRE)**[64] 1646 4-9-0 **94** .... PaulHanagan 12 94
(Richard Fahey) *lw: racd in far side gp: t.k.h: hld up in tch in midfield: effrt to ld gp and chsd ldrs overall over 1f out: no ex and wknd wl ins fnl f: 3rd of 15 in gp* **14/1**

46-2 **10** *nk* **Bertiewhittle**[41] 2254 5-9-3 **97** .... GrahamGibbons 10 97
(David Barron) *racd in far side gp: hld up towards rr: hdwy and squeezed through against far rail drvn and kpt on fnl f: no threat to wnr: 4th of 15 in gp* **16/1**

-303 **11** *1* **Dubawi Sound**[113] 834 5-9-10 **104** .... (t) JamieSpencer 29 101
(David Brown) *racd in stands' side gp: hld up in rr: clsd 2f out: rdn and hdwy over 1f out: kpt on fnl f: nvr trbld ldrs: 7th of 12 in gp* **40/1**

0103 **12** *¾* **Mezzotint (IRE)**[13] 3114 4-8-13 **93** .... MartinHarley 17 88
(Marco Botti) *racd in far side gp: hld up towards rr: rdn and hdwy wl over 1f out: kpt on same pce ins fnl f: no threat to wnr: 5th of 15 in gp* **28/1**

-001 **13** *nk* **Smarty Socks (IRE)**[7] 3300 9-9-0 **94** 5ex .... DanielTudhope 27 88
(David O'Meara) *lw: racd in stands' side gp: hld up in rr: rdn and hdwy over 2f out: drvn and no imp over 1f out: wknd ins fnl f: 8th of 12 in gp* **16/1**

-161 **14** *1 ½* **Mont Ras (IRE)**[29] 2592 6-9-0 **94** .... JosephO'Brien 28 84
(David O'Meara) *racd in stands' side gp: chsd overall ldr tl over 1f out: sn drvn and btn 1f out: wknd ins fnl f: 9th of 12 in gp* **25/1**

26-0 **15** *½* **Campanology**[27] 2679 4-8-12 **92** .... (t) JohnnyMurtagh 31 81
(J P Murtagh, Ire) *racd in stands' side gp: hld up towards rr: rdn and effrt 2f out: drvn and no hdwy over 1f out: kpt on same pce: 10th of 12 in gp* **12/1**

5322 **16** *hd* **Democretes**[42] 2207 4-8-11 **91** .... (b[1]) RichardHughes 11 79
(Richard Hannon) *racd in far side gp: hld up towards rr: clsd on ldrs 2f out: chsng gp ldrs and stl travelling wl whn nt clr run over 1f out: swtchd lft 1f out: kpt on but n.d: 6th of 15 in gp* **16/1**

60-0 **17** *¾* **Jamesie (IRE)**[27] 2679 5-9-1 **95** .... PatSmullen 20 81
(David Marnane, Ire) *racd in centre tl jnd stands' side gp 1/2-way: t.k.h: hld up in rr: rdn and effrt over 1f out: no imp: wknd ins fnl f: 11th of 12 in gp* **16/1**

-003 **18** *2* **Joe Packet**[8] 3249 6-8-8 **93** .... MatthewLawson(5) 4 74
(Jonathan Portman) *racd in far side gp: chsd gp ldrs and prom overall: led gp 3f out tl over 1f out: struggling whn pushed rt and hmpd 1f out: sn wknd: 7th of 15 in gp* **25/1**

41-4 **19** *1* **Emilio Largo**[42] 2207 5-9-2 **96** .... TomQueally 8 74
(James Fanshawe) *racd in far side gp: hld up in midfield: rdn and effrt 2f out: no imp over 1f out: wknd fnl f: 8th of 15 in gp* **9/1**[3]

0130 **20** *¾* **Maverik**[21] 2841 5-8-12 **92** .... HayleyTurner 21 68
(William Knight) *racd in centre tl jnd stands' side gp 1/2-way: in midfield: rdn and unable qck over 2f out: wknd over 1f out: 12th of 12 in gp* **66/1**

1-12 **21** *1* **Enrol**[13] 3114 4-8-13 **93** .... RyanMoore 1 71
(Sir Michael Stoute) *racd in far side gp: in tch in midfield: rdn and effrt 2f out: pressing gp ldrs but keeping on same pce whn pushed rt and hmpd 1f out: sn btn and eased: 9th of 15 in gp* **6/1**[1]

-401 **22** *2 ¼* **Highland Colori (IRE)**[14] 3060 5-9-5 **99** .... WilliamBuick 2 71
(Andrew Balding) *racd in far side gp: led gp tl 5f out: styd prom overall: rdn 2f out: keeping on same pce and struggling whn pushed rt and hmpd 1f out: sn btn and eased 10th of 15 in gp* **16/1**

2-56 **23** *¾* **Nassau Storm**[8] 3249 4-8-12 **92** .... JimCrowley 5 57
(William Knight) *racd in far side gp: racd in midfield: rdn and no hdwy 2f out: wknd over 1f out: 11th of 15 in gp* **20/1**

-023 **24** *3* **Anderiego (IRE)**[36] 2399 5-9-1 **95** ShaneFoley 19 56
(David O'Meara) *racd in far side gp: racd in midfield: rdn and struggling 3f out: wknd over 1f out: bhd fnl f: 12th of 15 in gp* **40/1**
4611 **25** *½* **Powerful Presence (IRE)**[13] 3088 7-8-11 **91** MickaelBarzalona 6 47
(David O'Meara) *racd in far side gp: t.k.h: chsd ldrs and prom overall: led gp 5f out tl 3f out: lost pl qckly 2f out: bhd fnl f: 13th of 15 in gp* **50/1**
0-15 **26** *¾* **Yair Hill (IRE)**[27] 2647 5-8-11 **91** PhillipMakin 18 45
(Kevin Ryan) *racd in far side gp: in tch in midfield: rdn and lost pl 2f out: wknd over 1f out: 14th of 15 in gp* **66/1**
1000 **27** *3 ½* **Thunderball**[20] 2868 7-8-10 **93** (p) BillyCray(3) 7 37
(Scott Dixon) *b: racd in far side gp: chsd gp ldrs and prom overall tl 3f out: sn dropped out: bhd over 1f out: 15th of 15 in gp* **100/1**

1m 26.31s (-1.29) **Going Correction** +0.075s/f (Good) **27** Ran SP% **137.6**
Speed ratings (Par 109): **110,108,108,108,107 106,106,105,104,104 103,102,102,100,99 99,98,96,95,94 93,90,89,86,85 84,8**
Tote Swingers 1&2 £96.90, 2&3 £100.50, 1&3 £287.60 CSF £175.92 CT £5889.11 TOTE £32.00: £7.40, £2.80, £11.70, £14.70; EX 295.40 Trifecta £10422.80 Part won. Pool: £13,897.16 - 0.41 winning tickets..
Owner Hambleton Racing Ltd XVIII **Bred** John Cullinan **Trained** Hambleton, N Yorks
■ Stewards' Enquiry : Joe Fanning two-day ban: careless riding (5, 7 July)

FOCUS
A hugely competitive edition of this handicap. The big field soon split into two groups and it was the dozen on the stands' side who emerged on top, mirroring the Albany Stakes in which high numbers had also been favoured. Personal bests from the first two.
T/Jkpt: Not won. T/Plt: £195.20 to a £1 stake. Pool: £744,922.54 - 2784.64 winning tickets.
T/Qpdt: £137.90 to a £1 stake. Pool: £25,778.80 - 138.32 winning tickets. SP

3274 GOODWOOD (R-H)
Friday, June 21

OFFICIAL GOING: Good (7.9)
First 2f of mile course out 5yds, Top bend out 3yds increasing distances by 10yds. Lower bend out 3yds increasing distances by 10yds.
Wind: strong breeze against in relation to straight Weather: sunny with cloudy periods

3528 "MTV STAYING ALIVE FOUNDATION" APPRENTICE H'CAP 1m 1f 192y
6:15 (6:15) (Class 5) (0-75,75) 3-Y-O **£3,234** (£962; £481; £240) **Stalls** Low

Form RPR
51-3 **1** **Rhombus (IRE)**[36] 2386 3-9-1 **74** OisinMurphy(5) 8 82
(Ismail Mohammed) *mde all: rdn 3f out: wandered sltly u.p whn hrd pressed ent fnl f: hld on gamely: all out* **7/2**[1]
1-15 **2** *nk* **Smileswithhiseyes (IRE)**[56] 1812 3-9-4 **75** DanielMuscutt(3) 4 82
(Gay Kelleway) *trckd ldrs: rdn to chse wnr over 2f out: str chal and upsides thrght fnl f: edgd rt: kpt on but no ex nr fin* **6/1**
5335 **3** *1 ½* **Bee Jay Kay**[5] 3376 3-8-4 **63** DanielCremin(5) 6 68
(Mick Channon) *trckd wnr tl rdn over 2f out: kpt chsng ldng pair: styd on same pce fnl f* **9/2**[3]
4133 **4** *6* **Hidden Link**[52] 1900 3-8-13 **70** (p) EDLinehan(3) 3 63
(Ronald Harris) *t.k.h in tch: rdn into 4th over 2f out: nt pce to get on terms: fdd fnl 120yds* **4/1**[2]
63P **5** *8* **Breccbennach**[8] 3241 3-9-0 **75** CameronHardie(7) 1 53
(Seamus Durack) *t.k.h in tch: rdn over 2f out: nt pce to chal: fdd fnl f* **11/1**
5150 **6** *shd* **Gambolling Den (IRE)**[52] 1900 3-8-8 **67** LewisWalsh(5) 5 45
(David Simcock) *restrained bk into last trio sn after s: rdn wl over 2f out: sn btn* **6/1**
65-0 **7** *4* **Exclusive Waters (IRE)**[18] 2938 3-8-9 **63** NicoleNordblad 2 33
(William Knight) *stdd into last pair sn after s: rdn over 3f out: sn btn* **8/1**
2-00 **8** *3 ½* **Anjuna Beach (USA)**[18] 2935 3-8-12 **69** NedCurtis(3) 7 33
(Gary Moore) *slowly away: t.k.h early: a last: rdn wl over 2f out: sn btn* **14/1**

2m 12.41s (4.31) **Going Correction** +0.20s/f (Good) **8** Ran SP% **115.1**
Speed ratings (Par 99): **90,89,88,83,77 77,74,71**
Tote Swingers 1&2 £3.40, 2&3 £6.00, 1&3 £2.30 CSF £24.92 CT £95.42 TOTE £3.40: £1.60, £2.00, £1.90; EX 29.20 Trifecta £53.90 Pool: £1,563.39 - 21.75 winning tickets..
Owner Sheikh Rashid Dalmook Al Maktoum **Bred** Ruskerne Ltd **Trained** Newmarket, Suffolk
■ Stewards' Enquiry : Daniel Muscutt seven-day ban: use of whip (11, -13, 15-28 July)

FOCUS
The first 2f of the 1m course were dolled out 5yds. Top bend was dolled out 3yds increasing distances by 10yds, and lower was dolled out 3yds increasing distances by 10yds. An uncompetitive apprentices' handicap and, with Rhombus allowed a totally uncontested lead, the first four finishers filled the first four places for most of the way. The bare form is pretty ordinary.

3529 THREE FRIDAY NIGHTS H'CAP 6f
6:50 (6:50) (Class 5) (0-70,70) 4-Y-O+ **£3,234** (£962; £481; £240) **Stalls** High

Form RPR
2324 **1** **Where's Reiley (USA)**[23] 2772 7-9-0 **63** (v) SebSanders 9 71
(Michael Attwater) *hmpd after 100yds: chsd ldrs: rdn 2f out: led ent fnl f: kpt on gamely* **7/2**[1]
2532 **2** *1* **Chevise (IRE)**[29] 2588 5-8-5 **59** (p) RyanTate(5) 11 64
(Steve Woodman) *squeezed up s: outpcd in last pair: swtchd rt and hdwy 2f out: chsd wnr ent fnl f: kpt on but a being hld* **15/2**
526 **3** *1* **One Last Dream**[18] 2918 4-8-7 **56** (b) WilliamCarson 4 57
(Ron Hodges) *sn swtchd to stands' side rail: led tl over 3f out: sn rdn: dropped to 5th but in tch jst over 1f out: kpt on again fnl 120yds to go 3rd nr fin* **5/1**
4055 **4** *¾* **Pharoh Jake**[6] 3325 5-7-12 **54** JoeyHaynes(7) 3 53
(John Bridger) *prom: rdn to ld 2f out tl ent fnl f: no ex fnl 120yds: lost 3rd nr fin* **16/1**
0304 **5** *2* **Elna Bright**[43] 2196 8-9-7 **70** PatDobbs 10 63
(Peter Crate) *wnt sltly lft s: in tch: pushed along and swtchd rt 2f out: sn rdn to chse ldrs: fdd fnl 120yds* **4/1**[2]
0022 **6** *¾* **Pelmanism**[20] 2884 6-9-0 **63** (b) DaleSwift 8 53
(Brian Ellison) *s.i.s: last: sn pushed along: nvr gng pce to get involved* **9/2**[3]
2002 **7** *1 ¾* **Belle Bayardo (IRE)**[18] 2918 5-8-13 **67** EDLinehan(5) 1 52
(Ronald Harris) *prom: rdn and ev ch 2 out: sn hld: wknd ins fnl f* **9/2**[3]
0-00 **8** *8* **Sir Geoffrey (IRE)**[100] 986 7-8-3 **55** (p) DarrenEgan(3) 7 14
(Scott Dixon) *prom: led over 3f out tl rdn 2f out: wknd ent fnl f* **20/1**

1m 13.11s (0.91) **Going Correction** +0.25s/f (Good) **8** Ran SP% **117.7**
Speed ratings (Par 103): **103,101,100,99,96 95,93,82**
Tote Swingers 1&2 £2.90, 2&3 £8.20, 1&3 £7.40 CSF £31.14 CT £133.04 TOTE £4.20: £1.70, £1.60, £2.30; EX 24.20 Trifecta £78.40 Pool: £1,302.59 - 12.44 winning tickets..
Owner J M Duggan & T P Duggan **Bred** Overbrook Farm **Trained** Epsom, Surrey
■ Stewards' Enquiry : William Carson two-day ban: careless riding (5, 7 July)

FOCUS
Not form to be positive about, with none of these appealing beforehand. The winner was 2lb below his turf best.

3530 BIBENDUM MAIDEN FILLIES' STKS 1m 1f
7:20 (7:24) (Class 5) 3-Y-O+ **£3,234** (£962; £481; £240) **Stalls** Low

Form RPR
03 **1** **Rock Choir**[17] 2960 3-9-0 0 SebSanders 6 88+
(William Haggas) *mid-div: swtchd lft 3f out: sn making hdwy: shkn up to ld jst over 1f out: drew clr: readily* **15/8**[2]
5-2 **2** *5* **Sunbula (USA)**[53] 1876 3-8-7 0 [1] DanielMuscutt(7) 9 74
(Charles Hills) *led: rdn 2f out: wandered sltly u.p: hdd jst over 1f out: kpt on but nt pce of ready wnr* **4/1**[3]
2 **3** *½* **Archive**[18] 2931 3-9-0 0 FrederikTylicki 3 73
(Lady Cecil) *trckd ldng trio: rdn wl over 2f out: nvr able to chal: kpt on same pce* **7/4**[1]
-564 **4** *3 ½* **Azelle**[14] 3039 3-9-0 67 KieranO'Neill 4 65
(Richard Hannon) *trckd ldrs: rdn over 2f out: kpt on same pce fnl f* **7/1**
06 **5** *3 ¼* **La Rosiere (USA)**[36] 2392 4-9-11 0 PatDobbs 7 59
(Pat Murphy) *hld up in last trio: rdn over 3f out: styd on steadily fnl f: nvr trbld ldrs* **25/1**
05- **6** *2* **Gwenelda**[249] 7112 4-9-11 0 JakeNoonan 2 55
(Andrew Balding) *mid-div: rdn over 3f out: nvr threatened: fdd ins fnl f* **25/1**
0- **7** *1 ¾* **Sweet Louise (IRE)**[237] 7403 3-8-11 0 DarrenEgan(3) 1 50
(Sean Curran) *squeezed up after 120yds: in last pair: rdn over 2f out: nvr any imp* **50/1**
00- **8** *16* **Zinnobar**[230] 7552 3-9-0 0 WilliamCarson 8 15
(Jonathan Portman) *hld up in last pair: struggling 4f out: wknd 2f out* **40/1**
60 **9** *8* **Youmaysee**[8] 3239 3-9-0 0 SamHitchcott 5
(Mick Channon) *tk str hold early: trckd ldrs: rdn 3f out: wknd 2f out: t.o* **25/1**

1m 57.78s (1.48) **Going Correction** +0.20s/f (Good)
WFA 3 from 4yo 11lb **9** Ran SP% **119.6**
Speed ratings (Par 100): **101,96,96,93,90 88,86,72,65**
Tote Swingers 1&2 £2.50, 2&3 £1.10, 1&3 £1.10 CSF £9.66 TOTE £3.20: £1.10, £1.80, £1.20; EX 11.00 Trifecta £16.70 Pool: £2,134.03 - 95.62 winning tickets..
Owner Cheveley Park Stud **Bred** Cheveley Park Stud Ltd **Trained** Newmarket, Suffolk

FOCUS
There was a major market drift on Archive and she duly failed to build on a promising debut performance. In contrast, Rock Choir, the one for all the money, confirmed earlier promise with a straightforward success. The winner was value for extra.

3531 GORDON'S STKS (H'CAP) 1m 6f
7:55 (7:55) (Class 3) (0-95,92) 4-Y-O+
£7,470 (£2,236; £1,118; £559; £279; £140) **Stalls** Low

Form RPR
4122 **1** **Duke Of Clarence (IRE)**[20] 2867 4-9-5 **90** RichardHughes 10 100
(Richard Hannon) *hld up: nudged along briefly 5f out: swtchd rt and hdwy over 2f out: cl up whn nt clr run over 1f out: chal ent fnl f: led fnl 12oyds: edgd lft whn rdn: hld on wl* **7/2**[1]
1310 **2** *nk* **Noble Silk**[62] 1689 4-9-0 **88** (p) DarrenEgan(3) 6 97
(Lucy Wadham) *hld up: swtchd lft over 2f out: sn rdn and hdwy: styd on wl for str chal fnl 75yds: hld nring fin* **10/1**
-332 **3** *¾* **Novirak (IRE)**[20] 2855 5-8-13 **84** FrederikTylicki 9 92
(James Fanshawe) *trckd ldrs: gng strly whn taking the ld 2f out: sn drvn: hdd fnl 120yds: no ex whn lost 2nd towards fin* **5/1**[2]
60-0 **4** *5* **Lyric Street (IRE)**[27] 2671 5-9-3 **88** SebSanders 4 89
(Jeremy Noseda) *hld up in last 3: hdwy 3f out: ev ch whn rdn 2f out: sn one pce* **15/2**
110- **5** *hd* **Signed Up**[259] 6833 4-9-7 **92** PatDobbs 1 93
(Amanda Perrett) *in tch: rdn wl over 2f out: nvr finding pce to threaten ldrs* **5/1**[2]
1461 **6** *2 ½* **Taglietelle**[13] 3118 4-8-5 **83** JoeyHaynes(7) 2 81
(Andrew Balding) *led for 1f: trckd ldr: rdn and ev ch 2f out: fdd ent fnl f* **6/1**[3]
/040 **7** *2 ½* **Topolski (IRE)**[42] 1547 7-8-5 **76** HarryBentley 5 70
(David Arbuthnot) *in tch: nudged along to hold pl over 5f out: rdn over 3f out: wknd ent fnl f* **28/1**
-320 **8** *2* **Red Orator**[34] 2451 4-9-1 **86** JoeFanning 7 77
(Mark Johnston) *s.i.s: rcvrd to ld after 1f: rdn and hdd 2f out: wknd ent fnl f* **7/2**[1]

3m 3.66s (0.06) **Going Correction** +0.20s/f (Good) **8** Ran SP% **116.4**
Speed ratings (Par 107): **107,106,106,103,103 102,100,99**
Tote Swingers 1&2 £9.40, 2&3 £5.50, 1&3 £4.30 CSF £40.32 TOTE £3.50: £1.70, £2.50, £2.20; EX 43.80 Trifecta £105.40 Pool: £1,437.50 - 10.22 winning tickets..
Owner D Dixon J Stunt J Fiyaz **Bred** Corduff Stud Ltd & J F Gribomont **Trained** East Everleigh, Wilts

FOCUS
A good staying handicap, and the pace looked plenty strong enough with the winner and runner-up filling the last two places for much of the journey. Decent form.

3532 TREVOR NELSON FILLIES' H'CAP 7f
8:25 (8:25) (Class 4) (0-85,84) 3-Y-O+ **£5,175** (£1,540; £769; £384) **Stalls** Low

Form RPR
-251 **1** **Saucy Minx (IRE)**[27] 2658 3-8-13 **78** (b1) PatDobbs 1 85
(Amanda Perrett) *mde all: rdn over 2f out: kpt on v gamely fnl f: drvn out* **9/2**[3]
3200 **2** *1* **Savanna Days (IRE)**[17] 2964 4-9-5 **75** (v1) MatthewDavies 7 82
(Mick Channon) *hld up: tk clsr order wl over 2f out: rdn wl over 1f out: kpt on ins fnl f: wnt 2nd fnl 100yds but a being hld* **16/1**
0-31 **3** *¾* **Broadway Duchess (IRE)**[13] 3116 3-9-1 **80** RichardHughes 5 82
(Richard Hannon) *trckd wnr: rdn 2f out: nvr quite pce to chal: no ex whn lost 2nd fnl 100yds* **6/4**[1]
116 **4** *½* **Sharp And Smart (IRE)**[41] 2253 4-9-6 **76** DaneO'Neill 2 80
(Hughie Morrison) *trckd ldrs: rdn 2f out: kpt on same pce fnl f* **3/1**[2]
-521 **5** *nse* **Malekat Jamal (IRE)**[11] 3158 4-9-0 **73** 6ex DarrenEgan(3) 4 76
(David Simcock) *hld up in tch: rdn 2f out: no imp tl r.o ins fnl f* **10/1**
0013 **6** *½* **Alice's Dancer (IRE)**[11] 3158 4-10-0 **84** WilliamCarson 8 86
(William Muir) *broke wl racd keenly and sn restrained in last: rdn to chse ldrs 2f out: kpt on ins fnl f* **16/1**

-014 7 2 1/4 **School Fees**41 2255 4-9-9 **79** JamesMcDonald 3 75
(Olly Stevens) *trckd ldrs: rdn jst over 2f out: kpt chsng ldrs tl fdd fnl 120yds* **6/1**

1m 27.96s (0.96) **Going Correction** +0.20s/f (Good)
WFA 3 from 4yo+ 9lb 7 Ran SP% **118.3**
Speed ratings (Par 102): **102,100,100,99,99 98,96**
Tote Swingers 1&2 £10.20, 2&3 £5.10, 1&3 £2.30 CSF £71.15 CT £157.53 TOTE £5.10: £2.10, £8.00; EX 78.60 Trifecta £935.20 Pool: £1,397.86 - 1.12 winning tickets..
Owner Mr & Mrs F Cotton, Mr & Mrs P Conway **Bred** Summerhill & J Osborne **Trained** Pulborough, W Sussex

FOCUS
This looked a clever front-running ride from Pat Dobbs aboard Saucy Minx, stacking the field up by setting a modest pace, and consequently the form needs treating with caution. The second and sixth help set the level.

3533 GOODWOOD FARM SHOP H'CAP 6f
8:55 (8:56) (Class 5) (0-75,71) 3-Y-O £3,408 (£1,006; £503) Stalls High

Form RPR
-603 1 **Barbs Princess**18 2919 3-9-2 **65** JamesMcDonald 6 75
(Charles Hills) *mde all: rdn clr over 1f out: in command fnl f: rdn out* **9/2**2
4120 2 2 1/4 **Red Gift (IRE)**64 1647 3-9-7 **70** DaleSwift 9 73
(Brian Ellison) *outpcd in last: hdwy ent fnl f: r.o wl to go 2nd fnl stride: nvr rching wnr* **9/2**2
1301 3 hd **The Black Jacobin**18 2919 3-9-5 **68** (b) LiamKeniry 8 70
(J S Moore) *trckd ldrs: rdn 2f out: kpt on to go 2nd ins fnl f: a being hld: lost 2nd fnl stride* **5/1**3
4-31 4 1 1/4 **My Sweet Lord**22 2791 3-8-12 **61** HarryBentley 2 59
(Mark Usher) *chsd ldrs: rdn wl over 2f out: kpt on same pce fnl f* **7/2**1
5632 5 1 3/4 **Buy Art**14 3050 3-9-6 **69** (p) PatDobbs 4 61
(Gary Moore) *pressed wnr: rdn and ev ch 2f out: sn hld: no ex ins fnl f* **9/2**2
3046 6 14 **Talqaa**13 3109 3-9-2 **65** (v) SamHitchcott 1 13
(Mick Channon) *chsd ldrs: rdn 3f out: wknd ent fnl f* **9/1**
62-0 7 8 **Pearl Noir**17 2962 3-8-11 **60** (p) JoeFanning 3
(Scott Dixon) *stmbld sn after leaving stalls: trckd ldrs: rdn 2f out: wknd over 1f out* **7/1**

1m 13.48s (1.28) **Going Correction** +0.25s/f (Good) 7 Ran SP% **115.9**
Speed ratings (Par 99): **101,98,97,96,93 75,64**
Tote Swingers 1&2 £6.30, 2&3 £7.10, 1&3 £3.50 CSF £25.58 TOTE £5.60: £2.90, £3.00; EX 23.40 Trifecta £93.30 Pool: £1,103.23 - 8.86 winning tickets..
Owner Mrs Barbara James **Bred** Mrs R Wilson **Trained** Lambourn, Berks

FOCUS
A moderate sprint handicap. The third and fourth set the level.
T/Plt: £271.30 to a £1 stake. Pool: £70,847.74 - 190.57 winning tickets. T/Qpdt: £70.40 to a £1 stake. Pool: £5,414.47 - 56.90 winning tickets. TM

3112 NEWMARKET (R-H)
Friday, June 21

OFFICIAL GOING: Good to firm (8.3)
Far side track used. Stalls on far side except 10f &12f: Centre. Bend into home straight repositioned, increasing distances of 10f & 12f races by 20m.
Wind: Light behind Weather: Overcast

3534 ADNAMS NEWMARKET NIGHTS APPRENTICE H'CAP 1m
5:50 (5:50) (Class 5) (0-70,69) 4-Y-O+ £3,234 (£962; £481; £240) Stalls High

Form RPR
3/46 1 **Hamble**28 2640 4-8-12 **55** (t) TobyAtkinson 5 63
(Marco Botti) *mde all: rdn over 1f out: jst hld on* **12/1**
000 2 shd **Action Front (USA)**23 2785 5-8-2 **50** (v) AdamMcLean(5) 6 58
(Derek Shaw) *hld up: hdwy u.p and hung lft over 1f out: r.o* **8/1**
6411 3 1/2 **Peak Storm**18 2920 4-9-10 **67** RobertTart 2 74
(John O'Shea) *chsd ldrs: rdn over 2f out: edgd lft over 1f out: styd on* **5/2**1
2-04 4 3/4 **Excellent Jem**18 2929 4-9-8 **65** (p) WilliamTwiston-Davies 12 70
(Jane Chapple-Hyam) *a.p: chsd ldr over 2f out: rdn over 1f out: sn ev ch: styd on same pce wl ins fnl f* **13/2**3
/26- 5 1 **Daneside (IRE)**379 2855 6-9-11 **68** JustinNewman 7 71
(Gary Harrison) *prom: pushed along 1/2-way: sn outpcd: rallied over 1f out: r.o* **12/1**
0-40 6 nk **Saskia's Dream**28 2638 5-9-6 **66** IanBurns(3) 11 68
(Jane Chapple-Hyam) *s.s: hdwy over 3f out: rdn over 1f out: styd on* **25/1**
4255 7 1 **Hierarch (IRE)**13 3087 6-9-3 **65** SiobhanMiller(5) 4 65
(David Simcock) *chsd ldrs: rdn over 1f out: no ex ins fnl f* **15/2**
5341 8 hd **Handheld**41 2273 6-9-7 **67** (p) ShelleyBirkett(3) 1 66
(Julia Feilden) *hld up: hdwy 1/2-way: rdn over 2f out: styd on same pce fnl f* **11/2**2
15-0 9 1/2 **Warden Bond**14 3063 5-8-4 **50** (p) NoelGarbutt(3) 9 48
(William Stone) *chsd ldr tl rdn over 2f out: no ex ins fnl f* **33/1**
3365 10 1/2 **Cyflymder (IRE)**10 3172 7-9-6 **68** AliRawlinson(5) 3 65
(David C Griffiths) *hld up: rdn over 2f out: nvr on terms* **20/1**
-026 11 46 **Rough Rock (IRE)**17 2964 8-9-4 **66** JoshCrane(5) 8
(Chris Dwyer) *s.i.s: sn mid-div: rdn over 2f out: sn wknd and eased: t.o* **8/1**

1m 39.66s (-0.34) **Going Correction** +0.05s/f (Good) 11 Ran SP% **118.2**
Speed ratings (Par 103): **103,102,102,101,100 100,99,99,98,98 52**
Tote Swingers 1&2 £15.30, 2&3 £6.40, 1&3 £7.20 CSF £102.55 CT £321.59 TOTE £19.20: £3.90, £2.80, £1.50; EX 160.00 Trifecta £524.90 Part won. Pool: £699.95 - 0.14 winning tickets..
Owner Paolo Benedetti **Bred** C A Cyzer **Trained** Newmarket, Suffolk
■ Stewards' Enquiry : Adam McLean four-day ban: use of whip (5, 7, 8, 9 July)

FOCUS
With regard to the ground, Ian Burns, jockey of Saskia's Dream, said: "It's good to firm but they are kicking the top off". They raced centre-field in this moderate handicap. The winner is capable of bettering this.

3535 NEWMARKETRACECOURSES.CO.UK CLASSIFIED STKS 1m 4f
6:25 (6:25) (Class 5) 3-Y-O £3,234 (£962; £481; £240) Stalls Centre

Form RPR
-612 1 **Special Meaning**17 2957 3-9-0 70 FrannyNorton 1 76+
(Mark Johnston) *mde all: rdn over 1f out: edgd rt ins fnl f: styd on wl* **4/5**1
6010 2 1 3/4 **Aficionado**8 3243 3-9-0 69 (v1) JimmyFortune 2 73
(Ed Dunlop) *s.i.s: hld up: hdwy over 3f out: rdn and hung lft over 1f out: styd on* **6/1**3
434 3 nse **Magika**14 3055 3-8-9 67 (t) RobertTart(5) 5 73
(Marco Botti) *hld up: hdwy over 4f out: rdn and ev ch whn hung lft ins fnl f: no ex towards fin* **8/1**
554 4 3 3/4 **Kingston Eucalypt**42 2231 3-9-0 70 AndreaAtzeni 4 67
(Ed Vaughan) *chsd ldrs: rdn over 2f out: styd on same pce fnl f* **12/1**
213- 5 1 1/4 **Stiff Upper Lip (IRE)**263 6732 3-8-9 70 WilliamTwiston-Davies(5) 3 65
(Richard Hannon) *chsd wnr tl rdn over 2f out: styd on same pce fr over 1f out* **4/1**2

2m 33.93s (1.03) **Going Correction** +0.05s/f (Good) 5 Ran SP% **108.6**
Speed ratings (Par 99): **98,96,96,94,93**
CSF £5.86 TOTE £1.80: £1.20, £2.80; EX 6.80 Trifecta £22.10 Pool: £792.65 - 26.80 winning tickets..
Owner Newsells Park Stud **Bred** Newsells Park Stud **Trained** Middleham Moor, N Yorks

FOCUS
A straightforward race to assess. The slow pace governs the potential merit of the form.

3536 MK SHIPPING MAIDEN STKS 6f
7:00 (7:00) (Class 4) 2-Y-O £3,881 (£1,155; £577; £288) Stalls High

Form RPR
1 **Figure Of Speech (IRE)** 2-9-5 0 AdamKirby 7 85+
(Saeed bin Suroor) *chsd ldr tl led over 1f out: sn rdn and edgd rt: r.o* **5/1**
2 2 4 **Whaleweigh Station**18 2925 2-9-5 0 RichardKingscote 5 73
(Tom Dascombe) *led: hdd over 1f out: no ex ins fnl f* **6/4**1
3 1 1/4 **Master Of Suspense** 2-9-5 0 ChrisCatlin 1 69+
(Peter Chapple-Hyam) *hld up: hdwy over 2f out: rdn over 1f out: styd on same pce* **7/2**2
4 1 **Peak Royale** 2-9-5 0 JimmyFortune 8 66+
(Richard Hannon) *chsd ldrs: pushed along 1/2-way: outpcd 2f out: styd on ins fnl f* **14/1**
5 1 1/4 **Headlong (IRE)** 2-9-5 0 FrankieDettori 6 63
(Brian Meehan) *chsd ldrs: rdn over 1f out: wknd ins fnl f* **4/1**3
6 1 1/4 **Alquimia (IRE)** 2-9-0 0 AndreaAtzeni 4 54+
(Ed Dunlop) *s.i.s: hld up: outpcd over 2f out: kpt on ins fnl f* **25/1**
7 11 **Arrowzone** 2-9-0 0 JustinNewman(5) 3 26
(Garry Moss) *hld up: rdn and wknd over 2f out* **66/1**
8 hd **Freddie Kilroy** 2-9-5 0 JimmyQuinn 2 25
(Ed Dunlop) *s.i.s: hld up: rdn and wknd over 2f out* **25/1**

1m 12.86s (0.36) **Going Correction** +0.05s/f (Good) 8 Ran SP% **114.7**
Speed ratings (Par 95): **99,93,92,90,89 87,72,72**
Tote Swingers 1&2 £3.00, 2&3 £1.90, 1&3 £3.80 CSF £12.81 TOTE £4.90: £1.90, £1.10, £1.40; EX 12.80 Trifecta £53.70 Pool: £991.06 - 13.82 winning tickets..
Owner Godolphin **Bred** Darley **Trained** Newmarket, Suffolk

FOCUS
They raced against the far rail in what was probably just a fair maiden for the track. The winner impressed and the second was 5lb off his debut figure.

3537 NGK SPARK PLUGS H'CAP 1m
7:30 (7:32) (Class 5) (0-75,76) 3-Y-O £3,234 (£962; £481; £240) Stalls High

Form RPR
-610 1 **Aussie Reigns (IRE)**18 2935 3-9-7 **74** (v) AdamKirby 13 87+
(William Knight) *racd far side: hld up: hdwy over 2f out: rdn to ld 1f out: drvn clr* **11/2**3
0000 2 2 1/4 **Ocean Applause**20 2866 3-9-4 **71** (p) DaraghO'Donohoe 3 79
(John Ryan) *racd centre: chsd ldrs: rdn and hung lft over 1f out: sn ev ch: styd on same pce ins fnl f: 1st of 4 in gp* **33/1**
-321 3 3/4 **Mushaakis (IRE)**7 3281 3-9-9 **76** 6ex FrannyNorton 8 82+
(Mark Johnston) *racd far side: chsd ldrs: rdn to ld overall and hung rt over 1f out: sn hdd: styd on same pce ins fnl f: 2nd of 8 in gp* **11/8**1
-253 4 2 **Lovesome**31 2546 3-9-5 **72** WilliamBuick 5 74
(Michael Bell) *overall ldr in centre tl rdn and hdd over 1f out: no ex ins fnl f: 2nd of 4 in gp* **20/1**
0-55 5 3/4 **Patently (IRE)**18 2931 3-9-5 **72** JimmyFortune 4 72
(Brian Meehan) *racd centre: chsd ldr: rdn over 1f out: styd on same pce: 3rd of 4 in gp* **12/1**
0634 6 2 **Napinda**24 2762 3-7-9 **55** oh2 NoelGarbutt(7) 6 50
(Philip McBride) *racd centre: hld up: pushed along over 3f out: styd on: nvr nrr: last of 4 in gp* **33/1**
22-4 7 4 1/2 **Soaring Spirits (IRE)**41 2272 3-9-7 **74** AndreaAtzeni 12 59
(Roger Varian) *racd far side: chsd ldrs: rdn over 2f out: wknd over 1f out: 3rd of 8 in gp* **4/1**2
035 8 1 3/4 **Persian Patriot**13 3116 3-9-3 **70** FrankieDettori 7 51
(William Jarvis) *racd far side: hld up: hdwy over 2f out: rdn and wknd over 1f out: 4th of 8 in gp* **14/1**
2-04 9 2 1/4 **Danz Choice (IRE)**17 2951 3-9-1 **73** WilliamTwiston-Davies(5) 11 49
(Richard Hannon) *racd far side: hld up: hdwy over 2f out: rdn and wknd over 1f out: 5th of 8 in gp* **20/1**
5263 10 3 1/4 **Sixties Queen**42 2215 3-8-6 **64** RobertTart(5) 9 32
(Alan Bailey) *racd far side: chsd ldr over 4f: rdn and wknd over 1f out: 6th of 8 in gp* **25/1**
3-32 11 5 **Not Rigg (USA)**12 3137 3-9-0 **67** (t) ShaneKelly 10 24
(Gary Harrison) *led far side: rdn over 2f out: hdd & wknd over 1f out: 7th of 8 in gp* **14/1**
250 12 25 **Minimee**52 1912 3-9-2 **69** (p) SilvestreDeSousa 2
(Phil McEntee) *s.s: swtchd to r far side sn after s: a in rr: wknd over 2f out: eased: t.o: last of 8 in gp* **20/1**

1m 39.56s (-0.44) **Going Correction** +0.05s/f (Good) 12 Ran SP% **122.5**
Speed ratings (Par 99): **104,101,101,99,98 96,91,90,87,84 79,54**
Tote Swingers 1&2 £19.60, 2&3 £18.90, 1&3 £3.10 CSF £186.13 CT £392.86 TOTE £7.60: £2.30, £9.70, £1.40; EX 222.20 Trifecta £810.60 Part won. Pool: £1,080.82 - 0.51 winning tickets..
Owner The Old Brokers **Bred** S Connolly **Trained** Patching, W Sussex
■ Stewards' Enquiry : Daragh O'Donohoe two-day ban: use of whip (5-7 July)

FOCUS
They split into two groups, with a smaller bunch of four racing centre-field, and there proved little between them. The winner and third rate better than the bare form.

3538 POPTELECOM.CO.UK H'CAP 7f
8:05 (8:05) (Class 3) (0-95,93) 3-Y-O+ £7,762 (£2,310; £1,154; £577) Stalls High

Form RPR
0-33 1 **The Confessor**29 2585 6-9-7 **90** CathyGannon 1 98
(Henry Candy) *mde all: set stdy pce tl qckng 2f out: rdn over 1f out: r.o gamely* **7/2**3
412- 2 nk **Famous Poet (IRE)**314 5094 4-9-10 **93** SilvestreDeSousa 2 100
(Saeed bin Suroor) *trckd ldrs: racd keenly: rdn and ev ch ins fnl f: r.o* **15/8**1

-632 3 hd **Zacynthus (IRE)**27 2665 5-9-7 **90**........ KierenFallon 6 97
(Luca Cumani) *trckd ldrs: rdn and ev ch ins fnl f: r.o* **9/4**2
0-R4 4 ½ **Ducal**27 2665 5-9-5 **88**........ ShaneKelly 4 94
(Mike Murphy) *s.s: hld up: hdwy and nt clr run fr over 1f out tl swtchd rt wl ins fnl f: r.o: nvr able to chal* **12/1**
0-36 5 ½ **Hefner (IRE)**21 2841 4-9-5 **88**........ AdamKirby 5 92
(Marco Botti) *hld up: rdn over 1f out: r.o: nt rch ldrs* **8/1**
6-00 6 3¼ **Common Touch (IRE)**14 3060 5-9-8 **91**........ StevieDonohoe 7 87
(Willie Musson) *prom: shkn up over 1f out: no ex ins fnl f* **20/1**
10-0 7 27 **Esprit De Midas**18 2937 7-8-11 **87**........ PaulBooth(7) 3 12
(Dean Ivory) *w wnr tl pushed along 2f out: sn hung lft and wknd* **40/1**
1m 27.04s (1.34) **Going Correction** +0.05s/f (Good) **7** Ran SP% **113.8**
Speed ratings (Par 107): **94,93,93,92,92 88,57**
Tote Swingers 1&2 £1.90, 2&3 £1.10, 1&3 £1.20 CSF £10.39 CT £16.88 TOTE £4.60: £2.40, £1.70; EX 10.40 Trifecta £19.70 Pool: £848.50 - 32.20 winning tickets..
Owner Six Too Many **Bred** Mrs C R D Wilson **Trained** Kingston Warren, Oxon
FOCUS
They raced centre-field and went just a steady gallop. A decnt handicap but the form can't rate any higher.

3539 PIPER-HEIDSIECK EBF MAIDEN STKS 1m 2f
8:40 (8:41) (Class 5) 3-Y-O **£3,881** (£1,155; £577; £288) **Stalls** Centre

Form RPR
2 1 **Endless Credit (IRE)**34 2456 3-9-5 0........ KierenFallon 6 86+
(Luca Cumani) *a.p: chsd ldr over 4f out: led over 2f out: rdn out* **15/8**1
2 1 **Obstacle** 3-9-5 0........ WilliamBuick 4 84+
(John Gosden) *a.p: pushed along 3f out: chsd wnr over 1f out: styd on* **9/4**2
06-2 3 9 **Forward March**18 2938 3-9-5 79........ ShaneKelly 3 65
(Gary Harrison) *led: racd keenly: hdd over 2f out: rdn over 1f out: wknd ins fnl f* **10/1**
4- 4 nk **Bourbon (IRE)**377 2929 3-9-5 0........ MickaelBarzalona 5 64
(Saeed bin Suroor) *hld up: hdwy over 2f out: rdn over 1f out: hung rt and wknd ins fnl f* **11/4**3
0 5 6 **Able Dash**8 3250 3-9-5 0........(p) TomMcLaughlin 1 53
(Ed Walker) *racd keenly: trckd ldr over 5f: rdn and wknd over 2f out* **66/1**
6 11 **Sheila's Heart** 3-9-5 0........ AnnelieHollstenius 2 32
(Julia Feilden) *s.s: hdwy over 5f out: wknd over 2f out* **50/1**
2m 7.7s (2.20) **Going Correction** +0.05s/f (Good) **6** Ran SP% **104.8**
Speed ratings (Par 99): **93,92,85,84,79 71**
Tote Swingers 1&2 £1.50, 2&3 £1.30, 1&3 £2.60 CSF £5.50 TOTE £2.10: £1.60, £1.40; EX 5.40 Trifecta £21.60 Pool: £1,000.63 - 34.65 winning tickets..
Owner Leonidas Marinopoulos **Bred** Roncon Churchtown Bloodstock & Lane Ltd **Trained** Newmarket, Suffolk
FOCUS
Two decent prospects drew clear in this maiden, and both are likely to rate higher.

3540 PIPER-HEIDSIECK H'CAP 5f
9:10 (9:10) (Class 5) (0-75,75) 3-Y-O **£3,234** (£962; £481; £240) **Stalls** High

Form RPR
U12 1 **Holley Shiftwell**62 1682 3-9-0 **68**........ AndreaAtzeni 5 77+
(Stuart Williams) *hmpd sn after s: chsd ldrs: led over 1f out: rdn and edgd rt ins fnl f: r.o* **5/1**3
3222 2 1¾ **Seven Of Clubs (IRE)**23 2779 3-9-7 **75**........(b) StevieDonohoe 4 78
(Noel Quinlan) *swtchd lft sn after s: chsd ldrs: rdn and ev ch over 1f out: styd on same pce ins fnl f* **11/4**2
116 3 1 **Secret Of Success**57 1784 3-8-12 **66**........ ChrisCatlin 3 65
(Rae Guest) *chsd ldr: rdn and ev ch over 1f out: no ex ins fnl f* **15/2**
0552 4 shd **Borough Boy (IRE)**6 3323 3-8-2 **56** oh2........(v) FrannyNorton 6 55
(Derek Shaw) *hmpd sn after s: hld up: hdwy 1/2-way: nt clr run over 1f out: styd on* **8/1**
1142 5 2 **Hit The Lights (IRE)**20 2888 3-9-3 **71**........ ShaneKelly 2 63
(Ollie Pears) *awkward leaving stalls: sn led: rdn and hdd over 1f out: no ex ins fnl f* **11/8**1
245 6 1 **Clock Opera (IRE)**23 2772 3-8-6 **60**........ CathyGannon 7 48
(William Stone) *hmpd sn after s: hld up: rdn over 1f out: nt trble ldrs* **14/1**
59.79s (0.69) **Going Correction** +0.05s/f (Good) **6** Ran SP% **115.0**
Speed ratings (Par 99): **96,93,91,91,88 86**
Tote Swingers 1&2 £1.02, 2&3 £8.80, 1&3 £14.00 CSF £19.71 TOTE £4.10: £2.70, £1.80; EX 10.10 Trifecta £50.20 Pool: £1,051.89 - 15.71 winning tickets..
Owner J W Parry **Bred** Mr & Mrs K W Grundy, Mr & Mrs P Hopper **Trained** Newmarket, Suffolk
■ Stewards' Enquiry : Stevie Donohoe seven-day ban: careless riding (11, 12, 13, 15 -18 July)
FOCUS
Just ordinary form, rated around the second and third.
T/Plt: £7.00 to a £1 stake. Pool: £50,900.39 - 5264.19 winning tickets. T/Qpdt: £3.10 to a £1 stake. Pool: £4,317.80 - 1024.40 winning tickets. CR

2751 REDCAR (L-H)
Friday, June 21
OFFICIAL GOING: Good to firm (firm in places; 9.9)
Wind: Virtually nil Weather: Grey cloud

3541 WIN A VIP DAY OUT @ REDCARRACING.CO.UK (S) STKS 7f
2:10 (2:11) (Class 6) 2-Y-O **£1,940** (£577; £288; £144) **Stalls** Centre

Form RPR
05 1 **Strictly Glitz (IRE)**14 3064 2-7-13 0........ JoeDoyle(7) 7 57
(John Quinn) *s.i.s: t.k.h and bhd: stdy hdwy to trck ldrs 1/2-way: slt ld on bit over 1f out: shkn up and rdn clr fnl f* **3/1**2
5 2 1¾ **Arthur's Melody**8 3255 2-8-4 0........ RyanWhile(7) 1 57
(Bill Turner) *prom: pushed along over 2f out: sltly outpcd and n.m.r wl over 1f out: sn swtchd rt and rdn: styd on fnl f: tk 2nd nr line* **16/1**
00 3 nk **Maupiti Express (FR)**7 3298 2-8-11 0........ TonyHamilton 5 56
(David O'Meara) *t.k.h: prom: effrt over 2f out: rdn to chal and edgd lft wl over 1f out: ev ch tl drvn and one pce ins fnl f* **5/1**3
0 4 1¾ **Tunnel Tiger (IRE)**4 3414 2-8-6 0........ LukeMorris 6 46
(J S Moore) *in tch: rdn along and edgd lft 3f out: kpt on u.p fnl f* **3/1**2
566 5 5 **Riley's Missile (IRE)**17 2947 2-8-11 0........(p) RobertWinston 2 38
(Charles Smith) *led: rdn along 2f out: hdd over 1f out and sn wknd* **20/1**
0 6 5 **Astral Pursuits**20 2883 2-8-3 0........(v1) DeclanCannon(3) 3 19
(Nigel Tinkler) *towards rr: rdn along 1/2-way: sn outpcd* **40/1**
3342 7 2 **Sherry For Nanny (IRE)**3 3440 2-8-1 0........(p) ShirleyTeasdale(5) 4 14
(Marjorie Fife) *trckd ldrs: rdn along wl over 2f out: sn wknd* **2/1**1
1m 27.52s (3.02) **Going Correction** -0.025s/f (Good) **7** Ran SP% **113.1**
Speed ratings (Par 91): **81,79,78,76,70 65,62**
Tote Swingers 1&2 £5.00, 2&3 £8.20, 1&3 £3.80 CSF £45.68 TOTE £3.90: £1.10, £5.90; EX 37.30 Trifecta £182.90 Pool: £1,866.86 - 7.65 winning tickets..There was no bid for the winner.
Owner Nigel S Cooper **Bred** Lynn Lodge Stud **Trained** Settrington, N Yorks
■ The first winner in Britain for 'Joe' Doyle, to go with four in Ireland.
FOCUS
The ground was officially good to firm, firm in places (watered). A weak 2yo seller, though a few of these were bred to be suited by the step up to 7f. The form has been given a chance of sorts.

3542 REDCAR RACECOURSE FOR YOUR WEDDING VENUE MAIDEN STKS 1m 2f
2:45 (2:45) (Class 5) 3-Y-O+ **£2,587** (£770; £384; £192) **Stalls** Low

Form RPR
0-32 1 **Paris Rose**16 2989 3-8-9 72........ PaulMulrennan 5 87+
(William Haggas) *mde all: pushed along wl over 2f out: rdn clr wl over 1f out: styd on strly: readily* **7/2**3
5-53 2 8 **Dance King**18 2931 3-9-0 80........ TedDurcan 1 81
(David Lanigan) *trckd ldng pair: hdwy 4f out: pushed along to chse wnr over 3f out: rdn and hung lft wl over 1f out: sn no imp* **11/8**1
0- 3 2 **Gamble**218 7721 3-8-9 0........ LukeMorris 6 68
(Michael Bell) *trckd wnr: pushed along 4f out: rdn 3f out: drvn and one pce fnl 2f* **7/1**
04 4 3 **Respect Me**15 3021 3-9-0 0........ RobertWinston 7 67
(Saeed bin Suroor) *trckd ldrs: effrt over 3f out: rdn along wl over 2f out: sn one pce* **2/1**2
3-5 5 7 **My Mum Mo**4 3398 5-9-7 0........ DuranFentiman 2 49
(Simon West) *hld up towards rr: sme hdwy 3f out: sn rdn along and nvr a factor* **40/1**
0 6 1¾ **Eium Mac**16 2989 4-9-7 0........ AdamCarter(5) 3 51
(Neville Bycroft) *chsd ldrs: rdn along 4f out: sn outpcd* **50/1**
7 12 **Sab Le Beau (FR)**33 4-9-9 0........ PaulPickard(3) 8 28
(Alan Brown) *dwlt: a in rr: bhd fnl 4f* **100/1**
0/0 8 ½ **Regy From Sedgy**48 2030 6-9-12 0........ PaddyAspell 4 27
(Frederick Watson) *a in rr: bhd fnl 4f* **150/1**
2m 6.02s (-1.08) **Going Correction** -0.10s/f (Good)
WFA 3 from 4yo+ 12lb **8** Ran SP% **116.2**
Speed ratings (Par 103): **100,93,92,89,84 82,73,72**
Tote Swingers 1&2 £2.00, 2&3 £1.80, 1&3 £3.20 CSF £8.94 TOTE £5.10: £1.10, £1.10, £1.70; EX 12.10 Trifecta £47.00 Pool: £2,888.00 - 46.02 winning tickets..
Owner Jaber Abdullah **Bred** Rabbah Bloodstock Limited **Trained** Newmarket, Suffolk
FOCUS
This maiden was all about the 3yos and the order barely changed. Probably not form to take at face value.

3543 JACK EVERSON MEMORIAL H'CAP 1m 2f
3:20 (3:20) (Class 5) (0-70,70) 4-Y-O+ **£2,587** (£770; £384; £192) **Stalls** Low

Form RPR
3115 1 **Size (IRE)**1 3506 4-8-11 **63**........ LeeTopliss(3) 3 73
(Richard Fahey) *trckd ldrs on inner: hdwy 3f out: cl up 2f out: rdn to ld over 1f out: edgd lft ins fnl f: kpt on* **5/4**1
0050 2 ¾ **Morocco**22 2798 4-9-1 **64**........ TomEaves 1 73
(David O'Meara) *in tch on inner: hdwy 3f out: trckd ldrs and nt clr run over 2f out: sn swtchd rt: rdn to chse wnr ent fnl f: n.m.r and swtchd rt again: kpt on towards fin* **20/1**
-304 3 nk **Ailsa Craig (IRE)**17 2956 7-8-9 **58** ow2........ PaulMulrennan 5 65
(Edwin Tuer) *trckd ldrs: hdwy on outer 1/2-way: cl up 3f out: effrt to chal over 2f out: sn rdn and ev ch tl drvn and kpt on same pce fnl f* **11/1**
0403 4 3¾ **Amazing Blue Sky**9 3195 7-8-4 **53**........ JamesSullivan 6 53
(Ruth Carr) *cl up: led 3f out: sn rdn: hdd and drvn over 1f out: wknd fnl f* **5/1**2
0-41 5 2 **Barton Bounty**16 2972 6-8-6 **55**........ PJMcDonald 12 52+
(Peter Niven) *hld up in rr: hdwy over 3f out: swtchd rt to outer over 2f out: sn rdn and no imp appr fnl f* **10/1**
-460 6 ¾ **Sinatramania**9 3195 6-8-4 **53** ow1........ RoystonFfrench 11 48+
(Tracy Waggott) *hld up: hdwy and in tch 3f out: rdn over 2f out and no imp* **20/1**
-543 7 nk **Tinseltown**11 2615 7-9-1 **67**........(p) LucyAlexander(3) 7 62
(Brian Rothwell) *sn slt ld: pushed along 4f out: rdn and hdd 3f out: grad wknd fnl 2f* **14/1**
-062 8 3¾ **Miss Ella Jade**9 3195 4-8-2 **51** oh3........ PaulQuinn 9 38
(Richard Whitaker) *trckd ldrs: pushed along and lost pl over 4f out: rdn along 3f out: n.d* **6/1**3
-000 9 3¾ **Striker Torres (IRE)**24 2753 7-8-8 **57**........(v) LukeMorris 8 37
(Ian McInnes) *a towards rr* **50/1**
0000 10 4½ **Quintain (IRE)**16 2986 5-8-2 **51** oh1........ DuranFentiman 2 23
(Tim Easterby) *a in rr* **40/1**
10-0 11 hd **Monthly Medal**20 2886 10-8-13 **62**........(t) AmyRyan 10 33
(Wilf Storey) *dwlt: a in rr* **66/1**
0-05 12 24 **Destination Aim**4 3397 6-9-7 **70**........ PaddyAspell 4
(Frederick Watson) *t.k.h: trckd ldng pair: pushed along over 3f out: sn lost pl and bhd: eased fnl f* **33/1**
2m 5.34s (-1.76) **Going Correction** -0.10s/f (Good) **12** Ran SP% **117.8**
Speed ratings (Par 103): **103,102,102,99,97 96,96,93,90,87 86,67**
Tote Swingers 1&2 £6.20, 2&3 £25.50, 1&3 £4.50 CSF £36.04 CT £205.57 TOTE £1.80: £1.02, £6.20, £4.30; EX 36.20 Trifecta £294.20 Pool: £2,475.24 - 6.30 winning tickets..
Owner Sir Robert Ogden **Bred** Manister House Stud **Trained** Musley Bank, N Yorks
FOCUS
A modest handicap. The third gives perspective to the form.

3544 ANDERSON BARROWCLIFF CELEBRATING 100 YEARS H'CAP (REDCAR STRAIGHT-MILE CHAMPIONSHIP QUALIFIER) 1m
4:00 (4:01) (Class 3) (0-90,88) 3-Y-O+ **£7,439** (£2,213; £1,106; £553) **Stalls** Centre

Form RPR
05-4 1 **The Rectifier (USA)**9 3207 6-10-0 **88**........(t) MickyFenton 4 96+
(Seamus Durack) *mde all: rdn wl over 1f out: edgd lft fnl f: kpt on wl* **5/2**2
0-10 2 2 **Forging The Path (USA)**20 2862 3-8-9 **79**........ TonyHamilton 3 81
(Richard Fahey) *trckd wnr: cl up 1/2-way: rdn along over 2f out: drvn over 1f out: kpt on same pce fnl f* **5/1**
-611 3 ½ **Ingleby Angel (IRE)**15 3027 4-9-10 **84**........ PaulMulrennan 7 87
(David O'Meara) *t.k.h: trckd ldrs: pushed along 3f out: sltly outpcd 2f out: sn rdn and kpt on fnl f* **15/8**1

310- **4** *nk* **Broctune Papa Gio**[19] 6881 6-8-11 **71**................................ TomEaves 5 73
(Keith Reveley) *trckd ldrs: hdwy 1/2-way: chsd wnr 2f out: sn rdn: drvn and one pce ins fnl f* **20/1**

30-0 **5** *shd* **Jo'Burg (USA)**[25] 2718 9-9-12 **86**.................................... AndrewMullen 6 88+
(David O'Meara) *dwlt and in rr: pushed along 3f out: hdwy and n.m.r over 1f out: swtchd lft and rdn: kpt on fnl f: nrst fin* **12/1**

1-40 **6** *3 ½* **Prophesy (IRE)**[35] 2431 4-9-4 **81**....................................... NeilFarley(3) 1 75
(Declan Carroll) *trckd ldng pair on outer: pushed along over 3f out: rdn over 2f out and sn wknd* **4/1**[3]

1m 38.8s (2.20) **Going Correction** -0.025s/f (Good)
WFA 3 from 4yo+ 10lb **6** Ran SP% **112.5**
Speed ratings (Par 107): **95,93,92,92,92 88**
Tote Swingers 1&2 £1.80, 2&3 £2.70, 1&3 £1.40 CSF £15.25 CT £26.92 TOTE £2.90: £2.00, £3.10; EX 17.00 Trifecta £37.70 Pool: £2,953.46 - 58.73 winning tickets..
Owner Mrs Anne Cowley **Bred** Ceka Ireland Ltd **Trained** Baydon, Wilts

FOCUS
A decent handicap, but with a smallish field it became a tactical event. The winner set his own tempo on a front runners' track and built on his latest promise.

3545 REDCAR RACECOURSE SHOWGROUND & OUTDOOR EVENTS CLASSIFIED CLAIMING STKS — 1m 2f
4:35 (4:38) (Class 6) 3-Y-O+ **£2,045** (£603; £302) **Stalls** Low

Form RPR

5-56 **1** **Yorksters Prince (IRE)**[85] 1222 6-8-11 47........(b) ShirleyTeasdale(5) 10 60
(Marjorie Fife) *mde all: pushed along 3f out: rdn 2f out: kpt on wl u.p fnl f* **28/1**

0-25 **2** *1 ¾* **Triple Eight (IRE)**[13] 3083 5-9-8 71........................(b) MichaelO'Connell 4 63
(Philip Kirby) *hld up: stdy hdwy over 4f out: effrt to chse wnr wl over 1f out: rdn to chal and ev ch ent fnl f: sn drvn and kpt on same pce* **5/1**[3]

3100 **3** *2 ½* **Matraash (USA)**[14] 3043 7-9-6 68...........................(be) JamesSullivan 1 56
(Daniel Mark Loughnane) *hld up in rr: swtchd to outer and hdwy 3f out: rdn 2f out: styd on appr fnl f: edgd lft and nrst fin* **20/1**

0-06 **4** *1 ½* **Tropical Duke (IRE)**[7] 3285 7-9-2 47.................. RoystonFfrench 8 49
(Ron Barr) *in rr: hdwy 3f out: rdn 2f out: kpt on appr fnl f: nrst fin* **66/1**

-010 **5** *1 ¾* **Valantino Oyster (IRE)**[9] 3195 6-9-2 61....................(p) BarryMcHugh 9 46
(Tracy Waggott) *chsd wnr: rdn along 3f out: drvn 2f out: grad wknd* **8/1**

0034 **6** *7* **West End Lad**[25] 2710 10-9-3 68...............................(b) MarkCoumbe(3) 6 36
(Roy Bowring) *trckd ldrs: hdwy on outer to chse ldng pair 1/2-way: rdn along 3f out: wknd over 2f out* **5/1**[3]

00-0 **7** *3 ¼* **Judicious**[36] 2383 6-9-8 71.. PaulMulrennan 7 32
(Noel Quinlan) *hld up towards rr: smooth hdwy on outer 4f out: cl up 3f out: sn rdn and wknd 2f out* **10/3**[1]

0-26 **8** *13* **Waltz Darling (IRE)**[53] 1567 5-9-12 68.............................. TomEaves 3 12
(Keith Reveley) *chsd ldrs: rdn along over 3f out: sn wknd* **8/1**

4-00 **9** *1 ¼* **Refractor (IRE)**[53] 1884 5-9-12 72... LukeMorris 5 9
(Michael Bell) *trckd ldrs: rdn along wl over 3f out: sn drvn and wknd* **7/2**[2]

06-0 **10** *5* **Distant Sunrise**[20] 2885 3-8-6 36..................................... PJMcDonald 2
(Ann Duffield) *chsd ldrs on inner: rdn along over 4f out: sn wknd* **40/1**

2m 5.89s (-1.21) **Going Correction** -0.10s/f (Good)
WFA 3 from 5yo+ 12lb **10** Ran SP% **113.0**
Speed ratings (Par 101): **100,98,96,95,94 88,85,75,74,70**
Tote Swingers 1&2 £16.40, 2&3 £10.80, 1&3 £23.50 CSF £154.08 TOTE £47.00: £10.10, £1.50, £5.60; EX 271.20 Trifecta £1498.80 Pool: £3,757.37 - 1.88 winning tickets..Judicious was claimed by Mr G A Harker for £8,000.
Owner Mrs Marion Turner **Bred** Lady Legard & Sir Tatton Sykes **Trained** Stillington, N Yorks

FOCUS
A moderate classified claimer and the third winner on the day to make all. It's unlikely the bare form is worth any more.

3546 FOLLOW REDCARRACING ON FACEBOOK & TWITTER H'CAP — 1m
5:10 (5:11) (Class 5) (0-70,70) 3-Y-O+ **£2,587** (£770; £384; £192) **Stalls** Centre

Form RPR

6465 **1** **Blue Maisey**[18] 2915 5-9-3 **59**.. PaulMulrennan 4 72
(Edwin Tuer) *midfield: pushed along 3f out: hdwy over 2f out: sn swtchd rt and rdn to ld wl over 1f out: drvn ins fnl f: jst hld on* **13/2**

6-21 **2** *shd* **Darkside**[32] 2501 3-8-7 **59**.. RoystonFfrench 5 70
(Tracy Waggott) *towards rr: swtchd rt to stands' rail 1/2-way: rdn along over 2f out: hdwy over 1f out: drvn and styd on strly fnl f: jst failed* **5/1**[2]

-135 **3** *6* **Red Paladin (IRE)**[18] 2916 3-9-4 **70**..........................(p) RobertWinston 8 69
(Kevin Ryan) *trckd ldrs: hdwy over 3f out: cl up over 2f out: sn rdn to chal and ev ch tl drvn and one pce ent fnl f* **6/1**[3]

6530 **4** *4 ½* **Illustrious Prince (IRE)**[3] 3445 6-9-2 **65**................. LukeLeadbitter(7) 1 54
(Declan Carroll) *cl up: led over 3f out: rdn and hdd wl over 1f out: wknd fnl f* **11/1**

-004 **5** *2 ¼* **Conjuror's Bluff**[4] 3395 5-8-7 **52**...................................... NeilFarley(3) 6 35
(Frederick Watson) *trckd ldrs: pushed along wl over 2f out: rdn wl over 1f out: sn one pce* **40/1**

4300 **6** *2 ¾* **Moral Issue**[9] 3192 5-8-12 **59**... JasonHart(5) 7 36
(Ian McInnes) *slt ld: pushed along and hdd over 3f out: rdn over 2f out: grad wknd* **33/1**

320- **7** *1* **Storma Norma**[210] 7840 3-9-1 **67**................................ DuranFentiman 10 40
(Tim Easterby) *nvr bttr than midfield* **33/1**

06-1 **8** *¾* **Blackball (USA)**[24] 2762 3-9-1 **67**...................................(b) TedDurcan 2 38
(David Lanigan) *hld up in rr: hdwy 3f out: in tch and rdn wl over 1f out: n.d* **9/4**[1]

-304 **9** *1* **Dialogue**[25] 2707 7-9-8 **64**..(p) TomEaves 3 35
(Geoffrey Harker) *a towards rr* **8/1**

-005 **10** *2* **Master Of Song**[30] 2575 6-9-2 **58**.................................(bt) LukeMorris 9 24
(Roy Bowring) *dwlt and towards rr: swtchd rt to stands' rail 1/2-way: rdn along whn n.m.r 3f out: sn bhd* **25/1**

04-0 **11** *2 ¾* **Team Challenge**[34] 2464 3-8-9 **61**.............................. JamesSullivan 13 19
(Tim Easterby) *a in rr* **33/1**

-550 **12** *¾* **Red Charmer (IRE)**[28] 2616 3-8-11 **63**.......................(p) PJMcDonald 12 19
(Ann Duffield) *prom: rdn along 1/2-way: sn wknd* **16/1**

44U3 **13** *1 ¾* **Solarmaite**[8] 3247 4-9-1 **60**..(b) MarkCoumbe(3) 11 14
(Roy Bowring) *cl up: rdn along 3f out: sn wknd* **18/1**

1m 37.17s (0.57) **Going Correction** -0.025s/f (Good)
WFA 3 from 4yo+ 10lb **13** Ran SP% **120.8**
Speed ratings (Par 103): **103,102,96,92,90 87,86,85,84,82 79,79,77**
Tote Swingers 1&2 £6.00, 2&3 £6.80, 1&3 £6.80 CSF £37.47 CT £210.43 TOTE £12.80: £4.10, £1.90, £3.00; EX 54.60 Trifecta £257.80 Pool: £2,085.33 - 6.06 winning tickets..
Owner Ontoawinner **Bred** Worksop Manor Stud **Trained** Birkby, N Yorks

FOCUS
A moderate handicap. The winner is rated back to last year's best.

3547 COME RACING TOMORROW ON LADIES' DAY MAIDEN H'CAP — 5f
5:40 (5:43) (Class 5) (0-70,60) 3-Y-O+ **£2,587** (£770; £384; £192) **Stalls** Centre

Form RPR

4025 **1** **A J Cook (IRE)**[24] 2756 3-9-2 **60**..................................(bt[1]) LMcNiff(5) 4 64
(David Barron) *slt ld: rdn along and hdd wl over 1f out: drvn ent fnl f: edgd rt: styd on wl to ld again on line* **11/8**[1]

00-0 **2** *nse* **Niceonemyson**[8] 3247 4-9-3 **50**....................................... PaddyAspell 1 56
(Christopher Wilson) *cl up: rdn to ld wl over 1f out: drvn and edgd rt fnl f: hdd on line* **11/2**[3]

50-0 **3** *2 ¼* **Isle Of Ellis (IRE)**[24] 2757 6-8-7 **45**.......................(v) ShirleyTeasdale(5) 2 43
(Ron Barr) *chsd ldng pair: rdn along 2f out: drvn and one pce fnl f* **13/2**

6304 **4** *nse* **Wotalad**[9] 3196 3-9-6 **59**.. AmyRyan 5 55
(Richard Whitaker) *chsd ldrs: rdn along wl over 1f out: drvn and one pce fnl f* **5/2**[2]

4-6 **5** *2 ¼* **Marmalade Moon**[20] 2870 4-9-6 **56**............................ RossAtkinson(3) 6 46
(Robert Cowell) *wnt rt s: in rr: rdn along 2f out: n.d* **7/1**

58.85s (0.25) **Going Correction** -0.025s/f (Good)
WFA 3 from 4yo+ 6lb **5** Ran SP% **111.9**
Speed ratings (Par 103): **97,96,93,93,89**
Tote Swinger 1&2 £10.80 CSF £9.50 TOTE £2.40: £1.40, £2.90; EX 10.80 Trifecta £33.90 Pool: £896.24 - 19.78 winning tickets..
Owner Norton Common Farm Racing **Bred** Francis Stynes **Trained** Maunby, N Yorks
■ Stewards' Enquiry : L McNiff two-day ban: use of whip (5, 7, July)

FOCUS
A poor maiden handicap and not much to take forward from this. The front pair duelled throughout.
T/Plt: £340.50 to a £1 stake. Pool: £49,702.02 - 106.53 winning tickets. T/Qpdt: £69.90 to a £1 stake. Pool: £2,828.13 - 29.9 winning tickets. JR

3548 - 3554a (Foreign Racing) - See Raceform Interactive

3522 ASCOT (R-H)
Saturday, June 22

OFFICIAL GOING: Good to firm (stands' side 9.4, centre 9.3, far side 9.5, round 8.2)
False rail on Round course removed, track at full width and distances as advertised.
Wind: Blustery; half against Weather: Sunny intervals with showers

3555 CHESHAM STKS (LISTED RACE) — 7f
2:30 (2:33) (Class 1) 2-Y-O
£34,026 (£12,900; £6,456; £3,216; £1,614; £810) **Stalls** Centre

Form RPR

3 **1** **Berkshire (IRE)**[36] 2411 2-9-3 0.. JimCrowley 21 106+
(Paul Cole) *w'like: scope: gd-bodied: stdd s: t.k.h and hld up in rr: gd hdwy over 2f out: rdn to ld wl over 1f out: styd on strly fnl f and gng away at fin: rdn out: quite impressive* **16/1**

1 **2** *2 ½* **Bunker (IRE)**[30] 2591 2-9-3 0.. RichardHughes 7 98+
(Richard Hannon) *lengthy: str: chsd ldrs: rdn and effrt 2f out: chsd wnr and edgd lft over 1f out: no imp and btn ins fnl f: kpt on to hold 2nd* **11/4**[1]

22 **3** *1 ½* **Ihtimal (IRE)**[15] 3057 2-8-12 0................................ SilvestreDeSousa 12 90+
(Saeed bin Suroor) *in tch in midfield: effrt whn n.m.r 2f out: swtchd sharply rt over 1f out: hdwy u.p to chse ldng pair ent fnl f: kpt on but no threat to wnr* **7/1**[3]

1 **4** *4* **Somewhat (USA)**[8] 3282 2-9-3 0..................................... JoeFanning 3 83+
(Mark Johnston) *unf: scope: tall: led: rdn and hdd 2f out: drvn and outpcd over 1f out: 4th and wl hld fnl f: plugged on* **5/1**[2]

1 **5** *¾* **Lone Warrior (IRE)**[11] 3175 2-9-3 0.............................. TomQueally 18 81
(David Evans) *leggy: in tch in midfield: rdn and outpcd 2f out: switching lft and rallying over 1f out: no threat to ldrs but kpt on u.p fnl f* **40/1**

3 **6** *hd* **Tinga (IRE)**[21] 2856 2-8-12 0... MartinHarley 6 76+
(Mick Channon) *neat: s.i.s: sn rcvrd and racd in midfield: rdn and outpcd over 2f out: no threat to ldrs but rallied and kpt on fnl f* **20/1**

02 **7** *1 ¼* **Sir Jack Layden**[9] 3233 2-9-3 0.................................... JamieSpencer 5 77
(David Brown) *w'like: hld up in rr: outpcd ent fnl 2f: bhd and swtchd lft over 1f out: no threat to ldrs but styd on past btn horses fnl f* **33/1**

8 *nk* **Calrissian (IRE)** 2-9-3 0... KierenFallon 20 77
(Alan Jarvis) *leggy: hld up in tch in midfield: rdn 3f out: drvn and outpcd over 1f out: n.d and kpt on same pce fnl f* **50/1**

9 *¾* **Friendship (IRE)**[20] 2898 2-9-3 0................................. JosephO'Brien 9 75
(A P O'Brien, Ire) *athletic: chsd ldrs: rdn to ld 2f out: sn hdd and no ex u.p: btn over 1f out: wknd fnl f* **8/1**

10 *½* **Shepherd Gate (USA)** 2-9-3 0....................................... WayneLordan 15 73
(J S Moore) *leggy: s.i.s: sn rcvrd and in tch in midfield: rdn and outpcd over 2f out: wl hld whn swtchd rt over 1f out: plugged on fnl f* **100/1**

5123 **11** *1 ¼* **Scargill**[32] 2553 2-9-3 0.. RyanMoore 2 70
(Brian Ellison) *stdd s: t.k.h: hld up towards rr: rdn and effrt 2f out: no imp over 1f out: plugged on same pce fnl f* **40/1**

1 **12** *1* **Autumn Lily (USA)**[10] 3205 2-8-12 0............................ WilliamBuick 8 63
(Saeed bin Suroor) *leggy: in tch in midfield: rdn and outpcd over 2f out: n.d and swtchd rt over 1f out: no imp* **14/1**

4 **13** *½* **Street Force (USA)**[8] 3290 2-9-3 0................................ JamesDoyle 13 66
(Clive Brittain) *w'like: in tch in midfield: rdn and struggling over 2f out: wknd over 1f out* **25/1**

2 **14** *½* **Bureau (IRE)**[8] 3290 2-8-12 0.. GrahamLee 17 60
(Mark Johnston) *leggy: in tch in midfield: rdn and unable qck 2f out: wkng and edgd rt over 1f out: fdd fnl f* **33/1**

131 **15** *3 ½* **Master Carpenter (IRE)**[32] 2553 2-9-3 0..................... AndreaAtzeni 10 56
(Rod Millman) *str: lw: pressed ldr: rdn and ev ch ent fnl 2f: sn struggling and wkng whn jostled over 1f out: fdd fnl f* **8/1**

16 *1* **Freedom Square (IRE)**[13] 3139 2-9-3 0...................(t) KevinManning 16 53
(J S Bolger, Ire) *athletic: lw: pressed ldrs: rdn and no ex 2f out: wkng whn jostling match w rival over 1f out: sn fdd* **14/1**

461 **17** *hd* **Know Your Name**[9] 3245 2-9-3 0.................................. WilliamCarson 1 53
(David Evans) *leggy: stdd s: hld up in tch towards rr: rdn and no prog ent fnl 2f: wknd u.p over 1f out* **80/1**

53 **18** *1* **Khee Society**[9] 3245 2-9-3 0.. AdamKirby 14 50
(David Evans) *w'like: in tch in midfield: rdn and lost pl over 2f out: bhd over 1f out* **100/1**

The Form Book Flat, Raceform Ltd, Compton, RG20 6NL.

19 *nse* **Citizen Kaine (IRE)** 2-9-3 0 CathyGannon 19 50
(Jo Hughes) *w'like: s.i.s: in tch in rr: rdn and outpcd over 2f out: bhd over 1f out* **100/1**

1m 28.46s (0.86) **Going Correction** +0.175s/f (Good) **19** Ran SP% **122.8**
Speed ratings (Par 101): **102,99,97,92,92 91,90,90,89,88 87,86,85,84,80 79,79,78,78**
toteswingers 1&2 £13.80, 1&3 £28.90, 2&3 £5.60 CSF £54.80 TOTE £21.80: £5.30, £1.80, £3.00; EX 104.00 Trifecta £1774.50 Pool: £10,108.34 - 4.27 winning units..
Owner H R H Sultan Ahmad Shah **Bred** Newsells Park Stud **Trained** Whatcombe, Oxon

FOCUS
The course was at full width with race distances as advertised. Restricted to the progeny of sires who won over at least 1m2f, the Chesham is often an ordinary Listed event, but subsequent Moyglare winner Maybe landed the 2011 running. Only time will show the true worth of this year's edition but the winner looks a decent prospect for good races. They raced up the middle of the track.

3556 HARDWICKE STKS (GROUP 2) 1m 4f
3:05 (3:05) (Class 1) 4-Y-0+

£120,962 (£45,859; £22,951; £11,432; £5,737; £2,879) **Stalls** Low

Form RPR

0-22 **1** **Thomas Chippendale (IRE)**[42] 2252 4-9-0 111 JohnnyMurtagh 8 119
(Lady Cecil) *hld up: hdwy to chse ldr 3f out: rdn to ld ent fnl 2f: edgd rt over 1f out: pressed by runner-up fnl 100yds: styd on gamely and in command towards fin: collapsed fatally after line* **8/1**

20-2 **2** *1* **Dandino**[49] 2020 6-9-0 113 FrankieDettori 9 117
(Marco Botti) *chsd ldrs: lft in 2nd pl over 7f out: lost 2nd 3f out: sn outpcd: rallied to regain 2nd ins fnl f: pressed wnr fnl 100yds: no ex towards fin* **10/1**

2111 **3** *2 1/2* **Universal (IRE)**[49] 2020 4-9-0 114 JoeFanning 2 113
(Mark Johnston) *lw: broke wl: led early: chsd clr ldr after: swvd to avoid loose horse whn lft in ld over 7f out: clr 4f out: rdn and hdd ent fnl 2f: nt qckn over 1f out: styd on for press towards fin* **10/1**

-341 **4** *shd* **Noble Mission**[28] 2656 4-9-0 111 TomQueally 1 113
(Lady Cecil) *s.i.s: hld up in rr: hdwy over 2f out: rdn to chse wnr and ev ch over 1f out: lost 2nd ins fnl f: no ex fnl 75yds: lost 3rd fnl stride* **12/1**

50-1 **5** *hd* **Mount Athos (IRE)**[43] 2212 6-9-0 117 JamieSpencer 5 113
(Luca Cumani) *lw: hld up: rdn and nt qckn over 2f out: u.p whn n.m.r and lost pl over 1f out: sn plld out: wanted to lug rt whn prog wl ins fnl f: r.o and gng on at fin* **11/4**[2]

30-1 **6** *1 3/4* **Songcraft (IRE)**[28] 2668 5-9-0 106 (p) SilvestreDeSousa 7 110
(Saeed bin Suroor) *hmpd s: hld up: effrt over 2f out: chsng ldrs for press whn n.m.r and lost pl over 1f out: one pce ins fnl f tl no ex towards fin* **20/1**

4-11 **7** *10* **Sir John Hawkwood (IRE)**[36] 2427 4-9-0 110 RyanMoore 6 98
(Sir Michael Stoute) *lw: chsd ldrs: outpcd and lost pl over 2f out: bhd and struggling after* **6/1**[3]

2-31 **S** **Ektihaam (IRE)**[42] 2252 4-9-0 115 PaulHanagan 4
(Roger Varian) *racd keenly: sn led: steadily drew clr after 2f: slipped up on bnd and uns rdr over 7f out* **9/4**[1]

2m 30.65s (-1.85) **Going Correction** +0.175s/f (Good) **8** Ran SP% **113.5**
Speed ratings (Par 115): **113,112,110,110,110 109,102,**
toteswingers 1&2 £10.20, 1&3 £10.50, 2&3 £8.60 CSF £81.88 TOTE £9.90: £2.50, £2.00, £2.30; EX 91.50 Trifecta £595.80 Pool: £16,074.95 - 20.35 winning units..
Owner Sir Robert Ogden **Bred** Premier Bloodstock **Trained** Newmarket, Suffolk

FOCUS
All but one of these were covered by 7lb on official ratings, so a competitive event, but whether the standard of the race was high enough to help the race gain Group 1 status in the near future is debatable. It rates an ordinary renewal with the runner-up the best guide. As predicted with two front-runners in the line-up there was a decent early gallop. There was drama early on as Ektihaam slipped on the turn before halfway and unshipped Paul Hanagan.

3557 DIAMOND JUBILEE STKS (BRITISH CHAMPIONS SERIES & GLOBAL SPRINT CHALLENGE) (GROUP 1) 6f
3:45 (3:46) (Class 1) 3-Y-0+

£283,550 (£107,500; £53,800; £26,800; £13,450; £6,750) **Stalls** Centre

Form RPR

30-2 **1** **Lethal Force (IRE)**[38] 2368 4-9-4 111 AdamKirby 15 123
(Clive Cox) *racd keenly: sn led and mde rest: rdn and qcknd 2 l clr wl over 1f out: hung lft u.p but styd on strly fnl f* **11/1**

15-1 **2** *2* **Society Rock (IRE)**[38] 2368 6-9-4 117 KierenFallon 8 117+
(James Fanshawe) *s.i.s: hld up in rr: swtchd lft 1/2-way: hdwy u.p over 1f out: chsd wnr ins fnl f: r.o but no imp* **4/1**[1]

-323 **3** *1 3/4* **Krypton Factor**[84] 1266 5-9-4 117 (b) LukeMorris 16 111
(Fawzi Abdulla Nass, Bahrain) *in tch in midfield: effrt and rdn 2f out: hrd drvn over 1f out: kpt on to go 3rd wl ins fnl f: no threat to wnr* **25/1**

4-03 **4** *1* **Gordon Lord Byron (IRE)**[38] 2368 5-9-4 117 WilliamBuick 4 108
(T Hogan, Ire) *lw: racd keenly: chsd ldrs: rdn 2f out: chsd ldng pair and drvn over 1f out: kpt on same pce ins fnl f* **15/2**[3]

11-4 **5** *nse* **Rosdhu Queen (IRE)**[63] 1676 3-8-8 107 RichardHughes 10 103
(William Haggas) *restless in stalls: stdd s: hld up in rr: hdwy in midfield: effrt and drvn wl over 1f out: edgd rt and no imp fnl f* **16/1**

2-44 **6** *3/4* **Hawkeyethenoo (IRE)**[38] 2368 7-9-4 112 GrahamLee 7 105+
(Jim Goldie) *s.i.s: hld up in rr: clsng but bhd a wall of horses 2f out: swtchd rt and hdwy u.p ent fnl f: styd on: nvr trbld ldrs* **12/1**

10-3 **7** *hd* **Slade Power (IRE)**[28] 2676 4-9-4 109 WayneLordan 17 105+
(Edward Lynam, Ire) *swtg: awkward leaving stalls and slowly away: t.k.h: hld up in tch in midfield: rdn and effrt 2f out: no imp but kpt on ins fnl f: no threat to ldrs* **10/1**

0- **8** *nk* **Sea Siren (AUS)**[28] 2684 5-9-1 115 (b) RyanMoore 13 101
(J O'Shea, Australia) *w'like: chsd ldrs: rdn to chse wnr 2f out but sn outpcd: drvn and no imp over 1f out: lost 2nd and wknd ins fnl f* **7/1**[2]

2-15 **9** *2* **Maarek**[6] 3380 6-9-4 112 JamieSpencer 5 97+
(David Peter Nagle, Ire) *lw: hld up in tch in last trio: rdn and effrt on towards far side over 1f out: no prog 1f out: nvr trbld ldrs* **14/1**

0-03 **10** *1/2* **Gammarth (FR)**[20] 2909 5-9-4 107 FabriceVeron 6 96
(H-A Pantall, France) *broke wl: sn stdd bk into midfield and t.k.h: rdn and effrt 2f out: sn outpcd and btn over 1f out* **66/1**

0/ **11** *hd* **Havelock (USA)**[49] 6-9-4 109 (t) FrankieDettori 9 95+
(Darrin Miller, U.S.A) *str: gd-bodied: lw: hld up in midfield: lost pl and towards rr: plenty to do but sme hdwy whn nt clr run 1f out: sn swtchd rt and kpt on but n.d* **33/1**

01-3 **12** *nk* **Intense Pink**[42] 2264 4-9-1 104 SebSanders 14 91
(Chris Wall) *hld up in tch towards rr: rdn and effrt wl over 1f out: no imp 1f out: wknd ins fnl f* **50/1**

3-04 **13** *3* **Sirius Prospect (USA)**[19] 2936 5-9-4 104 JimCrowley 12 84
(Dean Ivory) *hld up in tch in midfield: rdn and effrt 2f out: sn drvn and struggling: wknd over 1f out* **33/1**

0-00 **14** *nk* **Dandy Boy (ITY)**[28] 2676 7-9-4 108 PatDobbs 1 83
(David Marnane, Ire) *t.k.h: hld up in tch in midfield: rdn 2f out: no hdwy u.p over 1f out and wl hld whn sltly hmpd 1f out* **12/1**

2141 **15** *nk* **Zanetto**[36] 2415 3-8-11 109 LiamKeniry 2 81
(Andrew Balding) *chsd ldrs: rdn and outpcd 2f out: sn drvn and outpcd: wknd ent fnl f* **25/1**

1-03 **16** *3 1/2* **Mince**[19] 2936 4-9-1 110 JamesDoyle 11 76
(Roger Charlton) *chsd ldrs: rdn and struggling 2f out: sn outpcd and lost pl: wknd over 1f out* **10/1**

602- **17** *3 1/2* **Soul (AUS)**[259] 6867 6-9-4 115 SilvestreDeSousa 3 76
(Saeed bin Suroor) *lw: chsd wnr tl 2f out: sn rdn and btn: wkng whn short of room 1f out: eased ins fnl f* **16/1**

0025 **18** *7* **Reply (IRE)**[9] 3262 4-9-4 107 (v) JosephO'Brien 18 65
(A P O'Brien, Ire) *chsd ldrs: rdn 1/2-way: lost pl 2f out: bhd and eased 1f out* **33/1**

1m 13.36s (-1.14) **Going Correction** +0.175s/f (Good)
WFA 3 from 4yo+ 7lb **18** Ran SP% **124.6**
Speed ratings (Par 117): **114,111,109,107,107 106,106,105,103,102 102,101,97,97,97 92,87,78**
toteswingers 1&2 £12.20, 1&3 £61.50, 2&3 £15.00 CSF £51.60 TOTE £13.00: £3.90, £2.20, £10.60; EX 57.70 Trifecta £2168.10 Pool: £187,418.38 - 64.83 winning units..
Owner Alan G Craddock **Bred** Declan Johnson **Trained** Lambourn, Berks

FOCUS
The foreign challenge wasn't up to much this year, and the home-trained sprinters, as usual, looked an ordinary bunch, so this wasn't a strong renewal. Not form to rate too literally. They raced up the middle of the track, but the first three finishers were all positioned towards the near side of the group (like the winners of the Chesham and Wokingham) and may have been at an advantage. Lethal Force saved plenty before being committed and that helped him reverse recent York form with the held-up Society Rock. The time was 0.43 seconds quicker than the Wokingham. All things considered, this isn't form to get carried away with.

3558 WOKINGHAM STKS (HERITAGE H'CAP) 6f
4:25 (4:25) (Class 2) (0-110,109) 3-Y-0+

£93,375 (£27,960; £13,980; £6,990; £3,495; £1,755) **Stalls** Centre

Form RPR

6142 **1** **York Glory (USA)**[28] 2669 5-9-2 100 (b) JamieSpencer 22 114
(Kevin Ryan) *hld up stands' side: swtchd rt to r in main gp on far side after 1f: hdwy 2f out: swtchd lft over 1f out: r.o ins fnl f to ld fnl 150yds: in command cl home: 1st of 20 in gp* **14/1**

-424 **2** *1 3/4* **Shropshire (IRE)**[48] 2046 5-9-1 99 JamesMcDonald 18 107
(Charles Hills) *swtg: racd in main gp on far side: hdwy over 2f out: rdn to chal over 1f out: stl ev ch 150yds out: unable to go w wnr towards fin: 2nd of 20 in gp* **12/1**

0-03 **3** *1* **Dinkum Diamond (IRE)**[21] 2865 5-9-2 100 CathyGannon 15 105+
(Henry Candy) *racd in main gp on far side: midfield: hdwy 2f out: rdn over 1f out: styd on ins fnl f: nt quite get to front two: 3rd of 20 in gp* **22/1**

2061 **4** *3/4* **Khubala (IRE)**[19] 2937 4-9-0 98 5ex (b) FrankieDettori 29 101
(Hugo Palmer) *lw: racd stands' side: chsd ldrs: effrt to chal wl over 1f out: styd on: hld fnl 50yds: 1st of 6 in gp* **16/1**

5062 **5** *hd* **Glass Office**[14] 3103 3-8-12 103 JimCrowley 19 105
(David Simcock) *racd in main gp on far side: midfield: hdwy 3f out: led over 1f out: edgd lft ins fnl f: hdd fnl 150yds: styd on same pce fnl 75yds: 4th of 20 in gp* **20/1**

02 **6** *1 1/4* **Rex Imperator**[21] 2858 4-9-0 98 NeilCallan 21 96
(William Haggas) *lw: swtchd lft to r stands' side sn after s: swtchd rt to r in main gp on far side after 1f: hld up: hdwy 2f out: styd on ins fnl f: gng on at fin: 5th of 20 in gp* **8/1**[3]

-644 **7** *nk* **Elusivity (IRE)**[20] 2909 5-9-6 104 TomQueally 30 101
(David O'Meara) *lw: racd stands' side: chsd ldrs: effrt over 2f out: rdn and ch over 1f out: nt qckn ins fnl f: 2nd of 6 in gp* **25/1**

0151 **8** *3/4* **Duke Of Firenze**[21] 2865 4-9-4 102 5ex RyanMoore 31 97
(Sir Michael Stoute) *lw: racd stands' side: in rr: pushed along and outpcd 2f out: hdwy over 1f out: styd on ins fnl f: nt rch ldrs: one pce fnl 50yds: 3rd of 6 in gp* **7/1**[2]

31-2 **9** *hd* **Gabriel's Lad (IRE)**[48] 2046 4-8-12 96 KierenFallon 24 90
(Denis Coakley) *racd stands' side: swtchd rt to r in main gp on far side after 1f: chsd ldrs: led 2f out: rdn and hdd over 1f out: styd on same pce fnl 110yds: 6th of 20 in gp* **6/1**[1]

1032 **10** *3/4* **Prodigality**[29] 2621 5-9-3 101 LukeMorris 27 93
(Ronald Harris) *racd stands' side: chsd ldr: effrt and ch over 1f out: one pce fnl 100yds: 4th of 6 in gp* **20/1**

0-01 **11** *nk* **Mass Rally (IRE)**[38] 2366 6-9-6 104 (b) PaulMulrennan 6 95
(Michael Dods) *racd in main gp on far side: hld up: hdwy 2f out: styd on ins fnl f: nt rch ldrs: 7th of 20 in gp* **20/1**

20-6 **12** *1/2* **Louis The Pious**[38] 2366 5-9-2 100 (p) DanielTudhope 20 89
(David O'Meara) *racd in main gp on far side: chsd ldrs: pushed along 2f out: rdn over 1f out: kpt on ins fnl f: one pce towards fin: 8th of 20 in gp* **16/1**

02-0 **13** *nk* **Ladyship**[48] 2046 4-8-12 96 [1] RichardHughes 17 84
(Sir Michael Stoute) *racd in main gp on far side: midfield: effrt to chse ldrs over 2f out: one pce ins fnl f: no ex fnl 75yds: 9th of 20 in gp* **16/1**

6165 **14** *hd* **Regal Parade**[6] 3373 9-9-0 103 (t) MatthewLawson(5) 28 91
(Milton Bradley) *racd stands' side: in rr: hdwy over 2f out: rdn in midfield over 1f out: one pce and no imp ins fnl f: 5th of 6 in gp* **50/1**

2323 **15** *1* **Poole Harbour (IRE)**[19] 2937 4-8-7 95 ow1 WilliamTwiston-Davies(5) 8 80
(Richard Hannon) *racd in main gp on far side: led overall: rdn and hdd 2f out: wknd over 1f out: 10th of 20 in gp* **20/1**

0510 **16** *1 1/4* **Ancient Cross**[28] 2669 9-8-11 95 (t) MartinHarley 9 75
(Michael Easterby) *racd in main gp on far side: in tch: rdn to chse ldrs 2f out: wknd fnl 110yds: 11th of 20 in gp* **66/1**

00-0 **17** *1 1/4* **Rebellious Guest**[42] 2254 4-8-11 95 GrahamLee 11 71
(George Margarson) *racd in main gp on far side: midfield: pushed along over 2f out: sn outpcd: nvr a threat: 12th of 20 in gp* **33/1**

0-60 **18** *1/2* **Bapak Chinta (USA)**[38] 2366 4-8-11 95 AmyRyan 16 70
(Kevin Ryan) *racd in main gp on far side: chsd ldr tl rdn over 2f out: btn over 1f out: 13th of 20 in gp* **50/1**

4301 **19** *nse* **Hitchens (IRE)**[28] 2676 8-9-10 108 JohnnyMurtagh 5 83
(David Barron) *lw: racd in main gp on far side: hld up: rdn and kpt on steadily over 1f out: no imp on ldrs: eased fnl 75yds: 14th of 20 in gp* **16/1**

-060 **20** *1/2* **Secret Witness**[14] 3114 7-9-3 101 (b) JoeFanning 7 74
(Ronald Harris) *racd in main gp on far side: hld up: outpcd 3f out: nvr a threat: 15th of 20 in gp* **66/1**

/600 **21** 3/4 **Chandlery (IRE)**[30] 2585 4-8-13 **97** PatDobbs 13 68
(Richard Hannon) *racd in main gp on far side: chsd ldrs: pushed along over 2f out: wknd over 1f out: 16th of 20 in gp* **66/1**

00-0 **22** 3/4 **Zero Money (IRE)**[14] 3114 7-9-0 **98** (b) JamesDoyle 25 66
(Hugo Palmer) *lw: racd stands' side: led gp tl rdn and hdd fr 2f out: wknd ins fnl f: eased after: 6th of 6 in gp* **33/1**

1121 **23** 2 1/4 **Nocturn**[14] 3114 4-9-1 **99** 5ex (p) WilliamBuick 12 67
(Jeremy Noseda) *racd in main gp on far side: midfield: rdn over 2f out: btn ins fnl f: eased fnl 110yds: 17th of 20 in gp* **11/1**

60-2 **24** 3 1/4 **Royal Rock**[42] 2257 9-9-6 **104** GeorgeBaker 3 77
(Chris Wall) *lw: racd in main gp on far side: hld up in rr: rdn 2f out: nvr able to get on terms: eased fnl 110yds: 18th of 20 in gp* **33/1**

00-5 **25** 5 **Palace Moon**[19] 2936 8-9-3 **101** JimmyQuinn 1 36
(William Knight) *racd in main gp on far side: hld up: pushed along over 3f out: nvr on terms: 19th of 20 in gp* **33/1**

-304 **26** 7 **Our Jonathan**[28] 2667 6-9-4 **102** (v[1]) SilvestreDeSousa 10
(Tim Pitt) *racd in main gp on far side: midfield: outpcd and lost pl 3f out: bhd after: 20th of 20 in gp* **33/1**

1m 13.79s (-0.71) **Going Correction** +0.175s/f (Good)
WFA 3 from 4yo+ 7lb **26** Ran SP% **134.5**
Speed ratings (Par 109): **111,108,107,106,106 104,104,103,102,101 101,100,100,100,98 97,95,94,94,93 92,91,88,84,77 68**
toteswingers 1&2 £11.50, 1&3 £119.00, 2&3 £63.70 CSF £149.54 CT £3745.20 TOTE £14.90: £3.70, £3.10, £7.10, £4.10; EX 130.40 Trifecta £11592.10 Part won. Pool: £15,456.22 - 0.68 winning units..
Owner Salman Rashed & Mohamed Khalifa **Bred** Paget Bloodstock & Horse France **Trained** Hambleton, N Yorks

FOCUS
They shunned the far side here, with the main bunch racing more towards the middle and a smaller group of six racing stands' side. The first three raced in the larger group, and not many counted. The final time was 0.43sec slower than the Golden Jubilee. York Glory is rated up a length on his better recent runs.

3559 DUKE OF EDINBURGH H'CAP 1m 4f

5:00 (5:02) (Class 2) (0-105,105) 3-Y-0+

£46,687 (£13,980; £6,990; £3,495; £1,747; £877) **Stalls** Low

Form RPR

10-3 **1** **Opinion (IRE)**[48] 2044 4-9-0 **95** (t) RyanMoore 10 109
(Sir Michael Stoute) *chsd ldng trio: swtchd out lft 3f out and sn rdn to chal: led over 2f out: styd on wl u.p fnl f: drvn out* **8/1**

22-6 **2** 2 **Stencive**[48] 2044 4-9-3 **98** FrankieDettori 20 109+
(William Haggas) *lw: stdd after s: hld up in last trio: rdn and hdwy on outer over 2f out: str run but edging rt whn wnt 2nd 1f out: hrd drvn and ins fnl f: no ex fnl 100yds* **5/1**[1]

12-1 **3** 2 **Ustura (USA)**[33] 2520 4-8-11 **92** (tp) SilvestreDeSousa 6 100
(Saeed bin Suroor) *led for 2f: chsd ldr after tl rdn to ld over 2f out: immediately hdd and nt quite pce of wnr 2f out: lost 2nd whn bmpd and pushed rt 1f out: kpt on same pce after* **7/1**[3]

15-4 **4** 1 **Caravan Rolls On**[35] 2451 5-9-0 **95** JamieSpencer 17 101
(Peter Chapple-Hyam) *lw: chsd ldrs: rdn and effrt over 2f out: keeping on same pce and no imp whn pushed rt and sltly hmpd jst over 1f out: one pce fnl f* **11/2**[2]

2-02 **5** 1 3/4 **Lahaag**[38] 2365 4-9-5 **100** RichardHughes 4 103
(John Gosden) *lw: chsd ldrs: switching out lft and n.m.r briefly wl over 2f out: sn rdn and unable qck: kpt on same pce fr over 1f out* **15/2**

5300 **6** 1 1/4 **Sir Graham Wade (IRE)**[23] 2810 4-9-10 **105** JoeFanning 14 106
(Mark Johnston) *bustled along leaving stalls and sn chsd ldr: led after 2f: rdn and hdd over 2f out: sn drvn and unable qck: btn over 1f out: plugged on same pce fnl f* **16/1**

10-4 **7** nk **Blue Surf**[22] 2839 4-9-3 **98** PatDobbs 1 99
(Amanda Perrett) *chsd ldrs: swtchd lft and effrt over 2f out: sn drvn and outpcd by ldrs: pluged on same pce and no threat fr over 1f out* **14/1**

20- **8** 3/4 **Hammerfest**[16] 6-9-5 **100** JimCrowley 18 100
(J E Hammond, France) *hld up in tch in midfield hld but stuck wd: rdn and effrt over 2f out: drvn and no imp over 1f out: wknd ins fnl f* **12/1**

3-40 **9** nk **Silver Lime (USA)**[26] 2718 4-8-11 **92** [1] JamesDoyle 19 93+
(Roger Charlton) *stdd and dropped in bhd after s: hld up in last trio: hdwy on inner ent fnl 2f: keeping on same pce and no threat to ldrs whn nt clr run: swtchd lft and bmpd rival ins fnl f* **12/1**

1132 **10** nk **Beaumont's Party (IRE)**[36] 2407 6-9-0 **95** DaleSwift 15 94
(Brian Ellison) *t.k.h early: hld up in tch in midfield: rdn and unable qck over 1f out: drvn and no imp over 1f out* **14/1**

24-3 **11** 4 **Communicator**[43] 2212 5-9-1 **96** JimmyFortune 5 91+
(Andrew Balding) *hld up in tch in midfield: rdn and unable qck ent fnl 2f: plugged on same pce and wl hld whn pushed lft and hmpd ins fnl f: eased after* **20/1**

/451 **12** 1 1/4 **Highland Castle**[14] 3115 5-8-13 **94** LiamKeniry 3 97+
(David Elsworth) *taken down early: stdd s: t.k.h and hld up in rr: effrt and clsng but stl plenty to do whn bdly hmpd and snatched up 2f out: nt rcvr and no ch after* **12/1**

4003 **13** 3/4 **Art Scholar (IRE)**[92] 1110 6-9-1 **96** TomQueally 7 99+
(Michael Appleby) *hld up in tch in last quartet: effrt and hdwy but stl plenty to do whn bdly hmpd 2f out: rallied and sme hdwy but n.d whn bmpd: bdly hmpd again and stmbld ins fnl f: eased after* **33/1**

2102 **14** 6 **Hanoverian Baron**[36] 2427 8-8-12 **93** SebSanders 16 79+
(Tony Newcombe) *t.k.h early: hld up in tch in midfield: rdn and effrt over 2f out: sn outpcd and no prog u.p wl over 1f out: no ch whn pushed lft and hmpd ins fnl f: eased after* **25/1**

521- **15** 1/2 **Deia Sunrise (IRE)**[41] 6661 4-9-2 **97** (t) WilliamBuick 21 76
(Paul Webber) *stdd after s: t.k.h: hld up in rr: rdn and no prog over 2f out: lost tch wl over 1f out* **40/1**

1240 **16** 1 **Buckland (IRE)**[45] 2149 5-9-4 **104** NicoleNordblad(5) 2 81
(Hans Adielsson) *in tch in midfield: rdn and no prog over 2f out: losing pl whn squeezed for room 2f out: bhd and no ch after* **33/1**

2m 31.3s (-1.20) **Going Correction** +0.175s/f (Good) **16** Ran SP% **126.6**
Speed ratings (Par 109): **111,109,108,107,106 105,105,104,104,104 101,101,100,96,96 95**
toteswingers 1&2 £8.60, 1&3 £9.60, 2&3 £5.50 CSF £46.71 CT £307.25 TOTE £9.20: £2.30, £1.70, £2.20, £1.60; EX 50.40 Trifecta £343.70 Pool: £16,549.77 - 36.10 winning units..
Owner Highclere Thoroughbred Racing-Herring **Bred** Ballylinch Stud **Trained** Newmarket, Suffolk
■ Stewards' Enquiry : Jimmy Fortune two-day ban: careless riding (7-8 July)
Frankie Dettori two-day ban: careless riding (7-8 July)
James Doyle two-day ban: careless riding (7-8 July)

FOCUS
The bend where Ektihaam slipped in the Hardwicke, about 7f out, was reportedly spiked and sanded ahead of this race. This was another good running of the Duke of Edinburgh handicap, but six of the first seven finishers filled the first six positions for most of the way. The winner built on his reappearance.

3560 QUEEN ALEXANDRA STKS (CONDITIONS RACE) 2m 5f 159y

5:35 (5:39) (Class 2) 4-Y-0+

£37,350 (£11,184; £5,592; £2,796; £1,398; £702) **Stalls** Low

Form RPR

25-5 **1** **Chiberta King**[35] 2443 7-9-2 102 (p) JimmyFortune 16 91
(Andrew Balding) *lw: hld up: hdwy 10f out: trckd ldrs sn after: wnt 2nd 4f out: led over 2f out: edgd lft u.p over 1f out: rdr dropped rein whn hrd pressed ins fnl f: kpt finding more towards fin: hld on wl* **8/1**

10-6 **2** hd **Shahwardi (FR)**[27] 2695 7-9-2 109 FrankieDettori 5 91
(A De Royer-Dupre, France) *racd keenly in midfield: hdwy 4f out: str chal on outer fr 2f out: pressed wnr strly ins fnl f: hld fnl strides* **3/1**[1]

0-14 **3** 1 1/2 **Seaside Sizzler**[48] 2052 6-9-2 86 (vt) JimCrowley 18 90
(Ralph Beckett) *midfield: hdwy over 4f out: rdn to chal fr 2f out: stl ev ch ins fnl f: no ex cl home* **16/1**

-045 **4** nk **First Avenue**[21] 2867 8-9-2 80 JoeFanning 13 90
(Laura Mongan) *hld up: hdwy over 2f out: rdn and swtchd rt to chse ldrs over 1f out: styd on ins fnl f: no imp nr fin* **40/1**

00-5 **5** 3/4 **Cloudy Spirit**[37] 2402 8-8-11 77 JimmyQuinn 15 84
(Andrew Hollinshead) *hld up: hdwy on inner over 2f out: styd on ins fnl f: gng on at fin but nt quite get to ldrs* **40/1**

3-13 **6** nk **No Heretic**[14] 3115 5-9-2 96 JamieSpencer 19 89
(David Simcock) *lw: hld up in rr: hdwy on outer over 2f out: rdn to chse ldrs over 1f out: styd on and gng on towards fin: nt quite get to ldrs* **13/2**[3]

02-5 **7** 1/2 **Sohar**[28] 2654 5-8-11 84 KirstyMilczarek 12 83
(James Toller) *chsd ldrs: rdn over 3f out: chal fr 2f out: one pce fnl 100yds* **33/1**

4- **8** shd **Cul Baire (IRE)**[15] 3072 5-9-2 90 KevinManning 14 88
(J S Bolger, Ire) *racd keenly in midfield: in tch bhd ldrs after 8f: nt clr run and swtchd lft over 3f out: rdn and tried to cl over 2f out: chsd ldrs over 1f out: one pce fnl 100yds* **10/1**

31-4 **9** 8 **Mashaari (IRE)**[37] 2402 4-9-0 87 KierenFallon 1 82
(Brian Ellison) *racd keenly in midfield: pushed along and outpcd over 2f out: no imp over 1f out: eased whn btn ins fnl f* **12/1**

4510 **10** nk **Palazzo Bianco**[14] 3099 5-9-2 86 (p) DaleSwift 9 81
(Brian Ellison) *lw: chsd ldrs: pushed along whn nt clr run 4f out: outpcd over 2f out: one pce u.p over 1f out: no imp after* **33/1**

012- **11** 29 **Courtesy Call (IRE)**[51] 6493 4-9-0 88 NeilCallan 7 68
(Nicky Henderson) *prom: led over 4f out: rdn and hdd over 2f out: wknd over 1f out: eased whn wl btn ins fnl f: t.o* **6/1**[2]

-301 **12** 39 **Riptide**[15] 3065 7-9-2 76 (v) PaulMulrennan 4
(Michael Scudamore) *midfield: lost pl over 3f out: bhd over 2f out: eased whn wl btn fnl f: t.o* **66/1**

0-62 **13** 2 **Cosimo de Medici**[30] 2587 6-9-2 82 RichardHughes 3
(Hughie Morrison) *s.v.s: hld up: detached early: rdn over 3f out: nvr able to trble ldrs: eased whn btn over 1f out: t.o* **20/1**

0/3- **14** 4 **American Spin**[25] 521 9-9-2 69 (b[1]) PatDobbs 10
(Luke Dace) *led: rdn and hdd over 4f out: wknd over 3f out: eased whn wl btn fnl f: t.o* **33/1**

120/ **15** 17 **Junior**[30] 3013 10-9-2 91 (b) RyanMoore 17
(David Pipe) *drvn along early: racd on outer in midfield: lost pl over 8f out: struggling bhd sn after: eased fnl f: t.o* **10/1**

2 **16** 11 **Stopped Out**[35] 2465 8-9-2 0 (p) DanielTudhope 20
(Philip Kirby) *w ldr: rdn over 4f out: wknd over 3f out: eased whn wl btn fnl f: t.o* **25/1**

500- **17** 2 1/2 **Yazdi (IRE)**[44] 7032 4-9-0 76 (t) SilvestreDeSousa 11
(Charlie Mann) *in tch: rdn over 3f out: wknd over 2f out: sn eased whn btn: t.o* **66/1**

12R **18** 87 **Mad Moose (IRE)**[28] 2668 9-9-2 100 WilliamTwiston-Davies 2
(Nigel Twiston-Davies) *rel to r and s.v.s: drvn along bhd and tk little interest: in rr but ct up field 11f out: struggling 8f out: t.o: eased fnl f* **14/1**

006- **P** **Ocean's Minstrel**[232] 7522 7-9-2 83 GrahamLee 8
(John Ryan) *midfield: lost pl qckly whn smething amiss 5f out: wl bhd whn p.u over 4f out* **50/1**

4m 51.49s (2.09) **Going Correction** +0.175s/f (Good)
WFA 4 from 5yo+ 2lb **19** Ran SP% **129.4**
Speed ratings (Par 109): **103,102,102,102,102 101,101,101,98,98 88,73,73,71,65 61,60,29,**
toteswingers 1&2 £7.60, 1&3 £41.80, 2&3 £18.40 CSF £30.62 TOTE £10.60: £3.30, £2.00, £5.50; EX 32.30 Trifecta £959.80 Pool: £18,364.10 - 14.34 winning units..
Owner The Pink Hat Racing Partnership **Bred** Watership Down Stud **Trained** Kingsclere, Hants
■ Stewards' Enquiry : Jim Crowley two-day ban: use of whip (7-8 July)

FOCUS
As usual a mix of abilities in this marathon race. The pace wasn't strong and that led to the field being well bunched turning for home and a relative sprint to the line. There was trouble towards the inside as the leaders weakened and the principals all avoided it by sweeping around the outside. The finish was fought out by the two highest rated horses in the field. The first two were a stone off their best figures.
T/Jkpt: Not won. T/Plt: £844.90 to a £1 stake. Pool: £761,044.93 - 657.51 winning units T/Qpdt: £37.10 to a £1 stake. Pool: £36,507.58 - 727.80 winning units SP

2971 AYR (L-H)

Saturday, June 22

OFFICIAL GOING: Good to firm (good in places; 9.3)
Home bend and straight were 4m from innermost line adding about 12yds to races on Round course.
Wind: Fresh, half against Weather: Cloudy, bright

3561 SCOTTISH SUN MISS SCOTLAND H'CAP 5f

2:25 (2:27) (Class 3) (0-95,86) 3-Y-0+ **£9,703** (£2,887; £1,443; £721) **Stalls** High

Form RPR

0-03 **1** **Midnight Dynamo**[7] 3331 6-8-13 **73** AndrewElliott 5 82
(Jim Goldie) *dwlt: hld up: hdwy and swtchd lft over 1f out: edgd rt and led wl ins fnl f: r.o* **16/1**

02 **2** 1/2 **Jedward (IRE)**[7] 3331 6-9-9 **83** (b) PhillipMakin 8 90
(Kevin Ryan) *prom: smooth hdwy to ld over 1f out: rdn and hdd wl ins fnl f: no ex* **8/1**

-000 **3** *nk* **Crimson Knot (IRE)**[7] 3331 5-8-12 **72** RobertWinston 2 78
(Alan Berry) *hld up towards rr: rdn over 2f out: hdwy and edgd rt over 1f out: styd on ins fnl f: nrst fin* **22/1**

0401 **4** *1 ½* **Arctic Feeling (IRE)**[21] 2868 5-9-5 **86** LauraBarry(7) 6 87
(Richard Fahey) *cl up: rdn and led briefly 2f out: kpt on same pce fnl fulroung* **6/1**[3]

-020 **5** *1 ¼* **Flash City (ITY)**[7] 3334 5-9-2 **81** (vt) JustinNewman(5) 3 77
(Bryan Smart) *w ldrs: drvn 2f out: outpcd pce fnl f* **16/1**

0064 **6** *½* **Head Space (IRE)**[9] 3249 5-9-6 **80** JamesSullivan 1 74
(Ruth Carr) *hld up in tch: effrt and swtchd lft over 1f out: no imp fnl f* **10/3**[1]

2-16 **7** *½* **Silken Express (IRE)**[22] 2848 4-9-11 **85** ShaneKelly 7 77
(Robert Cowell) *trckd ldrs: drvn over 2f out: outpcd whn edgd rt over 1f out* **9/2**[2]

2030 **8** *1 ½* **Bosun Breese**[7] 3334 8-9-11 **85** GrahamGibbons 10 72
(David Barron) *led tl rdn and outpcd 2f out* **8/1**

0042 **9** *hd* **Tax Free (IRE)**[13] 3135 11-9-11 **85** TonyHamilton 11 71
(David Nicholls) *in tch: nt clr run over 2f out: rdn whn hmpd appr fnl f: sn btn* **8/1**

5210 **10** *2 ¼* **Rothesay Chancer**[7] 3334 5-9-5 **79** TomEaves 9 57
(Jim Goldie) *hld up: nt clr run fr 1/2-way to ins fnl f: nvr on terms* **8/1**

58.22s (-1.18) **Going Correction** -0.075s/f (Good) **10** Ran SP% **116.1**
Speed ratings (Par 107): **106,105,104,102,100 99,98,96,96,92**
toteswingers 1&2 £15.70, 1&3 £35.10, 2&3 £36.70 CSF £137.31 CT £2886.24 TOTE £10.20: £3.70, £3.30, £5.90; EX 62.90 Trifecta £676.20 Part won. Pool: £901.69 - 0.06 winning units..
Owner Lorimer Racing **Bred** E W Hyslop **Trained** Uplawmoor, E Renfrews

FOCUS
Home bend and straight 4m from innermost line adding approximately 12yds to race distances over 7f and further. A devilishly difficult, decent sprint handicap got proceedings underway on ground officially described as good to firm, good in the places, and it paid to come from off the four-way contested early pace.

3562 SCOTTISH SUN/EBF STALLIONS LAND O'BURNS FILLIES' STKS (LISTED RACE) 5f
3:00 (3:00) (Class 1) 3-Y-O+

£22,684 (£8,600; £4,304; £2,144; £1,076; £540) **Stalls** High

Form RPR

-203 **1** **My Propeller (IRE)**[15] 3046 4-9-3 99 RobertWinston 12 106
(Peter Chapple-Hyam) *prom: rdn and hdwy to ld ins fnl f: kpt on wl* **7/2**[2]

-502 **2** *1 ¼* **Jwala**[15] 3046 4-9-3 101 ShaneKelly 11 102
(Robert Cowell) *led: rdn and hdd ins fnl f: kpt on same pce towards fin* **10/3**[1]

0006 **3** *2* **I'm So Glad**[14] 3102 4-9-3 90 SamHitchcott 13 94
(Mick Channon) *hld up on ins: rdn 2f out: styd on fnl f: nt gng pce to chal* **20/1**

4-40 **4** *hd* **Excelette (IRE)**[15] 3046 4-9-3 102 RoystonFfrench 6 94
(Bryan Smart) *cl up tl rdn and nt qckn ins fnl f* **13/2**

0606 **5** *nk* **Jillnextdoor (IRE)**[3] 3478 3-8-11 84 (v[1]) AndrewElliott 8 91
(Mick Channon) *prom: rdn over 2f out: kpt on same pce ins fnl f* **20/1**

6006 **6** *2 ¾* **Jadanna (IRE)**[14] 3103 3-8-11 90 JamesSullivan 9 81
(James Given) *hld up: rdn whn nt clr run over 1f out: r.o ins fnl f: n.d* **20/1**

-002 **7** *½* **Ponty Acclaim (IRE)**[8] 3299 4-9-3 90 (t) GrahamGibbons 5 81
(Tim Easterby) *cl up on outside tl rdn and no ex over 1f out* **7/1**

010- **8** *nk* **Perfect Blossom**[273] 6495 6-9-3 85 StephenCraine 1 80
(Alan Berry) *hld up: effrt and swtchd lft 2f out: sn rdn: outpcd fnl f* **100/1**

53-5 **9** *1 ¾* **El Manati (IRE)**[78] 1362 3-8-11 102 FrannyNorton 10 71
(James Tate) *midfield: drvn and outpcd whn nt clr run over 1f out: n.d after* **10/1**

4-06 **10** *1 ¾* **Strange Magic (IRE)**[14] 3097 3-8-11 90 TonyHamilton 2 65
(Richard Fahey) *bhd: struggling wl over 2f out: nvr on terms* **33/1**

1212 **11** *nse* **Riskit Fora Biskit (IRE)**[33] 2521 3-8-11 91 TomEaves 7 65
(Michael Bell) *cl up tl rdn and wknd over 1f out* **9/2**[3]

57.74s (-1.66) **Going Correction** -0.075s/f (Good)
WFA 3 from 4yo+ 6lb **11** Ran SP% **116.6**
Speed ratings (Par 108): **110,108,104,104,104 99,98,98,95,92 92**
toteswingers 1&2 £5.40, 1&3 £15.40, 2&3 £24.00 CSF £14.28 TOTE £5.00: £2.00, £2.20, £6.10; EX 12.40 Trifecta £168.70 Pool: £1022.37- 4.54 winning units..
Owner Joseph Barton **Bred** D J & Mrs Brown **Trained** Newmarket, Suffolk

FOCUS
An intriguing Listed fillies' sprint in which they went an even gallop. The previous five runnings went to 3yos, including the very smart Margot Did in 2011. Decent form for the grade, the winner close to her best.

3563 SCOTTISH SUN ON SUNDAY H'CAP 1m
3:35 (3:35) (Class 2) (0-100,95) 3-Y-O

£15,562 (£4,660; £2,330; £1,165; £582; £292) **Stalls** Low

Form RPR

5-11 **1** **Off Art**[35] 2439 3-9-1 **89** GrahamGibbons 4 99
(Tim Easterby) *trckd ldr: rdn 2f out: styd on wl fnl f: led cl home* **5/2**[1]

-522 **2** *shd* **Party Royal**[3] 3464 3-8-7 **81** FrannyNorton 3 91
(Mark Johnston) *led at modest gallop: rdn 2f out: kpt on fnl f: hdd cl home* **9/1**

2614 **3** *1 ½* **Hay Dude**[21] 2857 3-9-7 **95** TomEaves 2 102
(Mrs K Burke) *taken early to post: trckd ldrs on ins: effrt whn nt clr run over 1f out: sn drvn: one pce ins fnl f* **7/1**

1453 **4** *nk* **Country Western**[14] 3117 3-8-12 **89** PatrickHills(3) 7 95
(Charles Hills) *t.k.h: trckd ldrs: effrt and drvn 2f out: kpt on same pce fnl f* **5/1**[2]

-102 **5** *1 ¼* **Royal Prize**[14] 3117 3-8-9 **83** ShaneKelly 1 87+
(Ralph Beckett) *hld up on ins: swtchd rt and n.m.r over 2f out: hdwy and rdn over 1f out: kpt on but no imp fnl f* **15/2**

2421 **6** *shd* **Sublimation (IRE)**[18] 2960 3-8-11 **85** RobertWinston 5 88
(David Barron) *hld up towards rr: rdn and hdwy over 2f out: kpt on same pce fnl f* **11/2**[3]

2503 **7** *1* **Luhaif**[9] 3235 3-9-4 **92** (v) SamHitchcott 8 92
(Mick Channon) *hld up: stdy hdwy over 3f out: sn drvn: outpcd fr over 1f out* **22/1**

1-55 **8** *½* **Steelriver (IRE)**[21] 2857 3-8-13 **87** AndrewElliott 6 86
(James Bethell) *dwlt: hld up: stdy hdwy on wd outside over 2f out: rdn and no imp fr over 1f out* **8/1**

0-26 **9** *2 ¾* **Flyman**[28] 2655 3-9-5 **93** TonyHamilton 10 86
(Richard Fahey) *in tch on outside tl rdn and wknd wl over 1f out* **16/1**

5-56 **10** *3 ½* **Steer By The Stars (IRE)**[4] 3443 3-9-0 **88** PhillipMakin 9 73
(Mark Johnston) *trckd ldrs tl rdn: hung lft and wknd 2f out* **33/1**

1m 40.68s (-3.12) **Going Correction** -0.35s/f (Firm) **10** Ran SP% **119.2**
Speed ratings (Par 105): **101,100,99,99,97 97,96,96,93,90**
toteswingers 1&2 £5.10, 1&3 £5.50, 2&3 £5.30 CSF £26.90 CT £132.34 TOTE £3.20: £1.40, £3.60, £2.60; EX 26.80 Trifecta £169.70 Pool: £1184.38- 5.23 winning units..
Owner D B Lamplough **Bred** D B Lamplough **Trained** Great Habton, N Yorks

FOCUS
The early gallop was relatively steady in this decent 3yo handicap, and it paid to race prominently. The form is rated around the third and fourth.

3564 PEOPLE'S POSTCODE LOTTERY H'CAP 1m
4:15 (4:15) (Class 2) (0-105,99) 4-Y-O+

£15,562 (£4,660; £2,330; £1,165; £582; £292) **Stalls** Low

Form RPR

0000 **1** **Capaill Liath (IRE)**[8] 3300 5-8-9 **87** (p) FrannyNorton 6 94
(Kevin Ryan) *t.k.h: hld up towards rr: rdn over 2f out: hdwy on outside over 1f out: led ins fnl f: kpt on strly* **22/1**

4436 **2** *hd* **Dubai Dynamo**[10] 3207 8-8-10 **88** JamesSullivan 8 95
(Ruth Carr) *hld up on ins: shkn up and hdwy over 1f out: ev ch ins fnl f: kpt on: hld cl home* **4/1**[3]

0065 **3** *1 ¼* **Beacon Lodge (IRE)**[7] 3335 8-9-3 **95** SamHitchcott 1 100+
(David Nicholls) *hld up: pushed along and hdwy over 2f out: kpt on fnl f: nvr able to chal* **20/1**

15-0 **4** *½* **Trail Blaze (IRE)**[49] 2029 4-8-6 **91** KevinStott(7) 4 94
(Kevin Ryan) *trckd ldrs: effrt and led briefly wl over 1f out: kpt on same pce ins fnl f* **8/1**

-404 **5** *hd* **Set The Trend**[7] 3335 7-9-7 **99** TonyHamilton 3 101
(David O'Meara) *in tch: hdwy to ld over 1f out: hdd ins fnl f: sn outpcd* **7/1**

-010 **6** *1 ¼* **Norse Blues**[7] 3339 5-9-1 **93** GrahamGibbons 9 92
(David Barron) *dwlt: t.k.h and sn rcvrd: chal after 2f: led over 2f out to wl over 1f out: no ex whn n.m.r ins fnl f* **7/2**[2]

-210 **7** *¾* **Strictly Silver (IRE)**[84] 1235 4-9-6 **98** PhillipMakin 2 95
(Alan Bailey) *trckd ldrs: nt clr run briefly over 2f out: rdn: and one pce appr fnl f* **3/1**[1]

0020 **8** *2 ¾* **Chosen Character (IRE)**[28] 2649 5-9-3 **95** (vt) StephenCraine 5 86
(Tom Dascombe) *t.k.h: led to over 2f out: sn rdn: wknd appr fnl f* **12/1**

3532 **9** *nk* **Extraterrestrial**[19] 2912 9-7-10 **81** oh3 ow1 (p) SamanthaBell(7) 10 71
(Richard Fahey) *hld up on outside: effrt and pushed along on outside over 2f out: edgd lft and wknd over 1f out* **14/1**

1m 39.08s (-4.72) **Going Correction** -0.35s/f (Firm) **9** Ran SP% **114.3**
Speed ratings (Par 109): **109,108,107,107,106 105,104,102,101**
toteswingers 1&2 £18.90, 1&3 £23.20, 2&3 £13.60 CSF £107.03 CT £1821.24 TOTE £32.40: £7.00, £2.20, £4.30; EX 182.40 Trifecta £1955.00 Part won. Pool: £2,606.73 - 0.25 winning units..
Owner T A Rahman **Bred** Stanley Estate & Stud Co & Mount Coote Stud **Trained** Hambleton, N Yorks

FOCUS
A good-quality handicap for older horses in which the they went a good clip from the outset, and the first three horses home raced towards the rear at that stage. The winner is rated pretty much back to his best.

3565 SUNSPORT/EBF MAIDEN STKS 6f
4:50 (4:51) (Class 4) 2-Y-O **£4,528** (£1,347; £673; £336) **Stalls** High

Form RPR

3 **1** **Queen Catrine (IRE)**[15] 3057 2-9-0 0 RobertWinston 2 82+
(Charles Hills) *hld up: smooth hdwy over 1f out: shkn up to ld ins fnl f: qcknd clr: readily* **7/4**[1]

202 **2** *5* **Tanseeb**[16] 3023 2-9-5 0 FrannyNorton 11 70
(Mark Johnston) *t.k.h early: trckd ldrs: effrt 2f out: chsd (clr) wnr wl ins fnl f: no imp* **5/2**[2]

5 **3** *½* **State Anthem**[15] 3035 2-9-0 0 SamHitchcott 10 64
(Mick Channon) *led: rdn and hdd over 1f out: kpt on same pce fnl f* **28/1**

6340 **4** *nk* **Donny Rover (IRE)**[15] 3044 2-9-5 0 (p) RoystonFfrench 4 68
(David C Griffiths) *dwlt: bhd: drvn along over 3f out: hdwy on outside over 1f out: kpt on fnl f: n.d* **33/1**

5 *½* **Straits Of Malacca** 2-9-5 0 PhillipMakin 3 66
(Kevin Ryan) *t.k.h: pressed ldr: led over 1f out to ins fnl f: sn outpcd* **16/1**

04 **6** *2 ¼* **Handwoven (IRE)**[19] 2925 2-9-5 0 AndrewElliott 8 59
(Mark Johnston) *hld up in tch: shkn up and outpcd 2f out: sn n.d* **20/1**

23 **7** *4* **Jacquotte Delahaye**[21] 2877 2-9-0 0 TomEaves 9 42
(Bryan Smart) *loaded rdrless into stall: trckd ldrs: rdn and edgd lft wl over 1f out: wknd fnl f* **10/3**[3]

8 *½* **Two Shades Of Grey (IRE)** 2-9-5 0 TonyHamilton 5 46
(Richard Fahey) *prom: drvn and rn green 1/2-way: hung lft and wknd over 1f out* **5/1**

1m 11.9s (-0.50) **Going Correction** -0.075s/f (Good) **8** Ran SP% **121.7**
Speed ratings (Par 95): **100,93,92,92,91 88,83,82**
toteswingers 1&2 £2.90, 1&3 £8.80, 2&3 £9.50 CSF £6.73 TOTE £2.60: £1.10, £1.10, £7.70; EX 6.50 Trifecta £139.10 Pool: £2766.67- 14.91 winning units..
Owner J Gompertz,Mrs G Galvin,Marston Stud **Bred** Mount Coote Stud **Trained** Lambourn, Berks

FOCUS
A good juvenile maiden in which they went a proper gallop. The winner was value for a little extra.

3566 LIDL SURPRISES H'CAP 6f
5:25 (5:27) (Class 4) (0-80,78) 3-Y-O **£5,175** (£1,540; £769; £384) **Stalls** High

Form RPR

4502 **1** **Sand Boy (IRE)**[18] 2959 3-9-1 **72** RobertWinston 4 82
(Charles Hills) *prom: nt clr run over 2f out to over 1f out: hdwy to ld ins fnl f: qcknd clr* **5/1**[3]

5421 **2** *1 ¾* **Someone's Darling**[25] 2756 3-8-7 **64** AndrewElliott 7 68
(Jim Goldie) *in tch: n.m.r over 2f out to over 1f out: hdwy to chse wnr ins fnl f: r.o* **6/1**

1602 **3** *1 ½* **Repetition**[18] 2951 3-8-12 **69** PhillipMakin 1 68
(Kevin Ryan) *cl up: led over 1f out to ins fnl f: kpt on same pce* **9/2**[2]

14 **4** *½* **Algar Lad**[21] 2888 3-8-9 **73** ConnorBeasley(7) 2 71
(Jim Goldie) *hld up in tch: hdwy and cl up over 1f out: kpt on same pce fnl f* **9/2**[2]

6224 **5** *2 ¼* **Mowhoob**[21] 2876 3-9-0 **74** LucyAlexander(3) 12 64
(Jim Goldie) *prom: pushed along whn n.m.r over 2f out to over 1f out: outpcd fnl f* **9/1**

2103 **6** *4 ½* **Right Touch**[29] 2626 3-9-7 **78** TonyHamilton 9 54
(Richard Fahey) *led to over 2f out: rdn and wknd 1f out* **11/4**[1]

40-0 **7** *1 ¼* **Cumbrian Craic**[17] 2987 3-8-12 **69** GrahamGibbons 8 41
(Tim Easterby) *w ldrs: led over 2f out to over 1f out: wknd fnl f* **12/1**

3606 **8** 1 3/4 **Opt Out**[9] 3234 3-9-2 **73**.................................... SamHitchcott 3 39
(Alistair Whillans) *w ldrs: ev ch tl wknd over 1f out* **22/1**
45-0 **9** 3 **Princess Cayan (IRE)**[43] 2218 3-7-10 **59** oh14 ow1 SamanthaBell(7) 10 17
(Linda Perratt) *reluctant to enter stalls: missed break: a bhd* **66/1**
000- **10** 4 **Vanessa**[323] 4767 3-8-8 **65**.................................... RoystonFfrench 13
(Ian Semple) *cl up tl lost pl over 2f out: sn struggling* **40/1**
1m 12.04s (-0.36) **Going Correction** -0.075s/f (Good) **10** Ran SP% **120.0**
Speed ratings (Par 101): **99,96,94,94,91 85,83,81,77,71**
toteswingers 1&2 £7.10, 1&3 £4.10, 2&3 £6.80 CSF £35.67 CT £147.50 TOTE £5.70: £2.30, £2.00, £2.00; EX 29.90 Trifecta £115.20 Pool: £2485.01- 16.16 winning units..
Owner Sir A Ferguson,Mr,Mrs J Cotton,J Hanson **Bred** P Kelly **Trained** Lambourn, Berks
FOCUS
A competitive if modest 3yo hcap. The winner seems to be getting his act together now.

3567 ARNOLD CLARK FILLIES' H'CAP 1m 2f
6:00 (6:00) (Class 3) (0-95,87) 4-Y-0+ **£9,703** (£2,887; £1,443; £721) **Stalls** Low

Form RPR
0223 **1** **Maven**[7] 3346 5-9-2 **82**.................................... GrahamGibbons 1 92
(Tim Easterby) *trckd ldrs: rdn to ld over 1f out: hld on wl fnl f* **7/4**[1]
631 **2** 3/4 **Star Lahib (IRE)**[14] 3095 4-9-7 **87**.................................... FrannyNorton 2 95
(Mark Johnston) *t.k.h early: prom: pushed along over 2f out: hdwy to chse wnr ins fnl f: kpt on u.p* **11/4**[2]
6420 **3** 2 1/2 **Act Your Shoe Size**[7] 3349 4-9-0 **80**.................................... TomEaves 4 83
(Keith Dalgleish) *pressed ldr: rdn along 2f out: kpt on same pce ins fnl f* **10/1**
-411 **4** 1 **Christmas Light**[7] 3349 6-8-8 **81**.................................... KevinStott(7) 3 82
(Brian Ellison) *hld up in last but in tch: effrt and pushed along 2f out: kpt on fnl f: no imp* **11/4**[2]
4563 **5** hd **Lady Macduff (IRE)**[3] 3468 4-8-6 **72**.................................... RoystonFfrench 5 73
(Mark Johnston) *led at stdy pce: rdn over 2f out: hdd over 1f out: sn outpcd* **15/2**[3]
2m 8.15s (-3.85) **Going Correction** -0.35s/f (Firm) **5** Ran SP% **110.6**
Speed ratings (Par 104): **101,100,98,97,97**
CSF £6.87 TOTE £2.50: £1.50, £1.50; EX 5.40 Trifecta £30.30 Pool: £1127.60- 27.85 winning units..
Owner Mrs Jennifer E Pallister **Bred** Habton Farms **Trained** Great Habton, N Yorks
FOCUS
It had started to rain quite steadily prior to this decent handicap for older fillies, but not for long enough to suggest it had got into the ground in any significant way, and they went quite steady early on. The winner deserved this and is rated to form.
T/Plt: £197.10 to a £1 stake. Pool of £79675.19 - 294.95 winning tickets. T/Qpdt: £23.00 to a £1 stake. Pool of £4283.32 - 137.80 winning tickets. RY

3231 HAYDOCK (L-H)
Saturday, June 22

OFFICIAL GOING: Good (good to firm in places; 7.8)
All races run on Inner home straight and races on Round course increased by 8yds.
Wind: Fresh; half against Weather: Changeable, occasional showers, cold and very windy, heavy rain last 2

3568 RITA ORA HERE ON 9TH AUGUST MAIDEN STKS 5f
6:50 (6:51) (Class 5) 2-Y-0 **£2,911** (£866; £432; £216) **Stalls** High

Form RPR
4 **1** **Mecca's Angel (IRE)**[35] 2458 2-9-0 0.................................... LeeTopliss 4 76+
(Michael Dods) *dwlt: sn led: edgd lft ins fnl f: drvn out* **10/11**[1]
3 **2** 1 1/2 **Flying Bear (IRE)**[24] 2771 2-9-5 0.................................... SteveDrowne 5 76
(Jeremy Gask) *chsd ldrs: wnt 2nd over 1f out: edgd lft ins fnl f: kpt on* **7/2**[2]
60 **3** 2 3/4 **Quincel**[30] 2591 2-9-5 0.................................... RichardKingscote 6 66+
(Tom Dascombe) *sn outpcd in last: rdn and hdwy over 2f out: 3rd 1f out: kpt on* **7/2**[2]
000 **4** 7 **Red Forever**[14] 3092 2-9-0 0.................................... SladeO'Hara(5) 3 41
(Alan Berry) *led early: chsd ldrs: wknd over 1f out* **33/1**
0 **5** 2 3/4 **Overstep (IRE)**[9] 3245 2-9-5 0.................................... LiamJones 2 31
(Mark Johnston) *dwlt: sn w ldrs on outer: drvn over 2f out: lost pl over 1f out* **11/1**[3]
6 15 **Etchy** 2-9-0 0.................................... JasonHart(5) 1
(Robin Bastiman) *chsd ldrs on outside: reminders over 3f out: lost pl over 2f out: sn wl bhd* **22/1**
1m 1.99s (1.19) **Going Correction** +0.20s/f (Good) **6** Ran SP% **112.5**
Speed ratings (Par 93): **98,95,91,80,75 51**
toteswingers 1&2 £1.50, 1&3 £1.20, 2&3 £2.60 CSF £4.42 TOTE £1.90: £1.10, £2.00; EX 4.70 Trifecta £8.80 Pool: £1,040.65 - 88.47 winning units..
Owner David T J Metcalfe **Bred** Yeomanstown Stud & Doc Bloodstock **Trained** Denton, Co Durham
FOCUS
Despite 5mm of overnight rain the ground was still good to firm as a strong wind helped dry it out, although runners did kick the top off in the opener. All races were on the inside home straight. This was a modest juvenile maiden.

3569 ABACUS SECURITIES ANNUAL H'CAP (JOCKEY CLUB GRASSROOTS SPRINT SERIES QUALIFIER) 5f
7:20 (7:21) (Class 5) (0-75,72) 3-Y-0+ **£2,911** (£866; £432; £216) **Stalls** High

Form RPR
1554 **1** **Script**[3] 3462 4-8-0 **53**.................................... JordanHibberd(7) 6 62
(Alan Berry) *chsd ldrs: led 1f out: hld on towards fin* **16/1**
1-05 **2** 3/4 **Diman Waters (IRE)**[9] 3236 6-9-7 **72**.................................... JasonHart(5) 8 78
(Eric Alston) *trckd ldrs: wnt 2nd 1f out: kpt on towards fin* **3/1**[1]
0613 **3** 1 3/4 **Methaaly (IRE)**[7] 3317 10-8-10 **59**....................(be) RyanClark(3) 1 59
(Michael Mullineaux) *in rr: swtchd outside and hdwy over 1f out: styd on to take 3rd fnl strides* **16/1**
0040 **4** hd **Commanche Raider (IRE)**[15] 3069 6-9-9 **69**..............(p) LeeTopliss 13 68
(Michael Dods) *mid-div: effrt over 2f out: kpt on same pce fnl f* **16/1**
2003 **5** nse **Royal Bajan (USA)**[32] 2550 5-9-9 **69**..............(b) RichardKingscote 14 68
(James Given) *wnt rt s: racd stands' side: sn w ldrs: led over 3f out: hdd 1f out: edgd lft: kpt on same pce* **7/1**[3]
4-20 **6** nse **Layla's Oasis**[14] 3097 3-9-4 **70**.................................... LiamJones 11 67
(Richard Fahey) *dwlt: hdwy over 2f out: sn drvn: kpt on same pce fnl f* **9/1**
1450 **7** 1 **Avonvalley**[36] 2410 6-9-1 **66**.................................... SladeO'Hara(5) 7 61
(Peter Grayson) *dwlt: sn detached in last: hdwy over 1f out: styng on wl at fin* **40/1**

3540 **8** nk **Song Of Parkes**[9] 3236 6-9-5 **65**.................................... AndreaAtzeni 10 59
(Peter Grayson) *rr-div: hdwy over 2f out: kpt on one pce fnl f* **14/1**
1-62 **9** 3 **Indian Trail**[39] 2343 13-9-7 **72**....................(b) ShirleyTeasdale(5) 12 55
(David Nicholls) *in rr: drvn 2f out: nvr a factor* **8/1**
-040 **10** 3 1/4 **Tom Sawyer**[22] 2832 5-9-5 **65**....................(be) SteveDrowne 15 37
(Julie Camacho) *hmpd s: racd stands' side: mid-div: rdn over 2f out: wknd over 1f out* **9/1**
00-1 **11** 1 1/4 **China Excels**[10] 3196 6-9-4 **64**.................................... RussKennemore 3 31
(Sue Smith) *led over 1f: wknd over 1f out* **5/1**[2]
00-2 **12** hd **Baby Queen (IRE)**[15] 3042 7-9-2 **69**.................................... GaryMahon(7) 4 36
(Brian Baugh) *w ldrs: lost pl over 1f out* **12/1**
4-60 **13** 7 **Almond Branches**[36] 2410 4-9-11 **71**....................(b[1]) PaddyAspell 2 12
(Sharon Watt) *in rr: bhd fnl 2f* **20/1**
1m 1.37s (0.57) **Going Correction** +0.20s/f (Good)
WFA 3 from 4yo+ 6lb **13** Ran SP% **124.5**
Speed ratings (Par 103): **103,101,99,98,98 98,96,96,91,86 84,84,72**
toteswingers 1&2 £52.00, 1&3 £35.20, 2&3 £9.40 CSF £66.22 CT £851.73 TOTE £20.50: £5.10, £1.20, £4.20; EX 70.50 Trifecta £551.90 Part won. Pool: £735.89 - 0.32 winning units..
Owner T Blane **Bred** Bearstone Stud **Trained** Cockerham, Lancs
FOCUS
A moderate sprint handicap and the main action developed down the middle of the course. A personal best from the winner.

3570 SOCKSHOP H'CAP 1m
7:50 (7:51) (Class 4) (0-85,85) 4-Y-0+ **£5,175** (£1,540; £769; £384) **Stalls** Low

Form RPR
0033 **1** **Postscript (IRE)**[5] 3411 5-9-7 **85**.................................... AndreaAtzeni 3 93
(David Simcock) *trckd ldrs: effrt 2f out: r.o to ld last 50yds* **2/1**[2]
0-66 **2** nk **Ewell Place (IRE)**[7] 3322 4-8-12 **76**.................................... PaddyAspell 1 83
(David Nicholls) *sn trcking ldr: led over 1f out: edgd lft ins fnl f: hdd and no ex clsng stages* **20/1**
504 **3** 1/2 **Basseterre (IRE)**[14] 3113 4-9-7 **85**.................................... SteveDrowne 7 91+
(Charles Hills) *hood removed late: dwlt: hld up in rr: hdwy on outside over 2f out: kpt on fnl f* **15/8**[1]
0-24 **4** shd **Le Chat D'Or**[43] 2220 5-8-12 **76**....................(bt) LeeTopliss 4 82
(Michael Dods) *hld up in mid-div on ins: effrt over 2f out: nt clr run and swtchd 4 horses wd jst ins fnl f: styd on towards fin* **8/1**
4101 **5** 2 1/4 **Copperwood**[10] 3193 8-8-12 **76**.................................... LiamJones 2 79+
(Mark Johnston) *drvn to ld: increased gallop over 3f out: hdd over 1f out: keeping on same pce whn bdly hmpd 100yds out* **11/1**
-340 **6** 1 3/4 **An Cat Dubh (IRE)**[14] 3094 4-9-1 **79**.................................... StevieDonohoe 5 75
(Ian Williams) *hld up in rr: effrt over 2f out: kpt on one pce* **7/1**[3]
-416 **7** nk **The Osteopath (IRE)**[35] 2463 10-8-12 **76**.................................... RichardKingscote 8 72
(John Davies) *t.k.h on outer: hld up towards rr: effrt 3f out: hung rt over 1f out: nvr a thyreat* **10/1**
1m 43.37s (-0.33) **Going Correction** +0.05s/f (Good) **7** Ran SP% **113.9**
Speed ratings (Par 105): **103,102,102,102,99 98,97**
toteswingers 1&2 £10.90, 1&3 £1.30, 2&3 £10.00 CSF £38.51 CT £85.26 TOTE £3.20: £2.10, £9.80; EX 44.20 Trifecta £103.30 Pool: £701.80 - 5.09 winning units..
Owner Dr Marwan Koukash **Bred** Darley **Trained** Newmarket, Suffolk
■ Stewards' Enquiry : Paddy Aspell two-day ban: careless riding (7-8 July)
FOCUS
A fair handicap. They went a sound pace and it saw a tight four-way finish. The form is rated around the runner-up and fourth.

3571 ABACUS SECURITIES H'CAP 1m
8:20 (8:21) (Class 4) (0-80,78) 3-Y-0 **£5,175** (£1,540; £769; £384) **Stalls** Low

Form RPR
053 **1** **Ready (IRE)**[18] 2951 3-8-13 **75**....................(p) JustinNewman(5) 7 83
(Garry Moss) *hld up in rr: drvn 4f out: hdwy on outside over 2f out: edgd lft fnl f: led last 100yds: jst hld on* **15/2**
11-0 **2** nse **Polar Chief**[82] 1293 3-9-6 **77**.................................... JamesSullivan 3 85+
(Kristin Stubbs) *t.k.h: trckd ldrs: led over 1f out: hdd last 100yds: carried lft and crowded: rallied and jst hld* **14/1**
6-00 **3** 4 1/2 **Hunting Rights (USA)**[36] 2432 3-9-4 **75**.................................... LiamJones 5 73
(Mark Johnston) *dwlt: sn chsng ldrs: drvn over 4f out: led briefly 2f out: one pce fnl f* **17/2**
5063 **4** 1 1/4 **Mandy's Boy (IRE)**[9] 3241 3-8-13 **70**.................................... StevieDonohoe 6 65
(Ian Williams) *rrd over and uns rdr s: sn chsng ldrs: rdn over 2f out: one pce whn n.m.r and swtchd rt ins fnl f* **3/1**[3]
22-0 **5** 1 **Jubilee Games**[10] 3207 3-9-7 **78**.................................... LeeTopliss 2 70
(Richard Fahey) *dwlt: sn chsng ldrs: rdn over 2f out: swtchd rt over 1f out: kpt on one pce* **12/1**
354 **6** hd **Kabbaas (IRE)**[8] 3289 3-9-3 **74**....................(b) AndreaAtzeni 4 66
(Roger Varian) *dwlt: sn trcking ldrs: drvn over 3f out: one pce fnl 2f* **11/4**[2]
031 **7** 2 1/2 **Brave Acclaim (IRE)**[15] 3047 3-9-7 **78**..............(p) RichardKingscote 1 64
(Tom Dascombe) *led: hdd 2f out: sn wknd* **5/2**[1]
1m 43.51s (-0.19) **Going Correction** +0.05s/f (Good) **7** Ran SP% **116.9**
Speed ratings (Par 101): **102,101,97,96,95 95,92**
toteswingers 1&2 £6.10, 1&3 £11.40, 2&3 £14.50 CSF £102.26 TOTE £10.00: £3.90, £4.10; EX 109.10 Trifecta £397.20 Pool: £641.54 - 1.21 winning units..
Owner Ron Hull **Bred** Kilshannig Stud **Trained** Tickhill, S Yorks
■ Stewards' Enquiry : Justin Newman caution: careless riding; seven-day ban: use of whip (6-12 July)
FOCUS
This looked a tight handicap, but the first pair came right away inside the final furlong. The pace was decent but the market leaders disappointed, so the form isn't straightforward.

3572 MADNESS MUSIC NIGHT HERE 20TH JULY MAIDEN STKS 1m
8:50 (8:54) (Class 5) 3-Y-0+ **£2,911** (£866; £432; £216) **Stalls** Low

Form RPR
4-43 **1** **Estifzaaz (IRE)**[18] 2953 3-9-2 77.................................... RichardKingscote 2 83
(Charles Hills) *led early: trckd ldrs: smooth hdwy on ins to ld over 2f out: styd on wl fnl f* **9/4**[2]
54-4 **2** 1 1/2 **Qawaafy (USA)**[21] 2885 3-8-11 72.................................... AndreaAtzeni 5 75
(Roger Varian) *trckd ldrs: 2nd 2f out: 1 1/2 l down whn rdr dropped whip over a f out: kpt on same pce* **5/2**[3]
2 **3** 4 **Response**[25] 2746 3-9-2 0.................................... LiamJones 6 70
(William Haggas) *trckd ldrs: effrt over 3f out: sn rdn and outpcd: kpt on to take modest 3rd 1f out* **13/8**[1]
6 **4** 4 1/2 **Ravensburg**[25] 2760 3-8-11 0.................................... SteveDrowne 3 55
(Chris Wall) *dwlt: sn chsng ldrs: drvn over 3f out: sn outpcd: wknd 2f out* **15/2**
-345 **5** 3/4 **Exclusive Predator**[33] 2507 4-9-12 62.................................... RussKennemore 4 60
(Geoffrey Oldroyd) *sn led: drvn 4f out: hdd over 2f out: wknd over 1f out* **25/1**

0- 6 36 **Smirfys Blackcat (IRE)**282 6154 4-9-4 0........................ RyanClark(3) 1
(Michael Mullineaux) *s.i.s: in rr: reminders after 1f: sn bhd: t.o whn rn wd bnd over 4f out: eased ins fnl f* **66/1**

1m 43.04s (-0.66) **Going Correction** +0.05s/f (Good)
WFA 3 from 4yo 10lb 6 Ran SP% **114.5**
Speed ratings (Par 103): **105,103,99,95,94 58**
toteswingers 1&2 £1.70, 1&3 £1.10, 2&3 £1.50 CSF £8.60 TOTE £3.10: £1.70, £2.40; EX 9.40 Trifecta £12.80 Pool: £1,098.46 - 64.22 winning units..
Owner Hamdan Al Maktoum **Bred** M Duffy **Trained** Lambourn, Berks

FOCUS
This was the pick of the C&D times and a slightly positive view has been taken of the form.

3573 HAYDOCK-PARK.CO.UK H'CAP — 1m 2f 95y
9:20 (9:20) (Class 4) (0-80,78) 3-Y-O+ **£5,175** (£1,540; £769; £384) **Stalls** Centre

Form RPR
00-3 **1** **Tuscan Fun**18 2957 3-8-6 **68**........................ AndreaAtzeni 11 82+
(Roger Varian) *trckd ldrs: 2nd over 3f out: led over 1f out: drvn rt out* **13/8**1

20-6 **2** *1* **Livia's Dream (IRE)**21 2855 4-9-9 **73**........................ TomMcLaughlin 8 85
(Ed Walker) *t.k.h: led after 1f: hdd over 1f out: kpt on same pce ins fnl f* **7/1**

4/0- **3** *11* **Diamond Penny (IRE)**220 7715 5-9-11 **75**.................... SteveDrowne 2 66
(Seamus Durack) *drvn early: sn mid-div: styd alone far side over 4f out: one pce and modest 3rd over 1f out* **16/1**

-334 **4** *1* **Gabrial The Thug (FR)**29 2624 3-8-2 **67**........................ NeilFarley(3) 7 56
(Richard Fahey) *hld up in rr: effrt over 4f out: one pce fnl 3f* **4/1**2

-130 **5** *½* **Significant Move**23 2808 6-9-8 **72**........................ RichardKingscote 3 60
(Stuart Kittow) *hld up in rr: effrt over 3f out: edgd lft and one pce fnl 2f* **5/1**3

-220 **6** *3 ½* **Skyfire**21 2889 6-9-3 **67**........................ MichaelStainton 6 49
(Nick Kent) *led 1f: chsd ldrs: wknd 2f out* **20/1**

2413 **7** *shd* **Day Of Destiny (IRE)**21 2886 8-9-5 **69**........................ JamesSullivan 10 50
(James Given) *t.k.h in rr: wnt 3rd 3f out: wknd fnl 2f* **7/1**

0-15 **8** *15* **Special Mix**15 3043 5-9-5 **69**........................ LiamJones 9 22
(Michael Easterby) *sn drvn along: hdwy to chse ldrs after 2f: lost pl 3f out: sn bhd* **10/1**

2m 14.82s (-0.68) **Going Correction** +0.05s/f (Good)
WFA 3 from 4yo+ 12lb 8 Ran SP% **119.5**
Speed ratings (Par 105): **104,103,94,93,93 90,90,78**
toteswingers 1&2 £5.60, 1&3 £9.70, 2&3 £8.60 CSF £14.68 CT £140.16 TOTE £2.70: £1.10, £2.30, £2.80; EX 17.30 Trifecta £95.10 Pool: £964.67 - 7.60 winning units..
Owner K Allen, R Marchant & G Jarvis **Bred** Highclere Stud **Trained** Newmarket, Suffolk

FOCUS
A modest handicap and the first pair came well clear nearing the furlong marker down the centre. The unexposed winner improved and should do better.
T/Plt: £755.50 to a £1 stake. Pool: £72,659.45 - 70.20 winning units T/Qpdt: £138.00 to a £1 stake. Pool: £4,020.79 - 21.55 winning units WG

3493 LINGFIELD (L-H)
Saturday, June 22
OFFICIAL GOING: Turf course - good to firm (8.9); all-weather - standard
Wind: Strong; half behind Weather: Overcast, drizzly

3574 VINES BMW MAIDEN AUCTION STKS — 7f
6:05 (6:07) (Class 6) 2-Y-O **£2,045** (£603; £302) **Stalls** High

Form RPR
42 **1** **Double Point (IRE)**11 3174 2-9-1 0........................ LukeMorris 5 81
(Paul Cole) *chsd ldrs but sn pushed along: vigorously rdn fr 1/2-way: picked up 2f out: clsd to ld jst ins fnl f: styd on wl* **4/7**1

2232 **2** *1 ¼* **Cockney Bob**4 3436 2-8-9 0........................ CathyGannon 1 72
(J S Moore) *pressed ldr: rdn over 2f out: led and edgd rt 1f out: sn hdd and one pce* **4/1**2

50 **3** *4* **Chance Of Romance (IRE)**29 2617 2-8-6 0........................ JohnFahy 2 58
(Clive Cox) *led and sn crossed to nr side rail: drvn 2f out: hdd and nudged 1f out: fdd* **33/1**

4 *1 ¾* **Ifrika** 2-8-4 0........................ RyanPowell(3) 8 56+
(Clive Brittain) *chsd ldrs against rail: rdn over 2f out: trying to keep on whn nt clr run 1f out: one pce* **14/1**

5 *1 ¾* **Cotton Club (IRE)** 2-9-1 0........................ AdamKirby 4 58+
(Rod Millman) *chsd ldrs: impeded 1/2-way and pushed along: no imp on ldrs 2f out: fdd* **10/1**3

6 *12* **Indie Star** 2-8-5 0........................ KierenFox 10 17
(Harry Dunlop) *s.i.s: outpcd in last: nvr on terms: t.o but passed rivals over 1f out* **20/1**

7 *2 ½* **Zambeasy** 2-8-11 0........................ JackMitchell 3 17
(Philip Hide) *s.s: rn green but quick prog to press ldng pair after 2f: wknd rapidly over 2f out: t.o* **33/1**

0 **8** *1 ½* **Bright Society (IRE)**11 3175 2-8-4 0........................ CharlotteJenner(7) 9 13
(J S Moore) *pushed along in rr after 3f: wknd over 2f out: t.o* **66/1**

54 **9** *3 ½* **Plucky Dip**31 2562 2-8-10 0........................ DaraghO'Donohoe 7
(John Ryan) *in tch: prog on outer 1/2-way: cl up 2f out: wknd rapidly and heavily eased* **14/1**

1m 23.11s (-0.19) **Going Correction** -0.175s/f (Firm) 9 Ran SP% **118.2**
Speed ratings (Par 91): **94,92,88,86,84 70,67,65,61**
toteswingers 1&2 £1.50, 1&3 £8.40, 2&3 £7.90 CSF £3.01 TOTE £1.70: £1.10, £1.40, £6.80; EX 3.80 Trifecta £60.60 Pool: £1,146.74 - 14.16 winning units..
Owner Black Run Racing **Bred** Victor Stud Bloodstock Ltd **Trained** Whatcombe, Oxon

FOCUS
Most of the field quickly congregated on the stands' side rail in this opener. The form has a sound feel with the first two clear.

3575 STUART WALTON BIRTHDAY H'CAP — 7f 140y
6:35 (6:35) (Class 5) (0-75,74) 4-Y-O+ **£2,726** (£805; £402) **Stalls** Centre

Form RPR
0360 **1** **Halling Dancer**17 2981 4-9-3 **70**........................ KierenFox 10 77
(Lee Carter) *mde all against nr side rail: drvn 2f out: kpt on wl u.p* **8/1**3

0000 **2** *1 ¼* **Chiswick Bey (IRE)**35 2450 5-9-7 **74**........................ AdamKirby 7 78
(Noel Quinlan) *prom: chsd wnr over 4f out: hrd rdn over 2f out: nvr quite able to chal: kpt on* **7/4**2

6000 **3** *hd* **Shifting Star (IRE)**10 3215 8-9-3 **70**........................(vt) KieranO'Neill 8 73
(John Bridger) *hld up towards rr: prog 2f out: drvn to dispute 2nd fnl f: kpt on same pce* **12/1**

01-0 **4** *2 ¼* **Eager To Bow (IRE)**11 3172 7-9-6 **73**........................ GeorgeBaker 4 71
(Patrick Chamings) *hld up in last pair and swtchd to rail: nt clr run 3f out tl swtchd to outer 2f out: rdn and kpt on same pce after* **12/1**

-011 **5** *1 ¾* **Darnathean**15 3052 4-9-2 **69**........................(p) JamesMcDonald 3 62
(Paul D'Arcy) *chsd ldrs on outer: rdn bef 1/2-way: prog and on terms 3f out: nt qckn 2f out: fdd fnl f* **6/4**1

00-0 **6** *1 ½* **My Learned Friend (IRE)**11 3181 9-8-9 **69**..............(p) RobHornby(7) 9 59
(Andrew Balding) *chsd wnr to over 4f out: styd cl up tl steadily wknd over 1f out* **33/1**

1-00 **7** *12* **Dana's Present**24 2780 4-9-1 **68**........................ PatCosgrave 6 28
(George Baker) *t.k.h: hld up in last pair: shkn up 3f out: sn wknd: t.o* **20/1**

2050 **8** *¾* **Warbond**25 2747 5-8-2 **55** oh6........................(v) CathyGannon 1 13
(Michael Madgwick) *chsd ldrs on outer: lost pl bef 1/2-way: t.o* **33/1**

1m 29.96s (-2.34) **Going Correction** -0.175s/f (Firm) 8 Ran SP% **113.5**
Speed ratings (Par 103): **104,102,102,100,98 97,85,84**
toteswingers 1&2 £3.70, 1&3 £6.50, 2&3 £4.90 CSF £21.92 CT £166.90 TOTE £9.00: £2.50, £1.10, £2.80; EX 23.10 Trifecta £374.00 Pool: £1,700.93 - 3.41 winning units..
Owner Tattenham Corner Racing IV **Bred** Meon Valley Stud **Trained** Epsom, Surrey

FOCUS
A race determined by who could grab the stands' rail first and a gamble foiled. The time was modest and the winner is rated to this year's AW form.

3576 CRANBROOK MAIDEN STKS — 6f
7:05 (7:05) (Class 5) 3-Y-O+ **£2,726** (£805; £402) **Stalls** High

Form RPR
62-4 **1** **Abated**61 1732 3-9-0 75........................ JamesDoyle 2 81
(Roger Charlton) *mde all and r against nr side rail: gng bttr than only serious rival fr over 2f out: rdn out fnl f* **5/4**2

3030 **2** *2 ¼* **Millers Wharf (IRE)**9 3242 3-9-0 74.........(b) WilliamTwiston-Davies(5) 4 79
(Richard Hannon) *hld up: chsd wnr 1/2-way: rdn and no imp over 1f out: wl hld after* **1/1**1

3-06 **3** *20* **Poitin**18 2951 3-9-0 66........................(b1) LukeMorris 1 36
(Harry Dunlop) *s.i.s: racd awkwardly: chsd wnr to 1/2-way: dropped away rapidly: t.o* **6/1**3

1m 9.44s (-1.76) **Going Correction** -0.175s/f (Firm)
WFA 3 from 4yo 7lb 3 Ran SP% **108.7**
Speed ratings (Par 103): **104,101,74**
CSF £2.92 TOTE £2.00; EX 3.00 Trifecta £2.80 Pool: £645.19 - 171.37 winning units..
Owner K Abdullah **Bred** Juddmonte Farms Ltd **Trained** Beckhampton, Wilts

FOCUS
Non-runners, most significantly Meridius, reduced the field of this maiden by half, but it was still an event of some merit with the first two having both already posted personal-best RPRs of 79 previously. Limited form though, which makes sense at face value.

3577 ST SHIPPING AND TRANSPORT H'CAP — 5f
7:35 (7:35) (Class 5) (0-75,79) 3-Y-O+ **£2,726** (£805; £402) **Stalls** High

Form RPR
2041 **1** **Dorback**2 3487 6-10-2 **79** 6ex........................(t) MartinHarley 5 88
(Violet M Jordan) *fast away and crossed to nr side rail: mde virtually all: in command over 1f out: rdn out* **9/4**1

5050 **2** *1 ½* **Welease Bwian (IRE)**7 3341 4-8-12 **61**........................ JamesMcDonald 2 65
(Stuart Williams) *hld up in 5th: waiting for room 2f out: prog to chse wnr 1f out: styd on but no great imp* **8/1**

0060 **3** *3* **Bubbly Ballerina**14 3093 4-9-11 **74**........................ AdamKirby 7 67
(Alan Bailey) *chsd ldrs: rdn 2f out: outpcd over 1f out: no ch after* **5/1**3

0-00 **4** *2* **Best Be Careful (IRE)**16 3018 5-9-5 **68**........................ LiamKeniry 4 54
(Mark Usher) *chsd ldng pair but racd on outer: rdn wl over 1f out: sn btn* **5/1**3

0046 **5** *shd* **Jarrow (IRE)**7 3341 6-9-10 **73**........................ SebSanders 3 58
(Milton Bradley) *hld up in last and crossed to nr side rail: pushed along bef 1/2-way: rdn and one pce over 1f out* **8/1**

10-5 **6** *1* **Howyadoingnotsobad (IRE)**50 1984 5-9-12 **75**.............. LukeMorris 6 57
(Karen George) *sn w wnr: nt qckn 2f out: lost 2nd and wknd 1f out* **3/1**2

-400 **7** *¾* **Multitask**26 2727 3-8-8 **63**........................ CathyGannon 8 40
(Michael Madgwick) *a in rr: struggling sn after 1/2-way* **16/1**

56.89s (-1.31) **Going Correction** -0.175s/f (Firm)
WFA 3 from 4yo+ 6lb 7 Ran SP% **117.2**
Speed ratings (Par 103): **103,100,95,92,92 90,89**
toteswingers 1&2 £3.40, 1&3 £3.40, 2&3 £8.30 CSF £21.86 CT £83.16 TOTE £3.50: £1.80, £2.90; EX 19.90 Trifecta £87.30 Pool: £1,054.74 - 9.05 winning units..
Owner Rakebackmypoker.com **Bred** Winterbeck Manor Stud **Trained** Moreton Morrell, Warwicks

FOCUS
An outcome very much like that of the two events which preceded it. Modest form, but the winner's best figure since 2011.

3578 PAYNE & CO. OXTED (S) STKS — 1m 4f (P)
8:05 (10:06) (Class 6) 3-Y-O **£2,045** (£603; £302) **Stalls** Low

Form RPR
54-4 **V** **Honey Haven (IRE)**156 237 3-8-0 45........................ NoelGarbutt(7) 2
(Mark Brisbourne) *r voided*

-640 **V** **Dark Justice (IRE)**39 2341 3-8-4 51........................ DarrenEgan(3) 3
(Tim Pitt) *r voided*

6-04 **V** **Helamis**9 3257 3-8-7 50........................ SaleemGolam 6
(Stuart Williams) *r voided*

3033 **V** **Rock Diamond (IRE)**4 3428 3-8-7 47........................ JackMitchell 1
(Sylvester Kirk) *r voided*

3310 **V** **Inessa Armand (IRE)**54 1885 3-8-12 61........................(p) LiamKeniry 7
(J S Moore) *r voided*

V **Chief Monolulu** 3-8-12........................ JamesDoyle 5
(Pat Phelan) *r voided*

FOCUS
Debutant Chief Monolulu broke a leg after 2f and was attended by vets near the winning post. The gelding had to be put down. The field was stopped by a yellow flag on the home turn and the race voided.

3579 FOREST ROW H'CAP — 1m 4f (P)
8:35 (8:36) (Class 5) (0-75,75) 4-Y-O+ **£2,726** (£805; £402) **Stalls** Low

Form RPR
0041 **1** **Standpoint**7 3330 7-9-0 **68**........................ HayleyTurner 5 78
(Conor Dore) *hld up in 7th: prog wl over 2f out: brought wd and clsd over 1f out: rdn to ld last 100yds: edgd lft and jst hld on* **5/1**

04/1 **2** *shd* **Cornish Beau (IRE)**11 3168 6-8-6 **60**........................ LukeMorris 7 70
(Dr Richard Newland) *wl in tch: rdn and prog to chse ldng pair over 2f out: led over 1f out: hdd last 100yds: styd on wl: jst hld* **11/4**2

0511 **3** *3* **Foxhaven**[31] 2569 11-9-6 **74**...(v) GeorgeBaker 2 79
(Patrick Chamings) *led 100yds: trckd ldr: led 3f out: rdn and hdd over 1f out: readily outpcd* **9/2**[3]

32 **4** *2 1/4* **Saint Helena (IRE)**[19] 2939 5-9-2 **70**... JamesDoyle 6 72
(Harry Dunlop) *hld up in last: prog over 2f out: no imp on ldrs over 1f out: outpcd after* **2/1**[1]

002/ **5** *1* **Canna (IRE)**[542] 3781 5-9-4 **72**... MartinHarley 1 72
(Ali Brewer) *chsd ldrs: rdn over 3f out: struggling whn short of room on inner over 2f out: wl btn after* **14/1**

2500 **6** *nse* **Total Obsession**[11] 3169 6-7-9 **56** oh7...(v) NoelGarbutt(7) 3 56
(Mark Hoad) *nvr gng that wl: lost pl 5f out and sn rdn: struggling over 2f out: no ch after: plugged on* **33/1**

3060 **7** *2 3/4* **Ajeeb (USA)**[56] 1849 5-9-2 **75**... WilliamTwiston-Davies(5) 4 71
(Michael Scudamore) *t.k.h: racd wd: in tch: prog to chse ldr wl over 2f out: wknd qckly over 1f out* **16/1**

6/0- **8** *2 1/4* **Proud Times (USA)**[47] 1880 7-9-2 **70**... AdamKirby 8 62
(Ali Brewer) *led after 100yds at gd pce: stdd 7f out: hdd 3f out: no rspnse u.p and sn dropped out* **25/1**

2m 32.36s (-0.64) **Going Correction** -0.10s/f (Stan) **8** Ran SP% **114.2**
Speed ratings (Par 103): **98,97,95,94,93 93,91,90**
toteswingers 1&2 £4.30, 1&3 £3.90, 2&3 £2.80 CSF £19.11 CT £65.57 TOTE £3.60: £1.10, £1.60, £2.60; EX 18.70 Trifecta £82.10 Pool: £680.86 - 6.21 winning units..
Owner Mrs Jennifer Marsh **Bred** Juddmonte Farms Ltd **Trained** Hubbert's Bridge, Lincs

FOCUS
A modest handicap. The winner might defy another small rise.

3580 HIGHURST H'CAP — 1m 2f (P)
9:05 (9:06) (Class 6) (0-65,65) 4-Y-O+ **£2,045** (£603; £302) **Stalls** Low

Form RPR

00-3 **1** **Hector's Chance**[17] 2982 4-9-7 **65**... GeorgeBaker 7 76
(Heather Main) *hld up in last pair: prog on outer over 4f out: more hdwy over 2f out to chse ldr wl over 1f out: clsd to ld last 150yds: sn clr* **5/1**[2]

0605 **2** *2 1/2* **Megalala (IRE)**[7] 3330 12-9-1 **59**...(p) KieranO'Neill 8 65
(John Bridger) *led at gd pce: rdn over 3f out: 3 l clr 2f out: hdd and one pce last 150yds* **20/1**

4304 **3** *nk* **Dolly Colman (IRE)**[10] 3213 5-8-2 **46** oh1...(p) CathyGannon 4 51
(Zoe Davison) *hld up in rr: stuck on inner over 2f out: plld out wd over 1f out: r.o fnl f to take 3rd nr fin* **20/1**

06-4 **4** *3/4* **Opera Buff**[29] 2640 4-9-7 **65**...(p) RenatoSouza 6 69
(Barry Brennan) *hld up in rr: drvn and struggling 3f out: no prog u.p over 1f out: fnlly r.o wl fnl f: tk 4th nr fin* **8/1**

1300 **5** *1/2* **Scamperdale**[26] 2710 11-9-6 **64**... KierenFox 9 67
(Brian Baugh) *hld up in last: prog on wd outside fr 4f out: clsd 2f out: chsd ldng pair jst over 1f but outpcd: one pce after* **16/1**

-240 **6** *3/4* **Grand Theft Equine**[36] 2417 5-9-5 **63**...(v[1]) PatCosgrave 11 64
(Jim Boyle) *hld up in midfield: prog over 3f out: tried to cl 2f out: one pce over 1f out* **7/1**

0426 **7** *1* **Chik's Dream**[58] 1797 6-7-11 **46**... RosieJessop(5) 12 45
(Derek Haydn Jones) *chsd ldng pair: rdn 3f out: lost pl over 2f out: plugged on one pce* **33/1**

6435 **8** *2* **Bit Windy**[10] 3222 4-8-4 **48**... HayleyTurner 10 43
(Chris Dwyer) *chsd ldr: drvn wl over 2f out: lost 2nd and wknd qckly wl over 1f out* **10/1**

6113 **9** *4* **Salient**[11] 3169 9-8-10 **54**... SebSanders 2 41
(Michael Attwater) *trckd ldrs on inner: rdn wl over 2f out: lost pl sn after and wl btn* **6/1**[3]

-560 **10** *1 1/4* **Derfenna Art (IRE)**[23] 2807 4-9-0 **63**...(t) WilliamTwiston-Davies(5) 13 48
(Seamus Durack) *wl in tch: drvn 3f out: lost pl over 2f out: sn btn* **6/1**[3]

23-0 **11** *25* **Russian Storm**[7] 3330 5-9-2 **60**... JamesDoyle 3
(Pat Phelan) *in tch tl rdn and wknd over 3f out: t.o* **10/1**

000/ **12** *16* **Bollywood (IRE)**[767] 7888 10-7-13 **46** oh1...(t) RyanPowell(3) 5
(Alison Batchelor) *chsd ldrs to 1/2-way: wknd rapidly and sn t.o* **50/1**

0-02 **U** **Lady Barastar (IRE)**[11] 3169 5-8-7 **51**...(b) LukeMorris 1
(Amanda Perrett) *rrd and uns rdr leaving stalls* **4/1**[1]

2m 4.28s (-2.32) **Going Correction** -0.10s/f (Stan) **13** Ran SP% **127.3**
Speed ratings (Par 101): **105,103,102,102,101 101,100,98,95,94 74,61,**
toteswingers 1&2 £15.10, 1&3 £23.20, 2&3 £50.00 CSF £111.15 CT £1894.37 TOTE £6.30: £2.60, £7.20, £5.40; EX 172.60 Trifecta £710.60 Part won. Pool: £947.53 - 0.71 winning units..
Owner M Scott Russell **Bred** Wickham Stud **Trained** Kingston Lisle, Oxon

FOCUS
A moderate handicap and drama at the start. The pace was good and the winner returned to form.
T/Plt: £46.50 to a £1 stake. Pool: £67,917.00 - 1,064.77 winning units T/Qpdt: £7.10 to a £1 stake. Pool: £4,586.97 - 472.90 winning units JN

[3534] NEWMARKET (R-H)
Saturday, June 22

OFFICIAL GOING: Good (7.8)
Far side track used. Stalls on far side except 13f: Centre. Bend into home straight repositioned, increasing distance of 13f race by 20m.
Wind: Light across Weather: Sunshine and showers

3581 HOUSE COLLECTION EBF MAIDEN STKS — 7f
2:15 (2:16) (Class 4) 2-Y-O **£4,528** (£1,347; £673; £336) **Stalls** High

Form RPR

1 **Outstrip** 2-9-5 0... MickaelBarzalona 2 84+
(Saeed bin Suroor) *s.i.s: hld up: hdwy and hung lft over 1f out: r.o u.p to ld wl ins fnl f* **4/1**[3]

2 *1 1/2* **True Story** 2-9-5 0... ChrisCatlin 6 80+
(Saeed bin Suroor) *s.i.s: hld up: hdwy over 2f out: rdn over 1f out: r.o* **3/1**[2]

3 **3** *nk* **Showpiece**[9] 3238 2-9-5 0... DaneO'Neill 13 79
(Richard Hannon) *chsd ldrs: led over 2f out: rdn and edgd lft over 1f out: hdd wl ins fnl f* **15/8**[1]

4 *1 1/2* **Sudden Wonder (IRE)** 2-9-5 0... MartinLane 8 75+
(Saeed bin Suroor) *chsd ldrs: rdn over 1f out: styd on* **16/1**

5 *1/2* **Gilbey's Mate** 2-9-5 0... RobertHavlin 10 74+
(John Gosden) *hld up: hdwy over 1f out: r.o: nt rch ldrs* **28/1**

6 *2* **Rainbow Rock (IRE)** 2-9-5 0... TedDurcan 5 69+
(Mark Johnston) *led to 1/2-way: rdn over 1f out: styd on same pce* **20/1**

7 *2 3/4* **Maxie T** 2-9-5 0... HayleyTurner 4 61+
(Mark Johnston) *chsd ldrs: rdn over 2f out: wknd over 1f out* **33/1**

5 **8** *nk* **Haayil**[15] 3044 2-9-5 0... NickyMackay 14 61
(John Gosden) *chsd ldrs: led 1/2-way: hdd over 2f out: rdn and wknd fnl f* **8/1**

9 *shd* **Drinkuptrig (IRE)** 2-9-5 0... PatCosgrave 3 60+
(Stuart Williams) *hld up: shkn up over 1f out: styd on ins fnl f: nvr nrr* **66/1**

0 **10** *nk* **Basil Berry**[25] 2758 2-9-5 0... SaleemGolam 12 60
(Chris Dwyer) *hld up: hdwy over 2f out: rdn and wknd over 1f out* **100/1**

11 *4 1/2* **Kinema (IRE)** 2-9-5 0... FergusSweeney 1 48
(Ed Dunlop) *s.i.s: hdwy 1/2-way: rdn and wknd over 1f out* **50/1**

12 *1* **Iconic Artist (USA)** 2-9-5 0... HarryBentley 9 45
(Andrew Balding) *s.s: hdwy 4f out: wknd over 2f out* **12/1**

13 *1 1/4* **Galab (IRE)** 2-9-5 0... MartinDwyer 15 42
(Conrad Allen) *s.i.s: a in rr: wknd over 2f out* **66/1**

1m 28.54s (2.84) **Going Correction** +0.125s/f (Good) **13** Ran SP% **121.6**
Speed ratings (Par 95): **88,86,85,84,83 81,78,77,77,77 72,71,69**
toteswingers 1&2 £3.60, 1&3 £4.70, 2&3 £4.80 CSF £15.94 TOTE £5.30: £1.90, £1.60, £1.20; EX 20.00 Trifecta £46.10 Pool: £1546.49 - 25.12 winning units..
Owner Godolphin **Bred** Darley **Trained** Newmarket, Suffolk

FOCUS
Probably a good contest, as it has produced a few above-average types down the years, including subsequent Group 2 winner Silver Grecian. A race that looks sure to produce winners.

3582 POETS HOUSE H'CAP — 7f
2:50 (2:51) (Class 4) (0-85,85) 3-Y-O **£5,175** (£1,540; £769; £384) **Stalls** High

Form RPR

6-06 **1** **Azrur (IRE)**[35] 2445 3-9-3 **81**...[1] HayleyTurner 3 92
(Michael Bell) *w ldrs tl led 5f out: rdn and hung rt over 1f out: jst hld on* **15/2**

01- **2** *nse* **Veeraya**[242] 7305 3-8-12 **76**... DaneO'Neill 9 86+
(William Haggas) *hld up: hdwy 2f out: chsd wnr over 1f out: sn rdn: ev ch ins fnl f: r.o* **6/1**[3]

-402 **3** *2 3/4* **Al Udeid (IRE)**[15] 3053 3-8-13 **77**... PatCosgrave 4 80
(Kevin Ryan) *chsd ldrs: rdn and ev ch over 1f out: styd on same pce ins fnl f* **14/1**

0-33 **4** *1 1/2* **Liberty Jack (IRE)**[39] 2346 3-8-7 **71**...[1] FergusSweeney 8 70
(Roger Charlton) *s.i.s: hdwy 1/2-way: hung lft 2f out: styng on same pce whn hung rt ins fnl f* **5/1**[2]

035 **5** *1 1/4* **Bold Prediction (IRE)**[29] 2626 3-8-6 **77**... JoeyHaynes(7) 7 73
(Mrs K Burke) *chsd ldrs: rdn over 1f out: styd on same pce* **20/1**

2-02 **6** *1/2* **Dance With Dragons (IRE)**[33] 2495 3-8-10 **79**... LauraPike(5) 6 73
(William Stone) *hld up: hdwy u.p over 1f out: styd on same pce ins fnl f* **9/2**[1]

1-41 **7** *shd* **Whipper Snapper (IRE)**[15] 3053 3-9-0 **78**... MickaelBarzalona 1 72
(William Knight) *sn pushed along in rr: hdwy over 1f out: styd on same pce ins fnl f* **5/1**[2]

2-00 **8** *3 1/4* **Dashing David (IRE)**[21] 2857 3-9-7 **85**... SeanLevey 2 70
(Richard Hannon) *s.i.s: sn prom: rdn over 1f out: wknd ins fnl f* **12/1**

0-65 **9** *2 1/2* **Banovallum**[16] 3020 3-9-2 **80**... HarryBentley 10 58
(Sylvester Kirk) *hld up: hdwy 1/2-way: rdn: hung lft and wknd over 1f out* **6/1**[3]

0456 **10** *3/4* **Triple Aitch (USA)**[13] 3137 3-7-13 **66** oh4... DarrenEgan(3) 5 42
(Gay Kelleway) *led 2f: chsd ldrs tl rdn and wknd over 1f out* **40/1**

6-6 **11** *1* **Hidden Talent**[65] 1645 3-9-7 **85**... MartinDwyer 11 59
(David Brown) *racd alone far side: up w the pce tl rdn and wknd over 1f out* **33/1**

1m 26.41s (0.71) **Going Correction** +0.125s/f (Good) **11** Ran SP% **116.4**
Speed ratings (Par 101): **100,99,96,95,93 93,92,89,86,85 84**
toteswingers 1&2 £10.00, 1&3 £27.20, 2&3 £24.20 CSF £50.42 CT £630.96 TOTE £6.90: £1.80, £2.80, £4.60; EX 63.20 Trifecta £1268.30 Part won. Pool: £1691.14 - 0.15 winning units..
Owner Saleh Al Homaizi & Imad Al Sagar **Bred** Kildaragh Stud **Trained** Newmarket, Suffolk

FOCUS
Nothing more than a fair contest considering plenty of these were exposed, and it appeared important to make your bid towards the stands' side. It was competitive and ther time wasn't bad.

3583 PADDOCKS HOUSE EBF FILLIES' H'CAP — 1m
3:25 (3:26) (Class 4) (0-85,79) 3-Y-O+ **£6,469** (£1,925; £962; £481) **Stalls** High

Form RPR

1-1 **1** **Ribbons**[44] 2195 3-9-4 **79**... HayleyTurner 1 90+
(James Fanshawe) *trckd ldrs: rdn over 1f out: r.o u.p to ld nr fin* **5/4**[1]

3-41 **2** *nk* **Zeyran (IRE)**[25] 2761 4-9-11 **76**... PatCosgrave 4 88
(Lady Cecil) *trckd ldr: plld hrd: led over 5f out: edgd rt over 1f out: rdn ins fnl f: hdd nr fin* **7/2**[3]

4-05 **3** *1* **Macchiara**[14] 3111 4-9-7 **72**... ChrisCatlin 5 82
(Rae Guest) *a.p: chsd ldr over 4f out: rdn over 1f out: unable qck towards fin* **25/1**

2661 **4** *9* **It's My Time**[14] 3098 4-9-2 **67**...(p) PatrickMathers 3 56
(Richard Fahey) *hld up: rdn over 2f out: wknd fnl f* **20/1**

51- **5** *3 1/2* **Snow Rose (USA)**[291] 5907 3-9-3 **78**... MickaelBarzalona 2 56
(Saeed bin Suroor) *led: hdd over 5f out: rdn over 2f out: wknd over 1f out* **5/2**[2]

1- **6** *1/2* **Keep The Secret**[183] 8201 3-9-1 **76**... TedDurcan 6 54
(William Knight) *hld up: rdn over 2f out: wknd over 1f out* **12/1**

1m 41.47s (1.47) **Going Correction** +0.125s/f (Good)
WFA 3 from 4yo 10lb **6** Ran SP% **111.5**
Speed ratings (Par 102): **97,96,95,86,83 82**
toteswingers 1&2 £1.50, 1&3 £5.00, 2&3 £7.60 CSF £5.90 TOTE £2.10: £1.70, £1.40; EX 6.00 Trifecta £56.30 Pool: £3223.91 - 42.90 winning units..
Owner Elite Racing Club **Bred** Elite Racing Club **Trained** Newmarket, Suffolk

FOCUS
A couple of these lacked the scope of their rivals, so it was encouraging to see something unexposed take the prize. The early pace was sedate, and the time and the third limit the form.

3584 AGRIBANK H'CAP — 5f
4:05 (4:05) (Class 2) (0-105,100) 3-Y-O
£12,450 (£3,728; £1,864; £932; £466; £234) **Stalls** High

Form RPR

501 **1** **Dutch Masterpiece**[14] 3097 3-9-5 **98**... SeanLevey 12 109
(Gary Moore) *chsd ldrs: rdn to ld and hung rt 1f out: r.o* **4/1**[1]

1001 **2** *1 1/4* **Aetna**[21] 2888 3-7-13 **81** oh1... NeilFarley(3) 6 88+
(Michael Easterby) *hld up: rdn and r.o to go 2nd wl ins fnl f: nt rch wnr* **6/1**[2]

5-30 **3** *1* **Cosmic Chatter**[7] 3348 3-9-1 **99**... LMcNiff(5) 4 102
(David Barron) *wnt rt s: chsd ldr tl c stands' side and led that pair over 3f out: hdd that side 2f out: rdn and ev ch 1f out: edgd lft: styd on same pce ins fnl f* **7/1**

-416 **4** *1/2* **Normal Equilibrium**[7] 3340 3-9-0 **93**... HarryBentley 7 96+
(Robert Cowell) *hld up: hdwy and nt clr run over 1f out: sn rdn: no imp towards fin* **6/1**[2]

The Form Book Flat, Raceform Ltd, Compton, RG20 6NL.

-030 **5** *nse* **Chilworth Icon**[7] 3348 3-9-2 **100** .... CharlesBishop(5) 11 101
(Mick Channon) *chsd ldrs: rdn over 1f out: nt clr run ins fnl f: styd on same pce* **10/1**

-155 **6** *½* **Dominate**[7] 3340 3-8-11 **90** .... DaneO'Neill 8 89
(Richard Hannon) *chsd ldrs: rdn and ev ch 1f out: no ex wl ins fnl f* **13/2**[3]

6555 **7** *nse* **Top Boy**[14] 3097 3-8-9 **88** .... MartinDwyer 10 87
(Derek Shaw) *hld up: shkn up over 1f out: nt clr run ins fnl f: r.o towards fin: nt rch ldrs* **7/1**

0100 **8** *1 ½* **Storm Moon (USA)**[7] 3348 3-8-10 **89** .... TedDurcan 2 83
(Mark Johnston) *bmpd s: chsd ldrs: c stands' side over 3f out: led overall 2f out: rdn and hdd 1f out: no ex ins fnl f* **8/1**

3040 **9** *1* **Equitania**[10] 3220 3-8-6 **85** .... HayleyTurner 9 79
(Alan Bailey) *overall ldr 3f: sn rdn: ev ch over 1f out: looked hld whn nt clr run and eased ins fnl f* **16/1**

0010 **10** *9* **Effie B**[22] 2848 3-9-0 **93** .... NickyMackay 5 66
(Mick Channon) *sn pushed along towards rr: rdn over 1f out: sn wknd: eased whn btn ins fnl f* **20/1**

58.96s (-0.14) **Going Correction** +0.125s/f (Good) **10** Ran SP% **117.8**
Speed ratings (Par 105): **106,104,102,101,101 100,100,98,96,82**
toteswingers 1&2 £6.50, 1&3 £23.50, 2&3 £23.50 CSF £27.91 CT £168.55 TOTE £4.30: £1.90, £1.90, £2.70; EX 29.70 Trifecta £269.30 Pool: £903.43 - 2.51 winning units..
Owner R A Green **Bred** Bumble Bloodstock Ltd **Trained** Lower Beeding, W Sussex

FOCUS
There was plenty of pace on early, as one would expect for a competitive sprint handicap. The form makes sense and the winner continues on the upgrade.

3585 BRIGADIER EBF MAIDEN STKS — 1m
4:40 (4:41) (Class 5) 3-Y-O **£3,881** (£1,155; £577; £288) **Stalls** High

Form RPR

2- **1** **Top Joker**[364] 3397 3-9-5 0 .... MickaelBarzalona 7 83
(Saeed bin Suroor) *s.i.s: hld up: hdwy over 2f out: rdn and edgd lft over 1f out: styd on to ld last strides* **11/10**[1]

06-2 **2** *nk* **Shaishee (USA)**[53] 1908 3-9-5 80 .... DaneO'Neill 10 82
(Charles Hills) *hld up in tch: led over 2f out: rdn over 1f out: hdd ins fnl f: rallied to ld nr fin: hdd last strides* **5/2**[2]

3 *nk* **Disco Inferno (IRE)** 3-9-5 0 .... (t) MartinLane 9 81
(Brian Meehan) *s.i.s: hdwy over 3f out: rdn to ld ins fnl f: hdd nr fin* **22/1**

0 **4** *3* **Top Set (IRE)**[25] 2760 3-9-0 0 .... RobertTart(5) 1 74+
(Marco Botti) *chsd ldrs: rdn over 2f out: sn outpcd: r.o ins fnl f* **18/1**

5 *½* **Akeed Dubawi** 3-9-5 0 .... HayleyTurner 6 73+
(William Haggas) *hld up: hdwy over 2f out: outpcd over 1f out: styd on ins fnl f* **11/2**[3]

6 *6* **Shamalad** 3-9-2 0 .... SimonPearce(3) 3 59
(Lydia Pearce) *chsd ldrs: rdn over 2f out: wkng whn hmpd 1f out* **25/1**

000 **7** *nse* **Kazak**[16] 3021 3-9-5 0 .... FergusSweeney 2 59
(Roger Charlton) *hld up: effrt over 2f out: wknd over 1f out* **12/1**

8 *½* **Red Warrior (IRE)** 3-9-5 0 .... TedDurcan 5 58
(Ismail Mohammed) *chsd ldrs: ev ch over 2f out: wknd over 1f out* **25/1**

9 *4 ½* **St Elmo's Fire** 3-9-5 0 .... RobertHavlin 8 48
(Peter Chapple-Hyam) *hld up: pushed along 3f out: wknd 2f out* **20/1**

0-0 **10** *10* **My Renaissance**[35] 2448 3-9-5 0 .... MartinDwyer 4 25
(Ben Case) *led over 5f: hung lft and wknd over 1f out* **66/1**

1m 41.91s (1.91) **Going Correction** +0.125s/f (Good) **10** Ran SP% **122.8**
Speed ratings (Par 99): **95,94,94,91,90 84,84,84,79,69**
toteswingers 1&2 £1.50, 2&3 £16.30, 1&3 £8.70 CSF £3.83 TOTE £2.00: £1.10, £1.30, £4.50; EX 4.80 Trifecta £75.30 Pool: £4102.62 - 40.86 winning units..
Owner Godolphin **Bred** Darley **Trained** Newmarket, Suffolk
■ Stewards' Enquiry : Dane O'Neill four-day ban: use of whip (7-10 July)

FOCUS
We are just about getting to the stage of the season where 3yo plus maidens start to look on the weak side and, although the contest produced subsequent Group performer Multidimensional in 2006, this was probably an ordinary maiden for the track.

3586 ECF H'CAP — 6f
5:15 (5:17) (Class 4) (0-85,83) 3-Y-O+ **£5,175** (£1,540; £769; £384) **Stalls** High

Form RPR

0053 **1** **My Kingdom (IRE)**[11] 3172 7-9-2 **73** .... (t) HarryBentley 14 85
(Stuart Williams) *chsd ldrs tl led over 1f out: sn rdn: r.o* **10/1**

21-2 **2** *nk* **Nardin**[15] 3058 3-9-2 **80** .... DaneO'Neill 10 89
(Ed Dunlop) *hld up: hdwy over 2f out: rdn to chse wnr over 1f out: sn ev ch: r.o* **4/1**[2]

0-00 **3** *1 ½* **Johnny Castle**[15] 3060 5-9-9 **83** .... DarrenEgan(3) 2 89
(Amanda Perrett) *hld up: hdwy over 2f out: rdn over 1f out: styd on: hung rt towards fin* **12/1**

4000 **4** *nk* **Showboating (IRE)**[7] 3351 5-9-3 **74** .... (tp) SeanLevey 13 79
(Alan McCabe) *chsd ldrs: rdn over 1f out: styd on u.p* **8/1**

00-1 **5** *nk* **Trojan Rocket (IRE)**[26] 2725 5-9-10 **81** .... MickaelBarzalona 1 85
(Michael Wigham) *hld up: rdn over 1f out: r.o ins fnl f: nvr nrr* **11/4**[1]

0110 **6** *nk* **Gabbiano**[21] 2868 4-9-6 **82** .... RobertTart(5) 7 85
(Jeremy Gask) *chsd ldrs: rdn over 1f out: edgd lft and styd on same pce ins fnl f* **5/1**[3]

4035 **7** *1* **Arctic Lynx (IRE)**[10] 3220 6-9-9 **80** .... HayleyTurner 5 80
(Robert Cowell) *hld up: hdwy over 1f out: sn rdn: styd on same pce ins fnl f* **20/1**

215 **8** *nk* **Albaqaa**[15] 3060 8-9-4 **80** .... NatashaEaton(5) 11 79
(P J O'Gorman) *chsd ldr tl rdn over 1f out: no ex ins fnl f* **25/1**

304 **9** *hd* **My Son Max**[28] 2663 5-9-10 **81** .... BrettDoyle 9 79
(P J O'Gorman) *hld up: rdn over 1f out: nt trble ldrs* **14/1**

6-00 **10** *1* **Emkanaat**[15] 3060 5-9-9 **80** .... MartinDwyer 12 75
(Amy Weaver) *led: rdn and hdd over 1f out: wknd ins fnl f* **33/1**

-430 **11** *1 ¼* **Living Leader**[48] 2046 4-9-7 **78** .... (t) TomMcLaughlin 6 69
(Nick Littmoden) *hld up: rdn over 2f out: nvr on terms* **18/1**

-000 **12** *2 ½* **Medici Time**[7] 3351 8-9-5 **76** .... (v) TedDurcan 3 59
(Tim Easterby) *dwlt: hld up: rdn over 1f out: a in rr* **18/1**

1m 13.0s (0.50) **Going Correction** +0.125s/f (Good)
WFA 3 from 4yo+ 7lb **12** Ran SP% **120.0**
Speed ratings (Par 105): **101,100,98,98,97 96,96,95,95,94 92,89**
toteswingers 1&2 £9.00, 1&3 £19.50, 2&3 £9.00 CSF £49.25 CT £506.97 TOTE £12.00: £2.80, £1.90, £3.30; EX 64.20 Trifecta £560.20 Pool: £3018.96 - 4.04 winning units..
Owner My Kingdom For A Horse **Bred** Irish National Stud **Trained** Newmarket, Suffolk

FOCUS
The field raced in a bunch towards the middle of the track early and pretty much stayed there until fanning out towards the end. Plenty finished close up, suggesting this isn't overly reliable form. The winner took advantage of a good mark.

3587 HOUSE COLLECTION H'CAP — 1m 5f
5:50 (5:50) (Class 5) (0-75,75) 4-Y-O+ **£3,234** (£962; £481; £240) **Stalls** Centre

Form RPR

-435 **1** **Porcini**[14] 3118 4-9-7 **75** .... (p) WilliamCarson 5 86
(Philip McBride) *mde all: rdn and hung lft fr over 1f out: styd on u.p* **8/1**[3]

3304 **2** *3 ½* **Flashman**[17] 2973 4-9-7 **75** .... PatrickMathers 4 80
(Richard Fahey) *chsd ldrs: rdn and edgd lft over 1f out: styd on same pce fnl f* **13/2**[2]

0610 **3** *nk* **Thecornishcowboy**[5] 3412 4-9-5 **73** .... (t) BrettDoyle 9 78
(John Ryan) *hld up: hdwy over 4f out: rdn over 1f out: styd on same pce fnl f* **20/1**

-230 **4** *5* **Silver Samba**[30] 2587 4-8-9 **70** .... DanielMuscutt(7) 1 68
(Andrew Balding) *prom: chsd wnr over 3f out tl rdn over 1f out: wknd fnl f* **5/2**[1]

5103 **5** *¾* **Beat Route**[44] 2197 6-8-13 **67** .... RobertHavlin 2 63
(Michael Attwater) *mid-div: hdwy over 4f out: rdn over 2f out: sn wknd* **20/1**

63/1 **6** *16* **Sancho Panza**[29] 2642 6-8-3 **64** .... ShelleyBirkett(7) 3 36
(Julia Feilden) *mid-div: hdwy 6f out: wknd over 3f out* **12/1**

/4-0 **7** *11* **Deceptive**[11] 21 5-9-0 **68** .... (p) MartinDwyer 10 24
(Paul Webber) *hld up: rdn over 5f out: wknd over 3f out: t.o* **25/1**

4421 **8** *2* **Admirable Duque (IRE)**[14] 3110 7-9-3 **71** .... (b) HayleyTurner 8 24
(Dominic Ffrench Davis) *hld up: rdn and wknd over 3f out: t.o* **8/1**[3]

1-22 **9** *9* **Passion Play**[14] 3110 5-9-4 **72** .... MickaelBarzalona 7
(William Knight) *prom tl rdn and wknd over 3f out: t.o* **5/2**[1]

0-34 **10** *30* **Mohanad (IRE)**[25] 2749 7-9-2 **70** .... (v[1]) FergusSweeney 6
(Philip Hide) *chsd wnr tl rdn over 3f out: sn wknd: t.o* **22/1**

2m 44.44s (0.44) **Going Correction** +0.125s/f (Good) **10** Ran SP% **118.1**
Speed ratings (Par 103): **103,100,100,97,97 87,80,79,73,55**
toteswingers 1&2 £17.70, 1&3 £3.00, 2&3 £17.70 CSF £56.09 CT £1013.78 TOTE £8.40: £2.40, £2.20, £3.80; EX 60.30 Trifecta £141.90 Pool: £316.01 - 1.66 winning units..
Owner PMRacing **Bred** Cheveley Park Stud Ltd **Trained** Newmarket, Suffolk

FOCUS
Plenty of these were in big trouble over 3f out, suggesting this was run at a strong pace. The top three in the weights dominated. The winner stepped up on last year's progressive sand form.
T/Plt: £14.90 to a £1 stake. Pool of £71573.38 - 3506.49 winning tickets. T/Qpdt: £4.50 to a £1 stake. Pool of £3732.94 - 607.25 winning tickets. CR

3541 REDCAR (L-H)
Saturday, June 22

OFFICIAL GOING: Good to firm (good in places; 9.1)
Wind: Fresh half behind Weather: Cloudy with sunny periods

3588 BRITISH STALLION STUDS EBF MARKET CROSS JEWELLERS MAIDEN STKS — 7f
2:05 (2:06) (Class 5) 2-Y-O **£2,911** (£866; £432; £216) **Stalls** Centre

Form RPR

402 **1** **Al Baz**[12] 3148 2-9-0 0 .... ThomasBrown(5) 7 78+
(James Tate) *mde all: rdn clr wl over 1f out: readily* **7/4**[1]

2 *5* **George The First** 2-9-5 0 .... PJMcDonald 1 65
(Kevin Ryan) *trckd ldrs: pushed along 3f out: rdn to chse wnr over 2f out: kpt on but no ch w wnr* **13/2**

0 **3** *4* **Street Boss (IRE)**[28] 2670 2-9-5 0 .... DuranFentiman 3 54+
(Tim Easterby) *t.k.h: green and towards rr: swtchd rt and hdwy 3f out: rdn over 2f out: sn chsng ldng pair: no imp* **14/1**

4 *1* **Champagne Rules** 2-9-5 0 .... PaddyAspell 2 51+
(Sharon Watt) *dwlt and green in rr: bhd and pushed along 1/2-way: rdn and hdwy 2f out: sn edgd bdly rt to stands' rail: kpt on fnl f* **20/1**

3 **5** *¾* **Irondale Express**[33] 2502 2-9-0 0 .... [1] BarryMcHugh 4 44
(Tony Coyle) *chsd ldrs: rdn along 3f out: outpcd fnl 2f* **11/2**[3]

6 *2* **Blue Atlantic (USA)** 2-9-5 0 .... FrederikTylicki 6 44
(Mark Johnston) *chsd ldrs: green and pushed along after 3f: rdn 3f out: sn outpcd* **2/1**[2]

0 **7** *3 ¼* **Frost In May (IRE)**[23] 2793 2-9-0 0 .... AndrewMullen 5 30
(David O'Meara) *cl up: rdn along 1/2-way: sn wknd* **33/1**

1m 25.23s (0.73) **Going Correction** -0.025s/f (Good) **7** Ran SP% **112.8**
Speed ratings (Par 93): **94,88,83,82,81 79,75**
toteswingers 1&2 £1.50, 1&3 £23.50, 2&3 £22.20 CSF £13.39 TOTE £2.60: £1.60, £3.30; EX 10.30 Trifecta £89.90 Pool: £1,283.79 - 10.70 winning units..
Owner Saif Ali **Bred** Norman Court Stud **Trained** Newmarket, Suffolk

FOCUS
Not much depth to this maiden.

3589 TEESSIDE HOSPICE FASHION SHOW H'CAP (DIV I) — 1m 6f 19y
2:40 (2:40) (Class 6) (0-65,63) 4-Y-O+ **£1,940** (£577; £288; £144) **Stalls** Low

Form RPR

-042 **1** **Maska Pony (IRE)**[21] 2887 9-8-6 **53** .... JasonHart(5) 8 62
(George Moore) *hld up: hdwy to trck ldrs 6f out: effrt and cl up 3f out: rdn to ld wl over 1f out: drvn fnl f and hld on gamely* **11/2**[3]

0353 **2** *nk* **Madrasa (IRE)**[21] 2860 5-9-7 **63** .... (bt) MickyFenton 4 71
(Keith Reveley) *hld up in midfield: stdy hdwy over 5f out: trckd ldrs whn swtchd rt and effrt 3f out: sn cl up: rdn and ev ch over 1f out: drvn and kpt on fnl f: jst hld* **7/2**[2]

35-6 **3** *2 ¾* **Sheila's Castle**[14] 3089 9-8-8 **55** .... DeclanBates(5) 10 59
(Sean Regan) *hld up in rr: stdy hdwy on inner 5f out: trckd ldrs 3f out: sn cl up: rdn and ev ch wl over 1f out: drvn and one pce fnl f* **12/1**

0310 **4** *1* **Amir Pasha (UAE)**[14] 3089 8-8-10 **52** .... (p) FrederikTylicki 7 55
(Micky Hammond) *hld up towards rr: hdwy on wd outside over 3f out: chsd ldrs over 2f out: sn rdn and kpt on fnl f: nrst fin* **8/1**

-031 **5** *2 ¾* **Sally Friday (IRE)**[26] 2721 5-8-13 **60** .... (p) GeorgeChaloner(5) 5 59
(Edwin Tuer) *trckd ldrs: hdwy 5f out: led 3f out: sn rdn: hdd and drvn wl over 1f out: wknd appr fnl f* **13/8**[1]

4460 **6** *4* **Brunello**[17] 2990 5-9-4 **60** .... (p) MichaelO'Connell 6 54
(Philip Kirby) *prom: led after 6f: rdn along 4f out: hdd 3f out: sn drvn and grad wknd* **9/1**

00-0 **7** *14* **Tenacity**[32] 2537 4-8-1 **50** .... (p) GemmaTutty(7) 3 24
(Karen Tutty) *led 2f: cl up: rdn along 1/2-way: wknd over 4f out* **25/1**

300- **8** *nk* **Joyful Motive**[267] 6626 4-8-5 **47** .... AndrewMullen 2 21
(Tom Tate) *chsd ldrs: rdn along over 6f out: sn lost pl and bhd* **25/1**

6-60 **9** *8* **Miss Mohawk (IRE)**[21] 2887 4-8-3 **45**........................ DuranFentiman 12
(Alan Brown) *midfield: rdn along over 6f out: sn wknd* **66/1**

0-00 **10** *5* **Nippy Nikki**[17] 2986 5-8-2 **47** ow2.. BillyCray(3) 9
(John Norton) *cl up: rdn along 5f out: wknd 4f out* **40/1**

0006 **11** *9* **Wesleydale (IRE)**[10] 3203 6-8-3 **45**.. PaulQuinn 11
(Simon West) *plld hrd: chsd ldrs on outer: led after 2f: wd and hdd 1/2-way: sn wknd and bhd* **40/1**

3m 3.19s (-1.51) **Going Correction** -0.025s/f (Good) **11** Ran SP% **118.6**
Speed ratings (Par 101): **103,102,101,100,99 96,88,88,84,81 76**
toteswingers 1&2 £2.80, 1&3 £4.70, 2&3 £16.00 CSF £24.20 CT £225.77 TOTE £6.10: £2.00, £1.50, £3.50; EX 23.00 Trifecta £761.50 Part won. Pool: £1,015.45 - 0.47 winning units..
Owner Diane Russell & Paul Blair **Bred** Twelve Oaks Stud Establishment **Trained** Middleham Moor, N Yorks
■ Stewards' Enquiry : Declan Bates four-day ban: use of whip (7-10 July)

FOCUS
This was wide open up the straight with several in the reckoning. Pretty straightforward form.

3590 H JARVIS 135TH ANNIVERSARY H'CAP 7f
3:15 (3:15) (Class 3) (0-90,90) 4-Y-0+ **£7,439** (£2,213; £1,106; £553) **Stalls** Centre

Form RPR

-445 **1** **Wannabe King**[10] 3207 7-8-13 **89**..............................(v) JordanNason(7) 5 96
(Geoffrey Harker) *prom: led after 2f: rdn along 2f out: kpt on gamely fnl f* **8/1**

3-00 **2** *½* **Orbit The Moon (IRE)**[14] 3087 5-8-6 **75**.......................(tp) PJMcDonald 6 81
(Michael Dods) *prom: effrt 2f out: sn rdn: chal ins fnl f: drvn and no ex towards fin* **14/1**

0202 **3** *shd* **Galician**[42] 2265 4-9-7 **90**.. FrederikTylicki 3 95
(Mark Johnston) *trckd ldrs: hdwy 2f out: sn rdn: drvn and styng on whn j. small piece of litter on trck wl ins fnl f: kpt on* **7/2**[3]

3-00 **4** *1* **Fayr Fall (IRE)**[14] 3087 4-8-3 **72**..................................(v) DuranFentiman 4 75
(Tim Easterby) *t.k.h: hld up: hdwy 3f out: chsd ldrs 2f out: rdn and ev ch ent fnl f: sn drvn and no ex last 75yds* **22/1**

1100 **5** *nse* **Khawatim**[21] 2868 5-9-3 **89**.. DeclanCannon(3) 2 92
(Noel Quinlan) *hld up in rr: hdwy over 2f out: rdn to chse ldrs over 1f out: n.m.r ins fnl f: kpt on: nrst fin* **13/2**

0543 **6** *5* **Chookie Royale**[7] 3335 5-8-7 **81**.....................................(b) JasonHart(5) 8 70
(Keith Dalgleish) *dwlt and t.k.h in rr: hdwy on outer to chse ldrs after 3f: rdn 2f out: drvn and wknd fnl f* **3/1**[2]

0352 **7** *14* **King Of Jazz (IRE)**[26] 2725 5-8-13 **87**...................... ThomasBrown(5) 1 38
(Michael Bell) *trckd ldrs: effrt 2f out: sn rdn whn sddle slipped: eased over 1f out* **2/1**[1]

0-40 **8** *25* **Outpost (IRE)**[58] 1796 5-8-3 **72**... PaulQuinn 7
(Alan Bailey) *led: hdd after 2f and sn rdn along: lost pl and bhd fr 1/2-way* **40/1**

1m 22.99s (-1.51) **Going Correction** -0.025s/f (Good) **8** Ran SP% **118.5**
Speed ratings (Par 107): **107,106,106,105,105 99,83,54**
toteswingers 1&2 £23.90, 1&3 £7.30, 2&3 £2.50 CSF £113.21 CT £467.04 TOTE £8.40: £2.40, £3.50, £1.80; EX 72.00 Trifecta £1122.30 Pool: £1,907.47 - 1.27 winning units..
Owner Mr & Mrs H Nensey, Saif Nensey **Bred** Chippenham Lodge Stud Ltd **Trained** Thirkleby, N Yorks
■ Stewards' Enquiry : Jordan Nason two-day ban: use of whip (7-8 July)

FOCUS
Not many of these came here at the top of their game and their was a compressed finish. The winner is rated up a length on this year's form.

3591 TEC4M BUILDING THE FUTURE H'CAP 5f
3:55 (3:56) (Class 4) (0-85,82) 3-Y-0 **£5,175** (£1,540; £769; £384) **Stalls** Centre

Form RPR

2313 **1** **Tumblewind**[17] 2987 3-8-12 **78**.................................. GeorgeChaloner(5) 8 89
(Richard Whitaker) *hld up towards rr: swtchd rt to outer and gd hdwy 2f out: rdn to ld over 1f out: kpt on wl* **4/1**[3]

-203 **2** *¾* **Almalekiah (IRE)**[17] 2983 3-8-10 **71**.......................... MichaelO'Connell 1 79
(J S Moore) *wnt rt and hmpd s: sn trcking ldrs on outer: effrt 2f out: sn chal and ev ch: drvn and edgd rt ins fnl f: no ex* **8/1**

0-05 **3** *3* **Mitchell**[9] 3234 3-8-9 **70**..(b[1]) BarryMcHugh 2 67
(David Thompson) *hmpd s and bhd: hdwy 1/2-way: rdn over 1f out: n.m.r and swtchd lft ins fnl f: kpt on* **25/1**

5203 **4** *½* **Boxing Shadows**[7] 3320 3-8-12 **73**.............................. RussKennemore 9 68
(Bryan Smart) *cl up: rdn 2f out and ev ch tl drvn and wknd ent fnl f* **8/1**

0502 **5** *1 ¾* **Bapak Sayang (USA)**[14] 3097 3-9-7 **82**......................... FrederikTylicki 6 71
(Kevin Ryan) *led: rdn along 2f out: hdd and drvn over 1f out: wknd fnl f* **5/2**[1]

6-00 **6** *1 ¼* **Blue Lotus (IRE)**[38] 2371 3-8-13 **74**........................... DuranFentiman 4 59
(Tim Easterby) *hld up: sme hdwy 2f out: sn rdn and no imp* **16/1**

0-60 **7** *nk* **Lady Poppy**[8] 3299 3-9-0 **75**.. PJMcDonald 3 59
(George Moore) *chsd ldrs: rdn along 2f out: sn wknd* **20/1**

-236 **8** *1* **Angus Og**[26] 2708 3-9-1 **81**..(e) ThomasBrown(5) 5 61
(Mrs K Burke) *trckd ldrs: pushed along 2f out: n.m.r and wknd ent fnl f* **11/4**[2]

-160 **9** *nk* **Bogsnog (IRE)**[14] 3104 3-9-3 **78**... MickyFenton 7 57
(Kristin Stubbs) *cl up: rdn along over 2f out: sn wknd* **14/1**

57.81s (-0.79) **Going Correction** -0.025s/f (Good) **9** Ran SP% **118.6**
Speed ratings (Par 101): **105,103,99,98,95 93,92,91,90**
toteswingers 1&2 £6.50, 1&3 £23.50, 2&3 £23.50 CSF £37.03 CT £721.51 TOTE £7.30: £2.50, £3.00, £9.90; EX 31.30 Trifecta £342.30 Pool: £2,076.20 - 4.54 winning units..
Owner Nice Day Out Partnership **Bred** Hellwood Stud Farm **Trained** Scarcroft, W Yorks

FOCUS
Reasonable handicap form. The winner continues to progress.

3592 LITCHFIELD GROUP SHEERFRAME CLAIMING STKS 7f
4:30 (4:32) (Class 5) 3-Y-0+ **£2,587** (£770; £384; £192) **Stalls** Centre

Form RPR

0001 **1** **All Or Nothin (IRE)**[25] 2752 4-9-5 80....................(v[1]) MichaelO'Connell 5 68
(John Quinn) *trckd ldr: cl up 3f out: led wl over 1f out: rdn and edgd rt ins fnl f: sn drvn and edgd lft and kpt on* **6/4**[1]

6-50 **2** *½* **My New Angel (IRE)**[109] 890 4-8-10 41.................... DuranFentiman 3 58
(Jason Ward) *in rr: hdwy over 2f out: rdn to chse ldrs over 1f out: styng on whn n.m.r and swtchd lft ins fnl f: kpt on wl towards fin* **33/1**

3 **3** *1 ¾* **Dual Mac**[10] 3191 6-9-11 0.. FrederikTylicki 4 68
(Neville Bycroft) *trckd ldng pair: rdn along 2f out: drvn and one pce fnl f* **10/1**

624 **4** *½* **Chookie Avon**[10] 3200 6-8-13 76............................(p) GeorginaBaxter(7) 9 62
(Keith Dalgleish) *trckd ldrs on outer: hdwy over 2f out: chal over 1f out and ev ch: rdn and wknd fnl f* **9/4**[2]

00-0 **5** *4 ½* **Abraham Monro**[25] 2756 3-7-13 54................................ RowanScott(7) 6 42
(Ann Duffield) *in tch: rdn along over 2f out: sn one pce* **20/1**

502/ **6** *¾* **King Of Dixie (USA)**[646] 6088 9-9-3 87............................ PJMcDonald 8 45
(Ruth Carr) *led: rdn along over 2f out: hdd wl over 1f out: sn wknd* **11/4**[3]

0-0 **7** *15* **Fairlie Dinkum**[10] 3195 5-8-7 54.................................... DeclanCannon(3) 2
(Andrew Crook) *chsd ldrs: rdn along 1/2-way: sn wknd and bhd* **40/1**

1m 24.93s (0.43) **Going Correction** -0.025s/f (Good)
WFA 3 from 4yo+ 9lb **7** Ran SP% **116.7**
Speed ratings (Par 103): **96,95,93,92,87 86,69**
toteswingers 1&2 £7.90, 1&3 £3.40, 2&3 £7.00 CSF £56.53 TOTE £2.10: £1.80, £8.00; EX 29.10 Trifecta £144.40 Pool: £2,257.77 - 11.72 winning units..
Owner Ross Harmon **Bred** Ballyhane Stud **Trained** Settrington, N Yorks

FOCUS
A weak claimer and shaky form. The pace collapsed and the winner scraped home.

3593 CAPTURE LE COEUR PHOTOGRAPHY MEDIAN AUCTION MAIDEN STKS 6f
5:05 (5:05) (Class 5) 3-5-Y-0 **£2,587** (£770; £384; £192) **Stalls** Centre

Form RPR

-322 **1** **Gold Beau (FR)**[19] 2916 3-9-5 66..................................(p) MickyFenton 8 70
(Kristin Stubbs) *mde all: jnd 2f out and sn rdn: drvn and edgd lft ins fnl f: kpt on wl towards fin* **15/8**[1]

24 **2** *½* **Adiator**[24] 2765 5-9-7 0.. FrederikTylicki 3 65
(Neville Bycroft) *trckd ldng pair: cl up after 2f: chal over 1f out: sn rdn and ev ch tl drvn and no ex wl ins fnl f* **15/8**[1]

3 *4 ½* **Dennis** 3-9-0 0.. DarylByrne(5) 7 54
(Tim Easterby) *dwlt: sn trcking ldrs: hdwy on outer 1/2-way: rdn 2f out and ev ch tl drvn and one pce ins fnl f* **12/1**[3]

2 **4** *5* **Idle Warrior**[21] 2861 3-9-5 0.. BarryMcHugh 1 38
(Richard Fahey) *hld up in rr: hdwy over 2f out: rdn to chse ldrs over 1f out: sn no imp* **3/1**[2]

5 *3 ¼* **Time For Crabbies (IRE)** 3-9-2 0............................ MarkCoumbe(3) 6 28
(Lisa Williamson) *dwlt: sn trcking ldrs: rdn along over 2f out: wknd over 1f out* **22/1**

60-6 **6** *4 ½* **Benidorm**[29] 2634 5-9-7 46...(v) AdamCarter(5) 5 11
(Neville Bycroft) *cl up: rdn along 1/2-way: wknd over 2f out* **33/1**

4-30 **7** *2 ¼* **Queen's Princess**[25] 2757 5-9-2 46.....................(p) GeorgeChaloner(5) 2
(Neville Bycroft) *chsd ldrs: rdn along 1/2-way: sn wknd* **20/1**

1m 11.51s (-0.29) **Going Correction** -0.025s/f (Good)
WFA 3 from 4yo+ 7lb **7** Ran SP% **114.3**
Speed ratings (Par 103): **100,99,93,86,82 76,73**
toteswingers 1&2 £1.10, 1&3 £17.70, 2&3 £17.00 CSF £5.47 TOTE £3.00: £2.00, £1.70; EX 5.10 Trifecta £35.60 Pool: £887.29 - 18.66 winning units..
Owner D Arundale **Bred** Haras Du Quesnay **Trained** Norton, N Yorks

FOCUS
A weak maiden, rated around the winner.

3594 LADIES AND GENTS EVENING, 24TH AUGUST H'CAP 5f
5:40 (5:45) (Class 6) (0-60,62) 3-Y-0 **£2,045** (£603; £302) **Stalls** Centre

Form RPR

1506 **1** **Lexington Place**[21] 2888 3-9-7 **60**.............................. MichaelO'Connell 3 67
(David O'Meara) *t.k.h early: trckd ldrs: hdwy 1/2-way: cl up wl over 1f out: rdn to ld and edgd lft ins fnl f: kpt on* **11/4**[1]

2000 **2** *½* **Megaleka**[18] 2962 3-8-12 **51**... FrederikTylicki 4 56
(Alan Bailey) *led: rdn along over 1f out: drvn and hdd ins fnl f: kpt on u.p* **20/1**

2341 **3** *½* **Confidential Creek**[17] 2996 3-8-10 **56**..................(p) JacobButterfield(7) 1 59
(Ollie Pears) *hld up towards rr: hdwy 2f out: rdn to chse ldrs over 1f out: much room whn hit in face by opponents whip last 100yds: no ex towards fin* **7/2**[2]

6633 **4** *¾* **Perfect Words (IRE)**[10] 3198 3-9-4 **62**......................(p) DeclanBates(5) 7 63
(Marjorie Fife) *trckd ldrs: effrt 2f out: sn rdn and one pce fnl f* **7/1**

40-5 **5** *¾* **Cymeriad**[7] 3323 3-8-13 **52**...(p) MickyFenton 10 50
(Michael Easterby) *hmpd s and towards rr: pushed along on outer and hdwy 1/2-way: rdn wl over 1f out: kpt on fnl f: nrst fin* **22/1**

0006 **6** *nk* **Moss The Boss (IRE)**[13] 3134 3-8-4 **46** oh1.............. DeclanCannon(3) 6 43
(Paul Midgley) *hld up in rr: hdwy 2f out: rdn over 1f out: kpt on fnl f: nrst fin* **33/1**

1500 **7** *1 ¼* **Windforpower (IRE)**[8] 3283 3-8-12 **58** ow1..................... JoshCrane(7) 8 50
(Tracy Waggott) *a towards rr* **20/1**

3322 **8** *2 ¼* **Chloe's Dream (IRE)**[13] 3134 3-9-7 **60**.........................(p) PJMcDonald 9 44
(Ann Duffield) *wnt rt s: cl up: rdn along over 2f out: sn wknd* **4/1**[3]

0043 **9** *1 ½* **Queen Flush (IRE)**[14] 3086 3-9-4 **57**............................(p) BarryMcHugh 2 36
(David Nicholls) *cl up: rdn along over 2f out: sn wknd* **8/1**

-642 **10** *4* **Only For You**[14] 3091 3-8-12 **56**.................................. ThomasBrown(5) 5 20
(Alan Brown) *midfield: n.m.r 1/2-way: sn rdn along and wknd* **12/1**

58.46s (-0.14) **Going Correction** -0.025s/f (Good) **10** Ran SP% **117.0**
Speed ratings (Par 97): **100,99,98,97,96 95,93,89,87,81**
toteswingers 1&2 £17.70, 1&3 £3.00, 2&3 £17.70 CSF £63.97 CT £188.56 TOTE £4.00: £1.80, £5.60, £2.00; EX 58.70 Trifecta £386.10 Pool: £1,427.13 - 2.77 winning units..
Owner Middleham Park Racing XXXI **Bred** Christopher & Annabelle Mason **Trained** Nawton, N Yorks

FOCUS
A moderate handicap. The well backed winner could have been rated upto 9lb higher.

3595 TEESSIDE HOSPICE FASHION SHOW H'CAP (DIV II) 1m 6f 19y
6:10 (6:11) (Class 6) (0-65,62) 4-Y-0+ **£1,940** (£577; £288; £144) **Stalls** Low

Form RPR

/525 **1** **Spiekeroog**[14] 3089 7-9-7 **62**..................................[1] MichaelO'Connell 11 71
(David O'Meara) *hld up in rr: hdwy 1/2-way: pushed along to chse ldrs 4f out: rdn over 2f out: led 1 1/2f out: drvn ins fnl f: jst hld on* **9/2**[2]

0651 **2** *shd* **Petella**[6] 3363 7-8-7 **55**..(p) JacobButterfield(7) 3 63
(George Moore) *in tch on inner: lost pl and towards rr 1/2-way: hdwy on inner over 4f out: swtchd rt to outer and rdn over 2f out: styd on wl fr over 1f out: drvn to chal ins fnl f: edgd lft and no ex nr line* **9/4**[1]

6263 **3** *1 ¾* **Blue Top**[17] 2986 4-8-11 **52**.. DuranFentiman 4 58
(Tim Walford) *trckd ldrs on inner: hdwy 4f out: swtchd rt and effrt to chal 2f out: sn rdn and ev ch tl drvn and one pce ins fnl f* **13/2**[3]

6030 **4** *5* **Light The City (IRE)**[9] 3231 6-8-13 **54**............................ MickyFenton 2 53
(Ruth Carr) *led 3f: cl up tl led again again over 7f out: hdd over 6f out: trckd ldr: hdwy and cl up 3f out: rdn to ld briefly 2f out: sn hdd and drvn: wknd ent fnl f* **18/1**

66-5 **5** *2* **Swift Encounter (IRE)**[18] 2961 4-9-5 **60**......................... PJMcDonald 6 56
(Ann Duffield) *trckd ldrs: hdwy 4f out: rdn along over 2f out: drvn wl over 1f out and sn wknd* **8/1**

06-5 **6** *nk* **Dimashq**[26] 2721 11-8-4 **45**.. AndrewMullen 12 40
(Richard Guest) *hld up: hdwy after 3f: sn trcking ldrs: led over 6f out: rdn and qckned over 3f out: hdd 2f out: sn drvn and grad wknd* **25/1**

0-54 **7** *9* **Uncut Stone (IRE)**17 2975 5-8-6 52....................(p) GeorgeChaloner(5) 10 35
(Peter Niven) *hld up: a bhd* **12/1**

24/3 **8** *9* **Miss Mysterious (FR)**26 2721 5-8-4 48.................... DeclanCannon(3) 9 18
(Philip Kirby) *cl up: rdn along and lost pl over 4f out: sn bhd: fin lame* **8/1**

0006 **9** *4* **Rolen Sly**17 2986 4-8-4 45.. PaulQuinn 1 10
(Brian Rothwell) *a bhd* **66/1**

-004 **10** *1* **Shirls Son Sam**21 2887 5-8-6 47.................................. BarryMcHugh 5 10
(Chris Fairhurst) *in tch: pushed along over 4f out: rdn wl over 3f out: sxoon wknd* **7/1**

0-00 **11** *44* **Roc Fort**22 2833 4-7-13 47 ow2.................................. GemmaTutty(7) 8
(James Moffatt) *midfie ld pulling hrd: sddle slipped and rapid hdwy to ld after 4f: hdd over 7f out: wknd over 4f out: sn bhd and eased* **66/1**

600- **12** *4 ½* **Hal Of A Lover**317 5022 5-8-3 47 ow2................................ BillyCray(3) 7
(Lisa Williamson) *a towards rr* **66/1**

3m 3.18s (-1.52) **Going Correction** -0.025s/f (Good) **12** Ran SP% **118.3**
Speed ratings (Par 101): **103,102,101,99,97 97,92,87,85,84 59,56**
toteswingers 1&2 £1.70, 1&3 £13.70, 2&3 £6.30 CSF £14.69 CT £64.97 TOTE £5.40: £1.10, £1.60, £3.10; EX 21.70 Trifecta £568.20 Part won. Pool: £757.66 - 0.42 winning units..
Owner G Schoeningh **Bred** M J Dawson **Trained** Nawton, N Yorks

FOCUS
Modest form, slightly weaker than division I. The winner's best effort since 2011.
T/Plt: £130.90 to a £1 stake. Pool: £64,212.47 - 357.97 winning units T/Qpdt: £34.20 to a £1 stake. Pool: £2,811.51 - 60.71 winning units JR

3596 - 3598a (Foreign Racing) - See Raceform Interactive

2851 DOWN ROYAL (R-H)
Saturday, June 22

OFFICIAL GOING: Good (good to yielding in places on round course)

3599a MAGNERS ULSTER DERBY (PREMIER H'CAP) 1m 4f 190y
4:00 (4:05) 3-Y-O+

£48,780 (£15,447; £7,317; £2,439; £1,626; £813)

RPR

1 **Sir Ector (USA)**22 2201 6-9-3 91......................................(b) ChrisHayes 7 100+
(J J Lambe, Ire) *chsd ldrs in 5th: t.k.h: 6th 1/2-way: clsd on outer fr 2f out to chal in 2nd: led 1f out and drvn clr towards fin* **14/1**

2 *2 ½* **Maggie Dalton (IRE)**13 3143 4-8-12 89.................. RonanWhelan(3) 12 94
(J S Bolger, Ire) *hld up in mid-div: clsr in 7th 1/2-way: wnt 4th 4f out and sn hdwy to almost get on terms: sn rdn and no imp on wnr in 3rd ins fnl f: kpt on u.p into 2nd fnl 50yds* **7/2**1

3 *½* **Scatter Dice (IRE)**10 3208 4-9-2 90...................................... FMBerry 11 94
(Mark Johnston) *led: narrow advantage 1/2-way: strly pressed fr 3f out: hdd 1f out and sn no ex u.p: dropped to 3rd fnl 50yds* **7/1**3

4 *1 ¾* **Buy Back Bob (IRE)**217 7040 6-8-13 87.................. SeamieHeffernan 10 88
(A J Martin, Ire) *in tch: rdn in 6th ent fnl f and sn wnt 4th: no imp on principals towards fin: kpt on same pce* **12/1**

5 *1 ¼* **Alhellal (IRE)**11 3184 7-8-12 86.............................. DeclanMcDonogh 2 86
(M Phelan, Ire) *chsd ldrs: cl 3rd 1/2-way: wnt 2nd 4f out and rdn 2f out and sn lost pl: kpt on same pce in 5th ins fnl f* **9/2**2

6 *¾* **Bayan (IRE)**26 1632 4-8-7 81..(t) DannyGrant 13 79
(Gordon Elliott, Ire) *in tch: 9th 1/2-way: rdn and n.m.r bhd horses over 1f out: kpt on wl towards fin into nvr nrr 6th cl home* **14/1**

7 *½* **Midnight Game**57 5980 6-9-12 100...................................... PatSmullen 6 98
(W P Mullins, Ire) *cl up: settled bhd ldrs in 3rd: rdn over 2f out and sn no imp in 6th ent fnl f: dropped to 7th cl home* **8/1**

8 *½* **Aladdins Cave**27 2686 9-9-5 93......................................(p) GaryCarroll 14 90
(C A Murphy, Ire) *in tch: 5th 1/2-way: rdn 2f out and sn no imp: one pce ins fnl f* **8/1**

9 *½* **Paddy The Celeb (IRE)**27 2686 7-9-7 95......................(p) ShaneFoley 9 91
(M Halford, Ire) *towards rr: tk clsr order in 8th 1/2-way: rdn and no ex ent fnl f: kpt on one pce* **7/1**3

10 *1 ¼* **Cry For The Moon (USA)**24 7584 7-8-10 84.......................... WJLee 8 78
(J H Culloty, Ire) *in rr of mid-div: 12th 1/2-way: rdn and no imp fr 2f out: kpt on one pce* **14/1**

11 *nk* **Macbeth (IRE)**13 3142 4-9-3 98......................................(v) ConnorKing(7) 4 92
(K J Condon, Ire) *towards rr: 13th 1/2-way: rdn and no imp fr 3f out* **25/1**

12 *11* **Muck 'N' Brass (IRE)**11 3184 4-9-0 88..............................(tp) BenCurtis 5 65
(J Larkin, Ire) *dwlt and racd towards rr: last 1/2-way: rdn and no imp fr 3f out* **33/1**

13 *2 ¾* **Hot Prospect**11 3184 6-8-13 94.................................. LiamMcKenna(7) 3 67
(J J Lambe, Ire) *towards rr: clsr in 10th 1/2-way: pushed along fr 4f out and sn no imp: wknd fnl 2f* **33/1**

14 *62* **Rich Coast**27 2686 5-9-1 96...1 LukeDempsey(7) 1
(J P Murtagh, Ire) *trckd ldr: cl 2nd 1/2-way: rdn and wknd qckly fr 4f out: completely t.o* **20/1**

2m 47.41s (167.41) **14** Ran SP% **129.8**
CSF £64.99 CT £394.46 TOTE £20.40: £5.00, £1.70, £2.30; DF 74.10.
Owner Dorightlys Syndicate **Bred** George Strawbridge Jnr **Trained** Kilmore, Co Armagh

FOCUS
With an increased prize pool of 100,000, it was hardly surprising that a maximum field showed up. The early gallop was generous and there didn't appear to be any hard-luck stories. The winner was much the best, and the standard is set by the third, fifth, eighth and ninth.

3600 - 3603a (Foreign Racing) - See Raceform Interactive

2910 DUSSELDORF (R-H)
Saturday, June 22

OFFICIAL GOING: Turf: good

3604a BMW PREIS DUSSELDORF (LISTED RACE) (3YO FILLIES) (TURF) 1m 2f 110y
4:10 (12:00) 3-Y-O **£9,756** (£3,577; £1,951; £975)

RPR

1 **Duchess Lemonade** 3-9-0 0.. AStarke 9 97
(P Harley, Germany) **6/1**2

2 *1* **Daytona Bay** 3-9-0 0..................................... LennartHammer-Hansen 4 95
(Ferdinand J Leve, Germany) **13/10**1

3 *nk* **Penelopa**20 2910 3-9-2 0.. APietsch 8 96
(M G Mintchev, Germany) **15/2**

4 *1 ¾* **Viletta (GER)**42 3-9-2 0.. MircoDemuro 1 93
(J Hirschberger, Germany) **116/10**

5 *1* **Savanna La Mar (USA)**301 5571 3-9-0 0.................... J-PGuillambert 10 89
(Sir Mark Prescott Bt) *got across fr wdst draw and trckd ldr on outer: rdn and ev ch on turn into st: outpcd by ldrs ins fnl 2f: styd on* **41/5**

6 *1 ¼* **La Sabara**230 7588 3-9-0 0.. EPedroza 2 87
(A Wohler, Germany) **141/10**

7 *1* **Betty Lou (GER)** 3-9-0 0... DPorcu 5 85
(Markus Klug, Germany) **202/10**

8 *nse* **Magali (GER)** 3-9-0 0.. SHellyn 3 85
(W Giedt, Germany) **113/10**

9 *½* **Aspidistra (GER)** 3-9-0 0.. RPiechulek 6 84
(W Giedt, Germany) **74/10**

10 *3 ½* **Hey Little Gorl (GER)**20 2905 3-9-0 0.............................. AHelfenbein 7 77
(Markus Klug, Germany) **69/10**3

2m 11.9s (131.90) **10** Ran SP% **132.4**
WIN (incl. 10 euro stake): 70. PLACES: 15, 13, 17. SF: 164.
Owner Gestut Brummerhof **Bred** Mrs F Delage & Earl Du Champ Gignoux **Trained** Germany

3064 PONTEFRACT (L-H)
Sunday, June 23

OFFICIAL GOING: Good (good to firm in places; 7.8)
False rail in place from 6f to Winning Post which adding 16yds to all race distances.
Wind: Fresh; half behind Weather: Changeable; very breezy

3605 TOTEPLACEPOT ON ALL UK MEETINGS / EBF MAIDEN FILLIES' STKS 6f
2:10 (2:11) (Class 5) 2-Y-O **£4,528** (£1,347; £673; £336) **Stalls** Low

Form RPR

02 **1** **Dutch Courage**37 2419 2-9-0 0.. TonyHamilton 5 86
(Richard Fahey) *trckd ldr: led over 1f out: styd on wl* **13/8**2

352 **2** *1 ¾* **Augusta Ada**26 2751 2-9-0 0.. PaulMulrennan 8 81
(Ollie Pears) *chsd ldrs: wnt 2nd appr fnl f: styd on same pce* **8/1**3

4 **3** *1 ¾* **Sunrise Star**16 3057 2-9-0 0.. TomQueally 9 76
(Lady Cecil) *in rr-div: hdwy over 2f out: 3rd appr fnl f: kpt on same pce* **6/5**1

4 *10* **Flighty Peaches (IRE)** 2-9-0 0...................................... RichardHughes 6 46
(Rebecca Curtis) *led: hdd over 1f out: sn wknd* **12/1**

00 **5** *1 ¾* **Madame Mirasol (IRE)**30 2625 2-8-7 0.............................. KevinStott(7) 1 40+
(Kevin Ryan) *in tch: outpcd 2f out* **66/1**

6 *1 ¾* **Moving Waves (IRE)** 2-9-0 0... ShaneKelly 3 35
(Ollie Pears) *s.s: sme hdwy over 1f out: nvr on terms* **40/1**

45 **7** *shd* **Shelley's Choice (IRE)**62 1718 2-9-0 0........................ RichardKingscote 7 35
(Tom Dascombe) *s.i.s: in rr: sme hdwy over 1f out: nvr a factor* **33/1**

8 *nk* **L'Artiste (IRE)** 2-9-0 0.. MickyFenton 11 34
(John Quinn) *chsd ldrs: wknd over 1f out* **50/1**

0 **9** *2 ¼* **Notts So Blue**16 3064 2-9-0 0...................................... DuranFentiman 13 27
(Shaun Harris) *in tch: lost pl after 2f* **100/1**

10 *1 ¾* **Lazy Sioux** 2-9-0 0.. RobbieFitzpatrick 10 22
(Richard Guest) *mid-div: drvn and outpcd over 2f out: sn wknd* **100/1**

11 *26* **Chantrea (IRE)** 2-9-0 0... PatCosgrave 14
(Lady Cecil) *in tch on outer: lost pl over 3f out: bhd whn heavily eased clsng stages: t.o* **16/1**

1m 18.34s (1.44) **Going Correction** +0.20s/f (Good) **11** Ran SP% **119.0**
Speed ratings (Par 90): **98,95,93,80,77 75,75,74,71,69 34**
toteswingers 1&2 £2.90, 1&3 £1.30, 2&3 £2.70 CSF £15.00 TOTE £1.90: £1.10, £1.90, £1.10; EX 16.30 Trifecta £37.40 Pool: £3,743.01 - 75.05 winning units..
Owner Cheveley Park Stud **Bred** Barton Bloodstock **Trained** Musley Bank, N Yorks

FOCUS
There was a false rail in place from the 6f bend to the winning post, adding 16yds to all races distances, and there was 1.5mm of overnight rain. A fair fillies' maiden and three of them finished clear. Improved form from the winner.

3606 BET TOTEPOOL ON ALL IRISH RACING MAIDEN STKS (THE SUNDAY £5K BONUS RACE) 1m 4f 8y
2:40 (2:42) (Class 5) 3-Y-O **£4,528** (£1,347; £673; £336) **Stalls** Low

Form RPR

6-2 **1** **Dare To Achieve**36 2442 3-9-5 0..................................... RichardHughes 3 96+
(William Haggas) *hld up in last: t.k.h early: smooth hdwy to trck ldrs 4f out: shkn up to ld over 1f out: nudged clr: v easily* **1/4**1

3 **2** *6* **Astorgs Galaxy**24 2803 3-9-0 0.................................. SilvestreDeSousa 2 72
(Sir Michael Stoute) *chsd ldrs: pushed along 5f out: 3rd 2f out: kpt on to take 2nd last 100yds* **11/1**3

232 **3** *2 ¾* **The Welsh Wizard (IRE)**75 1443 3-9-5 80........................ GrahamLee 1 73
(Charles Hills) *led 3f: drvn over 4f out: led over 2f out: hdd over 1f out: wknd last 100yds* **5/1**2

4 *11* **Diamonds A Dancing** 3-9-5 0................................. RichardKingscote 5 55
(Rebecca Curtis) *trckd ldrs: pushed along over 3f out: lost pl over 1f out* **66/1**

65 **5** *16* **Near Time**17 3021 3-9-0 0... JimmyFortune 6 38
(Andrew Balding) *w ldr: t.k.h: led after 3f: hdd over 2f out: lost pl wl over 1f out: sn bhd* **20/1**

2m 43.24s (2.44) **Going Correction** +0.20s/f (Good) **5** Ran SP% **111.3**
Speed ratings (Par 99): **99,95,93,85,75**
CSF £4.26 TOTE £1.20: £1.10, £3.00; EX 4.20 Trifecta £11.30 Pool: £2,863.48 - 189.54 winning units..
Owner B Kantor & M Jooste **Bred** Hascombe & Valiant Stud & Amarvilas Bstk **Trained** Newmarket, Suffolk

FOCUS
An interesting maiden, but the race somewhat fell apart and it was easy for the potentially smart winner. It's hard form to pin down.

3607 TOTEQUADPOT FOUR PLACES IN FOUR RACES H'CAP 1m 2f 6y
3:10 (3:10) (Class 3) (0-90,88) 3-Y-O+ **£12,938** (£3,850; £1,924; £962) **Stalls** Low

Form RPR

3253 **1** **Haylaman (IRE)**15 3094 5-9-13 87.............................. SilvestreDeSousa 6 97
(David Simcock) *in rr: drvn 4f out: hdwy to chse ldr 2f out: led jst ins fnl f: drvn clr* **7/2**2

0-34 **2** *7* **Gabrial The Great (IRE)**15 3115 4-10-0 88........................ GrahamLee 4 84+
(Luca Cumani) *hld up: hdwy to trck ldng pair over 5f out: led on bit over 2f out: hdd jst ins fnl f: no ex* **2/1**1

4/4- **3** *8* **Almagest**[323] 4821 5-9-12 **86**.. DanielTudhope 2 66
(David O'Meara) *hld up in rr: hdwy 3f out: hung lft and tk 3rd last 100yds* **9/1**

0-41 **4** *1 ½* **Carthaginian (IRE)**[22] 2885 4-9-3 **77**.............................. TonyHamilton 7 54
(Richard Fahey) *in rr: drvn over 3f out: sn outpcd: kpt on over 1f out: nvr a threat* **11/2**

2146 **5** *½* **Love Marmalade (IRE)**[22] 2879 3-8-4 **76**.......................... JoeFanning 1 52
(Mark Johnston) *chsd ldng pair: drvn 3f out: one pce* **4/1**[3]

2400 **6** *15* **Aquilonius (IRE)**[22] 2867 4-9-1 **75**..........................(t) RichardKingscote 3 35
(Stuart Williams) *set str pce: hdd over 2f out: sn wknd and bhd* **11/1**

0050 **7** *75* **Super Say (IRE)**[11] 3204 7-9-8 **82**...............................(t) AndrewMullen 8
(Michael Appleby) *w ldr: drvn 4f out: sn wknd and bhd: t.o 2f out: virtually p.u* **22/1**

2m 13.79s (0.09) **Going Correction** +0.20s/f (Good)
WFA 3 from 4yo+ 12lb **7** Ran SP% **113.6**
Speed ratings (Par 107): **107,101,95,93,93 81,21**
toteswingers 1&2 £2.60, 1&3 £5.00, 2&3 £5.20 CSF £10.80 CT £55.49 TOTE £4.80: £1.90, £1.70; EX 12.50 Trifecta £55.20 Pool: £1,244.26 - 16.89 winning units..
Owner Dr Marwan Koukash **Bred** M Morrin **Trained** Newmarket, Suffolk

FOCUS
This form is worth little as Aquilonius and Super Say had no chance after taking each other on up front, and the favourite got there too soon. It's been rated a bit cautiously.

3608 TOTEPOOL PONTEFRACT CASTLE STKS (LISTED RACE) 1m 4f 8y
3:40 (3:40) (Class 1) 4-Y-0+
£22,684 (£8,600; £4,304; £2,144; £1,076; £540) **Stalls** Low

Form RPR
230- **1** **Brown Panther**[238] 7431 5-9-1 113........................... RichardKingscote 2 114
(Tom Dascombe) *hld up: sn trcking ldrs: 2nd over 3f out: drvn over 2f out: led over 1f out: styd on* **11/8**[2]

34 **2** *3 ½* **Souviens Toi**[15] 3100 4-8-13 102.. NeilCallan 6 106
(Marco Botti) *led: rdn over 2f out: hdd over 1f out: kpt on same pce* **11/1**[3]

3-3 **3** *9* **Between Us**[22] 2855 4-8-10 85.. ChrisCatlin 5 89
(Sir Mark Prescott Bt) *hld up in last: effrt over 4f out: rdn 3f out: kpt on and modest 4th 1f out: tk 3rd nr fin* **28/1**

5-32 **4** *½* **Main Sequence (USA)**[24] 2811 4-9-1 110......................(p) TedDurcan 1 93
(David Lanigan) *trckd ldrs: t.k.h: rdn over 2f out: fnd little: lost modest 3rd nr fin* **1/1**[1]

05/5 **5** *7* **Saptapadi (IRE)**[37] 2427 7-9-1 94.................................... BarryMcHugh 4 82
(Brian Ellison) *hld up toward rr: t.k.h: hdwy to trck ldrs over 4f out: rdn over 2f out: wknd over 1f out* **20/1**

0-00 **6** *45* **Ed De Gas**[37] 2407 4-9-1 95.. SilvestreDeSousa 3
(Rae Guest) *t.k.h: trckd ldrs: lost pl 3f out: sn bhd: t.o*

2m 39.71s (-1.09) **Going Correction** +0.20s/f (Good) **6** Ran SP% **111.1**
Speed ratings (Par 111): **111,108,102,102,97 67**
toteswingers 1&2 £1.10, 1&3 £1.40, 2&3 £4.50 CSF £14.89 TOTE £2.40: £1.20, £2.40; EX 12.00 Trifecta £49.60 Pool: £2,125.17 - 32.11 winning units..
Owner A Black & Owen Promotions Limited **Bred** Owen Promotions Ltd **Trained** Malpas, Cheshire

FOCUS
The winner returned as good as ever, though his task was eased by a poor show from the favourite.

3609 TOTEPOOL MOBILE PONTEFRACT CUP (H'CAP) 2m 1f 216y
4:10 (4:10) (Class 4) (0-85,85) 4-Y-0+ **£6,469** (£1,925; £962; £481) **Stalls** Low

Form RPR
00-0 **1** **Herostatus**[39] 2369 6-9-8 **83**................................... SilvestreDeSousa 8 91
(Jason Ward) *hld up in last: hdwy on outside over 3f out: drvn to chse ldrs over 2f out: led appr fnl f: edgd lft: forged clr* **10/1**

1-04 **2** *3 ½* **Nashville (IRE)**[15] 3089 4-8-6 **68**.................................(p) BarryMcHugh 6 72
(Richard Fahey) *trckd ldrs: led over 2f out: hdd over 1f out: kpt on same pce* **12/1**

0-03 **3** *2 ½* **Art History (IRE)**[149] 378 5-9-10 **85**.......................... DanielTudhope 9 86
(David O'Meara) *hld up in rr: hdwy over 3f out: chsng ldrs over 2f out: kpt on to take 3rd nr fin* **7/1**[3]

6406 **4** *½* **Eagle Rock (IRE)**[8] 3345 5-9-0 **75**.................................... MickyFenton 4 76
(Tom Tate) *trckd ldrs: t.k.h: chal 4f out: one pce over 1f out: tk 4th nr fin* **3/1**[1]

22/0 **5** *1 ¼* **Mubrook (USA)**[27] 2706 8-8-8 **69**..................................(b) TomEaves 5 68
(Brian Ellison) *led after 1f: drvn over 4f out: hdd over 2f out: wknd clsng stages* **12/1**

040- **6** *18* **Orsippus (USA)**[43] 7367 7-9-2 **77**...................................... NeilCallan 2 57
(Michael Smith) *chsd ldrs: drvn 4f out: lost pl over 2f out* **3/1**[1]

5043 **7** *3 ¾* **Tartan Jura**[18] 2990 5-8-10 **71**..(p) JoeFanning 3 47
(Mark Johnston) *in rr: drvn over 5f out: lost pl over 2f out* **5/1**[2]

0434 **8** *1* **Kayef (GER)**[8] 3328 6-8-8 **69**.. PaulMulrennan 1 43
(Michael Scudamore) *led 1f: trckd ldrs: wknd 2f out* **10/1**

4m 8.02s (11.82) **Going Correction** +0.20s/f (Good)
WFA 4 from 5yo+ 1lb **8** Ran SP% **112.7**
Speed ratings (Par 105): **81,79,78,78,77 69,67,67**
toteswingers 1&2 £10.30, 1&3 £8.20, 2&3 £7.90 CSF £116.23 CT £891.84 TOTE £10.00: £2.60, £2.00, £2.20; EX 110.20 Trifecta £1151.40 Pool: £2,016.07 - 1.31 winning units..
Owner R Naylor **Bred** Darley **Trained** Middleham, N Yorks

FOCUS
An ordinary staying handicap in which they didn't go too quickly. The winner was back to his best.

3610 TOTETRIFECTA FILLIES' H'CAP 1m 2f 6y
4:40 (4:40) (Class 4) (0-85,83) 3-Y-0+ **£6,469** (£1,925; £962; £481) **Stalls** Low

Form RPR
235 **1** **Huffoof (IRE)**[24] 2803 3-8-5 **72**...............................(b) SilvestreDeSousa 2 82
(Roger Varian) *mde virtually all: qcknd pce 4f out: drvn over 2f out: styd on wl fnl f* **15/2**

31-1 **2** *1 ½* **Kikonga**[33] 2546 3-9-1 **82**.. RichardHughes 3 89
(Luca Cumani) *hld up in rr: hdwy and handy 3rd 2f out: chsd wnr over 1f out: sn rdn: styd on same pce* **11/10**[1]

16-2 **3** *1 ¾* **Miss Cap Estel**[13] 3158 4-9-13 **82**................................... JimmyFortune 4 86
(Andrew Balding) *hld up in rr: stdy hdwy over 2f out: 3rd over 1f out: kpt on same pce* **11/2**[3]

-235 **4** *5* **Bobs Her Uncle**[19] 2956 4-8-9 **64**................................... TedDurcan 6 57
(James Bethell) *trckd ldrs: drvn over 2f out: wknd appr fnl f* **14/1**

-126 **5** *1* **Of Course Darling**[31] 2586 3-9-2 **83**................................ GrahamLee 5 74
(Ed Dunlop) *hld up in rr: effrt over 2f out: wknd appr fnl f* **12/1**

-133 **6** *2* **Ingleby Symphony (IRE)**[40] 2342 3-8-4 **71**................... BarryMcHugh 1 58
(Richard Fahey) *sn w wnr: drvn over 2f out: rdr dropped whip over 1f out: sn wknd* **4/1**[2]

2m 16.07s (2.37) **Going Correction** +0.20s/f (Good)
WFA 3 from 4yo 12lb **6** Ran SP% **109.1**
Speed ratings (Par 102): **98,96,95,91,90 89**
toteswingers 1&2 £2.20, 1&3 £2.90, 2&3 £1.90 CSF £15.44 TOTE £9.10: £3.30, £1.60; EX 18.80 Trifecta £70.90 Pool: £2,678.44 - 28.32 winning units..
Owner Sheikh Ahmed Al Maktoum **Bred** Darley **Trained** Newmarket, Suffolk

FOCUS
A fair fillies' handicap run at an ordinary pace. The form has been taken at face value.

3611 TOTEEXACTA ON ALL RACES H'CAP 6f
5:10 (5:13) (Class 5) (0-75,75) 3-Y-O **£2,518** (£2,518; £577; £288) **Stalls** Low

Form RPR
3400 **1** **Ayasha**[19] 2959 3-8-10 **64**.. RoystonFfrench 5 73
(Bryan Smart) *led: drvn over 2f out: edgd rt ins fnl f: jnd on line* **20/1**

3431 **1** *dht* **Teetotal (IRE)**[8] 3323 3-8-11 **65**............................. SilvestreDeSousa 4 74
(Nigel Tinkler) *in rr: hdwy over 2f out: swtchd outside over 1f out: chsd wnr and hung lft 1f out: styd on to dead-heat on line* **5/1**[3]

4043 **3** *9* **Deepest Blue**[19] 2959 3-8-6 **67**................................ LukeLeadbitter(7) 7 47
(Declan Carroll) *t.k.h: sn chsng ldrs on outside: hung rt over 2f out: chsd wnr over 1f out: fdd fnl f* **8/1**

0006 **4** *1 ¼* **Blue Clumber**[15] 3082 3-8-2 **56** oh4..........................(t) DuranFentiman 1 32
(Shaun Harris) *chsd ldrs: drvn over 2f out: fdd appr fnl f* **33/1**

1404 **5** *¾* **My Name Is Rio (IRE)**[15] 3104 3-9-4 **72**........................ TomEaves 8 46
(Michael Dods) *t.k.h on outer: stdd and swtchd lft after s: outpcd over 2f out: kpt on fnl f* **4/1**[2]

40-0 **6** *8* **Scentpastparadise**[18] 2987 3-9-7 **75**...........................(p) PJMcDonald 2 23
(Ann Duffield) *chsd ldrs: drvn over 2f out: lost pl over 1f out* **10/1**

5062 **7** *2* **Magical Rose (IRE)**[9] 3289 3-9-6 **74**...............................(p) NeilCallan 9 16
(Paul D'Arcy) *swvd rt s: sn chsng ldrs: drvn over 2f out: wknd over 1f out* **3/1**[1]

46-0 **8** *13* **Ingleby Royale**[26] 2737 3-8-12 **66**................................ TonyHamilton 6
(Richard Fahey) *chsd ldrs: t.k.h: lost pl 2f out: bhd whn eased clsng stages* **28/1**

1m 19.19s (2.29) **Going Correction** +0.20s/f (Good) **8** Ran SP% **93.0**
TRI27 Owner.
Owner Raybould & Scott **Bred** T Jones **Trained** Langton, N Yorks
■ Chasing Dreams was withdrawn (7-2, ref to ent stalls). Deduct 20p in the £ under R4.
■ Stewards' Enquiry : Royston Ffrench four-day ban: use of whip (7-10 July)
Silvestre De Sousa two-day ban: use of whip (7th-8th July)

FOCUS
A modest sprint handicap in which long-time leader Ayasha was joined on the line by Teetotal and the pair, who pulled a long way clear, couldn't be separated. Both posted personal bests.
T/Plt: £83.90 to a £1 stake. Pool: £90,314.83 - 785.25 winning units T/Qpdt: £41.70 to a £1 stake. Pool: £3,872.50 - 68.70 winning units WG

DORTMUND (R-H)
Sunday, June 23

OFFICIAL GOING: Turf: good

3612a GROSSER PREIS DER WIRTSCHAFT (GROUP 3) (3YO+) (TURF) 1m 165y
4:15 (12:00) 3-Y-0+
£26,016 (£8,943; £4,471; £2,439; £1,626; £1,219)

RPR
1 **Neatico (GER)**[24] 6-9-1 0.. AStarke 6 109
(P Schiergen, Germany) *trckd ldr: rdn to chal 2f out: r.o: grad wore down eventual runner-up and led ins fnl f: asserted cl home: shade cosily* **13/10**[1]

2 *1 ¼* **Empire Storm (GER)**[47] 2146 6-9-1 0.............................. EPedroza 7 106
(A Wohler, Germany) *led: rdn and strly pressed fr 2f out: r.o but grad worn down by eventual wnr and hdd ins fnl f: no ex and hld cl home* **89/10**

3 *1 ½* **Global Thrill**[45] 2202 4-9-5 0.................................... MircoDemuro 9 107
(J Hirschberger, Germany) *prom on outer: rdn 2f out: wnt 3rd over 1f out: chsd ldng pair thrght fnl f but no imp* **19/5**[2]

4 *¾* **Wasimah (GER)**[15] 4-8-11 0.. WPanov 5 97
(H J Groschel, Germany) *midfield in tch: rdn 2f out: sn outpcd by ldrs: swtchd lft and r.o to go 4th ins fnl f* **111/10**

5 *1 ¼* **Next Green (GER)**[43] 3-8-3 0.................................... StefanieHofer 2 97
(P Schiergen, Germany) *prom on inner: rdn and ev ch 2f out: outpcd by ldng pair over 1f out: kpt on but dropped to 5th ins fnl f* **145/10**

6 *¾* **Samba Brazil (GER)**[13] 3165 4-9-0 0............................ AndreaAtzeni 3 96
(A Wohler, Germany) *hld up in last: rdn 2f out: kpt on but nvr gng pce to chal* **155/10**

7 *nk* **Saratino (GER)**[28] 2696 3-8-6 0...................................(p) AndreBest 1 98
(Mario Hofer, Germany) *midfield on inner: rdn over 2f out: sn outpcd: kpt on wout threatening* **4/1**[3]

8 *1 ¼* **Combat Zone (IRE)**[24] 7-9-7 0.. NRichter 8 100
(Mario Hofer, Germany) *t.k.h: hld up in last pair on outer: rdn over 2f out: outpcd in last and btn ent fnl f: nvr a factor* **26/5**

1m 46.64s (106.64)
WFA 3 from 4yo+ 11lb **8** Ran SP% **131.3**
Win (incl. 10 euro stake): 23. PLACES: 11, 18, 14. SF: 161.
Owner Gestut Ittlingen **Bred** Gestut Hof Ittlingen **Trained** Germany

The Form Book Flat, Raceform Ltd, Compton, RG20 6NL.

3613 - (Foreign Racing) - See Raceform Interactive

[2644]SAINT-CLOUD (L-H)

Sunday, June 23

OFFICIAL GOING: Turf: soft

3614a ABU DHABI PRIX DE MALLERET (GROUP 2) (3YO FILLIES) (TURF) 1m 4f

1:50 (12:00) 3-Y-O **£60,975** (£24,390; £18,292; £12,195; £6,097)

RPR

1 **Pacific Rim (IRE)**[13] 3-8-11 0 UmbertoRispoli 8 114
(M Delzangles, France) *trckd ldr on outer: shkn up to chal 2f out: rdn to ld over 1f out: styd on strly ins fnl f and asserted: readily* **11/2**[2]

2 2 ½ **Chalnetta (FR)**[29] 2682 3-8-11 0 JulienAuge 1 110
(C Ferland, France) *sn led: hdd after 3f but remained prom on inner: rdn over 2f out: swtchd off rail and styd on to go 2nd cl home: nt pce of wnr* **18/1**

3 ¾ **Orion Love**[21] 2905 3-8-11 0 (p) FabriceVeron 7 109
(H-A Pantall, France) *t.k.h: prom early but sn restrained in midfield: allowed to stride on and led over 6f out: rdn 2f out: strly pressed and hdd over 1f out: outpcd by wnr ins fnl f: styd on but dropped to 3rd cl home* **14/1**

4 3 **Ferevia (IRE)**[28] 2693 3-8-11 0 OlivierPeslier 6 104+
(C Laffon-Parias, France) *hld up in last trio on outer: rdn over 2f out: hung lft u.p but wnt 4th ent fnl f: styd on under hands and heels but no imp on ldrs* **5/2**[1]

5 1 ¼ **The Lark**[23] 2842 3-8-11 0 JamieSpencer 5 102+
(Michael Bell) *hld up in last trio on inner: swtchd out and rdn over 2f out: styd on to go 5th cl home: nvr threatened* **5/2**[1]

6 nk **La Banderilla (FR)**[42] 2296 3-8-11 0 Francois-XavierBertras 3 102
(J Heloury, France) *midfield in tch on inner: rdn over 2f out: styd on but nt pce to chal: dropped to 6th cl home* **20/1**

7 2 **Parle Moi (IRE)**[28] 2693 3-8-11 0 ChristopheSoumillon 10 98
(P Bary, France) *dwlt: qckly rcvrd and sn prom on outer: led after 3f out tl hdd over 6f out: trckd ldr on inner: rdn over 2f out: no ex and btn ent fnl f: fdd* **7/1**[3]

8 snk **Santa Ponsa (FR)**[39] 2381 3-8-11 0 FranckBlondel 4 98
(F Rossi, France) *t.k.h: midfield on outer: rdn over 2f out: outpcd by ldrs but keeping on whn squeezed for room and lost momentum over 1f out: plugged on after but nt rcvr* **7/1**[3]

9 6 **Contradict**[31] 2586 3-8-11 0 RyanMoore 9 88
(Mick Channon) *restless in stalls and slow to s: dropped in and hld up in last: rdn over 2f out: outpcd and btn ent fnl f: nvr a factor* **25/1**

10 2 **Eleuthera (FR)**[21] 2905 3-8-11 0 EddyHardouin 2 85
(P Demercastel, France) *plld hrd: prom early but sn restrained in midfield: rdn over 2f out: no ex and btn over 1f out: fdd and dropped to last* **10/1**

2m 34.63s (-5.77) **Going Correction** -0.325s/f (Firm) **10** Ran SP% **127.2**
Speed ratings: **106,104,103,101,101 100,99,99,95,94**
WIN (incl. 1 euro stake): 7.10. PLACES: 2.90, 5.80, 4.00. DF: 62.80. SF: 69.50.
Owner Wildenstein Stables Limited **Bred** Dayton Investments Ltd **Trained** France

FOCUS
They didn't go much pace.

3615a GRAND PRIX DE SAINT-CLOUD (GROUP 1) (4YO+) (TURF) 1m 4f

2:55 (12:00) 4-Y-O+ **£162,601** (£65,040; £48,780; £32,520; £16,260)

RPR

1 **Novellist (IRE)**[42] 2294 4-9-2 0 RyanMoore 6 119
(A Wohler, Germany) *midfield in tch: hdwy through gap created as ldr rn wd over 3f out: rdn to ld over 2f out: styd on strly to maintain advantage ins fnl 1 1/2f: drvn out* **7/2**[2]

2 1 ¼ **Dunaden (FR)**[22] 2864 7-9-2 0 JamieSpencer 7 117
(M Delzangles, France) *midfield: rdn 3f out: hld in and nt clr run over 2f out: styd on steadily once in the clr: wnt 2nd ins fnl 100yds: chsd wnr cl home but no real imp* **6/1**[3]

3 1 **Haya Landa (FR)**[21] 2908 5-8-13 0 FranckBlondel 3 112
(Mme L Audon, France) *slow to stride and pushed along to rcvr: sn prom on inner: 3rd whn swtchd off rail and rdn to chse ldrs over 2f out: styd on but nt pce to chal* **20/1**

4 1 **Meleagros (IRE)**[46] 2184 4-9-2 0 AdrienFouassier 11 114+
(A Couetil, France) *pushed along in rr early: last 3f out: rdn over 2f out: styd on to take n.d 4th cl home* **33/1**

5 1 ¼ **Cirrus Des Aigles (FR)**[246] 7239 7-9-2 0 OlivierPeslier 1 112+
(Mme C Barande-Barbe, France) *trckd ldr on inner: led whn ldr rn wd over 3f out: rdn and hdd over 2f out: styd on tl no ex and btn ins fnl f: fdd and dropped to 5th cl home* **1/1**[1]

6 ½ **Pirika (IRE)**[21] 2908 5-8-13 0 Pierre-CharlesBoudot 2 108
(A Fabre, France) *hld up towards rr: rdn and barging match w eventual runner-up over 2f out: edgd lft u.p: styd on but nt pce to chal* **11/1**

7 1 ¾ **Pagera (FR)**[13] 3165 5-8-13 0 (p) FabriceVeron 5 105
(H-A Pantall, France) *dwlt and slow to stride: pushed along in detached last early: sn rcvrd and tacked on to rr of main body of field on inner: rdn over 2f out: styd on but nvr a factor* **33/1**

8 2 **Sediciosa (IRE)**[30] 2644 4-8-13 0 ChristopheSoumillon 10 102
(Y Barberot, France) *dwlt: taken across fr wd draw and settled in midfield on inner: rdn over 2f out: styd on tl no ex and btn ins fnl f: fdd and eased* **25/1**

9 10 **Dalkala (USA)**[38] 2397 4-8-13 0 Christophe-PatriceLemaire 8 86
(A De Royer-Dupre, France) *midfield on outer: smooth hdwy on to heels of ldrs on turn into st: sn rdn and fnd little: btn over 1f out: eased ins fnl f* **9/1**

10 dist **Joshua Tree (IRE)**[22] 2864 6-9-2 0 FrankieDettori 9
(Ed Dunlop) *trckd ldr on outer: forced out whn ldr rn wd over 3f out: rdn to rcvr: no ex 2f out: fdd and eased over 1f out: t.o* **16/1**

11 9 **Lateran Accord (IRE)**[35] 2492 4-9-2 0 SHellyn 4
(W Hickst, Germany) *drvn along and reminder to go forward early: sn led: hdd whn taken wd to create gap for eventual wnr and interfered w rival over 3f out: nvr put under any press and fdd: dropped to last and t.o* **100/1**

2m 31.12s (-9.28) **Going Correction** -0.325s/f (Firm) 11 Ran SP% **126.2**
Speed ratings: **117,116,115,114,114 113,112,111,104,**
WIN (incl. 1 euro stake): 5.40 (Novellist coupled with Lateran Accord). PLACES: 2.40, 2.00, 4.30. DF: 13.00. SF: 22.00.
Owner Dr Christoph Berglar **Bred** Christoph Berglar **Trained** Germany

FOCUS
Previous races on the card had suggested it was tough to come from well off the pace. The form is rated around the winner and sixth.

[3147]SAN SIRO (R-H)

Sunday, June 23

OFFICIAL GOING: Turf: good

3616a PREMIO MARIO INCISA DELLA ROCCHETTA (GROUP 3) (3YO (FILLIES) (TURF) 1m 2f

5:35 (12:00) 3-Y-O **£28,455** (£12,520; £6,829; £3,414)

RPR

1 **Licia (ITY)**[28] 2697 3-8-11 0 CristianDemuro 3 97
(S Botti, Italy) *prom in main gp bhd clr ldrs: stdy hdwy fr over 2 1/2f out: led 1 1/2f out: clr ent fnl f: pushed out: won easing down* **19/10**[1]

2 3 ¼ **Shirley's Kitten (USA)**[56] 1866 3-8-11 0 GBietolini 9 95
(Gianluca Bietolini, Italy) *w.w towards rr: midfield and shkn up over 3f out: 5th and styng on u.p passing 2f marker: r.o u.p fnl f to take 2nd cl home: no ch w wnr* **18/5**[3]

3 ½ **Mangiapregaama (ITY)**[28] 2697 3-8-11 0 DarioVargiu 8 94
(B Grizzetti, Italy) *towards rr: swtchd outside and prog 2 1/2f out: sn rdn: styng on but wandered u.p over 1f out: r.o fnl f: tk 3rd cl home: nvr on terms* **17/5**[2]

4 hd **Lucky Serena (IRE)**[49] 3-8-11 0 MEsposito 4 94
(Agostino Affe', Italy) *midfield: shkn up and hdwy over 3f out: 3rd and hrd rdn 1 1/2f out: styd on to go 2nd ins fnl f: no ex fnl 50yds: lost two pls cl home* **23/5**

5 2 ¾ **Road Tosky (IRE)**[28] 2697 3-8-11 0 SSulas 11 88
(E Botti, Italy) *towards rr: hdwy 2 1/2f out: styd on ins fnl f: nvr in contention* **27/1**

6 nk **Danspi** 3-8-11 0 PierantonioConvertino 2 88
(B Grizzetti, Italy) *prom in main gp bhd clr ldrs: rdn and no hdwy 2 1/2f out: plugged on at one pce tl wknd ins fnl f* **17/5**[2]

7 nk **Night Of Light (IRE)**[28] 2697 3-8-11 0 SDiana 7 87
(F Camici, Italy) *chsd ldr: wnt on after 1 1/2f: sn 10 l clr: 5 l advantage but rdn over 2f out: hdd 1 1/2f out: sn wknd* **185/10**

8 10 **Air Mail (IRE)**[28] 2697 3-8-11 0 LManiezzi 1 67
(A Giorgi, Italy) *hld up on inner: rdn and no hdwy fr over 2f out: eased ins fnl f* **79/10**

9 8 **Miss Massucco (FR)**[386] 3-8-11 0 DPerovic 5 51
(B Vidovic, Croatia) *a among bkmarkers: rdn and no imp fnl 2f: eased ins fnl f* **39/1**

10 1 **Zamaya (ITY)** 3-8-11 0 SBasile 10 49
(M Grassi, Italy) *chsd clr ldrs: rdn and nt qckn 3f out: wknd ins fnl 2f* **73/10**

11 10 **Montevideo (GER)**[49] 3-8-11 0 AFresu 6 29
(S Botti, Italy) *led: hdd after 1 1/2f: chsd clr ldr: rdn and no imp over 2f out: sn wknd* **102/10**

2m 1.3s (-5.40) **11** Ran SP% **162.9**
WIN (incl. 1 euro stake): 2.86. PLACES: 1.44, 1.60, 1.76. DF: 14.08.
Owner Quafin Spa **Bred** Allevamente Dei Lagoni Srl **Trained** Italy

[3267]CHEPSTOW (L-H)

Monday, June 24

OFFICIAL GOING: Good to firm (good in places; 9.0)

Wind: Moderate behind Weather: Sunny spells

3617 BET365 H'CAP 1m 2f 36y

2:30 (2:30) (Class 5) (0-75,75) 4-Y-O+ **£2,587** (£770; £384; £192) **Stalls** Low

Form RPR

6-52 1 **Burnham**[27] 2739 4-9-7 **75** (p) RichardHughes 1 84+
(Hughie Morrison) *trckd ldrs: pushed along over 2f out: trckd ldr appr fnl f: drvn to ld fnl 110yds: readily* **5/4**[1]

3621 2 1 **Lady Bayside**[10] 3269 5-9-4 **72** JimCrowley 8 79
(Malcolm Saunders) *led for 1f: chsd ldrs: wnt 2nd over 2f out: sn rdn: styd on fnl f to take 2nd cl home: no imp on wnr* **3/1**[2]

1002 3 ¾ **Honey Of A Kitten (USA)**[11] 3156 5-8-10 **71** (v) EoinWalsh[(7)] 9 77
(David Evans) *led after 1f and t.k.h: pushed along ins fnl 3f: rdn fr 2f out: hdd fnl 110yds and sn outpcd by wnr: lost 2nd clsng stages* **14/1**

31 4 2 ¼ **Tyrur Ted**[26] 2785 8-8-5 **59** (t) LiamJones 6 60
(Frank Sheridan) *in tch: rdn and kpt on fr 3f out: styd on same pce fnl 2f* **10/1**

131- 5 1 ¼ **Ever Fortune (USA)**[237] 7469 4-9-0 **73** ThomasBrown[(5)] 5 72+
(Rae Guest) *in rr: hdwy on ins whn nt clr run 2f out: styd on again fnl f but nvr any ch* **6/1**[3]

-004 6 1 ¼ **Batchelors Star (IRE)**[21] 2920 5-8-9 **68** (t) WilliamTwiston-Davies[(5)] 3 64
(Seamus Durack) *s.i.s: in rr: drvn 3f out: sme prog fnl f* **20/1**

03 7 4 ½ **Dimitar (USA)**[21] 2920 4-9-0 **71** ow1 BrendanPowell[(3)] 2 58
(Brendan Powell) *in rr: rdn 3f out: mod prog over 2f out: wknd fnl f* **16/1**

1144 8 3 ½ **Waving**[94] 1117 4-9-4 **72** CathyGannon 7 52
(Tony Carroll) *chsd ldrs: wnt 2nd 5f out: rdn 4f out: wkng whn wnt lft 2f out* **25/1**

2m 11.04s (0.44) **Going Correction** +0.15s/f (Good) **8** Ran SP% **114.0**
Speed ratings (Par 103): **104,103,102,100,99 98,95,92**
toteswingers 1&2 £1.90, 1&3 £2.90, 2&3 £5.70 CSF £4.93 CT £32.18 TOTE £2.00: £1.10, £1.10, £3.80; EX 5.80 Trifecta £21.40 Pool: £1721.87 - 60.18 winning units..
Owner The Hill Stud **Bred** The Hill Stud **Trained** East Ilsley, Berks

FOCUS
A modest handicap but the winner rates a small personal best. It wasn't truly run.

3618 BET365.COM MEDIAN AUCTION MAIDEN STKS 1m 4f 23y

3:00 (3:00) (Class 5) 3-5-Y-O **£2,587** (£770; £384; £192) **Stalls** Low

Form RPR

1 **Java Rose**[52] 4-9-8 0 FergusSweeney 7 72
(Henry Candy) *in rr but in tch: pushed along and hdwy over 3f out: led over 2f out: drvn and styd on strly fnl f* **20/1**

060 2 ¾ **Halling's Treasure**[18] 3021 3-8-9 **75** ThomasBrown[(5)] 3 75
(Andrew Balding) *pressed ldr: drvn and upsides over 2f out: rdn and one pce ins fnl f: rallied clsng stages but a hld* **5/1**[3]

44 **3** 1 1/4 **Sultanah Heyam**[21] 2938 3-8-8 0 LiamJones 6 68
(William Haggas) *t.k.h: chsd ldrs: rdn over 3f out: styd on fnl f but nvr gng pce of ldng duo* **2/1**[2]

000 **4** 4 1/2 **Maraweh (IRE)**[32] 2605 3-8-13 73 DaneO'Neill 1 66
(J W Hills) *chsd ldrs: rdn and outpcd over 3f out: styd on again ins fnl f* **10/1**

4 **5** shd **Silk Train**[38] 2423 3-8-8 0 JimCrowley 2 61
(David Simcock) *led but hrd pressed: hdd over 2f out: wknd over 1f out* **1/1**[1]

0 **6** 4 1/2 **Hallingham**[21] 2938 3-9-0 0 ow1 SebSanders 8 59
(Jonathan Portman) *in rr: hdwy to get in tch 4f out: sn rdn: nvr rchd ldrs and wknd 2f out* **33/1**

6-0 **7** 3/4 **Primacy (IRE)**[10] 3272 4-9-4 0 ow1 RobertWilliams(5) 4 53?
(Neil Mulholland) *t.k.h: bhd most of way* **100/1**

2m 38.99s (-0.01) **Going Correction** +0.15s/f (Good)
WFA 3 from 4yo 14lb 7 Ran SP% **117.8**
Speed ratings (Par 103): **106,105,104,101,101 98,98**
toteswingers 1&2 £4.10, 1&3 £1.70, 2&3 £2.20 CSF £118.17 TOTE £10.20: £3.90, £3.60; EX 63.00 Trifecta £152.40 Pool: £2049.52 - 10.08 winning units..
Owner Mrs M D Low **Bred** Mrs David Low **Trained** Kingston Warren, Oxon

FOCUS
A modest maiden which was slowly run, and shaky form. The winner did it nicely but there are doubts over the race.

3619 BET365 MAIDEN STKS 1m 14y
3:30 (3:30) (Class 5) 3-Y-O+ **£2,587** (£770; £384; £192) **Stalls** Centre

Form RPR

62- **1** **Hekaayaat (USA)**[235] 7505 3-8-12 0 DaneO'Neill 6 82+
(Roger Varian) *t.k.h: early: trckd ldrs: drvn to ld over 1f out: kpt on wl fnl 110yds: a doing enough* **5/4**[1]

35 **2** nk **International Love (IRE)**[11] 3239 3-8-12 0 JakeNoonan 5 80
(Andrew Balding) *tk str hold and led 2f: styd chsng ldr tl over 2f out: rdn and styd on over 1f out: chsd wnr fnl 100yds: kpt on but a hld* **7/4**[2]

5 **3** 2 3/4 **Majesty (IRE)**[10] 3278 3-9-3 0 RichardHughes 4 79
(Richard Hannon) *led after 2f: rdn over 2f out: sn edging lft and hdd over 1f out: wknd fnl 110yds* **5/2**[3]

046 **4** 10 **Our Golden Girl**[27] 2742 3-8-5 55 DanielMuscutt(7) 2 51
(Shaun Lycett) *chsd ldrs tl rdn and wknd fr over 3f out* **33/1**

6/ **5** 26 **Blues Buddy**[1193] 928 6-9-1 0 JoeyHaynes(7) 1
(H Edward Haynes) *bhd fr 1/2-way* **100/1**

1m 33.63s (-2.57) **Going Correction** -0.275s/f (Firm)
WFA 3 from 6yo 10lb 5 Ran SP% **113.3**
Speed ratings (Par 103): **101,100,97,87,61**
CSF £3.93 TOTE £3.30: £2.00, £1.10; EX 5.00 Trifecta £6.60 Pool: £1454.19 - 161.78 winning units..
Owner Hamdan Al Maktoum **Bred** Shadwell Farm LLC **Trained** Newmarket, Suffolk

FOCUS
This modest maiden developed into something of a dash for home and there was a difference of opinion as to where the best ground was. The form trio were clear and the winner is entitled to do better.

3620 BET365 CLASSIFIED STKS 1m 14y
4:00 (4:00) (Class 5) 3-Y-O **£2,587** (£770; £384) **Stalls** Centre

Form RPR

1060 **1** **Reggae Star**[9] 3322 3-9-0 70 FrannyNorton 3 74
(Mark Johnston) *led towards in centre of crse: hdd 2f out: rallied u.p fnl f to ld again fnl 110yds: rdn out* **3/1**[3]

3-13 **2** nk **This Is Nice (IRE)**[13] 3179 3-9-0 70 JimCrowley 5 73
(Tom Dascombe) *trckd ldr and racd on stands' side: rdn: edgd lft and led 2f out: continued to edge fnl f and hdd fnl 110yds: no ex u.p* **10/11**[1]

23-3 **3** 3 1/4 **Watcheroftheskies**[25] 2788 3-9-0 70 SebSanders 4 66
(J W Hills) *racd in 3rd on stands' side thrght: rdn over 2f out and sn fnd no ex u.p* **5/2**[2]

1m 34.06s (-2.14) **Going Correction** -0.275s/f (Firm) 3 Ran SP% **106.0**
Speed ratings (Par 99): **99,98,95**
CSF £6.03 TOTE £4.30; EX 5.40 Trifecta £5.30 Pool: £1454.19 - 202.69 winning units..
Owner Hugh Hart **Bred** Mrs P Hart **Trained** Middleham Moor, N Yorks

FOCUS
Despite there being just three runners, this classified contest was run at a fair pace and it saw a tight finish more towards the centre of the track. Another muddling little race. The runner-up sets the standard.

3621 BET365.COM H'CAP 7f 16y
4:30 (4:31) (Class 5) (0-70,70) 3-Y-O **£2,587** (£770; £384; £192) **Stalls** Centre

Form RPR

6-02 **1** **Secret Rebel**[11] 3242 3-9-7 70 (t) RichardHughes 1 84
(Sylvester Kirk) *mde all: rdn and qcknd 2f out: c clr fnl f: unchal* **6/4**[1]

0166 **2** 4 1/2 **Jimmy Elder**[19] 2983 3-9-5 68 DaneO'Neill 2 69
(Richard Hannon) *chsd ldrs: wnt 2nd ins fnl 3f: rdn 2f out: kpt on but no imp on wnr fnl f* **12/1**

-043 **3** 1 3/4 **Admirable Art (IRE)**[11] 3242 3-9-2 65 JimCrowley 7 61
(Tony Carroll) *in tch: hdwy to chse ldrs 3f out: styd on for one pce 3rd over 1f out* **6/4**[1]

2326 **4** 13 **Green Special (ITY)**[49] 2094 3-9-0 62 ow1 (t) SebSanders 5 24
(Frank Sheridan) *chsd ldrs: rdn over 2f out: sn btn* **10/1**[3]

204- **5** 7 **Frosted Off**[228] 7649 3-8-11 60 CathyGannon 4
(John Spearing) *chsd wnr tl ins fnl 3f: sn wknd* **20/1**

6155 **6** 15 **Compton Silver**[4] 3495 3-8-6 60 (b) RyanTate(5) 6
(Hans Adielsson) *fly-jmpd after 1f: wl bhd fr 1/2-way* **8/1**[2]

1m 21.19s (-2.01) **Going Correction** -0.275s/f (Firm) 6 Ran SP% **112.7**
Speed ratings (Par 99): **100,94,92,78,70 52**
toteswingers 1&2 £2.50, 1&3 £1.50, 2&3 £3.60 CSF £21.57 TOTE £2.40: £3.20, £4.80; EX 17.80 Trifecta £40.50 Pool: £2840.89 - 52.57 winning units..
Owner J C Smith **Bred** Littleton Stud **Trained** Upper Lambourn, Berks

FOCUS
An ordinary 3-y-o handicap, run at a decent pace. The joint favourites were closely matched on Newbury form and the race has been rated cautiously.

3622 CASINO AT BET365 H'CAP 6f 16y
5:00 (5:00) (Class 5) (0-75,75) 3-Y-O+ **£2,587** (£770; £384; £192) **Stalls** Centre

Form RPR

4000 **1** **Jack My Boy (IRE)**[23] 2871 6-9-9 75 (b) DeclanBates(5) 11 83
(David Evans) *chsd ldrs: rdn and one pce 2f out: styd on u.p fnl f but edging rt: kpt on wl to ld last strides* **7/1**[2]

0020 **2** nk **Belle Bayardo (IRE)**[3] 3529 5-9-6 67 DaneO'Neill 1 74
(Ronald Harris) *chsd ldrs: rdn over 2f out: sn chsng ldr: led fnl 130yds: hdd last strides* **7/2**[1]

00-0 **3** 3/4 **Portrush Storm**[16] 3098 8-8-2 56 JoeyHaynes(7) 5 61
(Ray Peacock) *chsd ldr tl rdn over 2f out: rallied and styd on u.p ins fnl f to take 3rd last strides: no imp on ldng duo* **33/1**

0103 **4** shd **Edged Out**[14] 3160 3-8-13 67 CathyGannon 2 71
(Christopher Mason) *sn led: rdn over 2f out: hdd fnl 130yds: wknd clsng stages* **7/1**[2]

015 **5** 1/2 **Night Trade (IRE)**[27] 2745 6-9-4 70 (p) EDLinehan(5) 8 73
(Ronald Harris) *in rr: rdn and hdwy over 1f out: n.m.r ins fnl f: kpt on clsng stages* **14/1**

4026 **6** 1/2 **Kyllachy Storm**[40] 2364 9-8-4 56 oh1 RyanTate(5) 4 57
(Ron Hodges) *chsd ldrs: rdn and one pce over 2f out: kpt on same pce fnl f* **16/1**

2500 **7** 3/4 **Tidal's Baby**[9] 3315 4-8-12 64 GeorgeDowning(5) 3 67+
(Tony Carroll) *s.i.s: in rr: hdwy over 1f out and sn nt clr run: kpt on same pce* **8/1**[3]

2-40 **8** shd **Dream Catcher (FR)**[37] 2441 5-9-8 74 AmyScott(5) 9 72
(Henry Candy) *chsd ldrs: rdn 2f out: no ex fnl f* **7/2**[1]

2030 **9** 1/2 **Bussa**[27] 2736 5-9-3 71 (t) EoinWalsh(7) 7 68
(David Evans) *s.i.s: in rr: pushed along over 2f out: mod prog fnl f* **20/1**

-260 **10** 2 **Divine Call**[24] 2825 6-9-9 70 JimmyQuinn 6 60
(Milton Bradley) *chsd ldrs: rdn over 2f out: wknd ins fnl f* **8/1**[3]

0506 **11** 30 **Nellie Bly**[21] 2919 3-8-7 61 FrannyNorton 10
(Mark Johnston) *chsd ldrs: wknd ins fnl 2f and wknd qckly: eased fnl f* **20/1**

1m 9.66s (-2.34) **Going Correction** -0.275s/f (Firm)
WFA 3 from 4yo+ 7lb 11 Ran SP% **116.7**
Speed ratings (Par 103): **104,103,102,102,101 101,100,100,99,96 56**
toteswingers 1&2 £5.50, 1&3 £33.80, 2&3 £33.90 CSF £30.58 CT £776.36 TOTE £7.90: £4.70, £3.00, £18.70; EX 28.70 Trifecta £2156.80 Part won. Pool: £2875.78 - 0.93 winning units..
Owner T Earle & G Evans **Bred** Mrs Sheila Walker **Trained** Pandy, Monmouths

FOCUS
A moderate sprint handicap and it saw a typically tight finish for a race of its type. Routine form.

3623 POKER AT BET365 H'CAP 5f 16y
5:30 (5:30) (Class 6) (0-60,59) 3-Y-O+ **£1,940** (£577; £288; £144) **Stalls** Centre

Form RPR

11-0 **1** **Steel Rain**[66] 1665 5-9-5 59 RyanTate(5) 1 68
(Nikki Evans) *w ldr: led after 2f: rdn: hrd pressed fnl f: edgd rt clsng stages: hld on all out* **9/2**[3]

2-00 **2** shd **Griffin Point (IRE)**[9] 3317 6-9-4 58 (b) WilliamTwiston-Davies(5) 7 66
(William Muir) *led 2f: styd pressing wnr: str chal ins fnl f: pushed rt and no ex ins clsng stages* **8/1**

140 **3** 1/2 **Tooley Woods (IRE)**[27] 2747 4-9-3 52 CathyGannon 8 58
(Tony Carroll) *chsd ldrs: rdn and styd on wl fnl f: kpt on clsng stages but a hld by ldng duo* **7/2**[2]

4062 **4** 2 1/4 **Scommettitrice (IRE)**[6] 3425 5-8-9 51 (b) OisinMurphy(7) 4 49
(Mark Gillard) *chsd ldrs: outpcd 2f out: kpt on again fnl f* **3/1**[1]

0260 **5** hd **Diamond Vine (IRE)**[18] 3010 5-9-9 58 (p) DaneO'Neill 9 55
(Ronald Harris) *chsd ldrs: outpcd over 2f out: styd on again ins fnl f* **8/1**

0562 **6** 2 1/4 **Farmers Dream (IRE)**[10] 3268 6-8-6 48 (vt[1]) AdamMcLean(7) 5 37
(Derek Shaw) *chsd ldrs: rdn over 2f out: wknd over appr fnl f* **10/1**

-000 **7** 2 1/2 **Memphis Man**[10] 3270 10-9-1 50 (p) FrannyNorton 3 30
(Milton Bradley) *outpcd: sme prog fnl f* **33/1**

0-30 **8** 1 1/4 **Depden (IRE)**[11] 3246 5-8-11 46 AdamBeschizza 10 22
(Richard Price) *s.i.s: outpcd* **7/1**

0000 **9** 2 3/4 **Quan (IRE)**[9] 3326 4-8-11 46 JimmyQuinn 2 12
(Milton Bradley) *sn outpcd* **20/1**

58.79s (-0.51) **Going Correction** -0.275s/f (Firm)
WFA 3 from 4yo+ 6lb 9 Ran SP% **116.9**
Speed ratings (Par 101): **93,92,92,88,88 84,80,78,74**
toteswingers 1&2 £8.20, 1&3 £4.70, 2&3 £9.10 CSF £40.76 CT £141.84 TOTE £6.20: £2.70, £3.70, £1.10; EX 46.60 Trifecta £244.60 Pool: £2142.10 - 6.56 winning units..
Owner John Berry (Gwent) **Bred** L T Roberts **Trained** Pandy, Monmouths

FOCUS
This weak sprint handicap was run at a frantic pace and again they raced down the middle. Straightforward form.
T/Plt: £287.20 to a £1 stake. Pool: £74,103.53 - 188.35 winning tickets T/Qpdt: £35.60 to a £1 stake. Pool: £5,050.83 - 104.8 winning tickets ST

3439 THIRSK (L-H)
Monday, June 24

OFFICIAL GOING: Good (good to soft in places; 7.7)
Wind: Light 1/2 behind Weather: fine but overcast and quite cold

3624 WATCH RACING UK ON FREEVIEW 231 MAIDEN AUCTION STKS 6f
6:20 (6:22) (Class 6) 2-Y-O **£2,045** (£603; £302) **Stalls** High

Form RPR

1 **Announcement** 2-9-0 0 BarryMcHugh 13 73
(Karen Tutty) *chsd ldrs stands' rail: drvn over 2f out: upsides jst ins fnl f: styd on to ld towards fin* **33/1**

0 **2** 3/4 **Ticking Katie (IRE)**[17] 3044 2-9-0 0 DanielTudhope 5 71
(Mrs K Burke) *w ldrs: led over 2f out: jnd jst ins fnl f: no ex nr fin* **3/1**[1]

42 **3** 2 3/4 **Sartorialist (IRE)**[9] 3310 2-9-5 0 SeanLevey 6 68
(J S Moore) *s.i.s: hdwy over 2f out: swtchd to stands' rail ins fnl f: r.o to take 3rd nr line* **4/1**[2]

000 **4** 3/4 **Lady Liz**[20] 2955 2-8-7 0 ConnorBeasley(7) 12 60
(George Moore) *led tl over 1f out: kpt on same pce fnl f* **20/1**

6 **5** shd **De Repente (IRE)**[17] 3044 2-9-0 0 JoeFanning 2 60
(Paul Green) *sn chsng ldrs on outside: edgd lft over 1f out: kpt on same pce* **11/2**[3]

2 **6** 1/2 **Henke (IRE)**[23] 2883 2-8-12 0 DanielleMooney(7) 10 63+
(Nigel Tinkler) *mid-div: effrt over 2f out: kpt on: nvrr nr to chal* **8/1**

7 3 3/4 **Firecruise** 2-9-5 0 PhillipMakin 11 52
(David Barron) *dwlt: in rr: sme hdwy 2f out: nvr on terms* **6/1**

8 8 **Running Wolf (IRE)** 2-9-5 0 TomEaves 1 28+
(Michael Dods) *dwlt: in rr: bhd fnl 2f* **25/1**

9 6 **Pay The Greek** 2-9-5 0 GrahamLee 3 10
(Noel Quinlan) *dwlt: mid-div: hung lft and lost pl 2f out* **20/1**

0 **10** hd **Paparima (IRE)**[51] 2025 2-9-0 0 [1] JamesSullivan 8
(Paul Green) *s.i.s: swtchd rt after s: hdwy and hung bdly rt over 2f out: sn wknd* **80/1**

The Form Book Flat, Raceform Ltd, Compton, RG20 6NL.

11 1 1/2 **Shesadanser** 2-9-0 0 PJMcDonald 9
(Ann Duffield) *chsd ldrs: lost pl over 2f out: bhd whn eased ins fnl f: collapsed and died after r* **8/1**

0 12 19 **Bridge Of Avon**[94] 1108 2-9-0 0 PaulMulrennan 4
(Mel Brittain) *mid-div: lost pl over 2f out: wl bhd whn heavily eased clsng stages: t.o* **33/1**

1m 13.52s (0.82) **Going Correction** +0.25s/f (Good) **12** Ran SP% **117.4**
Speed ratings (Par 91): **104,103,99,98,98 97,92,81,73,73 71,46**
toteswingers 1&2 £56.70, 1&3 £27.50, 2&3 £4.20 CSF £122.31 TOTE £71.70: £14.40, £1.10, £2.50; EX 432.90 Trifecta £733.90 Part won. Pool: £978.53 - 0.01 winning units..
Owner Thoroughbred Homes Ltd **Bred** Kassala Limited **Trained** Osmotherley, N Yorks

FOCUS
Following 13mm of rain since lunchtime on Sunday, the ground was eased to "good, good to soft in places". Paul Mulrennan stated the ground was on the soft side of good. No more than a modest maiden. The gallop was sound throughout but only those up with the pace figured. Ordinary form

3625 WATCH RACING UK ON SKY 432 H'CAP 1m 4f
6:50 (6:51) (Class 6) (0-60,60) 4-Y-0+ **£1,940** (£577; £288; £144) **Stalls** High

Form RPR

-420 1 **Medieval Bishop (IRE)**[19] 2991 4-8-7 **51** (p) JasonHart(5) 6 63
(Tim Walford) *chsd ldrs: 2nd over 1f out: styd on to ld last 50yds: hld on wl towards fin* **9/1**

00-6 2 1/2 **Slide Show**[5] 3467 5-8-7 **46** oh1 PaulQuinn 12 57
(David Nicholls) *hld up towards rr: hdwy over 4f out: led 3f out: hdd wl ins fnl f: kpt on towards fin* **16/1**

5304 3 6 **Operateur (IRE)**[19] 2986 5-9-2 **55** PhillipMakin 5 57
(Ben Haslam) *mid-div: hdwy 4f out: kpt on to take modest 3rd last 100yds* **4/1**[2]

4 3/4 **Gunboat (IRE)**[192] 8125 5-8-11 **50** PaulMulrennan 8 50
(Ed Dunlop) *mid-div: effrt 3f out: chsng ldrs over 1f out: kpt on one pce* **9/2**[3]

/50- 5 1/2 **Queen Of Epirus**[110] 7869 5-9-2 **55** MickyFenton 10 55
(Brian Rothwell) *in rr: hdwy over 2f out: kpt on fnl f* **66/1**

/43 6 nk **Summerlea (IRE)**[24] 2831 7-9-2 **55** JoeFanning 13 54
(Patrick Holmes) *trckd ldrs: 2nd over 2f out: wknd over 1f out* **20/1**

6242 7 4 **Petrol**[19] 2986 4-9-7 **60** DanielTudhope 17 55
(David O'Meara) *swtchd lft after s: in rr: hdwy 4f out: chsng ldrs 2f out: wknd appr fnl f* **3/1**[1]

000- 8 1 3/4 **Jim Tango (FR)**[275] 6478 9-8-5 **51** (p) ConnorBeasley(7) 2 41
(Karen McLintock) *rr-div: sme hdwy whn hmpd over 4f out: kpt on fnl 2f: nvr on terms* **20/1**

-254 9 14 **Eijaaz (IRE)**[24] 2831 12-9-4 **57** (p) PJMcDonald 9 25
(Geoffrey Harker) *s.i.s: hdwy on ins 3f out: 9th and no ch whn heavily eased clsng stages* **25/1**

00-6 10 2 1/4 **The Lodge Road (IRE)**[20] 2961 5-9-7 **60** GrahamLee 11 24
(Martin Todhunter) *chsd ldrs: lost pl over 2f out: sn bhd* **12/1**

500- 11 3/4 **Ruby Glass (IRE)**[405] 2144 4-9-1 **54** JamesSullivan 15 17
(Ruth Carr) *stdd s: a in rr: bhd fnl 3f* **66/1**

-132 12 nse **Jewelled Dagger (IRE)**[7] 3406 9-9-3 **56** (t) PaddyAspell 16 19
(Sharon Watt) *chsd ldrs: led over 7f out: hdd 3f out: sn lost pl and bhd* **12/1**

564 13 12 **Croftamie**[34] 2555 4-9-1 **54** (p) RoystonFfrench 1
(Tracy Waggott) *chsd ldrs: drvn 5f out: lost pl over 3f out: wl bhd fnl 2f* **14/1**

-425 14 4 **Needwood Park**[41] 1217 5-8-12 **51** (p) TomEaves 4
(Ray Craggs) *led tl over 7f out: sn drvn: lost pl over 3f out: wl bhd fnl 2f* **40/1**

2m 39.38s (3.18) **Going Correction** +0.25s/f (Good) **14** Ran SP% **119.9**
Speed ratings (Par 101): **99,98,94,94,93 93,90,89,80,78 78,78,70,67**
toteswingers 1&2 £40.40, 1&3 £10.10, 2&3 £21.50 CSF £132.20 CT £671.97 TOTE £11.60: £4.60, £8.50, £1.90; EX 220.00 Trifecta £360.50 Part won. Pool: £480.73 - 0.02 winning units..
Owner Mr & Mrs K Hamilton,D Dickson,N Skinner **Bred** Keatly Overseas Ltd **Trained** Sheriff Hutton, N Yorks

FOCUS
Mainly exposed sorts in a moderate handicap in which not many figured. The gallop was ordinary until picking up turning for home and the first two pulled clear. The winner is rated in line with a best view of his post-2yo form.

3626 READ HAYLEY TURNER EVERY FRIDAY RACINGUK.COM MAIDEN STKS 5f
7:20 (7:25) (Class 5) 3-4-Y-O **£2,587** (£770; £384; £192) **Stalls** High

Form RPR

-352 1 **Sixty Minutes**[16] 3086 3-9-3 68 (t) SeanLevey 6 71
(David Brown) *wnt lft s: led: rdn over 2f out: edgd lft ins fnl f: kpt on* **15/8**[2]

2-5 2 1 **Pastureyes**[94] 1122 3-8-9 0 BillyCray(3) 3 63
(Scott Dixon) *trckd ldrs: t.k.h: upsides jst ins fnl f: no ex last 50yds* **10/1**

640- 3 hd **Shillito**[259] 6920 3-9-3 74 BarryMcHugh 8 67
(Tony Coyle) *chsd ldrs: rdn over 2f out: kpt on towards fin* **13/8**[1]

6044 4 2 3/4 **Beacon Tarn**[15] 3134 3-8-7 53 (p) JasonHart(5) 5 52
(Eric Alston) *bmpd s: w wnr: rdn 2f out: hung lft and fdd appr fnl f* **10/3**[3]

55-0 5 5 **Princess In Exile**[31] 2635 3-8-12 59 TomEaves 4 34
(Ian Semple) *sltly hmpd s: in rr: swtchd rt to stands' side rail after 1f: sn outpcd: sme hdwy over 1f out: sn wknd* **18/1**

1m 0.75s (1.15) **Going Correction** +0.25s/f (Good)
WFA 3 from 4yo 6lb **5** Ran SP% **110.3**
Speed ratings (Par 103): **100,98,98,93,85**
CSF £18.72 TOTE £2.10: £1.10, £5.10; EX 11.10 Trifecta £29.70 Pool: £614.05 - 15.46 winning units..
Owner J C Fretwell **Bred** Whitsbury Manor Stud & A W M Christie-Miller **Trained** Averham Park, Notts
■ Stewards' Enquiry : Billy Cray two-day ban: excessive use (8-9 July)

FOCUS
A weak maiden run at a reasonable gallop. The winner is rated to form.

3627 YORKSHIRE OUTDOORS ADVENTURE EXPERIENCES H'CAP 2m
7:50 (7:51) (Class 5) (0-70,70) 4-Y-0+ **£2,587** (£770; £384; £192) **Stalls** Low

Form RPR

1-66 1 **Estemaala (IRE)**[9] 3321 4-9-6 **69** DanielTudhope 8 76
(David O'Meara) *trckd ldrs: hdwy 3f out: sn chsng ldr: rdn over 1f out: drvn to chal ent fnl f: led last 50yds: kpt on gamely towards fin* **16/1**

0464 2 hd **Beat The Shower**[19] 2990 7-8-10 **59** GrahamLee 6 66
(Peter Niven) *hld up: hdwy 4f out: effrt on outer to chse ldng pair wl over 1f out: rdn to chal ent fnl f: sn drvn and kpt on: jst failed* **9/2**[3]

0100 3 nk **Mason Hindmarsh**[19] 2990 6-9-3 **66** PhillipMakin 5 73
(Karen McLintock) *chsd ldr: hdwy 3f out: rdn wl over 1f out: jnd and drvn ent fnl f: hdd and no ex last 50yds* **14/1**

0651 4 1 3/4 **Enchanted Garden**[23] 2887 5-9-3 **66** FrederikTylicki 2 71+
(Malcolm Jefferson) *tacked ldrs on inner: swtchd rt and hdwy whn nt clr run: hmpd wl over 2f out: sn rdn and kpt on fnl f: nrst fin* **9/4**[1]

1-12 5 shd **Zarosa (IRE)**[34] 2545 4-8-6 **62** NoelGarbutt(7) 9 66
(John Berry) *hld up in rr: hdwy 3f out: chsd ldrs wl over 1f out: sn rdn and kpt on same pce fnl f* **5/2**[2]

2-60 6 1 1/4 **My Destination (IRE)**[8] 3363 4-8-13 **65** NeilFarley(3) 7 68
(Declan Carroll) *hld up in rr: hdwy 4f out: n.m.r and swtchd lft over 2f out: sn rdn to chse ldrs: drvn and no imp fnl f* **22/1**

1100 7 8 **Full Speed (GER)**[10] 3301 8-8-13 **65** DeclanCannon(3) 3 58
(Philip Kirby) *trckd ldng pair: swtchd rt and rdn 3f out: sn wknd* **22/1**

6303 8 7 **La Bacouetteuse (FR)**[16] 3089 8-9-0 **68** (p) GarryWhillans(5) 11 53
(Iain Jardine) *sn in tch: effrt over 3f out: sn rdn along and n.d* **16/1**

06/5 9 3 1/4 **Wee Giant (USA)**[23] 2887 7-8-7 **56** BarryMcHugh 1 37
(Tony Coyle) *hld up: effrt and sme hdwy over 3f out: sn rdn along and btn over 2f out* **33/1**

60-6 10 21 **Authentication**[5] 3480 4-9-2 **65** (t) PaulMulrennan 4 32
(Mel Brittain) *set stdy pce: pushed along over 4f out: rdn and hdd over 3f out: sn wknd and bhd whn eased over 1f out* **14/1**

3m 36.84s (8.54) **Going Correction** +0.25s/f (Good) **10** Ran SP% **114.3**
Speed ratings (Par 103): **88,87,87,86,86 86,82,78,77,66**
toteswingers 1&2 £32.20, 1&3 £29.40, 2&3 £4.20 CSF £82.95 CT £1045.53 TOTE £14.70: £5.10, £1.90, £2.90; EX 79.10 TRIFECTA Part won. Pool: £719.70 - 0.59 winning units..
Owner Middleham Park Racing XLVI & Partners **Bred** Shadwell Estate Company Limited **Trained** Nawton, N Yorks
■ Stewards' Enquiry : Daniel Tudhope two-day ban: excessive use (8-9 July)

FOCUS
A modest staying handicap in which the gallop was on the steady side to the home straight and this bare form may not be entirely reliable, as they finished in a bunch.

3628 BET & WATCH WITH RACINGUK'S APP H'CAP 7f
8:20 (8:21) (Class 4) (0-80,78) 4-Y-0+ **£4,690** (£1,395; £697; £348) **Stalls** Low

Form RPR

5006 1 **Green Park (IRE)**[16] 3088 10-8-12 **72** (b) NeilFarley(3) 3 82
(Declan Carroll) *chsd ldrs: nt clr run over 1f out: styd on to ld last 75yds: drvn out* **25/1**

-606 2 1/2 **Kuwait Star**[23] 2889 4-8-12 **69** PJMcDonald 7 78
(Jason Ward) *in tch: drvn and hung lft over 2f out: swtchd rt over 1f out: styd on to take 2nd nr line* **8/1**[3]

-662 3 1 **Ewell Place (IRE)**[2] 3570 4-9-5 **76** TonyHamilton 6 82
(David Nicholls) *w ldrs: upsides 2f out: kpt on same pce last 100yds* **3/1**[2]

4435 4 1 3/4 **Paramour**[21] 2911 6-9-1 **72** (v[1]) DanielTudhope 1 73
(David O'Meara) *led: hdd ins fnl f: no ex* **11/4**[1]

610 5 1 1/4 **Steel Stockholder**[70] 1571 7-9-7 **78** PaulMulrennan 4 76
(Mel Brittain) *chsd ldrs: effrt over 2f out: one pce* **16/1**

-400 6 2 1/2 **Orpsie Boy (IRE)**[16] 3087 10-8-13 **70** AmyRyan 14 61+
(Ruth Carr) *swtchd lft after s: hld up in rr: kpt on fnl 2f: nvr a threat* **28/1**

3000 7 1/2 **New Leyf (IRE)**[24] 2834 7-9-3 **74** (p) PaulQuinn 2 64
(David Nicholls) *in tch: drvn 4f out: one pce* **20/1**

5511 8 3 **Running Reef (IRE)**[10] 3286 4-8-11 **68** BarryMcHugh 10 50
(Tracy Waggott) *mid-div: effrt over 2f out: edgd lft and wknd over 1f out* **8/1**[3]

-000 9 1 1/4 **Henry Bee**[16] 3090 4-8-8 **70** GeorgeChaloner(5) 12 48
(Richard Fahey) *mid-div: drvn 3f out: nvr a factor* **33/1**

0000 10 1 **Unex Michelangelo (IRE)**[9] 3345 4-9-3 **74** JamesSullivan 13 50
(Michael Easterby) *in rr-div: drvn over 4f out: nvr on terms* **16/1**

00-5 11 3/4 **Lolita Lebron (IRE)**[16] 3098 4-9-1 **77** (tp) JasonHart(5) 5 51
(Lawrence Mullaney) *s.s: sme hdwy over 2f out: sn wknd* **20/1**

-000 12 2 **Kuanyao (IRE)**[16] 3090 7-9-1 **72** JoeFanning 9 40
(David Nicholls) *reain r-div: nvr on terms* **10/1**

0506 13 hd **Aerodynamic (IRE)**[49] 2081 6-9-0 **71** PhillipMakin 8 39
(Michael Easterby) *s.i.s: a in rr: bhd fnl 2f* **14/1**

1m 28.2s (1.00) **Going Correction** +0.25s/f (Good) **13** Ran SP% **121.2**
Speed ratings (Par 105): **104,103,102,100,98 96,95,92,90,89 88,86,86**
toteswingers 1&2 £37.70, 1&3 £27.80, 2&3 £3.90 CSF £204.50 CT £791.86 TOTE £35.50: £10.70, £1.70, £2.50; EX 274.40 Trifecta £678.10 Part won. Pool: £904.21 - 0.12 winning units..
Owner G A Fixings Ltd **Bred** James Burns And A Moynan **Trained** Sledmere, E Yorks

FOCUS
A fair handicap comprising mainly exposed sorts. The gallop was soon sound but those held up were at a disadvantage. The form is rated around the second and third.

3629 DOWNLOAD THE FREE RACINGUK APP H'CAP 1m
8:50 (8:52) (Class 6) (0-65,65) 3-Y-0 **£2,045** (£603; £302) **Stalls** Low

Form RPR

1-05 1 **Aeronwyn Bryn (IRE)**[49] 2080 3-8-13 **64** ConnorBeasley(7) 1 75
(Michael Dods) *dwlt: pushed along on inner and sn trcking ldrs: n.m.r and sltly hmpd over 2f out: gd hdwy on inner to ld 1 1/2f out: rdn clr ent fnl f: styd on strly* **11/1**

-650 2 1 3/4 **Polar Forest**[44] 2274 3-8-10 **54** RobbieFitzpatrick 11 61
(Richard Guest) *in tch: hdwy on outer over 2f out: rdn over 1f out: edgd lft ins fnl f: kpt on* **50/1**

563 3 hd **Confusing**[6] 3445 3-9-7 **65** DanielTudhope 5 72
(David O'Meara) *towards rr: gd hdwy on inner 1/2-way: sn chsng ldrs: effrt and swtchd rt over 2f out: chsd wnr jst over 1f out: sn rdn and kpt on same pce* **5/2**[1]

62 4 3/4 **Excellent Addition (IRE)**[41] 2340 3-9-7 **65** GrahamLee 18 70+
(David O'Meara) *hld up and bhd: stdy hdwy on inner over 2f out: rdn over 1f out: kpt on fnl f* **3/1**[2]

0-54 5 2 **Sandy's Row (USA)**[11] 3254 3-9-4 **62** JoeFanning 7 63
(Mark Johnston) *dwlt and in rr: hdwy over 2f out: rdn wl over 1f out: styd on fnl f: nrst fin* **12/1**

3205 6 1 1/4 **Lucky Mountain**[47] 2175 3-8-3 **50** BillyCray(3) 13 48
(Scott Dixon) *towards rr: hdwy on wd outside over 3f out: rdn to chse ldrs over 2f out: sn drvn and no imp* **40/1**

205 7 1 1/2 **Royal Style (IRE)**[27] 2754 3-9-4 **62** PhillipMakin 17 56
(David Barron) *qckly away and sn led: clr 1/2-way: rdn along over 2f out: hdd 1 1/2f out: sn wknd* **12/1**

6560 8 nse **Out Of The Blocks**[16] 3082 3-8-7 **51** PJMcDonald 9 45
(Ruth Carr) *in tch: hdwy 3f out: rdn over 2f out: n.d* **14/1**

-554 9 5 **Relight My Fire**[16] 3082 3-9-4 **62** MickyFenton 14 45
(Tim Easterby) *nvr bttr than midfield* **11/1**

0-03 10 1 **Stand N Applaude**[19] 2992 3-8-9 **53** AndrewMullen 2 33
(David Nicholls) *chsd ldr: rdn along and wandered wl over 2f out: sn drvn: edgd rt and wknd* **33/1**

1462 **11** 2 1/4 **Shearian**[10] 3281 3-9-7 **65**.................................... BarryMcHugh 6 40
(Tracy Waggott) *in tch: hdwy to chse ldrs over 3f out: sn rdn and wknd* **8/1**[3]
2400 **12** 1 1/4 **Multisure**[35] 2501 3-8-12 **56**.................................... JamesSullivan 12 28
(Ruth Carr) *chsd ldng pair: rdn along 3f out: wknd over 2f out* **18/1**
0-40 **13** *nk* **Rosie Hall (IRE)**[35] 2507 3-8-9 **53**.................................... RoystonFfrench 8 25
(Bryan Smart) *a in rr* **25/1**
1m 43.18s (3.08) **Going Correction** +0.25s/f (Good) **13** Ran SP% **119.9**
Speed ratings (Par 97): **94,92,92,91,89 88,86,86,81,80 78,77,76**
toteswingers 1&2 £82.00, 1&3 £6.20, 2&3 £21.50 CSF £486.88 CT £1857.76 TOTE £15.80: £4.70, £12.80, £1.90; EX 1168.20 Trifecta £709.00 Part won. Pool: £945.45 - 0.03 winning units..
Owner Andrew Tinkler **Bred** Owenstown Stud **Trained** Denton, Co Durham
■ Stewards' Enquiry : Billy Cray two-day ban: excessive use (10-11 July)
FOCUS
A modest handicap run at a reasonable gallop. A length personal best from the winner.

3630 RACING UK YOUR RACING HOME FROM HOME H'CAP 6f
9:20 (9:21) (Class 6) (0-60,60) 3-Y-O+ **£2,045** (£603; £302) **Stalls** High

Form RPR
-050 **1** **Iceblast**[34] 2536 5-9-7 **55**....................................(v[1]) PaulMulrennan 16 65
(Michael Easterby) *in rr: hdwy over 2f out: nt clr run and swtchd lft appr fnl f: fin strly to ld nr fin* **7/2**[1]
4351 **2** 3/4 **Hab Reeh**[12] 3197 5-9-2 **57**....................................(t) GemmaTutty(7) 8 65+
(Ruth Carr) *in rr: hdwy on outside over 2f out: styd on to ld last 50yds: hdd nr fin* **10/1**
350 **3** 1/2 **Hazza The Jazza**[42] 2308 3-9-4 **59**....................(b) RobbieFitzpatrick 11 63
(Richard Guest) *mid-div: hdwy over 2f out: chsng ldrs 1f out: no ex clsng stages* **14/1**
-635 **4** *nk* **Ingenti**[28] 2702 5-9-9 **57**.................................... TomEaves 14 62
(Christopher Wilson) *chsd ldrs: led briefly 100yds out: no ex clsng stage* **12/1**
00-6 **5** *shd* **Sinai (IRE)**[24] 2835 4-9-3 **58**.................................... JordanNason(7) 12 63
(Geoffrey Harker) *dwlt and wnt rt s: hld up in rr: hdwy 2f out: chsng ldrs stands' side 1f out: kpt on same pce last 50yds* **20/1**
0-00 **6** *nk* **Layla's Hero (IRE)**[16] 3090 6-9-12 **60**....................(v) JoeFanning 1 64+
(David Nicholls) *s.s: hdwy on outside over 2f out: chsng ldrs 1f out: kpt on same pce* **16/1**
-050 **7** 3/4 **Rat Catcher (IRE)**[15] 3134 3-9-2 **60**....................(b) DeclanCannon(3) 15 59
(Andrew Crook) *chsd ldrs: led 2f out: hdd & wknd last 100yds* **33/1**
-330 **8** 3 **Mcmonagle (USA)**[17] 3068 5-9-12 **60**....................(bt) DaleSwift 18 52
(Alan Brown) *in tch: drvn over 2f out: one pce whn pushed lft over 1f out* **15/2**[3]
0-50 **9** 1 1/4 **Novalist**[18] 3026 5-9-2 **57**....................................(b) GaryMahon(7) 9 45
(Robin Bastiman) *prom: chsng ldrs 2f out: edgd rt and fdd jst ins fnl f* **14/1**
5203 **10** 3/4 **Captain Royale (IRE)**[6] 3446 8-9-10 **58**....................(p) BarryMcHugh 4 43
(Tracy Waggott) *in rr: hdwy over 1f out: nvr a factor* **12/1**
-662 **11** 6 **Lees Anthem**[10] 3286 6-9-3 **51**.................................... GrahamLee 20 17
(Michael Smith) *in tch stands' side: drvn over 2f out: lost pl over 1f out* **9/2**[2]
2-04 **12** 1 **Aussie Blue (IRE)**[11] 3246 9-9-12 **60**....................(p) MichaelStainton 2 23
(Charles Pogson) *in rr-div: hdwy on outer over 2f out: lost pl over 1f out: eased clsng stages* **33/1**
0000 **13** 1/2 **Dolly Diva**[18] 3030 4-9-4 **52**....................................(b[1]) MickyFenton 10 13
(Paul Midgley) *swtchd rt after s: led: hdd 2f out: sn wknd* **40/1**
3-00 **14** 3/4 **Skidby Mill (IRE)**[15] 3137 3-8-12 **60**....................(p) JoeDoyle(7) 6 17
(Brian Rothwell) *s.i.s: a in rr* **20/1**
200- **15** *hd* **Ursus**[264] 6786 8-9-6 **54**....................................(p) PJMcDonald 5 12
(Christopher Wilson) *chsd ldrs on outer: lost pl over 2f out* **50/1**
222 **16** 10 **Choc'A'Moca (IRE)**[12] 3190 6-9-5 **60**....................(v) DavidSimmonson(7) 3
(Paul Midgley) *awkward s: in rr: bhd whn eased ins fnl f* **14/1**
1m 14.05s (1.35) **Going Correction** +0.25s/f (Good)
WFA 3 from 4yo+ 7lb **16** Ran SP% **122.3**
Speed ratings (Par 101): **101,100,99,98,98 98,97,93,91,90 82,81,80,79,79 66**
toteswingers 1&2 £14.70, 1&3 £14.10, 2&3 £56.70 CSF £35.33 CT £468.05 TOTE £5.30: £2.00, £2.50, £4.70, £3.00; EX 51.80 TRIFECTA Part won. Pool: £897.42 - 0.39 winning units..
Owner B Padgett **Bred** A C M Spalding **Trained** Sheriff Hutton, N Yorks
FOCUS
A moderate handicap in which the gallop was strong. The winner's best turf form for two years.
T/Jkpt: Not won. T/Plt: £613.60 to a £1 stake. Pool: £86224.64 - 102.57 winning tickets T/Qpdt: £101.60 to a £1 stake. Pool: £5819.89 - 42.35 winning tickets WG

3412 WINDSOR (R-H)
Monday, June 24

OFFICIAL GOING: Good (8.1)
Wind: Light, behind Weather: Fine but cloudy

3631 CLIC SARGENT FOR CHILDREN WITH CANCER MEDIAN AUCTION MAIDEN STKS 6f
6:40 (6:42) (Class 5) 2-Y-O **£2,587** (£770; £384; £192) **Stalls** Low

Form RPR
1 **Hiking (USA)** 2-9-0 0.................................... JamesDoyle 4 84+
(Roger Charlton) *dwlt: off the pce in last trio: gd prog over 2f out to ld over 1f out: sn clr: easily* **12/1**
4 **2** 6 **Sebs Sensei (IRE)**[11] 3238 2-9-5 0.................................... RichardHughes 11 70
(Richard Hannon) *chsd ldng trio: shkn up over 2f out: wnt 2nd jst over 1f out: no ch w wnr* **11/10**[1]
3 1/2 **Jersey Cream (IRE)** 2-9-0 0.................................... RyanMoore 6 60
(Gary Moore) *towards rr early: sme prog whn swtchd out wd wl over 1f out: nudged along and styd on steadily to take 3rd* **16/1**
5 **4** 1 **Sleeping Venus (IRE)**[16] 3107 2-9-0 0.................................... PatCosgrave 8 57
(George Baker) *settled in midfield: shkn up over 2f out: rdn and sme prog over 1f out: one pce fnl f* **8/1**[3]
05 **5** 2 **Connaught Water (IRE)**[13] 3174 2-9-5 0.................... JamesMcDonald 5 56
(Jonathan Portman) *pressed ldr: led over 2f out to over 1f out: no ch w wnr after: wknd fnl f* **50/1**
6 3 1/4 **Aya's Gift** 2-9-5 0.................................... JamieSpencer 2 46
(Ed Walker) *slowest away: off the pce in last pair: pushed along 1/2-way: sme prog 2f out: no hdwy fnl f* **16/1**
7 2 1/2 **Dream Sika (IRE)** 2-9-5 0.................................... AdamKirby 9 39
(Clive Cox) *led but hanging lft: hdd over 2f out: hung lft and ended towards far side: wknd* **2/1**[2]

05 **8** 3 1/2 **Ivan B**[9] 3311 2-9-5 0.................................... MartinHarley 12 28
(Mick Channon) *s.i.s: sn rdn in rr: nvr a factor* **66/1**
9 1 3/4 **Desert Flute** 2-8-12 0.................................... JordanUys(7) 3 23
(Paul Cole) *sn outpcd and drvn in last: a bhd* **33/1**
0 **10** *nse* **Tidal Beauty**[19] 2978 2-9-0 0.................................... MartinLane 1 18
(Tony Carroll) *chsd ldrs early: rdn and wknd sn after 1/2-way* **100/1**
0 **11** 3 3/4 **Little Big Man**[70] 1580 2-9-5 0.................................... LiamKeniry 10 12
(Sylvester Kirk) *pressed ldr to 1/2-way: wknd rapidly* **66/1**
1m 12.87s (-0.13) **Going Correction** -0.10s/f (Good) **11** Ran SP% **120.4**
Speed ratings (Par 93): **96,88,87,86,83 79,75,71,68,68 63**
toteswingers 1&2 £2.70, 1&3 £6.60, 2&3 £6.10 CSF £26.17 TOTE £11.30: £2.20, £1.20, £5.00; EX 30.90 Trifecta £198.00 Pool: £1555.96 - 5.89 winning units..
Owner K Abdullah **Bred** Juddmonte Farms Inc **Trained** Beckhampton, Wilts
FOCUS
Inner of straight dolled out 17yds at 6f and 8yds at Winning Post. Top bend dolled out 11yds from normal configuration adding 45yds to races of 1m and beyond. In an otherwise routine maiden, the winner put in a stylish performance. She could be decent.

3632 WSM COMMUNICATIONS IN AID OF CLIC SARGENT MAIDEN STKS 1m 67y
7:10 (7:22) (Class 5) 3-Y-O **£2,587** (£770; £384; £192) **Stalls** Low

Form RPR
6-2 **1** **Star Pearl (USA)**[15] 3136 3-9-0 0.................................... JamieSpencer 7 76+
(Roger Varian) *mde all: clr 3f out: coasted home* **2/9**[1]
00- **2** 4 **Simple Joys**[244] 7306 3-8-9 0.................................... ThomasBrown(5) 6 60
(Andrew Balding) *s.s: sn chsd ldng pair: rdn over 2f out: kpt on to take modest 2nd ins fnl f* **12/1**[3]
00 **3** 3/4 **The Green Ogre**[21] 2938 3-9-5 0.................................... RyanMoore 8 63
(Gary Moore) *chsd wnr: drvn and no imp 2f out: lost 2nd ins fnl f* **14/1**
4 1 1/2 **Mcdelta** 3-9-5 0.................................... SebSanders 1 60
(Geoffrey Deacon) *s.s: hld up in last: pushed along 1/2-way: struggling over 2f out: clsd on plcd horses 1f out: one pce after* **40/1**
54 **5** *shd* **Red Red Wine**[17] 3047 3-9-5 0.................................... AndreaAtzeni 2 59
(Hugo Palmer) *hld up in 4th: pushed along 1/2-way: shkn up and one pce fnl 2f* **9/2**[2]
1m 46.19s (1.49) **Going Correction** -0.05s/f (Good) **5** Ran SP% **116.8**
Speed ratings (Par 99): **90,86,85,83,83**
CSF £5.07 TOTE £1.20: £1.02, £4.60; EX 4.60 Trifecta £12.90 Pool: £806.57 - 46.70 winning units..
Owner Pearl Bloodstock Ltd **Bred** Stephen E Quick **Trained** Newmarket, Suffolk
■ Gregori (9-2, unruly in stalls) & Quest For More (10-1, loose bef start) were withdrawn. Deduct 20p in the £ under R4.
FOCUS
What already looked a simple task for the winner was made even easier by the withdrawal of the second and third favourites. The winner didn't need to match her Nottingham latest.

3633 CORAL.CO.UK H'CAP 1m 67y
7:40 (7:44) (Class 4) (0-85,84) 3-Y-O **£4,851** (£1,443; £721; £360) **Stalls** Low

Form RPR
1P **1** **Ogbourne Downs**[32] 2603 3-9-2 **79**.................................... SteveDrowne 1 86
(Charles Hills) *sn trckd ldrs in 5th: prog to go 3rd 2f out: rdn and styd on fnl f to ld last 75yds* **20/1**
0531 **2** 1/2 **Harry Bosch**[21] 2935 3-8-12 **75**.................................... JamieSpencer 8 81
(Brian Meehan) *led: styd against rail in st: gng strly over 2f out: rdn over 1f out: worn down last 75yds* **8/1**
-525 **3** *nk* **Short Squeeze (IRE)**[24] 2846 3-8-11 **74**.................... MartinDwyer 7 79+
(Hugo Palmer) *dwlt: hld up in last pair: prog over 2f out: hrd rdn and styd on fr over 1f out to chal 3rd last strides: nrst fin* **10/1**
1264 **4** 1 1/4 **Strong Conviction**[32] 2584 3-8-13 **76**.................... MartinHarley 6 78
(Mick Channon) *prom: chsd ldr 3f out: drvn and no imp over 1f out: lost 2 pls fnl f* **25/1**
-422 **5** 5 **George Cinq**[26] 2776 3-9-7 **84**.................................... FrankieDettori 3 75
(Michael Bell) *hld up in rr: shkn up on outer 3f out: sme prog over 2f out: no hdwy and wl hld over 1f out* **11/4**[1]
-005 **6** 3 3/4 **The Gatling Boy (IRE)**[19] 2984 3-9-2 **79**.................... RichardHughes 5 61
(Richard Hannon) *chsd ldng trio to over 2f out: sn fdd: eased fnl f* **8/1**
0-15 **7** 2 **Derwent (USA)**[26] 2776 3-9-6 **83**.................................... JamesDoyle 9 61
(Roger Charlton) *hld up in last: sme prog and shkn up over 2f out: no ch of rching ldrs over 1f out and eased* **9/2**[3]
-130 **8** 17 **Hipster**[24] 2844 3-9-6 **83**....................................(b) JimCrowley 2 22
(Ralph Beckett) *chsd ldrs in 6th: pushed along over 3f out: lost pl and struggling over 2f out: eased and t.o* **12/1**
2-06 **9** 4 1/2 **Canadian Run (IRE)**[32] 2604 3-9-4 **81**.................... JimmyFortune 10
(Robert Mills) *chsd ldr to 3f out: wknd rapidly: t.o* **33/1**
61 **10** 11 **Messila Star**[55] 1908 3-9-5 **82**.................................... RyanMoore 4
(Jeremy Noseda) *a in rr: wknd 3f out: t.o* **7/2**[2]
1m 43.82s (-0.88) **Going Correction** -0.05s/f (Good) **10** Ran SP% **117.6**
Speed ratings (Par 101): **102,101,101,99,94 91,89,72,67,56**
toteswingers 1&2 £17.40, 1&3 £31.50, 2&3 £17.60 CSF £169.32 CT £1745.08 TOTE £26.80: £6.60, £1.80, £2.10; EX 111.10 Trifecta £398.40 Pool: £1503.75 - 2.83 winning units..
Owner S W Group Logistics Limited **Bred** Bumble Bloodstock & Mrs S Nicholls **Trained** Lambourn, Berks
FOCUS
This was a decent handicap for the money, but the first four home were at the lower end of the weights. The winner built on his C&D debut win.

3634 DOWNLOAD CORAL MOBILE FROM THE APP STORE H'CAP 6f
8:10 (8:10) (Class 4) (0-85,84) 3-Y-O **£4,851** (£1,443; £721; £360) **Stalls** Low

Form RPR
1002 **1** **Robot Boy (IRE)**[16] 3104 3-9-6 **83**.................................... JamieSpencer 4 96
(David Barron) *hld up in 5th and off the pce: plld out over 2f out: gd prog after to ld jst over 1f out: rdn and styd on wl* **6/4**[1]
46-1 **2** 2 **Noble Deed**[21] 2934 3-8-11 **74**.................................... RyanMoore 1 81
(William Haggas) *fractious bef gng to post: trckd ldng pair: swtchd lft wl over 1f out but wnr already gone by: styd on to take 2nd ins fnl f: no imp* **7/4**[2]
0003 **3** 2 **Miss Diva**[10] 3279 3-9-1 **83**.................... WilliamTwiston-Davies(5) 5 83
(Richard Hannon) *led: jnd 1/2-way: hdd over 1f out: wknd fnl f* **8/1**
1-60 **4** *hd* **Huntsmans Close**[16] 3104 3-9-5 **82**.................................... RichardHughes 6 82
(Michael Bell) *trckd ldr: upsides fr 1/2-way and appeared to be gng wl: shkn up and led briefly over 1f out: folded tamely after* **6/1**[3]
5020 **5** 1/2 **Laudation**[34] 2544 3-8-4 **67**.................................... MartinLane 2 65
(William Jarvis) *awkward s: off the pce in last: plld out wd and drvn over 2f out: one pce and no real prog* **20/1**

32-0 **6** 1 1/2 **Alcando (IRE)**68 1625 3-9-7 **84** ShaneKelly 3 77
(Denis Coakley) *trckd ldng pair: rdn and no imp 2f out: wknd over 1f out* **12/1**

1m 12.09s (-0.91) **Going Correction** -0.10s/f (Good) **6** Ran SP% **114.2**
Speed ratings (Par 101): **102,99,96,96,95 93**
toteswingers 1&2 £1.20, 1&3 £4.40, 2&3 £3.40 CSF £4.54 TOTE £2.50: £1.70, £1.20; EX 5.10 Trifecta £13.40 Pool: £1203.19 - 67.30 winning units..

Owner Qatar Racing Limited **Bred** Corduff Stud Ltd **Trained** Maunby, N Yorks

FOCUS
This wasn't the most competitive of sprints, but it was well run and the form makes sense. The winner is going from strength to strength.

3635 WINDSOR & ETON BREWERY FILLIES' H'CAP 1m 2f 7y
8:40 (8:42) (Class 5) (0-70,69) 4-Y-0+ **£2,587** (£770; £384; £192) **Stalls** Centre

Form RPR
202- **1** **Easter Diva (IRE)**191 8135 4-9-5 **67** RichardHughes 7 76
(Gerard Butler) *trckd ldrs: shkn up and clsd to ld jst over 1f out: pushed out: readily* **8/1**

-406 **2** 1 1/2 **Gaelic Ice**9 3314 4-8-5 **53** AndreaAtzeni 2 60
(Rod Millman) *wl in tch: pushed along over 2f out: nt clr run over 1f out: r.o fnl f to take 2nd nr fin: no ch to threaten wnr* **7/1**3

-002 **3** 1 **Langham Lily (USA)**9 3330 4-8-13 **61** SebSanders 10 65
(Chris Wall) *chsd ldrs: one of the first rdn over 3f out: styd on u.p over 1f out to take 2nd briefly ins fnl f* **9/2**1

2203 **4** 1 1/2 **Chrissycross (IRE)**9 3330 4-8-9 **57**(v) LiamKeniry 8 58
(Roger Teal) *hld up in last pair: pushed along over 2f out: reminders and r.o fnl f: nrst fin* **8/1**

2056 **5** hd **Ogaritmo**15 3138 4-8-12 **60**(p) PatCosgrave 4 61
(Alastair Lidderdale) *prom: trckd ldr over 2f out: rdn to ld briefly over 1f out: fdd fnl f* **20/1**

1330 **6** hd **If I Were A Boy (IRE)**11 3244 6-9-3 **65**(b) MartinLane 3 65
(Dominic Ffrench Davis) *hld up in last in modly run event: stl there over 2f out: shkn up and styd on fr over 1f out: no ch* **8/1**

-635 **7** 1/2 **Hip Hip Hooray**130 652 7-9-1 **63** RyanMoore 5 62
(Luke Dace) *a in midfield: rdn over 2f out: one pce and no prog* **11/2**2

0005 **8** 1 **Lily Edge**16 3106 4-8-11 **64** WilliamTwiston-Davies(5) 9 61
(John Bridger) *a towards rr: shkn up on wd outside over 2f out: no imp on ldrs over 1f out* **7/1**3

6253 **9** 3/4 **Dazzling Valentine**11 3258 5-9-7 **69** AdamKirby 6 65
(Alan Bailey) *chsd ldr: rdn over 3f out: lost pl and wknd over 2f out* **8/1**

3400 **10** 2 1/2 **Berwin (IRE)**16 3106 4-9-0 **62** JamesDoyle 12 53
(Sylvester Kirk) *awkward s but sn led at mod pce: hdd & wknd qckly over 1f out: eased* **20/1**

40-5 **11** 1 1/2 **Bladewood Girl**138 536 5-9-1 **63** JimmyFortune 1 51
(J R Jenkins) *v awkward s: towards rr: urged along 3f out: no prog and btn 2f out* **25/1**

-660 **12** 10 **Shirazz**90 1178 4-8-0 **53** 1 AmyScott(5) 11 21
(Alastair Lidderdale) *prom tl wknd 3f out: eased over 1f out* **25/1**

2m 10.1s (1.40) **Going Correction** -0.05s/f (Good) **12** Ran SP% **120.2**
Speed ratings (Par 100): **92,90,90,88,88 88,88,87,86,84 83,75**
toteswingers 1&2 £14.00, 1&3 £3.70, 2&3 £13.40 CSF £60.35 CT £285.22 TOTE £8.20: £2.30, £2.10, £2.60; EX 64.80 Trifecta £216.00 Pool: £1186.67 - 4.12 winning units..

Owner Kevin Quinn **Bred** Dr M V O'Brien **Trained** Newmarket, Suffolk

FOCUS
This was a routine fillies' handicap, with some regular AW runners switching to turf, but it was competitive enough. The first two have had fewer chances than most.

3636 CITI PRIVATE BANK SUPPORTING CLIC SARGENT H'CAP 1m 3f 135y
9:10 (9:11) (Class 5) (0-75,73) 3-Y-0 **£2,587** (£770; £384; £192) **Stalls** Centre

Form RPR
3421 **1** **Couloir Extreme (IRE)**7 3418 3-9-8 **73** 6ex RyanMoore 8 80
(Gary Moore) *trckd ldrs: quick move to ld 3f out: drvn fnl 2f: ld eroded nr fin but a in command* **5/4**1

-465 **2** 1 1/4 **Yul Finegold (IRE)**32 2603 3-9-7 **72** PatCosgrave 4 77
(George Baker) *hld up in rr: prog 3f out but wnr already gone for home: wnt 2nd over 1f out: drvn and grad clsd: a hld* **20/1**

-024 **3** 1 1/4 **Ivanhoe**11 3243 3-9-3 **68**(p) LiamKeniry 6 71
(Michael Blanshard) *hld up: in last pair 3f out: prog over 2f out: rdn and styd on wl fr over 1f out to take 3rd nr fin* **5/1**3

-343 **4** 1 **Bursledon (IRE)**24 2846 3-9-7 **72** RichardHughes 5 73
(Richard Hannon) *dwlt: sn prom: hanging lft bnd over 6f out to over 5f out and reminders: rdn 3f out: chsd ldng pair fnl f: pushed along and lost 3rd nr fin* **7/1**

4311 **5** 1/2 **Knight's Parade (IRE)**9 3313 3-9-6 **71** PatDobbs 1 71
(Amanda Perrett) *cl up: rdn to chal 3f out but no answer to wnr: chsd him after to over 1f out: one pce* **9/2**2

-516 **6** 7 **Jan De Heem**32 2600 3-9-0 **65**(v) JimCrowley 9 53
(Ralph Beckett) *hld up towards rr: sme prog over 2f out: no imp on ldrs over 1f out* **8/1**

0-06 **7** 3 **Lambert Pen (USA)**10 3281 3-8-9 **60** MartinHarley 7 43
(Mick Channon) *hld up and mostly in last pair: rdn 3f out: no prog and btn over 2f out* **33/1**

500 **8** 3/4 **Pursivere**33 2560 3-8-13 **64**(p) JimmyFortune 3 46
(Hughie Morrison) *led 3f: styd prom tl drvn and wknd 3f out* **25/1**

3140 **9** 4 1/2 **Strategic Strike (IRE)**17 3055 3-9-5 **70** MartinLane 2 44
(Paul Cole) *led after 3f to 3f out: wknd sn after* **16/1**

2m 30.84s (1.34) **Going Correction** -0.05s/f (Good) **9** Ran SP% **120.3**
Speed ratings (Par 99): **93,92,91,90,90 85,83,83,80**
toteswingers 1&2 £12.90, 1&3 £3.50, 2&3 £22.80 CSF £34.94 CT £105.65 TOTE £2.20: £1.20, £1.30, £2.30; EX 26.40 Trifecta £81.00 Pool: £1310.75 - 12.12 winning units..

Owner C E Stedman **Bred** Irish National Stud **Trained** Lower Beeding, W Sussex

FOCUS
This was just a middling handicap, won by an in-form improver, but the placed horses are also capable of winning a similar event. Couloir Extreme was not far off his C&D form.

T/Plt: £31.30 to a £1 stake. Pool: £105524.57 - 2455.28 winning tickets T/Qpdt: £15.20 to a £1 stake.Pool: £5783.74 - 281.15 winning tickets JN

2326 WOLVERHAMPTON (A.W) (L-H)
Monday, June 24

OFFICIAL GOING: Standard
Wind: Fresh across Weather: Cloudy with sunny spells

3637 BETVICTOR.COM AMATEUR RIDERS' (S) STKS 1m 4f 50y(P)
2:15 (2:15) (Class 6) 4-Y-0+ **£1,871** (£580; £290; £145) **Stalls** Low

Form RPR
-410 **1** **Underwritten**10 3287 4-11-0 63(v) NickSlatter(3) 2 66
(Donald McCain) *mde all: pushed along over 2f out: rdn clr fnl f* **6/1**3

5420 **2** 6 **Knox Overstreet**10 3284 5-10-12 66 MissSMDoolan(5) 5 56
(Mick Channon) *hld up: hdwy over 1f out: styd on to go 2nd nr fin: no ch w wnr* **15/8**2

5600 **3** 1/2 **Silver Marizah (IRE)**47 2159 4-10-0 40 MissRBIngram(7) 4 46
(Roger Ingram) *chsd wnr: rdn over 1f out: no ex fnl f: eased towards fin* **33/1**

32/0 **4** 6 **Waahej**21 2939 7-10-7 71 MissMEdden(5) 7 41
(Peter Hiatt) *hld up: hdwy over 4f out: pushed along over 2f out: wknd over 1f out* **11/10**1

4/0- **5** 2 3/4 **Kristallo (GER)**11 4904 8-10-5 58(p) MissSLewis(7) 9 37
(Dai Burchell) *hld up: hdwy over 7f out: wknd over 3f out* **14/1**

0405 **6** 9 **Heading To First**14 3151 6-10-7 40(p) MissMBryant(5) 3 22
(Paddy Butler) *trckd ldrs: racd keenly: wknd wl over 2f out* **50/1**

-500 **7** 18 **Visions Of Johanna (USA)**33 2575 8-10-12 43..(tp) MissSBrotherton 6
(Charles Smith) *prom: racd keenly: pushed along over 3f out: sn wknd: t.o* **12/1**

0060 **8** 21 **Dubai Emerald (USA)**11 3256 4-10-2 39(b1) MissKMargarson(5) 1
(Chris Dwyer) *reluctant to s: a t.o* **25/1**

2m 40.13s (-0.97) **Going Correction** -0.20s/f (Stan) **8** Ran SP% **119.8**
Speed ratings (Par 101): **95,91,90,86,84 78,66,52**
toteswingers 1&2 £2.30, 1&3 £11.50, 2&3 £12.80 CSF £18.43 TOTE £6.60: £1.80, £1.02, £8.30; EX 26.60 Trifecta £189.30 Pool: £2743.73 - 10.86 winning units..The winner was bought in for 3,200gns.

Owner D McCain Jnr **Bred** W And R Barnett Ltd **Trained** Cholmondeley, Cheshire

FOCUS
A desperately poor race, weakened substantially by the absence of likely market principal Right Stuff. However, the race developed at a relatively early stage. The winner sets the standard.

3638 BRIAN ECCLESHALL RETIREMENT H'CAP 5f 20y(P)
2:45 (2:47) (Class 5) (0-75,73) 3-Y-0 **£2,587** (£770; £384; £192) **Stalls** Low

Form RPR
5503 **1** **Silca's Dream**7 3400 3-8-5 **64** DanielCremin(7) 5 72
(Mick Channon) *a.p: pushed along to chse ldr over 1f out: rdn to ld ins fnl f: r.o* **7/2**2

1-06 **2** 2 1/4 **Saga Lout**12 3212 3-9-5 **71**(p) RichardKingscote 9 72
(Tom Dascombe) *chsd ldrs: pushed along and hung lft 1/2-way: rdn over 1f out: r.o to go 2nd post* **6/4**1

1360 **3** nse **Dangerous Age**15 3134 3-8-10 **62** MartinLane 7 63
(J W Hills) *a.p: chsd ldr 4f out tl led 1/2-way: rdn and hdd ins fnl f: styd on same pce* **12/1**

3400 **4** 2 **Lager Time (IRE)**56 1892 3-8-13 **65** TomQueally 1 60
(David Evans) *prom: racd keenly: rdn over 1f out: styd on* **7/1**3

66-5 **5** 3 1/2 **Max The Machine**7 3400 3-9-1 **67**(v1) MartinDwyer 3 50
(Derek Shaw) *hld up: hdwy over 1f out: sn rdn: nt trble ldrs* **14/1**

3153 **6** 3/4 **Balatina**20 2965 3-8-6 **58** SaleemGolam 4 39
(Chris Dwyer) *led to 1/2-way: sn rdn: wknd fnl f* **12/1**

31-6 **7** 4 **Twilight Pearl**84 1284 3-8-10 **62**(b) DuranFentiman 10 30
(Tim Easterby) *mid-div: lost pl over 3f out: in rr whn rdn and hung rt 2f out* **22/1**

60-0 **8** 1/2 **Time For Lambrini (IRE)**12 3212 3-8-13 **68** MarkCoumbe(3) 6 35
(Lisa Williamson) *s.i.s: outpcd* **16/1**

1334 **9** 3 **Miako (USA)**19 2994 3-9-4 **70** AndrewMullen 8 27
(Michael Appleby) *s.i.s: outpcd* **14/1**

1m 1.05s (-1.25) **Going Correction** -0.20s/f (Stan) **9** Ran SP% **113.7**
Speed ratings (Par 99): **102,98,98,95,89 88,81,81,76**
toteswingers 1&2 £2.10, 1&3 £7.00, 2&3 £5.00 CSF £8.93 CT £53.55 TOTE £3.40: £1.10, £1.10, £2.70; EX 10.40 Trifecta £74.20 Pool: £3052.84 - 30.83 winning units..

Owner Aldridge Racing Partnership **Bred** Aldridge Racing Partnership **Trained** West Ilsley, Berks

FOCUS
A low-grade handicap, but a fierce pace throughout. The winner's bset two runs have arguably come over C&D.

3639 £25 FREE BET AT BETVICTOR.COM CLAIMING STKS 5f 216y(P)
3:15 (3:15) (Class 5) 3-Y-0 **£2,587** (£770; £384; £192) **Stalls** Low

Form RPR
2060 **1** **Archie Stevens**16 3104 3-9-1 80 RichardKingscote 5 80
(Tom Dascombe) *chsd ldr tl led 1/2-way: shkn up over 1f out: pushed clr fnl f* **1/3**1

4043 **2** 4 **Dream Vale (IRE)**5 3475 3-8-6 65 DuranFentiman 1 58
(Tim Easterby) *s.i.s: hdwy over 3f out: rdn to go 2nd nr fin: no ch w wnr* **8/1**3

203- **3** 3/4 **Work Ethic (IRE)**195 8065 3-9-5 72(tp) NeilCallan 2 69
(Gerard Butler) *led to 1/2-way: rdn over 1f out: wknd ins fnl f: lost 2nd nr fin* **9/2**2

5030 **4** 1 1/2 **Annaley My Darling (IRE)**15 3134 3-8-0 50 NickyMackay 4 45?
(Mark Rimmer) *chsd ldrs: rdn over 1f out: styd on same pce* **20/1**

0 **5** 25 **Telamon (IRE)**16 3109 3-9-1 0 FrederikTylicki 3
(Milton Bradley) *chsd ldrs: pushed along and lost pl over 3f out: sn bhd: t.o* **66/1**

1m 13.8s (-1.20) **Going Correction** -0.20s/f (Stan) **5** Ran SP% **110.6**
Speed ratings (Par 99): **100,94,93,91,58**
CSF £3.85 TOTE £1.40: £1.10, £2.60; EX 3.70 Trifecta £6.70 Pool: £2557.81 - 285.08 winning units..Archie Stevens was claimed by Miss A Weaver for £10,000.

Owner L Bellman & Manor House Stables LLP **Bred** Howard Barton Stud **Trained** Malpas, Cheshire

■ Stewards' Enquiry : Frederik Tylicki caution: careless riding

FOCUS
A one-horse race according to the market and those that got involved at skinny prices were rewarded. The winner didn't need to match his winter best.

3640 IRISH STALLION FARMS EBF MAIDEN STKS 5f 216y(P)
3:45 (3:45) (Class 5) 2-Y-O £2,911 (£866; £432; £216) Stalls Low

Form RPR
5 1 **Chord Chart (IRE)**[11] 3245 2-9-5 0 MickaelBarzalona 3 83
(Saeed bin Suroor) *chsd ldrs: shkn up ld ins fnl f: r.o wl* **2/1**[2]
54 2 1 3/4 **Wickhambrook (IRE)**[9] 3350 2-9-5 0 SilvestreDeSousa 10 78
(Saeed bin Suroor) *led 1f: chsd ldr tl rdn to ld ins fnl f: sn hdd and unable qck* **7/4**[1]
22 3 1 1/2 **Bewitchment**[6] 3426 2-9-0 0 ChrisCatlin 1 68
(Sir Mark Prescott Bt) *led 5f out: rdn and hdd ins fnl f: styd on same pce* **11/4**[3]
6 4 3 1/4 **Black Geronimo**[24] 2823 2-9-5 0 TomQueally 2 63+
(David Evans) *chsd ldrs: rdn over 1f out: styd on same pce* **14/1**
5 5 nk **Resist**[6] 3426 2-9-0 0 NeilCallan 5 57+
(Tobias B P Coles) *chsd ldrs: rdn and ev ch over 1f out: edgd rt and wknd ins fnl f* **33/1**
6 4 **Ellalan** 2-9-5 0 MartinLane 4 50+
(David Simcock) *hld up: pushed along 1/2-way: styd on fr over 1f out: nvr nrr* **14/1**
4 7 2 3/4 **Global Explorer (USA)**[26] 2778 2-9-5 0 SaleemGolam 9 42
(Stuart Williams) *hld up: rdn over 1f out: nvr on terms* **40/1**
8 1 **Day Star Lad** 2-9-5 0 MartinDwyer 11 39+
(Derek Shaw) *s.s: rn green in rr: nvr nrr* **66/1**
0 9 1 1/4 **Jazri**[13] 3175 2-9-5 0 FrederikTylicki 6 35
(Milton Bradley) *sn pushed along in rr: sme hdwy over 2f out: sn rdn and wknd* **100/1**
6 10 1 1/4 **Big Kenny**[10] 3267 2-9-5 0 WilliamCarson 7 32
(David Evans) *s.i.s: a in rr* **66/1**
11 3/4 **Without Truth (IRE)** 2-9-5 0 ShaneKelly 12 29
(Ed McMahon) *mid-div: hdwy over 3f out: rdn over 2f out: sn wknd* **16/1**
0 12 4 **Spirit O Goodchild**[67] 1642 2-8-12 0 AaronJones(7) 8 17
(Alan McCabe) *mid-div: rdn over 2f out: sn wknd* **80/1**
1m 14.58s (-0.42) **Going Correction** -0.20s/f (Stan) 12 Ran SP% 126.2
Speed ratings (Par 93): **94,91,89,85,84 79,75,74,72,71 70,64**
toteswingers 1&2 £1.60, 1&3 £2.60, 2&3 £2.30 CSF £6.27 TOTE £2.20: £1.10, £1.30, £1.10; EX 5.70 Trifecta £16.90 Pool: £3665.04 - 162. winning units..
Owner Godolphin **Bred** Rathbarry Stud **Trained** Newmarket, Suffolk

FOCUS
Only three of these could be seriously considered for this juvenile contest, but there are reasons to be relatively positive about the form.

3641 DOWNLOAD THE BETVICTOR APP NOW MEDIAN AUCTION MAIDEN STKS 1m 141y(P)
4:15 (4:17) (Class 5) 3-Y-O £2,587 (£770; £384; £192) Stalls Low

Form RPR
4- 1 **Mount Tiger**[220] 7750 3-9-5 0 NeilCallan 7 85+
(James Tate) *a.p: chsd ldr over 6f out: led over 2f out: pushed out* **5/4**[1]
0-0 2 3 1/4 **Rabdaan**[35] 2507 3-9-5 0 FrederikTylicki 8 77
(James Fanshawe) *a.p: rdn and hung lft fr over 1f out: styd on to go 2nd wl ins fnl f: no ch w wnr* **25/1**
2-35 3 3 **Misfer**[42] 2322 3-9-5 72 (b) TomQueally 2 70
(Lady Cecil) *sn led: rdn and hdd over 2f out: wknd ins fnl f* **5/2**[2]
2-44 4 6 **Banreenahreenkah (IRE)**[11] 3241 3-9-0 67 ShaneKelly 9 51
(Denis Coakley) *prom: rdn over 3f out: wknd over 1f out* **9/2**[3]
2630 5 5 **Sixties Queen**[3] 3537 3-9-0 64 SamHitchcott 11 39
(Alan Bailey) *hld up: hdwy over 3f out: hmpd and wknd over 2f out* **20/1**
0- 6 1 **Somerton Star**[212] 7855 3-9-5 0 SilvestreDeSousa 6 42
(Pat Eddery) *s.i.s: hdwy over 6f out: rdn and wknd over 2f out* **33/1**
6 7 8 **Hattie Jacques**[10] 3278 3-9-0 0 MartinDwyer 10 19
(Mick Channon) *dwlt: sn pushed along and a in rr* **12/1**
0 8 1 3/4 **Pingit**[19] 2979 3-9-0 0 J-PGuillambert 5 15
(Alan McCabe) *sn pushed along and a in rr* **100/1**
0 9 1 3/4 **Ramata**[32] 2597 3-9-0 0 JohnFahy 4
(Harry Dunlop) *chsd ldr 2f: remained handy tl rdn and wknd over 2f out: t.o* **40/1**
10 15 **Green And White (ITY)** 3-9-5 0 MircoMimmocchi 1
(Frank Sheridan) *s.s: a bhd: t.o* **66/1**
00- 11 15 **Bella Bijou**[258] 6960 3-8-11 0 DarrenEgan(3) 3
(Christopher Kellett) *chsd ldrs tl wknd over 3f out: t.o* **200/1**
1m 47.4s (-3.10) **Going Correction** -0.20s/f (Stan) 11 Ran SP% 115.9
Speed ratings (Par 99): **105,102,99,94,89 88,81,80,78,65 51**
toteswingers 1&2 £8.50, 1&3 £8.50, 2&3 £9.30 CSF £42.04 TOTE £2.10: £1.10, £6.60, £1.30; EX 34.00 Trifecta £160.10 Pool: £4426.88 - 20.72 winning units..
Owner Saif Ali **Bred** Rabbah Bloodstock Limited **Trained** Newmarket, Suffolk

FOCUS
The well backed winner did this in good style. The bare form could be worth a bit more.

3642 BETVICTOR CASINO ON YOUR MOBILE H'CAP 1m 141y(P)
4:45 (4:45) (Class 6) (0-65,65) 4-Y-O+ £1,940 (£577; £288; £144) Stalls Low

Form RPR
1604 1 **Beauchamp Xerxes**[6] 3434 7-9-0 63 (t) NicoleNordblad(5) 6 74
(Hans Adielsson) *mde all: clr 5f out: shkn up over 1f out: unchal* **10/1**
64-0 2 2 1/4 **Opus Maximus (IRE)**[21] 2932 8-8-5 49 (p) JohnFahy 9 55
(Jennie Candlish) *stdd s: hld up: hdwy on outer over 1f out: rdn to go 2nd fnl f: r.o: nt rch wnr* **18/1**
5333 3 1/2 **Peter's Friend**[35] 2514 4-9-6 64 DaleSwift 12 69
(Michael Herrington) *prom: racd keenly: lost pl over 4f out: rdn over 1f out: r.o ins fnl f* **11/1**
0213 4 1/2 **Edgware Road**[16] 3106 5-9-5 63 WilliamCarson 3 67
(Sean Curran) *hld up: pushed along over 3f out: r.o u.p fnl f: nvr nrr* **5/1**[3]
2-40 5 1 **Tenessee**[38] 2417 6-9-7 65 SilvestreDeSousa 2 67
(Ben De Haan) *chsd ldrs: rdn over 3f out: styd on same pce fr over 1f out* **7/2**[2]
0000 6 3/4 **Tatting**[14] 2514 4-8-11 55 SaleemGolam 4 57
(Chris Dwyer) *mid-div: plld hrd: lost pl 5f out: rdn and r.o ins fnl f* **22/1**
2220 7 3 3/4 **John Potts**[89] 1214 8-8-11 55 (p) KierenFox 10 47
(Brian Baugh) *mid-div: hdwy 1/2-way: rdn over 2f out: wknd fnl f* **20/1**
4120 8 3/4 **William Van Gogh**[60] 1788 6-9-7 65 NeilCallan 7 56
(Michael Easterby) *hld up: rdn over 1f out: n.d* **3/1**[1]
/004 9 3/4 **Lady Tycoon**[19] 2974 4-7-10 47 ShelleyBirkett(7) 1 36
(Mark Brisbourne) *prom: pushed along over 3f out: wknd over 2f out* **40/1**
0336 10 1 1/2 **Mafi (IRE)**[25] 2807 5-9-7 65 (t) RobertHavlin 8 51
(Mark Hoad) *hld up: rdn over 1f out: nvr dangerous* **14/1**
3004 11 1 **Jumbo Prado (USA)**[17] 3054 4-9-5 63 ShaneKelly 5 47
(John Stimpson) *hld up: rdn over 1f out: a in rr* **7/1**
2514 12 1/2 **Just Five (IRE)**[33] 2575 7-8-9 53 (v) ChrisCatlin 13 36
(John Weymes) *mid-div: hdwy over 6f out: chsd wnr who was clr 5f out: rdn and wknd wl over 1f out* **20/1**
6000 13 2 1/2 **Firefly**[16] 3081 4-7-13 46 (b) DarrenEgan(3) 11 24
(John Weymes) *chsd ldrs: rdn over 3f out: sn wknd* **80/1**
1m 48.73s (-1.77) **Going Correction** -0.20s/f (Stan) 13 Ran SP% 123.3
Speed ratings (Par 101): **99,97,96,96,95 94,91,90,89,88 87,87,85**
toteswingers 1&2 £35.10, 1&3 £21.70, 2&3 £42.30 CSF £169.01 CT £2101.76 TOTE £12.70: £4.10, £5.70, £4.80; EX 248.50 Trifecta £2450.50 Part won. Pool: £3267.34 - 0.48 winning units..
Owner Erik Penser **Bred** E Penser **Trained** Kingston Lisle, Oxon

FOCUS
A competitive, if moderate handicap on paper in which the winner was allowed an easy lead. Hard to be confident about the form.

3643 TALK TO VICTOR H'CAP (DIV I) 7f 32y(P)
5:15 (5:16) (Class 6) (0-60,60) 3-Y-O+ £1,940 (£577; £288; £144) Stalls High

Form RPR
0602 1 **Whipphound**[11] 3247 5-9-7 55 GeorgeBaker 4 67
(Mark Brisbourne) *hld up: hdwy over 2f out: led 1f out: rdn out* **4/1**[1]
3030 2 2 1/4 **Penbryn (USA)**[17] 3054 6-9-11 59 TomMcLaughlin 10 65
(Nick Littmoden) *hld up: hdwy over 2f out: ev ch 1f out: sn rdn: styd on same pce ins fnl f* **14/1**
3622 3 1 1/2 **Mucky Molly**[33] 2575 5-9-7 55 (vt) RobertHavlin 2 57
(Alison Hutchinson) *w ldr tl led 4f out: rdn and hdd 1f out: styd on same pce* **4/1**[1]
-350 4 1 **Shomberg**[10] 3270 4-9-4 52 (p) SamHitchcott 8 51
(Dai Burchell) *chsd ldrs: rdn and ev ch over 1f out: no ex ins fnl f* **25/1**
-000 5 nk **Hinton Admiral**[45] 2236 9-9-4 52 NeilCallan 11 50
(Pat Eddery) *chsd ldrs: rdn over 2f out: styd on same pce fr over 1f out* **25/1**
2350 6 1 **Seamster**[9] 3329 6-9-10 58 (vt) SilvestreDeSousa 9 54
(Richard Ford) *s.i.s: hld up: nt clr run over 2f out: hdwy u.p over 1f out: no imp ins fnl f* **7/1**[2]
665 7 1 1/2 **Bill Of Rights**[35] 2499 3-8-11 57 DarrenEgan(3) 6 49
(Michael Bell) *hld up: rdn over 2f out: nvr on terms* **4/1**[1]
0004 8 1 1/2 **Marshall Art**[56] 1886 4-9-8 56 (tp) JohnFahy 1 44
(Ken Wingrove) *hld up: hdwy u.p over 1f out: wknd ins fnl f* **16/1**
6030 9 1 1/2 **Glenridding**[24] 2836 9-9-11 59 (p) DaleSwift 5 43
(James Given) *sn pushed along to chse ldrs: rdn over 2f out: wknd over 1f out* **9/1**[3]
1406 10 3/4 **Chambles**[97] 1079 4-9-2 57 GemmaTutty(7) 7 39
(Andrew Reid) *hld up: rdn over 1f out: n.d* **7/1**[2]
-206 11 1/2 **Bertie Blu Boy**[135] 587 5-9-3 54 (p) MarkCoumbe(3) 3 34
(Lisa Williamson) *sn led: hdd 4f out: rdn over 2f out: wknd fnl f* **16/1**
1m 28.73s (-0.87) **Going Correction** -0.20s/f (Stan)
WFA 3 from 4yo+ 9lb 11 Ran SP% 121.1
Speed ratings (Par 101): **96,93,91,90,90 89,87,85,83,83 82**
toteswingers 1&2 £9.60, 1&3 £3.50, 2&3 £9.60 CSF £66.99 CT £244.65 TOTE £3.80: £1.80, £4.10, £1.40; EX 63.60 Trifecta £231.80 Pool: £2445.98 - 7.91 winning units..
Owner W M Clare **Bred** Mrs B Skinner **Trained** Great Ness, Shropshire
■ Stewards' Enquiry : Mark Coumbe caution: careless riding

FOCUS
A wide-open low-grade handicap, run at a stern pace and that played very much into the hands of the winner and second.

3644 TALK TO VICTOR H'CAP (DIV II) 7f 32y(P)
5:45 (5:45) (Class 6) (0-60,59) 3-Y-O+ £1,940 (£577; £288; £144) Stalls High

Form RPR
0254 1 **Basle**[10] 3270 6-9-12 59 (t) RichardKingscote 9 67
(Michael Blake) *s.i.s: hld up: hdwy over 1f out: led ins fnl f: r.o wl* **4/1**[2]
0441 2 3/4 **Very First Blade**[19] 2998 4-8-12 52 (p) MatthewHopkins(7) 2 58
(Mark Brisbourne) *trckd ldrs: plld hrd: rdn and ev ch fr over 1f out: styd on* **10/1**
2205 3 1/2 **High On The Hog (IRE)**[12] 3210 5-9-11 58 TomMcLaughlin 11 63
(Mark Brisbourne) *chsd ldrs: rdn over 2f out: styd on* **14/1**
2200 4 hd **Kielty's Folly**[97] 1079 9-9-8 55 KierenFox 4 59
(Brian Baugh) *hld up: hdwy over 2f out: shkn up over 1f out: styd on* **14/1**
036 5 3/4 **Coastal Passage**[18] 3029 5-9-5 52 (t[1]) StephenCraine 5 54
(Charles Smith) *hld up: hdwy u.p over 1f out: edgd lft: r.o* **10/1**
260 6 1/2 **True Prince (USA)**[18] 3026 4-9-8 55 (b) SilvestreDeSousa 1 56
(Brian Ellison) *hld up: rdn over 2f out: r.o towards fin: nt rch ldrs* **9/4**[1]
0520 7 3/4 **Imtithal (IRE)**[12] 3203 4-9-7 54 (b) ChrisCatlin 8 53
(John Weymes) *prom: chsd ldr over 5f out: rdn and ev ch fr over 1f out tl no ex ins fnl f* **25/1**
00 8 nk **Spartic**[21] 2932 5-9-9 56 (p) NeilCallan 10 54
(Alan McCabe) *led: rdn over 1f out: hdd and unable qck ins fnl f* **5/1**[3]
U0/6 9 1/2 **Bond Artist (IRE)**[35] 2503 4-9-8 55 JohnFahy 6 52
(Geoffrey Oldroyd) *s.i.s: hld up: nvr nrr* **16/1**
-635 10 4 1/2 **Give Us A Belle (IRE)**[25] 2788 4-8-10 46 (bt[1]) DarrenEgan(3) 3 31
(Christine Dunnett) *chsd ldrs: rdn over 2f out: wknd over 1f out* **8/1**
1m 28.85s (-0.75) **Going Correction** -0.20s/f (Stan)
WFA 3 from 4yo+ 9lb 10 Ran SP% 119.8
Speed ratings (Par 101): **96,95,94,94,93 92,92,91,91,86**
toteswingers 1&2 £3.50, 1&3 £9.20, 2&3 £7.70 CSF £45.10 CT £528.90 TOTE £4.80: £1.40, £2.00, £4.40; EX 22.10 Trifecta £354.30 Pool: £2417.86 - 5.11 winning units..
Owner West Wilts Hockey Lads **Bred** W H R John And Partners **Trained** Trowbridge, Wilts

FOCUS
An active market for the second division of this handicap, which was more evenly run. Straightforward form.

T/Plt: £44.40 to a £1 stake. Pool: £73,485.57 - 1,206.47 winning tickets T/Qpdt: £12.50 to a £1 stake. Pool: £4,318.25 - 253.85 winning tickets CR

[3385] CHANTILLY (R-H)
Monday, June 24

OFFICIAL GOING: Turf: very soft

3645a PRIX RIDGWAY (LISTED RACE) (3YO COLTS & GELDINGS) (TURF) 1m 2f 110y
1:55 (12:00) 3-Y-O £22,357 (£8,943; £6,707; £4,471; £2,235)

RPR
1 **Buckwheat**[33] 3-8-11 0 .... MaximeGuyon 5 100
(A Fabre, France) **17/5**[3]
2 ¾ **Glacial Age (IRE)**[22] 2907 3-9-2 0 .... ThomasHenderson 6 104
(Jo Hughes) *led: shkn up 2f out: rdn and strly pressed ent fnl f: hdd ins fnl 150yds: styd on but hld* **24/1**
3 *hd* **Vanishing Cupid (SWI)**[23] 3-8-11 0 .... FabriceVeron 4 99
(H-A Pantall, France) **18/1**
4 1 **Art Contemporain (USA)**[43] 2297 3-9-2 0 .... ChristopheSoumillon 8 102
(P Bary, France) **33/10**[2]
5 ½ **Silver Trail**[23] 3-8-11 0 .... UmbertoRispoli 2 96
(M Delzangles, France) **2/1**[1]
6 ½ **Diyamindar (FR)**[41] 2355 3-8-11 0 ....(p) ThierryJarnet 7 95
(J Boisnard, France) **18/1**
7 ½ **Meneas (FR)**[307] 5471 3-8-11 0 .... OlivierPeslier 3 94
(C Laffon-Parias, France) **48/10**
8 10 **Face Surface (GER)**[41] 2357 3-8-11 0 .... Francois-XavierBertras 1 74
(F Rohaut, France) **14/1**

2m 12.56s (3.76) 8 Ran SP% **117.8**
WIN (incl. 1 euro stake): 4.40. PLACES: 2.20, 5.30, 4.40. DF: 50.80. SF: 73.10.
Owner Sheikh Mohammed **Bred** Darley **Trained** Chantilly, France

OSTEND (R-H)
Monday, June 24

OFFICIAL GOING: Turf: good

3647a PRIJS MODULAR (H'CAP) (4YO+) (TURF) 2m
6:30 (12:00) 4-Y-0+ £2,439 (£731; £365; £243; £121)

RPR
1 **If I Had Him (IRE)**[11] 3256 9-9-5 **0** ....(b) KClijmans 11 66
(George Baker) **3/1**[1]
2 ¾ **Agosto (GER)** 4-9-4 **0** .... FilipMinarik 8 64
(N Minner, Belgium) **43/10**[2]
3 1 ¾ **Killusty Fancy (IRE)**[565] 6-9-7 **0** .... MaximPecheur 9 65
(S Smrczek, Germany) **20/1**
4 2 ½ **Frederick William**[288] 5158 5-8-7 **0** ....(b) SHellyn 10 48
(Stal Klaverhof, Belgium) **35/1**
5 ¾ **Omokoroa (IRE)**[418] 7061 7-8-3 **0** .... DavidBreux 1 43
(Braem Horse Racing Sprl, Belgium) **11/1**
6 *snk* **All Dynamite (FR)**[176] 4-8-7 **0** ....(b) GlenBraem 6 47
(Braem Horse Racing Sprl, Belgium) **10/1**
7 1 **Sinbad The Sailor**[686] 4844 8-9-11 **0** ....(b) DPorcu 2 64
(George Baker) **68/10**[3]
8 1 ¾ **Frameit (IRE)**[441] 4633 6-8-11 **0** ....(b) ToonVanDenTroost 5 48
(R Ducasteele, France) **32/1**
9 3 **Bad Sir Brian (IRE)**[781] 1840 8-8-4 **0** .... MichelleSwinnens(4) 4 42
(M Ameye, Belgium) **46/1**
10 ¾ **Spark (GER)** 4-9-5 **0** .... APietsch 12 52
(C Von Der Recke, Germany) **9/1**
0 **Silver Gilt**[176] 13-7-13 **0** ....(b) ZoeVanDeVelde(1) 3
(D De Waele, France) **50/1**
0 **Urban Tiger (GER)**[768] 10-9-5 **0** ....(p) BartDeKoninck 7
(Ecurie'T Heyveld, Belgium) **30/1**

3m 41.8s (221.80) 12 Ran SP% **102.0**
PARI-MUTUEL (all including 1 euro stakes): WIN 4.00; PLACE 2.37, 2.35, 3.31; SF 22.37.
Owner Sir Alex Ferguson **Bred** Mrs J Morrissey **Trained** Manton, Wilts

[3189] BEVERLEY (R-H)
Tuesday, June 25

OFFICIAL GOING: Good (good to firm in places; 8.5)
Wind: Light half against Weather: Sunny

3648 BET AND WATCH WITH RACING UK'S APP MAIDEN AUCTION STKS 7f 100y
2:30 (2:32) (Class 6) 2-Y-O £2,264 (£673; £336; £168) Stalls Low

Form RPR
4426 1 **Atlantic Affair (IRE)**[17] 3092 2-8-6 0 .... JoeFanning 6 71
(Mark Johnston) *mde all: rdn clr 2f out: styd on* **13/8**[1]
552 2 *nk* **Shot In The Sun (IRE)**[12] 3255 2-8-4 0 .... BarryMcHugh 2 68
(Richard Fahey) *trckd ldng pair: hdwy to chse wnr over 2f out: rdn along wl over 1f out: styd on fnl f* **7/2**[2]
64 3 3 ¼ **Latenightrequest**[11] 3298 2-8-6 0 .... PatrickMathers 3 62
(Richard Fahey) *chsd ldrs: swtchd to outer and hdwy over 2f out: rdn wl over 1f out: kpt on fnl f: nrst fin* **7/1**[3]
30 4 *shd* **Chamberlain**[55] 1930 2-8-11 0 .... AndrewMullen 7 67
(Alan McCabe) *in tch: hdwy to chse ldrs 3f out: rdn wl over 1f out: kpt on same pce* **8/1**
0 5 2 ½ **Bertha Burnett (IRE)**[18] 3064 2-8-8 0 .... MickyFenton 8 58
(Brian Rothwell) *towards rr: hdwy 3f out: chsd ldrs wl over 1f out: sn rdn and no imp* **20/1**
6 2 ¾ **Hulcolt (IRE)** 2-8-11 0 .... RussKennemore 4 55
(Garry Moss) *chsd ldrs: rdn 2f out: wknd over 1f out* **14/1**
7 2 ¾ **Jacbequick** 2-8-9 0 .... JamesSullivan 1 46
(Karen Tutty) *s.i.s: a in rr* **10/1**
8 18 **Northern Reach** 2-8-4 0 .... PaulQuinn 12
(Geoffrey Harker) *hmpd s: a bhd* **33/1**
00 9 1 ½ **Sleaford**[69] 1606 2-8-9 0 .... PaulMulrennan 10
(Mel Brittain) *chsd wnr: rdn along wl over 2f out: sn wknd* **66/1**
5 10 6 **Mystic Angellina**[20] 2993 2-7-11 0 .... DanielleMooney(7) 11
(Michael Chapman) *rrd and wnt lft s: a wl bhd* **66/1**

1m 33.5s (-0.30) **Going Correction** -0.275s/f (Firm) **10** Ran SP% **110.4**
Speed ratings (Par 91): **90,89,85,85,82 79,76,56,54,47**
toteswingers 1&2 £1.40, 2&3 £2.80, 1&3 £3.00 CSF £5.96 TOTE £2.40: £1.10, £1.30, £1.80; EX 7.80 Trifecta £25.30 Pool: £3322.03 - 98.40 winning units..
Owner Atlantic Racing & R W Huggins **Bred** Airlie Stud **Trained** Middleham Moor, N Yorks
■ Colour Of The Wind was withdrawn (9-1, ref to enter stalls). Deduct 10p in the £ under R4.

FOCUS
All distances were as advertised. A moderate maiden that served up a decent test and straightforward form rated through the winner.

3649 GBI RACING LAUNCHES IN SWEDEN H'CAP 7f 100y
3:00 (3:00) (Class 5) (0-70,68) 3-Y-O+ £3,234 (£962; £481; £240) Stalls Low

Form RPR
1002 1 **Ted's Brother (IRE)**[7] 3444 5-9-9 **63** ....(e) RobbieFitzpatrick 3 71
(Richard Guest) *t.k.h: trckd ldng pair: effrt and nt clr run over 1f out tl squeezed through and rdn to ld last 50yds: jst hld on* **5/1**[2]
5-33 2 *shd* **Rex Romanorum (IRE)**[28] 2753 5-9-10 **64** .... DuranFentiman 1 72
(Patrick Holmes) *sn led: rdn along 2f out: drvn ent fnl f: edgd lft and hdd last 50yds: rallied nr line* **7/1**[3]
-06 3 1 **Dance For Georgie**[19] 3027 4-9-8 **62** .... PhillipMakin 6 68
(Ben Haslam) *trckd ldrs: hdwy 3f out: effrt 2f out: sn rdn and ev ch ent fnl f: sn drvn and kpt on same pce towards fin* **9/2**[1]
00-1 4 *nk* **Joyful Sound (IRE)**[17] 3081 5-9-4 **58** .... BarryMcHugh 5 63
(Brian Ellison) *trckd ldng pair: hdwy and cl up 3f out: rdn along 2f out and ev ch tl drvn and one pce fnl f* **5/1**[2]
034 5 ¾ **Last Destination (IRE)**[17] 3081 5-8-13 **53** ....(p) JamesSullivan 2 56+
(Nigel Tinkler) *dwlt and towards rr: hdwy on inner 2f out: effrt and nt clr run over 1f out: swtchd lft and rdn ent fnl f: kpt on: nrst fin* **8/1**
4500 6 1 ½ **Marshland**[11] 3289 3-9-2 **65** .... FrannyNorton 9 66+
(Mark Johnston) *dwlt and swtchd rt s: in rr: hdwy over 2f out: in tch and nt clr run wl over 1f out: swtchd rt and kpt on fnl f: nrst fin* **16/1**
-505 7 ½ **Sareeah (IRE)**[26] 2796 4-9-9 **63** .... DanielTudhope 4 61
(David O'Meara) *midfield: hdwy over 2f out: sn rdn along and no imp appr fnl f* **8/1**
1405 8 3 ½ **Powerful Pierre**[13] 3192 6-9-8 **62** ....(b) DaleSwift 13 51
(Ollie Pears) *dwlt and bhd tl sme late hdwy* **16/1**
1-05 9 *hd* **Monsieur Royale**[19] 3025 3-9-4 **67** ....(b) RussKennemore 8 56
(Geoffrey Oldroyd) *a in midfield* **14/1**
500 10 1 ¾ **Hussar Ballad (USA)**[21] 2961 4-9-5 **59** .... PaulMulrennan 10 43
(Mel Brittain) *a towards rr* **50/1**
-346 11 *shd* **Eeny Mac (IRE)**[13] 3192 6-8-13 **58** .... AdamCarter(5) 14 42
(Neville Bycroft) *chsd ldrs: hdwy on wd outside over 2f out: sn rdn and wknd* **14/1**
0-66 12 ¾ **Emperatriz**[40] 2387 3-9-3 **66** .... TomEaves 15 48
(John Holt) *midfield: sme hdwy 3f out: rdn along over 2f out: sn wknd* **20/1**
6000 13 10 **Gunner Will (IRE)**[59] 1842 4-8-12 **52** .... MickyFenton 12 9
(Paul Midgley) *a in rr* **40/1**
3000 14 7 **Thrust Control (IRE)**[13] 3192 6-9-5 **59** ....(p) JoeFanning 7
(Tracy Waggott) *cl up: disp ld 1/2-way: rdn along over 2f out: sn wknd* **20/1**

1m 31.33s (-2.47) **Going Correction** -0.275s/f (Firm)
WFA 3 from 4yo+ 9lb **14** Ran SP% **125.3**
Speed ratings (Par 103): **103,102,101,101,100 98,98,94,94,92 91,91,79,71**
toteswingers 1&2 £7.70, 2&3 £9.10, 1&3 £5.50 CSF £40.07 CT £175.46 TOTE £6.40: £1.90, £2.90, £1.40; EX 45.50 Trifecta £198.10 Pool: £2469.35 - 9.34 winning units..
Owner Mrs Alison Guest **Bred** T Counihan **Trained** Wetherby, W Yorks

FOCUS
A moderate handicap in which it paid to be handy and a low draw was an advantage.

3650 RACING UK PROFITS ALL RETURNED TO RACING MEDIAN AUCTION MAIDEN STKS 1m 100y
3:30 (3:32) (Class 5) 3-Y-O £3,408 (£1,006; £503) Stalls Low

Form RPR
2222 1 **Dairam (USA)**[11] 3278 3-9-5 75 .... DaneO'Neill 1 70
(Charles Hills) *trckd ldrs: hdwy and cl up 2f out: shkn up to ld 1 1/2f out: rdn and edgd rt over 1f out: clr ins fnl f: styd on* **30/100**[1]
0135 2 3 ¼ **Correggio**[21] 2960 3-9-5 70 .... PJMcDonald 6 63
(Micky Hammond) *trckd ldng pair: effrt over 2f out: rdn along wl over 1f out: styd on to chse wnr ins fnl f: no imp* **5/1**[2]
0-00 3 3 ¾ **Ella Motiva (IRE)**[12] 3232 3-9-0 49 .... RobbieFitzpatrick 5 50
(Mark Brisbourne) *t.k.h early: hld up: hdwy 2f out: sn rdn and kpt on same pce* **40/1**
3 4 3 ½ **Echo Of Lightning**[32] 2634 3-9-5 0 .... DuranFentiman 3 47
(Noel Wilson) *led: rdn along and jnd 2f out: hdd and drvn 1 1/2f out: wknd ent fnl f* **10/1**[3]
5 5 **Brother Duke** 3-9-0 0 .... JustinNewman(5) 2 36
(Garry Moss) *dwlt and green in rr: swtchd to outer and hdwy 3f out: rdn along 2f out: sn wknd* **33/1**
65- 6 8 **Prokeel (IRE)**[231] 7598 3-9-5 0 .... PaulMulrennan 4 19
(Tim Easterby) *chsd ldrs on inner: rdn along wl over 2f out: sn wknd* **14/1**

1m 46.52s (-1.08) **Going Correction** -0.275s/f (Firm) **6** Ran SP% **114.7**
Speed ratings (Par 99): **94,90,87,83,78 70**
toteswingers 1&2 £1.20, 2&3 £10.90, 1&3 £7.30 CSF £2.45 TOTE £1.40: £1.10, £1.50; EX 2.40 Trifecta £28.10 Pool: £4412.21 - 117.61 winning units..
Owner Hamdan Al Maktoum **Bred** Shadwell Farm LLC **Trained** Lambourn, Berks

FOCUS
A weak maiden and straightforward form but with the winner not needing to step up to score.

3651 SANDRA EVISON MEMORIAL H'CAP 1m 1f 207y
4:00 (4:00) (Class 4) (0-80,79) 4-Y-0+ £6,469 (£1,925; £962; £481) Stalls Low

Form RPR
0-21 1 **Hydrant**[8] 3397 7-8-6 **71** 6ex .... ConnorBeasley(7) 7 83
(Richard Guest) *sn led: pushed along and qcknd 3f out: jnd and rdn 2f out: styd on strly fnl f* **17/2**
2123 2 2 ½ **Saint Thomas (IRE)**[17] 3083 6-8-13 **71** .... JoeFanning 2 78
(John Mackie) *trckd ldng pair: cl up 3f out: chal 2f out: sn rdn and ev ch tl drvn and one pce ent fnl f* **4/1**[2]
-065 3 2 ¼ **Woodacre**[20] 2989 6-8-3 **61** .... JamesSullivan 1 64
(Richard Whitaker) *t.k.h: trckd wnr: plld hrd 1/2-way: rdn along 2f out: kpt on same pce appr fnl f* **16/1**
4110 4 1 ½ **Arc Light (IRE)**[11] 3301 5-9-0 **72** .... DuranFentiman 8 72+
(Tim Easterby) *hld up in rr: swtchd wd and hdwy wl over 2f out: rdn along wl over 1f out: kpt on fnl f: nrst fin* **13/2**[3]

3346 **5** *1* **Gala Casino Star (IRE)**[20] 2976 8-9-0 **79**................(p) JordanNason(7) 6 77
(Geoffrey Harker) *trckd ldrs: hdwy 3f out: rdn along over 2f out: sn one pce* **10/1**

5212 **6** *1½* **Reset City**[7] 3427 7-8-6 **64**.................................... FrannyNorton 5 59
(Mark Johnston) *dwlt and rdn along in rr sn after s: sme hdwy over 2f out: sn rdn and n.d* **7/4**[1]

1504 **7** *1¼* **Carragold**[27] 2766 7-9-1 **73**.................................... PaulMulrennan 4 66
(Mel Brittain) *chsd ldrs: rdn along 3f out: wknd over 2f out* **12/1**

-636 **8** *½* **Tartan Gigha (IRE)**[27] 2766 8-9-1 **73**.............................. PJMcDonald 3 65
(Geoffrey Harker) *a towards rr* **11/1**

0321 **9** *1½* **Honoured (IRE)**[16] 3138 6-8-9 **67**..........................(t) AndrewMullen 9 56
(Michael Appleby) *hld up: effrt wl over 2f out: sn rdn and btn* **14/1**

2m 4.51s (-2.49) **Going Correction** -0.275s/f (Firm) **9** Ran SP% **117.9**
Speed ratings (Par 105): **98,96,94,93,92 91,90,89,88**
toteswingers 1&2 £8.10, 2&3 £19.40, 1&3 £27.40 CSF £43.41 CT £543.77 TOTE £12.90: £2.50, £1.30, £5.60; EX 45.20 Trifecta £807.10 Pool: £2312.77 - 2.14 winning units..
Owner C Hatch **Bred** Lord Halifax **Trained** Wetherby, W Yorks

FOCUS
This looked a decent handicap for the class, but it was run at a crawling early pace and those held up stood no chance. The placed horses are the best guides with the second reliable here.

3652 WOLD TOP BREWERY "RACE SAUCE" H'CAP 1m 4f 16y
4:30 (4:30) (Class 5) (0-70,68) 4-Y-O+ **£3,234** (£962; £481; £240) **Stalls** Low

Form RPR

-103 **1** **Maybeme**[5] 3504 7-8-10 **57**..................................(p) AndrewElliott 8 63
(Neville Bycroft) *dwlt: sn in tch: hdwy 3f out: chal 2f out: rdn to ld over 1f out: drvn ins fnl f and kpt on gamely towards fin* **7/2**[2]

00-4 **2** *½* **Badea**[18] 3043 4-9-6 **67**...(v) TonyHamilton 7 72
(Richard Fahey) *dwlt and in rr: pushed along 3f out: rdn over 2f out: hdwy over 1f out: sn drvn and styd on wl fnl f* **4/1**[3]

50-0 **3** *¾* **Bavarian Nordic (USA)**[21] 2961 8-8-5 **57**...........(v) GeorgeChaloner(5) 5 61
(Richard Whitaker) *hld up in tch: hdwy 3f out: rdn wl over 1f out: chsd wnr ent fnl f: sn edgd rt and kpt on same pce* **16/1**

0-00 **4** *1¾* **Fossgate**[6] 3480 12-9-7 **68**.. AmyRyan 1 69+
(James Bethell) *s.i.s and bhd: hdwy over 4f out: rdn along wl over 2f out: styng on whn n.m.r and swtchd rt ent fnl f: kpt on towards fin* **12/1**

0105 **5** *9* **Valantino Oyster (IRE)**[4] 3545 6-9-0 **61**......................(p) JoeFanning 3 48
(Tracy Waggott) *led: rdn along and jnd 2f out: hdd and drvn over 1f out: wknd ent fnl f* **3/1**[1]

3202 **6** *2½* **Politibureau**[5] 3504 6-8-2 **49**.. JamesSullivan 4 32
(Michael Easterby) *cl up and pushed along after 1f: rn in snatches: rdn along over 5f out: wknd wl over 2f out* **11/2**

0200 **7** *2½* **Fine Kingdom**[24] 2887 4-8-3 **50**..................................(v[1]) BarryMcHugh 2 29
(Brian Ellison) *trckd ldrs: pushed along over 3f out: rdn over 2f out: sn wknd* **12/1**

-004 **8** *16* **Tribal Myth (IRE)**[17] 3083 6-8-4 **58**..........................(b) PaulMcGiff(7) 6 11
(Kevin Ryan) *cl up: rdn along 4f out: wknd over 3f out* **13/2**

2m 36.18s (-3.62) **Going Correction** -0.275s/f (Firm) **8** Ran SP% **117.2**
Speed ratings (Par 103): **101,100,100,99,93 91,89,79**
toteswingers 1&2 £3.70, 2&3 £15.10, 1&3 £12.70 CSF £18.47 CT £198.18 TOTE £4.90: £1.90, £2.10, £5.60; EX 19.90 Trifecta £142.40 Pool: £2587.32 - 18.16 winning units..
Owner Mrs J Dickinson **Bred** Harts Farm And Stud **Trained** Brandsby, N Yorks

FOCUS
A weak handicap. It was run at a frantic early pace with a three-way go for the lead. The winner is rated to her best form, backed up by the third.

3653 DOWNLOAD THE FREE RACING UK APP H'CAP 1m 4f 16y
5:00 (5:01) (Class 6) (0-65,64) 3-Y-O **£2,264** (£673; £336; £168) **Stalls** Low

Form RPR

5433 **1** **Wadacre Sarko**[8] 3394 3-9-7 64.................................... FrannyNorton 12 73+
(Mark Johnston) *trckd ldrs: swtchd rt to outer and hdwy wl over 1f out: rdn to chal and hung bdly rt ent fnl f: sn led: drvn out* **4/1**[2]

0-55 **2** *1¾* **Sunblazer (IRE)**[18] 3055 3-9-6 63.................................... PhillipMakin 6 69
(William Muir) *prom: cl up 3f out: rdn to ld over 1f out: drvn and hdd ent fnl f: hld whn n.m.r towards fin* **22/1**

232 **3** *¾* **Alshan Fajer**[33] 2599 3-9-7 64.. TonyHamilton 8 69+
(Roger Ingram) *hld up: hdwy 4f out: trckd ldrs 3f out: rdn to chal over 1f out: cl up and ev ch whn hmpd ent fnl f: kpt on towards fin* **5/2**[1]

-033 **4** *½* **Halfwaytocootehill (IRE)**[29] 2716 3-8-8 51....................(t) PJMcDonald 11 55
(Ollie Pears) *prom: rdn along wl over 1f out: styng on and ev ch whn hmpd ent fnl f: drvn and no ex towards fin* **13/2**

-652 **5** *1¾* **Attansky (IRE)**[13] 3194 3-9-0 57................................(p) DuranFentiman 7 58
(Tim Easterby) *led: rdn along over 3f out: drvn and hdd wl over 1f out: grad wknd* **11/1**

600- **6** *2* **Jebulani**[192] 8134 3-8-5 48.. AndrewMullen 1 46
(David O'Meara) *midfield: hdwy over 2f out: sn rdn and no imp* **11/1**

5114 **7** *1¾* **Precision Strike**[4] 2274 3-8-13 56.........................(tp) RobbieFitzpatrick 10 51
(Richard Guest) *hld up in rr: sme hdwy fnl 2f: n.d* **33/1**

5-06 **8** *hd* **Hurricane John (IRE)**[42] 2341 3-8-7 50.................................... PaulQuinn 9 45
(David Nicholls) *a towards rr* **33/1**

204 **9** *hd* **Duchess Of Dreams**[48] 2154 3-8-2 45.................................. JamesSullivan 3 40
(Richard Guest) *plld hrd: chsd ldrs on inner: rdn along over 3f out: sn wknd* **33/1**

1326 **10** *¾* **Niknad**[13] 3194 3-8-10 53..(p) TomEaves 2 47
(Brian Ellison) *hld up towards rr: hdwy on outer over 3f out: chsd ldrs whn hmpd wl over 1f out: wknd after* **6/1**[3]

00-0 **11** *18* **Tallaay (IRE)**[59] 1837 3-8-7 50.. JoeFanning 4 15
(Mark Johnston) *hld up in rr: sme hdwy 5f out: sn rdn and wknd 3f out* **15/2**

0-6 **12** *13* **Causeway Foot (USA)**[61] 1776 3-9-6 63...............(t) MichaelO'Connell 5 7
(Jedd O'Keeffe) *prom: rdn along over 4f out: wknd 3f out* **33/1**

2m 40.12s (0.32) **Going Correction** -0.275s/f (Firm) **12** Ran SP% **120.7**
Speed ratings (Par 97): **87,85,85,85,83 82,81,81,81,80 68,59**
toteswingers 1&2 £17.20, 2&3 £11.70, 1&3 £2.70 CSF £96.80 CT £258.55 TOTE £6.20: £2.90, £6.80, £1.40; EX 93.10 Trifecta £630.70 Pool: £3549.90 - 4.22 winning units..
Owner Wadacre Stud **Bred** Wadacre Stud **Trained** Middleham Moor, N Yorks

■ Stewards' Enquiry : Franny Norton one-day ban: careless riding (9 July)

FOCUS
Previous winning form was thin on the ground in this ordinary handicap. The form looks straightforward though, with the third the best guide.

3654 GO RACING IN YORKSHIRE FUTURE STARS APPRENTICE H'CAP (ROUND 4) 5f
5:30 (5:31) (Class 6) (0-60,60) 3-Y-O+ **£2,264** (£673; £336; £168) **Stalls** Low

Form RPR

-411 **1** **Bondi Beach Boy**[19] 3024 4-9-9 **56**.................................. JordanNason 6 65
(James Turner) *mde all: rdn wl over 1f out: drvn and wandered ins fnl f: kpt on wl towards fin* **4/1**[2]

0433 **2** *1½* **Pull The Pin (IRE)**[13] 3190 4-9-0 **52**........................ LukeLeadbitter(5) 9 56
(Declan Carroll) *trckd ldng pair: hdwy to chse wnr over 1f out: rdn and n.m.r ins fnl f: kpt on same pce towards fin* **5/2**[1]

0-04 **3** *nk* **See Vermont**[19] 3024 5-8-8 **46**.................................. GaryMahon(5) 8 49
(Robin Bastiman) *trckd ldrs: hdwy over 1f out: swtchd rt and rdn ent fnl f: kpt on: nrst fin* **12/1**

0522 **4** *¾* **Blue Noodles**[49] 2126 7-9-5 **55**..............................(v) KevinStott(3) 5 55+
(Neville Bycroft) *in rr: rdn along 2f out: swtchd to outer ent fnl f: fin strly* **11/2**[3]

300 **5** *½* **Lord Buffhead**[20] 2998 4-9-1 **55**..............................(b) LisaTodd(7) 2 53
(Richard Guest) *in tch: hdwy wl over 1f out: sn rdn and kpt on same pce fnl f* **14/1**

3600 **6** *nk* **Wicked Wilma (IRE)**[26] 2795 9-8-13 **51**.................. JordanHibberd(5) 12 48
(Alan Berry) *chsd ldrs: hdwy 2f out: rdn over 1f out: one pce fnl f* **14/1**

-300 **7** *shd* **Queen's Princess**[3] 3593 5-8-8 **46**..............................(p) PaulMcGiff(5) 3 43
(Neville Bycroft) *towards rr: hdwy wl over 1f out: sn rdn and no imp fnl f* **20/1**

0-06 **8** *¾* **Robyn**[48] 2169 3-8-6 **52** ow3.................................... KatieWatson(7) 14 46
(Scott Dixon) *dwlt and sltly hmpd s: sn in tch on outer: rdn to chse ldrs 2f out: sn one pce* **40/1**

5001 **9** *1* **Sophie's Beau (USA)**[13] 3190 6-8-13 **51**..........(b) DanielleMooney(5) 15 41
(Michael Chapman) *qckly away and wnt rt s: sn cl up: rdn along wl over 1f out: wknd appr fnl f* **16/1**

-000 **10** *½* **Lady Del Sol**[25] 2837 5-9-8 **60**.................................. LouisSteward(5) 13 48
(Marjorie Fife) *dwlt: a in rr* **20/1**

2030 **11** *hd* **Captain Royale (IRE)**[1] 3630 8-9-11 **58**..........................(p) JoshCrane 1 46
(Tracy Waggott) *chsd ldrs on inner: hdwy over 1f out: rdn whn n.m.r ins fnl f: wknd* **6/1**

4-50 **12** *1½* **Rio Sands**[32] 2611 8-8-6 **46**.................................. CaseyWilcox(7) 7 28
(Richard Whitaker) *a in rr* **25/1**

1m 2.31s (-1.19) **Going Correction** -0.20s/f (Firm)
WFA 3 from 4yo+ 6lb **12** Ran SP% **121.0**
Speed ratings (Par 101): **101,98,98,96,96 95,95,94,92,91 91,89**
toteswingers 1&2 £2.30, 2&3 £9.70, 1&3 £12.60 CSF £13.93 CT £113.59 TOTE £6.30: £2.80, £2.50, £2.40; EX 15.70 Trifecta £230.40 Pool: £2532.87 - 8.24 winning units..
Owner J R Turner **Bred** G R & H Turner **Trained** Norton-le-Clay, N Yorks

FOCUS
Not a bad sprint handicap for the lowly class, confined to apprentice riders. The second is rated close to recent C&D form.
T/Plt: £33.70 to a £1 stake. Pool of £80476.53 - 1738.91 winning tickets. T/Qpdt: £16.00 to a £1 stake. Pool of £5659.0 - 261.69 winning tickets JR

3425 BRIGHTON (L-H)
Tuesday, June 25

OFFICIAL GOING: Good to firm (8.0)
Wind: virtually nil Weather: bright spells

3655 BRIGHTON STREAMLINE TAXIS SUPPORTS THE MARTLETS H'CAP 1m 3f 196y
2:15 (2:16) (Class 6) (0-65,63) 4-Y-O+ **£1,940** (£577; £288; £144) **Stalls** High

Form RPR

-002 **1** **Beacon Lady**[15] 3151 4-8-4 **51**.................................. NicoleNordblad(5) 6 63+
(William Knight) *stdd s: hld up in last pair: effrt towards centre over 2f out: led over 1f out: sn clr: r.o wl: comf* **3/1**[2]

-054 **2** *6* **Steely**[14] 3168 5-9-4 **60**.. GeorgeBaker 3 62
(Gary Moore) *taken down early: led: reminders over 4f out: rdn and hdd over 1f out: sn no ch w wnr but kpt on for clr 2nd* **7/2**[3]

64-5 **3** *2¾* **Panettone (IRE)**[29] 2729 4-9-2 **63**..............................(b) ThomasBrown(5) 5 61
(Roger Varian) *chsd ldr: rdn and pressed ldr over 2f out: no ex u.p 2f out: 3rd and wknd over 1f out* **5/4**[1]

0-40 **4** *3¼* **Lindsay's Dream**[26] 2801 7-8-5 **47**..............................(p) RichardThomas 1 40
(Zoe Davison) *hld up in last pair: clsd 5f out: rdn and effrt on inner over 2f out: wknd over 1f out* **20/1**

5006 **5** *6* **Total Obsession**[3] 3579 6-8-7 **49**..............................(v) LukeMorris 4 32
(Mark Hoad) *chsd ldrs: rdn and unable qck 3f out: btn 2f out: sn wknd* **12/1**

6056 **6** *13* **Revert (USA)**[15] 3151 4-8-1 **46** ow1..........................(b) SimonPearce(3) 2
(Gerry Enright) *chsd ldrs tl lost pl and rdn 4f out: lost tch over 2f out* **66/1**

2m 33.17s (0.47) **Going Correction** +0.025s/f (Good) **6** Ran SP% **105.6**
Speed ratings (Par 101): **99,95,93,91,87 78**
toteswingers 1&2 £1.70, 2&3 £1.70, 1&3 £1.40 CSF £12.09 TOTE £3.00: £1.40, £1.70; EX 12.60 Trifecta £21.70 Pool: £2952.68 - 101.95 winning units..
Owner The Pro-Claimers **Bred** Ashley House Stud **Trained** Patching, W Sussex

FOCUS
Course at inner configuration and all distances were as advertised. A moderate handicap, run at a steady pace and not a race to be positive about.

3656 PIPECENTER.CO.UK H'CAP 1m 1f 209y
2:45 (2:47) (Class 6) (0-65,62) 4-Y-O+ **£1,940** (£577; £288; £144) **Stalls** High

Form RPR

4111 **1** **Green Earth (IRE)**[8] 3412 6-8-11 **57**.................................. JemmaMarshall(5) 1 67
(Pat Phelan) *chsd ldng trio: clsd 5f out: rdn and chsd clr ldr over 1f out: styd on to ld fnl 150yds: kpt on wl: rdn out* **2/1**[1]

0332 **2** *1* **Whinging Willie (IRE)**[17] 3106 4-9-7 **62**.................................. GeorgeBaker 7 68
(Gary Moore) *stdd s: t.k.h: hld up in last pair: clsd 5f out: swtchd rt and effrt 2f out: hdwy u.p over 1f out: styd on wl to go 2nd last strides* **5/2**[2]

00 **3** *shd* **St Ignatius**[71] 1585 6-9-3 **58**..(p) AdamKirby 4 64
(Alan Bailey) *chsd ldr: rdn 3f out: sn drvn and unable qck: rallied and kpt on wl ins fnl f* **6/1**[3]

6435 **4** *nse* **Standing Strong (IRE)**[13] 3218 5-9-7 **62**..........................(p) LiamKeniry 6 68
(Zoe Davison) *led: rdn and qcknd clr over 2f out: drvn and hdd fnl 150yds: kpt on same pce after: lost 2 pls last strides* **8/1**

5055 **5** 2½ **Having A Ball**[8] 3399 9-8-8 **49**.. ChrisCatlin 2 50
(Geoffrey Deacon) *hld up in midfield: clsd and in tch 5f out: rdn and effrt 2f out: styd on same pce ins fnl f* **7/1**

6001 **6** ½ **Hawaiian Freeze**[10] 3314 4-8-6 **47**.................................... LukeMorris 9 47
(John Stimpson) *hld up in last quartet: clsd and in tch 5f out: rdn and effrt over 2f out: styng on same pce whn n.m.r 1f out: no imp fnl f* **25/1**

660- **7** 1¾ **Hubood**[17] 5938 5-8-4 **45**... RichardThomas 8 42
(Zoe Davison) *stdd s: hld up in last pair: rdn and effrt ent fnl 2f: no imp: nvr trbld ldrs* **66/1**

4305 **8** ¾ **Mishrif (USA)**[18] 3054 7-9-6 **61**...............................(v) JamesMcDonald 5 57
(J R Jenkins) *chsd ldrs: rdn and unable qck over 2f out: wknd ent fnl f: eased whn no ch wl ins fnl f* **20/1**

4004 **9** 4½ **Hawk Moth (IRE)**[7] 3429 5-9-4 **59**.............................(p) SamHitchcott 3 46
(John Spearing) *hld up in midfield: clsd 5f out: lost pl u.p over 2f out: bhd 1f out* **25/1**

2m 4.59s (0.99) **Going Correction** +0.025s/f (Good) **9** Ran SP% **113.7**
Speed ratings (Par 101): **97,96,96,96,94 93,92,91,88**
toteswingers 1&2 £1.50, 2&3 £2.80, 1&3 £4.30 CSF £6.61 CT £23.68 TOTE £2.50: £1.20, £1.10, £1.70; EX 5.90 Trifecta £18.20 Pool: £2076.66 - 85.48 winning units..
Owner P Wheatley **Bred** Woodcote Stud Ltd **Trained** Epsom, Surrey

FOCUS
The pace was steady for this weak handicap. The winner had something in hand with the form straightforward in behind.

3657 WORSLEY PIPE CENTER H'CAP 7f 214y
3:15 (3:15) (Class 6) (0-55,55) 3-Y-0+ **£1,940** (£577; £288; £144) **Stalls** Low

Form RPR

0506 **1** **Lightning Spirit**[14] 3169 5-9-7 **52**...................................(p) GeorgeBaker 5 63+
(Gary Moore) *stdd s: hld up in rr: swtchd rt and hdwy 2f out: rdn and gd hdwy over 1f out: edging lft and led ins fnl f: sn clr: r.o wl: comf* **7/2**[2]

0000 **2** 1½ **Benandonner (USA)**[8] 3406 10-9-1 **53**......................(p) JoeyHaynes(7) 3 60
(Paddy Butler) *in tch: rdn and chsd ldrs 2f out: swtchd rt ins fnl f: styd on and wnt 2nd wl ins fnl f: r.o but no threat to wnr* **25/1**

3640 **3** 3 **Surrey Dream (IRE)**[10] 3326 4-9-1 **46**............................(tp) SeanLevey 13 46
(John Bridger) *wl in tch in midfield: rdn and effrt to chse ldr 2 out: drvn and pressing wnr but nt qckning over 1f out: wknd wl ins fnl f* **10/1**

1532 **4** 1¾ **Munaawib**[5] 3513 5-9-7 **52**...(bt) PatCosgrave 12 48
(Charles Smith) *led: rdn ent fnl 2f: drvn and hdd ins fnl f: sn btn and wknd* **3/1**[1]

6/00 **5** 1 **Mr Mallo**[34] 2576 4-9-1 **46** oh1... ShaneKelly 14 39
(John Stimpson) *dwlt: sn rcvrd and in tch in midfield: rdn to chse ldrs but hld hd high over 1f out: one pce fnl f* **50/1**

0/00 **6** shd **Keyhole Kate**[52] 2030 4-9-1 **46** oh1.................................(p) LiamKeniry 8 39
(Polly Gundry) *s.i.s: hld up in rr: swtchd rt and hdwy 2f out: styd on fnl f: nvr trbld ldrs* **40/1**

2350 **7** 3½ **Hellbender (IRE)**[24] 2884 7-9-10 **55**.............................(t) HarryBentley 4 43
(Shaun Harris) *wl in tch in midfield: rdn and effrt 2f out: no imp and sn outpcd: wknd 1f out* **5/1**[3]

00-0 **8** 4½ **Jackpot**[16] 3134 3-8-5 **46** oh1.. JimmyQuinn 2 21
(Brendan Powell) *taken down early: t.k.h: in tch in midfield: rdn and effrt on inner over 2f out: wknd over 1f out* **50/1**

00-0 **9** 2 **Mitch Rapp (USA)**[21] 2954 4-9-9 **54**........................ FergusSweeney 11 24
(Jamie Osborne) *t.k.h: chsd ldr for 2f: styd handy: rdn and no ex ent fnl 2f: wknd over 1f out* **8/1**

0005 **10** ¾ **Dancing Welcome**[11] 3269 7-9-3 **55**.............................(bt) WillPettis(7) 7 23
(Milton Bradley) *chsd ldrs: wnt 2nd 3f out tl 2f out: sn wknd* **16/1**

05-0 **11** 4½ **Sporting Club Girl**[17] 3116 3-8-2 **46** oh1................(v[1]) DarrenEgan(3) 10
(William Knight) *a towards rr: rdn and no hdwy over 2f out: wknd over 1f out* **20/1**

0-00 **12** 4 **Fault**[21] 2954 7-9-7 **52**..(t) FrankieMcDonald 9
(Zoe Davison) *hld up in tch: rdn and sme hdwy over 2f out: no prog wl over 1f out: sn wknd* **33/1**

2050 **13** 19 **Bougaloo**[34] 2576 3-8-11 **52**...(p[1]) HayleyTurner 1
(Alan McCabe) *pushed along and in tch: chsd ldr 4f out tl 3f out: sn lost pl: t.o and eased wl ins fnl f* **8/1**

0000 **14** ¾ **Confirmed**[111] 907 4-9-5 **50**...(t) LukeMorris 6
(Barry Brennan) *chsd ldr after 1f tl 4f out: sn lost pl: t.o and eased wl ins fnl f* **14/1**

1m 36.02s (0.02) **Going Correction** +0.025s/f (Good)
WFA 3 from 4yo+ 10lb **14** Ran SP% **125.7**
Speed ratings (Par 101): **100,98,95,93,92 92,89,84,82,81 77,73,54,53**
toteswingers 1&2 £21.30, 2&3 £59.00, 1&3 £8.80 CSF £101.75 CT £847.30 TOTE £3.60: £1.10, £7.70, £3.70; EX 117.80 Trifecta £514.40 Pool: £2984.83 - 4.35 winning units..
Owner Heart Of The South Racing **Bred** John And Caroline Penny **Trained** Lower Beeding, W Sussex

FOCUS
A low-grade but open handicap, run at a fierce gallop. The form looks sound for the level.

3658 PLATINUM LACE H'CAP 5f 59y
3:45 (3:46) (Class 4) (0-80,85) 3-Y-0+ **£4,690** (£1,395; £697; £348) **Stalls** Low

Form RPR

1530 **1** **Sandfrankskipsgo**[10] 3341 4-9-12 **79**.................................. ShaneKelly 2 88
(Peter Crate) *stdd s: t.k.h: hld up in tch in midfield: swtchd lft and effrt on inner 2f out: rdn to ld over 1f out: in command and kpt on wl fnl f* **7/2**[2]

5106 **2** 1 **Whitecrest**[9] 3371 5-9-12 **79**... ChrisCatlin 6 84
(John Spearing) *in tch in rr: rdn 1/2-way: hdwy u.p 1f out: styd on wl to go 2nd last strides* **7/1**

2424 **3** hd **Red Refraction (IRE)**[10] 3320 3-9-1 **79**........ WilliamTwiston-Davies(5) 4 82
(Richard Hannon) *chsd ldrs: rdn 2f out: chsd wnr over 1f out: styd on same pce ins fnl f: lost 2nd last strides* **5/4**[1]

4050 **4** 2¾ **Marvelino**[12] 3243 3-8-4 **63**...(b) CathyGannon 7 56
(Pat Eddery) *racd wd: in tch in midfield: rdn and effrt 2f out: edgd lft u.p and no imp over 1f out: one pce fnl f* **16/1**

0603 **5** ½ **Bubbly Ballerina**[3] 3577 4-9-2 **74**.............................. NatashaEaton(5) 5 67
(Alan Bailey) *in tch in last pair: rdn and effrt 2f out: styd on same pce fnl f* **6/1**[3]

1413 **6** 2½ **Monumental Man**[14] 3171 4-9-8 **75**..................................(p) AdamKirby 1 59
(James Unett) *dwlt: sn bustled along and rcvrd to ld: rdn and edgd rt ent fnl 2f: hdd over 1f out: no ex: wknd ins fnl f: eased towards fin* **7/1**

1200 **7** 8 **Billy Red**[14] 3171 9-9-6 **73**...(b) FergusSweeney 3 28
(J R Jenkins) *chsd ldr tl 2f out: lost pl over 1f out: bhd and heavily eased wl ins fnl f* **20/1**

1m 2.87s (0.57) **Going Correction** +0.025s/f (Good)
WFA 3 from 4yo+ 6lb **7** Ran SP% **116.6**
Speed ratings (Par 105): **96,94,94,89,88 84,72**
toteswingers 1&2 £4.80, 2&3 £2.90, 1&3 £2.20 CSF £28.69 CT £46.03 TOTE £4.10: £1.70, £3.00; EX 31.70 Trifecta £86.70 Pool: £3667.12 - 31.70 winning units..
Owner Peter Crate **Bred** Peter Crate **Trained** Newdigate, Surrey

FOCUS
A fair sprint handicap, run at a decent pace and straightforward form rated through the runner-up.

3659 GENTING CASINO BRIGHTON MAIDEN AUCTION STKS 5f 213y
4:15 (4:16) (Class 5) 2-Y-0 **£2,587** (£770; £384; £192) **Stalls** Low

Form RPR

0 **1** **Picks Pinta**[95] 1108 2-8-9 0... CathyGannon 6 68+
(Jo Hughes) *hmpd s: t.k.h: hld up in last pair: clsd to trck ldrs 2f out: swtchd lft and effrt on inner over 1f out: led 1f out: rn green and hung rt ins fnl f: styd on* **7/4**[1]

06 **2** ½ **Sakhee'Ssquirrel**[8] 3413 2-8-6 0..................................... SaleemGolam 3 63
(David Evans) *t.k.h: chsd ldrs: rdn and chal 2f out: led over 1f out: carried rt and styd on same pce ins fnl f* **14/1**

4 **3** 1¼ **G Man (IRE)**[15] 3148 2-9-2 0... HarryBentley 5 69+
(Olly Stevens) *hld up wl in tch in midfield: swtchd rt and effrt 2f out: chsd ldrs 1f out: keeping on same pce whn hmpd ins fnl f* **9/4**[2]

36 **4** 3¾ **Aweebitowinker**[63] 1749 2-8-9 0....................................... JohnFahy 10 50
(J S Moore) *bustled along leaving stalls: sn rcvrd to press ldr and t.k.h: rdn and unable qck 2f out: wknd fnl f* **16/1**

02 **5** ½ **Zafraaj**[19] 3009 2-8-11 0... LukeMorris 4 50
(Ronald Harris) *led: rdn 2f out: drvn and hdd over 1f out: wknd ins fnl f* **5/2**[3]

5 **6** 2 **Silver Starlet (IRE)**[15] 3155 2-8-5 0......................... SimonPearce(3) 7 44
(Alastair Lidderdale) *wnt lft s: chsd ldrs: effrt 2f out: pushed rt and sltly hmpd 2f out: wknd ent fnl f* **20/1**

50 **7** 1 **Dawnfromthepast (IRE)**[10] 3310 2-8-11 0................ FergusSweeney 1 41
(Jamie Osborne) *t.k.h: hld up in tch in rr: pushed rt and edgd lft over 1f out: wknd 1f out* **33/1**

1m 12.3s (2.10) **Going Correction** +0.025s/f (Good) **7** Ran SP% **116.0**
Speed ratings (Par 93): **87,86,84,79,79 76,75**
toteswingers 1&2 £4.90, 2&3 £4.10, 1&3 £2.10 CSF £28.33 TOTE £4.30: £4.10, £4.50; EX 32.40 Trifecta £136.40 Pool: £3700.40 - 20.33 winning units..
Owner Chester Racing Club Ltd **Bred** Heatherwold Stud **Trained** Lambourn. Berks

FOCUS
Not a strong maiden, run at a fair pace but the form is fluid and rated around the middle of race averages.

3660 PIPE CENTER H'CAP 5f 213y
4:45 (4:45) (Class 6) (0-60,58) 3-Y-0+ **£1,940** (£577; £288; £144) **Stalls** Low

Form RPR

0004 **1** **Hamis Al Bin (IRE)**[10] 3325 4-9-9 **55**................................ LukeMorris 9 66
(Milton Bradley) *hld up in tch towards rr: clsd and nt clr run over 1f out: rdn and hdwy 1f out: led ins fnl f: r.o wl* **12/1**

50-0 **2** 1¾ **Ridgeway Sapphire**[12] 3247 6-8-13 **45**.......................(v) HayleyTurner 7 50
(Mark Usher) *stdd s: hld up in last trio: clsd on inner and swtchd rt 2f out: 5th and drvn over 1f out: styd on to go 2nd wl ins fnl f* **14/1**

4333 **3** 1¼ **My Own Way Home**[13] 3223 5-9-10 **56**............................ AdamKirby 11 57
(David Evans) *in tch: rdn and effrt to ld 2f out: edgd lft u.p over 1f out: hdd ins fnl f: no ex and wknd towards fin* **2/1**[1]

0650 **4** 2½ **Amenable (IRE)**[13] 3190 6-9-11 **57**................................ MartinHarley 5 50
(Violet M Jordan) *hld up wl in tch in midfield: rdn and effrt to chal 2f out: ev ch over 1f out tl no ex ins fnl f: wknd fnl 100yds* **7/1**[3]

3004 **5** 1¾ **Johnny Splash (IRE)**[7] 3425 4-9-0 **51**....................(b) NathanAlison(5) 4 38
(Roger Teal) *chsd ldrs: rdn and ev ch 2f out: no ex 1f out: wkng whn short of room and hit rail ins fnl f* **12/1**

0430 **6** 3¼ **Alpha Tauri (USA)**[13] 3197 7-9-1 **47**...........................(t[1]) PatCosgrave 12 24
(Charles Smith) *hld up in rr: c wd and sme hdwy over 1f out: nvr trbld ldrs* **16/1**

0002 **7** 2¼ **Verus Delicia (IRE)**[19] 3026 4-9-9 **55**............................ ShaneKelly 2 53+
(Daniel Mark Loughnane) *in tch in midfield on inner: short of room and bdly hmpd over 2f out: n.d after: bhd and swtchd rt over 1f out: plugged on* **6/1**[2]

0000 **8** 1½ **Courageous (IRE)**[11] 3270 7-9-3 **56**............................(v) WillPettis(7) 10 21
(Milton Bradley) *s.i.s: bhd: rdn and effrt 2f out: plugging on but no ch whn hmpd over 1f out: wknd fnl f* **16/1**

3506 **9** ½ **Athwaab**[49] 2126 6-9-12 **58**... GeorgeBaker 6 21
(Simon Hodgson) *taken down early: in tch in midfield: effrt 2f out: wknd u.p over 1f out: no ch whn eased wl ins fnl f* **25/1**

/005 **10** 2 **Mousie**[15] 3154 4-8-13 **45**.. HarryBentley 1
(Alan McCabe) *led tl 1/2-way: rdn and struggling whn hmpd and lost pl jst over 2f out: n.d after: wknd over 1f out* **25/1**

00-0 **11** nk **Rio Royale (IRE)**[10] 3326 7-9-0 **46**................................(p) SeanLevey 3
(Amanda Perrett) *chsd ldrs: rdn and unable qck whn bdly hmpd jst over 2f out: sn lost pl and bhd* **16/1**

0431 **12** 5 **Russian Bullet**[7] 3425 4-9-0 **51** 6ex......................(b) RachealKneller(5) 14
(Jamie Osborne) *sn chsng ldrs fr wd draw: led 1/2-way tl 2f out: wknd qckly over 1f out: fdd fnl f* **8/1**

1m 10.95s (0.75) **Going Correction** +0.025s/f (Good) **12** Ran SP% **118.6**
Speed ratings (Par 101): **96,93,92,88,86 82,79,77,76,73 73,66**
toteswingers 1&2 £14.20, 2&3 £9.70, 1&3 £7.10 CSF £169.22 CT £476.75 TOTE £16.70: £4.80, £4.10, £1.50; EX 242.00 Trifecta £1618.70 Pool: £3161.23 - 1.46 winning units..
Owner Philip Banfield **Bred** Mrs H Owen **Trained** Sedbury, Gloucs
■ Stewards' Enquiry : Nathan Alison four-day ban: careless riding (9, 10, 11, 15 July)

FOCUS
Plenty of pace on for this modest handicap, with a number of runners suffering interference up the far rail 2f from home. The placed horses are pretty solid at this level, suggesting the form is reasonable.

3661 HARRINGTONS LETTINGS H'CAP 6f 209y
5:15 (5:15) (Class 5) (0-70,70) 3-Y-0+ **£2,587** (£770; £384; £192) **Stalls** Low

Form RPR

43 **1** **Decent Fella (IRE)**[17] 3087 7-9-2 **65**..........................(t) OisinMurphy(7) 3 78+
(Violet M Jordan) *in tch in midfield: pushed along and sltly outpcd 4f out: rdn and hdwy on inner to ld over 1f out: sn qcknd clr: r.o strly: readily* **2/1**[1]

0-05 **2** 5 **Kamchatka**[40] 2394 3-9-5 **70**.......................................(bt[1]) LiamKeniry 1 67
(Philip Hide) *in tch in midfield: rdn and effrt 2f out: kpt on 1f out: chsd clr wnr ins fnl f: no imp* **6/1**[2]

5012 **3** 1¾ **Wishformore (IRE)**[10] 3326 6-8-11 **53**....................(p) RichardThomas 7 48
(Zoe Davison) *t.k.h: chsd ldrs: rdn and unable qck 2f out: kpt on ins fnl f to go 3rd fnl 100yds: no ch w wnr* **9/1**

5301 **4** 2 **The Mongoose**[7] 3430 5-9-2 **65** 6ex............................(t) NoelGarbutt(7) 2 55
(David Evans) *led: rdn 2f out: hdd over 1f out and sn outpcd by wnr: lost 2 pls and wknd fnl f* **8/1**[3]

5026 **5** *hd* **Ishisoba**[26] 2802 3-8-8 **59** .... LukeMorris 4 46
(Alastair Lidderdale) *in tch in midfield: n.m.r and shuffled bk over 2f out: sme hdwy over 1f out: no threat to wnr and n.m.r again ins fnl f* **8/1**[3]

6-00 **6** *1* **Nubar Boy**[22] 2918 6-9-6 **62** .... (v) StevieDonohoe 8 49
(Ian Williams) *s.i.s: hld up in rr: rdn and effrt whn swtchd rt over 1f out: no imp* **10/1**

0040 **7** *4* **Blue Deer (IRE)**[7] 3433 5-8-13 **58** .... (b[1]) DarrenEgan(3) 5 35
(Lee Carter) *chsd ldr tl wl over 1f out: sn struggling u.p: wknd over 1f out* **25/1**

5460 **8** *11* **Orders From Rome (IRE)**[8] 3404 4-10-0 **70** .... ShaneKelly 9 18
(Eve Johnson Houghton) *in tch: swtchd rt and effrt 2f out: no imp and btn over 1f out: eased ins fnl f* **6/1**[2]

0-10 **9** *1 ½* **Alice Rose (IRE)**[29] 2711 4-9-11 **67** ....[1] NickyMackay 6 11
(Rae Guest) *in tch in last pair: effrt whn sltly hmpd 2f out: sn btn: bhd and eased ins fnl f* **10/1**

1m 22.67s (-0.43) **Going Correction** +0.025s/f (Good)
WFA 3 from 4yo+ 9lb **9 Ran SP% 116.2**
Speed ratings (Par 103): **103,97,95,93,92 91,87,74,72**
toteswingers 1&2 £3.90, 2&3 £12.60, 1&3 £4.90 CSF £14.10 CT £88.66 TOTE £2.90: £1.50, £1.80, £3.00; EX 17.80 Trifecta £127.90 Pool: £1880.59 - 11.02 winning units..
Owner Rakebackmypoker.com **Bred** Michael Dalton **Trained** Moreton Morrell, Warwicks

FOCUS
This handicap was run at a fair pace with the winner pulling clear. The winner is likely to do better and the form behind looks sensible.
T/Plt: £152.80 to a £1 stake. Pool of £88390.52 - 422.20 winning tickets. T/Qpdt: £43.70 to a £1 stake. Pool of £6712.69 - 113.60 winning tickets. SP

3237 NEWBURY (L-H)
Tuesday, June 25

OFFICIAL GOING: Good to firm
Wind: Nil Weather: Sunny spells

3662 PUMP TECHNOLOGY APPRENTICE H'CAP — 1m 3f 5y
6:20 (6:20) (Class 5) (0-70,74) 4-Y-0+ **£2,587** (£770; £384; £192) **Stalls** Centre

Form RPR

0411 **1** **Standpoint**[3] 3579 7-10-0 **74** 6ex .... RyanTate(3) 7 83
(Conor Dore) *hld up in rr: stdy hdwy fr 3f out: chal over 1f out: sn chsng ldr: drvn to ld fnl 110yds: r.o strly* **2/1**[1]

1240 **2** *1 ¾* **Shirataki (IRE)**[27] 2777 5-9-4 **64** .... ThomasGarner(3) 6 70
(Peter Hiatt) *s.i.s: in rr: stdy hdwy fr 3f out to ld over 1f out: sn rdn: hdd fnl 110yds: kpt on same pce* **16/1**

2-04 **3** *2 ¾* **Now What**[27] 2777 6-8-12 **60** .... DavidCoyle(5) 2 62
(Jonathan Portman) *led tl narrowly hdd over 5f out: styd upsides tl led again 3f out: drvn over 2f out: hdd over 1f out: outpcd by ldng duo ins fnl f* **9/2**[2]

1110 **4** *1 ¼* **Highlife Dancer**[8] 3412 5-9-12 **69** .... (v) CharlesBishop 5 69
(Mick Channon) *chsd ldrs: drvn ins fnl 3f: stl ev ch over 1f out: wknd ins fnl f* **7/1**[3]

0-00 **5** *hd* **Dicey Vows (USA)**[58] 883 5-8-8 **56** .... DavidParkes(5) 4 55
(Alan Jarvis) *trckd ldr: tk keen hodd: led over 5f out but hrd pressed tl hdd 3f out: drvn and ev ch over 1f out: wknd ins fnl f* **40/1**

4-60 **6** *shd* **Chasin' Rainbows**[14] 3169 5-8-7 **53** .... JoshBaudains(3) 1 52
(Sylvester Kirk) *t.k.h: sn in tch: drvn to chse ldrs over 2f out: wknd ins fnl f* **8/1**

-303 **7** *hd* **Transfer**[12] 3231 8-8-5 **51** .... DanielMuscutt(3) 8 50
(Richard Price) *t.k.h: trckd ldrs: rdn over 2f out: wknd ins fnl f* **8/1**

6052 **8** *½* **Bold Cross (IRE)**[10] 3312 10-9-2 **59** .... DeclanBates 10 57
(Edward Bevan) *s.i.s: t.k.h and sn in tch: pushed along 3f out: outpcd sn after: drvn and kpt on again ins fnl f* **15/2**

00-6 **9** *21* **Epsom Salts**[10] 3328 8-9-7 **69** .... SophieRalston(5) 9 34
(Pat Phelan) *plld hrd in rr: hung rt fr 3f out: a wl bhd* **14/1**

2m 23.39s (2.19) **Going Correction** -0.225s/f (Firm) **9 Ran SP% 113.0**
Speed ratings (Par 103): **83,81,79,78,78 78,78,78,62**
toteswingers 1&2 £10.10, 2&3 £18.60, 1&3 £3.20 CSF £36.77 CT £129.07 TOTE £3.20: £1.30, £5.20, £2.30; EX 55.90 Trifecta £181.50 Pool: £892.57 - 3.68 winning units..
Owner Mrs Jennifer Marsh **Bred** Juddmonte Farms Ltd **Trained** Hubbert's Bridge, Lincs
■ Golden Jubille was withdrawn (5-2, no suitable jockey available). Deduct 25p in the £ under R4.
■ Stewards' Enquiry : Charles Bishop one-day ban: careless riding (9 July)

FOCUS
Races on Round course increased in distance by about 4m. There was little pace on early and all apart from Epsom Salts were in contention with 2f to run. The first two are rated close to their 2012 form with the in-form fourth not far below recent efforts.

3663 PEGASUS PUMPS LTD MAIDEN AUCTION FILLIES' STKS — 6f 8y
6:55 (6:55) (Class 4) 2-Y-0 **£3,752** (£1,116; £557; £278) **Stalls** Low

Form RPR

3 **1** **Kendal Mint**[17] 3107 2-8-10 0 .... JamesDoyle 12 80+
(Clive Cox) *mde all: shkn up and qcknd over 1f out: reminder ins fnl f and readily strode clr: unchal* **4/5**[1]

2 *2 ½* **Secret Kode (IRE)** 2-8-8 0 .... WilliamCarson 15 70+
(Brendan Powell) *chsd ldrs: wnt 2nd over 2f out: sn rdn and kpt on wl but nvr any ch w wnr* **25/1**

3 *1 ¼* **Baars Causeway (IRE)** 2-8-6 0 .... MartinDwyer 6 64
(Alan Jarvis) *in tch: drvn to chse ldrs 2f out: wnt 3rd 1f out: styd on u.p but nvr gng pce of ldng duo* **8/1**[3]

4 *¾* **Warrendale** 2-8-8 0 .... FergusSweeney 8 64+
(Henry Candy) *towards rr on stands' side: pushed along and hdwy 2f out: styd on wl fnl f: gng on in clsng stages but nt rch ldrs* **9/2**[2]

5 *hd* **Oyster (IRE)** 2-8-4 0 .... JimmyQuinn 3 59+
(Gary Harrison) *in rr: pushed along over 2f out: hdwy over 1f out: styd on fnl f: nt rch ldrs* **33/1**

6 *1* **Castagna Girl** 2-8-6 0 .... CathyGannon 4 59+
(Denis Coakley) *slowly away: in rr: hdwy over 2f out: rn green and edgd lft ins fnl f: kpt on in clsng stages* **25/1**

7 *2 ¼* **Nimble Kimble** 2-8-1 0 .... RyanTate(5) 7 51+
(James Eustace) *in tch: drvn: green and outpcd over 1f out: kpt on again in clsng stages* **28/1**

00 **8** *1 ¾* **Mildenhall**[9] 3374 2-8-10 0 .... PatDobbs 14 49
(Richard Hannon) *chsd wnr tl over 2f out: wknd appr fnl f* **16/1**

64 **9** *1 ¾* **Lady Marl**[11] 3275 2-8-10 0 .... TomQueally 9 43
(Gary Moore) *t.k.h: in tch: drvn: hdwy but green and edgd lft 2f out: chsd ldrs over 1f out: wknd ins fnl f* **9/1**

0 **10** *¾* **Rural Affair**[14] 3174 2-8-4 0 .... LiamJones 16 35
(Harry Dunlop) *chsd ldrs: rdn over 2f out: wknd sn after* **50/1**

11 *½* **Morgans Bluff** 2-7-13 0 .... JemmaMarshall(5) 1 33
(Pat Phelan) *chsd ldrs: hung lft: green and wknd over 1f out* **66/1**

06 **12** *3 ¼* **Anya's Angel**[13] 3217 2-8-8 0 .... MartinLane 13 27
(David Simcock) *s.i.s: outpcd most of way* **40/1**

13 *½* **Mistress And Maid** 2-7-11 0 .... NoraLooby(7) 10 21
(Joseph Tuite) *chsd ldrs: rdn over 2f out: wknd ins fnl 2f* **66/1**

1m 14.59s (1.59) **Going Correction** +0.05s/f (Good) **13 Ran SP% 122.2**
Speed ratings (Par 92): **91,87,86,85,84 83,80,78,75,74 74,69,69**
toteswingers 1&2 £3.50, 2&3 £32.10, 1&3 £2.60 CSF £33.74 TOTE £1.70: £1.10, £4.80, £3.00; EX 28.70 Trifecta £415.10 Pool: £999.94 - 1.80 winning units..
Owner Hot To Trot Racing Club & Mrs J Scott **Bred** Glebe Stud **Trained** Lambourn, Berks

FOCUS
Two of the last five winners of this maiden auction for fillies have gone on to score at Group 3 level, including last year's victor Maureen who returned to this venue to take the Fred Darling at the spring meeting. A big field lined up this year, though traffic problems caused Pink Mirage to be withdrawn due to no suitable jockey being present. The winner scored well but this does not look a strong contest for the track.

3664 PUMPMATIC PUMP STATIONS BY PUMP TECHNOLOGY MAIDEN FILLIES' STKS — 7f (S)
7:25 (7:29) (Class 4) 2-Y-0 **£3,752** (£1,116; £557; £278) **Stalls** Low

Form RPR

4 **1** **Gold Top (IRE)**[28] 2740 2-9-0 0 .... RichardHughes 14 82
(Richard Hannon) *mde all: drvn and qcknd appr fnl f styd on strly* **7/2**[1]

2 *1 ½* **Autumn Sunrise (IRE)** 2-9-0 0 .... SeanLevey 5 78+
(Richard Hannon) *chsd ldrs: rdn to press wnr over 1f out: outpcd ins fnl f but hld on wl for 2nd* **33/1**

3 *nk* **Grevillea (IRE)** 2-9-0 0 .... MartinHarley 10 78+
(Mick Channon) *in rr: hdwy fr 2f out: nt much daylight over 1f tl shkn up and swtchd lft fnl 120yds: fin wl to press for 2nd but could nt trble wnr* **50/1**

4 *½* **Amber Isle (USA)** 2-9-0 0 .... JamesDoyle 13 76
(Roger Charlton) *trckd wnr: tl pushed along over 1f out: kpt on same pce in clsng stages* **13/2**

5 *1 ¾* **Redinha** 2-9-0 0 .... AdamKirby 8 71
(Clive Cox) *chsd ldrs: drvn 2f out: outpcd ins fnl f* **14/1**

6 *1 ¾* **Peacemaker (IRE)** 2-9-0 0 .... JohnFahy 9 67
(Eve Johnson Houghton) *in tch: chsd ldrs fr 1/2-way: rdn over 2f out: wknd ins fnl f* **50/1**

7 *½* **Amazing Maria (IRE)** 2-9-0 0 .... FrankieDettori 4 66
(Ed Dunlop) *in tch: hdwy to chse ldrs 2f out: wknd ins fnl f* **6/1**[3]

8 *¾* **Spring Carnival (USA)** 2-9-0 0 .... MickaelBarzalona 12 64
(Saeed bin Suroor) *chsd ldrs: rdn and wknd over 1f out* **4/1**[2]

9 *hd* **Nyanza (GER)** 2-9-0 0 .... FergusSweeney 3 63+
(Alan King) *s.i.s: hdwy and in tch over 2f out: wknd over 1f out* **50/1**

10 *1* **Pushkar** 2-9-0 0 .... TomQueally 7 61
(Lady Cecil) *chsd ldrs: rdn 2f out: wknd wl over 1f out* **4/1**[2]

11 *nk* **Miss Tweedy** 2-9-0 0 .... SteveDrowne 11 60
(Rod Millman) *towards rr most of way* **100/1**

12 *¾* **Ultraviolet (IRE)** 2-9-0 0 .... MartinLane 1 58
(David Simcock) *in rr: sme hdwy 3f out: n.d and sn wknd* **66/1**

13 *½* **Maysville (IRE)** 2-9-0 0 .... JamesMcDonald 6 57
(Charles Hills) *in tch: chsd ldrs over 2f out: wknd wl over 1f out* **25/1**

14 *½* **Hala Hala (IRE)** 2-9-0 0 .... JamieSpencer 2 55
(Michael Bell) *in rr: hdwy to cl on ldrs over 2f out: wknd qckly over 1f out* **16/1**

15 *½* **Starlight Princess (IRE)** 2-9-0 0 .... LiamJones 16 54
(J S Moore) *s.i.s: outpcd* **50/1**

1m 27.87s (2.17) **Going Correction** +0.05s/f (Good) **15 Ran SP% 119.5**
Speed ratings (Par 92): **89,87,86,86,84 82,81,80,80,79 79,78,77,77,76**
toteswingers 1&2 £12.70, 2&3 £100.10, 1&3 £46.00 CSF £130.13 TOTE £3.30: £1.10, £9.90, £23.40; EX 101.30 Trifecta £782.90 Part won. £1043.99 - 0.56 winning units..
Owner D Boocock **Bred** Top Row Partnership **Trained** East Everleigh, Wilts

FOCUS
This fillies' maiden has a history of producing smart types and the last three renewals have produced winners who have graduated to either the top of the ladder or one rung down. Last year's victor Just The Judge went on to better her second place finish in the 1000 Guineas with success in the Irish equivalent. On looks it was clear to see why some of these fillies' had been targeted at the race. This looks a pretty good contest and might prove better than rated.

3665 JUNG PUMPEN & PUMP TECHNOLOGY H'CAP — 1m 7y(R)
8:00 (8:01) (Class 5) (0-70,69) 3-Y-0 **£2,587** (£770; £384; £192) **Stalls** Low

Form RPR

0-15 **1** **Winslow Arizona (IRE)**[21] 2950 3-8-7 **55** .... JamieSpencer 7 63
(Michael Bell) *towards rr: hdwy fr 3f out: rdn to chal appr fnl f: styd on u.p to ld fnl 150yds: hld on all out* **4/1**[2]

0000 **2** *½* **Club House (IRE)**[14] 3178 3-8-13 **61** .... TomQueally 4 68
(Robert Mills) *s.i.s: in rr: hdwy over 2f out: chsd ldrs u.p appr fnl f: hrd drvn to cl on ldr fnl 110yds but a jst hld* **33/1**

-313 **3** *¾* **Shaolin (IRE)**[125] 731 3-9-6 **68** .... GeorgeBaker 2 73+
(Seamus Durack) *chsd ldrs: rdn to ld ins fnl 2f: kpt on u.p: hdd and one pce fnl 150yds* **16/1**

004 **4** *½* **Keene**[15] 3149 3-8-10 **58** .... WilliamCarson 8 62
(Philip McBride) *in tch: rdn and one pce 3f out: styd on again u.p ins fnl f* **20/1**

5051 **5** *1 ¼* **Imperial Glance**[9] 3376 3-8-8 **63** .... OisinMurphy(7) 3 64
(Andrew Balding) *led after 1f: rdn and hdd ins fnl 2f: wknd ins fnl f* **11/8**[1]

-525 **6** *2* **Fair Comment**[18] 3039 3-8-12 **60** .... LiamKeniry 10 57
(Michael Blanshard) *chsd ldrs: rdn and outpcd over 2f out: sme prog again fnl f* **20/1**

04-6 **7** *½* **Admirals Walk (IRE)**[22] 2935 3-9-3 **65** .... JamesDoyle 9 61
(Sylvester Kirk) *led 1f: chsd ldr: rdn over 2f out: wknd fnl f* **12/1**

4016 **8** *1 ¼* **Tagalaka (IRE)**[29] 2727 3-8-12 **60** .... JohnFahy 5 53
(Eve Johnson Houghton) *chsd ldrs: rdn over 2f out: wknd appr fnl f* **16/1**

-463 **9** *9* **Star Of Mayfair (USA)**[16] 3137 3-9-3 **65** .... JimCrowley 6 37
(Alan Jarvis) *s.i.s: reminders 4f out: sn btn* **9/2**[3]

6-64 **10** *20* **Gunning For Glory**[113] 877 3-9-1 **63** .... MartinLane 11
(Martin Bosley) *s.i.s: in rr but in tch 4f out: wknd 3f out* **66/1**

1m 38.53s (-0.17) **Going Correction** -0.225s/f (Firm) **10 Ran SP% 113.7**
Speed ratings (Par 99): **91,90,89,89,88 86,85,84,75,55**
toteswingers 1&2 £26.60, 2&3 £14.00, 1&3 £4.90 CSF £131.25 CT £1939.67 TOTE £5.30: £2.30, £9.30, £3.20; EX 149.40 Trifecta £556.20 Pool: £1097.69 - 1.48 winning units..
Owner Rathordan Partnership **Bred** Sir E J Loder **Trained** Newmarket, Suffolk

The Form Book Flat, Raceform Ltd, Compton, RG20 6NL.

FOCUS
The first of a string of three handicaps to close the card. The form looks fluid and might take time to settle.

3666 WIN RACES WITH JONATHAN PORTMAN FILLIES' H'CAP 1m 2f 6y
8:35 (8:36) (Class 4) (0-85,82) 3-Y-O **£4,690** (£1,395; £697; £348) **Stalls** Centre

Form RPR

1-12 **1** **Danat Al Atheer**[29] 2704 3-9-7 **82**.....(b[1]) JamesDoyle 7 90+
(William Haggas) *hld up in rr: pushed along and hdwy over 1f out: rdn and str run ins fnl f to ld fnl 30yds: won gng away* **11/4**[2]

3-50 **2** 1 1/2 **Super Cookie**[28] 2743 3-8-2 **63** oh1..... WilliamCarson 1 68
(Philip McBride) *chsd ldr: t.k.h: styd on u.p to chal wl over 1f out: led ins fnl f: hdd and outpcd fnl 30yds* **10/1**

1-4 **3** 1 3/4 **Light Rose (IRE)**[83] 1321 3-9-1 **76**..... SilvestreDeSousa 3 78
(Mark Johnston) *led: t.k.h and sn clr: stdd 3f out: jnd and rdn over 1f out: hdd ins fnl f: no ex* **6/1**[3]

-530 **4** 1/2 **Everleigh**[12] 3251 3-8-13 **74**..... RichardHughes 8 75
(Richard Hannon) *in rr: hdwy over 2f out: drvn to chse ldrs 2f out but no imp: styd on same pce ins fnl f* **8/1**

-450 **5** 1 3/4 **Starlight Symphony (IRE)**[33] 2586 3-8-13 **74**..... TomQueally 2 72
(Eve Johnson Houghton) *in tch: drvn to chse ldrs 3f out: wknd appr fnl f* **6/1**[3]

32-3 **6** 2 **Squeeze My Brain (IRE)**[33] 2606 3-8-13 **74**.....[1] JamieSpencer 5 68
(Ralph Beckett) *s.i.s: in rr: rdn 3f out: chsd ldrs u.p over 2f out: sn no imp and wknd over 1f out* **2/1**[1]

020 **7** shd **Kenny's Girl (IRE)**[12] 3237 3-8-9 **70**..... MartinDwyer 6 64
(William Muir) *chsd ldrs: rdn over 3f out: wknd 2f out* **16/1**

2m 6.81s (-1.99) **Going Correction** -0.225s/f (Firm) **7** Ran SP% **114.7**
Speed ratings (Par 98): **98,96,95,95,93 92,91**
toteswingers 1&2 £4.30, 2&3 £11.60, 1&3 £3.50 CSF £29.67 CT £152.41 TOTE £3.70: £1.80, £5.20; EX 47.30 Trifecta £525.20 Pool: £1643.45 - 2.34 winning units..
Owner Jaber Abdullah **Bred** Rabbah Bloodstock Limited **Trained** Newmarket, Suffolk

FOCUS
A decent handicap and the third race on the card to be confined to fillies. The third looks a reasonable guide to the level.

3667 AMANDA TAPLIN & JON BARKER 50TH BIRTHDAY H'CAP 5f 34y
9:05 (9:05) (Class 5) (0-70,68) 3-Y-O+ **£2,587** (£770; £384; £192) **Stalls** Low

Form RPR

0446 **1** **Crimson Queen**[120] 795 6-9-7 **66**.....(b) MarkCoumbe(3) 2 80
(Roy Brotherton) *mde all: drvn clr and edgd lft 2f out: unchal* **14/1**

30-0 **2** 4 **Ryan Style (IRE)**[33] 2588 7-9-11 **67**.....(p) AdamKirby 3 67
(Lisa Williamson) *sn chsng ldrs: rdn over 2f out: styd on to take 2nd fnl 110yds: no ch w wnr* **7/1**[3]

6105 **3** 1/2 **Dreams Of Glory**[10] 3341 5-9-7 **63**..... SilvestreDeSousa 1 61
(Ron Hodges) *chsd wnr: rdn and no imp fr 1/2-way: one pce into 3rd fnl 110yds* **5/2**[1]

5506 **4** 3/4 **Sole Danser (IRE)**[25] 2825 5-9-11 **67**.....(p) RichardKingscote 8 62+
(Milton Bradley) *in rr: hdwy and nt clr run appr fnl f: swtchd lft and styd on fnl f: nt rch ldrs* **9/2**[2]

0006 **5** hd **Charming (IRE)**[5] 3498 4-9-5 **61**.....(p[1]) SebSanders 4 55
(Olivia Maylam) *chsd ldrs: rdn 1/2-way: outpcd fnl f* **14/1**

4030 **6** 3/4 **Brandywell Boy (IRE)**[10] 3325 10-8-4 **49** oh2..... BillyCray(3) 5 41
(Dominic Ffrench Davis) *chsd ldrs: rdn 3f out: sn one pce* **20/1**

01 **7** 1/2 **Even Bolder**[15] 3154 10-8-10 **59**..... JoeyHaynes(7) 6 49
(Eric Wheeler) *in tch: chsd ldrs 1/2-way: edgd rt and wknd appr fnl f* **14/1**

004 **8** 3 1/2 **Best Be Careful (IRE)**[3] 3577 5-9-12 **68**..... LiamKeniry 10 45
(Mark Usher) *outpcd* **9/2**[2]

-200 **9** 2 **Superior Edge**[22] 2918 6-9-6 **62**.....(p) CathyGannon 7 32
(Christopher Mason) *early spd: sn outpcd* **12/1**

5-60 **10** 15 **Fathom Five (IRE)**[18] 3042 9-9-7 **63**..... GeorgeBaker 9
(Gary Moore) *outpcd: lost tch over 1f out: eased* **20/1**

1m 1.19s (-0.21) **Going Correction** +0.05s/f (Good) **10** Ran SP% **114.7**
Speed ratings (Par 103): **103,96,95,94,94 93,92,86,83,59**
toteswingers 1&2 £11.30, 2&3 £3.30, 1&3 £6.80 CSF £106.70 CT £290.97 TOTE £13.10: £2.90, £3.00, £1.50; EX 119.00 Trifecta £576.30 Pool: £960.51 - 1.24 winning units..
Owner Arthur Clayton **Bred** Cheveley Park Stud Ltd **Trained** Elmley Castle, Worcs

FOCUS
The final sprint handicap was the scene of a performance that was hard to predict coming in to the race. The winner is rated back to his best at least but not really form to take at face value.
T/Jkpt: £7,100.00 to a £1 stake. Pool of £25000.00 - 2.50 winning units. T/Plt: £150.30 to a £1 stake. Pool of £92251.54 - 447.85 winning tickets. T/Qpdt: 44.30 to a £1 stake. Pool of £6947.66 - 115.90 winning tickets. ST

3668 - 3672a (Foreign Racing) - See Raceform Interactive

3310 BATH (L-H)
Wednesday, June 26

OFFICIAL GOING: Firm (9.8)
Wind: Moderate ahead Weather: White cloud

3673 BRITISH STALLION STUDS EBF MAIDEN FILLIES' STKS 5f 161y
6:10 (6:10) (Class 5) 2-Y-O **£2,911** (£866; £432; £216) **Stalls** Centre

Form RPR

032 **1** **Sunset Shore**[6] 3510 2-9-0 0..... LukeMorris 2 73+
(Sir Mark Prescott Bt) *mde all: shkn up fnl f: a doing enough as 2nd clsd nr fin* **5/6**[1]

35 **2** nk **Princess Rose**[39] 2458 2-9-0 0..... LiamJones 3 72
(William Haggas) *sn trcking ldng duo in 3rd: wnt 2nd over 1f out: drvn and clsd on wnr nr fin but a readily hld* **2/1**[2]

3 4 **Yajamila** 2-9-0 0..... TomQueally 5 59
(James Tate) *sn chsng wnr: rdn over 2f out: dropped to one pce 3rd over 1f out* **7/1**[3]

4 4 **Reimpose (USA)** 2-9-0 0..... MartinHarley 1 46
(Pat Eddery) *s.i.s: a struggling and outpcd* **14/1**

1m 11.92s (0.72) **Going Correction** -0.20s/f (Firm) **4** Ran SP% **107.1**
Speed ratings (Par 90): **87,86,81,75**
CSF £2.68 TOTE £1.40; EX 2.90 Trifecta £3.60 Pool: £1,154.28 - 237.27 winning tickets..
Owner Miss K Rausing **Bred** Miss K Rausing **Trained** Newmarket, Suffolk

FOCUS
A fair small-field juvenile fillies' maiden in which they went a decent early gallop. The runner-up is rated a minor improver but the form behind is fluid.

3674 PERTEMPS PEOPLE DEVELOPMENT GROUP MAIDEN STKS 1m 3f 144y
6:40 (6:41) (Class 5) 3-Y-O+ **£2,587** (£770; £384; £192) **Stalls** Low

Form RPR

1 **Pitchoun (IRE)** 3-8-13 0..... SilvestreDeSousa 5 76+
(Mark Johnston) *mde all: qcknd clr under hand riding over 1f out: v easily* **6/4**[2]

6-44 **2** 6 **Society Pearl (IRE)**[13] 3239 3-8-8 72..... JamieSpencer 1 61
(Charles Hills) *t.k.h early: hld up in rr: stdy hdwy over 2f out: drvn to chse wnr wl over 1f out but nvr any ch and edgd lft u.p* **5/4**[1]

00 **3** 4 1/2 **Money Talks**[35] 2560 3-8-13 0..... LiamKeniry 2 59
(Michael Madgwick) *chsd ldrs: rdn and outpcd 3f out: rallied u.p fnl f to retake wl-hld 3rd clsng stages* **66/1**

0 **4** shd **Obaha (USA)**[13] 3239 3-8-8 0..... LiamJones 6 53
(J W Hills) *chsd wnr: rdn 3f out: dropped to 3rd u.p 2f out: no ch after and lost wl-hld 3rd clsng stages* **10/1**

-355 **5** 3/4 **Bin Manduro**[56] 1923 3-8-13 67..... TomQueally 4 57
(James Tate) *t.k.h: sn wl there: c wd bnd over 3f out: drvn to chse wnr 2f out but no imp: wknd over 1f out* **5/1**[3]

0 **6** 6 **Tammis**[13] 3239 3-8-8 0..... LukeMorris 3 42
(Ron Hodges) *rdn along 7f out: a in rr* **100/1**

2m 31.5s (0.90) **Going Correction** -0.20s/f (Firm) **6** Ran SP% **112.7**
Speed ratings (Par 103): **89,85,82,81,81 77**
Tote Swingers 1&2 £1.90, 2&3 £16.00, 1&3 £33.20 CSF £3.75 TOTE £2.10: £1.50, £1.40; EX 5.20 Trifecta £21.70 Pool: £1,078.36 - 37.12 winning tickets..
Owner Sheikh Hamdan Bin Mohammed Al Maktoum **Bred** Swettenham Stud & Scout Stable Llc **Trained** Middleham Moor, N Yorks

FOCUS
A fair middle-distance maiden in which they went steady initially under a canny front-running ride from Silvestre de Sousa. The time was moderate but the winner impressed, although the form is muddling.

3675 TOTAL PRODUCE H'CAP 1m 3f 144y
7:10 (7:10) (Class 6) (0-60,60) 3-Y-O **£2,045** (£603; £302) **Stalls** Low

Form RPR

640 **1** **World Map (IRE)**[19] 3055 3-9-2 **55**..... SilvestreDeSousa 7 61
(Mark Johnston) *in rr: rdn over 5f out: c wd bnd over 3f out: styd on u.p over 1f out: edging lft and rt but kpt on clsng stages to ld last strides* **5/1**[3]

-231 **2** shd **Alpine Mysteries (IRE)**[8] 3432 3-9-2 **60**..... ThomasBrown(5) 3 66
(Harry Dunlop) *towards rr: hdwy fr 3f out: chal 2f out: rdn to ld over 1f out: kpt on u.p: hdd last strides* **6/4**[1]

4445 **3** 1 1/4 **Dalaway (IRE)**[20] 3013 3-9-4 **57**..... MartinHarley 2 61
(Mick Channon) *hld up in rr: hdwy fr 2f out: drvn to dispute 2nd ins fnl f but fnd no ex u.p fnl 110yds* **12/1**

310V **4** 2 **Inessa Armand (IRE)**[4] 3578 3-9-5 **58**.....(p) LiamKeniry 5 58
(J S Moore) *chsd ldrs: wnt 2nd over 3f out: led 2f out: hdd over 1f out: wknd fnl f* **20/1**

3032 **5** 2 3/4 **Eyeline**[19] 3040 3-8-6 **50**..... JackDuern(5) 1 47
(Andrew Hollinshead) *chsd ldr tl over 3f out: styd chsng ldrs tl n.m.r on rails and eased whn hld ins fnl f* **16/1**

402 **6** nk **Uganda Glory (USA)**[8] 3428 3-9-2 **55**..... PatCosgrave 6 50
(George Baker) *in tch: drvn along over 5f out: chsd ldrs fr 2f out: nt much daylight over 1f out and sn btn* **8/1**

0-42 **7** 1 3/4 **Ebony Roc (IRE)**[9] 3403 3-8-13 **52**..... PatDobbs 4 44
(Amanda Perrett) *led tl hdd 2f out: wknd qckly over 1f out* **11/4**[2]

2m 29.2s (-1.40) **Going Correction** -0.20s/f (Firm) **7** Ran SP% **112.8**
Speed ratings (Par 97): **96,95,95,93,91 91,90**
Tote Swingers 1&2 £2.80, 2&3 £5.40, 1&3 £4.50 CSF £12.58 TOTE £6.80: £2.50, £1.60; EX 22.60 Trifecta £147.00 Pool: £750.96 - 3.83 winning tickets..
Owner Sheikh Hamdan Bin Mohammed Al Maktoum **Bred** Darley **Trained** Middleham Moor, N Yorks

FOCUS
A moderate middle-distance 3-y-o handicap rated around the winner and third.

3676 GRANDE JAGUAR SWINDON H'CAP 1m 5y
7:40 (7:40) (Class 5) (0-70,69) 4-Y-O+ **£2,587** (£770; £384; £192) **Stalls** Low

Form RPR

0054 **1** **Croquembouche (IRE)**[16] 3157 4-9-7 **69**..... LiamKeniry 6 78
(Ed de Giles) *mde all: drvn and qcknd over 2f out: styd on strly fnl f* **15/8**[1]

2122 **2** 1 3/4 **Ifan (IRE)**[23] 2920 5-8-11 **66**..... DanielMuscutt(7) 7 71
(Tim Vaughan) *chsd ldrs: rdn and outpcd 3f out: styd on u.p fnl f to take 2nd last strides but no ch w wnr* **2/1**[2]

0-35 **3** 1/2 **Lutine Charlie (IRE)**[79] 1426 6-9-1 **63**..... CathyGannon 2 67
(Pat Eddery) *chsd wnr: rdn 3f out: outpcd by wnr ins fnl 2f: no ex and lost 2nd last strides* **13/2**

4-14 **4** 3 3/4 **Precision Five**[155] 330 4-8-7 **55**.....(p) FergusSweeney 4 50
(Jeremy Gask) *in rr: rdn over 3f out: mod prog fr over 1f out* **12/1**

000 **5** 3 1/2 **Garrisson (IRE)**[13] 3244 4-8-12 **60**..... SteveDrowne 8 47
(Charles Hills) *s.i.s: rdn over 3f out: a in rr* **14/1**

034 **6** 6 **Lady Sylvia**[12] 3269 4-9-1 **63**.....(p) TomQueally 1 37
(Joseph Tuite) *chsd ldrs: rdn 4f out: wknd 3f out* **6/1**[3]

1m 40.73s (-0.07) **Going Correction** -0.20s/f (Firm) **6** Ran SP% **110.1**
Speed ratings (Par 103): **92,90,89,86,82 76**
Tote Swingers 1&2 £2.20, 2&3 £1.10, 1&3 £1.40 CSF £5.67 CT £16.03 TOTE £3.50: £2.10, £1.10; EX 7.40 Trifecta £30.40 Pool: £581.77 - 14.31 winning tickets..
Owner John Manser **Bred** Ballymacoll Stud Farm Ltd **Trained** Ledbury, H'fords

FOCUS
An ability to act properly on firm ground is a necessity if attempting to pick up a front-runner who revels in such conditions, and this modest handicap was a case in point. The third looks the best guide to the level.

3677 BEGBIES TRAYNOR H'CAP 5f 11y
8:10 (8:10) (Class 4) (0-85,80) 3-Y-O **£4,690** (£1,395; £697; £348) **Stalls** Centre

Form RPR

2032 **1** **Almalekiah (IRE)**[4] 3591 3-8-12 **71**..... LiamJones 4 82
(J S Moore) *chsd ldrs in 3rd: drvn to chal 2f out: led sn after and swtchd lft: kpt on u.p: edgd rt fnl 50yds* **7/4**[1]

10-3 **2** 1/2 **Smart Daisy K**[18] 3097 3-9-0 **73**..... ShaneKelly 3 82
(Andrew Hollinshead) *trckd ldrs in 4th: hdwy fr 2f out: swtchd rt to chse wnr appr fnl f: clsng whn pushed rt fnl 50yds: no ex* **4/1**[3]

5-21 **3** 6 **Daylight**[19] 3036 3-9-7 **80**..... LiamKeniry 2 67
(Andrew Balding) *chsd ldr: drvn to chal 2f out: one pce whn checked wl over 1f out: wknd fnl f* **2/1**[2]

321 **4** *hd* **Pixilated**[22] 2965 3-9-2 **80** .... RobertTart(5) 1 67
(Gay Kelleway) *led: drvn and jnd 2f out: sn hdd: n.m.r and wknd appr fnl f* **4/1**[3]

1m 1.37s (-1.13) **Going Correction** -0.20s/f (Firm) **4** Ran SP% **109.7**
Speed ratings (Par 101): **101,100,90,90**
CSF £8.72 TOTE £2.30; EX 6.70 Trifecta £11.80 Pool: £648.93 - 41.16 winning tickets..
Owner Sheikh Abdullah Almalek Alsabah **Bred** Mark Hanly **Trained** Upper Lambourn, Berks

FOCUS
A fair small-field 3yo handicap in which they went a strong, contested pace throughout. The winner is rated to her latest mark with the runner-up back to her juvenile best.

3678 BUGLER COACHES CLASSIFIED STKS 5f 161y
8:40 (8:40) (Class 5) 3-Y-O **£2,587** (£770; £384; £192) **Stalls** Centre

Form RPR
2222 **1** **Silverrica (IRE)**[19] 3036 3-9-0 68 .... MartinHarley 6 73
(Malcolm Saunders) *mde all: drvn and styd on wl thrght fnl f* **4/1**[3]
4236 **2** *1* **Hot Secret**[19] 3058 3-9-0 70 .... LiamKeniry 2 70
(Andrew Balding) *hld up in tch: hdwy over 1f out: styd on u.p to chse wnr fnl 75yds: no imp* **6/1**
3315 **3** *1 ¼* **Harbour Captain (IRE)**[21] 2994 3-9-0 69 .... CathyGannon 4 66
(Jo Hughes) *chsd ldrs: wnt 2nd 3f out: rdn 2f out: no imp over 1f out: no ex and dropped to 3rd fnl 75yds* **5/2**[2]
3036 **4** *3 ¾* **Little Choosey**[12] 3268 3-8-9 67 .... RyanTate(5) 3 53
(Clive Cox) *chsd wnr to 3f out: wknd wl over 1f out* **12/1**
-201 **5** *shd* **Alhaarth Beauty (IRE)**[22] 2962 3-8-9 69 .... ThomasBrown(5) 1 53+
(Ismail Mohammed) *chsd ldrs: rdn 3f out: n.m.r and wknd appr fnl 2f* **7/4**[1]
02-0 **6** *19* **Kodatish (IRE)**[14] 3212 3-9-0 68 .... LukeMorris 5
(Ronald Harris) *plunged s and rdr lost iron: rdn and effrt to cl 3f out but nvr any ch* **25/1**

1m 9.9s (-1.30) **Going Correction** -0.20s/f (Firm) **6** Ran SP% **110.8**
Speed ratings (Par 99): **100,98,97,92,91 66**
Tote Swingers 1&2 £7.90, 2&3 £1.80, 1&3 £3.80 CSF £26.42 TOTE £5.10: £1.60, £2.20; EX 24.70 Trifecta £73.30 Pool: £649.71 - 6.64 winning tickets..
Owner Mrs Ginny Nicholas **Bred** Miss A R Byrne **Trained** Green Ore, Somerset

FOCUS
A modest classified stakes, and another race where an ability to handle firm ground was paramount. The form is rated around the first two.

3679 UNIVERSITY OF THE WEST OF ENGLAND H'CAP 5f 161y
9:10 (9:11) (Class 6) (0-60,60) 3-Y-O **£2,045** (£603; £302) **Stalls** Centre

Form RPR
0501 **1** **Cara Gina**[11] 3316 3-9-3 **56** ....(b) LiamJones 7 65
(William Haggas) *hld up towards rr: swtchd rt and hdwy ins fnl 2f: led over 1f out: sn pushed clr: easily* **7/4**[1]
6-03 **2** *3* **Sunny Hollow**[20] 3016 3-9-1 **54** .... SilvestreDeSousa 8 53
(James Toller) *chsd ldrs: led appr fnl 2f: hdd over 1f out: sn no ch w wnr but styd on wl for 2nd* **9/2**[2]
0-04 **3** *1 ½* **Secret Success**[27] 2788 3-9-5 **58** ....(t) TomQueally 6 52+
(Paul Cole) *chsd ldrs after 2f: styd on for one pce 3rd fnl f* **11/2**[3]
0022 **4** *5* **Foie Gras**[11] 3316 3-8-13 **52** ....(b) MartinDwyer 1 30
(William Muir) *s.i.s: in rr: drvn and sme hdwy on outside fr 2f out: nvr rchd ldrs* **10/1**
-540 **5** *3 ¾* **Majestic Red (IRE)**[15] 3178 3-9-0 **53** .... MartinHarley 2 18
(Malcolm Saunders) *chsd ldrs to 2f out: wknd sn after* **10/1**
5036 **6** *2* **Outbid**[11] 3323 3-9-7 **60** ....(b[1]) FergusSweeney 4 19
(Jamie Osborne) *t.k.h in rr: hdwy over 2f out: sn rdn and btn* **20/1**
0644 **7** *4* **Vergality Ridge (IRE)**[12] 3268 3-8-10 **49** ....(be) LukeMorris 5
(Ronald Harris) *led tl hdd & wknd appr fnl 2f* **16/1**
1550 **8** *1* **Chelsea Grey (IRE)**[64] 1742 3-8-9 **48** .... SteveDrowne 3
(Ronald Harris) *chsd ldrs 3f* **33/1**
6-06 **9** *nk* **Dee Aitch Dove**[23] 2934 3-9-4 **57** .... PatCosgrave 9 16
(George Baker) *chsd ldrs: ev ch 2f out: hmpd and wknd over 1f out* **7/1**
04-0 **10** *2 ½* **Shes Ellie**[67] 1695 3-8-11 **57** .... JosephineGordon(7) 10
(Jo Hughes) *a outpcd* **22/1**
040 **11** *38* **Kaahen (USA)**[23] 2934 3-8-7 **46** oh1 ....(vt[1]) CathyGannon 11
(Pat Eddery) *s.i.s: a bhd: eased fnl 2f: t.o* **33/1**

1m 10.69s (-0.51) **Going Correction** -0.20s/f (Firm) **11** Ran SP% **121.5**
Speed ratings (Par 97): **95,91,89,82,77 74,69,68,67,64 13**
Tote Swingers 1&2 £2.60, 2&3 £8.20, 1&3 £1.50 CSF £9.15 CT £36.79 TOTE £2.40: £1.60, £3.00, £1.10; EX 15.70 Trifecta £43.00 Pool: £950.71 - 16.56 winning tickets..
Owner Mrs Deborah June James **Bred** Old Mill Stud & S Williams & J Parry **Trained** Newmarket, Suffolk

FOCUS
A moderate 3-y-o sprint handicap in which they went a decent gallop. The form is not solid with the runner-up to her latest Brighton mark the best guide.
T/Plt: £42.80 to a £1 stake. Pool: £57,083.15 - 972.77 winning tickets. T/Qpdt: £23.00 to a £1 stake. Pool: £4,189.00 - 134.6 winning tickets. ST

3391 CARLISLE (R-H)
Wednesday, June 26

OFFICIAL GOING: Good (good to firm in places; 7.7)
Wind: Fresh, half against Weather: Cloudy, bright

3680 BRITISH STALLION STUDS EBF MAIDEN STKS 5f 193y
2:00 (2:01) (Class 5) 2-Y-O **£2,911** (£866; £432; £216) **Stalls** Low

Form RPR
64 **1** **Atheera (IRE)**[14] 3206 2-9-0 0 .... JoeFanning 1 68
(Mark Johnston) *mde virtually all: rdn 2f out: edgd lft ins fnl f: kpt on fnl f* **7/1**[3]
62 **2** *nk* **Disclosure**[9] 3391 2-9-5 0 ....(p) TomEaves 5 72
(Bryan Smart) *cl up on outside: rdn over 2f out: kpt on fnl f: a hld* **7/2**[2]
22 **3** *hd* **Searchlight**[22] 2955 2-9-5 0 .... PhillipMakin 3 71
(Kevin Ryan) *t.k.h: trckd ldrs: effrt and rdn over 1f out: kpt on ins fnl f* **10/11**[1]
4 *1 ¼* **Boogangoo (IRE)** 2-9-0 0 .... PaulMulrennan 6 62+
(Keith Dalgleish) *bhd and sn rn green: rdn and hdwy over 1f out: kpt on fnl f: nrst fin* **7/1**[3]
0 **5** *1 ¾* **Mfiftythreedotcom (IRE)**[21] 2985 2-9-5 0 .... TonyHamilton 2 62
(Richard Fahey) *chsd ldng gp: rdn along and effrt over 2f out: no imp fnl f* **11/1**
0 **6** *2 ½* **Slanderous**[11] 3318 2-9-0 0 .... FrederikTylicki 4 49
(Scott Dixon) *disp ld to 2f out: sn rdn: wknd ent fnl f* **80/1**

7 *13* **Mrs J (IRE)** 2-9-0 0 .... DuranFentiman 7 7
(Tim Easterby) *s.i.s: rn green in rr: sme hdwy and hung lft over 2f out: sn btn* **33/1**

1m 14.89s (1.19) **Going Correction** +0.125s/f (Good) **7** Ran SP% **112.1**
Speed ratings (Par 93): **97,96,96,94,92 89,71**
Tote Swingers 1&2 £1.50, 2&3 £1.70, 1&3 £2.10 CSF £30.32 TOTE £5.70: £1.20, £2.80; EX 17.30 Trifecta £30.10 Pool: £2,607.89 - 64.81 winning tickets..
Owner Hamdan Al Maktoum **Bred** Shadwell Estate Company Limited **Trained** Middleham Moor, N Yorks

FOCUS
Old Stable bend and home straight moved out 4yds, adding 7yds to races of 7f & 1m. Rail also moved out 4yds from 12f to 1m adding 9yds to 1m 4f race. The ground was officially described as good, good to firm in places (GoingStick 7.7). Due to rail movement, races over 7f and 1m were run over an extra 7yds and over 1m3f an extra 9yds. An ordinary maiden and the front pair just about held those positions throughout.

3681 EDMUNDSON ELECTRICAL CARLISLE MAIDEN AUCTION STKS 5f
2:30 (2:33) (Class 5) 2-Y-O **£2,587** (£770; £384; £192) **Stalls** Low

Form RPR
6 **1** **Oasis Town**[12] 3280 2-8-6 0 .... AmyRyan 2 80+
(Kevin Ryan) *dwlt: hld up: hdwy on outside over 2f out: hung rt and led appr fnl f: rdn and r.o wl* **10/1**
4 **2** *2 ¼* **Simply Black (IRE)**[12] 3280 2-8-8 0 .... RoystonFfrench 4 74
(Bryan Smart) *t.k.h: w ldr: led over 2f out: sn rdn: hdd appr fnl f: kpt on same pce* **5/1**[3]
02 **3** *6* **Stoney Quine (IRE)**[7] 3461 2-8-7 0 ow1 .... TomEaves 1 51
(Keith Dalgleish) *led to over 2f out: sn rdn: edgd lft and outpcd by first two ins fnl f* **10/3**[2]
03 **4** *1 ¼* **Emily Davison (IRE)**[7] 3476 2-8-4 0 .... JoeFanning 7 44
(David C Griffiths) *cl up: rdn over 2f out: no ex over 1f out* **5/1**[3]
00 **5** *¾* **Kopkap**[19] 3044 2-8-9 0 .... GrahamGibbons 8 46
(Ed McMahon) *prom: drvn over 2f out: outpcd over 1f out* **14/1**
6 *¾* **Sassy Brown (IRE)** 2-8-11 0 .... DuranFentiman 5 46
(Tim Easterby) *towards rr: drvn along 1/2-way: nvr able to chal* **22/1**
7 *nse* **Back Lane** 2-8-9 0 .... TonyHamilton 6 43
(Richard Fahey) *prom: rdn over 2f out: edgd rt and wknd over 1f out* **9/4**[1]
8 *70* **Panzi Potter Too** 2-8-5 0 ow1 ....(p) PJMcDonald 9
(Michael Dods) *rn green in rr: lost tch after 1f: t.o* **33/1**

1m 1.28s (0.48) **Going Correction** +0.125s/f (Good) **8** Ran SP% **110.2**
Speed ratings (Par 93): **101,97,87,85,84 83,83,**
Tote Swingers 1&2 £10.00, 2&3 £3.50, 1&3 £7.10 CSF £54.83 TOTE £12.80: £3.20, £2.00, £1.60; EX 43.80 Trifecta £242.20 Pool: £1,465.24 - 4.53 winning tickets..
Owner M&S Beaumont,North,O'Farrell & Saunders **Bred** New Hall Stud & Vera Scott **Trained** Hambleton, N Yorks

FOCUS
Another modest maiden in which the first two pulled clear.

3682 TOTEPOOL MOBILE H'CAP 5f
3:00 (3:00) (Class 4) (0-85,85) 3-Y-O+ **£5,498** (£1,636; £817; £408) **Stalls** Low

Form RPR
0-12 **1** **Avon Breeze**[29] 2755 4-9-6 **77** .... AmyRyan 4 89+
(Richard Whitaker) *awkward s: hld up: stdy hdwy wl over 1f out: n.m.r briefly 1f out: led wl ins fnl f: r.o* **7/2**[1]
2320 **2** *shd* **Rylee Mooch**[11] 3341 5-8-13 **77** ....(e) ConnorBeasley(7) 11 87
(Richard Guest) *hld up in tch: rdn and hdwy over 1f out: led briefly ins fnl f: kpt on: jst hld* **11/2**[3]
5041 **3** *2 ¼* **Rusty Rocket (IRE)**[13] 3236 4-9-9 **80** .... JoeFanning 5 82
(Paul Green) *chsd ldr: rdn over 2f out: kpt on same pce ins fnl f* **10/1**
5306 **4** *nk* **Six Wives**[49] 2173 6-9-0 **71** ....(p) FrederikTylicki 1 72
(Scott Dixon) *led at decent gallop: rdn and hdd ins fnl f: sn one pce* **14/1**
6630 **5** *1 ¼* **Another Wise Kid (IRE)**[12] 3299 5-9-9 **85** .... ShirleyTeasdale(5) 8 81
(Paul Midgley) *midfield: rdn and edgd rt over 1f out: kpt on same pce ins fnl f* **4/1**[2]
0332 **6** *nse* **Ashpan Sam**[6] 3487 4-9-9 **80** .... RobertWinston 6 76
(John Spearing) *chsd ldrs: effrt and rdn over 1f out: kpt on same pce ins fnl f* **4/1**[2]
0600 **7** *1 ½* **Escape To Glory (USA)**[10] 3367 5-9-13 **84** ....(t) PaulMulrennan 7 75
(Michael Dods) *hld up: rdn over 2f out: kpt on fnl f: nvr able to chal* **14/1**
0100 **8** *2 ¼* **Towbee**[8] 3441 4-9-10 **81** .... JamesSullivan 9 64
(Michael Easterby) *towards rr on outside: rdn over 2f out: hung rt and wknd over 1f out* **28/1**
0060 **9** *1 ½* **Beau Mistral (IRE)**[13] 3236 4-8-13 **70** ....(v) TonyHamilton 10 47
(Paul Green) *chsd ldrs on outside: rdn and edgd lft over 2f out: wknd over 1f out* **18/1**
-510 **10** *½* **Just Like Heaven (IRE)**[13] 3236 4-8-12 **69** .... DuranFentiman 2 44
(Tim Easterby) *prom on ins: drvn over 2f out: wknd over 1f out* **14/1**

1m 0.61s (-0.19) **Going Correction** +0.125s/f (Good) **10** Ran SP% **115.4**
Speed ratings (Par 105): **106,105,102,101,99 99,97,93,91,90**
Tote Swingers 1&2 £5.40, 2&3 £6.30, 1&3 £4.70 CSF £22.59 CT £179.24 TOTE £4.60: £1.10, £2.00, £3.00; EX 22.20 Trifecta £144.40 Pool: £2,226.64 - 11.56 winning tickets..
Owner Grange Park Racing II & Partner **Bred** Hellwood Stud Farm **Trained** Scarcroft, W Yorks

FOCUS
A decent sprint handicap and no hanging about. The winner rates a shade better than the bare form.

3683 CARLISLE BELL CONSOLATION RACE (H'CAP) 7f 200y
3:30 (3:30) (Class 4) (0-85,80) 3-Y-O+ **£6,469** (£1,925; £962; £481) **Stalls** Low

Form RPR
5610 **1** **Lord Of The Dance (IRE)**[11] 3349 7-9-6 **78** .... RyanClark(3) 13 87
(Michael Mullineaux) *in tch: hdwy to ld over 1f out: rdn out fnl f* **25/1**
6532 **2** *1* **Hot Rod Mamma (IRE)**[8] 3443 6-9-2 **71** .... PJMcDonald 6 78+
(Dianne Sayer) *t.k.h in midfield: nt clr run over 2f out: rdn and hdwy over 1f out: chsd wnr ins fnl f: r.o* **11/2**[2]
1510 **3** *¾* **Baltic Prince (IRE)**[13] 3232 3-8-0 **65** .... JamesSullivan 7 68
(Paul Green) *t.k.h: cl up: effrt and drvn over 2f out: kpt on ins fnl f* **25/1**
1015 **4** *½* **Copperwood**[4] 3570 8-9-7 **76** .... JoeFanning 16 80
(Mark Johnston) *chsd ldrs: drvn and effrt over 2f out: kpt on same pce ins fnl f* **22/1**
0514 **5** *nse* **Day Of The Eagle (IRE)**[12] 3300 7-9-7 **76** .... GrahamGibbons 10 80+
(Michael Easterby) *hld up in tch: effrt whn nt clr run over 2f out: sn outpcd: rdn and styd on fnl f: nrst fin* **11/2**[2]
244 **6** *hd* **Chookie Avon**[4] 3592 6-9-7 **76** ....(p) TomEaves 17 79+
(Keith Dalgleish) *hld up on outside: n.m.r briefly over 2f out: hdwy on outside fr over 1f out: kpt on fnl f: nrst fin* **50/1**

6151 **7** 3/4 **Hakuna Matata**[6] 3506 6-9-3 **79** 6ex.....................(b) ConnorBeasley(7) 15 81
(Michael Dods) *dwlt: hld up: hdwy on outside over 2f out: chsd ldrs over 1f out: sn hung rt: rdn and outpcd fnl f* **11/2**[2]

000- **8** 1/2 **Ralphy Boy (IRE)**[251] 7202 4-8-10 **65**........................ MichaelO'Connell 5 65
(Alistair Whillans) *midfield on ins: rdn whn n.m.r briefly over 2f out: no imp fr over 1f out* **50/1**

3015 **9** 3/4 **It's A Mans World**[25] 2881 7-9-6 **78**........................ PaulPickard(3) 14 77
(Brian Ellison) *hld up in midfield on outside: drvn over 2f out: one pce fr over 1f out* **28/1**

2133 **10** 1/2 **No Dominion (IRE)**[14] 3193 4-9-8 **77**................................ GrahamLee 3 75
(James Given) *dwlt: hld up: rdn 3f out: kpt on fnl f: nt pce to chal* **14/1**

4132 **11** hd **Rawaafed (IRE)**[9] 3397 4-8-10 **65** ow1.........................(p) DanielTudhope 8 64+
(Keith Dalgleish) *chsd ldrs: nt clr run over 2f out and over 1f out: rdn and wknd fnl f* **12/1**

-221 **12** 1 **Bartack (IRE)**[20] 3011 3-9-1 **80**..(b) PhillipMakin 1 73
(Luca Cumani) *plld hrd towards rr on ins: n.m.r after 3f: rdn over 2f out: edgd rt and sn btn* **3/1**[1]

0000 **13** 1/2 **Hayek**[14] 3193 6-8-3 **65**..(b) GaryMahon(7) 11 59
(Tim Easterby) *s.i.s: bhd: rdn and effrt on outside over 2f out: sn no imp* **33/1**

3104 **14** 1/2 **World Record (IRE)**[13] 3235 3-8-10 **75**........................ TonyHamilton 12 65
(Paul Green) *led to over 1f out: sn rdn and wknd* **33/1**

0-05 **15** 2 1/4 **Barren Brook**[11] 3349 6-9-10 **79**.................................... PaulMulrennan 2 66
(Michael Easterby) *s.i.s: hld up: rdn whn n.m.r briefly over 2f out: sn wknd* **7/1**[3]

1m 40.15s (0.15) **Going Correction** -0.025s/f (Good)
WFA 3 from 4yo+ 10lb **15** Ran SP% **123.3**
Speed ratings (Par 105): **98,97,96,95,95 95,94,94,93,93 92,91,91,90,88**
Tote Swingers 1&2 £26.60, 2&3 £41.60, 1&3 £100.50 CSF £150.52 CT £3585.54 TOTE £38.50: £10.30, £3.10, £11.60; EX 154.40 Trifecta £1901.30 Part won. Pool: £2,535.18 - 0.24 winning tickets..
Owner H Clewlow **Bred** Bridgewater Equine Ltd **Trained** Alpraham, Cheshire

FOCUS
A competitive handicap, though the early pace didn't look that strong. A few took a grip and space was at a premium in the straight. This form is inconclusive overall, but the winner confirmed he is better than ever.

3684 BOOKMAKERS.CO.UK CARLISLE BELL (H'CAP) 7f 200y
4:05 (4:05) (Class 4) (0-85,85) 3-Y-0+ **£18,113** (£5,390; £2,693; £1,346) **Stalls** Low

Form RPR

-002 **1** **Silvery Moon (IRE)**[11] 3346 6-9-7 **85**........................ RobertWinston 11 94
(Tim Easterby) *hld up in tch: hdwy and hung into centre wl over 1f out: led ins fnl f: hld on gamely* **6/1**[2]

5436 **2** hd **Chookie Royale**[4] 3590 5-9-3 **81**.................................(p) TomEaves 6 89
(Keith Dalgleish) *in tch: effrt in centre over 1f out: disp ld ins fnl f: kpt on: hld nr fin* **33/1**

-221 **3** 1 3/4 **Pacific Heights (IRE)**[30] 2705 4-9-3 **84**........................ PaulPickard(3) 12 88+
(Brian Ellison) *hld up: rdn and hdwy in centre 2f out: kpt on fnl f: nt rch first two* **11/2**[1]

0034 **4** shd **Kalk Bay (IRE)**[11] 3349 6-9-2 **80**...............................(t) GrahamGibbons 15 84
(Michael Easterby) *hld up in midfield: effrt and rdn in centre 2f out: kpt on same pce ins fnl f* **10/1**

145- **5** 1/2 **Magic Destiny**[266] 6789 4-9-2 **80**.. AndrewElliott 4 83
(Mrs K Burke) *chsd ldr: carried lft over 2f out: rdn and led towards stands' side over 1f out to ins fnl f: kpt on same pce* **14/1**

5153 **6** 1/2 **Music In The Rain (IRE)**[39] 2463 5-9-7 **85**............ MichaelO'Connell 16 87
(David O'Meara) *in tch: rdn and edgd lft over 2f out: one pce fnl f* **16/1**

1212 **7** 1 1/4 **Karaka Jack**[25] 2881 6-9-5 **83**....................................... PaddyAspell 14 82
(David Nicholls) *hld up in tch: rdn centre over 2f out: one pce over 1f out* **10/1**

-014 **8** 3/4 **Best Trip (IRE)**[18] 3096 6-9-5 **83**....................................... BarryMcHugh 8 80
(Brian Ellison) *led: crossed over to stands' rail over 2f out: hdd over 1f out: one pce ins fnl f* **10/1**

-611 **9** 1 3/4 **Springheel Jake**[7] 3464 4-9-5 **83** 6ex............................. PJMcDonald 13 76
(Ann Duffield) *chsd ldrs: rdn along centre 2f out: outpcd appr fnl f* **17/2**

6113 **10** 2 1/4 **Ingleby Angel (IRE)**[5] 3544 4-9-6 **84**.............................. DanielTudhope 9 72
(David O'Meara) *hld up towards rr: drvn centre over 2f out: nvr able to chal* **7/1**[3]

-331 **11** 1/2 **Restaurateur (IRE)**[14] 3215 4-9-5 **83**................................(v) JoeFanning 2 70
(Andrew Balding) *hld up: rdn over 4f out: no imp centre fr over 2f out* **9/1**

-400 **12** 3 1/2 **Green Howard**[22] 2958 5-9-4 **82**.. GrahamLee 5 61
(Robin Bastiman) *midfield: drvn and styd far side fr 3f out: nvr on terms* **12/1**

6200 **13** hd **Docofthebay (IRE)**[18] 3096 9-9-2 **80**..........................(p) FrederikTylicki 3 58
(Scott Dixon) *dwlt: hld up: rdn and styd far side fr 3f out: sn btn* **33/1**

1000 **14** 1 1/2 **Gouray Girl (IRE)**[36] 2541 6-9-6 **84**................................. DaleSwift 7 59
(Brian Ellison) *hld up: styd towards far side and rdn 3f out: nvr on terms* **50/1**

5310 **15** 1 3/4 **Al Muheer (IRE)**[10] 3368 8-9-1 **84**...............................(b) JasonHart(5) 10 55
(Ruth Carr) *hld up: rdn and styd far side over 2f out: sn struggling* **25/1**

1m 38.48s (-1.52) **Going Correction** -0.025s/f (Good) **15** Ran SP% **121.9**
Speed ratings (Par 105): **106,105,104,103,103 102,101,100,99,96 96,92,92,91,89**
Tote Swingers 1&2 £34.90, 2&3 £29.40, 1&3 £6.50 CSF £202.75 CT £1190.90 TOTE £5.90: £1.90, £9.70, £1.30; EX 259.20 Trifecta £2625.50 Part won. Pool: £3,500.68 - 0.57 winning tickets..
Owner C H Stevens **Bred** Colin Kennedy **Trained** Great Habton, N Yorks
■ Stewards' Enquiry : Barry McHugh one-day ban: careless riding (10 July)
Tom Eaves four-day ban: use of whip (10, 11, 15 & 16 July)

FOCUS
The pace looked more solid than in the consolation event and the winning time was 1.67 seconds quicker. The complexion of the race changed when the leader Best Trip was brought across to the stands' rail over 2f from home, taking Magic Destiny with him, and a few of the others gradually migrated over towards the end. The winner rates pretty much back to his best.

3685 TOTEPOOL.COM CUMBERLAND PLATE (H'CAP) 1m 3f 107y
4:35 (4:35) (Class 4) (0-85,85) 3-Y-0+ **£18,113** (£5,390; £2,693; £1,346) **Stalls** High

Form RPR

002 **1** **Warlu Way**[11] 3345 6-9-7 **85**.. GrahamGibbons 17 95
(Michael Easterby) *hld up: hdwy in centre 2 out: led wl ins fnl f: hld on wl* **10/1**

0-00 **2** hd **Franciscan**[32] 2671 5-9-7 **85**... PhillipMakin 14 95
(Luca Cumani) *hld up: hdwy in centre over 2f out: effrt and ev ch wl ins fnl f: kpt on: jst hld* **16/1**

1416 **3** nk **Cousin Khee**[32] 2654 6-9-3 **81**...................................... RobertHavlin 10 90
(Hughie Morrison) *hld up: hdwy stands' rail over 2f out: ev ch fr over 1f out: kpt on fnl f: hld cl home* **13/2**[3]

6366 **4** shd **Mica Mika (IRE)**[18] 3118 5-8-11 **80**......................... GeorgeChaloner(5) 3 89
(Richard Fahey) *prom: effrt and led in centre over 2f out: hdd and no ex wl ins fnl f* **20/1**

3064 **5** 2 3/4 **Royal Peculiar**[8] 3442 5-9-2 **80**..................................... AndrewMullen 13 84
(Michael Appleby) *prom: effrt and styd far side over 2f out: kpt on same pce fnl f* **20/1**

00-4 **6** nk **Scrapper Smith (IRE)**[40] 2407 7-9-2 **85**.................... GarryWhillans(5) 9 89
(Alistair Whillans) *hld up: rdn and hdwy far side over 2f out: kpt on fnl f: nvr able to chal* **14/1**

3-54 **7** 2 **Eltheeb**[30] 2718 6-9-5 **83**...(v[1]) DanielTudhope 4 83
(David O'Meara) *midfield: hdwy and ev ch far side over 1f out: outpcd fnl f* **5/1**[2]

-034 **8** 1 **Calaf**[18] 3094 5-9-2 **83**.. PaulPickard(3) 16 82
(Brian Ellison) *t.k.h: cl up: ev ch and c stands' side over 2f out: outpcd over 1f out* **18/1**

-003 **9** 4 **War Poet**[8] 3442 6-9-4 **82**..(v) JoeFanning 15 74
(David O'Meara) *hld up towards rr: stdy hdwy 1/2-way: effrt towards stands' side over 2f out: edgd rt and wknd over 1f out* **14/1**

3-32 **10** 1 **Ethics Girl (IRE)**[24] 2385 7-8-10 **81**............................(t) NoelGarbutt(7) 12 71
(John Berry) *midfield: effrt in centre over 2f out: wknd over 1f out* **20/1**

3350 **11** 2 3/4 **Tappanappa (IRE)**[18] 3099 6-9-4 **82**..............................(b) TomEaves 6 68
(Brian Ellison) *dwlt: hld up: drvn along 4f out: wknd in centre 2f out* **14/1**

0353 **12** 11 **Demolition**[7] 3477 9-8-13 **82**... JasonHart(5) 2 49
(Noel Wilson) *chsd ldrs: drvn along in centre over 2f out: sn wknd* **28/1**

260- **13** 1 **Aazif (IRE)**[12] 7194 4-9-5 **83**..(t) GrahamLee 11 48
(Donald McCain) *prom: rdn over 3f out: wknd towards far side over 2f out* **4/1**[1]

2520 **14** 1 3/4 **Porgy**[32] 2654 8-9-7 **85**..(p) BarryMcHugh 8 47
(Brian Ellison) *hld up in tch: effrt towards stands' side over 2f out: sn wknd* **33/1**

6-10 **15** 20 **Classic Punch (IRE)**[28] 2766 10-9-4 **82**....................... PaulMulrennan 1
(Tim Etherington) *led: styd far side and hdd over 2f out: wknd and eased over 1f out* **33/1**

5224 **16** 1 3/4 **Northside Prince (IRE)**[33] 2633 7-9-7 **85**.................. RobertWinston 5
(Alan Swinbank) *in tch: rdn over 4f out: styd far side and wknd over 2f out* **18/1**

-600 **17** 3 3/4 **Spanish Duke (IRE)**[40] 2427 6-9-7 **85**.............................. DaleSwift 7
(Brian Ellison) *towards rr: niggled 1/2-way: lost tch 4f out: nvr on terms* **16/1**

2m 22.71s (-0.39) **Going Correction** -0.025s/f (Good) **17** Ran SP% **125.0**
Speed ratings (Par 105): **100,99,99,99,97 97,95,95,92,91 89,81,80,79,64 63,60**
Tote Swingers 1&2 £48.10, 2&3 £18.90, 1&3 £13.10 CSF £147.66 CT £1132.76 TOTE £9.70: £2.80, £3.40, £1.90, £6.00; EX 165.10 Trifecta £1473.30 Pool: £2,913.29 - 1.48 winning tickets..
Owner B Hoggarth & S Hollings **Bred** The Earl Cadogan **Trained** Sheriff Hutton, N Yorks

FOCUS
They went a decent pace in this and the field were spread right across the track coming to the last 2f. The first three came from well back, suggesting the leaders went off too quickly. The fourth helps set the standard.

3686 "CHOOSE EBF NOMINATED" FILLIES' H'CAP 6f 192y
5:05 (5:05) (Class 4) (0-80,79) 3-Y-0+ **£6,469** (£1,925; £962; £481) **Stalls** Low

Form RPR

-302 **1** **Elle Woods (IRE)**[9] 3396 3-9-2 **76**..............................(p) PaulMulrennan 3 85
(Michael Dods) *trckd ldrs: hdwy to ld over 1f out: rdn and edgd rt ins fnl f: r.o wl* **9/4**[1]

4-54 **2** 1 1/4 **Dusky Queen (IRE)**[44] 2309 3-9-5 **79**........................... TonyHamilton 2 84
(Richard Fahey) *trckd ldrs: drvn and chsd wnr over 1f out: kpt on ins fnl f* **5/2**[2]

0602 **3** 3/4 **Shesastar**[13] 3259 5-9-12 **77**.. GrahamGibbons 5 83
(David Barron) *hld up in tch: drvn along over 3f out: rallied over 1f out: r.o ins fnl f* **9/1**

1202 **4** 3/4 **Alluring Star**[9] 3395 5-8-13 **64**...................................... JamesSullivan 9 68
(Michael Easterby) *led: rdn and hdd over 1f out: kpt on same pce ins fnl f* **6/1**[3]

5000 **5** 1 1/4 **Delores Rocket**[13] 3234 3-9-0 **74**..(b) AmyRyan 7 72
(Kevin Ryan) *trckd ldr: rdn along over 2f out: no ex over 1f out* **14/1**

5000 **6** 3 1/4 **Queens Revenge**[21] 2988 4-9-5 **70**...................................... GrahamLee 6 62
(Tim Easterby) *hld up in tch: drvn and outpcd over 2f out: n.d after* **12/1**

-014 **7** 1 1/4 **Who's Shirl**[9] 3393 7-9-5 **70**... DuranFentiman 1 58
(Chris Fairhurst) *hld up on ins: n.m.r bnd over 4f out: sn n.d* **11/1**

6223 **8** 1 **Gift Of Silence**[22] 2963 4-8-9 **67**..................................(t) NoelGarbutt(7) 8 53
(John Berry) *hld up: hdwy on outside whn hung lft over 2f out: sn wknd* **11/1**

1m 27.05s (-0.05) **Going Correction** -0.025s/f (Good)
WFA 3 from 4yo+ 9lb **8** Ran SP% **114.7**
Speed ratings (Par 102): **99,97,96,95,94 90,89,88**
Tote Swingers 1&2 £2.40, 2&3 £4.70, 1&3 £5.40 CSF £8.09 CT £40.15 TOTE £2.60: £1.10, £1.70, £1.70; EX 10.80 Trifecta £68.80 Pool: £2,417.04 - 26.34 winning tickets..
Owner Andrew Tinkler **Bred** Ballylinch Stud **Trained** Denton, Co Durham

FOCUS
They didn't appear to go that quick in this fair fillies' handicap. The winner was well in on his C&D latest.
T/Jkpt: Not won. T/Plt: £384.10 to a £1 stake. Pool: £84,279.05 - 160.15 winning tickets. T/Qpdt: £65.80 to a £1 stake. Pool: £7,931.13 - 89.06 winning tickets. RY

3468 KEMPTON (A.W) (R-H)
Wednesday, June 26

OFFICIAL GOING: Standard
Wind: Moderate, half against Weather: Fine but cloudy, warm

3687 ORDIGINAL PARTNER PACESETTER APPRENTICE H'CAP 1m (P)
6:20 (6:21) (Class 6) (0-60,60) 4-Y-0+ **£1,940** (£577; £288; £144) **Stalls** Low

Form RPR

0-04 **1** **Wyndham Wave**[8] 3433 4-8-11 **55**................................(p[1]) PatMillman(5) 4 63
(Rod Millman) *trckd ldrs: prog to ld wl over 1f out but jnd: kpt on wl to hold narrow ld fnl f* **3/1**[1]

2245 **2** nk **Piccolo Mondo**[26] 2845 7-9-4 **60**.................................. ShelleyBirkett(3) 11 67
(Philip Hide) *racd wd early: pressed ldng pair: rdn to chal and w wnr wl over 1f out: nt qckn and a abt a nk down fnl f* **7/2**[2]

0-00 **3** 1 1/2 **Compton Bird**[9] 3399 4-9-1 **54**......................................(t) RosieJessop 5 58
(Hans Adielsson) *reluctant to go to post: slow and awkward s: detached in last early: prog fr last pair over 2f out: tk 3rd 1f out: styd on but unable to chal* **20/1**

-064 **4** 1/2 **Catchanova (IRE)**[9] 3399 6-9-6 **59** WilliamTwiston-Davies 6 62
(Eve Johnson Houghton) *chsd ldrs: shkn up and trying to cl whn squeezed out 2f out: nt rcvr but kpt on wl fnl f* **7/2**[2]

0000 **5** 3 **Vermeyen**[11] 3326 4-8-7 **46** oh1 DeclanBates 2 42
(Geoffrey Deacon) *in tch: effrt on inner over 2f out: no prog over 1f out: kpt on u.p fnl f* **14/1**

0200 **6** 3/4 **Karate (IRE)**[8] 3433 5-9-5 **58** (t) NicoleNordblad 8 52
(Hans Adielsson) *hld up in last pair: effrt on inner over 2f out: no prog over 1f out* **7/1**

404 **7** 1 1/2 **Deal Me In (IRE)**[91] 1213 4-9-4 **60** (p) GeorgeDowning(3) 1 50
(Ian Williams) *led to wl over 1f out: sn wknd* **9/2**[3]

0000 **8** 1 1/2 **Olynard (IRE)**[6] 3513 7-8-4 **46** (p) NoraLooby(3) 7 33
(Michael Mullineaux) *wl in tch: nt qckn over 2f out: steadily wknd over 1f out* **33/1**

00-0 **9** nk **Spanish Trail**[30] 2714 4-8-4 **46** oh1 DannyBrock(3) 3 32
(Christopher Kellett) *pressed ldr to 2f out: wknd qckly* **66/1**

2520 **10** 3 1/4 **Mcconnell (USA)**[37] 2514 8-8-11 **55** (b) OisinMurphy(5) 9 34
(Violet M Jordan) *racd wd towards rr: lost grnd whn v wd bnd 3f out: sn no ch* **12/1**

1m 40.35s (0.55) **Going Correction** +0.025s/f (Slow) **10** Ran SP% **123.7**
Speed ratings (Par 101): **98,97,96,95,92 91,90,88,88,85**
Tote Swingers 1&2 £3.90, 2&3 £16.90, 1&3 £9.70 CSF £14.38 CT £190.30 TOTE £4.10: £1.50, £1.50, £7.90; EX 14.90 Trifecta £389.30 Pool: £1,314.79 - 2.53 winning tickets..
Owner Kentisbeare Racing **Bred** Newsells Park Stud **Trained** Kentisbeare, Devon
■ Stewards' Enquiry : Shelley Birkett one-day ban: careless riding (10 July)

FOCUS
A moderate handicap for apprentice riders. They went a routine pace and it paid to be handy. A slight personal best from the winner with the second in line with recent form.

3688 CONOR MAYNARD LIVE AT KEMPTON 14.09.13 H'CAP 2m (P)
6:50 (6:50) (Class 6) (0-65,64) 4-Y-0+ **£1,940** (£577; £288; £144) **Stalls** Low

Form RPR

3343 **1** **Barachiel**[84] 1325 5-9-3 **60** RichardHughes 6 68
(Luke Dace) *stdd s: hld up in last trio: prog over 3f out: pushed along over 2f out: chsd ldr 1f out: rdn to ld ins fnl f* **3/1**[1]

66-5 **2** 1 1/4 **Lombok**[7] 3473 7-9-7 **64** (v) RyanMoore 8 71
(Gary Moore) *hld up in last trio: prog gng easily 6f out: trckd ldr over 2f out: drvn to ld over 1f out: hdd and one pce ins fnl f* **5/1**

0/35 **3** 1 **Star Alliance (IRE)**[33] 2642 5-9-2 **59** (b[1]) StevieDonohoe 9 64
(Ian Williams) *hld up: last of 8 but stl in tch 3f out: swtchd to inner and prog over 2f out: styd on to take 3rd ins fnl f: nt rch ldng pair* **4/1**[2]

2415 **4** 3 1/4 **Bold Adventure**[21] 2980 9-9-2 **59** NeilCallan 7 60
(Willie Musson) *hld up and last tl after 1/2-way: prog 3f out: rdn over 2f out: hung rt whn trying to cl over 1f out: one pce after* **9/2**[3]

0050 **5** 1 3/4 **Petersboden**[7] 3473 4-8-2 **45** JimmyQuinn 3 44
(Michael Blanshard) *cl up: trckd ldr 7f out: led 3f out and sn wnt for home: hdd & wknd over 1f out* **25/1**

3653 **6** 4 1/2 **Sommersturm (GER)**[7] 3473 9-9-0 **62** (t) DeclanBates(5) 1 56
(David Evans) *hld up in tch: trckd ldng pair 6f out to 3f out: wknd u.p over 2f out: b.b.v* **6/1**

1303 **7** 26 **Highly Likely (IRE)**[15] 3168 4-9-2 **59** JamesDoyle 2 31
(Steve Woodman) *t.k.h: trckd ldr: led after 7f: hdd & wknd 3f out: t.o* **6/1**

0-50 **8** 3/4 **Icebreaker Two**[33] 2642 4-8-9 **52** SamHitchcott 5 22
(John E Long) *chsd ldrs: shoved along bef 1/2-way: u.p 5f out: wknd rapidly wl over 2f out: t.o* **20/1**

4000 **9** 31 **If What And Maybe**[7] 3473 5-7-13 **45** (p) RyanPowell(3) 10
(John Ryan) *in tch: drvn and wknd 5f out: wl t.o* **50/1**

15-0 **10** 104 **Barathea Dancer (IRE)**[9] 3399 5-8-11 **54** (tp) KierenFox 4
(Christine Dunnett) *led 7f: wknd rapidly 7f out: wl t.o and virtually p.u 4f out* **33/1**

3m 30.69s (0.59) **Going Correction** +0.025s/f (Slow) **10** Ran SP% **121.9**
Speed ratings (Par 101): **99,98,97,96,95 93,80,79,64,**
Tote Swingers 1&2 £3.70, 2&3 £4.50, 1&3 £2.20 CSF £18.50 CT £62.78 TOTE £3.50: £2.20, £1.90, £1.60; EX 19.20 Trifecta £50.00 Pool: £876.79 - 13.13 winning tickets..
Owner Peter Gray & John Buchanan **Bred** Laundry Cottage Stud Farm **Trained** Five Oaks, W Sussex

FOCUS
A weak staying handicap in which the average early pace picked up as they went onto the far side. It is hard to see the winner as having improved to get off the mark.

3689 £200 FREE BETS AT BETDAQ MAIDEN STKS 7f (P)
7:20 (7:22) (Class 5) 2-Y-0 **£2,587** (£770; £384; £192) **Stalls** Low

Form RPR

2 **1** **Extra Noble**[32] 2653 2-9-5 0 JimCrowley 3 80
(Ralph Beckett) *prom: trckd ldr 3f out: rdn to cl 2f out: led over 1f out but drifted lft: drvn fnl f: jnd post* **1/1**[1]

64 **2** nse **Fire Fighting (IRE)**[13] 3233 2-9-5 0 NeilCallan 2 80
(Mark Johnston) *led: jinked lft after 1f: kicked on 3f out: hung lft fr 2f out: hdd over 1f out: rallied fnl f to force dead-heat last stride* **16/1**

3 2 3/4 **Snow Trouble (USA)** 2-9-5 0 HayleyTurner 8 73+
(Marcus Tregoning) *reminder sn after s and shoved along to rch midfield: outpcd fr 3f out: prog 2f out: styd on wl to take 3rd last 75yds* **20/1**

0353 **4** 1 1/4 **Seaham**[15] 3174 2-9-5 0 WilliamCarson 5 70
(Rod Millman) *t.k.h: trckd ldrs: chsd clr ldng pair over 2f out: no imp: one pce and lost 3rd last 75yds* **12/1**

5 3 **Dance Bid** 2-9-0 0 JamesDoyle 7 57
(Clive Brittain) *sn in midfield: outpcd fr 3f out: shkn up wl over 1f out: kpt on fnl f* **40/1**

6 1 1/4 **Adventure Seeker (IRE)** 2-9-5 0 GeorgeBaker 10 59
(Ed Vaughan) *s.s then hmpd: wl in rr: 9th over 2f out and wl outpcd: kpt on fr over 1f out* **33/1**

7 3/4 **Anglophile** 2-9-5 0 MickaelBarzalona 9 57
(Saeed bin Suroor) *towards rr and racd wd: rdn and struggling 1/2-way: no ch over 2f out: kpt on fnl f* **11/4**[2]

0 **8** 1 1/4 **Rising Dawn (IRE)**[20] 3017 2-9-5 0 RichardHughes 12 53
(Richard Hannon) *chsd ldrs: rdn and outpcd wl over 2f out: n.d after: fdd* **11/2**[3]

9 nk **Mezel** 2-9-5 0 DaneO'Neill 11 53
(Sir Michael Stoute) *dwlt: towards rr: 8th over 2f out: shkn up and sme prog on inner over 1f out: wknd fnl f* **20/1**

6 **10** 2 **Choral Clan (IRE)**[15] 3174 2-9-5 0 JackMitchell 4 47
(Philip Mitchell) *chsd ldr to 3f out: wknd qckly 2f out* **50/1**

11 11 **Turnbury** 2-9-5 0 FrankieDettori 6 19
(Robert Mills) *awkward s and rdr nrly off: a in last pair: t.o* **25/1**

12 5 **Miss Verdoyante** 2-9-0 0 ChrisCatlin 1
(Sir Mark Prescott Bt) *s.s: rn green and a in last pair: t.o* **50/1**

1m 26.82s (0.82) **Going Correction** +0.025s/f (Slow) **12** Ran SP% **128.3**
Speed ratings (Par 93): **96,95,92,91,87 86,85,84,83,81 69,63**WIN: EN £1.00, FF £12.30; PL: EN £1.10, FF £3.70, ST £2.40; EX: EN & FF £11.10, FF & EN £31.40; CSF: EN & FF £10.99, FF & EN £16.68; TRIF: EN, FF & ST £33.10, FF, EN & ST £495.90; SW: EN & FF £5.70, EN & ST £8.00, FF & ST £37.40, £27Owner Ballymore Downunder Syndicate Trifecta £Bred Mr & Mrs A E Pakenham Trained.

FOCUS
This juvenile maiden was run at a decent early tempo and the first pair had it to themselves from 2f out. A dead-heat was originally declared but changed following a review of the high definition photo-finish print. The runner-up sets the level rated to his debut form.

3690 BRITISH STALLION STUDS SUPPORTING BRITISH RACING EBF NOVICE STKS 6f (P)
7:50 (7:50) (Class 5) 2-Y-0 **£2,911** (£866; £432; £216) **Stalls** Low

Form RPR

21 **1** **Ligeia**[18] 3107 2-8-11 0 RichardHughes 1 86+
(Richard Hannon) *racd freely early: mde all: stretched on fr 2f out: clr whn shkn up briefly ins fnl f: comf* **4/7**[1]

41 **2** 3 1/2 **Razor Quest**[21] 2978 2-9-2 0 WilliamCarson 3 78
(Philip McBride) *trckd ldng pair: rdn 2f out: wnt 2nd over 1f out: no threat to wnr but kpt on* **6/1**[3]

210 **3** 2 **Tableforten**[8] 3424 2-9-2 0 AndreaAtzeni 2 72
(J S Moore) *chsd wnr: rdn and nt qckn 2f out: lost 2nd and one pce over 1f out* **11/4**[2]

4 1/2 **Merry Me (IRE)** 2-8-9 0 HayleyTurner 5 64
(Andrew Balding) *wnt lft s: in tch in 4th: outpcd and pushed along 2f out: n.d after but kpt on* **16/1**

5 14 **Pelagian (USA)** 2-9-0 0 JimCrowley 4 27
(Dean Ivory) *a last: rdn over 2f out: sn wknd: t.o* **33/1**

1m 13.38s (0.28) **Going Correction** +0.025s/f (Slow) **5** Ran SP% **113.4**
Speed ratings (Par 93): **99,94,91,91,72**
CSF £4.98 TOTE £1.70: £1.10, £2.40; EX 3.70 Trifecta £10.50 Pool: £1,114.31 - 79.49 winning tickets..
Owner Pineapple Stud **Bred** Plantation Stud **Trained** East Everleigh, Wilts

FOCUS
The winner was quite impressive in this novice stakes.

3691 WINNERS ARE WELCOME AT BETDAQ FILLIES' H'CAP 6f (P)
8:20 (8:20) (Class 4) (0-80,80) 3-Y-0+ **£4,690** (£1,395; £697; £348) **Stalls** Low

Form RPR

5-00 **1** **Badr Al Badoor (IRE)**[30] 2708 3-9-7 **80** (v[1]) JamesDoyle 8 89
(James Fanshawe) *dwlt: hld up in last: prog on inner 2f out: clsd over 1f out: drvn ahd last 150yds: won gng away* **7/2**[2]

1-0 **2** 1 1/2 **Angel Way (IRE)**[29] 2745 4-9-7 **73** NeilCallan 1 79
(Mike Murphy) *t.k.h: trckd ldng pair: rdn to chal 2f out: led briefly 1f out: outpcd last 100yds* **16/1**

-256 **3** 3/4 **Glastonberry**[34] 2596 5-9-3 **69** GeorgeBaker 5 73
(Geoffrey Deacon) *trckd ldng pair: moved up gng strly to ld wl over 1f out: sn rdn: hdd and nt qckn 1f out* **5/1**

-403 **4** 2 3/4 **Ray Of Joy**[13] 3259 7-9-10 **76** RyanMoore 6 71
(J R Jenkins) *hld up in last trio: rdn and sme prog 2f out: no imp on ldrs 1f out: wl hld after: dismntd after fin* **9/2**[3]

-103 **5** 2 **Red Larkspur (IRE)**[36] 2531 4-9-13 **79** RichardHughes 3 67
(Roger Teal) *hld up in last trio: shkn up and no rspnse wl over 1f out: wl btn fnl f* **5/1**

1131 **6** 5 **Above The Stars**[23] 2926 5-9-4 **75** RachealKneller(5) 7 47
(Jamie Osborne) *w ldr at brisk pce: led over 2f out to wl over 1f out: wknd qckly* **10/1**

2105 **7** 7 **Hard Walnut (IRE)**[21] 2983 3-9-2 **75** HarryBentley 2 23
(Olly Stevens) *mde most at brisk pce to over 2f out: wknd rapidly* **9/4**[1]

1m 12.19s (-0.91) **Going Correction** +0.025s/f (Slow)
WFA 3 from 4yo+ 7lb **7** Ran SP% **119.5**
Speed ratings (Par 102): **107,105,104,100,97 91,81**
Tote Swingers 1&2 £9.80, 2&3 £7.10, 1&3 £7.40 CSF £57.06 CT £285.44 TOTE £4.80: £2.80, £5.60; EX 76.80 Trifecta £539.30 Part won. Pool: £719.08 - 0.20 winning tickets..
Owner Mohamed Obaida **Bred** Con Harrington **Trained** Newmarket, Suffolk

FOCUS
A modest fillies' sprint handicap. There was no hanging about, which suited the closers. The winner built on her juvenile form in the first-time visor, while the placed horses set an ordinary standard.

3692 BETDAQ 1ST UK RACE COMMISSION FREE H'CAP (LONDON MIDDLE DISTANCE SERIES QUALIFIER) 1m 3f (P)
8:50 (8:50) (Class 4) (0-85,85) 4-Y-0+ **£4,690** (£1,395; £697; £348) **Stalls** Low

Form RPR

4030 **1** **Sir Boss (IRE)**[11] 3345 8-8-3 **74** JoeyHaynes(7) 4 82
(Michael Mullineaux) *trckd ldrs: clsd fr 2f out: rdn to ld jst over 1f out: hld on nr fin* **25/1**

1-43 **2** hd **Villoresi (IRE)**[10] 3370 4-9-2 **80** HayleyTurner 2 88+
(James Fanshawe) *hld up in last pair in slowly run r: plld out wd 2f out: prog over 1f out: clsng whn hung rt ins fnl f: r.o: jst failed* **6/4**[1]

1 **3** 1/2 **Cranach**[29] 2754 4-9-5 **83** JimmyQuinn 1 90
(Tom Keddy) *hld up in rr: prog on inner jst over 2f out: chal over 1f out: styd on fnl f: a hld* **10/1**

5060 **4** 3/4 **Takeitfromalady (IRE)**[26] 2841 4-9-0 **78** (b) KierenFox 3 83
(Lee Carter) *hld up in last trio in slowly run r: rdn 2f out: clsd 1f out and pressed for a pl: nt qckn after* **25/1**

-055 **5** 1/2 **Nordic Quest (IRE)**[23] 2939 4-8-10 **74** (p) NeilCallan 10 78
(Gerard Butler) *hld up in last in slowly run r: prog 2f out to chal over 1f out: one pce ins fnl f* **5/1**[3]

0031 **6** 1 3/4 **Mountain Range (IRE)**[21] 2982 5-8-6 **70** JamieMackay 11 72
(Willie Musson) *trckd ldr: led 2f out to jst over 1f out: fdd fnl f* **16/1**

1/5- **7** 1 1/4 **Waterclock (IRE)**[404] 2235 4-9-6 **84** JamesDoyle 9 83
(Roger Charlton) *trckd ldrs: rdn over 2f out: sn lost pl and btn* **12/1**

24-3 **8** 2 1/4 **Lucanin**[56] 1926 4-9-2 **80** RyanMoore 6 75
(Sir Michael Stoute) *trckd ldng pair: rdn and lost pl quite qckly 2f out: wl btn after* **11/4**[2]

260- **9** 2 1/4 **Freddy Q (IRE)**[247] 7300 4-9-1 **79** FrankieDettori 7 70
(Roger Teal) *led: set pedestrian pce: tried to kick on over 2f out: sn hdd & wknd* **14/1**

0-00 L **Halfsin (IRE)**[18] 3113 5-9-7 **85**........(t[1]) AndreaAtzeni 8
(Marco Botti) *rrd bef stalls opened and failed to emerge fr them* **20/1**
2m 28.56s (6.66) **Going Correction** +0.025s/f (Slow) **10** Ran SP% **125.1**
Speed ratings (Par 105): **76,75,75,74,74 73,72,70,69,**
Tote Swingers 1&2 £15.10, 2&3 £7.80, 1&3 £64.60 CSF £66.13 CT £441.35 TOTE £25.60: £4.90, £1.20, £2.80; EX 154.70 Trifecta £603.50 Pool: £804.70 - 0.22 winning tickets..
Owner Miss M Mullineaux, P Lawton, I Ross **Bred** Mrs E R Cantillon **Trained** Alpraham, Cheshire

FOCUS
A fair handicap that developed into a sprint from 2f out due to the dawdling early pace and it is suspect form.

3693 COMMISSION FREE 1ST MONTH AT BETDAQ H'CAP (LONDON MILE SERIES QUALIFIER) 1m (P)
9:20 (9:21) (Class 4) (0-85,84) 3-Y-0+ **£4,690** (£1,395; £697; £348) **Stalls** Low

Form RPR
2214 **1** **Sennockian Star**[12] 3276 3-8-10 **76**........(b) JamieSpencer 10 85
(Mark Johnston) *trckd ldrs: prog to go 2nd over 3f out: drvn and nt qckn 2f out: styd on over 1f out: clsd to ld last 75yds* **7/2**[2]
5-40 **2** ¾ **Net Whizz (USA)**[18] 3108 4-10-0 **84**........(p) FrankieDettori 6 93
(Jeremy Noseda) *trckd ldr: led 1/2-way: kicked on 2f out: drvn over 1f out: worn down last 75yds* **9/2**[3]
-503 **3** 1 ¾ **Ocean Tempest**[26] 2841 4-9-13 **83**........(p) BrettDoyle 3 88
(John Ryan) *trckd ldrs: rdn and outpcd over 2f out: kpt on to take 3rd over 1f out: nvr able to threaten* **11/2**
0-00 **4** 1 ¼ **Graphic (IRE)**[32] 2647 4-9-10 **80**........ RyanMoore 4 82+
(William Haggas) *w.w in midfield: outpcd and shkn up over 2f out: kpt on fr over 1f out: n.d* **2/1**[1]
2201 **5** 1 ¾ **Pategonia**[15] 3172 4-9-8 **78**........ RichardHughes 2 76
(John Gosden) *led to 1/2-way: drvn in 3rd over 2f out: one pce after* **6/1**
12-3 **6** ½ **Take A Note**[16] 3153 4-9-7 **77**........ JimCrowley 1 74
(Patrick Chamings) *trckd ldrs: outpcd and shkn up over 2f out: pushed along and no prog over 1f out* **12/1**
0-05 **7** ¾ **Mingun Bell (USA)**[20] 3019 6-9-12 **82**........(b) DaneO'Neill 7 77
(Ed de Giles) *s.s: prog fr last trio 1/2-way: rdn wl over 2f out: sn struggling* **25/1**
1000 **8** 1 ¾ **Brocklebank (IRE)**[14] 3215 4-9-5 **75**........ NeilCallan 5 66
(Simon Dow) *nvr bttr than midfield: u.p wl over 2f out: strugging in rr after* **50/1**
-416 **9** ½ **Great Expectations**[29] 2761 5-9-5 **75**........ GeorgeBaker 9 65
(J R Jenkins) *t.k.h: hld up in last trio: rdn and no prog over 2f out* **20/1**
1620 **10** 3 **Poetic Lord**[20] 3019 4-9-7 **77**........ JamesDoyle 8 60
(Sylvester Kirk) *hld up in last trio: jst pushed along and no prog fr over 2f out: eased fnl f* **16/1**
1m 39.12s (-0.68) **Going Correction** +0.025s/f (Slow)
WFA 3 from 4yo+ 10lb **10** Ran SP% **127.6**
Speed ratings (Par 105): **104,103,101,100,98 98,97,95,95,92**
Tote Swingers 1&2 £4.40, 2&3 £9.10, 1&3 £4.00 CSF £21.47 CT £92.38 TOTE £5.70: £2.10, £2.10, £1.70; EX 23.70 Trifecta £190.40 Pool: £1,654.37 - 6.51 winning tickets..
Owner The Vine Accord **Bred** Cheveley Park Stud Ltd **Trained** Middleham Moor, N Yorks

FOCUS
This was another race where those held up faced a stiff task due to the uneven pace and few got involved. A personal-best from the second with the third the best guide to the level.
T/Plt: £56.90 to a £1 stake. Pool: £68,772.56 - 881.96 winning tickets. T/Qpdt: £39.30 to a £1 stake. Pool: £4,502.73 - 84.69 winning tickets. JN

3370 SALISBURY (R-H)
Wednesday, June 26

OFFICIAL GOING: Good to firm (9.2)
Wind: virtually nil Weather: overcast but warm

3694 BRITISH STALLION STUDS EBF ASHBRITTLE STUD MAIDEN FILLIES' STKS 5f
2:20 (2:21) (Class 4) 2-Y-0 **£4,204** (£1,251; £625; £312) **Stalls** Low

Form RPR
0 **1** **Chutney (IRE)**[19] 3057 2-9-0 0........ RichardHughes 4 77
(Richard Hannon) *mde all: rdn over 1f out: r.o wl: pushed out fnl 120yds* **9/2**[3]
23 **2** 2 ¾ **Stellarta**[21] 2978 2-9-0 0........ LiamKeniry 6 67
(Michael Blanshard) *trckd wnr in disp 2nd tl wnt clr 2nd 2f out: sn rdn: kpt on but nt pce of wnr* **20/1**
3 ¾ **Trinity River** 2-8-11 0........ DarrenEgan(3) 8 64
(Daniel Kubler) *chsd ldrs: racd green and hung in bhd runner-up whn rdn 2f out: kpt on fnl f* **33/1**
23 **4** 1 ½ **Weisse Socken (IRE)**[20] 3023 2-9-0 0........ JimCrowley 9 59
(Ralph Beckett) *trckd ldrs: rdn 2f out: kpt on same pce fr over 1f out* **5/2**[2]
2 **5** hd **Meeting Waters**[12] 3288 2-9-0 0........ RyanMoore 7 58
(William Haggas) *trckd wnr in disp 2nd tl rdn 2f out: kpt on same pce* **10/11**[1]
40 **6** 1 **Paradise Child**[26] 2823 2-9-0 0........ LukeMorris 3 55
(Bill Turner) *in tch: sn pushed along: rdn over 2f out: nt pce to threaten: no ex fnl 120yds* **66/1**
7 2 ¼ **Spider Lily** 2-9-0 0........ JohnFahy 2 47
(Peter Makin) *wnt to s early: racd green: s.i.s: sn outpcd in last: n.d* **40/1**
8 ¾ **Dizzy Miss Lizzy (IRE)** 2-9-0 0........ SeanLevey 1 44
(Richard Hannon) *sn outpcd in last pair: nvr a factor: wknd over 1f out* **16/1**
9 6 **Warm Order** 2-9-0 0........ PatDobbs 5 22
(Tony Carroll) *s.i.s: sn in tch: outpcd after 1f: wknd over 1f out* **66/1**
1m 2.06s (1.06) **Going Correction** +0.175s/f (Good) **9** Ran SP% **118.1**
Speed ratings (Par 92): **98,93,92,90,89 88,84,83,73**
Tote Swingers 1&2 £9.60, 2&3 £48.20, 1&3 £32.80 CSF £84.12 TOTE £5.50: £1.10, £4.00, £13.60; EX 53.00 Trifecta £679.50 Pool: £4,185.38 - 4.61 winning tickets..
Owner R J McCreery **Bred** Simon Tindall **Trained** East Everleigh, Wilts

FOCUS
Enticing (2006) and Perfect Tribute (2010) are notable exceptions, but eight of the ten winners of this in the past mustered only one more victory between them from plenty of subsequent outings, suggesting you're either very good when landing this maiden, or going to struggle with the handicapper down the line.

3695 WESTOVER JAGUAR F-TYPE MAIDEN STKS 6f
2:50 (2:50) (Class 5) 2-Y-0 **£3,234** (£962; £481; £240) **Stalls** Low

Form RPR
2 **1** **Brown Sugar (IRE)**[18] 3112 2-9-5 0........ RichardHughes 3 87+
(Richard Hannon) *broke wl: mde all: qcknd clr over 1f out: readily* **30/100**[1]
2 5 **Harwoods Volante (IRE)** 2-9-5 0........ PatDobbs 2 71+
(Amanda Perrett) *trckd ldrs: rdn 2f out: sn chsng wnr: kpt on nicely but nvr any ch w ready wnr* **25/1**
3 4 ½ **Earl Of Menteith (IRE)** 2-9-5 0........ MickaelBarzalona 7 57
(Saeed bin Suroor) *trckd wnr tl rdn wl over 1f out: kpt on same pce* **5/1**[2]
4 1 ¾ **Zampa Manos (USA)** 2-9-5 0........ RyanMoore 5 51
(Andrew Balding) *slowly away: last but in tch: outpcd after 1f: hdwy into 4th wl over 1f out: no further imp fnl f* **10/1**[3]
5 7 **Three Peaks** 2-9-5 0........ JamesMcDonald 1 29
(Charles Hills) *little slowly away: cl up: racd green whn rdn 2f out: wknd ent fnl f* **16/1**
6 1 ½ **Lambeth Palace** 2-9-5 0........ LukeMorris 4 24
(Ronald Harris) *little slowly away: sn chsng ldrs: rdn over 2f out: wknd jst over 1f out* **100/1**
1m 15.31s (0.51) **Going Correction** +0.175s/f (Good) **6** Ran SP% **113.4**
Speed ratings (Par 93): **103,96,90,88,78 76**
Tote Swingers 1&2 £5.00, 2&3 £6.10, 1&3 £1.30 CSF £11.65 TOTE £1.20: £1.10, £11.10; EX 12.30 Trifecta £31.60 Pool: £3,943.89 - 93.39 winning tickets..
Owner De La Warr Racing **Bred** Ballylinch Stud **Trained** East Everleigh, Wilts

FOCUS
A contest that saw subsequent Group 2 winner Harbour Watch make his debut in 2011.

3696 SMITH & WILLIAMSON MAIDEN FILLIES' STKS 6f 212y
3:20 (3:21) (Class 5) 3-Y-0 **£3,234** (£962; £481; £240) **Stalls** Low

Form RPR
00- **1** **Lunette (IRE)**[196] 8070 3-9-0 0........ JimCrowley 5 69
(Ralph Beckett) *trckd ldr: rdn over 2f out: led narrowly over 1f out: remained hrd pressed: got the bttr of 3rd fnl 120yds: jst hld on fr late surge of runner-up* **10/1**
-0 **2** shd **Candy Kitten**[57] 1908 3-9-0 0........ LukeMorris 1 68
(Alastair Lidderdale) *trckd ldrs: pushed along 3f out: swtchd off rails over 2f out: sn drvn: r.o wl fnl 120yds: jst failed* **16/1**
-440 **3** 1 ½ **Secretly**[15] 3179 3-9-0 73........(v[1]) DaneO'Neill 2 64
(Henry Candy) *led: rdn whn hdd over 1f out: kpt pressing wnr w ev ch tl no ex fnl 120yds* **9/2**[3]
63 **4** 4 ½ **Meddling**[15] 3176 3-9-0 0........ RyanMoore 3 52
(Sir Michael Stoute) *awkward leaving stalls: last but in tch: nudged along 3f out: hdwy wl over 2f out: sn rdn: nt pce to chal: no ex fnl 120yds* **1/1**[1]
5 5 **Quantify (USA)** 3-9-0 0........ JamieSpencer 4 41
(Luca Cumani) *trckd ldrs: swtchd rt 2f out: sn rdn: wknd ins fnl f* **11/4**[2]
6 13 **Duchess Of Hygrove** 3-9-0 0........ SebSanders 6 14
(J W Hills) *slowly away: sn trcking ldrs: rdn wl over 2f out: btn whn hung rt over 1f out* **66/1**
1m 28.95s (0.35) **Going Correction** +0.175s/f (Good) **6** Ran SP% **111.3**
Speed ratings (Par 96): **105,104,103,98,92 77**
Tote Swingers 1&2 £6.60, 2&3 £3.70, 1&3 £4.30 CSF £131.01 TOTE £11.10: £4.10, £4.90; EX 103.30 Trifecta £619.80 Pool: £3,103.92 - 3.75 winning tickets..
Owner T D Rootes & O F Waller **Bred** Shutford Stud And O F Waller **Trained** Kimpton, Hants

FOCUS
Probably nothing more than a weak event of its type, and it paid to be handy. The first two in the market were both disappointing.

3697 MOLSON COORS NOEL CANNON MEMORIAL TROPHY H'CAP 1m
3:50 (3:54) (Class 2) (0-100,97) 3-Y-0+
£12,450 (£3,728; £1,864; £932; £466; £234) **Stalls** Low

Form RPR
60-0 **1** **Asatir (USA)**[26] 2841 4-9-9 **92**........(v[1]) SilvestreDeSousa 12 101
(Saeed bin Suroor) *racd keenly: swtchd to farside rail and led after 1f: rdn over 2f out: hld on v gamely fnl f: all out* **20/1**
-110 **2** hd **Rockalong (IRE)**[40] 2424 4-9-5 **88**........ JamieSpencer 5 97
(Luca Cumani) *led for 1f: trckd wnr: nudged along to cl over 3f out: rdn over 2f out: str chal ins fnl f: kpt on but no ex* **2/1**[1]
4224 **3** ¾ **Lord Ofthe Shadows (IRE)**[18] 3108 4-9-3 **86**........ RichardHughes 7 93+
(Richard Hannon) *mid-div: hdwy on far rail 2f out to trck ldrs: nt clr run whn rdn jst over 1f out: swtchd lft and r.o ins fnl f: wnt 3rd towards fin* **7/1**[3]
-401 **4** ¾ **Head Of Steam (USA)**[34] 2585 6-9-7 **90**........ PatDobbs 6 96
(Amanda Perrett) *mid-div: smooth hdwy to trck ldrs over 2f out: shkn up for effrt over 1f out: kpt on but nt quite pce to chal* **7/1**[3]
6-06 **5** shd **Commend**[20] 3019 4-8-12 **81**........(v) RyanMoore 2 86
(Sir Michael Stoute) *trckd ldrs: rdn in cl 3rd but nt best of runs over 1f out: no ex whe lost 2 pls fnl 75yds* **4/1**[2]
0610 **6** 2 ¾ **Bancnuanaheireann (IRE)**[11] 3339 6-9-8 **91**........ TomQueally 1 90
(Michael Appleby) *hld up towards rr: rdn and hdwy into midfield whn swtchd lft over 2f out: kpt on same pce fr over 1f out* **8/1**
-030 **7** 1 ¾ **Redact (IRE)**[7] 3458 4-9-9 **97**........ WilliamTwiston-Davies(5) 8 92
(Richard Hannon) *trckd ldrs: rdn over 3f out: one pce fnl 2f* **33/1**
4200 **8** ½ **Shavansky**[12] 3293 9-8-11 **87**........ PatMillman(7) 9 81
(Rod Millman) *stdd s: racd keenly towards rr: pushed along wl over 2f out: nvr any real imp on ldrs* **33/1**
0055 **9** 1 **Mabait**[12] 3300 7-9-1 **89**........ LauraPike(5) 11 81
(David Simcock) *towards rr: rdn and hdwy into midfield over 2f out but nvr a threat* **18/1**
31-0 **10** shd **Jacob Cats**[53] 2029 4-9-13 **96**........(bt[1]) HarryBentley 10 87
(Olly Stevens) *mid-div: hdwy over 3f out: rdn to chse ldrs over 2f out: wknd ent fnl f* **18/1**
00-0 **11** 2 ½ **Top Offer**[19] 3060 4-9-9 **92**........[1] JamesDoyle 3 78
(Roger Charlton) *hld up towards rr: swtchd lft 3f out: rdn 2f out: nvr any imp* **11/1**
1m 43.25s (-0.25) **Going Correction** +0.175s/f (Good)
WFA 3 from 4yo+ 10lb **11** Ran SP% **118.9**
Speed ratings (Par 109): **108,107,107,106,106 103,101,101,100,100 97**
Tote Swingers 1&2 £12.10, 2&3 £3.10, 1&3 £16.50 CSF £59.79 CT £329.60 TOTE £22.60: £6.20, £1.30, £2.20; EX 89.50 Trifecta £628.00 Pool: £4,720.30 - 5.63 winning tickets..
Owner Godolphin **Bred** Robert Raphaelson **Trained** Newmarket, Suffolk

FOCUS
A competitive handicap, but the early pace wasn't strong. The winner set steady fractions and the fourth sets the standard.

3698 ASHBRITTLE STUD BIBURY CUP (H'CAP) 1m 4f
4:25 (4:25) (Class 3) (0-95,88) 3-Y-O **£9,703** (£2,887; £1,443; £721) **Stalls** High

Form RPR
1-23 **1** **Cafe Society (FR)**[39] 2457 3-8-9 **76** JamieSpencer 2 85+
(David Simcock) *awkward leaving stalls: hld up in 5th: dropped to 6th but in tch 5f out: stl last but travelling wl whn swtchd to centre wl over 1f out: str run ent fnl f: drifted rt: led fnl 40yds: won gng away: pushed out* **9/4**[2]
3231 **2** 1 1/4 **Royal Signaller**[12] 3277 3-8-13 **80** (p) PatDobbs 4 87
(Amanda Perrett) *led: rdn whn jnd over 2f out: bk in clr ld jst ins fnl f: no ex whn hdd fnl 40yds* **7/1**
1114 **3** 1 1/4 **Poetic Verse**[34] 2602 3-8-10 **77** RyanMoore 3 82
(Rod Millman) *trckd ldng pair: rdn whn swtchd lft jst over 2f out: ch jst over 1f out: kpt on same pce ins fnl f* **12/1**
4032 **4** 1/2 **Snowy Dawn**[32] 2651 3-8-5 **72** JimmyQuinn 5 76
(Andrew Hollinshead) *trckd ldr: upsides gng the bttr jst over 2f out: sn rdn: ev ch tl ent fnl f: no ex* **4/1**[3]
12-1 **5** 3 **Ennistown**[19] 3048 3-9-7 **88** MickaelBarzalona 6 87
(Saeed bin Suroor) *racd keenly early: trckd ldng trio: rdn to dispute cl 3rd 2f out: fdd ins fnl f* **2/1**[1]
0315 **6** 2 1/4 **Isis Blue**[12] 3294 3-8-7 **74** AndreaAtzeni 1 70
(Rod Millman) *hld up in last: disp 4th 5f out: rdn wl over 2f out: fdd ent fnl f* **9/1**

2m 38.9s (0.90) **Going Correction** +0.175s/f (Good) **6** Ran SP% **114.3**
Speed ratings (Par 103): **104,103,102,102,100 98**
Tote Swingers 1&2 £3.80, 2&3 £3.80, 1&3 £2.60 CSF £18.38 TOTE £3.20: £1.90, £3.60; EX 18.10 Trifecta £79.70 Pool: £2,447.58 - 23.01 winning tickets..
Owner S Bamber J Barnett & M Caine **Bred** Haras Du Quesnay **Trained** Newmarket, Suffolk

FOCUS
Not form to take literally considering it was steadily run and the whole field held some sort of chance a furlong out. It has been rated slightly positively however.

3699 NEW FOREST FARM MACHINERY/JOHN DEERE FILLIES' H'CAP 6f
4:55 (4:55) (Class 5) (0-70,71) 3-Y-O **£2,911** (£866; £432; £216) **Stalls** Low

Form RPR
-061 **1** **Glossy Posse**[10] 3375 3-9-10 **71** 6ex RichardHughes 3 77
(Richard Hannon) *trckd ldrs on far rail: pushed along over 3f out: rdn over 2f out: gap appeared to ld jst over 1f out: kpt on w enough in hand fnl 120yds: rdn out* **3/1**[1]
0-05 **2** nk **Front Page News**[19] 3058 3-9-6 **67** AndreaAtzeni 14 72+
(Robert Eddery) *hld up bhd: stl last whn pushed along and swtchd lft 2f out: sn rdn: gd hdwy ent fnl f: str run fnl 120yds: a gng to be jst hld by wnr* **9/2**[2]
3560 **3** 1/2 **Tregereth (IRE)**[17] 3134 3-8-5 **57** ow1 MatthewLawson[(5)] 1 60
(Jonathan Portman) *mid-div: hdwy 2f out: sn rdn: edgd lft over 1f out: kpt on to go 3rd ins fnl f* **22/1**
2144 **4** 1 3/4 **Princess Cammie (IRE)**[15] 3178 3-8-3 **57** (p) JoeyHaynes[(7)] 6 55
(John Bridger) *led for 1f: trckd ldr: rdn and ev ch over 1f out: edgd lft: no ex ins fnl f* **11/1**
4440 **5** 1/2 **Starlight Angel (IRE)**[14] 3216 3-9-1 **67** ThomasBrown[(5)] 11 63
(Ronald Harris) *hld up towards rr: rdn into midfield over 2f out: kpt on ins fnl f* **20/1**
2203 **6** hd **Loulou Vuitton**[11] 3327 3-8-11 **58** (p) PatDobbs 9 54
(Frank Sheridan) *mid-div: rdn over 2f out: stdy prog over 1f out: kpt on ins fnl f* **33/1**
-404 **7** 3 1/4 **Roanne (USA)**[26] 2824 3-9-4 **65** (b[1]) AdamKirby 8 50
(Clive Cox) *racd keenly: trckd ldr: led after 1f: rdn: edgd off far rails and hdd jst over 1f out: wknd* **6/1**[3]
-166 **8** 2 1/4 **Elusive Gold (IRE)**[18] 3111 3-9-4 **65** SebSanders 10 43
(J W Hills) *mid-div: rdn over 3f out: chsd ldrs over 1f out: wknd ins fnl f* **8/1**
-000 **9** 3/4 **Lady Vermeer**[14] 3216 3-9-3 **64** (b[1]) JimCrowley 2 40
(Ralph Beckett) *s.i.s: sn mid-div: rdn over 2f out: wknd jst over 1f out* **12/1**
20-1 **10** 3 1/2 **Spray Tan**[26] 2829 3-9-2 **63** SeanLevey 7 27
(Tony Carroll) *trckd ldrs: rdn wl over 2f out: wknd over 1f out* **11/1**
00-0 **11** 2 1/2 **Chandelle Celeste**[22] 2950 3-8-4 **51** HarryBentley 13
(James Toller) *mid-div: effrt 3f out: wknd over 1f out* **7/1**
006- **12** 7 **Elounta**[193] 8138 3-7-13 **49** oh1 DarrenEgan[(3)] 5
(John Best) *racd keenly: stmbld after 2f: a towards rr: wknd over 1f out* **18/1**
5-54 **13** 1/2 **Emerald Sea**[29] 2763 3-9-7 **68** TedDurcan 12
(Chris Wall) *a towards rr* **8/1**

1m 14.92s (0.12) **Going Correction** +0.175s/f (Good) **13** Ran SP% **123.8**
Speed ratings (Par 96): **106,105,104,102,101 101,97,94,93,88 85,76,75**
Tote Swingers 1&2 £4.50, 2&3 £38.90, 1&3 £19.40 CSF £15.57 CT £270.56 TOTE £2.70: £1.10, £1.90, £9.60; EX 13.60 Trifecta £217.00 Pool: £2,414.47 - 8.34 winning tickets..
Owner J G Davis **Bred** J G Davis & Star Pointe Ltd **Trained** East Everleigh, Wilts

FOCUS
Quite a weak fillies' handicap. The winner arrived in form and built on her latest win.

3700 TRACKPATH LTD H'CAP (FOR GENTLEMAN AMATEUR RIDERS) 6f 212y
5:30 (5:31) (Class 6) (0-65,64) 4-Y-O+ **£2,495** (£774; £386; £193) **Stalls** Low

Form RPR
6-00 **1** **Loyal N Trusted**[28] 2781 5-10-9 **55** (p) MrMPrice[(3)] 7 63
(Richard Price) *in tch: rdn to chse ldrs over 2f out: styd on to ld fnl 140yds: kpt on wl* **9/1**
-603 **2** 1 **Graylyn Valentino**[13] 3246 4-11-6 **63** MrMarioBaratti 2 68
(Robert Eddery) *slowly away: in tch: hdwy u.p 3f out: lcd ont fnl f: no ex whn hdd fnl 140yds* **11/4**[2]
2031 **3** nk **Supa Seeker (USA)**[6] 3513 7-10-0 **46** MrChrisMartin[(3)] 11 50
(Tony Carroll) *bhd: swtchd to centre and hdwy fr 2f out: styd on ent fnl f: wnt 3rd ins fnl 120yds* **2/1**[1]
5304 **4** 1/2 **Khajaaly (IRE)**[20] 3015 6-10-9 **52** (b) MrRossBirkett 8 55
(Julia Feilden) *lost pl whn nt clr run after leaving stalls: hdwy to trck ldrs after 2f: led over 2f out: rdn and hdd ent fnl f: no ex* **12/1**
6430 **5** 5 **The Name Is Frank**[11] 3326 8-10-7 **55** (t) MrBenFfrenchDavis[(5)] 9 45
(Mark Gillard) *disp for 2f: in tch: rdn over 3f out: nvr bk on terms* **7/1**[3]
463 **6** hd **Jonnie Skull (IRE)**[8] 3430 7-11-0 **64** (vt) MrJAMcEntee[(7)] 3 53
(Phil McEntee) *chsd ldrs: prom after 2f: rdn and edgd lft over 2f out: wknd fnl f* **8/1**
0-04 **7** 6 **Beach Rhythm (USA)**[21] 2998 6-10-2 **48** MrFMitchell[(3)] 4 21
(Jim Allen) *prom: rdn over 3f out: wknd wl over 1f out* **20/1**
3550 **8** 3 3/4 **Flying Kitty**[50] 2125 4-9-11 **45** MrDLevey[(5)] 5 8
(John Bridger) *led for 1f: chsd ldrs tl wknd over 2f out* **50/1**
1016 **9** 3 1/2 **Shahrazad (IRE)**[9] 3404 4-10-4 **54** (t) JackGilligan[(7)] 1 7
(Patrick Gilligan) *disp: led after 1f: rdn over 3f out: hdd over 2f out: sn wknd* **15/2**
25-0 **10** 5 **Waspy**[19] 3052 4-10-12 **58** (t) MrKevinJones[(3)] 6
(Dr Jeremy Naylor) *chsd ldrs: sn pushed along: wknd over 2f out* **25/1**

1m 29.1s (0.50) **Going Correction** +0.175s/f (Good) **10** Ran SP% **123.6**
Speed ratings (Par 101): **104,102,102,101,96 96,89,84,80,75**
Tote Swingers 1&2 £7.80, 2&3 £3.00, 1&3 £6.20 CSF £35.54 CT £73.76 TOTE £9.20: £2.00, £1.80, £1.30; EX 47.10 Trifecta £208.00 Pool: £2,835.75 - 10.22 winning tickets..
Owner The Net Partnership & G Robinson **Bred** Mountgrange Stud Ltd **Trained** Ullingswick, H'fords

FOCUS
Not a result to take too seriously for various reasons. The winner is rated to his old turf best.
T/Plt: £1,051.10 to a £1 stake. Pool: £63,572.85 - 44.15 winning tickets. T/Qpdt: £313.30 to a £1 stake. Pool: £5,436.82 - 12.84 winning tickets. TM

3701 - 3707a (Foreign Racing) - See Raceform Interactive

3185 MAISONS-LAFFITTE (R-H)
Wednesday, June 26

OFFICIAL GOING: Turf: good

3708a PRIX DE L'ISLE ADAM (CLAIMER) (3YO) (TURF) 6f (S)
1:50 (1:51) 3-Y-O **£9,349** (£3,739; £2,804; £1,869; £934)

RPR
1 **Kalicamix**[68] 1668 3-9-4 0 OlivierPeslier 7 94
(Paul Cole) *broke wl: w ldrs on outside: cl 3rd and pushed along 1 1/2f out: rdn ent fnl f: led 100yds out: sn clr: a holding fast-fining runner-up* **18/5**[3]
2 1/2 **Perrecalla (FR)**[50] 3-8-10 0 ThibaultSpeicher[(6)] 1 90
(J Van Handenhove, France) **3/1**[1]
3 3/4 **Renny Storm (CZE)** 3-9-4 0 JaromirSafar 2 90
(J Michal, Czech Republic) **24/1**
4 3/4 **Vahiney (FR)**[165] 3-8-11 0 GregoryBenoist 5 81
(Mme Pia Brandt, France) **13/1**
5 hd **Shingueti (FR)**[51] 3-9-6 0 (p) MaximeGuyon 8 89
(C Baillet, France) **9/2**
6 snk **Baba O'Riley (IRE)**[71] 3-9-5 0 CesarPasserat[(3)] 3 90
(W Walton, France) **58/10**
7 1 1/2 **Sian Kaan (FR)**[77] 3-9-1 0 ChristopheSoumillon 6 79
(J-C Rouget, France) **7/2**[2]
8 1 1/4 **Tittle Tattle**[27] 3-8-8 0 MircoDemuro 4 68
(E J O'Neill, France) **42/1**

1m 11.7s (-1.70) **8** Ran SP% **115.3**
WIN (incl. 1 euro stake): 4.60. PLACES: 2.00, 1.80, 4.00. DF: 10.10. SF: 18.80.
Owner P F I Cole Ltd **Bred** Whatton Manor Stud **Trained** Whatcombe, Oxon

3461 HAMILTON (R-H)
Thursday, June 27

OFFICIAL GOING: Good (good to firm in places; 8.6)
Wind: Light across Weather: Overcast

3709 HAMILTON PARK LADY AMATEUR RIDERS' H'CAP (FOR SAINTS & SINNERS CHALLENGE CUP) 1m 5f 9y
6:20 (6:21) (Class 6) (0-65,63) 4-Y-O+ **£1,975** (£607; £303) **Stalls** High

Form RPR
-016 **1** **A Southside Boy (GER)**[15] 3199 5-10-2 **58** MissCWalton 7 66
(Jim Goldie) *hld up in tch: hdwy over 4f out: led 2f out: rdn appr fnl f: styd on wl* **9/2**[3]
5241 **2** 1 3/4 **Schmooze (IRE)**[8] 3467 4-10-2 **58** MrsCBartley 2 63
(Linda Perratt) *hld up in rr: effrt and nt clr run on inner over 3f out and sn swtchd lft: pushed along and hdwy over 2f out: sn rdn and styd on to chse wnr ins fnl f: no imp towards fin* **7/4**[1]
0-30 **3** 1 3/4 **Talk Of Saafend (IRE)**[13] 3287 8-9-9 **56** (p) MissRobynGray[(5)] 4 59
(Dianne Sayer) *led: rdn along 3f out: hdd 2f out: sn drvn and kpt on same pce* **16/1**
1536 **4** shd **Jan Smuts (IRE)**[7] 3504 5-10-2 **63** (tp) MissSMDoolan[(5)] 1 66
(Wilf Storey) *hld up in rr: hdwy on wd outside over 3f out: rdn to chse wnr wl over 1f out: drvn: edgd lft and one pce fnl f* **9/2**[3]
0400 **5** 2 1/2 **Raleigh Quay (IRE)**[23] 2961 6-9-13 **60** MissBeckySmith[(5)] 8 59
(Micky Hammond) *trckd ldrs: hdwy to trck ldr after 5f: rdn along 3f out: wknd wl over 1f out* **7/2**[2]
4-00 **6** 3/4 **Tropenfeuer (FR)**[29] 2540 6-9-1 **48** MissJoannaMason[(5)] 5 46
(James Moffatt) *hld up in tch: effrt and sme hdwy 4f out: rdn along 3f out: n.d* **20/1**
00/0 **7** 6 **Suprise Vendor (IRE)**[7] 3504 7-9-9 **54** MissJRRichards[(3)] 6 43
(Stuart Coltherd) *trckd ldrs: rdn along over 3f out: sn wknd* **33/1**
0-0 **8** 2 3/4 **Mystified (IRE)**[8] 3467 10-8-12 **45** MissLWilson[(5)] 3 30
(Alan Berry) *chsd ldrs: rdn along 4f out: sn wknd* **40/1**

2m 53.02s (-0.88) **Going Correction** -0.10s/f (Good) **8** Ran SP% **111.0**
Speed ratings (Par 101): **98,96,95,95,94 93,90,88**
toteswingers 1&2 £2.60, 1&3 £6.00, 2&3 £4.90 CSF £11.96 CT £106.32 TOTE £5.20: £1.30, £1.30, £3.30; EX 9.30 Trifecta £189.30 Pool: £1417.87 - 5.61 winning tickets..
Owner Connor & Dunne **Bred** Gestut Karlshof **Trained** Uplawmoor, E Renfrews

FOCUS
Rails realignment around the loop reduced distances on Round course by about 25yds. A modest lady amateurs' handicap best rated around the third and fourth.

3710 RACING UK ON SKY 432 MAIDEN AUCTION STKS 6f 5y
6:50 (6:51) (Class 5) 2-Y-O **£2,911** (£866; £432; £216) **Stalls** High

Form RPR
3 **1** **Mitchelton (FR)**[11] 3366 2-8-8 0 JoeFanning 5 80+
(Mark Johnston) *mde all: rdn clr 2f out: styd on strly* **13/8**[1]
2 **2** 5 **Gown (IRE)**[19] 3107 2-8-6 0 MartinLane 1 60
(Charles Hills) *trckd ldrs on outer: hdwy 1/2-way: chsd wnr 2f out: sn rdn and no imp* **15/8**[2]
6344 **3** nk **Princess Tamay (IRE)**[9] 3436 2-8-8 0 RobertHavlin 2 61
(Mark Johnston) *in rr: hdwy 1/2-way: rdn along over 2f out: kpt on u.p fnl f* **14/1**

The Form Book Flat, Raceform Ltd, Compton, RG20 6NL.

02 **4** 3 1/4 **Midnight Muscida (IRE)**[19] 3084 2-8-6 0 DuranFentiman 4 49
(Tim Easterby) *trckd ldrs on inner: rdn along wl over 2f out: sn one pce* **20/1**

2 **5** 2 **Khalice**[20] 3064 2-8-8 0 TonyHamilton 3 45
(Richard Fahey) *awkward s: t.k.h and sn chsng wnr: cl up after 2f: rdn along wl over 2f out: sn wknd and rr whn eased fnl f* **10/3**[3]

1m 12.7s (0.50) **Going Correction** +0.05s/f (Good) **5** Ran SP% **107.4**
Speed ratings (Par 93): **98,91,90,86,83**
CSF £4.69 TOTE £2.70: £1.50, £1.70; EX 4.40 Trifecta £51.20 Pool: £794.16 - 11.62 winning tickets..
Owner Gerry Ryan **Bred** Rashit Shaykhutdinov **Trained** Middleham Moor, N Yorks

FOCUS
Almost certainly an above-average 2-y-o maiden auction race with five fillies in opposition and a very impressive winner. The third is rated to pre-race form.

3711 IRN BRU OPEN MAIDEN STKS 1m 1f 36y
7:20 (7:21) (Class 5) 3-4-Y-0 **£3,234** (£962; £481; £240) **Stalls** Low

Form RPR
0022 **1** **Argaki (IRE)**[8] 3465 3-9-0 65 JoeFanning 1 68
(Keith Dalgleish) *trckd ldng pair: hdwy 3f out: chal 2f out: sn rdn: led appr fnl f: drvn clr* **2/1**[2]

3 **2** 5 **Gwael (USA)**[22] 2995 3-8-9 0 RobertWinston 3 52
(James Tate) *set stdy pce: qcknd over 3f out: rdn 2f out and sn jnd: drvn and hdd appr fnl f: sn one pce* **10/11**[1]

00 **3** 2 1/2 **Captain Rhyric**[10] 3398 4-9-8 0 LucyAlexander(3) 4 52
(James Moffatt) *hld up in rr: sme hdwy over 2f out: sn rdn and no imp* **40/1**

-055 **4** 7 **Three Glasses (IRE)**[14] 3232 3-9-0 67 DuranFentiman 5 36
(Tim Easterby) *trckd ldr: cl up 3f out: sn rdn along: wknd wl over 1f out* **4/1**[3]

1m 59.38s (-0.32) **Going Correction** -0.10s/f (Good)
WFA 3 from 4yo 11lb **4** Ran SP% **108.2**
Speed ratings (Par 103): **97,92,90,84**
CSF £4.22 TOTE £2.80; EX 4.50 Trifecta £38.30 Pool: £783.40 - 15.30 winning tickets..
Owner D G Savala **Bred** A Christodoulou **Trained** Carluke, S Lanarks

FOCUS
A modest maiden best rated through the winner to previous form.

3712 E B F CAPTAIN J.C. STEWART FILLIES' H'CAP 1m 65y
7:50 (7:50) (Class 4) (0-85,80) 3-Y-0+ **£6,469** (£1,925; £962; £481) **Stalls** Low

Form RPR
4203 **1** **Act Your Shoe Size**[5] 3567 4-10-0 80 RobertHavlin 2 87
(Keith Dalgleish) *trckd ldng pair: swtchd lft and hdwy 2f out: sn rdn: squeezed through ent fnl f: drvn to ld last 100yds: jst hld on* **5/1**

0-54 **2** nse **Simply Shining (IRE)**[11] 3369 3-8-12 74 TonyHamilton 4 79
(Richard Fahey) *pushed along in rr early: rdn along over 3f out: styd on u.p fr wl over 1f out: drvn to chal ins fnl f: kpt on wl towards fin: jst failed* **7/2**[2]

-234 **3** 2 1/2 **Tussie Mussie**[10] 3396 3-9-0 76 JoeFanning 1 75
(Mark Johnston) *trckd ldr: hdwy and cl up 3f out: rdn 2f out and ev ch tl drvn and one pce fnl f* **4/1**[3]

5322 **4** nk **Hot Rod Mamma (IRE)**[1] 3683 6-9-5 71 PJMcDonald 3 72
(Dianne Sayer) *hld up and t.k.h early: sn trcking ldrs: hdwy over 2f out: rdn to chal over 1f out: led ent fnl f: sn drvn: hdd and one pce last 100yds* **2/1**[1]

0-02 **5** 1 **New Falcon (IRE)**[20] 3039 3-8-13 75 (b) RobertWinston 5 71
(James Tate) *set stdy pce: qcknd 3f out: rdn and jnd 2f out: drvn and hdd ent fnl f: grad wknd* **10/1**

-101 **6** 6 **Spavento (IRE)**[22] 2974 7-9-2 73 JasonHart(5) 6 57
(Eric Alston) *hld up towards rr: pushed along 3f out: rdn over 2f out: sn btn* **8/1**

1m 46.54s (-1.86) **Going Correction** -0.10s/f (Good)
WFA 3 from 4yo+ 10lb **6** Ran SP% **112.4**
Speed ratings (Par 102): **105,104,102,102,101 95**
toteswingers 1&2 £2.90, 1&3 £4.90, 2&3 £3.40 CSF £22.64 TOTE £7.20: £2.10, £2.00; EX 37.70 Trifecta £314.20 Pool: £744.25 - 1.77 winning tickets..
Owner Gordon McDowall **Bred** Gordon McDowall **Trained** Carluke, S Lanarks

FOCUS
Quite a competitive and valuable fillies' handicap. The pace was sound and there were five in a line with 75 yards to go. The winner is exposed and an unlikely improver.

3713 WHOLESALEDOMESTIC.COM (S) STKS 5f 4y
8:20 (8:21) (Class 6) 3-Y-0+ **£2,045** (£603; £302) **Stalls** Centre

Form RPR
1140 **1** **Hamoody (USA)**[24] 2914 9-9-4 78 JasonHart(5) 4 82
(David Nicholls) *wnt rt s: trckd ldrs on inner: swtchd rt and hdwy to chal over 1f out: rdn to ld ins fnl f: kpt on strly towards fin* **5/2**[2]

3455 **2** 1 3/4 **Red Cape (FR)**[7] 3501 10-9-4 68 (b) PJMcDonald 6 71
(Ruth Carr) *led: rdn along wl over 1f out: drvn and hdd ins fnl f: no ex last 100yds* **11/2**[3]

4121 **3** 1 **Haajes**[20] 3069 9-9-4 76 (v) ShirleyTeasdale(5) 3 72
(Paul Midgley) *sltly hmpd s: cl up: rdn along wl over 1f out: drvn and one pce fnl f* **5/2**[2]

5024 **4** 2 1/2 **Mercers Row**[13] 3283 6-8-11 70 GemmaTutty(7) 1 58
(Karen Tutty) *trckd ldrs on outer: effrt 2f out: sn rdn and btn over 1f out* **9/4**[1]

5300 **5** hd **Rock Canyon (IRE)**[15] 3197 4-9-4 51 (p) PaulMulrennan 2 57
(Linda Perratt) *hld up: effrt and n.m.r wl over 1f out: sn rdn and btn* **25/1**

0-60 **6** 4 1/2 **Distant Sun (USA)**[13] 3283 9-9-4 56 (p) PhillipMakin 5 41
(Linda Perratt) *cl up: rdn along 2f out: sn wknd* **20/1**

59.6s (-0.40) **Going Correction** +0.05s/f (Good)
WFA 3 from 4yo+ 6lb **6** Ran SP% **111.9**
Speed ratings (Par 101): **105,102,100,96,96 89**
toteswingers 1&2 £1.60, 1&3 £2.20, 2&3 £2.00 CSF £16.22 TOTE £3.60: £1.90, £2.00; EX 11.40 Trifecta £54.90 Pool: £824.44 - 11.24 winning tickets..Hamoody was bought in for 4,800gns
Owner Hart Inn I **Bred** Ragged Mountain Farm **Trained** Sessay, N Yorks

FOCUS
Quite a competitive event by selling race standards. The runner-up is rated close to recent form.

3714 PATERSONS OF GREENOAKHILL H'CAP 6f 5y
8:50 (8:58) (Class 4) (0-80,79) 3-Y-0+ **£5,175** (£1,540; £769; £384) **Stalls** Centre

Form RPR
051 **1** **Sunraider (IRE)**[8] 3462 6-9-10 75 6ex MickyFenton 11 86
(Paul Midgley) *towards rr: gd hdwy over 2f out: rdn to ld jst over 1f out: drvn and styd on wl fnl f* **9/1**

-006 **2** 3/4 **Jinky**[12] 3331 5-9-5 70 TomEaves 4 78
(Linda Perratt) *trckd ldrs: effrt whn n.m.r wl over 1f out: squeezed through and rdn ent fnl f: ev ch tl drvn and no ex last 75yds* **20/1**

-002 **3** 1 3/4 **Sir Pedro**[12] 3351 4-9-13 78 TonyHamilton 12 81
(Charles Hills) *s.i.s and bhd: gd hdwy on inner wl over 1f out: nt clr run and swtchd rt ent fnl f: sn rdn and styd on strly towards fin* **4/1**[1]

0154 **4** shd **Bonnie Charlie**[12] 3351 7-9-12 77 PaulQuinn 8 79
(David Nicholls) *dwlt and in rr: swtchd rt towards outer and hdwy 2f out: rdn to chse ldrs over 1f out: edgd lft and one pce ins fnl f* **10/1**

6362 **5** 1/2 **Barkston Ash**[15] 3200 5-9-9 79 (p) JasonHart(5) 10 80
(Eric Alston) *trckd ldrs on inner: effrt and n.m.r over 1f out: sn rdn and one pce fnl f* **4/1**[1]

5-04 **6** 3 1/2 **Fol Hollow (IRE)**[7] 3505 8-8-13 64 PJMcDonald 1 53
(Stuart Coltherd) *in tch on wd outside: hdwy to chse ldrs over 1f out: sn rdn and no imp* **40/1**

0631 **7** 3/4 **Hopes N Dreams (IRE)**[15] 3200 5-9-10 78 BrianToomey(3) 2 65
(Kevin Ryan) *trckd ldrs: hdwy 1/2-way: led 2f out: sn rdn: hdd appr fnl f: sn wknd* **11/2**[3]

4463 **8** 3/4 **Bassett Road (IRE)**[28] 2797 5-8-4 62 (p) GeorginaBaxter(7) 7 47
(Keith Dalgleish) *led: rdn along wl over 2f out: sn hdd & wknd over 1f out* **16/1**

-035 **9** 2 1/4 **Findog**[8] 3462 3-8-12 70 PaulMulrennan 9 47
(Linda Perratt) *trckd ldrs: rdn along 2f out: sn wknd* **10/1**

2564 **10** 1 1/2 **Flexible Flyer**[15] 3215 4-9-9 74 (b[1]) RobertWinston 6 47
(Hughie Morrison) *cl up: rdn along 2f out: sn wknd* **9/2**[2]

3036 **11** 8 **Art Dzeko**[31] 2702 4-9-3 68 DuranFentiman 3 15
(Tim Easterby) *chsd ldrs: rdn along over 2f out: sn wknd* **40/1**

1m 11.7s (-0.50) **Going Correction** +0.05s/f (Good)
WFA 3 from 4yo+ 7lb **11** Ran SP% **117.3**
Speed ratings (Par 105): **105,104,101,101,100 96,95,94,91,89 78**
toteswingers 1&2 £50.40, 1&3 £9.00, 2&3 £10.20 CSF £174.10 CT £847.20 TOTE £11.30: £3.40, £4.40, £2.10; EX 215.20 Trifecta £751.90 Part won. Pool: £1002.56 - 0.06 winning tickets..
Owner R Wardlaw **Bred** Lodge Park Stud **Trained** Westow, N Yorks

FOCUS
An open-looking sprint handicap and it paid to come from off the pace. The winner built on his C&D win.

3715 SAINTS AND SINNERS H'CAP 1m 65y
9:20 (9:21) (Class 5) (0-75,75) 3-Y-0+ **£3,408** (£1,006; £503) **Stalls** Low

Form RPR
0040 **1** **Limit Up**[12] 3320 3-9-4 75 JoeFanning 5 80
(Mark Johnston) *mde all: set stdy pce: qcknd 2f out: rdn appr fnl f: kpt on strly* **4/1**[3]

0034 **2** 1 1/2 **Joshua The First**[8] 3466 4-9-3 64 TomEaves 2 68
(Keith Dalgleish) *trckd ldng pair: hdwy on inner 2f out: rdn to chse wnr ent fnl f: sn swtchd lft and drvn: no imp towards fin* **6/1**

-002 **3** 1 1/4 **Royal Straight**[8] 3466 8-9-6 67 (t) PhillipMakin 4 68
(Linda Perratt) *s.i.s and in rr: hdwy over 2f out: rdn over 1f out: drvn and no imp fnl f* **3/1**[2]

0006 **4** 1 **Rio Cobolo (IRE)**[19] 3090 7-8-13 60 (v) PaulMulrennan 6 58
(David Nicholls) *trckd ldrs: hdwy 3f out: rdn along 2f out: drvn and one pce fnl f* **13/2**

-340 **5** 1/2 **I'm Super Too (IRE)**[12] 3349 6-9-11 72 RobertWinston 3 69
(Alan Swinbank) *trckd wnr: hdwy and cl up on outer 3f out: rdn to chal over 2f out: drvn and wknd over 1f out* **7/4**[1]

1m 49.24s (0.84) **Going Correction** -0.10s/f (Good)
WFA 3 from 4yo+ 10lb **5** Ran SP% **109.0**
Speed ratings (Par 103): **91,89,88,87,86**
CSF £25.37 TOTE £4.10: £2.10, £2.20; EX 23.30 Trifecta £63.30 Pool: £666.82 - 7.89 winning tickets..
Owner Sheikh Hamdan Bin Mohammed Al Maktoum **Bred** Minster Stud **Trained** Middleham Moor, N Yorks

FOCUS
A weak-looking handicap which went to the only 3-y-o in the line-up under a fine tactical ride. He is rated to his AW form but little solid amongst the rest.
T/Plt: £168.50 to a £1 stake. Pool: £59,733.94 - 258.72 winning tickets. T/Qpdt: £74.90 to a £1 stake. Pool: £4229.00 - 41.75 winning tickets. JR

3487 LEICESTER (R-H)
Thursday, June 27

OFFICIAL GOING: Good to firm (good in places) changing to good after race 1 (6.10)
Wind: Light across Weather: Raining

3716 LANGHAM LADIES' H'CAP (LADY AMATEUR RIDERS) 5f 2y
6:10 (6:10) (Class 5) (0-75,72) 3-Y-0+ **£2,495** (£774; £386; £193) **Stalls** High

Form RPR
-000 **1** **Noodles Blue Boy**[40] 2441 7-10-7 72 MissSBrotherton 9 82
(Ollie Pears) *chsd ldrs: led over 3f out: rdn and hung rt fr over 1f out: styd on* **7/2**[2]

0253 **2** 1/2 **Haadeeth**[9] 3431 6-9-6 62 (t) MissHDoyle(5) 2 70
(David Evans) *chsd ldrs: rdn and ev ch ins fnl f: styd on: carried rt towards fin* **7/1**

00 **3** 1 1/2 **Storm Lightning**[15] 3215 4-10-2 70 MissBeckyBrisbourne(3) 3 73
(Mark Brisbourne) *led 1f: chsd ldrs: rdn and ev ch ins fnl f: n.m.r sn after: styd on same pce* **12/1**

0502 **4** 1/2 **Welease Bwian (IRE)**[5] 3577 4-9-5 61 MissKMargarson(5) 10 63
(Stuart Williams) *chsd ldrs: ev ch over 1f out: hung rt and no ex ins fnl f* **3/1**[1]

6133 **5** 3/4 **Methaaly (IRE)**[5] 3569 10-9-5 59 (be) MissMMullineaux(3) 7 58
(Michael Mullineaux) *s.s: outpcd: r.o ins fnl f* **8/1**

0-02 **6** 1/2 **Ryan Style (IRE)**[2] 3667 7-10-2 67 (p) MissZoeLilly 6 65
(Lisa Williamson) *mid-div: sn pushed along: hdwy 1/2-way: styd on same pce fnl f* **11/2**[3]

506 **7** 4 1/2 **Quality Art (USA)**[9] 3446 5-9-7 58 (p) MissADeniel 4 41
(Richard Guest) *prom: racd keenly: hung rt and wknd over 1f out* **8/1**

0010 **8** 1/2 **Sophie's Beau (USA)**[2] 3654 6-8-11 53 oh2 (b) AnnaHesketh(5) 1 35
(Michael Chapman) *s.i.s: rcvrd to ld 4f out: sn hdd: hung rt 1/2-way: sn wknd* **14/1**

/00- 9 6 **Heresellie (IRE)**[372] 3285 5-8-11 **53** oh8.................. MissAliceMills(5) 5 15
(Michael Chapman) *s.i.s: outpcd* **66/1**

1m 1.52s (1.52) **Going Correction** +0.10s/f (Good) **9** Ran SP% **113.2**
Speed ratings (Par 103): **91,90,87,87,85 85,77,77,67**
toteswingers 1&2 £2.50, 1&3 £11.80, 2&3 £11.80 CSF £27.60 CT £261.71 TOTE £4.50: £1.80, £2.80, £3.50; EX 28.80 Trifecta £187.80 Pool: £1108.70 - 4.42 winning tickets..
Owner Keith Taylor & Keith West **Bred** Fifehead Farms M C Denning **Trained** Norton, N Yorks

FOCUS
A weak sprint handicap, confined to lady amateur riders, which saw a tight finish down the centre of the track. The runner-up is rated in line with last year's form with the winner still below last season's best.

3717 OSBASTON MAIDEN AUCTION STKS 5f 218y
6:40 (6:40) (Class 5) 2-Y-O **£2,587** (£770; £384; £192) **Stalls** High

Form RPR
1 **Chess Valley** 2-8-11 0.................................... TomQueally 3 73+
(Rae Guest) *hld up: hdwy over 2f out: led over 1f out: pushed out* **8/1**[3]
4 2 2 ¾ **Brownsville (USA)**[8] 3461 2-8-13 0.......................... DarrenEgan(3) 5 70
(Mark Johnston) *led: rdn and hdd over 1f out: styd on same pce ins fnl f* **6/1**[2]
0 3 nk **Tubeanie (IRE)**[70] 1834 2-8-8 0.................................... JohnFahy 7 61
(Clive Cox) *sn pushed along to chse ldr: rdn over 1f out: styd on same pce ins fnl f* **14/1**
2 4 nk **Salford Secret (IRE)**[13] 3275 2-8-13 0.......................... AdamKirby 2 65
(Marco Botti) *trckd ldrs: shkn up over 1f out: styd on same pce ins fnl f* **4/6**[1]
5 1 ¼ **Craftsmanship (FR)** 2-8-11 0.......................... AndreaAtzeni 1 59+
(Robert Eddery) *sn pushed along in rr: styd on fnl f: nt trble ldrs* **16/1**
6 hd **Bognor (USA)** 2-8-13 0.. CathyGannon 6 61
(Jo Hughes) *hld up: hdwy 1/2-way: rdn over 1f out: styd on same pce* **9/1**
4 7 25 **Maximilianthefirst**[38] 2510 2-8-11 0.......................... MartinHarley 4
(P J O'Gorman) *uns rdr and got loose on the way to post: plld hrd and prom: rdn over 2f out: sn wknd* **50/1**

1m 14.33s (1.33) **Going Correction** +0.10s/f (Good) **7** Ran SP% **109.9**
Speed ratings (Par 93): **95,91,90,90,88 88,55**
toteswingers 1&2 £2.50, 1&3 £6.70, 2&3 £5.90 CSF £50.01 TOTE £9.70: £3.00, £2.40; EX 48.20 Trifecta £297.30 Pool: £1380.25 - 3.48 winning tickets..
Owner The Boot Sarratt Racing Syndicate **Bred** Rabbah Bloodstock Limited **Trained** Newmarket, Suffolk

FOCUS
An average juvenile maiden. The compressed field and modest time suggest this form is ordinary.

3718 KING'S NORTON FILLIES' H'CAP 7f 9y
7:10 (7:10) (Class 4) (0-85,85) 3-Y-O **£4,690** (£1,395; £697; £348) **Stalls** High

Form RPR
4-30 1 **Tantshi (IRE)**[27] 2848 3-9-7 **85**....................................[1] AndreaAtzeni 3 95
(Roger Varian) *racd stands' side: hld up: hdwy over 2f out: rdn to ld that trio 1f out: r.o u.p to ld overall post* **3/1**[3]
-310 2 nk **Maid A Million**[20] 3039 3-9-4 **82**.................................... SebSanders 1 91
(David Elsworth) *racd alone centre: overall ldr: rdn over 1f out: hdd post* **5/2**[2]
-241 3 5 **Tight Fit**[16] 3178 3-8-5 **69**.. CathyGannon 2 65
(Henry Candy) *racd stands' side: w ldr tl led that trio over 4f out: rdn and hdd 1f out: no ex: 2nd of 3 in gp* **11/8**[1]
3521 4 8 **Krupskaya (FR)**[40] 2464 3-8-9 **73**.................................. MartinHarley 5 47
(Mrs K Burke) *led stands' side over 2f: chsd ldr tl rdn 2f out: wknd fnl f: last of 3 in gp* **7/1**

1m 25.56s (-0.64) **Going Correction** +0.10s/f (Good) **4** Ran SP% **108.2**
Speed ratings (Par 98): **107,106,100,91**
CSF £10.45 TOTE £3.30; EX 8.50 Trifecta £16.80 Pool: £635.74 - 28.31 winning tickets..
Owner Sheikh Ahmed Al Maktoum **Bred** Darley **Trained** Newmarket, Suffolk

FOCUS
This was a fair little 3-y-o fillies' handicap which saw a difference of opinion as to where the best ground was. The runner-up is rated to her Yarmouth mark and sets the level.

3719 WELBY OSIERS H'CAP 1m 1f 218y
7:40 (7:40) (Class 5) (0-70,69) 4-Y-O+ **£2,587** (£770; £384; £192) **Stalls** Low

Form RPR
5-02 1 **Laughing Jack**[58] 1915 5-9-0 **67**.......................... GeorgeDowning(5) 2 84
(Tony Carroll) *mde all: t.k.h: clr 7f out: rdn and hung lft over 1f out: styd on: unchal* **10/1**[3]
55-1 2 2 ¼ **Mankini (IRE)**[20] 3063 4-9-2 **64**.......................... KirstyMilczarek 4 76+
(Luca Cumani) *hld up: hdwy over 6f out: chsd wnr over 2f out: rdn over 1f out: no imp ins fnl f* **4/5**[1]
4103 3 15 **Nolecce**[150] 418 6-8-2 **50** oh1..........................(p) PaoloSirigu 5 32
(Tony Forbes) *hld up: hdwy over 3f out: sn rdn: wknd over 1f out* **25/1**
0022 4 3 ¾ **Newnton Lodge**[7] 3507 4-8-12 **60**.......................... JamesDoyle 1 35
(Ian Williams) *dwlt: hld up: rdn over 2f out: sn wknd* **7/2**[2]
223 5 5 **Maakirr (IRE)**[36] 2576 4-9-2 **64**..........................(t) JimmyQuinn 8 29
(Roy Bowring) *trckd wnr: t.k.h: rdn over 2f out: wknd wl over 1f out* **12/1**
-464 6 9 **Kalily**[22] 2981 4-9-5 **67**.. AdamKirby 3 14
(Rae Guest) *chsd ldrs: rdn over 4f out: wknd over 2f out* **11/1**
-000 7 17 **Tevez**[16] 3172 8-9-7 **69**.. TomQueally 6
(Des Donovan) *prom: lost pl over 6f out: rdn over 4f out: wknd over 2f out* **20/1**

2m 7.9s **Going Correction** +0.10s/f (Good) **7** Ran SP% **111.5**
Speed ratings (Par 103): **104,102,90,87,83 76,62**
toteswingers 1&2 £2.50, 1&3 £36.70, 2&3 £6.70 CSF £17.66 CT £195.97 TOTE £5.80: £3.20, £1.20; EX 16.90 Trifecta £492.00 Pool: £1360.87 - 2.07 winning tickets..
Owner Paul Downing **Bred** Sir Thomas Pilkington **Trained** Cropthorne, Worcs

FOCUS
A moderate handicap in which the winner dominated. The winner is rated back to something near his early 2012 form.

3720 STAPLEFORD H'CAP 5f 218y
8:10 (8:10) (Class 3) (0-90,89) 3-Y-O+ **£7,439** (£2,213; £1,106; £553) **Stalls** High

Form RPR
4601 1 **Harrison George (IRE)**[14] 3249 8-9-7 **89**............(bt) NatashaEaton(5) 6 100
(P J O'Gorman) *hld up: hdwy 1/2-way: hung rt fr over 1f out: led ins fnl f: r.o* **5/1**[3]
-000 2 1 ¼ **Elusive Flame**[20] 3060 4-9-11 **88**.................................... SebSanders 4 95
(David Elsworth) *led: rdn over 1f out: hdd and unable qck ins fnl f* **10/3**[2]
1540 3 1 ¾ **Apollo D'Negro (IRE)**[10] 3415 5-9-4 **81**..........................(v) AdamKirby 7 82
(Clive Cox) *chsd ldrs: rdn over 1f out: styd on same pce ins fnl f* **11/2**
-021 4 1 ¾ **Fanrouge (IRE)**[10] 3407 4-9-10 **87** 6ex.......................... AndreaAtzeni 1 82
(Rod Millman) *s.i.s: hld up: rdn over 2f out: styd on ins fnl f: nvr nrr* **5/1**[3]

-502 5 hd **Piazza San Pietro**[15] 3220 7-9-5 **82**..........................(p) NeilCallan 3 77
(Zoe Davison) *chsd ldrs: pushed along 1/2-way: rdn over 1f out: styd on same pce fnl f* **16/1**
5-00 6 3 ¼ **L'Ami Louis (IRE)**[24] 2937 5-9-9 **86**..........................[1] DaneO'Neill 2 70
(Henry Candy) *chsd ldrs: rdn over 1f out: wknd ins fnl f* **3/1**[1]
2261 7 4 ½ **Noverre To Go (IRE)**[12] 3351 7-9-2 **79**..........................(p) SteveDrowne 5 49
(Ronald Harris) *trckd ldr: racd keenly: rdn over 1f out: wknd fnl f* **15/2**

1m 12.51s (-0.49) **Going Correction** +0.10s/f (Good) **7** Ran SP% **114.4**
Speed ratings (Par 107): **107,105,103,100,100 96,90**
toteswingers 1&2 £3.30, 1&3 £3.80, 2&3 £1.80 CSF £22.01 TOTE £6.60: £3.70, £2.40; EX 28.90 Trifecta £121.60 Pool: £972.77 - 5.99 winning tickets..
Owner Racing To The Max **Bred** R P Ryan **Trained** Newmarket, Suffolk

FOCUS
A fair sprint handicap rated through the third and close to form. They stuck to the centre and the majority looked held back by the deteriorating surface.

3721 BRUNTINGTHORPE H'CAP 1m 3f 183y
8:40 (8:41) (Class 6) (0-65,65) 4-Y-O+ **£1,940** (£577; £288; £144) **Stalls** Low

Form RPR
-504 1 **Kittens**[12] 3321 4-9-4 **62**.. SteveDrowne 4 69+
(William Muir) *mid-div: hdwy over 3f out: pushed along and nt clr run over 1f: rdn and r.o to ld wl ins fnl f* **7/1**
4/12 2 ¾ **Cornish Beau (IRE)**[5] 3579 6-9-2 **60**.......................... MartinHarley 1 65
(Dr Richard Newland) *chsd ldrs: led 3f out: rdn over 1f out: hdd wl ins fnl f* **7/4**[1]
0045 3 ½ **Torero**[22] 2986 4-8-10 **54**..........................(p) NeilCallan 8 58
(Kevin Ryan) *chsd ldr: rdn and ev ch fr over 2f out tl styd on same pce ins fnl f* **8/1**
5223 4 1 **Spanish Plume**[10] 3410 5-8-13 **62**..........................(b) JackDuern(5) 11 65
(Andrew Hollinshead) *hld up: hdwy on bit over 2f out: rdn ins fnl f: nt run on* **13/2**[3]
000- 5 1 ½ **Avon River**[204] 7997 6-9-7 **65**.. JamesDoyle 5 65
(Dean Ivory) *chsd ldrs: rdn over 2f out: no ex ins fnl f* **12/1**
0-14 6 3 **Iceman George**[20] 3037 9-8-13 **62**..........................(v) NatashaEaton(5) 6 57
(Alison Hutchinson) *hld up: rdn and nt clr run over 2f out: nvr trbld ldrs* **6/1**[2]
0-56 7 1 **Excellent News (IRE)**[14] 3231 4-8-4 **48**.......................... PaoloSirigu 9 42
(Tony Forbes) *prom: rdn over 2f out: edgd rt and wknd ins fnl f* **50/1**
000- 8 5 **Souter Point (USA)**[27] 8273 7-9-2 **60**.......................... AdamBeschizza 10 46
(William Kinsey) *hld up: rdn over 3f out: wknd over 1f out* **25/1**
61 9 ¾ **Monopoli**[31] 2709 4-9-3 **64**.. DarrenEgan(3) 2 49
(Daniel Kubler) *s.i.s: hld up: nt clr run over 2f out: wknd over 1f out* **10/1**
-065 10 5 **Marina Ballerina**[22] 2995 5-8-2 **46** oh1..........................(p) JimmyQuinn 7 23
(Roy Bowring) *sn led: hdd 3f out: rdn and wknd wl over 1f out* **28/1**

2m 37.36s (3.46) **Going Correction** +0.10s/f (Good) **10** Ran SP% **113.6**
Speed ratings (Par 101): **92,91,91,90,89 87,86,83,83,79**
toteswingers 1&2 £5.20, 1&3 £5.50, 2&3 £4.60 CSF £18.76 CT £100.42 TOTE £8.90: £2.40, £1.20, £2.70; EX 23.40 Trifecta £146.60 Pool: £969.49 - 4.95 winning tickets..
Owner Muir Racing Partnership - Chester **Bred** Moyns Park Estate And Stud Ltd **Trained** Lambourn, Berks

FOCUS
An ordinary handicap, run at a fair pace, with the winner doing well to overcome a troubled run and the second rated slightly below his AWw best.

3722 COLD OVERTON H'CAP 1m 60y
9:10 (9:10) (Class 5) (0-70,70) 3-Y-O **£2,587** (£770; £384; £192) **Stalls** Low

Form RPR
5641 1 **Woody Bay**[18] 3137 3-9-6 **69**.. JamesDoyle 1 78
(James Given) *s.i.s: sn pushed along in rr: hdwy over 4f out: rdn over 2f out: styd on u.p to ld nr fin* **2/1**[2]
6-63 2 1 ¼ **Visit Copenhagen (USA)**[20] 3047 3-9-6 **69**.......................... MartinHarley 7 75
(Mrs K Burke) *led: hdd over 6f out: chsd ldr tl rdn to ld over 2f out: hung rt and hdd ins fnl f: styd on same pce* **7/2**[3]
-243 3 3 **Wellingrove (IRE)**[8] 3466 3-9-4 **70**.......................... DarrenEgan(3) 2 70
(Mark Johnston) *led over 6f out: rdn and hdd over 2f out: no ex ins fnl f* **7/4**[1]
2300 4 6 **Beau Select (IRE)**[20] 3062 3-9-2 **65**..........................(b) AndreaAtzeni 4 50
(Robert Eddery) *hld up: outpcd over 3f out: n.d* **13/2**
6-05 5 shd **Refuse To Mambo**[7] 3488 3-8-2 **51** oh3.......................... CathyGannon 6 36
(Andrew Hollinshead) *chsd ldrs: swtchd centre to r alone over 3f out: rdn over 2f out: wknd over 1f out* **25/1**

1m 46.31s (1.21) **Going Correction** +0.10s/f (Good) **5** Ran SP% **109.1**
Speed ratings (Par 99): **97,95,92,86,86**
CSF £9.09 TOTE £3.10: £1.70, £2.10; EX 7.60 Trifecta £20.40 Pool: £751.07 - 27.60 winning tickets..
Owner J Barson **Bred** Cheveley Park Stud Ltd **Trained** Willoughton, Lincs

FOCUS
A moderate 3-y-o handicap with the runner-up rated to his latest turf form.
T/Plt: £573.50 to a £1 stake. Pool: £61,522.04 - 78.31 winning tickets. T/Qpdt: £33.20 to a £1 stake. Pool: £6874.70 - 152.80 winning tickets. CR

2883 NEWCASTLE (L-H)
Thursday, June 27

OFFICIAL GOING: Good (good to firm in places; 7.6)
Wind: Breezy, half against Weather: Overcast, showers

3723 BETFRED MOBILE LOTTO NOVICE STKS 6f
2:00 (2:02) (Class 5) 2-Y-O **£2,587** (£770; £384; £192) **Stalls** Centre

Form RPR
1 1 **Good Old Boy Lukey**[41] 2404 2-9-0 0.................. GeorgeChaloner(5) 4 89+
(Richard Fahey) *t.k.h: chsd ldr: shkn up to ld over 1f out: pushed along and styd on strly fnl f* **10/11**[1]
21 2 1 ¾ **Mr Matthews (IRE)**[10] 3391 2-9-2 0.......................... MichaelO'Connell 3 81
(Mrs K Burke) *reluctant to enter stalls: cl up: rdn over 2f out: rallied over 1f out: chsd wnr last 100yds: kpt on* **4/1**[3]
21 3 ¾ **Milly's Secret (IRE)**[20] 3064 2-8-11 0.......................... PJMcDonald 2 74
(Ann Duffield) *led: rdn: edgd lft and hdd over 1f out: lost 2nd and one pce last 100yds* **9/4**[2]
4 10 **Ofelia (IRE)** 2-8-9 0.. TomEaves 1 42+
(Brian Ellison) *dwlt: in tch: rdn and outpcd over 2f out: sn btn* **20/1**

1m 15.18s (0.58) **Going Correction** -0.075s/f (Good) **4** Ran SP% **107.9**
Speed ratings (Par 93): **93,90,89,76**
CSF £4.84 TOTE £1.70; EX 2.20 Trifecta £4.20 Pool: £1166.15 - 207.84 winning tickets..
Owner Leods Contracts Limited **Bred** Mrs Sarah Hamilton **Trained** Musley Bank, N Yorks

FOCUS
All rails moved back to original position to provide fresh ground and distances were as advertised. Three last-time-out winners in the field. It was run at an honest pace, with the runners racing up the centre. The winner can do better and the third is rated below her winning mark.

3724 BETFRED MOBILE SPORTS MEDIAN AUCTION MAIDEN STKS 6f
2:30 (2:31) (Class 5) 2-Y-O £2,587 (£770; £384; £192) **Stalls** Centre

Form RPR
225 **1** **Lily Rules (IRE)**[52] 2075 2-9-0 0 BarryMcHugh 2 73
(Tony Coyle) *cl up centre: led that gp fr 1/2-way: effrt and drvn 2f out: overall ldr ins fnl f: r.o* **10/1**
0 **2** ½ **Broadcaster (IRE)**[14] 3233 2-9-5 0 SeanLevey 12 77
(Ed McMahon) *chsd stands' side ldrs: smooth hdwy and overall ldr wl over 1f out: hdd ins fnl f: kpt on: hld nr fin* **9/1**
3 2 ¼ **Foxy Clarets (IRE)** 2-9-5 0 TonyHamilton 3 70
(Richard Fahey) *dwlt: chsd ldng gp centre: shkn up and hdwy 2f out: kpt on same pce fnl f: bttr for r* **6/1**[2]
254 **4** 3 **Rose Gloria (IRE)**[28] 2805 2-9-0 0 SamHitchcott 1 56
(Mick Channon) *trckd ldrs centre: drvn along over 2f out: rallied: one pce fr over 1f out* **8/1**
02 **5** ½ **Tautira (IRE)**[12] 3324 2-9-0 0 JamieSpencer 10 55
(Michael Bell) *led and overall ldr stands' rail: rdn and hdd wl over 1f out: outpcd fnl f* **2/1**[1]
0 **6** 5 **Lomond Lassie**[13] 3280 2-9-0 0 GrahamGibbons 9 40
(Keith Dalgleish) *chsd stands' side ldrs: rdn over 2f out: wknd over 1f out* **13/2**[3]
7 1 **Casper Lee (IRE)** 2-9-5 0 PaulMulrennan 6 42
(Nigel Tinkler) *dwlt: bhd and sn swtchd to stands' side: sme late hdwy: nvr on terms* **66/1**
55 **8** 3 ¾ **Lady Mai (IRE)**[13] 3298 2-9-0 0 AdamBeschizza 7 25
(William Kinsey) *t.k.h: chsd centre ldrs: rdn over 2f out: sn outpcd* **20/1**
5 **9** hd **Paddy's Bay**[13] 3282 2-9-5 0 PhillipMakin 5 30
(Kevin Ryan) *led centre gp to 1/2-way: edgd lft and wknd fr 2f out* **12/1**
0 **10** 4 **Under Approval**[23] 2955 2-9-5 0 DanielTudhope 11 18
(David O'Meara) *chsd ldng gp stands' side: rdn and hung lft over 2f out: wknd wl over 1f out* **33/1**
11 1 ¾ **Always Be Closing** 2-9-5 0 MichaelO'Connell 4 12
(John Quinn) *in tch centre tl rdn and wknd over 2f out* **28/1**
12 14 **Halloween Moon** 2-9-5 0 GrahamLee 8
(James Bethell) *chsd stands' side ldrs: drvn over 2f out: sn wknd: t.o* **18/1**

1m 16.27s (1.67) **Going Correction** -0.075s/f (Good) **12** Ran SP% **116.8**
Speed ratings (Par 93): **85,84,81,77,76 70,68,63,63,58 55,37**
toteswingers 1&2 £22.20, 1&3 £7.10, 2&3 £14.20 CSF £91.77 TOTE £8.30: £2.00, £2.90, £2.00; EX 131.80 Trifecta £2040.30 Pool: £2740.27 - 1.00 winning tickets..
Owner C E Whiteley **Bred** Lynn Lodge Stud **Trained** Norton, N Yorks

FOCUS
This maiden was run at a fair pace with the field splitting into two groups, before converging 3f out. The form fits in with recent race averages.

3725 BETFRED TV SEATON DELAVAL H'CAP 1m 3y(S)
3:00 (3:00) (Class 2) (0-105,101) 4-Y-0+
£12,450 (£3,728; £1,864; £932; £466; £234) **Stalls** Centre

Form RPR
0-40 **1** **My Freedom (IRE)**[126] 744 5-8-12 **92** SilvestreDeSousa 2 103
(Saeed bin Suroor) *prom: shkn up to ld over 1f out: kpt on strly fnl f* **6/1**[3]
15-6 **2** 2 ¼ **Validus**[64] 1768 4-9-7 **101** JamieSpencer 4 107
(Luca Cumani) *hld up: hdwy over 2f out: pressed wnr and rdn over 1f out: kpt on same pce ins fnl f* **10/3**[1]
240- **3** 1 ¾ **Balducci**[278] 6494 6-9-1 **95** MartinLane 8 97
(David Simcock) *led at stdy pce: rdn and hdd over 1f out: kpt on same pce fnl f* **50/1**
1020 **4** 1 ½ **Hi There (IRE)**[27] 2841 4-8-9 **89** TonyHamilton 6 88
(Richard Fahey) *t.k.h: hld up bhd ldng gp: rdn over 2f out: styd on fnl f: nt pce to chal* **10/1**
4362 **5** ½ **Dubai Dynamo**[5] 3564 8-8-8 **88** PJMcDonald 9 85
(Ruth Carr) *in tch: drvn over 2f out: one pce fr over 1f out* **9/2**[2]
6000 **6** 2 **Dance And Dance (IRE)**[42] 2399 7-9-2 **96** JoeFanning 5 89
(Ed Vaughan) *dwlt: hld up: stdy hdwy 3f out: rdn and outpcd fr over 1f out* **9/2**[2]
0230 **7** shd **Fort Belvedere**[12] 3346 5-8-10 **90** GrahamGibbons 1 83
(Keith Dalgleish) *chsd ldr: rdn over 2f out: wknd over 1f out* **16/1**
0000 **8** 2 **Memory Cloth**[39] 2477 6-8-7 **87** BarryMcHugh 3 75
(Brian Ellison) *cl up tl rdn and wknd wl over 1f out* **16/1**
-400 **9** 7 **Justonefortheroad**[42] 2399 7-8-9 **94** GeorgeChaloner(5) 10 66
(Richard Fahey) *chsd ldrs tl rdn and wknd over 2f out* **16/1**
2023 **10** 7 **Galician**[5] 3590 4-8-10 **90** GrahamLee 7 46
(Mark Johnston) *dwlt: hdwy and prom whn swtchd to r alone stands' rail 1/2-way: sn struggling* **13/2**

1m 40.94s (-2.46) **Going Correction** -0.075s/f (Good) **10** Ran SP% **115.8**
Speed ratings (Par 109): **109,106,105,103,103 101,100,98,91,84**
toteswingers 1&2 £5.80, 1&3 £30.60, 2&3 £24.00 CSF £26.09 CT £937.27 TOTE £6.90: £2.10, £3.50, £10.60; EX 32.40 Trifecta £799.10 Pool: £2695.40 - 2.52 winning tickets..
Owner Godolphin **Bred** Skymarc Farm **Trained** Newmarket, Suffolk

FOCUS
This decent contest was run at a steady pace, with the action taking place towards the centre/far rail. The form is rated through the third to last year's best.

3726 BETFRED SLATYFORD OLD BOYS H'CAP 2m 19y
3:30 (3:30) (Class 4) (0-80,80) 4-Y-0+ **£4,690** (£1,395; £697; £348) **Stalls** Centre

Form RPR
0-01 **1** **Big Time Billy (IRE)**[7] 2990 7-8-3 **62** (v) JoeFanning 3 75+
(Peter Bowen) *t.k.h early: prom on ins: smooth hdwy to ld over 2f out: sn rdn clr: kpt on strly* **4/5**[1]
2226 **2** 5 **Brasingaman Eric**[20] 3065 6-8-6 **65** PJMcDonald 9 72
(George Moore) *led at stdy pce: rdn and edgd rt over 2f out: sn hdd: kpt on same pce fr over 1f out* **22/1**
160 **3** 1 ¼ **Wyborne**[75] 1536 4-9-7 **80** DaleSwift 13 86+
(Brian Ellison) *hld up: rdn over 3f out: styd on fr 2f out: nrst fin* **33/1**
41 **4** hd **Mister Pagan**[22] 2971 5-9-3 **76** GrahamLee 4 81
(Jim Goldie) *hld up towards rr: rdn over 3f out: styd on fr over 1f out: nvr able to chal* **12/1**[3]
1310 **5** 1 ½ **Activate**[12] 3333 6-9-0 **73** (p) GrahamGibbons 10 76
(Keith Dalgleish) *prom: rdn over 2f out: one pce fr over 1f out* **14/1**
2441 **6** ½ **Capellanus (IRE)**[12] 3333 7-9-3 **76** JamesSullivan 1 79
(Brian Ellison) *t.k.h: hld up in midfield: rdn and effrt over 2f out: no imp fr over 1f out* **12/1**[3]
-534 **7** 1 **Come Here Yew (IRE)**[20] 3065 5-8-11 **73** NeilFarley(3) 8 75
(Declan Carroll) *chsd ldrs: rdn over 2f out: no ex fr over 1f out* **8/1**[2]
20-1 **8** hd **Rock Relief (IRE)**[37] 2540 7-8-11 **70** PaulMulrennan 5 71
(Chris Grant) *chsd ldrs: drvn over 4f out: outpcd fnl 2f* **20/1**
0-00 **9** 2 **Harrison's Cave**[26] 2855 5-9-6 **79** [1] DanielTudhope 6 78
(Chris Grant) *in tch: rdn and outpcd over 2f out: n.d after* **25/1**
114 **10** 4 **Mohawk Ridge**[34] 2615 7-9-4 **77** TomEaves 2 71
(Michael Dods) *t.k.h: cl up tl rdn and wknd 2f out* **33/1**
6640 **11** 2 ¼ **Bow To No One (IRE)**[35] 2587 7-9-0 **73** LeeTopliss 7 65
(Alan Jarvis) *dwlt: hld up: drvn over 3f out: nvr on terms* **20/1**
3030 **12** 1 **La Bacouetteuse (FR)**[3] 3627 8-8-9 **68** (p) SilvestreDeSousa 12 58
(Iain Jardine) *hld up: struggling wl over 3f out: sn btn: eased whn no ch fnl f* **25/1**
-162 **13** ½ **Singzak**[13] 3301 5-8-10 **76** MatthewHopkins(7) 11 66
(Michael Easterby) *hld up in tch: struggling 3f out: btn fnl 2f* **16/1**

3m 36.15s (-3.25) **Going Correction** -0.075s/f (Good) **13** Ran SP% **122.0**
Speed ratings (Par 105): **105,102,101,101,101 100,100,100,99,97 96,95,95**
toteswingers 1&2 £7.60, 1&3 £16.70, 2&3 £109.90 CSF £27.69 CT £372.92 TOTE £1.70: £1.10, £6.90, £12.20; EX 22.70 Trifecta £709.80 Pool: £3251.76 - 3.43 winning tickets..
Owner Miss R L Bryan **Bred** A And C Enterprises **Trained** Little Newcastle, Pembrokes

FOCUS
An interesting handicap run at an honest pace. The runner-up is rated to form, while the next six home were all close to their marks.

3727 BETFRED "RACING'S BIGGEST SUPPORTER" H'CAP (DIV I) 1m 2f 32y
4:00 (4:01) (Class 6) (0-60,60) 4-Y-0+ **£1,940** (£577; £288; £144) **Stalls** Centre

Form RPR
4034 **1** **Amazing Blue Sky**[6] 3543 7-9-2 **55** JamesSullivan 14 65
(Ruth Carr) *sn crossed over to r against ins rail: mde all: hrd pressed over 1f out: rdn and styd on wl fnl f* **4/1**[1]
0006 **2** 2 ¼ **Madame Blavatsky (FR)**[28] 2796 5-8-10 **49** (v) PaulMulrennan 10 54
(Karen McLintock) *midfield: rdn and hdwy over 2f out: chsd wnr ins fnl f: kpt on* **16/1**
00 **3** ½ **Mullins Way (USA)**[18] 3138 5-9-3 **56** J-PGuillambert 3 60
(Jo Hughes) *chsd wnr: shkn up and ev ch over 1f out: no ex and lost 2nd ins fnl f* **7/1**[3]
0-60 **4** 4 **The Lodge Road (IRE)**[3] 3625 5-9-7 **60** PhillipMakin 7 56+
(Martin Todhunter) *hld up: rdn and hdwy on outside 2f out: kpt on fnl f: nvr able to chal* **20/1**
4606 **5** nse **Sinatramania**[6] 3543 6-8-12 **51** (p) RoystonFfrench 15 47
(Tracy Waggott) *midfield: effrt and rdn over 2f out: one pce fr over 1f out* **8/1**
6005 **6** 3 ¼ **Aquarian Spirit**[10] 3395 6-9-4 **57** LeeTopliss 9 46
(Richard Fahey) *towards rr: rdn over 2f out: styd on fnl f: n.d* **16/1**
000- **7** nk **Oliver's Gold**[263] 6252 5-8-9 **48** (p) GrahamGibbons 8 37
(Tim Walford) *dwlt: bhd tl hung lft and hdwy over 2f out: styd on: nvr able to chal* **12/1**
-066 **7** dht **Tweedle Dee**[24] 2932 4-8-12 **51** PJMcDonald 12 40
(Noel Quinlan) *chsd ldrs tl rdn and wknd wl over 1f out* **8/1**
200- **9** ¾ **Inniscastle Boy**[257] 7062 4-9-1 **54** GrahamLee 5 41
(Jim Goldie) *hld up towards rr: rdn over 3f out: hdwy over 1f out: no imp* **7/1**[3]
00- **10** nk **Grammar**[167] 6103 4-8-10 **49** (e[1]) BarryMcHugh 1 36
(David Thompson) *dwlt: rdn in rr over 3f out: sme late hdwy: nvr on terms* **66/1**
0-00 **11** ½ **Miss Matiz**[10] 3398 6-8-4 **46** oh1 DeclanCannon(3) 4 32
(Alan Kirtley) *in tch tl rdn and wknd over 2f out* **100/1**
66/0 **12** ½ **Hartforth**[115] 53 5-8-11 **50** MichaelO'Connell 6 35
(Donald Whillans) *midfield: drvn and outpcd over 2f out: sn btn* **33/1**
20-0 **13** ¾ **Celtic Step**[23] 2961 9-9-0 **53** DaleSwift 13 36
(Peter Niven) *in tch: drvn and outpcd over 2f out: sn btn* **10/1**
06-0 **14** 1 **Korngold**[15] 3195 5-8-12 **58** JacobButterfield(7) 2 39
(Ollie Pears) *t.k.h in rr: struggling wl over 2f out: sn btn* **11/2**[2]

2m 10.45s (-1.45) **Going Correction** -0.075s/f (Good) **14** Ran SP% **121.3**
Speed ratings (Par 101): **102,100,99,96,96 93,93,93,93,92 92,92,91,90**
toteswingers 1&2 £18.70, 1&3 £9.50, 2&3 £38.00 CSF £70.28 CT £445.95 TOTE £3.50: £1.80, £6.70, £2.80; EX 84.70 Trifecta £1001.80 Pool: £1987.13 - 1.48 winning tickets..
Owner G Scruton, D Williamson & R Carr **Bred** Hong Kong Breeders Club **Trained** Huby, N Yorks
■ Stewards' Enquiry : James Sullivan one-day ban: careless riding (11 July)

FOCUS
This weak handicap was run at a sound pace and it paid to race handily. Few of these are solid, although a number look well handicapped at present.

3728 BETFRED "RACING'S BIGGEST SUPPORTER" H'CAP (DIV II) 1m 2f 32y
4:30 (4:30) (Class 6) (0-60,59) 4-Y-0+ **£1,940** (£577; £288; £144) **Stalls** Centre

Form RPR
-400 **1** **Bygones For Coins (IRE)**[31] 349 5-8-7 **45** AndrewMullen 13 58
(Robert Johnson) *trckd ldrs: hdwy to ld over 2f out: sn rdn: clr fnl f: kpt on wl* **25/1**
4360 **2** 3 ¼ **Outlaw Torn (IRE)**[26] 2889 4-9-7 **59** (e) DanielTudhope 2 66+
(Richard Guest) *hld up in midfield: effrt whn nt clr run wl over 2f out: rallied: chsd (clr) wnr ins fnl f: kpt on: no imp* **7/1**
-561 **3** 1 ¼ **Yorksters Prince (IRE)**[6] 3545 6-8-10 **53** 6ex (b) ShirleyTeasdale(5) 7 57
(Marjorie Fife) *led: rdn and hdd over 2f out: kpt on same pce fnl f* **7/2**[1]
4200 **4** 2 ¼ **Koo And The Gang (IRE)**[22] 2991 6-8-11 **52** PaulPickard(3) 3 52
(Brian Ellison) *chsd ldrs: drvn over 2f out: one pce over 1f out* **6/1**[3]
003 **5** nk **True Pleasure (IRE)**[10] 3399 6-8-11 **49** SilvestreDeSousa 6 48
(James Bethell) *hld up: rdn over 2f out: hdwy and edgd lft wl over 1f out: kpt on fnl f: nrst fin* **15/2**
4-05 **6** 4 ½ **Echo Of Footsteps**[14] 3252 4-9-5 **57** PaulMulrennan 4 47
(Michael Herrington) *hld up: rdn and hdwy 3f out: no imp wl over 1f out* **5/1**[2]
-624 **7** 1 **Essell**[15] 3222 4-8-12 **50** SamHitchcott 11 38
(Mick Channon) *midfield: hdwy on ins over 2f out: rdn and no further imp fr over 1f out* **14/1**
006- **8** 1 ½ **Touching History (IRE)**[217] 7822 4-8-7 **45** [1] JamesSullivan 1 30
(Tim Etherington) *hld up: hdwy over 4f out: rdn and hung lft wl over 2f out: sn btn* **40/1**
06-0 **9** 2 ¼ **Dean Iarracht (IRE)**[73] 1572 7-8-13 **51** (p) BarryMcHugh 9 31
(Tracy Waggott) *s.v.s: detached tl sme hdwy over 2f out: nvr on terms* **20/1**
0050 **10** 6 **Elizabeth Coffee (IRE)**[14] 3231 5-8-13 **51** (v[1]) GrahamGibbons 14 19
(John Weymes) *hld up in tch: drvn over 2f out: wknd wl over 1f out* **20/1**
35-0 **11** 4 ½ **Valentine's Gift**[22] 2986 5-8-6 **49** AdamCarter(5) 8 8
(Neville Bycroft) *hld up on outside: struggling over 2f out: sn btn* **33/1**

0610 **12** 1 3/4 **Cufflink**[22] 2972 4-9-6 **58**...........................(v) MichaelO'Connell 5 14
(Iain Jardine) *chsd ldrs: rdn over 3f out: wknd over 2f out* **13/2**
050- **13** 3 1/2 **Lady Gargoyle**[180] 6885 5-8-7 **45**............................... AndrewElliott 12
(Jim Goldie) *sn wl bhd: no ch fr 1/2-way* **40/1**
4050 **14** 32 **Bonnie Echo**[28] 2798 6-9-2 **54**...................................(p) TomEaves 10
(Michael Dods) *t.k.h: pressed ldr: wkng whn hmpd wl over 2f out: lost tch and eased over 1f out* **16/1**
2m 10.58s (-1.32) **Going Correction** -0.075s/f (Good) **14** Ran SP% **124.5**
Speed ratings (Par 101): **102,99,98,96,96 92,91,90,88,84 80,79,76,50**
toteswingers 1&2 £35.60, 1&3 £19.00, 2&3 £7.30 CSF £185.92 CT £782.56 TOTE £38.40: £7.60, £4.40, £1.10; EX 518.20 Trifecta £1905.80 Part won. Pool: £2541.12 - 0.55 winning tickets..
Owner Do Well Racing **Bred** Hong Kong Breeders Club **Trained** Newburn, Tyne & Wear
FOCUS
This modest yet open handicap was run at a fair pace. Once again it paid to race handily. The winner is rated to her turf best backed up by the second.

3729 BETFRED "FRED'S PUSHES" H'CAP 1m 2f 32y
5:00 (5:00) (Class 5) (0-75,80) 4-Y-0+ **£2,587** (£770; £384; £192) **Stalls** Centre

Form RPR
1-00 **1** **Oetzi**[21] 3022 5-9-2 **69**... LeeToplis 1 77
(Alan Jarvis) *s.i.s: hld up: squeezed through on ins fr over 2f out: led ins fnl f: r.o wl* **8/1**
0500 **2** 1 1/4 **Warcrown (IRE)**[13] 3301 4-8-9 **67**.........................(t) GeorgeChaloner(5) 6 72
(Richard Fahey) *cl up: led 2f out: rdn and hdd ins fnl f: kpt on same pce towards fin* **12/1**
/0-0 **3** 1 **Rock Supreme (IRE)**[31] 2705 4-9-6 **73**........................ PaulMulrennan 7 76
(Michael Dods) *hld up in tch: rdn over 2f out: hdwy over 1f out: kpt on ins fnl f* **14/1**
5- **4** 1 3/4 **Time Of My Life (IRE)**[285] 6240 4-9-5 **72**..................(t) DanielTudhope 8 72
(Patrick Holmes) *prom: rdn over 2f out: one pce fr over 1f out* **25/1**
-104 **5** hd **Exning Halt**[33] 2077 4-9-5 **72**...................................... MichaelO'Connell 4 71
(John Quinn) *hld up in tch: hdwy to chse ldrs whn n.m.r 2f out: one pce fnl f* **16/1**
60/ **6** 2 **Viva Colonia (IRE)**[84] 2034 8-8-7 **60**.............................. BarryMcHugh 2 55
(Brian Ellison) *led to over 2f out: rdn and wknd appr fnl f* **9/2**[3]
0-06 **7** 3/4 **Pivotman**[19] 3081 5-9-0 **67**... GrahamGibbons 3 61
(Michael Easterby) *hld up: rdn and outpcd over 2f out: rallied over 1f out: sn no imp* **6/1**
5041 **8** 3 **San Cassiano (IRE)**[8] 3477 6-9-13 **80** 6ex.................... JamesSullivan 5 68
(Ruth Carr) *t.k.h: cl up: outpcd 3f out: n.d after* **5/2**[1]
235- **9** nk **Cape Explorer**[31] 7353 4-9-6 **73**...................................... TomEaves 9 60
(Brian Ellison) *prom tl rdn and wknd over 2f out* **4/1**[2]
2m 10.61s (-1.29) **Going Correction** -0.075s/f (Good) **9** Ran SP% **116.2**
Speed ratings (Par 103): **102,101,100,98,98 97,96,94,93**
toteswingers 1&2 £11.80, 1&3 £18.20, 2&3 £14.40 CSF £98.92 CT £1322.49 TOTE £9.10: £2.20, £3.10, £3.70; EX 115.00 Trifecta £1185.80 Pool: £3402.10 - 2.15 winning tickets..
Owner Allen B Pope & Jarvis Associates **Bred** Jarvis Associates **Trained** Twyford, Bucks
FOCUS
Few came into this in much form. It was run at a fair pace. Improved efforts from the placed horses with the the fourth close to form.

3730 BETFRED MOBILE CASINO H'CAP 7f
5:30 (5:31) (Class 5) (0-75,72) 3-Y-0 **£2,587** (£770; £384; £192) **Stalls** Centre

Form RPR
4412 **1** **Black Rider (IRE)**[30] 2763 3-9-2 **67**.....................[1] PaulMulrennan 9 74
(Julie Camacho) *hld up: hdwy over 2f out: led appr fnl f: sn rdn and edgd lft: hld on towards fin* **11/2**[3]
2150 **2** hd **Surround Sound**[20] 3067 3-9-1 **66**............................ GrahamGibbons 6 72
(Tim Easterby) *t.k.h: in tch: rdn and hdwy to ld briefly over 1f out: hung lft: kpt on ins fnl f: jst hld* **7/2**[2]
60-0 **3** 1 1/2 **Perfect Pasture**[76] 1522 3-8-5 **56**................................ JamesSullivan 7 58+
(Michael Easterby) *dwlt: plld hrd in rr: rdn and hdwy wl over 1f out: r.o ins fnl f* **16/1**
20-0 **4** 1 1/2 **Storma Norma**[6] 3546 3-9-2 **67**................................ SilvestreDeSousa 4 65
(Tim Easterby) *chsd ldrs: rdn over 2f out: edgd lft: ev ch over 1f out: one pce ins fnl f* **16/1**
-212 **5** shd **Darkside**[6] 3546 3-8-8 **59**... RoystonFfrench 1 57+
(Tracy Waggott) *chsd ldr: outpcd and hung rt over 2f out: styd on fnl f: no imp* **11/4**[1]
26-4 **6** 1 1/4 **Kolonel Kirkup**[48] 2235 3-9-7 **72**.................................... TomEaves 5 66
(Michael Dods) *t.k.h: led to over 1f out: rdn and outpcd fnl f* **12/1**
1240 **7** 2 3/4 **Taxiformissbyron**[29] 2770 3-8-13 **64**............................ GrahamLee 8 51
(Michael Herrington) *hld up in tch: rdn over 2f out: no imp fr over 1f out* **25/1**
2160 **8** 1/2 **Brooke's Bounty**[26] 2876 3-9-2 **72**.................... GeorgeChaloner(5) 10 57
(Richard Fahey) *trckd ldrs: drvn over 2f out: btn over 1f out* **9/1**
1202 **9** hd **Red Gift (IRE)**[6] 3533 3-9-5 **70**.. DaleSwift 3 55
(Brian Ellison) *hld up in tch: struggling 2f out: sn btn* **11/2**[3]
5030 **10** 2 **Another Claret**[21] 3025 3-8-0 **58**.......................... SamanthaBell(7) 2 38
(Richard Fahey) *prom: rdn and hung lft 2f out: sn btn* **40/1**
1m 28.2s (0.40) **Going Correction** -0.075s/f (Good) **10** Ran SP% **115.4**
Speed ratings (Par 99): **94,93,92,90,90 88,85,85,84,82**
toteswingers 1&2 £6.20, 1&3 £18.30, 2&3 £16.10 CSF £24.79 CT £290.21 TOTE £8.20: £2.90, £2.00, £4.90; EX 31.90 Trifecta £388.20 Pool: £3346.60 - 6.46 winning tickets..
Owner Nigel Gravett **Bred** Patrick A Cassidy **Trained** Norton, N Yorks
FOCUS
This handicap was run at a sound gallop. The runner-up is rated to form with the fourth close to her juvenile marks.
T/Jkpt: Not won. T/Plt: £416.90 to a £1 stake. Pool: £74,655.06 - 130.70 winning tickets. T/Qpdt: £18.60 to a £1 stake. Pool: £6616.06 - 262.05 winning tickets. RY

3507 WARWICK (L-H)
Thursday, June 27

OFFICIAL GOING: Good to firm (8.3)
Wind: Virtually nil Weather: White cloud

3731 BROKERS MAIDEN STKS 7f 26y
2:10 (2:11) (Class 5) 3-Y-0+ **£2,587** (£770; £384; £192) **Stalls** Low

Form RPR
44 **1** **Ziekhani**[24] 2930 3-9-3 0.. RichardHughes 8 82+
(Hughie Morrison) *mde all: drvn over 1f out and sn strly pressed: fnd ex ins fnl f: kpt on wl clsng stages* **7/2**[2]
4 **2** nk **Muthmir (IRE)**[16] 3176 3-9-3 0.. DaneO'Neill 2 81+
(William Haggas) *chsd ldrs: wnt 2nd ins fnl 2f: chal appr fnl f and styd pressing wnr tl no ex clsng stages* **11/10**[1]
6460 **3** 4 **Sedenoo**[20] 3062 3-9-3 72... NeilCallan 9 70
(Marco Botti) *chsd wnr tl rdn ins fnl 2f: outpcd by ldng duo ins fnl f* **4/1**[3]
4 10 **Princess Quest** 4-9-7 0.. MartinHarley 3 41
(Mick Channon) *s.i.s: in rr: drvn along 3f out but styd on fr over 1f out to take mod 4th* **33/1**
0 **5** 1 1/2 **Petrify**[30] 2760 3-9-3 0... KirstyMilczarek 6 39
(Luca Cumani) *in rr: pushed along over 3f out: modest prog fnl f* **25/1**
2 **6** 4 1/2 **Saigon City**[16] 3176 3-9-0 0....................................... PatrickHills(3) 5 27
(Luca Cumani) *in tch: rdn and btn over 3f out* **5/1**
50 **7** 2 3/4 **Bridge Builder**[26] 2872 3-8-12 0...................................(v[1]) RyanTate(5) 4 19
(Peter Hedger) *chsd ldrs tl rdn and wknd 3f out* **50/1**
8 5 **Bahama Bay** 3-8-12 0.. SaleemGolam 1
(Stuart Williams) *t.k.h: sn bhd* **50/1**
0-05 **9** 3 1/2 **Rupeetoups**[16] 3170 5-9-7 39....................................... NathanAlison(5) 7
(Jim Boyle) *chsd ldrs to 1/2-way* **200/1**
1m 23.59s (-1.01) **Going Correction** -0.075s/f (Good)
WFA 3 from 4yo+ 9lb **9** Ran SP% **117.7**
Speed ratings (Par 103): **102,101,97,85,83 78,75,69,65**
toteswingers 1&2 £1.70, 1&3 £1.80, 2&3 £1.90 CSF £7.77 TOTE £4.30: £1.30, £1.10, £1.10; EX 9.80 Trifecta £24.80 Pool: £2062.49 - 62.23 winning tickets..
Owner The Fairy Story Partnership **Bred** Deepwood Farm Stud **Trained** East Ilsley, Berks
FOCUS
A modest-looking maiden. Enterprising tactics by Richard Hughes were rewarded. The winner is rated to his Leicester form and the third to his latest Newmarket mark.

3732 AFL PRIME H'CAP 5f
2:40 (2:40) (Class 5) (0-70,70) 3-Y-O **£2,587** (£770; £384) **Stalls** Low

Form RPR
6325 **1** **Buy Art**[6] 3533 3-9-7 **69**..(p) JimmyFortune 1 72
(Gary Moore) *trckd ldr: drvn to chal 1f out: led fnl 150yds: kpt on wl* **11/8**[2]
5031 **2** nk **Silca's Dream**[3] 3638 3-9-1 **70** 6ex.............................. DanielCremin(7) 3 72
(Mick Channon) *led: rdn over 1f out: sn jnd: hdd fnl 150yds: kpt on but nt quite pce of wnr* **11/10**[1]
0000 **3** 3/4 **Winnie Perry**[11] 3376 3-9-0 **62**...................................... AndreaAtzeni 2 61
(Rod Millman) *racd in 3rd: rdn and one pce over 2f out: kpt on wl fnl f: clsng on ldng duo nr fin but a hld* **11/2**[3]
1m 0.44s (0.84) **Going Correction** -0.075s/f (Good) **3** Ran SP% **105.1**
Speed ratings (Par 99): **90,89,88**
CSF £3.16 TOTE £2.00; EX 3.40 Trifecta £3.10 Pool: £838.36 - 199.80 winning tickets..
Owner R A Green **Bred** Mount Coote Stud & M & W Bell Racing **Trained** Lower Beeding, W Sussex
■ Stewards' Enquiry : Daniel Cremin four-day ban: use of whip (11, 15, 16, 17 July)
FOCUS
Three runners, but only two were seriously fancied in the betting and they are rated pretty much to form.

3733 ASSET FINANCE H'CAP (JOCKEY CLUB GRASSROOTS SPRINT SERIES QUALIFIER) 6f
3:10 (3:10) (Class 4) (0-80,79) 3-Y-0+ **£4,690** (£1,395; £697; £348) **Stalls** Low

Form RPR
5-46 **1** **Minalisa**[22] 2988 4-9-11 **76**... SteveDrowne 1 99
(Rae Guest) *mde all: rdn ins fnl f: kpt on wl* **11/4**[1]
-023 **2** 2 1/4 **Picture Dealer**[19] 3093 4-10-0 **79**................................. JimmyFortune 7 95
(Gary Moore) *hld up towards rr but in tch: hdwy ins fnl 2f to chse wnr appr fnl f but no imp* **4/1**[2]
130- **3** 3/4 **Ambitious Boy**[278] 6488 4-9-5 **70**.................................... ShaneKelly 4 83
(Andrew Hollinshead) *hld up in rr: hdwy appr fnl f and sn tk 3rd: kpt on u.p to cl on 2nd but no ch w wnr* **16/1**
0063 **4** 5 **Clear Praise (USA)**[12] 3315 6-9-9 **74**........................... SebSanders 6 71
(Simon Dow) *chsd ldrs: rdn fr 1/2-way and styd on same pce fnl 2f* **14/1**
3231 **5** 1 **Indian Affair**[20] 3050 3-9-1 **73**...................................... JimmyQuinn 2 67
(Milton Bradley) *chsd ldrs: rdn 3f out: wknd over 1f out* **7/1**[3]
5600 **6** 1/2 **Dark Lane**[11] 3371 7-8-13 **69**................................. DeclanBates(5) 5 62
(David Evans) *in rr but in tch: rdn 3f out: nvr gng pce to get into contention* **22/1**
24-0 **7** 1 3/4 **Mount Hollow**[19] 3093 8-9-8 **78**.................................(p) JackDuern(5) 3 65
(Andrew Hollinshead) *chsd ldrs: rdn over 2f out: wknd over 1f out* **33/1**
3023 **8** hd **Alnoomaas (IRE)**[10] 3415 4-9-11 **76**............................ RichardHughes 9 62
(Luke Dace) *disp 2nd: rdn over 2f out: wknd appr fnl f* **11/4**[1]
-000 **9** 1 **Lunar Deity**[23] 2964 4-9-12 **77**...(p) NeilCallan 8 60
(Eve Johnson Houghton) *chsd ldrs: rdn 3f out: wknd over 2f out* **8/1**
1m 10.53s (-1.27) **Going Correction** -0.075s/f (Good)
WFA 3 from 4yo+ 7lb **9** Ran SP% **116.8**
Speed ratings (Par 105): **105,102,101,94,93 92,90,89,88**
toteswingers 1&2 £4.00, 1&3 £10.60, 2&3 £11.40 CSF £13.98 CT £148.01 TOTE £5.60: £2.40, £1.10, £4.20; EX 16.40 Trifecta £124.70 Pool: £1866.28 - 11.21 winning tickets..
Owner C J Mills **Bred** C J Mills **Trained** Newmarket, Suffolk
FOCUS
A fair contest in which significant money came for the winner in the minutes leading up to the race. The placed horses are rated close to their marks.

3734 EBF STALLIONS/ARKLE FINANCE ETERNAL STKS (LISTED RACE) (FILLIES) 7f 26y
3:40 (3:40) (Class 1) 3-Y-O
£22,684 (£8,600; £4,304; £2,144; £1,076; £540) **Stalls** Low

Form RPR
2-34 **1** **Winning Express (IRE)**[53] 2047 3-9-2 107.................... JamesDoyle 7 105+
(Ed McMahon) *trckd ldrs: chal appr fnl f sn led and shkn up: styd on wl and in command fnl 110yds: comf* **10/11**[1]
3450 **2** 1 1/2 **Exactement (IRE)**[32] 2689 3-8-12 96............................. JimCrowley 8 97
(Mrs K Burke) *hld up in rr but in tch: hdwy fr 2f out: styd on wl fnl f to take 2nd clsng stages but no ch w wnr* **5/1**[3]
-642 **3** nk **Victrix Ludorum (IRE)**[24] 2936 3-8-12 100................. RichardHughes 2 96
(Richard Hannon) *sn led: drvn over 2f out: jnd by wnr appr fnl f: sn outpcd but kpt on tl lost 2nd clsng stages* **3/1**[2]
0400 **4** 1 **Sorella Bella (IRE)**[8] 3460 3-9-2 95............................ MartinHarley 4 97
(Mick Channon) *chsd ldr: rdn over 2f out: one pce into 4th appr fnl f* **11/1**
1-10 **5** hd **How's Life**[41] 2429 3-8-12 80.. AndreaAtzeni 6 93
(Rae Guest) *towards rr but in tch: drvn and hdwy 2f out: styd on same pce appr fnl f* **12/1**
-566 **6** 1 3/4 **Dream Maker (IRE)**[33] 2666 3-8-12 88........................ JimmyFortune 9 88?
(Tim Easterby) *s.i.s: in rr: rdn and hdwy ins fnl 2f: no imp on ldrs u.p appr fnl f* **66/1**

5436 **7** *6* **Lady Of The House (IRE)**[14] 3235 3-8-12 82..................(p) AmyRyan 5 72
(Kevin Ryan) *chsd ldrs: wknd 2f out* **50/1**

2230 **8** *6* **Senafe**[8] 3460 3-8-12 100.. NeilCallan 10 67
(Marco Botti) *chsd ldrs: wknd 2f out* **16/1**

1m 23.19s (-1.41) **Going Correction** -0.075s/f (Good) **8** Ran SP% **119.4**
Speed ratings (Par 104): **105,103,102,101,101 99,92,85**
toteswingers 1&2 £1.10, 1&3 £1.10, 2&3 £2.20 CSF £6.44 TOTE £1.90: £1.10, £1.50, £1.10; EX 7.70 Trifecta £19.60 Pool: £2600.47 - 99.49 winning tickets..
Owner Milton Express Limited **Bred** Yeomanstown Stud **Trained** Lichfield, Staffs

FOCUS
A decent fillies' Listed event rated around those in the frame behind the winner.

3735 CONSUMER CREDIT H'CAP (JOCKEY CLUB GRASSROOTS MIDDLE DISTANCE SERIES QUALIFIER) 1m 2f 188y

4:10 (4:10) (Class 5) (0-70,70) 3-Y-O **£2,587** (£770; £384; £192) **Stalls** Low

Form RPR

4-41 **1** **Al Thumama**[28] 2796 3-9-1 64...(p) NeilCallan 1 72
(Kevin Ryan) *mde all: rdn and qcknd bnd over 2f out: hrd pressed and edgd rt fnl 100yds: hld on gamely* **3/1**[2]

6042 **2** *shd* **Whitefall (USA)**[28] 2800 3-8-2 51...................................... AndreaAtzeni 6 59
(David Evans) *chsd ldrs: wnt 2nd over 2f out: chal on rail: edgd lft and bmpd fnl 110yds: no ex last strides* **7/2**[3]

30-6 **3** *4* **Uncle Bernie (IRE)**[22] 2989 3-8-9 58.................................. ShaneKelly 2 59
(Andrew Hollinshead) *chsd ldrs: rdn 2f out: styd on to chse ldng duo over 1f out: no imp and outpcd fnl f* **10/1**

1144 **4** *hd* **Echo Brava**[13] 3294 3-9-6 69... RichardHughes 5 70
(Luke Dace) *hld up in rr: drvn and hdwy 3f out: styd on same pce fr over 1f out* **5/2**[1]

00-2 **5** *4 1/2* **Lady Of Yue**[28] 2802 3-8-6 55.. WilliamCarson 7 48
(Eugene Stanford) *in rr: rdn and hdwy fr 2f out: nvr rchd ldrs and wknd fnl f* **9/1**

215 **6** *3 1/4* **Continental Divide (IRE)**[45] 2325 3-9-7 70.............. FergusSweeney 8 57
(Jamie Osborne) *chsd ldr tl wknd over 2f out* **11/2**

0-00 **7** *1 3/4* **Elvin**[9] 3428 3-7-13 51 oh3...(b[1]) DarrenEgan(3) 4 36
(Amanda Perrett) *chsd ldrs: wknd over 2f out* **33/1**

4300 **8** *11* **Silver Fawn (IRE)**[8] 3463 3-8-2 51...................................(be) JimmyQuinn 3 22
(John Weymes) *a in rr* **25/1**

2m 20.65s (-0.45) **Going Correction** -0.075s/f (Good) **8** Ran SP% **117.1**
Speed ratings (Par 99): **98,97,95,94,91 89,87,79**
toteswingers 1&2 £3.20, 1&3 £11.30, 2&3 £7.30 CSF £14.39 CT £92.87 TOTE £3.50: £1.10, £1.70, £3.30; EX 16.20 Trifecta £181.40 Pool: £2781.18 - 11.49 winning tickets..
Owner Mubarak Al Naemi **Bred** John James **Trained** Hambleton, N Yorks
■ Stewards' Enquiry : Neil Callan caution: careless riding

FOCUS
Just a modest event in which two pulled clear. The third and fourth are the best guides to the level.

3736 BARBARA CARRINGTON MEMORIAL APPRENTICE H'CAP 1m 22y

4:40 (4:40) (Class 5) (0-70,71) 4-Y-O+ **£2,587** (£770; £384; £192) **Stalls** Low

Form RPR

-132 **1** **Dutch Mistress**[19] 3098 4-9-4 67.................................... OisinMurphy(5) 1 75
(James Unett) *trckd ldr: chal fr over 4f out tl led over 3f out: hrd drvn ins fnl f: kpt on wl* **5/4**[1]

500- **2** *1* **Malih**[254] 7131 4-9-7 70.. JoeyHaynes(5) 5 76
(Ben De Haan) *in rr: hdwy 3f out: chsd wnr ins fnl 2f: kpt on u.p fnl f: no ex* **4/1**[3]

0350 **3** *5* **Rigid**[9] 3433 6-8-4 53 oh5 ow2.................................... AidenBlakemore(5) 6 48
(Tony Carroll) *chsd ldrs: pushed along and one pce over 2f out: styd on for wl-hld 3rd fnl f* **16/1**

000- **4** *3* **Quite A Catch (IRE)**[287] 6157 5-8-8 57 ow2..............(p) DavidCoyle(5) 3 45
(Jonathan Portman) *chsd ldrs: rdn over 2f out: wknd over 1f out* **33/1**

0021 **5** *1 1/4* **Paphos**[9] 3429 6-9-13 71 6ex...(v) DeclanBates 7 56
(David Evans) *led: jnd over 4f out: hdd over 3f out: wknd 2f out* **7/2**[2]

-004 **6** *1* **Tartan Trip**[15] 3210 6-9-11 69...................................(v) MatthewLawson 2 51
(Luke Dace) *s.i.s: in rr: rdn 3f out: brief effrt 2f out but nvr any ch and sn wknd* **15/2**

1m 41.18s (0.18) **Going Correction** -0.075s/f (Good) **6** Ran SP% **112.0**
Speed ratings (Par 103): **96,95,90,87,85 84**
toteswingers 1&2 £1.40, 1&3 £4.80, 2&3 £8.30 CSF £6.50 TOTE £2.00: £2.90, £1.40; EX 7.20 Trifecta £55.50 Pool: £3359.45 - 45.35 winning tickets..
Owner Gordon Kendrick **Bred** P And Mrs Venner And Trickledown Stud **Trained** Tedsmore Hall, Shropshire

FOCUS
The whole field were close together entering the home straight. The runner-up is rated to form for now.
T/Plt: £13.50 to a £1 stake. Pool: £49,846.79 - 2685.72 winning tickets. T/Qpdt: £3.80 to a £1 stake. Pool: £4452.20 - 864.99 winning tickets. ST

3253 YARMOUTH (L-H)

Thursday, June 27

OFFICIAL GOING: Good to firm (7.5)
Wind: fresh and blustery Weather: sunny but breezy; light rain from Race 5

3737 TRAFALGAR RESTAURANT AT GREAT YARMOUTH RACECOURSE MAIDEN STKS 6f 3y

2:20 (2:20) (Class 5) 2-Y-O **£2,587** (£770; £384; £192) **Stalls** Centre

Form RPR

2 **1** **Ertijaal (IRE)**[30] 2741 2-9-5 0... PaulHanagan 1 93+
(William Haggas) *mde all at decent pce: qcknd clr on bit over 1f out: impressive* **1/4**[1]

2 **2** *6* **Exceeder**[14] 3245 2-9-5 0.. FrankieDettori 3 73
(Marco Botti) *chsd wnr: rdn 2f out: easily hld after but a 2nd best* **6/1**[2]

3 *1 1/4* **Gilmer (IRE)** 2-9-5 0.. MickaelBarzalona 4 67+
(Saeed bin Suroor) *a 3rd: drvn over 2f out: kpt on steadily wout threatening after* **17/2**[3]

0 **4** *9* **Village Cricket**[14] 3245 2-9-5 0.. PatCosgrave 2 38
(Pam Sly) *awkward leaving stalls: a last: rdn and btn over 2f out* **200/1**

1m 12.83s (-1.57) **Going Correction** -0.325s/f (Firm) **4** Ran SP% **105.3**
Speed ratings (Par 93): **97,89,87,75**
CSF £1.98 TOTE £1.20; EX 2.20 Trifecta £2.10 Pool: £1786.20 - 635.49 winning tickets..
Owner Hamdan Al Maktoum **Bred** Shadwell Estate Company Limited **Trained** Newmarket, Suffolk

FOCUS
Bottom bend out 2m for fresh ground adding 12m to races on Round course. A fair maiden, despite the small field with the runner-up rated to his debut form and the winner different class.

3738 SEALIFE CENTRE H'CAP 6f 3y

2:50 (2:51) (Class 6) (0-65,65) 4-Y-O+ **£1,940** (£577; £288; £144) **Stalls** Centre

Form RPR

-400 **1** **Majestic Manannan (IRE)**[31] 2702 4-9-3 61.................. PaulHanagan 8 72
(David Nicholls) *mde all: a gng wl: pushed along to hold rival comf thrght fnl f* **17/2**[3]

2445 **2** *1 1/4* **Putin (IRE)**[9] 3431 5-8-13 62...................................(bt) RachealKneller(5) 6 69
(Phil McEntee) *pressed wnr: rdn and clr of rest 1f out: no imp fnl 100yds* **12/1**

0-00 **3** *1 3/4* **Coach Montana (IRE)**[12] 3326 4-8-2 46..........................(b) LukeMorris 7 47
(Jane Chapple-Hyam) *midfield: drvn after 2f: kpt on steadily ins fnl f but no threat to ldrs* **14/1**

045 **4** *1 3/4* **Ambitious Icarus**[15] 3200 4-9-4 62.......................(e) RobbieFitzpatrick 5 58
(Richard Guest) *taken down early: towards rr and racd awkwardly: rdn over 2f out: kpt on ins fnl f but no ch* **12/1**

4232 **5** *nk* **Aaranyow (IRE)**[14] 3246 5-8-4 53..................................... RobertTart(5) 4 48
(Clifford Lines) *pressed ldrs: rdn over 2f out: one pce and btn over 1f out* **3/1**[1]

4400 **6** *4 1/2* **Medam**[75] 1540 4-8-3 50 ow3..(v[1]) BillyCray(3) 10 30
(Shaun Harris) *sn urged along: towards rr: wl hld fnl 2f* **40/1**

0-55 **7** *2 1/2* **Jack Barker**[51] 2133 4-8-7 51.. FrederikTylicki 11 23
(Robin Bastiman) *pressed ldrs over 4f: rdn and sn lost pl* **16/1**

-360 **8** *3/4* **Sarah Berry**[7] 3498 4-8-13 60... RyanClark(3) 1 30
(Chris Dwyer) *midfield: rdn and btn 2f out* **20/1**

/61- **9** *11* **For Life (IRE)**[321] 5047 11-9-0 61............................ NataliaGemelova(3) 3
(John E Long) *taken down early: spd 4f: sn dropped rt out: t.o* **25/1**

30-5 **10** *30* **Isola Verde**[15] 3223 4-9-7 65.. HayleyTurner 2
(James Fanshawe) *taken down early: dwlt: drvn and struggling in last: t.o and virtually p.u over 1f out* **7/2**[2]

1m 12.12s (-2.28) **Going Correction** -0.325s/f (Firm) **10** Ran SP% **96.7**
Speed ratings (Par 101): **102,100,98,95,95 89,85,84,70,30**
toteswingers 1&2 £11.80, 1&3 £11.10, 2&3 £16.30 CSF £67.61 CT £724.02 TOTE £8.70: £2.30, £3.50, £4.60; EX 74.90 Trifecta £1504.80 Pool: £2055.13 - 1.02 winning tickets..
Owner Mark & Maureen Schofield **Bred** Curlew Partnership **Trained** Sessay, N Yorks

FOCUS
Those who raced on the pace were seen to advantage in what was a moderate sprint. The winner is rated close to his 3-y-o form.

3739 BBC RADIO NORFOLK H'CAP (DIV I) 7f 3y

3:20 (3:22) (Class 6) (0-65,65) 3-Y-O **£1,940** (£577; £288; £144) **Stalls** Centre

Form RPR

4100 **1** **Little Indian**[28] 2802 3-8-6 55.. DannyBrock(5) 2 63
(J R Jenkins) *t.k.h in rr: gd hdwy on outside 2f out: led over 1f out: edgd rt: hld on wl* **25/1**

1552 **2** *1 1/2* **Loucal**[20] 3041 3-9-1 59...(b) StevieDonohoe 7 63
(Noel Quinlan) *trckd ldrs: rdn to dispute ld 2f out: hdd over 1f out: ev ch and edgd lft ins fnl f: no ex fnl 50yds* **2/1**[1]

05-4 **3** *1/2* **Perpetual Ambition**[57] 1931 3-9-7 65..........................(p) FrederikTylicki 1 68+
(Paul D'Arcy) *chsd ldrs: drvn 1/2-way: tried to chal and n.m.r ins fnl f: swtchd lft and no imp after* **9/4**[2]

000- **4** *3 1/2* **Troy Boy**[241] 7441 3-8-2 49.. BillyCray(3) 8 42
(Robin Bastiman) *led: rdn and jnd 2f out: no ex over 1f out* **33/1**

00-5 **5** *nk* **Marju's Quest (IRE)**[14] 3254 3-9-4 62................................ LiamJones 5 57
(David Simcock) *immediately rdn: prom: ev ch 2f out: nt qckn over 1f out* **6/1**[3]

5340 **6** *7* **The Manx Missile**[23] 2962 3-8-13 57................................ LukeMorris 6 30
(Michael Bell) *chsd ldrs tl rdn and wknd over 2f out* **14/1**

03-4 **7** *6* **Clear Loch**[177] 4 3-9-6 64.. NickyMackay 10 21
(John Spearing) *s.i.s and stdd: a bhd: btn over 2f out* **16/1**

3550 **8** *4 1/2* **Red Star Lady (IRE)**[12] 3325 3-8-2 46 oh1...............(v[1]) ShelleyBirkett 9
(Shaun Harris) *prom tl rdn and wknd over 2f out: t.o* **50/1**

4006 **9** *8* **Mr Snooks**[14] 3246 3-8-7 51...(v) TedDurcan 4
(David Nicholls) *chsd ldrs: rdn over 2f out: sn btn: t.o* **16/1**

6212 **10** *43* **Claude Greenwood**[15] 3219 3-8-11 62 ow1..................(b) NedCurtis(7) 3
(Roger Curtis) *stmbld and s.s and hacked rnd in t.o last* **10/1**

1m 26.39s (-0.21) **Going Correction** -0.325s/f (Firm) **10** Ran SP% **114.7**
Speed ratings (Par 97): **88,86,85,81,81 73,66,61,52,3**
toteswingers 1&2 £9.80, 1&3 £12.30, 2&3 £2.10 CSF £73.11 CT £169.19 TOTE £26.00: £4.70, £1.50, £1.40; EX 34.30 Trifecta £537.20 Pool: £3926.57 - 5.48 winning tickets..
Owner Two Little Indians **Bred** D R Tucker **Trained** Royston, Herts
■ Stewards' Enquiry : Danny Brock two-day ban: careless riding (11,15 July)

FOCUS
They raced centre-to-stands' side in this low-grade handicap (time 0.59secs quicker than division two), with the main action unfolding against the rail late on. In contrast to the first two races, the winner came from behind this time. The placed horses are the best guides to the level.

3740 BBC RADIO NORFOLK H'CAP (DIV II) 7f 3y

3:50 (3:56) (Class 6) (0-65,65) 3-Y-O **£1,940** (£577; £288; £144) **Stalls** Centre

Form RPR

6346 **1** **Napinda**[6] 3537 3-8-2 53... NoelGarbutt(7) 5 58
(Philip McBride) *s.i.s and rdn: hdwy over 2f out: led 1f out: hld on gamely* **5/1**[3]

6-65 **2** *1/2* **Sakash**[14] 3253 3-8-6 50... LukeMorris 9 54
(J R Jenkins) *towards rr and racing awkwardly: hdwy and edging lft u.p fnl f: wnt 2nd nr fin but nt quite catch wnr* **7/1**

4560 **3** *1/2* **Triple Aitch (USA)**[5] 3582 3-8-13 62..............................[1] RobertTart(5) 8 64
(Gay Kelleway) *prom: slt ld 2f out tl 1f out: kpt on same pce: lost 2nd fnl strides* **8/1**

-260 **4** *3 1/2* **Tiger's Home**[45] 2331 3-8-6 57..................................... ShelleyBirkett(7) 2 50
(Julia Feilden) *t.k.h: cl up tl wknd 2f out* **25/1**

0-65 **5** *1 1/2* **True Spirit**[152] 396 3-9-7 65..(t) FrederikTylicki 7 54
(Paul D'Arcy) *slt ld for 5f: rdn and wknd over 1f out* **6/1**

0-64 **6** *nk* **Shamiana**[23] 2962 3-9-2 60..[1] HayleyTurner 3 48
(Gerard Butler) *plld hrd: w ldr 5f: rdn and sn btn* **4/1**[2]

-314 **7** *nse* **Next Door (IRE)**[54] 2010 3-9-7 65.................................. FrankieDettori 6 53
(David Barron) *lost gd pl after 2f: rdn and struggling 2f out* **2/1**[1]

5-00 **8** *6* **Grapes Hill**[19] 3116 3-9-0 58... NickyMackay 1 30
(Mark Rimmer) *s.s: a detached in last: no ch fnl 3f* **33/1**

1m 26.98s (0.38) **Going Correction** -0.325s/f (Firm) **8** Ran SP% **114.7**
Speed ratings (Par 97): **84,83,82,78,77 76,76,69**
toteswingers 1&2 £7.80, 1&3 £5.80, 2&3 £7.10 CSF £39.62 CT £278.31 TOTE £5.10: £1.40, £2.50, £2.30; EX 50.80 Trifecta £410.40 Pool: £4070.64 - 7.43 winning tickets..
Owner Peter Wagstaffe **Bred** Stuart McPhee Bloodstock Ltd **Trained** Newmarket, Suffolk

■ Stewards' Enquiry : Luke Morris one-day ban: careless riding (11 July)

FOCUS
Probably the lesser of the two divisions, and the time was 0.59secs slower. The winner is rated as having recorded a slight personal-best but nothing really solid behind.

3741 ASCO UK H'CAP — 7f 3y
4:20 (4:23) (Class 5) (0-75,75) 4-Y-0+ **£2,587** (£770; £384; £192) **Stalls** Centre

Form RPR

00-0 **1** **Fantasy Gladiator**[176] 25 7-8-11 **65**...........................(p) WilliamBuick 6 74
(John Quinn) *mounted on crse: hld up towards rr: urged along and gd run to ld 100yds out: jst hld on* **6/1**

-002 **2** *shd* **Orbit The Moon (IRE)**[5] 3590 5-9-0 **75**................(tp) ConnorBeasley(7) 8 84
(Michael Dods) *led: drvn and hdd 100yds out: kpt on gamely and almost regained advantage* **11/4**[1]

-400 **3** *1 1/4* **Comrade Bond**[33] 2665 5-9-7 **75**.. TedDurcan 2 80
(Mark H Tompkins) *racd far side and w ldr but sn isolated fr bunch: rdn and ev ch 1f out: no ex fnl 100yds* **9/2**[2]

-002 **4** *1/2* **First Class**[23] 2964 5-8-9 **63**.. HayleyTurner 4 67
(Rae Guest) *w ldrs: rdn over 1f out: nt qckn fnl 100yds* **11/2**[3]

-214 **5** *nse* **Secret City (IRE)**[9] 3441 7-9-4 **72**...........................(b) FrederikTylicki 5 76
(Robin Bastiman) *hld up and bhd: rdn 2f out: kpt on ins fnl f: unable to chal* **10/1**

00-0 **6** *3/4* **Evervescent (IRE)**[54] 2028 4-9-6 **74**...............................(p) LiamJones 7 76
(J S Moore) *racd keenly towards rr: drvn oven over 2f out: no rspnse and sn btn* **25/1**

-400 **7** *3/4* **Shamahan**[12] 3322 4-9-6 **74**... GeorgeBaker 3 74
(Gary Moore) *trckd ldrs gng wl: rdn 2f out: little rspnse and sn btn* **13/2**

0060 **8** *hd* **Woolfall Sovereign (IRE)**[15] 3220 7-9-0 **68**..................... LukeMorris 9 67
(George Margarson) *t.k.h: chsd ldrs tl drvn and no ex over 2f out* **20/1**

6145 **9** *3 3/4* **Olney Lass**[34] 2638 6-8-6 **63**.................................... SimonPearce(3) 1 52
(Lydia Pearce) *pressed ldrs tl rdn over 2f out: fading ins fnl f* **16/1**

1m 27.59s (0.99) **Going Correction** -0.325s/f (Firm) **9** Ran SP% **111.4**
Speed ratings (Par 103): **81,80,79,78,78 77,77,76,72**
toteswingers 1&2 £5.50, 1&3 £6.70, 2&3 £3.40 CSF £21.68 CT £78.89 TOTE £5.60: £1.70, £1.90, £1.30; EX 29.30 Trifecta £155.40 Pool: £4208.39 - 20.29 winning tickets..
Owner The Fantasy Fellowship **Bred** R S A Urquhart **Trained** Settrington, N Yorks
■ Stewards' Enquiry : Connor Beasley two-day ban: use of whip (11, 15 July)

FOCUS
A moderate time for the grade and muddling form.

3742 PLEASUREWOOD HILLS THEME PARK FILLIES' H'CAP — 1m 1f
4:50 (4:50) (Class 4) (0-85,80) 4-Y-0+ **£4,690** (£1,395; £697; £348) **Stalls** Low

Form RPR

644- **1** **Tuscania**[182] 8250 5-9-5 **78**... FrederikTylicki 4 86
(Lucy Wadham) *hld up in last: effrt over 2f out: drvn into ld 1f out: sn clr but idling: a gng to hold on* **9/2**

2-04 **2** *1* **Fulney**[17] 3158 4-9-6 **79**.. LukeMorris 3 85
(James Eustace) *t.k.h in 2nd: rdn wl over 1f out: ev ch 150yds out: hld after* **9/4**[2]

6153 **3** *hd* **Nimiety**[7] 3506 4-8-11 **70**.. LiamJones 1 76
(Mark Johnston) *led: drvn over 2f out: hdd 1f out: plugged on same pce ins fnl f* **7/4**[1]

0326 **4** *30* **Four Leaves (IRE)**[17] 3158 4-9-7 **80**...........................(p) FrankieDettori 5
(Marco Botti) *chsd ldr tl drvn over 2f out: fnd nil and sn btn and eased: t.o* **7/2**[3]

1m 55.51s (-0.29) **Going Correction** +0.05s/f (Good) **4** Ran SP% **107.5**
Speed ratings (Par 102): **103,102,101,75**
CSF £14.34 TOTE £8.00; EX 19.00 Trifecta £27.80 Pool: £1470.33 - 39.64 winning tickets..
Owner Mr And Mrs A E Pakenham **Bred** Juddmonte Farms Ltd **Trained** Newmarket, Suffolk

FOCUS
They went a fair gallop, but probably not form to put much faith in. The runner-up is rated to his old form with the third to his previous best.

3743 NELSON MONUMENT MEDIAN AUCTION MAIDEN STKS — 1m 2f 21y
5:20 (5:20) (Class 6) 3-Y-0 **£1,940** (£577; £288) **Stalls** Low

Form RPR

4323 **1** **Seamless**[20] 3059 3-9-5 84.. WilliamBuick 1 71+
(Charles Hills) *t.k.h: mde all: v slow pce: cantered clr w rdr persistently looking rnd fnl f: hrd hld* **1/50**[1]

0000 **2** *8* **Betty Boo (IRE)**[8] 3463 3-8-7 37............................. ConnorBeasley(7) 3 51?
(Shaun Harris) *chsd wnr: drvn over 2f out: completely lft bhd bef f marker* **66/1**[3]

3 *2 1/2* **She's A Honey** 3-8-7 0..[1] ShelleyBirkett(7) 2 46?
(Julia Feilden) *a last: shkn up and lost tch over 4f out: plugged on* **25/1**[2]

2m 13.92s (3.42) **Going Correction** +0.05s/f (Good) **3** Ran SP% **103.4**
Speed ratings (Par 97): **88,81,79**
CSF £3.40 TOTE £1.02; EX 2.90 Trifecta £2.40 Pool: £1229.80 - 375.03 winning tickets..
Owner K Abdullah **Bred** Juddmonte Farms Ltd **Trained** Lambourn, Berks

FOCUS
A race barely worth writing about, with the 1-50 favourite winning as expected.

3744 CONFERENCES AT GREAT YARMOUTH RACECOURSE H'CAP — 1m 6f 17y
5:50 (5:50) (Class 5) (0-70,75) 4-Y-0+ **£2,587** (£770; £384; £192) **Stalls** High

Form RPR

3435 **1** **Mediterranean Sea (IRE)**[44] 2349 7-9-7 **70**................ FrederikTylicki 1 79
(J R Jenkins) *t.k.h in last pair: stdy prog on rails fnl 3f: drvn into ld 1f out: kpt on steadily* **14/1**

4-36 **2** *1 1/4* **Green To Gold (IRE)**[31] 2721 8-9-0 **63**......................(b) HayleyTurner 2 70
(Don Cantillon) *hld up in last pair: effrt gng wl to chal on outer 3f out: rdn and outpcd over 1f out: rallied and styng on wl cl home* **11/2**[3]

3051 **3** *2 1/2* **Wild Desert (FR)**[7] 3512 8-9-12 **75** 6ex.......................... FrankieDettori 6 79
(Tony Carroll) *led: rdn 2f out: hdd 1f out: sn btn: lost 2nd ins fnl f* **4/5**[1]

0-03 **4** *4 1/2* **Eanans Bay (IRE)**[14] 3256 4-7-13 **51** oh6...............(b) SimonPearce(3) 3 48
(Mark H Tompkins) *disp 2nd: rdn over 2f out: btn wl over 1f out* **14/1**

506 **5** *30* **Reach The Beach**[61] 1837 4-8-3 **52**.................................(t) LukeMorris 5
(Brendan Powell) *racd keenly: disp 2nd tl rdn over 4f out: sn dropped out: t.o and eased wl over 1f out* **11/4**[2]

3m 6.64s (-0.96) **Going Correction** +0.05s/f (Good) **5** Ran SP% **110.9**
Speed ratings (Par 103): **104,103,101,99,82**
CSF £81.35 TOTE £10.40: £4.40, £1.90; EX 33.10 Trifecta £98.50 Pool: £1727.20 - 13.14 winning tickets..
Owner Mrs Wendy Jenkins **Bred** D H W Dobson **Trained** Royston, Herts

FOCUS
This was run at no more than a fair gallop and the form looks moderate. The fourth offers perspective despite being 6lb out of the handicap.
T/Plt: £977.40 to a £1 stake. Pool: £59,879.42 - 44.72 winning tickets. T/Qpdt: £44.20 to a £1 stake. Pool: £6786.90 - 113.55 winning tickets. IM

3745 - 3751a (Foreign Racing) - See Raceform Interactive

[922]DEAUVILLE (R-H)
Thursday, June 27

OFFICIAL GOING: Turf: good; fibresand: standard

3752a PRIX YACOWLEF (LISTED RACE) (UNRACED 2YO) (TURF) — 5f
3:40 (12:00) 2-Y-0 **£22,357** (£8,943; £6,707; £4,471; £2,235)

RPR

1 **Make It Reel (FR)** 2-9-2 0... ThierryThulliez 5 98
(P Bary, France) **137/10**

2 *1/2* **Stormyra (FR)** 2-8-13 0... ThierryJarnet 2 93
(J-P Gallorini, France) **78/10**

3 *snk* **Royale Du Buisson (IRE)** 2-8-13 0............................. OlivierPeslier 3 93
(F Head, France) **39/10**[3]

4 *1 1/2* **Oxanueva (FR)** 2-8-13 0... MaximeGuyon 4 87
(H-A Pantall, France) **73/10**

5 *nse* **Angel Spirit (IRE)** 2-8-13 0....................................... AntoineHamelin 6 87
(Matthieu Palussiere, France) **12/1**

6 *snk* **Complicit (IRE)** 2-9-2 0...................................... ChristopheSoumillon 7 90
(Paul Cole) *settled towards rr: hdwy on outside 1 1/2f out: cl 6th and rdn appr fnl f: no further imp and eased cl home* **2/1**[1]

7 *10* **Yankee Red** 2-9-2 0... Pierre-CharlesBoudot 8 54
(John Best) *prom on outside: 3rd and shkn up 2f out but unable qck: grad lost tch fr 1 1/2f out: eased ins fnl f* **17/1**

8 *3/4* **Fairwater (USA)** 2-8-13 0.. StephanePasquier 1 48
(Mme C Head-Maarek, France) **19/5**[2]

59.01s (1.51) **8** Ran SP% **118.0**
WIN (incl. 1 euro stake): 14.70. PLACES: 3.40, 2.60, 2.30. DF: 9.60. SF: 84.80.
Owner Mlle Emmeline De Waldner **Bred** Earl Haras Du Logis & J Ince **Trained** Chantilly, France

[3092]CHESTER (L-H)
Friday, June 28

OFFICIAL GOING: Good changing to good to soft after race 1 (6:15)
Wind: moderate 1/2 against Weather: overcast, frequent showers

3753 LIVERPOOL ONE MAIDEN FILLIES' STKS — 7f 2y
6:15 (6:16) (Class 4) 2-Y-0 **£6,469** (£1,925; £962; £481) **Stalls** Low

Form RPR

304 **1** **Heskin (IRE)**[27] 2856 2-9-0 0... TonyHamilton 1 70
(Richard Fahey) *trckd ldrs: drvn and outpcd over 2f out: hdwy on ins whn nt clr run and swtchd 3 wd jst ins fnl f: r.o to ld post* **5/2**[2]

53 **2** *shd* **Royal Connection**[14] 3275 2-9-0 0...................................... SeanLevey 4 70
(Richard Hannon) *t.k.h: led after 1f: drvn 3 l clr over 1f out: hdd post* **2/1**[1]

033 **3** *1/2* **Mimi Luke (USA)**[52] 2131 2-9-0 0................................. JimmyFortune 2 68
(Alan Bailey) *led 1f: chsd ldr: rdn and edgd lft 1f out: kpt on towards fin* **9/1**

4 *4 1/2* **Charlotte's Day** 2-9-0 0.. LukeMorris 6 57+
(Sir Mark Prescott Bt) *s.i.s: green and outpcd: hdwy 3f out: kpt on over 1f out: will improve* **15/2**

0634 **5** *5* **Dancing Sal (IRE)**[34] 2645 2-8-9 0.............................. DeclanBates(5) 9 44
(David Evans) *sn chsng ldrs: drvn 3f out: wknd over 1f out* **25/1**

0 **6** *2 1/4* **Hija**[16] 3211 2-8-7 0.. RyanWhile(7) 8 38
(Bill Turner) *mid-div: outpcd 3f out: wknd over 1f out* **66/1**

7 *7* **Dry Your Eyes (IRE)** 2-9-0 0.. SamHitchcott 5 20+
(Mark Johnston) *sn drvn along: sn chsng ldrs: hanging rt: wkng whn wd bnd and lost pl over 2f out* **7/2**[3]

8 *4 1/2* **Flower Arranger (IRE)** 2-8-9 0.................. WilliamTwiston-Davies(5) 7 8
(David Evans) *s.i.s: a outpcd and in rr: bhd fnl 3f* **22/1**

1m 31.94s (5.44) **Going Correction** +0.45s/f (Yiel) **8** Ran SP% **115.6**
Speed ratings (Par 92): **86,85,85,80,74 71,63,58**
toteswingers 1&2 £2.30, 1&3 £3.80, 2&3 £3.40 CSF £7.88 TOTE £3.70: £3.00, £1.30, £3.20; EX 8.40 Trifecta £38.00 Pool: £2023.48 - 39.87 winning tickets..
Owner David W Armstrong **Bred** Carpet Lady Partnership **Trained** Musley Bank, N Yorks

FOCUS
Course at inner configuration and all distances as advertised. A modest fillies' maiden with the winner rated to her mark.

3754 WREXHAM LAGER CLAIMING STKS — 7f 122y
6:50 (6:50) (Class 4) 4-Y-0+ **£6,469** (£1,925; £962; £481) **Stalls** Low

Form RPR

6000 **1** **Marcret (ITY)**[13] 3335 6-9-7 94.. TonyHamilton 5 103
(David Nicholls) *drvn: swtchd lft after s to ld: mde all: drvn 3 l clr over 1f out: unchal* **9/1**

6251 **2** *7* **Clockmaker (IRE)**[13] 3335 7-9-3 92.................................... SeanLevey 2 82
(Tim Easterby) *chsd wnr after 1f: drvn 3f out: kpt on: no imp* **13/8**[1]

1050 **3** *4 1/2* **Toto Skyllachy**[9] 3458 8-8-11 97................... WilliamTwiston-Davies(5) 1 69
(David O'Meara) *dwlt: hdwy to chse ldrs over 4f out: drvn 3f out: kpt on to take 3rd last 100yds* **9/4**[2]

2120 **4** *1 3/4* **Polar Kite (IRE)**[35] 2618 5-8-9 84................................ ThomasBrown(5) 6 63
(Sean Curran) *dwlt: hld up towards rr: hdwy over 2f out: kpt on to take 4th last 100yds* **4/1**[3]

0010 **5** *3* **Elusive Hawk (IRE)**[20] 3093 9-8-6 78...........................(v) DeclanBates(5) 7 52
(David Evans) *sn chsng ldrs: 3rd over 4f out: drvn 3f out: wknd last 150yds* **25/1**

0530 **6** *28* **Minty Jones**[14] 3268 4-8-8 45 ow2.....................................(v) RyanClark(3) 8
(Michael Mullineaux) *t.k.h in rr: wd bnd over 5f out: hung rt and bhd fnl 3f: t.o 2f out* **100/1**

0000 **7** *2 3/4* **Olynard (IRE)**[2] 3687 7-8-2 46.......................................(p) NoraLooby(7) 3
(Michael Mullineaux) *chsd ldrs: drvn and lost pl over 4f: sn bhd: t.o 2f out* **100/1**

000- **8** *7* **King Torus (IRE)**[310] 5492 5-9-7 95.............................. JimmyFortune 4 32
(Jamie Osborne) *mid-div: drvn 3f out: wknd 1f out: modest 6th whn heavily eased: virtually p.u: t.o* **12/1**

1m 36.09s (2.29) **Going Correction** +0.50s/f (Yiel) **8** Ran SP% **112.4**
Speed ratings (Par 105): **108,101,96,94,91 63,61,54**
toteswingers 1&2 £3.10, 1&3 £6.70, 2&3 £1.20 CSF £23.33 TOTE £11.90: £4.00, £1.10, £2.20; EX 20.10 Trifecta £85.80 Pool: £1550.41 - 13.54 winning tickets..Clockmaker was claimed by Mr C. R. Dore for £22,000. Marcret was claimed by Mr Mark Brisbourne for £30,000.
Owner Dr Marwan Koukash **Bred** Az Ag Antezzate Srl **Trained** Sessay, N Yorks

The Form Book Flat, Raceform Ltd, Compton, RG20 6NL.

FOCUS
The going was changed to good to soft after the first. A very strong race of its type and the winner is rated not far off his best form, having got an uncontested lead.

3755 BRITISH STALLION STUDS EBF FILLIES' H'CAP — 1m 2f 75y
7:25 (7:25) (Class 3) (0-90,88) 3-Y-0+ **£9,703** (£2,887; £1,443; £721) **Stalls** High

Form — RPR
5635 **1** **Lady Macduff (IRE)**[6] 3567 4-8-13 **72** FrannyNorton 1 78
(Mark Johnston) *mde all: qcknd pce over 2f out: drvn and styd on: unchal* **9/1**
-121 **2** *1 1/4* **Danat Al Atheer**[3] 3666 3-9-3 **88** 6ex (b) JimmyFortune 5 92+
(William Haggas) *swtchd lft after s: hld up in last: effrt and plld outside over 1f out: styd on to take 2nd fnl strides* **5/4**[1]
-040 **3** *hd* **Bridle Belle**[11] 3409 5-10-0 **87** TonyHamilton 2 90
(Richard Fahey) *chsd ldrs: kpt on same pce over 1f out* **9/2**[3]
6-23 **4** *nk* **Miss Cap Estel**[5] 3610 4-9-4 **82** ThomasBrown[(5)] 6 85
(Andrew Balding) *hld up: trckd ldrs 6f out: effrt and chsd wnr over 1f out: kpt on same pce* **85/40**[2]
2530 **5** *11* **Dazzling Valentine**[4] 3635 5-8-7 **71** oh2 NatashaEaton[(5)] 3 53
(Alan Bailey) *sn trcking wnr: t.k.h: lost pl over 1f out: bhd whn eased towards fin* **20/1**

2m 17.75s (6.55) **Going Correction** +0.55s/f (Yiel)
WFA 3 from 4yo+ 12lb — 5 Ran SP% **109.4**
Speed ratings (Par 104): **95,94,93,93,84**
CSF £20.74 TOTE £7.50: £3.00, £1.60; EX 22.20 Trifecta £57.80 Pool: £969.05 - 12.56 winning tickets..
Owner Sheikh Hamdan Bin Mohammed Al Maktoum **Bred** Mrs E Thompson **Trained** Middleham Moor, N Yorks

FOCUS
A fair fillies' handicap, run at an uneven pace and the winner made all. She is rated to this year's form while the third is rated close to her best mark at the trip.

3756 CHESTER STANDARD H'CAP — 1m 2f 75y
7:55 (7:55) (Class 4) (0-80,79) 3-Y-0 **£6,469** (£1,925; £962; £481) **Stalls** High

Form — RPR
0-12 **1** **Broughton (GER)**[8] 3502 3-9-7 **79** FrannyNorton 5 91+
(Mark Johnston) *swtchd lft after s: in rr: nt clr run on inner 2f out: sn swtchd rt: r.o wl to ld last 100yds: readily* **6/4**[1]
-125 **2** *1 3/4* **Endorsing (IRE)**[12] 3369 3-9-6 **78** SeanLevey 6 84
(Richard Hannon) *hld up in mid-div: hdwy over 2f out: led 1f out: sn hdd and no ex* **9/2**[2]
-130 **3** *3 1/4* **Wyldfire (IRE)**[42] 2432 3-8-13 **71** TonyHamilton 2 71
(Richard Fahey) *trckd ldrs: t.k.h: effrt over 2f out: kpt on same pce to take 3rd clsng stages* **6/1**
1144 **4** *1 3/4* **Gabrial's Wawa**[34] 2651 3-9-1 **78** GeorgeChaloner[(3)] 3 74
(Richard Fahey) *trckd ldrs: led over 1f out: sn hdd: fdd last 50yds* **11/2**[3]
1303 **5** *1 3/4* **Enzaal (USA)**[20] 3105 3-9-7 **79** SamHitchcott 1 72
(Mark Johnston) *led: hdd over 1f out: wknd last 150yds* **14/1**
2102 **6** *1/2* **Gabrial The Duke (IRE)**[8] 3497 3-8-4 **65** DarrenEgan[(3)] 8 57
(David Simcock) *sn chsng ldrs: drvn over 2f out: one pce* **13/2**
-604 **7** *18* **Mandy The Nag (USA)**[19] 3137 3-8-7 **65** LukeMorris 4 23
(Ian Williams) *toward rr: sn pushed along: drvn over 4f out: lost pl over 2f out: eased whn bhd* **16/1**

2m 18.1s (6.90) **Going Correction** +0.60s/f (Yiel) — 7 Ran SP% **113.7**
Speed ratings (Par 101): **96,94,92,90,89 88,74**
toteswingers 1&2 £3.10, 1&3 £2.10, 2&3 £6.00 CSF £8.34 CT £30.48 TOTE £1.70: £1.10, £1.20; EX 8.90 Trifecta £42.10 Pool: £619.54 - 11.03 winning tickets..
Owner Sheikh Hamdan Bin Mohammed Al Maktoum **Bred** Gestut Westerberg **Trained** Middleham Moor, N Yorks

FOCUS
Not a bad handicap rated around the pklaced horses, with the winner one to keep on-side.

3757 IG H'CAP — 7f 2y
8:25 (8:25) (Class 4) (0-85,85) 4-Y-0+ **£6,469** (£1,925; £962; £481) **Stalls** Low

Form — RPR
2120 **1** **Snow Bay**[27] 2882 7-9-0 **83** ShirleyTeasdale[(5)] 1 92
(Paul Midgley) *mde all: qcknd pce over 2f out: hrd rdn and hld on wl nr fin* **6/1**
2256 **2** *nk* **Kingscroft (IRE)**[13] 3335 5-9-4 **82** FrannyNorton 2 90
(Mark Johnston) *chsd ldrs: effrt 2f out: styd on to take 2nd over 1f out: chal ins fnl f: no ex nr fin* **7/2**[2]
6-61 **3** *1* **Magic City (IRE)**[35] 2618 4-9-2 **85** WilliamTwiston-Davies[(5)] 3 90
(Richard Hannon) *hld up in mid-div: hdwy over 2f out: kpt on to take 3rd last 50yds* **3/1**[1]
0020 **4** *1 1/2* **Alejandro (IRE)**[20] 3096 4-9-4 **82** (p) TonyHamilton 7 83
(Richard Fahey) *trckd wnr: kpt on same pce over 1f out* **16/1**
313 **5** *1/2* **Gabrial's Gift (IRE)**[13] 3322 4-8-5 **72** DarrenEgan[(3)] 5 72+
(David Simcock) *mid-div on outer: hdwy 3f out: sn drvn: kpt on ins fnl f* **4/1**[3]
0040 **6** *3 1/2* **Verse Of Love**[20] 3096 4-8-13 **82** DeclanBates[(5)] 4 72
(David Evans) *s.s: in rr: effrt on ins whn rdr dropped whip 2f out: wknd fnl f* **11/1**
3310 **7** *2 3/4* **Restaurateur (IRE)**[2] 3684 4-9-5 **83** (v) JimmyFortune 10 66
(Andrew Balding) *in rr: drvn 3f out: sme hdwy over 1f out: sn wknd* **11/1**
00-6 **8** *21* **Red Art (IRE)**[11] 3411 4-9-6 **84** SteveDrowne 9
(Charles Hills) *chsd ldrs: drvn over 3f out: lost pl 2f out: sn eased and bhd: t.o* **11/1**

1m 30.06s (3.56) **Going Correction** +0.65s/f (Yiel) — 8 Ran SP% **112.4**
Speed ratings (Par 105): **105,104,103,101,101 97,94,70**
toteswingers 1&2 £8.30, 1&3 £4.60, 2&3 £5.00 CSF £26.31 TOTE £9.50: £3.30, £1.50, £1.30; EX 26.80 Trifecta £100.30 Pool: £591.66 - 4.42 winning tickets..
Owner Snow Bay Partnership **Bred** West Dereham Abbey Stud **Trained** Westow, N Yorks
■ Stewards' Enquiry : Shirley Teasdale twenty-one day ban (seven days deferred for six weeks until 15 Sep 2013); used whip above permitted level (fifth offence since 10th Feb) (Jul 19-Jul 23, Jul 26-Aug 3)

FOCUS
A competitive handicap with the winner rated as having recorded his best effort since 2011 and the runner-up to his recent best.

3758 LIVERPOOL ONE BEST DRESSED LADY H'CAP — 7f 122y
9:00 (9:01) (Class 4) (0-80,80) 3-Y-0 **£6,469** (£1,925; £962; £481) **Stalls** Low

Form — RPR
-623 **1** **Mystical Man**[21] 3067 3-9-7 **80** LukeMorris 7 89
(James Tate) *edgd lft after s: mde all: drvn 4 l clr over 1f out: styd on: unchal* **6/1**[2]
2240 **2** *4* **Lightning Launch (IRE)**[15] 3234 3-8-12 **78** DanielCremin[(7)] 2 77
(Mick Channon) *trckd ldrs: 2nd over 1f out: kpt on: no imp* **8/1**
-323 **3** *3* **Majestic Moon (IRE)**[15] 3234 3-9-7 **80** TonyHamilton 1 72
(Richard Fahey) *dwlt: hld up towards rr: t.k.h: effrt and nt clr run 2f out: plld wd: kpt on ins fnl f: tk 3rd post* **11/8**[1]
5103 **4** *shd* **Baltic Prince (IRE)**[2] 3683 3-8-3 **65** RaulDaSilva[(3)] 8 56
(Paul Green) *chsd wnr: one pce over 1f out* **13/2**[3]
1040 **5** *1/2* **World Record (IRE)**[2] 3683 3-8-13 **75** DarrenEgan[(3)] 4 65
(Paul Green) *chsd ldrs: drvn 3f out: kpt on fnl f* **11/1**
6250 **6** *3 1/2* **Gabrial The Boss (USA)**[31] 2763 3-8-11 **70** FrannyNorton 5 51
(David Simcock) *hld up in rr: drvn over 3f out: kpt on fnl 2f: nvr a factor* **18/1**
-5S0 **7** *nk* **Elle Rebelle**[11] 3396 3-8-7 **66** PaulQuinn 6 47
(Mark Brisbourne) *s.i.s: in rr: kpt on over 1f out: nvr a factor* **20/1**
5323 **8** *1* **Clary (IRE)**[16] 3216 3-8-0 **66** OisinMurphy[(7)] 10 44
(James Unett) *wnt rt s: in rr: hdwy on outside over 3f out: one pce* **14/1**
1-06 **9** *15* **Red Cobra (IRE)**[22] 3025 3-8-7 **66** SteveDrowne 3 30
(Tim Easterby) *trckd ldrs: t.k.h: lost pl over 1f out: eased whn bhd* **16/1**

1m 38.7s (4.90) **Going Correction** +0.70s/f (Yiel) — 9 Ran SP% **111.7**
Speed ratings (Par 101): **103,99,96,95,95 91,91,90,75**
toteswingers 1&2 £6.70, 1&3 £1.80, 2&3 £2.90 CSF £50.62 TOTE £7.60: £1.90, £1.90, £1.50; EX 56.10 Trifecta £125.40 Pool: £939.15 - 5.61 winning tickets..
Owner Saeed Manana **Bred** Lady Hardy **Trained** Newmarket, Suffolk

FOCUS
This looked competitive, but it was yet another race on the night that produced a front-running winner. He recorded a personal-best while the second ran better with the headgear removed.
T/Plt: £3.20 to a £1 stake. Pool: £78772.98 - 17904.53 winning tickets T/Qpdt: £2.20 to a £1 stake. Pool: £4766.44 - 1553.70 winning tickets WG

3363 DONCASTER (L-H)
Friday, June 28

OFFICIAL GOING: Good to firm changing to good after race 3 (3:00)
Wind: Wind light, half behind Weather: Cloudy, rain after race 2 until 5th

3759 COMMUNICATION WORKERS UNION HUMANITARIAN AID MAIDEN STKS — 6f
2:00 (2:01) (Class 5) 3-Y-0+ **£2,587** (£770; £384; £192) **Stalls** Low

Form — RPR
44-2 **1** **Cape Of Hope (IRE)**[15] 3253 3-9-5 70 RichardHughes 2 77
(Peter Chapple-Hyam) *led: rdn whn hdd over 1f out: drvn ins fnl f: rallied to ld again towards fin* **15/8**[2]
5 **2** *nk* **Lulu The Zulu (IRE)**[16] 3191 5-9-7 0 AndrewMullen 1 72
(Michael Appleby) *trckd ldr: rdn over 2f out: led narrowly over 1f out: one pce: hdd towards fin* **25/1**
2 **3** *7* **Hi Filwah (USA)**[20] 3109 3-9-5 0 WilliamBuick 5 55
(Jeremy Noseda) *s.i.s: hld up: rdn over 2f out: wnt 3rd over 1f out: no threat to ldng pair* **7/4**[1]
4 *1/2* **Princess Loulou (IRE)** 3-9-0 0 AndreaAtzeni 4 49
(Roger Varian) *in tch: rdn and outpcd by ldng pair over 2f out: no threat after* **9/4**[3]
0 **5** *7* **Manatee Bay**[9] 3479 3-9-5 0 PaulMulrennan 3 33
(David Nicholls) *hld up in tch: pushed along over 2f out: wknd over 1f out* **40/1**
- **6** *32* **Rosy Ryan (IRE)** 3-9-0 0 BarryMcHugh 6
(Tina Jackson) *s.i.s: hld up: bhd 1/2-way* **100/1**

1m 12.27s (-1.33) **Going Correction** -0.125s/f (Firm)
WFA 3 from 5yo 7lb — 6 Ran SP% **109.2**
Speed ratings (Par 103): **103,102,93,92,83 40**
toteswingers 1&2 £2.20, 1&3 £1.10, 2&3 £2.10 CSF £33.71 TOTE £3.10: £1.90, £4.40; EX 23.10 Trifecta £45.70 Pool: £2484.31 - 40.70 winning tickets..
Owner Eledy Srl **Bred** Pendley Farm **Trained** Newmarket, Suffolk

FOCUS
Rail on round course was moved out from 1m2f to start of home straight. With two of the three market principals proving disappointing, this might not be very strong maiden form. The winner is rated to his mark.

3760 EBF CWU LEGAL SERVICES MAIDEN FILLIES' STKS — 6f
2:30 (2:35) (Class 5) 2-Y-0 **£2,911** (£866; £432; £216) **Stalls** Low

Form — RPR
6 **1** **Mahlah (IRE)**[21] 3049 2-9-0 0 DaneO'Neill 14 80+
(Richard Hannon) *mde all: rdn over 1f out: kpt on wl* **20/1**
5 **2** *1 3/4* **Musicora**[27] 2856 2-9-0 0 RichardHughes 1 75
(Richard Hannon) *in tch: rdn over 2f out: wnt 2nd ins fnl f: kpt on but a hld by wnr* **9/2**[3]
5 **3** *3/4* **Inyordreams**[14] 3295 2-9-0 0 DaleSwift 2 73
(James Given) *chsd ldr: rdn over 2f out: kpt on one pce* **15/2**
4 *3/4* **Lady Tiana** 2-9-0 0 LukeMorris 12 71
(Lucy Wadham) *dwlt: hld up in midfield: rdn and hdwy over 1f out: kpt on fnl f* **33/1**
5 *1/2* **Ivy Trump** 2-9-0 0 AndrewMullen 15 69
(Michael Appleby) *chsd ldr: rdn over 2f out: outpcd by wnr over 1f out: plugged on fnl f* **66/1**
6 *shd* **Merletta** 2-9-0 0 WilliamBuick 9 69+
(Jeremy Noseda) *dwlt: hld up: pushed along over 2f out: hdwy over 1f out: kpt on: nrst fin* **4/1**[2]
7 *1 1/4* **Western Sands (IRE)** 2-9-0 0 BarryMcHugh 11 65
(Richard Fahey) *hld up: pushed along 1/2-way: kpt on fnl f: nvr threatened* **50/1**
33 **8** *2* **Misty Sparkler**[30] 2774 2-9-0 0 FrankieDettori 5 59
(Brian Meehan) *chsd ldr: rdn over 2f out: sn lost pl: wknd over 1f out* **10/1**
9 *nk* **Savanna Spring (IRE)** 2-9-0 0 MartinDwyer 6 58
(Alan Jarvis) *s.i.s: hld up: pushed along 1/2-way: nvr threatened* **50/1**
4 **10** *nk* **Talent Spotter**[21] 3049 2-9-0 0 MickaelBarzalona 10 57
(Saeed bin Suroor) *in tch: rdn 1/2-way: wknd over 1f out* **3/1**[1]
11 *1/2* **Bruni Heinke (IRE)** 2-9-0 0 TonyHamilton 13 56
(Richard Fahey) *trckd ldr: dropped to midfield 1/2-way: wknd over 1f out* **15/2**
0 **12** *1 1/4* **Danzig In The Dark (IRE)**[13] 3350 2-9-0 0 DuranFentiman 7 52
(Tim Easterby) *hld up: a towards rr* **100/1**
13 *39* **River Goddess (IRE)** 2-9-0 0 JamesMcDonald 3
(Charles Hills) *dwlt: hld up: bhd over 2f out: eased* **40/1**

6 P **Francisca**[21] 3064 2-9-0 0 .... TomQueally 4
(James Given) *midfield: rdn over 2f out: wnt wrong over 1f out: p.u* **50/1**

1m 14.39s (0.79) **Going Correction** -0.125s/f (Firm) **14** Ran SP% **114.3**
Speed ratings (Par 90): **89,86,85,84,84 83,82,79,79,78 78,76,24,**
toteswingers 1&2 £12.40, 1&3 £16.80, 2&3 £5.70 CSF £94.37 TOTE £20.20: £5.00, £1.80, £1.90; EX 91.30 Trifecta £935.70 Pool: £3206.43 - 2.57 winning tickets..

Owner Saleh Al Homaizi & Imad Al Sagar **Bred** Rathbarry Stud **Trained** East Everleigh, Wilts

FOCUS
This is traditionally quite a strong maiden and there looked to be a host of interesting runners coming into it, but very few got into the race itself. The winner cost plenty and looks a fair prospect.

3761 SIMPSON MILLAR LEGAL SERVICES NOVICE STKS 7f
3:00 (3:02) (Class 4) 2-Y-O £3,752 (£1,116; £557; £278) **Stalls** Low

Form				RPR
012	1		**Malachim Mist (IRE)**[38] 2553 2-9-5 0 .... RichardHughes 4 (Richard Hannon) *trckd ldr: pushed along to press ldr 2f out: rdn over 1f out: led ins fnl f: sn drvn: edgd lft: kpt on* **1/3**[1]	86
100	2	1	**Lady Frances**[44] 2370 2-9-0 0 .... FrannyNorton 3 (Mark Johnston) *sn led: rdn 2f out: hdd ins fnl f: one pce and a hld by wnr* **10/1**[3]	78
1	3	1 ¾	**One Penny Piece**[15] 3255 2-8-9 0 .... WilliamBuick 1 (Philip McBride) *trckd ldr: pushed along over 2f out: rdn and one pce in 3rd fr over 1f out* **7/2**[2]	69
35	4	½	**Irondale Express**[6] 3588 2-8-9 0 .... BarryMcHugh 2 (Tony Coyle) *in tch in 4th: rdn 2f out: one pce and nvr threatened* **40/1**	67

1m 28.52s (2.22) **Going Correction** +0.30s/f (Good) **4** Ran SP% **108.8**
Speed ratings (Par 95): **99,97,95,95**
CSF £4.53 TOTE £1.30; EX 3.70 Trifecta £6.40 Pool: £3292.97 - 380.93 winning tickets..

Owner Michael Daniels **Bred** Guy O'Callaghan **Trained** East Everleigh, Wilts

FOCUS
A fair novice stakes and the winner was far from impressive. The second and third are rated close to their debut marks.

3762 GMB - BRITAIN'S GENERAL UNION H'CAP 6f
3:35 (3:36) (Class 5) (0-70,69) 3-Y-O £2,587 (£770; £384; £192) **Stalls** Low

Form				RPR
06-1	1		**Jubilee Dancer**[32] 2719 3-9-2 **64** .... PaulMulrennan 9 (Geoffrey Oldroyd) *mde all: rdn over 1f out: kpt on wl* **7/2**[2]	73+
5123	2	1 ¾	**Royal Guinevere**[35] 2623 3-9-5 **67** .... RichardHughes 8 (Dean Ivory) *hld up: rdn over 1f out: kpt on: wnt 2nd fnl 75yds: no threat wnr* **9/4**[1]	70
-450	3	1	**Whatwehavewehold**[10] 3446 3-8-10 **58** .... AndrewMullen 5 (Alan McCabe) *hld up: rdn and hdwy over 1f out: kpt on: wnt 3rd towards fin* **50/1**	58
11-4	4	½	**Hardy Blue (IRE)**[22] 3025 3-9-7 **69** .... TomQueally 6 (Danielle McCormick) *prom: rdn and ev ch over 1f out: wknd and lost 2 pls fnl 100yds* **7/1**	67
0433	5	¾	**Deepest Blue**[5] 3611 3-8-12 **67** .... LukeLeadbitter(7) 4 (Declan Carroll) *slowly away: racd keenly and sn in tch: rdn and ev ch over 1f out: wknd ins fnl f* **11/2**[3]	63
5201	6	1 ½	**Charlemagne Diva**[22] 3025 3-8-12 **60** .... RobbieFitzpatrick 10 (Richard Guest) *slowly away: hld up: rdn over 2f out: nvr threatened* **11/1**	51
0-34	7	1 ½	**Secret Empress**[38] 2556 3-8-5 **53** .... MartinDwyer 7 (Bryan Smart) *hld up: rdn over 2f out: nvr threatened* **14/1**	39
300-	8	½	**Ryedale Valley**[280] 6451 3-8-4 **52** .... DuranFentiman 3 (Tim Easterby) *prom towards far side: wknd over 1f out* **20/1**	37+
00-0	9	nk	**Starbotton**[14] 3281 3-9-0 **62** .... MickaelBarzalona 2 (James Bethell) *chsd ldrs towards far side: wknd over 1f out* **14/1**	46
5000	10	17	**Gold Roll (IRE)**[14] 3281 3-8-2 **50** oh1 .... (b[1]) PatrickMathers 1 (Ruth Carr) *chsd ldrs towards far side: pushed along 1/2-way: bhd fnl 2f* **12/1**	

1m 15.5s (1.90) **Going Correction** +0.30s/f (Good) **10** Ran SP% **117.0**
Speed ratings (Par 99): **99,96,95,94,93 91,89,89,88,65**
toteswingers 1&2 £2.70, 1&3 £24.30, 2&3 £18.60 CSF £11.81 CT £330.09 TOTE £4.80: £2.00, £1.10, £8.60; EX 15.10 Trifecta £519.10 Pool: £5155.02 - 7.44 winning tickets..

Owner Moneypenny Racing **Bred** Bond Thoroughbred Corporation **Trained** Brawby, N Yorks

FOCUS
A competitive race on paper, but it proved difficult for horses to make any telling impact from off the pace. The second is rated to form with the third and fourth close to their juvenile level.

3763 PRESERVE ACCESS TO JUSTICE H'CAP 1m (R)
4:10 (4:11) (Class 3) (0-95,91) 3-Y-O £7,439 (£2,213; £1,106; £553) **Stalls** Low

Form				RPR
2102	1		**Intrigo**[28] 2844 3-9-4 **88** .... RichardHughes 4 (Richard Hannon) *midfield: pushed along and hdwy over 1f out: qcknd to ld fnl 75yds: shade cosily* **5/2**[1]	98+
0-40	2	1	**Makafeh**[27] 2862 3-9-4 **88** .... JamesDoyle 5 (Luca Cumani) *hld up: hdwy over 2f out: rdn to ld appr fnl f: edgd rt: kpt on: hdd fnl 75yds* **13/2**[3]	96
121-	3	3 ¼	**Muharrib (IRE)**[230] 7687 3-9-7 **91** .... MickaelBarzalona 8 (Saeed bin Suroor) *dwlt: hld up: rdn and hdwy over 1f out: one pce fnl f* **13/2**[3]	91+
2-45	4	nk	**Swift Bounty**[36] 2584 3-8-8 **78** .... MartinDwyer 1 (Alan Jarvis) *hld up in rr: pushed along and hdwy over 2f out: rdn over 1f out: edgd rt fnl 100yds: kpt on* **15/2**	78
5-12	5	2 ¼	**Al Mukhdam**[48] 2259 3-9-2 **86** .... PaulMulrennan 6 (Peter Chapple-Hyam) *led: rdn over 2f out: hdd over 1f out: grad wknd* **4/1**[2]	80
5222	6	2	**Party Royal**[6] 3563 3-8-11 **81** .... J-PGuillambert 3 (Mark Johnston) *trckd ldr: rdn over 2f out: led wl over 1f out: sn hdd: no ex whn sltly hmpd fnl 100yds: eased* **9/1**	73
2-06	7	5	**Mutazamen**[22] 3020 3-9-3 **87** .... SteveDrowne 9 (Richard Hannon) *prom tl wknd over 2f out* **22/1**	65
1-22	8	11	**Jodies Jem**[36] 2603 3-9-3 **87** .... WilliamBuick 2 (William Jarvis) *midfield: rdn over 3f out: sn wknd* **13/2**[3]	40

1m 39.41s (-0.29) **Going Correction** +0.05s/f (Good) **8** Ran SP% **114.7**
Speed ratings (Par 103): **103,102,98,98,96 94,89,78**
toteswingers 1&2 £5.10, 1&3 £3.70, 2&3 £9.30 CSF £19.27 CT £93.79 TOTE £2.90: £2.20, £1.90, £2.10; EX 23.20 Trifecta £109.50 Pool: £5527.33 - 37.85 winning tickets..

Owner Gillian, Lady Howard De Walden **Bred** Gillian Lady Howard De Walden **Trained** East Everleigh, Wilts

FOCUS
A competitive race on paper. The winner looks progressive with the second generally solid.

3764 EBF TRADE UNION CONGRESS MAIDEN FILLIES' STKS 1m 2f 60y
4:45 (4:46) (Class 5) 3-Y-O+ £3,881 (£1,155; £577; £288) **Stalls** Low

Form				RPR
0-0	1		**Missed Call (IRE)**[24] 2953 3-8-12 0 .... TomQueally 7 (Lady Cecil) *hld up: smooth hdwy fr 3f out: rdn appr fnl f: led ins fnl f: kpt on* **16/1**	84+
6-4	2	1	**Soryah (IRE)**[23] 2979 3-8-12 0 .... RichardHughes 10 (Luca Cumani) *in tch: hdwy to trck ldr 3f out: rdn over 1f out: kpt on* **3/1**[1]	82+
5-4	3	1	**Familliarity**[23] 2989 3-8-12 0 .... PatCosgrave 1 (Roger Varian) *led: rdn over 1f out: hdd ins fnl f: no ex* **9/2**[3]	80
5	4	3 ½	**Pernica**[24] 2952 3-8-12 0 .... JohnFahy 6 (Lucy Wadham) *trckd ldr: rdn over 2f out: ev ch over 1f out: no ex fnl f* **11/2**	74
	5	½	**Palkin** 3-8-12 0 .... FrankieDettori 11 (William Haggas) *dwlt: midfield: pushed along over 2f out: kpt on fnl f* **6/1**	73
00	6	nk	**Sureness (IRE)**[29] 2803 3-8-12 0 .... PaoloSirigu 2 (Marco Botti) *trckd ldr: rdn over 2f out: sn one pce* **33/1**	72
	7	6	**Filia Regina** 3-8-12 0 .... JamesDoyle 5 (Ed Dunlop) *slowly away: hld up: pushed along over 3f out: nvr threatened* **4/1**[2]	61
	8	7	**Perivale (USA)** 3-8-12 0 .... SteveDrowne 12 (Saeed bin Suroor) *dwlt: hld up in rr: nvr threatened* **8/1**	47
0	9	2	**Snow Train**[12] 3364 3-8-12 0 .... DaleSwift 3 (James Given) *in tch: rdn over 3f out: wknd fnl 2f* **100/1**	44
	10	8	**Holli Deya** 3-8-12 0 .... MarcHalford 4 (Andi Brown) *midfield: rdn 3f out: sn wknd* **100/1**	28
	11	14	**Moreamore (IRE)** 3-8-12 0 .... MartinDwyer 9 (Alan Jarvis) *dwlt: hld up: pushed along over 4f out: sn btn: eased* **33/1**	

2m 14.55s (5.15) **Going Correction** +0.30s/f (Good) **11** Ran SP% **117.7**
Speed ratings (Par 100): **91,90,89,86,86 85,81,75,73,67 56**
toteswingers 1&2 £9.20, 1&3 £10.30, 2&3 £3.30 CSF £63.30 TOTE £13.70: £3.00, £1.30, £2.10; EX 64.00 Trifecta £286.80 Pool: £5378.74 - 14.06 winning tickets..

Owner Malcolm C Denmark **Bred** Francois Drion & Ptns **Trained** Newmarket, Suffolk

FOCUS
Some smart pedigrees on show here and an open maiden on paper given the form principals didn't set a particularly exacting standard. The form looks fluid, although the first two look potential improvers.

3765 MG LAW EDUCATION & SOCIAL CARE LAW H'CAP 1m 6f 132y
5:20 (5:20) (Class 4) (0-85,82) 4-Y-O+ £4,690 (£1,395; £697; £348) **Stalls** Low

Form				RPR
2611	1		**Mr Snoozy**[27] 2860 4-8-6 **72** .... (p) JasonHart(5) 5 (Tim Walford) *prom: led over 3f out: rdn clr over 2f out: kpt on wl* **7/2**[1]	85
-213	2	4	**Ashdown Lad**[13] 3321 4-9-0 **75** .... JamesDoyle 6 (William Jarvis) *hld up: hdwy 3f out: rdn to go 2nd 2f out: kpt on but no ch w wnr* **4/1**[2]	83
1-22	3	1 ¾	**Twelve Strings (IRE)**[13] 3333 4-9-7 **82** .... FrankieDettori 7 (Brian Ellison) *midfield: rdn over 3f out: kpt on fnl f: wnt 3rd post* **4/1**[2]	88
3-10	4	nk	**Sign Manual**[49] 2205 4-9-4 **79** .... [1] JamesMcDonald 1 (Michael Bell) *hld up: rdn and hdwy over 3f out: kpt on one pce* **7/1**	84
5056	5	½	**Gabrial's Star**[13] 3344 4-9-5 **80** .... (p) StephenCraine 9 (Ian Williams) *midfield: rdn over 3f out: one pce* **12/1**	85
0016	6	hd	**Rocktherunway (IRE)**[35] 2633 4-9-5 **80** .... (p) SteveDrowne 2 (Michael Dods) *hld up: pushed along and hdwy over 3f out: rdn over 2f out: one pce* **14/1**	84
-532	7	3 ¾	**Running Deer (IRE)**[13] 3321 4-8-11 **72** .... TomQueally 8 (Lady Cecil) *trckd ldng pair: rdn over 2f out: wknd fnl f* **6/1**[3]	72
1560	8	8	**Masterful Act (USA)**[34] 2648 6-9-3 **78** .... JohnFahy 4 (Alan McCabe) *sn led: rdn whn hdd over 3f out: sn wknd* **20/1**	67
60	9	26	**Mexicali (IRE)**[25] 2939 5-9-3 **78** .... [1] RichardHughes 3 (Dean Ivory) *trckd ldng pair: rdn over 3f out: wknd over 2f out: eased* **10/1**	33

3m 9.68s (2.28) **Going Correction** +0.30s/f (Good) **9** Ran SP% **117.2**
Speed ratings (Par 105): **105,102,101,101,101 101,99,95,81**
toteswingers 1&2 £3.90, 1&3 £4.10, 2&3 £4.10 CSF £17.84 CT £58.32 TOTE £5.20: £1.80, £1.80, £1.60; EX 16.60 Trifecta £73.90 Pool: £4224.35 - 42.86 winning tickets..

Owner T W Heseltine **Bred** J W Mursell **Trained** Sheriff Hutton, N Yorks

■ Stewards' Enquiry : Stephen Craine two-day ban; used whip above permitted level (19th-20th July).

FOCUS
This was won by the most progressive horse in the field. The third, fourth and fifth help set the level.

T/Plt: £26.20 to a £1 stake. Pool: £85340.69 - 2369.76 winning tickets. T/Qpdt: £3.10 to a £1 stake. Pool: £4917.54 - 1156.15 winning tickets AS

3331 MUSSELBURGH (R-H)
Friday, June 28

OFFICIAL GOING: Good (good to firm in places) changing to good (good to soft in places) after race 1 (2:10).
Wind: Fresh half against Weather: Overcast

3766 BRITISH STALLION STUDS EBF MAIDEN STKS 5f
2:10 (2:11) (Class 4) 2-Y-O £4,204 (£1,251; £625; £312) **Stalls** High

Form				RPR
04	1		**Viva Verglas (IRE)**[22] 3023 2-9-5 0 .... GrahamGibbons 5 (David Barron) *sn led: rdn and qcknd clr appr fnl f: readily* **6/4**[1]	83+
5	2	5	**The Dukkerer (IRE)**[14] 3280 2-9-0 0 .... DanielTudhope 1 (David O'Meara) *trckd ldrs: hdwy on outer over 2f out: rdn to chse wnr ent fnl f: kpt on: no ch w wnr* **13/2**	57
	3	shd	**Go Jamesway** 2-9-5 0 .... LeeTopliss 7 (Richard Fahey) *green and sn pushed along in rr: hdwy and n.m.r over 1f out: squeezed through on inner ent fnl f: sn rdn and kpt on wl towards fin* **3/1**[2]	64+
552	4	2 ¾	**Red House**[17] 3167 2-9-5 0 .... RoystonFfrench 6 (David C Griffiths) *trckd ldrs: effrt 2f out: sn rdn and one pce* **25/1**	52
	5	3 ½	**Chuckamental** 2-9-5 0 .... TomEaves 2 (Bryan Smart) *sn cl up: rdn along wl over 2f out: wknd ent fnl f* **10/1**	39
00	6	2 ¼	**Pavers Bounty**[22] 3023 2-9-5 0 .... AndrewElliott 4 (Noel Wilson) *chsd ldrs: swtchd rt to outer and hdwy wl over 1f out: sn rdn and wknd* **16/1**	31

0 7 12 **Baileys Celebrate**[42] 2419 2-9-0 0 .... JoeFanning 3
(Mark Johnston) *cl up: rdn along 2f out: sn wknd* **6/1**[3]

1m 3.11s (2.71) **Going Correction** +0.40s/f (Good) **7** Ran SP% **111.4**
Speed ratings (Par 95): **94,86,85,81,75 53,72**
toteswingers 1&2 £4.20, 1&3 £2.40, 2&3 £2.80 CSF £11.24 TOTE £2.20: £2.80, £1.40; EX 8.20 Trifecta £47.80 Pool: £1994.33 - 31.25 winning tickets..
Owner Raymond Miquel **Bred** Mrs Mary Coonan **Trained** Maunby, N Yorks

FOCUS
The rain had clearly got into the ground and Joe Fanning described it as "soft, maybe good to soft". They were running into a headwind, which may also help to explain the slow time of the opener. Quite a modest juvenile maiden but the winner scored easily and the form could rate a little higher.

3767 INVESTEC WEALTH & INVESTMENT EDINBURGH (S) STKS 5f
2:40 (2:40) (Class 4) 2-Y-O **£6,469** (£1,925; £962; £481) **Stalls** High

Form RPR
1230 1 **Scargill**[6] 3555 2-8-10 0 .... ConnorBeasley(7) 6 65
(Brian Ellison) *racd awkwardly thrght: chsd ldrs: pushed along and hdwy wl over 1f out: rdn to chal ent fnl f and sn hung rt: drvn and styd on wl to ld nr fin* **1/1**[1]

10 2 ½ **Baytown Kestrel**[9] 3459 2-8-12 0 .... GrahamLee 1 58
(Phil McEntee) *led and sn clr: rdn over 1f out: hdd ins fnl f: kpt on u.p towards fin* **9/4**[2]

433 3 shd **Marti's Girl**[11] 3414 2-8-0 0 .... CharlotteJenner(7) 3 53
(J S Moore) *chsd ldr: hdwy over 1f out: rdn to chal over 1f out: led ins fnl f: hdd and no ex last 50yds* **33/1**

440 4 1¼ **Bandolier**[24] 2955 2-8-12 0 .... LeeTopliss 5 53
(Richard Fahey) *chsd ldrs: rdn along 2f out: kpt on u.p fnl f* **15/2**[3]

5 ½ **Straight Gin** 2-8-12 0 .... TomEaves 4 52
(Alan Berry) *s.i.s: green and sn detached in rr: hdwy 1/2-way: rdn and styd on wl fnl f: nrst fin* **14/1**

6 17 **Rubylicious (IRE)** 2-8-7 0 .... JoeFanning 2
(J S Moore) *chsd ldrs: rdn along 2f out: wknd wl over 1f out* **8/1**

1m 3.44s (3.04) **Going Correction** +0.40s/f (Good) **6** Ran SP% **113.3**
Speed ratings (Par 95): **91,90,90,88,87 60**
toteswingers 1&2 £1.10, 1&3 £7.00, 2&3 £6.30 CSF £3.51 TOTE £1.70: £2.00, £1.90; EX 3.40 Trifecta £23.10 Pool: £1329.81 - 43.14 winning tickets..There was no bid for the winner.
Owner L S Keys **Bred** Imperial **Trained** Norton, N Yorks

FOCUS
A relatively valuable seller and it attracted two Royal Ascot also-rans. Predictably they finished one-two. The form is rated a little better than average for the grade.

3768 DOWNLOAD THE FREE RACING PLUS APP H'CAP 1m 4f 100y
3:10 (3:10) (Class 6) (0-65,65) 4-Y-0+ **£2,587** (£770; £384; £192) **Stalls** Low

Form RPR
5653 1 **Ebony Express**[16] 3199 4-9-4 **62** .... RobertWinston 3 69
(Alan Swinbank) *trckd ldng pair: hdwy over 2f out: swtchd lft and led wl over 1f out: sn rdn clr: styd on wl fnl f* **9/4**[2]

60-0 2 2¼ **Circle Of Angels**[39] 2511 5-8-13 **57** .... JoeFanning 1 61
(Mark Johnston) *sn trcking ldr: hdwy to ld over 3f out: rdn along and hdd wl over 1f out: swtchd lft and drvn ent fnl f: kpt on same pce* **11/4**[3]

3104 3 hd **Titus Bolt (IRE)**[35] 2630 4-9-7 **65** .... GrahamLee 2 68
(Jim Goldie) *hld up in rr: hdwy wl over 2f out: rdn to chse ldng pair wl over 1f out: drvn and wandered ins fnl f: sn one pce* **15/8**[1]

-361 4 1¾ **Grand Diamond (IRE)**[14] 3287 9-8-2 **53** .... SophieRobertson(7) 6 54
(Jim Goldie) *trckd ldrs: hdwy wl over 2f out: rdn wl over 1f out: one pce ent fnl f* **8/1**

000- 5 33 **Cadgers Brig**[193] 8146 5-9-0 **61** ....(p) LucyAlexander(3) 4 12
(Barry Murtagh) *led: rdn along and hdd over 3f out: sn hdd & wknd over 2f out* **14/1**

2m 48.81s (6.81) **Going Correction** +0.40s/f (Good) **5** Ran SP% **110.0**
Speed ratings (Par 101): **93,91,91,90,68**
CSF £8.77 TOTE £2.90: £1.30, £2.10; EX 10.40 Trifecta £21.20 Pool: £2623.74 - 92.51 winning tickets..
Owner Mrs T Blackett **Bred** Miss E J Wright **Trained** Melsonby, N Yorks

FOCUS
Moderate form best assessed through the winner.

3769 INVESTEC WEALTH & INVESTMENT H'CAP 5f
3:45 (3:49) (Class 4) (0-80,79) 3-Y-O+ **£6,469** (£1,925; £962; £481) **Stalls** High

Form RPR
2221 1 **Red Baron (IRE)**[14] 3283 4-8-13 **69** .... NeilFarley(3) 4 81+
(Eric Alston) *uns rdr and bolted bef s: qckly away: mde all: rdn ent fnl f: kpt on strly* **10/3**[1]

1040 2 2¼ **Chosen One (IRE)**[15] 3236 8-8-11 **64** .... PJMcDonald 9 66
(Ruth Carr) *a chsng wnr: rdn over 1f out: drvn and no imp ins fnl f* **12/1**

1213 3 ½ **Haajes**[1] 3713 9-9-9 **76** ....(v) MickyFenton 1 76
(Paul Midgley) *dwlt: hdwy on outer to chse ldrs 1/2-way: effrt over 1f out: sn rdn and kpt on fnl f* **7/1**[3]

0541 4 1¼ **The Nifty Fox**[13] 3331 9-9-11 **78** ....(p) JamesSullivan 2 75
(Tim Easterby) *t.k.h: hld up towards rr: effrt and nt clr run over 1f out: swtchd rt to outer and rdn ent fnl f: no imp* **8/1**

6060 5 nk **Opt Out**[6] 3566 3-9-0 **73** .... JoeFanning 8 69
(Alistair Whillans) *hld up towards rr: hdwy 2f out: nt clr run over 1f out: swtchd rt and rdn whn n.m.r ent fnl f: kpt on: nrst fin* **9/1**

0001 6 hd **Pavers Star**[35] 2632 4-8-7 **60** oh2 .... AndrewElliott 7 54
(Noel Wilson) *chsd ldng pair: rdn along wl over 1f out: grad wknd* **20/1**

0003 7 ¾ **Crimson Knot (IRE)**[6] 3561 5-9-5 **72** .... TomEaves 3 63
(Alan Berry) *trckd ldrs: effrt wl over 1f out: sn rdn and wknd ent fnl f* **7/2**[2]

2100 8 nk **Rothesay Chancer**[6] 3561 5-9-12 **79** .... GrahamLee 6 69
(Jim Goldie) *chsd ldrs: rdn along wl over 1f out: sn wknd* **10/3**[1]

1m 1.75s (1.35) **Going Correction** +0.40s/f (Good)
WFA 3 from 4yo+ 6lb **8** Ran SP% **114.4**
Speed ratings (Par 105): **105,101,100,98,98 97,96,96**
toteswingers 1&2 £10.40, 1&3 £2.20, 2&3 £5.60 CSF £42.95 CT £265.73 TOTE £4.20: £1.20, £3.10, £2.40; EX 56.10 Trifecta £201.50 Pool: £2050.33 - 7.63 winning tickets..
Owner J Stephenson **Bred** Mrs C A Moore **Trained** Longton, Lancs

FOCUS
Few got into this ordinary sprint. The winner impressed and can go on again.

3770 32RED.COM H'CAP 7f 30y
4:20 (4:22) (Class 5) (0-70,70) 4-Y-0+ **£3,234** (£962; £481; £240) **Stalls** Low

Form RPR
-565 1 **Silver Rime (FR)**[14] 3285 8-9-0 **63** .... PJMcDonald 1 75
(Linda Perratt) *in tch: hdwy over 2f out: rdn to chse ldr ent fnl f: styd on to ld last 75yds: drvn out* **9/1**

0013 2 1¼ **Dhhamaan (IRE)**[10] 3444 8-8-5 **54** ....(b) JamesSullivan 2 63
(Ruth Carr) *set str pce: rdn along over 2f out: drvn ent fnl f: hdd and no ex last 75yds* **9/2**[2]

0-23 3 hd **Circuitous**[11] 3393 5-9-4 **67** ....(v) JoeFanning 11 75
(Keith Dalgleish) *chsd ldng pair: hdwy on outer over 2f out: rdn to chse ldng pair over 1f out: drvn and kpt on fnl f: nrst fin* **9/2**[2]

3004 4 1½ **Goninodaethat**[14] 3286 5-7-13 **51** oh1 .... NeilFarley(3) 5 55
(Jim Goldie) *chsd clr ldr: cl up 1/2-way: rdn along wl over 2f out: drvn ent fnl f: wknd* **8/1**

3236 5 hd **Music Festival (USA)**[13] 3337 6-8-6 **55** .... AndrewElliott 6 59
(Jim Goldie) *hld up: hdwy wl over 2f out: sn rdn: styd on fnl f: nrst fin* **5/1**[3]

3-00 6 2½ **Berbice (IRE)**[46] 2319 8-8-4 **53** ow2 .... RoystonFfrench 10 50
(Linda Perratt) *dwlt and towards rr: hdwy on inner 2f out: sn rdn and kpt on same pce fnl f* **33/1**

1111 7 hd **Jebel Tara**[35] 2636 8-9-4 **70** ....(bt) PaulPickard(3) 8 67
(Alan Brown) *in tch: effrt 3f out: rdn along wl over 2f out: sn btn* **10/3**[1]

-602 8 8 **Weetentherty**[16] 3197 6-8-7 **56** ....(b) TomEaves 4 32
(Keith Dalgleish) *a in rr* **14/1**

-563 9 1¾ **Amno Dancer (IRE)**[14] 3286 6-8-0 **52** oh2 ow1 ....(p) DeclanCannon(3) 3 23
(Keith Dalgleish) *a towards rr* **9/1**

1m 32.02s (3.02) **Going Correction** +0.40s/f (Good) **9** Ran SP% **116.8**
Speed ratings (Par 103): **98,96,96,94,94 91,91,82,80**
toteswingers 1&2 £10.70, 1&3 £10.50, 2&3 £4.30 CSF £49.83 CT £210.79 TOTE £12.60: £4.00, £2.10, £1.70; EX 79.20 Trifecta £892.00 Pool: £4801.86 - 4.03 winning tickets..
Owner Ken McGarrity **Bred** Jean-Philippe Dubois **Trained** East Kilbride, S Lanarks

FOCUS
No hanging around in this low-grade handicap, but it still proved difficult to make up ground from behind. The fourth is rated close to recent efforts.

3771 BOOGIE IN MORNING H'CAP (QUALIFIER FOR £15K BETFAIR SCOTTISH STAYERS' SERIES FINAL) 2m
4:55 (4:55) (Class 6) (0-65,65) 4-Y-0+ **£2,587** (£770; £384; £192) **Stalls** Low

Form RPR
5364 1 **Dr Irv**[14] 3301 4-9-2 **63** .... DeclanCannon(3) 5 72
(Philip Kirby) *hld up towards rr: hdwy on inner 3f out: swtchd lft and effrt over 2f out: led wl over 1f out and sn rdn clr: styd on* **10/11**[1]

-560 2 2½ **Jeu De Roseau (IRE)**[20] 3089 9-9-0 **58** .... PJMcDonald 3 63
(Chris Grant) *trckd ldng pair: hdwy 3f out: led 2 1/2f out: sn rdn and hdd wl over 1f out: drvn and kpt on same pce fnl f* **8/1**[3]

4006 3 nk **Sohcahtoa (IRE)**[14] 3287 7-9-2 **65** .... LMcNiff(5) 4 70
(Andrew Crook) *hld up towards rr: hdwy 3f out: rdn to chse ldrs wl over 1f out: drvn and one pce fnl f* **10/1**

50-0 4 4½ **Bandanaman (IRE)**[32] 2720 7-9-2 **60** .... RobertWinston 1 59
(Alan Swinbank) *hld up in rr: hdwy on wd outside 3f out: rdn to chse ldrs 2f out: no imp appr fnl f* **12/1**

0553 5 10 **Geanie Mac (IRE)**[9] 3467 4-8-6 **50** ....(b) RoystonFfrench 6 37
(Linda Perratt) *slt ld: rdn along over 3f out: hdd 2 1/2f out and sn wknd* **4/1**[2]

6-00 6 4 **Hi Dancer**[27] 2887 10-8-2 **46** oh1 .... JamesSullivan 2 28
(Ben Haslam) *cl up: rdn along 3f out: sn wknd* **17/2**

0/00 7 26 **Grandad Bill (IRE)**[35] 2630 10-8-5 **49** ow1 .... AndrewElliott 7
(Jim Goldie) *trckd ldrs: effrt over 3f out: rdn along wl over 2f out: sn wknd* **25/1**

3m 39.58s (6.08) **Going Correction** +0.40s/f (Good) **7** Ran SP% **114.7**
Speed ratings (Par 101): **100,98,98,96,91 89,76**
toteswingers 1&2 £1.70, 1&3 £2.00, 2&3 £5.60 CSF £9.22 CT £45.80 TOTE £1.70: £1.10, £3.20; EX 7.80 Trifecta £37.80 Pool: £3591.08 - 71.14 winning tickets..
Owner Irvine Lynch **Bred** Whitsbury Manor Stud & Pigeon House Stud **Trained** Middleham, N Yorks

FOCUS
A weak staying handicap, run at a steady pace. The placed horses give the form a solid but limited feel.

3772 RACING UK-YOUR RACING HOME FROM HOME H'CAP (QUALIFIER FOR £15K BETFAIR SCOTTISH MILE SERIES FINAL) 1m
5:30 (5:31) (Class 6) (0-65,70) 3-Y-O **£2,587** (£770; £384; £192) **Stalls** Low

Form RPR
-051 1 **Aeronwyn Bryn (IRE)**[4] 3629 3-9-5 **70** 6ex .... ConnorBeasley(7) 6 84+
(Michael Dods) *midfield: hdwy over 3f out: led over 2f out: rdn clr appr fnl f: styd on wl* **6/4**[1]

0404 2 7 **Look On By**[9] 3463 3-8-9 **53** .... JamesSullivan 2 51
(Ruth Carr) *t.k.h: trckd ldrs: hdwy over 2f out: rdn to chse wnr over 1f out: drvn and kpt on fnl f: no ch w wnr* **7/2**[2]

-060 3 3 **Royal Caper**[11] 3405 3-9-1 **59** .... RobertWinston 1 50
(John Ryan) *chsd ldng pair: pushed along 3f out: rdn 2f out: drvn and one pce fr over 1f out* **9/1**

4-56 4 nk **Sakhees Romance**[9] 3463 3-8-6 **53** .... NeilFarley(3) 7 43
(Noel Wilson) *hld up in rr: hdwy 3f out: rdn to chse ldrs 2f out: drvn and one pce fnl f* **16/1**

3430 5 4 **Spider House**[31] 2756 3-9-2 **60** .... PJMcDonald 8 41
(David O'Meara) *towards rr tl sme late hdwy* **6/1**

4-60 6 2 **Baraboy (IRE)**[11] 3394 3-8-11 **58** .... LucyAlexander(3) 4 35
(Barry Murtagh) *dwlt and in rr tl sme late hdwy* **22/1**

0132 7 1 **Just A Pound (IRE)**[12] 3376 3-8-11 **62** .... JosephineGordon(7) 5 36
(Jo Hughes) *t.k.h: led: rn wd on home turn: rdn along and hdd over 2f out: grad wknd* **9/2**[3]

4000 8 5 **Riponian**[9] 3463 3-8-9 **53** .... PaddyAspell 10 16
(Susan Corbett) *prom: rdn along 3f out: sn wknd* **50/1**

5-00 9 11 **Princess Cayan (IRE)**[6] 3566 3-7-9 **46** oh1 .... SamanthaBell(7) 9
(Linda Perratt) *midfield: rdn along 1/2-way: sn wknd* **66/1**

00-0 10 1¼ **Vanessa**[6] 3566 3-9-2 **65** .... LMcNiff(5) 3
(Ian Semple) *a towards rr* **40/1**

1m 43.73s (2.53) **Going Correction** +0.40s/f (Good) **10** Ran SP% **120.8**
Speed ratings (Par 97): **103,96,93,92,88 86,85,80,69,68**
toteswingers 1&2 £2.20, 1&3 £6.20, 2&3 £6.00 CSF £6.88 CT £37.69 TOTE £1.90: £1.10, £2.20, £3.90; EX 8.60 Trifecta £71.60 Pool: £1894.08 - 19.38 winning tickets..
Owner Andrew Tinkler **Bred** Owenstown Stud **Trained** Denton, Co Durham

FOCUS
A weak handicap with the winner thrashing her rivals and value for more, although the form is rated conservatively.
T/Plt: £15.30 to a £1 stake. Pool: £57115.31 - 2720.43 winning tickets T/Qpdt: £9.90 to a £1 stake. Pool: £3988.90 - 295.60 winning tickets JR

[3723]NEWCASTLE (L-H)

Friday, June 28

OFFICIAL GOING: Good to soft (soft in places; 6.9)

Wind: Breezy, half against Weather: Overcast

3773 BETFRED ON 0800 221 221 CLASSIFIED STKS — 7f

6:05 (6:05) (Class 5) 3-Y-O — **£2,587** (£770; £384; £192) **Stalls** Centre

Form — RPR

1-40 **1** **Unknown Villain (IRE)**[13] 3342 3-9-0 75 .... GrahamGibbons 1 — 79
(Tom Dascombe) *in tch: rdn over 2f out: hdwy to ld ins fnl f: sn clr* **13/8**[2]

2-21 **2** 3 ³/₄ **Floating Along (IRE)**[20] 3109 3-9-0 75 .... PhillipMakin 2 — 69
(William Haggas) *led: rdn over 2f out: hdd ins fnl f: kpt on same pce* **11/8**[1]

4-02 **3** 3 ¹/₂ **Exzachary**[10] 3438 3-9-0 73 .... DanielTudhope 4 — 60
(Jo Hughes) *trckd ldr: rdn and ev ch briefly 2f out: edgd rt and wknd appr fnl f* **4/1**[3]

434- **4** 3 ¹/₂ **Mishaal (IRE)**[271] 6699 3-9-0 75 .... LeeTopliss 3 — 51
(Michael Herrington) *chsd ldrs: drvn and outpcd over 2f out: sn btn* **11/1**

1m 32.11s (4.31) **Going Correction** +0.35s/f (Good) **4** Ran SP% **108.5**
Speed ratings (Par 99): **89,84,80,76**
CSF £4.25 TOTE £2.70; EX 4.50 Trifecta £5.30 Pool: £467.98 - 65.62 winning tickets..
Owner Panarea Racing **Bred** Mrs Jan O'Dwyer **Trained** Malpas, Cheshire

FOCUS
Fresh ground provided on 7f of round course from Thursday. A small field and an ordinary 3-y-o handicap for those who had not won more than once. They came up the centre of the track and they finished tired. The form is rated cautiously.

3774 BETFRED TV MAIDEN FILLIES' STKS — 7f

6:40 (6:42) (Class 5) 3-Y-O+ — **£2,587** (£770; £384; £192) **Stalls** Centre

Form — RPR

1 **Zibelina (IRE)** 3-8-12 0 .... RobertHavlin 4 — 84+
(Saeed bin Suroor) *prom: smooth hdwy to ld over 1f out: qcknd and sn wl clr: eased ins fnl f* **5/1**[3]

3-30 **2** 10 **Graceful Act**[11] 3397 5-9-7 55 .... [1] PhillipMakin 1 — 56
(Ron Barr) *prom: effrt and led over 2f out: hdd over 1f out: kpt on: no ch w wnr* **20/1**

3 1 **Sugarcraft (USA)** 3-8-12 0 .... GrahamGibbons 12 — 50
(Saeed bin Suroor) *hld up: stdy hdwy over 2f out: rdn over 1f out: kpt on fnl f: no imp* **15/8**[2]

4 1 ³/₄ **Just Poppy (IRE)** 4-9-7 0 .... LeeTopliss 5 — 49
(Stuart Coltherd) *hld up: rdn and hdwy to chse ldrs over 2f out: nt qckn over 1f out* **20/1**

53 **5** 2 **Rufoof**[12] 3372 3-8-12 0 .... DaneO'Neill 7 — 41
(Charles Hills) *t.k.h: cl up: rdn over 2f out: wknd appr fnl f* **6/4**[1]

6 6 **Henpecked** 3-8-12 0 .... MichaelO'Connell 10 — 25
(Alistair Whillans) *hld up: rdn and outpcd wl over 2f out: sme late hdwy: nvr on terms* **22/1**

7 1 ¹/₄ **The Bay Tigress** 3-8-12 0 .... AmyRyan 8 — 22
(Lisa Williamson) *t.k.h: chsd ldrs tl rdn and wknd over 2f out* **66/1**

8 2 ¹/₄ **Sabrina's Secret** 3-8-12 0 .... MickyFenton 2 — 31
(Tom Tate) *plld hrd: hld up: hdwy to ld over 4f out: hdd over 2f out: sn btn* **14/1**

9 9 **Maillot Jaune (IRE)** 3-8-12 0 .... DuranFentiman 11
(Patrick Holmes) *missed break: bhd: hdwy over 4f out: rdn and wknd over 2f out* **66/1**

0 **10** 27 **Lilyofthevalley**[39] 2503 3-8-8 0 ow1 .... JustinNewman[(5)] 9
(John Weymes) *led to over 4f out: rdn and wknd 3f out: t.o* **100/1**

1m 30.6s (2.80) **Going Correction** +0.35s/f (Good)
WFA 3 from 4yo+ 9lb **10** Ran SP% **116.0**
Speed ratings (Par 100): **98,86,85,83,81 74,72,70,60,29**
toteswingers 1&2 £7.70, 1&3 £1.80, 2&3 £12.00 CSF £96.48 TOTE £4.20: £1.10, £3.40, £1.60; EX 85.10 Trifecta £469.80 Pool: £2065.53 - 3.29 winning tickets..
Owner Godolphin **Bred** Darley **Trained** Newmarket, Suffolk
■ Stewards' Enquiry : Graham Gibbons £140.00 fine; failed to arrive in time to weigh out.

FOCUS
A weak fillies' maiden again run into a strong headwind. They went no great pace, the slow time in keeping with the easy ground. A taking performance from the winner with the second setting a moderate standard.

3775 BETFRED/BRITISH STALLION STUDS EBF HOPPINGS STKS (LISTED RACE) (F&M) — 1m 2f 32y

7:15 (7:15) (Class 1) 3-Y-O+

£22,684 (£8,600; £4,304; £2,144; £1,076; £540) **Stalls** Centre

Form — RPR

0-00 **1** **Making Eyes (IRE)**[28] 2838 5-9-5 96 .... JoeFanning 5 — 104
(Hugo Palmer) *t.k.h: prom: smooth hdwy and ev ch over 1f out: sn rdn: led wl ins fnl f: hld on wl* **12/1**

3-53 **2** shd **Reckoning (IRE)**[34] 2652 4-9-5 99 .... (p) PaulMulrennan 4 — 104
(Jeremy Noseda) *trckd ldr: led gng wl over 2f out: jnd and rdn over 1f out: hdd wl ins fnl f: rallied: jst hld* **9/2**[2]

3-02 **3** 2 ³/₄ **Sound Hearts (USA)**[11] 3409 4-9-5 97 .... AndreaAtzeni 7 — 99
(Roger Varian) *led at stdy pce: rdn and hdd over 2f out: one pce fr over 1f out* **6/1**[3]

-153 **4** 2 ¹/₂ **Eastern Destiny**[44] 2365 4-9-5 86 .... LeeTopliss 1 — 94
(Richard Fahey) *in tch: rdn along over 2f out: rallied wl over 1f out: kpt on fnl f: no imp* **12/1**

2-25 **5** 2 ³/₄ **Prussian**[20] 3100 4-9-5 107 .... MickaelBarzalona 3 — 89
(Saeed bin Suroor) *trckd ldrs: rdn over 2f out: wknd fnl f* **5/4**[1]

00-4 **6** 2 ³/₄ **Falls Of Lora (IRE)**[155] 366 4-9-5 104 .... RobertHavlin 8 — 84
(Saeed bin Suroor) *t.k.h: hld up: hdwy over 2f out: rdn and wknd over 1f out* **6/1**[3]

-563 **7** 15 **Dark Orchid (USA)**[11] 3409 4-9-5 105 .... DaneO'Neill 9 — 68
(Saeed bin Suroor) *hld up in tch on outside: stmbld bdly after 1f: rdn over 2f out: wknd wl over 1f out* **12/1**

8 1 ¹/₂ **Magic Skyline (IRE)** 3-8-7 0 .... TomEaves 2 — 52
(Brian Ellison) *s.i.s: hld up: struggling wl over 3f out: nvr on terms* **100/1**

2m 13.94s (2.04) **Going Correction** +0.35s/f (Good)
WFA 3 from 4yo+ 12lb **8** Ran SP% **115.3**
Speed ratings (Par 111): **105,104,102,100,98 96,84,83**
toteswingers 1&2 £7.80, 1&3 £9.10, 2&3 £3.80 CSF £65.58 TOTE £11.70: £3.00, £2.10, £2.40; EX 53.40 Trifecta £736.50 Pool: £1378.20 - 1.40 winning tickets..
Owner Starter For Ten Partnership **Bred** F Dunne **Trained** Newmarket, Suffolk

FOCUS
Won in the past by subsequent Group 1 scorers Chorist and Lady Jane Digby, this fillies' Listed event did not appear to harbour any such performers of that quality and was run at a modest pace. It produced a tight finish. The winner recorded a personal-best with the second to form.

3776 BETFRED GOSFORTH PARK CUP (H'CAP) — 5f

7:45 (7:47) (Class 2) (0-105,102) 3-Y-O+

£12,450 (£3,728; £1,864; £932; £466; £234) **Stalls** Centre

Form — RPR

0-50 **1** **Magical Macey (USA)**[34] 2669 6-9-7 97 .... (b) PhillipMakin 5 — 107
(David Barron) *mde all: drvn over 1f out: hld on wl fnl f* **8/1**

5100 **2** ³/₄ **Ancient Cross**[6] 3558 9-9-5 95 .... (t) GrahamGibbons 8 — 103
(Michael Easterby) *hld up: stdy hdwy 2f out: chsd wnr ins fnl f: r.o* **5/1**[1]

1-41 **3** 1 ¹/₄ **Jack Luey**[39] 2505 6-8-10 86 .... AndreaAtzeni 9 — 89
(Lawrence Mullaney) *prom: effrt and drvn over 1f out: kpt on same pce wl ins fnl f* **7/1**[2]

0540 **4** ¹/₂ **Fitz Flyer (IRE)**[34] 2669 7-8-9 85 .... (v) JoeFanning 6 — 86
(David Nicholls) *hld up: hdwy over 2f out: rdn over 1f out: kpt on same pce ins fnl f* **10/1**

20-0 **5** 2 ¹/₄ **Mayoman (IRE)**[14] 3299 8-8-11 87 .... DanielTudhope 3 — 80
(David O'Meara) *towards rr on outside: drvn 1/2-way: hdwy over 1f out: kpt on fnl f: nvr able to chal* **15/2**[3]

0663 **6** ¹/₂ **Lady Gibraltar**[34] 2669 4-8-6 87 .... MichaelJMMurphy[(5)] 14 — 78
(Alan Jarvis) *prom: drvn along 2f out: outpcd fnl f* **15/2**[3]

0-55 **7** ³/₄ **Jiroft (ITY)**[21] 3046 6-9-12 102 .... GrahamLee 10 — 91
(Robert Cowell) *trckd ldrs: rdn over 1f out: edgd rt and wknd ent fnl f* **10/1**

-151 **8** hd **Lucky Numbers (IRE)**[20] 3093 7-8-13 89 .... AndrewMullen 12 — 77
(David O'Meara) *in tch: drvn along over 2f out: no imp fr over 1f out* **14/1**

-200 **9** ³/₄ **Captain Dunne (IRE)**[13] 3334 8-9-3 93 .... DuranFentiman 4 — 78
(Tim Easterby) *trckd ldrs: rdn over 2f out: wknd fnl f* **20/1**

6000 **10** ¹/₂ **Mister Manannan (IRE)**[13] 3334 6-8-11 87 .... (p) RobertHavlin 7 — 70
(David Nicholls) *hld up towards rr: drvn over 2f out: btn over 1f out* **20/1**

0000 **11** ¹/₂ **Cheviot (USA)**[13] 3334 7-9-7 97 .... (p) TomEaves 13 — 79
(Ian Semple) *hld up: drvn along over 2f out: nvr able to chal* **50/1**

4600 **12** 3 ³/₄ **Confessional**[13] 3334 6-9-8 98 .... (e) PaulMulrennan 15 — 66
(Tim Easterby) *towards rr: rdn and hdwy over 2f out: btn over 1f out* **8/1**

52-6 **13** 7 **Stone Of Folca**[13] 3334 5-9-5 95 .... DaneO'Neill 16 — 38
(John Best) *racd alone towards stands' side: cl up tl hung lft and wknd 2f out* **12/1**

-000 **14** 3 ¹/₄ **Ubetterbegood (ARG)**[13] 3334 5-9-0 90 .... MickaelBarzalona 2 — 21
(Robert Cowell) *bhd on outside: struggling over 2f out: sn btn* **16/1**

1m 0.87s (-0.23) **Going Correction** +0.20s/f (Good) **14** Ran SP% **124.8**
Speed ratings (Par 109): **109,107,105,105,101 100,99,99,97,97 96,90,79,73**
toteswingers 1&2 £18.00, 1&3 £12.80, 2&3 £7.50 CSF £48.42 CT £305.57 TOTE £10.80: £3.60, £2.80, £1.80; EX 70.70 Trifecta £538.40 Pool: £1740.33 - 2.42 winning tickets..
Owner K J Alderson **Bred** Silver Springs Stud Farm Inc & Mrs J Costelloe **Trained** Maunby, N Yorks

FOCUS
A decent sprint handicap. All bar one came up the centre of the track and it paid to be prominent. A marginal personal-best from the winner with the second recording his best figure since winning this in 2011.

3777 BETFRED "THE BONUS KING" H'CAP — 1m 3y(S)

8:15 (8:15) (Class 4) (0-85,80) 3-Y-O+ — **£4,690** (£1,395; £697; £348) **Stalls** Centre

Form — RPR

5562 **1** **Seattle Drive (IRE)**[38] 2551 5-9-9 75 .... GrahamLee 5 — 83
(Brian Ellison) *t.k.h: hld up in tch: hdwy 2f out: sn rdn: led wl ins fnl f: r.o* **15/2**[3]

-315 **2** ¹/₂ **Snooky**[49] 2240 4-9-12 78 .... LeeTopliss 4 — 85
(Richard Fahey) *hld up: stdy hdwy over 2f out: rdn to ld over 1f out: hdd wl ins fnl f: kpt on* **4/1**[2]

006- **3** 1 ¹/₂ **Dhaular Dhar (IRE)**[238] 7529 11-8-10 62 oh3 .... AndrewElliott 1 — 65
(Jim Goldie) *trckd ldrs: drvn and outpcd wl over 1f out: r.o ins fnl f* **33/1**

10-4 **4** nse **Broctune Papa Gio**[7] 3544 6-9-5 71 .... TomEaves 11 — 74
(Keith Reveley) *chsd ldr: led over 2f out to over 1f out: kpt on same pce ins fnl f* **25/1**

-022 **5** ³/₄ **Robert The Painter (IRE)**[13] 3349 5-9-9 75 .... (v) DanielTudhope 3 — 77
(David O'Meara) *in tch: rdn over 2f out: kpt on ins fnl f: nt pce to chal* **4/1**[2]

0150 **6** 3 ¹/₂ **It's A Mans World**[2] 3683 7-9-9 78 .... PaulPickard[(3)] 8 — 72
(Brian Ellison) *hld up: rdn over 2f out: hdwy over 1f out: wknd ins fnl f* **9/1**

31-2 **7** 9 **Elnadwa (USA)**[17] 3179 3-9-4 80 .... DaneO'Neill 2 — 51
(Saeed bin Suroor) *led at stdy pce: hung lft and hdd over 2f out: sn btn* **10/3**[1]

13-0 **8** 3 ¹/₂ **Dos Amigos (IRE)**[88] 1281 4-10-0 80 .... PaulMulrennan 10 — 45
(Michael Dods) *t.k.h: trckd ldrs: drvn and outpcd over 2f out: sn btn* **10/1**

1m 46.16s (2.76) **Going Correction** +0.35s/f (Good)
WFA 3 from 4yo+ 10lb **8** Ran SP% **100.7**
Speed ratings (Par 105): **100,99,98,97,97 93,84,81**
toteswingers 1&2 £5.60, 1&3 £20.00, 2&3 £16.10 CSF £28.55 CT £573.32 TOTE £7.80: £2.80, £1.90, £7.10; EX 34.70 Trifecta £480.80 Part won. Pool: £641.13 - 0.68 winning tickets..
Owner Steve May **Bred** Littleton Stud **Trained** Norton, N Yorks

FOCUS
A competitive handicap diminished by the defection of two non-runners and the withdrawal of the very well-backed Sound Advice who got worked up in the stalls. There was very little pace and, while largely unsatisfactory for form purposes, the winner took this on merit. They came up the centre of the track and the first four finished in a heap, so the form is rather muddling, with the first two probably the best guides.

3778 BETFRED.COM H'CAP — 6f

8:50 (8:51) (Class 5) (0-75,74) 3-Y-O+ — **£2,587** (£770; £384; £192) **Stalls** Centre

Form — RPR

4030 **1** **Mitchum**[10] 3444 4-9-2 64 .... (p) PhillipMakin 5 — 73
(Ron Barr) *awkward s: hld up: stdy hdwy 2f out: rdn ins fnl f: styd on to ld cl home* **16/1**

2451 **2** shd **Mutafaakir (IRE)**[20] 3090 4-9-9 71 .... PJMcDonald 11 — 80
(Ruth Carr) *in tch gng wl: hdwy 2f out: rdn to ld ins fnl f: kpt on: hdd cl home* **5/2**[1]

60-0 **3** 1 ³/₄ **Monel**[27] 2884 5-8-7 56 oh8 .... AndrewElliott 9 — 58
(Jim Goldie) *t.k.h: hld up: hdwy and swtchd rt over 1f out: styd on strly fnl f: nt rch first two* **25/1**

5441 **4** ³/₄ **Sunrise Dance**[10] 3446 4-9-4 71 6ex .... JasonHart[(5)] 1 — 72
(Robert Johnson) *t.k.h: led: rdn 2f out: hdd ins fnl f: kpt on same pce* **6/1**[2]

0226 **5** ¹/₂ **Here Now And Why (IRE)**[14] 3283 6-9-0 62 .... (p) DanielTudhope 12 — 61
(Iain Jardine) *hld up towards rr: rdn and hdwy over 1f out: kpt on same pce last 100yds* **16/1**

2510 **6** *1½* **Adam's Ale**[10] 3444 4-9-8 **70** MickyFenton 13 65
(Paul Midgley) *trckd ldr: rdn over 2f out: outpcd fnl f* **9/1**

00 **7** *nk* **Breezolini**[28] 2834 5-9-7 **69** RobertWinston 8 63
(Geoffrey Harker) *hld up: swtchd lft and hdwy over 2f out: no imp fnl f* **7/1**[3]

3100 **8** *1* **Mission Impossible**[35] 2614 8-9-9 **71** JoeFanning 16 61
(Tracy Waggott) *hld up: rdn over 2f out: styd on fnl f: nvr rchd ldrs* **7/1**[3]

2300 **9** *½* **Strong Man**[21] 3068 5-9-1 **63** GrahamGibbons 15 52
(Michael Easterby) *chsd ldrs: rdn over 2f out: nt qckn fr over 1f out* **16/1**

4050 **10** *1¼* **Hello Stranger (IRE)**[21] 3068 4-9-2 **64** DuranFentiman 3 49
(Tim Easterby) *trckd ldrs: rdn over 2f out: wknd over 1f out* **16/1**

1-50 **11** *nk* **Star City (IRE)**[48] 2278 4-8-12 **60** (be) TomEaves 14 44
(Michael Dods) *dwlt: sn in tch: rdn over 2f out: wknd over 1f out* **16/1**

414- **12** *1½* **Evanescent (IRE)**[312] 5415 4-9-12 **74** MichaelO'Connell 2 53
(John Quinn) *prom: rdn over 2f out: hung lft and wknd over 1f out* **16/1**

150- **13** *6* **I'll Be Good**[240] 7489 4-9-9 **71** GrahamLee 6 31
(Robert Johnson) *plld hrd: hld up towards rr: hdwy over 2f out: wknd over 1f out* **14/1**

1m 16.05s (1.45) **Going Correction** +0.35s/f (Good) **13** Ran SP% **123.7**
Speed ratings (Par 103): **104,103,101,100,99 97,97,96,95,93 93,91,83**
toteswingers 1&2 £15.80, 1&3 £37.10, 2&3 £32.10 CSF £57.74 TOTE £25.40: £5.90, £1.60, £9.30; EX 89.10 Trifecta £557.40 Part won. Pool: £743.21 - 0.09 winning tickets..
Owner A J Duffield **Bred** Conor J C Parsons & Brian M Parsons **Trained** Seamer, N Yorks

FOCUS
A competitive sprint handicap and the centre of the track was again the place to be. The form appears sound despite the third racing from out of the handicap.

3779 BETFRED ON 0800 221 221/KEVIN LEE MEMORIAL H'CAP 5f
9:20 (9:20) (Class 5) (0-75,75) 3-Y-O **£2,587** (£770; £384; £192) **Stalls** Centre

Form RPR

-301 **1** **Bondesire**[24] 2959 3-9-7 **75** DanielTudhope 7 82
(David O'Meara) *trckd ldr: rdn to ld ins fnl f: edgd rt: kpt on wl* **1/1**[1]

-450 **2** *1¼* **Our Diane (IRE)**[27] 2888 3-7-13 **60** SamanthaBell(7) 10 63
(Richard Fahey) *dwlt: in tch: effrt and hdwy 1/2-way: chsd wnr ins fnl f: kpt on same pce towards fin* **7/1**

2466 **3** *2* **Cracking Choice (IRE)**[16] 3198 3-8-1 **62** (b[1]) ConnorBeasley(7) 9 57
(Michael Dods) *led at decent gallop: rdn and hdd ins fnl f: kpt on same pce* **7/2**[2]

1-2 **4** *4* **Lucies Diamond (IRE)**[120] 828 3-8-13 **67** TomEaves 1 48
(Michael Dods) *in tch: rdn over 1f out: sn wknd* **4/1**[3]

4-50 **5** *4½* **Poppy Bond**[79] 1458 3-8-6 **60** RoystonFfrench 8 25
(Chris Fairhurst) *chsd ldrs: rdn over 2f out: sn wknd* **14/1**

1m 2.24s (1.14) **Going Correction** +0.20s/f (Good) **5** Ran SP% **111.4**
Speed ratings (Par 99): **98,96,92,86,79**
CSF £8.75 TOTE £2.10: £1.20, £3.60; EX 9.70 Trifecta £26.90 Pool: £590.34 - 16.44 winning tickets..
Owner Geoff & Sandra Turnbull **Bred** A C M Spalding **Trained** Nawton, N Yorks

FOCUS
Five non-runners reduced the field by half. They raced up the centre of the track in this modest sprint handicap. The pace was true but the form has little depth.
T/Jkpt: Not won. T/Plt: £713.70 to a £1 stake. Pool: £90096.46 - 92.15 winning tickets T/Qpdt: £75.00 to a £1 stake. Pool: £8610.75 - 84.85 winning tickets RY

3581 NEWMARKET (R-H)
Friday, June 28

OFFICIAL GOING: Good (8.4)
Wind: medium, half behind Weather: light rain

3780 NEWMARKETRACECOURSES.CO.UK H'CAP 1m
5:55 (5:55) (Class 5) (0-75,80) 3-Y-O+ **£3,234** (£962; £481; £240) **Stalls** High

Form RPR

4636 **1** **Azma (USA)**[14] 3292 3-8-10 **67** NeilCallan 1 74
(Conrad Allen) *racd down centre thrght: dwlt and bustled along early: chsd ldrs after 1f out: rdn to ld jst over 2f out: edging lft u.p and hld on wl fnl 100yds* **11/2**[3]

6101 **2** *½* **Aussie Reigns (IRE)**[7] 3537 3-9-9 **80** 6ex (v) AdamKirby 8 86+
(William Knight) *hld up in tch in midfield: rdn and hdwy between horses jst over 1f out: drvn and chsd wnr ins fnl f: kpt on but a gng to be hld* **13/8**[1]

-633 **3** *2½* **McCool Bannanas**[62] 1827 5-9-0 **61** StevieDonohoe 5 63
(James Unett) *racd in centre tl jnd far side 5f out: t.k.h: hld up wl in tch in midfield: rdn and chsd ldrs 2f out: no ex and outpcd fnl 100yds* **12/1**

-000 **4** *nk* **Fabled City (USA)**[49] 2232 4-9-9 **75** (t) RyanTate(5) 10 76
(Clive Cox) *taken down early: chsd ldrs: effrt u.p and chsd ldrs 2f out: no ex and outpcd fnl 100yds* **16/1**

5-01 **5** *1½* **Qanan**[35] 2640 4-9-12 **73** GeorgeBaker 9 71
(Chris Wall) *taken down early: led: rdn over 2f out: sn hdd: no ex and btn 1f out: wl hld and hung rt ins fnl f* **4/1**[2]

5533 **6** *3* **Mcbirney (USA)**[21] 3063 6-9-11 **72** FrederikTylicki 11 63
(Paul D'Arcy) *stdd s: hld up in tch in last quartet: switching out rt and effrt wl over 1f out: no imp 1f out: wknd fnl f* **12/1**

0200 **7** *½* **Norwegian Reward (IRE)**[88] 1297 5-8-9 **56** oh2 PaulHanagan 4 46
(Michael Wigham) *racd in centre tl jnd far side 5f out: stdd s: t.k.h: hld up in rr: rdn and effrt ent fnl 2f: no imp over 1f out: wknd fnl f* **20/1**

00-0 **8** *½* **Woolston Ferry (IRE)**[49] 2232 7-9-13 **74** FergusSweeney 6 63
(Henry Candy) *t.k.h: hld up in tch towards rr: rdn and effrt 2f out: no imp over 1f out: wknd fnl f* **25/1**

5-00 **9** *2½* **Warden Bond**[7] 3534 5-8-9 **56** oh6 (p) MartinHarley 2 39
(William Stone) *racd in centre tl jnd far side 5f out: chsd ldr: rdn and ev ch over 2f out: wknd over 1f out* **66/1**

0254 **10** *¾* **Greyfriarschorista**[24] 2964 6-9-5 **71** (p) RobertTart(5) 3 52
(Tom Keddy) *racd in centre tl jnd far side 5f out: lost pl and rdn ent fnl 2f: no rspnse and wknd over 1f out* **9/1**

1120 **11** *2¾* **Rezwaan**[29] 2808 6-9-3 **71** (p) NedCurtis(7) 7 46
(Murty McGrath) *stdd s: t.k.h: hld up in rr: rdn and no rspnse over 2f out: bhd 1f out* **40/1**

1m 39.9s (-0.10) **Going Correction** -0.025s/f (Good)
WFA 3 from 4yo+ 10lb **11** Ran SP% **117.3**
Speed ratings (Par 103): **99,98,96,95,94 91,90,90,87,86 84**
toteswingers 1&2 £2.70, 1&3 £7.80, 2&3 £5.40 CSF £14.22 CT £106.27 TOTE £8.00: £2.00, £1.10, £2.70; EX 23.30 Trifecta £135.60 Pool: £2064.72 - 11.41 winning tickets..
Owner A Al Hajri **Bred** Robert Raphaelson **Trained** Newmarket, Suffolk

FOCUS
Far side track used with stalls on Far side, except 10f &13f:, which was in the Centre. Bend into home straight reposition which increased distance of 10f &13f races by 20m. After some rain throughout the day the going was changed to good. A fair handicap. Most of the runners converged against the far rail but the winner raced alone under a positive ride down the centre of the track. The winner recorded a persoanl-best with the runner-up building on his recent C&D win and the third a few pounds off last year's best.

3781 BRITISH STALLION STUDS EBF MAIDEN FILLIES' STKS 6f
6:30 (6:31) (Class 4) 2-Y-O **£4,528** (£1,347; £673; £336) **Stalls** High

Form RPR

5 **1** **Lamar (IRE)**[21] 3057 2-9-0 0 NeilCallan 8 85
(James Tate) *mde all: rdn and fnd ex wl over 1f out: drvn ent fnl f: pressed fnl 100yds: hld on gamely and a jst holding runner-up* **5/4**[1]

2 *nk* **Artistic Charm** 2-9-0 0 JimCrowley 9 84
(David Simcock) *t.k.h early: chsd ldrs: chsd wnr 2f out and sn rdn: styd on and pressing wnr fnl 100yds: kpt on wl but a jst hld* **25/1**

3 *2¾* **Qawaasem (IRE)** 2-9-0 0 PaulHanagan 1 76+
(Charles Hills) *awkward leaving stalls: rn green: in tch in last trio: swtchd rt and effrt over 2f out: hdwy to chse ldng pair 1f out: stl showing greeness and edging lft fnl f: kpt on same pce* **14/1**

4 *1¾* **Brown Eyed Honey** 2-9-0 0 MartinHarley 4 71+
(William Haggas) *wnt rt s: hld up in tch in last trio: swtchd rt: rdn and hdwy over 1f out: styd on same pce fnl f* **25/1**

5 *nk* **Flippant (IRE)** 2-9-0 0 RyanMoore 2 70
(William Haggas) *chsd wnr tl 2f out: outpcd u.p over 1f out: kpt on same pce and no threat to ldrs fnl f* **5/1**[3]

6 *nk* **Spellbind** 2-9-0 0 HarryBentley 5 69+
(Saeed bin Suroor) *rn green: in tch in midfield: rdn and unable qck over 2f out: stl showing greenness and sltly outpcd over 1f out: no threat to ldrs but kpt on again ins fnl f* **4/1**[2]

7 *3* **Gentle Breeze (IRE)** 2-9-0 0 MartinLane 7 60
(Saeed bin Suroor) *in tch in midfield: rdn and unable qck 2f out: wknd u.p ent fnl f* **10/1**

8 *½* **Saffire Song** 2-9-0 0 FrederikTylicki 3 58
(Alan Bailey) *bmpd leaving stalls: hld up in tch in rr: rdn and unable qck over 2f out: wknd over 1f out* **66/1**

4 **9** *½* **Relation Alexander (IRE)**[19] 3132 2-9-0 0 AdamKirby 6 57
(Paul D'Arcy) *chsd ldrs: shkn up 1/2-way: rdn and lost pl over 2f out: bhd 1f out* **10/1**

1m 13.64s (1.14) **Going Correction** -0.025s/f (Good) **9** Ran SP% **115.1**
Speed ratings (Par 92): **91,90,86,84,84 83,79,79,78**
toteswingers 1&2 £7.20, 1&3 £4.80, 2&3 £41.40 CSF £41.65 TOTE £2.20: £1.10, £10.30, £4.70; EX 39.40 Trifecta £391.00 Pool: £1760.88 - 3.37 winning tickets..
Owner Saif Ali **Bred** Rabbah Bloodstock Limited **Trained** Newmarket, Suffolk

FOCUS
The experienced favourite put in gutsy front-running display in this maiden which involved a majority of newcomers. The ground seemed to be cutting up a bit. This looked a decent maiden in which several shaped well.

3782 KYOCERA DOCUMENT SOLUTIONS H'CAP 7f
7:05 (7:05) (Class 4) (0-80,79) 3-Y-O **£5,175** (£1,540; £769; £384) **Stalls** High

Form RPR

4100 **1** **Skytrain**[13] 3342 3-9-3 **75** NeilCallan 3 81
(Mark Johnston) *t.k.h: led and set stdy gallop: hdd 4f out: led again 2f out and sn rdn: edgd rt 1f out: grad asserted ins fnl f: styd on wl* **7/1**

-026 **2** *¾* **Dance With Dragons (IRE)**[6] 3582 3-9-2 **79** LauraPike(5) 2 83
(William Stone) *dwlt and bmpd leaving stall: sn pushed along and grad rcvrd to ld 4f out: hdd and rdn 2f out: ev ch after: no ex fnl 100yds* **11/2**

30-2 **3** *1¾* **Secret Beau**[72] 1612 3-9-2 **74** (v) JimCrowley 4 73
(Ralph Beckett) *t.k.h: chsd ldrs: swtchd lft towards far side 5f out: rdn and effrt 2f out: styd on same pce fnl f* **9/2**[3]

6441 **4** *¾* **Benoni**[14] 3289 3-9-2 **74** FergusSweeney 1 71
(Henry Candy) *t.k.h: hld up in tch in midfield: outpcd and rdn 2f out: rallied and styd on ins fnl f: no threat to ldng pair* **7/2**[1]

2214 **5** *½* **Firmdecisions (IRE)**[28] 2844 3-9-4 **76** (p) GeorgeBaker 8 72
(Brett Johnson) *stdd s: t.k.h: hld up in tch in rr: swtchd lft towards far side 5f out: rdn and no prog 2f out: hdwy ins fnl f: styd on towards fin: no threat to ldng pair* **13/2**

-600 **6** *1* **Vallarta (IRE)**[22] 3020 3-9-5 **77** MartinHarley 5 70
(Mick Channon) *in tch in midfield: rdn and chsd ldng trio over 1f out: no ex 1f out: wknd ins fnl f* **4/1**[2]

1255 **7** *2¾* **Admiralofthesea (USA)**[11] 3404 3-8-12 **70** AdamBeschizza 6 56
(Robert Eddery) *t.k.h: hld up in tch in midfield: swtchd lft towards far side 5f out: rdn and effrt 2f out: no imp and wl hld after* **12/1**

14-0 **8** *4* **Aye Aye Skipper (IRE)**[23] 2984 3-9-3 **75** [1] AdamKirby 7 50
(Dean Ivory) *rrd as stalls opened: t.k.h: hld up in tch in rr: outpcd and rdn 2f out: n.d after: eased towards fin* **25/1**

1m 26.47s (0.77) **Going Correction** -0.025s/f (Good) **8** Ran SP% **113.2**
Speed ratings (Par 101): **94,93,91,90,89 88,85,80**
toteswingers 1&2 £8.50, 1&3 £5.80, 2&3 £4.20 CSF £44.02 CT £191.59 TOTE £7.20: £1.90, £2.60, £1.90; EX 59.20 Trifecta £245.30 Pool: £1105.03 - 3.37 winning tickets..
Owner A D Spence **Bred** Brook Stud Bloodstock Ltd **Trained** Middleham Moor, N Yorks

FOCUS
They went a steady pace in this handicap. The hold-up runners struggled to get involved and the winner scored under another good ride from Neil Callan.

3783 DANWOOD.CO.UK PRINT SAVINGS H'CAP 1m 5f
7:35 (7:38) (Class 4) (0-80,85) 3-Y-O **£5,175** (£1,540; £769; £384) **Stalls** Centre

Form RPR

5122 **1** **Arbaah (USA)**[28] 2846 3-9-3 **76** PaulHanagan 7 86
(Brian Meehan) *mde all: rdn clr 2f out: in command after: styd on wl: rdn out* **9/2**[3]

15 **2** *5* **Deira Phantom (IRE)**[36] 2602 3-9-7 **80** HarryBentley 4 82
(Roger Varian) *chsd wnr: rdn and unable qck w wnr 2f out: wl hld after but plugged on to hold 2nd fnl f* **7/2**[2]

6-13 **3** *3¾* **Sioux Chieftain (IRE)**[42] 2432 3-9-3 **76** ShaneKelly 3 72
(Tim Pitt) *chsd ldrs: rdn and effrt over 2f out: 3rd and no imp whn edgd lft u.p over 1f out: plugged on* **13/8**[1]

-610 **4** *1½* **Getaway Car**[27] 2878 3-8-6 **65** (p) MartinLane 5 59
(Gerard Butler) *hld up in tch in last pair: hdwy to chse ldrs 5f out: struggling u.p over 3f out: 4th and wl hld over 1f out* **14/1**

4001 **5** *3¼* **Kuantan One (IRE)**[28] 2846 3-9-4 **77** JimCrowley 6 66
(Paul Cole) *hld up in tch: rdn and no hdwy over 2f out: 5th and wl btn over 1f out* **5/1**

014 **6** *33* **Song Light**[20] 3105 3-9-4 **77** .... SebSanders 8
(David Elsworth) *hld up in tch in rr: rdn and no rspnse over 2f out: lost tch 2f out: virtually p.u ins fnl f: t.o* **9/1**

2m 46.73s (2.73) **Going Correction** -0.025s/f (Good) **6** Ran SP% **111.8**
Speed ratings (Par 101): **90,86,84,83,81 61**
toteswingers 1&2 £3.10, 1&3 £2.50, 2&3 £1.30 CSF £20.23 CT £34.59 TOTE £4.00: £2.10, £2.60; EX 20.40 Trifecta £56.90 Pool: £1241.49 - 16.33 winning tickets..
Owner Hamdan Al Maktoum **Bred** Shadwell Farm LLC **Trained** Manton, Wilts

FOCUS
There was an emphatic front-running winner in this middle-distance handicap. The runner-up looks the best guide but this could be better than rated.

3784 BRITISH STALLION STUDS EBF FILLIES' CONDITIONS STKS 6f
8:05 (8:06) (Class 3) 3-Y-0+ **£9,056** (£2,695; £1,346; £673) **Stalls** High

Form RPR
4-20 **1** **City Girl (IRE)**[20] 3102 3-8-8 **95** .... JimCrowley 1 103
(Ralph Beckett) *racd down centre: chsd ldrs tl led 2f out: edgd lft u.p over 1f out: kpt on wl ins fnl f: drvn out* **8/1**

5443 **2** *1 ¾* **Miss Lahar**[12] 3373 4-8-12 **95** .... MartinHarley 6 96
(Mick Channon) *stdd s: t.k.h: hld up in tch in midfield: rdn and effrt 2f out: chsd wnr 1f out: styd on same pce fnl 100yds* **8/1**

0-14 **3** *1* **Hallelujah**[12] 3373 5-8-12 **101** .... FrederikTylicki 2 93
(James Fanshawe) *in tch in last pair: rdn 3f out: drvn: outpcd and looked wl hld over 1f out: rallied and styd on ins fnl f: no threat to wnr* **15/8**[1]

4463 **4** *1 ¼* **Mar Mar (IRE)**[20] 3103 3-8-8 **97** .... (b) WilliamBuick 4 90
(Saeed bin Suroor) *t.k.h: hld up wl in tch in midfield: rdn and unable qck over 1f out: edgd lft and plugged on same pce fnl f* **10/3**[2]

-064 **5** *shd* **Tassel**[28] 2848 3-8-9 **89** ow1 .... RyanMoore 7 90
(Richard Hannon) *sn pushed along to ld: rdn and hdd 2f out: no ex u.p ent fnl f: wknd and lost 2 pls ins fnl f* **8/1**

21-0 **6** *1* **Beautiful View**[13] 3342 3-8-8 **88** .... TomQueally 5 86
(Richard Hannon) *stdd s: t.k.h: hld up in tch in rr: rdn and no hdwy 2f out: n.d but plugged on same pce ins fnl f* **15/2**[3]

4-02 **7** *3 ¼* **Supernova Heights (IRE)**[25] 2928 3-8-8 **89** .... MartinLane 8 78
(Brian Meehan) *chsd ldr tl over 2f out: sn rdn and lost pl 2f out: bhd 1f out: wknd fnl f* **11/1**

1m 11.66s (-0.84) **Going Correction** -0.025s/f (Good)
WFA 3 from 4yo+ 7lb **7** Ran SP% **111.3**
Speed ratings (Par 104): **104,101,100,98,98 97,92**
toteswingers 1&2 £7.40, 1&3 £2.40, 2&3 £3.80 CSF £64.32 TOTE £8.60: £3.00, £3.20; EX 39.00 Trifecta £131.40 Pool: £1006.50 - 5.74 winning tickets..
Owner J C Smith **Bred** Littleton Stud **Trained** Kimpton, Hants

FOCUS
A useful conditions event for fillies. The winner battled bravely to score under a prominent ride, but again there seemed to be a pace bias and the form may not work out. The runner-up sets the standard with the fifth and sixth close to their marks.

3785 TURFTV H'CAP 1m 2f
8:40 (8:41) (Class 4) (0-80,78) 3-Y-0+
£4,980 (£1,491; £745; £372; £186; £93) **Stalls** Centre

Form RPR
-321 **1** **Paris Rose**[7] 3542 3-9-2 **78** 6ex .... RyanMoore 3 88+
(William Haggas) *chsd ldr: effrt u.p to ld wl over 1f out: in command and styd on wl ins fnl f* **13/8**[1]

-004 **2** *2* **Amoya (GER)**[20] 3095 6-9-10 **74** .... AdamBeschizza 5 80
(Philip McBride) *led: drvn and hdd wl over 1f out: hld and styd on same pce fnl f* **7/1**[2]

0510 **3** *2 ½* **Handsome Stranger (IRE)**[8] 3497 3-7-8 **63** .... (v) NoelGarbutt(7) 2 64
(Alan Bailey) *t.k.h: hld up in tch in midfield: rdn and effrt to chse ldng pair 2f out: styd on same pce fr over 1f out* **40/1**

3-11 **4** *8* **Tajheez (IRE)**[15] 3232 3-8-13 **75** .... PaulHanagan 1 60
(Roger Varian) *plld hrd: hld up in midfield: 4th and effrt u.p wl over 1f out: no prog and wl hld 1f out: wknd fnl f* **13/8**[1]

2-20 **5** *4 ½* **Three Choirs (IRE)**[14] 3277 3-8-7 **74** .... (p) RobertTart(5) 6 50
(William Stone) *chsd ldrs: rdn 4f out: lost pl u.p over 2f out: 5th and wknd over 1f out* **20/1**

5-44 **6** *9* **Odin (IRE)**[10] 378 5-10-0 **78** .... (p) LiamKeniry 4 36
(Don Cantillon) *stdd s: hld up in tch in rr: rdn over 2f out: sn btn and bhd over 1f out* **20/1**

3042 **7** *3 ¾* **Patriotic (IRE)**[31] 2761 5-9-11 **75** .... (p) AdamKirby 7 33
(Chris Dwyer) *stdd s: hld up in last pair: rdn and short-lived effrt over 2f out: wknd and bhd over 1f out* **9/1**[3]

2m 5.69s (0.19) **Going Correction** -0.025s/f (Good)
WFA 3 from 5yo+ 12lb **7** Ran SP% **110.7**
Speed ratings (Par 105): **98,96,94,88,84 74,77**
toteswingers 1&2 £2.80, 1&3 £4.40, 2&3 £22.20 CSF £13.05 TOTE £2.60: £1.60, £3.30; EX 14.20 Trifecta £228.40 Pool: £1513.10 - 4.96 winning tickets..
Owner Jaber Abdullah **Bred** Rabbah Bloodstock Limited **Trained** Newmarket, Suffolk

FOCUS
They raced near the stands' rail in this handicap. A progressive 3-y-o forged clear and was the first winner on the card to score from off the pace. The winner was well-in under a penalty and the second is rated a slight improver on this year's form.

3786 NEWMARKETEXPERIENCE.CO.UK H'CAP 5f
9:10 (9:11) (Class 4) (0-85,85) 3-Y-0+ **£5,175** (£1,540; £769; £384) **Stalls** High

Form RPR
0420 **1** **Tax Free (IRE)**[6] 3561 11-9-11 **85** .... TomQueally 4 96
(David Nicholls) *chsd ldrs: rdn over 1f out: hdwy u.p to ld fnl 75yds: hld on wl: all out* **8/1**

0330 **2** *shd* **Gladiatrix**[12] 3371 4-9-8 **82** .... (b) RyanMoore 6 93
(Rod Millman) *chsd ldr: rdn to ld jst over 1f out: drvn and hdd fnl 75yds: kpt on wl: jst hld* **7/2**[2]

-112 **3** *1* **Asian Trader**[12] 3371 4-9-5 **79** .... (t) FrankieDettori 5 86
(William Haggas) *hld up in midfield: clsd and swtchd rt over 1f out: sn rdn: chsd ldng pair ins fnl f: one pce fnl 100yds* **6/4**[1]

3446 **4** *1 ½* **Waseem Faris (IRE)**[14] 3299 4-9-3 **77** .... MartinHarley 2 79
(Mick Channon) *stdd s: hld up in last pair: clsd 2f out: drvn and effrt over 1f out: kpt on ins fnl f to snatch 4th last strides: no threat to ldrs* **9/1**

0400 **5** *nse* **Equitania**[6] 3584 3-9-5 **85** .... (p) FrederikTylicki 8 86
(Alan Bailey) *led: rdn wl over 1f out: hdd jst over 1f out: wknd fnl 100yds* **10/1**

0100 **6** *2 ¾* **Church Music (IRE)**[15] 3249 4-9-10 **84** .... (v) GeorgeBaker 7 76
(Michael Scudamore) *hld up in midfield: effrt u.p over 1f out: no prog 1f out: wknd ins fnl f* **25/1**

2062 **7** *1* **Rocket Rob (IRE)**[13] 3341 7-9-2 **76** .... WilliamBuick 1 64
(Willie Musson) *dwlt: sn swtchd lft and pushed along in detached last: n.d* **11/2**[3]

58.18s (-0.92) **Going Correction** -0.025s/f (Good)
WFA 3 from 4yo+ 6lb **7** Ran SP% **111.7**
Speed ratings (Par 105): **106,105,104,101,101 97,95**
toteswingers 1&2 £2.00, 1&3 £2.50, 2&3 £1.70 CSF £34.26 TOTE £7.10: £3.30, £2.50; EX 24.60 Trifecta £29.10 Pool: £1231.41 - 31.73 winning tickets..
Owner D Nicholls & Mrs J Love **Bred** Denis And Mrs Teresa Bergin **Trained** Sessay, N Yorks

FOCUS
They went a decent pace against the far rail in this sprint handicap and an admirable veteran recorded his 17th win. Cadeaux Pearl reared and went down in the stalls before being withdrawn. The first two are rated in line with recent efforts.
T/Plt: £215.60 to a £1 stake. Pool: £65227.28 - 220.82 winning tickets T/Qpdt: £56.10 to a £1 stake. Pool: £3777.00 - 49.80 winning tickets SP

3737 YARMOUTH (L-H)
Friday, June 28

OFFICIAL GOING: Good to firm (7.7)
Wind: light against Weather: overcast; 18 degrees

3787 EUROPEAN BREEDERS' FUND MAIDEN FILLIES' STKS 6f 3y
2:20 (2:22) (Class 5) 3-Y-0+ **£3,881** (£1,155; £577; £288) **Stalls** Centre

Form RPR
3 **1** **Ghasabah**[23] 2979 3-9-0 0 .... PaulHanagan 3 84+
(William Haggas) *t.k.h and pressed ldrs: wnt 2nd over 2f out: led gng best over 1f out: shkn up and in command after* **11/10**[1]

4-4 **2** *2 ¾* **Honeymoon Express (IRE)**[15] 3253 3-9-0 0 .... AnnelieHollstenius 7 70
(Julia Feilden) *prom: led wl over 2f out: rdn and hdd over 1f out: wkng fnl 100yds: jst hld on to 2nd* **66/1**

3 *½* **Arcadian Legend (USA)** 3-9-0 0 .... ShaneKelly 5 68+
(Jeremy Noseda) *s.s and rdn: bhd tl hdwy 2f out: wnt 3rd over 1f out: kpt on steadily and catching 2nd nr fin* **11/1**[3]

0-42 **4** *14* **Arbeel**[27] 2872 3-9-0 70 .... JamieSpencer 2 24
(Peter Chapple-Hyam) *led tl wl over 2f out: lost tch wl over 1f out* **5/4**[2]

040- **5** *2 ¾* **Cross Pattee (IRE)**[277] 6541 3-9-0 65 .... (e[1]) TedDurcan 1
(Ed Vaughan) *s.i.s: towards rr: struggling 1/2-way: t.o* **22/1**

0-0 **6** *2 ¾* **Grey Poppett**[15] 3253 3-8-11 0 .... RaulDaSilva(3) 6
(Chris Dwyer) *t.k.h: prom: rdn 1/2-way: fdd qckly over 2f out: t.o* **200/1**

00- **7** *23* **L'Ile Rousse**[412] 2085 4-9-0 0 .... JoshCrane(7) 4
(Chris Dwyer) *a towards rr: struggling 1/2-way: hopelessly t.o and eased* **250/1**

1m 12.14s (-2.26) **Going Correction** -0.30s/f (Firm)
WFA 3 from 4yo 7lb **7** Ran SP% **107.1**
Speed ratings (Par 100): **103,99,98,80,76 72,42**
toteswingers 1&2 £4.20, 1&3 £1.50, 2&3 £4.50 CSF £60.56 TOTE £1.80: £1.20, £15.90; EX 37.40 Trifecta £123.50 Pool: £2728.19 - 16.56 winning tickets..
Owner Hamdan Al Maktoum **Bred** Shadwell Estate Company Limited **Trained** Newmarket, Suffolk

FOCUS
Bottom bend out 2m for fresh ground, adding 12m to races on round course. A fairly weak fillies' maiden in which only two of the runners held a chance on all known form. However, there was no doubt about who was best on the day. The form is treated slightly negatively due to the proximity of the runner-up.

3788 VISITENGLAND.COM H'CAP 1m 3y
2:50 (2:50) (Class 6) (0-65,65) 4-Y-0+ **£1,940** (£577; £288; £144) **Stalls** Centre

Form RPR
4636 **1** **Jonnie Skull (IRE)**[2] 3700 7-9-6 **64** .... (vt) FrederikTylicki 9 71
(Phil McEntee) *mde all: rdn 1f out: kpt on v gamely* **6/1**

0-21 **2** *¾* **Pink Lips**[31] 2747 5-9-0 **58** .... TedDurcan 10 63
(J R Jenkins) *towards rr: drvn fr 1/2-way: stl plenty to do in 6th over 1f out: fin strly to snatch 2nd but wnr beyond recall* **7/2**[1]

10-5 **3** *½* **Enriching (USA)**[24] 2966 5-9-4 **62** .... ShaneKelly 8 66
(Gary Harrison) *pressed ldrs: rdn and n.m.r 2f out: chal 1f out and wnt 2nd 100yds out: nt qckn and lost 2nd nr fin* **11/2**[3]

0032 **4** *1 ½* **Spin Again (IRE)**[13] 3329 8-8-8 **52** .... KirstyMilczarek 2 53
(John Ryan) *t.k.h and prom: wnt 2nd over 2f out: sn rdn: lost 2nd and wkng fnl 100yds* **12/1**

4165 **5** *nk* **Monsieur Pontaven**[22] 3029 6-8-3 **49** ow2 .... (b) BillyCray(3) 6 50
(Robin Bastiman) *hld up and bhd: swtchd outside over 1f out: kpt on but no threat to ldrs although nrly snatched 4th* **18/1**

4654 **6** *¾* **Floralys (USA)**[13] 3326 4-8-12 **56** .... JamieSpencer 7 54
(Amy Weaver) *t.k.h towards rr: effrt 3f out: sn rdn w little rspnse: btn wl over 1f out* **11/2**[3]

265 **7** *¾* **Hail Promenader (IRE)**[35] 2640 7-9-2 **60** .... (p) WilliamCarson 3 57
(Anthony Carson) *chsd ldrs: rdn 1/2-way: one pce and no imp fnl 2f* **4/1**[2]

202- **8** *10* **Giorgio's Dragon (IRE)**[276] 6560 4-9-7 **65** .... AdamBeschizza 1 39
(Robert Stephens) *taken down early: plld hrd: swtchd rt after s: pressed wnr tl rdn and lost pl qckly over 2f out: wl bhd whn eased fnl f* **9/1**

0-00 **9** *4 ½* **Jessica's Gold**[31] 2746 4-8-2 **46** oh1 .... JimmyQuinn 5 9
(Christine Dunnett) *s.s: in last pair: struggling bdly 3f out: t.o and eased* **66/1**

1m 40.34s (-0.26) **Going Correction** +0.025s/f (Good) **9** Ran SP% **111.7**
Speed ratings (Par 101): **102,101,100,99,98 98,97,87,82**
toteswingers 1&2 £4.00, 1&3 £11.70, 2&3 £5.70 CSF £26.03 CT £110.78 TOTE £7.00: £2.30, £1.70, £2.10; EX 21.00 Trifecta £120.80 Pool: £2176.03 - 13.50 winning tickets..
Owner Eventmaker Racehorses **Bred** Canice Farrell Jnr **Trained** Newmarket, Suffolk
■ Stewards' Enquiry : Billy Cray two-day ban; used whip above permitted level.
Ted Durcan two-day ban; used whip above permitted level (15th-16th July).

FOCUS
A competitive, if only moderate handicap with over half of the field bringing previous course-winning form to the table. The third is rated back to form and sets the level.

3789 SEADELL SHOPS AND CHALETS AT HEMSBY H'CAP 5f 43y
3:20 (3:20) (Class 6) (0-60,60) 3-Y-0 **£1,940** (£577; £288; £144) **Stalls** Centre

Form RPR
6404 **1** **Green Monkey**[16] 3221 3-9-5 **58** .... FrederikTylicki 6 63+
(James Fanshawe) *settled in rr: effrt 2f out: rdn to ld on rails 1f out: hld on wl* **2/1**[1]

000 **2** *½* **Welsh Moonlight**[27] 2872 3-9-7 **60** .... SaleemGolam 4 63+
(Stuart Williams) *bhd: gd hdwy over 1f out: str run to go 2nd wl ins fnl f: too much to do* **7/2**[3]

4064 **3** ¾ **Imperial Spirit**[13] 3316 3-8-8 **50** ow2.......................(v) CharlesBishop(5) 8 51
(Mick Channon) *prom: led 2f out: drifted lft over 1f out and impeded rival: sn hdd: nt qckn after: lost 2nd nr fin* **10/3**[2]
040- **4** shd **Hellolini**[315] 5313 3-8-10 **52**.. BillyCray(3) 2 52
(Robin Bastiman) *prom: sn pushed along: ev ch but drifting rt over 1f out: nt qckn after* **33/1**
0-60 **5** 2 ½ **Marvelous Miss (IRE)**[35] 2643 3-8-7 **46** oh1.................. JimmyQuinn 1 37
(Christine Dunnett) *racd keenly on outside: pressed ldrs: rdn and short-lived effrt over 1f out* **66/1**
5005 **6** 1 ¼ **Lively Little Lady**[16] 3221 3-8-9 **48**.............................(v[1]) CathyGannon 7 38
(Tim Pitt) *slt ld 3f: rdn and wkng whn squeezed out over 1f out* **16/1**
-240 **7** hd **Senora Lobo (IRE)**[13] 3323 3-9-2 **55**.................................. TedDurcan 3 41
(Lisa Williamson) *towards rr: rdn and btn 2f out: eased cl home* **5/1**
5004 **8** 4 ½ **Viva L'Inghilterra (IRE)**[13] 3323 3-8-11 **50**....................(p) ShaneKelly 5 20
(Robert Cowell) *plld hrd: w ldrs over 3f out: sn wknd* **10/1**

1m 3.6s (0.90) **Going Correction** +0.025s/f (Good) **8** Ran SP% **114.7**
Speed ratings (Par 97): **93,92,91,90,86 84,84,77**
toteswingers 1&2 £3.70, 1&3 £2.60, 2&3 £3.20 CSF £9.21 CT £21.58 TOTE £2.80: £1.10, £2.50, £1.20; EX 13.60 Trifecta £40.50 Pool: £2313.56 - 42.82 winning tickets..
Owner Mr & Mrs P Hopper, Mr & Mrs M Morris **Bred** Jan & Peter Hopper **Trained** Newmarket, Suffolk
■ Stewards' Enquiry : Charles Bishop three-day ban; weight in heavy (15th-17th July).

FOCUS
A low-grade 3-y-o handicap and, although the first two are relatively unexposed, not form to go overboard about.

3790 GUIDE DOGS FOR THE BLIND H'CAP 2m
3:55 (3:56) (Class 5) (0-75,75) 4-Y-O+ **£2,587** (£770; £384; £192) **Stalls** Low

Form RPR
0-02 **1** **Bounty Seeker (USA)**[12] 3363 4-9-4 **70**............................ LiamJones 1 76
(Mark Johnston) *mde nrly all: pushed along at times fr 1/2-way: hmpd rival over 2f out and lft clr: a holding on after* **10/3**[2]
1000 **2** ¾ **Foster's Road**[23] 2990 4-9-1 **72**.................................. CharlesBishop(5) 2 77
(Mick Channon) *hld up last: effrt 4f out to go 2nd over 2f out: sn impeded and lost momentum: rallied gamely and clsng ins fnl f where regained 2nd: looked rather unlucky* **5/1**[3]
153 **3** 3 **Naburn**[38] 2540 5-8-13 **65**.. JimmyQuinn 7 66
(Alan Swinbank) *settled in 3rd tl qcknd to ld briefly 6f out: 3rd and rdn and one pce over 2f out: lft 2nd and plugged on wout clsng: lost 2nd ins fnl f* **10/3**[2]
-601 **4** 2 **Queen's Star**[25] 2922 4-8-10 **62**....................................... CathyGannon 4 60
(Andrew Balding) *hld up in 4th pl: rdn over 5f out: limited rspnse: plodded on and no real threat fnl 3f* **7/4**[1]
46-3 **5** 8 **Astrogold**[52] 2136 4-7-13 **54** oh1.................................. SimonPearce(3) 5 43
(Mark H Tompkins) *chsd ldr tl appr home turn: sn racd v awkwardly: rdn over 5f out: fdd wl over 2f out* **9/1**

3m 38.03s (5.63) **Going Correction** +0.10s/f (Good) **5** Ran SP% **109.2**
Speed ratings (Par 103): **89,88,87,86,82**
CSF £18.87 TOTE £3.80: £2.60, £2.70; EX 16.10 Trifecta £51.70 Pool: £2442.19 - 35.36 winning tickets..
Owner A D Spence **Bred** Arindel **Trained** Middleham Moor, N Yorks
■ Stewards' Enquiry : Liam Jones two-day ban; careless riding (15th-16th July).

FOCUS
A tactically run staying handicap, the form of which should be treated with a degree of caution. Front-runners are generally favoured in steadily run races, and that certainly proved the way of it on this occasion. The winner is rated to this year's form.

3791 ANGLIAN HOME IMPROVEMENT RAISING THE STANDARD H'CAP 1m 3f 101y
4:30 (4:30) (Class 4) (0-80,80) 4-Y-O+ **£4,690** (£1,395; £697; £348) **Stalls** Low

Form RPR
4-03 **1** **Colinca's Lad (IRE)**[27] 2867 11-8-12 **76**...................... RosieJessop(5) 1 84
(Peter Charalambous) *led at str pce: sn clr: 10 l ld on home turn: rdn 3f out: pressed 1f out: almost jnd fnl 100yds and looked v vulnerable but kpt battling and asserted nr fin* **4/1**[3]
-015 **2** ½ **Villa Royale**[23] 2973 4-9-7 **80**.. ShaneKelly 7 87+
(David O'Meara) *hld up: wnt 4th st: rdn 3f out: tk 2nd and gng clr of rest wl over 1f out: urged upsides on rails w 100yds to go: outbattled nr fin* **5/2**[1]
161 **3** 7 **Honest Deal**[77] 1523 5-9-7 **80**.. JimmyQuinn 3 76
(Alan Swinbank) *chsd wnr tl over 4f out: sn rdn: lost tch w ldng pair over 1f out: eased clsng stages* **18/1**
065 **4** 1 ¾ **Layline (IRE)**[9] 3480 6-8-4 **70**...................................... DanielMuscutt(7) 4 63
(Gay Kelleway) *last pair: rdn and outpcd 4f out: plodded on fnl 2f* **13/2**
112 **5** 4 ½ **Dandy (GER)**[18] 3150 4-9-5 **78**...(p) CathyGannon 6 64
(Andrew Balding) *settled in 3rd: rdn to go 2nd over 4f out: tk 2nd u.p 3f out tl wl over 1f out: wknd tamely* **6/1**
-204 **6** 3 ¾ **Aegaeus**[14] 3293 4-9-6 **79**.. JamieSpencer 5 59
(Ed Dunlop) *dropped out last: cajoled along 4f out: fnd nil and plodded on* **10/3**[2]
60-0 **7** 25 **Queen's Estate (GER)**[16] 3204 4-8-13 **72**......................... LiamJones 2 12
(Mark Johnston) *chsd ldrs: lost tch tamely over 4f out: t.o over 2f out* **11/1**

2m 28.4s (-0.30) **Going Correction** +0.10s/f (Good) **7** Ran SP% **112.9**
Speed ratings (Par 105): **105,104,99,98,95 92,74**
toteswingers 1&2 £3.70, 1&3 £9.80, 2&3 £6.10 CSF £14.04 TOTE £6.40: £2.60, £1.90; EX 22.30 Trifecta £248.40 Pool: £3421.72 - 10.33 winning tickets..
Owner P Charalambous **Bred** Peter Charles **Trained** Newmarket, Suffolk

FOCUS
A highly competitive handicap, despite the relatively small field, and an admirable effort by the veteran winner. The runner-up is rated to her recent Catterick mark.

3792 HOLIDAY ON THE NORFOLK BROADS H'CAP 1m 3f 101y
5:05 (5:06) (Class 6) (0-60,59) 4-Y-O+ **£1,940** (£577; £288; £144) **Stalls** Low

Form RPR
-003 **1** **Frosty Secret**[18] 3151 4-8-10 **48**..(b) LiamJones 5 57
(Jane Chapple-Hyam) *sn pushed into ld: rdn 3f out: 3 l clr 1f out: kpt on stoutly* **10/1**
0223 **2** 1 ¾ **Peace In Our Time**[27] 2875 4-9-7 **59**........................(b[1]) WilliamCarson 4 65
(Anthony Carson) *trckd ldrs: wnt 2nd over 3f out: rdn 2f out: no imp fnl f and easily hld* **2/1**[1]
4-05 **3** 1 ¼ **Astroscarlet**[17] 3168 4-8-7 **48**.................................... SimonPearce(3) 2 52
(Mark H Tompkins) *cl up: 4th st: sn rdn: no real rspnse: btn 2f out: wnt one pce 3rd cl home* **4/1**[3]
3005 **4** ¾ **Frosty Friday**[17] 3169 5-8-10 **48**.................................(p) TedDurcan 3 51
(J R Jenkins) *dropped out last tl rdn 4f out: prog to 3rd 2f out: no imp after: lost 3rd nr fin* **15/2**

0-00 **5** 6 **Omega Omega**[46] 2332 4-8-0 **45**.................................. ShelleyBirkett(7) 7 38
(Julia Feilden) *last trio: shkn up 4f out: sn struggling: eased fnl f* **14/1**
-051 **6** 10 **Josie's Dream (IRE)**[11] 3406 5-9-4 **56** 6ex...................... CathyGannon 1 33
(Jo Hughes) *last pair: rdn 4f out: struggling after: eased 1f out* **11/4**[2]
0-60 **7** ½ **Princess Palmer**[13] 3326 4-8-2 **45**.............................. RosieJessop(5) 6 22
(Lydia Pearce) *plld hrd in 2nd or 3rd: lost pl qckly over 3f out: eased 1f out: t.o* **33/1**

2m 30.79s (2.09) **Going Correction** +0.10s/f (Good) **7** Ran SP% **110.5**
Speed ratings (Par 101): **96,94,93,93,88 81,81**
toteswingers 1&2 £3.50, 1&3 £3.30, 2&3 £3.00 CSF £28.39 TOTE £12.70: £3.40, £1.50; EX 27.10 Trifecta £128.00 Pool: £4035.37 - 23.64 winning tickets..
Owner Simon Brewster **Bred** Langham Hall Stud **Trained** Dalham, Suffolk

FOCUS
Yarmouth had proved something of a front-runners' paradise at this meeting and history repeated itself in this handicap with Liam Jones getting the fractions right aboard the winner. The form looks ordinary rated around the principals.

3793 WEDDINGS AT GREAT YARMOUTH RACECOURSE H'CAP 1m 2f 21y
5:40 (5:41) (Class 5) (0-70,70) 3-Y-O **£2,587** (£770; £384; £192) **Stalls** Low

Form RPR
6-04 **1** **Tenor (IRE)**[53] 2093 3-9-4 **67**.. ChrisCatlin 9 72
(Roger Varian) *prom: drvn and outpcd briefly 3f out: rallied to 2nd over 1f out: edging lft after: urged ahd cl home* **2/1**[1]
-433 **2** nk **Zhuba (IRE)**[15] 3254 3-8-13 **62**.................................... WilliamCarson 1 66
(John Best) *sn led: almost jnd 3f out: rdn and kpt on wl tl hdd fnl 50yds* **5/1**[3]
045- **3** 3 **Runninglikethewind (IRE)**[273] 6645 3-9-2 **65**.................. TedDurcan 8 64
(Chris Wall) *plld hrd and prom: jnd ldr 3f out tl rdn 2f out: lost 2nd over 1f out: one pce* **5/1**[3]
040 **4** 1 **Duchess Of Dreams**[3] 3653 3-7-9 **51** oh6.................... NoelGarbutt(7) 4 48
(Richard Guest) *t.k.h: chsd ldrs: rdn over 2f out: no imp* **33/1**
-335 **5** nk **First Sargeant**[11] 3418 3-9-6 **69**....................................(p) JimmyQuinn 3 65
(Marco Botti) *t.k.h: pressed ldrs: shkn up 4f out: drvn 3f out: kpt on same pce and wl hld fnl 2f* **12/1**
-000 **6** 3 **Algorithmic (IRE)**[39] 2508 3-8-6 **55**............................... NickyMackay 5 46
(Michael Bell) *s.i.s: hld up towards rr: brief effrt on outer 3f out: rdn and nvr able to chal* **12/1**
4034 **7** 6 **Dark Templar**[10] 3438 3-9-7 **70**...................................... JamieSpencer 7 49
(Ed Vaughan) *stdd s: plld hrd in last: 10 l last on home turn: nvr on terms after* **4/1**[2]
3310 **8** 2 ½ **Two No Bids (IRE)**[79] 1487 3-9-5 **68**........................ KirstyMilczarek 2 42
(Phil McEntee) *t.k.h towards rr: rdn and btn 3f out* **25/1**
5-00 **9** 20 **Exempt**[20] 3116 3-9-1 **64**... ShaneKelly 6
(Jeremy Noseda) *nvr bttr than midfield: shkn up over 4f out: rdn and struggling 3f out: t.o and eased over 1f out* **14/1**

2m 11.41s (0.91) **Going Correction** +0.10s/f (Good) **9** Ran SP% **115.5**
Speed ratings (Par 99): **100,99,97,96,96 93,89,87,71**
toteswingers 1&2 £3.30, 1&3 £4.80, 2&3 £4.60 CSF £12.12 CT £43.57 TOTE £2.80: £1.30, £1.90, £2.00; EX 10.70 Trifecta £58.90 Pool: £2845.26 - 36.21 winning tickets..
Owner Highclere Thoroughbred Racing-JohnPorter **Bred** Epona Bloodstock Ltd And P A Byrne **Trained** Newmarket, Suffolk

FOCUS
An informative 3-y-o handicap on paper but, with very little in the way of pace on in the early stages, it remains to be seen how well the form holds up. The bare form is modest.
T/Plt: £97.40 to a £1 stake. Pool: £76111.21 - 570.08 winning tickets T/Qpdt: £23.60 to a £1 stake. Pool: £4487.38 - 140.62 winning tickets IM

3794 - 3795a (Foreign Racing) - See Raceform Interactive

3139 CURRAGH (R-H)
Friday, June 28

OFFICIAL GOING: Round course - good to firm (watering); straight course - good (good to firm in places)

3796a IRISH NATIONAL STUD GATHERING H'CAP 5f
6:30 (6:35) (60-90,92) 3-Y-O+ **£7,573** (£1,756; £768; £439)

RPR
1 **Yulong Baoju (IRE)**[23] 3000 3-9-10 **84**.....................(p) JohnnyMurtagh 4 93+
(Edward Lynam, Ire) *trckd ldr in centre of trck and overall 2nd 1/2-way: styd on wl to ld fnl 150yds: comf* **7/2**[2]
2 1 **Speed Dream (IRE)**[20] 3121 9-9-0 **75**...................... DylanRobinson(7) 3 82
(James M Barrett, Ire) *w.w: travelled wl in centre of trck in 3rd appr fnl f: styd on wl to go 2nd fnl 100yds: nt trble wnr* **8/1**[3]
3 2 ¼ **Powerful Wind (IRE)**[12] 3371 4-9-8 **76**......................... KevinManning 1 75
(Ronald Harris) *smartly away and sn disp in centre of trck: overall advantage 1/2-way tl wandered fr 1f out: hdd fnl 150yds* **11/1**
4 1 ¼ **Wicked Wench**[11] 3407 4-9-10 **78**...................................(p) WJLee 11 72
(Jeremy Gask) *w.w stands' side: nt clr run over 1f out and swtchd rt: kpt on wout threatening ldrs* **9/1**
5 ½ **Knock Stars (IRE)**[22] 3032 5-9-13 **81**............................(bt) ChrisHayes 9 74
(Patrick Martin, Ire) *racd in mid-div tl tk clsr order in 5th over 1f out: one pce fnl 100yds* **14/1**
6 ½ **Rigid Rock (IRE)**[84] 1376 6-8-13 **67**.. FMBerry 6 58
(J T Gorman, Ire) *trckd ldr in 2nd on stands' side: overall 4th over 1f out: sn one pce* **20/1**
7 nk **Stones Peak (IRE)**[247] 7336 6-9-8 **79**......................... RonanWhelan(3) 2 69
(Patrick Martin, Ire) *hld up towards rr: sme late hdwy* **16/1**
8 ½ **Pencil Hill (IRE)**[133] 679 8-9-7 **82**.......................... MeganCarberry(7) 13 70
(Tracey Collins, Ire) *slowly away and sn in rr: kpt on wl ins fnl f* **16/1**
9 nse **City Of Culture (IRE)**[14] 3306 5-8-6 **63**........................ ShaneBKelly(3) 10 51
(W McCreery, Ire) *chsd ldrs stands' side: short of room over 1f out: sn no ex* **25/1**
10 hd **Scatty Cat (IRE)**[1] 3746 3-9-4 **78**................................. MichaelHussey 5 63
(Peter McCreery, Ire) *chsd ldrs stands' side tl no imp 1f out: kpt on one pce* **20/1**
11 2 **Illustrate (IRE)**[2] 3702 3-10-4 **92** 5ex.............................(v) JosephO'Brien 8 70
(A P O'Brien, Ire) *led stands' side gp tl hdd 1/2-way: wknd appr fnl f* **15/8**[1]
12 1 ¼ **First In Command (IRE)**[19] 3135 8-9-11 **79**.................(t) PatSmullen 12 54
(Daniel Mark Loughnane) *chsd ldrs stands' side: short of room over 1f out: sn no ex* **9/1**
13 nk **Statue Of Dreams (IRE)**[20] 3121 7-9-4 **72**....................(tp) RoryCleary 7 46
(Noel Lawlor, Ire) *sn pushed along in rr: nvr a threat* **33/1**

57.85s (-5.05) **Going Correction** -0.825s/f (Hard)
WFA 3 from 4yo+ 6lb **13** Ran SP% **131.2**
Speed ratings: **107,105,101,99,99 98,97,96,96,96 93,91,90**
CSF £33.71 CT £247.78 TOTE £4.80: £1.80, £2.60, £2.80; DF 33.00.

Owner Zhang Yuesheng **Bred** Shadwell Estate Company Limited **Trained** Dunshaughlin, Co Meath
FOCUS
The lightly-raced Yulong Baoju won this in a fast time and looks useful. The runner-up beat those on his side by over three lengths.

3798a EFLOW "YOU FIRST" INTERNATIONAL STKS (GROUP 3) 1m 2f
7:30 (7:30) 3-Y-O+ **£31,707** (£9,268; £4,390; £1,463)

RPR
1 **Flying The Flag (IRE)**[8] 3517 3-8-12 109.............(p) SeamieHeffernan 1 112
(A P O'Brien, Ire) *chsd clr ldr in 2nd tl drvn to assert 1f out: sn clr and styd on wl* **21/10**[2]
2 4 **Aloof (IRE)**[19] 3142 4-9-9 103.. WayneLordan 3 103
(David Wachman, Ire) *led and sn 3 l clr: pressed appr fnl f and hdd: sn no match for wnr* **5/2**[3]
3 6 ½ **Most Improved (IRE)**[251] 7238 4-10-0 113.................. JosephO'Brien 2 95
(A P O'Brien, Ire) *settled in modest 3rd: nt qckn over 1f out: sn one pce* **5/4**[1]
4 ¾ **Uleavemebreathless**[9] 3460 3-8-9 93............................... ChrisHayes 4 87
(A Oliver, Ire) *a in rr: reminders 4f out: kpt on same pce fnl 2f* **16/1**

2m 4.09s (-5.21) **Going Correction** -0.725s/f (Hard)
WFA 3 from 4yo 12lb 4 Ran SP% **111.2**
Speed ratings: **111,107,102,102**
CSF £7.76 TOTE £3.20; DF 7.70.
Owner Mrs John Magnier & Michael Tabor & Derrick Smith **Bred** Orpendale, Chelston & Wynatt **Trained** Ballydoyle, Co Tipperary
FOCUS
Flying the Flag was the Ballydoyle horse most punters wanted to know about and he rewarded supporters with a convincing victory. The early pace was strong thanks to Aloof. The first two were always in front and have been rated to the lower end of the place averages for the race in non-Famous Name winning years.

3797 - 3800a (Foreign Racing) - See Raceform Interactive

3753 CHESTER (L-H)
Saturday, June 29

OFFICIAL GOING: Good to soft (good in places; 7.4)
Wind: moderate 1/2 against Weather: fine

3801 HOUSE RESTAURANT & BAR CHESTER NOVICE STKS 5f 16y
2:10 (2:11) (Class 4) 2-Y-O **£6,469** (£1,925; £962; £481) **Stalls** Low

Form RPR
145 1 **Suzi's Connoisseur**[21] 3079 2-9-2 0.............................. FrannyNorton 6 86
(Mark Johnston) *drvn early to chse ldrs: drvn over 2f out: styd on to ld last 50yds* **9/2**[2]
31 2 nk **Salford Red Devil**[21] 3092 2-9-5 0....................................... LeeTopliss 5 88
(Richard Fahey) *sltly hmpd and dropped bk last after 100yds: sn chsng ldrs on outside: effrt and hung lft 2f out: edgd lft and styd on to take 2nd clsng stages* **1/1**[1]
1444 3 1 **Orton Park (IRE)**[14] 3332 2-9-0 0...................................... HarryBentley 4 79
(Tobias B P Coles) *led: hdd and no ex clsng stages* **16/1**
0163 4 2 ¼ **Rosebay Coral (IRE)**[15] 3298 2-8-11 0.............................. AmyRyan 2 68
(Tony Coyle) *chsd ldrs on inner: effrt and edgd rt over 1f out: kpt on to take modest 4th clsng stages* **9/1**[3]
216 5 1 ¼ **Money Team (IRE)**[28] 2863 2-8-12 0............................... RyanWhile[(7)] 8 72
(Bill Turner) *swtchd lft after 100yds: w ldrs: wknd and crowded last 100yds* **9/1**[3]
240 6 1 **Limegrove**[31] 2767 2-8-11 0.. MartinLane 3 60
(David Evans) *awkward to s: sn outpcd and in rr: sme hdwy over 1f out: nvr a factor* **9/2**[2]

1m 3.88s (2.88) **Going Correction** +0.60s/f (Yiel) 6 Ran SP% **112.2**
Speed ratings (Par 95): **100,99,97,94,92 90**
toteswingers 1&2 £2.40, 1&3 £6.20, 2&3 £1.30 CSF £9.47 TOTE £5.60: £3.60, £1.10; EX 17.70 Trifecta £129.30 Pool: £1420.72 - 8.24 winning tickets..
Owner Greenstead Hall Racing Ltd **Bred** Greenstead Hall Racing Ltd **Trained** Middleham Moor, N Yorks
■ Stewards' Enquiry : Lee Topliss one-day ban; careless riding (15th July).
FOCUS
Rail between 6f and 1.5f moved out 3yds, adding 10yds to races 1 & 2, 13yds to race 3, 19yds to race 4, 14yds to race 5, 20yds to race 6 and 26yds to race 7. An interesting novice stakes considering all six runners were previous winners, the winner showed a good attitude while the second raced wide throughout and can do better.

3802 MA KELLY'S BLACKPOOL H'CAP 5f 16y
2:45 (2:48) (Class 3) (0-90,88) 3-Y-O+ **£7,762** (£2,310; £1,154; £577) **Stalls** Low

Form RPR
0413 1 **Rusty Rocket (IRE)**[3] 3682 4-9-4 80.................................. MartinLane 2 90
(Paul Green) *chsd ldrs on ins: led appr fnl f: drvn out* **4/1**[2]
-104 2 1 **Sir Maximilian (IRE)**[20] 3135 4-9-11 87.......................... LukeMorris 4 93+
(Ian Williams) *sn chsng ldrs: styd on to take 2nd last 50yds* **7/2**[1]
-540 3 2 **Secret Look**[21] 3097 3-9-6 88.. SeanLevey 10 85+
(Ed McMahon) *in rr: hdwy on outskide over 1f out: r.o to take 3rd towards fin* **20/1**
1000 4 1 **Storm Moon (USA)**[7] 3584 3-9-5 87............................... FrannyNorton 3 81
(Mark Johnston) *chsd ldrs: kpt on same pce fnl f* **5/1**[3]
2000 5 nk **Decision By One**[13] 3371 4-9-4 80.................................(vt[1]) StephenCraine 1 75
(Tom Dascombe) *led: hdd appr fnl f: kpt on one pce* **14/1**
2004 6 ¾ **Cruise Tothelimit (IRE)**[16] 3236 5-8-13 78................... RyanPowell[(3)] 6 70
(Ian Williams) *sn outpcd and in rr: hdwy over 1f out: nt clr run and edgd rt ins fnl f: nvr nr ldrs* **14/1**
4020 7 nk **Chooseday (IRE)**[15] 3299 4-9-9 85....................................(p) AmyRyan 7 81+
(Kevin Ryan) *dwlt: sn detached in last: hdwy on ins 2f out: keeping on whn nt clr run nr fin* **11/2**
5005 8 ½ **Doctor Parkes**[21] 3114 7-9-9 85.. HarryBentley 8 74
(Stuart Williams) *in rr: hdwy over 2f out: sn chsng ldrs: wknd fnl f* **8/1**
3000 9 1 **Silvanus (IRE)**[15] 3299 8-9-8 84................................ RussKennemore 9 69
(Paul Midgley) *chsd ldrs: wknd fnl f* **25/1**
-400 10 2 ¼ **Lady Ibrox**[14] 3340 3-9-6 88.. DaleSwift 5 63
(Alan Brown) *chsd ldrs: lost pl over 1f out* **8/1**

1m 2.81s (1.81) **Going Correction** +0.60s/f (Yiel)
WFA 3 from 4yo+ 6lb 10 Ran SP% **118.4**
Speed ratings (Par 107): **109,107,104,102,102 100,100,99,98,94**
toteswingers 1&2 £3.20, 1&3 £8.00, 2&3 £26.10 CSF £18.76 CT £257.54 TOTE £3.30: £1.70, £1.30, £4.60; EX 16.00 Trifecta £573.80 Pool: £1670.30 - 2.18 winning tickets..
Owner Seven Stars Racing **Bred** Mike Hyde **Trained** Lydiate, Merseyside
FOCUS
A competitive sprint handicap run at a furious pace.

3803 WRO WEST KIRBY H'CAP 7f 2y
3:20 (3:21) (Class 2) (0-100,99) 3-Y-**£12,602** (£3,772; £1,886; £944; £470) **Stalls** Low

Form RPR
-406 1 **Correspondent**[42] 2453 3-9-1 93.. MartinLane 1 101
(Brian Meehan) *trckd ldrs on inner: chsd ldr and edgd rt over 1f out: styd on to ld towards fin* **9/4**[1]
1033 2 ¾ **Rene Mathis (GER)**[22] 3066 3-8-4 82........................... PatrickMathers 6 88
(Richard Fahey) *swtchd lft after s: led: kpt on wl fnl f: hdd clsng stages* **13/2**
0604 3 2 ¼ **Queen Aggie (IRE)**[21] 3097 3-8-3 81................................ LukeMorris 9 81
(David Evans) *in rr: hdwy over 2f out: chsng ldrs over 1f out: kpt on same pce* **16/1**
0051 4 shd **Penny Garcia**[12] 3396 3-8-3 81.. AmyRyan 4 81
(Tim Easterby) *chsd ldrs: hmpd over 5f out: drvn over 2f out: kpt on same pce over 1f out* **9/1**
-114 5 1 ½ **Lord Ashley (IRE)**[16] 3234 3-8-5 83................................ HarryBentley 10 79
(Tom Dascombe) *in rr: hdwy on outer 2f out: styd on fnl f* **9/2**[2]
1-0 6 ¾ **Chelwood Gate (IRE)**[14] 3342 3-9-0 92............................ ChrisCatlin 3 86
(Roger Varian) *chsd ldrs on inner: drvn 2f out: one pce* **14/1**
211 7 2 ½ **Duke Cosimo**[17] 3212 3-8-3 81.. JimmyQuinn 12 68+
(Sir Michael Stoute) *sn chsng ldrs: rdn 2f out: wknd over 1f out* **5/1**[3]
-000 8 8 **Lady Phill**[14] 3340 3-8-7 85... KierenFox 2 50
(Bill Turner) *stdd s: sn detached: hung rt over 1f out: nvr on terms* **14/1**
0000 9 22 **Heavy Metal**[14] 3348 3-9-7 99.. FrannyNorton 5
(Mark Johnston) *mid-div: lost pl over 5f out: sn drvn and bhd: eased clsng stages: t.o* **10/1**

1m 29.09s (2.59) **Going Correction** +0.60s/f (Yiel) 9 Ran SP% **117.3**
Speed ratings (Par 105): **109,108,105,105,103 102,100,90,65**
toteswingers 1&2 £4.70, 1&3 £20.80, 2&3 £0.00 CSF £17.55 CT £191.47 TOTE £2.60: £1.10, £3.20, £7.80; EX 17.80 Trifecta £231.40 Pool: £1423.19 - 4.61 winning tickets..
Owner Mrs P Good **Bred** Mrs P Good **Trained** Manton, Wilts
FOCUS
A strong class 2 on paper for the feature race, with the top-rated just 1lb below the ceiling.

3804 MILL HOTEL & SPA CHESTER H'CAP 1m 3f 79y
3:55 (3:55) (Class 4) (0-85,85) 4-Y-O+ **£6,469** (£1,925; £962; £481) **Stalls** Low

Form RPR
-665 1 **Kiwayu**[17] 3208 4-9-2 80...(p) LukeMorris 1 88
(Ian Williams) *hld up in rr: hdwy to chse ldrs 6f out: shkn up over 4f out: styd on and 2nd 1f out: led last 50yds* **11/2**
0301 2 1 ¼ **Sir Boss (IRE)**[3] 3692 8-9-0 81 7ex.................................... RyanClark[(3)] 5 87
(Michael Mullineaux) *hld up in rr: smooth hdwy over 3f out: led 2f out: hdd and no ex clsng stages* **8/1**
0366 3 1 ¾ **Assizes**[14] 3349 4-9-0 78.. FrannyNorton 4 81
(Mark Johnston) *chsd ldrs: drvn and outpcd over 2f out: rallied ins fnl f: styd on to take 3rd nr fin* **5/2**[1]
25-4 4 ½ **Watts Up Son**[39] 2552 5-9-0 78..(v) HarryBentley 6 80
(Declan Carroll) *led: hdd 2f out: kpt on same pce* **6/1**
-002 5 1 ½ **Pintrada**[11] 3442 5-8-12 76... TedDurcan 8 75
(James Bethell) *stdd and swtchd lft s: hld up in rr: hdwy 4f out: drvn 2f out: one pce* **9/2**[3]
-050 6 9 **Kiama Bay (IRE)**[21] 3099 7-9-7 85....................................(p) SeanLevey 2 68
(John Quinn) *chsd ldrs: drvn over 3f out: lost pl appr fnl f* **4/1**[2]
20 7 14 **Duaiseoir (IRE)**[26] 2939 7-8-10 74.................................(b) SteveDrowne 9 32
(Venetia Williams) *drvn early to chse ldrs: drvn over 6f out: lost pl 4f out: sn bhd* **12/1**

2m 31.47s (6.67) **Going Correction** +0.60s/f (Yiel) 7 Ran SP% **115.2**
Speed ratings (Par 105): **99,98,96,96,95 88,78**
toteswingers 1&2 £14.50, 1&3 £10.80, 2&3 £8.40 CSF £48.10 CT £136.56 TOTE £7.40: £3.10, £6.70; EX 89.60 Trifecta £514.70 Pool: £1537.38 - 2.24 winning tickets..
Owner Paul Wildes **Bred** Fittocks Stud Ltd **Trained** Portway, Worcs
FOCUS
A fair middle-distance handicap.

3805 ALBERT SQUARE CHOPHOUSE MAIDEN STKS 1m 2f 75y
4:25 (4:26) (Class 4) 3-Y-O+ **£6,469** (£1,925; £962; £481) **Stalls** High

Form RPR
323 1 **Ducab (IRE)**[12] 3417 3-9-1 85.. SeanLevey 3 83
(Roger Varian) *dwlt: sn chsng ldr: chal over 3f out: led over 2f out: drvn out* **6/5**[1]
2253 2 2 ¼ **Khudoua**[25] 2952 3-9-1 77..(b) NickyMackay 4 79
(John Gosden) *hld up: drvn over 4f out: sn chsng ldrs: wnt 2nd over 1f out: kpt on: no imp* **11/4**[3]
3 3 ¾ **Bushel (USA)** 3-9-1 0... FrannyNorton 2 72
(Mark Johnston) *chsd ldrs: shkn up after 3f: drvn over 4f out: wknd last 150yds* **9/4**[2]
-006 4 28 **Speedy Utmost Meg**[22] 3047 3-8-3 48............................ ShelleyBirkett[(7)] 1 31
(William Kinsey) *led: continually thrashed tail: hdd over 2f out: wknd over 1f out: eased whn bhd clsng stages: t.o* **16/1**

2m 16.99s (5.79) **Going Correction** +0.60s/f (Yiel) 4 Ran SP% **108.8**
Speed ratings (Par 105): **100,98,95,72**
CSF £4.81 TOTE £1.60; EX 4.10 Trifecta £3.60 Pool: £1131.99 - 231.51 winning tickets..
Owner Sultan Ali **Bred** Watership Down Stud **Trained** Newmarket, Suffolk
FOCUS
A simple task for the favourite, who had plenty in hand on the figures.

3806 RED ALERT H'CAP 1m 4f 66y
4:55 (4:55) (Class 4) (0-85,83) 3-Y-O **£6,469** (£1,925; £962; £481) **Stalls** Low

Form RPR
2-42 1 **Muthmera (USA)**[16] 3237 3-9-3 79.....................................(p[1]) SeanLevey 2 86
(Roger Varian) *mde all: qcknd pce over 4f out: rdn and idled over 1f out: drvn out* **2/1**[1]
3102 2 2 ½ **Dali's Lover (IRE)**[14] 3313 3-8-10 72............................... SteveDrowne 1 75
(Charles Hills) *sn chsng ldrs: drvn over 4f out: chsd wnr 1f out: styd on same pce* **3/1**[2]
222 3 ½ **Street Artist (IRE)**[24] 2995 3-9-2 78............................... FrannyNorton 5 80
(Mark Johnston) *in rr: shkn up after 4f: drvn over 4f out: chsng ldrs 3f out: kpt on same pce appr fnl f* **3/1**[2]
1426 4 ¾ **Gabrial The Master (IRE)**[52] 2153 3-8-11 73.................... LeeTopliss 3 74
(Richard Fahey) *trckd ldrs: drvn over 4f out: kpt on one pce appr fnl f* **7/1**

-321 5 7 **Interior Minister**[17] 3214 3-9-7 **83**...... MartinLane 4 73
(Jo Hughes) *trckd ldrs: drvn over 4f out: lost pl over 1f out* **5/1**[3]

2m 46.33s (7.83) **Going Correction** +0.60s/f (Yiel) **5** Ran SP% **112.5**
Speed ratings (Par 101): **97,95,95,94,89**
CSF £8.48 TOTE £2.40: £2.10, £1.30; EX 11.20 Trifecta £21.30 Pool: £1037.25 - 36.40 winning tickets..
Owner Hamdan Al Maktoum **Bred** Shadwell Farm LLC **Trained** Newmarket, Suffolk

FOCUS
A closely-knit handicap.

3807 STELLA CIDRE H'CAP — 1m 7f 195y
5:25 (5:26) (Class 4) (0-85,80) 4-Y-0+ **£6,469** (£1,925; £962; £481) **Stalls** Low

Form RPR
-611 1 **Kashgar**[26] 2921 4-8-11 **70**...... MartinLane 3 80
(Bernard Llewellyn) *trckd ldr: led 2f out: styd on wl* **10/3**[2]
-123 2 4 **Gabrial's King (IRE)**[21] 3118 4-9-4 **77**...... FrannyNorton 6 82
(David Simcock) *stdd s: hld up in rr: effrt 3f out: sn outpcd: hdwy on ins to chse wnr over 1f out: styd on same pce* **5/4**[1]
5004 3 1 1/4 **Montaff**[14] 3333 7-9-6 **79**...... SamHitchcott 5 83
(Mick Channon) *hld up in rr: hdwy 3f out: 3rd over 1f out: kpt on same pce* **9/2**[3]
1144 4 1 1/4 **Hallstatt (IRE)**[20] 3133 7-8-7 **69**......(t) RaulDaSilva(3) 1 71
(John Mackie) *chsd ldrs: drvn over 2f out: 4th over 1f out: kpt on one pce* **8/1**
610- 5 2 1/4 **L Frank Baum (IRE)**[259] 5798 6-9-0 **80**...... OisinMurphy(7) 8 79
(Bernard Llewellyn) *drvn to r in useful ld: qcknd pce over 4f out: hdd 2f out: edgd rt and fdd appr fnl f* **16/1**
0-45 6 13 **Lifetime (IRE)**[34] 622 5-9-1 **74**......(t) SeanLevey 4 64
(Brian Ellison) *chsd ldrs: drvn over 4f out: lost pl 2f out: bhd whn eased 1f out* **10/1**

3m 41.51s (13.51) **Going Correction** +0.60s/f (Yiel) **6** Ran SP% **111.8**
Speed ratings (Par 105): **90,88,87,86,85 79**
toteswingers 1&2 £1.10, 1&3 £1.50, 2&3 £1.80 CSF £7.86 CT £16.76 TOTE £7.10: £2.90, £1.10; EX 9.30 Trifecta £25.90 Pool: £1209.98 - 34.99 winning tickets..
Owner Alex James & B J Llewellyn **Bred** J L C Pearce **Trained** Fochriw, Caerphilly

FOCUS
A progressive winner to follow in the finale and an excellent training performance too.
T/Plt: £111.90 to a £1 stake. Pool: £74,212.27 - 483.98 winning tickets T/Qpdt: £31.70 to a £1 stake. Pool: £2813.12 - 65.50 winning tickets WG

3759 DONCASTER (L-H)
Saturday, June 29

OFFICIAL GOING: Good (8.7)
Wind: Virtually nil Weather: Fine and dry

3808 EVEN BOB'S GOT TO GO SOMEWHERE SRP H'CAP — 1m 4f
5:30 (5:32) (Class 5) (0-75,77) 4-Y-0+ **£2,911** (£866; £432; £216) **Stalls** Low

Form RPR
1032 1 **El Bravo**[10] 3467 7-8-1 **58**...... NeilFarley(3) 2 65
(Shaun Harris) *set stdy pce: qcknd 3f out: rdn and qcknd 2f out: kpt on gamely u.p fnl f* **11/2**
2130 2 nk **Gran Maestro (USA)**[15] 3301 4-9-2 **75**......(b) LMcNiff(5) 4 81
(Ruth Carr) *trckd ldrs: hdwy 4f out: cl up 3f out: rdn to chal 2f out: sn ev ch: drvn ins fnl f: nt qckn nr fin* **4/1**[2]
0-00 3 shd **Dark Dune (IRE)**[11] 3442 5-9-4 **72**...... DuranFentiman 7 78
(Tim Easterby) *hld up in rr: hdwy on outer 4f out: cl up over 2f out: rdn to chal over 1f out and ev ch tl drvn and nt qckn towards fin* **5/1**
33-6 4 1 1/4 **Sedgwick**[20] 3133 11-8-1 **62**...... GaryMahon(7) 6 66
(Shaun Harris) *hld up in rr: hdwy on inner wl over 2f out: rdn to chse ldrs ent fnl f: n.m.r and kpt on same pce* **12/1**
4541 5 hd **Tetbury (USA)**[10] 3480 4-9-9 **77**......(v[1]) DougieCostello 8 81
(David O'Meara) *hld up in tch: hdwy over 3f out: trckd ldrs over 2f out: rdn wl over 1f out: one pce fnl f* **3/1**[1]
5430 6 shd **Tinseltown**[8] 3543 7-8-12 **66**......(p) MickyFenton 5 70
(Brian Rothwell) *trckd ldr: pushed along and outpcd whn pce qcknd 3f out: sn rdn: hdwy and n.m.r jst over 1f out: one pce* **11/1**
0204 7 nk **Silver Tigress**[16] 3231 5-8-6 **60**...... AndrewElliott 1 63
(George Moore) *trckd ldrs: pushed along and outpcd over 3f out: sn rdn: kpt on fnl f: nrst fin* **9/2**[3]
1236 8 5 **Tornado Force (IRE)**[58] 1956 5-9-2 **70**...... AndrewMullen 3 65
(Alan McCabe) *in tch: rdn along 3f out: sn wknd* **20/1**

2m 36.45s (1.55) **Going Correction** 0.0s/f (Good) **8** Ran SP% **116.0**
Speed ratings (Par 103): **94,93,93,92,92 92,92,89**
toteswingers 1&2 £3.40, 1&3 £7.90, 2&3 £6.50 CSF £28.20 CT £117.51 TOTE £6.20: £2.10, £1.40, £1.90; EX 28.30 Trifecta £296.00 Pool: £1935.23 - 4.90 winning tickets..
Owner www.nottinghamshireracing.co.uk (2) **Bred** D J And Mrs Deer **Trained** Carburton, Notts

FOCUS
The Rail on the round course was moved out from 10f to start of home straight. A fair handicap. They didn't go much of a gallop and that resulted in a bunched finish. The form cannot be rated any more than modest, with the sixth to form setting the level.

3809 PANELCRAFT ACCESS PANELS H'CAP — 1m 4f
6:05 (6:07) (Class 5) (0-70,68) 3-Y-0 **£2,911** (£866; £432; £216) **Stalls** Low

Form RPR
4431 1 **Chant (IRE)**[12] 3394 3-9-6 **67**...... PJMcDonald 10 77
(Ann Duffield) *prom: hdwy to trck ldr 1/2-way: effrt to ld over 3f out: rdn and hdd 2f out: rallied u.p to take slt ld again ent fnl f: sn drvn and kpt on gamely* **4/1**[2]
0034 2 nk **Duke Of Yorkshire**[17] 3194 3-8-12 **62**...... NeilFarley(3) 5 71
(Declan Carroll) *trckd ldr: effrt over 3f out: rdn to ld 2f out: drvn and hdd ent fnl f: edgd rt and ev ch tl no ex towards fin* **4/1**[2]
-433 3 2 1/2 **Rex Whistler (IRE)**[16] 3232 3-9-6 **67**...... PaulMulrennan 3 72
(Julie Camacho) *hld up in rr: hdwy 4f out: rdn over 2f out: drvn to chse ldng pair ent fnl f: kpt on same pce* **2/1**[1]
-001 4 5 **Choral Prince (IRE)**[12] 3403 3-9-2 **68**...... MichaelJMMurphy(5) 2 65
(Mike Murphy) *hld up in rr: hdwy over 3f out: rdn to chse ldrs 2f out: n.m.r and swtchd rt wl over 1f out: sn drvn: carried hd high and no imp* **12/1**
3344 5 1/2 **Gabrial The Thug (FR)**[7] 3573 3-9-5 **66**...... TonyHamilton 7 62
(Richard Fahey) *trckd ldrs: effrt over 3f out: rdn along over 2f out: drvn wl over 1f out and grad wknd* **9/1**[3]
006- 6 nk **Santa Fe Stinger**[287] 6257 3-8-2 **49** oh4...... JamesSullivan 1 45
(Tim Easterby) *in tch on inner: rdn along 3f out: drvn 2f out and sn no imp* **40/1**

3-30 7 6 **Grayswood**[17] 3214 3-9-5 **66**...... WilliamCarson 9 52
(William Muir) *led: rdn along and hdd over 3f out: wknd over 2f out* **9/1**[3]
-050 8 2 1/4 **Inovate (IRE)**[33] 2716 3-8-3 **50**......(b[1]) DuranFentiman 4 33
(Tim Easterby) *hld up towards rr: hdwy 4f out: rdn along 3f out: n.d* **14/1**
-605 9 5 **Lady Margaeux (IRE)**[17] 3202 3-9-1 **62**...... DaleSwift 6 37
(David O'Meara) *towards rr: n.m.r and hmpd after 2f: nvr a factor* **28/1**
6316 10 2 1/4 **Darakti (IRE)**[31] 2784 3-8-10 **57**......(v) AndrewMullen 8 28
(Alan McCabe) *midfield: hdwy to chse ldrs 1/2-way: rdn along over 4f out: sn wknd* **22/1**

2m 34.95s (0.05) **Going Correction** 0.0s/f (Good) **10** Ran SP% **117.9**
Speed ratings (Par 99): **99,98,97,93,93 93,89,87,84,82**
toteswingers 1&2 £2.20, 1&3 £3.60, 2&3 £3.40 CSF £20.25 CT £41.15 TOTE £4.80: £1.80, £1.60, £1.40; EX 23.90 Trifecta £49.60 Pool: £2355.60 - 35.61 winning tickets..
Owner Mrs Ann Starkie & Mrs I Starkie **Bred** Roger K Lee **Trained** Constable Burton, N Yorks

■ Stewards' Enquiry : Neil Farley four-day ban; used whip doen shoulder and above permitted level (15th-18th July).

FOCUS
Just a modest 3-y-o handicap. The gallop wasn't overly strong and the leading pair were both fairly handy from the off. The form is rated on the positive side with the placed horses setting the level.

3810 BEAVER 84 E B F MAIDEN STKS — 7f
6:40 (6:42) (Class 5) 2-Y-O **£2,911** (£866; £432; £216) **Stalls** High

Form RPR
6 1 **Speedy Approach**[16] 3238 2-9-5 0...... JamesMcDonald 1 80+
(Michael Bell) *trckd ldrs: swtchd rt and shkn up over 1f out: qckn wl to ld jst ins fnl f: edgd lft and sn clr: readily* **1/1**[1]
2 4 1/2 **Craggaknock** 2-9-5 0...... DuranFentiman 5 67+
(Tim Walford) *s.i.s and in rr: green and pushed along 1/2-way: hdwy over 2f out: rdn over 1f out: styd on wl fnl f: tk 2nd nr line* **25/1**
4 3 hd **Red Tide (IRE)**[13] 3366 2-9-5 0...... DanielTudhope 7 66
(Alan McCabe) *led: pushed along and hdd 3f out: led again 1 1/2f out: hdd jst ins fnl f: one pce: lost 2nd nr line* **9/2**[2]
4 4 3/4 **Sbraase**[15] 3291 2-9-5 0...... PaulMulrennan 6 64
(James Tate) *cl up: led 3f out: rdn along 2f out: sn hdd and one pce ent fnl f* **5/1**[3]
5 3 **Dolphin Club (IRE)** 2-9-5 0...... TonyHamilton 2 56
(Richard Fahey) *trckd ldrs: hdwy over 2f out: rdn and hung lft over 1f out: sn wknd* **7/1**
0 6 3 1/2 **Leaderene**[15] 3291 2-9-0 0...... GrahamLee 4 42
(Mark Johnston) *cl up: rdn along over 2f out: wkng whn carried sltly lft over 1f out* **12/1**
3404 7 2 1/2 **Donny Rover (IRE)**[7] 3565 2-9-5 0......(p) WilliamCarson 3 41
(David C Griffiths) *s.i.s: a in rr* **16/1**

1m 26.89s (0.59) **Going Correction** -0.075s/f (Good) **7** Ran SP% **114.8**
Speed ratings (Par 93): **93,87,87,86,83 79,76**
toteswingers 1&2 £11.90, 1&3 £1.50, 2&3 £18.20 CSF £30.54 TOTE £1.70: £1.20, £10.20; EX 32.60 Trifecta £95.50 Pool: £1877.09 - 14.72 winning tickets..
Owner Jaber Abdullah **Bred** Rabbah Bloodstock Limited **Trained** Newmarket, Suffolk

FOCUS
This may not have been a particularly strong maiden but it was still hard not to be impressed by the winner. The level is fluid but the winner can rate higher.

3811 ROSIE YUJI GILKS H'CAP — 6f
7:15 (7:16) (Class 4) (0-85,83) 3-Y-0+ **£5,175** (£1,540; £769; £384) **Stalls** High

Form RPR
0600 1 **Dark Castle**[14] 3351 4-9-5 **74**...... PJMcDonald 8 88
(Micky Hammond) *in tch: smooth hdwy 2f out: led jst over 1f out: rdn ins fnl f: kpt on wl* **7/1**[3]
150 2 3/4 **Albaqaa**[7] 3586 8-9-10 **79**...... WilliamCarson 2 91
(P J O'Gorman) *stdd s and hld up in rr: hdwy wl over 1f out: rdn and styd on to chal ins fnl f: sn drvn and nt qckn towards fin* **20/1**
0646 3 1 3/4 **Head Space (IRE)**[7] 3561 5-9-9 **78**...... JamesSullivan 12 84
(Ruth Carr) *trckd ldrs: hdwy 2f out: rdn to chal ent fnl f: sn drvn: edgd lft and one pce* **11/2**[1]
0340 4 1 1/2 **Mappin Time (IRE)**[15] 3300 5-9-11 **80**......(p) MickyFenton 9 82
(Tim Easterby) *trckd ldrs: hdwy over 2f out: sn cl up: rdn over 1f out: sn one pce* **14/1**
0400 5 nse **Barney McGrew (IRE)**[14] 3351 10-9-8 **77**...... PaulMulrennan 3 78
(Michael Dods) *hld up towards rr: hdwy 2f out: rdn over 1f out: styd on fnl f: nrst fin* **16/1**
0450 6 1/2 **Victoire De Lyphar (IRE)**[11] 3441 6-9-6 **75**......(b) GrahamLee 14 75
(Ruth Carr) *racd nr stands' rail: led: rdn along 2f out: hdd over 1f out: sn drvn and wknd fnl f* **11/2**[1]
2101 7 1/2 **Meandmyshadow**[11] 3441 5-9-12 **81**...... DaleSwift 1 79
(Alan Brown) *racd wd: cl up: rdn along 2f out: drvn over 1f out: wknd ent fnl f* **15/2**
0004 8 3/4 **Showboating (IRE)**[7] 3586 5-9-5 **74**......(tp) AndrewMullen 6 70
(Alan McCabe) *midfield: rdn along and outpcd over 2f out: styd on fnl f: nrst fin* **10/1**
5020 9 1/2 **Free Spin (IRE)**[21] 3096 4-10-0 **83**......(b[1]) GrahamGibbons 4 77
(David Barron) *racd wd: trckd ldrs: rdn along 2f out: sn drvn one pce appr fnl f* **13/2**[2]
0151 10 nk **Point North (IRE)**[31] 2780 6-9-4 **73**......(b) DanielTudhope 10 66
(John Balding) *racd towards stands' rail: in tch: rdn along 2f out: grad wknd* **15/2**
6060 11 4 1/2 **Sleepy Blue Ocean**[29] 2832 7-8-10 **65**......(p) TedDurcan 11 44
(John Balding) *racd towards stands' rail: prom: rdn along 2f out: sn wknd* **20/1**
61-3 12 11 **Belinsky (IRE)**[173] 95 6-8-10 **65**...... FrederikTylicki 13
(Julie Camacho) *racd nr stands' rail: chsd ldrs: rdn along wl over 2f out: sn wknd* **20/1**
4605 13 5 **Defence Council (IRE)**[14] 3351 5-9-8 **77**...... DuranFentiman 5
(Mel Brittain) *v.s.i.s and lost many l s: a t.o* **16/1**

1m 12.24s (-1.36) **Going Correction** -0.075s/f (Good) **13** Ran SP% **121.9**
Speed ratings (Par 105): **106,105,102,100,100 99,99,98,97,97 91,76,69**
toteswingers 1&2 £35.50, 1&3 £8.70, 2&3 £25.10 CSF £144.77 CT £844.44 TOTE £9.10: £3.10, £6.70, £2.20; EX 168.90 Trifecta £612.80 Part won. Pool: £817.18 - 0.35 winning tickets..
Owner J Cox and E Tasker **Bred** Hedsor Stud **Trained** Middleham Moor, N Yorks

FOCUS
A fairly useful sprint with a personal-best from the winner and the second to his Haydock mark.

3812 M & G ASBESTOS ABATEMENT SERVICES H'CAP 1m (R)
7:45 (7:46) (Class 3) (0-90,90) 4-Y-O+ £7,762 (£2,310; £1,154; £577) Stalls Low

Form RPR
4-05 1 **Storm King**14 3347 4-9-7 **90**............(p) PatCosgrave 9 100+
(Jane Chapple-Hyam) *hld up towards rr: gd hdwy over 3f out: swtchd rt to outer 2f out: rdn to ld over 1f out: edgd rt and kpt on strly* **9/2**1

6342 2 1 1/4 **Kakatosi**22 3060 6-9-1 **84**............ TedDurcan 4 91
(Mike Murphy) *hld up in rr: hdwy on outer 3f out: rdn to chse wnr wl over 1f out: swtchd lft and drvn ent fnl f: kpt on same pce* **6/1**3

55-3 3 nk **Bank On Me**13 3368 4-8-7 **76**............ WilliamCarson 5 82
(Philip McBride) *hld up in tch: hdwy over 2f out: clr run and swtchd lft to inner over 1f out: squeezed through and rdn ent fnl f: kpt on same pce* **9/2**1

0/60 4 2 1/4 **Karam Albaari (IRE)**29 2841 5-9-4 **87**............ FrederikTylicki 3 88
(J R Jenkins) *trckd ldrs: hdwy over 3f out: rdn to chal 2f out: ev ch tl drvn and one pce appr fnl f* **14/1**

-406 5 1 1/2 **Prophesy (IRE)**8 3544 4-8-7 **79**............ NeilFarley(3) 8 76
(Declan Carroll) *trckd ldng pair: hdwy 3f out: cl up over 2f out: sn rdn and grad wknd appr fnl f* **20/1**

3210 6 nse **Classic Colori (IRE)**14 3346 6-9-4 **87**............(v) DanielTudhope 2 84
(David O'Meara) *hld up towards rr: pushed along and sltly outpcd 3f out: rdn over 2f out: kpt on fnl f: nrst fin* **5/1**2

-012 7 1 1/2 **Legendary**17 3218 4-8-8 **77**............(b1) JimmyQuinn 6 71
(Ed Vaughan) *chsd ldr: hdwy and cl up 3f out: sn led: rdn 2f out: drvn and hdd over 1f out: grad wknd* **8/1**

0145 8 2 3/4 **Invincible Hero (IRE)**13 3368 6-8-8 **82**............ JasonHart(5) 7 69
(Declan Carroll) *led: rdn along 3f out: sn hdd & wknd* **5/1**2

521- 9 3 1/2 **True To Form (IRE)**189 8227 6-9-4 **87**............(p) GrahamLee 1 69
(Alan McCabe) *hld up in tch: hdwy on inner 2f out: sn rdn and wknd over 1f out* **10/1**

1m 38.16s (-1.54) **Going Correction** 0.0s/f (Good) 9 Ran SP% **115.6**
Speed ratings (Par 107): **107,105,105,103,101 101,100,97,93**
toteswingers 1&2 £2.90, 1&3 £6.40, 2&3 £1.80 CSF £31.55 TOTE £7.10: £2.70, £2.40, £1.10; EX 40.70 Trifecta £81.90 Pool: £1161.89 - 10.63 winning tickets..
Owner Norcroft Park Stud **Bred** Norcroft Park Stud And D Laidlaw **Trained** Dalham, Suffolk
■ Stewards' Enquiry : William Carson two-day ban; careless riding (15th-16th July).

FOCUS
Another fairly useful contest. The pace was a sound one and the form looks solid rated around the placed horses.

3813 JORDAN ROAD SURFACING H'CAP 5f 140y
8:15 (8:16) (Class 4) (0-85,83) 3-Y-O £5,175 (£1,540; £769; £384) Stalls High

Form RPR
-320 1 **Shrimper Roo**10 3478 3-9-2 **78**............(b1) DuranFentiman 2 87
(Tim Easterby) *hld up in rr: hdwy on outer 2f out: rdn to chal over 1f out: led ins fnl f: edgd rt and drvn out* **8/1**

6-10 2 1 1/2 **Time And Place**73 1625 3-9-3 **79**............ TonyHamilton 3 83
(Richard Fahey) *t.k.h: trckd ldrs: swtchd rt and hdwy to ld 1 1/2f out: sn rdn: hdd and drvn ins fnl f: edgd lft and kpt on same pce* **11/4**2

4311 3 nk **Teetotal (IRE)**6 3611 3-8-9 **71** 6ex............ PaulMulrennan 5 74
(Nigel Tinkler) *hld up: hdwy over 2f out: chsd ldrs over 1f out: swtchd rt ent fnl f: kpt on wl u.p towards fin* **7/1**3

3014 4 1 3/4 **Star Of Rohm**22 3053 3-8-13 **75**............ JamesMcDonald 1 72
(Michael Bell) *trckd ldrs: hdwy 2f out: sn cl up: rdn and ev ch over 1f out: drvn and hld whn n.m.r and one pce ins fnl f* **16/1**

5020 5 5 **Sejalaat (IRE)**15 3279 3-9-6 **82**............ PaulHanagan 8 62
(Ed Dunlop) *chsd ldrs: rdn along 2f out: sn wknd* **2/1**1

-600 6 5 **Lady Poppy**7 3591 3-8-10 **72**............ PJMcDonald 7 35
(George Moore) *cl up: rdn along 1/2-way: sn wknd* **12/1**

-403 7 2 3/4 **Rhagori Aur**10 3478 3-8-12 **79**............ JustinNewman(5) 4 33
(Bryan Smart) *t.k.h: disp ld: rdn along 2f out: sn wknd* **8/1**

10-0 8 3 1/2 **Avec Rose**64 1806 3-8-6 **75**............ JoshQuinn(7) 6 17
(Richard Fahey) *slt ld: rdn along 2f out: sn hdd & wknd* **14/1**

1m 7.78s (-1.02) **Going Correction** -0.075s/f (Good) 8 Ran SP% **115.0**
Speed ratings (Par 101): **103,101,100,98,91 84,81,76**
toteswingers 1&2 £4.10, 1&3 £6.90, 2&3 £4.50 CSF £30.52 CT £163.67 TOTE £10.90: £2.90, £1.40, £1.60; EX 44.80 Trifecta £176.30 Pool: £1303.62 - 5.54 winning tickets..
Owner Reality Partnerships IV **Bred** Ercan Dogan **Trained** Great Habton, N Yorks

FOCUS
The leading pair here are both pretty useful sorts and this should prove solid form for the grade, with the field finishing quite well strung out in behind. More to come from the runner-up with the third backing up previous Pontefract form.

3814 BEAVER 84 HIRE PLETTAC CUP FILLIES' H'CAP 1m 2f 60y
8:45 (8:46) (Class 5) (0-70,69) 4-Y-O+ £2,911 (£866; £432; £216) Stalls Low

Form RPR
-242 1 **Curly Come Home**22 3063 4-9-7 **69**............(t) TedDurcan 6 76
(Chris Wall) *trckd ldrs: hdwy over 3f out: led 2f out: sn rdn and kpt on strly* **6/4**1

0500 2 1 1/2 **Elizabeth Coffee (IRE)**2 3728 5-8-3 **51**............(v) JimmyQuinn 9 55
(John Weymes) *t.k.h: hld up in rr: hdwy wl over 2f out: rdn over 1f out: styd on wl fnl f: tk 2nd nr fin* **16/1**

0002 3 hd **Maybeagrey**10 3477 4-9-5 **67**............ DuranFentiman 8 71
(Tim Easterby) *t.k.h: trckd ldrs: hdwy on outer over 3f out: effrt over 2f out: rdn to chse wnr wl over 1f out: drvn and no imp fnl f: lost 2nd nr fin* **7/2**2

50-0 4 1 3/4 **Margo Channing**25 2956 4-7-13 **50** oh1............ NeilFarley(3) 2 51
(Micky Hammond) *hld up in tch: hdwy over 2f out: rdn to chse ldrs wl over 1f out: kpt on: nrst fin* **25/1**

2320 5 1 1/4 **Imaginary World (IRE)**25 2956 5-9-0 **62**............(p) DanielTudhope 4 60
(John Balding) *hld up in rr: hdwy 3f out: rdn over 2f out: kpt on appr fnl f: nrst fin* **13/2**3

26-0 6 1/2 **Taro Tywod (IRE)**22 3043 4-8-8 **56**............ PaulMulrennan 1 53
(Mark Brisbourne) *trckd ldrs on inner: hdwy 3f out: rdn along over 2f out: grad wknd* **9/1**

5-00 7 4 **Kathlatino**25 2961 6-8-6 **54** ow1............ PJMcDonald 3 44
(Micky Hammond) *led: rdn along over 3f out: drvn and hdd 2f out: sn wknd* **16/1**

-000 8 3 1/2 **Dansili Dutch (IRE)**28 1610 4-7-13 **50** oh5............ DeclanCannon(3) 5 33
(Andrew Crook) *a towards rr* **33/1**

15-0 9 7 **Gadobout Dancer**12 3397 6-8-4 **52**............ JamesSullivan 10 33
(Julie Camacho) *t.k.h: trckd ldrs: hdwy on outer to chse ldr over 6f out: rdn along 3f out: drvn over 2f out: wknd qckly wl over 1f out* **8/1**

2m 12.48s (3.08) **Going Correction** 0.0s/f (Good) 9 Ran SP% **115.2**
Speed ratings (Par 100): **87,85,85,84,83 82,79,76,76**
toteswingers 1&2 £6.70, 1&3 £2.20, 2&3 £2.60 CSF £29.18 TOTE £2.30: £1.10, £3.70, £1.70; EX 28.20 Trifecta £115.60 Pool: £1176.22 - 7.63 winning tickets..
Owner The Hut Partnership & Partner **Bred** Farmers Hill Stud **Trained** Newmarket, Suffolk

FOCUS
A modest fillies' event. The pace wasn't strong and the race did not really begin in earnest until the final 3f. The third to her latest mark sets the level.
T/Plt: £23.90 to a £1 stake. Pool: £84,567.18 - 2582.33 winning tickets T/Qpdt: £8.80 to a £1 stake. Pool: £7986.58 - 671.58 winning tickets JR

3574 LINGFIELD (L-H)
Saturday, June 29

OFFICIAL GOING: Turf course - good to firm (firm in places; 8.6); all-weather - standard
Wind: Almost nil Weather: Fine, warm

3815 AB COATINGS SUPPORTING BRITISH SOLDIERS EBF MAIDEN STKS 5f
5:45 (5:46) (Class 5) 2-Y-O £3,067 (£905; £453) Stalls High

Form RPR
2 1 **Banaadeer (IRE)**9 3490 2-9-5 0............ PatDobbs 1 77+
(Richard Hannon) *slowly away but sn rcvrd to press ldng pair: wnt 2nd wl over 1f out: rdn to ld jst ins fnl f: drvn out* **8/11**1

32 2 1/2 **Taquka (IRE)**12 3408 2-9-5 0............ RichardThomas 4 73
(Ralph Beckett) *led and racd against rail: drvn and hdd jst ins fnl f: kpt on but a hld* **6/1**3

64 3 1 1/2 **Minley**12 3413 2-9-5 0............ JohnFahy 3 68
(Rae Guest) *pressed ldr to wl over 1f out: kpt on same pce fnl f* **7/2**2

50 4 1 1/2 **Finn Class (IRE)**16 3245 2-9-5 0............ KieranO'Neill 7 62
(Michael Bell) *chsd ldrs against rail: plld out wd over 1f out: rdn and kpt on same pce* **10/1**

35 5 1 1/4 **Narborough**12 3413 2-9-0 0............ CharlesBishop(5) 6 58
(Mick Channon) *hld up in tch: rdn and effrt out wd over 1f out: sn no prog* **12/1**

40 6 3 1/4 **Global Explorer (USA)**5 3640 2-9-5 0............ AdamBeschizza 2 46
(Stuart Williams) *slowly away: outpcd in last: pushed along fr 1/2-way: nvr on terms* **50/1**

60 7 2 1/4 **Movie Magic**37 2583 2-8-7 0............ JoeyHaynes(7) 5 33
(John Bridger) *in tch tl wknd 2f out* **100/1**

58.86s (0.66) **Going Correction** -0.075s/f (Good) 7 Ran SP% **114.1**
Speed ratings (Par 93): **91,90,87,85,83 78,74**
toteswingers 1&2 £1.90, 1&3 £1.50, 2&3 £2.50 CSF £5.80 TOTE £1.40: £1.10, £3.10; EX 4.30 Trifecta £10.90 Pool: £2179.21 - 149.19 winning tickets..
Owner Hamdan Al Maktoum **Bred** Victor Stud And Brendan Cummins **Trained** East Everleigh, Wilts

FOCUS
The stands' rail remained three metres in from its original position. An ordinary juvenile maiden, but the winner can rate a lot higher and the second ran close to his previous mark.

3816 IMTECH MEICA H'CAP 5f
6:20 (6:20) (Class 5) (0-70,69) 3-Y-O+ £2,726 (£805; £402) Stalls High

Form RPR
4452 1 **Putin (IRE)**2 3738 5-8-13 **61**............(bt) NathanAlison(5) 4 69
(Phil McEntee) *trckd ldng pair: pushed along to take 2nd wl over 1f out: rdn to ld jst ins fnl f: styd on* **7/4**1

5400 2 1 **Song Of Parkes**7 3569 6-9-6 **63**............(p) JohnFahy 3 67
(Peter Grayson) *hld up in last and off the pce: shkn up 2f out: r.o fr over 1f out: tk 2nd nr fin and clsd on wnr* **8/1**

0-42 3 nk **Indian Tinker**14 3317 4-9-8 **68**............ RossAtkinson(3) 2 71
(Robert Cowell) *pressed ldr: led over 3f out: rdn and hdd jst ins fnl f: one pce* **3/1**2

0554 4 1 3/4 **Pharoh Jake**8 3529 5-8-8 **51**............ KieranO'Neill 7 48+
(John Bridger) *tried to ld against rail but lost out then hmpd after 100yds: effrt fr rr over 1f out: kpt on same pce fnl f* **5/1**

5-56 5 4 1/2 **Mossgo (IRE)**31 2779 3-8-12 **66**............ RyanTate(5) 6 47
(John Best) *won battle for nr side rail and hmpd rival after 100yds: hdd over 3f out: edgd lft and wknd over 1f out* **20/1**

3045 6 hd **Elna Bright**8 3529 8-9-12 **69**............ PatDobbs 5 49
(Peter Crate) *t.k.h: hld up bhd ldrs: pushed along 2f out: wknd over 1f out* **7/2**3

58.5s (0.30) **Going Correction** -0.075s/f (Good)
WFA 3 from 4yo+ 6lb 6 Ran SP% **116.1**
Speed ratings (Par 103): **94,92,91,89,81 81**
toteswingers 1&2 £5.40, 1&3 £1.30, 2&3 £4.20 CSF £17.29 TOTE £2.60: £1.60, £3.10; EX 16.10 Trifecta £147.50 Pool: £1202.60 - 6.11 winning tickets..
Owner Steve Jakes **Bred** D Llewelyn & J Runeckles **Trained** Newmarket, Suffolk
■ Stewards' Enquiry : Ryan Tate four-day ban; careless riding (15th-18th July).

FOCUS
A weak sprint handicap rated around the third to his latest mark.

3817 ADAPTO MEMORIAL LT. COL. DANNY BRYAN FILLIES' H'CAP 7f
6:55 (6:55) (Class 5) (0-75,73) 3-Y-O+ £2,726 (£805; £402) Stalls High

Form RPR
0614 1 **Moma Lee**30 2806 3-8-13 **67**............ RobertHavlin 5 73
(John Gosden) *mde all and racd against nr side rail: shkn up 2f out: in command fnl f: readily* **7/2**3

0123 2 1 1/2 **Wishformore (IRE)**4 3661 6-8-9 **54** oh1............(p) RichardThomas 8 59
(Zoe Davison) *t.k.h: hld up bhd ldrs against rail: rdn over 2f out: styd on fr over 1f out to take 2nd nr fin* **5/2**1

0-03 3 nk **Koharu**14 3316 3-7-8 **55** oh5 ow1............(t) JoeyHaynes(7) 3 56
(Peter Makin) *pressed wnr: rdn 2f out: nt qckn and hld over 1f out: lost 2nd nr fin* **20/1**

-406 4 2 1/4 **Saskia's Dream**8 3534 5-8-12 **64**............ IanBurns(7) 2 62
(Jane Chapple-Hyam) *racd wd: pressed ldng pair: rdn 2f out: steadily outpcd* **5/1**

-056 5 shd **Mystical Moment**16 3242 3-9-5 **73**............ PatDobbs 1 68
(Richard Hannon) *hld up and sn in last pair: rdn 2f out: one pce and nvr threatened ldrs* **3/1**2

/35 6 ½ **Madeira Girl (IRE)**[13] 3375 4-9-8 **67** GeorgeBaker 4 63
(Jonjo O'Neill) *wl in tch: rdn 2f out: nt qckn over 1f out and no imp after* **14/1**

-254 7 2 **Tomintoul Magic (IRE)**[21] 3086 3-9-1 **69** TomQueally 7 57
(Lady Cecil) *fractious bef gng to post: t.k.h: hld up in last pair: shkn up and nt qckn 2f out: no ch after* **8/1**

050- 8 ½ **Silvee**[193] 8156 6-8-9 **54** KieranO'Neill 6 44
(John Bridger) *trckd ldrs: rdn over 2f out: wknd over 1f out* **20/1**

1m 23.4s (0.10) **Going Correction** -0.075s/f (Good)
WFA 3 from 4yo+ 9lb 8 Ran SP% **119.8**
Speed ratings (Par 100): **96,94,93,91,91 90,88,87**
toteswingers 1&2 £2.80, 1&3 £11.90, 2&3 £11.80 CSF £13.42 CT £149.85 TOTE £4.00: £1.10, £1.90, £7.60; EX 13.90 Trifecta £172.08 Pool: £1620.11 - 7.03 winning tickets..
Owner Magnolia Racing LLC & Ms Rachel Hood **Bred** Newsells Park Stud **Trained** Newmarket, Suffolk

FOCUS
An ordinary fillies' handicap with the runner-up rated to his C&D form.

3818 PRIORY MECHANICAL SERVICES 40TH ANNIVERSARY H'CAP 7f
7:25 (7:25) (Class 5) (0-75,75) 3-Y-O **£2,726** (£805; £402) **Stalls** High

Form RPR

0001 1 **Jontleman (IRE)**[9] 3494 3-8-7 **66** CharlesBishop(5) 4 74
(Mick Channon) *trckd ldr 2f: styd cl up: pushed along over 2f out: clsd between rivals 1f out to ld last 150yds: styd on wl* **6/1**[3]

6030 2 1¾ **Ceelo**[14] 3342 3-9-7 **75** LiamKeniry 3 78
(Sylvester Kirk) *led against nr side rail: gng best and looked in command 2f out: drvn over 1f out: hdd and fdd last 150yds* **7/4**[2]

1 3 nse **Maria Lombardi**[16] 3253 3-8-12 **66** (t) JamesDoyle 1 69+
(Jeremy Noseda) *trckd ldr after 2f: drvn and nt qckn over 1f out: kpt on same pce after* **1/1**[1]

-000 4 7 **Santo Prince (USA)**[40] 2495 3-9-2 **70** TomQueally 2 54
(Michael Bell) *hld up in last: pushed along 3f out: no prog 2f out: wknd over 1f out* **7/1**

1m 22.62s (-0.68) **Going Correction** -0.075s/f (Good) 4 Ran SP% **113.1**
Speed ratings (Par 99): **100,98,97,89**
CSF £17.29 TOTE £6.30; EX 27.70 Trifecta £16.20 Pool: £516.54 - 23.83 winning tickets..
Owner Paul Corbett **Bred** Old Carhue & Graeng Bloodstock **Trained** West Ilsley, Berks

FOCUS
Just four runners, and only three really mattered, but not terrible form, with the winner to his juvenile form and the second to this year's mark.

3819 CARRY ON HUNTING (S) STKS 1m 4f (P)
8:00 (8:00) (Class 6) 3-Y-O+ **£2,045** (£603; £302) **Stalls** Low

Form RPR

1242 1 **Right Stuff (FR)**[39] 1513 10-9-13 79 (v) GeorgeBaker 5 72
(Gary Moore) *led after 1f: mde rest: stretched clr over 1f out: in n.d after: eased nr fin* **10/11**[1]

/0-0 2 2 **Proud Times (USA)**[7] 3579 7-9-8 60 (p) AdamKirby 4 64
(Ali Brewer) *in tch: rdn bef 1/2-way: outpcd over 2f out: styd on u.p after to take 2nd last 150yds* **7/1**

0306 3 3¼ **El Libertador (USA)**[18] 3180 7-9-1 55 (b) JoeyHaynes(7) 6 59
(Eric Wheeler) *trckd wnr after 3f: rdn over 2f out: outpcd over 1f out: lost 2nd last 150yds* **5/1**[3]

00-0 4 6 **Play Tiger (FR)**[12] 3402 4-9-8 55 LiamKeniry 7 49
(Peter Hiatt) *t.k.h: hld up in tch: prog to chse ldng pair wl over 2f out: wknd over 1f out* **20/1**

0105 5 4½ **Minority Interest**[21] 3110 4-9-13 59 (p) JimmyFortune 1 47
(Brett Johnson) *led 1f: trckd wnr to 9f out: pushed along over 4f out: wknd wl over 2f out* **7/2**[2]

030 6 ½ **Running Bull (IRE)**[12] 3403 3-8-8 43 RobertHavlin 9 41
(Linda Jewell) *hld up in last pair: effrt 3f out: wknd over 2f out* **33/1**

7 54 **Kid Wizzard (USA)**[35] 4-9-8 0 ShaneKelly 3
(David Flood) *dwlt: a in last pair: lost tch 5f out: wl t.o* **20/1**

2m 34.9s (1.90) **Going Correction** +0.20s/f (Slow)
WFA 3 from 4yo+ 14lb 7 Ran SP% **116.2**
Speed ratings (Par 101): **101,99,97,93,90 90,54**
toteswingers 1&2 £1.50, 1&3 £2.40, 2&3 £4.40 CSF £8.17 TOTE £1.80: £1.50, £2.40; EX 5.20 Trifecta £20.20 Pool: £1057.92 - 39.25 winning tickets..There was no bid for the winner
Owner The Ashden Partnership & Partners **Bred** N P Bloodstock Ltd **Trained** Lower Beeding, W Sussex

FOCUS
An uncompetitive seller and Right Stuff, who had been running to a reasonable level in defeat on the Flat and, most recently over hurdles, had upwards of 9lb in hand on RPRs. He was unimpressive here.

3820 SURREY ROYAL BRITISH LEGION H'CAP 1m 4f (P)
8:30 (8:30) (Class 6) (0-65,64) 3-Y-O **£2,045** (£603; £302) **Stalls** Low

Form RPR

00-4 1 **Duchess Of Gazeley (IRE)**[28] 2874 3-8-13 **56** ShaneKelly 11 63
(Gary Harrison) *trckd ldrs: prog to take 3rd 3f out: clsd to ld 1f out: hrd rdn and styd on* **6/1**

00-2 2 1¾ **Aloha**[32] 2762 3-9-5 **62** GeorgeBaker 12 66+
(Roger Varian) *stdd s: hld up in last trio: sme prog fr 3f out but plenty to do 2f out: rdn over 1f out: r.o to take 2nd nr fin: no ch to chal* **4/1**[2]

323 3 ¾ **Alshan Fajer**[4] 3653 3-9-7 **64** RobertHavlin 8 67
(Roger Ingram) *trckd ldr: rdn to ld over 2f out: hdd 1f out: one pce and lost 2nd nr fin* **7/2**[1]

2402 4 ¾ **Aphrodite Spirit (IRE)**[11] 3432 3-8-3 **46** CathyGannon 10 48
(Pat Eddery) *led to over 2f out: pressed ldr to jst over 1f out: one pce after* **20/1**

1654 5 ½ **Noor Al Haya (IRE)**[12] 3418 3-8-0 **50** DanielMuscutt(7) 6 51
(Mark Usher) *wnt lft s: hld up in midfield: sme prog into 5th over 2f out: rdn and nt qckn over 1f out: kpt on same pce after* **33/1**

3353 6 ¾ **Bee Jay Kay**[8] 3528 3-8-13 **63** DanielCremin(7) 5 63
(Mick Channon) *bmpd sn after s: towards rr: looking for room 3f out: rdn 2f out: styd on fr over 1f out: nrst fin* **16/1**

-503 7 ½ **See And Be Seen**[11] 3432 3-8-2 **45** FrankieMcDonald 3 44
(Sylvester Kirk) *hld up in midfield: lost pl over 3f out and pushed along: plenty to do whn rdn 2f out: kpt on fnl f: nrst fin* **50/1**

033V 8 nk **Rock Diamond (IRE)**[7] 3578 3-8-4 **47** JohnFahy 1 45
(Sylvester Kirk) *trckd ldrs on inner: sltly outpcd over 2f out: tried to cl over 1f out: one pce after* **25/1**

5-00 9 ½ **Exclusive Waters (IRE)**[8] 3528 3-9-3 **60** (v[1]) AdamKirby 4 58
(William Knight) *trckd ldrs: hrd rdn in 4th over 2f out: wknd jst over 1f out* **14/1**

0-50 10 9 **Point Of Control**[33] 2713 3-9-7 **64** TomQueally 13 47
(Michael Bell) *hld up in rr: rdn and no prog over 3f out: wl btn after* **14/1**

4064 11 ½ **Jacobella**[11] 3437 3-9-1 **63** MatthewLawson(5) 7 45
(Jonathan Portman) *s.s: hld up in last trio: effrt on wd outside over 3f out: no prog over 2f out: wknd* **12/1**

0054 12 4 **Little Alice**[14] 3319 3-8-2 **45** [1] KieranO'Neill 2 21
(Stuart Williams) *chsd ldng pair: rdn 5f out: lost pl over 3f out: wknd* **50/1**

5-20 13 3½ **Snoqualmie Chief**[37] 2600 3-9-5 **62** LiamKeniry 14 32
(David Elsworth) *stdd s: hld up in last trio: trying to make prog whn rn into trble over 2f out: no ch after* **14/1**

-320 14 8 **Hello Sailor**[31] 2784 3-9-4 **61** (b) JamesDoyle 9 19
(Ralph Beckett) *chsd ldrs: drvn 5f out: wknd over 3f out: eased over 2f out: t.o* **9/2**[3]

2m 32.58s (-0.42) **Going Correction** +0.20s/f (Slow) 14 Ran SP% **123.7**
Speed ratings (Par 97): **109,107,107,106,106 106,105,105,105,99 98,96,93,88**
toteswingers 1&2 £5.00, 1&3 £7.60, 2&3 £3.50 CSF £29.50 CT £99.85 TOTE £7.40: £2.60, £1.80, £1.70; EX 42.50 Trifecta £94.30 Pool: £961.20 - 7.64 winning tickets..
Owner Franconson Partners **Bred** Overbury Stallions Ltd And D Boocock **Trained** Newmarket, Suffolk

FOCUS
Moderate stuff, but the front two are lightly raced and going the right way. The third helps set the standard.

3821 BRITISH ARMED FORCES DAY MEDIAN AUCTION MAIDEN STKS 1m 2f (P)
9:00 (9:02) (Class 6) 3-4-Y-O **£2,045** (£603; £302) **Stalls** Low

Form RPR

2-42 1 **Fly Haaf (IRE)**[131] 709 4-10-0 65 AdamKirby 3 70
(William Knight) *sn trckd ldr: rdn to ld over 2f out: hrd drvn and edgd rt fnl f: hld on* **4/1**[3]

2300 2 ½ **Harbinger Lass**[37] 2586 3-8-6 76 CharlesBishop(5) 8 64
(Mick Channon) *led: tended to hang rt: rdn and hdd over 2f out: pressed wnr after: edgd rt fnl f: jst hld* **5/2**[2]

-604 3 1¾ **Muskat Link**[18] 3173 3-8-11 63 AmyScott(5) 1 66
(Henry Candy) *trckd ldng pair: outpcd over 2f out: kpt on fr over 1f out: nvr able to chal* **14/1**

4 1 **Al Guwair (IRE)** 3-9-2 0 TomQueally 7 64+
(Lady Cecil) *green in preliminaries: difficult to load into stall: dwlt: in tch in rr: rdn 3f out: sn outpcd: styd on fr over 1f out* **9/4**[1]

006 5 2½ **Faustinatheyounger (IRE)**[22] 3059 3-8-11 57 LiamKeniry 5 54
(David Elsworth) *sn trckd ldng pair: outpcd over 2f out: no imp fr over 1f out* **25/1**

45 6 1¼ **Viennese Verse**[26] 2930 3-9-2 0 CathyGannon 6 56
(Henry Candy) *hld up in last early: effrt over 3f out: outpcd over 2f out: nvr on terms after* **20/1**

7 3¼ **The Wizard Of Aus (IRE)** 3-9-2 0 (t) JimmyFortune 2 50
(Andrew Balding) *in tch: outpcd over 3f out: no ch fr 2f out: plugged on* **5/1**

8 22 **Loafer** 3-9-2 0 KieranO'Neill 9
(Olivia Maylam) *dwlt: a in rr: lost tch over 4f out: t.o* **66/1**

2m 9.12s (2.52) **Going Correction** +0.20s/f (Slow)
WFA 3 from 4yo 12lb 8 Ran SP% **112.8**
Speed ratings (Par 101): **97,96,95,94,92 91,88,71**
toteswingers 1&2 £4.10, 1&3 £5.10, 2&3 £11.30 CSF £13.93 TOTE £4.40: £1.50, £1.40, £2.40; EX 11.00 Trifecta £148.30 Pool: £1128.30 - 5.70 winning tickets..
Owner The Pheasant Rew Partnership **Bred** John O'Connor **Trained** Patching, W Sussex

FOCUS
An ordinary maiden and muddling form, with the runner-up rated well below her mark.
T/Plt: £87.50 to a £1 stake. Pool: £62,551.65 - 521.45 winning tickets T/Qpdt: £19.90 to a £1 stake. Pool: £6026.70 - 223.50 winning tickets JN

[3773]NEWCASTLE (L-H)
Saturday, June 29

OFFICIAL GOING: Good to soft (good in places; 7.0)
Wind: Fresh, half against Weather: Overcast

3822 BETFRED CHIPCHASE STKS (GROUP 3) 6f
2:05 (2:05) (Class 1) 3-Y-O+
£34,026 (£12,900; £6,456; £3,216; £1,614; £810) **Stalls** Centre

Form RPR

1064 1 **Jack Dexter**[11] 3420 4-9-3 110 GrahamLee 5 111
(Jim Goldie) *in tch: stdy hdwy 2f out: rdn and led last 100yds: hld on wl cl home* **4/5**[1]

-010 2 hd **Mass Rally (IRE)**[7] 3558 6-9-3 104 (b) PaulMulrennan 1 110
(Michael Dods) *hld up: stdy hdwy over 2f out: effrt and rdn over 1f out: kpt on wl fnl f: hld cl home* **15/2**

0-00 3 2½ **Mirza**[27] 2909 6-9-3 96 (p) SebSanders 7 102
(Rae Guest) *chsd ldr: rdn and led appr fnl f: edgd lft: hdd last 100yds: kpt on same pce* **33/1**

-024 4 1½ **Majestic Myles (IRE)**[63] 1835 5-9-3 105 PaulHanagan 4 98
(Richard Fahey) *chsd ldrs: drvn along over 2f out: kpt on same pce fnl f* **6/1**[2]

2032 5 nk **Justineo**[13] 3373 4-9-3 101 JimCrowley 2 97
(Roger Varian) *taken early to post: led tl rdn and hdd appr fnl f: one pce whn checked ins fnl f* **13/2**[3]

40 6 11 **Switcher (IRE)**[77] 1544 4-9-0 95 (v) DanielTudhope 9 58
(David O'Meara) *racd jst away fr main centre gp: hld up in tch: rdn over 2f out: sn wknd* **11/1**

2-06 7 nk **Free Zone**[22] 3046 4-9-3 101 TomEaves 8 67
(Bryan Smart) *racd jst away fr main centre gp: chsd ldrs tl rdn and wknd wl over 1f out* **20/1**

1m 13.83s (-0.77) **Going Correction** +0.05s/f (Good) 7 Ran SP% **111.0**
Speed ratings (Par 113): **107,106,103,101,101 86,85**
toteswingers 1&2 £2.90, 1&3 £7.30, 2&3 £28.30 CSF £6.95 TOTE £1.50: £1.20, £3.90; EX 7.30 Trifecta £83.80 Pool: £3001.08 - 26.83 winning tickets..
Owner Johnnie Delta Racing **Bred** Jim Goldie **Trained** Uplawmoor, E Renfrews

FOCUS
Fresh ground provided. The ground had dried a little overnight and was described after the first as "on the slow side" and "dead, tacky." The time was only 1.33sec outside the standard, suggesting it wasn't as soft as feared. Not a great deal of depth to this Group 3, in which Mayson finished fifth last year before winning the July Cup. The winner did not match his Royal Ascot mark and the runner-up helps set the level.

3823 BETFRED "WATCH FRED'S PUSHES ON BETFRED TV" H'CAP 6f
2:40 (2:40) (Class 2) (0-100,100) 3-Y-0+

£12,450 (£3,728; £1,864; £932; £466; £234) **Stalls** Centre

Form RPR

04 **1** **Baby Strange**[28] 2868 9-8-2 **81** oh2 AdamMcLean(7) 1 92
(Derek Shaw) *hld up: rdn and hdwy over 1f out: led ins fnl f: edgd rt: kpt on strly* **12/1**

3114 **2** 1 1/4 **Chester Aristocrat**[21] 3093 4-8-8 **85** JasonHart(5) 6 92
(Eric Alston) *cl up: rdn and ev ch over 1f out: led briefly ins fnl f: kpt on same pce towards fin* **9/1**

3066 **3** 3/4 **Rodrigo De Torres**[15] 3300 6-9-6 **92** AndrewMullen 4 97
(David Nicholls) *led: rdn and jnd over 1f out: hdd ins fnl f: kpt on same pce* **33/1**

02-0 **4** 1 **Gramercy (IRE)**[21] 3114 6-9-6 **92** JimCrowley 5 93
(David Simcock) *hld up: rdn and hdwy over 1f out: kpt on ins fnl f: nt pce to chal* **14/1**

0-15 **5** 1 **Trojan Rocket (IRE)**[7] 3586 5-8-9 **81** RobertWinston 11 79+
(Michael Wigham) *hld up: rdn and hdwy over 1f out: kpt on fnl f: nrst fin* **12/1**

0-06 **6** 1/2 **Pearl Ice**[35] 2647 5-9-4 **90** GrahamGibbons 10 87
(David Barron) *hld up in midfield: effrt and hdwy over 1f out: kpt on same pce last 100yds* **8/1**[3]

0-33 **7** 1 3/4 **Barracuda Boy (IRE)**[14] 3348 3-9-0 **93** TonyHamilton 8 84
(Tom Dascombe) *chsd ldrs: rdn over 2f out: no ex appr fnl f* **9/2**[1]

1130 **8** 3/4 **Tarooq (USA)**[17] 3220 7-8-13 **85** (t) AndreaAtzeni 14 74+
(Stuart Williams) *hld up: rdn 2f out: styd on fnl f: nvr able to chal* **16/1**

0322 **9** hd **Fast Shot**[24] 2988 5-9-3 **89** PaulMulrennan 12 77+
(Tim Easterby) *chsd ldrs: drvn and outpcd 2f out: no imp fnl f* **5/1**[2]

230/ **10** shd **Son Du Silence (IRE)**[242] 4-8-13 **85** (t) GrahamLee 7 73
(James Ewart) *chsd ldrs: rdn 2f out: wknd ins fnl f* **33/1**

2310 **11** 3/4 **Summerinthecity (IRE)**[21] 3114 6-9-4 **90** JoeFanning 9 75
(David Nicholls) *t.k.h in midfield: outpcd 2f out: n.d after* **16/1**

6110 **12** 3/4 **Powerful Presence (IRE)**[8] 3527 7-9-5 **91** DanielTudhope 15 74
(David O'Meara) *midfield: rdn and outpcd 2f out: sn n.d* **16/1**

0-00 **13** nk **Ahern**[14] 3348 3-9-7 **100** (b) PhillipMakin 3 82
(David Barron) *hld up: rdn over 2f out: edgd lft and btn over 1f out* **20/1**

1600 **14** 1/2 **Klynch**[13] 3367 7-9-4 **90** (b) JamesSullivan 2 70
(Ruth Carr) *prom tl rdn and wknd over 1f out* **25/1**

-201 **15** 1/2 **Spinatrix**[41] 2476 5-9-10 **96** (p) TomEaves 13 75
(Michael Dods) *cl up tl rdn and wknd wl over 1f out* **10/1**

0000 **16** 9 **Johannes (IRE)**[21] 3114 10-8-13 **85** PaulHanagan 16 35
(Richard Fahey) *taken early to post: hld up: rdn and outpcd over 2f out: sn struggling* **12/1**

1m 14.16s (-0.44) **Going Correction** +0.05s/f (Good)
WFA 3 from 4yo+ 7lb **16** Ran SP% **126.9**
Speed ratings (Par 109): **104,102,101,100,98 98,95,94,94,94 93,92,91,91,90 78**
toteswingers 1&2 £29.00, 1&3 £139.50, 2&3 £102.90 CSF £115.80 CT £2088.70 TOTE £13.90: £3.20, £2.60, £10.00, £3.30; EX 173.90 Trifecta £4336.80 Part won. Pool: £5782.46 - 0.84 winning tickets..
Owner Market Avenue Racing Club Ltd **Bred** Michael John Williamson **Trained** Sproxton, Leics

FOCUS
Not many got involved in this decent handicap, in which those drawn low dominated. The placed horses offer the best guide to the level.

3824 JOHN SMITH'S NORTHUMBERLAND PLATE (HERITAGE H'CAP) 2m 19y
3:15 (3:15) (Class 2) 3-Y-0+

£92,385 (£27,810; £10,417; £10,417; £3,480; £1,755) **Stalls** Centre

Form RPR

43-3 **1** **Tominator**[52] 2149 6-9-10 **102** GrahamLee 4 110+
(Jonjo O'Neill) *hld up and bhd: stdy hdwy whn n.m.r over 2f out: effrt over 1f out: styd on wl fnl f: led cl home* **8/1**[2]

5620 **2** shd **Oriental Fox (GER)**[21] 3099 5-9-3 **95** JoeFanning 6 103
(Mark Johnston) *hld up in rr: gd hdwy on wd outside to ld over 2f out: sn kicked clr: kpt on fnl f: hdd cl home* **20/1**

0534 **3** 1 1/4 **Mubaraza (IRE)**[11] 3423 4-9-0 **92** PaulHanagan 3 99
(Ed Dunlop) *hld up in midfield: lost pl 6f out: gd hdwy to chse ldr over 1f out to ins fnl f: kpt on same pce* **15/2**[1]

-034 **3** dht **Brockwell**[21] 3099 4-8-7 **90** JasonHart(5) 11 97+
(Tom Dascombe) *hld up in rr: hdwy whn nt clr run over 2f out: effrt over 1f out: edgd rt ins fnl f: kpt on: nrst fin* **20/1**

0033 **5** 1 1/4 **Scatter Dice (IRE)**[7] 3599 4-8-12 **90** PJMcDonald 19 95
(Mark Johnston) *hld up in midfield: effrt and hdwy on ins 2f out: kpt on same pce ins fnl f* **33/1**

-202 **6** 1 3/4 **Moidore**[44] 2402 4-8-12 **90** MichaelO'Connell 10 93
(John Quinn) *hld up in midfield: effrt on outside over 2f out: kpt on fnl f: nt gng pce to chal* **17/2**[3]

01-2 **7** shd **Noble Alan (GER)**[49] 2251 10-8-11 **89** PaulMulrennan 16 92
(Nicky Richards) *t.k.h: in tch: smooth hdwy over 2f out: rdn over 1f out: kpt on same pce* **20/1**

1-11 **8** 1/2 **Arch Villain (IRE)**[35] 2654 4-8-12 **90** AndreaAtzeni 22 92
(Amanda Perrett) *hld up: gd hdwy on outside to chse ldr over 2f out: sn edgd lft: lost 2nd and no ex over 1f out* **12/1**

6-46 **9** nk **Blue Bajan (IRE)**[11] 3423 11-9-3 **95** DanielTudhope 7 97
(David O'Meara) *hld up: stdy hdwy whn n.m.r briefly over 2f out: rdn over 1f out: kpt on fnl f: nt pce to chal* **16/1**

-000 **10** 1 **Crackentorp**[14] 3345 8-9-1 **93** GrahamGibbons 21 94
(Tim Easterby) *in tch: effrt and rdn over 2f out: one pce fr over 1f out* **33/1**

21-1 **11** 1/2 **Ardlui (IRE)**[63] 1841 5-9-6 **98** FergusSweeney 12 98
(Alan King) *chsd ldrs: rdn over 4f out: led briefly over 2f out: wknd fnl f* **9/1**

0-04 **12** nk **Ile De Re (FR)**[35] 2668 7-9-9 **101** JimCrowley 8 101
(Donald McCain) *hld up: rdn and hdwy over 2f out: edgd lft: no imp fr over 1f out* **12/1**

6005 **13** 2 **Party Line**[14] 3345 4-8-10 **88** RoystonFfrench 14 85
(Mark Johnston) *hld up towards rr: rdn and hdwy over 3f out: wknd 2f out* **25/1**

1-40 **14** 7 **Mashaari (IRE)**[7] 3560 4-8-9 **87** TomEaves 17 76
(Brian Ellison) *midfield on outside: hdwy and cl up over 6f out: rdn over 3f out: wknd 2f out* **8/1**[2]

0-13 **15** 5 **Address Unknown**[35] 2668 6-9-4 **101** GeorgeChaloner(5) 15 84
(Richard Fahey) *w ldr: led 1/2-way to over 2f out: sn rdn and wknd* **25/1**

0-12 **16** 2 1/2 **Ingleby Spirit**[52] 2149 6-9-1 **93** TonyHamilton 18 73
(Richard Fahey) *chsd ldrs tl rdn and wknd over 2f out* **14/1**

1-22 **17** 44 **Handsome Man (IRE)**[21] 3115 4-9-6 **98** RobertWinston 2 25
(Saeed bin Suroor) *trckd ldrs: drvn over 3f out: sn wknd: eased whn no ch: t.o* **15/2**[1]

0605 **18** 19 **Good Morning Star (IRE)**[14] 3333 4-9-1 **93** PhillipMakin 5
(Mark Johnston) *led to 1/2-way: lost pl qckly 6f out: lost tch fnl 3f: eased: t.o* **28/1**

3m 34.11s (-5.29) **Going Correction** -0.10s/f (Good) **18** Ran SP% **125.5**
Speed ratings (Par 109): **109,108,108,108,107 106,106,106,106,105 105,105,104,100,98 97,75,65**
Place: Mubaraza £2.50. Brockwell £4.30. CSF £165.63 TOTE £6.80: £2.20, £4.50; EX 185.60 TRIFECTA Trifecta T&OF&M £1,167.30; T&OF&B £2,272.30..
Owner P A Byrne **Bred** Mrs S L Brimble **Trained** Cheltenham, Gloucs

■ Stewards' Enquiry : Paul Mulrennan one-day ban; careless riding (15th July).
Andrea Atzeni three-day ban; careless riding (15th-17th July).
Jason Hart one-day ban; careless riding (15th July).

FOCUS
With fast ground anticipated earlier in the week leading fancies Tiger Cliff and Biographer were taken out, while in contrast Friday's rain on watered ground ruled out two more leading fancies in Montaser and Sun Central. It was still a good edition of this historic handicap, which produced a compressed finish in which the first dozen home were separated by around 7l at the line. The first two and a dead-heater for third all came from the lowest five stalls, the other two drawn in the bottom five finishing last and second-last. The pace was good and the first four came from off the pace but the form looks sound with the runner-up and fifth the best guides.

3825 BETFRED "STILL TREBLE ODDS ON LUCKY'S" H'CAP 7f
3:50 (3:51) (Class 2) (0-105,104) 3-Y-0+

£12,450 (£3,728; £1,864; £932; £466; £234) **Stalls** Centre

Form RPR

1-31 **1** **Diescentric (USA)**[28] 2858 6-9-6 **96** PaulMulrennan 3 111+
(Julie Camacho) *t.k.h early: hld up in tch: smooth hdwy 2f out: led gng wl ins fnl f: shkn up and qcknd: readily* **9/2**[2]

6-20 **2** 2 1/2 **Bertiewhittle**[8] 3527 5-9-7 **97** GrahamGibbons 11 105
(David Barron) *hld up: smooth hdwy 2f out: rdn and chsd wnr ins fnl f: kpt on: nt pce to chal* **3/1**[1]

5-04 **3** 2 **Trail Blaze (IRE)**[7] 3564 4-9-1 **91** PhillipMakin 9 94
(Kevin Ryan) *cl up: led 1/2-way to ins fnl f: sn outpcd by first two* **8/1**[3]

-030 **4** 3 3/4 **Gatepost (IRE)**[21] 3114 4-8-9 **85** PaulHanagan 6 78
(Richard Fahey) *prom: effrt and drvn over 2f out: outpcd fr over 1f out* **10/1**

6000 **5** nse **Compton**[16] 3249 4-9-0 **90** GrahamLee 8 83
(Robert Cowell) *t.k.h: chsd ldrs: outpcd 2f out: rallied ins fnl f: no imp* **10/1**

6-02 **6** 1/2 **Able Master (IRE)**[21] 3088 7-9-0 **90** DanielTudhope 7 81
(David O'Meara) *led to 1/2-way: sn pushed along: rallied: wknd fnl f* **11/1**

3004 **7** 2 1/4 **Santefisio**[8] 3527 7-10-0 **104** (b) JoeFanning 1 89
(Keith Dalgleish) *hld up: effrt and rdn along over 2f out: nvr able to chal* **10/1**

1200 **8** 2 1/4 **King Of Eden (IRE)**[35] 2665 7-8-8 **89** (p) JasonHart(5) 2 68
(Eric Alston) *dwlt: hld up: rdn and hung lft 2f out: sn btn* **16/1**

11-0 **9** 2 **Anton Chigurh**[97] 1168 4-9-1 **91** SebSanders 5 65
(Tom Dascombe) *t.k.h: hld up in tch: outpcd over 2f out: sn btn* **12/1**

0000 **10** 5 **Memory Cloth**[2] 3725 6-8-11 **87** TomEaves 14 47
(Brian Ellison) *midfield: stdy hdwy 1/2-way: drvn and outpcd 2f out: sn btn* **10/1**

-150 **11** 1 1/2 **Masteroftherolls (IRE)**[121] 836 5-9-13 **103** RobertWinston 12 68
(Saeed bin Suroor) *trckd ldrs: drvn over 2f out: wknd wl over 1f out* **11/1**

1m 26.31s (-1.49) **Going Correction** +0.05s/f (Good) **11** Ran SP% **120.9**
Speed ratings (Par 109): **110,107,104,100,100 99,97,94,92,86 85**
toteswingers 1&2 £3.50, 1&3 £6.50, 2&3 £7.90 CSF £18.95 CT £109.74 TOTE £5.20: £2.00, £1.70, £2.70; EX 18.90 Trifecta £1167.30 Pool: £106,572.84 - 34.23 winning tickets..
Owner Axom (XVIII) **Bred** Morgan's Ford Farm **Trained** Norton, N Yorks

FOCUS
A good handicap in which they finished spread out behind the impressive winner. The placed horses offer the best guides and the form could be rated a little higher.

3826 BETFRED MOBILE LOTTO / IRISH STALLION FARMS EBF MAIDEN STKS 5f
4:20 (4:22) (Class 4) 2-Y-0 **£4,075** (£1,212; £606; £303) **Stalls** Centre

Form RPR

4 **1** **Fast Track**[15] 3295 2-9-5 0 GrahamGibbons 10 83+
(David Barron) *t.k.h: cl up: shkn up to ld 1f out: qcknd: readily* **5/4**[1]

5 **2** 2 1/4 **Instant Attraction (IRE)**[14] 3350 2-9-5 0 PhillipMakin 7 72
(Kevin Ryan) *led: rdn and hdd 1f out: kpt on: nt pce of wnr* **5/2**[2]

0 **3** 2 1/2 **Another Royal**[32] 2751 2-9-0 0 RobertWinston 11 58
(Tim Easterby) *hld up in tch: hdwy to chse ldrs and edgd lft over 1f out: one pce fnl f* **10/1**[3]

60 **4** 2 **Please Let Me Go**[12] 3391 2-8-7 0 KevinStott(7) 8 51+
(Kevin Ryan) *hld up: rdn and hdwy over 1f out: kpt on fnl f: nrst fin* **50/1**

5 1/2 **Baltic Spirit (IRE)** 2-9-0 0 JoeFanning 3 49
(Keith Dalgleish) *dwlt: stdy hdwy and in tch 1/2-way: shkn up over 1f out: sn one pce* **10/1**[3]

62 **6** 1 3/4 **Bountiful Forest**[17] 3189 2-9-0 0 PaulHanagan 6 43
(Richard Fahey) *trckd ldrs tl edgd rt and wknd over 1f out* **10/1**[3]

0 **7** 1 1/2 **Imshivalla (IRE)**[35] 2670 2-8-7 0 SamanthaBell(7) 1 37
(Richard Fahey) *bhd: rdn over 2f out: nvr able to chal* **12/1**

6 **8** 3 3/4 **Dancing Juice**[12] 3408 2-9-5 0 JimCrowley 9 29
(Alan Jarvis) *t.k.h: hld up in tch: rdn over 2f out: btn over 1f out* **14/1**

0 **9** 2 **Mornin Mr Norris**[21] 3084 2-9-5 0 MichaelO'Connell 2 22
(John Quinn) *hld up bhd ldng gp: rdn over 2f out: sn outpcd: n.d after* **50/1**

00 **10** 6 **Who Followed Who**[21] 3084 2-8-12 0 DanielleMooney(7) 5
(Nigel Tinkler) *t.k.h: cl up tl edgd lft and wknd wl over 1f out* **50/1**

1m 1.6s (0.50) **Going Correction** +0.05s/f (Good) **10** Ran SP% **120.5**
Speed ratings (Par 95): **98,94,90,87,86 83,81,75,72,62**
toteswingers 1&2 £1.90, 1&3 £3.80, 2&3 £4.10 CSF £4.49 TOTE £1.90: £1.10, £1.50, £3.10; EX 5.10 Trifecta £24.60 Pool: £5324.65 - 161.97 winning tickets..
Owner Raymond Miquel **Bred** Jnp Bloodstock Ltd **Trained** Maunby, N Yorks

FOCUS
Just an ordinary maiden, but a nice performance from the winner. The runner-up probably progressed, and the next two certainly did.

3827 BETFRED TV H'CAP 1m 2f 32y
4:50 (4:50) (Class 4) (0-85,85) 4-Y-0+ £4,690 (£1,395; £697; £348) Stalls Centre

Form RPR
1161 **1** **Whispering Warrior (IRE)**[35] 2673 4-9-7 85 JimCrowley 11 96+
(David Simcock) *confidently rdn in rr: smooth hdwy 2f out: shkn up to ld ins fnl f: pushed out: readily* 6/4[1]
-610 **2** 2 **Spirit Of The Law (IRE)**[51] 2191 4-9-0 83 GeorgeChaloner(5) 4 90
(Richard Fahey) *prom: hdwy to ld 2f out: hdd ins fnl f: kpt on: no ch w wnr* 11/2[3]
1400 **3** 1 **Gold Show**[10] 3477 4-8-2 69 DeclanCannon(3) 12 74
(Edwin Tuer) *t.k.h in midfield: effrt over 2f out: one pce fr over 1f out* 16/1
0006 **4** 2 3/4 **Moheebb (IRE)**[10] 3466 9-7-9 66 oh7 (p) NoelGarbutt(7) 13 66
(Robert Johnson) *s.i.s: hld up: hdwy and in tch over 4f out: rdn and one pce fr 2f out* 28/1
0455 **5** 4 1/2 **Suffice (IRE)**[15] 3301 4-8-9 73 PaulHanagan 1 64
(Richard Fahey) *trckd ldrs: rdn and outpcd over 2f out: n.d after* 5/1[2]
30-0 **6** 3 3/4 **Tiger Reigns**[42] 2463 7-9-2 80 (t) PhillipMakin 7 64
(Michael Dods) *hld up: rdn 3f out: nvr able to chal* 12/1
1320 **7** 2 **Rawaafed (IRE)**[3] 3683 4-8-2 66 (p) AndreaAtzeni 6 46
(Keith Dalgleish) *hld up: pushed along over 2f out: nvr on terms* 14/1
6351 **8** nk **Lady Macduff (IRE)**[1] 3755 4-9-0 78 6ex JoeFanning 8 58
(Mark Johnston) *led tl rdn and hdd 2f out: sn btn* 15/2
6-00 **9** 2 **Indepub**[63] 1831 4-8-7 78 (p) KevinStott(7) 10 54
(Kevin Ryan) *chsd ldr: rdn over 2f out: wknd over 1f out* 14/1
4040 **10** 1/2 **Right Step**[28] 2867 6-9-2 80 (v) SebSanders 3 55
(Alan Jarvis) *hld up in tch: struggling over 2f out: sn btn: sddle slipped* 16/1

2m 12.41s (0.51) **Going Correction** -0.10s/f (Good) 10 Ran SP% 120.1
Speed ratings (Par 105): **93,91,90,88,84 81,80,79,78,77**
toteswingers 1&2 £3.80, 1&3 £9.60, 2&3 £32.00 CSF £10.11 TOTE £2.30: £1.10, £2.20, £4.90; EX 9.90 Trifecta £132.50 Pool: £2302.85 - 13.02 winning tickets..
Owner Daniel Pittack **Bred** Epona Bloodstock Ltd **Trained** Newmarket, Suffolk

FOCUS
A fair handicap run at a sound gallop and the placed horses set a solid standard.

3828 "PICK UP TOTEPOOL RETURNS AT ANY BETFRED SHOP" H'CAP 1m (R)
5:20 (5:20) (Class 4) (0-85,81) 3-Y-O £4,690 (£1,395; £697; £348) Stalls Centre

Form RPR
-041 **1** **Swift Cedar (IRE)**[16] 3242 3-9-2 75 JimCrowley 1 85
(Alan Jarvis) *hld up in tch: hdwy 2f out: drvn to ld ins fnl f: edgd lft: kpt on wl* 2/1[1]
355 **2** nk **Bold Prediction (IRE)**[7] 3582 3-9-2 75 RobertWinston 3 84
(Mrs K Burke) *trckd ldrs: led and hrd pressed fr over 2f out: hdd ins fnl f: sn blkd: kpt on: hld nr fin* 14/1
03-1 **3** 9 **Al Manaal**[19] 3149 3-9-0 80 AhmadAlSubousi(7) 7 71
(Saeed bin Suroor) *in tch on outside: smooth hdwy to dispute ld over 1f out: outpcd by first two and eased fnl 100yds* 7/2[3]
5-36 **4** 3/4 **Midnight Warrior**[40] 2506 3-8-9 68 RoystonFfrench 6 55
(Ron Barr) *chsd ldrs: drvn and outpcd over 2f out: n.d after* 14/1
00-6 **5** 9 **Winged Icarus (USA)**[28] 2876 3-8-8 67 (p) TomEaves 5 33
(Brian Ellison) *t.k.h: led tl hdd & wknd over 2f out* 20/1
-003 **6** 5 **Hunting Rights (USA)**[7] 3571 3-9-1 74 JoeFanning 2 28
(Mark Johnston) *cl up: drvn and outpcd over 2f out: btn over 1f out* 9/2
-401 **7** 62 **Unknown Villain (IRE)**[1] 3773 3-9-3 81 6ex DeclanBates(5) 4
(Tom Dascombe) *dwlt: bhd and nvr gng wl: lost tch fr 3f out: t.o* 3/1[2]

1m 44.35s (-0.95) **Going Correction** -0.10s/f (Good) 7 Ran SP% 116.8
Speed ratings (Par 101): **100,99,90,89,80 75,13**
toteswingers 1&2 £6.60, 1&3 £2.30, 2&3 £5.40 CSF £32.51 TOTE £3.30: £1.50, £4.30; EX 27.80 Trifecta £120.10 Pool: £1940.68 - 12.11 winning tickets..
Owner Cedars Partnership **Bred** Carlingford Breeding Syndicate **Trained** Twyford, Bucks
■ Stewards' Enquiry : Jim Crowley caution; careless riding.

FOCUS
The first two pulled clear in this fair handicap, which was run at a good pace. With a couple failing to give their running this form doesn't look strong, the runner-up being the best guide.
T/Jkpt: £5,461.50 to a £1 stake. Pool: £11388.84 - 6.50 winning tickets T/Plt: £77.80 to a £1 stake. Pool: £177272.64 - 1662.71 winning tickets T/Qpdt: £7.30 to a £1 stake. Pool: £12308.72 - 1241.04 winning tickets RY

3780 NEWMARKET (R-H)
Saturday, June 29

OFFICIAL GOING: Good (8.1)
Wind: virtually nil Weather: bright spells

3829 BET365 EMPRESS STKS (LISTED RACE) (FILLIES) 6f
2:20 (2:21) (Class 1) 2-Y-O
£14,744 (£5,590; £2,797; £1,393; £699; £351) Stalls High

Form RPR
2134 **1** **Fig Roll**[10] 3459 2-8-12 0 RichardHughes 9 94
(Richard Hannon) *hld up wl in tch in midfield: rdn and effrt 2f out: led ent fnl f: hdd and drvn fnl 150yds: kpt on wl to ld again wl ins fnl f: gng away at fin* 5/2[1]
3110 **2** 3/4 **Ventura Mist**[10] 3459 2-8-12 0 (p) DuranFentiman 1 92
(Tim Easterby) *t.k.h: chsd ldrs: rdn 2f out: outpcd and drvn over 1f out: rallied ins fnl f: styd on strly fnl 100yds to go 2nd towards fin* 12/1
31 **3** hd **Love In The Desert**[23] 3023 2-8-12 0 PatCosgrave 3 91
(Noel Quinlan) *chsd ldr tl over 1f out: sltly outpcd and drvn ent fnl f: rallied u.p fnl 100yds: kpt on to go 3rd nr fin* 14/1
221 **4** hd **Disko (IRE)**[14] 3324 2-8-12 0 JamesMcDonald 5 91
(Daniel Kubler) *racd keenly: led tl rdn and hdd ent fnl f: stl ev ch tl no ex fnl 100yds* 33/1
1 **5** hd **Majeyda (USA)**[14] 3318 2-8-12 0 MickaelBarzalona 10 90
(Saeed bin Suroor) *hld up in tch in midfield: rdn and hdwy ent fnl 2f: drvn to chal over 1f out: led and hung lft u.p ins fnl f: hdd wl ins fnl f: no ex and lost 3 pls towards fin* 5/2[1]
6002 **6** 1 1/2 **Rough Courte (IRE)**[42] 2458 2-8-12 0 FrederikTylicki 2 85
(Mick Channon) *in tch in midfield: effrt u.p 2f out: hdwy and drvn to chse ldrs 1f out: kpt on same pce ins fnl f* 50/1
1 **7** 3/4 **Lady Chantilly (IRE)**[9] 3510 2-8-12 0 CathyGannon 11 83
(Jo Hughes) *hld up in tch in last quartet: rdn and effrt 2f out: chsd ldrs and drvn over 1f out: no ex and no imp ins fnl f* 33/1
32 **8** 1/2 **Hoku (IRE)**[43] 2426 2-8-12 0 JamieSpencer 7 82
(Olly Stevens) *stdd s: hld up in tch in last quartet: clsd 2f out: rdn and fnd little for press ent fnl f: no imp after: wl hld and eased towards fin* 8/1[3]
1 **9** 6 **Sunny Harbor (IRE)**[32] 2751 2-8-12 0 RyanMoore 12 64
(David O'Meara) *s.i.s: in tch in last quartet: rdn 1/2-way: struggling and outpcd 2f out: wknd over 1f out* 5/1[2]
012 **10** nk **Lady Lydia (IRE)**[43] 2421 2-8-12 0 FrankieDettori 4 63
(Michael Wigham) *t.k.h: chsd ldrs: rdn and unable qck over 1f out: btn 1f out: fdd ins fnl f* 16/1
404 **11** 1 **Sweet Alibi (IRE)**[21] 3107 2-8-12 0 (p) LiamJones 6 60
(J S Moore) *awkward leaving stalls: in tch in last quartet: rdn and struggling 2f out: wknd over 1f out* 100/1

1m 11.62s (-0.88) **Going Correction** -0.05s/f (Good) 11 Ran SP% 114.0
Speed ratings (Par 98): **103,102,101,101,101 99,98,97,89,89 87**
toteswingers 1&2 £5.50, 1&3 £7.90, 2&3 £24.80 CSF £34.10 TOTE £2.40: £1.30, £2.80, £4.60; EX 26.70 Trifecta £227.60 Pool: £2601.99 - 7.02 winning tickets..
Owner Des Anderson **Bred** D J Anderson **Trained** East Everleigh, Wilts

FOCUS
Far side track used with stall on far side except 13f, which was in the centre. Bend into home straight repositioned which increased distance of 10f &12f races by 20m. This was a competitive Listed race for 2-y-o fillies and they went a solid pace. Despite the bunched finish the form looks up to standard, with the first two coming from decent efforts in the Queen Mary.

3830 BET365.COM FRED ARCHER STKS (LISTED RACE) 1m 4f
2:55 (2:55) (Class 1) 4-Y-O+ £20,982 (£7,955; £3,981; £1,983) Stalls Centre

Form RPR
335- **1** **Lost In The Moment (IRE)**[231] 7696 6-9-0 110 (p) MickaelBarzalona 4 112
(Saeed bin Suroor) *hld up in tch: swtchd lft to centre 4f out: rdn and effrt over 2f out: styng on and pressing ldrs whn squeezed out and hmpd 1f out: swtchd lft and rallied u.p to ld fnl 100yds: hld on wl towards fin* 9/2
4-6 **2** hd **I'm Your Man (FR)**[27] 2908 4-9-3 108 AntoineHamelin 2 114
(A De Royer-Dupre, France) *hld up in tch: swtchd lft to centre 4f out: rdn and outpcd over 2f out: rallied u.p 1f out: str chal fnl 100yds: r.o but jst hld* 11/4[2]
03-2 **3** 3 **Harris Tweed**[42] 2443 6-9-0 109 RichardHughes 3 106
(William Haggas) *led: styd against stands' rail and drvn over 2f out: hrd pressed and hung lft over 1f out: hdd fnl 100yds: no ex and sn btn* 11/8[1]
14-4 **4** nk **Cameron Highland (IRE)**[35] 2652 4-9-0 107 FrankieDettori 5 106
(Roger Varian) *t.k.h: chsd ldr: swtchd lft to centre 4f out: rdn over 2f out: hrd drvn and ev ch over 1f out tl fnl 100yds: no ex and sn btn* 7/2[3]

2m 28.93s (-3.97) **Going Correction** -0.05s/f (Good) 4 Ran SP% 109.2
Speed ratings (Par 111): **111,110,108,108**
CSF £30.50 TOTE £6.00; EX 20.20 Trifecta £30.50 Pool: £1441.86 - 35.35 winning tickets..
Owner Godolphin **Bred** Rockhart Trading Ltd **Trained** Newmarket, Suffolk
■ Stewards' Enquiry : Richard Hughes two-day ban; careless riding (15th-16th July).
Antoine Hamelin two-day ban; used whip above permitted level (15th-16th July).

FOCUS
A solid little race for the class. They went sound pace and developed down the centre late on in a tight finish. The winner is rated to last year's form and sets the level.

3831 BET365 CRITERION STKS (GROUP 3) 7f
3:30 (3:31) (Class 1) 3-Y-O+
£34,026 (£12,900; £6,456; £3,216; £1,614; £810) Stalls High

Form RPR
2014 **1** **Producer**[29] 2840 4-9-3 111 RichardHughes 5 114
(Richard Hannon) *chsd ldng trio: rdn and effrt whn swtchd lft 2f out: hdwy u.p to chse ldr 1f out: drvn to ld wl ins fnl f: r.o wl* 11/4[1]
0033 **2** 3/4 **Red Jazz (USA)**[21] 3101 6-9-3 109 JamesMcDonald 4 112
(Charles Hills) *led: rdn ent fnl 2f: hrd pressed and drvn over 1f out: kpt on wl tl hdd and no ex wl ins fnl f* 9/1
-042 **3** 1 1/4 **Pastoral Player**[21] 3101 6-9-3 111 GeorgeBaker 6 109
(Hughie Morrison) *taken down early: awkward as stalls opened and v.s.a: sn rcvrd and in tch in rr: effrt and swtchd lft over 1f out: drvn and hdwy 1f out: kpt on same pce ins fnl f* 10/3[2]
2-45 **4** 1 **Ultrasonic (USA)**[29] 2838 4-9-0 102 RyanMoore 8 103
(Sir Michael Stoute) *chsd ldrs: wnt 2nd 2f out: sn rdn and chalng: unable qck u.p 1f out: kpt on same pce ins fnl f* 7/1[3]
-446 **5** 3/4 **Hawkeyethenoo (IRE)**[7] 3557 7-9-3 110 JamieSpencer 7 104
(Jim Goldie) *stdd s: in tch in last trio: pushed along after 2f: rdn and hdwy 1/2-way: chal u.p and edgd lft over 1f out: no ex 1f out: wknd ins fnl f* 11/4[1]
050- **6** 1 **Instance**[220] 7809 5-9-0 93 (p) FrankieDettori 3 98
(Jeremy Noseda) *hld up in tch in last pair: rdn and no imp 2f out: rallied and styd on ins fnl f: no threat to ldrs* 33/1
4046 **7** 1/2 **Libranno**[11] 3419 5-9-11 111 PatCosgrave 2 108
(Richard Hannon) *chsd ldr tl 2f out: struggling to qckn u.p and n.m.r jst over 1f out: plugged on same pce and wl hld fnl f* 12/1
5-60 **8** 3 1/4 **The Taj (USA)**[64] 1808 3-8-8 97 DaneO'Neill 9 88
(Richard Hannon) *stdd and dropped in after s: hld up in midfield: rdn and effrt whn flashed tail u.p over 1f out: btn 1f out: fdd ins fnl f* 40/1
00-4 **9** 15 **Cocozza (USA)**[31] 2782 5-9-3 90 SaleemGolam 1 51
(K F Clutterbuck) *t.k.h early: in tch in midfield: lost pl and rdn 1/2-way: lost tch over 1f out: wl bhd and eased towards fin* 100/1

1m 23.09s (-2.61) **Going Correction** -0.05s/f (Good)
WFA 3 from 4yo+ 9lb 9 Ran SP% 113.0
Speed ratings (Par 113): **112,111,109,108,107 106,106,102,85**
toteswingers 1&2 £2.60, 1&3 £1.80, 2&3 £1.90 CSF £27.49 TOTE £3.90: £1.40, £2.20, £1.50; EX 30.80 Trifecta £98.10 Pool: £3112.01 - 23.76 winning tickets..
Owner J Palmer-Brown **Bred** Cheveley Park Stud Ltd **Trained** East Everleigh, Wilts

FOCUS
A tight Group 3 and sound form for the grade. There was a fair pace on and again the middle of the course was the place to be.

3832 CASINO AT BET365 H'CAP 1m 2f
4:05 (4:07) (Class 2) (0-100,98) 3-Y-O+ £12,938 (£3,850; £1,924; £962) Stalls Centre

Form RPR
0-32 **1** **Nabucco**[21] 3113 4-9-5 91 RyanMoore 5 101
(John Gosden) *chsd ldr: rdn and led wl over 1f out: styd on wl ins fnl f: rdn out* 9/4[1]
2100 **2** 1 1/4 **Strictly Silver (IRE)**[7] 3564 4-9-4 95 RobertTart(5) 3 103
(Alan Bailey) *t.k.h: hld up in tch in midfield: rdn and effrt 2f out: sltly outpcd over 1f out: rallied and styd on ins fnl f to go 2nd last strides* 11/1

1131 **3** *hd* **Awake My Soul (IRE)**[24] 2976 4-9-7 **93**........................ PatCosgrave 11 100
(David O'Meara) *led and stdy gallop: rdn and qcknd ent fnl 2f: hdd over 1f out: kpt on same pce u.p ins fnl f: lost 2nd last strides* **15/2**

211- **4** *1 ¾* **Viewpoint (IRE)**[185] 8242 4-9-5 **91**................................ RichardHughes 4 95
(Richard Hannon) *chsd ldrs: rdn 2f out: hrd drvn over 1f out: no ex and one pce ins fnl f* **10/1**

0122 **5** *nk* **Come On Blue Chip (IRE)**[19] 3157 4-9-2 **88**............(p) FrederikTylicki 2 91
(Paul D'Arcy) *hld up in tch in last quartet: rdn and effrt over 1f out: kpt on ins fnl f: no threat to wnr* **20/1**

-534 **6** *½* **Proud Chieftain**[30] 2811 5-9-11 **97**................................ JamieSpencer 9 99
(Clifford Lines) *hld up in tch in midfield: effrt u.p jst over 2f out: drvn and no ex 1f out: hld and one pce fnl f* **10/1**

4520 **7** *½* **Spifer (IRE)**[21] 3094 5-9-6 **92**...(p) DaneO'Neill 7 93
(Marco Botti) *hld up in tch in last quartet: rdn and effrt over 1f out: swtchd rt jst ins fnl f: styd on fnl 100yds: nvr trbld ldrs* **20/1**

30-3 **8** *1* **Beaufort Twelve**[21] 3113 4-9-3 **89**.................................. FrankieDettori 8 88
(William Jarvis) *chsd ldrs: rdn and effrt 2f out: pressing ldr over 1f out tl 1f out: wknd ins fnl f* **13/2**[3]

-432 **9** *¾* **Forgotten Hero (IRE)**[21] 3094 4-9-4 **90**.................... JamesMcDonald 1 88
(Charles Hills) *t.k.h: hld up in tch in midfield: rdn and effrt whn edgd lft 2f out: no imp over 1f out: wknd ins fnl f* **6/1**[2]

/0-0 **10** *1* **Cry Fury**[91] 1242 5-9-7 **93**... GeorgeBaker 6 89
(Roger Charlton) *stdd s: hld up in rr: rdn and effrt ent fnl 2f: no imp over 1f out: nvr trbld ldrs* **12/1**

22-1 **11** *4 ½* **Resurge (IRE)**[29] 2839 8-9-12 **98**...........................(t) MickaelBarzalona 10 85
(Stuart Kittow) *stdd s: t.k.h: hld up in last pair: swtchd lft and effrt u.p over 1f out: no prog: wl btn and eased wl ins fnl f* **16/1**

2m 3.89s (-1.61) **Going Correction** -0.05s/f (Good) **11** Ran SP% **119.8**
Speed ratings (Par 109): **104,103,102,101,101 100,100,99,99,98 94**
toteswingers 1&2 £3.60, 1&3 £4.80, 2&3 £12.40 CSF £29.31 CT £160.17 TOTE £3.10: £1.70, £2.70, £2.30; EX 33.60 Trifecta £121.70 Pool: £2763.18 - 17.01 winning tickets..
Owner HRH Princess Haya Of Jordan **Bred** Darley **Trained** Newmarket, Suffolk

FOCUS
This was a decent handicap, run at a routine sort of pace. The form is a bit fluid with the runner-up to his AW mark the best guide.

3833 BET365.COM MAIDEN STKS 7f
4:35 (4:35) (Class 4) 2-Y-O **£3,881** (£1,155; £577; £288) **Stalls** High

Form RPR

1 **Kingman** 2-9-5 0.. RyanMoore 5 96+
(John Gosden) *racd towards far side: dwlt: sn rcvrd and in midfield: clsd and gng wl whn nt clr run 3f out: gap opened and chsd wnr 2f out: rdn to ld over 1f out: sn clr and r.o strly: impressive* **11/4**[2]

0 **2** *6* **Adhwaa**[22] 3057 2-9-0 0... FrankieDettori 8 76
(J W Hills) *racd towards far side: chsd ldrs tl led 3f out: rdn and hdd over 1f out: no ch w wnr after but kpt on for clr 2nd* **40/1**

3 *5* **Sea The Skies** 2-9-5 0.. FrederikTylicki 6 68+
(Gerard Butler) *racd towards far side: in tch in midfield: rdn and effrt over 2f out: 3rd and wl hld over 1f out: plugged on fnl f* **25/1**

0 **4** *1 ¾* **Citizen Kaine (IRE)**[7] 3555 2-9-5 0.................................... CathyGannon 4 63
(Jo Hughes) *racd towards centre: overall ldr tl 3f out: rdn and no ex 2f out: 4th and wl btn over 1f out: plugged on* **66/1**

0 **5** *1 ¼* **Shepherd Gate (USA)**[7] 3555 2-9-5 0................................... LiamJones 1 60
(J S Moore) *racd towards centre: in tch in midfield: rdn and unable qck over 2f out: outpcd 2f out and wl btn after* **16/1**

6 *¾* **Mutawathea** 2-9-5 0... DaneO'Neill 2 58
(Richard Hannon) *racd towards far side: t.k.h: hld up in midfield: rdn and outpcd over 2f out: wknd over 1f out* **7/1**

2 **7** *3 ½* **Man Amongst Men (IRE)**[43] 2411 2-9-5 0......................... JamieSpencer 9 49
(Brian Meehan) *racd towards far side: chsd ldrs: rdn 3f out: outpcd and btn 2f out: no ch and eased wl ins fnl f* **2/1**[1]

8 *2 ¾* **Squire** 2-9-5 0.. MickaelBarzalona 7 42
(Saeed bin Suroor) *racd towards far side: in tch in midfield: rdn and lost pl 4f out: n.d after: bhd over 1f out* **7/2**[3]

9 *2 ¼* **Jeremos (IRE)** 2-9-5 0.. RichardHughes 10 36
(Richard Hannon) *racd towards far side: s.i.s: a in rr: rdn and no prog over 2f out: wl bhd over 1f out* **14/1**

10 *9* **Motamayezah** 2-9-0 0... PatCosgrave 3 8
(Ismail Mohammed) *racd towards nr side: rn green in rr: lost tch over 2f out: t.o fnl f* **50/1**

1m 24.3s (-1.40) **Going Correction** -0.05s/f (Good) **10** Ran SP% **117.0**
Speed ratings (Par 95): **106,99,93,91,90 89,85,82,79,69**
toteswingers 1&2 £13.40, 1&3 £12.60, 2&3 £25.80 CSF £114.02 TOTE £3.50: £1.50, £5.50, £4.70; EX 103.70 Trifecta £327.20 Pool: £4785.62 - 4.28 winning tickets..
Owner K Abdullah **Bred** Juddmonte Farms Ltd **Trained** Newmarket, Suffolk

FOCUS
This looked a fair 2-y-o maiden and it was a really impressive display from Kingman. He looks a future Group winner but the form behind will take time to settle.

3834 BET365 FILLIES' H'CAP 1m 4f
5:05 (5:05) (Class 3) (0-95,92) 3-Y-O+ **£8,409** (£2,502; £1,250; £625) **Stalls** Centre

Form RPR

4140 **1** **Alta Lilea (IRE)**[28] 2879 3-8-5 **83**... LiamJones 4 95
(Mark Johnston) *mde all: set stdy gallop tl shkn up and wnt clr over 2f out: clr and in command over 1f out: styd on wl: readily* **15/2**

-325 **2** *4* **Pompeia**[18] 3177 3-8-0 **78** oh1..(p) CathyGannon 5 84
(Ralph Beckett) *hld up in tch: rdn and effrt over 2f out: chsd clr wnr 2f out: no imp and edgd lft over 1f out: kpt on but no threat to wnr fnl f* **7/1**

3220 **3** *3 ½* **Heading North**[16] 3240 3-9-0 **92**.. RichardHughes 2 92
(Richard Hannon) *chsd ldrs: effrt u.p but nt qckn 2f out: 3rd and wl hld fnl f: plugged on* **4/1**[3]

1-33 **4** *1* **Princess Caetani (IRE)**[21] 3095 4-9-7 **85**........................... JamieSpencer 3 83
(David Simcock) *stdd s: t.k.h: hld up in rr: rdn and effrt ent fnl 2f: no hdwy: wl hld but kpt on fnl 100yds to snatch 4th cl home* **6/1**

1-13 **5** *nse* **Mama Quilla (USA)**[15] 3301 4-8-13 **77**..............................(p) RyanMoore 1 75
(William Haggas) *t.k.h: hld up in last pair: effrt u.p 3f out: no imp and wl hld over 1f out* **9/4**[1]

13 **6** *½* **Abilene**[59] 1933 3-8-10 **88**.. KirstyMilczarek 6 86
(Luca Cumani) *chsd wnr: rdn 3f out: lost 2nd and outpcd and btn 2f out: wl hld over 1f out* **7/2**[2]

2m 29.96s (-2.94) **Going Correction** -0.05s/f (Good)
WFA 3 from 4yo 14lb **6** Ran SP% **111.5**
Speed ratings (Par 104): **107,104,102,101,101 100**
toteswingers 1&2 £7.90, 1&3 £5.80, 2&3 £5.70 CSF £54.96 TOTE £10.00: £3.20, £2.20; EX 41.00 Trifecta £199.90 Pool: £3233.29 - 12.12 winning tickets..
Owner Mrs S Bianco & Ms J Bianco **Bred** Rockhart Trading Ltd **Trained** Middleham Moor, N Yorks

FOCUS
A fair fillies' handicap and the form is fluid but is taken at face value through the third.

3835 POKER AT BET365 EBF FILLIES' H'CAP 1m
5:35 (5:36) (Class 3) (0-95,90) 3-Y-O+ **£8,409** (£2,502; £1,250; £625) **Stalls** High

Form RPR

41-2 **1** **Great Timing (USA)**[15] 3292 3-9-4 **90**.................................. RyanMoore 3 98+
(Saeed bin Suroor) *chsd ldr: rdn and effrt 2f out: drvn to chal over 1f out: led jst ins fnl f: styd on strly and forged clr fnl 100yds: drvn out* **11/10**[1]

10-0 **2** *1 ¾* **Forgive**[14] 3339 4-10-0 **90**.. LiamJones 1 96
(Richard Hannon) *wnt rt s: sn rcvrd and led: rdn ent fnl 2f: drvn and hdd jst ins fnl f: no ex and btn fnl 100yds: hld on for 2nd cl home* **11/1**

13-1 **3** *hd* **Ghanaian (FR)**[18] 3179 3-9-0 **86**................................ MickaelBarzalona 2 90+
(Saeed bin Suroor) *chsd ldrs: effrt u.p over 1f out: drvn and kpt on same pce ins fnl f* **9/4**[2]

-341 **4** *2 ¼* **Sharqawiyah**[31] 2783 3-9-0 **86**.. KirstyMilczarek 4 85
(Luca Cumani) *hld up wl in tch in midfield: rdn and effrt 2f out: outpcd and edgd lft over 1f out: kpt on same pce fnl f* **11/2**[3]

20 **5** *15* **Majestic Oasis**[49] 2264 4-9-10 **86**.. JamieSpencer 6 63
(Robert Cowell) *hld up in tch in rr: shkn up ent fnl 2f: rdn and no imp over 1f out: sn btn: virtually p.u fnl 100yds* **20/1**

0-02 **6** *3* **Tosca (GER)**[31] 2783 3-8-11 **83**.. FrankieDettori 5 51
(Mrs Ilka Gansera-Leveque) *in tch: rdn over 2f out: drvn and struggling 2f out: sn lost pl and bhd over 1f out: virtually p.u ins fnl f* **16/1**

1m 38.5s (-1.50) **Going Correction** -0.05s/f (Good)
WFA 3 from 4yo 10lb **6** Ran SP% **112.8**
Speed ratings (Par 104): **105,103,103,100,85 82**
toteswingers 1&2 £2.20, 1&3 £1.10, 2&3 £4.10 CSF £14.62 TOTE £1.90: £1.20, £2.50; EX 12.60 Trifecta £35.00 Pool: £2416.51 - 51.72 winning tickets..
Owner Godolphin **Bred** Pin Oak Stud LLC **Trained** Newmarket, Suffolk

FOCUS
A decent little fillies' handicap in which the principals had it to themselves inside the final furlong. The winner looks smart and at least matched her reappearance effort, with the third to her Salisbury mark.
T/Plt: £1,178.20 to a £1 stake. Pool: £142794.23 - 88.47 winning tickets T/Qpdt: £130.60 to a £1 stake. Pool: £8916.54 - 50.50 winning tickets SP

3631 WINDSOR (R-H)
Saturday, June 29

OFFICIAL GOING: Good (good to firm in places; 8.2)
Wind: Moderate across Weather: Sunny

3836 INFINEUM COLLABORATION MAIDEN STKS 6f
2:30 (2:30) (Class 5) 2-Y-O **£2,587** (£770; £384; £192) **Stalls** Low

Form RPR

32 **1** **Rizal Park (IRE)**[35] 2645 2-9-0 0.................................... ThomasBrown(5) 13 75+
(Andrew Balding) *trckd ldrs: led over 1f out: shkn up and hrd pressed ins fnl f: asserted readily clsng stages* **7/2**[1]

00 **2** *nk* **Deeds Not Words (IRE)**[35] 2653 2-9-5 0......................... MatthewDavies 5 74
(Mick Channon) *trckd ldr: slt ld 3f out but hrd pressed tl hdd over 1f out: rallied to chal ins fnl f: readily outpcd clsng stages* **50/1**

44 **3** *2* **Killing Time (IRE)**[18] 3174 2-9-5 0...................................... MartinDwyer 1 68
(Ralph Beckett) *led tl narrowly hdd 3f out: styd chalng and upsides over 1f out: outpcd by ldng duo ins fnl f* **16/1**

4 *½* **Autopilot** 2-9-5 0.. NeilCallan 11 67+
(Brian Meehan) *towards rr: drvn and green over 3f out: stl green and edging lft fr 2f out: kpt on wl clsng stages* **12/1**

6 **5** *hd* **Aspirant**[19] 3155 2-9-5 0... JamesDoyle 12 66+
(Roger Charlton) *mid-div: hdwy to cl on ldrs fr 3f out: drvn 2f out: styd on same pce ins fnl f* **6/1**

0 **6** *shd* **Dont Have It Then**[23] 3017 2-9-5 0................................ J-PGuillambert 4 67+
(Willie Musson) *in tch: trckd ldrs and shkn up over 1f out: styd on wl clsng stages* **100/1**

2 **7** *3* **Rock Of Dreams (IRE)**[19] 3155 2-9-5 0......................... JimmyFortune 10 58
(Charles Hills) *chsd ldrs: rdn over 2f out: wknd appr fnl f* **9/2**[3]

0 **8** *nse* **Bowsers Bold**[13] 3374 2-9-5 0... ShaneKelly 3 56
(Marcus Tregoning) *chsd ldrs: rdn over 2f out: wknd wl over 1f out* **12/1**

9 *½* **Fear Or Favour (IRE)** 2-9-5 0.. AdamKirby 2 55
(Clive Cox) *outpcd in rr and green: styd on clsng stages* **8/1**

10 *1 ½* **Half Way** 2-9-5 0.. LiamKeniry 9 50
(Henry Candy) *s.i.s: outpcd: sme late prog* **20/1**

3 **11** *½* **Ice Slice (IRE)**[19] 3155 2-9-5 0... PatDobbs 7 49
(Richard Hannon) *in tch: rdn 1/2-way: wknd 2f out* **4/1**[2]

12 *7* **Penara** 2-9-0 0.. TomQueally 6 23
(Philip Hide) *outpcd* **66/1**

13 *nk* **Nick The Odds (IRE)** 2-9-5 0.. RenatoSouza 8 27
(Jo Hughes) *chsd ldrs 3f* **66/1**

1m 12.79s (-0.21) **Going Correction** -0.15s/f (Firm) **13** Ran SP% **117.8**
Speed ratings (Par 93): **95,94,91,91,91 90,86,86,86,84 83,74,73**
toteswingers 1&2 £42.50, 1&3 £20.40, 2&3 £42.50 CSF £197.98 TOTE £4.40: £1.40, £11.00, £3.50; EX 252.30 Trifecta £900.00 Part won. Pool: £1200.01 - 0.02 winning tickets..
Owner L L Register, Martin & Valerie Slade **Bred** Irish National Stud **Trained** Kingsclere, Hants

FOCUS
Top bend dolled out 2yds from normal inner configuration, adding 7yds to races of 1m and beyond. Rest of rail in normal position and course at maximum width. A fair maiden in which a few had already shown decent form, one of whom was the winner. The form behind is fluid though.

3837 TOTESCOOP6 MAIDEN STKS 6f
3:05 (3:06) (Class 5) 3-Y-O **£2,587** (£770; £384; £192) **Stalls** Low

Form RPR

0-4 **1** **Oasis Spirit**[12] 3401 3-8-9 0... ThomasBrown(5) 10 75+
(Andrew Balding) *trckd ldrs: led over 1f out: drvn and styd on wl fnl f: jst hld on* **14/1**

2 *nk* **Port Alfred** 3-9-5 0.. JamesDoyle 9 79+
(Saeed bin Suroor) *s.i.s: sn in tch: drvn and hdwy 2f out: chsd wnr fnl 100yds: kpt on strly and edgd lft clsng stages: nt quite get up* **3/1**[1]

0302 **3** *1 ½* **Millers Wharf (IRE)**[7] 3576 3-9-5 74.............................(b) PatDobbs 7 74
(Richard Hannon) *chsd ldrs: chal fr 2f out tl 1f out: styd chsng wnr tl no ex fnl 100yds* **9/2**

4 *nk* **Secret Weapon** 3-9-5 0.. MartinDwyer 11 73+
(William Muir) *s.i.s and bhd: pushed along and green 3f out: stl green and edging lft whn styd on appr fnl f: kpt on clsng stages* **25/1**

The Form Book Flat, Raceform Ltd, Compton, RG20 6NL.

0-2 **5** 1 1/4 **Meridius (IRE)**[18] 3170 3-9-5 0 ShaneKelly 2 69
(Gary Harrison) *chsd ldrs: led 2f out but hrd pressed: hdd over 1f out: wknd ins fnl f* **8/1**

5 **6** nk **Coire Gabhail**[21] 3109 3-9-0 0 JimmyFortune 1 63
(Hughie Morrison) *chsd ldrs: pushed along over 2f out: styd on same pce appr fnl f* **14/1**

5- **7** 2 1/2 **Golden Secret**[274] 6627 3-9-0 0 AdamKirby 3 55
(Clive Cox) *led to 2f out: wknd appr fnl f* **7/2**[2]

3 **8** 2 **Spiraea**[37] 2597 3-9-0 0 TomQueally 12 49
(Mark Rimell) *s.i.s: in rr tl hdwy 3f out: rdn 2f out: sn wknd* **4/1**[3]

9 1 1/2 **Joyous** 3-9-0 0 LiamKeniry 8 44
(Dean Ivory) *s.i.s: outpcd most of way* **50/1**

5 **10** 1 1/4 **High Tone**[61] 1875 3-9-0 0 JohnFahy 4 40
(Dean Ivory) *chsd ldrs over 3f* **66/1**

00- **11** 6 **Soubrette**[240] 7505 3-9-0 0 JamieMackay 5 21
(George Margarson) *s.i.s: outpcd* **100/1**

1m 12.03s (-0.97) **Going Correction** -0.15s/f (Firm) **11** Ran SP% **118.1**
Speed ratings (Par 99): **100,99,97,97,95 95,91,89,87,85 77**
toteswingers 1&2 £9.80, 1&3 £8.60, 2&3 £4.50 CSF £55.56 TOTE £15.70: £3.60, £1.80, £1.90; EX 69.00 Trifecta £458.60 Pool: £1590.88 - 2.60 winning tickets..
Owner George Strawbridge **Bred** George Strawbridge **Trained** Kingsclere, Hants

FOCUS
Just a fair 3-y-o maiden, though a few of these are likely to improve. The third looks the best guide and the form could rate a little higher.

3838 TOTEQUADPOT FOUR PLACES IN FOUR RACES H'CAP 1m 3f 135y
3:35 (3:36) (Class 2) (0-100,98) 4-Y-O+ **£12,938** (£3,850; £1,924; £962) **Stalls** Centre

Form RPR

1-30 **1** **Rawaki (IRE)**[21] 3115 5-8-8 **90** ThomasBrown(5) 1 101
(Andrew Balding) *in tch: hdwy fr 3f out to chse ldr 2f out: led over 1f out: styd on strly* **10/1**

035 **2** 1 3/4 **Vasily**[21] 3115 5-8-12 **89** LiamKeniry 3 97
(Robert Eddery) *chsd ldr: led 3f out: hdd u.p over 1f out: kpt on same pce: jst hld on for 2nd* **11/2**[2]

1-1 **3** nk **Clowance Estate (IRE)**[15] 3293 4-9-0 **91** JamesDoyle 8 99
(Roger Charlton) *t.k.h: hld up in rr: hdwy 3f out and sn rdn: styd on fr over 1f out: clsd on 2nd nr fin but no imp on wnr* **5/4**[1]

2531 **4** 3 1/2 **Haylaman (IRE)**[6] 3607 5-9-2 **93** 6ex ShaneKelly 2 95
(David Simcock) *in rr: pushed along 3f out: styd on fr over 1f out: kpt on clsng stages but nvr a threat* **7/1**[3]

3-10 **5** hd **Voodoo Prince**[43] 2407 5-9-4 **95** TomQueally 7 96
(Ed Dunlop) *in rr: pushed along and sme hdwy fr 3f out: nvr gng pce to get into contention* **10/1**

3-11 **6** 8 **Jupiter Storm**[26] 2939 4-8-13 **90** JimmyFortune 4 78
(Gary Moore) *led tl hdd 3f out: sn rdn: hung lft and wknd over 2f out* **7/1**[3]

/0-6 **7** 4 1/2 **Parlour Games**[21] 3115 5-9-7 **98** AdamKirby 6 78
(Saeed bin Suroor) *chsd ldrs: wknd 3f out* **8/1**

400/ **8** nk **Togiak (IRE)**[616] 7029 6-8-5 **82** MartinDwyer 9 61
(David Pipe) *in tch: rdn 3f out: sn btn* **40/1**

0-40 **9** 32 **Aldwick Bay (IRE)**[68] 1728 5-8-4 **81** KieranO'Neill 5
(Richard Hannon) *chsd ldrs tl wknd qckly fr 3f out* **25/1**

2m 23.79s (-5.71) **Going Correction** -0.275s/f (Firm) **9** Ran SP% **120.4**
Speed ratings (Par 109): **108,106,106,104,104 98,95,95,74**
toteswingers 1&2 £10.50, 1&3 £15.80, 2&3 £7.70 CSF £66.77 CT £118.46 TOTE £11.80: £2.60, £2.40, £1.10; EX 62.70 Trifecta £425.20 Pool: £1464.05 - 2.58 winning tickets..
Owner Kingsclere Racing CLub **Bred** Kingsclere Stud **Trained** Kingsclere, Hants

FOCUS
A decent handicap and the pace looked solid. They finished well spread out as a result. The runner-up is rated to last year's C&D win with a personal-best from the winner.

3839 TOTEPOOL KING SIZE POOLS MIDSUMMER STKS (LISTED RACE) 1m 67y
4:10 (4:10) (Class 1) 3-Y-O+ **£20,982** (£7,955; £3,981; £1,983) **Stalls** Low

Form RPR

201- **1** **French Navy**[238] 7558 5-9-7 107 AdamKirby 3 113
(Saeed bin Suroor) *trckd ldrs in cl 3rd: drvn 2f out: styd on to chal between horses ins fnl f: led fnl 100yds: readily* **6/4**[1]

2252 **2** 3/4 **Emell**[29] 2843 3-8-8 105 PatDobbs 1 106
(Richard Hannon) *led: pushed along and styd wl whn chal fr 3f out: rdn over 1f out: hdd and outpcd fnl 100yds* **11/4**[2]

-404 **3** 1 **Lockwood**[119] 869 4-9-4 108 JamesDoyle 2 106
(Saeed bin Suroor) *trckd ldr: chal fr 3f out: stl upsides u.p 1f out: no ex fnl 110yds* **3/1**[3]

4-30 **4** 4 **Questioning (IRE)**[14] 3347 5-9-4 107 (b[1]) RobertHavlin 4 97
(John Gosden) *chsd ldrs in 3rd: rdn over 2f out: sn btn* **4/1**

1m 39.81s (-4.89) **Going Correction** -0.275s/f (Firm) course record
WFA 3 from 4yo+ 10lb **4** Ran SP% **111.7**
Speed ratings (Par 111): **113,112,111,107**
CSF £6.07 TOTE £2.40; EX 5.20 Trifecta £9.50 Pool: £421.32 - 33.15 winning tickets..
Owner Godolphin **Bred** Darley **Trained** Newmarket, Suffolk

FOCUS
A disappointing turnout for this Listed event with just the four runners, two of whom were representing Godolphin. At least the runner-up made sure it was run at a true pace and they took 0.38sec off the course record set in this race two years ago. The form is rated around the first two.

3840 LIVE POOL INFORMATION AT TOTEPOOL.COM H'CAP 6f
4:40 (4:40) (Class 2) (0-105,105) 3-Y-O+
£18,675 (£5,592; £2,796; £1,398; £699; £351) **Stalls** Low

Form RPR

-012 **1** **Tropics (USA)**[26] 2937 5-9-3 **94** AdamKirby 12 110
(Dean Ivory) *trckd ldrs: led over 1f out: drvn out ins fnl f* **11/4**[1]

026 **2** 1 **Rex Imperator**[7] 3558 4-9-10 **101** (p) NeilCallan 7 114
(William Haggas) *in rr but in tch: hdwy 2f out: drvn to chse wnr fnl f but no imp clsng stages* **7/2**[2]

61-1 **3** 1 1/4 **Out Do**[17] 3220 4-9-0 **91** JamesDoyle 3 100
(Luca Cumani) *chsd ldrs: rdn 2f out: kpt on same pce u.p fnl f* **9/2**[3]

3230 **4** nse **Poole Harbour (IRE)**[7] 3558 4-8-13 **95** WilliamTwiston-Davies(5) 11 104
(Richard Hannon) *led: rdn 2f out: hdd over 1f out: one pce ins fnl f* **7/1**

4560 **5** 3/4 **Monsieur Chevalier (IRE)**[11] 3419 6-9-9 **100** (b) ShaneKelly 5 106
(P J O'Gorman) *in rr: rdn and hdwy over 1f out: kpt on ins fnl f* **20/1**

0026 **6** 1/2 **Intransigent**[21] 3114 4-9-0 **91** JimmyFortune 6 96
(Andrew Balding) *t.k.h in tch: rdn fr 2f out: styd on same pce fnl f* **8/1**

-523 **7** 2 1/4 **Picabo (IRE)**[13] 3367 5-9-2 **93** LiamKeniry 8 91
(Henry Candy) *in rr: drvn 2f out: hdwy appr fnl f: styd on same pce* **12/1**

01- **8** 2 **Magic Secret**[257] 7113 5-8-11 **88** MartinDwyer 10 79
(William Muir) *chsd ldrs: rdn over 2f out: wknd appr fnl f* **25/1**

0-40 **9** 1 1/2 **Seachantach (USA)**[112] 954 7-10-0 **105** (t[1]) PaoloSirigu 1 91
(Marco Botti) *chsd ldr to 2f out: sn btn* **33/1**

0-00 **10** 1/2 **Tioman Legend**[26] 2937 4-8-13 **90** RobertHavlin 14 75
(Roger Charlton) *stdd s and swtchd rt in rr: outpcd most of way* **33/1**

4-60 **11** shd **Baddilini**[14] 3342 3-8-1 **90** (p) NatashaEaton(5) 2 75
(Alan Bailey) *sn in tch: rdn and btn 2f out* **40/1**

0-50 **12** 7 **Palace Moon**[7] 3558 8-9-7 **98** TomQueally 4 60
(William Knight) *s.i.s: a in rr* **33/1**

305- **13** 1 1/2 **Mac's Power (IRE)**[261] 7010 7-9-6 **97** J-PGuillambert 9 54
(Willie Musson) *outpcd* **40/1**

1m 10.52s (-2.48) **Going Correction** -0.15s/f (Firm)
WFA 3 from 4yo+ 7lb **13** Ran SP% **120.7**
Speed ratings (Par 109): **110,108,107,106,105 105,102,99,97,96 96,87,85**
toteswingers 1&2 £3.80, 1&3 £3.20, 2&3 £4.50 CSF £11.23 CT £43.65 TOTE £3.80: £1.40, £1.50, £2.30; EX 13.10 Trifecta £42.20 Pool: £3010.52 - 53.41 winning tickets..
Owner Dean Ivory **Bred** D Konecny, S Branch & A Branch **Trained** Radlett, Herts

FOCUS
A hot sprint handicap and three of these ran in the Wokingham seven days earlier. Predictably there was no hanging about and the winner took another step up.

3841 BET TOTETRIFECTA ON ALL RACES H'CAP 6f
5:10 (5:13) (Class 5) (0-70,70) 3-Y-O+ **£2,726** (£805; £402) **Stalls** Low

Form RPR

4-44 **1** **Jay Bee Blue**[31] 2773 4-9-6 **62** (bt) JamesDoyle 2 72
(Sean Curran) *s.i.s: sn in tch: rdn and styd on over 1f out: drvn to ld ins fnl f: kpt on strly* **11/2**[3]

601 **2** 1 1/4 **Jubilant Queen**[16] 3246 3-9-7 **70** AdamKirby 3 74
(Clive Cox) *chsd ldrs: rdn 2f out: styd on to chse wnr ins fnl f but no imp* **5/2**[1]

000- **3** 3/4 **Alfresco**[339] 4468 9-9-2 **58** (b) RobertHavlin 1 62
(Martin Bosley) *led: rdn 2f out: hdd and one pce ins fnl f* **33/1**

0666 **4** 3/4 **Reginald Claude**[9] 3499 5-8-10 **57** RachealKneller(5) 10 58
(Mark Usher) *in rr: hdwy over 1f out: kpt on fnl f: nt rch ldrs* **16/1**

50 **5** nse **Gung Ho Jack**[21] 3090 4-9-12 **68** LiamKeniry 11 69
(John Best) *chsd ldrs: rdn over 2f out: no ex ins fnl f* **11/1**

-336 **6** nk **Fortrose Academy (IRE)**[122] 812 4-9-4 **65** ThomasBrown(5) 4 65
(Andrew Balding) *in tch: chsd ldrs 1/2-way: kpt on fnl f: nt rch ldrs* **5/1**[2]

5056 **7** 1/2 **Frognal (IRE)**[17] 3220 7-9-9 **70** (bt) WilliamTwiston-Davies(5) 9 68
(Paddy Butler) *s.i.s: in rr: rdn over 2f out: swtchd lft and styd on fnl f: nt rch ldrs* **16/1**

0266 **8** hd **Kyllachy Storm**[5] 3622 9-8-8 **55** PhilipPrince(5) 5 53
(Ron Hodges) *chsd ldrs: rdn over 2f out: wknd ins fnl f* **12/1**

5406 **9** 2 3/4 **The Strig**[11] 3431 6-9-4 **60** (v) J-PGuillambert 8 49
(Stuart Williams) *s.i.s: in rr: hdwy over 2f out: nvr rchd ldrs and wknd fnl f* **22/1**

0-00 **10** 2 1/2 **Uprise**[33] 2725 4-9-13 **69** (p) TomQueally 7 50
(George Margarson) *in rr: sme prog 1/2-way: sn btn* **6/1**

0602 **11** 2 1/4 **Kings 'n Dreams**[31] 2781 6-9-0 **56** (b) JimmyFortune 12 30
(Dean Ivory) *chsd ldrs tl wknd ins fnl 2f* **8/1**

1m 12.11s (-0.89) **Going Correction** -0.15s/f (Firm)
WFA 3 from 4yo+ 7lb **11** Ran SP% **121.1**
Speed ratings (Par 103): **99,97,96,95,95 94,94,93,90,86 83**
toteswingers 1&2 £3.50, 1&3 £34.80, 2&3 £46.30 CSF £20.21 CT £377.69 TOTE £6.40: £2.20, £1.30, £9.80; EX 20.70 Trifecta £1032.20 Pool: £1501.00 - 1.09 winning tickets..
Owner Scuderia Vita Bella **Bred** L A C Ashby Newhall Estate Farm **Trained** Hatford, Oxon

FOCUS
A competitive enough race for the grade, but the draw played its part with the first three starting from the three lowest stalls. The form looks sound.

3842 COLLECT TOTEPOOL WINNINGS AT BETFRED SHOPS FILLIES' H'CAP 1m 67y
5:40 (5:40) (Class 5) (0-75,77) 3-Y-O+ **£2,587** (£770; £384; £192) **Stalls** Low

Form RPR

2-52 **1** **Serenity Spa**[13] 3375 3-9-1 **72** JamesDoyle 2 79
(Roger Charlton) *in rr: hdwy 2f out: hrd drvn and styd on strly fnl f to ld last strides* **2/1**[1]

2002 **2** nk **Savanna Days (IRE)**[8] 3532 4-10-2 **77** (v) MatthewDavies 4 83
(Mick Channon) *in rr: hdwy fr 3f out: chsd ldrs 2f out: led jst ins fnl f: kpt on: hdd last strides* **8/1**

/1- **3** 3/4 **Dance Express (IRE)**[226] 7719 4-10-0 **75** AdamKirby 5 79
(Clive Cox) *trckd ldrs: rdn 3f out: led wl over 2f out: hdd jst ins fnl f: kpt on same pce* **4/1**[2]

1322 **4** 4 **Tilstarr (IRE)**[16] 3241 3-9-0 **71** LiamKeniry 8 66
(Roger Teal) *chsd ldr tl over 3f out: sn rdn: styd on same pce fnl 2f* **6/1**[3]

204 **5** 1 1/4 **Ellie In The Pink (IRE)**[21] 3111 5-8-13 **65** JemmaMarshall(5) 1 57
(Pat Phelan) *t.k.h: chsd ldrs to 3f out: wknd 2f out* **12/1**

0-35 **6** 10 **Fanzine**[44] 2389 3-9-1 **72** JimmyFortune 6 41
(Hughie Morrison) *led: hdd wl over 2f out: sn wknd* **4/1**[2]

0-14 **7** 59 **Beat Of The Drum (IRE)**[50] 2223 3-8-8 **70** WilliamTwiston-Davies(5) 3
(Richard Hannon) *chsd ldrs: wkng whn hmpd and stmbld bdly over 2f out: eased* **7/1**

1m 41.54s (-3.16) **Going Correction** -0.275s/f (Firm)
WFA 3 from 4yo+ 10lb **7** Ran SP% **118.9**
Speed ratings (Par 100): **104,103,102,98,97 87,28**
toteswingers 1&2 £2.80, 1&3 £2.50, 2&3 £26.50 CSF £20.23 CT £60.84 TOTE £3.10: £1.80, £3.30; EX 25.80 Trifecta £85.00 Pool: £1369.85 - 12.07 winning tickets..
Owner Seasons Holidays **Bred** Barry Hurley **Trained** Beckhampton, Wilts

FOCUS
An interesting fillies' handicap with a couple of unexposed sorts amongst the field. The pace was furious and it's probably no coincidence that the first two came from last and last-but-one. The winner built on her latest effort with the second recording a personal-best.

T/Plt: £31.40 to a £1 stake. Pool: £87,863.38 - 2038.83 winning tickets T/Qpdt: £7.40 to a £1 stake. Pool: £5027.79 - 798.06 winning tickets ST

3843 - (Foreign Racing) - See Raceform Interactive

[3794]CURRAGH (R-H)

Saturday, June 29

OFFICIAL GOING: Round course - good to firm; straight course - good

3844a DUBAI DUTY FREE MILLENIUM MILLIONAIRE CELEBRATION STKS (LISTED RACE) 1m

3:40 (3:40) 3-Y-O+ **£23,780** (£6,951; £3,292; £1,097)

RPR

1 **Count Of Limonade (IRE)**[22] 3074 3-9-0 104 ow1...... JosephO'Brien 9 110
(A P O'Brien, Ire) *prom: settled in cl 2nd: pushed along into st and led narrowly 2f out: strly pressed ins fnl f: kpt on wl u.p towards fin: all out* **7/2**[2]

2 ½ **Scintillula (IRE)**[9] 3515 3-8-8 104................................(t) KevinManning 1 103
(J S Bolger, Ire) *sn led: 1 l clr 1/2-way: pushed along and hdd narrowly 2f out: kpt on wl u.p ins fnl f to strly press wnr: hld* **5/1**[3]

3 ½ **Captain Joy (IRE)**[20] 3142 4-9-9 106............................. RonanWhelan 5 109+
(Tracey Collins, Ire) *chsd ldrs: pushed along in cl 5th after 1/2-way: rdn fr 2f out and clsd u.p on outer into 3rd cl home wout threatening principals: nrst fin* **8/1**

4 hd **Caponata (USA)**[62] 1862 4-9-7 110..................................... PatSmullen 6 106
(D K Weld, Ire) *chsd ldrs: t.k.h: cl 4th on outer 1/2-way: tk clsr order in 3rd 2f out: sn rdn and no ex u.p over 1f out: kpt on same pce towards fin* **2/1**[1]

5 nk **Elleval (IRE)**[91] 1264 3-8-13 106.. FMBerry 3 106
(David Marnane, Ire) *hld up: 7th 1/2-way: tk clsr order on inner fr 2f out: wnt 3rd u.p ins fnl f: sn no ex and dropped to 5th cl home* **8/1**

6 1 ½ **Brendan Brackan (IRE)**[9] 3517 4-9-9 104............. EmmetMcNamara 4 104
(G M Lyons, Ire) *cl up: settled bhd ldrs: cl 3rd on inner 1/2-way: rdn fr 2f out and sn no imp on principals: kpt on same pce u.p ins fnl f* **12/1**

7 13 **Flashy Approach**[30] 2815 3-8-13 .... DeclanMcDonogh 8 72
(John M Oxx, Ire) *hld up in tch: 6th 1/2-way: rdn into st and sn no imp on principals: eased ins fnl f* **13/2**

8 hd **Croi An Or (IRE)**[52] 2180 4-9-9 95.................................. WayneLordan 2 74
(T Stack, Ire) *towards rr: rdn and no imp fr 3f out: one pce fnl 2f* **25/1**

9 6 ½ **Hot Prospect**[7] 3599 6-9-9 90.. TadhgO'Shea 7 59
(J J Lambe, Ire) *towards rr: rdn and no imp fr 3f out: one pce fnl 2f* **50/1**

1m 35.65s (-10.35) **Going Correction** -1.00s/f (Hard)
WFA 3 from 4yo+ 10lb **9 Ran SP% 121.3**
Speed ratings: **111,110,110,109,109 108,95,94,88**
CSF £22.71 TOTE £3.50: £1.20, £2.10, £2.50; DF 17.10.
Owner Mrs John Magnier & Michael Tabor & Derrick Smith **Bred** K Lynch & S O'Sullivan **Trained** Ballydoyle, Co Tipperary

FOCUS

The decision to take the winner out of the Irish Derby and take in this race instead proved a very wise one as he was tough in landing this. They didn't go that slowly yet finished in a heap and it does lead one to conclude that it was far from a vintage race. The standard is set by the second, fifth and sixth.

3845a DUBAI DUTY FREE JUMEIRAH CREEKSIDE HOTEL SUMMER FILLIES H'CAP (PREMIER HANDICAP) 7f

4:15 (4:16) 3-Y-O+

£24,390 (£7,723; £3,658; £1,219; £813; £406)

RPR

1 **Majestic Queen (IRE)**[14] 3358 3-8-5 83..................... MichaelHussey 2 91+
(Tracey Collins, Ire) *chsd ldrs: 5th 1/2-way: hdwy to ld 1 1/2f out: wnt clr ins fnl f and styd on wl towards fin* **9/1**

2 2 ¼ **Liberating**[16] 3263 3-9-1 93...(p) KevinManning 4 94
(Mrs John Harrington, Ire) *hld up in rr of mid-div: prog on far side fr over 2f out to chse ldrs in 5th over 1f out: clsd u.p into 2nd fnl 100yds: kpt on same pce wout troubling wnr* **25/1**

3 shd **Slipper Orchid (IRE)**[14] 3358 4-9-7 90............................ ShaneFoley 3 94
(M Halford, Ire) *in tch: cl 10th after 1/2-way: hdwy fr 2f out to chse ldrs in 4th ent fnl f: kpt on same pce in 3rd towards fin wout ever troubling wnr* **8/1**

4 1 **Sharp And Smart (IRE)**[8] 3532 4-8-3 75.................... LeighRoche(3) 19 76
(Hughie Morrison) *chsd ldrs: 6th 1/2-way: rdn over 2f out and sn no imp on principals: kpt on same pce in 4th ins fnl f* **12/1**

5 ½ **Talitha Kum (IRE)**[24] 3000 3-8-11 89................................. ChrisHayes 6 86
(P D Deegan, Ire) *prom: sn led: narrow advantage 1/2-way: sn strly pressed and hdd 1 1/2f out: sn no ex: kpt on one pce fnl f* **33/1**

6 ½ **Queen Of The Sand (IRE)**[9] 3516 3-8-1 82.................... IJBrennan(3) 5 77
(G M Lyons, Ire) *trckd ldrs: cl 2nd 1/2-way: rdn and no ex fr under 2f out: kpt on one pce fnl f* **20/1**

7 nk **Curly Wee (IRE)**[15] 3305 3-8-10 88..................................(b[1]) FMBerry 13 83+
(David Wachman, Ire) *hld up towards rr: rdn fr 2f out and sme hdwy u.p over 1f out: wnt nvr threatening 7th ins fnl f and kpt on same pce towards fin* **7/1**[3]

8 hd **Hanky Panky (IRE)**[16] 3263 3-9-8 100........................ JosephO'Brien 17 94+
(A P O'Brien, Ire) *hld up: sme hdwy after 1/2-way: sn rdn and no ex over 1f out: kpt on same pce* **5/1**[1]

9 ¾ **Angela's Dream (IRE)**[9] 3516 3-8-4 82 oh2...............(p) TadhgO'Shea 14 74+
(G M Lyons, Ire) *hld up in mid-div: rdn and no imp fr 2f out: kpt on one pce fnl f* **20/1**

10 hd **Saratoga Baby (IRE)**[19] 3164 5-8-8 77..............(t) DeclanMcDonogh 21 71+
(Peter Fahey, Ire) *in rr of mid-div: 12th 1/2-way: rdn and no imp fr 2f out: kpt on one pce fnl f* **14/1**

11 ½ **Gathering Power (IRE)**[45] 2374 3-8-12 90.............. JohnnyMurtagh 10 80+
(Edward Lynam, Ire) *hld up: 13th 1/2-way: rdn and no imp fr 2f out: kpt on same pce ins fnl f* **6/1**[2]

12 nk **Akira (IRE)**[52] 2177 3-9-1 93.................................... NGMcCullagh 12 82+
(Eoin Doyle, Ire) *chsd ldrs: rdn and wknd fr 2f out* **16/1**

13 ¾ **Harmonic Note**[10] 3460 3-8-11 89.................................. GaryCarroll 11 76+
(G M Lyons, Ire) *chsd ldrs: 8th 1/2-way: rdn and no imp over 2f out: one pce fnl f* **25/1**

14 nk **Topadee (IRE)**[8] 3550 6-8-9 78... DannyGrant 8 67+
(Patrick J Flynn, Ire) *chsd ldrs early: rdn and wknd fr 2f out* **22/1**

15 nse **Royal Blue Star (IRE)**[17] 3225 5-8-12 91............(b[1]) CharlieElliott(10) 15 80+
(Mrs John Harrington, Ire) *in rr of mid-div: rdn and no imp fr over 2f out* **25/1**

16 shd **Ondeafears (IRE)**[62] 1858 6-9-9 97........................ MarcMonaghan(5) 7 86+
(M Halford, Ire) *in tch: 9th 1/2-way: rdn and wknd fr over 2f out* **14/1**

17 shd **Nini Ok (IRE)**[13] 3380 4-9-2 85.............................(b) SeamieHeffernan 18 74+
(John Joseph Murphy, Ire) *chsd ldrs: pushed along in 8th over 2f out and sn no ex: wknd fnl f* **20/1**

18 1 ¾ **Lily Of Kenmare (IRE)**[24] 3002 5-8-2 74...................(t) ConorHoban(3) 9 58+
(M Halford, Ire) *chsd ldrs: pushed along in 8th over 2f out: sn wknd* **16/1**

19 nk **Tropical Mist (IRE)**[30] 2814 3-8-8 89........................ RonanWhelan(3) 20 69+
(George J Kent, Ire) *chsd ldrs: cl 3rd 1/2-way: rdn and wknd fr 2f out* **16/1**

20 1 ½ **Core Element (IRE)**[16] 3263 6-8-13 89..................... LukeDempsey(7) 16 68+
(P J Prendergast, Ire) *in rr of mid-div: pushed along and no imp over 2f out: one pce fnl f* **25/1**

21 23 **Flic Flac (IRE)**[26] 2942 5-9-3 86..(bt) PatSmullen 1 3+
(D K Weld, Ire) *hld up in tch: 7th 1/2-way: rdn and wknd fr 2f out: eased fnl f* **25/1**

1m 22.23s (-8.57) **Going Correction** -1.00s/f (Hard)
WFA 3 from 4yo+ 9lb **21 Ran SP% 144.0**
Speed ratings: **108,105,105,104,103 103,102,102,101,101 100,100,99,99,99 99,98,96,96,94 68**
CSF £236.37 CT £1222.79 TOTE £15.00: £2.90, £8.40, £2.50, £3.30; DF 596.70.
Owner Majestic Queen Partnership **Bred** Sunderland Holdings Ltd **Trained** The Curragh, Co Kildare

FOCUS

The Collins sisters have proved themselves adept at winning this race and, handicaps aside, Tracey looks to have a smart filly on her hands in Majestic Queen. The fourth, fifth, sixth and seventh are the guide.

3846a PADDY POWER SPRINT (PREMIER H'CAP) 6f 63y

4:45 (4:51) 3-Y-O+

£48,780 (£15,447; £7,317; £2,439; £1,626; £813)

RPR

1 **Burn The Boats (IRE)**[35] 2679 4-8-8 87......................... GaryCarroll 25 93
(G M Lyons, Ire) *chsd ldrs: 6th 1/2-way: prog to chal ins fnl f: kpt on wl u.p to ld fnl 50yds* **7/1**[1]

2 ¾ **Whozthecat (IRE)**[13] 3367 6-8-3 92...................(v) LukeLeadbitter(10) 26 96
(Declan Carroll) *sn led: over 1 l clr 1/2-way: rdn and strly pressed over 1f out: hdd ins fnl f: kpt on wl towards fin wout matching wnr* **20/1**

3 ½ **Joe Eile (IRE)**[15] 3305 5-9-4 97............................(b) EmmetMcNamara 23 99
(G M Lyons, Ire) *chsd ldrs: cl 3rd 1/2-way: hdwy to chal over 1f out: led narrowly ins fnl f tl hdd fnl 50yds: no ex* **20/1**

4 shd **Dick Bos**[16] 3249 4-8-3 89.. LukeDempsey(7) 27 91
(David O'Meara) *chsd ldrs: hdwy fr 2f out: rdn in 3rd ins fnl f and sn no ex u.p: kpt on same pce* **10/1**[3]

5 ½ **Clancy Avenue (USA)**[21] 3103 3-8-11 97.............................[1] WJLee 13 95
(T Stack, Ire) *hld up: gd hdwy fr 1 1/2f out and clsd on principals ins fnl f: nrst fin* **22/1**

6 ½ **Mississippi**[13] 3367 4-8-9 88.. FMBerry 21 87
(David Barron) *in tch: rdn in 8th ent ins fnl f and kpt on wl u.p towards fin wout ever threatening* **7/1**[1]

7 nk **Seanie (IRE)**[26] 2942 4-8-11 90................................ SeamieHeffernan 30 88
(David Marnane, Ire) *chsd ldrs on nrside: 7th 1/2-way: rdn and no imp ent fnl f: kpt on same pce towards fin* **14/1**

8 ¾ **Bubbly Bellini (IRE)**[15] 3305 6-9-0 96..........................(p) IJBrennan(3) 5 92+
(Adrian McGuinness, Ire) *racd in mid-div: sme hdwy fr 2f out to chse ldrs over 1f out: kpt on same pce in 8th wl ins fnl f* **20/1**

9 ½ **Ask Dad**[26] 2941 3-8-6 92..(p) BenCurtis 28 84
(J P Murtagh, Ire) *chsd ldrs: cl 4th 1/2-way: sn pushed along and no imp on principals fr 2f out: kpt on one pce* **20/1**

10 nk **Via Ballycroy (IRE)**[34] 2690 4-8-12 91.............................[1] ShaneFoley 20 84
(M Halford, Ire) *hld up in tch: swtchd 1 1/2f out and sn no imp on principals: kpt on same pce ins fnl f* **12/1**

11 nk **Seal Rock**[315] 5370 5-9-0 93... DannyGrant 10 85+
(A Oliver, Ire) *hld up in tch: rdn fr 2f out and sn no imp on principals ent fnl f: kpt on same pce* **33/1**

12 1 **Arctic (IRE)**[35] 2676 6-9-8 104................................... RonanWhelan(3) 15 93+
(Tracey Collins, Ire) *prom far side rdn fr 2f out and sn no ex: one pce fnl f* **25/1**

13 ½ **Yeeoow (IRE)**[24] 2988 4-9-1 94... MartinHarley 9 81+
(Mrs K Burke) *in rr of mid-div: sme late hdwy ins fnl f: kpt on* **14/1**

14 nk **Strait Of Zanzibar (USA)**[15] 3305 4-8-3 85................. ConorHoban(3) 4 71+
(K J Condon, Ire) *chsd ldrs early: rdn and no imp fr 2f out: wknd fnl f* **33/1**

15 nk **Harry Trotter (IRE)**[24] 3000 4-8-5 91......................... ConnorKing(7) 29 76
(David Marnane, Ire) *racd in mid-div: rdn and no imp fr 2f out: one pce fnl f* **16/1**

16 shd **Prodigality**[7] 3558 5-9-8 101.. KevinManning 19 86
(Ronald Harris) *in tch: rdn fr 2f out and sn no ex: wknd ins fnl f* **14/1**

17 nse **An Saighdiur (IRE)**[34] 2690 6-9-0 93........................ DeclanMcDonogh 2 78+
(Andrew Slattery, Ire) *chsd ldrs: rdn and no imp fr 2f out: one pce fnl f* **25/1**

18 nk **Gabriel's Lad (IRE)**[7] 3558 4-9-3 96................................ JosephO'Brien 1 80+
(Denis Coakley) *nvr bttr than mid-div: rdn and no imp fr 2f out: kpt on one pce* **8/1**[2]

19 hd **Scotland Forever (IRE)**[45] 2374 3-8-5 91.................... TadhgO'Shea 22 72
(John Patrick Shanahan, Ire) *chsd ldrs early: pushed along in 10th bef 1/2-way and sn no imp: one pce ins fnl f* **16/1**

20 1 ¼ **Srucahan (IRE)**[34] 2690 4-8-11 90..................................(b) ChrisHayes 7 69+
(P D Deegan, Ire) *racd in mid-div: rdn fr over 2f out and no imp ent fnl f: one pce towards fin* **16/1**

21 ½ **Arbitrageur (IRE)**[34] 2690 4-8-6 85..................................(t) RoryCleary 3 63+
(Donal Kinsella, Ire) *hld up: rdn and no imp fr 2f out: one pce fnl f* **20/1**

22 nk **Reply (IRE)**[7] 3557 4-9-4 107......................................(v) AnaO'Brien(10) 6 84+
(A P O'Brien, Ire) *racd in mid-div: rdn fr 2f out and sn no ex: wknd ins fnl f* **16/1**

23 nse **Bajan Tryst (USA)**[14] 3334 7-8-12 91...........................(p) PatSmullen 11 67+
(Kevin Ryan) *in rr of mid-div: pushed along and no imp fr 2f out* **16/1**

24 1 ½ **Royal Empress (IRE)**[20] 3140 3-8-8 94....................... WayneLordan 18 64+
(David Wachman, Ire) *nvr bttr than mid-div: no imp fr 2f out: one pce fnl f* **25/1**

25 nk **Racy**[14] 3334 6-8-11 95.. ColinKeane(5) 12 66+
(Brian Ellison) *in rr of mid-div: rdn and no imp fr 2f out* **20/1**

26 1 **Angel's Pursuit (IRE)**[23] 3032 6-8-9 93................ MarcMonaghan(5) 17 61+
(David Marnane, Ire) *racd in mid-div: rdn and wknd fr 2f out* **25/1**

27 nk **Springinmystep (IRE)**[21] 3096 4-8-0 84............................ ShaneGray(5) 8 51+
(Ed de Giles) *hld up in mid-div: rdn and wknd fr 2f out* **25/1**

28 1 **Tarrsille (IRE)**[8] 3550 7-8-4 83...................................(b) NGMcCullagh 24 46
(A Oliver, Ire) *in tch: rdn in 12th fr 1/2-way and sn wknd* **25/1**

29 2 ½ **Evens And Odds (IRE)**[45] 2366 9-8-10 94................ SladeO'Hara(5) 14 49+
(Peter Grayson) *in rr of mid-div: rdn and no imp fr 2f out* **40/1**

30 *13* **Battleroftheboyne (IRE)**[8] 3550 4-8-5 **87**.................. ShaneBKelly(3) 16 1+
(Michael Mulvany, Ire) *a bhd: struggling after 1/2-way: nvr a factor* **33/1**

1m 12.95s (-6.15) **Going Correction** -0.775s/f (Hard)
WFA 3 from 4yo+ 7lb **30** Ran SP% **169.6**
Speed ratings: **110,109,108,108,107 106,106,105,104,104 104,102,102,101,101 101,101,100,100,98 98,97,97,95,95**
CSF £159.91 CT £2873.03 TOTE £12.70: £2.70, £5.90, £8.60, £3.80; DF 389.40.
Owner David Spratt **Bred** Anamoine Ltd **Trained** Dunsany, Co. Meath

FOCUS
Nothing like contrasts but in this cavalry charge high numbers in the draw dominated compared with low numbers in the 7f handicap previously. The first two set the standard.

3847a DUBAI DUTY FREE FULL OF SURPRISES RAILWAY STKS (GROUP 2) 6f

5:15 (5:18) 2-Y-O **£48,780** (£15,447; £7,317; £2,439; £1,626)

RPR

1 **Sudirman (USA)**[9] 3514 2-9-3 .... WayneLordan 1 107
(David Wachman, Ire) *trckd ldrs in cl 3rd: pushed along fr 2f out and tk clsr order on outer to chal ent fnl f: led narrowly ins fnl 100yds and styd on wl towards fin* **5/1**[3]

2 *1/2* **Big Time (IRE)**[45] 2373 2-9-3 .... ShaneFoley 2 106
(John Joseph Murphy, Ire) *disp early: cl 2nd 1/2-way: rdn to ld narrowly 1 1/2f out: sn strly pressed and hdd ins fnl 100yds: kpt on wl wout matching wnr towards fin* **9/2**[2]

3 *4 1/4* **Coach House (IRE)**[9] 3481 2-9-3 .... JosephO'Brien 7 93
(A P O'Brien, Ire) *w.w in rr: brought wd and hdwy on outer fr 2f out: rdn in 3rd ent fnl f and sn no imp on principals: kpt on same pce* **8/15**[1]

4 *13* **Muscle Beach (USA)**[21] 3119 2-9-3 .... FMBerry 5 54
(Charles O'Brien, Ire) *chsd ldrs in cl 4th: pushed along 1/2-way and sn no imp in rr: kpt on one pce into mod 4th fnl 100yds* **20/1**

5 *8* **Focus On Venice (IRE)**[76] 1554 2-9-3 .... KevinManning 4 48
(J S Bolger, Ire) *disp early: narrow advantage 1/2-way: pushed along over 2f out and hdd 1 1/2f out: sn no ex: eased ins fnl f and dropped to rr fnl 100yds* **9/1**

1m 11.73s (-3.77) **Going Correction** -0.775s/f (Hard) **5** Ran SP% **114.8**
Speed ratings: **94,93,87,70,59**
CSF £27.29 TOTE £5.10: £1.70, £1.80; DF 22.70.
Owner Mrs Fitri Hay/Mrs John Magnier **Bred** Kathryn Nikkel & Jeanne Canty **Trained** Goolds Cross, Co Tipperary

FOCUS
One juvenile that had looked genuinely progressive this season was Surdiman and he continued that by winning this. The runner-up was conceding experience to the winner and ran with a deal of credit.

3848a WOODIES D.I.Y. SAPPHIRE STKS (GROUP 3) 5f

5:50 (5:50) 3-Y-O+

£30,487 (£9,654; £4,573; £1,524; £1,016; £508)

RPR

1 **Slade Power (IRE)**[7] 3557 4-9-9 109.............................. WayneLordan 2 112
(Edward Lynam, Ire) *chsd ldrs: cl 4th 1/2-way: tk clsr order in 3rd over 1f out: rdn to ld on outer fnl 100yds and kpt on wl* **11/4**[1]

2 *1/2* **Russian Soul (IRE)**[35] 2676 5-9-9 107...........................(p) ShaneFoley 11 110
(M Halford, Ire) *trckd ldrs: cl 3rd 1/2-way: lost pl 2f out: rdn bhd ldrs over 1f out and sn hdwy u.p on inner into 2nd cl home wout really troubling wnr: nrst fin* **13/2**

3 *1/2* **Morawij**[14] 3340 3-9-3 .... WilliamBuick 4 106
(Roger Varian) *prom: settled bhd ldr in 2nd: hdwy to get on terms 1 1/2f out: sn led narrowly and edgd sltly rt ins fnl f: hdd fnl 100yds: no ex and dropped to 3rd cl home* **7/2**[2]

4 *1/2* **Move In Time**[11] 3420 5-9-9 .... JohnnyMurtagh 7 107
(David O'Meara) *in tch: cl 5th 1/2-way: rdn over 1f out and kpt on wl towards fin wout troubling principals* **7/2**[2]

5 *nse* **Medicean Man**[11] 3420 7-9-9 ....(p) WJLee 9 106
(Jeremy Gask) *in tch: cl 6th 1/2-way: rdn and no imp on principals ent fnl f: kpt on same pce* **6/1**[3]

6 *3/4* **Judge 'n Jury**[28] 2865 9-9-9 ....(t) KevinManning 8 104
(Ronald Harris) *sn led: 1 l clr 1/2-way: strly pressed fr 2f out and hdd ins fnl f: no ex u.p and dropped to 6th cl home* **16/1**

7 *shd* **Secret Witness**[7] 3558 7-9-9 ....(b) MartinHarley 10 103
(Ronald Harris) *in tch: cl 6th 1/2-way: rdn and no imp on principals ins fnl f: kpt on same pce* **25/1**

8 *1 3/4* **Parliament Square (IRE)**[10] 3455 3-9-3 101...........(b[1]) JosephO'Brien 5 95
(A P O'Brien, Ire) *w.w in rr: reminder early: pushed along fr 2f out: sn rdn and no ex in 8th u.p ins fnl f: kpt on* **14/1**

9 *1 3/4* **Antious (ARG)**[17] 3225 6-9-9 100.....................................(bt) PatSmullen 3 91
(David Marnane, Ire) *in tch: cl 7th 1/2-way: rdn and outpcd fr wl over 1f out: kpt on* **33/1**

10 *nk* **Red Dubawi (IRE)**[13] 3380 5-9-9 100.. FMBerry 1 90
(David Marnane, Ire) *towards rr thrght: rdn and no imp fr under 2f out: one pce fnl f* **12/1**

57.51s (-5.39) **Going Correction** -0.775s/f (Hard)
WFA 3 from 4yo+ 6lb **10** Ran SP% **125.8**
Speed ratings: **112,111,110,109,109 108,108,105,102,102**
CSF £23.33 TOTE £4.30: £1.50, £3.10, £2.30; DF 18.90.
Owner Mrs S Power **Bred** Mrs S Power **Trained** Dunshaughlin, Co Meath

FOCUS
Having not enjoyed a tremendous amount of luck on his first two starts, this fell right for Slade Power, who may well have put himself in line for a crack at the July Cup. The fourth helps set the standard.

3849a DUBAI DUTY FREE IRISH DERBY (GROUP 1) (ENTIRE COLTS & FILLIES) 1m 4f

6:30 (6:30) 3-Y-O

£589,430 (£193,089; £91,463; £30,487; £20,325; £10,162)

RPR

1 **Trading Leather (IRE)**[20] 3142 3-9-0 115...................... KevinManning 5 119+
(J S Bolger, Ire) *chsd ldrs on outer: mod 3rd 1/2-way: tk clsr order 3f out: hdwy u.p to ld 1 1/2f out: styd on wl u.p ins fnl f* **6/1**[3]

2 *1 3/4* **Galileo Rock (IRE)**[28] 2866 3-9-0 117............................ WayneLordan 1 116
(David Wachman, Ire) *hld up: prog fr over 4f out: tk clsr order in 5th into st: sn rdn and clsd into 2nd ins fnl f: kpt on same pce wout matching wnr* **9/1**

3 *1 3/4* **Festive Cheer (FR)**[28] 2866 3-9-0 109....................... SeamieHeffernan 9 115+
(A P O'Brien, Ire) *w.w in rr: hdwy fr 4f out into 6th 3f out: tk clsr order in 4th 2f out: sn short of room on inner and swtchd lft: kpt on wl into nvr threatening 3rd fnl 50yds* **33/1**

4 *1/2* **Cap O'Rushes**[9] 3486 3-9-0 .... PatSmullen 4 113
(Saeed bin Suroor) *prom: settled bhd ldr in 2nd: prog to ld under 3f out: strly pressed fr 2f out and sn hdd: no ex in 3rd ins fnl f and dropped to 4th fnl 50yds* **66/1**

5 *6* **Ruler Of The World (IRE)**[28] 2866 3-9-0 120...........(p) JosephO'Brien 8 103
(A P O'Brien, Ire) *w.w towards rr: sme hdwy fr 4f out: rdn in 7th over 2f out and sn no imp on principals in 5th: kpt on same pce towards fin* **4/5**[1]

6 *nk* **Little White Cloud (IRE)**[34] 2687 3-9-0 106........... DeclanMcDonogh 6 103
(John M Oxx, Ire) *chsd ldrs: mod 4th 1/2-way: tk clsr order into st: sn rdn and no ex in 6th ins fnl f: kpt on same pce* **16/1**

7 *1 3/4* **Ralston Road (IRE)**[8] 3526 3-9-0 93...........................(b[1]) TadhgO'Shea 7 100
(John Patrick Shanahan, Ire) *trckd ldrs early: hdwy to ld after 1f: over 4 l clr 1/2-way: reduced advantage bef st and strly pressed 3f out: sn hdd: no ex fnl 2f: kpt on one pce* **100/1**

8 *4 3/4* **Libertarian**[28] 2866 3-9-0 .... WilliamBuick 2 92
(Mrs K Burke) *hld up: niggled along in 7th fr 1/2-way: sn rdn and no imp into st: one pce fnl 2f* **7/2**[2]

9 *13* **Sugar Boy (IRE)**[64] 1811 3-9-0 112.. ChrisHayes 3 72
(P J Prendergast, Ire) *chsd ldrs on inner: pushed along in mod 5th after 1/2-way: wknd into st* **9/1**

2m 27.17s (-11.33) **Going Correction** -0.60s/f (Hard) **9** Ran SP% **123.4**
Speed ratings: **113,111,110,110,106 106,104,101,93**
CSF £61.76 CT £1676.53 TOTE £6.90: £2.00, £2.60, £7.10; DF 36.80.
Owner Mrs J S Bolger **Bred** J S Bolger **Trained** Coolcullen, Co Carlow

FOCUS
This will probably be seen as an ordinary Irish Derby, but unlike other Derbys that have borne similar descriptions, it's not hard to see some of the main protagonists coming out and winning more good races. The fourth and seventh, who both raced prominently, limit the form to some extent.

3752 DEAUVILLE (R-H)

Saturday, June 29

OFFICIAL GOING: Turf: good to soft; fibresand: standard

3851a PRIX DE RIS-ORANGIS (GROUP 3) (3YO+) (TURF) 6f

1:15 (12:00) 3-Y-O+ **£32,520** (£13,008; £9,756; £6,504; £3,252)

RPR

1 **Abu Sidra (FR)**[24] 4-9-0 0.................................... ChristopheSoumillon 8 114
(J-F Bernard, France) *trckd ldr: rdn to chal 1 1/2f out: led ins fnl 150yds: drvn out* **44/5**

2 *1* **Princedargent (FR)**[18] 3186 3-8-7 0................................ FabriceVeron 1 109
(H-A Pantall, France) *led on rail: rdn and strly pressed 1 1/2f out: hdd ins fnl 150yds: r.o* **13/2**[3]

3 *1/2* **Morache Music**[13] 3373 5-9-0 0.......................... Pierre-CharlesBoudot 3 109
(Peter Makin) *midfield in tch on inner: trapped bhd wall of horses and nt clr run tl swtchd rt ent fnl f: rdn and r.o to go 3rd fnl strides* **23/1**

4 *hd* **Tulips (IRE)**[28] 2897 4-8-10 0.. MaximeGuyon 10 105
(A Fabre, France) *midfield in tch: rdn and ev ch ent fnl f: r.o but sn no imp on ldr: dropped to 4th fnl strides* **3/1**[2]

5 *1/2* **American Devil (FR)**[28] 2897 4-9-0 0.......................... UmbertoRispoli 12 107
(J Van Handenhove, France) *hld up towards rr on outer: rdn and hdwy over 1f out: r.o but nt pce to chal* **11/1**

6 *hd* **Chopouest (FR)**[43] 6-9-0 0... FredericSpanu 7 107
(T Castanheira, France) *slow to s: hld up in rr on inner: shkn up 2f out: rdn ent fnl f and r.o to go 6th post: fin wl but nvr able to chal* **21/1**

7 *nk* **Myasun (FR)**[27] 2909 6-9-4 0.. OlivierPeslier 9 110
(C Baillet, France) *dwlt: t.k.h under restraint in rr and sn allowed to stride on: midfield on outer 3f out: rdn to chal and ev ch ent fnl f: kpt on tl no ex and lost multiple pls ins fnl 100yds* **15/2**

8 *1 1/4* **Fortune Hunter (FR)**[43] 4-8-10 0.................... Francois-XavierBertras 5 98
(F Rohaut, France) *midfield in tch: rdn 2f out: outpcd by ldrs whn nt clrest of runs over 1f out: swtchd lft and r.o to go 8th post* **21/1**

9 *nse* **Mariol (FR)**[18] 3187 10-9-0 0.. ThierryJarnet 11 101
(Robert Collet, France) *dwlt: hld up towards rr: hdwy into midfield over 2f out: rdn over 1f out: outpcd by ldrs ins fnl f: kpt on but dropped to 9th post* **24/1**

10 *4 1/2* **Gengis (FR)**[21] 3128 3-8-11 0...................................... StephanePasquier 2 89
(G Doleuze, France) *t.k.h: prom on inner: swtchd out and rdn 1 1/2f out: hanging and looked v awkward u.p: sn no ex and btn: fdd and eased* **14/5**[1]

11 *1* **Coup De Theatre (FR)**[28] 2897 4-9-0 0..... Christophe-PatriceLemaire 6 84
(P Van De Poele, France) *prom on outer: lost pl over 1f out: sn rdn and btn: fdd and eased: almost pipped for 11th post* **28/1**

12 *nse* **Indian Sly (FR)**[11] 8-9-0 0.. JimmyTastayre 4 84
(P Capelle, France) *midfield in tch: rdn and outpcd 2f out: last and btn ent fnl f: kpt gng all the way to fin and almost snatched 11th post* **97/1**

1m 10.69s (-0.31)
WFA 3 from 4yo+ 7lb **12** Ran SP% **116.7**
WIN (incl. 1 euro stake): 9.80. PLACES: 3.50, 3.20, 6.50. DF: 37.20. SF: 87.30.
Owner Mubarak Al Naemi **Bred** B Jeffroy, J-C Leclerc, P Le Baut & P Cochard **Trained** France

HAMBURG (R-H)

Saturday, June 29

OFFICIAL GOING: Turf: good to soft

3852a FRANZ-GUNTHER VON GAERTNER GEDACHTNISRENNEN (GROUP 3) (3YO+ FILLIES & MARES) (TURF) 1m

4:10 (12:00) 3-Y-O+

£26,016 (£8,943; £4,471; £2,439; £1,626; £1,219)

RPR

1 **Lady Jacamira (GER)**[34] 2698 4-9-0 0.................................. APietsch 8 103
(R Dzubasz, Germany) *midfield on outer: rdn over 2f out: hdwy to chal over 1f out: led ent fnl f: drew clr: pushed out: readily* **108/10**

2 2 **Akua'da (GER)**27 2910 3-8-10 0 EPedroza 6 102
(A Wohler, Germany) *led: rdn 2f out: strly pressed fr over 1f out: hdd ent fnl f: readily outpcd by wnr but kpt on wl for 2nd* **18/5**2

3 nk **Scoville (GER)**62 4-9-2 0 MarvinSuerland 11 100
(H Hesse, Germany) *bhd s and hld up in last pair on outer: rdn 2f out: r.o to go 3rd post: nrst fin* **222/10**

4 shd **Red Lips (GER)**27 2910 3-8-6 0 DPorcu 7 97
(Andreas Lowe, Germany) *midfield: rdn 2f out: nt clrest of runs ins fnl f but kpt on and wnt 3rd fnl strides: dropped to 4th post* **68/10**

5 nk **Julissima** 3-8-6 0 AStarke 4 97
(P Schiergen, Germany) *prom on inner: rdn and ev ch 2f out: kpt on one pce u.p ins fnl 1 1/2f: lost two pls fnl strides* **43/10**3

6 nk **Calyxa**27 2910 3-8-6 0 LennartHammer-Hansen 9 96
(Ferdinand J Leve, Germany) *prom on outer: rdn over 2f out: hdwy to chal over 1f out: ev ch ent fnl f: sn outpcd by wnr: kpt on but dropped to 6th cl home* **13/10**1

7 2 **Molly Mara (GER)**27 2910 3-8-6 0 MircoDemuro 1 92
(J Hirschberger, Germany) *settled in midfield on inner: rdn 2f out: nt clr run over 1f out: kpt on once in the clr but sn outpcd and fdd* **94/10**

8 ½ **Palomita (GER)**30 5-9-2 0 AndreBest 2 92
(Frau Nina Bach, Germany) *hld up towards rr on inner: rdn 2f out: outpcd by ldrs ent fnl f: kpt on but n.d* **229/10**

9 4½ **Soprana (GER)**34 4-9-0 0 AHelfenbein 5 80
(Markus Klug, Germany) *t.k.h: trckd ldr on outer: rdn and brief effrt to chal 2f out: no ex and btn whn squeezed for room over 1f out: fdd and eased ins fnl f* **27/1**

10 2½ **Ilena (GER)**237 4-9-0 0 (b) KClijmans 3 74
(Dr A Bolte, Germany) *hld up towards rr on outer: rdn over 2f out: outpcd and btn ent fnl f: eased* **68/1**

11 5 **Eleona (GER)**62 6-9-0 0 StefanieHofer 10 63
(Frau E Mader, Germany) *hld up in last pair on inner: rdn 2f out: no ex and btn ent fnl f: eased: nvr a factor* **37/1**

1m 36.98s (96.98)
WFA 3 from 4yo+ 10lb 11 Ran SP% **131.1**
WIN (incl. 10 euro stake): 118. PLACES: 38, 22, 48. SF: 546.
Owner Stall Zaster **Bred** Pegasus Europe Ag **Trained** Germany

3694 SALISBURY (R-H)

Sunday, June 30

OFFICIAL GOING: Good to firm (good in places between 7f & 5f; 8.9)
Wind: virtually nil Weather: sunney and very warm

3853 BATHWICK TYRES E B F BLAGRAVE MAIDEN STKS 6f 212y
2:30 (2:31) (Class 4) 2-Y-O **£4,851** (£1,443; £721; £360) **Stalls** Centre

Form RPR

1 **Cricklewood Green (USA)** 2-9-5 0 PatDobbs 11 77+
(Richard Hannon) *towards rr: pushed along whn swtchd lft 2f out: str run fr over 1f out to ld ins fnl f: drifted rt: r.o wl: readily* **6/1**2

6 2 1¼ **Truth Or Dare**14 3374 2-9-5 0 KieranO'Neill 7 75
(Richard Hannon) *trckd ldrs: shkn up 3f out: nt best of runs whn swtchd lft twice over 1f out: r.o ins fnl f: wnt 2nd nring fin* **9/4**1

0 3 ¾ **Solo Hunter**19 3174 2-9-5 0 TomQueally 3 72
(David Evans) *led: rdn whn jnd over 2f out: regained narrow advantage jst over 1f out: hdd ins fnl f: kpt on but no ex* **10/1**

6 4 shd **Mabdhool (IRE)**16 3290 2-9-5 0 PaulHanagan 5 72
(Marcus Tregoning) *little slowly away: sn pushed along to chse ldrs: rdn wl over 2f out: nt best of runs after but nt pce to get on terms: kpt on fnl f* **9/4**1

5 5 2 **Cotton Club (IRE)**8 3574 2-9-5 0 DaneO'Neill 1 66
(Rod Millman) *prom: rdn and ev ch fr over 2f out tl no ex ins fnl f* **17/2**3

0 6 2½ **Loving Your Work**20 3155 2-9-5 0 GeorgeBaker 9 60
(George Baker) *sn chsng ldrs: rn green whn rdn to dispute ld over 2f out tl hdd jst over 1f out: fdd fnl 120yds* **22/1**

7 3¼ **Almost Famous (IRE)** 2-9-5 0 FergusSweeney 6 51
(Jamie Osborne) *mid-div: pushed along over 2f out: nvr any imp* **33/1**

8 nk **Aristocracy** 2-9-5 0 SamHitchcott 8 50
(Mick Channon) *mid-div: drvn whn outpcd 1/2-way: nt a threat after* **12/1**

9 nk **My Anchor** 2-9-5 0 LiamKeniry 10 49
(Sylvester Kirk) *s.i.s: sme late prog: mainly towards rr* **40/1**

0 10 4½ **My Secret Dream (FR)**27 2917 2-9-0 0 GrahamLee 2 32
(Ron Hodges) *mid-div: rdn over 2f out: wknd over 1f out* **100/1**

11 6 **Just Rubie** 2-9-0 0 JohnFahy 12 16
(Michael Blanshard) *wnt lft s: a in rea* **66/1**

12 15 **Princess Tilly** 2-8-7 0 RyanWhile(7) 4
(Bill Turner) *prom tl rdn jst over 3f out: sn wknd* **16/1**

1m 29.54s (0.94) **Going Correction** +0.15s/f (Good) 12 Ran SP% **121.2**
Speed ratings (Par 95): **100,98,97,97,95 92,88,88,88,82 76,58**
toteswingers 1&2 £2.80, 1&3 £13.40, 2&3 £6.40 CSF £19.71 TOTE £7.40: £2.40, £1.40, £2.50; EX 23.30 Trifecta £340.50 Pool: £1977.22 - 4.35 winning tickets..
Owner Chris Wright & Andy MacDonald **Bred** Stratford Place Stud **Trained** East Everleigh, Wilts

FOCUS
Rail erected up straight up to 20ft off far side rail. Probably no more than a fair maiden. The time was just over 3.5sec outside the standard. It produced a 1-2 for the Richard Hannon stable but is rated towards the bottom end of race averages.

3854 BATHWICK TYRES H'CAP 1m 1f 198y
3:00 (3:00) (Class 5) (0-70,73) 4-Y-O+ **£3,234** (£962; £481; £240) **Stalls** High

Form RPR

2023 1 **Breakheart (IRE)**23 3043 6-8-7 63 (v) JackGarritty(7) 1 73
(Andrew Balding) *trckd ldrs: rdn to chal over 2f out: led over 1f out: styd on wl to assert fnl f: rdn out* **9/2**3

461 2 2¼ **Breaking The Bank**20 3156 4-9-5 68 MartinDwyer 7 73
(William Muir) *led: rdn wl over 2f out: hdd over 1f out: sn hld by wnr: kpt on same pce* **7/2**2

604- 3 6 **Ice Nelly (IRE)**246 7409 5-8-13 62 TomQueally 5 55
(Stuart Kittow) *s.i.s: pushed along early in last: rdn wl over 2f out: styd on steadily fnl 2f: wnt 3rd ent fnl f: no ch w ldng pair* **7/1**

0-31 4 2½ **Hector's Chance**8 3580 4-9-4 67 GeorgeBaker 4 55
(Heather Main) *hld up in tch: rdn to dispute 3rd over 2f out tl no ex ent fnl f* **6/1**

4111 5 ¾ **Standpoint**5 3662 7-9-10 73 LiamKeniry 3 60
(Conor Dore) *hld up in tch: rdn wl over 2f out: nvr gng pce to get involved whn swtchd lft jst over 1f out* **9/4**1

3455 6 ½ **Ice Tres**23 3037 4-8-5 54 SilvestreDeSousa 6 40
(Rod Millman) *trckd ldrs: rdn to chse ldr briefly over 1f out: sn hld in disp 3rd tl no ex ent fnl f* **11/1**

-605 7 42 **Sondeduro**15 3321 4-9-6 69 FergusSweeney 2
(Jamie Osborne) *trckd ldr tl over 3f out: sn rdn and hld: wknd over 2f out: eased fr over 1f out* **12/1**

2m 8.15s (-1.75) **Going Correction** -0.10s/f (Good) 7 Ran SP% **114.0**
Speed ratings (Par 103): **103,101,96,94,93 93,59**
toteswingers 1&2 £3.00, 1&3 £5.10, 2&3 £4.40 CSF £20.43 TOTE £5.00: £1.50, £2.40; EX 20.60 Trifecta £144.00 Pool: £2952.05 - 15.37 winning tickets..
Owner I A Balding **Bred** Littleton Stud **Trained** Kingsclere, Hants
■ Jack Garritty's first winner.

FOCUS
Not many figured in this modest handicap.

3855 DEREK BURRIDGE GOLF & RACING TROPHIES H'CAP (SENIORS' SPRINT) 5f
3:30 (3:30) (Class 4) (0-80,85) 6-Y-O+ **£5,175** (£1,540; £769; £384) **Stalls** Centre

Form RPR

5215 1 **Go Nani Go**15 3331 7-9-4 77 LiamKeniry 9 86
(Ed de Giles) *s.i.s: towards rr: smooth prog fr 3f out: rdn to ld fnl 100yds: r.o wl* **11/2**2

3064 2 1¾ **Six Wives**4 3682 6-8-12 71 (p) PaulHanagan 11 74+
(Scott Dixon) *travelled wl bhd ldng trio: led 2f out: sn rdn: no ex whn hdd fnl 100yds: jst hld on for 2nd* **7/1**

60-0 3 shd **Valmina**15 3315 6-8-11 75 (t) GeorgeDowning(5) 12 77
(Tony Carroll) *hld up towards rr: pushed along and hdwy fr 2f out: r.o fnl f: jst failed to snatch 2nd* **12/1**

20-0 4 ¾ **The Wee Chief (IRE)**36 2657 7-8-9 68 KieranO'Neill 8 68
(Jimmy Fox) *s.i.s: towards rr: rdn and hdwy 2f out: r.o fnl f* **25/1**

1640 5 ½ **Drawnfromthepast (IRE)**15 3315 8-9-4 77 FergusSweeney 4 75
(Jamie Osborne) *led chsng gp in 5th: rdn over 2f out: kpt on same pce fnl f* **25/1**

4205 6 ¾ **Triple Dream**15 3315 8-9-1 74 (tp) GrahamLee 13 69
(Milton Bradley) *mid-div: rdn over 2f out: little imp tl styd on ins fnl f* **20/1**

6006 7 1¼ **Dark Lane**3 3733 7-8-9 68 CathyGannon 10 62
(David Evans) *mid-div: rdn over 2f out: no imp* **14/1**

0555 8 ½ **Macdillon**14 3371 7-8-4 68 (bt) MichaelJMMurphy(5) 1 57+
(Stuart Kittow) *v awkwardly away: bhd: sn struggling: styd on past btn horses fnl f: nvr any danger* **3/1**1

411 9 3 **Dorback**8 3577 6-9-12 85 (t) GeorgeBaker 6 63
(Violet M Jordan) *led at decent pce: rdn and hdd 2f out: wknd fnl f* **13/2**3

3126 10 ¾ **Bronze Beau**17 3236 6-9-5 78 (t) JamesSullivan 7 53
(Kristin Stubbs) *pressed ldr tl rdn over 2f out: wknd fnl f* **12/1**

4530 11 2 **Wooden King (IRE)**15 3315 8-8-3 67 ow1 MatthewLawson(5) 2 35
(Malcolm Saunders) *mid-div: pushed along 3f out: running on whn nt clr run bhd wkng horses on far rails fr 2f out tl fin: nvr any ch to land a blow* **12/1**

306 12 6 **Taurus Twins**13 3415 7-9-5 78 (v1) TomQueally 3 25
(Richard Price) *pressed ldr tl 3f out: wknd over 1f out* **7/1**

1m 0.89s (-0.11) **Going Correction** +0.15s/f (Good) 12 Ran SP% **120.9**
Speed ratings: **106,103,103,101,101 99,97,97,92,91 87,78**
toteswingers 1&2 £9.10, 1&3 £11.60, 2&3 £17.80 CSF £43.58 CT £446.49 TOTE £5.90: £2.10, £3.00, £4.30; EX 49.80 Trifecta £729.80 Pool: £2845.48 - 2.92 winning tickets..
Owner T Gould **Bred** D J And Mrs Deer **Trained** Ledbury, H'fords

FOCUS
They went off hard in this modest handicap, confined to sprinters aged six plus, and a group of four were several lengths clear at halfway.

3856 H S LESTER MEMORIAL H'CAP 1m 6f 21y
4:05 (4:05) (Class 4) (0-85,85) 4-Y-O+ **£5,175** (£1,540; £769; £384) **Stalls** Far side

Form RPR

/40- 1 **Beyond (IRE)**55 7051 6-9-2 85 (tp) ThomasBrown(5) 5 94
(David Pipe) *chsd ldr in clr 2nd: rdn to ld 3f out: styd on wl fnl f: drvn out* **7/2**2

-300 2 1½ **Sula Two**27 2939 6-8-10 79 PhilipPrince(5) 8 86
(Ron Hodges) *disp 4th in chsng gp: hdwy over 3f out: sn rdn: chsd wnr over 2f out: nvr quite upsides: styd on but no ex fnl f* **12/1**

-301 3 1¾ **Sunny Future (IRE)**19 3180 7-8-3 71 ow1 MatthewLawson(5) 2 77
(Malcolm Saunders) *dwlt bdly: detached in last: jnd bk of chsng gp after 5f: hdwy over 3f out: rdn to chse ldng pair over 2f out: swtchd rt over 1f out: styd on same pce fnl f* **7/2**2

-431 4 3¾ **The Holyman (IRE)**24 3012 5-8-12 76 DaneO'Neill 7 75
(Jo Crowley) *chsd clr ldrs tl 3f out: sn rdn: one pce fnl 2f* **10/1**3

000- 5 21 **Fair Trade**49 6987 6-9-0 78 GrahamLee 3 48
(Alan King) *disp 4th in chsng gp: effrt to chse ldng pair 3f out: wknd over 1f out: t.o* **6/4**1

00-0 6 5 **Kangaroo Court (IRE)**22 3118 9-8-12 76 MickyFenton 4 39
(Emma Lavelle) *led at str pce tl hdd 3f out: wknd 2f out: t.o* **11/1**

3m 3.62s (-3.78) **Going Correction** -0.10s/f (Good) 6 Ran SP% **109.6**
Speed ratings (Par 105): **106,105,104,102,90 87**
toteswingers 1&2 £4.80, 1&3 £2.20, 2&3 £5.90 CSF £38.70 CT £142.75 TOTE £4.00: £1.70, £4.60; EX 44.00 Trifecta £140.60 Pool: £3043.85 - 16.23 winning tickets..
Owner W Frewen **Bred** Pat Fullam **Trained** Nicholashayne, Devon

FOCUS
They went a good gallop in this fair staying handicap, set by Kangaroo Court, who eventually dropped right out. It was a muddling race tactically and the form may not be entirely solid.

3857 BATHWICK TYRES AUCTION STKS (CONDITIONS RACE) (THE SUNDAY £5K BONUS RACE) 6f
4:40 (4:41) (Class 3) 2-Y-O **£7,762** (£2,310; £1,154; £577) **Stalls** Low

Form RPR

641 1 **Miracle Of Medinah**10 3493 2-8-6 0 SilvestreDeSousa 9 85
(Mark Usher) *sn trcking ldrs: chal jst over 3f out: led over 2f out: sn rdn: jst enough in hand ent fnl f to hold on fnl stride: all out* **7/1**

0 2 shd **Treaty Of Paris (IRE)**14 3374 2-8-6 0 CathyGannon 2 86+
(Henry Candy) *trckd ldrs: rdn whn sltly outpcd over 2f out: str run ins fnl f: jst failed* **8/1**

210 3 4½ **Midnite Angel (IRE)**9 3522 2-8-6 0 PaulHanagan 7 71
(Richard Hannon) *hld up in tch: rdn over 2f out: hdwy over 1f out: kpt on same pce fnl f* **7/4**1

031 4 ½ **Biography**16 3288 2-8-11 0 PatDobbs 3 75
(Richard Hannon) *led: rdn and hdd over 2f out: kpt chsng ldrs but sn hld: no ex ins fnl f* **9/2**3

5 1 **Needless Shouting (IRE)** 2-8-1 0 NickyMackay 5 62+
(Mick Channon) *s.i.s: towards rr: outpcd 3f out: r.o ent fnl f: nvr troubling ldrs* 12/1

2410 6 2 3/4 **Kidmenot (IRE)**[9] 3522 2-8-0 0 KieranO'Neill 1 52
(J S Moore) *trckd ldr tl squeezed up on rails after 2f: rdn over 3f out: one pce fnl 2f* 20/1

0 7 shd **Sheacheval (IRE)**[22] 3107 2-8-0 0 JamesSullivan 4 52
(J S Moore) *sn pushed along in last pair: nvr a threat* 66/1

40 8 1 **Vodka Chaser (IRE)**[69] 1724 2-7-11 0 RyanPowell(3) 8 49
(J S Moore) *w ldr: rdn 3f out: hld fr 2f out: edgd lft and wknd ent fnl f* 66/1

1 U **Intermath (IRE)**[14] 3374 2-8-7 0 TomQueally 6
(David Evans) *travelling wl bhd ldrs whn jinked at path and uns rdr over 3f out* 10/3[2]

1m 15.0s (0.20) **Going Correction** +0.15s/f (Good) 9 Ran SP% 116.7
Speed ratings (Par 97): **104,103,97,97,95 92,92,90,**
CSF £60.91 TOTE £7.30: £2.10, £2.70, £1.20; EX 65.80 Trifecta £312.00 Pool: £3454.45 - 8.30 winning tickets..
Owner The High Jinks Partnership **Bred** A C M Spalding **Trained** Upper Lambourn, Berks

FOCUS
This event has been won by the likes of Sir Percy and Milk It Milk, but it's unlikely there were any stars of that magnitude on show here. The first two finished clear but the form does not look that strong with the third and fourth a few pounds off.

3858 BATHWICK TYRES MAIDEN STKS 1m 1f 198y
5:10 (5:10) (Class 5) 3-Y-O+ £4,204 (£1,251; £625; £312) Stalls High

Form RPR
0- 1 **Venue**[226] 7750 3-9-0 0 MickyFenton 12 84+
(Lady Cecil) *s.i.s: towards rr: swtchd lft 3f out: sn pushed along for hdwy: rdn over 1f out to chse ldr: str run fnl 120yds: led neaering fin* 4/1[3]

-422 2 nk **Thouwra (IRE)**[26] 2953 3-9-0 80 (p) SilvestreDeSousa 2 83
(Saeed bin Suroor) *mid-div: hdwy over 2f out: led over 1f out: sn rdn: all out whn hdd nr fin* 10/11[1]

00 3 7 **Samoan (IRE)**[13] 3417 4-9-12 0 GrahamLee 9 69
(Brian Meehan) *mid-div: rdn and stdy prog fr over 2f out: styd on to go 3rd ent fnl f: no ch w ldng pair* 16/1

0- 4 2 **Ingot Of Gold**[227] 7720 3-8-9 0 JimCrowley 7 60
(Ralph Beckett) *trckd ldrs: disp ld over 3f out: rdn in to clr ld over 2f out: hdd over 1f out: no ex* 7/2[2]

40 5 1 3/4 **Miss Mitigate**[27] 2938 3-8-9 0 LiamKeniry 4 57
(Andrew Balding) *trckd ldr: disp ld over 3f out tl rdn over 2f out: hld whn edgd lft over 1f out: fdd fnl f* 25/1

6 1 **Wooly Bully** 3-9-0 0 FergusSweeney 1 60
(Alan King) *trckd ldrs: rdn over 2f out: edgd lft and fdd ent fnl f* 25/1

00 7 3 3/4 **Emerald Art (IRE)**[26] 2952 3-8-6 0 RyanClark(3) 10 47
(J W Hills) *towards rr: rdn into midfield 2f out: wknd ent fnl f* 50/1

-250 8 nk **Atlantis City (FR)**[16] 3294 3-9-0 67 PatDobbs 5 51
(Richard Hannon) *mid-div: hdwy to chse ldrs 3f out: sn rdn: wknd 1f out* 20/1

9 4 **Lady Cliche**[19] 4-9-0 0 NedCurtis(7) 8 38
(Roger Curtis) *s.i.s: reminders in rr: hdwy into midfield on bnd 6f out: wknd over 2f out* 150/1

10 4 **Autumn Draw** 3-9-0 0 RichardThomas 11 35
(Ralph Beckett) *s.i.s: t.k.h towards rr: rdn over 2f out: sn wknd* 16/1

50 11 22 **Dark Rumour (IRE)**[45] 2389 3-8-9 0 KieranO'Neill 3
(John Bridger) *led tl 3f out: sn wknd: t.o* 150/1

2m 9.08s (-0.82) **Going Correction** -0.10s/f (Good)
WFA 3 from 4yo 12lb 11 Ran SP% 122.1
Speed ratings (Par 103): **99,98,93,91,90 89,86,86,82,79 62**
CSF £7.96 TOTE £5.00: £1.20, £1.10, £4.90; EX 11.50 Trifecta £106.30 Pool: £3799.79 - 26.80 winning tickets..
Owner K Abdullah **Bred** Juddmonte Farms Ltd **Trained** Newmarket, Suffolk

FOCUS
This maiden went to subsequent Breeders' Cup Turf scorer Dangerous Midge back in 2009. The first two drew clear this time and winners should come out of the race.

3859 CGA RACING EXCELLENCE APPRENTICE H'CAP (WHIPS SHALL BE CARRIED BUT NOT USED) 1m
5:40 (5:44) (Class 6) (0-60,60) 3-Y-O £2,587 (£770; £384; £192) Stalls Low

Form RPR
5002 1 **The Scuttler (IRE)**[17] 3254 3-9-2 60 DanielCremin(5) 12 67
(Mick Channon) *mde all: pushed clr 2f out: strly pressed fnl 120yds: jst hld on* 10/3[2]

6456 2 shd **Loraine**[23] 3040 3-9-3 56 NedCurtis 2 63
(Jamie Osborne) *mid-div tl lost pl 4f out: swtchd lft and hdwy fr wl over 2f out: chsd wnr 1f out: str chal fnl 120yds: kpt on: jst hld* 8/1

5256 3 9 **Fair Comment**[5] 3665 3-9-2 60 OisinMurphy(5) 11 46
(Michael Blanshard) *towards rr: pushed along and stdy prog in centre fr 3f out: wnt 3rd ins fnl f: no ch w front pair* 5/2[1]

0503 4 1/2 **Just Isla**[23] 3040 3-8-0 46 (p) CameronHardie(7) 14 31
(Peter Makin) *mid-div: hdwy over 3f out: chsd wnr over 2f out tl ent fnl f: no ex whn lost 3rd sn after* 11/1

2056 5 1 **Lucky Mountain**[6] 3629 3-8-4 50 KatieWatson(7) 5 33
(Scott Dixon) *mid-div: rdn 3f out: nvr any real imp on ldrs* 12/1

006 6 1 **Toffee Shot**[14] 3372 3-9-3 56 ShelleyBirkett 8 36
(J W Hills) *s.i.s: towards rr: hdwy 3f out: styd on same pce fnl 2f* 14/1

0-00 7 5 **Terpsichore**[17] 3243 3-8-7 46 oh1 DanielMuscutt 6 15
(Sylvester Kirk) *chsd ldrs: rdn 3f out: wknd over 1f out* 14/1

-550 8 1/2 **So Lyrical**[26] 2950 3-8-0 46 oh1 (b[1]) JosephineGordon(7) 1 14
(Pat Murphy) *prom tl 3f out: wknd 2f out* 33/1

453 9 1/2 **Spanish Art**[10] 3488 3-8-9 55 BradleyBosley(7) 4 22
(Gay Kelleway) *chsd ldrs tl 3f out: wknd 2f out* 16/1

0-00 10 1 1/2 **Cool And Clear (IRE)**[26] 2950 3-8-7 49 (v[1]) EoinWalsh(3) 10 12
(Pat Eddery) *chsd ldrs tl rdn 3f out: wknd 2f out* 50/1

-456 11 1/2 **Thomasina**[24] 3013 3-8-9 48 TimClark 7 10
(Denis Coakley) *in tch tl over 3f out: sn wknd* 20/1

-060 12 2 1/4 **Penang Power**[12] 3428 3-8-13 57 (t) ThomasHemsley(5) 3 14
(Michael Bell) *s.i.s: a towards rr* 13/2[3]

1m 44.58s (1.08) **Going Correction** +0.15s/f (Good) 12 Ran SP% 121.0
Speed ratings (Par 97): **100,99,90,90,89 88,83,82,82,80 80,78**
CSF £30.53 CT £80.10 TOTE £4.40: £1.80, £3.10, £1.40; EX 27.60 Trifecta £151.40 Pool: £2144.36 - 10.61 winning tickets..
Owner Lord Ilsley Racing (Hern Syndicate) **Bred** J Hanly **Trained** West Ilsley, Berks

FOCUS
A weak apprentice handicap in which the first two pulled clear.
T/Plt: £279.20 to a £1 stake. Pool: £80349.67 - 210.06 winning tickets T/Qpdt: £46.80 to a £1 stake. Pool: £4608.68 - 72.80 winning tickets TM

[3836]WINDSOR (R-H)
Sunday, June 30

OFFICIAL GOING: Good to firm (good in places)
Wind: Behind, light becoming moderate Weather: Fine, very warm

3860 TOTEJACKPOT AT TOTEPOOL.COM MAIDEN FILLIES' STKS 1m 67y
2:20 (2:22) (Class 5) 3-5-Y-O £2,587 (£770; £384; £192) Stalls Low

Form RPR
4-23 1 **Close At Hand**[21] 3136 3-8-12 76 [1] RichardHughes 2 76
(John Gosden) *trckd ldng pair: wnt 2nd 3f out: shkn up 2f out: rdn to assert fnl f* 1/2[1]

5-45 2 2 **Cloudwalker (USA)**[22] 3116 3-8-12 75 JimmyFortune 10 71
(Ed Vaughan) *mde most to 2f out: styd on u.p: wl hld fnl f* 4/1[2]

0 3 2 1/4 **Calling**[17] 3237 3-8-12 0 SeanLevey 6 66
(Brian Meehan) *w ldr to 3f out: rdn and styd on same pce after* 16/1

0 4 7 **Roxy Lane**[17] 3250 4-9-8 0 WilliamCarson 3 52
(Peter Hiatt) *in tch: outpcd and pushed along fr 3f out: nvr on terms after: tk modest 4th fnl f* 66/1

30 5 1/2 **Timeless**[25] 2979 3-8-12 0 (t) MartinLane 4 49
(Tobias B P Coles) *trckd ldrs: outpcd 3f out: hrd rdn and no imp after* 16/1

0-4 6 1 1/2 **First Secretary**[16] 3278 3-8-12 0 JamesDoyle 9 45
(Roger Charlton) *awkward s and slowly away: effrt fr last pair whn outpcd 3f out: nvr on terms after* 9/2[3]

0- 7 1 3/4 **Wedding Speech (IRE)**[375] 3282 3-8-12 0 ShaneKelly 7 41
(James Fanshawe) *wl in tch: rdn and outpcd 3f out: steadily wknd after* 10/1

8 1 **My Peggy Sue** 3-8-7 0 RobertTart(5) 5 39
(Tom Keddy) *in last and struggling bef 1/2-way: lost tch over 3f out and looked like tailing off: kpt on fr over 1f out* 50/1

1m 43.75s (-0.95) **Going Correction** -0.325s/f (Firm)
WFA 3 from 4yo+ 10lb 8 Ran SP% 129.2
Speed ratings (Par 100): **91,89,86,79,79 77,76,75**
toteswingers 1&2 £1.30, 1&3 £5.50, 2&3 £15.10 CSF £3.76 TOTE £1.30: £1.02, £1.70, £6.60; EX 4.50 Trifecta £41.00 Pool: £2209.63 - 40.38 winning tickets..
Owner Normandie Stud Ltd **Bred** Hesmonds Stud Ltd **Trained** Newmarket, Suffolk

FOCUS
Top bend dolled out 2yds from normal inner configuration, adding 7yds to races of 1m and beyond. Rest of rail in normal position and course at maximum width. An ordinary fillies' maiden.

3861 KING SIZE POOLS AT TOTEPOOL.COM H'CAP 1m 67y
2:50 (2:50) (Class 5) (0-70,70) 3-Y-O £2,587 (£770; £384; £192) Stalls Low

Form RPR
606 1 **Orbison (IRE)**[32] 2765 3-9-5 68 [1] NeilCallan 3 77
(Roger Varian) *mde all: drew clr against nr side rail 3f out: drvn fnl 2f: kpt on and unchal* 7/2[1]

6340 2 2 3/4 **Jullundar (IRE)**[17] 3242 3-9-4 67 (v[1]) MatthewDavies 5 70
(Mick Channon) *hld up: in last tl prog fr 3f out: styd on wl to take 2nd ins fnl f: no ch to threaten wnr* 20/1

52-0 3 1 1/2 **Codebreaker**[60] 1923 3-9-5 68 JimmyFortune 1 68
(Hughie Morrison) *prom: rdn to chse wnr 3f out: no imp and hanging lft over 1f out: lost 2nd ins fnl f* 4/1[2]

260- 4 3/4 **Lisa's Legacy**[296] 6016 3-8-13 65 DarrenEgan(3) 10 63
(Daniel Kubler) *hld up in last trio: taken to outer and sme prog over 2f out: nt clr run over 1f out: pushed along and kpt on to take 4th nr fin* 20/1

0-05 5 3/4 **Haatefina**[17] 3241 3-9-3 66 (v) ShaneKelly 4 62
(Mark Usher) *hld up towards rr: effrt on wd outside 3f out: kpt on one pce fr over 1f out* 7/1

6146 6 1 3/4 **Zero Game (IRE)**[13] 3418 3-9-7 70 (e) LukeMorris 8 62
(Michael Bell) *stmbld s: chsd ldrs: u.p wl over 3f out: no prog over 2f out* 8/1

1022 7 5 **Girl Of Cadiz**[19] 3178 3-8-11 65 WilliamTwiston-Davies(5) 9 53
(Richard Hannon) *trckd ldrs: rdn to dispute 2nd 3f out to over 1f out: wknd qckly: eased* 9/2[3]

0-60 8 2 1/2 **Polly's Love (IRE)**[27] 2935 3-9-2 65 (p) AdamKirby 11 40
(Clive Cox) *chsd wnr: rdn 4f out: lost 2nd and wknd 3f out* 10/1

-150 9 2 **Al Enbess (IRE)**[19] 3173 3-9-3 66 MartinLane 7 36
(David Simcock) *in tch in midfield: hanging lft bnd 6f out: rdn wl over 3f out: sn struggling* 14/1

00-0 10 21 **Classic Art**[57] 2017 3-8-13 62 (p) SebSanders 6
(Roger Teal) *nvr bttr than midfield: rdn bef 1/2-way: wknd 3f out: t.o and eased over 1f out* 25/1

1m 43.21s (-1.49) **Going Correction** -0.325s/f (Firm) 10 Ran SP% 113.1
Speed ratings (Par 99): **94,91,89,89,88 86,81,79,77,56**
toteswingers 1&2 £17.40, 1&3 £4.20, 2&3 £13.60 CSF £74.90 CT £255.03 TOTE £5.20: £1.60, £6.50, £1.80; EX 84.50 Trifecta £343.10 Pool: £1255.41 - 2.74 winning tickets..
Owner A D Spence **Bred** P G Connolly **Trained** Newmarket, Suffolk

FOCUS
The winner stole this handicap but it's fair form for the grade.

3862 TOTEQUADPOT AT TOTEPOOL.COM H'CAP 1m 2f 7y
3:20 (3:20) (Class 3) (0-90,88) 3-Y-O £7,439 (£2,213; £1,106; £553) Stalls Centre

Form RPR
10- 1 **Flying Officer (USA)**[260] 7053 3-9-7 88 JimmyFortune 3 105+
(John Gosden) *s.i.s: trckd ldng pair after 3f: shkn up to chse ldr over 2f out: clsd to ld over 1f out: firmly pushed clr* 11/4[2]

2141 2 3 1/2 **Sennockian Star**[4] 3693 3-9-1 82 6ex (b) JoeFanning 6 92
(Mark Johnston) *hld up in last: rdn 3f out: styd on fr over 1f out to take 2nd nr fin: no ch w wnr* 11/2

-312 3 nk **Duroble Man**[16] 3294 3-9-3 84 NeilCallan 4 93
(Roger Varian) *led at mod pce: kicked on over 3f out: drvn and hdd over 1f out: one pce and lost 2nd nr fin* 9/4[1]

-345 4 11 **London Citizen (USA)**[29] 2862 3-9-6 87 RichardHughes 5 83
(Mrs K Burke) *mostly chsd ldr to 3f out: u.p whn squeezed out over 2f out: wknd over 1f out: eased* 7/2[3]

0-21 5 32 **Bedouin Invader (IRE)**[26] 2953 3-9-1 82 JamesDoyle 1
(Sir Michael Stoute) *hld up in tch: rdn to chse ldr 3f out to over 2f out: sn wknd: virtually p.u fnl f* 6/1

2m 5.26s (-3.44) **Going Correction** -0.325s/f (Firm) 5 Ran SP% 109.3
Speed ratings (Par 103): **100,97,96,88,62**
toteswingers 1&2 £6.30, 1&3 £2.60, 2&3 £5.50 CSF £16.92 TOTE £3.00: £1.90, £2.90; EX 19.70 Trifecta £45.80 Pool: £1453.32 - 23.78 winning tickets..
Owner George Strawbridge **Bred** George Strawbridge Jr **Trained** Newmarket, Suffolk

FOCUS
A decent handicap run at just an ordinary gallop.

3863 TOTEEXACTA AT TOTEPOOL.COM / E B F FILLIES' CONDITIONS STKS 5f 10y
3:55 (3:55) (Class 2) 2-Y-O
£10,271 (£3,075; £1,537; £768; £384; £193) Stalls Low

Form RPR
102 1 **Majestic Alexander (IRE)**[15] 3311 2-8-12 0 NeilCallan 7 89
(David Evans) *mde all: clr and in command fnl 2f: rdn out* 6/1[3]
2 3 ¼ **Along Again (IRE)** 2-8-7 0 JamesDoyle 1 72+
(Sir Michael Stoute) *chsd ldrs: rdn 1/2-way: wnt 2nd over 1f out: kpt on but no ch w wnr* 16/1
41 3 2 ¼ **Emperor's Hope (IRE)**[19] 3174 2-8-9 0 SeanLevey 4 66
(Richard Hannon) *chsd wnr over 3f out: rdn and no imp 2f out: lost 2nd over 1f out: one pce* 5/1[2]
4 hd **Thatchit (IRE)** 2-8-7 0 LukeMorris 5 63+
(Paul Cole) *dwlt: urged along in last early: rdn 2f out: kpt on fr over 1f out to press for 2nd nr fin* 5/1[2]
5100 5 11 **Outback Lover (IRE)**[53] 2147 2-8-9 0 LiamJones 3 26
(J S Moore) *s.i.s: in tch: rdn whn hung lft to centre of crse 1/2-way: wknd qckly over 1f out: t.o* 33/1
10 6 4 **Fast (IRE)**[11] 3459 2-8-12 0 RichardHughes 2 29
(Richard Hannon) *taken down early and v free to post: chsd wnr to over 3f out: nudged along and no rspnse 2f out: wknd and eased over 1f out: t.o* 5/6[1]

59.6s (-0.70) **Going Correction** -0.025s/f (Good) 6 Ran SP% 111.0
Speed ratings (Par 96): **104,98,95,94,77 70**
toteswingers 1&2 £6.30, 1&3 £2.60, 2&3 £5.50 CSF £80.78 TOTE £8.70: £2.60, £6.30; EX 68.60 Trifecta £150.30 Pool: £3162.33 - 15.77 winning tickets..
Owner Noel O'Callaghan **Bred** Victor Stud Bloodstock & Brendan Cummins **Trained** Pandy, Monmouths

FOCUS
A fair race of its type that could rate higher but will take time to settle.

3864 COLLECT TOTEPOOL WINNINGS AT BETFRED SHOPS H'CAP 1m 67y
4:30 (4:30) (Class 3) (0-90,90) 3-Y-O+ £7,439 (£2,213; £1,106; £553) Stalls Low

Form RPR
5633 1 **Gaul Wood (IRE)**[15] 3339 4-9-6 87 (p) DeclanBates[(5)] 1 99
(Tom Dascombe) *trckd ldr: lft in ld 5f out: drvn over 2f out: kpt on wl fr over 1f out* 2/1[1]
1341 2 2 ¼ **Ree's Rascal (IRE)**[22] 3108 5-9-4 85 NathanAllison[(5)] 4 92
(Jim Boyle) *hld up: pushed along and in tch whn nt clr run wl over 2f out: swtchd lft then edgd lft: kpt on fr over 1f out to take 2nd ins fnl f* 7/2[2]
-153 3 1 ½ **Kinglami**[39] 2573 4-8-10 72 oh1 [1] RichardHughes 3 75
(Brian Gubby) *led: hung lft and hdd bnd 5f out: shkn up and nt qckn over 2f out: no imp on wnr after: lost 2nd ins fnl f* 10/1
0004 4 4 ½ **First Post (IRE)**[13] 3416 6-8-12 74 NeilCallan 2 67
(Derek Haydn Jones) *trckd ldng pair: shkn up over 3f out: no imp u.p 2f out: wknd fnl f* 10/1
31-3 5 10 **Anya**[18] 3215 4-9-1 77 JamesDoyle 5 52
(Ed Walker) *hld up in last: rdn on outer 3f out: no prog 2f out: wknd and eased over 1f out* 9/2[3]
30-6 6 6 **Circumvent**[30] 2839 6-10-0 90 (p) ShaneKelly 7 51
(Paul Cole) *hld up: hrd rdn over 3f out: sn btn: wknd over 2f out: t.o* 9/2[3]

1m 40.62s (-4.08) **Going Correction** -0.325s/f (Firm) 6 Ran SP% 110.1
Speed ratings (Par 107): **107,104,103,98,88 82**
toteswingers 1&2 £2.80, 1&3 £3.80, 2&3 £3.40 CSF £8.77 TOTE £2.80: £1.80, £1.60; EX 11.80 Trifecta £71.80 Pool: £2170.04 - 22.64 winning tickets..
Owner Star Sports **Bred** Patrick J Monahan **Trained** Malpas, Cheshire

FOCUS
Not a bad handicap.

3865 TOTETRIFECTA AT TOTEPOOL.COM H'CAP 1m 3f 135y
5:00 (5:00) (Class 5) (0-70,68) 4-Y-O+ £2,726 (£805; £402) Stalls Centre

Form RPR
3532 1 **Nave (USA)**[19] 3180 6-9-6 67 MartinLane 6 81
(David Simcock) *s.i.s: sn trckd ldrs: wnt 2nd over 3f out: clsd to ld over 2f out: rdn wl clr over 1f out* 2/1[1]
-243 2 8 **Royal Etiquette (IRE)**[20] 3156 6-9-0 61 (v) LukeMorris 1 61
(Lawney Hill) *w.w in rr: rdn and prog fr 3f out: tk 2nd over 1f out: no ch w wnr* 12/1
0-04 3 3 ¾ **Star Date (IRE)**[25] 2982 4-9-0 66 WilliamTwiston-Davies[(5)] 5 60
(Michael Attwater) *trckd ldr: led after 4f: clr 5f out: drvn and hdd over 2f out: wknd and lost 2nd over 1f out* 9/2[3]
3 4 4 ½ **Tempuran**[16] 3273 4-9-7 68 RichardHughes 2 54
(David Bridgwater) *prom: chsd ldr 5f out to over 3f out: steadily wknd and sn no ch* 3/1[2]
5321 5 ¾ **Time Square (FR)**[13] 3399 6-9-2 63 AdamKirby 7 48
(Tony Carroll) *led 4f: reminder 4f out and lost pl: wl btn fr 3f out* 11/2
1045 6 22 **Linkable**[13] 3412 4-9-7 68 (t) SebSanders 8 16
(Brendan Powell) *in tch: nt gng wl bef 1/2-way where reminders: lost tch over 3f out: t.o* 8/1
060 7 13 **Shameless Man (IRE)**[13] 3417 6-7-9 49 oh1 (tp) NoelGarbutt[(7)] 4
(Anthony Middleton) *hld up in tch: rdn 4f out: sn wknd: t.o* 50/1

2m 27.12s (-2.38) **Going Correction** -0.325s/f (Firm) 7 Ran SP% 112.7
Speed ratings (Par 103): **94,88,86,83,82 68,59**
toteswingers 1&2 £4.60, 1&3 £2.30, 2&3 £5.00 CSF £26.25 CT £96.01 TOTE £3.00: £1.50, £1.60; EX 23.90 Trifecta £127.70 Pool: £1993.70 - 11.70 winning tickets..
Owner Anthony Hogarth **Bred** Mineola Farm II Llc Et Al **Trained** Newmarket, Suffolk

FOCUS
A moderate handicap and an easy winner.

3866 TCA ENGINEERING LTD FRIENDS OF RCS H'CAP 5f 10y
5:30 (5:31) (Class 5) (0-75,78) 3-Y-O £2,587 (£770; £384; £192) Stalls Low

Form RPR
00-5 1 **Tychaios**[51] 2224 3-8-3 57 ChrisCatlin 6 60
(Stuart Williams) *chsd ldrs: shkn up 2f out: clsd on outer over 1f out: drvn ahd last 75yds: styd on* 8/1
4-31 2 nk **Dream Cast (IRE)**[22] 3086 3-9-7 75 MartinLane 5 78
(David Simcock) *hld up in last pair: waiting for a split fr over 1f out: drvn and r.o fnl f to take 2nd nr fin: jst too late to chal* 11/4[2]
36-4 3 nk **Pal Of The Cat**[13] 3400 3-8-8 67 ow1 WilliamTwiston-Davies[(5)] 3 68
(Brian Gubby) *mde most on outer: drvn over 1f out: edgd rt fnl f: hdd and no ex last 75yds* 12/1
11-5 4 2 **Oscars Journey**[72] 1661 3-9-4 72 JimmyFortune 2 66
(J R Jenkins) *chsd ldng pair: wnt 2nd and chal jst over 1f out: nt qckn ins fnl f: fdd last 75yds* 9/2[3]
00-6 5 ¾ **Somethingboutmary**[10] 3509 3-8-8 62 ShaneKelly 1 53
(Tim Pitt) *w ldr to over 1f out: wknd fnl f* 22/1
4132 6 12 **Royal Challis**[13] 3400 3-9-10 78 RichardHughes 4 55
(Richard Hannon) *hld up in last pair: pushed along 2f out: wknd over 1f out: heavily eased* 6/5[1]

59.97s (-0.33) **Going Correction** -0.025s/f (Good) 6 Ran SP% 113.5
Speed ratings (Par 99): **101,100,100,96,95 76**
toteswingers 1&2 £4.20, 1&3 £9.60, 2&3 £2.40 CSF £30.66 TOTE £12.90: £3.90, £1.70; EX 46.60 Trifecta £198.90 Pool: £1,871.23 - 7.05 winning tickets..
Owner Panny Ellinas **Bred** L Ellinas & Old Mill Stud **Trained** Newmarket, Suffolk

FOCUS
An ordinary sprint handicap.
T/Plt: £282.40 to a £1 stake. Pool: £99675.29 - 257.60 winning tickets T/Qpdt: £97.50 to a £1 stake. Pool: £4295.67 - 32.60 winning tickets JN

3867 - (Foreign Racing) - See Raceform Interactive

[3843]CURRAGH (R-H)
Sunday, June 30

OFFICIAL GOING: Good to firm

3868a GRANGECON STUD STKS (GROUP 3) (FILLIES) 6f
2:35 (2:35) 2-Y-O £31,707 (£9,268; £4,390; £1,463)

RPR
1 **Bye Bye Birdie (IRE)**[11] 3459 2-9-0 (v[1]) JosephO'Brien 2 105
(A P O'Brien, Ire) *wnt sltly rt s: mde virtually all: over 2 l clr 1/2-way: rdn and in command over 1f out: styd on wl towards fin* 9/2[3]
2 3 **Heart Focus (IRE)**[9] 3522 2-9-0 KevinManning 8 96
(J S Bolger, Ire) *chsd ldr in 2nd: over 2 l bhd at 1/2-way: sn pushed along and no imp on wnr under 2f out: kpt on wl ins fnl f* 5/4[1]
3 2 ½ **Clenor (IRE)**[14] 3379 2-9-0 WayneLordan 1 89
(T Stack, Ire) *sltly hmpd s: chsd ldrs: 4th 1/2-way: rdn fr 1 1/2f out and no imp on wnr: sltly hmpd ins fnl f and wnt nvr threatening 3rd cl home* 7/2[2]
4 hd **Colour Blue (IRE)**[25] 2999 2-9-0 JohnnyMurtagh 5 88
(W McCreery, Ire) *chsd ldrs: 3rd 1/2-way: rdn and no imp on wnr fr 2f out: swtchd rt ins fnl f and hmpd rivals: no ex u.p and dropped to 4th cl home* 9/1
5 4 ¼ **Bluebell (IRE)**[15] 3352 2-9-0 SeamieHeffernan 4 77
(A P O'Brien, Ire) *chsd ldrs: 6th 1/2-way: sn pushed along and no ex u.p in 5th whn short of room ins fnl f and sn hmpd: kpt on same pce* 10/1
6 2 ¾ **Pearl Earing (IRE)**[15] 3352 2-9-0 WJLee 3 70
(David Wachman, Ire) *chsd ldrs: 5th 1/2-way: rdn fr 2f out and no imp on principals in 6th whn hmpd ins fnl f: eased nr fin* 11/1
7 6 ½ **Gwen Lady Byron (IRE)**[81] 1488 2-9-0 DannyGrant 6 47
(Michael Mulvany, Ire) *in rr: pushed along and struggling bef 1/2-way: nvr a factor* 20/1

1m 10.94s (-4.56) **Going Correction** -0.75s/f (Hard) 7 Ran SP% 117.0
Speed ratings: **100,96,92,92,86 83,74**
CSF £10.99 TOTE £4.40: £2.50, £1.02; DF 7.10 Trifecta £19.90.
Owner Mrs John Magnier & Michael Tabor & Derrick Smith **Bred** London Thoroughbred Services Ltd **Trained** Ballydoyle, Co Tipperary
■ Stewards' Enquiry : Johnny Murtagh four-day ban; careless riding (14th-17th July).

FOCUS
This was not the strongest of Group 3s, with only the favourite coming in with a RPR above 101. The race could be rated 3lb higher through the runner-up.

3869a IRISH FIELD H'CAP (PREMIER HANDICAP) 1m
3:05 (3:05) 3-Y-O+
£24,390 (£7,723; £3,658; £1,219; £813; £406)

RPR
1 **Ansgar (IRE)**[21] 3142 5-9-7 93 (t) RoryCleary 17 107+
(Sabrina J Harty, Ire) *prom: t.k.h: settled bhd ldr in 2nd: got on terms 1/2-way and sn led: wnt 2 l clr ent fnl f: kpt on wl towards fin* 20/1
2 2 ½ **Fortify (IRE)**[55] 2107 3-9-5 101 (p) JosephO'Brien 13 107
(A P O'Brien, Ire) *chsd ldrs: cl 5th 1/2-way: rdn fr 2f out and wnt mod 2nd ins fnl f: kpt on wl towards fin: a hld* 9/2[1]
3 2 ½ **Moran Gra (USA)**[11] 3458 6-9-6 95 (p) RonanWhelan[(3)] 16 97
(Ms Joanna Morgan, Ire) *chsd ldrs: cl 6th 1/2-way: rdn over 2f out and clsd u.p into 2nd ent fnl f: sn no ex and dropped to 3rd: kpt on same pce* 5/1[2]
4 1 ¾ **Hes Our Music (IRE)**[31] 2821 4-8-4 76 DannyGrant 12 74
(Patrick J Flynn, Ire) *chsd ldrs: cl 4th 1/2-way: rdn fr 2f out on far side: no imp on wnr 1f out: jst hld on for 4th* 8/1[3]
5 nse **Swiftly Done (IRE)**[15] 3346 6-9-4 90 (v) SeamieHeffernan 9 88+
(Declan Carroll) *in tch: 8th after 1/2-way: rdn 2f out and clsd u.p in nvr threatening 5th fnl 100yds: kpt on and jst failed for 4th* 16/1
6 ¾ **Akasaka (IRE)**[18] 3225 6-9-2 98 RPDowney[(10)] 15 94
(Edward Lynam, Ire) *hld up in mid-div: tk clsr order in 7th 3f out: rdn and no imp fr 2f out: kpt on same pce* 20/1
7 nk **Vastonea (IRE)**[53] 2180 5-9-3 96 GaryHalpin[(7)] 11 92
(Kevin Prendergast, Ire) *in rr of mid-div: pushed along in 10th 3f out: no ex u.p in 7th ins fnl f: kpt on same pce* 12/1
8 1 ½ **Regulation (IRE)**[36] 2679 4-8-13 90 MarcMonaghan[(5)] 6 82
(M Halford, Ire) *s.i.s and racd towards rr: rdn over 2f out and sme hdwy over 1f out: kpt on same pce in 8th towards fin* 5/1[2]
9 4 ¼ **Banna Boirche (IRE)**[10] 3517 7-10-1 101 ShaneFoley 5 83
(M Halford, Ire) *dwlt: w.w towards rr: sme late hdwy ins fnl f: nvr a factor* 16/1
10 1 **Maggie Dalton (IRE)**[8] 3599 4-9-4 90 KevinManning 14 70
(J S Bolger, Ire) *chsd ldrs: cl 3rd 1/2-way: rdn over 2f out and no imp in 5th ent fnl f: wknd* 5/1[2]
11 ¾ **Clondinnery (IRE)**[1099] 3488 5-9-9 95 ChrisHayes 2 73
(A Oliver, Ire) *sn led narrowly: jnd 1/2-way: sn hdd: rdn and wknd fr 2f out: eased fnl f* 25/1
12 3 ½ **Hujaylea (IRE)**[36] 2679 10-9-9 98 (p) ConorHoban[(3)] 4 68
(M Halford, Ire) *in rr of mid-div: rdn and no imp fr over 2f out* 25/1
13 4 ¼ **Back Burner (IRE)**[36] 2679 5-9-0 86 (t) FMBerry 1 47
(Edward Lynam, Ire) *hld up towards rr: rdn and no imp fr 2f out* 8/1[3]

14 *14* **Negotiate**[35] 2688 5-9-6 92..(t) PatSmullen 7 20
(Ms Joanna Morgan, Ire) *prom: sn settled bhd ldr on far side: pushed along fr 1/2-way and sn wknd: eased under 2f out* **12/1**

1m 35.68s (-10.32) **Going Correction** -1.05s/f (Hard)
WFA 3 from 4yo+ 10lb **14** Ran SP% **134.8**
Speed ratings: **109,106,104,102,102 101,101,99,95,94 93,90,85,71**
CSF £115.39 CT £439.61 TOTE £30.60: £6.60, £2.60, £2.30; DF 285.60 Trifecta £1204.40.

Owner Mrs Chynel Phelan/Shane Fox **Bred** Miss Chynel Phelan **Trained** Newbridge, Co Kildare

FOCUS
The third and fourth have been rated to their recent form.

3870a OXIGEN ENVIRONMENTAL PRETTY POLLY STKS (GROUP 1) (F&M) 1m 2f

3:35 (3:37) 3-Y-0+

£97,560 (£30,894; £14,634; £4,878; £3,252; £1,626)

RPR

1 **Ambivalent (IRE)**[22] 3100 4-9-10 .... JohnnyMurtagh 1 111
(Roger Varian) *mde virtually all: over 1 l clr 1/2-way: pushed along into st and jnd briefly fr 2f out: gained narrow advantage ent fnl f and styd on wl u.p towards fin: all out* **10/1**

2 *1/2* **Was (IRE)**[36] 2678 4-9-10 112.. JosephO'Brien 3 110+
(A P O'Brien, Ire) *wnt sltly lft s: chsd ldrs in 3rd: rdn and tk clsr order fr 2f out: styd on wl towards fin and wnt 2nd fnl 50yds: hld* **5/2**[1]

3 *nk* **Shirocco Star**[56] 2045 4-9-10 .... KierenFallon 9 109+
(Hughie Morrison) *chsd ldrs in 4th: rdn and tk clsr order on outer fr 2f out: kpt on wl u.p ins fnl f: nrst fin* **11/2**[3]

4 *1/2* **Harasiya (IRE)**[35] 2689 3-8-12 103........................... DeclanMcDonogh 5 108
(John M Oxx, Ire) *settled bhd ldr in 2nd: got on terms briefly fr 2f out: rdn and no ex in 2nd 1f out: dropped to 4th fnl 50yds* **14/1**

5 *hd* **Say (IRE)**[14] 3381 3-8-12 94... SeamieHeffernan 6 108
(A P O'Brien, Ire) *hld up in tch: t.k.h: rdn in 5th fr 2f out and clsd u.p ent fnl f: kpt on wl towards fin: nvr on terms* **20/1**

6 *3 3/4* **La Collina (IRE)**[36] 2678 4-9-10 108.................................... ChrisHayes 7 101
(Kevin Prendergast, Ire) *hld up towards rr: 8th 1/2-way: rdn fr 2f out and sn no imp on principals: wnt mod 6th fnl 100yds and kpt on same pce towards fin* **7/1**

7 *1 3/4* **Princess Highway (USA)**[46] 2375 4-9-10 114...........(b[1]) PatSmullen 10 97
(D K Weld, Ire) *hld up: t.k.h: 7th 1/2-way: hdwy fr 1/2-way to chse ldrs in 6th 2f out: sn rdn and no ex u.p: dropped to 7th fnl 100yds* **7/2**[2]

8 *4 3/4* **Rehn's Nest (IRE)**[9] 3524 3-8-12 107..........................(t) KevinManning 8 88
(J S Bolger, Ire) *hld up in rr: pushed along into st and sn no imp: kpt on one pce ins fnl f* **6/1**

9 *1/2* **Cruck Realta**[17] 3240 3-8-12 .... MartinHarley 4 87
(Mick Channon) *hld up in tch: t.k.h: 6th 1/2-way: rdn over 2f out and sn wknd* **16/1**

2m 4.83s (-4.47) **Going Correction** -0.575s/f (Hard)
WFA 3 from 4yo 12lb **9** Ran SP% **119.4**
Speed ratings: **114,113,113,112,112 109,108,104,104**
CSF £36.54 TOTE £11.40: £2.60, £1.70, £1.30; DF 53.40 Trifecta £148.85.

Owner Ali Saeed **Bred** Darley **Trained** Newmarket, Suffolk

FOCUS
This lost a key element of interest when Alive Alive Oh was withdrawn having come in season. Also taken out of her intended engagement in the Ribblesdale (on account of the ground), she had been a strong ante-post-fancy for this. There was some top-class Group 1 form on show here, but a number with apparently better credentials were eclipsed by the front-running winner. It paid to be on the pace and the fifth potentially limits the form.

3873a AT THE RACES CURRAGH CUP (GROUP 3) 1m 6f

5:15 (5:16) 3-Y-0+

£30,487 (£9,654; £4,573; £1,524; £1,016; £508)

RPR

1 **Ernest Hemingway (IRE)**[84] 1415 4-9-11 105......... SeamieHeffernan 1 116+
(A P O'Brien, Ire) *w.w: tk clsr order in 4th into st: sn lost pl and swtchd to outer: rdn in 5th 2f out and sn qcknd wl to ld fnl 200yds: gng away at fin: comf* **12/1**

2 *5* **Royal Diamond (IRE)**[44] 2428 7-10-0 111.................. JohnnyMurtagh 3 112
(J P Murtagh, Ire) *trckd ldr in 3rd: tk clsr order in 2nd fr 4f out: pushed along to ld over 3f out: rdn and strly pressed ent fnl f: sn hdd and no ch w wnr: kpt on wl* **5/1**

3 *1/2* **Voleuse De Coeurs (IRE)**[42] 2485 4-9-8 108.................... PatSmullen 5 105
(D K Weld, Ire) *hld up in rr: hdwy into 3rd under 3f out: rdn into 2nd fr 2f out: no ex u.p ins fnl f and dropped to 3rd: kpt on same pce* **6/4**[1]

4 *1 1/4* **El Salvador (IRE)**[10] 3483 4-9-11 108........................... JosephO'Brien 4 107
(A P O'Brien, Ire) *disp early: sn settled bhd ldrs in 6th: hdwy in 4th into st: sn rdn and no imp on principals fr 2f out: kpt on same pce* **7/1**

5 *10* **Glen's Diamond**[44] 2428 5-10-0 .... TonyHamilton 7 96
(Richard Fahey) *settled bhd ldrs in 4th: wnt 2nd 3f out: sn rdn and no ex u.p: dropped to mod 5th over 1f out: one pce towards fin* **9/2**[3]

6 *18* **Zafarqand (IRE)**[10] 3520 5-9-11 80..................................... GaryCarroll 6 67
(Patrick O Brady, Ire) *prom: sn trckd ldr in 2nd: pushed along and lost pl 4f out: sn dropped to rr: one pce fnl 2f and wnt remote 6th over 1f out* **66/1**

7 *3 1/2* **Mijhaar**[44] 2407 5-9-11 .... AndreaAtzeni 2 62
(Roger Varian) *dwlt: chsd ldrs early: gd hdwy on inner to sn ld after 1f: over 1 l clr 1/2-way: reduced advantage over 4f out: pushed along and hdd over 3f out: sn no ex: wknd qckly: eased* **7/2**[2]

2m 56.33s (-13.07) **Going Correction** -0.575s/f (Hard) **7** Ran SP% **118.8**
Speed ratings: **114,111,110,110,104 94,92**
CSF £73.34 TOTE £14.70: £4.50, £2.50; DF 69.40.

Owner Mrs John Magnier & Michael Tabor & Derrick Smith **Bred** Barronstown Stud **Trained** Ballydoyle, Co Tipperary

■ Stewards' Enquiry : Andrea Atzeni jockey said gelding weakened quickly and may not have acted on todays ground.

FOCUS
A strong Group 3 and Irish Leger trial run on pretty quick ground. At least one of these had credentials to be a plausible Gold Cup winner next year. The winner has been rated as a big improver while the second and third have been rated in line with their recent form.

3874 - (Foreign Racing) - See Raceform Interactive

3645 CHANTILLY (R-H)

Sunday, June 30

OFFICIAL GOING: Turf: good to soft

3875a PRIX DU BOIS (GROUP 3) (2YO) (TURF) 5f

1:00 (12:00) 2-Y-0 **£32,520** (£13,008; £9,756; £6,504; £3,252)

RPR

1 **Vedeux (IRE)**[30] 2-8-11 0... MarcLerner 4 106
(C Lerner, France) *led: narrowly hdd 1/2-way: scrubbed along and qcknd to regain ld 2f out: rdn and wnt 2 l clr over 1f out: r.o u.p fnl f* **7/1**

2 *1 1/4* **Another Party (FR)**[9] 2-8-11 0.................................. AntoineHamelin 6 101
(Matthieu Palussiere, France) *chsd ldrs on outer: lost pl appr 1/2-way: last and rdn over 2f out: styd on u.p ins fnl f: tk 2nd cl home: nvr on terms w wnr* **7/2**[1]

3 *hd* **Empreinte (USA)**[21] 2-8-8 0... FlavienPrat 5 98
(C Laffon-Parias, France) *tk a t.k.h and restrained towards rr: shkn up to chse ldrs over 1 1/2f out: rdn to dispute 2nd ins fnl f: r.o u.p: tk 2nd cl home but lost it almost immediately* **9/2**[2]

4 *hd* **Early Prime (FR)**[19] 3185 2-8-9 0 ow1.............................. MarcNobili 2 98
(Rod Collet, France) *trckd ldrs: rdn and r.o to dispute 2nd ins fnl f: no ex u.p last 50yds: lost two pls cl home* **14/1**

5 *1 1/4* **Ultradargent (FR)**[18] 2-8-8 0.. FabriceVeron 1 93
(H-A Pantall, France) *chsd ldrs on ins: tk narrow ld 1/2-way: rdn and hdd 2f out: sn outpcd by ldrs: one pce u.p fnl f* **7/1**

6 *nk* **My Sapphire (IRE)**[41] 2-8-8 0................................. StephanePasquier 3 91
(R Pritchard-Gordon, France) *towards rr: effrt on inner to chse ldrs over 2f out: sn rdn and nt qckn over 1f out: styd on again fnl 75yds* **11/1**

7 *1 1/4* **Oeil De Tigre (FR)**[19] 3185 2-8-11 0................................ MaximeGuyon 9 90
(H-A Pantall, France) *chsd ldrs on outside: rdn and nt qckn over 1 1/2f out: no imp u.p whn fly j. 75yds out and eased* **6/1**[3]

8 *5* **Victorianvalentine (FR)**[22] 2-8-8 0................................ ThierryJarnet 8 69
(Matthieu Palussiere, France) *prom towards outside: lost pl appr 1/2-way: hrd rdn and no imp over 1 1/2f out: sn wl btn and eased fnl 100yds* **11/1**

59.24s (0.94) **Going Correction** +0.225s/f (Good) **8** Ran SP% **103.0**
Speed ratings: **101,99,98,98,96 95,93,85**
WIN (incl. 1 euro stake): 6.80. PLACES: 2.00, 1.50, 1.90. DF: 10.30. SF: 26.80.

Owner P Hoze & Ecurie Haras Du Cadran **Bred** Ecurie Haras Du Cadran & P Hoze **Trained** France

3876a PRIX JEAN PRAT (GROUP 1) (3YO COLTS & FILLIES) (TURF) 1m

2:40 (12:00) 3-Y-0 **£162,601** (£65,040; £48,780; £32,520; £16,260)

RPR

1 **Havana Gold (IRE)**[36] 2677 3-9-2 0......................... MickaelBarzalona 6 113+
(Richard Hannon) *dwlt and pushed along to rcvr: hld up towards rr on inner: rdn and hdwy fr 3f out: swtchd lft for clr run 1 1/2f out: r.o to chal ins fnl f: drvn to ld cl home* **6/1**[3]

2 *snk* **San Marino Grey (FR)**[22] 3128 3-9-2 0......................... MaximeGuyon 5 113
(A Fabre, France) *midfield on outer: rdn and hdwy fr 2f out: r.o to chal ent fnl f: led 120yds out: drvn and kpt on but hdd cl home* **11/1**

3 *1 1/2* **Mondialiste (IRE)**[37] 3-9-2 0... FlavienPrat 7 109
(F Head, France) *dwlt and pushed along to rcvr: sn disputing ld on outer: led 5f out: 1 l ahd whn rdn 2f out: strly pressed ent fnl f: hdd 120yds: no ex and jst hld on for 3rd* **150/1**

4 *shd* **Style Vendome (FR)**[49] 2298 3-9-2 0......................... ThierryThulliez 10 109+
(N Clement, France) *stdd and hld up towards rr on outer: rdn and hdwy fr 2f out: outpcd by eventual wnr ent fnl f: edgd rt u.p but r.o and almost snatched 3rd post* **7/4**[1]

5 *hd* **Pearl Flute (IRE)**[11] 3455 3-9-2 0................................. UmbertoRispoli 4 109+
(F-H Graffard, France) *restrained in midfield: swtchd ins and hdwy whn hmpd on rail 2f out: sn in the clr and rdn: swtchd bk off rail ent fnl f and r.o to go 5th cl home: fin wl but nvr able to chal* **14/1**

6 *1 1/2* **Us Law (IRE)**[49] 2298 3-9-2 0......................... ChristopheSoumillon 12 105
(P Bary, France) *midfield in tch on outer: smooth hdwy to chal gng wl 2f out: rdn in 2nd and ev ch 1 1/2f out: kpt on tl no ex ins fnl f: fdd* **14/1**

7 *1/2* **Anodin (IRE)**[22] 3128 3-9-2 0... OlivierPeslier 9 104
(F Head, France) *t.k.h: stdd and hld up in last trio on inner: had to wait for run 3f out and trbld passage tl ins fnl f: ch gone but kpt on nicely under hands and heels cl home: wnt 7th fnl strides* **4/1**[2]

8 *shd* **Lines Of Battle (USA)**[21] 3142 3-9-2 0...........................(p) RyanMoore 8 104
(A P O'Brien, Ire) *dwlt and pushed along to rcvr: sn stdd and hld up in last: rdn and sltly detached 3f out: hdwy on outside fr over 2f out: swtchd ins ent fnl f: r.o but nt pce to chal: dropped to 8th fnl strides* **8/1**

9 *1 3/4* **Zenji (USA)**[19] 3186 3-9-2 0................................ Pierre-CharlesBoudot 11 100
(A Fabre, France) *bobbled s: dropped in and hld up in last pair on outer: rdn 2f out: outpcd by ldrs over 1f out: hung rt u.p ins fnl f and sn no ex and btn* **33/1**

10 *20* **Anna's Pearl**[16] 3278 3-9-2 0..(b) JamieSpencer 1 54
(Ralph Beckett) *broke wl and led early: sn restrained and trckd ldrs on outer: 2nd and ev ch 3f out: rdn 2f out and qckly btn: wknd and eased over 1f out: t.o* **16/1**

11 *20* **Peace At Last (IRE)**[41] 2526 3-9-2 0.................................. FabriceVeron 3 8
(H-A Pantall, France) *prom on inner: rdn and stl ev ch whn bdly hmpd 2f out: nt rcvr and immediately eased: dropped rt out and t.o* **12/1**

12 *6* **Top Chill (FR)**[19] 3-9-2 0.. YannickLetondeur 2
(N Clement, France) *t.k.h: dwlt and rousted along to rcvr: sn disputing ld on inner: hdd 5f out and trckd ldr: rdn 3f and sn btn: eased over 2f out and dropped to last: tailed rt off* **200/1**

1m 37.01s (-0.99) **Going Correction** +0.225s/f (Good) **12** Ran SP% **121.1**
Speed ratings: **113,112,111,111,111 109,109,108,107,87 67,61**
WIN (incl. 1 euro stake): 7.40 ((Havana Gold coupled with Anna's Pearl & Pearl Flute). PLACES: 3.50, 2.40, 10.60. DF: 25.60. SF: 80.10.

Owner Qatar Racing Limited & CSH **Bred** Sir Eric Parker **Trained** East Everleigh, Wilts

FOCUS
They went a good gallop, but the form looks average for the level.

3877a PRIX CHLOE (GROUP 3) (3YO FILLIES) (TURF) 1m 1f

3:10 (12:00) 3-Y-0 **£32,520** (£13,008; £9,756; £6,504; £3,252)

RPR

1 **Sparkling Beam (IRE)**[28] 2906 3-8-11 0.......................... ThierryJarnet 4 114+
(J E Pease, France) *midfield in tch on outer: smooth hdwy fr over 3f out: shkn up to chal 2f out: sn led and qcknd clr: rdn and r.o strly ins fnl f: impressive* **20/1**

2 3 **Pearlside (FR)**[14] 3385 3-8-11 0 StephanePasquier 5 108
(M Delcher Sanchez, France) *hld up in tch on outer: smooth hdwy fr 3f out: rdn and ev ch 2f out: sn outpcd by wnr: r.o and wnt 2nd cl home* **15/2**

3 nk **Table Ronde (IRE)**[47] 2356 3-8-11 0 ChristopheSoumillon 9 107
(J-C Rouget, France) *sn prom on outer: led after 3f tl hdd 5f out: trckd ldr: smooth hdwy to chal 2f out: rdn in 2nd but readily outpcd by wnr over 1f out: r.o but dropped to 3rd cl home* **5/2**[1]

4 1 1/4 **Snow Bell (FR)**[26] 2970 3-8-11 0 GregoryBenoist 2 105+
(N Clement, France) *dwlt and slow to stride: hld up in last: rdn and hanging u.p ent fnl f: r.o to go 4th post: nvr nrr* **7/2**[2]

5 shd **Intimhir (IRE)**[37] 3-8-11 0 OlivierPeslier 8 105
(F Head, France) *dwlt sltly: hld up in last pair: rdn and hdwy fr 2f out: r.o but nt pce to chal* **16/1**

6 hd **Ighraa (IRE)**[30] 2838 3-8-11 0 AntoineHamelin 7 104
(F-H Graffard, France) *broke wl and led: hdd after 3f but remained prom on inner: rdn 2f out: angled out ent fnl f: kpt on one pce* **12/1**

7 1/2 **Alumna (USA)**[35] 2693 3-8-11 0 MaximeGuyon 3 103
(A Fabre, France) *hld up in tch on inner: shkn up and hdwy on rail 2f out: rdn and nt qckn over 1f out: kpt on one pce ins fnl f and lost multiple pls cl home* **4/1**[3]

8 1/2 **Belonging**[25] 3008 3-8-11 0 MickaelBarzalona 6 102
(A Fabre, France) *plld hrd: prom tl led 5f out: rdn and strly pressed 2f out: sn hdd: no ex and btn ent fnl f: fdd* **7/1**

9 1/2 **Venturous Spirit (FR)**[25] 3008 3-8-11 0 (p) UmbertoRispoli 1 101
(M Delzangles, France) *t.k.h: midfield in tch on inner: rdn and ev ch 2f out: outpcd over 1f out: fdd and dropped to last ins fnl f* **12/1**

1m 50.79s (-0.31) **Going Correction** +0.225s/f (Good) 9 Ran SP% **121.1**
Speed ratings: **110,107,107,105,105 105,105,104,104**
WIN (incl. 1 euro stake): 28.00. PLACES: 4.40, 2.30, 1.70. DF: 80.00. SF: 146.30.
Owner George Strawbridge **Bred** George Strawbridge **Trained** Chantilly, France

3852 HAMBURG (R-H)

Sunday, June 30

OFFICIAL GOING: Turf: good

3879a IDEE HANSA-PREIS (GROUP 2) (3YO+) (TURF) 1m 4f

4:10 (12:00) 3-Y-0+ **£32,520** (£12,601; £5,284; £3,252; £2,032; £1,219)

RPR

1 **Berlin Berlin**[22] 4-9-3 0 AHelfenbein 3 104
(Markus Klug, Germany) *midfield in tch on inner: rdn 2f out: r.o to chal jst ins fnl f: sn jnd eventual runner-up and sustained battle to fin: drvn and jst prevailed on hd bob post* **22/1**

2 nse **Runaway (GER)**[31] 2822 6-9-6 0 SteveDrowne 2 107
(A Trybuhl, Germany) *w ldrs: trckd ldr after 5f: rdn to ld 2f out: r.o but jnd ins fnl f: sustained battle to fin: drvn and jst denied on hd bob post* **102/10**

3 1 1/4 **Girolamo (GER)**[31] 2822 4-9-6 0 EPedroza 5 105
(P Schiergen, Germany) *midfield in tch: rdn 2f out: wnt 3rd ent fnl f: styd on but nt pce of front pair* **1/2**[1]

4 1 1/2 **Silvaner (GER)**[31] 2822 5-9-6 0 MrDennisSchiergen 7 103
(P Schiergen, Germany) *hld up in last pair on inner: rdn in last 3f out: swtchd to wd outside on turn into st: styd on and wnt 4th ins fnl f: nt pce to chal* **195/10**

5 nk **Sir Lando**[19] 3188 6-9-6 0 PatCosgrave 9 102
(Wido Neuroth, Norway) *racd in snatches: slow to stride and pushed along to rcvr: hld up in last pair on outer: rdn 4f out: outpcd by ldrs fr 2f out: rallied u.p and styd on ins fnl f but n.d* **198/10**

6 2 1/2 **Baschar**[280] 6523 6-9-6 0 APietsch 1 98
(M G Mintchev, Germany) *broke wl and led early: w ldrs tl after 5f then prom on inner: rdn 2f out: outpcd ins fnl f: fdd* **81/10**

7 1 1/4 **Seismos (IRE)**[49] 2294 5-9-6 0 EddyHardouin 8 96
(A Wohler, Germany) *dwlt and in rr early: rapid hdwy on outer to join ldrs after 3f: settled in midfield after 5f: drvn to maintain position over 4f out: outpcd in last ent fnl f: rallied and styd on again cl home* **56/10**[2]

8 3 1/2 **Andolini (GER)**[31] 2822 4-9-6 0 JBojko 6 90
(A Wohler, Germany) *prom on outer: short of room and relegated to midfield after 3f: sent forward and again prom on outer after 6f: rdn to chal and ev ch 2f out: outpcd and btn ent fnl f: fdd and eased* **25/1**

9 3/4 **Wilddrossel (GER)**[31] 2822 4-9-3 0 DPorcu 4 86
(Markus Klug, Germany) *hld up towards rr: rapid hdwy to ld after 5f: rdn and hdd 2f out: no ex and btn over 1f out: fdd and dropped to last ins fnl f: eased* **63/10**[3]

2m 33.62s (-0.93) 9 Ran SP% **133.3**
WIN (incl. 10 euro stake): 230. PLACES: 26, 17, 11. SF: 2,514.
Owner Gestut Gorlsdorf **Bred** Mr & Mrs A E Pakenham **Trained** Germany

3616 SAN SIRO (R-H)

Sunday, June 30

OFFICIAL GOING: Turf: good

3880a PREMIO PRIMI PASSI (GROUP 3) (2YO) (TURF) 6f

3:00 (12:00) 2-Y-0 **£28,455** (£12,520; £6,829; £3,414)

RPR

1 **Arpinati** 2-8-11 0 MEsposito 5 105
(S Botti, Italy) *trckd ldr on outside: rdn over 1f out: r.o wl ins fnl f to ld last 100yds: pushed out* **7/2**[3]

2 1/2 **Omaticaya (IRE)**[28] 2-8-8 0 GFois 2 101
(Manila Illuminati, Italy) *broke wl and led: rdn and r.o over 1f out: hdd fnl 100yds: no ex* **1/1**[1]

3 2 1/2 **Quiz Evolution (ITY)**[21] 2-8-11 0 DarioVargiu 3 96
(B Grizzetti, Italy) *reluctant to enter stalls: trckd ldr: shkn up to press ldr 1 1/2f out: sn rdn and nt qckn: outpcd by first two ins fnl f* **6/4**[2]

4 3/4 **Grey Greezly (FR)** 2-8-11 0 CristianDemuro 1 94
(B Grizzetti, Italy) *last but wl in tch: rdn and effrt 1 1/2f out: kpt on at one pce u.p fnl f* **116/10**

5 12 **Seaside Runner (IRE)** 2-8-11 0 MircoDemuro 4 58
(R Brogi, Italy) *rrd leaving stalls: sn rcvrd to chse ldrs: rdn and wknd fr 2f out* **81/10**

1m 10.9s (-0.90) 5 Ran SP% **131.1**
WIN (incl. 1 euro stake): 4.49. PLACES: 1.90, 1.53. DF: 11.92.
Owner Dioscuri Srl **Bred** G.A.G. Equestrian **Trained** Italy

3881a PREMIO DEL GIUBILEO (GROUP 3) (3YO+) (TURF) 1m 1f

4:40 (12:00) 3-Y-0+ **£22,764** (£10,016; £5,463; £2,731)

RPR

1 **Pattaya (ITY)**[49] 2295 5-9-4 0 MEsposito 8 104
(S Botti, Italy) *hld up in rr: rdn and hdwy 2 1/2f out: swtchd outside and styd on wl u.p fnl f: led cl home* **363/100**[2]

2 1/2 **Storming Loose**[49] 2295 6-9-4 0 MircoDemuro 2 103
(B Grizzetti, Italy) *hld up towards rr: hdwy 2 1/2f out: 7th: rdn and swtchd ins 2f out: led ent fnl f: r.o u.p: hdd cl home: no ex* **22/5**

3 2 1/2 **Orpello (IRE)**[49] 2295 4-9-6 0 (b) FabioBranca 1 100
(S Botti, Italy) *midfield on inner: swtchd outside in st and prog to go 4th 2f out: outpcd ent fnl f: kpt on wout qckning fnl 100yds* **11/10**[1]

4 3/4 **Sciolina (IRE)**[49] 4-9-1 0 DPerovic 9 93
(Cristiana Signorelli, Italy) *towards rr: hdwy to chse ldrs 2f out: outpcd by ldrs ent fnl f: styd on last 150yds: nvr really on terms* **219/10**

5 1/2 **Vola E Va**[21] 3147 4-9-4 0 DarioVargiu 3 95
(B Grizzetti, Italy) *settled in 4th: 3rd and rdn 2f out: kpt on at one pce u.p fnl f* **22/5**

6 nse **Chardonney Tcheque (FR)**[623] 6905 5-9-4 0 PierantonioConvertino 5 95
(T Satra, Czech Republic) *trckd ldrs tl settled in midfield bef 1/2-way: smooth hdwy over 3f out: cl 2nd and ev ch 2f out: stl 2nd and hrd rdn ins fnl f: fdd last 100yds* **39/10**[3]

7 3 **Wild Wolf (IRE)**[21] 3147 4-9-4 0 (b) CColombi 6 89
(S Botti, Italy) *midfield on outer: tk clsr order to trck ldrs bef 1/2-way: jnd ldr 4f out: sn led: rdn appr last 2f: hdd ent fnl f: sn wknd and eased last 100yds* **11/10**[1]

8 10 **Billy Budd (IRE)**[400] 2521 5-9-4 0 CFiocchi 7 68
(S Bazzani, Italy) *midfield: rushed up on outside to ld after 1f: hdd over 4f out: grad dropped away fr 3f out: eased ins fnl f* **214/10**

9 dist **Branderburgo (IRE)**[49] 2295 6-9-4 0 CristianDemuro 4
(M Grassi, Italy) *led tl hdd after 1f: pressed ldr tl led again over 4f out: jnd 4f out and hdd sn after: sn wknd and bhd fr 2f out: eased ins fnl f* **69/10**

1m 48.5s (-9.40) 9 Ran SP% **195.8**
WIN (incl. 1 euro stake): 4.63. PLACES: 1.69, 3.28, 1.54. DF: 35.24.
Owner Dioscuri Srl **Bred** Azienda Agricola Al Deni S R L **Trained** Italy

FFOS LAS (L-H)

Monday, July 1

OFFICIAL GOING: Good to firm (8.4)
Wind: fresh against Weather: sunny spells

3882 RACING EXCELLENCE APPRENTICE TRAINING SERIES H'CAP 1m 4f (R)

6:15 (6:15) (Class 6) (0-65,64) 4-Y-0+ **£1,940** (£577; £288; £144) **Stalls** Low

Form RPR

4200 1 **Stag Hill (IRE)**[16] 3314 4-9-1 **53** JoeyHaynes 5 62
(Bernard Llewellyn) *in tch: rdn over 2f out: led over 1f out: rdn clr fnl f* **7/1**[3]

00-0 2 2 1/4 **Lisselan Pleasure (USA)**[16] 3314 6-8-8 **51** (t) SiobhanMiller(5) 8 56
(Bernard Llewellyn) *in tch towards outer: tk clsr order 4f out: rdn 3f out: chsd wnr ins fnl f: a being hld* **16/1**

4062 3 1 1/2 **Gaelic Ice**[7] 3635 4-8-12 **53** PatMillman(3) 4 56
(Rod Millman) *trckd ldr 4f: styd prom: wnt sltly wd bnd 4f out: rdn over 2f out: kpt on* **9/2**[2]

5621 4 1/2 **Automotive**[18] 3244 5-9-4 **56** ShelleyBirkett 7 58
(Julia Feilden) *prom: trckd ldr after 4f: tk narrow ld gng wl 3f out: hdd over 1f out: sn rdn: no ex and lost 2 pls ins fnl f* **3/1**[1]

3030 5 3/4 **Transfer**[6] 3662 8-8-13 **51** DanielMuscutt 9 52
(Richard Price) *hld up towards rr: hdwy 4f out: rdn 2f out: kpt on same pce* **8/1**

126/ 6 hd **Dark Spirit (IRE)**[53] 7244 5-9-5 **64** (p) JackGarritty(7) 6 65
(Evan Williams) *led tl hdd 3f out: sn pushed along and one pce* **9/2**[2]

-550 7 shd **Richo**[47] 703 7-8-2 **45** LouisSteward(5) 1 46
(Shaun Harris) *s.i.s: hld up last but in tch: effrt over 2f out: no real imp on ldrs* **50/1**

-232 8 1 1/2 **Liberty Love (IRE)**[156] 406 8-8-11 **54** (bt) OisinMurphy(5) 2 52
(Niall Moran, Ire) *hld up towards rr: rdn over 2f out: no imp on ldrs* **3/1**[1]

2m 36.67s (-0.73) **Going Correction** -0.175s/f (Firm) 8 Ran SP% **117.8**
Speed ratings (Par 101): **95,93,92,92,91 91,91,90**
toteswingers 1&2 £48.80, 1&3 £8.10, 2&3 £48.80 CSF £110.58 CT £563.03 TOTE £15.10: £6.50, £9.10, £2.10; EX 66.90 Trifecta £703.60 Pool: £1653.08 - 1.76 winning tickets..
Owner B W Parren **Bred** Tally-Ho Stud **Trained** Fochriw, Caerphilly

FOCUS
A moderate handicap, confined to apprentice riders.

3883 IRISH STALLION FARMS EBF MAIDEN STKS 5f

6:45 (6:45) (Class 5) 2-Y-0 **£2,911** (£866; £432; £216) **Stalls** Centre

Form RPR

3 1 **Captain Whoosh (IRE)**[24] 3045 2-9-5 0 LiamKeniry 6 73
(Tom Dascombe) *trckd ldr: rdn over 1f out: led early ins fnl f: drvn out* **6/4**[1]

4 2 2 **Dodger Marley (IRE)**[24] 3035 2-9-5 0 JamieSpencer 3 66
(Stuart Williams) *racd keenly: hld up in tch: rdn over 1f out: r.o ins fnl f: tk 2nd post* **2/1**[2]

003 3 shd **The Dandy Yank (IRE)**[14] 3413 2-9-5 0 FergusSweeney 5 65
(Jamie Osborne) *led: rdn over 1f out: hdd early ins fnl f: no ex and lost 2nd post* **10/1**

32 4 1 1/4 **Flying Bear (IRE)**[9] 3568 2-9-5 0 SteveDrowne 4 61
(Jeremy Gask) *chsd ldrs: rdn over 1f out: one pce* **5/1**[3]

00 5 1/2 **Caledonia Laird**[45] 2411 2-9-0 0 PhilipPrince(5) 1 59
(Jo Hughes) *in rr: sn outpcd: clsd and in tch 1/2-way: rdn 2f out: r.o ins fnl f* **20/1**

40 **6** *2* **Thrtypointstothree (IRE)**[13] 3422 2-8-12 0................ OisinMurphy(7) 2 52
(Nikki Evans) *chsd ldrs: rdn 2f out: wknd fnl f* **16/1**

57.74s (-0.56) **Going Correction** -0.25s/f (Firm) **6** Ran SP% **109.7**
Speed ratings (Par 94): **94,90,90,88,87 84**
toteswingers 1&2 £2.20, 1&3 £3.30, 2&3 £3.50 CSF £4.47 TOTE £2.20: £1.30, £1.40; EX 6.60 Trifecta £22.00 Pool: £1859.74 - 63.15 winning tickets..
Owner D Ward **Bred** J Cullen **Trained** Malpas, Cheshire

FOCUS
A modest 2-y-o maiden. There are grounds for rating the form either a few pounds higher or lower.

3884 IWEC ELECTRICAL H'CAP 2m (R)
7:15 (7:15) (Class 6) (0-60,66) 4-Y-0+ **£1,940** (£577; £288; £144) **Stalls** Low

Form RPR
34-4 **1** **Annaluna (IRE)**[28] 2922 4-8-9 **53**................(v) DeclanBates(5) 4 62
(David Evans) *trckd ldrs: pushed along 3f out: swtchd rt 2f out: led appr fnl f: styd on wl* **6/1**
0153 **2** *3 ¾* **Pass The Time**[17] 3271 4-8-11 **50**................(p) LiamKeniry 7 54
(Neil Mulholland) *led: rdn and jnd 3f out: hdd appr fnl f: styd on same pce u.p* **11/2**[3]
3/0 **3** *½* **Rock Peak (IRE)**[17] 3271 8-8-0 **46**................(b) JoeyHaynes(7) 1 49
(Bernard Llewellyn) *nvr far away: rdn over 2f out: styd on fnl f: wnt 3rd post* **20/1**
0025 **4** *hd* **Rowlestone Lad**[14] 3406 6-8-10 **56**................ DanielMuscutt(7) 6 59
(John Flint) *t.k.h: trckd ldrs: rdn and ev ch 2f out: no ex fnl f: lost 3rd post* **7/1**
413/ **5** *1 ½* **Schelm (GER)**[16] 3359 11-9-6 **59**................ ShaneKelly 3 60
(Ronald O'Leary, Ire) *in rr of mid-div: clsd 4f out: styd on u.p fnl 2f: nt rch ldrs* **20/1**
-050 **6** *1 ½* **Lucky Diva**[28] 2921 6-9-0 **58**................(v[1]) JakePayne(5) 9 58+
(Bill Turner) *s.s: hld up in rr: rdn 3f out: swtchd rt over 2f out: styd on one pce* **25/1**
4605 **7** *2 ¾* **Zafaraban (IRE)**[8] 1916 6-8-10 **54** ow2................(p) GeorgeDowning(5) 12 50
(Tony Carroll) *hld up in rr: rdn over 3f out: styd on fnl 2f: nvr trbld ldrs* **33/1**
/0-4 **8** *2* **Venir Rouge**[23] 3110 9-8-11 **55**................ RosieJessop(5) 2 49
(Harry Whittington) *in rr of mid-div: sme hdwy u.p 5f out: no further imp on ldrs fnl 3f* **20/1**
2221 **9** *2* **If I Had Him (IRE)**[7] 3647 9-9-13 **66** 6ex................(v) JamieSpencer 10 62
(George Baker) *trckd ldr: rdn to chal 3f out: no ex over 1f out: eased whn btn ins fnl f* **3/1**[1]
2425 **10** *4 ½* **Fuzzy Logic (IRE)**[17] 3271 4-8-2 **48**................ OisinMurphy(7) 8 34
(Bernard Llewellyn) *mid-div: rdn 5f out: wknd over 1f out* **7/2**[2]
006 **11** *1 ¾* **Celtic Legacy**[26] 2995 6-8-8 **52**................ MichaelJMMurphy(5) 5 36
(Michael Murphy) *chsd ldrs early: mid-div after 2f: effrt 4f out: wknd over 2f out* **33/1**
3440 **12** *4 ½* **Ctappers**[17] 3271 4-8-10 **56**................ DanielCremin(7) 11 35
(Mick Channon) *hld up in rr: rdn 4f out: struggling fnl 2f* **14/1**

3m 29.58s (-0.42) **Going Correction** -0.175s/f (Firm) course record **12** Ran SP% **120.1**
Speed ratings (Par 101): **94,92,91,91,91 90,88,87,86,84 83,81**
toteswingers 1&2 £5.50, 1&3 £27.80, 2&3 £14.20 CSF £35.24 CT £624.83 TOTE £7.30: £2.50, £2.40, £6.50; EX 43.00 Trifecta £781.40 Part won. Pool: £1041.90 - 0.40 winning tickets..
Owner Nick Shutts **Bred** Michael Dalton **Trained** Pandy, Monmouths

FOCUS
A weak staying handicap, run at an average pace until they straightened up for home. The first four were always prominent.

3885 THREE RIVERS H'CAP 1m (R)
7:45 (7:45) (Class 6) (0-60,58) 3-Y-0+ **£1,940** (£577; £288; £144) **Stalls** Low

Form RPR
-043 **1** **Greyemkay**[11] 3513 5-8-10 **49**................ DanielMuscutt(7) 5 57
(Richard Price) *mid-div: hdwy over 2f out: led over 1f out: rdn out to hold on* **3/1**[2]
0100 **2** *nk* **For Shia And Lula (IRE)**[11] 3513 4-9-9 **55**................(p) ShaneKelly 2 62
(Daniel Mark Loughnane) *hld up towards rr: clsd 3f out: nt clr run over 2f out: let down appr fnl f: r.o: jst hld* **12/1**
0-64 **3** *¾* **Choral Rhythm (IRE)**[24] 3041 3-7-11 **45**................ JoeyHaynes(7) 9 48
(Tony Carroll) *in rr: pushed along and hdwy 3f out: pressed wnr over 1f out: kpt on* **16/1**
6100 **4** *1 ½* **Spinning Ridge (IRE)**[11] 3513 8-9-11 **57**................(b) WilliamCarson 6 59
(Ronald Harris) *s.s: in rr: clsd 3f out: nt clr run over 1f out: kpt on fnl f* **25/1**
-041 **5** *2 ½* **Wyndham Wave**[5] 3687 4-9-1 **54**................(p) PatMillman(7) 1 50
(Rod Millman) *trckd ldrs: n.m.r after 2f: rdn 2f out: one pce* **5/2**[1]
-005 **6** *shd* **Wordismybond**[11] 3511 4-9-12 **58**................ SteveDrowne 4 54
(Peter Makin) *led after 1f: rdn 2f out: hdd over 1f out: wknd* **5/1**
0-03 **7** *9* **Maisie's Moon (USA)**[20] 3178 3-9-1 **56**................(p) LiamKeniry 7 29
(Hughie Morrison) *trckd ldrs: rdn over 2f out: wknd over 1f out* **7/2**[3]
0-20 **8** *14* **Mr Udagawa**[16] 3314 7-8-8 **47**................(p) OisinMurphy(7) 3
(Bernard Llewellyn) *led 1f: styd prom: drvn over 2f out: wknd over 1f out: t.o* **16/1**

1m 39.23s (-1.77) **Going Correction** -0.175s/f (Firm)
WFA 3 from 4yo+ 9lb **8** Ran SP% **115.8**
Speed ratings (Par 101): **101,100,99,98,95 95,86,72**
toteswingers 1&2 £5.50, 1&3 £27.80, 2&3 £14.20 CSF £38.66 CT £501.31 TOTE £4.70: £2.10, £1.30, £1.40; EX 30.70 Trifecta £482.50 Part won. Pool: £643.37 - 0.82 winning tickets..
Owner Richard Price & Maria Slade **Bred** Shade Oak Stud **Trained** Ullingswick, H'fords

FOCUS
An ordinary handicap.

3886 LONETREE LTD MCDONALDS H'CAP 1m (R)
8:15 (8:15) (Class 4) (0-80,80) 3-Y-0+ **£4,690** (£1,395; £697; £348) **Stalls** Low

Form RPR
0312 **1** **Cruiser**[11] 3492 5-9-11 **77**................(p) MartinDwyer 5 82
(William Muir) *in tch in 4th: rdn 3f out: r.o u.p fnl f to ld last strides* **3/1**[2]
3520 **2** *hd* **Storming (IRE)**[17] 3294 3-8-10 **71**................(p) JamieSpencer 2 73
(Andrew Balding) *led: rdn wl over 1f out: sn hrd pressed: battled on wl: hdd last strides* **9/4**[1]
0140 **3** *hd* **Prime Exhibit**[16] 3349 8-9-9 **75**................(t) ShaneKelly 7 79
(Daniel Mark Loughnane) *hld up in last: hdwy to chse ldrs 2f out: r.o ins fnl f: wnt 3rd last strides* **14/1**
0005 **4** *nk* **Yojimbo (IRE)**[23] 3108 5-9-12 **78**................ MatthewDavies 3 81
(Mick Channon) *chsd ldr: rdn over 2f out: r.o u.p fnl f: jst hld and lost 3rd last strides* **11/2**
4113 **5** *2* **Peak Storm**[10] 3534 4-9-2 **68**................ WilliamCarson 6 67
(John O'Shea) *towards rr: rdn and clsd on ldrs over 2f out: one pce fnl f* **9/2**[3]
0533 **6** *17* **Ertikaan**[23] 3108 6-9-11 **80**................(tp) BrendanPowell(3) 4 40
(Brendan Powell) *chsd ldrs tl rdn and nt qckn over 2f out: sn wknd: t.o* **5/1**

1m 38.41s (-2.59) **Going Correction** -0.175s/f (Firm)
WFA 3 from 4yo+ 9lb **6** Ran SP% **112.7**
Speed ratings (Par 105): **105,104,104,104,102 85**
toteswingers 1&2 £1.10, 1&3 £5.00, 2&3 £3.00 CSF £10.27 TOTE £2.40: £1.40, £2.80; EX 9.90 Trifecta £106.90 Pool: £838.92 - 5.88 winning tickets..
Owner C L A Edginton **Bred** The Hill Stud **Trained** Lambourn, Berks

FOCUS
This modest handicap was run at a decent pace and it saw a blanket four-way finish.

3887 WALTERS UK H'CAP 6f
8:45 (8:46) (Class 4) (0-80,81) 3-Y-0+ **£4,690** (£1,395; £697; £348) **Stalls** Centre

Form RPR
3655 **1** **Swendab (IRE)**[17] 3270 5-8-9 **62**................(v) FergusSweeney 6 75
(John O'Shea) *mde all: shkn up appr fnl f: edgd lft and r.o strly to draw clr* **3/1**[3]
5021 **2** *6* **Sand Boy (IRE)**[9] 3566 3-9-6 **79**................ SteveDrowne 1 72
(Charles Hills) *hld up in last: rdn to go 2nd over 1f out: sn edgd lft and outpcd by wnr* **1/1**[1]
0001 **3** *2 ¼* **Jack My Boy (IRE)**[7] 3622 6-9-9 **81** 6ex................(b) DeclanBates(5) 2 68
(David Evans) *racd in 3rd: rdn over 2f out: briefly disp 2nd over 1f out but sn outpcd by ldrs* **5/2**[2]
4230 **4** *8* **Novabridge**[24] 3042 5-8-13 **66**................(p) LiamKeniry 5 34
(Neil Mulholland) *chsd wnr: pushed along over 2f out: wknd over 1f out* **8/1**

1m 8.37s (-1.63) **Going Correction** -0.25s/f (Firm)
WFA 3 from 5yo+ 6lb **4** Ran SP% **114.7**
Speed ratings (Par 105): **100,92,89,78**
CSF £6.93 TOTE £5.10; EX 9.00 Trifecta £11.30 Pool: £468.77 - 30.97 winning tickets..
Owner The Cross Racing Club & Patrick Brady **Bred** P Brady **Trained** Elton, Gloucs

FOCUS
A modest sprint handicap. They went a fair pace and predictably kept the middle of the track.

3888 STRADEY PARK H'CAP 5f
9:15 (9:15) (Class 6) (0-65,70) 3-Y-0+ **£1,940** (£577; £288; £144) **Stalls** Centre

Form RPR
4111 **1** **Nafa (IRE)**[11] 3498 5-9-11 **63**................ ShaneKelly 5 78
(Daniel Mark Loughnane) *wl in tch: pushed along to ld appr fnl f: r.o strly* **6/1**[3]
-002 **2** *3* **Griffin Point (IRE)**[7] 3623 6-9-6 **58**................(b) MartinDwyer 6 62
(William Muir) *led 1f: styd prom: rdn 2f out: kpt on: outpcd by wnr fnl f* **7/1**
1-01 **3** *1 ¼* **Steel Rain**[7] 3623 5-9-6 **65** 6ex................ OisinMurphy(7) 2 65
(Nikki Evans) *chsd ldrs: rdn to ld over 1f out: sn hdd: kpt on* **4/1**[2]
-060 **4** *½* **Samba Night (IRE)**[11] 3499 4-9-0 **52**................(bt[1]) SteveDrowne 12 50
(Jeremy Gask) *in rr: rdn over 1f out: r.o ins fnl f: nvr nrr* **50/1**
0306 **5** *nk* **Brandywell Boy (IRE)**[6] 3667 10-8-4 **47**................ MichaelJMMurphy(5) 10 44
(Dominic Ffrench Davis) *in rr and sn chsd along: r.o ins fnl f: nvr trbld ldrs* **25/1**
5400 **6** *nk* **Ingleby Star (IRE)**[38] 2632 8-9-6 **63**................(p) DeclanBates(5) 11 59
(Daniel Mark Loughnane) *chsd ldrs: rdn and outpcd by principals over 1f out: styd on ins fnl f* **20/1**
4310 **7** *½* **Russian Bullet**[6] 3660 4-8-11 **49**................(b) FergusSweeney 8 43
(Jamie Osborne) *cl up: led after 1f: hdd over 1f out: sn hung rt and one pce* **16/1**
0003 **8** *nse* **Winnie Perry**[4] 3732 3-9-2 **59**................ LiamKeniry 9 53
(Rod Millman) *chsd ldrs: rdn over 1f out: one pce* **16/1**
2536 **9** *1 ½* **Spic 'n Span**[30] 2873 8-9-0 **52**................(be) WilliamCarson 7 40
(Ronald Harris) *taken to post early: s.s: sn racing keenly in tch: rdn over 1f out: kpt on same pce* **14/1**
0312 **10** *¾* **Silca's Dream**[4] 3732 3-9-6 **70** 6ex................ DanielCremin(7) 3 55
(Mick Channon) *mid-div: rdn 1/2-way: wknd ins fnl f* **7/2**[1]
-660 **11** *5* **Copper Leyf**[18] 3247 3-8-5 **51**................ RyanClark(3) 1 18
(Jeremy Gask) *in tch: rdn over 1f out: wknd fnl f* **40/1**
2532 **12** *2 ½* **Haadeeth**[4] 3716 6-9-3 **62**................ EoinWalsh(7) 4 20+
(David Evans) *taken to post early: got nose wedgd in bars of stall and missed break: rdn and edgd lft 1/2-way: nvr on terms* **7/2**[1]

56.63s (-1.67) **Going Correction** -0.25s/f (Firm)
WFA 3 from 4yo+ 5lb **12** Ran SP% **122.7**
Speed ratings (Par 101): **103,98,96,95,94 94,93,93,91,89 81,77**
toteswingers 1&2 £8.90, 1&3 £4.70, 2&3 £5.70 CSF £47.62 CT £193.23 TOTE £6.00: £1.60, £2.90, £1.50; EX 31.50 Trifecta £163.00 Pool: £831.59 - 3.82 winning tickets..
Owner Ian O'Connor **Bred** Basil Brindley **Trained** Baldwin's Gate, Staffs

FOCUS
A wide-open sprint handicap and again the centre was the place to be.
T/Jkpt: Not won. T/Plt: £648.80 to a £1 stake. Pool: £100,978.51 - 113.61 winning tickets T/Qpdt: £96.20 to a £1 stake. Pool: £8803.51 - 67.70 winning tickets RL

3605 PONTEFRACT (L-H)
Monday, July 1

OFFICIAL GOING: Good (good to firm in places)
Wind: moderate half behind Weather: Cloudy

3889 PATRICIA GEORGE MEMORIAL LADIES' H'CAP (LADY AMATEUR RIDERS) 1m 2f 6y
2:30 (2:31) (Class 5) (0-75,74) 3-Y-0+ **£3,119** (£967; £483; £242) **Stalls** Low

Form RPR
01-1 **1** **Tapis Libre**[38] 2629 5-10-3 **70**................ MissJCoward 6 78
(Michael Easterby) *trckd ldr on inner: effrt wl over 1f out: rdn and qcknd on inner to ld jst ins fnl f: hld on wl* **13/2**[3]
0321 **2** *¾* **El Bravo**[2] 3808 7-9-6 **64** 6ex................ AnnaHesketh(5) 8 71
(Shaun Harris) *trckd ldrs on inner: hdwy over 2f out: swtchd rt and rdn over 1f out: chal and n.m.r ent fnl f: squeezed through to chse wnr ins fnl f: kpt on* **8/1**
-064 **3** *1 ¼* **Rub Of The Relic (IRE)**[11] 3504 8-9-1 **59**................(v) MissHDukes(5) 5 63
(Paul Midgley) *led: pushed along 3f out: jnd and rdn wl over 1f out: drvn and hdd jst ins fnl f: kpt on u.p* **14/1**
4631 **4** *½* **Tenhoo**[18] 3231 7-10-3 **70**................ MissCWalton 2 73
(Eric Alston) *t.k.h early: hld up in rr: hdwy over 3f out: rdn to chse ldrs over 1f out: styd on fnl f: nrst fin* **10/3**[2]
1105 **5** *shd* **Jordaura**[18] 3231 7-9-10 **66**................ MissJRRichards(3) 1 69
(Alan Berry) *hld up and bhd: hdwy on inner 3f out: rdn over 1f out: squeezed through and styd on fnl f: nrst fin* **22/1**

6440 **6** 3 1/2 **Flag Of Glory**[23] 3106 6-9-2 **60** .... MissMEdden(5) 7 56
(Peter Hiatt) *trckd ldng pair: hdwy and cl up 3f out: rdn to chal wl over 1f out and ev ch tl wknd ins fnl f* **20/1**

6041 **7** 3 3/4 **Beauchamp Xerxes**[7] 3642 7-9-10 **68** 6ex .... (t) MissLCGriffiths(5) 9 56
(Hans Adielsson) *trckd ldrs: hdwy on outer 4f out: chsd ldng pair over 2f out: rdn along on outer wl over 1f out: grad wknd* **20/1**

00-1 **8** 3/4 **City Ground (USA)**[30] 2875 6-9-9 **62** .... MissSBrotherton 4 49
(Michael Easterby) *trckd ldrs: hdwy 4f out: rdn along over 2f out: sn wknd* **5/2**[1]

0230 **9** hd **Merchant Of Medici**[16] 3349 6-10-1 **68** .... MissADeniel 10 54
(Micky Hammond) *t.k.h early: hld up towards rr: hdwy over 4f out: rdn along on outer 3f out: wknd over 2f out* **7/1**

600/ **10** 3 1/4 **Winged Farasi**[475] 4605 9-8-13 **55** oh10 .... MissAliceMills(3) 11 35
(Joanne Foster) *a in rr* **100/1**

166- **11** 7 **Archie Rice (USA)**[461] 529 7-10-2 **74** .... MissKMargarson(5) 3 40
(Tom Keddy) *hld up towards rr: effrt and sme hdwy 4f out: rdn along over 3f out: sn wknd* **50/1**

2m 15.72s (2.02) **Going Correction** +0.05s/f (Good) 11 Ran SP% **112.1**
Speed ratings (Par 103): **93,92,91,91,90 88,85,84,84,81 76**
toteswingers 1&2 £5.20, 1&3 £10.60, 2&3 £13.90 CSF £50.61 CT £695.54 TOTE £7.20: £2.80, £4.10, £3.90; EX 54.60 Trifecta £617.00 Pool: £2142.73 - 2.60 winning tickets..
Owner Mrs Susan E Mason **Bred** Sedgecroft Stud **Trained** Sheriff Hutton, N Yorks
■ Stewards' Enquiry : Miss M Edden caution: careless riding

FOCUS
A modest lady amateurs' handicap, but the pace was solid.

3890 SPINDRIFTER CONDITIONS STKS 6f
3:00 (3:00) (Class 2) 2-Y-O **£9,337** (£2,796; £1,398; £699) **Stalls** Low

Form RPR
15 **1** **Cool Bahamian (IRE)**[30] 2863 2-8-12 0 .... JohnFahy 2 88
(Eve Johnson Houghton) *trckd ldrs: hdwy and cl up 3f out: led wl over 1f out: rdn and edgd rt and lft ins fnl f: styd on* **9/2**[2]

331 **2** nk **Fair Ranger**[15] 3366 2-8-10 0 .... PatDobbs 5 85
(Richard Hannon) *cl up on outer: pushed along and outpcd over 2f out: swtchd lft and rdn wl over 1f out: styd on to chal wl ins fnl f: ev ch tl drvn and nt qckn nr fin* **9/2**[2]

1 **3** 3/4 **Rufford (IRE)**[16] 3350 2-8-12 0 .... TonyHamilton 3 85
(Richard Fahey) *cl up: pushed along 3f out: hung rt on home turn: sn rdn to chal: drvn and ev ch ins fnl f: edgd lft and no ex last 50yds* **4/7**[1]

10 **4** 12 **Pigeon Pie**[30] 2877 2-8-7 0 .... SilvestreDeSousa 1 44
(Mark Johnston) *led: rdn along over 2f out: hdd wl over 1f out: sn wknd* **12/1**[3]

1m 17.94s (1.04) **Going Correction** +0.05s/f (Good) 4 Ran SP% **107.7**
Speed ratings (Par 100): **95,94,93,77**
CSF £21.50 TOTE £5.70; EX 20.70 Trifecta £23.60 Pool: £1437.36 - 45.62 winning tickets..
Owner L R Godfrey & R F Johnson Houghton **Bred** Kildaragh Stud **Trained** Blewbury, Oxon
■ Stewards' Enquiry : Pat Dobbs two-day ban: use of whip (15-16 July)

FOCUS
This event usually features a small but select field and it has been a good race for favourites, with seven of the last ten market leaders successful. However, those who supported the odds-on favourite this time got their fingers burnt. The pace looked decent and the form is up to scratch for the race.

3891 DAVID WATERS - A LIFETIME IN RACING FILLIES' H'CAP 1m 4f 8y
3:30 (3:30) (Class 4) (0-85,82) 3-Y-O+ **£5,175** (£1,540; £769; £384) **Stalls** Low

Form RPR
2-12 **1** **Centred (IRE)**[38] 2619 3-9-1 **82** .... FrannyNorton 5 95+
(Sir Michael Stoute) *trckd ldr: cl up 3f out: led 2f out: rdn over 1f out: kpt on strly u.p fnl f* **11/8**[1]

0406 **2** 2 1/2 **Bollin Greta**[17] 3284 8-9-4 **72** .... DuranFentiman 3 81
(Tim Easterby) *hld up in rr: tk clsr order over 3f out: effrt 2f out: sn rdn to chse wnr: drvn and no imp ins fnl f* **20/1**[3]

2351 **3** 5 **Huffoof (IRE)**[8] 3610 3-8-11 **78** 6ex .... (b) SilvestreDeSousa 1 81
(Roger Varian) *trckd ldng pair: hdwy on outer and cl up 2f out: sn rdn and one pce fr over 1f out* **11/8**[1]

0-33 **4** 13 **Wadaa (USA)**[17] 3272 3-8-9 **76** .... NeilCallan 4 67
(James Tate) *t.k.h: led: pushed along 3f out: rdn and hdd 2f out: sn wknd* **9/2**[2]

2m 40.13s (-0.67) **Going Correction** +0.05s/f (Good)
WFA 3 from 4yo+ 13lb 4 Ran SP% **107.2**
Speed ratings (Par 102): **104,102,99,90**
CSF £19.98 TOTE £2.00; EX 15.30 Trifecta £35.70 Pool: £1180.07 - 24.75 winning tickets..
Owner Ballymacoll Stud **Bred** Ballymacoll Stud Farm Ltd **Trained** Newmarket, Suffolk

FOCUS
Despite just the four runners, they appeared to go a decent pace and this looked a proper test at the trip.

3892 EBF/KYLE AKAM CYSTIC FIBROSIS TRUST MEMORIAL FILLIES' H'CAP 6f
4:00 (4:00) (Class 3) (0-90,90) 3-Y-O+
£9,337 (£2,097; £2,097; £699; £349; £175) **Stalls** Low

Form RPR
0330 **1** **Love Island**[15] 3367 4-9-1 **82** .... (p) GeorgeChaloner(5) 7 94
(Richard Whitaker) *slt ld on outer: rdn clr over 1f out: styd on strly* **6/1**

6440 **2** 4 **Misplaced Fortune**[18] 3249 8-9-9 **90** .... (v) JasonHart(5) 6 89
(Nigel Tinkler) *trckd ldrs: hdwy to chse ldng pair wl over 1f out: sn rdn: drvn and kpt on fnl f* **4/1**[3]

1-52 **2** dht **Rivas Rhapsody (IRE)**[14] 3407 5-9-9 **85** .... SilvestreDeSousa 3 84
(Rae Guest) *cl up on inner: rdn along over 2f out: drvn over 1f out: kpt on same pce* **7/2**[2]

-031 **4** 1 3/4 **Midnight Dynamo**[9] 3561 6-9-2 **78** .... GrahamLee 1 72
(Jim Goldie) *hld up in tch: hdwy 2f out: sn rdn and no imp fnl f* **4/1**[3]

10-0 **5** shd **Perfect Blossom**[9] 3562 6-9-9 **85** .... RobertWinston 4 78
(Alan Berry) *awkward s and in rr: hdwy 2f out: sn rdn and kpt on fnl f* **25/1**

0214 **6** 5 **Fanrouge (IRE)**[4] 3720 4-9-9 **85** .... DanielTudhope 2 62
(Rod Millman) *chsd ldng pair: rdn along 2f out: sn wknd* **3/1**[1]

4034 **7** 3 3/4 **Ray Of Joy**[5] 3691 7-8-11 **73** .... PatDobbs 5 38
(J R Jenkins) *a towards rr: rdn along over 2f out: sn outpcd* **14/1**

1m 16.9s **Going Correction** +0.05s/f (Good) 7 Ran SP% **112.0**
Speed ratings (Par 104): **102,96,96,94,94 87,82**Tote PL: MF £1.30, RR £0.80; EX: LI/MF £15.50, LI/RR £19.90; Trifecta: LI/MF/RR £93.50, LI/RR/MF £98.40; CSF LI/MF £14.38, LI/RR £13.02; toteswingers LI&MF £3.90, LI&RR £4.70, MF&RR £3.20 TOTE £6.70: £2.80 TRIFECTA Pool: £4338.38 - 17.39 winni27 Owner.
■ Stewards' Enquiry : George Chaloner rainer's representative said, regarding the apparent improvement of form, that the filly benefited from the application of first time cheek pieces

FOCUS
A decent prize for this fillies' handicap but, strangely for a sprint, they went no pace early and that played into the hands of those who raced prominently.

3893 WAYNE CONWAY MEMORIAL H'CAP 1m 4f 8y
4:30 (4:31) (Class 5) (0-70,70) 3-Y-O **£3,234** (£962; £481; £240) **Stalls** Low

Form RPR
425 **1** **Danehill Flyer (IRE)**[35] 2716 3-9-0 **63** .... MichaelO'Connell 4 76+
(Philip Kirby) *trckd ldng pair on inner: hdwy to ld over 2f out: rdn clr wl over 1f out: styd on strly* **7/2**[1]

3142 **2** 1 1/2 **Astrum**[18] 3232 3-9-4 **67** .... DanielTudhope 2 75
(Rod Millman) *hld up towards rr: stdy hdwy over 4f out: trckd ldrs 3f out: rdn to chse wnr over 1f out: kpt on u.p fnl f: nt trble wnr* **9/2**[2]

5534 **3** 3 3/4 **Attention Seaker**[14] 3394 3-9-0 **63** .... DuranFentiman 8 65
(Tim Easterby) *hld up towards rr: hdwy over 3f out: rdn over 2f out: styd on appr fnl f: nrst fin* **20/1**

-061 **4** 1 1/4 **Spats Colombo**[14] 3394 3-8-2 **51** .... FrannyNorton 12 51+
(Micky Hammond) *hld up: hdwy 3f out: rdn along 2f out: kpt on appr fnl f: nrst fin* **9/2**[2]

20-0 **5** 1/2 **Tobacco**[35] 2716 3-8-2 **51** oh2 .... PaulQuinn 1 50
(Tim Easterby) *hld up in rr: hdwy 3f out: in tch and rdn whn swtchd lft wl over 1f out: kpt on fnl f: nrst fin* **25/1**

401 **6** 2 3/4 **World Map (IRE)**[5] 3675 3-8-12 **61** 6ex .... SilvestreDeSousa 5 56
(Mark Johnston) *trckd ldrs: rdn along wl over 2f out: drvn and edgd lft wl over 1f out: sn btn* **5/1**[3]

2600 **7** 1 3/4 **Tinctoria**[12] 3463 3-8-6 **55** .... (p) AmyRyan 7 47
(Kevin Ryan) *led: rdn along 3f out: sn hdd: drvn wl over 1f out: grad wknd* **40/1**

00-6 **8** 8 **Star Of Missouri**[24] 3055 3-8-11 **60** .... GrahamLee 13 39
(Mark H Tompkins) *hld up towards rr: sme hdwy over 4f out: rdn along and wknd over 3f out* **14/1**

0334 **9** 5 **Halfwaytocootehill (IRE)**[6] 3653 3-7-13 **51** .... (t) NeilFarley(3) 10 22
(Ollie Pears) *t.k.h: chsd ldrs on outer rdn along 3f out: sn wknd* **11/2**

4-60 **10** 7 **Bahamamay**[18] 3232 3-8-13 **62** .... TonyHamilton 11 22
(Richard Fahey) *cl up: rdn along 3f out: wknd over 2f out* **33/1**

0-00 **11** 4 **Noosa Sound**[19] 3194 3-7-13 **51** oh2 .... DeclanCannon(3) 3
(John Davies) *chsd ldrs on inner: rdn along over 3f out: drvn over 2f out: grad wknd* **50/1**

6140 **12** 64 **Burgoyne (USA)**[49] 2322 3-9-7 **70** .... (b) RobertWinston 6
(Hughie Morrison) *a in rr: bhd and eased fnl 2f* **33/1**

2m 41.48s (0.68) **Going Correction** +0.05s/f (Good) 12 Ran SP% **116.2**
Speed ratings (Par 100): **99,98,95,94,94 92,91,86,82,78 75,32**
toteswingers 1&2 £4.20, 1&3 £11.10, 2&3 £8.30 CSF £17.13 CT £273.91 TOTE £4.40: £1.30, £1.60, £4.10; EX 20.40 Trifecta £235.20 Pool: £3535.49 - 11.26 winning tickets..
Owner Mrs Jayne Sivills **Bred** Edmond Kent **Trained** Middleham, N Yorks

FOCUS
A modest middle-distance handicap and, with the early pace not strong, the winning time was 1.35sec slower than the earlier fillies' handicap.

3894 WILFRED UNDERWOOD MEMORIAL CLASSIFIED STKS 6f
5:00 (5:00) (Class 5) 3-Y-O **£3,234** (£962; £481; £240) **Stalls** Low

Form RPR
6-12 **1** **Noble Deed**[7] 3634 3-9-0 74 .... SilvestreDeSousa 6 88+
(William Haggas) *cl up: led 1/2-way: rdn clr wl over 1f out: readily* **5/6**[1]

3212 **2** 4 1/2 **Nurpur (IRE)**[12] 3478 3-9-0 74 .... (v1) DanielTudhope 3 74
(David O'Meara) *hld up: hdwy on inner 2f out: rdn wl over 1f out: styd on fnl f: tk 2nd nr fin* **5/2**[2]

0105 **3** nk **Khelman (IRE)**[26] 2987 3-9-0 74 .... TonyHamilton 4 73
(Richard Fahey) *trckd ldrs: hdwy to chse wnr wl over 1f out: sn rdn and no imp: lost 2nd towards fin* **6/1**[3]

40-3 **4** 3 3/4 **Shillito**[7] 3626 3-9-0 74 .... GrahamLee 1 61
(Tony Coyle) *slt ld on inner: hdd 1/2-way and sn pushed along: rdn over 2f out: sn drvn and wknd* **14/1**

1-04 **5** 12 **Star Up In The Sky (USA)**[21] 3160 3-9-0 74 .... AmyRyan 2 23
(Kevin Ryan) *prom 2f: sn pushed along: outpcd and bhd fr over 2f out* **20/1**

1m 16.41s (-0.49) **Going Correction** +0.05s/f (Good) 5 Ran SP% **108.8**
Speed ratings (Par 100): **105,99,98,93,77**
CSF £3.02 TOTE £2.10: £1.70, £1.40; EX 3.30 Trifecta £6.70 Pool: £3723.14 - 415.61 winning tickets..
Owner Cheveley Park Stud **Bred** Cheveley Park Stud Ltd **Trained** Newmarket, Suffolk

FOCUS
An ordinary classified event in which all five runners were rated 74, but the differences in their respective abilities were plain to see. The winning time was the fastest of the three 6f races on the card.

3895 MICKY HAMMOND PROUDLY SPONSORED BY QUOTELINE DIRECT H'CAP 1m 4y
5:30 (5:30) (Class 5) (0-75,75) 3-Y-O+ **£3,234** (£962; £481; £240) **Stalls** Low

Form RPR
6011 **1** **Talent Scout (IRE)**[19] 3192 7-9-7 **75** .... (p) GemmaTutty(7) 2 88
(Karen Tutty) *t.k.h: set str pce: pushed clr wl over 1f out: rdn ent fnl f: jst hld on* **7/2**[1]

0331 **2** nk **Lord Franklin**[19] 3203 4-8-8 **60** .... JasonHart(5) 11 72
(Eric Alston) *trckd ldng pair: hdwy to chse wnr 2 1/2f out: rdn wl over 1f out: drvn and styd on wl fnl f: jst hld* **7/1**[3]

5234 **3** 8 **Cabal**[16] 3337 6-8-6 **56** oh2 .... (v1) NeilFarley(3) 10 50
(Andrew Crook) *hld up towards rr: hdwy over 2f out: rdn on wd outside over 1f out: styd on fnl f* **33/1**

5546 **4** 2 1/2 **Keep It Dark**[13] 3445 4-9-3 **64** .... GrahamLee 7 52
(Tony Coyle) *towards rr: hdwy on inner 2f out: sn rdn and n.d* **10/1**

0-02 **5** nk **Icy Blue**[28] 2911 5-8-4 **58** .... (p) NoelGarbutt(7) 12 45
(Richard Whitaker) *dwlt and in rr tl styd on fnl 2f: n.d* **9/1**

3650 **6** nk **Cyflymder (IRE)**[10] 3534 7-9-5 **66** .... KirstyMilczarek 4 52
(David C Griffiths) *nvr bttr than midfield* **33/1**

-001 **7** 1 1/4 **Dubious Escapade (IRE)**[14] 3395 4-9-8 **69** .... (p) PJMcDonald 3 55
(Ann Duffield) *in tch: rdn along wl over 2f out: n.m.r wl over 1f out: sn wknd* **8/1**

620 **8** 1 1/4 **Flying Applause**[67] 1775 8-9-7 **71** .... (b) MarkCoumbe(3) 8 52
(Roy Bowring) *dwlt and in rr: hdwy on outer to chse ldrs 1/2-way: rdn along 3f out: sn wknd* **33/1**

-350 **9** 1 **Eastlands Lad (IRE)**[38] 2616 4-8-12 **59** .... (p) TomEaves 1 37
(Micky Hammond) *chsd ldrs on inner: rdn along over 2f out: sn wknd* **20/1**

3032 **10** *1* **Cono Zur (FR)**^{11} 3506 6-9-1 **67** ... LMcNiff$^{(5)}$ 5 43
(Ruth Carr) *chsd ldrs: rdn along over 2f out: drvn and wknd wl over 1f out* **5/1^{2}**

25-0 **11** *6* **Daddy Warbucks (IRE)**^{16} 3349 4-10-0 **75** ... AndrewMullen 6 42
(David Nicholls) *cl up: rdn along over 3f out: sn wknd* **5/1^{2}**

5050 **12** *9* **Sareeah (IRE)**^{6} 3649 4-9-2 **63** ... (v^{1}) DanielTudhope 9
(David O'Meara) *midfield: rdn along 3f out: sn wknd* **11/1**

1m 45.38s (-0.52) **Going Correction** +0.05s/f (Good) **12** Ran SP% **120.2**
Speed ratings (Par 103): **104,103,95,93,92 92,91,90,89,88 82,73**
toteswingers 1&2 £6.30, 1&3 £26.80, 2&3 £19.10 CSF £27.24 CT £694.46 TOTE £4.10: £1.40, £3.10, £10.70; EX 34.00 Trifecta £424.90 Pool: £3091.73 - 5.45 winning tickets..
Owner Thoroughbred Homes Ltd **Bred** Johnston King **Trained** Osmotherley, N Yorks

FOCUS
Another race dominated by those who raced up with the pace.
T/Plt: £270.20 to a £1 stake. Pool: £68,458.62 - 184.90 winning tickets T/Qpdt: £9.10 to a £1 stake. Pool: £5441.41 - 439.61 winning tickets JR

3860 WINDSOR (R-H)

Monday, July 1

OFFICIAL GOING: Good to firm (good in places)
Wind: Moderate, half behind Weather: Fine, warm

3896 EBF/TOTEPOOL MOBILE TEXT TOTE TO 89660 FILLIES' MEDIAN AUCTION MAIDEN STKS 5f 10y
6:00 (6:01) (Class 5) 2-Y-O **£2,911** (£866; £432; £216) **Stalls** Low

Form RPR

1 **La Tinta Bay** 2-9-0 0 ... RyanMoore 7 72+
(Richard Hannon) *chsd ldng pair: pushed along 1/2-way: clsd fr 2f out: led and reminder 1f out: styd on: readily* **5/1^{2}**

443 **2** *½* **Prisca**^{16} 3318 2-9-0 0 ... RichardHughes 4 69
(Richard Hannon) *led against nr side rail: shkn up 2f out: hdd 1f out: kpt on but readily hld* **5/6^{1}**

3 *1 ½* **Ajig** 2-9-0 0 ... JoeFanning 2 64+
(Eve Johnson Houghton) *s.i.s: sn in tch on outer: shkn up 2f out: kpt on to take 3rd fnl f* **8/1**

4 *½* **Skinny Love** 2-9-0 0 ... JamesDoyle 1 62+
(Robert Cowell) *dwlt: prog fr last trio 1/2-way: shkn up to chse ldrs over 1f out: edgd lft and one pce fnl f* **10/1**

5 *2 ½* **Neuf Des Coeurs** 2-9-0 0 ... PatCosgrave 5 55+
(George Baker) *slowest away: off the pce in last pair: prog 2f out: rchd 5th fnl f but no ch: eased nr fin: nt disgracd* **20/1**

6 *2 ½* **Sing Out Sister** 2-9-0 0 ... SamHitchcott 6 44
(Mick Channon) *pressed ldr but rn green: lost 2nd wl over 1f out: wknd* **6/1^{3}**

50 **7** *1 ¾* **Mystic Angellina**^{6} 3648 2-9-0 0 ... RenatoSouza 3 38
(Michael Chapman) *chsd ldrs to 1/2-way: sn lost pl and btn* **200/1**

8 *8* **Clear Focus (IRE)** 2-9-0 0 ... JackMitchell 8 9
(Brendan Powell) *rn green: sn dropped to last pair and pushed along: t.o* **20/1**

1m 1.63s (1.33) **Going Correction** +0.025s/f (Good) **8** Ran SP% **115.7**
Speed ratings (Par 91): **90,89,86,86,82 78,75,62**
toteswingers 1&2 £1.80, 1&3 £8.00, 2&3 £2.90 CSF £9.54 TOTE £7.00: £1.70, £1.10, £2.40; EX 12.60 Trifecta £59.60 Pool: £12419.78 - 156.16 winning tickets..
Owner J R Shannon **Bred** J R Shannon **Trained** East Everleigh, Wilts

FOCUS
The going was good to firm, good in places. Only two of the field had experience in this fillies' maiden. The form is pitched towards the bottom end of the race averages.

3897 PROGRESSIVE CASINO JACKPOTS AT TOTEPOOL.COM (S) STKS 6f
6:30 (6:30) (Class 6) 3-Y-O+ **£1,940** (£577; £288; £144) **Stalls** Low

Form RPR

-556 **1** **Nenge Mboko**^{34} 2738 3-8-10 73 ... (v^{1}) RichardHughes 1 75+
(George Baker) *trckd ldrs: wnt 2nd 2f out: jnd ldr and gng wl jst over 1f out: cajoled along vigorously to take narrow ld ins fnl f* **10/11^{1}**

2000 **2** *shd* **We Have A Dream**^{14} 3415 8-9-2 70 ... GeorgeBaker 4 75
(William Muir) *led against nr side rail: rdn and jnd jst over 1f out: battled on wl but narrowly hdd and hld ins fnl f* **5/1^{3}**

3 *4 ½* **Battibecco (IRE)**^{24} 4-9-2 79 ... JimCrowley 3 61
(Robert Cowell) *dwlt: hld up in last pair: prog over 2f out: chal and upsides jst over 1f out: wknd fnl f* **7/2^{2}**

2420 **4** *3 ½* **Paradise Spectre**^{51} 2276 6-9-2 72 ... JamesDoyle 6 50
(Mrs K Burke) *dwlt: hld up in last pair: shkn up over 2f out: no imp over 1f out: wknd* **6/1**

2622 **5** *5* **Doctor Hilary**^{16} 3325 11-9-2 46 ... (v) JoeFanning 5 34
(Mark Hoad) *racd on outer: chsd ldr after 2f to 2f out: sn wknd* **25/1**

000/ **6** *5* **Baby Judge (IRE)**^{635} 3732 6-8-9 0 ... DanielleMooney$^{(7)}$ 2 18
(Michael Chapman) *t.k.h: chsd ldr 2f: wknd over 2f out* **100/1**

1m 12.26s (-0.74) **Going Correction** +0.025s/f (Good)
WFA 3 from 4yo+ 6lb **6** Ran SP% **110.4**
Speed ratings (Par 101): **105,104,98,94,87 80**
toteswingers 1&2 £1.70, 1&3 £1.30, 2&3 £2.00 CSF £5.74 TOTE £1.90: £1.10, £4.00; EX 6.80 Trifecta £13.50 Pool: £17647.47 - 977.42 winning tickets..Nenge Mboko was bought in for £6,600
Owner Russell Conrad Vail Wheeler Hippychick **Bred** Pigeon House Stud **Trained** Manton, Wilts

FOCUS
Not a bad race for the grade. It was run at a fair pace, with the front two fighting out a thrilling finish.

3898 YOUR FAVOURITE SPORTS AT TOTEPOOL.COM MAIDEN STKS 6f
7:00 (7:00) (Class 5) 3-4-Y-O **£2,587** (£770; £384; £192) **Stalls** Low

Form RPR

332 **1** **Realize**^{28} 2934 3-9-5 73 ... RichardHughes 3 75+
(Hughie Morrison) *w ldr: led 2f: shkn up 1f out: sn drew clr* **2/13^{1}**

0 **2** *5* **Trisara**^{26} 2979 3-9-0 0 ... JamesDoyle 5 54
(Harry Dunlop) *narrow ldr to 2f out: rdn and pressed wnr to jst over 1f out: wknd fnl f* **10/1^{2}**

64 **3** *2 ¼* **Mighty Mata**^{131} 729 3-9-5 0 ... RenatoSouza 2 52
(Mark Usher) *chsd ldng pair: outpcd 1/2-way: tried to cl over 1f out: lft bhd fnl f* **50/1**

4 *16* **Another Name (IRE)** 3-8-12 0 ... JordanUys$^{(7)}$ 4
(Paul Cole) *awkward s: slowly away and shoved along: in tch after 2f: wknd over 2f out: t.o* **12/1^{3}**

1m 13.31s (0.31) **Going Correction** +0.025s/f (Good)
WFA 3 from 4yo 6lb **4** Ran SP% **105.4**
Speed ratings (Par 103): **98,91,88,67**
CSF £2.09 TOTE £1.30; EX 3.40 Trifecta £15.40 Pool: £15576.95 - 754.23 winning tickets..
Owner Deborah Collett & M J Watson **Bred** M J Watson **Trained** East Ilsley, Berks

FOCUS
A desperately uncompetitive maiden, run at a steady pace.

3899 PLAY ROULETTE AND BLACKJACK AT TOTEPOOL.COM H'CAP 1m 2f 7y
7:30 (7:30) (Class 4) (0-85,83) 3-Y-O+ **£4,851** (£1,443; £721; £360) **Stalls** Centre

Form RPR

-332 **1** **Evangelist**^{18} 3235 3-8-9 **75** ... RyanMoore 1 84
(Sir Michael Stoute) *trckd ldr: dashed into narrow ld 3f out: hrd rdn 2f out: maintained narrow ld fr over 1f out* **7/4^{1}**

3-21 **2** *nk* **One Pekan (IRE)**^{68} 1769 3-9-3 **83** ... RichardHughes 7 91
(Roger Varian) *led: hdd and shkn up 3f out: rdn to press wnr fnl 2f: styd on but a jst hld* **2/1^{2}**

10-6 **3** *hd* **Glenard**^{74} 1641 3-8-12 **78** ... JamesDoyle 6 86
(Charles Hills) *t.k.h early: hld up in 4th: rdn over 2f out: grad clsd over 1f out: chal fnl f: kpt on but hld* **3/1^{3}**

6015 **4** *2 ½* **Emman Bee (IRE)**^{24} 3063 4-9-2 **71** ... JoeFanning 3 74
(Luke Dace) *hld up in last pair: sltly outpcd 3f out: shkn up 2f out: one pce fr over 1f out* **25/1**

1225 **5** *2 ¾* **Flamborough Breeze**^{81} 1500 4-9-7 **76** ... GeorgeBaker 5 74
(Ed Vaughan) *stdd s: hld up in last: taken to outer and shkn up over 2f out: nt qckn wl over 1f out: fdd fnl f* **16/1**

6043 **6** *7* **Tinshu (IRE)**^{17} 3293 7-9-10 **79** ... (p) PatCosgrave 2 66
(Derek Haydn Jones) *trckd ldng pair: rdn over 2f out: wknd over 1f out: eased fnl f* **12/1**

2m 5.84s (-2.86) **Going Correction** -0.125s/f (Firm)
WFA 3 from 4yo+ 11lb **6** Ran SP% **112.1**
Speed ratings (Par 105): **106,105,105,103,101 95**
toteswingers 1&2 £1.10, 1&3 £2.10, 2&3 £2.60 CSF £5.54 TOTE £2.60: £1.40, £2.10; EX 7.20 Trifecta £14.10 Pool: £15487.27 - 819.31 winning tickets..
Owner Philip Newton **Bred** Philip Newton **Trained** Newmarket, Suffolk

FOCUS
The pace was steady for this tight handicap.

3900 EXCLUSIVE OFFERS ON TOTEPOOL MOBILE FILLIES' H'CAP 1m 3f 135y
8:00 (8:01) (Class 5) (0-70,70) 3-Y-O+ **£2,587** (£770; £384; £192) **Stalls** Centre

Form RPR

3625 **1** **Choral Festival**^{18} 3244 7-10-0 **70** ... RichardHughes 8 79
(John Bridger) *hld up in 7th: waited tl over 1f out bef threading way through: produced to ld last 100yds: styd on wl* **5/1^{3}**

-525 **2** *½* **Just Darcy**^{18} 3243 3-8-12 **67** ... RyanMoore 5 75
(Sir Michael Stoute) *trckd ldng pair: shkn up over 2f out: drvn to ld and edgd rt 1f out: hdd and one pce last 100yds* **7/4^{1}**

-640 **3** *1* **Prospera (IRE)**^{30} 2874 3-8-7 **62** ... (b^{1}) JimmyQuinn 7 68
(Ralph Beckett) *hld up in midfield: pushed along 4f out: clsd on ldrs fr 2f out: in tch whn n.m.r jst ins fnl f: styd on* **16/1**

0-30 **4** *shd* **Montjess (IRE)**^{52} 2206 3-8-12 **67** ... (v^{1}) RichardKingscote 2 73
(Tom Dascombe) *mde most: hdd over 3f out to over 2f out: drvn and hdd 1f out: kpt on same pce after* **11/1**

3306 **5** *nk* **If I Were A Boy (IRE)**^{7} 3635 6-9-9 **65** ... (b) JamesDoyle 9 70
(Dominic Ffrench Davis) *hld up in last: prog on outer over 2f out: clsd on ldrs over 1f out: styd on same pce fnl f* **10/1**

1 **6** *6* **Pixie Cut (IRE)**^{11} 3488 3-8-9 **64** ... LiamJones 1 59
(J S Moore) *t.k.h: hld up in midfield: pushed along 4f out: in tch but u.p whn nt clr run over 1f out: wknd* **10/1**

5600 **7** *10* **Open Letter (IRE)**^{30} 2878 3-8-6 **61** ... JoeFanning 6 46
(Mark Johnston) *chsd ldng pair to wl over 2f out: sn wknd* **7/2^{2}**

-030 **8** *2 ¼* **Janie Runaway (IRE)**^{18} 3243 3-8-6 **61** ... MartinLane 3 49
(Brian Meehan) *pressed ldr: led over 3f out to over 2f out: beginning to weaken whn hmpd jst ins fnl f: eased* **14/1**

2m 27.68s (-1.82) **Going Correction** -0.125s/f (Firm)
WFA 3 from 6yo+ 13lb **8** Ran SP% **114.3**
Speed ratings (Par 100): **101,100,100,99,99 95,89,87**
toteswingers 1&2 £1.60, 1&3 £13.20, 2&3 £6.10 CSF £14.16 CT £128.41 TOTE £6.40: £1.60, £1.20, £4.90; EX 14.30 Trifecta £81.80 Pool: £6519.92 - 59.72 winning tickets..
Owner Mrs Liz Gardner **Bred** Cheveley Park Stud Ltd **Trained** Liphook, Hants

FOCUS
A fair handicap run at an honest pace with the winner scoring under a superb ride.

3901 PLAY DEAL OR NO DEAL AT TOTEPOOL.COM H'CAP 1m 67y
8:30 (8:38) (Class 5) (0-70,70) 3-Y-O+ **£2,587** (£770; £384; £192) **Stalls** Low

Form RPR

-220 **1** **Poor Duke (IRE)**^{41} 2549 3-9-5 **70** ... JamesDoyle 2 74
(Jamie Osborne) *trckd ldrs: rdn 2f out: sn in 2nd: drvn to ld 1f out: wandered but hld on nr fin* **3/1^{2}**

0003 **2** *½* **Shifting Star (IRE)**^{9} 3575 8-10-0 **70** ... (vt) RichardHughes 8 75
(John Bridger) *hld up in midfield: stdy prog over 2f out: chsd ldng pair jst over 1f out: plld out and drvn to chal ins fnl f: styd on* **10/1**

3312 **3** *shd* **On With The Dance (IRE)**^{28} 2935 3-9-5 **70** ... RyanMoore 3 73
(Ed Vaughan) *led to 5f out: drvn to ld again over 2f out: hdd u.p 1f out: kpt on but lost 2nd last stride* **2/1^{1}**

0-40 **4** *¾* **Mahadee (IRE)**^{28} 2920 8-9-13 **69** ... (b) LiamTreadwell 13 72
(Ed de Giles) *hld up towards rr: prog on outer over 2f out: clsd on ldrs and ch 1f out: drifted lft and nt qckn* **25/1**

056 **5** *3* **Bankroll**^{40} 2574 6-10-0 **70** ... (t) GeorgeBaker 10 66
(Jonjo O'Neill) *hld up in midfield: rdn and clsd on ldrs 2f out: nt qckn jst over 1f out: fdd* **12/1**

26-5 **6** *2 ¾* **Daneside (IRE)**^{10} 3534 6-9-6 **67** ... MatthewLawson$^{(5)}$ 4 57
(Gary Harrison) *taken down early: hld up in last pair early: plld way arnd field to ld 5f out: hdd over 2f out: wknd over 1f out* **6/1^{3}**

3023 **7** *½* **Strategic Action (IRE)**^{13} 3433 4-9-2 **58** ... RobertHavlin 11 47
(Linda Jewell) *hld up in last trio: pushed along over 2f out: kpt on same pce after: nvr involved* **20/1**

445- **8** *2 ¾* **Typography**^{288} 6275 4-10-0 **70** ... (t) PatCosgrave 5 52
(Alastair Lidderdale) *chsd ldr 3f: styd prom tl wknd wl over 1f out* **33/1**

0-00 **9** *2 ¼* **Switcharooney (IRE)**^{49} 2306 3-9-2 **67** ... RichardKingscote 1 42
(Tom Dascombe) *a in last trio: rdn and struggling 1/2-way: bhd after* **6/1^{3}**

-003 **10** *nk* **Uncle Fred**^{21} 3152 8-9-5 **61** ... LiamJones 9 37
(Patrick Chamings) *dwlt: hld up in last pair: taken to outer over 3f out: no prog over 2f out: sn wknd* **14/1**

1m 43.96s (-0.74) **Going Correction** -0.125s/f (Firm)
WFA 3 from 4yo+ 9lb **10** Ran SP% **121.9**
Speed ratings (Par 103): **98,97,97,96,93 90,90,87,85,85**
toteswingers 1&2 £5.90, 1&3 £3.00, 2&3 £2.80 CSF £34.00 CT £75.57 TOTE £4.00: £1.60, £2.60, £1.50; EX 42.20 Trifecta £187.70 Pool: £3199.29 - 12.78 winning tickets..
Owner The Duke's Partnership **Bred** Corrin Stud **Trained** Upper Lambourn, Berks

FOCUS
The race was delayed as Titan Triumph broke through the stalls a fraction before the other runners were dispatched and the starter flagged for a false start. Batchelors Star was very lit up and withdrawn alongside Titan Triumph. No R4.

3902 SYDNEY ARMS PUB CHELSEA & RACING CLUB MAIDEN STKS 1m 67y
9:00 (9:03) (Class 5) 3-Y-O £2,726 (£805; £402) Stalls Low

Form RPR
3 1 **Magistral**[18] 3250 3-9-5 0 RyanMoore 2 88+
(John Gosden) *mde all: set mod pce to 1/2-way: stretched on over 2f out: in command over 1f out: pushed out* 5/6[1]
2 3 1/4 **Commissioned (IRE)** 3-9-5 0 JoeFanning 7 80+
(Mark Johnston) *cl up: chsd wnr over 5f out: rdn over 2f out: one pce and no imp over 1f out* 9/2[3]
2325 3 1 3/4 **Caramack**[16] 3322 3-9-5 76 RichardHughes 3 76
(Richard Hannon) *hld up bhd ldrs: pushed along to dispute 2nd jst over 2f out: nt qckn over 1f out: one pce after* 11/4[2]
04- 4 4 1/2 **Quest For More (IRE)**[229] 7706 3-9-5 0 JamesDoyle 6 66
(Roger Charlton) *hld up in 5th: pushed along 3f out: wnt 4th 2f out: no imp after: nt knocked abt and fdd fnl f* 12/1
5 5 **Calon Lad (IRE)** 3-9-5 0 PatCosgrave 4 54
(George Baker) *chsd ldr tl hung lft bnd over 5f out: in tch tl wknd over 2f out* 40/1
0 6 13 **Feather Dancer**[17] 3278 3-9-0 0 RobertHavlin 1 19
(Jamie Poulton) *slowly away: a in last: lost tch over 3f out: t.o* 80/1

1m 45.18s (0.48) **Going Correction** -0.125s/f (Firm) 6 Ran SP% **110.8**
Speed ratings (Par 100): **92,88,87,82,77 64**
toteswingers 1&2 £2.80, 1&3 £1.30, 2&3 £1.10 CSF £4.93 TOTE £1.70: £1.40, £1.90; EX 6.10 Trifecta £9.00 Pool: £2064.05 - 171.46 winning tickets..
Owner HRH Princess Haya Of Jordan **Bred** Mr & Mrs R & P Scott **Trained** Newmarket, Suffolk
FOCUS
A fair maiden despite the small field, run at a sound gallop.
T/Plt: £3.30 to a £1 stake. Pool: £93,817.31 - 20,678.52 winning tickets T/Qpdt: £2.00 to a £1 stake. Pool: £7140.82 - 2605.47 winning tickets JN

3637 WOLVERHAMPTON (A.W) (L-H)
Monday, July 1

OFFICIAL GOING: Standard
Wind: Fresh behind Weather: Overcast

3903 TALK TO VICTOR H'CAP 5f 216y(P)
2:15 (2:16) (Class 6) (0-65,65) 3-Y-O £1,940 (£577; £288; £144) Stalls Low

Form RPR
0112 1 **Fossa**[11] 3499 3-9-4 **62** SebSanders 13 71+
(Dean Ivory) *hld up: hdwy on outer over 2f out: rdn to ld wl ins fnl f: r.o* 7/2[1]
3003 2 1 1/2 **Brynford**[14] 3405 3-8-12 **56** SaleemGolam 11 60
(Chris Dwyer) *prom: lost pl 5f out: hdwy over 3f out: rdn to ld ins fnl f: sn hdd and unable qck* 25/1
4314 3 1/2 **Eastern Dragon (IRE)**[68] 1759 3-9-2 **65** WilliamTwiston-Davies(5) 2 67+
(Michael Scudamore) *s.i.s: hld up: nt clr run over 2f out: hdwy over 1f out: r.o: nt rch ldrs* 7/2[1]
006 4 1 1/2 **Encapsulated**[20] 3176 3-9-2 **60** RobertHavlin 8 58
(Roger Ingram) *sn chsng ldr: led over 2f out: rdn: edgd rt and hdd ins fnl f: styd on same pce* 9/2[2]
3006 5 3/4 **Moe's Place (IRE)**[34] 2737 3-9-4 **62** DavidNolan 5 57
(Kristin Stubbs) *chsd ldrs: rdn over 1f out: styd on same pce fnl f* 9/1[3]
-540 6 3/4 **Ishi Honest**[14] 3407 3-9-5 **63** DaneO'Neill 12 56
(Mark Usher) *chsd ldrs: rdn over 1f out: no ex ins fnl f* 14/1
0-00 7 1 **Grace Hull**[31] 2829 3-9-7 **65** LiamJones 3 55
(J S Moore) *hld up: hdwy over 2f out: rdn over 1f out: wknd ins fnl f* 25/1
0406 8 1/2 **Carneades (IRE)**[11] 3495 3-8-2 **46** oh1 (t) LukeMorris 7 34
(Ed Walker) *hld up: drvn along 1/2-way: nvr nrr* 22/1
3-06 9 shd **Gallena**[27] 2959 3-9-7 **65** FrankieDettori 10 53
(William Haggas) *prom: rdn over 2f out: styd on same pce fr over 1f out* 7/2[1]
6-00 10 1 1/4 **Direct Trade**[20] 3178 3-8-3 **47** [1] JimmyQuinn 4 31
(Mark Usher) *s.i.s: hld up: rdn over 2f out: n.d* 33/1
0640 11 3 1/2 **Transluscent (IRE)**[20] 3178 3-9-0 **58** (t) JimmyFortune 1 30
(Andrew Balding) *prom: rdn and n.m.r over 1f out: sn wknd* 16/1
0000 12 3 3/4 **Gold Roll (IRE)**[3] 3762 3-8-5 **49** (b) JamesSullivan 6 9
(Ruth Carr) *led: hdd over 2f out: rdn and wknd over 1f out* 20/1

1m 14.32s (-0.68) **Going Correction** -0.075s/f (Stan) 12 Ran SP% **127.1**
Speed ratings (Par 98): **101,99,98,96,95 94,93,92,92,90 85,80**
toteswingers 1&2 £8.50, 1&3 £2.80, 2&3 £12.80 CSF £106.51 CT £348.98 TOTE £4.20: £1.40, £7.30, £1.20; EX 48.90 Trifecta £159.90 Pool: £4085.12 - 19.16 winning tickets..
Owner Geoff Copp **Bred** G B Turnbull Ltd **Trained** Radlett, Herts
FOCUS
A modest 3yo sprint handicap, but they went a solid pace with most of the principals finishing towards the centre of the track.

3904 £25 FREE BET AT BETVICTOR.COM (S) STKS 5f 20y(P)
2:45 (2:45) (Class 6) 3-Y-O+ £1,940 (£577; £288; £144) Stalls Low

Form RPR
4552 1 **Red Cape (FR)**[4] 3713 10-9-4 67 (b) JamesSullivan 6 74
(Ruth Carr) *a.p: chsd ldr over 3f out: shkn up over 1f out: rdn to ld ins fnl f: r.o* 11/2[3]
-062 2 2 1/4 **Saga Lout**[7] 3638 3-8-13 71 (p) RichardKingscote 3 64
(Tom Dascombe) *led: rdn over 1f out: hdd and nt qckn ins fnl f* 1/2[1]
1316 3 1/2 **Above The Stars**[5] 3691 5-8-13 75 RachealKneller(5) 5 64
(Jamie Osborne) *broke wl: lost pl after 1f: shkn up and r.o ins fnl f: nt rch ldrs* 4/1[2]
6020 4 3/4 **Steelcut**[25] 3024 9-9-4 61 (p) MartinDwyer 4 61
(Mark Buckley) *prom: pushed along 1/2-way: rdn over 1f out: edgd lft and styd on same pce fnl f* 20/1
5-43 5 3 3/4 **Coconut Kisses**[11] 3494 3-8-1 58 RyanWhile(7) 2 41
(Bill Turner) *chsd ldr tl over 3f out: remained handy: rdn over 1f out: wknd ins fnl f* 14/1
65 6 6 **Sextons House (IRE)**[11] 3507 5-8-13 43 (p) ShirleyTeasdale(5) 1 26
(Alan McCabe) *s.i.s: sn pushed along in rr: wknd 1/2-way* 100/1

1m 1.33s (-0.97) **Going Correction** -0.075s/f (Stan)
WFA 3 from 5yo+ 5lb 6 Ran SP% **114.5**
Speed ratings (Par 101): **104,100,99,98,92 82**
.There was no bid for the winner \n\x\x Above The Stars was bought by Mr C R Dore for £6000 \n\x\x Saga Lout was bought by Mr John P Evitt for £6000\n\x\x
Owner Middleham Park Racing LVI **Bred** Gilles And Mrs Forien **Trained** Huby, N Yorks
FOCUS
Not a bad little seller with a couple of these coming here in reasonable form.

3905 IRISH STALLION FARMS EBF MAIDEN STKS 7f 32y(P)
3:15 (3:16) (Class 5) 2-Y-O £2,911 (£866; £432; £216) Stalls High

Form RPR
1 **Claim The Roses (USA)** 2-9-5 0 JimmyFortune 2 75+
(Ed Vaughan) *plld hrd: trckd ldrs: shkn up to ld wl ins fnl f: edgd rt: r.o* 10/1[3]
40 2 3/4 **Clever Miss**[24] 3064 2-9-0 0 MartinDwyer 1 68
(Alan McCabe) *led: rdn and hung rt fr over 1f out: hdd wl ins fnl f* 7/1[2]
5423 3 2 **Ocean Storm (IRE)**[17] 3290 2-9-5 0 AdamKirby 5 69
(James Tate) *chsd wnr: shkn up over 2f out: rdn whn hmpd over 1f out: carried rt: styng on same pce whn nt clr run wl ins fnl f* 1/1[1]
00 4 3 **St Vincent (IRE)**[18] 3245 2-9-5 0 TedDurcan 8 61+
(David Lanigan) *chsd ldrs: rdn and hung lft over 1f out: no ex* 33/1
50 5 3/4 **May Whi (IRE)**[34] 2751 2-9-0 0 RichardKingscote 7 54
(Tom Dascombe) *hld up: shkn up over 1f out: nvr on terms* 33/1
0 6 3 1/2 **Chinese Jade**[18] 3233 2-9-5 0 LukeMorris 6 51+
(Sir Mark Prescott Bt) *dwlt and wnt lft s: sn pushed along in rr: shkn up over 1f out: eased fnl f* 25/1
0 7 nk **Laughing Musketeer (IRE)**[18] 3238 2-9-5 0 MartinLane 3 50
(Paul Cole) *plld hrd and prom: rdn over 3f out: wknd over 2f out* 20/1
8 1 1/4 **Ohio (IRE)** 2-9-0 0 J-PGuillambert 9 42
(Gary Harrison) *hld up: rdn over 2f out: sn wknd* 50/1

1m 31.31s (1.71) **Going Correction** -0.075s/f (Stan) 8 Ran SP% **88.0**
Speed ratings (Par 94): **87,86,83,80,79 75,75,73**
toteswingers 1&2 £2.30, 1&3 £1.70, 2&3 £2.20 CSF £34.35 TOTE £7.80: £1.70, £1.50, £1.02; EX 21.70 Trifecta £48.50 Pool: £1585.47 - 24.46 winning tickets..
Owner Salem Rashid **Bred** Woodford Thoroughbreds LLC **Trained** Newmarket, Suffolk
■ Stewards' Enquiry : Martin Dwyer three-day ban: careless riding (15, 16, 17 Jul)
FOCUS
Not a particularly competitive maiden, with the withdrawal of the Godolphin-trained Solidarity who played up in the stalls (2-1, deduct 30p in the £ under R4). The front three drifted towards the stands' side rail in the straight. The form matches the solid race averages.

3906 DOWNLOAD THE BETVICTOR APP NOW APPRENTICE CLAIMING STKS 7f 32y(P)
3:45 (3:45) (Class 6) 4-Y-O+ £1,940 (£577; £288; £144) Stalls High

Form RPR
0003 1 **Light From Mars**[11] 3507 8-9-1 81 EDLinehan(3) 5 78
(Ronald Harris) *s.i.s: sn chsng ldrs: led 2f out: rdn out* 7/2[3]
5024 2 2 1/2 **Mr David (USA)**[12] 3472 6-9-12 83 (b) NicoleNordblad 2 79+
(Jamie Osborne) *plld hrd and prom: hmpd 6f out: nt clr run and swtchd lft over 1f out: rdn to go 2nd wl ins fnl f: no ch w wnr* 7/4[1]
4530 3 1 **Flying Pickets (IRE)**[96] 1203 4-8-7 68 (be) AaronJones(5) 6 63
(Alan McCabe) *s.i.s: hld up: hdwy over 2f out: chsd wnr over 1f out tl rdn wl ins fnl f: one pce* 16/1
050- 4 4 1/2 **Ottavino (IRE)**[314] 5458 4-8-9 37 IanBurns(3) 8 50?
(Jane Chapple-Hyam) *hld up: styd on u.p fnl f: nvr nrr* 50/1
0-6 5 1 **El Camino Real (IRE)**[35] 2709 5-8-5 50 RyanHolmes(7) 1 48?
(Barry Leavy) *led 5f: wknd fnl f* 66/1
00-0 6 nk **Abi Scarlet (IRE)**[132] 715 4-8-6 78 CharlieBennett(5) 7 46
(Hughie Morrison) *hld up: hdwy on outer over 2f out: wknd over 1f out* 17/2
0050 7 1 1/4 **Dubawi Phantom**[19] 3204 6-9-4 76 (tp) WilliamTwiston-Davies 3 50
(Alan McCabe) *chsd ldr tl rdn over 2f out: wknd over 1f out* 10/3[2]
4010 8 20 **Mister Green (FR)**[52] 2228 7-8-12 69 (b) MatthewLawson 4
(David Flood) *chsd ldrs: pushed along 1/2-way: wknd over 2f out: t.o* 11/2

1m 28.86s (-0.74) **Going Correction** -0.075s/f (Stan) 8 Ran SP% **116.9**
Speed ratings (Par 101): **101,98,97,91,90 90,88,66**
toteswingers 1&2 £2.40, 1&3 £4.70, 2&3 £4.00 CSF £10.31 TOTE £4.60: £1.30, £1.10, £3.60; EX 11.80 Trifecta £50.60 Pool: £4079.70 - 60.35 winning tickets..Light From Mars was claimed by Mr T Dascombe for £8000
Owner Mrs N Macauley **Bred** Harts Farm And Stud **Trained** Earlswood, Monmouths
FOCUS
The front three finished clear in this claimer.

3907 BETVICTOR CASINO ON YOUR MOBILE MEDIAN AUCTION MAIDEN STKS 1m 4f 50y(P)
4:15 (4:15) (Class 6) 3-4-Y-O £1,940 (£577; £288; £144) Stalls Low

Form RPR
4233 1 **Could Be (IRE)**[14] 3402 3-9-0 70 (b[1]) AdamKirby 9 76
(David Simcock) *hld up: hdwy 1/2-way: r.o u.p to ld wl ins fnl f* 9/2[3]
-023 2 3/4 **White Month**[24] 3055 3-9-0 71 JimmyFortune 8 75
(Andrew Balding) *set stdy pce tl qcknd over 2f out: rdn over 1f out: hdd and unable qck wl ins fnl f* 6/5[1]
6 3 1 1/2 **Aiyana**[12] 3469 3-8-9 0 RobertHavlin 2 68
(Hughie Morrison) *chsd ldrs: wnt 2nd 2f out: sn rdn: styd on same pce fnl f* 8/1
6-00 4 3/4 **Rock God (IRE)**[19] 3214 3-9-0 76 DaneO'Neill 7 71
(Eve Johnson Houghton) *chsd ldrs: rdn over 2f out: hung lft over 1f out: styd on same pce fnl f* 7/2[2]
5 6 **Ocean Secret (IRE)** 3-9-0 0 SebSanders 1 62
(Jeremy Noseda) *hld up: hdwy over 2f out: wknd over 1f out* 6/1
04 6 1 3/4 **Qibtee (FR)**[14] 3402 3-9-0 0 TedDurcan 10 59
(Mick Channon) *chsd ldr tl rdn 2f out: wknd over 1f out* 22/1
3-0 7 nk **Camelopardalis**[26] 2971 4-9-8 0 MartinLane 4 54
(Tobias B P Coles) *hld up: rdn over 3f out: n.d* 50/1
0 8 28 **Green And White (ITY)**[7] 3641 3-9-0 0 (t) LukeMorris 6 14
(Frank Sheridan) *s.s: hld up: hdwy u.p over 3f out: wknd over 2f out: t.o* 100/1
6 9 25 **Grivola (GER)**[54] 2172 3-8-9 0 MartinDwyer 3
(Conrad Allen) *mid-div: lost pl 7f out: wknd over 3f out: t.o* 40/1
600- 10 2 1/4 **Thecornishwren (IRE)**[227] 7739 4-9-3 35 NatashaEaton(5) 5
(John Ryan) *chsd ldrs tl rdn and wknd over 3f out: t.o* 100/1

2m 39.31s (-1.79) **Going Correction** -0.075s/f (Stan)
WFA 3 from 4yo 13lb 10 Ran SP% **122.0**
Speed ratings (Par 101): **102,101,100,100,96 94,94,75,59,57**
toteswingers 1&2 £2.30, 1&3 £5.60, 2&3 £4.10 CSF £10.66 TOTE £5.50: £1.30, £1.10, £3.80; EX 15.50 Trifecta £85.60 Pool: £4563.30 - 39.95 winning tickets..
Owner Al Asayl Bloodstock Ltd **Bred** Sheikh Sultan Bin Khalifa Al Nayhan **Trained** Newmarket, Suffolk

The Form Book Flat, Raceform Ltd, Compton, RG20 6NL.

FOCUS
A fair maiden with the 'right' horses coming to the fore. Three of the front four had already qualified for marks in the 70s.

3908 **BETVICTOR.COM H'CAP** **1m 4f 50y(P)**
4:45 (4:45) (Class 4) (0-80,79) 3-Y-O **£4,690** (£1,395; £697; £348) **Stalls** Low

Form RPR
-632 **1** **Portmonarch (IRE)**[40] 2564 3-9-4 **76**...(p) TedDurcan 6 86+
(David Lanigan) *led after 1f: sn hdd: remained handy: led over 1f out: rdn and wandered ins fnl f: styd on* **4/1**[2]
51-4 **2** 1 3/4 **Alwilda**[19] 3214 3-9-1 **73**... LukeMorris 2 78
(Sir Mark Prescott Bt) *a.p: pushed along over 3f out: rdn to chse wnr ins fnl f: styd on* **6/1**[3]
6104 **3** 3/4 **Getaway Car**[3] 3783 3-8-7 **65**...(bt[1]) MartinLane 4 69
(Gerard Butler) *hld up: pushed along over 3f out: rdn and r.o wl ins fnl f: nt rch ldrs* **14/1**
522 **4** 1 1/4 **Bantam (IRE)**[18] 3239 3-9-3 **75**... FrankieDettori 9 77
(Ed Dunlop) *hld up: hdwy over 4f out: rdn over 1f out: styd on same pce ins fnl f* **6/5**[1]
1036 **5** 1 1/4 **King Muro**[17] 3276 3-9-5 **77**... JimmyFortune 8 77
(Andrew Balding) *chsd ldrs: led over 10f out: rdn and hdd over 1f out: no ex ins fnl f* **10/1**
55-0 **6** 2 **Revise (IRE)**[54] 2151 3-9-5 **77**... AdamKirby 7 74
(Marco Botti) *sn prom: chsd ldr over 9f out tl rdn over 2f out: wknd fnl f* **8/1**
11-6 **7** 5 **Paddy's Saltantes (IRE)**[70] 1729 3-8-12 **70**... LiamJones 1 59
(J S Moore) *hld up: rdn over 3f out: wknd over 1f out* **14/1**
1400 **8** 1 3/4 **Strategic Strike (IRE)**[7] 3636 3-8-9 **70**...(p) AshleyMorgan(3) 3 56
(Paul Cole) *led 1f: chsd ldrs: rdn over 2f out: wknd over 1f out* **40/1**
2m 38.43s (-2.67) **Going Correction** -0.075s/f (Stan) **8** Ran SP% **115.7**
Speed ratings (Par 102): **105,103,103,102,101 100,97,95**
toteswingers 1&2 £4.60, 1&3 £6.40, 2&3 £7.20 CSF £28.50 CT £305.24 TOTE £5.70: £1.90, £2.70, £4.40; EX 22.70 Trifecta £104.70 Pool: £3714.69 - 26.58 winning tickets..
Owner Robert V LaPenta **Bred** Smythson **Trained** Upper Lambourn, Berks
FOCUS
An interesting middle-distance 3yo handicap. The winning time was almost a second quicker than the 3yo maiden earlier on the card over the same trip.

3909 **FOLLOW US ON TWITTER @BETVICTORRACING H'CAP (DIV I)** **1m 141y(P)**
5:15 (5:16) (Class 6) (0-60,60) 3-Y-O+ **£1,940** (£577; £288; £144) **Stalls** Low

Form RPR
2065 **1** **Safwaan**[62] 1909 6-9-11 **57**... J-PGuillambert 3 65
(Gary Harrison) *hld up: hdwy over 1f out: r.o u.p to ld wl ins fnl f* **5/1**[2]
0504 **2** 3/4 **Men Don't Cry (IRE)**[20] 3169 4-9-4 **50**...(b) ChrisCatlin 12 56
(Ed de Giles) *chsd ldrs: rdn over 2f out: r.o* **11/1**
-500 **3** hd **King Of Wing (IRE)**[14] 3406 4-9-1 **47**...(be) AdamKirby 1 53
(Phil McEntee) *hld up: nt clr run wl over 2f out: hdwy u.p over 1f out: r.o wl: nt quite rch ldrs* **16/1**
4-02 **4** shd **Opus Maximus (IRE)**[7] 3642 8-9-3 **49**...(p) JimmyFortune 5 55
(Jennie Candlish) *chsd ldrs: wnt 2nd over 1f out: rdn to ld ins fnl f: sn hdd and unable qck* **2/1**[1]
0304 **5** 1 1/4 **Katmai River (IRE)**[28] 2932 6-8-10 **47**...(v) RachealKneller(5) 8 50
(Mark Usher) *chsd ldrs: rdn over 1f out: r.o* **14/1**
0300 **6** 1 **Glenridding**[7] 3643 9-9-13 **59**...(p) DaleSwift 6 59
(James Given) *led: rdn over 1f out: hdd and no ex ins fnl f* **12/1**
3005 **7** hd **Spirit Of Gondree (IRE)**[16] 3329 5-9-12 **58**...(b) LukeMorris 11 58
(Milton Bradley) *hld up: rdn over 1f out: styng on whn nt clr run ins fnl f: nvr nrr* **8/1**
5324 **8** nk **Munaawib**[6] 3657 5-9-2 **55**...(t) RyanWhile(7) 4 54
(Charles Smith) *mid-div: pushed along over 5f out: styd on fr over 1f out: nvr trbld ldrs* **13/2**[3]
-235 **9** 3/4 **Meglio Ancora**[19] 3203 6-9-4 **55**... AmyScott(5) 9 53
(Richard Ford) *s.s: in rr: hdwy over 2f out: sn rdn: styd on same pce fnl f* **20/1**
3060 **10** 1 1/4 **Guardi (IRE)**[13] 3433 4-9-6 **52**... TedDurcan 10 47
(Dean Ivory) *chsd ldr: rdn over 2f out: lost 2nd over 1f out: wknd ins fnl f* **16/1**
3000 **11** 6 **Silver Fawn (IRE)**[4] 3735 3-8-8 **50**...(be) JimmyQuinn 7 30
(John Weymes) *prom: rdn over 1f out: wknd fnl f* **20/1**
0066 **12** 4 **This Is Me**[19] 3222 5-10-0 **60**... DaneO'Neill 2 32
(Don Cantillon) *s.s: a in rr: rdn over 3f out: sn lost tch* **16/1**
1m 50.3s (-0.20) **Going Correction** -0.075s/f (Stan)
WFA 3 from 4yo+ 10lb **12** Ran SP% **124.3**
Speed ratings (Par 101): **97,96,96,96,94 94,93,93,92,91 86,82**
toteswingers 1&2 £10.00, 1&3 £26.70, 2&3 £36.80 CSF £62.37 CT £842.29 TOTE £4.90: £1.60, £4.80, £9.10; EX 54.60 Trifecta £1136.70 Pool: £3519.55 - 2.32 winning tickets..
Owner Maze Rattan Limited **Bred** Shadwell Estate Company Limited **Trained** Newmarket, Suffolk
■ Stewards' Enquiry : Adam Kirby two-day ban: use of whip (15-16 Jul)
FOCUS
A pretty weak handicap, but they went a decent pace thanks to a contested lead and the winning time was almost half a second quicker than the second division.

3910 **FOLLOW US ON TWITTER @BETVICTORRACING H'CAP (DIV II)** **1m 141y(P)**
5:45 (5:46) (Class 6) (0-60,60) 3-Y-O+ **£1,940** (£577; £288; £144) **Stalls** Low

Form RPR
5544 **1** **Crucis Abbey (IRE)**[56] 2072 5-9-2 **48**...(p) RobbieFitzpatrick 12 56
(Mark Brisbourne) *hld up: hdwy over 2f out: rdn ins fnl f: r.o to ld nr fin* **16/1**
2252 **2** 1/2 **Moment In The Sun**[11] 3496 4-9-9 **60**...(b) JemmaMarshall(5) 7 67
(David Flood) *chsd ldrs: wnt 2nd over 3f out: rdn to ld ins fnl f: hdd nr fin* **13/2**
-256 **3** 1 **Buaiteoir (FR)**[14] 3399 7-9-12 **58**... AdamKirby 2 63
(Nikki Evans) *hld up: hdwy over 2f out: sn rdn: ev ch wl ins fnl f: unable qck towards fin* **11/2**[3]
365 **4** 3 **Coastal Passage**[7] 3644 5-8-13 **52**...(b) RyanWhile(7) 9 50
(Charles Smith) *plld hrd: trckd ldr tl led 6f out: clr over 2f out: rdn over 1f out: wknd and hdd ins fnl f* **14/1**
6-00 **5** 1 **Marguerite St Just**[11] 3495 3-8-2 **49**... ShirleyTeasdale(5) 8 44
(Olivia Maylam) *mid-div: pushed along over 3f out: styd on fr over 1f out: nt trble ldrs* **16/1**
6534 **6** 4 1/2 **Adorable Choice (IRE)**[32] 2796 5-9-10 **56**...(vt) StephenCraine 6 41
(Tom Dascombe) *sn pushed along in rr: hdwy u.p over 1f out: swtchd rt ins fnl f: nt trble ldrs* **8/1**
005- **7** 1/2 **Kat Moon**[310] 5586 3-9-1 **57**... TedDurcan 11 40
(Tim Easterby) *sn pushed along in rr: nt clr run over 2f out: nvr on terms* **4/1**[1]
1610 **8** 2 **Downtown Boy (IRE)**[41] 2537 5-9-12 **58**...(p) DaleSwift 10 37
(Ray Craggs) *chsd ldrs: pushed along over 5f out: wknd over 1f out* **5/1**[2]
00-0 **9** 3 1/4 **Euroquip Boy (IRE)**[17] 3270 6-9-9 **55**... RussKennemore 13 27
(Michael Scudamore) *stdd s: a in rr* **40/1**
0100 **10** 3 1/4 **Dubara Reef (IRE)**[23] 3089 6-9-2 **48**...(p) LukeMorris 1 12
(Paul Green) *in rr: pushed along over 5f out: lost tch over 3f out* **12/1**
4465 **11** 4 **Impeccability**[22] 3137 3-8-5 **50**... RaulDaSilva(3) 5 4
(John Mackie) *chsd ldrs tl rdn and wknd over 2f out* **8/1**
3055 **12** 1 **Nonaynever**[13] 3445 5-9-3 **49**...(b) JamesSullivan 3
(Ruth Carr) *prom: nt clr run and lost pl over 3f out: nt rcvr* **10/1**
5200 **13** 24 **Imtithal (IRE)**[7] 3644 4-9-8 **54**...(b) ChrisCatlin 4
(John Weymes) *led over 2f: chsd ldr tl rdn over 3f out: sn wknd: t.o* **28/1**
1m 50.72s (0.22) **Going Correction** -0.075s/f (Stan)
WFA 3 from 4yo+ 10lb **13** Ran SP% **128.7**
Speed ratings (Par 101): **96,95,94,92,91 87,86,84,82,79 75,74,53**
toteswingers 1&2 £20.10, 1&3 £19.40, 2&3 £4.70 CSF £125.52 CT £690.70 TOTE £23.00: £5.80, £2.00, £3.70; EX 80.30 Trifecta £1005.30 Pool: £2855.51 - 2.13 winning tickets..
Owner Mark Brisbourne **Bred** M G Daly **Trained** Great Ness, Shropshire
FOCUS
A modest handicap, and although they went a solid pace, the winning time was almost half a second slower than the first division.
T/Plt: £8.10 to a £1 stake. Pool: £87,793.59 - 7871.52 winning tickets T/Qpdt: £3.60 to a £1 stake. Pool: £6231.74 - 1260.37 winning tickets CR

COMPIEGNE (L-H)
Monday, July 1

OFFICIAL GOING: Turf: very soft

3911a **PRIX DAPHNIS (GROUP 3) (3YO COLTS & GELDINGS) (TURF)** **1m 1f**
2:20 (12:00) 3-Y-O **£32,520** (£13,008; £9,756; £6,504; £3,252)

RPR
1 **Superplex (FR)**[29] 2907 3-8-11 0... MircoDemuro 6 110
(M Figge, Germany) *dwlt: sn rcvrd and hld up in rr but wl in tch: stdy hdwy on outside over 2f out: 3rd and shkn up 1 1/2f out: rdn and chal ldr ins fnl f: r.o wl to ld 60yds out: won gng away* **14/1**
2 1 1/2 **Pilote (IRE)**[26] 3007 3-8-11 0... OlivierPeslier 1 107
(A Fabre, France) *settled on ldr's quarters: led 1 1/2f out: rdn 1f out: r.o u.p ins fnl f: hdd last 60yds: no ex* **2/1**[2]
3 1 1/4 **Saint Thomas (FR)**[23] 3128 3-8-11 0... ThierryJarnet 4 104
(P Bary, France) *hld up towards rr but wl in tch: cl 4th and travelling wl 2f out:shkn up and swtchd outside under 1 1/2f out: sn hrd rdn and nt qckn ent fnl f: styd on wl u.p last 75yds: nt pce to chal* **6/1**[3]
4 1 1/2 **Lion D'Anvers (FR)**[29] 2907 3-8-11 0... UmbertoRispoli 2 101
(J Van Handenhove, France) *led: qcknd pce under 2 1/2f out: hdd 1 1/2f out: rdn and rallied to press ldr: hrd rdn and outpcd by ldrs ins fnl f: kpt on at same pce last 100yds* **12/1**
5 5 **Sefri (USA)**[85] 1419 3-8-11 0... ChristopheSoumillon 3 91
(J-C Rouget, France) *tk str hold and restrained in 3rd: rdn and swtchd outside over 1 1/2f out: no imp: wknd and eased ins fnl f* **4/5**[1]
1m 55.36s (115.36) **5** Ran SP% **117.5**
WIN (incl. 1 euro stake): 10.70. PLACES: 3.40, 1.70. SF: 39.40.
Owner Stall Eivissa **Bred** Lord Huntingdon **Trained** Germany

3912 - (Foreign Racing) - See Raceform Interactive

NANTES (R-H)
Monday, July 1

OFFICIAL GOING: Turf: good to soft

3913a **GRAND PRIX ANJOU BRETAGNE (LISTED RACE) (4YO+) (TURF)** **1m**
4:40 (12:00) 4-Y-O+ **£21,138** (£8,455; £6,341; £4,227; £2,113)

RPR
1 **Pinturicchio (IRE)**[29] 5-8-11 0... AnthonyCrastus 1 103
(E Lellouche, France) **29/10**[2]
2 nk **Zayade (FR)**[27] 2969 4-8-11 0... AlexandreRoussel 6 102
(J Boisnard, France) **17/2**
3 2 **Fire Ship**[16] 3339 4-9-1 0... AdrienFouassier 7 101
(William Knight) *shkn up fr wd draw to ld after 1f: jnd by rival on inner 1/2-way: rdn and led again over 2f out: hdd ins fnl f: kpt on gamely u.p to hold 3rd* **44/5**
4 nse **Foreign Tune**[15] 3387 4-8-11 0... JeromeClaudic 4 97
(C Laffon-Parias, France) **10/1**
5 3/4 **Polarix**[9] 7-8-11 0... FabriceVeron 5 96
(H-A Pantall, France) **7/1**
6 1 **Sommerabend**[32] 6-8-11 0... MaximeGuyon 3 93
(U Stoltefuss, Germany) **2/1**[1]
7 15 **Celebrissime (IRE)**[83] 1456 8-9-5 0... FlavienPrat 2 67
(F Head, France) **48/10**[3]
1m 38.01s (98.01) **7** Ran SP% **118.5**
WIN (incl. 1 euro stake): 3.90. PLACES: 2.10, 3.70. SF: 32.80.
Owner Mlle Julia Tokay **Bred** Dayton Investments Ltd **Trained** Lamorlaye, France

3673 BATH (L-H)
Tuesday, July 2

OFFICIAL GOING: Firm (10.3)
Wind: Moderate across Weather: Overcast

3914 **BET365.COM MAIDEN AUCTION STKS** **5f 11y**
6:00 (6:02) (Class 6) 2-Y-O **£1,940** (£577; £288; £144) **Stalls** Centre

Form RPR
633 **1** **Captain Ryan**[17] 3310 2-8-11 0...(e[1]) SteveDrowne 8 65
(Peter Makin) *trckd ldrs: chal fr 2f out: led 1f out: pushed out* **3/1**[2]
2 3/4 **Flicksta (USA)** 2-9-1 0... ShaneKelly 4 66
(Ronald Harris) *chsd ldrs: chal over 1f out: chsd wnr ins fnl f but no imp* **10/1**
35 **3** 1 **Brunhilde**[20] 3205 2-8-13 0... RichardKingscote 2 61
(Tom Dascombe) *chsd ldr: chal fr 2f out tl 1f out: outpcd ins fnl f* **5/4**[1]

0 **4** 1 ¼ **Debt Settler (IRE)**[15] 3413 2-8-8 0 SimonPearce(3) 7 58+
(Luke Dace) *s.i.s: in rr: hdwy over 2f out: clsng on ldrs on ins whn nt clr run appr fnl f: kpt on same pce fnl 150yds* **20/1**

364 **5** ½ **Aweebitowinker**[7] 3659 2-8-9 0 LiamJones 9 50
(J S Moore) *s.i.s: in rr: drvn and hdwy over 2f out: kpt on fnl f: nt pce to rch ldrs* **25/1**

062 **6** 1 **Sakhee'Ssquirrel**[7] 3659 2-8-6 0 CathyGannon 1 44
(David Evans) *led: jnd 2f out: hdd 1f out: sn wknd* **5/1**[3]

055 **7** 11 **Zac's Princess**[29] 2917 2-8-6 0 ow2 JohnFahy 5 4
(Milton Bradley) *spd to 1/2-way* **100/1**

6 **8** 5 **Notnow Penny**[29] 2917 2-8-4 0 FrannyNorton 3
(Milton Bradley) *s.i.s: outpcd* **100/1**

9 nk **Blunos (IRE)** 2-8-9 0 AndreaAtzeni 6
(Rod Millman) *s.i.s: a in rr* **10/1**

1m 2.28s (-0.22) **Going Correction** -0.125s/f (Firm) 9 Ran SP% **114.9**
Speed ratings (Par 92): **96,94,93,91,90 88,71,63,62**
Tote Swingers 1&2 £6.00, 2&3 £4.60, 1&3 £1.60 CSF £30.96 TOTE £2.90: £1.10, £2.30, £1.10; EX 26.10 Trifecta £109.00 Pool: £2,301.54 - 15.83 winning tickets..
Owner Og Partnership **Bred** Mrs C Lloyd **Trained** Ogbourne Maisey, Wilts

FOCUS
Only a handful of runners could be seriously considered for this juvenile contest on all known form. The winner found some improvement.

3915 BET365 MAIDEN STKS 5f 161y
6:30 (6:30) (Class 5) 3-Y-O **£2,587** (£770; £384; £192) **Stalls** Centre

Form RPR

20-6 **1** **Trinityelitedotcom (IRE)**[17] 3320 3-9-5 75 RichardKingscote 4 79+
(Tom Dascombe) *trckd ldr: chal fr 2f out tl led 1f out: pushed clr fnl 110yds* **4/6**[1]

2 **2** 2 ¼ **Hand Grenade (IRE)**[12] 3508 3-9-0 0 JohnFahy 3 64
(Eve Johnson Houghton) *led: jnd 2f out: sn drvn: narrowly hdd 1f out: outpcd fnl 110yds* **5/4**[2]

040- **3** 3 ½ **Black Eyed Girl (IRE)**[267] 6936 3-9-0 59 LiamJones 2 52
(J S Moore) *s.i.s: sn chsng ldrs: drvn over 3f out: pressed ldrs 2f out: wknd fnl f* **25/1**[3]

00 **4** 7 **Bustling Darcey**[21] 3176 3-8-7 0 OisinMurphy(7) 1 32
(Mark Gillard) *s.i.s: sn chsng ldrs: rdn 2f out and sn wknd* **100/1**

1m 11.52s (0.32) **Going Correction** -0.125s/f (Firm) 4 Ran SP% **109.3**
Speed ratings (Par 100): **92,89,84,75**
CSF £1.78 TOTE £2.00; EX 1.70 Trifecta £3.10 Pool: £1,063.88 - 257.06 winning tickets..
Owner Manor House Stables LLP **Bred** Natasha Newsome **Trained** Malpas, Cheshire

FOCUS
A desperately weak maiden, but straightforward form with the winner to his previous best.

3916 BET365.COM MAIDEN H'CAP 1m 5f 22y
7:00 (7:00) (Class 5) (0-70,68) 3-Y-O+ **£2,587** (£770; £384; £192) **Stalls** Low

Form RPR

-323 **1** **Deficit (IRE)**[19] 3257 3-8-11 **65** JamieSpencer 4 77
(Michael Bell) *mde all: shkn up 6f out: drvn and qcknd over 4f out: pushed along fr over 3f out: rdn over 2f out: hrd pressed ins fnl f: hld on all out* **7/4**[1]

2542 **2** nk **Zenafire**[19] 3231 4-9-1 **60** JackDuern(5) 6 71
(Andrew Hollinshead) *chsd ldrs: wnt 2nd 2f out: drvn and styd on fr over 1f out to cl on wnr ins fnl f: kpt on clsng stages but a hld* **9/2**[3]

-252 **3** 6 **Nateeja (IRE)**[19] 3257 3-8-10 **64** DaneO'Neill 3 66
(J W Hills) *sn chsng ldr: rdn whn pce qcknd 4f out: styd on same pce u.p and dropped to 3rd 2f out: btn fnl f* **5/2**[2]

/566 **4** 12 **Eshtyaaq**[24] 3110 6-10-0 **68** AdamKirby 7 52
(David Evans) *chsd ldrs: rdn 4f out: sn wknd* **7/1**

-520 **5** 2 ¼ **Moaning Butcher**[36] 2716 3-8-5 **59** FrannyNorton 5 40
(Mark Johnston) *chsd ldrs: wknd 6f out* **5/2**[2]

005 **6** 12 **Mr Blue Nose**[19] 2568 3-8-0 **54** oh1 (v[1]) JamieMackay 2 17
(Karen George) *a wl bhd* **66/1**

2m 49.14s (-2.86) **Going Correction** -0.125s/f (Firm)
WFA 3 from 4yo+ 14lb 6 Ran SP% **125.7**
Speed ratings (Par 103): **103,102,99,91,90 82**
Tote Swingers 1&2 £1.50, 2&3 £2.20, 1&3 £1.10 CSF £11.94 TOTE £2.80: £2.00, £1.20; EX 9.00 Trifecta £19.10 Pool: £1,584.71 - 62.16 winning tickets..
Owner Lawrie Inman **Bred** J Hanly, T Stewart & A Stroud **Trained** Newmarket, Suffolk

FOCUS
The winner was given a good front-running ride and rates a minor personal best.

3917 BET365 H'CAP 1m 2f 46y
7:30 (7:31) (Class 5) (0-75,75) 3-Y-O+ **£2,587** (£770; £384; £192) **Stalls** Low

Form RPR

-622 **1** **Duke Of Perth**[25] 3067 3-8-13 **71** JamieSpencer 5 83+
(Luca Cumani) *trckd ldrs: led 2f out: sn drvn and styd on wl u.p fnl f* **1/1**[1]

13-5 **2** 1 ½ **Stiff Upper Lip (IRE)**[11] 3535 3-8-2 **67** CameronHardie(7) 8 76
(Richard Hannon) *in rr but in tch: hdwy on outside over 2f out: chsd wnr 1f out: styd on but edgd lft fnl 100yds: no ex* **10/1**

3314 **3** 3 ½ **Perfect Cracker**[12] 3492 5-9-8 **74** RyanTate(5) 2 76
(Clive Cox) *in rr: hdwy over 3f out: chal u.p 2f out: wknd into 3rd fnl f* **9/2**[2]

-462 **4** 2 **Wilfred Pickles (IRE)**[27] 2981 7-10-0 **75** DaneO'Neill 1 74
(Jo Crowley) *in rr: in tch: drvn and hdwy to cl on ldrs over 2f out: sn rdn: wknd fnl f* **20/1**

2006 **5** 3 ½ **Flying Trader (USA)**[70] 1753 4-9-9 **70** AdamKirby 4 62
(Jane Chapple-Hyam) *led after 2f: rdn 3f out: hdd 2f out: sn wknd* **20/1**

0023 **6** 1 **Honey Of A Kitten (USA)**[8] 3617 5-9-3 **71** (v) EoinWalsh(7) 6 61
(David Evans) *chsd ldrs: rdn 3f out: wknd over 2f out* **16/1**

2425 **7** 3 **April Ciel**[18] 3273 4-9-8 **69** LukeMorris 9 53
(Ronald Harris) *led 2f: rdn 3f out: sn wknd* **20/1**

06-0 **8** 18 **Cio Cio San (IRE)**[20] 3216 3-8-4 **62** (p) CathyGannon 3 12
(Bill Turner) *a in rr* **50/1**

-545 **R** **Sandy's Row (USA)**[8] 3629 3-8-4 **62** FrannyNorton 7
(Mark Johnston) *ref to r* **5/1**[3]

2m 8.6s (-2.40) **Going Correction** -0.125s/f (Firm)
WFA 3 from 4yo+ 11lb 9 Ran SP% **123.8**
Speed ratings (Par 103): **104,102,100,98,95 94,92,78,**
Tote Swingers 1&2 £2.60, 2&3 £6.80, 1&3 £2.00 CSF £13.72 TOTE £1.70: £1.10, £2.90, £2.50; EX 11.50 Trifecta £58.50 Pool: £1,642.62 - 21.03 winning tickets..
Owner Fittocks Stud **Bred** Fittocks Stud **Trained** Newmarket, Suffolk

FOCUS
A fair race for the grade. The winner was due this and the second has good course form.

3918 CASINO AT BET365 H'CAP 1m 3f 144y
8:00 (8:00) (Class 6) (0-60,59) 3-Y-O **£1,940** (£577; £288; £144) **Stalls** Low

Form RPR

000- **1** **Portrait**[207] 8017 3-9-7 **59** LukeMorris 1 74+
(Sir Mark Prescott Bt) *chsd ldrs: drvn fr over 4f out: chal u.p 2f out: led over 1f out: drvn clr fnl f* **4/1**[3]

0063 **2** 5 **Dalliefour (IRE)**[26] 3013 3-9-1 **53** JamesDoyle 3 58
(Michael Bell) *hld up in rr but in tch: hdwy over 2f out: sn rdn: styd on fnl f to take 2nd last stride but no ch w wnr* **7/2**[2]

0325 **3** shd **Eyeline**[6] 3675 3-8-7 **50** JackDuern(5) 6 55
(Andrew Hollinshead) *led: rdn over 2f out: hdd over 1f out: outpcd by wnr fnl f: lost 2nd last strides* **8/1**

0422 **4** 10 **Whitefall (USA)**[5] 3735 3-9-0 **52** ow1 AdamKirby 7 41
(David Evans) *chsd ldrs: rdn 4f out: wknd ins fnl 2f* **6/4**[1]

00-2 **5** 2 ½ **Hail To Princess**[35] 2748 3-8-8 **46** FrannyNorton 2 31
(Patrick Chamings) *in rr: rdn and sme hdwy over 3f out: nvr rchd ldrs and sn wknd* **12/1**

-606 **6** 11 **Al Zein**[33] 2800 3-9-1 **53** SeanLevey 4 20
(Richard Hannon) *chsd ldrs: rdn 4f out: wknd 3f out* **16/1**

0040 **7** 86 **Culture Trip**[25] 3041 3-8-9 **47** (p) ShaneKelly 5
(Gary Moore) *in rr: pushed along 3f out: wknd qckly and virtually p.u 2f out* **14/1**

2m 27.73s (-2.87) **Going Correction** -0.125s/f (Firm) 7 Ran SP% **113.6**
Speed ratings (Par 98): **104,100,100,93,92 84,27**
Tote Swingers 1&2 £3.80, 2&3 £7.90, 1&3 £5.80 CSF £18.10 CT £104.78 TOTE £3.00: £2.20, £1.70; EX 14.50 Trifecta £64.30 Pool: £1,222.49 - 14.24 winning tickets..
Owner Denford Stud **Bred** Denford Stud Ltd **Trained** Newmarket, Suffolk

FOCUS
A moderate race littered with disappointing types, but the winner surely has more to come. Straightforward form.

3919 POKER AT BET365 H'CAP 1m 5y
8:30 (8:30) (Class 6) (0-55,55) 3-Y-O+ **£1,940** (£577; £288; £144) **Stalls** Low

Form RPR

0-02 **1** **Devon Diva**[17] 3314 7-8-7 **46** MichaelJMMurphy(5) 10 54
(John Gallagher) *mde all: drvn along fr 2f out: styd on wl u.p fnl f: rdn out* **8/1**[3]

5033 **2** nk **Offbeat Safaris (IRE)**[18] 3270 5-9-1 **54** EDLinehan(5) 13 62
(Ronald Harris) *chsd ldrs: wnt 2nd 2f out: styd on u.p fnl f but a jst hld by wnr* **4/1**[2]

4300 **3** 2 **The Great Gabrial**[15] 3410 4-9-7 **55** (b[1]) JamieSpencer 5 58
(Ian Williams) *s.i.s: t.k.h in rr: hdwy 3f out: drvn to chse ldrs 2f out: fnd no ex and styd on same pce fnl f* **12/1**

0604 **4** 2 **Sonnetation (IRE)**[14] 3428 3-8-5 **48** AndreaAtzeni 12 44
(Jim Boyle) *chsd ldrs: rdn over 2f out: styd on same pce* **10/1**

0-01 **5** ½ **Double Star**[25] 3040 3-8-6 **54** MatthewLawson(5) 8 49
(Jonathan Portman) *in rr: drvn along 4f out: hdwy on outside fr 2f out: kpt on but nvr gng pce to rch ldrs* **7/2**[1]

00-2 **6** 1 ¼ **The Bay Bandit**[27] 2305 6-9-2 **50** (p) AdamKirby 6 44
(Neil Mulholland) *in tch: hdwy and drvn 3f out: no prog u.p fnl 2f* **10/1**

0464 **7** 1 **Our Golden Girl**[8] 3619 3-8-7 **55** RobertTart(5) 7 45
(Shaun Lycett) *in rr: rdn 4f out: sme late prog fnl f* **20/1**

-204 **8** nk **Perfect Outlook**[17] 3314 5-8-8 **47** ow1 (p) WilliamTwiston-Davies(5) 4 38
(Charlie Longsdon) *chsd ldr: rdn and hung lft appr fnl 2f: sn btn* **7/2**[1]

00-0 **9** 10 **Buds Bruvver**[25] 3047 4-8-12 **46** oh1 [1] ShaneKelly 1 14
(Brian Baugh) *a outpcd* **66/1**

-160 **10** ½ **Poetry Writer**[15] 3399 4-9-6 **54** DaneO'Neill 3 21
(Michael Blanshard) *chsd ldrs: rdn and btn 3f out* **8/1**[3]

0/50 **11** 1 ¾ **Classic Voice (IRE)**[19] 3252 5-9-1 **52** (b[1]) MarkCoumbe(3) 2 15
(Roy Brotherton) *rdn 5f out: a in rr* **33/1**

1m 40.73s (-0.07) **Going Correction** -0.125s/f (Firm)
WFA 3 from 4yo+ 9lb 11 Ran SP% **121.7**
Speed ratings (Par 101): **95,94,92,90,90 88,87,87,77,77 75**
Tote Swingers 1&2 £10.70, 2&3 £22.80, 1&3 £31.30 CSF £40.89 CT £400.58 TOTE £11.50: £2.70, £2.00, £4.60; EX 71.80 Trifecta £721.90 Part won. Pool: £962.59 - 0.33 winning tickets..
Owner Miss Jennifer Dorey **Bred** East Burrow Farm **Trained** Chastleton, Oxon

FOCUS
A competitive, if modest handicap. Clearly limited form.

3920 BET365.COM FILLIES' H'CAP 5f 161y
9:00 (9:00) (Class 5) (0-75,70) 3-Y-O+ **£2,587** (£770; £384; £192) **Stalls** Centre

Form RPR

5011 **1** **Cara Gina**[6] 3679 3-8-12 **62** 6ex (b) LiamJones 1 76+
(William Haggas) *s.i.s: in rr: nt clr run over 2f out but sn squeezed through to chal and ld wl over 1f out: gng clr whn stmbld fnl 150yds: easily* **1/1**[1]

-300 **2** 3 ¾ **Comptonspirit**[24] 3078 9-9-2 **65** MatthewLawson(5) 5 67
(Brian Baugh) *in rr: drvn and hdwy on outer over 2f out: sn chsng ldrs: kpt on clsng stages to take 2nd but no ch w wnr* **20/1**

3333 **3** shd **My Own Way Home**[7] 3660 5-8-12 **56** CathyGannon 4 58
(David Evans) *in tch: drvn to chse ldrs over 2f out and edgd lft: kpt on to press for wl-hld 2nd fnl 110yds but nvr any ch w wnr* **5/2**[2]

155 **4** nk **Night Trade (IRE)**[8] 3622 6-9-7 **70** (p) EDLinehan(5) 3 71
(Ronald Harris) *chsd ldrs: drvn to dispute 2nd fnl 110yds but nvr any ch w wnr and styd on same pce for 4th* **8/1**[3]

0040 **5** ¾ **Best Be Careful (IRE)**[7] 3667 5-9-7 **65** DaneO'Neill 2 63
(Mark Usher) *led tl jnd 2f out: hdd sn after: no ch w wnr fnl f and outpcd fnl 110yds* **10/1**

6-0 **6** 5 **Mandy Lexi (IRE)**[64] 1892 3-8-12 **62** AndreaAtzeni 6 42
(Ian Williams) *chsd ldr: rdn over 2f out: btn sn after* **8/1**[3]

1m 10.71s (-0.49) **Going Correction** -0.125s/f (Firm)
WFA 3 from 5yo+ 6lb 6 Ran SP% **114.6**
Speed ratings (Par 100): **98,93,92,92,91 84**
Tote Swingers 1&2 £16.40, 2&3 £15.20, 1&3 £1.02 CSF £23.68 TOTE £1.50: £1.10, £8.80; EX 25.10 Trifecta £46.30 Pool: £1,492.15 - 24.14 winning tickets..
Owner Mrs Deborah June James **Bred** Old Mill Stud & S Williams & J Parry **Trained** Newmarket, Suffolk

FOCUS
A fair sprint handicap. The winner progressed again with the next three setting the level.
T/Plt: £39.60 to a £1 stake. Pool: £75,797.96 - 1,396.64 winning tickets. T/Qpdt: £17.40 to a £1 stake. Pool: £6,572.70 - 278.65 winning tickets. ST

[3655] BRIGHTON (L-H)

Tuesday, July 2

OFFICIAL GOING: Good to firm (good in places; 8.0) changing to good after race 4 (3:45)

Wind: medium, against Weather: overcast

3921 HARDINGS FIRST ATERERS H'CAP — 5f 59y

2:15 (2:15) (Class 5) (0-70,67) 3-Y-O+ £2,587 (£770; £384; £192) Stalls Low

Form RPR

0045 **1** nk **Johnny Splash (IRE)**[7] 3660 4-8-2 **50**.......................... OisinMurphy(7) 6 58
(Roger Teal) *outpcd in last pair and niggled along: clsd and edgd lft over 1f out: nt clr run and swtchd rt 1f out: stl n.m.r tl hdwy to chse wnr wl ins fnl f: r.o wl: nvr quite getting to wnr* **6/1**

3241 **2** 1 ½ **Where's Reiley (USA)**[11] 3529 7-9-12 **67**......................(v) SebSanders 1 69
(Michael Attwater) *dwlt: sn rcvrd to press ldrs: rdn and ev ch 2f out: no ex ins fnl f: wknd cl home* **2/1**[1]

4521 **3** hd **Putin (IRE)**[3] 3816 5-9-7 **67** 6ex................................(bt) NathanAlison(5) 4 68
(Phil McEntee) *racd keenly: pressed ldrs on outer: rdn and ev ch 2f out: outpcd ent fnl f: kpt on same pce after* **3/1**[2]

5030 **4** ½ **Little China**[22] 3154 4-8-11 **52**...(b) MartinDwyer 2 51
(William Muir) *sn bustled along to ld: rdn and hdd 2f out: unable qck ent fnl f: btn whn n.m.r and edgd lft fnl 100yds* **12/1**

0504 **5** 8 **Marvelino**[7] 3658 3-8-12 **63**..(b) PhilipPrince(5) 5 33
(Pat Eddery) *a outpcd in rr: rdn over 3f out: wknd over 1f out: burst blood vessel* **8/1**

4060 **D** **The Strig**[3] 3841 6-9-5 **60**.. J-PGuillambert 3 69
(Stuart Williams) *pressed ldrs tl led 2f out: sn rdn: kpt on u.p ins fnl f: pushed along and pressed towards fin: a holding on* **4/1**[3]

1m 3.64s (1.34) **Going Correction** +0.175s/f (Good)
WFA 3 from 4yo+ 5lb **6** Ran SP% **111.4**
Speed ratings (Par 103): **95,93,92,92,79 96**
Tote Swingers 1&2 £4.40, 2&3 £2.70, 1&3 £1.70 CSF £26.75 TOTE £5.30: £2.00, £2.90; EX 29.70 Trifecta £95.00 Pool: £2,862.13 - 22.58 winning tickets..
Owner Epping Racing **Bred** J Connolly **Trained** Ashtead, Surrey

FOCUS
This moderate sprint handicap was run at a strong pace and the main action was down the centre inside the final 2f. Ordinary form.

3922 3663 FIRST FOR FOOD SERVICE H'CAP — 5f 213y

2:45 (2:45) (Class 6) (0-55,55) 3-Y-O+ £1,940 (£577; £288; £144) Stalls Low

Form RPR

0335 **1** **Renoir's Lady**[26] 3015 5-9-2 **50**.. GeorgeBaker 3 61
(Simon Dow) *hld up off the pce in last trio: clsd 2f out: swtchd rt and effrt over 1f out: hanging lft but r.o to ld ins fnl f: stl hanging but kpt on* **6/1**

30-0 **2** ¾ **Excellent Aim**[150] 493 6-9-3 **51**...................................... RyanPowell(3) 11 63
(George Margarson) *chsd ldr: rdn to ld over 1f out: hdd and styd on same pce ins fnl f* **12/1**

6-00 **3** shd **Sweet Talking Guy (IRE)**[29] 2931 3-8-7 **50**...........(t) SimonPearce(3) 12 57
(Lydia Pearce) *midfield: clsd over 2f out: chsd ldrs u.p over 1f out: kpt on and pressed ldrs ins fnl f: one pce fnl 100yds* **16/1**

0-02 **4** 2 **Ridgeway Sapphire**[7] 3660 6-8-12 **46** oh1..................(v) HayleyTurner 2 48
(Mark Usher) *s.i.s: wl bhd: rdn 4f out: effrt on inner 2f out: swtchd rt 1f out: styd on but no threat to ldrs* **7/2**[2]

6403 **5** 1 ¼ **Surrey Dream (IRE)**[7] 3657 4-8-12 **46**.........................(tp) MartinDwyer 4 44
(John Bridger) *midfield: rdn 4f out: drvn and hdwy on inner over 1f out: no imp ins fnl f* **5/1**[3]

403 **6** 3 ¼ **Tooley Woods (IRE)**[8] 3623 4-9-4 **52**.............................. CathyGannon 6 40
(Tony Carroll) *hmpd s and slowly away: steadily rcvrd and in midfield after 2f: rdn and unable qck over 1f out: wknd 1f out* **3/1**[1]

2422 **7** 2 ¼ **Slatey Hen (IRE)**[22] 3154 5-9-7 **55**.................................(p) NeilCallan 10 35
(Violet M Jordan) *led: drvn and hdd 1f out: btn 1f out: fdd fnl f* **7/1**

0004 **8** 3 ¼ **Miakora**[56] 2133 5-8-9 **46**... RossAtkinson(3) 5 16
(Mick Quinn) *chsd ldrs: rdn and struggling over 2f out: wknd over 1f out* **25/1**

000 **9** 4 ½ **Bobbyow**[19] 3247 5-8-12 **46** oh1.. PatCosgrave 7
(K F Clutterbuck) *wnt lft s: hld up in rr: n.d* **50/1**

60-0 **10** 3 ¾ **Delphica (IRE)**[17] 3316 3-8-11 **51**.....................................(v[1]) SamHitchcott 9
(Gary Moore) *chsd ldrs tl rdn and lost pl over 2f out: wl bhd fnl f* **25/1**

0000 **R** **Sakhee's Alround**[17] 3325 3-8-3 **46** oh1......................(p) DarrenEgan(3) 1
(K F Clutterbuck) *ref to r* **66/1**

1m 11.13s (0.93) **Going Correction** +0.175s/f (Good)
WFA 3 from 4yo+ 6lb **11** Ran SP% **115.4**
Speed ratings (Par 101): **100,99,98,96,94 90,87,82,76,71**
Tote Swingers 1&2 £16.80, 2&3 £16.10, 1&3 £20.20 CSF £71.10 CT £1111.18 TOTE £7.40: £2.30, £4.00, £6.10; EX 73.10 Trifecta £1366.60 Part won. Pool: £1,822.23 - 0.41 winning tickets..
Owner Malcolm & Alicia Aldis **Bred** Laundry Cottage Stud Farm **Trained** Epsom, Surrey

FOCUS
A very ordinary sprint handicap, run at a strong early pace and again the action developed down the centre late on. The first and second's better turf form sets the level.

3923 EBF / BRIGHTON'S BIG SCREEN MAIDEN STKS — 1m 1f 209y

3:15 (3:16) (Class 5) 3-Y-O £3,881 (£1,155; £577; £288) Stalls High

Form RPR

4-3 **1** **Sadiq**[17] 3343 3-9-5 0.. JimCrowley 2 79+
(Saeed bin Suroor) *chsd ldrs: chal and rdn 2f out: drvn to ld 1f out: clr ins fnl f: kpt on* **11/4**[2]

2 1 **Apparently** 3-9-5 0.. MickaelBarzalona 4 78+
(Saeed bin Suroor) *hld up in tch in rr: effrt on outer and rn green over 3f out: stl green whn hung lft and hmpd over 1f out: hdwy but stl gng lft 1f out: r.o wl ins fnl f: wnt 2nd cl home* **5/4**[1]

23 **3** hd **Response**[10] 3572 3-9-5 0.. NeilCallan 5 75
(William Haggas) *hld up in tch: rdn and effrt 2f out: drvn and pressed ldrs 1f out: chsd wnr ins fnl f: kpt on but lost 2nd last strides* **7/2**[3]

3254 **4** 1 ¼ **Punditry**[28] 2952 3-9-5 73...(v[1]) RobertHavlin 1 73
(John Gosden) *led and set stdy gallop: rdn and qcknd 2f out: drvn and hdd 1f out: one pce and hld whn edgd rt towards fin* **8/1**

5 9 **Rocky Ride (IRE)** 3-9-0 0.. LiamKeniry 3 51
(Andrew Balding) *s.i.s: sn rcvrd and chsd ldng pair: rdn and lost pl over 2f out: wknd over 1f out* **25/1**

2m 6.4s (2.80) **Going Correction** +0.175s/f (Good) **5** Ran SP% **108.3**
Speed ratings (Par 100): **95,94,94,93,85**
CSF £6.39 TOTE £3.80: £1.30, £1.80; EX 8.00 Trifecta £13.30 Pool: £3,301.00 - 185.47 winning tickets..
Owner Godolphin **Bred** Darley **Trained** Newmarket, Suffolk

FOCUS
A good 3-y-o maiden by track standards, run at a steady pace. The winner perhaps didn't need to improve on his good Sandown run and the second was better than the bare facts.

3924 CATERING SERVICES INTERNATIONAL H'CAP — 1m 1f 209y

3:45 (3:46) (Class 6) (0-55,58) 4-Y-O+ £1,940 (£577; £288; £144) Stalls High

Form RPR

3021 **1** **Young Jackie**[21] 3169 5-8-10 **51**.............................(b) JordanVaughan(7) 7 60+
(George Margarson) *t.k.h: hld up in tch in midfield: rdn and clsd to ld over 1f out: clr and edgd lft ins fnl f: kpt on* **6/1**

0021 **2** 1 ½ **Beacon Lady**[10] 3655 4-9-4 **57** 6ex.............................. NicoleNordblad(5) 5 63
(William Knight) *stdd s: hld up in tch in rr: effrt on outer ent fnl 2f: hdwy u.p to chse ldrs 1f out: kpt on to go 2nd cl home* **6/4**[1]

-02U **3** nk **Lady Barastar (IRE)**[10] 3580 5-9-3 **51**..........................(b) GeorgeBaker 9 57
(Amanda Perrett) *stdd s: t.k.h: hld up in last trio: rdn and hdwy whn edgd lft over 1f out: chsd wnr ins fnl f: no imp: lost 2nd cl home* **9/2**[3]

0002 **4** 2 ½ **Benandonner (USA)**[7] 3657 10-8-8 **49**......................(p) JoeyHaynes(7) 2 50+
(Paddy Butler) *t.k.h: led and set stdy gallop: clr 4f out: rdn ent fnl 2f: hdd and unable qck over 1f out: one pce fnl f* **12/1**

0006 **5** 1 ½ **Tatting**[8] 3642 4-8-12 **53**... JoshCrane(7) 1 51
(Chris Dwyer) *t.k.h: chsd ldr tl 4f out: styd prom: wnt 2nd again 2f out: no ex u.p over 1f out: wknd ins fnl f* **25/1**

5061 **6** 3 ¾ **Lightning Spirit**[7] 3657 5-9-3 **58** 6ex...............................(p) NedCurtis(7) 4 49
(Gary Moore) *hld up in tch in last pair: rdn and clsd whn nt clr run and swtchd rt over 1f out: no prog and wl btn ins fnl f* **4/1**[2]

103 **7** nse **Ermyntrude**[26] 3015 6-9-2 **55**..(v) JemmaMarshall(5) 3 46
(Pat Phelan) *chsd ldrs: wnt 2nd 4f out tl 2f out: wknd over 1f out* **10/1**

/006 **8** 8 **Keyhole Kate**[7] 3657 4-8-12 **46** oh1................................(p) LiamKeniry 6 22
(Polly Gundry) *hld up in tch in midfield: rdn and lost pl over 2f out: bhd 1f out* **25/1**

2m 7.65s (4.05) **Going Correction** +0.175s/f (Good) **8** Ran SP% **116.9**
Speed ratings (Par 101): **90,88,88,86,85 82,82,75**
Tote Swingers 1&2 £2.20, 2&3 £3.00, 1&3 £4.50 CSF £15.83 CT £43.72 TOTE £4.80: £1.30, £1.20, £1.10; EX 19.20 Trifecta £73.30 Pool: £4,146.67 - 42.42 winning tickets..
Owner Miss J Kentish **Bred** M F Kentish **Trained** Newmarket, Suffolk

FOCUS
This was competitive for the class. They went steady early before the pace lifted turning for home and the principals came clear. Straightforward form. The winner can rate higher again.

3925 3663 H'CAP — 1m 3f 196y

4:15 (4:16) (Class 5) (0-70,70) 3-Y-O+ £2,587 (£770; £384; £192) Stalls High

Form RPR

3-13 **1** **Brigh (IRE)**[14] 3437 3-9-1 **70**.. HayleyTurner 2 90+
(David Simcock) *hld up in tch in rr: smooth hdwy to chse ldr and swtchd to r against stands' rail 2f out: led over 1f out: stormed clr fnl f: rdn out hands and heels* **6/4**[1]

6052 **2** 13 **Megalala (IRE)**[10] 3580 12-9-3 **59**...................................... KieranO'Neill 3 58
(John Bridger) *led: c towards stands' rail 3f out: rdn and hdd over 1f out: sn btn: no ch w wnr but plugged on to hold 2nd* **10/1**[3]

6-22 **3** 2 **Spieta (IRE)**[14] 3437 3-9-0 **69**.. KirstyMilczarek 4 65
(Luca Cumani) *hld up in tch in last pair: c towards stands' rail and effrt over 2f out: 3rd and no ch w wnr over 1f out: plugged on* **6/4**[1]

0250 **4** 1 ½ **Rossetti**[53] 2232 5-10-0 **70**.. GeorgeBaker 5 64
(Gary Moore) *t.k.h: chsd ldr: c to r against stands' rail 3f out: rdn and unable qck whn bdly hmpd 2f out: 4th and wl hld after* **5/1**[2]

640V **5** 40 **Dark Justice (IRE)**[10] 3578 3-7-11 **55** oh4...................... DarrenEgan(3) 1
(Tim Pitt) *chsd ldrs: rdn and lost pl over 2f out: sn lost tch: t.o fnl f* **33/1**

2m 30.72s (-1.98) **Going Correction** +0.175s/f (Good)
WFA 3 from 5yo+ 13lb **5** Ran SP% **108.7**
Speed ratings (Par 103): **113,104,103,102,75**
CSF £16.52 TOTE £2.80: £1.90, £2.90; EX 14.70 Trifecta £17.40 Pool: £3,656.03 - 157.12 winning tickets..
Owner Al Asayl Bloodstock Ltd **Bred** Sheikh Sultan Bin Khalifa Al Nayhan **Trained** Newmarket, Suffolk

FOCUS
The going was eased to good prior to this very modest handicap. The winner was in a different league, with the race rather falling apart in behind. The form could be rated 4-6lb better.

3926 WAR & PEACE REVIVAL, FOLKESTONE RACECOURSE H'CAP — 7f 214y

4:45 (4:45) (Class 5) (0-70,71) 4-Y-O+ £2,587 (£770; £384; £192) Stalls Centre

Form RPR

3001 **1** **Aqua Ardens (GER)**[26] 3015 5-9-4 **67**..............................(t) PatCosgrave 4 75
(George Baker) *stdd s: t.k.h: hld up wl in tch: waiting for gap over 1f out: gap opened and qcknd to chal ins fnl f: led wl ins fnl f: sn in command* **8/1**[3]

3230 **2** ½ **Exceedexpectations (IRE)**[13] 3472 4-9-7 **70**................ HayleyTurner 3 77
(Conor Dore) *led and set stdy gallop: rdn and qcknd ent fnl 2f: drvn and kpt on wl fr over 1f out tl hdd and no ex wl ins fnl f* **7/4**[2]

431 **3** ½ **Decent Fella (IRE)**[7] 3661 7-9-8 **71** 6ex..............................(t) NeilCallan 7 77
(Violet M Jordan) *stdd s: t.k.h: hld up in tch in rr: swtchd lft and effrt u.p over 1f out: ev ch ins fnl f: unable qck fnl 50yds* **11/10**[1]

052 **4** 4 **Fairy Mist (IRE)**[14] 3430 6-8-2 **51** oh5............................. KieranO'Neill 5 48
(John Bridger) *t.k.h: chsd ldr: rdn and ev ch 2f out tl outpcd and lost pl ent fnl f: wknd fnl 100yds* **33/1**

0-06 **5** ½ **My Learned Friend (IRE)**[10] 3575 9-8-9 **65**...............(p) RobHornby(7) 1 60
(Andrew Balding) *stdd s: t.k.h: hld up in tch in last pair: hdwy to chse ldrs 3f out: rdn and pressing ldrs 2f out: wknd ins fnl f* **33/1**

0020 **6** 6 **Saint Irene**[24] 3111 4-9-0 **63**... LiamKeniry 2 45
(Michael Blanshard) *t.k.h: hld up wl in tch: rdn and unable qck wl over 1f out: wknd 1f out* **10/1**

1m 37.7s (1.70) **Going Correction** +0.175s/f (Good) **6** Ran SP% **110.1**
Speed ratings (Par 103): **98,97,97,93,92 86**
Tote Swingers 1&2 £1.60, 2&3 £1.30, 1&3 £2.40 CSF £21.65 TOTE £8.00: £2.50, £1.20; EX 24.50 Trifecta £48.40 Pool: £3,792.63 - 58.74 winning tickets..
Owner M Khan X2 **Bred** Gestut Karlshof **Trained** Manton, Wilts

FOCUS
A moderate handicap, run at an average pace and again the runners came over to the nearside. The second is the best guide.

3927 DGH RECRUITMENT 15 YEAR ANNIVERSARY H'CAP 6f 209y
5:15 (5:15) (Class 5) (0-70,70) 3-Y-O £2,587 (£770; £384; £192) Stalls Low

Form RPR
-200 1 **Lionheart**[40] 2593 3-9-6 **69** KirstyMilczarek 1 80+
(Luca Cumani) *stdd after s: t.k.h: hld up in tch in last pair: effrt and qcknd to ld 1f out: edgd rt jst ins fnl f: r.o strly: drew wl clr fnl 100yds: readily* 9/2[3]
-132 2 3 **This Is Nice (IRE)**[8] 3620 3-9-7 **70** JimCrowley 8 73
(Tom Dascombe) *led and set stdy gallop: bought field to stands' rail 3f out: rdn and qcknd 2f out: hdd 1f out: outpcd by wnr but hld on for 2nd fnl 100yds* 2/1[2]
5-23 3 nse **Aglaophonos**[29] 2934 3-9-5 **68** NeilCallan 4 71
(Roger Varian) *t.k.h: chsd ldr: rdn and ev ch over 1f out: outpcd by wnr whn hmpd and swtchd lft jst ins fnl f: kpt on same pce after* 7/4[1]
0002 4 1 1/4 **Club House (IRE)**[7] 3665 3-8-12 **61** MartinDwyer 5 61
(Robert Mills) *stdd s: hld up in last pair: swtchd lft and effrt over 1f out: no imp 1f out: wknd ins fnl f* 7/1
3013 5 3/4 **The Black Jacobin**[11] 3533 3-9-5 **68** (b) LiamKeniry 6 66
(J S Moore) *t.k.h early: chsd ldrs: rdn and unable qck over 2f out: plugging on same pce and hld whn swtchd lft ins fnl f* 12/1
34-5 6 12 **New Rich**[29] 2919 3-8-13 **62** AdamBeschizza 7 29
(Sylvester Kirk) *t.k.h early: hld up in tch in midfield: rdn 4f out: dropped to last and struggling 3f out: lost tch over 1f out* 16/1

1m 24.63s (1.53) **Going Correction** +0.175s/f (Good) 6 Ran SP% **114.0**
Speed ratings (Par 100): **98,94,94,93,92 78**
Tote Swingers 1&2 £2.40, 2&3 £2.00, 1&3 £2.20 CSF £14.30 CT £20.89 TOTE £6.40: £2.20, £2.20; EX 14.00 Trifecta £35.50 Pool: £3,562.95 - 75.08 winning tickets..
Owner Fittocks Stud & Andrew Bengough **Bred** Fittocks Stud **Trained** Newmarket, Suffolk

FOCUS
A modest 3-y-o handicap. They went a routine sort of pace. The winner can do better if going the right way from this.
T/Plt: £127.20 to a £1 stake. Pool: £90,336.79 - 518.23 winning tickets. T/Qpdt: £13.00 to a £1 stake. Pool: £7,153.79 - 406.76 winning tickets. SP

3709 HAMILTON (R-H)
Tuesday, July 2

OFFICIAL GOING: Good (good to firm in places; 9.2) changing to good after race 4 (4:00)
Wind: Fresh, half behind Weather: Overcast, showers

3928 RACING UK ON SKY CHANNEL 432 MAIDEN STKS 6f 5y
2:30 (2:30) (Class 5) 2-Y-O £3,408 (£1,006; £503) Stalls High

Form RPR
05 1 **Overstep (IRE)**[10] 3568 2-9-5 0 JoeFanning 5 80+
(Mark Johnston) *mde all: rdn and qcknd over 1f out: kpt on strly fnl f: unchal* 25/1
3 2 4 **Morning Post**[18] 3295 2-9-5 0 PhillipMakin 1 68
(Kevin Ryan) *chsd ldr: rdn 2f out: kpt on same pce fnl f* 2/9[1]
3 2 **Black Treacle (IRE)** 2-9-5 0 SilvestreDeSousa 4 62
(Keith Dalgleish) *dwlt: sn in tch: hdwy 1/2-way: sn rdn: outpcd fr over 1f out* 8/1[2]
4 3 1/2 **Woodbridge** 2-9-5 0 TonyHamilton 6 52
(Richard Fahey) *s.i.s: bhd: stdy hdwy after 2f: rdn and outpcd fr wl over 1f out* 11/1[3]
6 5 13 **Spring Willow (IRE)**[78] 1565 2-9-0 0 JasonHart[(5)] 2 13
(Eric Alston) *chsd ldrs to 1/2-way: sn rdn and wknd* 50/1

1m 11.73s (-0.47) **Going Correction** -0.20s/f (Firm) 5 Ran SP% **107.1**
Speed ratings (Par 94): **95,89,87,82,65**
Tote Swinger 1&2 £3.90 CSF £30.91 TOTE £16.40: £6.20, £1.10; EX 32.60 Trifecta £76.60 Pool: £3,356.66 - 32.82 winning tickets..
Owner Sheikh Hamdan Bin Mohammed Al Maktoum **Bred** Darley **Trained** Middleham Moor, N Yorks

FOCUS
Due to the position of the rail on the loop, all races over distances further than 6f were approximately 25yds shorter than the official measurements. A tricky race to assess but the form has been given a chance.

3929 WEATHERBYS BANK CLAIMING STKS 5f 4y
3:00 (3:01) (Class 6) 3-5-Y-O £2,045 (£603; £302) Stalls Centre

Form RPR
0000 1 **Lady Del Sol**[7] 3654 5-8-4 60 (p) RaulDaSilva[(3)] 5 66
(Marjorie Fife) *taken early to post: mde all: rdn over 1f out: hld on wl fnl f* 7/2[3]
0-06 2 2 **Scentpastparadise**[9] 3611 3-8-8 75 (t) PJMcDonald 2 64
(Ann Duffield) *cl up: effrt and drvn over 1f out: kpt on same pce fnl f* 6/4[1]
3-30 3 2 **Done Dreaming (IRE)**[20] 3221 3-8-9 61 TonyHamilton 4 58
(Richard Fahey) *chsd ldrs: drvn along over 2f out: one pce fr over 1f out* 13/2
5541 4 1/2 **Script**[10] 3569 4-8-12 59 JordanHibberd[(7)] 1 62
(Alan Berry) *in tch: shkn up and hdwy over 2f out: drifted lft and one pce fnl f* 3/1[2]
56-0 5 5 **Lothian Countess**[31] 2888 3-8-4 57 [1] RoystonFfrench 3 33
(Ian Semple) *restless in stalls: dwlt and wnt rt s: bhd: sme hdwy and hung rt 2f out: sn n.d* 16/1
0-00 6 4 **Vanessa**[4] 3772 3-8-4 60 (b[1]) JamesSullivan 6 18
(Ian Semple) *taken early to post: chsd ldrs tl rdn and wknd 2f out* 22/1

58.56s (-1.44) **Going Correction** -0.20s/f (Firm) 6 Ran SP% **110.8**
WFA 3 from 4yo+ 5lb
Speed ratings (Par 101): **103,99,96,95,87 81**
Tote Swingers 1&2 £1.90, 2&3 £1.90, 1&3 £2.50 CSF £8.94 TOTE £4.80: £2.50, £1.40; EX 10.50 Trifecta £46.10 Pool: £4,086.79 - 66.41 winning tickets..The winner was claimed by Jo Hughes for £3,000.
Owner Mrs Sue Johnson **Bred** Bond Thoroughbred Corporation **Trained** Stillington, N Yorks

FOCUS
A moderate claimer with most struggling for form. The race could be rated up to 6lb higher.

3930 WEATHERBYS HAMILTON INSURANCE H'CAP 1m 4f 17y
3:30 (3:30) (Class 5) (0-75,73) 3-Y-O+ £3,881 (£1,155; £577; £288) Stalls Low

Form RPR
4331 1 **Wadacre Sarko**[7] 3653 3-8-13 **71** 6ex JoeFanning 7 79+
(Mark Johnston) *trckd ldrs: hdwy to ld over 2f out: rdn and r.o wl fr over 1f out* 6/5[1]
2412 2 1 **Schmooze (IRE)**[5] 3709 4-9-4 **63** LeeTopliss 1 69+
(Linda Perratt) *hld up last but in tch: stdy hdwy over 2f out: rdn to chse wnr over 1f out: kpt on ins fnl f: hld towards fin* 4/1[3]
-042 3 1 **Aleksandar**[18] 3284 4-9-13 **72** GrahamLee 2 76
(Jim Goldie) *disp ld: led 1/2-way to over 2f out: sn rdn and rallied: one pce fnl f* 7/2[2]
3561 4 2 **Pertuis (IRE)**[12] 3504 7-9-7 **66** PJMcDonald 5 67
(Micky Hammond) *in tch: effrt and cl up over 2f out: kpt on same pce fr over 1f out* 9/1
00/5 5 3/4 **Lochiel**[20] 3199 9-8-9 **54** TomEaves 3 54
(Ian Semple) *prom: rdn whn n.m.r and outpcd over 1f out: kpt on fnl f: no imp* 25/1
1/0- 6 9 **Red Eyes**[287] 6338 5-9-13 **72** AndrewMullen 4 58
(Chris Grant) *dwlt: t.k.h and sn chsng ldrs: lost pl over 4f out: sn struggling* 66/1
0-00 7 10 **Grandiloquent**[115] 948 4-9-11 **73** BrianToomey[(3)] 8 44
(Kevin Ryan) *led to 1/2-way: cl up: lost pl whn n.m.r over 2f out: sn btn* 10/1

2m 36.77s (-1.83) **Going Correction** -0.05s/f (Good)
WFA 3 from 4yo+ 13lb 7 Ran SP% **112.1**
Speed ratings (Par 103): **104,103,102,101,100 94,88**
Tote Swingers 1&2 £1.70, 2&3 £2.50, 1&3 £1.90 CSF £5.98 CT £12.25 TOTE £1.70: £1.10, £2.70; EX 6.80 Trifecta £19.30 Pool: £3,461.62 - 134.20 winning tickets..
Owner Wadacre Stud **Bred** Wadacre Stud **Trained** Middleham Moor, N Yorks

FOCUS
A modest handicap won in likeable fashion by the improving winner. The form is taken at face value.

3931 IRISH STALLION FARMS EBF CONDITIONS STKS 1m 65y
4:00 (4:00) (Class 3) 3-Y-O+ £9,703 (£2,887; £1,443; £721) Stalls Low

Form RPR
0230 1 **Galician**[5] 3725 4-9-4 92 JoeFanning 2 102+
(Mark Johnston) *mde all at stdy pce: qcknd wl over 1f out: kpt on strly fnl f* 6/1[2]
6012 2 3 1/4 **Quick Wit**[17] 3347 6-9-9 109 (p) SilvestreDeSousa 4 99
(Saeed bin Suroor) *t.k.h: pressed wnr: rdn over 2f out: kpt on same pce fnl f* 1/5[1]
0653 3 6 **Beacon Lodge (IRE)**[10] 3564 8-9-9 95 PaddyAspell 3 85
(David Nicholls) *t.k.h: prom: stdy hdwy over 3f out: rdn over 2f out: sn edgd rt and outpcd* 10/1[3]
360 4 15 **Bix (IRE)**[33] 2794 3-8-7 47 JordanHibberd[(7)] 1 47?
(Alan Berry) *trckd ldrs tl rdn and wknd wl over 2f out* 200/1

1m 46.35s (-2.05) **Going Correction** -0.05s/f (Good)
WFA 3 from 4yo+ 9lb 4 Ran SP% **107.2**
Speed ratings (Par 107): **108,104,98,83**
CSF £7.94 TOTE £5.30; EX 8.90 Trifecta £7.50 Pool: £2,074.22 - 206.41 winning tickets..
Owner Sheikh Hamdan Bin Mohammed Al Maktoum **Bred** Darley **Trained** Middleham Moor, N Yorks

FOCUS
A disappointing race for the money with only three realistic contenders, and the form is worth little. The winner dictated slow fractions.

3932 WEATHERBYS HAMILTON INSURANCE MAIDEN STKS 6f 5y
4:30 (4:33) (Class 5) 3-Y-O+ £3,234 (£962; £481; £240) Stalls Centre

Form RPR
04 1 **Shady McCoy (USA)**[36] 2719 3-9-5 0 RobertWinston 8 78
(David Barron) *in tch: smooth hdwy to ld over 1f out: pushed along and drew clr fnl f: easily* 2/1[1]
305 2 7 **Royal Duchess**[39] 2634 3-9-0 47 AmyRyan 10 52
(Lucy Normile) *led: rdn over 2f out: hdd over 1f out: kpt on: no ch w wnr* 10/1
503 3 1 **Lady Calantha**[53] 2241 3-9-0 51 PaddyAspell 11 49
(Alan Berry) *hld up in midfield: rdn and hdwy over 1f out: kpt on fnl f: nvr able to chal* 25/1
6-00 4 1 1/2 **Star Request**[13] 3463 3-9-0 57 JoeFanning 1 45
(Keith Dalgleish) *bhd tl hdwy 2f out: styd on fnl f: nvr on terms* 10/3[2]
6 5 7 **True That (IRE)**[13] 3479 3-9-5 0 PhillipMakin 4 29
(David Nicholls) *in tch tl rdn and wknd wl over 1f out* 17/2
0-06 6 1/2 **Myjestic Melody (IRE)**[18] 3286 5-8-13 44 EvaMoscrop[(7)] 7 22
(Noel Wilson) *chsd ldrs: rdn over 2f out: hung rt and wknd over 1f out* 28/1
-325 7 1 1/2 **Pastoral Prey**[20] 3198 3-9-5 57 (b[1]) TomEaves 5 23
(Ian Semple) *cl up tl rdn and wknd over 1f out* 11/2[3]
5 8 6 **Time For Crabbies (IRE)**[10] 3593 3-9-5 0 GrahamLee 3 5
(Lisa Williamson) *slowly away: outpcd in rr: sme late hdwy: nvr on terms* 12/1
0 9 3 **Cantara**[61] 1962 3-8-9 0 JasonHart[(5)] 6
(Eric Alston) *bhd and outpcd: no ch fr 1/2-way* 25/1
10 5 **Alfred The Great** 3-8-12 0 VictorSantos[(7)] 9
(Richard Ford) *chsd ldrs tl hung rt and wknd over 2f out* 40/1
55-0 11 2 3/4 **Mr Khan**[60] 1995 5-9-11 46 LeeTopliss 12
(Linda Perratt) *in tch: drvn over 2f out: sn wknd* 40/1

1m 10.5s (-1.70) **Going Correction** -0.20s/f (Firm)
WFA 3 from 5yo 6lb 11 Ran SP% **115.1**
Speed ratings (Par 103): **103,93,92,90,81 80,78,70,66,59 56**
Tote Swingers 1&2 £5.10, 2&3 £12.60, 1&3 £9.50 CSF £21.19 TOTE £3.50: £2.50, £2.70, £4.70; EX 22.80 Trifecta £289.70 Pool: £5,578.74 - 14.43 winning tickets..
Owner Allwins Stables **Bred** Bluegrass Hall Llc **Trained** Maunby, N Yorks

FOCUS
A weak maiden but the form is sound behind the easy winner.

3933 WEATHERBYS PRIVATE BANKING H'CAP 5f 4y
5:00 (5:02) (Class 5) (0-75,75) 3-Y-O+ £3,234 (£962; £481; £240) Stalls Centre

Form RPR
0625 1 **Imperial Legend (IRE)**[12] 3505 4-9-11 **74** (p) AndrewMullen 9 84
(David Nicholls) *cl up: rdn to ld over 1f out: edgd rt ins fnl f: kpt on strly* 7/1

-052 **2** 1 ¼ **Diman Waters (IRE)**[10] 3569 6-9-7 **75**............................ JasonHart(5) 5 81
(Eric Alston) *cl up: effrt and chsd wnr over 1f out: kpt on ins fnl f* **9/2**
4111 **3** ¾ **Bondi Beach Boy**[7] 3654 4-8-7 **56**............................ PJMcDonald 8 59
(James Turner) *prom: effrt and hdwy over 1f out: kpt on same pce wl ins fnl f* **11/4**[1]
03 **4** 2 **Captain Scooby**[13] 3462 7-9-0 **70**............................ ConnorBeasley(7) 2 66+
(Richard Guest) *bhd: rdn after 2f: hdwy on outside wl over 1f out: kpt on fnl f: no imp* **4/1**[3]
400 **5** ½ **Economic Crisis (IRE)**[19] 3236 4-9-8 **71**............................ PaddyAspell 3 65
(Alan Berry) *awkward s: hld up: rdn and hdwy wl over 1f out: kpt on fnl f: no imp* **22/1**
4121 **6** 1 ¾ **Salvatore Fury (IRE)**[15] 3392 3-8-9 **63**............................(p) JoeFanning 4 51
(Keith Dalgleish) *t.k.h: prom: n.m.r over 2f out: edgd lft and no ex over 1f out* **10/3**[2]
-606 **7** 1 **Distant Sun (USA)**[5] 3713 9-8-8 **57** ow1............................(p) TomEaves 6 41
(Linda Perratt) *in tch: rdn over 2f out: outpcd over 1f out* **33/1**
-030 **8** shd **Cayman Fox**[33] 2795 8-8-7 **56** oh5............................ RoystonFfrench 7 40
(Linda Perratt) *led tl rdn and hdd over 1f out: sn btn* **50/1**
0-06 **9** 17 **Sandwith**[31] 2880 10-9-0 **68**............................(p) LMcNiff(5) 1
(Ian Semple) *prom to 1/2-way: rdn and wknd over 2f out: t.o* **50/1**

58.38s (-1.62) **Going Correction** -0.20s/f (Firm)
WFA 3 from 4yo+ 5lb **9** Ran SP% **111.6**
Speed ratings (Par 103): **104,102,100,97,96 94,92,92,65**
Tote Swingers 1&2 £4.70, 2&3 £2.70, 1&3 £4.20 CSF £35.82 CT £105.94 TOTE £6.40: £1.30, £1.50, £2.50; EX 36.60 Trifecta £162.80 Pool: £4,533.01 - 20.88 winning tickets..
Owner Pinnacle Mujadil Partnership **Bred** Newlands House Stud **Trained** Sessay, N Yorks

FOCUS
An okay sprint handicap. Straightforward form, the winner close to his mark.

3934 BOBBY JONES MEMORIAL H'CAP 6f 5y
5:30 (5:30) (Class 6) (0-65,70) 3-Y-O+ **£2,045** (£603; £302) **Stalls** Centre

Form RPR
2240 **1** **Mandalay King (IRE)**[25] 3068 8-9-10 **63**............................(p) RaulDaSilva(3) 5 73
(Marjorie Fife) *in tch: hdwy to chal over 1f out: led ins fnl f: kpt on wl* **13/2**[3]
4001 **2** 2 ½ **Ayasha**[9] 3611 3-9-9 **70** 6ex............................ JustinNewman(5) 6 71
(Bryan Smart) *chsd ldrs: effrt and rdn over 1f out: chsd wnr ins fnl f: r.o* **7/1**
012 **3** nk **Insolenceofoffice (IRE)**[18] 3285 5-9-0 **57**............................(p) ConnorBeasley(7) 2 58
(Richard Ford) *cl up: rdn and led over 1f out: hdd ins fnl f: one pce* **15/2**
0-03 **4** 1 **Monel**[4] 3778 5-8-12 **48**............................ GrahamLee 3 46
(Jim Goldie) *dwlt: bhd: rdn and hdwy on outside over 1f out: kpt on: nvr able to chal* **3/1**[1]
3512 **5** 1 **Hab Reeh**[8] 3630 5-9-0 **57**............................(t) GemmaTutty(7) 12 52
(Ruth Carr) *dwlt: hld up: pushed along and hdwy over 1f out: kpt on fnl f: n.d* **3/1**[1]
0-65 **6** 1 ¾ **Sinai (IRE)**[8] 3630 4-9-8 **58**............................ SilvestreDeSousa 9 47
(Geoffrey Harker) *t.k.h: chsd ldrs tl edgd rt and wknd over 1f out* **9/2**[2]
3005 **7** ½ **Rock Canyon (IRE)**[5] 3713 4-9-1 **51**............................(p) TomEaves 8 38
(Linda Perratt) *cl up: led briefly 2f out: sn rdn: wknd fnl f* **20/1**
000/ **8** 3 ¼ **Durham Express (IRE)**[617] 7064 6-8-9 **45**............................ DuranFentiman 11 22
(Tina Jackson) *led tl rdn and hdd 2f out: sn wknd* **66/1**

1m 10.91s (-1.29) **Going Correction** -0.20s/f (Firm)
WFA 3 from 4yo+ 6lb **8** Ran SP% **112.0**
Speed ratings (Par 101): **100,96,96,94,93 91,90,86**
Tote Swingers 1&2 £5.80, 2&3 £6.20, 1&3 £6.80 CSF £48.75 CT £345.26 TOTE £10.80: £3.30, £2.70, £1.70; EX 41.00 Trifecta £97.00 Pool: £2,776.54 - 21.45 winning tickets..
Owner R W Fife **Bred** Forenaghts Stud And Dermot Cantillon **Trained** Stillington, N Yorks

FOCUS
A moderate sprint handicap but a reasonable race for the grade. The third is a decent guide.
T/Plt: £153.10 to a £1 stake. Pool: £60,749.45 - 289.58 winning tickets. T/Qpdt: £75.20 to a £1 stake. Pool: £4,007.06 - 39.40 winning tickets. RY

3085 CATTERICK (L-H)
Wednesday, July 3

OFFICIAL GOING: Good to firm (good in places; 9.0)
Wind: Light, across Weather: Cloudy with sunny periods

3942 BRITISH STALLION STUDS SUPPORTING BRITISH RACING EBF MAIDEN FILLIES' STKS 5f
2:30 (2:34) (Class 5) 2-Y-O **£2,911** (£866; £432; £216) **Stalls** Low

Form RPR
1 **Madagascar Moll (IRE)** 2-9-0 0............................ DanielTudhope 3 70+
(David O'Meara) *cl up: effrt 2f out: sn rdn: led and edgd rt ent fnl f: kpt on wl towards fin* **3/1**[1]
2 1 ¼ **Jamboree Girl** 2-9-0 0............................ DuranFentiman 4 66+
(Tim Easterby) *trckd ldrs on inner: pushed along 2f out: rdn over 1f out: styd on and ev ch ins fnl f: no ex last 75yds* **11/1**
3 hd **Birkacre (IRE)** 2-9-0 0............................ TonyHamilton 7 65+
(Richard Fahey) *dwlt: sn chsng ldrs: swtchd rt to outer after 2f: rdn 2f out: styd on appr fnl f* **10/3**[2]
55 **4** 2 **Resist**[9] 3640 2-9-0 0............................ RobertWinston 10 58
(Tobias B P Coles) *slt ld: pushed along 2f out: sn rdn: hdd and sltly hmpd ent fnl f: wknd* **7/1**
654 **5** 2 ½ **Noble Reach**[14] 3476 2-8-7 0............................ JordanNason(7) 9 49
(Geoffrey Harker) *chsd ldrs: rdn along 2f out: grad wknd* **20/1**
5 **6** ½ **Evie Jay (IRE)**[26] 3045 2-8-11 0............................[1] RaulDaSilva(3) 6 47
(Paul Green) *sn outpcd and bhd: rdn along 1/2-way: hdwy wl over 1f out: kpt on fnl f: nrst fin* **66/1**
7 1 ¼ **Flair For Fashion (IRE)** 2-9-0 0............................ SeanLevey 2 43
(Ed McMahon) *s.i.s: green and bhd: hdwy wl over 1f out: styd on fnl f: nrst fin* **4/1**[3]
35 **8** 33 **Reet Thicknstrong**[30] 2913 2-9-0 0............................ RoystonFfrench 8
(Bryan Smart) *chsd ldrs: lost pl after 1 1/2f: sn bhd and eased over 1f out* **5/1**

1m 1.33s (1.53) **Going Correction** +0.10s/f (Good) **8** Ran SP% **111.8**
Speed ratings (Par 91): **91,89,88,85,81 80,78,25**
toteswingers: 1&2 £7.80, 1&3 £3.00, 2&3 £7.30 CSF £34.67 TOTE £4.80: £1.70, £2.70, £2.00; EX 47.20 Trifecta £339.40 Pool: £2,656.58 - 5.87 winning units..
Owner Hambleton Racing XXVIII **Bred** Tom Radley **Trained** Nawton, N Yorks
■ Stewards' Enquiry : Sean Levey £140 fine: failed to report a reason for the poor performance

FOCUS
The pace was honest for this modest maiden, with three unraced fillies fighting out the finish. Straightforward form in terms of the race averages, with the first three all likely to rate higher.

3943 NORMAN JOHNSON IS SEVENTY MEDIAN AUCTION MAIDEN STKS 5f 212y
3:00 (3:00) (Class 5) 2-Y-O **£2,911** (£866; £432; £216) **Stalls** Low

Form RPR
5 **1** **Regiment**[17] 3366 2-9-5 0............................ TonyHamilton 1 77+
(Richard Fahey) *mde all: jnd 1/2-way: rdn wl over 1f out: drvn ent fnl f: hld on gamely* **15/8**[2]
30 **2** 1 ¼ **Oriental Relation (IRE)**[13] 3481 2-9-5 0............................ GrahamLee 6 73
(James Given) *trckd wnr: cl up 1/2-way: chal over 2f out: rdn wl over 1f out: drvn ins fnl f: no ex towards fin* **4/5**[1]
03 **3** 3 ¾ **Street Boss (IRE)**[11] 3588 2-9-5 0............................ DuranFentiman 2 62+
(Tim Easterby) *in tch: hdwy 2f out: sn rdn: styd on fnl f* **12/1**[3]
60 **4** 2 ¾ **Patisserie**[27] 3023 2-8-7 0............................(p) RowanScott(7) 7 49
(Ann Duffield) *t.k.h: chsd ldrs on outer: rdn along 2f out: wknd over 1f out* **20/1**
0 **5** nk **Autumn Tide (IRE)**[16] 3391 2-9-0 0............................ MichaelO'Connell 5 48
(John Quinn) *chsd ldrs: hdwy over 2f out: rdn wl over 1f out: sn btn* **50/1**
6 1 **Breakable** 2-8-9 0............................ DarylByrne(5) 4 45+
(Tim Easterby) *dwlt: green and sn outpcd in rr: hdwy wl over 1f out: styd on fnl f* **33/1**
40 **7** nse **Tricksome (IRE)**[19] 3280 2-9-0 0............................ PJMcDonald 3 44
(Ann Duffield) *chsd ldrs on inner: rdn along 2f out: grad wknd* **50/1**

1m 13.75s (0.15) **Going Correction** -0.125s/f (Firm) **7** Ran SP% **109.7**
Speed ratings (Par 94): **94,92,87,83,83 81,81**
toteswingers: 1&2 £1.20, 1&3 £2.00, 2&3 £2.30 CSF £3.33 TOTE £3.00: £1.20, £1.20; EX 5.00 Trifecta £15.60 Pool: £3,274.61 - 156.83 winning units..
Owner T G & Mrs M E Holdcroft **Bred** Bearstone Stud **Trained** Musley Bank, N Yorks

FOCUS
This looked a match on the book and the market leaders were in control from some way out. The three colts in the field were the first three home and the winner had a bit to spare.

3944 ST TERESA'S HOSPICE H'CAP 1m 7f 177y
3:30 (3:30) (Class 5) (0-75,72) 4-Y-O+ **£2,911** (£866; £432; £216) **Stalls** Centre

Form RPR
0430 **1** **Tartan Jura**[10] 3609 5-9-6 **71**............................(p) JoeFanning 7 77
(Mark Johnston) *mde all: pushed clr over 5f out: rdn along over 3f out: drvn wl over 1f out: kpt on* **3/1**[2]
3104 **2** 1 ½ **Amir Pasha (UAE)**[11] 3589 8-7-13 **53** oh2............................(v) NeilFarley(3) 1 56
(Micky Hammond) *hld up in rr: hdwy over 3f out: rdn 2f out: drvn and styd on wl fnl f* **10/1**
50/0 **3** ½ **Keep It Cool (IRE)**[15] 3442 9-9-7 **72**............................ DanielTudhope 2 75
(David O'Meara) *hld up in rr: hdwy over 4f out: rdn over 2f out: kpt on u.p fnl f: nrst fin* **8/1**
1 **4** 1 ½ **Miss Macnamara (IRE)**[25] 3089 4-8-12 **63**............................ PhillipMakin 4 64
(Martin Todhunter) *trckd wnr: pushed along 4f out: rdn over 2f out: drvn over 1f out: kpt on same pce* **11/4**[1]
5364 **5** nk **Jan Smuts (IRE)**[6] 3709 5-8-5 **63**............................(tp) ConnorBeasley(7) 3 63
(Wilf Storey) *hld up in rr: hdwy on outer over 3f out: rdn over 2f out: drvn and no imp fnl f* **9/2**[3]
-060 **6** 3 ¾ **Bijou Dan**[25] 3089 12-7-13 **53** oh5............................ DeclanCannon(3) 5 49
(George Moore) *chsd ldrs: rdn along 3f out: drvn 2f out: sn wknd* **40/1**
6224 **7** 35 **Zaplamation (IRE)**[17] 3363 8-8-11 **69**............................ JoeDoyle(7) 6 23
(John Quinn) *t.k.h: hld up towards rr: hdwy to chse wnr 1/2-way: rdn along over 4f out: sn wknd* **9/2**[3]

3m 27.65s (-4.35) **Going Correction** -0.125s/f (Firm) **7** Ran SP% **110.7**
Speed ratings (Par 103): **105,104,104,103,103 101,83**
toteswingers: 1&2 £4.60, 1&3 £3.70, 2&3 £5.90 CSF £29.81 CT £204.52 TOTE £4.00: £1.60, £4.70; EX 28.70 Trifecta £101.60 Pool: £2,441.80 - 18.01 winning units..
Owner Frank Bird **Bred** Newsells Park Stud **Trained** Middleham Moor, N Yorks

FOCUS
Plenty of pace on for this open staying handicap, with the winner making all under a fine ride. He is rated basically to form.

3945 WATCH RACING UK ON SKY 432 H'CAP 7f
4:00 (4:00) (Class 4) (0-80,78) 3-Y-O+ **£6,469** (£1,925; £962; £481) **Stalls** Centre

Form RPR
2151 **1** **West Leake Hare (IRE)**[15] 3444 4-9-2 **68**............................ PaulQuinn 15 81+
(David Nicholls) *dwlt and bhd: hdwy 1/2-way: swtchd rt to outer 2f out: rdn over 1f out: str run to ld ins fnl f: edgd lft and kpt* **5/1**[1]
3400 **2** 1 ¼ **Kung Hei Fat Choy (USA)**[16] 3416 4-9-7 **73**............................(b) GrahamLee 5 80
(James Given) *trckd ldrs: hdwy 2f out: n.m.r over 1f out: sn rdn and ev ch ent fnl f: kpt on same pce towards fin* **20/1**
0302 **3** ¾ **Our Boy Jack (IRE)**[16] 3411 4-9-12 **78**............................ TonyHamilton 8 83
(Richard Fahey) *trckd ldng pair: hdwy and cl up over 2f out: rdn wl over 1f out: led briefly jst ins fnl f: sn hdd and drvn: kpt on same pce* **6/1**[2]
105 **4** nk **Steel Stockholder**[9] 3628 7-9-12 **78**............................ JimmyQuinn 7 82
(Mel Brittain) *hld up: hdwy over 2f out: swtchd to outer and rdn over 1f out: kpt on fnl f* **20/1**
6310 **5** ½ **Smalljohn**[25] 3087 7-9-1 **72**............................(v) JustinNewman(5) 4 75
(Bryan Smart) *cl up: rdn along over 2f out: drvn wl over 1f out: wknd ins fnl f* **16/1**
2226 **6** shd **Llewellyn**[57] 2119 5-9-9 **75**............................ PaddyAspell 2 78
(David Nicholls) *sn led: rdn along over 2f out: edgd rt wl over 1f out: sn drvn: hdd jst ins fnl f: one pce* **11/1**
-004 **7** 1 **Fayr Fall (IRE)**[11] 3590 4-9-6 **72**............................(v) DuranFentiman 1 72
(Tim Easterby) *hld up towards rr: hdwy 2f out: rdn and kpt on fnl f: nrst fin* **11/1**
2500 **8** ¾ **Berlusca (IRE)**[13] 3506 4-9-6 **72**............................ DanielTudhope 3 70
(David O'Meara) *chsd ldrs on inner: rdn along 2f out: drvn over 1f out: grad wknd* **8/1**
446 **9** nk **Chookie Avon**[7] 3683 6-9-6 **72**............................(p) TomEaves 6 69
(Keith Dalgleish) *midfield: effrt 2f out: sn rdn along and no imp* **14/1**
4603 **10** nk **Beckermet (IRE)**[13] 3501 11-9-2 **68**............................ JamesSullivan 11 64
(Ruth Carr) *dwlt and towards rr: hdwy wl over 2f out: rdn to chse ldrs and n.m.r over 1f out: n.d* **33/1**
5034 **11** 3 ½ **Solar Spirit (IRE)**[25] 3088 8-9-11 **77**............................ JoeFanning 14 64
(Tracy Waggott) *stdd s: hld up: a towards rr* **8/1**
6062 **12** nse **Kuwait Star**[9] 3628 4-9-3 **69**............................ PJMcDonald 13 56
(Jason Ward) *s.i.s: a towards rr* **7/1**[3]
10-0 **13** ¾ **Complexity**[72] 1714 3-9-3 **77**............................ RobertWinston 12 62
(Charles Hills) *chsd ldrs: rdn along wl over 2f out: sn wknd* **20/1**

0041 **14** *1 1/4* **Indego Blues**[16] 3393 4-9-5 **71** .... AndrewMullen 9 52
(David Nicholls) *midfield: rdn along 3f out: sn wknd* **14/1**

03-0 **15** *nse* **Oil Strike**[16] 3392 6-9-2 **68** .... PhillipMakin 10 49
(Michael Easterby) *a towards rr* **20/1**

1m 25.23s (-1.77) **Going Correction** -0.125s/f (Firm)
WFA 3 from 4yo+ 8lb **15** Ran SP% **123.5**
Speed ratings (Par 105): **105,103,102,102,101 101,100,99,99,99 95,94,94,92,92**
toteswingers: 1&2 £30.90, 1&3 £6.00, 2&3 £30.50 CSF £112.68 CT £641.36 TOTE £6.20: £2.60, £11.10, £2.60; EX 189.90 Trifecta £953.70 Pool: £2,813.16 - 2.21 winning units..
Owner Neil Yeoman & Mrs Alex Nicholls **Bred** Churchtown House Stud **Trained** Sessay, N Yorks

FOCUS
Plenty of prominent racers in this wide open handicap. It was run at a fierce gallop. The winner rates value for a bit extra.

3946 GO RACING IN YORKSHIRE CLASSIFIED STKS 7f

4:30 (4:31) (Class 6) 3-Y-O+ **£2,385** (£704; £352) **Stalls** Centre

Form RPR

-645 **1** **Mrs Warren**[32] 2872 3-8-12 63 .... RobertWinston 4 64
(Charles Hills) *trckd ldrs on inner: hdwy 2f out: rdn over 1f out: styd on to ld ins fnl f: drvn out* **6/1**[3]

-502 **2** *1/2* **My New Angel (IRE)**[11] 3592 4-9-6 50 .... PJMcDonald 6 65
(Jason Ward) *in tch: hdwy to chse ldrs 2f out: swtchd rt and rdn over 1f out: styd on fnl f* **20/1**

-542 **3** *1 1/2* **Legal Bond**[14] 3475 4-9-6 65 .... (p) DanielTudhope 8 61
(David O'Meara) *led: rdn along 2f out: drvn over 1f out: edgd rt and hdd ins fnl f: one pce* **9/2**[2]

3-0 **4** *1 1/4* **Logans Legend (IRE)**[19] 3286 5-9-1 55 .... DarylByrne(5) 3 58
(Lawrence Mullaney) *trckd ldrs: hdwy on inner 2f out: rdn over 1f out: no imp fnl f* **66/1**

4205 **5** *2 3/4* **Mishhar (IRE)**[21] 3193 4-8-13 59 .... (v) DavidSimmonson(7) 9 51
(Tony Coyle) *dwlt and towards rr: hdwy over 2f out: rdn along wl over 1f out: styd on appr fnl f: nrst fin* **12/1**

2422 **6** *hd* **Duke Of Destiny (IRE)**[15] 3429 4-9-6 65 .... JoeFanning 7 50
(Ed Walker) *trckd ldrs: effrt 2f out: rdn wl over 1f out: drvn and wknd fnl f* **6/4**[1]

6420 **7** *6* **Only For You**[11] 3594 3-8-9 54 .... RaulDaSilva(3) 12 31
(Alan Brown) *cl up: rdn along over 2f out: drvn wl over 1f out: grad wknd* **66/1**

-040 **8** *1 1/4* **Fab Lolly (IRE)**[16] 3396 3-8-12 64 .... GrahamLee 13 27
(James Bethell) *towards rr: sme hdwy over 2f out: sn rdn and n.d* **14/1**

00-0 **9** *1/2* **Layla's King**[42] 2582 5-9-6 58 .... (p[1]) RoystonFfrench 14 29
(David C Griffiths) *in tch: rdn along 3f out: sn wknd* **25/1**

-000 **10** *3 1/4* **Easy Over (IRE)**[30] 2929 5-9-6 59 .... SeanLevey 11 20
(Ed McMahon) *a towards rr* **12/1**

0-00 **11** *4* **Balinka**[43] 2544 3-8-12 65 .... JimmyQuinn 2 7
(Mel Brittain) *in tch: rdn along wl over 2f out: sn wknd* **12/1**

5026 **12** *1 3/4* **Gladsome**[40] 2616 5-8-13 60 .... KieranSchofield(7) 15
(Jason Ward) *stmbld and rdr lost irons s: a towards rr* **25/1**

6-60 **13** *2 3/4* **Lady Bentinck (IRE)**[30] 2912 4-9-6 42 .... (p) PaddyAspell 5
(Alan Berry) *s.i.s: a towards rr* **100/1**

0-00 **14** *6* **Artillery Train (IRE)**[27] 3030 4-9-6 45 ....[1] JamesSullivan 1
(Tim Etherington) *a towards rr* **66/1**

1m 25.89s (-1.11) **Going Correction** -0.125s/f (Firm)
WFA 3 from 4yo+ 8lb **14** Ran SP% **120.1**
Speed ratings (Par 101): **101,100,98,97,94 93,87,85,85,81 76,74,71,64**
toteswingers: 1&2 £14.40, 1&3 £5.30, 2&3 £10.20 CSF £124.61 TOTE £6.40: £1.80, £3.30, £1.10; EX 117.70 Trifecta £638.30 Pool: £3,165.12 - 3.71 winning units..
Owner Mrs J K Powell & David F Powell **Bred** Freedom Farm Stud **Trained** Lambourn, Berks

FOCUS
This was not a race to get excited about. It was run at a sound gallop with few able to close. The winner is rated pretty much to form, but the runner-up is a doubt.

3947 RACING AGAIN NEXT WEDNESDAY H'CAP (QUALIFIER FOR THE 2013 CATTERICK TWELVE FURLONG SERIES FINAL) 1m 3f 214y

5:00 (5:00) (Class 6) (0-65,63) 4-Y-O+ **£3,408** (£1,006; £503) **Stalls** Low

Form RPR

0-62 **1** **Slide Show**[9] 3625 5-8-3 **45** .... PaulQuinn 5 62+
(David Nicholls) *hld up towards rr: stdy hdwy over 4f out: chsd ldrs 2f out: rdn to ld ent fnl f: sn clr: readily* **15/8**[1]

2420 **2** *6* **Petrol**[9] 3625 4-9-4 **60** .... (v[1]) DanielTudhope 10 64
(David O'Meara) *trckd ldrs: hdwy 4f out: rdn to chse ldr 2f out: drvn to ld briefly over 1f out: hdd ent fnl f and sn one pce* **4/1**[2]

4606 **3** *hd* **Brunello**[11] 3589 5-8-13 **58** .... (p) DeclanCannon(3) 4 62
(Philip Kirby) *trckd ldrs: hdwy 4f out: rdn over 2f out: drvn and kpt on same pce appr fnl f* **15/2**

3043 **4** *2 1/4* **Ailsa Craig (IRE)**[12] 3543 7-8-11 **60** .... KevinStott(7) 12 60
(Edwin Tuer) *in tch: hdwy 4f out: rdn along on outer 2f out: sn drvn to chse ldrs: no imp fnl f* **13/2**[3]

0304 **5** *2 1/2* **Light The City (IRE)**[11] 3595 6-8-11 **53** .... JamesSullivan 13 49
(Ruth Carr) *led 1 1/2f: trckd ldr tl tk clsr order over 4f out: led over 3f out: rdn 2f out: drvn and hdd over 1f out: grad wknd* **10/1**

00-0 **6** *1 1/4* **Cowslip**[25] 3089 4-8-0 **45** .... RaulDaSilva(3) 9 39
(George Moore) *in tch: rdn along over 3f out: drvn 2f out: plugged on: n.d* **33/1**

7 *1* **Apolskapart (IRE)**[33] 6682 5-8-11 **58** .... JasonHart(5) 8 51
(Michael Smith) *led after 1 1/2f: clr 1/2-way: rdn along and jnd 4f out: sn hdd: drvn and wknd fnl 2f* **10/1**

2540 **8** *3 3/4* **Eijaaz (IRE)**[9] 3625 12-9-1 **57** .... (p) DuranFentiman 2 44
(Geoffrey Harker) *hld up in rr: sme hdwy over 3f out: rdn along over 2f out: n.d* **16/1**

-064 **9** *5* **Tropical Duke (IRE)**[12] 3545 7-8-4 **46** .... RoystonFfrench 14 25
(Ron Barr) *chsd ldrs: rdn along 5f out: sn wknd* **33/1**

0060 **10** *22* **Rolen Sly**[11] 3595 4-8-3 **45** .... AndrewMullen 3
(Brian Rothwell) *prom: rdn along over 5f out: sn wknd* **100/1**

/-05 **11** *5* **Freddie Bolt**[21] 3201 7-8-0 **45** .... (t) NeilFarley(3) 11
(Frederick Watson) *a towards rr* **80/1**

30-6 **12** *4 1/2* **Jeer (IRE)**[176] 107 9-9-0 **63** .... (t) MatthewHopkins(7) 1
(Michael Easterby) *a towards rr* **20/1**

2m 36.76s (-2.14) **Going Correction** -0.125s/f (Firm) **12** Ran SP% **116.8**
Speed ratings (Par 101): **102,98,97,96,94 93,93,90,87,72 69,66**
toteswingers: 1&2 £2.90, 1&3 £4.60, 2&3 £5.60 CSF £8.29 CT £45.56 TOTE £3.70: £1.50, £1.50, £2.30; EX 11.60 Trifecta £90.50 Pool: £3,054.32 - 3.71 winning units..
Owner Seneca Racing **Bred** Floors Farming And Newbyth Stud **Trained** Sessay, N Yorks

FOCUS
Plenty of out-of-form performers in the field. The pace was sound with the favourite winning easily. The form is rated around the second and third.

T/Plt: £70.60 to a £1 stake. Pool: £69,041.98. 713.66 winning tickets. T/Qpdt: £34.00 to a £1 stake. Pool: £4,423.59. 96.17 winning tickets. JR

3617 CHEPSTOW (L-H)

Wednesday, July 3

OFFICIAL GOING: Good to firm (8.6)
Wind: Moderate, across Weather: Sunny spells

3948 EBF 32RED CASINO MAIDEN STKS 6f 16y

6:10 (6:10) (Class 5) 2-Y-O **£2,911** (£866; £432; £216) **Stalls** Centre

Form RPR

1 **Wee Jean** 2-9-0 0 .... SamHitchcott 6 83+
(Mick Channon) *in tch: gd hdwy over 2f out: led over 1f out: sn c clr: comf* **10/1**

2 *4 1/2* **Tobougg Happy** 2-9-0 0 .... NeilCallan 2 68
(James Tate) *trckd ldr: led wl over 2f out: drvn and hdd over 1f out: nt pce of wnr but kpt on wl for 2nd* **5/1**[2]

3 *2 1/4* **Storm Trooper (IRE)** 2-9-5 0 .... RichardHughes 8 66
(Richard Hannon) *chsd ldrs: pushed along over 2f out: one pce appr fnl f* **4/6**[1]

6 **4** *4* **Mersad (IRE)**[13] 3493 2-9-5 0 .... ShaneKelly 1 54
(James Tate) *in tch: hdwy to cl on ldrs over 2f out but nvr on terms: wknd fnl f* **14/1**

5 *shd* **Classic Pursuit** 2-9-5 0 .... SteveDrowne 7 54
(Ronald Harris) *towards rr: pushed along over 3f out: styd on fnl f to cl on 4th but nvr any ch* **20/1**

6 *3/4* **Gamgoom** 2-9-5 0 .... MartinLane 4 51
(Harry Dunlop) *sn outpcd: sme hdwy 3f out: nvr rchd ldrs and wknd fnl f* **6/1**[3]

60 **7** *2 1/4* **Big Kenny**[9] 3640 2-9-0 0 .... DeclanBates(5) 3 45
(David Evans) *outpcd* **50/1**

0 **8** *31* **Go Charlie**[33] 2823 2-9-0 0 .... EDLinehan(5) 5
(Ronald Harris) *led tl hdd wl over 2f out: wknd rapidly sn after* **25/1**

1m 10.57s (-1.43) **Going Correction** -0.15s/f (Firm) **8** Ran SP% **117.3**
Speed ratings (Par 94): **103,97,94,88,88 87,84,43**
toteswingers: 1&2 £5.80, 1&3 £2.50, 2&3 £2.40 CSF £59.01 TOTE £11.60: £2.70, £1.50, £1.10; EX 68.50 Trifecta £129.00 Pool: £2,236.39 - 12.99 winning units..
Owner B Robe **Bred** Mickley Stud & B Robe **Trained** West Ilsley, Berks

FOCUS
This 2yo maiden was run at a frantic early pace and the runners merged stands' side. It could work out to be a fair heat. The fourth and seventh help with the opening level.

3949 1ST SECURITY SOLUTIONS H'CAP 6f 16y

6:40 (6:41) (Class 6) (0-65,68) 3-Y-O+ **£1,940** (£577; £288; £144) **Stalls** Centre

Form RPR

0020 **1** **Verus Delicia (IRE)**[8] 3660 4-9-4 **55** .... ShaneKelly 5 67
(Daniel Mark Loughnane) *chsd ldrs: wnt 2nd and drvn 1f out: styd on u.p to ld clsng stages* **12/1**

6551 **2** *1/2* **Swendab (IRE)**[2] 3887 5-10-0 **68** 6ex .... (b) DarrenEgan(3) 1 78
(John O'Shea) *racd alone far side and led: rdn fnl f: hdd clsng stages* **3/1**[1]

2000 **3** *1 1/4* **Stonecrabstomorrow (IRE)**[18] 3317 10-9-8 **62** .... MarkCoumbe(3) 6 68
(Roy Brotherton) *towards rr but in tch: pushed along 3f out: styd on fr 2f out: r.o clsng stages to take 3rd nr fin but no imp on ldng duo* **50/1**

0002 **4** *3/4* **Consistant**[16] 3392 5-9-7 **58** .... NeilCallan 11 62
(Brian Baugh) *chsd ldrs: rdn 2f out: outpcd fnl f and lost 3rd clsng stages* **6/1**

3545 **5** *nk* **Catflap (IRE)**[13] 3498 4-8-13 **55** .... (p) RosieJessop(5) 14 58
(Derek Haydn Jones) *racd stands' side rail and chsd ldr on far side: rdn and ev ch 2f out: lost 2nd 1f out: wknd clsng stages* **25/1**

503 **6** *1/2* **Hazza The Jazza**[9] 3630 3-9-2 **59** .... (b) RobbieFitzpatrick 12 59
(Richard Guest) *towards rr: rdn 3f out: styd on u.p fnl f: kpt on cl home* **7/2**[2]

3014 **7** *shd* **The Mongoose**[8] 3661 5-9-12 **63** .... (t) RichardHughes 10 64
(David Evans) *in tch: rdn over 2f out: kpt on fnl f: nt rch ldrs* **5/1**[3]

0266 **8** *1 3/4* **Catalinas Diamond (IRE)**[18] 3315 5-9-10 **61** .... (t) SteveDrowne 7 56
(Pat Murphy) *s.i.s: in rr: rdn and hdwy over 2f out: kpt on fnl f: nt rch ldrs* **25/1**

2605 **9** *1/2* **Diamond Vine (IRE)**[9] 3623 5-9-2 **58** .... (p) PhilipPrince(5) 4 52
(Ronald Harris) *early spd: hrd drvn 3f out and sn outpcd* **20/1**

3-04 **10** *shd* **Trending (IRE)**[18] 3317 4-9-9 **60** .... (b) ChrisCatlin 9 53
(Jeremy Gask) *chsd ldrs: rdn 2f out: sn btn* **14/1**

/6-0 **11** *7* **Seraphiel**[18] 3325 4-9-4 **55** .... KirstyMilczarek 2 26
(Chris Down) *outpcd* **66/1**

4400 **12** *2* **Colourbearer (IRE)**[20] 3247 6-8-13 **53** .... (t) ThomasBrown(3) 8 17
(Milton Bradley) *outpcd* **16/1**

3030 **13** *1/2* **Dishy Guru**[41] 2596 4-9-10 **61** .... LiamKeniry 3 24
(Michael Blanshard) *spd to 1/2-way* **20/1**

-034 **14** *9* **Compton Prince**[13] 3499 4-9-11 **62** .... (b) RichardKingscote 13
(Milton Bradley) *spd 3f* **20/1**

1m 10.68s (-1.32) **Going Correction** -0.15s/f (Firm)
WFA 3 from 4yo+ 6lb **14** Ran SP% **123.8**
Speed ratings (Par 101): **102,101,99,98,98 97,97,95,94,94 85,82,81,69**
toteswingers: 1&2 £14.20, 1&3 £155.40, 2&3 £37.30 CSF £45.36 CT £1815.88 TOTE £16.40: £3.60, £1.20, £15.40; EX 86.20 Trifecta £1677.50 Part won. Pool: £2,236.73 - 0.13 winning units..
Owner R M Brilley **Bred** R Fagan **Trained** Baldwin's Gate, Staffs

FOCUS
A weak sprint handicap and this time the main action was more towards the far side of the track. The form is rated round the second to his Ffos Las level.

3950 DRAGON SIGNS AND PRINT CARDIFF MEDIAN AUCTION MAIDEN STKS 7f 16y

7:10 (7:10) (Class 6) 3-4-Y-O **£2,045** (£603; £302) **Stalls** Centre

Form RPR

6-40 **1** **Hidden Belief (IRE)**[25] 3116 3-8-12 77 ....[1] RichardHughes 1 78
(Ralph Beckett) *mde all: drvn appr fnl f: sn clr: readily* **10/11**[1]

64-2 **2** *7* **Martial Art (IRE)**[39] 2650 3-9-0 75 .... ThomasBrown(3) 2 64
(Andrew Balding) *trckd ldrs and chsd wnr fr 4f out: rdn and effrt 2f out but nvr on terms and easily outpcd fnl f* **5/4**[2]

05 **3** *2 1/4* **Logans Lad (IRE)**[91] 1323 3-9-3 0 .... (t) ShaneKelly 5 61
(Daniel Mark Loughnane) *disp 2nd 3f: styd cl 3rd tl pushed along and one pce over 1f out* **20/1**

0 **4** *5* **Eaton Oak**[21] 3201 3-9-3 0 SamHitchcott 4 45
(Lisa Williamson) *towards rr: drvn 4f out: a struggling to go pce but styd on fnl f to take poor 4th nr fin* **100/1**

4- **5** *2 ½* **Paddy Burke**[247] 7434 3-9-3 0 PatCosgrave 3 47
(Stuart Kittow) *chsd ldrs: rdn 3f out: sn struggling to go pce and wknd over 1f out: lost poor 4th nr fin* **10/1**[3]

1m 22.18s (-1.02) **Going Correction** -0.15s/f (Firm) **5** Ran SP% **111.7**
Speed ratings (Par 101): **99,91,88,82,79**
CSF £2.35 TOTE £1.70: £1.10, £1.40; EX 2.60 Trifecta £7.80 Pool: £939.82 - 89.91 winning units..
Owner Clipper Logistics **Bred** Nanallac Stud **Trained** Kimpton, Hants
FOCUS
A weak maiden and unconvincing form, the second finding nothing.

3951 FIRST CAFES H'CAP 1m 14y
7:40 (7:40) (Class 5) (0-75,75) 3-Y-O+ **£2,587** (£770; £384; £192) **Stalls** Centre

Form RPR
6430 **1** **Saint Jerome (IRE)**[20] 3241 3-9-5 **75** MartinDwyer 2 83
(Jamie Osborne) *slt ld after 2f: sn hrd pressed but kpt slt advantage: stl strly chal clsng stages: jst lasted* **4/1**[2]

10-2 **2** *nse* **Footstepsintherain (IRE)**[26] 3062 3-9-5 **75** TedDurcan 4 83+
(David Lanigan) *t.k.h: in tch: hdwy and pushed along 2f out: chsd wnr ins fnl f: str chal clsng stages: jst failed* **5/4**[1]

-030 **3** *2 ¼* **Equitissa (IRE)**[22] 3177 3-8-11 **67** KieranO'Neill 7 70
(Richard Hannon) *in rr: hdwy and drvn 2f out: styd on to take 3rd last strides but no imp on ldng duo* **14/1**

0236 **4** *nk* **Honey Of A Kitten (USA)**[1] 3917 5-9-10 **71** (v) RichardHughes 1 75
(David Evans) *led 2f: styd pressing wnr and stl upsides u.p ins fnl f: sn no ex and one pce: lost 3rd last strides* **5/1**

1135 **5** *3 ¾* **Peak Storm**[2] 3886 4-9-4 **68** DarrenEgan(3) 5 63
(John O'Shea) *chsd ldrs: rdn 2f out and sn btn* **9/2**[3]

060 **6** *8* **Fire King**[47] 2413 7-8-13 **60** (p) LiamKeniry 6 37
(Paul Burgoyne) *towards rr: sme hdwy 3f out: wknd fr 2f out* **20/1**

0005 **7** *1 ¼* **Boom To Bust (IRE)**[16] 3416 5-9-13 **74** ChrisCatlin 3 48
(Barry Brennan) *chsd ldrs 5f* **25/1**

1m 34.08s (-2.12) **Going Correction** -0.15s/f (Firm)
WFA 3 from 4yo+ 9lb **7** Ran SP% **114.6**
Speed ratings (Par 103): **104,103,101,101,97 89,88**
toteswingers: 1&2 £1.90, 1&3 £7.80, 2&3 £7.80 CSF £9.46 TOTE £5.40: £2.10, £1.50; EX 10.30 Trifecta £65.50 Pool: £952.71 - 10.90 winning units..
Owner Mrs F Walwyn **Bred** P Turley **Trained** Upper Lambourn, Berks
FOCUS
An ordinary handicap, run at a modest early pace as they stuck to the centre of the track and two 3yos fought it out. The winner has been rated back to his best.

3952 32RED H'CAP 2m 49y
8:10 (8:10) (Class 5) (0-75,73) 4-Y-O+ **£2,587** (£770; £384; £192) **Stalls** Low

Form RPR
031 **1** **Tijori (IRE)**[19] 3271 5-8-12 **64** (p) NeilCallan 2 71
(Bernard Llewellyn) *chsd ldrs in 4th: pushed along and hdwy to go 2nd appr fnl 2f: sn chalng: led appr fnl f and sn edgd lft u.p: styd on wl fnl 110yds but edgd lft again nr fin* **3/1**[2]

5-16 **2** *nk* **Filatore (IRE)**[28] 2990 4-9-4 **70** (p) MartinLane 8 76
(Bernard Llewellyn) *led: drvn along 4f out: kpt on whn pressed fr 2f out: hdd appr fnl f and sn n.m.r on rails: kpt on and bmpd clsng stages: jst failed* **7/4**[1]

4202 **3** *3 ¾* **Knox Overstreet**[9] 3637 5-8-7 **66** DanielCremin(7) 5 67
(Mick Channon) *chsd ldrs in 3rd: rdn and nt much daylight on inner over 2f out: readily outpcd by ldng duo fnl f* **8/1**

-023 **4** *1 ¼* **Double Cee**[25] 3110 4-9-7 **73** RichardHughes 1 73
(Warren Greatrex) *hld up in rr: drvn 3f out: styd on fr 2f out but nvr gng pce to get into contention: tk wl-hld 4th ins fnl f* **7/2**[3]

2332 **5** *1 ¼* **Jezza**[19] 3271 7-8-13 **65** (bt) TedDurcan 7 63
(Karen George) *s.i.s: in rr: hdwy 3f out: rdn to chse ldrs over 2f out: sn btn* **6/1**

/0-5 **6** *1 ¾* **Kristallo (GER)**[9] 3637 8-8-6 **58** (p) SamHitchcott 3 54
(Dai Burchell) *chsd ldr: rdn over 3f out: lost 2nd over 2f out: wknd sn after* **25/1**

3m 36.39s (-2.51) **Going Correction** -0.05s/f (Good) **6** Ran SP% **112.8**
Speed ratings (Par 103): **104,103,101,101,100 99**
toteswingers: 1&2 £5.20, 1&3 £5.60, 2&3 £1.70 CSF £8.79 CT £35.15 TOTE £5.30: £3.50, £1.90; EX 11.60 Trifecta £55.30 Pool: £558.90 - 7.57 winning units..
Owner G Robinson **Bred** Polish Belle Partnership **Trained** Fochriw, Caerphilly
FOCUS
A modest staying handicap which served up a proper test as they were strung out on the far side. The winner built on his C&D latest.

3953 WESTERN DAILY PRESS CHAMPION SINCE 1858 H'CAP 1m 4f 23y
8:40 (8:40) (Class 6) (0-60,59) 4-Y-O+ **£1,940** (£577; £288; £144) **Stalls** Low

Form RPR
-006 **1** **Bondi Mist (IRE)**[16] 3412 4-8-13 **56** (v) RyanTate(5) 8 65
(Jonathan Geake) *chsd ldrs: chal 4f out: led over 3f out: jnd appr fnl f: hdd fnl 150yds: styd upsides: led again u.p last strides* **14/1**

500- **2** *shd* **Lily Potts**[258] 7196 4-9-5 **57** SteveDrowne 3 66
(Chris Down) *in rr: hdwy 5f out: chsd ldrs 3f out: wnt 2nd 2f out: chal appr fnl f: slt ld fnl 150yds: hdd and no ex last strides* **16/1**

-054 **3** *5* **Red Current**[49] 2360 9-8-8 **49** DarrenEgan(3) 4 50
(Michael Scudamore) *in rr: hdwy 3f out: styd on u.p fnl f to take wl hld 3rd nr fin* **33/1**

-563 **4** *nk* **Arch Event**[18] 3312 8-8-11 **49** (p) MartinLane 7 50
(Bernard Llewellyn) *chsd ldrs: rdn 4f out: btn into 3rd fr 2f out: dropped to wl hld 4th nr fin* **8/1**[3]

44-6 **5** *6* **Picalily**[16] 3406 4-9-2 **57** BrendanPowell(3) 9 48
(Brendan Powell) *chsd ldrs: hdwy on outside to ld 5f out: hdd over 3f out: wknd over 2f out* **16/1**

2052 **6** *1 ¾* **Party Palace**[23] 2828 9-8-7 **50** NatashaEaton(5) 2 38
(Stuart Howe) *in rr: hdwy 6f out: chsd ldrs 4f out: wknd 3f out* **7/2**[1]

-342 **7** *3 ¼* **Minstrel Lad**[16] 3399 5-9-3 **55** RichardKingscote 11 38
(Jonjo O'Neill) *chsd ldrs: chal u.p 3f out: wknd over 2f out* **7/2**[1]

060/ **8** *7* **Stafford Charlie**[266] 1580 7-8-4 **45** RyanPowell(3) 1 17
(John O'Shea) *in rr: rn past btn horses fnl f* **66/1**

400- **9** *9* **Crystal Monarch (IRE)**[343] 4465 4-9-7 **59** PatCosgrave 5 16
(Lady Cecil) *s.i.s: sn in tch: rdn 5f out: btn 4f out* **4/1**[2]

10/1 **10** *53* **Acapulco Bay**[10] 2350 9-9-0 **52** (p) RichardHughes 10
(Dai Burchell) *led: hdd 5f out: wknd 3f out: virtually p.u clsng stages* **7/2**[1]

2m 37.85s (-1.15) **Going Correction** -0.05s/f (Good) **10** Ran SP% **120.6**
Speed ratings (Par 101): **101,100,97,97,93 92,90,85,79,44**
toteswingers: 1&2 £61.70, 1&3 £22.30, 2&3 £30.80 CSF £222.82 CT £7066.25 TOTE £17.40: £4.30, £4.70, £3.40; EX 161.80 Trifecta £861.10 Part won. Pool: £1,148.26 - 0.65 winning units..

Owner Double Kings Partnership **Bred** Akoya Syndicate **Trained** Marlborough, Wilts
■ Stewards' Enquiry : Richard Hughes one-day ban: careless riding (Jul 17)
FOCUS
This low-grade handicap was contested at an average pace and the first two dominated the final furlong. The winner's two best runs last year came here.

3954 32RED.COM H'CAP 1m 2f 36y
9:10 (9:12) (Class 6) (0-65,69) 4-Y-O+ **£1,940** (£577; £288; £144) **Stalls** Low

Form RPR
4-05 **1** **Certavi (IRE)**[16] 3410 4-8-13 **55** LiamKeniry 3 69
(Brendan Powell) *chsd ldrs: drvn to chal 2f out: sn led: rdn clr fnl 110yds* **7/2**[2]

0231 **2** *2 ¼* **Breakheart (IRE)**[3] 3854 6-9-6 **69** 6ex (v) JackGarritty(7) 2 78
(Andrew Balding) *hld up in rr: pushed along 3f out: styd on wl to take 2nd fnl 30yds but no ch w wnr* **6/4**[1]

-60 **3** *½* **Belle Park**[18] 3314 6-8-8 **50** KirstyMilczarek 1 58
(Karen George) *chsd ldrs: drvn to dispute ld over 1f out: outpcd fnl 110yds and lost 2nd fnl 30yds* **8/1**[3]

450 **4** *3 ½* **Drummond**[18] 3312 4-8-13 **55** (p) MartinLane 8 56
(Bernard Llewellyn) *led: rdn 3f out: hdd ins fnl 2f: wknd fnl f* **8/1**[3]

2134 **5** *6* **Edgware Road**[9] 3642 5-9-7 **63** RichardHughes 9 52
(Sean Curran) *in rr: hdwy 3f out: sn rdn: nvr rchd ldrs and wknd fr 2f out* **7/2**[2]

6003 **6** *5* **Madam Tessa (IRE)**[18] 3314 5-7-11 **46** ChloeIngram(7) 11 25
(Tim Vaughan) *chsd ldrs: wknd qckly fr 2f out* **16/1**

0000 **7** *3 ¾* **Delicious Patrica**[15] 3433 4-8-0 **45** DarrenEgan(3) 5 17
(Tony Carroll) *in tch early: rdn and btn 4f out* **50/1**

050/ **8** *1 ¾* **Desert Fairy**[860] 409 7-8-0 **45** RyanPowell(3) 7
(Trevor Wall) *chsd ldrs: rdn 3f out: sn btn* **50/1**

2m 10.43s (-0.17) **Going Correction** -0.05s/f (Good) **8** Ran SP% **116.5**
Speed ratings (Par 101): **98,96,95,93,88 84,81,79**
toteswingers 1&2 £1.10, 1&3 £7.30 2&3 £5.00 CSF £9.34 CT £37.26 TOTE £4.30: £1.70, £1.10, £2.00; EX 13.10 Trifecta £110.00 Pool: £1,327.72 - 9.05 winning units..
Owner Nigel M Davies **Bred** Anthony Jones **Trained** Upper Lambourn, Berks
FOCUS
A weak handicap, run at a sound pace. There could be a bit more to come from the winner.
T/Plt: £247.00 to a £1 stake. Pool: £79,101.64. 233.75 winning tickets T/Qpdt: £103.20 to a £1 stake. Pool: £5,274.71. 37.80 winning tickets ST

3687 KEMPTON (A.W) (R-H)
Wednesday, July 3

OFFICIAL GOING: Standard
Wind: Light, across Weather: Overcast

3955 IRISH NIGHT 10.07.13 APPRENTICE H'CAP 6f (P)
6:20 (6:21) (Class 5) (0-75,74) 4-Y-O+ **£2,587** (£770; £384; £192) **Stalls** Low

Form RPR
-401 **1** **Zhiggy's Stardust**[16] 3401 4-9-5 **74** OisinMurphy(5) 2 86+
(Henry Candy) *mde all: rdn and clr over 1f out: kpt on under hands and heels fnl f: comf* **1/2**[1]

6-02 **2** *1 ¼* **Fenella Fudge**[13] 3489 5-8-10 **63** (v) AdamMcLean(3) 1 70
(Derek Shaw) *hld up in tch in midfield: rdn and hdwy over 1f out: chsd wnr 1f out: kpt on but a hld* **8/1**[3]

0104 **3** *2 ¼* **Prince Of Passion (CAN)**[20] 3247 5-9-0 **64** RobertTart 8 64
(Derek Shaw) *chsd ldng pair: rdn and effrt 2f out: chsd wnr over 1f out tl 1f out: one pce fnl f* **8/1**[3]

6006 **4** *2* **South Kenter (USA)**[15] 3433 4-8-2 **55** oh9 (p) TimClark(3) 6 48
(Heather Main) *chsd wnr tl unable qck over 1f out: 4th and plugged on same pce fnl f* **50/1**

2260 **5** *¾* **Baby Dottie**[138] 665 6-8-4 **59** (t) SophieRalston(5) 7 50
(Pat Phelan) *dwlt: racd off the pce in last pair: rdn and effrt 2f out: kpt on ins fnl f: nvr trbld ldrs* **20/1**

0300 **6** *1 ¼* **Kellys Eye (IRE)**[16] 3415 6-9-6 **70** WilliamTwiston-Davies 5 57
(Zoe Davison) *chsd ldng trio: rdn and unable qck ent fnl 2f: wknd 1f out* **7/1**[2]

1-04 **7** *1* **Annes Rocket (IRE)**[18] 3315 8-9-3 **72** (p) CameronHardie(5) 3 56
(Jimmy Fox) *stdd s: hld up in rr: rdn and no real imp 2f out: n.d* **14/1**

1m 12.82s (-0.28) **Going Correction** +0.075s/f (Slow) **7** Ran SP% **114.8**
Speed ratings (Par 103): **104,102,99,96,95 94,92**
toteswingers: 1&2 £2.10, 1&3 £1.80, 2&3 £3.00 CSF £5.46 CT £16.42 TOTE £1.60: £1.70, £2.80; EX 7.00 Trifecta £24.60 Pool: £2,366.74 - 72.06 winning units..
Owner Henry Candy **Bred** Mr And Mrs L Baker **Trained** Kingston Warren, Oxon
FOCUS
Just an average race of its type and it revolved around one horse, who built on his C&D win.

3956 JOCKEY CLUB H'CAP (JOCKEY CLUB GRASSROOTS FLAT SPRINT SERIES QUALIFIER) 6f (P)
6:50 (6:50) (Class 5) (0-75,74) 3-Y-O **£2,587** (£770; £384; £192) **Stalls** Low

Form RPR
5622 **1** **Bosham**[13] 3509 3-8-8 **66** MichaelJMMurphy(5) 1 72
(William Jarvis) *chsd ldrs: rdn and effrt to chse ldr on inner wl over 1f out: swtchd lft over 1f out: r.o wl to ld fnl 50yds* **6/1**[2]

4450 **2** *½* **Surge Ahead (IRE)**[14] 3472 3-9-6 **73** GeorgeBaker 2 77
(Ed Walker) *led and set stdy gallop: rdn and qcknd but edgd rt wl over 1f out: kpt on wl tl hdd and no ex fnl 50yds* **13/2**[3]

0054 **3** *1 ¾* **Lucky Di**[23] 3159 3-9-7 **74** AdamKirby 3 73
(Peter Hedger) *in tch in midfield: hmpd 4f out: effrt u.p ent fnl 2f: styd on same pce ins fnl f: wnt 2nd last strides* **12/1**

313- **4** *hd* **Broughtons Charm (IRE)**[254] 7298 3-9-6 **73** WilliamBuick 7 71+
(Willie Musson) *wnt rt s: t.k.h and chsng ldr: rdn and effrt ent fnl 2f: 3rd and one pce ins fnl f: lost 3rd last strides* **8/1**

1-54 **5** *1 ¾* **Oscars Journey**[3] 3866 3-9-5 **72** JimmyFortune 4 64
(J R Jenkins) *stdd s: t.k.h: hld up in tch towards rr: effrt and hdwy on inner over 1f out: no imp fnl f* **6/1**[2]

405 **6** *1 ¼* **Scala Romana (IRE)**[28] 2979 3-9-0 **67** LukeMorris 8 55
(Sir Mark Prescott Bt) *hld up in tch in rr: effrt u.p 2f out: kpt on but no threat to ldrs fnl f* **33/1**

0-40 **7** *hd* **Blue Twister**[13] 3509 3-8-7 **60**..(v) HayleyTurner 5 48
(Andrew Balding) *in tch in midfield: rdn and outpcd over 2f out: rallied and kpt on again ins fnl f: no threat to ldrs* **20/1**

-152 **8** *1 ½* **Smokethatthunders (IRE)**[21] 3212 3-9-6 **73**........... SilvestreDeSousa 6 56+
(James Toller) *hmpd s: t.k.h and hld up in rr: hmpd 4f out: c v wd bnd 3f out: sn drvn and no real imp: nvr trbld ldrs* **15/8**[1]

1003 **9** *1 ¼* **El Mirage (IRE)**[21] 3212 3-9-7 **74**.. JimCrowley 9 53+
(Dean Ivory) *t.k.h: hld up towards rr: hdwy to chse ldrs 4f out: flashed tail and rdn 3f out: lost pl u.p 2f out: wknd over 1f out* **8/1**

1m 13.78s (0.68) **Going Correction** +0.075s/f (Slow) **9** Ran SP% **114.3**
Speed ratings (Par 100): **98,97,95,94,92 90,90,88,86**
toteswingers: 1&2 £11.90, 1&3 £20.40, 2&3 £26.10 CSF £44.12 CT £353.87 TOTE £6.50: £2.10, £2.40, £4.50; EX 52.50 Trifecta £842.50 Pool: £1,702.21 - 1.51 winning units..

Owner The Bosham Partnership **Bred** Rabbah Bloodstock Limited **Trained** Newmarket, Suffolk

FOCUS
Just an ordinary sprint handicap although the winner of this race in the last two years went on to be rated in the 80s so there could be some improvement to come from some of these. The first three home were drawn in the lowest three stalls. A length best from the winner.

3957 £200 FREE BETS AT BETDAQ MAIDEN STKS 1m 4f (P)
7:20 (7:21) (Class 5) 3-Y-O+ **£2,587** (£770; £384; £192) **Stalls** Centre

Form RPR

6-3 **1** **Astonishing (IRE)**[20] 3239 3-8-8 0.. PatDobbs 5 94+
(Sir Michael Stoute) *led for 1f: chsd ldng pair after: chal and carried rt wl over 1f out: pushed into ld 1f out: styd on wl under hands and heels: gng away at fin* **9/2**

044 **2** *1 ¾* **Respect Me**[12] 3542 3-8-13 80.............................. SilvestreDeSousa 10 94
(Saeed bin Suroor) *chsd ldr over 10f out: rdn to ld 2f out: sn carried rt: drvn and hdd 1f out: no ex and one pce ins fnl f* **4/1**[3]

-332 **3** *1* **Shwaiman (IRE)**[17] 3364 3-8-13 83.. JamesDoyle 7 92
(James Fanshawe) *chsd ldrs: rdn over 3f out: drvn to chal and hung rt wl over 1f out: no ex and btn ins fnl f: hld whn hmpd and wnt lft ins fnl f* **7/4**[1]

0444 **4** *7* **She's Late**[14] 3470 3-8-13 76..(b[1]) WilliamBuick 8 81
(John Gosden) *t.k.h: led after 1f: rdn over 2f out: hdd 2f out and sn btn: wknd over 1f out* **3/1**[2]

05 **5** *4 ½* **Midaz**[42] 2576 3-8-13 0.. JimmyFortune 9 76+
(Hughie Morrison) *stdd and dropped in bhd after s: hld up in rr: rdn and hdwy into modest 5th 2f out: no imp after* **66/1**

5 **6** *shd* **Phiz (GER)**[48] 2392 3-8-8 0.. NickyMackay 1 69
(John Gosden) *in tch in midfield: rdn and struggling wl over 2f out: sn wknd* **14/1**

0 **7** *11* **Mignonne**[14] 3469 3-8-3 0.. NicoleNordblad[(5)] 3 51
(Hans Adielsson) *stdd s: hld up in rr: struggling 3f out: no ch whn edgd rt 2f out* **100/1**

0 **8** *3 ¾* **Le Tigre De Bronze**[30] 2938 3-8-13 0.. HayleyTurner 2 50
(Hughie Morrison) *t.k.h: hld up in rr: hdwy into midfield 7f out: rdn and wknd over 2f out* **33/1**

0 **9** *5* **Achtung**[27] 3021 3-8-13 0..(p) FrankieDettori 4 42
(Jeremy Noseda) *t.k.h: hld up in last quartet: rdn and struggling over 3f out: wknd u.p over 2f out: t.o* **20/1**

00 **10** *7* **Mrs Mann (USA)**[42] 2560 3-8-1 0.. JosephineGordon[(7)] 6 26
(Jo Hughes) *in tch in midfield: steadily lost pl and bhd 5f out: sn lost tch* **100/1**

000- **11** *6* **Jambobo**[28] 3947 4-9-7 25..(tp) JemmaMarshall[(5)] 11 21
(Chris Down) *in tch in midfield on outer: rdn and lost pl over 3f out: bhd 2f out: t.o* **100/1**

2m 32.02s (-2.48) **Going Correction** +0.075s/f (Slow)
WFA 3 from 4yo 13lb **11** Ran SP% **118.4**
Speed ratings (Par 103): **111,109,109,104,101 101,94,91,88,83 79**
toteswingers: 1&2 £4.30, 1&3 £2.60, 2&3 £3.00 CSF £22.29 TOTE £3.10: £1.10, £2.00, £1.30; EX 23.70 Trifecta £61.20 Pool: £1,952.81 - 23.92 winning units..

Owner Lady Rothschild **Bred** Azienda Agricola Rosati Colarieti **Trained** Newmarket, Suffolk

FOCUS
A good maiden with the third setting the standard. The last time it was won by a filly it was the Group One-placed Vita Nova. The front four were nicely clear in both the betting and the race itself.

3958 LEONARD CURTIS/BRITISH STALLION STUDS EBF MAIDEN FILLIES' STKS 7f (P)
7:50 (7:52) (Class 5) 2-Y-O **£2,911** (£866; £432; £216) **Stalls** Low

Form RPR

6 **1** **Cornish Path**[22] 3175 2-9-0 0.. CathyGannon 5 73
(Henry Candy) *in tch in last quartet: swtchd rt and gd hdwy u.p over 1f out: r.o wl to ld wl ins fnl f: gng away at fin* **20/1**

0 **2** *¾* **Taleteller (USA)**[21] 3205 2-9-0 0.. MickaelBarzalona 10 71
(Saeed bin Suroor) *led and grad crossed to inner: rdn and hdd jst over 1f out: led again over 1f out and forged ahd u.p jst ins fnl f: hdd and no ex wl ins fnl f* **4/1**[2]

0 **3** *1 ¾* **Rayoumti (IRE)**[21] 3205 2-9-0 0.. AdamKirby 2 67
(Marco Botti) *awkward leaving stalls: sn in tch in midfield: rdn and chsd clr ldng pair over 1f out: kpt on u.p* **12/1**

4 *1 ¾* **Jacqueline Jouliac** 2-9-0 0.. WilliamBuick 8 62+
(John Gosden) *rn v green thrght: s.i.s: bhd: stl only 10th and no prog wl over 1f out: hdwy 1f out: kpt on wl fnl f: wnt 4th last strides: nvr trbld ldrs* **3/1**[1]

0 **5** *hd* **Sleeping Princess (IRE)**[58] 2090 2-9-0 0.. FrederikTylicki 4 61
(Clive Brittain) *chsd ldrs: wnt 2nd 4f and sn led: flashed tail u.p but stl ev ch tl no ex 1f out: wknd ins fnl f* **66/1**

6 *1 ½* **Palace Princess (FR)** 2-9-0 0.. JamesDoyle 11 58+
(Ed Dunlop) *rn green: in tch in last quartet: hdwy 1/2-way: rdn and wnt 5th over 1f out: styd on same pce fnl f* **20/1**

0 **7** *1* **Pastoral Witness**[75] 1669 2-9-0 0.. JimmyFortune 7 55
(Clive Brittain) *in tch in midfield: rdn over 3f out: drvn and outpcd over 2f out: plugged on fnl f but no threat to ldrs* **4/1**[2]

0 **8** *2* **Soiree D'Ete**[14] 3471 2-9-0 0.. LukeMorris 3 50
(Sir Mark Prescott Bt) *chsd ldr tl 4f out: rdn and struggling over 2f out: drvn and wknd over 1f out* **33/1**

9 *¾* **Habdab** 2-9-0 0.. PatDobbs 6 48
(Richard Hannon) *hld up in tch towards rr: rdn and no hdwy over 1f out: styd on same pce fr over 1f out* **8/1**[3]

10 *2 ½* **Last Echo (IRE)** 2-9-0 0.. JimCrowley 1 41
(Ralph Beckett) *s.i.s: hld up in rr: rdn and no hdwy over 2f out: n.d* **4/1**[2]

11 *4* **Star Anise (FR)** 2-9-0 0.. KierenFallon 9 31
(Harry Dunlop) *t.k.h: chsd ldrs: rdn and struggling over 2f out: wknd qckly 2f out: bhd and eased wl ins fnl f* **25/1**

1m 27.52s (1.52) **Going Correction** +0.075s/f (Slow) **11** Ran SP% **121.6**
Speed ratings (Par 91): **94,93,91,89,88 87,86,83,82,80 75**
toteswingers: 1&2 £11.00, 1&3 £41.40, 2&3 £10.00 CSF £97.05 TOTE £33.60: £6.30, £1.70, £3.90; EX 209.30 Trifecta £927.90 Part won. Pool: £1,237.22 - 0.23 winning units..

Owner The Cornish Path Partnership **Bred** Dunchurch Lodge Stud Co **Trained** Kingston Warren, Oxon

FOCUS
An ordinary fillies' maiden and those with experience came to the fore. It's rated towards the bottom end of the pre-race averages.

3959 COMMISSION FREE 1ST MONTH AT BETDAQ H'CAP 2m (P)
8:20 (8:20) (Class 3) (0-90,90) 4-Y-O+ **£7,439** (£2,213; £1,106; £553) **Stalls** Low

Form RPR

0-02 **1** **Dark Ranger**[25] 3118 7-8-9 **78**.. AndreaAtzeni 11 88+
(Tim Pitt) *in tch in midfield: rdn to chse ldr 2f out: led and qcknd clr over 1f out: styd on wl: rdn out* **12/1**

61 **2** *1 ¾* **Presto Volante (IRE)**[36] 2749 5-8-8 **77**..(p) PatDobbs 7 84
(Amanda Perrett) *hld up in tch in midfield: rdn and effrt over 2f out: styd on u.p over 1f out: chsd wnr ins fnl f: kpt on* **8/1**

/500 **3** *¾* **Theology**[25] 3099 6-9-2 **85**.. WilliamBuick 3 91
(Steve Gollings) *hld up in last trio: swtchd lft and effrt over 2f out: hdwy u.p over 1f out: styd on but no threat to wnr* **7/1**[3]

1-23 **4** *½* **Mutual Regard (IRE)**[19] 3284 4-9-2 **85**.. LukeMorris 10 91
(Sir Mark Prescott Bt) *chsd ldrs: rdn and effrt 2f out: drvn and chsd clr wnr 1f out: plugged on same pce and lost 2 pls ins fnl f* **5/2**[1]

-002 **5** *hd* **Spice Fair**[18] 3344 6-8-11 **80**.. JimmyFortune 1 85
(Mark Usher) *s.i.s: hld up in rr: hdwy u.p over 1f out: kpt on wl ins fnl f: nvr threatened ldrs* **14/1**

5-60 **6** *6* **Perennial**[46] 2451 4-9-7 **90**.. FrankieDettori 8 88
(Charles Hills) *led: rdn ent fnl 2f: hdd over 1f out and sn btn: wknd ins fnl f* **9/2**[2]

5100 **7** *½* **Fleur De La Vie (IRE)**[18] 3344 4-8-13 **82**.. JimCrowley 2 79
(Ralph Beckett) *in tch in midfield: unable qck u.p over 2f out: wknd over 1f out* **15/2**

-620 **8** *nk* **Cosimo de Medici**[11] 3560 6-8-11 **80**.. KierenFallon 12 77
(Hughie Morrison) *s.i.s: sn rcvrd and in tch in midfield: rdn and unable qck over 2f out: wknd over 1f out* **10/1**

-310 **9** *nk* **Desert Recluse (IRE)**[46] 2451 6-9-2 **85**.. GeorgeBaker 6 82
(Pat Eddery) *chsd ldr tl 2f out: sn struggling u.p: wknd over 1f out* **14/1**

1035 **10** *5* **Beat Route**[11] 3587 6-8-2 **76**.. NicoleNordblad[(5)] 5 67
(Michael Attwater) *in tch in midfield: shuffled bk on inner over 3f out: rdn and no hdwy 3f out: wl bhd over 1f out* **25/1**

00-0 **11** *29* **Ermyn Lodge**[54] 2205 7-8-11 **85**..(v) JemmaMarshall[(5)] 9
(Pat Phelan) *s.i.s: rdn along: grad rcvrd but a off the bridle: chsd ldrs 10f out: lost pl qckly 4f out: wl bhd fnl 2f: t.o* **33/1**

3m 29.23s (-0.87) **Going Correction** +0.075s/f (Slow) **11** Ran SP% **119.0**
Speed ratings (Par 107): **105,104,103,103,103 100,100,100,99,97 82**
toteswingers: 1&2 £11.30, 1&3 £15.60, 2&3 £11.90 CSF £105.90 CT £734.83 TOTE £14.10: £3.80, £3.40, £3.30; EX 105.40 Trifecta £1142.30 Part won. Pool: £1,523.08 - 0.82 winning units..

Owner Recycled Products Limited **Bred** Thomas G N Burrage **Trained** Newmarket, Suffolk

FOCUS
A competitive staying handicap with a few decent performers taking their chance. Perennial led at a sedate pace before fading out of it and it turned into a bit of a sprint. The winner is rated back to his best.

3960 BETDAQ 1ST UK RACE COMMISSION FREE-EVERYDAY H'CAP 1m 4f (P)
8:50 (8:51) (Class 3) (0-95,93) 4-Y-O+ **£7,439** (£2,213; £1,106; £553) **Stalls** Centre

Form RPR

21- **1** **Seal Of Approval**[308] 5745 4-9-2 **88**..[1] HayleyTurner 5 102+
(James Fanshawe) *t.k.h: hld up in last trio: swtchd rt and hdwy wl over 1f out: drvn to chal ins fnl f: led wl ins fnl f: in command and idling towards fin* **14/1**

1-56 **2** *½* **Castilo Del Diablo (IRE)**[25] 3099 4-8-12 **84**..(p) JimCrowley 3 97
(David Simcock) *hld up in tch in midfield: rdn and gd hdwy over 1f out: drvn to ld ins fnl f: hdd wl ins fnl f: kpt on but readily hld* **7/2**[2]

1-4 **3** *2 ¼* **Bishop Roko**[35] 2775 4-9-7 **93**.. JamesDoyle 8 102
(Roger Charlton) *w ldrs tl led over 9f out: hdd 6f out and allowed ldr to go clr: clsd and led again over 2f out: drvn over 1f out: hdd ins fnl f: wknd towards fin* **10/1**

1-30 **4** *1 ½* **Ruscello (IRE)**[49] 2365 4-9-6 **92**.. GeorgeBaker 2 99
(Ed Walker) *hld up in tch in last quartet: clsd over 2f out: rdn and effrt wl over 1f out: 4th and styd on same pce ins fnl f* **5/1**[3]

2-13 **5** *1 ¾* **Ustura (USA)**[11] 3559 4-9-7 **93**..(tp) SilvestreDeSousa 7 97
(Saeed bin Suroor) *t.k.h: chsd ldrs: rdn and chsd ldr 2f out: drvn and unable qck over 1f out: wknd ins fnl f* **7/4**[1]

5-30 **6** *hd* **Harvard N Yale (USA)**[39] 2648 4-8-13 **85**..(p) SebSanders 9 89
(Jeremy Noseda) *t.k.h: hld up in tch in midfield: hdwy to chse ldrs 7f out: rdn and unable qck ent fnl 2f: wknd 1f out* **9/1**

4-40 **7** *4 ½* **Maria's Choice (IRE)**[25] 3118 4-8-9 **81**.. RichardMullen 4 78
(Sir Michael Stoute) *led for 2f: in tch: midfield and rdn over 3f out: wknd 2f out* **25/1**

/34- **8** *3* **Halling's Quest**[417] 2080 4-9-4 **90**.. PatDobbs 6 82
(Hughie Morrison) *styd wd early: midfield tl hdwy to chse ldrs 10f out: wnt 2nd over 8f out tl 6f out: unable qck u.p 2f out: sn wknd* **20/1**

534- **9** *2 ¼* **Daliance (IRE)**[23] 7487 4-8-10 **82**..(v[1]) LukeMorris 1 70
(Lucy Wadham) *hld up in tch in last 4: rdn wl over 2f out: wknd 2f out* **33/1**

2022 **10** *3 ¾* **Reflect (IRE)**[41] 2590 5-7-13 **78**..(vt) AdamMcLean[(7)] 10 60
(Derek Shaw) *stdd and dropped in bhd after s: t.k.h: hld up in rr tl dashed up to ld 6f out: sn clr: hdd over 2f out: wknd wl over 1f out* **33/1**

2m 33.09s (-1.41) **Going Correction** +0.075s/f (Slow) **10** Ran SP% **115.5**
Speed ratings (Par 107): **107,106,105,104,103 102,99,97,96,93**
toteswingers: 1&2 £9.40, 1&3 £16.90, 2&3 £6.80 CSF £59.57 CT £518.24 TOTE £10.20: £2.90, £1.70, £3.10; EX 49.60 Trifecta £230.10 Pool: £1,320.16 - 4.30 winning units..

Owner T R G Vestey **Bred** T R G Vestey **Trained** Newmarket, Suffolk

FOCUS
Another above-average race. The pace was steady and the time was over a second slower than the maiden ran over the same distance earlier in the card, but a fairly positive view has been taken of the form.

3961 WINNERS ARE WELCOME AT BETDAQ H'CAP (LONDON MILE QUALIFIER) 1m (P)
9:20 (9:21) (Class 4) (0-85,84) 3-Y-0+ **£4,690** (£1,395; £697; £348) **Stalls** Low

Form RPR
-562 **1** **Shamdarley (IRE)**[16] 3416 5-9-13 **83**.....(p) AdamKirby 8 93
(Marco Botti) *chsd ldr tl led on bit over 2f out: rdn and clr over 1f out: r.o wl: comf* **6/1**
-054 **2** *1 ½* **Silverheels (IRE)**[16] 3411 4-10-0 **84**..... SilvestreDeSousa 5 91
(Paul Cole) *in tch in midfield: rdn and effrt 2f out: hdwy to chse ldr ins fnl f: r.o but no threat to wnr* **4/1**[2]
0 **3** *1 ¾* **Toga Tiger (IRE)**[63] 1922 6-9-5 **80**..... RobertTart[(5)] 2 83
(Jeremy Gask) *t.k.h: hld up in tch in midfield: rdn and effrt ent fnl 2f: styd on to go 3rd ins fnl f: no threat to wnr* **8/1**
-402 **4** *1 ¾* **Net Whizz (USA)**[7] 3693 4-10-0 **84**.....(p) FrankieDettori 7 83
(Jeremy Noseda) *chsd ldrs: rdn and effrt to chse wnr over 1f out: no imp: lost 2nd and wknd ins fnl f* **5/2**[1]
/0-0 **5** *hd* **Commissar**[34] 2813 4-9-5 **75**..... JamesDoyle 3 73+
(Ian Williams) *stdd s: hld up in tch in last trio: effrt towards inner over 1f out: styd on wl fnl 100yds: nvr trbld ldrs* **33/1**
-445 **5** *dht* **Living Desert**[25] 3117 3-8-12 **77**..... SebSanders 6 73+
(James Toller) *stdd s: t.k.h: hld up in rr: rdn and effrt on inner wl over 1f out: kpt on but nvr trbld ldrs* **10/1**
2411 **7** *½* **Hill Of Dreams (IRE)**[15] 3434 4-9-8 **78**.....(b) JimCrowley 9 75
(Dean Ivory) *hld up in tch in last trio: rdn and effrt on outer 2f out: kpt on but nvr trbld ldrs* **5/1**[3]
05-0 **8** *¾* **Dellbuoy**[19] 3293 4-9-8 **78**..... KierenFallon 4 73
(Pat Phelan) *chsd ldrs: rdn and effrt 2f out: no imp over 1f out: wknd ins fnl f* **10/1**
4-20 **9** *hd* **Pashan Garh**[46] 2450 4-9-3 **76**..... CharlesBishop[(3)] 1 71
(Pat Eddery) *led tl rdn and hdd over 1f out: wknd ent fnl f* **20/1**

1m 39.89s (0.09) **Going Correction** +0.075s/f (Slow)
WFA 3 from 4yo+ 9lb **9** Ran SP% **116.5**
Speed ratings (Par 105): **102,100,98,97,96 96,96,95,95**
toteswingers: 1&2 £8.00, 1&3 £10.40, 2&3 £8.90 CSF £30.53 CT £196.02 TOTE £12.20: £2.50, £1.60, £1.90; EX 35.60 Trifecta £262.70 Pool: £1,495.86 - 4.26 winning units..
Owner Andrew Tinkler **Bred** D Veitch & R O'Brien **Trained** Newmarket, Suffolk

FOCUS
A decent event to close the card. It was run at a fair gallop and the winner took it in fair style. He has improved on each start for Botti.
T/Plt: £280.50 to a £1 stake. Pool: £76,215.84. 198.35 winning tickets. T/Qpdt: £43.20 to a £1 stake. Pool: £6,418.82. 109.80 winning tickets. SP

3962 - 3963a (Foreign Racing) - See Raceform Interactive

3224 FAIRYHOUSE (R-H)
Wednesday, July 3

OFFICIAL GOING: Good (good to yielding in places)

3964a IRISH STALLION FARMS EUROPEAN BREEDERS FUND BROWNSTOWN STKS (GROUP 3) 7f
7:00 (7:02) 3-Y-0+ **£40,955** (£11,971; £5,670; £1,890)

RPR
1 **Fiesolana (IRE)**[20] 3263 4-9-11 105..... WJLee 9 114
(W McCreery, Ire) *led and disp: settled in 2nd fr 4f out: gng best and led 2f out: rdn 1f out and r.o strly ins fnl f: gamely* **5/1**[3]
2 *hd* **Along Came Casey (IRE)**[13] 3517 5-9-8 109..... PatSmullen 6 110
(D K Weld, Ire) *sn settled chsng ldrs in cl 3rd: rdn to chal 2f out: sn chsng wnr: 1 l down ent fnl f: kpt on wl u.p to cl deficit wl ins fnl f* **6/4**[1]
3 *1 ¾* **Snow Queen (IRE)**[12] 3524 3-9-0 105.....(b[1]) SeamieHeffernan 3 102+
(A P O'Brien, Ire) *chsd ldrs: pushed along in 4th over 2f out: nt qckn and relegated to 6th appr fnl f: kpt on wl again to go 3rd cl home* **16/1**
4 *shd* **Lily's Angel (IRE)**[20] 3262 4-9-11 106..... GaryCarroll 5 108+
(G M Lyons, Ire) *in rr of mid-div: pushed along in 7th wl over 2f out: r.o to go 3rd 1f out: no ex ins fnl f* **6/1**
5 *nk* **Hint Of A Tint (IRE)**[14] 3460 3-9-0 100..... FMBerry 8 101+
(David Wachman, Ire) *mid-div: rdn over 2f out and prog to go 4th over 1f out: r.o but no ex fnl f* **4/1**[2]
6 *1 ½* **Hanky Panky (IRE)**[4] 3845 3-9-0 100..... JosephO'Brien 7 97
(A P O'Brien, Ire) *restrained and hld up wl in rr: sltly detached: clsd up 3f out: sn rdn and sme prog: nt pce to chal* **10/1**
7 *2* **True Verdict (IRE)**[20] 3263 3-9-0 97.....(p) WayneLordan 1 92
(David Wachman, Ire) *bit slowly away: sn pushed along and settled in rr: rdn over 2f out and sn one pce* **25/1**
8 *2 ½* **Coolnagree (IRE)**[20] 3263 4-9-8 93.....(b) ShaneFoley 4 88
(W McCreery, Ire) *mid-div: rdn and wknd fr over 2f out* **50/1**
9 *4 ½* **Sentaril**[33] 2838 4-9-8 .....(b[1]) KevinManning 2 76
(William Haggas) *led and disp: def ldr fr 4f out: rdn over 2f out and sn hdd: wknd* **10/1**

1m 29.17s (-1.33)
WFA 3 from 4yo+ 8lb **9** Ran SP% **120.8**
CSF £13.55 TOTE £7.40: £2.00, £1.30, £2.90; DF 16.50.
Owner K Leavy/L Cribben/Mrs A McCreery **Bred** Robert De Vere Hunt **Trained** The Curragh, Co.Kildare

FOCUS
The hat-trick was achieved here by Fiesolana, and what a likeable mare she is. The runner-up helps set the standard, supported by the fourth, fifth and sixth.

3965 - 3968a (Foreign Racing) - See Raceform Interactive

3851 DEAUVILLE (R-H)
Wednesday, July 3

OFFICIAL GOING: Fibresand: standard

3969a PRIX DE COLOMBELLES (CONDITIONS) (4YO+) (FIBRESAND) 6f 110y
12:30 (12:00) 4-Y-0+ **£11,382** (£4,552; £3,414; £2,276; £1,138)

RPR
1 **Bravo Echo**[19] 3274 7-8-13 0..... RobertHavlin 2 100
(Michael Attwater) *mde all: rdn 2f out: r.o strly and asserted: pushed out* **123/10**
2 *1 ¼* **Ariete Arrollador**[132] 744 6-8-13 0..... IoritzMendizabal 4 97
(G Arizkorreta Elosegui, Spain) **53/10**
3 *1 ¼* **Mon Choix (FR)**[7] 4-8-9 0..... GregoryBenoist 1 89
(Y Barberot, France) **4/1**[3]
4 *1* **Zarras (GER)**[34] 4-8-13 0..... AnthonyCrastus 9 90
(J Hirschberger, Germany) **14/1**
5 *nk* **Bravia**[268] 4-8-9 0..... Francois-XavierBertras 6 85
(F Rohaut, France) **9/1**
6 *1 ¾* **Dutchessa**[38] 4-8-9 0..... OlivierPeslier 3 80
(C Ferland, France) **23/10**[1]
7 *2 ½* **Robin Du Nord (FR)**[60] 6-8-13 0..... Pierre-CharlesBoudot 10 77
(J-P Gauvin, France) **19/5**[2]
8 *1 ¾* **Dragstair (FR)**[7] 6-8-13 0..... TheoBachelot 8 72
(C Boillot, France) **39/1**
9 *3* **Colorful Notion (IRE)**[172] 4-8-9 0.....(p) UmbertoRispoli 7 59
(Mme J Bidgood, France) **31/1**

1m 17.72s (77.72) **9** Ran SP% **116.8**
WIN (incl. 1 euro stake): 13.30. PLACES: 3.70, 2.10, 1.70. DF: 23.70. SF: 62.70.
Owner Canisbay Bloodstock **Bred** Juddmonte Farms Ltd **Trained** Epsom, Surrey

3879 HAMBURG (R-H)
Wednesday, July 3

OFFICIAL GOING: Turf: good

3970a PREIS DER DEUTSCHEN AFRIKA-LINIEN/JOHN T ESSBERGER (HAMBURGER FLIEGER PREIS) (GROUP 3) (3YO+) (TURF) 6f
5:55 (12:00) 3-Y-0+
£26,016 (£8,943; £4,471; £2,439; £1,626; £1,219)

RPR
1 **Dabbitse (GER)**[24] 4-9-2 0..... AHelfenbein 10 106
(C Zschache, Germany) *midfield: rdn over 2f out: sustained stdy run fr over 1f out: led post* **12/1**
2 *hd* **Smooth Operator (GER)**[52] 7-9-0 0.....(b) StefanieHofer 4 103
(Mario Hofer, Germany) *hld up towards rr: rdn over 2f out: r.o to chal wl ins fnl f: led cl home: kpt on but hdd post* **5/1**[3]
3 *shd* **Best Regards (IRE)**[24] 3-8-7 0..... StephanePasquier 2 101
(P Harley, Germany) *wnt rt s: chsd ldr on inner: rdn 2f out: r.o to chal ent fnl f: led ins fnl 100yds: hdd cl home and dropped to 3rd post* **11/5**[1]
4 *¾* **Govinda (USA)**[22] 6-9-2 0..... EPedroza 3 102
(Vanja Sandrup, Sweden) *broke wl and led: shkn up 2f out: rdn and strly pressed ent fnl f: hdd ins fnl 100yds: no ex and dropped to 4th* **187/10**
5 *½* **Kolonel (GER)**[52] 4-9-2 0..... CristianDemuro 8 101
(Mario Hofer, Germany) *chsd ldr on outer: rdn and ev ch 2f out: nt qckn over 1f out: kpt on* **22/5**[2]
6 *1 ¼* **Baiadera (GER)**[62] 6-8-11 0 ow1..... APietsch 5 92
(R Dzubasz, Germany) *in tch on inner: swtchd out and rdn 2f out: outpcd by ldrs ins fnl f: kpt on* **51/10**
7 *1* **Calrissian (GER)**[22] 9-9-0 0..... DPorcu 9 91
(Fredrik Reuterskiold, Sweden) *dropped in and hld up in last pair on inner: rdn over 2f out: kpt on steadily but nt pce to chal* **143/10**
8 *hd* **The Call (FR)**[24] 4-9-2 0..... MircoDemuro 11 93
(J Hirschberger, Germany) *in tch on outer: rdn and outpcd by ldrs over 1f out: kpt on wout threatening* **108/10**
9 *½* **Charles Darwin (GER)**[38] 4-9-0 0..... CTessarin 7 89
(D Moser, Germany) *hld up towards rr on outer: rdn 2f out: sn outpcd: kpt on and sme mod late hdwy but nvr a factor* **34/1**
10 *1 ½* **Konig Concorde (GER)**[38] 8-9-2 0.....(p) LennartHammer-Hansen 12 86
(C Sprengel, Germany) *midfield on outer: rdn over 2f out: sn outpcd and btn: nvr a factor* **98/10**
11 *2* **Xenophanes (IRE)**[24] 3-8-8 0.....(p) KClijmans 1 77
(P Schiergen, Germany) *t.k.h: midfield on inner: rdn 2f out: no ex and btn ent fnl f: fdd: eased cl home* **206/10**
12 *4 ½* **Ferro Sensation (GER)**[38] 7-9-6 0..... SHellyn 6 70
(D Klomp, Holland) *dwlt sltly: hld up in last: rdn 2f out: no hdwy and sn btn: eased ins fnl f* **28/1**

1m 9.96s (-2.73)
WFA 3 from 4yo+ 6lb **12** Ran SP% **130.8**
WIN (incl. 10 euro stake): 130. PLACES: 23, 15, 14, 28. SF: 882.
Owner C Zschache **Bred** Gestut Ebbesloh **Trained** Germany

2862 EPSOM (L-H)
Thursday, July 4

OFFICIAL GOING: Good (good to firm in places; 8.3)
Wind: Moderate, half against Weather: Fine, warm

3971 STUBHUB TICKETS H'CAP 1m 4f 10y
6:05 (6:06) (Class 5) (0-75,75) 4-Y-0+ **£3,234** (£962; £481; £240) **Stalls** Centre

Form RPR
-503 **1** **Break Rank (USA)**[16] 3434 4-9-7 **75**..... JamieSpencer 7 83
(Ed de Giles) *trckd ldr after 3f: chal and upsides fr 3f out tl drvn ahd jst ins fnl f: hld on nr fin* **3/1**[1]
5326 **2** *nk* **Norfolk Sky**[48] 2418 4-9-0 **68**..... JackMitchell 9 75
(Laura Mongan) *hld up: prog and 5th st: rdn to take 3rd 2f out: styd on to take 2nd last 50yds and cl on wnr at fin* **16/1**

0010 **3** ¾ **Honourable Knight (IRE)**[26] 3110 5-8-9 **63**.................... RobertHavlin 5 69
(Mark Usher) *led: shkn up and jnd 3f out: hdd jst ins fnl f: kpt on but lost 2nd last 50yds* **33/1**

6103 **4** 3 ¼ **Thecornishcowboy**[12] 3587 4-9-4 **72**..............................(t) AdamKirby 8 73
(John Ryan) *hld up: 7th st: rdn 3f out: kpt on to take 4th over 1f out: no imp on ldrs* **5/1**[2]

0-53 **5** 1 ¼ **No Such Number**[24] 3150 5-9-4 **72**............................ RichardHughes 3 71
(Julia Feilden) *hld up: 8th st: pushed along and no prog 3f out: kpt on same pce fr over 1f out* **11/2**[3]

4-25 **6** 1 **Marcus Antonius**[39] 1018 6-8-11 **65**................................ PatCosgrave 1 62
(Jim Boyle) *trckd ldrs: 6th st: rdn 3f out: sn lost pl and btn: tried to rally 1f out: eased whn no ch nr fin* **12/1**

402- **7** 1 ½ **Reggie Perrin**[50] 7012 5-8-5 **64**............................(v) JemmaMarshall(5) 2 59
(Pat Phelan) *trckd ldr 3f: rdn 1/2-way: 3rd st: steadily wknd fnl 2f* **12/1**

0-02 **8** 1 ¾ **Circle Of Angels**[6] 3768 5-8-3 **57**............................ RoystonFfrench 4 49
(Mark Johnston) *dwlt: sn trckd ldrs: 4th st: chsd ldng pair briefly over 2f out: wknd over 1f out* **5/1**[2]

2-02 **9** 6 **Laser Blazer**[28] 3012 5-9-5 **73**..(p) GeorgeBaker 6 55
(Jeremy Gask) *taken steadily to post: stdd s: hld up in detached last: shkn up and no rspnse 3f out: bhd after* **5/1**[2]

2m 38.05s (-0.85) **Going Correction** -0.125s/f (Firm) 9 Ran SP% **114.6**
Speed ratings (Par 103): **97,96,96,94,93 92,91,90,86**
Tote Swingers: 1&2 £10.10, 1&3 £29.90, 2&3 £39.90 CSF £53.97 CT £1313.46 TOTE £3.70: £1.50, £5.90, £9.30; EX 59.30 Trifecta £950.40 Part won. Pool: £1,267.27 - 0.16 winning units..
Owner T Gould **Bred** Millsec Ltd **Trained** Ledbury, H'fords

FOCUS
This modest handicap was run at a steady early pace and it no doubt proved a big advantage to race handily. The winner's French form could be rated this highly.

3972 BRITISH STALLION STUDS JAMES LAING MEMORIAL E B F MEDIAN AUCTION MAIDEN STKS 7f
6:35 (6:36) (Class 5) 2-Y-O £3,881 (£1,155; £577; £288) Stalls Low

Form RPR

025 **1** **Zain Zone (IRE)**[26] 3092 2-9-5 0..(p) AdamKirby 5 76
(Gerard Butler) *fractious in stalls: broke wl and mde all: 3 l clr 2f out: rdn out: unchal* **7/2**[2]

43 **2** 3 ½ **G Man (IRE)**[9] 3659 2-9-5 0.. HarryBentley 3 67
(Olly Stevens) *prom: 3rd st: chsd wnr 3f out: no imp 2f out: one pce after* **8/1**

5 **3** 2 ¾ **The Alamo (IRE)**[20] 3290 2-9-5 0............................... RichardHughes 7 61+
(Richard Hannon) *trckd wnr 2f: restrained sn after: 4th st: rdn to chse ldng pair over 1f out: one pce after* **5/4**[1]

4 1 ¼ **Master Dancer** 2-9-5 0..[1] SteveDrowne 1 57+
(Philip Hide) *s.s: wl in rr: 6th st: prog to go 4th over 1f out: no hdwy after* **33/1**

54 **5** 7 **Tamayuz Dream (IRE)**[26] 3077 2-9-5 0........................ JamieSpencer 6 38
(Mark Johnston) *s.i.s: prog to chse wnr after 2f: lost 2nd 3f out: wknd wl over 1f out* **9/2**[3]

5 **6** ½ **The Wallace Line (IRE)**[20] 3291 2-9-5 0.................... MatthewDavies 4 37
(Mick Channon) *in tch: 5th st: sn rdn and no prog: wl btn after* **8/1**

7 22 **Sweeney Todd** 2-9-5 0... GeorgeBaker 8
(John Best) *prom early: lost pl rapidly: sn bhd: t.o* **20/1**

1m 24.13s (0.83) **Going Correction** -0.125s/f (Firm) 7 Ran SP% **114.8**
Speed ratings (Par 94): **90,86,82,81,73 72,47**
Tote Swingers: 1&2 £4.50, 1&3 £1.50, 2&3 £3.20 CSF £31.08 TOTE £5.30: £3.00, £3.50; EX 40.10 Trifecta £81.90 Pool: £1,771.49 - 16.21 winning units..
Owner Asaad Al Banwan **Bred** Tom Kelly **Trained** Newmarket, Suffolk

FOCUS
The pace lifted in this modest 2-y-o maiden nearing the home straight and, as with the preceding handicap, it paid to race prominently. With the favourite disappointing it's uncertain how much winning this took.

3973 TOTESUPERSCOOP6 H'CAP 6f
7:10 (7:10) (Class 3) (0-95,90) 3-Y-O+ £7,439 (£2,213; £1,106; £553) Stalls High

Form RPR

0031 **1** **Clear Spring (IRE)**[19] 3315 5-9-7 **83**........................... RichardHughes 4 91+
(John Spearing) *trckd ldng pair: no room between them so swtchd rt over 1f out: drvn and r.o fnl f: pushed out fnl strides to ld post* **3/1**[2]

6-26 **2** hd **La Fortunata**[33] 2865 6-9-8 **89**............................. MichaelJMMurphy(5) 1 96
(Mike Murphy) *led: more than 2 l clr 3f out: rdn over 1f out: kpt on wl but hdd last stride* **9/4**[1]

-613 **3** nk **Charlotte Rosina**[34] 2848 4-10-0 **90**............................. JamieSpencer 3 96
(Roger Teal) *chsd ldr: rdn 2f out: grad clsd fr over 1f out: nrly upsides last 75yds but wnr wnt by nr fin* **10/3**[3]

0000 **4** 5 **Amadeus Wolfe Tone (IRE)**[18] 3367 4-9-13 **89**...........(b[1]) AdamKirby 6 79
(Jamie Osborne) *hld up: chsd ldng trio 3f out: no imp 2f out: fdd over 1f out* **9/1**

0000 **5** ¾ **Lunar Deity**[7] 3733 4-9-1 **77**...(b) ChrisCatlin 5 65
(Eve Johnson Houghton) *t.k.h: hld up in last: pushed along and no prog 3f out: sn btn* **12/1**

4224 **6** ½ **Titus Gent**[22] 3220 8-9-6 **87**... RobertTart(5) 2 73
(Jeremy Gask) *missed break sltly: chsd ldng trio to 3f out: sn btn* **7/1**

1m 8.34s (-1.06) **Going Correction** -0.125s/f (Firm) 6 Ran SP% **109.0**
Speed ratings (Par 107): **102,101,101,94,93 93**
Tote Swingers: 1&2 £1.90, 1&3 £2.90, 2&3 £2.30 CSF £9.55 TOTE £3.10: £2.30, £1.20; EX 8.00 Trifecta £16.00 Pool: £901.76 - 42.02 winning units..
Owner H James **Bred** Rocal Bloodstock **Trained** Kinnersley, Worcs

FOCUS
A fair little sprint handicap and although it was another race where those held up were at a disadvantage, there was a tight three-way finish. The form looks pretty straightforward, rated around the second and third.

3974 WEATHERBYS HAMILTON INSURANCE H'CAP 7f
7:45 (7:45) (Class 4) (0-85,85) 3-Y-O+ £4,690 (£1,395; £697; £348) Stalls Low

Form RPR

34 **1** **Balty Boys (IRE)**[17] 3415 4-10-0 **85**.........................(b) RichardHughes 7 95
(Jamie Osborne) *led: rdn 2f out: narrowly hdd ins fnl f: kpt on wl to ld again post* **9/2**[2]

-541 **2** nse **Good Luck Charm**[24] 3153 4-9-9 **80**................................ GeorgeBaker 1 90
(Gary Moore) *trckd ldrs: 4th st: smooth prog to trck wnr 2f out: rdn to take narrow ld ins fnl f: idled and hdd post* **11/2**[3]

5000 **3** 1 ¾ **Spirit Of Sharjah (IRE)**[31] 2937 8-9-12 **83**.................(p) SteveDrowne 2 91+
(Julia Feilden) *t.k.h: hld up in midfield: 7th st: trapped bhd rivals fr 3f out tl swtchd rt over 1f out: pushed along and r.o to take 3rd last strides* **25/1**

0531 **4** hd **My Kingdom (IRE)**[12] 3586 7-9-6 **77**..............................(t) HarryBentley 3 82
(Stuart Williams) *trckd ldrs: 5th st: rdn to chse ldng pair over 1f out: no real imp: lost 3rd last strides* **7/2**[1]

0020 **5** 1 **Starwatch**[20] 3274 6-9-4 **80**..............................(v[1]) MichaelJMMurphy(5) 9 82
(John Bridger) *mostly chsd wnr to 2f out: kpt on one pce u.p after* **6/1**

4-50 **6** 3 ¼ **Hometown Glory**[47] 2450 4-9-7 **78**...........................(t) RichardMullen 5 71
(Brian Meehan) *hld up in rr: 9th st: prog against rail fr over 2f out: disp 3rd jst over 1f out: wknd last 150yds* **11/1**

0304 **7** 2 ¾ **Kimberella**[20] 3279 3-9-3 **82**... RobertHavlin 4 65
(Michael Attwater) *t.k.h: hld up in midfield: 8th st: shkn up and no prog over 2f out: nvr on terms after* **15/2**

3601 **8** nk **Halling Dancer**[12] 3575 4-9-2 **73**... KierenFox 8 58
(Lee Carter) *sn prom: 3rd and rdn st: disp 2nd fr 3f out to 2f out: wknd* **16/1**

-200 **9** 2 ¾ **Charitable Act (FR)**[28] 3019 4-9-4 **75**.............................. AdamKirby 12 53
(Gary Moore) *chsd ldrs: 6th st: shkn up over 2f out: steadily wknd* **20/1**

3-05 **10** ½ **Rondeau (GR)**[22] 3215 8-9-5 **76**...................................... MickyFenton 10 52
(Patrick Chamings) *stdd s: hld up in rr: 10th st: pushed along and no prog over 2f out: nvr involved* **25/1**

-105 **11** 17 **Golden Desert (IRE)**[20] 3274 9-9-3 **74**........................ JamieSpencer 11
(Simon Dow) *s.s: a in 11th and detached fr main body of field: no prog 3f out: t.o* **14/1**

1350 **12** 39 **Lowther**[19] 3339 8-9-12 **83**..(v) AmirQuinn 6
(Lee Carter) *hit hd against stall whn anticipating s: c out wl bhd and allowed to amble arnd* **20/1**

1m 21.96s (-1.34) **Going Correction** -0.125s/f (Firm)
WFA 3 from 4yo+ 8lb 12 Ran SP% **119.9**
Speed ratings (Par 105): **102,101,99,99,98 94,91,91,88,87 68,23**
Tote Swingers: 1&2 £4.90, 1&3 £18.20, 2&3 £28.20 CSF £28.10 CT £563.25 TOTE £5.00: £1.70, £2.20, £7.90; EX 31.80 Trifecta £504.40 Pool: £901.76 - 42.02 winning units..
Owner Dr Marwan Koukash **Bred** Lynn Lodge Stud **Trained** Upper Lambourn, Berks

FOCUS
A competitive handicap. It was run at an uneven pace with the winner making all. The thid rates better than the bare form.

3975 EBF ARTHUR BUDGETT MEMORIAL MAIDEN FILLIES' STKS 1m 4f 10y
8:20 (8:22) (Class 4) 3-4-Y-O £5,175 (£1,540; £769; £384) Stalls Centre

Form RPR

33- **1** **Rosie Probert**[24] 3100 4-9-11 0...................................... RichardHughes 1 80
(Nicky Henderson) *trckd ldng pair: wnt 2nd over 2f out: sn drvn: clsd fnl f to ld last 50yds: pushed out after* **7/1**

32 **2** nk **Shalwa**[57] 2164 3-8-12 0.. RobertHavlin 4 79
(Marco Botti) *led: stretched on 3f out: drvn over 1f out: hdd and hld last 50yds* **4/1**[3]

3 3 ¼ **Saddaqa (USA)** 3-8-12 0.. HarryBentley 5 74+
(Saeed bin Suroor) *s.i.s: hld up in last tl 5th st: prog on outer to go 3rd jst over 2f out: rn green and no imp on ldng pair after* **10/1**

5-4 **4** 3 ¼ **Fatima's Gift**[38] 2713 3-8-12 0.. RichardMullen 7 69
(David Simcock) *hld up in 6th: drvn and nt qckn wl over 2f out: plugged on into 4th over 1f out: no imp on ldrs after* **7/2**[2]

552 **5** 7 **Gertrude Gray (IRE)**[20] 3272 3-8-12 78........................... PatCosgrave 6 58
(Lady Cecil) *trckd ldr: rdn and nt qckn 3f out: sn lost 2nd: hung lft and wknd over 1f out* **3/1**[1]

0 **6** 7 **Ninja Lady**[15] 3469 3-8-12 0.. FrederikTylicki 2 47
(James Fanshawe) *s.i.s: in tch tl dropped to last and rdn st: sn btn* **25/1**

4-6 **7** 4 ½ **Pearl Street (USA)**[21] 3237 3-8-12 0............................. JamieSpencer 3 39
(Henry Candy) *trckd ldng trio: rdn 4f out: 4th st: sn wknd* **9/2**

2m 37.33s (-1.57) **Going Correction** -0.125s/f (Firm)
WFA 3 from 4yo 13lb 7 Ran SP% **110.8**
Speed ratings (Par 102): **100,99,97,95,90 86,83**
Tote Swingers: 1&2 £3.60, 1&3 £8.90, 2&3 £3.70 CSF £32.70 TOTE £5.40: £2.70, £2.70; EX 20.30 Trifecta £205.80 Pool: £1,257.22 - 4.58 winning units..
Owner Seasons Holidays **Bred** Seasons Holidays **Trained** Upper Lambourn, Berks

FOCUS
An ordinary looking fillies' maiden in which a couple disappointed, but the pace was decent. There's the prospect of more to come from the winner.

3976 KISS MIX H'CAP (JOCKEY CLUB GRASSROOTS MIDDLE DISTANCE FLAT SERIES) 1m 2f 18y
8:55 (8:55) (Class 4) (0-80,78) 3-Y-O+ £4,690 (£1,395; £697; £348) Stalls Low

Form RPR

1 **1** **Court Pastoral**[31] 2938 3-9-1 **76**... PatCosgrave 5 88+
(Lady Cecil) *trckd ldng pair: clsd on inner to ld over 2f out: jnd over 1f out: drvn and asserted last 100yds* **4/1**[2]

5316 **2** 3 **Frozen Over**[28] 3022 5-9-8 **72**... AdamKirby 2 80
(Stuart Kittow) *hld up: 5th st: prog to chse wnr 2f out and sn challenging: upsides jst ins fnl f: wknd qckly last 100yds* **9/2**[3]

0555 **3** 2 **Nordic Quest (IRE)**[8] 3692 4-9-10 **74**.........................(t[1]) FrederikTylicki 1 76
(Gerard Butler) *led: rdn and hdd over 2f out: lost 2nd sn after: one pce fr over 1f out* **13/2**

3530 **4** ¾ **Whitby Jet (IRE)**[80] 1585 5-9-8 **72**................................... GeorgeBaker 3 73
(Ed Vaughan) *hld up in 7th and off the pce: sme prog fr 3f out: shkn up over 1f out: kpt on but nvr involved* **10/1**

1-02 **5** 1 **Kelpie Blitz (IRE)**[28] 3022 4-10-0 **78**.............................(t) MickyFenton 8 77
(Seamus Durack) *hld up in detached last: pushed along on outer 3f out: mod prog only: reminders fnl f and kpt on: nvr remotely involved* **7/1**

3663 **6** 5 **Assizes**[5] 3804 4-10-0 **78**.. JamieSpencer 6 72
(Mark Johnston) *pressed ldr to wl over 2f out: sn btn: wknd over 1f out: eased fnl f* **5/2**[1]

10-0 **7** 41 **The Wonga Coup (IRE)**[14] 3499 6-8-4 **59**.............. JemmaMarshall(5) 4
(Pat Phelan) *in tch in 6th tl wknd rapidly over 3f out: t.o* **20/1**

0600 **8** 5 **Ajeeb (USA)**[12] 3579 5-9-5 **69**.. RichardHughes 7
(Michael Scudamore) *chsd ldng trio tl 3f out: sn wknd: virtually p.u 2f out* **12/1**

2m 7.11s (-2.59) **Going Correction** -0.125s/f (Firm)
WFA 3 from 4yo+ 11lb 8 Ran SP% **114.1**
Speed ratings (Par 105): **105,102,101,100,99 95,62,58**
Tote Swingers: 1&2 £4.50, 1&3 £6.30, 2&3 £6.60 CSF £22.25 CT £113.16 TOTE £3.30: £1.70, £1.70, £2.00; EX 29.20 Trifecta £77.80 Pool: £1,317.59 - 12.68 winning units..
Owner J Shack **Bred** Newsells Park Stud **Trained** Newmarket, Suffolk

FOCUS
A modest handicap where few got seriously involved off a sound pace. The winner proved much too good and it will be interesting to see how much better she can do.
T/Plt: £769.80 to a £1 stake. Pool: £92,836.72 - 88.03 winning tickets. T/Qpdt: £27.90 to a £1 stake. Pool: £8,150.47 - 215.94 winning tickets. JN

3568 HAYDOCK (L-H)

Thursday, July 4

OFFICIAL GOING: Good to firm (8.2)

Wind: moderate 1/2 against Weather: overcast, becoming fine and sunny

3977 RITEC "GOOD GLASS CAMPAIGN" H'CAP — 1m 2f 95y

2:20 (2:21) (Class 5) (0-70,70) 3-Y-O+ **£2,587** (£770; £384; £192) **Stalls** High

Form RPR

2605 **1** **King Kurt (IRE)**[22] 3195 5-9-12 **68** PhillipMakin 14 77
(Kevin Ryan) *led early: w ldrs: effrt over 3f out: led over 1f out: hld on nr fin* **5/1**[3]

00-0 **2** *hd* **Snow Hill**[75] 1673 5-10-0 **70** SebSanders 2 79
(Chris Wall) *trckd ldrs: chal 1f out: kpt on towards fin: jst hld* **4/1**[1]

0-06 **3** *4 1/2* **Supreme Luxury (IRE)**[38] 2704 4-9-12 **68** AmyRyan 9 68
(Kevin Ryan) *in rr-div: hdwy on ins over 2f out: n.m.r: swtchd rt and styd on to take 3rd last 100yds* **11/1**

400- **4** *3/4* **Voice From Above (IRE)**[252] 7358 4-9-9 **65** DuranFentiman 12 64
(Patrick Holmes) *mid-div: hdwy on outside over 2f out: styd on same pce fnl f* **66/1**

2306 **5** *3/4* **Brown Pete (IRE)**[22] 3218 5-10-0 **70** RobertWinston 7 69+
(Violet M Jordan) *s.i.s: hld up in rr: hdwy and n.m.r 2f out: styd on ins fnl f* **10/1**

5100 **6** *nk* **Going Grey (IRE)**[26] 3083 4-9-2 **58** (p) TonyHamilton 8 55
(Richard Fahey) *sn led: hdd over 1f out: wknd last 100yds* **16/1**

324 **7** *1* **Royal Sea (IRE)**[21] 3248 4-9-2 **61** (p) RyanClark(3) 10 56
(Michael Mullineaux) *hld up in rr: n.m.r on inner and swtchd outside over 1f out: styd on ins fnl f* **11/1**

0062 **8** *1/2* **Dama De La Noche (IRE)**[28] 3014 3-8-10 **63** PatDobbs 13 57
(Richard Hannon) *prom: n.m.r 2f out: one pce* **9/2**[2]

5-40 **9** *hd* **Thatcherite (IRE)**[19] 3337 5-9-5 **61** (tp) StephenCraine 11 54
(Tony Coyle) *s.i.s: hld up in rr: hdwy over 2f out: nvr trbld ldrs* **16/1**

0-30 **10** *nse* **Meshardal (GER)**[28] 3021 3-9-1 **68** PaulHanagan 6 61
(Richard Hannon) *mid-div: drvn 3f out: nvr a threat* **13/2**

-005 **11** *16* **Dicey Vows (USA)**[9] 3662 5-8-7 **56** DavidParkes(7) 3 19
(Alan Jarvis) *trckd ldrs: drvn 3f out: lost pl over 1f out: bhd whn eased: t.o* **25/1**

000- **12** *1 1/2* **Oriental Cavalier**[329] 5001 7-9-4 **60** (v) JimCrowley 16 23
(Mark Buckley) *mid-div: hdwy 3f out: sn chsng ldrs: lost pl over 1f out: eased whn bhd: t.o* **18/1**

0000 **13** *2 1/2* **Mataajir (USA)**[22] 3210 5-8-10 **52** (t) MartinDwyer 5
(Derek Shaw) *in rr: bhd and drvn over 6f out: t.o* **66/1**

2m 13.75s (-1.75) **Going Correction** -0.075s/f (Good)
WFA 3 from 4yo+ 11lb **13** Ran SP% **117.8**
Speed ratings (Par 103): **104,103,100,99,99 98,98,97,97,97 84,83,81**
toteswingers 1&2 £5.70, 1&3 £12.70, 2&3 £13.50 CSF £24.60 CT £211.02 TOTE £5.60: £1.60, £2.20, £4.10; EX 22.30 Trifecta £250.70 Pool: £1765.43 - 5.28 winning units..
Owner Matthew Taylor **Bred** Hong Kong Breeders Club **Trained** Hambleton, N Yorks

FOCUS
A competitive handicap, if only a modest one and, with little pace on, it developed into something of a 3f sprint. It's been rated around the winner's form this year.

3978 FLOAT GLASS INDUSTRIES EBF MAIDEN FILLIES' STKS — 6f

2:50 (2:53) (Class 5) 2-Y-O **£2,911** (£866; £432; £216) **Stalls** Centre

Form RPR

1 **Hot Coffee (IRE)** 2-9-0 0 RichardKingscote 4 88+
(Tom Dascombe) *in rr: hdwy over 1f out: swtchd lft and chsd ldr 1f out: led last 100yds: forged clr* **8/1**

0 **2** *4* **Lady Lara (IRE)**[13] 3522 2-9-0 0 JimCrowley 10 74
(Alan Jarvis) *led: hdd last 100yds: no ex* **2/1**[1]

3 *1 1/2* **Souville** 2-9-0 0 SebSanders 9 70+
(Chris Wall) *s.s: hdwy stands' side and nt clr run over 2f out: styd on to take 3rd last 100yds* **40/1**

4 *nk* **Flycatcher (IRE)** 2-9-0 0 TonyHamilton 7 68+
(Richard Fahey) *dwlt: hld up towards rr: hdwy over 1f out: styd on wl towards fin: will improve* **7/1**

5 *3* **Good Morning Lady** 2-9-0 0 SamHitchcott 2 58
(Mick Channon) *chsd ldrs: effrt over 2f out: wknd over 1f out* **25/1**

6 **6** *1* **Omanome (IRE)**[14] 3500 2-9-0 0 DanielTudhope 1 55
(David O'Meara) *chsd ldrs on outer: swtchd rt after 1f: drvn 2f out: sn wknd* **50/1**

7 *6* **Realistic** 2-9-0 0 MichaelStainton 8 36
(David Brown) *chsd ldrs: drvn and outpcd 3f out: lost pl 2f out* **20/1**

8 *nse* **Setai** 2-9-0 0 KierenFallon 5 36
(Brian Meehan) *chsd ldrs: lost pl over 1f out* **5/1**[3]

9 *3/4* **Romantic Bliss (IRE)** 2-9-0 0 RobertWinston 6 33
(Mrs K Burke) *chsd ldrs: lost pl wl over 1f out* **16/1**

10 *2 3/4* **Mumtaza** 2-9-0 0 PaulHanagan 11 24
(Richard Hannon) *dwlt: hdwy to chse ldrs over 4f out: drvn 2f out: sn lost pl* **7/2**[2]

00 **11** *6* **Volodina (IRE)**[21] 3245 2-9-0 0 MartinDwyer 3
(Alan McCabe) *trckd ldrs on outside: t.k.h: hung lft and lost pl over 2f out* **200/1**

1m 16.14s (2.34) **Going Correction** +0.30s/f (Good) **11** Ran SP% **115.2**
Speed ratings (Par 91): **96,90,88,88,84 82,74,74,73,70 62**
toteswingers 1&2 £5.10, 1&3 £44.30, 2&3 £15.50 CSF £22.95 TOTE £8.50: £2.60, £1.30, £7.00; EX 30.00 Trifecta £670.30 Pool: £5178.55 - 5.79 winning units..
Owner The MHS 2013 Partnership **Bred** Lodge Park Stud **Trained** Malpas, Cheshire

FOCUS
This looked a decent editions of what is often a good maiden, with a very impressive winner who rates a nice prospect.

3979 BOHLE 90TH ANNIVERSARY EBF MAIDEN STKS — 6f

3:20 (3:22) (Class 5) 2-Y-O **£2,911** (£866; £432; £216) **Stalls** Centre

Form RPR

1 **Zaraee (IRE)** 2-9-5 0 PaulHanagan 5 83+
(William Haggas) *hld up in last: hdwy over 2f out: chsng ldr over 1f out: shkn up to ld last 150yds: styd on strly: v readily* **15/8**[2]

0 **2** *1 1/2* **Rogue Wave (IRE)**[16] 3422 2-9-5 0 JimCrowley 2 77
(Alan Jarvis) *led: qcknd pce over 2f out: rdn over 1f out: hdd and no ex ins fnl f* **11/10**[1]

3 *3 1/2* **Day Of Conquest** 2-9-5 0 PatDobbs 3 66+
(Richard Hannon) *trckd ldr: drvn over 2f out: edgd lft and one pce fnl f* **7/2**[3]

4 *11* **Argent Touch** 2-9-5 0 MartinDwyer 4 31
(Derek Shaw) *trckd ldrs: effrt over 2f out: hung lft and lost pl over 1f out* **16/1**

1m 17.5s (3.70) **Going Correction** +0.30s/f (Good) **4** Ran SP% **110.5**
Speed ratings (Par 94): **87,85,80,65**
CSF £4.46 TOTE £2.40; EX 4.30 Trifecta £6.50 Pool: £2009.99 - 229.01 winning units..
Owner Hamdan Al Maktoum **Bred** London Thoroughbred Services Ltd **Trained** Newmarket, Suffolk

FOCUS
Non-runners reduced this to just the four runners and the time was 1.36 seconds slower than the fillies in the preceding maiden. The runner-up is rated close to his debut form.

3980 TUFFX H'CAP (JOCKEY CLUB GRASSROOTS SPRINT SERIES QUALIFIER) (DIV I) — 6f

3:50 (3:51) (Class 4) (0-80,80) 3-Y-O+ **£5,175** (£1,540; £769; £384) **Stalls** Centre

Form RPR

-011 **1** **Nasharra (IRE)**[55] 2222 5-9-3 **78** (tp) KevinStott(7) 4 89
(Kevin Ryan) *outpcd in rr: hdwy stands' side 2f out: led last 150yds: all out* **12/1**

4036 **2** *nse* **Al Khan (IRE)**[19] 3351 4-9-12 **80** RobertWinston 6 91
(Violet M Jordan) *dwlt: hdwy to trck ldrs over 3f out: led over 1f out: narrowly hdd last 150yds: rallied nr fin: jst failed* **11/2**

4512 **3** *5* **Mutafaakir (IRE)**[6] 3778 4-9-3 **71** PJMcDonald 3 66
(Ruth Carr) *hld up in mid-div: nt clr run 2f out and swtchd rt: 3rd 1f out: kpt on same pce* **7/4**[1]

040 **4** *1 1/2* **My Son Max**[12] 3586 5-9-11 **79** KierenFallon 1 69
(P J O'Gorman) *dwlt: in rr: hdwy 2f out: 4th 1f out: kpt on one pce* **5/1**[3]

-000 **5** *4 1/2* **Another Try (IRE)**[33] 2868 8-9-3 **78** DavidParkes(7) 9 54
(Alan Jarvis) *led 1f: w ldrs: led briefly wl over 1f out: sn wknd* **12/1**

1-44 **6** *2 1/4* **Hardy Blue (IRE)**[6] 3762 3-8-9 **69** DuranFentiman 2 38
(Danielle McCormick) *chsd ldrs on outer: edgd lft and lost pl over 1f out* **20/1**

3625 **7** *shd* **Barkston Ash**[7] 3714 5-9-6 **79** (p) JasonHart(5) 10 47
(Eric Alston) *reminders after s: hdwy to ld after 1f: hdd and hmpd wl over 1f out: sn wknd* **7/2**[2]

4000 **8** *3/4* **Lucky Dan (IRE)**[26] 3093 7-9-7 **75** JoeFanning 8 41
(Paul Green) *w ldrs: lost pl wl over 1f out* **22/1**

1m 14.99s (1.19) **Going Correction** +0.30s/f (Good)
WFA 3 from 4yo+ 6lb **8** Ran SP% **115.1**
Speed ratings (Par 105): **104,103,97,95,89 86,86,85**
toteswingers 1&2 £7.40, 1&3 £3.70, 2&3 £3.90 CSF £76.59 CT £173.30 TOTE £10.30: £2.30, £1.60, £1.40; EX 69.80 Trifecta £197.70 Pool: £3818.06 - 14.48 winning units..
Owner Mr & Mrs Julian And Rosie Richer **Bred** P McCutcheon **Trained** Hambleton, N Yorks

FOCUS
A fair sprint handicap, but the leaders may have gone off too quick as the trio who helped force it all stopped to nothing. in fact all four sprints on the card were won from the rear. The winner's best form since he was a 2yo.

3981 THE LEGEND THAT IS NELSON GRAHAM H'CAP (JOCKEY CLUB GRASSROOTS SPRINT SERIES QUALIFIER) (DIV II) — 6f

4:20 (4:20) (Class 4) (0-80,80) 3-Y-O+ **£5,175** (£1,540; £769; £384) **Stalls** Centre

Form RPR

0500 **1** **Pea Shooter**[19] 3351 4-9-8 **76** (p) GrahamLee 3 86
(Kevin Ryan) *dwlt: in rr: hdwy and edgd rt over 1f out: hung rt and led last 150yds: jst hld on* **7/2**[2]

6463 **2** *nse* **Head Space (IRE)**[5] 3811 5-9-10 **78** JamesSullivan 7 88
(Ruth Carr) *dwlt: hld up in rr: swtchd rt and hdwy stands' side 2f out: rdn and edgd lft fnl f: upsides last 100yds: jst hld* **5/2**[1]

-240 **3** *2 1/4* **Rich Again (IRE)**[131] 775 4-8-11 **65** RobertWinston 9 68
(James Bethell) *dwlt: hld up in rr: effrt over 2f out: chsng ldrs whn nt clr run ins fnl f: styd on to take 3rd nr fin* **15/2**

3404 **4** *nk* **Mappin Time (IRE)**[5] 3811 5-9-7 **80** (p) DarylByrne(5) 4 82
(Tim Easterby) *mid-div: effrt over 2f out: nt clr run over 1f out: swtchd lft jst ins fnl f: styd on to take 3rd last 50yds* **4/1**[3]

3200 **5** *2 1/4* **Tyfos**[26] 3093 8-9-11 **79** TomMcLaughlin 6 73
(Brian Baugh) *w ldrs: t.k.h: led briefly 1f out: sltly hmpd 100yds out: wknd and eased nr fin* **25/1**

36-5 **6** *1/2* **Imperator Augustus (IRE)**[16] 3441 5-9-4 **72** DuranFentiman 8 65
(Patrick Holmes) *dwlt: sn chsng ldrs: wknd over 1f out* **18/1**

2540 **7** *1/2* **Burnhope**[61] 2007 4-9-7 **75** (p) JamesDoyle 10 66
(Scott Dixon) *led: hdd 1f out: wkng whn sltly hmpd 100yds out* **14/1**

0226 **8** *3* **Pelmanism**[13] 3529 6-8-8 **62** (p) TomEaves 5 44
(Brian Ellison) *chsd ldrs: wkng whn hmpd over 1f out* **16/1**

0556 **9** *2* **Roker Park (IRE)**[22] 3200 8-9-10 **78** DanielTudhope 1 53
(David O'Meara) *mid-div: lost pl aver 4f out: sme hdwy over 2f out: sn wknd* **9/1**

1m 14.81s (1.01) **Going Correction** +0.30s/f (Good) **9** Ran SP% **114.2**
Speed ratings (Par 105): **105,104,101,101,98 97,97,93,90**
toteswingers 1&2 £4.00, 1&3 £4.90, 2&3 £3.80 CSF £12.51 CT £60.22 TOTE £4.00: £1.80, £1.10, £2.50; EX 13.20 Trifecta £66.20 Pool: £3385.30 - 38.33 winning units..
Owner Mrs Margaret Forsyth **Bred** R F And S D Knipe **Trained** Hambleton, N Yorks

FOCUS
A very similar race to the first division in that those who raced up with the pace didn't get home and the principals came from the back. The winning time was 0.18 seconds faster. The winner is rated to last September's form.

3982 DISTINCTION DOORS H'CAP — 1m 6f

4:50 (4:50) (Class 2) (0-100,88) 3-Y-O **£16,172** (£4,812; £2,405; £1,202) **Stalls** Low

Form RPR

0-61 **1** **Great Hall**[27] 3059 3-9-7 **88** KierenFallon 5 101+
(Brian Meehan) *in rr: drvn over 6f out: hdwy on outside over 2f out: led appr fnl f: hung lft: hld on wl towards fin* **13/2**[3]

3322 **2** *1* **Debdebdeb**[21] 3243 3-8-9 **76** MartinDwyer 10 87
(Andrew Balding) *t.k.h: trckd ldrs: lost pl over 6f out: hdwy on outer over 3f out: edgd lft and chsd ldrs over 1f out: upsides ins fnl f: crowded and no ex nr fin* **7/2**[2]

2-14 **3** *3/4* **Hawk High (IRE)**[14] 3502 3-8-7 **74** DavidAllan 8 84
(Tim Easterby) *dwlt: in rr: effrt on outer over 3f out: chsng ldrs over 1f out: keeping on same pce whn hmpd and eased nr fin* **12/1**

-122 **4** *2* **Argent Knight**[22] 3206 3-8-7 **74** ow1 (v[1]) TomEaves 6 82
(William Jarvis) *hld up in mid-div: effrt 4f out: lost pl and hmpd on ins wl over 1f out: swtchd rt: styd on: nt rch ldrs* **10/1**

2223 **5** *2 3/4* **Street Artist (IRE)**[5] 3806 3-8-11 **78** RichardKingscote 9 81
(Mark Johnston) *chsd ldrs: drvn 4f out: wknd over 1f out* **7/1**

3524 **6** *1 3/4* **Enaitch (IRE)**[20] 3272 3-8-8 **75** SamHitchcott 7 76
(Mick Channon) *t.k.h in rr: effrt on ins over 2f out: one pce whn hmpd over 1f out* **25/1**

-311 **7** *1* **Lion Beacon**[42] 2602 3-9-3 **84** PatDobbs 2 83
(Amanda Perrett) *trckd ldrs: 2nd 7f out: wknd over 1f out* **5/2**[1]
5250 **8** *4 ½* **Blue Wave (IRE)**[14] 3486 3-9-4 **85** (b) JoeFanning 4 78
(Mark Johnston) *led: clr after 3f tl 7f out: sent 3 l clr over 3f out: hdd & wknd appr fnl f* **7/1**
-534 **9** *12* **Dragon City**[20] 3277 3-8-10 **77** JamesDoyle 3 64
(Harry Dunlop) *trckd ldrs: drvn over 3f out: lost pl and eased wl over 1f out* **20/1**

2m 58.25s (-3.75) **Going Correction** -0.075s/f (Good) 9 Ran **SP% 114.5**
Speed ratings (Par 106): **107,106,106,104,103 102,101,99,92**
toteswingers 1&2 £5.70, 1&3 £11.30, 2&3 £10.20 CSF £29.25 CT £267.05 TOTE £6.00: £3.10, £1.50, £4.00; EX 27.00 Trifecta £274.60 Pool: £2925.88 - 7.99 winning units..
Owner Raymond Tooth **Bred** Aston House Stud **Trained** Manton, Wilts
FOCUS
A decent staying handicap in which the pace was strong. This was another contest dominated by those held up, but it was also rather a messy race. The form is rated on the positive side.

3983 SUPALITE TILED ROOF SYSTEM FILLIES' H'CAP 1m
5:20 (5:23) (Class 5) (0-75,75) 3-Y-O+ **£2,587** (£770; £384; £192) **Stalls** Low

Form RPR
1630 **1** **Goldstorm**[19] 3349 5-10-0 **75** GrahamLee 4 86
(Brian Baugh) *t.k.h in rr: effrt and nt clr run over 1f out: swtchd rt: styd on wl to ld last 100yds* **8/1**
32-3 **2** *3* **Trucanini**[27] 3062 3-9-5 **75** SebSanders 5 77
(Chris Wall) *t.k.h in rr-div: hdwy over 3f out: led over 1f out: hdd ins fnl f: no ex* **9/4**[1]
0-21 **3** *2 ¾* **Thankyou Very Much**[22] 3191 3-8-9 **65** AmyRyan 1 61
(James Bethell) *trckd ldrs: led and hung lft 2f out: hdd over 1f out: kpt on same pce* **16/1**
0-12 **4** *¾* **Emmuska**[20] 3269 4-9-7 **68** JamesDoyle 8 64
(Clive Cox) *led 1f: chsd ldrs: one pce over 1f out* **5/1**[3]
1321 **5** *1* **Dutch Mistress**[7] 3736 4-9-6 **67** PaulHanagan 7 61
(James Unett) *trckd ldrs: wknd fnl f* **5/2**[2]
1016 **6** *1 ¼* **Spavento (IRE)**[7] 3712 7-9-7 **73** JasonHart(5) 2 64
(Eric Alston) *chsd ldrs: drvn and outpcd over 3f out: chsd ldrs on inner 2f out: n.m.r: wknd last 75yds* **22/1**
-463 **7** *¾* **Silvas Romana (IRE)**[20] 3269 4-9-11 **72** TomMcLaughlin 3 63
(Mark Brisbourne) *s.i.s: in rr: hdwy over 2f out: sn chsng ldrs: 5th and hld whn eased last 50yds* **25/1**
0-00 **8** *3 ¼* **First Class Favour (IRE)**[14] 3506 5-9-3 **64** DavidAllan 6 46
(Tim Easterby) *led after 1f: hdd 2f out: wkng whn hmpd over 1f out* **33/1**
00-1 **9** *½* **Golden Causeway**[148] 532 3-9-1 **71** RobertWinston 9 50
(Charles Hills) *hld up in rr: effrt on outside over 3f out: lost pl over 1f out* **12/1**

1m 42.31s (-1.39) **Going Correction** -0.075s/f (Good)
WFA 3 from 4yo+ 9lb 9 Ran **SP% 111.8**
Speed ratings (Par 100): **103,100,97,96,95 94,93,90,89**
toteswingers 1&2 £4.00, 1&3 £8.90, 2&3 £6.00 CSF £24.94 CT £280.59 TOTE £10.60: £3.50, £1.10, £4.20; EX 38.50 Trifecta £502.60 Pool: £3816.35 - 5.69 winning units..
Owner Magnate Racing **Bred** Andrew Bailey **Trained** Audley, Staffs
FOCUS
A modest fillies' handicap, run at a good pace, and another race where the first two came from well back. A 4lb personal best from the winner.

3984 GLASS TIMES H'CAP 1m
5:50 (5:50) (Class 3) (0-95,94) 3-Y-O+ **£8,086** (£2,406; £1,202; £601) **Stalls** Low

Form RPR
1610 **1** **Mont Ras (IRE)**[13] 3527 6-10-0 **94** DanielTudhope 6 105
(David O'Meara) *led 1f: chsd ldrs: rallied over 1f out: led last 100yds: r.o gamely* **5/2**[1]
2562 **2** *1* **Kingscroft (IRE)**[6] 3757 5-9-2 **82** JoeFanning 8 90
(Mark Johnston) *trckd ldrs: 2nd over 4f out: led over 2f out: hdd and no ex ins fnl f* **7/2**[2]
5423 **3** *2 ½* **Dubai Hills**[22] 3207 7-9-8 **88** TomEaves 1 91
(Bryan Smart) *dwlt: in rr: hdwy over 3f out: styd on and 3rd 1f out: kpt on same pce* **6/1**[3]
-000 **4** *½* **Crius (IRE)**[33] 2858 4-9-7 **87** PatDobbs 4 89
(Richard Hannon) *t.k.h: trckd ldrs: outpcd over 3f out: hdwy on ins over 1f out: tk 4th last 100yds* **9/1**
0200 **5** *3* **Chosen Character (IRE)**[12] 3564 5-9-13 **93** (vt) RichardKingscote 7 88
(Tom Dascombe) *led after 1f: led over 2f out: wknd jst ins fnl f* **13/2**
6101 **6** *nk* **Lord Of The Dance (IRE)**[8] 3683 7-9-1 **84** 6ex RyanClark(3) 10 78
(Michael Mullineaux) *in rr: hdwy 3f out: sn drvn: wknd over 1f out* **9/1**
0206 **7** *¾* **No Poppy (IRE)**[14] 3503 5-9-0 **85** AdamCarter(5) 11 77
(Tim Easterby) *chsd ldrs: drvn over 2f out: wknd over 1f out* **25/1**
-250 **8** *12* **Weapon Of Choice (IRE)**[19] 3339 5-9-8 **88** KierenFallon 5 62
(Stuart Kittow) *in rr: hdwy 3f out: sn drvn: lost pl over 1f out: bhd whn eased* **7/1**

1m 41.33s (-2.37) **Going Correction** -0.075s/f (Good)
WFA 3 from 4yo+ 9lb 8 Ran **SP% 114.8**
Speed ratings (Par 107): **108,107,104,104,101 100,99,87**
toteswingers 1&2 £2.80, 1&3 £3.50, 2&3 £2.70 CSF £11.31 CT £46.61 TOTE £3.30: £1.20, £1.70, £2.30; EX 11.80 Trifecta £62.00 Pool: £2199.86 - 26.57 winning units..
Owner Colne Valley Racing **Bred** Patrick M Ryan **Trained** Nawton, N Yorks
FOCUS
A decent handicap and the front pair bucked the trend of most of the races at the meeting by racing handily and staying there. The form is rated around the second.
T/Jkpt: Not won. T/Plt: £58.60 to a £1 stake. Pool: £83,409.37 - 1037.74 winning tickets. T/Qpdt: £16.40 to a £1 stake. Pool: £4650.99 - 209.44 winning tickets. WG

3662 NEWBURY (L-H)
Thursday, July 4

OFFICIAL GOING: Good to firm
Wind: Moderate ahead Weather: Sunny

3985 KNIGHT FRANK APPRENTICE H'CAP 1m 3f 5y
6:20 (6:21) (Class 5) (0-70,73) 4-Y-O+ **£2,587** (£770; £384; £192) **Stalls** Centre

Form RPR
-021 **1** **Laughing Jack**[7] 3719 5-10-2 **73** 6ex GeorgeDowning 5 82
(Tony Carroll) *mde all: drvn over 2f out: styd on wl fnl f* **2/1**[1]
2466 **2** *2* **Comedy House**[11] 1899 5-8-13 **59** PhilipPrince(3) 6 64
(Michael Madgwick) *in rr: rdn over 2f out: styd on wl fnl f to take 2nd fnl 50yds but no imp on wnr* **16/1**
-431 **3** *1* **Golden Jubilee (USA)**[22] 3213 4-9-3 **60** (v[1]) WilliamTwiston-Davies 2 64
(Nigel Twiston-Davies) *in rr: hdwy 3f out: chsd wnr 1f out but no imp: one pce and dropped to 3rd fnl 50yds* **11/4**[2]
4446 **4** *½* **Hurakan (IRE)**[24] 3157 7-9-10 **67** (p) DeclanBates 1 70
(Richard Price) *chsd ldrs: rdn 4f out: no ex fr 1f out* **6/1**
222 **5** *2* **Pandorica**[26] 3095 5-9-6 **68** (p) OisinMurphy(5) 4 67
(Bernard Llewellyn) *chsd ldr: rdn fr 4f out: lost 2nd 1f out and sn btn* **7/2**[3]
1104 **6** *13* **Highlife Dancer**[9] 3662 5-9-12 **69** (v) CharlesBishop 3 45
(Mick Channon) *chsd ldrs: rdn and wknd qckly over 2f out* **10/1**

2m 21.18s (-0.02) **Going Correction** -0.10s/f (Good) 6 Ran SP% **111.5**
Speed ratings (Par 103): **96,94,93,93,92 82**
Tote Swingers: 1&2 £1.30, 1&3 £2.80, 2&3 £6.20 CSF £32.02 TOTE £3.10: £1.40, £8.40; EX 40.40 Trifecta £81.90 Pool: £1,126.71 - 10.31 winning units..
Owner Paul Downing **Bred** Sir Thomas Pilkington **Trained** Cropthorne, Worcs
■ Stewards' Enquiry : William Twiston-Davies four-day ban; used whip above permitted level (18th-21st July).
FOCUS
The going was good to firm on a watered track. The pace was not strong in this handicap but the favourite put in a brave front-running effort to score with something in hand.

3986 DENFORD STUD IRISH E B F MAIDEN FILLIES' STKS 6f 8y
6:50 (6:52) (Class 4) 2-Y-O **£4,075** (£1,212; £606; £303) **Stalls** High

Form RPR
1 **Baby Bush (IRE)** 2-9-0 0 FrankieDettori 16 79+
(Richard Hannon) *trckd ldr: chal 2f out: sn led: drvn out fnl f* **8/1**[3]
2 *2* **Heartstrings** 2-9-0 0 MartinHarley 14 73
(Mick Channon) *chsd ldrs: drvn 2f out: styd on fnl f and kpt on to take 2nd fnl 75yds but no imp on wnr* **10/1**
6 **3** *½* **Cay Dancer**[42] 2601 2-9-0 0 JimmyFortune 13 71
(Richard Hannon) *led: rdn and jnd 2f out: sn hdd: styd on fnl f tl no ex and lost 2nd fnl 75yds* **9/2**[2]
4 *1 ¼* **Djinni (IRE)** 2-9-0 0 KieranO'Neill 1 67
(Richard Hannon) *chsd ldrs: rdn over 2f out: one pce fnl f* **25/1**
0 **5** *2* **Green Music**[19] 3324 2-8-9 0 RyanTate(5) 5 61
(James Eustace) *chsd ldrs: drvn to chal 2f out: wknd ins fnl f* **20/1**
6 *1* **Mendacious Harpy (IRE)** 2-9-0 0 WilliamBuick 15 60+
(George Baker) *stmbld sn after s: green: bhd and continually flashed tail: shkn up and hdwy over 1f out: swtchd lft and hdwy ins fnl f: gng on clsng stages* **16/1**
7 *nk* **Raajis (IRE)** 2-9-0 0 DaneO'Neill 7 56+
(Richard Hannon) *s.i.s: in rr: hdwy over 2f out: nvr quite gng pce to rch ldrs: wknd ins fnl f* **3/1**[1]
8 *½* **Lunar Spirit** 2-9-0 0 JimCrowley 3 55
(Ralph Beckett) *s.i.s: in rr: sme hdwy 2f out: wknd fnl f* **9/2**[2]
9 *1* **Pink Mirage (IRE)** 2-8-11 0 DarrenEgan(3) 10 52
(Jonathan Portman) *in rr: pushed along and sme hdwy over 1f out: wknd ins fnl f* **20/1**
4 **10** *½* **Value (IRE)**[49] 2391 2-9-0 0 SeanLevey 9 50
(Richard Hannon) *chsd ldrs: rdn to chal over 2f out: wknd fnl f* **8/1**[3]
11 *1 ½* **Reflected Love (IRE)** 2-9-0 0 CathyGannon 11 45
(Mick Channon) *in tch: rdn 1/2-way and sn bhd* **20/1**
12 *3 ½* **Nakuti (IRE)** 2-8-11 0 ThomasBrown(3) 2 34
(Sylvester Kirk) *in tch: sme hdwy over 2f out: nvr rchd ldrs and wknd over 1f out* **50/1**
13 *hd* **Khloe** 2-9-0 0 LiamKeniry 6 33
(Michael Blanshard) *in tch to 1/2-way: sn rdn and btn* **40/1**
14 *1* **Come On Lila** 2-9-0 0 AndreaAtzeni 8 30
(Alex Hales) *chsd ldrs over 3f* **100/1**
15 *hd* **Currently Inlondon (IRE)** 2-8-11 0 CharlesBishop(3) 4 30
(Mick Channon) *in rr: rdn over 2f out: a outpcd* **33/1**

1m 15.0s (2.00) **Going Correction** +0.225s/f (Good) **15** Ran **SP% 125.0**
Speed ratings (Par 93): **95,92,91,90,87 86,85,84,83,82 80,76,76,74,74**
Tote Swingers: 1&2 £10.20, 1&3 £6.20, 2&3 £10.50 CSF £79.78 TOTE £6.30: £2.70, £3.80, £2.20; EX 70.80 Trifecta £204.70 Pool: £948.99 - 10.31 winning units..
Owner Malih Lahej Al Basti **Bred** Edward And Mrs S Hannigan **Trained** East Everleigh, Wilts
FOCUS
An interesting fillies' maiden, involving a majority of newcomers. Richard Hannon trained three of the first four home and the winner provided him with a fifth success in this race in the last eight years. Probably not a great renewal of the race.

3987 JLT CONDITIONS STKS 7f (S)
7:25 (7:25) (Class 4) 3-Y-O+ **£6,225** (£1,864; £932; £466; £233) **Stalls** High

Form RPR
5020 **1** **Tamayuz Star (IRE)**[15] 3455 3-8-8 **99** SeanLevey 4 92
(Richard Hannon) *disp 2nd tl chsd ldr ins fnl 3f: drvn wl over 1f out: styd on to ld fnl 120yds: hld on wl* **11/10**[1]
4610 **2** *hd* **Jalaa (IRE)**[14] 3484 3-8-8 **95** DaneO'Neill 5 91
(Richard Hannon) *led: rdn along and qcknd ins fnl 2f: jnd 1f out: hdd fnl 120yds: rallied cl home but a hld* **4/1**[2]
0300 **3** *2 ¼* **Redact (IRE)**[8] 3697 4-8-8 **95** WilliamTwiston-Davies(5) 1 85
(Richard Hannon) *hld up in rr but wl in tch: rdn 2f out: hdwy u.p over 1f out: styd on to take 3rd fnl 50yds but no ch w ldng duo* **11/2**
16-0 **4** *1 ¼* **Selkie's Friend**[54] 2266 4-8-13 **75** AndreaAtzeni 3 82
(Stuart Williams) *stdd s: in rr: rdn: hdwy and swtchd lft appr fnl f to take 3rd: sn hung lft and no imp: dropped to 4th fnl 50yds* **12/1**
5030 **5** *8* **Luhaif**[12] 3563 3-8-2 **90** (v) DarrenEgan(3) 2 60
(Mick Channon) *disp 2nd tl ins fnl 3f: rdn over 2f out: wknd u.p wl over 1f out* **5/1**[3]

1m 25.97s (0.27) **Going Correction** +0.225s/f (Good)
WFA 3 from 4yo 8lb 5 Ran **SP% 107.4**
Speed ratings (Par 105): **107,106,104,102,93**
CSF £5.39 TOTE £1.80: £1.10, £3.20; EX 4.90 Trifecta £5.80 Pool: £668.65 - 85.83 winning units..
Owner Abdulla Al Mansoori **Bred** John Malone **Trained** East Everleigh, Wilts
FOCUS
The leading form contender battled well to overhaul his stablemate in this decent conditions event. Richard Hannon had the third too.

3988 BETFAIR SUPPORTING THE MARY HARE FOUNDATION FILLIES' H'CAP 7f (S)
8:00 (8:00) (Class 4) (0-80,79) 3-Y-O+ **£4,851** (£1,443; £721; £360) **Stalls** High

Form RPR
-052 **1** **Front Page News**[8] 3699 3-8-8 **67** AndreaAtzeni 7 77
(Robert Eddery) *in tch: drvn and hdwy over 1f out: qcknd to ld fnl 120yds: kpt on strly* **5/2**[2]

The Form Book Flat, Raceform Ltd, Compton, RG20 6NL.

5231 **2** 2 1/4 **Sarangoo**[20] 3270 5-9-8 **73** CathyGannon 6 80
(Malcolm Saunders) *chsd ldrs: chal 2f out: sn drvn to ld: hdd and outpcd fnl 120yds* **8/1**

000- **3** 2 **Three Crowns**[292] 6227 3-8-13 **72** [1] MartinHarley 5 71
(Jonathan Portman) *s.i.s: in rr: drvn and hdwy u.p over 1f out: edgd lft and tk 3rd jst ins fnl f: no imp on ldng duo* **33/1**

2-53 **4** 3 1/2 **Lisiere (IRE)**[20] 3300 4-10-0 **79** SilvestreDeSousa 4 71
(Mrs K Burke) *chsd ldrs: rdn 2f out and over 1f out and sn btn* **9/4**[1]

-421 **5** 3 1/4 **Celestial Bay**[14] 3508 4-9-5 **70** WilliamBuick 3 53
(Sylvester Kirk) *towards rr but in tch: pushed along fr 3f out: rdn over 2f out: nvr in contention and sn btn* **6/1**[3]

063- **6** nk **Perfect Venture**[194] 8233 3-8-0 **64** ow2 RyanTate(5) 2 44
(Clive Cox) *led: jnd 2f: sn hdd: wknd wl over 1f out* **20/1**

5P11 **7** 15 **Amosite**[26] 3111 7-9-6 **71** (p) FrankieDettori 1 13
(J R Jenkins) *pressed ldrs: wknd qckly wl over 1f out: eased whn no ch* **13/2**

1-60 **8** 6 **Coincidently**[78] 1622 3-9-4 **77** (p) LiamKeniry 8
(Alan Bailey) *pressed ldrs to 3f out: wknd over 2f out: eased whn no ch* **12/1**

1m 26.91s (1.21) **Going Correction** +0.225s/f (Good)
WFA 3 from 4yo+ 8lb 8 Ran SP% **113.5**
Speed ratings (Par 102): **102,99,97,93,89 89,71,65**
Tote Swingers: 1&2 £6.50, 1&3 £23.70, 2&3 £14.50 CSF £22.43 CT £520.11 TOTE £3.90: £1.50, £2.50, £6.20; EX 24.10 Trifecta £536.20 Pool: £944.45 - 1.32 winning units..
Owner Gurnett, Rayment & Anderson **Bred** Helen Plumbly And Wendy Balding **Trained** Newmarket, Suffolk

FOCUS
Three last-time-out winners lined-up in this fair handicap. The went a decent pace and the winner powered clear.

3989 CHEVELEY PARK STUD MAIDEN STKS 1m 4f 5y
8:35 (8:35) (Class 5) 3-Y-0+ **£2,587** (£770; £384; £192) **Stalls** Centre

Form RPR

3-3 **1** **Hold On Tight (IRE)**[57] 2157 3-8-10 0 JimCrowley 8 72
(Ralph Beckett) *in rr but in tch: hdwy fr 4f out: drvn and kpt on over 1f out: styd on u.p to ld fnl 50yds: hld on all out* **5/2**[3]

-02 **2** shd **Fledged**[27] 3059 3-9-1 0 WilliamBuick 3 77+
(John Gosden) *toodk t.k.h: trckd ldrs: wnt 2nd over 7f out: slt ld 3f out: drvn: hung lft and hdd over 2f out: rallied ins fnl f: chal fnl stride: jst failed* **5/4**[1]

53-6 **3** 1/2 **Shamaheart (IRE)**[64] 1923 3-9-1 67 SeanLevey 4 76
(Richard Hannon) *chsd ldrs: led over 2f out: hrd drvn fnl f: hdd and dropped 2 pls fnl 50yds* **16/1**

52 **4** 1 **Battalion (IRE)**[14] 3491 3-9-1 0 SilvestreDeSousa 1 74
(William Haggas) *in rr: drvn and hdwy on outside over 2f out: chsd ldrs appr fnl f: styd on same pce* **9/4**[2]

6 **5** 1 1/4 **Silk Route**[21] 3239 3-8-10 0 DaneO'Neill 5 67
(Henry Candy) *in rr: hdwy 3f out: drvn 2f out: styd on same pce* **14/1**

06 **6** 2 3/4 **Hallingham**[10] 3618 3-9-1 0 MartinHarley 7 68
(Jonathan Portman) *in rr: pushed along and in tch 3f out: rdn over 2f out: sn btn* **50/1**

7 26 **Goldie Horn**[23] 5-9-4 0 (t) WilliamTwiston-Davies(5) 2 21
(Nigel Twiston-Davies) *led 1f: styd chsng ldr tl over 7f out: wknd over 3f out* **50/1**

5 **8** 2 1/2 **Lalinde**[122] 877 3-8-7 0 DarrenEgan(3) 6 17
(Daniel Kubler) *led after 1f: t.k.h: hdd 3f out: wknd qckly wl over 2f out* **40/1**

2m 34.68s (-0.82) **Going Correction** -0.10s/f (Good)
WFA 3 from 5yo 13lb 8 Ran SP% **122.7**
Speed ratings (Par 103): **98,97,97,96,96 94,76,75**
Tote Swingers: 1&2 £1.10, 1&3 £7.00, 2&3 £6.30 CSF £6.52 TOTE £3.30: £1.30, £1.10, £5.90; EX 6.80 Trifecta £37.80 Pool: £1,318.28 - 26.11 winning units..
Owner The Eclipse Partnership **Bred** Car Colston Hall Stud **Trained** Kimpton, Hants

FOCUS
There was a tight finish in this maiden which was run at a steady pace.

3990 SMITH & WILLIAMSON H'CAP 1m 4f 5y
9:10 (9:10) (Class 4) (0-85,89) 3-Y-0 **£4,851** (£1,443; £721; £360) **Stalls** Centre

Form RPR

1-3 **1** **Chesterfield (IRE)**[27] 3061 3-9-6 **83** SilvestreDeSousa 5 93+
(Saeed bin Suroor) *hld up in rr: gd hdwy over 2f out: rdn and str run fnl f to ld fnl 110yds: hld on wl* **11/4**[2]

1-35 **2** nk **Lady Pimpernel**[20] 3277 3-8-11 **74** DaneO'Neill 3 83
(Henry Candy) *chsd ldrs: chal fr 2f out: led u.p over 1f out: hdd fnl 110yds: kpt on but nt gng pce of wnr* **8/1**

6320 **3** 5 **Naru (IRE)**[13] 3526 3-9-7 **84** AndreaAtzeni 1 85
(James Tate) *chsd ldr: drvn to chal over 2f out and stl ev ch over 1f out: wknd ins fnl f* **15/2**

3434 **4** 2 3/4 **Bursledon (IRE)**[10] 3636 3-8-9 **72** SeanLevey 4 69
(Richard Hannon) *sn led: rdn and jnd over 2f out: hdd over 1f out: wknd fnl f* **22/1**

-626 **5** hd **Musikhani**[23] 3177 3-8-10 **73** LiamKeniry 6 70
(Andrew Balding) *in rr: hdwy and rdn over 2f out: nvr rchd ldrs: wknd wl over 1f out* **25/1**

16 **6** 26 **Premium**[57] 2148 3-9-7 **84** FrankieDettori 2 39
(Charles Hills) *trckd ldrs: rdn and wknd 3f out* **2/1**[1]

1401 **7** 1 1/2 **Alta Lilea (IRE)**[5] 3834 3-9-12 **89** 6ex WilliamBuick 7 42
(Mark Johnston) *in tch: pushed along and sme hdwy fr 4f out: wknd qckly fr 3f out* **7/2**[3]

2m 32.86s (-2.64) **Going Correction** -0.10s/f (Good) 7 Ran SP% **113.3**
Speed ratings (Par 102): **104,103,100,98,98 81,80**
Tote Swingers: 1&2 £3.50, 1&3 £4.70, 2&3 £4.40 CSF £24.10 TOTE £3.10: £2.00, £2.70; EX 22.00 Trifecta £160.20 Pool: £1,317.59 - 12.68 winning units..
Owner Godolphin **Bred** Darley **Trained** Newmarket, Suffolk

FOCUS
A decent handicap for 3yos. The pace was not strong but an unexposed type scored from some way back.
T/Plt: £42.10 to a £1 stake. Pool: £61,781.39 - 1,069.69 winning tickets. T/Qpdt: £6.20 to a £1 stake. Pool: £5,991.98 - 714.95 winning tickets. ST

3787 YARMOUTH (L-H)
Thursday, July 4

OFFICIAL GOING: Good to firm (7.5)
Wind: light, across Weather: dry and sunny spells

3991 BRITISH STALLION STUDS/BHEST EBF MAIDEN STKS 6f 3y
2:10 (2:10) (Class 5) 2-Y-0 **£3,072** (£914; £456; £228) **Stalls** Centre

Form RPR

563 **1** **Bahamian Heights**[20] 3291 2-9-5 0 BrettDoyle 2 81
(Clive Brittain) *mde all: rdn 2f out: hrd pressed and drvn ent fnl f: kpt on gamely and hld on wl fnl 100yds* **16/1**

0 **2** 1/2 **Mappa Mundi (USA)**[42] 2595 2-9-5 0 NeilCallan 5 79
(Eve Johnson Houghton) *t.k.h early: hld up in tch in midfield: rdn and effrt 2f out: hdwy to chse ldrs 1f out: kpt on u.p to chse wnr fnl 50yds: r.o* **9/1**

33 **3** nse **Major Crispies**[18] 3374 2-9-5 0 SteveDrowne 8 79
(James Eustace) *hld up in tch in last trio: rdn and gd hdwy over 1f out: styd on wl u.p fnl f: wnt 3rd towards fin* **7/2**[2]

0 **4** 1/2 **Speedfiend**[26] 3112 2-9-5 0 StevieDonohoe 7 77
(Noel Quinlan) *swtchd lft after s: hld up in tch in midfield: rdn and effrt over 1f out: chsd wnr jst ins fnl f: ev ch but nt qckning whn edgd lft u.p fnl 100yds: wknd and lost 2 pls towards fin* **11/8**[1]

33 **5** 2 1/4 **Meaning Of Life (IRE)**[22] 3211 2-9-5 0 LukeMorris 6 70
(Marco Botti) *in tch in midfield: rdn and effrt 2f out: chsd wnr over 1f out tl jst ins fnl f: wknd fnl 100yds* **10/1**

6 2 3/4 **Mathematics** 2-9-5 0 HarryBentley 4 61
(Saeed bin Suroor) *t.k.h: chsd wnr: ev ch and rdn 2f out: sn struggling and lost 2nd over 1f out: wknd fnl f* **6/1**[3]

7 2 **Island Remede** 2-9-0 0 HayleyTurner 3 50
(Ed Dunlop) *s.i.s: sn pushed along in rr: n.d but kpt on ins fnl f* **66/1**

0 **8** 2 **Barbary (IRE)**[18] 3366 2-9-5 0 FrederikTylicki 1 49
(James Fanshawe) *chsd ldrs: rdn and struggling over 2f out: wknd over 1f out* **25/1**

04 **9** nk **Village Cricket**[7] 3737 2-9-2 0 SimonPearce(3) 9 48
(Pam Sly) *a in last pair: rdn 1/2-way: n.d* **200/1**

1m 13.82s (-0.58) **Going Correction** -0.05s/f (Good) 9 Ran SP% **109.4**
Speed ratings (Par 94): **101,100,100,99,96 92,90,87,87**
toteswingers 1&2 £13.80, 1&3 £7.30, 2&3 £7.20 CSF £137.07 TOTE £15.40: £2.40, £2.60, £1.80; EX 109.00 Trifecta £429.20 Pool: £3840.77 - 6.71 winning units..
Owner Sheikh Juma Dalmook Al Maktoum **Bred** Pantile Stud **Trained** Newmarket, Suffolk
■ Bahrain-based Brett Doyle's first domestic winner of the season.

FOCUS
The bottom bend was dolled out 2m to provide fresh ground, adding on 12m to all races above 1m1f. A fair juvenile maiden in which they went a decent gallop on ground officially described as good to firm. However, there were early signs of the 4mm of water put on track the previous day having an effect, as the winner made all despite plenty of challengers attempting to quicken past him, and the first four home finished in a heap. Quite straightforward form.

3992 NELSON MONUMENT (S) STKS 6f 3y
2:40 (2:40) (Class 6) 2-Y-0 **£1,940** (£577; £288; £144) **Stalls** Centre

Form RPR

034 **1** **Flora Medici**[20] 3282 2-8-6 0 LukeMorris 2 66+
(Sir Mark Prescott Bt) *led for 2f: chsd ldr: rdn and edgd lft 2f out: led over 1f out and sn drvn clr: eased towards fin* **11/8**[2]

460 **2** 5 **My Little Friend**[20] 3298 2-8-11 0 (b[1]) NeilCallan 1 50
(Mark H Tompkins) *racd alone in centre to far side: wnt lft s: chsd ldr tl led 4f out: hdd and rdn over 1f out: sn btn: wl hld and hung rt ins fnl f* **7/1**[3]

050 **3** 6 **Ivan B**[10] 3631 2-8-4 0 DanielCremin(7) 3 31
(Mick Channon) *wnt rt s: chsd ldrs: rdn and struggling 1/2-way: wknd wl over 1f out* **16/1**

2234 **4** 28 **Gin Time (IRE)**[56] 2189 2-8-6 0 WilliamCarson 4
(David Evans) *s.i.s: in tch in rr but nvr looked to be gng wl: rdn and no rspnse over 2f out: sn btn: virtually p.u ins fnl f: t.o* **11/10**[1]

1m 15.31s (0.91) **Going Correction** -0.05s/f (Good) 4 Ran SP% **108.1**
Speed ratings (Par 92): **91,84,76,39**
CSF £9.93 TOTE £2.90; EX 10.60 Trifecta £32.80 Pool: £1785.06 - 40.79 winning units..Flora Medici was bought in for £6,200
Owner Neil Greig **Bred** W N Greig **Trained** Newmarket, Suffolk

FOCUS
A weak seller. There was a difference of opinion as to which strip of the centre of the course to race on. Improved form from the winner.

3993 HOLIDAYS ON THE NORFOLK BROADS H'CAP 7f 3y
3:10 (3:10) (Class 5) (0-75,72) 3-Y-0+ **£2,587** (£770; £384; £192) **Stalls** Centre

Form RPR

1-11 **1** **Levi Draper**[17] 3404 4-9-12 **70** HayleyTurner 1 81+
(James Fanshawe) *stdd and dropped in after s: hld up in last pair: effrt nrest stands' rail over 1f out: led and hung violently lft 1f out: kpt on under hands and heels and a holding runner-up* **2/1**[1]

0115 **2** nk **Darnathean**[12] 3575 4-9-11 **69** (p) FrederikTylicki 2 79
(Paul D'Arcy) *chsd ldrs: rdn to chal over 1f out: led ent fnl f: sn hdd and bmpd: drvn and drew clr w wnr ins fnl f: a hld* **4/1**[3]

0215 **3** 5 **Paphos**[7] 3736 6-9-6 **71** EoinWalsh(7) 4 68
(David Evans) *bustled along leaving stall: chsd ldr: rdn and ev ch over 2f out: 4th and btn 1f out: sn wknd: wnt 3rd fnl 50yds* **18/1**

0042 **4** 1 **Afkar (IRE)**[23] 3172 5-10-0 **72** NeilCallan 7 66
(Clive Brittain) *led: rdn ent fnl 2f: hdd ent fnl f and struggling whn short of room and hmpd 1f out: sn wknd* **3/1**[2]

0024 **5** 1 1/4 **First Class**[7] 3741 5-9-5 **63** MartinLane 8 53
(Rae Guest) *chsd ldrs: effrt u.p 2f out: edgd lft u.p and btn jst over 1f out: wknd fnl f* **5/1**

0-45 **6** 1 1/4 **Katy's Secret**[58] 2134 6-8-4 **55** NoelGarbutt(7) 6 42
(William Jarvis) *hld up in tch in midfield: effrt but stuck bhd horses over 2f out: rdn and outpcd jst over 1f out: sn wknd* **12/1**

050 **7** 14 **Diplomatic (IRE)**[16] 3434 8-9-1 **59** (p) JimmyQuinn 3 8
(Michael Squance) *s.i.s: nvr gng wl and sn rdn along in rr: lost tch over 2f out* **33/1**

1m 25.72s (-0.88) **Going Correction** -0.05s/f (Good) 7 Ran SP% **110.9**
Speed ratings (Par 103): **103,102,96,95,94 92,76**
toteswingers 1&2 £2.50, 1&3 £4.70, 2&3 £5.20 CSF £9.62 CT £100.41 TOTE £2.50: £1.10, £3.60; EX 10.60 Trifecta £55.40 Pool: £2722.59 - 36.80 winning units..
Owner Andrew & Julia Turner **Bred** Cheveley Park Stud Ltd **Trained** Newmarket, Suffolk
■ Stewards' Enquiry : Hayley Turner two-day ban; careless riding (18th-19th July).

FOCUS
A fair handicap in which they went a proper gallop. Ordinary form, but the first two came well clear and the winner is perhaps bit better than the bare form in coming from a bit off the pace.

3994 VISITENGLAND.COM H'CAP — 5f 43y
3:40 (3:42) (Class 6) (0-60,60) 3-Y-0+ £1,940 (£577; £288; £144) Stalls Centre

Form — RPR
-000 1 **Sir Geoffrey (IRE)**13 3529 7-9-0 50 ....(p) LukeMorris 8 58
(Scott Dixon) *chsd ldrs: rdn and effrt to ld 2f out: edgd lft u.p over 1f out: edgd bk rt 1f out: hld up u.p fnl 100yds* 12/1

0065 2 ½ **Charming (IRE)**9 3667 4-9-7 60 ....(p) MarkCoumbe(3) 2 67
(Olivia Maylam) *hld up in tch towards rr: hdwy and nt clr run over 1f out: hdwy u.p 1f out: chal ins fnl f: hld towards fin* 10/1

005 3 1¼ **Lord Buffhead**9 3654 4-8-12 55 ....(b) ConnorBeasley(7) 4 57
(Richard Guest) *in tch in midfield: rdn and effrt 2f out: chsd ldrs 1f out: kpt on same pce ins fnl f* 4/1[2]

-416 4 nk **Burnt Cream**16 3425 6-9-0 50 ....(t) StevieDonohoe 11 51
(Martin Bosley) *stdd and swtchd lft after s: hld up in rr: rdn and hdwy 2f out: ev ch 1f out: no ex and btn wl ins fnl f* 25/1

0643 5 1¾ **Imperial Spirit**6 3789 3-8-9 50 ....(v) NeilCallan 6 43
(Mick Channon) *chsd ldrs: rdn 2f out: no ex u.p 1f out: wknd ins fnl f* 9/2[3]

0223 6 1½ **Imaginary Diva**16 3425 7-9-3 56 .... RyanPowell(3) 5 45
(George Margarson) *in tch towards rr: rdn 1/2-way: drvn over 1f out: kpt on but nvr threatened ldrs* 6/1

3060 7 shd **Whiskey Junction**24 3154 9-9-1 51 .... LiamJones 9 40
(Mick Quinn) *sn rdn along towards rr: kpt on fnl f: nvr trbld ldrs* 16/1

4-65 8 1¼ **Marmalade Moon**13 3547 4-9-3 53 .... MartinLane 3 37
(Robert Cowell) *led tl rdn and hdd 2f out: btn over 1f out: wknd fnl f* 16/1

-060 9 hd **Robyn**9 3654 3-8-5 49 .... BillyCray(3) 10 31
(Scott Dixon) *a towards rr: rdn over 3f out: kpt on but no real imp fnl 2f* 14/1

0002 10 nse **Megaleka**12 3594 3-8-12 53 .... FrederikTylicki 1 38
(Alan Bailey) *chsd ldr tl 2f out: hung lft and btn ent fnl f: continued to hang bdly and eased fnl 100yds* 7/2[1]

1m 2.88s (0.18) **Going Correction** -0.05s/f (Good)
WFA 3 from 4yo+ 5lb — 10 Ran SP% **113.8**
Speed ratings (Par 101): **96,95,93,92,89 87,87,85,85,84**
toteswingers 1&2 £11.60, 1&3 £10.90, 2&3 £9.70 CSF £122.72 CT £582.11 TOTE £12.40: £3.20, £3.60, £2.10; EX 125.50 Trifecta £1126.80 Pool: £3001.94 - 1.99 winning units..
Owner Dixon, Howlett & The Chrystal Maze Ptn **Bred** P Rabbitte **Trained** Babworth, Notts

FOCUS
A moderate sprint handicap with recent form in short supply although most figured on god marks.

3995 RACING WELFARE H'CAP — 1m 1f
4:10 (4:12) (Class 4) (0-80,80) 3-Y-0 £4,690 (£1,395; £697; £348) Stalls Low

Form — RPR
-502 1 **Super Cookie**9 3666 3-8-3 62 .... WilliamCarson 4 70
(Philip McBride) *mde all: rdn and clr 2f out: tiring fnl 100yds but a jst holding on: gamely* 14/1

41 2 nk **Odeliz (IRE)**25 3136 3-9-6 79 .... LukeMorris 7 86+
(Mrs K Burke) *hld up in tch in rr: swtchd rt and effrt 3f out: 3rd and hrd drvn over 1f out: styd on to chse wnr ins fnl f: kpt on but edgd lft towards fin: nvr quite getting to wnr* 7/4[1]

2-22 3 ½ **Elhaame (IRE)**26 3105 3-9-7 80 .... NeilCallan 6 86+
(Luca Cumani) *hld up in tch in last pair: hdwy to chse ldrs 4f out: rdn and chsd clr wnr over 2f out: kpt on ins fnl f: nvr quite pce to rch wnr: hld and bmpd towards fin* 13/2

3-12 4 6 **Freeport**18 3369 3-9-4 77 .... MartinLane 1 71
(Brian Meehan) *chsd wnr tl 7f out: chsd ldrs after: drvn and unable qck 2f out: wknd ent fnl f* 5/2[2]

-215 5 1 **Aneedh**27 3062 3-9-2 75 .... LiamJones 3 67
(William Haggas) *wl in tch in midfield: rdn and effrt 3f out: lost pl and dropped to rr over 2f out: wknd over 1f out* 4/1[3]

0-00 6 11 **Jareeda (USA)**43 2560 3-8-11 70 .... JimmyQuinn 2 40
(Sir Michael Stoute) *rdn along briefly leaving stalls: chsd ldrs tl wnt 2nd 7f out tl over 2f out: sn dropped out: wl bhd and eased wl ins fnl f* 22/1

1m 54.97s (-0.83) **Going Correction** -0.05s/f (Good) — 6 Ran SP% **109.3**
Speed ratings (Par 102): **101,100,100,94,94 84**
toteswingers 1&2 £4.60, 1&3 £4.10, 2&3 £1.90 CSF £37.06 TOTE £18.00: £4.90, £1.70; EX 44.10 Trifecta £170.60 Pool: £2837.48 - 12.47 winning units..
Owner Peter Botham **Bred** Earle I Mack **Trained** Newmarket, Suffolk

FOCUS
A decent 3yo handicap in which William Carson gave the narrow, front-running winner an inspired ride. The winner is rated up a length on her latest form.

3996 TRAFALGAR RESTAURANT H'CAP — 1m 2f 21y
4:40 (4:40) (Class 5) (0-70,74) 3-Y-0+ £1,678 (£1,678; £384; £192) Stalls Low

Form — RPR
-211 1 **Hydrant**9 3651 7-9-11 74 6ex .... ConnorBeasley(7) 3 86
(Richard Guest) *led: rdn over 1f out: jnd 1f out: narrowly hdd ins fnl f: battled on gamely u.p and jnd ldr on line* 5/4[2]

61- 1 dht **Willow Beck**227 7787 4-9-9 65 .... NickyMackay 6 77+
(John Gosden) *s.i.s: hld up in tch in last pair: hdwy on bit to chse ldr 2f out: shkn up to chal 1f out: rdn to ld narrowly ins fnl f: jnd on line* 11/10[1]

0600 3 7 **Strike Force**26 3106 9-9-4 65 ....(t) TobyAtkinson(5) 5 63
(Alison Hutchinson) *chsd ldr tl 2f out: sn drvn and unable qck: wknd 1f out* 25/1

00-6 4 4½ **Land Hawk (IRE)**37 2764 7-8-9 54 .... SimonPearce(3) 2 43
(Lydia Pearce) *chsd ldrs: rdn and struggling 2f out: 4th and wknd over 1f out* 20/1

330 5 28 **Rubbamaa**45 2519 4-10-0 70 .... TedDurcan 1 35
(Clive Brittain) *hld up in rr: rdn and struggling over 3f out: wknd 2f out: bhd and heavily eased ins fnl f: t.o* 11/1[3]

2m 9.91s (-0.59) **Going Correction** -0.05s/f (Good)
WFA 3 from 4yo+ 11lb — 5 Ran SP% **109.0**
Speed ratings (Par 103): **100,100,94,90,68**
WIN: H £1.00, WB £1.20; EX: H/WB £1.20, WB/H £1.60; CSF: H/WB £1.43, WB/H £1.34; Trifecta: H/WB/SF £7.10, WB/H/SF £6.90 TRIFECTA Pool: £2347.82 - 122.45 winning units..
Owner C Hatch **Bred** Lord Halifax **Trained** Wetherby, W Yorks
Owner HRH Princess Haya Of Jordan **Bred** Worksop Manor Stud **Trained** Newmarket, Suffolk

FOCUS
A modest handicap lacking depth, in which the honours were shared after an engaging tussle in the final furlong. Hydrant was another front-runner to 'win' here.

3997 BBC RADIO NORFOLK "HANDS AND HEELS" APPRENTICE SERIES H'CAP (RACING EXCELLENCE INITIATIVE) — 1m 3f 101y
5:10 (5:10) (Class 6) (0-65,65) 4-Y-0+ £1,940 (£577; £288; £144) Stalls Low

Form — RPR
1035 1 **The Ducking Stool**36 2785 6-9-8 63 .... ShelleyBirkett 7 71
(Julia Feilden) *led for 1f: chsd ldng pair after: wnt 2nd again over 2f out: rdn and effrt over 1f out: led ins fnl f: r.o wl* 7/2[2]

2501 2 1¼ **Conducting**17 3410 5-9-5 63 .... DanielCremin(3) 1 69
(Gay Kelleway) *chsd ldr tl led after 1f: rdn 2f out: hdd and styd on same pce ins fnl f* 9/2[3]

0056 3 1¾ **Capriska**22 3213 4-8-5 46 oh1 .... JoeyHaynes 2 49
(Willie Musson) *in tch: chsd ldrs over 2f out: rdn and no imp over 1f out: styd on ins fnl f but no threat to ldrs* 6/1

/0-0 4 8 **Piers Gaveston (IRE)**26 3106 4-9-10 65 .... EoinWalsh 4 54
(George Baker) *t.k.h: hld up in tch in midfield: effrt ent fnl 2f: sn struggling and wknd over 1f out* 10/3[1]

5003 5 3¾ **King Of Wing (IRE)**3 3909 4-8-11 52 ....(be) ConnorBeasley 3 35
(Phil McEntee) *hld up in tch in rr: short-lived effrt over 2f out: wknd wl over 1f out* 11/2

044 6 20 **Flash Crash**17 3410 4-9-3 61 .... JackGarritty(3) 6 10
(Robert Cowell) *chsd ldrs tl jnd ldr after 2f: rdn and struggling 3f out: lost pl over 2f out: t.o fnl f* 11/2

6000 7 nse **Rasteau (IRE)**17 3399 5-8-2 46 oh1 .... JeanVanOvermeire(3) 5
(Tom Keddy) *hld up in tch in last pair: c centre st: wknd over 2f out: t.o fnl f* 66/1

2m 28.39s (-0.31) **Going Correction** -0.05s/f (Good) — 7 Ran SP% **110.0**
Speed ratings (Par 101): **99,98,96,91,88 73,73**
toteswingers 1&2 £3.20, 1&3 £3.60, 2&3 £3.90 CSF £17.97 TOTE £4.40: £1.80, £1.60; EX 15.00 Trifecta £48.90 Pool: £2187.92 - 33.55 winning units..
Owner Miss J Feilden **Bred** Cheveley Park Stud Ltd **Trained** Exning, Suffolk

FOCUS
A modest middle-distance handicap for apprentice riders in the 'Hands And Heels' series. The first pair were always 1-2 and the form is rated around them.
T/Plt: £170.90 to a £1 stake. Pool: £66,267.62 - 283.06 winning tickets. T/Qpdt: £21.70 to a £1 stake. Pool: £5316.76 - 180.50 winning tickets. SP

3998 - 4004a (Foreign Racing) - See Raceform Interactive

3648 BEVERLEY (R-H)
Friday, July 5

OFFICIAL GOING: Good to firm (good in places)
Wind: Light; half against Weather: Fine and sunny; very warm

4005 RACING AGAIN TOMORROW (S) STKS — 7f 100y
6:30 (6:30) (Class 6) 3-Y-0+ £2,264 (£673; £336; £168) Stalls Low

Form — RPR
5020 1 **Rasselas (IRE)**34 2889 6-9-3 58 ....(p) FrannyNorton 14 64
(David Nicholls) *t.k.h in midfield: hdwy and swtchd lft over 2f out: styd on to ld last 50yds* 12/1

3460 2 nk **Eeny Mac (IRE)**10 3649 6-9-3 58 .... AndrewElliott 5 63
(Neville Bycroft) *drvn to ld after 1f: edgd lft ins fnl f: hdd and no ex clsng stages* 4/1[2]

-014 3 3 **Jessie's Spirit (IRE)**15 3501 4-9-3 70 .... PJMcDonald 2 56
(Ann Duffield) *chsd ldrs: 2nd over 1f out: kpt on same pce* 5/2[1]

42/4 4 1¾ **Four Winds**15 3507 7-9-3 83 .... TomEaves 15 51
(Robert Cowell) *in rr: hdwy over 2f out: kpt on fnl f: nt rch ldrs* 6/1[3]

3034 5 1½ **Shamrocked (IRE)**16 3475 4-8-10 63 .... JacobButterfield(7) 11 47
(Ollie Pears) *rrd and s.s: in rr: kpt on fnl 2f: nvr nr ldrs* 6/1[3]

006 6 nk **Throwing Roses**46 2507 3-8-1 45 .... RaulDaSilva(3) 1 39
(Lawrence Mullaney) *chsd ldrs: one pce over 1f out* 25/1

3352 7 hd **Lil Sophella (IRE)**20 3337 4-8-5 48 .... JackGarritty(7) 12 41
(Patrick Holmes) *s.s and wnt rt s: in rr: hdwy on outside over 2f out: one pce over 1f out* 12/1

-000 8 5 **Miss Matiz**8 3727 6-8-9 45 .... DeclanCannon(3) 4 29
(Alan Kirtley) *mid-div: hdwy on inner over 2f out: wknd over 1f out* 100/1

4651 9 2¾ **Tony Hollis**21 3285 5-9-1 55 .... GemmaTutty(7) 3 32
(Karen Tutty) *led 1f: chsd ldrs: wknd over 1f out* 8/1

0050 10 1 **Bachelor Knight (IRE)**29 3029 5-9-3 47 .... DaleSwift 9 24
(Suzzanne France) *rrd and swvd rt s: sn chsng ldrs: lost pl over 1f out* 50/1

5224 11 3½ **Blue Noodles**10 3654 7-9-8 55 ....(v) MickyFenton 8 21
(Neville Bycroft) *hmpd s: in rr: bhd fnl 2f* 10/1

0000 12 4½ **Sairaam (IRE)**22 3246 7-8-12 52 .... PaulMulrennan 6
(Charles Smith) *chsd ldrs: lost pl 2f out* 40/1

1m 30.74s (-3.06) **Going Correction** -0.40s/f (Firm)
WFA 3 from 4yo+ 8lb — 12 Ran SP% **122.0**
Speed ratings (Par 101): **101,100,97,95,93 93,92,87,84,82 78,73**
toteswingers 1&2 £10.00, 1&3 £3.20, 2&3 £3.30 CSF £60.33 TOTE £16.60: £4.60, £1.90, £1.10; EX 69.80 Trifecta £691.60 Pool: £1,596.42 - 1.73 winning units.There was no bid for the winner.
Owner J P Honeyman **Bred** Lynch Bages Ltd **Trained** Sessay, N Yorks

FOCUS
The ground was officially described as good to firm, good in places after 3mm of water was applied to the back straight on the morning of the race. The time for the opener was 0.74 seconds above standard, suggesting conditions were fast. Doubts over many of these, and the form is rated around the winner.

4006 EBF AUNT BESSIE'S ROASTINESS RACE NOVICE STKS — 5f
7:00 (7:00) (Class 5) 2-Y-0 £3,234 (£962; £481) Stalls Low

Form — RPR
1 1 **Peter Mac (IRE)**23 3217 2-9-2 0 .... LeeTopliss 5 90+
(Richard Fahey) *hld up in last: effrt on inner over 2f out: swtchd lft and chsd wnr appr fnl f: rdn to ld last 100yds: r.o* 15/8[3]

3152 2 1 **Blockade (IRE)**17 3439 2-8-11 0 .... PaulMulrennan 4 81
(James Tate) *led: swtchd rt on to rail after 1f: rdn 1f out: hdd and no ex ins fnl f* 13/8[1]

3323 3 4 **Split Rock**20 3332 2-9-5 0 .... FrannyNorton 2 75
(Mark Johnston) *chsd ldr: rdn and bmpd appr fnl f: wknd last 150yds* 7/4[2]

1m 2.03s (-1.47) **Going Correction** -0.40s/f (Firm) — 3 Ran SP% **109.2**
Speed ratings (Par 94): **95,93,87**
CSF £5.12 TOTE £2.60; EX 3.70 Trifecta £7.30 Pool: £480.64 - 49.07 winning units.
Owner Middleham Park LXX & Partner **Bred** Tally-Ho Stud **Trained** Musley Bank, N Yorks
■ Stewards' Enquiry : Franny Norton one-day ban; careless riding (19th July).

FOCUS
Just the three runners lined up for this novice stakes, but the market said they were closely matched. The form is rated through the runner-up to his mark.

4007 JACKSON'S YORKSHIRE CHAMPION BREAD H'CAP — 7f 100y
7:30 (7:31) (Class 4) (0-80,80) 3-Y-0+ — **£6,469** (£1,925; £962; £481) — **Stalls** Low

Form — RPR

21-4 **1** **Altharoos (IRE)**[29] 3020 3-9-6 **80** .... DaneO'Neill 10 — 88+
(Sir Michael Stoute) *mid-div: hdwy 3f out: styd on to ld last 100yds* **7/4**[1]

0154 **2** 1 ½ **Copperwood**[9] 3683 8-9-10 **76** .... FrannyNorton 6 — 83
(Mark Johnston) *chsd ldrs: led narrowly appr fnl f: hdd and no ex ins fnl f* **10/1**

0132 **3** nk **Muftarres (IRE)**[23] 3192 8-8-11 **70** .... (t) GemmaTutty[(7)] 12 — 76
(Frank Sheridan) *hld up towards rr: hdwy and nt clr run 2f out tl swtchd lft 1f out: r.o wl towards fin* **11/1**

00-0 **4** 1 **Rich Forever (IRE)**[28] 3062 3-8-10 **70** .... (b[1]) RobertWinston 1 — 71
(James Bethell) *chsd ldrs: swtchd lft 1f out: kpt on same pce* **25/1**

0531 **5** ¾ **Ready (IRE)**[13] 3571 3-9-6 **80** .... (p) PhillipMakin 4 — 83+
(Garry Moss) *in rr: hdwy on inner over 2f out: nt clr run: hmpd and swtchd lft jst ins fnl f: r.o wl towards fin* **9/1**

-332 **6** ¾ **Rex Romanorum (IRE)**[10] 3649 5-8-12 **64** .... DuranFentiman 2 — 64
(Patrick Holmes) *chsd ldr: one pce fnl f* **11/2**[2]

4651 **7** ¾ **Blue Maisey**[14] 3546 5-9-0 **66** .... PaulMulrennan 5 — 64
(Edwin Tuer) *in tch: drvn over 3f out: hdwy on ins over 1f out: nvr nr to chal* **13/2**[3]

1600 **8** ½ **Mujaadel (USA)**[17] 3445 8-9-2 **68** .... (p) MichaelO'Connell 11 — 65
(David Nicholls) *hood removed late: s.i.s: hdwy over 2f out: n.m.r 1f out: kpt on ins fnl f* **28/1**

242 **9** 1 **Adiator**[13] 3593 5-8-9 **61** .... AndrewElliott 7 — 55
(Neville Bycroft) *swtchd rt s: in rr: kpt on ins fnl 2f: nvr a factor* **14/1**

004- **10** ½ **Polish World (USA)**[248] 7453 9-9-9 **75** .... MickyFenton 9 — 68
(Paul Midgley) *led: clr over 4f out: hdd & wknd appr fnl f* **25/1**

3324 **11** hd **Shadowtime**[23] 3193 8-9-12 **78** .... BarryMcHugh 8 — 70
(Tracy Waggott) *dwlt: hld up in rr: effrt and c on outside over 1f out: no imp whn pushed wd jst ins fnl f* **16/1**

5013 **12** 2 **Clubland (IRE)**[17] 3441 4-9-3 **69** .... JimmyQuinn 13 — 56
(Roy Bowring) *chsd ldrs: effrt on outer over 2f out: wkng whn pushed wd jst ins fnl f* **20/1**

1m 29.99s (-3.81) **Going Correction** -0.40s/f (Firm)
WFA 3 from 4yo+ 8lb — **12** Ran SP% **121.0**
Speed ratings (Par 105): **105,103,102,101,100 100,99,98,97,96 96,94**
toteswingers 1&2 £7.50, 1&3 £5.70, 2&3 £18.00 CSF £19.59 TOTE £2.80: £1.40, £3.30, £3.40; EX 23.70 Trifecta £132.00 Pool: £912.18 - 5.17 winning units.
Owner Hamdan Al Maktoum **Bred** Shadwell Estate Company Limited **Trained** Newmarket, Suffolk
■ Stewards' Enquiry : Robert Winston one-day ban; careless riding (19th July).

FOCUS
The winner rather stood out in this ordinary handicap. The third helps set the standard.

4008 SWAN INDUSTRIAL DRIVES H'CAP — 1m 100y
8:00 (8:01) (Class 6) (0-60,60) 3-Y-0 — **£2,385** (£704; £352) — **Stalls** Low

Form — RPR

3061 **1** **Rocket Ronnie (IRE)**[16] 3463 3-9-6 **59** .... BarryMcHugh 5 — 68+
(David Nicholls) *trckd ldrs: edgd lft over 1f out: led jst ins fnl f: drvn rt out* **3/1**[1]

4000 **2** ½ **Birdy Boy (USA)**[16] 3463 3-9-2 **55** .... FrannyNorton 2 — 63
(Mark Johnston) *led: jnd over 1f out: hdd and no ex last 30yds* **7/2**[2]

-000 **3** 2 **Khelac**[17] 3434 3-9-7 **60** .... (b[1]) TomEaves 4 — 63
(Philip Hide) *sn chsng ldrs: hmpd over 1f out: styd on same pce ins fnl f* **25/1**

4042 **4** ½ **Look On By**[7] 3772 3-9-0 **53** .... JamesSullivan 8 — 55
(Ruth Carr) *t.k.h: trckd ldrs: settled in mid-div after 2f: hdwy over 2f out: styd on same pce fnl f* **6/1**[3]

5110 **5** hd **Lexington Blue**[16] 3463 3-9-6 **59** .... DavidNolan 16 — 61
(David O'Meara) *mid-div: hdwy over 2f out: kpt on fnl f* **10/1**

3-53 **6** ½ **Multilicious**[16] 3463 3-9-2 **55** .... DavidAllan 11 — 56
(Tim Easterby) *mid-div: effrt 3f out: kpt on fnl f* **17/2**

-003 **7** 2 ¼ **Ella Motiva (IRE)**[10] 3650 3-8-10 **49** .... RobbieFitzpatrick 12 — 44
(Mark Brisbourne) *in rr: kpt on fnl 2f: nvr nr ldrs* **14/1**

5-33 **8** nk **Reggie Bond**[31] 2950 3-9-1 **54** .... (p) RussKennemore 14 — 49
(Geoffrey Oldroyd) *mid-div: effrt 3f out: kpt on fnl f* **7/1**

06-5 **9** shd **El Molino Blanco**[16] 3463 3-9-3 **56** .... PaulMulrennan 9 — 51+
(Michael Easterby) *in rr: nt clr run over 2f out: styd on: nvr a factor* **12/1**

0000 **10** 1 ½ **Moorway (IRE)**[22] 711 3-9-5 **58** .... (p) PhillipMakin 1 — 49
(Andrew Hollinshead) *in rr: effrt on outer over 2f out: nvr a threat* **40/1**

0050 **11** 1 ¾ **Ground Ginger**[18] 3405 3-8-10 **49** .... (b[1]) JimmyQuinn 6 — 36
(James Bethell) *in rr: effrt on ins 3f out: sn hmpd nvr on terms* **33/1**

0000 **12** 1 **Fishlake Rebel**[21] 3281 3-8-7 **46** .... PJMcDonald 3 — 31
(Ruth Carr) *chsd ldr: lost pl over 1f out* **18/1**

000- **13** 5 **Double Happiness**[336] 4778 3-8-4 **46** oh1 .... NeilFarley[(3)] 7 — 19
(Brian Rothwell) *in rr: drvn over 3f out: nvr on terms* **66/1**

0064 **14** 3 **Blue Clumber**[12] 3611 3-8-13 **52** .... (t) DuranFentiman 10 — 18
(Shaun Harris) *chsd ldrs: lost pl over 2f out* **33/1**

1m 44.92s (-2.68) **Going Correction** -0.40s/f (Firm) — **14** Ran SP% **126.9**
Speed ratings (Par 98): **97,96,94,94,93 93,91,90,90,89 87,86,81,78**
toteswingers 1&2 £5.80, 1&3 £30.40, 2&3 £46.90 CSF £13.40 CT £215.12 TOTE £4.90: £2.20, £1.90, £8.00; EX 21.90 Trifecta £304.10 Part won. Pool: £405.52 - 0.29 winning units..
Owner Mills, Fallon, Purchase & Love **Bred** Sandra Russell **Trained** Sessay, N Yorks

FOCUS
As often is the case at Beverley, it paid to be on the pace in this 3-yo handicap. The winner has his act together now and should do better.

4009 FERGUSON FAWSITT ARMS H'CAP — 5f
8:30 (8:30) (Class 6) (0-60,60) 3-Y-0+ — **£2,264** (£673; £336; £168) — **Stalls** Low

Form — RPR

1113 **1** **Bondi Beach Boy**[3] 3933 4-9-6 **56** .... PJMcDonald 6 — 75
(James Turner) *mde all: wnt clr over 1f out: styd on strly* **15/8**[1]

6354 **2** 3 ½ **Ingenti**[11] 3630 5-9-7 **57** .... PaulMulrennan 5 — 63
(Christopher Wilson) *chsd ldrs: tk 2nd last 100yds* **8/1**[3]

4332 **3** 1 ½ **Pull The Pin (IRE)**[10] 3654 4-8-9 **52** .... LukeLeadbitter[(7)] 4 — 53
(Declan Carroll) *chsd ldrs: styd on same pce over 1f out* **5/1**[2]

6324 **4** ½ **Headstight (IRE)**[29] 3026 4-9-3 **53** .... (p) LeeTopliss 14 — 52+
(Paul Midgley) *dwlt: mid-div: hdwy whn nt clr run 2f out: kpt on ins fnl f* **14/1**

3236 **5** 1 **Tuibama (IRE)**[42] 2611 4-9-9 **59** .... (p) FrannyNorton 10 — 55
(Tracy Waggott) *chsd wnr: kpt on same pce over 1f out* **10/1**

0000 **6** ¾ **Dolly Diva**[11] 3630 4-8-9 **52** .... (p) JordanNason[(7)] 1 — 45
(Paul Midgley) *mid-div: hdwy over 1f out: hmpd and swtchd rt ins fnl f: kpt on* **33/1**

0000 **7** nse **Ivestar (IRE)**[17] 3446 8-9-8 **58** .... (vt) JamesSullivan 12 — 51
(Michael Easterby) *in rr: hdwy and nt clr run over 1f out: swtchd ins: styd on* **50/1**

-600 **8** nk **Arch Walker (IRE)**[29] 3024 6-9-5 **55** .... (b) LukeMorris 8 — 47
(John Weymes) *in tch: drvn over 2f out: kpt on: nvr a threat* **25/1**

-065 **9** 1 **Little Jimmy Odsox (IRE)**[18] 3393 5-9-9 **59** .... (b) RobertWinston 9 — 47
(Tim Easterby) *towards rr: hdwy and swtchd lft jst ins fnl f: kpt on* **8/1**[3]

5034 **10** hd **Ace Master**[17] 3446 5-9-6 **56** .... (v[1]) JimmyQuinn 3 — 43
(Roy Bowring) *chsd ldrs: hmpd after wkng whn bmpd jst ins fnl f* **10/1**

0505 **11** hd **One Kool Dude**[42] 2643 4-9-6 **56** .... AndrewElliott 15 — 43
(Neville Bycroft) *in rr on outer: sme hdwy over 1f out: nvr a factor* **28/1**

4400 **12** hd **Baltic Bomber (IRE)**[23] 3190 4-9-10 **60** .... (v) MichaelO'Connell 11 — 46
(John Quinn) *in rr: sme hdwy over 1f out: nvr on terms* **20/1**

0-20 **13** 1 **Lady Kildare (IRE)**[29] 3026 5-9-5 **55** .... TomEaves 17 — 37
(Jedd O'Keeffe) *hood removed late: dwlt: a in rr* **25/1**

0300 **14** 1 ½ **Rio's Girl**[18] 3392 6-8-11 **54** ow2 .... (p) DavidSimmonson[(7)] 2 — 31
(Tony Coyle) *chsd ldrs on inner: n.m.r and lost pl after 1f* **25/1**

0016 **15** 1 **Pavers Star**[7] 3769 4-9-8 **58** .... BarryMcHugh 13 — 31
(Noel Wilson) *chsd ldrs on outer: lost pl over 1f out* **20/1**

005- **16** 8 **Piste**[240] 7634 7-9-3 **53** .... (e) DuranFentiman 7
(Tina Jackson) *s.i.s: in rr: bhd fnl 2f* **50/1**

1m 1.28s (-2.22) **Going Correction** -0.40s/f (Firm) — **16** Ran SP% **129.9**
Speed ratings (Par 101): **101,95,93,92,90 89,89,88,87,86 86,86,84,82,80 67**
toteswingers 1&2 £7.00, 1&3 £1.60, 2&3 £11.80 CSF £15.75 CT £72.47 TOTE £2.50: £1.20, £2.20, £1.80, £3.70; EX 25.00 Trifecta £69.60 Pool: £496.77 - 5.35 winning units..
Owner J R Turner **Bred** G R & H Turner **Trained** Norton-le-Clay, N Yorks

FOCUS
A big field lined up for this handicap run over the minimum trip that saw an in-form sprinter romp to victory. This rates a personal best.

4010 BEVERLEY MIDDLE DISTANCE SERIES H'CAP — 1m 4f 16y
9:00 (9:00) (Class 6) (0-60,59) 3-Y-0+ — **£2,587** (£770; £384; £192) — **Stalls** Low

Form — RPR

00-0 **1** **Grammar**[8] 3727 4-8-13 **49** .... (e) RaulDaSilva[(3)] 5 — 56
(David Thompson) *chsd ldrs: drvn over 3f out: upsides over 1f out: styd on to ld last stride* **33/1**

2633 **2** nse **Blue Top**[13] 3595 4-9-6 **53** .... (p) DuranFentiman 4 — 60
(Tim Walford) *w ldr: t.k.h: led 2f out: jnd 1f out: hdd post* **11/4**[1]

0453 **3** 3 **Torero**[8] 3721 4-9-7 **54** .... (v[1]) BrianHughes 9 — 56
(Kevin Ryan) *dwlt: reminders after s: hdwy 8f out: chsd ldrs over 4f out: edgd rt 1f out: styd on same pce* **11/2**

5-00 **4** ¾ **Valentine's Gift**[8] 3728 5-9-2 **49** .... (p) AndrewElliott 3 — 50
(Neville Bycroft) *trckd ldrs: effrt on inner over 2f out: kpt on one pce over 1f out* **25/1**

50-5 **5** 1 ½ **Queen Of Epirus**[11] 3625 5-9-8 **55** .... MickyFenton 7 — 54
(Brian Rothwell) *mid-div: lost pl 8f out: styd on fnl 2f* **16/1**

6-55 **6** nse **Swift Encounter (IRE)**[13] 3595 4-9-12 **59** .... PJMcDonald 6 — 58
(Ann Duffield) *mid-div: hdwy over 4f out: one pce fnl 2f* **5/1**[3]

5366 **7** ½ **Lacey**[18] 3410 4-9-7 **54** .... RussKennemore 8 — 52
(Andrew Hollinshead) *sn chsng ldrs: one pce fnl 2f* **4/1**[2]

6-00 **8** 1 **Dean Iarracht (IRE)**[8] 3728 7-9-4 **51** .... (p) BarryMcHugh 11 — 47
(Tracy Waggott) *hld up in rr: effrt outside over 2f out: nvr a threat* **12/1**

0-01 **9** 2 ¼ **Chankillo**[30] 2986 4-9-7 **54** .... LukeMorris 10 — 47
(Mark H Tompkins) *in rr-div: drvn and outpcd over 3f out* **5/1**[3]

00-0 **10** 7 **Ruby Glass (IRE)**[11] 3625 4-9-7 **54** .... JamesSullivan 1 — 41
(Ruth Carr) *set stdy pce: qcknd gallop over 3f out: hdd 2f out: wkng whn n.m.r 1f out: sn heavily eased* **28/1**

2m 39.09s (-0.71) **Going Correction** -0.40s/f (Firm) — **10** Ran SP% **119.2**
Speed ratings (Par 101): **86,85,83,83,82 82,82,81,79,75**
toteswingers 1&2 £33.90, 1&3 £52.20, 2&3 £2.20 CSF £123.50 CT £606.15 TOTE £51.60: £14.50, £1.90, £2.20; EX 253.50 Trifecta £383.50 Part won. Pool: £511.39 - 0.10 winning units..
Owner G T Carlton **Bred** Millsec Limited **Trained** Bolam, Co Durham

FOCUS
A poor middle-distance handicap. The form has been rated cautiously.
T/Plt: £24.60 to a £1 stake. Pool: £75,390.38 - 2,229.52 winning units T/Qpdt: £4.80 to a £1 stake. Pool: £6,334.66 - 961.48 winning units WG

3808 DONCASTER (L-H)
Friday, July 5

OFFICIAL GOING: Good to firm (9.4)
Wind: Virtually nil Weather: Sunny and dry

4011 JESSICA GAIGER & ELIZABETH STARKEY CARDSAVE MAIDEN STKS — 7f
2:00 (2:01) (Class 5) 3-Y-0 — **£2,587** (£770; £384; £192) — **Stalls** High

Form — RPR

33- **1** **Gold Hunter (IRE)**[409] 2376 3-9-5 0 .... FrederikTylicki 7 — 93+
(Saeed bin Suroor) *trckd ldrs: swtchd rt and smooth hdwy 2f out: led wl over 1f out: rdn clr ent fnl f: readily* **15/8**[1]

3 **2** 6 **Paradise Watch**[34] 2872 3-9-5 0 .... JamieSpencer 4 — 75
(Luca Cumani) *hld up in tch: hdwy wl over 2f out: swtchd lft and rdn over 1f out: edgd lft and kpt on fnl f: no ch w wnr* **5/1**

3 1 ¼ **Life Partner (IRE)** 3-9-5 0 .... [1] HarryBentley 2 — 72+
(Saeed bin Suroor) *hld up in tch: hdwy on outer 1/2-way: effrt and cl up 2f out: rdn over 1f out: edgd rt and one pce fnl f* **10/1**

03 **4** 3 ¾ **Tawtheeq (IRE)**[48] 2447 3-9-5 0 .... DaneO'Neill 3 — 62
(Richard Hannon) *prom: cl up 1/2-way: rdn along 2f out: drvn over 1f out and sn wknd* **3/1**[2]

0-2 **5** ¾ **Bastion (USA)**[74] 1722 3-9-5 0 .... AndreaAtzeni 6 — 59
(Roger Varian) *led: rdn along over 2f out: hdd wl over 1f out and sn wknd* **9/2**[3]

6 5 **Snap Music (USA)** 3-9-0 0 .... FrannyNorton 1 — 41
(Mark Johnston) *prom: rdn along over 3f out: sn wknd* **16/1**

7 4 ½ **Cruising Along** 3-9-5 0 .... RoystonFfrench 5 — 34
(Ed McMahon) *cl up: rdn along 3f out: wknd over 2f out* **66/1**

1m 24.19s (-2.11) **Going Correction** -0.225s/f (Firm) — **7** Ran SP% **111.1**
Speed ratings (Par 100): **103,96,94,90,89 83,78**
toteswingers 1&2 £2.90, 1&3 £4.40, 2&3 £4.70 CSF £10.99 TOTE £2.70: £1.90, £2.10; EX 14.40 Trifecta £82.30 Pool: £2,742.15 - 24.97 winning units.
Owner Godolphin **Bred** Airlie Stud And Sir Thomas Pilkington **Trained** Newmarket, Suffolk

FOCUS
Not the most competitive of maidens, but the winner looks useful. The runner-up is rated to his debut mark.

4012 ASHLEIGH RIACH & LEWIS SMITH CARDSAVE CLAIMING STKS 1m (S)
2:30 (2:30) (Class 5) 4-Y-0+ **£2,587** (£770; £384; £192) **Stalls** High

Form RPR
0-05 1 **Jo'Burg (USA)**[14] 3544 9-9-5 85 DanielTudhope 10 87
(David O'Meara) *dwlt: hld up: hdwy over 3f out: chsd clr ldr wl over 1f out: led ins fnl f: rdn and edgd rt towards fin* **6/4**[1]
5320 2 ¾ **Extraterrestrial**[13] 3564 9-8-10 76 (p) TonyHamilton 5 76
(Richard Fahey) *hld up in rr: hdwy wl over 2f out: rdn over 1f out: styd on to chse wnr ins fnl f: kpt on* **3/1**[2]
6200 3 3¼ **Flying Applause**[4] 3895 8-8-10 71 (b) MarkCoumbe(3) 3 72
(Roy Bowring) *led and sn clr: ten l advantage 1/2-way: pushed along over 2f out: rdn wl over 1f out: wknd and hdd ins fnl f* **20/1**
0011 4 4½ **All Or Nothin (IRE)**[13] 3592 4-9-3 77 (v) MichaelO'Connell 8 65
(John Quinn) *t.k.h: chsd clr ldr: rdn along over 2f out: sn one pce* **9/2**[3]
0600 5 1¾ **Mr Red Clubs (IRE)**[20] 3346 4-9-11 84 (b) ShaneKelly 6 69
(Tim Pitt) *t.k.h early: trckd ldrs: pushed along 3f out: rdn 2f out: sn wknd* **5/1**
5 6 1½ **Latin Rebel (IRE)**[81] 1570 6-8-13 0 AndrewElliott 9 54
(Jim Goldie) *trckd ldrs: pushed along 3f out: sn rdn and wknd* **22/1**
1m 37.84s (-1.46) **Going Correction** -0.225s/f (Firm) **6** Ran SP% **109.0**
Speed ratings (Par 103): **98,97,94,89,87 86**
toteswingers 1&2 £1.50, 1&3 £5.80, 2&3 £5.70 CSF £5.76 TOTE £2.30: £1.20, £1.80; EX 8.20 Trifecta £48.70 Pool: £3,106.57 - 47.77 winning units.
Owner Richard Walker **Bred** Tim Cooper **Trained** Nawton, N Yorks
FOCUS
A modest claimer in which the pace was good thanks to the aggressively ridden third horse.

4013 ROMERO INSURANCE BROKERS LTD MAIDEN FILLIES' STKS 7f
3:00 (3:01) (Class 5) 3-Y-0+ **£2,587** (£770; £384; £192) **Stalls** High

Form RPR
2 1 **Ethel**[30] 2979 3-9-0 0 RobertHavlin 2 73+
(John Gosden) *trckd ldrs: hdwy to ld wl over 1f out: sn rdn and edgd rt ent fnl f: kpt on wl towards fin* **7/2**[3]
0- 2 ½ **Nur Jahan (IRE)**[210] 8017 3-9-0 0 [1] TedDurcan 13 72+
(David Lanigan) *hld up in rr: hdwy on outer 1/2-way: effrt over 1f out: sn rdn and ev ch ins fnl f: nt qckn towards fin* **6/1**
5- 3 hd **Deserted**[351] 4246 3-9-0 0 KirstyMilczarek 9 71+
(Luca Cumani) *dwlt and in rr: hdwy over 2f out: rdn to chse ldrs over 1f out: kpt on ins fnl f: nrst fin* **10/3**[2]
4 1½ **Thorntoun Lady (USA)** 3-9-0 0 DanielTudhope 11 67+
(Jim Goldie) *hld up in tch: hdwy over 2f out and sn chsng ldrs: effrt over 1f out: rdn and ev ch ent fnl f: green: n.m.r and no ex last 150yds* **16/1**
05- 5 1½ **Dame Nellie Melba**[240] 7636 3-9-0 0 FrannyNorton 10 63+
(Mark Johnston) *dwlt and sltly hmpd after s: in rr: swtchd rt and hdwy wl over 1f out: kpt on fnl f: nrst fin* **14/1**
664 6 ¾ **Loved One**[26] 3136 3-9-0 74 FrederikTylicki 6 61
(James Fanshawe) *midfield: hdwy to chse ldrs over 2f out: rdn wl over 1f out and sn one pce* **2/1**[1]
7 2¼ **Sleek** 3-9-0 0 AndreaAtzeni 4 55
(Marco Botti) *dwlt and in rr tl sme late hdwy* **16/1**
8 2¾ **Valley Fire** 3-9-0 0 RoystonFfrench 8 47
(Ed McMahon) *trckd ldr: cl up 1/2-way: rdn along wl over 2f out and sn wknd* **50/1**
420/ 9 ½ **Enchanted Dream**[603] 7354 5-9-8 54 HarryBentley 12 49
(David C Griffiths) *chsd ldrs on outer: rdn along over 2f out: sn wknd* **66/1**
0 10 3¼ **Tumbleweed Finale**[22] 3253 3-9-0 0 SteveDrowne 1 37
(Rae Guest) *led: rdn along over 2f out: hdd wl over 1f out and sn wknd* **100/1**
0 11 nk **Maillot Jaune (IRE)**[7] 3774 3-9-0 0 DuranFentiman 3 37
(Patrick Holmes) *in tch on outer: hdwy to chse ldrs 1/2-way: rdn along over 2f out: sn wknd* **100/1**
0/0- 12 2¼ **Secret Lodge**[393] 2865 5-9-8 15 MickyFenton 5 33
(Garry Woodward) *t.k.h: chsd ldrs: rdn along 3f out: sn wknd* **150/1**
1m 26.55s (0.25) **Going Correction** -0.225s/f (Firm)
WFA 3 from 5yo 8lb **12** Ran SP% **117.4**
Speed ratings (Par 100): **89,88,88,86,84 83,81,78,77,73 73,71**
toteswingers 1&2 £2.00, 1&3 £2.40, 2&3 £3.00 CSF £24.60 TOTE £3.40: £1.40, £2.10, £1.30; EX 26.40 Trifecta £100.00 Pool: £3,184.73 - 23.88 winning units.
Owner Normandie Stud Ltd **Bred** Normandie Stud Ltd **Trained** Newmarket, Suffolk
FOCUS
They went no pace and the time was 2.36sec slower than the opening 3yo maiden, but a few caught the eye. The bare form can't be much better than this.

4014 REBECCA DADE & SAMANTHA PRICE CARDSAVE H'CAP 7f
3:35 (3:35) (Class 3) (0-90,88) 3-Y-0+ **£7,439** (£2,213; £1,106; £553) **Stalls** High

Form RPR
-204 1 **Glen Moss (IRE)**[34] 2858 4-9-13 87 JamesMcDonald 3 97
(Charles Hills) *trckd ldng pair: hdwy over 2f out: led wl over 1f out: drvn ins fnl f: kpt on wl towards fin* **5/2**[1]
-230 2 ½ **Fils Anges (IRE)**[62] 2022 3-9-6 88 HayleyTurner 5 94
(Michael Bell) *hld up in tch: hdwy on outer wl over 2f out: rdn over 1f out: chal ins fnl f and ev ch: drvn and no ex last 75yds* **7/1**
4316 3 ¾ **Defendant**[20] 3342 3-9-3 85 ShaneKelly 4 89
(Sir Michael Stoute) *trckd ldrs: hdwy over 2f out: rdn wl over 1f out: kpt on same pce fnl f* **9/2**[3]
0-02 4 2 **Otto The Great**[20] 3322 4-9-0 79 GeorgeChaloner(5) 1 80
(Richard Fahey) *led: pushed along wl over 2f out: rdn and hdd wl over 1f out: grad wknd appr fnl f* **13/2**
00-0 5 2 **Hadaj**[36] 2813 4-9-5 79 [1] RobertWinston 9 75
(Clive Brittain) *cl up: rdn along wl over 2f out: wknd over 1f out* **14/1**
-000 6 1¾ **Emkanaat**[13] 3586 5-9-3 77 DaneO'Neill 6 68
(Amy Weaver) *trckd ldrs: hdwy 1/2-way: rdn along over 2f out: sn btn* **40/1**
0101 7 1 **Creek Falcon (IRE)**[32] 2929 4-9-5 79 DanielTudhope 7 67
(David O'Meara) *hld up in rr: effrt and sme hdwy over 2f out: sn rdn and n.d* **11/4**[2]
0040 8 ¾ **Showboating (IRE)**[6] 3811 5-9-0 74 (vt) HarryBentley 8 60
(Alan McCabe) *a in rr* **16/1**
1m 23.42s (-2.88) **Going Correction** -0.225s/f (Firm)
WFA 3 from 4yo+ 8lb **8** Ran SP% **114.2**
Speed ratings (Par 107): **107,106,105,103,101 99,97,97**
toteswingers 1&2 £3.90, 1&3 £3.90, 2&3 £5.20 CSF £20.54 CT £73.95 TOTE £2.70: £1.10, £3.00, £2.30; EX 17.70 Trifecta £79.40 Pool: £3,147.78 - 29.72 winning units.
Owner John C Grant **Bred** Rathbarry Stud **Trained** Lambourn, Berks
FOCUS
A decent handicap and the pace was fair. Straightforward form.

4015 KIRSTY STORR & JOSH ALLISON CARDSAVE FILLIES' H'CAP 1m 4f
4:10 (4:10) (Class 4) (0-85,83) 3-Y-0+ **£4,690** (£1,395; £697; £348) **Stalls** Low

Form RPR
4062 1 **Bollin Greta**[4] 3891 8-9-3 72 DavidAllan 4 82
(Tim Easterby) *hld up towards rr: hdwy over 3f out: chsd ldrs 2f out: rdn to chal ent fnl f: styd on to ld last 100yds* **15/2**
310 2 1¼ **Fersah (USA)**[15] 3482 3-9-1 83 DaneO'Neill 3 91
(William Haggas) *trckd ldrs: smooth hdwy 4f out: led wl over 1f out: jnd and rdn ent fnl f: sn hdd and hung lft: drvn and one pce fnl 100yds* **7/2**[2]
12 3 1½ **Raushan (IRE)**[24] 3177 3-8-12 80 ShaneKelly 7 86
(Sir Michael Stoute) *trckd ldr: cl up 4f out: led 3f out: rdn along and hdd wl over 1f out: drvn and one pce fnl f* **11/4**[1]
61 4 5 **Controversy**[16] 3469 3-8-12 80 HarryBentley 2 78
(Saeed bin Suroor) *trckd ldrs: effrt 3f out: rdn along 2f out: drvn and one pce fr over 1f out* **7/1**
-210 5 ½ **Cosmic Halo**[30] 2976 4-9-4 73 TonyHamilton 6 70
(Richard Fahey) *hld up towards rr: hdwy over 3f out: rdn along to chse ldrs over 2f out: sn drvn and no imp* **20/1**
4321 6 ¾ **Looks Like Rain**[21] 3301 4-8-11 71 GeorgeChaloner(5) 8 67
(Brian Ellison) *hld up in rr: hdwy over 4f out: swtchd rt and effrt 3f out: sn rdn and n.d* **7/1**
2142 7 ½ **Hepworth**[22] 3258 4-9-12 81 (b) RobertHavlin 5 76
(John Gosden) *dwlt: midfield: pushed along after 3f: rdn along on inner over 5f out: keeping on whn n.m.r and hmpd over 2f out: in rr after* **10/1**
135- 8 31 **Little Dutch Girl**[59] 6964 4-9-11 80 (b) JamieSpencer 1 25
(Nicky Henderson) *led: rdn along over 4f out: hdd 3f out: wknd qckly: sn bhd and eased* **9/2**[3]
2m 31.07s (-3.83) **Going Correction** -0.225s/f (Firm)
WFA 3 from 4yo+ 13lb **8** Ran SP% **117.7**
Speed ratings (Par 102): **103,102,101,97,97 97,96,76**
toteswingers 1&2 £7.30, 1&3 £5.40, 2&3 £3.30 CSF £34.99 CT £91.79 TOTE £10.90: £3.50, £1.40, £1.10; EX 46.00 Trifecta £168.80 Pool: £3,569.36 - 15.85 winning units.
Owner Habton Farms **Bred** Sir Neil & Exors Of Late Lady Westbrook **Trained** Great Habton, N Yorks
FOCUS
A good fillies' handicap and they went a decent pace, which was very much to the advantage of the winner. She found a little on recent runs.

4016 WINNINGPOST.CO.UK HORSE RACING RESULTS H'CAP 1m 4f
4:45 (4:45) (Class 5) (0-70,70) 4-Y-0+ **£2,587** (£770; £384; £192) **Stalls** Low

Form RPR
5-12 1 **Mankini (IRE)**[8] 3719 4-9-1 64 KirstyMilczarek 8 81+
(Luca Cumani) *hld up: hdwy 4f out: led over 2f out: sn rdn clr: edgd rt ent fnl f: kpt on strly: unchal* **5/6**[1]
0402 2 9 **Muzhil (IRE)**[23] 3222 4-8-11 60 RobertWinston 2 63
(Clive Brittain) *led 1f: trckd ldr tl led again 3f out: sn hdd and rdn: drvn over 1f out: rallied to take modest 2nd ins fnl f* **11/1**[3]
2354 3 ¾ **Bobs Her Uncle**[12] 3610 4-9-1 64 TedDurcan 3 66
(James Bethell) *trckd ldrs: hdwy 4f out: rdn over 2f out: sn drvn to chse wnr and kpt on one pce: lost modest 2nd ins fnl f* **11/1**[3]
-604 4 5 **The Lodge Road (IRE)**[8] 3727 5-8-11 60 PhillipMakin 4 54
(Martin Todhunter) *hld up in rr: sme hdwy on outer over 3f out: sn rdn along and n.d* **33/1**
0502 5 3¾ **Morocco**[14] 3543 4-9-3 66 TomEaves 1 54
(David O'Meara) *hld up: sme hdwy 4f out: rdn along 3f out: n.d* **12/1**
0-42 6 ½ **Badea**[10] 3652 4-9-4 67 (v) TonyHamilton 5 54
(Richard Fahey) *trckd ldrs: pushed along 4f out: wknd 3f out* **11/2**[2]
5251 7 47 **Spiekeroog**[13] 3595 7-9-3 66 (v) DanielTudhope 7
(David O'Meara) *led after 1f: set stdy pce: rdn along 4f out: hdd 3f out: sn wknd and bhd whn heavily eased fnl f* **11/2**[2]
2m 30.8s (-4.10) **Going Correction** -0.225s/f (Firm) **7** Ran SP% **112.6**
Speed ratings (Par 103): **104,98,97,94,91 91,60**
toteswingers 1&2 £2.90, 1&3 £3.70, 2&3 £9.00 CSF £11.04 CT £60.11 TOTE £1.70: £1.50, £5.00; EX 11.20 Trifecta £81.10 Pool: £4,687.91 - 43.33 winning units.
Owner Leonidas Marinopoulos **Bred** Oak Hill Stud **Trained** Newmarket, Suffolk
FOCUS
The early pace didn't look strong in this ordinary handicap, but the winning time was 0.27sec faster than the preceding fillies' contest. It turned out to be a one-horse race and there's more to come from the winner despite a hefty rise for this. The second and third set an ordinary level.

4017 FREEBETS.CO.UK FILLIES' H'CAP 5f
5:15 (5:16) (Class 4) (0-80,82) 4-Y-0+ **£4,690** (£1,395; £697; £348) **Stalls** High

Form RPR
1101 1 **Cincinnati Kit**[20] 3317 4-8-10 66 (t) AndreaAtzeni 10 79
(Stuart Williams) *trckd ldrs: hdwy over 1f out: rdn and str run on stands' rail to chal ent fnl f: kpt on strly to ld last 100yds* **7/1**
-461 2 ¾ **Minalisa**[8] 3733 4-9-12 82 6ex SteveDrowne 3 92
(Rae Guest) *cl up: effrt wl over 1f out: rdn to chal over 1f out: led briefly jst ins fnl f: drvn: hdd and no ex last 100yds* **13/8**[1]
0032 3 1¾ **Sulis Minerva (IRE)**[22] 3236 6-9-1 74 RyanClark(3) 9 78
(Jeremy Gask) *towards rr: hdwy wl over 1f out: rdn and styd on fnl f: nrst fin* **13/2**[3]
4461 4 nk **Crimson Queen**[10] 3667 6-8-13 72 6ex (b) MarkCoumbe(3) 1 75
(Roy Brotherton) *led: rdn over 1f out: edgd lft ent fnl f: sn hdd & wknd last 100yds* **6/1**[2]
0120 5 ¾ **Mey Blossom**[28] 3069 8-8-3 64 (p) GeorgeChaloner(5) 6 64
(Richard Whitaker) *chsd ldrs on outer: rdn along and sltly outpcd over 2f out: kpt on u.p appr fnl f* **25/1**
2443 6 1¾ **Phoenix Clubs (IRE)**[15] 3505 4-9-2 72 (p) BarryMcHugh 2 66
(Paul Midgley) *chsd ldrs: rdn along wl over 1f out: drvn and wknd appr fnl f* **14/1**
-540 7 ¾ **Passionada**[27] 3078 4-8-12 68 RoystonFfrench 8 59
(Ed McMahon) *cl up: rdn along wl over 1f out: sn wknd* **22/1**
6-40 8 ¾ **Sunny Side Up (IRE)**[21] 3299 4-9-7 77 TonyHamilton 7 65
(Richard Fahey) *chsd ldrs: rdn along 1/2-way: sn wknd* **9/1**
-033 9 1 **Cats Eyes**[15] 3487 4-9-7 77 ShaneKelly 5 62
(Robert Cowell) *a in rr* **20/1**
02 10 ½ **Dreaming Of Rubies**[27] 3078 4-9-5 75 (t) HayleyTurner 4 58
(Ben Haslam) *a towards rr* **10/1**
58.2s (-2.30) **Going Correction** -0.225s/f (Firm) **10** Ran SP% **116.9**
Speed ratings (Par 102): **109,107,105,104,103 100,99,98,96,95**
toteswingers 1&2 £3.00, 1&3 £5.80, 2&3 £4.00 CSF £18.28 CT £81.19 TOTE £7.60: £2.20, £1.10, £2.60; EX 22.90 Trifecta £131.90 Pool: £4,012.71 - 22.80 winning units.

Owner J W Parry **Bred** Old Mill Stud & S Williams & J Parry **Trained** Newmarket, Suffolk
FOCUS
A fair fillies' sprint handicap and they went a serious pace. The winner is thriving.
T/Plt: £16.40 to £1 stake. Pool: £64,333.91 - 2,852.64 winning units T/Qpdt: £5.40 to a £1 stake. Pool: £6,252.87 - 853.44 winning units JR

3977 HAYDOCK (L-H)
Friday, July 5

OFFICIAL GOING: Good to firm (8.5)
Wind: Almost nil Weather: Hot and Sunny

4018 BETDAQ HAYDOCK PARK APPRENTICE TRAINING SERIES H'CAP (PART OF THE RACING EXCELLENCE INITIATIVE) 5f
6:45 (6:49) (Class 5) (0-75,75) 3-Y-O+ **£2,587** (£770; £384; £192) **Stalls** Centre

Form RPR
0000 **1** **Chunky Diamond (IRE)**[15] 3505 4-9-6 **71** KevinStott(4) 9 81
(Ruth Carr) *hld up: travelled wl: smooth hdwy fr 2f out: led 1f out: dashed clr and edgd lft ins fnl 150yds: r.o wl* **9/1**
3-00 **2** *3* **Wild Sauce**[58] 2173 4-9-12 **73** (bt) JustinNewman 6 72
(Bryan Smart) *trckd ldrs: effrt to take 2nd 2f out: chal jst ins fnl f: outpcd by wnr fnl 150yds* **6/1**
3130 **3** *½* **Spykes Bay (USA)**[17] 3441 4-9-5 **70** (b) RobJFitzpatrick(4) 1 67
(Mrs K Burke) *w ldrs: led over 2f out: rdn and hdd 1f out: kpt on same pce fnl 150yds* **3/1**[1]
0000 **4** *1 ¾* **Lucky Dan (IRE)**[1] 3980 7-9-10 **75** NicolaGrundy(4) 8 66
(Paul Green) *outpcd and bhd: prog and styd on ins fnl f: unable to rch ldrs* **16/1**
5414 **5** *2* **Script**[3] 3929 4-8-8 **59** JordanHibberd(4) 5 43
(Alan Berry) *hld up: rdn over 1f out: hdwy ent fnl f: kpt on: nvr able to trble ldrs* **9/2**[2]
0-00 **6** *shd* **Foxy Music**[42] 2614 9-10-0 **75** JasonHart 4 58
(Eric Alston) *racd keenly: led: rdn and hdd over 2f out: wl btn over 1f out* **10/1**
1500 **7** *1 ¾* **Liberty Ship**[20] 3317 8-8-10 **59** EDLinehan(2) 3 36
(Mark Buckley) *hld up: rdn and hdwy to chse ldrs over 1f out: no imp ins fnl f: fdd fnl 100yds* **40/1**
-206 **8** *2* **Layla's Oasis**[13] 3569 3-9-2 **70** (p) LauraBarry(2) 7 40
(Richard Fahey) *w ldrs: u.p and lost pl 2f out: wknd sn after* **15/2**
-646 **9** *½* **Amadeus Denton (IRE)**[16] 3462 4-9-0 **63** (p) ConnorBeasley(2) 2 31
(Michael Dods) *w ldrs: rdn over 2f out: wknd over 1f out* **5/1**[3]

1m 0.33s (-0.47) **Going Correction** +0.025s/f (Good)
WFA 3 from 4yo+ 5lb **9** Ran SP% **113.3**
Speed ratings (Par 103): **104,99,98,95,92 92,89,86,85**
toteswingers 1&2 £12.00, 1&3 £7.60, 2&3 £5.10 CSF £60.74 CT £201.75 TOTE £12.70: £3.70, £1.90, £1.50; EX 83.70 Trifecta £762.90 Part won. Pool: £1,017.22 - 0.95 winning units..
Owner The Bottom Liners & Mrs R Carr **Bred** Mrs E Comer **Trained** Huby, N Yorks
FOCUS
A total of 6mm of water had been put on the track since the previous day's racing, and the going was given as good to firm (GoingStick 8.5). All races were on the inner home straight, reducing race distances on the round course by 5yds. In-form horses looked thin on the ground here, but several looked well handicapped on their best. The third is the best guide.

4019 ADAPT (UK) TRAINING SERVICES CELEBRATION NURSERY H'CAP 6f
7:15 (7:16) (Class 4) 2-Y-O **£5,175** (£1,540; £769; £384) **Stalls** Centre

Form RPR
606 **1** **Woodland Girl**[23] 3205 2-8-1 **65** (p) PatrickMathers 5 68+
(Richard Fahey) *sn pushed along towards rr: hdwy over 1f out: r.o to ld wl ins fnl f* **20/1**
3654 **2** *nk* **Bounty Hunter (IRE)**[22] 3245 2-8-9 **73** HarryBentley 9 75
(Tom Dascombe) *a.p: w ldrs over 3f out: str chal fr over 1f out: r.o u.p ins fnl f: hld towards fin* **11/4**[1]
51 **3** *½* **Centre Haafhd**[16] 3461 2-8-11 **75** GrahamGibbons 6 75
(David Barron) *hung lft fr s: a.p: led over 2f out: rdn whn hrd pressed 1f out: hung lft ins fnl f: sn hdd: hld towards fin* **11/2**[3]
01 **4** *2 ¼* **Green Run**[34] 2869 2-8-11 **75** JamieSpencer 2 70
(Richard Hannon) *chsd ldrs: effrt and tried to chal fr over 1f out: abt 1 l down whn n.m.r and hmpd 150yds out: sn lost pl: n.d after* **10/1**
6623 **5** *nse* **The Smart One (IRE)**[20] 3311 2-8-11 **75** GrahamLee 4 68
(Mick Channon) *hld up bhd ldrs: effrt over 1f out: nt qckn ins fnl f: kpt on same pce fnl 100yds* **15/2**
505 **6** *3* **Dovil's Duel (IRE)**[51] 2359 2-8-0 **64** oh5 NickyMackay 3 47
(Rod Millman) *s.i.s: in rr: rdn and hung rt wl over 1f out: racd on stands' side fnl f: kpt on one pce* **25/1**
5145 **7** *¾* **Vine De Nada**[34] 2877 2-9-2 **80** JoeFanning 1 61
(Mark Johnston) *hld up: u.p over 2f out: one pce and no imp ins fnl f* **10/1**
31 **8** *3* **Secret Applause**[34] 2883 2-8-4 **75** ConnorBeasley(7) 11 46
(Michael Dods) *in tch: impr to r w ldrs over 3f out: rdn and wknd over 1f out* **8/1**
406 **9** *3* **Limegrove**[6] 3801 2-8-11 **80** [1] DeclanBates(5) 10 41
(David Evans) *prom: w ldrs over 3f out: rdn and wknd over 1f out* **20/1**
5160 **10** *8* **Corncockle**[16] 3459 2-9-7 **85** RichardHughes 8 21
(Richard Hannon) *racd keenly: led: rdn and hdd over 2f out: wknd wl over 1f out: eased whn wl btn and bhd wl ins fnl f* **9/2**[2]

1m 14.37s (0.57) **Going Correction** +0.025s/f (Good) **10** Ran SP% **114.7**
Speed ratings (Par 96): **97,96,95,92,92 88,87,83,79,69**
toteswingers 1&2 £20.10, 1&3 £19.50, 2&3 £5.20 CSF £71.77 CT £355.71 TOTE £22.30: £5.70, £1.70, £1.70; EX 115.00 Trifecta £528.60 Pool: £1,100.93 - 1.56 winning units.
Owner Peter Timmins **Bred** Jeremy Green And Sons **Trained** Musley Bank, N Yorks
FOCUS
The official ratings shown are estimated and for information only. They migrated centre to far side in this race, the first nursery of the season. Straightforward form.

4020 RITA ORA HERE ON 9TH AUGUST H'CAP 1m 3f 200y
7:45 (7:45) (Class 4) (0-85,85) 4-Y-O+ **£5,175** (£1,540; £769; £384) **Stalls** Centre

Form RPR
-330 **1** **Chancery (USA)**[50] 2402 5-8-12 **76** DanielTudhope 1 91
(David O'Meara) *hld up: swtchd lft to inner and hdwy over 2f out: rdn to ld over 1f out: styd on ins fnl f: in command towards fin* **6/1**[3]
-211 **2** *2 ¾* **Continuum**[19] 3370 4-9-7 **85** RichardHughes 2 96
(Lady Cecil) *hld up in tch in main pack: hdwy and effrt over 2f out: chal over 1f out: sn wnt 2nd: no imp on wnr fnl 150yds* **2/1**[2]
6-11 **3** *2 ¾* **Semeen**[20] 3321 4-9-5 **83** JamieSpencer 6 89
(Luca Cumani) *chsd ldrs: wnt 2nd and chsng clr ldr 3f out: chal over 1f out: sn lost 2nd: nt qckn ins fnl f: no ex fnl 100yds: all out to hold on for 3rd* **7/4**[1]
240 **4** *nk* **English Summer**[37] 2775 6-9-4 **82** (t) HayleyTurner 8 88
(David Simcock) *hld up in rr: rdn over 3f out: stdy hdwy over 1f out: styd on towards fin: nvr able to chal* **16/1**
1-40 **5** *4 ½* **Forget Me Not Lane (IRE)**[20] 3349 4-9-1 **79** GrahamLee 7 78
(Kevin Ryan) *led for 2f: chsd clr ldr after tl lost 2nd 3f out: sn rdn: wknd over 1f out* **7/1**
5560 **6** *¾* **Dancing Primo**[20] 3345 7-8-4 **73** JackDuern(5) 9 70
(Mark Brisbourne) *plld hrd: in tch: led after 2f: clr after 4f: stl abt 10 l clr 3f out: reduced advantage 2f out: hdd over 1f out: wknd ins fnl f* **33/1**
2006 **7** *2 ¾* **Flying Power**[17] 3442 5-8-10 **74** PaddyAspell 10 67
(John Norton) *hld up: rdn over 2f out: no imp: wl btn ins fnl f* **25/1**

2m 30.3s (-3.50) **Going Correction** -0.175s/f (Firm) **7** Ran SP% **109.2**
Speed ratings (Par 105): **104,102,100,100,97 96,94**
toteswingers 1&2 £3.50, 1&3 £2.60, 2&3 £1.50 CSF £16.74 TOTE £7.40: £2.80, £1.90; EX 21.10 Trifecta £34.60 Pool: £1,249.69 - 27.02 winning units.
Owner Hollowdean **Bred** Darley **Trained** Nawton, N Yorks
FOCUS
There was a bit of muddling early pace, with no-one really wanting to go on until the sixth raced clear. The winner was on a good mark on a best reading of his maiden form.

4021 BRITISH STALLION STUDS SUPPORTING BRITISH RACING EBF MAIDEN STKS 7f
8:15 (8:17) (Class 5) 2-Y-O **£2,911** (£866; £432; £216) **Stalls** Low

Form RPR
1 **Snow Squall** 2-9-5 0 HarryBentley 7 79+
(Saeed bin Suroor) *hld up: hdwy over 1f out: led fnl 150yds: r.o* **8/1**
4 **2** *¾* **Peak Royale**[14] 3536 2-9-5 0 RichardHughes 8 77
(Richard Hannon) *unsettled bef gng into stalls: trckd ldrs: led over 1f out: sn edgd lft: hdd fnl 150yds: hld towards fin* **15/8**[1]
5 **3** *¾* **Diplomatic Force (USA)**[15] 3490 2-9-5 0 GrahamLee 9 75
(Saeed bin Suroor) *hld up: rdn and hdwy over 1f out: ch jst ins fnl f: styd on: hld by front two towards fin* **6/1**
5 **4** *4 ½* **The Kid**[22] 3233 2-9-5 0 RichardKingscote 1 63
(Tom Dascombe) *led: pushed along 3f out: rdn and hdd over 1f out: wknd fnl 150yds* **9/2**[3]
5 **5** *3 ¾* **Our Gabrial (IRE)**[16] 3461 2-9-5 0 TonyHamilton 5 57+
(Richard Fahey) *trckd ldrs: shkn up over 2f out: nt clr run on inner sn after: nrly 2 l down whn n.m.r and hmpd over 1f out: sn lost grnd: n.d after* **12/1**
4 **6** *2 ¾* **Stars Over The Sea (USA)**[15] 3490 2-9-5 0 JoeFanning 4 45+
(Mark Johnston) *rrd s and completely missed break losing abt 12 l: a bhd: nvr on terms: allowed to coast home* **3/1**[2]
00 **7** *2 ½* **Hickster (IRE)**[65] 1930 2-9-5 0 StephenCraine 2 39
(Tom Dascombe) *w ldr: pushed along 3f out: rdn 2f out: wknd over 1f out* **50/1**

1m 29.84s (-0.86) **Going Correction** -0.175s/f (Firm) **7** Ran SP% **113.0**
Speed ratings (Par 94): **97,96,95,90,85 82,79**
toteswingers 1&2 £3.80, 1&3 £7.70, 2&3 £2.40 CSF £22.92 TOTE £10.00: £4.60, £1.80; EX 30.30 Trifecta £121.40 Pool: £1,218.15 - 7.51 winning units.
Owner Godolphin **Bred** Darley **Trained** Newmarket, Suffolk
FOCUS
Probably no more than a fair maiden but the winner was quite impressive.

4022 MADNESS MUSIC NIGHT 20TH JULY MAIDEN STKS 1m
8:45 (8:45) (Class 5) 3-Y-O+ **£2,587** (£770; £384; £192) **Stalls** Low

Form RPR
1 **Mulakim** 3-9-3 0 HarryBentley 6 88
(Saeed bin Suroor) *chsd ldrs: dropped to rr after 2f: pushed along 5f out: rn green: sltly outpcd over 3f out: rdn to improve 2f out: r.o to ld 1f out: in command fnl 100yds: pushed out* **4/1**[2]
3 **2** *3 ¼* **Disco Inferno (IRE)**[13] 3585 3-9-3 0 (t) KierenFallon 2 81
(Brian Meehan) *broke wl: led at stdy pce: pushed along over 2f out: rdn and hdd over 1f out: duelled for 2nd ins fnl f: no imp on wnr fnl 100yds* **8/13**[1]
3 *shd* **Lions Park (IRE)** 3-9-3 0 JoeFanning 1 81
(Mark Johnston) *chsd ldr: chal over 2f out: led over 1f out: sn hdd: duelled for 2nd ins fnl f: no imp on wnr fnl 100yds* **5/1**[3]
4 *3 ¾* **Court Life (IRE)** 3-9-3 0 PaddyAspell 5 72
(Ismail Mohammed) *hld up: effrt on inner over 2f out: nt clr run whn swtchd rt over 1f out: outpcd after* **11/1**

1m 45.13s (1.43) **Going Correction** -0.175s/f (Firm)
WFA 3 from 4yo 9lb **4** Ran SP% **106.9**
Speed ratings (Par 103): **85,81,81,77**
CSF £6.96 TOTE £4.20; EX 6.50 Trifecta £13.10 Pool: £584.78 - 33.25 winning units.
Owner Godolphin **Bred** Darley **Trained** Newmarket, Suffolk
FOCUS
Just the four runners and the early gallop was steady. Muddling form but the winner looks sure to do a fair bit better.

4023 FAMILY FUN DAY HERE 8TH AUGUST H'CAP 1m 2f 95y
9:15 (9:17) (Class 4) (0-85,85) 3-Y-O **£5,175** (£1,540; £769; £384) **Stalls** High

Form RPR
-461 **1** **Double Discount (IRE)**[27] 3105 3-9-4 **82** RichardKingscote 3 91+
(Tom Dascombe) *hld up: hdwy 3f out: led over 1f out: r.o and edgd lft ins fnl f: hld on wl towards fin* **7/2**[2]
51 **2** *½* **Velox**[32] 2930 3-9-5 **83** KierenFallon 4 91+
(Luca Cumani) *s.i.s: in rr: rdn on inner over 2f out: nt clr run whn swtchd rt over 1f out: prog ins fnl f: tk 2nd fnl 100yds: r.o towards fin: nt quite pce to chal wnr* **3/1**[1]
6-23 **3** *2* **Playbill**[39] 2713 3-8-10 **74** (v[1]) RichardHughes 2 78
(Sir Michael Stoute) *trckd ldrs: rdn over 1f out: kpt on u.p ins fnl f: one pce fnl 100yds* **5/1**[3]
1465 **4** *1 ¼* **Marhaba Malayeen (IRE)**[15] 3502 3-8-7 **71** (b) HarryBentley 5 73
(Kevin Ryan) *s.i.s: racd keenly: hld up: in tch after 3f: prom over 3f out: rdn and nt qckn over 1f out: kpt on same pce fnl 100yds* **20/1**
4026 **5** *3 ½* **Salutation (IRE)**[15] 3486 3-9-7 **85** JoeFanning 7 80
(Mark Johnston) *led: pushed along 2f out: rdn and hdd over 1f out: wknd fnl 100yds* **7/2**[2]
10-2 **6** *1* **Beat The Tide**[42] 2624 3-8-0 **71** ConnorBeasley(7) 6 64
(Michael Dods) *trckd ldrs: pushed along and outpcd over 2f out: no imp after* **13/2**

5214 **7** 1 ¾ **Dolphin Village (IRE)**[34] 2878 3-8-9 **73**........................ TonyHamilton 1 63
(Richard Fahey) *chsd ldr: ev ch 2f out: rdn over 1f out: wknd ins fnl f* **10/1**

2m 12.12s (-3.38) **Going Correction** -0.175s/f (Firm) **7** Ran SP% **113.3**
Speed ratings (Par 102): **106,105,104,103,100 99,98**
toteswingers 1&2 £2.30, 1&3 £6.40, 2&3 £2.20 CSF £14.15 TOTE £5.20: £2.30, £2.10; EX 22.20 Trifecta £78.10 Pool: £2,006.46 - 19.25 winning units.
Owner Laurence A Bellman **Bred** Bernard Cooke **Trained** Malpas, Cheshire

FOCUS
A nice little handicap featuring some improving sorts. The pace was fair and the first two came from the back of the field. Both are likely to do better, while the third and fourth were pretty much to form.
T/Plt: £251.50 to a £1 stake. Pool: £73,629.63 - 213.67 winning units T/Qpdt: £82.10 to a £1 stake. Pool: £4,880.79 - 43.95 winning units DO

3338 SANDOWN (R-H)
Friday, July 5

OFFICIAL GOING: Good to firm (good in places; 8.0)
Wind: Almost nil Weather: Fine; very warm

4024 LONDON'S RACE TRACKS RACINGANDMUSIC.CO.UK H'CAP 5f 6y
2:20 (2:22) (Class 3) (0-95,95) 3-Y-O+ **£9,703** (£2,887; £1,443; £721) **Stalls** Low

Form RPR
0050 **1** **Doctor Parkes**[6] 3802 7-9-2 **85**.. NeilCallan 2 96
(Stuart Williams) *chsd ldng pair: rdn to go 2nd 2f out: clsd to ld last 150yds: drvn out* **7/1**[3]
0030 **2** ½ **Joe Packet**[14] 3527 6-9-8 **91**.. JimCrowley 1 100
(Jonathan Portman) *nt wl away to hold pl on inner and sn in midfield: prog 2f out: wnt 3rd jst over 1f out: swtchd lft ins fnl f: r.o to take 2nd nr fin and gaining on wnr* **11/2**[1]
-514 **3** nse **Steps (IRE)**[32] 2937 5-9-9 **95**................................(b) ThomasBrown(3) 10 104
(Roger Varian) *lw: t.k.h: hld up in midfield: n.m.r over 3f out: swtchd to outer 2f out: rdn over 1f out: r.o wl fnl f: gaining at fin* **12/1**
-343 **4** ¾ **Fair Value (IRE)**[28] 3038 5-9-8 **91**.................................... KierenFallon 6 97
(Simon Dow) *led: gng strly 2f out: stretched on over 1f out: hdd & wknd last 150yds* **10/1**
-050 **5** ¾ **Taajub (IRE)**[34] 2865 6-9-12 **95**...................................... AdamKirby 3 101
(Peter Crate) *t.k.h: hld up in midfield: trbld passage fr 2f out whn trying to make prog: r.o last 100yds: nrst fin* **6/1**[2]
5-00 **6** nk **Dungannon**[32] 2937 6-9-5 **88**...................................... JimmyFortune 12 92
(Andrew Balding) *hld up in last quartet fr wd draw: nt clrest of runs whn making prog over 1f out: kpt on but nvr really threatened* **16/1**
3302 **7** nk **Gladiatrix**[7] 3786 4-8-13 **82**..................................(b) RichardHughes 7 83
(Rod Millman) *chsd ldrs: rdn over 2f out: one pce and lost pls fnl f* **6/1**[2]
0100 **8** 1 **Effie B**[13] 3584 3-9-3 **91**..(v[1]) MartinHarley 5 89
(Mick Channon) *racd against rail towards rr: rdn 2f out: n.m.r briefly sn after: no threat but kpt on fnl f* **33/1**
3202 **9** nk **Rylee Mooch**[9] 3682 5-8-8 **77**.................................(e) RobbieFitzpatrick 8 74
(Richard Guest) *chsd ldr: drvn and lost 2nd 2f out: wknd fnl f* **16/1**
5431 **10** hd **Lupo D'Oro (IRE)**[20] 3341 4-9-2 **85**................................ GrahamLee 15 81
(John Best) *hld up in last quartet fr wd draw: rdn over 1f out: styd on fnl f: nrst fin* **20/1**
0003 **11** 2 ½ **Pabusar**[21] 3299 5-9-12 **95**...................................... WilliamBuick 4 82
(Jamie Osborne) *lw: s.s: hld up in last: shkn up briefly and no prog over 1f out: passed 3 rivals nr fin: nvr involved* **8/1**
10-0 **12** ¾ **Edge Closer**[48] 2444 9-9-9 **92**... JamesDoyle 9 76
(Tony Carroll) *lw: chsd ldrs: rdn 2f out: lost pl jst over 1f out: wknd* **20/1**
-006 **13** 1 **Naabegha**[26] 3135 6-9-6 **89**... LiamKeniry 11 70
(Ed de Giles) *prom on outer tl wknd over 1f out: eased ins fnl f* **16/1**
0254 **14** ½ **Kyleakin Lass**[37] 2768 4-9-7 **95**........................... MichaelJMMurphy(5) 14 74
(Paul Fitzsimons) *hld up in last quartet: rdn over 1f out: no prog* **16/1**

59.93s (-1.67) **Going Correction** -0.125s/f (Firm)
WFA 3 from 4yo+ 5lb **14** Ran SP% **120.3**
Speed ratings (Par 107): **108,107,107,105,104 104,103,102,101,101 97,96,94,93**
toteswingers 1&2 £9.10, 1&3 £29.00, 2&3 £30.00 CSF £44.00 CT £476.27 TOTE £8.60: £3.40, £2.50, £4.00; EX 43.30 Trifecta £1024.20 Pool: £2,244.58 - 1.64 winning units.
Owner Mrs S Mason & Partners **Bred** Joseph Heler **Trained** Newmarket, Suffolk

FOCUS
On a warm, sunny day, the going was changed to good to firm, good in places before the first race. The jockeys described it as riding fast but "lovely". A good sprint handicap in which the draw played its part, with the pair drawn nearest the rail the first two home.

4025 CORAL DRAGON STKS (LISTED RACE) 5f 6y
2:50 (2:51) (Class 1) 2-Y-O
£14,461 (£5,482; £2,743; £1,366; £685; £344) **Stalls** Low

Form RPR
014 **1** **Ambiance (IRE)**[15] 3481 2-9-2 0...................................... MartinHarley 2 100
(Mick Channon) *lw: trckd ldng pair: gng strly 2f out: plld out over 1f out: drvn and r.o to ld last 150yds: sn clr* **7/2**[2]
3U1 **2** 1 ½ **Langavat (IRE)**[27] 3079 2-9-2 0.................................. RichardHughes 6 95+
(Richard Hannon) *wnt lft s: racd in 5th and struggling to stay w ldrs fr 1/2-way: drvn on outer over 1f out: styd on wl fnl f to take 2nd last stride* **4/1**[3]
1021 **3** shd **Majestic Alexander (IRE)**[5] 3863 2-8-11 0........................ NeilCallan 3 89
(David Evans) *disp ld against rail: rdn 2f out: def advantage over 1f out: hdd and no ex last 150yds: lost 2nd post* **5/1**
216 **4** 1 **Survived**[16] 3459 2-8-11 0.. GrahamLee 1 86
(William Haggas) *trckd ldng pair: shkn up over 1f out: rdn and styd on same pce fnl f* **3/1**[1]
21 **5** 3 **Fine 'n Dandy (IRE)**[57] 2189 2-9-2 0.......................... RichardKingscote 4 80
(Tom Dascombe) *lw: disp ld to 2f out: shkn up and nt qckn over 1f out: sn lost 2nd and fdd tamely* **3/1**[1]
4140 **6** 5 **Iseemist (IRE)**[14] 3522 2-8-11 0.............................[1] MichaelJMMurphy 5 57
(John Gallagher) *wnt rt s: immediately outpcd and wl bhd in last: nvr a factor but lost no grnd fr 1/2-way* **66/1**

1m 0.25s (-1.35) **Going Correction** -0.125s/f (Firm) **6** Ran SP% **110.4**
Speed ratings (Par 102): **105,102,102,100,96 88**
toteswingers 1&2 £2.00, 1&3 £2.40, 2&3 £3.00 CSF £17.03 TOTE £4.10: £2.00, £2.30; EX 16.10 Trifecta £72.90 Pool: £1,846.07 - 18.98 winning units.
Owner Prince A A Faisal **Bred** John McEnery **Trained** West Ilsley, Berks

FOCUS
A decent juvenile sprint, the best recent winner of which was the prolific and subsequent Group 2 winner Zebedee. The pace was good, setting things up for the closers, and the winner more than confirmed his Norfolk progress.

4026 IRISH STALLION FARMS EBF MAIDEN STKS 7f 16y
3:25 (3:26) (Class 5) 2-Y-O **£3,881** (£1,155; £577; £288) **Stalls** Low

Form RPR
1 **Emirates Galloper (IRE)** 2-9-5 0........................... SilvestreDeSousa 3 84+
(Saeed bin Suroor) *w'like: scope: well-made: swtg: slowest away: rn green in last pair: plld out and rdn over 2f out: gd prog and hrd drvn over 1f out: r.o to ld last 100yds: sn clr* **9/2**[2]
2 1 ¾ **Practising** 2-9-0 0.. RichardThomas 6 74
(Ralph Beckett) *leggy: prom: wnt 2nd over 3f out: led over 2f out: rdn over 1f out: hdd and outpcd last 100yds* **66/1**
3 ½ **Full Day** 2-9-0 0... JimCrowley 9 73
(Ralph Beckett) *w'like: bit bkwd: wl in tch: prog on outer over 2f out to chse ldr wl over 1f out: shkn up and lost 2nd ins fnl f: promising debut* **25/1**
43 **4** 1 ½ **Munjally**[27] 3112 2-9-5 0.. PaulHanagan 7 75
(Richard Hannon) *str: swtg: sltly awkward s: settled in rr: pushed along and prog whn nt clr run then squeezed out 2f out: nt rcvr but kpt on to take 4th last 100yds* **11/4**[1]
0 **5** 2 ¼ **Calrissian (IRE)**[13] 3555 2-9-0 0........................... MichaelJMMurphy(5) 4 68
(Alan Jarvis) *t.k.h: trckd ldrs: disp 2nd briefly wl over 1f out: wknd fnl f* **8/1**
0 **6** nse **Veya (USA)**[38] 2741 2-9-5 0... WilliamBuick 5 70+
(Ed Walker) *str: swtg: trckd ldr to over 3f out: lost pl over 2f out: bmpd wl over 1f out and lost further grnd: r.o again last 100yds* **11/1**
42 **7** 1 ½ **Brownsville (USA)**[8] 3717 2-9-5 0................................. JamesDoyle 10 64
(Mark Johnston) *w'like: str: mde most to over 2f out: steadily wknd* **14/1**
8 1 **Dover The Moon (IRE)** 2-9-5 0................................ RichardHughes 2 62+
(Richard Hannon) *w'like: scope: gd bodied: lw: settled in last trio: pushed along over 2f out: no real prog: nt knocked abt* **7/1**[3]
00 **9** 4 ½ **Cape Arrow**[22] 3238 2-9-5 0.. GrahamLee 12 50
(Paul Cole) *dwlt: mostly in last and rn green: bhd over 2f out* **66/1**
2 **P** **Diapenko**[21] 3291 2-9-5 0.. KierenFallon 8
(Brian Meehan) *trckd ldrs: pushed along and clsng whn broke down 2f out: p.u* **11/4**[1]

1m 31.53s (2.03) **Going Correction** -0.125s/f (Firm) **10** Ran SP% **117.0**
Speed ratings (Par 94): **83,81,80,78,76 76,74,73,68,**
toteswingers 1&2 £87.00, 1&3 £17.60, 2&3 £47.80 CSF £266.52 TOTE £4.80: £2.10, £13.60, £6.20; EX 620.90 Trifecta £2582.30 Part won. Pool: £3,443.10 - 0.67 winning units..
Owner Godolphin **Bred** Darley **Trained** Newmarket, Suffolk

FOCUS
This has proven a good maiden over the years, having recently produced most notably the Group 2 Celebration Mile scorer and Group 1 placed Zacinto. There were several interesting sorts in the line-up and the form was probably up to the recent race average.

4027 AMBANT GALA STKS (LISTED RACE) 1m 2f 7y
4:00 (4:00) (Class 1) 3-Y-O+
£20,982 (£7,955; £3,981; £1,983; £995; £499) **Stalls** Low

Form RPR
3-3 **1** **Mandour (USA)**[40] 2694 4-9-5 116............. Christophe-PatriceLemaire 3 114+
(A De Royer-Dupre, France) *w'like: hld up in 6th: rdn 2f out: prog to chse ldr jst over 1f out: r.o readily to ld last 75yds* **9/4**[1]
22-0 **2** ¾ **Afsare**[16] 3457 6-9-5 116.. JamesDoyle 5 113+
(Luca Cumani) *lw: trckd ldng trio: prog to ld over 2f out: drvn over 1f out: styd on but hdd and outpcd last 75yds* **9/2**[3]
120- **3** nk **Excess Knowledge**[279] 6671 3-8-8 102.......................... WilliamBuick 2 112+
(John Gosden) *sn trckd ldrs in 5th: rdn and outpcd over 2f out: prog over 1f out: styd on wl to take 3rd nr fin* **10/1**
3-05 **4** hd **David Livingston (IRE)**[16] 3458 4-9-5 102...................... PatCosgrave 1 112
(M F De Kock, South Africa) *hld up in 7th: pushed along and outpcd over 2f out: drvn and prog over 1f out: r.o fnl f: nrst fin* **16/1**
1303 **5** 1 **Van Der Neer**[15] 3485 3-8-11 110................................... RichardHughes 6 113
(Richard Hannon) *lw: trckd ldng pair: rdn and nt qckn 3f out: sn outpcd: kpt on u.p fnl 2f: nvr able to chal* **3/1**[2]
-550 **6** 1 **Dick Doughtywylie**[14] 3525 5-9-5 99............................. JimmyFortune 8 108
(John Gosden) *led: rdn and hdd over 2f out: fought on wl tl lost 2nd jst over 1f out: one pce after* **50/1**
0-10 **7** 7 **Mirsaale**[34] 2866 3-8-8 108... NeilCallan 10 95
(James Tate) *mostly chsd ldr to 3f out: wknd 2f out* **12/1**
110- **8** 3 **Black Spirit (USA)**[54] 6855 6-9-5 109................................(t) AdamKirby 9 89
(Clive Cox) *hld up in 8th: shkn up wl over 2f out and no prog: wl btn after* **16/1**
60-0 **9** 7 **Sri Putra**[35] 2840 7-9-5 115... FrankieDettori 11 76
(Roger Varian) *restrained into last trio: pushed along and no rspnse over 3f out: no ch after* **9/1**
/66- **10** 4 **World Domination (USA)**[419] 2081 5-9-5 95..............(b[1]) TomQueally 7 68
(Lady Cecil) *slowly away: t.k.h in last pair: sme prog on outer over 4f out: wknd qckly over 2f out* **33/1**
0-50 **11** 16 **Mendip (USA)**[118] 958 6-9-5 108...........................(p) SilvestreDeSousa 4 38
(Saeed bin Suroor) *swtg: slowly away: hld up in last pair: pushed along over 4f out: wknd over 3f out: eased and t.o* **20/1**

2m 7.29s (-3.21) **Going Correction** -0.125s/f (Firm)
WFA 3 from 4yo+ 11lb **11** Ran SP% **122.2**
Speed ratings (Par 111): **107,106,106,106,105 104,98,96,90,87 74**
toteswingers 1&2 £3.40, 1&3 £6.60, 2&3 £8.40 CSF £12.84 TOTE £3.50: £1.50, £1.50, £4.00; EX 12.90 Trifecta £106.30 Pool: £5,657.06 - 39.88 winning units.
Owner Princess Zahra Aga Khan **Bred** Princess Zahra Aga Khan **Trained** Chantilly, France

FOCUS
Subsequent Eclipse, Champion Stakes and Dubai Duty Free winner David Junior was the best recent winner of this Listed race. This looked a fair renewal, with three interesting 3-y-o contenders to add to the more established older horses. The pace did not look that strong but the first six came clear. The sixth is the key to the form.

4028 CORAL.CO.UK H'CAP 1m 2f 7y
4:35 (4:35) (Class 3) (0-95,93) 3-Y-O+
£12,450 (£3,728; £1,864; £932; £466; £234) **Stalls** Low

Form RPR
1-40 **1** **Code Of Honor**[41] 2661 3-9-0 **90**...................................... JamesDoyle 1 102+
(Henry Candy) *lw: trckd ldrs disputing 5th: rdn over 2f out: prog and drvn over 1f out: r.o to ld last 150yds: sn clr* **4/1**[2]

3213 **2** 3 **Mushaakis (IRE)**[14] 3537 3-8-4 **80** PaulHanagan 10 86
(Mark Johnston) *trckd ldr: led 2f out and sn wnt for home: hdd 150yds out: no ch w wnr but hld on for 2nd* **9/2**[3]

-021 **3** nk **Cashpoint**[29] 3022 8-9-2 **81** WilliamBuick 5 86
(Ian Williams) *trckd ldrs disputing 5th: effrt over 2f out: rdn to take 3rd fnl f: kpt on same pce after* **9/2**[3]

1-01 **4** nk **Al Saham**[23] 3208 4-9-13 **92** SilvestreDeSousa 3 97
(Saeed bin Suroor) *t.k.h: hld up in last quartet: stl there over 1f out: rdn and gd prog fnl f: nrst fin* **7/2**[1]

5055 **5** ½ **Benzanno (IRE)**[35] 2841 4-9-6 **88** ThomasBrown(3) 7 92
(Andrew Balding) *tk fierce hold: hld up in last quartet: pushed along 3f out: drvn and styd on fr over 1f out: nrst fin* **11/1**

0312 **6** 1½ **Tight Lipped (IRE)**[21] 3293 4-8-10 **80** RyanTate(5) 9 81
(James Eustace) *led: urged along 3f out: hdd 2f out: wknd fnl f* **14/1**

3203 **7** 2½ **Mawaakef (IRE)**[33] 2520 5-9-10 **89** FrankieDettori 2 85
(J R Jenkins) *trckd ldng pair: nt qckn over 2f out: sn lost pl and n.m.r: wl btn fnl f* **16/1**

-020 **8** 3¼ **Pilgrims Rest (IRE)**[35] 2839 4-9-9 **88** RichardHughes 4 78
(Richard Hannon) *t.k.h and hld up in last quartet: shkn up briefly 2f out: no hdwy fnl f: nvr involved and eased last 100yds* **10/1**

13-6 **9** 2½ **Jake's Destiny (IRE)**[69] 1848 4-10-0 **93** (t) PatCosgrave 8 78
(George Baker) *trckd ldrs: rdn over 2f out: sn wknd* **25/1**

1066 **10** 1¼ **Carazam (IRE)**[30] 2981 6-8-4 **74** oh2 MichaelJMMurphy(5) 6 57
(William Jarvis) *t.k.h: hld up in last quartet: pushed along in last 2f out: no ch whn nt clr run ins fnl f and eased: nvr involved* **25/1**

2m 10.69s (0.19) **Going Correction** -0.125s/f (Firm)
WFA 3 from 4yo+ 11lb **10** Ran SP% **116.3**
Speed ratings (Par 107): **94,91,91,91,90 89,87,84,82,81**
toteswingers 1&2 £4.20, 1&3 £5.50, 2&3 £4.80 CSF £22.34 CT £82.08 TOTE £4.90: £1.80, £1.90, £1.90; EX 24.10 Trifecta £104.40 Pool: £5,174.11 - 37.15 winning units.
Owner D B Clark/ J J Byrne **Bred** J Byrne And Partners **Trained** Kingston Warren, Oxon

FOCUS
Another good handicap but they went steady early on and the time was 3.4secs slower than the preceding Listed race, and the finish was dominated by the two 3-y-os. Subsequent St Leger winner Encke made a winning reappearance in this last season. The progressive Code Of Honor was quite impressive.

4029 TRAVIS LIVE ON 24TH JULY H'CAP 1m 6f
5:05 (5:05) (Class 4) (0-85,85) 3-Y-0+ **£6,469** (£1,925; £962; £481) **Stalls** Low

Form RPR

2341 **1** **Good Evans**[23] 3206 3-8-0 **72** oh1 KieranO'Neill 5 81+
(Tom Dascombe) *tried to match strides w ldr at furious pce for 2f: settled bhd him after and clr of rest: rdn to chal over 2f out: drvn ahd 150yds out: kpt on* **4/1**[3]

00-4 **2** 1¼ **Bolivia (GER)**[61] 2040 7-10-0 **85** DougieCostello 10 92
(Lucy Wadham) *hld up in 5th: shkn up over 2f out: prog and rdn over 1f out: styd on to take 2nd last 75yds: nt rch wnr* **20/1**

1-00 **3** 1½ **Australia Day (IRE)**[27] 2251 10-9-12 **83** MartinDwyer 3 88
(Paul Webber) *disp ld at furious pce tl allowed to dictate after 2f: rdn and pressed over 2f out: fought on wl but hdd last 150yds: lost 2nd nr fin* **12/1**

/0-0 **4** 4 **Sergeant Ablett (IRE)**[29] 3019 5-9-9 **80** LiamTreadwell 8 80
(Luke Dace) *hld up in 7th: pushed along over 2f out: kpt on one pce fr over 1f out to take 4th nr fin* **66/1**

-321 **5** 1½ **Auld Alliance (IRE)**[21] 3272 3-8-11 **83** JamesDoyle 11 81
(Sir Michael Stoute) *lw: chsd clr ldng pair: rdn over 3f out: no imp and lost 3rd over 1f out: fdd* **9/4**[1]

0012 **6** 1¼ **Dunhoy (IRE)**[19] 3370 5-9-10 **81** MartinHarley 9 77
(Tony Newcombe) *hld up in last trio: rdn and no prog over 3f out: modest late hdwy* **10/1**

5502 **7** ½ **Priors Gold**[57] 2197 6-9-2 **73** JackMitchell 1 69
(Laura Mongan) *hld up in last trio: rdn and no prog over 3f out: plugged on fnl f* **33/1**

-324 **8** 1 **Abundantly**[20] 3344 4-9-4 **75** RichardHughes 4 69
(Hughie Morrison) *hld up in 4th: rdn over 3f out: no imp on clr ldng pair: wknd over 1f out* **7/2**[2]

1-11 **9** ¾ **Albonny (IRE)**[45] 2545 4-8-11 **73** MichaelJMMurphy(5) 7 66
(Alan Jarvis) *hld up in last trio: drvn and no prog over 3f out: nvr a factor* **10/1**

10-3 **10** 27 **Saborido (USA)**[20] 3344 7-9-12 **83** JimCrowley 2 41
(Amanda Perrett) *hld up in midfield: pushed along 5f out: wknd 3f out: t.o* **10/1**

3m 0.32s (-4.18) **Going Correction** -0.125s/f (Firm)
WFA 3 from 4yo+ 15lb **10** Ran SP% **117.2**
Speed ratings (Par 105): **106,105,104,102,101 100,100,99,99,83**
toteswingers 1&2 £9.00, 1&3 £8.00, 2&3 £24.00 CSF £81.74 CT £889.35 TOTE £4.50: £3.00, £5.50, £3.10; EX 81.70 Trifecta £1908.10 Pool: £2,960.89 - 1.16 winning units.
Owner Rawhide Racing **Bred** Newsells Park Stud **Trained** Malpas, Cheshire

FOCUS
An interesting stayers' handicap made more so by some unexposed sorts, including a pair of 3yos towards the bottom of the weights, and one of those came out on top. The pace was fast and the winner deserves plenty of credit.
T/Jkpt: Not won. T/Plt: £2,078.50 to a £1 stake. Pool: £128,538.31 - 45.14 winning units T/Qpdt: £376.30 to a £1 stake. Pool: £6,866.31 - 13.50 winning units JN

3731 WARWICK (L-H)
Friday, July 5

OFFICIAL GOING: Good to firm (7.7)
Wind: Virtually nil Weather: Sunny

4030 FIAT 500 WORLD'S BEST RIDE (S) STKS 1m 2f 188y
2:10 (2:10) (Class 6) 3-Y-0 **£1,940** (£577; £288; £144) **Stalls** Low

Form RPR

5402 **1** **Curl (IRE)**[15] 3488 3-8-1 60 (b) ConnorBeasley(7) 3 51
(Michael Dods) *t.k.h: trckd ldrs: pushed along and outpcd 3f out: pushed along and rallied to chal 1f out: sn led: kpt on wl* **6/4**[2]

5644 **2** 1¾ **Azelle**[14] 3530 3-8-9 65 ow1 PatDobbs 4 49
(Richard Hannon) *trckd ldrs: wnt 2nd travelling ok over 2f out: sn chalng: drvn wl over 1f out: fnd no ex and one pce fr ins fnl f* **5/4**[1]

-000 **3** nk **Jomari (IRE)**[39] 2716 3-8-10 40 NeilFarley(3) 7 52?
(Declan Carroll) *led: rdn whn chal fr 2f out: hdd jst ins fnl f: styd on same pce* **40/1**

4 12 **Maximito** 3-8-13 0 PaoloSirigu 2 29
(Marco Botti) *s.i.s: in rr: hmpd after 2f: in rr but in tch: rdn over 3f out and sn wknd* **11/2**[3]

00-4 **5** 15 **Lilly May (IRE)**[63] 1982 3-8-3 44 NathanAlison(5) 6
(Phil McEntee) *t.k.h: chsd ldrs: rdn over 3f out: wknd sn after* **50/1**

600 **U** **Youmaysee**[14] 3530 3-8-1 38 DanielCremin(7) 1
(Mick Channon) *s.i.s: t.k.h and sn chsng ldrs tl fly-jmpd, slipped and uns rdr after 2f* **14/1**

2m 21.09s (-0.01) **Going Correction** +0.025s/f (Good) **6** Ran SP% **110.9**
Speed ratings (Par 98): **101,99,99,90,79**
toteswingers 1&2 £1.02, 1&3 £5.70, 2&3 £16.10 CSF £3.60 TOTE £2.00: £1.10, £1.30; EX 4.10 Trifecta £34.20 Pool: £1,703.15 - 37.28 winning units.There was no bid for the winner.
Owner Andrew Tinkler **Bred** Naiff Sa & Newtown Stud **Trained** Denton, Co Durham

FOCUS
A weak seller, with the six-strong field looking for their first success. It was run at a steady pace. The winner only needed to repeat her recent form.

4031 BRITISH STALLION STUDS SUPPORTING BRITISH RACING EBF NOVICE STKS 7f 26y
2:40 (2:40) (Class 5) 2-Y-0 **£2,911** (£866; £432; £216) **Stalls** Low

Form RPR

3312 **1** **Fair Ranger**[4] 3890 2-9-2 0 PatDobbs 4 85
(Richard Hannon) *led: rdn and jnd over 1f out: narrowly hdd fnl 110yds and rdr dropped reins: sn rallied to ld and kpt on wl* **5/6**[1]

2 nk **Brazos (IRE)** 2-9-0 0 SebSanders 2 82+
(Clive Brittain) *racd in cl 4th: drvn and gd hdwy over 2f out: j. path appr fnl f: slt ld fnl 110yds: sn hdd: nt quite pce of wnr* **7/1**[3]

01 **3** 1½ **Stormy Paradise (IRE)**[21] 3275 2-9-5 0 MartinLane 1 83
(Brian Meehan) *disp 2nd: rdn and stl pressing wnr 1f out: wknd fnl 75yds* **13/8**[2]

00 **4** 10 **Jazri**[11] 3640 2-9-0 0 LukeMorris 3 50
(Milton Bradley) *disp 2nd: rdn over 2f out: wknd wl over 1f out* **100/1**

1m 27.49s (2.89) **Going Correction** +0.025s/f (Good) **4** Ran SP% **106.1**
Speed ratings (Par 94): **84,83,81,70**
CSF £6.64 TOTE £1.70; EX 6.70 Trifecta £7.20 Pool: £1,284.77 - 133.48 winning units.
Owner D W Barker **Bred** D R Botterill **Trained** East Everleigh, Wilts

FOCUS
Not much pace on for this novice stakes. The winner had the run of the race and ran to form.

4032 MIDSHIRE BUSINESS SYSTEMS CLASSIC MAIDEN STKS 7f 26y
3:10 (3:10) (Class 5) 3-4-Y-0 **£2,587** (£770; £384; £192) **Stalls** Low

Form RPR

53 **1** **Majesty (IRE)**[11] 3619 3-9-5 0 PatDobbs 3 87+
(Richard Hannon) *mde all: drvn along fr 2f out: kpt on wl fnl f* **6/4**[2]

6-22 **2** 2¼ **Shaishee (USA)**[13] 3585 3-9-2 80 PatrickHills(3) 1 81
(Charles Hills) *racd in 4th tl hdwy 3f out and chsd wnr over 2f out: sn rdn: fnd no ex and wl hld fnl f* **4/5**[1]

4 **3** 10 **Mcdelta**[11] 3632 3-9-5 0 SebSanders 5 55
(Geoffrey Deacon) *racd in last pl tl pushed along fr 2f out to take mod 3rd fnl f* **9/1**[3]

0 **4** 4 **Nifty Kier**[18] 3417 4-9-10 0 BrendanPowell(3) 2 51
(Martin Bosley) *chsd ldrs: rdn 3f out: sn btn* **100/1**

0 **5** 2¾ **K Lightning (IRE)**[24] 3176 3-9-5 0 LiamJones 4 38
(J W Hills) *chsd wnr tl over 2f out: sn wknd* **40/1**

1m 23.78s (-0.82) **Going Correction** +0.025s/f (Good)
WFA 3 from 4yo 8lb **5** Ran SP% **109.0**
Speed ratings (Par 103): **105,102,91,86,83**
CSF £2.93 TOTE £1.80: £1.30, £1.10; EX 3.10 Trifecta £5.40 Pool: £2,150.12 - 293.31 winning units.
Owner Highclere Thoroughbred Racing - Archer **Bred** Round Hill Stud **Trained** East Everleigh, Wilts

FOCUS
This looked a match on the book and the market rivals pulled well clear up the straight. Not form to take too literally.

4033 500 GOES LARGE WITH NEW 500L H'CAP 6f
3:45 (3:45) (Class 4) (0-80,79) 3-Y-0 **£4,690** (£1,395; £697; £348) **Stalls** Low

Form RPR

21-4 **1** **Red Explorer (USA)**[16] 3474 3-9-2 **77** PatrickHills(3) 2 86+
(Charles Hills) *in tch: pushed along and hdwy over 2f out: chal u.p appr fnl f: led sn after: drvn clr clsng stages* **11/4**[1]

-430 **2** 3 **Gift Of Music (IRE)**[36] 2806 3-8-9 **67** CathyGannon 3 67
(James Eustace) *chsd ldr: drvn 3f out: styd on to ld over 1f out: hdd ins fnl f: sn outpcd by wnr* **9/1**

0115 **3** 1¾ **Clement (IRE)**[17] 3438 3-9-2 **74** FergusSweeney 1 72
(Eve Johnson Houghton) *in rr: hdwy on ins whn hmpd over 1f out: rallied and kpt on again ins fnl f: gng on cl home* **8/1**

5201 **4** 4 **Roland**[15] 3509 3-8-10 **71** (b) BrendanPowell(3) 4 54
(Kevin Ryan) *led: rdn over 2f out: hung rt u.p and hdd over 1f out: sn btn* **5/1**

1620 **5** 9 **Foxtrot Jubilee (IRE)**[27] 3104 3-9-7 **79** SebSanders 6 35
(Ralph Beckett) *in rr: drvn over 2f out: sn btn: eased whn no ch fnl f* **4/1**[3]

013- **U** **Ziggy's Secret**[325] 5202 3-9-3 **75** LukeMorris 5
(Lucy Wadham) *rrd and uns rdr s* **3/1**[2]

1m 11.17s (-0.63) **Going Correction** +0.025s/f (Good) **6** Ran SP% **109.4**
Speed ratings (Par 102): **105,101,98,93,81**
toteswingers 1&2 £5.10, 1&3 £2.30, 2&3 £11.80 CSF £25.19 TOTE £2.70: £1.30, £6.70; EX 27.00 Trifecta £129.70 Pool: £2,001.53 - 11.56 winning units.
Owner The Hon R J Arculli & Robert Ng **Bred** E Hernandez, K Hernandez & J Duvieilh **Trained** Lambourn, Berks
■ Stewards' Enquiry : Brendan Powell three-day ban; careless riding (19th-21st July).

FOCUS
The pace was honest for this fair handicap. There was drama at the start as the well-backed Ziggy's Secret, who had got unsettled in the stalls, reared leaving the gates and unseated her rider. Only three really mattered and the form is rated cautiously.

4034 NICK BILL MEMORIAL H'CAP (A JOCKEY CLUB GRASSROOTS SPRINT SERIES QUALIFIER) 5f 110y
4:20 (4:21) (Class 5) (0-70,70) 3-Y-0+ **£2,587** (£770; £384; £192) **Stalls** Low

Form RPR

5064 **1** **Sole Danser (IRE)**[10] 3667 5-9-9 **67** (p) SebSanders 8 76
(Milton Bradley) *wnt lft s and s.i.s: drvn and hdwy over 1f out: rdn to ld fnl 110yds: hld on wl* **3/1**[2]

003 **2** nk **Storm Lightning**[8] 3716 4-9-12 **70** TomMcLaughlin 6 78
(Mark Brisbourne) *sn chsng ldr: rdn to ld over 1f out: hdd fnl 110yds: one pce cl home* **7/1**

6-60 **3** 2¼ **Volito**[55] 2281 7-9-0 **58** SamHitchcott 7 58
(Anabel K Murphy) *bmpd s and s.i.s: sn rcvrd to chse ldrs: rdn 2f out: edgd lft and one pce fnl f* **16/1**

0202 **4** *nk* **Belle Bayardo (IRE)**[11] 3622 5-9-9 **67**.............................. LukeMorris 5 66
(Ronald Harris) *led: rdn over 2f out: hdd over 1f out: wknd u.p ins fnl f* **2/1**[1]

-140 **5** *nk* **Amber Heights**[28] 3042 5-9-6 **64**.............................. FergusSweeney 2 62
(Henry Candy) *in tch: hdwy to chse ldrs 2f out: chal u.p over 1f out: styd on same pce fnl f* **4/1**[3]

6006 **6** *2* **Rutterkin (USA)**[18] 3393 5-8-2 **53** oh3 ow2.................. VictorSantos(7) 1 43
(Richard Ford) *in rr: rdn and sme hdwy and rdn over 1f out: nvr rchd ldrs* **11/1**

5626 **7** *1 ¾* **Farmers Dream (IRE)**[11] 3623 6-8-7 **51** oh3.................(vt) MartinLane 3 35
(Derek Shaw) *s.i.s: sn chsd ldrs: wknd wl over 1f out* **20/1**

000/ **8** *10* **Emerald Girl (IRE)**[610] 7247 6-8-3 **52** oh1 ow1.............. JakePayne(5) 4
(Simon Hodgson) *chsd ldrs to 1/2-way* **40/1**

1m 6.21s (0.31) **Going Correction** +0.025s/f (Good) **8 Ran SP% 112.2**
Speed ratings (Par 103): **98,97,94,94,93 91,88,75**
toteswingers 1&2 £4.60, 1&3 £6.50, 2&3 £8.00 CSF £23.27 CT £241.11 TOTE £4.10: £1.10, £3.80, £3.50; EX 21.10 Trifecta £159.60 Pool: £4,134.65 - 19.42 winning units.

Owner E A Hayward **Bred** Airlie Stud **Trained** Sedbury, Gloucs

FOCUS
A modest contest, with three of the field out of the handicap. It was run at a fair pace, with the first two home coming up the stands rail. Straightforward form.

4035 BULMERS H'CAP — 1m 6f 213y
4:55 (4:56) (Class 6) (0-65,65) 3-Y-O+ **£1,940** (£577; £288; £144) **Stalls** Low

Form RPR

4435 **1** **Chapter Five**[32] 2922 6-9-1 **55**.............................. RyanPowell(3) 5 62
(Ian Williams) *chsd ldrs: wnt 2nd 3f out: sn rdn: slt ld jst ins fnl f: kpt on u.p: edgd rt cl home: all out* **7/2**[1]

4210 **2** *shd* **Miss Tiger Lily**[32] 2924 3-8-8 **62**.............................. LiamJones 14 69
(Harry Dunlop) *led: rdn 2f out: narrowly hdd jst ins fnl f: rallied u.p and edgd lft cl home: jst failed* **8/1**[3]

324 **3** *¾* **Danisa**[21] 3271 4-9-8 **64**..................(t) WilliamTwiston-Davies(5) 7 70+
(David Bridgwater) *hld up towards rr but in tch: hdwy fr 3f out: styd on to cl on ldrs ins fnl f: no ex clsng stages* **9/2**[2]

-065 **4** *hd* **Blackstone Vegas**[27] 2563 7-9-3 **54**..................(v) MartinLane 12 61+
(Derek Shaw) *in rr tl hdwy over 2f out: styd on wl fnl f: jst hld whn n.m.r cl home* **12/1**

0-34 **5** *nk* **Into The Wind**[24] 3180 6-9-7 **65**.............................. PatMillman(7) 4 70
(Rod Millman) *s.i.s: in rr: gd hdwy 4f out: chsd ldrs fr 2f out: kpt on fnl f tl no ex clsng stages* **9/1**

4016 **6** *1 ¾* **World Map (IRE)**[4] 3893 3-8-4 **61** 6ex.................. DarrenEgan(3) 2 64
(Mark Johnston) *chsd ldrs: rdn over 2f out: kpt on same pce fnl f* **9/2**[2]

0-04 **7** *4* **Boogie De Bispo**[32] 2924 3-8-0 **54** oh9.................. CathyGannon 10 52
(Stuart Kittow) *in rr: rdn along over 3f out: styd on fnl f: nvr a threat* **16/1**

323- **8** *2* **Sainglend**[9] 7077 8-9-10 **64**.............................. BrendanPowell(3) 13 59
(Sean Curran) *chsd ldrs: rdn over 3f out: wknd fr 2f out* **8/1**[3]

60-0 **9** *nk* **Star Hill**[18] 3406 6-8-13 **50**.............................. FergusSweeney 11 45
(Alan King) *chsd ldrs: wknd u.p over 2f out* **25/1**

0-00 **10** *1 ¾* **Falcun**[32] 2922 6-8-2 **46** oh1..............................(p) OisinMurphy(7) 3 39
(Nikki Evans) *s.i.s: a towards rr* **40/1**

-064 **11** *3 ½* **Mariet**[18] 3412 4-8-8 **52**.............................. RyanWhile(7) 8 40
(Suzy Smith) *chsd ldr: wknd fr ins fnl 3f* **16/1**

3m 19.97s (0.97) **Going Correction** +0.025s/f (Good)
WFA 3 from 4yo+ 17lb **11 Ran SP% 116.6**
Speed ratings (Par 101): **98,97,97,97,97 96,94,93,92,92 90**
toteswingers 1&2 £7.70, 1&3 £3.70, 2&3 £7.70 CSF £31.52 CT £128.67 TOTE £3.90: £1.20, £2.90, £2.10; EX 37.80 Trifecta £163.70 Pool: £3,419.79 - 15.66 winning units.

Owner Mr & Mrs Hutton & Mrs Laing **Bred** Mrs Lesley A Hutton **Trained** Portway, Worcs

■ Stewards' Enquiry : Brendan Powell four-day ban; used whip above permitted level (19th-22nd July).

Oisin Murphy five-day ban; used whip when out of contention (19th-23rd July).

FOCUS
An open yet modest staying contest that was run at a messy pace. It paid to race prominently and there was a blanket finish. The third and fourth are the best guides.

4036 FOLLOW US ON TWITTER @WARWICKRACES APPRENTICE H'CAP — 1m 4f 134y
5:25 (5:25) (Class 6) (0-60,60) 4-Y-O+ **£1,940** (£577; £288; £144) **Stalls** Low

Form RPR

00-2 **1** **On Stage**[52] 2350 4-9-2 **55**.............................. PatMillman 4 65+
(Stuart Kittow) *chsd ldrs: wnt 2nd 6f out: drvn to ld over 1f out: pushed out* **1/1**[1]

0206 **2** *3 ½* **Youm Jamil (USA)**[28] 3037 6-8-5 **52**.................. AidenBlakemore(8) 7 56
(Tony Carroll) *hld up in rr but in tch: wnt wl bnd 3f out: hdwy over 2f out: pushed along to chse wnr fnl f but sn fnd no ex* **5/1**[3]

33-6 **3** *½* **Finch Flyer (IRE)**[15] 3512 6-8-10 **49**..................(p) EoinWalsh 6 53
(Aytach Sadik) *chsd ldrs: lost position fr 4f out and n.m.r bnd 3f out: styd on over 1f out and tk 3rd fnl 110yds: nt rch ldng duo* **10/1**

4330 **4** *3* **Tram Express (FR)**[22] 3248 9-8-12 **54**..................(t) OisinMurphy(3) 1 53
(Shaun Lycett) *chsd ldrs: rdn 3f out: wknd wl over 1f out* **9/2**[2]

5 *1 ¼* **Up In Flames (IRE)**[53] 6858 4-9-4 **60**..................(b) JordanVaughan(3) 2 57
(Martin Keighley) *led: racd alone far side and hdd over 1f out: wknd qckly fnl f* **20/1**

050/ **6** *1* **Almowj**[575] 3716 10-8-4 **46** oh1.............................. DanielCremin(3) 5 41
(George Jones) *in rr: kpt on same pce fnl 2f and nvr nr ldrs* **100/1**

0040 **7** *30* **Lady Tycoon**[11] 3642 4-8-8 **47**.............................. MatthewHopkins 3
(Mark Brisbourne) *chsd ldr to 6f out: wkng whn n.m.r bnd 3f out* **7/1**

2m 46.91s (2.31) **Going Correction** +0.025s/f (Good) **7 Ran SP% 112.2**
Speed ratings (Par 101): **93,90,90,88,87 87,68**
toteswingers 1&2 £2.00, 1&3 £2.50, 2&3 £5.10 CSF £6.12 TOTE £1.70: £2.20, £2.00; EX 6.00 Trifecta £30.80 Pool: £2,655.83 - 64.46 winning units.

Owner Eric Gadsden **Bred** Mrs M Fairbairn And E Gadsden **Trained** Blackborough, Devon

FOCUS
Very few came here in any sort of form in this ordinary race. It was run at a steady pace and the form makes sense rated through the second and third.

T/Plt: £18.20 to a £1 stake. Pool: £36,577.58 - 1,466.46 winning units T/Qpdt: £9.50 to a £1 stake. Pool: £2,442.22 - 188.70 winning units ST

4037 - 4041a (Foreign Racing) - See Raceform Interactive

3970 HAMBURG (R-H)
Friday, July 5

OFFICIAL GOING: Turf: good

4042a GROSSER PREIS VON LOTTO HAMBURG (HAMBURG-TROPHY) (GROUP 3) (3YO+) (TURF) — 1m 2f
6:10 (12:00) 3-Y-O+

£26,016 (£8,943; £4,471; £2,439; £1,626; £1,219)

RPR

1 **Neatico (GER)**[12] 3612 6-9-4 0.............................. AStarke 6 113
(P Schiergen, Germany) *hld up in tch: swtchd to outer and rdn on turn into st: r.o to ld over 1f out: qcknd clr ins fnl f: pushed out: comf* **27/10**[1]

2 *7* **Petit Chevalier (FR)**[10] 3672 5-9-2 0.............................. EddyHardouin 2 97
(W Mongil, Germany) *midfield in tch on inner: swtchd out and rdn over 1f out: readily outpcd by wnr ent fnl f: styd on for remote 2nd* **57/10**

3 *1 ¾* **Russian Tango (GER)**[27] 6-9-2 0.............................. EPedroza 5 94
(A Wohler, Germany) *midfield in tch: rdn and ev ch 2f out: outpcd by wnr ent fnl f: styd on and wnt 3rd cl home* **16/5**[2]

4 *nk* **Quinindo (GER)**[62] 5-9-2 0.............................. SHellyn 4 93
(Elfie Schnakenberg, Germany) *pressed ldr on outer: jnd ldr 5f out: rdn 2f out: hdd over 1f out and readily outpcd by wnr: kpt on but dropped to 4th cl home* **176/10**

5 *3* **Technokrat (IRE)**[36] 2822 5-9-2 0..............................(b) APietsch 3 87
(W Hickst, Germany) *slow to stride and pushed along in rr: sn detached in last and drvn: wl bhd 2f out: consented to run on ent fnl f and wnt 5th towards fin: nvr a factor* **19/5**

6 *1 ¾* **Szoff (GER)** 3-8-3 0.............................. CristianDemuro 1 81
(W Giedt, Germany) *led: jnd 5f out: rdn 2f out: hdd over 1f out: no ex and btn ent fnl f: fdd and eased* **9/2**

7 *¾* **Destor (GER)**[26] 3-8-3 0.............................. JBojko 7 80
(U Stech, Germany) *midfield in tch on outer: rdn 2f out: sn outpcd and btn: fdd and dropped to last* **18/5**[3]

2m 6.69s (126.69)
WFA 3 from 5yo+ 11lb **7 Ran SP% 131.9**
WIN (incl. 10 euro stake): 37. PLACES: 29, 32. SF: 266.

Owner Gestut Ittlingen **Bred** Gestut Hof Ittlingen **Trained** Germany

3969 DEAUVILLE (R-H)
Friday, July 5

OFFICIAL GOING: Turf: good; fibresand: standard

4043a PRIX DE SAINT-PATRICK (LISTED RACE) (3YO COLTS & GELDINGS) (TURF) — 1m (R)
1:50 (12:00) 3-Y-O **£22,357** (£8,943; £6,707; £4,471; £2,235)

RPR

1 **Zhiyi (USA)**[31] 3-8-11 0.............................. StephanePasquier 8 105
(P Bary, France) **11/10**[1]

2 *¾* **Kapstadt (FR)**[30] 3007 3-8-11 0..................(p) IoritzMendizabal 5 103
(F Doumen, France) **15/1**

3 *1* **Star Prince (FR)**[239] 7664 3-8-11 0.............................. ChristopheSoumillon 1 101
(J-C Rouget, France) **19/5**[2]

4 *nk* **Pont Neuilly (FR)**[27] 3128 3-8-11 0.............................. Pierre-CharlesBoudot 9 100
(Y De Nicolay, France) **10/1**

5 *½* **Etalondes (FR)**[54] 2298 3-8-11 0.............................. GregoryBenoist 6 99
(J-C Rouget, France) **7/1**[3]

6 *snk* **Boomshackerlacker (IRE)**[35] 2843 3-8-11 0.............................. OlivierPeslier 4 99
(George Baker) *chsd ldr on inner: rdn 2f out: nt clr run on rail tl ins fnl f: kpt on once in the clr but nvr able to chal* **13/1**

7 *½* **Nabucco (GER)**[46] 2527 3-8-11 0..............................(p) AnthonyCrastus 3 97
(R Rohne, Germany) **52/1**

8 *1 ¼* **Far Afield**[52] 2357 3-8-11 0.............................. MaximeGuyon 7 94
(A Fabre, France) **10/1**

9 *shd* **El Dorado (FR)** 3-8-11 0.............................. NicolasPerret 2 94
(K Borgel, France) **19/1**

1m 41.45s (0.65) **9 Ran SP% 119.4**
WIN (incl. 1 euro stake): 2.10. PLACES: 1.30, 2.40, 1.50. DF: 14.60. SF: 17.10.

Owner Niarchos Family **Bred** Flaxman Holdings Limited **Trained** Chantilly, France

4005 BEVERLEY (R-H)
Saturday, July 6

OFFICIAL GOING: Good to firm (watered; 9.2)
Wind: Light across Weather: Hot and dry

4044 AWARD-WINNING COACHMAN CARAVANS MAIDEN AUCTION STKS — 7f 100y
1:55 (2:09) (Class 6) 2-Y-O **£2,385** (£704; £352) **Stalls** Low

Form RPR

5522 **1** **Shot In The Sun (IRE)**[11] 3648 2-7-12 0.............................. SamanthaBell(7) 4 69+
(Richard Fahey) *hld up in tch: hdwy over 2f out: chsd ldrs over 1f out: swtchd lft and rdn to chse ldr ins fnl f: styd on wl to ld nr fin* **6/1**

2322 **2** *hd* **Cockney Bob**[14] 3574 2-8-9 0.............................. JohnFahy 1 73
(J S Moore) *led: rdn along 2f out: drvn ins fnl f: hdd and no ex nr fin* **9/4**[1]

2 **3** *3 ½* **George The First**[14] 3588 2-8-12 0.............................. PhillipMakin 8 68
(Kevin Ryan) *trckd ldr: cl up 3f out: rdn along wl over 1f out: drvn and one pce fnl f* **4/1**[3]

5 **4** *1 ¼* **Crakehall Lad (IRE)**[37] 2793 2-9-0 0.............................. RobertWinston 6 67
(Alan Swinbank) *trckd ldrs: hdwy on outer over 2f out: sn rdn and kpt on fnl f* **11/2**

23 **5** *3 ½* **Supa U**[29] 3064 2-8-6 0.............................. DavidAllan 7 50
(Tim Easterby) *t.k.h: sn chsng ldng pair: effrt on outer and ev ch 2f out: sn rdn and wknd* **5/2**[2]

6 *6* **Captain Cleo (IRE)** 2-8-4 0..............................(t) JamesSullivan 2 34
(David Peter Nagle, Ire) *plld hrd: trckd ldrs: effrt on inner over 2f out: rdn along wl over 1f out: sn wknd* **25/1**

0 7 4 **Bar Shy**[35] 2883 2-8-10 0 DuranFentiman 9 30
(Tim Easterby) *dwlt: green and a bhd* **16/1**

1m 33.67s (-0.13) **Going Correction** -0.30s/f (Firm) 7 Ran SP% **118.7**
Speed ratings (Par 92): **88,87,83,82,78 71,66**
toteswingers 1&2 £3.50, 1&3 £3.40, 2&3 £2.00 CSF £21.05 TOTE £6.00: £3.50, £1.40; EX 20.10 Trifecta £36.80 Pool: £1046.71 - 21.31 winning units.
Owner Middleham Park Racing XXX & Partner **Bred** Henry O'Callaghan **Trained** Musley Bank, N Yorks
■ Samantha Bell's first winner in Britain, to go with ten in Ireland.

FOCUS
Nothing more than a modest event. There was a lengthy delay to the start as Bertha Burnett became upset in the stalls, when the field looked all set to be released, and eventually burst out underneath them. The remaining runners were taken out and reloaded when the track was clear. Straightforward form, the runner-up setting the level.

4045 ELTHERINGTON STKS (H'CAP) 7f 100y
2:30 (2:30) (Class 5) (0-70,70) 3-Y-0 **£3,234** (£962; £481; £240) **Stalls** Low

Form RPR
5011 1 **Just Paul (IRE)**[18] 3445 3-8-10 **62** DeclanCannon(3) 2 68
(Philip Kirby) *trckd ldrs: hdwy over 2f out: rdn to ld appr fnl f: drvn and hld on wl towards fin* **3/1**[1]

5540 2 nk **Relight My Fire**[12] 3629 3-8-11 **60** (b) DavidAllan 4 65
(Tim Easterby) *prom: effrt over 2f out: rdn and ev ch over 1f out: drvn and styng on whn n.m.r and swtchd rt wl ins fnl f: kpt on strly nr fin* **8/1**

5522 3 hd **Loucal**[9] 3739 3-8-11 **60** (b) PJMcDonald 6 64
(Noel Quinlan) *hld up towards rr: hdwy 2f out: rdn to chse ldrs and edgd lft over 1f out: styng on to chal whn edgd rt ins fnl f: drvn and kpt on wl towards fin* **9/2**[3]

1353 4 4 ½ **Red Paladin (IRE)**[15] 3546 3-9-6 **69** (p) PaulMulrennan 10 64
(Kevin Ryan) *wnt lft s: sn cl up: rdn to ld wl over 1f out: hdd appr fnl f: hld whn sltly hmpd last 100yds* **5/1**

630 5 ½ **My Claire**[19] 3418 3-7-13 **51** oh2 (p) NeilFarley(3) 5 43
(Nigel Tinkler) *hld up towards rr: hdwy over 2f out: rdn to chse ldrs over 1f out: sn no imp* **14/1**

624 6 1 ¾ **Excellent Addition (IRE)**[12] 3629 3-9-2 **65** DavidNolan 3 52
(David O'Meara) *led: rdn along over 2f out: hdd wl over 1f out: drvn and grad wknd appr fnl f* **10/3**[2]

2400 7 6 **Taxiformissbyron**[9] 3730 3-8-11 **60** TomEaves 9 32
(Michael Herrington) *hld up towards rr: hdwy on outer to chse ldrs wl over 2f out: rdn wl over 1f out: sn wknd* **33/1**

5314 8 3 ¾ **Botteen (IRE)**[57] 2229 3-9-7 **70** PhillipMakin 8 33
(William Haggas) *chsd ldrs: rdn along wl over 2f out: sn wknd* **9/1**

600- 9 5 **Joeluke**[273] 6889 3-7-13 **55** EvaMoscrop(7) 1
(Philip Kirby) *dwlt and outpcd and in rr: bhd and rdn whn hung bdly lft 2f out* **33/1**

1m 31.99s (-1.81) **Going Correction** -0.30s/f (Firm) 9 Ran SP% **116.6**
Speed ratings (Par 100): **98,97,97,92,91 89,82,78,72**
toteswingers 1&2 £12.90, 1&3 £1.50, 2&3 £12.90 CSF £27.97 CT £105.90 TOTE £3.40: £1.70, £2.40, £1.60; EX 39.20 Trifecta £91.00 Pool: £787.67 - 6.48 winning units.
Owner Mr and Mrs Paul Chapman **Bred** Oghill House Stud **Trained** Middleham, N Yorks
■ Stewards' Enquiry : David Nolan caution; careless riding.

FOCUS
A competitive contest for some modest types. A length personal best from the winner.

4046 BRITISH STALLION STUDS E B F LEISURE FURNISHINGS MAIDEN STKS 5f
3:05 (3:07) (Class 5) 2-Y-0 **£3,881** (£1,155; £577; £288) **Stalls** Low

Form RPR
0 1 **Tweety Pie (IRE)**[29] 3064 2-8-11 0 NeilFarley(3) 8 69
(Declan Carroll) *mde all: rdn over 1f out: drvn ins fnl f: hld on gamely towards fin* **50/1**

360 2 nk **Sefaat**[18] 3424 2-9-0 0 (t) TomEaves 9 68
(Brian Meehan) *chsd wnr: cl up over 1f out: rdn to chal ent fnl f: sn drvn and ev ch: no ex towards fin* **7/4**[1]

33 3 nse **Bounty Girl (IRE)**[16] 3500 2-9-0 0 DavidAllan 1 68
(Tim Easterby) *chsd ldng pair: effrt wl over 1f out: sn rdn to chal and ev ch ins fnl f: sn drvn and no ex towards fin* **11/4**[2]

6 4 1 ¼ **Le Laitier (FR)**[22] 3288 2-9-5 0 PJMcDonald 7 68
(Scott Dixon) *chsd ldrs: rdn wl over 1f out: kpt on fnl f: nrst fin* **28/1**

63 5 shd **Nelson's Pride**[17] 3461 2-9-0 0 PhillipMakin 5 63
(Kevin Ryan) *chsd ldrs: rdn along wl over 1f out: drvn and keeping on whn n.m.r and swtchd rt ins fnl f: one pce after* **11/2**[3]

05 6 ¾ **Mfiftythreedotcom (IRE)**[10] 3680 2-9-5 0 TonyHamilton 10 67+
(Richard Fahey) *towards rr: hdwy 2f out: rdn and kpt on fnl f: nrst fin* **16/1**

0 7 ½ **Two Shades Of Grey (IRE)**[14] 3565 2-9-5 0 LeeTopliss 3 65+
(Richard Fahey) *towards rr: pushed along 1/2-way: hdwy on inner over 1f out: rdn and styng on whn nt clr run and hmpd ins fnl f: nt rcvr* **12/1**

8 1 ¼ **Hoof's So Lucky** 2-8-10 0 GrahamGibbons 2 50+
(Michael Easterby) *dwlt and in rr tl styd on appr fnl f: nrst fin* **8/1**

9 nk **Snugfit Sam** 2-9-1 0 MichaelO'Connell 6 54+
(John Quinn) *dwlt: sn in midfield: rdn along 2f out: styd on appr fnl f: nrst fin* **16/1**

0 10 1 ½ **Laraaj (IRE)**[30] 3023 2-9-0 0 RobertWinston 13 47+
(David Barron) *a towards rr* **20/1**

11 15 **Reale Silenzio** 2-8-10 0 JamesSullivan 12
(John Weymes) *a in rr: bhd and eased over 1f out* **50/1**

12 3 ¾ **Tinsill** 2-8-12 0 DeclanCannon(3) 11
(Nigel Tinkler) *chsd ldrs: rdn along 1/2-way: sn wknd: bhd and eased fnl f* **40/1**

13 1 **Poco Piccolo** 2-8-12 0 BillyCray(3) 14
(Deborah Sanderson) *wnt lft s: a in rr: bhd and eased fnl f* **33/1**

1m 3.66s (0.16) **Going Correction** -0.175s/f (Firm) 13 Ran SP% **126.5**
Speed ratings (Par 94): **91,90,90,88,88 87,86,84,83,81 57,51,49**
toteswingers 1&2 £10.60, 1&3 £26.90, 2&3 £2.50 CSF £140.02 TOTE £55.20: £8.70, £1.20, £1.40; EX 373.70 Trifecta £1245.50 Part won. Pool: £1,660.77 - 0.01 winning units..
Owner J G Johnson **Bred** Team Valor International & Aron Wellman **Trained** Sledmere, E Yorks

FOCUS
A very ordinary maiden, rated around the second, third and fifth.

4047 COACHMAN CARAVANS QUALITY H'CAP 5f
3:40 (3:44) (Class 4) (0-85,85) 3-Y-0+ **£6,469** (£1,925; £962; £481) **Stalls** Low

Form RPR
/06- 1 **Ziggy Lee**[406] 2507 7-9-2 **82** JordanNason(7) 2 90
(Geoffrey Harker) *in tch: hdwy wl over 1f out: swtchd lft and rdn ent fnl f: led last 75yds* **11/1**

0205 2 ¾ **Flash City (ITY)**[14] 3561 5-9-7 **80** (vt) PaulMulrennan 3 85
(Bryan Smart) *trckd ldrs on inner: hdwy over 1f out: rdn to ld ent fnl f: sn drvn: edgd lft and hdd last 75yds: no ex* **12/1**

6250 3 nk **Waking Warrior**[21] 3351 5-8-10 **76** (tp) KevinStott(7) 11 80
(Kevin Ryan) *hld up in rr: hdwy on wd outside over 1f out: sn rdn and str run ins fnl f: hung rt and fin wl* **6/1**[3]

5404 4 nk **Fitz Flyer (IRE)**[8] 3776 7-9-11 **84** (v) TonyHamilton 6 87
(David Nicholls) *hld up in tch: hdwy over 1f out: nt clr run ins fnl f: sn rdn and kpt on wl towards fin* **4/1**[1]

2200 5 hd **Lenny Bee**[18] 3441 7-9-6 **79** (t) PhillipMakin 1 81
(Garry Moss) *cl up: led 1/2-way: rdn over 1f out: hdd and drvn ent fnl f: kpt on same pce* **14/1**

0000 6 1 ¼ **Caranbola**[21] 3351 7-8-13 **75** NeilFarley(3) 16 73
(Mel Brittain) *in tch on wd outside: rdn and hdwy over 1f out: n.m.r ins fnl f: kpt on: nrst fin* **20/1**

0-06 7 hd **Burning Thread (IRE)**[29] 3038 6-9-5 **78** (b[1]) AdamBeschizza 9 75
(Tim Etherington) *trckd ldrs: hdwy over 1f out: drvn and ch ent fnl f: kpt on same pce* **25/1**

-620 8 shd **Indian Trail**[14] 3569 13-8-11 **70** (b) PaulQuinn 12 67
(David Nicholls) *sltly hmpd s: sn swtchd rt and bhd: gd hdwy over 1f out: rdn and n.m.r whn swtchd rt ins fnl f: kpt on wl towards fin* **25/1**

1064 9 nk **Bedloe's Island (IRE)**[22] 3299 8-9-12 **85** DavidNolan 7 84+
(David O'Meara) *hld up towards rr: hdwy wl over 1f out: rdn and styng on whn nt clr run and hmpd ins fnl f: nt rcvr* **5/1**[2]

0001 10 2 ½ **Noodles Blue Boy**[9] 3716 7-9-4 **77** GrahamGibbons 5 63
(Ollie Pears) *chsd ldrs: rdn over 1f out: wknd ent fnl f* **17/2**

0-10 11 nse **China Excels**[14] 3569 6-8-0 **66** oh3 NoelGarbutt(7) 14 52
(Sue Smith) *wnt rt s and qckly away: led to 1/2-way: cl up tl rdn over 1f out and grad wknd* **20/1**

0214 12 nk **Lost In Paris (IRE)**[21] 3331 7-9-1 **74** (p) DavidAllan 4 59
(Tim Easterby) *hld up: a towards rr* **7/1**

2646 13 1 ¼ **Diamond Blue**[16] 3505 5-8-8 **67** ow1 (p[1]) TomEaves 10 48
(Richard Whitaker) *hld up towards rr: hdwy over 1f out: rdn and n.m.r ent fnl f: n.d* **14/1**

1250 14 1 ½ **Oldjoesaid**[42] 2669 9-9-7 **80** RussKennemore 13 55
(Paul Midgley) *dwlt and sltly hmpd s: a in rr* **20/1**

1000 15 hd **Towbee**[10] 3682 4-9-6 **79** JamesSullivan 8 54
(Michael Easterby) *nvr bttr than midfield* **33/1**

1m 1.78s (-1.72) **Going Correction** -0.175s/f (Firm) 15 Ran SP% **128.3**
Speed ratings (Par 105): **106,104,104,103,103 101,101,101,100,96 96,96,94,91,91**
toteswingers 1&2 £22.10, 1&3 £48.30, 2&3 £26.50 CSF £129.97 CT £908.43 TOTE £15.90: £5.10, £5.00, £2.50; EX 193.00 Trifecta £1168.40 Part won. Pool: £1,557.99 - 0.04 winning units..
Owner Rothmere Racing Limited **Bred** Ian Allan **Trained** Thirkleby, N Yorks

FOCUS
Being drawn low here was beneficial, as the first two home came from stalls two and three. However, each-way punters were left frustrated when two horses, both with wide draws, were taken out earlier in the day, meaning a 17-runner handicap ended up one short of the number required for four places. The second and fifth help set the standard.

4048 C.G.I. IN MEMORY OF AUDREY MOXON H'CAP 1m 100y
4:15 (4:15) (Class 5) (0-75,74) 3-Y-0 **£3,881** (£1,155; £577; £288) **Stalls** Low

Form RPR
0410 1 **Zaitsev (IRE)**[23] 3232 3-9-3 **70** RobertWinston 2 78
(Ollie Pears) *t.k.h early: mde all: pushed clr 2f out: rdn and kpt on wl fnl f* **3/1**[1]

-260 2 1 ¼ **Orions Hero (IRE)**[29] 3067 3-9-1 **68** (p) TonyHamilton 6 73
(Richard Fahey) *trckd ldrs: hdwy 2f out: rdn over 1f out: drvn and kpt on to chse wnr ins fnl f: no imp towards fin* **9/1**

4505 3 1 **Starlight Symphony (IRE)**[11] 3666 3-9-4 **71** (b[1]) JohnFahy 1 74
(Eve Johnson Houghton) *hld up towards rr: hdwy 2f out: sn rdn along: styd on u.p fnl f: nrst fin* **3/1**[1]

3242 4 ½ **Tanawar (IRE)**[21] 3327 3-9-0 **67** (b) PhillipMakin 8 69
(William Haggas) *trckd ldng pair: chsd wnr 3f out: rdn 2f out: drvn and one pce appr fnl f* **11/2**[3]

1 5 5 **Nonotnow**[24] 3191 3-9-3 **70** DavidAllan 5 60
(Tim Easterby) *hld up in rr: pushed along 3f out: effrt whn n.m.r and green 2f out: plugged on one pce after* **5/1**[2]

3250 6 4 ½ **Nordikhab (IRE)**[20] 3369 3-8-7 **67** [1] KevinStott(7) 7 47
(Kevin Ryan) *hld up in rr: effrt and sme hdwy on outer over 2f out: sn rdn and n.d* **7/1**

3030 7 2 ¼ **Old Man Clegg**[44] 2593 3-9-7 **74** JamesSullivan 4 49
(Michael Easterby) *sn chsng wnr: rdn along wl over 2f out: sn wknd* **12/1**

0-00 8 4 ½ **Cumbrian Craic**[14] 3566 3-8-13 **66** GrahamGibbons 3 30
(Tim Easterby) *t.k.h: chsd ldrs: rdn along on inner 3f out: sn wknd* **14/1**

1m 44.89s (-2.71) **Going Correction** -0.30s/f (Firm) 8 Ran SP% **118.9**
Speed ratings (Par 100): **101,99,98,98,93 88,86,82**
toteswingers 1&2 £5.80, 1&3 £11.10, 2&3 £11.60 CSF £32.74 CT £89.63 TOTE £5.10: £1.20, £2.70, £1.80; EX 38.90 Trifecta £344.70 Pool: £1651.44 - 3.59 winning units..
Owner Mrs Z Wentworth **Bred** J F Tuthill **Trained** Norton, N Yorks

FOCUS
An ordinary handicap in which the winner built on his Ripon victory, with the second back to his reappearance form.

4049 POWERPART FILLIES' H'CAP 1m 1f 207y
4:50 (4:50) (Class 5) (0-70,60) 3-Y-0 **£3,234** (£962; £481; £240) **Stalls** Low

Form RPR
545R 1 **Sandy's Row (USA)**[4] 3917 3-9-6 **59** J-PGuillambert 6 69
(Mark Johnston) *sn led: rdn along over 2f out and sn clr: kpt on strly u.p fnl f* **13/2**

0-26 2 2 ½ **Chloe's Image**[23] 3251 3-8-13 **55** DeclanCannon(3) 8 60
(Philip Kirby) *hld up in tch: hdwy 3f out: rdn to chse wnr over 1f out: sn drvn and no imp* **10/1**

-004 3 3 ½ **Bayan Kasirga (IRE)**[33] 2915 3-9-6 **59** TonyHamilton 1 57
(Richard Fahey) *hld up: hdwy wl over 2f out: rdn over 1f out: kpt on u.p fnl f* **9/1**

0-16 4 shd **Chocolate Block (IRE)**[16] 3497 3-9-3 **56** PhillipMakin 2 54
(William Haggas) *sn trcking wnr: effrt 3f out: rdn 2f out: drvn and one pce fr over 1f out* **2/1**[1]

404 5 1 **Duchess Of Dreams**[8] 3793 3-8-1 **47** NoelGarbutt(7) 7 43
(Richard Guest) *hld up towards rr: hdwy 3f out: rdn to chse ldrs over 2f out: sn drvn and one pce* **16/1**

4453 6 1 ¾ **Dalaway (IRE)**[10] 3675 3-9-4 **60** CharlesBishop(3) 3 52
(Mick Channon) *hld up in rr: sme hdwy wl over 2f out: rdn along wl over 1f out: n.d* **11/2**[3]

40-3 **7** *13* **Perfect Pose (IRE)**[19] 3398 3-9-6 **59**............................ PaulMulrennan 4 25
(Michael Dods) *towards rr whn stmbld after 1f: bhd after* **7/1**

0-02 **8** *2¼* **Isle Of Beauty**[17] 3463 3-8-10 **49**...................(p) GrahamGibbons 5 11
(Tom Dascombe) *trckd ldrs: effrt on inner 3f out: sn rdn along and wknd over 2f out* **5/1[2]**

0-50 **9** *7* **Lucky Prize**[27] 3137 3-8-3 **45**.. NeilFarley(3) 9
(Mel Brittain) *prom: rdn along over 3f out: sn wknd* **28/1**

2m 4.16s (-2.84) **Going Correction** -0.30s/f (Firm) **9** Ran SP% **119.6**
Speed ratings (Par 97): **99,97,94,94,93 91,81,79,74**
toteswingers 1&2 £5.70, 1&3 £17.90, 2&3 £17.90 CSF £71.65 CT £594.12 TOTE £8.90: £3.00, £3.30, £1.80; EX 91.70 Trifecta £1058.90 Part won. Pool: £1,411.94 - 0.01 winning units..
Owner Sheikh Hamdan Bin Mohammed Al Maktoum **Bred** Darley **Trained** Middleham Moor, N Yorks

FOCUS
The winner broke smartly before making all. She had refused to race only four days previously and this was a personal best. There are one or two doubts over the form.

4050 COACHMAN MAIDEN STKS — 5f
5:25 (5:25) (Class 5) 3-Y-O+ **£3,234** (£962; £481; £240) **Stalls** Low

Form RPR

4-02 **1** **Funding Deficit (IRE)**[17] 3479 3-9-5 73..................... GrahamGibbons 2 69
(David Barron) *mde all: rdn over 1f out: drvn ins fnl f: edgd lft and kpt on wl towards fin* **11/10[1]**

30- **2** *1½* **Meeting In Paris (IRE)**[271] 6936 3-9-0 0...................... TonyHamilton 6 58
(Richard Fahey) *chsd ldrs: rdn over 1f out: hdwy ent fnl f: sn swtchd rt and drvn: kpt on wl towards fin* **15/8[2]**

0-02 **3** *nse* **Niceonemyson**[15] 3547 4-9-3 54...................................... KevinStott(7) 7 65
(Christopher Wilson) *cl up: rdn over 1f out and ev ch ent fnl f: sn drvn and no ex last 75yds* **8/1**

06-P **4** *2¾* **Copper To Gold**[63] 2006 4-8-12 0..................................... GaryMahon(7) 9 50
(Robin Bastiman) *towards rr and sn pushed along: swtchd lft to outer after 2f: rdn 2f out: styd on wl fnl f: nrst fin* **33/1**

3 **5** *1½* **Dennis**[14] 3593 3-9-0 0... DarylByrne(5) 8 48
(Tim Easterby) *chsd ldrs: rdn 2f out: sn drvn and one pce* **7/1[3]**

0- **6** *2¾* **Lichen Angel**[339] 4710 3-9-0 0... PaulQuinn 10 33
(Richard Whitaker) *in tch: rdn along over 2f out: no hdwy* **20/1**

00- **7** *4½* **Misu Mac**[297] 6132 3-9-0 0.. AndrewElliott 3 17
(Neville Bycroft) *sn outpcd and a in rr* **28/1**

00 **8** *10* **Son Of Neptune**[39] 2752 3-9-2 0.............................. DeclanCannon(3) 4
(Nigel Tinkler) *sn outpcd and a in rr* **50/1**

9 *15* **Playful Promises (IRE)**[98] 1256 3-9-0 0........................ PhillipMakin 12
(David Peter Nagle, Ire) *cl up on outer: rdn along over 2f out: sn hung lft and lost pl: eased over 1f out* **16/1**

1m 2.0s (-1.50) **Going Correction** -0.175s/f (Firm)
WFA 3 from 4yo+ 5lb **9** Ran SP% **125.0**
Speed ratings (Par 103): **105,102,102,98,95 91,84,68,44**
toteswingers 1&2 £1.70, 1&3 £3.80, 2&3 £7.10 CSF £3.55 TOTE £2.00: £1.10, £1.50, £2.30; EX 4.50 Trifecta £17.20 Pool: £1374.95 - 59.94 winning units.
Owner D Pryde & J Callow **Bred** Rancho San Peasea S A **Trained** Maunby, N Yorks
■ Stewards' Enquiry : Kevin Stott two-day ban; used whip above permitted level (20th-21st July).

FOCUS
This race was won at the start, as the winner got away quickly and made all. Modest form, limited by the third, and the winner didn't need to be at his best.
T/Plt: £126.80 to a £1 stake. Pool: £77,468.91 - 445.86 winning units T/Qpdt: £85.70 to a £1 stake. Pool: £3754.20 - 32.40 winning units JR

3680 CARLISLE (R-H)
Saturday, July 6

OFFICIAL GOING: Good (good to firm in places) changing to good to firm (good in places) after race 3 (7.15)
Wind: fresh across Weather: sunny

4051 MADNESS IN CONCERT TONIGHT APPRENTICE H'CAP — 5f 193y
6:15 (6:16) (Class 5) (0-75,73) 4-Y-O+ **£2,587** (£770; £384; £192) **Stalls** Low

Form RPR

-233 **1** **Circuitous**[8] 3770 5-9-6 **67**...(v) LMcNiff 2 76
(Keith Dalgleish) *led narrowly: rdn whn hdd ent fnl f: kpt on: led again post* **9/4[1]**

5044 **2** *nse* **Holy Angel (IRE)**[18] 3444 4-8-13 **65**..................(e) RachelRichardson(5) 7 74
(Tim Easterby) *trckd ldrs: rdn to ld ent fnl f: hung rt: hdd post* **11/2**

0-03 **3** *3¼* **Ferdy (IRE)**[19] 3392 4-9-1 **65**............................... PhilipPrince(3) 1 63
(Paul Green) *dwlt: hld up: rdn and gd hdwy over 2f out: ev ch over 1f out: one pce fnl f* **13/2**

5125 **4** *2* **Hab Reeh**[4] 3934 5-8-9 **59**...(t) GemmaTutty(3) 3 51
(Ruth Carr) *t.k.h: hld up in tch: pushed along whn n.m.r over 2f out: kpt on fnl f: nvr threatened* **9/2[3]**

0404 **5** *1* **Commanche Raider (IRE)**[14] 3569 6-9-5 **69**.......(p) ConnorBeasley(3) 4 58
(Michael Dods) *t.k.h: w ldr: rdn over 2f out: wknd appr fnl f* **11/1**

2502 **6** *1¼* **Majestic Dream (IRE)**[17] 3462 5-9-7 **73**............(b) MatthewHopkins(5) 5 58
(Michael Easterby) *dwlt: hld up in tch towards outer: rdn over 2f out: no imp* **4/1[2]**

0000 **7** *2¾* **Unex Michelangelo (IRE)**[12] 3628 4-9-4 **65**.............. ShirleyTeasdale 6 41
(Michael Easterby) *prom towards outer: rdn over 2f out: wknd over 1f out* **11/1**

1m 13.33s (-0.37) **Going Correction** +0.075s/f (Good) **7** Ran SP% **114.3**
Speed ratings (Par 103): **105,104,100,97,96 94,91**
toteswingers 1&2 £4.70, 1&3 £3.80, 2&3 £5.40 CSF £15.01 CT £69.04 TOTE £3.10: £2.80, £3.00; EX 18.30 Trifecta £69.70 Pool: £790.66 - 8.50 winning units.
Owner Alison Walker Sarah Cousins **Bred** Deepwood Farm Stud **Trained** Carluke, S Lanarks

FOCUS
A total of 5-6mm of water had been put on the track the previous day and the going was good, good to firm in places (Going stick 7.8). Inside rail moved out on the stable bend adding around 9yds to 7f, 1m, and 1m1f races. A modest handicap in which it proved advantageous to race close to the pace. The winner rates a small personal best.

4052 BOOKMAKERS ON YOUR MOBILE WITH BOOKMAKERS.CO.UK H'CAP — 1m 1f 61y
6:45 (6:45) (Class 6) (0-60,60) 3-Y-O+ **£2,264** (£673; £336; £168) **Stalls** Low

Form RPR

035 **1** **True Pleasure (IRE)**[9] 3728 6-9-2 48................................ DaleSwift 8 61
(James Bethell) *dwlt: hld up: hdwy on outer 3f out: rdn to ld 2f out: edgd lft ins fnl f: kpt on* **20/1**

0221 **2** *¾* **Tectonic (IRE)**[17] 3466 4-9-13 59..................................(p) TomEaves 5 70
(Keith Dalgleish) *midfield: pushed along and hdwy over 2f out: chsd wnr over 1f out: drvn and carried hd high jst ins fnl f: swtchd rt fnl 100yds: kpt on but a hld* **9/2[3]**

6635 **3** *2* **Call Of Duty (IRE)**[17] 3466 8-10-0 60............................ PJMcDonald 4 67
(Dianne Sayer) *in tch: hdwy over 2f out: sn ev ch: one pce fr over 1f out* **11/2**

3602 **4** *4½* **Outlaw Torn (IRE)**[9] 3728 4-9-6 59.......................(e) ConnorBeasley(7) 9 56
(Richard Guest) *trckd ldr: rdn over 2f out: grad wknd fr over 1f out* **4/1[2]**

4001 **5** *2¾* **Bygones For Coins (IRE)**[9] 3728 5-9-1 52....................... LMcNiff(5) 11 43
(Robert Johnson) *trckd ldr: rdn over 2f out: grad wknd* **8/1**

0-00 **6** *1½* **Monthly Medal**[15] 3543 10-10-0 60.................................(t) PaddyAspell 6 47
(Wilf Storey) *hld up: pushed along over 1f out: nvr threatened* **40/1**

0062 **7** *hd* **Madame Blavatsky (FR)**[9] 3727 5-8-13 50.........(v) GeorgeChaloner(5) 1 37
(Karen McLintock) *midfield: rdn over 3f out: sn no imp* **6/1**

2400 **8** *7* **Landesherr (GER)**[22] 3287 6-9-3 49.................................. JoeFanning 2 21
(Thomas Cuthbert) *in tch: rdn over 2f out: wknd* **16/1**

0-14 **9** *1¾* **Joyful Sound (IRE)**[11] 3649 5-9-12 58........................... BarryMcHugh 10 26
(Brian Ellison) *sn led: rdn whn hdd 2f out: wknd* **7/2[1]**

-050 **10** *11* **One Of Twins**[56] 2273 5-9-4 50..............................(v[1]) DavidNolan 7
(Michael Easterby) *midfield: rdn over 5f out: wknd 4f out* **20/1**

4250 **11** *42* **Needwood Park**[12] 3625 5-9-0 46....................................(b) MickyFenton 12
(Ray Craggs) *hld up: rdn over 6f out: bhd 1/2-way: t.o* **66/1**

1m 57.61s (0.01) **Going Correction** +0.075s/f (Good) **11** Ran SP% **120.5**
Speed ratings (Par 101): **102,101,99,95,93 91,91,85,83,74 36**
toteswingers 1&2 £23.20, 1&3 £18.10, 2&3 £4.00 CSF £107.35 CT £582.42 TOTE £16.60: £4.60, £2.00, £2.30; EX 114.70 Trifecta £470.70 Part won. Pool: £627.66 - 0.03 winning units..
Owner Clarendon Thoroughbred Racing **Bred** Michael O'Mahony **Trained** Middleham Moor, N Yorks
■ Stewards' Enquiry : Tom Eaves two-day ban; used whip down shoulder

FOCUS
A modest but competitive handicap. The pace was solid and this suited those ridden with restraint. The first three finished clear and the form makes sense.

4053 ANDERSONS (DENTON HOLME) SAWMILLS CARLISLE MAIDEN AUCTION STKS — 5f 193y
7:15 (7:15) (Class 5) 2-Y-O **£2,587** (£770; £384; £192) **Stalls** Low

Form RPR

5352 **1** **Azagal (IRE)**[20] 3366 2-8-11 0...................................... DuranFentiman 1 75
(Tim Easterby) *trckd ldr: rdn to ld over 1f out: drvn and kpt on* **15/8[1]**

56 **2** *¾* **Evie Jay (IRE)**[3] 3942 2-8-3 0................................... RaulDaSilva(3) 4 68
(Paul Green) *hld up: rdn 1/2-way: r.o wl on outside fr over 1f out: wnt 2nd fnl 75yds* **50/1**

4 **3** *1¾* **Boogangoo (IRE)**[10] 3680 2-8-8 0...................................... TomEaves 12 65+
(Keith Dalgleish) *chsd ldr: rdn to ld 2f out: hdd over 1f out: one pce* **5/1[3]**

343 **4** *hd* **Ixelles Diamond (IRE)**[19] 3391 2-8-3 0.............. GeorgeChaloner(5) 11 64
(Richard Fahey) *midfield: pushed along 1/2-way: sn chsd ldrs: rdn and ev ch over 1f out: one pce ins fnl f* **14/1**

0 **5** *shd* **Camatini (IRE)**[17] 3476 2-8-1 0.............................. ConnorBeasley(7) 6 64
(Michael Dods) *midfield: rdn over 2f out: hdwy on outer over 1f out: kpt on fnl f* **33/1**

0026 **6** *1¼* **Rough Courte (IRE)**[7] 3829 2-8-4 0............................ DanielCremin(7) 3 63
(Mick Channon) *midfield on inner: pushed along whn n.m.r over 1f out: kpt on* **5/2[2]**

7 *3¾* **El Beau (IRE)** 2-8-11 0... MichaelO'Connell 5 52+
(John Quinn) *s.i.s: hld up: pushed along over 2f out: kpt on ins fnl f: nvr threatened* **25/1**

8 *½* **Toboggan Star** 2-8-11 0.. PJMcDonald 7 50
(Ann Duffield) *hld up: rdn over 2f out: wknd over 1f out* **25/1**

0 **9** *2¾* **Firecruise**[12] 3624 2-8-11 0.. DaleSwift 2 42
(David Barron) *midfield: pushed along and outpcd 1/2-way: no threat after: eased fnl 100yds* **12/1**

10 *½* **Kenny The Captain (IRE)** 2-9-2 0................................ MickyFenton 9 45
(Tim Easterby) *hld up: nvr threatened* **25/1**

304 **11** *¾* **Chamberlain**[11] 3648 2-8-11 0.. SeanLevey 10 38
(Alan McCabe) *in tch: rdn over 2f out: wknd over 1f out* **28/1**

12 *7* **Mister Uno (IRE)** 2-8-9 0.. RowanScott(7) 13 22
(Ann Duffield) *dwlt: sn pushed along in rr: a bhd* **40/1**

13 *17* **Absconder (IRE)** 2-9-2 0... JoeFanning 8
(Mark Johnston) *in tch: rdn whn hdd 2f out: wknd and eased* **10/1**

1m 14.18s (0.48) **Going Correction** +0.075s/f (Good) **13** Ran SP% **125.8**
Speed ratings (Par 94): **99,98,95,95,95 93,88,87,84,83 82,73,50**
toteswingers 1&2 £73.60, 1&3 £3.60, 2&3 £48.10 CSF £129.04 TOTE £2.90: £1.50, £11.00, £2.80; EX 134.00 Trifecta £538.30 Part won. Pool: £717.83 - 0.16 winning units..
Owner Roger Sidebottom **Bred** Robert Norton **Trained** Great Habton, N Yorks

FOCUS
No more than a fair maiden. The winner more than confirmed her Doncaster level.

4054 COMPARE BOOKMAKERS WITH BOOKMAKERS.CO.UK NURSERY H'CAP — 5f
7:45 (7:45) (Class 5) 2-Y-O **£2,587** (£770; £384; £192) **Stalls** Low

Form RPR

163 **1** **Innocently (IRE)**[18] 3439 2-8-7 **67**.................................. JulieBurke(3) 1 70
(David O'Meara) *mde all: pushed clr over 1f out: rdn out fnl f* **5/2[3]**

454 **2** *1¾* **Luckys Connoisseur**[33] 2913 2-8-6 **63**............................... JoeFanning 2 60
(Mark Johnston) *trckd wnr: rdn over 2f out: outpcd over 1f out: kpt on fnl f* **7/4[1]**

3231 **3** *nk* **Danfazi (IRE)**[21] 3310 2-9-7 **78**.. DavidNolan 4 74
(Kristin Stubbs) *in tch in 3rd: rdn over 2f out: one pce* **2/1[2]**

4204 **4** *nk* **Dotesy (IRE)**[18] 3440 2-7-8 **58**.................................(v[1]) JoeDoyle(7) 3 54
(John Quinn) *slowly away: hld up in 4th: rdn over 2f out: sn one pce: edgd rt ins fnl f* **6/1**

1m 2.79s (1.99) **Going Correction** +0.075s/f (Good) **4** Ran SP% **112.6**
Speed ratings (Par 94): **87,84,83,83**
CSF £7.54 TOTE £4.70; EX 4.90 Trifecta £12.30 Pool: £434.94 - 26.42 winning units.
Owner Hollowdean **Bred** Longfort Stud **Trained** Nawton, N Yorks

FOCUS
The official ratings shown are estimated and for information only. An ordinary nursery in which the winner was never headed. Straightforward form with the winner back to his debut level.

4055 STOBART SILVER CUP (H'CAP) — 7f 200y
8:15 (8:16) (Class 4) (0-85,84) 3-Y-O+ **£6,469** (£1,925; £962; £481) **Stalls** Low

Form RPR

1412 **1** **Sennockian Star**[6] 3862 3-9-3 **82**..............................(b) JoeFanning 10 90+
(Mark Johnston) *trckd ldr: led 3f out: rdn whn hdd over 1f out: rallied to ld again towards fin* **3/1[1]**

00-0 **2** *nk* **Lady Chaparral**[49] [2463] 6-9-3 **80** ConnorBeasley(7) 5 89
(Michael Dods) *hld up: rdn and gd hdwy on outer over 2f out: led over 1f out: drvn and one pce fnl f: hdd towards fin* **8/1**[3]
5062 **3** *nse* **Frog Hollow**[24] [3193] 4-9-10 **80** DavidNolan 6 89
(David O'Meara) *midfield: pushed along over 3f out: rdn and hdwy over 2f out: ev ch over 1f out: kpt on* **3/1**[1]
1104 **4** *1 1/4* **Arc Light (IRE)**[11] [3651] 5-9-1 **71** DuranFentiman 12 77
(Tim Easterby) *hld up: swtchd to outer over 2f out: rdn and kpt on fr over 1f out: nrst fin* **14/1**
3100 **5** *nse* **Al Muheer (IRE)**[10] [3684] 8-10-0 **84** (b) DaleSwift 13 90
(Ruth Carr) *stmbld leaving stalls: hld up: rdn over 2f out: angled towards outer over 1f out: kpt on: nrst fin* **33/1**
3224 **6** *1* **Hot Rod Mamma (IRE)**[9] [3712] 6-9-3 **73** [1] PJMcDonald 2 77
(Dianne Sayer) *dwlt: hld up in midfield: pushed along and hdwy over 1f out: n.m.r towards inner jst ins fnl f: kpt on* **13/2**[2]
021 **7** *1* **Ted's Brother (IRE)**[11] [3649] 5-8-11 **67** (e) RobbieFitzpatrick 8 69
(Richard Guest) *trckd ldr: rdn over 2f out: no ex ins fnl f* **16/1**
4362 **8** *1 3/4* **Chookie Royale**[10] [3684] 5-10-0 **84** (p) SeanLevey 1 82
(Keith Dalgleish) *midfield: rdn over 3f out: one pce* **9/1**
00-5 **9** *10* **Fazza**[82] [1576] 6-9-6 **76** PaulMulrennan 4 51
(Edwin Tuer) *midfield: rdn over 3f out: wknd fnl 2f* **20/1**
4302 **10** *12* **Kiwi Bay**[20] [3368] 8-9-7 **77** TomEaves 7 24
(Michael Dods) *trckd ldr: pushed along and lost pl whn short of room on inner 2f out: eased* **16/1**
2536 **11** *5* **Sardanapalus**[24] [3193] 4-9-3 **73** (p) BarryMcHugh 11
(Kevin Ryan) *in tch: rdn over 3f out: wknd fnl 2f* **20/1**
0405 **12** *7* **World Record (IRE)**[8] [3758] 3-8-4 **72** RaulDaSilva(3) 9
(Paul Green) *sn led: hdd 3f out: sn wknd* **20/1**

1m 39.26s (-0.74) **Going Correction** +0.075s/f (Good)
WFA 3 from 4yo+ 9lb **12** Ran SP% **120.1**
Speed ratings (Par 105): **106,105,105,104,104 103,102,100,90,78 73,66**
toteswingers 1&2 £4.50, 1&3 £2.90, 2&3 £3.00 CSF £26.46 CT £80.81 TOTE £4.00: £1.10, £4.40, £1.50; EX 29.90 Trifecta £208.80 Pool: £930.51 - 3.34 winning units.
Owner The Vine Accord **Bred** Cheveley Park Stud Ltd **Trained** Middleham Moor, N Yorks
■ Stewards' Enquiry : Connor Beasley caution; careless riding.
David Nolan four-day ban: used whip above permiited level (Aug 11-14)

FOCUS
A decent handicap in which the pace was strong and the form should work out. The winner did much the best of those who raced up with the pace.

4056 STOBART FEST COMES TO CARLISLE H'CAP 6f 192y
8:45 (8:46) (Class 4) (0-85,82) 3-Y-0 £4,690 (£1,395; £697; £348) **Stalls** Low

Form RPR
3021 **1** **Elle Woods (IRE)**[10] [3686] 3-9-7 **82** (p) PaulMulrennan 4 90+
(Michael Dods) *in tch: smooth hdwy over 2f out: pushed along to ld appr fnl f: rdn out ins fnl f* **7/4**[1]
2061 **2** *3/4* **Tatlisu (IRE)**[21] [3320] 3-8-12 **78** GeorgeChaloner(5) 6 84
(Richard Fahey) *midfield: pushed along 1/2-way: rdn over 2f out: chsd wnr appr fnl f: kpt on but a hld* **13/2**[3]
1034 **3** *1 1/4* **Baltic Prince (IRE)**[8] [3758] 3-8-1 **65** RaulDaSilva(3) 8 68
(Paul Green) *hld up: pushed along 1/2-way: rdn and hdwy 2f out: kpt on to go 3rd ins fnl f* **8/1**
2U01 **4** *3 1/4* **Order Of Service**[18] [3438] 3-9-3 **78** SeanLevey 7 72
(David Brown) *led: rdn over 2f out: hdd appr fnl f: wknd* **5/1**[2]
4023 **5** *hd* **Al Udeid (IRE)**[14] [3582] 3-9-2 **77** TomEaves 5 70
(Kevin Ryan) *trckd ldr: rdn over 2f out: wknd fnl f* **13/2**[3]
2402 **6** *6* **Lightning Launch (IRE)**[8] [3758] 3-9-3 **78** PJMcDonald 1 55
(Mick Channon) *hld up: rdn 3f out: nvr threatened* **5/1**[2]
-604 **7** *30* **Bachotheque (IRE)**[17] [3478] 3-9-7 **82** DuranFentiman 2
(Tim Easterby) *t.k.h in midfield: rdn 3f out: sn wknd* **9/1**

1m 27.39s (0.29) **Going Correction** +0.075s/f (Good) **7** Ran SP% **117.5**
Speed ratings (Par 102): **101,100,98,95,94 87,53**
toteswingers 1&2 £6.20, 1&3 £2.90, 2&3 £12.70 CSF £14.45 TOTE £1.90: £1.10, £4.60; EX 15.40 Trifecta £135.70 Pool: £880.89 - 4.86 winning units.
Owner Andrew Tinkler **Bred** Ballylinch Stud **Trained** Denton, Co Durham

FOCUS
A fair handicap and the pace was sound. The progressive winner is rated better than the bare form.
T/Plt: £51.80 to a £1 stake. Pool: £70,119.72 - 987.24 winning units T/Qpdt: £15.40 to a £1 stake. Pool: £4626.38 - 221.20 winning units AS

4018 HAYDOCK (L-H)
Saturday, July 6

OFFICIAL GOING: Good to firm (watered; 8.6)
Wind: light 1/2 against Weather: fine and sunny, very warm

4057 CASINO AT BET365.COM H'CAP 5f
1:45 (1:46) (Class 4) (0-85,85) 3-Y-0 £6,469 (£1,925; £962; £481) **Stalls** Centre

Form RPR
0-32 **1** **Smart Daisy K**[10] [3677] 3-8-13 **77** NeilCallan 3 89
(Andrew Hollinshead) *t.k.h: trckd ldrs: effrt 2f out: led last 150yds: edgd lft: kpt on wl* **8/1**
U121 **2** *1 3/4* **Holley Shiftwell**[15] [3540] 3-8-9 **73** AndreaAtzeni 5 79
(Stuart Williams) *trckd ldr: led appr fnl f: hdd jst ins fnl f: no ex* **7/2**[2]
2-42 **3** *1 1/4* **Dusty Storm (IRE)**[26] [3160] 3-9-1 **79** FrannyNorton 6 81
(Ed McMahon) *led: hdd appr fnl f: styd on same pce* **13/2**
3131 **4** *shd* **Tumblewind**[14] [3591] 3-9-2 **85** GeorgeChaloner(5) 7 86
(Richard Whitaker) *trckd ldr: drvn 2f out: kpt on same pce fnl f* **5/1**
212 **5** *hd* **The Art Of Racing (IRE)**[40] [2726] 3-9-7 **85** (t) HarryBentley 2 85
(Olly Stevens) *dwlt: hld up: swtchd lft appr fnl f: kpt on same pce* **11/4**[1]
312 **6** *2 1/4* **Dream Cast (IRE)**[6] [3866] 3-8-11 **75** JimCrowley 1 67
(David Simcock) *hld up in rr: t.k.h: effrt 2f out: wknd fnl f* **4/1**[3]

58.91s (-1.89) **Going Correction** -0.30s/f (Firm) **6** Ran SP% **110.0**
Speed ratings (Par 102): **103,100,98,98,97 94**
toteswingers 1&2 £5.30, 1&3 £6.00, 2&3 £4.70 CSF £34.18 TOTE £9.40: £3.30, £2.20; EX 37.80 Trifecta £1106.30 Part won. Pool: £1,475.16 - 0.99 winning units..
Owner Mr & Mrs D J Smart **Bred** D J And Mrs K D Smart **Trained** Upper Longdon, Staffs

FOCUS
The going was good to firm having been watered. The jockeys reported it was riding fast. A fair 3-y-o sprint handicap in which the four fillies filled the frame and the outsider came off best. The pace was decent and the winner posted a personal best.

4058 BET365.COM CONDITIONS STKS 6f
2:20 (2:21) (Class 2) 3-Y-0+
£15,562 (£4,660; £2,330; £1,165; £582; £292) **Stalls** Centre

Form RPR
0-60 **1** **Louis The Pious**[14] [3558] 5-8-11 **98** KierenFallon 1 103
(David O'Meara) *drvn and outpcd over 3f out: hdwy over 2f out: hrd drvn and styd on wl ins fnl f: led post* **3/1**[3]
5-20 **2** *shd* **Masamah (IRE)**[42] [2662] 7-8-11 **104** NeilCallan 4 103
(Marco Botti) *led: swtchd rt to stands' side rail after 1f: t.k.h and hung lft: hdd fnl stride* **5/2**[2]
3030 **3** *1 1/2* **Dubawi Sound**[15] [3527] 5-8-11 **102** (t) HarryBentley 6 98
(David Brown) *chsd ldrs: hmpd and swtchd lft over 3f out: effrt 2f out: n.m.r over 1f out: kpt on same pce* **15/8**[1]
0106 **4** *2 1/4* **Annunciation**[43] [2621] 3-8-5 **98** KieranO'Neill 3 90
(Richard Hannon) *outpcd over 3f out: hdwy over 2f out: chsng ldrs over 1f out: one pce* **13/2**
33 **5** *2* **Superboot (IRE)**[28] [3109] 3-8-5 **0** SilvestreDeSousa 2 83?
(Michael Wigham) *hld up: outpcd over 3f out: swtchd lft and hdwy over 2f out: chsng ldrs over 1f out: one pce* **33/1**
2-00 **6** *6* **Addictive Dream (IRE)**[163] [365] 6-8-11 **102** FrannyNorton 5 65
(David Nicholls) *w ldr: t.k.h: rdn and wknd appr fnl f* **11/1**

1m 11.63s (-2.17) **Going Correction** -0.30s/f (Firm)
WFA 3 from 5yo+ 6lb **6** Ran SP% **113.0**
Speed ratings (Par 109): **102,101,99,96,94 86**
toteswingers 1&2 £1.50, 1&3 £2.30, 2&3 £1.40 CSF £11.08 TOTE £3.50: £2.20, £2.30; EX 12.10 Trifecta £27.40 Pool: £1473.28 - 40.21 winning units..
Owner F Gillespie **Bred** Ashbrittle Stud **Trained** Nawton, N Yorks
■ Stewards' Enquiry : Neil Callan one-day ban; careless riding (20th July).

FOCUS
Normally a high-class conditions stakes won by the subsequent Sprint Cup and multiple Group 1 winner Somnus twice, with Stewards' Cup and subsequent Group 3 winner Genki another of several well-known names in domestic sprinting to take this. A small field for this year's renewal but a close finish, and the form has been rated a bit cautiously.

4059 BET365 LANCASHIRE OAKS (GROUP 2) (F&M) 1m 3f 200y
2:55 (2:55) (Class 1) 3-Y-0+
£51,039 (£19,350; £9,684; £4,824; £2,421; £1,215) **Stalls** Centre

Form RPR
05-6 **1** **Emirates Queen**[51] [2397] 4-9-5 **102** AndreaAtzeni 1 111
(Luca Cumani) *stdd to rr after 1f: hld up: hdwy to trck ldrs 7f out: effrt over 2f out: r.o to ld nr fin* **20/1**
2131 **2** *3/4* **Moment In Time (IRE)**[28] [3100] 4-9-5 **107** JimCrowley 8 110
(David Simcock) *dwlt: hld up in rr: hdwy whn nt clr run over 2f out: chsng ldrs 1f out: kpt on to take 2nd post* **5/1**[2]
1-15 **3** *shd* **Albasharah (USA)**[15] [3525] 4-9-5 **106** SilvestreDeSousa 2 110
(Saeed bin Suroor) *trckd ldrs: t.k.h: swtchd rt over 3f out: led over 1f out: hdd and no ex nr fin* **5/4**[1]
16-1 **4** *2 1/4* **Wannabe Loved**[43] [2619] 4-9-5 **96** RobertHavlin 5 106
(John Gosden) *led: qcknd pce over 4f out: hdd over 2f out: rallied and upsides over 1f out: fdd fnl 50yds* **10/1**
110 **5** *1/2* **Banoffee (IRE)**[36] [2842] 3-8-6 **93** KierenFallon 7 105
(Hughie Morrison) *trckd ldrs: t.k.h: effrt 4f out: one pce over 1f out* **6/1**[3]
64-1 **6** *3/4* **Midnight Soprano (IRE)**[20] [3381] 6-9-5 **106** ChrisHayes 4 104
(P D Deegan, Ire) *trckd ldr: led over 2f out: hdd over 1f out: fdd last 100yds* **8/1**
1-45 **7** *nk* **Gallipot**[19] [3409] 4-9-5 **100** DaneO'Neill 6 104
(John Gosden) *hld up in rr: effrt over 2f out: one pce* **10/1**
30-6 **8** *2 1/2* **Coquet**[63] [2012] 4-9-5 **103** PatDobbs 3 100
(Hughie Morrison) *trckd ldrs: drvn over 2f out: fdd over 1f out* **16/1**

2m 30.84s (-2.96) **Going Correction** -0.025s/f (Good)
WFA 3 from 4yo+ 13lb **8** Ran SP% **115.3**
Speed ratings (Par 115): **108,107,107,105,105 105,104,103**
toteswingers 1&2 £17.40, 1&3 £5.80, 2&3 £2.80 CSF £117.27 TOTE £22.90: £4.90, £1.80, £1.10; EX 120.40 Trifecta £269.50 Pool: £2197.83 - 6.11 winning units.
Owner Sheikh Mohammed Obaid Al Maktoum **Bred** Darley **Trained** Newmarket, Suffolk
■ Stewards' Enquiry : Andrea Atzeni two-day ban; used whip above permitted level (20th-21st July).

FOCUS
This long-established fillies' Group 2 saw John Gosden bidding for a third successive win with two representatives, but it was not to be. The form is sound and just about up to the race standard, with a length personal best from Emirates Queen.

4060 BET365 OLD NEWTON CUP (HERITAGE H'CAP) 1m 3f 200y
3:30 (3:31) (Class 2) 4-Y-0+
£62,250 (£18,640; £9,320; £4,660; £1,750; £1,750) **Stalls** Centre

Form RPR
12 **1** **Star Lahib (IRE)**[14] [3567] 4-8-8 **87** FrannyNorton 14 97
(Mark Johnston) *trckd ldrs: drvn over 3f out: styd on to ld last 100yds* **8/1**[3]
3236 **2** *3/4* **Tepmokea (IRE)**[35] [2867] 7-8-9 **88** JimCrowley 2 97
(Mrs K Burke) *w ldr: led 3f out: hdd and no ex last 100yds* **16/1**
4301 **3** *2 3/4* **Fennell Bay (IRE)**[18] [3442] 4-8-11 **90** NeilCallan 17 95
(Mark Johnston) *sn chsng ldrs: drvn over 2f out: kpt on same pce fnl f* **20/1**
4510 **4** *1/2* **Highland Castle**[14] [3559] 5-9-0 **93** LiamKeniry 7 97
(David Elsworth) *stdd after s: t.k.h mid-div on outer: effrt over 2f out: edgd lft: kpt on fnl f* **9/1**
-002 **5** *hd* **Franciscan**[10] [3685] 5-8-10 **89** SilvestreDeSousa 5 92
(Luca Cumani) *in tch: drvn 6f out: styd on same pce over 1f out* **7/1**[2]
0-31 **5** *dht* **Opinion (IRE)**[14] [3559] 4-9-10 **103** (t) KierenFallon 6 108+
(Sir Michael Stoute) *hld up in mid-div: drvn over 4f out: nt clr run 2f out tl swtchd rt jst ins fnl f: r.o wl (dht 5th)* **7/2**[1]
1020 **7** *nse* **Hanoverian Baron**[14] [3559] 8-8-7 **93** ConnorBeasley(7) 1 99+
(Tony Newcombe) *mid-div: nt clr run on inner over 2f out: hmpd and lost pl over 1f out: swtchd rt and styd on strly ins fnl f* **33/1**
1002 **8** *3/4* **Strictly Silver (IRE)**[7] [3832] 4-9-0 **98** RobertTart(5) 18 100
(Alan Bailey) *sn chsng ldrs: drvn over 2f out: one pce* **10/1**
1320 **9** *1* **Beaumont's Party (IRE)**[14] [3559] 6-9-1 **94** DaleSwift 12 95
(Brian Ellison) *in rr: hdwy on inner over 2f out: one pce over 1f out* **20/1**

3006 **10** *nk* **Sir Graham Wade (IRE)**[14] 3559 4-9-10 **103**.................... JoeFanning 8 103+
(Mark Johnston) *hld up in mid-div: nt clr run fr over 2f out: nt rcvr: eased clsng stages* **9/1**
1442 **11** *hd* **Icebuster**[24] 3208 5-8-8 **87**.. AndreaAtzeni 15 87
(Rod Millman) *s.i.s: hld up in rr: effrt over 2f out: nvr a factor* **16/1**
5314 **12** *1* **Haylaman (IRE)**[7] 3838 5-8-11 **90**.. MartinLane 9 88
(David Simcock) *s.i.s: hld up in rr: effrt 3f out: nvr a factor* **16/1**
5422 **13** *½* **Quixote**[22] 3297 4-8-11 **90**...(t) HayleyTurner 3 87
(Clive Brittain) *chsd ldrs: drvn 3f out: wknd qckly jst ins fnl f* **16/1**
3130 **14** *¾* **Roman Flight (IRE)**[18] 3423 5-8-8 **87**..........................(v) ChrisHayes 16 83
(David O'Meara) *hld up in rr: nt clr run over 2f out: nvr on terms* **16/1**
0335 **15** *1 ¼* **Scatter Dice (IRE)**[7] 3824 4-8-12 **91**.................................. RobertHavlin 4 85
(Mark Johnston) *mde most: hdd 3f out: wknd appr fnl f* **16/1**
0210 **16** *1* **Angel Gabrial (IRE)**[28] 3115 4-8-6 **90**.................. GeorgeChaloner(5) 13 83
(Ian Williams) *mid-div: effrt over 2f out: sn wknd* **16/1**
4-30 **17** *14* **Communicator**[14] 3559 5-9-1 **94**.................................. RichardMullen 10 64
(Andrew Balding) *in rr: drvn 3f out: nvr on terms: eased clsng stages* **20/1**
2m 30.49s (-3.31) **Going Correction** -0.025s/f (Good) **17** Ran SP% **133.3**
Speed ratings (Par 109): **110,109,107,107,107 107,107,106,106,105 105,105,104,104,103 102,93**
toteswingers 1&2 £53.00, 1&3 £54.60, 2&3 £88.50 CSF £134.18 CT £2533.53 TOTE £11.00: £2.40, £5.80, £5.30, £2.60; EX 203.90 Trifecta £6882.50 Pool: £60,622.37 - 6.60 winning units.
Owner Jaber Abdullah **Bred** Piercetown Stud **Trained** Middleham Moor, N Yorks
■ Stewards' Enquiry : Franny Norton two-day ban; used whip above permitted level (20th-21st July).
FOCUS
One of the hottest middle-distance handicaps of the season and Luca Cumani was bidding to win it for the fourth time in the last ten years. The time was only 0.35 secs faster than the preceding Lancashire Oaks and the first three were all in the first five turning for home. The form is not rated as positively as it might have been, with the pace not that strong.

4061 MOBILE AT BET365.COM NURSERY H'CAP 7f
4:05 (4:06) (Class 3) 2-Y-O **£7,439** (£2,213; £1,106; £553) **Stalls** Low

Form RPR
252 **1** **Culdaff (IRE)**[20] 3374 2-9-3 **76**.. SteveDrowne 3 81+
(Charles Hills) *trckd ldrs: effrt over 2f out: upsides over 1f out: styd on to ld last 150yds: drvn out* **2/1**[1]
2251 **2** *1* **Lily Rules (IRE)**[9] 3724 2-9-2 **75**.................................... BarryMcHugh 2 77
(Tony Coyle) *mid-div: drvn over 4f out: chsng ldrs on ins over 1f out: nt clr run tl swtchd rt ins fnl f: styd on wl to take 2nd nr fin* **7/1**
2022 **3** *¾* **Tanseeb**[14] 3565 2-9-7 **80**.. DaneO'Neill 7 80
(Mark Johnston) *wnt rt s: sn w ldr: led 2f out: hdd jst ins fnl f: styd on same pce* **4/1**[3]
033 **4** *2 ¼* **Party Ruler (IRE)**[42] 2645 2-9-1 **74**......................... RichardKingscote 6 69
(Tom Dascombe) *led: hdd 2f out: wknd last 100yds* **10/3**[2]
5501 **5** *½* **Jive**[37] 2805 2-8-11 **70**.. PatDobbs 1 63
(Richard Hannon) *trckd ldrs: t.k.h: drvn over 2f out: fdd fnl f* **15/2**
002 **6** *2 ¾* **Porteous**[19] 3414 2-8-7 **66**.. NickyMackay 4 52
(Mick Channon) *stdd s: hld up detached in last: hdwy over 3f out: chsng ldrs over 2f out: wknd appr fnl f* **16/1**
624 **7** *2 ¼* **Mitcd (IRE)**[19] 3391 2-8-6 **65**................................ SilvestreDeSousa 5 48
(Richard Fahey) *hld up in rr: hdwy to chse ldrs over 2f out: wknd appr fnl f: eased clsng stages* **9/1**
1m 31.73s (1.03) **Going Correction** -0.025s/f (Good) **7** Ran SP% **116.6**
Speed ratings (Par 98): **93,91,91,88,87 84,82**
toteswingers 1&2 £2.20, 1&3 £3.00, 2&3 £6.50 CSF £17.40 TOTE £3.10: £1.80, £2.60; EX 19.10 Trifecta £47.80 Pool: £1847.97 - 28.98 winning units.
Owner John C Grant **Bred** Knocktoran Stud & Tinnakill Bloodstock **Trained** Lambourn, Berks
FOCUS
The official ratings shown are estimated and for guidance only. A fair-looking nursery and there's every chance of more from the winner.

4062 BET365 H'CAP 7f
4:40 (4:41) (Class 2) (0-105,102) 3-Y-O+**£16,172** (£4,812; £2,405; £1,202) **Stalls** Low

Form RPR
-516 **1** **Ashaadd (IRE)**[21] 3339 3-8-13 **95**................................. AndreaAtzeni 12 101+
(Roger Varian) *swtchd lft after s: hld up in rr: hdwy on ins over 2f out: nt clr run over 1f out: swtchd rt ins fnl f: r.o to ld nr fin* **9/2**[2]
0550 **2** *½* **Mabait**[10] 3697 7-8-11 **85**... MartinLane 3 93
(David Simcock) *s.i.s: hdwy over 2f out: sn chsng ldrs: edgd rt over 1f out: styd on to take 2nd cl home* **11/1**
1010 **3** *½* **Shebebi (USA)**[16] 3484 3-8-10 **92**..................................... DaneO'Neill 9 96
(Mark Johnston) *hmpd s: sn trcking ldrs: led gng wl 2f out: hdd and no ex clsng stages* **7/1**
-R44 **4** *1 ½* **Ducal**[15] 3538 5-9-0 **88**.. PatDobbs 10 91
(Mike Murphy) *hmpd s: in rr: hdwy over 2f out: nt clr run over 1f out: swtchd rt and styd on ins fnl f* **16/1**
0120 **5** *½* **Capo Rosso (IRE)**[16] 3484 3-8-7 **89**...................... RichardKingscote 5 87
(Tom Dascombe) *mid-div: drvn over 3f out: hung lft and bmpd over 1f out: kpt on ins fnl f* **8/1**
0-22 **6** *hd* **Les Troyens**[140] 696 5-9-9 **97**........................... SilvestreDeSousa 4 98
(Saeed bin Suroor) *mid-div: drvn over 3f out: hmpd over 1f out: styd on ins fnl f* **18/1**
6533 **7** *1* **Beacon Lodge (IRE)**[4] 3931 8-9-7 **95**............................. BarryMcHugh 2 93
(David Nicholls) *led rdrless to s: led: hdd 2f out: fdd jst ins fnl f* **14/1**
-165 **8** *nk* **Tartiflette**[35] 2858 4-9-5 **93**.. FrannyNorton 1 90
(Ed McMahon) *trckd ldrs: effrt and chsng ldrs whn n.m.r over 1f out: one pce* **7/2**[1]
2-00 **9** *1 ¾* **Webbow (IRE)**[140] 690 11-9-6 **94**................................... LiamKeniry 13 86
(Julie Camacho) *in rr: swtchd lft after s: effrt on outer over 2f out: nvr a factor* **25/1**
2301 **10** *nk* **Galician**[4] 3931 4-9-8 **96** 6ex.. JoeFanning 6 88
(Mark Johnston) *chsd ldrs: outpcd over 3f out: sme hdwy over 1f out: no threat* **12/1**
2011 **11** *¾* **Boots And Spurs**[19] 3411 4-9-4 **92**.............................(v) JimCrowley 8 82
(Mrs K Burke) *wnt rt s: mid-div: effrt 3f out: lost pl over 1f out* **6/1**[3]
2030 **12** *1 ¾* **Laffan (IRE)**[29] 3060 4-9-1 **89**.. NeilCallan 7 74
(Kevin Ryan) *trckd ldr: t.k.h: wkng whn hmpd over 1f out: eased clsng stages* **16/1**
00 **13** *4 ½* **Pied A Terre (AUS)**[128] 838 5-9-7 **102**................ AhmadAlSubousi(7) 11 75
(Saeed bin Suroor) *in rr: rdn and hung bdly lft over 2f out: sn bhd* **28/1**
1m 29.14s (-1.56) **Going Correction** -0.025s/f (Good)
WFA 3 from 4yo+ 8lb **13** Ran SP% **125.3**
Speed ratings (Par 109): **107,106,105,104,103 103,102,101,99,99 98,96,91**
toteswingers 1&2 £17.30, 1&3 £8.20, 2&3 £14.70 CSF £56.55 CT £366.05 TOTE £6.10: £1.80, £4.10, £3.10; EX 66.80 Trifecta £341.30 Pool: £2463.65 - winning units.
Owner Sheikh Ahmed Al Maktoum **Bred** Socrates Partnership **Trained** Newmarket, Suffolk

FOCUS
This good handicap was soundly run and the time was 2.59secs faster than the preceding nursery. Sound form with the fourth setting the standard.

4063 BET365.COM H'CAP 1m 2f 95y
5:15 (5:16) (Class 2) (0-100,93) 3-Y-O **£16,172** (£4,812; £2,405) **Stalls** Centre

Form RPR
0200 **1** **Red Avenger (USA)**[16] 3484 3-9-4 **90**.............................. AndreaAtzeni 5 102
(Ed Dunlop) *trckd ldr: led 2f out: drvn clr fnl f* **5/2**[2]
-121 **2** *3* **Broughton (GER)**[8] 3756 3-9-0 **86**................................ FrannyNorton 1 92
(Mark Johnston) *led: qcknd pce 4f out: rdn over 2f out: sn hdd: btn over 1f out* **10/11**[1]
301 **3** *8* **Grandorio (IRE)**[22] 3296 3-9-7 **93**................................... KierenFallon 3 87
(David O'Meara) *hld up in last: shkn up 6f out: drvn over 4f out: no imp and hung lft over 1f out: eased fnl 75yds* **11/4**[3]
2m 14.53s (-0.97) **Going Correction** -0.025s/f (Good) **3** Ran SP% **107.6**
Speed ratings (Par 106): **102,99,93**
CSF £5.18 TOTE £3.50; EX 5.00 Trifecta £6.20 Pool: £2081.48 - 250.56 winning units.
Owner The Hon R J Arculli **Bred** Wedgewood Farm **Trained** Newmarket, Suffolk
FOCUS
A disappointing turnout for this valuable Class 2 handicap for 3-y-os and it turned out to be a straightforward affair with the winning rider completing a treble. Tricky to assess but the form has been rated at face value.
T/Plt: £119.30 to a £1 stake. Pool: £131,830.40 - 806.24 winning units T/Qpdt: £18.30 to a £1 stake. Pool: £9426.24 - 379.20 winning units WG

3716 LEICESTER (R-H)
Saturday, July 6

OFFICIAL GOING: Good to firm (good in places; watered; 8.8)
Wind: Almost nil Weather: Sunshine

4064 STRESSLESS AT FENWICK OF LEICESTER FILLIES' H'CAP 5f 218y
2:15 (2:15) (Class 5) (0-70,70) 3-Y-O+ **£4,528** (£1,347; £673; £336) **Stalls** Centre

Form RPR
6-02 **1** **Laughing Rock (IRE)**[31] 2996 3-8-6 **56**........................ AndrewMullen 9 68
(Michael Appleby) *chsd ldrs: rdn over 2f out: led and edgd rt fr over 1f out: styd on* **11/2**[3]
10-3 **2** *2 ¾* **Sakhee's Rose**[16] 3489 3-9-1 **65**................................ RoystonFfrench 8 68
(Ed McMahon) *sn pushed along in rr: hdwy u.p over 1f out: styd on same pce ins fnl f* **14/1**
5603 **3** *1* **Tregereth (IRE)**[10] 3699 3-8-8 **58**.................................. WilliamCarson 2 58
(Jonathan Portman) *prom: rdn over 2f out: styd on same pce ins fnl f* **5/1**[2]
5021 **4** *1* **Big Wave (IRE)**[16] 3489 5-9-11 **69**....................................(p) AdamKirby 1 67
(Alison Hutchinson) *sn led: rdn and hdd over 1f out: no ex ins fnl f* **11/4**[1]
2036 **5** *1 ½* **Loulou Vuitton**[10] 3699 3-8-6 **56**...................................(p) JimmyQuinn 5 48
(Frank Sheridan) *sn pushed along in rr: hdwy u.p over 1f out: no ex ins fnl f* **14/1**
2016 **6** *nk* **Charlemagne Diva**[8] 3762 3-8-5 **60**............................ PhilipPrince(5) 7 51
(Richard Guest) *chsd ldrs: rdn over 2f out: wknd ins fnl f* **8/1**
-320 **7** *2 ¾* **Avonrose**[163] 358 6-9-5 **70**...(v) AdamMcLean(7) 3 53
(Derek Shaw) *in tch: rdn over 2f out: hung rt over 1f out: wknd fnl f* **8/1**
-646 **8** *nk* **Shamiana**[9] 3740 3-8-7 **57**...(tp) MartinDwyer 4 43+
(Gerard Butler) *s.s: outpcd: sme hdwy over 1f out: eased ins fnl f* **6/1**
0-03 **9** *1 ½* **Portrush Storm**[12] 3622 8-8-5 **56**................................. JoeyHaynes(7) 6 33
(Ray Peacock) *chsd ldrs: rdn over 2f out: wknd over 1f out* **12/1**
1m 12.07s (-0.93) **Going Correction** -0.225s/f (Firm)
WFA 3 from 5yo+ 6lb **9** Ran SP% **116.3**
Speed ratings (Par 100): **97,93,92,90,88 88,84,84,82**
toteswingers 1&2 £1.60, 1&3 £5.70, 2&3 £6.60 CSF £78.82 CT £412.45 TOTE £5.30: £1.70, £3.10, £1.50; EX 39.40 Trifecta £120.30 Pool: £669.50 - 4.17 winning units.
Owner Michael Appleby **Bred** Moorpark Stud **Trained** Danethorpe, Notts
FOCUS
The going was good to firm, good in places on a watered track. The leaders went off fast in this sprint handicap and the first three came from off the pace. Modest form.

4065 FLOWFAYRE PLUMBING AND HEATING (S) STKS 5f 218y
2:50 (2:52) (Class 5) 2-Y-O **£2,587** (£770; £384; £192) **Stalls** Centre

Form RPR
3 **1** **Sakuramachi**[43] 2612 2-8-6 0.. SamHitchcott 4 61
(Mick Channon) *mde all: rdn over 1f out: styd on* **11/10**[1]
6633 **2** *¾* **Lady Captain (IRE)**[18] 3440 2-8-6 0........................... RoystonFfrench 8 59
(Kevin Ryan) *a.p: rdn to chse wnr over 1f out: ev ch ins fnl f: nt run on* **7/1**[3]
04 **3** *1 ¼* **Tunnel Tiger (IRE)**[15] 3541 2-7-13 0..................... CharlotteJenner(7) 11 55
(J S Moore) *hld up: hdwy and hung rt over 1f out: styd on same pce ins fnl f* **16/1**
06 **4** *6* **Hija**[8] 3753 2-8-1 0 ow2..(p) RyanWhile(7) 3 38
(Bill Turner) *chsd wnr tl rdn over 1f out: wknd ins fnl f* **10/1**
00 **5** *1 ¾* **Frost In May (IRE)**[14] 3588 2-8-6 0.............................. AndrewMullen 5 30
(David O'Meara) *sn pushed along and prom: lost pl 4f out: n.d after* **25/1**
023 **6** *2 ¼* **See Me Sometime**[23] 3255 2-8-8 0........................... AshleyMorgan(3) 9 28
(Mark H Tompkins) *chsd ldrs: rdn and edgd rt over 1f out: wknd fnl f* **16/1**
6 **7** *5* **Rubylicious (IRE)**[8] 3767 2-8-6 0.................................... LiamJones 1
(J S Moore) *prom: rdn over 2f out: wknd fnl f* **25/1**
06 **8** *nk* **Astral Pursuits**[15] 3541 2-7-13 0............................ DanielleMooney(7) 10
(Nigel Tinkler) *in rr and sn pushed along: nvr on terms* **66/1**
0 **9** *1 ¼* **Valued Opinion (IRE)**[45] 2562 2-8-11 0...................(t) WilliamCarson 2
(Tim Pitt) *hld up: pushed along over 3f out: hdwy and hung lft over 2f out: wknd wl over 1f out* **11/4**[2]
006 **10** *¾* **Jazzy Lady (IRE)**[48] 2474 2-8-6 0...............................(v) CathyGannon 6
(David Evans) *s.i.s: outpcd* **16/1**
1m 13.77s (0.77) **Going Correction** -0.225s/f (Firm) **10** Ran SP% **122.7**
Speed ratings (Par 94): **85,84,82,74,72 69,62,61,60,59**
toteswingers 1&2 £2.50, 1&3 £4.30, 2&3 £8.00 CSF £10.27 TOTE £2.10: £1.10, £2.60, £4.00; EX 9.70 Trifecta £46.70 Pool: £2457.39 - 39.46 winning units.There was no bid for the winner.
Owner Imperial **Bred** Imperial & Mike Channon Bloodstock Ltd **Trained** West Ilsley, Berks

The Form Book Flat, Raceform Ltd, Compton, RG20 6NL.

FOCUS
The hot favourite battled well to take advantage of a good opportunity in this seller. The first three were clear.

4066 E B F SLIDEROBES MAKE SPACE BE HAPPY FILLIES' H'CAP 1m 1f 218y
3:25 (3:25) (Class 4) (0-80,85) 3-Y-O **£7,561** (£2,263; £1,131; £566; £282) **Stalls** Low

Form RPR
-554 1 **Nemushka**[18] 3443 4-9-7 **73** .... JimmyQuinn 4 83
(Richard Fahey) *hld up: hdwy to ld over 1f out: rdn and edgd rt ins fnl f: r.o* **11/1**
44-1 2 1 1/4 **Tuscania**[9] 3742 5-10-0 **80** .... FrederikTylicki 2 87
(Lucy Wadham) *trckd ldrs: nt clr run over 2f out: rdn over 1f out: styd on to go 2nd nr fin* **11/2**[3]
3-11 3 hd **Lyric Ballad**[25] 3177 3-8-13 **76** .... AdamKirby 3 83
(Hughie Morrison) *hld up: hdwy over 2f out: led wl over 1f out: sn rdn and hdd: styng on same pce whn nt clr run and lost 2nd towards fin* **2/1**[2]
3211 4 3 1/2 **Paris Rose**[8] 3785 3-9-8 **85** .... LiamJones 6 85
(William Haggas) *led: rdn and hdd wl over 1f out: wknd wl ins fnl f* **11/8**[1]
41 5 13 **Ardingly (IRE)**[17] 3469 3-9-3 **80** .... ChrisCatlin 1 54
(Roger Varian) *trckd ldr: plld hrd: pushed along over 3f out: rdn and wknd over 1f out* **7/1**

2m 5.88s (-2.02) **Going Correction** -0.225s/f (Firm)
WFA 3 from 4yo+ 11lb **5** Ran SP% **111.7**
Speed ratings (Par 102): **99,98,97,95,84**
CSF £64.81 TOTE £11.60: £3.50, £2.20; EX 24.60 Trifecta £172.10 Pool: £1276.22 - 5.55 winning units.
Owner The G-Guck Group **Bred** Avenue Farm Stud **Trained** Musley Bank, N Yorks
■ Stewards' Enquiry : Frederik Tylicki one-day ban; careless riding (20th July).

FOCUS
The outsider beat four last-time-out winners in this fillies' handicap, although she was rated to win on her best form.

4067 YOU'LL BE GLAD YOU CHOSE STORMCLAD H'CAP 7f 9y
4:00 (4:00) (Class 3) (0-90,88) 3-Y-O **£9,451** (£2,829; £1,414; £708; £352) **Stalls** Centre

Form RPR
501 1 **Askaud (IRE)**[21] 3322 5-9-6 **80** ....(p) FrederikTylicki 1 90
(Scott Dixon) *mde all: rdn over 1f out: edgd rt ins fnl f: styd on* **11/4**[1]
4316 2 3/4 **Azrael**[20] 3368 5-9-3 **77** .... MartinDwyer 4 85
(Alan McCabe) *edgd lft s: chsd wnr: rdn over 2f out: lost 2nd over 1f out: styd on u.p to go 2nd again ins fnl f: nt quite rch wnr* **25/1**
0000 3 1 1/2 **Al's Memory (IRE)**[28] 3093 4-9-10 **84** .... CathyGannon 11 88
(David Evans) *stmbld s: hld up: rdn over 2f out: hdwy over 1f out: edgd rt ins fnl f: r.o: nt rch ldrs* **20/1**
246- 4 3/4 **Piddie's Power**[275] 6820 6-9-9 **83** .... RoystonFfrench 7 85
(Ed McMahon) *mid-div: rdn over 2f out: hdwy over 1f out: styd on: nt trble ldrs* **25/1**
6000 5 1 **Accession (IRE)**[19] 3411 4-9-7 **81** ....(b) AdamKirby 2 80
(Clive Cox) *prom: racd keenly: rdn to chse wnr over 1f out tl no ex ins fnl f* **7/2**[2]
4321 6 3 3/4 **Good Authority (IRE)**[22] 3274 6-10-0 **88** .... ChrisCatlin 10 77
(Karen George) *s.i.s: sn pushed along in rr: nvr nrr* **4/1**[3]
5314 7 1 **My Kingdom (IRE)**[2] 3974 7-9-3 **77** ....(t) SebSanders 9 63
(Stuart Williams) *hld up: shkn up over 2f out: nvr on terms* **11/2**
2000 8 1/2 **King Of Eden (IRE)**[7] 3825 7-9-8 **87** ....[1] JasonHart(5) 6 72
(Eric Alston) *chsd ldrs: rdn 4f out: wknd over 2f out* **9/1**
0040 9 25 **Nasri**[19] 3415 7-9-2 **76** .... FergusSweeney 8
(Milton Bradley) *prom: rdn 1/2-way: wknd wl over 2f out: t.o* **20/1**
1101 U **Midnight Feast**[24] 3210 5-8-12 **72** ....(v) KierenFox 5
(Lee Carter) *hmpd and uns rdr s* **12/1**

1m 23.93s (-2.27) **Going Correction** -0.225s/f (Firm) **10** Ran SP% **119.2**
Speed ratings (Par 107): **103,102,100,99,98 94,93,92,63,**
toteswingers 1&2 £19.00, 1&3 £2.00, 2&3 £34.00 CSF £81.54 CT £1173.58 TOTE £3.10: £1.10, £7.80, £4.70; EX 97.20 Trifecta £997.60 Part won. Pool: £1,330.16 - 0.05 winning units..
Owner Paul J Dixon **Bred** John P Jones **Trained** Babworth, Notts

FOCUS
The favourite made all in this decent handicap and not many got involved from off the pace. There was drama at the start when Midnight Feast swerved into a rival and unseated his rider. The winner is up a length on his best form of last year.

4068 BUNNY APPLIANCE WAREHOUSE RATING RELATED MAIDEN STKS 7f 9y
4:35 (4:36) (Class 5) 3-Y-O **£3,881** (£1,155; £577; £288) **Stalls** Centre

Form RPR
2534 1 **Lovesome**[15] 3537 3-8-8 70 ....[1] LouisSteward(7) 1 76
(Michael Bell) *chsd ldrs: led over 4f out: rdn and edgd rt over 1f out: pushed out* **13/2**
-334 2 nk **Liberty Jack (IRE)**[14] 3582 3-8-10 70 .... WilliamTwiston-Davies(5) 2 75
(Roger Charlton) *s.i.s: hdwy over 4f out: chsd wnr over 2f out: n.m.r fr over 1f out tl ins fnl f: sn rdn and ev ch: nt qckn towards fin* **11/4**[2]
3233 3 11 **Knight Owl**[20] 3365 3-9-1 69 .... FrederikTylicki 8 45
(James Fanshawe) *trckd ldrs: racd keenly: rdn over 2f out: wknd over 1f out* **5/2**[1]
4565 4 2 3/4 **Guishan**[25] 3179 3-9-1 62 .... AndrewMullen 4 38
(Michael Appleby) *prom: rdn over 2f out: wknd over 1f out* **20/1**
23-3 5 1 3/4 **Sky Garden**[36] 2824 3-9-1 70 ....(b[1]) LiamJones 7 33
(William Haggas) *plld hrd and prom: rdn over 2f out: wknd over 1f out* **7/1**
30-3 6 2 3/4 **North Pole**[18] 3438 3-9-1 67 .... ChrisCatlin 6 26
(Sir Mark Prescott Bt) *chsd ldrs: lost pl over 4f out: sn pushed along: rdn and wknd over 2f out* **16/1**
-044 7 nse **Mujarrad (USA)**[24] 3191 3-9-1 68 .... SebSanders 5 26
(J W Hills) *led: hdd over 4f out: rdn and wknd over 2f out* **14/1**
060- 8 7 **Desert Command**[288] 6443 3-9-1 68 .... CathyGannon 10 7
(Andrew Balding) *free to post: plld hrd: trckd ldrs: rdn over 2f out: sn wknd* **5/1**[3]

1m 23.59s (-2.61) **Going Correction** -0.225s/f (Firm) **8** Ran SP% **115.0**
Speed ratings (Par 100): **105,104,92,88,86 83,83,75**
toteswingers 1&2 £5.50, 1&3 £2.20, 2&3 £2.00 CSF £24.93 TOTE £8.80: £2.20, £1.10, £1.30; EX 18.50 Trifecta £52.80 Pool: £1464.16 - 20.77 winning units.
Owner Sheikh Marwan Al Maktoum **Bred** Darley **Trained** Newmarket, Suffolk
■ Stewards' Enquiry : Louis Steward one-day ban; careless riding (20th July).

FOCUS
The majority of runners were closely matched on official figures in this 0-70 maiden but the first two pulled a long way clear. A personal best from the winner and the time might be a bit better than it looks.

4069 HOPEWELLS THE FURNITURE STORE NOTTINGHAM H'CAP 5f 2y
5:05 (5:07) (Class 5) (0-70,70) 3-Y-O **£4,528** (£1,347; £673; £336) **Stalls** Centre

Form RPR
5061 1 **Lexington Place**[14] 3594 3-8-10 **64** .... DavidBergin(5) 8 76
(David O'Meara) *mde all: rdn over 1f out: edgd rt ins fnl f: styd on* **9/4**[1]
4004 2 3/4 **Lager Time (IRE)**[12] 3638 3-9-0 **63** .... WilliamCarson 1 72
(David Evans) *hld up: hdwy 2f out: chsd wnr over 1f out: sn rdn: styd on* **16/1**
2116 3 2 **Shirley's Pride**[36] 2829 3-9-4 **67** ....(t) AndrewMullen 2 69
(Michael Appleby) *s.i.s: sn pushed along in rr: hdwy u.p over 1f out: styd on same pce ins fnl f* **9/2**
4040 4 nk **Roanne (USA)**[10] 3699 3-9-0 **63** ....(bt) AdamKirby 7 64
(Clive Cox) *trckd ldrs: wnt 2nd over 3f out tl rdn over 1f out: styd on same pce ins fnl f* **4/1**[3]
2362 5 2 1/2 **Hot Secret**[10] 3678 3-9-7 **70** .... CathyGannon 6 62
(Andrew Balding) *chsd ldrs: rdn over 1f out: wknd ins fnl f* **11/4**[2]
605 6 3/4 **Dream Ally (IRE)**[32] 2959 3-9-5 **68** ....(p) FrederikTylicki 3 57
(Jedd O'Keeffe) *chsd wnr tl over 3f out: rdn 1/2-way: wknd ins fnl f* **6/1**

59.51s (-0.49) **Going Correction** -0.225s/f (Firm) **6** Ran SP% **115.8**
Speed ratings (Par 100): **94,92,89,89,85 83**
toteswingers 1&2 £14.70, 1&3 £1.10, 2&3 £6.20 CSF £37.03 CT £152.42 TOTE £3.20: £1.90, £3.90; EX 37.90 Trifecta £115.40 Pool: £1143.48 - 7.43 winning units.
Owner Middleham Park Racing XXXI **Bred** Christopher & Annabelle Mason **Trained** Nawton, N Yorks

FOCUS
There was a front-running winner in this minor sprint handicap for 3-y-os. He stepped up from his Redcar win.

4070 SANDICLIFFE YOUR GREAT MOTORING FAMILY H'CAP 1m 60y
5:35 (5:37) (Class 6) (0-65,63) 3-Y-O+ **£3,234** (£962; £481; £240) **Stalls** Low

Form RPR
3312 1 **Lord Franklin**[5] 3895 4-9-6 **60** .... JasonHart(5) 14 73
(Eric Alston) *chsd ldr tl led over 2f out: rdn over 1f out: edgd lft: styd on* **15/8**[1]
054 2 hd **Sacred Square (GER)**[23] 3250 3-9-5 **63** ....(v) FrederikTylicki 9 74
(William Haggas) *hld up: hdwy u.p over 2f out: hung rt and chsd wnr over 1f out: sn ev ch: styd on* **9/4**[2]
-353 3 5 **Lutine Charlie (IRE)**[10] 3676 6-9-13 **62** .... CathyGannon 8 63
(Pat Eddery) *chsd ldrs: rdn over 2f out: styd on same pce fnl f* **12/1**
0050 4 1 1/4 **Master Of Song**[15] 3546 6-9-6 **55** ....(p) JimmyQuinn 12 53+
(Roy Bowring) *hld up: hdwy over 3f out: nt clr run fr over 2f out tl swtchd lft ins fnl f: r.o: nvr able to chal* **33/1**
4000 5 2 3/4 **Multisure**[12] 3629 3-8-10 **54** .... SamHitchcott 3 44
(Ruth Carr) *chsd ldrs: rdn over 2f out: wknd ins fnl f* **50/1**
2452 6 3/4 **Piccolo Mondo**[10] 3687 7-9-5 **61** .... ShelleyBirkett(7) 4 51
(Philip Hide) *chsd ldrs: rdn over 2f out: wknd fnl f* **12/1**
00-5 7 1 3/4 **Tanforan**[16] 3513 11-9-5 **54** .... WilliamCarson 10 40
(Brian Baugh) *hld up in tch: plld hrd: rdn over 1f out: wknd fnl f* **25/1**
415- 8 1 3/4 **Angel Cake (IRE)**[204] 8111 4-9-5 **54** .... AndrewMullen 13 36
(Michael Appleby) *mid-div: hdwy over 3f out: rdn over 2f out: wknd over 1f out* **12/1**
345 9 1 1/2 **Last Destination (IRE)**[11] 3649 5-8-13 **53**(p) WilliamTwiston-Davies(5) 6 32
(Nigel Tinkler) *hld up: rdn over 3f out: n.d* **6/1**[3]
2235 10 6 **Maakirr (IRE)**[9] 3719 4-9-11 **63** ....(t) MarkCoumbe(3) 1 28
(Roy Bowring) *hld up: plld hrd: hdwy over 2f out: rdn and wknd over 1f out* **14/1**
60-0 11 6 **Ocean Power (IRE)**[178] 122 3-8-7 **51** ow1 .... FergusSweeney 11
(Richard Phillips) *s.i.s: a in rr* **50/1**
035- 12 1/2 **Lordship (IRE)**[244] 7318 9-8-9 **49** .... JakePayne(5) 7
(Tom Gretton) *led: rdn and hdd over 2f out: wknd over 1f out* **40/1**
-000 13 12 **Siouxperhero (IRE)**[40] 2728 4-10-0 **63** ....(b) MartinDwyer 5
(William Muir) *s.s: a bhd: t.o* **11/1**

1m 42.89s (-2.21) **Going Correction** -0.225s/f (Firm)
WFA 3 from 4yo+ 9lb **13** Ran SP% **131.1**
Speed ratings (Par 101): **102,101,96,95,92 92,90,88,87,81 75,74,62**
toteswingers 1&2 £1.90, 1&3 £3.50, 2&3 £5.60 CSF £6.56 CT £45.09 TOTE £2.60: £1.20, £1.60, £3.50; EX 8.40 Trifecta £45.70 Pool: £1747.33 - 28.62 winning units.
Owner Liam & Tony Ferguson **Bred** Tony Ferguson & Liam Ferguson **Trained** Longton, Lancs
■ Stewards' Enquiry : Jason Hart three-day; careless riding (20th-22nd July).

FOCUS
An ordinary handicap with little depth, but the two market leaders pulled clear and the form looks decent for the grade.
T/Plt: £202.70 to a £1 stake. Pool: £79,322.39 - 285.59 winning tickets T/Qpdt: £145.30 to a £1 stake. Pool: £5047.63 - 25.70 winning tickets CR

3245 NOTTINGHAM (L-H)
Saturday, July 6

OFFICIAL GOING: Good to firm (watered; 9.1)
Wind: virtually nil Weather: very warm

4071 AJA LADIES' H'CAP (FOR LADY AMATEUR RIDERS) 1m 2f 50y
6:00 (6:00) (Class 6) (0-60,60) 3-Y-O+ **£1,871** (£580; £290; £145) **Stalls** Low

Form RPR
4406 1 **Flag Of Glory**[5] 3889 6-10-2 **60** .... MissMEdden(5) 11 69
(Peter Hiatt) *racd wd: hld up in midfield: hdwy 2f out: styd on wl to ld ins fnl f: gng away at fin* **22/1**
0-55 2 1 1/2 **Hernando Torres**[16] 3504 5-10-0 **58** .... AnnaHesketh(5) 7 64
(Michael Easterby) *hld up wl in tch in midfield: effrt to chse ldr ent fnl f: ev ch briefly ins fnl f: styd on but outpcd by wnr fnl 100yds* **7/1**[3]
3430 3 1 1/4 **Rockweiller**[24] 3195 6-10-2 **55** ....(v) MissJCoward 2 59
(Steve Gollings) *sn led: rdn 2f out: hdd and no ex ins fnl f: wknd towards fin* **7/2**[1]
0643 4 3/4 **Rub Of The Relic (IRE)**[5] 3889 8-10-1 **59** ....(v) MissHDukes(5) 4 61
(Paul Midgley) *chsd ldr: rdn ent fnl 2f: styd on same pce ent fnl f: u.p after* **10/1**
002 5 3/4 **Action Front (USA)**[15] 3534 5-9-13 **52** ....(v) MissADeniel 1 53
(Derek Shaw) *in tch in midfield: effrt on inner to chse ldrs 2f out: one pce u.p fr over 1f out* **6/1**[2]

5042 **6** ½ **Men Don't Cry (IRE)**[5] 3909 4-9-4 **46** oh1..............(v) MissAliceMills(3) 8 46
(Ed de Giles) *chsd ldrs: rdn and unable qck 2f out: plugged on same pce fr over 1f out* **12/1**

-500 **7** 1¾ **Ma Kellys (IRE)**[46] 2536 4-9-3 **47**......................... MissBeckySmith(5) 16 44
(Micky Hammond) *hld up in midfield: rdn and effrt 2f out: no imp over 1f out* **40/1**

0211 **8** 1¼ **Young Jackie**[4] 3924 5-9-13 **57** 6ex....................(b) MissKMargarson(5) 6 51
(George Margarson) *v.s.a: bhd: hdwy into midfield but stl plenty to do 3f out: rdn and kpt on fr over 2f out: nvr trbld ldrs* **6/1**[2]

-540 **9** hd **Laconicos (IRE)**[16] 3504 11-10-0 **58**..........................(t) MissCScott(5) 15 52
(William Stone) *taken down early: bhd: rdn 3f out: no imp tl styd on ins fnl f: nvr trbld ldrs* **33/1**

3536 **10** nse **Who's That Chick (IRE)**[16] 3496 4-9-7 **53**................ MissEllaSmith(7) 9 47
(Ralph Smith) *t.k.h: hld up in midfield: rdn and hdwy over 2f out: no imp over 1f out* **33/1**

0204 **11** ¾ **Iguacu**[19] 3406 9-9-12 **51**...(p) MissSBrotherton 3 43
(Richard Price) *chsd ldrs: rdn and effrt 3f out: struggling and lost pl ent fnl 2f: wknd over 1f out* **8/1**

4000 **12** 1 **Follow The Flag (IRE)**[32] 2966 9-9-7 **51**..........(v) MissPhillipaTutty(5) 13 41
(Alan McCabe) *in tch in midfield: rdn and struggling over 3f out: n.d fnl 2f* **20/1**

6-50 **13** ½ **Barbsiz (IRE)**[39] 2762 3-8-9 **52**............................. MissNMcCaffrey(7) 14 42
(Mark H Tompkins) *stdd and dropped in bhd after s: hld up in rr: sme hdwy over 2f out: no imp* **50/1**

2030 **14** ¾ **Al Furat (USA)**[16] 3504 5-10-0 **58**................................ MrsVDavies(5) 10 46
(Ron Barr) *racd wd: a towards rr: rdn and no prog over 2f out: n.d* **12/1**

0020 **15** hd **Market Puzzle (IRE)**[21] 3314 6-9-9 **51**......(p) MissBeckyBrisbourne(3) 12 39
(Mark Brisbourne) *t.k.h: hld up towards rr: rdn and effrt ent fnl 2f: bhd and swtchd rt 1f out: n.d* **22/1**

6003 **16** 6 **Silver Marizah (IRE)**[12] 3637 4-9-0 **46** oh1.............. MissRBIngram(7) 5 22
(Roger Ingram) *t.k.h: chsd ldrs tl over 2f out: sn dropped out: bhd 1f out* **33/1**

2m 10.02s (-4.28) **Going Correction** -0.375s/f (Firm)
WFA 3 from 4yo+ 11lb **16** Ran SP% **125.6**
Speed ratings (Par 101): **102,100,99,99,98 98,96,95,95,95 95,94,93,93,93 88**
toteswingers 1&2 £36.90, 1&3 £22.70, 2&3 £5.30 CSF £162.34 CT £690.01 TOTE £34.80: £5.80, £2.10, £1.90, £2.40; EX 296.70 Trifecta £2027.80 Part won. Pool: £2,703.80 - 0.79 winning units..
Owner N D Edden **Bred** Follow The Flag Partnership **Trained** Hook Norton, Oxon

FOCUS
This was run at no more than a sensible gallop. The winner is rated back to his best form of the past year.

4072 WINNING WAY WITH DG CARS (S) STKS 6f 15y
6:30 (6:30) (Class 6) 3-4-Y-O **£1,940** (£577; £288; £144) **Stalls** High

Form RPR

5561 **1** **Nenge Mboko**[5] 3897 3-9-1 73.......................................(v) PatCosgrave 2 81
(George Baker) *chsd ldrs: rdn and effrt to ld jst over 1f out: edgd rt but sn clr: eased towards fin: comf* **6/5**[1]

-001 **2** 3 **Planetex (IRE)**[17] 3475 4-8-9 69.................................... OisinMurphy(7) 4 66
(John Quinn) *pressed ldr tl led ent fnl 2f: rdn and hdd jst over 1f out: nt qckn and pushed rt jst ins fnl f: sn btn* **7/4**[2]

10-0 **3** 10 **Albert Tatlock (IRE)**[29] 3068 4-9-2 68............................(p) AdamKirby 3 34
(John Butler) *led: rdn and hdd ent fnl 2f: flashed tail u.p and btn over 1f out: wknd 1f out* **7/1**[3]

4 **4** 2¾ **Princess Quest**[9] 3731 4-8-11 0....................................... MartinHarley 5 21
(Mick Channon) *taken down early: t.k.h: chsd ldrs: ev ch and rdn 2f out: struggling over 1f out: wknd 1f out* **7/1**[3]

0363 **5** 7 **Rooknrasbryripple**[29] 3052 4-8-6 46.................................... RyanTate(5) 1
(Ralph Smith) *taken down early: wnt lft s: bhd: rdn and clsd to press ldrs 1/2-way: wknd 2f out: wl bhd fnl f* **33/1**

1m 12.36s (-2.34) **Going Correction** -0.325s/f (Firm)
WFA 3 from 4yo 6lb **5** Ran SP% **109.8**
Speed ratings (Par 101): **102,98,84,81,71**
CSF £3.53 TOTE £2.20: £2.00, £1.10; EX 3.20 Trifecta £4.10 Pool: £1251.11 - 224.31 winning units.Nenge Mboko was bought in for 5,200gns
Owner Russell Conrad Vail Wheeler Hippychick **Bred** Pigeon House Stud **Trained** Manton, Wilts

FOCUS
There wasn't much between the main protagonists on adjusted ratings in this weak seller. The winner is rated to form.

4073 MOST RELIABLE BET DG TAXIS MAIDEN AUCTION FILLIES' STKS 5f 13y
7:00 (7:05) (Class 5) 2-Y-O **£3,234** (£962; £481; £240) **Stalls** High

Form RPR

5 **1** **Hopefilly (IRE)**[35] 2869 2-8-8 0...................................... HayleyTurner 12 75
(Ed Walker) *racd nr stands' rail: in tch in midfield: effrt to chse clr ldr ent fnl f: rn and hung lft but clsd and str chal ins fnl f: r.o wl to ld nr fin* **8/1**

3522 **2** hd **Memory Styx**[22] 3280 2-8-8 0....................................... MartinHarley 3 74
(Mick Channon) *racd in centre: led: drvn and clr ent fnl f: hrd pressed ins fnl f: r.o tl hdd and no ex nr fin* **3/1**[2]

00 **3** 5 **Fredricka**[38] 2767 2-8-4 0.. AndrewMullen 5 52
(Garry Moss) *racd in centre: racd freely: chsd wnr tl 3rd and btn ent fnl f: outpcd by ldng pair but battled on to hold 3rd* **16/1**

5 **4** 1¼ **Heroique (IRE)**[30] 3023 2-8-12 0.................................... DavidAllan 2 56
(Tim Easterby) *racd in centre: chsd ldrs: rdn 1/2-way: outpcd and btn over 1f out: wl hld but plugged on fnl f* **12/1**

6 **5** shd **Lady In Blue (IRE)**[57] 2204 2-8-12 0.............................. LiamJones 6 55
(William Haggas) *racd in centre: in tch in midfield: rdn 1/2-way: outpcd and btn wl over 1f out: wl hld but plugged on fnl f* **6/4**[1]

6 1¾ **Rosita** 2-7-13 0.. AmyScott(5) 11 41+
(Henry Candy) *led rdrless to s: racd towards stands' rail: s.i.s: bhd: hdwy over 1f out: kpt on steadily fnl f: nvr trbld ldrs* **12/1**

0420 **7** 1¼ **Wiki Tiki**[22] 3295 2-8-12 0.. HarryBentley 10 44
(Stuart Williams) *racd against stands' rail: chsd ldrs: rdn and btn over 1f out: fdd fnl f* **6/1**[3]

8 2½ **Britain (IRE)** 2-8-4 0.. KirstyMilczarek 7 27
(David C Griffiths) *in tch in midfield: rn green and outpcd wl over 1f out: sn wknd* **40/1**

0 **9** 1¼ **Biscuiteer**[20] 3366 2-8-2 0 ow1..................................... BillyCray(3) 1 24
(Scott Dixon) *taken down early: restless in stalls: wnt lft s: racd in centre: a towards rr: n.d* **66/1**

00 **10** 2¾ **Sands Legends**[19] 3413 2-8-4 0.................................... JamesSullivan 9 13
(James Given) *in tch in midfield tl lost pl u.p 1/2-way: bhd over 1f out* **66/1**

11 2¾ **Hoofs (IRE)** 2-8-4 0.. JimmyQuinn 4 3
(Gary Harrison) *racd in centre: a in rr: n.d* **40/1**

12 11 **Artistic Acclaim (IRE)** 2-8-4 0 ow3................................ RyanClark(3) 8
(John Weymes) *wnt rt s: sn outpcd: t.o fr 1/2-way* **50/1**

59.67s (-1.83) **Going Correction** -0.325s/f (Firm) 2y crse rec **12** Ran SP% **121.5**
Speed ratings (Par 91): **101,100,92,90,90 87,85,81,79,75 70,53**
toteswingers 1&2 £7.60, 1&3 £15.80, 2&3 £11.00 CSF £32.54 TOTE £11.30: £2.70, £1.30, £3.40; EX 52.60 Trifecta £506.50 Pool: £1420.29 - 2.10 winning units.
Owner Laurence A Bellman **Bred** Mount Coote Stud & M & W Bell Racing **Trained** Newmarket, Suffolk

FOCUS
The front two pulled nicely clear and the form can be rated around the consistent runner-up. The form is sound.

4074 FOR YOUR COMFORT DG CARS 01159500500 H'CAP 5f 13y
7:30 (7:32) (Class 5) (0-70,69) 3-Y-0+ **£2,587** (£770; £384; £192) **Stalls** High

Form RPR

0600 **1** **Sleepy Blue Ocean**[7] 3811 7-9-5 **62**................................(p) JimCrowley 2 71
(John Balding) *in tch in midfield: clsd and swtchd lft over 1f out: rdn to ld ins fnl f: drvn out* **7/1**

0244 **2** nk **Mercers Row**[9] 3713 6-9-12 **69**.. JimmyQuinn 8 77
(Karen Tutty) *racd in midfield: rdn and effrt over 1f out: str run to chse wnr fnl 100yds: clsng but nvr quite getting to wnr* **6/1**[3]

3-00 **3** 2¼ **Errigal Lad**[23] 3246 8-8-7 **50** oh1.................................. KirstyMilczarek 7 50
(Garry Woodward) *sn outpcd in last trio: rdn 1/2-way: hdwy u.p 1f out: styd on strly fnl f to go 3rd last strides: nvr trbld ldrs* **13/2**

0035 **4** hd **Royal Bajan (USA)**[14] 3569 5-9-12 **69**............................(b) GrahamLee 4 68
(James Given) *chsd ldr: rdn and ev ch over 1f out: chsd wnr and no ex ins fnl f: wknd towards fin* **7/1**

3131 **5** nk **Black Annis Bower**[28] 3078 5-9-11 **68**.......................... JamesSullivan 5 66
(Michael Easterby) *dwlt: pushed along early and rcvrd to chse ldrs after 1f out: effrt u.p over 1f out: pressed ldrs ins fnl f: no ex and wknd fnl 75yds* **5/1**[2]

4001 **6** ½ **Majestic Manannan (IRE)**[9] 3738 4-9-10 **67**................ AndrewMullen 6 63
(David Nicholls) *led: drvn ent fnl f: hdd ins fnl f: wknd fnl 75yds* **10/3**[1]

0-20 **7** 1 **Baby Queen (IRE)**[14] 3569 7-9-11 **68**........................ TomMcLaughlin 1 61
(Brian Baugh) *chsd ldrs: rdn and effrt 2f out: no ex ent fnl f: wknd ins fnl f* **16/1**

1400 **8** nse **Divertimenti (IRE)**[23] 3246 9-9-1 **61**.........................(b) MarkCoumbe(3) 9 54
(Roy Bowring) *sn outpcd and rdn along in last trio: clsd u.p and switching lft jst ins fnl f: kpt on but nvr trbld ldrs* **11/1**

40 **9** 31 **My Time**[39] 2757 4-8-6 **52**...(p) RyanClark(3) 3
(Michael Mullineaux) *sn totally outpcd in last: t.o fr 1/2-way* **9/1**

59.45s (-2.05) **Going Correction** -0.325s/f (Firm) **9** Ran SP% **116.6**
Speed ratings (Par 103): **103,102,98,98,98 97,95,95,46**
toteswingers 1&2 £8.30, 1&3 £10.30, 2&3 £6.70 CSF £49.00 CT £290.67 TOTE £9.40: £3.30, £1.60, £2.60; EX 48.20 Trifecta £827.40 Pool: £1357.55 - 1.23 winning units.
Owner Tykes And Terriers Racing Club **Bred** Exors Of The Late N Ahamad & P C Scott **Trained** Scrooby, Notts

FOCUS
They went hard up front, so much so that the speedy Divertimenti couldn't get into it, and, unsurprisingly, the pace didn't hold up. The time was only marginally faster than the previous seller and the form isn't particularly trustworthy. The winner bounced back from a couple of lesser efforts.

4075 LIN & DICK GETTING CLOSE TO YO H'CAP 1m 2f 50y
8:00 (8:00) (Class 4) (0-80,80) 3-Y-0+ **£6,469** (£1,925; £962; £481) **Stalls** Low

Form RPR

1166 **1** **Take Two**[24] 3208 4-10-0 **80**.. HayleyTurner 3 88
(Alex Hales) *in tch in midfield: clsd to chse ldr 2f out: drvn to ld jst ins fnl f: hld on wl: rdn out* **6/1**[2]

4006 **2** ½ **Aquilonius (IRE)**[13] 3607 4-9-6 **72**..............................(t) HarryBentley 8 79
(Stuart Williams) *led after 1f and set stdy gallop: qcknd 3f out: hdd and drvn jst ins fnl f: kpt on but a hld* **8/1**

-041 **3** 1½ **Tenor (IRE)**[8] 3793 3-8-8 **71**.. AndreaAtzeni 4 75+
(Roger Varian) *hld up in tch in midfield: rdn 3f out: n.m.r over 2f out: unable qck over 1f out: swtchd rt and styd on ins fnl f to go 3rd last strides* **10/11**[1]

1320 **4** hd **Purple 'n Gold (IRE)**[17] 3468 4-9-5 **76**......(v) WilliamTwiston-Davies(5) 2 80
(David Pipe) *in tch in last pair: clsd but nt clr run on inner over 2f out: chsd ldng pair: swtchd rt and drvn jst ins fnl f: one pce after and lost 3rd last strides* **20/1**

1330 **5** 2¾ **No Dominion (IRE)**[10] 3683 4-9-10 **76**.......................... GrahamLee 5 75
(James Given) *s.i.s: hld up in tch: rdn and effrt over 2f out: no ex 1f out: wknd ins fnl f* **9/1**

3510 **6** 4 **Lady Macduff (IRE)**[7] 3827 4-9-10 **76**............................ FrannyNorton 1 67
(Mark Johnston) *chsd ldr tl 2f out: sn struggling u.p: wknd 1f out* **15/2**[3]

5006 **7** 6 **Marshland**[11] 3649 3-8-1 **64**.. NickyMackay 6 44
(Mark Johnston) *t.k.h: led for 1f: chsd ldng pair tl lost pl 3f out: wknd over 1f out* **14/1**

2m 9.62s (-4.68) **Going Correction** -0.375s/f (Firm)
WFA 3 from 4yo+ 11lb **7** Ran SP% **111.0**
Speed ratings (Par 105): **103,102,101,101,99 95,91**
toteswingers 1&2 £6.50, 1&3 £2.10, 2&3 £2.40 CSF £48.46 CT £78.59 TOTE £8.00: £3.40, £4.40; EX 59.80 Trifecta £101.50 Pool: £945.07 - 6.97 winning units.
Owner S P Bloodstock **Bred** Steven & Petra Wallace **Trained** Edgcote, Northants

FOCUS
With the pace being no stronger than leisurely, this probably isn't very strong form for the grade. The winner rates a small personal best.

4076 SAFE BET DG TAXIS 01159500500 H'CAP (JOCKEY CLUB GRASSROOTS MIDDLE DISTANCE SERIES QUALIFIER) 1m 2f 50y
8:30 (8:32) (Class 5) (0-75,74) 3-Y-O **£2,587** (£770; £384; £192) **Stalls** Low

Form RPR

0542 **1** **Invincible Cara (IRE)**[20] 3365 3-9-5 **72**......................... AdamKirby 1 84+
(Ed Dunlop) *t.k.h: hld up in tch: trckd ldrs but nt enough room against rail fr 2f out: gap opened and readily qcknd to ld wl ins fnl f: sn in command* **5/1**[3]

6502 **2** ½ **Polar Forest**[12] 3629 3-8-2 **55**....................................... FrannyNorton 5 63
(Richard Guest) *t.k.h: chsd ldrs tl hdwy to ld after 2f and settled in front: set stdy gallop: rdn over 2f out: drvn 1f out: hdd and outpcd wl ins fnl f* **20/1**

4-61 **3** 1¼ **Fast Pace**[23] 3251 3-9-7 **74**.. JimCrowley 3 80
(Amanda Perrett) *in tch: clsd to press ldr gng wl 2f out: sn rdn: unable qck and one pce fnl 100yds* **3/1**[2]

-264 **4** 1¾ **Manchestar**[22] 3281 3-9-2 **69**.. TonyHamilton 6 71+
(Richard Fahey) *taken down early: stdd s: t.k.h: hld up in tch in rr: swtchd rt and nt clr run 2f out: in the clr and styd on u.p fnl f: no threat to ldrs* **8/1**

435 5 1/2 **Jazz Master**[29] 3059 3-9-6 **73** KierenFallon 2 74
(Luca Cumani) *dwlt: niggled along in last trio: rdn 4f out: swtchd rt and sme hdwy 2f out: hung lft over 1f out: one pce fnl f* **9/4**[1]

0-04 6 1 1/2 **Marlborough House**[23] 3232 3-8-9 **62** RichardKingscote 8 61
(James Given) *led for 2f: chsd ldr tl 3f: lost pl u.p over 2f out: plugged on but no threat to ldrs after* **11/2**

-220 7 nk **Cash Is King**[22] 3294 3-9-4 **71** GrahamLee 4 69
(Jonjo O'Neill) *chsd ldr for 2f: styd chsng ldrs tl wnt 2nd again 3f out tl 2f out: btn 1f out: wknd ins fnl f* **8/1**

2m 10.89s (-3.41) **Going Correction** -0.375s/f (Firm) **7** Ran SP% **114.8**
Speed ratings (Par 100): **98,97,96,95,94 93,93**
toteswingers 1&2 £13.00, 1&3 £3.10, 2&3 £21.70 CSF £89.56 TOTE £3.30: £1.30, £10.60; EX 50.50 Trifecta £330.20 Pool: £924.29 - 2.09 winning units.
Owner Windflower Overseas Holdings Inc **Bred** Windflower Overseas **Trained** Newmarket, Suffolk

FOCUS
Another steadily run affair, indeed the time was even slower than the previous race, and once again the market leader proved disappointing. The form makes some sense, however.

4077 ODDS ON FAVOURITE DG TAXIS 01159500500 H'CAP 1m 75y
9:00 (9:03) (Class 5) (0-70,73) 3-Y-O+ **£2,587** (£770; £384; £192) **Stalls** Centre

Form RPR

-320 1 **Not Rigg (USA)**[15] 3537 3-9-5 **70** (t) ShaneKelly 5 75
(Gary Harrison) *broke wl: led for 2f: allowed ldr to go clr: clsd and led 2f out: clr and drvn 1f out: a holding on: rdn out* **10/1**

0021 2 nk **The Scuttler (IRE)**[6] 3859 3-8-11 **62** MartinHarley 3 66
(Mick Channon) *chsd ldrs: rdn and effrt 2f out: drvn and chsd wnr ins fnl f: r.o and clsng towards fin: nvr quite getting to wnr* **6/4**[1]

6411 3 1 1/2 **Woody Bay**[9] 3722 3-9-8 **73** GrahamLee 7 74
(James Given) *in tch: clsd on ldr 3f out: rdn and chsd wnr over 1f out: no imp and lost 2nd ins fnl f: no ex* **2/1**[2]

0346 4 2 1/2 **West End Lad**[15] 3545 10-9-8 **67** (b) MarkCoumbe(3) 4 64
(Roy Bowring) *dwlt: in rr: hdwy on outer bnd 5f out: rdn 3f out: outpcd 2f out: no threat to ldrs but kpt on again ins fnl f* **8/1**

-264 5 1/2 **Cheers Big Ears (IRE)**[16] 3513 7-8-9 **51** oh4 AndreaAtzeni 1 47
(Richard Price) *t.k.h: chsd ldrs tl stdd to rr 5f out: rdn and effrt 3f out: no real imp: kpt on* **7/1**[3]

100 6 3/4 **Two No Bids (IRE)**[8] 3793 3-8-12 **63** (p) JimCrowley 2 55
(Phil McEntee) *chsd ldrs and styd wd early: led after 2f and sn clr: hdd 2f and fnd little for press: wknd 1f out* **20/1**

1m 45.17s (-3.83) **Going Correction** -0.375s/f (Firm)
WFA 3 from 7yo+ 9lb **6** Ran SP% **110.8**
Speed ratings (Par 103): **104,103,102,99,99 98**
toteswingers 1&2 £2.10, 1&3 £2.10, 2&3 £1.10 CSF £24.98 TOTE £4.10: £1.10, £2.50; EX 31.60 Trifecta £52.20 Pool: £975.47 - 13.99 winning units.
Owner Franconson Partners **Bred** Galleria Bloodstock **Trained** Newmarket, Suffolk

FOCUS
Two No Bids went tearing off, but the others seemed to ignore him and the pace for the main body of runners was fairly sedate. Shaky form.
T/Plt: £768.20 to a £1 stake. Pool: £63,545.36 - 60.38 winning units T/Qpdt: £126.10 to a £1 stake. Pool: £5540.87 - 32.50 winning units SP

4024 SANDOWN (R-H)
Saturday, July 6

OFFICIAL GOING: Good to firm (firm in places; round course 8.5, sprint course 8.6)
Wind: Almost nil Weather: Fine, very warm

4078 MALCOLM PALMER MEMORIAL H'CAP 7f 16y
1:30 (1:32) (Class 3) (0-95,89) 3-Y-O **£9,337** (£2,796; £1,398; £699; £349; £175) **Stalls** Low

Form RPR

-202 1 **Beach Club**[23] 3234 3-9-5 **87** SeanLevey 5 94
(David Brown) *mde all: 4 l clr after 3f: rdn 2f out: gap whittled away fnl f but hld on wl* **10/1**

1-00 2 nk **Related**[140] 697 3-8-12 **80** LukeMorris 1 86
(Clive Cox) *chsd wnr: 4 l down after 3f: drvn 2f out: grad clsd fnl f: jst hld* **10/1**

-114 3 nk **Pythagorean**[21] 3342 3-9-7 **89** JamesDoyle 6 98+
(Roger Charlton) *hld up in last: stl long way off the pce whn rn into trble over 1f out: prog sn after: r.o strly fnl f: clsng fast at fin: too much to do* **15/8**[1]

21 4 2 1/4 **Plover**[31] 2979 3-9-6 **88** RyanMoore 8 87
(Sir Michael Stoute) *wore net-muzzle: hld up in 5th: rdn over 2f out: prog to chse clr ldng pair over 1f out: one pce after: lost 3rd nr fin* **7/2**[3]

0310 5 1 1/2 **Kyllachy Rise**[16] 3484 3-9-1 **83** RichardHughes 4 78
(Richard Hannon) *hld up in last trio: n.m.r on inner wl over 2f out: styd on same pce fr over 1f out: n.d* **10/3**[2]

-660 6 3 1/2 **Operation Chariot (IRE)**[35] 2857 3-9-5 **87**[1] JakeNoonan 2 73
(Andrew Balding) *sn chsd clr ldng pair: drvn and no imp over 2f out: wknd over 1f out* **20/1**

1001 7 4 **Skytrain**[8] 3782 3-8-7 **78** DarrenEgan(3) 3 53
(Mark Johnston) *chsd ldng trio: rdn over 2f out: wknd wl over 1f out* **12/1**

0-00 8 2 3/4 **Annie's Fortune (IRE)**[17] 3460 3-9-1 **88**[1] MichaelJMMurphy(5) 7 55
(Alan Jarvis) *t.k.h: hld up in last trio: shkn up over 2f out: wknd wl over 1f out* **16/1**

1m 27.23s (-2.27) **Going Correction** -0.30s/f (Firm) **8** Ran SP% **116.6**
Speed ratings (Par 104): **100,99,99,96,95 91,86,83**
toteswingers 1&2 £5.30, 1&3 £6.00, 2&3 £4.70 CSF £105.04 CT £272.74 TOTE £12.60: £2.70, £2.50, £1.20; EX 115.00 Trifecta £388.00 Pool: £2556.35 - 4.94 winning units.
Owner J C Fretwell **Bred** Mill House Stud **Trained** Averham Park, Notts

FOCUS
Just 2.5mm of water was added to the track overnight and on a hot and sunny day the going was given as good to firm, firm in places (GoingStick: Round 8.5; Sprint 8.6). The round course was at its innermost configuration. They didn't go that quick early here and the 1-2 were always the front pair. The winner is progressive and has been given some credit, but the third was unlucky.

4079 CORAL CHARGE (REGISTERED AS THE SPRINT STKS) (GROUP 3) 5f 6y
2:05 (2:06) (Class 1) 3-Y-O+
£34,026 (£12,900; £6,456; £3,216; £1,614; £810) **Stalls** Low

Form RPR

-105 1 **Tickled Pink (IRE)**[23] 3263 4-9-4 108 TomQueally 2 112
(Lady Cecil) *fast away: led against far rail: narrowly hdd after 2f: drvn wl over 1f out: rallied to ld jst ins fnl f: edgd lft but styd on wl* **5/2**[1]

-210 2 1 **Kingsgate Native (IRE)**[18] 3420 8-9-9 112 ShaneKelly 6 114
(Robert Cowell) *hld up in last trio: prog 2f out: trying to cl whn nt clr run briefly and swtchd lft ins fnl f: r.o to take 2nd last strides* **15/2**

-030 3 nk **Mince**[14] 3557 4-9-0 107 (b[1]) JamesDoyle 3 103
(Roger Charlton) *sn pressed wnr: narrow ldr after 2f: drvn over 1f out: hdd and nt qckn jst ins fnl f: lost 2nd last strides* **5/1**[3]

-400 4 3/4 **Bungle Inthejungle**[18] 3420 3-8-12 105 MartinHarley 8 102
(Mick Channon) *chsd ldng pair: rdn 1/2-way: lost pl and struggling over 1f out: styd on again last 150yds* **9/1**

0230 5 nse **Hoyam**[18] 3420 3-8-9 102 JamesMcDonald 1 98
(Michael Bell) *chsd ldng pair: rdn 2f out: keeping on but hld whn carried lft ins fnl f* **12/1**

1510 6 1 1/4 **Duke Of Firenze**[14] 3558 4-9-3 101 RyanMoore 4 99
(Sir Michael Stoute) *hld up in last trio: pushed along and no prog 2f out: kpt on fnl f: n.d* **3/1**[2]

5510 7 2 1/4 **Spirit Quartz (IRE)**[18] 3420 5-9-9 110 (p) JamieSpencer 5 97
(Robert Cowell) *a in last trio and sn struggling to go the pce: no prog over 1f out: wl btn after* **11/2**

59.27s (-2.33) **Going Correction** -0.175s/f (Firm)
WFA 3 from 4yo+ 5lb **7** Ran SP% **115.1**
Speed ratings (Par 113): **111,109,108,107,107 105,102**
toteswingers 1&2 £3.80, 1&3 £3.30, 2&3 £5.60 CSF £21.99 TOTE £3.20: £2.00, £2.90; EX 20.50 Trifecta £75.40 Pool: £3557.76 - 35.34 winning units.
Owner Trevor C Stewart **Bred** T Stewart **Trained** Newmarket, Suffolk

FOCUS
The sprint course was realigned four yards in from its full width. The Classic generation had taken five of the last eight runnings of this Group 3 sprint, but the two 3yos here were the outsiders and this was one for the older fraternity. Pretty straightforward form, Tickled Pink rated back to her Newmarket win.

4080 CORAL CHALLENGE (H'CAP) 1m 14y
2:40 (2:40) (Class 2) 3-Y-O+
£46,687 (£13,980; £6,990; £3,495; £1,747; £877) **Stalls** Low

Form RPR

020 1 **Prince Of Johanne (IRE)**[17] 3458 7-9-10 **100** (p) GrahamLee 2 110
(Tom Tate) *hld up in midfield disputing 8th: stdy prog against rail fr 2f out: rdn to chse ldr jst ins fnl f: r.o wl to ld last 50yds* **16/1**

0205 2 1/2 **Es Que Love (IRE)**[15] 3527 4-9-9 **99** OlivierPeslier 5 108
(Mark Johnston) *led at gd pce: 2 l clr and rdn 1f out: styd on but hdd and outpcd last 50yds* **16/1**

1-34 3 3/4 **Wentworth (IRE)**[16] 3484 3-8-13 **98** RichardHughes 16 103
(Richard Hannon) *chsd ldrs in 4th: drvn over 2f out: wnt 3rd wl over 1f out: nt qckn after but styd on: unable to chal* **11/4**[1]

0-55 4 shd **Trader Jack**[21] 3339 4-8-12 **88** JamesDoyle 14 95
(Roger Charlton) *hld up in last quartet: prog jst over 2f out: drvn and styd on fr over 1f out: nrly snatched 3rd* **14/1**

0-01 5 1 1/4 **Asatir (USA)**[10] 3697 4-9-5 **95** (v) MickaelBarzalona 11 99
(Saeed bin Suroor) *dwlt: towards rr in 11th: pushed along 1/2-way: rdn and prog on inner fr 2f out: styd on fnl f: nvr able to chal* **20/1**

5-22 6 3/4 **Danchai**[21] 3339 4-9-2 **92** (p) WilliamBuick 8 94+
(William Haggas) *settled in 10th: drvn on outer over 2f out: styd on fr over 1f out: nrst fin* **7/1**[3]

1006 7 1 1/4 **St Moritz (IRE)**[32] 2958 7-9-2 **92** DanielTudhope 6 91
(David O'Meara) *trckd ldrs in 6th: rdn on inner 2f out: kpt on same pce after: no imp* **25/1**

1156 8 3/4 **Windhoek**[16] 3485 3-9-5 **104** RyanMoore 1 100
(Mark Johnston) *trckd ldng pair: drvn to chse ldr jst over 2f out: no imp over 1f out: lost 2nd and wknd jst ins fnl f* **7/2**[2]

-110 9 1 1/2 **Directorship**[17] 3458 7-9-9 **99** GeorgeBaker 3 93
(Patrick Chamings) *hld up in midfield disputing 8th: shkn up and nt qckn 2f out: n.d after: kpt on same pce* **14/1**

0331 10 7 **Postscript (IRE)**[14] 3570 5-8-8 **87** DarrenEgan(3) 12 65
(David Simcock) *settled in last quartet: rdn and tried to make prog on outer over 2f out: no hdwy over 1f out: wknd* **40/1**

4611 11 3/4 **Roserrow**[21] 3339 4-9-5 **95** JimmyFortune 17 71
(Andrew Balding) *chsd ldr to jst over 2f out: sn wknd qckly* **9/1**

3622 12 3/4 **Tigers Tale (IRE)**[30] 3019 4-8-11 **87** (v) MartinHarley 10 62
(Roger Teal) *racd wd early: in tch: drvn and struggling over 2f out: sn wknd* **20/1**

1102 13 1/2 **Rockalong (IRE)**[10] 3697 4-9-0 **90** JamieSpencer 4 64
(Luca Cumani) *sn in last trio and pushed along: modest prog u.p over 1f out: no ch and eased ins fnl f* **11/1**

6331 14 3/4 **Gaul Wood (IRE)**[6] 3864 4-8-12 **93** 6ex (p) DeclanBates(5) 9 65
(Tom Dascombe) *chsd ldrs in 5th: hrd rdn over 2f out: sn wknd* **16/1**

0001 15 19 **Capaill Liath (IRE)**[14] 3564 5-9-0 **90** (p) PaulHanagan 15 18
(Kevin Ryan) *mostly in last: lost tch 3f out: t.o* **66/1**

1m 38.87s (-4.43) **Going Correction** -0.30s/f (Firm) course record
WFA 3 from 4yo+ 9lb **15** Ran SP% **128.0**
Speed ratings (Par 109): **110,109,108,108,107 106,105,104,103,96 95,94,94,93,74**
toteswingers 1&2 £37.10, 1&3 £16.80, 2&3 £15.50 CSF £249.13 CT £951.86 TOTE £22.10: £4.20, £5.50, £2.20; EX 152.90 Trifecta £2573.80 Pool: £6534.06 - 1.90 winning units.
Owner David Storey **Bred** T J Rooney And Corduff Stud **Trained** Tadcaster, N Yorks

FOCUS
A good-quality well-contested handicap run at a decent gallop on fast ground, and it resulted in the course record being lowered by 0.21sec. The market was dominated by the two 3yos in the line-up, but with only one success from 24 runners over the past ten years the Classic generation have a pretty ordinary record in the race, and it was the older horses that once again came to the fore, with the top weight coming out on top. Prince Of Johannes is rated back to his 2012 Royal Hunt Cup win with the runner-up pretty much to his best 3yo form.

4081 CORAL DISTAFF (LISTED RACE) (FILLIES) 1m 14y
3:15 (3:15) (Class 1) 3-Y-O

£20,982 (£7,955; £3,981; £1,983; £995; £499) Stalls Low

Form RPR

1 **1** **Integral**[36] 2850 3-8-12 88 RyanMoore 4 107+
(Sir Michael Stoute) *hld up in last and wl off the pce early: stl in last pair whn swtchd to outer wl over 1f out: gd prog after: swept into ld 100yds out: pushed out firmly: impressive* **4/1**[2]

2-06 **2** 1 1/2 **Light Up My Life (IRE)**[17] 3460 3-8-12 99 RichardHughes 8 101
(Richard Hannon) *led: rdn 2f out: fought on wl but hdd and outpcd last 100yds* **7/1**

0-6 **3** 1/2 **Private Alexander (IRE)**[41] 2687 3-8-12 87 DanielTudhope 5 100
(David O'Meara) *trckd ldng pair: chsd ldr 2f out: styd on but lost 2nd ins fnl f* **33/1**

1112 **4** nk **Auction (IRE)**[17] 3460 3-8-12 96 FrankieDettori 1 101+
(Ed Dunlop) *hld up in 7th early: rchd 5th 1/2-way: nt clr run 2f out and lost pl: styd on again fnl f: gng on at fin* **13/2**

6-00 **5** 3/4 **Ollie Olga (USA)**[15] 3524 3-9-4 99 MartinHarley 7 103
(Mick Channon) *hld up in abt 6th: rdn on inner 2f out: styd on fnl f: nt pce to threaten* **20/1**

1313 **6** 1/2 **Woodland Aria**[17] 3460 3-8-12 98 WilliamBuick 9 96
(John Gosden) *hld up in 8th: tried to make prog on outer fr 2f out: styd on but nvr gng pce to threaten* **9/2**[3]

-120 **7** 3 1/4 **Lovely Pass (IRE)**[15] 3524 3-9-1 103 (p) MickaelBarzalona 3 92
(Saeed bin Suroor) *chsd ldng trio: pushed along 3f out: effrt u.p 2f out: stl ch of a pl 1f out: wknd qckly* **14/1**

2-04 **8** 3 **Nargys (IRE)**[17] 3460 3-8-12 107 JamieSpencer 2 82
(Luca Cumani) *trckd ldrs: drvn and tried to cl fr 2f out: chalng for a pl 1f out: wknd qckly* **2/1**[1]

1000 **9** 4 1/2 **Masarah (IRE)**[15] 3524 3-8-12 100 JamesDoyle 6 72
(Clive Brittain) *chsd ldr to 2f out: wknd qckly* **25/1**

1m 39.85s (-3.45) **Going Correction** -0.30s/f (Firm) 9 Ran SP% **115.6**
Speed ratings (Par 105): **105,103,103,102,101 101,98,95,90**
toteswingers 1&2 £7.00, 1&3 £23.90, 2&3 £25.60 CSF £31.11 TOTE £4.80: £1.80, £2.20, £6.50; EX 36.50 Trifecta £793.00 Pool: £4729.86 - 4.47 winning units.
Owner Cheveley Park Stud **Bred** Cheveley Park Stud Ltd **Trained** Newmarket, Suffolk

FOCUS
They didn't hang about in this fillies' Listed event and the nine runners were soon well spread out. The winner looks potentially a very nice filly indeed, for all that the pre-race standard was not great and the favourite was disappointing. The second and fourth set the standard.

4082 CORAL-ECLIPSE (BRITISH CHAMPIONS SERIES) (GROUP 1) 1m 2f 7y
3:50 (3:51) (Class 1) 3-Y-O+

£241,017 (£91,375; £45,730; £22,780; £11,432; £5,737) Stalls Low

Form RPR

-111 **1** **Al Kazeem**[17] 3457 5-9-7 126 JamesDoyle 2 126
(Roger Charlton) *trckd ldng pair: wnt 2nd over 2f out: chal wl over 1f out: drvn to ld jst ins fnl f: in command whn hung rt 100yds out: styd on wl* **15/8**[1]

-151 **2** 2 **Declaration Of War (USA)**[18] 3419 4-9-7 118 JosephO'Brien 6 122
(A P O'Brien, Ire) *hld up in 4th: shkn up and nt qckn over 2f out: styd on u.p to go 3rd fnl f and hung rt: lft in 2nd pl last 75yds* **4/1**[2]

5-12 **3** 1 1/4 **Mukhadram**[17] 3457 4-9-7 125 PaulHanagan 1 123+
(William Haggas) *led at fair pce: kicked on 3f out: hrd pressed over 1f out: drvn and hdd jst ins fnl f: keeping on but hld whn hmpd 100yds out: snatched up and sn lost 2nd pl* **15/2**

-663 **4** 3/4 **Mars (IRE)**[18] 3421 3-8-10 117[1] RyanMoore 5 119+
(A P O'Brien, Ire) *trckd ldr: tried to chal 4f out: drvn and nt qckn 3f out: sn lost 2nd: hmpd ins fnl f: kpt on* **9/2**[3]

1435 **5** 4 1/2 **Miblish**[17] 3457 4-9-7 116 (t) RichardHughes 3 109
(Clive Brittain) *hld up in last trio: shkn up and no prog wl over 2f out: one pce and no imp on ldrs after* **66/1**

4-10 **6** 3 **Pastorius (GER)**[48] 2494 4-9-7 0 OlivierPeslier 4 103
(Mario Hofer, Germany) *hld up in last trio: wl bhd and btn over 2f out* **12/1**

23-3 **7** 1 **The Fugue**[17] 3457 4-9-4 116 WilliamBuick 7 98
(John Gosden) *hld up in last trio: shkn up and no prog over 2f out: no ch after: wknd and eased fnl f* **5/1**

2m 4.35s (-6.15) **Going Correction** -0.30s/f (Firm)
WFA 3 from 4yo+ 11lb 7 Ran SP% **110.6**
Speed ratings (Par 117): **112,110,109,108,105 102,102**
toteswingers 1&2 £2.70, 1&3 £2.90, 2&3 £5.00 CSF £8.83 TOTE £2.00: £1.30, £3.10; EX 6.90 Trifecta £20.20 Pool: £17161.88 - 636.33 winning units.
Owner D J Deer **Bred** D J And Mrs Deer **Trained** Beckhampton, Wilts
■ Stewards' Enquiry : James Doyle five-day ban; careless riding (20th-24th July).

FOCUS
With the first three from the Prince of Wales's taken on by the winners of the Queen Anne and the Ganay, and the Classic generation represented by the St James's Palace third, this had the look of solid and informative Group 1. The early pace wasn't strong but things hotted up in the straight as Paul Hanagan kicked on aboard Mukhadram (quickest sectional was from 4f out to 3f out). The form makes a fair bit of sense and Al Kazeem, who improved again, is an up-to-standard Eclipse winner.

4083 CORAL MARATHON (REGISTERED AS THE ESHER STKS) (LISTED RACE) 2m 78y
4:25 (4:26) (Class 1) 4-Y-O+

£20,982 (£7,955; £3,981; £1,983; £995; £499) Stalls Centre

Form RPR

01-2 **1** **Caucus**[66] 1920 6-9-0 108 WilliamBuick 2 113
(John Gosden) *trckd ldr 6f: pushed along 4f out: prog to ld over 2f out: sn hrd pressed: styd on strly to assert ins fnl f* **13/8**[1]

21-4 **2** 3/4 **Biographer**[49] 2451 4-9-0 103 TedDurcan 7 112
(David Lanigan) *hld up in last: smooth prog on outer 3f out to press wnr jst over 2f out: gd battle after tl wandered lft and rt fnl f: no ex* **2/1**[2]

5-51 **3** 8 **Chiberta King**[14] 3560 7-9-0 102 (p) JimmyFortune 1 103
(Andrew Balding) *chsd ldrs in 4th: rdn over 3f out: lft bhd over 2f out: plugged on to take modest 3rd nr fin* **10/1**

46-0 **4** 1 3/4 **Repeater**[16] 3483 4-9-0 106 LukeMorris 6 100
(Sir Mark Prescott Bt) *hld up in 5th: nt clr run over 2f out: drvn to chse ldng pair over 1f out but easily lft bhd by them: wknd and lost 3rd nr fin* **12/1**

1430 **5** nse **Model Pupil**[16] 3483 4-9-0 109 JamesMcDonald 4 100
(Charles Hills) *trckd ldr after 6f to 3f out: shkn up and nt qckn: fdd fnl 2f* **6/1**[3]

6-42 **6** 2 1/2 **Bite Of The Cherry**[42] 2668 4-8-9 98 JamieSpencer 3 92
(Michael Bell) *led at decent pce and mostly 4 l clr: hdd & wknd over 2f out* **10/1**

3m 29.38s (-9.32) **Going Correction** -0.30s/f (Firm) course record 6 Ran SP% **111.6**
Speed ratings (Par 111): **111,110,106,105,105 104**
toteswingers 1&2 £1.40, 1&3 £2.90, 2&3 £2.60 CSF £5.04 TOTE £2.40: £1.30, £2.00; EX 5.90 Trifecta £25.10 Pool: £4150.96 - 123.85 winning units.
Owner Normandie Stud Ltd **Bred** Normandie Stud Ltd **Trained** Newmarket, Suffolk

FOCUS
The Listed staying event was run at a solid pace and they took 0.48sec off the course record set in this race three years ago. The first pair pulled clear and the winner's Sagaro form could be rated this high.

4084 CORAL BACKING MACMILLAN CANCER SUPPORT H'CAP 1m 2f 7y
5:00 (5:00) (Class 4) (0-85,85) 3-Y-O £6,469 (£1,925; £962; £481) Stalls Low

Form RPR

032 **1** **Circus Turn (USA)**[32] 2952 3-9-3 81 RyanMoore 1 90+
(Sir Michael Stoute) *mde all: pressed 3f out but gng strly: shkn up 2f out: drvn fnl f but a holding rivals* **5/1**[3]

-000 **2** 3/4 **Mundahesh (IRE)**[21] 3338 3-9-4 82 PaulHanagan 4 89+
(William Haggas) *hld up in last: prog against rail 2f out: drvn over 1f out: styd on to take 2nd last strides: nvr able to chal* **12/1**

1252 **3** hd **Endorsing (IRE)**[8] 3756 3-9-2 80 JimmyFortune 2 87
(Richard Hannon) *trckd ldng pair after 1f: drvn 2f out: chsd wnr ins fnl f: styd on but a hld: lost 2nd last strides* **13/2**

3231 **4** 1 3/4 **Seamless**[9] 3743 3-9-6 84 JamesMcDonald 5 88
(Charles Hills) *trckd wnr after 1f: tried to chal 3f out: btn off 2f out: lost 2nd and fdd ins fnl f* **13/2**

-251 **5** 1 **Ningara**[21] 3338 3-8-10 77 ThomasBrown[(3)] 3 79
(Andrew Balding) *trckd wnr 1f: sn restrained into 5th: rdn and nt qckn jst over 2f out: one pce and no imp after* **7/2**[2]

3220 **6** 2 1/2 **Number One London (IRE)**[16] 3486 3-9-4 82 FrankieDettori 8 79
(Brian Meehan) *hld up in last pair: effrt on wd outside over 2f out: no prog over 1f out: wl btn after* **11/2**

2250 **7** 8 **Carry On Sydney**[16] 3486 3-9-7 85 RichardHughes 7 71
(Richard Hannon) *racd on outer: trckd ldrs: drvn over 2f out: wknd over 1f out: eased* **11/4**[1]

2m 7.37s (-3.13) **Going Correction** -0.30s/f (Firm) 7 Ran SP% **115.3**
Speed ratings (Par 102): **100,99,99,97,97 95,88**
toteswingers 1&2 £9.10, 1&3 £5.20, 2&3 £12.90 CSF £60.76 CT £394.11 TOTE £4.20: £3.00, £5.10; EX 73.90 Trifecta £270.20 Pool: £3016.00 - 8.37 winning units.
Owner The Queen **Bred** Darley **Trained** Newmarket, Suffolk

FOCUS
The winning time was over three seconds slower than the Eclipse, but even allowing for the gulf in class it still shows that this handicap wasn't run at a strong pace. The winner made all for another clear best, with the third setting the standard.
T/Jkpt: Not won. T/Plt: £126.10 to a £1 stake. Pool: £224,953.55 - 1301.93 winning units T/Qpdt: £14.80 to a £1 stake. Pool: £12,430.34 - 618.06 winning units JN

4085 - 4091a (Foreign Racing) - See Raceform Interactive

4042 HAMBURG (R-H)
Saturday, July 6

OFFICIAL GOING: Turf: good

4092a ALMASED-CUP (HAMBURGER STUTEN-PREIS) (GROUP 3 (3YO FILLIES) (TURF) 1m 3f
4:25 (12:00) 3-Y-O

£26,016 (£8,943; £4,471; £2,439; £1,626; £1,219)

RPR

1 **Daytona Bay**[14] 3604 3-9-2 0 LennartHammer-Hansen 1 102
(Ferdinand J Leve, Germany) *sn led and mde rest: rdn whn chal 2f out: styd on strly and asserted: readily* **2/1**[1]

2 1 3/4 **Quilita (GER)**[27] 3146 3-9-2 0 AStarke 6 99
(P Schiergen, Germany) *trckd ldr: rdn to chal 2f out: no imp on wnr fr over 1f out: styd on* **125/10**

3 1/2 **Ars Nova (GER)**[27] 3146 3-9-2 0 CristianDemuro 7 98
(W Figge, Germany) *hld up in midfield on outer: rdn over 2f out: styd on and wnt 3rd fnl strides: no ch w wnr* **5/1**[2]

4 nk **Wild Silva** 3-9-2 0 DPorcu 8 97
(Markus Klug, Germany) *hld up in midfield on inner: rdn over 2f out: styd on and wnt 4th fnl strides: no ch w wnr* **12/1**

5 nk **Lady Liberty (IRE)** 3-9-2 0 AHelfenbein 2 97
(Andreas Lowe, Germany) *prom on inner: rdn and ev ch 2f out: sn no imp on wnr: styd on but dropped to 5th fnl strides* **218/10**

6 shd **Oriental Lady (GER)**[27] 3146 3-9-2 0 MircoDemuro 4 97
(J Hirschberger, Germany) *stdd and hld up in last: rdn 3f out: stl towards rr and hanging u.p ent fnl f: styd on towards fin and wnt 6th fnl strides: nvr nrr* **31/5**

7 3/4 **Thunderstruck (GER)** 3-9-2 0 APietsch 5 95
(R Dzubasz, Germany) *midfield on inner: rdn 2f out: kpt on one pce: n.d* **9/1**

8 shd **Daksha (FR)**[27] 3146 3-9-2 0 FranckBlondel 12 95
(W Hickst, Germany) *hld up in last quartet on outer: rdn over 3f out: sn outpcd: plugged on and sme late hdwy but nvr a factor* **19/2**

9 nk **Agama (GER)**[34] 2910 3-9-2 0 (p) KClijmans 11 95
(C Sprengel, Germany) *hld up in last trio on inner: rdn over 2f out: plugged on u.p but nvr a factor* **79/1**

10 nk **Quaduna** 3-9-2 0 EPedroza 9 94
(A Wohler, Germany) *midfield on outer: rdn over 2f out: hdwy and wnt 4th ent fnl f: kpt on tl no ex and lost multiple pls cl home* **101/10**

11 nk **Betty Lou (GER)**[14] 3604 3-9-2 0 AndreBest 10 94
(Markus Klug, Germany) *hld up in last trio: last and rdn 2f out: sn btn: nvr a factor* **45/1**

The Form Book Flat, Raceform Ltd, Compton, RG20 6NL.

12 1 1/2 **Beatrice**[34] 2910 3-9-2 0........ FabriceVeron 3 91
(H-A Pantall, France) *prom on outer: rdn over 2f out: sn outpcd by ldrs: steadily fdd: eased whn btn cl home and dropped to last* **53/10**[3]

2m 19.08s (-5.62) **12** Ran SP% **131.2**
WIN (incl. 10 euro stake): 30. PLACES: 13, 19, 15, 19. SF: 434.
Owner Gestut Haus Ittlingen **Bred** Gestut Haus Ittlingen **Trained** Germany

3165 LONGCHAMP (R-H)

Saturday, July 6

OFFICIAL GOING: Turf: good

4093a PRIX DE LA PORTE MAILLOT (GROUP 3) (3YO+) (TURF) 7f
5:30 (12:00) 3-Y-0+ **£32,520** (£13,008; £9,756; £6,504; £3,252)

RPR

1 **Moonlight Cloud**[245] 7575 5-8-11 0........ ThierryJarnet 6 117+
(F Head, France) *hld up towards rr on outer: smooth hdwy fr 2f out: shkn up and qcknd sharply to ld ins fnl f: pushed out: impressive* **9/10**[1]

2 2 1/2 **Amarillo (IRE)**[28] 3101 4-9-4 0........ UmbertoRispoli 9 115
(P Schiergen, Germany) *midfield: rdn to chal over 1f out: led ent fnl f: sn hdd and readily outpcd by wnr: kpt on* **13/1**

3 3/4 **So Long Malpic (FR)**[14] 6-8-11 0........ StephanePasquier 7 106+
(T Lemer, France) *hld up towards rr on inner: swtchd out and rdn over 1f out: r.o to go 3rd cl home: no ch w wnr* **8/1**[3]

4 3/4 **Sir Patrick Moore (FR)**[21] 3347 3-8-7 0.... Christophe-PatriceLemaire 5 105
(Harry Dunlop) *prom on outer: cl 2nd 2f out: rdn to chal over 1f out: sn outpcd by front pair: kpt on but dropped to 4th cl home* **15/1**

5 1/2 **Guajaraz (FR)**[28] 3128 3-8-7 0........ IoritzMendizabal 1 104
(J-C Rouget, France) *prom on inner: shuffled bk whn angled off rail and lost pl over 2f out: rdn over 1f out: r.o but n.d* **15/1**

6 1/2 **Spoil The Fun (FR)**[20] 3387 4-9-1 0........ JulienAuge 2 105
(C Ferland, France) *midfield on inner: swtchd off rail and rdn over 1f out: nt clrest of runs ins fnl f: kpt on but n.d* **13/1**

7 1 **Blue Soave (FR)**[35] 2897 5-9-1 0........ ThierryThulliez 4 103
(F Chappet, France) *t.k.h: led: rdn and strly pressed over 1f out: hdd ent fnl f: no ex and btn: fdd* **44/1**

8 snk **Kendam (FR)**[35] 2897 4-8-11 0........ MaximeGuyon 8 98
(H-A Pantall, France) *towards rr early: hdwy into midfield on outer 4f out: rdn and nt qckn over 1f out: no ex ins fnl f: fdd* **20/1**

9 2 1/2 **Silas Marner (FR)**[35] 2897 6-9-4 0........ ChristopheSoumillon 10 98
(J-C Rouget, France) *got across fr wdst draw and trckd ldr: ev ch whn nt clr run on rail fr 2f out: sn lost pl: eased whn ch gone ins fnl f* **4/1**[2]

10 nk **Nova Neyev (FR)**[9] 5-9-1 0........ JimmyTastayre 3 95
(P Capelle, France) *midfield early: towards rr 4f out: rdn 2f out: outpcd in last ent fnl f: sn btn* **126/1**

1m 20.43s (-0.27)
WFA 3 from 4yo+ 8lb **10** Ran SP% **118.3**
WIN (incl. 1 euro stake): 1.90. PLACES: 1.20, 2.70, 1.80. DF: 13.60. SF: 16.80.
Owner George Strawbridge **Bred** George Strawbridge **Trained** France

4094 - (Foreign Racing) - See Raceform Interactive

OVREVOLL (R-H)

Saturday, July 6

OFFICIAL GOING: Turf: soft

4095a SUBARU OSLO CUP (GROUP 3) (3YO+) (TURF) 1m 4f
7:05 (12:00) 3-Y-0+ **£44,247** (£22,123; £10,619; £7,079; £4,424)

RPR

1 **Touz Price (FR)**[730] 5-9-4 0........ JacobJohansen 5 103
(Rune Haugen, Norway) *mde all: rdn and wnt clr over 2f out: drvn out ins fnl f: won easing down: unchal* **234/10**

2 6 1/2 **Touch Of Hawk (FR)**[25] 3188 7-9-4 0........ EspenSki 3 93
(Wido Neuroth, Norway) *a.p: chsd eventual wnr fr 2 1/2f out: rdn and no imp fr 1 1/2f out: kpt on at same pce u.p fnl f* **26/1**

3 1/2 **Bank Of Burden (USA)**[25] 3188 6-9-6 0........ Per-AndersGraberg 1 94
(Niels Petersen, Norway) *w.w towards rr: hdwy 3f out: 3rd and rdn 2f out: no imp on wnr but chalng for 2nd whnshort of room and swtchd outside ins fnl f: no ex* **2/5**[1]

4 1 1/2 **Jumeirah (DEN)**[331] 5-9-4 0........ AndersBager 2 89
(Lone Bager, Denmark) *midfield on inner: chsd ldr between horses 3 1/2f out: sn rdn and lost pl 2 1/2f out: styd on to go 4th appr fnl f: kpt on u.p but nt pce to chal* **104/1**

5 4 1/2 **Without Fear (FR)**[25] 3188 5-9-6 0........ ElioneChaves 8 84
(Niels Petersen, Norway) *hld up towards rr: shkn up and hdwy on outside over 5f out: lost pl 3 1/2f out: last and rdn 2f out: r.o appr fnl f: styd on wl wout ever threatening ldrs* **29/10**[2]

6 3 **Plantagenet (SPA)**[25] 3188 6-9-6 0........ RafaelSchistl 4 79
(Niels Petersen, Norway) *hld up in rr detached fr main gp: tk clsr order 3 1/2f out: 5th and hrd rdn over 2f out: plugged on at one pce* **146/10**

7 1 **Dramatic Act**[50] 5-9-4 0........ Jan-ErikNeuroth 7 76
(Arne O Karlsen, Norway) *midfield on outer: rdn and no imp fnl 2 1/2f* **31/1**

8 1 1/2 **Berling (IRE)**[25] 3188 6-9-4 0........ ManuelMartinez 6 73
(Jessica Long, Sweden) *trckd ldr: rdn and outpcd under 2 1/2f out: wknd appr fnl f* **89/10**[3]

9 9 1/2 **Bomar (IRE)**[25] 3188 4-9-4 0........ CarlosLopez 9 58
(Wido Neuroth, Norway) *hld up towards rr: rdn and no imp fr 3f out: eased fnl f* **233/10**

2m 32.4s (-1.70) **9** Ran SP% **129.6**
PARI-MUTUEL (all including 1krone stakes): WIN 24.35; PLACE 4.59, 2.61, 1.39; DF 140.55.
Owner Stall Nor & Lagulise Racing **Bred** Ecurie De La Rehoraie & P Brecheteau **Trained** Norway

3561 AYR (L-H)

Sunday, July 7

OFFICIAL GOING: Good to firm (good in places; 9.2) changing to good to firm after race 2 (2.30)

Wind: Light; half against Weather: Cloudy; warm

4096 BET TOTEJACKPOT AT TOTEPOOL.COM MAIDEN STKS 7f 50y
2:00 (2:00) (Class 5) 2-Y-0 **£3,234** (£962; £481) **Stalls** Low

Form RPR

020 1 **Sir Jack Layden**[15] 3555 2-9-5 0........ GrahamLee 2 79
(David Brown) *t.k.h: w ldr: led over 4f out: rdn and hdd over 1f out: rallied and led ins fnl f: hld on wl* **4/6**[1]

4 2 nk **Lyn Valley**[65] 1989 2-9-5 0........ JoeFanning 5 78
(Mark Johnston) *t.k.h: led to over 4f out: pressed wnr: shkn up and led over 1f out: hdd ins fnl f: kpt on: hld towards fin* **9/4**[2]

3 2 1/4 **Longton** 2-9-5 0........ TonyHamilton 3 73+
(Richard Fahey) *chsd ldrs: rdn and outpcd wl over 1f out: kpt on ins fnl f: improve* **5/1**[3]

1m 31.47s (-1.93) **Going Correction** -0.35s/f (Firm) **3** Ran SP% **107.4**
Speed ratings (Par 94): **97,96,94**
CSF £2.43 TOTE £1.40; EX 2.50 Trifecta £2.30 Pool: £1,742.68 - 550.27 winning units.
Owner Ron Hull, David Brown & Clive Watson **Bred** Clive Dennett **Trained** Averham Park, Notts

FOCUS
There had been 20.8mm of rain during the week, but with the weather dry and sunny the going was still good to firm, good in places (GoingStick 9.2). Jockeys returning after the first said the ground was "fast and pretty quick". The stands' rail was in 3m, while the rest of the track was on its innermost line. Only half the runners declared turned up in this opening maiden, but it was probably still a fair contest. The winner is rated just to form.

4097 KING SIZE POOLS AT TOTEPOOL.COM FILLIES' H'CAP 7f 50y
2:30 (2:30) (Class 4) (0-85,83) 4-Y-0+ **£5,175** (£1,540; £769; £384) **Stalls** Low

Form RPR

45-5 1 **Magic Destiny**[11] 3684 4-9-4 **80**........ DanielTudhope 1 90+
(Mrs K Burke) *trckd ldrs: led gng wl over 1f out: qcknd clr on bridle ins fnl f: easily* **6/5**[1]

0-60 2 2 **Jeannie Galloway (IRE)**[25] 3200 6-8-11 **73**........ JoeFanning 2 76
(Keith Dalgleish) *led at modest gallop: rdn over 2f out: hdd over 1f out: kpt on fnl f: no ch w wnr* **7/1**

0136 3 nk **Alice's Dancer (IRE)**[16] 3532 4-9-7 **83**........ GrahamLee 3 85
(William Muir) *t.k.h: in tch: hdwy on outside over 2f out: rdn wl over 1f out: kpt on same pce ins fnl f* **4/1**[3]

6023 4 1/2 **Shesastar**[11] 3686 5-9-1 **77**........ GrahamGibbons 4 78
(David Barron) *trckd ldr: drvn over 2f out: one pce fr over 1f out* **5/2**[2]

1m 30.09s (-3.31) **Going Correction** -0.35s/f (Firm) **4** Ran SP% **106.5**
Speed ratings (Par 102): **104,101,101,100**
CSF £8.96 TOTE £1.50; EX 10.00 Trifecta £19.80 Pool: £1,550.02 - 58.64 winning units.
Owner Ray Bailey **Bred** Ray Bailey **Trained** Middleham Moor, N Yorks

■ Stewards' Enquiry : Daniel Tudhope one-day ban; careless riding (21st July).

FOCUS
This proved very straightforward for the winner.

4098 TOTEQUADPOT AT TOTEPOOL.COM H'CAP 1m 2f
3:00 (3:00) (Class 4) (0-85,82) 3-Y-0+ **£5,175** (£1,540; £769; £384) **Stalls** Low

Form RPR

0221 1 **Argaki (IRE)**[10] 3711 3-7-11 **65**........ RaulDaSilva(3) 1 73+
(Keith Dalgleish) *trckd ldrs: led against ins rail over 1f out: sn qcknd: kpt on wl fnl f* **4/1**[2]

2126 2 1 3/4 **Reset City**[12] 3651 7-9-3 **71**........ FrannyNorton 4 75
(Mark Johnston) *hld up: rdn and hdwy wl over 1f out: styd on to go 2nd nr fin: no ch w wnr* **7/1**

1320 3 hd **Eutropius (IRE)**[18] 3477 4-9-6 **74**........ AndrewMullen 5 78
(Alan Swinbank) *t.k.h early: hld up towards rr: rdn and hdwy on outside to chse wnr over 1f out: kpt on fnl f: lost 2nd cl home* **14/1**

0351 4 3/4 **Now My Sun**[25] 3204 4-9-10 **78**........ DanielTudhope 2 80
(Mrs K Burke) *dwlt: t.k.h in rr: effrt whn nt clr run over 2f out: rdn and hdwy over 1f out: no imp fnl f* **85/40**[1]

0-50 5 hd **High Resolution**[51] 2406 6-9-2 **70**........ PhillipMakin 6 72
(Linda Perratt) *s.i.s: hld up: rdn and hdwy on outside wl over 1f out: kpt on ins fnl f: no imp* **25/1**

0410 6 shd **San Cassiano (IRE)**[10] 3729 6-10-0 **82**........ JamesSullivan 3 84
(Ruth Carr) *led: rdn and hdd over 1f out: rallied: outpcd ins fnl f* **8/1**

6614 7 3/4 **It's My Time**[15] 3583 4-8-13 **67**........ TonyHamilton 7 67
(Richard Fahey) *taken early to post: t.k.h: in tch: rdn 2f out: outpcd ins fnl f* **20/1**

1460 8 5 **Ofcoursewecan (USA)**[21] 3365 3-8-4 **69**........ JoeFanning 9 59
(Mark Johnston) *in tch: rdn over 2f out: wknd over 1f out* **12/1**

106- 9 2 1/2 **Full Toss**[282] 6638 7-10-0 **82**........ GrahamLee 8 67
(Jim Goldie) *cl up: rdn and ev ch over 2f out: wknd over 1f out* **13/2**[3]

2m 7.78s (-4.22) **Going Correction** -0.35s/f (Firm)
WFA 3 from 4yo+ 11lb **9** Ran SP% **111.9**
Speed ratings (Par 105): **102,100,100,99,99 99,99,95,93**
toteswingers 1&2 £5.00, 1&3 £9.00, 2&3 £15.30 CSF £30.68 CT £348.40 TOTE £4.20: £1.50, £1.80, £3.30; EX 34.80 Trifecta £212.00 Pool: £2,685.63 - 9.49 winning units.
Owner D G Savala **Bred** A Christodoulou **Trained** Carluke, S Lanarks

FOCUS
A solidly run handicap.

4099 TRY A TOTETRIFECTA AT TOTEPOOL.COM H'CAP 1m 2f
3:30 (3:34) (Class 6) (0-60,60) 4-Y-0+ **£2,045** (£603; £302) **Stalls** Low

Form RPR

-415 1 **Barton Bounty**[16] 3543 6-9-2 **55**........ TomEaves 5 61
(Peter Niven) *prom: rdn over 3f out: rallied over 2f out: led ins fnl f: hld on wl u.p* **7/2**[2]

2350 2 shd **Meglio Ancora**[6] 3909 6-8-13 **52**........ GrahamLee 2 57
(Richard Ford) *chsd ldrs: led over 2f out: sn rdn: hdd ins fnl f: rallied: jst hld* **10/1**

003 3 3 **St Ignatius**[12] 3656 6-9-0 **58**........(p) NatashaEaton(5) 3 57
(Alan Bailey) *cl up: led briefly over 2f out: sn rdn: rallied: kpt on same pce ins fnl f* **5/1**[3]

003 4 3/4 **Captain Rhyric**[10] 3711 4-8-11 **50**........ PhillipMakin 6 48
(James Moffatt) *hld up towards rr: rdn 3f out: kpt on ins fnl f: nvr able to chal* **28/1**

0-05 **5** *hd* **Miss Blink**[61] 2137 6-9-7 **60** DanielTudhope 4 57
(Robin Bastiman) *hld up towards rr: pushed along and hdwy over 2f out: effrt whn nt clr run over 1f out: kpt on same pce ins fnl f* **6/1**

5002 **6** *shd* **Elizabeth Coffee (IRE)**[8] 3814 5-9-0 **53** (v) GrahamGibbons 7 50
(John Weymes) *missed break: bhd: stdy hdwy over 4f out: effrt and rdn 2f out: n.m.r briefly ins fnl f: one pce* **12/1**

0341 **7** *7* **Amazing Blue Sky**[10] 3727 7-9-7 **60** JamesSullivan 1 43
(Ruth Carr) *led: rdn and hdd over 2f out: wknd over 1f out* **13/8**[1]

-500 **8** *1 1/2* **Carla Allegra**[25] 3203 4-8-7 **46** oh1 JoeFanning 8 26
(Jim Goldie) *hld up in tch: rdn over 3f out: wknd over 2f out* **40/1**

2m 7.63s (-4.37) **Going Correction** -0.35s/f (Firm) **8** Ran SP% **113.9**
Speed ratings (Par 101): **103,102,100,99,99 99,94,92**
toteswingers 1&2 £5.30, 1&3 £3.90, 2&3 £6.60 CSF £37.48 CT £173.27 TOTE £5.00: £1.70, £2.60, £1.70; EX 42.10 Trifecta £289.00 Pool: £1,691.69 - 5.00 winning units.
Owner Francis Green Racing Ltd **Bred** Mrs M L Parry **Trained** Barton-le-Street, N Yorks
■ Stewards' Enquiry : Natasha Eaton two-day ban; careless riding (21st-22nd July).

FOCUS
Two came clear in this ordinary handicap.

4100 GRAHAM PIATCZANYN 50TH BIRTHDAY CELEBRATION H'CAP 1m
4:00 (4:03) (Class 5) (0-75,75) 3-Y-0+ **£3,234** (£962; £481; £240) **Stalls** Low

Form RPR

1110 **1** **Jebel Tara**[9] 3770 8-9-6 **70** (bt) PaulPickard(3) 6 79+
(Alan Brown) *hld up: smooth hdwy on outside over 2f out: led and rdn over 1f out: edgd lft: kpt on wl fnl f* **12/1**

-461 **2** *1/2* **Corton Lad**[25] 3202 3-9-0 **70** (bt) TomEaves 8 74
(Keith Dalgleish) *trckd ldrs: rdn over 2f out: chsd wnr over 1f out: kpt on ins fnl f* **8/1**

1533 **3** *1/2* **Nimiety**[10] 3742 4-9-9 **70** JoeFanning 5 75
(Mark Johnston) *trckd ldrs: rdn and effrt whn n.m.r wl over 1f out: kpt on ins fnl f* **5/2**[1]

2433 **4** *1 3/4* **Wellingrove (IRE)**[10] 3722 3-8-13 **69** FrannyNorton 3 68
(Mark Johnston) *t.k.h: hld up: effrt 2f out: kpt on ins fnl f: nvr able to chal* **3/1**[2]

0-60 **5** *2 1/2* **Fine Altomis**[58] 2219 4-8-7 **61** (b[1]) ConnorBeasley(7) 2 56
(Michael Dods) *t.k.h: pressed ldr: led over 2f out to over 1f out: sn outpcd* **6/1**[3]

0342 **6** *2 3/4* **Joshua The First**[10] 3715 4-9-3 **64** (t) GrahamLee 4 53
(Keith Dalgleish) *hld up in tch: effrt and pushed along over 2f out: wknd over 1f out* **6/1**[3]

0200 **7** *3/4* **Silverware (USA)**[43] 2659 5-10-0 **75** DavidNolan 7 62
(Kristin Stubbs) *led to over 2f out: rallied: wknd over 1f out* **9/1**

2-00 **8** *12* **Red Joker (IRE)**[51] 2408 3-9-5 **75** (b[1]) AndrewMullen 1 33
(Alan Swinbank) *bhd: outpcd 4f out: sn struggling: nvr on terms* **28/1**

1m 40.12s (-3.68) **Going Correction** -0.35s/f (Firm)
WFA 3 from 4yo+ 9lb **8** Ran SP% **114.4**
Speed ratings (Par 103): **104,103,103,101,98 96,95,83**
toteswingers 1&2 £13.10, 1&3 £7.60, 2&3 £4.20 CSF £102.62 CT £318.84 TOTE £14.50: £3.00, £2.30, £1.20; EX 101.70 Trifecta £879.90 Pool: £1,766.99 - 1.50 winning units.
Owner Miss E Johnston **Bred** Mrs G P Booth And J Porteous **Trained** Yedingham, N Yorks

FOCUS
They went a good gallop here and that set things up for a closer.

4101 COLLECT TOTEPOOL WINNINGS AT BETFRED SHOPS H'CAP (THE SUNDAY £5K BONUS RACE) 1m
4:30 (4:30) (Class 3) (0-95,90) 3-Y-0+ **£9,703** (£2,887; £1,443; £721) **Stalls** Low

Form RPR

-026 **1** **Able Master (IRE)**[8] 3825 7-9-13 **89** DanielTudhope 3 97+
(David O'Meara) *mde all at stdy pce: rdn and qcknd over 1f out: hld on wl fnl f* **3/1**[1]

0654 **2** *1/2* **Osteopathic Remedy (IRE)**[33] 2958 9-9-7 **90** ConnorBeasley(7) 5 97
(Michael Dods) *hld up: hdwy over 2f out: rdn and chsd wnr ins fnl f: kpt on fin* **4/1**[3]

0264 **3** *1* **Another For Joe**[18] 3464 5-8-13 **75** GrahamLee 6 80
(Jim Goldie) *t.k.h early: hld up on ins: rdn and hdwy over 1f out: disp 2nd pl briefly ins fnl f: one pce* **7/1**

2031 **4** *5* **Act Your Shoe Size**[10] 3712 4-9-6 **82** TomEaves 2 75
(Keith Dalgleish) *chsd wnr to over 2f out: rdn and outpcd over 1f out* **8/1**

0401 **5** *3/4* **Limit Up**[10] 3715 3-8-7 **78** JoeFanning 4 67+
(Mark Johnston) *t.k.h: trckd ldrs: effrt and chsd wnr over 2f out to ins fnl f: sn wknd* **10/3**[2]

1-43 **6** *3* **Light Rose (IRE)**[12] 3666 3-8-5 **76** FrannyNorton 7 59
(Mark Johnston) *in tch: rdn and effrt on outside over 2f out: wknd over 1f out* **9/2**

0-00 **7** *2 1/2* **Kay Gee Be (IRE)**[29] 3094 9-8-11 **80** JordanHibberd(7) 1 59
(Alan Berry) *trckd ldrs on ins tl rdn and wknd over 2f out* **33/1**

1m 39.43s (-4.37) **Going Correction** -0.35s/f (Firm)
WFA 3 from 4yo+ 9lb **7** Ran SP% **112.8**
Speed ratings (Par 107): **107,106,105,100,99 96,94**
toteswingers 1&2 £2.30, 1&3 £4.50, 2&3 £5.10 CSF £14.85 TOTE £4.10: £1.80, £3.00; EX 16.40 Trifecta £77.60 Pool: £1,757.68 - 16.97 winning units.
Owner Rasio Cymru Racing 1 & Partners **Bred** Scuderia Miami Di Sandro Guerra And Co **Trained** Nawton, N Yorks

FOCUS
Not a bad handicap.

4102 WESTERN HOUSE HOTEL AMATEUR RIDERS' H'CAP 5f
5:00 (5:04) (Class 6) (0-65,64) 4-Y-0+ **£1,975** (£607; £303) **Stalls** Low

Form RPR

1034 **1** **Foreign Rhythm (IRE)**[25] 3197 8-10-5 **60** MrsVDavies(5) 3 68
(Ron Barr) *hld up: gd hdwy over 1f out: kpt on strly fnl f to ld nr fin* **6/1**[3]

-005 **2** *hd* **Ryedane (IRE)**[19] 3446 11-10-6 **61** (b) MrWEasterby(5) 5 68
(Tim Easterby) *bhd: plenty to do 2f out: styd on strly fnl f: jst hld* **10/1**

00-5 **3** *hd* **Saxonette**[44] 2632 5-9-11 **50** MrJHamilton(3) 6 56
(Linda Perratt) *prom: hdwy to ld over 1f out: kpt on fnl f: hdd nr fin* **14/1**

6006 **4** *2 1/4* **Wicked Wilma (IRE)**[12] 3654 9-9-8 **49** MrJamesHughes(5) 10 47
(Alan Berry) *midfield centre: edgd lft and hdwy to chse ldrs over 1f out: one pce ins fnl f* **10/1**

2265 **5** *hd* **Here Now And Why (IRE)**[9] 3778 6-10-10 **60** (p) MissSBrotherton 13 57
(Iain Jardine) *bhd and outpcd: gd hdwy fnl f: kpt on: nrst fin* **4/1**[1]

1335 **6** *1* **Methaaly (IRE)**[10] 3716 10-10-5 **58** (be) MissMMullineaux(3) 12 52
(Michael Mullineaux) *dwlt: bhd and outpcd: gd hdwy fnl f: nvr able to chal* **16/1**

0053 **7** *shd* **Lord Buffhead**[3] 3994 4-10-1 **54** (b) MissJRRichards(3) 9 48
(Richard Guest) *towards rr: pushed along 1/2-way: r.o fnl f: nvr rchd ldrs* **9/1**

6060 **8** *1/2* **Distant Sun (USA)**[5] 3933 9-10-2 **55** (p) MissBeckyBrisbourne(3) 8 47
(Linda Perratt) *midfield: pushed along over 2f out: r.o fnl f: no imp* **28/1**

0-60 **9** *shd* **Black Douglas**[40] 2757 4-10-1 **51** MrsCBartley 14 42
(Jim Goldie) *bhd and outpcd: no imp tl styd on fnl f* **10/1**

0402 **10** *1 3/4* **Chosen One (IRE)**[9] 3769 8-10-9 **64** MrRColley(5) 2 49
(Ruth Carr) *led at str pce: edgd lft and hdd over 1f out: wknd and eased last 100yds* **11/2**[2]

4630 **11** *3/4* **Bassett Road (IRE)**[10] 3714 5-10-10 **60** (p) MrWHogg 11 42
(Keith Dalgleish) *w ldrs: edgd lft and led briefly over 1f out: wknd ins fnl f* **6/1**[3]

-066 **12** *3/4* **Myjestic Melody (IRE)**[5] 3932 5-9-4 **45** AnnaHesketh(5) 7 25
(Noel Wilson) *chsd ldrs tl edgd lft and wknd over 1f out* **33/1**

0300 **13** *2* **Cayman Fox**[5] 3933 8-9-10 **51** MrBenFfrenchDavis(5) 4 23
(Linda Perratt) *w ldrs tl wknd fr 2f out* **22/1**

1m 0.19s (0.79) **Going Correction** -0.35s/f (Firm) **13** Ran SP% **124.5**
Speed ratings (Par 101): **79,78,78,74,74 72,72,71,71,68 67,66,63**
toteswingers 1&2 £7.40, 1&3 £14.20, 2&3 £27.30 CSF £66.41 CT £589.37 TOTE £6.60: £2.70, £3.90, £4.70; EX 63.70 Trifecta £1658.10 Part won. Pool: £2,210.89 - 0.68 winning units..
Owner R E Barr **Bred** Yeomanstown Stud **Trained** Seamer, N Yorks
■ Stewards' Enquiry : Mr W Easterby one-day ban; careless riding (24th July).
Miss Becky Brisbourne two-day ban; careless riding (24th,27th July).
Mr R Colley caution; failing to take all reasonable measures to obtain best possible postions.

FOCUS
The leaders went off too quick here and the closers had their day.
T/Plt: £173.80 to a £1 stake. Pool: £93,119.11 - 391.03 winning units T/Qpdt: £35.60 to a £1 stake. Pool: £7,848.20 - 162.81 winning units RY

4092 HAMBURG (R-H)
Sunday, July 7

OFFICIAL GOING: Turf: good

4103a SPARDA DEUTSCHES DERBY (GROUP 1) (3YO COLTS & FILLIES) (TURF) 1m 4f
3:30 (3:33) 3-Y-0 **£243,902** (£81,300; £48,780; £24,390; £8,130)

RPR

1 **Lucky Speed (IRE)**[42] 2696 3-9-2 0 AStarke 15 108
(P Schiergen, Germany) *settled towards rr: stdy hdwy into midfield 3f out: rdn and c wd into st over 2f out: styd on u.p to go 4th on outside 1f out: r.o to ld last 50yds: drvn out* **7/1**[3]

2 *3/4* **Tres Blue (IRE)**[21] 3386 3-9-2 0 FabriceVeron 5 107
(H-A Pantall, France) *midfield travelling wl: gd hdwy on ins fr 3f out: 3rd and shkn up 2f out: swtchd outside and r.o to ld appr fnl f: sn hrd rdn and kpt on gamely: hdd 50yds out: no ex* **14/1**

3 *nk* **Nordvulkan (GER)**[42] 2696 3-9-2 0 JBojko 12 107
(R Dzubasz, Germany) *towards rr: reminders over 3f out: prog whn forced wd fnl bnd over 2f out: styd on u.p ins fnl 1 1/2f: nvr quite on terms* **100/1**

4 *nk* **Quinzieme Monarque (USA)**[21] 3389 3-9-2 0 MircoDemuro 10 106
(J Hirschberger, Germany) *in rr: one fr last: rdn and forced wdst of all fnl bnd over 2f out: hdwy over 1 1/2f out: styd on u.p fnl f: nt pce to chal* **40/1**

5 *1/2* **Global Bang (GER)**[48] 2526 3-9-2 0 AndreaAtzeni 8 105
(Mario Hofer, Germany) *hld up towards rr: rdn and hdwy 2f out: hrd rdn and edgd rt whn r.o to go 3rd over 1f out: chal ldr ins fnl f: run flattened out fnl 110yds* **12/1**

6 *1/2* **Saratino (GER)**[14] 3612 3-9-2 0 FrederikTylicki 14 104
(Mario Hofer, Germany) *midfield: short of room and shuffled bk on fnl bnd over 2f out: rdn and styd on fr 1 1/2f out: wnt 4th appr fnl f: one pce u.p fnl f* **66/1**

7 *1 1/4* **Limario (GER)**[14] 3-9-2 0 HarryBentley 3 102
(R Dzubasz, Germany) *trckd ldr on inner: eased outside and shkn up to ld 2f out: rdn over 1 1/2f out: hdd appr fnl f: fdd ins fnl f* **40/1**

8 *3 1/2* **Ivanhowe (GER)**[21] 3389 3-9-2 0 CristianDemuro 1 97
(W Giedt, Germany) *hld up towards rr: shkn up and hdwy on outside 4f out: 4th and styng on over 2f out: hrd rdn and no further imp over 1f out: fdd and eased ins fnl f* **15/8**[1]

9 *2 1/2* **Samos (GER)**[42] 2696 3-9-2 0 APietsch 9 93
(W Hickst, Germany) *chsd ldng gp: scrubbed along to hold pl 3f out: rdn and outpcd 2f out: one pce fnl f* **16/1**

10 *1 3/4* **Erlkonig (GER)**[14] 3-9-2 0 DPorcu 7 90
(Markus Klug, Germany) *towards rr: rdn and no imp over 2f out: styd on ins fnl f: nvr in contention* **66/1**

11 *2 1/2* **See The Rock (IRE)**[14] 3-9-2 0 MickaelBarzalona 6 86
(A Wohler, Germany) *midfield on inner: pushed along appr 2 1/2f out: styd on to go 5th ins fnl 2f: sn hrd rdn and no further imp: wknd fr 1f out* **33/1**

12 *5* **Schulz (GER)**[21] 3389 3-9-2 0 AHelfenbein 19 78
(Markus Klug, Germany) *pressed ldr on outer: tk narrow ld appr 1/2-way: hdd over 3f out: wknd u.p fr over 1 1/2f out* **10/1**

13 *3* **Empoli (GER)**[21] 3389 3-9-2 0 EPedroza 13 73
(P Schiergen, Germany) *chsd ldng gp: prog on ins to ld over 3f out: rdn and hdd 2f out: sn wknd* **12/1**

14 *nse* **Nicolosio (IRE)**[48] 3-9-2 0 WilliamBuick 18 73
(W Hickst, Germany) *midfield: sme hdwy on outside whn hmpd over 5f out: rcvrd to chse ldrs 4f out: rdn and outpcd 2 1/2f out: wknd over 1f out: eased ins fnl f* **9/2**[2]

15 *1 1/2* **Vif Monsieur (GER)**[42] 2696 3-9-2 0 KClijmans 16 71
(J Hirschberger, Germany) *trckd ldrs: lost pl 4f out: rdn and btn fr 2f out* **33/1**

16 *3 1/2* **Bermuda Reef (IRE)**[14] 3-9-2 0 FrankieDettori 11 65
(P Schiergen, Germany) *midfield: lost pl over 3f out: sn rdn and btn over 1 1/2f out* **50/1**

17 *4* **Noble Galileo (GER)**[21] 3389 3-9-2 0 FredericSpanu 17 59
(Mario Hofer, Germany) *a towards rr: last and detached over 2f out: nvr in contention* **66/1**

18 *3/4* **Flamingo Star (GER)**[42] 2696 3-9-2 0 LennartHammer-Hansen 2 58
(R Dzubasz, Germany) *led on rail: narrowly hdd appr 1/2-way: rdn and began to lose pl over 3f out: sn wknd and eased fnl f* **33/1**

19 *6* **Probably (IRE)**[26] 3-9-2 0 KierenFallon 4 48
(Rune Haugen, Norway) *chsd ldng gp: dropped to midfield 1/2-way: hdwy on outside to chse ldrs 2 1/2f out: sn rdn and wknd u.p fr 2f out: eased ins fnl f* **11/1**

2m 27.87s (-6.68) **19** Ran SP% **132.0**
WIN (incl. 10 euro stake): 59. PLACES: 20, 38, 80, 59. SF: 777.
Owner Stall Hornoldendorf **Bred** Gestut Hof Ittlingen **Trained** Germany

3708 MAISONS-LAFFITTE (R-H)

Sunday, July 7

OFFICIAL GOING: Turf: good

4104a PRIX MESSIDOR (GROUP 3) (3YO+) (TURF) 1m (S)

2:40 (12:00) 3-Y-O+ £32,520 (£13,008; £9,756; £6,504; £3,252)

RPR

1 **Intello (GER)**35 2907 3-9-1 0 OlivierPeslier 2 118+
(A Fabre, France) *settled in 3rd: shkn up and hdwy under 2f out: qcknd to ld ins fnl f: pushed out: comf* **2/7**1

2 1 1/2 **Mainsail**21 3387 4-9-5 0 ChristopheSoumillon 4 112
(P Bary, France) *settled in 4th: rdn and prog 1 1/2f out: r.o to go 2nd 50yds out: nvr on terms w wnr* **11/2**2

3 1/2 **Don Bosco (FR)**42 2694 6-9-7 0 GregoryBenoist 3 113
(D Smaga, France) *t.k.h and trckd ldr: shkn up to chal 1 1/2f out: tk narrow ld 1f out: hdd sn after: r.o u.p* **8/1**3

4 1 3/4 **Prince D'Alienor (IRE)**91 5-9-1 0 (p) FlavienPrat 5 103
(A Fabre, France) *led field in single file: rdn and hdd 1f out: one pce fnl f* **100/1**

5 1 **Poupee Flash (USA)**21 3387 4-8-11 0 StephanePasquier 1 97
(P Bary, France) *hld up in 5th: rdn and tk clsr order 1 1/2f out: kpt on ins fnl f: no imp* **16/1**

6 hd **King Air (FR)**36 2897 6-9-1 0 JamieSpencer 6 100
(R Pritchard-Gordon, France) *w.w in rr: shkn up and tk clsr order 1 1/2f out: kpt on fr 1f out: no imp* **40/1**

1m 34.0s (-8.30) 6 Ran SP% 113.6
WFA 3 from 4yo+ 9lb
WIN (incl. 1 euro stake): 1.20 (Intello coupled with Prince D'Alienor). PLACES: 1.10, 1.30. SF: 3.70.
Owner Wertheimer & Frere **Bred** Wertheimer Et Frere **Trained** Chantilly, France

3390 HOLLYWOOD PARK (L-H)

Sunday, July 7

OFFICIAL GOING: Cushion track: fast

4106a HOLLYWOOD GOLD CUP H'CAP (GRADE 1) (3YO+) (CUSHION TRACK) 1m 2f (D)

1:00 (1:17) 3-Y-O+ £184,049 (£61,349; £36,809; £18,404; £6,134)

RPR

1 **Game On Dude (USA)**77 6-9-1 0 (b) MESmith 2 125+
(Bob Baffert, U.S.A) *broke wl and mde all: shkn up and qcknd over 1 1/2f out: pushed out fnl f: a holding runner-up* **30/100**1

2 1 **Kettle Corn (USA)**35 6-8-4 0 (b1) RBejarano 4 112
(John W Sadler, U.S.A) *in rr: hdwy on ins over 2f out: chsd ldr into st: rdn and r.o gamely fnl f: a hld by wnr* **104/10**

3 6 3/4 **Sky Kingdom (USA)**77 4-8-4 0 (b) MGarcia 5 99
(Bob Baffert, U.S.A) *trckd ldr on outside: rdn and nt qckn 2f out: one pce fnl f* **9/1**3

4 1/2 **Clubhouse Ride (USA)**35 5-8-7 0 (b) JTalamo 1 101
(Craig A Lewis, U.S.A) *settled in 3rd on rail: 2nd and rdn over 2f out: no imp fr over 1 1/2f out: fdd ins fnl f* **17/5**2

5 2 1/2 **Oilisblackgold (USA)**35 6-8-6 0 ow3 EMaldonado 3 95
(Craig Dollase, U.S.A) *settled in 4th: pushed along and tk clsr order 3f out: sn rdn and wknd ins fnl 2f* **26/1**

2m 1.88s (121.88) 5 Ran SP% 122.1
PARI-MUTUEL (all including $2 stakes): WIN 2.60; PLACE (1-2) 2.20, 5.20; SHOW (1-2-3) 2.10, 3.40, 3.80; DF 9.40; SF 11.40.
Owner Diamond Pride LLC, Lanni Family Trust et al **Bred** Adena Springs **Trained** USA

4096 AYR (L-H)

Monday, July 8

OFFICIAL GOING: Good to firm (watered; 9.3)

Stands side rail 3m inwards, rest of track at innermost configuration and al distances as advertised.
Wind: Light; half against Weather: Sunny; hot

4107 IRISH STALLION FARMS EBF / WILLIAM HILL MAIDEN STKS 5f

2:30 (2:30) (Class 5) 2-Y-O £3,234 (£962; £481; £240) Stalls High

Form RPR

5 1 **Straits Of Malacca**16 3565 2-9-5 0 PhillipMakin 8 71
(Kevin Ryan) *mde all: shkn up and hung lft 1f out: hld on wl towards fin* **11/8**1

330 2 hd **Captain Midnight (IRE)**34 2955 2-9-5 0 GrahamLee 4 70
(David Brown) *cl up: effrt 2f out: ev ch whn carried lft 1f out: swtchd rt ins fnl f: r.o: jst hld* **4/1**2

04 3 1 **Beltor**20 3439 2-9-5 0 TomEaves 7 67+
(Michael Dods) *dwlt: t.k.h in rr: shkn up and hdwy over 1f out: kpt on wl fnl f: nvr nr to chal: improve* **66/1**

4 1 1/2 **Kano's Ghirl (IRE)** 2-9-0 0 PaulMulrennan 3 56
(Keith Dalgleish) *t.k.h: prom: rdn and hung lft over 1f out: kpt on same pce run-in* **16/1**

3 5 1 **Go Jamesway**10 3766 2-9-5 0 TonyHamilton 6 58
(Richard Fahey) *chsd ldrs: rdn and effrt over 1f out: sn one pce* **9/2**3

6 4 **Ibecke** 2-9-0 0 JoeFanning 2 38
(Mark Johnston) *chsd ldrs tl rdn and wknd over 1f out* **7/1**

7 1 **Captain Gee** 2-9-5 0 MichaelO'Connell 5 40
(John Quinn) *trckd ldrs: rdn over 2f out: wknd over 1f out* **7/1**

59.76s (0.36) **Going Correction** 0.0s/f (Good) 7 Ran SP% 112.7
Speed ratings (Par 94): **97,96,95,92,91 84,83**
toteswingers 1&2 £2.10, 1&3 £6.70, 2&3 £11.00 CSF £6.84 TOTE £1.90: £1.10, £4.00; EX 7.40 Trifecta £144.70 Pool: £2,814.84 - 14.58 winning units.
Owner JCG Chua & CK Ong **Bred** Whitsbury Manor Stud **Trained** Hambleton, N Yorks

FOCUS
The jockeys after the first said the ground was quick, but safe. An ordinary juvenile maiden, but a close finish between the market leaders. The runner-up is rated back towards his debut form.

4108 WILLIAM HILL DOWNLOAD THE APP NURSERY H'CAP 7f 50y

3:00 (3:02) (Class 5) 2-Y-O £3,234 (£962; £481; £240) Stalls Low

Form RPR

643 1 **Latenightrequest**13 3648 2-8-10 68 TonyHamilton 2 70+
(Richard Fahey) *pressed ldr: rdn to ld over 1f out: kpt on gamely fnl f* **4/1**3

1 2 nk **Homestretch**28 3155 2-9-5 77 GrahamLee 3 78+
(Mick Channon) *trckd ldrs: drvn and outpcd over 2f out: rallied over 1f out: kpt on to chse wnr ins fnl f: kpt on: hld nr fin* **15/8**1

4261 3 3 **Atlantic Affair (IRE)**13 3648 2-9-7 79 JoeFanning 4 72
(Mark Johnston) *t.k.h: led to over 1f out: rallied: lost 2nd and outpcd ins fnl f* **2/1**2

1 4 2 1/4 **Angel Rosa**39 2793 2-8-8 66 TomEaves 5 53
(Keith Dalgleish) *checked s and s.i.s: hld up: hdwy over 2f out: rdn: edgd lft and no imp over 1f out* **13/2**

000 5 7 **It's All A Game**24 3298 2-7-7 58 (p) NoelGarbutt(7) 1 27
(Richard Guest) *prom: rdn over 3f out: wknd over 2f out* **14/1**

1m 30.62s (-2.78) **Going Correction** -0.475s/f (Firm) 5 Ran SP% 108.1
Speed ratings (Par 94): **96,95,92,89,81**
CSF £11.48 TOTE £2.60: £3.20, £1.10; EX 14.70 Trifecta £39.30 Pool: £2,524.33 - 48.11 winning units.
Owner Middleham Park Racing XVI & Partner **Bred** Mrs S J Walker **Trained** Musley Bank, N Yorks

FOCUS
The official ratings shown are estimated and for information only. A small-field nursery in which the winner has improved with racing and there is more to come from the second.

4109 WILLIAM HILL IPHONE, IPAD, IPAD MINI H'CAP 1m

3:30 (3:31) (Class 6) (0-60,60) 3-Y-O+ £1,940 (£577; £288; £144) Stalls Low

Form RPR

2212 1 **Tectonic (IRE)**2 4052 4-9-11 59 (p) TomEaves 9 69
(Keith Dalgleish) *t.k.h: hld up in tch: hdwy and edgd lft 2f out: led ent fnl f: edgd rt: drvn out* **9/4**1

0-60 2 nk **Eilean Mor**26 3197 5-8-5 46 NoelGarbutt(7) 7 55
(R Mike Smith) *hld up towards rr: rdn and hdwy over 2f out: led over 1f out to ent fnl f: kpt on: hld nr fin* **66/1**

2365 3 1 3/4 **Music Festival (USA)**10 3770 6-9-6 54 JoeFanning 4 59
(Jim Goldie) *hld up in midfield: hdwy to chse ldrs over 1f out: kpt on same pce wl ins fnl f* **9/2**3

0020 4 3/4 **Flipping**26 3203 6-9-7 55 GrahamLee 11 59
(Nicky Richards) *hld up in midfield: rdn and hdwy over 1f out: kpt on fnl f: nvr able to chal* **14/1**

1655 5 hd **Monsieur Pontaven**10 3788 6-8-6 47 (b) GaryMahon(7) 8 50
(Robin Bastiman) *hld up: effrt and hdwy on wd outside 2f out: edgd rt: kpt on fnl f: nrst fin* **16/1**

0550 6 2 1/4 **Nonaynever**7 3910 5-9-1 49 (b) PJMcDonald 1 47
(Ruth Carr) *chsd ldr: rdn and ev ch over 2f out to over 1f out: outpcd fnl f* **16/1**

-203 7 1 3/4 **Cross The Boss (IRE)**32 3030 6-9-10 58 (t) DavidNolan 13 52
(David O'Meara) *dwlt: hld up: rdn over 3f out: hdwy over 1f out: kpt on fnl f: nrst fin* **11/2**

6024 8 2 1/4 **Outlaw Torn (IRE)**2 4052 4-9-4 59 (e) ConnorBeasley(7) 14 48
(Richard Guest) *t.k.h: led to over 1f out: sn wknd* **4/1**2

-006 9 5 **Berbice (IRE)**10 3770 8-9-2 50 LeeTopliss 3 27
(Linda Perratt) *dwlt: sn midfield on ins: effrt whn nt clr run over 2f out: sn rdn: wknd over 1f out* **22/1**

050- 10 3/4 **Princess Gail**311 5804 5-8-12 46 oh1 PaulMulrennan 10 22
(Mark Brisbourne) *prom: rdn over 2f out: wknd over 1f out* **33/1**

60/0 11 hd **Mr Dream Maker (IRE)**23 3314 5-9-2 53 DeclanCannon(3) 6 28
(Noel Wilson) *chsd ldrs tl edgd lft and wknd wl over 1f out* **25/1**

6100 12 hd **Cufflink**11 3728 4-9-3 56 (v) GarryWhillans(5) 2 31
(Iain Jardine) *prom: rdn over 2f out: edgd lft: wknd wl over 1f out* **25/1**

0-06 13 20 **Pendle Lady (IRE)**21 3395 4-9-1 52 RyanClark(3) 5
(Mark Brisbourne) *hld up: drvn wl over 2f out: sn wknd: t.o* **40/1**

1m 39.61s (-4.19) **Going Correction** -0.475s/f (Firm) 13 Ran SP% 121.7
Speed ratings (Par 101): **101,100,98,98,98 95,94,91,86,86 85,85,65**
toteswingers 1&2 £53.90, 1&3 £3.50, 2&3 £76.90 CSF £216.20 CT £656.01 TOTE £2.30: £1.10, £33.00, £2.30; EX 237.00 Trifecta £798.40 Pool: £2,757.39 - 2.59 winning units.
Owner Mrs L A Ogilvie **Bred** W Maxwell Ervine **Trained** Carluke, S Lanarks

FOCUS
A big field for this moderate 1m handicap and another good finish. A similar effort from the winner to his recent Carlisle run.

4110 WILLIAM HILL IN THE APP STORE H'CAP 1m 5f 13y

4:00 (4:00) (Class 4) (0-85,80) 4-Y-O+ £4,851 (£1,443; £721; £360) Stalls Low

Form RPR

5262 1 **Hawdyerwheesht**24 3287 5-8-9 68 JoeFanning 2 81
(Jim Goldie) *t.k.h: hld up in tch: smooth hdwy to ld over 1f out: sn rdn and edgd lft: kpt on strly to go clr fnl f* **5/1**2

0225 2 6 **Muharrer**20 3442 4-9-7 80 PaulMulrennan 1 84
(Michael Dods) *trckd ldrs: effrt and pushed along over 2f out: chsd (clr) wnr over 1f out: kpt on fnl f: no imp* **2/1**1

0-41 3 3/4 **Forrest Flyer (IRE)**33 2975 9-8-7 66 AndrewElliott 6 69
(Jim Goldie) *led to 3f out: sn drvn and outpcd: styd on fnl f: no imp* **5/1**2

0010 4 1 1/4 **Cosmic Sun**23 3345 7-9-1 74 (t) TonyHamilton 5 75
(Richard Fahey) *dwlt: hld up: rdn over 3f out: hdwy over 1f out: nvr able to chal* **5/1**2

3105 5 1 **Activate**11 3726 6-8-13 72 (b) TomEaves 8 72
(Keith Dalgleish) *prom: hdwy on outside to ld 3f out: sn edgd lft: rdn and hdd over 1f out: sn outpcd* **5/1**2

0520 6 10 **Teenage Idol (IRE)**20 3442 9-8-7 66 PJMcDonald 4 51
(Dianne Sayer) *pressed ldr: chal over 5f out to over 3f out: rdn and wknd over 2f out* **12/1**3

7 2 **Sendiym (FR)**34 6-8-8 74 ConnorBeasley(7) 3 56
(Dianne Sayer) *hld up: rdn along over 3f out: wknd over 2f out* **25/1**

2m 50.7s (-3.30) **Going Correction** -0.475s/f (Firm) 7 Ran SP% 111.5
Speed ratings (Par 105): **91,87,86,86,85 79,78**
toteswingers 1&2 £3.30, 1&3 £4.20, 2&3 £2.10 CSF £14.66 CT £50.05 TOTE £5.70: £2.30, £1.50; EX 17.70 Trifecta £36.80 Pool: £2,507.22 - 51.02 winning units.
Owner J S Morrison **Bred** Baldernock Bloodstock Ltd **Trained** Uplawmoor, E Renfrews

FOCUS
They went a steady early pace in this fair staying handicap, but the winner scored emphatically. The form is taken at face value, but with reservations.

4111 WILLIAM HILL BET ON THE MOVE H'CAP — 7f 50y
4:30 (4:30) (Class 4) (0-85,85) 3-Y-0+ **£4,851** (£1,443; £721; £360) **Stalls** Low

Form RPR

6530 **1** **Rasaman (IRE)**[22] 3367 9-9-4 **75**........ GrahamLee 1 84
(Jim Goldie) *t.k.h early: prom: nt clr run over 2f out: squeezed through to ld ins fnl f: rdn and r.o strly* **8/1**[3]

0062 **2** 1 1/2 **Jinky**[11] 3714 5-9-2 **73**........ TomEaves 9 78
(Linda Perratt) *hld up: rdn and hdwy over 2f out: chsd wnr last 100yds: kpt on towards fin* **10/1**

2100 **3** 3/4 **Fieldgunner Kirkup (GER)**[23] 3335 5-9-7 **85**........ GemmaTutty(7) 8 89+
(David Barron) *t.k.h: hld up: stdy hdwy whn n.m.r briefly over 2f out: styd on fnl f: nvr able to chal* **9/1**

5622 **4** 1/2 **Kingscroft (IRE)**[4] 3984 5-9-13 **84**........ JoeFanning 3 86
(Mark Johnston) *t.k.h: prom: effrt and rdn over 2f out: sltly outpcd over 1f out: r.o ins fnl f* **5/4**[1]

4006 **5** shd **Orpsie Boy (IRE)**[14] 3628 10-8-8 **68**........ JulieBurke(3) 6 69
(Ruth Carr) *t.k.h: hld up in tch: effrt on outside wl over 1f out: kpt on same pce fnl f* **14/1**

0022 **6** 3/4 **Orbit The Moon (IRE)**[11] 3741 5-9-0 **78**........(tp) ConnorBeasley(7) 7 77
(Michael Dods) *t.k.h: w ldr: rdn 2f out: no ex ins fnl f* **7/2**[2]

3320 **7** nk **Polish Crown**[24] 3279 3-8-2 **67**........ DuranFentiman 2 66
(Mark Johnston) *led: rdn 2f out: hdd ins fnl f: sn btn* **10/1**

1m 30.14s (-3.26) **Going Correction** -0.475s/f (Firm)
WFA 3 from 5yo+ 8lb **7** Ran SP% **112.6**
Speed ratings (Par 105): **99,97,96,95,95 94,94**
toteswingers 1&2 £7.50, 1&3 £9.90, 2&3 £11.00 CSF £78.55 CT £730.07 TOTE £12.80: £5.40, £6.50; EX 68.60 Trifecta £408.30 Pool: £3,715.40 - 6.82 winning units.
Owner Paul Moulton **Bred** Rasana Partnership **Trained** Uplawmoor, E Renfrews

FOCUS
This older-horse handicap was run a comparatively modest 0.48secs faster than the earlier nursery. A compressed finish to an ordinary race.

4112 WILLIAM HILL EXCLUSIVE MOBILE BONUSES H'CAP — 5f
5:00 (5:00) (Class 3) (0-95,93) 3-Y-0 **£7,762** (£2,310; £1,154; £577) **Stalls** High

Form RPR

0004 **1** **Storm Moon (USA)**[9] 3802 3-8-13 **85**........ JoeFanning 1 91
(Mark Johnston) *pressed ldr: rdn to ld over 1f out: edgd lft ins fnl f: hld on wl* **2/1**[2]

2360 **2** hd **Angus Og**[16] 3591 3-8-8 **80**........ TomEaves 4 85
(Mrs K Burke) *led: rdn and hdd over 1f out: rallied ins fnl f: kpt on wl towards fin: jst hld* **13/2**

4164 **3** 2 **Normal Equilibrium**[16] 3584 3-9-7 **93**........ JamieSpencer 3 91
(Robert Cowell) *trckd ldrs: effrt and swtchd lft over 1f out: sn rdn: kpt on same pce ins fnl f* **6/4**[1]

3201 **4** 1 1/2 **Shrimper Roo**[9] 3813 3-8-12 **84**........(b) DuranFentiman 2 77
(Tim Easterby) *prom: rdn over 2f out: one pce fr over 1f out* **7/2**[3]

58.67s (-0.73) **Going Correction** 0.0s/f (Good) **4** Ran SP% **108.9**
Speed ratings (Par 104): **105,104,101,99**
CSF £13.09 TOTE £3.50; EX 11.60 Trifecta £23.60 Pool: £1,848.69 - 58.51 winning units.
Owner Sheikh Hamdan Bin Mohammed Al Maktoum **Bred** Darley **Trained** Middleham Moor, N Yorks

FOCUS
A small field for the feature race on the card and the time was over a second faster than the juvenile maiden. The winner may not have had to match his best.

4113 WILLIAMHILL.COM APP APPRENTICE H'CAP — 7f 50y
5:30 (5:33) (Class 6) (0-65,65) 3-Y-0 **£2,045** (£603; £302) **Stalls** Low

Form RPR

5402 **1** **Relight My Fire**[2] 4045 3-9-4 **60**........(b) DarylByrne(3) 11 71
(Tim Easterby) *chsd ldr: led and rdn over 2f out: hld on wl fnl f* **11/4**[1]

6430 **2** 2 **Marcus Caesar (IRE)**[49] 2501 3-9-0 **58**........ GemmaTutty(5) 7 64
(David Barron) *t.k.h: led: hung rt bnd over 3f out: hdd over 2f out: kpt on fnl f: nt rch wnr* **6/1**[2]

5036 **3** 1/2 **Hazza The Jazza**[5] 3949 3-9-2 **60**........(b) ConnorBeasley(5) 12 65
(Richard Guest) *t.k.h: prom: effrt and pushed along over 2f out: kpt on same pce fnl f* **11/4**[1]

04-0 **4** nk **Diddy Eric**[75] 1759 3-8-10 **49**........ DeclanCannon 9 53
(Micky Hammond) *hld up towards rr: pushed along over 2f out: hdwy wl over 1f out: styd on fnl f: nrst fin* **25/1**

-004 **5** 8 **Star Request**[6] 3932 3-8-11 **57**........ GeorginaBaxter(7) 8 40
(Keith Dalgleish) *bhd: detached after 3f: styd on wl fr 2f out: nvr able to chal* **16/1**

06 **6** 2 1/4 **West Beat**[34] 2960 3-8-7 **51** ow1........ DavidBergin(5) 1 28
(David O'Meara) *towards rr: rdn and hdwy over 2f out: no imp over 1f out* **9/1**[3]

2406 **7** 1/2 **Ceekay's Girl**[41] 2748 3-8-0 **46** oh1........ DanielleMooney(7) 6 22
(R Mike Smith) *towards rr: drvn along over 3f out: sme late hdwy: nvr on terms* **40/1**

5S00 **8** 4 **Elle Rebelle**[10] 3758 3-9-9 **62**........ RyanClark 5 27
(Mark Brisbourne) *plld hrd: prom tl rdn and wknd over 2f out* **12/1**

-000 **9** 7 **Princess Cayan (IRE)**[10] 3772 3-8-7 **46** oh1........ JulieBurke 10
(Linda Perratt) *bhd: struggling 1/2-way: nvr on terms* **66/1**

5600 **10** 9 **Out Of The Blocks**[14] 3629 3-8-10 **49** ow1........(b) LeeTopliss 2
(Ruth Carr) *in tch: rdn 3f out: wknd 2f out* **6/1**[2]

1m 30.75s (-2.65) **Going Correction** -0.475s/f (Firm) **10** Ran SP% **113.3**
Speed ratings (Par 98): **96,93,93,92,83 81,80,75,67,57**
toteswingers 1&2 £3.40, 1&3 £2.30, 2&3 £4.00 CSF £18.68 CT £49.13 TOTE £3.50: £1.20, £3.10, £1.10; EX 17.10 Trifecta £55.80 Pool: £2,837.72 - 38.11 winning units.
Owner Jonathan Gill **Bred** J Gill **Trained** Great Habton, N Yorks
■ Stewards' Enquiry : David Bergin four-day ban: weighed in 2lb heavy (22-25 Jul)

FOCUS
The early pace looked strong in this apprentice handicap, but the time was slowest of the three races over the trip on the day. That said, the first three were always in the leading group. The second and third help with the level.
T/Plt: £207.70 to a £1 stake. Pool: £60,981.14 - 214.25 winning units T/Qpdt: £122.90 to a £1 stake. Pool: £5,080.48 - 30.57 winning units RY

[3500]RIPON (R-H)
Monday, July 8

OFFICIAL GOING: Good to firm (good in places; watered; 8.5)
Rail on bend from back straight to home straight moved out 3m adding 7yds to races on Round course.
Wind: Virtually nil Weather: Fine and dry

4114 KIRKGATE H'CAP — 6f
6:50 (6:51) (Class 6) (0-65,65) 3-Y-0 **£2,587** (£770; £384; £192) **Stalls** High

Form RPR

3140 **1** **Next Door (IRE)**[11] 3740 3-9-5 63........ GrahamGibbons 4 74
(David Barron) *prom: led after 1f: rdn 2f out: clr whn intimidated by loose horse and carried rt ent fnl f: kpt on* **7/1**

0-05 **2** 1 1/2 **Abraham Monro**[16] 3592 3-8-6 50........ JamesSullivan 13 56
(Ruth Carr) *led 1f: cl up: rdn along and sltly outpcd wl over 2f out: kpt on u.p fnl f: tk 2nd towards fin* **20/1**

0-03 **3** 3/4 **Perfect Pasture**[11] 3730 3-8-13 57........ KierenFallon 9 61+
(Michael Easterby) *in rr: pushed along bef 1/2-way: sn swtchd rt to outer and hdwy over 2f out: rdn wl over 1f out: kpt on fnl f: nrst fin* **7/2**[1]

0206 **4** 1 **Flighty Clarets (IRE)**[21] 3396 3-9-1 64........ GeorgeChaloner(5) 5 65
(Richard Fahey) *trckd ldrs: hdwy to chse wnr 1/2-way: rdn along 2f out: drvn and one pce ent fnl f* **6/1**[3]

2600 **5** 2 1/2 **Annie Gogh**[24] 3281 3-9-0 58........ DavidAllan 12 51+
(Tim Easterby) *towards rr: pushed along and hdwy on inner whn nt clr run wl over 1f out: kpt on fnl f: nrst fin* **7/1**

6550 **6** 1/2 **Rose Of May (IRE)**[33] 2997 3-8-7 51........ AndrewMullen 8 42
(David O'Meara) *chsd ldrs: rdn along over 2f out: grad wknd* **16/1**

0251 **7** 2 **A J Cook (IRE)**[17] 3547 3-9-2 65........(bt) LMcNiff(5) 3 50
(David Barron) *hmpd s: t.k.h: a towards rr* **10/1**

56-0 **8** hd **Bapak Pesta (IRE)**[82] 1608 3-9-4 62........ PhillipMakin 7 46
(Kevin Ryan) *midfield: hdwy and in tch over 2f out: sn rdn and btn* **11/2**[2]

00-0 **9** 1 1/2 **Ryedale Valley**[10] 3762 3-8-5 49........ FrannyNorton 10 28
(Tim Easterby) *a towards rr* **18/1**

0310 **10** 5 **Little Eli**[26] 3198 3-8-8 57........ JasonHart(5) 11 20
(Eric Alston) *chsd ldrs: rdn along wl over 2f out: sn wknd* **12/1**

0-20 **U** **Lucy Minaj**[30] 3082 3-8-8 52........ PaulHanagan 1
(Bryan Smart) *wnt lft: stmbld and uns rdr s* **16/1**

1m 12.06s (-0.94) **Going Correction** -0.20s/f (Firm) **11** Ran SP% **115.5**
Speed ratings (Par 98): **98,96,95,93,90 89,87,86,84,78**
toteswingers 1&2 £50.20, 1&3 £2.80, 2&3 £11.40 CSF £134.48 CT £583.81 TOTE £7.70: £2.30, £4.20, £1.80; EX 70.90 Trifecta £363.40 Pool: £729.13 - 1.50 winning units.
Owner Oghill House Stud & Partner **Bred** Oghill House Stud **Trained** Maunby, N Yorks

FOCUS
Few got into this moderate sprint handicap and the form is nothing to take much notice of going forward, although it was relatively the best C&D time. They raced stands' side.

4115 RACING AGAIN SATURDAY 20TH JULY MAIDEN AUCTION FILLIES' STKS — 6f
7:20 (7:21) (Class 5) 2-Y-0 **£3,234** (£962; £481; £240) **Stalls** High

Form RPR

5 **1** **Oyster (IRE)**[13] 3663 2-8-4 0........ JimmyQuinn 1 62+
(Gary Harrison) *carried rt s: sn trcking ldrs on outer: hdwy and cl up 2f out: chal over 1f out: rdn and slt advantage jst ins fnl f: drvn and edgd lft last 75yds: kpt on* **7/2**[3]

0 **2** nk **Where The Boys Are (IRE)**[26] 3205 2-8-10 0........ FrannyNorton 5 67
(Ed McMahon) *cl up: led over 2f out: jnd and rdn over 1f out: drvn and edgd rt jst ins fnl f: narrowly hdd and stl ev ch whn bmpd and hmpd last 75yds: no ex nr fin* **9/4**[1]

00 **3** 2 **Imshivalla (IRE)**[9] 3826 2-8-10 0........ PaulHanagan 6 61
(Richard Fahey) *chsd ldrs: pushed along and n.m.r wl over 1f out: swtchd rt to outer and rdn ent fnl f: kpt on* **5/1**

00 **4** 2 1/4 **Elualla (IRE)**[50] 2475 2-8-7 0........ AndrewMullen 2 50
(Nigel Tinkler) *dwlt: sn chsng ldrs: rdn along wl over 1f out: kpt on same pce appr fnl f* **100/1**

52 **5** nse **The Dukkerer (IRE)**[10] 3766 2-8-10 0........ KierenFallon 7 53
(David O'Meara) *trckd ldrs: cl up 1/2-way: rdn 2f out: hld whn n.m.r ins fnl f: wknd* **3/1**[2]

6 1/2 **Ladies In Waiting** 2-8-4 0........[1] PatrickMathers 3 46
(Richard Fahey) *dwlt and in rr: sme hdwy whn n.m.r wl over 1f out: n.d* **16/1**

5 **7** 1 1/2 **Witchy Woman**[26] 3217 2-8-0 0........ JoeyHaynes(7) 8 50+
(Mrs K Burke) *a towards rr* **12/1**

6 **8** 8 **Sassy Brown (IRE)**[12] 3681 2-8-13 0........ DavidAllan 4 24
(Tim Easterby) *sn led: rdn along 1/2-way: hdd over 2f out and sn wknd* **16/1**

1m 13.41s (0.41) **Going Correction** -0.20s/f (Firm) **8** Ran SP% **115.1**
Speed ratings (Par 91): **89,88,85,82,82 82,80,69**
toteswingers 1&2 £3.30, 1&3 £2.50, 2&3 £2.40 CSF £11.91 TOTE £3.00: £1.50, £1.10, £1.30; EX 10.50 Trifecta £42.60 Pool: £1,180.54 - 20.78 winning units.
Owner Franconson Partners **Bred** Peter McCutcheon **Trained** Newmarket, Suffolk
■ Stewards' Enquiry : Kieren Fallon caution: careless riding

FOCUS
Quite a modest juvenile maiden, but the winner should receive a fair mark for nurseries.

4116 FOLLOW @ATTHERACES ON TWITTER H'CAP — 1m 4f 10y
7:50 (7:52) (Class 4) (0-80,72) 3-Y-0 **£4,851** (£1,443; £721) **Stalls** Low

Form RPR

0342 **1** **Duke Of Yorkshire**[9] 3809 3-8-11 **65**........ NeilFarley(3) 3 71
(Declan Carroll) *trckd ldng pair: hdwy on bit and cl up 3f out: slt ld 2f out: shkn up ent fnl f: sn rdn: kpt on wl towards fin* **5/4**[2]

2153 **2** 1/2 **Ambleside**[31] 3048 3-9-7 **72**........(b) FrannyNorton 2 77
(Mark Johnston) *dwlt: t.k.h and rapid hdwy to ld after 2 1/2f: m in snatches: pushed along 3f out: rdn and hdd 2f out: drvn and rallied ins fnl f: ev ch tl no ex towards fin* **11/10**[1]

2024 **3** 25 **Hamla**[23] 3313 3-8-10 **61**........ KierenFallon 1 39
(Mark Johnston) *set stdy pce: hdd after 2 1/2f: trckd ldr: cl up over 3f out: rdn along wl over 2f out: sn wknd and eased* **5/1**[3]

2m 39.96s (3.26) **Going Correction** -0.20s/f (Firm) **3** Ran SP% **108.7**
Speed ratings (Par 102): **81,80,64**
CSF £3.04 TOTE £2.40; EX 2.70 Trifecta £2.00 Pool: £351.83 - 125.90 winning units.
Owner M Stewart **Bred** Redhill Bloodstock & Tweenhills Stud **Trained** Sledmere, E Yorks

The Form Book Flat, Raceform Ltd, Compton, RG20 6NL.

FOCUS
Just the three runners and it was a messy race, with no pace on. The first two have been rated to form.

4117 SUMMER SPRINT TROPHY H'CAP — 6f
8:20 (8:20) (Class 3) (0-90,88) 3-Y-O **£7,561** (£2,263; £1,131; £566; £282) **Stalls** High

Form RPR
-021 **1** **Pipers Note**[19] 3478 3-9-0 **86** .... GeorgeChaloner(5) 4 96
(Richard Whitaker) *trckd ldrs: hdwy over 2f out: led 1 1/2f out: sn rdn: styd on wl fnl f* **7/2[2]**
0066 **2** 1 1/2 **Jadanna (IRE)**[16] 3562 3-9-6 **87** .... DaleSwift 7 92
(James Given) *trckd ldrs: pushed along 1/2-way: effrt and n.m.r wl over 1f out: sn swtchd rt and rdn: keeping on whn n.m.r and swtchd rt again ent fnl f: sn drvn and kpt on* **8/1**
3011 **3** shd **Bondesire**[10] 3779 3-8-12 **79** .... PaulHanagan 6 84
(David O'Meara) *trckd ldrs: slt ld after 1f: rdn along and hdd 1 1/2f out: drvn and edgd rt ins fnl f: no ex* **7/2[2]**
4030 **4** 1 1/2 **Rhagori Aur**[9] 3813 3-8-10 **77** ....(b[1]) PaulMulrennan 8 77
(Bryan Smart) *t.k.h: hld up towards rr: effrt and n.m.r wl over 1f out: swtchd rt and rdn appr fnl f: kpt on: nrst fin* **22/1**
2014 **5** 1/2 **Line Of Reason (IRE)**[22] 3367 3-9-7 **88** .... KierenFallon 5 87
(Paul Midgley) *hld up: in rr: swtchd rt and hdwy 2f out: rdn to chse ldrs over 1f out: one pce fnl f* **11/4[1]**
1215 **6** nk **Antonio Gramsci**[23] 3320 3-8-13 **80** .... GrahamGibbons 3 78
(David Barron) *led 1f: cl up on stands' rail: effrt 2f out and sn rdn: drvn appr fnl f: sn hung rt and wknd* **4/1[3]**
-006 **7** 6 **Blue Lotus (IRE)**[16] 3591 3-8-4 **71** .... PaulQuinn 2 49
(Tim Easterby) *cl up: rdn along 1/2-way: wknd 2f out* **20/1**
0-00 **8** 2 1/2 **Avec Rose**[9] 3813 3-7-12 **72** .... SamanthaBell(7) 1 42
(Richard Fahey) *wnt rt s: hld up: effrt and sme hdwy on outer 1/2-way: sn rdn and wknd* **33/1**

1m 11.1s (-1.90) **Going Correction** -0.20s/f (Firm) **8 Ran SP% 114.3**
Speed ratings (Par 104): **104,102,101,99,99 98,90,87**
toteswingers 1&2 £9.80, 1&3 £2.70, 2&3 £2.70 CSF £30.03 CT £103.95 TOTE £3.90: £1.80, £2.20, £1.70; EX 35.70 Trifecta £101.90 Pool: £985.33 - 7.25 winning units.
Owner Six Iron Partnership & Partner **Bred** Wadacre Stud **Trained** Scarcroft, W Yorks

FOCUS
A decent 3yo sprint and the winner continues on the upgrade. He's rated up 5lb.

4118 SIS LIVE MAIDEN STKS — 1m
8:50 (8:51) (Class 5) 3-Y-O+ **£3,234** (£962; £481; £240) **Stalls** Low

Form RPR
53 **1** **Cupertino**[58] 2279 3-9-3 0 .... PhillipMakin 4 76+
(Kevin Ryan) *mde all: jnd 2f out: sn rdn: drvn ins fnl f: styd on wl towards fin* **15/8[1]**
2 1 3/4 **Iptisam** 4-9-12 0 .... PaulMulrennan 1 74+
(James Tate) *t.k.h: trckd ldrs: hdwy to chse wnr over 4f out: chal 2f out: sn rdn and ev ch: drvn ins fnl f: no ex towards fin* **5/1[3]**
23 **3** 5 **Primary Route (IRE)**[19] 3465 3-8-12 0 .... GrahamGibbons 7 55
(David Barron) *in tch: hdwy to chse ldrs wl over 2f out: rdn along wl over 1f out: kpt on same pce fnl f* **6/1**
0-4 **4** 2 1/4 **Obboorr**[21] 3398 4-9-12 0 .... MickyFenton 8 57
(Brian Rothwell) *towards rr: hdwy on outer 3f out: rdn along 2f out: styd on fnl f: nrst fin* **16/1**
06 **5** nse **Eium Mac**[17] 3542 4-9-7 0 .... AdamCarter(5) 6 57
(Neville Bycroft) *trckd ldrs on inner: pushed along 3f out: swtchd rt and rdn over 2f out: drvn and one pce fr wl over 1f out* **28/1**
6 1 1/4 **Slip Of A Girl (IRE)** 3-8-12 0 .... RussKennemore 10 47
(Patrick Holmes) *s.i.s and in rr: hdwy 3f out: rdn 2f out: styd on fnl f: nrst fin* **50/1**
6- **7** hd **Hartlebury**[230] 7796 3-9-3 0 .... JimmyQuinn 3 51
(James Bethell) *trckd ldr 3f: cl up: on outer: rdn along wl over 2f out: grad wknd* **20/1**
8 1 1/4 **Young Jay** 3-9-3 0 .... FrannyNorton 5 49+
(Mark Johnston) *chsd ldrs: rdn along 3f out: sn wknd* **8/1**
3 **9** 1/2 **Helterskelter Girl**[19] 3479 3-8-12 0 .... PJMcDonald 2 42
(Ann Duffield) *midfield: hdwy on inner and in tch over 3f out: rdn along to chse ldrs over 2f out: wknd wl over 1f out* **20/1**
04 **10** nk **Card High (IRE)**[19] 3479 3-9-3 0 .... JamesSullivan 12 47
(Wilf Storey) *a towards rr* **66/1**
11 6 **Jimsneverright**[180] 5-9-12 0 .... PaulQuinn 11 35
(Geoffrey Harker) *s.i.s: a in rr* **80/1**
12 32 **Outset (USA)** 3-9-3 0 .... KierenFallon 13
(Mark Johnston) *green and sn pushed along in rr: outpcd over 3f out: sn bhd and eased* **9/2[2]**

1m 40.65s (-0.75) **Going Correction** -0.20s/f (Firm)
WFA 3 from 4yo+ 9lb **12 Ran SP% 118.6**
Speed ratings (Par 103): **95,93,88,86,85 84,84,83,82,82 76,44**
toteswingers 1&2 £4.30, 1&3 £3.00, 2&3 £8.60 CSF £10.26 TOTE £2.80: £1.50, £2.20, £2.00; EX 13.50 Trifecta £45.50 Pool: £755.72 - 12.43 winning units.
Owner S C B Limited **Bred** Boyce Bloodstock **Trained** Hambleton, N Yorks
■ Stewards' Enquiry : Adam Carter one-day ban: careless riding (22 Jul)

FOCUS
The front pair had it to themselves from quite a way out in what was a maiden lacking depth. The winner was entitled to progress but the opposition was shaky.

4119 YORKSHIRE RACING SUMMER FESTIVAL COMING SOON H'CAP — 1m
9:20 (9:20) (Class 5) (0-70,70) 3-Y-O+ **£3,234** (£962; £481; £240) **Stalls** Low

Form RPR
6544 **1** **Border Bandit (USA)**[21] 3397 5-8-10 **52** .... BarryMcHugh 1 64
(Tracy Waggott) *trckd ldr 3f: cl up on inner: effrt 2f out swtchd lft and hdwy jst over 1f out: rdn to ld ent fnl f: kpt on strly* **6/1[2]**
3300 **2** 1 1/4 **Mcmonagle (USA)**[14] 3630 5-9-2 **58** ....(tp) DaleSwift 7 67
(Alan Brown) *prom: chsd ldr 5f out: led 2f out: sn rdn: hdd and drvn ent fnl f: kpt on same pce* **20/1**
-252 **3** 2 3/4 **Triple Eight (IRE)**[17] 3545 5-10-0 **70** ....(b) MichaelO'Connell 9 73
(Philip Kirby) *hld up towards rr: hdwy on outer 3f out: chsd ldrs 2f out: sn rdn and kpt on fnl f: nrst fin* **12/1**
0305 **4** nse **The Blue Banana (IRE)**[32] 3027 4-8-11 **53** ....(b) PJMcDonald 12 56
(Edwin Tuer) *hld up in tch: hdwy 3f out: trckd ldrs 2f out: rdn to chal and ev ch over 1f out: drvn and one pce fnl f: lost 3rd nr line* **16/1**
3300 **5** 3/4 **Cheers For Thea (IRE)**[39] 2796 8-9-8 **64** ....(bt) DavidAllan 8 65
(Tim Easterby) *trckd ldrs: hdwy 3f out: rdn along 2f out: drvn appr fnl f and sn one pce* **20/1**
3500 **6** 2 1/4 **Fraserburgh (IRE)**[20] 3434 3-9-5 **70** .... FrannyNorton 6 66+
(Mark Johnston) *hld up in rr: hdwy 3f out: swtchd lft 2f out: styng on whn n.m.r ent fnl f: kpt on towards fin* **16/1**
5225 **7** nse **Bunce (IRE)**[21] 3392 5-9-13 **69** .... KierenFallon 11 65+
(David O'Meara) *s.i.s and bhd: hdwy over 3f out: swtchd lft and chsd ldrs 2f out: sn rdn and one pce appr fnl f* **10/1**
-025 **8** 1 3/4 **Icy Blue**[7] 3895 5-8-9 **58** ....(p) NoelGarbutt(7) 3 52
(Richard Whitaker) *dwlt: sn in midfield: effrt on inner 3f out: sn rdn: n.m.r wl over 1f out: n.d* **6/1[2]**
0-23 **9** nse **Dubai Celebration**[160] 435 5-9-3 **59** .... PaulMulrennan 4 50
(Julie Camacho) *trckd ldrs on inner: pushed along 3f out: rdn wl over 1f out: sn btn* **4/1[1]**
0002 **10** nk **District Attorney (IRE)**[30] 3081 4-8-11 **53** .... DuranFentiman 2 44
(Chris Fairhurst) *in tch: rdn along 3f out: hld whn n.m.r wl over 1f out* **8/1[3]**
2215 **11** 3/4 **Clock On Tom**[30] 3082 3-9-1 **66** .... GrahamGibbons 5 55
(Michael Easterby) *sn led: rdn along 3f out: hdd 2f out: sn drvn and wknd* **4/1[1]**
400 **12** 2 **Thatcherite (IRE)**[4] 3977 5-9-4 **60** ....(bt[1]) StephenCraine 10 44
(Tony Coyle) *s.i.s: hdwy 1/2-way: chsd ldrs 3f out: rdn along 2f out: n.m.r and hmpd over 1f out: sn wknd* **20/1**

1m 39.03s (-2.37) **Going Correction** -0.20s/f (Firm)
WFA 3 from 4yo+ 9lb **12 Ran SP% 122.5**
Speed ratings (Par 103): **103,101,99,98,98 95,95,94,94,93 93,91**
toteswingers 1&2 £32.90, 1&3 £16.00, 2&3 £69.30 CSF £126.13 CT £1396.60 TOTE £3.60: £1.60, £5.00, £5.90; EX 160.70 Trifecta £683.60 Part won. Pool: £911.55 - 0.02 winning units..
Owner Elsa Crankshaw Gordon Allan **Bred** Darley **Trained** Spennymoor, Co Durham

FOCUS
They went a good gallop and the time was decent. The winner was close to last year's best run, which came here.
T/Plt: £128.30 to a £1 stake. Pool: £83,920.80 - 477.38 winning units T/Qpdt: £33.20 to a £1 stake. Pool: £5,020.18 - 111.70 winning units JR

3896 WINDSOR (R-H)
Monday, July 8

OFFICIAL GOING: Good to firm (watered; 8.7)
Inner of straight dolled out 5yds at 6f and 2yds at Winning Post. Top bend dolled out 2yds adding 9yds to races of 1m and beyond
Wind: Moderate; against Weather: Fine; very warm

4120 IRISH RACENIGHT HERE ON JULY 29TH APPRENTICE H'CAP — 6f
6:00 (6:01) (Class 5) (0-75,75) 4-Y-O+ **£2,587** (£770; £384; £192) **Stalls** Low

Form RPR
5000 **1** **Tidal's Baby**[14] 3622 4-8-12 **64** .... GeorgeDowning(3) 7 74
(Tony Carroll) *hld up in last pair and off the pce: prog over 2f out: drvn to chse ldr jst over 1f out: styd on wl to ld post* **10/1**
5512 **2** shd **Swendab (IRE)**[5] 3949 5-9-5 **68** 6ex ....(v) DarrenEgan 1 78
(John O'Shea) *led against nr side rail: clr over 2f out: drvn over 1f out: looked like holding on tl wknd nr fin: hdd post* **2/1[1]**
6311 **3** 1 3/4 **Commanche**[20] 3431 4-9-7 **75** .... JoshCrane(5) 6 79+
(Chris Dwyer) *w.w in midfield: prog 2f out: rdn to dispute 2nd briefly jst over 1f out: styd on but unable to chal* **5/1[2]**
05 **4** 4 **Gung Ho Jack**[9] 3841 4-9-4 **67** .... ThomasBrown 8 59
(John Best) *prom: rdn to chse ldr 2f out to jst over 1f out: wknd* **8/1**
0300 **5** 1 1/2 **Bussa**[14] 3622 5-9-0 **68** ....(t) EoinWalsh(5) 2 55
(David Evans) *slowest away: off the pce in last pair: rdn and prog over 2f out: kpt on one pce over 1f out* **25/1**
2325 **6** nk **Aaranyow (IRE)**[11] 3738 5-8-4 **56** oh3 .... NathanAlison(3) 10 42
(Clifford Lines) *a in midfield: rdn over 2f out: one pce and no imp* **25/1**
5024 **7** 2 **Welease Bwian (IRE)**[11] 3716 4-8-7 **61** .... ShelleyBirkett(5) 12 40
(Stuart Williams) *prom: trckd ldr after 2f to 2f out: folded tamely and edgd rt fnl f* **20/1**
0310 **8** 1/2 **Black Cadillac (IRE)**[135] 775 5-9-4 **72** .... OisinMurphy(5) 4 50
(Andrew Balding) *dwlt: wl in rr: trying to make prog but no ch whn hmpd against nr side rail over 1f out: hmpd again ins fnl f* **14/1**
0-04 **9** 1/2 **Oh So Spicy**[26] 3223 6-9-9 **72** .... AshleyMorgan 11 48
(Chris Wall) *racd wdst of all: hld up in midfield: nt qckn over 2f out: steadily wknd* **12/1**
5322 **10** 1 **Chevise (IRE)**[17] 3529 5-8-8 **60** ....(p) RyanTate(3) 5 33
(Steve Woodman) *chsd ldr 2f: lost pl sn after 1/2-way: no ch fnl 2f* **14/1**
00-4 **11** 2 1/4 **Judd Street**[27] 3181 11-9-0 **70** ....(v) CharlieBennett(7) 3 36
(Eve Johnson Houghton) *chsd ldrs to 1/2-way: losing pl whn hmpd against nr side rail over 1f out: bdly hmpd ins fnl f* **25/1**
013- **12** 9 **Golden Compass**[312] 5775 5-9-4 **70** .... MichaelJMMurphy(3) 9
(Giles Bravery) *chsd ldrs but sn u.p: wknd bef 1/2-way: t.o* **15/2[3]**

1m 11.75s (-1.25) **Going Correction** -0.10s/f (Good) **12 Ran SP% 119.3**
Speed ratings (Par 103): **104,103,101,96,94 93,91,90,89,88 85,73**
toteswingers 1&2 £6.70, 1&3 £11.00, 2&3 £2.80 CSF £28.93 CT £114.58 TOTE £6.60: £1.30, £1.90, £3.60; EX 48.70 Trifecta £494.60 Pool: £2,710.80 - 4.11 winning units.
Owner Mrs Bernadette Quinn **Bred** Mr & Mrs J Quinn **Trained** Cropthorne, Worcs
■ Stewards' Enquiry : Shelley Birkett three-day ban: careless riding (22-24 Jul)

FOCUS
Following another sweltering, hot afternoon and despite a watered track, the going changed to good to firm (from good to firm, good in places) prior to the opening contest, a weak sprint handicap for apprentice riders. The early pace was strong and they came up the stands' side. This is up there with the winner's best efforts.

4121 BRITISH STALLION STUDS EBF MAIDEN STKS — 6f
6:30 (6:30) (Class 5) 2-Y-O **£2,911** (£866; £432; £216) **Stalls** Low

Form RPR
1 **Nezar (IRE)** 2-9-5 0 .... WilliamBuick 2 78+
(William Haggas) *trckd ldrs in 5th: prog over 1f out: chsd ldr fnl f: clsd to ld last 100yds: pushed out to hold on* **6/1[3]**
2 hd **Smart Salute** 2-9-5 0 .... GeorgeBaker 9 77+
(Ed Walker) *pressed ldr: shkn up to ld over 1f out: hdd last 100yds: styd on but jst hld* **4/1[2]**
00 **3** 2 1/2 **Bowsers Bold**[9] 3836 2-9-5 0 .... HayleyTurner 5 70
(Marcus Tregoning) *trckd ldng pair: looking for room 2f out: shkn up and styd on same pce to take 3rd wl ins fnl f* **16/1**
324 **4** 1/2 **Bonjour Steve**[27] 3175 2-9-5 0 .... LiamKeniry 6 68
(J S Moore) *led against nr side rail but set mod pce: rdn and hdd over 1f out: one pce* **8/1**

5 1 ¼ **Captain Bob (IRE)** 2-9-5 0 JamesMcDonald 3 65+
(Charles Hills) *slowly away: off the pce in last quartet: shkn up and prog wl over 1f out: pushed along to take 5th fnl f* **4/1**[2]

0 6 ¾ **Drinkuptrig (IRE)**[16] 3581 2-9-5 0 AndreaAtzeni 7 62
(Stuart Williams) *in tch on outer in 6th: pushed along and cl enough over 1f out: fdd fnl f* **12/1**

7 4 **Shyron** 2-9-5 0 TomQueally 1 50+
(George Margarson) *slowly away: wl in rr and rn green: no ch over 1f out* **16/1**

8 ¾ **Canary Lad (IRE)** 2-9-0 0 MichaelJMMurphy(5) 4 48
(Alan Jarvis) *s.i.s: rn green in fnl pair: reminders over 2f out: last 1f out: r.o nr fin* **33/1**

9 1 ½ **Kickboxer (IRE)** 2-9-5 0 MartinHarley 10 44
(Mick Channon) *slowly away: a wl in rr: no prog over 1f out* **20/1**

10 ½ **Grass Green** 2-9-0 0 RyanMoore 8 37
(William Haggas) *trckd ldng pair: shkn up to try to chal 2f out: wknd qckly over 1f out: eased* **10/3**[1]

1m 13.74s (0.74) **Going Correction** -0.10s/f (Good) **10** Ran SP% **115.6**
Speed ratings (Par 94): **91,90,87,86,85 84,78,77,75,75**
toteswingers 1&2 £5.30, 1&3 £15.90, 2&3 £9.20 CSF £29.97 TOTE £7.80: £2.30, £1.40, £3.60; EX 42.20 Trifecta £400.10 Pool: £2,021.00 - 3.78 winning units.

Owner Saleh Al Homaizi & Imad Al Sagar **Bred** Edgeridge Ltd And Glenvale Stud **Trained** Newmarket, Suffolk

FOCUS
Only a trio had previous experience and there were plenty of respected yards represented in what looked an ordinary juvenile maiden. The early pace was not strong and the finish was dominated by two debutants. The form is rated at the bottom end of the pre-race averages.

4122 FAMILY FUN DAY ON SUNDAY AUGUST 11 CLAIMING STKS 1m 2f 7y
7:00 (7:01) (Class 6) 3-Y-O **£1,940** (£577; £288; £144) **Stalls** Centre

Form RPR

3355 1 **First Sargeant**[10] 3793 3-8-9 67 (p) MartinHarley 6 64
(Marco Botti) *trckd ldng pair: plld out and rdn jst over 2f out: led over 1f out: edgd rt and drvn out* **6/4**[1]

5-00 2 1 **Bold And Free**[21] 3418 3-9-2 65 (p) WilliamCarson 4 69
(David Elsworth) *led but pressed: rdn 2f out: hdd over 1f out: kpt on same pce* **7/1**

16 3 hd **Pixie Cut (IRE)**[7] 3900 3-8-3 64 LiamJones 5 56
(J S Moore) *pressed ldr: rdn and upsides over 2f out tl wnr wnt by over 1f out: n.m.r sn after: one pce* **9/4**[2]

10V4 4 9 **Inessa Armand (IRE)**[12] 3675 3-8-1 58 (p) RyanTate(5) 8 41
(J S Moore) *chsd ldng pair: rdn and nt qckn over 3f out: sn struggling* **9/2**[3]

2264 5 ½ **Winter Music (IRE)**[18] 3488 3-8-0 59 (v) JackGarritty(7) 3 41
(Andrew Balding) *hld up in last pair: hanging and no prog fr 4f out: nvr threatened* **10/1**

-500 6 11 **Dancing Chief (IRE)**[47] 2566 3-8-4 42 (v[1]) MichaelJMMurphy(5) 9 21
(Alan Jarvis) *rousted along early: in tch: effrt to press ldrs 4f out: wknd 3f out: t.o* **33/1**

2m 4.64s (-4.06) **Going Correction** -0.375s/f (Firm) **6** Ran SP% **113.5**
Speed ratings (Par 98): **101,100,100,92,92 83**
toteswingers 1&2 £2.30, 1&3 £1.60, 2&3 £2.90 CSF £12.97 TOTE £2.20: £1.40, £2.30; EX 11.40 Trifecta £22.90 Pool: £1,475.99 - 48.23 winning units.

Owner Rothmere Racing Limited **Bred** Rothmere Racing Ltd **Trained** Newmarket, Suffolk

FOCUS
A trio of non-runners made this weak claimer even more uncompetitive, in which they went off quite quickly for the level and the front-runners were picked off. The time was quite quick but the form is rated a bit cautiously.

4123 CORAL.CO.UK H'CAP 5f 10y
7:30 (7:30) (Class 4) (0-85,85) 3-Y-O+ **£4,851** (£1,443; £721; £360) **Stalls** Low

Form RPR

-613 1 **Blanc De Chine (IRE)**[29] 3135 4-9-12 85 RyanMoore 6 95
(Peter Makin) *trckd ldng pair gng wl: led on outer wl over 1f out: edgd rt after: drvn out* **11/4**[1]

3-26 2 1 **Angelito**[41] 2755 4-9-5 78 SeanLevey 7 84+
(Ed McMahon) *slowly away: racd in last pair tl prog against nr side rail 2f out: clsng and looked dangerous whn sddle slipped over 1f out: chsd wnr fnl f: unable to throw down a chal* **7/2**[2]

0046 3 1 **Cruise Tothelimit (IRE)**[9] 3802 5-9-3 76 RichardHughes 4 79
(Ian Williams) *towards rr: prog wl over 1f out: rdn and styd on to take 3rd ins fnl f: unable to chal* **7/2**[2]

5301 4 1 ¼ **Sandfrankskipsgo**[13] 3658 4-9-10 83 ShaneKelly 8 81
(Peter Crate) *t.k.h: hld up bhd ldrs: clsd to chal 2f out: nt qckn over 1f out: one pce after* **14/1**

1062 5 1 ½ **Whitecrest**[13] 3658 5-9-7 80 ChrisCatlin 3 75+
(John Spearing) *trckd ldrs: trying to mount an effrt but pl prospects only whn squeezed out jst ins fnl f: nt rcvr* **20/1**

4464 6 nse **Waseem Faris (IRE)**[10] 3786 4-9-3 76 MartinHarley 9 69
(Mick Channon) *nudged by rival over 3f out and dropped to last: nvr on terms after: kpt on fnl f* **7/1**

0-56 7 3 ½ **Howyadoingnotsobad (IRE)**[16] 3677 5-9-0 73 AdamKirby 5 53
(Karen George) *led to over 3f out: sing to lose pl whn squeezed out jst over 1f out* **25/1**

6033 8 nk **West Coast Dream**[22] 3371 6-9-5 81 MarkCoumbe(3) 2 60
(Roy Brotherton) *pressed ldr: led over 3f out to wl over 1f out: wknd fnl f* **6/1**[3]

0-05 9 2 **Royal Award**[21] 3407 4-9-1 74 TomQueally 1 46
(Jonathan Portman) *trckd ldrs: struggling to hold pl whn short of room wl over 1f out: no ch after* **25/1**

59.39s (-0.91) **Going Correction** -0.10s/f (Good) **9** Ran SP% **117.0**
Speed ratings (Par 105): **103,101,99,97,95 95,89,89,86**
toteswingers 1&2 £3.50, 1&3 £2.80, 2&3 £4.00 CSF £12.28 CT £32.97 TOTE £3.60: £1.40, £1.60, £2.10; EX 13.60 Trifecta £46.80 Pool: £1,317.71 - 21.11 winning units.

Owner R P Marchant & Mrs E Lee **Bred** Newlands House Stud **Trained** Ogbourne Maisey, Wilts

■ Stewards' Enquiry : Chris Catlin caution: careless riding

FOCUS
A reasonably competitive, low-grade sprint handicap, with plenty of early pace. There were a couple of hard-luck stories but the market proved correct and the form should hold up. The winner continues to progress, though things went her way here.

4124 DOWNLOAD CORAL MOBILE FROM THE APP STORE H'CAP 1m 67y
8:00 (8:00) (Class 4) (0-85,82) 3-Y-O+ **£4,851** (£1,443; £721; £360) **Stalls** Low

Form RPR

-031 1 **Consign**[31] 3062 3-8-13 76 (v) WilliamBuick 5 86+
(Jeremy Noseda) *trckd ldrs in 4th: rdn and clsd fr 2f out: led jst ins fnl f: drvn out* **2/1**[2]

5412 2 1 ¼ **Good Luck Charm**[4] 3974 4-9-12 80 RyanMoore 1 89
(Gary Moore) *broke wl but stdd bhd ldng pair: clsd fr 2f out: drvn to chal 1f out: nt qckn fnl f and a hld by wnr* **5/4**[1]

022- 3 1 ½ **Multi Bene**[200] 8181 4-9-12 80 SeanLevey 9 86
(Ed McMahon) *sn chsd ldr: clsd fr 2f out: drvn to chal jst over 1f out: kpt on same pce* **14/1**

0256 4 ¾ **Noble Bull (IRE)**[24] 3294 3-8-11 74 (b) SteveDrowne 2 76
(Charles Hills) *racd freely: sn led: drew clr over 3f out: hdd and fdd jst ins fnl f* **14/1**

6200 5 3 ¼ **Poetic Lord**[12] 3693 4-9-5 73 LiamKeniry 3 69
(Sylvester Kirk) *a abt same pl: outpcd over 3f out: sn rdn: kpt on fnl 2f but nvr able to threaten* **33/1**

0032 6 3 ½ **Shifting Star (IRE)**[7] 3901 8-9-2 70 (vt) RichardHughes 6 58+
(John Bridger) *hld up in last pair: plenty to do after pce lifted over 3f out: nudged along and no prog sn after: stuck bhd rival 2f out: nvr in it* **6/1**[3]

-610 7 5 **Red Seventy**[37] 2858 4-9-11 79 TomQueally 4 56
(Harry Dunlop) *stdd s: hld up in last pair: plenty to do after pce lifted over 3f out: no prog after* **12/1**

1300 8 shd **Hipster**[14] 3633 3-8-10 80 (p) JaneElliott(7) 8 55
(Ralph Beckett) *chsd ldrs: pushed along bef 1/2-way: lft bhd over 3f out: no ch after* **25/1**

1m 41.57s (-3.13) **Going Correction** -0.375s/f (Firm)
WFA 3 from 4yo+ 9lb **8** Ran SP% **119.9**
Speed ratings (Par 105): **100,98,97,96,93 89,84,84**
toteswingers 1&2 £1.50, 1&3 £1.60, 2&3 £5.20 CSF £5.15 CT £25.90 TOTE £2.90: £1.10, £1.20, £2.50; EX 6.10 Trifecta £24.60 Pool: £1,616.07 - 49.13 winning units.
Owner Miss Yvonne Jacques **Bred** Natton House Thoroughbreds & Mark Woodall **Trained** Newmarket, Suffolk

FOCUS
A fair handicap although not one of the field was within 5lb of the ceiling. The pace was honest and the market proved correct. The winner could get a biggish rise for this.

4125 FLORIDITA CUBAN RACENIGHT HERE ON JULY 15 MAIDEN FILLIES' STKS 1m 67y
8:30 (8:32) (Class 5) 3-4-Y-O **£2,587** (£770; £384; £192) **Stalls** Low

Form RPR

1 **Velvety (USA)** 3-9-0 0 AdamKirby 3 81+
(Saeed bin Suroor) *hld up in 5th: pushed along whn pce lifted over 3f out: clsd on outer 2f out: shkn up to ld over 1f out: wl on top and pushed out fnl f* **5/2**[2]

2 2 **Endless Light** 3-9-0 0 RyanMoore 1 76
(Jeremy Noseda) *led at mod pce: kicked on over 3f out: hdd and outpcd over 1f out* **5/1**[3]

35- 3 1 ½ **Raskova (USA)**[318] 5550 3-9-0 0 JamesMcDonald 5 73
(William Jarvis) *t.k.h: w ldr: shkn up and lost 2nd over 2f out: one pce over 1f out* **7/1**

00 4 3 ½ **Marmalady (IRE)**[22] 3372 3-9-0 0 TomQueally 6 65?
(Gary Moore) *tk fierce hold: trckd ldng pair: wnt 2nd and chal over 2f out: wknd over 1f out* **33/1**

5 1 ¾ **Pearl Queen (USA)** 3-9-0 0[1] HarryBentley 2 61
(Chris Wall) *trckd ldng pair: pushed along whn pce lifted over 3f out: no imp after: eased ins fnl f* **20/1**

6 ½ **Snow Powder (IRE)** 3-9-0 0 WilliamBuick 4 60
(John Gosden) *s.i.s: rn green and a last: struggling over 3f out: kpt on fnl f* **9/4**[1]

1m 44.6s (-0.10) **Going Correction** -0.375s/f (Firm) **6** Ran SP% **96.2**
Speed ratings (Par 100): **85,83,81,78,76 75**
toteswingers 1&2 £1.80, 1&3 £3.60, 2&3 £4.70 CSF £10.67 TOTE £2.80: £1.40, £2.00; EX 14.20 Trifecta £55.70 Pool: £624.52 - 8.39 winning units.
Owner Godolphin **Bred** Darley **Trained** Newmarket, Suffolk

FOCUS
The withdrawal of Princess Loulou, who failed to enter the stalls, left just two who had previous experience in this modest fillies' 3yo maiden, which contained some runners with respected connections. They went no pace early on but the winner might be useful. She bettered the established race average at this stage.

4126 SCOUTING FOR GIRLS LIVE ON AUGUST 24 H'CAP 1m 2f 7y
9:00 (9:03) (Class 5) (0-75,75) 3-Y-O+ **£2,587** (£770; £384; £192) **Stalls** Centre

Form RPR

1305 1 **Significant Move**[16] 3573 6-9-5 71 (b[1]) MichaelJMMurphy(5) 4 81
(Stuart Kittow) *sn prom: wnt 2nd 3f out gng strly: drvn to ld jst over 1f out: styd on* **14/1**

6305 2 1 ¼ **Greylami (IRE)**[28] 3157 8-9-9 75 RyanTate(5) 6 82
(Clive Cox) *sn prom: rdn to chal 2f out: drifted lft after: chsd wnr fnl f: nt qckn* **5/1**[2]

2453 3 nk **Jewelled**[63] 2070 7-9-11 72 (p) SebSanders 12 78
(Lady Herries) *hld up in midfield: trckd ldrs over 4f out: waiting bhd them gng strly over 2f out: drvn over 1f out: nt qckn and kpt on same pce after* **16/1**

0211 4 nse **Laughing Jack**[4] 3985 5-9-9 75 GeorgeDowning(5) 2 81
(Tony Carroll) *led but a pestered: tried to kick on over 3f out: drifted lft fr 2f out: hdd and one pce jst over 1f out* **9/4**[1]

-213 5 ½ **Silver Dixie (USA)**[113] 1053 3-8-13 71 WilliamBuick 8 76+
(Jeremy Noseda) *hld up in 9th: rdn on outer wl over 2f out: styd on after: nrst fin but nvr able to threaten* **9/4**[1]

612 6 3 **Breaking The Bank**[8] 3854 4-9-7 68 MartinDwyer 11 67
(William Muir) *trckd ldrs: lost pl sn after 1/2-way: shkn up over 3f out: no imp 2f out: kpt on after* **6/1**[3]

00-0 7 7 **Divea**[72] 1836 4-9-2 63 WilliamCarson 10 48
(Anthony Carson) *hld up in last pair: shkn up and no prog 4f out: modest late hdwy: nvr a factor* **66/1**

0001 8 5 **Super Duplex**[27] 2954 6-8-10 62 JemmaMarshall(5) 9 37
(Pat Phelan) *mostly chsd ldr to 3f out: sn wknd* **25/1**

2000 **9** *3* **Bajan Story**[20] 3434 4-8-2 **56** .... OisinMurphy(7) 1 25
(Michael Blanshard) *in tch: rdn on outer wl over 3f out: sn struggling and btn* **66/1**

1440 **10** *nse* **Waving**[14] 3617 4-9-6 **67** .... AdamKirby 7 36
(Tony Carroll) *nvr bttr than midfield: shoved along 4f out: sn lft bhd* **33/1**

0050 **11** *3 ½* **Lily Edge**[14] 3635 4-9-2 **63** .... RichardHughes 5 25
(John Bridger) *hld up in midfield: in tch at rr of main gp over 3f out: sn shkn up and wknd* **16/1**

003- **12** *½* **No Compromise**[15] 6798 4-9-13 **74** .... (t) FergusSweeney 3 35
(Richard Phillips) *hld up in last pair: drvn and struggling 4f out: sn bhd* **50/1**

2m 3.92s (-4.78) **Going Correction** -0.375s/f (Firm)
WFA 3 from 4yo+ 11lb **12** Ran SP% **122.7**
Speed ratings (Par 103): **104,103,102,102,102 99,94,90,87,87 85,84**
CSF £83.24 CT £1161.15 TOTE £15.90: £4.00, £2.10, £2.70; EX 119.30 Trifecta £946.70 Pool: £1,737.13 - 1.37 winning units.
Owner Midd Shire Racing **Bred** Juddmonte Farms Ltd **Trained** Blackborough, Devon

FOCUS
It paid to be up with the pace for this ordinary handicap. The pace was solid and the first three were spread across the track. The place to be all night was three wide from the stands' rail and that looked to help the winner. He's rated back to his C&D reappearance form.
T/Plt: £42.40 to a £1 stake. Pool: £102,427.46 - 1,759.51 winning units T/Qpdt: £6.20 to a £1 stake. Pool: £8,670.50 - 1,033.29 winning units JN

4127 - 4133a (Foreign Racing) - See Raceform Interactive

3889 PONTEFRACT (L-H)
Tuesday, July 9

OFFICIAL GOING: Good to firm (good in places; 7.8)
False rail from 6f bend to Winning Post adding 16yds to all race distances.

4134 DIANNE NURSERY H'CAP — 6f
2:30 (2:33) (Class 4) 2-Y-O **£4,528** (£1,347; £673; £336) **Stalls** Low

Form RPR

13 **1** **One Penny Piece**[11] 3761 2-9-2 **74** .... WilliamCarson 2 74
(Philip McBride) *trckd ldr: rdn over 1f out: led fnl 75yds: sn drvn: hld on all out* **8/1**[3]

213 **2** *hd* **Milly's Secret (IRE)**[12] 3723 2-9-7 **79** .... PJMcDonald 1 78
(Ann Duffield) *hld up in tch: rdn and hdwy over 1f out: ev ch ins fnl f: kpt on: jst hld* **3/1**[1]

2301 **3** *nk* **Scargill**[11] 3767 2-8-13 **78** .... ConnorBeasley(7) 3 76
(Brian Ellison) *racd keenly: trckd ldr: led over 2f out: sn rdn: hdd fnl 75yds: one pce* **3/1**[1]

10 **4** *5* **Arabda**[18] 3522 2-9-6 **78** .... PaulHanagan 4 61
(Mark Johnston) *led: rdn whn hdd over 2f out: wknd fnl f* **9/2**[2]

1 **5** *1 ¼* **Cascadia (IRE)**[21] 3440 2-7-13 **64** .... JoeyHaynes(7) 5 43
(Mrs K Burke) *dwlt: hld up: rdn over 2f out: sn no imp on ldrs* **17/2**

0321 **6** *2 ¾* **Sunset Shore**[13] 3673 2-9-6 **78** .... LukeMorris 6 49
(Sir Mark Prescott Bt) *midfield: pushed along 1/2-way: drvn 2f out: sn btn* **9/2**[2]

024 **7** *1* **Midnight Muscida (IRE)**[12] 3710 2-8-9 **67** .... JamesSullivan 7 35
(Tim Easterby) *in tch on outer: rdn over 2f out: sn wknd* **25/1**

1m 19.8s (2.90) **Going Correction** +0.325s/f (Good) **7** Ran SP% **111.8**
Speed ratings (Par 96): **93,92,92,85,84 80,79**
Tote Swingers: 1&2 £4.40, 1&3 £5.20, 2&3 £2.50 CSF £30.76 TOTE £9.70: £3.70, £2.40; EX 35.90 Trifecta £101.50 Pool: £3,000.72 - 22.15 winning units..
Owner P J McBride **Bred** Mrs Sarah Hamilton **Trained** Newmarket, Suffolk

FOCUS
The rail was out from the 6f marker to the winning post, adding around 16yds to the distance of all races. Paul Hanagan described the ground as "pretty quick". The front three drew a little way clear in what was an ordinary nursery. The second and third help with the level.

4135 RACING UK YOUR RACING HOME FROM HOME H'CAP — 1m 2f 6y
3:00 (3:00) (Class 5) (0-75,72) 3-Y-O+ **£3,234** (£962; £481; £240) **Stalls** Low

Form RPR

-020 **1** **Circle Of Angels**[5] 3971 5-8-13 **57** .... FrannyNorton 2 67
(Mark Johnston) *dwlt: hld up: rdn and gd hdwy over 2f out: led 1f out: kpt on wl* **15/2**

3420 **2** *2 ½* **Rock Song**[27] 3204 4-9-13 **71** .... GrahamGibbons 3 76
(John Mackie) *midfield: rdn and hdwy over 2f out: led appr fnl f: sn hdd: one pce* **9/2**[2]

0601 **3** *shd* **King Of Paradise (IRE)**[27] 3199 4-9-5 **68** .... JasonHart(5) 6 73
(Eric Alston) *led: clr 9f out tl 3f out: rdn over 2f out: hdd appr fnl f: one pce* **7/1**[3]

0006 **4** *9* **Queens Revenge**[13] 3686 4-9-6 **64** .... DavidAllan 7 52
(Tim Easterby) *hld up: rdn and hdwy on outer over 2f out: chsd ldr over 1f out: wknd fnl f* **25/1**

0-30 **5** *2 ½* **Yorkshireman (IRE)**[83] 1608 3-9-3 **72** .... GrahamLee 5 55
(David Brown) *midfield: rdn over 5f out: wknd over 2f out* **12/1**

2256 **6** *1 ¼* **Eastward Ho**[19] 3506 5-9-8 **66** .... KierenFallon 1 47
(Jason Ward) *chsd clr ldr: rdn over 2f out: wknd over 1f out* **7/1**[3]

251 **7** *4* **Danehill Flyer (IRE)**[8] 3893 3-8-11 **69** 6ex .... DeclanCannon(3) 4 42
(Philip Kirby) *chsd clr ldr: rdn over 3f out: wknd fnl 2f* **6/4**[1]

0-00 **8** *dist* **Queen's Estate (GER)**[11] 3791 4-9-12 **70** .... JoeFanning 8
(Mark Johnston) *hld up: rdn over 4f out: sn btn: eased and t.o fnl 2f* **25/1**

2m 14.77s (1.07) **Going Correction** +0.05s/f (Good)
WFA 3 from 4yo+ 11lb **8** Ran SP% **110.3**
Speed ratings (Par 103): **97,95,94,87,85 84,81,**
Tote Swingers: 1&2 £5.30, 1&3 £7.50, 2&3 £3.00 CSF £38.16 CT £232.53 TOTE £8.10: £1.80, £1.90, £1.50; EX 38.70 Trifecta £301.10 Pool: £2,155.85 - 5.36 winning units..
Owner R S Brookhouse **Bred** R S Brookhouse **Trained** Middleham Moor, N Yorks

FOCUS
This was run at a good gallop, with King Of Paradise tearing off, and the race set up nicely for the closers. Straightforward form, with the first three clear.

4136 JEFF AND MARGARET SMITH MEMORIAL H'CAP — 5f
3:30 (3:30) (Class 5) (0-75,72) 3-Y-O **£3,234** (£962; £481; £240) **Stalls** Low

Form RPR

2121 **1** **Jofranka**[41] 2779 3-9-2 **67** .... GrahamGibbons 8 76+
(David Barron) *mde all: rdn over 1f out: kpt on wl* **7/4**[1]

0430 **2** *1 ¼* **Queen Flush (IRE)**[17] 3594 3-8-3 **54** .... (b[1]) JoeFanning 1 58
(David Nicholls) *trckd ldng pair: rdn to chse wnr over 1f out: kpt on but a hld* **15/2**

3113 **3** *1* **Teetotal (IRE)**[10] 3813 3-9-2 **72** .... JasonHart(5) 6 73
(Nigel Tinkler) *s.i.s: hld up: rdn 2f out: swtchd rt jst ins fnl f: r.o wl: nrst fin* **5/1**[3]

5000 **4** *shd* **Windforpower (IRE)**[17] 3594 3-8-4 **55** .... FrannyNorton 4 55
(Tracy Waggott) *midfield on inner: n.m.r 2f out: rdn over 1f out: kpt on one pce* **25/1**

03-3 **5** *½* **Work Ethic (IRE)**[15] 3639 3-9-4 **69** .... (tp) LukeMorris 7 67
(Gerard Butler) *hld up: rdn 1/2-way: kpt on one pce* **12/1**

6006 **6** *3* **Lady Poppy**[10] 3813 3-9-3 **68** .... PJMcDonald 9 55
(George Moore) *pressed ldr: rdn 2f out: wknd appr fnl f* **20/1**

5-10 **7** *1* **Rangooned**[67] 1988 3-9-0 **72** .... RowanScott(7) 2 56
(Ann Duffield) *dwlt: hld up: pushed along 1/2-way: nvr threatened* **9/1**

2034 **8** *¾* **Boxing Shadows**[17] 3591 3-9-6 **71** .... PaulMulrennan 5 52
(Bryan Smart) *chsd ldng pair: pushed along and lost pl 1/2-way: wknd over 1f out* **7/2**[2]

1m 4.97s (1.67) **Going Correction** +0.325s/f (Good) **8** Ran SP% **113.3**
Speed ratings (Par 100): **99,97,95,95,94 89,88,86**
Tote Swingers: 1&2 £3.00, 1&3 £2.20, 2&3 £5.20 CSF £15.40 CT £55.32 TOTE £2.10: £1.10, £2.50, £1.80; EX 14.90 Trifecta £81.30 Pool: £2,961.04 - 27.29 winning units..
Owner M Dalby **Bred** Harrowgate Bloodstock Ltd **Trained** Maunby, N Yorks

FOCUS
Few got into this. Straightforward form, with the winner the type to find a bit more.

4137 WEATHERBYS VAT SERVICES PIPALONG STKS (LISTED RACE) (F&M) — 1m 4y
4:00 (4:01) (Class 1) 4-Y-O+
£22,684 (£8,600; £4,304; £2,144; £1,076; £540) **Stalls** Low

Form RPR

1-12 **1** **Gifted Girl (IRE)**[39] 2838 4-8-12 **106** .... TomQueally 6 110+
(Paul Cole) *hld up in rr: gd hdwy 2f out: pushed along to ld ins fnl f: kpt on: shade cosily* **9/4**[1]

3362 **2** *2* **Ladys First**[20] 3456 4-8-12 **110** .... PaulHanagan 8 104
(Richard Fahey) *trckd ldng pair: rdn over 2f out: led over 1f out: hdd ins fnl f: kpt on but no ch w wnr* **4/1**[3]

-454 **3** *nk* **Ultrasonic (USA)**[10] 3831 4-8-12 **101** .... RyanMoore 2 105+
(Sir Michael Stoute) *trckd ldng pair: stl gng wl whn short of room on inner over 1f out: swtchd rt: nt clr tl ins fnl f: r.o wl fnl 100yds* **3/1**[2]

01-6 **4** *2* **Hippy Hippy Shake**[66] 2015 4-8-12 **95** .... KierenFallon 1 99
(Luca Cumani) *s.i.s: sn midfield: rdn over 2f out: chsd ldr over 1f out: one pce fnl f* **9/2**

-003 **5** *7* **Dutch Rose (IRE)**[21] 3443 4-8-12 **89** .... LukeMorris 9 83
(David O'Meara) *prom: rdn over 2f out: wknd over 1f out* **50/1**

0-30 **6** *2 ¼* **Sweetnessandlight**[20] 3456 4-8-12 **95** .... GrahamLee 4 78
(Jason Ward) *led: rdn whn hdd over 1f out: wknd* **28/1**

4-34 **7** *1* **Oojooba**[52] 2440 4-8-12 **95** .... [1] AndreaAtzeni 3 75
(Roger Varian) *hld up in midfield: rdn over 3f out: sn btn* **9/1**

5-00 **8** *4 ½* **Semayyel (IRE)**[54] 2397 4-8-12 **99** .... (b) BrettDoyle 7 65
(Clive Brittain) *hld up: rdn 3f out: nvr threatened* **40/1**

0-02 **9** *4 ½* **Forgive**[10] 3835 4-8-12 **90** .... PatDobbs 10 55
(Richard Hannon) *midfield: rdn over 3f out: sn wknd* **28/1**

1m 44.05s (-1.85) **Going Correction** +0.05s/f (Good) **9** Ran SP% **115.2**
Speed ratings (Par 111): **111,109,108,106,99 97,96,91,87**
Tote Swingers: 1&2 £2.50, 1&3 £2.10, 2&3 £2.20 CSF £11.15 TOTE £3.00: £1.10, £1.80, £1.50; EX 9.20 Trifecta £22.50 Pool: £4,093.90 - 136.08 winning units..
Owner A D Spence **Bred** Airlie Stud **Trained** Whatcombe, Oxon

FOCUS
They appeared to go a fair gallop and the market leaders drew clear. Solid form for the grade, with the winner more than confirming her latest form.

4138 KING RICHARD III STKS (H'CAP) — 6f
4:30 (4:30) (Class 3) (0-90,89) 3-Y-O+ **£7,762** (£2,310; £1,154; £577) **Stalls** Low

Form RPR

6001 **1** **Dark Castle**[10] 3811 4-9-3 **80** .... PJMcDonald 3 89
(Micky Hammond) *midfield on inner: rdn over 1f out: r.o wl to ld fnl 50yds* **9/2**[2]

-001 **2** *½* **Links Drive Lady**[39] 2848 5-9-8 **85** .... KierenFallon 10 93
(Dean Ivory) *midfield: rdn over 2f out: hdwy over 1f out: led jst ins fnl f: kpt on: hdd fnl 50yds* **7/1**[3]

4632 **3** *hd* **Head Space (IRE)**[5] 3981 5-9-1 **78** .... (p) JamesSullivan 2 85
(Ruth Carr) *hld up in rr: stl plenty to do ent fnl f: r.o wl towards wd outside fnl 100yds: nrst fin* **4/1**[1]

0511 **4** *2 ¼* **Sunraider (IRE)**[12] 3714 6-9-3 **80** .... MickyFenton 8 80
(Paul Midgley) *dwlt: hld up: pushed along 1/2-way: hdwy over 1f out: one pce fnl f* **14/1**

6050 **5** *nk* **Defence Council (IRE)**[10] 3811 5-9-0 **77** .... PaulHanagan 4 76
(Mel Brittain) *dwlt: hld up: smooth hdwy on outer 2f out: rdn to chse ldr jst ins fnl f: no ex fnl 100yds* **20/1**

1142 **6** *shd* **Chester Aristocrat**[10] 3823 4-9-6 **88** .... JasonHart(5) 5 87+
(Eric Alston) *led: rdn whn hdd jst ins fnl f: no ex* **4/1**[1]

6000 **7** *5* **Klynch**[10] 3823 7-9-11 **88** .... (b) TomEaves 9 72
(Ruth Carr) *prom on outer: rdn and ev ch over 1f out: wknd fnl f* **40/1**

-000 **8** *hd* **Last Bid**[25] 3299 4-9-0 **77** .... DavidAllan 1 60
(Tim Easterby) *hld up in midfield: pushed along 1/2-way: nvr threatened* **33/1**

1005 **9** *shd* **Khawatim**[17] 3590 5-9-12 **89** .... MartinHarley 7 72
(Mrs K Burke) *trckd ldng pair: rdn over 2f out: wknd over 1f out* **8/1**

0340 **10** *9* **Solar Spirit (IRE)**[6] 3945 8-9-0 **77** .... FrannyNorton 6 33
(Tracy Waggott) *midfield: rdn over 2f out: sn wknd* **8/1**

1010 **11** *3 ½* **Meandmyshadow**[10] 3811 5-9-4 **81** .... TomQueally 12 27
(Alan Brown) *pressed ldr tl wknd qckly over 2f out* **16/1**

1m 17.69s (0.79) **Going Correction** +0.325s/f (Good) **11** Ran SP% **115.6**
Speed ratings (Par 107): **107,106,106,103,102 102,95,95,95,83 78**
Tote Swingers: 1&2 £8.50, 1&3 £3.30, 2&3 £7.10 CSF £34.62 CT £138.86 TOTE £6.90: £2.70, £2.40, £1.20; EX 42.50 Trifecta £139.70 Pool: £3,430.43 - 18.40 winning units..
Owner J Cox and E Tasker **Bred** Hedsor Stud **Trained** Middleham Moor, N Yorks

■ Stewards' Enquiry : Jason Hart one-day ban: failed to keep straight from the stalls (23 July)

FOCUS
Several held their chance in the straight as the runners fanned across the track. The form looks sound, with the in-form runners coming to the fore as the pace collapsed.

4139 RED SHIRT NIGHT BEER FESTIVAL 19TH JULY MAIDEN STKS 1m 4f 8y
5:00 (5:00) (Class 5) 3-Y-0+ **£3,234** (£962; £481; £240) **Stalls** Low

Form RPR
0 **1** **Silk Sari**[20] 3469 3-8-9 0 .... KierenFallon 5 83+
(Luca Cumani) *midfield: pushed along over 3f out: hdwy to ld wl over 2f out: hdd appr fnl f: rallied to ld again fnl 50yds* **9/4**[1]
2 *1* **Statutory (IRE)** 3-9-0 0 .... FrannyNorton 6 86+
(Mark Johnston) *hld up: rdn and hdwy to chse ldr over 2f out: led narrowly appr fnl f: one pce: hdd fnl 50yds: hld nr fin* **7/2**[3]
23 **3** *11* **Arr' Kid (USA)**[27] 3201 3-9-0 0 .... TomEaves 3 69
(Keith Dalgleish) *led: rdn over 3f out: hdd wl over 2f out: sn btn* **5/1**
4 *½* **Mansoreen** 3-9-0 0 .... PaulHanagan 4 68+
(Saeed bin Suroor) *trckd ldr: rdn 3f out: wknd fnl 2f* **5/2**[2]
0 **5** *5* **Bollin Bob**[22] 3398 4-9-6 0 .... GaryMahon(7) 2 60
(Tim Easterby) *hld up: rdn over 3f out: nvr threatened* **50/1**
05 **6** *28* **Moscow Circus (IRE)**[165] 373 3-9-0 0 .... JoeFanning 1 15
(Mark Johnston) *trckd ldr: pushed along over 4f out: sn wknd* **9/1**

2m 40.32s (-0.48) **Going Correction** +0.05s/f (Good)
WFA 3 from 4yo 13lb **6** Ran SP% **110.2**
Speed ratings (Par 103): **103,102,95,94,91 72**
Tote Swingers: 1&2 £2.20, 1&3 £2.50, 2&3 £3.30 CSF £10.05 TOTE £2.10: £1.10, £2.90; EX 8.60 Trifecta £41.00 Pool: £2,657.27 - 48.54 winning units..
Owner Fittocks Stud & Andrew Bengough **Bred** Fittocks Stud Ltd & Arrow Farm Stud **Trained** Newmarket, Suffolk

FOCUS
The front pair pulled a long way clear and are probably useful handicappers in the making. The third helps with the opening level.

4140 THREE SCORE YEAR AND TEN H'CAP 1m 4y
5:30 (5:30) (Class 5) (0-70,69) 3-Y-0 **£3,234** (£962; £481; £240) **Stalls** Low

Form RPR
0212 **1** **The Scuttler (IRE)**[3] 4077 3-9-0 **62** .... MartinHarley 3 71
(Mick Channon) *chsd ldr: led jst over 1f out: drvn out and r.o ins fnl f* **9/4**[1]
5022 **2** *1 ¼* **Polar Forest**[3] 4076 3-8-7 **55** .... FrannyNorton 7 61
(Richard Guest) *sn led: rdn and hdd jst over 1f out: continued to chal ins fnl f: no ex and hld towards fin* **7/2**[3]
4620 **3** *nk* **Shearian**[15] 3629 3-9-1 **63** .... BarryMcHugh 4 68
(Tracy Waggott) *chsd ldrs: effrt on inner over 1f out: nt quicken and edgd rt jst ins fnl f: kpt on towards fin* **16/1**
6-46 **4** *7* **Kolonel Kirkup**[12] 3730 3-9-0 **69** .... ConnorBeasley(7) 1 58
(Michael Dods) *hld up: effrt over 2f out: nvr able to trble ldrs and no imp fr over 1f out* **11/4**[2]
-103 **5** *2 ¾* **War Lord (IRE)**[25] 3281 3-9-3 **65** .... KierenFallon 8 48
(David O'Meara) *chsd ldrs: pushed along over 3f out: outpcd over 2f out: sn wl btn* **9/2**
05-0 **6** *7* **Kat Moon**[8] 3910 3-8-9 **57** .... DavidAllan 2 24
(Tim Easterby) *hld up: sme hdwy on outer 4f out: u.p over 2f out: sn wknd* **18/1**
1600 **7** *14* **Blazeofenchantment (USA)**[59] 2272 3-8-10 **58** ....(p) TomEaves 6
(Mrs K Burke) *stdd s: hld up: outpcd fr 2f out: wl bhd over 1f out: nvr a threat* **28/1**
0-00 **8** *7* **Threepence**[56] 2342 3-8-2 **50** .... PaulQuinn 5
(Richard Whitaker) *in rr: niggled along 5f out: bhd fnl 2f* **50/1**

1m 47.13s (1.23) **Going Correction** +0.05s/f (Good) **8** Ran SP% **114.4**
Speed ratings (Par 100): **95,93,93,86,83 76,62,55**
Tote Swingers: 1&2 £1.70, 1&3 £6.20, 2&3 £7.10 CSF £10.05 TOTE £2.40: £1.10, £2.20, £4.80; EX 11.90 Trifecta £82.00 Pool: £1,699.00 - 15.52 winning units..
Owner Lord Ilsley Racing (Hern Syndicate) **Bred** J Hanly **Trained** West Ilsley, Berks

FOCUS
A race in which it paid to race prominently, with the first trio pulling right away having soon been up there. The winner was pretty much back to his best.
T/Plt: £60.80 to a £1 stake. Pool: £94,640.29 - 1,136.26 winning tickets. T/Qpdt: £3.90 to a £1 stake. Pool: £6,881.76 - 1,300.31 winning tickets. AS

2991 SOUTHWELL (L-H)
Tuesday, July 9

OFFICIAL GOING: Standard
Wind: Virtually nil Weather: Fine and dry

4141 JD ARNOLD FARRIERS FOR SHAUN HARRIS NURSERY H'CAP 5f (F)
6:05 (6:05) (Class 6) 2-Y-0 **£1,940** (£577; £288; £144) **Stalls** High

Form RPR
41 **1** **Mecca's Angel (IRE)**[17] 3568 2-9-7 **78** .... PaulMulrennan 3 100
(Michael Dods) *sn led: rdn and qcknd clr 2f out: unchal* **5/2**[2]
0033 **2** *12* **The Dandy Yank (IRE)**[8] 3883 2-9-2 **73** .... FergusSweeney 5 52+
(Jamie Osborne) *prom: sn chsng wnner: rdn along 2f out: drvn and edgd lft wl over 1f out: one pce* **7/2**[3]
410 **3** *½* **Sandsman's Girl (IRE)**[20] 3459 2-9-7 **78** .... GrahamLee 2 55+
(James Given) *in tch: pushed along and outpcd after 1 1/2f: rdn 1/2-way: styd on u.p fnl f* **9/4**[1]
064 **4** *¾* **Faye Belle**[28] 3167 2-7-11 **59** oh12 .... RaulDaSilva(3) 7 31
(Derek Shaw) *racd nr stands' rail: sn rdn along and outpcd: bhd 1/2-way: sme hdwy fnl f* **33/1**
0050 **5** *¾* **Chilly In Rio (IRE)**[22] 3414 2-8-0 **57** oh6 ....(p) CathyGannon 4 29
(William Muir) *broke wl and led early: hdd after 1f: prom: rdn along 1/2-way: sn drvn and wknd: hung rt fnl f* **25/1**
050 **6** *3 ½* **Creative Spirit**[24] 3318 2-8-2 **59** .... NickyMackay 1 18
(David Brown) *dwlt: a in rr* **8/1**
020 **7** *¾* **Kitty Brown (IRE)**[22] 3414 2-7-10 **60** .... NoelGarbutt(7) 6 16
(David Evans) *sn outpcd and bhd fr 1/2-way* **8/1**

59.68s (-0.02) **Going Correction** -0.025s/f (Stan) **7** Ran SP% **110.6**
Speed ratings (Par 92): **99,79,79,77,76 71,69**
Tote Swingers: 1&2 £2.20, 1&3 £1.30, 2&3 £2.00 CSF £10.87 TOTE £2.80: £1.10, £2.40; EX 11.40 Trifecta £14.90 Pool: £2,002.27 - 100.75 winning units..
Owner David T J Metcalfe **Bred** Yeomanstown Stud & Doc Bloodstock **Trained** Denton, Co Durham

FOCUS
Plenty of unexposed types in this nursery. It was run at a fair pace, with the field well strung out from an early stage. There's a doubt the winner can reproduce this sort of big figure elsewhere. Everything else was below form.

4142 EBF QUARRYDALE ACADEMY HAPPILY SUPPORTING NOTTINGHAMSHIRE RACING MAIDEN STKS 5f (F)
6:35 (6:35) (Class 5) 2-Y-0 **£3,408** (£1,006; £503) **Stalls** High

Form RPR
3 **1** **Bushcraft (IRE)**[25] 3288 2-9-5 0 .... GeorgeBaker 4 83+
(Ed Walker) *cl up: led 2f out: rdn clr over 1f out: readily* **10/11**[1]
03 **2** *4 ½* **Anytimeatall (IRE)**[19] 3510 2-8-9 0 .... NatashaEaton(5) 7 59
(Alan Bailey) *led: pushed along 1/2-way: hdd 2f out and sn rdn: drvn and one pce fnl f* **10/1**
4 **3** *hd* **Boston Alex (IRE)**[24] 3324 2-9-0 0 .... HayleyTurner 9 58
(Conor Dore) *in tch: pushed along 1/2-way: rdn wl over 1f out: kpt on wl fnl f: nrst fin* **6/1**[2]
45 **4** *1 ¾* **She Can Jig**[19] 3510 2-9-0 0 .... PhillipMakin 5 52
(Kevin Ryan) *chsd ldrs: rdn along 2f out: drvn over 1f out and sn wknd* **7/1**[3]
33 **5** *2 ¾* **Yellow Lady (IRE)**[22] 3408 2-9-0 0 ....(t) HarryBentley 6 42
(Olly Stevens) *wore a net muzzle: prom: rdn along 2f out: wknd over 1f out* **10/1**
0 **6** *½* **Without Truth (IRE)**[15] 3640 2-9-5 0 .... SeanLevey 3 45
(Ed McMahon) *chsd ldrs: rdn along 2f out: grad wknd* **8/1**
0 **7** *7* **Phoenix Angel**[21] 3436 2-9-5 0 .... PatrickMathers 8 20
(Derek Shaw) *a towards rr* **66/1**
00 **8** *2 ¼* **Spirit O Goodchild**[15] 3640 2-9-5 0 .... AndrewMullen 10 17
(Alan McCabe) *towards rr whn rdn along and hung bdly lft fr 1/2-way* **80/1**
50 **9** *1 ¼* **John Lea (IRE)**[27] 3211 2-9-0 0 .... RobertTart(5) 1 7
(Derek Shaw) *s.i.s: a in rr* **66/1**
10 *½* **Rocky Hill Ridge** 2-9-0 0 .... ShirleyTeasdale(5) 2 6
(Alan McCabe) *dwlt: sn outpcd and a in rr* **33/1**

1m 1.2s (1.50) **Going Correction** -0.025s/f (Stan) **10** Ran SP% **115.6**
Speed ratings (Par 94): **87,79,79,76,72 71,60,56,54,53**
Tote Swingers: 1&2 £2.80, 1&3 £1.50, 2&3 £3.80 CSF £11.01 TOTE £1.30: £1.02, £3.30, £2.50; EX 8.10 Trifecta £32.70 Pool: £1,360.32 - 31.19 winning units..
Owner Laurence A Bellman **Bred** L Fox **Trained** Newmarket, Suffolk

FOCUS
The pace was honest for this modest maiden, with the action taking place up the centre. The winner impressed and the placed horses dictate the level.

4143 CASTLE HOMES SUPPORTING CLUMBER PARK RACING CLAIMING STKS 1m (F)
7:05 (7:06) (Class 6) 3-Y-0 **£2,045** (£603; £302) **Stalls** Low

Form RPR
6040 **1** **Mandy The Nag (USA)**[11] 3756 3-8-12 62 .... JoeFanning 9 82+
(Ian Williams) *led 2f: cl up: led again over 3f out: rdn clr 2f out: easily* **3/1**[2]
0250 **2** *4 ½* **Mixed Message (IRE)**[30] 3137 3-9-4 68 .... GrahamLee 6 76
(John Mackie) *trckd ldrs: hdwy over 3f out: rdn to chse wnr wl over 1f out: drvn and no imp fnl f* **7/2**[3]
500 **3** *10* **Minimee**[18] 3537 3-9-0 67 ....(v) DannyBrock(5) 10 54
(Phil McEntee) *dwlt and towards rr: swtchd to outer after 2f: hdwy to chse ldrs over 3f out: rdn to chse ldng pair 2f out: sn one pce* **11/1**
0002 **4** *6* **Betty Boo (IRE)**[12] 3743 3-8-5 35 .... NeilFarley(3) 11 29
(Shaun Harris) *chsd ldrs: hdwy to chse wnr 3f out: rdn over 2f out: sn drvn and wknd* **66/1**
0030 **5** *2* **Big John Cannon (IRE)**[27] 3194 3-8-9 57 .... GrahamGibbons 8 25
(David Barron) *in tch: swtchd to outer and reminders after 1f: sn rdn along and lost pl: in rr after* **11/4**[1]
55 **6** *1 ¼* **Father Fred**[19] 3494 3-8-11 0 .... SaleemGolam 3 24
(Chris Dwyer) *a towards rr* **66/1**
-350 **7** *1* **Reconsider Baby (IRE)**[22] 3396 3-8-8 66 .... LukeMorris 1 19
(Mrs K Burke) *chsd ldrs on inner: rdn along 3f out: drvn and wknd over 2f out* **5/1**
0-06 **8** *nk* **Windsor Rose (IRE)**[27] 3219 3-7-7 44 .... NoelGarbutt(7) 5
(Mark Brisbourne) *a towards rr* **100/1**
0500 **9** *1 ¾* **Bougaloo**[14] 3657 3-8-11 64 ....(p) SeanLevey 2
(Alan McCabe) *cl up: slt ld after 2f: rdn and hdd over 3f out: sn wknd* **28/1**
-300 **10** *3 ½* **Cinderslipper (IRE)**[22] 3396 3-9-4 63 ....(p) PJMcDonald 7
(Ann Duffield) *s.i.s: a bhd* **10/1**

1m 43.41s (-0.29) **Going Correction** +0.10s/f (Slow) **10** Ran SP% **115.4**
Speed ratings (Par 98): **105,100,90,84,82 81,80,79,78,74**
Tote Swingers: 1&2 £2.30, 1&3 £7.80, 2&3 £10.70 CSF £13.63 TOTE £3.60: £1.50, £1.90, £2.50; EX 14.50 Trifecta £155.20 Pool: £1,249.62 - 6.03 winning units..
Owner Dr Marwan Koukash **Bred** Randal Family Trust Et Al **Trained** Portway, Worcs

FOCUS
A fair pace for this claimer. They came home at long intervals, with the first two well clear, but this isn't form to go overboard about.

4144 WILLASPOONS "BEST PUB IN THORNE" NOTTINGHAMSHIRERACING.CO.UK MAIDEN H'CAP 1m (F)
7:35 (7:36) (Class 6) (0-60,60) 3-Y-0+ **£2,045** (£603; £302) **Stalls** Low

Form RPR
-406 **1** **Exclusion (USA)**[21] 3428 3-8-10 **53** ....(b) PJMcDonald 9 60
(Noel Quinlan) *in rr and pushed along whn swtchd to outer after 2f: bhd and rdn along 1/2-way: wd st and hdwy wl over 2f out: sn rdn: styd on strly u.p appr fnl f: led fnl 50yds* **33/1**
6-26 **2** *½* **Bapak Muda (USA)**[62] 2167 3-9-3 **60** .... PhillipMakin 1 66+
(Kevin Ryan) *cl up: led 1/2-way: jnd and rdn 2f out: drvn ent fnl f: edgd rt: hdd and no ex last 50yds* **5/1**[2]
0-36 **3** *1 ¾* **My Gigi**[28] 3178 3-9-3 **60** ....(be[1]) GeorgeBaker 6 62
(Gary Moore) *prom gng wl: cl up 3f out: chal over 2f out: rdn wl over 1f out and ev ch: drvn and hung rt to stands' rail ent fnl f: kpt on same pce* **10/1**
4U30 **4** *6* **Solarmaite**[18] 3546 4-9-9 **60** ....(p) MarkCoumbe(3) 12 50
(Roy Bowring) *in tch: hdwy and wd st: rdn to chse ldrs 2f out: sn drvn and no imp* **14/1**
05-3 **5** *3 ¼* **Hidden Asset**[50] 2512 3-8-10 **53** .... AndrewMullen 4 34
(Michael Appleby) *chsd ldrs: rdn along 3f out: drvn 2f out and sn one pce* **8/1**[3]
6305 **6** *8* **Sixties Queen**[15] 3641 3-8-12 **60** .... RobertTart(5) 14 22
(Alan Bailey) *chsd ldrs: rdn along wl over 2f out: sn outpcd* **20/1**

The Form Book Flat, Raceform Ltd, Compton, RG20 6NL.

5-06 **7** nse **Silvio Dante (USA)**57 2330 3-9-1 **58** DavidNolan 2 20
(David O'Meara) *slt ld to 1/2-way: cl up: rdn along wl over 2f out and sn wknd* **9/1**

6546 **8** 2 **Floralys (USA)**11 3788 4-9-1 **56** (be) ConnorBeasley(7) 7 15
(Amy Weaver) *a in rr* **8/1**3

4305 **9** 1/2 **Spider House**11 3772 3-8-13 **59** JulieBurke(3) 13 15
(David O'Meara) *nvr a factor* **12/1**

-546 **10** 14 **Attain**19 3513 4-8-12 **53** (p) ShelleyBirkett(7) 5
(Julia Feilden) *a bhd* **12/1**

3455 **11** 3 1/2 **Exclusive Predator**17 3572 4-9-12 **60** SilvestreDeSousa 11
(Geoffrey Oldroyd) *a in rr* **7/2**1

-304 **12** 3 3/4 **First Serve (IRE)**85 1578 3-8-8 **58** GemmaTutty(7) 8
(Karen Tutty) *chsd ldrs 3f: sn lost pl and bhd* **40/1**

2050 **13** 14 **Royal Style (IRE)**15 3629 3-9-1 **58** GrahamGibbons 10
(David Barron) *chsd ldrs: rdn along and lost pl 1/2-way: sn bhd* **8/1**3

1m 44.7s (1.00) **Going Correction** +0.10s/f (Slow)
WFA 3 from 4yo 9lb **13** Ran SP% **123.5**
Speed ratings (Par 101): **99,98,96,90,87 79,79,77,76,62 59,55,41**
Tote Swingers: 1&2 £59.50, 1&3 £104.40, 2&3 £1.90 CSF £195.04 CT £1876.75 TOTE £35.10: £6.50, £1.10, £4.10; EX 232.20 Trifecta £470.70 Pool: £1,304.68 - 2.07 winning units..
Owner Newtown Anner Stud Farm Ltd **Bred** Shortleaf Stable **Trained** Newmarket, Suffolk

FOCUS
A modest yet wide-open maiden handicap, run at a strong gallop. The first three were clear, and the form is limited.

4145 JENNIFER WALLACE MEMORIAL FILLIES' H'CAP 7f (F)
8:05 (8:06) (Class 5) (0-75,75) 3-Y-O+ **£2,587** (£770; £384; £192) **Stalls** Low

Form RPR

3126 **1** **Yahilwa (USA)**23 3375 3-9-5 **74** PaulMulrennan 9 83
(James Tate) *trckd ldrs: smooth hdwy on outer 3f out: cl up 2f out: shkn up to ld wl over 1f out: rdn and styd on wl fnl f* **9/2**2

6421 **2** 1/2 **Combustible (IRE)**104 1202 3-9-1 **70** ShaneKelly 10 78
(Daniel Mark Loughnane) *cl up: chal 3f out: rdn 2f out: sltly outpcd over 1f out: drvn: rallied and ch ins fnl f: no ex towards fin* **5/2**1

/356 **3** 2 1/4 **Madeira Girl (IRE)**10 3817 4-9-3 **64** GeorgeBaker 4 69+
(Jonjo O'Neill) *sn outpcd and bhd: rdn and hdwy wl over 2f out: styd on appr fnl f: nrst fin* **20/1**

6-00 **4** 3 3/4 **Last Supper**39 2836 4-8-10 **57** (p) SilvestreDeSousa 2 52
(James Bethell) *chsd ldrs: rdn along 3f out: drvn over 2f out and sn one pce* **40/1**

1-12 **5** 3/4 **Miss Avonbridge (IRE)**27 3216 3-9-5 **74** RichardKingscote 3 64
(Tom Dascombe) *in tch on inner: rdn along 3f out: sn no imp* **5/2**1

50-0 **6** nse **Shes Rosie**23 3375 5-9-8 **69** LiamTreadwell 11 62
(Ed de Giles) *s.i.s and bhd: hdwy wl over 2f out: edgd lft wl over 1f out: kpt on fnl f: nrst fin* **40/1**

2032 **7** 1 **Spark Of Genius**35 2949 4-9-4 **70** (v) WilliamTwiston-Davies(5) 1 60
(Alan McCabe) *cl up on inner: rdn wl over 2f out: drvn wl over 1f out: grad wknd* **20/1**

1100 **8** 3 1/2 **Hannahs Turn**50 2521 3-9-4 **73** HayleyTurner 8 51
(Chris Dwyer) *led: rdn along 3f out: hdd 2f out: grad wknd* **11/1**

-334 **9** 1/2 **Glan Lady (IRE)**21 3431 7-8-4 **56** oh10 TobyAtkinson(5) 5 36
(Michael Appleby) *midfield: rdn along over 3f out: sn outpcd* **33/1**

2343 **10** 3 1/2 **Tussie Mussie**12 3712 3-9-6 **75** JoeFanning 6 43
(Mark Johnston) *s.i.s: a in rr* **7/1**3

6223 **11** 2 1/2 **Mucky Molly**15 3643 5-8-9 **56** oh1 (vt) TomEaves 7 20
(Alison Hutchinson) *a towards rr* **20/1**

1m 30.58s (0.28) **Going Correction** +0.10s/f (Slow)
WFA 3 from 4yo+ 8lb **11** Ran SP% **118.3**
Speed ratings (Par 100): **102,101,98,94,93 93,92,88,87,83 81**
Tote Swingers: 1&2 £5.60, 1&3 £23.20, 2&3 £21.50 CSF £14.74 CT £206.01 TOTE £5.30: £1.70, £1.60, £5.70; EX 20.20 Trifecta £301.60 Pool: £1,274.42 - 3.16 winning units..
Owner Sheikh Juma Dalmook Al Maktoum **Bred** Avalon Farms Inc **Trained** Newmarket, Suffolk

FOCUS
An open fillies' handicap run at a decent pace. It paid to race handy and the form is fair.

4146 CHATSWORTH FINANCIAL SOUTHWELL RACECOURSE OWNERS GROUP H'CAP 6f (F)
8:35 (8:35) (Class 5) (0-70,68) 3-Y-O+ **£2,587** (£770; £384; £192) **Stalls** Low

Form RPR

3323 **1** **Pull The Pin (IRE)**4 4009 4-8-12 **61** LukeLeadbitter(7) 3 70
(Declan Carroll) *led: rdn along over 2f out: hung rt fr over 1f out: drvn along on stands' rail ins fnl f: kpt on gamely towards fin* **7/2**2

1350 **2** 1 **King Bertie (IRE)**25 3289 3-9-6 **68** ShaneKelly 6 73
(Peter Chapple-Hyam) *trckd ldrs: hdwy to chse ldng pair wl over 2f out: rdn to chse wnr over 1f out: sn swtchd lft and drvn: ev ch ins fnl f tl no ex nr fin* **3/1**1

0360 **3** nk **Art Dzeko**12 3714 4-9-10 **66** DavidAllan 9 71
(Tim Easterby) *chsd wnr: effrt and cl up 2f out: sn rdn: drvn and kpt on same pce fnl f* **9/1**

-006 **4** 5 **Layla's Hero (IRE)**15 3630 6-9-4 **60** (v) PaulMulrennan 10 49
(David Nicholls) *stdd s and hld up: hdwy and pushed along bef 1/2-way: wd st: rdn over 2f out: no imp fr over 1f out* **5/1**3

4434 **5** 4 **Fairy Wing (IRE)**50 2515 6-9-9 **65** GeorgeBaker 4 41
(Violet M Jordan) *trckd ldrs: effrt over 2f out: sn rdn along and no imp* **11/1**

1160 **6** 3/4 **Whisky Bravo**41 2780 4-9-11 **67** SilvestreDeSousa 7 41
(David Brown) *dwlt and in rr: wd st: sme hdwy over 2f out: sn rdn and n.d* **8/1**

-002 **7** 1 1/4 **Mistress Shy**34 2992 6-9-0 **56** (t) AndrewMullen 2 26
(Michael Appleby) *chsd ldrs on outer: rdn along bef 1/2-way: wd st and sn outpcd* **28/1**

5303 **8** 1 **Flying Pickets (IRE)**8 3906 4-9-5 **68** (be) AaronJones(7) 5 35
(Alan McCabe) *sn rdn along and a in rr* **16/1**

1043 **9** 2 1/4 **Prince Of Passion (CAN)**6 3955 5-9-8 **64** JoeFanning 1 23
(Derek Shaw) *chsd ldng pair on inner: rdn along 1/2-way: sn wknd* **6/1**

1m 16.19s (-0.31) **Going Correction** +0.10s/f (Slow)
WFA 3 from 4yo+ 6lb **9** Ran SP% **116.9**
Speed ratings (Par 103): **106,104,104,97,92 91,89,88,85**
Tote Swingers: 1&2 £3.00, 1&3 £1.40, 2&3 £10.60 CSF £14.67 CT £87.40 TOTE £3.00: £1.20, £2.20, £3.60; EX 14.20 Trifecta £126.00 Pool: £722.60 - 4.29 winning units..
Owner C Harding **Bred** T J Ryan **Trained** Sledmere, E Yorks

FOCUS
Not a strong contest, run at a sound pace. Once again few were able to close from behind. Straightforward form, rated around the third.

4147 TEST & MAINTENANCE PROUD OWNER SHAUNHARRISRACING.CO.UK H'CAP 1m 6f (F)
9:05 (9:05) (Class 6) (0-65,63) 4-Y-O+ **£2,045** (£603; £302) **Stalls** Low

Form RPR

0-02 **1** **Proud Times (USA)**10 3819 7-9-2 **58** (p) GeorgeBaker 3 70+
(Ali Brewer) *hld up in tch: smooth hdwy to join ldrs 4f out: led over 2f out: rdn clr over 1f out: kpt on* **5/1**3

4506 **2** 4 **Soweto Star (IRE)**26 3256 5-8-11 **53** LukeMorris 4 58
(John Best) *cl up: led after 2f: hdd 1/2-way: cl up: rdn and ev ch over 2f out: drvn to chse wnr wl over 1f out: no imp* **10/1**

600 **3** 2 1/4 **Miss Mohawk (IRE)**17 3589 4-8-0 **45** RaulDaSilva(3) 5 46
(Alan Brown) *dwlt and in rr: pushed along over 5f out: rdn over 3f out: hdwy u.p 2f out: styd on appr fnl f: nrst fin* **33/1**

4451 **4** 3 1/2 **Barnacle**34 2991 4-8-8 **50** (vt) CathyGannon 2 46
(Pat Eddery) *led 2f: trckd ldrs: effrt 3f out: sn rdn along and plugged on same pce fnl 2f* **9/4**1

4101 **5** 1/2 **Underwritten**15 3637 4-9-7 **63** (v) GrahamLee 9 59
(John Weymes) *chsd ldrs: rdn along over 4f out: drvn 3f out and grad wknd* **7/1**

00-0 **6** 5 **Souter Point (USA)**12 3721 7-8-8 **57** ConnorBeasley(7) 1 46
(William Kinsey) *chsd ldrs on inner: rdn along over 3f out: drvn and wknd wl over 2f out* **9/1**

614- **7** 5 **Irish Jugger (USA)**237 7710 6-9-6 **62** AndrewMullen 8 45
(Michael Appleby) *trckd ldrs: hdwy and cl up after 4f: led 1/2-way: rdn along over 3f out: hdd over 2f out: sn drvn and wknd* **5/2**2

0 **8** 2 1/4 **Blewit (IRE)**22 3406 5-8-13 **55** (p) AdamBeschizza 7 35
(William Kinsey) *dwlt: a in rr: rdn along and outpcd 5f out: sn bhd* **22/1**

3m 12.12s (3.82) **Going Correction** +0.10s/f (Slow) **8** Ran SP% **114.9**
Speed ratings (Par 101): **93,90,89,87,87 84,81,80**
Tote Swingers: 1&2 £10.80, 1&3 £14.90, 2&3 £1.80 CSF £53.29 CT £1478.86 TOTE £5.30: £2.00, £3.30, £6.30; EX 61.50 Trifecta £378.90 Pool: £1,238.75 - 2.45 winning units..
Owner Miss Ali Brewer **Bred** Timothy Thornton & Meg & Mike Buckley **Trained** Eastbury, Berks

FOCUS
A weak handicap run at a fair pace. The winner has a fine record here and was totally dominant.
T/Plt: £19.90 to a £1 stake. Pool: £91,724.61 - 3,362.47 winning units. T/Qpdt: £12.70 to a £1 stake. Pool: £6,059.25 - 351.70 winning units. JR

3903 WOLVERHAMPTON (A.W) (L-H)
Tuesday, July 9

OFFICIAL GOING: Standard
Wind: Light against Weather: Sunny

4148 BETVICTOR.COM H'CAP 5f 216y(P)
1:45 (1:45) (Class 6) (0-60,60) 3-Y-O+ **£1,940** (£577; £288; £144) **Stalls** Low

Form RPR

3003 **1** **The Great Gabrial**7 3919 4-9-3 **55** (b) JamieSpencer 8 65+
(Ian Williams) *chsd ldrs: rdn to ld ins fnl f: r.o* **11/4**1

0650 **2** 1/2 **Little Jimmy Odsox (IRE)**4 4009 5-9-7 **59** (b) DuranFentiman 1 67
(Tim Easterby) *sn led: rdn over 1f out: hdd ins fnl f: styd on* **11/2**2

410- **3** 2 3/4 **Maltease Ah**231 7794 4-9-7 **59** JimCrowley 7 59
(Andrew Reid) *chsd ldr: rdn over 1f out: no ex ins fnl f* **16/1**

6021 **4** 1 3/4 **Whipphound**15 3643 5-9-8 **60** GeorgeBaker 9 55
(Mark Brisbourne) *chsd ldrs: shkn up over 1f out: no ex fnl f* **11/4**1

-020 **5** 2 **Irish Boy (IRE)**27 3196 5-9-7 **59** (tp) TomMcLaughlin 12 48
(Christine Dunnett) *mid-div: pushed along over 2f out: rdn and hung lft over 1f out: styd on same pce* **40/1**

0050 **6** 1 **Dancing Welcome**14 3657 7-9-1 **60** (bt) WillPettis(7) 6 46
(Milton Bradley) *chsd ldrs: rdn over 3f out: wknd fnl f* **40/1**

1050 **7** 1/2 **Loyal Royal (IRE)**19 3498 10-9-6 **58** (bt) SilvestreDeSousa 10 42
(Milton Bradley) *hld up: rdn over 1f out: nvr trbld ldrs* **25/1**

6050 **8** 3 **Diamond Vine (IRE)**6 3949 5-9-0 **57** (p) PhilipPrince(5) 13 32
(Ronald Harris) *sn pushed along in rr: nvr on terms* **16/1**

5-41 **9** nk **Queen Hermione (IRE)**25 3268 5-8-12 **55** (vt) RobertTart(5) 11 29
(Derek Shaw) *s.i.s: outpcd* **15/2**3

2100 **10** 1/2 **Almaty Express**27 3197 11-9-2 **54** (b) KieranO'Neill 2 27
(John Weymes) *prom: rdn over 2f out: wknd over 1f out* **16/1**

1660 **11** 1 3/4 **Sweet Ovation**19 3499 4-9-4 **56** MichaelO'Connell 5 24
(Mark Usher) *s.i.s: rdn over 2f out: a in rr* **14/1**

3260 **12** 9 **Code Six (IRE)**26 3246 4-9-2 **54** (v1) TomEaves 4
(Bryan Smart) *s.i.s: pushed along 1/2-way: a in rr* **20/1**

1m 14.66s (-0.34) **Going Correction** +0.075s/f (Slow) **12** Ran SP% **118.3**
Speed ratings (Par 101): **105,104,100,98,95 94,93,89,89,88 86,74**
Tote Swingers: 1&2 £3.90, 1&3 £10.60, 2&3 £16.84 CT £206.58 TOTE £5.20: £2.20, £2.40, £8.10; EX 27.60 Trifecta £196.00 Pool: £1,439.68 - 5.50 winning units..
Owner Dr Marwan Koukash **Bred** Juddmonte Farms Ltd **Trained** Portway, Worcs

FOCUS
A moderate sprint handicap to start the card and it was dominated by those who raced handily. Fair form for the grade, backed up by the time.

4149 £25 FREE BET AT BETVICTOR.COM CLASSIFIED CLAIMING STKS 5f 216y(P)
2:15 (2:15) (Class 5) 3-Y-O+ **£2,587** (£770; £384; £192) **Stalls** Low

Form RPR

2260 **1** **Pelmanism**5 3981 6-8-10 62 (p) SilvestreDeSousa 4 77
(Brian Ellison) *sn drvn along in rr: hdwy u.p over 1f out: edgd lft and r.o to ld wl ins fnl f: eased nr fin* **5/1**3

0543 **2** 1 1/2 **Amethyst Dawn (IRE)**19 3496 7-8-10 66 (t) JimCrowley 5 73
(Andrew Reid) *a.p: chsd ldr over 2f out: rdn to ld ins fnl f: sn hdd and unable qck* **9/1**

2334 **3** 1 1/2 **Wicked Wench**11 3796 4-8-13 70 (b1) RobertTart(5) 7 76
(Jeremy Gask) *s.i.s: in rr: hdwy u.p over 1f out: r.o: nt rch ldrsi* **5/2**1

5320 **4** 1 1/4 **Haadeeth**8 3888 6-8-1 70 (t) NoelGarbutt(7) 3 63
(David Evans) *s.i.s: hld up: hdwy and nt clr run over 2f out: rdn over 1f out: styng on same pce whn n.m.r wl ins fnl f* **7/1**

5521 **5** shd **Red Cape (FR)**8 3904 10-8-10 67 (b) DaleSwift 1 64
(Ruth Carr) *led: clr 2f out: rdn over 1f out: hdd and no ex ins fnl f* **4/1**2

2522 **6** 4 1/2 **Moment In The Sun**8 3910 4-8-13 60 (b) JemmaMarshall(5) 8 58
(David Flood) *sn pushed along in rr: nvr nrr* **28/1**

0432 **7** 1 1/4 **Dream Vale (IRE)**15 3639 3-8-6 62 DuranFentiman 11 49
(Tim Easterby) *prom: rdn over 2f out: wknd over 1f out* **20/1**

-640 **8** 3 ½ **Uncomplicated**[23] 3375 3-8-4 67................................(p[1]) NickyMackay 10 36
(Jim Boyle) *prom: pushed along over 4f out: wknd over 1f out* **16/1**

666 **9** 6 **Showtime Girl (IRE)**[27] 3190 3-8-6 62............................ ChrisCatlin 12 20
(Tim Easterby) *s.i.s: a in rr: wknd over 2f out* **50/1**

2-06 **10** 1 ¼ **Kodatish (IRE)**[13] 3678 3-7-12 65 ow1......................(b[1]) PhilipPrince(5) 6 13
(Ronald Harris) *prom: chsd ldr over 4f out tl rdn: hung rt and wknd over 2f out: eased* **33/1**

-056 **11** 10 **Parisian Pyramid (IRE)**[22] 3392 7-9-4 65..................(p) JamieSpencer 9
(Patrick Morris) *chsd ldr tl over 4f out: remained handy: nt clr run over 2f out: sn rdn and wknd: eased ins fnl f* **8/1**

1m 14.58s (-0.42) **Going Correction** +0.075s/f (Slow)
WFA 3 from 4yo+ 6lb **11** Ran SP% **117.8**
Speed ratings (Par 103): **105,103,101,99,99 93,91,86,78,77 63**
Tote Swingers: 1&2 £9.40, 1&3 £4.40, 2&3 £7.40 CSF £47.35 TOTE £8.20: £2.60, £3.80, £1.70; EX 65.90 Trifecta £221.80 Pool: £2,735.14 - 9.24 winning units..Amethyst Dawn claimed by Mr Tom Malone for £6,000.
Owner Koo's Racing Club **Bred** Guy Reed **Trained** Norton, N Yorks

FOCUS
The winning time was 0.08sec quicker than the opening handicap, but this time the majority of the principals were outpaced early, suggesting the leaders went off too quick. The winner is rated back to his 2012 peak.

4150 NEAL WOOD FOURTH ANNIVERSARY MEMORIAL H'CAP 1m 4f 50y(P)
2:45 (2:45) (Class 5) (0-75,74) 3-Y-O+ **£2,587** (£770; £384; £192) **Stalls** Low

Form RPR

6-31 **1** **Velvetina (IRE)**[48] 2560 3-9-0 **73**.. TedDurcan 3 84+
(Harry Dunlop) *a.p: led over 1f out: shkn up ins fnl f: r.o wl: eased nr fin* **9/2**[3]

0-42 **2** 2 ½ **Thorpe (IRE)**[54] 2386 3-9-1 **74**.. JimCrowley 2 81
(Ralph Beckett) *chsd ldrs: rdn and ev ch over 1f out: styd on same pce ins fnl f* **3/1**[2]

0064 **3** 1 ¼ **Brigadoon**[52] 2435 6-9-9 **69**.. MichaelO'Connell 1 74
(Philip Kirby) *mid-div: hdwy over 3f out: rdn and swtchd rt over 1f out: styd on same pce ins fnl f* **6/4**[1]

1-50 **4** 1 ¾ **Felix Fabulla**[53] 2416 3-9-1 **74**.................................. SilvestreDeSousa 7 76
(Hughie Morrison) *trckd ldrs: racd keenly: wnt 2nd over 7f out: rdn and ev ch over 1f out: no ex ins fnl f* **8/1**

-403 **5** hd **Sweet Martoni**[26] 3251 3-8-10 **69**............................... MickaelBarzalona 4 71
(William Knight) *mid-div: rdn over 2f out: styd on: nt trble ldrs* **16/1**

4630 **6** 3 ¼ **Mirth**[19] 3497 3-7-11 **59** oh1.. DarrenEgan(3) 6 55
(Mark Johnston) *led: rdn and hdd over 1f out: wknd ins fnl f* **33/1**

6536 **7** 6 **Sommersturm (GER)**[13] 3688 9-8-9 **62**......................... EoinWalsh(7) 5 49
(David Evans) *hld up: rdn over 2f out: nt clr run wl over 1f out: n.d* **50/1**

510 **8** shd **He's No Angel (IRE)**[25] 3273 4-9-10 **70**............................... AdamKirby 9 57
(Clive Cox) *hld up: hdwy over 3f out: sn rdn: wknd fnl f* **8/1**

5402 **9** nse **Star Of Namibia (IRE)**[36] 2924 3-8-6 **65**......................(b) LiamJones 10 52
(J S Moore) *hld up: a in rr: rdn and wknd over 2f out* **12/1**

2360 **10** 9 **Tornado Force (IRE)**[10] 3808 5-9-3 **68**........ WilliamTwiston-Davies(5) 8 40
(Alan McCabe) *hld up: a in rr: rdn over 2f out: sn wknd* **25/1**

1000 **11** 40 **Full Speed (GER)**[15] 3627 8-8-13 **66**.......................... EvaMoscrop(7) 11
(Philip Kirby) *chsd ldr tl over 7f out: remained handy tl wknd 4f out: t.o* **33/1**

2m 39.14s (-1.96) **Going Correction** +0.075s/f (Slow)
WFA 3 from 4yo+ 13lb **11** Ran SP% **130.7**
Speed ratings (Par 103): **109,107,106,105,105 103,99,98,98,92 66**
Tote Swingers: 1&2 £4.20, 1&3 £4.10, 2&3 £2.40 CSF £20.19 CT £31.70 TOTE £6.40: £2.30, £2.50, £1.02; EX 19.50 Trifecta £71.10 Pool: £2,611.40 - 27.54 winning units..
Owner Windflower Overseas Holdings Inc **Bred** Windflower Overseas **Trained** Lambourn, Berks

FOCUS
An ordinary middle-distance handicap run at a modest pace, but the winner and second look progressive so the form is rated slightly positively.

4151 DOWNLOAD THE BETVICTOR APP NOW MAIDEN STKS (DIV I) 1m 1f 103y(P)
3:15 (3:16) (Class 5) 3-4-Y-O **£2,587** (£770; £384; £192) **Stalls** Low

Form RPR

40- **1** **Winterlude (IRE)**[276] 6872 3-9-3 0.............................. MickaelBarzalona 7 96+
(Saeed bin Suroor) *led 2f: chsd ldrs: led over 1f out: rdn clr ins fnl f* **2/1**[2]

32- **2** 7 **Nickels And Dimes (IRE)**[259] 7312 3-8-12 0............... WilliamBuick 12 78
(John Gosden) *chsd ldrs: led over 7f out: sn hdd: remained handy: nt clr run over 1f out: styd on same pce ins fnl f* **11/8**[1]

0-3 **3** 2 **Inaad (IRE)**[38] 2885 3-9-3 0....................................... SilvestreDeSousa 11 77
(Saeed bin Suroor) *s.i.s: sn prom: chsd ldr 7f out tl led over 4f out: rdn and hdd over 1f out: hung lft and wknd ins fnl f* **5/1**[3]

04 **4** 2 **Top Set (IRE)**[17] 3585 3-8-12 0... RobertTart(5) 6 73+
(Marco Botti) *hld up: hdwy over 1f out: r.o to go 4th nr fin: nvr nr to chal* **12/1**

5 nk **Successful Year** 3-9-3 0... AdamKirby 3 72
(Mark Johnston) *sn prom: chsd ldr over 3f out: rdn and ev ch over 1f out: wknd ins fnl f* **20/1**

6 2 **Perfect Summer (IRE)** 3-8-12 0...................................... JamieSpencer 8 63
(Lady Cecil) *s.i.s: hld up: pushed along 1/2-way: styd on ins fnl f: nvr nrr* **20/1**

05 **7** ½ **Royal Marskell**[26] 3250 4-9-8 0.. LauraPike(5) 5 67
(K F Clutterbuck) *hld up: hdwy over 3f out: rdn and wknd over 1f out* **50/1**

0 **8** 2 ½ **Capetown Kid**[132] 815 3-9-3 0... LiamKeniry 2 62
(Sylvester Kirk) *prom: rdn over 2f out: wknd over 1f out* **125/1**

0- **9** 6 **Captain Caroline**[244] 7627 3-8-12 0................................ TedDurcan 10 44
(Mike Murphy) *s.i.s: hld up: racd keenly early: a in rr* **66/1**

05 **10** 4 ½ **Able Dash**[18] 3539 3-9-3 0.. TomMcLaughlin 9 40
(Ed Walker) *hld up: rdn over 3f out: a in rr* **100/1**

0 **11** 10 **Mme Sans Gene**[22] 3417 3-8-12 0...................................... JimCrowley 1 14
(Ralph Beckett) *prom: lost pl over 7f out: hdwy over 6f out: wknd over 3f out: t.o* **33/1**

00-0 **12** 5 **Modern Society**[22] 3403 3-9-3 33...................................(b) MartinDwyer 4
(Andrew Reid) *prom: led 7f out: hdd over 4f out: wknd wl over 3f out: t.o* **150/1**

2m 1.96s (0.26) **Going Correction** +0.075s/f (Slow)
WFA 3 from 4yo 10lb **12** Ran SP% **118.2**
Speed ratings (Par 103): **101,94,93,91,90 89,88,86,81,77 68,63**
Tote Swingers: 1&2 £1.50, 1&3 £2.60, 2&3 £2.20 CSF £4.75 TOTE £3.70: £1.40, £1.10, £1.70; EX 6.80 Trifecta £21.10 Pool: £4,771.40 - 27.54 winning units..
Owner Godolphin **Bred** Darley **Trained** Newmarket, Suffolk

FOCUS
An ordinary maiden in which only a couple had shown any worthwhile form. The winner looks a nice type but the second was a little below form.

4152 DOWNLOAD THE BETVICTOR APP NOW MAIDEN STKS (DIV II) 1m 1f 103y(P)
3:45 (3:45) (Class 5) 3-4-Y-O **£2,587** (£770; £384; £192) **Stalls** Low

Form RPR

556 **1** **Spirit Rider (USA)**[26] 3250 3-9-3 73.................................. WilliamBuick 3 78
(John Gosden) *chsd ldrs: rdn to ld ins fnl f: edgd lft: r.o* **7/2**[3]

2 nk **Desert Revolution** 3-9-3 0.. AdamKirby 2 79+
(Mark Johnston) *a.p: pushed along over 3f out: nt clr run and lost pl over 2f out: rallied over 1f out: rdn and r.o wl* **8/1**

5 **3** ½ **Akeed Dubawi**[17] 3585 3-9-3 0.................................. SilvestreDeSousa 4 76
(William Haggas) *s.i.s: sn chsng ldrs: rdn to ld on outer over 2f out: hdd ins fnl f: styd on* **11/4**[2]

06 **4** 2 **Dukes Delight (IRE)**[40] 2804 3-8-12 0................................ TedDurcan 7 68+
(David Lanigan) *hld up: hdwy and edgd rt over 1f out: styd on: nt trble ldrs* **25/1**

5 ½ **Entrenched (USA)** 3-9-3 0.. MickaelBarzalona 1 72
(Saeed bin Suroor) *chsd ldrs: nt clr run over 2f out: rdn over 1f out: no ex ins fnl f* **2/1**[1]

6-0 **6** 1 ¼ **Don Padeja**[54] 2384 3-9-3 0.. KirstyMilczarek 5 69+
(Luca Cumani) *mid-div: pushed along over 3f out: hdwy over 2f out: no ex fnl f* **11/1**

0-04 **7** 14 **Play Tiger (FR)**[10] 3819 4-9-13 51...................................... LiamKeniry 8 43
(Peter Hiatt) *sn led: rdn and hdd over 2f out: styd on same pce fnl f* **100/1**

0 **8** 3 **Never Too Much (IRE)**[22] 3417 3-9-0 0.................. AshleyMorgan(3) 11 37
(Chris Wall) *hld up: rdn over 3f out: wkng whn hung lft over 1f out* **100/1**

9 1 ¾ **Karitza (FR)** 3-8-12 0.. RichardKingscote 9 29
(Jeremy Gask) *s.s: rdn 1/2-way: a bhd* **50/1**

55-6 **10** 1 ½ **Common Courtesy**[111] 1089 3-8-12 0.............................. JamieSpencer 10 26
(John Butler) *hld up: plld hrd: hdwy over 2f out: wkng whn carried rt wl over 1f out* **28/1**

0- **11** ½ **Szabo's Art**[262] 7244 3-8-12 0... ChrisCatlin 6 25
(Sir Mark Prescott Bt) *hld up: pushed along 1/2-way: a in rr: wknd over 3f out* **33/1**

2m 2.53s (0.83) **Going Correction** +0.075s/f (Slow)
WFA 3 from 4yo 10lb **11** Ran SP% **115.8**
Speed ratings (Par 103): **99,98,98,96,96 94,82,79,78,76 76**
Tote Swingers: 1&2 £5.00, 1&3 £2.50, 2&3 £4.90 CSF £29.00 TOTE £3.30: £1.50, £2.60, £1.10; EX 36.30 Trifecta £101.40 Pool: £2,988.31 - 22.08 winning units..
Owner Magnolia Racing LLC & Ms Rachel Hood **Bred** John Bowers, Jr **Trained** Newmarket, Suffolk

FOCUS
This looked the weaker of the two divisions and the winning time was over half a second slower. The winner is rated just a length up on his pre-race figure.

4153 BETVICTOR CASINO ON YOUR MOBILE (S) STKS 1m 141y(P)
4:15 (4:15) (Class 6) 3-Y-O+ **£1,940** (£577; £288; £144) **Stalls** Low

Form RPR

2253 **1** **Pravda Street**[24] 3349 8-9-8 72.................................. SilvestreDeSousa 1 70
(Brian Ellison) *chsd ldrs: pushed along over 2f out: rdn to ld ins fnl f: r.o* **13/8**[1]

2/44 **2** 1 **Four Winds**[4] 4005 7-9-8 83.. JimCrowley 6 68
(Robert Cowell) *chsd ldrs: rdn and hung lft ins fnl f: r.o* **11/4**[2]

1-44 **3** ½ **Abbraccio**[29] 3156 5-9-3 66..........................(t) WilliamTwiston-Davies(5) 8 67
(Fergal O'Brien) *chsd ldr tl led over 2f out: rdn over 1f out: hdd ins fnl f: styd on same pce* **8/1**

6205 **4** hd **Fred Willetts (IRE)**[26] 2929 5-9-8 71...................................(b) AdamKirby 5 67
(David Evans) *prom: rdn over 2f out: r.o u.p* **9/2**[3]

0224 **5** 3 ½ **Newnton Lodge**[12] 3719 4-9-8 60.................................... JamieSpencer 4 58
(Ian Williams) *hld up: plld hrd: hdwy over 1f out: sn hung lft: nt trble ldrs* **13/2**

3504 **6** 3 ¼ **Shomberg**[15] 3643 4-9-8 50...(p) SamHitchcott 7 51
(Dai Burchell) *led: rdn and hdd over 2f out: wknd ins fnl f* **50/1**

1004 **7** 10 **Spinning Ridge (IRE)**[8] 3885 8-9-9 57.............................(b) EDLinehan(5) 2 34
(Ronald Harris) *s.i.s: hld up: effrt over 2f out: wknd over 1f out* **25/1**

/500 **8** 13 **Classic Voice (IRE)**[7] 3919 5-9-5 52...........................(p) MarkCoumbe(3) 9
(Roy Brotherton) *sn pushed along and prom: wknd 3f out: t.o* **66/1**

05 **9** 2 ½ **Telamon (IRE)**[15] 3639 3-8-7 0.................................. MatthewLawson(5) 3
(Milton Bradley) *hld up: pushed along 5f out: wknd over 3f out: t.o* **125/1**

1m 51.47s (0.97) **Going Correction** +0.075s/f (Slow)
WFA 3 from 4yo+ 10lb **9** Ran SP% **115.5**
Speed ratings (Par 101): **98,97,96,96,93 90,81,70,67**
Tote Swingers: 1&2 £2.20, 1&3 £3.90, 2&3 £3.80 CSF £6.10 TOTE £1.80: £1.02, £1.50, £2.50; EX 8.30 Trifecta £29.10 Pool: £1,892.87 - 48.73 winning units..There was no bid for the winner.
Owner Koo's Racing Club **Bred** R A Instone **Trained** Norton, N Yorks

FOCUS
A moderate seller. The winner was fully entitled to win at these weights, and this might overrate him.

4154 TALK TO VICTOR MAIDEN AUCTION STKS 7f 32y(P)
4:45 (4:46) (Class 5) 2-Y-O **£2,587** (£770; £384; £192) **Stalls** High

Form RPR

402 **1** **Clever Miss**[8] 3905 2-8-7 0.. MickaelBarzalona 11 77+
(Alan McCabe) *chsd ldrs: led over 1f out: r.o wl* **9/2**[3]

433 **2** 4 **Lucky Visione**[21] 3436 2-8-10 0......................................(p) JackMitchell 8 70
(Gay Kelleway) *prom: rdn and hung lft over 1f out: chsd wnr fnl f: no imp* **4/1**[2]

3 5 **Captain Secret** 2-8-6 0.. PaoloSirigu 2 57+
(Marco Botti) *chsd ldrs: cl up and styng on whn nt clr run and hmpd over 1f out: nt rcvr* **6/1**

0236 **4** 3 ½ **Classy Lassy (IRE)**[38] 2883 2-8-6 0.......................... SilvestreDeSousa 3 45
(Brian Ellison) *led: rdn and hdd over 1f out: edgd lft: wknd fnl f* **9/4**[1]

0 **5** 2 **Day Star Lad**[15] 3640 2-8-11 0.. MartinDwyer 4 45
(Derek Shaw) *prom: pushed along 4f out: wknd over 1f out* **40/1**

6 nk **Sheila's Footsteps** 2-8-10 0.. LiamKeniry 5 44
(J S Moore) *chsd ldr: rdn over 2f out: wknd over 1f out* **16/1**

6 **7** 1 ¾ **Indie Star**[17] 3574 2-8-2 0... DarrenEgan(3) 9 34
(Harry Dunlop) *mid-div: sn pushed along: rdn over 2f out: sn wknd* **50/1**

8 7 **Escarlata Rossa** 2-8-5 0 ow1.. JohnFahy 1 17
(J S Moore) *s.i.s: outpcd* **33/1**

9 ½ **Secret Ocean (IRE)** 2-8-12 0.. LiamJones 6 23
(J S Moore) *sn pushed along in rr: hdwy 1/2-way: wknd 2f out* **20/1**

The Form Book Flat, Raceform Ltd, Compton, RG20 6NL.

6 **10** ½ **Meconopsis**[22] 3391 2-8-10 0 DuranFentiman 10 20
(Tim Easterby) *s.i.s: sn pushed along in rr: hdwy over 2f out: wknd over 1f out* **33/1**

0 **11** ¾ **My Anchor**[9] 3853 2-8-9 0 ChrisCatlin 7 17
(Sylvester Kirk) *s.i.s: outpcd* **8/1**

0 **12** 3¼ **Crazy Brenda (IRE)**[40] 2805 2-8-5 0 KirstyMilczarek 12 5
(Sylvester Kirk) *sn outpcd* **50/1**

1m 30.95s (1.35) **Going Correction** +0.075s/f (Slow) **12 Ran SP% 117.2**
Speed ratings (Par 94): **95,90,84,80,78 78,76,68,67,66 66,62**
Tote Swingers: 1&2 £4.00, 1&3 £8.00, 2&3 £6.80 CSF £21.09 TOTE £6.20: £2.10, £1.90, £2.60; EX 17.10 Trifecta £88.90 Pool: £3,272.49 - 27.58 winning units..
Owner Khalifa Dasmal **Bred** Newsells Park Stud & Strategic B'Stock **Trained** Averham Park, Notts

FOCUS
The field finished well spread out in this modest maiden auction event. The runner-up guides the form.

4155 FOLLOW US ON TWITTER @BETVICTORRACING H'CAP 7f 32y(P)
5:15 (5:16) (Class 6) (0-60,60) 3-Y-O+ **£1,940** (£577; £288; £144) **Stalls** High

Form RPR

36-5 **1** **Menelik (IRE)**[40] 2807 4-9-5 **60** RichardKingscote 10 69+
(Tom Dascombe) *chsd ldrs: rdn over 1f out: r.o to ld wl ins fnl f* **3/1**[1]

3006 **2** 1¼ **Glenridding**[8] 3909 9-9-2 **57** (p) DaleSwift 6 63
(James Given) *led: rdn over 1f out: hdd wl ins fnl f* **12/1**

0300 **3** nk **Youhavecontrol (IRE)**[22] 3392 5-9-5 **60** (tp) AdamKirby 5 65
(Nicky Vaughan) *hld up: hdwy u.p over 1f out: edgd lft: r.o wl* **33/1**

1000 **4** ½ **Bang Tidy (IRE)**[21] 3444 4-9-4 **59** (t) SilvestreDeSousa 3 63
(Brian Ellison) *in rr: hdwy u.p over 1f out: r.o: nt rch ldrs* **6/1**[3]

2-2 **5** 1¾ **Phils Wish (IRE)**[67] 1999 4-9-2 **57** MickaelBarzalona 12 56
(John C McConnell, Ire) *a.p: chsd ldr over 2f out: rdn over 1f out: styd on same pce ins fnl f* **4/1**[2]

0302 **6** nk **Penbryn (USA)**[15] 3643 6-9-4 **59** SebSanders 8 57
(Nick Littmoden) *hld up: hdwy on outer over 3f out: gng wl over 1f out: rdn ins fnl f: fnd nil* **7/1**

6030 **7** ¾ **George Benjamin**[19] 3511 6-8-13 **57** (tp) DarrenEgan(3) 2 53
(Christopher Kellett) *outpcd: rdn over 1f out: r.o wl ins fnl f: nt rch ldrs* **20/1**

6233 **8** ½ **Silly Billy (IRE)**[71] 1887 5-8-9 **57** (p) RyanWhile(7) 1 52
(Bill Turner) *chsd ldrs: rdn over 2f out: no ex fnl f* **10/1**

2506 **9** ¾ **Gaelic Wizard (IRE)**[19] 3511 5-8-10 **58** (p) JoshBaudains(7) 9 51
(Dominic Ffrench Davis) *chsd ldr tl rdn over 2f out: no ex fnl f* **20/1**

3604 **10** 4 **Unlimited**[11] 11-8-13 **57** AmyBaker(3) 4 39
(Tony Carroll) *chsd ldrs: rdn over 2f out: wknd fnl f* **14/1**

2053 **11** 7 **High On The Hog (IRE)**[15] 3644 5-9-3 **58** TomMcLaughlin 11 21
(Mark Brisbourne) *mid-div: rdn and hdwy over 2f out: wknd wl over 1f out* **16/1**

50-0 **12** 1¾ **All Right Now**[56] 2345 6-9-5 **60** LiamKeniry 7 18
(Tony Newcombe) *prom: lost pl over 4f out: wknd and eased over 1f out* **11/1**

1m 30.42s (0.82) **Going Correction** +0.075s/f (Slow) **12 Ran SP% 121.9**
Speed ratings (Par 101): **98,96,96,95,93 93,92,91,91,86 78,76**
Tote Swingers: 1&2 £13.10, 1&3 £21.90, 2&3 £92.50 CSF £40.81 CT £1035.99 TOTE £4.00: £1.90, £4.30, £12.70; EX 54.30 Trifecta £2201.20 Part won. Pool: £2,934.93 - 0.90 winning units..
Owner Laurence A Bellman **Bred** Irish National Stud **Trained** Malpas, Cheshire

FOCUS
A moderate handicap, though the pace was honest. The winner could go on now and the second did well after setting the pace.
T/Jkpt: £11,833.30 to a £1 stake. Pool: £25,000.00 - 1.50 winning tickets. T/Plt: £12.70 to a £1 stake. Pool: £94,446.52 - 5,396.67 winning tickets. T/Qpdt: £1.70 to a £1 stake. Pool: £8,339.97 - 3,438.86 winning tickets. CR

3942 CATTERICK (L-H)
Wednesday, July 10

OFFICIAL GOING: Good to firm (firm in places; 9.3)
Wind: Virtually nil Weather: Grey cloud

4156 YORKSHIRE-OUTDOORS.CO.UK CLAIMING STKS 5f
2:20 (2:20) (Class 6) 2-Y-O **£2,385** (£704; £352) **Stalls** Low

Form RPR

2165 **1** **Money Team (IRE)**[11] 3801 2-8-9 0 RyanWhile(7) 10 80
(Bill Turner) *cl up on wd outside travelling wl: smooth hdwy to ld wl over 1f out: pushed clr ent fnl f: readily* **6/5**[1]

405 **2** 5 **Porsh Herrik**[28] 3189 2-8-11 0 (v[1]) MichaelO'Connell 1 55
(John Quinn) *sn led on inner: rdn along 2f out: hdd wl over 1f out: drvn and edgd rt ent fnl f: kpt on same pce* **22/1**

3 **3** ¾ **Black Treacle (IRE)**[8] 3928 2-9-7 0 JoeFanning 7 62
(Keith Dalgleish) *wnt rt s: cl up: rdn along 2f out: drvn appr fnl f: one pce* **5/1**[3]

006 **4** nk **Kindanyce (IRE)**[26] 3298 2-8-7 0 TonyHamilton 8 47
(Richard Fahey) *sltly hmpd s and towards rr: hdwy 1/2-way: sn swtchd rt to outer and rdn: kpt on fnl f: nrst fin* **14/1**

0 **5** ½ **Lady Alaska (IRE)**[21] 3476 2-7-12 0 JoeDoyle(7) 2 43
(John Quinn) *cl up: rdn 2f out: drvn wl over 1f out: grad wknd* **25/1**

05 **6** 1½ **Barleycorn**[52] 2475 2-8-6 0 RachelRichardson(7) 9 49+
(Tim Easterby) *dwlt and sltly hmpd s: in rr: pushed along and hdwy wl over 1f out: swtchd lft to inner and kpt on wl fnl f: nrst fin* **50/1**

604 **7** 2½ **Patisserie**[7] 3943 2-8-11 0 (p) PJMcDonald 5 35
(Ann Duffield) *cl up: rdn along 2f out: sn wknd* **7/1**

8 1¾ **Madame Giry (IRE)** 2-8-11 0[1] DanielTudhope 3 29+
(David O'Meara) *in tch: pushed along 1/2-way: sn rdn and wknd wl over 1f out* **9/2**[2]

9 9 **Marsden Cuckoo (IRE)** 2-8-8 0 JulieBurke(3) 6
(David O'Meara) *sn outpcd in rr: bhd fr 1/2-way* **14/1**

(0.20) **Going Correction** -0.10s/f (Good) **9 Ran SP% 116.3**
Speed ratings (Par 92): **94,86,84,84,83 81,77,74,59**
toteswingers 1&2 £7.20, 1&3 £2.40, 2&3 £7.50 CSF £35.68 TOTE £2.00: £1.10, £4.60, £4.00; EX 29.10 Trifecta £84.20 Pool: £2591.2 - 23.05 winning units..Money Team was claimed by Mr P Rolls for £10,000
Owner A C Elliott **Bred** Mrs Claire Doyle **Trained** Sigwells, Somerset

FOCUS
With the two newcomers making no impression, this looks weak form behind the winner.

4157 33 RACECOURSES LIVE ON SKY 432 MEDIAN AUCTION MAIDEN STKS 1m 3f 214y
2:50 (2:50) (Class 5) 3-4-Y-O **£2,911** (£866; £432; £216) **Stalls** Low

Form RPR

4 **1** **Northern Meeting (IRE)**[58] 2321 3-8-9 0 KierenFallon 1 77+
(Sir Michael Stoute) *t.k.h: hld up on inner towards rr: tk cl order over 5f out: swtchd rt and hdwy 3f out: led wl over 1f out: sn pushed clr: easily* **10/11**[1]

2 5 **Saffron Town (IRE)**[147] 4-9-13 0 (t) AndrewMullen 2 71
(Alan Swinbank) *fly-leapt and dwlt s: in rr and t.k.h: hdwy 5f out: effrt on outer to ld 3f out: sn rdn: edgd lft and hdd wl over 1f out: kpt on same pce* **33/1**

3 3¾ **Copybook** 3-8-9 0 JoeFanning 8 60
(Mark Johnston) *trckd ldrs: hdwy on outer to join ldr 1/2-way: cl up: rdn along 3f out: drvn 2f out and sn one pce* **11/4**[2]

-442 **4** 1¼ **Society Pearl (IRE)**[14] 3674 3-8-9 **71** RobertWinston 4 58
(Charles Hills) *trckd ldrs on inner: effrt 3f out and sn pushed along: rdn and outpcd over 2f out: swtchd rt and drvn wl over 1f out: plugged on one pce* **6/1**[3]

0 **5** 4 **Magic Skyline (IRE)**[12] 3775 3-8-9 0 BarryMcHugh 5 52
(Brian Ellison) *in tch: pushed along over 4f out: rdn 3f out: outpcd fnl 2f* **50/1**

00 **6** 6 **Snow Train**[12] 3764 3-8-9 0 DaleSwift 3 42
(James Given) *chsd ldrs: rdn along over 5f out: sn wknd: bhd fnl 3f* **100/1**

00-4 **7** ½ **Wynyard Boy**[52] 2480 3-9-0 **54** DavidAllan 7 46
(Tim Easterby) *chsd ldr: rdn along over 5f out: sn lost pl and bhd fnl 3f* **33/1**

3002 **8** 1½ **Harbinger Lass**[11] 3821 3-8-9 **75** GrahamLee 6 39
(Mick Channon) *set stdy pce: jnd and qcknd 1/2-way: pushed along 4f out: rdn and hdd 3f out: sn wknd* **6/1**[3]

2m 36.35s (-2.55) **Going Correction** -0.10s/f (Good)
WFA 3 from 4yo 13lb **8 Ran SP% 116.5**
Speed ratings (Par 103): **104,100,98,97,94 90,90,89**
toteswingers 1&2 £6.00, 1&3 £1.50, 2&3 £5.40 CSF £41.52 TOTE £1.90: £1.40, £3.90, £1.10; EX 28.80 Trifecta £100.70 Pool: £3445.52 - 25.63 winning units..
Owner Ballymacoll Stud **Bred** Ballymacoll Stud Farm Ltd **Trained** Newmarket, Suffolk

FOCUS
A modest maiden and easy for the winner with her main form rivals both disappointing again.

4158 GO RACING IN YORKSHIRE SUMMER FESTIVAL H'CAP 7f
3:20 (3:20) (Class 5) (0-75,75) 3-Y-O **£2,911** (£866; £432; £216) **Stalls** Centre

Form RPR

500 **1** **Absolute Diamond**[42] 2765 3-7-13 **56** oh1 (p) RaulDaSilva(3) 2 61
(John Quinn) *trckd ldng pair on inner: hdwy 2f out: rdn over 1f out: led ent fnl f: sn drvn and kpt on gamely towards fin* **20/1**

0-04 **2** nk **Rich Forever (IRE)**[5] 4007 3-9-2 **70** (p) RobertWinston 5 74
(James Bethell) *trckd ldrs: effrt 2f out: nt clr run and swtchd lft to inner over 1f out: sn rdn: styd on to chal ins fnl f: ev ch tl drvn and no ex nr fin* **11/4**[3]

1-15 **3** nk **Silkelly**[23] 3396 3-9-7 **75** DanielTudhope 1 78
(David O'Meara) *led 1f: cl up: led again 2f out: rdn and edgd rt over 1f out: hdd ent fnl f and sn drvn: ev ch tl no ex towards fin* **2/1**[2]

4056 **4** 7 **Scala Romana (IRE)**[7] 3956 3-8-8 **67** RosieJessop(5) 4 51
(Sir Mark Prescott Bt) *cl up: led after 1f: rdn along: edgd rt and hdd 2f out: sn wknd* **12/1**

0111 **5** 4 **Just Paul (IRE)**[4] 4045 3-8-11 **68** 6ex DeclanCannon(3) 6 41
(Philip Kirby) *t.k.h: trckd ldng pair on outer: effrt over 2f out: rdn wl over 1f out: sn edgd lft and wknd* **7/4**[1]

1m 26.43s (-0.57) **Going Correction** -0.10s/f (Good) **5 Ran SP% 108.8**
Speed ratings (Par 100): **99,98,98,90,85**
CSF £71.05 TOTE £24.80: £3.50, £2.00; EX 53.80 Trifecta £155.50 Pool: £1795.63 - 8.65 winning units..
Owner A Turton, J Blackburn, R Bond & C Bond **Bred** Bond Thoroughbred Corporation **Trained** Settrington, N Yorks

FOCUS
Solid enough form at a modest level, rated around the second.

4159 5TH REGIMENT ROYAL ARTILLERY HEIMDALL H'CAP (FOR THE TURMERIC CHALLENGE TROPHY) 1m 7f 177y
3:50 (3:50) (Class 4) (0-85,85) 3-Y-O+ **£6,469** (£1,925; £962; £481) **Stalls** Centre

Form RPR

3641 **1** **Dr Irv**[12] 3771 4-8-8 **68** DeclanCannon(3) 2 76+
(Philip Kirby) *hld up in tch: hdwy over 2f out: qcknd through on inner to ld appr fnl f: sn rdn clr: kpt on wl* **5/1**[3]

0423 **2** 1 **Aleksandar**[8] 3930 4-9-1 **72** GrahamLee 3 78
(Jim Goldie) *trckd ldng pair: effrt 2f out: sn n.m.r and swtchd rt over 1f out: rdn to chse wnr ins fnl f: styd on* **7/2**[2]

3200 **3** 1 **Red Orator**[19] 3531 4-10-0 **85** JoeFanning 5 90
(Mark Johnston) *stmbld s: hld up in rr: hdwy on outer and cl up after 7f: chal over 3f out: rdn over 2f out: drvn and ev ch over 1f out: one pce fnl f* **6/4**[1]

-030 **4** ½ **Major Domo (FR)**[35] 2990 5-8-9 **66** AndrewMullen 6 70
(Alan Swinbank) *hld up in tch: hdwy on outer 3f out: rdn 2f out: drvn and one pce ent fnl f* **15/2**

0/03 **5** 2¾ **Keep It Cool (IRE)**[7] 3944 9-9-1 **72** DanielTudhope 7 73
(David O'Meara) *trckd ldng pair: effrt over 3f out: sn rdn along: drvn wl over 1f out and sn wknd* **9/1**

-021 **6** 2¼ **Bounty Seeker (USA)**[12] 3790 4-9-2 **73** LiamJones 4 71
(Mark Johnston) *set stdy pce: pushed along 4f out: rdn 3f out: drvn 2f out: hdd over 1f out: sn wknd* **7/1**

3m 30.57s (-1.43) **Going Correction** -0.10s/f (Good) **6 Ran SP% 113.2**
Speed ratings (Par 105): **99,98,98,97,96 95**
toteswingers 1&2 £3.50, 1&3 £2.70, 2&3 £2.40 CSF £22.92 CT £37.77 TOTE £5.20: £3.40, £3.20; EX 24.90 Trifecta £60.80 Pool: £2360.78 - 29.07 winning units..
Owner Irvine Lynch **Bred** Whitsbury Manor Stud & Pigeon House Stud **Trained** Middleham, N Yorks

FOCUS
There wasn't much early pace in this, and everything held a chance turning into the home straight for the final time. Muddling form, but the winner is still on the upgrade.

4160 READ HAYLEY TURNER EVERY FRIDAY RACINGUK.COM H'CAP (DIV I) 7f
4:20 (4:22) (Class 6) (0-65,64) 3-Y-O+ **£2,385** (£704; £352) **Stalls** Centre

Form RPR
-250 **1** **Just The Tonic**[34] 3027 6-9-10 **62**.................... RaulDaSilva(3) 7 71
(Marjorie Fife) *towards rr: hdwy on outer 2f out: rdn to chse ldrs over 1f out: led ins fnl f: kpt on* **7/1**
3040 **2** *1 ½* **Dialogue**[19] 3546 7-9-7 **63**....................(t) JordanNason(7) 6 68
(Geoffrey Harker) *dwlt and in rr: swtchd rt to outer and rdn wl over 1f out: str run fnl f: tk 2nd nr fin* **8/1**
6620 **3** *1* **Lees Anthem**[16] 3630 6-9-2 **51**.................... PaulMulrennan 13 53
(Michael Smith) *towards rr: hdwy and midfield 1/2-way: rdn 2f out: styd on appr fnl f: nrst fin* **20/1**
3-04 **4** *1 ¼* **Logans Legend (IRE)**[7] 3946 5-9-6 **55**....................(p) DanielTudhope 3 54+
(Lawrence Mullaney) *trckd ldng pair: swtchd rt and hdwy to chal over 2f out: rdn to ld over 1f out: drvn and hdd ins fnl f: wknd towards fin* **10/1**
5510 **5** *nk* **Jupiter Fidius**[26] 3286 6-9-5 **61**.................... GemmaTutty(7) 9 59
(Karen Tutty) *in tch: hdwy to chse ldrs 2f out: swtchd rt and rdn wl over 1f out: kpt on same pce* **16/1**
0100 **6** *¾* **Needy McCredie**[23] 3393 7-9-10 **59**.................... GrahamLee 8 55
(James Turner) *s.i.s and in rr: hdwy and n.m.r 2f out: rdn wl over 1f out: styd on fnl f: nrst fin* **18/1**
0-55 **7** *1 ½* **Cymeriad**[18] 3594 3-8-8 **51**....................(p) JamesSullivan 5 40
(Michael Easterby) *cl up: chal 3f out: rdn and slt ld 2f out: drvn and hdd over 1f out: wknd fnl f* **20/1**
0000 **8** *¾* **Forever Janey**[58] 2326 4-8-10 **45**.................... TonyHamilton 2 35
(Paul Green) *chsd ldrs on inner: rdn 3f out: wknd fnl 2f* **100/1**
0000 **9** *1* **Thrust Control (IRE)**[15] 3649 6-9-3 **57**....................(v[1]) JasonHart(5) 10 44
(Tracy Waggott) *sn led: rdn along 3f out: drvn and hdd 2f out: grad wknd fr over 1f out* **18/1**
0201 **10** *nk* **Rasselas (IRE)**[5] 4005 6-9-8 **64** 6ex....................(p) ConnorBeasley(7) 11 53
(David Nicholls) *hld up and bhd: effrt and hdwy on inner whn nt clr run and hmpd 1f out: n.d* **7/2**[1]
0620 **11** *½* **Pippy**[29] 3178 3-9-3 **60**....................(p) GrahamGibbons 1 42
(Tom Dascombe) *midfield: rdn along 1/2-way: sn wknd* **9/2**[3]
00/0 **12** *hd* **Durham Express (IRE)**[8] 3934 6-8-10 **45**.................... DuranFentiman 4 30
(Tina Jackson) *chsd ldrs: rdn wl over 2f out: wknd wl over 1f out* **100/1**
0002 **13** *4 ½* **Birdy Boy (USA)**[5] 4008 3-8-12 **55**.................... JoeFanning 12 24
(Mark Johnston) *chsd ldrs: rdn along over 3f out: sn wknd* **4/1**[2]

1m 26.12s (-0.88) **Going Correction** -0.10s/f (Good)
WFA 3 from 4yo+ 8lb **13** Ran SP% **121.0**
Speed ratings (Par 101): **101,99,98,96,96 95,93,92,91,91 90,90,85**
toteswingers 1&2 £13.70, 1&3 £27.70, 2&3 £31.10 CSF £60.97 TOTE £7.70: £2.40, £3.60, £6.50; EX 54.00 Trifecta £1335.80 Pool: £3670.28 - 2.06 winning units..
Owner R W Fife **Bred** West Dereham Abbey Stud **Trained** Stillington, N Yorks
■ Stewards' Enquiry : Gemma Tutty 1st incident; three-day ban: careless riding (Jul 24-26); (2nd) one-day ban: careless riding (Jul 28)
Graham Gibbons one-day ban: careless riding (Jul 24)

FOCUS
The leaders went off far too quickly, so those settled off the gallop had the advantage. There were plenty of horses that suffered trouble in running. Gemma Tutty on Jupiter Fidius picked up two separate bans for careless riding, while Graham Gibbons also collected a ban for the same offence. The winner's best form since her 2012 reappearabce.

4161 READ HAYLEY TURNER EVERY FRIDAY RACINGUK.COM H'CAP (DIV II) 7f
4:50 (4:50) (Class 6) (0-65,64) 3-Y-O+ **£2,385** (£704; £352) **Stalls** Centre

Form RPR
3000 **1** **Strong Man**[12] 3778 5-9-10 **60**....................(b) GrahamGibbons 9 76+
(Michael Easterby) *led: qcknd clr over 2f out: rdn and kpt on strly fnl f* **9/2**[2]
0132 **2** *5* **Dhhamaan (IRE)**[12] 3770 8-9-5 **55**....................(b) JamesSullivan 7 55
(Ruth Carr) *dwlt: t.k.h and towards rr: stdy hdwy 1/2-way: rdn 2f out: kpt on appr fnl f: no ch w wnr* **9/2**[2]
6510 **3** *1 ¾* **Tony Hollis**[5] 4005 5-8-12 **55**.................... GemmaTutty(7) 6 50
(Karen Tutty) *midfield: hdwy 3f out: rdn 2f out: styd on u.p fnl f* **9/1**
-500 **4** *nk* **Star City (IRE)**[12] 3778 4-9-8 **58**....................(be) PaulMulrennan 2 52
(Michael Dods) *chsd wnr: rdn along over 2f out: drvn wl over 1f out: sn one pce* **9/2**[2]
0454 **5** *nse* **Blue Shoes (IRE)**[23] 3392 4-9-7 **64**.................... GaryMahon(7) 10 58
(Tim Easterby) *trckd ldng pair: hdwy 3f out and cl up: rdn over 2f out and grad wknd* **4/1**[1]
0-46 **6** *1 ¼* **Don't Tell**[40] 2836 3-8-2 **46**.................... AndrewMullen 1 36
(George Moore) *chsd ldrs: rdn along 3f out: drvn 2f out: grad wknd* **12/1**
4450 **7** *3 ¾* **Karate Queen**[23] 3393 8-8-8 **49**....................(p) ShirleyTeasdale(5) 13 29
(Ron Barr) *dwlt and towards rr: sme hdwy fnl 2f: n.d* **50/1**
40-0 **8** *½* **Prince Of Vasa (IRE)**[21] 3462 6-9-12 **62**....................(t) GrahamLee 11 41
(Michael Smith) *t.k.h: hld up: a towards rr* **20/1**
000 **9** *½* **Whistle We Go (GER)**[27] 3250 5-8-9 **45**.................... PJMcDonald 4 23
(Nick Kent) *a towards rr* **40/1**
0000 **10** *¾* **Dansili Dutch (IRE)**[11] 3814 4-8-6 **45**.................... NeilFarley(3) 3 21
(Andrew Crook) *a towards rr* **33/1**
11 *4* **Refuse Colette (IRE)**[96] 1376 4-8-9 **45**.................... JoeFanning 5 10
(Paul Green) *chsd ldrs: rdn over 2f out: sn wknd* **6/1**[3]

1m 25.82s (-1.18) **Going Correction** -0.10s/f (Good)
WFA 3 from 4yo+ 8lb **11** Ran SP% **118.6**
Speed ratings (Par 101): **102,96,94,93,93 92,88,87,87,86 81**
toteswingers 1&2 £3.40, 1&3 £6.20, 2&3 £4.10 CSF £24.46 TOTE £7.00: £1.40, £1.70, £3.60; EX 27.20 Trifecta £193.60 Pool: £2254.81 - 8.73 winning units..
Owner Mrs Jean Turpin **Bred** Mrs Jean Turpin **Trained** Sheriff Hutton, N Yorks

FOCUS
Nothing more than a moderate sprint. The winner was allowed to lead and wasn't really hassled. He's worth more at face value.

4162 RACING AGAIN NEXT WEDNESDAY 17TH JULY H'CAP 5f 212y
5:20 (5:20) (Class 5) (0-75,75) 3-Y-O **£2,911** (£866; £432; £216) **Stalls** Low

Form RPR
4335 **1** **Deepest Blue**[12] 3762 3-8-12 **66**.................... GrahamLee 6 71
(Declan Carroll) *trckd ldrs: pushed along 2f out: swtchd rt and rdn ent fnl f: drvn and styd on wl to ld nr fin* **7/2**[2]

6334 **2** *nk* **Perfect Words (IRE)**[18] 3594 3-8-3 **62**....................(p) ShirleyTeasdale(5) 2 66
(Marjorie Fife) *t.k.h: trckd ldr: hdwy 2f out: sn chalng: rdn over 1f out: edgd rt ins fnl f: sn drvn and edgd lft: slt ld last 50yds: hdd and no ex nr fin* **9/2**[3]
4110 **3** *½* **Sylvia Pankhurst (IRE)**[33] 3058 3-9-2 **75**....................(p) LMcNiff(5) 1 77
(David C Griffiths) *led: rdn along 2f out: drvn and edgd rt ins fnl f: hdd and no ex last 40yds* **3/1**[1]
0011 **4** *2* **Jontleman (IRE)**[11] 3818 3-9-2 **70**.................... PaulMulrennan 7 76+
(Mick Channon) *trckd ldrs: effrt over 1f out: chalng and ev ch whn bdly hmpd ins fnl f: no ch after* **7/2**[2]
0004 **5** *1 ½* **Windforpower (IRE)**[1] 4136 3-8-2 **56** oh1.................... JoeFanning 4 47
(Tracy Waggott) *towards rr: pushed along and outpcd 1/2-way: rdn over 2f out: kpt on fnl f: n.d* **12/1**
0500 **6** *2 ¾* **Rat Catcher (IRE)**[16] 3630 3-8-1 **58**....................(b) NeilFarley(3) 5 40
(Andrew Crook) *chsd ldrs: rdn along on outer over 2f out: drvn and wknd over 1f out* **13/2**
0-04 **7** *18* **Storma Norma**[13] 3730 3-8-12 **66**.................... DuranFentiman 3
(Tim Easterby) *dwlt: towards rr: rdn along and detached bef 1/2-way: bhd after* **12/1**

1m 12.27s (-1.33) **Going Correction** -0.10s/f (Good) **7** Ran SP% **116.3**
Speed ratings (Par 100): **104,103,102,100,98 94,70**
toteswingers 1&2 £3.50, 1&3 £2.50, 2&3 £4.00 CSF £20.21 TOTE £4.00: £3.20, £2.40; EX 17.90 Trifecta £104.80 Pool: £1967.08 - 14.06 winning units..
Owner Mr & Mrs I H Bendelow **Bred** Mr & Mrs J Laws **Trained** Sledmere, E Yorks
■ Stewards' Enquiry : Shirley Teasdale two-day ban: careless riding (Jul 24-25)

FOCUS
A modest handicap. Limited form, a small personal best from the winner.
T/Plt: £155.50 to a £1 stake. Pool: £66,056.98 - 309.91 winning tickets. T/Qpdt: £111.70 to a £1 stake. Pool: £3366.28 - 22.30 winning tickets. JR

3955 KEMPTON (A.W) (R-H)
Wednesday, July 10

OFFICIAL GOING: Standard
Wind: Brisk ahead Weather: Sunny early

4163 BETDAQ 1ST UK RACE COMMISSION FREE APPRENTICE H'CAP 7f (P)
6:20 (6:20) (Class 5) (0-70,67) 4-Y-O+ **£2,587** (£770; £384; £192) **Stalls** Low

Form RPR
0-03 **1** **Sheikh The Reins (IRE)**[20] 3511 4-9-12 **67**....................(v) RyanTate 4 76
(John Best) *mde virtually all: drvn and styd on strly fr over 1f out* **4/1**[2]
3400 **2** *2* **Welsh Inlet (IRE)**[62] 2196 5-9-1 **56**.................... MichaelJMMurphy 5 60
(John Bridger) *sn chsng ldrs: rdn 2f out: styd on fnl f to take 2nd clsng stages but no impeession on wnr* **18/1**
-044 **3** *¾* **Excellent Jem**[19] 3534 4-9-10 **65**....................(p) WilliamTwiston-Davies 1 67
(Jane Chapple-Hyam) *chsd ldrs: rdn to go 2nd ins fnl 2f: no imp on wnr fnl f and outpcd into 3rd clsng stages* **2/1**[1]
-022 **4** *1* **Fenella Fudge**[7] 3955 5-9-3 **63**....................(v) AdamMcLean(5) 11 62+
(Derek Shaw) *stdd s: in rr: drvn over 2f out: styd on u.p fnl f to take 4th nr fin* **8/1**
1134 **5** *hd* **Bold Ring**[41] 2792 7-9-3 **63**.................... CharlotteJenner(5) 6 61
(Edward Creighton) *in tch: hdwy 2f out: sn rdn: styd on same pce fnl f* **10/1**
5620 **6** *¾* **West Leake (IRE)**[23] 3404 7-9-8 **63**.................... CharlesBishop 9 59
(Paul Burgoyne) *stdd s: in rr: drvn and hdwy 2f out: one pce and no imp on ldrs fnl f* **11/1**
00 **7** *nk* **Gracie's Games**[37] 2918 7-8-4 **48** oh2....................(p) IanBurns(3) 3 44
(John Spearing) *t.k.h: chsd ldrs: chal over 2f out: wknd qckly fnl 110yds* **66/1**
5005 **8** *nk* **The Guru Of Gloom (IRE)**[22] 3430 5-9-5 **63**......(b[1]) ThomasGarner(3) 2 58
(William Muir) *s.i.s: in rr: hdwy over 2f out: sn rdn to chse ldrs: wknd appr fnl f* **6/1**[3]
1123 **9** *2 ¼* **Teen Ager (FR)**[23] 3404 9-9-4 **64**....................(p) OisinMurphy(5) 8 53
(Paul Burgoyne) *stdd s: in rr: hdwy over 2f out: styd on same pce fnl f* **13/2**
0-65 **10** *6* **El Camino Real (IRE)**[9] 3906 5-8-2 **50**.................... RyanHolmes(7) 7 22
(Barry Leavy) *chsd ldr but a wd: wknd over 2f out* **66/1**

1m 26.34s (0.34) **Going Correction** +0.075s/f (Slow) **10** Ran SP% **117.7**
Speed ratings (Par 103): **101,98,97,96,96 95,95,94,92,85**
toteswingers 1&2 £14.20, 1&3 £2.70, 2&3 £10.10 CSF £73.73 CT £184.58 TOTE £5.20: £1.50, £4.00, £1.50; EX 93.60 Trifecta £388.80 Pool: £1394.30 - 2.68 winning units..
Owner Splinter Group **Bred** M Enright **Trained** Hucking, Kent

FOCUS
A weak handicap, confined to apprentice riders. It was run at a routine pace and those held up were at a disadvantage. The winner is rated a length off his old form.

4164 BYRNE GROUP/IRISH STALLION FARMS EBF MAIDEN FILLIES' STKS 6f (P)
6:50 (6:50) (Class 5) 2-Y-O **£2,911** (£866; £432; £216) **Stalls** Low

Form RPR
52 **1** **Musicora**[12] 3760 2-9-0 0.................... RichardHughes 12 82
(Richard Hannon) *broke wl: mde all: drvn and qcknd appr fnl 2f: sn clr: unchal* **11/4**[2]
50 **2** *5* **Got To Dance**[47] 2625 2-9-0 0.................... JimCrowley 7 67
(Ralph Beckett) *chsd ldrs: wnt 2nd 4f out: drvn over 2f out and nt qckn w wnr: styd on same pce and jst hld on for 2nd* **3/1**[3]
4 **3** *shd* **Thatchit (IRE)**[10] 3863 2-9-0 0.................... TomQueally 6 67
(Paul Cole) *chsd ldrs: rdn over 2f out: styd on fnl f to press for 2nd clsng stages but nvr any ch w wnr* **9/4**[1]
4 *1 ¾* **Starlit Cantata** 2-9-0 0.................... JohnFahy 11 61
(Eve Johnson Houghton) *in rr: drvn and hdwy over 2f out: kpt on fnl f* **66/1**
5 *nk* **More Aspen (USA)** 2-9-0 0.................... AndreaAtzeni 10 61+
(Marco Botti) *s.i.s: in rr: pushed along 2f out: hdwy appr fnl f: styd on wl clsng stages* **14/1**
0 **6** *2* **Maysville (IRE)**[15] 3664 2-9-0 0.................... MartinHarley 5 55
(Charles Hills) *chsd ldrs: rdn over 2f out: wknd ins fnl f* **33/1**
7 *nk* **Johara (IRE)** 2-9-0 0.................... HayleyTurner 4 54
(Chris Wall) *in rr: n.m.r towards inner over 2f out: kpt on fnl f: nvr a threat* **50/1**
8 *¾* **Threetimesalady** 2-9-0 0.................... LukeMorris 1 51
(Sir Mark Prescott Bt) *in tch: rdn along over 2f out: styd on same pce fnl f* **16/1**
4 **9** *3 ¾* **Jalebi**[42] 2771 2-9-0 0.................... PatCosgrave 8 40
(Jim Boyle) *in rr: n.m.r over 3f out: outpcd most of way* **33/1**

The Form Book Flat, Raceform Ltd, Compton, RG20 6NL.

56 **10** *hd* **Silver Starlet (IRE)**^{15} [3659] 2-9-0 0 .... FergusSweeney 2 40
(Alastair Lidderdale) *chsd ldrs 4f* **50/1**

5 **11** *nk* **Mimbleberry**^{25} [3318] 2-9-0 .... RichardKingscote 9 39
(Tom Dascombe) *s.i.s: outpcd* **13/2**

00 **12** *5* **Tidal Beauty**^{16} [3631] 2-8-9 0 .... GeorgeDowning$^{(5)}$ 3 24
(Tony Carroll) *t.k.h: sn chsng ldrs: rdn 2f out: hung lft and wknd sn after* **100/1**

1m 13.4s (0.30) **Going Correction** +0.075s/f (Slow) **12** Ran SP% **120.6**
Speed ratings (Par 91): **101,94,94,91,91 88,88,87,82,82 81,75**
toteswingers 1&2 £3.20, 1&3 £1.80, 2&3 £3.20 CSF £11.32 TOTE £3.10: £1.20, £1.60, £1.60; EX 16.60 Trifecta £29.30 Pool: £1658.31 - 42.35 winning units..
Owner The Three Points Partnership **Bred** Sir Eric Parker **Trained** East Everleigh, Wilts

FOCUS
This looked to be a modest fillies' maiden. The winner might be worth more but the second and some others help guide the level.

4165 £200 FREE BETS AT BETDAQ H'CAP 6f (P)
7:20 (7:20) (Class 4) (0-80,80) 3-Y-O+ **£4,690** (£1,395; £697; £348) **Stalls** Low

Form RPR

0350 **1** **Arctic Lynx (IRE)**^{18} [3586] 6-9-4 **79** .... JimCrowley 5 88
(Robert Cowell) *chsd ldrs: drvn and hdwy on ins over 1f out: styd on u.p to ld cl home* **9/2**^{1}

1063 **2** *nk* **Tagula Night (IRE)**^{25} [3341] 7-9-3 **78** ....(bt) RichardHughes 9 86
(Dean Ivory) *trckd ldr: drvn to chal 2f out: slt ld appr fnl f: hdd and no ex u.p cl home* **6/1**^{3}

-105 **3** *shd* **The Tichborne (IRE)**^{44} [2724] 5-9-2 **77** ....(v) JackMitchell 4 85+
(Roger Teal) *in rr: drvn and hdwy over 1f out: styd on wl fnl f to take 3rd cl home but nt quite rch ldng duo* **6/1**^{3}

1311 **4** *nk* **Desert Strike**^{29} [3171] 7-9-4 **79** ....(p) HayleyTurner 11 86
(Conor Dore) *sn led: rdn and styd on whn chal 2f out: narrowly hdd appr fnl f: styd pressing ldrs tl no ex clsng stages* **14/1**

5025 **5** *2 ½* **Ocean Legend (IRE)**^{21} [3472] 8-8-12 **78** .... GeorgeDowning$^{(5)}$ 1 77
(Tony Carroll) *t.k.h: trckd ldrs: rdn appr 1f out: kpt on same pce* **12/1**

3326 **6** *nk* **Ashpan Sam**^{14} [3682] 4-9-5 **80** .... LukeMorris 10 78
(John Spearing) *chsd ldrs: rdn ins fnl 2f: outpcd fnl f* **16/1**

4300 **7** *1* **Living Leader**^{18} [3586] 4-9-3 **78** ....(v^{1}) TomMcLaughlin 7 73+
(Nick Littmoden) *s.i.s: in rr: drvn and styd on appr fnl f: kpt on clsng stages* **5/1**^{2}

0005 **8** *½* **Decision By One**^{11} [3802] 4-9-3 **78** ....(t) RichardKingscote 8 71+
(Tom Dascombe) *in rr: drvn and hdwy over 1f out: styd on clsng stages* **5/1**^{2}

0456 **9** *1* **Elna Bright**^{11} [3816] 8-9-4 **79** .... ShaneKelly 3 69
(Peter Crate) *chsd ldrs: n.m.r on inner appr fnl f: sn btn* **25/1**

6600 **10** *2 ½* **Heartsong (IRE)**^{24} [3371] 4-8-11 **77** ....(v^{1}) MichaelJMMurphy$^{(5)}$ 6 59
(John Gallagher) *towards rr but in tch: sme hdwy over 2f out: sn rdn: wknd over 1f out* **40/1**

02-0 **11** *2 ¼* **Jocasta Dawn**^{44} [2724] 4-9-2 **77** .... FergusSweeney 2 52
(Henry Candy) *outpcd* **10/1**

1m 12.8s (-0.30) **Going Correction** +0.075s/f (Slow) **11** Ran SP% **115.7**
Speed ratings (Par 105): **105,104,104,104,100 100,99,98,97,93 90**
toteswingers 1&2 £7.10, 1&3 £7.10, 2&3 £8.80 CSF £30.71 CT £166.41 TOTE £6.10: £2.10, £1.90, £2.10; EX 33.60 Trifecta £171.30 Pool: £1042.87 - 4.56 winning units..
Owner Heading For The Rocks Partnership **Bred** Derek Veitch And Saleh Ali Hammadi **Trained** Six Mile Bottom, Cambs

■ Stewards' Enquiry : Jim Crowley one-day ban: careless riding (Jul 24)

FOCUS
An open sprint handicap, run at a sound pace and with a blanket four-way finish. Routine form with the winner back to his best.

4166 BYRNE GROUP H'CAP 2m (P)
7:50 (7:50) (Class 5) (0-75,74) 4-Y-O+ **£2,587** (£770; £384; £192) **Stalls** Low

Form RPR

600 **1** **Mexicali (IRE)**^{12} [3765] 5-9-7 **74** .... SebSanders 9 84
(Dean Ivory) *trckd ldr: led 4f out: drvn clr appr fnl f: pushed out clsng stages* **20/1**

032 **2** *1 ¾* **Story Writer**^{25} [3328] 4-9-1 **68** .... RyanMoore 10 76
(William Knight) *chsd ldrs: drvn ins fnl 3f: chsd wnr 2f out: kpt on but a readily hld* **10/3**^{1}

3431 **3** *3 ¾* **Barachiel**^{14} [3688] 5-8-11 **64** .... RichardHughes 12 67
(Luke Dace) *hld up in rr: hdwy over 3f out: drvn and styd on fr 2f out to take 3rd over 1f out but nvr gng pce to rch ldng duo* **9/2**^{2}

003- **4** *6* **Ascalon**^{223} [7927] 9-9-2 **69** .... JimmyFortune 3 65
(Pat Eddery) *chsd ldrs: rdn to dispute: one pce in 2nd over 2f out: sn btn* **12/1**

1441 **5** *2* **Arashi**^{21} [3473] 7-9-2 **69** ....(v) MartinDwyer 7 63
(Derek Shaw) *in rr: rdn and hdwy over 2f out: kpt on fnl f but nvr nr ldrs* **10/1**

54 **6** *4* **All Annalena (IRE)**^{40} [2849] 7-9-7 **74** ....(p) LukeMorris 2 63
(Lucy Wadham) *chsd ldrs: drvn along 6f out: wknd ins fnl 2f* **16/1**

5054 **7** *5* **Robin Hood (IRE)**^{26} [3273] 5-9-5 **72** .... JackMitchell 8 55
(Philip Mitchell) *in rr: hdwy fr 4f out: in tch 3f out: rdn: hung rt and wknd sn after* **12/1**

6014 **8** *1* **Queen's Star**^{12} [3790] 4-8-8 **61** .... LiamKeniry 4 43
(Andrew Balding) *in rr: hdwy 5f out: rdn 3f out: sn btn* **16/1**

6035 **9** *¾* **Between The Lines (IRE)**^{36} [2968] 4-8-4 **57** ....(t) FrannyNorton 6 38
(Anthony Middleton) *chsd ldrs: rdn over 3f out: wknd qckly fr 2f out* **33/1**

3-63 **10** *5* **Joe The Coat**^{25} [3328] 4-8-12 **65** .... TomQueally 11 40
(Mark H Tompkins) *mid-div: rdn 4f out: sn btn* **8/1**

0002 **11** *nk* **Foster's Road**^{12} [3790] 4-9-7 **74** .... MartinHarley 1 49
(Mick Channon) *mid-div: rdn and sme hdwy over 3f out: nvr rchd ldrs and sn btn* **11/2**^{3}

0620 **12** *6* **Fulgora**^{25} [3328] 5-9-2 **69** .... RichardKingscote 13 36
(Brendan Powell) *a in rr* **25/1**

0156 **13** *29* **Shalambar (IRE)**^{35} [2982] 7-9-2 **69** ....(v) JimCrowley 14 2
(Tony Carroll) *stdd s: a in rr: eased fnl 2f* **16/1**

4/54 **14** *15* **Paintball (IRE)**^{20} [3512] 6-9-0 **67** ....(v^{1}) SamHitchcott 5
(Charlie Longsdon) *led to 4f out: sn wknd: eased fnl 2f* **25/1**

3m 28.58s (-1.52) **Going Correction** +0.075s/f (Slow) **14** Ran SP% **125.3**
Speed ratings (Par 103): **106,105,103,100,99 97,94,94,93,91 91,88,73,66**
toteswingers 1&2 £22.70, 1&3 £29.20, 2&3 £2.20 CSF £85.91 CT £373.92 TOTE £35.40: £8.90, £1.70, £1.70; EX 180.00 Trifecta £601.10 Part won. Pool: £801.50 - 0.28 winning units..
Owner Geoff Copp & Dean Ivory **Bred** Darley **Trained** Radlett, Herts

FOCUS
A moderate staying handicap, run at a fair pace. The winner is rated back to her Ascot May form.

4167 COMMISSION FREE 1ST MONTH AT BETDAQ H'CAP (LONDON MIDDLE DISTANCE SERIES QUALIFIER) 1m 3f (P)
8:20 (8:20) (Class 4) (0-80,82) 3-Y-O+ **£4,690** (£1,395; £697; £348) **Stalls** Low

Form RPR

4323 **1** **Zamoyski**^{37} [2927] 3-9-2 **80** .... RichardHughes 1 92
(Jeremy Noseda) *trckd ldrs: drvn to go 2nd over 1f out: styd on wl to ld fnl 110yds: kpt on wl* **11/4**^{2}

1-32 **2** *¾* **Autun (USA)**^{21} [3470] 3-9-2 **80** .... TomQueally 8 91
(Lady Cecil) *trckd ldrs: led appr fnl 2f: drvn over 1f out: hdd and no ex fnl 110yds* **9/4**^{1}

/0-3 **3** *3 ¾* **Diamond Penny (IRE)**^{18} [3573] 5-9-6 **72** ....(p^{1}) JamesDoyle 3 76
(Seamus Durack) *in tch: hdwy 4f out: styd on to take 3rd appr fnl f: no imp on ldng duo* **33/1**

00-0 **4** *hd* **Bobbyscot (IRE)**^{41} [2808] 6-9-7 **73** .... RyanMoore 12 77
(Gary Moore) *in rr: drvn over 3f out: hdwy over 2f out: styd on to press for 3rd ins fnl f but no ch w ldng duo* **12/1**

-400 **5** *6* **Aldwick Bay (IRE)**^{11} [3838] 5-9-5 **76** .... WilliamTwiston-Davies$^{(5)}$ 4 69
(Richard Hannon) *in tch: rdn 3f out: no imp on ldrs over 2f out and no ch after* **20/1**

0-31 **6** *½* **Tuscan Fun**^{18} [3573] 3-8-12 **76** .... AndreaAtzeni 9 68+
(Roger Varian) *in rr: rdn 3f out: mod prog fr 2f out* **11/4**^{2}

00 **7** *1 ¾* **Top Diktat**^{23} [3416] 5-8-13 **72** .... NedCurtis$^{(7)}$ 2 61
(Gary Moore) *chsd ldrs: rdn and no prog whn hmpd over 2f out* **50/1**

2122 **8** *nk* **King Olav (UAE)**^{21} [3468] 8-9-8 **74** .... JimCrowley 7 63
(Tony Carroll) *led: hdd over 2f out: wknd qckly over 1f out* **11/1**^{3}

065 **9** *½* **La Rosiere (USA)**^{19} [3530] 4-8-7 **64** oh1 .... PhilipPrince$^{(5)}$ 5 52
(Pat Murphy) *in rr: rdn over 2f out: mod late prog* **66/1**

14/3 **10** *shd* **West Brit (IRE)**^{17} [2234] 5-9-8 **74** ....(t) SamHitchcott 11 62
(Charlie Longsdon) *chsd ldrs: rdn 3f out: wknd and hung lft over 2f out* **25/1**

4516 **11** *1 ½* **Scottish Boogie (IRE)**^{99} [1302] 6-9-10 **76** .... WilliamBuick 10 61
(Seamus Durack) *a in rr* **33/1**

2m 21.51s (-0.39) **Going Correction** +0.075s/f (Slow)
WFA 3 from 4yo+ 12lb **11** Ran SP% **118.1**
Speed ratings (Par 105): **104,103,100,100,96 95,94,94,94,93 92**
toteswingers 1&2 £2.00, 1&3 £16.40, 2&3 £20.60 CSF £8.71 CT £164.66 TOTE £5.00: £1.70, £1.50, £3.50; EX 11.60 Trifecta £166.10 Pool: £1413.24 - 6.37 winning units..
Owner Mrs Susan Roy **Bred** N C Appleton & Cheveley Park Stud **Trained** Newmarket, Suffolk

FOCUS
This was a fair handicap for the grade and the form looks solid, with the first pair clear.

4168 WINNERS ARE WELCOME AT BETDAQ H'CAP (LONDON MILE SERIES QUALIFIER) 1m (P)
8:50 (8:50) (Class 4) (0-85,82) 3-Y-O **£4,690** (£1,395; £697; £348) **Stalls** Low

Form RPR

1-16 **1** **Noble Gift**^{25} [3338] 3-9-4 **79** ....^{1} WilliamBuick 4 84+
(William Knight) *awkward s and sn detached: clsd up 4f out: drvn over 2f out: outpcd and dropped to last pl appr fnl f: rallied u.p fnl 110yds to ld cl home* **13/8**^{1}

2-36 **2** *nk* **Mr Fitzroy (IRE)**^{33} [3061] 3-8-12 **73** .... JimmyFortune 5 77
(Andrew Balding) *chsd ldrs: rdn over 1f out: slt ld u.p fnl 50yds: hdd cl home* **7/1**^{3}

0036 **3** *nk* **Hunting Rights (USA)**^{11} [3828] 3-8-11 **72** .... RyanMoore 7 75
(Mark Johnston) *chsd ldrs: drvn to chal fnl 150yds: one pce clsng stages* **7/1**^{3}

0601 **4** *½* **Reggae Star**^{16} [3620] 3-8-10 **71** .... FrannyNorton 6 73
(Mark Johnston) *led: rdn and kpt slt advantage tl hdd and no ex fnl 50yds* **9/1**

2-40 **5** *nk* **Soaring Spirits (IRE)**^{19} [3537] 3-8-11 **72** ....(b^{1}) AndreaAtzeni 3 73
(Roger Varian) *chsd ldrs: drvn 2f out: kpt on fnl f but nvr quite gng pce to chal* **11/4**^{2}

0-00 **6** *1* **Rebel Magic**^{26} [3292] 3-9-7 **82** .... RichardHughes 2 81
(Richard Hannon) *in rr: drvn and hdwy over 1f out: styd on fnl f but nvr quite gng pce to chal* **14/1**

0160 **7** *¾* **Tagalaka (IRE)**^{15} [3665] 3-8-2 **63** .... CathyGannon 1 60
(Eve Johnson Houghton) *in tch: drvn to chse ldrs 2f out: chal jst ins fnl f: wknd clsng stages* **16/1**

1m 40.49s (0.69) **Going Correction** +0.075s/f (Slow) **7** Ran SP% **112.3**
Speed ratings (Par 102): **99,98,98,97,97 96,95**
toteswingers 1&2 £3.90, 1&3 £3.80, 2&3 £8.90 CSF £13.18 TOTE £2.80: £1.70, £5.20; EX 14.00 Trifecta £61.40 Pool: £1018.48 - 12.43 winning units..
Owner Gail Brown Racing (V) **Bred** Theakston Stud **Trained** Patching, W Sussex

FOCUS
A modest 3yo handicap that saw a tight finish. Given the lack of pace the form may not be entirely reliable.

4169 CONOR MAYNARD LIVE AT KEMPTON 14.09.13 H'CAP 1m (P)
9:20 (9:23) (Class 6) (0-65,65) 3-Y-O+ **£1,940** (£577; £288; £144) **Stalls** Low

Form RPR

00/1 **1** **Two Minds (FR)**^{22} [3433] 6-9-6 **60** .... WilliamCarson 4 69
(Eugene Stanford) *chsd ldrs: drvn to chal fnl f: led fnl 110yds: all out* **3/1**^{1}

1335 **2** *hd* **South Cape**^{55} [2395] 10-9-0 **61** .... JayneFarwell$^{(7)}$ 7 69
(Gary Moore) *t.k.h: trckd ldrs: pushed along to chal fnl 110yds: no ex last strides* **20/1**

60-4 **3** *½* **Lisa's Legacy**^{10} [3861] 3-9-2 **65** .... JimmyFortune 13 69
(Daniel Kubler) *chsd ldrs: drvn 2f out: styd on to take 3rd ins fnl f: nt quite pce of ldng duo* **8/1**

0-33 **4** *½* **Dandarrell**^{39} [2889] 6-9-9 **63** .... FrederikTylicki 3 68
(Julie Camacho) *chsd ldr: chal 3f out: slt ld u.p 2f out: jnd fnl f: hdd and outpcd fnl 110yds* **5/1**^{3}

0-50 **5** *1 ½* **Bladewood Girl**^{16} [3635] 5-9-6 **60** .... RichardHughes 11 62
(J R Jenkins) *in tch: hdwy 2f out: drvn to chse ldrs 1f out: wknd fnl 110yds* **16/1**

0436 **6** *1* **Divine Rule (IRE)**^{25} [3330] 5-9-6 **60** ....(v) JackMitchell 8 59
(Laura Mongan) *in rr: hdwy over 2f out: styd on fnl f: nt pce to trble ldrs* **20/1**

-405 **7** *3* **Tenessee**^{16} [3642] 6-9-10 **64** .... LukeMorris 6 57
(Jamie Osborne) *led: jnd 3f out: hdd 2f out: wknd over 1f out* **6/1**

0550 **8** *nk* **Kindia (IRE)**^{42} [2773] 5-9-5 **59** ....(p) SebSanders 10 51
(Michael Attwater) *in rr: pushed along over 2f out: nvr rchd ldrs* **25/1**

400 **9** *shd* **Baltic Blade (IRE)**^{39} [2872] 3-9-2 **65** .... RyanMoore 12 55
(Gary Moore) *in rr: rdn over 2f out: mod prog fnl f* **4/1**^{2}

2006 **10** *1* **Karate (IRE)**[14] 3687 5-8-11 **56**..............................(t) NicoleNordblad(5) 14 45
(Hans Adielsson) *outpcd most of way* **25/1**

0415 **11** *2 ¼* **Wyndham Wave**[9] 3885 4-8-10 **57**..............................(p) PatMillman(7) 1 41
(Rod Millman) *chsd ldrs: wknd over 1f out* **12/1**

540/ **12** *3 ¾* **Barnmore**[637] 6789 5-9-8 **62**..............................[1] TomMcLaughlin 9 38
(Peter Hedger) *s.i.s: a in rr* **50/1**

000 **13** *19* **Cocohatchee**[23] 3404 5-9-4 **58**..............................(p) FergusSweeney 5
(Pat Phelan) *chsd ldrs: rdn 3f out: wknd over 2f out: eased whn no ch* **40/1**

1m 40.31s (0.51) **Going Correction** +0.075s/f (Slow)
WFA 3 from 4yo+ 9lb **13** Ran SP% **122.3**
Speed ratings (Par 101): **100,99,99,98,97 96,93,93,92,91 89,85,66**
toteswingers 1&2 £13.00, 1&3 £11.20, 2&3 £44.80 CSF £72.80 CT £466.06 TOTE £4.30: £1.80, £5.00, £2.70; EX 69.70 Trifecta £847.80 Part won. Pool: £1130.53 - 0.34 winning units..
Owner Lemberg Stables **Bred** John Stevens & John Morgan **Trained** Newmarket, Suffolk

FOCUS
It paid to race handily in this moderate handicap. Straightforward form.
T/Jkpt: Not won. T/Plt: £8.80 to a £1 stake. Pool: £88,708.13 - 7309.70 winning tickets. T/Qpdt: £6.10 to a £1 stake. Pool: £5638.90 - 676.00 winning tickets. ST

3815 LINGFIELD (L-H)
Wednesday, July 10

OFFICIAL GOING: Turf - firm; all weather - standard
Wind: Light, half against Weather: Fine, very warm

4170 VINES BMW H'CAP — 1m 1f
2:00 (2:00) (Class 6) (0-60,60) 3-Y-O **£2,045** (£603; £302) **Stalls** Low

Form RPR

0003 **1** **Khelac**[5] 4008 3-9-7 **60**..............................(b) LiamKeniry 8 71+
(Philip Hide) *pressed ldrs: wnt 2nd over 3f out: led over 2f out gng easily: shkn up and sn clr: 5 l up 1f out: heavily eased nr fin* **5/1**[2]

0-00 **2** *2 ¼* **Kensington Gardens**[31] 3136 3-9-4 **57**.............................. TomQueally 7 61+
(Michael Bell) *hld up in 5th: plenty to do fr 4f out: rdn and prog over 2f out: styd on to take 2nd ins fnl f: no ch w wnr* **8/1**[3]

6-06 **3** *2 ¼* **Dawn Rock**[33] 3041 3-8-8 **47**.............................. LukeMorris 9 46
(Simon Dow) *chsd ldr to over 5f out: sn dropped to 4th and rdn: outpcd over 3f out: kpt on again to take 3rd fnl f* **25/1**

5606 **4** *1 ¼* **East Texas Red (IRE)**[27] 3254 3-9-7 **60**.............................. AndreaAtzeni 10 56
(Mick Quinn) *prom: prog to chse ldr over 5f out to over 3f out: sn rdn and clr of rest in 3rd: no ch w wnr 2f out: one pce* **5/1**[2]

4562 **5** *hd* **Loraine**[10] 3859 3-9-3 **56**.............................. FergusSweeney 5 52
(Jamie Osborne) *hld up in 7th: plenty to do 4f out: tried to make prog u.p over 2f out: n.d* **11/4**[1]

1-40 **6** *shd* **Pink Mischief**[34] 3013 3-8-12 **51**.............................. RichardHughes 6 47
(Harry Dunlop) *led to over 2f out: no ch w wnr after: wknd fnl f* **8/1**[3]

-060 **7** *¾* **Lambert Pen (USA)**[16] 3636 3-9-5 **58**.............................. MartinHarley 1 52
(Mick Channon) *hld up in 6th: plenty to do fr 4f out: sn rdn: no imp on ldrs fnl 2f* **10/1**

5-03 **8** *½* **Planchette**[28] 3219 3-8-3 **49**.............................. IanBurns(7) 3 42
(Jane Chapple-Hyam) *hld up in last pair: urged along over 4f out and wl bhd: plugged on fr over 1f out* **20/1**

0-00 **9** *3 ¼* **Delphica (IRE)**[8] 3922 3-8-12 **51**..............................(v) SeanLevey 4 37
(Gary Moore) *hld up in 8th: plenty to do 4f out: pushed along and modest prog 3f out: reminder 2f out: nvr involved and eased fnl f* **66/1**

-015 **10** *½* **Double Star**[8] 3919 3-8-10 **54**.............................. MatthewLawson(5) 2 39
(Jonathan Portman) *hld up and a in last pair: rdn and no prog over 3f out* **5/1**[2]

1m 56.08s (-0.52) **Going Correction** -0.275s/f (Firm) **10** Ran SP% **118.1**
Speed ratings (Par 98): **91,89,87,85,85 85,84,84,81,81**
toteswingers 1&2 £4.30, 1&3 £13.60, 2&3 £27.80 CSF £44.23 TOTE £5.90: £2.10, £2.90, £7.90; EX 37.00 Trifecta £628.10 Pool: £1159.75 - 1.38 winning units..
Owner Stephen Ho **Bred** Brook Stud Bloodstock Ltd **Trained** Findon, W Sussex

FOCUS
The going on the turf course, given as good to firm, firm in places (GoingStick 9.0) was quickly changed to firm after the first. Luke Morris described it as "good to firm, but with no jar" while Liam Keniry said it was "quite fast". An ordinary handicap with doubts over the field. The winner is rated back to his 2yo best.

4171 BHEST RACING TO SCHOOL (S) STKS — 1m 2f
2:30 (2:30) (Class 6) 3-Y-O+ **£2,045** (£603; £302) **Stalls** Low

Form RPR

1003 **1** **Matraash (USA)**[19] 3545 7-9-12 68..............................(be) ShaneKelly 1 62
(Daniel Mark Loughnane) *trckd ldr: chal 3f out: shkn up to ld narrowly 2f out: rdn to assert fnl f* **11/4**[3]

0 **2** *½* **Hilden**[27] 3417 4-9-1 0..............................(b) MartinDwyer 5 50
(William Muir) *led: edgd rt fr 3f out: rdn and narrowly hdd 2f out: pressed wnr after tl no ex last 150yds* **25/1**

5103 **3** *2* **Handsome Stranger (IRE)**[12] 3785 3-8-9 60..............................(v) AndreaAtzeni 4 51
(Alan Bailey) *hld up in 4th: pushed along to dispute 3rd 3f out: nt qckn and no imp on ldng pair 2f out: kpt on fnl f* **6/4**[1]

600U **4** *7* **Youmaysee**[5] 4030 3-8-4 38.............................. SamHitchcott 3 32
(Mick Channon) *t.k.h: hld up in last: shoved along and no prog 3f out: no ch after* **25/1**

4466 **5** *6* **Delightful Sleep**[39] 2875 5-9-12 60.............................. RichardHughes 2 47
(David Evans) *trckd ldng pair: pushed along 3f out: no imp u.p wl over 1f out: heavily eased fnl f: lame* **7/4**[2]

2m 10.75s (0.25) **Going Correction** -0.275s/f (Firm)
WFA 3 from 4yo+ 11lb **5** Ran SP% **110.7**
Speed ratings (Par 101): **88,87,86,80,75**
CSF £46.78 TOTE £4.70: £2.00, £6.30; EX 13.50 Trifecta £114.60 Pool: £891.72 - 5.83 winning units..There was no bid for the winner.
Owner Mrs C Loughnane **Bred** Shadwell Farm LLC **Trained** Baldwin's Gate, Staffs

FOCUS
A weak seller, and they went a steady pace early. The form is rated cautiously.

4172 HENRY STREETER LTD FILLIES' H'CAP — 1m 3f 106y
3:00 (3:00) (Class 5) (0-70,70) 3-Y-O+ **£3,234** (£962; £481; £240) **Stalls** High

Form RPR

5305 **1** **Dazzling Valentine**[12] 3755 5-9-4 **67**.............................. TimClark(7) 3 73
(Alan Bailey) *stdd s: hld up in last: shkn up over 3f out: prog on outer over 2f out: rdn to chal fnl f: styd on to ld last strides* **16/1**

5544 **2** *shd* **Kingston Eucalypt**[19] 3535 3-8-13 **67**.............................. AndreaAtzeni 1 73
(Ed Vaughan) *mostly trckd ldng pair: rdn to go 2nd 2f out: clsd to ld jst ins fnl f: styd on but hdd last strides* **7/2**[3]

06-4 **3** *1 ¼* **Candoluminescence**[24] 3372 3-9-2 **70**.............................. JamesDoyle 5 74+
(Roger Charlton) *sn pressed ldr: led over 3f out gng strly: rdn 2f out: hdd and nt qckn jst ins fnl f* **6/4**[1]

041 **4** *2 ¼* **Kittens**[13] 3721 4-9-12 **68**.............................. MartinDwyer 2 68
(William Muir) *hld up in last: pair: rdn 3f out: tried to cl 2f out: nt qckn and no imp after* **5/1**

460- **5** *½* **Flashy Star**[49] 5989 4-9-0 **56**.............................. ShaneKelly 6 55
(Sheena West) *hld up in 4th: dropped to last 3f out but gng wl enough: reminders over 1f out: r.o fnl f: nrst fin* **20/1**

0023 **6** *5* **Langham Lily (USA)**[16] 3635 4-9-5 **61**.............................. SebSanders 4 52
(Chris Wall) *pushed up to ld: shkn up and hdd over 3f out: steadily wknd fr 2f out* **3/1**[2]

2m 28.37s (-3.13) **Going Correction** -0.275s/f (Firm)
WFA 3 from 4yo+ 12lb **6** Ran SP% **114.5**
Speed ratings (Par 100): **100,99,99,97,97 93**
toteswingers 1&2 £9.50, 1&3 £8.20, 2&3 £2.20 CSF £71.96 TOTE £20.60: £6.00, £2.30; EX 85.60 Trifecta £329.60 Pool: £1320.96 - 3.00 winning units..
Owner The Glenbuccaneers **Bred** Chippenham Lodge Stud Ltd **Trained** Newmarket, Suffolk

FOCUS
This was run in a fair time and the winner was basically to form.

4173 ANTARES 5TH ANNIVERSARY CELEBRATION H'CAP — 2m
3:30 (3:30) (Class 6) (0-60,60) 4-Y-O+ **£2,045** (£603; £302) **Stalls** Low

Form RPR

-433 **1** **Hi Note**[20] 3512 5-9-2 **60**.............................. HarryPoulton(5) 1 75
(Sheena West) *pressed ldr: led over 5f out: shkn up and drew clr 3f out: in n.d after: rdn out* **5/4**[1]

5451 **2** *10* **Baan (USA)**[27] 3256 10-8-11 **55**.............................. RyanTate(5) 3 58
(James Eustace) *trckd ldng pair: wnt 2nd 4f out: lft bhd by wnr fr 3f out: one pce after* **2/1**[2]

6050 **3** *11* **Zafaraban (IRE)**[9] 3884 6-8-8 **52**..............................(p) GeorgeDowning(5) 6 42
(Tony Carroll) *awkward s but sn led: pushed along and hdd over 5f out: lost 2nd 4f out: sn wl btn* **7/1**

/0-0 **4** *2* **Go Amwell**[49] 1721 10-8-2 **46** oh1..............................(v) DannyBrock(5) 2 33
(J R Jenkins) *s.s: sn in tch in last pair: cajoled along and lft wl bhd fr 3f out* **25/1**

200- **5** *36* **Imperial Stargazer**[8] 1590 4-9-2 **55**.............................. ChrisCatlin 5
(Sheena West) *hld up in last pair: rdn and lost tch 1/2-way: sn wl t.o* **9/2**[3]

3m 33.91s (-0.89) **Going Correction** -0.275s/f (Firm) **5** Ran SP% **112.3**
Speed ratings (Par 101): **91,86,80,79,61**
CSF £4.14 TOTE £1.90: £1.20, £1.40; EX 5.10 Trifecta £11.90 Pool: £1207.62 - 76.00 winning units..
Owner Gerald West **Bred** J A And Mrs Duffy **Trained** Falmer, E Sussex

FOCUS
A rather uncompetitive small-field stayers' race. The form is taken at something like face value.

4174 LINGFIELD PARK OWNERS GROUP NURSERY H'CAP — 5f (P)
4:00 (4:01) (Class 5) 2-Y-O **£2,726** (£805; £402) **Stalls** High

Form RPR

1 **1** **Scruffy Tramp (IRE)**[23] 3408 2-9-7 **79**.............................. SeanLevey 1 84+
(Michael Wigham) *t.k.h: trckd ldr 1f: styd cl up: rdn to chal on inner 1f out: gd battle w runner-up after: led last strides* **3/1**[3]

41 **2** *shd* **Umneyati**[29] 3167 2-8-10 **68**.............................. AndreaAtzeni 5 73+
(James Tate) *trckd ldr after 1f: rdn to ld 1f out but immediately jnd: hdd last strides* **6/4**[1]

3425 **3** *3 ½* **Queen Of The Tarts**[26] 3275 2-8-10 **68**.............................. MickaelBarzalona 3 60
(Olly Stevens) *pushed along to stay in tch after 2f: outpcd 2f out: kpt on to take modest 3rd nr fin* **6/1**

2304 **4** *½* **M'Selle (IRE)**[37] 2933 2-9-3 **75**.............................. LukeMorris 2 66
(Ronald Harris) *led: rdn 2f out: hdd & wknd 1f out* **14/1**

406 **5** *1* **Paradise Child**[14] 3694 2-7-13 **60**.............................. DarrenEgan(3) 4 47
(Bill Turner) *in tch tl wknd wl over 1f out* **33/1**

1003 **U** **Kodafine (IRE)**[26] 3267 2-9-1 **73**.............................. RichardHughes 7
(David Evans) *rrd as stalls opened: emerged sme time after wout rdr* **11/4**[2]

1m 1.42s (2.62) **Going Correction** +0.40s/f (Slow) **6** Ran SP% **115.6**
Speed ratings (Par 94): **95,94,89,88,86**
toteswingers 1&2 £1.60, 1&3 £2.20, 2&3 £2.20 CSF £8.28 CT £24.00 TOTE £4.70: £2.10, £1.10; EX 9.50 Trifecta £33.60 Pool: £1929.04 - 42.98 winning units..
Owner D Hassan & B Green **Bred** Edmond Kent **Trained** Newmarket, Suffolk

FOCUS
The official ratings shown are estimated and for information only. The two last-time-out winners drew clear in this nursery, looking ahead of their marks. Not much depth to the race.

4175 HOOVES & GROOVES MAIDEN AUCTION STKS — 6f (P)
4:30 (4:31) (Class 5) 2-Y-O **£2,726** (£805; £402) **Stalls** Low

Form RPR

1 **Cape Factor (IRE)** 2-8-7 0.............................. ChrisCatlin 5 62
(Rae Guest) *in tch: pushed along and prog to chse ldrs 1/2-way: urged along to cl over 1f out: styd on to ld last 75yds: hld on* **6/1**[3]

2 *shd* **Krackerjill (IRE)** 2-8-7 0.............................. JohnFahy 6 61
(Mark Usher) *chsd ldrs: cajoled along over 2f out: clsd over 1f out: chal and upsides ins fnl f: jst hld* **16/1**

2 **3** *shd* **Flicksta (USA)**[8] 3914 2-9-1 0.............................. LukeMorris 10 69
(Ronald Harris) *t.k.h: pressed ldr: led over 1f out and tried to go clr: hdd u.p last 75yds: styd on* **1/1**[1]

4 *¾* **Officer Drivel (IRE)** 2-8-12 0.............................. SeanLevey 2 67+
(Luke Dace) *dwlt: sn in midfield: looking for room on inner over 2f out: prog over 1f out: styd on to press ldrs last 100yds: nvr quite able to chal* **12/1**

5 *4 ½* **Royal River** 2-8-9 0.............................. LiamKeniry 12 46+
(J S Moore) *s.s: t.k.h and hld up in last trio: stl t.k.h in rr over 2f out: r.o over 1f out to take 5th nr fin: should do considerably bttr* **10/1**

0 **6** *1* **Society Diva (IRE)**[35] 2978 2-8-7 0.............................. KieranO'Neill 1 41
(George Baker) *mostly chsd ldng pair: rdn over 2f out: wknd qckly fnl f* **33/1**

7 *1* **M'Lady Ermyn** 2-7-13 0.............................. JemmaMarshall(5) 4 35+
(Pat Phelan) *dwlt: hld up in last pair and racd wd thrght: no ch over 2f out: shkn up and styd on fnl f* **66/1**

0 **8** *½* **Mistress And Maid**[15] 3663 2-8-4 0.............................. CathyGannon 11 33
(Joseph Tuite) *towards rr: pushed along and nt on terms 1/2-way: no ch after: kpt on fnl f* **33/1**

40 **9** *¾* **Maximilianthefirst**[13] 3717 2-8-12 0.............................. J-PGuillambert 9 39
(P J O'Gorman) *led to over 1f out: wknd qckly* **25/1**

10 1 **Syrian Pearl** 2-8-10 0 WilliamBuick 8 34
(Chris Wall) *dwlt: hld up in last pair: pushed along 2f out: nvr a factor* **9/2**[2]

0 11 4 **Redy To Rumble**[22] 3436 2-8-9 0 ShaneKelly 3 20
(Michael Attwater) *nvr beyond midfield: wknd 2f out* **50/1**

12 1 3/4 **Black Sceptre (IRE)** 2-8-12 0 MarcHalford 7 17
(Edward Creighton) *s.s: a towards rr: pushed along 1/2-way: wknd 2f out* **50/1**

1m 15.17s (3.27) **Going Correction** +0.40s/f (Slow) 12 Ran SP% **120.3**
Speed ratings (Par 94): **94,93,93,92,86 85,84,83,82,81 75,73**
toteswingers 1&2 £13.60, 1&3 £2.40, 2&3 £4.90 CSF £90.31 TOTE £7.30: £1.80, £2.20, £1.50; EX 152.60 Trifecta £358.70 Pool: £3053.26 - 6.38 winning units..
Owner Derek J Willis **Bred** Nanallac Stud **Trained** Newmarket, Suffolk

FOCUS
A modest maiden run at a steady pace. The fourth was arguably unlucky.

4176 SHOVELSTRODE RACING STABLES MEDIAN AUCTION MAIDEN STKS 6f (P)
5:00 (5:02) (Class 6) 3-4-Y-0 **£2,045** (£603; £302) **Stalls** Low

Form RPR

3 1 **Arcadian Legend (USA)**[12] 3787 3-9-0 0 WilliamBuick 2 54+
(Jeremy Noseda) *pressed ldr: pushed along 2f out: rdn to ld 1f out: steadily asserted* **1/2**[1]

6435 2 1 3/4 **Imperial Spirit**[6] 3994 3-9-5 50 (v) MartinHarley 5 53
(Mick Channon) *led: rdn 2f out: hdd 1f out: styd on same pce* **8/1**[3]

3 1 1/4 **Copper Trade** 3-9-5 0 JohnFahy 8 49+
(Eve Johnson Houghton) *wl in tch: chsd ldng pair over 2f out: rdn and styd on fnl f: nvr able to threaten* **5/1**[2]

50 4 2 1/4 **High Tone**[11] 3837 3-9-0 0 LiamKeniry 7 37
(Dean Ivory) *in tch: chsd ldng trio over 2f out: drvn and no imp over 1f out* **50/1**

0-00 5 5 **Daneglow (IRE)**[68] 1986 3-8-9 36 GeorgeDowning(5) 4 21
(Mike Murphy) *restless in stalls: sn wl bhd and urged along: nvr a factor: kpt on fr over 1f out* **50/1**

3- 6 nk **Lars Krister (IRE)**[380] 3452 3-9-0 0 (p) NicoleNordblad(5) 6 25
(Hans Adielsson) *slowly away: nvr quite on terms in 6th: outpcd fr 1/2-way: no real hdwy after* **8/1**[3]

50 7 4 1/2 **Immediately**[23] 3401 3-9-0 0 ShaneKelly 9 5
(Robert Cowell) *racd wd: pressed ldng pair tl wknd rapidly over 2f out* **20/1**

8 6 **Violetgrace** 3-8-11 0 DarrenEgan(3) 3
(Michael Madgwick) *s.v.s: rn green and a wl bhd* **33/1**

050- 9 47 **Aurens (IRE)**[347] 4582 4-9-11 67 SebSanders 1
(Michael Attwater) *rel to r: a wl t.o* **16/1**

1m 14.03s (2.13) **Going Correction** +0.40s/f (Slow)
WFA 3 from 4yo 6lb 9 Ran SP% **123.1**
Speed ratings (Par 101): **101,98,97,94,87 86,80,72,10**
toteswingers 1&2 £2.20, 1&3 £2.00, 2&3 £3.30 CSF £5.90 TOTE £1.70: £1.10, £1.90, £1.80; EX 6.00 Trifecta £19.40 Pool: £4080.26 - 157.49 winning units..
Owner A Ferguson **Bred** Joe Murphy **Trained** Newmarket, Suffolk

FOCUS
A weak race and the winner did not need to improve on her debut effort.
T/Plt: £291.20 to a £1 stake. Pool: £46,755.33 - 117.18 winning tickets. T/Qpdt: £21.90 to a £1 stake. Pool: £4835.78 - 163.28 winning tickets. JN

3991 YARMOUTH (L-H)
Wednesday, July 10

OFFICIAL GOING: Good to firm (7.6)
Back straight and bottom bend dolled out 3m adding 15m to races on Round course.
Wind: medium, behind Weather: bright spells

4177 BBC RADIO NORFOLK MAIDEN AUCTION STKS 5f 43y
2:10 (2:10) (Class 6) 2-Y-0 **£1,940** (£577; £288; £144) **Stalls** Centre

Form RPR

32 1 **Hay Chewed (IRE)**[28] 3217 2-8-8 0 RobertHavlin 1 76+
(Peter Chapple-Hyam) *led for 1f: chsd ldr tl led again over 2f out: shkn up and asserted over 1f out: in command and kpt up to work ins fnl f: eased towards fin* **2/5**[1]

35 2 2 1/4 **Hatti (IRE)**[25] 3324 2-8-4 0 (p) KirstyMilczarek 4 64
(John Ryan) *chsd ldrs: chsd wnr and rdn 2f out: kpt on same pce and hld fnl f* **7/1**[3]

04 3 3 1/2 **Debt Settler (IRE)**[8] 3914 2-8-6 0 SimonPearce(3) 2 56
(Luke Dace) *in tch in rr: rdn and outpcd over 2f out: wnt modest 3rd over 1f out: no imp* **5/1**[2]

0 4 13 **Britain (IRE)**[4] 4073 2-8-4 0 WilliamCarson 3 5
(David C Griffiths) *awkward leaving stalls and slowly away: hung lft thrght: sn rcvrd and led after 1f: hdd over 2f out: sn dropped out: wl bhd fnl f* **25/1**

1m 0.42s (-2.28) **Going Correction** -0.525s/f (Hard) 4 Ran SP% **104.4**
Speed ratings (Par 92): **97,93,87,67**
CSF £3.27 TOTE £1.20; EX 2.60 Trifecta £4.70 Pool: £1947.77 - 305.08 winning units..
Owner John C Davies **Bred** Newlands House Stud **Trained** Newmarket, Suffolk

FOCUS
A disappointing turnout for this juvenile contest and it proved a relatively straightforward task for the short-priced favourite. A messy little race, and the winner's previous form could be rated this high.

4178 NORFOLK CHAMBER OF COMMERCE (S) STKS 1m 3f 101y
2:40 (2:40) (Class 6) 3-4-Y-0 **£1,940** (£577; £288; £144) **Stalls** Low

Form RPR

-04V 1 **Helamis**[18] 3578 3-8-9 50 JamieSpencer 5 53
(Stuart Williams) *chsd ldr tl led after 2f: mde rest: drvn over 1f out: asserted ins fnl f: in command fnl 100yds* **10/11**[1]

-005 2 3 **Omega Omega**[12] 3792 4-9-7 42 (b[1]) AdamBeschizza 4 48
(Julia Feilden) *in tch in last pair: rdn and effrt over 3f out: kpt on u.str.p: chsd wnr ins fnl f: no ex and btn fnl 100yds* **11/1**

530 3 2 1/4 **Spanish Art**[10] 3859 3-8-7 55 ShelleyBirkett(7) 6 49
(Gay Kelleway) *hld up in last pair early: hdwy to chse wnr 6f out tl 4f out: rdn and chsd wnr again 3f out: no ex 1f out: lost 2nd and wknd ins fnl f* **5/1**[3]

-010 4 2 1/4 **Chankillo**[5] 4010 4-10-3 54 PaulHanagan 3 50
(Mark H Tompkins) *led for 2f: chsd wnr tl 6f out: rdn to chse wnr again 4f out tl 3f out: wknd u.p over 1f out* **5/2**[2]

-000 5 29 **Jessica's Gold**[12] 3788 4-9-7 37 AdamKirby 1
(Christine Dunnett) *t.k.h early: chsd ldrs tl stdd bk to rr after 3f out: rdn 4f out: sn lost tch: t.o* **50/1**

2m 31.55s (2.85) **Going Correction** -0.175s/f (Firm)
WFA 3 from 4yo 12lb 5 Ran SP% **107.9**
Speed ratings (Par 101): **82,79,78,76,55**
CSF £11.15 TOTE £2.10: £4.40, £2.60; EX 9.60 Trifecta £23.00 Pool: £2125.65 - 69.17 winning units..The winner was bought by John Mangan for 6,200gns
Owner D A Shekells **Bred** Shadwell Estate Company Limited **Trained** Newmarket, Suffolk
■ Stewards' Enquiry : Adam Beschizza two-day ban: used whip above permitted level (July 24-25)

FOCUS
A desperately weak race, even by selling standards, and it's hard to get too excited by the victory of the well-supported favourite. Shaky form.

4179 ESSEX AND SUFFOLK WATER H'CAP 1m 6f 17y
3:10 (3:11) (Class 5) (0-70,67) 4-Y-0+ **£2,587** (£770; £384; £192) **Stalls** High

Form RPR

5103 1 **Meetings Man (IRE)**[19] 3085 6-9-7 67 (p) AdamKirby 2 74
(Ali Brewer) *prom: chsd ldr 12f out tl 9f out: wnt 2nd again 5f out: rdn and ev ch 3f out: led 2f out: sn hdd: hung rt but kpt on to ld wl ins fnl f* **9/4**[1]

-146 2 nk **Iceman George**[13] 3721 9-8-10 61 (v) PhilipPrince(5) 4 67
(Alison Hutchinson) *t.k.h: hld up in tch in rr: hdwy and c centre st: jnd ldrs 3f out: rdn and led over 1f out: sn hung rt: hdd and no ex wl ins fnl f* **12/1**

2401 3 2 1/2 **Dr Finley (IRE)**[36] 2968 6-9-2 65 (v) SimonPearce(3) 5 68
(Lydia Pearce) *t.k.h: hld up in tch in rr: hdwy to ld 9f out: jnd and rdn 3f out: hdd 2f out: styd pressing ldrs tl no ex and one pce ins fnl f* **5/1**[3]

33-0 4 2 1/4 **Outback (IRE)**[61] 1586 4-9-5 65 (p) MartinLane 6 65
(Neil King) *in tch in midfield: rdn and outpcd over 3f out: plugged on but no threat to ldrs fnl f* **7/1**

-053 5 2 1/4 **Astroscarlet**[12] 3792 4-8-2 48 NickyMackay 1 45
(Mark H Tompkins) *chsd ldr tl 12f out: styd chsng ldrs tl lost pl and rdn along 5f out: hdwy u.p over 2f out: no ex 1f out: wknd ins fnl f* **8/1**

4-53 6 4 **Panettone (IRE)**[15] 3655 4-9-1 61 DominicFox 7 52
(Roger Varian) *sn led: hdd 9f out: chsd ldr tl 5f out: rdn and lost pl 4f out: wknd and bhd 2f out* **7/2**[2]

3-00 7 17 **Native Colony**[64] 1502 5-9-1 61 (b) JimmyQuinn 3 28
(Neil King) *dwlt: in tch in last trio: rdn and no rspnse over 3f out: bhd 2f out* **10/1**

3m 9.75s (2.15) **Going Correction** -0.175s/f (Firm) 7 Ran SP% **110.1**
Speed ratings (Par 103): **86,85,84,83,81 79,69**
toteswingers 1&2 £6.90, 1&3 £2.20, 2&3 £10.00 CSF £27.58 TOTE £2.30: £1.50, £7.20; EX 33.20 Trifecta £185.70 Pool: £2364.58 - 9.54 winning units..
Owner Miss Ali Brewer **Bred** Hakan Keles **Trained** Eastbury, Berks

FOCUS
There were holes to be picked in the majority of these on paper and, with the race run at a steady tempo, it's debatable as to how well the form will work out. The winner did not need to find much on this year's form.

4180 WATERAID CHARITY FILLIES' H'CAP 1m 1f
3:40 (3:41) (Class 5) (0-70,70) 3-Y-0+ **£2,587** (£770; £384; £192) **Stalls** Low

Form RPR

4-42 1 **Qawaafy (USA)**[18] 3572 3-9-4 70 [1] PaulHanagan 3 83
(Roger Varian) *hmpd s: chsd ldng pair: rdn and chsd clr ldr 2f out: clsd u.p to ld ins fnl f: styd on wl and gng away at fin* **9/4**[2]

-632 2 1 1/2 **Visit Copenhagen (USA)**[13] 3722 3-9-4 70 AdamKirby 4 80
(Mrs K Burke) *taken down early: wnt lft s: led: rdn and clr ent fnl 2f: hdd ins fnl f: no ex and sn brushed aside by wnr: eased cl home* **15/2**

-223 3 3 1/4 **Waveguide (IRE)**[22] 3427 4-10-0 70 JamieSpencer 5 74
(David Simcock) *hld up wl off the pce in rr: rdn and effrt but stl plenty to do over 2f out: wnt modest 3rd jst over 1f out: one pce and no imp after* **13/2**[3]

11 4 3/4 **Drahem**[27] 3254 3-9-4 70 FrederikTylicki 6 71
(James Fanshawe) *hld up in last trio: rdn and effrt wl over 2f out: no real imp and plugged on same pce fnl f* **5/4**[1]

4605 5 6 **Maughami**[43] 2762 3-8-6 58 PaoloSirigu 2 46
(Marco Botti) *chsd wnr tl outpcd u.p ent fnl 2f: wknd and wl bhd fnl f* **33/1**

00-1 6 4 **Entrance**[33] 3056 5-8-2 51 oh1 ShelleyBirkett(7) 1 31
(Julia Feilden) *hld up in last trio: dropped to rr and rdn over 3f out: bhd fnl 2f* **20/1**

1m 53.52s (-2.28) **Going Correction** -0.175s/f (Firm)
WFA 3 from 4yo+ 10lb 6 Ran SP% **108.0**
Speed ratings (Par 100): **103,101,98,98,92 89**
toteswingers 1&2 £2.40, 1&3 £2.20, 2&3 £1.70 CSF £17.30 TOTE £3.10: £1.60, £1.90; EX 12.30 Trifecta £33.80 Pool: £2315.07 - 51.24 winning units..
Owner Hamdan Al Maktoum **Bred** Shadwell Farm LLC **Trained** Newmarket, Suffolk

FOCUS
Ordinary fillies' form with the favourite disappointing, but much to like about the performance of the winner.

4181 NORFOLK AND SUFFOLK ANIMAL TRUST H'CAP 7f 3y
4:10 (4:10) (Class 3) (0-90,85) 3-Y-0 **£7,246** (£2,168; £1,084; £542; £270) **Stalls** Centre

Form RPR

0010 1 **Skytrain**[4] 4078 3-8-13 78 SilvestreDeSousa 3 81
(Mark Johnston) *mde all: rdn 1/2-way: hrd pressed and drvn over 1f out: kpt on wl and asserted fnl 75yds* **11/4**[2]

-031 2 3/4 **Poisson D'Or**[27] 3259 4-9-9 80 TedDurcan 1 84
(Rae Guest) *hld up wl in tch in last pair: hdwy to chse wnr wl over 1f out: rdn and str chal ent fnl f: no ex and btn fnl 75yds* **2/1**[1]

1455 3 4 **Light Burst (USA)**[23] 3411 4-9-8 82 ThomasBrown(3) 5 75
(Ismail Mohammed) *hld up wl in tch in last pair: rdn and effrt over 2f out: swtchd rt and chsd ldng pair wl over 1f out: no ex and wknd fnl f* **4/1**

1-11 4 4 1/2 **Admiralty**[93] 1430 4-10-0 85 HarryBentley 4 66
(Ismail Mohammed) *chsd wnr: j. path over 5f out: rdn and unable qck over 2f out: 4th and btn over 1f out: wknd 1f out* **7/2**[3]

205 5 11 **Majestic Oasis**[11] 3835 4-9-9 80 JamieSpencer 2 40
(Robert Cowell) *chsd ldng pair: rdn and no rspnse ent fnl 2f: unbalanced and wl btn over 1f out: bhd and eased ins fnl f* **14/1**

1m 23.01s (-3.59) **Going Correction** -0.525s/f (Hard)
WFA 3 from 4yo+ 8lb 5 Ran SP% **108.9**
Speed ratings (Par 107): **99,98,93,88,75**
CSF £8.46 TOTE £2.80: £1.10, £2.20; EX 10.00 Trifecta £31.40 Pool: £1845.45 - 43.98 winning units..
Owner A D Spence **Bred** Brook Stud Bloodstock Ltd **Trained** Middleham Moor, N Yorks

FOCUS
A competitive handicap on paper despite the small field, but the winner got an easy lead and stepped up on his Newmarket win.

4182 SCROBY SANDS WINDFARM MEDIAN AUCTION MAIDEN STKS 1m 3y
4:40 (4:41) (Class 5) 3-Y-0 **£2,587** (£770; £384; £192) **Stalls** Centre

Form RPR
0002 1 **Ocean Applause**[19] 3537 3-9-5 72..............................(tp) BrettDoyle 10 82
(John Ryan) *hld up in tch in midfield: hdwy to chse ldr 2f out: clsd and upsides over 1f out: led 1f and sn rdn clr: comf* **9/4**[2]
2 3 1/2 **Bejeweled (IRE)** 3-9-0 0.. JimmyQuinn 9 71+
(Lady Cecil) *chsd ldrs: wnt 2nd 3f out tl 2f out: rn green and hung lft over 1f out: swtchd rt 1f out: no threat to wnr but kpt on to go 2nd again fnl 50yds* **6/1**[3]
0-02 3 1 1/2 **Jadesnumberone (IRE)**[28] 3201 3-9-0 75.................. JamieSpencer 5 66
(Michael Bell) *led and sn clr: rdn and hdd 1f out: sn btn: wknd and lost 2nd fnl 50yds* **6/4**[1]
05 4 6 **Petrify**[13] 3731 3-9-5 0.. KirstyMilczarek 2 57+
(Luca Cumani) *t.k.h: hld up wl in tch in midfield: pushed along and outpcd 2f out: wl hld 4th but plugged on fnl f* **33/1**
5 1 1/2 **Mylington Light** 3-9-0 0.. DominicFox 3 48+
(Roger Varian) *rn green in rr: rdn and struggling over 3f out: modest hdwy past btn horses over 1f out: nvr trbld ldrs* **22/1**
26 6 4 1/2 **Saigon City**[13] 3731 3-9-2 0.. PatrickHills(3) 7 43
(Luca Cumani) *in tch in midfield: rdn and lost pl 5f out: bhd and struggling 3f out: bhd fnl 2f* **10/1**
5 7 6 **Tornado Battle**[140] 729 3-9-5 0.............................. SilvestreDeSousa 6 29
(Mark Johnston) *t.k.h: chsd ldr tl 3f out: sn dropped out: wl bhd and eased ins fnl f* **10/1**
8 14 **One In A Thousand (IRE)** 3-9-0 0.............................. SaleemGolam 1
(Chris Dwyer) *t.k.h: rn green and a bhd: lost tch 3f out: t.o over 1f out* **125/1**
0 9 13 **Bahama Bay**[13] 3731 3-9-0 0.. HarryBentley 8
(Stuart Williams) *plld hrd: chsd ldrs tl lost pl qckly 1/2-way: t.o over 1f out* **100/1**

1m 36.03s (-4.57) **Going Correction** -0.525s/f (Hard) 9 Ran SP% **112.3**
Speed ratings (Par 100): **101,97,96,90,88 84,78,64,51**
toteswingers 1&2 £2.80, 1&3 £1.70, 2&3 £3.50 CSF £15.22 TOTE £2.60: £1.10, £3.00, £1.70; EX 18.10 Trifecta £41.10 Pool: £3497.91 - 63.69 winning units..
Owner W McLuskey **Bred** R G Levin **Trained** Newmarket, Suffolk
FOCUS
It's unlikely this maiden took a great deal of winning with the favourite disappointing again. The winner is rated in line with the better view of his Newmarket run.

4183 GREAT YARMOUTH TOURIST AUTHORITY H'CAP 1m 3y
5:10 (5:13) (Class 5) (0-75,75) 3-Y-0+ **£2,587** (£770; £384; £192) **Stalls** Centre

Form RPR
-053 1 **Macchiara**[18] 3583 4-9-10 73.............................. SilvestreDeSousa 2 84
(Rae Guest) *chsd ldng pair: rdn and chsd ldr 3f out: led 2f out: sn hdd but drew clr w rival ent fnl f: led again ins fnl f: kpt on* **10/3**[2]
0-22 2 hd **Footstepsintherain (IRE)**[7] 3951 3-9-3 75...................... TedDurcan 6 83
(David Lanigan) *t.k.h: hld up in tch in last pair: hdwy over 2f out: rdn to ld wl over 1f out: drvn and hdd ins fnl f: one pce u.p fnl 100yds* **8/11**[1]
361 3 6 **Jonnie Skull (IRE)**[12] 3788 7-9-4 67......................(vt) FrederikTylicki 3 63
(Phil McEntee) *led tl rdn and hdd 2f out: outpcd and btn jst over 1f out: no ch w ldrs but hld 3rd fnl f* **13/2**[3]
33- 4 1 **Red Shuttle**[348] 4541 6-9-3 71..............................[1] RobertTart(5) 5 65
(Andi Brown) *taken down early: stdd s: hld up in tch in last pair: rdn and effrt over 2f out: no ex and btn jst over 1f out* **10/1**
0260 5 3/4 **Rough Rock (IRE)**[19] 3534 8-8-13 65.............................. RyanClark(3) 4 57
(Chris Dwyer) *chsd ldr: rdn over 2f out: no ex and btn over 1f out: wl hld fnl f* **20/1**

1m 35.59s (-5.01) **Going Correction** -0.525s/f (Hard)
WFA 3 from 4yo+ 9lb 5 Ran SP% **108.2**
Speed ratings (Par 103): **104,103,97,96,96**
CSF £5.98 TOTE £3.60: £1.90, £1.10; EX 5.90 Trifecta £15.80 Pool: £3058.59 - 144.59 winning units..
Owner Mrs Linda P Fish **Bred** Horizon Bloodstock Limited **Trained** Newmarket, Suffolk
FOCUS
The market spoke heavily in favour of Footstepsintherain, but those that got involved in the 3yo at skinny prices were once again left licking their wounds. The time was decent for the small field and the first two were clear.
T/Plt: £45.50 to a £1 stake. Pool: £57,431.59 - 919.76 winning tickets. T/Qpdt: £14.60 to a £1 stake. Pool: £3592.18 - 181.51 winning tickets. SP

3914 BATH (L-H)
Thursday, July 11

OFFICIAL GOING: Firm (11.6)
Wind: Moderate behind Weather: Sunny

4191 MILLER CONSTRUCTION MAIDEN FILLIES' STKS 5f 11y
6:10 (6:11) (Class 5) 2-Y-0 **£2,587** (£770; £384; £192) **Stalls** Centre

Form RPR
1 **Blue Mood (IRE)** 2-9-0 0.. RobertHavlin 2 82+
(Saeed bin Suroor) *trckd ldrs: chal 2f out and sn led: c clr in own time fnl f: v easily* **2/1**[1]
4 2 6 **Flighty Peaches (IRE)**[18] 3605 2-9-0 0.............................. J-PGuillambert 3 60
(Rebecca Curtis) *led: jnd 2f out: sn hdd and rdn: no ch w wnr fnl f but hld on wl for 2nd* **6/1**
53 3 1 1/2 **State Anthem**[19] 3565 2-9-0 0.. SamHitchcott 6 55
(Mick Channon) *sn rdn and outpcd in rr: hdwy u.p 2f out: styd on to take wl hld 3rd fnl f* **4/1**[3]
4 1 **Eleventh Hour (IRE)** 2-9-0 0.. ChrisCatlin 1 51+
(Saeed bin Suroor) *sn green: wl bhd and sn drvn: stl struggling 2f out: styd on fnl f and gng on cl home but nvr any ch* **5/1**
025 5 2 1/4 **Tautira (IRE)**[14] 3724 2-9-0 0.. LukeMorris 4 43
(Michael Bell) *chsd ldrs in 3rd: rdn over 2f out: wknd appr fnl f* **11/4**[2]

1m 0.55s (-1.95) **Going Correction** -0.20s/f (Firm) 5 Ran SP% **111.0**
Speed ratings (Par 91): **107,97,95,93,89**
CSF £14.04 TOTE £3.20: £1.30, £3.80; EX 14.70 Trifecta £60.60 Pool: £1280.62 - 15.84 winning units..
Owner Godolphin **Bred** David Eiffe **Trained** Newmarket, Suffolk
FOCUS
An interesting maiden. It was run at a fast pace and a well-backed Godolphin newcomer scored in great style. The outsider Brean Splash Susie was withdrawn after falling down in the stalls.

4192 BATH BUSINESS RACEDAY JULY 16TH H'CAP 1m 5f 22y
6:40 (6:40) (Class 6) (0-60,54) 4-Y-0+ **£1,940** (£577; £288; £144) **Stalls** High

Form RPR
15 1 **Speed Steed (IRE)**[22] 671 6-9-7 54..........................(v[1]) CathyGannon 5 62
(Tim Vaughan) *trckd ldr: rdn over 3f out: chal u.p 2f out tl led appr fnl f: styd on wl* **9/2**
6334 2 3 **Glens Wobbly**[26] 3312 5-8-7 45.. RyanTate(5) 4 49
(Jonathan Geake) *led: rdn and jnd 2f out: hdd appr fnl f: styd on same pce u.p* **9/4**[1]
0303 3 1 3/4 **Fushicho**[28] 3252 4-9-0 47.. ChrisCatlin 1 48
(Brendan Powell) *chsd ldrs in 3rd: rdn over 3f out: styd on same pce u.p fnl 2f* **7/2**[3]
500- 4 1 1/4 **Nicky Nutjob (GER)**[18] 4988 7-8-12 45..........................(p) LukeMorris 2 44
(John O'Shea) *in rr: rdn over 3f out: mod hdwy 2f out: styd on same pce* **9/1**
6000 5 6 **Numen (IRE)**[11] 3213 9-8-7 47..............................(p) JoshBaudains(7) 3 37
(Barry Brennan) *in rr: hdwy after 5f: rdn over 3f out: nvr rchd ldrs and wknd over 1f out* **25/1**
0543 6 3 1/2 **Red Current**[8] 3953 9-8-11 49...................... WilliamTwiston-Davies(5) 6 34
(Michael Scudamore) *in tch: rdn and effrt over 3f out: nvr rchd ldrs and wknd 2f out* **11/4**[2]

2m 54.91s (2.91) **Going Correction** -0.20s/f (Firm) 6 Ran SP% **111.7**
Speed ratings (Par 101): **83,81,80,79,75 73**
toteswingers 1&2 £2.10, 2&3 £1.70, 1&3 £1.10 CSF £14.89 TOTE £3.50: £1.10, £1.80; EX 15.40 Trifecta £42.20 Pool: £835.76 - 14.85 winning units..
Owner J H Frost **Bred** Michael Thornton **Trained** Aberthin, Vale of Glamorgan
FOCUS
They went a steady pace in this weak handicap. The first two were always prominent and the hold-up performers couldn't get involved. The runner-up is the best guide.

4193 EXCALIBUR COMMUNICATIONS (S) STKS 1m 5y
7:10 (7:10) (Class 6) 3-4-Y-0 **£1,940** (£577; £288; £144) **Stalls** Low

Form RPR
3153 1 **Harbour Captain (IRE)**[15] 3678 3-9-3 68.............................. CathyGannon 4 69
(Jo Hughes) *mde all: rdn fr 2f out: styd on strly fnl f* **4/1**[3]
1002 2 4 **For Shia And Lula (IRE)**[10] 3885 4-9-7 55(p) WilliamTwiston-Davies(5) 1 62
(Daniel Mark Loughnane) *in rr but in tch: rdn 3f out: hdwy over 1f out: styd on to take 2nd fnl 110yds but no ch w wnr* **6/1**
2245 3 2 **Newnton Lodge**[2] 4153 4-9-6 60.. LiamJones 7 51
(Ian Williams) *pressed wnr early: styd in 2nd and rdn 3f out: outpcd fr over 1f out: wknd and dropped to 3rd fnl 110yds* **2/1**[2]
1334 4 3 3/4 **Hidden Link**[20] 3528 3-9-3 69..............................(p) LukeMorris 3 47
(Ronald Harris) *chsd ldrs: rdn over 3f out: styd on u.p in 3rd 2f out: wknd fnl f* **7/4**[1]
6036 5 2 1/2 **Grey Gazelle**[21] 3488 3-8-6 60.. SamHitchcott 6 30
(Mick Channon) *s.i.s: in rr: rdn over 3f out: mod prog over 2f out: sn btn* **20/1**
0400 6 6 **Kaahen (USA)**[15] 3679 3-8-8 37..............................(p) CharlesBishop(3) 5 21
(Pat Eddery) *chsd ldrs: rdn over 3f out: sn btn* **100/1**
0 7 shd **Kid Wizzard (USA)**[12] 3819 4-9-1 0..........................(bt[1]) EDLinehan(5) 2 23
(David Flood) *rdn 4f out: a in rr* **66/1**

1m 39.71s (-1.09) **Going Correction** -0.20s/f (Firm)
WFA 3 from 4yo 9lb 7 Ran SP% **111.2**
Speed ratings (Par 101): **97,93,91,87,84 78,78**
toteswingers 1&2 £3.20, 2&3 £3.50, 1&3 £2.00 CSF £25.63 TOTE £4.40: £1.80, £3.80; EX 22.00 Trifecta £89.80 Pool: £936.55 - 7.82 winning units..The winner was bought in 7,500gns.
Owner Jo Hughes & James Hearne **Bred** Paul Kavanagh **Trained** Lambourn, Berks
FOCUS
There was an emphatic all-the-way winner in this seller and the top two in the market were disappointing. The runner-up sets the standard.

4194 CREST NICHOLSON BATH RIVERSIDE H'CAP 1m 2f 46y
7:40 (7:40) (Class 4) (0-85,85) 3-Y-0+ **£4,690** (£1,395; £697; £348) **Stalls** Low

Form RPR
-312 1 **Big Thunder**[30] 3173 3-8-7 75.. LukeMorris 1 88+
(Sir Mark Prescott Bt) *sn drvn along: in tch: chsd ldrs and rdn 5f out: wnt 2nd u.p 2f out: chal and rdn appr fnl f: sn slt advantage: a jst doing enough under hrd riding* **10/11**[1]
0265 2 nk **Salutation (IRE)**[6] 4023 3-9-3 85.. LiamJones 2 97
(Mark Johnston) *pressed ldr: led over 4f out: hrd drvn and jnd over 1f out: sn narrowly hdd: styd pressing wnr tl no ex in clsng stages* **9/4**[2]
3143 3 10 **Perfect Cracker**[9] 3917 5-8-12 74.. RyanTate(5) 4 66
(Clive Cox) *chsd ldrs: rdn to cl on ldng duo 3f out: wknd over 1f out* **4/1**[3]
3533 4 47 **Lutine Charlie (IRE)**[5] 4070 6-8-9 66 oh4...................... CathyGannon 3
(Pat Eddery) *led tl hdd over 4f out: wknd 3f out: eased whn no ch* **16/1**

2m 7.34s (-3.66) **Going Correction** -0.20s/f (Firm)
WFA 3 from 5yo+ 11lb 4 Ran SP% **109.0**
Speed ratings (Par 105): **106,105,97,60**
CSF £3.25 TOTE £1.50; EX 3.30 Trifecta £4.70 Pool: £481.60 - 76.06 winning units..
Owner John Brown & Megan Dennis **Bred** Stanley House Stud **Trained** Newmarket, Suffolk
FOCUS
The went a decent pace in this fair handicap and the two market leaders pulled clear. The winner continues to progress, while the second rates a small personal best.

4195 EVENCO GOLD H'CAP 1m 2f 46y
8:10 (8:10) (Class 6) (0-60,60) 3-Y-0+ **£1,940** (£577; £288; £144) **Stalls** Low

Form RPR
6-06 1 **Taro Tywod (IRE)**[12] 3814 4-9-8 54.............................. TomMcLaughlin 7 64
(Mark Brisbourne) *led tl hdd 7f out: styd trcking ldr: chal 2f out: led and edgd lft appr fnl f: kpt on wl* **9/2**[3]
033 2 3/4 **St Ignatius**[4] 4099 6-9-5 58..............................(p) TimClark(7) 5 67
(Alan Bailey) *pushed along to chse ldr and led 7f out: rdn and jnd 2f out: hdd: n.m.r and swtchd rt appr fnl f: kpt on wl in clsng stages: a hld by wnr but wl clr of 3rd* **10/3**[1]
003 3 10 **Mullins Way (USA)**[14] 3727 5-9-10 56.............................. J-PGuillambert 2 45
(Jo Hughes) *in tch: drvn to take 3rd over 2f out: nvr rchd ldng duo and wknd over 1f out* **10/3**[1]
0016 4 1 1/4 **Hawaiian Freeze**[16] 3656 4-9-1 47.............................. StevieDonohoe 8 33
(John Stimpson) *in rr: pushed along and styd on over 2f out: tk mod 4th u.p over 1f out* **12/1**

The Form Book Flat, Raceform Ltd, Compton, RG20 6NL.

004- **5** 2 **Santadelacruze**[214] 8049 4-9-13 **59**...(p) WilliamCarson 6 41
(Gary Moore) *in rr: drvn and hdwy on outside over 3f out: nvr rchd ldrs and wknd ins fnl 2f* **8/1**

46-0 **6** ½ **Edgeworth (IRE)**[24] 3410 7-9-9 **60**...(p) WilliamTwiston-Davies(5) 4 41
(David Bridgwater) *sn in tch: chsd ldrs 6f out: rdn 3f out: wknd over 2f out* **4/1**[2]

0-00 **7** 9 **Endura**[27] 3272 3-8-3 **46** oh1... LukeMorris 3 9
(Harry Dunlop) *chsd ldrs: ridd 6f out: wknd 3f out* **10/1**

0300 **8** 1 **Rapid Water**[23] 3433 7-9-6 **52**...(p) CathyGannon 1 13
(Pat Eddery) *t.k.h: chsd ldrs: rdn 3f out: wknd over 2f out* **25/1**

2m 8.92s (-2.08) **Going Correction** -0.20s/f (Firm)
WFA 3 from 4yo+ 11lb **8** Ran SP% **116.1**
Speed ratings (Par 101): **100,99,91,90,88 88,81,80**
toteswingers 1&2 £2.60, 2&3 £2.30, 1&3 £3.80 CSF £20.25 CT £56.13 TOTE £6.80: £1.70, £1.40, £1.60; EX 31.80 Trifecta £70.80 Pool: £676.92 - 7.16 winning units..
Owner Rasio Cymru Racing 1 **Bred** Pat Fullam **Trained** Great Ness, Shropshire

FOCUS
They went a steady gallop in this low-grade handicap and the two pacesetters pulled a long way clear. The form is not rated as positively as it might have been given the grade and ground.

4196 NFU MUTUAL CLIFTON H'CAP 1m 3f 144y
8:40 (8:40) (Class 6) (0-65,65) 3-Y-O **£1,940** (£577; £288; £144) **Stalls** Low

Form RPR

00-1 **1** **Portrait**[9] 3918 3-9-9 **65** 6ex... LukeMorris 5 76+
(Sir Mark Prescott Bt) *chsd ldr: rdn along 5f out: u.p fr 3f out: led 2f out: hrd drvn fr over 1f out: a doing enough in clsng stages* **1/4**[1]

3536 **2** ½ **Bee Jay Kay**[12] 3820 3-9-7 **63**... SamHitchcott 3 73
(Mick Channon) *racd in 4th: rdn and hdwy 3f out: chsd wnr over 1f out: kpt on wl to cl u.p fnl f but a hld in clsng stages* **10/1**[3]

-351 **3** 11 **Sovereign Power**[23] 3428 3-9-3 **62**... AshleyMorgan(3) 2 53
(Paul Cole) *led: rdn and hdd 2f out: wknd over 1f out* **7/1**[2]

5030 **4** 3¼ **See And Be Seen**[12] 3820 3-8-3 **45**... CathyGannon 4 31
(Sylvester Kirk) *racd in 3rd: rdn over 3f out: wknd 2f out* **16/1**

2m 28.44s (-2.16) **Going Correction** -0.20s/f (Firm) **4** Ran SP% **107.5**
Speed ratings (Par 98): **99,98,91,89**
CSF £3.39 TOTE £1.10; EX 3.00 Trifecta £2.90 Pool: £527.99 - 132.76 winning units..
Owner Denford Stud **Bred** Denford Stud Ltd **Trained** Newmarket, Suffolk

FOCUS
The hot odds-on favourite had to work hard to defy a penalty in this middle-distance handicap. No depth to this race, the level of which revolves around the second.

4197 GRANGE JAGUAR SWINDON H'CAP 5f 161y
9:10 (9:10) (Class 5) (0-70,70) 3-Y-O+ **£2,587** (£770; £384; £192) **Stalls** Centre

Form RPR

3002 **1** **Comptonspirit**[9] 3920 9-9-2 **65**... MatthewLawson(5) 1 76
(Brian Baugh) *chsd ldrs: led wl over 1f: drvn out fnl f* **7/1**

4305 **2** 2½ **The Name Is Frank**[15] 3700 8-8-3 **54**...(t) OisinMurphy(7) 3 56
(Mark Gillard) *chsd ldrs: rdn to dispute 2nd fnl 110yds: chsd wnr in clsng stages but no imp* **9/2**[2]

0041 **3** shd **Hamis Al Bin (IRE)**[16] 3660 4-9-3 **61**... LukeMorris 8 63
(Milton Bradley) *in rr: hdwy over 2f out: styd on u.p to dispute 2nd fnl 110yds: no imp on wnr and dropped to 3rd in clsng stages* **7/4**[1]

0604 **4** 2½ **Samba Night (IRE)**[10] 3888 4-8-8 **52**...(bt) SteveDrowne 4 46
(Jeremy Gask) *in tch: rdn and hdwy over 1f out: styd on to take n.d 4th last strides* **16/1**

5543 **5** ½ **Volcanic Dust (IRE)**[21] 3498 5-8-10 **54**...(t) CathyGannon 6 46
(Milton Bradley) *pressed ldr: slt ld 2f out: hdd wl over 1f out: wknd fnl f and lost 4th last strides* **12/1**

1605 **6** 5 **Alpha Delta Whisky**[35] 3010 5-9-12 **70**... ChrisCatlin 2 45
(John Gallagher) *slt ld tl hdd 2f out: wknd wl over 1f out* **13/2**

2660 **7** 4 **Kyllachy Storm**[12] 3841 9-8-5 **54**... PhilipPrince(5) 10 15
(Ron Hodges) *outpcd* **5/1**[3]

5060 **8** 7 **Athwaab**[16] 3660 6-8-11 **55**...(t) WilliamCarson 7
(Simon Hodgson) *outpcd* **33/1**

1m 10.32s (-0.88) **Going Correction** -0.20s/f (Firm) **8** Ran SP% **113.6**
Speed ratings (Par 103): **97,93,93,90,89 82,77,68**
toteswingers 1&2 £11.10, 2&3 £2.50, 1&3 £4.30 CSF £37.86 CT £78.91 TOTE £5.50: £2.50, £2.20, £1.10; EX 31.70 Trifecta £156.40 Pool: £606.32 - 2.90 winning units..
Owner G B Hignett **Bred** Mrs F Wilson **Trained** Audley, Staffs

FOCUS
It was fast and furious in this competitive sprint handicap and the first four came from off the pace. The winner rates to her form from this time last year.
T/Plt: £55.00 to a £1 stake. Pool of £56710.13 - 752.36 winning tickets. T/Qpdt: £8.20 to a £1 stake. Pool of £4546.34 - 406.75 winning tickets. ST

4011 DONCASTER (L-H)
Thursday, July 11

OFFICIAL GOING: Good to firm (9.6)
Rail out on Round course from 10f to entrance to home straight.
Wind: Light half behind Weather: Fine and dry

4198 FREEBETS.CO.UK EXCLUSIVE WILLIAM HILL FREE BET H'CAP 7f
2:00 (2:00) (Class 5) (0-75,75) 3-Y-O+ **£2,587** (£770; £384; £192) **Stalls** High

Form RPR

4506 **1** **Victoire De Lyphar (IRE)**[12] 3811 6-9-12 **73**...(e) PJMcDonald 3 85
(Ruth Carr) *trckd ldrs: hdwy 2f out: rdn to ld appr fnl f: kpt on strly* **5/1**[2]

5304 **2** 2½ **Illustrious Prince (IRE)**[20] 3546 6-8-12 **64**... JasonHart(5) 8 69
(Declan Carroll) *cl up: led wl over 2f out: rdn over 1f out: hdd appr fnl f: sn drvn and kpt on* **7/1**

4005 **3** 1 **Barney McGrew (IRE)**[12] 3811 10-10-0 **75**... PaulMulrennan 4 77
(Michael Dods) *hld up in tch: hdwy 2f out: rdn fnl f: kpt on: nrst fin* **8/1**

0-06 **4** nk **Evervescent (IRE)**[14] 3741 4-9-11 **72**...(b[1]) SeanLevey 10 73
(J S Moore) *chsd ldrs: rdn along wl over 1f out: drvn and one pce fnl f* **16/1**

3221 **5** 2¼ **Gold Beau (FR)**[19] 3593 3-8-12 **67**...(p) MickyFenton 6 59
(Kristin Stubbs) *led: rdn along and hdd wl over 2f out: drvn over 1f out and grad wknd* **8/1**

0140 **6** shd **Who's Shirl**[15] 3686 7-9-9 **70**... TedDurcan 1 65
(Chris Fairhurst) *in rr: pushed along 3f out: rdn over 2f out: styd on fnl f: nrst fin* **20/1**

6-56 **7** hd **Imperator Augustus (IRE)**[7] 3981 5-9-11 **72**... DuranFentiman 11 67
(Patrick Holmes) *hld up towards rr: hdwy wl over 2f out: rdn wl over 1f out: kpt on same pce fnl f* **14/1**

-354 **8** 1¾ **Fame Again**[21] 3506 5-9-10 **71**... PhillipMakin 5 61
(Michael Easterby) *cl up: rdn along wl over 2f out: sn wknd* **9/2**[1]

2125 **9** 1¾ **Darkside**[14] 3730 3-8-9 **64**... RoystonFfrench 2 46+
(Tracy Waggott) *in rr and swtchd rt to r alone stands' rail after 2f: rdn along 3f out: nvr a factor* **6/1**[3]

0-00 **10** 1½ **Clumber Place**[23] 3445 7-9-0 **61**... DaleSwift 7 42
(James Given) *in tch: rdn along 3f out: sn wknd* **66/1**

0210 **11** 1 **Ptolemy**[26] 3337 4-9-0 **61**... GrahamGibbons 12 39
(David Barron) *a towards rr* **8/1**

-500 **12** ¾ **Bayleyf (IRE)**[31] 3153 4-10-0 **75**... DavidNolan 9 51
(John Best) *chsd ldrs: rdn along wl over 2f out: sn wknd* **50/1**

1m 23.88s (-2.42) **Going Correction** -0.40s/f (Firm)
WFA 3 from 4yo+ 8lb **12** Ran SP% **115.7**
Speed ratings (Par 103): **97,94,93,92,90 89,89,87,85,84 82,82**
toteswingers 1&2 £6.90, 2&3 £9.50, 1&3 £10.40 CSF £38.33 CT £280.37 TOTE £5.60: £2.30, £2.00, £3.20; EX 38.50 Trifecta £235.40 Pool: £2245.40 - 7.15 winning units..
Owner Middleham Park Racing Xviii **Bred** Mrs Monica Hackett **Trained** Huby, N Yorks

FOCUS
Despite extensive watering over the previous four days the ground was quick. After the opener the consensus amongst the riders was that it was very quick. They raced in one group towards the centre, with one exception. The form is taken at face value with the second close to form.

4199 FREEBETS.CO.UK MOBILE BETTING EBF MAIDEN STKS 6f
2:30 (2:30) (Class 5) 2-Y-O **£2,911** (£866; £432; £216) **Stalls** High

Form RPR

0 **1** **Mezel**[15] 3689 2-9-5 0... DaneO'Neill 7 77+
(Sir Michael Stoute) *t.k.h early: trckd ldrs: effrt 2f out: squeezed through ent fnl f: sn led: rdn and kpt on towards fin* **11/8**[1]

2 ¾ **Free Code (IRE)** 2-9-5 0... PaulMulrennan 6 75+
(James Tate) *cl up: led 2f out: rdn over 1f out: hdd ins fnl f: sn drvn and kpt on* **4/1**[2]

64 **3** 3½ **Sakhalin Star (IRE)**[21] 3500 2-9-5 0... MichaelO'Connell 1 63
(John Quinn) *t.k.h: trckd ldrs: cl up on outer 1/2-way: rdn and ev ch over 1f out: drvn and one pce fnl f* **8/1**

4 shd **Tez** 2-9-5 0... PaoloSirigu 4 63+
(Marco Botti) *t.k.h: trckd ldrs: effrt and green 2f out: rdn over 1f out: kpt on fnl f* **9/2**[3]

00 **5** 9 **Princess Myla (IRE)**[71] 1930 2-9-0 0... MickyFenton 5 29
(Paul Midgley) *dwlt and in rr: hdwy and cl up 1/2-way: rdn along over 2f out: sn wknd* **40/1**

6 nse **Desert Colours** 2-9-5 0... PhillipMakin 2 34
(Kevin Ryan) *led: rdn along and hdd 2f out: wknd over 1f out* **11/2**

7 10 **Elsie Bond** 2-9-0 0... DavidAllan 3
(Tim Easterby) *prom: pushed along 1/2-way: sn wknd* **20/1**

1m 13.78s (0.18) **Going Correction** -0.40s/f (Firm) **7** Ran SP% **114.0**
Speed ratings (Par 94): **82,81,76,76,64 64,50**
toteswingers 1&2 £1.80, 2&3 £4.70, 1&3 £3.60 CSF £7.05 TOTE £2.10: £1.20, £2.50; EX 8.40 Trifecta £39.20 Pool: £2184.78 - 41.72 winning units..
Owner Hamdan Al Maktoum **Bred** Shadwell Estate Company Limited **Trained** Newmarket, Suffolk

FOCUS
Previous form was thin on the ground but this was almost certainly an above-average maiden.

4200 FREEBETS.CO.UK DOWNLOAD THE APP MAIDEN STKS 6f
3:05 (3:06) (Class 5) 3-Y-O+ **£2,587** (£770; £384; £192) **Stalls** High

Form RPR

42 **1** **Muthmir (IRE)**[14] 3731 3-9-5 0... DaneO'Neill 8 94+
(William Haggas) *trckd ldrs: smooth hdwy over 2f out: rdn and qcknd to ld appr fnl f: readily* **11/8**[2]

2 **2** 1¼ **Port Alfred**[12] 3837 3-9-5 0... HarryBentley 6 85
(Saeed bin Suroor) *cl up: led over 3f out: rdn and edgd lft over 1f out: sn hdd and kpt on same pce* **5/4**[1]

52 **3** 2¾ **Lulu The Zulu (IRE)**[13] 3759 5-9-6 0... AndrewMullen 2 72
(Michael Appleby) *t.k.h: trckd ldrs: hdwy 2f out: rdn to chse ldng pair over 1f out: sn no imp* **6/1**[3]

4 6 **Pilates (IRE)** 3-9-0 0... PaulMulrennan 5 52
(Mark Johnston) *towards rr: hdwy wl over 2f out: rdn wl over 1f out: no imp* **16/1**

56 **5** 1½ **Coire Gabhail**[12] 3837 3-9-0 0... SeanLevey 7 47
(Hughie Morrison) *dwlt and in rr: hdwy over 2f out: sn pushed along and n.d* **33/1**

0 **6** 13 **Sabrina's Secret**[13] 3774 3-9-0 0... MickyFenton 1
(Tom Tate) *sn led: hdd over 3f out: rdn along wl over 2f out: sn wknd* **100/1**

3- **7** ¾ **Hanalei Bay (IRE)**[301] 6175 3-9-2 0... RaulDaSilva(3) 4
(Keith Dalgleish) *cl up: rdn along 1/2-way: sn wknd* **10/1**

8 ¾ **Wishing Gate (IRE)** 3-9-5 0... GrahamGibbons 3
(David Barron) *prom: rdn along wl over 2f out: sn wknd* **50/1**

1m 10.21s (-3.39) **Going Correction** -0.40s/f (Firm)
WFA 3 from 5yo 6lb **8** Ran SP% **121.7**
Speed ratings (Par 103): **106,104,100,92,90 73,72,71**
toteswingers 1&2 £1.50, 2&3 £2.00, 1&3 £3.40 CSF £3.73 TOTE £2.80: £1.10, £1.30, £1.40; EX 5.10 Trifecta £15.30 Pool: £4027.24 - 196.61 winning units..
Owner Hamdan Al Maktoum **Bred** Sunderland Holdings Ltd **Trained** Newmarket, Suffolk

FOCUS
Again an above-average maiden, run in a fast time. The winner impressed and the first two should rate higher on pedigree.

4201 FREEBETS.CO.UK FREE BETS FILLIES' H'CAP 1m (R)
3:40 (3:40) (Class 4) (0-85,84) 3-Y-O+ **£4,690** (£1,395; £697; £348) **Stalls** Low

Form RPR

1431 **1** **Oddysey (IRE)**[23] 3443 4-10-0 **84**... LeeTopliss 2 92
(Michael Dods) *trckd ldrs: hdwy on outer wl over 2f out: rdn over 1f out: drvn to chal ent fnl f: kpt on to ld last 50yds* **6/4**[1]

4360 **2** nk **Lady Of The House (IRE)**[14] 3734 3-9-3 **82**...(p) PhillipMakin 3 87
(Kevin Ryan) *led: qcknd 3f out: rdn wl over 1f out: drvn ent fnl f: hdd and no ex last 50yds* **13/2**[3]

-542 **3** 3½ **Simply Shining (IRE)**[14] 3712 3-8-10 **75**... TonyHamilton 4 72
(Richard Fahey) *trckd ldr: hdwy over 2f out: rdn wl over 1f out: drvn and one pce fnl f* **13/8**[2]

0166 **4** ¾ **Spavento (IRE)**[7] 3983 7-9-3 **73**... DavidAllan 1 71
(Eric Alston) *trckd ldng pair: pushed along on inner 3f out: rdn 2f out: drvn and wknd appr fnl f* **16/1**

06-0 **5** *3* **Certral**[26] 3349 5-9-3 **76** .... PaulPickard(3) 5 67
(Mel Brittain) *hld up in rr: effrt 3f out: rdn 2f out: sn no imp* **8/1**
1m 36.82s (-2.88) **Going Correction** -0.25s/f (Firm)
WFA 3 from 4yo+ 9lb **5** Ran SP% **108.4**
Speed ratings (Par 102): **104,103,100,99,96**
CSF £10.93 TOTE £2.80: £1.70, £1.80; EX 8.30 Trifecta £13.60 Pool: £2145.29 - 117.75 winning units..
Owner Pearson & Lowthian **Bred** Darling Smile Syndicate **Trained** Denton, Co Durham
FOCUS
A good-class fillies' handicap and the first two pulled clear. The winner rates a small personal best.

4202 BONUS.CO.UK CASINO BONUS H'CAP 1m 4f
4:15 (4:15) (Class 4) (0-85,85) 3-Y-0+ **£4,690** (£1,395; £697; £348) **Stalls** Low

Form RPR
12 **1** **Renew (IRE)**[54] 2457 3-9-1 **85** .... [1] DaneO'Neill 2 95
(Marco Botti) *trckd ldr: cl up 4f out: led 3f out: rdn 2f out: hdd over 1f out: drvn to ld again ent fnl f: kpt on wl* **7/2**[2]
1- **2** *¾* **Wadi Al Hattawi (IRE)**[292] 6501 3-8-12 **82** .... HarryBentley 5 90+
(Saeed bin Suroor) *dwlt: green and hld up in rr: hdwy on outer 3f out: chsd ldng pair and edgd lft 2f out: rdn and styng on whn hmpd over 1f out: swtchd lft and styng on whn n.m.r ins fnl f: kpt on wl towards fin* **11/10**[1]
0123 **3** *nk* **Masquerading (IRE)**[22] 3470 3-9-0 **84** .... TedDurcan 6 91
(David Lanigan) *trckd ldng pair: hdwy 3f out: cl up 2f out: rdn to take slt ld whn hung rt jst over 1f out: hdd ent fnl f: sn drvn and edgd lft: no ex last 100yds* **7/2**[2]
0123 **4** *shd* **Reve De Nuit (USA)**[26] 3345 7-9-9 **80** .... ShaneKelly 4 87
(Mrs K Burke) *trckd ldrs: hdwy on inner wl over 2f out: rdn wl over 1f out: n.m.r ent fnl f: sn drvn and one pce* **12/1**[3]
0645 **5** *12* **Royal Peculiar**[15] 3685 5-9-8 **79** .... AndrewMullen 1 67
(Michael Appleby) *t.k.h: trckd ldng pair: effrt on inner 4f out: rdn along 3f out: sn drvn and btn* **14/1**
-003 **6** *4* **Dark Dune (IRE)**[12] 3808 5-9-2 **73** .... DavidAllan 3 55
(Tim Easterby) *led: pushed along 4f out: rdn and hdd 3f out: sn wknd* **40/1**
3012 **7** *4* **Sir Boss (IRE)**[12] 3804 8-9-6 **84** .... JoeyHaynes(7) 7 59
(Michael Mullineaux) *hld up: effrt and hdwy over 3f out: rdn wl over 2f out: sn btn* **33/1**
2m 30.02s (-4.88) **Going Correction** -0.25s/f (Firm)
WFA 3 from 5yo+ 13lb **7** Ran SP% **111.8**
Speed ratings (Par 105): **106,105,105,105,97 94,91**
toteswingers 1&2 £1.90, 2&3 £2.00, 1&3 £2.20 CSF £7.36 TOTE £3.80: £1.90, £1.60; EX 10.30 Trifecta £25.70 Pool: £3738.82 - 109.06 winning units..
Owner Giuliano Manfredini **Bred** Premier Bloodstock **Trained** Newmarket, Suffolk
FOCUS
An interesting handicap which makes fair bit of sense on paper. Decent form, rated around the third.

4203 WINNINGPOST.CO.UK HORSE RACING RESULTS H'CAP 5f
4:50 (4:51) (Class 5) (0-75,75) 3-Y-0+ **£2,587** (£770; £384; £192) **Stalls** High

Form RPR
6001 **1** **Sleepy Blue Ocean**[5] 4074 7-9-5 **68** 6ex .... (p) RobertWinston 11 80
(John Balding) *cl up on outer: hdwy wl over 1f out: rdn to ld ent fnl f: kpt on wl* **11/1**
0522 **2** *¾* **Diman Waters (IRE)**[9] 3933 6-9-7 **75** .... JasonHart(5) 5 84
(Eric Alston) *a.p: cl up 2f out: rdn to chal wl over 1f out and ev ch tl drvn and nt qckn ins fnl f* **6/1**[3]
4136 **3** *½* **Monumental Man**[16] 3658 4-9-10 **73** .... (p) DaneO'Neill 3 80
(James Unett) *led: rdn wl over 1f out: hdd and drvn ent fnl f: kpt on same pce* **25/1**
1111 **4** *3¾* **Nafa (IRE)**[10] 3888 5-9-6 **69** 6ex .... ShaneKelly 7 63
(Daniel Mark Loughnane) *chsd ldrs: hdwy 2f out: sn rdn and ch tl drvn appr fnl f and sn one pce* **5/1**[2]
0001 **5** *shd* **Chunky Diamond (IRE)**[6] 4018 4-9-1 **71** .... KevinStott(7) 10 64
(Ruth Carr) *hld up towards rr: hdwy on outer 2f out: rdn and hung bdly lft over 1f out: one pce after* **2/1**[1]
6005 **6** *1* **Lady Royale**[29] 3190 5-9-2 **65** .... (b) PaulMulrennan 2 55
(Geoffrey Oldroyd) *towards rr: pushed along over 2f out: sn rdn and styd on fnl f: nrst fin* **25/1**
0-54 **7** *1* **Eland Ally**[21] 3487 5-9-12 **75** .... MickyFenton 1 61
(Tom Tate) *prom: rdn along on outer 2f out: sn drvn and wknd over 1f out* **20/1**
1205 **8** *1¼* **Mey Blossom**[6] 4017 8-8-10 **64** .... (p) GeorgeChaloner(5) 8 46
(Richard Whitaker) *nvr bttr than midfield* **25/1**
50-0 **9** *1* **I'll Be Good**[13] 3778 4-9-3 **69** .... MarkCoumbe(3) 4 47
(Robert Johnson) *chsd ldrs: rdn along over 2f out: sn wknd* **50/1**
2442 **10** *1½* **Mercers Row**[5] 4074 6-8-13 **69** .... GemmaTutty(7) 6 42
(Karen Tutty) *a in rr: outpcd fr 1/2-way* **6/1**[3]
-313 **11** *hd* **Flirtinaskirt**[36] 2994 3-9-5 **73** .... SeanLevey 9 43
(Ed McMahon) *a in rr* **7/1**
57.95s (-2.55) **Going Correction** -0.40s/f (Firm)
WFA 3 from 4yo+ 5lb **11** Ran SP% **117.7**
Speed ratings (Par 103): **104,102,102,96,95 94,92,90,89,86 86**
toteswingers 1&2 £7.30, 2&3 £15.10, 1&3 £20.70 CSF £70.34 CT £1660.11 TOTE £14.50: £3.20, £2.00, £6.70; EX 71.40 Trifecta £1448.20 Pool: £3623.11 - 1.87 winning units..
Owner Tykes And Terriers Racing Club **Bred** Exors Of The Late N Ahamad & P C Scott **Trained** Scrooby, Notts
FOCUS
The first three finished clear. Straightforward form to an ordinary handicap.

4204 AMATEUR JOCKEYS' ASSOCIATION H'CAP (FOR AMATEUR RIDERS) 2m 110y
5:25 (5:25) (Class 6) (0-65,65) 4-Y-0+ **£1,871** (£580; £290; £145) **Stalls** Low

Form RPR
-362 **1** **Green To Gold (IRE)**[14] 3744 8-11-0 **65** .... (b) MrSWalker 3 75
(Don Cantillon) *hld up towards rr: stdy hdwy 6f out: trckd ldrs 3f out: effrt whn n.m.r and squeezed through to chal wl over 1f out: sn rdn: styd on to ld ent fnl f: drvn out* **11/4**[2]
00-0 **2** *hd* **Joyful Motive**[19] 3589 4-9-2 **46** oh1 .... MissEmilyBullock(7) 13 55
(Tom Tate) *chsd ldrs and wd bnd after 1f: hdwy over 4f out: cl up 3f out: rdn over 2f out: slt ld wl over 1f out: hdd ent fnl f: kpt on gamely tl no ex nr fin* **66/1**
05-0 **3** *5* **Strikemaster (IRE)**[33] 3089 7-9-9 **51** .... (t) MrAaronJames(5) 6 54
(Lee James) *hld up towards rr: hdwy on outer over 4f out: rdn along wl over 2f out: styd on appr fnl f: nrst fin* **25/1**
4005 **4** *nse* **Raleigh Quay (IRE)**[14] 3709 6-10-2 **58** .... MissBeckySmith(5) 2 61
(Micky Hammond) *in tch: hdwy over 3f out: rdn to chse ldrs over 2f out: sn ev ch on inner tl styd on same pce appr fnl f* **16/1**
2223 **5** *4½* **Kodicil (IRE)**[25] 3363 5-11-0 **65** .... (p) MissJCoward 7 63
(Tim Walford) *prom: effrt on inner to dispute ld 3f out: rdn and led briefly 2f out: sn hdd and drvn wl over 1f out: grad wknd* **9/4**[1]
0-00 **6** *1½* **Tenacity**[19] 3589 4-9-5 **47** .... AnnaHesketh(5) 11 43
(Karen Tutty) *in tch: hdwy on inner to chse ldrs 1/2-way: pushed along and sltly outpcd over 4f out: plugged on fnl 2f* **40/1**
0040 **7** *nk* **Shirls Son Sam**[19] 3595 5-9-6 **46** .... MrJHamilton(3) 5 42
(Chris Fairhurst) *t.k.h: in tch: hdwy to trck ldrs after 4f: trckd ldr over 6f out: effrt to ld over 3f out: sn rdn: hdd 2f out and grad wknd* **25/1**
0050 **8** *1¼* **Maid Of Meft**[34] 3065 6-10-2 **58** .... MissHDukes(5) 1 52
(Paul Midgley) *hld up towards rr: hdwy over 5f out: rdn and in tch 3f out: sn drvn and btn* **15/2**
5506 **9** *5* **Merrjanah**[28] 3244 5-9-2 **46** oh1 .... MrAFrench(7) 4 34
(Neville Bycroft) *hld up: a in rr* **40/1**
5602 **10** *2½* **Jeu De Roseau (IRE)**[13] 3771 9-10-2 **58** .... MrRSmith(5) 12 43
(Chris Grant) *midfield: hdwy to chse ldrs over 5f out: rdn along over 3f out: wknd over 2f out* **14/1**
0421 **11** *18* **Maska Pony (IRE)**[19] 3589 9-9-12 **56** .... MissKHowden(7) 9 20+
(George Moore) *dwlt: racd wd: a bhd* **6/1**[3]
0516 **12** *1* **Josie's Dream (IRE)**[13] 3792 5-10-0 **56** .... MrJamesHughes(5) 8 19
(Jo Hughes) *led: rdn along over 4f out: hdd over 3f out: sn wknd* **20/1**
5/ **13** *19* **Cloudgazer (IRE)**[194] 8027 5-10-7 **65** .... MrWDegnan(7) 10 5
(Giles Bravery) *chsd ldrs: rdn along 5f out: sn wknd: bhd fnl 2f* **18/1**
3m 36.29s (-4.11) **Going Correction** -0.25s/f (Firm) **13** Ran SP% **120.1**
Speed ratings (Par 101): **99,98,96,96,94 93,93,92,90,89 80,80,71**
toteswingers 1&2 £34.90, 2&3 £117.00, 1&3 £18.30 CSF £200.90 CT £3825.35 TOTE £3.10: £1.80, £20.60, £7.70; EX 170.10 Trifecta £2353.00 Part won. Pool: £3137.42 - 0.39 winning units..
Owner Sir Alex Ferguson & Sotirios Hassiakos **Bred** Dominic O'Neill And Julie White **Trained** Newmarket, Suffolk
■ Stewards' Enquiry : Miss Becky Smith four-day ban: used whip above permitted level (Jul 27,30,31,Aug 2)
FOCUS
A modest amateur riders' handicap and the first two pulled clear after what had been a strong gallop for the grade. A Flat personal best from the winner.
T/Plt: £45.00 to a £1 stake. Pool of £68420.08 - 1107.76 winning tickets. T/Qpdt: £10.50 to a £1 stake. Pool of £4264.48 - 298.80 winning tickets. JR

3971 EPSOM (L-H)
Thursday, July 11

OFFICIAL GOING: Good to firm (8.5)
Rail out from 1m to Winning Post, up to 8yds from 8f to 6f and 3yds from 6f to finish.
Wind: Light, half behind Weather: Sunny, warm

4205 STEVE DONOGHUE APPRENTICE H'CAP 1m 2f 18y
6:20 (6:21) (Class 5) (0-75,73) 4-Y-0+ **£3,234** (£962; £481; £240) **Stalls** Low

Form RPR
3034 **1** **Xinbama (IRE)**[22] 3468 4-9-6 **72** .... (t) ShelleyBirkett(5) 2 82
(J W Hills) *trckd ldr and clr of rest to 1/2-way: shkn up to ld over 2f out: styd on strly fnl f* **4/1**[3]
31-5 **2** *1½* **Ever Fortune (USA)**[17] 3617 4-9-12 **73** .... ThomasBrown 6 80+
(Rae Guest) *hld up: prog and 4th st: rdn wl over 2f out: prog to chse wnr over 1f out: styd on but no imp last 150yds* **2/1**[1]
0522 **3** *4* **Megalala (IRE)**[9] 3925 12-8-9 **59** .... MichaelJMMurphy(3) 3 58
(John Bridger) *led at gd pce: hdd over 2f out: lost 2nd and fdd over 1f out* **5/1**
3262 **4** *1½* **Norfolk Sky**[7] 3971 4-9-0 **68** .... AaronChave(7) 4 64
(Laura Mongan) *hld up: chsd clr ldng pair 1/2-way: clsd ent st: rdn and no imp over 2f out: fdd over 1f out* **3/1**[2]
4354 **5** *2½* **Standing Strong (IRE)**[16] 3656 5-9-1 **62** .... (p) RossAtkinson 7 53
(Zoe Davison) *hld up in last: urged along and no prog 3f out: modest late hdwy* **14/1**
030 **6** *¾* **Ermyntrude**[9] 3924 6-8-1 **55** .... SophieRalston(7) 5 45
(Pat Phelan) *a in rr: 5th st: pushed along and no prog over 2f out* **25/1**
-203 **7** *3¾* **Bert The Alert**[118] 1010 5-9-5 **71** .... NedCurtis(5) 1 53
(Gary Moore) *chsd clr ldng pair to 1/2-way: 6th and losing pl st: sn struggling* **14/1**
2m 9.3s (-0.40) **Going Correction** 0.0s/f (Good) **7** Ran SP% **112.2**
Speed ratings (Par 103): **101,99,96,95,93 92,89**
toteswingers 1&2 £1.40, 2&3 £2.70, 1&3 £3.10 CSF £11.95 TOTE £4.50: £1.80, £2.10; EX 15.80 Trifecta £82.20 Pool: £1409.97 - 12.86 winning units..
Owner Tony Waspe Partnership **Bred** P Heffernan **Trained** Upper Lambourn, Berks
FOCUS
Following a dry night and a warm day, the ground was officially good to firm. Racing began with a competitive, if moderate, apprentices' handicap. The winner is rated in line with his AW best.

4206 SUTTON MAIDEN AUCTION STKS 6f
6:50 (6:50) (Class 5) 2-Y-0 **£3,881** (£1,155; £577; £288) **Stalls** High

Form RPR
0 **1** **Reflected Love (IRE)**[7] 3986 2-8-6 0 .... NickyMackay 1 62+
(Mick Channon) *sn hld up: could nt handle hill wl and detached in last in st: shkn up 3f out: prog on outer 2f out: led and edgd rt jst ins fnl f: styd on wl* **11/2**[3]
2 *2* **Hot Amber (USA)** 2-8-8 0 .... SilvestreDeSousa 3 58
(Robert Cowell) *prog on outer to chse ldr over 4f out: rdn to ld 2f out: hdd jst ins fnl f: short of room sn after: one pce* **5/2**[2]
3 **3** *nse* **Jersey Cream (IRE)**[17] 3631 2-8-11 0 .... PatDobbs 2 60
(Gary Moore) *trckd ldrs: 3rd st: chsd ldr over 1f out: upsides jst ins fnl f: hld whn short of room sn after: one pce* **5/6**[1]
0 **4** *2½* **Morgans Bluff**[16] 3663 2-7-13 0 .... JemmaMarshall(5) 4 45
(Pat Phelan) *chsd ldr to over 4f out: sn in 4th: renewed effrt on inner 2f out: one pce over 1f out* **25/1**
5 **5** *3¼* **Unfashionable (IRE)**[66] 2067 2-8-6 0 .... MartinLane 5 37
(Stuart Kittow) *mde most to 2f out: steadily wknd* **8/1**
1m 11.25s (1.85) **Going Correction** 0.0s/f (Good) **5** Ran SP% **113.5**
Speed ratings (Par 94): **87,84,84,80,76**
CSF £20.00 TOTE £7.30: £2.60, £1.50; EX 28.10 Trifecta £77.00 Pool: £962.72 - 9.36 winning units..
Owner Living Legend Racing Partnership 1 **Bred** L Queally **Trained** West Ilsley, Berks

The Form Book Flat, Raceform Ltd, Compton, RG20 6NL.

FOCUS
No great depth to this small-field auction maiden, in which all five runners were fillies.

4207 TOTEPOOL MOBILE H'CAP 1m 114y
7:20 (7:20) (Class 4) (0-85,82) 3-Y-0+ £6,469 (£1,925; £962; £481) Stalls Low

Form RPR
1542 **1** **Copperwood**[6] 4007 8-9-8 **76** SilvestreDeSousa 3 84
(Mark Johnston) *mde all: shkn up over 2f out: hrd pressed after: styd on stoutly fr over 1f out* **3/1**[2]

-040 **2** ¾ **Uppercut**[49] 2592 5-10-0 **82** (v[1]) PatCosgrave 1 88
(Stuart Kittow) *trckd ldng pair: pushed along on inner 3f out: could nt qckn wl over 1f out: squeezed through and styd on fnl f to take 2nd last strides: unable to chal* **7/1**

-225 **3** hd **Highland Duke (IRE)**[35] 3022 4-9-10 **78** AdamKirby 2 84
(Clive Cox) *chsd ldrs: 4th st: drvn over 2f out: prog to press wnr 1f out: nt qckn and hld ins fnl f: lost 2nd nr fin* **11/4**[1]

0054 **4** 2 ½ **Yojimbo (IRE)**[10] 3886 5-9-10 **78** MartinHarley 5 78
(Mick Channon) *trckd wnr: rdn to chal and upsides 2f out: nt qckn and lost 2nd 1f out: fdd* **4/1**[3]

0205 **5** 2 ½ **Starwatch**[7] 3974 6-9-7 **80** (v) MichaelJMMurphy[(5)] 8 74
(John Bridger) *racd wd: hld up: 5th st: sn shkn up: nt on terms after and wl btn 2f out* **7/1**

5336 **6** 1 ¼ **Ertikaan**[10] 3886 6-9-9 **80** (tp) BrendanPowell[(3)] 7 71
(Brendan Powell) *stdd s: hld up: 6th st: gng wl enough over 2f out: shkn up and fnd nil wl over 1f out: wknd fnl f* **25/1**

052 **7** 19 **Kamchatka**[16] 3661 3-8-6 **70** (bt) HayleyTurner 4 18
(Philip Hide) *hld up: last st: sn lost tch: wl bhd whn eased over 1f out* **13/2**

1m 44.58s (-1.52) **Going Correction** 0.0s/f (Good)
WFA 3 from 4yo+ 10lb 7 Ran SP% **113.8**
Speed ratings (Par 105): **106,105,105,102,100 99,82**
toteswingers 1&2 £2.00, 2&3 £3.20, 1&3 £3.20 CSF £23.72 CT £62.79 TOTE £3.30: £1.60, £3.10; EX 26.00 Trifecta £61.20 Pool: £842.47 - 10.31 winning units..
Owner Ready To Run Partnership **Bred** Hertford Offset Press **Trained** Middleham Moor, N Yorks

FOCUS
A fair handicap, with an 82-rated top weight and it looked competitive. The winner's recent turf form is a match for his AW best.

4208 STUBHUB TICKETS H'CAP 1m 4f 10y
7:55 (7:56) (Class 4) (0-80,80) 4-Y-0+ £5,822 (£1,732; £865; £432) Stalls Centre

Form RPR
5321 **1** **Nave (USA)**[11] 3865 6-9-0 **73** 6ex MartinLane 4 85
(David Simcock) *hld up and detached in last pair early: 5th st: smooth prog to ld over 2f out: clr over 1f out: pushed out* **7/4**[1]

2564 **2** 4 **Tingo In The Tale (IRE)**[25] 3370 4-8-11 **70** HayleyTurner 6 76
(David Arbuthnot) *sn restrained into detached last pair: 6th st: rdn and sme prog over 2f out: styd on after to take 2nd ins fnl f: no ch w wnr* **12/1**

430- **3** 2 ½ **Mighty Clarets (IRE)**[8] 6120 6-8-3 **62** (v) SilvestreDeSousa 7 64
(Peter Bowen) *led 100yds: sn in 4th: pushed along 1/2-way: rousted on outer and prog to ld over 3f out: hdd over 2f out: hrd rdn and no ch w wnr after: lost 2nd ins fnl f* **5/1**[3]

-152 **4** 3 ¾ **Paloma's Prince (IRE)**[41] 2849 4-9-4 **77** PatCosgrave 1 73
(Jim Boyle) *hld up in tch: 4th st: hmpd and snatched up 3f out: rdn to dispute 3rd 2f out: fdd over 1f out* **6/1**

4062 **5** 13 **Balady (IRE)**[24] 3412 4-8-8 **67** JimmyQuinn 5 42
(Dominic Ffrench Davis) *taken down early: trckd ldrs: wnt 2nd 5f out tl ent st: sn wknd and bhd* **16/1**

-031 **6** 10 **Colinca's Lad (IRE)**[13] 3791 11-9-2 **80** RosieJessop[(5)] 2 39
(Peter Charalambous) *led after 100yds: hdd over 3f out: sn wknd: t.o* **4/1**[2]

-020 **7** 34 **Gold Mine**[30] 3180 5-9-0 **73** (t) LiamKeniry 3
(Andrew Balding) *chsd ldr after 100yds tl 5f out: hanging bdly and dropped to last st: sn wl t.o* **7/1**

2m 37.98s (-0.92) **Going Correction** 0.0s/f (Good) 7 Ran SP% **113.4**
Speed ratings (Par 105): **103,100,98,96,87 80,58**
toteswingers 1&2 £3.80, 2&3 £4.20, 1&3 £2.10 CSF £24.01 TOTE £2.50: £1.80, £5.20; EX 20.90 Trifecta £186.30 Pool: £1295.48 - 5.21 winning units..
Owner Anthony Hogarth **Bred** Mineola Farm II Llc Et Al **Trained** Newmarket, Suffolk

FOCUS
Easy pickings for favourite backers in this one-sided handicap. The winner's best figure since 2011, and he may do better still.

4209 KISS MIX H'CAP 1m 2f 18y
8:25 (8:28) (Class 5) (0-75,73) 3-Y-0 £3,881 (£1,155; £577; £288) Stalls Low

Form RPR
3-63 **1** **Shamaheart (IRE)**[7] 3989 3-9-1 **67** PatDobbs 5 74+
(Richard Hannon) *trckd ldr: led over 2f out: pressed sn after: shkn up and readily asserted over 1f out: comf* **11/8**[1]

3402 **2** 2 ½ **Jullundar (IRE)**[11] 3861 3-9-1 **67** (v) MartinHarley 4 69
(Mick Channon) *hld up in 4th: prog to chal and w wnr 2f out: styd on but readily hld fr over 1f out* **7/1**

-301 **3** 1 ¾ **Typhon (USA)**[25] 3365 3-9-7 **73** TedDurcan 3 72
(David Lanigan) *hld up in last in modly run r: prog to go 3rd wl over 1f out: hd high and no imp on ldng pair* **3/1**[2]

5332 **4** 3 ¾ **Hawaiian Dream (IRE)**[99] 1321 3-8-9 **61** LiamKeniry 1 53
(Roger Teal) *trckd ldng pair to 2f out: hanging and fdd fr 2f out* **14/1**

5-60 **5** 1 ½ **Nile Knight**[26] 3338 3-9-2 **68** (p) HayleyTurner 2 57
(Marcus Tregoning) *led: set mod pce: tried to kick on 3f out: hdd & wknd over 2f out* **10/3**[3]

2m 14.75s (5.05) **Going Correction** 0.0s/f (Good) 5 Ran SP% **109.4**
Speed ratings (Par 100): **79,77,75,72,71**
CSF £11.18 TOTE £2.30: £1.40, £2.40; EX 9.50 Trifecta £22.70 Pool: £1015.25 - 33.40 winning units..
Owner Dragon Gate **Bred** Gus Roche **Trained** East Everleigh, Wilts

FOCUS
A modest handicap, with a 73-rated top weight and the pace was far from exacting. The form is a bit muddling, but the second helps with the standard.

4210 MIKE & THE MECHANICS LIVE 18.7.13 H'CAP (JOCKEY CLUB GRASSROOTS SPRINT FLAT SERIES QUALIFIER) 6f
8:55 (8:56) (Class 4) (0-85,85) 3-Y-0+ £5,822 (£1,732; £865; £432) Stalls High

Form RPR
0140 **1** **School Fees**[20] 3532 4-9-6 **79** HayleyTurner 3 90
(Olly Stevens) *hld up and sn detached in last: drvn and gd prog on outer fr 2f out: sustained chal and urged along to ld last 75yds* **13/2**

-012 **2** ½ **Freddy With A Y (IRE)**[27] 3279 3-9-6 **85** GeorgeBaker 4 93
(Gary Moore) *pressed ldr to 2f out: pressed new ldr after: drvn and styd on to ld last 100yds: sn hdd: kpt on* **5/2**[1]

-131 **3** hd **Langley Vale**[35] 3010 4-9-2 **75** SebSanders 8 84
(Roger Teal) *racd on outer: chsd ldng trio: clsd to ld wl over 1f out: drvn and hdd last 100yds: kpt on* **7/2**[2]

5214 **4** 3 ½ **Putin (IRE)**[9] 3921 5-8-0 **66** oh1 (bt) ShelleyBirkett[(7)] 7 64
(Phil McEntee) *racd on outer: led after 1f: wd into st: hdd wl over 1f out: fdd fnl f* **12/1**

0202 **5** ½ **Baldemar**[23] 3441 8-9-2 **75** BarryMcHugh 1 71
(Richard Fahey) *pushed along early in rr: 7th st: no real prog 2f out: plugged on nr fin* **4/1**[3]

-135 **6** 1 **Aye Aye Digby (IRE)**[24] 3415 8-9-3 **76** LiamKeniry 2 69
(Patrick Chamings) *led 1f: pressed ldng pair to 2f out: steadily wknd* **7/1**

0064 **7** 1 ¾ **Perfect Pastime**[24] 3404 5-9-1 **74** (p) PatCosgrave 6 61
(Jim Boyle) *chsd ldrs in 5th: rdn and no prog over 2f out: sn fdd* **20/1**

2413 **8** 9 **Where's Reiley (USA)**[9] 3921 7-8-8 **67** (v) JimmyQuinn 5 25
(Michael Attwater) *a towards rr: 6th st: wknd over 2f out: t.o* **12/1**

1m 8.39s (-1.01) **Going Correction** 0.0s/f (Good)
WFA 3 from 4yo+ 6lb 8 Ran SP% **116.8**
Speed ratings (Par 105): **106,105,105,100,99 98,96,84**
toteswingers 1&2 £5.80, 2&3 £3.40, 1&3 £4.00 CSF £23.70 CT £67.65 TOTE £8.60: £2.60, £1.60, £1.90; EX 33.60 Trifecta £96.80 Pool: £1005.80 - 7.78 winning units..
Owner Elias, Mitchell & Newton **Bred** Benjamin Newton And Graycroft Farm **Trained** Chiddingfold, Surrey

FOCUS
On paper, an ultra-competitive finale. There seemed a significant delay before the stalls opened and some jockeys thought that against them. The form looks sound with a trio clear.
T/Plt: £145.70 to a £1 stake. Pool of £62931.18 - 315.18 winning tickets. T/Qpdt: £10.10 to a £1 stake. Pool of £5620.08 - 410.0 winning tickets. JN

3829 NEWMARKET (R-H)
Thursday, July 11

OFFICIAL GOING: Good to firm (overall 8.3, stands' side 8.3, centre 8.2, far side 8.1)
Stands side track used for first time this year. Stalls Far side except 10f, 12, &13f: Centre
Wind: light. half against Weather: dry and sunny

4211 BAHRAIN TROPHY (GROUP 3) 1m 5f
1:40 (1:43) (Class 1) 3-Y-0
£34,026 (£12,900; £6,456; £3,216; £1,614; £810) Stalls Centre

Form RPR
1452 **1** **Feel Like Dancing**[20] 3526 3-9-0 **99** (p) WilliamBuick 5 101
(John Gosden) *chsd ldr: effrt to chal ent fnl 2f: rdn to ld over 1f out: hrd pressed but hld on wl fnl f* **3/1**[2]

1434 **2** nk **Jathabah (IRE)**[28] 3240 3-8-11 **90** JamesDoyle 4 98
(Clive Brittain) *chsd ldr tl rdn to ld ent fnl 2f: hdd over 1f out: ev ch after: kpt on wl but a jst hld fnl f* **33/1**

-435 **3** hd **Havana Beat (IRE)**[20] 3523 3-9-0 **100** LiamKeniry 6 102+
(Andrew Balding) *chsd ldrs: gng wl but stuck bhd horses fr over 2f out: swtchd lft and gap fnlly opened wl ins fnl f: r.o wl u.p towards fin: unlucky* **5/1**[3]

61 **4** ½ **Testudo (IRE)**[35] 3021 3-9-0 **88** KierenFallon 2 100
(Brian Meehan) *in tch in midfield: rdn and effrt ent fnl 2f: chsd ldrs 1f out: kpt on u.p fnl f: nvr quite gng pce to chal* **16/1**

6-21 **5** 3 **Dare To Achieve**[18] 3606 3-9-0 **95** RichardHughes 1 95+
(William Haggas) *lw: taken down early: stdd s: t.k.h: swtchd lft 5f out: rdn and effrt on outer over 2f out: chsd ldrs 1f out: no ex ins fnl f: wknd fnl 100yds* **2/1**[1]

5010 **6** hd **Dashing Star**[20] 3526 3-9-0 **89** RyanMoore 8 95
(David Elsworth) *taken down early: t.k.h: hld up in last pair: swtchd lft and hdwy into midfield on outer 5f out: rdn 4f out: lost pl 2f out: plugged on same pce after* **10/1**

1525 **7** ½ **Ray Ward (IRE)**[20] 3526 3-9-0 **97** GrahamLee 7 94
(David Simcock) *in tch in midfield: lost pl but stl wl in tch whn rdn 2f out: sme hdwy over 1f out: outpcd fnl f* **11/1**

2103 **8** 14 **Boite (IRE)**[20] 3526 3-9-0 **97** JamieSpencer 3 81
(Peter Chapple-Hyam) *lw: led tl rdn and hdd ent fnl 2f: wknd and bhd 1f out: eased wl ins fnl f* **15/2**

2m 45.35s (1.35) **Going Correction** -0.10s/f (Good) 8 Ran SP% **113.0**
Speed ratings (Par 110): **91,90,90,90,88 88,88,79**
toteswingers 1&2 £11.30, 2&3 £24.70, 1&3 £2.60 CSF £85.41 TOTE £3.30: £1.20, £7.20, £2.00; EX 87.20 Trifecta £516.00 Pool: £4115.15 - 5.98 winning units..
Owner Lady Bamford **Bred** Lady Bamford **Trained** Newmarket, Suffolk

FOCUS
This contest is often seen as an early trial for the St Leger, so it's worth noting that recent winners who went for the final domestic Classic finished 1st (Masked Marvel), 3rd (Corsica) and 2nd (Kite Wood). The opening fractions were not overly quick and the gallop quickened up from about the 4f marker. This looked a lesser renewal of the race and it's hard to rate the form much higher. The runner-up is the doubt.

4212 PORTLAND PLACE PROPERTIES JULY STKS (GROUP 2) (C&G) 6f
2:10 (2:13) (Class 1) 2-Y-0
£45,368 (£17,200; £8,608; £4,288; £2,152; £1,080) Stalls High

Form RPR
01 **1** **Anjaal**[33] 3077 2-8-12 **0** PaulHanagan 5 108
(Richard Hannon) *s.i.s: hld up in tch in last trio: rdn over 1f out: no imp tl str run ins fnl f to ld last strides* **14/1**

1 **2** nk **Figure Of Speech (IRE)**[20] 3536 2-8-12 **0** MickaelBarzalona 4 107+
(Saeed bin Suroor) *w'like: scope: dwlt: hld up in rr: stl in last and looking to switch rt over 1f out: switching lft and gd hdwy 1f out: led fnl 100yds but kpt gng lft: hdd last strides* **7/2**[2]

5315 **3** hd **Jallota**[23] 3422 2-8-12 **0** MartinHarley 7 107
(Mick Channon) *chsd ldrs and swtchd sltly rt over 1f out: drvn and led ins fnl f: sn hdd and unable qck towards fin* **20/1**

3 **4** ¾ **Sir John Hawkins (USA)**[23] 3422 2-8-12 **0** RyanMoore 6 104
(A P O'Brien, Ire) *chsd ldrs: rdn and effrt over 1f out: drvn and ev ch ins fnl f: no ex and wknd towards fin* **9/4**[1]

22 **5** 1 **Whaleweigh Station**[20] 3536 2-8-12 **0** RichardKingscote 2 101
(Tom Dascombe) *unf: t.k.h: hld up in tch in midfield: rdn and hdwy whn swtchd lft over 1f out: styd on same pce fnl 100yds* **33/1**

1 **6** *nk* **Astaire (IRE)**47 2670 2-8-12 0 NeilCallan 6 100
(Kevin Ryan) *unf: scope: lw: t.k.h: w ldr: rdn and ev ch over 1f out: led 1f out: sn hdd and no ex: wknd wl ins fnl f* **6/1**

631 **7** *1 1/4* **Bahamian Heights**7 3991 2-8-12 0 BrettDoyle 8 97
(Clive Brittain) *led: rdn 2f out: hdd and no ex 1f out: wknd fnl 100yds* **80/1**

1310 **8** *1 3/4* **Master Carpenter (IRE)**19 3555 2-8-12 0 GrahamLee 11 91
(Rod Millman) *in tch in midfield: rdn and effrt 2f out: no imp 1f out: wknd ins fnl f* **33/1**

1U **9** *2 1/2* **Intermath (IRE)**11 3857 2-8-12 0 TomQueally 9 84
(David Evans) *in tch in midfield: rdn and unable qck ent fnl 2f: wknd 1f out* **66/1**

21 **10** *3/4* **Brown Sugar (IRE)**15 3695 2-8-12 0 RichardHughes 3 82
(Richard Hannon) *w'like: scope: lw: plld hrd: chsd ldrs: rdn and btn over 1f out: wknd fnl f* **5/1**3

1 **11** *3/4* **Canyari (IRE)**59 2307 2-8-12 0 JimmyFortune 10 79
(Richard Fahey) *str: lw: a in rr: in tch: rdn and no hdwy ent fnl 2f: wknd jst over 1f out* **7/1**

1m 11.21s (-1.29) **Going Correction** -0.10s/f (Good) **11** Ran SP% **116.5**
Speed ratings (Par 106): **104,103,103,102,101 100,98,96,93,92 91**
toteswingers 1&2 £9.30, 2&3 £17.40, 1&3 £27.80 CSF £59.87 TOTE £19.30: £3.90, £1.60, £5.30; EX 83.80 Trifecta £631.60 Pool: £5295.26 - 6.28 winning.

Owner Hamdan Al Maktoum **Bred** Carmel Stud **Trained** East Everleigh, Wilts

FOCUS

The July Stakes has been won by some top-class horses in its very long history, but only the 2009 winner Arcano has gone on to Group 1 success (Prix Morny) in the past ten years and you have to go back to Noverre in 2000 to find the last winner of this to make an impact at the highest level as an older horse. Despite the stalls being placed against the far rail, the runners soon switched to come down the centre. They may have gone off quick enough, though, as the first two came from well off the pace. The field finished compressed and this is rated among the lesser renewals of the race.

4213 PRINCESS OF WALES'S BOYLESPORTS.COM STKS (GROUP 2) 1m 4f

2:40 (2:44) (Class 1) 3-Y-O+

£56,710 (£21,500; £10,760; £5,360; £2,690; £1,350) **Stalls** Centre

Form RPR

1113 **1** **Universal (IRE)**19 3556 4-9-5 114 JoeFanning 2 117
(Mark Johnston) *mde all: set stdy gallop: grad qcknd fr 3f out: rdn and 2 l clr jst over 1f out: in command and styd on wl fnl f* **3/1**1

2212 **2** *2 1/2* **Ahzeemah (IRE)**103 1263 4-9-2 111 (p) MickaelBarzalona 3 110
(Saeed bin Suroor) *lw: chsd ldrs: rdn and effrt over 2f out: kpt on u.p to chse wnr jst ins fnl f: no imp* **13/2**

-315 **3** *2* **Cavalryman**42 2810 7-9-2 115 SilvestreDeSousa 7 107
(Saeed bin Suroor) *t.k.h: trckd ldrs: rdn and effrt 3f out: chsd wnr over 2f out: unable qck over 1f out: 3rd and one pce fnl f* **7/2**3

112- **4** *nk* **Grandeur (IRE)**208 4-9-5 0 WilliamBuick 5 109
(Jeremy Noseda) *stdd s: hld up in tch in last pair: swtchd lft and effrt ent fnl 2f: no imp and one pce fnl f* **7/1**

4-03 **5** *3 1/4* **Wigmore Hall (IRE)**68 2020 6-9-2 114 JamieSpencer 4 101
(Michael Bell) *swtg: stdd s: t.k.h: hld up in rr: rdn and effrt over 2f out: no ex and btn over 1f out: hung lft ins fnl f* **5/1**

1-15 **6** *3 1/2* **Danadana (IRE)**42 2811 5-9-2 111 RyanMoore 6 96
(Luca Cumani) *lw: chsd wnr tl over 2f out: lost pl u.p over 1f out: wknd fnl f* **10/3**2

2m 28.45s (-4.45) **Going Correction** -0.10s/f (Good) **6** Ran SP% **112.8**
Speed ratings (Par 115): **110,108,107,106,104 102**
toteswingers 1&2 £3.50, 2&3 £4.40, 1&3 £2.50 CSF £22.50 TOTE £3.10: £1.80, £3.00; EX 14.30 Trifecta £39.50 Pool: £5490.26 - 104.11 winning.

Owner Abdulla Al Mansoori **Bred** Grangecon Stud **Trained** Middleham Moor, N Yorks

FOCUS

With only one true front-runner in the line-up this had the potential to be tactical. Universal is rated in line with his Jockey Club Stakes win, but had plenty in his favour and this form can't be taken too literally.

4214 BOYLESPORTS.COM DOWNLOAD OUR APP H'CAP 1m 2f

3:15 (3:17) (Class 2) (0-105,97) 3-Y-O

£43,575 (£13,048; £6,524; £3,262; £1,631; £819) **Stalls** Centre

Form RPR

1110 **1** **Maputo**21 3484 3-9-5 95 GrahamLee 9 115+
(Mark Johnston) *lw: chsd ldrs: clsd smoothly to ld 1f out: sn rdn and qcknd clr: r.o strly: readily* **8/1**2

2001 **2** *6* **Red Avenger (USA)**5 4063 3-9-6 96 6ex RyanMoore 8 104
(Ed Dunlop) *hld up off the pce towards rr: rdn and effrt 2f out: hdwy u.p over 1f out: styd on fnl f to snatch 2nd last strides: no ch w wnr* **8/1**2

1-02 **3** *nk* **Tarikhi (USA)**21 3484 3-9-5 95 SilvestreDeSousa 15 102
(Saeed bin Suroor) *lw: stdd s: t.k.h off the pce in rr: hdwy u.p on far side over 1f out: chsd clr wnr ins fnl f: styd on but no imp: lost 2nd last strides* **11/2**1

1-41 **4** *shd* **Goodwood Mirage (IRE)**27 3276 3-8-13 89 FrankieDettori 3 96+
(William Knight) *lw: stdd s: t.k.h: hld up off the pce in rr: hdwy u.p over 1f out: styd on fnl 100yds: no ch w wnr* **8/1**2

413 **5** *1/2* **Matrooh (USA)**40 2857 3-8-11 87 PaulHanagan 11 93
(William Haggas) *hld up off the pce towards rr: hdwy but stl plenty to do whn nt clr run and swtchd rt over 1f out: styd on ins fnl f: no ch w wnr* **11/2**1

-212 **6** *3/4* **One Pekan (IRE)**10 3899 3-8-7 83 1 AndreaAtzeni 1 88
(Roger Varian) *hld up in midfield: rdn and effrt over 2f out: no imp tl styd on u.p ins fnl f: no ch w wnr* **12/1**

1110 **7** *1/2* **Sea Shanty (USA)**21 3484 3-9-1 91 RichardHughes 12 95
(Richard Hannon) *stdd s: hld up off the pce in rr: rdn 3f out: no imp tl styd on past btn horses ins fnl f: nvr trbld ldrs* **10/1**

2650 **8** *3/4* **Greeleys Love (USA)**21 3486 3-8-8 84 JoeFanning 7 86
(Mark Johnston) *lean: in tch in midfield: rdn and effrt to chse ldrs over 2f out: no ex u.p ent fnl f: wnt modest 2nd briefly ins fnl f: fdd fnl 100yds* **18/1**

2226 **9** *nk* **Party Royal**13 3763 3-8-1 82 ow1 RobertTart(5) 16 84
(Mark Johnston) *led and set fast gallop: rdn over 1f out: hdd 1f out: sn brushed aside by wnr: fdd ins fnl f* **33/1**

2162 **10** *1* **Space Ship**21 3486 3-9-4 94 WilliamBuick 2 94
(John Gosden) *hld up off the pce in towards rr: rdn over 2f out: no imp tl plugged on ins fnl f: nvr trbld ldrs* **8/1**2

3343 **11** *hd* **Rouge Nuage (IRE)**26 3338 3-7-7 76 oh4 (b1) NoelGarbutt(7) 13 75
(Conrad Allen) *t.k.h: hld up in midfield early: hdwy to chse ldrs 8f out: wnt 2nd 6f out tl over 1f out: sn btn and fdd fnl f* **66/1**

4310 **12** *1 1/4* **Pasaka Boy**21 3486 3-8-12 88 RichardKingscote 14 85
(Jonathan Portman) *hld up in midfield: effrt u.p over 1f out: no imp whn carried sltly lft over 1f out: nvr trbld ldrs* **25/1**

-110 **13** *shd* **Soviet Rock (IRE)**21 3486 3-9-1 94 ThomasBrown(3) 6 91
(Andrew Balding) *chsd ldrs: lost pl and rdn ent fnl 2f: wknd over 1f out* **9/1**3

1025 **14** *1/2* **Royal Prize**19 3563 3-8-6 82 JimmyQuinn 4 78
(Ralph Beckett) *hld up off the pce towards rr: rdn and no prog over 2f out: n.d* **25/1**

-160 **15** *20* **Le Deluge (FR)**21 3484 3-8-7 83 MickaelBarzalona 5
(John Best) *lw: wnt freely to post: chsd ldr tl 6f out: lost pl qckly 3f out: t.o fnl f* **50/1**

2m 0.91s (-4.59) **Going Correction** -0.10s/f (Good) course record **15** Ran SP% **121.3**
Speed ratings (Par 106): **114,109,108,108,108 107,107,106,106,105 105,104,104,104,88**
toteswingers 1&2 £13.20, 2&3 £10.40, 1&3 £8.60 CSF £67.59 CT £390.06 TOTE £8.10: £3.10, £3.40, £2.50; EX 73.50 Trifecta £492.50 Pool: £10489.09 - 15.95 winning.

Owner Sheikh Hamdan Bin Mohammed Al Maktoum **Bred** Darley **Trained** Middleham Moor, N Yorks

FOCUS

A hot handicap and the first three home all ran in the Britannia. Again the runners came up the centre of the track and the pace was relentless, resulting in them shaving 0.06sec off the course record. Maputo impressed in pulling clear of some progressive types and the form is rated on the positive side.

4215 THREE CHIMNEYS EBF MAIDEN FILLIES' STKS 6f

3:50 (3:50) (Class 4) 2-Y-O

£6,469 (£1,925; £962; £481) **Stalls** High

Form RPR

3 **1** **Qawaasem (IRE)**13 3781 2-9-0 0 PaulHanagan 1 84
(Charles Hills) *tall: athletic: lw: wl in tch in midfield: effrt to chse ldr over 1f out: rdn to chal and drew clr w rival ins fnl f: r.o u.p to ld wl ins fnl f* **4/1**2

2 *1/2* **Valonia** 2-9-0 0 FergusSweeney 6 83+
(Henry Candy) *lengthy: scope: well made: chsd ldr tl led 2f out: rdn and edgd lft ent fnl f: drew clr w wnr wl ins fnl f: r.o wl tl hdd and no ex wl ins fnl f* **33/1**

230 **3** *2 3/4* **Oriel**22 3459 2-9-0 0 RichardHughes 4 74
(Richard Hannon) *taken down early: hld up wl in tch in midfield: rdn and effrt over 1f out: drvn and hdwy to chse ldng pair ins fnl f: edgd lft and no imp fnl 100yds* **9/4**1

0 **4** *1 1/2* **Dry Your Eyes (IRE)**13 3753 2-9-0 0 JoeFanning 11 70
(Mark Johnston) *w'like: t.k.h: chsd ldrs: rdn and unable qck over 1f out: hld and plugged on same pce fnl f* **14/1**

5 *1/2* **Crown Pleasure (IRE)** 2-9-0 0 JamesDoyle 8 68+
(Clive Brittain) *athletic: in tch in rr: shkn up: rn green and outpcd over 1f out: rallied and styd on wl ins fnl f: nvr trbld ldrs* **33/1**

3 **6** *3/4* **Grevillea (IRE)**16 3664 2-9-0 0 MartinHarley 12 66
(Mick Channon) *wl in tch in midfield: rdn and effrt 2f out: outpcd u.p over 1f out: plugged on same pce ins fnl f* **15/2**

4 **7** *nse* **Manderley (IRE)**43 2774 2-9-0 0 RyanMoore 9 66
(Richard Hannon) *w'like: tall: nt rt s: hld up wl in tch in midfield: effrt u.p over 1f out: unable qck 1f out: plugged on same pce fnl f* **6/1**3

8 *1/2* **Amnesia (IRE)** 2-9-0 0 GrahamLee 5 64
(William Haggas) *w'like: hld up in tch in last quartet: rdn and sme hdwy over 1f out: kpt on steadily fnl f: nvr trbld ldrs* **8/1**

9 *hd* **Lucky Surprise** 2-9-0 0 JackMitchell 15 64
(Gay Kelleway) *str: b.bwkd: chsd ldrs: rdn and effrt 2f out: drvn and no ex over 1f out: wknd ins fnl f* **40/1**

10 *1* **Spirit Of Alsace (IRE)** 2-9-0 0 AndreaAtzeni 13 61
(Roger Varian) *w'like: scope: gd bodied: short of room and swtchd lft sn after s: hld up in tch in midfield: rdn and effrt over 1f out: no ex 1f out: wknd ins fnl f* **11/1**

11 *2* **Musalaha (IRE)** 2-9-0 0 WilliamBuick 3 55
(Ed Dunlop) *lengthy: rn green in rr: in tch: rdn 2f out: no real imp: n.d* **25/1**

4 **12** *1* **Shamardyh (IRE)**26 3318 2-9-0 0 NeilCallan 16 52+
(James Tate) *w'like: tall: in tch in midfield: clsd and chsd ldrs 2f out: rdn and no ex jst over 1f out: wknd ins fnl f* **16/1**

0 **13** *2 1/4* **Saffire Song**13 3781 2-9-0 0 LiamKeniry 7 45
(Alan Bailey) *t.k.h: hld up in tch in last quartet: rdn 2f out: sn struggling and wknd over 1f out* **66/1**

14 *11* **Zaftual** 2-9-0 0 JimmyQuinn 14 12
(K F Clutterbuck) *w'like: b.bkwd: racd keenly: led tl 2f out: sn dropped out: bhd fnl f* **150/1**

1m 12.23s (-0.27) **Going Correction** -0.10s/f (Good) **14** Ran SP% **123.1**
Speed ratings (Par 93): **97,96,92,90,90 89,88,88,88,86 84,82,79,65**
toteswingers 1&2 £38.10, 2&3 £31.30, 1&3 £2.30 CSF £145.83 TOTE £5.40: £1.80, £13.90, £1.10; EX 197.60 Trifecta £1113.20 Pool: £7419.12 - 4.99 winning units..

Owner Hamdan Al Maktoum **Bred** Shadwell Estate Company Limited **Trained** Lambourn, Berks

FOCUS

Plenty of nice fillies have won this contest down the years, including Certify in 2012.

4216 INSURE PINK STUBBS STKS (LISTED RACE) 1m

4:25 (4:25) (Class 1) 3-Y-O

£22,684 (£8,600; £4,304; £2,144) **Stalls** High

Form RPR

-312 **1** **Montiridge (IRE)**22 3455 3-9-6 111 RichardHughes 2 117
(Richard Hannon) *lw: led tl hdd but stl on bit wl over 1f out: rdn to ld again 1f out and sn qckd clr: pushed out ins fnl f: comf* **4/7**1

114- **2** *2* **Ashdan**271 7050 3-9-3 107 1 WilliamBuick 1 109
(John Gosden) *t.k.h: trckd ldng pair: wnt 2nd over 2f out: rdn to ld wl over 1f out: hdd 1f out and sn outpcd: kpt on to hold 2nd fnl f* **10/3**2

2-54 **3** *1* **Alhebayeb (IRE)**47 2661 3-9-3 106 PaulHanagan 3 107
(Richard Hannon) *hld up in rr: effrt to chse ldng pair 2f out: sn rdn: outpcd and btn 1f out: plugged on fnl f* **15/2**3

0-56 **4** *7* **Fantastic Moon**20 3523 3-9-3 100 RyanMoore 6 93
(Jeremy Noseda) *chsd wnr tl over 2f out: lost pl 2f out and sn struggling u.p: wknd 1f out* **15/2**3

1m 37.42s (-2.58) **Going Correction** -0.10s/f (Good) **4** Ran SP% **110.3**
Speed ratings (Par 108): **108,106,105,98**
CSF £2.87 TOTE £1.70; EX 2.70 Trifecta £4.70 Pool: £3523.29 - 560.24 winning.

Owner M Clarke,J Jeffries,R Ambrose,B Reilly **Bred** Century Bloodstock **Trained** East Everleigh, Wilts

FOCUS
They only went a steady early pace in this small-field Listed event and things didn't quicken up until the runner-up was committed entering the last 2f. This looks improved form from Montiridge.

4217 FRONTLINE BATHROOMS H'CAP 5f
5:00 (5:01) (Class 3) (0-90,90) 3-Y-0+ **£9,703** (£2,887; £1,443; £721) **Stalls** High

Form RPR
0251 **1** **Last Sovereign**[21] 3501 9-9-5 **90**..........................(b) JacobButterfield[(7)] 6 99
(Ollie Pears) *chsd ldrs: wnt 2nd jst over 2f out: rdn and effrt to ld over 1f out: styd on wl fnl f: rdn out* **9/1**
0501 **2** *3/4* **Doctor Parkes**[6] 4024 7-9-12 **90** 6ex.................................... NeilCallan 5 96
(Stuart Williams) *taken down early: t.k.h: trckd ldrs: rdn and effrt to chal 1f out: unable qck u.p towards fin* **9/2**[2]
121 **3** *nk* **Avon Breeze**[15] 3682 4-9-4 **82**....................................... FrankieDettori 11 87+
(Richard Whitaker) *lw: chsd ldrs: rdn and effrt over 1f out: ev ch 1f out: no ex fnl 50yds* **7/2**[1]
3261 **4** *nk* **Rebecca Romero**[25] 3371 6-9-4 **82**................................ JamesDoyle 4 86
(Denis Coakley) *wnt rt s: hld up in tch in last quartet: rdn and effrt to chse ldrs 1f out: drvn and kpt on same pce ins fnl f* **11/2**[3]
404 **5** *1 1/4* **My Son Max**[7] 3980 5-8-10 **79**................................ NatashaEaton[(5)] 9 78
(P J O'Gorman) *chsd ldrs: hrd drvn over 1f out: unable qck ins fnl f: outpcd fnl 100yds* **11/1**
0620 **6** *1* **Rocket Rob (IRE)**[13] 3786 7-8-12 **76**...........................(b) WilliamBuick 3 72
(Willie Musson) *sn niggled along in rr: styd on ins fnl f: nvr trbld ldrs* **14/1**
-600 **7** *shd* **Baddilini**[12] 3840 3-9-4 **87**..(p) RichardHughes 2 82
(Alan Bailey) *in tch in midfield: clsd to chse ldrs 2f out: rdn and unable qck over 1f out: wknd ins fnl f* **16/1**
0300 **8** *1* **Bosun Breese**[19] 3561 8-9-0 **83**.. LMcNiff[(5)] 1 75
(David Barron) *led tl rdn and hdd over 1f out: struggling whn carried lft over 1f out: wknd ins fnl f* **16/1**
4534 **9** *2 1/4* **Fratellino**[117] 1032 6-9-12 **90**................................(t) MickaelBarzalona 10 74
(Alan McCabe) *taken down early: chsd ldr tl ent fnl 2f out: sn struggling u.p: wknd 1f out* **15/2**
331- **10** *3/4* **Midnight Rider (IRE)**[280] 6820 5-9-7 **85**......................... GeorgeBaker 7 66
(Chris Wall) *stdd s: hld up in rr: n.d* **8/1**
351/ **11** *6* **Appointee (IRE)**[259] 4-9-3 **81**.. JamieSpencer 8 40
(Robert Cowell) *bkwd: hld up in last trio: rdn over 1f out: sn struggling and wknd over 1f out* **33/1**

58.34s (-0.76) **Going Correction** -0.10s/f (Good)
WFA 3 from 4yo+ 5lb **11** Ran SP% **118.4**
Speed ratings (Par 107): **102,100,100,99,97 96,96,94,90,89 80**
toteswingers 1&2 £8.40, 2&3 £3.40, 1&3 £9.30 CSF £49.60 CT £175.78 TOTE £12.10: £3.60, £1.80, £1.80; EX 59.60 Trifecta £394.40 Pool: £5566.60 - 10.63 winning.
Owner Richard Walker **Bred** Gestut Hof Ittlingen & Cheveley Park Stud Ltd **Trained** Norton, N Yorks
FOCUS
A fair sprint for the class. An exposed field and straightforward form, the winner better than ever.
T/Jkpt: Not won. T/Plt: £85.60 to a £1 stake. Pool of £194963.28, 1661.54 winning tickets.
T/Qpdt: £9.90 to a £1 stake. Pool of £8854.45 - 659.64 winning tickets. SP

4030 WARWICK (L-H)
Thursday, July 11
OFFICIAL GOING: Good to firm (firm in places; 8.1)
Wind: Light across Weather: Fine

4218 ANIXTER I P ASSURED EBF MEDIAN AUCTION MAIDEN STKS 7f 26y
2:20 (2:22) (Class 5) 2-Y-O **£2,911** (£866; £432; £216) **Stalls** Low

Form RPR
0 **1** **Chriselliam (IRE)**[48] 2625 2-9-0 0.............................. JamesMcDonald 4 81+
(Charles Hills) *chsd ldr 2f: remained handy: rdn over 1f out: led ins fnl f: qcknd clr* **5/1**[3]
24 **2** *2 1/2* **Art Official (IRE)**[25] 3374 2-9-5 0.. PatDobbs 9 79
(Richard Hannon) *led: rdn: edgd rt and hdd ins fnl f: styd on same pce* **7/4**[1]
5 **3** *4 1/2* **Gilbey's Mate**[19] 3581 2-9-5 0.. RobertHavlin 10 67
(John Gosden) *prom: chsd ldr 5f out: rdn and ev ch over 1f out: no ex ins fnl f* **3/1**[2]
0 **4** *3 1/2* **Greed Is Good**[26] 3350 2-9-5 0... FrederikTylicki 3 57
(Mrs K Burke) *mid-div: pushed along 1/2-way: hdwy u.p 2f out: no ex fnl f* **17/2**
0 **5** *2 1/4* **Fair Flutter (IRE)**[22] 3461 2-9-5 0.................................. BarryMcHugh 11 51+
(Richard Fahey) *hld up: pushed along 1/2-way: nvr trbld ldrs* **14/1**
2 **6** *1/2* **Lady Red Oak**[29] 3205 2-9-0 0.. JimCrowley 1 45+
(Tom Dascombe) *hld up: rdn over 1f out: n.d* **11/2**
6230 **7** *1 1/4* **Sartori**[35] 3017 2-9-5 0..(v[1]) SamHitchcott 6 47
(Mick Channon) *chsd ldrs: rdn over 2f out: wknd over 1f out* **33/1**
0 **8** *hd* **Half Way**[12] 3836 2-9-5 0... CathyGannon 8 46+
(Henry Candy) *s.i.s: hld up: a in rr* **28/1**
9 *hd* **Mariners Moon (IRE)** 2-9-5 0.. FrannyNorton 7 46
(Mark Johnston) *mid-div: pushed along and lost pl after 2f: n.d after* **33/1**
00 **10** *shd* **Basil Berry**[19] 3581 2-9-5 0.. SaleemGolam 5 45+
(Chris Dwyer) *s.i.s: a in rr* **100/1**
0 **11** *5* **Miss Tweedy**[16] 3664 2-9-0 0.. SteveDrowne 2 27
(Rod Millman) *prom: rdn over 2f out: sn wknd* **100/1**

1m 22.74s (-1.86) **Going Correction** -0.10s/f (Good) 2y crse rec **11** Ran SP% **116.2**
Speed ratings (Par 94): **106,103,98,94,91 90,89,89,88,88 83**
toteswingers 1&2 £4.80, 2&3 £1.70, 1&3 £6.20 CSF £13.62 TOTE £4.50: £1.80, £1.10, £1.50; EX 14.00 Trifecta £71.10 Pool: £1254.07 - 13.21 winning units..
Owner W Carson, Miss E Asprey, C Wright **Bred** Ballylinch Stud **Trained** Lambourn, Berks
FOCUS
The opening contest was a fair juvenile maiden, and they went a decent gallop on ground officially described as good to firm, firm in places. The first three horses raced in the first three throughout.

4219 CDI GROUP EBF FILLIES' H'CAP 7f 26y
2:55 (2:56) (Class 4) (0-80,80) 3-Y-O+ **£6,469** (£1,925; £962; £481) **Stalls** Low

Form RPR
-212 **1** **Floating Along (IRE)**[13] 3773 3-9-1 **75**............................ FrannyNorton 1 81+
(William Haggas) *mde all: rdn and edgd rt over 1f out: styd on* **6/4**[1]
3-13 **2** *1 1/4* **Al Manaal**[12] 3828 3-8-13 **80**.................................... AhmadAlSubousi[(7)] 2 82
(Saeed bin Suroor) *chsd wnr: rdn over 1f out: styd on* **5/2**[2]
3-34 **3** *1* **Icon Dance**[25] 3375 3-9-0 **74**.. JohnFahy 3 73
(Ben De Haan) *s.i.s: sn pushed along in rr: rdn over 1f out: r.o ins fnl f: nt trble ldrs* **8/1**

-310 **4** *3/4* **Finesse**[33] 3098 4-9-10 **76**.. JimCrowley 4 76
(Ralph Beckett) *chsd ldrs: pushed along over 2f out: rdn over 1f out: no ex ins fnl f* **11/4**[3]

1m 24.65s (0.05) **Going Correction** -0.10s/f (Good)
WFA 3 from 4yo 8lb **4** Ran SP% **106.3**
Speed ratings (Par 102): **95,93,92,91**
CSF £5.30 TOTE £2.30; EX 5.40 Trifecta £11.80 Pool: £862.18 - 54.61 winning units..
Owner Lael Stable **Bred** Wentworth Racing **Trained** Newmarket, Suffolk
FOCUS
A fair small-field fillies' handicap run at a muddling early gallop, and in a slow time. The winner should be capable of significantly better.

4220 N G BAILEY H'CAP 6f
3:30 (3:30) (Class 5) (0-75,75) 3-Y-O+ **£2,587** (£770; £384; £192) **Stalls** Low

Form RPR
4-00 **1** **Mount Hollow**[14] 3733 8-9-7 **75**..................................(p) JackDuern[(5)] 7 85
(Andrew Hollinshead) *chsd ldrs: rdn to ld over 1f out: r.o u.p* **14/1**
0001 **2** *3/4* **Tidal's Baby**[3] 4120 4-8-10 **64**.............................. GeorgeDowning[(5)] 6 72
(Tony Carroll) *dwlt: hld up: hdwy over 1f out: rdn to chse wnr ins fnl f: sn ev ch styd on* **6/4**[1]
642 **3** *1/2* **John Coffey (IRE)**[23] 3446 4-8-3 **57** oh3 ow1............. TobyAtkinson[(5)] 2 63
(Michael Appleby) *chsd ldrs: rdn over 2f out: r.o u.p* **4/1**[3]
-035 **4** *hd* **Generalyse**[44] 2736 4-9-7 **70**.......................................(p) JohnFahy 5 75
(Ben De Haan) *led: rdn and hdd over 1f out: edgd lft: styd on same pce ins fnl f* **9/2**
0465 **5** *4 1/2* **Jarrow (IRE)**[19] 3577 6-9-7 **70**...............................(p) SteveDrowne 8 61
(Milton Bradley) *stdd s: hld up: rdn over 1f out: styd on same pce* **20/1**
0002 **6** *3/4* **We Have A Dream**[10] 3897 8-9-7 **70**.................................. JimCrowley 1 59
(William Muir) *chsd ldr tl rdn over 1f out: wknd ins fnl f* **7/2**[2]

1m 11.34s (-0.46) **Going Correction** +0.025s/f (Good)
WFA 3 from 4yo+ 6lb **6** Ran SP% **111.8**
Speed ratings (Par 103): **104,103,102,102,96 95**
toteswingers 1&2 £7.60, 2&3 £1.70, 1&3 £23.50 CSF £35.48 CT £102.26 TOTE £14.60: £4.50, £1.30; EX 45.00 Trifecta £104.10 Pool: £1494.04 - 10.75 winning units..
Owner Paul Shaw **Bred** G Robinson **Trained** Upper Longdon, Staffs
■ Stewards' Enquiry : Jack Duern two-day ban: used whip above shoulder height (Jul 25-26)
FOCUS
An ordinary sprint handicap in which there was no hanging about. The winner is rated to his turf best.

4221 ROYCE COMMUNICATIONS PREMIER PARTNER H'CAP 5f
4:05 (4:06) (Class 4) (0-85,82) 3-Y-O **£4,690** (£1,395; £697; £348) **Stalls** Low

Form RPR
0300 **1** **New Fforest**[33] 3097 3-8-11 **79**.................................... OisinMurphy[(7)] 5 94
(Andrew Balding) *a.p: chsd ldr over 3f out: led over 1f out: sn rdn: r.o wl* **11/4**[2]
1163 **2** *3* **Shirley's Pride**[5] 4069 3-8-3 **67**...............................(t) DarrenEgan[(3)] 2 71
(Michael Appleby) *hld up: hdwy 2f out: rdn and ev ch over 1f out: styd on same pce ins fnl f* **11/4**[2]
0111 **3** *1 3/4* **Cara Gina**[9] 3920 3-8-11 **72** 6ex..................................(b) LiamJones 3 70
(William Haggas) *in tch and sn pushed along: rdn 1/2-way: edgd lft over 1f out: styd on same pce: fnl f* **9/4**[1]
1-01 **4** *3* **Royal Acquisition**[24] 3400 3-8-13 **74**................................. JimCrowley 4 61
(Robert Cowell) *led: rdn and hdd over 1f out: wknd fnl f* **11/2**[3]
3120 **5** *3/4* **Silca's Dream**[10] 3888 3-8-9 **70**.................................... FrannyNorton 7 54
(Mick Channon) *chsd ldr tl over 3f out: sn rdn: wknd fnl f* **17/2**

59.42s (-0.18) **Going Correction** +0.025s/f (Good) **5** Ran SP% **110.0**
Speed ratings (Par 102): **102,97,94,89,88**
CSF £10.60 TOTE £3.90: £2.10, £1.50; EX 12.20 Trifecta £37.30 Pool: £2184.06 - 43.85 winning units..
Owner Elite Racing Club **Bred** Elite Racing Club **Trained** Kingsclere, Hants
FOCUS
A decent small-field 3yo sprint handicap. The winner rates a length personal best, with the second to form.

4222 BSCL MANAGING DIRECTOR IS ACTUALLY HERE H'CAP 1m 6f 213y
4:40 (4:41) (Class 5) (0-70,68) 3-Y-O **£2,587** (£770; £384; £192) **Stalls** Low

Form RPR
0-05 **1** **Tobacco**[10] 3893 3-8-2 **49**... PaulQuinn 2 53
(Tim Easterby) *hld up: swtchd rt and hdwy over 1f out: rdn to ld wl ins fnl f: styd on* **7/2**[2]
6545 **2** *nk* **Noor Al Haya (IRE)**[12] 3820 3-8-2 **49**.............................. FrannyNorton 4 53
(Mark Usher) *chsd ldrs: rdn over 2f out: hung lft and ev ch ins fnl f: hung rt towards fin: styd on* **7/1**[3]
-000 **3** *1* **Crystal Mist**[28] 3243 3-9-1 **62**....................................(b) LiamJones 7 64
(Harry Dunlop) *led after 1f: rdn: edgd rt and hdd 2f out: ev ch and hung lft ins fnl f: styd on same pce* **7/2**[2]
5-56 **4** *1/2* **Pearl Spice (IRE)**[116] 1053 3-9-1 **65**......................(b[1]) DarrenEgan[(3)] 3 67
(Tim Pitt) *hld up: rdn over 2f out: styd on fr over 1f out: nt trble ldrs* **28/1**
143 **5** *1/2* **Akdam (IRE)**[28] 2312 3-9-7 **68**... JimCrowley 5 69+
(Tony Carroll) *prom: rdn over 2f out: nt clr run ins fnl f: styd on* **9/4**[1]
0003 **6** *1* **Jomari (IRE)**[6] 4030 3-7-13 **49** oh4.................................. NeilFarley[(3)] 8 49
(Declan Carroll) *led 1f: chsd ldr: rdn to ld and bmpd 2f out: hdd and no ex wl ins fnl f* **7/1**[3]
466 **7** *1 1/4* **Dawn Beat**[27] 3272 3-8-5 **57** ow1............................... MatthewLawson[(5)] 1 55
(Jonathan Portman) *s.i.s: in rr: rdn over 2f out: no imp fnl f* **11/1**

3m 20.1s (1.10) **Going Correction** -0.10s/f (Good) **7** Ran SP% **112.0**
Speed ratings (Par 100): **93,92,92,92,91 91,90**
toteswingers 1&2 £2.90, 2&3 £3.90, 1&3 £2.80 CSF £26.49 CT £89.56 TOTE £4.60: £2.90, £2.80; EX 26.50 Trifecta £126.30 Pool: £4106.60 - 24.37 winning units..
Owner Patrick Milmo **Bred** Meon Valley Stud **Trained** Great Habton, N Yorks
■ Stewards' Enquiry : Paul Quinn two-day ban: used whip above permitted level (Jul 25-26)
FOCUS
A modest staying 3yo handicap in which there was a contested early pace, but the tempo slowed down the back straight. They finished in a bunch and the form is limited.

4223 COMMSCOPE SOLUTIONS YOUR TRUSTED ADVISOR MAIDEN STKS 1m 2f 188y
5:15 (5:16) (Class 5) 3-Y-O+ **£2,587** (£770; £384; £192) **Stalls** Low

Form RPR
5-22 **1** **Sunbula (USA)**[20] 3530 3-8-9 72.................................... SteveDrowne 1 77
(Charles Hills) *mde all: rdn and edgd rt fr over 1f out: styd on* **4/1**[2]
3 **2** *1/2* **Bushel (USA)**[12] 3805 3-9-0 0... FrannyNorton 11 81+
(Mark Johnston) *a.p: chsd wnr 9f out: rdn and nt clr run over 1f out: styng on whn n.m.r wl ins fnl f* **5/2**[1]

6- **3** 1 3/4 **National Poet (IRE)**[314] 5797 3-9-0 0 JimCrowley 4 78
(Saeed bin Suroor) *chsd ldrs: rdn over 2f out: styd on same pce ins fnl f* **7/1**[3]

4 1 **Cosmic Curious (GER)** 3-9-0 0 RichardMullen 6 76+
(Lady Cecil) *hld up: hdwy over 2f out: styd on: nt rch ldrs* **14/1**

6-0 **5** 2 1/4 **Happy Families**[28] 3237 3-8-9 0 JohnFahy 5 67
(Heather Main) *chsd wnr 2f: remained handy: rdn over 2f out: no ex fnl f* **100/1**

0-3 **6** hd **Gamble**[20] 3542 3-8-9 0 StevieDonohoe 10 67+
(Michael Bell) *hld up: shkn up over 2f out: hdwy over 1f out: no imp fnl f* **14/1**

26- **7** 1 1/2 **Ikhtisas (USA)**[260] 7332 3-9-0 0 FrederikTylicki 7 69+
(Saeed bin Suroor) *hld up in tch: plld hrd: rdn and nt clr run over 2f out: styd on same pce fr over 1f out* **5/2**[1]

04 **8** 2 **Perfect Spell**[21] 3491 3-8-7 0 OisinMurphy(7) 8 65
(Andrew Balding) *prom: lost pl 4f out: n.d after* **22/1**

00 **9** 2 3/4 **Achtung**[8] 3957 3-8-11 0 (p) DarrenEgan(3) 12 60
(Jeremy Noseda) *prom: rdn over 2f out: wknd over 1f out* **50/1**

6/5 **10** 9 **Blues Buddy**[17] 3619 6-9-7 0 AdamBeschizza 3 39
(H Edward Haynes) *prom tl rdn and wknd over 2f out* **150/1**

11 1/2 **Scala Santa** 4-9-2 0 ThomasGarner(5) 2 38
(Martin Bosley) *s.i.s: rn green and a in rr: wknd 3f out* **100/1**

0 **12** hd **Mickelson (IRE)**[115] 1069 7-9-12 0 AidanColeman 9 43
(Jonjo O'Neill) *s.i.s: a in rr: wknd 3f out* **50/1**

2m 19.96s (-1.14) **Going Correction** -0.10s/f (Good)
WFA 3 from 4yo+ 12lb **12** Ran SP% **113.9**
Speed ratings (Par 103): **100,99,98,97,96 95,94,93,91,84 84,84**
toteswingers 1&2 £2.80, 2&3 £4.60, 1&3 £6.50 CSF £13.41 TOTE £5.60: £1.40, £1.20, £2.00; EX 14.30 Trifecta £76.50 Pool: £2903.00 - 28.42 winning units..
Owner Hamdan Al Maktoum **Bred** Shadwell Farm LLC **Trained** Lambourn, Berks

FOCUS
An ordinary middle-distance maiden which was steadily run, and has been rated around the winner. The fifth is the doubt.
T/Plt: £59.20 to a £1 stake. Pool of £44796.71 - 552.34 winning tickets. T/Qpdt: £17.20 to a £1 stake. Pool of £2438.08 - 104.36 winning tickets. CR

4224 - 4230a (Foreign Racing) - See Raceform Interactive

3555
ASCOT (R-H)
Friday, July 12

OFFICIAL GOING: Good to firm (watered) (straight 9.0, round 8.2)
Rail realignment added 10yds to Old Mile, 14yds to 10f and 16yds to 12f.

4231 HELICAL BAR EBF MAIDEN STKS 6f
2:00 (2:00) (Class 3) 2-Y-O **£7,762** (£2,310; £1,154; £577) **Stalls High**

Form RPR

02 **1** **Mappa Mundi (USA)**[8] 3991 2-9-5 0 SebSanders 3 83
(Eve Johnson Houghton) *mostly pressed ldr: shkn up to ld jst over 1f out: styd on wl fnl f* **15/2**

2 1 **Tanzeel (IRE)** 2-9-5 0 DaneO'Neill 5 80+
(Charles Hills) *slowest away: hld up in rr: gd prog fr 2f out: rdn and styd on fnl f to take 2nd nr fin* **12/1**

3 shd **Toofi (FR)** 2-9-5 0 JimmyFortune 4 79+
(Roger Varian) *dwlt: hld up in rr: looking for room jst over 2f out: gd prog over 1f out: r.o fnl f: nrly snatched 2nd* **11/2**[3]

56 **4** shd **Crowdmania**[28] 3295 2-9-5 0 JoeFanning 8 79
(Mark Johnston) *mde most: rdn and hdd jst over 1f out: kpt on but lost 2 pls nr fin* **10/3**[2]

0 **5** 1/2 **Lincoln (IRE)**[28] 3295 2-9-5 0 MartinHarley 2 78
(Mick Channon) *trckd ldrs: shkn up 2f out: styd on fnl f but nvr able to chal* **9/4**[1]

6 2 1/2 **Bold Spirit** 2-9-5 0 PatDobbs 1 70+
(Richard Hannon) *wl in tch: pushed along and outpcd fr 2f out: n.d after* **16/1**

7 1 3/4 **Lawyer (IRE)** 2-9-5 0 KirstyMilczarek 6 64
(Luca Cumani) *pressed ldrs tl wknd wl over 1f out* **25/1**

8 shd **Gloss (IRE)** 2-9-5 0 SteveDrowne 7 64+
(Richard Hannon) *w ldrs tl wknd wl over 1f out* **25/1**

9 1 3/4 **Wilde Inspiration (IRE)** 2-9-5 0 RichardThomas 11 58
(Ralph Beckett) *prom over 2f: struggling in rr over 2f out* **33/1**

10 4 1/2 **Stomp** 2-9-5 0 GeorgeBaker 12 44
(Roger Charlton) *lost prom pl over 4f out: struggling in rr sn after 1/2-way* **10/1**

11 2 **If (GER)** 2-9-5 0 LiamKeniry 10 37
(Andrew Balding) *a in rr: struggling fr 1/2-way* **66/1**

1m 14.41s (-0.09) **Going Correction** -0.05s/f (Good) **11** Ran SP% **115.8**
Speed ratings (Par 98): **98,96,96,96,95 92,90,89,87,81 78**
Tote Swingers: 1&2 £13.80, 1&3 £9.60, 2&3 £11.50 CSF £88.10 TOTE £6.40: £2.10, £3.90, £2.30; EX 87.60 Trifecta £394.30 Pool: £1,801.19 - 3.45 winning units..
Owner Anthony Pye-Jeary & the late Mel Smith **Bred** Rockhart Trading Ltd **Trained** Blewbury, Oxon

FOCUS
The rail was in 3yds on the round course, increasing to 9yds in the home straight. As a result actual distances on the round course were 1m10yds, 1m4f16yds and 1m6f18yds. The ground had quickened up slightly from that advertised and was officially good to firm all over. The consensus amongst the jockeys after the opener was that conditions were fast. This looked just a fair maiden, but it should produce future winners. The winning time was a fraction over two seconds outside standard.

4232 COMMERCIAL PROPERTY LAW BY DARBYS SOLICITORS NURSERY H'CAP 6f
2:35 (2:35) (Class 4) 2-Y-O **£6,469** (£1,925; £962; £481) **Stalls High**

Form RPR

423 **1** **Sartorialist (IRE)**[18] 3624 2-8-0 **69** DarrenEgan(3) 7 72
(J S Moore) *mde virtually all: rdn to assert over 1f out: styd on fnl f: hld on nr fin* **20/1**

1 **2** nk **Grecian (IRE)**[30] 3211 2-8-13 **79** JimmyFortune 5 81+
(Paul Cole) *t.k.h: hld up bhd ldrs: shkn up over 1f out: hrd rdn and r.o to go 2nd last 100yds: clsng on wnr fin* **9/4**[1]

352 **3** 1 1/4 **Princess Rose**[16] 3673 2-8-9 **75** MartinHarley 8 73
(William Haggas) *trckd ldrs: rdn over 1f out: styd on same pce fnl f: nvr able to chal* **14/1**

046 **4** 1 **Handwoven (IRE)**[20] 3565 2-8-4 **70** JoeFanning 3 65
(Mark Johnston) *w wnr tl nt qckn over 1f out: fdd fnl f* **14/1**

51 **5** hd **A Childs Dream (IRE)**[44] 2771 2-8-4 **70** KieranO'Neill 1 64+
(Richard Hannon) *settled in last: rdn and struggling 2f out: styd on fnl f: nrly snatched 4th* **16/1**

51 **6** 1 1/4 **Chord Chart (IRE)**[18] 3640 2-9-4 **84** DaneO'Neill 2 74
(Saeed bin Suroor) *t.k.h early: trckd ldng pair and racd on outer: rdn and wknd over 1f out* **5/2**[2]

2210 **7** 2 1/4 **Beau Nash (IRE)**[24] 3424 2-9-2 **87** WilliamTwiston-Davies(5) 4 70+
(Richard Hannon) *a towards rr: rdn and wknd 2f out* **4/1**[3]

426 **8** nk **Primitorio (IRE)**[50] 2595 2-8-3 **69** MartinLane 6 51
(Ralph Beckett) *dwlt: sn trckd ldrs: rdn and wknd 2f out* **10/1**

1m 14.61s (0.11) **Going Correction** -0.05s/f (Good) **8** Ran SP% **112.4**
Speed ratings (Par 96): **97,96,94,93,93 91,88,88**
Tote Swingers: 1&2 £3.70, 1&3 £14.20, 2&3 £20.50 CSF £63.06 CT £668.92 TOTE £26.40: £5.00, £1.30, £2.70; EX 69.00 Trifecta £622.10 Pool: £2,676.86 - 3.22 winning units..
Owner Kieron Badger & J S Moore **Bred** Padraic Connolly **Trained** Upper Lambourn, Berks
■ Stewards' Enquiry : Darren Egan two-day ban: used whip above permitted level (Jul 26,28)

FOCUS
They dawdled for the first half-mile of this nursery and that played into the hands of the winner. The winning time was 0.2sec slower than the opener.

4233 CLOSE BROTHERS PROPERTY FINANCE H'CAP 1m 6f
3:05 (3:06) (Class 3) (0-95,95) 3-Y-O+
£7,158 (£2,143; £1,071; £535; £267; £134) **Stalls Low**

Form RPR

-400 **1** **Silver Lime (USA)**[20] 3559 4-9-10 **91** GeorgeBaker 4 101+
(Roger Charlton) *trckd ldng trio: wnt 3rd 4f out: smooth prog to ld over 1f out: shkn up to assert whn briefly pressed ins fnl f* **11/2**[2]

5-44 **2** 3/4 **Caravan Rolls On**[20] 3559 5-10-0 **95** HarryBentley 8 104
(Peter Chapple-Hyam) *hld up in last trio: prog jst over 2f out: rdn to chse wnr jst ins fnl f: tried to chal and r.o but readily hld* **5/4**[1]

3102 **3** 2 1/2 **Noble Silk**[21] 3531 4-9-8 **92** (p) DarrenEgan(3) 9 97
(Lucy Wadham) *hld up disputing 6th: lost pl fr 4f out and in last pair over 2f out: drvn and styd on over 1f out: tk 3rd last stride* **9/1**

-420 **4** nse **Suegioo (FR)**[34] 3115 4-9-7 **88** (p) MartinHarley 10 93+
(Marco Botti) *trckd ldng trio: rdn over 2f out: impeded over 1f out: styd on same pce fnl f and nrly won battle for 3rd* **8/1**[3]

0-00 **5** nse **Softsong (FR)**[24] 3423 5-9-10 **91** ChrisCatlin 1 96
(Philip Hobbs) *hld up disputing 6th: prog 3f out: cl up and shifted rt over 1f out: outpcd fnl f: kpt on* **33/1**

406/ **6** 2 **Sadler's Risk (IRE)**[98] 5271 5-9-9 **90** JoeFanning 3 92
(Mark Johnston) *trckd ldr 2f and again 6f out: led over 2f out: rdn and hdd over 1f out: wknd ins fnl f* **8/1**[3]

4616 **7** 3/4 **Taglietelle**[21] 3531 4-8-8 **82** OisinMurphy(7) 5 83
(Andrew Balding) *trckd ldr after 2f to 6f out: pushed along 4f out: lost pl over 2f out: steadily fdd* **14/1**

-143 **8** hd **Sizzler**[30] 3206 3-8-0 **82** oh2 MartinLane 2 85
(Ralph Beckett) *awkward s: squeezed out and snatched up after 1f: effrt on inner fr last trio over 3f out: no prog 2f out: sn btn* **14/1**

50-1 **9** 1 1/4 **Swinging Hawk (GER)**[48] 2648 7-8-6 **76** oh1 RyanPowell(3) 7 75
(Ian Williams) *hld up in last trio: rdn and no prog whn wd into st 3f out: n.d after* **20/1**

3/00 **10** 8 **Investissement**[24] 3423 7-9-5 **91** (t) WilliamTwiston-Davies(5) 6 81
(David Pipe) *rousted after s to ld: hdd over 2f out: wkng whn hmpd over 1f out* **20/1**

3m 1.05s (181.05)
WFA 3 from 4yo+ 15lb **10** Ran SP% **117.8**
Tote Swingers: 1&2 £2.50, 1&3 £14.40, 2&3 £3.90 CSF £12.53 CT £62.59 TOTE £6.60: £2.10, £1.10, £2.10; EX 15.40 Trifecta £113.20 Pool: £2,528.46 - 16.74 winning units..
Owner K Abdullah **Bred** Millsec Ltd **Trained** Beckhampton, Wilts
■ Stewards' Enquiry : Chris Catlin three-day ban: careless riding (Jul 26,28,29)

FOCUS
A decent staying handicap over a rarely used trip, but the pace wasn't that strong so not a true test of stamina.

4234 CUSHMAN & WAKEFIELD FILLIES' H'CAP (FOR JOHN TRAVERS MEMORIAL TROPHY) 1m 4f
3:40 (3:41) (Class 3) (0-95,88) 3-Y-O+ **£8,409** (£2,502; £1,250; £625) **Stalls Low**

Form RPR

1-12 **1** **Kikonga**[19] 3610 3-8-12 **85** KirstyMilczarek 2 98+
(Luca Cumani) *trckd ldng pair and sn clr of rest: wnt 2nd over 3f out: led over 2f out and sn clr: rdn and r.o wl: unchal* **7/2**[2]

-234 **2** 4 **Miss Cap Estel**[14] 3755 4-9-8 **82** JimmyFortune 8 89
(Andrew Balding) *hld up in last and sn wl off the pce: gng wl whn nt clr run over 2f out and wnr already gone: prog over 1f out: r.o to take 2nd last 100yds: no ch* **9/1**

0-64 **3** 3/4 **Saint Hilary**[25] 3409 4-10-0 **88** MartinDwyer 1 93
(William Muir) *s.i.s: sn chsd clr ldrs in 5th: clsd fr 4f out: rdn to chse clr wnr 2f out: kpt on but no imp: lost 2nd last 100yds* **20/1**

-040 **4** 5 **Lady Rosamunde**[27] 3344 5-9-10 **84** (p) HayleyTurner 5 81
(Marcus Tregoning) *hld up in 6th and sn wl off the pce: rdn and prog over 2f out: disp 2nd briefly over 1f out: wknd fnl f* **8/1**

0050 **5** 1 3/4 **Party Line**[13] 3824 4-9-11 **85** JoeFanning 7 79
(Mark Johnston) *hld up in last trio and sn wl off the pce: rdn over 2f out: modest prog only and fdd over 1f out* **5/1**[3]

1143 **6** 4 **Poetic Verse**[16] 3698 3-8-4 **77** NickyMackay 6 65
(Rod Millman) *chsd clr ldng trio: rdn over 2f out: pressed for a pl over 1f out: sn wknd* **14/1**

-421 **7** 11 **Muthmera (USA)**[13] 3806 3-8-10 **83** (p) DaneO'Neill 4 53
(Roger Varian) *led at str pce: hdd & wknd qckly over 2f out: t.o* **2/1**[1]

324 **8** 3/4 **Saint Helena (IRE)**[20] 3579 5-9-5 **79** GeorgeBaker 3 48
(Harry Dunlop) *hld up in last trio and sn wl off the pce: effrt on inner over 2f out: sn no prog: wknd over 1f out: t.o* **10/1**

0154 **9** 17 **Emman Bee (IRE)**[11] 3899 4-8-8 **71** SimonPearce(3) 9 13
(Luke Dace) *chsd ldr to over 3f out: wknd rapidly: wl t.o* **28/1**

2m 30.48s (-2.02) **Going Correction** -0.05s/f (Good)
WFA 3 from 4yo+ 13lb **9** Ran SP% **117.3**
Speed ratings (Par 104): **104,101,100,97,96 93,86,85,74**
Tote Swingers: 1&2 £7.20, 1&3 £27.80, 2&3 £33.40 CSF £35.59 CT £554.33 TOTE £4.40: £2.00, £2.20, £5.50; EX 36.90 Trifecta £403.70 Pool: £2,876.17 - 5.34 winning units..
Owner Fittocks Stud **Bred** Fittocks Stud Ltd **Trained** Newmarket, Suffolk

The Form Book Flat, Raceform Ltd, Compton, RG20 6NL.

FOCUS
This fillies' handicap was run at a strong pace and the form looks rock solid.

4235 LAND SECURITIES H'CAP 6f
4:15 (4:16) (Class 3) (0-90,90) 3-Y-O+ **£7,439** (£2,213; £1,106; £553) **Stalls** High

Form RPR
0362 **1** **Al Khan (IRE)**[8] 3980 4-9-4 **80** .... MartinHarley 1 90
(Violet M Jordan) *hld up towards rr: gd prog towards nr side fr 2f out: led over 1f out: hrd pressed last 100yds: hld on wl* **4/1**[2]
1106 **2** *nk* **Gabbiano**[20] 3586 4-9-0 **81** .... RobertTart(5) 10 90
(Jeremy Gask) *hld up in last trio: rdn and gd prog wl over 1f out towards nr side: chsd wnr fnl f: str chal last 100yds: jst hld* **7/2**[1]
14-0 **3** *1 ¾* **Signor Sassi**[55] 2444 4-9-7 **83** ....[1] ShaneKelly 9 86+
(William Knight) *hld up in last pair: rdn 2f out: gd prog towards nr side jst over 1f out: r.o to take 3rd nr fin* **6/1**
5403 **4** *½* **Apollo D'Negro (IRE)**[15] 3720 5-8-13 **80** .... RyanTate(5) 2 82
(Clive Cox) *t.k.h: w ldrs: upsides and disp briefly wl over 1f out: sn outpcd* **10/1**
0230 **5** *¾* **Crew Cut (IRE)**[41] 2868 5-9-9 **85** ....(b) DaneO'Neill 3 84
(Jeremy Gask) *hld up in tch on outer: nt qckn 2f out: n.d after: plugged on* **11/1**
0230 **6** *shd* **Alnoomaas (IRE)**[15] 3733 4-8-11 **76** .... SimonPearce(3) 5 75
(Luke Dace) *racd freely: led 2f: styd prom: disp briefly wl over 1f out: sn outpcd* **16/1**
1100 **7** *1 ½* **Powerful Presence (IRE)**[13] 3823 7-10-0 **90** .... DavidNolan 11 84
(David O'Meara) *t.k.h: prom: led after 2f to wl over 2f out: wl there over 1f out: fdd* **25/1**
0015 **8** *nk* **Chunky Diamond (IRE)**[1] 4203 4-8-9 **71** .... HayleyTurner 4 64
(Ruth Carr) *trckd ldng quartet: clsd to chal wl over 1f out: wknd fnl f* **7/1**
5025 **9** *shd* **Piazza San Pietro**[15] 3720 7-9-6 **82** ....(p) JoeFanning 8 75
(Zoe Davison) *awkward s and slowly away: a in rr: rdn and no prog 2f out* **16/1**
0023 **10** *6* **Sir Pedro**[15] 3714 4-9-2 **78** .... SteveDrowne 6 52
(Charles Hills) *rrd s: tk fierce hold and sn prom: led wl over 2f out: hdd & wknd rapidly wl over 1f out* **5/1**[3]

1m 13.61s (-0.89) **Going Correction** -0.05s/f (Good) **10** Ran SP% **118.7**
Speed ratings (Par 107): **103,102,100,99,98 98,96,96,95,87**
Tote Swingers: 1&2 £4.50, 1&3 £3.90, 2&3 £5.80 CSF £18.81 CT £86.18 TOTE £4.70: £1.80, £1.80, £1.80; EX 17.30 Trifecta £110.00 Pool: £3,157.00 - 21.52 winning units..
Owner Rakebackmypoker.com **Bred** Galadari Sons Stud Company Limited **Trained** Moreton Morrell, Warwicks

FOCUS
An interesting handicap featuring a couple of horses already due significant rises in their marks, but it was a very strange race for a sprint as they went no pace for the first-half of the race and the form is dubious. Despite that, the front three all came from behind.

4236 DELANCEY H'CAP 1m (R)
4:50 (4:51) (Class 3) (0-90,88) 3-Y-O **£7,439** (£2,213; £1,106; £553) **Stalls** Low

Form RPR
-621 **1** **Morpheus**[29] 3250 3-9-1 **82** .... MartinHarley 2 90+
(Lady Cecil) *difficult to load into stalls: hld up in 6th: looking for room and edgd lft 2f out: only 5th jst over 1f out: drvn and r.o fnl f to ld post* **2/1**[1]
214 **2** *nse* **Stableford**[27] 3338 3-9-2 **83** .... JimmyFortune 1 90
(Brian Meehan) *hld up in last: gd prog on outer and edgd rt 2f out: led 1f out: drvn fnl f: hdd post* **9/2**[3]
-431 **3** *nk* **Estifzaaz (IRE)**[20] 3572 3-8-10 **77** .... DaneO'Neill 5 83
(Charles Hills) *dwlt: rcvrd to ld after 1f: kicked on over 2f out and sn 2 l clr: hdd 1f out: styd on* **9/1**
3211 **4** *hd* **Secret Art (IRE)**[27] 3342 3-9-4 **85** .... MartinDwyer 3 91
(Ralph Beckett) *chsd ldng pair: rdn over 2f out: styd on after but nvr quite able to chal* **4/1**[2]
3130 **5** *2* **You Da One (IRE)**[22] 3484 3-9-7 **88** .... HayleyTurner 7 89
(Andrew Balding) *wnt lft s: led 1f: chsd ldr to over 1f out: kpt on tl no ex last 150yds* **8/1**
0-63 **6** *13* **Private Alexander (IRE)**[6] 4081 3-9-6 **87** .... DavidNolan 4 60+
(David O'Meara) *hld up in 5th: shkn up and sing to struggle whn bdly bmpd 2f out: sn bhd* **6/1**
-125 **7** *8* **Al Mukhdam**[14] 3763 3-9-5 **86** .... JoeFanning 6 42+
(Peter Chapple-Hyam) *chsd ldrs: rdn and losing pl whn hmpd and snatched up 2f out: sn bhd* **12/1**

1m 40.05s (-0.65) **Going Correction** -0.05s/f (Good) **7** Ran SP% **114.6**
Speed ratings (Par 104): **101,100,100,100,98 85,77**
Tote Swingers: 1&2 £2.50, 1&3 £4.40, 2&3 £4.80 CSF £11.27 CT £64.40 TOTE £2.60: £1.30, £2.90; EX 14.30 Trifecta £60.00 Pool: £3,289.31 - 41.07 winning units..
Owner K Abdullah **Bred** Juddmonte Farms Ltd **Trained** Newmarket, Suffolk
■ Stewards' Enquiry : Martin Harley three-day ban: careless riding (Jul 26,28,29)

FOCUS
Another handicap featuring a couple who were well in compared with their revised marks and, as in the previous contest, one of those was the winner. It was something of a rough race and the pace was ordinary, but even so the first two were last and last-but-one turning for home.

4237 JOHN SIMS MEMORIAL APPRENTICE H'CAP 7f
5:25 (5:25) (Class 4) (0-85,80) 4-Y-O+ **£6,145** (£1,828; £913; £456) **Stalls** High

Form RPR
0000 **1** **Brocklebank (IRE)**[16] 3693 4-9-0 **73** .... JackDuern(5) 9 81
(Simon Dow) *awkward s and impeded: wl in rr: rdn 3f out: prog but hanging rt 2f out: sn chsd ldr: drvn and styd on wl to ld last strides* **40/1**
1533 **2** *nk* **Kinglami**[12] 3864 4-8-12 **71** .... EDLinehan(5) 6 78
(Brian Gubby) *mde most: rdn 2f out: kpt on wl fr over 1f out: hdd last strides* **8/1**
-004 **3** *nk* **Graphic (IRE)**[16] 3693 4-9-9 **80** .... RobertTart(3) 4 86
(William Haggas) *prom: rdn to chse ldr briefly 2f out: sn nt qckn: styd on wl again last 150yds: clsng at fin* **9/2**[3]
0004 **4** *6* **Rocky Reef**[28] 3274 4-9-9 **77** ....(v) ThomasBrown 7 67
(Philip Hide) *chsd ldrs: rdn over 2f out: sn outpcd: no threat in 4th fr over 1f out* **7/1**
1152 **5** *2 ¼* **Darnathean**[8] 3993 4-8-10 **69** ....(p) PhilipPrince(5) 8 53
(Paul D'Arcy) *dwlt: towards rr: rdn over 2f out: sn outpcd: n.d after* **11/4**[1]
3230 **6** *1 ½* **Prince Of Burma (IRE)**[32] 3157 5-9-5 **76** ....(b) NicoleNordblad(3) 3 56
(Jeremy Gask) *towards rr on outer: effrt over 2f out: wknd over 1f out* **16/1**
3650 **7** *2* **Caldercruix (USA)**[76] 1849 6-9-5 **76** ....(v) GeorgeDowning(3) 2 51
(James Evans) *chsd ldrs: prog to go 2nd 3f out to 2f out: sn wknd* **20/1**
0-01 **8** *5* **Fantasy Gladiator**[15] 3741 7-8-12 **69** ....(p) WilliamTwiston-Davies(3) 1 30
(John Quinn) *wnt rt s: a in rr: n.d fnl 2f* **8/1**
-065 **9** *4 ½* **My Learned Friend (IRE)**[10] 3926 9-8-4 **65** ....(p) JonathanWilletts(7) 11 14
(Andrew Balding) *wnt rt s: w ldr to 3f out: wknd qckly* **50/1**
/1-3 **10** *54* **Dance Express (IRE)**[13] 3842 4-9-6 **77** .... RyanTate(3) 5
(Clive Cox) *dwlt: sn chsd ldrs: rdn and wknd rapidly over 2f out: t.o and eased* **7/2**[2]

1m 26.08s (-1.52) **Going Correction** -0.05s/f (Good) **10** Ran SP% **116.8**
Speed ratings (Par 105): **106,105,105,98,95 94,91,86,81,19**
Tote Swingers: 1&2 £32.00, 2&3 £7.30 CSF £329.11 CT £1788.66 TOTE £41.10: £7.40, £2.40, £2.00; EX 361.80 Trifecta £2334.50 Part won. Pool: £3,112.74 - 0.38 winning units..
Owner J C G Chua **Bred** Vincent Reen **Trained** Epsom, Surrey
■ Stewards' Enquiry : Jack Duern two-day ban: used whip above shoulder height (Jul 28-29)

FOCUS
A decent event of its type and the pace was fair. The first three pulled well clear.
T/Plt: £55.80 to a £1 stake. Pool: £84,117.67 -1,099.06 winning tickets. T/Qpdt: £8.30 to a £1 stake. Pool: £6,345.27 - 562.02 winning tickets. JN

3948 CHEPSTOW (L-H)
Friday, July 12

OFFICIAL GOING: Good to firm (8.9)
Wind: Virtually nil Weather: Sunny

4238 BREWIN DOLPHIN APPRENTICE TRAINING SERIES H'CAP (PART OF THE RACING EXCELLENCE INITIATIVE) 1m 4f 23y
6:10 (6:10) (Class 5) (0-70,69) 4-Y-O+ **£2,587** (£770; £384; £192) **Stalls** Low

Form RPR
2304 **1** **Silver Samba**[20] 3587 4-9-9 **69** .... OisinMurphy(3) 8 78
(Andrew Balding) *chsd ldrs: chal 2f out: sn led: drvn and styd on wl fnl f* **6/4**[1]
5634 **2** *2* **Arch Event**[9] 3953 8-8-7 **50** oh1 ....(p) NoelGarbutt 1 56
(Bernard Llewellyn) *in tch: rdn and one pce 3f out: rallied fr 2f out and chsd wnr ins fnl f but a hld* **10/1**
-052 **3** *2 ¼* **Taste The Wine (IRE)**[17] 3133 7-9-3 **65** .... LouisSteward(5) 5 67
(Bernard Llewellyn) *in rr but in tch: hdwy 5f out: drvn to chal 2f out: outpcd fnl f* **5/2**[2]
-043 **4** *1 ¼* **Now What**[17] 3662 6-8-11 **59** .... DavidCoyle(5) 6 59
(Jonathan Portman) *sn narrow ldr: jnd fr 6f out: rdn 3f out: hd ins fnl 2f: styd wl there tl wknd fnl 100yds* **6/1**[3]
-360 **5** *2 ¾* **Captain Sharpe**[17] 3271 5-8-13 **61** ....(bt) SiobhanMiller(5) 4 57
(Bernard Llewellyn) *trckd ldr: chal fr 6f out and stl upsides 3f out: wknd 2f out* **12/1**
015- **6** *37* **Captain Cardington (IRE)**[125] 7490 4-9-5 **65** .... CiaranMckee(3) 3
(John O'Shea) *a in rr: lost tch over 4f out: t.o* **8/1**

2m 37.63s (-1.37) **Going Correction** -0.025s/f (Good) **6** Ran SP% **110.8**
Speed ratings (Par 103): **103,101,100,99,97 72**
toteswingers 1&2 £4.30, 1&3 £1.20, 2&3 £4.90 CSF £16.64 CT £33.10 TOTE £2.20: £1.50, £4.90; EX 19.30 Trifecta £45.80 Pool: £1094.09 - 17.88 winning units..
Owner BA Racing **Bred** Ptarmigan Bloodstock Ltd **Trained** Kingsclere, Hants

FOCUS
A weak handicap.

4239 BRITISH STALLION STUDS SUPPORTING BRITISH RACING EBF NOVICE STKS 5f 16y
6:40 (6:40) (Class 4) 2-Y-O **£5,013** (£1,491; £745) **Stalls** Centre

Form RPR
3312 **1** **Meritocracy (IRE)**[56] 2433 2-9-5 0 .... ChrisCatlin 3 95
(Paul Cole) *mde virtually all: pushed clr over 1f out: easily* **8/11**[1]
3044 **2** *5* **M'Selle (IRE)**[2] 4174 2-9-0 0 .... WilliamCarson 2 71
(Ronald Harris) *disp cl 2nd: rdn over 2f out: styd on to chse wnr jst ins fnl f but nvr any ch* **12/1**[3]
413 **3** *1 ¼* **Emperor's Hope (IRE)**[12] 3863 2-8-11 0 .... PatDobbs 1 64
(Richard Hannon) *disp cl 2nd: drvn over 1f out and no ch w wnr: one pce ins fnl f* **11/8**[2]

58.65s (-0.65) **Going Correction** -0.25s/f (Firm) **3** Ran SP% **107.7**
Speed ratings (Par 96): **95,87,85**
CSF £6.68 TOTE £1.70; EX 5.40 Trifecta £6.20 Pool: £534.30 - 63.75 winning units..
Owner Mrs Fitri Hay **Bred** Oghill House Stud **Trained** Whatcombe, Oxon

FOCUS
An impressive win for Meritocracy whose French form fully entitled him to win this.

4240 DISCOUNT TYRES FILLIES' H'CAP 1m 14y
7:10 (7:10) (Class 5) (0-70,70) 3-Y-O **£2,587** (£770; £384; £192) **Stalls** Centre

Form RPR
0303 **1** **Equitissa (IRE)**[9] 3951 3-9-4 **67** .... PatDobbs 8 75
(Richard Hannon) *towards rr tl hdwy to cl on ldrs over 3f out: wnt 2nd 2f out: drvn to chal fnl f and edgd lft: eventually got on top cl home and pushed out* **7/4**[1]
-204 **2** *hd* **Oilinda**[30] 3202 3-8-11 **67** .... LouisSteward(7) 2 74
(Michael Bell) *led: rdn and jnd fnl f: kpt on wl tl outpcd cl home* **7/2**[3]
0265 **3** *6* **Ishisoba**[17] 3661 3-8-8 **57** .... SteveDrowne 6 50
(Alastair Lidderdale) *chsd ldrs: drvn along to chse ldr over 3f out: easily outpcd by ldng duo fnl f* **8/1**
2-30 **4** *1* **Baltic Gin (IRE)**[57] 2394 3-8-12 **61** .... CathyGannon 7 52
(Malcolm Saunders) *in rr but wl in tch: hdwy to cl on ldrs 3f out: rdn to chal 2f out: easily outpcd fnl f* **10/3**[2]
4-36 **5** *1 ¾* **Perfect Calm (USA)**[37] 2979 3-9-7 **70** .... KieranO'Neill 5 57
(Richard Hannon) *in rr and sn detached: pushed along over 4f out: sme hdwy 2f out but nvr rchd ldrs and no ch after* **11/2**
060 **6** *9* **Shikamoo**[25] 3401 3-7-13 **51** .... DarrenEgan(3) 4 17
(Dr Jeremy Naylor) *trckd ldr tl over 3f out: wknd sn after* **25/1**

1m 33.64s (-2.56) **Going Correction** -0.25s/f (Firm) **6** Ran SP% **112.0**
Speed ratings (Par 97): **102,101,95,94,93 84**
toteswingers 1&2 £1.20, 1&3 £3.40, 2&3 £1.70 CSF £8.09 CT £35.87 TOTE £1.80: £1.10, £2.30; EX 9.20 Trifecta £29.80 Pool: £889.90 - 22.32 winning units..
Owner Mrs Philip Snow **Bred** Corrin Stud **Trained** East Everleigh, Wilts

FOCUS
A moderate fillies' race.

4241 HIGOS INSURANCE SERVICES H'CAP 1m 14y
7:40 (7:40) (Class 5) (0-70,70) 3-Y-O+ **£2,587** (£770; £384; £192) **Stalls** Centre

Form RPR
-000 **1** **Dana's Present**[20] 3575 4-9-9 **65** .... PatCosgrave 4 74
(George Baker) *sn led: travelling best 2f out: shkn up over 1f out: strly pressed fnl 150yds: hld on all out* **33/1**

0332 **2** *nse* **Offbeat Safaris (IRE)**[10] 3919 5-8-12 **54**........................ WilliamCarson 5 63
(Ronald Harris) *in tch: drvn and hdwy to chse wnr fr 2f out: chal u.p and upsides fnl 150yds: jst failed* **15/2**[3]

0542 **3** *2 1/2* **Sacred Square (GER)**[6] 4070 3-8-12 **63**..................(b[1]) FrederikTylicki 3 64
(William Haggas) *chsd ldrs: rdn and outpcd over 3f out: rallied u.p fnl f to take 3rd fnl 110yds but nvr any ch w ldng duo* **1/1**[1]

00-0 **4** *1 3/4* **Another Squeeze**[52] 2534 5-8-9 **51** oh2........................ CathyGannon 8 50
(Peter Hiatt) *chsd ldrs tl rdn 3f out and sn outpcd: styd on again clsng stages to take wl-hld 4th* **25/1**

1355 **5** *1/2* **Peak Storm**[9] 3951 4-9-12 **68**..............................(p) ChrisCatlin 2 66
(John O'Shea) *chsd ldrs: rdn to chal 2f out: wknd appr fnl f* **10/1**

2121 **6** *2 3/4* **The Scuttler (IRE)**[3] 4140 3-9-0 **68** 6ex........................ CharlesBishop(3) 1 58
(Mick Channon) *pressed ldrs: rdn 3f out: wknd appr fnl f* **2/1**[2]

1m 34.02s (-2.18) **Going Correction** -0.25s/f (Firm)
WFA 3 from 4yo+ 9lb **6** Ran SP% **111.0**
Speed ratings (Par 103): **100,99,97,95,95 92**
toteswingers 1&2 £18.20, 1&3 £6.50, 2&3 £1.60 CSF £238.21 TOTE £35.60: £9.40, £3.00; EX 230.80 Trifecta £472.10 Pool: £701.04 - 1.11 winning units..
Owner Whitsbury Racing Club **Bred** Newsells Park Stud **Trained** Manton, Wilts

FOCUS
An ordinary handicap.

4242 WESTERN DAILY PRESS H'CAP 1m 14y
8:10 (8:10) (Class 2) (0-100,92) 3-Y-O+ **£12,291** (£3,657; £1,827; £913) **Stalls** Centre

Form RPR

3310 **1** **Postscript (IRE)**[6] 4080 5-9-6 **87**........................ DarrenEgan(3) 1 96
(David Simcock) *trckd ldrs: hdwy 2f out: chsd ldr appr fnl f and led sn after: rdn and r.o strly fnl 110yds* **7/1**

1405 **2** *3/4* **Shahdaroba (IRE)**[27] 3342 3-9-5 **92**........................ DaneO'Neill 2 97
(Rod Millman) *led: rdn 2f out: jnd over 1f out and hdd sn after: kpt on but nt gng pce of wnr fnl 110yds* **9/2**[3]

1550 **3** *2 3/4* **Fehaydi**[22] 3484 3-9-5 **92**........................ SteveDrowne 6 91
(William Haggas) *in rr but in tch: drvn 3f out: little rspnse tl styd on u.p to take 3rd fnl 110yds but no ch w ldng duo* **10/11**[1]

5330 **4** *1* **Flashlight (IRE)**[42] 2844 3-8-12 **85**........................ MartinLane 4 81
(Mark Johnston) *sn chsng ldr: rdn to chal ins fnl 3f: wknd u.p over 1f out* **7/2**[2]

041- **5** *9* **The Cayterers**[307] 5535 11-8-13 **82**........................ PhilipPrince(5) 3 60
(Ronald Harris) *t.k.h early and chsd ldrs: wknd ins fnl 2f* **20/1**

1m 32.67s (-3.53) **Going Correction** -0.25s/f (Firm)
WFA 3 from 5yo+ 9lb **5** Ran SP% **110.0**
Speed ratings (Par 109): **107,106,103,102,93**
CSF £36.11 TOTE £8.10: £2.20, £2.50; EX 23.80 Trifecta £19.80 Pool: £444.65 - 16.80 winning units..
Owner Dr Marwan Koukash **Bred** Darley **Trained** Newmarket, Suffolk

FOCUS
A fair little handicap.

4243 DISCOUNT TYRES H'CAP 7f 16y
8:40 (8:40) (Class 4) (0-85,82) 3-Y-O+ **£4,690** (£1,395; £697; £348) **Stalls** Centre

Form RPR

-000 **1** **Dashing David (IRE)**[20] 3582 3-9-6 **82**........................ PatDobbs 4 90
(Richard Hannon) *in rr but in tch: rdn over 2f out str run u.p ins fnl f to ld last strides* **4/1**[3]

2312 **2** *nk* **Sarangoo**[8] 3988 5-9-5 **73**........................ CathyGannon 1 83
(Malcolm Saunders) *led: rdn 2f out and sn hrd pressed: kpt slt advantage and styd on wl fnl 50yds: hdd last strides* **2/1**[1]

3-55 **3** *nk* **Angelic Upstart (IRE)**[174] 272 5-9-2 **70**........................ LiamKeniry 6 79
(Andrew Balding) *chsd ldr: rdn to chal appr fnl f: no ex fnl 50yds and outpcd in 3rd clsng stages* **4/1**[3]

1-20 **4** *3 1/2* **Elnadwa (USA)**[14] 3777 3-9-4 **80**........................ DaneO'Neill 3 77
(Saeed bin Suroor) *in tch: rdn over 2f out and no imp: wknd ins fnl f* **11/4**[2]

5400 **5** *nk* **Corporal Maddox**[36] 3019 6-9-10 **78**..........................(p) SteveDrowne 2 77
(Ronald Harris) *chsd ldrs: rdn 2f out: wknd fnl f* **9/1**

1m 21.47s (-1.73) **Going Correction** -0.25s/f (Firm)
WFA 3 from 5yo+ 8lb **5** Ran SP% **110.0**
Speed ratings (Par 105): **99,98,98,94,93**
CSF £12.38 TOTE £5.50: £2.10, £1.10; EX 12.90 Trifecta £46.20 Pool: £276.86 - 4.48 winning units..
Owner Sir David Seale **Bred** Hascombe And Valiant Studs **Trained** East Everleigh, Wilts

FOCUS
Not a bad handicap.

4244 COUNTY MARQUEES H'CAP 6f 16y
9:10 (9:10) (Class 5) (0-70,68) 3-Y-O **£2,587** (£770; £384; £192) **Stalls** Centre

Form RPR

1662 **1** **Jimmy Elder**[18] 3621 3-9-5 **66**........................ PatDobbs 1 75
(Richard Hannon) *hld up in tch: hdwy to ld jst ins fnl 2f: drvn and kpt on wl whn chal fr over 1f out: drvn to assert clsng stages* **9/2**[3]

0042 **2** *1* **Lager Time (IRE)**[6] 4069 3-9-2 **63**........................ WilliamCarson 8 69
(David Evans) *in rr early: hdwy fr 3f out: chal fr ins fnl 2f tl no ex clsng stages* **10/3**[1]

4405 **3** *1 3/4* **Starlight Angel (IRE)**[16] 3699 3-9-0 **66**........................ PhilipPrince(5) 4 66
(Ronald Harris) *s.i.s: sn rcvrd to chse ldrs: rdn and outpcd over 2f out: styd on again fnl f to take 3rd fnl 75yds but no ch w ldng duo* **10/1**

0135 **4** *nk* **The Black Jacobin**[10] 3927 3-9-7 **68**..........................(b) LiamKeniry 7 67
(J S Moore) *in tch: drvn 3f out: styd on under prssure to press for 3rd fnl 50yds but nvr any ch w ldng duo* **6/1**

004 **5** *1 1/2* **Khefyn (IRE)**[52] 2544 3-9-7 **68**........................ SteveDrowne 6 62
(Ronald Harris) *in rr but in tch: drvn over 2f out: styd on same pce ins fnl f* **7/1**

4352 **6** *nk* **Imperial Spirit**[2] 4176 3-8-0 **50**..........................(v) DarrenEgan(3) 2 43
(Mick Channon) *pressed ldrs: rdn 2f out: wknd over 1f out* **14/1**

1034 **7** *1 3/4* **Edged Out**[18] 3622 3-9-6 **67**........................ CathyGannon 5 55
(Christopher Mason) *pressed ldr: led 3f out: hdd jst ins fnl 2f: wknd over 1f out* **4/1**[2]

5405 **8** *7* **Majestic Red (IRE)**[16] 3679 3-8-3 **50**........................ KieranO'Neill 3 15
(Malcolm Saunders) *led to 1/2-way: wknd ins fnl 2f* **20/1**

-500 **9** *3 1/2* **Bheleyf (IRE)**[51] 2572 3-8-13 **60**........................ DaneO'Neill 9 14
(Joseph Tuite) *outpcd* **16/1**

1m 10.5s (-1.50) **Going Correction** -0.25s/f (Firm) **9** Ran SP% **114.4**
Speed ratings (Par 100): **100,98,96,95,93 93,91,81,77**
toteswingers 1&2 £2.50, 1&3 £10.80, 2&3 £5.30 CSF £19.70 TOTE £4.60: £1.40, £2.40, £3.20; EX 16.30 Trifecta £42.10 Pool: £629.29 - 11.20 winning units..
Owner Pineapple Stud **Bred** Mrs R Ablett **Trained** East Everleigh, Wilts

FOCUS
A moderate 3-y-o handicap.

T/Plt: £613.20 to a £1 stake. Pool: £54,994.82 - 65.46 winning tickets T/Qpdt: £69.10 to a £1 stake. Pool: £4,960.35 - 53.10 winning tickets ST

3801 CHESTER (L-H)
Friday, July 12

OFFICIAL GOING: Good to firm (good in places; watered; 8.0)
Rail between 6f and 1.5f moved out 6yds adding 20yds to races 2,3, 4 & 5, 24yds to race 1, 26yds to race 7, and 38yds to race 6
Wind: Light, against Weather: Hot and Sunny

4245 MOCOCO H'CAP (FOR LADY AMATEUR RIDERS) 7f 122y
6:20 (6:23) (Class 4) (0-80,80) 4-Y-O+ **£6,586** (£2,026; £1,013) **Stalls** Low

Form RPR

0406 **1** **Verse Of Love**[14] 3757 4-10-2 **80**........................ MissHDoyle(5) 1 90
(David Evans) *mde all: rdn over 1f out: hrd pressed ins fnl f: all out towards fin* **9/2**[1]

5-54 **2** *nk* **My Single Malt (IRE)**[45] 2761 5-9-6 **70**........................ MissLWilson(5) 4 79
(Julie Camacho) *chsd ldrs: rdn to take 2nd 1f out: sn chal wnr: r.o: jst hld* **6/1**[3]

6432 **3** *1 3/4* **Hoppy's Flyer (FR)**[24] 3445 5-9-3 **61** oh1 ow1.. MissBeckyBrisbourne 3 67
(Mark Brisbourne) *midfield: hdwy on outert 2f out: rdn to chse ldrs over 1f out: styd on ins fnl f: nt quite able to chal front two* **5/1**[2]

-242 **4** *3/4* **Kakapuka**[22] 3511 6-9-8 **72**........................ MissJoannaMason(5) 10 75
(Anabel K Murphy) *chsd wnr: ev ch 3f out: rdn and nt qckn whn lost 2nd 1f out: sn edgd lft: kpt on same pce fnl 75yds* **17/2**

6510 **5** *3/4* **Space War**[42] 2845 6-9-6 **70**........................ AnnaHesketh(5) 9 71
(Michael Easterby) *hld up: nt clr run 2f out: sn swtchd lft and hdwy: styd on towards fin: nt quite rch ldrs* **12/1**

6506 **6** *shd* **Cyflymder (IRE)**[11] 3895 7-9-7 **66**........................ MissSBrotherton 12 67
(David C Griffiths) *in tch: clsd to chse ldrs over 2f out: effrt over 1f out: kpt on ins fnl f but nvr able to chal* **11/1**

000- **7** *4 1/2* **Kyllachy Star**[258] 7415 7-10-3 **76**........................ MissADeniel 11 65
(Richard Fahey) *hld up: rdn over 1f out: kpt on ins fnl f: nvr a threat* **7/1**

5360 **8** *3 1/4* **Sardanapalus**[6] 4055 4-9-9 **73**..........................(b) MissSMDoolan(5) 7 54
(Kevin Ryan) *midfield: lost pl 5f out: outpcd over 2f out: n.d after* **11/1**

3356 **9** *1* **Methaaly (IRE)**[5] 4102 10-9-2 **61** oh3..................(be) MissMMullineaux 5 40
(Michael Mullineaux) *towards rr: pushed along over 2f out: nvr a threat* **33/1**

0004 **10** *3/4* **Lucky Dan (IRE)**[7] 4018 7-9-11 **75**........................ MissAimeeMKing(5) 2 52
(Paul Green) *chsd ldrs: effrt on outer 4f out: sn chalng: rdn and wknd over 2f out* **16/1**

0000 **11** *1/2* **Hayek**[16] 3683 6-8-12 **62**..............................(b) MissKMargarson(5) 8 38
(Tim Easterby) *dwlt: a bhd: nvr a threat* **11/1**

1m 35.58s (1.78) **Going Correction** +0.25s/f (Good) **11** Ran SP% **113.7**
Speed ratings (Par 105): **101,100,98,98,97 97,92,89,88,87 87**
toteswingers 1&2 £7.00, 1&3 £3.30, 2&3 £4.00 CSF £29.94 CT £124.71 TOTE £6.00: £1.20, £2.10, £1.90; EX 26.60 Trifecta £76.70 Pool: £1128.18 - 11.02 winning units..
Owner Wayne Clifford **Bred** Mrs S Clifford **Trained** Pandy, Monmouths

FOCUS
The seven-race card kicked off with a handicap for lady amateur riders. After a dry, sunny day the ground was described as good to firm, good in places. They went without Frognal, who refused to enter the stalls.

4246 MINSTRELL RECRUITMENT NURSERY H'CAP 7f 2y
6:50 (6:51) (Class 4) 2-Y-O **£6,469** (£1,925; £962; £481) **Stalls** Low

Form RPR

504 **1** **Finn Class (IRE)**[13] 3815 2-8-10 **66**........................ LukeMorris 6 68+
(Michael Bell) *midfield: pushed along over 3f out: rdn over 2f out: prog whn nt clr run and swtchd rt wl ins fnl f: str run towards fin: got up fnl stride* **9/2**[2]

0334 **2** *hd* **Party Ruler (IRE)**[6] 4061 2-9-4 **74**........................ JimCrowley 1 75
(Tom Dascombe) *led: rdn over 1f out: hrd pressed ins fnl f: hdd fnl stride* **3/1**[1]

6345 **3** *1/2* **Dancing Sal (IRE)**[14] 3753 2-8-7 **63**........................ AndrewElliott 4 63
(David Evans) *racd keenly: chsd ldrs: wnt 2nd over 1f out: str chal ins fnl f: hld fnl strides* **25/1**

3041 **4** *2* **Heskin (IRE)**[14] 3753 2-9-2 **72**........................ BarryMcHugh 3 66+
(Richard Fahey) *bmpd s: hld up: hdwy to trck ldrs over 4f out: rdn and nt qckn over 1f out: kpt on ins fnl f: one pce towards fin* **3/1**[1]

4610 **5** *shd* **Know Your Name**[20] 3555 2-9-2 **77**........................ DeclanBates(5) 8 71
(David Evans) *in rr: outpcd over 2f out: hrd at work wl over 1f out: hung lft and styd on ins fnl f: nrst fin* **12/1**

4040 **6** *1/2* **Donny Rover (IRE)**[13] 3810 2-9-2 **72**..........................(p) RoystonFfrench 2 65
(David C Griffiths) *bmpd s: in rr: a rdn along: nt clr run over 1f out: plugged on: nvr able to trble ldrs* **20/1**

653 **7** *1 1/2* **Shimba Hills**[28] 3282 2-8-13 **69**........................ GrahamGibbons 7 58
(Mick Channon) *hld up: impr to take cl 2nd after 2f: rdn and lost 2nd over 1f out: wknd ins fnl f* **9/1**[3]

641 **8** *nk* **Atheera (IRE)**[16] 3680 2-9-2 **72**........................ FrannyNorton 5 61
(Mark Johnston) *chsd ldr for 2f: remained handy: pushed along over 3f out: rdn 2f out: wknd over 1f out* **9/2**[2]

1m 30.01s (3.51) **Going Correction** +0.25s/f (Good) **8** Ran SP% **112.7**
Speed ratings (Par 96): **89,88,88,85,85 85,83,83**
toteswingers 1&2 £3.40, 1&3 £29.10, 2&3 £17.50 CSF £17.84 CT £297.41 TOTE £7.20: £2.80, £1.30, £9.00; EX 28.50 Trifecta £383.30 Pool: £1162.58 - 2.27 winning units..
Owner Saif Ali **Bred** Rabbah Bloodstock Limited **Trained** Newmarket, Suffolk

FOCUS
The official ratings shown are estimated and for information only. A fair nursery.

4247 CSP AUDIO VISUAL H'CAP 5f 16y
7:20 (7:20) (Class 2) (0-105,99) 3-Y-**£12,602** (£3,772; £1,886; £944; £470) **Stalls** Low

Form RPR

2120 **1** **Riskit Fora Biskit (IRE)**[20] 3562 3-8-13 **91**........................ LukeMorris 1 101
(Michael Bell) *mde all: rdn over 1f out: r.o ins fnl f: in command fnl 75yds* **4/1**[3]

1314 **2** *2* **Tumblewind**[6] 4057 3-8-7 **85**........................ FrannyNorton 3 88
(Richard Whitaker) *chsd ldrs: wnt 2nd over 1f out: tried to chal ins fnl f: no imp on wnr fnl 75yds* **11/2**

321 **3** *1 1/4* **Smart Daisy K**[6] 4057 3-8-5 **83** 6ex........................ BarryMcHugh 2 82
(Andrew Hollinshead) *plld hrd: prom: rdn over 1f out: nt qckn ins fnl f* **11/4**[1]

-303 **4** *4* **Cosmic Chatter**[20] 3584 3-9-7 **99** GrahamGibbons 4 83
(David Barron) *in rr: pushed along 2f out: one pce fnl f: nvr able to trble ldrs* **4/1**[3]

2031 **5** *1 3/4* **Brazen**[23] 3474 3-8-9 **87** (b[1]) JimCrowley 5 65
(David Simcock) *in tch: prom over 3f out: ev ch 2f out: rdn over 1f out: wknd ins fnl f* **3/1**[2]

6065 **6** *1* **Jillnextdoor (IRE)**[20] 3562 3-8-9 **87** (v) RoystonFfrench 6 61
(Mick Channon) *hld up: pushed along 3f out: sn rdn: outpcd fnl f* **20/1**

1m 1.28s (0.28) **Going Correction** +0.25s/f (Good) **6** Ran SP% **111.8**
Speed ratings (Par 106): **107,103,101,95,92 91**
toteswingers 1&2 £6.00, 1&3 £1.10, 2&3 £5.60 CSF £25.23 TOTE £5.80: £4.20, £6.40; EX 27.60 Trifecta £109.50 Pool: £876.07 - 5.99 winning units..
Owner Chris Wright & The Hon Mrs J M Corbett **Bred** Edmond Kent **Trained** Newmarket, Suffolk

FOCUS
Not the strongest sprint handicap for the grade.

4248 BRITISH STALLION STUDS/HOBBS CHESTER EBF CONDITIONS STKS 5f 16y
7:50 (7:50) (Class 2) 2-Y-O **£12,938** (£3,850; £1,924; £962) **Stalls** Low

Form RPR

312 **1** **Salford Red Devil**[13] 3801 2-9-0 0 JimCrowley 2 87
(Richard Fahey) *hld up in rr: pushed along over 2f out: rdn and hdwy on inner over 1f out: r.o ins fnl f: led fnl strides* **7/4**[1]

1150 **2** *hd* **Quatuor (IRE)**[23] 3459 2-8-13 0 GrahamGibbons 4 85
(Tom Dascombe) *w ldr: rdn over 1f out: led narrowly wl ins fnl f: hdd fnl strides* **13/2**

5140 **3** *3/4* **Ifwecan**[22] 3481 2-9-0 0 FrannyNorton 5 84
(Mark Johnston) *chsd ldrs: sn pushed along: rdn over 1f out: tried to chal ins fnl f: styd on: nt qckn and hld towards fin* **3/1**[2]

1260 **4** *1* **Blithe Spirit**[23] 3459 2-8-9 0 JasonHart 3 75
(Eric Alston) *led: rdn over 1f out: edgd rt and hdd wl ins fnl f: no ex towards fin* **10/1**

1140 **5** *2 1/2* **Steventon Star**[24] 3424 2-9-3 0 LukeMorris 1 74
(Richard Hannon) *chsd ldrs: rdn over 1f out: one pce ins fnl f* **10/3**[3]

0266 **6** *2* **Rough Courte (IRE)**[6] 4053 2-8-6 0 RoystonFfrench 6 56
(Mick Channon) *in rr: pushed along 3f out: outpcd sn after: nvr a threat* **28/1**

1m 2.36s (1.36) **Going Correction** +0.25s/f (Good) **6** Ran SP% **110.3**
Speed ratings (Par 100): **99,98,97,95,91 88**
toteswingers 1&2 £2.00, 1&3 £3.00, 2&3 £4.50 CSF £13.17 TOTE £2.20: £1.40, £1.10; EX 10.60 Trifecta £39.40 Pool: £935.93 - 17.79 winning units..
Owner Dr Marwan Koukash **Bred** Wickfield Stud & Roan Rocket Partnership **Trained** Musley Bank, N Yorks

FOCUS
Plenty of depth in this conditions event for two-year-olds, with five of the six runners holding form that would have been good enough to win an average renewal.

4249 VEUVE CLICQUOT H'CAP 1m 4f 66y
8:20 (8:21) (Class 3) (0-90,90) 3-Y-O **£8,086** (£2,406; £1,202) **Stalls** Low

Form RPR

61-0 **1** **Shrewd**[22] 3486 3-9-6 **89** LukeMorris 1 92
(Michael Bell) *hld up in last pl: pushed along over 2f out: swtchd lft to chal on inner over 1f out: led ins fnl f: r.o wl: in command ins fnl 100yds* **7/2**[3]

1 **2** *2 1/4* **Pitchoun (IRE)**[16] 3674 3-9-7 **90** FrannyNorton 3 90
(Mark Johnston) *led: rdn over 1f out: hdd ins fnl f: outpcd and unable to go w wnr ins fnl 100yds* **10/11**[1]

3121 **3** *1/2* **Edwyn Ralph**[111] 1145 3-8-8 **77** JimCrowley 2 76
(David Simcock) *racd in cl 2nd pl: rdn and ch over 1f out: nt qckn ins fnl f* **2/1**[2]

2m 43.29s (4.79) **Going Correction** +0.25s/f (Good) **3** Ran SP% **107.9**
Speed ratings (Par 104): **94,92,92**
CSF £7.08 TOTE £3.60; EX 6.30 Trifecta £8.40 Pool: £392.38 - 34.71 winning units..
Owner Sheikh Marwan Al Maktoum **Bred** Darley **Trained** Newmarket, Suffolk

FOCUS
Just three runners but this was still an interesting 1m4f handicap for three-year-olds.

4250 LINDOP TOYOTA H'CAP 7f 2y
8:50 (8:50) (Class 4) (0-80,77) 3-Y-O+ **£6,469** (£1,925; £962; £481) **Stalls** Low

Form RPR

-033 **1** **Ferdy (IRE)**[6] 4051 4-8-11 **65** JasonHart(5) 1 74
(Paul Green) *chsd ldr tl over 2f out: rdn to go 2nd again over 1f out: sn 2 l down: plld off rail ins fnl f: rallied and r.o towards fin: led fnl stride* **11/2**[3]

6000 **2** *hd* **One Scoop Or Two**[48] 2659 7-9-6 **69** (v) GrahamGibbons 13 77
(Andrew Hollinshead) *wnt lft s and crossed the whole field: led: rdn and hung lft over 1f out: sn 2 l clr: all out towards fin: hdd fnl stride* **20/1**

-141 **3** *2 3/4* **See The Storm**[22] 3511 5-9-8 **71** FrannyNorton 3 72
(Ian Williams) *chsd ldrs: rdn over 1f out: styd on ins fnl f: one pce fnl 75yds* **2/1**[1]

1323 **4** *nk* **Muftarres (IRE)**[7] 4007 8-9-0 **70** (t) DanaZamecnikova(7) 6 70+
(Frank Sheridan) *hmpd sn after s: hld up: nt clr run wl over 1f out: hdwy ins fnl f: styd on towards fin* **8/1**

0140 **5** *1 3/4* **The Mongoose**[9] 3949 5-8-9 **63** (t) DeclanBates(5) 5 59
(David Evans) *hmpd sn after s: hld up: rdn and hdwy over 1f out: one pce fnl 100yds* **25/1**

3406 **6** *1 1/4* **An Cat Dubh (IRE)**[20] 3570 4-10-0 **77** LukeMorris 8 69
(Nicky Vaughan) *hmpd sn after s: prom: wnt 2nd wl over 2f out: sn ev ch: rdn and lost 2nd over 1f out: no ex ins fnl f* **16/1**

0061 **7** *1/2* **Green Park (IRE)**[18] 3628 10-9-10 **76** (b) NeilFarley(3) 4 67
(Declan Carroll) *racd keenly: in tch: effrt over 1f out: no ex fnl 100yds* **6/1**

135 **8** *3/4* **Gabrial's Gift (IRE)**[14] 3757 4-9-8 **71** JimCrowley 9 60
(David Simcock) *rrd s: hld up: rdn over 1f out: no imp* **3/1**[2]

564- **9** *18* **Nezami (IRE)**[244] 7685 8-9-6 **69** (b) RussKennemore 12
(Patrick Clinton) *hmpd s: hld up: pushed along and outpcd over 2f out: sn lft bhd* **50/1**

1m 28.15s (1.65) **Going Correction** +0.25s/f (Good) **9** Ran SP% **115.6**
Speed ratings (Par 105): **100,99,96,96,94 92,92,91,70**
toteswingers 1&2 £14.80, 1&3 £4.40, 2&3 £11.10 CSF £106.18 CT £293.96 TOTE £8.50: £3.10, £6.00, £1.30; EX 97.10 Trifecta £304.60 Pool: £670.38 - 1.65 winning units..
Owner Men Behaving Badly Two **Bred** David And Elizabeth Kennedy **Trained** Lydiate, Merseyside
■ Stewards' Enquiry : Graham Gibbons six-day ban: careless riding (Jul 27,29-31,Aug 1-2)

FOCUS
Competitive stuff in this handicap.

4251 TRINITY MIRROR CHESHIRE H'CAP 1m 2f 75y
9:20 (9:20) (Class 4) (0-85,88) 3-Y-O **£6,469** (£1,925; £962; £481) **Stalls** High

Form RPR

3035 **1** **Enzaal (USA)**[14] 3756 3-9-1 **76** FrannyNorton 1 82
(Mark Johnston) *mde all: rdn over 2f out: hrd pressed ins fnl f: gamely fnd ex nr fin* **9/2**[3]

4611 **2** *shd* **Double Discount (IRE)**[7] 4023 3-9-8 **88** 6ex DeclanBates(5) 4 93
(Tom Dascombe) *hld up: effrt 3 wd 3f out: rdn and str chal upsides wnr ins fnl f: r.o* **1/1**[1]

2221 **3** *1 1/4* **Dairam (USA)**[17] 3650 3-9-0 **75** JimCrowley 3 78
(Charles Hills) *racd keenly: chsd wnr: rdn and str chal ins fnl f: no ex towards fin* **9/4**[2]

3445 **4** *shd* **Gabrial The Thug (FR)**[13] 3809 3-8-4 **65** (t) BarryMcHugh 5 68
(Richard Fahey) *hld up bhd ldrs: pushed along over 2f out: effrt on inner over 1f out: styd on ins fnl f: no imp towards fin* **8/1**

2m 18.74s (7.54) **Going Correction** +0.25s/f (Good) **4** Ran SP% **110.1**
Speed ratings (Par 102): **79,78,77,77**
CSF £9.75 TOTE £3.30; EX 5.40 Trifecta £14.70 Pool: £578.39 - 29.35 winning units..
Owner Hamdan Al Maktoum **Bred** Shadwell Farm LLC **Trained** Middleham Moor, N Yorks
■ Stewards' Enquiry : Declan Bates two-day ban: used whip above permitted level (Jul 26,28)

FOCUS
Only four runners but with two last-time-out winners in the field, this was an interesting contest.
T/Plt: £198.90 to a £1 stake. Pool: £72,502.92 - 266.07 winning tickets T/Qpdt: £68.60 to a £1 stake. Pool: £4,163.34 - 44.90 winning tickets DO

4211 NEWMARKET (R-H)
Friday, July 12

OFFICIAL GOING: Good to firm (watered) (overall 7.9, stands' side 7.9, centre 7.8, far side 8.0)
Stands side track used Stalls Stands side except 10f: Centre
Wind: virtually nil Weather: sunny and warm

4252 PIPER-HEIDSIECK EBF FILLIES' H'CAP 7f
1:40 (1:43) (Class 2) (0-100,96) 3-Y-O
£15,562 (£4,660; £2,330; £1,165; £582; £292) **Stalls** Low

Form RPR

2-22 **1** **Indignant**[27] 3342 3-9-1 **90** RichardHughes 5 100
(Richard Hannon) *lw: led tl 1/2-way: pressed ldr tl led again over 2f out: rdn and qcknd 2 l clr over 1f out: r.o wl fnl f* **7/2**[1]

-301 **2** *1 1/4* **Tantshi (IRE)**[15] 3718 3-8-13 **88** AndreaAtzeni 10 95
(Roger Varian) *stdd s: hld up in tch in rr: swtchd lft and hdwy over 1f out: drvn and chsd ldrs 1f out: kpt on to go 2nd fnl 75yds: no threat to wnr* **8/1**

1-22 **3** *nk* **Nardin**[20] 3586 3-8-8 **83** PaulHanagan 6 89
(Ed Dunlop) *t.k.h: hld up wl in tch in midfield: swtchd lft and hdwy wl over 1f out: chsd wnr over 1f out: styd on same pce and lost 2nd fnl 75yds* **13/2**

2-40 **4** *1* **Lizzie Tudor**[23] 3460 3-8-8 **86** ThomasBrown(3) 3 89
(Andrew Balding) *in tch in midfield: shuffled bk to rr and nt clr run 2f out: swtchd rt and rallied ent fnl f: styd on u.p but no threat to wnr* **11/1**

-123 **5** *shd* **Jubilante**[35] 3058 3-8-8 **83** RyanMoore 9 86
(Hughie Morrison) *in tch in midfield: effrt u.p to chse ldrs over 1f out: no ex u.p and btn ins fnl f: wkng towards fin* **9/2**[3]

-050 **6** *1* **Califante**[23] 3460 3-8-13 **88** JamesDoyle 13 88
(William Muir) *stdd s: hld up in tch in rr: rdn and hdwy to chse ldrs over 1f out: no ex 1f out: wknd ins fnl f* **20/1**

-101 **7** *1/2* **Milly's Gift**[37] 2983 3-8-10 **85** JohnFahy 1 84
(Clive Cox) *t.k.h: hld up in tch in midfield: clsd on ldrs over 2f out: chsd wnr 2f out and sn rdn: no ex ent fnl f: wknd ins fnl f* **25/1**

13 **8** *2 3/4* **Dream Wild**[57] 2390 3-8-3 **78** SilvestreDeSousa 2 69
(Sir Michael Stoute) *dwlt: in tch towards rr: rdn and sme hdwy wl over 2f out: outpcd and btn over 1f out: wl hld and plugged on same pce fnl f* **4/1**[2]

1-06 **9** *3/4* **Beautiful View**[14] 3784 3-8-13 **88** TomQueally 14 77
(Richard Hannon) *chsd ldrs: rdn and chsd wnr over 2f out tl 2f out: sn lost pl: wknd fnl f* **20/1**

4004 **10** *5* **Sorella Bella (IRE)**[15] 3734 3-9-7 **96** WilliamBuick 7 72
(Mick Channon) *racd keenly: chsd ldr tl 4f out: lost pl and rdn over 2f out: bhd 1f out* **16/1**

-020 **11** *5* **Supernova Heights (IRE)**[14] 3784 3-9-0 **89** KierenFallon 8 51
(Brian Meehan) *lw: t.k.h: in tch in midfield: hdwy to ld 1/2-way tl over 2f out: sn lost pl u.p: bhd 1f out* **16/1**

1m 23.88s (-1.82) **Going Correction** -0.20s/f (Firm) **11** Ran SP% **118.3**
Speed ratings (Par 103): **102,100,100,99,98 97,97,94,93,87 81**
Tote Swingers: 1&2 £5.40, 1&3 £3.00, 2&3 £8.10 CSF £31.09 CT £179.83 TOTE £4.00: £1.60, £2.90, £2.30; EX 38.30 Trifecta £164.70 Pool: £3,469.07 - 15.79 winning units..
Owner Theakston Stud Syndicate **Bred** Theakston Stud **Trained** East Everleigh, Wilts

FOCUS
There was 6mm of water applied to the course, but on another hot, sunny day, the ground would have been drying all the time, and although a few of the jockeys felt it was riding better than the previous day, they still concurred it was fast. Solid form, with some progressive fillies coming to the fore. They raced centre-field for much of the race, but ended up drifting more towards the far side late on. Another step forward from the winner and a good effort from the second.

4253 DUCHESS OF CAMBRIDGE STKS SPONSORED BY BETFRED (GROUP 2) (FILLIES) 6f
2:10 (2:11) (Class 1) 2-Y-O
£45,368 (£17,200; £8,608; £4,288; £2,152; £1,080) **Stalls** Low

Form RPR

116 **1** **Lucky Kristale**[21] 3522 2-8-12 0 TomQueally 2 110
(George Margarson) *hld up in tch in last trio: clsd and travelling wl whn nt clr run 2f out: gap opened jst over 1f out and qcknd to ld jst ins fnl f: sn clr and r.o wl* **20/1**

5111 **2** *2 1/4* **Rizeena (IRE)**[23] 3459 2-9-1 0 JamesDoyle 5 106
(Clive Brittain) *stdd and stmbld leaving stalls: in tch in midfield: rdn over 2f out: chsng ldrs whn carried lft over 1f out: hung lft but styd on to chse wnr ins fnl f: no imp* **11/10**[1]

31 **3** *3/4* **Queen Catrine (IRE)**[20] 3565 2-8-12 0 JamesMcDonald 4 101
(Charles Hills) *t.k.h: hld up in midfield: rdn and effrt to chse ldr whn edgd lft over 1f out: unable qck 1f out: kpt on same pce fnl f* **7/1**

1341 **4** ½ **Fig Roll**[13] 3829 2-8-12 0 RichardHughes 1 99
(Richard Hannon) *lw: chsd ldrs: rdn and effrt to ld over 1f out: drvn and hdd jst ins fnl f: sn outpcd by wnr: no ex and lost 2 pls fnl 100yds* **6/1**[3]

10 **5** 1¼ **Princess Noor (IRE)**[21] 3522 2-8-12 0 WilliamBuick 8 95
(Roger Varian) *wnt lft s: hld up in tch in last trio: effrt and rdn 2f out: outpcd and wandered rt over 1f out: no imp fnl f* **33/1**

01 **6** 1¼ **Bye Bye Birdie (IRE)**[12] 3868 2-8-12 0 (v) RyanMoore 3 91
(A P O'Brien, Ire) *lw: chsd ldr and sn crossed to r against stands' rail: chsd ldr tl wl over 1f out: wknd u.p fnl f* **4/1**[2]

10 **7** 5 **Fire Blaze (IRE)**[23] 3459 2-8-12 0 MickaelBarzalona 6 75
(Saeed bin Suroor) *racd keenly: led tl rdn and hdd over 1f out: sn btn: fdd ins fnl f* **12/1**

613 **8** 21 **One Chance (IRE)**[23] 3459 2-8-12 0 AndreaAtzeni 7 8
(Tim Pitt) *in tch in rr: rdn over 3f out: btn 2f and sn lost tch: virtually p.u ins fnl f: t.o* **25/1**

1m 10.76s (-1.74) **Going Correction** -0.20s/f (Firm) 8 Ran SP% **113.6**
Speed ratings (Par 103): **103,100,99,98,96 95,88,60**
Tote Swingers: 1&2 £5.10, 1&3 £10.60, 2&3 £2.70 CSF £41.73 TOTE £25.20: £6.50, £1.02, £2.30; EX 71.30 Trifecta £435.90 Pool: £5,669.01 - 9.75 winning units..
Owner Graham Lodge Partnership **Bred** Lilac Bloodstock & Redmyre Bloodstock **Trained** Newmarket, Suffolk

FOCUS
A new identity for this race, previously run as the Cherry Hinton Stakes. It looked an up-to-standard edition and they went a good, even pace. The time was quick, just 0.56sec slower than standard. All bar one of the field had run at Royal Ascot, five of them in the Queen Mary Stakes, but it was the Albany Stakes sixth who emerged on top. The fourth and the race averages guide the opening level of the form. Rizeena was 5lb off her Ascot level.

4254 ETIHAD AIRWAYS FALMOUTH STKS (BRITISH CHAMPIONS SERIES) (GROUP 1) (F&M) 1m
2:40 (2:41) (Class 1) 3-Y-O+ **£102,078** (£38,700; £19,368; £9,648) **Stalls** Low

Form RPR

23-4 **1** **Elusive Kate (USA)**[24] 3419 4-9-5 115 WilliamBuick 1 117
(John Gosden) *mde all: set stdy gallop tl rdn and qcknd 2f out: kpt hanging lft after but r.o wl and a holding runner-up ins fnl f* **3/1**[2]

-211 **2** nk **Sky Lantern (IRE)**[21] 3524 3-8-10 119 RichardHughes 2 114
(Richard Hannon) *lw: chsd wnr: rdn whn gallop qcknd 2f out: chal but carried lft fr over 1f out: struck by rival's whip jst ins fnl f: r.o u.p but a jst hld ins fnl f* **4/7**[1]

2-34 **3** 2 **Giofra**[75] 1870 5-9-5 115 (t) ChristopheSoumillon 4 111+
(A De Royer-Dupre, France) *chsd ldng pair: rdn and swtchd rt over 1f out: outpcd by ldng pair 1f out and edgd lft fnl f* **5/1**[3]

20-0 **4** 1½ **Purr Along**[21] 3524 3-8-10 109 FrankieDettori 3 106
(William Muir) *stdd and dropped in bhd after s: rdn and effrt wl over 1f out: outpcd by ldng pair 1f out: wknd ins fnl f* **22/1**

1m 40.54s (0.54) **Going Correction** -0.20s/f (Firm)
WFA 3 from 4yo+ 9lb 4 Ran SP% **109.7**
Speed ratings (Par 117): **89,88,86,85**
CSF £5.30 TOTE £3.30; EX 5.70 Trifecta £10.50 Pool: £15,881.90 - 1,128.01 winning units..
Owner Teruya Yoshida **Bred** Clovelly Farms **Trained** Newmarket, Suffolk
■ Stewards' Enquiry : William Buick three-day ban: careless riding (Jul 26,28,29)

FOCUS
Just the four runners, but three of them were genuine Group 1 fillies and the big two in the market fought out a controversial finish. The placings were unaltered following an enquiry. Tactically the race played out as anticipated. The form is not that solid given the unsatisfactory nature of the race, but Elusive Kate is rated close to her best and Sky Lantern a few pounds off her Ascot form.

4255 BETFRED "THE BONUS KING" (HERITAGE H'CAP) 6f
3:15 (3:15) (Class 2) (0-105,103) 3-Y-O
£62,250 (£18,640; £9,320; £4,660; £2,330; £1,170) **Stalls** Low

Form RPR

0114 **1** **Heaven's Guest (IRE)**[27] 3348 3-8-12 94 RyanMoore 15 105+
(Richard Fahey) *racd far side tl gps merged over 2f out: rdn and effrt over 1f out: str chal fnl f: led fnl 50yds: hld on wl cl home* **7/1**[2]

0112 **2** hd **Moviesta (USA)**[27] 3348 3-9-2 98 PaulMulrennan 14 108+
(Bryan Smart) *racd in nr side gp: in tch: clsd to press ldrs jst over 1f out: rdn to ld ins fnl f: sn hrd pressed: hdd fnl 50yds: r.o: jst hld* **6/1**[1]

0332 **3** 2 **Rene Mathis (GER)**[13] 3803 3-8-3 85 PatrickMathers 18 89
(Richard Fahey) *racd far side tl gps merged over 2f out: overall ldr: rdn 2f out: hdd ins fnl f: no ex fnl 100yds* **33/1**

-130 **4** 1½ **Ninjago**[23] 3455 3-9-7 103 RichardHughes 16 102+
(Richard Hannon) *lw: swtchd rt after s: racd in nr side gp: towards rr: rdn and effrt 2f out: styng on whn nt clr run and swtchd rt ins fnl f: styd on: nvr trbld ldrs* **8/1**[3]

1-10 **5** hd **Secretinthepark**[55] 2452 3-8-9 91 SeanLevey 7 90+
(Ed McMahon) *racd in nr side gp: stdd s: sn in midfield: effrt u.p over 1f out: kpt on but no threat to ldrs fnl f* **9/1**

-000 **6** nse **Ahern**[13] 3823 3-8-13 95 (b) TomQueally 17 93
(David Barron) *racd far side tl gps merged over 2f out: hld up in rr: effrt and hdwy u.p over 1f out: kpt on same pce ins fnl f* **20/1**

0021 **7** nk **Robot Boy (IRE)**[18] 3634 3-8-8 90 JamieSpencer 1 87+
(David Barron) *lw: racd in nr side gp: hld up towards rr: swtchd rt and effrt nrest stands' rail over 1f out: kpt on ins fnl f: nvr trbld ldrs* **10/1**

1-25 **8** ½ **Regal Dan (IRE)**[63] 2208 3-8-6 88 AndreaAtzeni 12 84
(Charles Hills) *racd in nr side gp: chsd ldrs overall: rdn and unable qck over 1f out: one pce and btn ins fnl f* **16/1**

3000 **9** shd **Threes Grand**[26] 3367 3-8-0 82 JamieMackay 19 77
(Scott Dixon) *racd far side tl gps merged over 2f out: chsd overall ldr: upsides and rdn 2f out: btn 1f out: fdd ins fnl f* **33/1**

4105 **10** 1¼ **Rivellino**[27] 3340 3-8-9 91 WilliamBuick 8 82+
(Mrs K Burke) *swtg: racd in nr side gp: rdn and no hdwy over 1f out: swtchd lft and plugged on ins fnl f: nvr trbld ldrs* **14/1**

342- **11** shd **Tennessee Wildcat (IRE)**[30] 3225 3-9-2 98 GaryCarroll 20 89
(G M Lyons, Ire) *racd far side tl gps merged over 2f out: hld up in rr: rdn and hdwy 2f out: no ex 1f out: wknd ins fnl f* **16/1**

-350 **12** hd **Mary's Daughter**[27] 3348 3-7-13 88 SamanthaBell(7) 11 79
(Richard Fahey) *racd in nr side gp: chsd ldrs: rdn 2f out: wknd ent fnl f* **50/1**

1362 **13** ½ **Purcell (IRE)**[23] 3474 3-8-3 85 JimmyQuinn 2 74
(Andrew Balding) *racd in nr side gp: chsd ldrs: rdn and unable qck wl over 1f out: wknd 1f out* **14/1**

-330 **14** ½ **Barracuda Boy (IRE)**[13] 3823 3-8-11 93 RichardKingscote 9 80
(Tom Dascombe) *racd in nr side gp: in tch: rdn and outpcd over 1f out: wknd fnl f* **11/1**

5550 **15** 1¾ **Top Boy**[20] 3584 3-7-13 88 ow1 AdamMcLean(7) 4 70
(Derek Shaw) *swtg: racd in nr side gp: t.k.h: hld up in rr: n.d* **25/1**

-060 **16** ½ **Mutazamen**[14] 3763 3-8-1 83 PaulHanagan 5 63
(Richard Hannon) *racd in nr side gp: a bhd: n.d* **25/1**

0305 **17** 1¼ **Chilworth Icon**[20] 3584 3-9-4 100 SamHitchcott 10 76
(Mick Channon) *racd in nr side gp: in tch tl rdn and lost pl 2f out: bhd fnl f* **25/1**

-211 **18** 1¼ **Equity Risk (USA)**[29] 3234 3-8-6 88 SilvestreDeSousa 3 60
(Kevin Ryan) *swtg: racd in nr side gp: in tch in midfield: rdn 1/2-way: wknd u.p over 1f out* **7/1**[2]

1m 10.14s (-2.36) **Going Correction** -0.20s/f (Firm) 18 Ran SP% **127.1**
Speed ratings (Par 106): **107,106,104,102,101 101,101,100,100,98 98,98,97,97,94 94,92,90**
Tote Swingers: 1&2 £7.00, 1&3 £55.60, 2&3 £32.80 CSF £45.88 CT £1345.93 TOTE £8.80: £2.10, £1.80, £7.20, £2.90; EX 48.10 Trifecta £1140.60 Pool: £6,607.76 - 4.34 winning units..
Owner J K Shannon & M A Scaife **Bred** Yeomanstown Stud **Trained** Musley Bank, N Yorks

FOCUS
A valuable and suitably competitive sprint handicap. Prix de l'Abbaye winner Total Gallery took this in 2009 and sprinters of the calibre of Deacon Blues and Mince have finished unplaced more recently. They split into two groups leaving the stalls and it was the five-strong bunch towards the far side where the pace was, the winner and third both coming from there. The first four home were all drawn high, with the two groups converging not long after halfway. Six of these contested a similar race at York last month, the Macmillan Charity Sprint, and two of them fought out the finish here. Solid form, with the third the best guide.

4256 WEATHERBYS EBF MAIDEN STKS 7f
3:50 (4:00) (Class 4) 2-Y-O **£6,469** (£1,925; £962; £481) **Stalls** Low

Form RPR

2 **1** **True Story**[20] 3581 2-9-5 0 SilvestreDeSousa 9 90+
(Saeed bin Suroor) *swtg: str: stdd s: hld up in tch towards rr: rdn and gd hdwy to ld jst over 1f out: rn green in front but sn drvn clr: r.o: readily* **1/1**[1]

4 **2** 3¾ **Expert (IRE)**[58] 2358 2-9-5 0 SeanLevey 3 80
(Richard Hannon) *w'like: well made: led: rn green and edgd lft whn rdn 2f out: hdd jst over 1f out: outpcd by wnr but kpt on for clr 2nd fnl f* **14/1**

3 1¾ **Voice Of A Leader (IRE)** 2-9-5 0 JamieSpencer 13 75+
(Peter Chapple-Hyam) *w'like: scope: in tch: swtchd lft and hdwy ent fnl 2f: ev ch over 1f out: outpcd by wnr 1f out: wknd ins fnl f* **11/2**[3]

4 ½ **Rock 'N' Roll Star** 2-9-5 0 JamesMcDonald 1 74+
(Charles Hills) *stdd and swtchd lft s: in tch in last pair: switching lft and sme hdwy over 1f out: wnt 4th ins fnl f: kpt on but no threat to wnr* **33/1**

5 1¼ **Postponed (IRE)** 2-9-5 0 AndreaAtzeni 10 70+
(Luca Cumani) *str: scope: in tch in midfield: rdn and outpcd 2f out: rdn and rallied ent fnl f: kpt on but no threat to ldrs* **50/1**

33 **6** 1¼ **Edge (IRE)**[27] 3350 2-9-5 0 RichardHughes 6 67
(Richard Hannon) *athletic: chsd ldrs: rdn ent fnl 2f: outpcd by ldng trio ent fnl f: wknd ins fnl f* **5/1**[2]

7 6 **Mantonize (USA)** 2-9-5 0 KierenFallon 5 51
(Brian Meehan) *cmpt: in tch in midfield: rdn ent fnl 2f: struggling and outpcd 2f out: wknd over 1f out* **33/1**

8 ¾ **Punk** 2-9-5 0 RichardKingscote 8 49
(Fawzi Abdulla Nass, Bahrain) *awkward leaving stalls: in tch towards rr: rdn and hdwy jst over 2f out: no ex over 1f out: sn wknd* **66/1**

9 1½ **Good Value** 2-9-5 0 RyanMoore 4 45
(Sir Michael Stoute) *str: rn green: s.i.s: in tch in rr: rdn ent fnl 2f: sn outpcd and bhd* **16/1**

0 **10** ¾ **Collaboration**[28] 3290 2-9-5 0 TomQueally 12 43
(Andrew Balding) *chsd ldr tl over 2f out: sn lost pl u.p: bhd fnl f* **20/1**

1m 25.06s (-0.64) **Going Correction** -0.20s/f (Firm) 10 Ran SP% **108.7**
Speed ratings (Par 96): **95,90,88,88,86 85,78,77,75,75**
Tote Swingers: 1&2 £4.30, 1&3 £2.00, 2&3 £10.10 CSF £13.70 TOTE £2.10: £1.10, £3.10, £2.20; EX 19.40 Trifecta £76.60 Pool: £10,695.31 - 104.68 winning units..
Owner Godolphin **Bred** Darley **Trained** Newmarket, Suffolk
■ Right Of Appeal was withdrawn after bursting out of the stalls (10-1, deduct 5p in the £ under R4.)

FOCUS
Probably just an ordinary maiden by course standards, albeit one that should produce winners. There was no doubt about the superiority of the favourite.

4257 CELEBRATING NEWMARKET - HISTORIC HOME OF HORSE RACING MAIDEN STKS 1m 2f
4:25 (4:32) (Class 4) 3-Y-O **£6,469** (£1,925; £962; £481) **Stalls** Centre

Form RPR

1 **Urban Dance (IRE)** 3-9-5 0 MickaelBarzalona 2 95+
(Saeed bin Suroor) *w'like: scope: gd bodied: t.k.h early: hld up in last pair: rdn over 3f out: hdwy u.p over 1f out: led ins fnl f: sn in command and styd on wl* **4/1**[3]

2 1½ **Refectory (IRE)** 3-9-5 0 RyanMoore 5 92+
(Andrew Balding) *tall: angular: stdd s: hld up in rr: rdn 3f out: outpcd and struggling 2f out: plenty to do whn swtchd lft and rallied 1f out: styd on strly to go 2nd cl home: no threat to wnr* **16/1**

020 **3** ½ **Toast Of The Town (IRE)**[29] 3237 3-9-0 84 WilliamBuick 8 86
(John Gosden) *lw: chsd ldr tl 5f out: styd chsng ldrs tl led and travelling wl jst over 2f out: rdn over 1f out: drvn and hdd ins fnl f: no ex: lost 2nd cl home* **3/1**[2]

2 **4** 2 **Vermont (IRE)**[27] 3343 3-9-5 0 KierenFallon 6 87
(Luca Cumani) *str: restless in stalls: awkward leaving stalls and slowly away: hdwy into midfield 8f out: chsd ldr 5f out: rdn and ev ch 2f out: edgd lft and unable qck over 1f out: outpcd fnl f* **15/8**[1]

50 **5** 1 **Phaenomena (IRE)**[29] 3237 3-9-0 0 TomQueally 7 80
(Lady Cecil) *t.k.h early: hld up in tch in midfield: clsd to chse ldrs whn carried lft over 1f out: sn rdn and one pce: wknd fnl 1000yds: eased nr fin* **14/1**

3 **6** 5 **Lions Park (IRE)**[7] 4022 3-9-5 0 SilvestreDeSousa 1 76
(Mark Johnston) *w'like: rn in snatches: chsd ldrs: clsd and rdn to chal 2f out: no ex 1f out: edgd lft and fdd ins fnl f* **5/1**

7 7 **Mount Macedon** 3-9-3 0 ow1 PatrickHills(3) 4 64
(Luca Cumani) *t.k.h early: in tch in midfield: rdn and lost pl over 2f out: bhd over 1f out* **66/1**

20 **8** nk **Gold Medal (IRE)**[55] 2442 3-9-5 0 SeanLevey 3 62
(Richard Hannon) *ld tl jst over 2f out: sn drvn and lost pl: bhd ent fnl f* **25/1**

2m 4.83s (-0.67) **Going Correction** -0.20s/f (Firm) 8 Ran SP% **114.3**
Speed ratings (Par 102): **94,92,92,90,90 86,80,80**
Tote Swingers: 1&2 £10.80, 1&3 £3.10, 2&3 £8.20 CSF £63.41 TOTE £3.60: £1.30, £3.80, £1.80; EX 56.60 Trifecta £282.20 Pool: £12,261.98 - 32.58 winning units..
Owner Godolphin **Bred** Darley **Trained** Newmarket, Suffolk

The Form Book Flat, Raceform Ltd, Compton, RG20 6NL.

FOCUS
A maiden that doesn't tend to produce stars, but is usually a decent race. A number of these looked like they'd improve for the outing but there were some excellent pedigrees on show. The initial pace was slow but it picked up with around half a mile to run. They shunned the inside in the long straight. The form could have been rated 2lb higher.

4258 ROBINSONS MERCEDES-BENZ H'CAP 1m
5:35 (5:38) (Class 3) (0-90,89) 3-Y-O+ £9,703 (£2,887; £1,443; £721) Stalls Low

Form RPR

043 1 **Basseterre (IRE)**[20] 3570 4-9-10 **85**.......................... JamesMcDonald 6 96
(Charles Hills) *hld up in tch in last trio: swtchd lft and hdwy over 1f out: led fnl 100yds: hld on wl towards fin* 7/1

2302 2 *hd* **Fils Anges (IRE)**[7] 4014 3-9-4 **88**.......................... JamieSpencer 5 97
(Michael Bell) *lw: stdd s: hld up in tch in rr: clsd and swtchd rt over 1f out: hung lft u.str.p but str chal fnl 100yds: hld on wl cl home* 11/2

2213 3 *1* **Henry The Aviator (USA)**[22] 3492 3-8-13 **83**.......... SilvestreDeSousa 4 89
(Mark Johnston) *lw: led tl rdn and hdd 2f out: battled on to ld again and edgd lft over 1f out: hdd and one pce fnl 100yds* 9/4[1]

2243 4 *1 3/4* **Lord Ofthe Shadows (IRE)**[16] 3697 4-9-11 **86**.......(b) RichardHughes 1 90
(Richard Hannon) *lw: t.k.h: chsd ldrs: shuffled bk and nt clr run whn swtchd rt over 1f out: chsng ldrs and keeping on whn squeezed for room and hmpd ins fnl f: no ex* 9/2[3]

02 5 *1 1/2* **Albaqaa**[13] 3811 8-9-8 **83**.......................... J-PGuillambert 8 84
(P J O'Gorman) *t.k.h: chsd ldrs: rdn and ev ch over 1f out: struggling to qckn whn hmpd 1f out: wknd ins fnl f* 16/1

1-11 6 *3/4* **Bassara (IRE)**[26] 3368 4-9-10 **85**.......................... TedDurcan 3 84
(Chris Wall) *stdd s: t.k.h: hld up in tch in rr: hdwy 3f out: rdn and ev ch over 1f out: btn whn carried lft ins fnl f: wknd fnl 100yds* 4/1[2]

-006 7 *nk* **Common Touch (IRE)**[21] 3538 5-10-0 **89**....................(p) KierenFallon 9 87
(Willie Musson) *lw: in tch: rdn and effrt to chal over 1f out: edgd rt ent fnl f: unable qck and carried lft 1f out: wknd ins fnl f* 20/1

6361 8 *1* **Azma (USA)**[14] 3780 3-8-3 **73**.......................... AndreaAtzeni 7 67
(Conrad Allen) *chsd ldr: rdn to ld 2f out: hdd over 1f out and struggling whn squeezed for room and hmpd 1f out: wknd fnl f* 11/1

45-5 9 *27* **Exotic Guest**[102] 1295 3-8-2 **72**.......................... PaulHanagan 2
(George Margarson) *stdd s: t.k.h: hld up in tch in midfield: rdn and lost pl 2f: sn btn: eased fnl f* 33/1

1m 38.63s (-1.37) **Going Correction** -0.20s/f (Firm)
WFA 3 from 4yo+ 9lb 9 Ran SP% 118.8
Speed ratings (Par 107): **98,97,96,95,93 92,92,91,64**
Tote Swingers: 1&2 £6.60, 1&3 £4.90, 2&3 £4.00 CSF £46.56 CT £115.67 TOTE £8.40: £2.50, £2.50, £1.60; EX 46.60 Trifecta £272.90 Pool: £3,778.02 - 10.38 winning units..
Owner H R Mould **Bred** D G Hardisty Bloodstock **Trained** Lambourn, Berks
■ James McDonald's final ride of a successful stint in Britain.
■ Stewards' Enquiry : Jamie Spencer two-day ban: careless riding (Jul 26,28)

FOCUS
A fair handicap, run at just a steady pace early, but they got racing a fair way out and the front pair came from just off the pace.
T/Jkpt: Not won. T/Plt: £54.90 to a £1 stake. Pool: £189,435.77 - 2,517.18 winning tickets. T/Qpdt: £27.10 to a £1 stake. Pool: £6,288.86 - 171.60 winning tickets. SP

3345 YORK (L-H)
Friday, July 12

OFFICIAL GOING: Good to firm (overall 7.7, stands' side 7.4, centre 7.6, far side 7.5)
Races on inside line around home bend and races of a mile and beyond reduced by 24yds.
Wind: almost nil Weather: fine and sunny, very warm

4259 CAKEMARK EBF MAIDEN STKS 5f 89y
1:50 (1:50) (Class 3) 2-Y-O £7,115 (£2,117; £1,058; £529) Stalls Centre

Form RPR

426 1 **Royal Mezyan (IRE)**[22] 3481 2-9-5 0.......................... NeilCallan 6 94
(William Haggas) *t.k.h: w ldrs: crowded after 1f: led over 2f out: drvn clr appr fnl f: rdn out* 4/7[1]

333 2 *6* **Bounty Girl (IRE)**[6] 4046 2-9-0 0.......................... DavidAllan 4 67
(Tim Easterby) *w ldrs: rdn and outpcd over 2f out: edgd rt and kpt on totake 2nd 1f out: no ch w wnr* 20/1

002 3 *1 1/2* **Deeds Not Words (IRE)**[13] 3836 2-9-5 0.......................... TedDurcan 2 67+
(Mick Channon) *sn drvn along: wl outpcd and last: hdwy over 1f out: styd on wl to go 3rd nr fin* 14/1

3 4 *hd* **Trinity River**[16] 3694 2-9-0 0.......................... GrahamLee 7 61
(Daniel Kubler) *outpcd after 1f: mid-div: hdwy over 2f out: chsng ldrs 1f out: kpt on same pce* 20/1

3 5 *1 1/4* **Birkacre (IRE)**[9] 3942 2-9-0 0.......................... TonyHamilton 1 56
(Richard Fahey) *led 1f: sn outpcd and mid-div: hdwy over 2f out: one pce* 10/1

0 6 *3 3/4* **Dream Sika (IRE)**[18] 3631 2-9-5 0.......................... AdamKirby 8 48
(Clive Cox) *t.k.h: edgd lft and led after 1f: hdd over 2f out: wknd fnl f* 11/2[2]

7 *3/4* **Noble Asset** 2-9-5 0.......................... MichaelO'Connell 5 45
(John Quinn) *t.k.h early: n.m.r and outpcd after 1f: mid-div: sme hdwy over 2f out: wknd fnl f* 8/1[3]

0 8 *2 3/4* **My Boy Bob**[27] 3350 2-9-5 0.......................... LeeTopliss 3 35
(Richard Fahey) *drvn along and sn wl outpcd: hung lft thrght: a bhd* 33/1

1m 4.59s (0.49) **Going Correction** +0.05s/f (Good) 8 Ran SP% 118.4
Speed ratings (Par 98): **98,88,86,85,83 77,76,72**
Tote Swingers: 1&2 £1.80, 1&3 £1.90, 2&3 £16.10 CSF £18.54 TOTE £1.50: £1.10, £2.80, £3.40; EX 12.80 Trifecta £52.40 Pool: £1,436.59 - 20.55 winning units..
Owner Sheikh Juma Dalmook Al Maktoum **Bred** Mark Salmon **Trained** Newmarket, Suffolk

FOCUS
A dry and warm run up to a meeting staged on fast ground. Racing took place on the inside racing line around the home bend reducing the race distances of a mile and beyond by 24 yards. Ted Durcan stated: "It's beautiful ground, like a carpet". Not much strength in depth but a reasonable gallop and very useful performance from the favourite. Straightforward form, the winner entitled to win.

4260 32RED SUMMER STKS (GROUP 3) 6f
2:25 (2:25) (Class 1) 3-Y-O+
£34,026 (£12,900; £6,456; £3,216; £1,614; £810) Stalls Centre

Form RPR

1105 1 **Ladies Are Forever**[34] 3102 5-9-2 103..........................(b[1]) GrahamLee 1 110
(Geoffrey Oldroyd) *trckd ldrs on outer: effrt over 2f out: rn to ld wl ins fnl f* 16/1

0-22 2 *1 1/2* **Gracia Directa (GER)**[34] 3102 5-9-2 101.......................... RobertWinston 3 105
(D Moser, Germany) *trckd ldrs: led over 1f out: edgd rt: hdd and no ex last 75yds* 10/1

1-12 3 *nk* **March**[27] 3340 3-8-10 97.......................... LukeMorris 9 103
(Marco Botti) *dwlt and wnt rt s: drvn along in rr: hdwy stands' side 2f out: edgd lft and styd on fnl f* 6/1[3]

00-3 4 *1 1/2* **Restiadargent (FR)**[62] 2270 4-9-2 108.......................... DanielTudhope 7 99
(William Haggas) *chsd ldrs: effrt over 2f out: kpt on same pce fnl f* 7/1

-134 5 *nk* **Place In My Heart**[29] 3263 4-9-2 103.......................... AdamKirby 5 98
(Clive Cox) *w ldrs: led 3f out: hdd over 1f out: keeping on one pce whn checked last 50oyds* 12/1

1-51 6 *2 1/4* **Body And Soul (IRE)**[27] 3348 3-8-10 101.......................... DuranFentiman 10 90
(Tim Easterby) *hld up: hdwy over 2f out: sn drvn: chsng ldrs 1f out: one pce* 7/2[2]

-201 7 *3* **City Girl (IRE)**[14] 3784 3-8-10 103.......................... JimCrowley 6 81
(Ralph Beckett) *chsd ldrs: drvn over 2f out: wknd last 100yds* 12/1

044 8 *1* **Sound Of Guns**[27] 3340 3-8-10 100..........................(b[1]) TomMcLaughlin 4 77
(Ed Walker) *s.i.s: t.k.h: sn trcking ldrs: wknd over 1f out* 33/1

5666 9 *4 1/2* **Dream Maker (IRE)**[15] 3734 3-8-10 88.......................... DavidAllan 2 63
(Tim Easterby) *led 3f: wknd over 1f out* 100/1

1-03 10 *hd* **Sandreamer (IRE)**[27] 3340 3-8-10 99..........................(v) TedDurcan 11 62
(Mick Channon) *sltly hmpd s: a outpcd and in rr* 40/1

1-45 11 *3 3/4* **Rosdhu Queen (IRE)**[20] 3557 3-8-10 107.......................... NeilCallan 8 50
(William Haggas) *plunged s: in rr: hdwy stands' side over 2f out: wknd over 1f out: eased ins fnl f* 2/1[1]

1m 10.53s (-1.37) **Going Correction** +0.05s/f (Good)
WFA 3 from 4yo+ 6lb 11 Ran SP% 119.1
Speed ratings (Par 113): **111,109,108,106,106 103,99,97,91,91 86**
Tote Swingers: 1&2 £15.30, 1&3 £21.40, 2&3 £8.20 CSF £166.88 TOTE £14.80: £3.00, £3.00, £2.20; EX 99.40 Trifecta £835.60 Pool: £2,015.68 - 1.80 winning units..
Owner R C Bond **Bred** Bond Thoroughbred Corporation **Trained** Brawby, N Yorks

FOCUS
A competitive Group 3 but one that didn't take as much winning as seemed likely with the two market leaders disappointing to varying degrees. The gallop was sound, the field raced in the centre (first two home raced towards the far side of the bunch) and the two that had taken the corresponding race in 2011 and last year filled the first two placings. The winner is rated basically to her mark wuth the runner-up fitting in.

4261 HAYLIN STKS (NURSERY H'CAP) 5f
2:55 (2:57) (Class 3) 2-Y-O £7,439 (£2,213; £1,106; £553) Stalls Centre

Form RPR

041 1 **Viva Verglas (IRE)**[14] 3766 2-9-7 **88**.......................... GrahamGibbons 5 89
(David Barron) *rrd s: sn chsng wnr: edgd lft and styd on fnl f: led post* 9/2[2]

102 2 *nse* **Baytown Kestrel**[14] 3767 2-8-5 **72**.......................... LukeMorris 2 73
(Phil McEntee) *led: edgd lft fnl f: hdd last stride* 8/1

1631 3 *nk* **Innocently (IRE)**[6] 4054 2-8-3 **79** 6ex.......................... JulieBurke[(3)] 3 73
(David O'Meara) *sn outpcd: hdwy over 1f out: kpt on last 150yds* 11/2[3]

2031 4 *hd* **Hello Beautiful (IRE)**[23] 3476 2-8-1 **68**.......................... JamesSullivan 1 67
(Ann Duffield) *mid-div: hdwy over 1f out: carried lft ins fnl f: styng on whn squeezed out clsng stages* 17/2

1634 5 *2* **Rosebay Coral (IRE)**[13] 3801 2-8-5 **72**.......................... BarryMcHugh 6 64
(Tony Coyle) *dwlt: outpcd in last: kpt on to take 5th nr line: nvr a threat* 11/1

21 6 *nk* **Classical Diva**[28] 3280 2-8-7 **77**.......................... NeilFarley[(3)] 7 68
(Declan Carroll) *dwlt: sn chsng ldrs: drvn along over 2f out: lost pl over 1f out* 10/3[1]

1m 0.05s (0.75) **Going Correction** +0.05s/f (Good) 6 Ran SP% 86.6
Speed ratings (Par 98): **96,95,95,95,91 91**
Tote Swingers: 1&2 £4.50, 1&3 £2.60, 2&3 £4.40 CSF £21.99 TOTE £4.40: £2.10, £2.90; EX 20.80 Trifecta £65.00 Pool: £478.09 - 5.51 winning units..
Owner Raymond Miquel **Bred** Mrs Mary Coonan **Trained** Maunby, N Yorks
■ Stewards' Enquiry : Graham Gibbons two-day ban: used whip above permitted level (Jul 26,28)

FOCUS
The official ratings shown are estimated and for information only. A competitive nursery in which all were previous winners and one in which the gallop was strong throughout. The principals drifted from the centre to the far side from halfway. Market leader Lord Clyde was withdrawn after refusing to enter the stalls (11-4, deduct 25p in the £ under R4).

4262 GROCERYAID CHAIRMAN'S CHARITY CUP (H'CAP) 1m 4f
3:30 (3:30) (Class 2) (0-100,100) 3-Y-O+ £12,291 (£3,657; £1,827; £913) Stalls Centre

Form RPR

6651 1 **Kiwayu**[13] 3804 4-8-13 **85**..........................(p) LukeMorris 5 93
(Ian Williams) *hld up in rr: drvn over 3f out: hdwy over 1f out: edgd lft and styd on to ld nr fin* 13/2

0403 2 *nk* **Bridle Belle**[14] 3755 5-8-9 **86**.......................... GeorgeChaloner[(5)] 1 93
(Richard Fahey) *led: qcknd pce over 4f out: rdn 2f out: r.o gamely: hdd fnl strides* 13/2

0-00 3 *1 3/4* **Ithoughtitwasover (IRE)**[155] 555 5-10-0 **100**.......................... LiamJones 6 104
(Mark Johnston) *chsd ldrs: chal over 2f out: styd on same pce fnl f* 10/1

3020 4 *3* **High Office**[28] 3297 7-8-9 **81**.......................... TonyHamilton 2 81
(Richard Fahey) *chsd ldrs: effrt over 3f out: edgd rt over 1f out: one pce* 8/1

0030 5 *3 3/4* **Art Scholar (IRE)**[20] 3559 6-9-10 **96**.......................... AndrewMullen 4 90
(Michael Appleby) *trckd ldrs: effrt over 3f out: one pce whn n.m.r and swtchd lft over 1f out: sn wknd* 8/1

0031 6 *2 1/4* **Nanton (USA)**[27] 3345 11-8-13 **85**.......................... GrahamLee 8 75
(Jim Goldie) *hld up in last: effrt 4f out: nvr a factor* 6/1[3]

0621 7 *2 1/2* **Bollin Greta**[7] 4015 8-8-9 **81** 6ex.......................... DavidAllan 7 67
(Tim Easterby) *dwlt: hld up in rr: effrt on ins over 3f out: wknd over 1f out* 5/1[2]

021 **8** *5* **Warlu Way**[16] 3685 6-9-4 **90** GrahamGibbons 3 68
(Michael Easterby) *trckd ldrs: effrt over 3f out: wknd 2f out* **7/2**[1]
2m 27.93s (-5.27) **Going Correction** -0.40s/f (Firm) **8** Ran SP% **111.2**
Speed ratings (Par 109): **101,100,99,97,95 93,91,88**
Tote Swingers: 1&2 £40.40, 1&3 £40.40, 2&3 £4.80 CSF £45.16 CT £403.97 TOTE £7.20: £2.10, £2.00, £2.90; EX 45.20 Trifecta £410.90 Pool: £1,207.07 - 2.20 winning units..
Owner Paul Wildes **Bred** Fittocks Stud Ltd **Trained** Portway, Worcs
FOCUS
A very useful handicap featuring several last-time-out winners. An ordinary gallop only picked up in the last 3f.

4263 CRANSWICK PLC FOOD GROUP STKS (H'CAP) 5f
4:05 (4:05) (Class 2) (0-100,96) 3-Y-O+ **£12,291** (£3,657; £1,827; £913) **Stalls** Centre

Form RPR
0030 **1** **Secret Asset (IRE)**[35] 3046 8-9-12 **96** (p[1]) MichaelO'Connell 13 105
(Jane Chapple-Hyam) *wnt rt s: chsd ldrs stands' side: styd on to ld post* **20/1**
3301 **2** *shd* **Love Island**[11] 3892 4-8-12 **87** 6ex (p) GeorgeChaloner(5) 11 96
(Richard Whitaker) *chsd ldrs centre: styd on to ld last 30yds: hdd fnl stride* **10/1**
6636 **3** *½* **Lady Gibraltar**[14] 3776 4-8-12 **87** MichaelJMMurphy(5) 6 94
(Alan Jarvis) *w ldrs towards far side: led jst ins fnl f: hdd and no ex last 30yds* **5/1**[1]
4201 **4** *¾* **Tax Free (IRE)**[14] 3786 11-9-1 **90** JasonHart(5) 15 94
(David Nicholls) *w ldrs stands' side: kpt on same pce last 150yds* **12/1**
1-21 **5** *shd* **Demora**[33] 3135 4-9-6 **90** AndrewMullen 16 94
(Michael Appleby) *w ldrs stands' side: sltly outpcd over 2f out: kpt on wl ins fnl f* **13/2**[2]
4014 **6** *shd* **Arctic Feeling (IRE)**[20] 3561 5-8-9 **86** LauraBarry(7) 4 89
(Richard Fahey) *chsd ldrs far side: edgd lft: kpt on same pce last 150yds* **16/1**
0000 **7** *½* **Cheviot (USA)**[14] 3776 7-9-10 **94** (p) TomEaves 7 96
(Ian Semple) *chsd ldrs towards far side: kpt on same pce fnl f* **28/1**
1105 **8** *¾* **Mayfield Girl (IRE)**[23] 3478 3-8-10 **85** DavidAllan 2 82
(Mel Brittain) *w ldrs far side: led over 1f out: hdd jst ins fnl f: fdd towards fin* **14/1**
4044 **9** *nse* **Fitz Flyer (IRE)**[6] 4047 7-9-0 **84** (v) TonyHamilton 14 83+
(David Nicholls) *hmpd s: hdwy towards stands' side over 1f out: styd on clsng stages* **9/1**[3]
2-60 **10** *nk* **Stone Of Folca**[14] 3776 5-9-10 **94** LukeMorris 5 92
(John Best) *overall ldr towards far side: hdd over 1f out: one pce* **9/1**[3]
110 **11** *1 ¼* **Dorback**[12] 3855 6-9-1 **85** (t) GrahamLee 10 78
(Violet M Jordan) *chsd ldrs: wknd appr fnl f* **25/1**
0020 **12** *nse* **Ponty Acclaim (IRE)**[20] 3562 4-9-6 **90** (t) RobertWinston 1 83
(Tim Easterby) *swtchd rt s: sn chsng ldrs: wknd over 1f out* **13/2**[2]
-000 **13** *1 ½* **Hazelrigg (IRE)**[55] 2461 8-8-12 **82** DanielTudhope 9 70+
(Tim Easterby) *hood removed late: s.s: a in rr* **25/1**
-600 **14** *1 ½* **Bapak Chinta (USA)**[20] 3558 4-9-7 **91** PhillipMakin 8 73
(Kevin Ryan) *a towards rr towards far side* **9/1**[3]
0000 **15** *2 ¼* **Ubetterbegood (ARG)**[14] 3776 5-9-4 **88** NeilCallan 12 62
(Robert Cowell) *in rr towards stands' side and sn drvn along: nvr on terms* **20/1**
58.34s (-0.96) **Going Correction** +0.05s/f (Good)
WFA 3 from 4yo+ 5lb **15** Ran SP% **123.3**
Speed ratings (Par 109): **109,108,108,106,106 106,105,104,104,103 101,101,99,97,93**
Tote Swingers: 1&2 £52.40, 1&3 £38.80, 2&3 £9.10 CSF £199.15 CT £1198.23 TOTE £29.50: £7.10, £3.20, £2.10; EX 411.90 Trifecta £789.40 Part won. Pool: £1,052.59 - 0.21 winning units..

Owner Simon & Mrs Jeanette Pierpoint **Bred** Mrs C Hartery **Trained** Dalham, Suffolk
■ Stewards' Enquiry : George Chaloner two-day ban: used whip above permitted level (Jul 26,28)
FOCUS
A very useful and competitive sprint but, although the gallop was sound throughout, not many got into it from off the pace. The field fanned across the track but the first two raced in the centre. A bunch finish and the bare form can't be rated any higher.

4264 ACTURIS STKS (H'CAP) 1m 2f 88y
4:40 (4:40) (Class 4) (0-85,91) 3-Y-O+ **£7,439** (£2,213; £1,106; £553) **Stalls** Low

Form RPR
3301 **1** **Chancery (USA)**[7] 4020 5-9-11 **82** 6ex DanielTudhope 9 97+
(David O'Meara) *hld up in rr: smooth hdwy on outer over 2f out: edgd lft and led over 1f out: wnt clr: v readily* **11/4**[1]
050 **2** *3 ¾* **Barren Brook**[16] 3683 6-9-7 **78** PhillipMakin 12 84
(Michael Easterby) *s.s: in rr: hdwy on outer 3f out: chsd wnr jst ins fnl f: no imp* **14/1**
4065 **3** *2 ½* **Prophesy (IRE)**[13] 3812 4-9-3 **77** NeilFarley(3) 6 78+
(Declan Carroll) *trckd ldr: led over 2f out: edgd rt and hdd over 1f out: kpt on one pce* **20/1**
-540 **4** *½* **Eltheeb**[16] 3685 6-9-11 **82** (v) PJMcDonald 11 82
(David O'Meara) *hld up towards rr: hdwy over 2f out: swtchd lft over 1f out: kpt on* **17/2**
4114 **5** *½* **Christmas Light**[20] 3567 6-9-10 **81** DaleSwift 3 80
(Brian Ellison) *hld up in rr: hdwy on outer 3f out: kpt on fnl f* **9/1**
/4-3 **6** *½* **Almagest**[19] 3607 5-9-8 **84** DavidBergin(5) 7 82
(David O'Meara) *chsd ldrs: one pce whn edgd lft over 1f out* **25/1**
1151 **7** *3* **Size (IRE)**[21] 3543 4-8-13 **70** LeeTopliss 4 63+
(Richard Fahey) *trckd ldng pair: drvn over 3f out: one pce whn n.m.r over 1f out: crowded and wknd 150yds out* **13/2**[3]
-001 **8** *1 ¼* **Oetzi**[15] 3729 5-8-12 **74** MichaelJMMurphy(5) 2 64
(Alan Jarvis) *mid-div: effrt 4f out: sn outpcd: kpt on over 1f out: nvr a factor* **14/1**
1043 **9** *½* **Titus Bolt (IRE)**[14] 3768 4-8-9 **66** oh1 GrahamLee 13 55
(Jim Goldie) *hld up in rr: hdwy over 2f out: nt clr run and swtchd lft over 1f out: sn wknd* **16/1**
5-00 **10** *1 ½* **Daddy Warbucks (IRE)**[11] 3895 4-8-11 **75** ConnorBeasley(7) 5 62
(David Nicholls) *led: hdd over 2f out: lost pl over 1f out* **14/1**
2231 **11** *¾* **Maven**[20] 3567 5-9-9 **85** DarylByrne(5) 1 70
(Tim Easterby) *hld up in rr: hdwy on ins over 3f out: wknd 2f out* **9/2**[2]
5040 **12** *3 ¾* **Carragold**[17] 3651 7-9-1 **72** DavidAllan 10 50
(Mel Brittain) *mid-div: effrt 4f out: lost pl 2f out* **33/1**
2m 6.78s (-5.72) **Going Correction** -0.40s/f (Firm) **12** Ran SP% **116.1**
Speed ratings (Par 105): **106,103,101,100,100 99,97,96,96,94 94,91**
Tote Swingers: 1&2 £37.30, 1&3 £10.50, 2&3 £12.30 CSF £41.60 CT £647.20 TOTE £3.00: £1.30, £4.90, £6.10; EX 38.70 Trifecta £615.90 Pool: £2,707.97 - 3.29 winning units..
Owner Hollowdean **Bred** Darley **Trained** Nawton, N Yorks

FOCUS
A useful handicap run at a sound gallop and the winner looks a decent prospect. There's nothing wrong with the form in behind.

4265 ELECTROLUX APPLIANCES STKS (APPRENTICE H'CAP) 7f
5:10 (5:11) (Class 3) (0-95,92) 3-Y-O **£7,439** (£2,213; £1,106; £553) **Stalls** Low

Form RPR
3233 **1** **Majestic Moon (IRE)**[14] 3758 3-9-0 **80** LeeTopliss 2 90+
(Richard Fahey) *drvn to ld: jnd over 1f out: kpt on wl ins fnl f* **4/1**[3]
0514 **2** *2* **Penny Garcia**[13] 3803 3-8-11 **80** DarylByrne(3) 3 85
(Tim Easterby) *trckd wnr: t.k.h: upsides over 1f out: edgd lft and fdd last 75yds* **14/1**
1145 **3** *½* **Lord Ashley (IRE)**[13] 3803 3-9-2 **85** RossAtkinson 6 85
(Tom Dascombe) *hld up in rr: t.k.h: effrt over 3f out: edgd lft and styd on fnl furlonmg: tk 2nd nr fin* **7/1**
-121 **4** *3 ½* **Noble Deed**[11] 3894 3-8-11 **82** 6ex ConnorBeasley(5) 5 76
(William Haggas) *t.k.h: trckd ldrs: stmbld over 5f out: wknd fnl f* **6/4**[1]
-043 **5** *2 ¼* **George Rooke (IRE)**[36] 3028 3-8-12 **83** KevinStott(5) 1 71
(Kevin Ryan) *trckd ldrs: effrt over 2f out: wknd fnl f* **7/2**[2]
-340 **6** *3 ¼* **Georgian Bay (IRE)**[48] 2661 3-9-7 **92** JoeyHaynes(5) 7 71
(Mrs K Burke) *swtchd lft after s: hld up in rr: effrt on ins over 2f out: wknd over 1f out* **10/1**
1m 23.72s (-1.58) **Going Correction** -0.10s/f (Good) **6** Ran SP% **110.5**
Speed ratings (Par 104): **105,102,102,98,95 91**
Tote Swingers: 1&2 £3.10, 1&3 £3.90, 2&3 £9.30 CSF £49.94 TOTE £5.20: £2.40, £2.70; EX 32.00 Trifecta £122.60 Pool: £3,561.57 - 21.78 winning units..
Owner James Gaffney **Bred** Tony Cosgrave **Trained** Musley Bank, N Yorks
FOCUS
Only six runners, but a useful apprentice handicap in which the gallop was on the steady side. The winner got the run of the race this may not be form to take too literally.
T/Plt: £635.90 to a £1 stake. Pool: £90,599.80 - 104.00 winning tickets. T/Qpdt: £167.50 to a £1 stake. Pool: £4,961.85 - 21.90 winning tickets. WG

4266 - 4273a (Foreign Racing) - See Raceform Interactive

3875 CHANTILLY (R-H)
Thursday, July 11
OFFICIAL GOING: Turf: good to soft; polytrack: standard

4274a PRIX BLUSHING GROOM (CONDITIONS) (3YO) (POLYTRACK) 6f 110y
2:20 (12:00) 3-Y-O **£15,040** (£6,016; £4,512; £3,008; £1,504)

RPR
1 **Dibajj (FR)**[17] 3-8-8 0 AntoineHamelin 5 91
(A De Royer-Dupre, France) **4/1**[2]
2 *1 ¼* **Zejel**[112] 3-8-8 0 JulienAuge 8 87
(C Ferland, France) **6/1**[3]
3 *½* **Rapideur (FR)**[42] 3-8-11 0 EddyHardouin 10 89
(S Smrczek, Germany) **3/1**[1]
4 *¾* **Bluegrass Blues (IRE)**[27] 3279 3-8-11 0 OlivierPeslier 3 87
(Paul Cole) *stdd and hld up towards rr: rdn 2f out: r.o and stl ev ch whn squeezed for room and lost momentum ins fnl f: nt rcvr but fin wl and wnt 4th cl home* **63/10**
5 *½* **Damsah (USA)**[92] 1495 3-8-8 0 IoritzMendizabal 9 82
(D De Watrigant, France) **9/1**
6 *1 ½* **Zor (FR)**[43] 3-8-13 0 ow2 (b) ChristopheSoumillon 4 83
(T Larriviere, France) **9/1**
7 *½* **Holly Filly (IRE)**[58] 2356 3-8-8 0 MlleLilyLePemp 2 77
(D Guillemin, France) **38/1**
8 *1 ¾* **You're Golden (IRE)**[37] 3-8-11 0 Christophe-PatriceLemaire 11 75
(E Legrix, France) **12/1**
9 *¾* **Asteria (FR)**[59] 2334 3-8-8 0 StephanePasquier 6 69
(J E Pease, France) **78/10**
10 *¾* **Julius Quercus (IRE)**[111] 3-8-11 0 AnthonyCrastus 7 70
(F Chappet, France) **38/1**
1m 18.37s (78.37) **10** Ran SP% **117.2**
WIN (incl. 1 euro stake): 3.60 (Dibajj coupled with You're Golden). PLACES: 1.70, 2.00, 1.50. DF: 18.40. SF: 26.40.
Owner A Al Maddah **Bred** C Humphris **Trained** Chantilly, France

4231 ASCOT (R-H)
Saturday, July 13
OFFICIAL GOING: Good to firm changing to good to firm (firm in places) after race 5 (4.15)
Rail realignment added 10yds to Old Mile, 14yds to 10f and 16yds to 12f.
Wind: Almost nil Weather: Fine, hot

4275 BETFRED MOBILE SPORTS H'CAP 5f
1:55 (1:59) (Class 2) 3-Y-O+
£62,250 (£18,640; £9,320; £4,660; £2,330; £1,170) **Stalls** High

Form RPR
-202 **1** **Masamah (IRE)**[7] 4058 7-9-2 **100** (p) DarrenEgan(3) 11 111
(Marco Botti) *led nr side gp thrght: overall ldr over 1f out: edgd to rail ins fnl f: styd on* **14/1**
0120 **2** *½* **Racy**[14] 3846 6-9-0 **95** HarryBentley 17 104
(Brian Ellison) *hld up in rr nr side: gd prog fr 2f out: chsd wnr ins fnl f: trying to chal whn short of room against rail last 100yds: styd on* **20/1**
0-00 **3** *1 ½* **Zero Money (IRE)**[21] 3558 7-9-0 **95** (b) MartinDwyer 8 99
(Hugo Palmer) *overall ldr in centre: hung lft over 1f out and sn hdd: one pce fnl f* **33/1**
2-04 **4** *½* **Long Awaited (IRE)**[28] 3334 5-8-13 **94** (b) PaulHanagan 20 96
(David Barron) *chsd ldrs nr side: rdn and styd on fr over 1f out: nvr able to chal* **9/1**[3]
53-6 **5** *shd* **Ahtoug**[175] 290 5-9-1 **96** JoeFanning 5 98+
(Saeed bin Suroor) *trckd ldrs in centre: shkn up over 1f out: styd on: nt pce to chal* **14/1**
3-02 **6** *hd* **Goldream**[58] 2396 4-8-12 **93** JamesDoyle 10 94+
(Robert Cowell) *chsd ldr in centre: hung lft fr over 1f out: hrd rdn and one pce after* **9/1**[3]
4432 **7** *¾* **Miss Lahar**[15] 3784 4-9-0 **95** MartinHarley 12 93
(Mick Channon) *chsd wnr nr side to jst ins fnl f: fdd* **28/1**

5143 **8** ½ **Steps (IRE)**[8] 4024 5-8-13 **97**....(b) ThomasBrown(3) 1 93
(Roger Varian) *chsd ldrs in centre: effrt 2f out: edgd lft and kpt on same pce* **12/1**

0302 **9** ¾ **Joe Packet**[8] 4024 6-8-12 **93**.... WilliamCarson 3 87+
(Jonathan Portman) *towards rr in centre and off the pce: effrt 2f out: keeping on but no ch whn nt clr run and swtchd lft ins fnl f* **16/1**

3-10 **10** nse **Ajjaadd (USA)**[42] 2865 7-8-12 **98**.... WilliamTwiston-Davies(5) 2 92
(Ted Powell) *wl in rr in centre: prog on wd outside 2f out: kpt on one pce fnl f* **25/1**

0505 **11** ½ **Taajub (IRE)**[8] 4024 6-9-0 **95**.... ShaneKelly 18 87
(Peter Crate) *hld up in midfield in centre: effrt 2f out: one pce over 1f out* **7/1**[1]

3204 **12** nk **Move In Time**[14] 3848 5-9-10 **105**.... WilliamBuick 19 96
(David O'Meara) *chsd wnr nr side to over 1f out: losing pl whn short of room ins fnl f* **7/1**[1]

1002 **13** 2¼ **Ancient Cross**[15] 3776 9-9-3 **98**....(t) JamesSullivan 7 81
(Michael Easterby) *towards rr in centre: no real prog over 1f out* **20/1**

4060 **14** 1¼ **Face The Problem (IRE)**[28] 3334 5-9-6 **101**.... JamieSpencer 15 79
(Jamie Osborne) *sn last of nr side gp: nvr on terms* **12/1**

0063 **15** nk **Barnet Fair**[28] 3334 5-8-10 **91**.... KierenFox 14 68
(Richard Guest) *wnt rt s: towards rr nr side: hung rt to centre 1/2-way: n.d after* **8/1**[2]

3434 **16** hd **Fair Value (IRE)**[8] 4024 5-8-10 **91**.... HayleyTurner 9 67
(Simon Dow) *chsd ldr in centre to over 1f out: wknd qckly* **25/1**

0030 **17** 2½ **Pabusar**[8] 4024 5-9-0 **95**.... FergusSweeney 6 62
(Jamie Osborne) *sn last of centre gp: nvr on terms* **25/1**

-550 **18** 1 **Jiroft (ITY)**[15] 3776 6-9-5 **100**.... JimmyFortune 13 64
(Robert Cowell) *hmpd s: racd freely and sn chsd nr side ldrs: wknd 2f out* **33/1**

4-50 **19** 3 **Prohibit**[25] 3420 8-9-6 **101**....(p) GeorgeBaker 4 54
(Robert Cowell) *chsd ldrs in centre tl wknd 2f out: eased* **20/1**

59.31s (-1.19) **Going Correction** +0.025s/f (Good) 19 Ran SP% **125.9**
Speed ratings (Par 109): **110,109,106,106,105 105,104,103,102,102 101,100,97,95,94 94,90,88,84**
Tote Swingers: 1&2 £41.10 CSF £275.69 CT £8934.03 TOTE £20.60: £4.50, £6.50, £5.80, £2.80; EX 498.30 Trifecta £1962.90 Part won. Pool: £2,617.24 - 0.01 winning units..
Owner Dr Marwan Koukash **Bred** Stanley Estate & Stud Co & Mount Coote Stud **Trained** Newmarket, Suffolk
■ Confessional was withdrawn (20-1, ref to ent stalls).
■ Stewards' Enquiry : Darren Egan one-day ban: careless riding (Jul 29)

FOCUS
Rail realignment added 10yds to Old Mile, 14yds to 10f and 16yds to 12f. The jockeys seemed happy with the ground which was described variously as "good to firm", "fast" and "quick." Run later in July last season, this very valuable and highly competitive event was worth more than no fewer than 15 races at the recent Royal meeting. They spilt from the stalls into two groups before converging latterly, with the principals ending up on the stands' side. Not many got involved, with the winner and third making all in their groups. Masamah's best form since his 2011 peak.

4276 FRED COWLEY MBE MEMORIAL SUMMER MILE STKS (GROUP 2) 1m (R)

2:30 (2:35) (Class 1) 4-Y-0+
£56,710 (£21,500; £10,760; £5,360; £2,690; £1,350) **Stalls** Low

Form RPR

-232 **1** **Aljamaaheer (IRE)**[25] 3419 4-9-1 116.... PaulHanagan 5 119+
(Roger Varian) *hld up disputing 8th: prog on outer over 2f out: rdn to ld jst ins fnl f: sn in comand: readily* **6/4**[1]

1-15 **2** 1 **Mull Of Killough (IRE)**[55] 2494 7-9-1 116.... WilliamBuick 13 117
(Jane Chapple-Hyam) *trckd ldrs in 5th: pushed along 3f out: prog on outer to ld wl over 1f out: drvn and hdd jst ins fnl f: styd on* **7/1**[2]

2221 **3** ½ **Guest Of Honour (IRE)**[61] 2323 4-9-1 110....(p) MartinHarley 4 116+
(Marco Botti) *hld up in midfield: trckd ldrs gng strly 2f out and waiting for a run: rdn over 1f out: styd on fnl f to take 3rd nr fin* **9/1**[3]

1145 **4** hd **Trade Storm**[25] 3419 5-9-4 113.... JamieSpencer 6 118
(David Simcock) *stdd s: hld up in 10th: prog on outer 2f out: chsd ldng pair ins fnl f: effrt flattened out and lost 3rd nr fin* **9/1**[3]

1330 **5** 3½ **Gabrial (IRE)**[25] 3419 4-9-1 110.... HayleyTurner 12 107
(Richard Fahey) *s.s: hld up in last: no prog tl wl over 1f out: styd on to take modest 5th nr fin* **25/1**

-100 **6** 1 **Trumpet Major (IRE)**[25] 3419 4-9-4 114....(p) PatDobbs 10 108
(Richard Hannon) *chsd clr ldr: clsd to chal 2f out: sn outpcd and btn* **20/1**

-400 **7** 1¾ **Aesop's Fables (USA)**[105] 1267 4-9-1 113....(p) HarryBentley 7 101
(Saeed bin Suroor) *chsd ldng trio: clsd to chal 2f out: wknd over 1f out* **16/1**

12-2 **8** 1½ **Famous Poet (IRE)**[22] 3538 4-9-1 94.... TedDurcan 9 97
(Saeed bin Suroor) *led: clr after 2f: hdd & wknd wl over 1f out* **33/1**

0332 **9** nk **Red Jazz (USA)**[14] 3831 6-9-1 109.... WilliamCarson 11 97
(Charles Hills) *nvr bttr than midfield: struggling and no prog 2f out* **25/1**

5602 **10** ½ **Premio Loco (USA)**[24] 3458 9-9-1 111.... GeorgeBaker 3 95
(Chris Wall) *chsd ldng pair to over 2f out: wknd* **16/1**

0423 **11** 2 **Pastoral Player**[14] 3831 6-9-1 111.... JimmyFortune 8 91
(Hughie Morrison) *rrd s: a in rr: btn 2f out* **16/1**

1m 38.51s (-2.19) **Going Correction** +0.025s/f (Good) 11 Ran SP% **105.5**
Speed ratings (Par 115): **111,110,109,109,105 104,103,101,101,100 98**
Tote Swingers: 1&2 £2.70, 1&3 £3.70, 2&3 £8.30 CSF £8.53 TOTE £2.00: £1.10, £2.20, £2.20; EX 9.90 Trifecta £39.90 Pool: £1,710.54 - 32.11 winning units..
Owner Hamdan Al Maktoum **Bred** Corrin Stud & Sean O'Keeffe **Trained** Newmarket, Suffolk
■ Afsare was withdrawn (6-1, ref to ent stalls). Deduct 10p in the £ under R4.

FOCUS
This event was switched to the King George card last season, when this particular fixture wasn't held. It was a bigger field than usual, despite the late withdrawal of Afsare, and a classy and well contested one too. The pace was decent and the time quick, 1.49sec inside the standard. The form makes a fair bit of sense among the principals, with a small personal best from Aljamaaheer.

4277 RUDDY FILLIES' NURSERY H'CAP 7f

3:05 (3:06) (Class 4) 2-Y-0 **£6,469** (£1,925; £962; £481) **Stalls** High

Form RPR

10 **1** **Autumn Lily (USA)**[21] 3555 2-9-6 **81**.... WilliamBuick 3 92+
(Saeed bin Suroor) *w.w in midfield: smooth prog on outer over 2f out: led over 1f out: pushed out: comf* **13/8**[1]

3336 **2** 3¼ **Senorita Guest (IRE)**[28] 3324 2-8-4 **65**.... KieranO'Neill 6 67
(Mick Channon) *trckd ldrs: rdn over 2f out: styd on to chse wnr fnl f: no imp* **12/1**

532 **3** 2½ **Royal Connection**[15] 3753 2-8-11 **72**.... PatDobbs 4 67
(Richard Hannon) *wl in tch in midfield: rdn and prog 2f out: disp 2nd 1f out: kpt on one pce* **7/2**[2]

1002 **4** 2¼ **Lady Frances**[15] 3761 2-9-7 **82**.... JoeFanning 5 71
(Mark Johnston) *racd freely: led after 2f to over 1f out: wknd* **5/1**[3]

4040 **5** ½ **Sweet Alibi (IRE)**[14] 3829 2-8-3 **67**....(p) DarrenEgan(3) 8 55
(J S Moore) *hld up in last pair: rdn wl over 1f out: flashed tail and one pce after* **14/1**

0341 **6** 10 **Flora Medici**[9] 3992 2-8-7 **68**.... ChrisCatlin 7 29
(Sir Mark Prescott Bt) *led 2f: chsd ldr to over 2f out: wknd qckly* **12/1**

333 **7** 9 **Mimi Luke (USA)**[15] 3753 2-8-9 **70**.... PaulHanagan 1 7
(Alan Bailey) *prom: chsd ldr briefly over 2f out: wknd rapidly over 1f out* **7/1**

4106 **P** **Kidmenot (IRE)**[13] 3857 2-8-11 **72**.... JamesDoyle 2
(J S Moore) *hld up in last pair: prog 2f out: drvn to dispute 2nd and styng on whn broke down 1f out: p.u* **16/1**

1m 28.22s (0.62) **Going Correction** +0.025s/f (Good) 8 Ran SP% **117.4**
Speed ratings (Par 93): **97,93,90,87,87 75,65,**
Tote Swingers: 1&2 £6.00, 1&3 £1.40, 2&3 £5.20 CSF £24.12 CT £63.28 TOTE £2.50: £1.10, £3.40, £1.50; EX 27.20 Trifecta £169.70 Pool: £1,635.99 - 7.22 winning units..
Owner Godolphin **Bred** Darley **Trained** Newmarket, Suffolk

FOCUS
The official ratings shown are estimated and for information only. All eight were making their handicap debut in this fillies' nursery.

4278 NORMAN COURT STUD FILLIES' H'CAP 1m (S)

3:40 (3:42) (Class 3) (0-90,89) 3-Y-0+ **£8,409** (£2,502; £1,250; £625) **Stalls** High

Form RPR

-210 **1** **Butterfly McQueen (USA)**[30] 3240 3-8-12 **85**.... ThomasBrown(3) 6 100
(Andrew Balding) *pressed ldr and clr of rest: led over 2f out: shkn up and drew clr wl over 1f out: unchal* **5/1**

-030 **2** 6 **Princess Of Orange**[36] 3060 4-10-0 **89**.... JamieSpencer 5 92
(Rae Guest) *s.s: hld up in detached last: nt asked to make prog tl over 1f out whn wnr already gone: rdn and r.o to take 2nd ins fnl f* **9/1**

21-1 **3** 1 **Jabhaat (USA)**[87] 1608 3-9-1 **85**.... PaulHanagan 1 84
(Ed Dunlop) *chsd clr ldng pair: rdn over 2f out: chsd wnr over 1f out: no imp: lost 2nd ins fnl f* **2/1**[1]

1-25 **4** 3¼ **Love Magic**[43] 2844 3-9-0 **84**.... JamesDoyle 3 75
(Sir Michael Stoute) *nvr on terms w ldrs disputing 4th: rdn and no prog over 2f out* **5/2**[2]

0022 **5** 7 **Savanna Days (IRE)**[14] 3842 4-9-5 **80**....(v) MartinHarley 2 57
(Mick Channon) *nvr on terms w ldrs disputing 4th: rdn over 2f out: wknd over 1f out* **12/1**

1644 **6** 7 **Sharp And Smart (IRE)**[14] 3845 4-9-1 **76**.... JimmyFortune 4 42
(Hughie Morrison) *led and clr w wnr: hdd over 2f out: wknd rapidly over 1f out* **9/2**[3]

1m 39.36s (-1.44) **Going Correction** +0.025s/f (Good)
WFA 3 from 4yo 9lb 6 Ran SP% **114.4**
Speed ratings (Par 104): **108,102,101,97,90 83**
Tote Swingers: 1&2 £24.90, 1&3 £3.70, 2&3 £5.90 CSF £46.85 TOTE £6.10: £2.60, £4.00; EX 43.50 Trifecta £255.70 Pool: £1,977.24 - 5.79 winning units..
Owner Sir A Ferguson, G Mason & P Done **Bred** Pollock Farms **Trained** Kingsclere, Hants

FOCUS
A decent fillies' handicap, the equivalent race to which was won by the smart Dank last season. The leader went off fast and the race rather fell apart, leading to doubts over how literally the form should be taken, but the winner has been accorded a large personal best.

4279 NEPTUNE INVESTMENT MANAGEMENT H'CAP 1m 4f

4:15 (4:15) (Class 2) (0-105,94) 3-Y-0
£31,125 (£9,320; £4,660; £2,330; £1,165; £585) **Stalls** Low

Form RPR

0113 **1** **Bold Sniper**[23] 3486 3-9-6 **93**.... JamesDoyle 4 105
(Sir Michael Stoute) *stdd s: hld up in 7th: prog on inner over 2f out: chsd ldr over 1f out: drvn to chal fnl f: edgd ahd last 100yds: hld on* **15/8**[1]

-231 **2** nk **Cafe Society (FR)**[17] 3698 3-8-11 **84**.... JamieSpencer 9 97+
(David Simcock) *stdd s: hld up in last: smooth prog on inner jst over 2f out to trck ldng trio over 1f out: swtchd arnd them sn after: pushed along and clsd to take 2nd last stride: too much to do* **9/2**[2]

111 **3** hd **London Bridge (USA)**[23] 3502 3-9-2 **89**.... PaulHanagan 7 100
(Jo Hughes) *prom: led after 3f: pushed along 5f out: drvn and kpt finding fr over 2f out: hdd last 100yds: lost 2nd post* **9/2**[2]

3-21 **4** 1¾ **Prairie Ranger**[57] 2416 3-8-13 **89**.... ThomasBrown(3) 2 97
(Andrew Balding) *hld up in 6th: rdn and prog on outer over 2f out: chal and upsides 1f out: nt qckn and hld last 150yds* **7/1**

1245 **5** 6 **Another Cocktail**[23] 3486 3-9-7 **94**.... JimmyFortune 1 93
(Hughie Morrison) *pushed along early: chsd ldrs: drvn to go 2nd over 2f out to over 1f out: wknd qckly* **12/1**

1212 **6** 1½ **Broughton (GER)**[7] 4063 3-8-13 **86**.... JoeFanning 3 82
(Mark Johnston) *trckd ldr 3f: cl up tl shkn up and wknd 2f out* **13/2**[3]

-662 **7** 2½ **Linguine (FR)**[29] 3277 3-8-8 **84**.... DarrenEgan(3) 8 76
(Seamus Durack) *trckd ldrs on outer: rdn and wknd over 3f out* **16/1**

610 **8** 6 **Federal Blue (USA)**[22] 3526 3-8-12 **85**.... MartinDwyer 5 68
(Mark Johnston) *led 3f: chsd ldr to over 2f out: wknd qckly* **25/1**

2m 30.2s (-2.30) **Going Correction** +0.025s/f (Good) 8 Ran SP% **114.4**
Speed ratings (Par 106): **108,107,107,106,102 101,99,95**
Tote Swingers: 1&2 £3.30, 2&3 £2.70 CSF £10.34 CT £32.50 TOTE £2.60: £1.10, £2.00, £1.70; EX 9.70 Trifecta £30.80 Pool: £3,154.76 - 76.78 winning units..
Owner The Queen **Bred** The Queen **Trained** Newmarket, Suffolk

FOCUS
A valuable handicap, run at a good gallop and featuring some progressive 3yos. The font four were all ahead of their marks to pull clear of the rest. The form is rated on the positive side.

4280 TARA & PIPPA H'CAP 1m 2f

4:50 (4:53) (Class 3) (0-90,90) 3-Y-0+ **£8,409** (£2,502; £1,250; £625) **Stalls** Low

Form RPR

1465 **1** **Love Marmalade (IRE)**[20] 3607 3-8-2 **75**.... JoeFanning 10 89
(Mark Johnston) *mde all and sn crossed fr wd draw: rdn over 2f out: styd on stoutly to draw clr over 1f out* **9/2**[2]

1225 **2** 4 **Come On Blue Chip (IRE)**[14] 3832 4-9-12 **88**....(p) MartinHarley 4 94
(Paul D'Arcy) *chsd ldng trio: rdn over 2f out: styd on fr over 1f out to take 2nd last 100yds: no ch w wnr* **9/1**

-521 **3** 1 **Burnham**[19] 3617 4-9-4 **80**....(p) JimmyFortune 2 84
(Hughie Morrison) *chsd ldng pair: rdn over 2f out: lost 3rd briefly 1f out: kpt on last 100yds: n.d* **6/1**[3]

-065 **4** hd **Commend**[17] 3697 4-9-4 **80**....(p) WilliamBuick 6 84
(Sir Michael Stoute) *chsd wnr: drvn to try to chal jst over 2f out: nt qckn and lft bhd over 1f out: lost 2 pls last 100yds* **9/2**[2]

1P1 **5** 2 1/2 **Ogbourne Downs**[19] 3633 3-8-9 **82** JamesDoyle 9 81
(Charles Hills) *trckd ldrs in 5th: clsd over 3f out: drvn over 2f out: nt qckn and no imp over 1f out* **2/1**[1]
2030 **6** *hd* **Mawaakef (IRE)**[8] 4028 5-9-12 **88** JamieSpencer 3 86
(J R Jenkins) *a abt same pl: rdn and no prog over 2f out: no ch after* **22/1**
-025 **7** 2 1/4 **Kelpie Blitz (IRE)**[9] 3976 4-9-2 **78** (t) GeorgeBaker 8 72
(Seamus Durack) *awkward leaving stalls: hld up in 8th: shkn up on outer 2f out: no real prog* **14/1**
0002 **8** 3 1/4 **Muffin McLeay (IRE)**[64] 2240 5-9-13 **89** PaulHanagan 5 76
(David Barron) *hld up in 7th: shkn up over 2f out: no prog and nvr figured* **9/1**
00-0 **9** *68* **King Torus (IRE)**[15] 3754 5-10-0 **90** HayleyTurner 7
(Jamie Osborne) *hld up in last: pushed along and no prog 3f out: eased and t.o* **33/1**

2m 6.07s (-1.33) **Going Correction** +0.025s/f (Good)
WFA 3 from 4yo+ 11lb 9 Ran SP% **117.9**
Speed ratings (Par 107): **106,102,102,101,99 99,97,95,40**
Tote Swingers: 1&2 £9.40, 1&3 £8.00, 2&3 £6.80 CSF £45.45 CT £247.60 TOTE £5.30: £2.10, £2.40, £1.80; EX 61.20 Trifecta £338.20 Pool: £4,789.65 - 10.61 winning units..
Owner Crone Stud Farms Ltd **Bred** Stonethorn Stud Farms Ltd **Trained** Middleham Moor, N Yorks

FOCUS
The ground was officially amended to good to firm, firm in places before this race. This fair handicap was run at a decent pace and the winner was back on his game to post a clear personal best. The next three set a sound standard.

4281 MITIE TOTAL SECURITY MANAGEMENT H'CAP 7f
5:25 (5:26) (Class 4) (0-85,90) 3-Y-0+ **£6,469** (£1,925; £962; £481) **Stalls** High

Form RPR
5211 **1** **Labienus**[24] 3472 3-9-4 **83** TedDurcan 10 94
(David Lanigan) *sltly impeded s: in rr: pushed along and prog jst over 2f out: clsd to ld jst over 1f out: rdn clr: readily* **9/4**[1]
0-13 **2** 2 1/2 **Tidentime (USA)**[29] 3274 4-9-8 **79** MartinHarley 7 86
(Mick Channon) *trckd ldrs: rdn 2f out: prog to chal and upsides jst over 1f out: chsd wnr after but readily outpcd* **9/1**
4414 **3** 3/4 **Benoni**[15] 3782 3-8-8 **73** FergusSweeney 5 75+
(Henry Candy) *prom: rdn to ld briefly over 1f out: one pce fnl f* **8/1**
6153 **4** *hd* **Forceful Appeal (USA)**[36] 3060 5-9-10 **81** PaulHanagan 12 85
(Simon Dow) *in tch: rdn and nt qckn 2f out: styd on again fnl f: gng on at fin* **7/1**[3]
1300 **5** 1/2 **Tarooq (USA)**[14] 3823 7-9-11 **82** (t) WilliamBuick 11 85
(Stuart Williams) *sn detached in last: sme prog and swtchd rt to wd outside over 1f out: drvn and styd on same pce fnl f* **8/1**
341 **6** *1* **Balty Boys (IRE)**[9] 3974 4-10-5 **90** (b) JamieSpencer 8 90
(Jamie Osborne) *led: rdn and hanging fr 2f out: hdd and nt qckn over 1f out: one pce* **7/1**[3]
2236 **7** 1 1/2 **Jack Of Diamonds (IRE)**[29] 3274 4-9-9 **80** (p) GeorgeBaker 4 76
(Roger Teal) *racd alone in centre to 1/2-way: in tch: prog to chal and upsides over 1f out: fdd fnl f* **5/1**[2]
101U **8** *7* **Midnight Feast**[7] 4067 5-9-1 **72** (v) KierenFox 6 53
(Lee Carter) *t.k.h: trckd ldr: upsides over 1f out: sn wknd* **20/1**
00-0 **9** *19* **Rustic Deacon**[26] 3411 6-9-11 **82** ShaneKelly 1 24
(Willie Musson) *dwlt: trckd ldrs tl wknd rapidly jst over 2f out: t.o* **18/1**
-036 **10** 1 3/4 **Jungle Bay**[31] 3215 6-9-5 **76** (p) ChrisCatlin 9
(Jane Chapple-Hyam) *sltly impeded s: chsd ldrs: wknd 3f out: t.o* **16/1**

1m 25.9s (-1.70) **Going Correction** +0.025s/f (Good)
WFA 3 from 4yo+ 8lb 10 Ran SP% **120.6**
Speed ratings (Par 105): **110,107,106,106,105 104,102,94,72,70**
Tote Swingers 1&2 £5.10, 2&3 £14.40, 1&3 £5.40 CSF £24.60 CT £147.13 TOTE £3.30: £1.50, £3.40, £2.10; EX 28.00 Trifecta £363.50 Pool: £2,684.86 - 5.53 winning units..
Owner B E Nielsen **Bred** Mrs S L Gibson Fleming **Trained** Upper Lambourn, Berks

FOCUS
An ordinary handicap for the track, contested by a number who are more associated with the AW. This form is a length off his Polytrack best, with the next two to form.
T/Plt: £251.00 to a £1 stake. Pool: £137,985.64 - 401.22 winning units. T/Qpdt: £35.30 to a £1 stake. Pool: £7,306.95 - 152.80 winning units. JN

4245 CHESTER (L-H)
Saturday, July 13

OFFICIAL GOING: Good to firm (8.4)
The rail between the 6f and 1 1/2f point was moved out by a further three yards after Friday's racing (9yds in total)
Wind: Light, half against Weather: Hot and Sunny

4282 CORBETTSPORTS.COM MOBILE/BRITISH STALLION STUDS EBF MAIDEN STKS 5f 16y
2:15 (2:15) (Class 4) 2-Y-0 **£6,469** (£1,925; £962; £481) **Stalls** Low

Form RPR
234 **1** **Weisse Socken (IRE)**[17] 3694 2-9-0 0 RichardKingscote 4 70
(Ralph Beckett) *wnt rt s: trckd ldrs: effrt to chal on inner over 1f out: sn led: edgd rt wl ins fnl f: r.o: pushed out cl home* **3/1**[1]
55 **2** 3/4 **Our Gabrial (IRE)**[8] 4021 2-9-5 0 LeeTopliss 3 72+
(Richard Fahey) *bmpd s: pushed along in tch: rdn and hdwy over 1f out: r.o to take 2nd cl home: nt quite able to chal wnr* **3/1**[1]
0 **3** *nk* **Extreme Supreme**[23] 3481 2-8-12 0 AdamMcLean(7) 2 71
(Derek Shaw) *bmpd s: prom: led after 1f: rdn over 1f out: sn hdd: continued to chal ins fnl f: one pce fnl strides* **9/2**[3]
4 *5* **Signore Piccolo** 2-9-0 0 JasonHart(5) 7 53+
(Eric Alston) *s.i.s and rdn early: wl bhd and outpcd: kpt on fnl f: nvr able to trble ldrs* **25/1**
5 **5** *shd* **Offshore Bond**[39] 2955 2-9-5 0 MichaelO'Connell 3 53
(Jedd O'Keeffe) *led for 1f: remained w ldr: rdn 2f out: nt qckn whn rdr got unbalanced over 1f out: btn ins fnl f* **5/1**
60 **6** *1* **Dancing Juice**[14] 3826 2-9-0 0 MichaelJMMurphy(5) 5 49
(Alan Jarvis) *carried rt s: chsd ldrs: upsides and 3 wd over 3f out: rdn over 1f out: wknd fnl f* **25/1**
2532 **7** 2 3/4 **Urban Dreamer (IRE)**[36] 3035 2-9-5 0 CathyGannon 6 39
(Rod Millman) *carried rt s: outpcd and bhd: nvr on terms* **7/2**[2]

1m 2.91s (1.91) **Going Correction** +0.225s/f (Good) 7 Ran SP% **114.8**
Speed ratings (Par 96): **93,91,91,83,83 81,77**
Tote Swingers: 1&2 £1.40, 1&3 £1.10, 2&3 £7.70 CSF £12.35 TOTE £2.80: £2.10, £2.20; EX 7.80 Trifecta £23.30 Pool: £1,065.08 - 34.24 winning units..
Owner Mrs Emma Kennedy **Bred** Cooneen Stud **Trained** Kimpton, Hants

FOCUS
After a warm morning the ground had become quicker than that advertised and it was good to firm all over. After the opener the jockeys felt the ground was quick and safe.

4283 KATHLEEN CORBETT MEMORIAL H'CAP 6f 18y
2:50 (2:50) (Class 4) (0-80,85) 3-Y-0 **£6,469** (£1,925; £962; £481) **Stalls** Low

Form RPR
1103 **1** **Sylvia Pankhurst (IRE)**[3] 4162 3-8-11 **75** (p) LMcNiff(5) 3 80
(David C Griffiths) *chsd ldrs: rdn to ld over 1f out: r.o: eased whn in command cl home* **4/1**[3]
1-41 **2** 3/4 **Red Explorer (USA)**[8] 4033 3-9-9 **85** PatrickHills(3) 2 88
(Charles Hills) *hld up: pushed along 2f out: effrt over 1f out: styd on to take 2nd wl ins fnl f: unable to trble wnr* **11/8**[1]
4243 **3** 3/4 **Red Refraction (IRE)**[18] 3658 3-9-7 **80** RichardMullen 5 81
(Richard Hannon) *chsd ldrs: pushed along over 2f out: rdn and swtchd lft over 1f out: sn wnt 2nd: no imp on wnr ins fnl f: sn lost 2nd: no ex fnl 75yds* **6/1**
3641 **4** *3* **Clearing**[23] 3499 3-7-13 **63** NathanAlison(5) 6 54
(Jim Boyle) *chsd ldr tl rdn over 1f out: hung lft ins fnl f: one pce after* **20/1**
2060 **5** 3/4 **Layla's Oasis**[8] 4018 3-8-9 **68** CathyGannon 1 57
(Richard Fahey) *led: rdn over 2f out: hdd over 1f out: one pce ins fnl f* **10/1**
0-06 **6** *7* **Joey's Destiny (IRE)**[29] 3279 3-9-2 **75** MartinLane 4 41
(George Baker) *s.i.s: bhd: pushed along and hung sltly rt over 3f out: outpcd over 2f out: eased whn wl btn over 1f out* **7/2**[2]

1m 15.68s (1.88) **Going Correction** +0.225s/f (Good) 6 Ran SP% **112.5**
Speed ratings (Par 102): **96,95,94,90,89 79**
Tote Swingers: 1&2 £1.02, 1&3 £3.30, 2&3 £1.90 CSF £10.01 CT £30.60 TOTE £5.20: £1.90, £1.10; EX 15.40 Trifecta £39.60 Pool: £1,770.93 - 33.51 winning units..
Owner Norton Common Farm Racing **Bred** T Cahalan & D Cahalan **Trained** Bawtry, S Yorks

FOCUS
A decent 3yo handicap. The pace was solid and the first three pulled clear. The winner is rated close to her AW mark.

4284 RAYMOND CORBETT MEMORIAL CITY PLATE (LISTED RACE) 7f 2y
3:25 (3:26) (Class 1) 3-Y-0+
£20,982 (£7,955; £3,981; £1,983; £995; £499) **Stalls** Low

Form RPR
2-00 **1** **Ladyship**[21] 3558 4-8-11 94 CathyGannon 3 95
(Sir Michael Stoute) *hld up: hdwy over 2f out: r.o to ld wl ins fnl f: in command fnl strides* **7/2**[3]
-522 **2** 1/2 **Rivas Rhapsody (IRE)**[12] 3892 5-8-11 85 RichardKingscote 2 94
(Rae Guest) *hld up in rr: pushed along 2f out: hdwy on inner over 1f out: r.o to chal ins fnl f: tk 2nd fnl stride but hld* **12/1**
1115 **3** *hd* **Dr Red Eye**[42] 2868 5-9-2 95 (p) BillyCray 6 98
(Scott Dixon) *led: pushed along 3f out: rdn and edgd lft over 1f out: hdd wl ins fnl f: r.o u.p: hld cl home* **15/2**
4061 **4** 3 1/2 **Correspondent**[14] 3803 3-8-8 98 MartinLane 5 86
(Brian Meehan) *chsd ldrs: pushed along 3f out: tried to chal over 1f out: nt qckn ins fnl f: sn edgd rt and no ex* **3/1**[2]
0-10 **5** 2 1/4 **Navajo Chief**[24] 3458 6-9-5 104 MichaelJMMurphy 1 85
(Alan Jarvis) *hld up: nt clr run under 3f out: sn u.p and outpcd: kpt on ins fnl f wout threatening* **6/1**
0244 **6** *7* **Majestic Myles (IRE)**[14] 3822 5-9-2 102 LeeTopliss 4 64
(Richard Fahey) *chsd ldr: rdn and hung rt over 2f out: sn lost 2nd: wknd 1f out* **5/2**[1]
-600 **7** *7* **The Taj (USA)**[14] 3831 3-8-8 95 RichardMullen 7 42
(Richard Hannon) *in tch: rdn over 2f out: sn wknd* **20/1**

1m 27.57s (1.07) **Going Correction** +0.225s/f (Good)
WFA 3 from 4yo+ 8lb 7 Ran SP% **114.3**
Speed ratings (Par 111): **102,101,101,97,94 86,78**
Tote Swingers: 1&2 £6.20 CSF £42.75 TOTE £5.10: £1.70, £6.10; EX 58.20 Trifecta £333.70 Pool: £2,048.34 - 4.60 winning units..
Owner Cheveley Park Stud **Bred** Cheveley Park Stud Ltd **Trained** Newmarket, Suffolk
■ Stewards' Enquiry : Cathy Gannon one-day ban: careless riding (Jul 28)
Billy Cray 26-day ban; used whip above permitted level, fifth suspension within six months (Aug 3, 5-21); eight days deferred until Oct 21st

FOCUS
Not the strongest of Listed contests but it was run at a good pace. With the market 1-2 disappointing, the winner did not need to improve on her 3yo form. The form is rated around the third.

4285 LIVERPOOL ONE H'CAP 6f 18y
4:00 (4:01) (Class 2) (0-105,95) 3-Y-0+ **£12,938** (£3,850; £1,924; £962) **Stalls** Low

Form RPR
0003 **1** **Al's Memory (IRE)**[7] 4067 4-8-10 **84** DeclanBates(5) 1 93
(David Evans) *mde all: rdn over 1f out: r.o ins fnl f: doing enough towards fin* **9/1**
320 **2** 1/2 **El Viento (FR)**[59] 2366 5-9-9 **92** LeeTopliss 2 99
(Richard Fahey) *in tch: trckd ldrs over 3f out: rdn over 1f out: wnt 2nd wl ins fnl f: r.o to press wnr towards fin* **5/1**[2]
0266 **3** 1 1/4 **Intransigent**[14] 3840 4-9-7 **90** RichardMullen 9 93+
(Andrew Balding) *hld up: rdn and hdwy over 1f out: styd on towards fin: nt quite rch ldrs* **17/2**
3100 **4** 1/2 **Summerinthecity (IRE)**[14] 3823 6-9-6 **89** CathyGannon 4 90
(David Nicholls) *a.p: rdn over 1f out: ev ch and kpt on ins fnl f: no ex towards fin* **5/1**[2]
1042 **5** *nk* **Sir Maximilian (IRE)**[14] 3802 4-9-6 **89** RichardKingscote 7 89
(Ian Williams) *midfield: rdn and nt pick up over 1f out: styd on towards fin: nt quite gng pce to chal* **3/1**[1]
1426 **6** 1 1/2 **Chester Aristocrat**[4] 4138 4-9-0 **88** JasonHart(5) 11 84+
(Eric Alston) *missed break: hld up: rdn over 1f out: kpt on ins fnl f: nvr trbld ldrs* **6/1**[3]
00-0 **7** 3/4 **West Leake Diman (IRE)**[105] 1232 4-9-6 **92** [1] PatrickHills(3) 6 85
(Charles Hills) *hld up: rdn and hdwy over 1f out: nt rch ldrs: no imp fnl 100yds* **25/1**
003- **8** 1/2 **Grissom (IRE)**[245] 7691 7-9-0 **88** DarylByrne(5) 5 80
(Tim Easterby) *prom: pushed along over 2f out: rdn and nt qckn over 1f out: one pce ins fnl f* **20/1**
-0 **9** *nk* **Mehdi (IRE)**[84] 1688 4-9-7 **90** (t) PaddyAspell 10 84
(David Nicholls) *n.m.r s: hld up: nt clr run over 1f out: no imp ins fnl f* **25/1**
0000 **10** 3 3/4 **Heavy Metal**[14] 3803 3-9-6 **95** LiamJones 3 73
(Mark Johnston) *midfield: pushed along 3f out: outpcd u.p over 1f out: wl btn ins fnl f* **12/1**

4131 **11** *22* **Rusty Rocket (IRE)**[14] 3802 4-9-2 **85**................................ MartinLane 12
(Paul Green) *wnt lft s: sddle slipped and racd wd: in midfield: dropped wl bhd and eased over 2f out* **12/1**

1m 15.67s (1.87) **Going Correction** +0.225s/f (Good)
WFA 3 from 4yo+ 6lb **11** Ran SP% **121.0**
Speed ratings (Par 109): **96,95,93,93,92 90,89,88,88,83 54**
Tote Swingers: 1&2 £18.60, 1&3 £18.60, 2&3 £4.10 CSF £53.81 CT £408.78 TOTE £8.10: £2.70, £3.30, £1.30; EX 39.20 Trifecta £359.50 Pool: £1,408.04 - 2.93 winning units..
Owner Will Dawson **Bred** Brian Miller **Trained** Pandy, Monmouths

FOCUS
An open handicap in which the draw played a big part, with the first two home coming out of stalls one and two. The pace held up and only the third made any ground from the rear.

4286 ABODE HOTEL CHESTER H'CAP — 1m 6f 91y
4:35 (4:35) (Class 3) (0-95,90) 3-Y-O **£8,086** (£2,406; £1,202; £601) **Stalls** Low

Form RPR
0324 **1** **Snowy Dawn**[17] 3698 3-8-3 **72**..(p) JimmyQuinn 3 83+
(Andrew Hollinshead) *hld up: hdwy 3f out: led 1f out: styd on wl and in command fnl 150yds* **5/2**[2]

4010 **2** *2 1/4* **Alta Lilea (IRE)**[9] 3990 3-9-7 **90**... LiamJones 4 98
(Mark Johnston) *led: kicked on over 2f out: rdn and hdd 1f out: no imp on wnr fnl 150yds* **11/1**

3411 **3** *1/2* **Good Evans**[8] 4029 3-8-9 **78**...................................... RichardKingscote 2 85
(Tom Dascombe) *chsd ldr: pushed along 5f out: rdn over 3f out: lost 2nd over 1f out: kpt on u.p ins fnl f but hld* **5/4**[1]

4264 **4** *6* **Gabrial The Master (IRE)**[14] 3806 3-8-3 **72**.................. CathyGannon 1 71
(Richard Fahey) *in tch: rdn over 3f out: outpcd over 2f out: no imp after* **7/1**

152 **5** *12* **Deira Phantom (IRE)**[15] 3783 3-8-11 **80**........................... MartinLane 5 62
(Roger Varian) *missed break: hld up in tch: pushed along 5f out: wknd over 2f out: lft bhd over 1f out* **9/2**[3]

3m 10.33s (3.33) **Going Correction** +0.225s/f (Good) **5** Ran SP% **112.0**
Speed ratings (Par 104): **99,97,97,94,87**
CSF £26.15 TOTE £3.90: £1.20, £8.00; EX 33.50 Trifecta £72.50 Pool: £1,611.65 - 16.66 winning units..
Owner Mrs Christine Stevenson **Bred** Southcourt Stud **Trained** Upper Longdon, Staffs

FOCUS
They went a stop start gallop in this 3yo handicap. The winner ran to his best, with the second back to her Newmarket form.

4287 BET AT CORBETTSPORTS.COM H'CAP — 1m 2f 75y
5:10 (5:10) (Class 4) (0-80,79) 4-Y-O+ **£6,469** (£1,925; £962; £481) **Stalls** High

Form RPR
-424 **1** **Stellar Express (IRE)**[35] 3098 4-9-4 **76**......................... AndrewMullen 2 86
(Michael Appleby) *mde all: rdn 2f out: r.o wl and a in control fnl f* **4/1**[1]

3212 **2** *1 3/4* **El Bravo**[12] 3889 7-8-6 **67**.. NeilFarley(3) 8 74
(Shaun Harris) *a.p: chsd wnr 2f out: rdn over 1f out: no imp ins fnl f* **9/1**[3]

0-62 **3** *3/4* **Livia's Dream (IRE)**[21] 3573 4-9-7 **79**...................... TomMcLaughlin 10 85+
(Ed Walker) *hld up: rdn and hdwy over 3f out: chsd ldrs over 1f out: styd on ins fnl f: nt quite able to mount serious chal* **4/1**[1]

240 **4** *1 1/4* **Royal Sea (IRE)**[9] 3977 4-7-9 **60**............................(be[1]) JoeyHaynes(7) 1 63
(Michael Mullineaux) *midfield: pushed along 5f out: rdn over 3f out: kpt on ins fnl f: nvr able to trble ldrs* **20/1**

1262 **5** *3* **Reset City**[6] 4098 7-8-13 **71**.. LiamJones 3 69+
(Mark Johnston) *in rr: pushed along 4f out: outpcd over 2f out: hrd at work to get on terms: nvr able to trble ldrs* **4/1**[1]

-131 **6** *shd* **Dolphin Rock**[49] 2646 6-9-7 **79**.. MartinLane 9 76
(Brian Ellison) *chsd wnr: rdn over 3f out: lost 2nd 2f out: wknd ins fnl f* **4/1**[1]

4000 **7** *1 1/2* **Knowe Head (NZ)**[28] 3349 6-8-12 **70**.......................(v) AdamBeschizza 5 64
(James Unett) *hld up: rdn and edgd lft over 1f out: nvr able to chal* **10/1**

6623 **8** *3 1/2* **Ewell Place (IRE)**[19] 3628 4-9-5 **77**.................................. CathyGannon 4 65
(David Nicholls) *racd keenly: trckd ldrs: pushed along over 3f out: outpcd over 1f out: wl btn ins fnl f* **8/1**[2]

2m 12.0s (0.80) **Going Correction** +0.225s/f (Good) **8** Ran SP% **115.0**
Speed ratings (Par 105): **105,103,103,102,99 99,98,95**
Tote Swingers: 1&2 £2.70, 1&3 £12.90, 2&3 £3.00 CSF £41.88 CT £152.54 TOTE £7.40: £1.40, £2.10, £3.20; EX 35.10 Trifecta £216.20 Pool: £2,321.44 - 8.04 winning units..
Owner Dallas Racing **Bred** Adrian Purvis **Trained** Danethorpe, Notts

FOCUS
A fair handicap, and the winner made all at what looked a good pace. The form is rated around the second.

4288 CRUISE NIGHTCLUB APPRENTICE H'CAP — 7f 122y
5:45 (5:46) (Class 4) (0-80,80) 3-Y-O **£6,469** (£1,925; £962; £481) **Stalls** Low

Form RPR
0343 **1** **Baltic Prince (IRE)**[7] 4056 3-8-11 **65**................................... JasonHart 4 67
(Paul Green) *mde all: rdn and edgd lft fr over 1f out: kpt on wl towards fin* **8/1**

043 **2** *1/2* **Queen Aggie (IRE)**[14] 3803 3-9-12 **80**............................ DeclanBates 7 81
(David Evans) *hld up: hdwy over 1f out: wnt 2nd ins fnl f: r.o and pressed wnr towards fin* **5/1**[3]

4121 **3** *1/2* **Black Rider (IRE)**[16] 3730 3-9-1 **72**......................... ConnorBeasley(3) 2 72+
(Julie Camacho) *hld up in rr: effrt over 1f out: edgd rt u.p ins fnl f: styd on towards fin* **2/1**[1]

-425 **4** *hd* **Excuse To Linger**[33] 3153 3-9-12 **80**.................................. RobertTart 3 79
(Jeremy Noseda) *chsd ldrs: wnt 2nd 2f out: rdn over 1f out: chal on inner ins fnl f: no ex towards fin* **4/1**[2]

4266 **5** *7* **Keene's Pointe**[25] 3438 3-9-8 **76**.......................................(p) RyanClark 6 58
(J W Hills) *chsd wnr tl rdn 2f out: wknd 1f out* **16/1**

1m 35.89s (2.09) **Going Correction** +0.225s/f (Good) **5** Ran SP% **87.0**
Speed ratings (Par 102): **98,97,97,96,89**
CSF £26.52 TOTE £3.40: £2.40, £1.30; EX 19.80 Trifecta £55.80 Pool: £481.26 - 6.46 winning units..
Owner A Mills **Bred** William Pilkington **Trained** Lydiate, Merseyside
■ Gabrial's Wawa was withdrawn on vet's advice; (3-1, deduct 25p in the £ under R4.)

FOCUS
A fair apprentice handicap and the third race on the card in which the winner made all. A bunch finish and the winner rates a length personal best.

T/Plt: £511.20 to £1 stake. Pool: £137,985.64 - 401.22 winning tickets. T/Qpdt: £79.00 to £1 stake. Pool: £3,172.76 - 29.70 winning tickets. DO

3928 HAMILTON (R-H)
Saturday, July 13

OFFICIAL GOING: Good to firm (good in places; watered; 8.4)
Rail realignment around the loop reduced advertised distances on the Round course by 25yds.
Wind: Breezy, across Weather: Cloudy, warm

4289 RACING UK ON SKY 432 MAIDEN AUCTION STKS — 5f 4y
6:40 (7:06) (Class 5) 2-Y-O **£3,408** (£1,006; £503) **Stalls** Low

Form RPR
5222 **1** **Memory Styx**[7] 4073 2-8-8 0... AndrewElliott 8 74
(Mick Channon) *trckd ldrs: hdwy to ld over 1f out: rdn out fnl f* **2/1**[1]

42 **2** *1* **Simply Black (IRE)**[17] 3681 2-8-8 0............................ RoystonFfrench 6 70
(Bryan Smart) *dwlt: chsd ldng gp: hdwy over 1f out: chsd wnr ins fnl f: kpt on: hld nr fin* **4/1**[2]

52 **3** *2 3/4* **Instant Attraction (IRE)**[14] 3826 2-8-13 0......................... PhillipMakin 3 68
(Kevin Ryan) *t.k.h: led: hung rt thrght: hdd over 3f out: rallied whn n.m.r briefly appr fnl f: kpt on same pce ins fnl f* **2/1**[1]

4 *hd* **Gym Shoes** 2-8-11 0 ow3.. JustinNewman(5) 5 68+
(Richard Fahey) *trckd ldrs: effrt and edgd rt over 1f out: kpt on same pce ins fnl f* **8/1**[3]

225 **5** *1/2* **Inciting Incident (IRE)**[37] 3017 2-8-13 0............................ TomEaves 1 63
(Ed McMahon) *t.k.h: cl up: led over 3f out: hdd over 1f out: outpcd fnl f* **14/1**

0 **6** *15* **Absconder (IRE)**[7] 4053 2-9-0 0.................................... J-PGuillambert 4 10
(Mark Johnston) *in tch: rdn over 2f out: wknd wl over 1f out* **33/1**

7 *14* **Boy Ranger (IRE)** 2-8-10 0.. RaulDaSilva(3) 7
(Ann Duffield) *s.i.s: bhd and rn green: no ch fr 1/2-way* **28/1**

Going Correction -0.20s/f (Firm) **7** Ran SP% **110.8**
Speed ratings (Par 94): **92,90,86,85,84 60,38**
toteswingers 1&2 £2.60, 1&3 £1.10, 2&3 £1.90 CSF £9.69 TOTE £2.30: £1.70, £1.30; EX 10.30 Trifecta £24.60 Pool: £1712.20 - 52.14 winning units..
Owner Mrs Ann C Black **Bred** Exors Of The Late John Breslin **Trained** West Ilsley, Berks

FOCUS
Racing was delayed due to an accident on the M74. Rail realignment around the loop reduced advertised distances on the Round course by 25yds. Fair form in this maiden, the winner confirming her recent improvement.

4290 BILL AND DAVID MCHARG MEMORIAL H'CAP — 5f 4y
7:15 (7:36) (Class 6) (0-65,70) 3-Y-O **£1,940** (£577; £288; £144) **Stalls** Centre

Form RPR
0611 **1** **Lexington Place**[7] 4069 3-9-7 **70**..................................... DavidBergin(5) 7 78
(David O'Meara) *dwlt: hld up: smooth hdwy 1/2-way: led and rdn over 1f out: kpt on wl fnl f* **6/4**[1]

1216 **2** *1/2* **Salvatore Fury (IRE)**[11] 3933 3-9-4 **62**...............................(p) TomEaves 2 68
(Keith Dalgleish) *t.k.h: prom: effrt and rdn over 1f out: ev ch ins fnl f: hld towards fin* **11/4**[2]

3220 **3** *1* **Chloe's Dream (IRE)**[21] 3594 3-9-1 **59**.........................(p) PJMcDonald 5 61
(Ann Duffield) *t.k.h: led to over 1f out: kpt on same pce ins fnl f* **4/1**[3]

3250 **4** *nk* **Pastoral Prey**[11] 3932 3-8-12 **56** ow1..............................(p) PhillipMakin 4 57
(Ian Semple) *prom: rdn and edgd lft over 1f out: kpt on same pce ins fnl f* **11/1**

5310 **5** *2* **Ichimoku**[46] 2756 3-8-11 **60**.......................................(t) JustinNewman(5) 1 54
(Bryan Smart) *plld hrd: cl up: rdn 2f out: outpcd fnl f* **10/1**

033 **6** *1/2* **Lady Calantha**[11] 3932 3-7-9 **46**................................. JordanHibberd(7) 3 38
(Alan Berry) *prom: outpcd and edgd rt over 2f out: kpt on fnl f: no imp* **28/1**

-505 **7** *3* **Poppy Bond**[15] 3779 3-8-11 **55**..................................... RoystonFfrench 6 37
(Chris Fairhurst) *chsd ldrs: lost pl over 3f out: sn struggling* **25/1**

59.74s (-0.26) **Going Correction** -0.20s/f (Firm) **7** Ran SP% **111.4**
Speed ratings (Par 98): **94,93,91,91,87 87,82**
CSF £5.41 TOTE £2.10: £1.50, £2.50; EX 5.90 Trifecta £14.00 Pool: £1529.75 - 81.93 winning units..
Owner Middleham Park Racing XXXI **Bred** Christopher & Annabelle Mason **Trained** Nawton, N Yorks

FOCUS
A decidedly modest contest.

4291 HAMILTON-PARK.CO.UK H'CAP (QUALIFIER FOR THE £15,000 BETFAIR SCOTTISH SPRINT FINAL) — 6f 5y
7:50 (8:10) (Class 5) (0-70,74) 3-Y-O+ **£3,234** (£962; £481; £240) **Stalls** Centre

Form RPR
000- **1** **Gran Canaria Queen**[227] 7914 4-8-8 **51**.......................... PJMcDonald 8 62
(Tim Easterby) *wnt rt s: mde all centre: shkn up over 1f out: kpt on strly fnl f* **16/1**

-013 **2** *1 3/4* **Feel The Heat**[31] 3197 6-9-4 **66**...............................(v) JustinNewman(5) 6 71
(Bryan Smart) *bmpd s: sn cl up: effrt and towards stands' rail over 1f out: sn chsng wnr: kpt on ins fnl f* **9/4**[1]

0350 **3** *nk* **Findog**[16] 3714 3-9-6 **69**.. PhillipMakin 5 72
(Linda Perratt) *hmpd s: in tch: effrt towards stands' side over 1f out: no imp fnl f* **6/1**

-053 **4** *1 1/4* **Mitchell**[21] 3591 3-9-6 **69**...(b) BarryMcHugh 4 68
(David Thompson) *chsd wnr in centre to over 1f out: sn rdn: kpt on same pce ins fnl f* **4/1**[3]

2401 **5** *1/2* **Mandalay King (IRE)**[11] 3934 8-9-9 **69**.....................(p) RaulDaSilva(3) 2 67
(Marjorie Fife) *prom centre: effrt and rdn 2f out: outpcd fnl f* **5/2**[2]

0151 **6** *2 3/4* **Secret Advice**[31] 3198 3-9-1 **64**.. TomEaves 3 53
(Keith Dalgleish) *plld hrd early: trckd centre ldrs: rdn and edgd lft over 1f out: edgd rt and wknd fnl f* **7/1**

1m 11.26s (-0.94) **Going Correction** -0.20s/f (Firm)
WFA 3 from 4yo+ 6lb **6** Ran SP% **112.0**
Speed ratings (Par 103): **98,95,95,93,92 89**
toteswingers 1&2 £6.80, 1&3 £12.70, 2&3 £2.40 CSF £51.88 CT £246.35 TOTE £16.10: £3.70, £1.90; EX 54.50 Trifecta £208.10 Pool: £786.68 - 2.83 winning units..
Owner M Gillies **Bred** H Moszkowicz And Whitsbury Manor Stud **Trained** Great Habton, N Yorks

FOCUS
A run-of-the-mill handicap. The second and third both got slightly hampered at the start but it would be hard to argue it affected the result.

4292 BOOK NOW FOR MID-FAIR FRIDAY NIGHT (S) H'CAP 6f 5y
8:20 (8:40) (Class 6) (0-65,60) 3-5-Y-O **£2,045** (£603; £302) **Stalls** Centre

Form RPR
0-53 **1** **Saxonette**[6] 4102 5-9-2 **50** PJMcDonald 3 60
(Linda Perratt) *hld up in tch: stdy hdwy over 2f out: led over 1f out: edgd rt ins fnl f: drvn out* **3/1**[2]

0-40 **2** *1* **Lothair (IRE)**[57] 2409 4-9-2 **50** RobertWinston 1 57
(Alan Swinbank) *t.k.h: cl up: led over 2f out: rdn: hung rt and hdd over 1f out: rallied: one pce ins fnl f* **9/2**

006 **3** *¾* **Busy Bimbo (IRE)**[24] 3475 4-8-11 **45** TomEaves 6 49
(Alan Berry) *bhd: struggling over 3f out: gd hdwy over 1f out: r.o ins fnl f: nrst fin* **20/1**

0050 **4** *7* **Rock Canyon (IRE)**[11] 3934 4-9-3 **51** (p) PhillipMakin 2 33
(Linda Perratt) *led to over 2f out: rdn and wknd over 1f out* **11/2**

4000 **5** *shd* **Baltic Bomber (IRE)**[8] 4009 4-9-10 **58** (v) MichaelO'Connell 5 40
(John Quinn) *trckd ldrs: hmpd over 3f out: outpcd over 2f out: no imp fnl f* **7/2**[3]

6-05 **6** *7* **Lothian Countess**[11] 3929 3-9-0 **54** RoystonFfrench 4 12
(Ian Semple) *plld hrd: chsd ldrs: blkd over 3f out: rdn and wknd over 1f out* **22/1**

0001 **7** *4½* **Lady Del Sol**[11] 3929 5-9-12 **60** (p) J-PGuillambert 7 5
(Jo Hughes) *hld up in tch: hdwy and hung rt over 3f out: wknd 2f out* **11/4**[1]

1m 10.8s (-1.40) **Going Correction** -0.20s/f (Firm)
WFA 3 from 4yo+ 6lb **7 Ran SP% 116.6**
Speed ratings (Par 101): **101,99,98,89,89 79,73**
toteswingers 1&2 £3.70, 1&3 £6.50, 2&3 £6.70 CSF £17.50 TOTE £4.10: £2.50, £2.90; EX 20.00 Trifecta £590.50 Pool: £900.55 - 1.14 winning units..There was no bid for the winner.
Owner John Murphy **Bred** Mike Channon Bloodstock Ltd **Trained** East Kilbride, S Lanarks

FOCUS
Another low-grade sprint on the card.

4293 FOLLOW @HAMILTONPARKRC ON TWITTER H'CAP 1m 3f 16y
8:50 (9:10) (Class 5) (0-75,72) 3-Y-0+ **£3,881** (£1,155; £577; £288) **Stalls** Low

Form RPR
6121 **1** **Special Meaning**[22] 3535 3-9-2 **72** FrannyNorton 2 85+
(Mark Johnston) *mde all: rdn and qcknd clr over 1f out: readily* **1/1**[1]

2211 **2** *3¾* **Argaki (IRE)**[6] 4098 3-9-1 **71** 6ex TomEaves 4 75
(Keith Dalgleish) *trckd ldrs: rdn over 2f out: chsd (clr) wnr over 1f out: no imp ins fnl f* **9/2**[3]

2432 **3** *nk* **Eric The Grey (IRE)**[28] 3336 3-9-0 **70** BarryMcHugh 5 74
(Richard Fahey) *hld up: effrt whn nt clr run over 2f out and over 1f out: kpt on ins fnl f: nvr able to chal* **3/1**[2]

0023 **4** *1¾* **Royal Straight**[16] 3715 8-9-10 **68** (t) PhillipMakin 6 68
(Linda Perratt) *hld up in tch: stdy hdwy on outside over 2f out: rdn over 1f out: sn outpcd* **22/1**

6531 **5** *4* **Ebony Express**[15] 3768 4-9-9 **67** RobertWinston 7 60
(Alan Swinbank) *prom: smooth hdwy to press wnr over 2f out: rdn over 1f out: fnd little and sn btn* **7/1**

-000 **6** *3* **Indepub**[14] 3827 4-10-0 **72** (b) BrianHughes 3 60
(Kevin Ryan) *pressed wnr: rdn over 3f out: wknd fr 2f out* **22/1**

2m 21.48s (-4.12) **Going Correction** -0.325s/f (Firm)
WFA 3 from 4yo+ 12lb **6 Ran SP% 114.4**
Speed ratings (Par 103): **101,98,98,96,93 91**
toteswingers 1&2 £2.30, 1&3 £1.30, 2&3 £3.70 CSF £6.20 TOTE £2.00: £1.40, £1.40; EX 4.40 Trifecta £13.70 Pool: £755.26 - 41.15 winning units..
Owner Newsells Park Stud **Bred** Newsells Park Stud **Trained** Middleham Moor, N Yorks

FOCUS
A one-sided handicap.

4294 DOWNLOAD FREE RACING UK APP H'CAP (QUALIFIER FOR £15,000 BETFAIR SCOTTISH MILE SERIES FINAL) 1m 65y
9:20 (9:37) (Class 5) (0-70,70) 3-Y-0+ **£3,234** (£962; £481; £240) **Stalls** Low

Form RPR
5651 **1** **Silver Rime (FR)**[15] 3770 8-9-11 **67** PhillipMakin 4 79
(Linda Perratt) *hld up in tch: stdy hdwy over 3f out: effrt and chsd ldr 1f out: styd on to ld last 50yds* **8/1**

4612 **2** *nk* **Corton Lad**[6] 4100 3-9-5 **70** (bt) TomEaves 2 79
(Keith Dalgleish) *dwlt: sn rdn to ld: t.k.h: led: rdn over 2f out: kpt on: hdd last 50yds* **15/8**[1]

00-0 **3** *6* **Ralphy Boy (IRE)**[17] 3683 4-9-8 **64** MichaelO'Connell 1 61
(Alistair Whillans) *trckd ldrs: effrt and rdn over 2f out: kpt on same pce fr over 1f out* **7/1**

033 **4** *6* **Mullins Way (USA)**[2] 4195 5-9-0 **56** (p) J-PGuillambert 3 39
(Jo Hughes) *sn pushed along to chse ldr: rdn over 3f out: wknd over 1f out* **4/1**[2]

0010 **5** *2½* **Dubious Escapade (IRE)**[12] 3895 4-9-13 **69** (p) PJMcDonald 7 47
(Ann Duffield) *prom: rdn and outpcd over 3f out: rallied over 2f out: wknd over 1f out* **4/1**[2]

4440 **6** *7* **Dakota Canyon (IRE)**[28] 3349 4-9-13 **69** (b) BarryMcHugh 6 31
(Richard Fahey) *sn niggled in rr: struggling 4f out: nvr on terms* **11/2**[3]

1m 45.18s (-3.22) **Going Correction** -0.325s/f (Firm)
WFA 3 from 4yo+ 9lb **6 Ran SP% 113.8**
Speed ratings (Par 103): **103,102,96,90,88 81**
toteswingers 1&2 £1.80, 1&3 £8.60, 2&3 £4.00 CSF £24.00 TOTE £10.70: £3.80, £1.60; EX 22.10 Trifecta £90.30 Pool: £845.66 - 7.01 winning units..
Owner Ken McGarrity **Bred** Jean-Philippe Dubois **Trained** East Kilbride, S Lanarks

FOCUS
A modest handicap. The runner-up set what looked no more than a fair gallop.

T/Plt: £22.40 to a £1 stake. Pool: £64995.59 - 2117.42 winning tickets T/Qpdt: £8.40 to a £1 stake. Pool: £3753.85 - 327.95 winning tickets RY

[4252]NEWMARKET (R-H)
Saturday, July 13

OFFICIAL GOING: Good to firm (watered) (overall 7.8, stands' side 7.7, centre 7.9, far side 7.6)
Stands side track used Stalls Stands side except 10f: Centre
Wind: virtually nil Weather: sunny and hot

4295 32RED CASINO H'CAP 1m
2:05 (2:08) (Class 2) (0-100,100) 3-Y-O
£12,450 (£3,728; £1,864; £932; £466; £234) **Stalls** Low

Form RPR
-500 **1** **Law Enforcement (IRE)**[23] 3484 3-9-7 **100** DaneO'Neill 3 110
(Richard Hannon) *stdd s: hld up in tch in last pair: swtchd lft and effrt 2f out: led 1f out: r.o wl fnl f: rdn out* **9/1**

21-3 **2** *1½* **Muharrib (IRE)**[15] 3763 3-8-12 **91** MickaelBarzalona 1 98
(Saeed bin Suroor) *stdd s: hld up wl in tch in midfield: rdn over 2f out: hdwy u.p over 1f out: chsd wnr ins fnl f: r.o but a hld* **9/2**[2]

3163 **3** *1¾* **Defendant**[8] 4014 3-8-6 **85** RyanMoore 2 88
(Sir Michael Stoute) *chsd ldrs: rdn over 2f out: drvn to ld over 1f out: hdd and unable qck 1f out: styd on same pce fnl f* **3/1**[1]

114 **4** *1½* **Stepping Ahead (FR)**[29] 3296 3-8-12 **91** NeilCallan 8 90
(Mrs K Burke) *chsd ldr: rdn and ev ch briefly wl over 1f out: sn drvn and outpcd ent fnl f: one pce fnl f* **6/1**[3]

-550 **5** *1¼* **Steelriver (IRE)**[21] 3563 3-8-6 **85** JohnFahy 5 81
(James Bethell) *t.k.h: hld up wl in tch in midfield: effrt u.p 2f out: outpcd and no imp fr over 1f out* **20/1**

1012 **6** *2½* **Aussie Reigns (IRE)**[15] 3780 3-8-6 **85** (v) LukeMorris 6 75
(William Knight) *hld up wl in tch in midfield: rdn and effrt 2f out: hrd drvn and outpcd over 1f out: wknd fnl f* **9/1**

531 **7** *2½* **Prince's Trust**[56] 2456 3-8-9 **88** RichardHughes 4 73
(Richard Hannon) *led and set stdy gallop: jnd and rdn ent fnl 2f: hdd over 1f out and sn btn: wknd 1f out* **9/2**[2]

5130 **8** *10* **Jammy Guest (IRE)**[24] 3455 3-9-3 **96** TomQueally 10 58
(George Margarson) *wnt lft s: hld up in tch in rr: rdn and effrt 2f out: sn hung lft and btn: bhd and eased ins fnl f* **13/2**

1m 37.61s (-2.39) **Going Correction** -0.125s/f (Firm) **8 Ran SP% 113.7**
Speed ratings (Par 106): **106,104,102,101,100 97,95,85**
Tote Swingers: 1&2 £7.50, 1&3 £4.70, 2&3 £2.90 CSF £48.55 CT £142.03 TOTE £10.70: £2.80, £1.60, £1.60; EX 56.90 Trifecta £209.30 Pool: £3,660.70 - 13.11 winning units..
Owner Mohamed Saeed Al Shahi **Bred** Mrs E J O'Grady **Trained** East Everleigh, Wilts

FOCUS
A total of 6mm of water was applied overnight, leaving the going officially good to firm (GoingStick 7.8; Stands' side 7.7, Centre 7.9, Far side7.6), but with the temperature high from early in the morning the moisture was soon out of the ground and jockeys returning after the first declared it to be riding fast. They went a steady early gallop here, which in theory should have suited those racing to the fore, but the first two came from off the pace. The winner is rated back to his 2yo best, with the next two open to improvement.

4296 32RED.COM SUPERLATIVE STKS (GROUP 2) 7f
2:40 (2:42) (Class 1) 2-Y-O
£45,368 (£17,200; £8,608; £4,288; £2,152; £1,080) **Stalls** Low

Form RPR
11 **1** **Good Old Boy Lukey**[16] 3723 2-9-0 0 RyanMoore 4 104
(Richard Fahey) *chsd ldr: rdn to chal and edgd rt over 1f out: led ent fnl f: battled on gamely u.p and hld on wl fnl f: drvn out* **7/2**[2]

14 **2** *hd* **Somewhat (USA)**[21] 3555 2-9-0 0 JohnnyMurtagh 8 103
(Mark Johnston) *led: rdn and edgd rt over 1f out: hdd ent fnl f: ev ch and battled on gamely u.p fnl f: a jst hld* **11/4**[1]

1 **3** *2* **Washaar (IRE)**[30] 3233 2-9-0 0 DaneO'Neill 1 98
(Richard Hannon) *hld up wl in tch in midfield: rdn and effrt to chse ldrs whn swtchd lft over 1f out: styd on same pce fnl f: eased nr fin* **7/2**[2]

40 **4** *2½* **Street Force (USA)**[21] 3555 2-9-0 0 TomQueally 9 91
(Clive Brittain) *t.k.h: chsd ldrs: edgd rt u.p and unable qck over 1f out: no imp fnl f* **33/1**

0310 **5** *¾* **Rosso Corsa**[25] 3422 2-9-0 0 KierenFallon 2 89
(Mick Channon) *stdd s: t.k.h: hld up in tch in last trio: rdn and hdwy 2f out: struggling to qckn whn squeezed for room ent fnl f: one pce and n.d after* **11/1**

21 **6** *nse* **Vigor (IRE)**[25] 3426 2-9-0 0 NeilCallan 5 89
(David Simcock) *hld up wl in tch in midfield: lost pl and rdn whn short of room and swtchd lft over 1f out: kpt on but no threat to ldrs fnl f* **8/1**

1 **7** *3* **Noble Metal**[23] 3490 2-9-0 0 RichardHughes 7 81
(Peter Chapple-Hyam) *stdd s: t.k.h: hld up in rr: swtchd lft and short-lived effrt over 1f out: wknd fnl f* **16/1**

1 **8** *5* **Recanted (USA)**[30] 3238 2-9-0 0 FrankieDettori 3 68
(Brian Meehan) *taken down early and ponied to s: stdd s: hld up in tch in last trio: rdn and effrt ent fnl 2f: wknd jst over 1f out* **9/2**[3]

1m 24.58s (-1.12) **Going Correction** -0.125s/f (Firm) **8 Ran SP% 117.6**
Speed ratings (Par 106): **101,100,98,95,94 94,91,85**
Tote Swingers: 1&2 £2.50, 1&3 £3.30, 2&3 £2.70 CSF £14.04 TOTE £3.80: £1.20, £1.40, £1.50; EX 16.00 Trifecta £55.30 Pool: £8,802.30 - 119.27 winning units..
Owner Leods Contracts Limited **Bred** Mrs Sarah Hamilton **Trained** Musley Bank, N Yorks

FOCUS
Usually a strong juvenile Group 2 in which three of the last ten winners, Dubawi, Horatio Nelson and Olympic Glory, went on to score at the highest level. Incidentally all of their successes at that level were gained in either France or Ireland. This looked quite a weak renewal, although all but one of the runners were previous winners. They went steady for a couple of furlongs before winding up the pace, the first four held those positions throughout and the first two had it between them from the Dip. The form is rated towards the bottom end of the race averages.

4297 32RED BUNBURY CUP (HERITAGE H'CAP) 7f
3:15 (3:17) (Class 2) 3-Y-O+
£62,250 (£18,640; £9,320; £4,660; £2,330; £1,170) **Stalls** Low

Form RPR
5606 **1** **Field Of Dream**[24] 3458 6-9-7 **98** (b) AdamKirby 20 109
(Jamie Osborne) *taken down early: racd far side: in tch in midfield: rdn and effrt to chse ldng pair over 1f out: r.o u.p to ld wl ins fnl f* **14/1**

2052 **2** *1* **Es Que Love (IRE)**[7] 4080 4-9-10 **101** JohnnyMurtagh 19 109
(Mark Johnston) *racd far side: chsd overall ldr: rdn to ld 1f out: drvn fnl f: hdd and no ex wl ins fnl f* **15/2**[2]

The Form Book Flat, Raceform Ltd, Compton, RG20 6NL.

0063 **3** 1 1/4 **I'm So Glad**[21] 3562 4-8-12 **92**.................................. CharlesBishop[(3)] 17 97
(Mick Channon) *racd far side: overall ldr tl rdn and hdd over 1f out: no ex ins fnl f* **25/1**

0006 **4** *nse* **Dance And Dance (IRE)**[16] 3725 7-9-3 **94**....................(b[1]) RyanMoore 8 102+
(Ed Vaughan) *racd in centre: stdd s: hld up in rr: hdwy whn gap clsd and hmpd over 1f out: rallied and r.o wl ins fnl f: nt rch ldrs* **14/1**

-410 **5** *nk* **Redvers (IRE)**[22] 3527 5-9-4 **95**..(b) NeilCallan 16 99
(Ed Vaughan) *racd in centre: hld up towards rr: rdn and effrt 2f out: forced way between horses and hdwy over 1f out: styd on wl fnl f: nt rch ldrs* **8/1**[3]

4010 **6** *1* **Highland Colori (IRE)**[22] 3527 5-9-8 **99**............................ LiamKeniry 5 100
(Andrew Balding) *racd nr side: chsd ldrs overall: rdn 2f out: edgd lft and styd on same pce fr over 1f out* **12/1**

-360 **7** *1* **Burwaaz**[24] 3458 4-9-6 **97**.. DaneO'Neill 11 95
(Ed Dunlop) *racd in centre: chsd ldrs overall: 4th and edgd lft u.p over 1f out: wknd ins fnl f and flashed tail towards fin* **33/1**

/00- **8** *shd* **Best Of Order (IRE)**[17] 6-9-3 **94**...............................(p) LukeMorris 2 92
(E J O'Neill, France) *racd nr side: in tch in midfield: effrt u.p 2f out: edgd lft and styd on same pce fr over 1f out* **33/1**

41 **9** *hd* **Burn The Boats (IRE)**[14] 3846 4-9-5 **96**........................... GaryCarroll 13 93
(G M Lyons, Ire) *racd in centre: chsd ldrs overall: rdn and unable qck whn edgd lft over 1f out: btn and one pce fnl f* **13/2**[1]

3010 **10** *nk* **Galician**[7] 4062 4-9-1 **92**.. NickyMackay 4 89
(Mark Johnston) *racd nr side: in tch in midfield: rdn and effrt over 2f out: edgd lft and plugged on fnl f: no threat to ldrs* **25/1**

1030 **11** 1 1/4 **Mezzotint (IRE)**[22] 3527 4-9-2 **93**....................................... PaoloSirigu 9 86
(Marco Botti) *racd in centre: chsd gp ldrs and wl in tch overall: rdn and unable qck over 1f out: wknd ins fnl f: eased towards fin* **28/1**

-401 **12** *nse* **My Freedom (IRE)**[16] 3725 5-9-8 **99**...................... MickaelBarzalona 15 92
(Saeed bin Suroor) *racd in centre: chsd gp ldrs and in tch overall: effrt 2f out: no prog and edgd lft over 1f out: wknd ins fnl f* **16/1**

2-04 **13** 1 1/4 **Gramercy (IRE)**[14] 3823 6-9-1 **92**................................. StevieDonohoe 6 82
(David Simcock) *racd in centre: t.k.h: hld up towards rr: effrt and racd awkwardly u.p 2f out: wknd over 1f out* **25/1**

0201 **14** 1/2 **Belgian Bill**[24] 3458 5-9-10 **101**....................................(tp) FrankieDettori 1 89
(George Baker) *racd nr side: hld up towards rr: rdn and no hdwy over 1f out: nvr trbld ldrs* **10/1**

0-10 **15** *nk* **Excellent Guest**[24] 3458 6-9-7 **98**..................................... TomQueally 10 86
(George Margarson) *racd in centre: hld up in tch in midfield: rdn 2f out: no hdwy and pushed lft over 1f out: wknd fnl f* **12/1**

1-40 **16** *nk* **Emilio Largo**[22] 3527 5-9-4 **95**...................................... FrederikTylicki 7 82
(James Fanshawe) *racd in centre: in tch in midfield overall: rdn and no hdwy 2f out: wknd fnl f* **14/1**

6124 **17** *shd* **George Guru**[28] 3339 6-9-2 **93**... KierenFallon 18 82
(Michael Attwater) *racd far side: towards rr: rdn 1/2-way: wknd over 1f out* **16/1**

-202 **18** *4* **Bertiewhittle**[14] 3825 5-9-6 **97**....................................... RichardHughes 12 76
(David Barron) *racd in centre: hld up in midfield overall: rdn and effrt jst over 2f out: no prog whn pushed lft over 1f out: sn btn and eased ins fnl f* **15/2**[2]

0500 **19** *21* **Brae Hill (IRE)**[28] 3346 7-9-3 **94**........................... ChristopheSoumillon 14
(Richard Fahey) *taken down early: racd in centre: s.i.s: a bhd: lost tch over 1f out: eased fnl f: t.o* **16/1**

1m 23.09s (-2.61) **Going Correction** -0.125s/f (Firm) **19** Ran SP% **131.0**
Speed ratings (Par 109): **109,107,106,106,106 104,103,103,103,103 101,101,100,99,99 98,98,94,70**
Tote Swingers: 1&2 £8.50, 1&3 £166.00, 2&3 £64.50 CSF £112.37 CT £1591.73 TOTE £20.80: £3.80, £2.20, £8.10, £3.00; EX 128.70 Trifecta £5106.90 Pool: £67,617.03 - 9.93 winning units..
Owner K J P Gundlach **Bred** Grundy Bloodstock Srl **Trained** Upper Lambourn, Berks
■ Stewards' Enquiry : Adam Kirby four-day ban: used whip above permitted (Jul 28-30, Aug 1)
Gary Carroll one-day ban: careless riding (Jul 28)

FOCUS
A highly competitive race on paper (9lb covered the entire field), and they were racing for double the prize-money handed out last year, but there was a draw bias, with those positioned high proving favoured. The first three were drawn in the top four stalls. The time was half a second outside the course record. The first two are rated to form.

4298 DARLEY JULY CUP (BRITISH CHAMPIONS SERIES AND GLOBAL SPRINT CHALLENGE) (GROUP 1) 6f
3:50 (3:52) (Class 1) 3-Y-O+
£283,550 (£107,500; £53,800; £26,800; £13,450; £6,750) **Stalls** Low

Form RPR

0-21 **1** **Lethal Force (IRE)**[21] 3557 4-9-5 120.................................. AdamKirby 4 124
(Clive Cox) *mde all: rdn 2f out: fnd ex and clr ent fnl f: in command and r.o wl ins fnl f: readily* **9/2**[3]

5-12 **2** 1 1/2 **Society Rock (IRE)**[21] 3557 6-9-5 117.............................. KierenFallon 1 119
(James Fanshawe) *in tch in midfield: pushed along 1/2-way: effrt u.p jst over 2f out: chsd wnr jst ins fnl f: styd on but no imp* **11/2**

-301 **3** 3/4 **Slade Power (IRE)**[14] 3848 4-9-5 109.............................. WayneLordan 2 117
(Edward Lynam, Ire) *chsd wnr: drvn and unable qck w wnr over 1f out: kpt on same pce u.p fnl f* **16/1**

0112 **4** *nk* **Shea Shea (SAF)**[25] 3420 6-9-5 120.................... ChristopheSoumillon 8 116+
(M F De Kock, South Africa) *stdd after s and hld up in last quartet: clsd and switching lft 2f out: swtchd lft and wnt between horses jst over 1f out: drvn and chsd ldng trio 1f out: styd on same pce fnl f* **3/1**[1]

4141 **5** *hd* **Sole Power**[25] 3420 6-9-5 117...................................... JohnnyMurtagh 11 115+
(Edward Lynam, Ire) *stdd and swtchd rt after s: hld up in rr: rdn and clsd over 1f out: n.m.r and swtchd lft ins fnl f: sn rdn and styd on same pce fnl 100yds* **15/2**

-421 **6** *2* **Gale Force Ten**[24] 3455 3-8-13 114...............................(b[1]) RyanMoore 6 108
(A P O'Brien, Ire) *hld up in tch in midfield: rdn 2f out: struggling to qckn whn pushed lft jst over 1f out: keeping on one pce whn pushed lft again ins fnl f: wknd towards fin* **4/1**[2]

0 **7** 1/2 **Shamexpress (NZ)**[25] 3420 4-9-5 115....................(t) MickaelBarzalona 3 107
(Danny O'Brien, Australia) *stdd s: hld up in rr: clsd and swtchd lft over 1f out: sn rdn and no hdwy: nvr trbld ldrs* **20/1**

-411 **8** 3 3/4 **Hamza (IRE)**[45] 2768 4-9-5 109...................................(b) NeilCallan 12 95
(Kevin Ryan) *chsd ldrs: struggling u.p wl over 1f out: btn 1f out and fdd ins fnl f* **12/1**

4220 **9** 2 3/4 **Sovereign Debt (IRE)**[25] 3419 4-9-5 112.......................... TomQueally 9 86
(Michael Bell) *wl in tch in midfield: drvn and struggling over 2f out: wknd over 1f out* **25/1**

1410 **10** *7* **Zanetto**[21] 3557 3-8-13 109... LiamKeniry 10 63
(Andrew Balding) *dwlt: sn rcvrd and in tch in midfield: rdn and lost pl ent fnl 2f: bhd and eased ins fnl f* **50/1**

0/0 **11** 1/2 **Havelock (USA)**[21] 3557 6-9-5 109...............................(t) FrankieDettori 7 62
(Darrin Miller, U.S.A) *stdd s: hld up in last quartet: swtchd lft and effrt in centre ent fnl 2f: sn struggling and btn: bhd and eased ins fnl f* **50/1**

1m 9.11s (-3.39) **Going Correction** -0.125s/f (Firm) course record
WFA 3 from 4yo+ 6lb **11** Ran SP% **116.4**
Speed ratings (Par 117): **117,115,114,113,113 110,110,105,101,92 91**
Tote Swingers: 1&2 £4.50, 1&3 £15.80, 2&3 £23.30 CSF £28.03 CT £292.61 TOTE £5.70: £1.70, £2.40, £4.80; EX 20.00 Trifecta £332.00 Pool: £12,253.96 - 27.67 winning units..
Owner Alan G Craddock **Bred** Declan Johnson **Trained** Lambourn, Berks
■ Stewards' Enquiry : Adam Kirby four-day ban: used whip above permitted level (Aug 2,4-6)

FOCUS
One of the top 6f sprints of the European season and traditionally won by horses that have gone on to become champion sprinter in the region, five of the previous ten winners having earned that title. This year's contest was truly international, with half of the field emanating from overseas, although Bahrain's representative Krypton Factor had to be withdrawn after bursting out of the stalls. Unlike the preceding race, with the stalls placed on the stands' rail the field came to race there, and the winner broke the course record. Lethal Force rates up with the better recent July Cup winners and is the current leading European sprinter. This rates a pound higher than his Ascot win.

4299 ROSSDALES EBF CONDITIONS STKS 6f
4:25 (4:25) (Class 2) 2-Y-O **£12,938** (£3,850; £1,924) **Stalls** Low

Form RPR

15 **1** **Emirates Flyer**[23] 3481 2-9-1 0.................................. MickaelBarzalona 3 95
(Saeed bin Suroor) *broke wl: sn stdd bk to 3rd and niggled along: rdn and swtchd lft over 2f out: carried lft but drvn to chal 1f out: led and stmbld fnl 100yds: hld on: drvn out* **8/11**[1]

226 **2** *nk* **Sacha Park (IRE)**[25] 3424 2-8-13 0............................. RichardHughes 1 92
(Richard Hannon) *chsd ldrs: upsides and rdn 2f out: led and edging lft 1f out: hdd fnl 100yds: r.o but a jst hld* **7/4**[2]

410 **3** 1 1/2 **Green Door (IRE)**[23] 3481 2-9-1 0............................... JohnnyMurtagh 4 89
(Olly Stevens) *wnt lft s: sn led and t.k.h: rdn and edgd lft jst over 1f out: hdd 1f out: btn whn continued hanging lft and hmpd nr fin* **13/2**[3]

1m 11.36s (-1.14) **Going Correction** -0.125s/f (Firm) **3** Ran SP% **107.6**
Speed ratings (Par 100): **102,101,99**
CSF £2.29 TOTE £1.40; EX 1.60 Trifecta £1.30 Pool: £2,470.30 - 1,331.86 winning units..
Owner Godolphin **Bred** Carmel Stud **Trained** Newmarket, Suffolk

FOCUS
Disappointingly, for the second year running this conditions event was a three-runner affair. The early pace was strong enough thanks to the free-going Green Door, but they all finished bunched up and there were no stars here.

4300 SPA AT BEDFORD LODGE HOTEL NURSERY H'CAP 7f
5:00 (5:00) (Class 2) 2-Y-O **£12,938** (£3,850; £1,924; £962) **Stalls** Low

Form RPR

021 **1** **Dutch Courage**[20] 3605 2-9-5 **87**.. RyanMoore 1 92+
(Richard Fahey) *hld up wl in tch in last pair: stuck bhd rivals and nt clr run 2f out: hmpd jst over 1f out: swtchd lft and gap opened ins fnl f: qcknd under hands and heels to ld fnl 75yds: gng away at fin* **5/4**[1]

0121 **2** *1* **Malachim Mist (IRE)**[15] 3761 2-9-7 **89**........................ RichardHughes 5 88
(Richard Hannon) *chsd ldng pair: rdn over 2f out: styd on to chse wnr jst over 1f out: drvn to ld ins fnl f: hdd fnl 75yds: no ex* **9/4**[2]

412 **3** *hd* **Razor Quest**[17] 3690 2-8-12 **80**....................................(t) WilliamCarson 3 79
(Philip McBride) *hld up wl in tch in last pair: n.m.r 2f out: rdn and hmpd jst over 1f out: swtchd lft and hdwy to press ldrs ins fnl f: one pce fnl 100yds* **7/1**

2103 **4** 3 1/2 **Tableforten**[17] 3690 2-8-9 **77**... KierenFallon 4 66
(J S Moore) *chsd ldr: rdn to ld and hung rt over 1f out: hdd ins fnl f: sn wknd* **12/1**

4021 **5** *10* **Al Baz**[21] 3588 2-9-1 **83**... NeilCallan 2 45
(James Tate) *racd keenly: led tl rdn and hdd over 1f out: bdly hmpd sn after: sn bhd and wknd fnl f* **5/1**[3]

1m 25.86s (0.16) **Going Correction** -0.125s/f (Firm) **5** Ran SP% **112.1**
Speed ratings (Par 100): **94,92,92,88,77**
CSF £4.42 TOTE £1.90: £1.10, £1.80; EX 4.20 Trifecta £14.50 Pool: £2,946.86 - 151.58 winning units..
Owner Cheveley Park Stud **Bred** Barton Bloodstock **Trained** Musley Bank, N Yorks
■ Stewards' Enquiry : Richard Hughes two-day ban: careless riding (Jul 28-29)

FOCUS
The official ratings shown are estimated and for information only. A very messy race, but the best horse still won in the end.

4301 EGERTON HOUSE STABLES H'CAP 1m 4f
5:35 (5:41) (Class 3) (0-90,90) 3-Y-O+ **£9,703** (£2,887; £1,443; £721) **Stalls** Centre

Form RPR

2-1 **1** **Havana Cooler (IRE)**[77] 1845 3-8-8 **83**.............................. KierenFallon 6 99
(Luca Cumani) *restless in stalls: s.i.s: steadily rcvrd and midfield after 4f: chsd ldr over 2f out: drvn and ev ch 1f out: led ins fnl f: pushed out and styd on wl towards fin* **5/1**[2]

-120 **2** 3/4 **Pether's Moon (IRE)**[23] 3486 3-9-1 **90**.......................... RichardHughes 4 104
(Richard Hannon) *chsd ldrs: rdn and effrt to chse ldng pair 2f out: drvn to ld 1f out: hdd and one pce ins fnl f* **6/4**[1]

11-4 **3** 3 3/4 **Cat O'Mountain (USA)**[36] 3061 3-8-13 **88**............. MickaelBarzalona 11 96
(Saeed bin Suroor) *styd wd: chsd ldr tl led over 2f out: edgd rt fr 2f out: hdd 1f out: wknd ins fnl f* **6/1**[3]

0-30 **4** 4 1/2 **Beaufort Twelve**[14] 3832 4-9-12 **88**.................................. FrankieDettori 1 89
(William Jarvis) *hld up in last quartet: effrt u.p over 2f out: wnt modest 4th over 1f out: plugged on same pce fnl f* **25/1**

51 **5** 1 3/4 **Poyle Thomas**[26] 3402 4-9-0 **76**... SebSanders 9 74+
(Ralph Beckett) *stdd s: hld up in rr: rdn and effrt over 2f out: outpcd and no threat to ldrs over 1f out: plugged on fnl f* **16/1**

43-0 **6** *6* **Willie Wag Tail (USA)**[69] 2044 4-10-0 **90**................. JohnnyMurtagh 10 78
(Ed Walker) *t.k.h: chsd ldrs tl lost pl u.p over 2f out: wl btn over 1f out* **6/1**[3]

4163 **7** 2 1/2 **Cousin Khee**[17] 3685 6-9-9 **85**.. RyanMoore 7 69
(Hughie Morrison) *hld up in last trio: effrt u.p but no hdwy over 2f out: wl btn over 1f out* **10/1**

2500 **8** 3/4 **Blue Wave (IRE)**[9] 3982 3-8-9 **84**..................................(v[1]) NeilCallan 2 67
(Mark Johnston) *led tl rdn and hdd over 2f out: drvn and outpcd by ldng pair 2f out: wknd over 1f out* **12/1**

0025 **9** 1 3/4 **Pintrada**[14] 3804 5-9-0 **76**.. DaneO'Neill 3 56
(James Bethell) *rrd as stalls opened and s.i.s: hld up in last trio: effrt u.p over 2f out: no hdwy and wknd over 1f out* **25/1**

1410 **10** *hd* **Harry Buckle**[140] 777 4-9-11 **87**........................ WilliamCarson 8 67
(Philip McBride) *in tch in midfield: no hdwy u.p over 2f out: wknd over 1f out* **33/1**

2m 28.91s (-3.99) **Going Correction** -0.125s/f (Firm)
WFA 3 from 4yo+ 13lb **10** Ran SP% **118.5**
Speed ratings (Par 107): **108,107,105,102,100 96,95,94,93,93**
Tote Swingers: 1&2 £2.30, 1&3 £5.10, 2&3 £3.70 CSF £12.83 CT £47.09 TOTE £6.10: £1.90, £1.30, £1.80; EX 15.40 Trifecta £69.80 Pool: £5,267.38 - 56.53 winning units..
Owner Leonidas Marinopoulos **Bred** Ammerland Verwaltung Gmbh **Trained** Newmarket, Suffolk

FOCUS
A decent middle-distance handicap in which 4yos have the best recent record, but this year's finish was dominated by the 3yos. The winner was a big improver and the first three finished clear.
T/Plt: £33.40 to a £1 stake. Pool: £203,464.39 - 4,443.58 winning tickets. T/Qpdt: £18.80 to a £1 stake. Pool: £7,654.32 - 299.77 winning tickets. SP

3853 SALISBURY (R-H)
Saturday, July 13

OFFICIAL GOING: Good to firm (firm between 1m & 7f starts and on loop section for 1m 4f start; watered; 9.1)
Rail erected up straight up to 15ft off far side rail between 6.5f and 2f.
Wind: virtually nil Weather: sunny

4302 4COM PLC NOVICE AUCTION STKS 6f
6:25 (6:25) (Class 5) 2-Y-O **£3,234** (£962; £481; £240) **Stalls** High

Form RPR
021 **1** **Our Queenie (IRE)**[50] 2617 2-8-9 0........................ PatDobbs 5 83
(Richard Hannon) *trckd ldr: shkn up to ld over 1f out: r.o wl and in control fnl f* **2/5**[1]

2 **2** *2 1/4* **Secret Kode (IRE)**[18] 3663 2-8-7 0........................ MartinDwyer 6 74
(Brendan Powell) *cl up: nudged along over 3f out: rdn over 2f out: kpt on same pce* **6/1**[2]

451 **3** *1 1/2* **Talksalot (IRE)**[25] 3436 2-8-4 0........................ CharlotteJenner(7) 2 73
(J S Moore) *led and rs freely tl rdn over 1f: kpt on same pce* **12/1**

4 *1 1/2* **Jersey Brown (IRE)** 2-8-7 0........................ SamHitchcott 1 64+
(Mick Channon) *hld up in last pair but wl in tch: rdn over 2f out: sn one pce* **16/1**

5 **5** *9* **Royal River**[3] 4175 2-8-9 0........................ JohnFahy 3 37
(J S Moore) *trckd ldrs: rdn over 2f out: sn wknd* **9/1**[3]

6 *1 1/4* **Touche De Rouge (IRE)** 2-8-4 0........................ KieranO'Neill 4 28
(Peter Makin) *hld up but wl in tch in last pair: rdn over 2f out: sn btn* **40/1**

1m 14.59s (-0.21) **Going Correction** -0.175s/f (Firm) **6** Ran SP% **111.7**
Speed ratings (Par 94): **94,91,89,87,75 73**
toteswingers 1&2 £1.20, 1&3 £1.90, 2&3 £2.20 CSF £3.28 TOTE £1.40: £1.10, £2.00; EX 3.00 Trifecta £8.10 Pool: £1889.76 - 174.39 winning units..
Owner N A Woodcock **Bred** Liam Brennan **Trained** East Everleigh, Wilts

FOCUS
Not a bad novice event.

4303 DANNY MCNAB 50 YEARS AT SALISBURY H'CAP 6f
6:55 (6:55) (Class 5) (0-75,75) 3-Y-O+ **£2,911** (£866; £432; £216) **Stalls** High

Form RPR
3652 **1** **Mambo Spirit (IRE)**[28] 3315 9-9-0 **63**........................ MartinDwyer 10 73
(Tony Newcombe) *mid-div: nudged along and hdwy over 1f out: str run ent fnl f: led towards fin: readily* **12/1**

0-34 **2** *1/2* **Bajan Bear**[28] 3322 5-8-13 **67**........................ WilliamTwiston-Davies(5) 1 75
(Michael Blanshard) *trckd ldrs: rdn 2f out: led over 1f out: kpt on but no ex whn hdd towards fin* **9/1**

0641 **3** *2 3/4* **Sole Danser (IRE)**[8] 4034 5-9-7 **70**........................(p) JohnFahy 2 69
(Milton Bradley) *mid-div: rdn over 1f out: r.o ins fnl f: wnt 3rd towards fin* **8/1**

302 **4** *nk* **Ceelo**[14] 3818 3-9-6 **75**........................(p) LiamKeniry 3 72
(Sylvester Kirk) *led: rdn and hdd over 1f out: no ex ins fnl f* **4/1**[2]

3322 **5** *1/2* **The Dark Wizard (IRE)**[26] 3401 3-9-1 **70**........................ JamesDoyle 8 66
(Roger Charlton) *rrd leaving stalls: in last pair: rdn and stdy prog fr 2f out: r.o but nvr gng pce to threaten* **5/2**[1]

0-04 **6** *1* **The Wee Chief (IRE)**[13] 3855 7-9-4 **67**........................ KieranO'Neill 11 60
(Jimmy Fox) *hld up in last pair: nudged along and stdy prog whn clr run over 1f out: kpt on fnl f but nvr gng pce to threaten* **10/1**

0060 **7** *3/4* **Dark Lane**[13] 3855 7-9-4 **67**........................ AidanColeman 9 58
(David Evans) *trckd ldrs: rdn 3f out: sn one pce* **16/1**

0144 **8** *1/2* **Star Of Rohm**[14] 3813 3-9-5 **74**........................ HayleyTurner 12 62
(Michael Bell) *prom: rdn over 2f out: hld over 1f out: fdd fnl f* **6/1**[3]

0634 **9** *1* **Clear Praise (USA)**[16] 3733 6-9-10 **73**........................ PatDobbs 7 59
(Simon Dow) *towards rr: rdn over 2f out: nvr gng pce to threaten* **12/1**

50-0 **10** *6* **Silvee**[14] 3817 6-8-7 **56** oh4........................ SamHitchcott 4 23
(John Bridger) *chsd ldrs: rdn over 2f out: wknd over 1f out* **50/1**

5000 **11** *nk* **Pick A Little**[28] 3315 5-9-7 **70**........................ HarryBentley 5 36
(Michael Blake) *mid-div: rdn over 2f out: wknd over 1f out* **25/1**

1m 13.33s (-1.47) **Going Correction** -0.175s/f (Firm)
WFA 3 from 5yo+ 6lb **11** Ran SP% **120.1**
Speed ratings (Par 103): **102,101,97,97,96 95,94,93,92,84 83**
toteswingers 1&2 £14.00, 1&3 £8.40, 2&3 £19.20 CSF £118.02 CT £947.09 TOTE £11.40: £4.10, £4.00, £2.60; EX 121.90 Trifecta £625.00 Part won. Pool: £833.36 - 0.07 winning units..
Owner Nigel Hardy **Bred** R Warren **Trained** Yarnscombe, Devon

FOCUS
A modest sprint handicap.

4304 BATHWICK TYRES BRITISH STALLION STUDS EBF MAIDEN STKS 6f 212y
7:30 (7:30) (Class 4) 2-Y-O **£4,204** (£1,251; £625; £312) **Stalls** Centre

Form RPR
62 **1** **Truth Or Dare**[13] 3853 2-9-5 0........................ RichardHughes 8 86+
(Richard Hannon) *trckd ldrs: pushed along whn edgd lft and led over 1f out: r.o wl: readily* **5/4**[1]

3 **2** *3* **Istimraar (IRE)**[23] 3490 2-9-5 0........................ WilliamBuick 9 77
(Saeed bin Suroor) *led: rdn and hdd over 1f out: kpt on wl but nt pce of ready wnr* **2/1**[2]

03 **3** *5* **Solo Hunter**[13] 3853 2-9-5 0........................ SaleemGolam 1 63
(David Evans) *cl up: rdn 2f out: kpt on but nt gng pce of ldng pair* **10/1**

4 *nk* **Festival Theatre (IRE)** 2-9-5 0........................ PatDobbs 2 63+
(Sir Michael Stoute) *s.i.s: in last pair: pushed along and hdwy to chse ldrs over 1f out: styd on same pce fnl f: improve* **7/1**[3]

0 **5** *8* **Aristocracy**[13] 3853 2-9-5 0........................ SamHitchcott 3 41
(Mick Channon) *s.i.s: towards rr: rdn 3f out: nvr gng pce to get involved* **25/1**

6 *3/4* **Man Of Law (USA)** 2-9-5 0........................ JamesDoyle 5 39
(Ralph Beckett) *cl up: rdn over 2f out: wknd ent fnl f* **7/1**[3]

0 **7** *3 1/2* **Blunos (IRE)**[11] 3914 2-9-5 0........................ LiamKeniry 10 30
(Rod Millman) *sn trcking ldrs: rdn over 2f out: wknd over 1f out* **50/1**

600 **8** *4 1/2* **Movie Magic**[14] 3815 2-9-0 0........................ KieranO'Neill 4
(John Bridger) *in tch: struggling 3f out: nvr a danger: wknd over 1f out* **100/1**

1m 27.59s (-1.01) **Going Correction** -0.175s/f (Firm) **8** Ran SP% **118.7**
Speed ratings (Par 96): **98,94,88,88,79 78,74,69**
CSF £4.09 TOTE £2.20: £1.10, £1.30, £2.60; EX 4.30 Trifecta £14.60 Pool: £1137.01 - 58.37 winning units..
Owner Carmel Stud **Bred** D G Hardisty Bloodstock **Trained** East Everleigh, Wilts

FOCUS
A fair 2yo maiden.

4305 CHAPEL NIGHTCLUB H'CAP 1m 4f
8:05 (8:05) (Class 5) (0-75,75) 3-Y-O+ **£2,911** (£866; £432; £216) **Stalls** High

Form RPR
3013 **1** **Sunny Future (IRE)**[13] 3856 7-9-10 **71**........................ RichardHughes 2 78
(Malcolm Saunders) *led: pushed along over 3f out: rdn and hdd 2f out: rallied gamely to take narrow ld jst ins fnl f: styd on wl fnl 120yds to assert* **6/4**[1]

00/- **2** *1 1/4* **Dumbarton (IRE)**[253] 7534 5-9-5 **71**........................ WilliamTwiston-Davies(5) 1 76
(Philip Hobbs) *trckd ldrs jnd wnr jst over 2f out travelling wl: sn shkn up to ld: rdn whn hdd jst ins fnl f: no ex fnl 120yds* **5/1**

3-24 **3** *9* **Neamour**[43] 2846 3-8-11 **71**........................ WilliamBuick 4 62
(David Simcock) *trckd ldng trio: rdn over 2f out: wknd ent fnl f* **2/1**[2]

0602 **4** *1/2* **Halling's Treasure**[19] 3618 3-8-12 **75**........................ ThomasBrown(3) 3 65
(Andrew Balding) *trckd ldr tl rdn over 2f out: wknd ent fnl f* **7/2**[3]

2m 34.57s (-3.43) **Going Correction** -0.175s/f (Firm)
WFA 3 from 5yo+ 13lb **4** Ran SP% **112.2**
Speed ratings (Par 103): **104,103,97,96**
CSF £9.13 TOTE £2.00; EX 7.50 Trifecta £27.10 Pool: £440.85 - 12.18 winning units..
Owner M S Saunders **Bred** Mrs G Stanga **Trained** Green Ore, Somerset

FOCUS
A tight handicap.

4306 FERNDENE FARM H'CAP 1m
8:35 (8:36) (Class 4) (0-85,80) 3-Y-O **£4,851** (£1,443; £721; £360) **Stalls** High

Form RPR
3-41 **1** **Monsieur Rieussec**[35] 3117 3-9-6 **79**........................ TedDurcan 3 86+
(Jonathan Portman) *stdd s: trckd ldrs: rdn whn edgd lft jst over 1f out: styd on wl ins fnl f: led fnl 100yds: rdn out* **6/4**[1]

2644 **2** *1 1/4* **Strong Conviction**[19] 3633 3-9-2 **75**........................ SamHitchcott 2 78
(Mick Channon) *trckd ldr tl rdn to ld over 2f out: styd on but no ex whn hdd fnl 100yds* **9/1**

4111 **3** *1 1/2* **Kohlaan (IRE)**[27] 3369 3-9-7 **80**........................ WilliamBuick 1 79
(Roger Varian) *led: rdn and hdd 2f out: kpt pressing ldrs tl no ex ins fnl f* **13/8**[2]

1-34 **4** *12* **Gracious George (IRE)**[30] 3242 3-9-0 **73**........................ PatDobbs 5 44
(Jimmy Fox) *trckd ldrs: swtchd to far rails after 3f: rdn wl over 2f out: wknd over 1f out* **7/2**[3]

1m 41.58s (-1.92) **Going Correction** -0.175s/f (Firm) **4** Ran SP% **110.3**
Speed ratings (Par 102): **102,100,99,87**
CSF £12.95 TOTE £2.30; EX 12.00 Trifecta £18.10 Pool: £480.11 - 19.86 winning units..
Owner J T Habershon-Butcher **Bred** Mrs James Wigan **Trained** Upper Lambourn, Berks

FOCUS
A fair little 3-y-o handicap.

4307 BRITISH STALLION STUDS EBF FILLIES' H'CAP 1m
9:05 (9:06) (Class 3) (0-95,93) 3-Y-O **£8,733** (£2,598; £1,298) **Stalls** High

Form RPR
6421 **1** **Magic Of Reality (FR)**[27] 3372 3-9-1 **87**........................ TomQueally 4 92+
(Lady Cecil) *racd keenly: trckd ldrs: jnd ldrs over 3f out: shkn up over 1f out: led ins fnl f: styd on wl: pushed out* **11/8**[2]

2511 **2** *hd* **Saucy Minx (IRE)**[22] 3532 3-8-10 **82**........................(b) PatDobbs 5 86
(Amanda Perrett) *trckd ldr: jnd ldr over 3f out: led jst over 2f out: hdd ins fnl f: styd on gamely u.p: jst hld nring fin* **5/1**[3]

2-10 **3** *7* **Fleeting Smile (USA)**[24] 3460 3-9-7 **93**........................ RichardHughes 1 81
(Richard Hannon) *racd keenly: led: rdn whn hdd jst over 2f out: kpt pressing ldrs tl fdd ent fnl f* **11/10**[1]

1m 42.61s (-0.89) **Going Correction** -0.175s/f (Firm) **3** Ran SP% **106.4**
Speed ratings (Par 101): **97,96,89**
CSF £6.51 TOTE £2.40; EX 6.30 Trifecta £4.90 Pool: £373.04 - 56.65 winning units..
Owner Niarchos Family **Bred** Suc S Niarchos **Trained** Newmarket, Suffolk

FOCUS
The complexion of this fillies' handicap was completely changed by the pair of non-runners.
T/Plt: £91.50 to a £1 stake. Pool: £67,841.84 - 540.99 winning tickets T/Qpdt: £19.60 to a £1 stake. Pool: £4,400.28 - 165.70 winning tickets TM

4259 YORK (L-H)
Saturday, July 13

OFFICIAL GOING: Good to firm (overall 7.8, stands' side 7.6, centre 7.7, far side 7.7)
Races on inside line around home bend and races of a mile and beyond reduced by 24yds.
Wind: light 1/2 against Weather: fine and sunny, very warm

4308 JOHN SMITH'S RACING STKS (H'CAP) 1m
1:45 (1:48) (Class 3) (0-95,95) 3-Y-O+ **£16,172** (£4,812; £2,405; £1,202) **Stalls** Low

Form RPR
5-41 **1** **The Rectifier (USA)**[22] 3544 6-9-11 **92**........................(t) MickyFenton 10 102
(Seamus Durack) *hld up in rr: hdwy on outside over 2f out: led narrowly jst ins fnl f: hld on nr fin* **14/1**

0010 **2** *hd* **Smarty Socks (IRE)**[22] 3527 9-10-0 **95**........................ DanielTudhope 14 104
(David O'Meara) *lw: swtchd lft after s: hld up in rr: hdwy over 2f out: swtchd outside over 1f out: upsides last 100yds: jst hld* **8/1**[3]

1005 **3** *shd* **Al Muheer (IRE)**[7] 4055 8-9-3 **84**........................(b) DaleSwift 4 93
(Ruth Carr) *swtg: in tch: t.k.h: hdwy over 1f out: upsides last 50yds: no ex* **25/1**

2525 **4** 2 ¾ **Lord Aeryn (IRE)**[28] 3346 6-9-3 **89**.......................... GeorgeChaloner(5) 8 92
(Richard Fahey) *lw: in rr: drvn and hdwy 4f out: led 1f out: sn hdd: one pce* **10/1**
2060 **5** 2 ¼ **No Poppy (IRE)**[9] 3984 5-8-10 **82**.................................. AdamCarter(5) 6 80
(Tim Easterby) *mid-div: lost pl and drvn after 3f: kpt on fnl 2f* **20/1**
0111 **6** 1 **Talent Scout (IRE)**[12] 3895 7-8-9 **83**......................(p) GemmaTutty(7) 15 78
(Karen Tutty) *swtg: trckd ldr: led briefly over 1f out: one pce* **16/1**
0060 **7** 1 **St Moritz (IRE)**[7] 4080 7-9-10 **91**.. DavidNolan 2 84
(David O'Meara) *in tch: droven over 3f out: n.m.r 2f out: one pce* **9/1**
0230 **8** hd **Anderiego (IRE)**[22] 3527 5-9-9 **95**................................ DavidBergin(5) 3 87
(David O'Meara) *chsd ldrs: drvn over 2f out: fdd fnl f* **9/2**[2]
0106 **9** nk **Norse Blues**[21] 3564 5-9-11 **92**................................. GrahamGibbons 12 84
(David Barron) *led: hdd over 1f out: grad wknd* **14/1**
221- **10** 1 **Nine Realms**[411] 2553 4-9-12 **93**.. GrahamLee 5 82
(William Haggas) *hld up in rr: hdwy on ins over 2f out: wknd over 1f out* **3/1**[1]
-002 **11** 1 ¼ **Nameitwhatyoulike**[29] 3300 4-9-9 **90**............................ PhillipMakin 13 77
(Michael Easterby) *t.k.h: sn trcking ldrs: wknd over 1f out* **14/1**
3152 **12** hd **Snooky**[15] 3777 4-8-13 **80**.. TonyHamilton 11 66
(Richard Fahey) *dwlt: swtchd lft after s: nvr a factor* **9/1**
000- **13** 14 **Arabian Star (IRE)**[287] 6674 5-9-8 **89**................................. SebSanders 9 43
(Alan McCabe) *trckd ldrs: lost pl over 1f out: eased ins fnl f* **40/1**
3203 **14** 1 **Eutropius (IRE)**[6] 4098 4-8-9 **76** oh2........................... RobertWinston 1 28
(Alan Swinbank) *trckd ldrs: lost pl over 1f out: bhd whn eased ins fnl f* **12/1**

1m 35.14s (-3.86) **Going Correction** -0.275s/f (Firm) course record 14 Ran SP% **128.0**
Speed ratings (Par 107): **108,107,107,104,102 101,100,100,100,99 97,97,83,82**
Tote Swingers: 1&2 £18.80, 1&3 £103.30, 2&3 £57.10 CSF £127.00 CT £2881.78 TOTE £16.20: £4.30, £2.40, £9.90; EX 131.70 Trifecta £1310.10 Part won. Pool: £1,746.90 - 0.40 winning units..
Owner Mrs Anne Cowley **Bred** Ceka Ireland Ltd **Trained** Baydon, Wilts
■ Stewards' Enquiry : Daniel Tudhope two-day ban: used whip down shoulder in the forehand (Jul 28-29)

FOCUS
They were racing on the inside line and distances in races over 1m and more were reduced by 24 yards. Tony Hamilton felt the ground was "a little bit quicker" than the previous day, but still "lovely". This looked more open than the market suggested and it produced a tight finish. It was strongly run and the first two were both on good marks based on their old form.

4309 JOHN SMITH'S SILVER CUP (H'CAP) (LISTED RACE) 1m 6f
2:20 (2:21) (Class 1) (0-110,109) 3-Y-0+

£22,684 (£8,600; £4,304; £2,144; £1,076; £540) **Stalls** Low

Form RPR
0-12 **1** **Sun Central (IRE)**[35] 3099 4-9-5 **100**.............................(p) SebSanders 6 110
(William Haggas) *swtg: hld up towards rr: effrt over 3f out: chsng ldrs over 1f out: styd on strly to ld last 75yds: drvn clr* **3/1**[2]
0-16 **2** 3 ¼ **Songcraft (IRE)**[21] 3556 5-9-11 **106**......................(p) SilvestreDeSousa 3 111
(Saeed bin Suroor) *t.k.h: hld up: effrt over 2f out: chal over 1f out: styd on same pce wl ins fnl f* **7/2**[3]
-420 **3** 1 ½ **Number Theory**[23] 3483 5-9-13 **108**........................ GrahamGibbons 7 111
(John Holt) *lw: trckd ldrs: led narrowly over 1f out: hdd and no ex wl ins fnl f* **16/1**
0-60 **4** nse **Guarantee**[57] 2428 4-9-7 **102**.. PhillipMakin 5 105
(William Haggas) *trckd ldr: led over 2f out: hdd over 1f out: one pce* **8/1**
20-1 **5** 4 **Montaser (IRE)**[29] 3297 4-9-6 **101**...................................... JimCrowley 2 98
(David Simcock) *swtg: s.s: hld up in last: smooth hdwy on outside3f out: chal over 1f out: sn rdn: edgd lft and wknd last 150yds* **11/4**[1]
3-40 **6** 2 ¼ **Tenenbaum**[105] 1263 4-10-0 **109**.. GrahamLee 1 103
(Saeed bin Suroor) *sn trcking ldrs: effrt over 3f out: wknd over 1f out* **10/1**
0060 **7** hd **Sir Graham Wade (IRE)**[7] 4060 4-9-8 **103**.................... FrannyNorton 4 97
(Mark Johnston) *hld up towards rr: drvn over 3f out: lost pl over 1f out* **8/1**
20-6 **8** 30 **Albamara**[57] 2407 4-9-1 **96**... AndreaAtzeni 8 48
(Sir Mark Prescott Bt) *led and sn clr: jnd whn qcknd pce 4f out: hdd over 2f out: sn lost pl: heavily eased ins fnl f: t.o* **16/1**

2m 56.68s (-3.52) **Going Correction** -0.275s/f (Firm) 8 Ran SP% **117.0**
Speed ratings (Par 111): **99,97,96,96,93 92,92,75**
Tote Swingers: 1&2 £3.30, 1&3 £58.30, 2&3 £16.90 CSF £14.38 CT £143.40 TOTE £3.70: £1.40, £1.50, £3.60; EX 13.00 Trifecta £98.00 Pool: £1,512.72 - 11.56 winning units..
Owner Lael Stable **Bred** Lael Stables **Trained** Newmarket, Suffolk

FOCUS
Albamara had soon established a clear lead, but they went just a fair gallop, with the others being happy to let her get on with it. The winners continues on the upgrade.

4310 54TH JOHN SMITH'S CUP (HERITAGE H'CAP) 1m 2f 88y
2:55 (2:57) (Class 2) 3-Y-0+

£93,375 (£27,960; £13,980; £6,990; £3,495; £1,755) **Stalls** Low

Form RPR
-226 **1** **Danchai**[7] 4080 4-8-11 **92**..(p) AndreaAtzeni 16 104
(William Haggas) *lw: trckd ldr: led over 1f out: hld on towards fin* **10/1**
2-62 **2** nk **Stencive**[21] 3559 4-9-3 **98**.. GrahamLee 21 110+
(William Haggas) *lw: in rr: gd hdwy on outer 2f out: styd on wl to take 2nd last 50yds: jst denied* **6/1**[1]
2213 **3** 1 ½ **Tres Coronas (IRE)**[43] 2839 6-8-9 **90**.......................... RobertWinston 4 99
(David Barron) *mid-div: t.k.h: effrt 3f out: styd on same pce appr fnl f* **20/1**
1313 **4** ½ **Awake My Soul (IRE)**[14] 3832 4-8-12 **93**.................. DanielTudhope 11 101
(David O'Meara) *mid-div: hdwy over 3f out: kpt on same pce appr fnl f* **14/1**
3-11 **5** 1 ¼ **Clon Brulee (IRE)**[47] 2718 4-8-12 **93**.......................... GrahamGibbons 6 99
(David Barron) *lw: mid-div: hdwy over 3f out: kpt on same pce appr fnl f* **13/2**[2]
2100 **6** ½ **Angel Gabrial (IRE)**[7] 4060 4-8-9 **90**................................ TomEaves 8 95+
(Ian Williams) *rrd s: sn in mid-div: outpcd over 3f out: hdwy 2f out: nt muh room and swtchd lft ins fnl f: styng on at fin* **50/1**
5/55 **7** hd **Saptapadi (IRE)**[20] 3608 7-8-13 **94**................................. BarryMcHugh 5 98
(Brian Ellison) *hld up in rr: hdwy 3f out: one pce over 1f out* **16/1**
121 **8** shd **Star Lahib (IRE)**[7] 4060 4-8-11 **92** 5ex......................... FrannyNorton 18 96+
(Mark Johnston) *in rr: drvn over 3f out: styd on fnl 2f* **12/1**
3200 **9** hd **Beaumont's Party (IRE)**[7] 4060 6-9-0 **95**........................... DaleSwift 9 99
(Brian Ellison) *chsd ldrs: drvn 3f out: one pce over 1f out* **25/1**
1010 **10** ¾ **Educate**[24] 3458 4-9-5 **100**... PhillipMakin 7 102
(Ismail Mohammed) *mid-div: t.k.h: hdwy over 2f out: nvr threatened* **15/2**[3]
04-1 **11** ½ **Expert Fighter (USA)**[45] 2775 4-9-0 **95**.................. SilvestreDeSousa 15 96
(Saeed bin Suroor) *chsd ldrs: drvn 3f out: one pce* **14/1**
3013 **12** 3 ¾ **Fennell Bay (IRE)**[7] 4060 4-8-10 **91** 5ex.......................... PJMcDonald 1 85
(Mark Johnston) *w ldr: led 3f out: hdd & wknd over 1f out* **20/1**
4320 **13** 1 ¼ **Forgotten Hero (IRE)**[14] 3832 4-8-9 **90**.......................... SteveDrowne 20 82
(Charles Hills) *mid-div: t.k.h: effrt over 3f out: wknd over 1f out* **33/1**
2-11 **14** 1 **Niceofyoutotellme**[35] 3113 4-8-11 **92**............................... JimCrowley 14 82
(Ralph Beckett) *s.i.s: hld up in rr: sme hdwy over 3f out: wknd 2f out* **6/1**[1]
5-62 **15** 2 **Validus**[16] 3725 4-9-6 **101**.. PaulMulrennan 12 87
(Luca Cumani) *in tch: t.k.h: hdwy on inner over 3f out: sn trcking ldrs: lost pl over 1f out* **18/1**
0-40 **16** 1 **King's Warrior (FR)**[57] 2427 6-9-5 **100**.......................... RobertHavlin 17 84
(Peter Chapple-Hyam) *lw: s.i.s: in rr: sme hdwy over 3f out: wknd 2f out* **25/1**
0-01 **17** nk **Garde Cotiere (USA)**[45] 2766 5-8-9 **90**........................ TonyHamilton 22 74
(Richard Fahey) *trckd ldrs: t.k.h: lost pl over 1f out* **33/1**
0503 **18** 13 **Toto Skyllachy**[15] 3754 8-8-9 **97**.............................. JacobButterfield(7) 3 56
(David O'Meara) *mid-div: t.k.h: hdwy over 3f out: lost pl 2f out* **50/1**
1421 **19** 20 **Area Fifty One**[35] 3094 5-9-5 **105**.............................. GeorgeChaloner(5) 13
(Richard Fahey) *mde most: hdd 3f out: sn lost pl: bhd whn eased ins fnl f: t.o* **16/1**

2m 7.79s (-4.71) **Going Correction** -0.275s/f (Firm) **19** Ran SP% **127.8**
Speed ratings (Par 109): **107,106,105,105,104 103,103,103,103,102 102,99,98,97,95 95,94,84,68**
Tote Swingers: 1&2 £11.40, 1&3 £34.90, 2&3 £19.80 CSF £63.95 CT £1214.35 TOTE £12.50: £3.20, £1.60, £5.30, £3.60; EX 65.40 Trifecta £1682.00 Pool: £3,895.23 - 1.73 winning units..
Owner Saleh Al Homaizi & Imad Al Sagar **Bred** Brook Stud Bloodstock Ltd **Trained** Newmarket, Suffolk

FOCUS
They went fairly steady up front early, resulting in quite a few taking a keen hold, but there's little doubt the two best horses at the weights emerged. Strong form, although they finished quite congested behind the progressive William Haggas 1-2.

4311 JOHN SMITH'S CITY WALLS STKS (LISTED RACE) 5f
3:30 (3:30) (Class 1) 3-Y-0+

£22,684 (£8,600; £4,304; £2,144; £1,076; £540) **Stalls** Centre

Form RPR
5022 **1** **Jwala**[21] 3562 4-8-9 101.. SteveDrowne 9 107
(Robert Cowell) *lw: racd stands' side: styd on fnl f: led nr fin* **16/1**
1426 **2** nk **Heeraat (IRE)**[25] 3420 4-9-0 107.. GrahamLee 1 111
(William Haggas) *lw: overall ldr far side: shkn up 1f out: hdd towards fin* **15/8**[1]
-404 **3** shd **Excelette (IRE)**[21] 3562 4-8-9 100............................ RoystonFfrench 5 106
(Bryan Smart) *chsd ldrs centre: drvn 2f out: styd on last 100yds: no ex nr fin* **20/1**
3311 **4** nk **Kingsgate Choice (IRE)**[28] 3334 6-9-0 109........................ JimCrowley 3 110
(Ed de Giles) *lw: trckd other 2 far side: drvn over 2f out: styd on same pce last 50yds* **4/1**[2]
2031 **5** 1 ½ **My Propeller (IRE)**[21] 3562 4-8-13 102...................... RobertWinston 10 104
(Peter Chapple-Hyam) *chsd ldrs stands' side: effrt 2f out: edgd lft and kpt on fnl 100yds* **8/1**
000- **6** shd **Borderlescott**[260] 7390 11-9-0 108.............................. PaulMulrennan 6 104
(Robin Bastiman) *chsd ldrs centre: drvn over 2f out: kpt on fnl f* **20/1**
/55- **7** nk **Hoof It**[378] 3633 6-9-0 112.. GrahamGibbons 11 103
(Michael Easterby) *dwlt: chsd ldrs stands' side over 3f out: kpt on same pce fnl f* **4/1**[2]
0450 **8** ¾ **Stepper Point**[25] 3420 4-9-0 104.................................... PhillipMakin 7 100
(William Muir) *dwlt: chsd ldrs centre: effrt over 2f out: one pce fnl f* **25/1**
-130 **9** 2 ¼ **Tangerine Trees**[49] 2662 8-9-0 106..................................(v) TomEaves 4 92
(Bryan Smart) *chsd ldr far side: drvn 2f out: wknd fnl f* **15/2**[3]

58.12s (-1.18) **Going Correction** +0.05s/f (Good) 9 Ran SP% **116.9**
Speed ratings (Par 111): **111,110,110,109,107 107,106,105,102**
Tote Swingers: 1&2 £15.10, 1&3 £9.80, 2&3 £29.00 CSF £45.86 TOTE £21.40: £4.20, £1.10, £6.10; EX 63.50 Trifecta £903.60 Pool: £1,601.24 - 1.32 winning units..
Owner Manor Farm Stud & Miss S Hoare **Bred** Manor Farm Stud (rutland) **Trained** Six Mile Bottom, Cambs

FOCUS
The runners raced spread across the track and there was little between the front four at the line, and this is ordinary form for the grade, albeit sound enough.

4312 JOHN SMITH'S MEDIAN AUCTION MAIDEN STKS 6f
4:05 (4:05) (Class 3) 2-Y-0 **£7,439** (£2,213; £1,106; £553) **Stalls** Centre

Form RPR
1 **The Grey Gatsby (IRE)** 2-9-5 0.. GrahamLee 8 90+
(Kevin Ryan) *w'like: scope: in rr: shkn up after 1f: hdwy over 2f out: chsng ldr ins fnl fn hung lft: styd on to ld towards fin* **11/4**[2]
2 **2** ¾ **Brazos (IRE)**[8] 4031 2-9-5 0... BrettDoyle 9 87
(Clive Brittain) *athletic: led: crowded: no ex and hdd clsng stages* **4/1**[3]
3 4 **Ventura Quest (USA)** 2-9-5 0.. DavidNolan 6 74
(Richard Fahey) *w'like: w ldrs: one pce fnl f* **20/1**
4 2 ½ **Royal Banker** 2-9-5 0.. SilvestreDeSousa 5 66
(Jedd O'Keeffe) *in rr: hung lft and hdwy over 2f out: sn chsng ldrs: fdd last 100yds* **10/1**
2 **5** shd **Bahamian C**[28] 3350 2-9-5 0..................................... TonyHamilton 1 66
(Richard Fahey) *w'like: rrd and wnt lft s: t.k.h: wknd fnl 100yds* **5/2**[1]
62 **6** 1 **Song Of Rowland (IRE)**[29] 3298 2-9-5 0...................... DanielTudhope 3 63
(David O'Meara) *trckd ldrs: effrt over 1f out: fdd last 100yds* **12/1**
42 **7** 3 ¾ **Ahoy There (IRE)**[23] 3500 2-9-5 0.................................. MickyFenton 10 51
(Tom Tate) *w'like: lw: chsd ldrs: lost pl over 1f out* **16/1**
8 2 ¼ **The Grumpy Gnome (IRE)** 2-9-5 0.............................. PatrickMathers 2 43
(Richard Fahey) *str: chsd ldrs: drvn over 2f out: lost pl over 1f out* **8/1**
06 **9** 2 ¾ **Network Perfection**[30] 3233 2-8-12 0................... MatthewHopkins(7) 7 35
(Michael Easterby) *str: trckd ldrs: drvn 2f out: sn wknd* **50/1**
0 **10** 7 **Casper Lee (IRE)**[16] 3724 2-9-5 0.............................. PaulMulrennan 4 12
(Nigel Tinkler) *s.i.s: bhd fnl 2f* **25/1**

1m 12.05s (0.15) **Going Correction** +0.05s/f (Good) **10** Ran SP% **119.6**
Speed ratings (Par 98): **101,100,94,91,91 89,84,81,78,68**
Tote Swingers: 1&2 £3.60, 1&3 £48.90, 2&3 £48.40 CSF £14.38 TOTE £4.10: £1.60, £1.80, £4.10; EX 16.00 Trifecta £259.90 Pool: £1,209.14 - 3.48 winning units..
Owner F Gillespie **Bred** M Parrish **Trained** Hambleton, N Yorks

FOCUS
The front pair pulled clear in what was probably a decent maiden.

4313 JOHN SMITH'S STAYERS' (H'CAP) 2m 88y
4:40 (4:41) (Class 3) (0-95,93) 4-Y-0+ **£8,409** (£2,502; £1,250; £625) **Stalls** Low

Form RPR
4064 **1** **Eagle Rock (IRE)**[20] 3609 5-8-2 **74** oh1.......................(p) FrannyNorton 8 85
(Tom Tate) *mde all: qcknd pce over 5f out: jnd jst ins fnl f: fnd ex nr fin* **7/1**[3]

4-60 **2** *hd* **Mawaqeet (USA)**[25] 3423 4-9-0 **86**.....(v) JimCrowley 13 96
(Sir Michael Stoute) *swtchd lft after s: hld up in rr: hdwy 7f out: edgd lft over 1f out: chal jst ins fnl f: jst hld* **13/2**[2]

1232 **3** *2 1/4* **Gabrial's King (IRE)**[14] 3807 4-8-5 **77**..... KirstyMilczarek 10 84
(David Simcock) *sn trcking ldrs: nt clr run fr over 2f out trill ins fnl f: styd on to take 3rd last 50yds* **12/1**

-011 **4** *hd* **Big Time Billy (IRE)**[16] 3726 7-8-2 **74**.....(v) SilvestreDeSousa 5 82+
(Peter Bowen) *chsd ldrs: drvn and outpcd over 3f out: rallied to chse ldrs whn nt clr run over 1f out: styd on wl to take 4th nr fin* **9/4**[1]

1603 **5** *1 1/2* **Wyborne**[16] 3726 4-8-8 **80**..... DaleSwift 14 85
(Brian Ellison) *lw: swtchd lft after s: hld up in rr: hdwy on outside 3f out: chsng ldrs 1f out: edgd lft and kpt on same pce* **12/1**

3/05 **6** *shd* **All The Aces (IRE)**[29] 3297 8-9-2 **88**..... AndreaAtzeni 12 93
(Nicky Henderson) *chsd wnr: drvn 4f out: chal over 2f out: one pce* **16/1**

4-13 **7** *1* **Jonny Delta**[28] 3333 6-8-9 **81** ow1..... GrahamLee 11 85
(Jim Goldie) *dwlt: swtchd lft after s: hld up in rr: effrt 3f out: nt clr run over 1f out: swtchd lft and styd on ins fnl f* **9/1**

-033 **8** *1 1/2* **Art History (IRE)**[20] 3609 5-8-12 **84**.....(v) DavidNolan 4 86
(David O'Meara) *chsd ldrs: drvn over 4f out: one pce fnl 2f* **25/1**

0-01 **9** *3/4* **Herostatus**[20] 3609 6-9-3 **89**..... TonyHamilton 6 90
(Jason Ward) *chsd ldrs: chal over 2f out: one pce* **12/1**

-460 **10** *1* **Blue Bajan (IRE)**[14] 3824 11-9-7 **93**..... DanielTudhope 2 93
(David O'Meara) *swtg: rr-div: hdwy 7f out: swtchd rt over 2f out: nvr a threat* **9/1**

-103 **11** *1 1/2* **Itlaaq**[29] 3297 7-9-6 **92**.....(t) GrahamGibbons 3 90
(Michael Easterby) *hld up towards rr: hdwy 7f out: nt clr run fr over 2f out: eased fnl 50yds* **14/1**

3664 **12** *4* **Mica Mika (IRE)**[17] 3685 5-8-7 **84**..... GeorgeChaloner(5) 7 77
(Richard Fahey) *in tch: drvn over 4f out: lost pl over 1f out* **20/1**

1620 **13** *2* **Singzak**[16] 3726 5-7-12 **75**..... ShirleyTeasdale(5) 1 66
(Michael Easterby) *in rr: lost pl over 1f out: nvr a factor* **40/1**

-002 **14** *13* **Choisan (IRE)**[24] 3480 4-8-3 **75**..... DuranFentiman 9 50
(Tim Easterby) *trckd ldrs: t.k.h: drvn 4f out: lost pl 2f out* **33/1**

3m 31.02s (-3.48) **Going Correction** -0.275s/f (Firm) **14** Ran SP% **126.2**
Speed ratings (Par 107): **97,96,95,95,94 94,94,93,93,92 92,90,89,82**
Tote Swingers: 1&2 £20.30, 1&3 £10.20, 2&3 £8.40 CSF £52.58 CT £557.47 TOTE £9.30: £3.00, £2.40, £3.70; EX 75.80 Trifecta £1236.90 Pool: £3,359.58 - 2.03 winning units..
Owner The Ivy Syndicate **Bred** Silk Fan Syndicate **Trained** Tadcaster, N Yorks

FOCUS
A decent staying handicap. The winner is rated back to his early-season form, and the second was to form too.

4314 JOHN SMITH'S STKS (NURSERY H'CAP) 6f
5:15 (5:15) (Class 2) 2-Y-O **£9,703** (£2,887; £1,443; £721) **Stalls** Low

Form RPR

303 **1** **Tiger Twenty Two**[30] 3233 2-8-6 **77**..... GeorgeChaloner(5) 5 81+
(Richard Fahey) *swvd rt s: chsd ldrs racing towards stands' side: rdn over 1f out: styd on to ld towards fin* **17/2**

210 **2** *hd* **Lanark (IRE)**[25] 3422 2-9-7 **87**..... SilvestreDeSousa 2 90
(Mark Johnston) *lw: chsd ldrs: sn drvn along: outpcd over 2f out: rallied over 1f out: led last 50yds: hdd nr fin* **13/8**[1]

212 **3** *3/4* **Mr Matthews (IRE)**[16] 3723 2-9-0 **80**..... DanielTudhope 3 81+
(Mrs K Burke) *lw: trckd ldrs gng wl: led over 1f out: rdn and hdd wl ins fnl f: no ex* **9/4**[2]

223 **4** *3* **Searchlight**[17] 3680 2-8-11 **77**..... GrahamLee 1 68
(Kevin Ryan) *t.k.h: led tl over 2f out: wknd fnl 50yds* **6/1**

010 **5** *3 1/4* **Neighbother**[42] 2863 2-8-13 **79**..... TonyHamilton 4 60
(Richard Fahey) *w ldr: led over 2f out: hdd over 1f out: sn wknd* **4/1**[3]

1m 12.31s (0.41) **Going Correction** +0.05s/f (Good) **5** Ran SP% **113.7**
Speed ratings (Par 100): **99,98,97,93,89**
CSF £23.62 TOTE £7.80: £2.50, £1.50; EX 25.60 Trifecta £72.40 Pool: £2,193.40 - 22.71 winning units..
Owner P D Smith Holdings Ltd **Bred** P D Smith Holdings Ltd **Trained** Musley Bank, N Yorks

FOCUS
The official ratings shown are estimated and for information only. Fair nursery form.
T/Jkpt: Not won. T/Plt: £749.80 to a £1 stake. Pool: £200,771.80 - 195.47 winning tickets.
T/Qpdt: £69.90 to a £1 stake. Pool: £11,401.12 - 120.60 winning tickets. WG

4315 - 4323a (Foreign Racing) - See Raceform Interactive

4093 LONGCHAMP (R-H)
Saturday, July 13

OFFICIAL GOING: Turf: good

4324a PRIX MAURICE DE NIEUIL (GROUP 2) (4YO+) (TURF) 1m 6f
5:40 (12:00) 4-Y-O+ **£60,243** (£23,252; £11,097; £7,398; £3,699)

RPR

1 **Verema (FR)**[48] 2695 4-8-9 0..... Christophe-PatriceLemaire 2 115+
(A De Royer-Dupre, France) *midfield: gng best 2f out: shkn up 1 1/2f out: hdwy to ld jst ins fnl f: rdn and styd on strly: readily* **4/1**[3]

2 *3/4* **La Pomme D'Amour**[50] 2644 5-8-9 0..... Pierre-CharlesBoudot 5 113+
(A Fabre, France) *hld up in last: rdn over 2f out: stl last ent fnl f: styd on u.p and wnt 2nd ins fnl 120yds: chsd wnr but no real imp* **13/2**

3 *1 1/4* **Goldtara (FR)**[19] 3646 5-8-9 0..... ThierryJarnet 4 111
(A Lyon, France) *hld up in last pair: rdn over 2f out: styd on but nt pce to chal* **6/1**

4 *1 3/4* **Last Train**[23] 3483 4-8-13 0..... MaximeGuyon 1 113
(A Fabre, France) *trckd ldr in 2nd: rdn over 2f out: readily outpcd by wnr ent fnl f: plugged on* **7/4**[1]

5 *1 1/2* **Les Beaufs (FR)**[48] 2695 4-8-13 0..... AdrienFouassier 3 111
(Mme V Seignoux, France) *led: 5 l ahd 3f out: rdn over 2f out: clsd down and hdd jst ins fnl f: no ex: fdd and dropped to last* **3/1**[2]

3m 0.01s (180.01) **5** Ran SP% **109.0**
WIN (incl. 1 euro stake): 4.70. PLACES: 2.40, 3.40. SF: 18.70.
Owner H H Aga Khan **Bred** The Aga Khan's Studs Sc **Trained** Chantilly, France

FOCUS
It turned into a sprint and the first two came from off the pace. The winner is likely to rate higher.

4325a JUDDMONTE GRAND PRIX DE PARIS (GROUP 1) (3YO COLTS & FILLIES) (TURF) 1m 4f
6:20 (12:00) 3-Y-O **£278,731** (£111,512; £55,756; £27,853; £13,951)

RPR

1 **Flintshire**[27] 3386 3-9-2 0..... MaximeGuyon 6 121+
(A Fabre, France) *t.k.h: hld up in last trio on outer: shkn up and hdwy 2f out: led over 1f out: qcknd clr and sn in full command: eased cl home: impressive* **5/4**[1]

2 *1 1/2* **Manndawi (FR)**[27] 3386 3-9-2 0..... Christophe-PatriceLemaire 7 116
(A De Royer-Dupre, France) *midfield in tch on outer: rdn to chal 2f out: readily outpcd by wnr ent fnl f: wnt 2nd 100yds out: styd on wl cl home but flattered by proximity to easy wnr* **14/1**

3 *1* **Ocovango**[42] 2866 3-9-2 0..... Pierre-CharlesBoudot 1 114
(A Fabre, France) *prom on inner: shkn up 2f out: sltly short of room over 1f out: rdn and styd on to go 3rd ins fnl 100yds: no ch w wnr* **5/2**[2]

4 *nk* **Singing (FR)**[9] 3-9-2 0..... OlivierPeslier 2 114
(C Laffon-Parias, France) *midfield on inner: rdn 2f out: angled out and styd on to go 4th cl home: no ch w wnr* **33/1**

5 *1 1/4* **Au Revoir (IRE)**[29] 3309 3-9-2 0..... FlavienPrat 8 112
(A Fabre, France) *trckd ldr: rdn to chal 3f out: jnd ldr over 2f out: hdd over 1f out and readily outpcd by wnr: kpt on tl no ex wl ins fnl f: fdd and dropped to 5th* **20/1**

6 *1 1/4* **Park Reel (FR)**[27] 3386 3-9-2 0..... GregoryBenoist 4 110
(E Lellouche, France) *led: rdn and jnd over 2f out: hdd over 1f out: sn no ex and btn: steadily fdd* **18/1**

7 *nk* **Battle Of Marengo (IRE)**[22] 3523 3-9-2 0.....(b[1]) JosephO'Brien 5 110
(A P O'Brien, Ire) *t.k.h: hld up in last pair on outer: rdn 2f out: sn outpcd: plugged on but nvr a factor* **10/3**[3]

8 *3* **Max Dynamite (FR)**[41] 2907 3-9-2 0..... AntoineHamelin 3 105
(J Van Handenhove, France) *t.k.h: hld up in last pair on inner: rdn in last 2f out: sn outpcd and btn: nvr a factor* **66/1**

2m 28.57s (-1.83) **Going Correction** -0.10s/f (Good) **8** Ran SP% **117.2**
Speed ratings: **102,101,100,100,99 98,98,96**
WIN (incl. 1 euro stake): 1.70. PLACES: 1.10, 1.60, 1.40. DF: 6.30. SF: 8.80.
Owner K Abdullah **Bred** Juddmonte Farms Ltd **Trained** Chantilly, France

FOCUS
In all truth there wasn't a huge amount of depth to this, a race that is now commonly viewed as the 'real' French Derby.

4326 - 4336a (Foreign Racing) - See Raceform Interactive

1708 KREFELD (R-H)
Sunday, July 14

OFFICIAL GOING: Turf: good

4333a GROSSER PREIS DER SWK STADTWERKE KREFELD - MEILEN TROPHY (GROUP 2) (3YO+) (TURF) 1m 110y
3:40 (3:47) 3-Y-O+
£32,520 (£12,601; £5,284; £3,252; £2,032; £1,219)

RPR

1 **Felician (GER)**[45] 5-9-2 0..... LennartHammer-Hansen 2 109
(Ferdinand J Leve, Germany) *midfield: swtchd outside 2f out: rdn and hdwy to chal under 1 1/2f out: r.o to ld ent fnl f: drvn out and a holding runner-up* **8/5**[1]

2 *1* **Global Thrill**[21] 3612 4-9-2 0..... SHellyn 4 107
(J Hirschberger, Germany) *trckd ldr: chal on outside fr 2f out: sn rdn and jst got bttr of ldr whn passed by eventual wnr ent fnl f: kpt on but a hld by wnr* **18/5**[3]

3 *1 1/2* **Gereon (GER)**[45] 5-9-2 0..... AHelfenbein 7 104
(C Zschache, Germany) *led: rdn whn pressed fr 2f out: rallied gamely: hdd ent fnl f: kpt on at same pce* **87/10**

4 *1 1/4* **Combat Zone (IRE)**[21] 3612 7-9-5 0..... NRichter 1 104
(Mario Hofer, Germany) *trckd ldrs: rdn and outpcd 2f out: short of room and swtchd outside over 1f out: styd on ins fnl f: nt pce to chal* **78/10**

5 *3/4* **Quixote (GER)**[74] 3-8-6 0..... AStarke 5 98
(P Schiergen, Germany) *settled towards rr: effrt on ins 2f out: sn no imp on ldrs: one pce fnl f* **2/1**[2]

6 *1* **Royal Fox**[55] 2526 3-8-6 0..... FilipMinarik 3 96
(P Schiergen, Germany) *midfield on inner: rdn to chse ldrs fr 2f out: one pce fnl f: eased fnl 50yds* **61/10**

7 *41* **Rock Rose (SWE)** 7-8-13 0..... MiguelLopez 6 4
(R Hirschfeld, Germany) *last: rdn and lost tch over 3f: wl bhd fr 2f out: t.o* **52/1**

1m 43.07s (-3.53)
WFA 3 from 4yo+ 9lb **7** Ran SP% **131.2**
WIN (incl. 10 euro stake): 26. PLACES: 18, 20. SF: 105.
Owner Gestut Haus Ittlingen **Bred** Gestut Haus Ittlingen **Trained** Germany

[4107]AYR (L-H)

Monday, July 15

OFFICIAL GOING: Good to firm (9.4)

Wind: Breezy, half against Weather: Overcast

4337 BETVICTOR 8 PLACES ON THE OPEN MEDIAN AUCTION MAIDEN STKS 6f

2:30 (2:33) (Class 6) 2-Y-0 **£1,940** (£577; £288; £144) **Stalls** Low

Form RPR

02 **1** **Ticking Katie (IRE)**[21] 3624 2-9-0 0 DanielTudhope 2 73
(Mrs K Burke) *excitable in paddock: slt ld tl edgd rt and hdd over 1f out: rallied and regained ld wl ins fnl f: kpt on wl* **6/5**[2]

02 **2** *nk* **Broadcaster (IRE)**[18] 3724 2-9-5 0 GrahamGibbons 3 77
(Ed McMahon) *noisy in paddock: t.k.h: trckd ldrs: smooth hdwy to ld over 1f out: edgd lft and hdd wl ins fnl f: jst hld* **11/10**[1]

3 *9* **Malraaj** 2-9-5 0 TonyHamilton 1 48+
(Richard Fahey) *green in paddock: trckd ldrs: rdn over 2f out: outpcd by first two over 1f out* **13/2**[3]

5 **4** *12* **Straight Gin**[17] 3767 2-9-5 0 PhillipMakin 4 10
(Alan Berry) *w wnr: rdn over 2f out: one pce whn nt clr run over 1f out: sn btn* **20/1**

1m 12.98s (0.58) **Going Correction** +0.05s/f (Good) **4** Ran SP% **111.2**

Speed ratings (Par 92): **98,97,85,69**

CSF £2.98 TOTE £3.50; EX 3.30 Trifecta £5.40 Pool: £2007.76 - 277.17 winning units..

Owner Ontoawinner, M Hulin & E Burke **Bred** Tally-Ho Stud **Trained** Middleham Moor, N Yorks

FOCUS

A fair maiden despite the small field size and run at a steady pace, with the front two fighting out a thrilling finish. The form is taken at face value for now. Home & back straights moved out 2yds. Home bend moved out 4m adding about 12yds to races on Round course.

4338 PRINCESS ROYAL CONFERENCE CENTRE H'CAP (QUALIFIER FOR THE £15,000 BETFAIR SCOTTISH SPRINT) 6f

3:00 (3:00) (Class 5) (0-75,75) 3-Y-0+ **£2,587** (£770; £384; £192) **Stalls** Low

Form RPR

4002 **1** **Diamondhead (IRE)**[28] 3393 4-9-7 70 LiamKeniry 7 80
(Ed de Giles) *cl up: led over 2f out: rdn over 1f out: kpt on wl fnl f* **7/2**[1]

6030 **2** *1 ¼* **Beckermet (IRE)**[12] 3945 11-9-4 67 JamesSullivan 6 73
(Ruth Carr) *in tch: rdn over 2f out: styd on fnl f to take 2nd towards fin* **12/1**

005 **3** *nk* **Economic Crisis (IRE)**[13] 3933 4-9-7 70 PaddyAspell 11 75
(Alan Berry) *trckd ldrs: effrt 2f out: edgd lft 1f out: kpt on: lost 2nd cl home* **66/1**

2331 **4** *1 ¼* **Circuitous**[9] 4051 5-9-7 70 (v) JoeFanning 4 71
(Keith Dalgleish) *hld up in tch: rdn and hdwy over 1f out: edgd lft: kpt on fnl f: nt pce to chal* **5/1**[3]

2403 **5** *1 ½* **Rich Again (IRE)**[11] 3981 4-9-2 65 GrahamLee 1 61
(James Bethell) *hld up in tch: n.m.r briefly over 2f out: effrt and rdn over 1f out: kpt on same pce fnl f* **5/1**[3]

-000 **6** *1 ½* **Partner (IRE)**[42] 2914 7-9-3 73 JoeyHaynes(7) 3 64
(Noel Wilson) *bhd tl rdn and hdwy over 1f out: kpt on fnl f: nvr able to chal* **25/1**

2-15 **7** *hd* **Colbyor**[165] 453 4-9-0 68 GeorgeChaloner(5) 13 59
(Richard Fahey) *prom: rdn over 2f out: no ex fnl f* **12/1**

5050 **8** *1 ¼* **Lupin Pooter**[30] 3331 4-9-10 73 GrahamGibbons 5 60
(David Barron) *stdd s: hld up: rdn and effrt wl over 1f out: sn no imp* **8/1**

600 **9** *nse* **Oneladyowner**[49] 2725 5-9-12 75 DanielTudhope 2 62
(David O'Meara) *in tch: rdn wl over 1f out: sn outpcd* **4/1**[2]

6300 **10** *2 ½* **Bassett Road (IRE)**[8] 4102 5-8-4 60 (p) GeorginaBaxter(7) 9 39
(Keith Dalgleish) *t.k.h: led to over 2f out: rdn and wknd over 1f out* **40/1**

0605 **11** *7* **Opt Out**[17] 3769 3-8-12 70 JulieBurke(3) 12 26
(Alistair Whillans) *hld up: rdn 2f out: sn wknd* **18/1**

1m 12.02s (-0.38) **Going Correction** +0.05s/f (Good)

WFA 3 from 4yo+ 6lb **11** Ran SP% **115.1**

Speed ratings (Par 103): **104,102,101,100,98 96,96,94,94,90 81**

toteswingers 1&2 £9.60, 1&3 £34.90, 2&3 £82.70 CSF £44.80 CT £2317.97 TOTE £4.70: £1.30, £3.80, £14.20; EX 54.20 Trifecta £1304.50 Part won. Pool: £1739.43 - 0.85 winning units..

Owner T Gould **Bred** J Joyce **Trained** Ledbury, H'fords

FOCUS

The pace was honest for this competitive sprint handicap yet it paid to race handy. Straightforward form rated around the first two.

4339 BETVICTOR OPEN CHAMPIONSHIP 8 PLACES EXCLUSIVE H'CAP 7f 50y

3:30 (3:31) (Class 6) (0-65,66) 3-Y-0+ **£2,045** (£603; £302) **Stalls** High

Form RPR

0044 **1** **Goninodaethat**[17] 3770 5-9-1 50 GrahamLee 2 61
(Jim Goldie) *plld hrd early: chsd ldrs: stdy hdwy over 2f out: shkn up to ld over 1f out: drvn and kpt on wl fnl f* **7/1**

0001 **2** *1* **Strong Man**[5] 4161 5-10-3 66 6ex (b) GrahamGibbons 6 74
(Michael Easterby) *t.k.h: led: rdn and hdd over 1f out: rallied: kpt on same pce towards fin* **9/4**[1]

615- **3** *4* **Burnwynd Boy**[308] 6106 8-9-8 57 PJMcDonald 1 55
(Keith Dalgleish) *hld up in tch: shkn up and swtchd rt wl over 1f out: kpt on but nt pce of first two fnl f* **9/2**[2]

-602 **4** *4* **Eilean Mor**[7] 4109 5-8-4 46 GemmaTutty(7) 8 33
(R Mike Smith) *towards rr: rdn and hdwy over 2f out: edgd lft over 1f out: no imp fnl f* **8/1**

0060 **5** *nk* **Berbice (IRE)**[7] 4109 8-9-1 50 PhillipMakin 5 36
(Linda Perratt) *hld up: shkn up wl over 1f out: sn btn* **28/1**

0-05 **6** *½* **Military Call**[40] 2977 6-8-11 49 (p) RaulDaSilva(3) 7 34
(Alistair Whillans) *prom: rdn over 3f out: rallied: wknd over 1f out* **14/1**

4060 **7** *1 ½* **Ceekay's Girl**[7] 4113 3-7-13 45 JulieBurke(3) 3 22
(R Mike Smith) *hld up: rdn over 3f out: nvr able to chal* **66/1**

003- **8** *3 ¾* **Foolbythepool**[307] 6121 3-9-6 63 JoeFanning 4 30
(Keith Dalgleish) *s.i.s: bhd: struggling 1/2-way: nvr on terms* **8/1**

1322 **9** *nk* **Dhhamaan (IRE)**[5] 4161 8-9-6 55 (b) JamesSullivan 10 25
(Ruth Carr) *sn pressing ldr: rdn and hung lft 2f out: sn btn* **5/1**[3]

06-0 **10** *7* **Touching History (IRE)**[18] 3728 4-8-10 45 AndrewElliott 9
(Tim Etherington) *prom tl drvn and wknd over 2f out* **66/1**

1m 30.99s (-2.41) **Going Correction** -0.30s/f (Firm)

WFA 3 from 4yo+ 8lb **10** Ran SP% **113.4**

Speed ratings (Par 101): **101,99,95,90,90 89,88,83,83,75**

toteswingers 1&2 £4.00, 1&3 £5.80, 2&3 £2.80 CSF £22.26 CT £80.07 TOTE £8.20: £3.20, £1.10, £1.60; EX 22.90 Trifecta £69.90 Pool: £2409.64 - 25.82 winning units..

Owner Caledonia Racing **Bred** W G H Barrons **Trained** Uplawmoor, E Renfrews

FOCUS

This moderate handicap was run at a sound gallop. Again it paid to race prominently.

4340 BETVICTOR.COM H'CAP 7f 50y

4:00 (4:00) (Class 4) (0-85,85) 3-Y-0+ **£4,851** (£1,443; £721; £360) **Stalls** High

Form RPR

0204 **1** **Alejandro (IRE)**[17] 3757 4-9-5 81 GeorgeChaloner(5) 4 90
(Richard Fahey) *t.k.h: pressed ldr: led 2f out: rdn and hung lft over 1f out: asserted wl ins fnl f* **7/1**

3023 **2** *1 ¼* **Our Boy Jack (IRE)**[12] 3945 4-9-7 78 TonyHamilton 5 84
(Richard Fahey) *led: hdd and rdn 2f out: styd upsides: one pce wl ins fnl f* **13/2**[3]

1-15 **3** *2* **Twenty One Choice (IRE)**[75] 1922 4-9-10 81 LiamKeniry 2 82
(Ed de Giles) *t.k.h: trckd ldrs: rdn over 2f out: kpt on same pce fr over 1f out* **11/8**[1]

0622 **4** *½* **Jinky**[7] 4111 5-9-2 73 GrahamLee 6 73
(Linda Perratt) *hld up in tch: rdn and hdwy wl over 1f out: sn no imp* **8/1**

0065 **5** *1 ½* **Orpsie Boy (IRE)**[7] 4111 10-8-8 68 JulieBurke(3) 9 64
(Ruth Carr) *hld up: rdn over 2f out: hdwy over 1f out: kpt on fnl f: nvr able to chal* **33/1**

5414 **6** *¾* **The Nifty Fox**[17] 3769 9-9-7 78 (p) JamesSullivan 3 72
(Tim Easterby) *dwlt: t.k.h in rr: rdn over 2f out: sme hdwy over 1f out: nvr rchd ldrs* **28/1**

6-51 **7** *1 ¼* **Menelik (IRE)**[6] 4155 4-8-9 66 6ex RichardKingscote 1 56
(Tom Dascombe) *hld up in tch: rdn wl over 2f out: no imp fr over 1f out* **5/1**[2]

1003 **8** *3 ¾* **Fieldgunner Kirkup (GER)**[7] 4111 5-9-7 85 GemmaTutty(7) 8 66
(David Barron) *hld up: hdwy on outside over 2f out: rdn and wknd over 1f out* **12/1**

2245 **9** *½* **Mowhoob**[23] 3566 3-8-7 72 (v[1]) AndrewElliott 7 48
(Jim Goldie) *chsd ldrs tl rdn and wknd over 2f out* **16/1**

1m 30.11s (-3.29) **Going Correction** -0.30s/f (Firm)

WFA 3 from 4yo+ 8lb **9** Ran SP% **115.7**

Speed ratings (Par 105): **106,104,102,101,100 99,97,93,92**

toteswingers 1&2 £6.80, 1&3 £3.50, 2&3 £2.70 CSF £51.89 CT £98.69 TOTE £8.60: £3.30, £2.30, £1.02; EX 37.70 Trifecta £212.20 Pool: £2805.18 - 9.91 winning units..

Owner F L F S Ltd **Bred** Yeomanstown Stud **Trained** Musley Bank, N Yorks

FOCUS

Plenty of pace on for this handicap, with the first two home always in command.

4341 WESTERN HOUSE HOTEL H'CAP (QUALIFIER FOR THE £15,000 BETFAIR SCOTTISH MILE SERIES FINAL) 1m

4:30 (4:31) (Class 5) (0-75,76) 3-Y-0+ **£2,587** (£770; £384; £192) **Stalls** Low

Form RPR

351 **1** **True Pleasure (IRE)**[9] 4052 6-8-9 53 PJMcDonald 2 65+
(James Bethell) *prom: hdwy to ld appr fnl f: drvn out* **11/2**[3]

00 **2** *1 ½* **Oratory (IRE)**[42] 2929 7-9-7 65 PhillipMakin 5 72
(Mrs K Burke) *hld up: shkn up and hdwy 2f out: chsd wnr ins fnl f: r.o* **7/2**[1]

4354 **3** *1 ¾* **Paramour**[21] 3628 6-9-13 71 (v) DanielTudhope 8 74
(David O'Meara) *t.k.h: cl up: led over 2f out to appr fnl f: kpt on same pce* **9/2**[2]

4460 **4** *¾* **Chookie Avon**[12] 3945 6-10-0 72 (p) JoeFanning 7 73
(Keith Dalgleish) *hld up: effrt and pushed along whn nt clr run and swtchd rt over 1f out: kpt on fnl f: no imp* **12/1**

5346 **5** *nk* **Adorable Choice (IRE)**[14] 3910 5-8-11 55 (vt) RichardKingscote 1 56
(Tom Dascombe) *led tl rdn and hdd over 2f out: rallied: one pce fnl f* **11/1**

1101 **6** *1 ¼* **Jebel Tara**[8] 4100 8-10-1 76 6ex (bt) PaulPickard(3) 6 74
(Alan Brown) *hld up in tch: stdy hdwy over 2f out: rdn and no imp fr over 1f out* **6/1**

3200 **7** *¾* **Rawaafed (IRE)**[16] 3827 4-9-7 65 (p) GrahamGibbons 3 61
(Keith Dalgleish) *dwlt: hld up in tch: rdn over 2f out: no imp over 1f out* **17/2**

2602 **8** *¾* **Orions Hero (IRE)**[9] 4048 3-9-3 70 (p) TonyHamilton 4 64
(Richard Fahey) *t.k.h: chsd ldrs tl rdn and wknd fr 2f out* **9/2**[2]

1m 40.93s (-2.87) **Going Correction** -0.30s/f (Firm)

WFA 3 from 4yo+ 9lb **8** Ran SP% **114.8**

Speed ratings (Par 103): **102,100,98,98,97 96,95,94**

toteswingers 1&2 £6.50, 1&3 £3.00, 2&3 £4.90 CSF £25.19 CT £94.57 TOTE £5.60: £1.90, £2.30, £1.40; EX 28.50 Trifecta £215.90 Pool: £2488.06 - 8.63 winning units..

Owner Clarendon Thoroughbred Racing **Bred** Michael O'Mahony **Trained** Middleham Moor, N Yorks

FOCUS

This handicap was run at a steady pace.

4342 POLYFLOR H'CAP 1m

5:00 (5:00) (Class 2) (0-100,95) 3-Y-0+

£12,450 (£3,728; £1,864; £932; £466; £234) **Stalls** Low

Form RPR

4121 **1** **Sennockian Star**[9] 4055 3-8-11 85 (v[1]) JoeFanning 8 93
(Mark Johnston) *trckd ldr: rdn to ld over 1f out: r.o strly fnl f* **5/2**[1]

0261 **2** *2 ¾* **Able Master (IRE)**[8] 4101 7-10-2 95 6ex DanielTudhope 2 99
(David O'Meara) *trckd ldrs: drvn over 2f out: rallied over 1f out: chsd wnr ins fnl f: kpt on* **9/1**

0-16 **3** *½* **Suits Me**[30] 3346 10-10-0 93 PhillipMakin 5 96
(David Barron) *led: rdn and hdd over 1f out: kpt on same pce fnl f* **13/2**

3625 **4** *½* **Dubai Dynamo**[18] 3725 8-9-11 90 PJMcDonald 6 92
(Ruth Carr) *hld up in tch: effrt and edgd lft over 1f out: kpt on same pce fnl f* **11/2**[3]

-541 **5** *1 ¾* **Ginger Jack**[25] 3503 6-9-10 89 GrahamGibbons 1 87
(Geoffrey Harker) *hld up in tch: rdn and effrt over 2f out: no imp over 1f out* **7/2**[2]

0204 **6** *nk* **Hi There (IRE)**[18] 3725 4-9-9 88 LeeTopliss 4 85
(Richard Fahey) *dwlt: hld up: rdn and effrt on outside over 2f out: no ex over 1f out* **8/1**

3620 **7** *1 ¼* **Chookie Royale**[9] 4055 5-9-5 84 (p) GrahamLee 3 78
(Keith Dalgleish) *t.k.h: hld up: rdn and effrt over 2f out: no imp over 1f out* **12/1**

-560 **8** *7* **Steer By The Stars (IRE)**[23] 3563 3-8-11 85 RichardKingscote 7 61
(Mark Johnston) *prom tl rdn and wknd over 2f out* **33/1**

1m 39.73s (-4.07) **Going Correction** -0.30s/f (Firm)

WFA 3 from 4yo+ 9lb **8** Ran SP% **111.3**

Speed ratings (Par 109): **108,105,104,104,102 102,100,93**

toteswingers 1&2 £3.10, 1&3 £4.40, 2&3 £5.30 CSF £24.30 CT £125.77 TOTE £2.80: £1.10, £2.30, £1.70; EX 23.00 Trifecta £97.50 Pool: £2752.15 - 21.16 winning units..

Owner The Vine Accord **Bred** Cheveley Park Stud Ltd **Trained** Middleham Moor, N Yorks

FOCUS
A decent contest. The pace was solid, with once again the prominent runners at a distinct advantage.

4343 OPEN CHAMPIONSHIP 8 PLACES AT BETVICTOR APPRENTICE H'CAP 1m 5f 13y
5:30 (5:30) (Class 6) (0-65,65) 4-Y-0+ **£2,045** (£603; £302) **Stalls** Low

Form RPR
3614 1 **Grand Diamond (IRE)**[17] 3768 9-8-11 53.................(p) JordanNason(3) 9 62
(Jim Goldie) *hld up: hdwy over 2f out: rdn to ld ins fnl f: kpt on wl towards fin* 5/1[2]
0050 2 ½ **Altnaharra**[33] 3199 4-8-0 46 oh1..........................(v) SophieRobertson(7) 6 54
(Jim Goldie) *prom: hdwy to ld over 2f out: rdn and hdd ins fnl f: rallied: hld nr fin* 20/1
5535 3 2½ **Geanie Mac (IRE)**[17] 3771 4-8-8 47...............................(v) SamanthaBell 3 51
(Linda Perratt) *chsd clr ldr: stdy hdwy and ev ch over 2f out: one pce appr fnl f* 9/1
60/6 4 ½ **Viva Colonia (IRE)**[18] 3729 8-9-4 60.............................. KevinStott(3) 10 63+
(Brian Ellison) *hld up and bhd: rdn over 3f out: styd on fnl 2f: nvr able to chal* 6/4[1]
5-66 5 ½ **Vittachi**[40] 2975 6-8-6 50.. RowanScott(5) 8 53
(Alistair Whillans) *hld up: hdwy over 3f out: effrt over 2f out: edgd lft and one pce over 1f out* 10/1
0300 6 hd **La Bacouetteuse (FR)**[18] 3726 8-9-12 65........................(b) DavidBergin 1 67
(Iain Jardine) *hld up: rdn and hdwy over 2f out: edgd lft over 1f out: sn no imp* 15/2
1320 7 6 **Jewelled Dagger (IRE)**[21] 3625 9-9-5 58..............(t) DavidSimmonson 2 51
(Sharon Watt) *chsd ldrs: drvn over 2f out: sn outpcd* 7/1[3]
5120 8 4 **Kingarrick**[26] 3467 5-9-2 60...................................... RobJFitzpatrick(5) 7 47
(Noel Wilson) *midfield: rdn and outpcd 2f out: n.d after* 12/1
-000 9 12 **Roc Fort**[23] 3595 4-8-7 46 oh1... GemmaTutty 4 15
(James Moffatt) *hld up: rdn over 5f out: struggling fnl 3f* 66/1
00-0 10 11 **Rare Coincidence**[22] 2313 12-8-2 46 oh1................ JordanHibberd(5) 5
(Alan Berry) *led and sn clr: hdd over 2f out: wknd qckly* 66/1

2m 52.09s (-1.91) **Going Correction** -0.30s/f (Firm) 10 Ran SP% **115.5**
Speed ratings (Par 101): **93,92,91,90,90 90,86,84,76,70**
toteswingers 1&2 £17.30, 1&3 £5.60, 2&3 £17.20 CSF £97.29 CT £870.34 TOTE £5.50: £2.20, £5.30, £3.90; EX 50.90 Trifecta £500.60 Pool: £2396.89 - 3.59 winning units..
Owner Caledonia Racing **Bred** Newberry Stud Company **Trained** Uplawmoor, E Renfrews
FOCUS
This moderate handicap confined to apprentice riders, was run at a sound gallop.
T/Jkpt: Not won. T/Plt: £75.50 to a £1 stake. Pool: £77,771.38 - 751.79 winning tickets T/Qpdt: £6.70 to a £1 stake. Pool: £6,835.93 - 752.65 winning tickets RY

4120 WINDSOR (R-H)
Monday, July 15

OFFICIAL GOING: Good to firm (8.6)
Wind: Almost nil Weather: Fine, hot

4344 CASTLEMEAD CARE APPRENTICE H'CAP 5f 10y
6:00 (6:00) (Class 5) (0-75,75) 3-Y-0+ **£2,587** (£770; £384; £192) **Stalls** Low

Form RPR
5455 1 **Catflap (IRE)**[12] 3949 4-8-9 56 oh2...............................(p) RosieJessop 6 64
(Derek Haydn Jones) *led to post 20 mins bef s wout jockey aboard: loaded into stalls wout jockey aboard: nrly anticipated s: trckd ldrs: shkn up and clsd to ld jst ins fnl f: pushed out* 4/1[2]
-560 2 1 **Howyadoingnotsobad (IRE)**[7] 4123 5-9-10 73........... RyanWhile(2) 4 77
(Karen George) *racd freely: led: rdn over 1f out: hdd and no ex jst ins fnl f* 8/1[3]
2056 3 nk **Triple Dream**[15] 3855 8-9-7 72...............................(tp) WillPettis(4) 5 75
(Milton Bradley) *pressed ldr: rdn and upsides over 1f out tl nt qckn jst ins fnl f* 8/1[3]
0022 4 1¼ **Griffin Point (IRE)**[14] 3888 6-8-13 60......................(b) GeorgeDowning 3 59
(William Muir) *towards rr: shkn up and tried to cl fr 2f out: nt qckn over 1f out: one pce after* 7/2[1]
-026 5 hd **Ryan Style (IRE)**[18] 3716 7-9-6 67...................(v) WilliamTwiston-Davies 7 65
(Lisa Williamson) *w.w in rr: effrt to chse ldrs over 1f out: nt qckn and no imp after* 4/1[2]
6405 6 3¼ **Drawnfromthepast (IRE)**[15] 3855 8-9-12 75................ EDLinehan(2) 8 61
(Jamie Osborne) *pressed ldrs tl rdn and wknd over 1f out* 4/1[2]
1065 7 nk **Danzoe (IRE)**[34] 3171 6-9-11 72.............................. MichaelJMMurphy 1 57
(Christine Dunnett) *pushed along in rr over 3f out: effrt against nr side rail 2f out: hanging and wknd over 1f out* 14/1
0100 8 shd **Sophie's Beau (USA)**[18] 3716 6-8-5 56 oh5.......(b) DanielleMooney(4) 9 41
(Michael Chapman) *dwlt: rcvrd to press ldrs on outer: lost pl 1/2-way: sn btn* 33/1

59.43s (-0.87) **Going Correction** -0.05s/f (Good) 8 Ran SP% **114.1**
Speed ratings (Par 103): **104,102,101,99,99 94,93,93**
toteswingers 1&2 £9.40, 1&3 £6.80, 2&3 £10.90 CSF £35.40 CT £242.67 TOTE £6.10: £1.60, £2.60, £3.10; EX 47.00 Trifecta £283.00 Pool: £1122.56 - 2.97 winning units..
Owner Llewelyn Newman & Runeckles **Bred** D Llewelyn & J Runeckles **Trained** Efail Isaf, Rhondda C Taff
FOCUS
They were making a print on the watered ground, which was given as good to firm (GoingStick 8.6). The inner of the straight was dolled out 5yds at 6f and 2yds at the winning post, while the top bend was dolled out 2yds from its normal inner configuration, adding 9yds to race distances of 1m plus. An ordinary sprint handicap.

4345 MACDONALDS HOTELS AND RESORTS LTD (S) STKS 1m 2f 7y
6:30 (6:30) (Class 6) 3-4-Y-0 **£1,940** (£577; £288; £144) **Stalls** Centre

Form RPR
33V0 1 **Rock Diamond (IRE)**[16] 3820 3-8-5 46.........................(p) CathyGannon 2 51
(Sylvester Kirk) *chsd ldng pair: pushed along 4f out: rdn and responded fr over 2f out to ld over 1f out: hld on wl* 11/2[3]
6442 2 ½ **Azelle**[10] 4030 3-7-12 64..................................... CameronHardie(7) 5 50
(Richard Hannon) *t.k.h: hld up in 5th: steadily clsd on clr ldrs fr 4f out: rdn over 1f out: chal fnl f: nt qckn nr fin* 5/2[1]
1540 3 1½ **Sutton Sid**[25] 3495 3-8-10 56.......................... WilliamTwiston-Davies(5) 7 57
(Chris Gordon) *sn in last: pushed along over 4f out: rdn and grad clsd fr 3f out: styd on to take 3rd ins fnl f: nvr able to chal* 16/1
-400 4 1½ **Day In Day Out**[29] 3376 3-8-10 60..................................(b[1]) JimCrowley 3 49
(Ralph Beckett) *pressed ldr: rdn to ld over 2f out: hdd and no ex over 1f out* 9/2[2]
02 5 4 **Hilden**[5] 4171 4-9-2 0..(b) SteveDrowne 6 36
(William Muir) *led at gd pce: rdn and hdd over 2f out: pressed ldr to over 1f out: wknd qckly* 6/1
500 6 37 **Dark Rumour (IRE)**[15] 3858 3-8-2 22......................(v[1]) SimonPearce(3) 1
(John Bridger) *in tch tl wknd qckly over 4f out: t.o* 66/1
0510 7 7 **Brick Rising**[53] 2599 3-9-1 58...(t) WilliamBuick 4
(Andrew Balding) *hld up in rr: rdn and no rspnse 1/2-way: sn t.o* 5/2[1]

2m 5.44s (-3.26) **Going Correction** -0.25s/f (Firm)
WFA 3 from 4yo 11lb 7 Ran SP% **112.4**
Speed ratings (Par 101): **103,102,101,100,97 67,61**
toteswingers 1&2 £5.00, 1&3 £16.00, 2&3 £10.20 CSF £18.96 TOTE £6.80: £3.30, £1.60; EX 22.20 Trifecta £45.70 Pool: £1893.80 - 2.91 winning units..The winner was sold to Brendan Powell for £7,500. Azelle was claimed by Mr T. J. Norman £6,000.
Owner Ron Gander & Barbara Matalon **Bred** L Butler & M Gaffney **Trained** Upper Lambourn, Berks
■ Stewards' Enquiry : William Twiston-Davies two-day ban: used whip above permitted level (Jul 29-30)
FOCUS
Weak form.

4346 BREEDERS' BACKING RACING EBF MAIDEN STKS 5f 10y
7:00 (7:01) (Class 5) 2-Y-0 **£2,911** (£866; £432; £216) **Stalls** Low

Form RPR
222 1 **Speed The Plough**[28] 3413 2-9-5 0.................................... RyanMoore 1 74
(Richard Hannon) *led or disp thrght and racd against nr side rail: rdn 2f out: maintained narrow advantage ins fnl f: drvn out* 5/4[1]
322 2 nk **Taquka (IRE)**[16] 3815 2-9-5 0... JimCrowley 5 73
(Ralph Beckett) *w wnr mostly: rdn over 1f out: nt qckn and jst hld ins fnl f* 7/4[2]
232 3 ¾ **Stellarta**[19] 3694 2-9-0 0... TomQueally 2 65
(Michael Blanshard) *dwlt: sn chsd ldrs against rail: swtchd lft over 1f out: drvn and tried to cl on ldng pair fnl f: nvr quite able to chal* 9/1
4 1½ **Elite Freedom (IRE)** 2-9-0 0.. CathyGannon 3 60+
(Jo Hughes) *sn pushed along in last: kpt on fr over 1f out to take 4th ins fnl f: nvr nrr* 33/1
4 5 3½ **Skinny Love**[14] 3896 2-9-0 0.. JamesDoyle 4 47
(Robert Cowell) *chsd ldrs: rdn and sing to struggle whn sltly impeded over 1f out* 8/1[3]
6 6 **Gulland Rock** 2-9-5 0.. SteveDrowne 6 31
(William Muir) *dwlt: chsd ldrs on outer tl wknd wl over 1f out* 12/1

59.97s (-0.33) **Going Correction** -0.05s/f (Good) 6 Ran SP% **112.6**
Speed ratings (Par 94): **100,99,98,95,90 80**
toteswingers 1&2 £1.02, 1&3 £1.60, 2&3 £3.70 CSF £3.68 TOTE £2.20: £1.10, £2.00; EX 3.80 Trifecta £9.30 Pool: £1652.21 - 132.89 winning units..
Owner Martin Hughes & Michael Kerr-Dineen **Bred** Clive Dennett **Trained** East Everleigh, Wilts
FOCUS
The first two in the betting had a good battle from the 2f marker. The form looks straightforward.

4347 BRITISH STALLION STUDS EBF MAIDEN STKS 6f
7:30 (7:35) (Class 5) 2-Y-0 **£2,911** (£866; £432; £216) **Stalls** Low

Form RPR
0 1 **Trading Profit**[29] 3374 2-9-5 0....................................... RyanMoore 10 83
(Andrew Balding) *pressed ldr: rdn to ld over 1f out: sn clr: r.o wl* 5/2[1]
5 2 4 **Classic Pursuit**[12] 3948 2-9-5 0.................................... TomQueally 8 70
(Ronald Harris) *chsd ldng trio: rdn wl over 1f out: styd on to chse clr wnr ins fnl f: stl green and no imp but jst hld on for 2nd* 25/1
3 nk **Retrofit** 2-9-5 0... SteveDrowne 9 69+
(William Muir) *pushed along to chse clr ldng quintet after 2f: stl pushed along and styd on encouragingly fr 2f out: tk 3rd ins fnl f and pressed runner-up nr fin* 16/1
4 2½ **Xanthos** 2-9-5 0... GeorgeBaker 4 61
(Ed Walker) *dwlt: sn chsd ldrs in 5th and clr of rest: reminder over 1f out: kpt on one pce after* 25/1
42 5 1 **Dodger Marley (IRE)**[14] 3883 2-9-5 0............................ HarryBentley 3 58
(Stuart Williams) *led: edgd lft fr 2f out: hdd over 1f out: wknd fnl f* 9/2[3]
320 6 3 **Llyrical**[31] 3290 2-9-5 0.. PatCosgrave 2 48
(Derek Haydn Jones) *fractious bef ent stalls: chsd ldng pair to over 1f out: wknd* 12/1
7 3½ **Bajan Beauty (IRE)** 2-9-0 0... FrankieDettori 6 41+
(Charles Hills) *dwlt: pushed along and wl off the pce in rr gp: nvr threatened* 15/2
8 2½ **Happy Clappy (IRE)** 2-9-5 0.. WilliamBuick 11 29
(Michael Bell) *slowly away: rn green and a wl off the pce* 10/1
9 2½ **Sandy Cove** 2-9-5 0.. JamesDoyle 5 21+
(Roger Charlton) *sn pushed along and wl off the pce in rr gp: nvr a factor* 4/1[2]
10 9 **Concrete Mac** 2-9-5 0.. JimCrowley 1
(Hughie Morrison) *slowly away: rn green and sn t.o* 16/1
0 11 1½ **Currently Inlondon (IRE)**[11] 3986 2-9-0 0...................... SamHitchcott 7
(Mick Channon) *nvr on terms wknd sn after 1/2-way: t.o* 66/1

1m 12.93s (-0.07) **Going Correction** -0.05s/f (Good) 11 Ran SP% **116.3**
Speed ratings (Par 94): **98,92,92,88,87 83,78,75,72,60 58**
toteswingers 1&2 £23.50, 1&3 £9.90, 2&3 £43.00 CSF £73.96 TOTE £3.00: £1.10, £8.50, £5.90; EX 71.80 Trifecta £1015.60 Part won. Pool: £1354.17 - 0.52 winning units..
Owner Another Bottle Racing 2 **Bred** D J And Mrs Deer **Trained** Kingsclere, Hants
FOCUS
They went pretty quick from the start here. The form is rated on the cautious side of the average for the level.

4348 CORAL.CO.UK FILLIES' H'CAP 1m 67y
8:00 (8:00) (Class 4) (0-80,79) 3-Y-0+ **£4,851** (£1,443; £721; £360) **Stalls** Low

Form RPR
5053 1 **Starlight Symphony (IRE)**[9] 4048 3-8-11 71.................(b) JohnFahy 6 78
(Eve Johnson Houghton) *chsd ldrs: rdn in 4th 3f out: responded wl to cl and wnt 2nd over 1f out: drvn to ld ins fnl f: a jst holding on* 16/1
02-1 2 shd **Easter Diva (IRE)**[21] 3635 4-9-8 73.................................. RyanMoore 5 81
(Gerard Butler) *pressed ldr: shkn up to ld over 2f out: drvn over 1f out: hdd ins fnl f: rallied but a jst hld* 8/1
-521 3 1½ **Serenity Spa**[16] 3842 3-9-2 76.. JamesDoyle 1 79+
(Roger Charlton) *hld up in last trio: rdn wl over 2f out: styd on to take 3rd fnl f: swtchd lft sn after: nt pce to chal* 5/2[2]
2313 4 2½ **Oratorio's Joy (IRE)**[103] 1321 3-8-12 72.................... FergusSweeney 2 69
(Jamie Osborne) *hld up in last: plenty to do fr 1/2-way: single reminder over 1f out: kpt on to take 4th ins fnl f: nvr involved* 33/1
-412 5 1 **Zeyran (IRE)**[23] 3583 4-10-0 79.. TomQueally 4 76
(Lady Cecil) *t.k.h: trckd ldng pair: rdn and cl enough 2f out: wknd jst over 1f out* 2/1[1]

21 **6** *1* **Ethel**[10] 4013 3-9-2 **76** WilliamBuick 3 69
(John Gosden) *led but pressed: pushed along 1/2-way: hdd over 2f out: wknd over 1f out* **11/4**[3]
1011 **7** *18* **Refreshestheparts (USA)**[96] 1479 4-9-10 **75** (t) PatCosgrave 7 42
(George Baker) *hld up in last trio: shkn up wl over 2f out: hanging lft and wknd qckly over 1f out: t.o* **33/1**

1m 41.9s (-2.80) **Going Correction** -0.25s/f (Firm)
WFA 3 from 4yo 9lb **7** Ran SP% **111.4**
Speed ratings (Par 102): **104,103,102,99,98 97,79**
toteswingers 1&2 £8.50, 1&3 £6.40, 2&3 £3.70 CSF £126.08 TOTE £20.20: £6.70, £3.50; EX 82.10 Trifecta £320.10 Pool: £1289.40 - 3.02 winning units..
Owner Brian & Liam McNamee, Les & Ian Dawson **Bred** Patrick Byrnes **Trained** Blewbury, Oxon
FOCUS
Not a bad little race but a bit of a turn-up.

4349 DOWNLOAD CORAL MOBILE FROM THE APP STORE H'CAP 1m 3f 135y
8:30 (8:30) (Class 4) (0-85,81) 3-Y-O **£4,851** (£1,443; £721; £360) **Stalls** Centre

Form RPR
-552 **1** **Sunblazer (IRE)**[20] 3653 3-8-5 **65** HarryBentley 3 75
(William Muir) *trckd ldr: clsd to chal over 2f out: shkn up to ld over 1f out: pushed out and a in command fnl f* **8/1**
0-63 **2** *1* **Glenard**[14] 3899 3-9-6 **80** JamesDoyle 5 89+
(Charles Hills) *hld up in 4th: clsd fr 3f out: drvn over 1f out: styd on to take 2nd nr fin: no real threat to wnr* **7/4**[2]
211 **3** *hd* **Thwart**[27] 3437 3-8-12 **72** JimCrowley 6 80
(Ralph Beckett) *led at mostly decent pce: tried to kick on 3f out: drvn and hdd over 1f out: kpt on but lost 2nd nr fin* **5/1**[3]
1140 **4** *2 ¾* **Red Runaway**[25] 3486 3-9-7 **81** RyanMoore 2 85+
(Ed Dunlop) *trckd ldng pair: tried to cl fr 3f out: pushed along and nt qckn wl over 1f out: fdd* **11/8**[1]
5 *21* **Innoko (FR)**[86] 3-9-5 **79** TomQueally 1 47
(Tony Carroll) *hld up: a last: pushed along and lost tch over 2f out: t.o* **25/1**

2m 26.64s (-2.86) **Going Correction** -0.25s/f (Firm) **5** Ran SP% **110.1**
Speed ratings (Par 102): **99,98,98,96,82**
CSF £22.48 TOTE £7.80: £3.50, £1.10; EX 24.80 Trifecta £74.30 Pool: £1057.38 - 10.66 winning units..
Owner Mrs D Edginton **Bred** Michael G Daly **Trained** Lambourn, Berks
FOCUS
There were one or two improvers in the line-up, but it went the way of one of the more exposed runners.

4350 BOOK JIM LAWLESS THROUGH CELEBRITY SPEAKERS H'CAP 1m 2f 7y
9:00 (9:00) (Class 6) (0-65,65) 4-Y-O+ **£1,940** (£577; £288; £144) **Stalls** Centre

Form RPR
1055 **1** **Minority Interest**[16] 3819 4-8-9 **53** (b[1]) KieranO'Neill 10 66
(Brett Johnson) *led and stretched field: pushed along 3f out: drvn and hdd wl over 1f out: rallied to ld ins fnl f: styd on wl* **16/1**
-051 **2** *½* **Certavi (IRE)**[12] 3954 4-9-3 **61** WilliamBuick 2 73
(Brendan Powell) *trckd ldng pair: moved up to chal over 2f out: led wl over 1f out: sn drvn: hdd ins fnl f: styd on but hld nr fin* **7/4**[1]
0565 **3** *3 ½* **Ogaritmo**[21] 3635 4-9-1 **59** (p) PatCosgrave 4 64
(Alastair Lidderdale) *trckd ldrs in 5th: clsd over 2f out gng strly: rdn and nt qckn wl over 1f out: kpt on to take 3rd fnl f* **16/1**
5012 **4** *1* **Conducting**[11] 3997 5-9-7 **65** FrankieDettori 1 68
(Gay Kelleway) *trckd ldr: shkn up 3f out: rdn to chal 2f out: wknd jst over 1f out* **7/2**[2]
6350 **5** *nse* **Hip Hip Hooray**[21] 3635 7-9-4 **62** JamesDoyle 6 65
(Luke Dace) *hld up in midfield and off the pce: weaved abt looking for room 2f out: drvn over 1f out: styd on same pce* **6/1**[3]
2425 **6** *5* **Cane Cat (IRE)**[30] 3314 6-8-10 **59** (t) GeorgeDowning[(5)] 5 52
(Tony Carroll) *awkward s: hld up in last trio and wl off the pce: rdn and prog on outer over 2f out: wknd over 1f out* **6/1**[3]
3043 **7** *1* **Dolly Colman (IRE)**[23] 3580 5-8-2 **46** (p) CathyGannon 9 37
(Zoe Davison) *hld up in last trio and wl off the pce: rdn and trying out make prog whn nt clr run wl over 1f out: n.d after* **20/1**
-005 **8** *2 ¼* **Arte Del Calcio**[128] 737 4-8-9 **53** HarryBentley 3 39
(Tony Carroll) *stdd s: hld up in last trio and wl off the pce: shuffled along over 2f out: nvr remotely involved* **40/1**
106/ **9** *½* **Appyjack**[623] 7198 5-8-11 **55** SteveDrowne 8 40
(Tony Carroll) *hld up in 8th and off the pce: shkn up over 2f out: nvr involved* **25/1**
0005 **10** *1 ¼* **Princess Spirit**[27] 3433 4-8-6 **50** ow1 (p) JohnFahy 12 33
(Edward Creighton) *hld up off the pce in midfield: hrd rdn and nt qckn over 2f out: sn btn* **16/1**
5-00 **11** *19* **Waspy**[19] 3700 4-8-12 **56** (t) RichardThomas 11
(Dr Jeremy Naylor) *chsd ldng trio tl wknd rapidly wl over 2f out: t.o* **50/1**

2m 5.67s (-3.03) **Going Correction** -0.25s/f (Firm) **11** Ran SP% **117.8**
Speed ratings (Par 101): **102,101,98,98,97 93,93,91,90,89 74**
toteswingers 1&2 £6.20, 1&3 £9.50, 2&3 £7.40 CSF £43.04 CT £483.49 TOTE £17.40: £4.20, £1.50, £4.00; EX 75.00 Trifecta £489.50 Pool: £835.37 - 1.27 winning units..
Owner J Daniels **Bred** Juddmonte Farms Ltd **Trained** Epsom, Surrey
■ Stewards' Enquiry : James Doyle two-day ban: careless riding (Jul 29-30)
FOCUS
The well-backed favourite was turned over here by the long-time leader.
T/Plt: £768.60 to a £1 stake. Pool: £88,082.98 - 83.65 winning tickets T/Qpdt: £134.70 to a £1 stake. Pool: £7630.34 - 41.89 winning tickets JN

4148 WOLVERHAMPTON (A.W) (L-H)
Monday, July 15

OFFICIAL GOING: Standard
Wind: Light half-against Weather: Overcast

4351 BETVICTOR.COM MAIDEN AUCTION STKS 5f 216y(P)
6:20 (6:25) (Class 5) 2-Y-O **£2,587** (£770; £384; £192) **Stalls** Low

Form RPR
1 **Pull The Plug (IRE)** 2-8-4 0 DuranFentiman 9 66+
(Declan Carroll) *chsd ldrs: shkn up over 1f out: r.o to ld wl ins fnl f* **66/1**
24F **2** *2* **Cheeky Peta'S**[26] 3476 2-8-6 0 SilvestreDeSousa 8 62
(James Given) *chsd ldr: led over 1f out: rdn and hdd wl ins fnl f: styd on same pce* **25/1**
24 **3** *½* **Salford Secret (IRE)**[18] 3717 2-8-13 0 DaneO'Neill 6 68+
(Marco Botti) *s.i.s: hdwy u.p over 2f out: rdn and hung lft ins fnl f: r.o: nt rch ldrs* **3/1**[2]
4 *2 ¼* **Chorlton Manor (IRE)** 2-9-1 0 NeilCallan 3 63
(Kevin Ryan) *led: rdn: hung lft and hdd over 1f out: no ex ins fnl f* **6/1**[3]
5 *1 ¾* **Gold Club** 2-8-9 0 FrannyNorton 7 54+
(Ed McMahon) *chsd ldrs: nt clr run over 1f out: wknd ins fnl f* **25/1**
4 **6** *1* **Autopilot**[16] 3836 2-9-1 0 KierenFallon 5 55
(Brian Meehan) *prom: pushed along 1/2-way: styd on same pce fr over 1f out* **11/10**[1]
0 **7** *1* **Nick The Odds (IRE)**[16] 3836 2-8-10 0 ow1 J-PGuillambert 11 47
(Jo Hughes) *prom: rdn 1/2-way: styd on same pce appr fnl f* **100/1**
64 **8** *2 ¾* **Black Geronimo**[21] 3640 2-8-8 0 DeclanBates[(5)] 13 41+
(David Evans) *hld up: shkn up over 2f out: nvr nr to chal* **20/1**
9 *1* **Black Vale (IRE)** 2-9-1 0 (p) PaulMulrennan 4 40
(James Tate) *hmpd s: hld up: rdn over 1f out: n.d* **33/1**
10 *1 ½* **Rockie Road (IRE)** 2-8-4 0 JasonHart[(5)] 2 30
(Paul Green) *s.i.s: sn given reminders: a in rr* **10/1**
11 *2 ¼* **Miss Acclaimed (IRE)** 2-8-10 0 DaleSwift 1 24
(Brian Ellison) *s.s: a in rr* **40/1**
12 *18* **Gravy Dipper (IRE)** 2-8-13 0 MichaelO'Connell 10
(John Quinn) *sn outpcd* **66/1**

1m 14.32s (-0.68) **Going Correction** -0.25s/f (Stan) **12** Ran SP% **117.8**
Speed ratings (Par 94): **94,91,90,87,85 84,82,79,77,75 72,48**
toteswingers 1&2 £71.30, 1&3 £51.80, 2&3 £10.10 CSF £1164.03 TOTE £122.30: £37.40, £6.30, £2.10; EX 753.30 Trifecta £1327.00 Part won. Pool: £1769.41 - 0.09 winning units..
Owner C Harding **Bred** Peter Molony **Trained** Sledmere, E Yorks
FOCUS
In all probability this was a modest maiden, especially with the favourite disappointing. Those who raced on the pace were favoured. The form could be rated higher through the third.

4352 WOLVERHAMPTON-RACECOURSE.CO.UK H'CAP 1m 5f 194y(P)
6:50 (6:51) (Class 6) (0-65,65) 3-Y-O **£2,264** (£673; £336; £168) **Stalls** Low

Form RPR
2523 **1** **Nateeja (IRE)**[13] 3916 3-9-6 **64** PaulHanagan 4 77
(J W Hills) *a.p: chsd ldr 9f out: led over 5f out: rdn clr fr over 1f out: styd on strly* **4/1**[2]
233 **2** *7* **Alshan Fajer**[16] 3820 3-9-7 **65** RobertHavlin 9 68
(Roger Ingram) *chsd ldrs: wnt 2nd over 5f out: rdn over 2f out: no ex fnl f* **5/1**[3]
0-22 **3** *¾* **Aloha**[16] 3820 3-9-7 **65** DaneO'Neill 10 67
(Roger Varian) *hld up: hdwy over 6f out: rdn over 3f out: styd on same pce fnl 2f* **5/2**[1]
4-4V **4** *16* **Honey Haven (IRE)**[23] 3578 3-7-9 **46** oh1 NoelGarbutt[(7)] 5 26
(Mark Brisbourne) *hld up: rdn over 7f out: wnt remote 4th over 2f out: n.d* **50/1**
6-36 **5** *3 ¾* **Vandross (IRE)**[32] 3257 3-9-0 **58** (b) SebSanders 3 32
(Chris Wall) *hld up: drvn along over 7f out: nvr on terms* **14/1**
4024 **6** *21* **Aphrodite Spirit (IRE)**[16] 3820 3-8-2 **46** DuranFentiman 1
(Pat Eddery) *chsd ldr 5f: remained handy tl rdn and wknd 4f out* **22/1**
2355 **7** *12* **Bold Assertion**[32] 3257 3-9-7 **65** LukeMorris 2
(John Best) *in rr: drvn along over 8f out: lost tch fnl 5f* **16/1**
5205 **8** *1 ¼* **Moaning Butcher**[13] 3916 3-8-13 **57** FrannyNorton 8
(Mark Johnston) *sn outpcd* **50/1**
000- **9** *23* **Many Levels**[234] 7840 3-8-4 **48** JimmyQuinn 7
(John Quinn) *chsd ldrs: rdn over 5f out: wknd over 3f out* **8/1**
4650 **10** *2 ¼* **Jawinski (IRE)**[32] 2924 3-8-6 **50** (v[1]) SilvestreDeSousa 6
(David Evans) *set str pce tl hdd over 5f out: wknd over 4f out* **15/2**

3m 0.06s (-5.94) **Going Correction** -0.25s/f (Stan) **10** Ran SP% **111.7**
Speed ratings (Par 98): **106,102,101,92,90 78,71,70,57,56**
toteswingers 1&2 £5.00, 1&3 £2.00, 2&3 £3.70 CSF £22.57 CT £57.50 TOTE £5.70: £2.70, £1.20, £1.10; EX 21.10 Trifecta £45.70 Pool: £874.77 - 14.34 winning units..
Owner Hamdan Al Maktoum **Bred** Shadwell Estate Company Limited **Trained** Upper Lambourn, Berks
FOCUS
This was run at a true gallop and the form looks sound for the grade, with the first three clear.

4353 BETVICTOR OPEN CHAMPIONSHIP 8 PLACES EXCLUSIVE (S) STKS 5f 20y(P)
7:20 (7:20) (Class 6) 3-4-Y-O **£1,940** (£577; £288; £144) **Stalls** Low

Form RPR
0305 **1** **Little China**[13] 3921 4-9-0 59 (b) SilvestreDeSousa 3 67
(William Muir) *chsd ldrs: rdn over 1f out: r.o u.p to ld post* **5/1**[2]
0601 **2** *hd* **Archie Stevens**[21] 3639 3-9-5 80 HayleyTurner 4 74
(Amy Weaver) *chsd ldr: shkn up to ld ins fnl f: sn rdn: hdd post* **1/4**[1]
-435 **3** *2* **Coconut Kisses**[14] 3904 3-8-9 55 PaulMulrennan 6 57
(Bill Turner) *led: rdn and hdd ins fnl f: styd on same pce* **12/1**[3]
6440 **4** *4 ½* **Vergality Ridge (IRE)**[19] 3679 3-9-0 47 (be) LukeMorris 2 46
(Ronald Harris) *chsd ldrs: sn drvn along: wknd fnl f* **22/1**
5500 **5** *1 ¼* **Red Star Lady (IRE)**[18] 3739 3-8-9 43 [1] DuranFentiman 1 36
(Shaun Harris) *in rr: rdn over 1f out: no imp fnl f* **66/1**
0/ **6** *6* **Lady Cricketer**[618] 7292 4-9-0 0 (b[1]) AdamBeschizza 5 17
(Michael Squance) *s.i.s: outpcd* **40/1**

1m 1.66s (-0.64) **Going Correction** -0.25s/f (Stan)
WFA 3 from 4yo 5lb **6** Ran SP% **112.6**
Speed ratings (Par 101): **95,94,91,84,82 72**
toteswingers 1&2 £71.30, 1&3 £51.80, 2&3 £10.10 CSF £6.78 TOTE £7.40: £1.80, £1.02; EX 7.10 Trifecta £17.50 Pool: £151.57 - 64.74 winning units..There was no bid for the winner. Archie Stevens was claimed by Mr Michael Wigham for £6,000.
Owner S Lamb **Bred** Stephen Lamb **Trained** Lambourn, Berks
FOCUS
Bit of a turn up in this uncompetitive seller.

4354 DOWNLOAD THE BETVICTOR APP NOW H'CAP 7f 32y(P)
7:50 (7:50) (Class 5) (0-75,75) 3-Y-O **£3,234** (£962; £481; £240) **Stalls** High

Form RPR
0522 **1** **Future Reference (IRE)**[27] 3434 3-9-4 **72** (t) SilvestreDeSousa 11 85
(Saeed bin Suroor) *chsd ldr: rdn and hung rt ins fnl f: r.o to ld nr fin* **7/4**[1]
-023 **2** *½* **Exzachary**[17] 3773 3-9-0 **73** PhilipPrince[(5)] 8 84
(Jo Hughes) *led: rdn and hung rt ins fnl f: hdd nr fin* **25/1**
-502 **3** *2 ¾* **Summer Dream (IRE)**[46] 2806 3-9-6 **74** (b) MartinHarley 10 78
(Marco Botti) *chsd ldrs: rdn over 1f out: styd on same pce ins fnl f* **11/1**
2001 **4** *1* **Lionheart**[13] 3927 3-9-7 **75** KirstyMilczarek 6 76+
(Luca Cumani) *plld hrd and prom: swtchd rt over 1f out: sn rdn: styd on* **3/1**[2]
-445 **5** *1 ¼* **Megamunch (IRE)**[55] 2544 3-9-0 **68** DavidNolan 2 66
(Kristin Stubbs) *hld up: swtchd rt and hdwy over 1f out: sn rdn and hung lft: nt rch ldrs* **18/1**

4045 **6** *3/4* **My Name Is Rio (IRE)**[22] 3611 3-9-2 **70**.................... PaulMulrennan 5 66
(Michael Dods) *chsd ldrs: rdn over 1f out: wknd ins fnl f* **20/1**

-050 **7** *hd* **Iberis**[38] 3062 3-9-5 **73**.................................... HayleyTurner 7 68
(Lady Cecil) *s.i.s: hld up: nt clr run over 1f out: nvr nrr* **25/1**

2251 **8** *6* **Hornboy**[30] 3327 3-9-7 **75**..................................(p) JimmyFortune 9 54
(Jeremy Noseda) *prom: rdn over 2f out: wknd over 1f out* **14/1**

6023 **9** *3 3/4* **Repetition**[23] 3566 3-9-5 **73**.................................... NeilCallan 4 42
(Kevin Ryan) *s.i.s: hdwy and hung rt 1/2-way: rdn and wknd over 1f out* **5/1**[3]

2315 **10** *6* **Indian Affair**[18] 3733 3-9-5 **73**.............................. LukeMorris 3 26
(Milton Bradley) *hld up: rdn over 2f out: wknd wl over 1f out* **25/1**

2400 **11** *1 3/4* **Lewamy (IRE)**[27] 3454 3-9-6 **74**.......................... FrederikTylicki 1 22
(John Best) *plld hrd and prom: nt clr run and lost pl 6f out: rdn over 2f out: sn wknd* **50/1**

1m 27.46s (-2.14) **Going Correction** -0.25s/f (Stan) **11** Ran SP% **116.6**
Speed ratings (Par 100): **102,101,98,97,95 94,94,87,83,76 74**
toteswingers 1&2 £8.80, 1&3 £4.70, 2&3 £59.30 CSF £57.98 CT £345.45 TOTE £2.00: £1.10, £8.80, £3.40; EX 56.00 Trifecta £323.30 Pool: £864.25 - 2.00 winning units..
Owner Godolphin **Bred** Darley **Trained** Newmarket, Suffolk
■ Stewards' Enquiry : Philip Prince one-day ban: careless riding (Jul 29)

FOCUS
Modest handicap form and little got involved from off the pace. The front pair ended up drifting to the stands' rail.

4355 OPEN CHAMPIONSHIP 8 PLACES AT BETVICTOR CLASSIFIED CLAIMING STKS 1m 4f 50y(P)
8:20 (8:20) (Class 6) 3-Y-0+ **£2,264** (£673; £336; £168) **Stalls** Low

Form RPR

300- **1** **Langley**[257] 7474 6-8-11 56..............................(vt) OisinMurphy(7) 6 70
(Tim Vaughan) *hld up: pushed along and hdwy over 3f out: led over 1f out: rdn clr* **9/2**[2]

50-4 **2** *15* **Anginola (IRE)**[38] 3056 4-9-2 57.............................. RyanPowell(3) 12 49+
(John Ryan) *hld up: hdwy u.p over 1f out: wnt 2nd ins fnl f: no ch w wnr* **16/1**

-560 **3** *3* **Excellent News (IRE)**[18] 3721 4-8-13 51...................... JackDuern(5) 11 41
(Tony Forbes) *led: clr over 4f out tl rdn and hdd over 1f out: wknd fnl f* **20/1**

-056 **4** *1* **Echo Of Footsteps**[18] 3728 4-9-7 55........................(p) PaulMulrennan 2 43
(Michael Herrington) *prom: rdn over 2f out: wknd over 1f out* **8/1**

/60- **5** *1/2* **Art Thief**[529] 389 5-9-4 51..................................(p) AndrewMullen 7 39
(Michael Appleby) *chsd ldr: rdn over 2f out: wknd over 1f out* **10/1**

400 **6** *2* **Daniel Thomas (IRE)**[25] 3513 11-9-2 56.....................(tp) MartinHarley 4 34
(Violet M Jordan) *hld up: sme hdwy over 1f out: sn rdn and wknd* **5/1**[3]

3660 **7** *3 1/4* **Lacey**[10] 4010 4-9-7 53.. RussKennemore 8 33
(Andrew Hollinshead) *chsd ldrs: rdn over 3f out: wknd over 2f out* **7/1**

0036 **8** *1* **Madam Tessa (IRE)**[12] 3954 5-8-9 46.......................... ChloeIngram(7) 9 27
(Tim Vaughan) *s.i.s: hld up: rdn over 2f out: sn wknd* **40/1**

314 **9** *14* **Tyrur Ted**[21] 3617 8-9-2 59..........................(t) DanaZamecnikova(7) 5 21
(Frank Sheridan) *hld up: pushed along over 5f out: wkng whn nt clr run over 2f out* **5/2**[1]

00-5 **10** *54* **Cadgers Brig**[17] 3768 5-9-5 57..............................(bt[1]) LukeMorris 1
(Barry Murtagh) *chsd ldrs: rdn over 4f out: wknd over 2f out: eased* **10/1**

2m 37.77s (-3.33) **Going Correction** -0.25s/f (Stan) **10** Ran SP% **118.3**
Speed ratings (Par 101): **101,91,89,88,88 86,84,83,74,38**
toteswingers 1&2 £35.50, 1&3 £52.10, 2&3 £55.90 CSF £74.73 TOTE £4.30: £1.20, £3.70, £3.30; EX 145.00 Trifecta £449.60 Part won. Pool: £559.59 - 0.07 winning units..
Owner C Davies **Bred** Gestut Hof Ittlingen **Trained** Aberthin, Vale of Glamorgan

FOCUS
What had looked quite an open claimer was blown apart by Langley.

4356 HOLIDAY INN WOLVERHAMPTON MEDIAN AUCTION MAIDEN STKS 1m 1f 103y(P)
8:50 (8:52) (Class 6) 3-4-Y-0 **£1,940** (£577; £288; £144) **Stalls** Low

Form RPR

33-3 **1** **Capella's Song (IRE)**[70] 2099 3-8-12 72.......................... HayleyTurner 5 75+
(Michael Bell) *chsd ldrs: shkn up to ld ins fnl f: r.o: comf* **1/1**[1]

2 *2 1/4* **Le Grande Cheval (IRE)** 3-9-3 0.................................. LukeMorris 10 70
(Harry Dunlop) *sn prom: chsd ldr over 5f out: rdn to ld and hung lft over 1f out: hdd and unable qck ins fnl f* **14/1**

3056 **3** *3 3/4* **Sixties Queen**[6] 4144 3-8-5 60.................................. TimClark(7) 4 57
(Alan Bailey) *led: rdn: edgd rt and hdd over 1f out: no ex ins fnl f* **10/1**

3230 **4** *3 1/4* **Clary (IRE)**[17] 3758 3-8-12 65.................................. StevieDonohoe 7 50
(James Unett) *hld up in tch: plld hrd: lost pl over 4f out: n.d after* **13/2**[3]

5 **5** *1* **Brother Duke**[20] 3650 3-8-12 0.............................. JustinNewman(5) 9 53
(Garry Moss) *in rr: hdwy over 5f out: rdn over 2f out: wknd fnl f* **50/1**

00 **6** *3* **Green And White (ITY)**[14] 3907 3-8-10 0.........(t) DanaZamecnikova(7) 2 47
(Frank Sheridan) *dwlt: hdwy over 2f out: rdn over 1f out: wknd fnl f* **150/1**

7 *3 1/2* **Denote** 3-9-3 0.. ChrisCatlin 1 40+
(Paul Cole) *sn pushed along and rn green in rr: effrt over 2f out: sn wknd* **5/2**[2]

0 **8** *3* **The Bay Tigress**[17] 3774 3-8-12 0.................................. DaleSwift 8 28
(Lisa Williamson) *hld up: hdwy over 5f out: rdn and wknd over 2f out* **100/1**

560- **9** *17* **Beauchamp Astra**[221] 8006 3-8-7 40.......................... NicoleNordblad(5) 6
(Hans Adielsson) *chsd ldr 4f: rdn and wknd over 2f out* **33/1**

10 *89* **All Black Rose** 3-8-12 0.. PaulMulrennan 3
(Ann Duffield) *s.s: outpcd* **25/1**

2m 0.55s (-1.15) **Going Correction** -0.25s/f (Stan) **10** Ran SP% **118.1**
Speed ratings (Par 101): **95,93,89,86,85 83,80,77,62,**
toteswingers 1&2 £2.60, 1&3 £1.70, 2&3 £17.00 CSF £17.80 TOTE £2.10: £1.10, £3.00, £2.70; EX 17.20 Trifecta £76.40 Pool: £1087.80 - 10.67 winning units..
Owner P A Philipps & C E L Philipps **Bred** Churchtown, Lane & Orpendale Bloodstock **Trained** Newmarket, Suffolk

FOCUS
A moderate maiden lacking depth.

4357 BETVICTOR 8 PLACES ON THE OPEN H'CAP 1m 141y(P)
9:20 (9:20) (Class 6) (0-60,66) 3-Y-0+ **£1,940** (£577; £288; £144) **Stalls** Low

Form RPR

2601 **1** **Pelmanism**[6] 4149 6-10-1 **66** 6ex..........................(p) AidanColeman 3 83
(Brian Ellison) *hld up: hdwy over 2f out: led 1f out: r.o wl* **7/1**

-000 **2** *4 1/2* **Save The Bees**[37] 3081 5-9-4 **60**.............................. JasonHart(5) 4 67
(Declan Carroll) *chsd ldrs: rdn over 3f out: styd on same pce fnl f* **11/2**[3]

-000 **3** *1 1/4* **Warden Bond**[17] 3780 5-9-4 **60**..............................(p) LauraPike(5) 11 64
(William Stone) *a.p: rdn over 1f out: styd on same pce fnl f* **18/1**

0050 **4** *1 1/2* **Spirit Of Gondree (IRE)**[14] 3909 5-9-7 **58**..................(b) LukeMorris 5 59
(Milton Bradley) *s.i.s: hld up: hdwy over 1f out: sn rdn: r.o: nt trble ldrs* **14/1**

2000 **5** *hd* **Norwegian Reward (IRE)**[17] 3780 5-9-2 **53**........... SilvestreDeSousa 1 53
(Michael Wigham) *hld up: r.o ins fnl f: nvr nrr* **11/2**[3]

3555 **6** *1* **Arabian Flight**[110] 1211 4-9-5 **56**.................................[1] AndrewMullen 8 54
(Michael Appleby) *chsd ldrs: rdn and ev ch over 1f out: wknd ins fnl f* **14/1**

0062 **7** *2* **Glenridding**[6] 4155 9-9-6 **57**......................................(p) DaleSwift 6 50
(James Given) *sn pushed along to ld: rdn and hdd 1f out: sn wknd* **4/1**[2]

4665 **8** *2 3/4* **Delightful Sleep**[5] 4171 5-9-4 **60**.......................... DeclanBates(5) 10 47
(David Evans) *hld up: rdn over 1f out: nt trble ldrs* **14/1**

0300 **9** *3/4* **George Benjamin**[6] 4155 6-9-1 **57**.........................(t) JackDuern(5) 12 42
(Christopher Kellett) *hld up: hdwy 1/2-way: rdn over 2f out: wknd over 1f out* **25/1**

54/6 **10** *5* **Thewinningmachine**[68] 2155 4-9-4 **55**.......................... J-PGuillambert 7 29
(Jo Hughes) *hld up: a in rr* **66/1**

0530 **11** *1 1/2* **High On The Hog (IRE)**[6] 4155 5-9-7 **58**.................(b[1]) JimmyQuinn 2 28
(Mark Brisbourne) *plld hrd and prom: rdn over 2f out: sn wknd* **33/1**

5004 **12** *3/4* **Star City (IRE)**[5] 4161 4-9-7 **58**..........................(be) PaulMulrennan 9 26
(Michael Dods) *prom: rdn over 2f out: wknd over 1f out* **3/1**[1]

2200 **13** *1* **John Potts**[21] 3642 8-9-3 **54**.....................................(p) KierenFox 13 20
(Brian Baugh) *chsd ldrs: forced to r wd: rdn over 3f out: wknd over 2f out* **28/1**

1m 48.39s (-2.11) **Going Correction** -0.25s/f (Stan) **13** Ran SP% **125.3**
Speed ratings (Par 101): **99,95,93,92,92 91,89,87,86,82 80,80,79**
toteswingers 1&2 £11.00, 1&3 £27.20, 2&3 £23.60 CSF £46.26 CT £710.06 TOTE £11.50: £3.20, £2.90, £4.10; EX 54.30 Trifecta £389.70 Pool: £1283.61 - 2.46 winning units..
Owner Koo's Racing Club **Bred** Guy Reed **Trained** Norton, N Yorks
■ Stewards' Enquiry : Laura Pike two-day ban: used whip above permitted level (Jul 29-30)

FOCUS
Weak handicap form.
T/Plt: £53.10 to a £1 stake. Pool: £82373.67 - 1131.91 winning tickets T/Qpdt: £12.00 to a £1 stake. Pool: £6383.89 - 393.60 winning tickets CR

4358 - 4362a (Foreign Racing) - See Raceform Interactive

4191
BATH (L-H)
Tuesday, July 16

OFFICIAL GOING: Firm (11.9)
Wind: Gentle breeze across Weather: Sunny

4363 EXCALIBUR BUSINESS MOBILES NURSERY H'CAP 5f 11y
2:15 (2:15) (Class 5) 2-Y-0 **£2,587** (£770; £384; £192) **Stalls** Centre

Form RPR

1040 **1** **Zalzilah**[28] 3424 2-9-7 **79**..(p) NeilCallan 6 86+
(James Tate) *sn led: drvn and qckng over 1f out: sn clr: readily* **1/1**[1]

3216 **2** *4* **Sunset Shore**[7] 4134 2-9-6 **78**.................................. ChrisCatlin 5 71
(Sir Mark Prescott Bt) *drvn to chse ldrs and t.k.h: nt clr run on rails and lost pl bnd over 3f out: swtchd rt and hdwy fr 2f out: edgd lft and styd on fnl f to take 2nd fnl 110yds: no ch w wnr* **9/2**[2]

554 **3** *hd* **Resist**[13] 3942 2-8-5 **63**.. HarryBentley 3 55
(Tobias B P Coles) *chsd wnr over 3f out: rdn and no imp wl over 1f out: lost 2nd fnl 110yds but kpt pressing for that position tl no ex cl home* **5/1**[3]

505 **4** *3/4* **Oxlip**[29] 3414 2-8-0 **58** oh2.. KieranO'Neill 1 47
(Richard Hannon) *outpcd: rdn over 2f out: nt clr run over 1f out: swtchd rt ins fnl f and kpt on in clsng stages: nvr a threat* **11/1**

400 **5** *2* **Vodka Chaser (IRE)**[16] 3857 2-7-11 **58** oh4.................. DarrenEgan(3) 4 43
(J S Moore) *in rr and outpcd: rdn over 2f out: sme hdwy whn nt clr run 1f out: no ch after* **14/1**

355 **6** *4 1/2* **Narborough**[17] 3815 2-8-7 **65**................................ SamHitchcott 2 31
(Mick Channon) *chsd ldr tl over 3f out: rdn 2f out: wkng whn hmpd jst ins fnl f* **8/1**

1m 1.68s (-0.82) **Going Correction** -0.225s/f (Firm) **6** Ran SP% **111.0**
Speed ratings (Par 94): **97,90,90,89,85 78**
toteswingers 1&2 £1.80, 2&3 £2.00, 1&3 £1.60 CSF £5.63 TOTE £2.00: £1.40, £1.60; EX 4.30 Trifecta £10.10 Pool: £2112.71 - 156.70 winning units..
Owner Sheikh Juma Dalmook Al Maktoum **Bred** Heather Raw **Trained** Newmarket, Suffolk

FOCUS
The going was fast and the jockeys said it was riding quite rough with not much grass. Just a fair nursery, but turned into a procession by the well-backed favourite, who looks capable of better.

4364 TOTALBATH.COM H'CAP 5f 11y
2:45 (2:45) (Class 4) (0-85,82) 3-Y-0+ **£4,690** (£1,395; £697; £348) **Stalls** Centre

Form RPR

-060 **1** **Burning Thread (IRE)**[10] 4047 6-9-2 **77**...(b) WilliamTwiston-Davies(5) 1 90
(Tim Etherington) *chsd clr ldr: rdn to ld 1f out: drvn clr* **8/1**

0625 **2** *7* **Whitecrest**[8] 4123 5-9-10 **80**.................................... ChrisCatlin 2 68
(John Spearing) *disp 3rd bhd clr ldrs: drvn and styd on fr 2f out: tk wl hld 2nd fnl 110yds* **8/1**

0405 **3** *3/4* **Best Be Careful (IRE)**[14] 3920 5-8-7 **63** oh1.............. HayleyTurner 6 48
(Mark Usher) *sn disputing 3rd bhd clr ldr: rdn 2f out: styd on to take wl hld 3rd fnl 75yds* **11/2**[3]

4646 **4** *2 1/4* **Waseem Faris (IRE)**[8] 4123 4-9-6 **76**.......................... MartinHarley 4 53
(Mick Channon) *sn disputing 3rd bhd clr ldr: hrd rdn over 1f out: btn ins fnl f* **6/4**[1]

5103 **5** *3 1/4* **Powerful Wind (IRE)**[18] 3796 4-9-1 **76**...................... PhilipPrince(5) 3 41
(Ronald Harris) *led: sn wl clr and c wd bnd 3f out: rdn 2f out: hdd 1f out: wknd qckly ins fnl f* **5/2**[2]

/04- **6** *17* **Billyrayvalentine (CAN)**[348] 4723 4-9-12 **82**..........(t) PatCosgrave 5
(George Baker) *restless in stalls: rrd and lost all ch s: a wl bhd* **16/1**

1m 0.6s (-1.90) **Going Correction** -0.225s/f (Firm) **6** Ran SP% **112.1**
Speed ratings (Par 105): **106,94,93,90,84 57**
toteswingers 1&2 £5.40, 2&3 £3.80, 1&3 £4.70 CSF £65.18 TOTE £5.30: £2.30, £5.50; EX 54.80 Trifecta £400.20 Pool: £1995.50 - 3.73 winning units..
Owner Tim Etherington **Bred** James Lombard **Trained** Norton, N Yorks

FOCUS
Not a bad little sprint handicap and the time was over a second faster than the preceding nursery. The winner is rated to somewhere near last year's peak.

4365 EXCALIBUR BUSINESS LANDLINES H'CAP 1m 3f 144y
3:15 (3:15) (Class 6) (0-60,58) 3-Y-0+ **£1,940** (£577; £288; £144) **Stalls** Low

Form RPR

0520 **1** **Bold Cross (IRE)**[21] 3662 10-9-11 **58**.......................... ThomasBrown(3) 1 71
(Edward Bevan) *hld up in rr: stdy hdwy over 3f out: led jst ins fnl 2f: pushed clr over 1f out: easily* **3/1**[2]

0505 **2** *11* **Petersboden**[20] 3688 4-9-1 **45** FergusSweeney 6 40
(Michael Blanshard) *chsd ldrs: led 3f out: rdn and hdd jst ins fnl 2f: sn no ch w wnr but kpt on wl to hold 2nd* **20/1**

00-4 **3** *2 ½* **Nicky Nutjob (GER)**[5] 4192 7-8-12 **45** (p) DarrenEgan(3) 2 36
(John O'Shea) *pressed ldrs fr 9f out tl led 7f out: hdd 3f out: btn ins fnl 2f but hld on for wl hld 3rd* **12/1**

66/5 **4** *1 ¾* **Faith Jicaro (IRE)**[23] 3180 6-9-5 **49** StevieDonohoe 5 38
(James Unett) *led: jnd fr 9f out tl hdd 7f out: sn rdn: hung rt bnd 3f out and no ch after* **7/2**[3]

3342 **5** *10* **Glens Wobbly**[5] 4192 5-9-1 **45** HarryBentley 4 18
(Jonathan Geake) *chsd ldrs: disp ld 9f out to 7f out: wknd u.p ins fnl 3f* **6/4**[1]

1-06 **6** *1 ¼* **Inffiraaj (IRE)**[96] 1502 4-9-12 **56** MartinHarley 3 27
(Mick Channon) *in rr: sme hdwy over 3f out: sn rdn and wknd* **6/1**

2m 29.01s (-1.59) **Going Correction** -0.10s/f (Good) 6 Ran SP% **114.0**
Speed ratings (Par 101): **101,93,92,90,84 83**
toteswingers 1&2 £7.60, 2&3 £9.20, 1&3 £5.30 CSF £52.42 TOTE £2.80: £1.30, £8.70; EX 61.90 Trifecta £220.40 Pool: £2422.98 - 8.24 winning units..
Owner E G Bevan **Bred** M Hosokawa **Trained** Ullingswick, H'fords

FOCUS
A moderate handicap, but a heartwarming success for a horse running for the 100th time. The form is treated cautiously.

4366 FOREVER FRIENDS APPEAL H'CAP 1m 5y
3:45 (3:45) (Class 4) (0-80,77) 3-Y-0+ £4,690 (£1,395; £697; £348) Stalls Low

Form RPR

5-66 **1** **African Oil (FR)**[59] 2439 3-9-2 **77** SteveDrowne 4 85+
(Charles Hills) *in rr and sltly hmpd 6f out: drvn over 3f out: styd on to ld 1f out: forged clr fnl 110yds* **3/1**[2]

2-36 **2** *2 ¼* **Take A Note**[20] 3693 4-9-8 **75** JimCrowley 1 79
(Patrick Chamings) *chsd ldr 6f out: chal over 2f out: slt ld sn after: hdd 1f out: sn no ch w wnr but hld on wl for 2nd* **3/1**[2]

0541 **3** *shd* **Croquembouche (IRE)**[20] 3676 4-9-6 **73** LiamKeniry 2 77
(Ed de Giles) *sn led: rdn and jnd over 2f out: narrowly hdd sn after: outpcd by wnr fnl f: styd pressing for 2nd tl no ex last strides and dropped to 3rd* **5/4**[1]

-064 **4** *7* **Evervescent (IRE)**[5] 4198 4-9-2 **72** (b) DarrenEgan(3) 3 59
(J S Moore) *plld hrd: in tch: sltly hmpd 6f out: chsd ldrs fr 4f out: rdn fr 3f out: wknd over 1f out* **8/1**[3]

2153 **P** **Paphos**[12] 3993 6-9-3 **70** (v) MartinHarley 5
(David Evans) *chsd ldr tl wnt bdly lame and p.u 6f out* **10/1**

1m 40.16s (-0.64) **Going Correction** -0.10s/f (Good)
WFA 3 from 4yo+ 8lb 5 Ran SP% **114.6**
Speed ratings (Par 105): **99,96,96,89,**
CSF £12.80 TOTE £5.50: £3.40, £1.10; EX 17.30 Trifecta £32.00 Pool: £2141.43 - 50.17 winning units..
Owner R A Pegum **Bred** S C A De La Perrigne **Trained** Lambourn, Berks

FOCUS
A tightly knit contest on paper, but a nice success for the 3-y-o, who recorded a personal best.

4367 EXCALIBUR IT SOLUTIONS H'CAP 5f 161y
4:15 (4:15) (Class 3) (0-95,91) 3-Y-0 £7,439 (£2,213; £1,106; £553) Stalls Centre

Form RPR

-030 **1** **Tartary (IRE)**[41] 2983 3-8-6 **76** HayleyTurner 2 81
(Roger Charlton) *chsd ldr: led 3f out: rdn whn chal over 1f out: styd on wl to assert fnl 75yds* **7/2**[3]

0656 **2** *nk* **Jillnextdoor (IRE)**[4] 4247 3-9-3 **87** MartinHarley 3 91
(Mick Channon) *chsd ldrs: drvn to chal fr over 1f out tl no ex u.p fnl 75yds* **5/1**

125 **3** *2 ½* **The Art Of Racing (IRE)**[10] 4057 3-9-1 **85** (t) HarryBentley 1 80
(Olly Stevens) *t.k.h: trckd ldrs: rdn over 2f out: no imp and wknd ins fnl f* **6/5**[1]

2-06 **4** *4 ½* **Alcando (IRE)**[22] 3634 3-8-10 **80** PatCosgrave 5 60
(Denis Coakley) *led: hdd 3f out: styd pressing ldrs tl wl over 1f out: sn hung lft and btn* **3/1**[2]

1m 10.57s (-0.63) **Going Correction** -0.225s/f (Firm) 4 Ran SP% **109.3**
Speed ratings (Par 104): **95,94,91,85**
CSF £18.40 TOTE £3.80; EX 13.00 Trifecta £36.80 Pool: £974.84 - 19.82 winning units..
Owner Lady Rothschild **Bred** The Rt Hon Lord Rothschild **Trained** Beckhampton, Wilts

FOCUS
The feature race on the card and a close finish.

4368 BATH BUSINESS NEWS FILLIES' H'CAP 5f 161y
4:45 (4:45) (Class 5) (0-75,75) 3-Y-0+ £2,587 (£770; £384; £192) Stalls Centre

Form RPR

-030 **1** **Ginzan**[40] 3018 5-9-5 **75** RyanWhile(7) 1 81
(Malcolm Saunders) *disp 2nd tl chsd ldr over 2f out: drvn and styd on wl fnl f to ld cl home* **9/4**[1]

2110 **2** *½* **Maria Montez**[28] 3431 4-8-10 **66** ShelleyBirkett(7) 2 70
(J W Hills) *led: rdn over 1f out: hdd and no ex cl home* **3/1**[3]

2660 **3** *nk* **Catalinas Diamond (IRE)**[13] 3949 5-8-11 **60** (t) SteveDrowne 4 63
(Pat Murphy) *rrd stalls and lost 5 l: hdwy over 2f out: styd on wl to take 3rd in clsng stages: nt quite rch ldng duo* **14/1**

0323 **4** *nk* **Sulis Minerva (IRE)**[11] 4017 6-9-8 **74** RyanClark(3) 6 76
(Jeremy Gask) *in tch: hdwy to chse ldrs over 1f out: styd on fnl f but nvr gng pce to chal* **5/2**[2]

6033 **5** *¾* **Tregereth (IRE)**[10] 4064 3-8-1 **58** DarrenEgan(3) 3 57
(Jonathan Portman) *chsd ldrs: rdn 2f out: outpcd ins fnl f* **7/1**

1554 **6** *11* **Night Trade (IRE)**[14] 3920 6-9-1 **69** (p) EDLinehan(5) 5 31
(Ronald Harris) *disp 2nd tl rdn over 2f out: wknd qckly appr fnl f* **8/1**

1m 10.95s (-0.25) **Going Correction** -0.225s/f (Firm)
WFA 3 from 4yo+ 5lb 6 Ran SP% **114.6**
Speed ratings (Par 100): **92,91,90,90,89 74**
toteswingers 1&2 £1.70, 2&3 £8.10, 1&3 £7.20 CSF £9.67 TOTE £3.20: £2.10, £1.90; EX 13.90 Trifecta £79.50 Pool: £2296.30 - 21.63 winning units..
Owner Paul Nicholas **Bred** Hedsor Stud **Trained** Green Ore, Somerset

FOCUS
This fillies' handicap was run 0.38secs slower than the preceding contest for 3-y-os. The form is ordinary with the placed horses the best indicators of the level.

4369 EXCALIBUR BUSINESS BROADBAND H'CAP 5f 11y
5:15 (5:15) (Class 6) (0-65,69) 3-Y-0+ £1,940 (£577; £288; £144) Stalls Centre

Form RPR

1053 **1** **Dreams Of Glory**[21] 3667 5-9-10 **63** HarryBentley 5 73
(Ron Hodges) *mde all: rdn over 1f out: hld on wl in clsng stages* **2/1**[1]

5300 **2** *¾* **Wooden King (IRE)**[16] 3855 8-9-7 **65** PhilipPrince(5) 3 72
(Malcolm Saunders) *chsd wnr: rdn over 1f out: kpt on u.p in clsng stages but a jst hld by wnr* **9/2**[3]

-603 **3** *¾* **Volito**[11] 4034 7-9-4 **57** AidanColeman 2 62
(Anabel K Murphy) *in rr: pushed along and hdwy over 1f out: kpt on ins fnl f to take 3rd cl home but nt rch ldng duo* **7/1**

0021 **4** *nk* **Comptonspirit**[5] 4197 9-9-11 **69** 6ex MatthewLawson(5) 1 73
(Brian Baugh) *chsd ldrs: drvn 2f out: disp 2nd u.p fnl f: no ex in clsng stages* **3/1**[2]

0/1- **5** *1 ¼* **Charismas Birthday (IRE)**[19] 3747 5-8-9 **48** (b) J-PGuillambert 8 47
(Philip M Byrne, Ire) *pressed ldrs: rdn over 2f out: outpcd ins fnl f* **8/1**

010 **6** *1* **Even Bolder**[21] 3667 10-8-13 **59** JoeyHaynes(7) 7 54
(Eric Wheeler) *chsd ldrs: drvn fr 2f out: wknd ins fnl f* **18/1**

4050 **7** *6* **Majestic Red (IRE)**[4] 4244 3-8-7 **50** (p) KieranO'Neill 4 24
(Malcolm Saunders) *s.i.s: outpcd* **12/1**

5000 **8** *7* **Bheleyf (IRE)**[4] 4244 3-8-10 **60** (v[1]) ShelleyBirkett(7) 6 9
(Joseph Tuite) *outpcd fr 1/2-way* **25/1**

1m 2.31s (-0.19) **Going Correction** -0.225s/f (Firm)
WFA 3 from 5yo+ 4lb 8 Ran SP% **116.9**
Speed ratings (Par 101): **92,90,89,89,87 85,75,64**
toteswingers 1&2 £3.60, 2&3 £6.10, 1&3 £3.10 CSF £11.66 CT £52.79 TOTE £3.40: £1.50, £1.80, £1.60; EX 12.40 Trifecta £45.00 Pool: £2342.78 - 39.01 winning units..
Owner P E Axon **Bred** P E Axon **Trained** Charlton Mackrell, Somerset

FOCUS
This moderate sprint was the slowest of the three races over the trip on the day. The winner is rated to last year's C&D win.
T/Plt: £581.70 to a £1 stake. Pool of £70728.69 - 88.75 winning tickets. T/Qpdt: £82.10 to a £1 stake. Pool of £5527.69 - 49.80 winning tickets. ST

4044 BEVERLEY (R-H)
Tuesday, July 16

OFFICIAL GOING: Good to firm (9.5)
Wind: Virtually nil Weather: Fine and dry

4370 33 RACECOURSES LIVE ON SKY 432 MAIDEN AUCTION STKS 5f
2:00 (2:01) (Class 5) 2-Y-0 £3,234 (£962; £481; £240) Stalls Low

Form RPR

1 **Belayer (IRE)** 2-8-9 0 PaulMulrennan 4 77+
(Kevin Ryan) *hld up towards rr: hdwy 1/2-way: swtchd lft and hdwy jst over 1f out: rdn and styd on strly ins fnl f to ld on line* **6/1**[3]

0 **2** *nse* **Back Lane**[20] 3681 2-8-9 0 TonyHamilton 6 77
(Richard Fahey) *qckly away and sn led: rdn over 1f out: drvn ins fnl f: hdd on line* **11/1**

2 **3** *½* **Jamboree Girl**[13] 3942 2-8-4 0 DuranFentiman 2 70
(Tim Easterby) *trckd ldrs: hdwy on inner 2f out: swtchd lft and effrt jst over 1f out: sn rdn and styd on to chal wl ins fnl f: no ex towards fin* **5/2**[1]

4 *2 ½* **Born To Fly (IRE)** 2-8-4 0 JimmyQuinn 1 61
(Gary Harrison) *towards rr: hdwy on inner 2f out: effrt and n.m.r over 1f out: kpt on fnl f: nrst fin* **7/1**

2220 **5** *hd* **Lilo Lil**[69] 2147 2-8-4 0 (p) JoeFanning 7 60
(David C Griffiths) *cl up: rdn wl over 1f out: drvn appr fnl f and grad wknd* **4/1**[2]

26 **6** *3 ¼* **Bajan Rebel**[31] 3350 2-8-4 0 JamesSullivan 5 49
(Michael Easterby) *trckd ldng pair: swtchd lft and hdwy 1/2-way: rdn over 1f out: sn wknd* **4/1**[2]

00 **7** *3 ¼* **Fuel Injection**[92] 1573 2-8-11 0 BarryMcHugh 3 44
(Paul Midgley) *a in rr* **20/1**

8 *2 ¼* **Shikari** 2-9-2 0 RobertWinston 9 41
(Robin Bastiman) *wnt lft s: sn chsng ldng pair: rdn along over 2f out: sn wknd* **20/1**

1m 2.79s (-0.71) **Going Correction** -0.35s/f (Firm) 8 Ran SP% **113.2**
Speed ratings (Par 94): **91,90,90,86,85 80,75,71**
toteswingers 1&2 £13.90, 2&3 £5.10, 1&3 £3.90 CSF £66.89 TOTE £6.50: £1.50, £2.40, £1.40; EX 66.30 Trifecta £408.00 Pool: £2147.69 - 3.94 winning units..
Owner Mrs J Ryan **Bred** M Phelan **Trained** Hambleton, N Yorks

FOCUS
The rail around the bottom bend was moved in to provide fresh ground, adding 12yds to all races except 5f. Just an ordinary maiden with the fifth the guide rated a little below her early season form.

4371 RACING UK HAS MADE LEE'S DAY H'CAP (DIV I) 5f
2:30 (2:33) (Class 6) (0-60,60) 3-Y-0+ £2,264 (£673; £336; £168) Stalls Low

Form RPR

20 **1** **Choc'A'Moca (IRE)**[22] 3630 6-9-10 **60** (v) MickyFenton 2 69
(Paul Midgley) *mde all: rdn over 1f out: drvn ins fnl f: kpt on strly* **6/1**

063 **2** *¾* **Busy Bimbo (IRE)**[3] 4292 4-8-10 **46** oh1 PaddyAspell 10 52
(Alan Berry) *towards rr: hdwy on outer wl over 1f out: sn rdn and str run ins fnl f: drvn: hung rt and no ex last 75yds* **40/1**

-043 **3** *hd* **See Vermont**[21] 3654 5-8-10 **46** RobertWinston 8 52
(Robin Bastiman) *trckd ldrs: effrt over 1f out: swtchd lft and rdn ent fnl f: ev ch tl drvn: n.m.r and no ex last 75yds* **7/1**

3542 **4** *4 ½* **Ingenti**[11] 4009 5-9-7 **57** PaulMulrennan 6 46
(Christopher Wilson) *cl up: rdn to chal wl over 1f out: ev ch tl drvn and wknd ent fnl f* **9/4**[1]

0503 **5** *¾* **You'relikemefrank**[31] 3325 7-8-10 **46** (p) GrahamLee 1 33
(Richard Ford) *chsd ldrs on inner: rdn along wl over 1f out: sn one pce* **11/2**[3]

3244 **6** *1 ¼* **Headstight (IRE)**[11] 4009 4-9-2 **52** (p) LeeTopliss 11 34
(Paul Midgley) *chsd ldrs: rdn along over 2f out: sn no imp* **4/1**[2]

-303 **7** *shd* **Done Dreaming (IRE)**[14] 3929 3-8-13 **58** GeorgeChaloner(5) 9 40
(Richard Fahey) *towards rr: rdn along 1/2-way: n.d* **10/1**

4035 **8** *nk* **Chester Deelyte (IRE)**[110] 1221 5-8-11 **47** (p) PJMcDonald 4 28
(Lisa Williamson) *dwlt: a in rr* **25/1**

0000 **9** *1 ¼* **Ivestar (IRE)**[11] 4009 8-9-6 **56** (vt) GrahamGibbons 12 32
(Michael Easterby) *chsd ldrs: prom on outer 1/2-way: sn rdn and wknd wl over 1f out* **18/1**

0500 **10** *½* **Scarlet Strand**[130] 923 3-8-7 **47** AndrewMullen 5 21
(Andrew Hollinshead) *cl up: rdn along wl over 1f out: sn wknd* **50/1**

1m 2.01s (-1.49) **Going Correction** -0.35s/f (Firm)
WFA 3 from 4yo+ 4lb 10 Ran SP% **115.5**
Speed ratings (Par 101): **97,95,95,88,87 85,84,84,82,81**
toteswingers 1&2 £34.00, 2&3 £22.10, 1&3 £7.40 CSF £218.56 CT £1758.74 TOTE £7.10: £2.70, £9.00, £1.80; EX 148.90 Trifecta £1184.80 Pool: £2977.86 - 1.88 winning units..
Owner John Milburn - Andrew Stephenson **Bred** Yeomanstown Stud **Trained** Westow, N Yorks

FOCUS
The first leg of a moderate sprint handicap. The winner goes well at this time of year and has the scope to rate higher.

4372 128TH YEAR OF THE WATT MEMORIAL H'CAP 2m 35y
3:00 (3:00) (Class 4) (0-85,78) 3-Y-O+ **£6,469** (£1,925; £962; £481) **Stalls** Low

Form RPR
0-60 **1** **Body Language (IRE)**[38] 3099 5-9-11 **77**.....................(p) GrahamLee 4 87
(Ian Williams) *hld up in rr: hdwy over 4f out: pushed along 3f out: rdn over 1f out: swtchd to outer and styd on strly fnl f to ld last 75yds* **11/4**[1]
215 **2** 2 ¼ **Platinum (IRE)**[32] 3284 6-9-12 **78**.....................(p) RussKennemore 3 85
(Philip Kirby) *trckd ldng pair: hdwy and cl up over 2f out: sn chal and rdn: drvn to ld jst ins fnl f: hdd and one pce last 75yds* **13/2**
-042 **3** 2 **Nashville (IRE)**[23] 3609 4-9-2 **68**.................................. TonyHamilton 1 73
(Richard Fahey) *trckd ldng pair on inner: pushed along 7f out: rdn and outpcd over 2f out: styd on u.p ent fnl f: sn drvn and one pce* **3/1**[2]
4301 **4** 2 **Tartan Jura**[13] 3944 5-9-9 **75**...(p) JoeFanning 5 77
(Mark Johnston) *trckd ldr: cl up 1/2-way: pushed along over 3f out: rdn over 2f out: drvn and one pce fr over 1f out* **10/3**[3]
43-5 **5** shd **Mojolika**[9] 3065 5-9-8 **74**.. GrahamGibbons 2 76
(Tim Easterby) *sn led: jnd and pushed along over 3f out: rdn 2f out: drvn over 1f out: hdd & wknd ins fnl f* **5/1**
3-60 **6** 20 **Up Ten Down Two (IRE)**[27] 3480 4-8-11 **70**......... MatthewHopkins(7) 6 48
(Michael Easterby) *in tch: pushed along over 7f out: rdn and outpcd fr wl over 3f out* **16/1**

3m 30.72s (-9.08) **Going Correction** -0.40s/f (Firm) **6** Ran SP% **110.6**
Speed ratings (Par 105): **106,104,103,102,102 92**
toteswingers 1&2 £3.60, 2&3 £5.30, 1&3 £3.00 CSF £19.88 TOTE £4.10: £1.70, £2.50; EX 20.30 Trifecta £51.90 Pool: £1574.02 - 22.71 winning units..
Owner Farranamanagh **Bred** Michael Morrissey **Trained** Portway, Worcs

FOCUS
An ordinary staying handicap and the visual impression was that Mojolika (winner of this race in 2011, second last year) went fast enough up front, hassled by Tartan Jura, and the pace collapsed in the straight. The form makes sense though rated around the htird, fourth and fifth.

4373 G1RACINGTRENDS.COM H'CAP 1m 100y
3:30 (3:30) (Class 4) (0-80,80) 3-Y-O+ **£4,690** (£1,395; £697; £348) **Stalls** Low

Form RPR
0225 **1** **Robert The Painter (IRE)**[18] 3777 5-9-9 **75**.............(v) DanielTudhope 5 84
(David O'Meara) *sn trcking ldr: cl up 3f out: chal over 2f out: rdn and slt ld appr fnl f: sn drvn: carried lft and sltly hmpd towards fin: kpt on wl* **9/2**[2]
0320 **2** nk **Cono Zur (FR)**[15] 3895 6-9-0 **66**..................................... JamesSullivan 7 74
(Ruth Carr) *sn led: jnd over 2f out and sn rdn: narrowly hdd appr fnl f: drvn and edgd lft last 100yds: no ex* **11/1**
05-5 **3** 1 **Dame Nellie Melba**[11] 4013 3-8-8 **68**.................................. JoeFanning 4 72
(Mark Johnston) *trckd ldng pair: swtchd lft and hdwy over 1f out: rdn ent fnl f: kpt on same pce* **9/2**[2]
4003 **4** 2 **Gold Show**[17] 3827 4-9-3 **69**... PaulMulrennan 1 70
(Edwin Tuer) *trckd ldrs on inner: effrt over 2f out: sn rdn and no imp appr fnl f* **6/1**[3]
3240 **5** hd **Shadowtime**[11] 4007 8-9-11 **77**.. BarryMcHugh 6 78
(Tracy Waggott) *hld up: hdwy 3f out: rdn to chse ldrs wl over 1f out: sn drvn and no imp fnl f* **12/1**
6-56 **6** 1 **Daneside (IRE)**[15] 3901 6-8-13 **65**.................................... RobertWinston 2 63
(Gary Harrison) *hld up in rr: effrt and sme hdwy over 2f out: rdn along wl over 1f out: n.d* **7/1**
0344 **7** 2 ¼ **Kalk Bay (IRE)**[20] 3684 6-10-0 **80**..............................(t) GrahamGibbons 3 73
(Michael Easterby) *trckd ldrs: rdn along over 2f out: drvn over 1f out: sn btn* **2/1**[1]

1m 43.75s (-3.85) **Going Correction** -0.40s/f (Firm)
WFA 3 from 4yo+ 8lb **7** Ran SP% **112.5**
Speed ratings (Par 105): **103,102,101,99,99 98,96**
toteswingers 1&2 £7.50, 2&3 £7.40, 1&3 £4.70 CSF £48.86 TOTE £4.80: £2.00, £6.00; EX 37.70 Trifecta £112.10 Pool: £2471.46 - 16.52 winning units..
Owner Stephen Humphreys **Bred** Ballylinch Stud **Trained** Nawton, N Yorks
■ Stewards' Enquiry : James Sullivan two-day ban: careless riding (Jul 30-Aug 1)

FOCUS
There wasn't much change to the running positions with the winner sat second before overhauling the long-time leader, while the third was always in bronze medal spot, but the form looks fair enough rated around the placed horses.

4374 TIMMY BEAR IS 50 H'CAP 1m 1f 207y
4:00 (4:01) (Class 6) (0-65,65) 3-Y-O **£2,385** (£704; £352) **Stalls** Low

Form RPR
-600 **1** **Bahamamay**[15] 3893 3-9-0 **58**.. LeeTopliss 2 65
(Richard Fahey) *sn led: rdn 2f out: hdd narrowly ent fnl f: drvn and rallied to ld again last 100yds: kpt on wl* **11/2**[3]
0611 **2** ½ **Rocket Ronnie (IRE)**[11] 4008 3-9-6 **64**............................ BarryMcHugh 6 70+
(David Nicholls) *trckd ldrs: hdwy 3f out: swtchd to outer and effrt to chse wnr over 2f out: rdn to chal wl over 1f out: drvn and slt ld ent fnl f: hdd and no ex last 110yds* **15/8**[1]
-002 **3** 2 ½ **Bold And Free**[8] 4122 3-9-7 **65**.. MickyFenton 8 66
(David Elsworth) *hld up and bhd: hdwy on wd outside wl over 2f out: rdn wl over 1f out: styd on u.p fnl f: nrst fin* **7/2**[2]
060- **4** ¾ **Bollin Billy**[334] 5254 3-8-2 **46** oh1...................................... DuranFentiman 1 46
(Tim Easterby) *trckd ldrs on inner: hdwy 4f out: rdn along over 2f out: drvn and one pce appr fnl f* **33/1**
400- **5** 1 ¼ **Smooth Handle**[306] 6156 3-8-2 **46**............................(b[1]) JamesSullivan 4 43
(Danielle McCormick) *plld hrd: in tch: lost pl and towards rr 1/2-way: hdwy over 2f out: sn rdn and one pce* **66/1**
0540 **6** nk **Lexi's Dancer**[34] 3194 3-8-12 **56**...................................... GrahamLee 3 53
(Ian Williams) *t.k.h: chsd wnr: pushed along and sltly outpcd over 3f out: rdn over 2f out: sn drvn and wknd wl over 1f out* **7/2**[2]
6-50 **7** 1 ½ **El Molino Blanco**[11] 4008 3-8-11 **55**.............................. GrahamGibbons 7 49
(Michael Easterby) *dwlt and wnt lft s: towards rr: hdwy to trck ldrs over 3f out: effrt over 2f out: sn rdn and wknd wl over 1f out* **7/1**
0000 **8** 13 **Riponian**[18] 3772 3-8-2 **46**.. JoeFanning 5 15
(Susan Corbett) *prom on outer: chsd wnr 1/2-way: rdn along wl over 2f out: sn wknd* **25/1**

2m 5.43s (-1.57) **Going Correction** -0.40s/f (Firm) **8** Ran SP% **115.4**
Speed ratings (Par 98): **90,89,87,87,86 85,84,74**
toteswingers 1&2 £2.60, 2&3 £2.30, 1&3 £4.80 CSF £16.25 CT £41.19 TOTE £6.10: £2.10, £1.30, £1.30; EX 16.70 Trifecta £48.40 Pool: £3541.70 - 54.85 winning units..
Owner Benatom Racing 1 **Bred** Trebles Holford Farm Thoroughbreds **Trained** Musley Bank, N Yorks

FOCUS
This wasn't much of a race with the fourth, fifth and sixth giving the contest perspective.

4375 RACING REPLAY, ALL TODAY'S RACING SKY432 H'CAP 7f 100y
4:30 (4:30) (Class 5) (0-75,72) 3-Y-O+ **£3,234** (£962; £481; £240) **Stalls** Low

Form RPR
4021 **1** **Relight My Fire**[8] 4113 3-8-10 **61**.......................................(b) DavidAllan 1 73+
(Tim Easterby) *trckd ldrs: hdwy 2f out: rdn to ld appr fnl f: sn clr: readily* **9/4**[1]
6510 **2** 3 ¼ **Blue Maisey**[11] 4007 5-9-7 **65**.. PaulMulrennan 10 72
(Edwin Tuer) *trckd ldrs on inner: swtchd lft and hdwy wl over 1f out: rdn to chse wnr ent fnl f: sn drvn and no imp* **17/2**
3540 **3** ¾ **Fame Again**[5] 4198 5-9-13 **71**.. JamesSullivan 6 76
(Michael Easterby) *dwlt and sltly hmpd s: t.k.h and hld up towards rr: hdwy on inner 2f out: nt clr run and swtchd lft over 1f out: rdn and styd on wl fnl f: nrst fin* **10/1**
4602 **4** ¾ **Eeny Mac (IRE)**[11] 4005 6-9-3 **61**...................................... AndrewElliott 4 63
(Neville Bycroft) *cl up: rdn to dispute ld 2f out: drvn wl over 1f out: sn one pce* **9/2**[2]
6500 **5** hd **Summer Dancer (IRE)**[34] 3192 9-9-3 **61**......................... MickyFenton 9 63
(Paul Midgley) *s.i.s and bhd: gd hdwy over 3f out: rdn wl over 1f out: kpt on fnl f: nrst fin* **20/1**
-050 **6** ¾ **Destination Aim**[25] 3543 6-9-2 **65**................................... JasonHart(5) 5 65
(Frederick Watson) *slt ld: rdn 2f out: drvn over 1f out: hdd appr fnl f: grad wknd* **40/1**
6000 **7** 1 **Mujaadel (USA)**[11] 4007 8-9-10 **68**...............................(p) JoeFanning 3 66
(David Nicholls) *dwlt and towards rr: hdwy 2f out: sn rdn and kpt on one pce appr fnl f* **9/1**
3450 **8** nk **Last Destination (IRE)**[10] 4070 5-8-9 **53** oh2............ GrahamGibbons 7 50
(Nigel Tinkler) *a towards rr* **8/1**
2501 **9** ½ **Just The Tonic**[6] 4160 6-9-7 **68** 6ex.................................. RaulDaSilva(3) 2 64
(Marjorie Fife) *in tch: rdn along wl over 2f out: sn wknd* **6/1**[3]
14-0 **10** shd **Evanescent (IRE)**[18] 3778 4-10-0 **72**............................. MichaelO'Connell 8 68
(John Quinn) *chsd ldng pair: rdn along 3f out: sn wknd* **33/1**

1m 30.65s (-3.15) **Going Correction** -0.40s/f (Firm)
WFA 3 from 4yo+ 7lb **10** Ran SP% **114.1**
Speed ratings (Par 103): **102,98,97,96,96 95,94,94,93,93**
toteswingers 1&2 £4.40, 2&3 £16.00, 1&3 £7.10 CSF £21.11 CT £161.32 TOTE £2.60: £1.70, £3.00, £3.20; EX 18.80 Trifecta £102.00 Pool: £3017.11 - 22.18 winning units..
Owner Jonathan Gill **Bred** J Gill **Trained** Great Habton, N Yorks
■ Stewards' Enquiry : Jason Hart three-day ban: careless riding (Jul 30,Aug 1-2)

FOCUS
Just a modest handicap but a pretty good pace and the form looks decent for the level, rated around the third and fourth.

4376 DOROTHY LAIRD MEMORIAL TROPHY H'CAP (LADIES RACE) 1m 1f 207y
5:00 (5:00) (Class 6) (0-65,65) 4-Y-O+ **£2,385** (£704; £352) **Stalls** Low

Form RPR
0-10 **1** **City Ground (USA)**[15] 3889 6-10-2 **60**........................ MissSBrotherton 3 70
(Michael Easterby) *set stdy pce: qcknd over 3f out: rdn along 2f out: drvn clr ent fnl f: kpt on strly* **5/1**
-552 **2** 3 ¼ **Hernando Torres**[10] 4071 5-9-10 **59**.........................(p) AnnaHesketh(5) 6 63
(Michael Easterby) *t.k.h: trckd ldrs: hdwy to chse wnr 1/2-way: cl up over 2f out: rdn along wl over 1f out: drvn and one pce ent fnl f* **9/2**[3]
2343 **3** nse **Cabal**[15] 3895 6-9-10 **54**..(v) MissCWalton 4 58
(Andrew Crook) *midfield: hdwy on inner 2f out: rdn over 1f out: n.m.r and styd on u.p fnl f: nrst fin* **11/1**
3502 **4** nk **Meglio Ancora**[9] 4099 6-9-8 **52**.. LucyAlexander 2 55
(Richard Ford) *t.k.h: trckd ldrs: hdwy to chse ldng pair 2f out: rdn over 1f out: drvn and one pce fnl f* **4/1**[2]
2234 **5** 1 ¾ **Spanish Plume**[19] 3721 5-10-4 **62**.................................(b) MrsCBartley 8 62
(Andrew Hollinshead) *t.k.h: hld up towards rr: swtchd lft and effrt wl over 1f out: sn rdn and kpt on fnl f: nrst fin* **13/2**
060- **6** 1 ¼ **Embsay Crag**[78] 3564 7-10-7 **65**....................................... EvaMoscrop 9 62
(Philip Kirby) *hld up towards rr: hdwy on wd outside wl over 2f out: rdn wl over 1f out: edgd rt and no imp fnl f* **10/1**
-004 **7** 3 ½ **Valentine's Gift**[11] 4010 5-9-3 **47**..................................(p) JulieBurke 10 38
(Neville Bycroft) *chsd ldrs: rdn along wl over 2f out: wknd wl over 1f out* **22/1**
2300 **8** shd **Merchant Of Medici**[15] 3889 6-10-2 **65**................. MissBeckySmith(5) 7 56
(Micky Hammond) *t.k.h: trckd ldrs on outer: effrt wl over 2f out: rdn along wl over 1f out: sn wknd* **7/2**[1]
4000 **9** 5 **Landesherr (GER)**[10] 4052 6-9-2 **46** oh1.................. MissHCuthbert 11 27
(Thomas Cuthbert) *a towards rr* **40/1**
00-0 **10** 2 **Grethel (IRE)**[41] 2974 9-9-2 **46** oh1........................... MissJRRichards 1 23
(Alan Berry) *s.i.s: a in rr* **80/1**
0600 **11** ¾ **Rolen Sly**[13] 3947 4-9-2 **46** oh1................................... ShirleyTeasdale 5 22
(Brian Rothwell) *cl up: rdn along over 3f out: sn wknd* **66/1**

2m 6.28s (-0.72) **Going Correction** -0.40s/f (Firm) **11** Ran SP% **117.3**
Speed ratings (Par 101): **86,83,83,83,81 80,77,77,73,72 71**
toteswingers 1&2 £5.30, 2&3 £10.60, 1&3 £13.90 CSF £27.11 CT £238.64 TOTE £6.30: £3.70, £1.30, £3.00; EX 22.00 Trifecta £248.40 Pool: £3109.93 - 9.38 winning units..
Owner Steve Hull **Bred** Mrs E Scott Jr & Mrs L Macelree **Trained** Sheriff Hutton, N Yorks

FOCUS
Form to treat with caution due to the slow pace, although it looks straightforward enough rated around the placed horses.

4377 RACING UK HAS MADE LEE'S DAY H'CAP (DIV II) 5f
5:35 (5:35) (Class 6) (0-60,60) 3-Y-O+ **£2,264** (£673; £336; £168) **Stalls** Low

Form RPR
-023 **1** **Niceonemyson**[10] 4050 4-8-11 **54**.................................... KevinStott(7) 3 64
(Christopher Wilson) *slt ld 2f: cl up: rdn wl over 1f out: drvn ent fnl f: kpt on to ld last 75yds* **4/1**[2]
0001 **2** nk **Sir Geoffrey (IRE)**[12] 3994 7-9-4 **54**..........................(p) JamesSullivan 2 63
(Scott Dixon) *cl up: led after 2f: rdn along wl over 1f out: drvn ent fnl f: hdd and no ex last 75yds* **9/1**
55-0 **3** nk **Emily Hall**[69] 2170 4-8-11 **47**.. RoystonFfrench 6 56+
(Bryan Smart) *dwlt and towards rr: hdwy 2f out: sn swtchd rt to inner: effrt and swtchd lft jst over 1f out: kpt on wl fnl f* **20/1**
1600 **4** 3 ¾ **Edith Anne**[40] 3025 3-9-6 **60**.. MickyFenton 1 54
(Paul Midgley) *chsd ldrs: rdn to chse ldng pair over 1f out: sn drvn and one pce* **16/1**
0050 **5** 1 **Mousie**[21] 3660 4-8-10 **46** oh1.. AndrewElliott 7 37
(Alan McCabe) *prom: rdn along 2f out: drvn over 1f out: grad wknd* **50/1**
2240 **6** shd **Blue Noodles**[11] 4005 7-8-13 **54**................................(v) AdamCarter(5) 10 44+
(Neville Bycroft) *bhd: rdn along over 2f out: kpt on u.p fnl f: nrst fin* **14/1**

The Form Book Flat, Raceform Ltd, Compton, RG20 6NL.

423 **7** 3/4 **John Coffey (IRE)**[5] 4220 4-9-3 **53** AndrewMullen 5 41
(Michael Appleby) *chsd ldrs: rdn along 2f out: drvn wl over 1f out: sn btn* **15/8**[1]
040 **8** *hd* **Trending (IRE)**[13] 3949 4-9-8 **58** (p) JoeFanning 4 45
(Jeremy Gask) *towards rr: hdwy 2f out: sn rdn and n.d* **9/2**[3]
665- **9** 3 1/4 **Too Ambitious**[337] 5177 4-8-5 **46** JackDuern(5) 11 21
(Andrew Hollinshead) *dwlt and swvd lft s: sddle slipped: a towards rr* **40/1**
0064 **10** 1 **Wicked Wilma (IRE)**[9] 4102 9-8-13 **49** GrahamLee 8 21
(Alan Berry) *chsd ldrs on wd outside: effrt 2f out: sn rdn and wknd* **8/1**
0-03 **11** 4 1/2 **Isle Of Ellis (IRE)**[25] 3547 6-8-5 **46** oh1 (v) ShirleyTeasdale(5) 9
(Ron Barr) *chsd ldrs: rdn along over 2f out: sn wknd* **25/1**

1m 1.55s (-1.95) **Going Correction** -0.35s/f (Firm)
WFA 3 from 4yo+ 4lb **11 Ran SP% 119.6**
Speed ratings (Par 101): **101,100,100,94,92 92,91,90,85,83 76**
toteswingers 1&2 £8.40, 2&3 £27.70, 1&3 £13.30 CSF £38.90 CT £653.36 TOTE £6.20: £1.90, £3.10, £5.90; EX 36.10 Trifecta £387.00 Pool: £2195.03 - 4.25 winning units..
Owner David Bartlett **Bred** Mrs Andrea Bartlett **Trained** Manfield, N Yorks

FOCUS
The second division of a moderate sprint handicap and the first two had the race to themselves for most of the way, disputing the lead clear of the others. They help to set the level.
T/Plt: £200.20 to a £1 stake. Pool of £69138.74 - 252.07 winning tickets. T/Qpdt: £38.30 to a £1 stake. Pool of £5235.74 - 100.90 winning tickets. JR

4163 KEMPTON (A.W) (R-H)

Tuesday, July 16

OFFICIAL GOING: Standard (watered)
Wind: virtually nil Weather: very warm and sunny

4378 SPARKS MEDICAL RESEARCH CLASSIFIED STKS 6f (P)

5:30 (5:30) (Class 5) 3-Y-O **£1,940** (£577; £288; £144) **Stalls** Low

Form RPR
-262 **1** **Bapak Muda (USA)**[7] 4144 3-9-0 60 NeilCallan 6 72+
(Kevin Ryan) *mde all: rdn ent fnl 2f: pressed and drvn ins fnl f: styd on wl fnl 100yds: drvn out* **5/4**[1]
1660 **2** 1 1/4 **Elusive Gold (IRE)**[20] 3699 3-9-0 63 WilliamBuick 3 68
(J W Hills) *chsd ldrs: effrt and hung rt over 2f out: sn swtchd lft and hdwy: chsd wnr 1f out: one pce and no imp fnl 100yds* **7/1**
3143 **3** 1 **Eastern Dragon (IRE)**[15] 3903 3-8-9 65 WilliamTwiston-Davies(5) 4 65
(Michael Scudamore) *in tch in midfield: effrt and rdn 2f out: styd on to go 3rd ins fnl f: nvr gng pce to threaten wnr* **11/4**[2]
5603 **4** 1 3/4 **Triple Aitch (USA)**[19] 3740 3-9-0 62 (b[1]) JamesDoyle 1 60
(Gay Kelleway) *chsd wnr for 1f: chsd ldrs after tl drvn to chse wnr again over 1f out tl 1f out: wknd ins fnl f* **13/2**[3]
-000 **5** 2 1/2 **Grace Hull**[15] 3903 3-9-0 62 (b[1]) TomQueally 8 53
(J S Moore) *s.i.s: hld up in tch in rr: rdn over 2f out: sme hdwy 2f out: no prog over 1f out* **16/1**
1444 **6** 3/4 **Princess Cammie (IRE)**[20] 3699 3-8-9 56 (p) MichaelJMMurphy(5) 7 50
(John Bridger) *chsd ldr after 1f tl over 1f out: wknd ins fnl f* **20/1**
6-40 **7** 7 **Just Past Andover (IRE)**[138] 828 3-9-0 64 KierenFox 2 29
(Lee Carter) *t.k.h: hld up in tch towards rr: drvn 2f out: sn wknd* **33/1**
-000 **8** 1 1/4 **Cool And Clear (IRE)**[16] 3859 3-8-11 43 (v) RyanPowell(3) 5 26
(Pat Eddery) *hld up in tch in last pair: rdn and struggling over 2f out: wknd over 1f out* **66/1**

1m 13.65s (0.55) **Going Correction** +0.125s/f (Slow) **8 Ran SP% 112.0**
Speed ratings (Par 100): **101,99,98,95,92 91,82,80**
toteswingers 1&2 £2.50, 2&3 £3.80, 1&3 £1.40 CSF £10.23 TOTE £1.80: £1.10, £3.00, £1.10; EX 12.60 Trifecta £27.40 Pool: £2661.36 - 72.65 winning units..
Owner T A Rahman **Bred** Flaxman Holdings Limited **Trained** Hambleton, N Yorks

FOCUS
This moderate classified event for 3-y-os. The winner is going the right way.

4379 SPARKS INNOVATION FUND/BRITISH STALLION STUDS EBF MAIDEN STKS 6f (P)

6:00 (6:01) (Class 5) 2-Y-O **£2,911** (£866; £432; £216) **Stalls** Low

Form RPR
1 **About Turn** 2-9-5 0 MickaelBarzalona 1 78+
(Saeed bin Suroor) *trckd ldrs: rdn and effrt on inner over 1f out: led ins fnl f: r.o strly and gng away at fin* **5/2**[1]
22 **2** 1 3/4 **Exceeder**[19] 3737 2-9-5 0 SilvestreDeSousa 5 73
(Marco Botti) *chsd ldr: rdn and ev ch ent fnl 2f: led narrowly over 1f out: hung rt and hdd ins fnl f: no ex* **7/2**[2]
4 **3** 1 1/2 **Steele Ranger**[49] 2741 2-9-5 0 WilliamBuick 3 70
(Peter Chapple-Hyam) *led: rdn ent fnl 2f: hdd but stl ev ch over 1f out: jst beginning to struggle whn squeezed for room and hmpd ins fnl f* **7/2**[2]
4 3 1/2 **Stella Clavisque (IRE)** 2-9-5 0 NeilCallan 6 58+
(Brian Meehan) *chsd ldrs: rdn 2f out: n.d to ldrs but kpt on same pce after* **50/1**
6 **5** 1 1/4 **Aya's Gift**[22] 3631 2-9-5 0 TomMcLaughlin 7 54+
(Ed Walker) *in tch in midfield: rdn and effrt jst over 2f out: outpcd and btn over 1f out: plugged on same pce after* **40/1**
06 **6** 1/2 **Dont Have It Then**[17] 3836 2-9-5 0 TomQueally 4 53
(Willie Musson) *in tch in midfield: rdn and outpcd 2f out: no threat to ldrs and one pce after* **12/1**[3]
0 **7** 1/2 **Fiftyshadesfreed (IRE)**[30] 3374 2-9-5 0 DaneO'Neill 10 51
(George Baker) *s.i.s: in tch in last trio: rdn over 4f out: sme late hdwy: nvr trbld ldrs* **50/1**
8 1 **Buy And Sell (IRE)** 2-9-5 0 SeanLevey 8 48
(Ed McMahon) *hld up in midfield: rdn and outpcd over 2f out: n.d after* **33/1**
5 **9** 1/2 **Headlong (IRE)**[25] 3536 2-9-5 0 KierenFallon 9 47
(Brian Meehan) *chsd ldrs: rdn over 2f out: btn 2f out and sn wknd* **7/2**[2]
10 3 1/4 **Picanight** 2-9-0 0 JohnFahy 2 32
(Eve Johnson Houghton) *s.i.s: a towards rr: effrt on inner ent fnl 2f: sn wknd* **25/1**
11 13 **Symphony Of Pearls** 2-8-11 0 RyanPowell(3) 12
(Dai Burchell) *s.i.s: a bhd: lost tch 2f out* **100/1**

1m 13.99s (0.89) **Going Correction** +0.125s/f (Slow) **11 Ran SP% 117.1**
Speed ratings (Par 94): **99,96,94,90,88 87,87,85,85,80 63**
toteswingers 1&2 £3.00, 2&3 £2.20, 1&3 £3.30 CSF £10.82 TOTE £2.60: £1.10, £1.10, £2.00; EX 14.60 Trifecta £26.00 Pool: £1778.28 - 51.19 winning units..
Owner Godolphin **Bred** Cheveley Park Stud Ltd **Trained** Newmarket, Suffolk
■ Stewards' Enquiry : Silvestre De Sousa caution: careless riding

FOCUS
This rates just a fair 2-y-o maiden with the principals coming clear. The winner can improve on the bare form.

4380 BETVICTOR OPEN CHAMPIONSHIPS 8 PLACES EXCLUSIVE H'CAP 2m (P)

6:30 (6:31) (Class 6) (0-60,64) 4-Y-O+ **£1,940** (£577; £288; £144) **Stalls** Low

Form RPR
/353 **1** **Star Alliance (IRE)**[20] 3688 5-9-7 **59** (b) WilliamBuick 14 66
(Ian Williams) *towards rr: hdwy to chse ldrs 12f out: clsd on ldng trio 5f out: wnt 2nd 3f out: rdn and ev ch over 2f out: led ins fnl f: doing little in front and drvn: a doing enough: styd on* **7/2**[1]
0542 **2** 3/4 **Steely**[21] 3655 5-9-7 **59** TomQueally 11 65
(Gary Moore) *chsd ldr: led 10f out: rdn and hrd pressed 2f out: hdd ins fnl f: no ex fnl 100yds* **10/1**
4 **3** 3/4 **Gunboat (IRE)**[22] 3625 5-8-11 **49** JamesDoyle 6 54
(Ed Dunlop) *chsd ldrs: clsd and wl in tch 5f out: pressing ldrs and swtchd rt over 1f out: kpt on same pce ins fnl f* **9/2**[2]
0350 **4** *nk* **Between The Lines (IRE)**[6] 4166 4-9-0 **57** ThomasGarner(5) 2 62
(Anthony Middleton) *hld up in rr: clsd on ldrs 5f out: hdwy on outer to chse ldrs over 3f out: drvn and pressing ldrs 2f out: one pce fnl f* **25/1**
-021 **5** 3 1/2 **Proud Times (USA)**[7] 4147 7-9-12 **64** 6ex (p) GeorgeBaker 13 65
(Ali Brewer) *chsd ldrs: clsd and trcking ldrs 4f out: rdn and outpcd 2f out: plugged on same pce after* **7/1**
0-00 **6** 1 **Layla's King**[13] 3946 5-9-3 **55** DaneO'Neill 7 54
(David C Griffiths) *stdd s: hld up in rr: clsd and wl in tch 5f out: effrt and carried v wd bnd 3f out: rallied u.p and modest 7th 2f out: kpt on but no threat to ldrs* **9/1**
1446 **7** 12 **Midnight Sequel**[31] 3312 4-9-1 **53** RichardKingscote 4 38
(Michael Blake) *hld up off the pce in midfield: clsd and wl in tch 5f out: rdn and struggling over 2f out: drvn and wknd 2f out* **8/1**
0-56 **8** 13 **Kristallo (GER)**[13] 3952 8-9-1 **53** (b) JohnFahy 5 22
(Dai Burchell) *sn rdn along to ld: stdd gallop 12f out: hdd 10f out: chsd ldrs after tl wknd over 2f out: eased ins fnl f* **20/1**
1200 **9** 20 **Gladstone (IRE)**[29] 3406 5-9-1 **53** LiamKeniry 1
(Polly Gundry) *hld up off the pce towards rr: clsd and wl in tch 5f out: drvn 3f out: sn wknd: t.o and eased fnl f* **12/1**
0000 **10** 13 **If What And Maybe**[20] 3688 5-8-2 **45** (v) NatashaEaton(5) 10
(John Ryan) *stdd and swtchd rt after s: a bhd: rdn and lost tch 6f out: t.o 3f out* **100/1**
-115 **11** 7 **Hoonose**[103] 1348 4-9-6 **58** (v) RyanMoore 8
(Pat Eddery) *chsd ldrs: wnt 2nd over 8f out tl jst over 3f out: sn hung lft and dropped out: rdr looking down and eased after: t.o fnl 2f* **11/2**[3]
/0-0 **12** 15 **Crystal High**[33] 3252 5-8-12 **50** (t) TomMcLaughlin 9
(Mrs Ilka Gansera-Leveque) *t.k.h early: hld up off the pce in midfield: clsd and wl in tch 5f out: rdn 3f out: sn wknd: t.o 2f out: eased* **50/1**
00/0 **13** 11 **Bollywood (IRE)**[14] 3580 10-8-4 **45** RyanPowell(3) 3
(Alison Batchelor) *chsd ldrs tl lost pl qckly 9f out: t.o fnl 5f out* **66/1**

3m 32.32s (2.22) **Going Correction** +0.125s/f (Slow) **13 Ran SP% 119.2**
Speed ratings (Par 101): **99,98,98,98,96 95,89,83,73,66 63,55,50**
toteswingers 1&2 £7.80, 2&3 £11.40, 1&3 £3.00 CSF £37.74 CT £163.24 TOTE £4.90: £1.70, £4.80, £2.60; EX 37.50 Trifecta £231.00 Pool: £1827.12 - 5.92 winning units..
Owner Ian Williams **Bred** Noel Carter **Trained** Portway, Worcs
■ Stewards' Enquiry : Natasha Eaton five-day ban: used whip when out of contention (Jul 30-31,Aug 1-3)

FOCUS
An ordinary staying handicap, run at a fair pace. The likes of the fourth highlight the limitations.

4381 £25 FREE BET AT BETVICTOR.COM MAIDEN STKS (DIV I) 1m (P)

7:00 (7:02) (Class 5) 3-Y-O+ **£2,587** (£770; £384; £192) **Stalls** Low

Form RPR
2 **1** **Noble Protector**[30] 3372 3-9-0 0 NeilCallan 8 85
(Stuart Kittow) *chsd ldr tl rdn to ld over 2f out: edgd lft 2f out: clr over 1f out: r.o strly: readily* **8/1**
3 **2** 3 **Don't Stare**[49] 2760 3-9-5 0 HayleyTurner 5 83
(James Fanshawe) *in tch in midfield: rdn and swtchd lft over 2f out: swtchd bk rt and chsd wnr 2f out: kpt on but no imp on wnr* **11/4**[2]
20 **3** 5 **Severiano (USA)**[92] 1570 3-9-5 0 JimmyFortune 11 72
(Roger Varian) *chsd ldrs: rdn and wnt 3rd 2f out: no ex and btn ent fnl f: wknd but hld on for 3rd fnl f* **25/1**
4 **4** 3/4 **Ruffled**[38] 3116 3-9-0 0 WilliamBuick 7 65
(John Gosden) *dwlt: hld up towards rr: hmpd after 2f: hdwy u.p 2f out: sn no imp and one pce after* **7/4**[1]
60 **5** 3/4 **Dambuster (IRE)**[29] 3417 3-9-5 0 RyanMoore 6 68+
(Sir Michael Stoute) *s.i.s: towards rr and pushed along early: plenty to and rdn 2f out: hdwy over 1f out: styng on whn n.m.r ins fnl f: no threat to ldrs but gng on fin* **15/2**[3]
2- **6** 1/2 **Catch The Cider**[252] 7613 3-9-5 0 GeorgeBaker 1 67+
(Hans Adielsson) *dwlt: hld up wl in rr: swtchd lft and stl plenty to do wl over 1f out: kpt on fnl f: nvr trbld ldrs* **8/1**
7 *nse* **Evermore (IRE)** 3-9-0 0 SilvestreDeSousa 12 62+
(Mark Johnston) *in tch in midfield on outer: effrt and rdn ent fnl 2f: drvn and no imp over 1f out: plugged on same pce after* **16/1**
0 **8** 9 **Polish Rider**[35] 3176 3-9-5 0 SeanLevey 14 46
(Richard Hannon) *hld up in midfield on outer: dropped to rr 1/2-way: rdn and wknd over 2f out: no ch whn hmpd and swtchd lft 1f out* **50/1**
5 **9** 1 **Rocky Ride (IRE)**[14] 3923 3-9-0 0 LiamKeniry 4 39
(Andrew Balding) *dwlt and pushed along early: rdn and effrt jst over 2f out: sn btn: no ch whn rn green and hung lft ins fnl f* **40/1**
10 4 **Up Tipp** 3-9-5 0 RichardMullen 9 35
(Mike Murphy) *dwlt: rn green: hmpd and lost pl after 2f: sn swtchd rt: rdn and wknd wl over 2f out* **66/1**
11 4 **Crystal Tiger** 3-9-0 0 JimCrowley 3 20
(Alan Jarvis) *t.k.h: chsd ldrs tl rdn ent fnl 2f: sn btn and fdd* **33/1**
0 **12** 3 1/4 **Babushka's Girl**[53] 2628 4-9-5 0 MarkCoumbe(3) 2 13
(Lisa Williamson) *led tl over 2f out: sn btn: fdd over 1f out* **100/1**
13 13 **Webby's Boy**[314] 5-9-10 0 RyanPowell(3) 10
(Dai Burchell) *a towards rr: rdn and dropped to last 3f out: sn wl bhd: t.o* **100/1**

1m 40.3s (0.50) **Going Correction** +0.125s/f (Slow)
WFA 3 from 4yo+ 8lb **13 Ran SP% 117.6**
Speed ratings (Par 103): **102,99,94,93,92 92,91,82,81,77 73,70,57**
toteswingers 1&2 £5.70, 2&3 £11.00, 1&3 £19.10 CSF £28.82 TOTE £6.70: £1.80, £1.50, £6.00; EX 23.80 Trifecta £407.50 Pool: £1683.68 - 3.09 winning units..
Owner The Black Type Partnership III **Bred** D R Tucker **Trained** Blackborough, Devon

FOCUS
They went an ordinary pace in this interesting maiden and most took a keen hold. The first two were clear, with the winner building on a pleasing debut.

4382 £25 FREE BET AT BETVICTOR.COM MAIDEN STKS (DIV II) 1m (P)
7:30 (7:50) (Class 5) 3-Y-0+ £2,587 (£770; £384; £192) Stalls Low

Form RPR

53- **1** **Breden (IRE)**[263] 7363 3-9-5 0 WilliamBuick 2 83+
(John Gosden) *chsd ldrs: nt clr run and sltly outpcd over 1f out: swtchd lft and rallied to chse ldr 1f out: led ins fnl f: sn in command and r.o wl: readily* **11/8**[1]

25 **2** 1 ½ **Dawn Of Empire (USA)**[37] 3136 3-9-0 0 JamesDoyle 11 73
(Roger Charlton) *chsd ldrs: rdn to ld 2f out: drvn over 1f out: hdd and one pce ins fnl f* **8/1**

3 **3** 2 ½ **I'm Fraam Govan**[41] 2989 5-9-13 0 (t) PatCosgrave 6 74
(George Baker) *in tch in midfield: effrt u.p 2f out: chsd ldng pair jst over 1f out: no imp fnl f* **3/1**[2]

4 1 ½ **Alegra** 3-9-0 0 TomQueally 7 65+
(Lady Cecil) *dwlt: pushed along and rn green in last trio: hdwy and edging lft over 1f out: kpt on steadily fnl f: nvr trbld ldrs* **10/1**

0 **5** 2 ¼ **Sweet Marwell (IRE)**[28] 3435 3-9-0 0 (t) FergusSweeney 4 58
(Jo Crowley) *chsd ldr: rdn and effrt ent fnl 2f: 4th and btn ent fnl f: wknd* **100/1**

60- **6** 1 ¼ **Red Pilgrim (IRE)**[284] 6845 3-9-5 0 KirstyMilczarek 10 60+
(James Toller) *s.i.s: hld up in last trio: rdn over 2f out: sme hdwy fnl f: nvr trbld ldrs* **50/1**

7 2 ¾ **Mu'Ajiza** 3-9-0 0 SilvestreDeSousa 3 49
(Mark Johnston) *s.i.s: in tch in midfield: rdn and struggling over 2f out: wknd wl over 1f out* **14/1**

6 **8** 1 **Gregori (IRE)**[59] 2447 3-9-5 0 KierenFallon 1 52
(Brian Meehan) *led tl rdn and hdd 2f out: sn btn: wknd over 1f out* **7/1**[3]

0-0 **9** ¾ **Szabo's Art**[7] 4152 3-9-0 0 ChrisCatlin 14 45
(Sir Mark Prescott Bt) *in tch in midfield: rdn 1/2-way: lost pl bnd 3f out: n.d but plugged on after* **100/1**

0 **10** 2 ¾ **Sleek**[11] 4013 3-9-0 0 MartinHarley 5 39
(Marco Botti) *wl in tch in midfield: rdn and effrt ent fnl 2f: fnd little and sn btn* **33/1**

0 **11** 11 **Get Going**[35] 3176 3-9-5 0 GeorgeBaker 13 18
(Hughie Morrison) *dropped to rr over 6f out and nvr travelling wl after: lost tch over 2f out* **40/1**

12 18 **Presumido (IRE)** 3-9-5 0 NeilCallan 12
(Simon Dow) *plld hrd: hld up in midfield: rdn: hung lft and nt run on over 2f out: sn bhd: t.o* **66/1**

1m 40.37s (0.57) **Going Correction** +0.125s/f (Slow)
WFA 3 from 5yo 8lb **12** Ran SP% **117.3**
Speed ratings (Par 103): **102,100,98,96,94 93,90,89,88,85 74,56**
toteswingers 1&2 £2.00, 2&3 £4.40, 1&3 £2.20 CSF £12.96 TOTE £2.20: £1.10, £1.70, £1.80; EX 11.80 Trifecta £24.40 Pool: £1503.72 - 46.05 winning units..
Owner Lady Rothschild **Bred** Mrs C L Weld **Trained** Newmarket, Suffolk

FOCUS
The second division of the 1m maiden was marginally slower than the first leg after a steady gallop. A notable step up from the winner on last year's form.

4383 DOWNLOAD THE BETVICTOR APP NOW H'CAP (LONDON MILE SERIES QUALIFIER) 1m (P)
8:00 (8:18) (Class 5) (0-75,81) 3-Y-0 £2,587 (£770; £384; £192) Stalls Low

Form RPR

212- **1** **Progenitor (IRE)**[262] 7414 3-8-13 **67** TomQueally 14 76+
(David Lanigan) *hld up in rr: stl last whn effrt on inner 2f out: str run and switching lft ins fnl f: led last strides* **13/2**[2]

-440 **2** hd **Magique (IRE)**[35] 3173 3-9-4 **72** RyanMoore 13 81
(Jeremy Noseda) *hld up towards rr: stl plenty to and effrt u.p 2f out: str run 1f out to ld fnl 50yds: hdd last strides* **16/1**

0401 **3** 1 ¾ **Mandy The Nag (USA)**[7] 4143 3-9-0 **68** 6ex KierenFallon 11 73
(Ian Williams) *chsd ldr: rdn to ld 2f out: forged in front and looked likely wnr ins fnl f: hdd and lost 2 pls fnl 50yds* **8/1**

3123 **4** hd **On With The Dance (IRE)**[15] 3901 3-9-2 **70** WilliamBuick 12 74+
(Ed Vaughan) *s.i.s: bhd: swtchd to outer after 2f: hdwy on outer over 1f out: styd on wl ins fnl f* **7/1**[3]

5202 **5** 1 **Storming (IRE)**[15] 3886 3-9-5 **73** (p) JimmyFortune 3 75
(Andrew Balding) *led: rdn and hdd 2f out: battled on wl tl no ex jst ins fnl f: wknd towards fin* **5/1**[1]

6023 **6** shd **Avatar Star (IRE)**[42] 2949 3-8-12 **66** (tp) MartinHarley 8 68
(Marco Botti) *chsd ldrs: effrt u.p 2f out: keeping on same pce and hld whn hmpd wl ins fnl f* **14/1**

-200 **7** ¾ **Nelson Quay (IRE)**[43] 2916 3-9-4 **72** (p) SteveDrowne 5 72
(Jeremy Gask) *t.k.h: hld up in midfield: rdn and lost pl over 3f out: rallied u.p 1f out: styd on u.p fnl f* **20/1**

540- **8** ½ **Unison (IRE)**[241] 7779 3-8-13 **67** NeilCallan 7 66
(Peter Makin) *in tch in midfield: rdn and effrt 2f out: styd on same pce after and hld whn hmpd fnl 100yds* **33/1**

0-65 **9** hd **Cherry Tiger**[40] 3011 3-8-11 **65** KirstyMilczarek 1 63
(James Toller) *chsd ldrs: drvn and pressed ldrs 2f out: no ex u.p 1f out: wknd fnl 100yds* **33/1**

0021 **10** 1 ¼ **Ocean Applause**[6] 4182 3-9-13 **81** 6ex (tp) BrettDoyle 9 77
(John Ryan) *in tch in midfield: rdn and outpcd 2f out: plugged on but no threat to ldrs fnl f* **5/1**[1]

32-1 **11** 1 **Captain Starlight (IRE)**[195] 14 3-9-7 **75** FergusSweeney 10 68
(Jo Crowley) *chsd ldrs: 5th and outpcd u.p 2f out: wknd ins fnl f* **12/1**

0-56 **12** 7 **Mick Duggan**[35] 3173 3-9-0 **68** DaneO'Neill 4 45
(Simon Hodgson) *a towards rr: rdn and struggling over 2f out: n.d* **20/1**

1-6 **13** 13 **Keep The Secret**[24] 3583 3-9-6 **74** JimCrowley 2 21
(William Knight) *s.i.s: sn rcvrd and in tch in midfield: rdn and btn 2f out: bhd and eased fnl f* **8/1**

3-33 **14** 3 **Watcherofthe skies**[22] 3620 3-9-6 **74** (p) JamesDoyle 6 14
(J W Hills) *in tch towards rr: lost pl over 2f out: bhd and eased ins fnl f* **25/1**

1m 40.34s (0.54) **Going Correction** +0.125s/f (Slow) **14** Ran SP% **120.9**
Speed ratings (Par 100): **102,101,100,99,98 98,98,97,97,96 95,88,75,72**
toteswingers 1&2 £28.60, 2&3 £37.40, 1&3 £11.70 CSF £98.07 CT £601.96 TOTE £7.00: £2.10, £3.40, £2.40; EX 151.90 Trifecta £607.40 Pool: £1289.93 - 1.59 winning units..
Owner B E Nielsen **Bred** Rathasker Stud **Trained** Upper Lambourn, Berks
■ Stewards' Enquiry : Tom Queally (1st incident) one-day ban: careless riding (Jul 30), (2nd) one-day ban: careless riding (Aug 1)

FOCUS
A modest 3-y-o handicap run in a similar time to the two divisions of the maiden that preceded it. The pace collapsed and the form has an ordinary feel to it.

4384 OPEN CHAMPIONSHIP 8 PLACES AT BETVICTOR H'CAP (LONDON MIDDLE DISTANCE SERIES QUALIFIER) 1m 3f (P)
8:30 (8:47) (Class 4) (0-80,80) 3-Y-0 £4,690 (£1,395; £697; £348) Stalls Low

Form RPR

1 **1** **Pomology (USA)**[29] 3417 3-9-7 **80** WilliamBuick 8 91+
(John Gosden) *hld up in last trio: rdn and effrt to chal over 1f out: led 1f out: in command and r.o wl ins fnl f: comf* **11/8**[1]

-105 **2** 1 ½ **Lamusawama**[34] 3214 3-9-6 **79** PaulHanagan 9 84
(Ed Dunlop) *t.k.h: hld up in tch in midfield: rdn and effrt to ld over 1f out: hdd 1f out: kpt on but nt gng pce of wnr* **4/1**[3]

3156 **3** 1 ½ **Isis Blue**[20] 3698 3-8-13 **72** (p) SteveDrowne 7 75
(Rod Millman) *hld up in last trio: n.m.r jst over 2f out: swtchd lft and hdd ent fnl f: kpt on u.p: no threat to wnr* **20/1**

0455 **4** 1 **Master Ming (IRE)**[31] 3338 3-9-7 **80** (b) KierenFallon 3 81
(Brian Meehan) *chsd ldrs: wnt 2nd 8f out tl rdn to ld 2f out: drvn and hdd over 1f out: wknd ins fnl f* **8/1**

41-6 **5** 1 ¼ **Aussie Lyrics (FR)**[54] 2584 3-9-3 **76** JimCrowley 2 75
(George Baker) *chsd ldr tl 8f out: rdn and swtchd lft 2f out: outpcd over 1f out: no threat to ldrs and one pce fnl f* **3/1**[2]

6-23 **6** 4 ½ **Forward March**[25] 3539 3-9-6 **79** J-PGuillambert 4 70
(Gary Harrison) *t.k.h: led tl rdn and hdd 2f out: struggling u.p over 1f out: wknd ins fnl f* **25/1**

-350 **7** hd **Guilded Spirit**[29] 3418 3-8-9 **68** RichardKingscote 10 59
(Stuart Kittow) *stdd and dropped in bhd after s: hld up in rr: effrt on inner 2f out: sn struggling: wknd over 1f out* **25/1**

-033 **8** nk **Dark Ocean (IRE)**[56] 2538 3-8-10 **69** TomQueally 1 60
(Jedd O'Keeffe) *t.k.h: hld up in midfield: rdn and unable qck ent fnl 2f: wknd over 1f out* **16/1**

2m 22.36s (0.46) **Going Correction** +0.125s/f (Slow) **8** Ran SP% **116.6**
Speed ratings (Par 102): **103,101,100,100,99 95,95,95**
toteswingers 1&2 £3.20, 2&3 £15.30, 1&3 £10.40 CSF £7.10 CT £70.12 TOTE £1.90: £1.20, £1.30, £4.40; EX 4.80 Trifecta £80.80 Pool: £1083.50 - 10.04 winning units..
Owner HRH Princess Haya Of Jordan **Bred** Dr John A Chandler **Trained** Newmarket, Suffolk

FOCUS
They didn't go much of an early pace here. The winner was value for extra.

4385 BETVICTOR 8 PLACES ON THE OPEN FILLIES' H'CAP 7f (P)
9:00 (9:14) (Class 5) (0-70,70) 3-Y-0+ £2,587 (£770; £384; £192) Stalls Low

Form RPR

1345 **1** **Bold Ring**[6] 4163 7-9-0 **63** JenniferFerguson(7) 9 72
(Edward Creighton) *hld up in tch in last quartet: gd hdwy to chse ldrs 2f out: nt clr run and swtchd rt over 1f out: r.o wl to ld ins fnl f: rdn out* **25/1**

00-1 **2** ½ **Lunette (IRE)**[20] 3696 3-9-7 **70** JimCrowley 6 75+
(Ralph Beckett) *hmpd s: hld up in tch towards rr: hdwy u.p over 1f out: r.o wl ins fnl f to go 2nd cl home: nt quite rch wnr* **7/2**[1]

103 **3** nk **Azenzar**[32] 3292 3-9-5 **68** JamesDoyle 8 72
(Roger Varian) *chsd ldrs: rdn and chal 2f out: led over 1f out: hdd and styd on same pce ins fnl f: lost 2nd cl home* **4/1**[2]

2563 **4** ¾ **Glastonberry**[20] 3691 5-9-13 **69** HayleyTurner 14 74
(Geoffrey Deacon) *t.k.h: hld up towards rr: rdn and hdwy over 1f out: styd on ins fnl f: nt rch ldrs* **9/1**

-541 **5** ½ **Fiducia**[34] 3216 3-9-5 **68** TomQueally 12 69
(Simon Dow) *stdd after s: t.k.h: hld up in tch in rr: hdwy u.p 1f out: styd on wl fnl f: nt rch ldrs* **16/1**

3-10 **6** ¾ **Two In The Pink (IRE)**[56] 2544 3-9-1 **64** (t) JimmyFortune 13 63
(Hugo Palmer) *hld up in tch in last pair: rdn and effrt ent fnl f: hdwy 1f out: styd on but no threat to ldrs* **20/1**

6141 **7** ½ **Moma Lee**[17] 3817 3-9-7 **70** WilliamBuick 11 67
(John Gosden) *hld up in tch in midfield: swtchd lft and effrt 2f out: kpt on fnl f: nvr trbld ldrs* **9/2**[3]

50 **8** hd **Mojo Bear**[30] 3376 3-8-13 **62** LiamKeniry 2 59
(Sylvester Kirk) *in tch: effrt over 1f out: styd on u.p fnl f: nvr trbld ldrs* **20/1**

6404 **9** 1 ½ **Commandingpresence (USA)**[26] 3498 7-9-3 **59** KieranO'Neill 4 55
(John Bridger) *taken down early: chsd ldr tl rdn to ld 2f out: hdd over 1f out: wknd ins fnl f* **33/1**

4500 **10** 1 **Avonvalley**[24] 3569 6-9-4 **65** SladeO'Hara(5) 3 58
(Peter Grayson) *taken down early: chsd ldrs: effrt on inner 2f out: stl pressing ldrs over 1f out: wknd ins fnl f* **33/1**

2541 **11** 2 ¾ **Basle**[22] 3644 6-9-6 **62** (t) RichardKingscote 5 48
(Michael Blake) *taken down early: wnt and stdd s: t.k.h: hld up in tch: rdn and no hdwy 2f out: wknd jst over 1f out* **16/1**

114- **12** shd **Silver Lace (IRE)**[256] 7530 4-9-10 **66** GeorgeBaker 10 52
(Chris Wall) *towards rr on outer: rdn and effrt over 2f out: no real imp: nvr trbld ldrs* **9/2**[3]

0200 **13** 6 **Nepalese Pearl**[29] 3405 3-8-5 **54** KirstyMilczarek 1 24
(Pat Eddery) *led tl rdn and hdd 2f out: sn wknd: fdd fnl f* **66/1**

1m 26.68s (0.68) **Going Correction** +0.125s/f (Slow)
WFA 3 from 4yo+ 7lb **13** Ran SP% **121.1**
Speed ratings (Par 100): **101,100,100,99,98 97,97,97,95,94 91,90,84**
toteswingers 1&2 £21.30, 2&3 £5.30, 1&3 £39.30 CSF £106.08 CT £443.75 TOTE £34.10: £10.20, £3.30, £1.10; EX 161.10 Trifecta £902.00 Part won. Pool: £1202.71 - 0.69 winning units..
Owner Miss Charlotte Harper **Bred** J A Pickering & T Pears **Trained** Wormshill, Kent

FOCUS
A competitive fillies' handicap for the class, run at a fair pace and there was a tight finish. The winner is rated back to her best.

T/Jkpt: £11,833.30 to a £1 stake. Pool of £25,0000 - 1.50 winning tickets. T/Plt: £17.70 to a £1 stake. Pool of £79,073.71 - 3257.73 winning tickets. T/Qpdt: £15.80 to a £1 stake. Pool of £6,021.12 - 281.50 winning tickets. SP

[4177]YARMOUTH (L-H)

Tuesday, July 16

OFFICIAL GOING: Good to firm (firm in places)

Wind: very light breeze Weather: hot and sunny; 22 degrees

4386 IRISH STALLION FARMS EBF / 4HEAD MAIDEN STKS 7f 3y

5:50 (5:51) (Class 5) 2-Y-O £2,911 (£866; £432; £216) Stalls Centre

Form RPR

20 **1** **Bureau (IRE)**[24] 3555 2-9-0 0 FrannyNorton 2 78
(Mark Johnston) *pressed ldr: led over 2f out: sn rdn but responding: pushed along and in command fnl f* **8/11**[1]

06 **2** 2 ½ **Chinese Jade**[15] 3905 2-9-5 0 LukeMorris 4 76
(Sir Mark Prescott Bt) *racd in 3rd tl pushed along to go 2nd 2f out: sn edging lft: one pce and wl hld fnl f* **25/1**

3 ¾ **Art Wave (IRE)** 2-9-0 0 RobertTart(5) 1 74+
(Marco Botti) *slowly in stride: pushed along 1/2-way: drvn on outer and tried to chal over 1f out: sn no imp* **5/1**[3]

04 **4** 6 **Citizen Kaine (IRE)**[17] 3833 2-9-5 0 CathyGannon 5 58
(Jo Hughes) *racd freely in ld: rdn and hdd over 2f out: sn dropped out* **3/1**[2]

5 32 **Nabstarlini** 2-9-5 0 ShaneKelly 3
(Ed Vaughan) *s.s: rdn and v green in detached last: t.o over 1f out: eased* **12/1**

1m 24.96s (-1.64) **Going Correction** -0.325s/f (Firm) **5** Ran SP% **111.1**
Speed ratings (Par 94): **96,93,92,85,48**
CSF £19.57 TOTE £1.50: £1.10, £5.60; EX 10.20 Trifecta £25.10 Pool: £1436.16 - 42.80 winning units..
Owner Sheikh Hamdan Bin Mohammed Al Maktoum **Bred** Darley **Trained** Middleham Moor, N Yorks

FOCUS
Back straight and bottom bend dolled out 3m adding about 15m to races on Round course.A weak juvenile maiden and, with Citizen Kaine appearing to run a long way below expecations, it certainly made life easier for the strongly fancied favourite. The pre-race profiles were not that strong and the time supports this level.

4387 IBULEVE (S) NURSERY H'CAP 7f 3y

6:20 (6:20) (Class 6) 2-Y-O £1,940 (£577; £288; £144) Stalls Centre

Form RPR

0026 **1** **Porteous**[10] 4061 2-9-7 **64** MartinLane 5 64
(Mick Channon) *trckd ldrs: led 2f out: pushed along and in command 1f out: v confidently handled as rivals clsd again nr fin* **6/5**[1]

0060 **2** nk **Jazzy Lady (IRE)**[10] 4065 2-8-9 **52** CathyGannon 2 51
(David Evans) *stmbld sltly leaving stalls: drvn along and sn cl up: bdly outpcd over 2f out: swtchd rt and rallied ins fnl f: snatched 2nd but flattered by proximity to wnr* **10/1**

040 **3** ½ **Red Dakota (IRE)**[40] 3023 2-9-0 **57** LukeMorris 1 55
(Alan McCabe) *taken down early: pressed ldrs: drvn 2f out: racing awkwardly after: one pce and wl hld fnl f* **2/1**[2]

060 **4** nk **Astral Pursuits**[10] 4065 2-8-2 **47** JimmyQuinn 3 42
(Nigel Tinkler) *slt ld tl over 3f out: drvn 2f out: nt qckn ins fnl f* **16/1**

0200 **5** ½ **Kitty Brown (IRE)**[7] 4141 2-8-12 **60** (v[1]) DeclanBates(5) 4 56
(David Evans) *2nd tl led over 3f out: drvn and hdd 2f out: fnd little fnl f* **5/1**[3]

1m 27.81s (1.21) **Going Correction** -0.325s/f (Firm) **5** Ran SP% **110.4**
Speed ratings (Par 92): **80,79,79,78,78**
CSF £13.44 TOTE £2.00: £1.20, £2.70; EX 10.70 Trifecta £35.60 Pool: £1109.12 - 23.34 winning units..The winner was bought in for 5,400gns.
Owner Imperial **Bred** Imperial & Mike Channon Bloodstock Ltd **Trained** West Ilsley, Berks

FOCUS
The official ratings shown are estimated and for information only. A desperately weak race, even accounting for the grade, and just a length and a half covering the five.

4388 AEROPAK H'CAP 6f 3y

6:50 (6:52) (Class 6) (0-60,59) 3-Y-O+ £1,940 (£577; £288; £144) Stalls Centre

Form RPR

-003 **1** **Sweet Talking Guy (IRE)**[14] 3922 3-8-8 **51** (t) SimonPearce(3) 5 57
(Lydia Pearce) *settled trcking ldrs: pushed along and effrt 2f out: led jst ins fnl f: a gng to hold on after* **9/4**[2]

5340 **2** ¾ **Amis Reunis**[43] 2932 4-9-9 **58** (p) MartinLane 9 63
(Anthony Carson) *stdd s: t.k.h and sn pressing ldr: rdn 2f out: no imp ins fnl f* **7/4**[1]

6000 **3** ¾ **Arch Walker (IRE)**[11] 4009 6-9-4 **53** (b) JimmyQuinn 6 55
(John Weymes) *taken down early: led at brisk pce: rdn 2f out: hdd jst ins fnl f: sn btn* **5/1**

00-3 **4** 2 ½ **Alfresco**[17] 3841 9-9-9 **58** (b) RobertHavlin 1 52
(Martin Bosley) *cl up tl drvn 2f out: fnd nil and sn wl btn* **7/2**[3]

0-60 **5** 3 **Mystical Witch**[156] 600 4-8-10 **45** CathyGannon 4 30
(Christine Dunnett) *sn in last: rdn and struggling bdly over 2f out* **16/1**

1m 12.43s (-1.97) **Going Correction** -0.325s/f (Firm)
WFA 3 from 4yo+ 5lb **5** Ran SP% **111.9**
Speed ratings (Par 101): **100,99,98,94,90**
CSF £6.75 TOTE £3.10: £2.20, £1.70; EX 7.50 Trifecta £18.50 Pool: £669.20 - 27.10 winning units..
Owner Killarney Glen **Bred** Churchtown House Stud **Trained** Newmarket, Suffolk

FOCUS
They went off hard in this moderate handicap and it appeared to play into the hands of the winner. Very limited form.

4389 DIOMED GOLDEN ANNIVERSARY H'CAP 6f 3y

7:20 (7:22) (Class 3) (0-90,90) 3-Y-O+ £8,086 (£2,406; £1,202; £601) Stalls Centre

Form RPR

4612 **1** **Minalisa**[11] 4017 4-9-9 **85** SebSanders 5 99+
(Rae Guest) *mde all: shkn up 2f out: wnt clr 1f out: v readily* **11/8**[1]

0311 **2** 3 ¼ **Clear Spring (IRE)**[12] 3973 5-9-10 **86** NickyMackay 6 90
(John Spearing) *s.i.s: rdn and effrt 2f out: kpt on gamely to go 2nd ins fnl f: no ch w easy wnr* **4/1**[3]

-560 **3** nk **Nassau Storm**[25] 3527 4-10-0 **90** ShaneKelly 4 93
(William Knight) *cl up: drvn to go 2nd over 2f out: outpcd by wnr 1f out: lost 2nd fnl 100yds* **5/2**[2]

6 **4** 2 ½ **Maglietta Fina (IRE)**[44] 4-9-9 **85** RobertHavlin 3 80
(Robert Cowell) *t.k.h: prom: rdn 2f out: wknd ins fnl f* **28/1**

0250 **5** 1 **Piazza San Pietro**[4] 4235 7-9-2 **81** (p) SimonPearce(3) 1 73
(Zoe Davison) *chsd ldrs: drvn 1/2-way: wknd over 1f out* **10/1**

1-02 **6** nk **Angel Way (IRE)**[20] 3691 4-8-12 **74** MartinLane 2 65
(Mike Murphy) *stdd in last: rdn and effrt on outer 2f out: wknd 1f out* **16/1**

5400 **7** 6 **Burnhope**[12] 3981 4-8-10 **72** (p) LukeMorris 7 44
(Scott Dixon) *pressed wnr tl rdn and lost pl rapidly over 2f out: eased in clsng stages* **20/1**

1m 11.28s (-3.12) **Going Correction** -0.325s/f (Firm)
WFA 3 from 4yo+ 5lb **7** Ran SP% **113.9**
Speed ratings (Par 107): **107,102,102,98,97 97,89**
toteswingers 1&2 £1.20, 2&3 £3.30, 1&3 £1.50 CSF £7.22 CT £11.91 TOTE £2.10: £1.70, £2.20; EX 7.90 Trifecta £19.90 Pool: £1235.26 - 46.49 winning units..
Owner C J Mills **Bred** C J Mills **Trained** Newmarket, Suffolk

FOCUS
A decent turn out for the feature race on the card and it was a hugely impressive display from the heavily supported favourite. The winner wasn't flattered and is clearly improving fast.

4390 FREEDERM H'CAP 5f 43y

7:50 (7:54) (Class 5) (0-70,65) 3-Y-O £2,587 (£770; £384; £192) Stalls Centre

Form RPR

2-23 **1** **Blessing Box**[26] 3509 3-9-7 **65** SebSanders 2 77+
(Chris Wall) *stdd in last and t.k.h: effrt 2f out: sn drvn: led fnl 100yds: jst hld on* **11/8**[1]

4041 **2** hd **Green Monkey**[18] 3789 3-9-2 **60** FrederikTylicki 1 71+
(James Fanshawe) *pressed ldr tl rdn to ld 2f out: drvn and hdd 100yds out: kpt on gamely: jst hld* **10/3**[2]

4-42 **3** 1 ½ **Honeymoon Express (IRE)**[18] 3787 3-9-7 **65** AdamBeschizza 4 71
(Julia Feilden) *chsd ldr: rdn and outpcd 2f out: rallied fnl 100yds and fin strly to snatch 3rd* **4/1**[3]

-565 **4** 1 ¼ **Mossgo (IRE)**[17] 3816 3-9-5 **63** LukeMorris 6 64
(John Best) *led: hrd drvn and hdd 2f out: btn 1f out: lost 3rd cl home* **16/1**

-605 **5** 8 **Marvelous Miss (IRE)**[18] 3789 3-8-2 **46** oh1 JimmyQuinn 7 19
(Christine Dunnett) *cl up tl lost pl rapidly over 2f out: sn racing v awkwardly* **22/1**

-102 **6** 1 **Hand In Glove**[42] 2965 3-9-5 **63** ShaneKelly 5 32
(Robert Cowell) *last away: struggling bdly fnl 2f* **9/2**

1m 2.16s (-0.54) **Going Correction** -0.325s/f (Firm) **6** Ran SP% **113.6**
Speed ratings (Par 100): **91,90,88,86,73 71**
toteswingers 1&2 £1.10, 2&3 £1.10, 1&3 £2.20 CSF £6.37 CT £13.80 TOTE £2.00: £1.60, £1.80; EX 5.90 Trifecta £12.00 Pool: £705.19 - 43.87 winning units..
Owner M Sinclair **Bred** Farmers Hill Stud **Trained** Newmarket, Suffolk
■ Stewards' Enquiry : Seb Sanders two-day ban: used whip above permitted level (Jul 30,Aug 1)

FOCUS
A lively betting heat and it was won by the strongly supported favourite. An ordinary race but the first two are progressive.

4391 ADIOS H'CAP 1m 1f

8:20 (8:21) (Class 6) (0-55,55) 3-Y-O £1,940 (£577; £288; £144) Stalls Low

Form RPR

0-00 **1** **Artful Prince**[59] 2464 3-9-0 **48** (b[1]) DaleSwift 2 56
(James Given) *rdn much of way: cl up in slowly run r: drvn to chse clr ldr over 5f out: led over 1f out: kpt on u.p despite awkward hd carriage: all out* **20/1**

0565 **2** 1 ¼ **Lucky Mountain**[16] 3859 3-8-7 **46** RobertTart(5) 12 51
(Scott Dixon) *bhd briefly: dashed up to ld 7f out: 6 l clr over 5f out: drvn over 2f out: hdd over 1f out: kpt on same pce* **10/1**

-652 **3** 2 ¼ **Sakash**[19] 3740 3-9-3 **51** FrederikTylicki 5 52
(J R Jenkins) *sn dropped to rr: lot to to do 5f out: drvn and plugged on w awkward hd carriage fr 2f out: wnt 3rd 1f out: unable to chal* **9/2**[2]

0632 **4** 1 **Dalliefour (IRE)**[14] 3918 3-9-7 **55** LukeMorris 4 54
(Michael Bell) *t.k.h: led at mod pce tl hdd 7f out: drvn and v one pce fr 2f out* **6/4**[1]

-065 **5** 4 **Smart Alice**[28] 3428 3-8-13 **47** SebSanders 6 37
(Chris Wall) *bhd early: rdn 4f out: plugged on nvr looked like getting on terms fnl 2f* **7/1**

4-60 **6** ½ **The Ginger Berry**[37] 3137 3-9-7 **55** RobertHavlin 3 44
(Dr Jon Scargill) *midfield: rdn over 2f out: sn btn: plodded on* **20/1**

305 **7** 10 **My Claire**[10] 4045 3-9-0 **48** (p) AdamBeschizza 10 16
(Nigel Tinkler) *chsd ldrs: rdn over 3f out: sn btn: t.o* **8/1**

66-0 **8** 7 **Iffley Fields**[29] 3405 3-9-7 **55** JimmyQuinn 9 8
(Michael Squance) *bhd: last st: t.o fnl 4f* **40/1**

0030 **9** 13 **Ella Motiva (IRE)**[11] 4008 3-8-13 **47** ShaneKelly 7
(Mark Brisbourne) *chsd ldrs tl rdn and wknd tamely over 3f out: t.o and eased* **6/1**[3]

-000 **10** 7 **Grapes Hill**[19] 3740 3-9-4 **52** (p) FrannyNorton 1
(Mark Rimmer) *midfield: rdn 6f out: no rspnse: t.o over 2f out: eased* **33/1**

1m 55.64s (-0.16) **Going Correction** -0.075s/f (Good) **10** Ran SP% **120.1**
Speed ratings (Par 98): **97,95,93,93,89 89,80,73,62,56**
toteswingers 1&2 £50.60, 2&3 £17.50, 1&3 £21.30 CSF £202.38 CT £1099.85 TOTE £27.40: £8.50, £3.00, £1.90; EX 437.20 Trifecta £619.10 Part won. Pool: £825.48 - 0.01 winning units..
Owner Ingram Racing **Bred** Graham Wilson **Trained** Willoughton, Lincs

FOCUS
This race was all about one horse, but with the strongly supported Dalliefour failing to run up to expectations, it was the seemingly unfancied winner who benefited the most. Low-grade form, rated slightly conservatively.

4392 BAZUKA H'CAP 1m 6f 17y

8:50 (8:50) (Class 5) (0-70,65) 3-Y-O+ £2,587 (£770; £384; £192) Stalls High

Form RPR

0014 **1** **Choral Prince (IRE)**[17] 3809 3-9-0 **65** ShaneKelly 3 72+
(Mike Murphy) *hld up in last tl swtchd rt to make effrt over 1f out: led on bit fnl 120yds: nvr out of a canter* **7/4**[2]

3-04 **2** 1 ¼ **Outback (IRE)**[6] 4179 4-10-0 **65** (p) MartinLane 5 68
(Neil King) *pressed ldr: drvn 4f out: remained w ev ch tl wnr cruised past fnl 120yds: v flattered by proximity* **3/1**[3]

4013 **3** nk **Dr Finley (IRE)**[6] 4179 6-9-11 **65** (v) SimonPearce(3) 2 68
(Lydia Pearce) *settled in 3rd: rdn over 3f out: jnd ldr 2f out tl 1f out: edgd rt and nt qckn after* **6/4**[1]

1015 **4** nk **Underwritten**[7] 4147 4-9-12 **63** (b) JimmyQuinn 4 65
(John Weymes) *led at v modest pce: rdn over 3f out: jnd 2f out tl 1f out: hdd 120yds out and plodded on* **10/1**

3m 10.11s (2.51) **Going Correction** -0.075s/f (Good)
WFA 3 from 4yo+ 14lb **4** Ran SP% **110.5**
Speed ratings (Par 103): **89,88,88,87**
CSF £7.29 TOTE £3.10; EX 9.30 Trifecta £11.40 Pool: £323.01 - 21.16 winning units..
Owner The Oratorios **Bred** Stonethorn Stud Farms Ltd **Trained** Westoning, Beds

FOCUS
A tactically run affair and that made the winner's performance all the more impressive.

T/Plt: £16.90 to a £1 stake. Pool of £61228.08 -2632.63 winning tickets. T/Qpdt: £9.50 to a £1 stake. Pool of £6435.63 - 499.99 winning tickets. IM

4393 - 4397a (Foreign Racing) - See Raceform Interactive

[4156]CATTERICK (L-H)

Wednesday, July 17

OFFICIAL GOING: Good to firm (firm in places; 9.4)

Wind: Light half against Weather: Sunny and warm

4398 YORKSHIRE-OUTDOORS.CO.UK (S) STKS 5f 212y

2:10 (2:10) (Class 6) 3-Y-O+ £2,385 (£704; £352) Stalls Low

Form RPR

5215 1 **Red Cape (FR)**[8] 4149 10-9-6 67..................................(b) JamesSullivan 2 71
(Ruth Carr) *mde all: pushed clr over 2f out: rdn over 1f out: drvn ins fnl f: kpt on* **7/4**[2]

1-00 2 ¾ **Fathsta (IRE)**[32] 3322 8-9-0 77.................................. JoeFanning 6 62
(Ian Williams) *dwlt: sn trcking ldrs on inner: hdwy over 2f out: chsd wnr wl over 1f out and sn rdn: drvn ent fnl f: kpt on towards fin* **8/11**[1]

4500 3 4½ **Karate Queen**[7] 4161 8-8-9 49..................................(p) DaleSwift 3 43
(Ron Barr) *sn rdn along and outpcd in rr: detached 1/2-way: hdwy 2f out: styd on u.p appr fnl f: nrst fin* **50/1**

-550 4 3¾ **Cymeriad**[7] 4160 3-7-13 51..................................(p) ShirleyTeasdale(5) 5 30
(Michael Easterby) *cl up on outer: effrt to chse wnr over 2f out: sn rdn and wknd over 1f out* **9/1**[3]

0660 5 9 **Myjestic Melody (IRE)**[10] 4102 5-8-9 42.................. DuranFentiman 4 2
(Noel Wilson) *cl up: rdn along over 2f out: sn wknd* **125/1**

1m 12.1s (-1.50) **Going Correction** -0.225s/f (Firm)

WFA 3 from 5yo+ 5lb 5 Ran SP% 107.0

Speed ratings (Par 101): **101,100,94,89,77**

CSF £3.12 TOTE £3.00: £1.10, £2.00; EX 3.50 Trifecta £13.90 Pool: £1,841.17 - 99.43 winning units..There was no bid for the winner.

Owner Middleham Park Racing LVI **Bred** Gilles And Mrs Forien **Trained** Huby, N Yorks

FOCUS

The rail on the bend had been moved out slightly which added 8yds to all the races except the 5f race. A weak seller in which the two geldings had plenty in hand over the females on official ratings.

4399 RACING UK ICARD FOR TODAY'S RACECARDS NURSERY H'CAP 5f 212y

2:40 (2:41) (Class 4) 2-Y-O £3,881 (£1,155; £577; £288) Stalls Low

Form RPR

4140 1 **Diamond Lady**[28] 3459 2-9-0 75.................................. FrannyNorton 1 81+
(Jo Hughes) *trckd ldrs on inner: effrt and swtchd rt ent fnl f: rdn to ld last 100yds: kpt on wl* **11/4**[2]

51 2 1¾ **Regiment**[14] 3943 2-9-7 82.................................. TonyHamilton 2 82
(Richard Fahey) *led: rdn along wl over 1f out: drvn ins fnl f: hdd and no ex last 100yds* **6/4**[1]

562 3 1½ **Evie Jay (IRE)**[11] 4053 2-8-8 72.................................. RaulDaSilva(3) 5 67
(Paul Green) *sn rdn along in rr: outpcd and detached after 2f: hdwy on wd outside over 2f out: styd on u.p fnl f* **12/1**

023 4 1 **Stoney Quine (IRE)**[21] 3681 2-8-5 66.................................. PJMcDonald 4 58
(Keith Dalgleish) *trckd wnr on outer: effrt and cl up 2f out: sn rdn: drvn over 1f out: wknd fnl f* **6/1**

330 5 1½ **Tamayuz Magic (IRE)**[42] 2985 2-8-7 68.................................. JoeFanning 3 55
(Mark Johnston) *trckd ldrs: effrt over 2f out: sn rdn and wknd over 1f out* **7/2**[3]

1m 13.06s (-0.54) **Going Correction** -0.225s/f (Firm) 5 Ran SP% 110.9

Speed ratings (Par 96): **94,91,89,88,86**

CSF £7.38 TOTE £3.50: £2.30, £1.30; EX 6.60 Trifecta £29.00 Pool: £1,935.84 - 50.00 winning units..

Owner B Bedford P Hanly D Bird D Bedford **Bred** Mickley Stud **Trained** Lambourn, Berks

FOCUS

The official ratings shown are estimated and for information only. Despite the small field this was an interesting nursery and this probably rates as fair form. They were almost a second slower than the older horses in the opening seller.

4400 GO RACING IN YORKSHIRE SUMMER FESTIVAL MEDIAN AUCTION MAIDEN STKS 7f

3:10 (3:14) (Class 6) 3-5-Y-O £2,385 (£704; £352) Stalls Centre

Form RPR

6 1 **Snap Music (USA)**[12] 4011 3-9-0 0.................................. JoeFanning 9 64
(Mark Johnston) *cl up: chal 2f out: rdn over 1f out: led ins fnl f: drvn and kpt on wl towards fin* **4/1**[2]

35 2 ½ **Dennis**[11] 4050 3-9-0 0.................................. DarylByrne(5) 10 67
(Tim Easterby) *sn led: jnd and rdn 2f out: drvn over 1f out: hdd ins fnl f: kpt on u.p* **14/1**

-302 3 2¼ **Graceful Act**[19] 3774 5-9-7 55.................................. PhillipMakin 8 59
(Ron Barr) *prom: rdn along over 2f out: drvn over 1f out: kpt on same pce* **7/1**

34-4 4 2¾ **Mishaal (IRE)**[19] 3773 3-9-5 72.................................. TomEaves 2 54
(Michael Herrington) *t.k.h: chsd ldrs on inner: hdwy 2f out: sn swtchd rt and rdn: kpt on same pce fr over 1f out* **5/1**[3]

0-36 5 ½ **North Pole**[11] 4068 3-9-5 65..................................(b[1]) ChrisCatlin 1 52
(Sir Mark Prescott Bt) *dwlt and bhd: hdwy on inner over 2f out: swtchd rt and rdn wl over 1f out: kpt on wl fnl f* **7/2**[1]

3500 6 2¾ **Eastlands Lad (IRE)**[16] 3895 4-9-12 55..................................(p) FrannyNorton 5 48
(Micky Hammond) *trckd ldrs: pushed along 3f out: rdn 2f out: sn no imp* **4/1**[2]

30 7 ½ **Helterskelter Girl**[9] 4118 3-9-0 0.................................. PJMcDonald 4 39
(Ann Duffield) *hld up: a towards rr* **40/1**

34 8 8 **Echo Of Lightning**[22] 3650 3-9-5 0.................................. DuranFentiman 6 22
(Noel Wilson) *t.k.h: chsd ldrs: rdn along wl over 2f out: sn wknd* **14/1**

0-66 9 2½ **Benidorm**[25] 3593 5-9-7 46..................................(v) AdamCarter(5) 7 18
(Neville Bycroft) *a in rr* **150/1**

34- 10 7 **Indie Banned**[296] 6524 3-9-5 0.................................. GrahamLee 3
(Ben Haslam) *in tch: rdn along 1/2-way: sn wknd* **14/1**

0-45 11 8 **Lilly May (IRE)**[12] 4030 3-9-0 44..................................(v[1]) PaddyAspell 11
(Phil McEntee) *in tch: hdwy on outer to chse ldrs 1/2-way: rdn along wl over 2f out: sn wknd* **150/1**

1m 25.28s (-1.72) **Going Correction** -0.225s/f (Firm)

WFA 3 from 4yo+ 7lb 11 Ran SP% 115.2

Speed ratings (Par 101): **100,99,96,93,93 90,89,80,77,69 60**

Tote Swingers: 1&2 £5.70, 1&3 £8.80, 2&3 £11.10 CSF £57.21 TOTE £4.50: £1.70, £4.30, £2.20; EX 44.80 Trifecta £296.30 Pool: £3,217.99 - 8.14 winning units..

Owner Sheikh Hamdan Bin Mohammed Al Maktoum **Bred** Darley **Trained** Middleham Moor, N Yorks

FOCUS

All of these had experience of the racecourse and on all evidence this is probably only a modest maiden, with the third the best guide.

4401 EAT SLEEP DRINK AT NAGS HEAD PICKHILL H'CAP (QUALIFIER FOR CATTERICK TWELVE FURLONG SERIES FINAL) 1m 3f 214y

3:40 (3:40) (Class 5) (0-70,70) 3-Y-O £3,881 (£1,155; £577; £288) Stalls Low

Form RPR

1026 1 **Gabrial The Duke (IRE)**[19] 3756 3-8-12 61.................................. FrannyNorton 1 67+
(David Simcock) *trckd ldrs: smooth hdwy on inner 3f out: led over 2f out: rdn over 1f out: kpt on wl fnl f* **11/10**[1]

0043 2 1½ **Bayan Kasirga (IRE)**[11] 4049 3-8-10 59.................................. TonyHamilton 3 62
(Richard Fahey) *trckd ldrs on inner: hdwy 3f out: swtchd rt and hdwy to chal 2f out: drvn and edgd lft fnl f: no ex towards fin* **15/2**[3]

1140 3 nk **Precision Strike**[22] 3653 3-8-5 57 ow2..................................(v) BillyCray(3) 5 57
(Richard Guest) *hld up in rr: hdwy on inner 2f out: rdn to chse wnr over 1f out: drvn and n.m.r ins fnl f: no ex towards fin* **20/1**

00-6 4 4½ **Jebulani**[22] 3653 3-7-13 51 oh5.................................. JulieBurke(3) 7 46
(David O'Meara) *trckd ldr: cl up 3f out: rdn along 2f out: sn drvn and wknd appr fnl f* **9/1**

-411 5 8 **Al Thumama**[20] 3735 3-9-7 70..................................(p) PhillipMakin 2 52
(Kevin Ryan) *led: rdn along 3f out: hdd 2f out: sn drvn and wknd over 1f out* **11/4**[2]

-536 6 12 **Multilicious**[12] 4008 3-8-5 54.................................. DuranFentiman 4 17
(Tim Easterby) *trckd ldrs: pushed along over 4f out: rdn 3f out: wknd 2f out* **8/1**

2m 35.64s (-3.26) **Going Correction** -0.225s/f (Firm) 6 Ran SP% 111.9

Speed ratings (Par 100): **101,100,99,96,91 83**

Tote Swingers: 1&2 £1.90, 1&3 £6.30, 2&3 £10.70 CSF £10.12 TOTE £1.70: £1.10, £4.00; EX 8.40 Trifecta £99.80 Pool: £2,449.58 - 18.39 winning units..

Owner Dr Marwan Koukash **Bred** Old Carhue & Graeng Bloodstock **Trained** Newmarket, Suffolk

■ Stewards' Enquiry : Billy Cray three-day ban: weighed in 2lb heavy (Aug 1,2,4)

FOCUS

A range of abilities on show in this moderate race. The form is limited judged around those in the frame behind the winner.

4402 READ HAYLEY TURNER EVERY FRIDAY RACINGUK.COM H'CAP 5f

4:10 (4:10) (Class 4) (0-85,83) 3-Y-O £6,469 (£1,925; £962; £481) Stalls Low

Form RPR

6111 1 **Lexington Place**[4] 4290 3-8-9 76 6ex.................................. DavidBergin(5) 4 82+
(David O'Meara) *trckd ldrs: hdwy 2f out: rdn to ld ent fnl f: sn edgd lft and kpt on* **11/4**[2]

0506 2 ¾ **Satsuma**[39] 3104 3-9-6 82.................................. GrahamLee 3 85
(David Brown) *cl up: rdn and ev ch wl over 1f out: drvn and n.m.r ins fnl f: kpt on* **2/1**[1]

-021 3 1½ **Funding Deficit (IRE)**[11] 4050 3-8-11 73.................................. GrahamGibbons 2 71
(David Barron) *sn led: rdn along 2f out: drvn and hdd ent fnl f: sn one pce* **2/1**[1]

-100 4 ½ **Rangooned**[8] 4136 3-8-10 72.................................. PJMcDonald 6 68
(Ann Duffield) *sn rdn along and outpcd in rr: hdwy wl over 1f out: chsd ldrs whn n.m.r ins fnl f: kpt on same pce towards fin* **11/1**

0066 5 1½ **Lady Poppy**[8] 4136 3-8-3 68.................................. DeclanCannon(3) 5 58
(George Moore) *cl up: pushed along bef 1/2-way: rdn over 2f out: wknd over 1f out* **10/1**[3]

58.32s (-1.48) **Going Correction** -0.225s/f (Firm) 5 Ran SP% 110.8

Speed ratings (Par 102): **102,100,98,97,95**

CSF £8.73 TOTE £3.90: £2.20, £1.20; EX 8.90 Trifecta £13.60 Pool: £2.217.20 - 121.70 winning units..

Owner Middleham Park Racing XXXI **Bred** Christopher & Annabelle Mason **Trained** Nawton, N Yorks

FOCUS

Nominally the best race on the card, but it lost a bit of interest when Sharaarah was pulled out in the morning due to worries over the fast ground. It was not the most competitive or strongest race for the grade, but it was a decent time recorded by the in-form winner.

4403 BETFAIR NOVICE FLAT AMATEUR RIDERS' H'CAP (FOR NOVICE AMATEUR RIDERS) 1m 3f 214y

4:40 (4:40) (Class 6) (0-65,64) 4-Y-O+ £2,183 (£677; £338; £169) Stalls Low

Form RPR

-564 1 **Gucci D'Oro (USA)**[42] 2991 4-10-7 53.................................. MrAlexFerguson(3) 1 67
(David Simcock) *hld up in tch: smooth hdwy 2f out: swtchd rt over 1f out: rdn to ld jst ins fnl f: sn clr* **17/2**[3]

-621 2 4½ **Slide Show**[14] 3947 5-10-10 56.................................. MrDPCostello(3) 14 63
(David Nicholls) *hld up towards rr: hdwy over 4f out: cl up 2f out: sn led: rdn and hdd jst ins fnl f: one pce* **5/2**[1]

5-53 3 1¾ **Candelita**[80] 714 6-11-2 59.................................. MrJamesHughes 10 63
(Jo Hughes) *hld up and bhd: hdwy and wd st: rdn 2f out: styd on fnl f: nrst fin* **5/1**[2]

4061 4 ½ **Flag Of Glory**[11] 4071 6-11-7 64.................................. MissMEdden 13 67
(Peter Hiatt) *trckd ldrs early: settled in midfield after 3f: hdwy 3f out: swtchd to outer 2f out and sn rdn: kpt on appr fnl f: nrst fin* **14/1**

6434 5 ¾ **Rub Of The Relic (IRE)**[11] 4071 8-11-3 60..................................(v) MissHDukes 7 62
(Paul Midgley) *led: rdn along 3f out: hdd over 2f out: sn drvn and kpt on same pce appr fnl f* **11/1**

026- 6 ½ **Only You Maggie (IRE)**[404] 2867 6-11-4 64..................................(v) MrWDegnan(3) 2 65
(Gary Harrison) *hld up and bhd: hdwy and wd st: rdn wl over 1f out: kpt on: nrst fin* **25/1**

1031 7 nse **Maybeme**[22] 3652 7-11-3 60..................................(p) MrSebSpencer 6 61
(Neville Bycroft) *hld up towards rr: hdwy 4f out: effrt over 2f out: sn rdn to chse ldrs: drvn and wknd over 1f* **10/1**

6332 8 2 **Blue Top**[12] 4010 4-10-13 56..................................(p) MissETodd 11 54
(Tim Walford) *cl up: rdn to chal 3f out: led briefly over 2f out: sn hdd & wknd* **17/2**[3]

1042 9 nk **Amir Pasha (UAE)**[14] 3944 8-10-10 53..................................(v) MissBeckySmith 8 50
(Micky Hammond) *trckd ldrs: rdn along 3f out: drvn 2f out: sn wknd* **11/1**

0-01 10 1¼ **Grammar**[12] 4010 4-10-10 53..................................(e) MrSmith 4 48
(David Thompson) *trckd ldrs: effrt 3f out: rdn along wl over 2f out: sn wknd* **22/1**

0035 11 5 **King Of Wing (IRE)**[13] 3997 4-10-7 53..................................(be) MrJAMcEntee(3) 12 40
(Phil McEntee) *nvr bttr than midfield* **66/1**

3045 12 8 **Light The City (IRE)**[14] 3947 6-10-9 52.................................. MrRColley 9 27
(Ruth Carr) *cl up: rdn along over 3f out: drvn wl over 2f out: sn wknd* **10/1**

2m 36.4s (-2.50) **Going Correction** -0.225s/f (Firm) 12 Ran SP% 117.5

Speed ratings (Par 101): **99,96,94,94,94 93,93,92,92,91 87,82**

Tote Swingers: 1&2 £8.90, 1&3 £10.10, 2&3 £4.40 CSF £29.11 CT £121.14 TOTE £12.20: £3.00, £1.70, £2.10; EX 49.50 Trifecta £498.70 Pool: £2,401.53 - 3.61 winning unit..

Owner Mrs John Ferguson **Bred** Donna Tullner & Stephen Glessner **Trained** Newmarket, Suffolk

The Form Book Flat, Raceform Ltd, Compton, RG20 6NL.

FOCUS
Just modest form but not a bad race of its type with a few of these coming here on good terms with themselves. The third helps set the level and is close to his AW form.
T/Plt: £17.70 to a £1 stake. Pool: £46,925.47 - 1,932.28 winning tickets. T/Qpdt: £17.70 to a £1 stake. Pool: £2,632.50 - 2,632.50 winning tickets. JR

4170 LINGFIELD (L-H)

Wednesday, July 17

OFFICIAL GOING: Turf course - good to firm (firm in places; watered; 8.9); all-weather course - standard
Wind: virtually nil Weather: hot and sunny

4404 BRITANIACREST MAIDEN STKS — 1m 1f
2:00 (2:01) (Class 5) 3-4-Y-0 — £2,726 (£805; £402) Stalls Low

Form — RPR
5-43 **1** **Familliarity**[19] 3764 3-9-0 73 .... DaneO'Neill 1 — 77
(Roger Varian) *chsd ldr: rdn and clsd to ld over 1f out: clr 1f out: styd on wl* — 3/1[3]
233 **2** 2 1/4 **Response**[15] 3923 3-9-5 75 .... JamesDoyle 4 — 77
(William Haggas) *led: rdn 2f out: hdd and unable qck over 1f out: one pce u.p fnl f* — 5/2[2]
3 5 **Bostonian** 3-9-5 0 .... SilvestreDeSousa 2 — 66+
(Mark Johnston) *chsd ldng pair: drvn and effrt over 2f out: no ex and btn over 1f out: plugged on fnl f* — 9/2
6- **4** 1/2 **Qareenah (USA)**[273] 7159 3-9-0 0 .... PaulHanagan 3 — 60
(Sir Michael Stoute) *chsd ldng trio: rdn and effrt ent fnl 2f: disputing 3rd and outpcd over 1f out: plugged on* — 2/1[1]
60 **5** 3 1/4 **Hattie Jacques**[23] 3641 3-9-0 0 .... MartinHarley 8 — 53
(Mick Channon) *racd off the pce in midfield: outpcd by ldrs 4f out: no ch after but kpt on steadily fnl f* — 25/1
0 **6** 7 **Hispania (IRE)**[60] 2456 3-8-7 0 .... ThomasHemsley(7) 9 — 37
(Michael Bell) *stdd s: hld up off the towards rr: hung rt bnd 7f out: outpcd 4f out: no ch fnl 3f* — 33/1
6 **7** 8 **Glassenbury Lass**[29] 3435 3-9-0 0 .... RobertHavlin 5 — 20
(Mark Hoad) *racd off the pce in midfield: outpcd 4f out: no ch 3f out: wknd* — 100/1
8 25 **Aster's Approval** 3-9-5 0 .... CathyGannon 7
(Tim Vaughan) *wnt rt and v.s.a: a in rr: lost tch 5f out: t.o fnl 4f* — 33/1
9 9 **Patino Kash** 3-9-0 0 .... MarcHalford 6
(Richard Rowe) *s.i.s: sn pushed along and bhd: lost tch 1/2-way: t.o fnl 5f* — 100/1

1m 54.81s (-1.79) **Going Correction** -0.30s/f (Firm) — 9 Ran SP% 116.8
Speed ratings (Par 103): **95,93,88,88,85 79,71,49,41**
Tote Swingers: 1&2 £1.50, 1&3 £3.00, 2&3 £2.70 CSF £10.77 TOTE £3.00: £1.10, £1.40, £1.30; EX 11.60 Trifecta £33.70 Pool: £3,338.97 - 74.23 winning units..
Owner Helena Springfield Ltd **Bred** Meon Valley Stud **Trained** Newmarket, Suffolk

FOCUS
Only four counted in this modest maiden according to the market and they were the only ones to figure.

4405 OILFIELD INSURANCE AGENCIES LTD H'CAP — 1m 3f 106y
2:30 (2:31) (Class 6) (0-60,60) 3-Y-0 — £2,045 (£603; £302) Stalls High

Form — RPR
423 **1** **Kastini**[34] 3243 3-9-4 57 .... KierenFallon 11 — 70+
(Denis Coakley) *in tch in midfield: hdwy to chse ldrs 4f out: chsd ldr 2f out: rdn to ld jst over 1f out: idled and drvn to assert fnl 100yds: styd on wl* — 6/4[1]
5-56 **2** 1 3/4 **Nullarbor Sky (IRE)**[34] 3243 3-9-5 58 .... (p) FrederikTylicki 1 — 68
(Lucy Wadham) *sn bustled up to ld: hdd 8f out: chsd ldrs after tl wnt 2nd again over 4f out: rdn to ld ent fnl 2f: hdd jst over 1f out: no ex and btn fnl 100yds* — 11/4[2]
1033 **3** 5 **Handsome Stranger (IRE)**[7] 4171 3-9-0 60 .... (v) TimClark(7) 6 — 62
(Alan Bailey) *t.k.h: chsd ldrs tl led 7f out: rdn and hdd jst over 2f out: wknd u.p 1f out* — 14/1
-005 **4** 3 1/2 **Sugar Coated (IRE)**[35] 3194 3-9-1 54 .... LukeMorris 12 — 50
(Michael Bell) *s.i.s: sn rcvrd and wl in tch in midfield: drvn and clr in ldng quintet over 3f out: wknd wl over 1f out* — 6/1[3]
0-63 **5** 1 3/4 **Uncle Bernie (IRE)**[20] 3735 3-9-5 58 .... ShaneKelly 8 — 51
(Andrew Hollinshead) *wl in tch: hdwy to chse ldrs 5f out: drvn and struggling over 2f out: wknd over 1f out* — 7/1
4536 **6** 4 **Dalaway (IRE)**[11] 4049 3-9-6 59 .... MartinHarley 3 — 45
(Mick Channon) *stdd s: t.k.h: hld up in rr: lost tch w ldng quintet 4f out: modest 6th 3f out: no imp* — 12/1
000 **7** 5 **Pure Flight (IRE)**[33] 3272 3-9-0 56 .... RachaelGreen(3) 9 — 34
(Anthony Honeyball) *t.k.h: hld up in last pair: lost tch w ldng quintet 4f out: n.d* — 50/1
4044 **8** 4 **Booktheband (IRE)**[48] 2800 3-9-0 53 .... TomQueally 5 — 24
(Clive Brittain) *chsd ldrs tl 1/2-way: steadily lost pl: bhd fnl 3f* — 14/1
5-00 **9** 6 **Sporting Club Girl**[22] 3657 3-8-7 46 oh1 .... (v) HarryBentley 7
(William Knight) *hld up in tch towards rr: lost tch 4f out: bhd fnl 3f: t.o* — 66/1
0000 **10** 46 **Hats Off**[27] 3495 3-8-7 46 oh1 .... PaulHanagan 10
(John Best) *chsd ldr tl led 8f out tl over 6f out: btn 4f out: sn dropped out: wl t.o and eased fnl f* — 66/1

2m 28.52s (-2.98) **Going Correction** -0.30s/f (Firm) — 10 Ran SP% 119.4
Speed ratings (Par 98): **98,96,93,90,89 86,82,79,75,42**
Tote Swingers: 1&2 £1.80, 1&3 £4.00, 2&3 £7.50 CSF £5.73 CT £40.39 TOTE £2.40: £1.30, £1.40, £3.10; EX 6.80 Trifecta £60.50 Pool: £2,480.90 - 30.74 winning units..
Owner West Ilsley Racing **Bred** J W Ford **Trained** West Ilsley, Berks

FOCUS
A moderate 3yo handicap in which only one of these had hit the target before.

4406 EMERSON CRANES H'CAP — 2m
3:00 (3:00) (Class 5) (0-75,74) 3-Y-0+ — £2,726 (£805; £402) Stalls Low

Form — RPR
2102 **1** **Miss Tiger Lily**[12] 4035 3-8-1 64 .... LukeMorris 1 — 78
(Harry Dunlop) *mde all: jnd and drvn 2f out: battled on u.str.p and forged ahd ins fnl f: styd on wl* — 9/4[2]
4331 **2** 1 3/4 **Hi Note**[7] 4173 5-9-1 66 6ex .... HarryPoulton(5) 2 — 78
(Sheena West) *hld up in tch: wnt 2nd 4f out: upsides wnr and stl on bit 2f out: drvn and over 1f out: no ex and btn fnl 100yds* — 2/1[1]
0020 **3** 10 **Foster's Road**[7] 4166 4-9-7 74 .... OisinMurphy(7) 4 — 74
(Mick Channon) *hld up in tch in rr: effrt to chse ldng pair over 3f out: sn outpcd and wl btn fnl 2f* — 8/1
-100 **4** 18 **Rapid Heat Lad (IRE)**[42] 2990 4-9-5 65 .... (p) TomQueally 6 — 50
(Andrew Hollinshead) *chsd ldrs: rdn to press ldr over 5f out tl 4f out: dropped to last over 3f out: sn wknd: eased ins fnl f* — 7/2[3]

3m 33.11s (-1.69) **Going Correction** -0.30s/f (Firm)
WFA 3 from 4yo+ 17lb — 4 Ran SP% 97.4
Speed ratings (Par 103): **92,91,86,77**
CSF £5.59 TOTE £2.60; EX 5.30 Trifecta £8.80 Pool: £557.33 - 47.03 winning units..
Owner Mr & Mrs D Hearson **Bred** Granham Farm Partnership **Trained** Lambourn, Berks

FOCUS
A modest staying handicap, weakened further by the late withdrawal of Cape Alex, and dominated by the two market leaders.

4407 PAUL KELLEWAY MEMORIAL H'CAP — 2m
3:30 (3:30) (Class 3) (0-95,88) 3-Y-0+ — £7,439 (£2,213; £1,106; £553) Stalls Low

Form — RPR
0062 **1** **Aquilonius (IRE)**[11] 4075 4-9-1 75 .... (t) HarryBentley 6 — 84
(Stuart Williams) *t.k.h: mde all: set stdy gallop and allowed to go clr early on: 15 l clr 6f out: 2 l in front and rdn 2f out: kpt on and a in command fnl f* — 5/1[3]
15-4 **2** 1 **Teak (IRE)**[17] 3118 6-9-1 75 .... JamesDoyle 5 — 83
(Ian Williams) *chsd wnr: allowed wnr to go clr fr 11f out: clsd 5f out: drvn and 2 l down 2f out: kpt on but a hld by wnr fnl f* — 6/4[1]
0043 **3** 6 **Montaff**[18] 3807 7-9-4 78 .... MartinHarley 2 — 79
(Mick Channon) *hld up in rr: clsd on wnr 5f out: wnt 3rd over 3f out: drvn and no imp 2f out* — 3/1[2]
0454 **4** 10 **First Avenue**[25] 3560 8-9-5 86 .... AaronChave(7) 4 — 75
(Laura Mongan) *t.k.h: hld up in last pair: clsd on ldr but dropped to last 4f out: sn struggling: no ch fnl 2f* — 3/1[2]
010/ **5** 8 **Rain Mac**[38] 5700 5-10-0 88 .... PaulHanagan 1 — 67
(Donald McCain) *t.k.h: chsd ldng pair: clsd on wnr 5f out: rdn and lost pl over 3f out: sn wknd: bhd fnl 2f* — 10/1

3m 39.09s (4.29) **Going Correction** -0.30s/f (Firm) — 5 Ran SP% 115.8
Speed ratings (Par 107): **77,76,73,68,64**
CSF £13.76 TOTE £6.10: £1.90, £1.30; EX 10.90 Trifecta £33.60 Pool: £1,408.59 - 31.35 winning units..
Owner T W Morley & Mrs J Morley **Bred** Redmondstown Stud **Trained** Newmarket, Suffolk

FOCUS
This race was two classes higher than the preceding handicap over the same trip, but they went no pace at all early here and the winning time was almost six seconds slower. The result was a very tactical affair and all the plaudits go to Harry Bentley for a fabulously judged front-running ride aboard the winner.

4408 EMERSON CRANES/BRITISH STALLION STUDS EBF MAIDEN FILLIES' STKS (DIV I) — 6f (P)
4:00 (4:02) (Class 5) 2-Y-O — £3,067 (£905; £453) Stalls Low

Form — RPR
2 **1** **Along Again (IRE)**[17] 3863 2-9-0 0 .... RyanMoore 3 — 76+
(Sir Michael Stoute) *chsd ldr: rdn to ld 1f out: r.o wl u.p whn pressed ins fnl f: rdn out* — 10/11[1]
2 1/2 **Much Promise** 2-9-0 0 .... WilliamBuick 9 — 75+
(John Gosden) *chsd ldrs: rdn and effrt 2f out: hdwy to chse wnr jst ins fnl f: pressing ldr fnl 100yds: r.o wl but a hld* — 14/1
63 **3** 3 1/4 **Gender Agenda**[28] 3471 2-9-0 0 .... TomQueally 5 — 65+
(Michael Bell) *chsd ldrs: rdn and unable qck over 1f out: rallied ins fnl f: wnt 3rd wl ins fnl f: styd on* — 25/1
53 **4** 1 **Cockney Belle**[32] 3324 2-9-0 0 .... DaneO'Neill 4 — 62
(Marco Botti) *chsd ldrs on inner: effrt u.p over 1f out: chsd ldng pair and drvn jst ins fnl f: sn outpcd and lost 3rd wl ins fnl f* — 20/1
0 **5** 2 **Setai**[13] 3978 2-9-0 0 .... KierenFallon 1 — 56
(Brian Meehan) *led: rdn wl over 1f out: drvn and hdd 1f out: wknd ins fnl f* — 8/1[3]
0 **6** 3/4 **Threetimesalady**[7] 4164 2-9-0 0 .... LukeMorris 8 — 54+
(Sir Mark Prescott Bt) *outpcd in last trio and pushed along early: clsd and hdwy into midfield and on bridle over 3f out: outpcd wl over 1f out: plugged on* — 66/1
320 **7** nk **Hoku (IRE)**[18] 3829 2-9-0 0 .... HarryBentley 7 — 53+
(Olly Stevens) *v.s.a and lost 10 l: clsd on to bk of field and in tch 4f out: effrt but forced wd bnd 2f out: no imp over 1f out* — 5/2[2]
40 **8** 1/2 **Talent Spotter**[19] 3760 2-9-0 0 .... MickaelBarzalona 6 — 51
(Saeed bin Suroor) *s.i.s: sn rdn and outpcd in last trio: clsd and in tch 4f out: rdn and struggling over 2f out: outpcd wl over 1f out* — 12/1
9 2 1/4 **Letthemusictakeus (IRE)** 2-9-0 0 .... JimCrowley 10 — 44
(Ralph Beckett) *in tch in midfield: rdn and outpcd ent fnl 2f: wknd over 1f out* — 33/1
10 nse **Rosina Jay (IRE)** 2-9-0 0 .... AdamKirby 11 — 44
(Clive Cox) *in tch in midfield on outer: dropped to rr and rn green bnd 2f out: n.d after* — 50/1

1m 13.88s (1.98) **Going Correction** +0.175s/f (Slow) — 10 Ran SP% 121.4
Speed ratings (Par 91): **93,92,88,86,84 83,82,81,78,78**
Tote Swingers: 1&2 £4.40, 1&3 £7.10, 2&3 £17.00 CSF £16.51 TOTE £1.80: £1.30, £2.30, £2.80; EX 18.00 Trifecta £217.20 Pool: £3,498.66 - 12.07 winning units..
Owner Ballymore Thoroughbred Ltd **Bred** Dayton Investments Ltd **Trained** Newmarket, Suffolk

FOCUS
An interesting fillies' maiden featuring a few with previous form and a couple of well-bred newcomers. The winner showed improved form with a nice debut from the runner-up.

4409 EMERSON CRANES/BRITISH STALLION STUDS EBF MAIDEN FILLIES' STKS (DIV II) — 6f (P)
4:30 (4:31) (Class 5) 2-Y-O — £3,067 (£905; £453) Stalls Low

Form — RPR
54 **1** **Inspiriter**[27] 3510 2-9-0 0 .... SilvestreDeSousa 9 — 76
(Saeed bin Suroor) *pushed rt s: rcvrd and hdwy to chse ldr after 2f: rdn and chal over 1f out: kpt on wl u.p to ld last strides* — 7/1
0 **2** hd **Gentle Breeze (IRE)**[19] 3781 2-9-0 0 .... MickaelBarzalona 6 — 75
(Saeed bin Suroor) *chsd ldr tl led after 1f: rdn wl over 1f out: kpt on u.p fnl f tl hdd last strides* — 3/1[2]
4 **3** 1 1/4 **Lady Tiana**[19] 3760 2-9-0 0 .... LukeMorris 3 — 72
(Lucy Wadham) *t.k.h: broke fast and led for 1f: chsd ldrs after: drvn and effrt over 1f out: n.m.r and styd on same pce ins fnl f* — 7/2[3]
4 2 1/4 **Dorothy B (IRE)** 2-9-0 0 .... WilliamBuick 4 — 65+
(John Gosden) *in tch in last trio: swtchd lft and hdwy wl over 1f out: chsd ldng trio whn rn green and hung rt jst ins fnl f: kpt on steadily* — 11/4[1]
46 **5** 1 1/2 **Herbah**[32] 3318 2-9-0 0 ....[1] PaulHanagan 11 — 60
(Roger Varian) *pushed rt s: hld up in tch in last trio: hdwy on outer whn sltly hmpd wl over 1f out: kpt on fnl f: no threat to ldrs* — 6/1

0 **6** *nk* **River Goddess (IRE)**[19] 3760 2-9-0 0........ SteveDrowne 8 60+
(Charles Hills) *dwlt and sltly hmpd s: t.k.h: hld up in midfield: swtchd rt and effrt bnd 2f out: no imp* **40/1**

7 *2¼* **Spiritual Flame** 2-9-0 0........ RyanMoore 5 53
(William Haggas) *bhd: effrt on inner over 1f out: no imp* **8/1**

8 *1* **Golly Miss Molly** 2-9-0 0........ RichardKingscote 7 50
(Jeremy Gask) *wnt rt s: t.k.h: chsd ldrs: rdn and unable qck wl over 1f out: wknd ent fnl f* **33/1**

0 **9** *1¾* **Island Remede**[13] 3991 2-9-0 0........ JamesDoyle 1 45
(Ed Dunlop) *in tch in midfield: rdn 1/2-way: lost pl wl over 1f out: sn wknd* **50/1**

1m 13.68s (1.78) **Going Correction** +0.175s/f (Slow) **9** Ran SP% **119.1**
Speed ratings (Par 91): **95,94,93,90,88 87,84,83,81**
Tote Swingers: 1&2 £5.70, 1&3 £5.10, 2&3 £3.30 CSF £29.02 TOTE £5.90: £2.30, £2.00, £1.90; EX 18.00 Trifecta £117.20 Pool: £61.45 - 1,99352 winning units..
Owner Godolphin **Bred** Darley **Trained** Newmarket, Suffolk

FOCUS
The winning time was 0.2sec quicker than the first division and it produced a 1-2 for Godolphin. The front three were up with the pace throughout. Average form for the race.

4410 OILFIELD OFFSHORE UNDERWRITING LTD H'CAP — 6f (P)
5:00 (5:00) (Class 6) (0-65,65) 3-Y-O — **£2,045** (£603; £302) **Stalls Low**

Form — RPR

63-6 **1** **Perfect Venture**[13] 3988 3-9-2 **60**........ AdamKirby 3 70
(Clive Cox) *mde all: rdn and qcknd clr 2f out: in command after: r.o wl* **6/1**

0030 **2** *2½* **Winnie Perry**[16] 3888 3-9-0 **58**........ RichardKingscote 1 60
(Rod Millman) *chsd ldr: rdn and unable qck w wnr 2f out: kpt on for 2nd but no threat to wnr* **16/1**

-063 **3** *3* **Poitin**[25] 3576 3-9-7 **65**........ JamesDoyle 2 57
(Harry Dunlop) *hld up wl in tch: effrt u.p on inner over 1f out: wnt 3rd 1f out: styd on but no imp* **12/1**

6600 **4** *2* **Copper Leyf**[16] 3888 3-8-3 **47**........(t) CathyGannon 6 33
(Jeremy Gask) *bhd: hdwy but stl plenty to do over 1f out: styd on: nvr trbld ldrs* **50/1**

0064 **5** *1* **Encapsulated**[16] 3903 3-9-0 **58**........(p) RobertHavlin 4 41
(Roger Ingram) *chsd ldrs tl squeezed for room: hmpd and dropped to rr after 1f: hdwy on outer 2f out: styd on fnl f: nvr trbld ldrs* **5/1**[3]

4503 **6** *¾* **Whatwehavewehold**[19] 3762 3-8-13 **57**........ AndrewMullen 7 37
(Alan McCabe) *taken down early: t.k.h: chsd ldrs: rdn and struggling ent fnl 2f: wl btn over 1f out: wknd fnl f* **4/1**[2]

6034 **7** *nk* **Triple Aitch (USA)**[1] 4378 3-9-4 **62**........(b) LukeMorris 8 41
(Gay Kelleway) *chsd ldrs: drvn and outpcd 2f out: btn over 1f out: fdd fnl f* **7/1**

2046 **8** *2¾* **Angels Calling**[35] 3216 3-8-12 **56**........(p) JimCrowley 10 27
(Mrs K Burke) *in tch in midfield on outer: lost pl and bhd 2f out: n.d after* **8/1**

40-3 **9** *½* **Black Eyed Girl (IRE)**[15] 3915 3-8-13 **57**........[1] ShaneKelly 5 26
(J S Moore) *hld up in last trio: outpcd over 2f out: n.d fnl 2f* **25/1**

-314 **10** *½* **My Sweet Lord**[26] 3533 3-9-3 **61**........(p) HayleyTurner 9 28
(Mark Usher) *sn rdn along in last trio: n.d* **3/1**[1]

1503 **11** *2¼* **Idle Curiosity (IRE)**[30] 3405 3-8-11 **55**........ PatCosgrave 11 15
(Jim Boyle) *in tch in midfield: rdn and struggling ent fnl 2f: sn lost pl: bhd ins fnl f* **20/1**

1m 13.31s (1.41) **Going Correction** +0.175s/f (Slow) **11** Ran SP% **123.7**
Speed ratings (Par 98): **97,93,89,87,85 84,84,80,79,79 76**
Tote Swingers: 1&2 £20.60, 1&3 £11.90, 2&3 £14.30 CSF £99.87 CT £802.23 TOTE £8.30: £3.70, £5.20, £2.10; EX 99.50 Trifecta £1429.20 Part won. Pool: £1,905.65 - 0.55 winning units..

Owner Mildmay Racing **Bred** Mildmay Bloodstock Ltd **Trained** Lambourn, Berks

FOCUS
A moderate sprint handicap and another race on the Polytrack favouring prominent racers. The runner-up sets the level, rated to his Warwick form.

4411 JOHN DUTTON 65TH BIRTHDAY H'CAP — 1m 2f (P)
5:30 (5:32) (Class 6) (0-60,66) 3-Y-O+ — **£2,045** (£603; £302) **Stalls Low**

Form — RPR

-144 **1** **Precision Five**[21] 3676 4-9-4 **55**........(p) JamesDoyle 9 65
(Jeremy Gask) *hld up in tch in midfield: rdn and effrt to chse ldrs over 2f out: swtchd rt and chsd ldr 1f out: led and racd awkwardly fnl 100yds: drvn out* **5/1**[3]

3050 **2** *¾* **Mishrif (USA)**[22] 3656 7-9-9 **60**........(v) SilvestreDeSousa 2 68
(J R Jenkins) *broke wl: led: drvn clr over 1f out: hdd fnl 100yds: tried to rally but no ex towards fin* **16/1**

0031 **3** *1¾* **Khelac**[7] 4170 3-9-5 **66** 6ex........(b) LiamKeniry 1 71
(Philip Hide) *chsd ldrs: wnt 2nd and travelling wl 3f out: drvn and fnd little over 1f out: 3rd and btn 1f out: wknd ins fnl f* **5/2**[1]

0262 **4** *2¼* **Princess Willow**[35] 3213 5-9-4 **55**........ KirstyMilczarek 4 55
(John E Long) *t.k.h: chsd ldr for 1f: chsd ldrs after: rdn and unable qck 2f out: plugged on same pce after* **7/2**[2]

0-42 **5** *2¾* **Anginola (IRE)**[2] 4355 4-9-3 **57**........ RyanPowell(3) 10 52
(John Ryan) *s.i.s: bhd: sme hdwy 5f out: rdn and past btn horses over 2f out: styd on but nvr trbld ldrs* **12/1**

-P00 **6** *¾* **Mr Fickle (IRE)**[30] 3416 4-9-6 **57**........ ShaneKelly 8 50
(Gary Moore) *bhd: rdn 4f out: hdwy past btn horses over 2f out: plugged on fnl f: nvr trbld ldrs* **25/1**

2406 **7** *2¾* **Signora Frasi (IRE)**[30] 3409 8-9-4 **55**........ RichardKingscote 3 43
(Tony Newcombe) *in tch in midfield: rdn and struggling over 2f out: wknd over 1f out* **12/1**

050- **8** *13* **Allanit (GER)**[359] 4405 9-9-4 **55**........ MickyFenton 5 17
(Des Donovan) *taken down early and led to s: t.k.h: chsd ldr after 1f tl 3f out: sn dropped out: wl bhd and eased ins fnl f* **16/1**

606 **9** *2½* **Fire King**[14] 3951 7-8-11 **55**........(p) OisinMurphy(7) 13 12
(Paul Burgoyne) *hld up in midfield: rdn 4f out: wknd over 2f out: bhd and eased ins fnl f* **8/1**

000- **10** *69* **My Manekineko**[260] 7470 4-9-4 **55**........ AdamKirby 12
(J R Jenkins) *racd wd and hung rt on bnds: in tch in midfield tl lost pl bnd 4f out: lost tch and eased 3f out: wl t.o and virtually p.u fnl f* **16/1**

3-00 **11** *2¼* **Russian Storm**[25] 3580 5-9-2 **58**........ JemmaMarshall(5) 7
(Pat Phelan) *taken down early: a bhd: lost tch over 3f out: wl t.o and virtually p.u fnl f* **33/1**

1130 **12** *¾* **Salient**[25] 3580 9-9-3 **54**........ SebSanders 11
(Michael Attwater) *sn rdn and along in last quartet: lost tch over 2f out: wl t.o and virtually p.u fnl f* **12/1**

2m 7.04s (0.44) **Going Correction** +0.175s/f (Slow)
WFA 3 from 4yo+ 10lb **12** Ran SP% **126.1**
Speed ratings (Par 101): **105,104,103,101,99 98,96,85,83,28 26,26**
Tote Swingers 1&2 £16.10, 2&3 £8.10, 1&3 £4.40 CSF £88.11 CT £254.16 TOTE £5.10: £1.90, £4.80, £1.90; EX 101.30 Trifecta £336.30 Pool: £2,428.17 - 5.41 winning units..
Owner Calne Engineering Ltd **Bred** Edward J G Young **Trained** Sutton Veny, Wilts

FOCUS
Another moderate handicap and several of these didn't appear to be enjoying themselves. The runner-up is rated to this year's form and sets the level.
T/Jkpt: £3,550.00 to a £1 stake. Pool: £25,000.00 - 5.00 winning tickets. T/Plt: £26.00 to a £1 stake. Pool: £71,615.13 - 2,006.08 winning tickets. T/Qpdt: £12.20 to a £1 stake. Pool: £3,947.83 - 238.60 winning tickets. SP

4078 SANDOWN (R-H)
Wednesday, July 17

OFFICIAL GOING: Good to firm (watered; 8.4)
Wind: Almost Nil Weather: Hot and humid

4412 DEVINE HOMES MAIDEN STKS — 5f 6y
6:05 (6:05) (Class 5) 2-Y-O — **£3,234** (£962; £481; £240) **Stalls Low**

Form — RPR

3 **1** **Storm Trooper (IRE)**[14] 3948 2-9-5 0........ RichardHughes 5 83+
(Richard Hannon) *mde all: pushed clr wl over 1f out: reminder ins fnl f: eased last strides* **1/4**[1]

0 **2** *4* **Kickboxer (IRE)**[9] 4121 2-9-5 0........ MartinHarley 2 69+
(Mick Channon) *dwlt: settled in last: pushed along after 2f: prog between rivals to go 2nd jst ins fnl f: styd on but no ch w wnr* **7/1**[2]

44 **3** *6* **Hot Stock (FR)**[72] 2082 2-9-5 0........ JackMitchell 4 47
(Pat Murphy) *chsd ldng pair: rdn to dispute 2nd over 1f out to jst ins fnl f: wknd* **15/2**[3]

00 **4** *1¾* **Little Big Man**[23] 3631 2-9-5 0........ DaneO'Neill 6 41
(Sylvester Kirk) *in tch: rdn to chse wnr jst over 2f out: no imp: wknd fnl f* **40/1**

400 **5** *7* **Maximilianthefirst**[7] 4175 2-9-5 0........ TomQueally 7 16
(P J O'Gorman) *chsd wnr to jst over 2f out: wknd rapidly: t.o* **16/1**

1m 1.7s (0.10) **Going Correction** -0.05s/f (Good) **5** Ran SP% **112.6**
Speed ratings (Par 94): **97,90,81,78,67**
CSF £2.84 TOTE £1.20: £1.10, £1.90; EX 2.60 Trifecta £4.90 Pool: £1,659.78 - 252.31 winning units..
Owner M Tabor, D Smith & Mrs J Magnier **Bred** M Fahy & Rathbarry Stud **Trained** East Everleigh, Wilts

FOCUS
Rail on Sprint course 3yds in, Round course at inner configuration and all distances as advertised. Martin Harley described the ground as "good to firm, but perfect". A modest juvenile maiden for the course, lacking depth, and the short-price favourite scored with ease. There is little depth to the form but the winner scored in straightforward fashion.

4413 STUBHUB TICKETS H'CAP — 5f 6y
6:35 (6:35) (Class 4) (0-85,84) 3-Y-O — **£4,690** (£1,395; £697; £348) **Stalls Low**

Form — RPR

3214 **1** **Pixilated**[21] 3677 3-9-1 **78**........ RyanMoore 6 84
(Gay Kelleway) *mde virtually all and grad crossed towards far rail fr outside draw: jnd over 1f out: drvn fnl f jst hld on* **8/1**

43-4 **2** *nk* **Exceptionelle**[40] 3058 3-9-7 **84**........ RichardHughes 1 93+
(Roger Varian) *hld up and sn in 5th against rail: gng easily but looking for room fr 1/2-way: swtchd bk to rail fnl f: rdn w animation last 100yds and tried to squeeze though on wnr's ins: couldn't get there in time* **10/11**[1]

2145 **3** *nk* **Firmdecisions (IRE)**[19] 3782 3-8-12 **75**........(v) KierenFallon 3 79
(Brett Johnson) *sn outpcd and pushed along in last: prog on outer wl over 1f out: kpt on wl fnl f: jst lacked pce to chal* **8/1**

0033 **4** *1* **Miss Diva**[23] 3634 3-9-0 **82**........ WilliamTwiston-Davies(5) 2 82
(Richard Hannon) *prom: pressed wnr jst over 2f out: upsides over 1f out tl nt qckn jst ins fnl f* **13/2**[3]

-213 **5** *1¾* **Daylight**[21] 3677 3-9-2 **79**........ JimmyFortune 4 73
(Andrew Balding) *taken down early: chsd ldrs: rdn over 2f out: cl enough over 1f out: fdd fnl f* **9/2**[2]

0000 **6** *1¾* **Lady Phill**[18] 3803 3-9-5 **82**........(p) KierenFox 5 70
(Bill Turner) *chsd wnr to jst over 2f out: sn lost pl and btn* **20/1**

1m 1.5s (-0.10) **Going Correction** -0.05s/f (Good) **6** Ran SP% **110.9**
Speed ratings (Par 102): **98,97,97,95,92 89**
Tote Swingers: 1&2 £3.20, 1&3 £3.30, 2&3 £2.70 CSF £15.52 TOTE £5.30: £2.40, £1.20; EX 18.40 Trifecta £69.20 Pool: £1,257.18 - 36.61 winning units..
Owner Patricia Crook & Francis Aspin **Bred** A Christou **Trained** Exning, Suffolk

FOCUS
Just a fair sprint handicap, not run at the furious early pace anticipated with several potential front-runners in the field. The runner-up endured a nightmare run through and would have won readily otherwise. The form looks messy.

4414 ROBERT DYAS MAIDEN AUCTION STKS — 7f 16y
7:10 (7:13) (Class 5) 2-Y-O — **£3,234** (£962; £481; £240) **Stalls Low**

Form — RPR

1 **Shifting Power** 2-9-1 0........ RichardHughes 12 84+
(Richard Hannon) *mde all: gng easily over 2f out: stretched away over 1f out: comf* **4/1**[1]

6 **2** *3¼* **Ellalan**[23] 3640 2-8-13 0........ MartinLane 15 74
(David Simcock) *racd alone and wd early: sn chsd wnr: shkn up 2f out: kpt on but n.d over 1f out* **33/1**

5 **3** *1* **Needless Shouting (IRE)**[17] 3857 2-8-9 0........ MartinHarley 7 67
(Mick Channon) *chsd ldng pair: shkn up over 2f out: kpt on same pce after* **4/1**[1]

3 **4** *½* **Top Of The Glas (IRE)**[56] 2562 2-8-11 0........ JimCrowley 2 68+
(Alan Jarvis) *dwlt: wl in tch: prog over 2f out: shkn up to chse ldrs over 1f out: kpt on same pce after* **5/1**[2]

5 *2* **Ninety Minutes (IRE)** 2-8-13 0........ FrederikTylicki 9 64
(John Best) *chsd ldng trio: shkn up over 2f out: one pce over 1f out: fdd nr fin* **33/1**

00 **6** *2* **Rising Dawn (IRE)**[21] 3689 2-9-1 0........ RyanMoore 16 61+
(Richard Hannon) *dwlt: wl in rr: only one bhd him over 2f out: styd on fr over 1f out: nrst fin* **8/1**

7 *hd* **Photography (IRE)** 2-8-13 0........................[1] PatCosgrave 13 59+
(Hugo Palmer) *wl in tch in midfield: shkn up over 2f out: sn outpcd: kpt on fnl f* **16/1**

60 8 *nk* **Choral Clan (IRE)**[21] 3689 2-8-9 0........................ JackMitchell 3 54
(Philip Mitchell) *hld up in rr: pushed along and kpt on one pce fnl 2f: nvr involved* **100/1**

9 *1 1/4* **Winter Spice (IRE)** 2-9-1 0........................ AdamKirby 8 57+
(Clive Cox) *hld up wl in rr: nudged along and one pce fnl 2f: n.d* **15/2**[3]

5 10 *shd* **Craftsmanship (FR)**[20] 3717 2-8-11 0........................ NickyMackay 4 52
(Robert Eddery) *chsd ldrs disputing 6th: shkn up over 2f out: wknd over 1f out* **12/1**

11 *hd* **Polar Express** 2-8-11 0........................ WilliamCarson 1 52
(Jonathan Portman) *hld up and wl in rr: pushed along over 2f out: nvr involved* **20/1**

6 12 *nse* **Bognor (USA)**[20] 3717 2-8-13 0........................ CathyGannon 6 54
(Jo Hughes) *t.k.h: chsd ldrs in 5th: shkn up 2f out: wknd jst over 1f out* **8/1**

13 *1/2* **Nice Arty (IRE)** 2-8-11 0........................ FergusSweeney 10 50
(Jamie Osborne) *slowly away: a wl in rr: kpt on fnl f on inner* **33/1**

14 *5* **Trip To Paris (IRE)** 2-8-13 0........................ JamesDoyle 14 39
(Ed Dunlop) *restless in stalls: chsd ldrs disputing 6th: shkn up and wknd qckly over 2f out* **16/1**

15 *1/2* **Benoordenhout (IRE)** 2-8-5 0 ow1....................[1] MatthewLawson(5) 11 35
(Jonathan Portman) *slowly away: rn green and a bhd* **50/1**

0 16 *19* **Desert Flute**[23] 3631 2-8-4 0........................ JordanUys(7) 5
(Paul Cole) *awkward s: rn green on outer in midfield: veered bdly lft and wknd 2f out: t.o* **66/1**

1m 30.7s (1.20) **Going Correction** -0.20s/f (Firm) **16** Ran SP% **128.1**
Speed ratings (Par 94): **85,81,80,79,77 75,74,74,73,72 72,72,72,66,65 44**
Tote Swingers: 1&2 £52.20, 1&3 £5.10, 2&3 £43.90 CSF £155.70 TOTE £5.60: £2.30, £10.90, £1.60; EX 211.60 Trifecta £1034.70 Part won. Pool: £1,379.60 - 0.26 winning units..
Owner Ms Elaine Chivers & Potensis Ltd **Bred** John And Susan Davis **Trained** East Everleigh, Wilts

FOCUS
Ordinary maiden form, with them going a very steady gallop, and it was a huge advantage to race on the speed. The winner has the scope to do better with the fourth the best from the rear.

4415 XL GROUP H'CAP 1m 14y
7:40 (7:45) (Class 3) (0-90,90) 3-Y-0+ **£7,439** (£2,213; £1,106; £553) **Stalls** Low

Form RPR

1-15 1 **Ehtedaam (USA)**[39] 3113 4-9-10 **86**........................(p) PaulHanagan 7 102
(Saeed bin Suroor) *trckd ldng pair tl moved up to ld over 6f out: mde rest: shkn up 2f out: drvn and grad drew clr over 1f out* **11/10**[1]

025 2 *5* **Albaqaa**[5] 4258 8-9-2 **83**........................ RobertTart(5) 3 87
(P J O'Gorman) *hld up in 4th: sed pulling after 2f: disp 2nd fr 1/2-way: rdn and nt qckn 2f out: one pce after* **10/1**

253- 3 *2 1/2* **Beedee**[264] 7374 3-9-3 **87**........................ RichardHughes 5 83
(Richard Hannon) *hld up in last: rdn over 2f out: plugged on fr over 1f out to take 3rd ins fnl f* **8/1**

3121 4 *2* **Cruiser**[16] 3886 5-9-2 **78**........................(p) RyanMoore 2 72
(William Muir) *led to over 6f out: chsd wnr: rdn over 2f out: wknd jst over 1f out* **11/4**[2]

0044 5 *13* **First Post (IRE)**[17] 3864 6-8-10 **72**........................ DaneO'Neill 4 47
(Derek Haydn Jones) *t.k.h: trckd ldr 1f: styd cl up tl wknd jst over 2f out: eased* **6/1**[3]

1m 40.2s (-3.10) **Going Correction** -0.20s/f (Firm)
WFA 3 from 4yo+ 8lb **5** Ran SP% **108.8**
Speed ratings (Par 107): **107,102,99,97,84**
CSF £12.17 TOTE £2.00: £1.50, £3.20; EX 14.20 Trifecta £49.30 Pool: £1,352.73 - 20.54 winning units..
Owner Godolphin **Bred** Grapestock Llc **Trained** Newmarket, Suffolk

FOCUS
Not a particularly competitive heat and it was yet another all-the-way winner on the night. He is likely to be hit hard by the handicapper for this, and needs to improve further.

4416 DEVINE HOMES H'CAP 1m 2f 7y
8:15 (8:17) (Class 4) (0-80,79) 3-Y-0 **£4,690** (£1,395; £697; £348) **Stalls** Low

Form RPR

1- 1 **Mighty Yar (IRE)**[231] 7899 3-9-4 **76**........................ TomQueally 5 91+
(Lady Cecil) *hld up in last: plenty to do 3f out: gd prog over 2f out: edgd rt and reminder over 1f out: stened and r.o to ld last 150yds: sn in command: impressive* **11/4**[1]

1-43 2 *3 3/4* **Leitrim Pass (USA)**[31] 3369 3-9-4 **76**........................ ShaneKelly 2 83
(William Haggas) *led: dashed for home over 3f out: kpt on wl fr 2f out: hdd last 150yds: no ch w wnr after* **11/4**[1]

-454 3 *1* **Swift Bounty**[19] 3763 3-9-5 **77**........................ JimCrowley 1 82
(Alan Jarvis) *t.k.h: trckd ldng pair after 2f: chsd ldr wl over 2f out: trying to cl whn wnr swept by fnl f: no ex after* **6/1**

0-11 4 *6* **Pleasure Bent**[34] 3241 3-9-6 **78**........................ KierenFallon 4 71
(Luca Cumani) *hld up in 6th: shoved along 4f out: sme prog u.p over 2f out: modest 4th fr over 1f out* **9/2**[3]

-205 5 *6* **Three Choirs (IRE)**[19] 3785 3-8-10 **73**........................(tp) LauraPike(5) 3 54
(William Stone) *chsd ldr 2f: sn in 4th: shkn up wl over 3f out: no hdwy after: wknd fnl f* **33/1**

4-1 6 *8* **Mount Tiger**[23] 3641 3-9-7 **79**........................ NeilCallan 7 44
(James Tate) *plld hrd: trckd ldr after 2f tl wl over 2f out: wknd qckly* **7/2**[2]

423 7 *4 1/2* **Fearless Lad (IRE)**[145] 748 3-8-10 **68**........................(t) FrederikTylicki 8 24
(John Best) *hld up in 5th: wknd qckly over 2f out* **20/1**

2m 7.8s (-2.70) **Going Correction** -0.20s/f (Firm) **7** Ran SP% **115.7**
Speed ratings (Par 102): **102,99,98,93,88 82,78**
Tote Swingers: 1&2 £3.60, 1&3 £4.90, 2&3 £2.70 CSF £10.80 CT £40.84 TOTE £3.30: £2.00, £2.10; EX 13.00 Trifecta £48.80 Pool: £1,385.25 - 21.27 winning units..
Owner R A H Evans **Bred** Gerry Flannery Developments **Trained** Newmarket, Suffolk

FOCUS
This looked a strong 3yo handicap beforehand and, although run at a steady gallop, it produced a really taking winner. The runner-up is rated in line with his better efforts , while the third is rated close to his 1m form.

4417 KISS MIX H'CAP 1m 6f
8:50 (8:51) (Class 5) (0-75,74) 3-Y-0 **£3,234** (£962; £481; £240) **Stalls** Low

Form RPR

1224 1 **Argent Knight**[13] 3982 3-9-7 **74**........................(v) SteveDrowne 1 86
(William Jarvis) *trckd ldng pair: shkn up to go 2nd over 2f out: led over 1f out: rdn and hld on wl fnl f* **5/2**[2]

-304 2 *nk* **Montjess (IRE)**[16] 3900 3-9-1 **68**........................(v) RichardKingscote 5 79
(Tom Dascombe) *led: rdn over 2f out: hdd over 1f out: rallied wl fnl f: a jst hld* **16/1**

01 3 *1* **Madame Vestris (IRE)**[27] 3491 3-9-4 **71**........................ RyanMoore 3 81
(Sir Michael Stoute) *trckd ldrs in 5th: shkn up 3f out: chsd ldng pair 2f out: drvn and styd on: nvr quite able to chal* **6/4**[1]

4343 4 *7* **Magika**[26] 3535 3-9-1 **68**........................(t) AdamKirby 2 68
(Marco Botti) *hld up in 6th: prog to dispute 3rd 2f out: sn rdn and wknd* **8/1**[3]

5246 5 *1 1/2* **Enaitch (IRE)**[13] 3982 3-9-6 **73**........................ MartinHarley 7 71
(Mick Channon) *chsd ldr: tried to chal 9f out: lost 2nd over 2f out: wknd over 1f out* **12/1**

-053 6 *nk* **Halling's Wish**[27] 3497 3-8-2 **55** oh1........................ CathyGannon 8 53
(John Best) *hld up in 7th: rdn 3f out: no prog and btn 2f out: fdd* **25/1**

4344 7 *3 1/4* **Bursledon (IRE)**[13] 3990 3-9-4 **71**........................ RichardHughes 6 64
(Richard Hannon) *rrd s and slowly away: hld up in last: rdn 3f out: no prog 2f out: sn wknd* **10/1**

1022 8 *1/2* **Dali's Lover (IRE)**[18] 3806 3-9-5 **72**........................ WilliamCarson 4 64
(Charles Hills) *cl up in 4th: rdn and disp 3rd over 3f out: wknd over 2f out* **8/1**[3]

3m 3.4s (-1.10) **Going Correction** -0.20s/f (Firm) **8** Ran SP% **117.3**
Speed ratings (Par 100): **95,94,94,90,89 89,87,87**
Tote Swingers 1&2 £8.90, 2&3 £10.90, 1&3 £2.00 CSF £42.30 CT £79.46 TOTE £3.90: £1.40, £2.80, £1.30; EX 54.00 Trifecta £234.70 Pool: £1,470.65 - 4.69 winning units..
Owner Dr J Walker **Bred** Mr & Mrs A E Pakenham **Trained** Newmarket, Suffolk

FOCUS
Another race run at a steady enough gallop and it again paid to race prominently. The runner-up sets the level, rated to the best view of her latest form.
T/Plt: £9.20 to a £1 stake. Pool: £69,662.56 - 5,470.29 winning tickets. T/Qpdt: £6.50 to a £1 stake. Pool: £5,710.63 - 646.11 winning tickets. JN

4418 - 4420a (Foreign Racing) - See Raceform Interactive

4362 VICHY
Wednesday, July 17

OFFICIAL GOING: Turf: soft

4421a GRAND PRIX DE VICHY-AUVERGNE (GROUP 3) (3YO+) (TURF) 1m 2f
7:53 (12:00) 3-Y-0+ **£32,520** (£13,008; £9,756; £6,504; £3,252)

RPR

1 **Saga Dream (FR)**[37] 3165 7-9-6 0........................ ChristopheSoumillon 4 115
(F Lemercier, France) **47/10**[3]

2 *nk* **Vally Jem (FR)**[43] 2969 4-8-13 0........................(p) ArnaudBourgeais 1 107
(D Sepulchre, France) **47/1**

3 *2 1/2* **Shamalgan (FR)**[53] 2683 6-9-2 0........................ Roberto-CarlosMontenegro 2 105
(X Thomas-Demeaulte, France) **9/1**

4 *1/4* **Pump Pump Boy (FR)**[32] 3362 5-9-2 0........................ FranckBlondel 3 105
(M Pimbonnet, France) **24/1**

5 *nk* **Making Eyes (IRE)**[19] 3775 5-8-13 0........................ IoritzMendizabal 8 101
(Hugo Palmer) **27/1**

6 *1/4* **Saonois (FR)**[45] 2908 4-9-2 0........................ AntoineHamelin 9 103
(J-P Gauvin, France) **6/4**[1]

7 *1/2* **Nutello (USA)**[53] 2683 4-9-2 0........................(p) FlavienPrat 5 102
(C Laffon-Parias, France) **14/1**

8 *3/4* **Albion**[37] 3165 4-9-2 0........................(b[1]) MaximeGuyon 6 101
(A Fabre, France) **39/10**[2]

9 *5* **Harem Lady (FR)**[37] 3165 4-8-13 0........................ GregoryBenoist 7 88
(D Smaga, France) **68/10**

2m 7.79s (-0.81) **9** Ran SP% **117.1**
WIN (incl. 1 euro stake): 5.70. PLACES: 2.10, 7.30, 2.90. DF: 114.70. SF: 196.00.
Owner Freddy Lemercier **Bred** A Audouinm, F Landais, A Oger & B Audouin **Trained** France

3921 BRIGHTON (L-H)
Thursday, July 18

OFFICIAL GOING: Firm (8.7)
Wind: light, behind Weather: hot and sunny

4422 LIFESTYLE MOTOR GROUP MEDIAN AUCTION MAIDEN STKS 5f 213y
2:20 (2:22) (Class 6) 2-Y-0 **£1,940** (£577; £288; £144) **Stalls** Centre

Form RPR

2 1 **Tobougg Happy**[15] 3948 2-9-0 0........................ NeilCallan 3 83+
(James Tate) *mde all: shkn and readily drew clr over 1f out: eased towards fin: v easily* **4/11**[1]

352 2 *7* **Hatti (IRE)**[8] 4177 2-9-0 0........................(p) KirstyMilczarek 2 61
(John Ryan) *chsd ldng pair: chsd wnr over 2f out: rdn and btn over 1f out: kpt on for clr 2nd* **4/1**[2]

0 3 *4 1/2* **Fine Art Fair (IRE)**[34] 3288 2-9-5 0........................ GeorgeBaker 4 51
(Gary Moore) *in tch: rdn and c towards centre over 2f out: outpcd and modest 3rd whn edgd lft 1f out* **10/1**[3]

4 *2* **Smart Payer** 2-9-5 0........................ CathyGannon 1 44
(Jo Hughes) *v.s.a: sn rcvrd and in tch in rr: rdn and struggling 2f out: sn wknd* **20/1**

6 5 *6* **Chanceuse**[36] 3189 2-9-0 0........................ LukeMorris 5 20
(Gay Kelleway) *chsd wnr tl over 2f out: sn rdn and struggling: wknd and bhd over 1f out* **50/1**

1m 8.82s (-1.38) **Going Correction** -0.35s/f (Firm) **5** Ran SP% **109.1**
Speed ratings (Par 92): **95,85,79,77,69**
CSF £2.09 TOTE £1.40: £1.10, £1.50; EX 1.90 Trifecta £4.80 Pool: £1915.83 - 297.67 winning units..
Owner Saif Ali **Bred** Capt A L Smith-Maxwell **Trained** Newmarket, Suffolk

FOCUS
Railed dolled out from 6f to 2.5f as at last meeting. A modest small-field juvenile maiden in which the odds-on favourite appeared to have a gilt-edged opportunity if handling ground officially described as firm, and she duly obliged. She looks pretty useful and is another to compliment the Wee Jean Chepstow form.

4423 CHUBE COOL NEW BREATHALYSER H'CAP (DIV I) 6f 209y
2:50 (2:50) (Class 6) (0-55,55) 3-Y-0+ **£1,940** (£577; £288; £144) **Stalls** Centre

Form RPR

5034 1 **Just Isla**[18] 3859 3-8-5 **46** oh1........................(p) LukeMorris 9 52
(Peter Makin) *chsd ldrs: chal u.p over 1f out: hrd drvn to ld 1f out: edgd lft and styd on wl fnl f* **3/1**[1]

030- 2 *1/2* **Squirrel Wood (IRE)**[239] 7816 5-9-6 **54**........................ GeorgeBaker 10 62
(George Baker) *chsd ldr: edgd out rt and effrt ent fnl 2f: ev ch fr over 1f out: edgd lft and unable qck ins fnl f* **4/1**[3]

2226 **3** 1 ½ **Do More Business (IRE)**[51] 2747 6-9-3 **51**....................(bt) ShaneKelly 6 55
(Liam Corcoran) *stdd s: t.k.h: hld up in tch in midfield: effrt u.p over 1f out: wnt 3rd and edgd lft ins fnl f: no imp* **7/2**[2]

-024 **4** 1 ¼ **Ridgeway Sapphire**[16] 3922 6-8-5 **46**......................(v) ShelleyBirkett(7) 1 47
(Mark Usher) *hld up in tch in midfield: stmbld over 4f out: effrt and styd towards inner over 2f out: chsng ldrs whn stmbld again over 1f: no ex: wknd fnl 100yds* **3/1**[1]

000- **5** 2 ¼ **Copper Rag**[208] 8224 3-8-6 **47**.. JohnFahy 2 39
(J S Moore) *chsd ldrs: outpcd and rdn 2f out: styd on same pce u.p fnl f* **50/1**

4300 **6** 1 ½ **Otto The First**[44] 2950 3-8-10 **51**.. JimmyQuinn 5 38
(John Best) *hld up in tch in last pair: styd towards inner and effrt 2f out: no imp: nvr trbld ldrs* **16/1**

0000 **7** 1 ¼ **Courageous (IRE)**[23] 3660 7-8-13 **54**.................................. WillPettis(7) 7 41
(Milton Bradley) *led: rdn over 1f out: hdd 1f out: fdd ins fnl f* **16/1**

0400 **8** 1 ½ **Blue Deer (IRE)**[23] 3661 5-9-7 **55**.. KierenFox 4 38
(Lee Carter) *in tch in midfield tl shuffled bk to rr after 2f: rdn and effrt 2f out: no hdwy* **10/1**

0/6- **9** ¾ **Lady Valtas**[48] 1791 5-8-7 **46** oh1.........................(vt¹) JemmaMarshall(5) 3 27
(Martin Bosley) *hld up in last trio: rdn 1/2-way: wknd over 1f out* **100/1**

1m 21.46s (-1.64) **Going Correction** -0.35s/f (Firm)
WFA 3 from 4yo+ 7lb **9** Ran SP% **116.0**
Speed ratings (Par 101): **95,94,92,91,88 87,85,83,83**
Tote Swingers 1&2 £3.50, 2&3 £3.40, 1&3 £3.60 CSF £15.37 CT £43.22 TOTE £3.10: £2.90, £1.40, £1.60; EX 16.80 Trifecta £53.50 Pool: £1896.42 - 26.56 winning units..
Owner D A Poole **Bred** David Poole **Trained** Ogbourne Maisey, Wilts
■ Stewards' Enquiry : Will Pettis one-day ban: failed to ride to draw (Aug 1)
Luke Morris one-day ban: careless riding (Aug 1)

FOCUS
A moderate handicap in which the pace was on from the outset. The winner did not need to find much on her poor previous form, and the level is sound.

4424 CHUBE COOL NEW BREATHALYSER H'CAP (DIV II) 6f 209y
3:20 (3:20) (Class 6) (0-55,55) 3-Y-0+ **£1,940** (£577; £288; £144) **Stalls** Centre

Form RPR

00-3 **1** **Gypsy Rider**[189] 143 4-8-12 **53**.. NedCurtis(7) 8 63
(Roger Curtis) *hld up in tch towards rr: hdwy and sltly hmpd over 1f out: str run ins fnl f to ld cl home* **14/1**

0040 **2** *nk* **Hawk Moth (IRE)**[23] 3656 5-9-7 **55**................................(b¹) LukeMorris 2 64
(John Spearing) *hld up in tch towards rr: swtchd lft and hdwy over 1f out: drvn to ld 1f out: r.o u.p: hdd and no ex cl home* **10/1**

-033 **3** *nk* **Koharu**[19] 3817 3-8-13 **54**...(t) NeilCallan 5 59
(Peter Makin) *chsd ldrs: rdn and effrt 2f out: drvn to ld ent fnl f: sn hdd: ev ch after: no ex towards fin* **3/1**[2]

3351 **4** ¾ **Renoir's Lady**[16] 3922 5-9-6 **54**.. GeorgeBaker 9 60
(Simon Dow) *hld up wl in tch: clsd to press ldrs over 1f out: styd on same pce u.p ins fnl f* **2/1**[1]

0-02 **5** 5 **Our Three Graces (IRE)**[44] 2950 3-9-0 **55**...................... JamesDoyle 7 45
(Gary Moore) *w ldr: drvn to ld over 1f out: sn hdd: wknd ins fnl f* **11/2**[3]

0-00 **6** 1 ¾ **Rio Royale (IRE)**[23] 3660 7-8-12 **46** oh1..........................(p) PatDobbs 4 34
(Amanda Perrett) *hld up in tch in rr: rdn and effrt over 1f out: no imp* **20/1**

0-00 **7** 2 ¾ **Jackpot**[23] 3657 3-8-5 **46** oh1.. CathyGannon 3 24
(Brendan Powell) *t.k.h: hld up in tch in midfield: rdn and effrt nrest far rail 2f out: sn struggling and wknd ent fnl f* **50/1**

-406 **8** 2 **Pink Mischief**[8] 4170 3-8-10 **51**.. SeanLevey 6 23
(Harry Dunlop) *led: rdn and hdd over 1f out: sn racd awkwardly and btn: bhd and eased ins fnl f* **6/1**

0030 **9** 44 **Dvinsky (USA)**[41] 3052 12-8-12 **46** oh1..........................(b) JimmyQuinn 1
(Roger Ingram) *broke okay but sn rdn and dropped himself to last: nvr travelling: lost tch 1/2-way: eased fnl 2f: t.o* **20/1**

1m 21.74s (-1.36) **Going Correction** -0.35s/f (Firm)
WFA 3 from 4yo+ 7lb **9** Ran SP% **115.2**
Speed ratings (Par 101): **93,92,92,91,85 83,80,78,28**
Tote Swingers 1&2 £11.30, 2&3 £4.90, 1&3 £8.90 CSF £139.39 CT £539.27 TOTE £17.10: £4.00, £2.30, £2.20; EX 113.50 Trifecta £790.10 Pool: £2723.51 - 2.58 winning units..
Owner The Racing 4 Fun Partnership **Bred** Mr And Mrs L Baker **Trained** Lambourn, Berks

FOCUS
The second division of a moderate handicap, and slightly the slower. Similar form.

4425 CHUBE SUPPORTS ARMS AROUND THE CHILD CHARITY H'CAP 1m 1f 209y
3:50 (3:51) (Class 4) (0-80,80) 3-Y-0+ **£4,690** (£1,395; £697) **Stalls** High

Form RPR

4-31 **1** **Sadiq**[16] 3923 3-8-8 **77**.. AhmadAlSubousi(7) 4 89+
(Saeed bin Suroor) *t.k.h: chsd ldr tl led 5f out: drew clr 2f out: eased ins fnl f: v easily* **6/4**[2]

2210 **2** 11 **Bartack (IRE)**[22] 3683 3-9-4 **80**..............................(p) LukeMorris 2 77
(Luca Cumani) *in tch in 3rd: chsd wnr over 3f out and sn rdn: fnd little and wl btn over 1f out: eased ins fnl f* **4/7**[1]

5000 **3** 31 **Bayleyf (IRE)**[7] 4198 4-9-9 **75**......................................(t) GeorgeBaker 5
(John Best) *led tl 5f out: dropped to last 3f out: rdn and btn 2f out: heavily eased fnl f* **20/1**[3]

1m 59.99s (-3.61) **Going Correction** -0.35s/f (Firm)
WFA 3 from 4yo+ 10lb **3** Ran SP% **108.4**
Speed ratings (Par 105): **100,91,66**
CSF £2.82 TOTE £2.40; EX 2.80 Trifecta £2.20 Pool: £1284.33 - 421.59 winning units..
Owner Godolphin **Bred** Darley **Trained** Newmarket, Suffolk
■ Ahmad Al Subousi's first winner.

FOCUS
A fair small-field handicap in which they went a sedate gallop early on. They finished at wide margins and it's hard to know quite what the winner achieved.

4426 BECHUBE.COM H'CAP 7f 214y
4:20 (4:20) (Class 5) (0-75,75) 3-Y-0+ **£2,587** (£770; £384) **Stalls** Centre

Form RPR

0005 **1** **Lunar Deity**[14] 3973 4-9-5 **73**.. NeilCallan 1 82
(Eve Johnson Houghton) *t.k.h: mde all: rdn 2f out: styd on wl u.p 1f out: in command and pushed out fnl 100yds* **5/2**[3]

0011 **2** 2 **Aqua Ardens (GER)**[16] 3926 5-9-3 **71**..........................(t) PatCosgrave 3 75
(George Baker) *hld up in 3rd: rdn over 2f out: hung lft and racing against far rail 1f out: chsd wnr ins fnl f: no imp* **6/4**[1]

-506 **3** 2 ¼ **Hometown Glory**[14] 3974 4-9-7 **75**..............................(tp) SeanLevey 2 74
(Brian Meehan) *chsd wnr: rdn and effrt 2f out: no ex 1f out: wknd ins fnl f* **7/4**[2]

1m 32.37s (-3.63) **Going Correction** -0.35s/f (Firm) **3** Ran SP% **104.9**
Speed ratings (Par 103): **104,102,99**
CSF £6.13 TOTE £4.50; EX 4.20 Trifecta £7.60 Pool: £1197.37 - 117.27 winning units..
Owner Eden Racing (III) **Bred** Hermes Services Ltd **Trained** Blewbury, Oxon

FOCUS
A straightforward, fair small-field handicap. The winner is rated similar to his last winning form.

4427 DRIVING, SPORT, LEARNING, LIFE...BECHUBE H'CAP 5f 59y
4:50 (4:51) (Class 6) (0-55,55) 3-Y-0+ **£1,940** (£577; £288; £144) **Stalls** Centre

Form RPR

0-02 **1** **Excellent Aim**[16] 3922 6-9-7 **55**.. TomQueally 3 64+
(George Margarson) *chsd ldr: rdn to ld over 1f out: r.o wl and clr ins fnl f: eased towards fin* **5/2**[1]

4220 **2** 1 ½ **Slatey Hen (IRE)**[16] 3922 5-9-7 **55**..............................(p) JimmyQuinn 4 59
(Violet M Jordan) *chsd ldrs: effrt and drvn to chse wnr ent fnl f: no ex and btn fnl 100yds* **8/1**[3]

4164 **3** 2 **Burnt Cream**[14] 3994 6-9-1 **49**..(t) DavidProbert 6 46
(Martin Bosley) *chsd ldrs: n.m.r over 1f out: sn rdn and bmpd: no ex u.p and btn ins fnl f* **20/1**

0452 **4** *nk* **Johnny Splash (IRE)**[16] 3921 4-9-4 **52**.............................. SeanLevey 2 48
(Roger Teal) *chsd ldrs: drvn and chsd ldrs over 1f out: no ex and btn ins fnl f* **4/1**[2]

3052 **5** 2 **The Name Is Frank**[7] 4197 8-8-13 **54**...........................(t) OisinMurphy(7) 7 43
(Mark Gillard) *in tch towards rr: rdn over 2f out: no imp tl plugged on ins fnl f: nvr trbld ldrs* **4/1**[2]

06-0 **6** ½ **Elounta**[22] 3699 3-8-3 **46** oh1.. RobertTart(5) 8 33
(John Best) *stdd s: t.k.h: hld up in tch in rr: swtchd rt and effrt wl over 1f out: kpt on but no threat to ldrs* **33/1**

0020 **7** 4 ½ **Megaleka**[14] 3994 3-8-10 **53**.. NatashaEaton(5) 1 24
(Alan Bailey) *led: rdn and hdd over 1f out: sn bmpd by loose horse and btn: wknd fnl f* **10/1**

5435 **8** 15 **Volcanic Dust (IRE)**[7] 4197 5-8-13 **54**...........................(t) WillPettis(7) 5
(Milton Bradley) *anticipated s and hit front of stalls: wnt bk as stalls opened and v.s.a: nt rcvr and nvr on terms* **12/1**

500- **9** 16 **Ladydolly**[274] 7157 5-9-4 **52**..(p) GeorgeBaker 10
(Roy Brotherton) *hld up in tch in last trio: shkn up and no rspnse 2f out: sn btn and eased fnl f* **25/1**

5360 **U** **Spic 'n Span**[17] 3888 8-9-2 **50**..(be) LukeMorris 9
(Ronald Harris) *j. v awkwardly leaving stalls and uns rdr* **14/1**

1m 0.9s (-1.40) **Going Correction** -0.35s/f (Firm)
WFA 3 from 4yo+ 4lb **10** Ran SP% **114.7**
Speed ratings (Par 101): **97,94,91,90,87 86,79,55,30,**
Tote Swingers 1&2 £4.20, 2&3 £9.70, 1&3 £6.40 CSF £22.18 CT £324.46 TOTE £2.50: £1.10, £3.10, £5.20; EX 20.60 Trifecta £245.00 Pool: £2728.49 - 8.34 winning units..
Owner Graham Lodge Partnership **Bred** Norcroft Park Stud **Trained** Newmarket, Suffolk

FOCUS
An eventful moderate sprint handicap with Spic 'N Span anticipating the start, jumping forward as the stalls opened, and depositing his jockey Luke Morris on the turf, whilst Volcanic Dust was rearing back on her haunches and got left a distance behind a strong gallop set by Megaleka. The winner built on his C&D latest.

4428 CHUBE SELF TESTING BREATHALYSER KIT H'CAP 5f 213y
5:20 (5:21) (Class 5) (0-70,70) 3-Y-0+ **£2,587** (£770; £384; £192) **Stalls** Centre

Form RPR

4-21 **1** **Cape Of Hope (IRE)**[20] 3759 3-9-5 **70**.............................. RobertHavlin 1 79
(Peter Chapple-Hyam) *chsd ldr tl 1/2-way: effrt on inner over 1f out: rdn hands and heels and led ins fnl f: r.o wl* **8/11**[1]

0003 **2** 1 ½ **Stonecrabstomorrow (IRE)**[15] 3949 10-8-13 **62**..... AshleyMorgan(3) 3 67
(Roy Brotherton) *chsd ldrs: hdwy to join ldr 1/2-way: drvn to ld jst over 1f out: hdd ins fnl f: no ex fnl 75yds* **8/1**

-000 **3** *nk* **Uprise**[19] 3841 4-9-6 **66**.. TomQueally 2 70
(George Margarson) *hld up in tch in rr: rdn and effrt jst over 1f out: pressed ldrs and drvn ins fnl f: no ex and btn fnl 75yds* **11/4**[2]

2024 **4** 3 **Belle Bayardo (IRE)**[13] 4034 5-9-8 **68**.............................. LukeMorris 5 62
(Ronald Harris) *t.k.h: led: jnd 1/2-way: hdd and drvn over 1f out: struggling whn n.m.r ins fnl f: sn wknd* **5/1**[3]

1m 9.13s (-1.07) **Going Correction** -0.35s/f (Firm)
WFA 3 from 4yo+ 5lb **4** Ran SP% **112.3**
Speed ratings (Par 103): **93,91,90,86**
CSF £7.26 TOTE £1.50; EX 8.90 Trifecta £13.90 Pool: £1816.40 - 97.47 winning units..
Owner Eledy Srl **Bred** Pendley Farm **Trained** Newmarket, Suffolk

FOCUS
A modest handicap, and the winning time was ordinary, but the youngest competitor won readily. Doubts over how solid the form is.

4429 LIFESTYLEEUROPE.CO.UK APPRENTICE H'CAP 1m 3f 196y
5:55 (5:56) (Class 6) (0-60,60) 4-Y-0+ **£1,940** (£577; £288; £144) **Stalls** High

Form RPR

332 **1** **St Ignatius**[7] 4195 6-9-0 **58**..(p) TimClark(5) 2 65
(Alan Bailey) *mde all: set stdy gallop tl rdn and qcknd wl over 2f out: hrd pressed over 1f out: kpt on wl: rdn out* **11/10**[1]

0212 **2** ½ **Beacon Lady**[16] 3924 4-9-4 **60**.. NicoleNordblad(3) 1 66
(William Knight) *hld up in last: rdn and effrt over 2f out: chal over 1f out: ev ch fnl f: no ex and btn towards fin* **11/10**[1]

00-0 **3** 3 ¼ **Novel Dancer**[37] 417 5-8-5 **49**..................................(t) ShelleyBirkett(5) 4 50
(Lydia Richards) *chsd ldr: rdn and effrt over 2f out: ev ch over 1f tl 1f out: outpcd ins fnl f* **12/1**[2]

5500 **4** ¾ **Richo**[11] 3882 7-8-0 **46** oh1.. JackGarritty(7) 5 46
(Shaun Harris) *s.i.s: sn rcvrd and chsd ldng pair: rdn and effrt over 2f out: ev ch over 1f out tl 1f out: outpcd ins fnl f* **20/1**[3]

2m 36.94s (4.24) **Going Correction** -0.35s/f (Firm) **4** Ran SP% **107.7**
Speed ratings (Par 101): **71,70,68,68**
Tote Swinger 1&2 £1.40 CSF £2.51 TOTE £1.80; EX 2.90 Trifecta £3.20 Pool: £802.53 - 182.60 winning units..
Owner A J H **Bred** Simon And Helen Plumbly **Trained** Newmarket, Suffolk

FOCUS
A moderate middle-distance handicap for apprentice riders and the field was decimated by non-runners. It was slowly run and the winner didn't need to improve on recent form.

T/Plt: £124.10 to a £1 stake. Pool: £57,532.27 - 338.39 winning tickets. T/Qpdt: £88.20 to a £1 stake. Pool: £2,683.80 - 22.5 winning tickets. SP

The Form Book Flat, Raceform Ltd, Compton, RG20 6NL.

[4198]DONCASTER (L-H)

Thursday, July 18

OFFICIAL GOING: Firm (good to firm in places; 10.9)

Wind: Light behind Weather: Fine and dry

4430 FREEBETS.CO.UK MOBILE BETTING APPRENTICE H'CAP 5f

5:50 (5:56) (Class 6) (0-65,64) 3-Y-0+ **£1,940** (£577; £288; £144) **Stalls** High

Form RPR

0205 **1** **Irish Boy (IRE)**[9] 4148 5-9-11 **64**..........(tp) EoinWalsh(3) 5 73
(Christine Dunnett) *trckd ldrs: hdwy 2f out: rdn to chal ins fnl f: kpt on wl to ld last 40yds* **12/1**

0160 **2** ½ **Pavers Star**[13] 4009 4-9-7 **57**.......... JoeyHaynes 4 64
(Noel Wilson) *prom: led 1/2-way: rdn over 1f out: jnd and drvn ins fnl f: hdd and no ex last 40yds* **14/1**

4006 **3** 2 ¼ **Ingleby Star (IRE)**[17] 3888 8-9-4 **61**..........(be) AaronFallon(7) 10 60
(Daniel Mark Loughnane) *prom: cl up and rdn along wl over 1f out: one pce fnl f* **10/1**

-000 **4** *hd* **Fidget**[35] 3247 3-8-6 **51**.......... ClaireMurray(5) 13 48+
(David Brown) *in tch nr stands' rail: rdn along 2f out: kpt on u.p appr fnl f: nrst fin* **18/1**

0031 **5** ½ **The Great Gabrial**[9] 4148 4-9-9 **59** 6ex..........(b) DavidBergin 1 56
(Ian Williams) *chsd ldrs on outer: effrt and cl up 2f out: sn rdn and grad wknd appr fnl f* **2/1**[1]

0-60 **6** *hd* **Mysterious Wonder**[61] 2464 3-9-0 **57**.......... EvaMoscrop(3) 3 52+
(Philip Kirby) *towards rr: hdwy wl over 1f out: sn rdn and kpt on fnl f: nrst fin* **20/1**

0052 **7** *hd* **Ryedane (IRE)**[11] 4102 11-9-6 **61**..........(b) RachelRichardson(5) 12 56
(Tim Easterby) *towards rr: pushed along 1/2-way: rdn and hdwy over 1f out: kpt on fnl f: nrst fin* **13/2**[2]

6460 **8** *nk* **Amadeus Denton (IRE)**[13] 4018 4-9-11 **61**..........(p) ConnorBeasley 8 55
(Michael Dods) *towards rr: hdwy and in tch over 2f out: sn rdn and no imp appr fnl f* **7/1**[3]

05-0 **9** 1 ¾ **Piste**[13] 4009 7-8-9 **50**..........(e) RobJFitzpatrick(5) 2 38
(Tina Jackson) *dwlt: sn in tch: rdn along over 2f out and sn wknd* **33/1**

0006 **10** ¾ **Dolly Diva**[13] 4009 4-8-10 **49**..........(p) JordanNason(3) 11 34
(Paul Midgley) *a towards rr* **14/1**

6200 **11** ½ **Roy's Legacy**[89] 1681 4-9-2 **57**.......... GaryMahon(5) 7 40
(Shaun Harris) *led: pushed along and hdd 1/2-way: sn rdn and wknd wl over 1f out* **10/1**

0066 **12** *nk* **Moss The Boss (IRE)**[26] 3594 3-8-5 **45**.......... SamanthaBell 6 26
(Paul Midgley) *a towards rr* **18/1**

58.81s (-1.69) **Going Correction** -0.60s/f (Hard)
WFA 3 from 4yo+ 4lb 12 Ran SP% **116.6**
Speed ratings (Par 101): **89,88,84,84,83 83,82,82,79,78 77,77**
Tote Swingers 1&2 £15.90, 2&3 £18.20, 1&3 £10.80 CSF £166.41 CT £1765.32 TOTE £12.80: £3.30, £3.60, £3.10; EX 153.30 Trifecta £1513.20 Pool: £2,620.52 - 1.29 winning tickets..
Owner Annwell Inn Syndicate **Bred** Seamus McMullan **Trained** Hingham, Norfolk

FOCUS
Rail out on Round course from 1m2f to entrance to home straight. Despite extensive watering the ground was very quick, especially on the round course. Good recent form was thin on the ground in this weak 5f apprentice handicap. The first two are rated to their best.

4431 D C TRAINING AND DEVELOPMENT SERVICES LTD FILLIES' NURSERY H'CAP 6f

6:20 (6:21) (Class 4) 2-Y-0 **£3,752** (£1,116; £557; £278) **Stalls** High

Form RPR

1401 **1** **Diamond Lady**[1] 4399 2-9-8 **81** 6ex.......... EDLinehan(5) 4 84+
(Jo Hughes) *mde most: overall ldr centre: pushed clr 2f out: rdn ent fnl f: edgd rt and kpt on wl* **5/2**[1]

3523 **2** 1 ¾ **Princess Rose**[6] 4232 2-9-7 **75**.......... MartinHarley 7 72
(William Haggas) *racd nr stands' rail: trckd ldr: hdwy to ld that gp over 2f out: sn rdn to chse wnr: drvn and kpt on fnl f: nt rch wnr: 1st of 2 in gp* **5/2**[1]

003 **3** 4 **Fredricka**[12] 4073 2-8-6 **67**.......... ConnorBeasley(7) 3 52
(Garry Moss) *chsd ldng pair in centre: rdn along over 2f out: drvn and kpt on same pce fnl f: 2nd of 4 in gp* **7/1**

201 **4** 3 ¼ **Musical Molly (IRE)**[40] 3084 2-9-0 **68**.......... DaneO'Neill 2 42
(Brian Ellison) *towards rr centre: rdn along wl over 2f out: sn drvn and n.d: 3rd of 4 in gp* **6/1**[3]

365 **5** 5 **Evacusafe Lady**[30] 3436 2-8-7 **61**..........(p) WilliamCarson 1 19
(John Ryan) *cl up: centre: rdn along wl over 2f out: sn drvn and wknd: 4th of 4 in gp* **16/1**

541 **6** ¾ **Honey Meadow**[42] 3017 2-9-2 **70**.......... AndreaAtzeni 6 26
(Robert Eddery) *blind removed late and dwlt: sn led stands' rail gp: rdn along 1/2-way: hdd over 2f out and sn wknd: 2nd of 2 in gp* **10/3**[2]

1m 10.7s (-2.90) **Going Correction** -0.60s/f (Hard) 2y crse rec 6 Ran SP% **112.9**
Speed ratings (Par 93): **95,92,87,83,76 75**
Tote Swingers 1&2 £2.40, 2&3 £2.50, 1&3 £4.10 CSF £9.07 TOTE £4.10: £2.20, £1.50; EX 9.30 Trifecta £32.70 Pool: £1,359.06 - 31.16 winning tickets..
Owner B Bedford P Hanly D Bird D Bedford **Bred** Mickley Stud **Trained** Lambourn, Berks

FOCUS
The official ratings shown are estimated and for information only. They split into two distinct groups in this fillies' nursery. The winner was one of four to race centre to far side, the runner-up was led by one other against the stands' side rail. The form is rated around the second.

4432 FREEBETS.CO.UK FREE BETS BRITISH STALLION STUDS EBF MAIDEN FILLIES' STKS 7f

6:50 (6:50) (Class 5) 2-Y-0 **£2,911** (£866; £432; £216) **Stalls** High

Form RPR

02 **1** **Adhwaa**[19] 3833 2-9-0 0.......... PaulHanagan 3 83+
(J W Hills) *a.p: cl up 1/2-way: led wl over 2f out: rdn over 1f out: narrowly hdd jst ins fnl f: rallied gamely u.p to ld last 75yds* **3/1**[2]

36 **2** *hd* **Tinga (IRE)**[26] 3555 2-9-0 0.......... MartinHarley 1 82+
(Mick Channon) *cl up: effrt 2f out: rdn and slt ld jst ins fnl f: edgd lft: hdd and no ex last 75yds* **13/8**[1]

3 3 ½ **Halljoy (IRE)** 2-9-0 0.......... WilliamCarson 11 73+
(Clive Brittain) *in tch: green and pushed along over 3f out: hdwy wl over 2f out: rdn to chse ldng pair and green ent fnl f: sn edgd lft and kpt on same pce* **33/1**

5 **4** 1 ¼ **Flippant (IRE)**[20] 3781 2-9-0 0.......... AndreaAtzeni 2 70
(William Haggas) *led: rdn along and hdd wl over 2f out: edgd lft over 1f out: kpt on same pce* **6/1**[3]

02 **5** 5 **Taleteller (USA)**[15] 3958 2-9-0 0.......... MickaelBarzalona 4 57
(Saeed bin Suroor) *t.k.h: chsd ldrs: hdwy 3f out: rdn along 2f out: sn one pce* **6/1**[3]

6 1 ¼ **Thurayaat** 2-9-0 0.......... DaneO'Neill 6 54+
(Roger Varian) *dwlt: sn chsng ldrs: rdn along wl over 2f out: sn wknd* **12/1**

7 7 **Opera Fan (FR)** 2-9-0 0.......... SilvestreDeSousa 5 36
(Mark Johnston) *dwlt: t.k.h and sn chsng ldrs: pushed along 1/2-way: sn rdn and wknd* **10/1**

8 *nk* **Shirocco Passion** 2-9-0 0.......... BarryMcHugh 9 35
(Tony Coyle) *a towards rr* **66/1**

9 9 **That Be Grand** 2-9-0 0.......... DuranFentiman 12 11
(Shaun Harris) *s.i.s: a in rr* **66/1**

1m 24.48s (-1.82) **Going Correction** -0.60s/f (Hard) 9 Ran SP% **114.4**
Speed ratings (Par 91): **86,85,81,80,74 73,65,64,54**
Tote Swingers 1&2 £2.20, 2&3 £23.80, 1&3 £17.70 CSF £8.10 TOTE £3.70: £1.10, £1.20, £7.10; EX 8.80 Trifecta £176.70 Pool: £1,904.14 - 8.08 winning tickets..
Owner Hamdan Al Maktoum **Bred** Shadwell Estate Company Limited **Trained** Upper Lambourn, Berks

FOCUS
The first two had a head-to head and they pulled clear of the strong finishing third in this decent maiden 2yo fillies' race. Both the first two improved, the winner boosting the Kingman form.

4433 TERRY BELLAS MEMORIAL CONDITIONS STKS 1m (S)

7:25 (7:25) (Class 3) 4-Y-0+ **£7,439** (£2,213; £1,106) **Stalls** High

Form RPR

0122 **1** **Quick Wit**[16] 3931 6-8-9 **109**..........(p) SilvestreDeSousa 3 105+
(Saeed bin Suroor) *set stdy pce: rdn and qcknd wl over 1f out: rdn clr fnl f: readily* **5/6**[1]

-306 **2** 3 ¼ **Sweetnessandlight**[9] 4137 4-8-4 **95**.......... PaulHanagan 1 93
(Jason Ward) *t.k.h early: hld up: hdwy wl over 1f out: sn rdn: swtchd lft and drvn ent fnl f: kpt on to take 2nd last 100yds: no ch w wnr* **9/1**[3]

3230 **3** 1 ¾ **Fulbright**[110] 1267 4-9-5 **113**.......... MickaelBarzalona 4 104
(Saeed bin Suroor) *trckd wnr: pushed along to take clsr order 2f out: sn rdn: drvn and one pce fnl f: lost 2nd last 100yds* **11/8**[2]

1m 34.95s (-4.35) **Going Correction** -0.60s/f (Hard) course record 3 Ran SP% **106.7**
Speed ratings (Par 107): **97,93,92**
CSF £6.25 TOTE £1.70; EX 6.70 Trifecta £11.60 Pool: £994.25 - 63.75 winning tickets..
Owner Godolphin **Bred** Ptarmigan Bloodstock Limited **Trained** Newmarket, Suffolk

FOCUS
Just the three runners with two of them representing Godolphin. Even so, they managed to lower the straight 1m track record. The winner had an easy task and the second is rated to this year's form.

4434 PDM GROUP CONNECT 2013 NOVICE STKS 6f

7:55 (7:55) (Class 5) 2-Y-0 **£3,752** (£1,116; £557; £278) **Stalls** High

Form RPR

120 **1** **Andhesontherun (IRE)**[30] 3424 2-9-5 0.......... AndreaAtzeni 4 91+
(Roger Varian) *trckd ldng pair: cl up after 2f: led wl over 2f out: rdn ent fnl f: kpt on strly* **11/8**[2]

1 **2** 1 ½ **Zaraee (IRE)**[14] 3979 2-9-5 0.......... PaulHanagan 3 86
(William Haggas) *hld up: hdwy 1/2-way: effrt and cl up wl over 1f out: sn chal: rdn and ev ch ent fnl f: sn rn green and edgd lft: one pce towards fin* **1/1**[1]

4314 **3** ½ **Left Defender (IRE)**[34] 3267 2-9-2 0.......... FrannyNorton 1 82?
(Jo Hughes) *led 1 1/2f: cl up: rdn wl over 1f out: ev ch tl drvn and one pce ins fnl f* **33/1**

31 **4** 11 **Captain Whoosh (IRE)**[17] 3883 2-9-5 0.......... LiamKeniry 2 49
(Tom Dascombe) *t.k.h early: chsd ldr: led after 1 1/2f: hdd wl over 2f out: sn rdn along and wknd wl over 1f out* **6/1**[3]

1m 10.87s (-2.73) **Going Correction** -0.60s/f (Hard) 2y crse rec 4 Ran SP% **109.3**
Speed ratings (Par 94): **94,92,91,76**
CSF £3.15 TOTE £2.40; EX 3.00 Trifecta £11.50 Pool: £718.07 - 46.47 winning tickets..
Owner H H Sheikh Mohammed Bin Khalifa Al Thani **Bred** John Hutchinson **Trained** Newmarket, Suffolk

FOCUS
A fair little novice event, and straightforward form around the first pair. Big improvement from the third.

4435 HAPPY BIRTHDAY JOY MILLER H'CAP 1m 2f 60y

8:30 (8:30) (Class 4) (0-85,85) 4-Y-0+ **£4,690** (£1,395; £697; £348) **Stalls** Low

Form RPR

-100 **1** **Classic Punch (IRE)**[22] 3685 10-9-3 **81**.......... PaulHanagan 6 88
(Tim Etherington) *trckd ldng pair: hdwy on inner to ld 3f out: rdn 2f out: drvn and edgd rt ins fnl f: kpt on wl towards fin* **14/1**

4321 **2** 1 ¼ **Manomine**[72] 2137 4-8-4 **68**.......... NickyMackay 9 73
(Clive Brittain) *hld up in tch: hdwy on outer over 3f out: chsd wnr wl over 1f out: rdn and swtchd lft ins fnl f: sn drvn and kpt on* **5/1**[3]

/604 **3** ½ **Karam Albaari (IRE)**[19] 3812 5-9-7 **85**.......... FrederikTylicki 3 89
(J R Jenkins) *hld up towards rr: hdwy 3f out: chsd ldrs 2f out: sn rdn: drvn and styd on fnl f: nrst fin* **5/2**[1]

-00L **4** *shd* **Halfsin (IRE)**[22] 3692 5-9-7 **85**..........[1] AndreaAtzeni 7 88
(Marco Botti) *trckd ldrs: hdwy 3f out: rdn and sltly outpcd 2f out: styd on u.p fnl f* **14/1**

136 **5** 1 ½ **Discay**[76] 1993 4-8-3 **67**.......... SilvestreDeSousa 8 68+
(Mark Johnston) *stmbld bdly and almost uns rdr s: bhd: gd hdwy on wd outside over 2f out: rdn to chse ldrs over 1f out: no imp ins fnl f* **6/1**

0000 **6** 2 ½ **Hit The Jackpot (IRE)**[36] 3207 4-9-5 **83**.......... DanielTudhope 2 79
(David O'Meara) *trckd ldrs: hdwy on inner 3f out: rdn to chse ldrs 2f out: drvn and wknd appr fnl f* **11/4**[2]

/0-6 **7** 8 **Red Eyes**[16] 3930 5-8-2 **66** oh1..........(v) DuranFentiman 4 47
(Chris Grant) *trckd ldr: effrt over 3f out: rdn along wl over 2f out: sn wknd* **33/1**

00-0 **8** 11 **Venutius**[44] 2958 6-9-5 **83**.......... FrannyNorton 5 43
(Philip Kirby) *dwlt and towards rr: rdn along 3f out: sn btn* **10/1**

320- **9** 4 **Ay Tay Tate (IRE)**[453] 1525 7-8-2 **66**..........(p) KieranO'Neill 1 18
(Noel Wilson) *led: rdn along 4f out: hdd 3f out and sn wknd* **25/1**

2m 7.64s (-1.76) **Going Correction** -0.025s/f (Good) 9 Ran SP% **115.4**
Speed ratings (Par 105): **106,105,104,104,103 101,94,86,82**
Tote Swingers 1&2 £16.30, 2&3 £3.00, 1&3 £9.90 CSF £82.37 CT £236.61 TOTE £8.90: £2.00, £2.10, £1.50; EX 67.00 Trifecta £836.20 Part won. Pool: £1,115.04 - 0.25 winning tickets..
Owner Mrs Brown's Boys **Bred** Granham Farm **Trained** Norton, N Yorks

FOCUS
A fair middle-distance handicap and nearly 2sec quicker than the next. Pretty ordinary for the grade.

4436 BONUS.CO.UK CASINO BONUS H'CAP 1m 2f 60y
9:00 (9:00) (Class 5) (0-70,66) 3-Y-O £2,587 (£770; £384; £192) Stalls Low

Form RPR
6403 1 **Prospera (IRE)**[17] 3900 3-9-4 63 (b) JimCrowley 1 75
(Ralph Beckett) *trckd ldng pair: hdwy to chse ldr wl over 2f out: rdn wl over 1f out: drvn to chal ent fnl f: kpt on gamely to ld nr fin* 3/1[2]
006 2 nk **Sureness (IRE)**[20] 3764 3-9-7 66 (t) MartinHarley 7 77
(Marco Botti) *set stdy pce: pushed along and qcknd over 3f out: rdn 2f out: drvn over 1f out: hdd and no ex nr fin* 9/2[3]
45-3 3 5 **Runninglikethewind (IRE)**[20] 3793 3-9-6 65 TedDurcan 3 67
(Chris Wall) *trckd ldrs: hdwy to chse ldng pair wl over 2f out: rdn wl over 1f out: sn one pce* 3/1[2]
-002 4 8 **Kensington Gardens**[8] 4170 3-8-12 57 PaulHanagan 2 43
(Michael Bell) *hld up in rr: pushed along 3f out: sme hdwy 2f out: sn rdn and n.d* 11/4[1]
-364 5 1 1/4 **Midnight Warrior**[19] 3828 3-9-0 66 ConnorBeasley(7) 5 50
(Ron Barr) *t.k.h: chsd ldr: rdn along over 3f out: sn wknd* 13/2
00-0 6 8 **Joeluke**[12] 4045 3-8-3 55 EvaMoscrop(7) 8 24
(Philip Kirby) *t.k.h in rr: hdwy on outer after 3f and sn chsng ldrs: prom on outer over 4f out: rdn along wl over 3f out: sn wknd* 50/1

2m 9.62s (0.22) **Going Correction** -0.025s/f (Good) 6 Ran SP% 110.1
Speed ratings (Par 100): **98,97,93,87,86 79**
Tote Swingers 1&2 £3.30, 2&3 £4.80, 1&3 £1.80 CSF £15.97 CT £39.33 TOTE £4.20: £3.40, £5.30; EX 17.80 Trifecta £52.20 Pool: £1,095.20 - 15.70 winning tickets..
Owner The Millennium Madness Partnership **Bred** Mount Coote Stud **Trained** Kimpton, Hants
FOCUS
The gallop was steady until the final half-mile and the first two home were one-two throughout. It was almost 2sec slower than the previous race for older horses. The winner is rated to her early best, with the first two clear.
T/Jkpt: Not won. T/Plt: £229.20 to a £1 stake. Pool: £71,636.46 - 228.12 winning tickets. T/Qpdt: £12.30 to a £1 stake. Pool: £5,802.31 - 346.74 winning tickets. JR

4205 EPSOM (L-H)
Thursday, July 18

OFFICIAL GOING: Good to firm (firm in places back straight; 8.7)
Wind: Nil Weather: Sunny

4437 THE KISS MIX LADIES' DERBY H'CAP (FOR LADY AMATEUR RIDERS) 1m 4f 10y
6:10 (6:12) (Class 4) (0-80,80) 4-Y-O+ £4,991 (£1,548; £773; £387) Stalls Centre

Form RPR
1-11 1 **Tapis Libre**[17] 3889 5-10-0 75 (p) MissJoannaMason(5) 6 83
(Michael Easterby) *in tch: trckd ldr over 6f out: pushed along to chal 2f out: kpt on wl fnl f to ld fnl 75yds: drvn out* 9/4[2]
231- 2 nk **Sky Khan**[9] 7131 4-10-7 80 (p) MissHBethell(3) 1 87
(Philip Kirby) *chsd ldr after 2f tl over 6f out: styd chsng ldrs: chal over 2f out: slt ld and rdn along over 1f out: hdd and no ex fnl 75yds* 6/5[1]
-535 3 1 1/2 **No Such Number**[14] 3971 5-9-12 71 (p) MissHayleyMoore(3) 3 76
(Julia Feilden) *hld up in rr: hdwy over 3f out: rdn and hung rt over 2f out: sn outpcd: drvn and styd on again fnl f* 11/2
0-60 4 3 1/4 **Epsom Salts**[23] 3662 8-9-9 65 (p) MissSBrotherton 2 65
(Pat Phelan) *in tch: rapid hdwy to ld over 4f out: jnd and rdn over 2f out: hdd over 1f out: wknd ins fnl f* 5/1[3]
0000 5 35 **Jakeys Girl**[64] 2332 6-8-12 61 oh16 (v[1]) MissLWilliams(7) 5
(Pat Phelan) *slowly away: sn rcvrd to ld: hdd over 4f out: wknd qckly* 100/1

2m 43.64s (4.74) **Going Correction** -0.125s/f (Firm) 5 Ran SP% 109.3
Speed ratings (Par 105): **79,78,77,75,52**
Tote Swinger 1&2 £3.40 CSF £5.26 TOTE £3.10: £1.60, £1.50; EX 6.00 Trifecta £8.90 Pool: £1,222.71 - 101.98 winning tickets..
Owner Mrs Susan E Mason **Bred** Sedgecroft Stud **Trained** Sheriff Hutton, N Yorks
FOCUS
Rail out from 1m to Winning Post, up to 6yds from 8f to 6f and 7yds from 6f to finish increasing races over 1m by 20yds and 8yds to 7f races. A modest little handicap, confined to lady amateur riders. Another best from the winner.

4438 STUBHUB TICKETS CLAIMING STKS 7f
6:40 (6:40) (Class 5) 3-Y-O+ £3,234 (£962; £481; £240) Stalls Low

Form RPR
3000 1 **Ortac Rock (IRE)**[34] 3274 4-9-0 80 RichardHughes 2 79
(Richard Hannon) *trckd ldr after 2f: chal over 2f out tl led over 1f out: hrd drvn ins fnl f: rdn out* 13/8[2]
1204 2 nk **Polar Kite (IRE)**[20] 3754 5-9-6 82 JamesDoyle 1 84
(Sean Curran) *trckd ldr 2f: styd in cl 3rd: rdn 2f out: hdwy to chse wnr appr fnl f: no ex u.p and a hld fnl 75yds* 11/8[1]
-103 3 1 1/4 **Raging Bear (USA)**[51] 2737 3-8-11 76 PatDobbs 3 76
(Richard Hannon) *reminder sn after s: in rr: rdn over 2f out: styd on to take 3rd fnl f: kpt on clsng stages: nt trble ldng duo* 4/1[3]
5000 4 9 **Seek The Fair Land**[68] 2266 7-9-10 79 (p) AdamKirby 4 69
(Jim Boyle) *led: jnd over 2f out: hdd over 1f out and sn wknd* 9/1

1m 21.82s (-1.48) **Going Correction** -0.125s/f (Firm)
WFA 3 from 4yo+ 7lb 4 Ran SP% 110.2
Speed ratings (Par 103): **103,102,101,90**
CSF £4.34 TOTE £2.20; EX 4.10 Trifecta £7.00 Pool: £610.85 - 65.03 winning tickets..Ortac Rock was claimed by Richard Fahey for £8,000.
Owner Carmichael Simmons Humber **Bred** Liam Queally **Trained** East Everleigh, Wilts
FOCUS
Not a bad little claimer, and straightforward form at face value.

4439 IRISH STALLION FARMS EBF MAIDEN STKS 7f
7:15 (7:15) (Class 5) 2-Y-O £3,881 (£1,155; £577; £288) Stalls Low

Form RPR
641 1 **Fire Fighting (IRE)**[22] 3689 2-9-5 0 NeilCallan 2 88
(Mark Johnston) *mde all: drvn clr fnl 2f: unchal* 7/4[2]
42 2 5 **Peak Royale**[13] 4021 2-9-5 0 RichardHughes 4 75
(Richard Hannon) *trckd ldrs: wnt 2nd 3f out: rdn: hung lft and no imp fr ins fnl 2f* 6/5[1]
3 3 2 **Mime Dance**[63] 2391 2-9-5 0 JimmyFortune 7 70
(Andrew Balding) *chsd ldrs: rdn to take 3rd over 2f out: nvr any ch w wnr and styd on same pce fr over 1f out* 8/1[3]
50 4 3 1/4 **Double Czech (IRE)**[35] 3238 2-9-5 0 PatDobbs 6 61
(Amanda Perrett) *chsd wnr to 3f out: wknd fr 2f out* 14/1
5 5 3 **Mawzoona**[29] 3471 2-9-0 0 SamHitchcott 5 49
(Mick Channon) *in rr: rdn and sme hdwy over 3f out: nvr in contention and sn wknd* 16/1
0 6 1 1/4 **Almost Famous (IRE)**[18] 3853 2-9-5 0 FergusSweeney 3 50
(Jamie Osborne) *outpcd most of way* 33/1
0 7 10 **Haines**[34] 3290 2-9-5 0 DavidProbert 1 24
(Brett Johnson) *a outpcd in rr* 66/1

1m 21.82s (-1.48) **Going Correction** -0.125s/f (Firm) 7 Ran SP% 109.9
Speed ratings (Par 94): **103,97,95,91,87 86,75**
Tote Swingers 1&2 £1.10, 2&3 £2.50, 1&3 £2.90 CSF £3.80 TOTE £2.80: £1.70, £1.40; EX 4.40 Trifecta £14.80 Pool: £1,156.10 - 58.35 winning tickets..
Owner A D Spence **Bred** P Bellaiche **Trained** Middleham Moor, N Yorks
FOCUS
A modest 2-y-o maiden but the form makes sense, with improvement from the easy winner.

4440 TOTEPOOL H'CAP 7f
7:45 (7:45) (Class 4) (0-85,85) 3-Y-O+ £6,469 (£1,925; £962; £481) Stalls Low

Form RPR
-613 1 **Magic City (IRE)**[20] 3757 4-10-0 85 RichardHughes 5 95+
(Richard Hannon) *trckd ldrs: drvn and qcknd over 1f out to ld fnl 150yds: styd on strly* 13/8[1]
0004 2 1 1/2 **Amadeus Wolfe Tone (IRE)**[14] 3973 4-10-0 85 (b) AdamKirby 2 91
(Jamie Osborne) *chsd ldrs: chal between horses fr 2f out tl led appr fnl f: hdd and outpcd fnl 150yds* 8/1
-400 3 3 **Dream Catcher (FR)**[24] 3622 5-9-1 72 CathyGannon 1 70
(Henry Candy) *led: chal 2f out: hdd appr fnl f sn outpcd* 8/1
0005 4 shd **Another Try (IRE)**[14] 3980 8-8-13 75 MichaelJMMurphy(5) 4 73
(Alan Jarvis) *chsd ldr: rdn to chal 2f out: outpcd fnl f* 16/1
0003 5 3/4 **Spirit Of Sharjah (IRE)**[14] 3974 8-9-5 83 (p) ShelleyBirkett(7) 6 79
(Julia Feilden) *in tch: hdwy and n.m.r over 2f out: sn swtchd rt: styd on again clsng stages* 11/2[2]
0044 6 3/4 **Rocky Reef**[6] 4237 4-9-6 77 (v) PatDobbs 3 71
(Philip Hide) *in tch: rdn and one pce fnl 3f* 13/2[3]
3100 7 7 **Restaurateur (IRE)**[20] 3757 4-9-8 79 (v) JimmyFortune 7 54
(Andrew Balding) *a outpcd* 8/1
0602 8 34 **Capitol Gain (IRE)**[35] 3244 4-8-11 68 NeilCallan 8
(Brian Meehan) *in rr: rdn over 3f out: nvr any ch: eased fnl f* 12/1

1m 21.31s (-1.99) **Going Correction** -0.125s/f (Firm) 8 Ran SP% 113.7
Speed ratings (Par 105): **106,104,100,100,99 99,91,52**
Tote Swingers 1&2 £2.40, 2&3 £7.00, 1&3 £4.30 CSF £15.17 CT £81.07 TOTE £2.20: £1.80, £2.30, £2.10; EX 16.00 Trifecta £162.40 Pool: £1,578.72 - 7.28 winning tickets..
Owner Barker, Ferguson, Mason, Hassiakos, Done **Bred** Miss Annmarie Burke **Trained** East Everleigh, Wilts
FOCUS
A fair handicap and it was run at an honest pace. A small personal best from the winner.

4441 WEATHERBYS HAMILTON INSURANCE H'CAP 1m 2f 18y
8:20 (8:21) (Class 4) (0-80,81) 3-Y-O+ £5,175 (£1,540; £769; £384) Stalls Low

Form RPR
0341 1 **Xinbama (IRE)**[7] 4205 4-9-2 72 (t) ShelleyBirkett(7) 2 83
(J W Hills) *trckd ldrs: wnt 2nd 4f out: drvn to ld appr fnl f: kpt on strly cl home* 4/1[2]
4651 2 2 1/4 **Love Marmalade (IRE)**[5] 4280 3-9-8 81 6ex NeilCallan 5 88
(Mark Johnston) *led: rdn over 2f out: hdd appr fnl f: styd on same pce* 1/2[1]
3065 3 3 1/2 **Brown Pete (IRE)**[14] 3977 5-9-0 70 OisinMurphy(7) 4 70
(Violet M Jordan) *s.i.s: hld up in rr: hdwy 3f out: rdn 2f out: hung lft and tk 3rd fnl f: nvr any ch w ldng duo* 16/1
0010 4 3 **Super Duplex**[10] 4126 6-8-8 62 JemmaMarshall(5) 1 56
(Pat Phelan) *in tch: chsd ldrs 4f out: styd on same pce fnl 3f* 25/1
1125 5 17 **Dandy (GER)**[20] 3791 4-10-0 77 (p) JimmyFortune 3 54
(Andrew Balding) *chsd ldrs: rdn 3f out: wknd over 2f out* 10/1[3]
0-00 6 7 **Claude Monet (BRZ)**[38] 3157 4-9-5 70 GeorgeBaker 6
(Simon Dow) *chsd ldr to 4f out: sn wknd* 25/1

2m 7.46s (-2.24) **Going Correction** -0.125s/f (Firm)
WFA 3 from 4yo+ 10lb 6 Ran SP% 109.3
Speed ratings (Par 105): **103,101,98,96,82 76**
Tote Swingers 1&2 £1.02, 2&3 £5.40, 1&3 £5.40 CSF £6.04 TOTE £4.00: £1.80, £1.10; EX 6.80 Trifecta £19.70 Pool: £1,428.77 - 54.28 winning tickets..
Owner Tony Waspe Partnership **Bred** P Heffernan **Trained** Upper Lambourn, Berks
FOCUS
A moderate handicap dominated by the first pair. A bit better again fronm the winner, with the second basically to form.

4442 TOTAL DATA MANAGEMENT H'CAP 1m 114y
8:50 (8:51) (Class 5) (0-75,75) 3-Y-O £3,881 (£1,155; £577; £288) Stalls Low

Form RPR
0363 1 **Hunting Rights (USA)**[8] 4168 3-9-4 72 AdamKirby 2 81
(Mark Johnston) *in tch: hdwy 3f out: chsd wnr u.p wl over 1f out: hrd drvn to ld ins fnl f: rdn out* 7/2[2]
-060 2 2 1/4 **Canadian Run (IRE)**[24] 3633 3-9-7 75 [1] JimmyFortune 1 79
(Robert Mills) *led: hrd pressed fr over 3f out: kpt advantage u.p tl hdd ins fnl f: wknd clsng stages* 15/2
-025 3 3 **New Falcon (IRE)**[21] 3712 3-9-6 74 (b) NeilCallan 3 71
(James Tate) *chsd ldrs: rdn and one pce fnl 2f* 13/2
0313 4 hd **Khelac**[1] 4411 3-8-5 66 6ex (b) ShelleyBirkett(7) 7 62
(Philip Hide) *chsd ldr: chal fr over 3f out tl 2f out: wknd appr fnl f* 4/1[3]
3253 5 5 **Caramack**[17] 3902 3-9-7 75 RichardHughes 4 60
(Richard Hannon) *in tch: rdn and btn over 2f out* 15/8[1]
3324 6 3/4 **Hawaiian Dream (IRE)**[7] 4209 3-8-0 61 OisinMurphy(7) 6 44
(Roger Teal) *chsd ldrs: wknd fr 3f out* 20/1
0000 7 1/2 **Lady Vermeer**[22] 3699 3-8-6 60 (b) MartinDwyer 5 42
(Ralph Beckett) *unruly stalls: a towards rr* 20/1

1m 44.75s (-1.35) **Going Correction** -0.125s/f (Firm) 7 Ran SP% 111.6
Speed ratings (Par 100): **101,99,96,96,91 91,90**
Tote Swingers 1&2 £4.80, 2&3 £7.00, 1&3 £3.00 CSF £27.80 TOTE £3.30: £1.50, £4.10; EX 44.10 Trifecta £211.60 Pool: £1,475.96 - 5.23 winning tickets..
Owner Sheikh Hamdan Bin Mohammed Al Maktoum **Bred** Darley **Trained** Middleham Moor, N Yorks
FOCUS
This ordinary handicap was run at a routine pace. The race lacked depth but the winner is rated back to his 2yo best.
T/Plt: £18.50 to a £1 stake. Pool: £52,113.23 - 2051.01 winning tickets. T/Qpdt: £5.10 to a £1 stake. Pool: £5,015.05 - 722.25 winning tickets. ST

[4289]HAMILTON (R-H)

Thursday, July 18

OFFICIAL GOING: Good to firm (good in places; 8.4)

Wind: Light, half behind Weather: Sunny, hot

4443 IRISH STALLION FARMS EBF MAIDEN STKS 6f 5y

2:00 (2:00) (Class 5) 2-Y-O **£3,408** (£1,006; £503) **Stalls** High

Form RPR

43 **1** **Boogangoo (IRE)**[12] 4053 2-9-0 0 PaulMulrennan 1 73+
(Keith Dalgleish) *t.k.h early: w ldrs: led after 2f: rdn and edgd rt over 1f out: kpt on strly fnl f* **1/1**[1]

65 **2** *3 ¾* **Soul Instinct**[28] 3500 2-9-5 0 PhillipMakin 5 66
(Kevin Ryan) *t.k.h early: w ldrs: effrt and rdn over 1f out: kpt on same pce fnl f* **7/4**[2]

6 **3** *9* **Ibecke**[10] 4107 2-9-0 0 JoeFanning 2 32
(Mark Johnston) *in tch: rdn and edgd rt over 2f out: sn outpcd: n.d after* **9/2**[3]

00 **4** *15* **Under Approval**[21] 3724 2-9-5 0 DanielTudhope 3
(David O'Meara) *t.k.h: led 2f: cl up tl rdn and wknd fr over 2f out* **33/1**

1m 12.5s (0.30) **Going Correction** +0.025s/f (Good) **4** Ran SP% **107.5**
Speed ratings (Par 94): **99,94,82,62**
CSF £2.99 TOTE £1.70; EX 2.30 Trifecta £2.50 Pool: £771.50 - 224.13 winning units..
Owner Middleham Park Racing II **Bred** Marie & Mossy Fahy **Trained** Carluke, S Lanarks

FOCUS
Rail realignment around the loop reduced advertised distances on the Round course by 25yds. The favourite had won all three previous runnings of this maiden and that trend continued. This was all very straightforward and the quartet finished well spread out. Not the easiest form to gauge and the winner might be better than rated.

4444 ROBERT MCKELLAR - A LIFETIME IN RACING CLAIMING STKS 6f 5y

2:30 (2:30) (Class 6) 3-Y-O+ **£2,045** (£603; £302) **Stalls** Centre

Form RPR

6310 **1** **Hopes N Dreams (IRE)**[21] 3714 5-9-2 78 PaulMulrennan 2 86
(Kevin Ryan) *t.k.h early: mde all and sn tacked over to stands' rail: qcknd clr over 1f out: shkn up and kpt on strly: unchal* **5/4**[1]

5114 **2** *7* **Sunraider (IRE)**[9] 4138 6-9-5 80 MickyFenton 4 67
(Paul Midgley) *dwlt: chsd ldrs: wnt 2nd 1/2-way: effrt and edgd rt over 1f out: kpt on same pce fnl f* **11/8**[2]

530- **3** *1* **Oor Jock (IRE)**[42] 3032 5-9-12 84 TadhgO'Shea 5 70
(John Patrick Shanahan, Ire) *in tch: effrt and drvn on outside over 2f out: no imp over 1f out* **4/1**[3]

4600 **4** *2 ¼* **Spread Boy (IRE)**[43] 2977 6-8-9 45 ow3 SladeO'Hara(5) 3 51
(Alan Berry) *chsd wnr to 1/2-way: rdn and wknd fr 2f out* **100/1**

1m 11.62s (-0.58) **Going Correction** +0.025s/f (Good) **4** Ran SP% **107.5**
Speed ratings (Par 101): **104,94,93,90**
CSF £3.26 TOTE £2.20; EX 2.50 Trifecta £3.70 Pool: £789.17 - 156.54 winning units..
Owner JCG Chua & CK Ong **Bred** J & Mrs Brennan & Edward & Mrs O'Regan **Trained** Hambleton, N Yorks

FOCUS
Only three mattered in this claimer, and the second and third were below form. The winner ran to her mark.

4445 NEILSLAND AND EARNOCK MAIDEN STKS 1m 3f 16y

3:00 (3:00) (Class 5) 3-Y-O+ **£3,234** (£962; £481; £240) **Stalls** Low

Form RPR

2 **1** **Statutory (IRE)**[9] 4139 3-9-3 0 JoeFanning 2 89+
(Mark Johnston) *in tch: hdwy to chse ldr after 4f: led over 3f out: rdn over 1f out: hld on wl towards fin* **1/1**[1]

22 **2** *hd* **Bomber Thorn**[36] 3209 3-9-3 0 RichardKingscote 3 86
(Tom Dascombe) *prom: niggled 1/2-way: effrt and nt handle trck fr over 4f out: chsd wnr and continued to hang rt fr 3f out: sn drvn: kpt on wl towards fin: jst hld* **13/8**[2]

3 *11* **Wee Willy Wilfords (IRE)**[60] 2488 3-9-3 0 TadhgO'Shea 4 66
(John Patrick Shanahan, Ire) *prom: effrt and rdn over 3f out: edgd rt and outpcd by first two fr 2f out* **4/1**[3]

60 **4** *16* **Yourholidayisover (IRE)**[32] 3364 6-10-0 0 RussKennemore 1 37
(Patrick Holmes) *hld up in tch: hung rt and rdn over 3f out: sn wknd* **100/1**

500/ **5** *6* **Eila Wheeler**[631] 7105 6-9-4 42 (t) SladeO'Hara(5) 5 21
(Maurice Barnes) *t.k.h: led to over 3f out: rdn and wknd over 2f out* **100/1**

2m 20.24s (-5.36) **Going Correction** -0.375s/f (Firm)
WFA 3 from 4yo+ 11lb **5** Ran SP% **110.1**
Speed ratings (Par 103): **104,103,95,84,79**
Tote Swinger 1&2 £1.90 CSF £2.90 TOTE £1.60: £1.10, £1.20; EX 3.60 Trifecta £4.20 Pool: £1275.53 - 225.97 winning units..
Owner Sheikh Hamdan Bin Mohammed Al Maktoum **Bred** Darley **Trained** Middleham Moor, N Yorks

FOCUS
This maiden featured a couple of promising 3yos who fought out the finish, a long way clear. The winner could leave this behind.

4446 TOTEPOOL.COM H'CAP 1m 1f 36y

3:30 (3:31) (Class 4) (0-80,76) 3-Y-O+ **£5,175** (£1,540; £769; £384) **Stalls** Low

Form RPR

/05- **1** **Prince Jock (USA)**[45] 2942 6-10-0 76 TadhgO'Shea 1 84
(John Patrick Shanahan, Ire) *led 2f: cl up: led again over 3f out: rdn and hld on wl fnl f* **12/1**

2112 **2** *hd* **Argaki (IRE)**[5] 4293 3-8-11 71 6ex RaulDaSilva(3) 5 78+
(Keith Dalgleish) *hld up in tch: stdy hdwy over 3f out: rdn and edgd rt whn n.m.r over 2f out: kpt on fnl f: hld nr fin* **5/2**[1]

06-3 **3** *2 ¼* **Dhaular Dhar (IRE)**[20] 3777 11-8-13 61 GrahamLee 7 64
(Jim Goldie) *hld up: stdy hdwy whn n.m.r over 2f out and over 1f out: sn rdn: kpt on fnl f: nt rch first two* **11/1**[3]

3121 **4** *¾* **Lord Franklin**[12] 4070 4-9-0 67 JasonHart(5) 6 68
(Eric Alston) *chsd ldrs on outside: effrt and drvn over 2f out: one pce fnl f* **5/2**[1]

6122 **5** *1* **Corton Lad**[5] 4294 3-8-13 70 (bt) TomEaves 3 68
(Keith Dalgleish) *trckd ldrs: drvn over 2f out: outpcd fnl f* **13/5**[2]

-505 **6** *1 ¼* **High Resolution**[11] 4098 6-9-8 70 PhillipMakin 4 66
(Linda Perratt) *hld up: stdy hdwy over 2f out: rdn and outpcd fr over 1f out* **12/1**

0-03 **7** *1 ¾* **Ralphy Boy (IRE)**[5] 4294 4-9-2 64 MichaelO'Connell 2 56
(Alistair Whillans) *cl up: led and stdd gallop after 2f: rdn and hdd over 3f out: wknd over 1f out* **20/1**

1m 55.58s (-4.12) **Going Correction** -0.375s/f (Firm)
WFA 3 from 4yo+ 9lb **7** Ran SP% **113.4**
Speed ratings (Par 105): **103,102,100,100,99 98,96**
Tote Swingers 1&2 £10.40, 2&3 £6.40, 1&3 £12.60 CSF £41.51 TOTE £18.50: £6.80, £2.80; EX 66.90 Trifecta £680.00 Pool: £1235.04 - 1.36 winning units..
Owner Thistle Bloodstock Limited **Bred** Clover Leaf Farms II Inc **Trained** Danesfort, Co. Kilkenny

FOCUS
A good handicap and the pace was just fair with the lead changing hands on a couple of occasions. The winner is rated to last year's form.

4447 RACING UK THIS WAY THAT WAY H'CAP 1m 5f 9y

4:00 (4:00) (Class 4) (0-85,82) 3-Y-O+ **£6,469** (£1,925; £962; £481) **Stalls** Low

Form RPR

2621 **1** **Hawdyerwheesht**[10] 4110 5-9-6 74 6ex GrahamLee 2 83+
(Jim Goldie) *hld up in midfield: stdy hdwy to chse ldrs 2f out: effrt and swtchd lft 1f out: led wl ins fnl f: pushed out* **5/1**[3]

3215 **2** *1 ¼* **Interior Minister**[19] 3806 3-9-1 82 PaulMulrennan 5 88
(Jo Hughes) *led: rdn over 2f out: hdd wl ins fnl f: kpt on same pce* **13/2**

6314 **3** *nse* **Tenhoo**[17] 3889 7-8-11 70 JasonHart(5) 1 76
(Eric Alston) *hld up: hdwy over 2f out: sn rdn: kpt on ins fnl f* **8/1**

4122 **4** *1* **Schmooze (IRE)**[16] 3930 4-8-12 66 LeeTopliss 6 70+
(Linda Perratt) *hld up: hdwy whn nt clr run over 1f out: effrt whn checked 1f out: kpt on same pce* **8/1**

5415 **5** *4 ½* **Tetbury (USA)**[19] 3808 4-9-9 77 DanielTudhope 8 75
(David O'Meara) *chsd ldrs: rdn: edgd rt and outpcd 2f out: no imp after* **15/2**

2235 **6** *½* **Street Artist (IRE)**[14] 3982 3-8-10 77 (b[1]) JoeFanning 3 74
(Mark Johnston) *in tch: hdwy to press ldr after 3f: effrt and ev ch 3f out to over 1f out: wknd ins fnl f* **3/1**[1]

4311 **7** *nk* **Chant (IRE)**[19] 3809 3-8-5 71 ow1 PJMcDonald 4 68
(Ann Duffield) *chsd ldrs: rdn over 4f out: outpcd over 2f out: n.d after* **9/2**[2]

4- **8** *3* **Queen Of Alba (IRE)**[20] 3797 4-9-4 72 TadhgO'Shea 7 64
(John Patrick Shanahan, Ire) *hld up in tch: rdn 4f out: wknd over 2f out* **14/1**

2m 47.28s (-6.62) **Going Correction** -0.375s/f (Firm)
WFA 3 from 4yo+ 13lb **8** Ran SP% **113.8**
Speed ratings (Par 105): **105,104,104,103,100 100,100,98**
Tote Swingers 1&2 £10.20, 2&3 £8.10, 1&3 £23.30 CSF £36.81 CT £254.36 TOTE £4.40: £2.20, £2.90, £2.60; EX 46.10 Trifecta £794.40 Pool: £1148.56 - 1.08 winning units..
Owner J S Morrison **Bred** Baldernock Bloodstock Ltd **Trained** Uplawmoor, E Renfrews
■ Stewards' Enquiry : Graham Lee three-day ban: careless riding (Aug 1,2,4)

FOCUS
A decent staying handicap, but it was also a rough race with the winner causing a domino effect when switched left for his run over a furlong from home. The winner was better than ever.

4448 DOWNLOAD THE FREE RACING UK APP H'CAP 5f 4y

4:30 (4:31) (Class 6) (0-60,66) 3-Y-O+ **£1,940** (£577; £288; £144) **Stalls** Centre

Form RPR

5424 **1** **Ingenti**[2] 4371 5-9-0 57 KevinStott(7) 11 66
(Christopher Wilson) *cl up stands' side gp: hdwy and overall ldr over 1f out: rdn and r.o strly fnl f* **3/1**[1]

2203 **2** *1 ¼* **Chloe's Dream (IRE)**[5] 4290 3-9-5 59 [1] PJMcDonald 6 62
(Ann Duffield) *led centre gp: rdn and chsd wnr over 1f out: kpt on ins fnl f* **11/2**[3]

4145 **3** *nk* **Script**[13] 4018 4-9-9 59 PaddyAspell 5 62
(Alan Berry) *cl up centre: rdn over 2f out: rallied over 1f out: kpt on ins fnl f* **20/1**

6504 **4** *½* **Amenable (IRE)**[23] 3660 6-9-6 56 (p) RobertWinston 2 57
(Violet M Jordan) *hld up in tch centre: effrt wl over 1f out: hung lft ins fnl f: kpt on* **7/1**

5 *2 ¾* **Dancing Cosmos (IRE)**[36] 3226 3-9-6 60 TadhgO'Shea 12 50
(John Patrick Shanahan, Ire) *bhd and pushed along stands' side: hdwy over 1f out: styng on but no imp whn checked ins fnl f* **15/2**

0504 **6** *nk* **Rock Canyon (IRE)**[5] 4292 4-9-1 51 (p) GrahamLee 4 41
(Linda Perratt) *cl up centre tl rdn and no ex over 1f out* **16/1**

2655 **7** *1 ¾* **Here Now And Why (IRE)**[11] 4102 6-9-10 60 (v) GrahamGibbons 8 44
(Iain Jardine) *hld up stands' side gp: rdn and hung rt 2f out: sn no imp* **5/1**[2]

0600 **8** *1 ½* **Distant Sun (USA)**[11] 4102 9-9-4 54 PaulMulrennan 9 32
(Linda Perratt) *dwlt: bhd stands' side: rdn over 2f out: no imp over 1f out* **40/1**

3052 **9** *¾* **Royal Duchess**[16] 3932 3-8-4 47 RaulDaSilva(3) 7 22
(Lucy Normile) *chsd stands' side ldrs tl rdn and wknd over 1f out* **8/1**

201 **10** *hd* **Choc'A'Moca (IRE)**[2] 4371 6-10-2 66 6ex (v) MickyFenton 1 41
(Paul Midgley) *outpcd and drvn along in centre: no ch fr 1/2-way* **9/1**

3000 **11** *¾* **Cayman Fox**[11] 4102 8-9-1 51 TomEaves 10 23
(Linda Perratt) *led and overall ldr stands' side: rdn and hdd over 1f out: sn btn* **33/1**

59.82s (-0.18) **Going Correction** +0.025s/f (Good)
WFA 3 from 4yo+ 4lb **11** Ran SP% **118.5**
Speed ratings (Par 101): **102,100,99,98,94 93,91,88,87,87 85**
Tote Swingers 1&2 £3.80, 2&3 £8.10, 1&3 £13.60 CSF £18.90 CT £289.18 TOTE £4.40: £1.50, £1.90, £4.30; EX 17.90 Trifecta £253.90 Pool: £2660.45 - 7.85 winning units..
Owner David Bartlett **Bred** Mrs Andrea Bartlett **Trained** Manfield, N Yorks

FOCUS
A moderate sprint handicap in which they split into two groups early, with the nearside bunch always appearing to hold the edge. A pesonal best from the winner, helped by the rider's claim.

4449 RACING UK SKY CHANNEL 432 H'CAP 1m 65y

5:00 (5:01) (Class 6) (0-65,61) 3-Y-O **£1,940** (£577; £288; £144) **Stalls** Low

Form RPR

5500 **1** **Red Charmer (IRE)**[27] 3546 3-9-7 61 PJMcDonald 2 77
(Ann Duffield) *cl up: rdn to ld over 1f out: kpt on strly fnl f* **7/1**

2 *3* **Minot Street (CAN)**[64] 2379 3-8-5 45 (bt[1]) JoeFanning 6 54
(John C McConnell, Ire) *hld up in tch: stdy hdwy over 2f out: chsd wnr over 1f out: edgd lft ins fnl f: r.o* **12/1**

4-04 **3** *3 ¾* **Diddy Eric**[10] 4113 3-8-9 49 TomEaves 1 49
(Micky Hammond) *hld up: rdn and outpcd over 3f out: rallied over 1f out: kpt on: no imp* **7/2**[3]

-630 **4** *1 ½* **Hello Gorgeous**[36] 3203 3-8-11 51 JamesSullivan 4 48
(Keith Dalgleish) *led 2f: cl up: outpcd and hung rt over 2f out: no imp fnl f* **6/1**

1105 **5** *1* **Lexington Blue**^{13} [4008] 3-9-4 **58**........ TonyHamilton 7 52
(David O'Meara) *hld up in tch: rdn over 2f out: outpcd wl over 1f out: sn n.d* **3/1**^{2}
0222 **6** *1* **Polar Forest**^{9} [4140] 3-9-3 **57**........ RobbieFitzpatrick 5 49
(Richard Guest) *led after 2f: rdn and hdd over 1f out: wknd ins fnl f* **5/2**^{1}
0-50 **7** *27* **Oh Boy Oh Boy**^{31} [3394] 3-8-2 **45**........(p) RaulDaSilva$^{(3)}$ 3
(James Moffatt) *dwlt: bhd: rdn and wandered over 2f out: sn lost tch* **33/1**
1m 45.36s (-3.04) **Going Correction** -0.375s/f (Firm) **7** Ran SP% **113.2**
Speed ratings (Par 98): **100,97,93,91,90 89,62**
Tote Swingers 1&2 £7.50, 2&3 £10.00, 1&3 £4.20 CSF £80.62 TOTE £12.30: £4.70, £5.90; EX 115.20 Trifecta £642.80 Pool: £2005.79 - 2.34 winning units..
Owner I Farrington & R Chapman **Bred** Tally-Ho Stud **Trained** Constable Burton, N Yorks
FOCUS
This did not look a great race and the favourite disappointed. The winner belatedly built on his 2yo form.
T/Plt: £103.50 to a £1 stake. Pool: £41,905.30 - 295.45 winning tickets. T/Qpdt: £23.40 to a £1 stake. Pool: £3,086.00 - 97.5 winning tickets. RY

4064 LEICESTER (R-H)
Thursday, July 18

OFFICIAL GOING: Good to firm (good in places; 9.0)
Wind: Almost nil Weather: Fine

4450 TRACK YOUR FAVOURITE HORSES AT ATTHERACES.COM (S) STKS — 5f 2y
2:10 (2:11) (Class 6) 2-Y-O **£1,940** (£577; £288; £144) **Stalls** Centre

Form RPR
600 **1** **Touch The Clouds**^{34} [3298] 2-8-11 0........ JamieSpencer 6 59
(Kevin Ryan) *chsd ldrs: shkn up to ld ins fnl f: pushed out* **7/4**^{2}
05 **2** *1* **Autumn Tide (IRE)**^{15} [3943] 2-8-6 0........ SilvestreDeSousa 3 50
(John Quinn) *prom: sn pushed along: rdn over 1f out: r.o ins fnl f: nt rch wnr* **5/4**^{1}
0 **3** *1 1/4* **Tinsill**^{12} [4046] 2-8-8 0........(v^{1}) DeclanCannon$^{(3)}$ 5 51
(Nigel Tinkler) *chsd ldrs: led over 1f out: rdn and hdd ins fnl f: styd on same pce* **25/1**
60 **4** *9* **Rubylicious (IRE)**^{12} [4065] 2-7-13 0........ CharlotteJenner$^{(7)}$ 4 13
(J S Moore) *sn led: rdn and hdd over 1f out: wknd fnl f* **40/1**
60 **5** *6* **Denby Dale**^{56} [2595] 2-8-6 0........(tp) JakePayne$^{(5)}$ 1
(Bill Turner) *chsd ldrs: pushed along 3f out: rdn and wknd over 1f out* **6/1**^{3}
0503 **6** *8* **Ivan B**^{14} [3992] 2-8-11 0........ SamHitchcott 2
(Mick Channon) *sn outpcd* **12/1**
1m 1.71s (1.71) **Going Correction** -0.125s/f (Firm) **6** Ran SP% **109.1**
Speed ratings (Par 92): **81,79,77,63,53 40**
Tote Swingers 1&2 £1.10, 2&3 £4.90, 1&3 £5.30 CSF £4.00 TOTE £2.50: £1.40, £1.80; EX 4.70 Trifecta £39.30 Pool: £2335.43 - 44.48 winning units..There was no bid for the winner.
Owner Matt & Lauren Morgan 1 **Bred** Stuart McPhee Bloodstock Ltd **Trained** Hambleton, N Yorks
FOCUS
A weak juvenile seller and unconvincing form set around the second.

4451 AT THE RACES ON FACEBOOK NURSERY H'CAP — 5f 2y
2:40 (2:45) (Class 5) 2-Y-O **£3,234** (£962; £481; £240) **Stalls** Centre

Form RPR
21 **1** **Excel's Beauty**^{39} [3132] 2-9-7 **74**........ RyanMoore 5 82+
(James Tate) *a.p: chsd ldr 1/2-way: shkn up to ld 1f out: pushed out* **2/5**^{1}
4504 **2** *3 1/4* **Anfield**^{36} [3217] 2-8-0 **53** oh4........ PaoloSirigu 2 49
(Mick Quinn) *led: rdn and hdd 1f out: styd on same pce* **25/1**
1005 **3** *7* **Sleepy Joe (IRE)**^{34} [3267] 2-8-10 **63**........ SamHitchcott 4 34
(Mick Channon) *sn pushed along in rr: outpcd fr 1/2-way* **8/1**^{3}
0332 **4** *3/4* **The Dandy Yank (IRE)**^{9} [4141] 2-9-6 **73**........ FergusSweeney 3 41
(Jamie Osborne) *chsd ldr to 1/2-way: rdn and wknd over 1f out* **11/2**^{2}
1m 0.04s (0.04) **Going Correction** -0.125s/f (Firm) **4** Ran SP% **101.8**
Speed ratings (Par 94): **94,88,77,76**
CSF £8.78 TOTE £1.40; EX 14.20 Trifecta £25.00 Pool: £1819.11 - 54.38 winning units..
Owner Sheikh Juma Dalmook Al Maktoum **Bred** Glebe Stud, J F Dean & Lady Trenchard **Trained** Newmarket, Suffolk
FOCUS
The official ratings shown are estimated and for information only. A modest nursery, numerically depleted when Kodafine unseated her rider and bolted away from the stalls. Probably not form to go overboard about, with the runner-up the key.

4452 AT THE RACES SKY 415 CONDITIONS STKS — 1m 1f 218y
3:10 (3:10) (Class 3) 3-Y-O **£7,561** (£2,263; £1,131) **Stalls** Low

Form RPR
21- **1** **Telescope (IRE)**^{294} [6596] 3-9-3 0........ RyanMoore 3 115+
(Sir Michael Stoute) *led: hdd over 8f out: trckd ldr tl led again 3f out: pushed clr fnl 2f* **1/2**^{1}
1 **2** *24* **Mulakim**^{13} [4022] 3-9-3 0........ SilvestreDeSousa 2 67+
(Saeed bin Suroor) *prom: rdn to chse wnr over 2f out: sn outpcd: eased over 1f out* **3/1**^{2}
120 **3** *20* **Centurius**^{28} [3485] 3-9-3 97........ DaneO'Neill 1 27+
(Marco Botti) *led over 8f out: hung lft almost thrght: hdd 3f out: sn wknd and eased* **5/1**^{3}
2m 2.5s (-5.40) **Going Correction** -0.125s/f (Firm) **3** Ran SP% **108.3**
Speed ratings (Par 104): **116,96,80**
CSF £2.32 TOTE £1.30; EX 2.10 Trifecta £2.30 Pool: £1098.91 - 344.26 winning units..
Owner Highclere Thoroughbred Racing -Wavertree **Bred** Barronstown Stud **Trained** Newmarket, Suffolk
FOCUS
Just a trio of runners, but a fascinating conditions event nonetheless, with all the contestants boasting useful form. The pace looked decent. Telescope is worth a big figure although the form is hard to pin down.

4453 BRITISH STALLION STUDS EBF AT THE RACES FILLIES' H'CAP — 7f 9y
3:40 (3:41) (Class 4) (0-80,80) 3-Y-O **£7,561** (£2,263; £1,131; £566; £282) **Stalls** Centre

Form RPR
31 **1** **Ghasabah**^{20} [3787] 3-9-3 **76**........ PaulHanagan 1 87+
(William Haggas) *hld up: hdwy over 2f out: led over 1f out: r.o wl* **11/4**^{1}
4-10 **2** *2 3/4* **Burning Dawn (USA)**^{41} [3058] 3-9-0 **73**........(t) JamieSpencer 3 77
(David Brown) *stdd s: hld up: hdwy u.p and hung rt fr over 1f out: r.o to go 2nd wl ins fnl f: nt rch wnr* **4/1**^{3}
0620 **3** *2 1/4* **Magical Rose (IRE)**^{25} [3611] 3-9-0 **73**........(p) FrederikTylicki 7 71
(Paul D'Arcy) *a.p: chsd ldr over 2f out tl rdn over 1f out: styd on same pce ins fnl f* **25/1**
5341 **4** *nse* **Lovesome**^{12} [4068] 3-8-6 **72**........ LouisSteward$^{(7)}$ 6 70
(Michael Bell) *chsd ldr tl led over 5f out: hdd over 1f out: styd on same pce ins fnl f* **4/1**^{3}
-021 **5** *1 1/2* **Laughing Rock (IRE)**^{12} [4064] 3-8-4 **63**........ AndrewMullen 5 57
(Michael Appleby) *chsd ldrs: rdn over 1f out: no ex ins fnl f* **12/1**
0-41 **6** *1 3/4* **Oasis Spirit**^{19} [3837] 3-8-12 **74**........ ThomasBrown$^{(3)}$ 2 63
(Andrew Balding) *prom: rdn over 1f out: wknd ins fnl f* **8/1**
432 **7** *1 1/4* **Queen Aggie (IRE)**^{5} [4288] 3-9-7 **80**........ RyanMoore 4 66
(David Evans) *led: hdd over 5f out: chsd ldr tl rdn over 2f out: wknd over 1f out* **3/1**^{2}
1m 24.86s (-1.34) **Going Correction** -0.125s/f (Firm) **7** Ran SP% **114.3**
Speed ratings (Par 99): **102,98,96,96,94 92,91**
Tote Swingers 1&2 £2.90, 2&3 £14.50, 1&3 £9.30 CSF £14.10 CT £221.04 TOTE £3.00: £1.70, £2.10; EX 15.60 Trifecta £306.40 Pool: £2742.25 - 6.71 winning units..
Owner Hamdan Al Maktoum **Bred** Shadwell Estate Company Limited **Trained** Newmarket, Suffolk
FOCUS
A fair fillies' handicap, with a top weight officially rated 80. There looks more to come from the winner.

4454 ATTHERACES.COM EXCLUSIVE HUGH TAYLOR TIPPING MAIDEN STKS — 1m 1f 218y
4:10 (4:10) (Class 4) 3-4-Y-O **£4,851** (£1,443; £721; £360) **Stalls** Low

Form RPR
54 **1** **Pernica**^{20} [3764] 3-8-12 0........ FrederikTylicki 3 78
(Lucy Wadham) *led: hdd over 8f out: remained handy: rdn to chse ldr over 1f out: styd on to ld nr fin* **20/1**
4222 **2** *nk* **Thouwra (IRE)**^{18} [3858] 3-9-3 82........(p) SilvestreDeSousa 2 82
(Saeed bin Suroor) *a.p: chsd ldr over 6f out: led over 2f out: rdn over 1f out: hdd nr fin* **10/11**^{1}
32 **3** *4* **Bushel (USA)**^{7} [4223] 3-9-3 0........ FrannyNorton 4 74
(Mark Johnston) *led over 8f out: rdn and hdd over 2f out: no ex ins fnl f* **7/2**^{2}
6- **4** *3* **Everlasting Light**^{245} [7720] 3-8-12 0........ JamieSpencer 5 65
(Luca Cumani) *chsd ldrs: rdn and hung rt fr over 1f out: eased whn btn ins fnl f* **6/1**
5 **5** *9* **Entrenched (USA)**^{9} [4152] 3-9-3 0........ MickaelBarzalona 1 57
(Saeed bin Suroor) *awkward leaving stalls: bhd: tk clsr order 1/2-way: hdwy over 2f out: wknd over 1f out* **5/1**^{3}
2m 6.27s (-1.63) **Going Correction** -0.125s/f (Firm) **5** Ran SP% **110.3**
Speed ratings (Par 105): **101,100,97,95,87**
CSF £39.82 TOTE £22.50: £7.10, £1.50; EX 63.50 Trifecta £71.40 Pool: £2233.66 - 23.43 winning units..
Owner Mr And Mrs A E Pakenham **Bred** Mr & Mrs A E Pakenham **Trained** Newmarket, Suffolk
■ Stewards' Enquiry : Frederik Tylicki two-day ban: used whip above permitted level (Aug 1-2)
FOCUS
On paper, a competitive maiden, despite the small field. A 3lb best from the winner, with the second to his latest.

4455 ATTHERACES.COM EXCLUSIVE WILLIAM BUICK BLOG H'CAP — 1m 3f 183y
4:40 (4:41) (Class 5) (0-75,71) 4-Y-O+ **£3,234** (£962; £481; £240) **Stalls** Low

Form RPR
2625 **1** **Reset City**^{5} [4287] 7-9-7 **71**........ FrannyNorton 1 82
(Mark Johnston) *hld up: hdwy to chse ldr over 3f out: led over 1f out: rdn out* **11/8**^{1}
-000 **2** *5* **Grandiloquent**^{16} [3930] 4-9-2 **66**........(b) JamieSpencer 3 69
(Kevin Ryan) *led after 1f and racd wd to 1/2-way: qcknd 4f out: rdn and hdd over 1f out: styd on same pce* **4/1**^{3}
1462 **3** *3 1/2* **Iceman George**^{8} [4179] 9-8-6 **61**........(v) PhilipPrince$^{(5)}$ 2 58
(Alison Hutchinson) *chsd ldrs: rdn over 3f out: edgd rt fr over 2f out: no ex fnl f* **2/1**^{2}
130- **4** *10* **Fleeting Fashion**^{354} [4626] 4-8-7 **57**........ AndrewMullen 4 38
(Michael Appleby) *led 1f: chsd ldr to over 3f out: rdn and wknd over 1f out* **7/1**
2m 31.41s (-2.49) **Going Correction** -0.125s/f (Firm) **4** Ran SP% **107.9**
Speed ratings (Par 103): **103,99,97,90**
CSF £6.93 TOTE £1.50; EX 5.90 Trifecta £8.50 Pool: £1692.23 - 148.77 winning units..
Owner R S Brookhouse **Bred** R S Brookhouse **Trained** Middleham Moor, N Yorks
FOCUS
A modest small-field handicap, in which the top weight was rated 71. The form is rated a bit conservatively around the winner.

4456 FOLLOW AT THE RACES ON TWITTER APPRENTICE H'CAP — 5f 218y
5:10 (5:11) (Class 6) (0-65,66) 3-Y-O+ **£1,940** (£577; £288; £144) **Stalls** Centre

Form RPR
0012 **1** **Strong Man**^{3} [4339] 5-10-3 **66** 6ex........(b) MatthewHopkins$^{(3)}$ 10 76
(Michael Easterby) *chsd ldrs: rdn over 1f out: styd on to ld towards fin* **6/4**^{1}
0201 **2** *1* **Verus Delicia (IRE)**^{15} [3949] 4-10-0 **60**........ PhilipPrince 8 67
(Daniel Mark Loughnane) *hld up: hdwy over 1f out: rdn to ld ins fnl f: hdd towards fin* **4/1**^{3}
4000 **3** *1/2* **Divertimenti (IRE)**^{12} [4074] 9-9-10 **59**........(b) AdamMcLean$^{(3)}$ 9 64
(Roy Bowring) *chsd ldrs: led over 1f out: sn rdn and hung rt: hdd ins fnl f: styd on same pce* **11/1**
0000 **4** *2 1/4* **Sairaam (IRE)**^{13} [4005] 7-9-1 **47**........ JackDuern 7 45
(Charles Smith) *chsd ldrs: rdn over 2f out: styd on same pce ins fnl f* **20/1**
4050 **5** *hd* **Powerful Pierre**^{23} [3649] 6-10-0 **60**........(p) JacobButterfield 5 57
(Ollie Pears) *s.i.s: hld up: hdwy and nt clr run over 1f out: nt trble ldrs* **7/2**^{2}
5000 **6** *nk* **The Bendy Fella (IRE)**^{120} [1093] 5-8-11 **46**........(p) CharlotteJenner$^{(3)}$ 3 42
(Mark Usher) *sn pushed along in rr: hdwy over 2f out: rdn over 1f out: styd on same pce ins fnl f* **25/1**
003 **7** *nse* **Errigal Lad**^{12} [4074] 8-9-3 **49**........ GemmaTutty 2 45
(Garry Woodward) *sn outpcd: hdwy over 1f out: nt trble ldrs* **7/1**
1000 **8** *5* **Sophie's Beau (USA)**^{3} [4344] 6-9-2 **51**........(b) DanielleMooney$^{(3)}$ 6 31
(Michael Chapman) *racd keenly: sn led: rdn and hdd over 1f out: wknd fnl f* **33/1**
1m 12.77s (-0.23) **Going Correction** -0.125s/f (Firm)
WFA 3 from 4yo+ 5lb **8** Ran SP% **114.6**
Speed ratings (Par 101): **96,94,94,91,90 90,90,83**
Tote Swingers 1&2 £1.70, 2&3 £8.40, 1&3 £1.70 CSF £7.47 CT £46.52 TOTE £2.40: £1.10, £1.50, £3.80; EX 7.90 Trifecta £40.80 Pool: £3003.62 - 55.18 winning units..
Owner Mrs Jean Turpin **Bred** Mrs Jean Turpin **Trained** Sheriff Hutton, N Yorks
■ Stewards' Enquiry : Adam McLean two-day ban: used whip above permitted level (Aug 1-2)
Charlotte Jenner two-day ban: used whip above permitted level (Aug 1-2)
FOCUS
A seemingly competitive finale, even though the quality of runners was not great. The winner is rated to his mark.

T/Plt: £11.50 to a £1 stake. Pool: £41,260.70 - 2607.02 winning tickets. T/Qpdt: £10.50 to a £1 stake. Pool: £1,942.81 - 135.86 winning tickets. CR

4457 - 4461a (Foreign Racing) - See Raceform Interactive

[4224]LEOPARDSTOWN (L-H)

Thursday, July 18

OFFICIAL GOING: Good to firm (good last 2f)

4462a SILVER FLASH STKS (GROUP 3) 7f

7:00 (7:00) 2-Y-O **£31,707** (£9,268; £4,390; £1,463)

RPR

1 **Wonderfully (IRE)**[27] 3522 2-9-0 ....(v[1]) JosephO'Brien 2 104
(A P O'Brien, Ire) *mde all: rdn clr under 2f out: stdy on wl though advantage reduced cl home* **13/8[1]**

2 *1* **Perhaps (IRE)**[14] 4000 2-9-0 .... SeamieHeffernan 6 101+
(A P O'Brien, Ire) *w.w: pushed along in 5th over 2f out: swtchd rt ent fnl f: styd on strly to go 2nd cl home* **11/2**

3 *½* **Avenue Gabriel**[20] 3794 2-9-0 .... ChrisHayes 5 100
(P D Deegan, Ire) *chsd ldr in 3rd: pushed along in 4th appr fnl f: styd on wl into 2nd fnl 100yds: dropped to 3rd cl home* **9/2[3]**

4 *¾* **Heart Focus (IRE)**[18] 3868 2-9-0 .... KevinManning 4 98
(J S Bolger, Ire) *trckd ldr in cl 2nd tl pushed along 2f out and nt qckn w ldr over 1f out and dropped to 4th: kpt on same pce fnl f* **2/1[2]**

5 *1* **Simple Love (USA)**[15] 3962 2-9-0 .... PatSmullen 3 96
(D K Weld, Ire) *chsd ldrs in 4th: pushed along to chse ldr in 2nd over 1f out: sn no imp: dropped to 5th ins fnl f* **8/1**

6 *20* **Wafer Ice (IRE)** 2-9-0 .... WayneLordan 1 44
(Ms Joanna Morgan, Ire) *slowly away: sn reminders in rr: detached over 2f out* **33/1**

1m 26.65s (-2.05) **Going Correction** -0.05s/f (Good) **6** Ran SP% **119.0**
Speed ratings: **109,107,107,106,105 82**
CSF £12.13 TOTE £3.30: £1.70, £2.50; DF 14.00.
Owner Michael Tabor & Derrick Smith & Mrs John Magnier **Bred** Massarra Syndicate **Trained** Ballydoyle, Co Tipperary

FOCUS
A decent renewal containing the Albany fourth and seventh as well as two unbeaten fillies. New tactics were deployed on the winner, who made all and always looked like holding on up the home straight. The form fits the race averages.

4465a IRISH STALLION FARMS EUROPEAN BREEDERS FUND "NASRULLAH" H'CAP (PREMIER HANDICAP) 1m 2f

8:35 (8:37) 3-Y-0+

£48,780 (£15,447; £7,317; £2,439; £1,626; £813)

RPR

1 **Tandem**[116] 1168 4-9-3 **94**..............................(v[1]) PatSmullen 6 103
(D K Weld, Ire) *chsd ldrs: tk clsr order in 3rd over 2f out: led over 1f out and pushed clr: hld on wl cl home* **6/1[3]**

2 *¾* **Fortify (IRE)**[18] 3869 3-9-4 **105**..............................(p) JosephO'Brien 10 113+
(A P O'Brien, Ire) *hld up towards rr: plenty to do in 11th home turn: kpt on into 7th 1f out: styd on strly into 2nd clsng stages: nt trble wnr* **9/2[2]**

3 *2* **Dane Street (USA)**[26] 3600 4-9-0 **94**..............................(p) RonanWhelan[(3)] 4 97
(Mrs John Harrington, Ire) *trckd ldr in 2nd tl nt qckn ent fnl f: kpt on same pce and dropped to 3rd clsng stages* **12/1**

4 *½* **Brog Deas (IRE)**[16] 3939 4-9-3 **94**..............................(v[1]) DannyGrant 14 96
(Patrick J Flynn, Ire) *w.w: prog over 2f out: kpt on into 4th ent fnl f: nvr on terms* **25/1**

5 *shd* **Strandfield Lady (IRE)**[4] 4330 8-7-11 **81** oh3.............. ConnorKing[(7)] 2 83
(H Rogers, Ire) *hld up in rr: prog on inner early in st: wnt 3rd 1f out: sn no ex and dropped to 5th ins fnl f* **12/1**

6 *shd* **Opera Gloves (IRE)**[10] 4132 3-8-11 **98**.............................. ShaneFoley 5 100+
(M Halford, Ire) *hld up towards rr: plenty to do home turn: kpt on wl fr over 1f out: nvr nrr* **10/1**

7 *1½* **Stronger Than Me (IRE)**[20] 3799 5-8-4 **81**..............(p) ChrisHayes 13 80
(W T Farrell, Ire) *hld up towards rr: plenty to do home turn and appr fnl f: kpt on wl: nvr nrr* **16/1**

8 *2* **Barack (IRE)**[20] 3799 7-8-6 **86**..............................(b) ShaneBKelly[(3)] 11 81
(W McCreery, Ire) *w.w towards rr: prog under 2f out: no imp ent fnl f* **28/1**

9 *6* **Bunairgead (IRE)**[10] 4132 3-9-2 **103** 5ex.............. KevinManning 15 86
(J S Bolger, Ire) *chsd ldrs tl clsd in 3rd 3f out: pushed along early in st and nt qckn: sn no ex* **4/1[1]**

10 *¾* **Levanto (IRE)**[8] 4190 3-8-2 **95** ow1.............................. LukeDempsey[(7)] 3 77
(W P Mullins, Ire) *trckd ldr in 3rd tl pushed along off home turn: sn no imp and wknd appr fnl f* **10/1**

11 *½* **Long Journey Home (IRE)**[35] 3265 5-8-4 **81** oh1........ WayneLordan 9 61
(Daniel William O'Sullivan, Ire) *led tl hdd over 1f out: wknd qckly* **16/1**

12 *1¾* **Vastonea (IRE)**[18] 3869 5-9-2 **96**.............................. SamJames[(3)] 1 73
(Kevin Prendergast, Ire) *racd in mid-div: nt qckn under 2f out: sn no imp* **25/1**

13 *nk* **Cyclone**[26] 3601 3-8-4 **91** oh1.............................. NGMcCullagh 16 67
(J P Murtagh, Ire) *racd in mid-div tl nt qckn over 2f out: sn no imp* **7/1**

14 *2* **Abbey Vale (IRE)**[14] 4002 3-8-1 **91** oh3..............(p) IJBrennan[(3)] 8 63
(G M Lyons, Ire) *nvr bttr than mid-div: no threat under 2f out* **12/1**

15 *4¼* **Sindjara (USA)**[54] 2678 4-9-2 **93**.............................. DeclanMcDonogh 12 57
(John M Oxx, Ire) *nvr bttr than mid-div: no imp 2f out: eased ins fnl f* **14/1**

16 *3* **Ottoman Empire (FR)**[27] 3525 7-9-12 **103**.............................. FMBerry 7 61
(John Butler) *trckd ldrs in 4th tl squeezed for room under 3f out and lost position: sn no ex* **9/1**

2m 6.44s (-1.76) **Going Correction** +0.075s/f (Good)
WFA 3 from 4yo+ 10lb **16** Ran SP% **145.8**
Speed ratings: **110,109,107,107,107 107,106,104,99,99 98,97,97,95,92 89**
CSF £39.26 CT £350.28 TOTE £7.90: £1.40, £1.40, £3.00, £5.70; DF 44.40.
Owner K Abdullah **Bred** Juddmonte Farms Ltd **Trained** The Curragh, Co Kildare

FOCUS
Fiercely competitive, which is hardly surprising given the money on offer. The form looks rock-solid and can be trusted, the standard set around the third, sixth and seventh. The first two might have seen the last of handicaps.

4466 - (Foreign Racing) - See Raceform Interactive

[3454]DIEPPE (R-H)

Thursday, July 18

OFFICIAL GOING: Turf: good

4467a PRIX FLOWERS (CLAIMER) (4YO+) (LADY RIDERS) (TURF) 1m 1f

2:05 (12:00) 4-Y-0+ **£6,504** (£2,601; £1,951; £1,300; £650)

RPR

1 **Casquito (IRE)**[59] 5-10-1 0..............................(b) MlleBarbaraGuenet 6 92
(F Chappet, France) **79/10**

2 *snk* **Glamour Star (GER)**[38] 4-9-4 0.............................. MissSilkeBruggemann 12 81
(W Mongil, Germany) **14/1**

3 *1½* **Zaungast (IRE)**[81] 9-9-4 0..............................(p) MlleAlexandraRosa 14 78
(W Hickst, Germany) **83/10**

4 *nse* **Blazon (FR)**[32] 6-9-12 0.............................. MlleDelphineGarcia-Dubois 5 86
(P Van De Poele, France) **73/10[3]**

5 *½* **Heraclius**[32] 5-9-11 0.............................. MissMPlat 8 84
(J-M Beguigne, France) **16/1**

6 *¾* **Primera Vista**[32] 7-9-8 0..............................(b) MlleJadeyPietrasiewicz 3 79
(Mario Hofer, Germany) **78/10**

7 *hd* **Chock Dee (FR)**[32] 8-9-4 0..............................(b) MlleAlisonMassin 9 75
(Y Barberot, France) **78/10**

8 *1* **Mrs Miller (GER)**[12] 5-9-7 0.............................. MlleSandrineHagenbach 15 76
(S Smrczek, Germany) **14/1**

9 *¾* **San Martin**[32] 6-10-6 0.............................. MlleCelineMonfort 4 87
(P Monfort, France) **11/2[2]**

10 *nse* **Curro Perote (FR)**[15] 6-9-3 0..............................(p) MlleMarieRollando[(4)] 13 74
(X Nakkachdji, France) **48/10[1]**

11 **Do It Yourself (IRE)** 5-9-4 0.............................. FrauVanessaBaltromei[(4)] 7
(Andreas Lowe, Germany) **50/1**

12 **My Grand Duke (USA)**[370] 6-9-0 0.............................. MlleMarionBas[(4)] 11
(R Schoof, Belgium) **107/1**

13 **Happy Valley (ARG)**[48] 7-9-4 0.............................. MissAZetterholm 1
(Mlle H Mennessier, France) **64/1**

14 **Arluno (FR)**[14] 4-9-0 0..............................(b) MlleMarieArtu[(4)] 10
(J-Y Artu, France) **40/1**

15 **Irons On Fire (USA)**[49] 2794 5-9-0 0..(b) MissAnne-SophieCrombez[(4)] 2
(Gay Kelleway) *midfield on inner: lost pl and dropped to last over 2f out: sn bhd and btn: eased and t.o* **62/1**

1m 52.03s (112.03) **15** Ran SP% **117.1**
WIN (incl. 1 euro stake): 8.90. Places: 2.90, 4.10, 2.80. DF: 54.60. SF: 145.50..
Owner P Roussillon & J Schenk **Bred** Stall Sohrenhof **Trained** France

[4421]VICHY

Thursday, July 18

OFFICIAL GOING: Turf: good to soft

4468a PRIX MADAME JEAN COUTURIE (LISTED RACE) (3YO FILLIES) (TURF) 1m 2f

1:20 (12:00) 3-Y-0 **£22,357** (£8,943; £6,707; £4,471; £2,235)

RPR

1 **Siljan's Saga (FR)**[18] 3-8-11 0.............................. Pierre-CharlesBoudot 12 109
(J-P Gauvin, France) **76/10**

2 *4* **Venturous Spirit (FR)**[18] 3877 3-8-11 0..............(b[1]) UmbertoRispoli 1 101
(M Delzangles, France) **73/10[3]**

3 *2* **Miss You Too**[48] 2842 3-8-11 0.............................. MartinLane 4 97
(David Simcock) *t.k.h: led: clr of all bar 2nd 1/2-way: rdn 3f out: racd alone against far side rail in st: steadily clsd down and hdd ins fnl f: no ex and dropped to 3rd* **7/1[2]**

4 *5* **Akemi (IRE)**[28] 3521 3-8-11 0.............................. MaximeGuyon 5 87
(X Thomas-Demeaulte, France) **7/2[1]**

5 *nse* **Savanna La Mar (USA)**[26] 3604 3-8-11 0.............. StephanePasquier 9 87
(Sir Mark Prescott Bt) *midfield: dropped to last and rdn 3f out: styd on u.p to take n.d 5th towards fin* **44/5**

6 *2* **Audacia (IRE)**[49] 2804 3-8-11 0.............................. IoritzMendizabal 6 83
(Hugo Palmer) *chsd ldr: clr of remainder 1/2-way: rdn over 2f out: no ex ent fnl f: fdd and dropped to 6th towards fin* **10/1**

7 *¾* **Princesse Fiona (FR)**[47] 3-8-11 0.............................. AntoineHamelin 3 81
(J-P Gallorini, France) **22/1**

8 *4* **Red Shot (FR)**[83] 1816 3-8-11 0.............................. Christophe-PatriceLemaire 7 73
(H-A Pantall, France) **29/1**

9 *¾* **Kathinka (GER)**[28] 3521 3-8-11 0.............................. FilipMinarik 11 72
(M Munch, Germany) **41/1**

10 *½* **Amarysia (FR)**[99] 3-8-11 0.............................. AnthonyCrastus 8 71
(C Laffon-Parias, France) **7/2[1]**

0 **Day For Night (IRE)**[83] 1816 3-8-11 0.............................. FabriceVeron 2
(H-A Pantall, France) **28/1**

0 **Endio (FR)**[32] 3385 3-8-11 0.............................. FranckBlondel 10
(Mme L Audon, France) **31/1**

2m 4.17s (-4.43) **12** Ran SP% **116.6**
WIN (incl. 1 euro stake): 8.60. Places: 3.10, 2.80, 2.70. DF: 27.50. SF: 52.00..
Owner E Palluat De Besset & E Tassin **Bred** Mme P Ouvry **Trained** France

[4443]HAMILTON (R-H)

Friday, July 19

OFFICIAL GOING: Good to firm (good in places; 8.3)
Wind: Breezy, half behind Weather: Sunny, hot

4469 BOOK NOW FOR LADIES NIGHT APPRENTICE SERIES H'CAP (ROUND 3 OF HAMILTON PARK APPRENTICE SERIES) 1m 65y

6:10 (6:11) (Class 6) (0-60,57) 4-Y-0+ **£2,045** (£603; £302) Stalls Low

Form RPR

53-2 1 **Idyllic Star (IRE)**[83] 1842 4-9-7 **57**..............................(p) JasonHart 3 73+
(Keith Dalgleish) *cl up: led over 2f out: rdn clr fr over 1f out* **2/1[1]**

0-00 **2** *8* **Triskaidekaphobia**[43] 3030 10-8-9 **45**......(t) JulieBurke 2 42
(Wilf Storey) *led: rdn and hdd over 2f out: no ch w wnr fr over 1f out* **66/1**

-403 **3** *½* **Remember Rocky**[59] 2537 4-8-13 **49**......(v) GemmaTutty 8 45
(Lucy Normile) *hld up: outpcd and struggling over 4f out: styd on fr over 1f out: nrst fin* **12/1**

3520 **4** *1¼* **Lil Sophella (IRE)**[14] 4005 4-8-7 **48**...... JackGarritty(5) 6 41
(Patrick Holmes) *dwlt: hld up: hdwy to chse ldrs 1/2-way: rdn and outpcd fr 2f out* **13/2**

6024 **5** *1¼* **Eilean Mor**[4] 4339 5-8-10 **46**...... NoelGarbutt 7 36
(R Mike Smith) *t.k.h: hld up towards rr: drvn and edgd rt over 2f out: sn no imp* **13/2**

4500 **6** *7* **Last Destination (IRE)**[3] 4375 5-9-1 **51**......(v[1]) LeeTopliss 4 25
(Nigel Tinkler) *missed break: hld up: hdwy after 2f: rdn and outpcd over 2f out: sn btn* **4/1**[2]

3433 **7** *2½* **Cabal**[3] 4376 6-9-4 **54**......(b) DarylByrne 9 22
(Andrew Crook) *dwlt: hld up on outside: stdy hdwy 4f out: rdn and wknd over 2f out* **5/1**[3]

-056 **8** *1¼* **Military Call**[4] 4339 6-8-8 **49**......(b[1]) RowanScott(5) 1 15
(Alistair Whillans) *prom: drvn and outpcd over 3f out: wknd fnl 2f* **16/1**

1m 44.7s (-3.70) **Going Correction** -0.425s/f (Firm) **8** Ran SP% **111.7**
Speed ratings (Par 101): **101,93,92,91,90 83,80,79**
toteswingers 1&2 £15.80, 2&3 £37.80, 1&3 £3.80 CSF £121.69 CT £1258.76 TOTE £2.00: £1.10, £5.50, £3.10; EX 90.90 Trifecta £318.50 Pool: £2458.57 - 5.78 winning units..
Owner Mac Asphalt Ltd **Bred** Coleman Bloodstock Limited **Trained** Carluke, S Lanarks
■ Stewards' Enquiry : Noel Garbutt one-day ban: careless riding (Aug 2)

FOCUS
Due to the rail position on the loop, all races over 1m or further were approximately 25yds shorter than the official measurements. An extremely weak handicap. The form is pitched towards the lower end of the possibilities.

4470 BRITISH STALLION STUDS E B F MAIDEN STKS 6f 5y
6:40 (6:40) (Class 5) 2-Y-O **£3,881** (£1,155; £577; £288) **Stalls** High

Form RPR

622 **1** **Disclosure**[23] 3680 2-9-5 0......(p) TomEaves 5 74+
(Bryan Smart) *t.k.h early: mde all: rdn over 1f out: styd on wl fnl f* **15/8**[2]

66 **2** *¾* **Omanome (IRE)**[15] 3978 2-9-0 0...... DanielTudhope 2 67+
(David O'Meara) *t.k.h early: chsd ldrs: effrt and chsd wnr 1f out: edgd rt: kpt on: hld nr fin* **7/1**[3]

6 **3** *6* **Emaad (USA)**[30] 3461 2-9-5 0...... JoeFanning 1 52+
(Mark Johnston) *chsd wnr: rdn over 2f out: lost 2nd and outpcd by first two fnl f* **11/8**[1]

4 *2* **Chookie's Lass** 2-8-9 0...... JasonHart(5) 3 41+
(Keith Dalgleish) *dwlt: in tch on outside: effrt over 2f out: outpcd fnl f* **14/1**

5 *24* **Toogoodtobegood (FR)** 2-9-5 0...... PhillipMakin 4
(Kevin Ryan) *plld hrd early: in tch: effrt and rn green over 2f out: lost tch wl over 1f out* **8/1**

1m 12.81s (0.61) **Going Correction** -0.075s/f (Good) **5** Ran SP% **107.2**
Speed ratings (Par 94): **92,91,83,80,48**
CSF £13.58 TOTE £4.60: £1.10, £4.10; EX 10.10 Trifecta £14.70 Pool: £1285.85 - 65.59 winning units..
Owner T G & Mrs M E Holdcroft **Bred** Bearstone Stud **Trained** Hambleton, N Yorks

FOCUS
A modest juvenile maiden. The winner showed good speed to see off the improved runner-up.

4471 JOHN SMITH'S EXTRA SMOOTH H'CAP 6f 5y
7:15 (7:15) (Class 5) (0-70,67) 3-Y-O+ **£3,234** (£962; £481; £240) **Stalls** Centre

Form RPR

2162 **1** **Salvatore Fury (IRE)**[6] 4290 3-9-2 **62**......(p) JoeFanning 1 72+
(Keith Dalgleish) *stdd in tch: stdy hdwy and poised to chal over 1f out: shkn up and qcknd to ld ins fnl f: comf* **13/8**[1]

6-06 **2** *2½* **Tongalooma**[59] 2542 7-9-2 **57**...... GrahamLee 4 57
(James Moffatt) *pressed ldr: led over 2f out: sn rdn: hdd ins fnl f: kpt on: nt gng pce of wnr* **25/1**

-531 **3** *2* **Saxonette**[6] 4292 5-9-1 **56** 6ex...... TomEaves 3 50
(Linda Perratt) *prom: rdn and ev ch over 1f out: one pce fnl f* **4/1**[3]

0600 **4** *2¼* **Dark Lane**[6] 4303 7-9-7 **67**...... DeclanBates(5) 7 53
(David Evans) *prom: rdn over 2f out: wknd over 1f out* **9/2**

5 **5** *¾* **Dancing Cosmos (IRE)**[1] 4448 3-9-0 **60**...... TadhgO'Shea 5 43
(John Patrick Shanahan, Ire) *trckd ldrs: hdwy 1/2-way: rdn and wknd over 1f out* **3/1**[2]

050- **6** *2½* **Carrie's Magic**[272] 7251 6-8-7 **48**...... AndrewElliott 6 24
(Alistair Whillans) *t.k.h: led to over 2f out: rdn and wknd over 1f out* **12/1**

1m 11.02s (-1.18) **Going Correction** -0.075s/f (Good)
WFA 3 from 4yo+ 5lb **6** Ran SP% **112.8**
Speed ratings (Par 103): **104,100,98,95,94 90**
toteswingers 1&2 £8.00, 2&3 £9.40, 1&3 £1.50 CSF £40.30 TOTE £1.80: £1.10, £9.00; EX 19.90 Trifecta £61.40 Pool: £1249.43 - 15.26 winning units..
Owner Prestige Thoroughbred Racing **Bred** Ken Harris & Dr Brid Corkery **Trained** Carluke, S Lanarks

FOCUS
A moderate sprint handicap. The winner was value for extra.

4472 JOHN SMITH'S SCOTTISH STEWARDS' CUP (H'CAP) 6f 5y
7:45 (7:48) (Class 2) (0-105,93) 3-Y-O+
£20,542 (£6,151; £3,075; £1,537; £768; £386) **Stalls** Centre

Form RPR

0663 **1** **Rodrigo De Torres**[20] 3823 6-9-12 **93**...... TonyHamilton 14 98
(David Nicholls) *mde all stands' side: overall ldr 1/2-way: rdn and hld on wl fnl f* **22/1**

3220 **2** *shd* **Fast Shot**[20] 3823 5-9-7 **88**...... TomEaves 13 93
(Tim Easterby) *hld up bhd ldng gp stands' side: rdn over 2f out: hdwy over 1f out: kpt on wl fnl f: jst hld* **20/1**

5301 **3** *shd* **Rasaman (IRE)**[11] 4111 9-9-0 **81** 6ex...... PhillipMakin 4 85
(Jim Goldie) *hld up in centre: rdn and hdwy over 1f out: kpt on wl fnl f: jst hld* **25/1**

0031 **4** *shd* **Al's Memory (IRE)**[6] 4285 4-9-4 **90** 6ex...... DeclanBates(5) 1 94
(David Evans) *cl up centre: effrt and rdn over 2f out: kpt on wl fnl f: hld cl home* **25/1**

226 **5** *½* **Mississippi**[20] 3846 4-9-7 **88**...... GrahamGibbons 5 91+
(David Barron) *hld up in tch centre: smooth hdwy 2f out: effrt and cl up ins fnl f: kpt on: hld nr fin* **9/4**[1]

0000 **6** *1¾* **Johannes (IRE)**[20] 3823 10-8-11 **83**...... GeorgeChaloner(5) 6 80
(Richard Fahey) *taken early to post: sn pushed along in rr centre: hdwy over 1f out: kpt on: nrst fin* **16/1**

4402 **7** *½* **Misplaced Fortune**[18] 3892 8-9-9 **90**......(v) DaleSwift 9 85
(Nigel Tinkler) *in tch centre: drvn and outpcd over 2f out: rallied fnl f: nrst fin* **28/1**

0630 **8** *hd* **Barnet Fair**[6] 4275 5-9-3 **91**...... ConnorBeasley(7) 11 86
(Richard Guest) *t.k.h: hld up stands' side: rdn and effrt over 1f out: kpt on fnl f: no imp* **10/1**

5100 **9** *½* **Yeeoow (IRE)**[20] 3846 4-9-12 **93**...... DanielTudhope 7 86
(Mrs K Burke) *hld up on outside of stands' side gp: rdn over 2f out: edgd lft and styd on fnl f: n.d* **8/1**[3]

1-13 **10** *nk* **Out Do**[20] 3840 4-9-10 **91**...... GrahamLee 12 83
(Luca Cumani) *trckd stands' side ldrs: stdy hdwy over 2f out: rdn over 1f out: wknd ins fnl f* **3/1**[2]

0041 **11** *1¼* **Storm Moon (USA)**[11] 4112 3-9-5 **91** 6ex...... JoeFanning 3 79
(Mark Johnston) *chsd ldrs centre: rdn over 2f out: wknd ins fnl f* **18/1**

4266 **12** *2* **Chester Aristocrat**[6] 4285 4-9-2 **88**...... JasonHart(5) 8 70
(Eric Alston) *chsd stands' side ldr tl rdn and wknd 2f out* **9/1**

6-30 **13** *¾* **Scotland Forever (IRE)**[20] 3846 3-9-4 **90**......(b[1]) TadhgO'Shea 2 69
(John Patrick Shanahan, Ire) *led and overall ldr centre to 1/2-way: wknd 2f out* **20/1**

1000 **14** *15* **Rothesay Chancer**[21] 3769 5-8-11 **78**...... AndrewElliott 10 9
(Jim Goldie) *in tch stands' side: rdn and lost pl over 2f out: lost tch over 1f out* **40/1**

1m 10.44s (-1.76) **Going Correction** -0.075s/f (Good)
WFA 3 from 4yo+ 5lb **14** Ran SP% **124.6**
Speed ratings (Par 109): **108,107,107,107,106 104,103,103,103,102 100,98,97,77**
toteswingers 1&2 £108.70, 2&3 £103.60, 1&3 £108.70 CSF £389.05 TOTE £24.80: £5.20, £5.70, £5.70; EX 289.00 Trifecta £1922.40 Part won. Pool: £2563.31 - 0.43 winning units..
Owner Brian Morton **Bred** Worksop Manor Stud **Trained** Sessay, N Yorks
■ Stewards' Enquiry : Declan Bates two-day ban: used whip above permitted level (Aug 2,4)

FOCUS
The top weight was rated 12lb below the race ceiling of 105, which was pretty poor, but this was still a seriously competitive handicap. They split into two groups early, but there was no major pace/track bias, for while the first two were drawn in the top two boxes and challenged towards the fence, the close fourth was drawn lowest and raced up the middle. Straightforward form.

4473 E B F STALLIONS GLASGOW STKS (LISTED RACE) 1m 3f 16y
8:15 (8:16) (Class 1) 3-Y-O **£23,680** (£8,956; £4,476; £2,236) **Stalls** Low

Form RPR

1101 **1** **Maputo**[8] 4214 3-9-3 95...... JoeFanning 2 107
(Mark Johnston) *trckd ldrs: smooth hdwy over 2f out: led appr fnl f: drvn and styd on wl* **30/100**[1]

0102 **2** *1¼* **Alta Lilea (IRE)**[6] 4286 3-8-12 90...... LiamJones 6 100
(Mark Johnston) *led: rdn over 2f out: hdd appr fnl f: rallied: kpt on same pce towards fin* **16/1**

4244 **3** *2¼* **Mister Impatience**[28] 3526 3-9-3 97...... MichaelO'Connell 5 101
(Mark Johnston) *chsd ldr: rdn 3f out: sn outpcd: kpt on ins fnl f: nt rch first two* **6/1**[2]

5210 **4** *2¼* **Cruck Realta**[19] 3870 3-9-2 97...... GrahamLee 1 97
(Mick Channon) *in tch: rdn and edgd rt over 2f out: no imp over 1f out* **10/1**[3]

5 *¾* **Hold The Line (IRE)**[42] 3074 3-9-3 93...... TadhgO'Shea 3 97
(John Patrick Shanahan, Ire) *hld up in tch: rdn along over 2f out: no ex wl over 1f out* **20/1**

2m 20.01s (-5.59) **Going Correction** -0.425s/f (Firm) **5** Ran SP% **110.9**
Speed ratings (Par 108): **103,102,100,98,98**
CSF £6.80 TOTE £1.10: £1.02, £6.40; EX 6.00 Trifecta £18.30 Pool: £1243.68 - 50.86 winning units..
Owner Sheikh Hamdan Bin Mohammed Al Maktoum **Bred** Darley **Trained** Middleham Moor, N Yorks

FOCUS
This should have been easy enough for Maputo, who had upwards of 13lb in hand on RPRs, but he made hard work of it and was short of his best. He did not need to hit the heights to see off a pair of stablemates, and the form could be rated up to 5lb higher.

4474 JOHN SMITH'S H'CAP 1m 3f 16y
8:45 (8:45) (Class 6) (0-65,71) 3-Y-O **£1,940** (£577; £288; £144) **Stalls** Low

Form RPR

5362 **1** **Bee Jay Kay**[8] 4196 3-9-5 **63**...... GrahamLee 1 78+
(Mick Channon) *in tch: niggled 1/2-way: hdwy to chse ldr over 2f out: led ins fnl f: styd on wl* **7/5**[1]

5001 **2** *2¾* **Red Charmer (IRE)**[1] 4449 3-9-2 **67** 6ex...... RowanScott(7) 4 77
(Ann Duffield) *cl up: led over 2f out: rdn and edgd rt over 1f out: hdd ins fnl f: kpt on same pce* **4/1**[3]

4224 **3** *9* **Whitefall (USA)**[17] 3918 3-8-7 **56**...... DeclanBates(5) 5 50
(David Evans) *trckd ldrs: effrt over 2f out: no imp whn edgd rt over 1f out* **11/2**

045 **4** *3½* **Duchess Of Dreams**[13] 4049 3-7-12 **47**...... PhilipPrince(5) 9 35
(Richard Guest) *taken early to post: led at stdy pce: rdn and hdd over 2f out: outpcd over 1f out* **20/1**

0614 **5** *1½* **Spats Colombo**[18] 3893 3-8-11 **55**...... TomEaves 3 40
(Micky Hammond) *prom: niggled 1/2-way: lost pl and hung rt over 3f out: n.d after* **3/1**[2]

-500 **6** *10* **Hayley**[35] 3281 3-8-2 **46** oh1...... JoeFanning 2 13
(Jim Goldie) *hld up in tch: drvn along over 3f out: wknd 2f out* **33/1**

0600 **7** *1* **Ceekay's Girl**[4] 4339 3-7-9 **46** oh1...... NoelGarbutt(7) 8 11
(R Mike Smith) *hld up: rdn along and edgd rt over 2f out: sn btn* **33/1**

2m 21.3s (-4.30) **Going Correction** -0.425s/f (Firm) **7** Ran SP% **112.7**
Speed ratings (Par 98): **98,96,89,86,85 78,77**
toteswingers 1&2 £2.00, 2&3 £5.20, 1&3 £1.10 CSF £7.05 TOTE £1.60: £1.90, £2.70; EX 6.90 Trifecta £21.90 Pool: £864.32 - 29.53 winning units..
Owner M Channon **Bred** Mike Channon Bloodstock Ltd **Trained** West Ilsley, Berks

FOCUS
A couple of in-form horses pulled well clear in this moderate handicap. The form has been given a chance and could easily be better than rated.

4475 DOWNLOAD THE FREE RACING UK APP H'CAP 1m 1f 36y
9:15 (9:15) (Class 5) (0-75,72) 3-Y-O+ **£3,234** (£962; £481; £240) **Stalls** Low

Form RPR

4334 **1** **Wellingrove (IRE)**[12] 4100 3-9-2 **69**...... JoeFanning 6 74
(Mark Johnston) *mde all at stdy pce: qcknd over 1f out: kpt on wl fnl f: unchal* **5/2**[1]

2 *1* **Janna's Jingle (IRE)**[23] 3706 3-9-2 **69**...... TadhgO'Shea 3 72+
(John Patrick Shanahan, Ire) *in tch: effrt whn nt clr run over 2f out: effrt on outside over 1f out: chsd wnr ins fnl f: r.o* **3/1**[3]

The Form Book Flat, Raceform Ltd, Compton, RG20 6NL.

2121 **3** 2 1/4 **Tectonic (IRE)**[11] 4109 4-9-11 **69** 6ex................................(p) TomEaves 1 69
(Keith Dalgleish) *trckd ldrs: effrt and chsd wnr over 1f out to ins fnl f: one pce* **11/4**[2]
-050 **4** 1 3/4 **Euston Square**[37] 3199 7-8-13 **57**... DaleSwift 4 53
(Alistair Whillans) *prom: effrt and rdn 2f out: one pce appr fnl f* **25/1**
06-5 **5** 1/2 **Change The Subject (USA)**[183] 239 5-9-7 **72**...... ConnorBeasley(7) 7 67
(Richard Guest) *stdd s: hld up in last: effrt and hdwy on ins over 1f out: no imp fnl f* **11/2**
5056 **6** 3 **High Resolution**[1] 4446 6-9-12 **70**.................................... PhillipMakin 2 59
(Linda Perratt) *hld up bhd ldng gp: effrt on outside 2f out: sn no imp* **8/1**
2364 **7** 11 **Honey Of A Kitten (USA)**[16] 3951 5-9-8 **71**.............(v) DeclanBates(5) 5 39
(David Evans) *chsd wnr: rdn over 2f out: wknd wl over 1f out* **14/1**

1m 58.57s (-1.13) **Going Correction** -0.425s/f (Firm)
WFA 3 from 4yo+ 9lb 7 Ran SP% **117.2**
Speed ratings (Par 103): **88,87,85,83,83 80,70**
toteswingers 1&2 £4.10, 2&3 £3.30, 1&3 £1.90 CSF £10.82 TOTE £3.00: £2.20, £2.10; EX 14.60 Trifecta £23.70 Pool: £1947.09 - 61.59 winning units..
Owner Sheikh Hamdan Bin Mohammed Al Maktoum **Bred** Hascombe And Valiant Studs **Trained** Middleham Moor, N Yorks

FOCUS
The winner was allowed his own way and basically ran to his pre-race best. Straightforward form.
T/Plt: £103.60 to a £1 stake. Pool of £41180.74 - 290.16 winning tickets. T/Qpdt: £62.40 to a £1 stake. Pool of £4057.22 - 48.10 winning tickets. RY

4057 HAYDOCK (L-H)
Friday, July 19

OFFICIAL GOING: Good to firm (8.2)
Wind: light 1/2 behind Weather: fine and sunny, very warm

4476 WKD H'CAP 1m 3f 200y
2:10 (2:12) (Class 4) (0-85,83) 3-Y-O **£5,175** (£1,540; £769) **Stalls** Centre

Form RPR
0-1 **1** **Venue**[19] 3858 3-9-7 **83**.. TomQueally 3 94
(Lady Cecil) *hld up in last: effrt 4f out: chal 2f out: rdn to ld 1f out: hung lft and wnt clr: readily* **15/8**[2]
6221 **2** 2 **Duke Of Perth**[17] 3917 3-9-2 **78**... KierenFallon 1 86
(Luca Cumani) *led 1f: led over 6f out: qcknd pce 4f out: hdd 1f out: styd on same pce* **10/3**[3]
0-1 **3** 4 1/2 **Vital Evidence (USA)**[34] 3343 3-9-7 **83**............................ RyanMoore 2 88
(Sir Michael Stoute) *led after 1f: hdd over 6f out: drvn 4f out: chal over 2f out: rdn over 1f out: eased whn wl hld in clsng stages* **11/10**[1]

2m 31.04s (-2.76) **Going Correction** -0.325s/f (Firm) 3 Ran SP% **105.5**
Speed ratings (Par 102): **96,94,91**
CSF £6.85 TOTE £3.10; EX 6.80 Trifecta £9.90 Pool: £1328.20 - 99.77 winning units..
Owner K Abdullah **Bred** Juddmonte Farms Ltd **Trained** Newmarket, Suffolk

FOCUS
All races on Inner home straight and races on Round course increased in distance by 1yd. The going was good to firm, but the jockeys reported it was "nice ground" and riding "quick but safe." A small field for this 3yo handicap, with all three trained in Newmarket. Not the easiest to quantify but the form is taken at face value.

4477 BRITISH STALLION STUDS SUPPORTING BRITISH RACING EBF MAIDEN STKS 6f
2:40 (2:43) (Class 5) 2-Y-O **£2,911** (£866; £432; £216) **Stalls** Centre

Form RPR
4 **1** **Zarwaan**[41] 3112 2-9-5 0... DaneO'Neill 7 85+
(Ed Dunlop) *hld up: hdwy to trck ldrs over 2f out: shkn up to ld appr fnl f: r.o strly: v readily* **4/6**[1]
2 2 1/4 **Strategical (USA)** 2-9-5 0... HarryBentley 2 78+
(Saeed bin Suroor) *dwlt: hdwy to chse ldrs whn n.m.r over 2f out: chsd wnr last 150yds: no imp* **11/4**[2]
65 **3** 3 3/4 **De Repente (IRE)**[25] 3624 2-9-0 0.. TomQueally 3 60
(Paul Green) *mde most: hdd appr fnl f: one pce* **50/1**
65 **4** 3 1/4 **Aspirant**[20] 3836 2-9-5 0.. GeorgeBaker 4 55+
(Roger Charlton) *t.k.h: sn w ldr: wknd fnl f* **28/1**
420 **5** 5 **Brownsville (USA)**[14] 4026 2-9-5 0.................................... JoeFanning 6 39
(Mark Johnston) *chsd ldrs: drvn over 2f out: lost pl wl over 1f out* **12/1**[3]
0 **6** 3/4 **Thataboy (IRE)**[42] 3044 2-9-5 0....................................... RobertWinston 1 36+
(Tom Dascombe) *chsd ldrs: outpcd over 3f out: hdwy and hung lft over 2f out: wknd over 1f out* **33/1**
7 2 1/4 **Roseburg (IRE)** 2-9-5 0.. RyanMoore 5 29
(Luca Cumani) *s.s: sn detached in last: reminders after 1f: nvr on terms* **12/1**[3]

1m 12.57s (-1.23) **Going Correction** -0.175s/f (Firm) 7 Ran SP% **110.4**
Speed ratings (Par 94): **101,98,93,88,82 81,78**
toteswingers 1&2 £1.50, 2&3 £10.80, 1&3 £6.20 CSF £2.37 TOTE £1.60: £1.20, £1.90; EX 2.90 Trifecta £47.00 Pool: £4207.74 - 67.01 winning units..
Owner Hamdan Al Maktoum **Bred** Haras D'Haspel **Trained** Newmarket, Suffolk

FOCUS
This juvenile maiden has thrown up a couple of subsequent Listed winners in Playfellow and Professor, plus several useful handicappers. The betting concerned only two and they dominated the finish. The third and sixth fit in.

4478 RITA ORA HERE 9TH AUGUST H'CAP 6f
3:15 (3:16) (Class 4) (0-85,83) 3-Y-O **£5,175** (£1,540; £769; £384) **Stalls** Centre

Form RPR
3-14 **1** **Secondo (FR)**[53] 2708 3-9-7 **83**... GeorgeBaker 5 94+
(Roger Charlton) *stdd s: sn trcking ldrs: 2nd over 2f out: led on bit appr fnl f: eased nr fin: v easily* **15/8**[2]
0304 **2** 3/4 **Rhagori Aur**[11] 4117 3-9-1 **77**.....................(b) PaulMulrennan 4 80
(Bryan Smart) *led: hdd appr fnl f: kpt on: no ch w wnr* **12/1**
6006 **3** 2 1/2 **Vallarta (IRE)**[21] 3782 3-8-13 **75**.. SamHitchcott 3 70
(Mick Channon) *dwlt: hdwy to chse ldrs 3f out: one pce over 1f out* **5/1**[3]
2502 **4** 2 1/4 **Fortinbrass (IRE)**[34] 3320 3-9-6 **82**.................................(t) RyanMoore 2 70
(Ralph Beckett) *chsd ldrs: wknd over 1f out* **6/4**[1]
1133 **5** 2 **Teetotal (IRE)**[10] 4136 3-8-10 **72**.. TomQueally 1 53
(Nigel Tinkler) *chsd ldrs: drvn and outpcd over 3f out: edgd lft 2f out: sn wknd* **10/1**

1m 12.07s (-1.73) **Going Correction** -0.175s/f (Firm) 5 Ran SP% **108.2**
Speed ratings (Par 102): **104,103,99,96,94**
CSF £20.50 TOTE £2.70: £1.20, £3.80; EX 21.80 Trifecta £74.80 Pool: £2959.81 - 29.63 winning units..
Owner D J Deer **Bred** John Deer **Trained** Beckhampton, Wilts

FOCUS
A fair 3yo sprint handicap, but again just a small field and the winner totally dominated. The time was half a second faster than the preceding juvenile contest. The form is rated around the second and the winner could have been rated higher.

4479 FAMILY FUN DAY HERE 8TH AUGUST H'CAP 5f
3:50 (3:51) (Class 4) (0-80,79) 3-Y-O+ **£5,175** (£1,540; £769; £384) **Stalls** Centre

Form RPR
0011 **1** **Sleepy Blue Ocean**[8] 4203 7-9-6 **73** 6ex...................(p) RobertWinston 7 82
(John Balding) *half-rrd s: in rr: drvn and hdwy over 2f out: r.o to ld last 100yds* **8/1**
6251 **2** 3/4 **Imperial Legend (IRE)**[17] 3933 4-9-11 **78**..............(p) PaulMulrennan 11 84
(David Nicholls) *trckd ldrs: led jst ins fnl f: hdd and no ex last 100yds* **11/2**[3]
-002 **3** 1/2 **Wild Sauce**[14] 4018 4-9-1 **73**...................................(bt) JustinNewman(5) 3 78
(Bryan Smart) *dwlt: in rr: hdwy farside 2f out: styd on ins fnl f: tk 3rd nr fin* **12/1**
0-1 **4** 1 **Bilash**[49] 2825 6-8-10 **68**.. JackDuern(5) 6 69
(Andrew Hollinshead) *w ldrs: led over 1f out: hdd jst ins fnl f: kpt on same pce* **20/1**
4044 **5** 1/2 **Mappin Time (IRE)**[15] 3981 5-9-12 **79**.............................(p) DavidAllan 2 78
(Tim Easterby) *drvn: outpcd and lost pl after 1f: kpt on fnl f* **11/2**[3]
0600 **6** nk **Beau Mistral (IRE)**[23] 3682 4-8-9 **67**.......................... PhilipPrince(5) 5 65
(Paul Green) *chsd ldrs: drvn and outpcd over 2f out: hdwy and edgd lft over 1f out: kpt on same pce* **22/1**
2005 **7** 1/2 **Tyfos**[15] 3981 8-9-10 **77**... GeorgeBaker 1 73
(Brian Baugh) *led over 1f: w ldrs: wknd in clsng stages* **18/1**
0642 **8** 1 1/2 **Six Wives**[19] 3855 6-9-4 **71**..(p) TomQueally 9 62
(Scott Dixon) *dwlt: in rr: hdwy over 1f out: nvr a factor* **9/2**[2]
2211 **9** hd **Red Baron (IRE)**[21] 3769 4-9-6 **76**.................................. NeilFarley(3) 10 66
(Eric Alston) *sn w ldrs: led over 3f out: hdd over 1f out: hung lft and wknd ins fnl f* **4/1**[1]
4020 **10** 3 1/4 **Chosen One (IRE)**[12] 4102 8-8-11 **64**................................ PJMcDonald 4 42
(Ruth Carr) *chsd ldrs: drvn 2f out: sn wknd* **25/1**
1062 **11** nk **Another Citizen (IRE)**[29] 3505 5-9-2 **76**....................(b) GaryMahon(7) 8 53
(Tim Easterby) *w ldrs: lost pl over 1f out* **12/1**

59.3s (-1.50) **Going Correction** -0.175s/f (Firm) 11 Ran SP% **113.7**
Speed ratings (Par 105): **105,103,103,101,100 100,99,96,96,91 90**
toteswingers 1&2 £5.20, 2&3 £10.10, 1&3 £20.90 CSF £48.30 CT £533.22 TOTE £7.30: £2.70, £2.30, £3.90; EX 35.00 Trifecta £382.60 Pool: £2818.61 - 5.52 winning units..
Owner Tykes And Terriers Racing Club **Bred** Exors Of The Late N Ahamad & P C Scott **Trained** Scrooby, Notts

FOCUS
An ordinary sprint handicap, but featuring several recent scorers and the winner was one of those. Straightforward form off a fast pace.

4480 BROWN SHIPLEY WEALTH WELL MANAGED H'CAP 1m 6f
4:25 (4:25) (Class 4) (0-85,82) 3-Y-O **£5,175** (£1,540; £769) **Stalls** Low

Form RPR
-143 **1** **Hawk High (IRE)**[15] 3982 3-9-2 **77**.. DavidAllan 1 86+
(Tim Easterby) *led early: trckd ldng pair: swtchd 3 wd over 3f out: rdn to ld 2f out: edgd lft: styd on* **7/4**[2]
1532 **2** 1 3/4 **Ambleside**[11] 4116 3-8-11 **72**.. LiamJones 2 78
(Mark Johnston) *dwlt: sn drvn into ld: qcknd pce over 6f out: hdd 2f out: n.m.r and swtchd rt ins fnl f: kpt on to take 2nd nr fin* **4/1**[3]
3215 **3** nk **Auld Alliance (IRE)**[14] 4029 3-9-7 **82**...............................(v) RyanMoore 3 88
(Sir Michael Stoute) *sn trcking ldr: chal over 2f out: sn rdn: one pce* **1/1**[1]

3m 2.4s (0.40) **Going Correction** -0.325s/f (Firm) 3 Ran SP% **106.4**
Speed ratings (Par 102): **85,84,83**
CSF £7.09 TOTE £2.70; EX 5.70 Trifecta £6.40 Pool: £1526.00 - 177.40 winning units..
Owner Trevor Hemmings **Bred** Gleadhill House Stud Ltd **Trained** Great Habton, N Yorks

FOCUS
Subsequent Ascot Gold Cup winner Colour Vision won this race in 2011. Improvement from the winner and the runner-up is consistent.

4481 LANCASHIRE LIFE MAIDEN STKS 1m
5:00 (5:00) (Class 5) 3-Y-O+ **£2,587** (£770; £384; £192) **Stalls** Low

Form RPR
2 **1** **Desert Revolution**[10] 4152 3-9-5 0...................................... LiamJones 5 84+
(Mark Johnston) *chsd ldrs: 2nd 6f out: effrt over 3f out: led 2f out: edgd lft and styd on ins fnl f* **10/11**[1]
-222 **2** 1 1/2 **Shaishee (USA)**[14] 4032 3-9-5 80.................................(p) DaneO'Neill 1 81
(Charles Hills) *led: qcknd pce over 3f out: hdd 2f out: kpt on same pce ins fnl f: hld whn crowded nr fin* **11/10**[2]
05 **3** 13 **Bollin Bob**[10] 4139 4-9-6 0.. GaryMahon(7) 2 54
(Tim Easterby) *chsd ldr: drvn over 3f out: sn wl outpcd* **50/1**
5 **4** 13 **Duke Of Grazeon (IRE)**[30] 3479 3-9-0 0............................ LMcNiff(5) 4 21
(Mrs Ilka Gansera-Leveque) *s.v.s: a hopelessly detached in last* **20/1**[3]

1m 41.2s (-2.50) **Going Correction** -0.325s/f (Firm)
WFA 3 from 4yo 8lb 4 Ran SP% **106.7**
Speed ratings (Par 103): **99,97,84,71**
CSF £2.12 TOTE £2.00; EX 2.20 Trifecta £5.70 Pool: £2797.48 - 367.16 winning units..
Owner Sheikh Hamdan Bin Mohammed Al Maktoum **Bred** Darley **Trained** Middleham Moor, N Yorks

FOCUS
An uncompetitive maiden in which there was not much between the principals in the market and that was reflected in the race. Straightforward form, with better to come from the winner.

4482 BETDAQ HAYDOCK PARK APPRENTICE TRAINING SERIES H'CAP (PART OF THE RACING EXCELLENCE INITIATIVE) 1m
5:30 (5:30) (Class 5) (0-75,75) 4-Y-O+ **£2,587** (£770; £384; £192) **Stalls** Low

Form RPR
3202 **1** **Cono Zur (FR)**[3] 4373 6-9-3 **66**.. LMcNiff 4 74
(Ruth Carr) *drvn early: in rr: hdwy over 2f out: n.m.r and swtchd lft jst ins fnl f: styd on to ld towards fin* **7/4**[1]
4630 **2** nk **Silvas Romana (IRE)**[15] 3983 4-9-4 **70**............................ JackDuern(3) 3 77
(Mark Brisbourne) *trckd ldrs: effrt on outside over 2f out: upsides over 1f out: edgd lft: styd on to take 2nd nr fin* **22/1**
6333 **3** nk **McCool Bannanas**[21] 3780 5-8-7 **61**.................................. KevinStott(5) 6 67
(James Unett) *s.i.s: hld up: hdwy 4f out: chal over 2f out: led jst ins fnl f: no ex and hdd in clsng stages* **7/2**[3]
5000 **4** 1/2 **Berlusca (IRE)**[16] 3945 4-9-4 **70**...................................... DavidBergin(3) 9 75
(David O'Meara) *trckd ldr: t.k.h: narrow ld over 2f out: hdd jst ins fnl f: kpt on same pce in clsng stages* **9/1**
0002 **5** 3 **Chiswick Bey (IRE)**[27] 3575 5-9-6 **74**............................. EvaMoscrop(5) 2 72
(Philip Kirby) *led: hdd over 2f out: wknd and eased in clsng stages* **3/1**[2]

0000 6 8 **Hayek**[7] 4245 6-8-8 62..........(b) RachelRichardson(5) 5 42
(Tim Easterby) *s.i.s: hdwy on inner to chse ldrs 4f out: sn outpcd and lost pl: sn bhd* **16/1**
0064 7 1 3/4 **Rio Cobolo (IRE)**[22] 3715 7-8-4 58..........(v) JordanNason(5) 1 34
(David Nicholls) *trckd ldrs: t.k.h: lost pl 3f out: sn bhd* **16/1**
1m 40.19s (-3.51) **Going Correction** -0.325s/f (Firm) 7 Ran SP% **109.7**
Speed ratings (Par 103): **104,103,103,102,99 91,90**
toteswingers 1&2 £5.30, 2&3 £7.50, 1&3 £2.80 CSF £38.02 CT £112.40 TOTE £2.20: £1.60, £6.90; EX 31.10 Trifecta £113.70 Pool: £1954.04 - 12.88 winning units..
Owner Ruth Carr Racing **Bred** J P Dubois **Trained** Huby, N Yorks
FOCUS
This apprentice handicap was run just over a second faster than the preceding maiden. Ordinary form, the winner rated to this year's level.
T/Plt: £138.30 to a £1 stake. Pool of £44612.55 - 235.42 winning tickets. T/Qpdt: £50.10 to a £1 stake. Pool of £2996.79 - 44.20 winning tickets. WG

3985 NEWBURY (L-H)

Friday, July 19

OFFICIAL GOING: Good to firm changing to good to firm (firm in places) after race 3 (2.50)
Wind: Moderate behind Weather: Sunny

4483 HIGHCLERE THOROUGHBRED RACING EBF MAIDEN STKS 7f (S)
1:50 (1:52) (Class 4) 2-Y-O **£4,528** (£1,347; £673; £336) **Stalls** Centre

Form RPR
1 **Muwaary** 2-9-5 0.......... WilliamBuick 10 81+
(John Gosden) *trckd ldrs: shkn up and green over 1f out: pushed along and qcknd fnl f to ld fnl 110yds: readily* **6/1**[3]
2 1/2 **Torrid** 2-9-5 0.......... PatDobbs 15 80+
(Amanda Perrett) *chsd ldrs: kpt on to take 3rd fnl f: r.o u.p to take 2nd last strides but no imp on wnr* **25/1**
5 3 nk **Captain Bob (IRE)**[11] 4121 2-9-5 0.......... FrankieDettori 11 79
(Charles Hills) *sn led: rdn along 2f out: jnd fr 2f out: kpt slt advantage tl hdd fnl 110yds: sn outpcd by wnr: lost 2nd last strides* **9/2**[2]
4 3 1/4 **Mount Logan (IRE)** 2-9-5 0.......... KirstyMilczarek 6 70+
(Luca Cumani) *in rr: pushed along over 2f out: styd on ins fnl f to take 4th last strides but nt trble ldng duo* **25/1**
0 5 nk **Jeremos (IRE)**[20] 3833 2-9-5 0.......... SteveDrowne 8 69
(Richard Hannon) *in tch: hdwy 3f out: pressed ldrs 2f out: wknd fnl 110yds* **14/1**
05 6 nse **Calrissian (IRE)**[14] 4026 2-9-5 0.......... JimCrowley 3 69
(Alan Jarvis) *chsd ldrs: chal and drvn fr 2f out to 1f out: wknd ins fnl f* **8/1**
7 2 1/4 **What About Carlo (FR)** 2-9-5 0.......... JimmyFortune 4 63+
(Eve Johnson Houghton) *s.i.s: in rr: hdwy to cl on ldrs over 2f out: wknd fnl f* **20/1**
0 8 1 **Cabaan (IRE)**[33] 3374 2-9-5 0.......... MartinLane 2 60
(Brian Meehan) *chsd ldrs: rdn and ev ch 2f out: wknd over 1f out* **16/1**
9 1 1/4 **Always Resolute** 2-8-12 0.......... DavidParkes(7) 7 57
(Alan Jarvis) *in tch: hdwy to chse ldrs over 2f out: wknd wl over 1f out* **100/1**
0 10 3 1/2 **Ferngrove (USA)**[63] 2411 2-9-0 0.......... MatthewLawson(5) 13 48
(Jonathan Portman) *chsd ldrs: wknd 2f out* **100/1**
11 1 1/2 **Ghaawy** 2-9-5 0.......... PaulHanagan 1 46+
(Sir Michael Stoute) *s.i.s: in rr: hdwy 3f out to trck ldrs over 2f out: sn pushed along: hung lft and green: wknd qckly over 1f out* **7/2**[1]
12 1 **Cosette (IRE)** 2-8-9 0.......... AmyScott(5) 12 36+
(Henry Candy) *spd over 3f* **50/1**
13 10 **Filosofo (IRE)** 2-9-5 0.......... SeanLevey 9 14
(Richard Hannon) *slowly away: in rr: sme hdwy to cl on main gp 1/2-way: sn wknd* **20/1**
14 2 **Jersey Royal** 2-9-5 0.......... RichardHughes 14 8
(Richard Hannon) *s.i.s: sn in tch w main gp: rdn and wknd qckly 1/2-way* **9/2**[2]
1m 24.66s (-1.04) **Going Correction** -0.25s/f (Firm) 14 Ran SP% **117.7**
Speed ratings (Par 96): **95,94,94,90,90 89,87,86,84,80 79,77,66,64**
toteswingers 1&2 £37.20, 2&3 £21.60, 1&3 £9.70 CSF £151.28 TOTE £6.80: £2.20, £6.70, £1.80; EX 184.50 Trifecta £661.60 Part won. Pool: £882.19 - 0.36 winning units..
Owner Hamdan Al Maktoum **Bred** Shadwell Estate Company Limited **Trained** Newmarket, Suffolk
FOCUS
Rail between 8f and 5f moved out adding 12m to races on Round course. An informative maiden that had been taken by smart performers Montiridge and Ektihaam in the past two seasons. They went an average pace down the centre and the principals were nicely clear at the finish. The winner looks a nice recruit and the form should be sound.

4484 COOLMORE STUD EXCELEBRATION EBF MAIDEN FILLIES' STKS 6f 8y
2:20 (2:22) (Class 4) 2-Y-O **£4,528** (£1,347; £673; £336) **Stalls** Centre

Form RPR
1 **J Wonder (USA)** 2-9-0 0.......... MartinLane 12 84+
(Brian Meehan) *trckd ldrs: wnt 2nd jst ins fnl f: fin strly to ld fnl 50yds* **16/1**
2 2 3/4 **Autumn Sunrise (IRE)**[24] 3664 2-9-0 0.......... RichardHughes 9 82
(Richard Hannon) *led: drvn over 1f out: kpt on fnl f tl hdd and outpcd fnl 50yds* **7/4**[1]
0 3 nk **Amazing Maria (IRE)**[24] 3664 2-9-0 0.......... FrankieDettori 18 81+
(Ed Dunlop) *sn chsng ldrs: rdn over 1f out: kpt on wl fnl f to take 3rd fnl 75yds: gng on in clsng stages* **9/2**[2]
4 1 **Isabella Bird** 2-9-0 0.......... MartinHarley 11 77
(Mick Channon) *chsd ldrs: rdn to dispute 2nd appr fnl f: styd on same pce fnl 110yds* **7/1**
3 5 1 1/2 **Baars Causeway (IRE)**[24] 3663 2-8-9 0.......... MichaelJMMurphy(5) 16 73+
(Alan Jarvis) *towards rr: pushed along over 2f out: stl green but styd on wl fnl f: gng on in clsng stages* **14/1**
6 6 1 1/2 **Mendacious Harpy (IRE)**[15] 3986 2-9-0 0.......... WilliamBuick 13 68
(George Baker) *chsd ldr: rdn 2f out: wknd ins fnl f* **12/1**
7 1 3/4 **Kanz** 2-8-11 0.......... CharlesBishop(3) 10 62+
(Mick Channon) *in tch: rdn along over 2f out: styd on same pce* **25/1**
8 3 **Terhaab (USA)** 2-9-0 0.......... PaulHanagan 5 53
(John Gosden) *s.i.s: in rr: hdwy 3f out: clsd on ldrs over 2f out: wknd appr fnl f* **6/1**[3]
9 1 **Polar Eyes** 2-9-0 0.......... PatCosgrave 2 49
(Peter Chapple-Hyam) *s.i.s: in rr and nt much daylight over 2f out: green but sme late prog fnl f* **50/1**
10 2 1/4 **Saxon Princess (IRE)** 2-9-0 0.......... JimCrowley 1 42
(Roger Charlton) *s.i.s: outpcd most of way: mod prog fnl f* **25/1**
11 nk **Sweet Amaalie (IRE)** 2-9-0 0.......... SebSanders 3 41
(William Haggas) *outpcd most of way* **25/1**
12 nk **Black Rodded** 2-9-0 0..........[1] JimmyFortune 15 40
(Hughie Morrison) *chsd ldrs: hung lft and wknd 2f out* **50/1**
13 1 1/4 **Emerald Breeze (IRE)** 2-9-0 0.......... SteveDrowne 14 36
(Charles Hills) *chsd ldrs: n.m.r: green and wknd 2f out* **33/1**
0 14 3/4 **Starlight Princess (IRE)**[24] 3664 2-9-0 0.......... LiamKeniry 8 34
(J S Moore) *s.i.s: outpcd* **100/1**
15 9 **Lady Emmuska** 2-9-0 0.......... PatDobbs 6 5
(Richard Hannon) *chsd ldrs: rdn 3f out: wknd qckly over 2f out* **33/1**
1m 11.24s (-1.76) **Going Correction** -0.25s/f (Firm) 15 Ran SP% **123.9**
Speed ratings (Par 93): **101,100,99,98,96 94,91,87,86,83 83,82,81,80,68**
toteswingers 1&2 £7.30, 2&3 £2.70, 1&3 £24.50 CSF £42.36 TOTE £31.20: £6.90, £1.10, £2.20; EX 93.20 Trifecta £1328.60 Pool: £3110.03 - 1.75 winning units..
Owner Andrew Rosen **Bred** Canterbury Lace Syndicate **Trained** Manton, Wilts
FOCUS
A fair fillies' maiden. It was run at a sound pace with the action again developing down the centre, and the time was decent. The form is rated in line with the race averages and the runner-up is a solid guide to the form.

4485 JOHN SUNLEY MEMORIAL T.B.A. FILLIES' H'CAP 1m 2f 6y
2:50 (2:52) (Class 3) (0-90,85) 3-Y-O **£9,703** (£2,887; £1,443; £721) **Stalls** Centre

Form RPR
031 1 **Rock Choir**[28] 3530 3-9-4 82.......... SebSanders 2 99+
(William Haggas) *trckd ldr tl over 6f out: styd trcking ldrs: pushed along to ld over 2f out: c clr appr fnl f: easily* **5/2**[1]
321 2 4 1/2 **Wall Of Sound**[30] 3465 3-9-3 81.......... RichardKingscote 4 88
(Tom Dascombe) *sn led: jnd 4f out: hdd over 2f out: sn outpcd by wnr but styd on wl for clr 2nd* **11/4**[2]
3414 3 6 **Sharqawiyah**[20] 3835 3-9-7 85.......... KirstyMilczarek 6 81
(Luca Cumani) *stdd s and wnt lft: in rr: hdwy over 2f out: drvn to take wl hld 3rd ins fnl 2f* **5/1**[3]
5421 4 4 **Invincible Cara (IRE)**[13] 4076 3-9-0 78 ow1.......... AdamKirby 7 66
(Ed Dunlop) *stdd s and swtchd lft: in rr but in tch: hdwy 3f out: hanging lft u.p and btn qckly 2f out*
2-3U 5 2 **Martinas Delight (USA)**[40] 3136 3-8-6 75.......... MichaelJMMurphy(5) 3 59
(Alan Jarvis) *s.i.s: in rr: sme hdwy and c wd into st bnd 5f out: sn rdn and brief effrt 4f out: nvr on terms and sn btn* **12/1**
-055 6 2 1/2 **Haatefina**[19] 3861 3-7-9 66 oh2..........(v) JoeyHaynes(7) 5 45
(Mark Usher) *chsd ldrs: rdn 3f out: sn btn* **33/1**
104 7 14 **Perfect Haven**[38] 3179 3-9-0 78.......... JimCrowley 1 31
(Ralph Beckett) *stdd s tk str hold: plld way through to chse ldr 6f out: chal 4f out: wknd qckly over 2f out* **7/1**
2m 6.9s (-1.90) **Going Correction** -0.25s/f (Firm) 7 Ran SP% **111.7**
Speed ratings (Par 101): **97,93,88,85,83 81,70**
toteswingers 1&2 £2.00, 2&3 £3.00, 1&3 £1.40 CSF £9.16 TOTE £3.30: £2.30, £1.80; EX 10.10 Trifecta £30.30 Pool: £2171.78 - 53.59 winning units..
Owner Cheveley Park Stud **Bred** Cheveley Park Stud Ltd **Trained** Newmarket, Suffolk
FOCUS
This looked a fair 3yo fillies' handicap, but it was steadily run and a number were keen. The winner is thriving though.

4486 ROSE BOWL STKS - SPONSORED BY COMPTON BEAUCHAMP ESTATES LTD (LISTED RACE) 6f 8y
3:25 (3:25) (Class 1) 2-Y-O **£14,461** (£5,482; £2,743; £1,366; £685) **Stalls** Centre

Form RPR
6411 1 **Miracle Of Medinah**[19] 3857 2-9-0 0.......... LiamKeniry 2 99
(Mark Usher) *mde all: rdn and hung rt fr over 1f out: drvn clr fnl f: styd on strly* **33/1**
021 2 3 3/4 **Mappa Mundi (USA)**[7] 4231 2-9-0 0.......... SebSanders 4 87
(Eve Johnson Houghton) *chsd wnr thrght: hrd pressed for 2nd fr over 2f out tl ins fnl f: kpt on but nvr any ch* **14/1**
2164 3 1 **Survived**[14] 4025 2-8-9 0.......... MartinHarley 3 79
(William Haggas) *chsd ldrs: drvn to dispute 2nd over 2f out tl ins fnl f: nvr nr wnr and sn one pce into 3rd* **3/1**[2]
151 4 3/4 **Cool Bahamian (IRE)**[18] 3890 2-9-0 0.......... JohnFahy 1 81
(Eve Johnson Houghton) *s.i.s: in rr: pushed along over 2f out and sme hdwy but nvr nr ldrs and sn wknd* **8/1**[3]
1114 5 2 3/4 **Thunder Strike**[31] 3422 2-9-3 0.......... RichardHughes 5 76
(Richard Hannon) *in tch: rdn over 2f out and sn btn* **1/2**[1]
1m 11.61s (-1.39) **Going Correction** -0.25s/f (Firm) 5 Ran SP% **112.4**
Speed ratings (Par 102): **99,94,92,91,88**
CSF £329.65 TOTE £15.90: £5.10, £4.20; EX 66.10 Trifecta £1082.80 Pool: £2169.65 - 1.50 winning units..
Owner The High Jinks Partnership **Bred** A C M Spalding **Trained** Upper Lambourn, Berks
FOCUS
This Listed 2yo contest was run at a fair pace, with the field sticking to the centre early on. The third and fifth were below par so there were doubts over the form, but there appeared no fluke about the winner's effort, which fits the race average.

4487 STARLIGHT CHARITY H'CAP 5f 34y
4:00 (4:00) (Class 5) (0-75,75) 3-Y-O+ **£2,587** (£770; £384; £192) **Stalls** Centre

Form RPR
0563 1 **Triple Dream**[4] 4344 8-9-2 72..........(tp) WillPettis(7) 4 82
(Milton Bradley) *chsd ldrs: chal jst ins fnl f: slt ld fnl 100yds: hld on all out* **16/1**
5122 2 shd **Swendab (IRE)**[11] 4120 5-9-8 71..........(v) FrankieDettori 10 81
(John O'Shea) *in tch: hdwy fr 2f out: slt ld jst ins fnl f: narrowly hdd fnl 100yds: kpt on but a jst hld* **4/1**[3]
61 3 nk **Trinityelitedotcom (IRE)**[17] 3915 3-9-8 75.......... RichardKingscote 3 82
(Tom Dascombe) *slt ld but hrd pressed fr 3f out: narrowly hdd jst ins fnl f: styd chalng: no ex in clsng stages* **3/1**[2]
5550 4 1 3/4 **Macdillon**[19] 3855 7-8-13 67..........(t) MichaelJMMurphy(5) 1 70
(Stuart Kittow) *chsd ldrs: pushed along and kpt on fr over 1f out: nvr quite gng pce of ldng trio ins fnl f* **9/4**[1]
6-43 5 shd **Pal Of The Cat**[19] 3866 3-9-1 68.......... RichardHughes 2 68
(Brian Gubby) *pressed ldr: chal fr 3f out: stl upsides ins fnl f: wknd fnl 110yds* **8/1**
0032 6 2 1/2 **Storm Lightning**[14] 4034 4-9-9 72..........(b) TomMcLaughlin 6 65
(Mark Brisbourne) *in rr: swtchd rt to stands' rail 2f out: sn drvn and no imp on ldrs: styd on in clsng stages* **14/1**
4614 7 2 1/4 **Crimson Queen**[14] 4017 6-9-11 74..........(b) ChrisCatlin 8 59
(Roy Brotherton) *chsd ldrs: rdn 2f out: wknd over 1f out* **14/1**
1405 8 3 1/4 **Amber Heights**[14] 4034 5-8-13 62.......... JimmyFortune 7 35
(Henry Candy) *outpcd most of way* **20/1**

3100 **9** *7* **Black Cadillac (IRE)**[11] 4120 5-9-9 **72**.........................(v) WilliamBuick 5 20
(Andrew Balding) *slowly away: a wl bhd* **12/1**
050 **10** *9* **Danziger (IRE)**[42] 3042 4-9-3 **66**... AdamKirby 9
(David Evans) *a in rr* **33/1**
59.53s (-1.87) **Going Correction** -0.25s/f (Firm)
WFA 3 from 4yo+ 4lb **10** Ran SP% **121.5**
Speed ratings (Par 103): **104,103,103,100,100 96,92,87,76,62**
toteswingers 1&2 £25.60, 2&3 £2.40, 1&3 £8.00 CSF £82.44 CT £259.17 TOTE £21.70: £4.10, £1.20, £1.80; EX 87.30 Trifecta £1076.00 Pool: £2112.49 - 1.47 winning units..
Owner J M Bradley **Bred** Hesmonds Stud Ltd **Trained** Sedbury, Gloucs
■ The first winner for Will Pettis.
FOCUS
A modest sprint handicap, and straightforward form.

4488 PERTEMPS SHERIDAN MAINE H'CAP 1m 2f 6y
4:35 (4:35) (Class 3) (0-95,91) 3-Y-O+
£7,158 (£2,143; £1,071; £535; £267; £134) **Stalls** Centre

Form RPR
-342 **1** **Gabrial The Great (IRE)**[26] 3607 4-9-10 **87**...................... AdamKirby 5 97+
(Luca Cumani) *hld up in rr: stdy hdwy over 2f out: qcknd ins fnl f to ld and hung lft fnl 110yds: readily* **7/4**[1]
-120 **2** *1 ½* **Opera Box**[65] 2369 5-9-6 **83**... FrankieDettori 1 90
(Marcus Tregoning) *led: drvn and qcknd over 2f out: hrd pressed ins fnl f: hdd and outpcd fnl 110yds: jst hld on for 2nd* **6/1**
-304 **3** *nse* **Ruscello (IRE)**[16] 3960 4-9-11 **88**.................................. WilliamBuick 4 95
(Ed Walker) *in tch: hdwy over 2f out: chal jst ins fnl f: styng on same pce whn crossed fnl 110yds: nt qckn after* **4/1**[2]
3/00 **4** *2 ¼* **Prompter**[41] 3094 6-9-13 **90**....................................... RichardKingscote 8 93
(Jonjo O'Neill) *mid-div: hdwy 4f out: rdn to chal 3f out tl over 1f out: wknd fnl 110yds* **20/1**
2434 **5** *½* **Lord Ofthe Shadows (IRE)**[7] 4258 4-9-9 **86**...........(b) RichardHughes 2 88
(Richard Hannon) *chsd ldrs: rdn 2f out and sn hung lft: wknd ins fnl f* **11/2**[3]
2-50 **6** *2 ½* **Jack's Revenge (IRE)**[28] 3527 5-10-0 **91**....................(bt) PatCosgrave 9 88
(George Baker) *stdd and swtchd lft s: hdwy on ins to chse ldrs 2f out but sn hanging lft: wknd fnl f* **6/1**
4420 **7** *1 ¼* **Icebuster**[13] 4060 5-9-10 **87**... JimmyFortune 7 82
(Rod Millman) *swtchd lft s: in rr: rdn over 2f out: mod prog fnl f* **14/1**
00/0 **8** *2* **Togiak (IRE)**[20] 3838 6-9-0 **77**... LiamKeniry 6 68
(David Pipe) *a towards rr* **66/1**
3-60 **9** *shd* **Jake's Destiny (IRE)**[14] 4028 4-10-0 **91**.....................(t) AidanColeman 3 82
(George Baker) *chsd ldr to 3f out: wknd qckly 2f out* **33/1**
2m 5.42s (-3.38) **Going Correction** -0.25s/f (Firm) **9** Ran SP% **116.2**
Speed ratings (Par 107): **103,101,101,99,99 97,96,94,94**
toteswingers 1&2 £3.80, 2&3 £6.10, 1&3 £2.60 CSF £12.61 CT £37.29 TOTE £3.00: £1.30, £2.00, £1.40; EX 15.70 Trifecta £66.70 Pool: £5965.61 - 67.02 winning units..
Owner Dr Marwan Koukash **Bred** Sarl Elevage Du Haras De Bourgeauville **Trained** Newmarket, Suffolk
■ Stewards' Enquiry : Adam Kirby caution: careless riding.
FOCUS
A fair handicap. It was run at a solid early pace, but slowed up shortly after they turned for home and was muddling overall. The winner can do better again and the second is rated to his mark.

4489 STARLIGHT APPRENTICE H'CAP 1m 3f 5y
5:10 (5:10) (Class 5) (0-75,75) 4-Y-O+ **£2,587** (£770; £384; £192) **Stalls** Centre

Form RPR
2402 **1** **Shirataki (IRE)**[24] 3662 5-9-2 **65**.. EoinWalsh 6 73
(Peter Hiatt) *in tch: hdwy in centre of crse over 3f out: drvn to ld 2f out: hung lft over 1f out: hung rt ins fnl f: drvn out* **9/2**[3]
5304 **2** *1 ¼* **Whitby Jet (IRE)**[15] 3976 5-9-1 **71**.......................... CameronHardie(7) 4 77
(Ed Vaughan) *in rr and t.k.h: hdwy 2f out: styd on fnl f to take 2nd cl home but no imp on wnr* **9/4**[1]
2421 **3** *hd* **Curly Come Home**[20] 3814 4-9-5 **75**.......................(t) SamuelClarke(7) 2 81
(Chris Wall) *in rr: hdwy 3f out: chsd wnr ins fnl 2f: no imp fnl f and lost 2nd cl home* **3/1**[2]
404- **4** *2 ¾* **Mister Fizz**[388] 3472 5-8-13 **65**............................... DanielCremin(3) 3 66
(Miss Imogen Pickard) *led: hdd 4f out: styd pressing ldrs and rdn 3f out: wknd fnl f* **12/1**
1206 **5** *nse* **Wordiness**[33] 3370 5-9-12 **75**..................................... JordanVaughan 1 76
(Brendan Powell) *chsd ldrs: rdn 2f out: n.m.r and wknd appr fnl f* **5/1**
5606 **6** *14* **Dancing Primo**[14] 4020 7-9-10 **73**............................. MatthewHopkins 5 52
(Mark Brisbourne) *t.k.h: c wd into st and led 4f out: hdd 2f out and sn wknd* **6/1**
2m 24.66s (3.46) **Going Correction** -0.25s/f (Firm) **6** Ran SP% **112.6**
Speed ratings (Par 103): **77,76,75,73,73 63**
toteswingers 1&2 £2.10, 2&3 £1.70, 1&3 £1.80 CSF £15.15 TOTE £5.10: £2.40, £1.90; EX 15.60 Trifecta £34.40 Pool: £2529.17 - 55.00 winning units..
Owner Carl Demczak **Bred** Deerfield Farm **Trained** Hook Norton, Oxon
FOCUS
An ordinary handicap for apprentice riders, run at an uneven pace, and it's form to treat with some caution. The winner's previous course second could be rated this high.
T/Jkpt: Not won. T/Plt: £333.80 to a £1 stake. Pool of £75366.33 - 164.80 winning tickets.
T/Qpdt: £66.00 to a £1 stake. Pool of £4518.35 - 50.62 winning tickets. ST

4295 NEWMARKET (R-H)
Friday, July 19

OFFICIAL GOING: Good to fiem (8.4)
Wind: light, half against Weather: hot and sunny

4490 JUST RECRUITMENT ANNIVERSARY H'CAP (JOCKEY CLUB GRASSROOTS MIDDLE DISTANCE SERIES QUALIFIER) 1m 2f
5:45 (5:49) (Class 5) (0-75,74) 3-Y-O+ **£3,234** (£962; £481; £240) **Stalls** Centre

Form RPR
2135 **1** **Silver Dixie (USA)**[11] 4126 3-9-1 **71**................................ PaulHanagan 6 81+
(Jeremy Noseda) *hld up in tch in rr: smooth hdwy to ld 3f out: rdn clr over 1f out: r.o wl: comf* **10/11**[1]
4355 **2** *3* **Jazz Master**[13] 4076 3-9-1 **71**... LukeMorris 4 75
(Luca Cumani) *hld up in tch in last pair: hdwy and cl up whn rdn 3f out: chsd wnr over 2f out: drvn and btn over 1f out: plugged on fnl f* **11/4**[2]
5400 **3** *2* **Laconicos (IRE)**[13] 4071 11-8-7 **58** ow1.........................(t) LauraPike(5) 9 59
(William Stone) *taken down early: led tl hdd 3f out: sn rdn and outpcd 2f out: no ch w wnr but plugged on fnl f* **25/1**

1034 **4** *11* **Thecornishcowboy**[15] 3971 4-9-12 **72**...............................(tp) NeilCallan 2 52
(John Ryan) *t.k.h: rdn over 2f out: sn outpcd and btn wl over 1f out: wknd* **6/1**[3]
5336 **5** *9* **Mcbirney (USA)**[21] 3780 6-9-11 **71**................................ FrederikTylicki 1 34
(Paul D'Arcy) *chsd ldr tl 3f out: ev ch and rdn over 2f out: btn and wknd qckly over 1f out: fdd fnl f* **8/1**
2m 8.04s (2.54) **Going Correction** +0.025s/f (Good)
WFA 3 from 4yo+ 10lb **5** Ran SP% **108.3**
Speed ratings (Par 103): **90,87,86,77,70**
CSF £3.46 TOTE £1.80: £1.10, £1.60; EX 3.60 Trifecta £36.70 Pool: £2656.56 - 54.24 winning units..
Owner Mrs Susan Roy **Bred** Lantern Hill Farm Llc **Trained** Newmarket, Suffolk
FOCUS
Stands' side track used Stalls Stands' side except 1m2f & 1m4f: Centre. The going was good to firm on a watered track. This handicap was weakened by several withdrawals, but they went a decent pace and a progressive 3yo scored in good style. Thwe form could be rated 5lb higher but a safer view has been taken.

4491 POPTELECOM.CO.UK MAIDEN FILLIES' STKS 7f
6:20 (6:21) (Class 5) 2-Y-O **£3,234** (£962; £481; £240) **Stalls** High

Form RPR
1 **Folk Melody (IRE)** 2-9-0 0.................................... MickaelBarzalona 14 89+
(Saeed bin Suroor) *hld up wl in tch in midfield: hdwy to trck ldrs 1/2-way: led ent fnl 2f: rdn and qcknd clr over 1f out: r.o wl* **3/1**[1]
6 **2** *2 ¾* **Enraptured (IRE)**[30] 3471 2-9-0 0.................................... RobertHavlin 2 81
(John Gosden) *chsd ldrs: clsd and upsides wnr ent fnl 2f: rdn and unable qck w wnr over 1f out: hung lft and one pce fnl f* **7/2**[2]
3 *2* **Makruma** 2-9-0 0... MartinDwyer 3 76+
(J W Hills) *s.i.s: hld up in tch in rr: clsng whn nt clr run over 2f out: pushed along and hdwy over 1f out: styd on wl under hands and heels fnl f: gng on fin* **12/1**
22 **4** *2* **Dancealot**[30] 3471 2-9-0 0... KierenFallon 17 71
(Clive Brittain) *led tl rdn and hdd ent fnl 2f: drvn and outpcd over 1f out: edgd lft 1f out: wknd ins fnl f* **7/2**[2]
0 **5** *hd* **Ultraviolet (IRE)**[24] 3664 2-9-0 0..................................... MartinLane 10 70
(David Simcock) *wnt rt s: w ldrs: rdn and unable qck ent fnl 2f: hung rt and outpcd over 1f out: plugged on but no threat to ldrs fnl f* **50/1**
6 *½* **Ejadah (IRE)** 2-9-0 0.. PaulHanagan 15 69+
(Roger Varian) *t.k.h: hld up wl in tch in midfield: hdwy to chse ldrs 1/2-way: rdn and outpcd wl over 1f out: keeping on same pce and hld whn sltly hmpd and swtchd rt jst ins fnl f* **8/1**[3]
7 *1 ¼* **Anipa** 2-8-9 0... LauraPike(5) 9 66+
(Ed Dunlop) *pushed rt s: t.k.h: hld up wl in tch: rdn and outpcd over 2f out: styng on same pce and wl hld whn hmpd jst ins fnl f* **25/1**
8 *nk* **Cordial** 2-8-7 0... JoeyHaynes(7) 6 65+
(John Gosden) *s.i.s: t.k.h: hld up in tch in rr: nt clr run but stl travelling strly 1/2-way: hdwy and rn green over 1f out: kpt on same pce after* **20/1**
9 *1 ¾* **Dalmatia (IRE)** 2-9-0 0.. RyanMoore 18 61+
(Sir Michael Stoute) *hld up in tch in rr: rdn and hdwy over 2f out: no imp over 1f out: n.d but plugged on fnl f* **9/1**
10 *½* **Turin (IRE)** 2-9-0 0.. NeilCallan 8 59+
(Saeed bin Suroor) *bmpd leaving stalls: hld up in tch in midfield: rdn and unable qck and rn green over 1f out: n.d but plugged on fnl f* **14/1**
0 **11** *½* **Nyanza (GER)**[24] 3664 2-9-0 0.. TedDurcan 5 58
(Alan King) *chsd ldrs: rdn and struggling over 2f out: outpcd and btn over 1f out: plugged on fnl f* **33/1**
12 *6* **Speedbird One** 2-9-0 0.. SteveDrowne 4 42
(Peter Chapple-Hyam) *in tch in midfield: lost pl and rdn 3f out: bhd over 1f out* **50/1**
13 *2 ½* **Trinity Lorraine (IRE)** 2-9-0 0.................................. FrederikTylicki 7 36
(Alan Bailey) *hld up in rr: rdn and struggling over 2f out: bhd whn hung lft over 1f out* **66/1**
0 **14** *2 ¼* **Ohio (IRE)**[18] 3905 2-9-0 0.. J-PGuillambert 1 30
(Gary Harrison) *hld up in tch in midfield: rdn and lost pl 2f out: sn wknd: bhd fnl f* **80/1**
15 *1 ½* **Percys Princess** 2-9-0 0.. DavidProbert 13 26
(Ed Vaughan) *in tch in midfield: rdn and lost pl wl over 2f out: bhd over 1f out* **33/1**
16 *17* **Gower Princess** 2-9-0 0... LukeMorris 16
(Ronald Harris) *t.k.h: chsd ldrs tl 3f out: sn hung lft and dropped out: t.o and eased ins fnl f* **66/1**
1m 27.21s (1.51) **Going Correction** +0.025s/f (Good) **16** Ran SP% **127.5**
Speed ratings (Par 91): **92,88,86,84,84 83,82,81,79,79 78,71,68,66,64 45**
toteswingers 1&2 £4.20, 2&3 £19.20, 1&3 £14.00 CSF £12.92 TOTE £3.60: £1.80, £1.90, £5.60; EX 19.20 Trifecta £161.00 Pool: £1599.35 - 7.44 winning units..
Owner Godolphin **Bred** Darley **Trained** Newmarket, Suffolk
FOCUS
A fascinating fillies' maiden, which was by Rainbow View in 2008. They raced centre to stands' side and a well-backed Godolphin newcomer powered clear from one of her main market rivals. She looks a good prospect, and the race should produce winners.

4492 NGK SPARK PLUGS H'CAP 7f
6:50 (6:51) (Class 4) (0-85,84) 3-Y-O **£5,175** (£1,540; £769; £384) **Stalls** High

Form RPR
2331 **1** **Majestic Moon (IRE)**[7] 4265 3-9-3 **80**............................ PaulHanagan 5 96
(Richard Fahey) *mde all: rdn and edgd rt over 1f out: edgd bk lft u.p but styd on wl fnl f* **13/8**[1]
01-2 **2** *1 ½* **Veeraya**[27] 3582 3-9-5 **82**..(p) RyanMoore 2 94
(William Haggas) *hld up in tch in rr: effrt to chse ldng pair and swtchd lft over 1f out: chsd wnr fnl 100yds: no imp* **9/4**[2]
3102 **3** *1 ½* **Maid A Million**[22] 3718 3-9-7 **84**..................................... SebSanders 7 92
(David Elsworth) *t.k.h: chsd ldrs: chsd wnr 2f out and sn rdn: no ex 1f out: lost 2nd and one pce fnl 100yds* **13/2**
0262 **4** *5* **Dance With Dragons (IRE)**[21] 3782 3-8-12 **80**.............. LauraPike(5) 1 75
(William Stone) *t.k.h: hld up in tch in midfield: rdn and effrt to chse ldrs over 2f out: wknd ent fnl f* **12/1**
441 **5** *3 ¾* **Ziekhani**[22] 3731 3-9-3 **80**.. KierenFallon 4 65
(Hughie Morrison) *chsd ldr tl 2f out: sn struggling u.p: wknd jst over 1f out* **9/2**[3]
520 **6** *9* **Kamchatka**[8] 4207 3-8-7 **70**...(bt) MartinDwyer 3 32
(Philip Hide) *awkward leaving stalls and s.i.s: hld up in tch in last pair: rdn and struggling over 2f out: wknd wl over 1f out: bhd and eased ins fnl f* **40/1**
1m 25.11s (-0.59) **Going Correction** +0.025s/f (Good) **6** Ran SP% **110.5**
Speed ratings (Par 102): **104,102,100,94,90 80**
toteswingers 1&2 £1.10, 2&3 £3.00, 1&3 £1.90 CSF £5.31 TOTE £2.70: £1.70, £1.60; EX 6.10 Trifecta £16.10 Pool: £1533.51 - 71.17 winning units..

Owner James Gaffney **Bred** Tony Cosgrave **Trained** Musley Bank, N Yorks

FOCUS

The favourite scored with something in hand under a positive ride in this steadily run handicap, and is rated similar to his York run.

4493 INVESCO PERPETUAL CONDITIONS STKS 5f

7:25 (7:25) (Class 3) 3-Y-O+

£8,715 (£2,609; £1,304; £652; £326; £163) **Stalls** High

Form RPR

0325 **1** **Justineo**[20] 3822 4-8-9 101 WilliamBuick 4 104
(Roger Varian) *chsd ldr tl led after 2f: mde rest: rdn over 1f out: forged clr ins fnl f: styd on wl* **7/4**[1]

2 1 1/2 **Bern Me Baby (USA)**[72] 3-8-0 100 PaoloSirigu 2 93
(Marco Botti) *hld up in tch in last pair: rdn and effrt jst over 1f out: kpt on u.p fnl 100yds to go 2nd towards fin: no threat to wnr* **10/1**

4500 **3** hd **Stepper Point**[6] 4311 4-8-9 104 (p) MartinDwyer 5 98
(William Muir) *hld up in tch in last pair: hdwy to join ldrs 2f out: unable qck w wnr jst ins fnl f: one pce fnl 100yds* **10/3**[3]

-006 **4** 3/4 **Addictive Dream (IRE)**[13] 4058 6-8-9 98 PaulHanagan 3 95
(David Nicholls) *broke wl: led tl 3f out: pressed wnr after: rdn and ev ch over 1f out: no ex and btn ins fnl f: wknd towards fin* **10/1**

5400 **5** 3 3/4 **Pandar**[33] 3373 4-8-9 98 NeilCallan 6 82
(Robert Cowell) *chsd ldrs: rdn and unable qck 2f out: wknd u.p ent fnl f* **16/1**

-262 **6** hd **La Fortunata**[15] 3973 6-7-11 90 JoeyHaynes(7) 1 76
(Mike Murphy) *chsd ldrs: rdn 2f out: lost pl over 1f out: sn wknd* **11/4**[2]

58.1s (-1.00) **Going Correction** +0.025s/f (Good)
WFA 3 from 4yo+ 4lb **6** Ran SP% **110.2**
Speed ratings (Par 107): **109,106,106,105,99 98**
toteswingers 1&2 £4.50, 2&3 £4.50, 1&3 £1.70 CSF £18.93 TOTE £2.60: £1.60, £2.70; EX 18.30 Trifecta £38.00 Pool: £1195.63 - 23.57 winning units..
Owner Saleh Al Homaizi & Imad Al Sagar **Bred** Saleh Al Homaizi & Imad Al Sagar **Trained** Newmarket, Suffolk

FOCUS

They went a good pace in this decent conditions event and the favourite scored with something in hand. The winner is the best guide and the third fits.

4494 DAVID HANLON MEMORIAL H'CAP (JOCKEY CLUB GRASSROOTS SPRINT SERIES QUALIFIER) 6f

7:55 (7:55) (Class 4) (0-80,79) 3-Y-O+ **£5,175** (£1,540; £769; £384) **Stalls** High

Form RPR

0232 **1** **Picture Dealer**[22] 3733 4-9-12 79 RyanMoore 1 96+
(Gary Moore) *stdd s: hld up in tch in rr: hdwy nrest stands' rail to ld ent fnl f: clr and r.o wl fnl f: readily* **6/4**[1]

-410 **2** 4 **Whipper Snapper (IRE)**[27] 3582 3-9-6 78 AdamKirby 2 80
(William Knight) *hld up in last pair: effrt whn nt clr run and hmpd wl over 1f out: stl bhd and swtchd rt jst over 1f out: r.o wl to go 2nd towards fin: no ch w wnr* **6/1**[3]

2610 **3** 3/4 **Noverre To Go (IRE)**[22] 3720 7-9-12 79 (p) SteveDrowne 4 81
(Ronald Harris) *in tch in midfield: rdn and effrt over 1f out: kpt on u.p and chsd clr wnr ins fnl f: no imp and lost 2nd towards fin* **14/1**

2242 **4** 1/2 **Peace Seeker**[53] 2724 5-9-12 79 WilliamBuick 8 79
(Anthony Carson) *sn w ldr: ev ch and rdn wl over 1f out: outpcd by wnr and btn 1f out: one pce fnl f* **5/1**[2]

0006 **5** hd **Emkanaat**[14] 4014 5-9-7 74 MartinDwyer 9 73
(Amy Weaver) *racd keenly: led: rdn over 1f out: hdd and outpcd by wnr ent fnl f: plugged on same pce and lost 3 pls ins fnl f* **33/1**

4005 **6** shd **Corporal Maddox**[7] 4243 6-9-11 78 [1] LukeMorris 5 79+
(Ronald Harris) *dwlt and rdn along leaving stalls: in tch in midfield: effrt u.p 2f out: keeping on but no ch w wnr whn nt clr run ins fnl f: swtchd rt and styd on towards fin* **20/1**

3113 **7** 2 **Commanche**[11] 4120 4-9-1 75 JoshCrane(7) 10 68
(Chris Dwyer) *rrd as stalls opened: sn in tch in midfield: rdn and unable qck over 1f out: wknd fnl f* **8/1**

1326 **8** 5 **Royal Challis**[19] 3866 3-9-6 78 SeanLevey 3 53
(Richard Hannon) *chsd ldrs: rdn and btn whn carried lft jst over 1f out: sn wknd* **25/1**

3366 **9** 1 **Fortrose Academy (IRE)**[20] 3841 4-8-11 64 DavidProbert 6 37
(Andrew Balding) *chsd ldrs: struggling u.p ent fnl 2f: wknd over 1f out* **14/1**

0601 **10** shd **The Strig**[17] 3921 6-8-10 63 J-PGuillambert 13 36
(Stuart Williams) *racd far side: chsd ldrs overall tl rdn and wknd over 1f out: fdd fnl f* **20/1**

2144 **11** 2 1/4 **Putin (IRE)**[8] 4210 5-8-12 65 (bt) KierenFallon 7 31
(Phil McEntee) *dwlt: sn wl in tch in midfield: rdn and struggling 2f out: sn wknd: bhd fnl f* **16/1**

0300 **12** 35 **Sans Loi (IRE)**[48] 2882 4-9-12 79 (p) ShaneKelly 12
(Brian Ellison) *racd on far side: chsd ldrs overall tl rdn and btn 2f out: bhd and virtually p.u fnl f: t.o* **20/1**

1m 11.81s (-0.69) **Going Correction** +0.025s/f (Good)
WFA 3 from 4yo+ 5lb **12** Ran SP% **122.4**
Speed ratings (Par 105): **105,99,98,98,97 97,94,88,86,86 83,37**
toteswingers 1&2 £5.20, 2&3 £8.20, 1&3 £7.30 CSF £9.69 CT £98.26 TOTE £2.30: £1.30, £2.30, £4.20; EX 14.80 Trifecta £160.50 Pool: £1092.07 - 5.10 winning units..
Owner R A Green **Bred** L Ellinas & Old Mill Stud **Trained** Lower Beeding, W Sussex

FOCUS

Most of the runners raced down the centre of the track in this sprint handicap. The pace was decent and the favourite powered clear, showing improved form. Low numbers came out on top.

4495 PIPER-HEIDSIECK MAIDEN STKS 1m

8:25 (8:26) (Class 5) 3-Y-O **£3,234** (£962; £481; £240) **Stalls** High

Form RPR

00 **1** **Investment Expert (IRE)**[62] 2456 3-9-5 0 SebSanders 5 81
(Jeremy Noseda) *hld up in tch in rr: swtchd rt and effrt 2f out: chal and carried hd high jst ins fnl f: racd awkwardly and hung lft fnl f: led cl home* **10/1**

53 **2** 1/2 **Akeed Dubawi**[10] 4152 3-9-5 0 NeilCallan 7 80
(William Haggas) *led: rdn over 1f out: hrd pressed and carried lft fnl f: hdd and no ex cl home* **7/4**[1]

3 1 1/2 **For Posterity** 3-9-5 0 MickaelBarzalona 6 76+
(Saeed bin Suroor) *chsd ldrs: rdn and effrt to chse ldr 2f out tl 1f out: stl pressing ldrs ins fnl f: no ex and wknd fnl 50yds* **7/4**[1]

4 3 1/2 **Electra Spectra** 3-9-0 0 KierenFallon 4 63
(Luca Cumani) *in tch in last pair: rdn and effrt 3f out: chsd ldr over 2f out tl 2f out: wknd u.p over 1f out* **9/2**[2]

5 15 **Meet Marhaba (IRE)** 3-9-0 0 PaulHanagan 2 27
(J W Hills) *chsd ldr tl over 2f out: sn lost pl: bhd 1f out* **8/1**[3]

1m 40.95s (0.95) **Going Correction** +0.025s/f (Good) **5** Ran SP% **111.1**
Speed ratings (Par 100): **96,95,94,90,75**
CSF £28.24 TOTE £10.10: £2.90, £1.80; EX 31.40 Trifecta £48.80 Pool: £729.72 - 11.21 winning units..
Owner Nigel O'Sullivan **Bred** Floors Farming **Trained** Newmarket, Suffolk

FOCUS

There was a tight finish in this maiden and the outsider just denied the main form contender. The runner-up and the race averages guide the form, which could be rated a bit higher.

4496 PIPER-HEIDSIECK H'CAP 7f

8:55 (8:55) (Class 5) (0-75,75) 4-Y-O+ **£3,234** (£962; £481; £240) **Stalls** High

Form RPR

3042 **1** **Illustrious Prince (IRE)**[8] 4198 6-8-7 64 NeilFarley(3) 8 74
(Declan Carroll) *chsd ldrs: jnd ldrs 3f out tl rdn to ld ins fnl f: r.o wl: comf* **4/1**[2]

2540 **2** 2 **Greyfriarschorista**[21] 3780 6-8-11 70 LauraPike(5) 6 75
(Tom Keddy) *hld up in tch in last trio: swtchd rt and hdwy 2f out: chsng ldrs and edgd lft ins fnl f: chsd wnr fnl 75yds: no imp* **9/1**

1-04 **3** 3/4 **Eager To Bow (IRE)**[27] 3575 7-9-4 72 DavidProbert 7 75
(Patrick Chamings) *in tch in midfield: gd hdwy to chse ldr wl over 2f out: kpt on same pce ins fnl f* **15/2**

4064 **4** nk **Saskia's Dream**[20] 3817 5-8-1 62 (v[1]) IanBurns(7) 5 64
(Jane Chapple-Hyam) *rrd in stalls and slowly away: hld up in rr: rdn and gd hdwy to ld wl over 2f out: hdd and no ex ins fnl f: wknd towards fin* **15/2**

313 **5** 2 1/2 **Decent Fella (IRE)**[17] 3926 7-9-7 75 (t) MartinHarley 3 71
(Violet M Jordan) *hld up in tch in last trio: hdwy u.p and swtchd lft over 1f out: no imp ins fnl f* **7/2**[1]

6-5 **6** hd **Trulee Scrumptious**[100] 1480 4-8-2 56 oh6 LukeMorris 1 51+
(Peter Charalambous) *chsd ldrs: rdn and ev ch 3f out: hrd drvn and outpcd over 1f out: n.d but kpt on again ins fnl f* **25/1**

3256 **7** nk **Aaranyow (IRE)**[11] 4120 5-7-11 56 oh3 NathanAlison(5) 11 50
(Clifford Lines) *t.k.h: hld up in tch in midfield: effrt to ld 3f out: sn hdd: chsd ldrs and no ex u.p over 1f out: wknd ins fnl f* **16/1**

4140 **8** 5 **Valdaw**[45] 2964 5-9-2 70 NeilCallan 2 51
(Mike Murphy) *in tch in midfield: lost pl u.p over 2f out: wknd over 1f out* **7/1**

-100 **9** 1/2 **Alice Rose (IRE)**[24] 3661 4-8-12 66 MartinDwyer 9 46
(Rae Guest) *chsd ldr: ev ch 3f out: sn struggling: wknd qckly jst over 1f out* **16/1**

3613 **10** 16 **Jonnie Skull (IRE)**[9] 4183 7-8-13 67 (vt) KierenFallon 10 6
(Phil McEntee) *led tl 3f out: sn dropped out and bhd: eased ins fnl f* **11/2**[3]

1m 26.33s (0.63) **Going Correction** +0.025s/f (Good) **10** Ran SP% **119.2**
Speed ratings (Par 103): **97,94,93,93,90 90,90,84,83,65**
toteswingers 1&2 £9.90, 2&3 £7.80, 1&3 £6.20 CSF £40.97 TOTE £5.10: £1.70, £3.00, £2.30; EX 49.60 Trifecta £160.90 Pool: £1211.52 - 5.64 winning units..
Owner Ray Flegg **Bred** Rathbarry Stud **Trained** Sledmere, E Yorks

FOCUS

They went a decent pace in this handicap and the winner can be marked up for scoring in a race where the other prominent runners dropped away. They edged to the far rail this time.

T/Plt: £12.10 to a £1 stake. Pool of £51890.74 - 3111.72 winning tickets. T/Qpdt: £5.00 to a £1 stake. Pool of £3340.74 - 490.18 winning tickets. SP

4071 NOTTINGHAM (L-H)

Friday, July 19

OFFICIAL GOING: Good to firm (firm in places; 9.0)

Wind: Light behind Weather: Hot and dry

4497 32RED CASINO IRISH EBF MAIDEN STKS 6f 15y

2:00 (2:00) (Class 5) 2-Y-O **£3,234** (£962; £481; £240) **Stalls** High

Form RPR

3 **1** **Brave Boy (IRE)**[59] 2543 2-9-5 0 SilvestreDeSousa 5 91+
(Saeed bin Suroor) *sn swtchd lft to outer and trck ldrs: hdwy to ld 1/2-way: qcknd clr wl over 1f out: pushed out* **2/5**[1]

2 1 1/4 **Music Theory (IRE)** 2-9-5 0 MickaelBarzalona 4 87+
(Saeed bin Suroor) *wnt lft s: towards rr: hdwy 1/2-way: chsd wnr over 1f out: sn rdn and kpt on: no imp towards fin* **6/1**[2]

64 **3** 7 **Le Laitier (FR)**[13] 4046 2-9-5 0 JamesDoyle 3 65
(Scott Dixon) *led: pushed along and hdd 1/2-way: rdn 2f out: grad wknd* **33/1**

05 **4** 1/2 **Centrality**[65] 2358 2-9-5 0 FrannyNorton 7 63
(Mark Johnston) *chsd ldrs on inner: rdn along over 2f out: sn one pce* **20/1**

5 6 **Exceed Areeda (IRE)** 2-9-0 0 NeilCallan 1 39
(James Tate) *trckd ldng pair: sn chsng ldr: rdn along over 2f out: wknd wl over 1f out* **20/1**

5 **6** 1 1/2 **Ivy Trump**[21] 3760 2-9-0 0 AndrewMullen 2 34
(Michael Appleby) *chsd ldr: pushed along after 2f: sn rdn and lost pl 1/2-way: bhd fnl 2f* **8/1**[3]

5 **7** 2 1/2 **Holystones (IRE)**[29] 3493 2-9-5 0 AndreaAtzeni 6 31
(Marco Botti) *a towards rr* **100/1**

1m 11.75s (-2.95) **Going Correction** -0.50s/f (Hard) **7** Ran SP% **110.3**
Speed ratings (Par 94): **99,97,88,87,79 77,74**
toteswingers 1&2 £1.70, 2&3 £6.90, 1&3 £3.10 CSF £2.68 TOTE £1.50: £1.10, £2.10; EX 4.30 Trifecta £26.60 Pool: £1411.58 - 39.67 winning units..
Owner Godolphin **Bred** Darley **Trained** Newmarket, Suffolk

FOCUS

Outer track used. Rail on inner line except home bend 2yds off inner which added 6yds to races on round course. A one-horse race according the market and that proved correct. The first two were clear. The form looks fluid and will take time to settle.

4498 £32 BONUS AT 32RED.COM NURSERY H'CAP 6f 15y

2:30 (2:30) (Class 5) 2-Y-O **£3,234** (£962; £481; £240) **Stalls** High

Form RPR

0223 **1** **Tanseeb**[13] 4061 2-9-7 80 FrannyNorton 2 87
(Mark Johnston) *mde all: qcknd over 2f out: rldden wl over 1f out: edgd lft and kpt on strly ins fnl f* **11/8**[2]

643 **2** 3 **Minley**[20] 3815 2-8-12 71 SilvestreDeSousa 1 68
(Rae Guest) *trckd wnr: cl up 1/2-way: rdn along over 2f out: drvn and ch over 1f out: edgd rt and one pce fnl f* **11/10**[1]

5015 **3** 3/4 **Jive**[13] 4061 2-8-11 **70** .... JamesDoyle 4 65
(Richard Hannon) *trckd ldng pair: effrt over 2f out: rdn wl over 1f out: sn one pce* **11/2**[3]

1335 **4** 9 **Loma Mor**[31] 3439 2-8-10 **69** .... MartinDwyer 3 35
(Alan McCabe) *t.k.h: chsd ldng pair: rdn along over 2f out: sn outpcd* **33/1**

1m 12.45s (-2.25) **Going Correction** -0.50s/f (Hard) **4** Ran SP% **108.1**
Speed ratings (Par 94): **95,91,90,78**
CSF £3.23 TOTE £1.50; EX 4.00 Trifecta £4.60 Pool: £1568.62 - 254.57 winning units..
Owner Hamdan Al Maktoum **Bred** Mildmay Bloodstock Ltd **Trained** Middleham Moor, N Yorks

FOCUS
A fair nursery and a lot to like about the winning performance. The placed horses help set the level.

4499 32REDPOKER.COM H'CAP 6f 15y
3:00 (3:00) (Class 5) (0-70,70) 3-Y-O **£3,234** (£962; £481; £240) **Stalls** High

Form RPR

4603 **1** **Sedenoo**[22] 3731 3-9-7 **70** .... AndreaAtzeni 2 82+
(Marco Botti) *trckd ldrs: swtchd lft to outer 2f out: sn chsng ldr: rdn to chal over 1f out: led ins fnl f: kpt on* **2/1**[1]

0-25 **2** 2 1/2 **Meridius (IRE)**[20] 3837 3-9-7 **70** .... ShaneKelly 9 74
(Gary Harrison) *sn trcking ldrs on inner: hdwy 1/2-way: led 2f out: jnd and rdn jst over 1f out: hdd ins fnl f: one pce* **7/1**

0632 **3** 4 1/2 **Rock Up (IRE)**[38] 3171 3-9-3 **66** ....(b) MickaelBarzalona 4 56
(David Elsworth) *cl up: led 1/2-way: rdn along and hdd 2f out: sn drvn and one pce* **6/1**[3]

3-35 **4** nk **Work Ethic (IRE)**[10] 4136 3-9-6 **69** ....(b) JamesDoyle 3 58
(Gerard Butler) *hld up: hdwy over 2f out: rdn wl over 1f out: kpt on fnl f* **8/1**

0363 **5** 1 **Hazza The Jazza**[11] 4113 3-8-10 **59** ....(b) RobbieFitzpatrick 6 44
(Richard Guest) *s.i.s: rdn along and hdwy wl over 2f out: swtchd lft over 1f out: n.d* **9/1**

4200 **6** 1 1/4 **Only For You**[16] 3946 3-8-1 **53** .... RaulDaSilva(3) 8 34
(Alan Brown) *led: hdd 1/2-way: sn rdn along and grad wknd fnl 2f* **20/1**

5-60 **7** 2 1/2 **Kwanto**[59] 2528 3-8-5 **54** .... AndrewMullen 1 27
(Michael Appleby) *dwlt: sn chsng ldrs on outer: rdn along wl over 2f out: sn wknd* **33/1**

-050 **8** 8 **Monsieur Royale**[24] 3649 3-9-1 **64** ....(b) SilvestreDeSousa 7 18
(Geoffrey Oldroyd) *cl up: rdn along bef 1/2-way: sn lost pl and bhd fnl 2f* **3/1**[2]

1m 11.66s (-3.04) **Going Correction** -0.50s/f (Hard) **8** Ran SP% **113.9**
Speed ratings (Par 100): **100,96,90,90,88 87,83,73**
toteswingers 1&2 £2.80, 2&3 £4.00, 1&3 £3.70 CSF £16.59 CT £71.49 TOTE £4.00: £1.10, £3.40, £1.40; EX 24.20 Trifecta £111.70 Pool: £1453.79 - 9.75 winning units..
Owner Scuderia Rencati Srl **Bred** Chegwidden Systems Ltd **Trained** Newmarket, Suffolk

FOCUS
An ordinary handicap but the form looks sound with the first two clear.

4500 32REDBINGO.COM FILLIES' MAIDEN STKS 1m 2f 50y
3:35 (3:35) (Class 5) 3-Y-O **£3,234** (£962; £481; £240) **Stalls** High

Form RPR

-023 **1** **Lemon Pearl**[43] 3021 3-9-0 76 .... JamieSpencer 6 80
(Ralph Beckett) *t.k.h early: trckd ldrs tl led after 2f: jnd and pushed along 3f out: rdn over 2f out: drvn over 1f out: hrd drvn ins fnl f: hld on gamely towards fin* **3/1**[3]

4 **2** nk **Bonanza Creek (IRE)**[36] 3237 3-9-0 0 ....(b) AndreaAtzeni 1 79
(Luca Cumani) *t.k.h early: trckd ldrs: swtchd rt and hdwy 3f out: effrt wl over 1f out: rdn to chse wnr appr fnl f: sn ev ch tl drvn and nt qckn nr fin* **9/4**[2]

3 2 1/2 **Annawi** 3-9-0 0 .... FergusSweeney 7 75+
(Henry Candy) *hld up: hdwy on outer over 3f out: chsd ldrs 2f out: rdn and ev ch over 1f out: kpt on same pce fnl f* **10/1**

35-3 **4** 1 3/4 **Raskova (USA)**[11] 4125 3-9-0 0 .... JamesDoyle 9 71
(William Jarvis) *t.k.h: in tch: hdwy 4f out: sn cl up: rdn over 2f out: sn drvn and wknd appr fnl f* **20/1**

0 **5** 8 **Cherokee Princess (IRE)**[40] 3136 3-9-0 0 .... ShaneKelly 2 56
(Tim Pitt) *dwlt and towards rr: sme hdwy over 2f out: sn rdn and n.d* **100/1**

6 nk **Fossola (USA)** 3-9-0 0 .... MickaelBarzalona 5 56+
(Saeed bin Suroor) *t.k.h early: hld up: hdwy on outer to trck ldrs after 3f: cl up 4f out: rdn over 2f out: sn wknd* **2/1**[1]

0065 **7** 1 **Faustinatheyounger (IRE)**[20] 3821 3-9-0 57 .... WilliamCarson 4 54
(David Elsworth) *led 2f: chsd ldrs: rdn along over 3f out: sn wknd* **66/1**

5 **8** 9 **Palkin**[21] 3764 3-9-0 0 .... SilvestreDeSousa 3 37
(William Haggas) *dwlt: a towards rr* **12/1**

04- **9** 2 3/4 **Pearla**[210] 8200 3-9-0 0 .... AdamBeschizza 8 31
(Robert Stephens) *prom: chsd ldrs whn n.m.r and hmpd on inner 1/2-way: rdn along wl over 3f out: sn wknd* **66/1**

2m 8.29s (-6.01) **Going Correction** -0.675s/f (Hard) course record **9** Ran SP% **114.6**
Speed ratings (Par 97): **97,96,94,93,86 86,85,78,76**
toteswingers 1&2 £2.00, 2&3 £2.30, 1&3 £6.20 CSF £9.92 TOTE £3.80: £1.30, £1.10, £3.60; EX 11.90 Trifecta £65.60 Pool: £2012.25 - 23.00 winning units..
Owner Pearl Bloodstock Ltd & N H Wrigley **Bred** Baron F Von Oppenheim **Trained** Kimpton, Hants

FOCUS
JUst fair fillies' maiden and they came home fairly well strung out. The winner is rated to form.

4501 32RED H'CAP 1m 2f 50y
4:10 (4:10) (Class 2) (0-105,97) 3-Y-O+ **£16,172** (£4,812; £2,405; £1,202) **Stalls** High

Form RPR

352 **1** **Vasily**[20] 3838 5-9-8 **91** .... AndreaAtzeni 1 101
(Robert Eddery) *t.k.h: sn led and set str pce: jnd and rdn 3f out: drvn wl over 1f out: kpt on gamely u.p towards fin* **4/1**[3]

-554 **2** 3/4 **Trader Jack**[13] 4080 4-9-6 **89** .... JamesDoyle 4 98
(Roger Charlton) *hld up in rr: tk clsr order 4f out: effrt 2f out: rdn to chse wnr over 1f out: drvn to chal ins fnl f: ev ch tl edgd lft and no ex nr fin* **11/10**[1]

0130 **3** 4 **Fennell Bay (IRE)**[6] 4310 4-9-7 **90** .... FrannyNorton 5 91
(Mark Johnston) *trckd ldng pair: effrt 3f out: sn rdn along: drvn wl over 1f out: kpt on same pce* **7/1**

12 **4** 1/2 **Pitchoun (IRE)**[7] 4249 3-8-11 **90** .... SilvestreDeSousa 8 90
(Mark Johnston) *trckd wnr: hdwy over 4f out: sn cl up: chal over 2f out: sn rdn and ev ch: drvn appr fnl f and sn wknd* **7/2**[2]

0305 **5** 1 1/4 **Art Scholar (IRE)**[7] 4262 6-9-13 **96** ....(p) AndrewMullen 2 94
(Michael Appleby) *hld up in tch: hdwy 4f out: rdn along wl over 2f out: sn one pce* **11/1**

2m 7.13s (-7.17) **Going Correction** -0.675s/f (Hard) course record
WFA 3 from 4yo+ 10lb **5** Ran SP% **110.7**
Speed ratings (Par 109): **101,100,97,96,95**
CSF £8.98 TOTE £4.50: £1.80, £1.20; EX 9.20 Trifecta £20.90 Pool: £1186.05 - 42.47 winning units..
Owner Owen O'Brien & David Bannon **Bred** Cheveley Park Stud Ltd **Trained** Newmarket, Suffolk

FOCUS
A course record. Some likeable types in the line-up for this feature handicap and, with the race run at a solid pace throughout, the form looks almost certain to work out. The form could rate slightly higher.

4502 32RED.COM H'CAP 1m 75y
4:45 (4:45) (Class 4) (0-85,85) 3-Y-O+ **£6,469** (£1,925; £962; £481) **Stalls** Centre

Form RPR

3-36 **1** **Ajmany (IRE)**[48] 2857 3-9-6 **85** ....(b) JamesDoyle 3 96+
(Luca Cumani) *hld up in tch: hdwy over 3f out: rdn 2f out: drvn to chal and edgd lft ent fnl f: kpt on to ld last 100yds* **5/6**[1]

4241 **2** 3 1/4 **Stellar Express (IRE)**[6] 4287 4-9-11 **82** 6ex .... AndrewMullen 4 87
(Michael Appleby) *chsd ldr: hdwy and cl up over 3f out: rdn 2f out: sn drvn and ev ch: n.m.r ent fnl f: kpt on u.p towards fin* **3/1**[2]

-436 **3** nk **Light Rose (IRE)**[12] 4101 3-8-11 **76** .... FrannyNorton 5 78
(Mark Johnston) *led: pushed along 3f out: jnd and rdn 2f out: drvn ent fnl f: hdd & wknd last 100yds: lost 2nd nr fin* **7/1**[3]

2003 **4** 2 3/4 **Flying Applause**[14] 4012 8-8-13 **70** ....(b) JimmyQuinn 2 68
(Roy Bowring) *t.k.h early: chsd ldng pair: rdn along and outpcd wl over 2f out: kpt on u.p fnl f* **25/1**

-050 **5** 1 1/4 **Mingun Bell (USA)**[23] 3693 6-9-6 **77** ....(b) LiamTreadwell 1 72
(Ed de Giles) *s.i.s and bhd: hdwy and in tch 5f out: effrt on inner to chse ldrs 3f out: sn rdn along and wknd fnl 2f* **14/1**

2000 **6** 3 1/2 **Shavansky**[23] 3697 9-9-7 **85** .... PatMillman(7) 6 71
(Rod Millman) *s.i.s and bhd: in tch 5f out: hdwy to chse ldrs on outer over 3f out: sn rdn and wknd fnl 2f* **10/1**

1m 42.26s (-6.74) **Going Correction** -0.675s/f (Hard) course record
WFA 3 from 4yo+ 8lb **6** Ran SP% **111.7**
Speed ratings (Par 105): **106,102,102,99,98 94**
toteswingers 1&2 £1.40, 2&3 £1.90, 1&3 £1.60 CSF £3.46 TOTE £1.50: £1.10, £2.70; EX 5.00 Trifecta £12.10 Pool: £2389.49 - 146.96 winning units..
Owner Sheikh Mohammed Obaid Al Maktoum **Bred** Rockfield Farm **Trained** Newmarket, Suffolk

FOCUS
Decent form backed up by a solid pace, and the form could rate slightly higher.

4503 32REDBET.COM H'CAP (DIV I) 1m 75y
5:20 (5:21) (Class 6) (0-65,65) 3-Y-O+ **£2,045** (£603; £302) **Stalls** Centre

Form RPR

3464 **1** **West End Lad**[13] 4077 10-10-0 **65** ....(b) JimmyQuinn 3 76
(Roy Bowring) *hld up towards rr: gd hdwy on inner 3f out: squeezed through 2f out: sn rdn: led ent fnl f: styd on strly* **7/1**

005 **2** 3 1/2 **Special Report (IRE)**[34] 3319 3-7-9 **47** oh1 ow1 .... ShelleyBirkett(7) 8 48
(Peter Hiatt) *cl up: rdn and slt ld 3f out: drvn over 1f out: hdd ent fnl f: kpt on same pce* **16/1**

3002 **3** 1 **Mcmonagle (USA)**[11] 4119 5-9-4 **58** ....(tp) PaulPickard(3) 10 59
(Alan Brown) *trckd ldrs on outer: hdwy 3f out: cl up over 2f out: sn rdn and ev ch tl drvn: edgd lft and one pce fnl f* **9/4**[2]

0-43 **4** 1 3/4 **Lisa's Legacy**[9] 4169 3-9-6 **65** .... JamesDoyle 4 59
(Daniel Kubler) *led 2f: cl up: rdn along over 2f out: drvn wl over 1f out: wknd appr fnl f* **7/4**[1]

4-60 **5** 2 3/4 **Admirals Walk (IRE)**[24] 3665 3-8-10 **62** .... JoshBaudains(7) 5 50
(Sylvester Kirk) *in tch: rdn along 3f out: drvn and no hdwy fnl 2f* **5/1**[3]

000- **6** 4 1/2 **Gadreel (IRE)**[17] 4457 4-8-6 **46** oh1 ....(p) RaulDaSilva(3) 1 25
(Anthony Middleton) *dwlt: sn in tch: hdwy to chse ldrs 5f out: rdn along 3f out: hld whn n.m.r and sltly hmpd 2f out: sn one pce* **50/1**

0-00 **7** 4 1/2 **Spanish Trail**[23] 3687 4-8-9 **46** oh1 .... FrankieMcDonald 6 14
(Christopher Kellett) *a towards rr* **100/1**

0-60 **8** 5 **Queen Cassiopeia**[73] 2133 4-8-5 **47** .... DannyBrock(5) 9 3
(J R Jenkins) *s.i.s and in rr: hdwy on inner 3f out: rdn along over 2f out: sn n.m.r and wknd* **28/1**

6-00 **9** 7 **Aureolin Gulf**[160] 587 4-8-13 **50** .... ShaneKelly 2
(Andrew Hollinshead) *t.k.h: chsd ldrs on inner tl led after 2f: rdn along 4f out: hdd 3f out: wkng whn n.m.r and hmpd 2f out: sn bhd* **25/1**

1m 43.06s (-5.94) **Going Correction** -0.675s/f (Hard) course record
WFA 3 from 4yo+ 8lb **9** Ran SP% **112.4**
Speed ratings (Par 101): **102,98,97,95,93 88,84,79,72**
toteswingers 1&2 £5.80, 2&3 £4.90, 1&3 £3.60 CSF £98.59 CT £331.02 TOTE £6.70: £2.40, £5.10, £1.10; EX 59.10 Trifecta £207.00 Pool: £3106.02 - 11.24 winning units..
Owner K Nicholls **Bred** Keith Nicholls **Trained** Edwinstowe, Notts

FOCUS
A relatively weak race, even accounting for the modest grade, and it served up something of a slow-motion finish. The winner is rated to this year's form.

4504 32REDBET.COM H'CAP (DIV II) 1m 75y
5:50 (5:51) (Class 6) (0-65,64) 3-Y-O+ **£2,045** (£603; £302) **Stalls** Centre

Form RPR

0-53 **1** **Enriching (USA)**[21] 3788 5-9-12 **62** .... ShaneKelly 7 71
(Gary Harrison) *in tch: hdwy 3f out: rdn to ld jst over 1f out: clr ins fnl f* **11/4**[2]

0024 **2** 2 **Club House (IRE)**[17] 3927 3-9-1 **64** .... RobertTart(5) 5 66
(Robert Mills) *dwlt and in rr: hdwy over 3f out: effrt 2f out: sn rdn and n.m.r over 1f out: drvn and kpt on fnl f* **3/1**[3]

025 **3** nk **Action Front (USA)**[13] 4071 5-8-9 **52** ....(v) AdamMcLean(7) 6 55
(Derek Shaw) *hld up towards rr: hdwy on outer 3f out: rdn to chse ldrs 2f out and sn ev ch: drvn over 1f out and kpt on same pce* **5/2**[1]

/0-0 **4** 2 **Secret Lodge**[14] 4013 5-8-9 **45** .... AndrewMullen 2 44
(Garry Woodward) *led: pushed along 3f out: rdn 2f out: drvn and hdd jst over 1f out: wknd fnl f* **50/1**

5126 **5** 1 1/2 **Chosen Forever**[104] 1394 8-9-7 **57** ....(p) DavidNolan 8 52
(Geoffrey Oldroyd) *hld up in tch: swtchd wd and hdwy wl over 2f out: sn rdn and plugged on: nvr rchd ldrs* **7/1**

100- **6** 1/2 **First Glance**[273] 7222 4-8-7 **48** .... TobyAtkinson(5) 9 42
(Michael Appleby) *t.k.h: chsd ldng pair: hdwy and cl up 4f out: rdn along wl over 2f out: drvn and wandered wl over 1f out: sn wknd* **8/1**

0000 **7** nk **Miss Chardonay**[36] 3252 6-8-9 **45** ....(t) JimmyQuinn 1 38
(Mandy Rowland) *chsd ldrs on inner: pushed along 3f out: rdn over 2f out: sn swtchd rt and wknd* **50/1**

-040 **8** *35* **Aussie Blue (IRE)**[25] 3630 9-9-9 **59**............................ MichaelStainton 3
(Charles Pogson) *chsd ldr: rdn along 4f out: sn wknd and bhd whn eased over 1f out* **25/1**

1m 45.0s (-4.00) **Going Correction** -0.675s/f (Hard)
WFA 3 from 4yo+ 8lb **8** Ran SP% **111.6**
Speed ratings (Par 101): **93,91,90,88,87 86,86,51**
toteswingers 1&2 £3.30, 2&3 £2.20, 1&3 £2.50 CSF £10.80 CT £21.24 TOTE £3.30: £1.70, £1.60, £1.20; EX 13.20 Trifecta £39.20 Pool: £1017.40 - 19.43 winning units..
Owner Franconson Partners **Bred** Adena Springs **Trained** Newmarket, Suffolk

FOCUS
The second division of this handicap looked marginally stronger than the first and there was plenty to like about the winning effort.
T/Plt: £10.80 to a £1 stake. Pool of £35441.81- 2377.27 winning tickets. T/Qpdt: £3.80 to a £1 stake. Pool of £3362.09 - 651.80 winning tickets. JR

4134 PONTEFRACT (L-H)
Friday, July 19

OFFICIAL GOING: Good to firm (7.8)
Wind: light across Weather: Cloudy, hot

4505 COUNTRYWIDE FREIGHT MAIDEN AUCTION STKS 6f
6:30 (6:32) (Class 4) 2-Y-O **£4,528** (£1,347; £673; £336) **Stalls** Low

Form RPR
02 **1** **Treaty Of Paris (IRE)**[19] 3857 2-8-11 0.................... FergusSweeney 1 86
(Henry Candy) *mde all: rdn over 1f out: kpt on to go clr* **4/6**[1]

54 **2** *5* **Heroique (IRE)**[13] 4073 2-8-8 0.. DavidAllan 10 67
(Tim Easterby) *prom: rdn over 2f out: kpt on one pce: no ch w wnr fnl f* **16/1**

3 *1 ½* **Braidley (IRE)** 2-8-11 0.. PJMcDonald 6 65+
(James Bethell) *dwlt: hld up: stl plenty to do over 1f out: r.o wl fnl f: edgd lft: nrst fin* **33/1**

04 **4** *1 ½* **Dry Your Eyes (IRE)**[8] 4215 2-8-8 0........................ SilvestreDeSousa 7 57
(Mark Johnston) *chsd ldrs: rdn 1/2-way: outpcd 2f out: plugged on fnl f* **5/1**[2]

5 *1 ¾* **Aeolus** 2-8-9 0.. RoystonFfrench 3 53
(Ed McMahon) *dwlt: sn chsd ldrs: rdn over 2f out: grad wknd fnl f* **7/1**[3]

6 **6** *nk* **Moving Waves (IRE)**[26] 3605 2-8-9 0 ow1........................ RobertWinston 13 52
(Ollie Pears) *midfield on outer: pushed along over 1f out: kpt on: nvr threatened* **66/1**

60 **7** *1 ¾* **Sassy Brown (IRE)**[11] 4115 2-8-6 0.......................... DuranFentiman 9 43
(Tim Easterby) *in tch: pushed along 1/2-way: wknd over 1f out* **80/1**

06 **8** *½* **Drinkuptrig (IRE)**[11] 4121 2-8-13 0............................ PaulMulrennan 14 49+
(Stuart Williams) *hld up: pushed along and sme hdwy over 1f out: nvr threatened ldrs* **25/1**

0 **9** *3 ¾* **Arrowzone**[28] 3536 2-8-13 0.. MickyFenton 11 37
(Garry Moss) *hld up: nvr threatened* **80/1**

0 **10** *2 ¾* **Nip A Bear**[64] 2382 2-8-11 0... WilliamCarson 12 26
(John Holt) *midfield on outer: wknd 2f out* **66/1**

5 **11** *7* **Good Morning Lady**[15] 3978 2-8-6 0.............................. SamHitchcott 2
(Mick Channon) *midfield on inner: rdn over 2f out: wknd over 1f out* **14/1**

0 **12** *¾* **Hoof's So Lucky**[13] 4046 2-8-8 0.................................. JamesSullivan 8
(Michael Easterby) *hld up in midfield: rdn over 2f out: sn wknd* **33/1**

0 **13** *1 ½* **Jacbequick**[24] 3648 2-8-9 0.. BarryMcHugh 4
(Karen Tutty) *slowly away: a bhd* **66/1**

1m 18.51s (1.61) **Going Correction** +0.25s/f (Good) **13** Ran SP% **118.4**
Speed ratings (Par 96): **99,92,90,88,86 85,83,82,77,73 64,63,61**
toteswingers 1&2 £3.20, 2&3 £58.20, 1&3 £11.40 CSF £13.05 TOTE £1.50: £1.02, £3.30, £11.50; EX 9.80 Trifecta £190.90 Pool: £1773.66 - 6.96 winning units..
Owner One Too Many Partners **Bred** John Malone **Trained** Kingston Warren, Oxon

FOCUS
False rail between 6f bend and Winning Post added about 16yds to advertised distances. Not much depth to this maiden and nothing got into it from off the pace. The easy winner was the clear pre-race pick.

4506 TOTEPOOL FILLIES' H'CAP 1m 4f 8y
7:00 (7:00) (Class 4) (0-85,78) 3-Y-O+ **£5,175** (£1,540; £769; £384) **Stalls** Low

Form RPR
1211 **1** **Special Meaning**[6] 4293 3-9-6 **78** 6ex...................... SilvestreDeSousa 1 92+
(Mark Johnston) *mde all: rdn over 2f out: firmly in command over 1f out: kpt on* **10/11**[1]

1 **2** *3 ¾* **Java Rose**[25] 3618 4-9-11 **71**.. FergusSweeney 5 79+
(Henry Candy) *hld up: hdwy over 4f out: rdn to chse wnr over 2f out: kpt on but no ch w wnr fr over 1f out* **10/1**[3]

-233 **3** *3 ¼* **Playbill**[14] 4023 3-9-2 **74**..(v) FrannyNorton 2 77
(Sir Michael Stoute) *trckd ldr: rdn over 2f out: sn one pce in 3rd* **7/4**[2]

0023 **4** *27* **Maybeagrey**[20] 3814 4-9-9 **69**.. DuranFentiman 4 29
(Tim Easterby) *t.k.h early: hld up in tch: rdn over 3f out: sn wknd* **16/1**

3216 **5** *16* **Looks Like Rain**[14] 4015 4-9-11 **71**............................(p) BarryMcHugh 3 5
(Brian Ellison) *slowly away: hld up: hdwy to trck ldr over 7f out: wknd qckly 3f out: eased* **20/1**

2m 40.51s (-0.29) **Going Correction** +0.175s/f (Good)
WFA 3 from 4yo 12lb **5** Ran SP% **108.5**
Speed ratings (Par 102): **107,104,102,84,73**
CSF £10.30 TOTE £3.10: £1.10, £3.10; EX 6.70 Trifecta £15.00 Pool: £900.69 - 44.76 winning units..
Owner Newsells Park Stud **Bred** Newsells Park Stud **Trained** Middleham Moor, N Yorks

FOCUS
This looked quite a competitive little handicap despite the small field, but it became a one-horse race with the winner granted a pretty soft lead. This confirmed the runner-up's maiden win was no fluke.

4507 BETFRED H'CAP 5f
7:35 (7:37) (Class 3) (0-95,91) 3-Y-O+
£9,337 (£2,796; £1,398; £699; £349; £175) **Stalls** Low

Form RPR
6305 **1** **Another Wise Kid (IRE)**[23] 3682 5-9-5 **84**...................... MickyFenton 4 93
(Paul Midgley) *midfield: pushed along 1/2-way: hdwy over 1f out: led ins fnl f: kpt on wl* **6/1**[3]

0-50 **2** *2 ¼* **Singeur (IRE)**[65] 2366 6-9-11 **90**.................................. RobertWinston 11 91
(Robin Bastiman) *dwlt: hld up: rdn 1/2-way: hdwy on outer over 1f out: kpt on: wnt 2nd fnl 50yds* **11/1**

2500 **3** *1 ¼* **Oldjoesaid**[13] 4047 9-8-13 **78**.. PJMcDonald 6 74
(Paul Midgley) *chsd ldrs: rdn 1/2-way: ev ch ins fnl f: one pce* **25/1**

2005 **4** *nk* **Lenny Bee**[13] 4047 7-8-13 **78**...................................(t) RoystonFfrench 5 73
(Garry Moss) *prom: towards inner: rdn 1/2-way: one pce* **16/1**

0000 **5** *1* **Silvanus (IRE)**[20] 3802 8-9-3 **82**................................ RussKennemore 9 74
(Paul Midgley) *led narrowly towards outer: rdn 1/2-way: hdd ins fnl f: wknd* **16/1**

0-05 **6** *½* **Perfect Blossom**[18] 3892 6-8-13 **83**.............................. SladeO'Hara[(5)] 10 73
(Alan Berry) *slowly away: hld up in rr: pushed along 1/2-way: kpt on fnl f: nvr threatened* **20/1**

0010 **7** *1 ½* **Noodles Blue Boy**[13] 4047 7-8-12 **77**.....................(p) SilvestreDeSousa 8 62
(Ollie Pears) *pressed ldr: rdn 1/2-way: wknd ins fnl f* **20/1**

2000 **8** *2* **Captain Dunne (IRE)**[21] 3776 8-9-12 **91**...................................... DavidAllan 2 68+
(Tim Easterby) *stdd s: hld up: nvr threatened* **3/1**[1]

2052 **9** *shd* **Flash City (ITY)**[13] 4047 5-9-2 **81**..............................(vt) PaulMulrennan 1 58
(Bryan Smart) *dwlt: hld up: nvr threatened* **11/2**[2]

5340 **10** *hd* **Fratellino**[8] 4217 6-9-4 **90**..(t) AaronJones[(7)] 3 66
(Alan McCabe) *sn pushed along in midfield: wknd over 1f out* **12/1**

1m 3.61s (0.31) **Going Correction** +0.25s/f (Good) **10** Ran SP% **95.8**
Speed ratings (Par 107): **107,103,101,100,99 98,96,92,92,92**
toteswingers 1&2 £7.10, 2&3 £53.40, 1&3 £18.60 CSF £44.12 TOTE £5.30: £1.90, £3.60, £3.80; EX 41.80 Trifecta £334.50 Part won. Pool: £446.06 - 0.22 winning units..
Owner Michael Ng **Bred** Paul Kavanagh **Trained** Westow, N Yorks

FOCUS
Competitive stuff but they went hard up front and the pace didn't hold up. A 3lb best from the winner and the form could be rated up to 3lb higher.

4508 COLSTROPE CUP H'CAP 1m 4y
8:05 (8:06) (Class 4) (0-85,83) 3-Y-O **£5,175** (£1,540; £769; £384) **Stalls** Low

Form RPR
2133 **1** **Henry The Aviator (USA)**[7] 4258 3-9-7 **83**.............. SilvestreDeSousa 4 93+
(Mark Johnston) *mde all: rdn over 1f out: drvn ins fnl f: kpt on wl* **11/10**[1]

5315 **2** *2* **Ready (IRE)**[14] 4007 3-8-13 **80**................................(p) JustinNewman[(5)] 1 85
(Garry Moss) *hld up: hdwy over 2f out: rdn to chse wnr appr fnl f: kpt on but a hld* **8/1**

552 **3** *shd* **Bold Prediction (IRE)**[20] 3828 3-9-4 **80**...................... RobertWinston 6 85
(Mrs K Burke) *trckd ldng pair: rdn over 2f out: ev ch appr fnl f: one pce* **6/1**[2]

1352 **4** *¾* **Correggio**[24] 3650 3-8-5 **67**.. PJMcDonald 2 70
(Micky Hammond) *hld up in tch: rdn and outpcd over 2f out: kpt on ins fnl f: nvr threatened* **18/1**

-124 **5** *½* **Freeport**[15] 3995 3-9-1 **77**... PaulMulrennan 7 79
(Brian Meehan) *half-rrd s: hld up in tch: rdn and outpcd over 2f out: kpt on ins fnl f: nvr threatened* **13/2**[3]

6203 **6** *3 ¼* **Shearian**[10] 4140 3-8-2 **64** oh1.................................... RoystonFfrench 3 58
(Tracy Waggott) *trckd ldng pair: rdn over 2f out: wknd over 1f out* **12/1**

5021 **7** *hd* **Super Cookie**[15] 3995 3-8-4 **66**... WilliamCarson 5 60
(Philip McBride) *prom: rdn over 2f out: wknd fnl f* **7/1**

1m 46.58s (0.68) **Going Correction** +0.175s/f (Good) **7** Ran SP% **111.8**
Speed ratings (Par 102): **103,101,100,100,99 96,96**
toteswingers 1&2 £4.00, 2&3 £3.30, 1&3 £2.00 CSF £10.12 TOTE £1.40: £1.10, £5.40; EX 11.20 Trifecta £35.70 Pool: £945.93 - 19.82 winning units..
Owner Crone Stud Farms Ltd **Bred** Summer Wind Farm **Trained** Middleham Moor, N Yorks

FOCUS
A fair handicap with the winner again making all on this pace-favouring track. He's a typically progressive Johnston 3yo.

4509 HIGHBANK STUD MAIDEN H'CAP 1m 2f 6y
8:35 (8:37) (Class 5) (0-70,70) 3-Y-O+ **£3,234** (£962; £481; £240) **Stalls** Low

Form RPR
-436 **1** **Arlecchino (IRE)**[29] 3502 3-9-4 **70**..........................(b[1]) RoystonFfrench 1 77
(Ed McMahon) *trckd ldng pair: rdn over 2f out: led over 1f out: styd on* **7/2**[2]

046 **2** *3* **Qibtee (FR)**[18] 3907 3-8-10 **62**.. SamHitchcott 5 63
(Mick Channon) *w ldr: rdn to ld over 2f out: hdd over 1f out: one pce* **15/2**

0500 **3** *3* **Inovate (IRE)**[20] 3809 3-8-0 **52** oh4...........................(b) DuranFentiman 2 47
(Tim Easterby) *dwlt: racd keenly: sn midfield: rdn over 2f out: kpt on to go 3rd appr fnl f: one pce* **16/1**

0050 **4** *2 ¾* **Azabitmour (FR)**[41] 3129 3-8-12 **64**.....................(v[1]) SilvestreDeSousa 3 54
(John Best) *trckd ldng pair: rdn and outpcd over 2f out: plugged on fr over 1f out* **13/2**[3]

0-04 **5** *5* **Margo Channing**[20] 3814 4-8-9 **51** oh2............................ PJMcDonald 6 32
(Micky Hammond) *hld up: pushed along over 3f out: nvr threatened* **16/1**

5506 **6** *6* **Nonaynever**[11] 4109 5-8-9 **51** oh2.................................... JamesSullivan 8 20
(Ruth Carr) *hld up in rr: nvr threatened* **7/1**

3333 **7** *1 ¼* **Peter's Friend**[25] 3642 4-9-8 **64**...................................... PaulMulrennan 4 31
(Michael Herrington) *led narrowly: rdn whn hdd over 2f out: sn wknd* **11/4**[1]

2305 **8** *12* **High Time Too (IRE)**[36] 3251 3-9-4 **70**..................(b[1]) RobertWinston 7 14
(Hugo Palmer) *midfield: rdn over 2f out: wknd over 1f out: eased* **13/2**[3]

2m 14.85s (1.15) **Going Correction** +0.175s/f (Good)
WFA 3 from 4yo+ 10lb **8** Ran SP% **111.6**
Speed ratings (Par 103): **102,99,97,95,91 86,85,75**
toteswingers 1&2 £4.40, 2&3 £18.30, 1&3 £13.10 CSF £28.18 TOTE £5.00: £1.90, £1.60, £3.90; EX 44.70 Trifecta £391.70 Pool: £867.67 - 1.66 winning units..
Owner The LAM Partnership **Bred** Airlie Stud **Trained** Lichfield, Staffs

FOCUS
A very moderate race in which the winner is rated back towards his better 2yo form.

4510 MOOR TOP FARM HEMSWORTH FARM SHOP H'CAP 6f
9:05 (9:05) (Class 5) (0-75,73) 3-Y-O+ **£3,234** (£962; £481; £240) **Stalls** Low

Form RPR
5106 **1** **Adam's Ale**[21] 3778 4-9-6 **69**.. MickyFenton 7 77
(Paul Midgley) *prom on outer: rdn over 2f out: led over 1f out: jnd ins fnl f: kpt on* **16/1**

0442 **2** *nk* **Holy Angel (IRE)**[13] 4051 4-8-11 **67**..................(e) RachelRichardson[(7)] 6 74
(Tim Easterby) *racd keenly: hld up: smooth hdwy on outer 1/2-way: pushed along to chal over 1f out: upsides ins fnl f: one pce: hld nr fin* **13/2**[3]

0012 **3** *2 ¾* **Ayasha**[17] 3934 3-8-11 **70**... JustinNewman[(5)] 5 67
(Bryan Smart) *led narrowly: rdn whn hdd over 1f out: no ex fnl f* **7/2**[2]

1406 **4** *¾* **Who's Shirl**[8] 4198 7-9-7 **70**...................................... PaulMulrennan 4 66
(Chris Fairhurst) *hld up in rr: rdn over 2f out: kpt on fnl f: nrst fin* **15/2**

5123 **5** *shd* **Mutafaakir (IRE)**[15] 3980 4-9-10 **73**.............................. PJMcDonald 1 68
(Ruth Carr) *hld up: pushed along and stl plenty to do over 1f out: kpt on one pce fnl f* **11/8**[1]

6460 **6** *1 ¼* **Diamond Blue**[13] 4047 5-9-2 **65**................................(p) SilvestreDeSousa 3 56
(Richard Whitaker) *chsd ldrs: rdn over 2f out: wknd fnl f* **9/1**

2145 **7** *15* **Secret City (IRE)**[22] 3741 7-9-8 **71**..............................(b) RobertWinston 2 14
(Robin Bastiman) *trckd ldrs: rdn over 2f out: sn wknd: eased* **11/1**

1m 17.93s (1.03) **Going Correction** +0.25s/f (Good)
WFA 3 from 4yo+ 5lb **7** Ran SP% **113.6**
Speed ratings (Par 103): **103,102,98,97,97 96,76**
toteswingers 1&2 £16.60, 2&3 £5.60, 1&3 £7.90 CSF £111.48 TOTE £17.90: £6.50, £3.90; EX 139.40 Trifecta £292.30 Pool: £793.81 - 2.03 winning units..
Owner Mrs M Hills **Bred** Mrs M J Hills **Trained** Westow, N Yorks

FOCUS
Nothing got into this from off the pace and the front two had it between them from the top of the straight.Straightforward form, the winner a minor improver.
T/Plt: £295.00 to a £1 stake. Pool of £46023.99 - 113.86 winning tickets. T/Qpdt: £203.00 to a £1 stake. Pool of £3306.70 - 12.05 winning tickets. AS

4476 HAYDOCK (L-H)

Saturday, July 20

OFFICIAL GOING: Good to firm (watered; 8.1)
Wind: Light behind Weather: Cloudy with sunny periods

4511 TUSCAR UTILITIES & CIVIL ENGINEERING NURSERY H'CAP 5f
6:25 (6:25) (Class 5) 2-Y-O **£2,911** (£866; £432; £216) **Stalls** Centre

Form RPR
0401 **1** **Zalzilah**[4] 4363 2-9-13 **85** 6ex..(p) PaulMulrennan 1 88
(James Tate) *led: jnd and rdn wl over 1f out: edgd lft and narrowly hdd ent fnl f: sn drvn and rallied to ld again last 75yds: edgd rt nr fin* **5/6**[1]

6313 **2** *nk* **Innocently (IRE)**[8] 4261 2-8-12 **73**.................................... JulieBurke(3) 3 75
(David O'Meara) *chsd wnr: cl up 2f out: sn rdn and tk slt advantage ent fnl f: drvn and hdd last 75yds: no ex towards fin* **7/2**[2]

034 **3** *1 1/4* **Emily Davison (IRE)**[24] 3681 2-8-6 **64**.......................... AndrewMullen 5 61
(David C Griffiths) *chsd ldrs: hdwy to chse ldng pair 2f out: rdn over 1f out: styng on whn edgd lft ins fnl f: kpt on same pce* **20/1**

450 **4** *3/4* **Shelley's Choice (IRE)**[27] 3605 2-8-7 **65**.......... RichardKingscote 4 60
(Tom Dascombe) *chsd ldng pair: pushed along and outpcd 1/2-way: sn rdn: styd on fnl f: nrst fin* **11/2**[3]

04 **5** *nse* **Red Forever**[28] 3568 2-8-0 **58** oh1.. PaulQuinn 2 53
(Alan Berry) *in rr: pushed along over 2f out: sn rdn: kpt on fnl f: nrst fin* **20/1**

5623 **6** *1/2* **Evie Jay (IRE)**[3] 4399 2-8-11 **72**....................................... RaulDaSilva(3) 6 65
(Paul Green) *racd wd: chsd ldrs: hdwy over 2f out: sn rdn and one pce fr over 1f out* **8/1**

1m 0.66s (-0.14) **Going Correction** -0.35s/f (Firm) **6** Ran SP% **112.8**
Speed ratings (Par 94): **87,86,84,83,83 82**
toteswingers 1&2 £1.30, 1&3 £5.30, 2&3 £16.00 CSF £4.06 TOTE £1.70: £1.20, £2.10; EX 3.50 Trifecta £24.00 Pool: £1192.55 - 37.15 winning units..
Owner Sheikh Juma Dalmook Al Maktoum **Bred** Heather Raw **Trained** Newmarket, Suffolk

FOCUS
The official ratings shown are estimated and for information only. All races on Inner home straight and races on Round course increased in distance by 1yd. There was no great strength in depth here, but the winner is above average for a nursery performer and the others can all make their mark.

4512 INSPIRED ENERGY H'CAP 1m 6f
7:00 (7:00) (Class 4) (0-80,80) 4-Y-O+ **£5,175** (£1,540; £769; £384) **Stalls** Low

Form RPR
5422 **1** **Zenafire**[18] 3916 4-8-4 **63**..(p) PaulQuinn 4 74+
(Andrew Hollinshead) *trckd ldrs: smooth hdwy 4f out: led 2f out: rdn clr ent fnl f: styd on wl* **10/3**[2]

0021 **2** *3* **Merchant Of Dubai**[36] 3284 8-9-2 **75**................................ GrahamLee 8 82
(Jim Goldie) *trckd ldr: hdwy and cl up over 4f out: chal wl over 3f out: led briefly over 2f out: sn rdn and hdd: drvn and kpt on same pce fnl f* **9/4**[1]

0506 **3** *2* **Kiama Bay (IRE)**[21] 3804 7-9-7 **80**.................................... BrianHughes 5 84
(Richard Fahey) *trckd ldng pair: effrt 3f out: rdn along over 2f out: drvn and edgd lft fnl f: no imp* **13/2**

6210 **4** *6* **Bollin Greta**[8] 4262 8-9-3 **76**... DuranFentiman 3 72
(Tim Easterby) *hld up in tch: hdwy over 4f out: rdn along wl over 2f out: sn drvn and one pce* **14/1**

1444 **5** *1* **Hallstatt (IRE)**[21] 3807 7-8-9 **68**...............................(t) RichardKingscote 7 62
(John Mackie) *trckd ldng pair: pushed along on outer 4f out: rdn 3f out: drvn and one pce fnl 2f* **9/1**

6455 **6** *hd* **Royal Peculiar**[9] 4202 5-9-5 **78**....................................... AndrewMullen 1 72
(Michael Appleby) *led: rdn along and jnd wl over 3f out: drvn and hdd over 2f out: sn wknd* **5/1**[3]

14-0 **7** *7* **Jawaab (IRE)**[11] 2673 9-8-7 **73**.. EvaMoscrop(7) 2 57
(Philip Kirby) *a in rr* **25/1**

-006 **8** *20* **Rock A Doodle Doo (IRE)**[36] 2590 6-9-5 **78**.............. PaulMulrennan 6 34
(Sally Hall) *a in rr: outpcd and bhd fnl 2f* **9/1**

2m 56.6s (-5.40) **Going Correction** -0.35s/f (Firm) **8** Ran SP% **114.4**
Speed ratings (Par 105): **101,99,98,94,94 94,90,78**
toteswingers 1&2 £1.40, 1&3 £3.00, 2&3 £5.00 CSF £11.27 CT £44.61 TOTE £4.90: £1.80, £1.30, £2.30; EX 10.50 Trifecta £46.20 Pool: £792.75 - 12.84 winning units..
Owner E Coquelin R Moseley **Bred** R J R Moseley & Mrs E Coquelin **Trained** Upper Longdon, Staffs

FOCUS
This was a middling stayers' event, won by a maiden who was suited by the greater test of stamina. The winner has more to offer.

4513 EXCALON LTD EBF MAIDEN STKS 7f
7:30 (7:31) (Class 5) 2-Y-O **£2,911** (£866; £432; £216) **Stalls** Low

Form RPR
1 **Silent Bullet (IRE)** 2-9-5 0.. DaneO'Neill 2 81+
(Saeed bin Suroor) *hld up: hdwy on inner to trck ldng pair 4f out: swtchd rt and hdwy 2f out: led jst over 1f out: rdn: rn green and edgd lft jst ins fnl f: kpt on wl: readily* **5/4**[1]

06 **2** *2 1/2* **Veya (USA)**[15] 4026 2-9-5 0.. RichardKingscote 1 72
(Ed Walker) *cl up on inner: led 1/2-way: rdn along 2f out: hdd appr fnl f: drvn and kpt on: no ch w wnr* **6/4**[2]

3 *5* **Archibald Thorburn (IRE)** 2-9-5 0.. GrahamLee 7 58+
(Ed McMahon) *towards rr: hdwy on outer 3f out: pushed along wl over 1f out: rdn and kpt on fnl f* **12/1**

05 **4** *2 1/2* **Aristocracy**[7] 4304 2-9-5 0.. SamHitchcott 5 51
(Mick Channon) *chsd ldrs: rdn along over 2f out: drvn and wknd over 1f out* **25/1**

0 **5** *1 3/4* **Rockie Road (IRE)**[5] 4351 2-9-2 0............................... RaulDaSilva(3) 6 46
(Paul Green) *sn led: pushed along and hdd 1/2-way: cl up tl rdn along 2f out and sn wknd* **16/1**

6 *3 1/2* **Strassman** 2-9-5 0.. JoeFanning 4 37
(Mark Johnston) *chsd ldrs: rdn along 4f out: sn lost pl and bhd fnl 2f* **6/1**[3]

00 **7** *24* **Paparima (IRE)**[26] 3624 2-9-0 0...................................... PaulMulrennan 3
(Paul Green) *green and hung rt bnd after 1f: hdwy on inner 1/2-way: rdn along wl over 2f out: sn wknd: bhd and eased fnl f* **66/1**

1m 28.44s (-2.26) **Going Correction** -0.35s/f (Firm) **7** Ran SP% **117.6**
Speed ratings (Par 94): **98,95,89,86,84 80,53**
toteswingers 1&2 £1.10, 1&3 £2.90, 2&3 £2.90 CSF £3.56 TOTE £2.10: £1.30, £1.60; EX 3.60 Trifecta £15.20 Pool: £874.38 - 43.02 winning units..
Owner Godolphin **Bred** Darley **Trained** Newmarket, Suffolk
■ Stewards' Enquiry : Dane O'Neill caution: careless riding.

FOCUS
There were some well-bred runners in this maiden, but the debutant winner outclassed the opposition. He looks the type to rate higher.

4514 MEDIA Q LTD CONDITIONS STKS 7f
8:00 (8:00) (Class 3) 3-Y-O+ **£8,086** (£2,406; £1,202; £601) **Stalls** Low

Form RPR
4045 **1** **Set The Trend**[28] 3564 7-9-9 98...................................... DanielTudhope 2 107
(David O'Meara) *cl up: led over 3f out: rdn and hdd 2f out: drvn and rallied ent fnl f: kpt on to ld last 100yds* **5/2**[3]

5-51 **2** *1 1/2* **Magic Destiny**[13] 4097 4-8-10 88............................ RichardKingscote 1 90
(Mrs K Burke) *trckd ldng pair: smooth hdwy to ld 2f out: shkn up over 1f out: rdn ent fnl f: hdd and no ex last 100yds* **7/4**[2]

00-0 **3** *7* **Bannock (IRE)**[142] 838 4-9-1 106.. GrahamLee 3 76
(Saeed bin Suroor) *sn led: hdd over 3f out: rdn 2f out: drvn and wknd over 1f out* **5/4**[1]

604 **4** *18* **Bix (IRE)**[18] 3931 3-8-4 47.. JordanHibberd(7) 4 27
(Alan Berry) *a in rr: outpcd and bhd fr wl over 2f out* **66/1**

1m 25.95s (-4.75) **Going Correction** -0.35s/f (Firm) course record
WFA 3 from 4yo+ 7lb **4** Ran SP% **110.9**
Speed ratings (Par 107): **113,111,103,82**
CSF £7.41 TOTE £4.20; EX 8.30 Trifecta £9.10 Pool: £872.11 - 71.84 winning units..
Owner Corbett Stud **Bred** Old Suffolk Stud **Trained** Nawton, N Yorks

FOCUS
There was a disappointing turnout for this, with the two highest-rated runners not at their best in recent races. The race looks confusing from a form perspective. The winner is rated close to last year's C&D win.

4515 MARKET AVENUE RACING H'CAP 1m
8:30 (8:30) (Class 5) (0-75,74) 3-Y-O **£2,911** (£866; £432; £216) **Stalls** Low

Form RPR
2122 **1** **Nurpur (IRE)**[19] 3894 3-9-7 **74**.. DanielTudhope 2 81+
(David O'Meara) *hld up in rr: swtchd rt to outer and hdwy 2f out: rdn to chse ldrs 1f out: drvn and styd on to ld nr fin* **5/2**[1]

4454 **2** *nk* **Gabrial The Thug (FR)**[8] 4251 3-8-12 **65**..................(t) PaulMulrennan 6 71
(Richard Fahey) *cl up: disp ld over 2f out: rdn to ld wl over 1f out: drvn ins fnl f: hdd and no ex nr fin* **7/2**[2]

320- **3** *1 3/4* **Madame Elizabeth**[266] 7406 3-9-3 **70**.................................. GrahamLee 5 72
(Andrew Hollinshead) *trckd ldrs: hdwy over 2f out: rdn over 1f out: n.m.r ins fnl f: kpt on* **9/1**

5006 **4** *2* **Fraserburgh (IRE)**[12] 4119 3-9-1 **68**................................... JoeFanning 4 65
(Mark Johnston) *slt ld: rdn along 3f out: drvn and hdd wl over 1f out: wknd fnl f* **7/2**[2]

-000 **5** *4 1/2* **Switcharooney (IRE)**[19] 3901 3-8-10 **63**............(tp) RichardKingscote 1 50
(Tom Dascombe) *sn pushed along to chse ldng pair on inner: rdn over 3f out: drvn and wknd fnl 2f* **13/2**[3]

4022 **6** *9* **Jullundar (IRE)**[9] 4209 3-9-0 **67**...................................(v) SamHitchcott 3 33
(Mick Channon) *a towards rr: rdn and outpcd fnl 2f* **13/2**[3]

15-0 **7** *2 1/4* **Cardmaster (IRE)**[94] 1612 3-9-3 **70**..................................... DaneO'Neill 8 31
(Eve Johnson Houghton) *chsd ldrs: rdn along wl over 2f out: sn wknd* **25/1**

1m 41.34s (-2.36) **Going Correction** -0.35s/f (Firm) **7** Ran SP% **113.5**
Speed ratings (Par 100): **97,96,94,92,88 79,77**
CSF £11.25 TOTE £3.70: £2.10, £2.10; EX 12.20 Trifecta £76.80 Pool: £528.18 - 5.15 winning units..
Owner Middleham Park Racing XXIX & Partners **Bred** B P Hayes **Trained** Nawton, N Yorks

FOCUS
They went a decent gallop here, which helped the hold-up tactics of the winner. The first two are rated to form.

4516 STEWART AND WOODBRIDGE H'CAP 1m 2f 95y
9:00 (9:00) (Class 5) (0-75,76) 3-Y-O+ **£2,911** (£866; £432; £216) **Stalls** Centre

Form RPR
3121 **1** **Big Thunder**[9] 4194 3-9-5 **76**.. LukeMorris 5 93+
(Sir Mark Prescott Bt) *rdn along s to trck ldr: hdwy and cl up 4f out: led over 3f out: rdn wl over 1f out: drvn fnl f and hld on wl* **1/1**[1]

-114 **2** *1 1/2* **Tajheez (IRE)**[22] 3785 3-9-4 **75**......................................[1] DaneO'Neill 1 89
(Roger Varian) *trckd ldrs: hdwy 3f out: chsd wnr 2f out and sn rdn: drvn ins fnl f: kpt on same pce towards fin* **6/4**[2]

404 **3** *8* **Royal Sea (IRE)**[7] 4287 4-8-5 **59**..............................(be) JoeyHaynes(7) 3 58
(Michael Mullineaux) *trckd ldng pair: effrt over 3f out: rdn along wl over 2f out: drvn and one pce fr wl over 1f out* **16/1**

4151 **4** *1* **Barton Bounty**[13] 4099 6-8-12 **59**... GrahamLee 6 56
(Peter Niven) *in rr: hdwy on outer over 3f out: sn rdn along and n.d* **7/1**[3]

5 *25* **Shukhov (IRE)**[15] 4039 4-9-9 **70**................................(b) DanielTudhope 4 34
(J F Levins, Ire) *set str pce: rdn along and hdd over 3f out: sn wknd* **25/1**

2m 10.81s (-4.69) **Going Correction** -0.35s/f (Firm)
WFA 3 from 4yo+ 10lb **5** Ran SP% **112.2**
Speed ratings (Par 103): **104,102,96,91,71**
CSF £2.83 TOTE £2.00: £1.40, £1.30; EX 2.70 Trifecta £10.90 Pool: £1266.64 - 87.05 winning units..
Owner John Brown & Megan Dennis **Bred** Stanley House Stud **Trained** Newmarket, Suffolk

FOCUS
Two decent sorts fought out the finish of this strongly run race, and both are likely to make further progress, although this is tricky form to pin down.
T/Plt: £21.00 to a £1 stake. Pool of £53,538.26 - 1860.81 winning tickets. T/Qpdt: £10.40 to a £1 stake. Pool of £2676.18 - 189.00 winning tickets. JR

4404 LINGFIELD (L-H)

Saturday, July 20

OFFICIAL GOING: Turf course - firm (good to firm in places; watered; 9.4); all-weather course - standard

Wind: light, half against Weather: cloudy, brighter spells, muggy

4517 ITM 10TH ANNIVERSARY H'CAP 7f

5:30 (5:32) (Class 6) (0-65,70) 3-Y-0+ £2,045 (£603; £302) Stalls High

Form RPR

3333 1 **My Own Way Home**[18] 3920 5-9-3 54 AdamKirby 3 64
(David Evans) *mde all and sn crossed to r against stands' rail: rdn clr over 1f out: r.o wl: comf* 5/1[3]

0001 2 2 1/4 **Dana's Present**[8] 4241 4-10-5 70 PatCosgrave 5 74
(George Baker) *chsd wnr thrght: rdn and unable qck over 1f out: styd on same pce but hld 2nd fnl f* 8/1

0-32 3 shd **Takitwo**[43] 3052 10-9-7 58 SebSanders 6 62
(Geoffrey Deacon) *in tch in last trio and niggled along early: nt clr run 2f out: swtchd rt and hdwy 1f out: kpt on and battling for 2nd fnl 100yds: no threat to wnr* 8/1

0524 4 1 3/4 **Fairy Mist (IRE)**[18] 3926 6-8-6 46 SimonPearce(3) 7 45
(John Bridger) *chsd ldrs: rdn and effrt 2f out: outpcd by wnr over 1f out: wknd fnl 100yds* 25/1

0413 5 2 1/4 **Hamis Al Bin (IRE)**[9] 4197 4-9-3 61 WillPettis(7) 2 54
(Milton Bradley) *stdd and swtchd rt after s: t.k.h: hld up in tch in midfield: effrt and rdn to chse ldrs 2f out: wknd ent fnl f* 8/1

4035 6 3 3/4 **Surrey Dream (IRE)**[18] 3922 4-8-9 46 oh1 (tp) KierenFox 1 29
(John Bridger) *in tch towards rr: rdn 1/2-way: drvn and no rspnse over 2f out: sn wl btn* 20/1

0-20 7 2 **Wise Venture (IRE)**[59] 2565 4-9-5 61 MichaelJMMurphy(5) 9 38
(Alan Jarvis) *in tch in midfld: sltly hmpd and lost pl after 2f: sn pushed along and nvr gng wl in rr after: drvn and wknd over 2f out* 7/4[1]

1002 8 2 1/4 **Flavius Victor (IRE)**[43] 3051 4-10-0 65 GeorgeBaker 8 36
(Patrick Chamings) *t.k.h: chsd ldrs: stdd bk and swtchd rt to trck ldrs after 2f: hung lft and btn over 1f out: bhd and eased wl ins fnl f* 7/2[2]

1m 22.21s (-1.09) **Going Correction** -0.10s/f (Good)
WFA 3 from 4yo+ 7lb 8 Ran SP% **117.2**
Speed ratings (Par 101): **102,99,99,97,94 90,88,85**
toteswingers 1&2 £5.00, 2&3 £5.80, 1&3 £8.40 CSF £45.26 CT £317.68 TOTE £4.30: £1.40, £2.40, £2.70; EX 33.30 Trifecta £96.70 Pool: £1762.40 - 13.66 winning units..
Owner Trevor Gallienne **Bred** Theresa Fitsall **Trained** Pandy, Monmouths

FOCUS
A minor handicap. The pace was not very strong and there was an all-the-way winner, who grabbed the rail. The form is taken at something like face value.

4518 ITM PENSCOPE / IRISH STALLION FARMS EBF MAIDEN STKS 7f

6:00 (6:00) (Class 5) 2-Y-0 £3,067 (£905; £453) Stalls High

Form RPR

03 1 **Faintly (USA)**[32] 3426 2-9-5 0 GeorgeBaker 2 86+
(Amanda Perrett) *mde all: cruised clr on bit over 1f out: v easily: nt extended* 7/4[2]

2 7 **Goleador (USA)** 2-9-5 0 AdamKirby 4 64+
(Marco Botti) *rn green: t.k.h: chsd ldng pair: rdn ent fnl 2f: sn swtchd lft: chsd wnr over jst over 1f out: sn brushed aside but plugged on* 5/4[1]

56 3 6 **The Wallace Line (IRE)**[16] 3972 2-9-5 0 TedDurcan 1 54
(Mick Channon) *taken down early: chsd wnr: rdn 1/2-way: drvn and no ex 2f out: lost 2nd jst over 1f out: wl btn and eased fnl 100yds* 7/2[3]

4 16 **Ormer** 2-8-9 0 DeclanBates(5) 3
(David Evans) *sn rdn and outpcd in rr: lost tch 1/2-way: t.o* 14/1

1m 24.6s (1.30) **Going Correction** -0.10s/f (Good) 4 Ran SP% **109.7**
Speed ratings (Par 94): **88,80,73,54**
CSF £4.40 TOTE £4.20; EX 4.70 Trifecta £6.40 Pool: £779.38 - 91.32 winning units..
Owner K Abdullah **Bred** Juddmonte Farms Inc **Trained** Pulborough, W Sussex

FOCUS
This looked an ordinary small-field maiden but the well-bred winner was quite impressive under a front-running ride against the rail. The race had little depth.

4519 ITM EDAART NURSERY H'CAP 6f

6:35 (6:36) (Class 5) 2-Y-0 £2,726 (£805; £402) Stalls High

Form RPR

4260 1 **Primitorio (IRE)**[8] 4232 2-8-7 66 (b[1]) MartinLane 5 69
(Ralph Beckett) *mde all: rdn 2f out: sustained duel w rival fr over 1f out: r.o wl: jst prevailed* 8/1[3]

516 2 shd **Chord Chart (IRE)**[8] 4232 2-9-7 80 SilvestreDeSousa 3 83
(Saeed bin Suroor) *in tch in midfield: sltly hmpd after 1f out: hdwy to chse ldr and travelling wl ent fnl 2f: rdn and ev ch over 1f out: sustained duel w wnr after: r.o: jst hld* 5/4[1]

5056 3 1/2 **Dovil's Duel (IRE)**[15] 4019 2-8-0 59 (p) KieranO'Neill 1 60
(Rod Millman) *stdd and swtchd rt after s: t.k.h: hld up bhd: swtchd lft and hdwy but stl plenty to do over 1f out: swtchd rt and chsd clr ldrs ins fnl f: swtchd lft and r.o strly fnl 100yds* 16/1

304 4 2 1/2 **Tyrsal (IRE)**[81] 1910 2-8-1 60 NickyMackay 7 53
(Robert Eddery) *racd in last trio: rdn along and outpcd 1/2-way: sme hdwy over 1f out: kpt on fnl f: no threat to ldrs* 25/1

3400 5 nk **Intense Feeling (IRE)**[32] 3424 2-9-2 75 AdamKirby 6 67
(David Evans) *chsd ldrs: rdn and chsd ldng pair 2f out: no ex and btn ent 1f out: wknd ins fnl f* 8/1[3]

001 6 3 3/4 **Cafetiere**[68] 2320 2-9-4 77 ChrisCatlin 4 57
(Paul Cole) *chsd ldrs early: rdn and lost pl 1/2-way: wknd wl over 1f out* 12/1

3244 7 7 **Bonjour Steve**[12] 4121 2-8-9 68 LiamJones 2 26
(J S Moore) *chsd ldr and sn crossed to r nr stands' rail: rdn: hung lft and lost 2nd ent fnl 2f: wknd over 1f out: fdd fnl f* 8/1[3]

31 8 5 **Sakuramachi**[14] 4065 2-8-10 69 TedDurcan 8 11
(Mick Channon) *a in rr: lost tch over 2f out: wl bhd fnl f* 7/2[2]

1m 10.4s (-0.80) **Going Correction** -0.10s/f (Good) 8 Ran SP% **117.4**
Speed ratings (Par 94): **101,100,100,96,96 91,82,75**
toteswingers 1&2 £3.10, 1&3 £16.50, 2&3 £2.80 CSF £19.01 CT £164.94 TOTE £12.20: £3.30, £1.10, £5.50; EX 27.30 Trifecta £392.80 Pool: £1526.32 - 2.91 winning units..
Owner Thurloe Thoroughbreds XXXI **Bred** Manister House Stud **Trained** Kimpton, Hants

FOCUS
There was a tight finish in this nursery and the favourite was just denied. Another winner to bag the rail, but the second was the moral winner.

4520 ITM EASE AUTO ENROLMENT SOLUTION H'CAP 6f

7:10 (7:10) (Class 6) (0-65,64) 3-Y-0+ £2,045 (£603; £302) Stalls High

Form RPR

4002 1 **Song Of Parkes**[21] 3816 6-9-7 64 (p) SladeO'Hara(5) 4 74
(Peter Grayson) *chsd ldrs and swtchd rt to r against stands' rail sn after s: in tch: travelling wl and waiting for gap 2f out: rdn and qcknd to chal 1f out: led ins fnl f: r.o wl* 6/1

00-3 2 1 1/2 **Ghost Train (IRE)**[30] 3499 4-9-3 60 (p) RobertTart(5) 5 65
(Tim McCarthy) *hld up in tch in last pair: switching lft and hdwy over 2f out: rdn and led 1f out: edgd rt and hdd ins fnl f: one pce* 4/1[2]

2542 3 2 3/4 **Proper Charlie**[135] 916 5-8-10 48 KierenFox 1 44
(Lee Carter) *chsd ldrs: rdn to chse ldr 2f out: pressing ldr and unable qck over 1f out: outpcd by ldrs fnl f: kpt on* 6/1

/1-5 4 3/4 **Charismas Birthday (IRE)**[4] 4369 5-8-10 48 (b) CathyGannon 7 42
(Philip M Byrne, Ire) *w ldr tl rdn to ld 2f out: hdd and no ex 1f out: wknd fnl 100yds* 8/1

000 5 2 1/2 **Kasbhom**[63] 2456 3-9-6 63 WilliamCarson 3 49
(Anthony Carson) *in tch in last pair: effrt and hdwy over 2f out: no imp u.p over 1f out: wknd ins fnl f* 20/1

0315 6 shd **The Great Gabrial**[2] 4430 4-9-8 60 (b) SilvestreDeSousa 2 46
(Ian Williams) *chsd ldrs: shuffled bk but stl wl in tch whn swtchd lft and drvn over 1f out: no hdwy: wknd ins fnl f* 7/4[1]

200- 7 10 **Ansells Pride (IRE)**[288] 6837 10-9-7 64 (p) JakePayne(5) 8 18
(Bill Turner) *taken down early: led tl rdn and hdd 2f out: sn btn and dropped out: wknd qckly fnl f* 5/1[3]

1m 10.4s (-0.80) **Going Correction** -0.10s/f (Good)
WFA 3 from 4yo+ 5lb 7 Ran SP% **117.5**
Speed ratings (Par 101): **101,99,95,94,91 90,77**
toteswingers 1&2 £2.80, 1&3 £4.30, 2&3 £4.60 CSF £31.30 CT £152.32 TOTE £7.40: £3.10, £2.40; EX 27.10 Trifecta £153.50 Pool: £1329.36 - 6.49 winning units..
Owner E Grayson **Bred** Joseph Heler **Trained** Formby, Lancs

FOCUS
The leaders went off fast in this handicap and first two came from some way back. The form is rated around the winner's best.

4521 EPORTAL CLAIMING STKS 1m (P)

7:45 (7:46) (Class 6) 3-5-Y-0 £2,045 (£603; £302) Stalls High

Form RPR

0-00 1 **King Torus (IRE)**[7] 4280 5-9-10 80 (b) AdamKirby 1 89
(Jamie Osborne) *mde all: drvn and qcknd clr ent fnl f: hung rt u.p 1f out: a doing enough: rdn out* 8/1

2306 2 1 1/2 **Prince Of Burma (IRE)**[8] 4237 5-8-12 75 (bt) RyanClark(3) 3 77
(Jeremy Gask) *s.i.s and bustled along leaving stalls: sn rcvrd and in midfield: hdwy to chse ldrs whn nt clr run 2f out: drvn to go 3rd over 1f out: chsd wnr ins fnl f: kpt on* 3/1[2]

0022 3 4 **For Shia And Lula (IRE)**[9] 4193 4-9-3 68 (p) ShaneKelly 5 70
(Daniel Mark Loughnane) *trckd ldng pair: nt clr run and hmpd on inner bnd 2f out: sn rdn to chse clr wnr: no imp: lost 2nd and wknd ins fnl f* 10/1

5226 4 1 1/4 **Moment In The Sun**[11] 4149 4-8-4 61 (b) RobertTart(5) 6 59
(David Flood) *t.k.h: chsd ldrs: rdn and nt qckn 2f out: plugged on but wl hld fr over 1f out* 6/1[3]

0-6 5 3 1/4 **Estibdaad (IRE)**[47] 2931 3-8-11 0 SteveDrowne 10 59
(Anthony Honeyball) *s.i.s: bhd tl styd on past btn horses fnl f: nvr trbld ldrs* 20/1

6-00 6 nk **Cio Cio San (IRE)**[18] 3917 3-7-7 60 (p) NoelGarbutt(7) 7 48
(Bill Turner) *in tch in midfield but stuck on outer: drvn and outpcd over 2f out: wl btn over 1f out* 66/1

000- 7 1 **Yasir (USA)**[290] 6776 5-9-3 79 (p) GeorgeBaker 8 56
(Conor Dore) *hld up off the pce in last quartet: shkn up and no rspnse jst over 2f out: n.d* 6/4[1]

8 2 **Watson Sama**[39] 3-8-13 75 (p) SilvestreDeSousa 2 54
(Amy Weaver) *chsd wnr: outpcd and hung rt bnd wl over 1f out: sn wknd* 12/1

-040 9 7 **Play Tiger (FR)**[11] 4152 4-9-0 47 WilliamCarson 9 33
(Peter Hiatt) *s.i.s: a bhd: lost tch wl over 2f out* 50/1

54-0 10 7 **Rioja Day (IRE)**[81] 1900 3-9-2 65 SebSanders 4 25
(J W Hills) *a last quartet: rdn and lost tch wl over 2f out* 20/1

1m 37.78s (-0.42) **Going Correction** +0.15s/f (Slow)
WFA 3 from 4yo+ 8lb 10 Ran SP% **120.2**
Speed ratings (Par 101): **108,106,102,101,98 97,96,94,87,80**
toteswingers 1&2 £6.10, 1&3 £6.50, 2&3 £4.90 CSF £32.22 TOTE £10.50: £2.40, £1.60, £2.90; EX 44.50 Trifecta £62.70 Pool: £1685.66 - 20.13 winning units..King Torus was claimed by Ruth Carr for £15000; Prince of Burma was claimed by David Evans for £6000
Owner Dr Marwan Koukash **Bred** Whisperview Trading Ltd **Trained** Upper Lambourn, Berks

FOCUS
There was a front-running winner in this decent claimer and the first two pulled clear. The winner was not far off last summer's form.

4522 ITM EMEMBER CLASSIFIED (S) STKS 1m 2f (P)

8:15 (8:15) (Class 6) 3-Y-0+ £2,045 (£603; £302) Stalls Low

Form RPR

0031 1 **Matraash (USA)**[10] 4171 7-9-11 68 (bc) ShaneKelly 5 82+
(Daniel Mark Loughnane) *hld up in last pair: trckd ldrs fr 5f out: jnd ldr on bit over 1f out: led ins fnl f and sn cruised clr: nt extended* 10/11[1]

0046 2 2 1/2 **Tartan Trip**[23] 3736 6-9-5 67 LiamTreadwell 4 68
(Luke Dace) *t.k.h: chsd ldr tl led 3f out: rdn over 1f out: sn jnd by cantering wnr: hdd ins fnl f: immediately btn* 7/2[3]

2/04 3 4 **Waahej**[26] 3637 7-9-5 65 ChrisCatlin 1 60
(Peter Hiatt) *broke wl: sn stdd bk and hld up in last pair: hdwy and rdn to press ldrs 2f out: outpcd over 1f out: wknd fnl f* 3/1[2]

0005 4 21 **Vermeyen**[24] 3687 4-9-0 43 DeclanBates(5) 6 18
(Geoffrey Deacon) *t.k.h: sn chsd ldr tl rdn and hdd 3f out: styd pressing ldrs tl wknd qckly over 1f out: fdd bdly fnl f: t.o* 14/1

5006 5 58 **Dark Rumour (IRE)**[5] 4345 3-8-6 22 (v) SimonPearce(3) 3
(John Bridger) *chsd ldrs: rdn after 2f: dropped to last over 4f out: sn lost tch and wl t.o fnl 3f* 33/1

2m 7.83s (1.23) **Going Correction** +0.15s/f (Slow)
WFA 3 from 4yo+ 10lb 5 Ran SP% **109.2**
Speed ratings (Par 101): **101,99,95,79,32**
CSF £4.34 TOTE £1.70: £1.20, £1.50; EX 4.20 Trifecta £7.60 Pool: £570.78 - 55.84 winning units..
Owner Mrs C Loughnane **Bred** Shadwell Farm LLC **Trained** Baldwin's Gate, Staffs

FOCUS
They went a steady pace in this seller but the odds-on favourite was hardly off the bridle and scored with plenty in hand under a confident ride. Not form to be confident about.

4523 E-DATA DICTIONARY FILLIES' H'CAP 1m 2f (P)
8:45 (8:45) (Class 5) (0-75,75) 3-Y-O+ **£3,067** (£905; £453) **Stalls** Low

Form RPR
-613 **1** **Fast Pace**[14] 4076 3-9-3 **74**................................ RobertHavlin 7 82
(Amanda Perrett) *t.k.h: in tch on outer: clsd to press ldrs 3f out: rdn and ev ch 2f out: led 1f out: r.o strly and clr ins fnl f* **9/2**[2]
0-63 **2** 2 ¼ **Mesmerized (IRE)**[50] 2850 3-8-10 **67**................................ NeilCallan 1 70
(Marco Botti) *t.k.h: chsd ldrs: effrt and rdn ent fnl 2f: kpt on u.p fnl f: snatched 2nd last stride* **5/1**[3]
2034 **3** shd **Chrissycross (IRE)**[26] 3635 4-9-6 **67**................................(v) AdamKirby 2 70
(Roger Teal) *in tch in rr: rdn and qcknd on outer to chal over 2f out: ev ch over 1f out: nt pce of wnr ins fnl f: lost 2nd last stride* **10/1**
02-0 **4** 1 **Signature Dish (IRE)**[36] 3292 3-8-12 **69**................................ MartinDwyer 8 70
(Andrew Balding) *t.k.h: chsd ldr: rdn and ev ch jst over 2f out: drvn to ld wl over 1f out: hdd 1f out: outpcd ins fnl f* **9/2**[2]
1405 **5** ¾ **Diletta Tommasa (IRE)**[68] 2331 3-8-7 **64**................................ CathyGannon 4 64
(John Stimpson) *broke wl: sn stdd and hld up in last trio: hdwy u.p ent fnl f: edgd lft and kpt on: no threat to wnr* **33/1**
2144 **6** ¾ **Movementneverlies**[47] 2935 3-9-4 **75**................................ SteveDrowne 3 73
(Charles Hills) *wl in tch in midfield: rdn and effrt jst over 2f out: outpcd over 1f out: wknd ins fnl f* **6/1**
5252 **7** nk **Just Darcy**[19] 3900 3-8-13 **70**................................(p) PatDobbs 6 67
(Sir Michael Stoute) *sn led and set stdy gallop: rdn and qcknd jst over 2f out: hdd wl over 1f out: sn drvn and unable qck: wknd ins fnl f* **7/2**[1]
2255 **8** 2 ½ **Flamborough Breeze**[19] 3899 4-10-0 **75**................................(t) GeorgeBaker 5 67
(Ed Vaughan) *t.k.h: hld up wl in tch in last trio: stuck bhd horses over 1f out: rdn and effrt over 1f out: keeping on but no threat to wnr whn carried lft ins fnl f: nt clr run after* **5/1**[3]

2m 8.13s (1.53) **Going Correction** +0.15s/f (Slow)
WFA 3 from 4yo 10lb 8 Ran SP% **118.2**
Speed ratings (Par 100): **99,97,97,96,95 95,94,92**
toteswingers 1&2 £7.00, 1&3 £5.50, 2&3 £4.60 CSF £28.24 CT £216.47 TOTE £7.00: £2.40, £2.40, £2.30; EX 20.90 Trifecta £218.20 Pool: £799.36 - 2.74 winning units..
Owner K Abdullah **Bred** Juddmonte Farms Ltd **Trained** Pulborough, W Sussex

FOCUS
The pace was steady in this competitive fillies' handicap but the winner scored in decent style. The finish was compressed and the form can only be rated as ordinary.
T/Plt: £56.80 to a £1 stake. Pool of £45,832.08 - 588.40 winning tickets. T/Qpdt: £6.50 to a £1 stake. Pool of £5086.55 - 574.60 winning tickets. SP

4483 NEWBURY (L-H)
Saturday, July 20

OFFICIAL GOING: Good to firm (firm in places; 7.6)
Wind: Moderate behind Weather: Overcast

4524 RACING UK PROFITS ALL RETURNED TO RACING CONDITIONS STKS 7f (S)
1:35 (1:36) (Class 4) 2-Y-O **£4,668** (£1,398; £699; £349) **Stalls** Centre

Form RPR
2102 **1** **Lanark (IRE)**[7] 4314 2-8-13 0................................ SilvestreDeSousa 5 97+
(Mark Johnston) *mde all: pushed along and qcknd fr 2f out: styd on strly fnl f: unchal* **1/1**[1]
3105 **2** 2 ¾ **Rosso Corsa**[7] 4296 2-8-13 0................................ MartinLane 1 90
(Mick Channon) *trckd wnr: jnd for 2nd over 2f out: sn rdn: no imp over 1f out: styd on same pce* **11/2**[3]
41 **3** nk **Gold Top (IRE)**[25] 3664 2-8-8 0................................ RichardHughes 4 84
(Richard Hannon) *trckd ldrs: chal for 2nd over 2f out: sn drvn: edgd lft over 1f out and no imp: dropped to 3rd clsng stages* **6/4**[2]
05 **4** 14 **Shepherd Gate (USA)**[21] 3833 2-8-10 0................................ LiamJones 2 50
(J S Moore) *in tch: rdn and effrt over 2f out: wknd u.p over 1f out* **25/1**

1m 24.27s (-1.43) **Going Correction** -0.275s/f (Firm) 4 Ran SP% **109.2**
Speed ratings (Par 96): **97,93,93,77**
CSF £6.75 TOTE £1.80; EX 6.00 Trifecta £7.50 Pool: £1596.83 - 158.61 winning units..
Owner Sheikh Hamdan Bin Mohammed Al Maktoum **Bred** Norelands Stallions **Trained** Middleham Moor, N Yorks

FOCUS
With just the four remaining runners, this was always likely to be tactical. The winner bossed it and this was a step up however viewed. The second posted a good advert for the Superlative level.

4525 "CHOOSE EBF NOMINATED" FILLIES' H'CAP 1m (S)
2:05 (2:05) (Class 2) (0-100,99) 3-Y-O+ **£12,450** (£3,728; £1,864; £932; £466; £234) **Stalls** Centre

Form RPR
0100 **1** **Galician**[7] 4297 4-9-7 **92**................................ SilvestreDeSousa 8 102
(Mark Johnston) *chsd ldrs: drvn to ld appr fnl 2f: rdn and edgd lft ins fnl f: kpt on wl* **4/1**[3]
-003 **2** 2 **Arsaadi (IRE)**[31] 3458 4-10-0 **99**................................(b) LiamJones 2 104
(William Haggas) *led: rdn and hdd appr fnl 2f: styd chsng wnr but no imp fnl f* **9/4**[1]
-020 **3** 1 ¼ **Forgive**[11] 4137 4-9-5 **90**................................ RichardHughes 7 92
(Richard Hannon) *in rr: hrd drvn 1/2-way and little rspnse: hdwy u.p appr fnl f: styd on for 3rd sn after: no imp fnl 110yds* **5/1**
1363 **4** 1 ¼ **Alice's Dancer (IRE)**[13] 4097 4-8-11 **82**................................ WilliamCarson 1 81
(William Muir) *chsd ldrs: rdn over 2f out: no ex ins fnl f* **14/1**
0040 **5** 3 **Sorella Bella (IRE)**[8] 4252 3-9-1 **94**................................ MartinLane 3 84
(Mick Channon) *chsd ldr to 3f out: wknd u.p over 1f out* **8/1**
4311 **6** 12 **Oddysey (IRE)**[9] 4201 4-9-3 **88**................................ LeeTopliss 4 62
(Michael Dods) *s.i.s: sn pushed along and in tch: rdn 3f out: btn ins fnl 2f* **3/1**[2]

1m 36.15s (-3.55) **Going Correction** -0.275s/f (Firm)
WFA 3 from 4yo 8lb 6 Ran SP% **110.2**
Speed ratings (Par 96): **106,104,102,101,98 86**
toteswingers 1&2 £2.20, 1&3 £3.30, 2&3 £3.10 CSF £12.91 CT £41.01 TOTE £4.70: £2.40, £1.50; EX 12.40 Trifecta £46.50 Pool: £1888.17 - 30.43 winning units..
Owner Sheikh Hamdan Bin Mohammed Al Maktoum **Bred** Darley **Trained** Middleham Moor, N Yorks

FOCUS
Rail between 8f and 5f moved out adding 12m to races on Round course. This looked a weak handicap for the prize money on offer, with a few of these fillies either not running to form or looking iffy. The second was shade off her Hunt Cup mark.

4526 SHARPS BREWERY STEVENTON STKS (LISTED RACE) 1m 2f 6y
2:40 (2:40) (Class 1) 3-Y-O+
£20,982 (£7,955; £3,981; £1,983; £995; £499) **Stalls** Centre

Form RPR
1220 **1** **Royal Empire (IRE)**[140] 873 4-9-4 112................................ SilvestreDeSousa 1 112+
(Saeed bin Suroor) *hld up towards rr swtchd rt and hdwy fr 3f out: drvn to ld jst ins fnl f: readily* **9/4**[1]
3-64 **2** 1 ½ **Al Waab (IRE)**[51] 2812 3-8-9 98 ow1................................ NeilCallan 2 110
(Lady Cecil) *sn chsng ldr: led 3f out: rdn 2f out: hdd jst ins fnl f and sn outpcd* **7/1**
5506 **3** 4 ½ **Dick Doughtywylie**[15] 4027 5-9-4 102................................ WilliamBuick 4 100
(John Gosden) *in tch: chsd ldrs fr 4f out: rdn 3f out: styd on u.p to take 3rd 1f out but nvr any ch w ldng duo* **4/1**[3]
10-0 **4** 1 **Black Spirit (USA)**[15] 4027 6-9-4 109................................(t) AdamKirby 5 98
(Clive Cox) *sn chsng ldrs: rdn over 2f out: wknd fnl f* **6/1**
10/0 **5** shd **Ocean War**[29] 3525 5-9-4 106................................ PaulHanagan 6 98
(Saeed bin Suroor) *t.k.h in rr: rdn and edgd lft 2f out: no further prog* **7/2**[2]
1-50 **6** 3 ¾ **Mobaco (FR)**[29] 3525 4-9-4 102................................ RichardHughes 3 90
(Luca Cumani) *led: hdd 3f out: wknd ins fnl 2f* **8/1**

2m 6.33s (-2.47) **Going Correction** -0.275s/f (Firm)
WFA 3 from 4yo+ 10lb 6 Ran SP% **110.9**
Speed ratings (Par 111): **98,96,93,92,92 89**
toteswingers 1&2 £2.90, 1&3 £2.10, 2&3 £5.50 CSF £17.77 TOTE £2.60: £1.90, £3.10; EX 16.70 Trifecta £44.10 Pool: £1935.36 - 32.88 winning units..
Owner Godolphin **Bred** Twelve Oaks Stud **Trained** Newmarket, Suffolk

FOCUS
An interesting Listed race, though the early pace didn't look that strong. Ordinary form for the grade, the winner perhaps a bit better than the bare form.

4527 GT EXHIBITIONS HACKWOOD STKS (GROUP 3) 6f 8y
3:15 (3:15) (Class 1) 3-Y-O+ **£34,026** (£12,900; £6,456; £3,216; £1,614) **Stalls** Centre

Form RPR
4262 **1** **Heeraat (IRE)**[7] 4311 4-9-4 107................................ PaulHanagan 5 116
(William Haggas) *ledf after 2f: racd on stands' side and pushed along 2f out: qcknd fnl f: edgd lft: r.o strly* **3/1**[3]
4110 **2** 1 ¾ **Hamza (IRE)**[7] 4298 4-9-4 109................................(b) NeilCallan 1 110
(Kevin Ryan) *led 2f towards centre of crse: styd pressing wnr and c over to stands' side 2f out: stl ev ch 1f out: outpcd by wnr ins fnl f: hld on wl for 2nd* **2/1**[2]
3233 **3** nk **Krypton Factor**[28] 3557 5-9-4 115................................(b) LukeMorris 6 109
(Fawzi Abdulla Nass, Bahrain) *chsd wnr towards stands' side: rdn over 2f out: hrd rdn appr fnl f: clsd on 2nd nr fin but no ch w wnr* **13/8**[1]
4-14 **4** 2 ½ **Bettolle (ITY)**[62] 2491 4-9-5 102................................ AdamKirby 4 102
(Marco Botti) *chsd ldrs: rdn over 1f out: swtchd rt and btn ins fnl f* **20/1**
5523 **5** 7 **Shamaal Nibras (USA)**[29] 3527 4-9-4 99................................(p) WilliamBuick 2 88
(Ismail Mohammed) *chsd ldr towards centre of crse: rdn 1/2-way: wknd 2f out* **10/1**

1m 10.48s (-2.52) **Going Correction** -0.275s/f (Firm)
WFA 3 from 4yo+ 5lb 5 Ran SP% **110.3**
Speed ratings (Par 113): **105,102,102,98,89**
CSF £9.44 TOTE £4.00: £1.90, £1.40; EX 9.40 Trifecta £13.50 Pool: £2626.97 - 145.45 winning units..
Owner Hamdan Al Maktoum **Bred** John McEnery **Trained** Newmarket, Suffolk

FOCUS
The Hackwood Stakes has been won by some high-class sprinters in the past ten years, including Somnus, Pastoral Pursuits, Fayr Jag, Regal Parade and Deacon Blues. This was a disappointing field though, but the winner has been credited with a personal best. Despite there only being five runners this time, they split into two groups for the first half of the contest, with the winner leading a pair up the nearside rail and the runner-up leading one rival up the middle.

4528 WEATHERBYS SUPER SPRINT 5f 34y
3:50 (3:52) (Class 2) 2-Y-O
£122,925 (£52,275; £24,600; £14,750; £9,825; £7,375) **Stalls** Centre

Form RPR
121 **1** **Peniaphobia (IRE)**[32] 3439 2-8-8 0................................ PaulHanagan 10 100+
(Richard Fahey) *trckd ldrs: rdn over 1f out: str run fnl f to ld last strides* **5/1**[3]
121 **2** nk **Lilbourne Lass**[35] 3311 2-8-1 0................................ JimmyQuinn 1 92+
(Richard Hannon) *racd far side and led overall: rdn 2f out: stl 1 l up ins fnl f: hdd last strides* **4/1**[1]
61 **3** 1 **Oasis Town**[24] 3681 2-8-0 0................................ DavidProbert 24 87
(Kevin Ryan) *racd stands' side and led that side and 2nd overall: rdn over 2f out: kpt on same pce for 3rd fnl f* **20/1**
1330 **4** 2 ¼ **Haikbidiac (IRE)**[32] 3424 2-8-12 0................................(p) LiamJones 4 91
(William Haggas) *racd towards far side: rdn 1/2-way: outpcd ins fnl f* **10/1**
1310 **5** ½ **Alutiq (IRE)**[31] 3459 2-8-0 0................................ CathyGannon 18 77
(Eve Johnson Houghton) *racd towards stands' side: mid-div and rdn 1/2-way: kpt on wl clsng stages: nt rch ldrs* **9/2**[2]
10 **6** ½ **Eccleston**[30] 3481 2-8-4 0................................ BarryMcHugh 13 79
(Richard Fahey) *racd towards centre: rdn over 2f out: hdwy fnl f and hung lft: kpt on cl home* **16/1**
41 **7** ¾ **Yorkshire Relish (IRE)**[36] 3298 2-8-3 0................................ SilvestreDeSousa 14 76
(Kevin Ryan) *towards rr: hdwy toward centre of crse fr 2f out: styng on whn hmpd ins fnl f: wnt lft and kpt on cl home* **16/1**
51 **8** nk **Hopefilly (IRE)**[14] 4073 2-8-0 0................................ MartinLane 9 72
(Ed Walker) *pressed ldrs in centre of crse: rdn 1/2-way: wknd ins fnl f* **16/1**
3 **9** 1 ½ **Foxy Clarets (IRE)**[23] 3724 2-8-7 0................................ WilliamCarson 5 73
(Richard Fahey) *racd far side: sn rdn and outpcd: styd on again clsng stages* **50/1**
32 **10** nse **Morning Post**[18] 3928 2-9-1 0................................ PhillipMakin 15 81
(Kevin Ryan) *in rr: hdwy towards centred and clsd on ldrs 2f out: wknd fnl f* **40/1**
4443 **11** ½ **Orton Park (IRE)**[21] 3801 2-8-2 0................................ FrankieMcDonald 20 66
(Tobias B P Coles) *racd on stands' side: rdn and sme hdwy 1/2-way: wknd fnl f* **66/1**
5320 **12** ½ **Urban Dreamer (IRE)**[7] 4282 2-8-8 0................................ FergusSweeney 12 72
(Rod Millman) *in tch: hdwy 2f out: styng on same pce whn hmpd and wknd ins fnl f* **80/1**

25 **13** *1 ¼* **Khalice**[23] 3710 2-8-1 0 ow1 RichardThomas 25 58
(Richard Fahey) *racd stands' side and outpcd: sme late hdwy* **66/1**
1522 **14** *nk* **Blockade (IRE)**[15] 4006 2-8-0 0 LukeMorris 6 57
(James Tate) *racd far side: chsd ldrs: rdn and btn 2f out* **33/1**
2221 **15** *1 ¼* **Memory Styx**[7] 4289 2-8-1 0 KieranO'Neill 22 53
(Mick Channon) *chsd ldrs towards stands' side: wknd 2f out* **40/1**
2313 **16** *1 ¾* **Danfazi (IRE)**[14] 4054 2-8-5 0 JohnFahy 7 51
(Kristin Stubbs) *chsd ldrs towards centre of crse to 1/2-way* **100/1**
0314 **17** *½* **Biography**[20] 3857 2-8-10 0 RichardHughes 23 54
(Richard Hannon) *in tch on stands' side: rdn 2f out: sn btn* **14/1**
1 **18** *1 ¼* **Bird Of Light (IRE)**[75] 2067 2-8-5 0 HarryBentley 21 45
(Richard Hannon) *in rr on stands' side: a outpcd* **25/1**
2341 **19** *nk* **Weisse Socken (IRE)**[7] 4282 2-8-11 0 (p) WilliamBuick 3 50
(Ralph Beckett) *racd far side: chsd ldrs over 3f* **40/1**
422 **20** *6* **Proclamationofwar**[35] 3332 2-8-12 0 NeilCallan 16 32
(Kevin Ryan) *s.i.s: sn outpcd* **50/1**
3121 **21** *1* **Meritocracy (IRE)**[8] 4239 2-9-1 0 ChrisCatlin 17 28
(Paul Cole) *pressed ldrs towards centre of crse tl wknd qckly 2f out* **16/1**
1421 **22** *1* **Lexington Rose**[35] 3332 2-8-1 0 RoystonFfrench 19 11
(Bryan Smart) *outpcd* **10/1**
4 **23** *2* **Gym Shoes**[7] 4289 2-8-6 0 RichardMullen 2 9
(Richard Fahey) *racd far side: outpcd* **66/1**
10 **24** *7* **Der Blaue Reiter (IRE)**[32] 3424 2-8-7 0 (p) TedDurcan 8
(George Baker) *early spd centre of crse: sn wknd* **66/1**

59.5s (-1.90) **Going Correction** -0.275s/f (Firm) 24 Ran SP% **134.2**
Speed ratings (Par 100): **104,103,101,98,97 96,95,95,92,92 91,90,88,88,86 83,82,80,80,70 69,67,64,53**
toteswingers 1&2 £3.90, 1&3 £72.60, 2&3 £49.20 CSF £24.05 TOTE £6.40: £2.50, £2.40, £7.70; EX 34.90 Trifecta £739.00 Pool: £4581.98 - 4.65 winning units..
Owner P Timmins & A Rhodes Haulage **Bred** Aidan Fogarty **Trained** Musley Bank, N Yorks

FOCUS
Half of this year's 24-strong field for the Weatherbys Super Sprint were either trained by Richard Fahey (5), Kevin Ryan (4) or Richard Hannon (3). The majority of the runners raced centre to nearside, while six raced against the far rail, but that group provided two of the first four home, suggesting there was no great bias. Straightforward form, fitting the solid race average. Peniaphobia progressed again.

4529 LUCK GREAYER BLOODSTOCK SHIPPING CONDITIONS STKS 7f (S)
4:25 (4:25) (Class 3) 3-Y-O **£7,158** (£2,143; £1,071; £535; £267) **Stalls** Centre

Form RPR
5-00 **1** **The Gold Cheongsam (IRE)**[31] 3460 3-8-7 102 (t) WilliamBuick 4 105
(Jeremy Noseda) *in tch: hdwy over 2f out: chsd ldr wl over 1f out: hrd drvn ins fnl f: styd on gamely to ld cl home* **3/1**[2]
-125 **2** *½* **Music Master**[31] 3455 3-8-9 103 FergusSweeney 3 106
(Henry Candy) *trckd ldr: led over 2f out: rdn and kpt on fnl f: hdd and no ex cl home* **10/11**[1]
6102 **3** *6* **Jalaa (IRE)**[16] 3987 3-8-12 95 PaulHanagan 1 92
(Richard Hannon) *led: hdd over 2f out: wknd over 1f out* **9/2**[3]
-230 **4** *4* **Pearl Sea (IRE)**[31] 3455 3-8-4 93 HarryBentley 5 74
(David Brown) *disp 2nd: rdn over 2f out: sn btn* **8/1**
1013 **5** *21* **Hartwright**[53] 2756 3-8-12 78 RichardHughes 2 25
(Michael Bell) *stmbld s: sn rcvrd: wknd fr 3f out: eased whn no ch* **25/1**

1m 22.4s (-3.30) **Going Correction** -0.275s/f (Firm) 5 Ran SP% **110.5**
Speed ratings (Par 104): **107,106,99,95,71**
CSF £6.21 TOTE £3.70: £1.60, £1.10; EX 6.20 Trifecta £13.10 Pool: £2314.65 - 132.36 winning units..
Owner Arashan Ali **Bred** Tally-Ho Stud **Trained** Newmarket, Suffolk

FOCUS
A decent conditions event and official ratings got it about right. The form pair were clear.

4530 OAKLEY COACHBUILDERS H'CAP 2m
5:00 (5:07) (Class 4) (0-80,80) 4-Y-O+ **£4,851** (£1,443; £721; £360) **Stalls** High

Form RPR
3002 **1** **Sula Two**[20] 3856 6-9-2 **80** PhilipPrince(5) 2 88
(Ron Hodges) *hld up towards rr but in tch: hdwy 2f out: led 1f out: drvn clr ins fnl f* **3/1**[2]
-112 **2** *2 ¾* **Our Folly**[43] 3065 5-9-1 **74** (t) NeilCallan 7 79
(Stuart Kittow) *trckd ldrs: drvn to take slt ld 2f out: hdd 1f out: one pce ins fnl f* **5/2**[1]
3312 **3** *nk* **Hi Note**[3] 4406 5-8-10 **69** FergusSweeney 6 73
(Sheena West) *trckd ldr: chal fr 6f out tl slt ld 3f out: rdn and narrowly hdd 2f out: styd on same pce fnl f* **3/1**[2]
0234 **4** *2 ¾* **Double Cee**[17] 3952 4-8-13 **72** RichardHughes 8 73
(Warren Greatrex) *led: jnd 6f out: narrowly hdd 3f out: styd pressing ldrs: wknd fnl f* **9/2**[3]
4340 **5** *4 ½* **Kayef (GER)**[27] 3609 6-8-7 **66** PaulHanagan 1 62
(Michael Scudamore) *chsd ldrs: rdn 3f out: wknd fr 2f out* **6/1**

3m 35.26s (3.26) **Going Correction** -0.275s/f (Firm) 5 Ran SP% **111.0**
Speed ratings (Par 105): **80,78,78,77,74**
CSF £10.95 TOTE £4.00: £2.20, £1.50; EX 9.50 Trifecta £18.20 Pool: £1417.50 - 58.15 winning units..
Owner Richard Prince **Bred** D R Tucker **Trained** Charlton Mackrell, Somerset

FOCUS
They didn't go much of a pace in this staying handicap and there were four in a line coming to the last furlong. A small personal best from the winner, with the second running at least as well as ever.
T/Plt: £63.40 to a £1 stake. Pool of £96,963.98 - 1115.98 winning tickets. T/Qpdt: £9.10 to a £1 stake. Pool of £5854.39 - 471.94 winning tickets. ST

4490 NEWMARKET (R-H)
Saturday, July 20

OFFICIAL GOING: Good to firm (8.4)
Wind: Light across Weather: Overcast

4531 POPTELECOM.CO.UK H'CAP 1m
1:50 (1:52) (Class 2) (0-105,105) 3-Y-O+ **£28,012** (£8,388; £4,194; £2,097; £1,048; £526) **Stalls** Low

Form RPR
3234 **1** **Snowboarder (USA)**[112] 1264 3-8-13 **102** MickaelBarzalona 1 110+
(Saeed bin Suroor) *a.p: swtchd lft over 1f out: rdn to ld ins fnl f: r.o: eased nr fin* **13/2**
0-31 **2** *1* **Sam Sharp (USA)**[35] 3346 7-8-11 **92** RichardKingscote 3 99
(Ian Williams) *hld up: hdwy u.p and hung lft fr over 1f out: r.o: nt rch wnr* **9/2**[3]
0522 **3** *¾* **Es Que Love (IRE)**[7] 4297 4-9-10 **105** RyanMoore 8 110
(Mark Johnston) *a.p: chsd ldr over 2f out: rdn and carried lft fr over 1f out: ev ch ins fnl f: no ex towards fin* **5/2**[1]
0103 **4** *½* **Shebebi (USA)**[14] 4062 3-8-5 **94** MartinDwyer 7 96
(Mark Johnston) *led: rdn and hung lft fr over 1f out: hdd and unable qck ins fnl f* **4/1**[2]
40 **5** *8* **Kitten On The Run (USA)**[30] 3485 3-8-13 **102** KierenFallon 4 86
(Luca Cumani) *hld up: pushed along over 3f out: wknd over 1f out* **9/2**[3]
-043 **6** *nk* **Trail Blaze (IRE)**[21] 3825 4-8-9 **90** KirstyMilczarek 6 75
(Kevin Ryan) *chsd ldr tl rdn over 2f out: wknd over 1f out* **9/1**
0-06 **7** *21* **Kinglet (USA)**[142] 836 4-9-8 **103** AhmedAjtebi 5 40
(Saeed bin Suroor) *s.i.s: hld up: rdn over 3f out: wknd and eased 2f out* **16/1**

1m 38.68s (-1.32) **Going Correction** +0.10s/f (Good)
WFA 3 from 4yo+ 8lb 7 Ran SP% **114.2**
Speed ratings (Par 109): **110,109,108,107,99 99,78**
toteswingers 1&2 £9.30, 2&3 £2.50, 1&3 £1.70 CSF £35.33 CT £92.28 TOTE £8.10: £3.20, £2.70; EX 40.00 Trifecta £81.10 Pool: £1639.57 - 15.16 winning units..
Owner Godolphin **Bred** Fares Farm Llc **Trained** Newmarket, Suffolk

FOCUS
Stands' side track used with stalls on stands' side, except 1m2f & 1m4f: Centre. A decent handicap and the form makes a fair bit of sense.

4532 NEWSELLS PARK STUD STKS (REGISTERED AS THE APHRODITE STAKES) (LISTED RACE) (F&M) 1m 4f
2:25 (2:25) (Class 1) 3-Y-O+
£22,684 (£8,600; £4,304; £2,144; £1,076; £540) **Stalls** Centre

Form RPR
0-15 **1** **Waila**[30] 3482 3-8-6 101 ow2 [1] RyanMoore 2 110
(Sir Michael Stoute) *sn chsng ldrs: shkn up and nt clr run over 2f out: led over 1f out: rdn clr fnl f* **5/4**[1]
1206 **2** *10* **Gertrude Versed**[30] 3482 3-8-4 91 NickyMackay 7 92
(John Gosden) *hld up: hdwy over 3f out: rdn over 1f out: wknd ins fnl f* **9/1**
00 **3** *1* **Soho Dancer**[37] 3240 3-8-4 0 KirstyMilczarek 5 90
(James Toller) *plld hrd and sn prom: lost pl over 7f out: swtchd lft and hdwy u.p over 2f out: hung lft and wknd ins fnl f* **40/1**
3-33 **4** *¾* **Between Us**[27] 3608 4-9-2 85 RichardKingscote 3 89
(Sir Mark Prescott Bt) *led after 1f: clr 1/2-way: rdn and hdd over 1f out: wknd ins fnl f* **9/1**
433 **5** *1 ½* **Whippy Cream (IRE)**[55] 2697 3-8-4 102 DarrenEgan 8 87
(Marco Botti) *prom: rdn over 4f out: wknd over 1f out* **11/1**
2-1 **6** *39* **La Arenosa (IRE)**[33] 3409 4-9-5 104 MickaelBarzalona 6
(Saeed bin Suroor) *hld up: plld hrd: rdn over 2f out: wknd and eased over 1f out* **10/3**[2]
-023 **7** *8* **Sound Hearts (USA)**[22] 3775 4-9-2 95 [1] FrankieDettori 4
(Roger Varian) *led 1f: chsd ldr tl rdn over 3f out: wknd over 2f out: eased* **13/2**[3]

2m 31.23s (-1.67) **Going Correction** +0.10s/f (Good)
WFA 3 from 4yo+ 12lb 7 Ran SP% **111.6**
Speed ratings (Par 111): **109,102,101,101,100 74,68**
toteswingers 1&2 £3.30, 2&3 £27.70, 1&3 £14.30 CSF £12.96 TOTE £2.00: £1.60, £4.30; EX 12.00 Trifecta £172.40 Pool: £2039.05 - 8.86 winning units..
Owner Sir Evelyn De Rothschild **Bred** Southcourt Stud **Trained** Newmarket, Suffolk

FOCUS
With La Arenosa running as though something was amiss, and third-placed Soho Dancer hanging all over the track (would otherwise have finished a well-beaten second), there wasn't much depth to this race. The impressive winner progressed again, though.

4533 LETTERGOLD MAIDEN STKS 7f
3:05 (3:05) (Class 4) 2-Y-O **£3,881** (£1,155) **Stalls** Low

Form RPR
2 **1** **Safety Check (IRE)**[43] 3044 2-9-5 0 MickaelBarzalona 3 87+
(Saeed bin Suroor) *mde all: clr 5f out: canter* **1/25**[1]
2 *24* **Rudi Five One (FR)** 2-9-5 0 NickyMackay 2 22
(Robert Eddery) *dwlt: a in last: outpcd fnl 5f* **14/1**[2]

1m 27.82s (2.12) **Going Correction** +0.10s/f (Good) 2 Ran SP% **102.8**
Speed ratings (Par 96): **91,63**
TOTE £1.10.
Owner Godolphin **Bred** Malih Al Basti **Trained** Newmarket, Suffolk

FOCUS
Two non-runners left a mismatch, with the winner in total command.

4534 TAMDOWN GROUP EBF FILLIES' H'CAP 6f
3:40 (3:40) (Class 3) (0-95,93) 3-Y-O+
£8,715 (£2,609; £1,304; £652; £326; £163) **Stalls** Low

Form RPR
1-51 **1** **Midnight Flower (IRE)**[43] 3058 3-8-7 **82** DarrenEgan(3) 2 98
(David Simcock) *trckd ldrs: led over 1f out: sn rdn: r.o wl u.p* **10/3**[1]
0012 **2** *3 ½* **Links Drive Lady**[11] 4138 5-9-6 **87** KierenFallon 7 93
(Dean Ivory) *s.i.s: sn pushed along in rr: hdwy over 1f out: rdn to chse wnr ins fnl f: styd on same pce* **4/1**[2]
0002 **3** *1 ¾* **Elusive Flame**[23] 3720 4-9-9 **90** RyanMoore 8 90
(David Elsworth) *led: rdn and hdd over 1f out: no ex ins fnl f* **4/1**[2]
6133 **4** *4 ½* **Charlotte Rosina**[16] 3973 4-9-9 **90** SebSanders 9 76
(Roger Teal) *prom: racd keenly: rdn and ev ch over 1f out: wknd ins fnl f* **8/1**
0645 **5** *¾* **Tassel**[22] 3784 3-9-4 **90** MickaelBarzalona 3 73
(Richard Hannon) *prom: rdn and ev ch over 1f out: wknd ins fnl f* **14/1**
5-20 **6** *nk* **Poetic Dancer**[49] 2858 4-9-3 **89** RyanTate(5) 1 72
(Clive Cox) *chsd ldrs: rdn and ev ch over 1f out: wknd ins fnl f* **4/1**[2]
0633 **7** *5* **I'm So Glad**[7] 4297 4-9-9 **93** CharlesBishop(3) 5 60
(Mick Channon) *chsd ldr tl pushed along over 2f out: wknd over 1f out* **6/1**[3]

1m 11.98s (-0.52) **Going Correction** +0.10s/f (Good)
WFA 3 from 4yo+ 5lb 7 Ran SP% **115.1**
Speed ratings (Par 104): **107,102,100,94,93 92,85**
toteswingers 1&2 £1.60, 2&3 £2.50, 1&3 £3.60 CSF £17.11 CT £54.21 TOTE £5.00: £2.90, £1.60; EX 19.00 Trifecta £87.80 Pool: £1514.48 - 12.92 winning units..
Owner Saeed Suhail **Bred** Rabbah Bloodstock Limited **Trained** Newmarket, Suffolk

The Form Book Flat, Raceform Ltd, Compton, RG20 6NL.

FOCUS
Perhaps not that strong a race, but a decent winner who stepped up on her previous C&D win.

4535 TAMDOWN SHELL & CORE MAIDEN STKS 7f
4:15 (4:15) (Class 5) 3-Y-O **£3,234** (£962; £481; £240) **Stalls** Low

Form RPR
43 **1** **Narmin (IRE)**[42] 3116 3-9-0 0 RobertHavlin 2 89
(John Gosden) *hld up: hdwy over 2f out: shkn up to chse ldr over 1f out: rdn to ld wl ins fnl f: sn clr* **9/4**[1]

5 **2** *3 ¼* **Satwa Story**[89] 1727 3-9-5 0 MickaelBarzalona 1 85
(Saeed bin Suroor) *chsd ldrs tl led 1/2-way: rdn over 1f out: hdd and unable qck wl ins fnl f* **9/4**[1]

0- **3** *3 ¾* **Muthafar (IRE)**[337] 5303 3-9-5 0 MartinDwyer 3 75
(William Haggas) *prom: rdn and edgd lft over 1f out: no ex fnl f* **11/2**[3]

4 **4** *3 ¼* **Pilates (IRE)**[9] 4200 3-9-0 0 RyanMoore 6 61
(Mark Johnston) *hld up: swtchd rt over 5f out: pushed along 4f out: rdn over 1f out: nvr on terms* **3/1**[2]

05 **5** *11* **Quintet (IRE)**[39] 3176 3-9-0 0 [1] FrankieDettori 5 32
(Ralph Beckett) *chsd ldrs: racd alone towards centre fr over 5f out tl jnd main gp 1/2-way: rdn over 2f out: sn edgd lft: wknd over 1f out* **8/1**

000R **6** *3* **Sakhee's Alround**[18] 3922 3-9-0 42 AdamBeschizza 4 24
(K F Clutterbuck) *led to 1/2-way: wknd over 2f out* **100/1**

1m 25.8s (0.10) **Going Correction** +0.10s/f (Good) **6 Ran SP% 114.0**
Speed ratings (Par 100): **103,99,95,91,78 75**
toteswingers 1&2 £1.10, 2&3 £2.90, 1&3 £4.00 CSF £7.78 TOTE £3.00: £1.90, £1.70; EX 7.50 Trifecta £16.10 Pool: £1685.62 - 78.23 winning units..

Owner Hamdan Al Maktoum **Bred** Shadwell Estate Company Limited **Trained** Newmarket, Suffolk

FOCUS
An ordinary maiden, but it was run at a good pace and the form is rated on the positive side.

4536 JOE & SARAH MEMORIAL H'CAP 5f
4:50 (4:50) (Class 3) (0-95,95) 3-Y-O+ **£7,762** (£2,310; £1,154; £577) **Stalls** Low

Form RPR
1011 **1** **Cincinnati Kit**[15] 4017 4-8-4 **76** oh4 (t) DarrenEgan[(3)] 3 87
(Stuart Williams) *hld up in tch: plld hrd: nt clr run over 1f out: rdn to ld and hung lft ins fnl f: r.o* **8/1**

2014 **2** *½* **Tax Free (IRE)**[8] 4263 11-9-7 **90** RyanMoore 5 99
(David Nicholls) *led: rdn over 1f out: hung lft and hdd ins fnl f: styd on* **4/1**[3]

2511 **3** *1 ¼* **Last Sovereign**[9] 4217 9-9-4 **94** (b) JacobButterfield[(7)] 2 99
(Ollie Pears) *chsd ldrs: rdn and ev ch over 1f out: styd on same pce ins fnl f* **7/2**[2]

-026 **4** *¾* **Goldream**[7] 4275 4-9-9 **92** FrankieDettori 7 94
(Robert Cowell) *sn chsng ldrs: rdn and ev ch over 1f out: no ex ins fnl f* **13/8**[1]

0300 **5** *½* **Pabusar**[7] 4275 5-9-11 **94** MartinDwyer 6 94
(Jamie Osborne) *hld up: rdn and nt clr run over 1f out: nvr able to chal* **12/1**

0060 **6** *¾* **Naabegha**[15] 4024 6-9-4 **87** (p) LiamKeniry 9 84
(Ed de Giles) *hld up: effrt over 1f out: styd on same pce ins fnl f* **11/1**

3140 **7** *½* **Mata Hari Blue**[36] 3299 7-8-8 **82** (t) TobyAtkinson[(5)] 4 78
(Michael Appleby) *chsd ldrs: rdn and ev ch over 1f out: wknd ins fnl f* **16/1**

58.78s (-0.32) **Going Correction** +0.10s/f (Good) **7 Ran SP% 113.3**
Speed ratings (Par 107): **106,105,103,102,101 100,99**
toteswingers 1&2 £2.20, 2&3 £3.20, 1&3 £1.90 CSF £38.99 CT £132.46 TOTE £6.20: £2.80, £2.20; EX 24.90 Trifecta £65.30 Pool: £3249.26 - 37.31 winning units..

Owner J W Parry **Bred** Old Mill Stud & S Williams & J Parry **Trained** Newmarket, Suffolk

FOCUS
A decent enough sprint handicap. The winner continues on the upgrade.

4537 TRICONNEX H'CAP 1m 2f
5:20 (5:20) (Class 2) (0-100,99) 3-Y-O
£12,450 (£3,728; £1,864; £932; £466; £234) **Stalls** Centre

Form RPR
0-20 **1** **Tha'ir (IRE)**[29] 3523 3-9-7 **99** MickaelBarzalona 1 109
(Saeed bin Suroor) *hld up: hdwy over 3f out: led over 1f out: rdn out* **11/4**[1]

1211 **2** *½* **Sennockian Star**[5] 4342 3-8-13 **91** 6ex (v) FrederikTylicki 4 100
(Mark Johnston) *led: wnt towards centre and racd alone fr 8f out: hdd over 2f out: rallied and ev ch fr over 1f out: styd on* **3/1**[2]

21 **3** *5* **Endless Credit (IRE)**[29] 3539 3-8-9 **87** KierenFallon 6 86
(Luca Cumani) *sn prom: led over 2f out: sn edgd rt: rdn and hdd over 1f out: edgd lft and styd on same pce fnl f* **10/3**[3]

1212 **4** *nk* **Danat Al Atheer**[22] 3755 3-8-11 **89** (b) FrankieDettori 5 87
(William Haggas) *prom: plld hrd: nt clr run and lost pl over 3f out: rdn and stl nt clr run over 1f out: styd on ins fnl f: nt trble ldrs* **8/1**

0321 **5** *½* **Circus Turn (USA)**[14] 4084 3-8-7 **85** RyanMoore 2 82
(Sir Michael Stoute) *chsd ldr: rdn over 2f out: nt clr run and swtchd lft over 1f out: no ex fnl f* **9/2**

6500 **6** *7* **Greeleys Love (USA)**[9] 4214 3-8-5 **83** (v) MartinDwyer 3 66
(Mark Johnston) *s.i.s: hld up: hdwy over 4f out: rdn over 2f out: sn edgd lft: wknd over 1f out* **10/1**

2m 7.45s (1.95) **Going Correction** +0.10s/f (Good) **6 Ran SP% 113.1**
Speed ratings (Par 106): **96,95,91,91,90 85**
toteswingers 1&2 £2.30, 2&3 £2.40, 1&3 £2.40 CSF £11.48 TOTE £3.70: £2.00, £2.20; EX 9.90 Trifecta £31.20 Pool: £2645.75 - 63.52 winning units..

Owner Godolphin **Bred** Lodge Park Stud **Trained** Newmarket, Suffolk

FOCUS
A good handicap with the first pair clear. The winner is rated back to his best 2yo form.

T/Plt: £91.80 to a £1 stake. Pool of £75444.28 - 599.59 winning tickets. T/Qpdt: £10.30 to a £1 stake. Pool of £3520.79 - 251.40 winning tickets. CR

4114 RIPON (R-H)
Saturday, July 20

OFFICIAL GOING: Good to firm (good in places; 8.5)
Wind: Breezy, half behind Weather: Overcast

4538 DOBSONS GASKETS 50TH ANNIVERSARY (S) STKS 6f
2:00 (2:00) (Class 6) 2-Y-O **£2,587** (£770; £384; £192) **Stalls** High

Form RPR
6332 **1** **Lady Captain (IRE)**[14] 4065 2-8-8 0 ow2 JamieSpencer 1 61
(Kevin Ryan) *cl up on outside: pushed along fr 1/2-way: cajoled to ld ins fnl f: hld on cl home* **6/4**[1]

004 **2** *hd* **Elualla (IRE)**[12] 4115 2-8-6 0 AndrewMullen 13 58
(Nigel Tinkler) *w ldrs: led 2f out to ins fnl f: rallied u.p: jst hld* **8/1**

50 **3** *2 ¼* **Witchy Woman**[12] 4115 2-7-13 0 JoeyHaynes[(7)] 9 51
(Mrs K Burke) *trckd ldrs: rdn and edgd rt over 1f out: kpt on same pce ins fnl f* **7/2**[2]

0600 **4** *4 ½* **Highland Princess (IRE)**[31] 3461 2-8-3 0 DeclanCannon[(3)] 6 37
(Paul Midgley) *prom: rdn and outpcd over 2f out: kpt on fnl f: no imp* **66/1**

056 **5** *hd* **Barleycorn**[10] 4156 2-8-11 0 DavidAllan 7 41
(Tim Easterby) *led to 2f out: rdn and wknd appr fnl f* **10/1**

0 **6** *2 ½* **Boy Ranger (IRE)**[7] 4289 2-8-4 0 RowanScott[(7)] 5 33+
(Ann Duffield) *bhd: pushed along over 3f out: styd on fr over 1f out: nvr able to chal* **40/1**

6040 **7** *1 ¼* **Patisserie**[10] 4156 2-8-6 0 PJMcDonald 8 24
(Ann Duffield) *in tch: rdn and outpcd over 2f out: sn btn* **11/2**[3]

0 **8** *4* **Always Be Closing**[23] 3724 2-8-11 0 (v[1]) MichaelO'Connell 12 16
(John Quinn) *in tch: drvn and outpcd 1/2-way: btn over 1f out* **28/1**

0 **9** *2 ¼* **Elsie Bond**[9] 4199 2-8-6 0 (b[1]) DuranFentiman 3 4
(Tim Easterby) *dwlt: bhd: drvn 1/2-way: sn btn* **33/1**

0 **10** *3 ¾* **Marsden Cuckoo (IRE)**[10] 4156 2-8-6 0 JoeFanning 10
(David O'Meara) *bhd and sn pushed along: hung rt and struggling fr 1/2-way* **40/1**

0 **11** *11* **Madame Giry (IRE)**[10] 4156 2-8-3 0 JulieBurke[(3)] 4
(David O'Meara) *rrd s: bhd: struggling over 3f out: sn btn* **11/1**

1m 13.42s (0.42) **Going Correction** -0.15s/f (Firm) **11 Ran SP% 118.9**
Speed ratings (Par 92): **91,90,87,81,81 78,76,71,68,63 48**
toteswingers 1&2 £1.70, 2&3 £9.50, 1&3 £1.50 CSF £14.15 TOTE £1.70: £1.10, £3.20, £1.60; EX 9.60 Trifecta £74.20 Pool: £671.61 - 6.78 winning units..There was no bid for the winner.

Owner Mrs J Ryan **Bred** Noel O'Callaghan **Trained** Hambleton, N Yorks

FOCUS
Rail on bend from back straight to home straight moved out 3m adding 7yds to races on Round course. The going was described as good to firm, good in places. After riding in the opener Andrew Mullen said it was good, fast ground. They raced near side in this uncompetitive 2yo seller. Routine selling form. The winner is progressing.

4539 EBF YORKSHIRE.COM MAIDEN STKS 5f
2:35 (2:40) (Class 4) 2-Y-O **£5,175** (£1,540; £769; £384) **Stalls** High

Form RPR
6 **1** **Complicit (IRE)**[23] 3752 2-9-5 0 GrahamLee 8 84+
(Paul Cole) *rdr lost iron sn after s: towards rr: hdwy into midfield 1/2-way: effrt and drvn over 1f out: led wl ins fnl f: r.o* **5/2**[2]

22 **2** *nk* **Genuine Quality (USA)**[35] 3318 2-9-0 0 JamieSpencer 2 78
(Ed Vaughan) *led and sn crossed over to stands' rail: rdn over 1f out: sn hrd pressed: hdd wl ins fnl f: kpt on* **6/4**[1]

3 *¾* **Northern Water** 2-9-5 0 DanielTudhope 5 80+
(Mrs K Burke) *trckd ldrs: effrt and ev ch over 1f out to ins fnl f: kpt on same pce towards fin* **9/1**

4 *1 ¼* **Lucy Parsons (IRE)** 2-9-0 0 GrahamGibbons 11 71+
(David Barron) *prom: effrt and pushed along over 1f out: kpt on same pce wl ins fnl f* **12/1**

5 *2 ¼* **See The Sun** 2-9-0 0 AdamCarter[(5)] 12 68+
(Tim Easterby) *in tch: rdn over 2f out: n.m.r briefly over 1f out: sn one pce* **40/1**

03 **6** *2 ½* **Another Royal**[21] 3826 2-9-0 0 DavidAllan 7 54
(Tim Easterby) *midfield: drvn over 2f out: no imp fr over 1f out* **7/1**[3]

4 **7** *½* **Signore Piccolo**[7] 4282 2-9-2 0 NeilFarley[(3)] 9 57
(Eric Alston) *bhd: rdn and outpcd after 2f: sme late hdwy: nvr on terms* **33/1**

4 **8** *½* **Alaskan Night (IRE)**[68] 2314 2-9-5 0 RobertWinston 10 55
(Kevin Ryan) *t.k.h: chsd ldr: rdn and edgd rt over 1f out: wknd ins fnl f* **20/1**

00 **9** *1* **Two Shades Of Grey (IRE)**[14] 4046 2-9-5 0 TonyHamilton 6 52+
(Richard Fahey) *bhd and sn outpcd: nvr on terms* **16/1**

10 *6* **Nu Form Fire (IRE)** 2-9-5 0 PaulMulrennan 3 30
(Nigel Tinkler) *bhd on outside: struggling after 2f: sn btn* **100/1**

00 **11** *3 ¼* **Baileys Celebrate**[22] 3766 2-9-0 0 JoeFanning 4 13
(Mark Johnston) *midfield on outside: struggling over 2f out: sn wknd* **50/1**

59.48s (-0.52) **Going Correction** -0.15s/f (Firm) **11 Ran SP% 117.7**
Speed ratings (Par 96): **98,97,96,94,90 86,85,85,83,73 68**
toteswingers 1&2 £1.40, 2&3 £8.60, 1&3 £12.20 CSF £6.31 TOTE £3.30: £1.60, £1.10, £2.40; EX 8.80 Trifecta £66.20 Pool: £1785.20 - 20.19 winning units..

Owner P F I Cole Ltd **Bred** Barouche Stud Ireland Ltd **Trained** Whatcombe, Oxon

FOCUS
Little depth to this maiden and the first pair had the best form on offer. The impression was that the winner was better than the bare form on the day.

4540 INFINITY ECOMAX TYRES H'CAP 1m
3:10 (3:13) (Class 4) (0-85,85) 3-Y-O+ **£6,301** (£1,886; £943; £472; £235) **Stalls** Low

Form RPR
0542 **1** **Silverheels (IRE)**[17] 3961 4-9-11 **85** AshleyMorgan[(3)] 7 94
(Paul Cole) *t.k.h early: trckd ldrs: edgd rt and led over 1f out: hld on wl fnl f* **8/1**

3305 **2** *¾* **No Dominion (IRE)**[14] 4075 4-9-3 **74** GrahamLee 8 81
(James Given) *hld up towards rr: hdwy over 2f out: drvn and chsd wnr ins fnl f: kpt on* **20/1**

3304 **3** *nk* **Flashlight (IRE)**[8] 4242 3-9-4 **83** JoeFanning 3 88
(Mark Johnston) *early ldr: pressed ldr: led over 2f out to over 1f out: rallied: kpt on same pce ins fnl f* **7/2**[2]

1130 **4** *½* **Ingleby Angel (IRE)**[24] 3684 4-9-13 **84** DanielTudhope 5 89
(David O'Meara) *dwlt: t.k.h in rr: rdn and hdwy over 2f out: kpt on ins fnl f* **9/1**

02 **5** 1 ¾ **Oratory (IRE)**[5] 4341 7-8-2 **66** oh1 .... JoeyHaynes(7) 6 67
(Mrs K Burke) *t.k.h early: trckd ldrs: rdn and hung rt over 1f out: kpt on same pce* **5/2**[1]

1510 **6** *shd* **Hakuna Matata**[24] 3683 6-9-0 **78** ....(b) ConnorBeasley(7) 2 79
(Michael Dods) *t.k.h: prom: nt clr run over 2f out to over 1f out: sn lost pl: styd on ins fnl f* **9/2**[3]

0-50 **7** 3 ½ **Fazza**[14] 4055 6-9-2 **73** .... JamesSullivan 9 66
(Edwin Tuer) *hld up in tch: outpcd over 3f out: n.d after* **50/1**

0200 **8** 4 ½ **Discression**[38] 3207 4-9-11 **82** .... PaulMulrennan 1 65
(Kevin Ryan) *sn led: rdn and hdd over 2f out: wknd over 1f out* **6/1**

0301 **9** *nse* **Mitchum**[22] 3778 4-8-10 **67** ....(p) DaleSwift 10 50
(Ron Barr) *hld up: rdn on outside over 2f out: hung rt and sn wknd* **25/1**

1m 39.35s (-2.05) **Going Correction** -0.10s/f (Good)
WFA 3 from 4yo+ 8lb **9** Ran SP% **114.9**
Speed ratings (Par 105): **106,105,104,104,102 102,99,94,94**
toteswingers 1&2 £15.60, 2&3 £8.40, 1&3 £4.10 CSF £148.79 CT £665.40 TOTE £6.90: £2.10, £3.70, £1.60; EX 56.10 Trifecta £278.20 Pool: £1689.97 - 4.55 winning units..
Owner Black Run Racing **Bred** Castlemartin Stud And Skymarc Farm **Trained** Whatcombe, Oxon

FOCUS
A competitive handicap and the pace was fair enough. The winner is rated in line with his best form since he was a 2yo.

4541 RIPON BELL-RINGER H'CAP — 1m 4f 10y
3:45 (3:45) (Class 2) (0-100,93) 3-Y-0 **£15,562** (£4,660; £2,330; £1,165; £582) **Stalls** Low

Form RPR

2652 **1** **Salutation (IRE)**[9] 4194 3-8-13 **85** .... JoeFanning 2 95
(Mark Johnston) *chsd ldr 3f: cl up: smooth hdwy to ld over 3f out: rdn and edgd rt over 1f out: kpt on strly fnl f* **9/4**[2]

3454 **2** 1 ½ **London Citizen (USA)**[20] 3862 3-9-0 **86** .... DanielTudhope 1 93
(Mrs K Burke) *led 3f: chsd ldr: effrt and ev ch over 3f out to 2f out: sn drvn: kpt on fnl f: nt rch wnr* **6/1**

1-01 **3** 1 ½ **Shrewd**[8] 4249 3-9-7 **93** .... JamieSpencer 3 98
(Michael Bell) *in tch: effrt and rdn over 2f out: edgd rt over 1f out: kpt on same pce ins fnl f* **11/4**[3]

3102 **4** 4 ½ **Fersah (USA)**[15] 4015 3-8-13 **85** .... DaneO'Neill 4 82
(William Haggas) *hld up in tch: effrt and pushed along over 2f out: outpcd fr over 1f out* **2/1**[1]

3140 **5** 19 **Contradict**[27] 3614 3-9-1 **87** .... SamHitchcott 5 65
(Mick Channon) *t.k.h: hld up in tch on outside: hdwy to ld after 3f and sn clr: hdd over 3f out: wknd 2f out: t.o* **14/1**

2m 33.76s (-2.94) **Going Correction** -0.10s/f (Good) **5** Ran SP% **111.7**
Speed ratings (Par 106): **105,104,103,100,87**
CSF £15.47 TOTE £5.60: £1.10, £3.90; EX 15.70 Trifecta £35.00 Pool: £736.49 - 15.75 winning units..
Owner Sheikh Hamdan Bin Mohammed Al Maktoum **Bred** Foursome Thoroughbreds, Muir & Waldron **Trained** Middleham Moor, N Yorks

FOCUS
A decent staying handicap for 3yos, run at a good pace. The winner is rated around his Bath run, with the second to form.

4542 SKYBET SUPPORTING THE YORKSHIRE RACING SUMMER FESTIVAL H'CAP — 1m 1f 170y
4:20 (4:20) (Class 4) (0-85,85) 3-Y-0+ **£6,301** (£1,886; £943; £472; £235) **Stalls** Low

Form RPR

2132 **1** **Mushaakis (IRE)**[15] 4028 3-9-0 **81** .... DaneO'Neill 9 93+
(Mark Johnston) *trckd ldr: rdn to ld 2f out: sn edgd rt: kpt on wl fnl f* **7/4**[1]

6140 **2** 2 ¾ **It's My Time**[13] 4098 4-8-9 **66** .... TonyHamilton 3 72
(Richard Fahey) *taken early to post: trckd ldrs: effrt over 2f out: chsd wnr 1f out: kpt on: nt gng pce to chal* **20/1**

2523 **3** *hd* **Triple Eight (IRE)**[12] 4119 5-8-12 **69** ....(b) MichaelO'Connell 4 75
(Philip Kirby) *prom: rdn 3f out: hdwy over 1f out: kpt on ins fnl f* **12/1**

4106 **4** ½ **San Cassiano (IRE)**[13] 4098 6-9-11 **82** .... JamesSullivan 8 87
(Ruth Carr) *led at ordinary gallop: rdn and hdd 2f out: kpt on same pce appr fnl f* **9/1**

1044 **5** 1 ¾ **Arc Light (IRE)**[14] 4055 5-9-0 **71** .... DuranFentiman 5 72
(Tim Easterby) *taken early to post: t.k.h: hld up: rdn over 2f out: plugged on fnl f: no imp* **9/2**[3]

2206 **6** *hd* **Number One London (IRE)**[14] 4084 3-9-0 **81** ....(b[1]) PaulMulrennan 1 82
(Brian Meehan) *hld up in tch: rdn over 2f out: no imp fr wl over 1f out* **5/2**[2]

051 **7** 8 **Jo'Burg (USA)**[15] 4012 9-10-0 **85** .... DanielTudhope 6 75
(David O'Meara) *taken early to post: hld up in tch: rdn over 2f out: sn wknd* **10/1**

2m 2.97s (-2.43) **Going Correction** -0.10s/f (Good)
WFA 3 from 4yo+ 10lb **7** Ran SP% **114.7**
Speed ratings (Par 105): **105,102,102,102,100 100,94**
toteswingers 1&2 £2.00, 2&3 £0.00, 1&3 £2.50 CSF £37.71 CT £328.43 TOTE £1.70: £1.10, £4.30; EX 42.40 Trifecta £159.30 Pool: £912.89 - 4.29 winning units..
Owner Hamdan Al Maktoum **Bred** Shadwell Estate Company Limited **Trained** Middleham Moor, N Yorks

FOCUS
Not that competitive for the grade. The pace was steady and the winner was too good. The form is rated around the fourth.

4543 AGE UK FIT AS A FIDDLE H'CAP — 1m 4f 10y
4:55 (4:55) (Class 4) (0-80,77) 3-Y-0+ **£5,175** (£1,540; £769; £384) **Stalls** Low

Form RPR

0015 **1** **Kuantan One (IRE)**[22] 3783 3-9-1 **76** ....(b[1]) PJMcDonald 8 84
(Paul Cole) *trckd ldrs: hdwy to ld over 5f out: sn kicked wl clr: styd on strly fnl f: unchal* **7/1**[3]

3311 **2** 1 ½ **Wadacre Sarko**[18] 3930 3-9-2 **77** .... JoeFanning 6 83
(Mark Johnston) *trckd ldr to over 6f out: cl up: effrt and chsd (clr) wnr over 3f out: rdn over 2f out: styd on fnl f: nt rch wnr* **11/8**[1]

1055 **3** 2 ¼ **Valantino Oyster (IRE)**[25] 3652 6-8-9 **58** ....(p) DaleSwift 1 60
(Tracy Waggott) *led at stdy gallop to over 6f out: rdn over 3f out: kpt on same pce fnl 2f* **20/1**

0036 **4** *nk* **Dark Dune (IRE)**[9] 4202 5-9-9 **72** .... DavidAllan 5 74
(Tim Easterby) *hld up: rdn and hdwy on outside over 2f out: edgd rt over 1f out: kpt on fnl f: no imp* **14/1**

5614 **5** 1 ¾ **Pertuis (IRE)**[18] 3930 7-8-10 **66** .... ConnorBeasley(7) 2 65
(Micky Hammond) *hld up: rdn over 3f out: hdwy wl over 1f out: kpt on fnl f: nvr able to chal* **17/2**

1133 **6** 1 ½ **Bright Applause**[31] 3480 5-9-5 **73** .... GeorgeChaloner(5) 9 69
(Tracy Waggott) *in tch: rdn over 3f out: no imp fr 2f out* **8/1**

-004 **7** *nk* **Fossgate**[25] 3652 12-9-3 **66** .... GrahamLee 3 62
(James Bethell) *hld up in tch: outpcd over 3f out: rallied and edgd rt over 1f out: sn no imp* **11/1**

0434 **8** 5 **Ailsa Craig (IRE)**[17] 3947 7-8-11 **60** .... JamesSullivan 4 48
(Edwin Tuer) *hld up in tch: rdn and outpcd wl over 2f out: sn btn* **20/1**

1302 **9** 6 **Gran Maestro (USA)**[21] 3808 4-9-8 **76** ....(b) LMcNiff(5) 7 54
(Ruth Carr) *chsd ldrs: hdwy to ld over 6f out to over 5f out: wknd over 2f out* **13/2**[2]

261/ **10** 1 ¼ **High On A Hill (IRE)**[514] 6749 6-9-5 **73** .... GarryWhillans(5) 10 49
(Iain Jardine) *hld up: struggling wl over 3f out: sn btn* **20/1**

2m 39.64s (2.94) **Going Correction** -0.10s/f (Good)
WFA 3 from 4yo+ 12lb **10** Ran SP% **118.9**
Speed ratings (Par 105): **86,85,83,83,82 81,80,77,73,72**
toteswingers 1&2 £1.60, 2&3 £19.60, 1&3 £0.00 CSF £16.81 CT £181.56 TOTE £11.30: £3.70, £1.02, £7.90; EX 17.90 Trifecta £262.40 Pool: £984.87 - 2.81 winning units..
Owner H R H Sultan Ahmad Shah **Bred** Manister House Stud **Trained** Whatcombe, Oxon
■ Stewards' Enquiry : P J McDonald caution: careless riding.

FOCUS
A fair handicap run at a steady pace. The first three were to the fore throughout and the form isn't rated too positively.

4544 CHS VEHICLES MAIDEN H'CAP — 6f
5:25 (5:27) (Class 5) (0-70,70) 3-Y-0+ **£3,234** (£962; £481; £240) **Stalls** High

Form RPR

-052 **1** **Abraham Monro**[12] 4114 3-8-2 **51** oh1 .... JamesSullivan 6 58
(Ruth Carr) *prom: effrt whn n.m.r briefly over 1f out: swtchd lft and hdwy to ld wl ins fnl f: r.o* **9/1**

3526 **2** ½ **Imperial Spirit**[8] 4244 3-7-11 **51** oh1 ....(v) NathanAlison(5) 10 56
(Mick Channon) *cl up: led over 2f out: sn rdn: hdd wl ins fnl f: hld nr fin* **22/1**

535 **3** 2 ¼ **Rufoof**[22] 3774 3-9-7 **70** .... DaneO'Neill 12 68+
(Charles Hills) *hld up in tch: rdn over 2f out: styd on wl last 100yds: nrst fin* **7/2**[1]

4 1 ¼ **Monakova (IRE)**[38] 3226 3-8-12 **66** .... DavidBergin(5) 3 60
(David O'Meara) *in tch: pushed along after 2f: hdwy and cl up 2f out: sn rdn: one pce fnl f* **14/1**

033 **5** 1 ¼ **Perfect Pasture**[12] 4114 3-8-8 **57** .... GrahamGibbons 9 47+
(Michael Easterby) *blindfold slow to remove and missed break: bhd: hdwy and drvn wl over 2f out: edgd rt and kpt on fnl f: nrst fin* **9/2**[2]

6005 **6** ½ **Annie Gogh**[12] 4114 3-8-8 **57** .... DavidAllan 7 46
(Tim Easterby) *hld up: rdn over 2f out: hdwy over 1f out: styng on whn n.m.r briefly ins fnl f: no imp* **6/1**[3]

4663 **7** *shd* **Cracking Choice (IRE)**[22] 3779 3-8-4 **60** ....(b) ConnorBeasley(7) 4 48
(Michael Dods) *led to over 2f out: rdn and outpcd fnl f* **9/1**

3450 **8** ½ **Puteri Nur Laila (IRE)**[51] 2806 3-8-10 **59** ....(bt) PJMcDonald 2 46
(Paul Cole) *towards rr: drvn over 2f out: sme hdwy over 1f out: nt gng pce to chal* **20/1**

0300 **9** 2 ¼ **Another Claret**[23] 3730 3-8-5 **54** .... PatrickMathers 14 33
(Richard Fahey) *prom: rdn over 3f out: no imp fnl 2f* **20/1**

6246 **10** ¾ **Excellent Addition (IRE)**[14] 4045 3-9-2 **65** ....(v[1]) DanielTudhope 13 42
(David O'Meara) *w ldrs: rdn over 2f out: wknd fnl f* **7/2**[1]

0-00 **11** ¾ **Majestic Angel (IRE)**[38] 3196 4-8-0 **51** oh6 .... DanielleMooney(7) 8 26
(Brian Rothwell) *towards rr: drvn over 2f out: sn btn* **66/1**

00-0 **12** 1 ¾ **Zoom In**[53] 2757 5-8-4 **51** oh6 ....(t) DeclanCannon(3) 11 20
(Lee James) *bhd: struggling 1/2-way: nvr on terms* **40/1**

-20U **13** 6 **Lucy Minaj**[12] 4114 3-8-3 **52** .... JamieMackay 1
(Bryan Smart) *racd alone centre 2f: sn jnd main gp on outside: prom tl wknd over 1f out* **28/1**

406- **14** 28 **Colours Of Nature**[356] 4625 3-8-10 **62** .... NeilFarley(3) 5
(Eric Alston) *hld up on outside: struggling wl over 2f out: sn wknd: t.o* **33/1**

1m 12.03s (-0.97) **Going Correction** -0.15s/f (Firm)
WFA 3 from 4yo+ 5lb **14** Ran SP% **127.8**
Speed ratings (Par 103): **100,99,96,94,93 92,92,91,88,87 86,84,76,38**
toteswingers 1&2 £8.60, 2&3 £15.60, 1&3 £9.80 CSF £201.63 CT £865.44 TOTE £11.40: £2.40, £6.70, £1.60; EX 165.60 Trifecta £730.90 Part won..
Owner Irvine Lynch **Bred** Mrs Fiona Denniff **Trained** Huby, N Yorks
■ Stewards' Enquiry : Nathan Alison two-day ban: used whip above permitted level (Aug 4-5)

FOCUS
The first two pulled a little way clear in this maiden handicap. The winner is rated up slightly on his C&D latest.
T/Plt: £22.30 to a £1 stake. Pool of £51083.23 - 1665.25 winning tickets. T/Qpdt: £16.30 to a £1 stake. Pool of £3262.30 - 147.50 winning tickets. RY

3867 CURRAGH (R-H)
Saturday, July 20

OFFICIAL GOING: Good to firm

4547a JEBEL ALI RACECOURSE & STABLES ANGLESEY STKS (GROUP 3) — 6f 63y
4:40 (4:40) 2-Y-O **£31,707** (£9,268; £4,390; £1,463)

RPR

1 **Wilshire Boulevard (IRE)**[32] 3424 2-9-3 95 .... SeamieHeffernan 2 109
(A P O'Brien, Ire) *sn trckd ldrs in 4th towards outer: clsd to press ldr in 2nd 2f out: led appr fnl f: styd on wl* **7/1**[3]

2 ¾ **Oklahoma City**[10] 4184 2-9-3 ....(b[1]) JosephO'Brien 7 106
(A P O'Brien, Ire) *slowly away but sn rcvrd to ld: pushed along under 2f out: hdd appr fnl f: rallied wl: no imp fnl 100yds* **1/1**[1]

3 ½ **Mansion House (IRE)**[16] 3999 2-9-3 .... WJLee 1 105
(David Wachman, Ire) *w.w towards outer: pushed along under 2f out: kpt on wl into 3rd fnl 100yds* **12/1**

4 1 ¼ **Jallota**[9] 4212 2-9-3 .... MartinHarley 3 101
(Mick Channon) *trckd ldr in 2nd tl pushed along under 2f out and dropped to 3rd appr fnl f: one pce and dropped to 4th fnl 100yds* **9/4**[2]

5 1 ¼ **Home School (IRE)**[12] 4127 2-9-3 89 ....(t) KevinManning 5 97
(J S Bolger, Ire) *chsd ldrs: 5th 1/2-way: nt qckn under 2f out: kpt on one pce* **12/1**

6 2 ¼ **Dai Bando (IRE)**[20] 3867 2-9-3 .... ChrisHayes 4 91
(P J Prendergast, Ire) *racd in rr: swtchd rt under 2f out: kpt on same pce: nvr on terms* **33/1**

7 *nk* **Tarn**[21] 3843 2-9-0 .... WayneLordan 6 87
(T Stack, Ire) *trckd ldrs: 3rd 1/2-way: nt qckn over 1f out: sn no ex* **9/1**

1m 15.78s (-3.32) **Going Correction** -0.45s/f (Firm) **7** Ran SP% **121.6**
Speed ratings: **104,103,102,100,99 96,95**
CSF £15.71 TOTE £11.50: £3.20, £1.20; DF 20.70.
Owner Derrick Smith & Mrs John Magnier & Michael Tabor **Bred** Denis Brosnan **Trained** Ballydoyle, Co Tipperary

The Form Book Flat, Raceform Ltd, Compton, RG20 6NL.

FOCUS
Fascinating stuff. The favourite looked all about speed at Naas but fluffed his lines at the start and had to fight for early supremacy. The generous early gallop set it up for a closer. Probably an ordinary renewal, but the front three were all improvers.

4549a INVESCO PENSION CONSULTANTS MINSTREL STKS (GROUP 3) 7f
5:40 (5:40) 3-Y-0+ £33,292 (£9,731; £4,609; £1,536)

RPR

1 **Darwin (USA)**[24] 3705 3-9-2 JosephO'Brien 2 114+
(A P O'Brien, Ire) *trckd ldr in 2nd: travelled wl to ld under 2f out: sn qcknd clr: styd on strly* **8/11**[1]

2 1 ¾ **Gordon Lord Byron (IRE)**[28] 3557 5-10-0 115 WayneLordan 4 117+
(T Hogan, Ire) *w.w in 4th: pushed along in 3rd under 2f out: strly rdn to go 2nd fnl 100yds: nt trble wnr* **6/4**[2]

3 1 ¼ **Leitir Mor (IRE)**[32] 3421 3-9-5 109 (tp) KevinManning 3 109
(J S Bolger, Ire) *led tl hdd under 2f out: sn nt qckn w wnr: dropped to 3rd fnl 100yds* **9/1**[3]

4 1 ¼ **Bold Thady Quill (IRE)**[30] 3517 6-9-9 104 (p) ShaneFoley 6 105+
(K J Condon, Ire) *hld up in rr: pushed along 2f out: kpt on to go 4th clsng stages* **33/1**

5 ½ **True Verdict (IRE)**[17] 3964 3-8-13 97 (p) WJLee 1 98+
(David Wachman, Ire) *trckd ldrs in 3rd on inner tl nt qckn under 2f out: one pce and dropped to 5th clsng stages* **33/1**

1m 24.08s (-6.72) **Going Correction** -0.70s/f (Hard)
WFA 3 from 4yo+ 7lb **5** Ran SP% **113.8**
Speed ratings: **110,108,106,105,104**
CSF £2.18 TOTE £1.90: £1.40, £1.02; DF 3.40.
Owner Derrick Smith & Mrs John Magnier & Michael Tabor **Bred** Lansdon Robbins & Tom Hansen **Trained** Ballydoyle, Co Tipperary

FOCUS
One of the most intriguing duels of the Irish Flat season so far saw genuine Group 1 7f specialist Gordon Lord Byron lock horns with up and coming star Darwin. The race itself didn't disappoint and the winner is a colt of serious potential. This was another big step up. The early pace was decent, if not spectacular, and quickened considerably from the 3f pole.

4550a DARLEY IRISH OAKS (GROUP 1) (FILLIES) 1m 4f
6:15 (6:15) 3-Y-0
£188,617 (£61,788; £29,268; £9,756; £6,504; £3,252)

RPR

1 **Chicquita (IRE)**[34] 3385 3-9-0 JohnnyMurtagh 1 114+
(A De Royer-Dupre, France) *trckd ldr in 2nd then 3rd after 3f: pushed along appr fnl f: hung bdly lft but styd on strly to ld cl home* **9/2**[3]

2 ½ **Venus De Milo (IRE)**[24] 3704 3-9-0 SeamieHeffernan 2 113+
(A P O'Brien, Ire) *w.w: pushed along under 3f out: wnt 5th ent fnl f: styd on strly to snatch 2nd on line* **6/1**

3 nk **Just Pretending (USA)**[30] 3482 3-9-0 107 JosephO'Brien 3 112
(A P O'Brien, Ire) *led at stdy pce: clly pressed fr 3f out: rallied wl fr under 2f out: hdd and dropped to 3rd cl home* **8/1**

4 nk **Scintillula (IRE)**[21] 3844 3-9-0 104 (t) KevinManning 6 112
(J S Bolger, Ire) *chsd ldrs in 4th: pushed along and nt qckn appr fnl f in 6th: styd on strly clsng stages to go 4th on line* **10/1**

5 ½ **Riposte**[30] 3482 3-9-0 TomQueally 5 111
(Lady Cecil) *chsd ldrs early: gd hdwy to trck ldr in cl 2nd after 3f: on terms over 2f out: no ex fnl 100yds and dropped to 5th cl home* **9/4**[1]

6 3 ½ **Magical Dream (IRE)**[34] 3381 3-9-0 105 (v[1]) MichaelHussey 7 105
(A P O'Brien, Ire) *hld up in rr: gd hdwy on inner into 4th appr fnl f: sn no imp* **20/1**

7 7 **Talent**[50] 2842 3-9-0 JimCrowley 4 94
(Ralph Beckett) *hld up in rr: pushed along 3f out: no imp 2f out and dropped to rr* **11/4**[2]

2m 35.01s (-3.49) **Going Correction** -0.025s/f (Good) **7** Ran SP% **114.9**
Speed ratings: **110,109,109,109,108 106,101**
CSF £31.40 CT £209.06 TOTE £3.80: £1.80, £3.60; DF 22.00.
Owner Paul Makin **Bred** Ecurie Des Monceaux & Skymarc Farm Inc **Trained** Chantilly, France
■ A sixth Irish Oaks for Johnny Murtagh.

FOCUS
It was no surprise to see Alive Alive Oh withdrawn because of the ground, while Secret Gesture was ruled out by Ralph Beckett earlier in the week. Despite the absence of that talented duo, this looked an up-to-scratch renewal, with the impressive Investec Oaks winner facing the Ribblesdale victor and an unbeaten filly from Ballydoyle. There was a tight finish and a stewards' enquiry before the result was confirmed. The form is rated towards the top of the place averages, with improvement from Chicquita and Venus De Milo. The third is the best guide.

4548 - 4555a (Foreign Racing) - See Raceform Interactive

3588 REDCAR (L-H)
Sunday, July 21

OFFICIAL GOING: Good to firm (firm in places; 9.5)
Wind: light across Weather: fine and sunny

4556 BRITISH STALLION STUDS EBF YORKSHIRE REGIMENT MAIDEN STKS 7f
2:10 (2:11) (Class 5) 2-Y-0 £2,911 (£866; £432; £216) Stalls Centre

Form RPR

2 1 **New Street (IRE)**[37] 3282 2-9-5 0 TonyHamilton 2 73+
(Richard Fahey) *trckd ldrs travelling strly: shkn up to ld appr fnl f: drvn out* **4/9**[1]

6 2 1 ¼ **Blue Atlantic (USA)**[29] 3588 2-9-5 0 JoeFanning 4 68+
(Mark Johnston) *led tl over 3f out: led over 2f out: hdd appr fnl f: styd on same pce* **3/1**[2]

3 2 ½ **Newgate Queen** 2-9-0 0 BarryMcHugh 5 56
(Tony Coyle) *chsd ldrs: outpcd over 3f out: kpt on to take 3rd over 1f out* **33/1**

00 4 2 ¾ **Bar Shy**[15] 4044 2-9-0 0 AdamCarter[(5)] 8 53
(Tim Easterby) *wnt rt s: t.k.h: trckd ldrs: led over 3f out: hdd over 2f out: wknd over 1f out* **20/1**

5 1 **Chivers (IRE)** 2-9-5 0 DavidAllan 3 51
(Tim Easterby) *dwlt: in rr and sn pushed along: sme hdwy over 2f out: wknd over 1f out* **10/1**[3]

0 6 11 **Reale Silenzio**[15] 4046 2-9-0 0 JamesSullivan 6 16
(John Weymes) *chsd ldrs: drvn over 3f out: lost pl over 1f out: bhd whn eased clsng stages* **100/1**

1m 26.95s (2.45) **Going Correction** +0.075s/f (Good) **6** Ran SP% **112.0**
Speed ratings (Par 94): **89,87,84,81,80 67**
toteswingers 1&2 £1.10, 1&3 £4.20, 2&3 £7.40 CSF £2.00 TOTE £3.50: £1.10, £1.10; EX 2.20 Trifecta £14.70 Pool: £3021.89 - 153.41 winning units..
Owner David W Armstrong **Bred** New Deal Partnership **Trained** Musley Bank, N Yorks

FOCUS
This looked an ordinary maiden and the winner won as he was entitled to. He was value for extra and may have more to offer.

4557 REDCAR CRICKET CLUB H'CAP (DIV I) 1m 1f
2:40 (2:40) (Class 6) (0-60,60) 3-Y-0+ £1,940 (£577; £288; £144) Stalls Low

Form RPR

0023 1 **Mcmonagle (USA)**[2] 4503 5-9-5 60 (tp) JacobButterfield[(7)] 9 69
(Alan Brown) *mde all: kpt on wl fnl 2f* **7/2**[2]

-230 2 1 ½ **Dubai Celebration**[13] 4119 5-9-9 57 PaulMulrennan 4 63
(Julie Camacho) *chsd wnr: drvn 3f out: styd on same pce fnl f* **7/2**[2]

5022 3 1 ½ **My New Angel (IRE)**[18] 3946 4-9-5 60 ConnorBeasley[(7)] 2 62
(Jason Ward) *s.i.s: in rr: hdwy on inner over 3f out: nt clr run and swtchd rt 2f out: kpt on to take 3rd clsng stages* **3/1**[1]

5103 4 1 ½ **Tony Hollis**[11] 4161 5-8-13 54 GemmaTutty[(7)] 1 53
(Karen Tutty) *chsd ldrs: one pce fnl 2f* **16/1**

2055 5 4 ½ **Mishhar (IRE)**[18] 3946 4-9-8 56 (v) StephenCraine 3 45
(Tony Coyle) *hld up in rr: hdwy whn nt clr run over 2f out: swtchd lft: fdd fnl f* **11/1**[3]

5-06 6 3 ¼ **Kat Moon**[12] 4140 3-8-9 52 DuranFentiman 5 33
(Tim Easterby) *mid-div: effrt 3f out: lost pl over 1f out* **25/1**

5441 7 9 **Border Bandit (USA)**[13] 4119 5-9-10 58 BarryMcHugh 6 20
(Tracy Waggott) *s.i.s: drvn 4f out: chsng ldrs over 2f out: lost pl over 1f out: eased ins fnl f* **3/1**[1]

0000 8 6 **Miss Matiz**[16] 4005 6-8-5 46 oh1 LouisSteward[(7)] 8
(Alan Kirtley) *t.k.h on outer: mid-div: lost pl over 4f out: sn bhd* **80/1**

1m 52.33s (-0.67) **Going Correction** -0.075s/f (Good)
WFA 3 from 4yo+ 9lb **8** Ran SP% **113.7**
Speed ratings (Par 101): **99,97,96,95,91 88,80,74**
toteswingers 1&2 £4.60, 1&3 £2.00, 2&3 £4.50 CSF £16.01 CT £39.98 TOTE £4.70: £1.10, £1.20, £1.50; EX 16.80 Trifecta £58.20 Pool: £1218.09 - 15.68 winning units..
Owner Don Ellis **Bred** Christopher Grosso **Trained** Yedingham, N Yorks

FOCUS
Three of the first four finishers filled the first three places for much of the way, with the winner making all in an uncontested lead, so suspect form.

4558 SKYBET SUPPORTING THE YORKSHIRE RACING SUMMER FESTIVAL H'CAP 5f
3:10 (3:12) (Class 5) (0-70,70) 3-Y-0 £2,587 (£770; £384; £192) Stalls Centre

Form RPR

6-11 1 **Jubilee Dancer**[23] 3762 3-9-7 70 PaulMulrennan 3 80
(Geoffrey Oldroyd) *wnt lft s: mde all: shkn up appr fnl f: r.o* **15/8**[1]

1516 2 1 **Secret Advice**[8] 4291 3-9-1 64 JoeFanning 2 70
(Keith Dalgleish) *dwlt: hld up: hdwy and edgd lft 2f out: styd on same pce fnl f* **4/1**[2]

3413 3 ½ **Confidential Creek**[29] 3594 3-8-1 57 (p) ConnorBeasley[(7)] 6 62
(Ollie Pears) *hld up: hdwy 2f out: kpt on same pce fnl f* **4/1**[2]

13-0 4 5 **Mandy Layla (IRE)**[37] 3283 3-9-1 69 JustinNewman[(5)] 7 56
(Bryan Smart) *wnt lft s: sn chsng ldrs: rdn over 2f out: wknd over 1f out* **17/2**

4302 5 3 ½ **Queen Flush (IRE)**[12] 4136 3-8-6 55 (b) BarryMcHugh 1 29
(David Nicholls) *trckd ldrs: wknd over 1f out* **7/1**[3]

0665 6 2 **Lady Poppy**[4] 4402 3-9-2 65 PJMcDonald 4 32
(George Moore) *chsd ldrs: drvn 2f out: sn lost pl* **8/1**

40-4 7 1 ¼ **Hellolini**[23] 3789 3-8-0 52 oh1 ow1 NeilFarley[(3)] 8 14
(Robin Bastiman) *chsd ldrs: drvn and wknd 2f out* **28/1**

59.02s (0.42) **Going Correction** +0.10s/f (Good) **7** Ran SP% **112.4**
Speed ratings (Par 100): **100,98,97,89,84 80,78**
toteswingers 1&2 £2.40, 1&3 £2.10, 2&3 £3.00 CSF £9.14 CT £25.43 TOTE £2.50: £2.00, £1.80; EX 9.40 Trifecta £23.00 Pool: £2447.61 - 79.54 winning units..
Owner Moneypenny Racing **Bred** Bond Thoroughbred Corporation **Trained** Brawby, N Yorks

FOCUS
Just a modest sprint handicap.

4559 DOWNLOAD THE FREE RACING UK APP CLAIMING STKS 1m 2f
3:40 (3:41) (Class 6) 3-Y-0+ £2,045 (£603; £302) Stalls Low

Form RPR

3530 1 **Demolition**[25] 3685 9-8-13 81 JoeyHaynes[(7)] 1 80
(Noel Wilson) *trckd ldr: effrt over 3f out: chal over 1f out: led last 75yds: drvn rt out* **11/10**[1]

1055 2 2 **Activate**[13] 4110 6-9-8 71 (b) JoeFanning 4 78
(Keith Dalgleish) *led: qcknd pce over 3f out: drvn 2f out: hdd and no ex ins fnl f* **11/10**[1]

0064 3 8 **Moheebb (IRE)**[22] 3827 9-9-6 61 (b) KirstyMilczarek 5 60
(Robert Johnson) *s.s: t.k.h: sn trcking ldrs: drvn over 4f out: one pce fnl 2f* **10/1**[2]

1000 4 10 **Cufflink**[13] 4109 4-9-1 54 (b[1]) DavidAllan 6 35
(Iain Jardine) *chsd ldrs: drvn over 4f out: lost pl over 2f out* **25/1**[3]

5 16 **Inka Express** 3-8-5 0 (t) PatrickMathers 7 3
(Mike Sowersby) *s.i.s: drvn along and sn detached in last: bhd fnl 3f* **66/1**

2m 5.06s (-2.04) **Going Correction** -0.075s/f (Good)
WFA 3 from 4yo+ 10lb **5** Ran SP% **109.7**
Speed ratings (Par 101): **105,103,97,89,76**
CSF £2.45 TOTE £2.30: £1.10, £1.10; EX 3.00 Trifecta £4.80 Pool: £1872.32 - 288.21 winning units..
Owner M Wormald **Bred** P D And Mrs Player **Trained** Middleham, N Yorks

FOCUS
An uncompetitive claimer.

4560 INFINITY ECOMAX TYRES H'CAP 6f
4:10 (4:11) (Class 4) (0-85,85) 3-Y-0+ £6,469 (£1,925; £962; £481) Stalls Centre

Form RPR

6323 1 **Head Space (IRE)**[12] 4138 5-9-7 80 (p) JamesSullivan 1 89
(Ruth Carr) *hld up: hdwy 2f out: led jst ins fnl f: drvn out* **5/2**[1]

0000 2 ½ **Medici Time**[29] 3586 8-9-0 73 PhillipMakin 2 80
(Tim Easterby) *in rr: hdwy 2f out: styd on to take 2nd last 100yds: no ex* **20/1**

3621 3 ¾ **Al Khan (IRE)**[9] 4235 4-9-12 85 RobertWinston 6 90
(Violet M Jordan) *chsd ldrs: drvn over 2f out: styd on fnl f: tk 3rd last strides* **3/1**[2]

-430 4 hd **Cocktail Charlie**[36] 3351 5-9-1 74 DavidAllan 10 78
(Tim Easterby) *w ldrs: led over 2f out: hdd jst ins fnl f: kpt on same pce* **15/2**

6250 5 1 ¼ **Barkston Ash**[17] 3980 5-9-2 78 (p) NeilFarley[(3)] 3 78
(Eric Alston) *w ldrs: one pce appr fnl f* **16/1**

0341 **6** 3/4 **Foreign Rhythm (IRE)**[14] 4102 8-8-4 **66** oh2................ RaulDaSilva(3) 4 64
(Ron Barr) *chsd ldrs: kpt on one pce over 1f out* **18/1**

6000 **7** 1 1/4 **Escape To Glory (USA)**[25] 3682 5-9-8 **81**................(t) PaulMulrennan 8 75
(Michael Dods) *hld up in rr: hdwy to trck ldrs whn nt clr run 1f out: fdd last 100yds* **11/1**

4035 **8** 4 1/2 **Rich Again (IRE)**[6] 4338 4-8-7 **66** oh1...........................(p) PJMcDonald 7 45
(James Bethell) *chsd ldrs: lost pl over 1f out* **6/1**[3]

0226 **9** 1/2 **Orbit The Moon (IRE)**[13] 4111 5-8-12 **78**...........(tp) ConnorBeasley(7) 5 56
(Michael Dods) *led tl over 2f out: lost pl over 1f out* **17/2**

0000 **10** 1 3/4 **Last Bid**[12] 4138 4-9-0 **73**...........................(t) DuranFentiman 9 45
(Tim Easterby) *chsd ldrs: lost pl over 1f out* **33/1**

1m 12.01s (0.21) **Going Correction** +0.10s/f (Good) **10** Ran SP% **117.3**
Speed ratings (Par 105): **102,101,100,100,98 97,95,89,89,86**
toteswingers 1&2 £11.90, 1&3 £2.20, 2&3 £9.30 CSF £55.57 CT £163.35 TOTE £3.40: £1.30, £5.50, £1.50; EX 57.30 Trifecta £147.20 Pool: £2873.08 - 14.63 winning units..
Owner The Bottom Liners & Mrs R Carr **Bred** Castlemartin Stud And Skymarc Farm **Trained** Huby, N Yorks

FOCUS
A fair sprint handicap.

4561 HELP FOR HEROES FILLIES' H'CAP 1m
4:40 (4:40) (Class 5) (0-75,72) 3-Y-O+ **£2,587** (£770; £384; £192) **Stalls** Centre

Form RPR

5215 **1** **Malekat Jamal (IRE)**[30] 3532 4-10-0 **72**........................... JoeFanning 2 79
(David Simcock) *hld up: trckd ldrs over 3f out: led over 1f out: edgd lft: drvn out* **11/10**[1]

1664 **2** 1 1/4 **Spavento (IRE)**[10] 4201 7-10-0 **72**........................... DavidAllan 1 76
(Eric Alston) *chsd ldrs: drvn over 3f out: upsides 1f out: kpt on same pce* **14/1**

6322 **3** 1 **Visit Copenhagen (USA)**[11] 4180 3-9-6 **72**................ DanielTudhope 4 72
(Mrs K Burke) *w ldr: led over 4f out: hdd over 1f out: one pce* **15/8**[2]

3023 **4** 5 **Graceful Act**[4] 4400 5-8-11 **55**........................... PhillipMakin 3 45
(Ron Barr) *led tl over 4f out: wknd over 1f out* **9/2**[3]

2000 **5** 9 **Tom's Anna (IRE)**[34] 3396 3-8-3 **62**........................... GaryMahon(7) 6 30
(Tim Easterby) *hld up in last: effrt 3f out: sn rdn and wknd* **25/1**

1m 38.16s (1.56) **Going Correction** +0.10s/f (Good)
WFA 3 from 4yo+ 8lb **5** Ran SP% **111.1**
Speed ratings (Par 100): **103,101,100,95,86**
CSF £16.52 TOTE £2.00: £2.30, £3.70; EX 10.20 Trifecta £29.70 Pool: £1578.52 - 39.82 winning units..
Owner Saeed Manana **Bred** Adrian Purvis & Luke Barry **Trained** Newmarket, Suffolk

FOCUS
A weak fillies' handicap.

4562 REDCAR CRICKET CLUB H'CAP (DIV II) 1m 1f
5:10 (5:13) (Class 6) (0-60,60) 3-Y-O+ **£1,940** (£577; £288; £144) **Stalls** Low

Form RPR

5613 **1** **Yorksters Prince (IRE)**[24] 3728 6-9-4 **55**................(b) RaulDaSilva(3) 1 63
(Marjorie Fife) *led after 1f: 5 l clr 4f out: hrd drvn over 1f out: lasted home* **13/8**[1]

-061 **2** 3/4 **Taro Tywod (IRE)**[10] 4195 4-9-12 **60**........................... TomMcLaughlin 5 66
(Mark Brisbourne) *led 1f: chsd wnr: drvn 4f out: rdn over 2f out: kpt on ins fnl f* **9/2**[3]

-525 **3** 4 1/2 **Maggie Mey (IRE)**[33] 3444 5-9-4 **52**........................... JoeFanning 6 48
(Lawrence Mullaney) *chsd ldrs: one pce fnl 2f* **12/1**

4000 **4** 3/4 **Thatcherite (IRE)**[13] 4119 5-9-9 **57**................(bt) StephenCraine 4 52
(Tony Coyle) *mid-div: awkward and lost grnd bnd over 5f out: hdwy over 3f out: kpt on one pce over 1f out* **16/1**

6065 **5** 3 1/2 **Sinatramania**[24] 3727 6-9-0 **48**........................... RoystonFfrench 7 35
(Tracy Waggott) *chsd ldrs: drvn over 3f out: wknd over 1f out* **9/1**

2030 **6** 3/4 **Cross The Boss (IRE)**[13] 4109 6-9-9 **57**................(t) DanielTudhope 2 42
(David O'Meara) *dwlt: sme hdwy 3f out: nvr nr ldrs* **3/1**[2]

0640 **7** 6 **Tropical Duke (IRE)**[18] 3947 7-8-12 **46** oh1................ PhillipMakin 8 18
(Ron Barr) *s.i.s: in rr: sme hdwy over 2f out: wknd fnl f* **25/1**

0000 **8** 1 3/4 **Roc Fort**[6] 4343 4-8-12 **46** oh1...........................(p) PaddyAspell 3 14
(James Moffatt) *chsd ldrs: lost pl 3f out* **80/1**

006 **9** 17 **Daniel Thomas (IRE)**[6] 4355 11-9-8 **56**................(tp) RobertWinston 9
(Violet M Jordan) *s.i.s: bhd and drvn over 4f out: eased ins fnl f* **25/1**

1m 52.0s (-1.00) **Going Correction** -0.075s/f (Good) **9** Ran SP% **113.8**
Speed ratings (Par 101): **101,100,96,95,92 91,86,85,69**
toteswingers 1&2 £2.70, 1&3 £5.20, 2&3 £6.40 CSF £8.82 CT £63.45 TOTE £2.70: £1.20, £1.80, £2.30; EX 10.30 Trifecta £54.00 Pool: £1936.33 - 26.88 winning units..
Owner Mrs Marion Turner **Bred** Lady Legard & Sir Tatton Sykes **Trained** Stillington, N Yorks

FOCUS
Not much of a race.

4563 GO RACING IN YORKSHIRE FUTURE STARS APPRENTICE H'CAP (ROUND 5) 1m 6f 19y
5:40 (5:40) (Class 5) (0-70,66) 4-Y-O+ **£2,587** (£770; £384; £192) **Stalls** Low

Form RPR

3532 **1** **Madrasa (IRE)**[29] 3589 5-9-11 **65**................(bt) JacobButterfield 2 75
(Keith Reveley) *trckd ldrs: drvn over 2f out: led on ins over 1f out: forged clr ins fnl f* **2/1**[1]

0315 **2** 3 3/4 **Sally Friday (IRE)**[29] 3589 5-9-6 **60**................(p) SamanthaBell 3 65
(Edwin Tuer) *hld up in rr: nt clr run fr over 3f out tl swtchd outside 2f out: styd on wl fnl f: edgd lft and tk 2nd nr fin* **13/2**[3]

6-03 **3** 1/2 **Golden Future**[55] 2720 10-8-13 **53**........................... DavidBergin 10 57
(Peter Niven) *swtchd lft s: led: qcknd pce over 4f out: narrowly hdd over 3f out: rallied and upsides over 1f out: styd on same pce* **12/1**

0300 **4** *nse* **Al Furat (USA)**[15] 4071 5-9-3 **57**...........................(p) NoelGarbutt 1 61
(Ron Barr) *dwlt: sn trcking ldrs: t.k.h: kpt on same pce over 1f out: crowded clsng stages* **7/1**

0420 **5** 1 1/2 **Amir Pasha (UAE)**[4] 4403 8-8-13 **53**................(p) DavidSimmonson 7 55
(Micky Hammond) *trckd ldrs: slt ld over 3f out: hdd over 1f out: fdd towards fin* **14/1**

6512 **6** *nk* **Petella**[29] 3595 7-9-4 **58**...........................(p) ConnorBeasley 8 59
(George Moore) *hld up towards rr: hdwy over 3f out: edgd lft and styd on fnl f* **4/1**[2]

0600 **7** 3 1/4 **Patavium (IRE)**[31] 3504 10-9-6 **60**........................... GemmaTutty 4 57
(Edwin Tuer) *t.k.h in mid-div: hdwy to chse ldrs over 3f out: rdn and outpcd over 2f out: wknd over 1f out* **40/1**

2510 **8** 3/4 **Spiekeroog**[16] 4016 7-9-5 **66**........................... JoshDoyle(7) 6 62
(David O'Meara) *hld up in rr: effrt over 2f out: nvr a factor* **8/1**

-000 **9** 2 1/4 **Dean Iarracht (IRE)**[16] 4010 7-8-3 **48**................(p) DanielleMooney(5) 5 41
(Tracy Waggott) *t.k.h in rr: outpcd over 3f out: sme hdwy over 2f out: sn wknd* **25/1**

0063 **10** 1 1/4 **Sohcahtoa (IRE)**[23] 3771 7-9-10 **64**........................... JackDuern 9 55
(Andrew Crook) *mid-div: effrt 4f out: lost pl over 2f out* **25/1**

3m 11.95s (7.25) **Going Correction** -0.075s/f (Good) **10** Ran SP% **114.8**
Speed ratings (Par 103): **76,73,73,73,72 72,70,70,68,68**
toteswingers 1&2 £3.20,1&3 £7.60, 2&3 £9.20 CSF £14.62 CT £123.11 TOTE £2.10: £1.30, £2.20, £4.10; EX 12.50 Trifecta £88.40 Pool: £1359.50 - 11.52 winning units..
Owner M W Joyce **Bred** Paget Bloodstock **Trained** Lingdale, Redcar & Cleveland

FOCUS
An ordinary race run at what looked a pretty modest pace.
T/Jkpt: £555.60 to a £1 stake. Pool of £121,860.41 - 155.72 winning tickets. T/Plt: £7.90 to a £1 stake. Pool of £67,669.79 - 6212.11 winning tickets. T/Qpdt: £4.50 to a £1 stake. Pool of £3257.30 - 529.65 winning tickets. WG

4564 - 4566a (Foreign Racing) - See Raceform Interactive

4545 CURRAGH (R-H)
Sunday, July 21

OFFICIAL GOING: Good to firm

4567a KILBOY ESTATE STKS (GROUP 2) (F&M) 1m 1f
3:45 (3:47) 3-Y-O+ **£52,845** (£15,447; £7,317; £2,439)

RPR

1 **Dank**[32] 3456 4-9-9 .... RyanMoore 1 113
(Sir Michael Stoute) *trckd ldrs in 3rd on inner tl clsd to press ldr in 2nd under 2f out: sn led and qcknd clr ent fnl f: styd on strly* **5/4**[1]

2 1 3/4 **Say (IRE)**[21] 3870 3-9-0 107...........................[1] JosephO'Brien 4 108
(A P O'Brien, Ire) *w.w: pushed along to chse ldrs under 2f out in 5th: styd on wl into 2nd ins fnl f: nt trble wnr* **8/1**

3 2 1/4 **Caponata (USA)**[22] 3844 4-9-9 109........................... PatSmullen 7 105+
(D K Weld, Ire) *hld up in rr: pushed along and nt qckn over 2f out in 6th: styd on wl ins fnl f to go 3rd on line* **7/1**[3]

4 *nk* **Aloof (IRE)**[23] 3798 4-9-9 103........................... WayneLordan 3 104
(David Wachman, Ire) *trckd ldr in 2nd tl led 2f out: sn pressed and hdd over 1f out: kpt on one pce: dropped to 4th on line* **14/1**

5 *nk* **Mizzava (IRE)**[30] 3524 3-9-0 106........................... ShaneFoley 5 102+
(M Halford, Ire) *w.w: pushed along 3f out: kpt on u.str-driving fr over 1f out* **7/1**[3]

6 *nk* **Fiesolana (IRE)**[18] 3964 4-9-9 110........................... WJLee 6 103
(W McCreery, Ire) *trckd ldrs in 4th: travelled wl 2f out in 3rd: sn pushed along and nt qckn: wknd ins fnl f* **7/2**[2]

7 1 **Bible Belt (IRE)**[332] 5518 5-9-9 107........................... FMBerry 8 101
(Mrs John Harrington, Ire) *hld up in rr: nvr on terms but kpt on steadily fr over 1f out: nt hrd-rdn* **14/1**

8 1 3/4 **What Style (IRE)**[56] 2689 3-9-0 99........................... DeclanMcDonogh 2 96
(John M Oxx, Ire) *led tl hdd 2f out: sn wknd* **25/1**

1m 51.29s (-3.61) **Going Correction** -0.10s/f (Good)
WFA 3 from 4yo+ 9lb **8** Ran SP% **120.0**
Speed ratings: **112,110,108,108,107 107,106,105**
CSF £13.28 TOTE £1.60: £1.10, £2.90, £1.90; DF 6.70.
Owner James Wigan **Bred** London Thoroughbred Services Ltd **Trained** Newmarket, Suffolk

FOCUS
The first running of this race as a Group 2 event was won in good style by Dank. The winner and fourth help set the standard.

4568 - 4570a (Foreign Racing) - See Raceform Interactive

3146 HOPPEGARTEN (R-H)
Sunday, July 21

OFFICIAL GOING: Turf: good

4571a GROSSER PREIS VON BERLIN (GROUP 1) (3YO+) (TURF) 1m 4f
3:35 (12:00) 3-Y-O+ **£81,300** (£32,520; £16,260; £8,130; £4,065)

RPR

1 **Nymphea (IRE)**[43] 3100 4-9-3 0........................... MrDennisSchiergen 6 116
(P Schiergen, Germany) *mde all: sn wl clr: at least 15 l clr whn rdn 2f out: styd on: reduced advantage cl home but nvr in any danger: unchal* **16/5**[3]

2 3 **Temida (IRE)**[343] 5145 5-9-3 0........................... FilipMinarik 5 111+
(M G Mintchev, Germany) *chsd clr ldr: rdn to try and cl 3f out: styd on but no real imp on wnr tl wl ins fnl f: nvr nr to chal* **37/10**

3 1 1/2 **Meandre (FR)**[63] 2494 5-9-6 0........................... MircoDemuro 4 112+
(A Savujev, Czech Republic) *midfield: 3rd whn rdn to try and cl 3f out: styd on but no real imp on wnr tl wl ins fnl f: nvr nr to chal* **14/5**[1]

4 4 **Girolamo (GER)**[21] 3879 4-9-6 0........................... ASuborics 1 105+
(P Schiergen, Germany) *midfield on inner: rdn 3f out: plugged on for 4th but nvr a factor* **31/10**[2]

5 *nk* **Donn Halling (IRE)**[49] 5-9-6 0........................... PetrForet 2 105+
(V Luka Jr, Czech Republic) *hld up in last: rdn 3f out: plugged on for 5th but nvr a factor* **98/10**

6 6 **Nordvulkan (GER)**[14] 4103 3-8-8 0........................... JBojko 7 95+
(R Dzubasz, Germany) *midfield on outer: rdn 3f out: dropped to last and btn over 1f out: nvr a factor* **33/10**

2m 26.3s (-3.00)
WFA 3 from 4yo+ 12lb **6** Ran SP% **128.3**
WIN (incl. 10 euro stake): 42. PLACES: 21, 30. SF: 223.
Owner Stall Nizza **Bred** Juergen Imm **Trained** Germany

4104 MAISONS-LAFFITTE (R-H)
Sunday, July 21

OFFICIAL GOING: Turf: good

4572a PRIX ROBERT PAPIN (GROUP 2) (2YO COLTS & FILLIES) (TURF) 5f 110y
1:30 (12:00) 2-Y-O **£60,243** (£23,252; £11,097; £7,398; £3,699)

RPR

1 **Vorda (FR)**[40] 3185 2-8-13 0........................... GregoryBenoist 8 108+
(P Sogorb, France) *restrained early and hld up in tch: shkn up 2f out: swtchd rt and hdwy over 1f out: qcknd to ld ins fnl f and drvn clr: readily* **3/1**[1]

2 1 1/2 **Omaticaya (IRE)**[21] 3880 2-8-13 0........................... CristianDemuro 5 103
(Manila Illuminati, Italy) *led: rdn over 2f out: strly pressed and hdd 1f out: rallied u.p and got bk up for 2nd cl home: nt pce of wnr* **12/1**

3 snk **Vedeux (IRE)**21 3875 2-9-2 0 MarcLerner 6 106
(C Lerner, France) *t.k.h: trckd ldr on rail: rdn 2f out: led 1f out: hdd ins fnl f and outpcd by wnr: kpt on but dropped to 3rd cl home* **7/2**2

4 3/4 **Muharaaj (IRE)**40 3185 2-9-2 0 AntoineHamelin 1 103
(Matthieu Palussiere, France) *midfield in tch on inner: rdn 2f out: r.o to snatch 4th post: nt pce to chal* **14/1**

5 shd **Anticipated (IRE)**33 3424 2-9-2 0 RichardHughes 7 103
(Richard Hannon) *trckd ldr on outer: rdn and ev ch 2f out: r.o but dropped to 5th post* **6/1**

6 1 1/4 **Ambiance (IRE)**16 4025 2-9-2 0 MartinHarley 2 99
(Mick Channon) *midfield in tch: rdn 2f out: ev ch ent fnl f: nt qckn: kpt on but dropped to 6th* **6/1**

7 1 1/2 **Another Party (FR)**21 3875 2-9-2 0 ChristopheSoumillon 3 94
(Matthieu Palussiere, France) *midfield in tch: rdn 2f out: carried rt by wnr over 1f out: sn no ex and btn: fdd* **10/1**

8 1/2 **Lady Chantilly (IRE)**22 3829 2-8-13 0 ThomasHenderson 4 89
(Jo Hughes) *t.k.h: dwlt: sn rcvrd to be prom on outer: rdn over 2f out: no ex and btn ent fnl f: fdd* **33/1**

9 7 **Extortionist (IRE)**33 3424 2-9-2 0 JamieSpencer 9 69
(Olly Stevens) *plld hrd: dwlt: hld up and nvr out of last: rdn 2f out: bhd and btn 1f out: eased ins fnl f: nvr a factor* **5/1**3

1m 5.0s (-2.30) **9 Ran SP% 118.9**
WIN (incl. 1 euro stake): 2.70. PLACES: 1.50, 3.40, 1.90. DF: 25.60. SF: 37.40.
Owner G Augustin-Normand & R Picamau **Bred** Edy S.R.L. **Trained** France

FOCUS
A solid renewal. The fifth and sixth, and the race averages back the form up.

4573a PRIX EUGENE ADAM (GRAND PRIX DE MAISONS-LAFFITTE) (GROUP 2) (3YO) (TURF) 1m 2f (S)
2:40 (12:00) 3-Y-0 **£60,243** (£23,252; £11,097; £7,398; £3,699)

RPR

1 **Triple Threat (FR)**68 2355 3-8-11 0 Pierre-CharlesBoudot 8 115+
(A Fabre, France) *stdd and hld up in last pair: last 1/2-way: shkn up and hdwy on wd outside fr 2f out: rdn to chal over 1f out: led ins fnl f: pushed clr: comf* **11/1**

2 2 **Pilote (IRE)**20 3911 3-8-11 0 OlivierPeslier 6 112
(A Fabre, France) *hld up in last trio: smooth hdwy on outer fr 3f out: rdn to chal 2f out: led over 1f out: hdd ins fnl f and readily outpcd by wnr: kpt on* **8/1**3

3 3/4 **Dalwari (USA)**49 2907 3-8-11 0 ChristopheSoumillon 7 110
(J-C Rouget, France) *hld up in last quartet: swtchd rt and hdwy fr 4f out: rdn to chal over 2f out: hung lft u.p but cl 3rd and ev ch ent fnl f: sn outpcd by front pair: kpt on* **4/1**2

4 1 1/2 **Meneas (FR)**27 3645 3-8-11 0 AnthonyCrastus 5 107
(C Laffon-Parias, France) *dwlt: hld up in last trio on inner: rdn over 2f out: styd on and wnt 4th ins fnl f: nt pce to chal* **14/1**

5 1/2 **Shikarpour (IRE)**31 3485 3-8-11 0 Christophe-PatriceLemaire 3 106
(A De Royer-Dupre, France) *midfield on outer: rdn and lost pl 3f out: rallied u.p and styd on steadily ins fnl 2f but v one-pced* **6/4**1

6 4 **Glacial Age (IRE)**27 3645 3-8-11 0 ThomasHenderson 9 98
(Jo Hughes) *got across fr wdst draw and led: rdn 3f out: strly pressed and hdd over 1f out: sn no ex and btn: fdd* **20/1**

7 12 **Buckwheat**27 3645 3-8-11 0 MaximeGuyon 2 74
(A Fabre, France) *midfield on inner: rdn 3f out: no ex and btn over 1f out: fdd and eased* **4/1**2

8 1/2 **Saint Thomas (FR)**20 3911 3-8-11 0 ThierryJarnet 4 73
(P Bary, France) *trckd ldr on outer: rdn over 2f out: no ex and btn over 1f out: fdd and eased* **16/1**

9 1 1/2 **Mutin (FR)**32 3455 3-8-11 0 IoritzMendizabal 1 70
(J-C Rouget, France) *trckd ldr on inner: swtchd out and rdn to chal 3f out: no ex and btn 2f out: fdd and dropped to last over 1f out: eased* **14/1**

2m 2.4s **9 Ran SP% 123.4**
WIN (incl. 1 euro stake): 11.20. PLACES: 2.80, 2.40, 2.30. DF: 23.70. SF: 68.70.
Owner Team Valor Llc/ G Barber **Bred** Team Valour & G Barber **Trained** Chantilly, France

FOCUS
They seemed to go fairly steady early and they were well bunched turning in. The principals all came from off the pace.

4575a PRIX DU BUISSON RICHARD (CLAIMER) (3YO) (YOUNG JOCKEYS & APPRENTICES) (TURF) 1m 2f (S)
3:45 (12:00) 3-Y-0 **£9,349** (£3,739; £2,804; £1,869; £934)

RPR

1 **Teolagi (IRE)**34 3418 3-8-8 0 SoufyaneMoulin(3) 6 73
(J S Moore) *midfield on outer: rdn to chal 2f out: continually hung rt u.p but jnd ldr over 1f out: duelled thrght fnl f: styd on and edgd ahd cl home* **42/10**

2 nk **Clef D'Or (FR)** 3-9-1 0 EnzoCorallo(3) 5 79
(Y Durepaire, France) **2/1**1

3 5 **Soul Sacrifice**49 3-9-1 0 (b) AntoineCoutier(3) 3 69
(A De Mieulle, France) **15/2**

4 1 **La Messalina (FR)** 3-8-6 0 SebastienMartino(5) 4 60
(Alex Fracas, France) **9/1**

5 1/2 **Gingka (FR)**8 3-9-2 0 AntoineWerle(3) 7 67
(Mme P Butel, France) **19/5**3

6 20 **Litian Rocket (FR)**39 3-9-1 0 AlexandreChampenois(5) 8 28
(M Boutin, France) **7/2**2

2m 6.7s (4.30) **6 Ran SP% 117.4**
WIN (incl.1 euro stake): 5.20. PLACES: 1.80, 1.30, 2.00. DF: 6.20. SF: 15.60.
Owner Mrs Fitri Hay **Bred** Mrs Fitriani Hay **Trained** Upper Lambourn, Berks

4337 AYR (L-H)
Monday, July 22

OFFICIAL GOING: Good to firm (watered; 9.3)
Wind: Breezy, half behind Weather: Hazy, humid

4576 EBF/33 RACECOURSES LIVE ON SKY 432 MAIDEN STKS 7f 50y
2:00 (2:00) (Class 4) 2-Y-0 **£4,528** (£1,347; £673) **Stalls Low**

Form RPR

46 1 **Stars Over The Sea (USA)**17 4021 2-9-5 0 JoeFanning 1 85+
(Mark Johnston) *trckd ldr: shkn up and hdwy to ld over 2f out: edgd lft: kpt on strly fnl f* **1/2**1

3 2 3 **Longton**15 4096 2-9-5 0 TonyHamilton 3 77+
(Richard Fahey) *t.k.h early: led: rdn and hdd over 2f out: kpt on same pce fnl f* **2/1**2

3 15 **Beautiful Stranger (IRE)** 2-9-5 0 TomEaves 2 38
(Keith Dalgleish) *chsd ldrs: rdn 3f out: sn wknd* **16/1**3

1m 30.68s (-2.72) **Going Correction** -0.30s/f (Firm) **3 Ran SP% 105.9**
Speed ratings (Par 96): **103,99,82**
CSF £1.73 TOTE £1.40; EX 1.90 Trifecta £1.60 Pool: £1230.76 - 563.17 winning units..
Owner R S Brookhouse **Bred** W S Farish & Watership Down Stud **Trained** Middleham Moor, N Yorks

FOCUS
Home bend moved out 6m adding about 18yds to races on Round course. There was no depth to this race, but the only previous performance of the runner-up and the manner of the winner's victory suggests it was up to standard for the course. The first two are both entitled to be better than this.

4577 BET & WATCH WITH RACING UK'S APP H'CAP (QUALIFIER FOR £15,000 BETFAIR SCOTTISH MILE SERIES FINAL) 7f 50y
2:30 (2:30) (Class 5) (0-75,75) 3-Y-0+ **£2,587** (£770; £384; £192) **Stalls Low**

Form RPR

0053 1 **Barney McGrew (IRE)**11 4198 10-9-13 74 PaulMulrennan 7 83
(Michael Dods) *hld up in tch: stdy hdwy on outside over 2f out: led and hrd pressed over 1f out: hld on wl towards fin* **9/2**2

1511 2 hd **West Leake Hare (IRE)**19 3945 4-10-0 75 PaulQuinn 3 83
(David Nicholls) *t.k.h: hld up in last pl: shkn up and hdwy on outside over 2f out: rdn and disp ld over 1f out: kpt on: hld cl home* **11/8**1

4604 3 2 3/4 **Chookie Avon**7 4341 6-9-11 72 (p) TomEaves 1 73
(Keith Dalgleish) *trckd ldrs: effrt and ev ch over 1f out: outpcd by first two fnl f* **9/1**

0302 4 3 3/4 **Beckermet (IRE)**7 4338 11-9-6 67 JamesSullivan 6 59
(Ruth Carr) *cl up: led over 2f out to over 1f out: sn wknd* **9/2**2

-423 5 2 **Strictly Ballroom (IRE)**45 3053 3-9-7 75 JoeFanning 2 58
(Mark Johnston) *dwlt: in tch: rdn over 2f out: edgd lft and wknd over 1f out* **11/2**3

0045 6 2 **Conjuror's Bluff**31 3546 5-8-6 56 oh8 DeclanCannon(3) 5 37
(Frederick Watson) *prom tl rdn and wknd fr 2f out* **100/1**

2000 7 2 1/2 **Silverware (USA)**15 4100 5-9-11 72 DavidNolan 4 47
(Kristin Stubbs) *t.k.h: led to over 2f out: sn rdn: wknd over 1f out* **16/1**

1m 30.6s (-2.80) **Going Correction** -0.30s/f (Firm)
WFA 3 from 4yo+ 7lb **7 Ran SP% 110.7**
Speed ratings (Par 103): **104,103,100,96,94 91,88**
toteswingers 1&2 £2.40, 1&3 £4.00, 2&3 £3.80 CSF £10.38 TOTE £4.20: £1.40, £1.80; EX 8.50 Trifecta £59.20 Pool: £2505.81 - 31.71 winning units..
Owner N A Riddell **Bred** Mrs H B Raw **Trained** Denton, Co Durham

FOCUS
Some decent performers, including two still-useful veterans, contested this 0-75. The early pace was quick and the first two came from the rear. This was close to the winner's form from last year.

4578 WATCH RACING UK ON SKY 432 H'CAP (QUALIFIER FOR £15,000 BETFAIR SCOTTISH STAYERS' SERIES FINAL) 1m 5f 13y
3:05 (3:05) (Class 5) (0-70,66) 3-Y-0+ **£2,587** (£770; £384) **Stalls Low**

Form RPR

6141 1 **Grand Diamond (IRE)**7 4343 9-8-8 53 (p) JordanNason(7) 1 61
(Jim Goldie) *chsd ldr: smooth hdwy and ev ch over 2f out: rdn to ld over 1f out: r.o wl* **11/4**3

1224 2 2 1/4 **Schmooze (IRE)**4 4447 4-9-7 66 ConnorBeasley(7) 4 71
(Linda Perratt) *chsd ldrs: hdwy to ld over 2f out: sn rdn: hdd over 1f out: kpt on same pce ins fnl f* **11/8**1

-413 3 3 3/4 **Forrest Flyer (IRE)**14 4110 9-10-0 66 GrahamLee 2 65
(Jim Goldie) *led: niggled after 4f: drvn and hdd over 2f out: sn outpcd: n.d after* **6/4**2

2m 54.94s (0.94) **Going Correction** -0.30s/f (Firm) **3 Ran SP% 108.8**
Speed ratings (Par 103): **85,83,81**
CSF £6.67 TOTE £3.20; EX 8.20 Trifecta £7.30 Pool: £1048.74 - 106.44 winning units..
Owner Caledonia Racing **Bred** Newberry Stud Company **Trained** Uplawmoor, E Renfrews

FOCUS
The quality of the runners in this race was fine for the grade, and the pace was generous considering the small field, but the turnout was disappointing. Similar form to last week's C&D win from Grand Diamond.

4579 RACING UK YOUR RACING HOME FROM HOME H'CAP 5f
3:40 (3:40) (Class 4) (0-85,83) 3-Y-0+ **£5,175** (£1,540; £769; £384) **Stalls Low**

Form RPR

0440 1 **Fitz Flyer (IRE)**10 4263 7-9-12 83 (v) JoeFanning 1 92
(David Nicholls) *in tch: n.m.r briefly over 2f out: shkn up and hdwy to ld ent fnl f: pushed out* **11/8**1

053 2 1 3/4 **Economic Crisis (IRE)**7 4338 4-8-13 70 PaddyAspell 3 73
(Alan Berry) *cl up: rdn 1/2-way: led over 1f out to ent fnl f: kpt on same pce* **10/1**

5222 3 1 1/4 **Diman Waters (IRE)**11 4203 6-9-2 78 DarylByrne(5) 4 76
(Eric Alston) *prom: effrt and pushed along wl over 1f out: kpt on same pce ins fnl f* **4/1**3

0314 4 nk **Midnight Dynamo**21 3892 6-9-7 78 GrahamLee 2 75
(Jim Goldie) *chsd ldrs: drvn wl over 1f out: kpt on same pce fnl f* **11/4**2

1260 5 2 **Bronze Beau**22 3855 6-9-6 77 (t) JamesSullivan 5 67
(Kristin Stubbs) *led tl rdn and hdd over 1f out: sn btn* **7/1**

59.03s (-0.37) **Going Correction** -0.175s/f (Firm) **5 Ran SP% 110.4**
Speed ratings (Par 105): **95,92,90,89,86**
CSF £15.16 TOTE £2.10: £1.10, £8.80; EX 12.20 Trifecta £83.50 Pool: £2188.16 - 19.64 winning units..
Owner Mike Browne **Bred** Colin Kennedy **Trained** Sessay, N Yorks

FOCUS
This went to the class act in the line-up.

4580 RACING REPLAY, ALL TODAY'S RACING SKY 432 FILLIES' H'CAP 6f
4:15 (4:15) (Class 4) (0-85,83) 3-Y-0+ **£5,175** (£1,540; £769; £384) **Stalls Low**

Form RPR

4212 1 **Someone's Darling**30 3566 3-8-4 66 AndrewElliott 3 73
(Jim Goldie) *chsd ldrs: effrt and hdwy to ld over 1f out: idled ins fnl f: drvn out* **7/4**2

2210 2 hd **Dancheur (IRE)**35 3407 4-9-7 78 PJMcDonald 4 85
(Mrs K Burke) *led tl rdn and hdd over 1f out: rallied and ev ch wl ins fnl f: jst hld* **13/8**1

-056 3 4 **Perfect Blossom**3 4507 6-9-7 83 SladeO'Hara(5) 1 77
(Alan Berry) *in tch: rdn and hdwy on ins wl over 1f out: wknd last 75yds* **8/1**

-400 **4** 4 **Sunny Side Up (IRE)**17 4017 4-9-4 **75**........................ TonyHamilton 2 56
(Richard Fahey) *chsd ldr tl rdn and wknd over 1f out* **7/2**3

1m 10.86s (-1.54) **Going Correction** -0.175s/f (Firm)
WFA 3 from 4yo+ 5lb **4** Ran SP% **107.8**
Speed ratings (Par 102): **103,102,97,92**
CSF £4.93 TOTE £6.00; EX 3.70 Trifecta £9.80 Pool: £1528.78 - 116.20 winning units..
Owner The McMaster Springford Partnership **Bred** W G H Barrons **Trained** Uplawmoor, E Renfrews
■ Stewards' Enquiry : P J McDonald two-day ban: used whip above permitted level (Aug 5-6)

FOCUS
With two of the four runners out of form beforehand, this race has a shallow look. The winner continues on the upgrade.

4581 LUKE CURRIE MEMORIAL H'CAP 1m
4:45 (4:45) (Class 3) (0-95,82) 3-Y-O **£7,762** (£2,310; £1,154) **Stalls** Low

Form RPR
5523 **1** **Bold Prediction (IRE)**3 4508 3-8-9 **80**........................ JoeyHaynes(7) 1 85
(Mrs K Burke) *mde all: rdn 2f out: edgd lft and bmpd rival ins fnl f: kpt on wl towards fin* **9/2**3

0511 **2** ½ **Aeronwyn Bryn (IRE)**24 3772 3-8-11 **82**........................ ConnorBeasley(7) 3 86
(Michael Dods) *chsd ldrs: effrt and disp ld over 1f out: bmpd ins fnl f: kpt on: hld nr fin* **15/8**2

2260 **3** 11 **Party Royal**11 4214 3-9-3 **81**........................ JoeFanning 2 67
(Mark Johnston) *chsd wnr to over 2f out: sn wknd: eased whn btn ins fnl f* **10/11**1

1m 40.15s (-3.65) **Going Correction** -0.30s/f (Firm) **3** Ran SP% **105.3**
Speed ratings (Par 104): **106,105,94**
CSF £11.51 TOTE £5.20; EX 5.40 Trifecta £7.50 Pool: £985.22 - 97.76 winning units..
Owner M Saunders & Mrs E Burke **Bred** Mountarmstrong Stud **Trained** Middleham Moor, N Yorks
■ Stewards' Enquiry : Joey Haynes two-day ban: careless riding (Aug 5-6)

FOCUS
The first two in this small-field event are both progressing well. The pace, set by the winner, was ordinary. The form is rated cautiously around the second.

4582 DOWNLOAD THE FREE RACING UK APP H'CAP (QUALIFIER FOR £15,000 BETFAIR SCOTTISH SPRINT SERIES) 6f
5:15 (5:16) (Class 6) (0-65,65) 3-Y-O+ **£2,045** (£603; £302) **Stalls** Low

Form RPR
100 **1** **Dartrix**45 3068 4-9-4 **64**........................ ConnorBeasley(7) 9 74
(Michael Dods) *hld up: gd hdwy on outside to ld over 1f out: r.o ins fnl f* **7/2**2

5313 **2** 1¼ **Saxonette**3 4471 5-9-0 **53**........................ PJMcDonald 6 59
(Linda Perratt) *trckd ldrs: effrt 2f out: chsd wnr fnl f: kpt on: hld nr fin* **11/4**1

1453 **3** 1 **Script**4 4448 4-9-6 **59**........................ PaddyAspell 2 62
(Alan Berry) *cl up: led over 2f out to over 1f out: kpt on same pce fnl f* **13/2**

-600 **4** 1¼ **Black Douglas**15 4102 4-8-11 **50**........................ GrahamLee 3 49
(Jim Goldie) *in tch: rdn over 2f out: kpt on same pce fnl f* **6/1**

4400 **5** 1½ **Compton Heights**38 3283 4-9-7 **60**........................ PhillipMakin 1 54
(Jim Goldie) *hld up: rdn over 2f out: kpt on fnl f: nt pce to chal* **14/1**

1254 **6** 1 **Hab Reeh**16 4051 5-8-12 **58**........................(t) GemmaTutty(7) 4 49
(Ruth Carr) *hld up: pushed along over 2f out: sme hdwy over 1f out: nvr rchd ldrs* **4/1**3

0-06 **7** 2 **Cara's Delight (AUS)**63 2504 6-8-4 **46** oh1............(t) DeclanCannon(3) 5 30
(Frederick Watson) *led to over 2f out: rdn and wknd over 1f out* **100/1**

060- **8** 7 **Hills Of Dakota**310 6260 5-9-12 **65**........................ TomEaves 8 27
(Keith Dalgleish) *chsd ldr to over 2f out: sn rdn and wknd* **9/1**

0000 **9** nse **Princess Cayan (IRE)**14 4113 3-7-9 **46** oh1............ SamanthaBell(7) 7 7
(Linda Perratt) *dwlt: bhd: rdn along over 2f out: sn btn* **100/1**

1m 11.03s (-1.37) **Going Correction** -0.175s/f (Firm)
WFA 3 from 4yo+ 5lb **9** Ran SP% **115.2**
Speed ratings (Par 101): **102,100,99,97,95 94,91,82,81**
toteswingers 1&2 £3.70, 1&3 £4.50, 2&3 £3.90 CSF £13.52 CT £58.68 TOTE £5.10: £1.60, £1.20, £2.50; EX 19.10 Trifecta £83.00 Pool: £2400.13 - 21.67 winning units..
Owner K Knox **Bred** T K & Mrs P A Knox **Trained** Denton, Co Durham

FOCUS
This was the biggest field of the day, but it was just a modest contest. The winner is still on the upgrade.
T/Plt: £218.60 to a £1 stake. Pool of £52,403.29 - 174.95 winning tickets. T/Qpdt: £101.80 to a £1 stake. Pool of £2697.46 - 19.60 winning tickets. RY

4370 BEVERLEY (R-H)
Monday, July 22

OFFICIAL GOING: Good to firm (watered; 9.3)
Wind: Moderate behind Weather: Cloudy with sunny periods

4583 GO RACING IN YORKSHIRE SUMMER FESTIVAL CLAIMING STKS 5f
6:30 (6:31) (Class 6) 2-Y-O **£2,385** (£704; £352) **Stalls** Low

Form RPR
33 **1** **Black Treacle (IRE)**12 4156 2-8-13 0........................(p) SilvestreDeSousa 6 64
(Keith Dalgleish) *sltly hmpd shortly after s: sn trcking ldr: cl up 1/2-way: rdn to ld ent fnl f: kpt on* **5/6**1

0064 **2** 1½ **Kindanyce (IRE)**12 4156 2-8-3 0........................ BarryMcHugh 8 49
(Richard Fahey) *qckly away and swtchd rt towards inner: led: rdn along wl over 1f out: hdd ent fnl f: kpt on same pce* **7/2**2

3 2¾ **Nowinaminute (IRE)** 2-8-2 0........................ NeilFarley(3) 5 41+
(Tony Coyle) *chsd ldrs: rdn along 2f out: kpt on fnl f* **11/1**

60 **4** 2¾ **Red Tiger Lily**86 1839 2-7-11 0........................ DanielleMooney(7) 2 30
(Nigel Tinkler) *towards rr and pushed along 1/2-way: swtchd lft and rdn 2f out: kpt on fnl f* **66/1**

4052 **5** 2 **Porsh Herrik**12 4156 2-8-9 0........................(v) MichaelO'Connell 7 28
(John Quinn) *dwlt: sn cl up: rdn along 1/2-way: sn wknd* **8/1**

05 **6** 4 **Gerdani**52 2830 2-8-4 0........................ AndrewMullen 1 8
(Michael Easterby) *a towards rr* **33/1**

064 **7** 3¾ **Hija**16 4065 2-8-3 0........................(p) LukeMorris 4
(Bill Turner) *a outpcd in rr* **7/1**3

1m 2.57s (-0.93) **Going Correction** -0.35s/f (Firm) **7** Ran SP% **113.2**
Speed ratings (Par 92): **93,90,86,81,78 72,66**
toteswingers 1&2 £1.20, 1&3 £2.60, 2&3 £5.20 CSF £3.86 TOTE £1.70: £1.40, £3.10; EX 5.50 Trifecta £26.70 Pool: £1621.27 - 45.45 winning units..Nowinaminute was claimed by Mr J Given for £6000
Owner Straightline Construction Ltd **Bred** Tally-Ho Stud **Trained** Carluke, S Lanarks
■ Stewards' Enquiry : Barry McHugh one-day ban: careless riding (Aug 5)

FOCUS
Rail around bottom bend moved for fresh ground adding 12yds to races beyond 5f. Modest but straightforward form in this claimer.

4584 RICHARD AND CAROL HUDSON H'CAP 1m 1f 207y
7:00 (7:00) (Class 5) (0-75,71) 3-Y-O+ **£3,234** (£962; £481; £240) **Stalls** Low

Form RPR
0310 **1** **Maybeme**5 4403 7-9-3 **60**........................(p) SilvestreDeSousa 3 69
(Neville Bycroft) *in rr and pushed along briefly after s: hld up: niggled along over 3f out: gd hdwy on outer over 2f out: rdn to ld over 1f out: sn edgd rt and kpt on wl towards fin* **7/2**3

2105 **2** 1 **Cosmic Halo**17 4015 4-9-9 **71**........................ GeorgeChaloner(5) 1 78
(Richard Fahey) *t.k.h: trckd ldrs on inner: effrt and n.m.r wl over 1f out: rdn to chal appr fnl f: sn drvn and kpt on same pce* **9/2**

6003 **3** 2½ **Strike Force**18 3996 9-9-1 **63**........................(t) TobyAtkinson(5) 4 65
(Alison Hutchinson) *hld up in rr: hdwy whn n.m.r wl over 1f out: sn rdn and kpt on fnl f: nrst fin* **33/1**

1232 **4** 2½ **Saint Thomas (IRE)**27 3651 6-10-0 **71**........................ FrannyNorton 2 68
(John Mackie) *led 1f: cl up: chal 3f out: rdn over 2f out and ev ch tl drvn and wknd appr fnl f* **15/8**1

3543 **5** ¾ **Bobs Her Uncle**17 4016 4-9-6 **63**........................(b1) DaleSwift 6 59
(James Bethell) *plld hrd: hdwy to ld after 1 1/2f: pushed along 3f out: rdn 2f out: drvn and hdd over 1f out: sn wknd* **10/1**

2312 **6** 3¾ **Alpine Mysteries (IRE)**26 3675 3-8-13 **66**........................ LukeMorris 5 54
(Harry Dunlop) *trckd ldrs on outer: pushed along over 4f out: rdn and hdwy 3f out: sn cl up: drvn and wknd wl over 1f out* **3/1**2

2m 4.01s (-2.99) **Going Correction** -0.25s/f (Firm)
WFA 3 from 4yo+ 10lb **6** Ran SP% **112.2**
Speed ratings (Par 103): **101,100,98,96,95 92**
toteswingers 1&2 £3.10, 1&3 £3.10, 2&3 £12.60 CSF £19.25 TOTE £4.30: £1.90, £2.20; EX 20.30 Trifecta £407.20 Pool: £1264.19 - 2.32 winning units..
Owner Mrs J Dickinson **Bred** Harts Farm And Stud **Trained** Brandsby, N Yorks

FOCUS
Not a particularly strong race for the grade. The pace steadied early, not really quickening appreciably until the final 4f. The winner's best since she was a 3yo.

4585 SKYBET SUPPORTING THE YORKSHIRE RACING SUMMER FESTIVAL H'CAP 7f 100y
7:30 (7:30) (Class 6) (0-65,70) 3-Y-O **£2,264** (£673; £336; £168) **Stalls** Low

Form RPR
0211 **1** **Relight My Fire**6 4375 3-9-13 **70** 6ex........................(b) DavidAllan 3 78
(Tim Easterby) *mde all: clr wl over 2f out: easily* **4/6**1

-340 **2** 2 **Secret Empress**24 3762 3-8-7 **50**........................ RoystonFfrench 1 50
(Bryan Smart) *sn chsng wnr: rdn along over 2f out: drvn wl over 1f out: no imp* **12/1**

0005 **3** 3¾ **Multisure**16 4070 3-8-5 **51**........................ JulieBurke(3) 5 42
(Ruth Carr) *chsd ldrs: pushed along 3f out: rdn 2f out: sn one pce* **8/1**3

00-4 **4** 6 **Troy Boy**25 3739 3-7-13 **49**........................ GaryMahon(7) 4 25
(Robin Bastiman) *hld up in rr whn edgd rt to rail after 1 1/2f: outpcd and pushed along over 4f out: rdn wl over 2f out: styd on fnl f: n.d* **8/1**3

-466 **5** 3½ **Don't Tell**12 4161 3-8-3 **46**........................ DuranFentiman 6 13
(George Moore) *chsd wnr 2f: prom: rdn along 3f out: sn edgd rt and wknd* **33/1**

3461 **6** 4½ **Napinda**25 3740 3-8-6 **56**........................ NoelGarbutt(7) 2 12+
(Philip McBride) *hld up in rr whn bdly hmpd and almost fell after 1 1/2f: bhd after* **7/2**2

1m 31.22s (-2.58) **Going Correction** -0.25s/f (Firm) **6** Ran SP% **115.1**
Speed ratings (Par 98): **104,101,97,90,86 81**
toteswingers 1&2 £2.90, 1&3 £2.50, 2&3 £5.70 CSF £10.84 TOTE £1.40: £1.10, £4.10; EX 6.70 Trifecta £38.20 Pool: £1360.82 - 26.68 winning units..
Owner Jonathan Gill **Bred** J Gill **Trained** Great Habton, N Yorks
■ Stewards' Enquiry : Gary Mahon six-day ban: careless riding (Aug 5-10)

FOCUS
A one-sided handicap, the winner bolting up, his task made even easier with his main market rival effectively out of the contest from an early stage. An improved effort from the winner on the face of things.

4586 INFINITY ECOMAX TYRES H'CAP 1m 100y
8:00 (8:00) (Class 4) (0-80,76) 3-Y-O **£6,469** (£1,925; £962; £481) **Stalls** Low

Form RPR
1363 **1** **Declamation (IRE)**33 3464 3-9-2 **72**........................ SilvestreDeSousa 4 76
(Mark Johnston) *t.k.h early: chsd ldr on outer: cl up 1/2-way: chal wl over 2f out: sn rdn: drvn jst over 1f out: styd on u.p to ld last 100yds: edgd rt towards fin* **11/10**1

4-0 **2** ½ **Hard Core Debt**36 3382 3-9-6 **76**........................ BarryMcHugh 1 79
(Brian Ellison) *trckd ldng pair on inner: smooth hdwy 2f out: sn cl up: rdn over 1f out and ev ch tl drvn and no ex nr fin* **14/1**

4101 **3** 1¼ **Zaitsev (IRE)**16 4048 3-9-5 **75**........................ RobertWinston 2 75
(Ollie Pears) *led: pushed along 3f out: rdn 2f out and sn edgd lft: drvn appr fnl f: hdd and no ex last 100yds* **7/4**2

-153 **4** 6 **Silkelly**12 4158 3-9-5 **75**........................(t1) DanielTudhope 3 61
(David O'Meara) *trckd ldrs: effrt 2f out: rdn wl over 1f out: sn one pce* **9/2**3

1m 45.24s (-2.36) **Going Correction** -0.25s/f (Firm) **4** Ran SP% **108.8**
Speed ratings (Par 102): **101,100,99,93**
CSF £13.58 TOTE £5.00; EX 17.90 Trifecta £25.90 Pool: £569.89 - 16.45 winning units..
Owner Sheikh Hamdan Bin Mohammed Al Maktoum **Bred** Darley **Trained** Middleham Moor, N Yorks

FOCUS
Another handicap on the card which was hardly a strong race of its type. The gallop was pretty sedate, the race not beginning in earnest until the final 3f. The winner is rated back to his maiden win.

4587 YORKSHIRE RADIO MAIDEN H'CAP 2m 35y
8:30 (8:31) (Class 6) (0-65,63) 3-Y-O **£2,264** (£673; £336; £168) **Stalls** Low

Form RPR
5343 **1** **Attention Seaker**21 3893 3-9-7 **63**........................ DuranFentiman 4 72
(Tim Easterby) *hld up towards rr: pushed along over 3f out: hdwy wl over 2f out: led wl over 1f out: sn rdn and kpt on strly fnl f* **10/3**2

0-64 **2** 3 **Jebulani**5 4401 3-8-1 **46**........................ JulieBurke(3) 2 51
(David O'Meara) *trckd ldng pair: hdwy over 2f out: rdn to chse wnr over 1f out: drvn and no imp fnl f* **11/4**1

6525 **3** 1½ **Attansky (IRE)**27 3653 3-9-0 **56**........................(p) DavidAllan 1 59
(Tim Easterby) *hld up towards rr: hdwy over 3f out: rdn along over 2f out: drvn wl over 1f out: kpt on fnl f: nrst fin* **9/2**

2050 **4** 1 1/2 **Moaning Butcher**[7] 4352 3-9-1 **57**....................(b[1]) SilvestreDeSousa 6 58
(Mark Johnston) *t.k.h early: trck ldrs: niggled along after 4f: rn in snatches after: rdn 4f out: drvn over 2f out: sn one pce* **8/1**

0036 **5** 4 **Jomari (IRE)**[11] 4222 3-8-0 **45**.................... NeilFarley(3) 3 42
(Declan Carroll) *led: rdn along over 3f out: drvn 2f out: sn hdd and grad wknd* **8/1**

06-6 **6** nk **Santa Fe Stinger**[23] 3809 3-8-3 **45**.................... PaulQuinn 9 41
(Tim Easterby) *awkward: wnt lft and lost several l s: bhd tl tk clsr order 1/2-way: rdn along to chse ldrs wl over 2f out: sn no imp* **12/1**

-000 **7** 72 **Noosa Sound**[21] 3893 3-8-5 **47**.................... RoystonFfrench 8
(John Davies) *chsd ldr: rdn along over 4f out: wknd 3f out: sn in rr and eased wl over 1f out* **50/1**

0003 **8** 28 **Crystal Mist**[11] 4222 3-9-6 **62**....................(b) LukeMorris 7
(Harry Dunlop) *reminders after s: chsd ldrs: rdn along on outer 1/2-way: sn lost pl and bhd: t.o fnl 3f* **4/1**[3]

3m 35.5s (-4.30) **Going Correction** -0.25s/f (Firm) **8** Ran SP% **119.8**
Speed ratings (Par 98): **100,98,97,97,95 94,58,44**
toteswingers 1&2 £10.50, 1&3 £2.40, 2&3 £6.10 CSF £13.71 CT £42.19 TOTE £4.10: £1.20, £1.80, £1.40; EX 22.40 Trifecta £56.00 Pool: £827.51 - 11.07 winning units..
Owner Ryedale Partners No 6 **Bred** Ryedale Partners No 6 **Trained** Great Habton, N Yorks
■ Stewards' Enquiry : Julie Burke two-day ban: careless riding (Aug 5-6)

FOCUS
Clearly an ordinary contest, but the winner is going the right way. The gallop looked sound enough in the main. The form is sound enough.

4588 BEVERLEY FASHION WEEK 22 - 27 JULY H'CAP 5f
9:00 (9:02) (Class 5) (0-75,75) 3-Y-O+ **£3,234** (£962; £481; £240) **Stalls** Low

Form RPR

3-00 **1** **Oil Strike**[19] 3945 6-9-5 **68**....................(b[1]) GrahamGibbons 3 85
(Michael Easterby) *trckd ldr: cl up 1/2-way: rdn to ld over 1f out: drvn out* **15/2**

2050 **2** 3 **Mey Blossom**[11] 4203 8-8-8 **62**....................(p) GeorgeChaloner(5) 4 68
(Richard Whitaker) *trckd ldrs: hdwy 2f out: rdn over 1f out: styd on to chse wnr ins fnl f: sn drvn and no imp* **16/1**

6200 **3** 2 1/4 **Indian Trail**[16] 4047 13-8-13 **69**....................(b) KevinStott(7) 7 67
(David Nicholls) *dwlt and swtchd rt to inner: bhd: hdwy 2f out: rdn over 1f out: styd on ins fnl f: tk 3rd nr fin* **16/1**

0000 **4** nk **Come On Dave (IRE)**[37] 3331 4-9-12 **75**.................... AndrewMullen 1 72
(David Nicholls) *led: rdn along 2f out: drvn and hdd over 1f out: wknd fnl f* **5/1**[3]

6420 **5** 2 3/4 **Six Wives**[3] 4479 6-9-8 **71**....................(p) LukeMorris 2 58
(Scott Dixon) *chsd ldrs: rdn along 2f out: sn drvn and btn over 1f out* **9/4**[1]

3323 **6** hd **Miss Bunter**[123] 1102 4-9-9 **72**.................... DanielTudhope 9 58
(David O'Meara) *chsd ldrs on outer: rdn along 2f out: sn drvn and wknd over 1f out* **10/1**

0006 **7** 1 **Caranbola**[16] 4047 7-9-11 **74**.................... SilvestreDeSousa 8 57
(Mel Brittain) *sn rdn along and a towards rr* **10/3**[2]

-400 **8** 1 **Master Rooney (IRE)**[37] 3351 7-9-5 **75**.................... JordanNason(7) 6 54
(Geoffrey Harker) *a in rr* **10/1**

5100 **9** 9 **Just Like Heaven (IRE)**[26] 3682 4-9-5 **68**....................(b[1]) DuranFentiman 5 15
(Tim Easterby) *chsd ldng pair: rdn along 1/2-way: sn wknd* **20/1**

1m 1.13s (-2.37) **Going Correction** -0.35s/f (Firm) **9** Ran SP% **117.0**
Speed ratings (Par 103): **104,99,95,95,90 90,88,87,72**
toteswingers 1&2 £16.60, 1&3 £36.50, 2&3 £21.60 CSF £119.10 CT £1865.59 TOTE £9.70: £3.40, £3.30, £2.80; EX 77.30 Trifecta £720.50 Pool: £1244.14 - 1.29 winning units..
Owner A Saha **Bred** Cobhall Court Stud **Trained** Sheriff Hutton, N Yorks

FOCUS
A sprint which few threatened to get into. The runner-up is the best guide.
T/Plt: £76.00 to a £1 stake. Pool of £63,257.20 - 607.07 winning tickets. T/Qpdt: £26.10 to a £1 stake. Pool of £4393.47 - 124.20 winning tickets. JR

4344 WINDSOR (R-H)
Monday, July 22

OFFICIAL GOING: Good to firm (watered; 8.9)
Wind: virtually nil Weather: hot and sunny

4589 BRITISH STALLION STUDS EBF MAIDEN FILLIES' STKS 6f
6:20 (6:20) (Class 5) 2-Y-O **£2,911** (£866; £432; £216) **Stalls** Low

Form RPR

4 **1** **Djinni (IRE)**[18] 3986 2-9-0 0.................... RichardHughes 9 83+
(Richard Hannon) *in tch in midfield: hdwy to chse ldrs 1/2-way: pushed into ld 1f out: gng clr and edgd rt ins fnl f: r.o wl: eased cl home: comf* **5/4**[1]

43 **2** 3 1/4 **Thatchit (IRE)**[12] 4164 2-9-0 0.................... TomQueally 5 70
(Paul Cole) *pressed ldrs tl led 4f out: rdn over 1f out: hdd 1f out and sn outpcd by wnr: kpt on to hold 2nd* **5/1**[3]

223 **3** 1/2 **Bewitchment**[28] 3640 2-9-0 0.................... RyanMoore 1 68
(Sir Mark Prescott Bt) *w ldr: rdn and ev ch ent fnl 2f: outpcd by wnr jst ins fnl f: kpt on same pce after* **5/2**[2]

4 1 **Alfie Lunete (IRE)** 2-9-0 0.................... LiamJones 3 65
(J S Moore) *hld up in tch in midfield: effrt to chse ldrs 1/2-way: switching lft jst over 1f out: kpt on same pce* **50/1**

0 **5** 1 3/4 **Pink Mirage (IRE)**[18] 3986 2-8-9 0.................... MatthewLawson(5) 10 59
(Jonathan Portman) *s.i.s: bhd: hdwy on outer 1/2-way: rdn 2f out: kpt on same pce after* **33/1**

6 hd **Zawiyah** 2-9-0 0.................... KierenFallon 11 59+
(Luca Cumani) *s.i.s: bhd: stl plenty to do whn nt clr run over 1f out: swtchd lft and hdwy 1f out: edging bk rt but styd on wl under hands and heels ins fnl f* **16/1**

3 **7** 2 **Ajig**[21] 3896 2-9-0 0.................... JohnFahy 7 52
(Eve Johnson Houghton) *in tch in midfield: rdn and lost pl 1/2-way: no threat to ldrs but kpt on again ins fnl f* **12/1**

0 **8** 2 1/4 **Acquaint (IRE)**[33] 3471 2-9-0 0.................... SeanLevey 2 45+
(Richard Hannon) *led for 2f: lost pl 1/2-way: bhd 1f out* **33/1**

6 **9** 7 **Sing Out Sister**[21] 3896 2-9-0 0.................... MartinHarley 8 23
(Mick Channon) *in tch towards rr: rdn and little rspnse over 2f out: wknd and bhd 1f out* **25/1**

10 4 **Stagewise (IRE)** 2-9-0 0.................... WilliamCarson 4 10+
(Jonathan Portman) *v s.i.s: a wl bhd: rn green and hung lft 1/2-way* **100/1**

11 nk **Tamarasha** 2-9-0 0.................... AdamKirby 6 9
(Clive Cox) *t.k.h early: in tch in midfield: rdn and lost pl 1/2-way: wknd over 2f out and sn bhd* **20/1**

1m 11.96s (-1.04) **Going Correction** 0.0s/f (Good) **11** Ran SP% **120.7**
Speed ratings (Par 91): **106,101,101,99,97 97,94,91,82,76 76**
toteswingers 1&2 £1.90, 1&3 £1.50, 2&3 £2.10 CSF £7.65 TOTE £2.20: £1.20, £1.70, £1.10; EX 8.50 Trifecta £20.90 Pool: £1590.56 - 56.81 winning units..
Owner Gillian, Lady Howard De Walden **Bred** Avington Manor Stud **Trained** East Everleigh, Wilts

FOCUS
Inner of straight dolled out 11yds at 6f and 6yds at winning post, and top bend dolled out 5yds, adding 22yds to races of 1m and over. This fillies' maiden has produced subsequent scorers at Listed and Group 3 level in recent years, but Richard Hannon has the best record, having trained three of the preceding five winners. The second and third help with the level.

4590 MAPPIN & WEBB MAIDEN STKS 1m 2f 7y
6:50 (6:52) (Class 5) 3-4-Y-O **£2,587** (£770; £384; £192) **Stalls** Centre

Form RPR

2-20 **1** **Regal Silk**[87] 1813 3-8-12 **78**.................... RyanMoore 10 85+
(Jeremy Noseda) *chsd ldrs tl led over 2f out: rdn and readily wnt clr over 1f out: styd on strly: comf* **5/4**[1]

2-4 **2** 5 **Hassle (IRE)**[35] 3417 4-9-13 0.................... AdamKirby 2 80
(Clive Cox) *chsd ldrs early: settled in midfield after 2f: rdn and effrt 3f out: chsd ldrs and swtchd lft over 1f out: chsd clr wnr ins fnl f: no imp* **2/1**[2]

3 1 1/2 **Al Arish (IRE)** 3-9-3 0.................... TomQueally 11 77
(Lady Cecil) *dwlt: rcvrd to press ldr after 2f out: led 6f out tl rdn and hdd over 3f out: outpcd 2f out: no threat to wnr but kpt on again ins fnl f: wnt 3rd cl home* **10/1**

0-4 **4** 1/2 **Ingot Of Gold**[22] 3858 3-8-12 0.................... JimCrowley 6 71
(Ralph Beckett) *chsd ldr for 2f: styd chsng ldrs: rdn and chsd wnr 2f out: no ex and btn over 1f out: wknd ins fnl f and lost 2 pls towards fin* **6/1**[3]

5 hd **Angus Glens** 3-9-3 0.................... SteveDrowne 8 76+
(Ali Brewer) *dwlt: hld up off the pce in midfield: hdwy whn rn green and wnt lft 2f out: kpt on ins fnl f: snatched 4th last strides: no threat to ldrs* **20/1**

0 **6** 3 1/2 **The Wizard Of Aus (IRE)**[23] 3821 3-9-3 0.................... JimmyFortune 4 69
(Andrew Balding) *chsd ldrs: rdn and unable qck over 2f out: struggling whn short of room 2f out: sn wknd: eased wl ins fnl f* **20/1**

5 **7** 2 **Calon Lad (IRE)**[21] 3902 3-9-3 0.................... PatCosgrave 12 65
(George Baker) *racd wl off the pce in last trio: rdn 2f out: modest hdwy over 1f out: sn no imp and nvr trbld ldrs* **66/1**

0-0 **8** nse **Wedding Speech (IRE)**[22] 3860 3-8-12 0.................... FrederikTylicki 9 60
(James Fanshawe) *in tch in midfield: rdn over 2f out: no hdwy and outpcd 2f out: wknd over 1f out* **33/1**

00 **9** 5 **Capetown Kid**[13] 4151 3-9-3 0.................... LiamKeniry 5 55
(Sylvester Kirk) *wl off the pce in last trio: pushed along and no hdwy over 2f out: wknd over 1f out* **50/1**

0-0 **10** 8 **Sweet Louise (IRE)**[31] 3530 3-8-12 0.................... JohnFahy 1 34
(Barry Brennan) *led tl 6f out: rdn to ld again over 3f out tl hdd over 2f out: sn btn and fdd* **100/1**

04 **11** 3/4 **Roxy Lane**[22] 3860 4-9-8 0.................... WilliamCarson 7 32
(Peter Hiatt) *t.k.h: hld up wl off the pce in midfield: rdn and no hdwy over 2f out: bhd and swtchd lft 1f out* **25/1**

12 27 **Just Gets Better (IRE)** 4-9-13 0....................[1] CathyGannon 3
(Sean Curran) *v.s.a and rdn along early: clsd to rr of field and t.k.h at bnd 7f out: rdn and btn 4f out: eased fr over 1f out: t.o: sddle slipped* **66/1**

2m 4.56s (-4.14) **Going Correction** -0.35s/f (Firm)
WFA 3 from 4yo 10lb **12** Ran SP% **123.4**
Speed ratings (Par 103): **102,98,96,96,96 93,91,91,87,81 80,59**
toteswingers 1&2 £1.10, 1&3 £4.20, 2&3 £3.80 CSF £3.65 TOTE £2.30: £1.10, £1.30, £3.00; EX 4.40 Trifecta £25.90 Pool: £1785.75 - 51.55 winning units..
Owner Cheveley Park Stud **Bred** Cheveley Park Stud Ltd **Trained** Newmarket, Suffolk

FOCUS
A couple of interesting newcomers in this maiden and they both ran well without being a match for the favourite. The winner could prove better than the bare form.

4591 CORAL.CO.UK H'CAP 1m 2f 7y
7:20 (7:20) (Class 5) (0-70,70) 3-Y-O+ **£2,587** (£770; £384; £192) **Stalls** Centre

Form RPR

3-52 **1** **Stiff Upper Lip (IRE)**[20] 3917 3-9-4 **70**.................... RichardHughes 9 80
(Richard Hannon) *in tch in midfield: pushed along briefly over 4f out: rdn and effrt on outer over 2f out: chsd ldr over 1f out: r.o u.p to ld fnl 50yds* **6/4**[1]

363- **2** hd **Heezararity**[222] 8080 5-9-4 **65**.................... RyanTate(5) 10 74
(Jonathan Geake) *t.k.h: hld up in tch in midfield: hdwy to ld 3f out: drvn 2f out: hrd pressed ins fnl f: hdd fnl 50yds: r.o but jst hld* **20/1**

00-2 **3** 3 **Malih**[25] 3736 4-9-13 **69**.................... FrankieDettori 7 72
(Jamie Osborne) *t.k.h: led tl hdd 3f out: rdn and chsd ldr after tl over 1f out: edgd lft and styd on same pce ins fnl f* **7/1**

4000 **4** 3/4 **Strategic Strike (IRE)**[21] 3908 3-8-13 **65**....................(t) JimCrowley 3 67
(Paul Cole) *hld up wl in tch in midfield: rdn and effrt over 2f out: chsd ldng pair jst ins fnl f: no ex and btn whn squeezed for room ins fnl f: wknd towards fin* **7/1**

260- **5** 3 3/4 **Spiritual Art**[259] 6950 7-8-13 **55**....................(b) SeanLevey 11 49
(Luke Dace) *chsd ldr tl over 5f out: rdn and ev ch 3f out: no ex u.p 2f out: wknd 1f out* **50/1**

13-0 **6** 4 **Geeaitch**[67] 2383 4-9-9 **65**.................... WilliamCarson 2 51
(Anthony Carson) *stdd s: hld up in tch in last trio: effrt 3f out: wnt lft and no hdwy 2f out: sn wknd* **6/1**[3]

605- **7** 2 1/4 **Norphin**[269] 7373 3-8-12 **64**.................... TomQueally 5 46
(Denis Coakley) *t.k.h: chsd ldrs: n.m.r over 2f out: rdn and no hdwy 2f out: sn wknd* **7/2**[2]

0-00 **8** 1 1/2 **The Wonga Coup (IRE)**[18] 3976 6-8-11 **58**.................... JemmaMarshall(5) 1 37
(Pat Phelan) *taken down early: stdd s: hld up in tch in rr: rdn and short-lived effrt over 2f out: wknd over 1f out* **33/1**

4400 **9** 3 1/4 **Waving**[14] 4126 4-9-3 **62**....................(t) MarkCoumbe(3) 4 34
(Tony Carroll) *dwlt: sn rdn along in last trio: lost tch over 2f out* **33/1**

U50- **10** 11 **Urban Space**[283] 7018 7-9-12 **68**.................... CathyGannon 8 18
(Tony Carroll) *chsd ldrs: rapid to join ldr over 5f out tl rdn and lost pl 3f out: wl bhd and eased ins fnl f* **20/1**

2m 4.46s (-4.24) **Going Correction** -0.35s/f (Firm)
WFA 3 from 4yo+ 10lb **10** Ran SP% **118.9**
Speed ratings (Par 103): **102,101,99,98,95 92,90,89,87,78**
toteswingers 1&2 £5.70, 1&3 £2.40, 2&3 £15.90 CSF £40.65 CT £173.65 TOTE £2.70: £1.40, £4.00, £1.70; EX 22.90 Trifecta £173.70 Pool: £1114.33 - 4.80 winning units..
Owner Richard Hitchcock Alan King **Bred** B Kennedy **Trained** East Everleigh, Wilts

FOCUS
This modest handicap was run a tenth of a second faster than the preceding maiden. Slight improvement from the winner.

4592 VARIETY - THE CHILDREN'S CHARITY H'CAP 6f
7:50 (7:50) (Class 4) (0-85,85) 3-Y-O £4,851 (£1,443; £721; £360) Stalls Low

Form RPR
5611 1 **Nenge Mboko**[16] 4072 3-9-2 80 ....(v) PatCosgrave 6 87
(George Baker) *stdd s: hld up wl in tch in last pair: clsd and trckd ldrs 2f out: swtchd lft and effrt 1f out: rdn: hands and heels and qckd ins fnl f to ld nr fin: cleverly* 6/1[3]
0114 2 nk **Jontleman (IRE)**[12] 4162 3-8-6 70 .... SamHitchcott 1 76
(Mick Channon) *t.k.h: hld up wl in tch in last pair: swtchd lft over 2f out: effrt and rdn to chal over 1f out: led 1f out: r.o u.p tl hdd and no ex nr fin* 7/1
3321 3 1 **Realize**[21] 3898 3-8-11 75 .... RichardHughes 5 78
(Hughie Morrison) *chsd ldr: rdn and ev ch over 1f out: no ex fnl 100yds: btn and eased cl home* 11/4[2]
-412 4 1 3/4 **Red Explorer (USA)**[9] 4283 3-9-4 85 .... PatrickHills(3) 2 82
(Charles Hills) *chsd ldrs: shuffled bk 1/2-way and stuck bhd horses over 2f out: effrt and hung lft 1f out: one pce ins fnl f* 5/2[1]
5161 5 1 1/4 **Exotic Isle**[42] 3160 3-9-2 80 .... JamieSpencer 4 73
(Ralph Beckett) *t.k.h: hld up wl in tch in midfield tl hdwy to ld and qcknEd gallop over 3f out: drvn and hrd pressed over 1f out: hdd 1f out: wknd ins fnl f* 11/4[2]
015- 6 1 **Bobby Two Shoes**[204] 8293 3-8-10 74 .... WilliamCarson 3 64
(Brett Johnson) *led and set stdy gallop tl over 3f out: styd chsng ldrs tl lost pl u.p over 1f out: wknd ins fnl f* 33/1
1m 12.65s (-0.35) **Going Correction** 0.0s/f (Good) 6 Ran SP% **111.6**
Speed ratings (Par 102): **102,101,100,97,96 94**
toteswingers 1&2 £3.00, 1&3 £3.00, 2&3 £1.90 CSF £44.44 TOTE £7.10: £3.30, £3.50; EX 46.20 Trifecta £226.70 Pool: £896.78 - 2.96 winning units..
Owner Russell Conrad Vail Wheeler Hippychick **Bred** Pigeon House Stud **Trained** Manton, Wilts
FOCUS
The feature event on the card and a decent 3yo sprint, despite the small field. The winner could possibly do better still.

4593 DOWNLOAD CORAL MOBILE FROM THE APP STORE H'CAP 1m 67y
8:20 (8:20) (Class 5) (0-75,75) 3-Y-O+ £2,587 (£770; £384; £192) Stalls Low

Form RPR
04-4 1 **Quest For More (IRE)**[21] 3902 3-8-13 68 .... SteveDrowne 8 75+
(Roger Charlton) *awkward leaving stalls: in tch in last quartet: nt clr run and swtchd lft over 1f out: gap opened 1f out: str run u.p fnl 100yds to ld cl home: rn green and pricking ears in front* 14/1
-165 2 hd **Aint Got A Scooby (IRE)**[41] 3173 3-8-12 72 .... RyanTate(5) 7 79
(Clive Cox) *hld up in tch in last quartet: effrt on outer over 2f out: chal and edgd rt over 1f out: led jst ins fnl f: edgd rt u.p fnl 100yds: hdd and no ex cl home* 4/1[3]
0000 3 1 **Siouxperhero (IRE)**[16] 4070 4-9-2 63 ....(b) JimCrowley 6 70
(William Muir) *hld up in tch in midfield: hdwy to chse ldrs 3f out: swtchd lft and hdwy over 1f out: edgd rt and pressing ldrs ins fnl f: styd on same pce fnl 100yds* 33/1
130 4 nse **Emulating (IRE)**[39] 3241 3-9-3 72 .... RichardHughes 5 78
(Richard Hannon) *hld up wl in tch in midfield: switching lft and effrt whn squeezed for room and pushed lft over 1f out: drvn and hdwy 1f out: one pce fnl 100yds* 7/2[2]
3-02 5 1/2 **Jack Who's He (IRE)**[182] 311 4-10-0 75 .... MartinDwyer 1 80
(William Muir) *chsd ldr tl rdn to ld ent fnl 2f: edgd lft u.p over 1f out: hdd ins fnl f: stl pressing ldr but styng on same pce whn carried rt and hmpd ins fnl f: no ex* 16/1
0-00 6 1 1/4 **Woolston Ferry (IRE)**[24] 3780 7-9-10 71 .... DaneO'Neill 10 74
(Henry Candy) *hld up in tch in rr: swtchd lft and hdwy jst over 1f out: kpt on ins fnl f: nvr trbld ldrs* 20/1
-404 7 1 3/4 **Mahadee (IRE)**[21] 3901 8-9-7 68 ....(b) LiamTreadwell 11 67
(Ed de Giles) *hld up in tch in last quartet: hdwy on outer 3f out: rdn and unable qck 2f out: wknd ins fnl f* 20/1
2201 8 3 **Poor Duke (IRE)**[21] 3901 3-9-3 72 .... FergusSweeney 9 64
(Jamie Osborne) *wl in tch in midfield: rdn and chsng ldrs over 2f out: keeping on same pce whn pushed lft over 1f out: wknd ins fnl f* 6/1
6061 9 6 **Orbison (IRE)**[22] 3861 3-9-6 75 .... NeilCallan 3 51
(Roger Varian) *chsd ldrs: rdn and effrt over 2f out: btn ent fnl f: wandered and rdr looking down ins fnl f: eased fnl 75yds* 5/2[1]
0565 10 6 **Bankroll**[21] 3901 6-9-6 67 ....(t) GeorgeBaker 2 31
(Jonjo O'Neill) *led tl rdn and hdd ent fnl 2f: sn dropped out: bhd ins fnl f* 16/1
10-0 11 2 **Majestic Zafeen**[40] 3215 4-9-9 70 .... MartinHarley 4 29
(Alastair Lidderdale) *chsd ldrs: rdn and lost pl over 2f out: bhd fnl f* 33/1
1m 40.99s (-3.71) **Going Correction** -0.35s/f (Firm)
WFA 3 from 4yo+ 8lb 11 Ran SP% **118.9**
Speed ratings (Par 103): **104,103,102,102,102 101,99,96,90,84 82**
toteswingers 1&2 £7.30, 1&3 £40.40, 2&3 £15.90 CSF £67.07 CT £1836.12 TOTE £14.80: £3.70, £1.70, £5.60; EX 52.30 Trifecta £952.50 Part won. Pool: £1270.06 - 0.48 winning units..
Owner H R H Sultan Ahmad Shah **Bred** Epona Bloodstock Ltd **Trained** Beckhampton, Wilts
■ Stewards' Enquiry : Ryan Tate three-day ban: careless riding (Aug 5-7)
FOCUS
An ordinary handicap which was sound run, but quite a rough race in the closing stages. Improvement from the winner.

4594 CORAL.CO.UK BEST PRICE ON HORSE RACING FILLIES' H'CAP 1m 3f 135y
8:50 (8:50) (Class 4) (0-85,79) 3-Y-O £4,690 (£1,395; £697; £348) Stalls Centre

Form RPR
5224 1 **Bantam (IRE)**[21] 3908 3-9-2 75 .... RyanMoore 4 86+
(Ed Dunlop) *hld up in tch in last pair: swtchd lft and effrt ent fnl 2f: chal over 1f out: edgd rt and led ins fnl f: styd on wl* 10/3[3]
322 2 1 1/4 **Shalwa**[18] 3975 3-9-3 76 .... MartinHarley 5 85
(Marco Botti) *led: rdn wl over 2f out: hdd jst ins fnl f: no ex and btn fnl 100yds: one pce after* 11/4[2]
3-31 3 1 1/2 **Hold On Tight (IRE)**[18] 3989 3-9-6 79 .... JimCrowley 1 86
(Ralph Beckett) *chsd ldng pair tl wnt 2nd 5f out: drvn and edging lft over 1f out: 3rd and styd on same pce fnl f* 9/2
4-05 4 5 **Just One Kiss**[73] 2206 3-9-4 77 .... TomQueally 3 75
(Lady Cecil) *t.k.h: hld up wl in tch in last pair: effrt u.p jst over 2f out: no ex and btn jst over 1f out: wknd ins fnl f* 7/1
32-2 5 4 **Nickels And Dimes (IRE)**[13] 4151 3-9-6 79 .... WilliamBuick 2 73
(John Gosden) *t.k.h: chsd ldr tl 5f out: rdn wl over 2f out: wknd over 1f out: bhd and eased towards fin* 2/1[1]
2m 25.84s (-3.66) **Going Correction** -0.35s/f (Firm) 5 Ran SP% **113.8**
Speed ratings (Par 99): **98,97,96,92,90**
CSF £13.23 TOTE £3.30: £1.30, £1.50; EX 10.20 Trifecta £32.30 Pool: £861.28 - 19.99 winning units..
Owner Brooke Kelly Partnership **Bred** Airlie Stud And Sir Thomas Pilkington **Trained** Newmarket, Suffolk
FOCUS
A fair fillies' handicap with just 4lb covering the entire field, and the bottom weight prevailed. She is rated back to her Newbury maiden form.
T/Jkpt: Part won. £17,750.00 to a £1 stake. Pool of £25,000.00 - 0.50 winning units. T/Plt: £181.90 to a £1 stake. Pool of £130,130.18 - 522.04 winning tickets. T/Qpdt: £103.90 to a £1 stake. Pool of £6746.49 - 48.04 winning tickets. SP

4595 - 4598a (Foreign Racing) - See Raceform Interactive

3911 COMPIEGNE (L-H)
Monday, July 22

OFFICIAL GOING: Turf: good to soft

4599a PRIX DE L'AILETTE (CLAIMER) (2YO) (TURF) 7f
1:50 (12:00) 2-Y-O £10,975 (£4,390; £3,292; £2,195; £1,097)

RPR
1 **Benodet (FR)**[12] 2-8-8 0 .... ThierryThulliez 7 76
(C Boutin, France) 11/2[3]
2 2 **Cockney Bob**[16] 4044 2-8-13 0 ow2 .... ChristopheSoumillon 3 76
(J S Moore) *bmpd leaving stalls: trckd ldr in share of 2nd: chal on outside over 2f out: rdn and r.o 1 1/2f out: jst getting bttr of ldr whn hdd and sltly hmpd by eventual wnr 75yds out: no ex* 9/10[1]
3 1 1/2 **Blu Axara (ITY)**[22] 2-8-9 0 .... AntoineCoutier(6) 4 74
(F Chappet, France) 48/1
4 2 1/2 **Monsieur Bachir (FR)** 2-8-11 0 .... CesarPasserat(4) 5 67
(C Lerner, France) 10/1
5 2 **Mystical Rock (FR)**[12] 2-8-11 0 .... Pierre-CharlesBoudot 9 58
(D Windrif, France) 23/1
6 4 **Thalie De La Vis (FR)**[12] 2-8-8 0 .... DavidBreux 1 45
(Mme C Barande-Barbe, France) 37/1
7 nk **Easy De Glanville (FR)** 2-8-11 0 .... OlivierPeslier 6 47
(Y Barberot, France) 15/1
8 3 **Donibane (FR)** 2-8-8 0 .... AlexisBadel 2 36
(Mlle V Dissaux, France) 42/1
9 10 **Striving (GER)**[90] 2-8-11 0 ....(p) MaximeGuyon 8 13
(H-A Pantall, France) 4/1[2]
10 3 **Manchu (FR)**[31] 2-9-1 0 .... AlexandreChampenois(3) 10 12
(F Chappet, France) 26/1
1m 25.77s (85.77) 10 Ran SP% **118.2**
WIN (incl. 1 euro stake): 6.50. PLACES: 1.70, 1.20, 6.00. DF: 6.50. SF: 17.90.
Owner Guy Pariente **Bred** Le Thenney **Trained** France

4601a PRIX DU BRAS D'OR (CONDITIONS) (4YO+) (TURF) 1m 2f
3:25 (12:00) 4-Y-O+ £12,195 (£4,878; £3,658; £2,439; £1,219)

RPR
1 **Esles (FR)**[16] 5-8-13 0 .... ChristopheSoumillon 4 98
(C Laffon-Parias, France) 1/1[1]
2 3/4 **Linda Radlett (IRE)**[23] 4-8-9 0 .... MaximeGuyon 6 92
(A Fabre, France) 5/1[3]
3 1 1/2 **Swing Alone (IRE)**[32] 3503 4-9-2 0 .... Pierre-CharlesBoudot 3 96
(Gay Kelleway) *broke wl and led: pushed along whn pressed 1 1/2f out: sn rdn and hdd over 1f out: kpt on tl no ex fnl 75yds: 3rd and hld whn eased cl home* 11/1
4 1 3/4 **Perfect Son**[16] 6-8-13 0 .... TonyPiccone 1 90
(C Zeitz, Germany) 11/1
5 8 **Propulsion (IRE)**[37] 3362 4-9-2 0 .... OlivierPeslier 2 77
(F Head, France) 2/1[2]
2m 9.48s (129.48) 5 Ran SP% **116.7**
WIN (incl. 1 euro stake): 2.00. PLACES: 1.30, 1.80. SF: 5.80.
Owner Mme Georgiana Cabrero **Bred** Janus Bloodstock Inc **Trained** Chantilly, France

4600 - 4601a (Foreign Racing) - See Raceform Interactive

3882 FFOS LAS (L-H)
Tuesday, July 23

OFFICIAL GOING: Good to firm (9.0)
Wind: very light, half against Weather: dry

4602 BRITISH STALLION STUDS EBF / WALTERS UK MAIDEN STKS 5f
6:05 (6:06) (Class 5) 2-Y-O £2,911 (£866; £432; £216) Stalls Centre

Form RPR
6542 1 **Bounty Hunter (IRE)**[18] 4019 2-9-5 0 ....(p) RichardKingscote 1 76
(Tom Dascombe) *mde all: rdn and readily asserted 1f out: clr and r.o wl fnl 150yds: comf* 4/6[1]
4 2 3 1/2 **Golden Spear**[64] 2497 2-9-5 0 .... StevieDonohoe 2 63
(Noel Quinlan) *dwlt: sn rcvrd and chsd ldng pair: rdn and hung lft over 1f out: outpcd by wnr and wnt bk rt ins fnl f: snatched 2nd last stride* 7/4[2]
025 3 shd **Zafraaj**[28] 3659 2-9-5 0 .... LukeMorris 3 63
(Ronald Harris) *in tch in last and pushed along: swtchd lft and effrt over 1f out: chsd wnr ent fnl f but sn outpcd by wnr: kpt on one pce and lost 2nd last stride* 25/1
4 hd **Bob Masnicken** 2-9-5 0 .... AdamKirby 4 62+
(Scott Dixon) *taken down early: chsd wnr: rdn and unable qck over 1f out: outpcd by wnr but ev ch of 2nd whn edgd lft ins fnl f: one pce* 12/1[3]
59.16s (0.86) **Going Correction** -0.20s/f (Firm) 4 Ran SP% **107.9**
Speed ratings (Par 94): **85,79,79,78**
CSF £2.06 TOTE £1.30; EX 2.10 Trifecta £4.90 Pool: £1154.24 - 176.61 winning units..
Owner D Ward **Bred** B Holland, S Hillen & J Cullinan **Trained** Malpas, Cheshire

The Form Book Flat, Raceform Ltd, Compton, RG20 6NL.

FOCUS
The course had seen no rain and selective watering had been applied, with another 5mm put down in the morning. The winner ran to his mark.

4603 DAVIES CHEMISTS "LLANELLI" FILLIES' H'CAP 6f
6:35 (6:35) (Class 5) (0-75,75) 3-Y-0+ **£2,587** (£577; £577; £192) **Stalls** Centre

Form RPR
3331 **1** **My Own Way Home**[3] 4517 5-8-6 **60** 6ex DeclanBates(5) 4 69
(David Evans) *racd nr stands' rail: mde all: rdn over 1f out: kpt on wl ins fnl f* **4/1**[3]
2-41 **2** ¾ **Abated**[31] 3576 3-9-7 **75** GeorgeBaker 2 81
(Roger Charlton) *racd far side: chsd wnr: rdn and effrt over 1f out: hung rt ins fnl f: one pce fnl 100yds* **5/4**[1]
2012 **2** *dht* **Verus Delicia (IRE)**[5] 4456 4-8-11 **60** ShaneKelly 3 67
(Daniel Mark Loughnane) *racd far side: chsd ldrs: rdn and effrt over 1f out: drvn and kpt on same pce ins fnl f* **15/8**[2]
0-00 **4** 2¾ **Madame Kintyre**[37] 3375 5-8-7 **56** oh4 (b) DavidProbert 6 54
(Rod Millman) *racd towards stands' rail: chsd ldrs: rdn and unable qck over 1f out: wknd ins fnl f* **40/1**
060- **5** 7 **Ivor's Princess**[291] 6842 4-9-7 **70** AndreaAtzeni 5 45
(Rod Millman) *racd towards stands' rail: a in rr: rdn 1/2-way: lost tch ent fnl f* **14/1**

1m 9.61s (-0.39) **Going Correction** -0.20s/f (Firm)
WFA 3 from 4yo+ 5lb 5 Ran SP% **108.3**
Speed ratings (Par 100): **94,93,93,89,80**
PL: Abated £0.90, Verus Delicia £0.50 EX: My Own Way Home/Abated £4.70 MOWH/VD £5.10 CSF: MOWH/A £4.60 MOWH/VD £5.77 TOTE £4.70: £1.90 TRIFECTA MOWH/A/VD £8.00 MOWH/VD/A £8.70.
Owner Trevor Gallienne **Bred** Theresa Fitsall **Trained** Pandy, Monmouths

FOCUS
A moderate fillies' sprint handicap. There was a contrasting opinion as to the best ground with three of the five coming stands' side and the winner was in that trio, but it didn't look to be a great bias. The dead-heaters for second are rated to form.

4604 32RED.COM H'CAP 1m 2f (R)
7:05 (7:05) (Class 6) (0-60,60) 3-Y-0+ **£1,940** (£577; £288; £144) **Stalls** Low

Form RPR
4313 **1** **Golden Jubilee (USA)**[19] 3985 4-9-11 **60**(v) WilliamTwiston-Davies(3) 6 67
(Nigel Twiston-Davies) *hld up wl in tch in midfield: effrt to chse ldr 2f out: chalng whn hung lft u.p: hit rail and rdr unbalanced over 1f out: rallied ins fnl f and rdn to ld wl ins fnl f: r.o wl* **7/2**[1]
2001 **2** *nk* **Stag Hill (IRE)**[22] 3882 4-9-8 **59** RobertWilliams(5) 2 65
(Bernard Llewellyn) *trckd ldrs tl rdn to ld 2f out: hrd pressed whn lft 1 l clr over 1f out: hdd wl ins fnl f: r.o gamely but a jst hld* **11/2**
3322 **3** *nk* **Offbeat Safaris (IRE)**[11] 4241 5-9-12 **58** LukeMorris 5 63
(Ronald Harris) *dwlt: hld up wl in tch in rr: rdn and effrt over 2f out: hdwy u.p over 1f out: kpt on wl fnl 100yds but nvr quite getting to ldng pair* **4/1**[2]
0431 **4** 1 **Greyemkay**[22] 3885 5-8-12 **51** DanielMuscutt(7) 9 54
(Richard Price) *hld up in tch in last trio: rdn and effrt over 2f out: hdwy to chse ldrs 1f out: kpt on same pce fnl 100yds* **9/2**[3]
4260 **5** *nk* **Chik's Dream**[31] 3580 6-8-9 **46** oh1 RosieJessop(5) 3 48
(Derek Haydn Jones) *chsd ldrs: rdn 2f out: unable qck 1f out: styd on same pce and lost 2 pls ins fnl f* **20/1**
0360 **6** 3¾ **Madam Tessa (IRE)**[8] 4355 5-9-0 **46** (v[1]) DavidProbert 8 41
(Tim Vaughan) *dwlt and rdn along early: hld up in tch in last trio: rdn and effrt over 2f out: styd on same pce fnl f* **14/1**
010- **7** 1½ **Pindar (GER)**[90] 7596 9-9-13 **59** AdamKirby 4 51
(Neil Mulholland) *led: rdn and hdd 2f out: no ex and btn ent fnl f: wknd ins fnl f: eased towards fin* **16/1**
5400 **8** 7 **Sweet Alabama**[37] 3376 3-8-5 **47** (b) AndreaAtzeni 11 25
(Rod Millman) *chsd ldr: ev ch and rdn 3f out: struggling ent fnl 2f and sn btn: wknd over 1f out* **9/1**
504 **9** 3½ **Drummond**[20] 3954 4-9-7 **53** (p) MartinLane 10 24
(Bernard Llewellyn) *in tch in midfield: rdn 1/2-way: lost pl 4f out: bhd fnl 2f* **13/2**

2m 5.88s (-3.52) **Going Correction** -0.45s/f (Firm)
WFA 3 from 4yo+ 10lb 9 Ran SP% **116.4**
Speed ratings (Par 101): **96,95,95,94,94 91,90,84,81**
toteswingers 1&2 £6.00, 2&3 £4.30, 1&3 £4.40 CSF £23.17 CT £80.10 TOTE £7.50: £2.90, £2.80, £1.02; EX 15.10 Trifecta £65.40 Pool: £704.29 - 8.06 winning units..
Owner Mrs J K Powell **Bred** Dixiana Farms Llc **Trained** Naunton, Gloucs

FOCUS
An ordinary handicap. They went a fair pace and the form is solid for the class. The winner was up a length on previous form.

4605 32RED CASINO H'CAP 1m 4f (R)
7:35 (7:35) (Class 6) (0-55,59) 4-Y-0+ **£1,940** (£577; £288; £144) **Stalls** Low

Form RPR
0426 **1** **Men Don't Cry (IRE)**[17] 4071 4-8-9 **46** oh1 (b) MarkCoumbe(3) 9 60
(Ed de Giles) *chsd ldr tl led over 2f out: sn rdn and wnt wl clr over 1f out: in command and styd on wl fnl f* **9/1**
-606 **2** 5 **Chasin' Rainbows**[28] 3662 5-9-3 **51** LiamKeniry 1 57
(Sylvester Kirk) *chsd ldrs: rdn and chsd wnr ent fnl 2f: outpcd and btn over 1f out: no ch w wnr but kpt on for clr 2nd* **16/1**
500/ **3** 2¼ **Cabuchon (GER)**[909] 301 6-9-0 **48** (t) AdamKirby 10 50
(David Evans) *hld up in tch in rr: rdn and clsd to chse ldrs: rdn and outpcd whn hung lft wl over 1f out: 3rd and wl hld after* **9/4**[2]
00-1 **4** 7 **Langley**[8] 4355 6-9-11 **59** 6ex (vt) DavidProbert 8 50
(Tim Vaughan) *led tl over 2f out: sn rdn and btn: wknd and wl btn over 1f out* **2/1**[1]
0623 **5** 3¾ **Gaelic Ice**[22] 3882 4-9-7 **55** AndreaAtzeni 4 40
(Rod Millman) *t.k.h early: hld up in tch in midfield: rdn and struggling over 3f out: 5th and wl btn fnl 2f* **5/1**[3]
5436 **6** 5 **Red Current**[12] 4192 9-8-10 **47** WilliamTwiston-Davies(3) 7 24
(Michael Scudamore) *awkward leaving stalls and s.i.s: hld up in tch in last trio: rdn and effrt over 3f out: sn outpcd and wl btn over 2f out* **20/1**
1312 **7** ½ **I'm Harry**[56] 2764 4-9-6 **54** (tp) AidanColeman 5 30
(George Baker) *hld up in last trio: rdn over 5f out: bhd over 2f out: n.d* **8/1**
500- **8** 7 **Tallulah Mai**[369] 4244 6-9-3 **51** LukeMorris 3 16
(Matthew Salaman) *chsd ldrs: rdn over 6f out: lost pl and bhd 3f out: sn lost tch* **25/1**

2m 31.58s (-5.82) **Going Correction** -0.45s/f (Firm) course record 8 Ran SP% **116.4**
Speed ratings (Par 101): **101,97,96,91,89 85,85,80**
toteswingers 1&2 £34.80, 2&3 £10.60, 1&3 £6.60 CSF £138.55 CT £435.43 TOTE £7.30: £2.70, £2.70, £1.60; EX 79.80 Trifecta £632.70 Part won. Pool: £843.70 - 0.98 winning units..
Owner Clarke, King & Lewis **Bred** Ecurie Des Monceaux **Trained** Ledbury, H'fords

FOCUS
A weak handicap in which they trailed home in Indian file behind a clear-cut winner, who set a new course record. He's rated in line with his AW best.

4606 BET LIVE WITH PETE SUTTON TONIGHT H'CAP 2m (R)
8:05 (8:05) (Class 4) (0-85,85) 4-Y-0+ **£4,690** (£1,395; £697; £348) **Stalls** Low

Form RPR
-234 **1** **Mutual Regard (IRE)**[20] 3959 4-9-7 **85** (p) LukeMorris 5 96+
(Sir Mark Prescott Bt) *t.k.h: hld up in tch in last pair: rdn and qcknd to ld 1f out: hung lft but sn in command: r.o wl: comf* **6/4**[1]
664 **2** ¾ **Eshtyaaq**[21] 3916 6-8-2 **66** oh1 CathyGannon 2 74
(David Evans) *stdd and sltly hmpd s: t.k.h: hld up in tch in rr: effrt u.p on inner to ld over 1f out: hdd 1f out: styd on same pce fnl f: hld whn swtchd rt towards fin* **16/1**
/5-0 **3** 1¾ **Waterclock (IRE)**[27] 3692 4-9-4 **82** GeorgeBaker 1 88
(Roger Charlton) *chsd ldng pair tl shuffled bk and stuck bhd horses over 2f out: swtchd rt and effrt jst over 1f out: 3rd and no imp fnl 100yds* **3/1**[3]
6160 **4** 1½ **Taglietelle**[11] 4233 4-9-3 **81** (p) DavidProbert 6 85
(Andrew Balding) *chsd ldrs: clsd and upsides ldr over 2f out: drvn and ev ch over 1f out: unable qck whn sltly hmpd 1f out: btn and one pce after* **2/1**[2]
10-5 **5** 3½ **L Frank Baum (IRE)**[24] 3807 6-9-0 **78** MartinLane 3 78
(Bernard Llewellyn) *led: rdn over 3f out: drvn over 2f out: hdd and btn over 1f out: wknd fnl f* **11/1**

3m 30.59s (0.59) **Going Correction** -0.45s/f (Firm) 5 Ran SP% **112.5**
Speed ratings (Par 105): **80,79,78,78,76**
CSF £23.26 TOTE £2.00: £1.20, £4.10; EX 26.70 Trifecta £66.10 Pool: £722.27 - 8.19 winning units..
Owner Moyglare Stud Farm **Bred** Moyglare Stud Farm Ltd **Trained** Newmarket, Suffolk

FOCUS
Not a bad little staying handicap. A step up from the winner on this year's form.

4607 32RED H'CAP 6f
8:35 (8:37) (Class 6) (0-55,55) 3-Y-0 **£1,940** (£577; £288; £144) **Stalls** Centre

Form RPR
5030 **1** **Idle Curiosity (IRE)**[6] 4410 3-9-7 **55** AndreaAtzeni 9 61
(Jim Boyle) *racd nrest stands' rail: in tch: rdn and effrt over 1f out: led ins fnl f: kpt on wl: all out* **13/2**
50-0 **2** *nk* **Our Sweet Art**[49] 2962 3-9-4 **52** GeorgeBaker 6 57
(John Best) *hld up in tch in rr: hdwy over 1f out: drvn and ev ch ins fnl f: unable qck cl home* **6/1**[3]
6-50 **3** 2¾ **Compton Albion (IRE)**[40] 3246 3-8-13 **52** (p) RobertTart(5) 5 48
(Jeremy Gask) *w ldr: rdn and ev ch over 1f out tl ins fnl f: outpcd by ldng pair fnl 100yds* **10/1**
5262 **4** *hd* **Imperial Spirit**[3] 4544 3-8-13 **50** (v) CharlesBishop(3) 8 45
(Mick Channon) *led: rdn ent fnl 2f: hdd and outpcd ins fnl f* **7/4**[1]
2400 **5** 1¾ **Senora Lobo (IRE)**[25] 3789 3-9-5 **53** AdamKirby 7 43
(Lisa Williamson) *in tch in midfield: drvn and unable qck over 1f out: one pce fnl f* **8/1**
0224 **6** 2¾ **Foie Gras**[27] 3679 3-9-4 **52** (b) LukeMorris 1 33
(William Muir) *dwlt: sn revcovered and chsd ldrs in centre: rdn and no ex 2f out: wknd fnl f* **4/1**[2]
-000 **7** *hd* **Direct Trade**[22] 3903 3-8-5 **46** oh1 DanielMuscutt(7) 2 26
(Mark Usher) *in tch: effrt to chse ldrs and rdn over 1f out: hung lft and btn 1f out: wknd fnl f* **22/1**
004 **8** 11 **Bustling Darcey**[21] 3915 3-8-12 **46** oh1 DavidProbert 10
(Mark Gillard) *in tch in midfield: rdn and struggling over 2f out: lost tch over 1f out* **40/1**
006 **9** 2½ **Deva Victrix**[38] 3327 3-8-12 **46** oh1 (b[1]) SamHitchcott 4
(Lisa Williamson) *a in rr: struggling u.p over 2f out: lost tch 2f out* **66/1**
43-0 **10** 1½ **Tristessa**[91] 1742 3-9-1 **54** RosieJessop(5) 3
(Derek Haydn Jones) *bhd: struggling u.p 1/2-way: sn hung lft and wl bhd* **25/1**

1m 10.25s (0.25) **Going Correction** -0.20s/f (Firm) 10 Ran SP% **116.3**
Speed ratings (Par 98): **90,89,85,85,83 79,79,64,61,59**
toteswingers 1&2 £11.20, 2&3 £94.30, 1&3 £18.20 CSF £43.37 CT £389.28 TOTE £2.00: £1.10, £3.90, £4.20; EX 58.00 Trifecta £609.90 Part won. Pool: £813.33 - 0.81 winning units..
Owner Inside Track Racing Club **Bred** Mountarmstrong Stud **Trained** Epsom, Surrey

FOCUS
A very weak 3yo sprint handicap. The 1-2 raced nearer the stands' rail than most. The winner rates a small personal best.

4608 £32 FREE AT 32RED.COM H'CAP 5f
9:05 (9:05) (Class 5) (0-70,67) 3-Y-0+ **£2,587** (£770; £384; £192) **Stalls** Centre

Form RPR
360U **1** **Spic 'n Span**[5] 4427 8-8-9 **50** (b) LukeMorris 9 59
(Ronald Harris) *chsd ldr and racing against stands' rail: led 1/2-way: drvn over 1f out: kpt on wl ins fnl f: hld on wl towards fin: drvn out* **14/1**
0422 **2** ½ **Lager Time (IRE)**[11] 4244 3-9-7 **66** AdamKirby 6 72
(David Evans) *s.i.s: niggled along in rr of main gp: hdwy and nt clr run jst over 1f out: wnt 2nd and swtchd lft fnl 100yds: sn pressing wnr: hld cl home* **5/2**[2]
5654 **3** 2¼ **Mossgo (IRE)**[7] 4390 3-9-4 **63** GeorgeBaker 8 61
(John Best) *t.k.h: hld up wl in tch in midfield: chsd wnr 1f out: sn rdn and fnd little: lost 2nd fnl 100yds: wknd towards fin* **20/1**
0265 **4** *nk* **Ryan Style (IRE)**[8] 4344 7-9-12 **67** (p) SamHitchcott 7 65
(Lisa Williamson) *in tch in midfield: rdn 1/2-way: no imp tl kpt on u.p fnl 100yds: nt pce to threaten ldrs* **12/1**
0063 **5** *nk* **Ingleby Star (IRE)**[5] 4430 8-9-6 **61** (be) ShaneKelly 1 58
(Daniel Mark Loughnane) *chsd ldrs: unable qck u.p ent fnl f: wknd ins fnl f* **5/1**[3]
1-54 **6** 1 **Charismas Birthday (IRE)**[3] 4520 5-8-7 **48** (b) CathyGannon 3 41
(Philip M Byrne, Ire) *led tl over 2f: struggling u.p over 1f out: wknd ins fnl f* **10/1**
3005 **7** ½ **Bussa**[15] 4120 5-9-7 **67** (t) DeclanBates(5) 2 58+
(David Evans) *v.s.a: detached in last: styd on ins fnl f: n.d* **20/1**
4551 **8** 5 **Catflap (IRE)**[8] 4344 4-8-8 **54** (p) RosieJessop(5) 5 27
(Derek Haydn Jones) *led to s: dwlt: hld up in rr of main gp: rdn and no rspnse over 1f out: wknd fnl f* **6/4**[1]

56.95s (-1.35) **Going Correction** -0.20s/f (Firm)
WFA 3 from 4yo+ 4lb 8 Ran SP% **118.2**
Speed ratings (Par 103): **102,101,97,97,96 95,94,86**
CSF £50.95 CT £713.52 TOTE £15.70: £3.40, £1.10, £5.10; EX 58.50 Trifecta £432.40 Pool: £790.63 - 1.37 winning units..
Owner P Nurcombe **Bred** C A Cyzer **Trained** Earlswood, Monmouths

FOCUS
This wasn't a bad sprint handicap for the grade. The field came stands' side and went hard. The winner is rated to last year's turf form.
T/Jkpt: £8,875.00 to a £1 stake. Pool of £25,000.00 - 2.00 winning tickets. T/Plt: £129.20 to a £1 stake. Pool of £76,818.69 - 433.76 winning tickets. T/Qpdt: £211.00 to a £1 stake. Pool of £5,789.29 - 20.30 winning tickets. SP

3766 MUSSELBURGH (R-H)

Tuesday, July 23

OFFICIAL GOING: Good to firm (good in places; 8.1)
Wind: Light, half behind Weather: Overcast

4609 32RED H'CAP — 1m 1f
2:00 (2:00) (Class 5) (0-70,67) 4-Y-0+ **£3,234** (£962; £481; £240) **Stalls** Low

Form RPR
2021 **1** **Cono Zur (FR)**[4] 4482 6-9-6 **66**........................ JamesSullivan 3 76
(Ruth Carr) *mde all: set stdy pce: rdn and hung lft wl over 1f out: kpt on wl fnl f* **9/4**[1]
0234 **2** *2 ¾* **Royal Straight**[10] 4293 8-9-7 **67**........................(t) PhillipMakin 1 71
(Linda Perratt) *hld up in tch: effrt and hdwy over 2f out: chsd wnr over 1f out: kpt on fnl f* **12/1**
3511 **3** *shd* **True Pleasure (IRE)**[8] 4341 6-8-13 **59** 6ex........................ PJMcDonald 6 63
(James Bethell) *t.k.h: in tch: effrt and swtchd lft over 1f out: kpt on ins fnl f* **3/1**[3]
1213 **4** *hd* **Tectonic (IRE)**[4] 4475 4-9-3 **63**........................(p) TomEaves 4 66
(Keith Dalgleish) *t.k.h: trckd ldrs: shkn up and hung rt over 1f out: kpt on same pce fnl f* **11/4**[2]
55 **5** *4 ½* **Jordaura**[22] 3889 7-9-6 **66**........................ RobertWinston 5 59
(Alan Berry) *hld up in last but in tch: drvn and outpcd over 3f out: rallied over 1f out: sn no imp* **12/1**
0064 **6** *6* **Queens Revenge**[14] 4135 4-9-0 **60**........................(t) DavidAllan 2 40
(Tim Easterby) *trckd wnr: rdn over 2f out: wknd over 1f out* **6/1**
1m 52.98s (-0.92) **Going Correction** -0.05s/f (Good) **6 Ran SP% 112.1**
Speed ratings (Par 103): **102,99,99,99,95 89**
toteswingers 1&2 £2.90, 2&3 £4.50, 1&3 £1.90 CSF £28.23 TOTE £2.20: £1.10, £6.50; EX 24.60 Trifecta £109.70 Pool: £1930.38 - 13.19 winning units..
Owner Ruth Carr Racing **Bred** J P Dubois **Trained** Huby, N Yorks

FOCUS
Following a heavy downpour in the morning, the ground had eased to good to firm, good in places, but the consensus amongst the jockeys after the opener was that the going was nearer good. An ordinary handicap, but with the early pace so steady the winner was rather gifted it. The form is sound enough.

4610 BRITISH STALLION STUDS EBF MAIDEN STKS — 7f 30y
2:30 (2:30) (Class 4) 2-Y-0 **£4,204** (£1,251; £625; £312) **Stalls** Low

Form RPR
4 **1** **Brown Eyed Honey**[25] 3781 2-9-0 0........................ GrahamLee 1 75+
(William Haggas) *t.k.h early: trckd ldr: rdn and led over 1f out: sn hrd pressed: kpt on wl towards fin* **8/13**[1]
2 *½* **Gallic Breeze (FR)** 2-9-5 0........................ MichaelO'Connell 2 78+
(John Quinn) *t.k.h early: trckd ldrs: hdwy to chal whn hung lft ins fnl f: kpt on: hld nr fin* **14/1**[3]
0406 **3** *5* **Donny Rover (IRE)**[11] 4246 2-9-5 0........................(p) RobertWinston 3 65
(David C Griffiths) *led: rdn over 2f out: hdd over 1f out: wknd ins fnl f* **16/1**
4 *8* **Damaah (USA)** 2-9-0 0........................ PaulHanagan 5 39+
(Mark Johnston) *rn green thrght: chsd ldrs on outside: outpcd whn rn wd bnd ent st: no imp after* **2/1**[2]
4 **5** *2 ¾* **Ofelia (IRE)**[26] 3723 2-9-0 0........................ TomEaves 4 32
(Brian Ellison) *dwlt: t.k.h early: hld up in tch: rdn and outpcd over 2f out: sn btn* **20/1**
1m 29.35s (0.35) **Going Correction** -0.05s/f (Good) **5 Ran SP% 112.6**
Speed ratings (Par 96): **96,95,89,80,77**
CSF £11.11 TOTE £1.60: £1.10, £5.50; EX 11.00 Trifecta £43.70 Pool: £1778.31 - 30.51 winning units..
Owner M S Bloodstock Ltd **Bred** Mike Smith **Trained** Newmarket, Suffolk

FOCUS
Only two mattered in this maiden according to the market, but with one of them flopping and the hot favourite making hard work of it, the form doesn't look anything special. This narrow win should help the winner's mark.

4611 ROTECH H'CAP — 5f
3:00 (3:00) (Class 6) (0-65,70) 3-Y-0 **£1,940** (£577; £288; £144) **Stalls** High

Form RPR
5162 **1** **Secret Advice**[2] 4558 3-9-7 **64**........................ TomEaves 1 72
(Keith Dalgleish) *pressed ldr: led over 1f out: drvn out fnl f* **11/5**[2]
1621 **2** *2 ¼* **Salvatore Fury (IRE)**[4] 4471 3-9-13 **70** 6ex........................(p) JoeFanning 2 70
(Keith Dalgleish) *trckd ldrs: effrt and wnt 2nd 1f out: kpt on same pce last 100yds* **1/1**[1]
0200 **3** *1 ½* **Megaleka**[5] 4427 3-8-10 **53**........................ GrahamLee 4 48
(Alan Bailey) *led to over 1f out: kpt on same pce fnl f* **6/1**[3]
660 **4** *¾* **Showtime Girl (IRE)**[14] 4149 3-9-3 **60**........................(b[1]) DavidAllan 6 52
(Tim Easterby) *trckd ldrs: rdn over 2f out: one pce over 1f out* **11/1**
0336 **5** *8* **Lady Calantha**[10] 4290 3-8-2 **45**........................ JamesSullivan 5 8
(Alan Berry) *unruly s: bhd and sn detached: hung rt 1/2-way: nvr on terms* **22/1**
59.56s (-0.84) **Going Correction** -0.15s/f (Firm) **5 Ran SP% 108.2**
Speed ratings (Par 98): **100,96,94,92,80**
CSF £4.60 TOTE £3.40: £1.40, £1.30; EX 4.60 Trifecta £10.50 Pool: £2432.85 - 172.26 winning units..
Owner G L S Partnership **Bred** G L S Partnership **Trained** Carluke, S Lanarks

FOCUS
A weak sprint handicap with the Keith Dalgleish pair dominating both the market and the race. The winner was always struggling to get to his improved stablemate.

4612 PAUL MERRITT'S 60TH BRITISH RACECOURSE H'CAP — 1m 4f 100y
3:30 (3:30) (Class 5) (0-70,69) 4-Y-0+ **£3,234** (£962; £481; £240) **Stalls** Low

Form RPR
0643 **1** **Brigadoon**[14] 4150 6-9-7 **69**........................ MichaelO'Connell 3 82
(Philip Kirby) *hld up in tch: smooth hdwy to ld 2f out: sn rdn: kpt on strly fnl f* **9/4**[1]
2000 **2** *3 ½* **Rawaafed (IRE)**[8] 4341 4-9-3 **65**........................ JoeFanning 1 72
(Keith Dalgleish) *hld up: stdy hdwy to chse ldrs over 2f out: effrt and chsd wnr fnl f: one pce last 100yds* **25/1**
3321 **3** *2* **St Ignatius**[5] 4429 6-8-12 **60**........................(p) GrahamLee 7 63
(Alan Bailey) *chsd clr ldr: effrt and ev ch 2f out: kpt on same pce fnl f* **6/1**[3]
6212 **4** *1* **Slide Show**[6] 4403 5-8-8 **56**........................ PaulQuinn 4 58
(David Nicholls) *hld up in tch: smooth hdwy to chse ldrs 3f out: rdn and outpcd 2f out: n.d after* **9/4**[1]
6013 **5** *5* **King Of Paradise (IRE)**[14] 4135 4-9-1 **68**........................ JasonHart(5) 2 62
(Eric Alston) *led and sn clr: rdn over 3f out: hdd 2f out: sn wknd* **5/2**[2]
-303 **6** *7* **Talk Of Saafend (IRE)**[20] 3709 8-8-8 **56**........................ PJMcDonald 5 39
(Dianne Sayer) *hld up towards rr: drvn and outpcd over 5f out: sn struggling* **20/1**
2m 41.84s (-0.16) **Going Correction** -0.05s/f (Good) **6 Ran SP% 113.0**
Speed ratings (Par 103): **98,95,94,93,90 85**
toteswingers 1&2 £6.10, 2&3 £6.50, 1&3 £2.60 CSF £49.64 TOTE £2.90: £1.40, £5.80; EX 69.10 Trifecta £120.20 Pool: £2445.97 - 15.25 winning units..
Owner Robin Oliver **Bred** Biddestone Stud **Trained** Middleham, N Yorks

FOCUS
This handicap was run at a strong early pace and the first two came from last and last-but-one. The form is rated around the second.

4613 WATCH RACING UK ON SKY 432 H'CAP — 5f
4:00 (4:01) (Class 4) (0-80,83) 3-Y-0+ **£5,175** (£1,540; £769; £384) **Stalls** High

Form RPR
2110 **1** **Red Baron (IRE)**[4] 4479 4-9-6 **76**........................ NeilFarley(3) 2 87+
(Eric Alston) *mde all and sn crossed to stands' rail: rdn over 1f out: kpt on strly* **4/1**[3]
503 **2** *1 ½* **Findog**[10] 4291 3-8-12 **69**........................ PaulMulrennan 5 74+
(Linda Perratt) *hmpd sn after s: t.k.h in rr: hdwy over 1f out: chsd wnr ins fnl f: one pce towards fin* **8/1**
000- **3** *1 ¼* **Gottcher**[340] 5294 5-8-8 **61**........................ JoeFanning 8 62
(Keith Dalgleish) *t.k.h: pressed wnr: rdn over 1f out: edgd rt and one pce ins fnl f* **50/1**
2512 **4** *nk* **Imperial Legend (IRE)**[4] 4479 4-9-12 **79**........................(p) AndrewMullen 3 79
(David Nicholls) *in tch: effrt and rdn wl over 1f out: kpt on same pce ins fnl f* **9/4**[1]
4146 **5** *1 ½* **The Nifty Fox**[8] 4340 9-9-11 **78**........................(p) JamesSullivan 4 73
(Tim Easterby) *hld up in tch: rdn over 2f out: kpt on fnl f: no imp* **16/1**
0-00 **6** *4* **I'll Be Good**[12] 4203 4-8-13 **66**........................ GrahamLee 7 46
(Robert Johnson) *chsd ldrs tl rdn and wknd wl over 1f out* **33/1**
0601 **7** *1 ¾* **Burning Thread (IRE)**[7] 4364 6-10-2 **83** 6ex........................(b) AdamBeschizza 9 57
(Tim Etherington) *prom tl rdn and wknd fr 1/2-way* **10/3**[2]
0030 **8** *7* **Crimson Knot (IRE)**[25] 3769 5-9-7 **74**........................ TomEaves 6 51
(Alan Berry) *towards rr on ins: rdn 1/2-way: edgd rt and sn btn: rdr looking down and eased fr over 1f out* **14/1**
58.89s (-1.51) **Going Correction** -0.15s/f (Firm)
WFA 3 from 4yo+ 4lb **8 Ran SP% 102.4**
Speed ratings (Par 105): **106,103,101,101,98 92,89,78**
CSF £27.82 CT £954.10 TOTE £3.40: £1.60, £2.30, £7.20; EX 33.30 Trifecta £859.70 Pool: £1505.03 - 1.31 winning units..
Owner J Stephenson **Bred** Mrs C A Moore **Trained** Longton, Lancs
■ Go Go Green was withdrawn (7-1, unruly in stalls). Deduct 10p in the £ under R4.

FOCUS
A decent sprint handicap. The winner continues to thrive and had a bit in hand.

4614 32RED CASINO H'CAP — 2m
4:30 (4:30) (Class 6) (0-65,65) 4-Y-0+ **£2,587** (£770; £384; £192) **Stalls** High

Form RPR
3006 **1** **La Bacouetteuse (FR)**[8] 4343 8-9-7 **65**........................(b) DavidAllan 5 73
(Iain Jardine) *hld up: rdn along 3f out: hdwy and swtchd lft over 1f out: led ins fnl f: kpt on wl* **8/1**[3]
-314 **2** *2* **Goldan Jess (IRE)**[53] 2328 9-8-12 **56**........................ RussKennemore 4 62
(Philip Kirby) *led: rdn over 2f out: hdd ins fnl f: kpt on same pce towards fin* **9/5**[1]
50-0 **3** *¾* **Lady Gargoyle**[19] 3728 5-7-9 **46** oh1........................ SophieRobertson(7) 8 51
(Jim Goldie) *rdr slow to remove blindfold: dwlt: t.k.h and hdwy to join ld after 2f: shkn up 2f out: one pce ins fnl f* **18/1**
-665 **4** *¾* **Vittachi**[8] 4343 6-8-6 **50**........................ PJMcDonald 6 54
(Alistair Whillans) *in tch on ins: rdn over 3f out: kpt on same pce fr over 1f out* **9/1**
5353 **5** *nk* **Geanie Mac (IRE)**[8] 4343 4-7-10 **47**........................(v) SamanthaBell(7) 2 51
(Linda Perratt) *trckd ldrs: rdn over 2f out: one pce fnl f* **9/2**[2]
6/00 **6** *4* **Hartforth**[26] 3727 5-8-3 **47** oh1 ow1........................ AndrewMullen 9 46
(Donald Whillans) *trckd ldrs: rdn over 3f out: outpcd whn checked over 1f out* **28/1**
0054 **7** *1 ½* **Raleigh Quay (IRE)**[12] 4204 6-8-13 **57**........................ GrahamLee 7 54
(Micky Hammond) *in tch: rdn over 5f out: outpcd fr over 2f out* **9/2**[2]
/00- **8** *16* **Solis (GER)**[20] 4869 10-7-13 **46** oh1........................(e) NeilFarley(3) 3 24
(Dianne Sayer) *hld up: struggling over 5f out: sn n.d* **12/1**
350- **9** *1 ½* **Tigerino (IRE)**[397] 3307 5-8-2 **46** oh1........................ JamesSullivan 10 22
(Chris Fairhurst) *t.k.h: hld up towards rr: effrt on outside 4f out: wknd over 2f out* **25/1**
3m 32.36s (-1.14) **Going Correction** -0.05s/f (Good) **9 Ran SP% 113.4**
Speed ratings (Par 101): **100,99,98,98,98 96,95,87,86**
toteswingers 1&2 £3.80, 2&3 £8.10, 1&3 £13.40 CSF £22.36 CT £253.42 TOTE £10.90: £3.00, £1.20, £3.50; EX 28.70 Trifecta £475.70 Pool: £2099.79 - 3.31 winning units..
Owner The Gold Cup In Mind **Bred** Sarl Classic Breeding & Maria R Mendes **Trained** Bonchester Bridge, Borders
■ Stewards' Enquiry : David Allan one-day ban: careless riding (Aug 6)

FOCUS
A modest staying handicap. The winner is rated to this year's form.

4615 32RED.COM H'CAP — 7f 30y
5:00 (5:01) (Class 5) (0-70,64) 3-Y-0+ **£3,234** (£962; £481; £240) **Stalls** Low

Form RPR
3-21 **1** **Idyllic Star (IRE)**[4] 4469 4-9-2 **57**........................(p) JasonHart(5) 6 75+
(Keith Dalgleish) *trckd ldrs: led over 2f out: drvn clr fr over 1f out* **8/13**[1]
15-3 **2** *4 ½* **Burnwynd Boy**[8] 4339 8-9-7 **57**........................ JoeFanning 2 61
(Keith Dalgleish) *t.k.h early: prom: hdwy to chse (clr) wnr over 1f out: edgd rt and one pce ins fnl f* **9/2**[2]
0605 **3** *nk* **Berbice (IRE)**[8] 4339 8-8-6 **45**........................ JulieBurke(3) 1 48
(Linda Perratt) *dwlt: hld up: stdy hdwy over 2f out: effrt and swtchd lft over 1f out: one pce ins fnl f* **22/1**
5066 **4** *1 ¾* **Cyflymder (IRE)**[11] 4245 7-9-11 **64**........................ LucyAlexander(3) 9 63
(David C Griffiths) *prom: effrt and rdn over 2f out: one pce over 1f out* **9/1**[3]
0603 **5** *4* **Royal Caper**[25] 3772 3-8-13 **56**........................(v[1]) MichaelO'Connell 5 41
(John Ryan) *trckd ldr: rdn over 2f out: wknd over 1f out* **18/1**

6550 **6** ½ **Here Now And Why (IRE)**[5] 4448 6-9-9 **59**..................(p) DavidAllan 10 46
(Iain Jardine) *hld up: rdn and sme hdwy over 1f out: nvr able to chal* **33/1**

-144 **7** ¾ **Whispered Times (USA)**[35] 3445 6-9-13 **63**.............(p) BarryMcHugh 7 48
(Tracy Waggott) *hld up towards rr: effrt and rdn over 2f out: edgd rt and wknd over 1f out* **12/1**

6203 **8** 3 **Lees Anthem**[13] 4160 6-9-1 **51**........................ RoystonFfrench 3 28
(Michael Smith) *midfield: n.m.r 4f out: sn drvn: struggling fr over 2f out* **20/1**

0-00 **9** 6 **Prince Of Vasa (IRE)**[13] 4161 6-9-10 **60**.................. PaulMulrennan 8 22
(Michael Smith) *led to over 2f out: rdn and wknd over 1f out* **50/1**

1m 28.08s (-0.92) **Going Correction** -0.05s/f (Good)
WFA 3 from 4yo+ 7lb 9 Ran SP% **117.1**
Speed ratings (Par 103): **103,97,97,95,90 90,89,86,79**
toteswingers 1&2 £1.80, 2&3 £7.50, 1&3 £5.30 CSF £3.40 CT £30.72 TOTE £1.40: £1.02, £1.90, £5.40; EX 5.00 Trifecta £43.60 Pool: £3613.78 - 62.14 winning units..
Owner Mac Asphalt Ltd **Bred** Coleman Bloodstock Limited **Trained** Carluke, S Lanarks

FOCUS
A modest handicap and a one-horse race as the market suggested. This was the second 1-2 of the afternoon for trainer Keith Dalgleish. The winner was 10lb well in.
T/Plt: £92.80 to a £1 stake. Pool of £64917.74 - 510.17 winning tickets. T/Qpdt: £40.90 to a £1 stake. Pool of £5340.67 - 96.40 winning tickets. RY

4398 CATTERICK (L-H)
Wednesday, July 24

OFFICIAL GOING: Good to firm (good in places; 8.7)
Wind: Virtually nil Weather: Cloudy and sunny periods

4616 BRITISH STALLION STUDS SUPPORTING BRITISH RACING EBF MAIDEN STKS 5f 212y
2:00 (2:00) (Class 5) 2-Y-O £2,911 (£866; £432; £216) **Stalls** Low

Form RPR

3522 **1** **Augusta Ada**[31] 3605 2-9-0 0........................ PaulMulrennan 7 69+
(Ollie Pears) *trckd ldng pair on outer: awkward home turn: sn cl up: pushed ahd over 1f out: rdn ins fnl f: edgd lft and sn clr* **4/6**[1]

0 **2** 2¾ **Sukari Gold (IRE)**[46] 3077 2-9-0 0........................ GrahamLee 2 58
(Kevin Ryan) *chsd ldr: rdn along over 2f out: sltly outpcd over 1f out: drvn and kpt on fnl f: tk 2nd nr line* **25/1**

35 **3** shd **Goadby**[35] 3476 2-9-0 0........................ GrahamGibbons 1 58
(John Holt) *led: rdn along and jnd over 2f out: hdd over 1f out: drvn and n.m.r ins fnl f: sn one pce* **25/1**

6 **4** shd **Breakable**[21] 3943 2-8-9 0........................ DarylByrne(5) 4 58+
(Tim Easterby) *sn pushed along to chse ldrs: rdn 3f out: styd on u.p fnl 2f: nrst fin* **33/1**

626 **5** 4½ **Song Of Rowland (IRE)**[11] 4312 2-9-5 0........................ DanielTudhope 5 48
(David O'Meara) *chsd ldrs: rdn along over 2f out: drvn wl over 1f out and sn wknd* **2/1**[2]

0 **6** 2¾ **Romantic Bliss (IRE)**[20] 3978 2-8-7 0........................ JoeyHaynes(7) 6 34
(Mrs K Burke) *a towards rr* **25/1**

60 **7** 8 **Meconopsis**[15] 4154 2-9-5 0........................ DuranFentiman 3 14
(Tim Easterby) *s.i.s: hdwy to chse ldrs 1/2-way: rdn wl over 2f out: sn wknd* **50/1**

8 ½ **Pure Amber (IRE)** 2-9-5 0........................ FrannyNorton 8 12
(Mark Johnston) *sn outpcd and a bhd* **7/1**[3]

1m 14.29s (0.69) **Going Correction** +0.10s/f (Good) 8 Ran SP% **122.3**
Speed ratings (Par 94): **99,95,95,95,89 85,74,74**
toteswingers 1&2 £5.50, 1&3 £4.70, 2&3 £21.30 CSF £28.01 TOTE £1.80: £1.02, £5.20, £4.80; EX 23.90 Trifecta £165.60 Pool: £2940.24 - 13.31 winning units..
Owner Timothy O'Gram **Bred** L C And Mrs A E Sigsworth **Trained** Norton, N Yorks
■ Stewards' Enquiry : Daryl Byrne caution: careless riding

FOCUS
Apart from the winner, this looked a modest event. The winner wouldn't have had to match her Pontefract form.

4617 DOWNLOAD THE FREE RACING UK APP (S) STKS 7f
2:30 (2:33) (Class 6) 2-Y-O £2,385 (£704; £352) **Stalls** Centre

Form RPR

4 **1** **Smart Payer**[6] 4422 2-8-11 0........................ FrannyNorton 1 67+
(Jo Hughes) *sn led: pushed clr 1/2-way: rdn and edgd rt fnl f: unchal* **11/10**[1]

00 **2** 10 **Mr Childrey (IRE)**[43] 3174 2-8-11 0....................(b[1]) GrahamLee 5 40
(J S Moore) *prom on outer: chsd wnr bef 1/2-way: rdn wl over 2f out: drvn wl over 1f out: plugged on: no ch w wnr* **5/2**[2]

0 **3** 1½ **Artistic Acclaim (IRE)**[18] 4073 2-8-6 0........................ JamesSullivan 6 31
(John Weymes) *outpcd and rdn along early: hdwy 1/2-way: rdn to chse ldrs 2f out: sn drvn and plugged on one pce* **28/1**

005 **4** nk **Frost In May (IRE)**[18] 4065 2-8-3 0........................ JulieBurke(3) 3 30
(David O'Meara) *sn rdn along and outpcd in rr: hdwy on inner over 2f out: sn drvn: n.m.r on inner fnl f: kpt on to take 4th nr line* **8/1**

0604 **5** nk **Astral Pursuits**[8] 4387 2-8-3 0........................ DeclanCannon(3) 2 29
(Nigel Tinkler) *chsd wnr over 2f: rdn along 1/2-way: drvn over 2f out: plugged on: edgd lft fnl f: lost 4th nr fin* **7/1**[3]

00 **6** 26 **Currently Inlondon (IRE)**[9] 4347 2-8-6 0........................ SamHitchcott 4
(Mick Channon) *chsd ldrs: rdn along after 2f: sn lost pl and bhd: t.o fnl 2f* **12/1**

1m 28.17s (1.17) **Going Correction** +0.10s/f (Good) 6 Ran SP% **110.9**
Speed ratings (Par 92): **97,85,83,83,83 53**
toteswingers 1&2 £1.30, 1&3 £6.50, 2&3 £8.20 CSF £3.89 TOTE £1.80: £1.10, £1.50; EX 5.10 Trifecta £37.40 Pool: £2388.91 - 47.80 winning units..The winner bought in for 5,500gns.
Owner Mrs Joanna Hughes **Bred** Llety Stud **Trained** Lambourn, Berks

FOCUS
It paid to follow market support in this weak contest, but the winner slammed them and is rated to the upper end of the race averages.

4618 PIN POINT RECRUITMENT NURSERY H'CAP 7f
3:00 (3:01) (Class 5) 2-Y-O £2,911 (£866; £432; £216) **Stalls** Centre

Form RPR

3416 **1** **Flora Medici**[11] 4277 2-8-9 **68**........................ ChrisCatlin 3 72
(Sir Mark Prescott Bt) *cl up: slt ld wl over 2f out: drvn over 1f out: edgd lft ins fnl f: kpt on* **22/1**

643 **2** 1¾ **Sakhalin Star (IRE)**[13] 4199 2-8-0 **62**........................ RaulDaSilva(3) 1 63+
(John Quinn) *slt ld on inner: rdn along and hdd wl over 2f out: cl up and drvn over 1f out: hld whn sltly hmpd ins fnl f: kpt on* **9/2**[3]

050 **3** nse **Baltic Fire (IRE)**[58] 2712 2-7-7 **61** oh14....................(b[1]) JoeyHaynes(7) 5 58
(Mrs K Burke) *in rr and outpcd 1/2-way: swtchd wd and rdn 2f out: hdwy over 1f out: styd on strly fnl f* **50/1**

3362 **4** ½ **Senorita Guest (IRE)**[11] 4277 2-8-9 **68**........................ SamHitchcott 6 66
(Mick Channon) *dwlt and towards rr: hdwy to trck ldrs 4f out: swtchd lft to inner and rdn to chse ldng pair 2f out: sn swtchd rt: drvn and one pce fnl f* **12/1**

2132 **5** 1¼ **Milly's Secret (IRE)**[15] 4134 2-9-7 **80**........................ PJMcDonald 4 75
(Ann Duffield) *trckd ldrs: rdn along 2f out: drvn over 1f out: kpt on same pce* **10/3**[2]

564 **6** ¾ **Crowdmania**[12] 4231 2-9-4 **77**........................ FrannyNorton 2 81+
(Mark Johnston) *dwlt: hdwy on inner to chse ldng pair whn hmpd and lost pl after 2f: hdwy whn hmpd and lost pl again 1/2-way: rdn and styng on wl to chse ldng pair whn hmpd again wl ins fnl f: nt rcvr* **11/10**[1]

025 **7** nk **Kraka Gym (IRE)**[71] 2337 2-8-3 **62**........................ JamesSullivan 9 54+
(Michael Easterby) *stdd s and hld up: a in rr* **22/1**

033 **8** 2¾ **Street Boss (IRE)**[21] 3943 2-8-10 **69**........................ DuranFentiman 7 53
(Tim Easterby) *trckd ldrs on outer: hdwy 1/2-way: chsd ldng pair over 2f out: sn rdn and wknd* **16/1**

1m 27.91s (0.91) **Going Correction** +0.10s/f (Good) 8 Ran SP% **113.1**
Speed ratings (Par 94): **98,96,95,95,93 93,92,89**
toteswingers 1&2 £12.10, 1&3 £35.20, 2&3 £23.40 CSF £114.59 CT £4904.84 TOTE £27.00: £4.70, £1.40, £9.00; EX 157.10 Trifecta £1909.30 Part won. Pool: £2545.77 - 0.87 winning units..
Owner Neil Greig **Bred** W N Greig **Trained** Newmarket, Suffolk
■ Stewards' Enquiry : Chris Catlin three-day ban: careless riding (Aug 7-9)

FOCUS
A slightly messy affair with the winner arguably unlucky. The form is rated around the second fourth.

4619 INFINITY ECOSIS TYRES CLAIMING STKS 5f
3:30 (3:31) (Class 6) 3-Y-O+ £2,385 (£704; £352) **Stalls** Low

Form RPR

1401 **1** **Hamoody (USA)**[27] 3713 9-9-2 78........................ JasonHart(5) 3 85
(David Nicholls) *dwlt: sn trcking ldrs: smooth hdwy on inner 2f out: led 1 1/2f out: sn rdn clr* **7/4**[2]

0600 **2** 4 **Lexi's Hero (IRE)**[46] 3093 5-9-4 77....................(p) FrannyNorton 5 67
(David Nicholls) *trckd ldng pair: pushed along 2f out: swtchd rt and rdn over 1f out: kpt on to take 2nd towards fin* **6/4**[1]

2151 **3** hd **Red Cape (FR)**[7] 4398 10-8-12 67....................(b) JamesSullivan 1 61
(Ruth Carr) *slt ld: rdn along 2f out: sn edgd rt: hdd and drvn 1 1/2f out: kpt on same pce: lost 2nd nr fin* **3/1**[3]

0300 **4** 1¼ **Captain Royale (IRE)**[29] 3654 8-8-2 56................(p) ConnorBeasley(7) 2 53
(Tracy Waggott) *cl up: ev ch 2f out: sn rdn and wknd ent fnl f* **20/1**

0000 **5** 1¼ **Ivestar (IRE)**[8] 4371 8-8-4 56........................ MatthewHopkins(7) 6 51
(Michael Easterby) *wnt rt s: in rr: hdwy 2f out: sn rdn and no imp fnl f* **50/1**

0-6 **6** 2¼ **Lichen Angel**[18] 4050 3-8-7 0........................ PJMcDonald 4 42
(Richard Whitaker) *chsd ldrs: pushed along over 2f out: sn rdn and btn* **80/1**

59.16s (-0.64) **Going Correction** 0.0s/f (Good)
WFA 3 from 5yo+ 4lb 6 Ran SP% **109.3**
Speed ratings (Par 101): **105,98,98,96,94 90**
toteswingers 1&2 £1.60, 1&3 £1.10, 2&3 £1.70 CSF £4.45 TOTE £1.90: £1.70, £1.20; EX 6.00 Trifecta £9.20 Pool: £2546.71 - 206.28 winning units..
Owner Hart Inn I **Bred** Ragged Mountain Farm **Trained** Sessay, N Yorks

FOCUS
The first three were the first three in the betting. The winner clocked a faster time than the following handicap and is rated close to his AW winter best.

4620 SKYBET SUPPORTING THE YORKSHIRE RACING SUMMER FESTIVAL H'CAP 5f
4:00 (4:00) (Class 4) (0-85,82) 3-Y-O+ £6,469 (£1,925; £962; £481) **Stalls** Low

Form RPR

2140 **1** **Lost In Paris (IRE)**[18] 4047 7-9-4 **74**....................(p) DavidAllan 3 84
(Tim Easterby) *mde all: jnd and rdn wl over 1f out: styd on wl u.p fnl f* **7/2**[2]

4414 **2** 2 **Sunrise Dance**[26] 3778 4-8-8 **71**........................ ConnorBeasley(7) 4 74
(Robert Johnson) *chsd wnr: hdwy 2f out: sn chal: rdn and ev ch over 1f out tl drvn ent fnl f and kpt on same pce* **13/2**

0005 **3** 1¼ **Silvanus (IRE)**[5] 4507 8-9-12 **82**........................ PaulMulrennan 7 80
(Paul Midgley) *trckd ldrs: hdwy 2f out: rdn to chse ldng pair ent fnl f: sn drvn and kpt on same pce* **6/1**[3]

532 **4** 1 **Economic Crisis (IRE)**[2] 4579 4-9-0 **70**........................ PaddyAspell 2 65
(Alan Berry) *trckd ldrs: rdn along and sltly outpcd wl over 1f out: kpt on u.p fnl f* **12/1**

-262 **5** hd **Angelito**[16] 4123 4-9-10 **80**........................ FrannyNorton 6 74
(Ed McMahon) *t.k.h: trckd ldrs and stmbld after 1 1/2f: effrt and n.m.r over 1f out: sn rdn and kpt on fnl f: nrst fin* **6/4**[1]

0150 **6** 3 **Chunky Diamond (IRE)**[12] 4235 4-9-5 **75**........................ PJMcDonald 5 58
(Ruth Carr) *dwlt and towards rr: hdwy on wd outside 2f out: sn rdn: edgd lft and n.d* **11/1**

0000 **7** ½ **Towbee**[18] 4047 4-9-7 **77**........................ JamesSullivan 1 58
(Michael Easterby) *trckd ldrs on inner: pushed along 1/2-way: rdn 2f out: sn wknd* **40/1**

140 **8** 3½ **Tango Sky (IRE)**[46] 3093 4-9-6 **76**........................ SamHitchcott 8 45
(David Nicholls) *sn outpcd and a in rr* **14/1**

59.36s (-0.44) **Going Correction** 0.0s/f (Good) 8 Ran SP% **115.0**
Speed ratings (Par 105): **103,99,97,96,95 91,90,84**
toteswingers 1&2 £4.30, 1&3 £2.70, 2&3 £4.90 CSF £26.59 CT £132.37 TOTE £5.60: £1.70, £1.80, £2.20; EX 27.70 Trifecta £111.80 Pool: £1387.30 - 9.30 winning units..
Owner W H Ponsonby **Bred** Yeomanstown Stud **Trained** Great Habton, N Yorks

FOCUS
Solid form for the Class. The winner showed similar form as when winning this last year.

4621 YORKSHIRE RADIO H'CAP 5f 212y
4:30 (4:30) (Class 6) (0-60,58) 3-Y-O+ £2,264 (£673; £336; £168) **Stalls** Low

Form RPR

1000 **1** **Almaty Express**[15] 4148 11-8-5 **46**....................(b) ConnorBeasley(7) 3 55
(John Weymes) *trckd ldrs on inner: swtchd rt and effrt over 1f out: squeezed through and rdn ent fnl f: qcknd to ld last 100yds* **22/1**

5006 **2** 1½ **Rat Catcher (IRE)**[14] 4162 3-9-0 **56**....................(b) DeclanCannon(3) 6 59
(Andrew Crook) *in tch: hdwy on outer 2f out: rdn over 1f out: str run to ld ent fnl f: sn edgd lft and drvn: hdd and one pce last 100yds* **9/1**

632 **3** 1 **Busy Bimbo (IRE)**[8] 4371 4-8-11 **45**........................ PaddyAspell 5 46
(Alan Berry) *chsd ldr: effrt and cl up 2f out: sn rdn: drvn and ev ch ent fnl f: one pce last 100yds* **7/1**[3]

0064 **4** *hd* **Layla's Hero (IRE)**[15] 4146 6-9-10 **58**.........................(v) PaulMulrennan 2 58+
(David Nicholls) *dwlt and in rr: swtchd lft towards inner and hdwy wl over 1f out: rdn to chse ldrs and n.m.r over 1f out: swtchd rt ins fnl f: kpt on: nrst fin* **11/4**[1]

-656 **5** *1 1/2* **Sinai (IRE)**[22] 3934 4-9-2 **57**..[1] JordanNason(7) 9 52
(Geoffrey Harker) *dwlt and towards rr: hdwy on outer 1/2-way: rdn to chse ldrs wl over 1f out: no imp fnl f* **15/2**

2006 **6** *1* **Only For You**[5] 4499 3-9-0 **53**.. DaleSwift 7 44
(Alan Brown) *chsd ldrs: hdwy 2f out: rdn wl over 1f out: drvn and one pce whn n.m.r and swtchd lft ins fnl f* **16/1**

5506 **7** *3/4* **Rose Of May (IRE)**[16] 4114 3-8-10 **49**...................(b[1]) GrahamGibbons 8 41
(David O'Meara) *swtchd rt and rdn along s: towards rr: sme hdwy 2f out: sn drvn and n.d* **7/1**[3]

030- **8** *2 1/4* **Baybshambles (IRE)**[267] 7456 9-9-1 **54**........................... JasonHart(5) 10 37
(Tina Jackson) *chsd ldng pair: rdn along over 2f out: drvn and wknd over 1f out* **20/1**

-200 **9** *shd* **Lady Kildare (IRE)**[19] 4009 5-9-6 **54**.................................. TomEaves 12 36
(Jedd O'Keeffe) *qckly away sn led and swtchd lft to inner: rdn along 2f out: drvn over 1f out: hdd & wknd ent fnl f* **10/1**

0045 **10** *1 3/4* **Windforpower (IRE)**[14] 4162 3-9-1 **54**.......................... FrannyNorton 1 30
(Tracy Waggott) *a in rr* **5/1**[2]

0-00 **11** *2 1/4* **Jay Kay**[48] 3030 4-8-12 **46**.. DuranFentiman 4 15
(Danielle McCormick) *midfield: rdn along over 2f out: sn wknd* **28/1**

1m 13.95s (0.35) **Going Correction** +0.10s/f (Good)
WFA 3 from 4yo+ 5lb **11** Ran SP% **117.6**
Speed ratings (Par 101): **101,99,97,97,95 94,93,90,89,87 84**
toteswingers 1&2 £44.40, 1&3 £30.90, 2&3 £14.70 CSF £203.20 CT £1544.94 TOTE £40.40: £8.20, £4.50, £2.50; EX 300.50 Trifecta £1605.80 Part won. Pool: £2141.17 - 0.45 winning units..
Owner Highmoor Racing 4 & Tag Racing **Bred** P G Airey **Trained** Middleham Moor, N Yorks
FOCUS
A weak race in which the winner showed his first real turf form for a couple of years.

4622 YORKSHIRE-OUTDOORS.CO.UK APPRENTICE TRAINING SERIES H'CAP (PART OF RACING EXCELLENCE INITIATIVE) 1m 3f 214y
5:00 (5:01) (Class 6) (0-65,59) 4-Y-O+ **£2,385** (£704; £352) **Stalls** Low

Form RPR

0/00 **1** **Mr Dream Maker (IRE)**[16] 4109 5-8-7 **45**................. LukeLeadbitter(5) 3 50
(Noel Wilson) *mde all: pushed along over 2f out: rdn over 1f out: kpt on wl towards fin* **20/1**

-063 **2** *shd* **Volcanic Jack (IRE)**[176] 432 5-9-7 **57**......................... EvaMoscrop(3) 8 62
(Philip Kirby) *t.k.h early: hld up: hdwy on outer 2f out: rdn to chse ldng pair whn edgd lft ent fnl f: styd on wl towards fin: jst failed* **2/1**[1]

5-03 **3** *1 1/4* **Strikemaster (IRE)**[13] 4204 7-9-3 **50**................................(t) NoelGarbutt 6 53
(Lee James) *hld up in rr: tk clsr order over 3f out: effrt 2f out: sn rdn: kpt on fnl f: nrst fin* **10/1**

2040 **4** *1* **Silver Tigress**[25] 3808 5-9-12 **59**.................................. ConnorBeasley 7 60
(George Moore) *trckd ldng pair: hdwy 3f out: chsd wnr 2f out: sn rdn: drvn and kpt on same pce ins fnl f* **9/4**[2]

-006 **5** *2 1/4* **Tenacity**[13] 4204 4-8-9 **45**... KevinStott(3) 2 43
(Karen Tutty) *trckd ldr: niggled along on inner 4f out: rdn over 2f out: sn drvn and one pce* **11/2**

4205 **6** *1* **Amir Pasha (UAE)**[3] 4563 8-8-13 **53**.......................(p) KatieDowson(7) 1 49
(Micky Hammond) *t.k.h early: trckd ldrs on inner: effrt and pushed along wl over 2f out: rdn wl over 1f out: sn one pce* **4/1**[3]

2m 41.85s (2.95) **Going Correction** +0.10s/f (Good) **6** Ran SP% **113.3**
Speed ratings (Par 101): **94,93,93,92,90 90**
toteswingers 1&2 £5.80, 1&3 £7.30, 2&3 £2.10 CSF £61.29 CT £440.10 TOTE £23.70: £10.40, £1.90; EX 89.40 Trifecta £1137.80 Pool: £2230.27 - 1.47 winning units..
Owner The Blue Celery Racing Partnership **Bred** Garry Chong **Trained** Middleham, N Yorks
FOCUS
Not form to trust considering they went a modest early gallop, the winner given an easy lead. This was his first form since 2011.
T/Plt: £212.20 to a £1 stake. Pool: £52,563.99 - 180.77 winning tickets T/Qpdt: £43.90 to a £1 stake. Pool: £3,402.30 - 57.30 winning tickets JR

4450 LEICESTER (R-H)
Wednesday, July 24

OFFICIAL GOING: Good (good to soft in places in straight; straight 7.7; round 8.0)
Wind: Almost nil Weather: Fine

4623 BETFAIR AMATEUR H'CAP (FOR NOVICE AMATEUR RIDERS) 7f 9y
5:40 (5:40) (Class 6) (0-60,60) 4-Y-O+ **£1,975** (£607; £303) **Stalls** Centre

Form RPR

0526 **1** **Boy The Bell**[36] 3444 6-10-12 **51**...............................(be) MissHDukes 17 60
(Ollie Pears) *chsd ldrs: rdn over 1f out: styd on to ld and edgd rt wl ins fnl f* **8/1**

0640 **2** *1/2* **Rio Cobolo (IRE)**[5] 4482 7-11-2 **58**.............................. MrDPCostello(3) 8 66
(David Nicholls) *s.i.s: sn rcvrd to ld: hdd over 4f out: rdn and ev ch fr over 1f out: styd on* **17/2**

5204 **3** *nk* **Lil Sophella (IRE)**[5] 4469 4-10-6 **48**........................ MissAChadwick(3) 14 55
(Patrick Holmes) *s.i.s: swtchd rt sn after s: hdwy over 2f out: led over 1f out: edgd lft and hdd wl ins fnl f* **5/1**[3]

2420 **4** *3 1/4* **Adiator**[19] 4007 5-11-7 **60**......................................(p) MrSebSpencer 5 58
(Neville Bycroft) *s.i.s and bmpd s: sn prom: rdn over 1f out: no ex ins fnl f* **7/2**[1]

650 **5** *3/4* **Hail Promenader (IRE)**[26] 3788 7-11-5 **58**........(p) MrGrahamCarson 11 55
(Anthony Carson) *s.i.s: hdwy over 1f out: r.o: nvr nrr* **11/1**

6234 **6** *1 1/4* **Ishiamiracle**[34] 3496 4-10-7 **49**................................(p) MrJAMcEntee(3) 10 42
(Phil McEntee) *chsd ldrs: rdn over 1f out: no ex fnl f* **22/1**

0403 **7** *nse* **Stormbound (IRE)**[36] 3429 4-11-7 **60**.................................. MrJHarding 15 53
(Paul Cole) *hld up: hdwy over 2f out: rdn over 1f out: no ex fnl f* **4/1**[2]

-240 **8** *1 1/4* **Arachnophobia (IRE)**[107] 1426 7-10-9 **51**.......................(v) MrZBaker(3) 12 41
(Martin Bosley) *prom: rdn over 2f out: wknd fnl f* **18/1**

0004 **9** *2 1/2* **Sairaam (IRE)**[6] 4456 7-10-8 **47**..................................... AnnaHesketh 3 30
(Charles Smith) *chsd ldrs: led over 4f out: rdn and hdd over 1f out: wknd fnl f* **14/1**

35-0 **10** *nk* **Lordship (IRE)**[18] 4070 9-10-9 **48**..................................... MissETodd 1 31
(Tom Gretton) *chsd ldrs: rdn over 2f out: wknd fnl f* **50/1**

0350 **11** *2 1/2* **King Of Wing (IRE)**[7] 4403 4-10-11 **53**..........................(v) MrTBurke(3) 2 29
(Phil McEntee) *sn pushed along in rr: n.d* **33/1**

0024 **12** *2 1/2* **Benandonner (USA)**[22] 3924 10-10-13 **52**.....................(p) MissMBryant 4 22
(Paddy Butler) *mid-div: bhd fr 1/2-way* **22/1**

624/ **13** *shd* **Harting Hill**[22] 6938 8-10-13 **55**.......................................(bt) MrJJInsole(3) 6 24
(Violet M Jordan) *s.i.s and bmpd s: sn chsng ldrs: rdn and wknd over 2f out* **20/1**

060- **14** *1* **Wing N Prayer (IRE)**[462] 1436 6-10-4 **46** oh1.................... MrAFrench(3) 7 13
(Neville Bycroft) *s.i.s: sn prom: lost pl over 5f out: n.d after* **66/1**

1m 26.05s (-0.15) **Going Correction** -0.125s/f (Firm) **14** Ran SP% **120.6**
Speed ratings (Par 101): **95,94,94,90,89 88,88,86,83,83 80,77,77,76**
toteswingers 1&2 £18.80, 1&3 £10.40, 2&3 £13.00 CSF £68.60 CT £390.16 TOTE £8.40: £2.70, £2.80, £2.70; EX 81.20 Trifecta £381.70 Part won. Pool: £508.94 - 0.88 winning units..
Owner K C West **Bred** D J P Turner **Trained** Norton, N Yorks
■ Stewards' Enquiry : Miss H Dukes one-day ban: careless riding (Aug 8)
FOCUS
The runners were spread across the track in this moderate handicap and it was those who raced towards the stands' side who emerged.

4624 MOLYNEUX H'CAP 5f 218y
6:10 (6:10) (Class 5) (0-70,76) 3-Y-O **£2,587** (£770; £384; £192) **Stalls** Centre

Form RPR

6031 **1** **Sedenoo**[5] 4499 3-9-8 **76** 6ex....................................... TobyAtkinson(5) 7 83
(Marco Botti) *a.p: rdn over 2f out: led ins fnl f: r.o: edgd rt towards fin* **8/15**[1]

250- **2** *3/4* **Dumbarton Rock**[229] 8016 3-9-4 **67**.................................. JoeFanning 4 72
(William Jarvis) *chsd ldrs: rdn and ev ch ins fnl f: styd on* **14/1**[3]

5406 **3** *1* **Ishi Honest**[23] 3903 3-8-5 **61**.................................. DanielMuscutt(7) 3 62
(Mark Usher) *led: hdd over 4f out: led again over 2f out: rdn over 1f out: hdd and unable qck ins fnl f* **20/1**

0-34 **4** *2 1/4* **Shillito**[23] 3894 3-9-6 **69**.. BarryMcHugh 8 63
(Tony Coyle) *hld up: rdn over 2f out: nt trble ldrs* **20/1**

3351 **5** *1* **Deepest Blue**[14] 4162 3-9-6 **69**....................................... GrahamLee 6 60
(Declan Carroll) *s.i.s: hld up: rdn and edgd rt over 1f out: no ex ins fnl f* **10/3**[2]

305 **6** *3 1/4* **Timeless**[24] 3860 3-9-0 **63**...(t) MartinLane 1 44
(Tobias B P Coles) *s.i.s: racd keenly: hdwy to ld over 4f out: rdn and hdd over 2f out: wknd fnl f* **20/1**

1m 12.5s (-0.50) **Going Correction** -0.125s/f (Firm) **6** Ran SP% **109.3**
Speed ratings (Par 100): **98,97,95,92,91 87**
toteswingers 1&2 £1.80, 1&3 £3.00, 2&3 £7.30 CSF £8.30 CT £61.78 TOTE £1.40: £1.10, £3.70; EX 8.50 Trifecta £72.70 Pool: £1862.34 - 19.18 winning units..
Owner Scuderia Rencati Srl **Bred** Chegwidden Systems Ltd **Trained** Newmarket, Suffolk
FOCUS
Moderate form.

4625 SUTTON (S) STKS 1m 60y
6:40 (6:42) (Class 6) 3-Y-O **£1,940** (£577; £288; £144) **Stalls** Low

Form RPR

0564 **1** **Scala Romana (IRE)**[14] 4158 3-8-6 62.............................. ChrisCatlin 2 62
(Sir Mark Prescott Bt) *led 1f: chsd ldr tl led again over 2f out: rdn over 1f out: styd on* **3/1**[2]

3500 **2** *3/4* **Reconsider Baby (IRE)**[15] 4143 3-8-6 65.......................... BarryMcHugh 6 60
(Mrs K Burke) *a.p: rdn to chse wnr over 1f out: edgd rt and styd on same pce ins fnl f* **7/4**[1]

5436 **3** *3* **Suspension**[38] 3376 3-8-6 51...(tp) JohnFahy 8 53
(Hughie Morrison) *a.p: chsd wnr over 2f out tl rdn over 1f out: styd on same pce fnl f* **5/1**[3]

50 **4** *2 1/4* **Tornado Battle**[14] 4182 3-8-11 0....................................(b[1]) GrahamLee 1 53
(Phil McEntee) *hld up: hdwy over 3f out: rdn over 1f out: no ex fnl f* **28/1**

2506 **5** *1/2* **Nordikhab (IRE)**[18] 4048 3-8-11 63.................................... PhillipMakin 7 52
(Kevin Ryan) *hld up: rdn over 2f out: no imp fnl f* **3/1**[2]

0000 **6** *2 1/2* **Moorway (IRE)**[19] 4008 3-8-6 55.................................(p) JackDuern(5) 3 46
(Andrew Hollinshead) *pushed along to ld after 1f: clr 5f out: rdn and hdd over 2f out: wknd fnl f* **20/1**

0 **7** *50* **One In A Thousand (IRE)**[14] 4182 3-8-6 0......................... SaleemGolam 5
(Chris Dwyer) *s.i.s: hld up: hdwy over 3f out: rdn and wknd over 2f out* **100/1**

1m 44.8s (-0.30) **Going Correction** -0.125s/f (Firm) **7** Ran SP% **112.2**
Speed ratings (Par 98): **96,95,92,90,89 87,37**
toteswingers 1&2 £2.20, 1&3 £3.30, 2&3 £2.20 CSF £8.31 TOTE £4.00: £1.80, £1.50; EX 13.10 Trifecta £36.00 Pool: £2005.03 - 41.70 winning units..There was no bid for the winner.
Owner Mr & Mrs John Kelsey-Fry **Bred** John Kelsey-Fry **Trained** Newmarket, Suffolk
FOCUS
The front pair drew clear in what had looked quite a competitive seller.

4626 TOM CRIBB H'CAP 1m 3f 183y
7:15 (7:15) (Class 4) (0-85,82) 4-Y-O+ **£4,851** (£1,443; £721) **Stalls** Low

Form RPR

-121 **1** **Mankini (IRE)**[19] 4016 4-9-1 **76**.............................. KirstyMilczarek 2 89+
(Luca Cumani) *racd keenly: trckd ldr tl over 8f out: remained handy: led over 2f out: shkn up and clr over 1f out: comf* **1/2**[1]

414 **2** *3* **Kittens**[14] 4172 4-8-6 **67**.. FrannyNorton 1 73
(William Muir) *s.i.s: chsd ldr over 8f out tl led over 3f out: rdn and hdd over 2f out: styd on same pce appr fnl f* **9/1**[3]

4-36 **3** *2 3/4* **Almagest**[12] 4264 5-9-7 **82**.. DanielTudhope 4 84
(David O'Meara) *led: hdd over 3f out: sn rdn: styd on same pce fnl 2f* **9/4**[2]

2m 33.55s (-0.35) **Going Correction** -0.125s/f (Firm) **3** Ran SP% **107.4**
Speed ratings (Par 105): **96,94,92**
CSF £4.71 TOTE £1.50; EX 3.90 Trifecta £5.20 Pool: £823.95 - 117.67 winning units..
Owner Leonidas Marinopoulos **Bred** Oak Hill Stud **Trained** Newmarket, Suffolk
FOCUS
With Nave defecting, this was left to look a straightforward opportunity for Mankini, and he duly obliged at short odds.

4627 THISTLETON GAP MAIDEN STKS 5f 2y
7:45 (7:47) (Class 5) 3-Y-O+ **£2,587** (£770; £384; £192) **Stalls** Centre

Form RPR

22 **1** **Port Alfred**[13] 4200 3-9-5 0...................................... MickaelBarzalona 4 87+
(Saeed bin Suroor) *mde all: clr fr 1/2-way: shkn up over 1f out: unchal* **1/6**[1]

5-0 **2** *4* **Golden Secret**[25] 3837 3-8-9 0.. RyanTate(5) 7 68
(Clive Cox) *hld up: hdwy over 1f out: wnt 2nd ins fnl f: no ch w wnr* **12/1**

22 **3** *1* **Hand Grenade (IRE)**[22] 3915 3-9-0 0................................... JohnFahy 3 64
(Eve Johnson Houghton) *chsd wnr: rdn over 1f out: no ex ins fnl f* **8/1**[3]

4 *6* **Random Success (IRE)** 3-9-0 0.. DaneO'Neill 2 42
(Roger Charlton) *s.i.s: hdwy over 3f out: wknd fnl f* **7/1**[2]

5 *1* **Lady Rain** 4-8-11 0... WillPettis(7) 6 39
(Milton Bradley) *prom: pushed along: edgd rt and wknd 1/2-way* **100/1**

The Form Book Flat, Raceform Ltd, Compton, RG20 6NL.

0-0 **6** 19 **Swift Code (IRE)**[109] 1392 3-9-5 0 AndrewMullen 1
(Nigel Tinkler) *chsd ldrs 2f: sn bhd* **100/1**

59.41s (-0.59) **Going Correction** -0.125s/f (Firm)
WFA 3 from 4yo+ 4lb **6** Ran SP% **119.0**
Speed ratings (Par 103): **99,92,91,81,79 49**
CSF £4.55 TOTE £1.10: £1.10, £5.20; EX 5.00 Trifecta £8.60 Pool: £1419.68 - 123.76 winning units..
Owner Godolphin **Bred** Templeton Stud **Trained** Newmarket, Suffolk

FOCUS
A straightforward opportunity for the red-hot favourite.

4628 RAY HAWLEY 90TH BIRTHDAY H'CAP 7f 9y
8:20 (8:21) (Class 4) (0-80,80) 3-Y-0+ **£5,175** (£1,540; £769; £384) **Stalls** Centre

Form RPR

0421 **1** **Illustrious Prince (IRE)**[5] 4496 6-9-1 **70** 6ex NeilFarley(3) 2 80
(Declan Carroll) *led 1f: chsd ldr: led again over 1f out: rdn out* **6/1**

-542 **2** 1 ½ **My Single Malt (IRE)**[12] 4245 5-9-6 **72** (p) PaulMulrennan 6 78
(Julie Camacho) *s.i.s: hld up: rdn and hdwy over 1f out: r.o: nt rch wnr* **11/2**[3]

0105 **3** hd **Elusive Hawk (IRE)**[26] 3754 9-9-2 **73** DeclanBates(5) 4 78
(David Evans) *hld up: hdwy and nt clr run over 1f out: r.o: nt rch ldrs* **33/1**

0-44 **4** nse **Broctune Papa Gio**[26] 3777 6-9-4 **70** TomEaves 11 75
(Keith Reveley) *hld up: rdn over 1f out: r.o ins fnl f: nrst fin* **16/1**

3534 **5** 3 **Red Paladin (IRE)**[18] 4045 3-8-8 **67** (b[1]) MartinLane 10 61
(Kevin Ryan) *chsd ldrs: led 1/2-way: rdn: edgd rt and hdd over 1f out: styd on same pce ins fnl f* **10/1**

034 **6** 2 ¼ **Tawtheeq (IRE)**[19] 4011 3-9-5 **78** DaneO'Neill 7 69
(Richard Hannon) *s.i.s: hld up: hdwy over 2f out: rdn over 1f out: wknd ins fnl f: eased nr fin* **8/1**

0101 **7** 3 **Skytrain**[14] 4181 3-9-7 **80** JoeFanning 9 60
(Mark Johnston) *chsd ldrs: rdn over 1f out: wknd ins fnl f* **3/1**[2]

0400 **8** 3 **Nasri**[18] 4067 7-9-1 **74** WillPettis(7) 5 49
(Milton Bradley) *led 6f out: pushed along and hdd 1/2-way: wknd over 1f out* **40/1**

1010 **9** ¾ **Creek Falcon (IRE)**[19] 4014 4-9-13 **79** DanielTudhope 1 58
(David O'Meara) *chsd ldrs: rdn over 2f out: wknd over 1f out* **5/2**[1]

1m 24.39s (-1.81) **Going Correction** -0.125s/f (Firm)
WFA 3 from 4yo+ 7lb **9** Ran SP% **114.7**
Speed ratings (Par 105): **105,103,103,103,99 97,93,90,89**
toteswingers 1&2 £1.80, 1&3 £20.40, 2&3 £14.60 CSF £38.63 CT £999.90 TOTE £7.30: £1.70, £2.00, £8.00; EX 51.10 Trifecta £607.40 Part won. Pool: £809.93 - 0.14 winning units..
Owner Ray Flegg **Bred** Rathbarry Stud **Trained** Sledmere, E Yorks

FOCUS
Fair handicap form.

4629 MELTON MOWBRAY H'CAP 1m 1f 218y
8:50 (8:50) (Class 5) (0-70,73) 3-Y-0 **£2,587** (£770; £384; £192) **Stalls** Low

Form RPR

5-53 **1** **Dame Nellie Melba**[8] 4373 3-9-7 **68** JoeFanning 4 78+
(Mark Johnston) *chsd ldr tl led over 3f out: shkn up and clr over 1f out: styd on* **15/8**[1]

12-1 **2** 1 ¼ **Progenitor (IRE)**[8] 4383 3-9-12 **73** 6ex TedDurcan 7 80
(David Lanigan) *hld up: hdwy 3f out: rdn over 1f out: hung rt and wnt 2nd ins fnl f: nt rch wnr* **2/1**[2]

054 **3** 3 **Petrify**[14] 4182 3-8-13 **60** KirstyMilczarek 2 61
(Luca Cumani) *hld up: plld hrd: hdwy to chse wnr over 3f out: rdn over 1f out: no ex ins fnl f* **7/2**[3]

35-0 **4** 3 ¼ **Lucky Black Star (IRE)**[37] 3418 3-9-2 **63** PatCosgrave 1 58
(George Baker) *s.i.s: plld hrd and sn prom: rdn over 3f out: wknd over 1f out* **40/1**

-046 **5** 2 **Marlborough House**[18] 4076 3-8-13 **60** (b[1]) TomEaves 5 51
(James Given) *prom: rdn over 2f out: sn wknd* **13/2**

066 **6** 66 **West Beat**[16] 4113 3-8-0 **50** JulieBurke(3) 3
(David O'Meara) *hld up: plld hrd: sddle slipped over 8f out: hdd over 3f out: eased and sn lost tch* **25/1**

2m 9.53s (1.63) **Going Correction** -0.125s/f (Firm) **6** Ran SP% **110.0**
Speed ratings (Par 100): **88,87,84,82,80 27**
CSF £5.68 TOTE £5.10: £2.60, £1.10; EX 5.70 Trifecta £11.00 Pool: £956.19 - 67.74 winning units..
Owner Miss K Rausing **Bred** Miss K Rausing **Trained** Middleham Moor, N Yorks

FOCUS
This was dominated by the three progressive types who headed up the market and the form looks solid. The saddle slipped on West Beat and she was largely ignored in front, although they still got racing a fair way out.
T/Plt: £33.90 to a £1 stake. Pool: £65173.31 - 1399.73 winning tickets T/Qpdt: £7.70 to a £1 stake. Pool: £5316.27 - 507.30 winning tickets CR

4517 LINGFIELD (L-H)
Wednesday, July 24

OFFICIAL GOING: Standard
Wind: very light, half behind Weather: sunny and warm

4630 VINES BMW CLAIMING STKS 6f (P)
2:10 (2:27) (Class 6) 2-Y-0 **£2,045** (£603; £302) **Stalls** Low

Form RPR

523 **1** **Instant Attraction (IRE)**[11] 4289 2-9-4 0 NeilCallan 5 78+
(Kevin Ryan) *mde all: rdn 2f out: drvn and wnt clr over 1f out: r.o wl* **1/2**[1]

060 **2** 3 ½ **Limegrove**[19] 4019 2-8-9 0 TomQueally 3 58
(David Evans) *taken down early: chsd wnr: drvn and unable qck w wnr wl over 1f out: kpt on same pce after* **7/4**[2]

3 6 **Hannah Louise (IRE)** 2-8-6 0 (t) CathyGannon 4 36
(Olivia Maylam) *taken down early: s.i.s and pushed along early: in tch after 2f: outpcd but wnt modest 3rd 2f out: no imp* **50/1**

0 **4** 3 ¼ **M'Lady Ermyn**[14] 4175 2-7-13 0 JemmaMarshall(5) 6 23
(Pat Phelan) *chsd ldrs on outer: rdn and outpcd over 2f out: wknd wl over 1f out* **33/1**[3]

00 **5** 13 **Bright Society (IRE)**[32] 3574 2-8-9 0 (b[1]) LiamJones 1
(J S Moore) *in tch: rdn and dropped to last 1/2-way: lost tch 2f out* **50/1**

1m 13.62s (1.72) **Going Correction** +0.10s/f (Slow) **5** Ran SP% **109.9**
Speed ratings (Par 92): **92,87,79,75,57**
CSF £1.59 TOTE £1.50: £1.10, £1.20; EX 1.90 Trifecta £5.90 Pool: £1307.91 - 165.09 winning units..
Owner Mrs J Ryan **Bred** Mrs Julia Hayes **Trained** Hambleton, N Yorks

FOCUS
An uncompetitive juvenile claimer with only two having any real claims based on previous form. The winner is rated towards the best of his previous efforts.

4631 LINGFIELD PARK OWNERS GROUP MAIDEN AUCTION STKS 7f (P)
2:40 (2:41) (Class 6) 2-Y-O **£2,045** (£603; £302) **Stalls** Low

Form RPR

0 **1** **Trip To Paris (IRE)**[7] 4414 2-9-3 0 (b[1]) RyanMoore 13 76
(Ed Dunlop) *t.k.h: chsd ldrs: effrt to chse ldr wl over 1f out: drvn to ld ins fnl f: styd on u.p: drvn out* **7/1**[3]

55 **2** 1 ¾ **Floating Ballerino (IRE)**[41] 3238 2-9-1 0 HarryBentley 4 69
(Olly Stevens) *led: rdn jst over 1f out: hdd ins fnl f: sn btn and edgd rt: wknd towards fin* **11/10**[1]

6 **3** 1 ¼ **Sheila's Footsteps**[15] 4154 2-8-11 0 LiamKeniry 1 62
(J S Moore) *in tch in midfield: 5th and drvn over 2f out: styd on u.p to go 3rd ins fnl f: kpt on steadily* **16/1**

00 **4** 2 **Rural Affair**[29] 3663 2-8-6 0 DavidProbert 6 52
(Harry Dunlop) *chsd ldr tl wl over 1f out: no ex u.p over 1f out: lost 3rd ins fnl f: wknd towards fin* **25/1**

06 **5** shd **Mount Cheiron (USA)**[36] 3436 2-9-3 0 JimmyFortune 2 62
(Brian Meehan) *chsd ldrs: rdn over 4f out: outpcd u.p over 2f out: kpt on again ins fnl f but no threat to wnr* **16/1**

6 4 **Moonspring (IRE)** 2-8-6 0 HayleyTurner 7 40
(Tobias B P Coles) *dwlt and rdn along early: hdwy into midfield after 1f: 6th and outpcd u.p over 2f out: wl hld fnl 2f* **20/1**

7 2 ¼ **Charleys Angel** 2-7-13 0 JemmaMarshall(5) 5 32
(Pat Phelan) *racd off the pce in midfield: struggling over 3f out: kpt on past btn horses fnl f: n.d* **100/1**

00 **8** hd **My Anchor**[15] 4154 2-8-9 0 CathyGannon 3 37
(Sylvester Kirk) *racd in midfield: u.p and struggling over 3f out: n.d fr 1/2-way* **50/1**

5 **9** 4 **Hostile Takeover (IRE)**[56] 2771 2-8-8 0 (t) CharlesBishop(3) 12 28
(Olly Stevens) *hld up wl off the pce in last quartet: rdn and effrt on inner over 2f out: no real hdwy: n.d* **33/1**

10 hd **Lupara** 2-8-4 0 FrankieMcDonald 8 20
(Paul Fitzsimons) *in tch in midfield for 2f: sn struggling u.p: wknd 1/2-way* **100/1**

11 1 ½ **Walta (IRE)** 2-8-11 0 LukeMorris 9 23
(Ronald Harris) *dwlt: sn in midfield: rdn over 4f out: struggling over 3f out: wknd and no ch 2f out* **33/1**

12 4 **Yellow Emperor (IRE)** 2-9-3 0 WilliamBuick 11 19
(Jeremy Noseda) *v.s.a: a wl off the pce in last trio: nvr on terms* **9/4**[2]

0 **13** 8 **Storm Of Choice**[40] 3291 2-8-9 0 RobertHavlin 10
(Michael Attwater) *dwlt: sn rdn and struggling in last trio: nvr on terms* **100/1**

14 1 ½ **Commanding Force** 2-8-9 0 KieranO'Neill 14
(John Bridger) *sn rdn and struggling in rr: nvr on terms* **100/1**

1m 26.35s (1.55) **Going Correction** +0.10s/f (Slow) **14** Ran SP% **123.1**
Speed ratings (Par 92): **95,93,91,89,89 84,82,81,77,77 75,70,61,59**
toteswingers 1&2 £4.30, 1&3 £16.40, 2&3 £5.20 CSF £14.63 TOTE £11.40: £2.40, £1.10, £3.40; EX 17.20 Trifecta £362.80 Pool: £2709.52 - 5.60 winning units..
Owner La Grange Partnership **Bred** Paul Monaghan & T J Monaghan **Trained** Newmarket, Suffolk

FOCUS
An uncompetitive maiden in which few were involved. The winner's effort fits the race averages.

4632 PORTO RACING MAIDEN STKS (DIV I) 1m 4f (P)
3:10 (3:10) (Class 5) 3-Y-O+ **£2,726** (£805; £402) **Stalls** Low

Form RPR

1 **Buchanan** 3-9-1 0 DaneO'Neill 5 88+
(Henry Candy) *hld up in tch in last quartet over 2f out: hdwy into midfield 1/2-way: chsd ldrs and effrt over 2f out: chal 1f out: led ins fnl f: r.o strly and hld on wl after* **10/1**

2 hd **Economy** 3-9-1 0 RyanMoore 11 87+
(Sir Michael Stoute) *t.k.h: hld up in tch in midfield: hdwy to chse ldrs 5f out: rdn ent ent fnl 2f: led 1f out: sn hdd: r.o strly and sustained duel w wnr after: jst hld* **3/1**[2]

3 5 **Exploratory (USA)** 3-9-1 0 SilvestreDeSousa 13 79
(Saeed bin Suroor) *chsd ldrs: wnt 2nd 8f out: drvn and ev ch over 1f out tl 1f out: sn outpcd by ldng pair: plugged on* **9/2**[3]

36 **4** 2 **Lions Park (IRE)**[12] 4257 3-9-1 0 NeilCallan 8 76
(Mark Johnston) *led and set stdy gallop: rdn and qcknd wl over 2f out: hrd pressed and drvn over 1f out: hdd 1f out: wknd fnl 150yds* **7/1**

6-3 **5** 5 **National Poet (IRE)**[13] 4223 3-9-1 0 MickaelBarzalona 4 68
(Saeed bin Suroor) *chsd ldr tl 8f out: chsd ldrs after: cl 4th and rdn over 2f out: btn over 1f out: fdd fnl f* **2/1**[1]

6 1 ½ **Martagon Lily** 3-8-10 0 [1] WilliamBuick 10 61+
(John Gosden) *dwlt: in tch in rr: sme hdwy over 3f out: pushed along and outpcd over 2f out: rn wd bnd 2f out: no ch but kpt on fnl f* **16/1**

0 **7** hd **Filia Regina**[26] 3764 3-8-10 0 PaulHanagan 2 60+
(Ed Dunlop) *t.k.h: hld up in tch in last quartet: effrt over 2f out but sn outpcd by ldrs: wl hld but kpt on fnl f* **14/1**

0 **8** ½ **Mystery Drama**[41] 3239 3-8-10 0 FergusSweeney 1 59+
(Alan King) *led for 1f: grad stdd bk and hld up in midfield: shuffled bk on inner over 3f out: pushed along ent fnl 2f: n.d but kpt on fnl f* **100/1**

0 **9** 6 **Holli Deya**[26] 3764 3-8-10 0 MarcHalford 12 50
(Andi Brown) *chsd ldrs: rdn and outpcd over 2f out: rn green and hung rt bnd 2f out: sn fdd* **100/1**

-006 **10** 3 ½ **Parsons Green**[98] 1611 4-9-8 40 RobertHavlin 6 44
(Michael Attwater) *hld up wl in tch in midfield: rdn wl over 2f out and sn outpcd: wknd 2f out and wl bhd fnl f* **100/1**

11 10 **Storm Quest**[97] 6-9-8 0 LukeMorris 7 28
(Robin Dickin) *s.i.s and rdn in detached last early: clsd and in tch 9f out: rdn and btn over 3f out: sn lost tch: t.o* **100/1**

4 **12** 2 ¼ **Tee It Up Tommo (IRE)**[63] 2576 4-9-13 0 GeorgeBaker 9 30
(Michael Wigham) *t.k.h: hld up in tch towards rr: rdn and btn over 3f out: sn lost tch: t.o* **16/1**

13 2 ¼ **Tarmo (IRE)** 3-9-1 0 AndreaAtzeni 3 26
(Marco Botti) *in tch: rdn and lost pl over 3f out: wl bhd 2f out: t.o* **66/1**

2m 33.73s (0.73) **Going Correction** +0.10s/f (Slow)
WFA 3 from 4yo+ 12lb **13** Ran SP% **122.0**
Speed ratings (Par 103): **101,100,97,96,92 91,91,91,87,85 78,76,75**
toteswingers 1&2 £8.30, 1&3 £7.70, 2&3 £4.80 CSF £41.26 TOTE £15.40: £2.50, £1.80, £1.80; EX 58.10 Trifecta £295.90 Pool: £2743.39 - 6.95 winning units..
Owner Thomas Barr **Bred** Lady Bamford **Trained** Kingston Warren, Oxon

FOCUS
Probably a fair maiden with some powerful yards represented. The pace was only modest, resulting in a time just over two seconds slower than the second division, but the front two pulled clear in the closing stages and look above-average types who should do better.

4633 PORTO RACING MAIDEN STKS (DIV II) 1m 4f (P)
3:40 (3:41) (Class 5) 3-Y-0+ £2,726 (£805; £402) Stalls Low

Form RPR

-022 **1** **Fledged**[20] 3989 3-9-1 84 WilliamBuick 7 93
(John Gosden) *t.k.h: chsd ldrs: wnt 2nd 6f out tl led wl over 2f out: rdn and clr w rival over 2f out: kpt on and a jst holding rival ins fnl f* **7/4**[1]

3 **2** *nk* **Saddaqa (USA)**[20] 3975 3-8-10 0 SilvestreDeSousa 2 87
(Saeed bin Suroor) *t.k.h: hld up wl in tch in midfield: hdwy to press ldr and wnt clr 2f out: ev ch but kpt wanting to edge lft u.p fr over 1f out: a jst hld fnl f* **9/2**[3]

3 **3** *13* **Maypole Lass**[55] 2804 3-8-10 0 RyanMoore 4 66
(Sir Michael Stoute) *chsd ldr over 10f out tl 9f out: styd chsng ldrs: 3rd and no ex u.p 2f out: wknd over 1f out* **11/4**[2]

4 *3* **Certification (IRE)** 3-9-1 0 NeilCallan 5 67
(Mark Johnston) *chsd ldrs: 4th and outpcd whn rn green and hung rt bnd 2f out: sn wknd* **25/1**

0-3 **5** *6* **Are You Mine (IRE)**[35] 3469 3-8-10 0 JimCrowley 8 52
(Ralph Beckett) *t.k.h: hld up in tch in rr: hdwy over 3f out: 5th and no hdwy jst over 2f out: wknd 2f out* **12/1**

6 **6** *shd* **Dumbfounded (FR)**[72] 2321 5-9-13 0 AdamKirby 11 57
(Lady Herries) *sltly hmpd s: hld up in tch in rr: lost tch over 3f out: no ch but passed btn horses ins fnl f* **66/1**

6043 **7** *½* **Muskat Link**[25] 3821 3-8-10 65 AmyScott(5) 3 56
(Henry Candy) *led tl over 10f out: stdd bk and wl in tch in midfield after: rdn and wknd over 2f out* **50/1**

2/5 **8** *9* **Fragonard**[35] 3469 4-9-8 TomQueally 12
(Lady Cecil) *sltly hmpd s: t.k.h early: hld up in tch in last quartet: hdwy into midfield 1/2-way: wknd wl over 2f out: eased fnl f* **8/1**

4 **9** *17* **Mansoreen**[15] 4139 3-9-1 0 MickaelBarzalona 10 14
(Saeed bin Suroor) *wnt sltly rt s: chsd ldr tl led over 10f out 3f out: sn btn and fdd: t.o and virtually p.u fnl f* **10/1**

5 **10** *21* **Sunday Meadow (IRE)**[40] 3272 4-9-8 0 HayleyTurner 13
(William Knight) *chsd ldrs: wnt 2nd 9f out tl 6f out: rdn and lost pl qckly over 4f out: t.o fnl 3f* **66/1**

6 **11** *14* **Wooly Bully**[24] 3858 3-9-1 0 FergusSweeney 6
(Alan King) *in tch towards rr: pushed along 7f out: rdn and lost tch 4f out: t.o over 2f out* **100/1**

0 **12** *1* **Lady Cliche**[24] 3858 4-9-1 0 NedCurtis(7) 9
(Roger Curtis) *swtchd lft after s: in tch in rr: rdn 8f out: lost tch 4f: t.o fnl 3f* **100/1**

2m 31.5s (-1.50) **Going Correction** +0.10s/f (Slow)
WFA 3 from 4yo+ 12lb **12 Ran SP% 119.9**
Speed ratings (Par 103): **109,108,100,98,94 94,93, ,76,62 53,52**
toteswingers 1&2 £2.40, 1&3 £2.60, 2&3 £3.40 CSF £9.84 TOTE £2.60: £1.20, £2.00, £1.70; EX 8.60 Trifecta £27.60 Pool: £3904.02 - 105.80 winning units..
Owner K Abdullah **Bred** Juddmonte Farms Ltd **Trained** Newmarket, Suffolk

FOCUS
There were more runners with form in the book for the second division of the 1m4f maiden and it was run at a more even tempo than the first division, resulting in a time just over two seconds quicker. As had been the case with the earlier leg, the front two pulled well clear. The form is rated on the positive side.

4634 JANICE WOOLACOTT LONGHAUL H'CAP 1m 4f (P)
4:10 (4:10) (Class 5) (0-75,75) 3-Y-0 £2,726 (£805; £402) Stalls Low

Form RPR

0-41 **1** **Duchess Of Gazeley (IRE)**[25] 3820 3-8-8 62 ShaneKelly 1 74
(Gary Harrison) *chsd ldrs: wnt 2nd over 3f out tl led 2f out: rdn and readily wnt clr over 1f out: in command and rdn out ins fnl f* **5/1**[2]

1422 **2** *1¼* **Astrum**[23] 3893 3-9-2 70 AndreaAtzeni 3 80
(Rod Millman) *led for 1f: hld up wl in tch after: chsd ldng pair over 2f out: chsd wnr jst over 1f out: r.o but no imp fnl 75yds* **7/2**[1]

-221 **3** *4½* **Sunbula (USA)**[13] 4223 3-9-7 75 PaulHanagan 8 78
(Charles Hills) *dwlt: hdwy to ld after 1f: jnd and rdn over 2f out: hdd 2f out: no ex u.p and lost 2nd jst over 1f out: wknd ins fnl f: jst hld 3rd* **6/1**[3]

60-5 **4** *nse* **Slip Of The Tongue**[36] 3432 3-8-5 59 LukeMorris 5 62
(Sir Mark Prescott Bt) *t.k.h: chsd ldrs: rdn over 4f out: no ex u.p ent 2f out: wknd over 1f out: almost snatched 3rd* **7/2**[1]

443 **5** *nk* **Sultanah Heyam**[30] 3618 3-8-13 67 RyanMoore 4 69
(William Haggas) *t.k.h: hld up wl in tch in last pair: stuck bhd horses 3f out: rdn and effrt over 2f out: no imp over 1f out: plugged on* **7/2**[1]

405 **6** *7* **Miss Mitigate**[24] 3858 3-8-4 58 DavidProbert 2 49
(Andrew Balding) *wl in tch in midfield: rdn over 4f out: styd wl in tch tch tl btn wl 1f out: sn wknd* **6/1**[3]

1-60 **7** *23* **Paddy's Saltantes (IRE)**[23] 3908 3-9-0 68 LiamJones 6 22
(J S Moore) *rn in snatches: in tch in last pair: lost tch 2f out: sn eased: t.o* **20/1**

003 **8** *11* **Money Talks**[28] 3674 3-9-0 68 LiamKeniry 7
(Michael Madgwick) *rn in snatches: in tch tl hdwy to chse ldr over 9f out tl over 3f out: sn dropped out: bhd and eased over 1f out: t.o* **66/1**

2m 32.58s (-0.42) **Going Correction** +0.10s/f (Slow) **8 Ran SP% 118.2**
Speed ratings (Par 100): **105,104,101,101,100 96,80,73**
toteswingers 1&2 £4.30, 1&3 £5.10, 2&3 £4.20 CSF £23.72 CT £108.87 TOTE £6.70: £2.70, £1.70, £2.70; EX 26.60 Trifecta £125.20 Pool: £2454.30 - 14.70 winning units..
Owner Franconson Partners **Bred** Overbury Stallions Ltd And D Boocock **Trained** Newmarket, Suffolk

FOCUS
A fair middle-distance handicap for 3yos with a mixture of horses making their handicap debuts taking on rivals with solid recent handicap form, and it was from the latter group that the front two emerged. The first two progressed again.

4635 LINGFIELD PARK SUPPORTS YOUNG EPILEPSY H'CAP 5f (P)
4:40 (4:41) (Class 6) (0-65,64) 3-Y-0+ £2,045 (£603; £302) Stalls High

Form RPR

3603 **1** **Dangerous Age**[30] 3638 3-9-5 61 RyanMoore 1 76
(J W Hills) *chsd ldr: rdn 2f out: drvn to ld 1f out: r.o strly and sn clr: readily* **5/4**[1]

10-3 **2** *3¼* **Maltease Ah**[15] 4148 4-9-7 59 JimCrowley 4 63
(Andrew Reid) *chsd ldrs: rdn and effrt over 1f out: no ch w wnr but styd on to go 2nd wl ins fnl f* **5/1**[2]

0-61 **3** *2¼* **Pucon**[34] 3498 4-9-12 64 LiamKeniry 8 60
(Roger Teal) *led: rdn over 1f out: hdd 1f out and sn brushed aside by wnr: wknd and lost 2nd wl ins fnl f* **8/1**

5544 **4** *nse* **Pharoh Jake**[25] 3816 5-9-5 57 SeanLevey 10 53
(John Bridger) *chsd ldrs: outpcd bnd 2f out: no ch w wnr but kpt on u.p ins fnl f* **14/1**

0652 **5** *1¼* **Charming (IRE)**[20] 3994 4-9-7 62 (p) MarkCoumbe(3) 7 54
(Olivia Maylam) *taken down early: t.k.h: hld up wl in tch in midfield: outpcd bnd 2f out: sn rdn and styd on same pce after* **6/1**[3]

-040 **6** *¾* **Beach Rhythm (USA)**[28] 3700 6-8-7 45 CathyGannon 9 34
(Jim Allen) *s.i.s: racd off the pce in last quartet: n.d* **16/1**

0400 **7** *3¾* **Ishetoo**[63] 2578 9-8-7 45 (p) AndreaAtzeni 2 20
(Peter Grayson) *in tch in midfield tl 1/2-way: sn bhd* **25/1**

0000 **8** *2* **Time Medicean**[154] 728 7-9-8 60 RobertWinston 5 28
(Tony Carroll) *a outpcd in last quartet: n.d* **7/1**

006- **9** *22* **Cashel's Missile (IRE)**[222] 8108 3-8-13 55 LukeMorris 6
(John Spearing) *a off the pce in last quartet: lost tch and eased fr over 1f out: t.o* **33/1**

59.61s (0.81) **Going Correction** +0.10s/f (Slow)
WFA 3 from 4yo+ 4lb **9 Ran SP% 118.3**
Speed ratings (Par 101): **97,91,88,88,86 84,78,75,40**
CSF £7.89 CT £36.87 TOTE £1.80: £1.30, £1.70, £1.90; EX 9.80 Trifecta £34.50 Pool: £3191.42 - 69.33 winning units..
Owner R Hunter, D Klein, M Hoodless **Bred** Mrs T Brudenell **Trained** Upper Lambourn, Berks

FOCUS
A moderate sprint handicap, but the well-backed winner landed this in good style. The runner-up helps set the standard.

4636 AURORA FIREWORKS H'CAP 6f (P)
5:10 (5:10) (Class 5) (0-70,70) 3-Y-0+ £2,726 (£805; £402) Stalls Low

Form RPR

60-0 **1** **Desert Command**[18] 4068 3-9-4 67 DavidProbert 10 78
(Andrew Balding) *taken down early: sn pressing ldr: rdn and clr w ldr 2f out: drvn to ld 1f out: styd on wl: rdn out* **12/1**

3-61 **2** *1* **Perfect Venture**[7] 4410 3-9-3 66 6ex AdamKirby 2 74
(Clive Cox) *led: rdn and wnt clr w wnr bnd 2f out: hdd 1f out: no ex and one pce fnl 100yds* **7/2**[3]

1121 **3** *2¼* **Fossa**[23] 3903 3-9-5 68 SebSanders 4 69+
(Dean Ivory) *t.k.h early: hld up in midfield: rdn and effrt on inner jst over 2f out: kpt on to go 3rd fnl 100yds: no threat to ldng pair* **3/1**[2]

5000 **4** *nse* **Avonvalley**[8] 4385 6-9-2 65 SladeO'Hara(5) 9 67+
(Peter Grayson) *mounted on crse and taken down early: racd off the pce in last trio: rdn and hdwy ent fnl f: r.o wl: nt rch ldrs* **33/1**

1360 **5** *1½* **Malaysian Boleh**[69] 2394 3-9-3 66 HarryBentley 1 62
(Simon Dow) *chsd ldng pair: rdn and unable to quickken 2f out: 3rd btn over 1f out: wknd ins fnl f* **8/1**

0540 **6** *1¾* **Rigolleto (IRE)**[34] 3511 5-9-9 67 JimmyFortune 6 58
(Anabel K Murphy) *chsd ldrs: rdn and unable qck wl over 1f out: wknd fnl f* **33/1**

-252 **7** *¾* **Meridius (IRE)**[5] 4499 3-9-7 70 ShaneKelly 5 58
(Gary Harrison) *hld up in tch in midfield: rdn and effrt wl over 1f out: no prog* **2/1**[1]

3163 **8** *¾* **Above The Stars**[23] 3904 5-9-11 69 HayleyTurner 11 55
(Conor Dore) *in tch in midfield on outer: rdn and outpcd jst over 2f out: sn btn and wknd over 1f out* **33/1**

0000 **9** *2¼* **Hatta Stream (IRE)**[43] 3172 7-9-4 65 SimonPearce(3) 7 44
(Lydia Pearce) *dwlt: a in rr: n.d* **25/1**

01-3 **10** *21* **Winter Song (IRE)**[75] 2572 3-9-3 66 SteveDrowne 3
(Charles Hills) *sn pushed along and outpcd in ast trio: bhd over 2f out: t.o fnl f* **10/1**

1m 12.5s (0.60) **Going Correction** +0.10s/f (Slow)
WFA 3 from 5yo+ 5lb **10 Ran SP% 121.1**
Speed ratings (Par 103): **100,98,95,95,93 91,90,89,86,58**
CSF £54.28 CT £165.71 TOTE £24.30: £3.90, £1.70, £1.50; EX 101.60 Trifecta £392.90 Pool: £2716.67 - 5.18 winning units..
Owner J C Smith **Bred** Littleton Stud **Trained** Kingsclere, Hants

FOCUS
A modest sprint handicap and the front two filled those positions throughout. The winner could go on from here.

4637 SHOVELSTRODE RACING H'CAP 7f (P)
5:35 (5:36) (Class 5) (0-70,70) 3-Y-0+ £2,726 (£805; £402) Stalls Low

Form RPR

-510 **1** **Menelik (IRE)**[9] 4340 4-9-7 64 (p) RichardKingscote 9 73
(Tom Dascombe) *t.k.h: chsd ldrs: rdn and effrt over 1f out: r.o wl to ld wl ins fnl f: r.o wl* **9/2**[2]

5432 **2** *¾* **Amethyst Dawn (IRE)**[15] 4149 7-9-9 66 DavidProbert 11 73
(Alan McCabe) *rn wout declared tongue tie: chsd ldr tl rdn to ld 2f out: kpt on wl u.p tl hdd and no ex wl ins fnl f* **16/1**

3451 **3** *2¼* **Bold Ring**[8] 4385 7-9-4 68 6ex JenniferFerguson(7) 6 69
(Edward Creighton) *hld up in tch in midfield: shuffled bk 3f out: rallied and hdwy to chse ldrs 1f out: styd on same pce ins fnl f* **14/1**

0640 **4** *1½* **Perfect Pastime**[13] 4210 5-9-12 69 (v) SebSanders 4 66
(Jim Boyle) *hld up in tch towards rr: rdn and hdwy on inner over 1f out: no imp ins fnl f: nvr trbld ldrs* **16/1**

0265 **5** *shd* **Athletic**[36] 3434 4-9-6 63 (p) SteveDrowne 13 60
(Andrew Reid) *stdd and swtchd lft after s: t.k.h: hld up in tch in rr: rdn and hdwy ent fnl f: no imp fnl 100yds* **8/1**

3-00 **6** *1* **David's Secret**[72] 2324 3-9-2 66 JimmyFortune 1 57
(Hughie Morrison) *hld up in tch towards rr: effrt and nt clr run on inner 2f out: swtchd rt and hmpd over 1f out: hdwy 1f out: kpt on: nvr trbld ldrs* **14/1**

1050 **7** *1½* **Golden Desert (IRE)**[20] 3974 9-9-11 68 HarryBentley 3 58
(Simon Dow) *s.i.s: bhd but in tch: rdn over 2f out: styd on ins fnl f: nvr trbld ldrs* **5/1**[3]

0326 **8** *2¾* **Shifting Star (IRE)**[16] 4124 8-9-13 70 SeanLevey 8 52
(John Bridger) *in tch in midfield: rdn and unable qck ent fnl 2f: btn over 1f out: wknd fnl f* **8/1**

2500 **9** *nk* **Zaheeb**[39] 3329 5-9-3 60 (b) WilliamCarson 12 42
(Dave Morris) *chsd ldrs after 2f: 3rd and nt qckn u.p ent fnl 2f: btn over 1f out: wknd ins fnl f* **50/1**

005- **10** *3¼* **Carlarajah**[285] 7020 3-9-6 70 LukeMorris 2 40
(Michael Bell) *in tch in midfield: rdn over 4f out: drvn and no rspnse wl over 1f out: sn wknd* **11/4**[1]

0-34 **11** 2 **Olympic Jule**[42] 3216 3-9-5 **69** CathyGannon 10 33
(Harry Dunlop) *led tl hdd 2f out: no ex u.p and btn over 1f out: fdd ins fnl f* **14/1**

324 **12** ½ **Spin Again (IRE)**[26] 3788 8-9-2 **64** (p) NatashaEaton(5) 14 30
(John Ryan) *hld up in tch towards rr: rdn and no hdwy over 2f out: nvr trbld ldrs* **20/1**

030 **13** 3½ **Titan Triumph**[43] 3172 9-9-8 **65** (t) RobertHavlin 7 22
(Michael Attwater) *chsd ldrs: rdn and lost pl 3f out: bhd and eased wl ins fnl f* **25/1**

1m 26.18s (1.38) **Going Correction** +0.10s/f (Slow)
WFA 3 from 4yo+ 7lb **13** Ran SP% **126.1**
Speed ratings (Par 103): **96,95,92,90,90 89,87,84,84,80 78,77,73**
toteswingers 1&2 £12.70, 1&3 £16.00, 2&3 £15.70 CSF £77.53 CT £966.66 TOTE £5.60: £2.10, £2.70, £4.50; EX 84.30 Trifecta £501.50 Pool: £2269.55 - 3.39 winning units..
Owner Laurence A Bellman **Bred** Irish National Stud **Trained** Malpas, Cheshire

FOCUS
A competitive, if low-grade handicap. Few got involved. The winner built on his Wolverhampton win.
T/Plt: £9.30 to a £1 stake. Pool: £74943.50 - 5879.47 winning tickets T/Qpdt: £6.80 to a £1 stake. Pool: £4723.82 - 510.35 winning tickets SP

4412 SANDOWN (R-H)
Wednesday, July 24

OFFICIAL GOING: Good to firm (good in places on round course; round 8.3; sprint 8.5)
Wind: Light, against Weather: Fine, very warm

4638 SLUG AND LETTUCE 2-4-1 COCKTAILS APPRENTICE H'CAP 1m 2f 7y
5:50 (5:50) (Class 5) (0-75,75) 4-Y-0+ **£3,234** (£962; £481; £240) Stalls Low

Form RPR

2312 **1** **Breakheart (IRE)**[21] 3954 6-9-2 **70** (v) JackGarritty(5) 1 80+
(Andrew Balding) *led after 2f: mde rest: pushed along 2f out: rdn and kpt on steadily fnl f* **7/4**[1]

2106 **2** 1½ **Ishikawa (IRE)**[35] 3468 5-9-2 **70** RobJFitzpatrick(5) 6 77
(Mrs K Burke) *trckd ldng pair: rdn to chse wnr wl over 2f out: sn clr of rest: kpt on but nvr able to chal* **6/1**

0-35 **3** 3¼ **Raamz (IRE)**[34] 3496 6-9-2 **65** DarrenEgan 5 66
(Kevin Morgan) *in tch: rdn over 2f out: outpcd sn after: wnt 3rd over 1f out: no real imp* **8/1**

/442 **4** 1¼ **Four Winds**[15] 4153 7-9-7 **70** TimClark 4 68
(Robert Cowell) *led 2f: chsd wnr to wl over 2f out: edgd lft u.p and outpcd after* **5/1**[3]

4005 **5** 3 **Aldwick Bay (IRE)**[14] 4167 5-9-12 **75** WilliamTwiston-Davies 2 67
(Richard Hannon) *a in 4th or 5th: rdn and no prog over 2f out: sn outpcd and btn* **5/2**[2]

66-0 **6** 7 **Archie Rice (USA)**[23] 3889 7-9-9 **72** RossAtkinson 7 50
(Tom Keddy) *slowly away: a in last: rdn and no prog over 3f out: t.o* **33/1**

2m 8.71s (-1.79) **Going Correction** -0.075s/f (Good) **6** Ran SP% **109.9**
Speed ratings (Par 103): **104,102,100,99,96 91**
toteswingers 1&2 £1.80, 1&3 £3.50, 2&3 £6.90 CSF £12.14 CT £59.13 TOTE £2.30: £1.40, £2.80; EX 12.90 Trifecta £31.70 Pool: £735.84 - 17.37 winning units..
Owner I A Balding **Bred** Littleton Stud **Trained** Kingsclere, Hants

FOCUS
The going was good to firm, good in places on round course (GoingStick: Round 8.3; Sprint 8.5). The rail was out 3yds from 1m1f to the winning post on the round course, adding 5yds to round course distances. Most of these had plenty to prove on current form.

4639 SLUG AND LETTUCE BOOK NOW FOR CHRISTMAS NURSERY H'CAP 5f 6y
6:20 (6:20) (Class 5) 2-Y-0 **£3,234** (£962; £481; £240) Stalls Low

Form RPR

31 **1** **Bushcraft (IRE)**[15] 4142 2-9-7 **82** GeorgeBaker 2 88
(Ed Walker) *lobbed along in narrow ld against rail: def advantage fr 2f out: pushed along and wl in command fnl f* **1/1**[1]

3602 **2** 2½ **Sefaat**[18] 4046 2-9-0 **75** (t) PaulHanagan 1 72
(Brian Meehan) *hld up in last: chsd wnr wl over 1f out: sn rdn: styd on but nvr able to threaten* **9/4**[2]

6331 **3** 17 **Captain Ryan**[22] 3914 2-8-10 **71** (e) SilvestreDeSousa 3 7
(Peter Makin) *wnt lft s: t.k.h: w wnr to 2f out: wknd rapidly and t.o* **7/2**[3]

1005 **4** 2¼ **Outback Lover (IRE)**[24] 3863 2-8-1 **65** (b[1]) DarrenEgan(3) 4
(J S Moore) *s.i.s: sn w ldng pair on outer: wknd rapidly 2f out: t.o* **20/1**

1m 2.01s (0.41) **Going Correction** -0.075s/f (Good) **4** Ran SP% **107.8**
Speed ratings (Par 94): **93,89,61,58**
CSF £3.49 TOTE £1.80; EX 3.30 Trifecta £2.80 Pool: £335.30 - 89.34 winning units..
Owner Laurence A Bellman **Bred** L Fox **Trained** Newmarket, Suffolk

FOCUS
The first two finished a mile clear. Not a race to rate highly.

4640 SLUG AND LETTUCE HAPPY MONDAYS EBF MAIDEN STKS 7f 16y
6:55 (6:56) (Class 5) 2-Y-0 **£3,881** (£1,155; £577; £288) Stalls Low

Form RPR

3 **1** **Sea The Skies**[25] 3833 2-9-5 0 NeilCallan 6 78+
(Gerard Butler) *trckd ldng trio: wnt 3rd over 2f out: stoked up and clsd to ld jst over 1f out: styd on wl* **4/1**[2]

04 **2** 2¼ **Greed Is Good**[13] 4218 2-9-5 0 MartinHarley 5 72
(Mrs K Burke) *trckd ldr: chal fr 3f out upsides whn wnr wnt by jst over 1f out: kpt on to win battle for 2nd* **20/1**

2 **3** hd **Pearl Spectre (USA)**[41] 3238 2-9-5 0 JamieSpencer 2 71
(Andrew Balding) *led at mod pce: jnd 3f out: tried to kick on over 2f out: hdd and outpcd jst over 1f out* **4/6**[1]

4 1¼ **Raise Your Gaze** 2-9-5 0 AdamKirby 9 68+
(Clive Cox) *t.k.h: trckd ldrs in 5th: shkn up whn pce lifted over 2f out: kpt on same pce after: nt disgracd* **16/1**

0 **5** ½ **Kinema (IRE)**[32] 3581 2-9-5 0 WilliamBuick 3 67+
(Ed Dunlop) *trckd ldng pair to over 2f out: shkn up and one pce fr over 1f out* **25/1**

6 nk **Son Of Feyan (IRE)** 2-9-5 0 RobertWinston 10 66+
(Roger Teal) *hld up in midfield: rn green whn asked for effrt over 2f out: nt on terms after but kpt on steadily ins fnl f* **66/1**

64 **7** 1 **Mabdhool (IRE)**[24] 3853 2-9-5 0 (b[1]) PaulHanagan 1 63
(Marcus Tregoning) *dwlt: t.k.h: hld up in midfield: outpcd 2f out: wandered after and no imp* **10/1**

8 hd **Maid Of Tuscany (IRE)** 2-9-0 0 DavidProbert 8 58
(Mark Usher) *dwlt: hld up in rr: effrt on outer whn nudged by rival 2f out: no imp after but kpt on ins fnl f* **80/1**

9 4 **All Talk N No Do (IRE)** 2-9-5 0 MickyFenton 4 52
(Seamus Durack) *a in last pair: shkn up 1/2-way: struggling after* **80/1**

10 1½ **Lord Lexington** 2-9-5 0 RyanMoore 7 48
(Richard Hannon) *slowly away: detached in last early and rn green: nvr any prog* **13/2**[3]

1m 32.84s (3.34) **Going Correction** -0.075s/f (Good) **10** Ran SP% **120.9**
Speed ratings (Par 94): **77,74,74,72,72 71,70,70,65,64**
toteswingers 1&2 £11.10, 1&3 £1.50, 2&3 £3.30 CSF £82.36 TOTE £5.70: £1.60, £3.90, £1.10; EX 74.30 Trifecta £222.30 Pool: £1342.83 - 4.52 winning units..
Owner A D Spence **Bred** Highclere Stud & Hmh Management **Trained** Newmarket, Suffolk

FOCUS
They didn't go a great pace early and once again it paid to race prominently.

4641 SLUG AND LETTUCE WEYBRIDGE H'CAP 7f 16y
7:30 (7:31) (Class 3) (0-90,90) 3-Y-0 **£7,439** (£2,213; £1,106; £553) Stalls Low

Form RPR

234 **1** **Yourartisonfire**[48] 3028 3-8-12 **81** MartinHarley 3 89
(Mrs K Burke) *trckd ldr: clsd to ld over 2f out: rdn over 1f out: styd on wl and gng away at fin* **4/1**

-021 **2** 2 **Secret Rebel**[30] 3621 3-8-13 **82** (t) FrankieDettori 4 84
(Sylvester Kirk) *led at decent pce: hdd and shkn up over 2f out: pressed wnr to 1f out: one pce and wl hld after* **3/1**[2]

1-14 **3** 2 **Mission Approved**[64] 2554 3-8-13 **82** RyanMoore 1 79
(Sir Michael Stoute) *awkward s: hld up in last: pushed along over 2f out: wnt 3rd 1f out: shkn up and no imp last 150yds* **11/8**[1]

0411 **4** ¾ **Swift Cedar (IRE)**[25] 3828 3-8-12 **81** NeilCallan 6 76
(Alan Jarvis) *stdd s: hld up in 3rd: clsd on ldng pair 2f out: nt qckn sn after: fdd* **7/2**[3]

1m 29.84s (0.34) **Going Correction** -0.075s/f (Good) **4** Ran SP% **109.3**
Speed ratings (Par 104): **95,92,90,89**
CSF £15.38 TOTE £5.50; EX 13.20 Trifecta £44.30 Pool: £705.37 - 11.93 winning units..
Owner J O'Shea, W Rooney & Ontoawinner **Bred** J A And Mrs M A Knox **Trained** Middleham Moor, N Yorks

FOCUS
Just the four runners, but an interesting tactical race.

4642 SLUG AND LETTUCE STAINES H'CAP 1m 14y
8:05 (8:05) (Class 4) (0-85,83) 3-Y-0+ **£5,175** (£1,540; £769; £384) Stalls Low

Form RPR

5253 **1** **Short Squeeze (IRE)**[30] 3633 3-8-12 **75** MartinDwyer 3 89+
(Hugo Palmer) *plld hrd early: hld up in 5th: plld wd and gd prog 2f out to ld over 1f out: drvn clr and in n.d fnl f* **6/1**

-002 **2** 3 **Related**[18] 4078 3-9-6 **83** AdamKirby 6 90
(Clive Cox) *trckd ldr: led over 2f out and sent for home: hdd over 1f out: one pce and no ch w wnr* **5/1**[3]

-663 **3** 1¾ **Lutine Bell**[53] 2858 6-9-13 **82** RyanMoore 7 85
(Mike Murphy) *hld up in 7th: pushed along jst over 2f out: prog over 1f out: chsd ldng pair jst ins fnl f: rdn and one pce after* **6/1**

4313 **4** 2 **Estifzaaz (IRE)**[12] 4236 3-9-0 **77** PaulHanagan 2 75
(Charles Hills) *trckd ldng pair: rdn to dispute 2nd briefly 2f out: steadily fdd over 1f out* **7/2**[2]

0311 **5** nk **Consign**[16] 4124 3-9-5 **82** (v) WilliamBuick 8 80
(Jeremy Noseda) *hld up in 6th: shkn up on outer 2f out: nt qckn and nvr threatened: plugged on nr fin* **5/2**[1]

3 **6** 2¾ **Toga Tiger (IRE)**[21] 3961 6-9-11 **80** RobertWinston 1 71
(Jeremy Gask) *s.s: hld up in last: rdn and detached over 2f out: no ch after: kpt on fnl f* **25/1**

0531 **7** shd **Macchiara**[14] 4183 4-9-9 **78** SilvestreDeSousa 5 69
(Rae Guest) *t.k.h early: trckd ldrs: rdn to dispute 2nd briefly 2f out: sn wknd* **10/1**

-042 **8** 2¾ **Fulney**[27] 3742 4-9-10 **79** LukeMorris 4 64
(James Eustace) *led at fair pce to over 2f out: wknd* **20/1**

1m 41.68s (-1.62) **Going Correction** -0.075s/f (Good)
WFA 3 from 4yo+ 8lb **8** Ran SP% **113.7**
Speed ratings (Par 105): **105,102,100,98,97 95,95,92**
toteswingers 1&2 £7.70, 1&3 £5.10, 2&3 £10.40 CSF £35.50 CT £187.80 TOTE £8.30: £2.20, £1.80, £2.40; EX 53.10 Trifecta £926.70 Pool: £1370.38 - 1.10 winning units..
Owner W A L Duff Gordon **Bred** Des Swan **Trained** Newmarket, Suffolk

FOCUS
A competitive little heat.

4643 STUBHUB TICKETS H'CAP 1m 6f
8:40 (8:41) (Class 4) (0-80,80) 4-Y-0+ **£4,690** (£1,395; £697; £348) Stalls Low

Form RPR

4351 **1** **Porcini**[32] 3587 4-9-7 **80** (p) WilliamCarson 3 89
(Philip McBride) *led 1f: chsd clr ldr: clsd to ld over 3f out and drvn for home: edgd lft fr 2f out: hld on wl* **3/1**[2]

-345 **2** 1¾ **Into The Wind**[19] 4035 6-8-6 **65** AndreaAtzeni 6 72
(Rod Millman) *hld up in chsng gp: prog to dispute 2nd fr 3f out: kpt on u.p but nvr able to chal wnr: edgd rt ins fnl f* **16/1**

200 **3** 1¼ **Cosimo de Medici**[21] 3959 6-9-5 **78** GeorgeBaker 4 83
(Hughie Morrison) *prom in chsng gp: rdn to dispute 2nd over 2f out to 1f out: one pce after* **6/1**

0025 **4** 1¼ **Spice Fair**[21] 3959 6-9-7 **80** JimmyFortune 2 84
(Mark Usher) *stdd s: hld up in last: plenty to do 4f out: prog on inner over 2f out: styng on and ch of a pl whn nowhere to go and snatched up 150yds out* **7/1**

213- **5** 2¾ **Bridgehampton**[351] 4930 4-9-1 **74** JamieSpencer 7 73
(Michael Bell) *stdd s: hld up in 7th: plenty to do and pushed along 4f out: prog to dispute 2nd 2f out: no imp after: wknd fnl f* **11/4**[1]

4210 **6** 4½ **Admirable Duque (IRE)**[32] 3587 7-8-11 **70** (b) NeilCallan 8 63
(Dominic Ffrench Davis) *in tch in chsng gp: drvn over 2f out: hanging and nt qckn: wl btn over 1f out* **25/1**

404 **7** 5 **English Summer**[19] 4020 6-9-7 **80** (t) SilvestreDeSousa 1 66
(David Simcock) *prom in chsng gp: drvn to dispute 2nd 3f out to 2f out: wknd over 1f out* **7/2**[3]

030- **8** 57 **Good Boy Jackson**[247] 3594 5-9-4 **77** MickyFenton 5
(Emma Lavelle) *plld way into ld after 1f and sn clr: 20 l up after 5f: wknd and hdd over 3f out: t.o* **33/1**

3m 1.48s (-3.02) **Going Correction** -0.075s/f (Good) **8** Ran SP% **113.3**
Speed ratings (Par 105): **105,104,103,102,101 98,95,63**
toteswingers 1&2 £7.00, 1&3 £3.90, 2&3 £11.70 CSF £47.63 CT £269.67 TOTE £3.70: £1.60, £2.40, £1.90; EX 44.40 Trifecta £299.60 Pool: £1211.40 - 3.03 winning units..
Owner PMRacing **Bred** Cheveley Park Stud Ltd **Trained** Newmarket, Suffolk

T/Plt: £229.10 to a £1 stake. Pool: £65046.63 - 207.25 winning tickets T/Qpdt: £48.60 to a £1 stake. Pool: £6496.72 - 98.84 winning tickets JN

4184 NAAS (L-H)
Wednesday, July 24

OFFICIAL GOING: Good to firm

4647a DARK ANGEL EUROPEAN BREEDERS FUND SWEET MIMOSA STKS (LISTED RACE) 6f
7:25 (7:26) 3-Y-O+ **£28,536** (£8,341; £3,951; £1,317)

RPR

1 **Miss Lahar**[11] 4275 4-9-5 .... JohnnyMurtagh 10 102
(Mick Channon) *cl up: settled bhd ldrs in 3rd: clsr in 2nd over 2f out: rdn over 1f out and sn on terms: kpt on best u.p towards fin to ld fnl strides* **15/2**

2 *hd* **Minalisa**[8] 4389 4-9-5 .... FMBerry 8 101
(Rae Guest) *prom: sn trckd ldr in 2nd: led narrowly bef 1/2-way: strly pressed fr 2f out and jnd ent fnl f: kpt on wl towards fin: hdd fnl strides* **11/4**[1]

3 *3 ½* **Boston Rocker (IRE)**[10] 4328 3-9-0 102........ DeclanMcDonogh 6 89
(Edward Lynam, Ire) *dwlt sltly and racd in mid-div: t.k.h: n.m.r and swtchd rt after 1/2-way: clsd u.p into mod 3rd ins fnl f: kpt on same pce: nvr trbld ldrs* **7/2**[2]

4 *1 ¼* **Hanky Panky (IRE)**[21] 3964 3-9-0 100........ MichaelHussey 3 85
(A P O'Brien, Ire) *prom early: sn settled in rr of mid-div: hdwy fr 1/2-way to chse ldrs in 4th over 2f out: sn rdn and no ex u.p: kpt on same pce* **8/1**

5 *1 ¼* **Mount McLeod (IRE)**[14] 4186 4-9-5 57........(b[1]) DannyGrant 4 82?
(Patrick J Flynn, Ire) *hld up towards rr: prog far side fr over 2f out: rdn in 5th ent fnl f and sn no ex: kpt on same pce* **100/1**

6 *1* **Via Ballycroy (IRE)**[10] 4329 4-9-5 90........ ShaneFoley 9 79
(M Halford, Ire) *chsd ldrs: 4th 1/2-way: rdn and no imp on ldrs fr 2f out: dropped to 6th over 1f out and kpt on same pce* **9/1**

7 *1 ¼* **Roseraie (IRE)**[38] 3380 3-9-0 91........(b[1]) ChrisHayes 7 74
(Kevin Prendergast, Ire) *chsd ldrs: 5th bef 1/2-way: sn lost pl: rdn and no ex u.p fr over 2f out: kpt on one pce* **16/1**

8 *¾* **Legal Lyric (IRE)**[6] 4466 4-9-5 81........ WJLee 5 72
(W P Mullins, Ire) *hld up in tch: pushed along in 6th fr 1/2-way: sn lost pl and rdn: no imp in 8th ent fnl f: kpt on one pce* **16/1**

9 *3 ¼* **Mironica (IRE)**[361] 4577 3-9-0 ....(t) WayneLordan 1 61
(David Wachman, Ire) *hld up in rr of mid-div: rdn and no imp fr 2f out* **12/1**

10 *24* **Allegra Tak (ITY)**[66] 2484 7-9-5 92........(tp) PatSmullen 11
(H Rogers, Ire) *sn led on nrside: hdd bef 1/2-way: sn pushed along and wknd fnl 2f: eased* **25/1**

11 *82* **Snow Queen (IRE)**[21] 3964 3-9-0 104........(b) JosephO'Brien 2
(A P O'Brien, Ire) *reluctant to jump off and wl bhd thrght: nvr a factor: completely t.o* **4/1**[3]

1m 10.81s (-2.39)
WFA 3 from 4yo+ 5lb **11 Ran SP% 126.1**
CSF £30.54 TOTE £8.60: £2.20, £1.50, £1.50; DF 26.50.
Owner Barry Walters Catering **Bred** Barry Walters **Trained** West Ilsley, Berks

FOCUS
Despite looking to have a bit to do on BHA ratings, Miss Lahar and Minalisa dominated the contest and pulled clear of their slightly more vaunted home rivals. It's been rated around the first two to their best.

4648 - 4650a (Foreign Racing) - See Raceform Interactive

4572 MAISONS-LAFFITTE (R-H)
Wednesday, July 24

OFFICIAL GOING: Turf: good

4651a PRIX ILLINOIS II (MAIDEN) (2YO) (TURF) 5f 110y
12:00 (12:00) 2-Y-O **£9,756** (£3,902; £2,926; £1,951; £975)

RPR

1 **My Catch (IRE)**[36] 3424 2-9-2 0........ ChristopheSoumillon 6 101
(David Brown) *mde all: crossed to rail 1/2-way: rdn 2f out: r.o strly and asserted: pushed out cl home: readily* **3/5**[1]

2 *2 ½* **Royale Du Buisson (IRE)**[27] 3752 2-8-13 0........ OlivierPeslier 3 89
(F Head, France) **7/2**[2]

3 *2* **Oxanueva (FR)**[27] 3752 2-8-13 0........ FabriceVeron 4 82
(H-A Pantall, France) **9/2**[3]

4 *2* **Yuki (IRE)**[30] 2-8-13 0........ Pierre-CharlesBoudot 1 75
(B Goudol, France) **34/1**

5 *2* **My Dear Watson** 2-9-2 0........ AntoineHamelin 8 72
(Matthieu Palussiere, France) **26/1**

6 *¾* **Almond Grace**[15] 2-8-13 0........ AlexisBadel 5 66
(Mme M Bollack-Badel, France) **28/1**

7 *nse* **Petits Potins (IRE)**[16] 2-8-13 0........(p) ThierryThulliez 2 66
(Rod Collet, France) **32/1**

8 *8* **Tumaini (IRE)** 2-8-13 0........(p) Christophe-PatriceLemaire 7 39
(U Suter, France) **74/1**

9 *7* **Timbergold (FR)**[19] 2-8-13 0........ UmbertoRispoli 9 15
(J-V Toux, France) **38/1**

1m 4.6s (-2.70) **9 Ran SP% 119.8**
WIN (incl. 1 euro stake): 1.60. PLACES: 1.10, 1.10, 1.10. DF: 3.10. SF: 5.90.
Owner Qatar Racing Limited **Bred** D Noonan & Loughphilip Bloodstock **Trained** Averham Park, Notts

4652 - (Foreign Racing) - See Raceform Interactive

4363 BATH (L-H)
Thursday, July 25

OFFICIAL GOING: Firm (11.0)
Wind: mild breeze Weather: cloudy with sunny periods and shower

4653 BRITISH STALLION STUDS/AKZONOBEL EBF NOVICE STKS 5f 11y
2:10 (2:10) (Class 4) 2-Y-O **£4,075** (£1,212; £606) **Stalls** Centre

Form RPR

106 1 **Fast (IRE)**[25] 3863 2-9-0 0........ PatDobbs 3 93
(Richard Hannon) *led to s early: mde all: edgd rt briefly whn shkn up over 1f out: kpt on wl* **7/2**[2]

11 2 *2 ¼* **Scruffy Tramp (IRE)**[15] 4174 2-9-4 0........ SeanLevey 1 89
(Michael Wigham) *trckd wnr: rdn wl over 1f out: kpt on but nt pce to chal* **7/1**[3]

1 3 *1 ½* **Blue Mood (IRE)**[14] 4191 2-9-0 0........ RobertHavlin 2 80
(Saeed bin Suroor) *played up gng to s: s.i.s: sn trcking wnr: rdn wl over 1f out: nt qckn: kpt on same pce fnl f* **4/11**[1]

1m 2.36s (-0.14) **Going Correction** -0.05s/f (Good) **3 Ran SP% 108.0**
Speed ratings (Par 96): **99,95,93**
CSF £15.62 TOTE £3.90; EX 10.50 Trifecta £15.20 Pool: £1579.42 - 77.79 winning units..
Owner Mrs J Wood **Bred** Ringfort Stud **Trained** East Everleigh, Wilts

FOCUS
There was 7mm of rain overnight, but the going remained officially firm (GoingStick 11.0). The subsequent triple Group 3 winner Amour Propre saw off two rivals in this novice event in 2008 so it can produce a good one, but the most significant pointers to the result of this year's renewal were pre-race.

4654 MINISTRY OF CAKE H'CAP 5f 11y
2:40 (2:40) (Class 5) (0-70,66) 3-Y-O **£2,587** (£770; £384; £192) **Stalls** Centre

Form RPR

0340 1 **Edged Out**[13] 4244 3-9-7 **66**........ CathyGannon 3 71
(Christopher Mason) *mde all: rdn wl over 1f out: kpt on wl: rdn out* **7/2**[2]

0364 2 *2 ½* **Little Choosey**[29] 3678 3-9-2 **66**........(p) RyanTate(5) 5 62
(Clive Cox) *pressed wnr tl rdn and hung sltly lft wl over 1f out: kpt on same pce fnl f* **5/1**

4-56 3 *2 ½* **New Rich**[23] 3927 3-8-12 **57**........ ShaneKelly 4 44
(Eve Johnson Houghton) *dwlt: sn pushed along in sltly detached last: rdn over 2f out: no imp tl styd on fr over 1f out: wnt 3rd ins fnl f* **5/1**

0-10 4 *1 ½* **Spray Tan**[29] 3699 3-9-4 **63**........ SeanLevey 2 45
(Tony Carroll) *trckd ldrs: rdn over 2f out: kpt on same pce fr over 1f out* **4/1**[3]

6-06 5 *1 ¾* **Elounta**[7] 4427 3-8-2 **47** oh2........ LukeMorris 6 22
(John Best) *chsd ldrs: rdn over 2f out: nt pce to chal: fdd ins fnl f* **14/1**

-032 6 *4* **Sunny Hollow**[29] 3679 3-8-10 **55**........ KirstyMilczarek 1 16
(James Toller) *chsd ldrs: rdn over 2f out: wknd jst over 1f out* **11/4**[1]

1m 2.4s (-0.10) **Going Correction** -0.05s/f (Good) **6 Ran SP% 108.9**
Speed ratings (Par 100): **98,94,90,87,84 78**
toteswingers 1&2 £3.30, 1&3 £4.10, 2&3 £3.80 CSF £19.54 TOTE £5.10: £1.90, £2.40; EX 5.70 Trifecta £95.70 Pool: £1491.93 - 11.68 winning units..
Owner Christopher & Annabelle Mason **Bred** Christopher & Annabelle Mason **Trained** Caewent, Monmouthshire

FOCUS
A modest sprint handicap with another all-the-way winner. The time was marginally slower than the 2-y-os in the opener.

4655 DOCMAIL H'CAP 1m 5f 22y
3:15 (3:16) (Class 6) (0-65,62) 4-Y-O+ **£1,940** (£577; £288; £144) **Stalls** High

Form RPR

-533 1 **Candelita**[8] 4403 6-9-4 **59**........ FrannyNorton 1 67
(Jo Hughes) *trckd ldrs: led over 5f out: strly pressed fr wl over 2f out: sn rdn: styd on strly to assert ent fnl f: edgd rt: rdn out* **15/8**[1]

151 2 *2 ¼* **Speed Steed (IRE)**[14] 4192 6-9-5 **60**........(v) CathyGannon 7 65
(Tim Vaughan) *t.k.h: trckd ldr: led after 4f: hdd over 5f out: rdn for str chal fr wl over 2f out tl no ex ent fnl f* **2/1**[2]

2345 3 *1 ¾* **Spanish Plume**[9] 4376 5-9-7 **62**........(e[1]) MartinDwyer 5 64
(Andrew Hollinshead) *stdd s: last but wl in tch: tk clsr order over 5f out: rdn wl over 2f out: wnt clr 3rd over 1f out: styd on same pce fnl f* **4/1**[3]

0506 4 *1 ¾* **Lucky Diva**[24] 3884 6-8-11 **57**........(v) JakePayne(5) 2 56
(Bill Turner) *racd in cl 4th: rdn wl over 2f out: styd on same pce* **10/1**

60-5 5 *8* **Flashy Star**[15] 4172 4-8-12 **53**........ ShaneKelly 4 43
(Sheena West) *led for 4f: trckd ldrs: rdn wl over 2f out: wknd ent fnl f* **6/1**

2m 54.93s (2.93) **Going Correction** -0.05s/f (Good) **5 Ran SP% 111.5**
Speed ratings (Par 101): **88,86,85,84,79**
CSF £6.07 TOTE £2.40: £2.60, £1.10; EX 5.60 Trifecta £9.30 Pool: £1271.11 - 102.45 winning units..
Owner Paul & David Bedford **Bred** Pedro Rosas **Trained** Lambourn. Berks

FOCUS
A moderate handicap, but they went a fair pace.

4656 TRENT SERVICES FILLIES' H'CAP 1m 2f 46y
3:50 (3:50) (Class 5) (0-70,70) 3-Y-O **£2,587** (£770; £384; £192) **Stalls** Low

Form RPR

0-11 1 **Portrait**[14] 4196 3-9-7 **70**........ LukeMorris 2 86+
(Sir Mark Prescott Bt) *mde all: pushed along early: shkn up to go clr wl over 2f out: a in command after: comf* **30/100**[1]

-444 2 *5* **Banreenahreenkah (IRE)**[31] 3641 3-9-4 **67**........ ShaneKelly 4 70
(Denis Coakley) *t.k.h: trckd ldrs: wnt 2nd 5f out: rdn wl over 2f out: kpt on for clr 2nd but sn readily hld by wnr* **8/1**[3]

5442 3 *12* **Kingston Eucalypt**[15] 4172 3-9-6 **69**........ SteveDrowne 1 54
(Ed Vaughan) *chsd wnr tl 5f out: sn rdn in 3rd: hld fr over 2f out: wknd fnl f* **5/1**[2]

-020 4 *2 ¼* **Isle Of Beauty**[19] 4049 3-8-2 **51** oh2........ CathyGannon 5 27
(Tom Dascombe) *nvr really travelling in last but wl in tch: rdn over 3f out: nvr any imp: wknd ent fnl f* **25/1**

2m 8.01s (-2.99) **Going Correction** -0.05s/f (Good) **4 Ran SP% 108.5**
Speed ratings (Par 97): **109,105,95,93**
CSF £3.36 TOTE £1.20; EX 2.40 Trifecta £5.00 Pool: £2575.76 - 381.65 winning units..
Owner Denford Stud **Bred** Denford Stud Ltd **Trained** Newmarket, Suffolk

FOCUS
An uncompetitive fillies' handicap and it was all very straightforward for long odds-on backers this time.

4657 ASCENTRIC H'CAP 1m 2f 46y
4:25 (4:25) (Class 6) (0-60,58) 3-Y-O £1,940 (£577; £288) Stalls Low

Form RPR
064- 1 **Alzavola**[247] 7796 3-9-7 **58** .... LukeMorris 2 67+
(Sir Mark Prescott Bt) *mde all: rdn wl over 2f out: styd on wl to draw clr ent fnl f: eased towards fin* **1/2**[1]

052 2 *10* **Special Report (IRE)**[6] 4503 3-8-1 **45** .... ShelleyBirkett[(7)] 4 38
(Peter Hiatt) *broke wl: sn restrained trcking wnr and sddle slipped: lost 2nd over 2f out tl regained pl over 1f out: no ch w wnr but jst hld on for 2nd despite rdr being unable to ride out because of sddle* **2/1**[2]

00-0 3 *nk* **Soubrette**[26] 3837 3-8-8 **45** .... JamieMackay 1 34
(George Margarson) *chsd ldng pair: rdn to chse wnr over 2f out tl over 1f out: kpt on same pce* **10/1**[3]

2m 11.83s (0.83) **Going Correction** -0.05s/f (Good) **3** Ran SP% **109.1**
Speed ratings (Par 98): **94,86,85**
CSF £1.85 TOTE £1.20; EX 1.70 Trifecta £1.70 Pool: £1680.84 - 701.79 winning units..
Owner Miss K Rausing **Bred** Miss K Rausing **Trained** Newmarket, Suffolk

FOCUS
Handicaps don't come any less competitive than this. The winner recorded a time 3.82 seconds slower than stablemate and fellow 3-y-o filly Portrait took to win the preceding contest.

4658 ADMIRAL GROUP H'CAP 1m 5y
5:00 (5:00) (Class 6) (0-60,60) 3-Y-O+ £1,940 (£577; £288; £144) Stalls Low

Form RPR
6044 1 **Sonnetation (IRE)**[23] 3919 3-8-4 **46** oh1 .... CathyGannon 4 54
(Jim Boyle) *disp ld: rdn over 4f out: outrt ldr 3f out: fnd plenty whn chal fnl 120yds: drvn out* **5/1**[2]

5441 2 *1* **Crucis Abbey (IRE)**[24] 3910 5-8-12 **46** oh1 ....(p) TomMcLaughlin 6 54
(Mark Brisbourne) *trckd ldrs: rdn wl over 2f out: styd on to chal briefly fnl 120yds: sn no ex* **8/1**[3]

2263 3 *3* **Do More Business (IRE)**[7] 4423 6-8-12 **51** ....(bt) EDLinehan[(5)] 8 52
(Liam Corcoran) *in tch: rdn wl over 2f out: hdwy fr over 1f out: styd on to go 3rd towards fin* **5/1**[2]

-021 4 *½* **Devon Diva**[23] 3919 7-8-11 **50** .... MichaelJMMurphy[(5)] 1 50
(John Gallagher) *disp ld tl rdn 3f out: kpt chsng wnr tl no ex ent fnl f* **3/1**[1]

004 5 *1* **Marmalady (IRE)**[17] 4125 3-9-4 **60** .... AidanColeman 9 56
(Gary Moore) *awkwardly away: sn in tch: rdn over 2f out: hdwy on rails over 1f out to chse ldrs: no ex fnl 120yds* **8/1**[3]

30-2 6 *2* **Squirrel Wood (IRE)**[7] 4423 5-9-6 **54** .... RichardKingscote 2 47
(Mary Hambro) *trckd ldrs: rdn over 2f out: nt pce to chal: no ex fnl f* **3/1**[1]

3006 7 *5* **Otto The First**[7] 4423 3-8-9 **51** .... LukeMorris 3 31
(John Best) *trckd ldrs: rdn wl over 2f out: wknd fnl f* **20/1**

00-6 8 *1 ¼* **Gadreel (IRE)**[6] 4503 4-8-12 **46** oh1 ....(p) SteveDrowne 5 25
(Anthony Middleton) *in tch: rdn over 4f out: wknd over 2f out* **50/1**

0060 9 *½* **Keyhole Kate**[23] 3924 4-8-12 **46** oh1 ....(p) KirstyMilczarek 10 24
(Polly Gundry) *rdn over 3f out: a last: nvr any imp* **33/1**

1m 40.05s (-0.75) **Going Correction** -0.05s/f (Good)
WFA 3 from 4yo+ 8lb **9** Ran SP% **115.2**
Speed ratings (Par 101): **101,100,97,96,95 93,88,87,86**
toteswingers 1&2 £6.30, 1&3 £6.00, 2&3 £4.50 CSF £43.18 CT £210.16 TOTE £5.90: £1.80, £2.40, £1.50; EX 59.50 Trifecta £228.60 Pool: £2215.35 - 7.26 winning units..
Owner The 'In Recovery' Partnership **Bred** Dr Dean Harron **Trained** Epsom, Surrey

FOCUS
A moderate handicap.

4659 QBE H'CAP 5f 161y
5:30 (5:32) (Class 6) (0-65,65) 3-Y-O+ £1,940 (£577; £288; £144) Stalls Centre

Form RPR
3500 1 **Brown Volcano (IRE)**[41] 3268 4-8-13 **52** .... LukeMorris 5 59+
(John O'Shea) *trckd ldrs: pushed along whn squeezed out and lost pl over 1f out: rdn whn swtchd lft ent fnl f: str run to ld fnl 40yds* **16/1**

0404 2 *nk* **Roanne (USA)**[19] 4069 3-8-12 **61** ....(bt) RyanTate[(5)] 1 66
(Clive Cox) *trckd ldrs: rdn to ld 2f out: sn drifted rt: kpt on: hdd fnl 40yds* **11/4**[1]

6603 3 *shd* **Catalinas Diamond (IRE)**[9] 4368 5-9-7 **60** ....(t[1]) SteveDrowne 6 66
(Pat Murphy) *in tch: hdwy whn nt clr run and hmpd over 1f out: sn rdn: kpt on* **5/1**[3]

3002 4 *1 ¾* **Wooden King (IRE)**[9] 4369 8-9-7 **65** .... MatthewLawson[(5)] 9 65
(Malcolm Saunders) *trckd ldrs: rdn 2f out: sn ev ch: no ex ins fnl f* **7/2**[2]

6033 5 *1 ½* **Volito**[9] 4369 7-9-4 **57** .... AidanColeman 8 52
(Anabel K Murphy) *in tch: pushed along to chse ldrs over 1f out: sn rdn: fdd fnl 120yds* **10/1**

3065 6 *1 ½* **Brandywell Boy (IRE)**[24] 3888 10-8-2 **46** oh1 .... MichaelJMMurphy[(5)] 3 36
(Dominic Ffrench Davis) *chsd ldrs: rdn over 2f out: nvr gng pce to threaten* **14/1**

0525 7 *2 ¼* **The Name Is Frank**[7] 4427 8-8-8 **54** ....(t) OisinMurphy[(7)] 4 36
(Mark Gillard) *prom tl rdn wl over 2f out: chsd ldrs tl wknd fnl f* **7/1**

65-0 8 *4 ½* **Too Ambitious**[9] 4377 4-8-7 **46** .... MartinDwyer 7 13+
(Andrew Hollinshead) *wnt to s early: prom: rdn over 2f out: chsng ldr whn bdly hmpd over 1f out: wknd fnl f* **50/1**

0244 9 *¾* **Ridgeway Sapphire**[7] 4423 6-8-0 **46** ....(v) ShelleyBirkett[(7)] 10 10
(Mark Usher) *dwlt: a bhd* **15/2**

5035 10 *½* **You'relikemefrank**[9] 4371 7-8-7 **46** ....(p) CathyGannon 2 9
(Richard Ford) *led: rdn and hdd 2f out: wknd over 1f out* **12/1**

1m 11.12s (-0.08) **Going Correction** -0.05s/f (Good)
WFA 3 from 4yo+ 5lb **10** Ran SP% **121.1**
Speed ratings (Par 101): **98,97,97,95,93 91,88,82,81,80**
toteswingers 1&2 £11.80, 1&3 £22.40, 2&3 £4.50 CSF £62.30 CT £271.38 TOTE £28.30: £6.00, £2.60, £1.60; EX 129.80 Trifecta £1307.10 Pool: £2399.43 - 1.37 winning units..
Owner Acousta Foam Limited **Bred** P Brady **Trained** Elton, Gloucs
■ Stewards' Enquiry : Ryan Tate one-day ban: careless riding (Aug 8)

FOCUS
A moderate sprint handicap and a rough race, with the runner-up causing a concertina effect as she hung right over a furlong out.
T/Plt: £167.70 to a £1 stake. Pool: £42,279.75 - 183.99 winning tickets T/Qpdt: £7.20 to a £1 stake. Pool: £3800.38 - 388.09 winning tickets TM

4422 BRIGHTON (L-H)
Thursday, July 25

OFFICIAL GOING: Firm (watered; 8.6)
Wind: light, across Weather: sunny and warm

4660 BRIGHTONCARBOOTSALE.CO.UK EVERY SUNDAY (S) H'CAP 5f 213y
5:15 (5:15) (Class 6) (0-60,54) 3-Y-O+ £2,045 (£603; £302) Stalls Centre

Form RPR
0356 1 **Surrey Dream (IRE)**[5] 4517 4-9-1 **45** ....(tp) KieranO'Neill 5 52
(John Bridger) *pressed ldr: rdn to ld ent fnl f: forged clr ins fnl f: kpt on* **9/2**

3066 2 *1 ¼* **Chester'Slittlegem (IRE)**[35] 3501 4-9-3 **47** .... LiamJones 1 50
(Jo Hughes) *led: rdn over 1f out: hdd ent fnl f: no ex and one pce fnl 100yds* **11/4**[2]

2330 3 *½* **Silly Billy (IRE)**[16] 4155 5-8-10 **47** ....(v) RyanWhile[(7)] 7 48
(Bill Turner) *chsd ldng pair: rdn and sltly outpcd over 1f out: rallied ins fnl f: styd on fnl 100yds: no threat to wnr* **7/2**[3]

0000 4 *½* **Flaxen Lake**[84] 1951 6-8-12 **45** ....(p) DarrenEgan[(3)] 4 45
(Milton Bradley) *chsd ldng quartet: effrt u.p on inner ent fnl f: no ex and one pce fnl 100yds* **20/1**

0000 5 *1* **Courageous (IRE)**[7] 4423 7-9-3 **54** .... WillPettis[(7)] 3 51
(Milton Bradley) *chsd ldng trio: hdwy to press ldng pair and rdn over 1f out: no ex ins fnl f: wknd towards fin* **8/1**

/6-0 6 *4 ½* **Lady Valtas**[7] 4423 5-8-12 **45** ....(vt) CharlesBishop[(3)] 6 27
(Martin Bosley) *sn outpcd and rdn along: modest prog fnl f but nvr on terms* **50/1**

3654 7 *28* **Coastal Passage**[24] 3910 5-9-2 **51** ....(t) RobertTart[(5)] 2
(Charles Smith) *stmbld bdly as stalls opened and lost all ch: continued t.o thrght* **5/2**[1]

1m 11.51s (1.31) **Going Correction** -0.025s/f (Good) **7** Ran SP% **113.5**
Speed ratings (Par 101): **90,88,87,87,85 79,42**
Tote Swingers: 1&2 £3.10, 1&3 £1.90, 2&3 £3.80 CSF £17.01 TOTE £6.60: £5.30, £2.40; EX 36.10 Trifecta £101.60 Pool: £951.96 - 7.02 winning units..Silly Billy was claimed by Mr Brian Ellison for £6,000. No bid for the winner.
Owner P Cook **Bred** Trois Graces Syndicate **Trained** Liphook, Hants

FOCUS
Rail dolled out from 6f to 2.5f as at last two meetings. After problems with the watering machine the staff were out on the track until 4am. The ground was very quick. A poor race even by selling-race standards further weakened by the favourite blowing the start. They raced in one group towards the far side.

4661 PAPA JOHN'S PIZZA IN BRIGHTON H'CAP 5f 213y
5:50 (5:51) (Class 5) (0-75,76) 3-Y-O £2,726 (£805; £402) Stalls Centre

Form RPR
6221 1 **Bosham**[22] 3956 3-8-13 **68** .... DarrenEgan[(3)] 4 73
(William Jarvis) *t.k.h: chsd ldr tl led wl over 1f out: rdn over 1f out: hrd pressed fnl 100yds: r.o wl and holding runner-up after: rdn out* **3/1**[2]

-211 2 *nk* **Cape Of Hope (IRE)**[7] 4428 3-9-10 **76** 6ex .... RobertHavlin 3 80
(Peter Chapple-Hyam) *chsd ldrs: rdn and effrt to chse wnr over 1f out: hrd drvn and str chal ins fnl f: r.o but hld fnl 50yds* **4/11**[1]

-050 3 *9* **Knight Charm**[48] 3050 3-9-2 **68** .... JohnFahy 2 43
(Eve Johnson Houghton) *led tl rdn and hdd wl over 1f out: btn ent fnl f: wknd* **10/1**[3]

1m 9.84s (-0.36) **Going Correction** -0.025s/f (Good) **3** Ran SP% **107.4**
Speed ratings (Par 100): **101,100,88**
CSF £4.73 TOTE £2.40; EX 4.80 Trifecta £3.60 Pool: £855.98 - 177.50 winning units..
Owner The Bosham Partnership **Bred** Rabbah Bloodstock Limited **Trained** Newmarket, Suffolk

FOCUS
The winner found a little on his latest form in this weak event.

4662 HARRINGTONS LETTINGS MAIDEN STKS 6f 209y
6:20 (6:20) (Class 5) 2-Y-O £2,587 (£770; £384) Stalls Centre

Form RPR
062 1 **Chinese Jade**[9] 4386 2-9-5 0 .... ChrisCatlin 4 76+
(Sir Mark Prescott Bt) *mde all: rdn ent fnl f: styd on wl and in command fnl 75yds* **5/4**[2]

0 2 *1* **Anglophile**[29] 3689 2-8-12 0 .... AhmadAlSubousi[(7)] 2 73
(Saeed bin Suroor) *stdd s: chsd ldrs: pushed along: effrt but edging lft down camber fr over 1f out: pressed wnr ins fnl f: no ex fnl 75yds* **10/11**[1]

542 3 *3 ½* **Island Kingdom (IRE)**[50] 2978 2-9-5 0 .... LiamJones 5 64
(J S Moore) *chsd wnr: drvn and unable qck over 1f out: lost 2nd and wknd fnl 150yds* **8/1**[3]

1m 25.21s (2.11) **Going Correction** -0.025s/f (Good) **3** Ran SP% **107.9**
Speed ratings (Par 94): **86,84,80**
CSF £2.79 TOTE £2.20; EX 2.40 Trifecta £3.10 Pool: £491.14 - 115.48 winning units..
Owner Lady O'Reilly **Bred** Castlemartin Sky & Skymarc Farm **Trained** Newmarket, Suffolk

FOCUS
The sea fret was rolling in ahead of this fair 2-y-o maiden for the course, and visibility was down to 4f. The winner set a fair standard.

4663 BRIGHTONBOATSALES.CO.UK FILLIES' H'CAP 1m 3f 196y
6:55 (6:56) (Class 4) (0-80,79) 4-Y-O+ £4,690 (£1,395; £697) Stalls High

Form RPR
2122 1 **Beacon Lady**[7] 4429 4-7-13 **60** .... DarrenEgan[(3)] 4 68
(William Knight) *stdd s: chsd ldr tl 9f out: in tch in 3rd tl rdn and effrt to chal over 1f out: led fnl 75yds: r.o wl* **9/4**[2]

6251 2 *1 ½* **Reset City**[7] 4455 7-9-5 **77** 6ex .... ChrisCatlin 5 83
(Mark Johnston) *stdd s: hld up in last tl chsd ldr 9f out: led and rdn 2f out: drvn ent fnl 2f: hdd and no ex fnl 75yds* **10/11**[1]

3051 3 *11* **Dazzling Valentine**[15] 4172 5-8-13 **71** ow1 .... SebSanders 2 64
(Alan Bailey) *led tl rdn and hdd 2f out: drvn and btn over 1f out: wl hld and eased ins fnl f* **3/1**[3]

2m 35.68s (2.98) **Going Correction** -0.025s/f (Good) **3** Ran SP% **108.2**
Speed ratings (Par 102): **89,88,80**
TOTE £2.40; EX 3.80 Trifecta £3.20 Pool: £488.28 - 112.01 winning units..
Owner The Pro-Claimers **Bred** Ashley House Stud **Trained** Patching, W Sussex

FOCUS
Visibility down to 2f. A depleted field for this fillies' handicap and the pace was just steady. The first two both rate small personal bests.

4664 DOMESTIC & GENERAL H'CAP 1m 3f 196y
7:25 (7:26) (Class 6) (0-60,58) 3-Y-O £2,045 (£603; £302) Stalls High

Form RPR
0304 1 **See And Be Seen**[14] 4196 3-8-8 45 RenatoSouza 4 53
(Sylvester Kirk) *chsd ldng pair: rdn and ev ch ent fnl 2f: led over 1f out: r.o wl: holding runner up fnl 100yds* **9/1**
4026 2 *hd* **Uganda Glory (USA)**[29] 3675 3-9-3 54 KieranO'Neill 3 61
(George Baker) *hld up in last pair: clsd 6f out: rdn and effrt to chal wl over 1f out: edgd lft to rail and sustained duel w wnr fnl f: r.o but a jst hld* **15/8**[1]
-200 3 *6* **Snoqualmie Chief**[26] 3820 3-9-7 58 (p[1]) WilliamCarson 2 55
(David Elsworth) *chsd ldr tl led over 2f out: rdn ent fnl 2f: hdd over 1f out: no ex and wknd ins fnl f* **5/2**[2]
5403 4 *1 1/2* **Sutton Sid**[10] 4345 3-9-2 56 WilliamTwiston-Davies(3) 1 51
(Chris Gordon) *hld up in last pair: clsd 6f out: effrt u.p 2f out: no imp and edgd lft over 1f out: wknd ins fnl f* **11/4**[3]
00U4 5 *37* **Youmaysee**[15] 4171 3-8-7 47 ow2 CharlesBishop(3) 6
(Mick Channon) *led tl rdn and hdd wl over 2f out: wkng whn sltly hmpd ent fnl 2f: sn wl btn: virtually p.u ins fnl f: t.o* **12/1**
-000 6 *30* **Sporting Club Girl**[8] 4405 3-8-5 45 DarrenEgan(3) 5
(William Knight) *chsd ldng trio tl dropped to rr 6f out: sn toiling: lost tch 3f out: t.o and virtually p.u fr over 1f out* **28/1**

2m 34.03s (1.33) **Going Correction** -0.025s/f (Good) 6 Ran SP% **111.2**
Speed ratings (Par 98): **94,93,89,88,64 44**
Tote Swingers: 1&2 £4.90, 1&3 £2.40, 2&3 £2.10 CSF £25.86 TOTE £9.50: £2.80, £2.20; EX 15.50 Trifecta £66.60 Pool: £972.27 - 10.94 winning units..
Owner Timothy Pearson **Bred** Exors Of The Late T E Pocock **Trained** Upper Lambourn, Berks
■ Stewards' Enquiry : Renato Souza two-day ban: used whip above permitted level (Aug 8-9)

FOCUS
The sea fret had disappeared ahead of this rock-bottom handicap, which was run at a sound pace. The first two were clear and the winner found a bit on his recent form.

4665 LIFESTYLE MOTOR GROUP H'CAP 1m 1f 209y
8:00 (8:01) (Class 5) (0-70,70) 3-Y-O+ £2,726 (£805; £402) Stalls High

Form RPR
0-55 1 **Marju's Quest (IRE)**[28] 3739 3-8-7 62 DarrenEgan(3) 2 68
(David Simcock) *stdd s: t.k.h: hld up in tch in rr: clsd to trck ldrs 2f out: rdn and chal between horses over 1f out: led 1f out: drvn and r.o wl ins fnl f* **9/4**[2]
1236 2 *3/4* **Mizyen (IRE)**[54] 2874 3-9-2 68 [1] NeilCallan 3 73
(James Tate) *chsd ldng pair: effrt on inner and rdn to ld over 1f out: hdd 1f out: ev ch u.p ins fnl f: no ex and btn fnl 50yds* **5/4**[1]
33-4 3 *nk* **Red Shuttle**[15] 4183 6-9-9 70 RobertTart(5) 5 74
(Andi Brown) *stdd s: t.k.h: hld up in tch in last pair: hdwy to chse ldrs 1f out: awkward hd carriage: no imp tl kpt on towards fin* **5/1**[3]
5223 4 *12* **Megalala (IRE)**[14] 4205 12-9-3 59 KieranO'Neill 1 39
(John Bridger) *led: rdn over 2f out: drvn and hdd over 1f out: sn btn and wknd fnl f* **8/1**
3004 5 *1 1/4* **Beau Select (IRE)**[28] 3722 3-8-11 63 (v) NickyMackay 4 40
(Robert Eddery) *chsd ldr tl lost pl ent fnl 2f: bhd whn hung lft 1f out* **8/1**

2m 2.41s (-1.19) **Going Correction** -0.025s/f (Good)
WFA 3 from 6yo+ 10lb 5 Ran SP% **114.1**
Speed ratings (Par 103): **103,102,102,92,91**
CSF £5.74 TOTE £7.10: £3.10, £1.20; EX 10.30 Trifecta £25.10 Pool: £544.72 - 16.22 winning units..
Owner Favourites Racing **Bred** Derrinstown Stud Ltd **Trained** Newmarket, Suffolk

FOCUS
A fair gallop and the unexposed winner came from last to first. The form is rated around the second.

4666 EF LANGUAGE TRAVEL BRIGHTON H'CAP 6f 209y
8:35 (8:35) (Class 6) (0-60,60) 3-Y-O £2,045 (£603; £302) Stalls Centre

Form RPR
0341 1 **Just Isla**[7] 4423 3-8-12 51 6ex (p) SebSanders 2 57
(Peter Makin) *stdd s: hld up in tch: jnd ldr on bit over 1f out: rdn 1f out: led and rn green ins fnl f: kpt on and a doing enough* **10/11**[1]
0-50 2 *1/2* **Speedfit Boy (IRE)**[43] 3221 3-9-7 60 NeilCallan 6 64
(George Margarson) *hld up in tch in rr: effrt u.p to chse ldng pair jst over 1f out: chsd wnr wl ins fnl f: hld towards fin* **7/1**
6200 3 *1 1/4* **Pippy**[15] 4160 3-9-5 58 (v) RichardKingscote 9 59
(Tom Dascombe) *led: rdn and jnd over 1f out: hdd and no ex ins fnl f: outpcd towards fin* **11/4**[2]
4446 4 *7* **Princess Cammie (IRE)**[9] 4378 3-9-3 56 (p) KieranO'Neill 7 38
(John Bridger) *chsd ldr: rdn and unable qck 2f out: wknd ent fnl f* **6/1**[3]
-000 5 *1 1/4* **Jackpot**[7] 4424 3-8-0 46 oh1 DanielMuscutt(7) 5 25
(Brendan Powell) *hld up in tch in midfield: effrt u.p over 1f out: sn no hdwy: wknd fnl f* **33/1**
U060 6 *7* **Forceful Flame**[51] 2962 3-9-2 55 NickyMackay 4 15
(Robert Eddery) *restless in stalls: in tch in last pair: rdn and no hdwy wl over 1f out: wknd and hung lft 1f out* **22/1**

1m 23.44s (0.34) **Going Correction** -0.025s/f (Good) 6 Ran SP% **113.1**
Speed ratings (Par 98): **97,96,95,87,85 77**
Tote Swingers 1&2 £2.40, 2&3 £4.60, 1&3 £1.10 CSF £8.36 CT £13.11 TOTE £1.70: £1.10, £4.70; EX 9.60 Trifecta £13.20 Pool: £672.18 - 37.97 winning units..
Owner D A Poole **Bred** David Poole **Trained** Ogbourne Maisey, Wilts

FOCUS
A low-grade 3-y-o handicap run at a sound pace. The winner found a bit on her latest C&D win.
T/Plt: £221.70 to a £1 stake. Pool: £34,304.00 - 112.92 winning tickets T/Qpdt: £27.20 to a £1 stake. Pool: £2,782.00 - 75.60 winning tickets SP

4430 DONCASTER (L-H)
Thursday, July 25
OFFICIAL GOING: Good to firm (good in places; 9.0)
Wind: Light half against Weather: Cloudy with sunny periods

4667 SAINT GOBAIN WEBER MAIDEN STKS 1m (S)
5:35 (5:36) (Class 5) 3-Y-O+ £2,587 (£770; £384; £192) Stalls High

Form RPR
3 1 **Life Partner (IRE)**[20] 4011 3-9-4 0 SilvestreDeSousa 3 92+
(Saeed bin Suroor) *dwlt: plld hrd and swtchd wd: led after 1 1/2f: stdd pce briefly over 3f out: pushed along and qcknd over 2f out: rdn over 1f out: kpt on wl fnl f* **7/4**[1]
2 *2 1/2* **China Creek (IRE)** 3-8-13 0 JoeFanning 7 81
(Mark Johnston) *led 1 1/2f: prom: effrt to chse wnr 3f out: rdn and ch whn rn green and edgd lft over 1f out: kpt on same pce fnl f* **25/1**
02 3 *3* **Cosseted**[65] 2548 3-8-13 0 TomQueally 9 74
(James Fanshawe) *towards rr: hdwy 3f out: rdn to chse ldrs 2f: sn drvn and one pce* **11/4**[2]
32 4 *1 1/2* **Disco Inferno (IRE)**[20] 4022 3-9-4 0 (t) KierenFallon 1 76
(Brian Meehan) *trckd ldrs: swtchd wd to trck wnr after 1f: effrt wl over 2f out: sn rdn and one pce fr over 1f out* **3/1**[3]
4- 5 *nk* **Spirit Of Rio (IRE)**[370] 4310 3-9-4 0 GrahamGibbons 6 75
(David Barron) *hld up in rr: hdwy wl over 2f out: rdn to chse ldrs wl over 1f out: kpt on fnl f: nrst fin* **13/2**
64 6 *3/4* **Glanely (IRE)**[52] 2934 3-9-4 0 MartinLane 8 73
(James Fanshawe) *towards rr: hdwy and in tch over 3f out: rdn along over 2f out: grad wknd* **16/1**
7 *12* **It Must Be Faith** 3-9-4 0 AndrewMullen 4 46
(Michael Appleby) *s.i.s and in rr: hdwy on outer 1/2-way: chsd ldrs over 3f out: rdn along over 2f out: sn wknd* **80/1**
6-0 8 *1* **Hartlebury**[17] 4118 3-9-4 0 GrahamLee 2 43
(James Bethell) *trckd ldrs: hdwy 1/2-way: rdn along wl over 2f out: sn wknd* **50/1**
0 9 *3 1/2* **Jimsneverright**[17] 4118 5-9-5 0 JordanNason(7) 10 37
(Geoffrey Harker) *chsd ldrs: rdn along 1/2-way: sn wknd* **150/1**
6-00 10 *2 1/4* **Touching History (IRE)**[10] 4339 4-9-12 40 (b[1]) JamesSullivan 5 32
(Tim Etherington) *s.i.s: a in rr* **150/1**

1m 38.97s (-0.33) **Going Correction** -0.125s/f (Firm)
WFA 3 from 4yo+ 8lb 10 Ran SP% **115.6**
Speed ratings (Par 103): **96,93,90,89,88 87,75,74,71,69**
Tote Swingers: 1&2 £6.10, 1&3 £2.40, 2&3 £5.20 CSF £50.21 TOTE £3.40: £1.10, £2.90, £1.60; EX 37.10 Trifecta £120.70 Pool: £2,080.11 - 12.92 winning units..
Owner Godolphin **Bred** Gigginstown House **Trained** Newmarket, Suffolk

FOCUS
Rail out on Round course from 1m2f to entrance to home straight. A fair maiden but the form pair (third and fourth) were a bit disappointing.

4668 CROWNHOTEL-BAWTRY.COM MAIDEN AUCTION FILLIES' STKS 7f
6:10 (6:11) (Class 5) 2-Y-O £2,587 (£770; £384; £192) Stalls High

Form RPR
3 1 **Captain Secret**[16] 4154 2-8-5 0 AndreaAtzeni 8 75+
(Marco Botti) *mde all: rdn clr over 1f out: drvn and edgd rt ins fnl f: hld on wl towards fin* **7/2**[2]
2 2 *nk* **Practising**[20] 4026 2-8-5 0 MartinLane 6 74
(Ralph Beckett) *hld up: hdwy to trck ldrs 3f out: effrt 2f out and sn rdn: drvn and styd on wl to chal ins fnl f: ev ch tl no ex towards fin* **8/11**[1]
3 *1 1/4* **Illuminating Dream (IRE)** 2-8-12 0 HarryBentley 9 78+
(David Brown) *hld up: hdwy3f out: chsd ldrs 2f out: rdn: green and edgd rt over 1f out: kpt on fnl f: nrst fin* **8/1**[3]
4 *1 1/4* **Singapore Secret (IRE)** 2-8-4 0 JamesSullivan 5 66
(James Given) *sltly hmpd s and sn t.k.h in rr: hdwy wl over 2f out: swtchd lft to outer and rdn over 1f out: kpt on fnl f: nrst fin* **33/1**
0 5 *2 1/4* **L'Artiste (IRE)**[32] 3605 2-8-8 0 MichaelO'Connell 3 64
(John Quinn) *trckd ldrs: rdn to chse wnr over 2f out: drvn and wknd over 1f out* **25/1**
00 6 *2 1/2* **My My My Diliza**[47] 3107 2-8-4 0 SilvestreDeSousa 7 53
(J S Moore) *chsd wnr: rdn along over 3f out: wknd over 2f out* **33/1**
7 *hd* **Miss Sophisticated** 2-8-6 0 AndrewMullen 4 55
(David Barron) *hld up: a towards rr* **14/1**
8 *11* **Olymnia** 2-8-10 0 KierenFallon 2 29
(Robert Eddery) *s.i.s and in rr: swtchd lft to outer and rapid hdwy to chse wnr over 4f out: rdn along 3f out: sn wknd* **10/1**

1m 27.15s (0.85) **Going Correction** -0.125s/f (Firm) 8 Ran SP% **116.7**
Speed ratings (Par 91): **90,89,88,86,84 81,81,68**
Tote Swingers: 1&2 £1.50, 1&3 £3.00, 2&3 £2.00 CSF £6.43 TOTE £5.80: £1.60, £1.02, £2.20; EX 9.40 Trifecta £41.40 Pool: £2,219.91 - 40.19 winning units..
Owner Scuderia Blueberry **Bred** R G Percival **Trained** Newmarket, Suffolk

FOCUS
A modest 2yo fillies' maiden in which the winner stepped up from her debut.

4669 ESQUIRES COFFEE PARTNERED WITH DONCASTER KNIGHTS H'CAP 6f
6:45 (6:46) (Class 5) (0-70,70) 4-Y-O+ £2,726 (£805; £402) Stalls High

Form RPR
0130 1 **Clubland (IRE)**[20] 4007 4-9-5 68 JimmyQuinn 7 81+
(Roy Bowring) *trckd ldrs: smooth hdwy and cl up 2f out: led appr fnl f: sn rdn clr* **9/2**[2]
0224 2 *2 1/4* **Fenella Fudge**[15] 4163 5-8-7 63 (v) AdamMcLean(7) 2 69
(Derek Shaw) *towards rr: swtchd lft and rdn wl over 1f out: styd on wl fnl f: nrst fin* **12/1**
5464 3 *3/4* **Keep It Dark**[24] 3895 4-9-1 64 GrahamLee 10 67
(Tony Coyle) *in tch: hdwy over 2f out: rdn to chse ldrs over 1f out: drvn and kpt on same pce fnl f* **6/1**
0132 4 *1* **Feel The Heat**[12] 4291 6-8-12 66 (v) JustinNewman(5) 5 66
(Bryan Smart) *slt ld: jnd and rdn 2f out: drvn and hdd jst over 1f out: wknd ins fnl f* **4/1**[1]
0030 5 *3 1/2* **Errigal Lad**[7] 4456 8-8-2 51 oh2 AndrewMullen 3 40
(Garry Woodward) *midfield: pushed along and outpcd after 1 1/2f: sn bhd tl styd on strly fr wl over 1f out: nrst fin* **28/1**
0354 6 *1* **Generalyse**[14] 4220 4-9-7 70 JoeFanning 8 56
(Ben De Haan) *chsd ldng pair: rdn along 2f out: wknd over 1f out* **5/1**[3]

The Form Book Flat, Raceform Ltd, Compton, RG20 6NL.

0500 **7** 2 1/2 **Hello Stranger (IRE)**[27] 3778 4-8-13 **62**........................ DuranFentiman 6 40
(Tim Easterby) *dwlt: hdwy 1/2-way: in tch over 2f out: sn rdn and wknd* **14/1**

0003 **8** 3/4 **Divertimenti (IRE)**[7] 4456 9-8-7 **59**..........................(b) MarkCoumbe(3) 4 34
(Roy Bowring) *cl up: rdn along wl over 2f out: sn wknd* **14/1**

1-30 **9** 4 **Belinsky (IRE)**[26] 3811 6-8-6 **62**.................................. RichardOliver(7) 1 25
(Julie Camacho) *dwlt: a in rr* **22/1**

0003 **10** 3 3/4 **Uprise**[7] 4428 4-9-3 **66**.. TomQueally 11 17
(George Margarson) *midfield: effrt over 2f out: sn rdn and wknd* **4/1**[1]

1m 12.29s (-1.31) **Going Correction** -0.125s/f (Firm) **10** Ran SP% **118.0**
Speed ratings (Par 103): **103,100,99,97,93 91,88,87,82,77**
Tote Swingers: 1&2 £10.30, 1&3 £7.30, 2&3 £8.20 CSF £58.03 CT £337.72 TOTE £4.70: £1.60, £3.30, £2.20; EX 61.20 Trifecta £696.40 Pool: £1,070.29 - 3.24 winning units..
Owner S R Bowring **Bred** Mrs Sharon Slattery **Trained** Edwinstowe, Notts

FOCUS
An ordinary sprint handicap. A clear personal best from the winner, and no fluke.

4670 JAMES PEARSON 80TH BIRTHDAY H'CAP 6f
7:15 (7:15) (Class 4) (0-80,80) 3-Y-O **£4,690** (£1,395; £697; £348) **Stalls** High

Form RPR

1232 **1** **Royal Guinevere**[27] 3762 3-8-9 **68**................................ JimmyQuinn 1 80
(Dean Ivory) *trckd ldrs on outer: cl up over 2f out: chal wl over 1f out: led ins fnl f: kpt on* **3/1**[1]

-604 **2** 1 1/4 **Huntsmans Close**[31] 3634 3-9-0 **80**.................... LouisSteward(7) 3 88
(Michael Bell) *led: rdn wl over 1f out: hdd ins fnl f: kpt on same pce* **4/1**[3]

050- **3** 4 1/2 **My Boy Bill**[268] 7463 3-8-8 **67**................................ GrahamGibbons 6 61
(Michael Easterby) *a.p: chsd ldng pair 2f out: sn rdn and no imp* **12/1**

2550 **4** 1 1/4 **Admiralofthesea (USA)**[27] 3782 3-8-9 **68**.................... AndreaAtzeni 2 58
(Robert Eddery) *hld up in rr: hdwy 2f out: sn rdn and no imp fnl f* **5/1**

1031 **5** *hd* **Sylvia Pankhurst (IRE)**[12] 4283 3-9-2 **78**..................(p) LMcNiff(3) 8 67
(David C Griffiths) *racd alone nr stands' rail: prom: rdn along 2f out: grad wknd* **10/3**[2]

-446 **6** 3 1/4 **Hardy Blue (IRE)**[21] 3980 3-8-10 **69** ow2........................ TomQueally 4 48
(Danielle McCormick) *prom: rdn along over 2f out: sn wknd* **16/1**

045 **7** 3 **Star Up In The Sky (USA)**[24] 3894 3-8-11 **70**..............(p) GrahamLee 5 39
(Kevin Ryan) *a in rr* **16/1**

0534 **8** 9 **Mitchell**[12] 4291 3-8-8 **67**.. BarryMcHugh 7 7
(David Thompson) *trckd ldrs: effrt over 2f out: sn rdn and wknd* **8/1**

1m 11.83s (-1.77) **Going Correction** -0.125s/f (Firm) **8** Ran SP% **115.3**
Speed ratings (Par 102): **106,104,98,96,96 92,88,76**
Tote Swingers: 1&2 £3.90, 1&3 £9.90, 2&3 £13.70 CSF £15.42 CT £124.60 TOTE £3.10: £1.50, £1.60, £2.90; EX 14.20 Trifecta £253.30 Pool: £1,097.29 - 3.24 winning units..
Owner M J Yarrow **Bred** Plantation Stud **Trained** Radlett, Herts

FOCUS
A modest 3yo sprint handicap. The winner is progressing now and the first two were clear.

4671 SKY BET SUPPORTING YORKSHIRE RACING SUMMER FESTIVAL FILLIES' H'CAP 7f
7:50 (7:51) (Class 3) (0-90,89) 3-Y-O+ **£7,439** (£2,213; £1,106; £553) **Stalls** High

Form RPR

0234 **1** **Shesastar**[18] 4097 5-9-0 **75**.. SilvestreDeSousa 3 85
(David Barron) *towards rr: sn rdn along and detached: gd hdwy u.p on wd outside over 2f out: led appr fnl f: sn drvn and edgd rt: kpt on* **7/2**[1]

0035 **2** 1/2 **Dutch Rose (IRE)**[16] 4137 4-10-0 **89**........................... DanielTudhope 9 97
(David O'Meara) *trckd ldrs: effrt wl over 1f out: sn rdn: styd on to chal ins fnl f: drvn and no ex towards fin* **9/2**[2]

0211 **3** 3/4 **Elle Woods (IRE)**[19] 4056 3-9-5 **87**..........................(p) PaulMulrennan 7 90
(Michael Dods) *trckd ldrs: n.m.r and lost pl 2f out: swtchd rt and rdn over 1f out: styd on fnl f: nrst fin* **7/2**[1]

00-0 **4** 1 1/2 **Batgirl**[182] 354 6-8-9 **70** oh3.. TedDurcan 6 72
(Martin Smith) *hld up towards rr: hdwy over 2f out: swtchd lft and effrt to chal whn n.m.r over 1f out: rdn and kpt on fnl f* **33/1**

46-4 **5** 1/2 **Piddie's Power**[19] 4067 6-9-8 **83**..................................... RoystonFfrench 8 84
(Ed McMahon) *trckd ldrs on outer: pushed along and sltly outpcd 2f out: sn rdn: styd on fnl f: nrst fin* **8/1**[3]

-401 **6** 1/2 **Hidden Belief (IRE)**[22] 3950 3-8-7 **75**............................. AndreaAtzeni 5 72
(Ralph Beckett) *trckd ldrs: effrt over 2f out: sn rdn and wknd appr fnl f* **9/2**[2]

3430 **7** 1 3/4 **Tussie Mussie**[16] 4145 3-8-5 **73**.. JoeFanning 1 65
(Mark Johnston) *prom: hdwy to ld wl over 2f out: rdn and hdd over 1f out: sn wknd* **12/1**

1010 **8** 3 1/2 **Available (IRE)**[40] 3322 4-9-4 **79**..............................(p) GrahamGibbons 4 64
(John Mackie) *led: rdn along and hdd wl over 2f out: sn drvn and wknd* **16/1**

0200 **9** 2 1/4 **Supernova Heights (IRE)**[13] 4252 3-9-5 **87**..................(t) KierenFallon 2 63
(Brian Meehan) *chsd ldrs: rdn along wl over 2f out: sn wknd* **10/1**

1m 24.79s (-1.51) **Going Correction** -0.125s/f (Firm)
WFA 3 from 4yo+ 7lb **9** Ran SP% **117.5**
Speed ratings (Par 104): **103,102,101,99,99 98,96,92,90**
Tote Swingers: 1&2 £3.30, 1&3 £3.50, 2&3 £2.50 CSF £19.68 CT £59.49 TOTE £4.10: £1.80, £2.20, £1.40; EX 14.50 Trifecta £80.80 Pool: £1,559.56 - 14.46 winning units..
Owner Star Alliance 4 - Lancs 2 Lincs **Bred** The Welcome Alliance **Trained** Maunby, N Yorks

FOCUS
A fair fillies' handicap. The winner found a little on last year's form.

4672 INFINITY ECOSIS TYRES H'CAP 1m 2f 60y
8:25 (8:25) (Class 5) (0-75,74) 3-Y-O **£2,587** (£770; £384; £192) **Stalls** Low

Form RPR

26-0 **1** **Ikhtisas (USA)**[14] 4223 3-9-5 **72**............................. SilvestreDeSousa 5 81+
(Saeed bin Suroor) *hld up and bhd: hdwy on outer 3f out: rdn to chse ldrs and edgd lft wl over 1f out: drvn to chal and edgd lft wl ins fnl f: kpt on strly to ld nr fin* **6/1**

-235 **2** *nk* **Gioia Di Vita**[36] 3470 3-9-5 **72**.. AndreaAtzeni 7 80
(Marco Botti) *set stdy pce: qcknd over 3f out: rdn and qcknd again 2f out: drvn ent fnl f: hdd and no ex nr fin* **2/1**[1]

2155 **3** 1 1/4 **Aneedh**[21] 3995 3-9-5 **72**...(p) DanielTudhope 3 78
(William Haggas) *trckd ldrs on inner: swtchd rt and hdwy 3f out: chsd ldng pair 2f out: sn rdn: drvn and ev ch ent fnl f tl no ex last 75yds* **4/1**[2]

15 **4** 2 **Nonotnow**[19] 4048 3-9-1 **68**.. DavidAllan 6 70
(Tim Easterby) *hld up towards rr: hdwy 3f out: swtchd to inner and rdn over 2f out: styd on fnl f: nrst fin* **20/1**

3013 **5** 1 **Typhon (USA)**[14] 4209 3-9-6 **73**... TedDurcan 8 73
(David Lanigan) *trckd ldrs: smooth hdwy on outer 3f out: rdn to chse ldrs wl over 1f out: drvn and ev ch ent fnl f: wknd last 100yds* **6/1**

4652 **6** 3 **Yul Finegold (IRE)**[31] 3636 3-9-7 **74**................................. PatCosgrave 2 68
(George Baker) *trckd ldr: effrt 3f out: rdn along 2f out: sn drvn and wknd over 1f out* **9/2**[3]

00-5 **7** 7 **Smooth Handle**[9] 4374 3-8-2 **55** oh9.............................. JamesSullivan 1 36
(Danielle McCormick) *in tch: rdn along over 3f out: sn wknd* **50/1**

4600 **8** 17 **Ofcoursewecan (USA)**[18] 4098 3-8-13 **66**........................ JoeFanning 4 15
(Mark Johnston) *trckd ldrs: rdn along over 3f out: wknd over 2f out* **12/1**

2m 12.61s (3.21) **Going Correction** +0.20s/f (Good) **8** Ran SP% **114.5**
Speed ratings (Par 100): **95,94,93,92,91 88,83,69**
Tote Swingers 1&2 £6.60, 2&3 £4.90, 1&3 CSF £18.47 CT £53.67 TOTE £4.80: £1.90, £1.20, £1.70; EX 25.20 Trifecta £101.90 Pool: £1,208.12 - 8.88 winning units..
Owner Godolphin **Bred** Darley **Trained** Newmarket, Suffolk

FOCUS
A moderate 3yo handicap. The second sets the standard.

4673 1STSECURITYSOLUTIONS.CO.UK H'CAP 1m 4f
8:55 (8:55) (Class 5) (0-75,72) 4-Y-O+ **£2,587** (£770; £384; £192) **Stalls** Low

Form RPR

0060 **1** **Flying Power**[20] 4020 5-9-6 **71**.. PaddyAspell 3 78
(John Norton) *trckd ldng pair: hdwy and cl up 4f out: led 3f out: rdn clr 2f out: drvn fnl f: kpt on gamely towards fin* **3/1**[1]

/035 **2** 1/2 **Keep It Cool (IRE)**[15] 4159 9-9-5 **70**............................. DanielTudhope 5 76
(David O'Meara) *trckd ldr: pushed along 3f out: rdn 2f out: sn n.m.r and sltly outpcd wl over 1f out: drvn and styd on to chse wnr ins fnl f: jst hld* **3/1**[1]

0026 **3** 5 **Elizabeth Coffee (IRE)**[18] 4099 5-8-2 **53**......................(v) JimmyQuinn 1 51
(John Weymes) *hld up in rr: hdwy on outer over 3f out: rdn to chse ldrs 2f out: drvn over 1f out: sn one pce* **5/1**[2]

-020 **4** 5 **Laser Blazer**[21] 3971 5-9-7 **72**..(p) GrahamLee 4 62
(Jeremy Gask) *set stdy pce: rdn along 4f out: hdd 3f out: wknd 2f out* **3/1**[1]

0/66 **5** *shd* **Layla's Dancer**[87] 1889 6-8-8 **59**.................................... AndrewMullen 2 49
(Michael Appleby) *trckd ldrs: hdwy over 3f out: rdn to chse wnr 2f out: sn drvn and wknd appr fnl f* **10/1**

0500 **6** 12 **Sareeah (IRE)**[24] 3895 4-8-6 **60**....................................... JulieBurke(3) 6 31
(David O'Meara) *a in rr: outpcd and bhd fnl 3f* **6/1**[3]

2m 36.4s (1.50) **Going Correction** +0.20s/f (Good) **6** Ran SP% **115.0**
Speed ratings (Par 103): **103,102,99,96,95 87**
Tote Swingers 1&2 £2.80, 2&3 £1.10, 1&3 £4.80 CSF £12.55 TOTE £4.80: £2.40, £2.10; EX 11.30 Trifecta £95.20 Pool: £958.60 - 7.54 winning units..
Owner Jaffa Racing Syndicate **Bred** Rabbah Bloodstock Limited **Trained** High Hoyland, S Yorks

FOCUS
An ordinary handicap. The winner only had to match his recent form.
T/Jkpt: Part won. £8,341.20 to a £1 stake. Pool: £11,748.00 - 0.50 winning tickets. T/Plt: £16.00 to a £1 stake. Pool: £94,331.00 - 4,301.95 winning tickets T/Qpdt: £10.90 to a £1 stake. Pool: £7,239.00 - 487.84 winning tickets JR

4437 EPSOM (L-H)
Thursday, July 25

OFFICIAL GOING: Good to firm (derby course - 8.4, sprint course 8.7)
Wind: Fresh, across Weather: Fine, warm

4674 STUBHUB TICKETS H'CAP 5f
6:00 (6:00) (Class 4) (0-80,82) 3-Y-O **£5,175** (£1,540; £769) **Stalls** High

Form RPR

1212 **1** **Holley Shiftwell**[19] 4057 3-9-6 **75**................................... RichardHughes 2 82+
(Stuart Williams) *led 1f: w ldr after: led again over 1f out: shkn up to assert ins fnl f: cleverly* **4/9**[1]

1111 **2** 1/2 **Lexington Place**[8] 4402 3-9-13 **82** 6ex.............................. JimmyFortune 3 87
(David O'Meara) *awkward s: racd against rail: led after 1f: narrowly hdd over 1f out: styd on wl but a hld* **9/4**[2]

0-65 **3** 4 **Somethingboutmary**[25] 3866 3-7-13 **59**...................(b[1]) RosieJessop(5) 1 50
(Tim Pitt) *chsd other pair: on terms on outer 1/2-way: rdn 2f out: outpcd over 1f out* **12/1**[3]

55.91s (0.21) **Going Correction** -0.025s/f (Good) **3** Ran SP% **107.7**
Speed ratings (Par 102): **97,96,89**
CSF £1.74 TOTE £1.60; EX 1.50 Trifecta £2.40 Pool: £572.60 - 174.81 winning units..
Owner J W Parry **Bred** Mr & Mrs K W Grundy, Mr & Mrs P Hopper **Trained** Newmarket, Suffolk

FOCUS
5mm of rain fell overnight but, after a dry day, the ground was described as "good to firm". The rail was out 3-4yds from the mile start to the winning post, adding 7yds to race distances. Effectively a match between the two at the head of the market and a race run at just an ordinary gallop. The first two rate small personal bests.

4675 INDIGENOUS H'CAP 5f
6:35 (6:35) (Class 4) (0-85,83) 4-Y-O+ **£6,469** (£1,925; £962; £481) **Stalls** High

Form RPR

1363 **1** **Monumental Man**[14] 4203 4-8-13 **75**.............................(p) DavidProbert 8 85
(James Unett) *mde all and sn 2 l clr against rail: pressed 2f out: drifted lft after: rdn clr again fnl f* **12/1**

5602 **2** 2 1/2 **Howyadoingnotsobad (IRE)**[10] 4344 5-8-9 **71** ow1.. RichardHughes 3 72
(Karen George) *chsd wnr: clsd to chal 2f out: looking hld whn short of room over 1f out: kpt on* **6/1**

3014 **3** *hd* **Sandfrankskipsgo**[17] 4123 4-9-6 **82**.................................. AdamKirby 5 82+
(Peter Crate) *hld up towards rr: plld wd and prog over 1f out: styd on fnl f: nrly snatched 2nd* **4/1**[2]

1-00 **4** *hd* **Muhdiq (USA)**[49] 3018 4-9-0 **76**.. PatDobbs 4 76+
(Mike Murphy) *hld up and detached in last: prog over 1f out: styd on to press plcd horses nr fin: nvr a threat* **5/1**[3]

1440 **5** *nk* **Putin (IRE)**[6] 4494 5-7-12 **65**.................................(bt) NathanAlison(5) 7 63
(Phil McEntee) *trckd ldrs against rail: shkn up and nt qckn wl over 1f out: hanging and one pce after* **16/1**

100 **6** 1 1/4 **Dorback**[13] 4263 6-9-7 **83**...(t) MartinHarley 6 77
(Violet M Jordan) *awkward s: hld up in last trio: trying to make prog whn hmpd jst over 1f out: no ch after* **8/1**

2151 **7** 3/4 **Go Nani Go**[25] 3855 7-9-6 **82**.. LiamKeniry 2 73
(Ed de Giles) *trckd ldng pair: clsd and on terms 2f out: rdn and wknd jst over 1f out* **5/2**[1]

-423 **8** 4 1/2 **Indian Tinker**[26] 3816 4-8-6 **68**................................. MickaelBarzalona 1 43
(Robert Cowell) *racd wd and nvr on terms w ldrs: rdn after 2f: wknd 2f out* **6/1**

54.79s (-0.91) **Going Correction** -0.025s/f (Good) **8** Ran SP% **118.5**
Speed ratings (Par 105): **106,102,101,101,100 98,97,90**
toteswingers 1&2 £3.90, 1&3 £8.50, 2&3 £5.10 CSF £84.39 CT £348.93 TOTE £10.60: £3.70, £2.90, £1.50; EX 135.70 Trifecta £737.00 Pool: £1462.53 - 1.48 winning units..

Owner P Fetherston-Godley **Bred** Christopher Chell **Trained** Tedsmore Hall, Shropshire

FOCUS

Mainly exposed sorts in a fairly useful handicap. The gallop was sound (over 1 second quicker than the previous race) but this suited those up with the pace. The winner is possibly worth more at face value.

4676 BRITISH STALLION STUDS EBF MAIDEN STKS 6f

7:05 (7:05) (Class 5) 2-Y-O **£3,881** (£1,155; £577; £288) **Stalls** High

Form RPR

242 **1** **Art Official (IRE)**[14] 4218 2-9-5 0 .... RichardHughes 1 88+
(Richard Hannon) *mde all: pushed clr wl over 1f out: comf* **2/9**[1]

3 **2** *5* **Gilmer (IRE)**[28] 3737 2-9-5 0 .... MickaelBarzalona 3 76
(Saeed bin Suroor) *outpcd early: rcvrd to chse wnr after 2f: rdn 1/2-way: cl enough 2f out: sn readily lft bhd* **3/1**[2]

53 **3** *21* **Music Stop**[66] 2510 2-8-9 0 ....(bt[1]) NathanAlison(5) 2
(Phil McEntee) *chsd wnr 2f: wknd rapidly 2f out: t.o* **50/1**[3]

4 *26* **Nunkie Bill** 2-9-5 0 .... DavidProbert 4
(James Unett) *green to post: slowly away: rn green and sn wl t.o* **66/1**

1m 10.06s (0.66) **Going Correction** -0.025s/f (Good) **4** Ran SP% **110.3**

Speed ratings (Par 94): **94,87,59,24**

CSF £1.28 TOTE £1.20; EX 1.40 Trifecta £2.50 Pool: £896.69 - 262.29 winning units..

Owner Chris Giles,Potensis Ltd,J Palmer-Brown **Bred** Lisieux Stud **Trained** East Everleigh, Wilts

FOCUS

The fifth running of a race won in 2009 by Group 2 winner Frozen Power and this year's renewal was a most uncompetitive event. The gallop was no more than fair and the winner only had to run to his mark.

4677 TOTEPOOL HOME OF KING SIZE POOLS H'CAP 7f

7:40 (7:40) (Class 4) (0-85,85) 3-Y-O+ **£6,469** (£1,925; £962; £481) **Stalls** Low

Form RPR

2424 **1** **Kakapuka**[13] 4245 6-9-1 72 .... MartinHarley 7 81
(Anabel K Murphy) *mde all: drvn 2f out: hld on gamely last 100yds* **4/1**[3]

1534 **2** *1* **Forceful Appeal (USA)**[12] 4281 5-9-9 80 .... RichardHughes 1 86
(Simon Dow) *trckd ldng pair on inner: rdn 2f out: wnt 2nd fnl f and eased off rail: clsd on wnr but nt qckn and hld last 75yds* **6/4**[1]

0020 **3** *½* **Top Cop**[39] 3371 4-9-11 82 .... DavidProbert 6 87
(Andrew Balding) *chsd wnr: shkn up 2f out: nt qckn and lost 2nd 1f out: kpt on nr fin* **7/1**

51/0 **4** *2½* **Appointee (IRE)**[14] 4217 4-9-8 79 .... MickaelBarzalona 3 77
(Robert Cowell) *a in 4th: rdn and no imp over 2f out* **25/1**

0042 **5** *¾* **Amadeus Wolfe Tone (IRE)**[7] 4440 4-10-0 85 ....(b) AdamKirby 5 81
(Jamie Osborne) *s.s: a last: rdn and no prog jst over 2f out: n.d after* **7/4**[2]

50-0 **R** **Aurens (IRE)**[15] 4176 4-8-10 67 .... LiamKeniry 9
(Michael Attwater) *ref to r: tk no part* **66/1**

1m 23.09s (-0.21) **Going Correction** -0.025s/f (Good)

WFA 3 from 4yo+ 7lb **6** Ran SP% **114.2**

Speed ratings (Par 105): **100,98,98,95,94**

toteswingers 1&2 £1.10, 1&3 £4.20, 2&3 £3.30 CSF £10.76 CT £39.15 TOTE £4.50: £2.00, £1.40; EX 13.80 Trifecta £38.40 Pool: £924.67 - 18.01 winning units..

Owner Mrs E Mills & A Murphy **Bred** Paradime Ltd **Trained** Wilmcote, Warwicks

FOCUS

Another fairly useful handicap but a steady gallop means this bare form isn't reliable. The winner is rated back to his old turf best.

4678 BRITISH STALLION STUDS EBF FILLIES' H'CAP 1m 2f 18y

8:10 (8:10) (Class 4) (0-80,78) 3-Y-O+ **£6,469** (£1,925; £962; £481) **Stalls** Low

Form RPR

6-42 **1** **Soryah (IRE)**[27] 3764 3-9-1 75 .... RichardHughes 1 90+
(Luca Cumani) *trckd ldrs: wnt 2nd st: shkn up to ld wl over 1f out: sn clr: eased last 75yds* **7/4**[1]

0241 **2** *4½* **Play Street**[41] 3273 4-9-12 76 .... MartinHarley 3 80
(Jonathan Portman) *led 150yds: in tch: 4th st: clsd on ldng pair over 2f out: sn rdn and outpcd: kpt on to take 2nd nr fin* **12/1**

3513 **3** *hd* **Huffoof (IRE)**[24] 3891 3-9-4 78 ....(b) SeanLevey 2 82
(Roger Varian) *pushed up to ld after 150yds: rdn and hdd wl over 1f out: no ch w wnr after: lost 2nd nr fin* **5/2**[2]

331- **4** *18* **Willowing (USA)**[313] 6253 3-9-3 77 .... AhmedAjtebi 4 58
(Saeed bin Suroor) *sn in last: detached fr rest 4f out: shkn up and no prog over 2f out: sn wknd and eased: t.o* **7/1**

614 **5** *78* **Controversy**[20] 4015 3-9-4 78 .... MickaelBarzalona 5
(Saeed bin Suroor) *trckd ldr after 1f: lost 2nd ent st and wknd bdly: sn t.o and virtually p.u* **3/1**[3]

2m 8.34s (-1.36) **Going Correction** -0.025s/f (Good)

WFA 3 from 4yo 10lb **5** Ran SP% **110.1**

Speed ratings (Par 102): **104,100,100,85,23**

CSF £21.05 TOTE £1.90: £1.10, £7.30; EX 26.50 Trifecta £38.50 Pool: £601.67 - 11.70 winning units..

Owner Sheikh Mohammed Obaid Al Maktoum **Bred** Liam Queally **Trained** Newmarket, Suffolk

FOCUS

A fair fillies' handicap in which five of the six runners were previous winners. The gallop was on the steady side but the winner won with plenty in hand and is still improving.

4679 SIX MILE HILL H'CAP 1m 4f 10y

8:45 (8:45) (Class 5) (0-70,70) 3-Y-O+ **£3,234** (£962; £481; £240) **Stalls** Centre

Form RPR

-605 **1** **Nile Knight**[14] 4209 3-8-11 65 ....(b[1]) ShaneKelly 9 74
(Marcus Tregoning) *hld up in tch: 6th st: prog to ld over 2f out: rdn and styd on wl fr over 1f out* **4/1**[2]

2504 **2** *2* **Rossetti**[23] 3925 5-9-5 68 .... NedCurtis(7) 4 75+
(Gary Moore) *hld up in tch: 7th st: prog to chse wnr 2f out: hanging bdly lft after and couldn't sustain a proper chal: kpt on* **16/1**

-602 **3** *½* **May Be Some Time**[41] 3273 5-9-6 67 ....(t) MichaelJMMurphy(5) 3 72
(Stuart Kittow) *prom: cl 4th st: nt qckn w ldng pair fr 2f out: styd on fnl f* **6/1**[3]

6006 **4** *13* **Cherry Princess**[38] 3403 3-8-2 56 oh9 ow2 .... DavidProbert 8 40
(Stuart Williams) *hld up: 8th and rdn st: sme prog 2f out but no ch w ldrs: edgd lft but tk modest 4th fnl f* **25/1**

563- **5** *nk* **Superciliary**[90] 7251 4-9-6 62 .... RichardHughes 6 46
(Chris Gordon) *hld up in detached last: rdn 3f out: sn outpcd: plugged on to press for modest 4th nr fin* **10/1**

3115 **6** *3½* **Knight's Parade (IRE)**[31] 3636 3-9-2 70 .... PatDobbs 7 48
(Amanda Perrett) *led 2f: w ldr: led ent st and tried to kick on: hdd over 2f out: sn wknd* **6/4**[1]

0104 **7** *1¾* **Super Duplex**[7] 4441 6-9-1 62 .... JemmaMarshall(5) 1 37
(Pat Phelan) *hld up in tch: 5th st: pushed along and wknd over 2f out* **20/1**

-256 **8** *17* **Marcus Antonius**[21] 3971 6-9-8 64 .... AdamKirby 5 12
(Jim Boyle) *pressed ldrs: urged along sn after 1/2-way: 3rd st: sn wknd: t.o* **8/1**

-043 **9** *15* **Star Date (IRE)**[25] 3865 4-9-6 65 .... WilliamTwiston-Davies(3) 2
(Michael Attwater) *mde most after 2f tl ent st: wknd rapidly: wl t.o* **8/1**

2m 38.77s (-0.13) **Going Correction** -0.025s/f (Good)

WFA 3 from 4yo+ 12lb **9** Ran SP% **120.1**

Speed ratings (Par 103): **99,97,97,88,88 86,84,73,63**

toteswingers 1&2 £17.60, 1&3 £7.00, 2&3 £20.30 CSF £67.71 CT £388.42 TOTE £9.00: £2.50, £2.50, £1.90; EX 79.90 Trifecta £479.70 Part won. Pool: £639.60 - 0.49 winning units..

Owner R C C Villers **Bred** Mr & Mrs Pakenham, F Hines & J James **Trained** Whitsbury, Hants

FOCUS

A modest finale. The gallop was on the steady side to the home straight but the first three deserve credit for pulling clear of the rest.The winner returned to form in the blinkers.

T/Plt: £52.30 to a £1 stake. Pool: £40,762.03 - 567.87 winning tickets T/Qpdt: £11.90 to a £1 stake. Pool: £2766.20 - 171.80 winning tickets JN

4638 SANDOWN (R-H)

Thursday, July 25

OFFICIAL GOING: Round course - good (good to firm in places; 8.5); sprint course - good to firm (8.6)

Wind: Moderate ahead Weather: Cloudy, humid

4680 BRITISH STALLION STUDS EBF MAIDEN STKS 5f 6y

2:00 (2:00) (Class 5) 2-Y-O **£3,881** (£1,155; £577; £288) **Stalls** Low

Form RPR

1 **Shamshon (IRE)** 2-9-5 0 .... FrankieDettori 1 82+
(Richard Hannon) *mde all: shkn up and qckd clr fnl f: easily* **8/11**[1]

06 **2** *6* **Dream Sika (IRE)**[13] 4259 2-9-5 0 .... AdamKirby 3 60
(Clive Cox) *trckd ldrs: drvn to chse wnr jst ins fnl f but nvr any ch* **6/1**[3]

0 **3** *2* **Grass Green**[17] 4121 2-9-0 0 .... RyanMoore 2 48
(William Haggas) *chsd wnr 2f: sn rdn and outpcd: edgd lft and kpt on same pce fr 3rd fnl f* **3/1**[2]

4 *4½* **Drive On (IRE)** 2-9-5 0 .... NeilCallan 4 37
(Eve Johnson Houghton) *chsd wnr after 2f: sn rdn: wknd fnl f* **7/1**

1m 3.29s (1.69) **Going Correction** +0.20s/f (Good) **4** Ran SP% **109.7**

Speed ratings (Par 94): **94,84,81,74**

CSF £5.55 TOTE £1.60; EX 5.80 Trifecta £10.40 Pool: £1002.80 - 72.28 winning units..

Owner HE Sh Joaan Bin Hamad Al Thani **Bred** Stonethorn Stud Farms Ltd **Trained** East Everleigh, Wilts

FOCUS

The rail was out 3yds from 1m1f to the winning post, adding 5yds to distances on the round course. There was reportedly 10mm of rain between 3am and 5am on race day and, while the ground was still described on the quick side on both the round and straight courses, the times were relatively slow. Little to go on, but the form is rated towards the top end of the race averages.

4681 WEATHERBYS VAT SERVICES H'CAP 1m 6f

2:30 (2:30) (Class 3) (0-90,83) 3-Y-O **£7,439** (£2,213; £1,106; £553) **Stalls** Low

Form RPR

3222 **1** **Debdebdeb**[21] 3982 3-9-4 80 .... DavidProbert 5 91
(Andrew Balding) *hld up in rr but in tch: hdwy 2f out: n.m.r and swtchd lft wl over 1f out: drvn and styd on wl to ld fnl 110yds: won gng away* **11/4**[2]

-352 **2** *2* **Lady Pimpernel**[21] 3990 3-9-2 78 .... DaneO'Neill 3 86
(Henry Candy) *led tl narrowly hdd 9f out: led again 7f out: jnd fr 3f out: styd on gamely u.p to hold ld tl hdd and outpcd fnl 110yds* **5/2**[1]

6321 **3** *2¼* **Portmonarch (IRE)**[24] 3908 3-9-6 82 ....(p) RyanMoore 4 87
(David Lanigan) *in rr: pushed along 3f out: hdwy over 1f out: styd on to take 3rd ins fnl f but no imp on ldng duo* **9/2**[3]

1430 **4** *nk* **Sizzler**[13] 4233 3-9-3 79 .... JamesDoyle 1 83
(Ralph Beckett) *chsd ldrs: rdn 3f out: styd on same pce fnl 2f* **10/1**

3231 **5** *1¼* **Deficit (IRE)**[23] 3916 3-8-9 71 .... WilliamBuick 2 74
(Michael Bell) *chsd ldrs: led 9f out to 7f out: pressed ldr 3f out tl over 1f out: wknd qckly fnl 110yds* **7/1**

1221 **6** *9* **Arbaah (USA)**[27] 3783 3-9-7 83 .... PaulHanagan 6 73
(Brian Meehan) *chsd ldr 5f: styd wl there: drvn to chal 3f out: wkng whn pushed lft wl over 1f out* **5/1**

3m 5.26s (0.76) **Going Correction** +0.20s/f (Good) **6** Ran SP% **111.7**

Speed ratings (Par 104): **105,103,102,102,101 96**

toteswingers 1&2 £3.30, 1&3 £2.80, 2&3 £2.00 CSF £9.94 TOTE £3.20: £1.90, £1.90; EX 6.90 Trifecta £29.80 Pool: £1407.87 - 35.39 winning units..

Owner C C Buckley **Bred** C C And Mrs D J Buckley **Trained** Kingsclere, Hants

■ Stewards' Enquiry : David Probert one-day ban: careless riding (Aug 8)

FOCUS

A reasonable staying handicap in which plenty wanted to race prominently, and the winner stayed on from last. Solid form, the winner from a Haydock race that's working out really well.

4682 IRISH STALLION FARMS EBF STAR STKS (LISTED RACE) 7f 16y

3:05 (3:14) (Class 1) 2-Y-O

£17,013 (£6,450; £3,228; £1,608; £807; £405) **Stalls** Low

Form RPR

15 **1** **Majeyda (USA)**[26] 3829 2-8-12 0 .... MickaelBarzalona 7 98
(Saeed bin Suroor) *trckd ldr: chal 2f out tl led u.p fnl 150yds: styd on wl clsng stages* **3/1**[2]

31 **2** *nk* **Qawaasem (IRE)**[14] 4215 2-8-12 0 .... PaulHanagan 1 97
(Charles Hills) *chsd ldrs: slt ld fr 2f out but hrd pressed: narrowly hdd fnl 150yds: no ex clsng stages* **9/4**[1]

51 **3** *2½* **Lamar (IRE)**[27] 3781 2-8-12 0 .... NeilCallan 5 90
(James Tate) *in tch: drvn and styd on fr 2f out: kpt on wl for 3rd clsng stages but no ch w ldng duo* **5/1**

1 **4** *shd* **Feedyah (USA)**[36] 3471 2-8-12 0 .... WilliamBuick 3 90+
(Saeed bin Suroor) *s.i.s: in rr: hdwy on outside fr 2f out: styd on to dispute 3rd ins fnl f but no imp on ldng duo: dropped to 4th last strides* **8/1**

10 **5** *1¾* **Rasheeda**[34] 3522 2-8-12 0 .... FrankieDettori 8 85
(Marco Botti) *in rr: drvn over 2f out: styd on same pce fr over 1f out* **10/1**

211 **6** *7* **Ligeia**[29] 3690 2-8-12 0 .... RichardHughes 4 67+
(Richard Hannon) *t.k.h: led: rdn and hdd 2f out: sn btn* **4/1**[3]

0120 **7** *1¾* **Lady Lydia (IRE)**[26] 3829 2-8-12 0 .... DaneO'Neill 2 62
(Michael Wigham) *in tch: rdn and sme hdwy over 2f out: nvr rchd ldrs and sn btn* **50/1**

1m 32.57s (3.07) **Going Correction** +0.20s/f (Good) **7** Ran SP% **114.6**

Speed ratings (Par 102): **90,89,86,86,84 76,74**

toteswingers 1&2 £2.40, 1&3 £4.10, 2&3 £3.20 CSF £10.26 TOTE £3.50: £2.00, £1.90; EX 10.60 Trifecta £41.00 Pool: £2872.48 - 52.42 winning units..

Owner Godolphin **Bred** Darley **Trained** Newmarket, Suffolk

The Form Book Flat, Raceform Ltd, Compton, RG20 6NL.

■ Stewards' Enquiry : Frankie Dettori one-day ban: careless riding (Aug 8)

FOCUS
The 2005 running of this Listed event went to Confidential Lady, who later landed the Prix de Diane, but the last five winners have all failed to win again. This year's race didn't look particularly strong, rated at the lower end of the averages, and it paid to be handy.

4683 WEATHERBYS VAT RETURNS SERVICE H'CAP 1m 2f 7y
3:40 (3:40) (Class 4) (0-85,85) 3-Y-0+ £5,175 (£1,540; £769; £384) Stalls Low

Form RPR
2515 1 **Ningara**[19] 4084 3-8-10 **77** DavidProbert 3 88
(Andrew Balding) *chsd ldrs: rdn to chal and edgd rt 2f out: sn led: styd on wl u.p thrght fnl f* **9/2**[3]
-311 2 1 1/4 **Sadiq**[7] 4425 3-9-2 **83** 6ex MickaelBarzalona 4 92
(Saeed bin Suroor) *in rr: rdn along 3f out: hdwy 2f out: chsd wnr ins fnl f but a hld* **6/4**[1]
0/-2 3 2 1/4 **Dumbarton (IRE)**[12] 4305 5-9-0 **71** (p) FrankieDettori 6 75
(Philip Hobbs) *hld up in rr: hdwy on outside 3f out: rdn: edgd rt and hd high fr 2f out: nt resolute but tk 3rd ins fnl f* **9/1**
4004 4 2 3/4 **Scottish Star**[49] 3022 5-9-3 **79** RosieJessop(5) 1 78
(James Eustace) *led: rdn 2f out and sn hdd: wknd fnl f* **12/1**
4554 5 5 **Master Ming (IRE)**[9] 4384 3-8-13 **80** (b) DaneO'Neill 2 69
(Brian Meehan) *chsd ldrs: rdn over 2f out: sn wknd* **12/1**
3231 6 1 1/2 **Ducab (IRE)**[26] 3805 3-9-4 **85** RyanMoore 5 71
(Roger Varian) *chsd ldr: rdn 3f out: wknd 2f out* **3/1**[2]
3/0- 7 30 **Arabian Heights**[144] 2248 5-9-11 **82** [1] SebSanders 7
(Anthony Middleton) *s.i.s: sn in tch: wknd ins fnl 4f* **66/1**

2m 10.76s (0.26) **Going Correction** +0.20s/f (Good)
WFA 3 from 5yo 10lb 7 Ran SP% **110.1**
Speed ratings (Par 105): **106,105,103,101,97 95,71**
toteswingers 1&2 £3.50, 1&3 £12.10, 2&3 £4.10 CSF £10.77 TOTE £7.50: £2.60, £1.40; EX 17.70 Trifecta £83.60 Pool: £1933.68 - 17.33 winning units..
Owner G B Russell **Bred** S R Hope **Trained** Kingsclere, Hants

FOCUS
A fair handicap in which a couple of progressive 3yos finished one-two. The winner gave the fifth a much bigger beating than here last month.

4684 DEANS CARLING CHALLENGE MAIDEN STKS 1m 14y
4:15 (4:15) (Class 5) 3-4-Y-0 £3,234 (£962; £481; £240) Stalls Low

Form RPR
-252 1 **Persepolis (IRE)**[41] 3276 3-9-3 86 [1] RyanMoore 1 91
(Sir Michael Stoute) *mde all: drvn clr over 2f out: kpt up to work fnl f: unchal* **1/5**[1]
2/45 2 12 **Key Appointment**[89] 1849 4-9-11 77 RichardHughes 2 65
(Paul Cole) *chsd wnr thrght: rdn and no ch fr over 2f out but kpt on for clr but wl hld 2nd* **9/2**[2]
00 3 13 **Polish Rider**[9] 4381 3-9-0 0 WilliamTwiston-Davies(3) 3 34
(Richard Hannon) *dropped to 4th after 2f: no ch whn hanging rt u.p fr 3f out: tk poor 3rd fr tired rival last strides* **50/1**
4 hd **Primo D'Oro (USA)** 3-9-3 0 DaneO'Neill 4 33
(Richard Hannon) *wnt 3rd after 2f: chsd ldrs: rdn over 3f out: edgd rt and wknd over 2f out: tired fnl f and lost poor 3rd last strides* **25/1**[3]

1m 45.38s (2.08) **Going Correction** +0.20s/f (Good)
WFA 3 from 4yo 8lb 4 Ran SP% **107.3**
Speed ratings (Par 103): **97,85,72,71**
CSF £1.42 TOTE £1.10; EX 1.40 Trifecta £7.60 Pool: £1884.32 - 185.74 winning units..
Owner Highclere Thoroughbred Racing - Sloan **Bred** Avington Manor Stud **Trained** Newmarket, Suffolk

FOCUS
This wasn't much of a contest and the easy winner is rated in line with his previous form.

4685 LUBRICATORS H'CAP 7f 16y
4:50 (4:50) (Class 5) (0-75,74) 3-Y-0+ £3,234 (£962; £481; £240) Stalls Low

Form RPR
2413 1 **Tight Fit**[28] 3718 3-9-2 **69** DaneO'Neill 3 76+
(Henry Candy) *chsd ldrs: chal 2f out: led u.p over 1f out: hld on all out* **11/4**[1]
2000 2 nse **Charitable Act (FR)**[21] 3974 4-9-10 **70** RyanMoore 2 80
(Gary Moore) *in tch: hdwy fr 2f out: hrd drvn to chse wnr fnl f: styd on strly last strides: jst failed* **6/1**[2]
0-35 3 2 **George Baker (IRE)**[52] 2920 6-9-11 **74** ThomasBrown(3) 9 81+
(George Baker) *hld up in rr: hdwy 2f out: nt clr run over 1f out and swtchd rt fnl f: fin wl to take 3rd clsng stages: nt rch ldng duo* **12/1**
234 4 1 **Muftarres (IRE)**[13] 4250 8-9-10 **70** (t) FrankieDettori 7 72
(Frank Sheridan) *chsd ldrs: rdn and styd on same pce fnl 2f* **8/1**
-322 5 1/2 **It's Taboo**[47] 3111 3-9-5 **72** DavidProbert 6 70
(Mark Usher) *in rr: drvn over 2f out: styd on fnl f but nvr gng pce to rch ldrs* **6/1**[2]
1433 6 3/4 **Eastern Dragon (IRE)**[9] 4378 3-8-13 **66** ow1 SebSanders 4 62
(Michael Scudamore) *towards rr: rdn and hdwy to chse ldrs 2f out: wknd ins fnl f* **16/1**
-500 7 2 **Scottish Glen**[38] 3416 7-9-10 **70** (p) GeorgeBaker 1 63
(Patrick Chamings) *chsd ldrs: rdn over 2f out: sn btn* **8/1**
0255 8 nk **Ocean Legend (IRE)**[15] 4165 8-9-10 **70** AdamKirby 8 62
(Tony Carroll) *sn led: hdd after 2f: led again 2f out: hdd over 1f out: wknd qckly fnl 110yds* **10/1**
040 9 1 1/4 **Annes Rocket (IRE)**[22] 3955 8-9-12 **72** (p) PatDobbs 5 61
(Jimmy Fox) *s.i.s: in rr: sme prog over 2f out: nvr nr ldrs* **20/1**
-031 10 2 **Sheikh The Reins (IRE)**[15] 4163 4-9-11 **71** (v) JamesDoyle 10 55
(John Best) *led after 2f: hdd 2f out: btn sn after* **7/1**[3]

1m 31.89s (2.39) **Going Correction** +0.20s/f (Good)
WFA 3 from 4yo+ 7lb 10 Ran SP% **117.4**
Speed ratings (Par 103): **94,93,91,90,89 89,86,86,85,82**
toteswingers 1&2 £4.00, 1&3 £5.70, 2&3 £12.60 CSF £19.00 CT £175.19 TOTE £3.60: £1.30, £2.80, £2.30; EX 21.80 Trifecta £196.70 Pool: £3819.00 - 14.55 winning units..
Owner W M Lidsey & H Candy **Bred** W M Lidsey **Trained** Kingston Warren, Oxon

FOCUS
An ordinary but competitive handicap. The winner resumed her progress.
T/Plt: £16.70 to a £1 stake. Pool: £53,612.32 - 2339.75 winning tickets T/Qpdt: £5.40 to a £1 stake. Pool: £4317.28 - 583.23 winning tickets ST

4386 YARMOUTH (L-H)
Thursday, July 25

OFFICIAL GOING: Good to firm (7.7)
Wind: very light breeze Weather: hot and sunny; 25 degrees

4686 FOLLOW US ON TWITTER @GTYARMOUTHRACES MAIDEN AUCTION STKS 6f 3y
2:20 (2:21) (Class 5) 2-Y-0 £2,587 (£770; £384; £192) Stalls Centre

Form RPR
65 1 **Lady In Blue (IRE)**[19] 4073 2-8-11 0 HayleyTurner 3 75
(William Haggas) *stdd s: gng wl in last: smooth run to go 2nd over 1f out: pushed into ld ins fnl f: drvn out cl home* **4/6**[1]
00 2 1/2 **Pastoral Witness**[22] 3958 2-8-11 0 BrettDoyle 5 73
(Clive Brittain) *led: rdn wl over 1f out: hdd ins fnl f: kpt on wl but a jst hld after* **11/2**[3]
3 3 1/4 **Kiss From A Rose** 2-8-7 0 [1] TedDurcan 2 59
(Rae Guest) *t.k.h in 3rd: wnt 2nd over 2f out tl rdn over 1f out: green and racd awkwardly whn wl hld fnl f* **12/1**
2 4 8 **Hot Amber (USA)**[14] 4206 2-8-11 0 FrederikTylicki 1 37
(Robert Cowell) *pressed ldr: hrd drvn wl over 2f out: floundering on grnd fnl 2f* **3/1**[2]

1m 15.45s (1.05) **Going Correction** +0.10s/f (Good) 4 Ran SP% **108.1**
Speed ratings (Par 94): **97,96,92,81**
CSF £4.69 TOTE £2.00; EX 4.50 Trifecta £20.00 Pool: £1599.08 - 59.90 winning units..
Owner The Duchess Syndicate **Bred** John Foley **Trained** Newmarket, Suffolk

FOCUS
Back straight and bottom bend dolled out 3m. A desperately weak juvenile contest.

4687 BOOK FAMILY FUNDAY SUNDAY 25TH AUGUST MAIDEN FILLIES' STKS 6f 3y
2:50 (2:52) (Class 5) 3-4-Y-0 £2,587 (£770; £384; £192) Stalls Centre

Form RPR
32 1 **Dodina (IRE)**[56] 2788 3-9-0 0 JamieSpencer 7 74
(Peter Chapple-Hyam) *settled trcking ldrs: led over 2f out: clr over 1f out: v easily* **11/4**[2]
2 2 3/4 **Teeline (IRE)** 3-9-0 0 AhmedAjtebi 8 65
(Saeed bin Suroor) *taken down early: hld up in last pair: effrt and rn green and outpcd briefly 2f out: rallied and rdn to chse v easy wnr over 1f out* **4/1**[3]
0-2 3 12 **Nur Jahan (IRE)**[20] 4013 3-9-0 0 TedDurcan 2 56+
(David Lanigan) *hld up in last pair: effrt to go 2nd over 2f out: sn rdn and nt striding out and wl btn: heavily eased 1f out* **4/6**[1]
0-06 4 8 **Grey Poppett**[27] 3787 3-9-0 20 [1] SaleemGolam 1
(Chris Dwyer) *prom: rdn and racing awkwardly over 2f out: qckly dropped out: t.o* **150/1**
00-0 5 hd **L'lle Rousse**[27] 3787 4-9-2 0 (v[1]) RyanClark(3) 5
(Chris Dwyer) *led tl hdd and lost pl rapidly over 2f out: t.o* **150/1**
0 6 26 **Raymond's Dream**[76] 2226 3-8-9 0 DannyBrock(5) 3
(J R Jenkins) *cl up tl 1/2-way: rdn and sn fdd rapidly: hopelessly t.o* **66/1**

1m 13.75s (-0.65) **Going Correction** +0.10s/f (Good)
WFA 3 from 4yo 5lb 6 Ran SP% **109.5**
Speed ratings (Par 100): **108,104,88,77,77 42**
toteswingers 1&2 £1.10, 1&3 £1.10, 2&3 £1.30 CSF £13.02 TOTE £4.20: £1.70, £2.10; EX 11.00 Trifecta £12.30 Pool: £4061.88 - 246.29 winning units..
Owner Eledy Srl **Bred** Rathbarry Stud **Trained** Newmarket, Suffolk

FOCUS
Only three of these could be given any kind of chance beforehand.

4688 RACING WELFARE H'CAP 1m 3f 101y
3:25 (3:28) (Class 6) (0-65,65) 3-Y-0 £1,940 (£577; £288; £144) Stalls Low

Form RPR
-562 1 **Nullarbor Sky (IRE)**[8] 4405 3-9-0 **58** (p) FrederikTylicki 5 64
(Lucy Wadham) *mde all: hrd drvn over 1f out: kpt finding ex fnl f* **1/1**[1]
04V1 2 1 3/4 **Helamis**[15] 4178 3-8-3 **52** ow2 TobyAtkinson(5) 8 55
(Alison Hutchinson) *t.k.h and cl up: wnt 2nd over 4f out: pressed wnr after: drvn and no imp fnl f* **14/1**
4332 3 1 **Zhuba (IRE)**[27] 3793 3-9-7 **65** TedDurcan 6 66
(John Best) *pressed wnr tl over 4f out: drvn along fnl 3f: one pce: btn over 1f out* **5/1**[3]
-023 4 3/4 **Hermosa Vaquera (IRE)**[49] 3014 3-9-4 **62** JamieSpencer 2 62
(Peter Chapple-Hyam) *a 3rd or 4th: rdn 2f out: fnd little and plugged on same pce fr over 1f out* **9/2**[2]
000- 5 3 **Roy Rocket (FR)**[247] 7796 3-8-0 **47** oh1 ow1 SimonPearce(3) 4 42
(John Berry) *same pl thrght: rdn 2f out: one pce and sn wl hld* **33/1**
-030 6 4 **Planchette**[15] 4170 3-7-12 **49** oh1 ow3 IanBurns(7) 3 37
(Jane Chapple-Hyam) *same pl thrght: rdn 3f out: struggling after: edgd rt fnl f* **28/1**
1403 7 hd **Precision Strike**[8] 4401 3-8-5 **54** (v) PhilipPrince(5) 1 42
(Richard Guest) *last pair: hrd drvn 4f out: nvr gng wl enough after* **10/1**
3105 8 6 **Entrapping**[56] 2802 3-8-12 **56** HayleyTurner 7 34
(John E Long) *last pair: hrd drvn 4f out: no rspnse and no ch after* **16/1**

2m 30.57s (1.87) **Going Correction** +0.10s/f (Good) 8 Ran SP% **112.9**
Speed ratings (Par 98): **97,95,95,94,92 89,89,84**
toteswingers 1&2 £5.90, 1&3 £1.40, 2&3 £5.50 CSF £16.96 CT £49.93 TOTE £2.10: £1.40, £3.40, £1.40; EX 21.30 Trifecta £84.90 Pool: £3044.67 - 26.88 winning units..
Owner Tim Wood **Bred** Vincent Hannon **Trained** Newmarket, Suffolk

FOCUS
A low-grade handicap.

4689 VIKING FAMILY SUPPORT GROUP FILLIES' H'CAP 1m 3y
4:00 (4:00) (Class 5) (0-70,69) 3-Y-0+ £2,587 (£770; £384; £192) Stalls Centre

Form RPR
4-32 1 **Clear Pearl (USA)**[58] 2760 3-9-6 **69** JamieSpencer 3 75+
(Ed Vaughan) *stdd to r in last: effrt over 2f out: rdn to ld over 1f out: clr whn hung bdly rt fnl 100yds* **11/8**[1]
-212 2 1 1/2 **Pink Lips**[27] 3788 5-9-4 **59** FrederikTylicki 2 64
(J R Jenkins) *trckd ldrs: rdn to dispute ld 2f out tl over 1f out: one pce ins fnl f* **9/4**[2]
2000 3 nk **Sinaadi (IRE)**[42] 3242 3-9-4 **67** BrettDoyle 1 69
(Clive Brittain) *cl up and moving wl tl led over 3f out: jnd 2f out: rdn and hdd over 1f out: no ex ins fnl f* **10/3**[3]
0563 4 17 **Sixties Queen**[10] 4356 3-7-13 **55** NoelGarbutt(7) 6 18
(Alan Bailey) *cl up: drvn over 3f out: sn struggling: t.o over 1f out* **14/1**

34 5 1/2 **Una Bella Cosa**66 2512 3-8-0 52.........................(v) NataliaGemelova(3) 5 14
(Alan McCabe) *sn led: drvn and hdd over 3f out: t.o over 1f out* **33/1**

1m 40.12s (-0.48) **Going Correction** +0.10s/f (Good)
WFA 3 from 4yo+ 8lb **5 Ran SP% 105.6**
Speed ratings (Par 100): **106,104,104,87,86**
CSF £4.26 TOTE £1.70: £1.30, £1.20; EX 4.00 Trifecta £5.50 Pool: £2182.17 - 297.23 winning units..
Owner Pearl Bloodstock Ltd **Bred** Northwest Farms Llc **Trained** Newmarket, Suffolk

FOCUS
A fair race for the grade with a couple of improving fillies in the line-up.

4690 JME LTD H'CAP 6f 3y
4:35 (4:38) (Class 4) (0-85,84) 3-Y-0+ **£4,690** (£1,395; £697; £348) **Stalls** Centre

Form RPR
-410 1 **Shafaani**99 1620 3-9-6 83.........................(t1) BrettDoyle 1 91
(Clive Brittain) *cl up: chal over 1f out: rdn to ld ins fnl f: kpt on wl: edgd rt clsng stages* **7/2**2

3501 2 1 1/4 **Arctic Lynx (IRE)**15 4165 6-9-9 81......................... FrederikTylicki 5 86+
(Robert Cowell) *stmbld bdly s and given plenty of time to rcvr: clsd 2f out: rdn to chal over 1f: n.m.r briefly whn ev ch jst ins fnl f: nt qckn last 75yds and edgd rt nr fin* **5/2**1

0214 3 1 1/4 **Big Wave (IRE)**19 4064 5-8-6 69......................... TobyAtkinson(5) 3 70
(Alison Hutchinson) *did nt parade in paddock and wnt down early: led and 3 l clr: rdn over 1f out: sn hung lft: hdd ins fnl f: nt qckn after* **7/2**2

600 4 4 1/2 **Coincidently**21 3988 3-8-5 75.........................(p) TimClark(7) 2 61
(Alan Bailey) *t.k.h early and sn 2nd: rdn and wknd over 1f out: eased fnl 100yds* **5/1**

0-00 5 20 **Cheveton**42 3249 9-9-12 84......................... JamieSpencer 6
(Richard Price) *stdd s: struggling 1/2-way: t.o and virtually p.u 1f out* **4/1**3

1m 13.99s (-0.41) **Going Correction** +0.10s/f (Good)
WFA 3 from 4yo+ 5lb **5 Ran SP% 109.7**
Speed ratings (Par 105): **106,104,102,96,70**
CSF £12.45 TOTE £4.50: £2.90, £1.10; EX 9.50 Trifecta £20.50 Pool: £2927.17 - 107.08 winning units..
Owner Saeed Manana **Bred** Rabbah Bloodstock Limited **Trained** Newmarket, Suffolk

FOCUS
Only a small field for this feature handicap but there was plenty of drama.

4691 GRANGE FREEHOUSE AT ORMESBY H'CAP 6f 3y
5:10 (5:10) (Class 6) (0-60,59) 3-Y-0+ **£1,940** (£577; £288; £144) **Stalls** Centre

Form RPR
0040 1 **Miakora**23 3922 5-8-11 46......................... PaoloSirigu 9 54
(Mick Quinn) *prom: rdn to chal but wnt lft 2f out: sustained effrt u.p fnl f: led fnl stride* **20/1**

0003 2 nse **Arch Walker (IRE)**9 4388 6-9-4 53.........................(b) JamieSpencer 2 61
(John Weymes) *taken down early: broke v fast and sn 3 l clr: pressed fr 2f out: hrd drvn fnl f: jst pipped* **7/2**3

6524 3 1 1/2 **Rambo Will**107 1452 5-9-10 59......................... HayleyTurner 5 62
(J R Jenkins) *prom chsng clr ldr: rdn 2f out: kpt on wout threatening ldng pair fnl f: uns rdr after fin* **3/1**2

300 4 1/2 **Depden (IRE)**31 3623 5-8-3 45......................... JoeyHaynes(7) 8 46
(Richard Price) *pressed ldrs: racing v awkwardly whn drvn over 2f out: kpt on but no ch w ldrs ins fnl f* **9/1**

3402 5 1 **Amis Reunis**9 4388 4-9-4 58.........................(p) PhilipPrince(5) 3 56
(Anthony Carson) *bhd and plenty to do: rdn 1/2-way: gd prog 2f out to chal for 3rd ins fnl f: no further imp fnl 75yds* **5/2**1

0600 6 2 **Whiskey Junction**21 3994 9-8-11 49......................... RossAtkinson(3) 7 41
(Mick Quinn) *chsd ldrs: drvn along bef 1/2-way: wl btn 2f out* **25/1**

065/ 7 7 **Edin Burgher (FR)**1247 682 12-8-5 45.........................(b1) TobyAtkinson(5) 4 14
(Michael Murphy) *missed break and immediately outpcd* **40/1**

000- 8 7 **Tracks Of My Tears**250 7777 3-7-12 45......................... IanBurns(7) 10
(Giles Bravery) *sn wl bhd: t.o fr 1/2-way* **28/1**

050- 9 3 **Fit For A King (IRE)**223 8108 3-8-10 50......................... FrederikTylicki 6
(John Best) *taken down early: chsd clr ldr tl 1/2-way: dropped out rapidly: t.o* **7/1**

1m 14.98s (0.58) **Going Correction** +0.10s/f (Good)
WFA 3 from 4yo+ 5lb **9 Ran SP% 112.8**
Speed ratings (Par 101): **100,99,97,97,95 93,83,74,70**
toteswingers 1&2 £8.70, 1&3 £13.00, 2&3 £2.90 CSF £84.08 CT £277.00 TOTE £36.50: £5.00, £1.10, £1.70; EX 114.70 Trifecta £1702.20 Pool: £2673.04 - 1.17 winning units..
Owner M Quinn **Bred** Henry And Mrs Rosemary Moszkowicz **Trained** Newmarket, Suffolk
■ The first winner in Britain for Italian jockey Paolo Sirigu.

FOCUS
A modest handicap.

4692 GO RACING IN NORFOLK H'CAP 2m
5:40 (5:40) (Class 5) (0-75,75) 4-Y-0+ **£2,587** (£770; £384; £192) **Stalls** High

Form RPR
0154 1 **Underwritten**9 4392 4-8-9 63.........................(b) JamieSpencer 5 70
(John Weymes) *sn led: sent 5 l clr home turn: in n.d after: rdn 2f out: heavily eased ins fnl f* **4/1**3

-042 2 8 **Outback (IRE)**9 4392 4-8-7 64.........................(p) SimonPearce(3) 2 60
(Neil King) *2nd tl 3rd and rdn 7f out: nvr nr ldr fnl 5f but drvn to plug into 2nd wl over 1f out: v flattered by proximity to wnr* **15/8**2

1/0- 3 1 1/2 **Ibn Hiyyan (USA)**205 7454 6-7-11 58 oh1 ow2......................... JoeyHaynes(7) 4 53
(Conor Dore) *wnt 2nd 6f out: rdn and struggling to keep up w wnr 4f out: gng v slowly in 3rd fr wl over 1f out* **17/2**

4351 4 18 **Mediterranean Sea (IRE)**28 3744 7-9-7 75......................... FrederikTylicki 1 48
(J R Jenkins) *hld up last: rdn to chal for 2nd 4f out: no imp after: eased over 1f out: t.o* **11/8**1

3m 34.44s (2.04) **Going Correction** +0.10s/f (Good) **4 Ran SP% 107.4**
Speed ratings (Par 103): **98,94,93,84**
CSF £11.57 TOTE £3.60; EX 8.30 Trifecta £27.00 Pool: £820.01 - 22.74 winning units..
Owner Thoroughbred Partners **Bred** W And R Barnett Ltd **Trained** Middleham Moor, N Yorks

FOCUS
A closely knit staying handicap on paper .but it was turned into a procession by the enterprisingly ridden winner.

T/Plt: £27.80 to a £1 stake. Pool: £54,588.18 - 1431.75 winning tickets T/Qpdt: £4.20 to a £1 stake. Pool: £4873.53 - 849.39 winning tickets IM

4460 LEOPARDSTOWN (L-H)
Thursday, July 25

OFFICIAL GOING: Good to firm changing to good (good to yielding last 2 furlongs) after race 1 (5.45) changing to yielding (soft last 2 furlongs) after race 4 (7.20)

4694a KOREAN RACING AUTHORITY TYROS STKS (GROUP 3) 7f
6:15 (6:16) 2-Y-0 **£31,707** (£9,268; £4,390; £1,463)

RPR
1 **Exogenesis (IRE)**21 3999 2-9-3......................... GaryCarroll 5 106
(G M Lyons, Ire) *trckd ldr in 2nd: 2 l bhd at 1/2-way: hdwy fr 1 1/2f out and clsd to chal ins fnl f: rdn to ld fnl 50yds and styd on wl* **11/8**2

2 1/2 **Home School (IRE)**5 4547 2-9-3 94.........................(t) KevinManning 6 104
(J S Bolger, Ire) *attempted to make all: 2 l clr 1/2-way: pushed along fr 2f out and reduced advantage u.p ent fnl f: sn chal and hdd fnl 50yds: no ex* **8/1**3

3 1 1/4 **Sir John Hawkins (USA)**14 4212 2-9-3.........................(b1) JosephO'Brien 1 101
(A P O'Brien, Ire) *chsd ldrs in 3rd: hdwy on outer gng wl fr 2f out: sn rdn and no imp on ldrs u.p ins fnl f: kpt on same pce wout threatening principals* **11/10**1

4 2 1/2 **Simple Love (USA)**7 4462 2-9-0......................... PatSmullen 3 91
(D K Weld, Ire) *hld up in tch: 4th 1/2-way: niggled along under 3f out: sn rdn and no imp on ldrs: kpt on same pce* **9/1**

D 9 1/2 **Gone Viral (IRE)**41 3304 2-9-3......................... RoryCleary 2 68
(Ms Sheila Lavery, Ire) *dwlt and racd in rr: rdn over 2f out and no imp: wknd: fin 5th: disq* **66/1**

1m 30.5s (1.80) **Going Correction** -0.075s/f (Good) **5 Ran SP% 112.3**
Speed ratings: **86,85,84,81,81**
CSF £12.44 TOTE £2.00: £1.02, £3.40; DF 8.80.
Owner Sean Jones **Bred** Mrs Jacqueline Donnelly **Trained** Dunsany, Co. Meath
■ Stewards' Enquiry : Rory Cleary sever caution: failed to weigh-in.

FOCUS
The front-running runner-up puts a slight question mark on the form, but the average ratings for the race suggest it's at least this good.

4696a JOCKEY CLUB OF TURKEY MELD STKS (GROUP 3) 1m 1f
7:20 (7:20) 3-Y-0+ **£31,707** (£9,268; £4,390; £1,463)

RPR
1 **Scintillula (IRE)**5 4550 3-8-11 112.........................(t) KevinManning 2 113+
(J S Bolger, Ire) *disp early: sn led: over 1 l clr 1/2-way: pushed along into st and sn strly pressed: rdn and styd on best ins fnl f: gng away at fin* **6/1**3

2 2 3/4 **Mars (IRE)**19 4082 3-9-0 118......................... JosephO'Brien 5 110
(A P O'Brien, Ire) *disp early: sn settled bhd ldr in 2nd: hdwy to chal 1 1/2f out: rdn and sn no imp on wnr ins fnl f: kpt on same pce* **8/11**1

3 3 1/4 **Along Came Casey (IRE)**22 3964 5-9-6 109......................... PatSmullen 3 101
(D K Weld, Ire) *hld up in tch: 5th 1/2-way: wnt 3rd into st: sn rdn and no imp on ldrs: kpt on same pce* **7/2**2

4 6 **Sweet Lightning**36 3458 8-9-9 108.........................(t) JohnnyMurtagh 6 93
(J P Murtagh, Ire) *hld up towards rr: 6th 1/2-way: prog 3f out and wnt 4th 2f out: sn no ex: kpt on same pce ins fnl f* **16/1**

5 2 **Elleval (IRE)**26 3844 3-9-0 107......................... FMBerry 1 87
(David Marnane, Ire) *dwlt and racd in rr: sme hdwy over 2f out into mod 5th: kpt on same pce ins fnl f* **16/1**

6 9 **La Collina (IRE)**25 3870 4-9-6 108......................... ChrisHayes 4 66
(Kevin Prendergast, Ire) *chsd ldrs: cl 4th 1/2-way: pushed along appr st and sn rdn in mod 5th: wknd over 1f out* **16/1**

7 32 **Dane Street (USA)**7 4465 4-9-6 95.........................(p) RonanWhelan 7
(Mrs John Harrington, Ire) *chsd ldrs: cl 3rd 1/2-way: pushed along over 3f out: sn wknd: eased fnl f* **40/1**

1m 52.64s (-1.46) **Going Correction** +0.125s/f (Good)
WFA 3 from 4yo+ 9lb **7 Ran SP% 114.5**
Speed ratings: **111,108,105,100,98 90,62**
CSF £10.83 TOTE £6.20: £3.30, £1.10; DF 15.80.
Owner Miss K Rausing & Mrs J S Bolger **Bred** J S Bolger **Trained** Coolcullen, Co Carlow

FOCUS
Having run a big race in the previous Saturday's Irish Oaks, it was a brave enough decision to bring Scintillula here but she repaid it handsomely. The first three held those positions throughout. It has been rated in line with the top end of the averages for the race.

4695 - 4699a (Foreign Racing) - See Raceform Interactive

4274 CHANTILLY (R-H)
Thursday, July 25

OFFICIAL GOING: Turf: good

4700a PRIX DE BAGATELLE (LISTED RACE) (3YO FILLIES) (TURF) 1m
1:20 (12:00) 3-Y-0 **£22,357** (£8,943; £6,707; £4,471; £2,235)

RPR
1 **Siyenica (FR)**34 3524 3-8-11 0......................... Christophe-PatriceLemaire 6 109
(A De Royer-Dupre, France) **1/1**1

2 2 1/2 **Nuit D'Amour (FR)**326 3-8-11 0......................... MaximeGuyon 2 103
(Mme Pia Brandt, France) **48/10**3

3 5 **Her Star (USA)**51 2970 3-8-11 0......................... StephanePasquier 5 92
(P Bary, France) **14/1**

4 shd **More Than Sotka (FR)**123 1166 3-8-11 0......................... AntoineHamelin 3 92
(Matthieu Palussiere, France) **29/1**

5 1 1/4 **Flawless Beauty**36 3460 3-8-11 0.........................(b) ThierryJarnet 7 89
(Hugo Palmer) *prom on outer: smooth hdwy to chal over 2f out: sn rdn: w ldrs and ev ch 1 1/2f out: no ex ent fnl f: fdd and dropped to 5th* **35/1**

6 1 3/4 **Shahad (IRE)**53 2905 3-8-11 0......................... OlivierPeslier 9 85
(F Head, France) **11/1**

7 snk **Bayargal (USA)**28 3-8-11 0......................... Pierre-CharlesBoudot 8 84
(A Fabre, France) **4/1**2

8 15 **Grand Treasure (IRE)**53 3-9-2 0......................... UmbertoRispoli 4 55
(G Colella, Italy) **10/1**

9 6 **Shenliyka (FR)**13 3-8-11 0......................... NJeanpierre 1 36
(A De Royer-Dupre, France) **50/1**

1m 36.82s (-1.18) **9 Ran SP% 119.4**
WIN (incl. 1 euro stake): 2.00. PLACES: 1.40, 1.70, 2.60. DF: 6.30. SF: 7.70.
Owner H H Aga Khan **Bred** Haras De Son Altesse L' Aga Khan Scea **Trained** Chantilly, France

The Form Book Flat, Raceform Ltd, Compton, RG20 6NL.

4701 - (Foreign Racing) - See Raceform Interactive

4275 ASCOT (R-H)

Friday, July 26

OFFICIAL GOING: Good (stands' side 8.0, centre 7.9, far side 8.2, round 7.7)

Wind: Almost nil Weather: Fine but cloudy, warm

4702 JOHN GUEST EBF MAIDEN FILLIES' STKS — 7f

2:00 (2:00) (Class 4) 2-Y-O — **£6,469** (£1,925; £962; £481) **Stalls** Centre

Form — RPR

1 **Lilyfire (USA)** 2-9-0 0 ..... JamesDoyle 6 — 79+
(Roger Charlton) *trckd ldrs: pushed along over 2f out: rdn and clsd over 1f out: gd burst to ld last 100yds: styd on* — **8/1**

2 ½ **Psychometry (FR)** 2-9-0 0 ..... RyanMoore 14 — 80+
(Sir Michael Stoute) *settled in last quartet: pushed along over 2f out: prog whn nt clr run and swtchd lft over 1f out: gd hdwy fnl f: tk 2nd and pressed wnr last 75yds* — **9/2**[1]

3 ½ **Gratzie** 2-8-11 0 ..... CharlesBishop(3) 5 — 76
(Mick Channon) *hld up in midfield: prog on far side of gp over 2f out: clsd on ldrs over 1f out: rdn to ld briefly ins fnl f: outpcd after* — **100/1**

4 nse **Tea In Transvaal (IRE)** 2-9-0 0 ..... RichardHughes 11 — 76
(Richard Hannon) *hld up towards rr: stdy prog fr 3f out: trckd ldrs over 1f out: swtchd lft sn after: r.o but outpcd by ldng pair last 100yds* — **12/1**

5 1 **Crowley's Law** 2-9-0 0 ..... MartinDwyer 7 — 75
(Tom Dascombe) *slowly away: plld hrd early and hld up wl in rr: prog on far side of gp over 2f out: n.m.r against rail over 1f out and swtchd lft: styd on fnl f* — **14/1**

6 ½ **Lovelocks (IRE)** 2-9-0 0 ..... SteveDrowne 15 — 72+
(Charles Hills) *s.s: in last quartet tl prog over 2f out: clsng whn nt clr run ins fnl f: swtchd and styd on wl nr fin* — **25/1**

0 **7** ¾ **Raajis (IRE)**[22] 3986 2-9-0 0 ..... PaulHanagan 2 — 70
(Richard Hannon) *mde most: rdn over 1f out: hdd & wknd ins fnl f* — **7/1**

8 nse **Lady Sparkler (IRE)** 2-9-0 0 ..... NeilCallan 3 — 70
(Roger Varian) *slowly away: sn wl plcd bhd ldrs: wnt 2nd over 1f out: upsides ins fnl f: wknd last 100yds* — **33/1**

9 shd **Bright Cecily (IRE)** 2-9-0 0 ..... AdamKirby 13 — 70
(Clive Cox) *mostly in midfield: pushed along fr 3f out: styd on same pce fnl 2f: nvr able to chal* — **25/1**

10 shd **Likelihood (USA)** 2-9-0 0 ..... RobertHavlin 18 — 69
(John Gosden) *towards rr: pushed along bef 1/2-way: rdn and kpt on fnl 2f: nvr gng pce to threaten* — **6/1**[3]

11 1¼ **Mutatis Mutandis (IRE)** 2-9-0 0 ..... [1] TomMcLaughlin 9 — 66
(Ed Walker) *hld up in midfield: pushed along fr 1/2-way: struggling over 2f out: tried to rally over 1f out: no prog after* — **40/1**

3 **12** 1¼ **Full Day**[21] 4026 2-9-0 0 ..... DavidProbert 16 — 63
(Ralph Beckett) *chsd ldrs: rdn 1/2-way: sn struggling: steadily wknd over 2f out* — **5/1**[2]

13 nk **Mollasses** 2-9-0 0 ..... [1] RichardKingscote 17 — 62
(Jonathan Portman) *sn in last pair and rn green: nvr a factor but styd on ins fnl f* — **66/1**

6 **14** 1¼ **Palace Princess (FR)**[23] 3958 2-9-0 0 ..... SebSanders 10 — 58
(Ed Dunlop) *trckd ldrs to 2f out: wknd after* — **33/1**

15 1 **Stealth Missile (IRE)** 2-9-0 0 ..... BrettDoyle 4 — 56
(Clive Brittain) *pressed ldr to over 1f out: wknd qckly* — **40/1**

2 **16** 1¼ **Heartstrings**[22] 3986 2-9-0 0 ..... SamHitchcott 8 — 52
(Mick Channon) *chsd ldrs: rdn 3f out: lost pl fr over 2f out: no ch whn no room 1f out* — **7/1**

17 1½ **Placidia (IRE)** 2-9-0 0 ..... TedDurcan 1 — 48+
(David Lanigan) *slowly away: rn green and a wl in rr* — **25/1**

18 13 **Division Belle** 2-9-0 0 ..... JoeFanning 12 — 13
(William Muir) *nvr beyond midfield: wknd rapidly over 2f out: t.o* — **100/1**

1m 29.37s (1.77) **Going Correction** +0.10s/f (Good) — **18 Ran SP% 125.4**

Speed ratings (Par 93): **93,92,91,91,90 90,89,89,89,88 87,86,85,84,83 81,80,65**

toteswingers 1&2 £10.70, 1&3 £150.70, 2&3 £83.00 CSF £41.04 TOTE £10.40: £3.50, £2.20, £14.70; EX 75.40 Trifecta £2294.60 Part won. Pool: £3059.51 - 0.39 winning units..

Owner K Abdullah **Bred** Juddmonte Farms Inc **Trained** Beckhampton, Wilts

FOCUS

The jockeys reckoned the ground was riding as advertised, rather than anything faster. A big field for this maiden, which was run at a solid pace. They bunched down the centre before drifting over to the far side with a couple of furlongs left. Only four of these fillies had run previously, and it was the newcomers who dominated. It's a race that's sure to produce winners, although there was a blanket finish and the bare form can't be rated much higher.

4703 HOUGHTON STONE NURSERY H'CAP — 6f

2:35 (2:36) (Class 4) 2-Y-O — **£6,469** (£1,925; £962; £481) **Stalls** Centre

Form — RPR

013 **1** **Stormy Paradise (IRE)**[21] 4031 2-9-7 **83** ..... RyanMoore 2 — 86
(Brian Meehan) *hld up in last trio: prog on far side of gp over 2f out: rdn to ld over 1f out: styd on wl* — **9/2**[3]

21 **2** ½ **Banaadeer (IRE)**[27] 3815 2-9-2 **78** ..... PaulHanagan 6 — 80
(Richard Hannon) *bmpd s: cl up: trckd ldr jst over 2f out: rdn to chal over 1f out: pressed wnr fnl f: nt qckn* — **6/4**[1]

2150 **3** ½ **Far Gaze (IRE)**[55] 2863 2-9-4 **80** ..... LiamJones 3 — 80
(J S Moore) *hld up in last: prog over 2f out: drvn and cl enough over 1f out: styd on same pce* — **40/1**

321 **4** ½ **Rizal Park (IRE)**[27] 3836 2-8-13 **78** ..... ThomasBrown(3) 1 — 76
(Andrew Balding) *chsd ldr to jst over 2f out: sn rdn: styd on again fnl f: nvr able to chal* — **5/1**

2123 **5** nk **Mr Matthews (IRE)**[13] 4314 2-9-6 **82** ..... (p) AdamKirby 7 — 81
(Mrs K Burke) *wnt rt s and bmpd rival: hld up in last trio: rdn over 1f out: styng on u.p and may have fin 3rd whn veered sharply lft last 50yds* — **3/1**[2]

0464 **6** 1¼ **Handwoven (IRE)**[14] 4232 2-8-6 **68** ..... JoeFanning 5 — 61
(Mark Johnston) *led to over 1f out: steadily fdd* — **10/1**

005 **7** ½ **Caledonia Laird**[25] 3883 2-8-6 **68** ..... KieranO'Neill 4 — 60
(Jo Hughes) *plld hrd early: trckd ldrs to over 2f out: sn lost pl and btn* — **33/1**

1m 15.23s (0.73) **Going Correction** +0.10s/f (Good) — **7 Ran SP% 114.3**

Speed ratings (Par 96): **99,98,97,97,96 94,94**

toteswingers 1&2 £2.30, 1&3 £12.60, 2&3 £8.30 CSF £11.69 TOTE £6.20: £3.00, £1.20; EX 15.80 Trifecta £228.40 Pool: £4,855.94 - 15.93 winning units..

Owner Decadent Racing **Bred** Rodger O'Dwyer **Trained** Manton, Wilts

FOCUS

A decent little nursery, but a compressed finish and it's hard to rate the form positively.

4704 JOHN GUEST BROWN JACK STKS (H'CAP) — 2m

3:10 (3:12) (Class 2) (0-100,93) 3-Y-O+ **£14,231** (£4,235; £2,116; £1,058) **Stalls** Low

Form — RPR

1352 **1** **Broxbourne (IRE)**[91] 1805 4-9-2 **81** ..... JoeFanning 1 — 91
(Mark Johnston) *trckd ldng pair: rdn over 3f out: wnt 2nd over 2f out: led over 1f out: clr fnl f: styd on wl* — **12/1**

-510 **2** 3½ **Homeric (IRE)**[38] 3423 4-9-11 **90** ..... RyanMoore 6 — 96
(Ed Dunlop) *hld up in 5th: clsd on ldrs over 2f out: rdn and nt qckn over 1f out: kpt on same pce to chse wnr fnl f: no imp* — **7/4**[1]

5104 **3** nk **Highland Castle**[20] 4060 5-10-0 **93** ..... LiamKeniry 2 — 99
(David Elsworth) *stdd s: t.k.h and sn in 4th: urged along over 2f out: rdn to chse ldng pair 2f out: nt qckn over 1f out: kpt on fnl f* — **11/2**[3]

-235 **4** 2¼ **Mysterious Man (IRE)**[38] 3423 4-9-9 **88** ..... DavidProbert 3 — 91
(Andrew Balding) *led: stdd pce after 6f: tried to kick on 6f out: hdd and fdd over 1f out* — **9/4**[2]

3100 **5** 5 **Desert Recluse (IRE)**[23] 3959 6-9-4 **83** ..... AdamKirby 5 — 80
(Pat Eddery) *chsd ldr to over 2f out: wknd over 1f out* — **20/1**

-602 **6** 2 **Mawaqeet (USA)**[13] 4313 4-9-11 **90** ..... (v) PaulHanagan 4 — 85
(Sir Michael Stoute) *stdd s: hld up in last: urged along and no rspnse 4f out: toiling after* — **11/2**[3]

3m 27.75s (-1.25) **Going Correction** -0.025s/f (Good) — **6 Ran SP% 110.4**

Speed ratings (Par 109): **102,100,100,98,96 95**

toteswingers 1&2 £3.60, 1&3 £4.50, 2&3 £2.50 CSF £32.45 TOTE £6.30: £2.50, £1.60; EX 18.30 Trifecta £123.90 Pool: £4690.65 - 28.37 winning units..

Owner Ready To Run Partnership **Bred** Mount Coote Stud And M Johnston **Trained** Middleham Moor, N Yorks

FOCUS

This good staying handicap was won by subsequent Cesarewitch winner Darley Sun in 2009, while Colour Vision was runner-up in 2011 before winning the Gold Cup the following year, but this didn't look the strongest edition. It was run at a bit of a stop-start gallop but the pace was a sound one for the final 6f or so. The form is taken at face value.

4705 WOODCOTE STUD EBF VALIANT STKS (LISTED RACE) (F&M) — 1m (R)

3:45 (3:46) (Class 1) 3-Y-O+

£22,684 (£8,600; £4,304; £2,144; £1,076; £540) **Stalls** Low

Form — RPR

1 **1** **Zibelina (IRE)**[28] 3774 3-8-7 0 ..... AhmedAjtebi 5 — 103
(Saeed bin Suroor) *t.k.h: trckd ldr in slowly run r: led wl over 1f out: sn jnd and u.p: styd on wl fnl f* — **14/1**

4543 **2** 1½ **Ultrasonic (USA)**[17] 4137 4-9-1 102 ..... RyanMoore 10 — 102
(Sir Michael Stoute) *trckd ldng trio: urged along and moved up to join wnr over 1f out: rdn and outbattled fnl f* — **5/2**[1]

26-0 **3** ½ **Winter's Night (IRE)**[37] 3458 5-9-1 97 ..... AdamKirby 6 — 101
(Clive Cox) *hld up in 5th in slowly run r: rdn and prog wl over 1f out: wnt 3rd ins fnl f: styd on but unable to chal* — **14/1**

-611 **4** 1½ **Annecdote**[37] 3460 3-8-11 97 ..... RichardKingscote 11 — 99
(Jonathan Portman) *hld up in 6th in slowly run r: rdn 2f out: pressed for a pl 1f out: one pce after* — **5/1**[3]

-120 **5** ½ **Westwiththenight (IRE)**[41] 3346 4-9-1 92 ..... JoeFanning 1 — 96
(William Haggas) *trckd ldng pair: shkn up and nt qckn over 1f out: one pce after* — **9/1**

0-46 **6** shd **Falls Of Lora (IRE)**[28] 3775 4-9-1 100 ..... MickaelBarzalona 8 — 96
(Saeed bin Suroor) *hld up in last pair in slowly run r: prog on outer jst over 2f out: drvn and one pce over 1f out* — **10/1**

3062 **7** nk **Sweetnessandlight**[8] 4433 4-9-1 92 ..... TedDurcan 7 — 95
(Jason Ward) *hld up in 7th in slowly run r: shkn up over 2f out: in last pair 1f out: styd on nr fin* — **100/1**

5630 **8** hd **Dark Orchid (USA)**[28] 3775 4-9-1 95 ..... [1] FrederikTylicki 9 — 95+
(Saeed bin Suroor) *hld up in last pair in slowly run r: looking for room on inner 2f out: stl same pl 1f out: r.o nr fin: no ch* — **40/1**

1124 **9** 1¾ **Auction (IRE)**[20] 4081 3-8-7 99 ..... PaulHanagan 3 — 89+
(Ed Dunlop) *s.s: mostly in last trio in slowly run r: rdn 2f out: no prog and btn over 1f out* — **7/2**[2]

-062 **10** 2¼ **Light Up My Life (IRE)**[20] 4081 3-8-7 99 ..... (p) RichardHughes 4 — 84
(Richard Hannon) *led at mod pce: tried to kick on over 2f out: hdd over 1f out: wknd qckly fnl f: eased* — **11/2**

1m 39.67s (-1.03) **Going Correction** -0.025s/f (Good)

WFA 3 from 4yo+ 8lb — **10 Ran SP% 118.7**

Speed ratings (Par 111): **104,102,102,100,100 99,99,99,97,95**

toteswingers 1&2 £6.50, 1&3 £15.10, 2&3 £8.50 CSF £50.03 TOTE £12.70: £2.90, £1.60, £3.60; EX 51.90 Trifecta £705.80 Pool: £8637.52 - 9.17 winning units..

Owner Godolphin **Bred** Darley **Trained** Newmarket, Suffolk

FOCUS

This decent Listed race was spoiled considerably by a very steady gallop, meaning the race boiled down to a sprint. There's no doubting the winner's potential though. The level is set around the third to fifth.

4706 NEWSMITH OCTOBER CLUB CHARITY H'CAP — 1m 2f

4:20 (4:20) (Class 2) (0-100,97) 3-Y-O+ **£12,450** (£3,728; £1,864; £932) **Stalls** Low

Form — RPR

2112 **1** **Sennockian Star**[6] 4537 3-9-4 **91** 6ex ..... (v) JoeFanning 4 — 106
(Mark Johnston) *trckd ldr: rdn 2f out: clsd to ld jst over 1f out: forged clr* — **10/11**[1]

521 **2** 3½ **Vasily**[7] 4501 5-10-1 **97** 6ex ..... RobertTart(5) 2 — 105
(Robert Eddery) *led: had rest off the bridle 2f out: rdn over 1f out: sn hdd and one pce* — **4/1**[3]

11-4 **3** 5 **Viewpoint (IRE)**[27] 3832 4-10-0 **91** ..... RichardHughes 3 — 89
(Richard Hannon) *hld up bhd ldng pair: rdn and cl enough 2f out: disp 2nd jst ins fnl f: wknd and eased last 100yds* — **5/2**[2]

4132 **4** 99 **Tenure**[94] 1753 4-8-10 **73** ..... MickaelBarzalona 1
(Amy Weaver) *trckd ldng pair: rdn and lost tch 1/2-way: t.o and virtually p.u fnl 2f* — **14/1**

2m 5.06s (-2.34) **Going Correction** -0.025s/f (Good)

WFA 3 from 4yo+ 10lb — **4 Ran SP% 107.6**

Speed ratings (Par 109): **108,105,101,22**

CSF £4.79 TOTE £1.70; EX 5.20 Trifecta £9.90 Pool: £2923.00 - 220.25 winning units..

Owner The Vine Accord **Bred** Cheveley Park Stud Ltd **Trained** Middleham Moor, N Yorks

FOCUS
Just a small field for this fairly valuable handicap, but an interesting race nevertheless, run at a sound pace. The weights were raised 8lb. The winner may not have finished yet, and the runner-up rates a personal best for his good claimer.

4707 JOHN GUEST H'CAP — 5f
4:50 (4:51) (Class 4) (0-85,85) 3-Y-0+ — **£5,175** (£1,540; £769; £384) **Stalls** Centre

Form — RPR

1062 **1** **Gabbiano**[14] 4235 4-9-5 **85** .... RobertTart(5) 10 — 96
(Jeremy Gask) *hld up in rr: prog over 2f out: rdn to press ldrs over 1f out: r.o to ld last 75yds: hld on* **5/2**[1]

3020 **2** *shd* **Gladiatrix**[21] 4024 4-9-5 **85** .... MichaelJMMurphy(5) 6 — 96
(Rod Millman) *pressed ldrs: rdn over 1f out: chal ins fnl f: r.o: jst hld last strides* **5/1**[2]

4053 **3** *hd* **Best Be Careful (IRE)**[10] 4364 5-7-12 **66** oh4 .... JoeyHaynes(7) 9 — 76
(Mark Usher) *pressed ldrs: drvn to ld narrowly 1f out: edgd rt u.p: hdd last 75yds* **14/1**

1040 **4** *1 1/2* **Diamond Charlie (IRE)**[50] 3018 5-9-8 **83** .... MickaelBarzalona 12 — 88
(Simon Dow) *hld up in rr: gng strly but plenty to do 2f out: drvn over 1f out: styd on to take 4th nr fin: no ch to threaten* **8/1**[3]

2020 **5** *1* **Rylee Mooch**[21] 4024 5-9-5 **80** ....(e) MartinDwyer 8 — 85
(Richard Guest) *mde most: drvn and hdd 1f out: cl 4th but hld whn squeezed out 100yds out* **8/1**[3]

6252 **6** *2 1/4* **Whitecrest**[10] 4364 5-9-4 **79** .... AdamKirby 11 — 72
(John Spearing) *chsd ldrs: rdn and no imp 2f out: outpcd over 1f out: one pce after* **10/1**

1313 **7** *1 1/2* **Langley Vale**[15] 4210 4-9-2 **77** .... RichardMullen 1 — 64
(Roger Teal) *taken down early: pressed ldrs on far side of gp: wknd over 1f out* **5/1**[2]

2051 **8** *1 1/2* **Irish Boy (IRE)**[8] 4430 5-8-2 **66** oh2 ....(tp) RaulDaSilva(3) 13 — 48
(Christine Dunnett) *taken down early: a in rr: rdn and no prog wl over 1f out* **12/1**

4130 **9** *3/4* **Where's Reiley (USA)**[15] 4210 7-8-5 **66** ....(v) LiamJones 4 — 45
(Michael Attwater) *pressed ldr to 2f out: sn lost pl and btn* **25/1**

6040 **10** *1* **Lujeanie**[84] 1984 7-8-9 **70** .... ShaneKelly 7 — 46
(Peter Crate) *stdd s: t.k.h and hld up in last: pushed along and no prog over 1f out* **25/1**

-435 **11** *3* **Overrider**[133] 1008 3-8-7 **72** ....(t) JamieMackay 2 — 37
(Alastair Lidderdale) *dwlt: t.k.h and sn in tch: lost pl rapidly and detached in last over 1f out* **40/1**

465 **12** *1 1/4* **Rowe Park**[50] 3018 10-9-7 **82** ....(p) SaleemGolam 3 — 42
(Linda Jewell) *pressed ldrs: drvn and sing to lose pl whn squeezed out over 1f out: wknd* **16/1**

1m 0.23s (-0.27) **Going Correction** +0.10s/f (Good)
WFA 3 from 4yo+ 4lb — **12** Ran SP% **123.6**
Speed ratings (Par 105): **106,105,105,103,101 97,95,93,91,90 85,83**
toteswingers 1&2 £4.80, 1&3 £12.00, 2&3 £14.10 CSF £14.74 CT £153.45 TOTE £3.20: £1.70, £2.30, £3.90; EX 14.90 Trifecta £189.10 Pool: £6047.19 - 23.98 winning units..
Owner Tony Bloom **Bred** Mrs R J Gallagher **Trained** Sutton Veny, Wilts
■ Stewards' Enquiry : Joey Haynes two-day ban: careless riding (Aug 9-10)

FOCUS
An ordinary handicap with a tight finish, the principals ending up towards the far side. The winner progress again.
T/Plt: £41.10 to a £1 stake. Pool: £112206.76 - 1989.23 winning tickets T/Qpdt: £9.70 to a £1 stake. Pool: £8101.02 - 617.29 winning tickets JN

4238 CHEPSTOW (L-H)
Friday, July 26

OFFICIAL GOING: Good to firm (watered; 7.9)
Wind: fresh beeze Weather: sunny

4708 SOUTH WALES ARGUS MAIDEN AUCTION STKS — 6f 16y
5:45 (5:46) (Class 5) 2-Y-0 — **£2,587** (£770; £384; £192) **Stalls** Centre

Form — RPR

06 **1** **Threetimesalady**[9] 4408 2-8-6 0 .... RosieJessop(5) 6 — 72+
(Sir Mark Prescott Bt) *s.i.s: bhd: hdwy fr 3f out: rdn to ld jst ins fnl f: sn edgd lft: kpt on* **16/1**

0 **2** *nk* **Concrete Mac**[11] 4347 2-8-6 0 .... CharlieBennett(7) 2 — 71
(Hughie Morrison) *chsd ldrs: rdn over 2f out: ev ch whn drifted rt fnl 120yds: kpt on* **50/1**

3 **3** *3/4* **Yajamila**[30] 3673 2-8-11 0 .... SeanLevey 4 — 66
(James Tate) *chsd ldrs: rdn 2f out: r.o to chal whn carried rt fnl 120yds: hld nring fin* **25/1**

6 **4** *1* **Castagna Girl**[31] 3663 2-8-4 0 .... CathyGannon 1 — 56
(Denis Coakley) *trckd ldrs: rdn 2f out: kpt on same pce fnl f* **9/4**[2]

6 **5** *3/4* **Rosita**[20] 4073 2-7-13 0 ....(b[1]) AmyScott(5) 9 — 54
(Henry Candy) *wnt to s early: led: rdn wl over 1f out: edgd lft and hdd jst ins fnl f: fdd* **7/1**

2 **6** *4 1/2* **Krackerjill (IRE)**[16] 4175 2-8-4 0 .... JohnFahy 3 — 39
(Mark Usher) *towards rr: sme late prog: nvr trbld ldrs* **5/1**[3]

6 **7** *11* **Lambeth Palace**[30] 3695 2-8-13 0 .... WilliamCarson 5 — 13
(Ronald Harris) *towards rr: squeezed up over 2f out: sn rdn: wknd over 1f out* **66/1**

3534 **8** *shd* **Seaham**[30] 3689 2-8-11 0 .... PatCosgrave 10 — 11
(Rod Millman) *s.i.s: towards rr: rdn wl over 2f out: no imp: wknd over 1f out* **2/1**[1]

9 *1/2* **Solicitation (IRE)** 2-8-9 0 .... RichardThomas 7 — 7
(Ralph Beckett) *chsd ldrs: rdn wl over 2f out: sn btn* **10/1**

1m 11.92s (-0.08) **Going Correction** -0.10s/f (Good) — **9** Ran SP% **115.5**
Speed ratings (Par 94): **96,95,94,93,92 86,71,71,70**
toteswingers 1&2 £15.90, 1&3 £14.90, 2&3 £22.70 CSF £590.97 TOTE £16.80: £4.30, £15.00, £4.20; EX 354.10 Trifecta £780.80 Part won. Pool: £1,041.15 - 0.70 winning units..
Owner Bluehills Racing Limited **Bred** Bluehills Racing Limited **Trained** Newmarket, Suffolk
■ Stewards' Enquiry : Charlie Bennett caution: careless riding.

FOCUS
They went a fast pace in this maiden and three big-priced runners filled the first three places. Tricky form to rate. The winner will be interesting for nurseries.

4709 FESTIVAL RACING FILLIES' H'CAP — 7f 16y
6:20 (6:20) (Class 5) (0-70,70) 3-Y-0+ — **£2,587** (£770; £384; £192) **Stalls** Centre

Form — RPR

0-12 **1** **Lunette (IRE)**[10] 4385 3-9-7 **70** .... RichardThomas 1 — 75
(Ralph Beckett) *led for 3f: prom: rdn for persistent chal fr 2f out: kpt on to ld fnl 50yds* **5/4**[1]

036 **2** *shd* **Tooley Woods (IRE)**[24] 3922 4-8-11 **53** .... CathyGannon 3 — 61
(Tony Carroll) *prom: led after 3f: rdn whn strly pressed fr 2f out: hdd fnl 50yds: kpt on* **9/2**[3]

4-20 **3** *2 1/4* **Cape Crossing**[183] 347 4-8-10 **52** ....(t) LiamKeniry 2 — 54
(Andrew Balding) *t.k.h: trckd ldrs: rdn 2f out: kpt on same pce ins fnl f* **10/1**

0506 **4** *1/2* **Dancing Welcome**[17] 4148 7-8-9 **51** oh1 ....(bt) JohnFahy 5 — 52
(Milton Bradley) *trckd ldrs: rdn 2f out: kpt on fnl 120yds: wnt 4th nring fin* **20/1**

4323 **5** *nk* **Hoppy's Flyer (FR)**[14] 4245 5-9-4 **60** .... RussKennemore 7 — 60
(Mark Brisbourne) *cl up: rdn over 2f out: kpt on same pce fnl f* **10/3**[2]

4215 **6** *19* **Celestial Bay**[22] 3988 4-9-13 **69** .... SeanLevey 6 — 17
(Sylvester Kirk) *cl up: rdn 3f out: wknd 2f out* **7/1**

1m 22.45s (-0.75) **Going Correction** -0.10s/f (Good)
WFA 3 from 4yo+ 7lb — **6** Ran SP% **112.1**
Speed ratings (Par 100): **100,99,97,96,96 74**
toteswingers 1&2 £2.10, 1&3 £2.60, 2&3 £4.20 CSF £7.22 TOTE £2.00: £1.20, £1.40; EX 6.60 Trifecta £34.60 Pool: £686.20 - 14.87 winning units..
Owner T D Rootes & O F Waller **Bred** Shutford Stud And O F Waller **Trained** Kimpton, Hants

FOCUS
The favourite battled well to deliver in this minor fillies' handicap. They raced near the stands' rail and the first two were always prominent. The winner should do a bit better yet.

4710 ADVANCED POWER SOLUTIONS H'CAP — 7f 16y
6:50 (6:50) (Class 5) (0-75,74) 3-Y-0 — **£2,587** (£770; £384; £192) **Stalls** Centre

Form — RPR

6645 **1** **Countryman**[42] 3279 3-8-10 **70** .... CharlieBennett(7) 2 — 78+
(Hughie Morrison) *trckd ldrs: led 2f out: sn rdn: idling ent fnl f: fnd more whn chal fnl 120yds: hld on wl* **7/4**[2]

0-23 **2** *nk* **Secret Beau**[28] 3782 3-9-7 **74** .... RichardKingscote 5 — 78
(Ralph Beckett) *set decent pce: rdn whn hdd 2f out: edgd lft over 1f out: rallied to chal ins fnl f: kpt on but hld nring fin* **6/4**[1]

2506 **3** *2 1/4* **Gabrial The Boss (USA)**[28] 3758 3-8-12 **65** .... WilliamCarson 1 — 63
(David Simcock) *s.i.s: sn outpcd in last: hdwy 3f out: chal for 2nd briefly jst ins fnl f: no ex fnl 120yds* **12/1**

3150 **4** *shd* **Indian Affair**[11] 4354 3-8-13 **73** .... WillPettis(7) 6 — 71
(Milton Bradley) *w ldr tl rdn over 2f out: chsd ldrs: kpt on ins fnl f: nrly snatched 3rd fnl stride* **9/1**

-040 **5** *1 1/4* **Danz Choice (IRE)**[35] 3537 3-9-5 **72** .... SeanLevey 4 — 66
(Richard Hannon) *s.i.s: in last pair: hdwy over 3f out: sn rdn to chse ldrs: fdd fnl 120yds* **9/2**[3]

1m 21.67s (-1.53) **Going Correction** -0.10s/f (Good) — **5** Ran SP% **112.2**
Speed ratings (Par 100): **104,103,101,100,99**
CSF £4.90 TOTE £3.80: £1.80, £1.20; EX 5.40 Trifecta £37.20 Pool: £561.87 - 11.32 winning units..
Owner H Scott-Barrett, S de Zoete & A Pickford **Bred** P And Mrs A G Venner **Trained** East Ilsley, Berks

FOCUS
The two market leaders filled the first two places in this fair handicap, which was run at a good pace. The race lacked improvers and the winner is rated to form.

4711 FREE BETS FREEBETS.CO.UK H'CAP — 1m 14y
7:20 (7:20) (Class 5) (0-70,70) 3-Y-0+ — **£2,587** (£770; £384; £192) **Stalls** Centre

Form — RPR

4013 **1** **Mandy The Nag (USA)**[10] 4383 3-9-4 **68** .... AidanColeman 5 — 78+
(Ian Williams) *mde all: jnd over 3f out tl shkn up wl over 1f out: clr ent fnl f: readily* **11/4**[2]

3555 **2** *2 1/4* **Peak Storm**[14] 4241 4-9-7 **66** .... ThomasBrown(3) 4 — 71
(John O'Shea) *cl up: rdn over 2f out: kpt on but nt pce to chal: wnt 2nd jst ins fnl f but a being comf hld by wnr* **4/1**[3]

3223 **3** *1/2* **Offbeat Safaris (IRE)**[3] 4604 5-9-2 **58** .... WilliamCarson 6 — 62
(Ronald Harris) *trckd wnr: jnd wnr over 3f out: rdn over 2f out: hld over 1f out: no ex whn lost 2nd jst ins fnl f* **7/4**[1]

0-04 **4** *1* **Another Squeeze**[14] 4241 5-8-9 **51** oh3 ....[1] CathyGannon 8 — 53
(Peter Hiatt) *trckd ldrs: rdn over 2f out: kpt on same pce* **8/1**

6/00 **5** *5* **Ernest Speak (IRE)**[85] 1951 4-8-9 **51** oh6 .... SeanLevey 7 — 41
(David Evans) *little slowly away: sn rcvrd to trck ldrs: racd keenly: rdn over 2f out: wknd ins fnl f* **33/1**

5653 **6** *6* **Ogaritmo**[11] 4350 4-9-3 **59** ....(p) PatCosgrave 2 — 35
(Alastair Lidderdale) *last but wl in tch: tk clsr order 3f out: rdn over 2f out: wknd over 1f out* **7/1**

1m 34.72s (-1.48) **Going Correction** -0.10s/f (Good)
WFA 3 from 4yo+ 8lb — **6** Ran SP% **109.6**
Speed ratings (Par 103): **103,100,100,99,94 88**
toteswingers 1&2 £3.60, 1&3 £1.80, 2&3 £1.70 CSF £13.31 CT £20.98 TOTE £3.90: £1.50, £2.70; EX 16.60 Trifecta £30.70 Pool: £401.44 - 9.80 winning units..
Owner Dr Marwan Koukash **Bred** Randal Family Trust Et Al **Trained** Portway, Worcs

FOCUS
They went a steady pace in this handicap and the winner scored with plenty in hand under a front-running ride. Modest and muddling form.

4712 REID LIFTING H'CAP — 5f 16y
7:50 (7:50) (Class 5) (0-70,68) 3-Y-0+ — **£2,587** (£770; £384; £192) **Stalls** Centre

Form — RPR

4222 **1** **Lager Time (IRE)**[3] 4608 3-8-13 **66** .... EoinWalsh(7) 2 — 74
(David Evans) *a.p: qcknd to ld wl over 1f out: rdn ent fnl f: jst hld on* **5/4**[1]

-200 **2** *shd* **Baby Queen (IRE)**[20] 4074 7-9-5 **66** .... MatthewLawson(5) 6 — 74
(Brian Baugh) *trckd ldrs: rdn 2f out: str run ins fnl f: jst failed* **16/1**

0244 **3** *1 1/4* **Belle Bayardo (IRE)**[8] 4428 5-9-12 **68** .... WilliamCarson 1 — 72
(Ronald Harris) *towards rr: rdn 2f out: hdwy over 1f out: r.o ins fnl f: wnt 3rd towards fin* **4/1**[2]

6-06 **4** *nk* **Mandy Lexi (IRE)**[24] 3920 3-8-13 **59** .... RichardKingscote 5 — 60
(Ian Williams) *led: rdn over 2f out: hdd wl over 1f out: kpt chsng wnr tl jst ins fnl f: no ex whn lost 3rd towards fin* **8/1**

6056 **5** *2 1/4* **Alpha Delta Whisky**[15] 4197 5-9-7 **68** .... MichaelJMMurphy(5) 9 — 62
(John Gallagher) *trckd ldrs: rdn 2f out: hung lft fr over 1f out: one pce fnl f* **8/1**

4655 **6** *hd* **Jarrow (IRE)**[15] 4220 6-9-5 **68** ....(p) WillPettis(7) 3 — 62
(Milton Bradley) *in tch: effrt 2f out: one pce fnl f* **9/1**

0032 **7** *2* **Stonecrabstomorrow (IRE)**[8] 4428 10-9-3 **62** .... MarkCoumbe(3) 4 — 48
(Roy Brotherton) *s.i.s: sn outpcd in last pair: hdwy 3f out: wknd ent fnl f* **7/1**[3]

0000 8 7 **Memphis Man**[32] 3623 10-8-7 **49** oh1 ....(p) CathyGannon 8 10
(Milton Bradley) *hmpd s: sn outpcd in rr: nvr any danger* **25/1**

58.76s (-0.54) **Going Correction** -0.10s/f (Good)
WFA 3 from 4yo+ 4lb 8 Ran SP% **118.9**
Speed ratings (Par 103): **100,99,97,97,93 93,90,79**
toteswingers 1&2 £6.10, 1&3 £2.00, 2&3 £15.80 CSF £26.09 CT £69.64 TOTE £2.30: £1.10, £3.30, £1.90; EX 35.70 Trifecta £99.20 Pool: £605.05 - 4.57 winning units..
Owner Mrs E Evans & C W Racing **Bred** Polish Belle Partnership **Trained** Pandy, Monmouths

FOCUS
The favourite was a narrow winner under a prominent ride in this sprint handicap. The winner did not need to find much on recent form.

4713 TRAVIS PERKINS H'CAP 2m 49y
8:20 (8:20) (Class 6) (0-60,56) 3-Y-O+ **£1,940** (£577; £288; £144) **Stalls** Low

Form RPR
5452 1 **Noor Al Haya (IRE)**[15] 4222 3-8-6 **51** .... KieranO'Neill 3 59
(Mark Usher) *hld up 4th: hdwy to chse ldr over 2f out: rdn to ld over 1f out: hung lft: styd on wl to assert fnl 175yds* **5/2**[3]
6342 2 2 ½ **Arch Event**[14] 4238 8-9-1 **50** ....(p) JoeyHaynes(7) 2 55
(Bernard Llewellyn) *trckd ldrs: wnt 2nd 5f out: led over 3f out: rdn and hdd over 1f out: kpt pressing ldr tl no ex ins fnl f* **2/1**[1]
1532 3 4 ½ **Pass The Time**[3] 3884 4-9-9 **51** ....(p) LiamKeniry 4 51
(Neil Mulholland) *led tl rdn over 3f out: hld in disp 3rd fr over 2f out: styd on same pce* **9/4**[2]
3-04 4 ½ **Descaro (USA)**[5] 1979 7-9-7 **56** ....(v) CiaranMckee(7) 5 55
(John O'Shea) *trckd ldr tl rdn 5f out: hld in disp 3rd fr over 2f out: styd on same pce* **5/1**

3m 33.0s (-5.90) **Going Correction** -0.375s/f (Firm)
WFA 3 from 4yo+ 17lb 4 Ran SP% **109.3**
Speed ratings (Par 101): **99,97,95,95**
CSF £7.85 TOTE £1.40; EX 7.00 Trifecta £11.60 Pool: £299.55 - 19.34 winning units..
Owner Imran Butt & High Five Racing **Bred** Victor Stud Bloodstock Ltd **Trained** Upper Lambourn, Berks

FOCUS
There was a tight market for this weak staying handicap. The first two were both ridden patiently off the fair pace and pulled clear. A step up from the winner.

4714 MOTORCARE MOTOR FACTORS LTD H'CAP 1m 4f 23y
8:55 (8:55) (Class 6) (0-65,67) 3-Y-O+ **£1,940** (£577; £288; £144) **Stalls** Low

Form RPR
200- 1 **Bohemian Rhapsody (IRE)**[110] 6971 4-10-0 **65** .... ConorO'Farrell 4 77
(Seamus Durack) *racd keenly: trckd ldrs: shkn up to ld over 2f out: styd on strly: pushed out* **10/1**
0261 2 2 **Gabrial The Duke (IRE)**[9] 4401 3-9-4 **67** 6ex .... WilliamCarson 14 75
(David Simcock) *in tch: hdwy 3f out: sn rdn: chsd wnr 2f out but a being hld* **7/4**[1]
0-04 3 4 **Piers Gaveston (IRE)**[22] 3997 4-9-13 **64** .... PatCosgrave 10 66
(George Baker) *mid-div: pushed along 4f out: hdwy 3f out: styd on fnl 2f but nvr trbld ldng pair* **16/1**
5201 4 hd **Bold Cross (IRE)**[10] 4365 10-9-10 **64** 6ex .... ThomasBrown(3) 12 65
(Edward Bevan) *hld up bhd: rdn and hdwy over 2f out: styd on to dispute hld 3rd over 1f out: nvr threatened ldrs* **8/1**
5166 5 6 **Jan De Heem**[32] 3636 3-9-1 **64** ....(b[1]) RichardKingscote 3 56
(Ralph Beckett) *trckd ldrs: rdn over 2f out: styd on same pce* **11/2**[2]
0523 6 ½ **Taste The Wine (IRE)**[14] 4238 7-9-8 **64** .... RobertWilliams(5) 1 55
(Bernard Llewellyn) *trckd ldrs: rdn jst ins 3f out: styd on same pce fnl 2f* **6/1**[3]
000 7 1 ¼ **Brave Helios**[50] 3021 3-8-8 **62** .... MatthewLawson(5) 2 51
(Jonathan Portman) *mid-div: rdn and hdwy over 2f out: styd on same pce fr over 1f out* **14/1**
536 8 nk **James Pollard (IRE)**[73] 2348 8-9-6 **64** ....(t) DanielMuscutt(7) 6 52
(Bernard Llewellyn) *s.i.s: towards rr of midfield: rdn and hdwy 3f out: styd on same pce fnl 2f* **16/1**
6600 9 hd **Shirazz**[32] 3635 4-8-13 **50** ....(p) LiamKeniry 13 38
(Alastair Lidderdale) *hld up towards rr: rdn wl over 3f out: styd on fr over 1f out: nvr a danger* **25/1**
5360 10 1 ¼ **Sommersturm (GER)**[17] 4150 9-9-2 **60** ....(t) EoinWalsh(7) 8 46
(David Evans) *a towards rr* **20/1**
0-00 11 1 ¾ **Euroquip Boy (IRE)**[25] 3910 6-8-13 **50** .... RussKennemore 15 33
(Michael Scudamore) *mid-div: hdwy 3f out: sn rdn: wknd over 1f out* **50/1**
-560 12 nk **Kristallo (GER)**[10] 4380 8-9-2 **53** ....(b) JohnFahy 7 36
(Dai Burchell) *led: rdn and hdd over 2f out: sn wknd* **20/1**
3200 13 2 **Jewelled Dagger (IRE)**[11] 4343 9-9-6 **57** ....(t) PaddyAspell 9 37
(Sharon Watt) *trckd ldr tl rdn 3f out: sn wknd* **20/1**

2m 36.52s (-2.48) **Going Correction** -0.375s/f (Firm)
WFA 3 from 4yo+ 12lb 13 Ran SP% **124.8**
Speed ratings (Par 101): **93,91,89,88,84 84,83,83,83,82 81,81,79**
toteswingers 1&2 £6.50, 1&3 £19.90, 2&3 £11.10 CSF £27.01 TOTE £11.40: £3.10, £1.50, £6.30; EX 34.50 Trifecta £426.60 Part won. Pool: £568.89 - 0.23 winning units..
Owner A A Byrne **Bred** Sweetmans Bloodstock **Trained** Baydon, Wilts
■ A first Flat winner for Conor O'Farrell.

FOCUS
This looked a competitive handicap but they finished quite well strung out. The winner is rated back to his Flat best.
T/Plt: £514.00 to a £1 stake. Pool £47,075.99 - 66.85 winning units T/Qpdt: £10.10 to a £1 stake. Pool £5,810.09 - 422.60 winning units TM

4531 NEWMARKET (R-H)
Friday, July 26

OFFICIAL GOING: Good (7.5)
Wind: Nil Weather: Cloudy

4715 JULY COURSE FILLIES' H'CAP 1m 2f
5:35 (5:36) (Class 5) (0-70,68) 3-Y-O+ **£3,234** (£962; £481; £240) **Stalls** Centre

Form RPR
0062 1 **Sureness (IRE)**[8] 4436 3-9-2 **66** ....(t) NeilCallan 1 74
(Marco Botti) *a.p: chsd ldr over 3f out: led over 2f out: rdn over 1f out: all out* **5/4**[1]
56 2 ¾ **Trulee Scrumptious**[7] 4496 4-8-10 **50** ....(be) JimmyQuinn 5 56
(Peter Charalambous) *led: rdn and hdd over 2f out: styd on* **12/1**
0620 3 1 ¼ **Dama De La Noche (IRE)**[22] 3977 3-8-12 **62** .... PatDobbs 4 66
(Richard Hannon) *hld up: rdn over 4f out: styd on u.p fr over 1f out: nt rch ldrs* **8/1**[3]
-140 4 ¾ **Srinagar Girl**[48] 3106 4-9-11 **65** .... JamesDoyle 8 67
(Clive Cox) *hld up: hdwy over 3f out: rdn over 2f out: styd on same pce ins fnl f* **17/2**
5406 5 2 **Lexi's Dancer**[10] 4374 3-8-6 **56** .... KirstyMilczarek 2 54
(Ian Williams) *chsd ldr tl rdn over 3f out: hung lft over 2f out: no ex fnl f* **10/1**
-231 6 17 **Empowermentofwomen (IRE)**[167] 590 3-9-3 **67** .... TomQueally 7 31
(Michael Bell) *hld up: hdwy over 6f out: rdn over 2f out: sn wknd* **9/2**[2]
0-10 7 7 **Golden Causeway**[22] 3983 3-9-4 **68** ....[1] SteveDrowne 6 18
(Charles Hills) *prom: lost pl over 6f out: rdn over 4f out: sn wknd* **12/1**
0054 8 2 ½ **Frosty Friday**[28] 3792 5-8-4 **49** oh2 ....(p) DannyBrock(5) 3
(J R Jenkins) *s.i.s: hld up: rdn over 4f out: sn wknd* **28/1**

2m 6.26s (0.76) **Going Correction** +0.05s/f (Good)
WFA 3 from 4yo+ 10lb 8 Ran SP% **112.2**
Speed ratings (Par 100): **98,97,96,95,94 80,75,73**
toteswingers 1&2 £3.80, 1&3 £3.40, 2&3 £8.50 CSF £17.24 TOTE £2.10: £1.20, £2.40, £2.00; EX 17.20 Trifecta £82.90 Pool: £2,143.53 - 19.39 winning units..
Owner Augusto Cati **Bred** Alberto Panetta **Trained** Newmarket, Suffolk

FOCUS
Far side track used. Stalls far side except 1m2f & 1m4f: centre. The repositioning of bend into home straight increased 1m2f &1m4f races by 16m. The ground was described as good before the opening fillies' handicap with the GoingStick reading 7.5. A slow-motion finish from this modest bunch after they started racing well over 3f from home. The winner stood out but made hard work of it and is rated to her latest form.

4716 THANK YOU BILL SCOTT MEDIAN AUCTION MAIDEN STKS 6f
6:10 (6:10) (Class 5) 2-Y-O **£3,234** (£962; £481; £240) **Stalls** High

Form RPR
2 1 **Tanzeel (IRE)**[14] 4231 2-9-5 0 .... PaulHanagan 2 89+
(Charles Hills) *trckd ldrs: led over 1f out: styd on wl* **8/13**[1]
30 2 4 ½ **Ice Slice (IRE)**[27] 3836 2-9-5 0 .... RichardHughes 1 77
(Richard Hannon) *sn led: rdn and hdd over 1f out: styd on same pce fnl f* **7/1**[3]
50 3 3 ½ **Headlong (IRE)**[10] 4379 2-9-5 0 .... NeilCallan 7 63
(Brian Meehan) *chsd ldrs: rdn and ev ch over 1f out: no ex fnl f* **10/1**
0 4 3 ½ **Shyron**[18] 4121 2-9-5 0 .... TomQueally 3 52
(George Margarson) *chsd ldrs: rdn and ev ch over 1f out: wknd fnl f* **20/1**
0 5 nk **Freddie Kilroy**[35] 3536 2-9-5 0 .... JamesDoyle 5 51
(Ed Dunlop) *s.i.s and n.m.r s: hld up: pushed along 1/2-way: rdn over 1f out: sn wknd* **33/1**
6 1 ¾ **Penny Sixpence (FR)** 2-9-0 0 .... FrankieDettori 6 41
(John Gosden) *edgd rt s: rn green in rr: shkn up 1/2-way: n.d* **11/4**[2]
0 7 1 ¼ **Pay The Greek**[32] 3624 2-9-5 0 .... StevieDonohoe 8 42
(Noel Quinlan) *hld up: pushed along over 2f out: rdn and wknd over 1f out* **50/1**
8 15 **Spreadable (IRE)** 2-9-5 0 .... SebSanders 4
(Nick Littmoden) *sn pushed along in rr: rdn and wknd over 2f out* **50/1**

1m 13.22s (0.72) **Going Correction** +0.05s/f (Good) 8 Ran SP% **121.8**
Speed ratings (Par 94): **97,91,86,81,81 78,77,57**
toteswingers 1&2 £1.30, 1&3 £1.90, 2&3 £2.50 CSF £6.37 TOTE £1.80: £1.02, £2.10, £2.30; EX 5.70 Trifecta £18.10 Pool: £2,013.23 - 83.01 winning units..
Owner Hamdan Al Maktoum **Bred** Norelands Stallions **Trained** Lambourn, Berks

FOCUS
The favourite set a high standard for the newcomers and was followed home by two who had shown only modest form so far. The form seems to make sense on the face of things.

4717 NEWMARKETRACECOURSES.CO.UK NURSERY H'CAP 7f
6:40 (6:40) (Class 4) 2-Y-O **£3,881** (£1,155; £577; £288) **Stalls** High

Form RPR
5041 1 **Finn Class (IRE)**[14] 4246 2-8-10 **69** .... TomQueally 7 73
(Michael Bell) *sn led: hdd over 4f out: chsd ldr: rdn over 1f out: led ins fnl f: sn hdd: rallied to ld nr fin* **3/1**[2]
61 2 nk **Cornish Path**[23] 3958 2-9-1 **74** .... FergusSweeney 4 77
(Henry Candy) *s.i.s: sn prom: rdn over 1f out: led wl ins fnl f: hdd nr fin* **9/1**
3143 3 1 ¼ **Left Defender (IRE)**[8] 4434 2-8-9 **68** .... PaulHanagan 1 68
(Jo Hughes) *chsd ldrs: led 3f out: rdn over 1f out: hdd ins fnl f: styd on same pce* **5/2**[1]
2521 4 ½ **Culdaff (IRE)**[20] 4061 2-9-7 **80** .... SteveDrowne 3 78
(Charles Hills) *hld up: hdwy over 1f out: sn rdn and hung lft: swvd rt jst ins fnl f: swvd lft wl ins fnl f: nt trble ldrs* **10/3**[3]
1 5 nk **La Tinta Bay**[25] 3896 2-9-2 **75** .... RichardHughes 5 72
(Richard Hannon) *plld hrd: trckd ldr tl led over 4f out: hdd 3f out: rdn over 1f out: styd on same pce ins fnl f* **7/1**
1 6 5 **Claim The Roses (USA)**[25] 3905 2-9-7 **80** .... JamesDoyle 2 69
(Ed Vaughan) *hld up: effrt over 1f out: sn hung lft and eased* **15/2**

1m 27.6s (1.90) **Going Correction** +0.05s/f (Good) 6 Ran SP% **110.9**
Speed ratings (Par 96): **91,90,89,88,88 82**
toteswingers 1&2 £5.80, 1&3 £2.50, 2&3 £4.70 CSF £27.60 TOTE £4.10: £2.30, £2.30; EX 31.90 Trifecta £121.10 Pool: £1,082.05 - 6.69 winning units..
Owner Saif Ali **Bred** Rabbah Bloodstock Limited **Trained** Newmarket, Suffolk

FOCUS
The whole field came into this nursery on the back of wins or career-best performances. The winner progressed and the overall form could be rated higher.

4718 TURFTV H'CAP 1m
7:10 (7:10) (Class 5) (0-75,75) 4-Y-O+ **£3,234** (£962; £481; £240) **Stalls** High

Form RPR
-544 1 **On My Own (TUR)**[49] 3063 4-9-2 **70** .... SebSanders 6 83
(J W Hills) *chsd ldrs: led over 1f out: rdn clr ins fnl f* **7/1**
5100 2 3 ¼ **Sir Mike**[42] 3274 4-9-7 **75** .... PatDobbs 5 81
(Amanda Perrett) *hld up in tch: rdn over 1f out: chsd wnr ins fnl f: styd on same pce* **4/1**[2]
4624 3 2 ½ **Wilfred Pickles (IRE)**[24] 3917 7-9-7 **75** .... FergusSweeney 10 75
(Jo Crowley) *prom: racd keenly: rdn and n.m.r over 1f out: no ex ins fnl f* **14/1**
3000 4 hd **Living Leader**[16] 4165 4-9-6 **74** ....(v) TomMcLaughlin 8 74
(Nick Littmoden) *led 2f: chsd ldr tl led again 3f out: rdn and hdd over 1f out: no ex ins fnl f* **12/1**
1-52 5 1 ¾ **Ever Fortune (USA)**[15] 4205 4-9-7 **75** .... TomQueally 4 71
(Rae Guest) *hld up: rdn over 1f out: r.o ins fnl f: nvr nrr* **3/1**[1]
0004 6 nk **Fabled City (USA)**[28] 3780 4-9-1 **74** ....(t) RyanTate(5) 9 69
(Clive Cox) *chsd ldr tl led 5f out: hdd 3f out: rdn over 1f out: wknd ins fnl f* **5/1**[3]
0456 7 1 ¼ **Authoritarian**[39] 3416 4-9-4 **72** .... RichardHughes 2 64
(Richard Hannon) *hld up: effrt over 2f out: wknd fnl f* **7/1**

5402 **8** 1 1/4 **Greyfriarschorista**[7] 4496 6-8-11 **70** LauraPike(5) 7 59
(Tom Keddy) *hld up: hdwy over 2f out: rdn and wknd over 1f out* **9/1**
5-31 **9** 3 1/2 **Jamaica Grande**[44] 3222 5-8-2 **56** oh3 DavidProbert 1 37
(Dave Morris) *hld up: rdn over 2f out: hung lft and wknd over 1f out* **20/1**
6000 **10** 1 **Monzino (USA)**[39] 3412 5-7-9 **56** oh7 DanielleMooney(7) 3 35
(Michael Chapman) *s.i.s: hld up: rdn and wknd over 2f out* **100/1**
1m 39.5s (-0.50) **Going Correction** +0.05s/f (Good) **10** Ran SP% **116.8**
Speed ratings (Par 103): **104,100,98,98,96 96,94,93,90,89**
toteswingers 1&2 £3.70, 1&3 £18.60, 2&3 £10.50 CSF £35.21 CT £395.95 TOTE £9.40: £2.90, £1.90, £5.10; EX 41.20 Trifecta £359.60 Pool: £964.30 - 2.01 winning units..
Owner Mehmet Kurt **Bred** Turk Cimentosu Ve Kireci A S **Trained** Upper Lambourn, Berks
FOCUS
A modest handicap in which it proved impossible to make up ground from off the pace. A clear personal best from the winner, with the next two close to recent marks.

4719 ADNAMS NEWMARKET NIGHTS MAIDEN STKS 1m 4f
7:40 (7:43) (Class 5) 3-Y-O **£3,234** (£962; £481; £240) **Stalls** Centre

Form RPR
04 **1** **Asbaab (USA)**[49] 3059 3-9-5 0 PaulHanagan 3 92
(Brian Meehan) *led: rdn over 2f out: hung lft and hdd over 1f out: rallied u.p to ld wl ins fnl f: styd on* **4/6**[1]
3 **2** 2 **Bostonian**[9] 4404 3-9-5 0 JoeFanning 2 89
(Mark Johnston) *chsd wnr: led and edgd lft over 1f out: sn rdn: hdd and unable qck wl ins fnl f* **7/2**[2]
0 **3** 12 **Mount Macedon**[14] 4257 3-9-2 0 PatrickHills(3) 1 70
(Luca Cumani) *prom: rdn over 3f out: wknd over 2f out* **25/1**
65 **4** 8 **Silk Route**[22] 3989 3-9-0 0 FergusSweeney 6 52
(Henry Candy) *trckd ldrs: racd keenly: rdn over 3f out: wknd over 2f out* **4/1**[3]
0 **5** 19 **My Peggy Sue**[26] 3860 3-9-0 0 JimmyQuinn 4 21
(Tom Keddy) *s.i.s: hld up: rdn and wknd over 3f out* **66/1**
6 24 **Ernest Defarge** 3-9-5 0 TomQueally 5
(Michael Bell) *dwlt: hld up: pushed along 5f out: rdn and wknd over 3f out* **25/1**
2m 33.39s (0.49) **Going Correction** +0.05s/f (Good) **6** Ran SP% **111.4**
Speed ratings (Par 100): **100,98,90,85,72 56**
toteswingers 1&2 £1.10, 1&3 £2.30, 2&3 £6.30 CSF £3.22 TOTE £1.20: £1.10, £2.10; EX 3.00 Trifecta £22.20 Pool: £1,583.81 - 53.28 winning units..
Owner Hamdan Al Maktoum **Bred** Shadwell Farm LLC **Trained** Manton, Wilts
FOCUS
Little strength in this maiden for 3-y-os and the front pair pulled a long way clear of some thorough plodders. The winner brought good form to race and was to entitled improve a bit.

4720 HOME OF RACING H'CAP 1m 4f
8:10 (8:13) (Class 3) (0-90,89) 3-Y-O+ **£7,439** (£2,213; £1,106; £553) **Stalls** Centre

Form RPR
-113 **1** **Semeen**[21] 4020 4-9-8 **83** RichardHughes 6 92+
(Luca Cumani) *stdd s: hld up: hdwy over 2f out: shkn up over 1f out: rdn to ld wl ins fnl f* **7/4**[1]
06/6 **2** 1/2 **Sadler's Risk (IRE)**[14] 4233 5-10-0 **89** JoeFanning 1 96
(Mark Johnston) *led: rdn over 1f out: hdd wl ins fnl f* **15/2**
-432 **3** hd **Villoresi (IRE)**[30] 3692 4-9-9 **84** JamesDoyle 2 91
(James Fanshawe) *hld up: hdwy over 8f out: chsd ldr 3f out: rdn and ev ch over 1f out: edgd rt ins fnl f: unable qck towards fin* **7/2**[2]
-020 **4** 3 1/4 **The Quarterjack**[41] 3344 4-8-10 **71** DavidProbert 3 73
(Ron Hodges) *chsd ldrs: rdn over 2f out: styd on same pce fnl f* **16/1**
3-02 **5** nk **Royal Dutch**[71] 2383 4-8-12 **73** TomQueally 4 74
(Denis Coakley) *hld up: hdwy u.p over 1f out: styd on same pce ins fnl f* **4/1**[3]
1420 **6** 23 **Hepworth**[21] 4015 4-9-6 **81** (b) FrankieDettori 7 64
(John Gosden) *hld up: rdn over 2f out: wknd over 1f out: eased* **8/1**
13 **P** **Cranach**[30] 3692 4-9-10 **85** JimmyQuinn 5
(Tom Keddy) *chsd ldr tl pushed along 3f out: sn wknd and eased: bhd whn p.u and dismntd over 1f out* **16/1**
2m 34.91s (2.01) **Going Correction** +0.05s/f (Good) **7** Ran SP% **113.2**
Speed ratings (Par 107): **95,94,94,92,92 76,**
toteswingers 1&2 £3.40, 1&3 £2.10, 2&3 £3.80 CSF £15.41 TOTE £2.10: £1.50, £2.50; EX 11.50 Trifecta £73.90 Pool: £1,111.21 - 11.27 winning units..
Owner Sheikh Mohammed Obaid Al Maktoum **Bred** Darley **Trained** Newmarket, Suffolk
FOCUS
A strong handicap, although it was steadily run and the absence of a 3-y-o detracted slightly from the interest. The first and third improved again, with the second back to his old handicap best.

4721 NEWMARKETEXPERIENCE.CO.UK H'CAP (LONDON MILE QUALIFIER) 1m
8:45 (8:45) (Class 5) (0-75,73) 3-Y-O **£3,234** (£962; £481; £240) **Stalls** High

Form RPR
0-24 **1** **Mazaaher**[50] 3011 3-9-4 **70** PaulHanagan 6 80
(J W Hills) *hld up in tch: shkn up to ld over 1f out: rdn out* **9/2**[2]
4402 **2** 1 **Magique (IRE)**[10] 4383 3-9-6 **72** JamesDoyle 1 79
(Jeremy Noseda) *hld up: hdwy 2f out: sn rdn: styd on* **7/2**[1]
3610 **3** 3/4 **Azma (USA)**[14] 4258 3-9-7 **73** NeilCallan 2 78
(Conrad Allen) *chsd ldr tl led over 2f out: rdn and hdd over 1f out: styng on same pce whn nt clr run ins fnl f* **7/2**[1]
-555 **4** 1 1/4 **Patently (IRE)**[35] 3537 3-9-4 **70** (t) FrankieDettori 7 72
(Brian Meehan) *chsd ldrs: rdn over 1f out: styd on same pce fnl f* **11/2**[3]
6035 **5** 1/2 **Royal Caper**[3] 4615 3-8-4 **56** (v) KirstyMilczarek 4 57
(John Ryan) *awkward leaving stalls: hld up: hdwy over 2f out: rdn over 1f out: styd on same pce fnl f* **28/1**
5223 **6** 3 1/2 **Loucal**[20] 4045 3-8-9 **61** (b) StevieDonohoe 3 54
(Noel Quinlan) *hld up: hdwy over 2f out: rdn over 1f out: no ex fnl f* **11/2**[3]
6064 **7** 4 1/2 **East Texas Red (IRE)**[16] 4170 3-8-6 **58** PaoloSirigu 10 41
(Mick Quinn) *hld up: effrt over 2f out: wknd over 1f out* **14/1**
1466 **8** hd **Zero Game (IRE)**[26] 3861 3-9-2 **68** [1] PatDobbs 8 50
(Michael Bell) *mid-div: pushed along over 2f out: wknd over 1f out* **12/1**
006 **9** 1 1/2 **Two No Bids (IRE)**[20] 4077 3-8-7 **59** (p) DavidProbert 9 38
(Phil McEntee) *led over 5f: wknd over 1f out* **33/1**
0340 **10** 34 **Triple Aitch (USA)**[9] 4410 3-8-10 **62** TomQueally 5
(Gay Kelleway) *hld up: rdn over 3f out: sn wknd* **25/1**
1m 39.58s (-0.42) **Going Correction** +0.05s/f (Good) **10** Ran SP% **118.0**
Speed ratings (Par 100): **104,103,102,101,100 97,92,92,90,56**
toteswingers 1&2 £3.30, 1&3 £3.40, 2&3 £3.80 CSF £20.50 CT £63.28 TOTE £4.20: £2.00, £1.90, £2.00; EX 15.80 Trifecta £28.20 Pool: £1,016.70 - 26.95 winning units..
Owner Hamdan Al Maktoum **Bred** Shadwell Estate Company Limited **Trained** Upper Lambourn, Berks
FOCUS
A fair 3-y-o handicap to close the card, and sound form.

T/Plt: £23.60 to a £1 stake. Pool: £48,068.97 - 1,481.87 winning units T/Qpdt: £38.30 to a £1 stake. Pool: £3,555.80 - 68.60 winning units CR

3624 THIRSK (L-H)
Friday, July 26

OFFICIAL GOING: Good to firm (9.7)
Wind: light 1/2 behind Weather: fine and sunny, very warm

4722 SKYBET SUPPORTING THE YORKSHIRE RACING SUMMER FESTIVAL (S) H'CAP 7f
2:10 (2:12) (Class 6) (0-65,65) 3-Y-O **£2,264** (£673; £336; £168) **Stalls** Low

Form RPR
4302 **1** **Marcus Caesar (IRE)**[18] 4113 3-9-0 **58** PhillipMakin 4 69
(David Barron) *mde all: kpt on u.p fnl 2f: unchal* **11/4**[1]
0460 **2** 1 1/4 **Angels Calling**[9] 4410 3-8-12 **56** RobertWinston 6 64
(Mrs K Burke) *chsd ldrs: 2nd over 1f out: kpt on: no imp* **16/1**
0065 **3** 3 **Moe's Place (IRE)**[25] 3903 3-8-11 **55** TonyHamilton 2 55
(Kristin Stubbs) *chsd ldrs: wnt 3rd 1f out: one pce* **12/1**
2460 **4** 1 **Excellent Addition (IRE)**[6] 4544 3-9-7 **65** DanielTudhope 11 62+
(David O'Meara) *hld up in rr: hdwy and swtchd outside over 1f out: kpt on to take 4th nr fin* **5/1**[3]
5504 **5** 3/4 **Cymeriad**[9] 4398 3-8-5 **49** JamesSullivan 5 44
(Michael Easterby) *chsd ldrs: one pce fnl 2f* **25/1**
5652 **6** hd **Lucky Mountain**[10] 4391 3-8-2 **46** LukeMorris 1 41
(Scott Dixon) *chsd ldrs: drvn over 2f out: one pce* **10/3**[2]
3040 **7** 1 1/2 **First Serve (IRE)**[17] 4144 3-8-11 **55** BarryMcHugh 3 46
(Karen Tutty) *half-rrd s: t.k.h in mid-div: effrt over 2f out: nvr trbld ldrs* **40/1**
0053 **8** 1 **Multisure**[4] 4585 3-8-7 **51** PJMcDonald 12 39+
(Ruth Carr) *mid-div: effrt over 2f out: nvr a factor* **8/1**
0060 **9** 1/2 **Panama Cat (USA)**[67] 2501 3-8-7 **51** (p) FrannyNorton 7 38
(Kevin Ryan) *in rr: hdwy on inner over 2f out: wknd last 150yds* **17/2**
040 **10** 14 **Woodley Wonder (IRE)**[52] 2960 3-7-13 **46** NeilFarley(3) 9
(Ben Haslam) *sn bhd: t.o 2f out* **28/1**
0-00 **11** 2 3/4 **Ryedale Valley**[18] 4114 3-8-3 **47** DuranFentiman 8
(Tim Easterby) *mid-div: reminders after 2f: rdn over 2f out: sn lost pl and bhd: t.o* **33/1**
120 **12** 8 **Claude Greenwood**[29] 3739 3-8-10 **61** (b) NedCurtis(7) 10
(Roger Curtis) *s.i.s: reminders after s: bhd fnl 3f: t.o* **20/1**
1m 26.58s (-0.62) **Going Correction** -0.025s/f (Good) **12** Ran SP% **119.1**
Speed ratings (Par 98): **102,100,97,96,95 94,93,92,91,75 72,63**
toteswingers 1&2 £7.10, 1&3 £9.10, 2&3 £21.70 CSF £45.49 CT £466.45 TOTE £3.40: £1.40, £4.40, £3.90; EX 43.30 Trifecta £564.50 Pool: £1350.40 - 1.79 winning units..There was no bid for the winner. Excellent Addition was claimed by Mr Declan Carroll £6,000.
Owner Gareth Fawcett **Bred** Kevin O'Reilly **Trained** Maunby, N Yorks
FOCUS
Both bends moved off inner line which added 15yds to races on Round course. A moderate selling handicap in which ten of the line-up were maidens. The pace held up and the winner is rated up a length.

4723 BRITISH STALLION STUDS EBF MAIDEN FILLIES' STKS 7f
2:45 (2:46) (Class 4) 2-Y-O **£4,075** (£1,212; £606; £303) **Stalls** Low

Form RPR
4 **1** **Chesturo (IRE)**[64] 2583 2-9-0 0 GrahamLee 7 79+
(Mick Channon) *trckd ldrs: chal over 1f out: styd on to ld towards fin* **5/1**
53 **2** 1/2 **Inyordreams**[28] 3760 2-9-0 0 DaleSwift 8 76
(James Given) *led: jnd over 1f out: no ecxtra and hdd nr fin* **11/4**[1]
63 **3** 4 **Miaplacidus (IRE)**[44] 3205 2-9-0 0 TonyHamilton 5 66
(Richard Fahey) *trckd ldrs: t.k.h: effrt over 2f out: one pce over 1f out* **8/1**
4 **4** hd **Charlotte's Day**[28] 3753 2-9-0 0 LukeMorris 4 65+
(Sir Mark Prescott Bt) *slipped s: in rr: hdwy over 2f out: kpt on same pce fnl f* **4/1**[3]
4 **5** 4 1/2 **Eleventh Hour (IRE)**[15] 4191 2-9-0 0 SilvestreDeSousa 1 53
(Saeed bin Suroor) *trckd ldrs: drvn and outpcd 3f out: kpt on fnl f* **7/2**[2]
0 **6** 1/2 **Musalaha (IRE)**[15] 4215 2-9-0 0 DaneO'Neill 3 52+
(Ed Dunlop) *s.i.s: sn chsng ldrs: outpcd 3f out: no threat after* **25/1**
7 nk **Modify** 2-9-0 0 RoystonFfrench 10 51
(Bryan Smart) *mid-div: effrt on wd outside over 2f out: kpt on ins fnl f* **33/1**
8 3/4 **Kashstaree** 2-9-0 0 DavidAllan 2 49+
(David Barron) *dwlt: in rr: sme hdwy on inner over 2f out: nvr a factor* **50/1**
9 1/2 **Scottish Academy** 2-9-0 0 FrannyNorton 9 51+
(Mark Johnston) *hmpd s: sn bhd: kpt on fnl 2f: nvr on terms* **20/1**
10 22 **Power Of Good News (FR)** 2-9-0 0 PhillipMakin 6
(Kevin Ryan) *s.i.s: hdwy to chse ldrs over 3f out: lost pl over 2f out: sn bhd: eased fnl f: virtually p.u: t.o* **33/1**
1m 27.66s (0.46) **Going Correction** -0.025s/f (Good) **10** Ran SP% **113.1**
Speed ratings (Par 93): **96,95,90,90,85 84,84,83,83,58**
toteswingers 1&2 £3.50, 1&3 £3.20, 2&3 £6.80 CSF £17.40 TOTE £5.40: £1.70, £1.90, £3.10; EX 22.10 Trifecta £169.70 Pool: £1635.18 - 7.22 winning units..
Owner Jaber Abdullah **Bred** Barry Noonan And Denis Noonan **Trained** West Ilsley, Berks
FOCUS
A fair fillies' maiden and the first two pulled clear. The form is rated around the second and third.

4724 BREEDERS BACKING RACING EBF MAIDEN STKS 5f
3:20 (3:20) (Class 5) 2-Y-O **£2,911** (£866; £432; £216) **Stalls** High

Form RPR
2 **1** **Free Code (IRE)**[15] 4199 2-9-5 0 PaulMulrennan 9 77+
(James Tate) *chsd ldrs: 2nd over 1f out: edgd lft and led last 75yds: drvn out* **4/11**[1]
2 2 **City Zen (IRE)** 2-9-0 0 BarryMcHugh 1 64+
(Tony Coyle) *dwlt: sn trcking ldrs: led over 1f out: hdd and no ex ins fnl f* **22/1**
3 1 1/2 **Thornaby Princess** 2-9-0 0 DanielTudhope 8 59+
(Marjorie Fife) *s.i.s: towards rr: hdwy over 2f out: nt clr run and swtchd rt over 1f out: edgd lft and styd on fnl f* **33/1**
5 **4** nk **Chuckamental**[28] 3766 2-9-5 0 (t) RoystonFfrench 10 63
(Bryan Smart) *led: hdd over 1f out: kpt on ins fnl f* **20/1**
5 1 1/4 **Danzki (IRE)** 2-9-5 0 LukeMorris 11 59
(Gay Kelleway) *chsd ldrs stands' side: edgd lft over 1f out: one pce* **18/1**[3]
6 1 1/4 **Eddiemaurice (IRE)** 2-9-5 0 RobbieFitzpatrick 5 54
(Richard Guest) *dwlt: detached in last: hdwy over 1f out: styd on ins fnl f* **100/1**
03 **7** 1 **Tinsill**[8] 4450 2-9-2 0 (v) DeclanCannon(3) 7 50
(Nigel Tinkler) *t.k.h: w ldrs: edgd lft over 1f out: fdd* **66/1**

The Form Book Flat, Raceform Ltd, Compton, RG20 6NL.

0 **8** 1 ½ **Captain Gee**[18] 4107 2-9-5 0 .... MichaelO'Connell 6 45
(John Quinn) *chsd ldrs: lost pl over 1f out* **33/1**
9 ½ **Bashiba (IRE)** 2-9-5 0 .... SilvestreDeSousa 4 43
(Nigel Tinkler) *s.i.s: sn drvn along: hdwy on outer to chse ldrs 2f out: sn wknd* **7/1**[2]
00 **10** 5 **Mornin Mr Norris**[27] 3826 2-8-12 0 .... JoeDoyle(7) 3 25
(John Quinn) *mid-div: sn drvn along: outpcd and lost pl 3f out* **80/1**
6 **11** ½ **Desert Colours**[15] 4199 2-9-5 0 .... PhillipMakin 2 23
(Kevin Ryan) *chsd ldrs on outside: edgd rt and lost pl over 1f out* **7/1**[2]

59.52s (-0.08) **Going Correction** -0.20s/f (Firm) **11** Ran SP% **122.3**
Speed ratings (Par 94): **92,88,86,85,83 81,80,77,77,69 68**
toteswingers 1&2 £11.80, 1&3 £7.80, 2&3 £49.30 CSF £17.33 TOTE £1.20: £1.02, £7.50, £10.20; EX 19.60 Trifecta £363.50 Pool: £1985.37 - 4.09 winning units..
Owner Sheikh Rashid Dalmook Al Maktoum **Bred** Rory O'Brien **Trained** Newmarket, Suffolk

FOCUS
An ordinary maiden. The winner did not need to improve but should do better in time.

4725 INFINITY ECOSIS TYRES H'CAP 7f
3:55 (3:56) (Class 4) (0-80,80) 3-Y-O **£5,175** (£1,540; £769; £384) **Stalls** Low

Form RPR
041 **1** **Shady McCoy (USA)**[24] 3932 3-8-13 **72** .... RobertWinston 1 87+
(David Barron) *dwlt: sn trcking ldrs: nt clr run over 2f out tl chsd ldr jst ins fnl f: qcknd to ld clsng stages: readily* **11/4**[1]
-542 **2** 1 ¼ **Dusky Queen (IRE)**[30] 3686 3-9-6 **79** .... TonyHamilton 2 89
(Richard Fahey) *trckd ldrs: led over 1f out: hdd and no ex last 30yds* **11/4**[1]
5142 **3** 4 ½ **Penny Garcia**[14] 4265 3-9-7 **80** .... DuranFentiman 3 78
(Tim Easterby) *chsd ldrs: upsides over 1f out: kpt on one pce* **9/2**[2]
0612 **4** 2 ½ **Tatlisu (IRE)**[20] 4056 3-9-7 **80** .... LeeTopliss 7 71
(Richard Fahey) *in rr and sn drvn along: hdwy over 3f out: chsng ldrs over 1f out: one pce* **6/1**[3]
2150 **5** 1 **Clock On Tom**[18] 4119 3-8-6 **65** .... JamesSullivan 6 53
(Michael Easterby) *led: hung rt: hdd over 1f out: sn wknd* **16/1**
-042 **6** ¾ **Rich Forever (IRE)**[16] 4158 3-8-12 **71** ....(b) GrahamLee 8 57
(James Bethell) *trckd ldrs: t.k.h: chal 2f out: sn rdn and hmpd: fdd appr fnl f* **9/1**
6020 **7** 1 ¾ **Dream Scenario**[38] 3445 3-8-10 **69** .... PaulMulrennan 9 51
(Mel Brittain) *hld up in rr: kpt on fnl 2f: nvr on terms* **14/1**
0005 **8** ½ **Delores Rocket**[30] 3686 3-8-6 **72** ....(b) PaulMcGiff(7) 4 52
(Kevin Ryan) *mid-div: lost pl over 4f out: hdwy on outer over 2f out: one pce* **40/1**
210 **9** 6 **Iggy**[74] 2308 3-8-2 **68** ....(t) MatthewHopkins(7) 5 32
(Michael Easterby) *hld up in rr: detached in last over 3f out* **40/1**

1m 26.77s (-0.43) **Going Correction** -0.025s/f (Good) **9** Ran SP% **113.2**
Speed ratings (Par 102): **101,99,94,91,90 89,87,87,80**
toteswingers 1&2 £2.80, 1&3 £2.50, 2&3 £2.90 CSF £9.73 CT £30.87 TOTE £2.60: £1.60, £1.60, £2.10; EX 11.70 Trifecta £34.10 Pool: £2134.43 - 46.87 winning units..
Owner Allwins Stables **Bred** Bluegrass Hall Llc **Trained** Maunby, N Yorks

FOCUS
This competitive handicap was run at an ordinary pace and the first two pulled clear. Both improved.

4726 THIRSK LADIES' DAY SATURDAY 7TH SEPTEMBER NURSERY H'CAP 6f
4:30 (4:30) (Class 3) 2-Y-O **£6,469** (£1,925; £962; £481) **Stalls** High

Form RPR
3521 **1** **Azagal (IRE)**[20] 4053 2-9-3 **79** .... DavidAllan 4 86+
(Tim Easterby) *dwlt: in last: hdwy 2f out: nt clr run and swtchd lft twice: qcknd to ld last 100yds: styd on strly: readily* **15/8**[1]
01 **2** 1 ¾ **Tweety Pie (IRE)**[20] 4046 2-8-7 **72** .... NeilFarley(3) 5 72
(Declan Carroll) *drvn to ld: hdd and no ex ins fnl f* **10/1**
003 **3** 1 ½ **Imshivalla (IRE)**[18] 4115 2-8-5 **67** .... BarryMcHugh 6 62
(Richard Fahey) *chsd ldrs: outpcd over 2f out: kpt on ins fnl f: tk 3rd nr fin* **7/1**
4011 **4** nk **Diamond Lady**[8] 4431 2-9-6 **87** 12ex .... PhilipPrince(5) 2 81
(Jo Hughes) *chsd ldr: rdn over 1f out: kpt on same pce* **11/4**[2]
15 **5** 1 ½ **One Boy (IRE)**[72] 2370 2-9-2 **78** .... TomEaves 3 67
(Michael Dods) *hld up: hdwy over 2f out: kpt on same pce over 1f out* **15/2**
251 **6** 1 ¾ **Muspelheim**[53] 2913 2-9-7 **83** .... PJMcDonald 1 67
(Ann Duffield) *wnt lft s: hdwy to chse ldrs over 2f out: hung lft and wknd jst ins fnl f* **5/1**[3]

1m 11.45s (-1.25) **Going Correction** -0.20s/f (Firm) **6** Ran SP% **111.5**
Speed ratings (Par 98): **100,97,95,95,93 90**
toteswingers 1&2 £4.10, 1&3 £3.80, 2&3 £5.50 CSF £20.52 TOTE £2.90: £1.60, £3.30; EX 15.70 Trifecta £74.60 Pool: £3007.14 - 30.22 winning units..
Owner Roger Sidebottom **Bred** Robert Norton **Trained** Great Habton, N Yorks

FOCUS
A fair nursery which was run at a good pace. The third helps with the standard.

4727 MARGARET LEETE MEMORIAL FILLIES' H'CAP 6f
5:00 (5:01) (Class 5) (0-70,70) 3-Y-O+ **£2,587** (£770; £384; £192) **Stalls** High

Form RPR
0166 **1** **Charlemagne Diva**[20] 4064 3-8-9 **59** ....(t) PhilipPrince(5) 1 67
(Richard Guest) *swtchd rt after s: sn chsng ldr: led over 1f out: fnd ex towards fin* **10/1**
4034 **2** ½ **See Clearly**[39] 3407 4-9-11 **65** ....(p) RobertWinston 2 72
(Tim Easterby) *chsd ldrs: drvn over 2f out: chsd wnr 1f out: no ex clsng stages* **9/2**[2]
001 **3** 1 **Dartrix**[4] 4582 4-9-11 **70** 6ex .... ConnorBeasley(5) 5 74+
(Michael Dods) *dwlt: hld up in rr: hdwy on outside over 2f out: chsng ldng pair 1f out: edgd rt: kpt on same pce last 75yds* **15/8**[1]
-000 **4** 3 ½ **Balinka**[23] 3946 3-9-3 **62** ....(v[1]) PJMcDonald 10 54
(Mel Brittain) *led: hdd over 1f out: grad wknd* **14/1**
5003 **5** ½ **Karate Queen**[9] 4398 8-8-0 **47** ....(p) NoelGarbutt(7) 7 38
(Ron Barr) *mid-div: rdn and outpcd over 2f out: kpt on fnl f* **25/1**
0056 **6** 3 ¼ **Lady Royale**[15] 4203 5-9-9 **63** ....[1] SilvestreDeSousa 4 44
(Geoffrey Oldroyd) *sn outpcd in rr: reminders after 1f: hdwy on outer over 2f out: chsd ldrs over 1f out: sn wknd* **9/2**[2]
20/0 **7** 1 **Enchanted Dream**[21] 4013 5-9-0 **54** .... AndrewMullen 6 31
(David C Griffiths) *chsd ldrs: drvn over 2f out: wknd over 1f out* **25/1**
0-6 **8** 1 ¼ **Shesnotforturning (IRE)**[85] 1962 3-7-13 **47** oh2 .... NeilFarley(3) 9 19
(Ben Haslam) *chsd ldrs: sn drvn along: lost pl over 1f out* **40/1**
4545 **9** 2 ¼ **Blue Shoes (IRE)**[16] 4161 4-9-2 **63** .... GaryMahon(7) 3 29
(Tim Easterby) *in rr: hdwy on outer over 2f out: chsng ldrs over 1f out: sn lost pl and edgd rt* **10/1**

1-24 **10** 9 **Lucies Diamond (IRE)**[28] 3779 3-9-7 **66** .... TomEaves 8
(Michael Dods) *s.s: in rr: bhd fnl 2f* **9/1**[3]

1m 11.44s (-1.26) **Going Correction** -0.20s/f (Firm)
WFA 3 from 4yo+ 5lb **10** Ran SP% **116.1**
Speed ratings (Par 100): **100,99,98,93,92 88,87,85,82,70**
toteswingers 1&2 £5.90, 1&3 £4.60, 2&3 £3.10 CSF £53.37 CT £122.63 TOTE £11.20: £2.70, £1.30, £1.70; EX 48.60 Trifecta £185.00 Pool: £3675.12 - 14.89 winning units..
Owner Chris Penney **Bred** Marston Stud And Fleming Thoroughbreds **Trained** Wetherby, W Yorks

FOCUS
A modest handicap run at a good pace. A clear personal best from the winner.

4728 RACING EXCELLENCE "HANDS AND HEELS" APPRENTICE SERIES H'CAP 5f
5:25 (5:25) (Class 5) (0-75,75) 3-Y-O+ **£2,587** (£770; £384; £192) **Stalls** High

Form RPR
001 **1** **Oil Strike**[4] 4588 6-9-13 **74** 6ex ....(b) MatthewHopkins 11 86+
(Michael Easterby) *t.k.h: led over 1f: led 2f out: edgd lft ins fnl f: hld on towards fin* **5/2**[1]
0463 **2** ½ **Cruise Tothelimit (IRE)**[18] 4123 5-9-11 **75** .... PaulMcGiff(3) 9 82
(Ian Williams) *s.i.s: in rr: hdwy stands' side 2f out: styd on fnl f: tk 2nd line* **4/1**[3]
1131 **3** nse **Bondi Beach Boy**[21] 4009 4-9-5 **66** .... JordanNason 5 73
(James Turner) *w wnr: led narrowly over 3f out: carried hd high: hdd over 1f out: edgd rt and kpt on ins fnl f* **7/2**[2]
34 **4** 1 ¼ **Captain Scooby**[24] 3933 7-9-8 **69** .... ConnorBeasley 10 71
(Richard Guest) *chsd ldrs: drvn and outpcd over 2f out: kpt on fnl f* **10/1**
2003 **5** nk **Indian Trail**[4] 4588 13-9-8 **69** ....(b) OisinMurphy 8 70
(David Nicholls) *towards rr: kpt on fnl 2f: nvr trbld ldrs* **20/1**
4422 **6** hd **Holy Angel (IRE)**[7] 4510 4-9-3 **67** ....(e) RachelRichardson(3) 4 74+
(Tim Easterby) *s.i.s: swtchd rt after s: bhd: hdwy stands' side over 1f out: styng on at fin* **9/2**
0060 **7** 4 **Elusive Bonus (IRE)**[36] 3505 4-9-3 **69** .... JoshDoyle(5) 2 55
(David O'Meara) *chsd ldrs: lost pl over 1f out* **50/1**
0354 **8** nk **Royal Bajan (USA)**[20] 4074 5-9-7 **68** ....(b) KevinStott 3 53
(James Given) *chsd ldrs on outer: edgd lft and lost pl 1f out* **14/1**
3236 **9** 1 ¼ **Miss Bunter**[4] 4588 4-9-8 **72** .... JackGarritty(3) 1 53
(David O'Meara) *t.k.h: chsd ldrs on outside: edgde rt and lost pl appr fnl f* **25/1**

58.61s (-0.99) **Going Correction** -0.20s/f (Firm) **9** Ran SP% **115.3**
Speed ratings (Par 103): **99,98,98,96,95 95,88,88,86**
toteswingers 1&2 £3.30, 1&3 £3.50, 2&3 £3.50 CSF £12.31 CT £34.51 TOTE £3.00: £1.10, £2.10, £2.00; EX 17.10 Trifecta £71.80 Pool: £2945.64 - 30.73 winning units..
Owner A Saha **Bred** Cobhall Court Stud **Trained** Sheriff Hutton, N Yorks
■ Stewards' Enquiry : Paul McGiff caution: careless riding

FOCUS
Quite a competitive apprentices' sprint handicap. The winner is in fine form and this was arguably more convincing than Beverley.
T/Plt: £13.00 to a £1 stake. Pool: £60961.97 - 3407.11 winning tickets T/Qpdt: £3.00 to a £1 stake. Pool: £3617.60 - 882.80 winning tickets WG

4308 YORK (L-H)
Friday, July 26

OFFICIAL GOING: Good to firm (watered; 7.8)
Wind: Virtually nil Weather: Cloudy with sunny periods

4729 FUTURE CLEANING SERVICES APPRENTICE STKS (H'CAP) 1m
6:00 (6:00) (Class 4) (0-80,80) 3-Y-O **£5,175** (£1,540; £769; £384) **Stalls** Low

Form RPR
1221 **1** **Nurpur (IRE)**[6] 4515 3-9-9 **80** 6ex .... DavidBergin(3) 4 88+
(David O'Meara) *hld up in tch: hdwy on outer over 2f out: led appr fnl f: sn rdn and kpt on* **3/1**[2]
5221 **2** 2 **Future Reference (IRE)**[11] 4354 3-9-5 **78** 6ex ....(t) AhmadAlSubousi(5) 3 81
(Saeed bin Suroor) *trckd ldrs: effrt and nt clr run over 2f out: sn swtchd lft and led briefly 1 1/2f out: sn hdd and rdn: edgd lft and one pce nfl f* **9/4**[1]
5423 **3** nse **Simply Shining (IRE)**[15] 4201 3-9-4 **75** ....(p) SamanthaBell(3) 9 78
(Richard Fahey) *trckd ldng pair: hdwy and cl up 2f out: sn rdn and ev ch tl one pce fnl f* **13/2**
4301 **4** shd **Saint Jerome (IRE)**[23] 3951 3-9-12 **80** .... WilliamTwiston-Davies 7 83
(Jamie Osborne) *led: jnd and rdn 3f out: drvn and hdd wl over 1f out: cl up tl one pce fnl f* **4/1**[3]
0605 **5** 3 ¼ **Woodstock (IRE)**[40] 3365 3-8-8 **65** .... JacobButterfield(3) 2 61
(Brian Ellison) *hld up in tch: pushed along 3f out: sn rdn and outpcd 2f out: styd on u.p fnl f* **10/1**
4-02 **6** 6 **Hard Core Debt**[4] 4586 3-9-1 **76** .... RichardOliver(7) 6 58
(Brian Ellison) *chsd ldr: hdwy and cl up 3f out: rdn 2f out: wknd 1 1/2f out* **15/2**

1m 37.29s (-1.71) **Going Correction** -0.175s/f (Firm) **6** Ran SP% **110.0**
Speed ratings (Par 102): **101,99,98,98,95 89**
toteswingers 1&2 £1.60, 1&3 £3.50, 2&3 £2.90 CSF £9.73 CT £35.13 TOTE £3.70: £2.40, £1.40; EX 7.30 Trifecta £31.50 Pool: £1,722.31 - 40.92 winning units..
Owner Middleham Park Racing XXIX & Partners **Bred** B P Hayes **Trained** Nawton, N Yorks

FOCUS
A dry and warm run up to a meeting that saw 3mm of water applied overnight. The rail on the home bend from 9f to the entrance to the home straight was moved to provide a fresh racing line - race distances for races of 1m and over were reduced by 20 yards. A fairly useful and competitive apprentice handicap on paper but a ready winner, who deserves extra credit given she was held up off a steady gallop.

4730 TOUR DE FRANCE YORKSHIRE GRAND DEPART STKS (H'CAP) 6f
6:30 (6:31) (Class 4) (0-80,85) 4-Y-O+ **£5,175** (£1,540; £769; £384) **Stalls** Centre

Form RPR
2321 **1** **Picture Dealer**[7] 4494 4-9-12 **85** 6ex .... GeorgeBaker 19 95
(Gary Moore) *stdd s and hld up in rr: swtchd rt to outer and gd hdwy 2f out: str run ent fnl f: led last 50yds* **11/4**[1]
5313 **2** ½ **Mon Brav**[41] 3351 6-9-7 **80** .... DaneO'Neill 6 88
(Brian Ellison) *hld up and bhd: swtchd rt over 2f out: rdn on wd outside over 2f out: styd on wl fnl f* **12/1**
0056 **3** nk **Corporal Maddox**[7] 4494 6-9-3 **76** .... LukeMorris 12 83
(Ronald Harris) *hld up towards rr: hdwy over 2f out: swtchd rt and rdn wl over 1f out: styd on to chal ins fnl f: no ex towards fin* **25/1**
6-00 **4** shd **Bop It**[44] 3200 4-9-4 **77** .... DanielTudhope 15 84
(David O'Meara) *trckd ldrs: hdwy 2f out: rdn ent fnl f: sn ev ch tl drvn and no ex towards fin* **18/1**

2223 **5** 1/2 **Diman Waters (IRE)**[4] [4579] 6-9-0 **78**............................ JasonHart(5) 14 83
(Eric Alston) *cl up: led 2f out: rdn wl over 1f out: sn drvn: hdd ins fnl f: no ex towards fin* **20/1**

0-05 **6** nk **Hadaj**[21] [4014] 4-9-4 **77**............................ JamesSullivan 1 81
(Ruth Carr) *in tch on wd outside: hdwy 2f out: rdn to chse ldrs over 1f out: drvn and one pce ins fnl f* **33/1**

3005 **7** hd **Tarooq (USA)**[13] [4281] 7-9-7 **80**............................(t) AndreaAtzeni 10 84
(Stuart Williams) *chsd ldrs: hdwy and cl up 2f out: sn rdn and kpt on same pce fnl f* **10/1**[3]

0100 **8** 1 1/4 **Meandmyshadow**[17] [4138] 5-9-7 **80**............................ DaleSwift 13 80
(Alan Brown) *led: pushed along and hdd 2f out: sn rdn and cl up tl drvn and wknd fnl f* **20/1**

0060 **9** 1 1/2 **Caranbola**[4] [4588] 7-9-1 **74**............................ PJMcDonald 16 69
(Mel Brittain) *prom: rdn along 2f out: edgd lft appr fnl f: grad wknd* **50/1**

1142 **10** 1/2 **Sunraider (IRE)**[8] [4444] 6-9-7 **80**............................ MickyFenton 17 73
(Paul Midgley) *midfield: pushed along over 2f out: sn rdn and no hdwy* **33/1**

0445 **11** 1 1/2 **Mappin Time (IRE)**[7] [4479] 5-9-6 **79**............................(p) DavidAllan 9 67
(Tim Easterby) *towards rr: rdn along and sme hdwy over 2f out: n.d* **16/1**

0604 **12** 1/2 **Sound Amigo (IRE)**[94] [1746] 5-9-4 **80**............................ NeilFarley(3) 11 67
(Declan Carroll) *chsd ldrs: rdn along 2f out: sn wknd* **20/1**

1544 **13** 1/2 **Bonnie Charlie**[29] [3714] 7-9-4 **77**............................ FrannyNorton 7 62
(David Nicholls) *dwlt: a towards rr* **10/1**[3]

5001 **14** 1/2 **Pea Shooter**[22] [3981] 4-9-6 **79**............................(p) GrahamLee 4 63
(Kevin Ryan) *in tch: hdwy 2f out: sn rdn and chsd ldrs on outer over 1f out: wknd fnl f* **7/1**[2]

0002 **15** 1 3/4 **Medici Time**[5] [4560] 8-9-0 **73**............................(v) PhillipMakin 20 51
(Tim Easterby) *hld up in rr: hdwy on wd outside 1/2-way: rdn along wl over 1f out: sn wknd* **16/1**

2025 **16** nk **Baldemar**[15] [4210] 8-9-1 **74**............................ LeeTopliss 2 51
(Richard Fahey) *midfield: rdn along 2f out: n.d* **28/1**

0000 **17** 12 **Trade Secret**[38] [3441] 6-9-7 **80**............................ TomEaves 8 19
(Mel Brittain) *midfield: rdn along over 2f out: sn wknd* **50/1**

-001 **18** 1 3/4 **Mount Hollow**[15] [4220] 8-9-6 **79**............................(p) AndrewMullen 18 12
(Andrew Hollinshead) *in tch: rdn along over 2f out: wkng whn hmpd over 1f out: sn bhd* **33/1**

0230 **19** 7 **Sir Pedro**[14] [4235] 4-9-4 **77**............................ RobertWinston 5
(Charles Hills) *s.i.s: a towards rr: bhd and eased fr wl over 1f out* **12/1**

0505 **R** **Defence Council (IRE)**[17] [4138] 5-9-2 **75**............................ SilvestreDeSousa 3
(Mel Brittain) *ref to r: tk no part* **20/1**

1m 10.56s (-1.34) **Going Correction** -0.05s/f (Good) **20** Ran SP% **128.8**
Speed ratings (Par 105): **106,105,104,104,104 103,103,101,99,99 97,96,95,95,92 92,76,74,64,**
toteswingers 1&2 £5.80, 1&3 £28.10, 2&3 £92.60 CSF £30.41 CT £740.84 TOTE £3.80: £1.70, £3.60, £7.50, £3.30; EX 48.30 Trifecta £873.20 Pool: £2,045.15 - 1.75 winning units..
Owner R A Green **Bred** L Ellinas & Old Mill Stud **Trained** Lower Beeding, W Sussex

FOCUS
After riding in the first race open to fully-fledged jockeys David Allan said: "It is a fraction on the quick side of good"; Andrea Atzeni said: "It is good ground"; Luke Morris said: "It is beautiful good, fast ground" and George Baker said: "They have done a very good job - it is quick but extremely safe." A useful handicap run at a sound gallop. The field converged in the centre but, although the first three finished more towards the near side of the group, there didn't seem much in the draw.

4731 BATLEYS CASH AND CARRY MEDIAN AUCTION MAIDEN STKS 7f
7:00 (7:02) (Class 4) 2-Y-O **£5,175** (£1,540; £769; £384) **Stalls** Low

Form RPR

6 **1** **Il Paparazzi**[42] [3291] 2-9-5 0............................ LukeMorris 6 89+
(Daniel Kubler) *trckd ldr: hdwy and cl up 1/2-way: led wl over 2f out: rdn clr wl over 1f out: edgd lft fnl f: kpt on strly* **9/1**

2 5 **Erroneous (IRE)** 2-9-5 0............................ MartinLane 8 76+
(David Simcock) *towards rr: hdwy on inner 1/2-way: rdn to chse wnr over 2f out: drvn over 1f out: no imp* **9/1**

3 3/4 **Bremner** 2-9-5 0............................ GrahamLee 5 74+
(Kevin Ryan) *towards rr: hdwy 4f out: effrt over 2f out and rn green: sn rdn and kpt on appr fnl f* **11/2**

4 4 1/2 **Master Of Finance (IRE)** 2-9-5 0............................ FrannyNorton 11 62+
(Mark Johnston) *chsd ldng pair: rdn along wl over 2f out: drvn wl over 1f out: sn one pce* **8/1**

26 **5** 3 **Henke (IRE)**[32] [3624] 2-9-2 0............................ DeclanCannon(3) 1 55
(Nigel Tinkler) *chsd ldrs on inner: hdwy 3f out: rdn over 2f out: sn wknd* **12/1**

6 1/2 **Giant Samurai (USA)** 2-9-5 0............................ MichaelO'Connell 4 53
(John Quinn) *chsd ldrs: rdn along wl over 2f out: sn wknd* **5/1**[3]

7 3/4 **Kalahari Kingdom (IRE)** 2-9-5 0............................ TonyHamilton 9 51
(Richard Fahey) *chsd ldrs: hdwy 3f out: rdn along: green and edgd lft wl over 2f out: sn wknd* **9/2**[2]

8 10 **Sandfield (IRE)** 2-9-5 0............................ MickyFenton 10 25
(Paul Midgley) *s.i.s: a bhd* **40/1**

9 nk **Hartnell** 2-9-5 0............................ SilvestreDeSousa 7 25
(Mark Johnston) *sn outpcd in rr: rdn along 1/2-way: sn bhd* **7/2**[1]

0 **10** 7 **How Rude**[41] [3350] 2-9-0 0............................ DavidAllan 2
(Mel Brittain) *led: rdn along 1/2-way: hdd wl over 2f out: sn wknd and bhd* **16/1**

1m 24.53s (-0.77) **Going Correction** -0.075s/f (Good) **10** Ran SP% **119.6**
Speed ratings (Par 96): **101,95,94,89,85 85,84,73,72,64**
toteswingers 1&2 £20.40, 1&3 £15.40, 2&3 £11.10 CSF £89.40 TOTE £11.20: £2.90, £3.20, £2.50; EX 90.10 Trifecta £337.20 Pool: £1,447.13 - 3.21 winning units..
Owner Capture The Moment **Bred** Highclere Stud **Trained** Whitsbury, Hants

FOCUS
The pick of the previous winners was subsequent Breeders' Cup Juvenile winner Vale Of York in 2009. Those with previous experience had looked modest at best but the winner posted a useful effort. The gallop was ordinary to halfway but the field finished well strung out. The winner showed big improvement and the fifth set the standard.

4732 BRITISH STALLION STUDS SUPPORTING BRITISH RACING EBF LYRIC FILLIES' STKS (LISTED RACE) 1m 2f 88y
7:30 (7:31) (Class 1) 3-Y-O+ **£22,792** (£8,708; £4,412; £2,252; £1,184) **Stalls** Low

Form RPR

1-64 **1** **Hippy Hippy Shake**[17] [4137] 4-9-4 **97**............................ KierenFallon 7 105
(Luca Cumani) *hld up in rr: hdwy 3f out: cl up over 1f out: rdn to ld ins fnl f: drvn out* **7/1**[3]

-023 **2** 1 **Lady Nouf**[43] [3240] 3-8-8 **94**............................(p) AndreaAtzeni 9 103
(William Haggas) *trckd ldrs: hdwy 4f out: sn cl up: rdn to ld wl over 2f out: drvn and hdd ins fnl f: kpt on* **7/1**[3]

3622 **3** 6 **Ladys First**[17] [4137] 4-9-4 **106**............................ TonyHamilton 6 92
(Richard Fahey) *set stdy pce: hdd afer 3f: trckd ldr: hdwy and cl up 3f out: sn slt ld: rdn and hdd 2f out: sn drvn and kpt on same pce* **5/1**[2]

-636 **4** 10 **Private Alexander (IRE)**[14] [4236] 3-8-8 **98**............................ FrannyNorton 2 73
(David O'Meara) *chsd ldng pair: rdn along over 3f out: sn wknd* **33/1**

-532 **5** 1/2 **Reckoning (IRE)**[28] [3775] 4-9-4 **99**............................(p) GrahamLee 4 72
(Jeremy Noseda) *trckd ldr: led after 3f: rdn along over 3f out: hdd wl over 2f out and sn wknd* **10/1**

-153 **U** **Albasharah (USA)**[20] [4059] 4-9-4 **108**............................[1] SilvestreDeSousa 5
(Saeed bin Suroor) *blind removed late: rrd and uns rdr s* **4/5**[1]

2m 8.23s (-4.27) **Going Correction** -0.175s/f (Firm)
WFA 3 from 4yo 10lb **6** Ran SP% **109.3**
Speed ratings (Par 108): **110,109,104,96,96**
toteswingers 1&2 £4.70, 1&3 £4.10, 2&3 £3.90 CSF £49.39 TOTE £5.70: £2.10, £3.10; EX 50.80 Trifecta £151.10 Pool: £1,995.36 - 9.89 winning units..
Owner Helena Springfield Ltd **Bred** Meon Valley Stud **Trained** Newmarket, Suffolk

FOCUS
A depleted field and drama at the start of this Listed Fillies' event. The pace was steady and, although the first two pulled clear, this form isn't reliable. The first two finished clear and showed improved form, worth more at face value.

4733 SKY BET SUPPORTING THE YORKSHIRE RACING FESTIVAL STKS (H'CAP) 1m
8:00 (8:01) (Class 3) (0-90,92) 3-Y-O+ **£8,086** (£2,406; £1,202; £601) **Stalls** Low

Form RPR

0623 **1** **Frog Hollow**[20] [4055] 4-9-6 **82**............................ DanielTudhope 10 95
(David O'Meara) *trckd ldrs: smooth hdwy 3f out: led 1 1/2f out: rdn and kpt on strly fnl f* **6/1**[3]

1-41 **2** 3 **Altharoos (IRE)**[21] [4007] 3-9-2 **86**............................ DaneO'Neill 2 90+
(Sir Michael Stoute) *trckd ldrs on inner: nt clr run and swtchd rt wl over 2f out: rdn wl over 1f out: styd on to chse wnr fnl f: no imp* **2/1**[2]

0510 **3** 1 1/4 **Jo'Burg (USA)**[6] [4542] 9-9-4 **85**............................ DavidBergin(5) 3 88
(David O'Meara) *dwlt and in rr: hdwy over 2f out: sn rdn and styd on fnl f: nrst fin* **25/1**

0605 **4** 1 3/4 **No Poppy (IRE)**[13] [4308] 5-8-13 **80**............................ AdamCarter(5) 8 79
(Tim Easterby) *trckd ldr: hdwy 1/2-way: cl up 3f out: sn rdn and ev ch tl drvn and one pce appr fnl f* **20/1**

054 **5** 1/2 **Steel Stockholder**[23] [3945] 7-9-1 **77**............................ DavidAllan 5 75
(Mel Brittain) *hld up towards rr: hdwy on wd outside over 2f out: rdn to chse ldrs over 12f out: drvn and one pce fnl f* **40/1**

-151 **6** 1/2 **Ehtedaam (USA)**[9] [4415] 4-10-2 **92** 6ex............................(p) SilvestreDeSousa 9 89
(Saeed bin Suroor) *sn led: rdn along 3f out: hdd wl over 1f out: drvn and grad wknd* **6/4**[1]

4000 **7** 1 **Green Howard**[30] [3684] 5-9-4 **80**............................ RobertWinston 4 75
(Robin Bastiman) *trckd ldrs: hdwy over 3f out: rdn 2f out: sn drvn and wknd* **33/1**

4233 **8** 3 **Dubai Hills**[22] [3984] 7-9-9 **88**............................ WilliamTwiston-Davies(3) 6 76
(Bryan Smart) *hld up towards rr: hdwy on outer 3f out: rdn to chse ldrs wl over 1f out: sn drvn and wknd* **12/1**

5254 **9** 1/2 **Lord Aeryn (IRE)**[13] [4308] 6-9-12 **88**............................ TonyHamilton 1 75
(Richard Fahey) *trckd ldr: rdn along over 3f out: wknd over 2f out* **14/1**

1m 36.2s (-2.80) **Going Correction** -0.175s/f (Firm)
WFA 3 from 4yo+ 8lb **9** Ran SP% **116.0**
Speed ratings (Par 107): **107,104,102,101,100 100,99,96,95**
toteswingers 1&2 £4.10, 1&3 £8.00, 2&3 £15.50 CSF £17.81 CT £282.55 TOTE £7.80: £2.00, £1.80, £4.30; EX 24.40 Trifecta £284.00 Pool: £1,434.45 - 3.78 winning units..
Owner Dab Hand Racing **Bred** Reid & Shriver **Trained** Nawton, N Yorks

FOCUS
A useful handicap in which the gallop was just an ordinary one to the 3f marker. The winner is rated back to his best.

4734 PINSENT MASONS LLP STKS (H'CAP) 5f 89y
8:30 (8:31) (Class 4) (0-85,85) 3-Y-O **£5,175** (£1,540; £769; £192; £192) **Stalls** Centre

Form RPR

10- **1** **Foxy Forever (IRE)**[321] [6022] 3-8-11 **75**............................ FrannyNorton 10 93+
(Michael Wigham) *hld up: gd hdwy 2f out: rdn and str run to ld appr fnl f: sn edgd lft and clr* **12/1**

-423 **2** 3 **Dusty Storm (IRE)**[20] [4057] 3-9-1 **79**............................ RoystonFfrench 11 86
(Ed McMahon) *cl up: rdn wl over 1f out: ev ch tl drvn and one pce fnl f* **12/1**

1211 **3** nk **Jofranka**[17] [4136] 3-8-4 **73**............................ JasonHart(5) 3 79
(David Barron) *sn led: rdn along wl over 1f out: drvn and hdd appr fnl f: kpt on same pce* **4/1**[1]

-102 **4** 1 1/2 **Time And Place**[27] [3813] 3-9-3 **81**............................ TonyHamilton 1 82
(Richard Fahey) *in tch: hdwy 2f out: sn rdn: styd on fnl f: nrst fin* **11/2**[3]

3142 **4** dht **Tumblewind**[14] [4247] 3-9-7 **85**............................ TomEaves 13 86
(Richard Whitaker) *sltly hmpd s and in rr: hdwy 2f out: swtchd rt and rdn over 1f out: styd on fnl f: nrst fin* **8/1**

5062 **6** 1 3/4 **Satsuma**[9] [4402] 3-9-4 **82**............................ GrahamLee 4 77
(David Brown) *trckd ldr: effrt 2f out: sn rdn: drvn and wknd fnl f* **5/1**[2]

6562 **7** 1 1/4 **Jillnextdoor (IRE)**[10] [4367] 3-9-6 **84**............................ DaneO'Neill 7 74
(Mick Channon) *in rr: rdn and sme hdwy 2f out: n.d* **8/1**

1004 **8** 1 1/2 **Rangooned**[9] [4402] 3-8-6 **70**............................ PJMcDonald 5 55
(Ann Duffield) *chsd ldrs: rdn along over 2f out: grad wknd* **28/1**

1600 **9** 1 3/4 **Bogsnog (IRE)**[34] [3591] 3-8-12 **76**............................ JamesSullivan 6 55
(Kristin Stubbs) *in tch: pushed along and lost pl 1/2-way: swtchd lft and rdn 2f out: n.d* **20/1**

2014 **10** 1 **Shrimper Roo**[18] [4112] 3-9-6 **84**............................(b) DuranFentiman 2 59
(Tim Easterby) *dwlt: a in rr* **14/1**

1050 **11** 4 1/2 **Mayfield Girl (IRE)**[14] [4263] 3-9-6 **84**............................ DavidAllan 9 44
(Mel Brittain) *cl up: rdn along 2f out: sn drvn and wknd* **12/1**

5025 **12** 4 **Bapak Sayang (USA)**[34] [3591] 3-8-11 **82**............................ KevinStott(7) 12 28
(Kevin Ryan) *wnt rt s: chsd ldrs: rdn along 2f out: sn wknd* **9/1**

1m 3.51s (-0.59) **Going Correction** -0.05s/f (Good) **12** Ran SP% **122.2**
Speed ratings (Par 102): **102,97,96,94,94 91,89,87,84,82 75,69**
toteswingers 1&2 £35.00, 1&3 £10.30, 2&3 £8.60 CSF £152.63 TOTE £10.80: £3.10, £4.80, £2.10; EX 213.10 Trifecta £963.80 Pool: £1,519.31 - 1.18 winning units..
Owner D Hassan, J Cullinan **Bred** Tally-Ho Stud **Trained** Newmarket, Suffolk

FOCUS
A useful sprint and one in which the gallop was sound throughout. Solid form, with a useful effort from the winner.

T/Jkpt: Not won. T/Plt: £575.80 to a £1 stake. Pool: £98,429.87 - 124.77 winning units T/Qpdt: £103.10 to a £1 stake. Pool £4,977.30 - 35.70 winning units JR

The Form Book Flat, Raceform Ltd, Compton, RG20 6NL.

4702 ASCOT (R-H)

Saturday, July 27

OFFICIAL GOING: Good to firm (good in places; stands' side 8.6, centre 8.4, far side 8.4, round 8.0)

Wind: Almost nil Weather: Fine, becoming cloudy from race 4 onwards; warm and humid

4742 PRINCESS MARGARET JUDDMONTE STKS (GROUP 3) (FILLIES) 6f

2:05 (2:08) (Class 1) 2-Y-O

£28,355 (£10,750; £5,380; £2,680; £1,345; £675) **Stalls** Centre

Form RPR

105 **1** **Princess Noor (IRE)**[15] 4253 2-8-12 94.....................(b[1]) AndreaAtzeni 6 107
(Roger Varian) *trckd ldng pair: clsd to ld 2f out: drifted rt fr over 1f out but styd on wl* **25/1**

313 **2** 2 **Queen Catrine (IRE)**[15] 4253 2-8-12 98.......................... OlivierPeslier 4 101
(Charles Hills) *hld up in last quartet: prog wl over 1f out: chsd wnr fnl f: styd on but no imp* **5/1**[2]

21 **3** ¾ **Along Again (IRE)**[10] 4408 2-8-12 83................................ RyanMoore 2 98
(Sir Michael Stoute) *chsd ldrs: rdn and on terms 2f out: nt qckn over 1f out: styd on same pce after* **9/1**

313 **4** 1 ¼ **Love In The Desert**[28] 3829 2-8-12 92........................ StevieDonohoe 3 94
(Noel Quinlan) *led 1f: chsd ldr: upsides 2f out: chsd wnr to 1f out: fdd* **20/1**

413 **5** nse **Wind Fire (USA)**[37] 3481 2-8-12 103.............................. JamieSpencer 9 94
(David Brown) *hld up in last quartet: prog over 1f out: struggling to cl on ldrs whn hung lft and lost all ch ins fnl f: kpt on nr fin* **15/8**[1]

02 **6** nk **Lady Lara (IRE)**[23] 3978 2-8-12 0....................................... NeilCallan 10 93
(Alan Jarvis) *dwlt: hld up in last: stl there over 1f out: drvn and kpt on after: n.d* **33/1**

1 **7** nk **Wee Jean**[24] 3948 2-8-12 0.. MartinHarley 7 92
(Mick Channon) *chsd ldrs in 6th: rdn over 2f out: one pce and no imp over 1f out* **6/1**

61 **8** 4 **Mahlah (IRE)**[29] 3760 2-8-12 84.. DaneO'Neill 8 79
(Richard Hannon) *racd freely: led after 1f to 2f out: wknd* **25/1**

3414 **9** nse **Fig Roll**[15] 4253 2-8-12 97.. RichardHughes 5 79
(Richard Hannon) *hld up in last quartet: rdn 2f out: hanging and unable to make prog over 1f out* **11/2**[3]

10 2 ½ **Chroussa (IRE)**[6] 4566 2-8-12 0.................................... KevinManning 1 71
(J S Bolger, Ire) *s.i.s: sn prom: rdn and nrly upsides 2f out: wknd qckly over 1f out* **9/1**

1m 12.74s (-1.76) **Going Correction** -0.175s/f (Firm) **10** Ran SP% **116.5**
Speed ratings (Par 101): **104,101,100,98,98 98,97,92,92,89**
toteswingers 1&2 £19.20, 1&3 £20.00, 2&3 £7.40 CSF £140.20 TOTE £29.80: £6.30, £1.80, £2.60; EX 144.30 Trifecta £1217.40 Pool: £7,659.24 - 4.71 winning units..
Owner Saleh Al Homaizi & Imad Al Sagar **Bred** Lynch Bages Ltd & Camas Park Stud **Trained** Newmarket, Suffolk

FOCUS
The going was Good to firm, good in places, after a dry night. The jockeys said the ground was fast. Usually a good fillies' Group 3, although not necessarily a long-term guide, with Lady Of The Desert and Soar the only recent winners to score at a higher level in Europe. They raced more or less up the centre of the track but the first three ended up finishing closer to the far side. Princess Noor reversed Newmarket form with Queen Catrine, but the form makes a fair bit of sense at face value.

4743 DELOITTE H'CAP 1m (S)

2:40 (2:41) (Class 2) 3-Y-O

£28,012 (£8,388; £4,194; £2,097; £1,048; £526) **Stalls** Centre

Form RPR

021 **1** **Yeager (USA)**[54] 2931 3-8-3 83......................................(t) JimmyQuinn 14 97+
(Jeremy Noseda) *s.i.s: hld up towards rr: prog on nr side of gp 2f out: shkn up to ld jst ins fnl f: sn clr: styd on wl* **20/1**

6 **2** 2 ¼ **Machete Mark (IRE)**[37] 3484 3-8-9 89.............................. GaryCarroll 15 98
(G M Lyons, Ire) *t.k.h: trckd ldrs: moved up on nr side of gp to ld 2f out: hdd and outpcd jst ins fnl f* **8/1**[3]

1021 **3** ¾ **Intrigo**[29] 3763 3-9-0 94... RichardHughes 12 101
(Richard Hannon) *hld up in last trio: rdn and prog on nr side wl over 1f out: tk 3rd ins fnl f: nvr able to chal* **5/1**[2]

2114 **4** 1 **Secret Art (IRE)**[15] 4236 3-8-5 85...................................... MartinLane 10 90
(Ralph Beckett) *chsd ldng pair: rdn wl over 2f out: kpt on same pce u.p: nvr able to chal* **10/1**

2101 **5** 1 ¼ **Butterfly McQueen (USA)**[14] 4278 3-9-0 97.......... ThomasBrown(3) 16 99
(Andrew Balding) *mde most to 2f out: fdd fnl f* **8/1**[3]

-402 **6** ½ **Makafeh**[29] 3763 3-8-12 92... NeilCallan 8 93
(Luca Cumani) *hld up in midfield: trckd ldrs gng strly over 2f out: rdn and nt qckn over 1f out: fdd fnl f* **10/1**

5503 **7** 1 ¼ **Fehaydi**[15] 4242 3-8-12 92.. GrahamLee 11 90
(William Haggas) *a in midfield: rdn 3f out: struggling after: kpt on same pce fr over 1f out* **8/1**[3]

0201 **8** shd **Tamayuz Star (IRE)**[23] 3987 3-9-5 99................................ RyanMoore 9 98
(Richard Hannon) *hld up in last trio: rdn and sme prog fr over 1f out: nvr rchd ldrs: no hdwy fnl 100yds* **16/1**

-023 **9** ¾ **Tarikhi (USA)**[16] 4214 3-9-1 95................................. MickaelBarzalona 4 91
(Saeed bin Suroor) *hld up towards rr: prog on far side of gp over 2f out: hanging and wknd over 1f out* **4/1**[1]

12-3 **10** 2 ½ **Yarroom (IRE)**[92] 1809 3-8-11 91...................................... AndreaAtzeni 7 81
(Roger Varian) *prom: rdn to chal jst over 2f out: wknd qckly over 1f out* **14/1**

1633 **11** 2 **Defendant**[14] 4295 3-8-1 86 ow1.. RobertTart(5) 3 72
(Sir Michael Stoute) *pressed ldrs: rdn to chal jst over 2f out: wknd qckly over 1f out* **20/1**

12 1 ¼ **Zalty (FR)**[24] 3963 3-8-7 87... RichardMullen 1 70
(David Marnane, Ire) *s.s: t.k.h in last trio: rdn and modest prog 2f out: wknd over 1f out* **33/1**

1331 **13** 3 ¼ **Henry The Aviator (USA)**[8] 4508 3-8-8 88....................... JoeFanning 2 63
(Mark Johnston) *w ldr to over 2f out: wknd rapidly* **17/2**

1m 37.78s (-3.02) **Going Correction** -0.175s/f (Firm) course record **13** Ran SP% **123.7**
Speed ratings (Par 106): **108,105,105,104,102 102,101,100,100,97 95,94,91**
toteswingers 1&2 £40.40, 1&3 £23.00, 2&3 £9.90 CSF £174.51 CT £696.89 TOTE £30.70: £6.10, £3.20, £2.20; EX 333.50 Trifecta £3434.80 Pool: £6,949.68 - 1.51 winning units..
Owner C Fox & B Wilson **Bred** Cloverleaf Farms II Llc **Trained** Newmarket, Suffolk

FOCUS
This line-up looked full of promising sorts, and the winner can definitely go on to hold his own at a higher level, although it's worth noting the first three tended to race towards the stands' side of the pack with high draws dominant. Strong form with the winner progressing well now.

4744 CASH OUT MULTIPLES ONLY ON BETFAIR INTERNATIONAL (HERITAGE H'CAP) 7f

3:15 (3:16) (Class 2) 3-Y-O+

£62,250 (£18,640; £9,320; £4,660; £2,330; £1,170) **Stalls** Centre

Form RPR

1001 **1** **Galician**[7] 4525 4-8-11 95 5ex.. JoeFanning 29 106
(Mark Johnston) *trckd ldng pair nr side: led gp 2f out: overall ldr over 1f out: clr of gp fnl f: drvn out* **33/1**

0436 **2** ½ **Trail Blaze (IRE)**[7] 4531 4-8-6 90..............................(b[1]) DavidProbert 10 99
(Kevin Ryan) *pressed far side ldr: led gp wl over 1f out and overall ldr briefly: styd on fnl f: jst hld: 1st of 10 in gp* **40/1**

-206 **3** nk **Loving Spirit**[36] 3527 5-8-5 94.. RobertTart(5) 5 103
(James Toller) *trckd far side ldrs: rdn and prog over 1f out: chsd ldr and swtchd lft jst ins fnl f: drifted lft but styd on wl: 2nd of 10 in gp* **12/1**

2041 **4** 1 ¾ **Glen Moss (IRE)**[22] 4014 4-8-6 90 3ex.................... MickaelBarzalona 24 94
(Charles Hills) *trckd nr side ldrs: rdn to chal 2f out: chsd wnr after: one pce fnl f: 2nd of 19 in gp* **20/1**

6061 **5** ½ **Field Of Dream**[14] 4297 6-9-3 101 3ex...............................(b) AdamKirby 2 104
(Jamie Osborne) *taken down early: hld up in last of far side gp: prog over 1f out: styd on fnl f to take 3rd of 10 in gp nr fin* **12/1**

6224 **6** ¾ **Don't Call Me (IRE)**[38] 3458 6-9-7 105......................(t) RichardMullen 17 105
(David Nicholls) *chsd nr side ldrs: drvn over 2f out: kpt on fr over 1f out: nvr able to threaten: 3rd of 19 in gp* **20/1**

0060 **7** nse **Common Touch (IRE)**[15] 4258 5-8-5 89.............................(b) JohnFahy 1 89
(Willie Musson) *hld up towards rr far side: prog 2f out: styd on same pce fnl f: 4th of 10 in gp* **66/1**

0303 **8** ½ **Dubawi Sound**[21] 4058 5-9-4 102...................................(t) HarryBentley 6 101
(David Brown) *walked to post: led far side gp: overall ldr 2f out: sn hdd: fdd fnl f: 5th of 10 in gp* **40/1**

5223 **9** hd **Es Que Love (IRE)**[7] 4531 4-9-1 99................................ OlivierPeslier 19 97
(Mark Johnston) *led nr side gp to 2f out: wknd fnl f: 4th of 19 in gp* **9/1**[2]

5235 **10** hd **Shamaal Nibras (USA)**[7] 4527 4-8-12 99..............(p) ThomasBrown(3) 3 97
(Ismail Mohammed) *chsd ldng pair far side: fdd fr over 1f out: 6th of 10 in gp*

4105 **11** nk **Redvers (IRE)**[14] 4297 5-8-11 95..............................(b) RichardHughes 4 92
(Ed Vaughan) *s.s: last of far side gp: prog 2f out: one pce fnl f: n.d: 7th of 10 in gp* **10/1**[3]

-100 **12** ½ **Excellent Guest**[14] 4297 6-9-0 98....................................... DaneO'Neill 25 94
(George Margarson) *wl in rr of nr side gp: drvn on outer over 2f out: kpt on u.p fr over 1f out: 5th of 19 in gp* **25/1**

0110 **13** nk **Boots And Spurs**[21] 4062 4-8-1 92............................(v) JoeyHaynes(7) 16 87
(Mrs K Burke) *chsd nr side ldrs: drvn over 2f out: no imp over 1f out: one pce fnl f: 6th of 19 in gp* **50/1**

201 **14** shd **Prince Of Johanne (IRE)**[21] 4080 7-9-5 103 3ex..(p) JohnnyMurtagh 21 98
(Tom Tate) *hld up towards rr nr side and off the pce: rdn and kpt on fr 2f out: n.d: 7th of 19 in gp* **12/1**

4465 **15** nse **Hawkeyethenoo (IRE)**[28] 3831 7-9-10 108........................ GrahamLee 18 103
(Jim Goldie) *racd nr side: nvr bttr than midfield and nt on terms w the pce: rdn 2f out: no imp on ldrs: 8th of 19 in gp* **12/1**

5161 **16** ½ **Ashaadd (IRE)**[21] 4062 3-8-7 98 3ex................................ AndreaAtzeni 23 88
(Roger Varian) *w.w wl in rr nr side: drvn 2f out: kpt on fr over 1f out: nvr gng pce to chal: 9th of 19 in gp* **12/1**

4014 **17** ¾ **Head Of Steam (USA)**[31] 3697 6-8-6 90............................ LukeMorris 9 81
(Amanda Perrett) *chsd far side ldrs tl wknd wl over 1f out: 8th of 10 in gp* **25/1**

3001 **18** ¾ **Lightning Cloud (IRE)**[36] 3527 5-9-2 100............................ NeilCallan 7 89
(Kevin Ryan) *slowly away: in rr of far side gp: rdn and sme prog over 2f out: wknd over 1f out: 9th of 10 in gp* **14/1**

2020 **19** shd **Bertiewhittle**[14] 4297 5-8-13 97.. FMBerry 13 86
(David Barron) *wl off the pce in last pair nr side: sme prog into midfield 2f out: no imp fr over 1f out: 10th of 19 in gp* **25/1**

-365 **20** nk **Hefner (IRE)**[36] 3538 4-8-3 87.. MartinLane 20 75
(William Jarvis) *chsd nr side ldrs: u.p fr 1/2-way: steadily wknd fnl 2f: 11th of 19 in gp* **33/1**

0040 **21** ¾ **Santefisio**[28] 3825 7-9-6 104.......................................(b) JimmyFortune 27 90
(Keith Dalgleish) *chsd nr side ldrs: no prog 2f out: wknd over 1f out: 12th of 19 in gp* **25/1**

1133 **22** 4 ½ **Queensberry Rules (IRE)**[37] 3484 3-8-9 100................. RyanMoore 22 71
(William Haggas) *nvr gng the pce in nr side gp: struggling over 2f out: 13th of 19 in gp* **11/2**[1]

R444 **23** 1 ½ **Ducal**[21] 4062 5-8-4 88.. KieranO'Neill 8 58
(Mike Murphy) *s.s: racd far side: nvr beyond midfield: wknd over 2f out: last of 10 in gp* **33/1**

0-00 **24** nse **Rebellious Guest**[35] 3558 4-8-5 92............................. RyanPowell(3) 26 62
(George Margarson) *racd nr side: a in rr: struggling on outer over 2f out: 14th of 19 in gp* **40/1**

-331 **25** 2 ¼ **The Confessor**[36] 3538 6-8-8 92.................................... CathyGannon 14 56
(Henry Candy) *pressed nr side ldrs to over 2f out: sn wknd qckly: 15th of 19 in gp* **33/1**

4000 **26** 3 ¾ **Justonefortheroad**[30] 3725 7-8-8 92.............................. JimmyQuinn 12 46
(Richard Fahey) *racd nr side: a wl in rr: wl bhd 2f out: 16th of 19 in gp* **66/1**

-500 **27** hd **Palace Moon**[28] 3840 8-8-11 95.......................................(t) TedDurcan 11 48
(William Knight) *mostly in last pair nr side: a bhd: 17th of 19 in gp* **66/1**

01-0 **28** 1 ¼ **Sacrosanctus**[94] 1765 5-8-3 90.. BillyCray(3) 15 40
(Scott Dixon) *pressed nr side ldr tl wknd rapidly over 2f out: 18th of 19 in gp* **100/1**

0005 **29** 7 **Compton**[28] 3825 4-8-4 88.. AdamBeschizza 28 19
(Robert Cowell) *chsd nr side ldrs: wknd rapidly over 2f out: t.o: last of 19 in gp* **33/1**

1m 24.28s (-3.32) **Going Correction** -0.175s/f (Firm) course record
WFA 3 from 4yo+ 7lb **29** Ran SP% **136.9**
Speed ratings (Par 109): **111,110,110,108,107 106,106,106,105,105 105,104,104,104,104 103,102,101,101,101 100,95,93,93,9**
toteswingers 1&2 £269.10, 1&3 £128.10, 2&3 not won CSF £1026.48 CT £15503.65 TOTE £43.90: £8.30, £12.10, £4.00, £6.50; EX 2484.40 Trifecta £6641.60 Part won. Pool: £8,855.57 - 0.05 winning units..
Owner Sheikh Hamdan Bin Mohammed Al Maktoum **Bred** Darley **Trained** Middleham Moor, N Yorks

■ Stewards' Enquiry : Dane O'Neill two-day ban: used whip above permitted level (Aug 10-11)
David Probert two-day ban: used whip above permitted level (Aug 11-12)

FOCUS
One of a series of hot handicaps run here and three of the first four from the Victoria Cup in May plus six of the first seven from the Buckingham Palace Handicap at the Royal Meeting were re-opposing. They split into two groups and there seemed no advantage to either side, but the winner broke the track record. Galician showed her Newbury win to be no fluke. Solid form but the race lacked improvers.

4745 KING GEORGE VI AND QUEEN ELIZABETH STKS SPONSORED BY BETFAIR (BRITISH CHAMPIONS SERIES) (GROUP 1) 1m 4f
3:50 (3:51) (Class 1) 3-Y-O+

£603,961 (£228,975; £114,594; £57,084; £28,648; £14,377) **Stalls** Low

Form RPR
1-11 **1** **Novellist (IRE)**[34] 3615 4-9-7 119 JohnnyMurtagh 3 128
(A Wohler, Germany) *t.k.h early: hld up in 4th: clsd on ldng pair fr 3f out: drvn to ld 2f out: stormed clr: impressive* **13/2**

2311 **2** *5* **Trading Leather (IRE)**[28] 3849 3-8-9 118 KevinManning 6 120
(J S Bolger, Ire) *t.k.h: trckd ldng pair: wnt 2nd over 3f out: rdn to chal and upsides 2f out as wnr swept by: kpt on but no ch after* **9/2**[2]

-221 **3** *¾* **Hillstar**[36] 3523 3-8-9 111 RyanMoore 8 119
(Sir Michael Stoute) *hld up in 6th: rdn and prog on outer over 2f out: styd on to take 3rd and press runner-up ins fnl f: no ch w wnr* **5/1**[3]

12-5 **4** *3* **Cirrus Des Aigles (FR)**[34] 3615 7-9-7 131 ChristopheSoumillon 1 114
(Mme C Barande-Barbe, France) *hld up in 5th: moved into 4th over 2f out: sn rdn and nt qckn: fdd over 1f out* **6/4**[1]

1131 **5** *hd* **Universal (IRE)**[16] 4213 4-9-7 115 JoeFanning 4 114
(Mark Johnston) *chsd ldr: chal fr 1/2-way despite fast pce: rdn to ld 4f out: hdd 2f out: steadily wknd* **14/1**

2300 **6** *5* **Red Cadeaux**[38] 3457 7-9-7 116 GrahamLee 7 106
(Ed Dunlop) *hld up in last and wl off the pce: no prog 3f out: nvr a factor* **25/1**

3 **7** *7* **Very Nice Name (FR)**[119] 1268 4-9-7 118 OlivierPeslier 5 94
(A De Mieulle, France) *hld up in 7th: no prog and wl btn over 2f out* **14/1**

-31S **8** *36* **Ektihaam (IRE)**[35] 3556 4-9-7 115 DaneO'Neill 2 37
(Roger Varian) *led at str pce but pestered: drvn and hdd 4f out: wknd qckly and eased: t.o* **10/1**

2m 24.6s (-7.90) **Going Correction** -0.175s/f (Firm) course record
WFA 3 from 4yo+ 12lb **8** Ran SP% **114.5**
Speed ratings (Par 117): **119,115,115,113,113 109,105,81**
toteswingers 1&2 £5.10, 1&3 £4.90, 2&3 £4.10 CSF £35.78 CT £158.37 TOTE £5.20: £1.40, £2.70, £2.60; EX 35.00 Trifecta £86.40 Pool: £18,535.43 - 160.84 winning units..
Owner Dr Christoph Berglar **Bred** Christoph Berglar **Trained** Germany
■ A course record time by 2sec.

FOCUS
Quite where this renewal of one of the most prestigious 1m4f races in the world will rest in the annals of history is open to debate, although it's fair to say it was only missing the recently retired (due to injury) St Nicholas Abbey and Eclipse winner Al Kazeem, who never really had this on his agenda, to make it a stronger contest. However, the facts show it contained five Group 1 winners, which includes Very Nice Name's top-flight successes in Qatar, and the current highest-rated horse in the world. It wasn't a strong race on pre-race figures, 5-6lb below the usual pre-race standard, but this rates a clear personal best from Novellist, up to the race's recent standard, with the next two close to their pre-race marks.

4746 LONGINES H'CAP (LADIES' RACE) (FOR LADY AMATEUR RIDERS) 7f
4:25 (4:26) (Class 3) (0-90,90) 3-Y-O+ **£8,110** (£2,515; £1,257; £629) **Stalls** Centre

Form RPR
1016 **1** **Lord Of The Dance (IRE)**[23] 3984 7-9-13 82 MissMMullineaux(3) 6 96
(Michael Mullineaux) *s.i.s: towards rr: prog on far side of gp to ld jst over 2f out: sn rdn wl clr* **16/1**

2120 **2** *7* **Karaka Jack**[31] 3684 6-10-2 82 MissADeniel 3 78
(David Nicholls) *prom in chsng gp: rdn over 2f out: kpt on to chse clr wnr fnl f: no imp* **5/1**[2]

4034 **3** *¾* **Apollo D'Negro (IRE)**[15] 4235 5-9-13 79 MissRachelKing 15 73
(Clive Cox) *wl in rr: prog nr side of gp fr 2f out: styd on to take 3rd nr fin* **11/1**

0043 **4** *¾* **Graphic (IRE)**[15] 4237 4-10-2 82 MissSBrotherton 10 74
(William Haggas) *prom in chsng gp: lost pl and rdn over 2f out: n.d after: kpt on fnl f* **9/4**[1]

5105 **5** *nk* **Space War**[15] 4245 6-9-0 71 oh2 (t) AnnaHesketh(5) 16 62
(Michael Easterby) *s.s: sn prom in chsng gp: rdn over 2f out: one pce after* **16/1**

4513 **6** *hd* **Bold Ring**[3] 4637 7-9-2 71 oh9 MissJRRichards(3) 11 62
(Edward Creighton) *wl in rr: prog 2f out: kpt on one pce fr over 1f out* **33/1**

0065 **7** *¾* **Emkanaat**[8] 4494 5-9-1 72 MissSAGrassick(5) 4 61
(Amy Weaver) *clr ldr: hdd jst over 2f out: steadily wknd* **25/1**

2146 **8** *1 ½* **Fanrouge (IRE)**[26] 3892 4-10-2 85 MissAliceMills(3) 7 70
(Rod Millman) *trckd ldrs: clsd and poised to chal jst over 2f out: sn rdn and fdd* **33/1**

0010 **9** *¾* **Capaill Liath (IRE)**[21] 4080 5-10-7 90 (p) MissHayleyMoore(3) 5 73
(Kevin Ryan) *chsd clr ldr: clsd to chal and upsides jst over 2f out: wknd over 1f out* **16/1**

6100 **10** *½* **Red Seventy**[19] 4124 4-9-11 77 (b[1]) MlleAlexandraRosa 14 59
(Harry Dunlop) *racd alone against nr side rail: on terms to 3f out: bmpd along vigorously after: unbalanced and fdd fnl 2f* **14/1**

2643 **11** *2 ¼* **Another For Joe**[20] 4101 5-9-9 75 MrsCBartley 2 51
(Jim Goldie) *a in rr: rdn and no prog over 2f out* **14/1**

6521 **12** *1* **Mambo Spirit (IRE)**[14] 4303 9-9-5 71 oh3 MissCWalton 1 44
(Tony Newcombe) *v awkward s and nrly uns rdr: a wl in rr* **25/1**

5621 **13** *9* **Seattle Drive (IRE)**[29] 3777 5-9-9 78 MissJoannaMason(3) 9 28
(Brian Ellison) *a in rr: wl bhd fnl 2f: t.o* **10/1**

1413 **14** *shd* **See The Storm**[15] 4250 5-9-5 71 MissJMMangan 12 20
(Ian Williams) *wl pl in chsng gp tl wknd rapidly over 2f out: t.o* **11/2**[3]

-100 **15** *3 ¾* **Magical Speedfit (IRE)**[58] 2790 8-9-0 71 oh3 MissKMargarson(5) 8 11
(George Margarson) *chsd ldrs tl wknd rapidly over 2f out: t.o* **50/1**

1m 27.8s (0.20) **Going Correction** -0.175s/f (Firm) **15** Ran SP% **126.8**
Speed ratings (Par 107): **91,83,82,81,80 80,79,78,77,76 74,73,62,62,58**
toteswingers 1&2 £21.40, 1&3 £25.70, 2&3 £10.40 CSF £94.08 CT £975.76 TOTE £15.30: £4.20, £2.40, £3.40; EX 82.30 Trifecta £1328.00 Pool: £6,689.25 - 3.77 winning units..
Owner H Clewlow **Bred** Bridgewater Equine Ltd **Trained** Alpraham, Cheshire
■ Stewards' Enquiry : Miss Joanna Mason five-day ban: used whip when out of contention (Aug 12,15-17,19)

FOCUS
This traditional race for lady amateurs was not surprisingly run 3.52secs slower than the earlier feature handicap after they went steady early on. Nevertheless, it has proved a decent guide to the following season's big handicaps, with Castles In The Air winning the International Handicap the season after taking this and Captain Ramius doing likewise in the Ayr Gold Cup. Hard to know what to make of this form, this wasy out of line with the winner's profile.

4747 TITANIC BELFAST WINKFIELD STKS (LISTED RACE) 7f
5:00 (5:01) (Class 1) 2-Y-O

£14,461 (£5,482; £2,743; £1,366; £685; £344) **Stalls** Centre

Form RPR
13 **1** **Washaar (IRE)**[14] 4296 2-9-2 0 DaneO'Neill 2 103
(Richard Hannon) *trckd ldr: led after 3f: rdn to assert wl over 1f out: in command fnl f* **11/4**[3]

151 **2** *1 ½* **Emirates Flyer**[14] 4299 2-9-2 101 RyanMoore 3 98
(Saeed bin Suroor) *hld up in last: prog on outer wl over 2f out: drvn and kpt on to take 2nd ins fnl f: no imp on wnr* **7/4**[1]

15 **3** *½* **Lone Warrior (IRE)**[35] 3555 2-9-2 85 AdamKirby 1 97
(David Evans) *hld up: prog to trck ldrs 1/2-way: drvn and nt qckn over 2f out: lost pl sn after: rallied u.p fnl f: pressed runner-up nr fin* **14/1**

10 **4** *4 ½* **Dubawi Fun**[39] 3422 2-9-2 0 NeilCallan 6 82
(Ismail Mohammed) *t.k.h: hld up in tch: outpcd fr over 2f out: n.d after: tk modest 4th last strides* **20/1**

21 **5** *hd* **Safety Check (IRE)**[7] 4533 2-9-2 0 MickaelBarzalona 5 82
(Charlie Appleby) *led at stdy pce for 3f: mostly chsd wnr to fnl f: hanging and wknd: eased nr fin* **5/2**[2]

2666 **6** *1* **Rough Courte (IRE)**[15] 4248 2-8-11 79 MartinHarley 4 73
(Mick Channon) *v free to post: plld hrd early: hld up in tch: rdn over 2f out: sn wknd* **33/1**

404 **7** *4* **Street Force (USA)**[14] 4296 2-9-2 92 KevinManning 7 66
(Clive Brittain) *in tch: dropped to last and struggling over 2f out: no ch after* **10/1**

1m 28.98s (1.38) **Going Correction** -0.175s/f (Firm) **7** Ran SP% **115.1**
Speed ratings (Par 102): **85,83,82,77,77 76,71**
toteswingers 1&2 £1.70, 1&3 £4.90, 2&3 £3.60 CSF £8.10 TOTE £4.10: £2.10, £1.20; EX 7.80 Trifecta £42.20 Pool: £4,653.00 - 82.59 winning units..
Owner Hamdan Al Maktoum **Bred** Gerard Corry & Cristian Healy **Trained** East Everleigh, Wilts

FOCUS
A couple of above-average types have taken this in the past, namely Toronado and Ravens Pass. This doesn't look like a better renewal, rated around the first two.

4748 CANISBAY BLOODSTOCK H'CAP 1m 4f
5:35 (5:35) (Class 4) (0-85,86) 3-Y-O **£6,469** (£1,925; £962; £481) **Stalls** Low

Form RPR
1211 **1** **Big Thunder**[7] 4516 3-9-8 86 LukeMorris 3 100
(Sir Mark Prescott Bt) *mde all: hanging lft bnd 3f out: sn drvn for home: edgd rt u.p fr over 1f out but a finding enough* **5/4**[1]

-632 **2** *2 ½* **Glenard**[12] 4349 3-9-4 82 RyanMoore 4 92
(Charles Hills) *hld up in last: prog to chse wnr over 2f out: drvn and cl enough over 1f out: hld whn forced to switch lft ins fnl f* **13/8**[2]

0-31 **3** *5* **Rosaceous**[44] 3237 3-9-2 80 MickaelBarzalona 1 82
(Daniel Kubler) *hld up in 3rd: moved up to dispute 2nd whn bmpd 4f out and dropped to last: kpt on one pce fnl 2f* **5/1**[3]

1156 **4** *2 ¾* **Knight's Parade (IRE)**[2] 4679 3-8-3 70 RyanPowell(3) 2 68
(Amanda Perrett) *chsd wnr: swtchd outside 4f out: lost 2nd and wknd over 2f out* **10/1**

2m 32.54s (0.04) **Going Correction** -0.175s/f (Firm) **4** Ran SP% **108.3**
Speed ratings (Par 102): **92,90,87,85**
CSF £3.58 TOTE £2.00; EX 3.60 Trifecta £3.90 Pool: £1,940.04 - 371.10 winning units..
Owner John Brown & Megan Dennis **Bred** Stanley House Stud **Trained** Newmarket, Suffolk
■ Stewards' Enquiry : Ryan Powell two-day ban: careless riding (Aug 10-11)

FOCUS
Just a small field for this fair 3yo handicap and they finished in racecard and market order. The winner continues to thrive but there wasn't great depth to this.
T/Jkpt: Not won. T/Plt: £2,656.70 to a £1 stake. Pool: £291,006.44 - 79.96 winning units T/Qpdt: £166.10 to a £1 stake. Pool: £14,708.94 - 65.50 winning units JN

4630 LINGFIELD (L-H)
Saturday, July 27

OFFICIAL GOING: Turf course - firm (good to firm in places; 9.3); all-weather course - standard
Wind: Light; across Weather: Unsettled

4749 LEE HANSON TO RECEPTION PLEASE MAIDEN AUCTION STKS 5f
5:20 (5:20) (Class 6) 2-Y-O **£2,045** (£603; £302) **Stalls** High

Form RPR
2205 **1** **Lilo Lil**[11] 4370 2-8-4 65 (p) DavidProbert 4 60+
(David C Griffiths) *fast away: mde all: hld on wl whn chal fnl f: drvn out* **10/11**[1]

4005 **2** *nk* **Vodka Chaser (IRE)**[11] 4363 2-8-7 54 ow1 SeanLevey 5 62
(J S Moore) *chsd wnr: drvn to chal ent fnl f: jst hld nr fin* **6/1**[3]

4 **3** *½* **Douneedahand**[42] 3310 2-8-5 0 KieranO'Neill 1 58
(Seamus Mullins) *sn pushed along in 4th: hdwy to chse ldng pair over 1f out: kpt on* **12/1**

4 *7* **Shrewd Bob (IRE)** 2-9-0 0 AndreaAtzeni 3 42+
(Robert Eddery) *chsd ldrs: rdn over 2f out: edgd bdly lft and wknd over 1f out* **7/4**[2]

58.29s (0.09) **Going Correction** -0.225s/f (Firm) **4** Ran SP% **110.7**
Speed ratings (Par 92): **90,89,88,77**
CSF £6.80 TOTE £2.10; EX 5.80 Trifecta £15.90 Pool: £906.03 - 42.60 winning units..
Owner Mickley Stud,D C Griffiths & D Clarke **Bred** S And R Ewart **Trained** Bawtry, S Yorks

FOCUS
A very weak maiden and the winner was well below her best.

4750 LAURA BRETT 21ST BIRTHDAY CELEBRATION MEDIAN AUCTION MAIDEN STKS 7f
5:55 (5:55) (Class 6) 3-5-Y-O **£2,045** (£603; £302) **Stalls** High

Form RPR
3342 **1** **Liberty Jack (IRE)**[21] 4068 3-9-5 71 (p) GeorgeBaker 4 82
(Roger Charlton) *sn led: mde virtually all: drew clr on bit over 1f out: v easily* **4/11**[1]

-343 **2** *7* **Icon Dance**[16] 4219 3-9-0 72 AndreaAtzeni 3 58
(Ben De Haan) *a 2nd: rdn 2f out: sn btn and no ch w wnr* **9/4**[2]

The Form Book Flat, Raceform Ltd, Compton, RG20 6NL.

504 **3** *12* **Tornado Battle**[3] 4625 3-9-5 0..(b) DavidProbert 2 31
(Phil McEntee) *chsd ldrs: rdn over 2f out: sn btn* **20/1**[3]
0 **4** *32* **Violetgrace**[17] 4176 3-8-9 0.. PhilipPrince(5) 1
(Michael Madgwick) *outpcd in 4th: lost tch over 2f out: sn wl bhd* **50/1**
1m 20.98s (-2.32) **Going Correction** -0.225s/f (Firm) **4** Ran SP% **110.8**
Speed ratings (Par 101): **104,96,82,45**
CSF £1.53 TOTE £5.20; EX 1.60 Trifecta £2.10 Pool: £1,751.73 - 599.97 winning units..
Owner D J Deer **Bred** D J And Mrs Deer **Trained** Beckhampton, Wilts

FOCUS
Only two mattered here and this turned into a cakewalk for the winner, who scored in a decent time.

4751 FREDDIE PARKER WINNING FASHION H'CAP 7f
6:25 (6:25) (Class 5) (0-70,70) 3-Y-O **£2,726** (£805; £402) **Stalls** High

Form RPR
-120 **1** **Bright Glow**[58] 2806 3-9-7 **70**..(p) TedDurcan 5 77
(David Lanigan) *chsd ldr: led on stands' rail over 2f out: drvn to hold on ins fnl f* **11/4**[2]
1142 **2** *nk* **Jontleman (IRE)**[5] 4592 3-9-7 **70**.. GeorgeBaker 3 76
(Mick Channon) *t.k.h in 3rd: effrt and gng wl towards centre 2f out: rdn to chal over 1f out: jst hld nr fin* **11/10**[1]
-365 **3** *1 1/4* **North Pole**[10] 4400 3-8-9 **63**..(b) RosieJessop(5) 2 66
(Sir Mark Prescott Bt) *dwlt: bhd: effrt and swtchd into centre 1f out: styd on: nvr nrr* **4/1**[3]
4000 **4** *2 3/4* **Multitask**[35] 3577 3-8-6 **60**.. PhilipPrince(5) 4 55
(Michael Madgwick) *led tl over 2f out: wknd over 1f out* **40/1**
-424 **5** *1/2* **Arbeel**[29] 3787 3-9-7 **70**.. GrahamLee 1 64
(Peter Chapple-Hyam) *swtchd rt to stands' rail s: plld hrd in 4th: rdn wl over 1f out: fnd little* **7/1**
1m 22.12s (-1.18) **Going Correction** -0.225s/f (Firm) **5** Ran SP% **109.2**
Speed ratings (Par 100): **97,96,95,92,91**
CSF £6.10 TOTE £3.80: £1.20, £1.60; EX 7.50 Trifecta £19.90 Pool: £1,406.57 - 52.77 winning units..
Owner Bjorn Nielsen & Lord Lloyd Webber **Bred** Watership Down Stud **Trained** Upper Lambourn, Berks

FOCUS
A decent race for the grade with the runner-up bang in form, but the time was relatively slow. The form makes sense at face value.

4752 BOWERS & WILKINS H'CAP 7f 140y
7:00 (7:02) (Class 6) (0-65,67) 3-Y-O+ **£2,045** (£603; £302) **Stalls** Centre

Form RPR
0402 **1** **Hawk Moth (IRE)**[9] 4424 5-9-6 **57**..(b) GrahamLee 8 67
(John Spearing) *chsd ldrs on stands' rail: effrt and squeezed through 1f out: drvn to chal ins fnl f: led fnl strides* **8/1**
-531 **2** *shd* **Enriching (USA)**[8] 4504 5-10-2 **67**.. ShaneKelly 10 77
(Gary Harrison) *pressed ldr: led wl over 1f out: hrd rdn fnl f: jst ct* **7/4**[1]
0245 **3** *2* **First Class**[23] 3993 5-9-11 **62**..(p) DavidProbert 5 67
(Rae Guest) *mid-div: hrd rdn and hdwy over 1f out: edgd lft: unable qck ins fnl f* **3/1**[2]
5000 **4** *2 1/4* **Zaheeb**[3] 4637 5-9-4 **55**..(p) AdamBeschizza 1 54
(Dave Morris) *led and sn got across to stands' rail: hdd wl over 1f out: one pce* **16/1**
0-31 **5** *4* **Gypsy Rider**[9] 4424 4-8-12 **56**.. NedCurtis(7) 2 45
(Roger Curtis) *prom towards centre tl wknd jst over 1f out* **7/1**
1232 **6** *2* **Wishformore (IRE)**[28] 3817 6-9-3 **54**..(p) RobertHavlin 3 38
(Zoe Davison) *stmbld s: towards rr: mod effrt over 2f out: n.d* **6/1**[3]
005 **7** *1 1/2* **Marguerite St Just**[26] 3910 3-8-3 **48**.. AndreaAtzeni 9 26
(Olivia Maylam) *prom: rdn 3f out: wknd wl over 1f out* **16/1**
2630 **8** *1 1/4* **Byrd In Hand (IRE)**[57] 2845 6-9-3 **54**.. SeanLevey 6 31
(John Bridger) *hld up in rr: rdn and n.d fnl 2f* **10/1**
3600 **9** *4* **Sarah Berry**[30] 3738 4-9-3 **57**.. RyanClark(3) 7 24
(Chris Dwyer) *a in rr: no ch fnl 2f* **33/1**
1m 29.94s (-2.36) **Going Correction** -0.225s/f (Firm)
WFA 3 from 4yo+ 8lb **9** Ran SP% **123.1**
Speed ratings (Par 101): **102,101,99,97,93 91,90,88,84**
CSF £23.97 CT £55.56 TOTE £8.40: £2.40, £2.00, £1.90; EX 20.60 Trifecta £75.40 Pool: £1,444.58 - 14.35 winning units..
Owner Kinnersley Partnership **Bred** Dr D Harron **Trained** Kinnersley, Worcs

FOCUS
The winner was not far off his old turf best and the second continued his improvement.

4753 GAIL MELMOE SEXY AT SIXTY BIRTHDAY H'CAP 1m 5f (P)
7:30 (7:32) (Class 5) (0-70,71) 3-Y-O **£3,234** (£721; £721; £240) **Stalls** Low

Form RPR
1021 **1** **Miss Tiger Lily**[10] 4406 3-9-8 **71**.. LukeMorris 3 77
(Harry Dunlop) *mde all: jnd and rdn 2f out: strly pressed after: hld on gamely* **7/2**[3]
-300 **2** *1/2* **Grayswood**[28] 3809 3-9-2 **65**.. GeorgeBaker 5 70
(William Muir) *prom: w wnr fnl 2f: kpt on u.p: jst unable to get on top* **5/1**
163 **2** *dht* **Pixie Cut (IRE)**[19] 4122 3-8-11 **60**.. AndreaAtzeni 2 65
(J S Moore) *mid-div on inner: hrd rdn and hdwy over 1f out: pressed ldrs ins fnl f: r.o* **16/1**
3550 **4** *3 1/2* **Bold Assertion**[12] 4352 3-9-0 **63**..(v[1]) TedDurcan 4 64
(John Best) *dwlt: hld up in rr: rdn over 2f out: styd on fr over 1f out* **33/1**
-305 **5** *2* **Yorkshireman (IRE)**[18] 4135 3-9-7 **70**.. GrahamLee 7 69
(David Brown) *mid-div: hdwy on outer 6f out: rdn over 3f out: btn 2f out* **16/1**
00-0 **6** *nse* **Katie Gale**[80] 2157 3-8-2 **51** oh4.. KieranO'Neill 6 50
(Tim Pitt) *chsd ldrs: outpcd and lost pl 4f out: kpt on again fnl f* **40/1**
4020 **7** *3/4* **Star Of Namibia (IRE)**[18] 4150 3-9-0 **63**..(b) DavidProbert 1 61
(J S Moore) *hld up in rr: rdn 3f out: n.d* **8/1**
4200 **8** *1 1/4* **El Massivo (IRE)**[50] 3055 3-9-4 **67**.. RobertHavlin 9 63
(William Jarvis) *hld up towards rr: rdn and hdwy on outer 3f out: wnt cl 3rd over 2f out: wknd over 1f out* **9/4**[1]
005 **9** *14* **Hero's Story**[42] 3343 3-8-12 **61**.. SeanLevey 8 41
(Amanda Perrett) *chsd ldr: rdn 3f out: sn wknd* **3/1**[2]
2m 47.33s (1.33) **Going Correction** +0.325s/f (Slow) **9** Ran SP% **122.9**
Speed ratings (Par 100): **108,107,107,105,104 104,103,103,94**
Places: Grayswood: £2.20, Pixie Cut: £3.40; Tote Exacta: MTL, G: £18.00, MTL, PC: £11.60; CSF: MTL, G: £11.54, MTL, PC: £30.68; Tricast: MTL, G, PC: 8.39, MTL, PC, G: £144.86 TOTE £3.50: £1.30 TRIFECTA 1-4-8 £73.70 1-8-4 £165.50.

FOCUS
The winner built on her previous turf win and may do better still.

4754 ADAM & MICKAELLA H'CAP 2m (P)
8:00 (8:01) (Class 5) (0-70,68) 4-Y-O+ **£2,726** (£805; £402) **Stalls** Low

Form RPR
4662 **1** **Comedy House**[23] 3985 5-8-11 **63**.. PhilipPrince(5) 3 69
(Michael Madgwick) *in tch: effrt on outer over 2f out: led 1f out: drvn out* **16/1**
0103 **2** *1/2* **Honourable Knight (IRE)**[23] 3971 5-9-7 **68**.. DavidProbert 5 73
(Mark Usher) *hld up in rr: rdn 3f out: r.o fr over 1f out: clsng at fin* **8/1**[3]
0423 **3** *hd* **Nashville (IRE)**[11] 4372 4-9-7 **68**.. J-PGuillambert 4 73
(Richard Fahey) *prom: rdn over 4f out: outpcd over 2f out: rallied and r.o fnl f* **1/1**[1]
1223 **4** *nk* **Guards Chapel**[67] 1348 5-9-7 **68**..(v) GeorgeBaker 6 72
(Gary Moore) *hld up and bhd: rdn and r.o fnl 2f: nrst fin* **4/1**[2]
02-0 **5** *hd* **Reggie Perrin**[23] 3971 5-8-9 **61**..(v) JemmaMarshall(5) 7 65
(Pat Phelan) *trckd ldrs: sltly outpcd and rdn over 4f out: rallied 1f out: one pce* **20/1**
53/0 **6** *1/2* **Sinbad The Sailor**[33] 3647 8-9-4 **65**..(v) AidanColeman 11 69
(George Baker) *mid-div: hdwy on outer 6f out: led over 3f out tl 1f out: wknd fnl 100yds* **12/1**
2264 **7** *5* **Moment In The Sun**[7] 4521 4-8-13 **60**.. AndreaAtzeni 8 58
(David Flood) *sn led: hdd over 3f out: w ldrs tl wknd ent fnl f* **16/1**
330- **8** *1* **Ampleforth**[253] 7744 5-9-3 **67**..(v) WilliamTwiston-Davies(3) 9 63
(Ian Williams) *prom: jnd ldr 5f out: wknd 1f out* **8/1**[3]
-066 **9** *3 1/2* **Inffiraaj (IRE)**[11] 4365 4-8-5 **52**.. KieranO'Neill 10 44
(Mick Channon) *rdn 3f out: a bhd* **33/1**
1150 **10** *6* **Hoonose**[11] 4380 4-8-11 **58**..(v) GrahamLee 2 43
(Pat Eddery) *in tch on inner: outpcd over 3f out: sn struggling* **33/1**
3m 29.4s (3.70) **Going Correction** +0.325s/f (Slow) **10** Ran SP% **122.3**
Speed ratings (Par 103): **103,102,102,102,102 102,99,99,97,94**
toteswingers 1&2 £27.20, 1&3 £3.30, 2&3 £3.50 CSF £141.10 CT £249.35 TOTE £7.50: £2.70, £2.60, £1.10; EX 89.40 Trifecta £345.60 Pool: £1,337.61 - 2.90 winning units..
Owner Los Leader **Bred** Giles W Pritchard-Gordon (farming) Ltd **Trained** Denmead, Hants

FOCUS
An open handicap run at a steady pace, backed up by the very slow overall time, and not form to take too literally as they finished in a heap.

4755 TANDRIDGE H'CAP 1m 2f (P)
8:30 (8:32) (Class 6) (0-65,65) 3-Y-O+ **£2,045** (£603; £302) **Stalls** Low

Form RPR
4055 **1** **Diletta Tommasa (IRE)**[7] 4523 3-9-1 **62**.. AndreaAtzeni 1 68
(John Stimpson) *prom: drvn to ld ins fnl f: all out* **20/1**
0V44 **2** *shd* **Inessa Armand (IRE)**[19] 4122 3-9-0 **61**..(p) DavidProbert 5 67
(J S Moore) *sn led: hrd rdn and hdd ins fnl f: r.o* **33/1**
064 **3** *hd* **Dukes Delight (IRE)**[18] 4152 3-9-3 **64**.. TedDurcan 4 70+
(David Lanigan) *in tch: rdn to chse ldrs over 1f out: r.o* **6/4**[1]
6-44 **4** *hd* **Opera Buff**[35] 3580 4-10-0 **65**..(p) AidanColeman 6 70
(Sean Curran) *chsd ldrs on outer: outpcd 2f out: rallied and r.o fnl f* **8/1**[3]
4000 **5** *1 1/2* **Baltic Blade (IRE)**[17] 4169 3-9-2 **63**.. GeorgeBaker 10 65
(Gary Moore) *trckd ldr: rdn 2f out: no ex fnl f* **12/1**
0651 **6** *hd* **Safwaan**[26] 3909 6-9-8 **59**.. J-PGuillambert 3 61
(Gary Harrison) *hld up towards rr: rdn and hdwy over 1f out: styd on steadily* **6/1**[2]
043 **7** *1/2* **Royal Sea (IRE)**[7] 4516 4-9-2 **58**..(be) RobertTart(5) 11 59
(Michael Mullineaux) *mid-div: rdn 3f out: styd on fnl f* **8/1**[3]
3-40 **8** *1 1/2* **Posh Boy (IRE)**[44] 3254 3-8-13 **63**.. AshleyMorgan(3) 14 61
(Chris Wall) *mid-div on outer tl outpcd and btn 2f out* **8/1**[3]
0504 **9** *nk* **Spirit Of Gondree (IRE)**[12] 4357 5-9-6 **57**..(b) LukeMorris 7 54
(Milton Bradley) *dwlt: bhd: mod effrt over 1f out: nt trble ldrs* **14/1**
4-24 **10** *2* **Pat's Legacy (USA)**[68] 2514 7-9-8 **64**.. JemmaMarshall(5) 8 57
(Pat Phelan) *dwlt: t.k.h in rr: rdn wl over 1f out: nvr nr ldrs* **12/1**
000 **11** *1/2* **Uncle Dermot (IRE)**[40] 3416 5-10-0 **65**.. GrahamLee 13 57
(Brendan Powell) *hld up towards rr: modest effrt on inner 2f out: sn btn* **12/1**
0500 **12** *hd* **Lily Edge**[19] 4126 4-10-0 **65**.. SeanLevey 2 57
(John Bridger) *in tch on rail: hrd rdn and wknd over 1f out* **20/1**
2m 10.6s (4.00) **Going Correction** +0.325s/f (Slow)
WFA 3 from 4yo+ 10lb **12** Ran SP% **129.8**
Speed ratings (Par 101): **97,96,96,96,95 95,94,93,93,91 91,91**
toteswingers 1&2 £36.00, 1&3 £26.70, 2&3 £29.00 CSF £590.18 CT £1606.83 TOTE £49.60: £8.50, £10.30, £1.50; EX 206.30 Trifecta £718.10 Part won. Pool: £957.52 - 0.41 winning units..
Owner J T Stimpson **Bred** Ms Sheila Lavery **Trained** Butterton, Staffs

FOCUS
Another steadily run affair, rated modestly.
T/Plt: £7.20 to a £1 stake. Pool: £49,245.51 - 4,939.73 winning units T/Qpdt: £2.70 to a £1 stake. Pool: £6,746.68 - 1,829.80 winning units LM

3822 NEWCASTLE (L-H)
Saturday, July 27

OFFICIAL GOING: Good to firm (8.4)
Wind: Breezy; half behind Weather: Warm; sunny

4756 COLLINGWOOD INSURANCE COMPANY MAIDEN AUCTION STKS 7f
1:55 (1:56) (Class 4) 2-Y-O **£3,881** (£1,155; £577; £288) **Stalls** Centre

Form RPR
4 **1** **Xanthos**[12] 4347 2-8-11 0.. TomMcLaughlin 1 80+
(Ed Walker) *t.k.h: w ldr: led over 2f out: rdn clr fr over 1f out* **12/1**
0 **2** *3 3/4* **Miss Acclaimed (IRE)**[12] 4351 2-8-7 0.. DaleSwift 4 66
(Brian Ellison) *chsd ldrs: effrt and wnt 2nd wl over 1f out: kpt on fnl f: nt pce of wnr* **66/1**
0 **3** *1 1/2* **El Beau (IRE)**[21] 4053 2-8-7 0.. RaulDaSilva(3) 7 65
(John Quinn) *sn pushed along towards rr: effrt and hdwy over 2f out: edgd lft: kpt on fnl f: nrst fin* **16/1**
53 **4** *2* **Needless Shouting (IRE)**[10] 4414 2-8-9 0.. SamHitchcott 2 58
(Mick Channon) *led to over 2f out: rdn and outpcd fr over 1f out* **11/4**[2]
0 **5** *1/2* **Maxie T**[35] 3581 2-8-11 0.. LiamJones 5 59
(Mark Johnston) *midfield: effrt on outside over 2f out: drvn and no imp fr over 1f out* **2/1**[1]
6 *1* **Penhill** 2-8-11 0.. PJMcDonald 3 56+
(James Bethell) *noisy and green in paddock: dwlt: sn in tch: pushed along over 2f out: one pce fr over 1f out: improve* **33/1**

235 **7** 1 **Supa U**[21] 4044 2-8-4 66 .... [1] DuranFentiman 11 47
(Tim Easterby) *plld hrd: hld up: rdn over 2f out: nvr able to chal* **8/1**[3]
8 1 **Emerahldz (IRE)** 2-8-5 0 .... BarryMcHugh 12 45
(Richard Fahey) *missed break: hld up: rdn and outpcd over 2f out: sn btn* **8/1**[3]
05 **9** 3 **Fair Flutter (IRE)**[16] 4218 2-8-12 0 .... LeeTopliss 6 47
(Richard Fahey) *hld up in tch: pushed along over 2f out: wknd over 1f out* **20/1**
36 **10** 8 **Nevada Blue**[49] 3079 2-8-11 0 .... MickyFenton 10 21
(Tony Coyle) *midfield: pushed along over 2f out: wknd over 1f out* **8/1**[3]
11 9 **Vosne Romanee** 2-8-9 0 .... TomEaves 8
(Keith Dalgleish) *missed break: bhd: struggling 3f out: nvr on terms* **40/1**
0 **12** 3 **Mrs J (IRE)**[31] 3680 2-8-5 0 .... (b[1]) PaulQuinn 9
(Tim Easterby) *dwlt: bhd and sn pushed along: struggling fr 1/2-way* **33/1**
1m 24.47s (-3.33) **Going Correction** -0.40s/f (Firm) **12** Ran SP% **121.5**
Speed ratings (Par 96): **103,98,97,94,94 93,91,90,87,78 67,64**
CSF £656.20 TOTE £15.20: £3.10, £10.90, £6.50; EX 604.30 TRIFECTA Not won..
Owner Matthew Cottis **Bred** G A E & J Smith Bloodstock Ltd **Trained** Newmarket, Suffolk

FOCUS
Rail on bend into home straight moved in 2yds. A bumper eight-race card got underway with a fair juvenile maiden in which they went a decent gallop on ground officially described as good to firm. The time was decent and the winner rates up with the best one of the recent winners of this race.

4757 COLLINGWOOD FLEET INSURANCE H'CAP 6f
2:30 (2:30) (Class 3) (0-90,88) 3-Y-0 **£9,056** (£2,695; £1,346; £673) **Stalls** Centre

Form RPR
1214 **1** **Noble Deed**[15] 4265 3-9-3 **84** .... LiamJones 1 94
(William Haggas) *pressed ldr: rdn and led over 1f out: hld on wl fnl f* **13/8**[1]
-223 **2** 1 **Nardin**[15] 4252 3-9-4 **85** .... PJMcDonald 5 91
(Ed Dunlop) *trckd ldrs: rdn and ev ch over 1f out: kpt on ins fnl f: hld last 75yds* **13/8**[1]
6660 **3** 1 ¾ **Dream Maker (IRE)**[15] 4260 3-9-7 **88** .... DuranFentiman 4 88
(Tim Easterby) *t.k.h: prom: rdn and outpcd wl over 1f out: kpt on ins fnl f: nt rch first two* **12/1**[3]
0113 **4** 1 **Bondesire**[19] 4117 3-8-8 **80** .... DavidBergin(5) 3 77
(David O'Meara) *t.k.h: led tl rdn and hdd over 1f out: outpcd ins fnl f* **11/4**[2]
1m 10.77s (-3.83) **Going Correction** -0.40s/f (Firm) **4** Ran SP% **110.5**
Speed ratings (Par 104): **109,107,105,104**
CSF £4.68 TOTE £2.40; EX 4.70 Trifecta £19.00 Pool: £1,743.24 - 68.51 winning units..
Owner Cheveley Park Stud **Bred** Cheveley Park Stud Ltd **Trained** Newmarket, Suffolk

FOCUS
A small field assembled for this decent 3yo handicap, but a particularly honest gallop produced another quick time. The second is the best guide.

4758 COLLINGWOOD LEARNER DRIVER INSURANCE "BEESWING" H'CAP 7f
3:05 (3:05) (Class 3) (0-95,95) 3-Y-0+ **£11,644** (£3,465; £1,731; £865) **Stalls** Centre

Form RPR
2213 **1** **Pacific Heights (IRE)**[31] 3684 4-9-3 **84** .... DaleSwift 7 95+
(Brian Ellison) *chsd ldr: hdwy to ld over 1f out: drvn and styd on strly fnl f* **5/2**[1]
2612 **2** 2 **Able Master (IRE)**[12] 4342 7-10-0 **95** .... DavidNolan 2 101
(David O'Meara) *taken early to post: led and clr to 1/2-way: rdn and hdd over 1f out: kpt on ins fnl f* **9/1**
0300 **3** ½ **Laffan (IRE)**[21] 4062 4-9-6 **87** .... TomEaves 5 92
(Tim Easterby) *hld up bhd ldng gp: effrt and rdn 2f out: kpt on ins fnl f: nrst fin* **16/1**
0001 **4** ½ **Ortac Rock (IRE)**[9] 4438 4-8-6 **78** .... GeorgeChaloner(5) 3 81
(Richard Fahey) *prom: rdn and ev ch over 1f out: kpt on same pce ins fnl f* **11/1**
0304 **5** ¾ **Gatepost (IRE)**[28] 3825 4-9-2 **83** .... BarryMcHugh 4 84
(Richard Fahey) *sweating and on toes in paddock: t.k.h: in tch: hdwy and ev ch over 1f out: outpcd ins fnl f* **5/1**[3]
6254 **6** 1 ½ **Dubai Dynamo**[12] 4342 8-9-8 **89** .... JamesSullivan 9 86
(Ruth Carr) *hld up bhd ldng gp: rdn and edgd lft 2f out: sn no imp* **6/1**
5061 **7** 3 **Victoire De Lyphar (IRE)**[16] 4198 6-8-13 **80** .... (e) PJMcDonald 8 69
(Ruth Carr) *taken early to post: chsd ldrs tl hung lft and wknd 2f out* **11/4**[2]
-150 **8** 2 **Yair Hill (IRE)**[36] 3527 5-9-9 **90** .... StephenCraine 10 74
(Noel Wilson) *stdd s: hld up: rdn and hung lft 2f out: sn btn* **16/1**
1m 23.59s (-4.21) **Going Correction** -0.40s/f (Firm) **8** Ran SP% **116.3**
Speed ratings (Par 107): **108,105,105,104,103 102,98,96**
toteswingers 1&2 £6.30, 1&3 £13.90, 2&3 £7.80 CSF £26.16 CT £302.08 TOTE £3.60: £1.50, £2.80, £4.50; EX 27.90 Trifecta £168.10 Pool: £1,647.92 - 7.34 winning units..
Owner A Barnes **Bred** Smythson **Trained** Norton, N Yorks

FOCUS
The feature race on the card, and a decent handicap won in another quick time off a strong gallop, with four horses fighting it out across the track over 1f out. The winner delivered on his early promise.

4759 COLLINGWOOD ANNUAL LEARNER DRIVER INSURANCE H'CAP 2m 19y
3:40 (3:40) (Class 5) (0-75,75) 4-Y-0+ **£2,587** (£770; £384; £192) **Stalls** Centre

Form RPR
0304 **1** **Major Domo (FR)**[17] 4159 5-8-12 **66** .... AndrewMullen 9 73+
(Alan Swinbank) *t.k.h: cl up: led over 5f out to over: hdd over 2f out: rallied: led wl ins fnl f: r.o gamely* **9/2**[3]
5126 **2** hd **Petella**[6] 4563 7-8-4 **58** .... (p) JamesSullivan 1 65
(George Moore) *chsd ldrs: stdy hdwy over 3f out: rdn to ld over 1f out: hdd wl ins fnl f: kpt on: hld nr fin* **9/2**[3]
0643 **3** 1 ½ **Moheebb (IRE)**[6] 4559 9-8-0 **61** .... (p) JackGarritty(7) 10 66
(Robert Johnson) *hld up: hdwy and in tch over 3f out: rdn and edgd lft over 1f out: kpt on: nt pce of first two* **20/1**
0352 **4** 2 ½ **Keep It Cool (IRE)**[2] 4673 9-8-11 **70** .... DavidBergin(5) 6 72
(David O'Meara) *rrd s: in tch: smooth hdwy to ld over 2f out: rdn and hdd over 1f out: wknd ins fnl f* **9/5**[1]
-000 **5** 1 **Harrison's Cave**[30] 3726 5-9-2 **75** .... JasonHart(5) 3 76
(Chris Grant) *taken early to post: cl up: drvn and outpcd over 3f out: kpt on fnl f: no imp* **7/2**[2]
1003 **6** 2 ½ **Mason Hindmarsh**[33] 3627 6-8-13 **67** .... TomEaves 4 65
(Karen McLintock) *led to over 5f out: rdn and outpcd wl over 2f out: n.d after* **8/1**
-000 **7** 1 ½ **Mr Crystal (FR)**[50] 3065 9-8-8 **62** .... DaleSwift 7 58
(Micky Hammond) *hld up: drvn and struggling wl over 2f out: sn btn* **16/1**
3m 33.17s (-6.23) **Going Correction** -0.60s/f (Hard) **7** Ran SP% **116.1**
Speed ratings (Par 103): **91,90,90,88,88 87,86**
toteswingers 1&2 £5.70, 1&3 £19.50, 2&3 not won CSF £25.61 CT £367.36 TOTE £4.70: £3.10, £2.50; EX 20.90 Trifecta £210.80 Pool: £1,960.78 - 6.97 winning units..
Owner G Brogan **Bred** Langham Hall Stud **Trained** Melsonby, N Yorks
■ Stewards' Enquiry : Andrew Mullen four-day ban: used whip above permitted level down the shoulder in the forehand (Aug 10-13)

FOCUS
A fair staying handicap for older horses in which they went a sedate gallop until the tempo increased at the end of the back straight. The winner has more to offer.

4760 COLLINGWOOD TAXI INSURANCE/EBF FILLIES' H'CAP 1m 4f 93y
4:15 (4:15) (Class 4) (0-85,83) 4-Y-0+ **£6,469** (£1,925; £962; £481) **Stalls** Low

Form RPR
623 **1** **Livia's Dream (IRE)**[14] 4287 4-9-3 **79** .... TomMcLaughlin 5 85+
(Ed Walker) *t.k.h: chsd clr ldr: clsd 1/2-way: led and shkn up over 2f out: pushed clr fnl f* **4/6**[1]
0015 **2** 4 ½ **Bygones For Coins (IRE)**[21] 4052 5-7-9 **64** oh13 .... JackGarritty(7) 4 63
(Robert Johnson) *led and clr to 1/2-way: rdn and hdd over 2f out: kpt on fnl f: no ch w wnr* **10/1**
0234 **3** 3 ½ **Maybeagrey**[8] 4506 4-8-7 **69** .... DuranFentiman 1 62
(Tim Easterby) *hld up in tch: effrt and rdn over 2f out: hdwy over 1f out: sn no imp* **4/1**[3]
0314 **4** 7 **Act Your Shoe Size**[20] 4101 4-9-6 **82** .... TomEaves 2 64
(Keith Dalgleish) *chsd ldrs: drvn and outpcd over 2f out: btn over 1f out* **7/2**[2]
2m 36.9s (-8.70) **Going Correction** -0.60s/f (Hard) **4** Ran SP% **111.3**
Speed ratings (Par 102): **105,102,99,95**
CSF £7.92 TOTE £1.70; EX 7.30 Trifecta £14.80 Pool: £1,243.72 - 62.67 winning units..
Owner Mrs Olivia Hoare **Bred** Mount Coote Stud And M H Dixon **Trained** Newmarket, Suffolk

FOCUS
A good small-field middle-distance fillies' handicap, and they went a perfectly respectable gallop. Shaky, muddling form though, with the second 13lb wrong.

4761 COLLINGWOOD SHORT TERM LEARNER DRIVER INSURANCE H'CAP (DIV I) 5f
4:50 (4:50) (Class 6) (0-60,62) 3-Y-0+ **£2,587** (£770; £384; £192) **Stalls** Centre

Form RPR
3004 **1** **Captain Royale (IRE)**[3] 4619 8-9-6 **56** .... (p) BarryMcHugh 3 64
(Tracy Waggott) *cl up: effrt and ev ch over 1f out: drvn and led ins fnl f: hld on wl* **12/1**
4241 **2** ½ **Ingenti**[9] 4448 5-9-5 **62** .... KevinStott(7) 11 68
(Christopher Wilson) *led: rdn and edgd lft fr over 1f out: hdd ins fnl f: rallied: hld towards fin* **11/4**[2]
323 **3** nk **Busy Bimbo (IRE)**[3] 4621 4-8-11 **47** .... PaddyAspell 2 52
(Alan Berry) *hld up bhd ldng gp: rdn along 2f out: edgd rt and styd on fnl f: nrst fin* **6/1**[3]
0032 **4** shd **Arch Walker (IRE)**[2] 4691 6-8-12 **53** .... (b) GeorgeChaloner(5) 6 58+
(John Weymes) *dwlt: sn rdn and prom: effrt and drvn over 1f out: kpt on ins fnl f* **9/4**[1]
3000 **5** 2 ¼ **Rio's Girl**[22] 4009 6-8-8 **51** .... LauraBarry(7) 4 48
(Tony Coyle) *cl up: drvn and outpcd over 2f out: rallied fnl f: no imp* **14/1**
5506 **6** nk **Here Now And Why (IRE)**[4] 4615 6-9-3 **58** .... (p) GarryWhillans(5) 8 54
(Iain Jardine) *hld up: rdn along 1/2-way: kpt on fnl f: n.d* **8/1**
5-00 **7** ½ **Piste**[9] 4430 7-8-5 **48** .... (e) LukeLeadbitter(7) 7 42
(Tina Jackson) *prom: drvn and outpcd 1/2-way: n.d after* **18/1**
2000 **8** ½ **Roy's Legacy**[9] 4430 4-9-0 **55** .... (t) JasonHart(5) 1 47
(Shaun Harris) *disp ld to 1/2-way: rdn and wknd over 1f out* **12/1**
0005 **9** ¾ **Baltic Bomber (IRE)**[14] 4292 4-9-6 **56** .... MickyFenton 5 45
(John Quinn) *t.k.h: in rr: rdn whn hmpd over 2f out: sn struggling* **9/1**
59.27s (-1.83) **Going Correction** -0.40s/f (Firm)
WFA 3 from 4yo+ 4lb **9** Ran SP% **120.1**
Speed ratings (Par 101): **98,97,96,96,92 92,91,90,89**
toteswingers 1&2 Not won, 1&3 £29.10, 2&3 £29.10 CSF £47.04 CT £229.33 TOTE £13.70: £3.60, £1.50, £1.60; EX 63.80 Trifecta £166.00 Pool: £1,512.55 - 6.83 winning units..
Owner H Conlon **Bred** Skymarc Farm Inc **Trained** Spennymoor, Co Durham

FOCUS
The first division of a moderate sprint handicap in which they went a contested gallop. Regulation form.

4762 COLLINGWOOD SHORT TERM LEARNER DRIVER INSURANCE H'CAP (DIV II) 5f
5:25 (5:25) (Class 6) (0-60,60) 3-Y-0+ **£2,587** (£770; £384; £192) **Stalls** Centre

Form RPR
2365 **1** **Tuibama (IRE)**[22] 4009 4-9-8 **58** .... (p) DaleSwift 5 65
(Tracy Waggott) *wnt lft s: t.k.h: cl up: rdn to ld appr fnl f: hld on wl* **6/1**
0433 **2** ½ **See Vermont**[11] 4371 5-8-6 **47** .... (p) JasonHart(5) 7 52
(Robin Bastiman) *prom: effrt and rdn 2f out: chsd wnr ins fnl f: kpt on: hld nr fin* **5/1**[3]
0640 **3** 1 **Wicked Wilma (IRE)**[11] 4377 9-8-11 **47** .... PaddyAspell 6 49
(Alan Berry) *in tch: effrt and edgd lft over 1f out: kpt on same pce ins fnl f* **14/1**
0231 **4** 1 **Niceonemyson**[11] 4377 4-9-2 **59** .... KevinStott(7) 2 57
(Christopher Wilson) *slt ld to appr fnl f: kpt on same pce* **3/1**[2]
00-1 **5** ½ **Gran Canaria Queen**[14] 4291 4-9-1 **56** .... GeorgeChaloner(5) 11 52+
(Tim Easterby) *missed break: sn drvn along: hdwy and in tch 2f out: kpt on fnl f* **15/8**[1]
-606 **6** 3 **Mysterious Wonder**[9] 4430 3-8-9 **56** .... EvaMoscrop(7) 9 41
(Philip Kirby) *s.i.s: bhd and outpcd: styd on fnl f: nvr rchd ldrs* **14/1**
1602 **7** nk **Pavers Star**[9] 4430 4-9-10 **60** .... StephenCraine 8 44
(Noel Wilson) *disp ld to 2f out: sn rdn and wknd* **10/1**
0-0 **8** 3 **Imperial Bond**[204] 59 4-8-10 **46** oh1 .... TomEaves 3 20
(Jason Ward) *checked s: sn bhd and outpcd: no ch fr 1/2-way* **20/1**
59.47s (-1.63) **Going Correction** -0.40s/f (Firm)
WFA 3 from 4yo+ 4lb **8** Ran SP% **117.9**
Speed ratings (Par 101): **97,96,94,93,92 87,86,82**
toteswingers 1&2 £6.50, 1&3 £8.20, 2&3 £12.90 CSF £37.13 CT £407.68 TOTE £9.50: £2.00, £1.90, £1.80; EX 39.10 Trifecta £895.40 Pool: £1,269.14 - 1.06 winning units..
Owner H Conlon **Bred** J F Tuthill **Trained** Spennymoor, Co Durham
■ Stewards' Enquiry : Stephen Craine one-day ban: careless riding (Aug 10)

FOCUS
The second division of a moderate sprint handicap in which trainer Tracy Waggott completed a quickfire double. The winning time was a shade slower than the first division. The winner is rated to this year's form.

4763 COLLINGWOOD.GI APPRENTICE H'CAP 1m 2f 32y
6:00 (6:00) (Class 6) (0-60,60) 3-Y-0+ **£1,940** (£577; £288; £144) **Stalls** Centre

Form RPR
0240 **1** **Outlaw Torn (IRE)**[19] 4109 4-9-11 **57**...............................(e) JoshCrane 3 65
(Richard Guest) *taken early to post: t.k.h: led at stdy gallop after 2f: qcknd clr 3f out: unchal* **2/1**[1]
0000 **2** *6* **Dean Iarracht (IRE)**[6] 4563 7-8-12 **48**...........................(p) PaulMcGiff(4) 6 45
(Tracy Waggott) *s.i.s: hld up: hdwy to chse (clr) wnr over 2f out: rdn and no imp over 1f out* **7/1**
0620 **3** *4 1/2* **Madame Blavatsky (FR)**[21] 4052 5-9-3 **49**......................(v) KevinStott 8 37
(Karen McLintock) *ld at stdy pce for 2f: chsd wnr: rdn 3f out: outpcd fnl 2f* **5/2**[2]
0-06 **4** *2 1/2* **Joeluke**[9] 4436 3-8-10 **52**...[1] EvaMoscrop 1 35
(Philip Kirby) *t.k.h: in tch: rdn and outpcd 3f: nt danger after* **14/1**
00-0 **5** *14* **Many Levels**[12] 4352 3-8-2 **46**.. JoeDoyle(2) 2 3
(John Quinn) *t.k.h: in tch: shortlived effrt over 3f out: sn btn* **5/1**[3]
5000 **6** *2* **Ma Kellys (IRE)**[21] 4071 4-8-10 **46** oh1..................... LukeLeadbitter(4) 4
(Micky Hammond) *t.k.h: prom tl rdn and wknd fr 3f out* **5/1**[3]

2m 9.43s (-2.47) **Going Correction** -0.60s/f (Hard)
WFA 3 from 4yo+ 10lb **6** Ran SP% **114.4**
Speed ratings (Par 101): **85,80,76,74,63 61**
toteswingers 1&2 £2.90, 1&3 £3.00, 2&3 £1.02 CSF £16.84 CT £35.68 TOTE £2.70: £1.90, £3.20; EX 13.80 Trifecta £21.20 Pool: £775.27 - 27.38 winning units..
Owner James S Kennerley **Bred** Derek Veitch & Rory O'Brien **Trained** Wetherby, W Yorks

FOCUS
A weak handicap for apprentice riders in which the gallop was not a strong one, and most of the horses refused to settle to the detriment of their prospects. The winner had a soft lead.
T/Plt: £1,463.60 to a £1 stake. Pool: £77,714.10 - 38.76 winning units T/Qpdt: £18.30 to a £1 stake. Pool: £5,708.55 - 230.35 winning units RY

4715 NEWMARKET (R-H)
Saturday, July 27

OFFICIAL GOING: Good to firm (7.9)
Wind: Very light; half against Weather: Warm and muggy

4764 ADNAMS SOUTHWOLD BITTER EBF MAIDEN STKS 7f
2:10 (2:10) (Class 4) 2-Y-O **£4,528** (£1,347; £673; £336) **Stalls** Low

Form RPR
42 **1** **Expert (IRE)**[15] 4256 2-9-5 0.. PatDobbs 3 85+
(Richard Hannon) *mde all: shkn up 2f out: gng clr but hung bdly lft to far rail between 2f out and 1f out: r.o wl: comf* **15/8**[1]
2 *2 1/4* **Madeed** 2-9-5 0.. KierenFallon 7 79
(Brian Meehan) *chsd ldrs: rdn to chse wnr ent fnl 2f: outpcd by wnr over 1f out: no threat to wnr but kpt on to hold 2nd fnl f* **9/1**
6 **3** *1/2* **Newmarket Warrior (IRE)**[37] 3490 2-9-5 0..................... LiamKeniry 2 78
(Michael Bell) *hld up in tch in midfield: hdwy ent fnl 2f: wnt 3rd and sn chalng for 2nd jst ins fnl f: kpt on but no threat to wnr* **40/1**
4 *4* **Meteoroid (USA)** 2-9-5 0.. TomQueally 5 67+
(Lady Cecil) *dwlt: in tch in midfield: rdn and effrt over 2f out: outpcd and btn over 1f out: wl hld but plugged on fnl f* **9/2**[3]
5 *1/2* **Grandest** 2-9-5 0.. RobertHavlin 6 65
(John Gosden) *chsd ldrs: rdn and unable qck wl over 1f out: 3rd and btn 1f out: wknd fnl f* **9/4**[2]
6 *5* **Never To Be (USA)** 2-9-5 0...(t) NickyMackay 8 52
(John Gosden) *t.k.h: chsd wnr tl ent fnl 2f: sn rdn: rn green and hung lft: wknd over 1f out: fdd fnl f* **16/1**
0 **7** *10* **Stalactite (IRE)**[49] 3112 2-9-5 0................................ SilvestreDeSousa 4 25
(Charlie Appleby) *dwlt: a in last pair and nvr travelling: lost tch 2f out* **7/1**
8 *1 1/2* **Frederic Chopin** 2-9-5 0.. JamesDoyle 9 21
(Stuart Williams) *s.i.s: rn green and a in rr: lost tch 2f out* **66/1**

1m 25.95s (0.25) **Going Correction** -0.025s/f (Good) **8** Ran SP% **116.0**
Speed ratings (Par 96): **97,94,93,89,88 83,71,69**
toteswingers 1&2 £4.40, 1&3 £3.80, 2&3 £21.70 CSF £20.27 TOTE £2.70: £1.10, £2.60, £5.80; EX 22.40 Trifecta £448.10 Pool: £602.92 - 1.00 winning unit..
Owner Mrs J Wood **Bred** Edgeridge Ltd **Trained** East Everleigh, Wilts

FOCUS
Far side track used with stalls on stands' side, except 1m2f & 1m4f: centre. The repositioning of bend into home straight increased 1m2f &1m5f races by 16m. Forecast showers failed to arrive and the ground had dried out, meaning that the going was changed before racing from an overnight good. The jockeys agreed that it was riding quick. This maiden has been won by some decent performers in the past decade, most notably the Group 1 winner Farhh three years ago. This was probably not a strong renewal, with the errant winner knowing too much for the newcomers.

4765 ADNAMS SPINDRIFT H'CAP 1m 2f
2:45 (2:45) (Class 3) (0-95,93) 3-Y-0+
£9,337 (£2,796; £1,398; £699; £349; £175) **Stalls** Centre

Form RPR
-260 **1** **Clayton**[42] 3346 4-10-0 **93**.. TomQueally 8 102
(Kevin Ryan) *chsd ldr tl led 3f out: drvn and hrd pressed over 1f out: r.o gamely and forged ahd ins fnl f: all out* **15/2**
/10- **2** *nk* **Greek War (IRE)**[380] 4009 4-9-12 **91**................................ AhmedAjtebi 1 99+
(Charlie Appleby) *t.k.h: hld up in tch in last trio: clsd and nt clr run wl over 1f out: drvn and wnt between horses ins fnl f: chsd wnr wl ins fnl f: clsng towards fin but nvr quite getting to wnr* **20/1**
1020 **3** *3/4* **Rockalong (IRE)**[21] 4080 4-9-11 **90**................................. KierenFallon 6 97
(Luca Cumani) *stdd s: sn in tch in midfield: rdn to chal wl over 1f out: chsd wnr but unable qck ins fnl f: lot 2nd and styd on same pce wl ins fnl f* **5/1**[3]
5-33 **4** *nk* **Bank On Me**[28] 3812 4-8-11 **76**...................................... WilliamCarson 2 82
(Philip McBride) *hld up in tch in last trio: effrt towards centre 2f out: pressed ldrs but unable qck 1f out: styd on same pce fnl f* **9/1**
-014 **5** *1/2* **Al Saham**[22] 4028 4-9-13 **92**...[1] SilvestreDeSousa 4 97
(Saeed bin Suroor) *stdd s: t.k.h: hld up in tch in last trio: hdwy 4f out: pressing ldrs and rdn wl over 1f out: unable qck 1f out: one pce after* **11/4**[1]
31 **6** *1 1/2* **Magistral**[26] 3902 3-8-10 **85**.. RobertHavlin 7 87
(John Gosden) *t.k.h: chsd ldng pair tl chsd wnr ent fnl 2f: drvn and ev ch wl over 1f out: no ex and lost 2nd ins fnl f: wknd fnl 75yds* **4/1**[2]
2126 **7** *2 1/4* **One Pekan (IRE)**[16] 4214 3-8-10 **85**.............................(t[1]) JamesDoyle 3 83
(Roger Varian) *chsd ldrs tl lost pl and rdn 3f out: bhd and styd on same pce fnl f* **4/1**[2]
0351 **8** *3/4* **Enzaal (USA)**[15] 4251 3-8-4 **79**.. FrannyNorton 5 75
(Mark Johnston) *led tl rdn and hdd 3f out: lost pl u.p ent fnl 2f: bhd ins fnl f* **20/1**

2m 5.91s (0.41) **Going Correction** -0.025s/f (Good)
WFA 3 from 4yo 10lb **8** Ran SP% **114.6**
Speed ratings (Par 107): **97,96,96,95,95 94,92,91**
toteswingers 1&2 £28.70, 1&3 £6.40, 2&3 £38.60 CSF £137.39 CT £814.44 TOTE £10.00: £2.60, £4.80, £1.50; EX 161.70 Trifecta £601.30 Pool: £1,195.07 - 1.49 winning units..
Owner Exors of The Late Guy Reed **Bred** G Reed **Trained** Hambleton, N Yorks

FOCUS
Re-positioning of the bend into the home straight added 16m to the distance of this race. This was a decent handicap, but it was steadily run and they finished in a heap. The time was 4.41sec slower than standard. The form makes a fair bit of sense, however, with the winner back to his best.

4766 ADNAMS GHOST SHIP FILLIES' H'CAP 7f
3:20 (3:22) (Class 2) (0-100,96) 3-Y-0+ **£16,172** (£4,812; £2,405; £1,202) **Stalls** Low

Form RPR
2151 **1** **Malekat Jamal (IRE)**[6] 4561 4-8-7 **78** 6ex..................... DarrenEgan(3) 8 87+
(David Simcock) *restless in stalls: stdd and dropped in bhd after s: hld up in tch in rr: swtchd lft and effrt u.p over 1f out: sustained run ins fnl f to ld towards fin* **20/1**
311 **2** *nk* **Ghasabah**[9] 4453 3-8-8 **83**.. PatDobbs 9 88+
(William Haggas) *hld up in tch in last quartet: rdn and effrt in centre 2f out: chsd ldr u.p over 1f out: sustained effrt to chal ins fnl f: kpt on wl* **5/2**[1]
4634 **3** *1/2* **Mar Mar (IRE)**[29] 3784 3-9-7 **96**.............................(b) SilvestreDeSousa 4 100
(Saeed bin Suroor) *t.k.h: led: rdn and fnd ex over 1f out: drvn ins fnl f: kpt on wl tl hdd and lost 2 pls towards fin* **10/1**
0-55 **4** *1 1/2* **Tipping Over (IRE)**[77] 2253 3-8-4 **86**............................ NoelGarbutt(7) 2 86
(Hugo Palmer) *chsd ldr: rdn 2f out: lolst 2nd over 1f out: 4th and styd on same pce u.p ins fnl f* **25/1**
214 **5** *3/4* **Plover**[21] 4078 3-8-13 **88**.. JamesDoyle 5 86
(Sir Michael Stoute) *t.k.h: hld up in tch in last quartet: rdn ent fnl 2f: no imp and hrd drvn over 1f out: styd on fnl 100yds: nvr trbld ldrs* **10/1**
3012 **6** *hd* **Tantshi (IRE)**[15] 4252 3-9-2 **91**.. KierenFallon 3 88
(Roger Varian) *t.k.h: hld up wl in tch in midfield: rdn and effrt to chse ldrs wl over 1f out: no ex 1f out: wknd fnl 100yds* **9/2**[3]
0312 **7** *2* **Poisson D'Or**[17] 4181 4-8-12 **80**... TomQueally 1 75
(Rae Guest) *t.k.h: hld up in tch in last quartet: rdn and unable qck over 1f out: no imp fnl f* **4/1**[2]
1650 **8** *1* **Tartiflette**[21] 4062 4-9-10 **92**.. FrannyNorton 6 84
(Ed McMahon) *hld up wl in tch in midfield: effrt u.p 2f out: no ex ent fnl f: wknd fnl 150yds* **5/1**
0506 **9** *1 3/4* **Califante**[15] 4252 3-8-12 **87**.. MartinDwyer 7 72
(William Muir) *chsd ldrs: no ex u.p wl over 1f out: lost pl over 1f out: wknd fnl f* **20/1**

1m 25.15s (-0.55) **Going Correction** -0.025s/f (Good)
WFA 3 from 4yo 7lb **9** Ran SP% **115.0**
Speed ratings (Par 96): **102,101,101,99,98 98,96,94,92**
toteswingers 1&2 £7.90, 1&3 £28.00, 2&3 £4.30 CSF £68.02 CT £552.19 TOTE £25.40: £4.60, £1.30, £2.50; EX 64.30 Trifecta £326.00 Pool: £1,334.03 - 3.06 winning units..
Owner Saeed Manana **Bred** Adrian Purvis & Luke Barry **Trained** Newmarket, Suffolk

FOCUS
A good fillies' handicap run at a reasonable gallop. The form looks sound, with no fluke despite the winner's improved effort. The third is the key.

4767 ADNAMS BROADSIDE H'CAP 6f
3:55 (3:55) (Class 2) (0-105,101) 3-Y-O **£32,345** (£9,625; £4,810; £2,405) **Stalls** Low

Form RPR
2240 **1** **Lucky Beggar (IRE)**[42] 3348 3-9-5 **99**........................... WilliamCarson 9 108
(Charles Hills) *mde all: rdn and wnt clr over 1f out: drvn and hrd pressed fnl 100yds: hld on gamely towards fin: all out* **33/1**
511 **2** *nk* **Midnight Flower (IRE)**[7] 4534 3-8-9 **92**........................ DarrenEgan(3) 4 100
(David Simcock) *chsd wnr: rdn and sltly outpcd whn edgd lft over 1f out: rallied to press wnr fnl 100yds: r.o but hld towards fin* **7/2**[2]
-105 **3** *1* **Secretinthepark**[15] 4255 3-8-10 **90**................................ SteveDrowne 8 95
(Ed McMahon) *fly-jmpd as stalls opened: in tch in midfield: rdn and effrt to chse ldrs over 1f out: styd on to press wnr fnl 100yds: no ex towards fin* **9/1**
33-1 **4** *nk* **Gold Hunter (IRE)**[22] 4011 3-8-12 **92**..................... SilvestreDeSousa 12 96
(Saeed bin Suroor) *racd in centre tl over 2f out: hld up in midfield: hdwy to chse ldrs 2f out: wnt lft u.p 1f out: styd on to press wnr fnl 100yds: no ex towards fin* **11/4**[1]
3323 **5** *nk* **Rene Mathis (GER)**[15] 4255 3-8-6 **86**........................ PatrickMathers 3 89
(Richard Fahey) *taken down early: t.k.h: chsd ldrs: outpcd u.p and edgd lft over 1f out: rallied ins fnl f: styd on fnl 100yds* **16/1**
3-53 **6** *2 1/2* **Burning Blaze**[42] 3342 3-8-9 **89**.. JamieSpencer 1 84
(Kevin Ryan) *hld up in last quartet: rdn and effrt against stands' rail over 1f out: no imp 1f out: nvr trbld ldrs* **7/2**[2]
0210 **7** *3 1/2* **Robot Boy (IRE)**[15] 4255 3-8-10 **90**................................ TomQueally 7 74
(David Barron) *awkward leaving stalls and s.i.s: hld up in last quartet: rdn and effrt over 1f out: no prog and sn btn: wknd fnl f* **12/1**
-141 **8** *1/2* **Secondo (FR)**[8] 4478 3-8-12 **92**.. JamesDoyle 10 74
(Roger Charlton) *racd in centre tl over 2f out: t.k.h: hld up in last quartet: rdn and effrt 2f out: no hdwy u.p over 1f out: wknd and hung rt ins fnl f* **7/1**[3]
2 **9** *1/2* **Bern Me Baby (USA)**[8] 4493 3-9-0 **99**........................ TobyAtkinson(5) 6 79
(Marco Botti) *stdd s: t.k.h: hld up in tch in rr: effrt and rdn 2f out: rn fnl 2f: rdn and no hdwy over 1f out: wl hld and carried rt ins fnl f* **50/1**
0000 **10** *10* **Heavy Metal**[14] 4285 3-8-12 **92**..................................(v[1]) FrannyNorton 13 40
(Mark Johnston) *racd in centre tl over 2f out: chsd ldrs tl struggling u.p over 2f out: wknd wl over 1f out: bhd fnl f* **25/1**

1m 11.35s (-1.15) **Going Correction** -0.025s/f (Good) **10** Ran SP% **115.9**
Speed ratings (Par 106): **106,105,104,103,103 100,95,94,94,80**
toteswingers 1&2 £6.40, 1&3 £24.30, 2&3 £7.10 CSF £143.55 CT £1162.04 TOTE £14.80: £3.00, £2.10, £3.00; EX 144.90 Trifecta £986.70 Part won. Pool: £1,315.70 - 0.68 winning units..

Owner Hon Mrs Corbett, C Wright, Mrs B W Hills **Bred** Mrs Cherry Faeste **Trained** Lambourn, Berks
■ Stewards' Enquiry : Darren Egan two-day ban: used whip above permitted level (Aug 10-11)

FOCUS
A valuable and well contested handicap, although the race was weakened a little with the withdrawal of the top two. They split into two groups early on, the majority near the stands' side with three down the centre. The first two home were always prominent in the larger group. A surprise winner with the form rated at face value for now.

4768 ADNAMS SOLE STAR EBF CONDITIONS STKS 6f
4:30 (4:30) (Class 3) 2-Y-O £8,409 (£2,502; £1,250; £625) Stalls Low

Form RPR
16 1 **Astaire (IRE)**[16] 4212 2-9-5 0 JamieSpencer 1 108
(Kevin Ryan) *mde all: gng best 2f out: rdn and readily asserted jst over 1f out: pushed out fnl f: comf* 5/6[1]
10 2 2 3/4 **Coulsty (IRE)**[37] 3481 2-9-3 0 PatDobbs 3 97
(Richard Hannon) *chsd ldng pair: rdn and effrt to chse wnr 2f out: drvn and unable qck ent fnl f: kpt on same pce after* 9/4[2]
216 3 5 **Vigor (IRE)**[14] 4296 2-9-5 90 SilvestreDeSousa 2 84
(David Simcock) *hld up in tch in last: rdn and effrt to chse ldng pair wl over 1f out: drvn and btn ent fnl f: wknd fnl 150yds* 9/2[3]
051 4 13 **Overstep (IRE)**[25] 3928 2-9-5 0 FrannyNorton 4 44
(Mark Johnston) *chsd wnr: rdn and unable qck ent fnl 2f: dropped to last wl over 1f out: sn wknd* 14/1

1m 12.29s (-0.21) **Going Correction** -0.025s/f (Good) 4 Ran SP% 110.2
Speed ratings (Par 98): **100,96,89,72**
CSF £3.06 TOTE £1.60; EX 3.10 Trifecta £3.60 Pool: £1,205.76 - 250.47 winning units..
Owner Mrs Angie Bailey **Bred** John O'Connor **Trained** Hambleton, N Yorks

FOCUS
This conditions event went to the top-class Excelebration in 2009 and the smart filly Ollie Olga won it a year ago. It looked a warm little race, with three of them dropping back in grade after contesting Group 2s last time. The winner made all in a good time and progressed, with the second to his debut form.

4769 ADNAMS FIRST RATE GIN H'CAP 1m
5:05 (5:06) (Class 3) (0-90,89) 3-Y-O
£9,337 (£2,796; £1,398; £699; £349; £175) Stalls Low

Form RPR
6543 1 **Top Notch Tonto (IRE)**[43] 3296 3-9-5 87 SilvestreDeSousa 1 98
(Brian Ellison) *in tch in midfield: rdn and effrt to chse ldr wl over 1f out: styd on u.p to ld fnl 100yds: jnd towards fin: jst prevailed on nod* 9/4[1]
0250 2 nse **Royal Prize**[16] 4214 3-8-13 81 JamesDoyle 5 92
(Ralph Beckett) *hld up in tch in rr: swtchd lft and effrt u.p wl over 1f out: r.o to chal wl ins fnl f: upsides wnr towards fin: jst btn on nod* 4/1[3]
6-21 3 2 1/4 **Star Pearl (USA)**[33] 3632 3-8-10 78 JamieSpencer 4 84
(Roger Varian) *led: gng best 2f out: rdn over 1f out: drvn and hdd ins fnl f: wknd towards fin* 11/4[2]
-350 4 2 3/4 **Gabrial's Kaka (IRE)**[63] 2661 3-9-7 89 PatrickMathers 7 89
(Richard Fahey) *in tch in midfield: rdn and effrt to chse ldng pair over 1f out: no ex 1f out: wknd ins fnl f* 14/1
-155 5 1 3/4 **Dark Emerald (IRE)**[43] 3276 3-9-5 87 (t) KierenFallon 2 82
(Brendan Powell) *in tch in last pair: swtchd lft and rdn ent fnl 2f: styng on same pce whn nt clr run and hmpd over 1f out: n.d after* 7/1
0-40 6 nk **Miss Marjurie (IRE)**[43] 3292 3-8-9 77 TomQueally 8 72
(Denis Coakley) *chsd ldr tl drvn and unable qck wl over 1f out: struggling whn edgd rt u.p over 1f out: sn wknd* 20/1
3631 7 2 1/4 **Hunting Rights (USA)**[9] 4442 3-8-10 78 FrannyNorton 3 68
(Mark Johnston) *stmbld leaving stalls: sn rcvrd and chsd ldrs: rdn and lost pl 1/2-way: bhd over 1f out: wknd* 8/1

1m 38.46s (-1.54) **Going Correction** -0.025s/f (Good) 7 Ran SP% 112.5
Speed ratings (Par 104): **106,105,103,100,99 98,96**
toteswingers 1&2 £2.30, 1&3 £2.00, 2&3 £3.50 CSF £11.17 CT £24.28 TOTE £3.00: £2.10, £2.20; EX 12.70 Trifecta £38.80 Pool: £2,607.15 - 50.35 winning units..
Owner Keith Brown **Bred** Seamus Finucane **Trained** Norton, N Yorks

FOCUS
A fair handicap. The winner is rated back to his best, with the second up a length.

4770 ROBERT PALMER MEMORIAL H'CAP 1m 5f
5:40 (5:40) (Class 4) (0-80,80) 3-Y-O £6,469 (£1,925; £962; £481) Stalls Centre

Form RPR
1111 1 **Alcaeus**[44] 3257 3-9-7 80 ChrisCatlin 1 95
(Sir Mark Prescott Bt) *led tl 11f out: chsd ldr tl led again and gng best over 2f out: rdn and edgd rt over 1f out: clr and styd on wl fnl f: eased cl home* 6/4[1]
1023 2 3 **Divergence (IRE)**[37] 3502 3-9-5 78 JamieSpencer 2 86
(Michael Bell) *hld up in 3rd: rdn 3f out: drvn over 1f out and plugged on to chse wnr fnl 100yds: no imp* 5/1[3]
3011 3 3/4 **Pivotal Silence**[37] 3497 3-8-12 71 JamesDoyle 3 78
(Amanda Perrett) *chsd ldr tl led 11f out: rdn and hdd over 2f out: unable qck whn sltly hmpd and swtchd lft over 1f out: one pce and lost 2nd fnl 100yds* 7/4[2]
3421 4 5 **Duke Of Yorkshire**[19] 4116 3-8-5 67 NeilFarley(3) 5 66
(Declan Carroll) *hld up in tch in rr: rdn 3f out: drvn and no imp over 1f out: wknd fnl f* 11/2

2m 45.87s (1.87) **Going Correction** -0.025s/f (Good) 4 Ran SP% 108.4
Speed ratings (Par 102): **93,91,90,87**
CSF £8.71 TOTE £1.90; EX 8.80 Trifecta £8.50 Pool: £827.75 - 72.94 winning units..
Owner Ne'er Do Wells IV **Bred** Miss K Rausing **Trained** Newmarket, Suffolk

FOCUS
Re-positioning of the bend into the home straight added 16m to the distance of this race. An interesting handicap. The early pace looked decent but the tempo soon eased once they were in the long home straight. A sound standard for a small field.
T/Plt: £273.80 to a £1 stake. Pool: £89,967.29 - 239.80 winning units T/Qpdt: £27.00 to a £1 stake. Pool: £3,730.80 101.90 winning units SP

4302 SALISBURY (R-H)
Saturday, July 27

OFFICIAL GOING: Good to firm (firm in places) changing to good after race 2 (6.40)
Wind: Quite strong against Weather: Heavy rain

4771 JRL GROUP "CARNARVON" H'CAP (FOR GENTLEMAN AMATEUR RIDERS) 1m
6:10 (6:10) (Class 5) (0-70,70) 3-Y-O+ £2,807 (£870; £435; £217) Stalls Centre

Form RPR
1531 1 **Harbour Captain (IRE)**[16] 4193 3-10-6 68 MrJamesHughes(5) 2 75
(Jo Hughes) *mde all: rdn and drifted lft fr over 1f out: racd up stands' side rails ent fnl f: qckly diminishing advantage but enough in hand to jst hold on* 5/2[1]
0056 2 hd **Wordismybond**[26] 3885 4-10-6 55 MrSWalker 4 63
(Peter Makin) *trckd ldrs: rdn over 2f out: drifted to stands' side rails jst over 1f out: str run fnl 120yds: jst failed* 9/2[3]
0-00 3 1 3/4 **Bountiful Girl**[57] 2845 4-10-8 64 MrAFrench(7) 8 68
(Neville Bycroft) *trckd ldrs: rdn over 2f out: sn chsng wnr: lost 2nd and no ex fnl 120yds* 20/1
-323 4 1 1/2 **Takitwo**[7] 4517 10-10-4 58 MrJHarding(5) 3 59
(Geoffrey Deacon) *trckd ldrs: rdn over 2f out: kpt on same pce fnl f* 7/1
-566 5 4 1/2 **Daneside (IRE)**[11] 4373 6-10-7 63 MrWDegnan(7) 7 54
(Gary Harrison) *little awkwardly away: hld up: hdwy 3f out: sn rdn to chse ldrs: one pce and edgd lft fnl f* 9/2[3]
-001 6 20 **Loyal N Trusted**[31] 3700 5-10-8 60 (p) MrMPrice(3) 5 23
(Richard Price) *reluctant to go to s: trckd ldrs: rdn 2f out: wknd jst over 1f out: eased whn btn* 4/1[2]
2030 7 3 **Bert The Alert**[16] 4205 5-10-11 65 MrGeorgeCrate(5) 6 21
(Gary Moore) *awkwardly away: sn trcking ldrs: rdn over 2f out: sn wknd* 20/1
2005 8 44 **Poetic Lord**[19] 4124 4-11-2 70 MrJReddington(5) 1
(Sylvester Kirk) *prom tl sddle slipped after 1f: unrideable after and nvr rcvrd: t.o* 11/1

1m 47.09s (3.59) **Going Correction** +0.30s/f (Good)
WFA 3 from 4yo+ 8lb 8 Ran SP% 115.3
Speed ratings (Par 103): **94,93,92,90,86 66,63,19**
toteswingers 1&2 £3.20, 1&3 £14.20, 2&3 £15.90 CSF £14.06 CT £176.95 TOTE £3.50: £1.50, £1.70, £3.70; EX 21.80 Trifecta £315.20 Pool: £825.49 - 1.96 winning units..
Owner Jo Hughes & James Hearne **Bred** Paul Kavanagh **Trained** Lambourn. Berks

FOCUS
Rail erected up straight up to 1m4ft off far side rail. A moderate handicap, confined to gentleman amateur riders. The form isn't too solid.

4772 FAMOUS GROUSE CLASSIFIED CLAIMING STKS 6f 212y
6:40 (6:40) (Class 5) 3-4-Y-O £2,749 (£818; £408; £204) Stalls Centre

Form RPR
1153 1 **Clement (IRE)**[22] 4033 3-8-11 74 JohnFahy 1 80
(Eve Johnson Houghton) *trckd ldr: chal 2f out: sn hrd drvn: tk narrow advantage fnl 120yds: asserting at fin* 5/2[2]
2406 2 1/2 **Small Fury (IRE)**[40] 3407 3-8-6 74 CathyGannon 4 74
(Jo Hughes) *led: rdn whn strly pressed 2f out: battled on gamely: narrowly hdd fnl 120yds: no ex nring fin* 7/2[3]
5640 3 3 1/2 **Flexible Flyer**[30] 3714 4-9-0 72 [1] JimmyFortune 2 68
(Hughie Morrison) *rrd leaving stalls: trckd ldng trio: pushed along over 3f out: rdn into 3rd ent fnl f but nt pce to chal* 7/2[3]
6621 4 7 **Jimmy Elder**[15] 4244 3-8-11 72 RichardHughes 3 50
(Richard Hannon) *racd keenly: trckd ldng pair: rdn 2f out: lost 3rd ent fnl f: fdd fnl 120yds* 7/4[1]

1m 31.21s (2.61) **Going Correction** +0.30s/f (Good)
WFA 3 from 4yo 7lb 4 Ran SP% 109.4
Speed ratings (Par 103): **97,96,92,84**
CSF £10.94 TOTE £3.50; EX 10.00 Trifecta £23.30 Pool: £580.04 - 18.61 winning units..Clement was claimed by Mr J. G. M. O'Shea £18,000
Owner Mrs R F Johnson Houghton **Bred** P Kelly **Trained** Blewbury, Oxon

FOCUS
Each of the four runners in this were making their debut in claiming company. Dubious form, but it's taken at face value.

4773 BATHWICK TYRES BRITISH STALLION STUDS EBF MAIDEN STKS 6f
7:15 (7:15) (Class 4) 2-Y-O £4,204 (£1,251; £625; £312) Stalls High

Form RPR
2 1 **Harwoods Volante (IRE)**[31] 3695 2-9-5 0 JimmyFortune 9 78+
(Amanda Perrett) *wnt sltly rt s: travelled wl trcking ldrs: led over 3f out: nudged clr over 1f out: qcknd up nicely whn asked fnl 100yds: readily* 7/4[2]
2 1 1/4 **After The Goldrush** 2-9-5 0 DaneO'Neill 7 73
(Richard Hannon) *trckd ldng 4: tk clsr order 2f out: sn rdn: chsd wnr ent fnl f: kpt on but a being readily hld* 6/1[3]
3 3 1/2 **Glebe Spirit (IRE)** 2-9-5 0 RichardHughes 3 62+
(Richard Hannon) *trckd ldrs: rdn over 1f out: edgd rt whn gng 3rd ins fnl f: no ex fnl 75yds* 5/4[1]
0 4 3 1/4 **Jersey Royal**[8] 4483 2-9-5 0 MartinDwyer 4 51
(Richard Hannon) *pushed into early ld: hdd over 3f out: sn rdn: one pce fnl f* 14/1
06 5 15 **Loving Your Work**[27] 3853 2-9-5 0 CathyGannon 2 3
(George Baker) *sn outpcd in last pair but in tch: wknd jst over 1f out* 20/1
00 6 4 1/2 **Bold Jack Donahue (IRE)**[41] 3374 2-9-5 0 MartinLane 8
(Ralph Beckett) *prom: rdn over 3f out: wknd over 1f out* 16/1
7 9 **Shock** 2-9-5 0 SteveDrowne 1
(Daniel Kubler) *s.i.s: a outpcd in last* 33/1

1m 16.36s (1.56) **Going Correction** +0.30s/f (Good) 7 Ran SP% 115.3
Speed ratings (Par 96): **101,99,94,90,70 64,52**
toteswingers 1&2 £2.90, 1&3 £1.10, 2&3 £2.30 CSF £13.08 TOTE £3.10: £1.80, £3.30; EX 11.50 Trifecta £23.50 Pool: £936.73 - 29.80 winning units..
Owner Harwoods Racing Club **Bred** Gerry And John Rowley **Trained** Pulborough, W Sussex

The Form Book Flat, Raceform Ltd, Compton, RG20 6NL.

FOCUS
Not a bad 2yo maiden, but it's rated towards the bottom end of the race averages.

4774 BATHWICK TYRES MAIDEN STKS 6f
7:45 (7:47) (Class 5) 3-Y-0+ **£3,234** (£962; £481; £240) **Stalls** High

Form RPR
4 **1** **Secret Weapon**[28] 3837 3-9-5 0........................ MartinDwyer 3 87
(William Muir) *trckd ldrs: swtchd lft over 2f out: sn pushed into ld: r.o strly to draw clr fnl f: readily* **3/1**[2]
6253 **2** *9* **Marjong**[41] 3375 3-9-0 76........................ RichardHughes 1 53
(Simon Dow) *trckd ldrs: rdn to chse wnr wl over 1f out: readily outpcd fnl f* **11/10**[1]
3 **3** *½* **Copper Trade**[17] 4176 3-9-5 0........................ JohnFahy 7 57
(Eve Johnson Houghton) *hld up bhd ldrs: hdwy over 2f out: rdn to chse wnr briefly sn after: kpt on same pce fnl f* **14/1**
0340 **4** *3 ¾* **Dark Templar**[29] 3793 3-9-5 68........................ JimmyFortune 5 45
(Ed Vaughan) *bmpd leaving stalls: trckd ldrs: led over 3f out tl rdn 2f out: kpt on same pce* **9/2**[3]
325/ **5** *13* **Royal Trix**[663] 6573 4-9-5 66........................ DaneO'Neill 4
(Marcus Tregoning) *j. awkwardly: led tl over 3f out: sn pushed along: wknd over 1f out* **8/1**
6 *6* **Dreaming Again** 3-9-5 0........................ JimmyQuinn 6
(Jimmy Fox) *s.i.s: a outpcd in rr* **66/1**
0 **7** *15* **Cruising Along**[22] 4011 3-9-5 0........................ SteveDrowne 2
(Ed McMahon) *prom tl rdn over 2f out: sn wknd: t.o* **25/1**

1m 15.73s (0.93) **Going Correction** +0.30s/f (Good)
WFA 3 from 4yo 5lb 7 Ran SP% **113.9**
Speed ratings (Par 103): **105,93,92,87,70 62,42**
toteswingers 1&2 £1.20, 1&3 £6.50, 2&3 £2.30 CSF £6.62 TOTE £3.40: £2.30, £1.10; EX 5.50 Trifecta £23.70 Pool: £1,013.26 - 32.00 winning units..
Owner Carmel Stud **Bred** Carmel Stud **Trained** Lambourn, Berks

FOCUS
A modest 3-y-o maiden, rated around the second. The winner did it well.

4775 GINGER GROUSE BY FAMOUS GROUSE H'CAP 1m 6f 21y
8:15 (8:15) (Class 5) (0-75,73) 3-Y-0+ **£2,911** (£866; £432; £216) **Stalls** Far side

Form RPR
0131 **1** **Sunny Future (IRE)**[14] 4305 7-10-0 73........................ RichardHughes 1 81
(Malcolm Saunders) *mde all: pushed along over 2f out: rdn ins fnl f: a holding runner-up: styd on wl* **8/11**[1]
4351 **2** *¾* **Chapter Five**[22] 4035 6-8-10 58........................ RyanPowell(3) 4 64
(Ian Williams) *trckd wnr: chal 3f out: sn rdn: styd on but a being hld fnl f* **3/1**[2]
4464 **3** *1 ¾* **Hurakan (IRE)**[23] 3985 7-9-4 66........................(p) ThomasBrown(3) 2 70
(Richard Price) *trckd ldng pair: rdn wl over 2f out: styd on but nt quite pce to mount chal* **6/1**[3]
00-2 **4** *8* **Lily Potts**[24] 3953 4-9-2 61........................ SteveDrowne 3 55
(Chris Down) *trckd ldng trio: rdn to dispute cl 3rd wl over 2f out: fdd fnl 120yds* **7/1**

3m 22.92s (15.52) **Going Correction** +0.30s/f (Good) 4 Ran SP% **109.7**
Speed ratings (Par 103): **67,66,65,61**
CSF £3.24 TOTE £1.50; EX 2.30 Trifecta £5.50 Pool: £425.83 - 57.19 winning units..
Owner M S Saunders **Bred** Mrs G Stanga **Trained** Green Ore, Somerset

FOCUS
A modest little staying handicap.

4776 BATHWICK TYRES H'CAP 6f 212y
8:45 (8:45) (Class 4) (0-85,84) 3-Y-0 **£5,175** (£1,540; £769) **Stalls** Centre

Form RPR
0001 **1** **Dashing David (IRE)**[15] 4243 3-9-7 84........................ RichardHughes 4 91
(Richard Hannon) *trckd ldr: shkn up over 2f out: led narrowly over 1f out: drvn whn strly pressed fnl 170yds: edgd rt: hld on: all out* **4/5**[1]
-344 **2** *hd* **Gracious George (IRE)**[14] 4306 3-8-9 72........................ JimmyQuinn 3 78
(Jimmy Fox) *dwlt: chsd ldng pair: rdn over 2f out: str chal fnl 170yds: jst hld* **3/1**[3]
-204 **3** *2 ¼* **Elnadwa (USA)**[15] 4243 3-9-1 78........................(v[1]) DaneO'Neill 1 78
(Saeed bin Suroor) *led: 2 l clr 3f out: rdn 2f out: narrowly hdd over 1f out: remained w ev ch tl fnl 120yds: hld whn squeezed up sn after* **5/2**[2]

1m 30.15s (1.55) **Going Correction** +0.30s/f (Good) 3 Ran SP% **109.1**
Speed ratings (Par 102): **103,102,100**
CSF £3.44 TOTE £1.60; EX 2.80 Trifecta £3.30 Pool: £414.33 - 92.73 winning units..
Owner Sir David Seale **Bred** Hascombe And Valiant Studs **Trained** East Everleigh, Wilts

FOCUS
A 3-y-o handicap weakened by the non-runners. The winner built on his Chespstow victory.
T/Plt: £29.30 to a £1 stake. Pool: £53,064.94 - 1,320.84 winning units T/Qpdt: £4.60 to a £1 stake. Pool: £3,883.77 - 612.77 winning units TM

4729 YORK (L-H)
Saturday, July 27

OFFICIAL GOING: Good to firm (7.9)
Wind: Light; half behind Weather: Changeable; mostly fine and warm

4777 SKY BET EBF FILLIES' H'CAP 1m 2f 88y
1:50 (1:50) (Class 3) (0-90,85) 3-Y-0+ **£16,172** (£4,812; £2,405; £1,202) **Stalls** Low

Form RPR
61- **1** **Our Obsession (IRE)**[294] 6876 3-9-3 84........................ FrankieDettori 3 96+
(William Haggas) *sn trcking ldrs: t.k.h: pushed along over 4f out: chal over 2f out: led over 1f out: styd on strly* **11/4**[1]
4-12 **2** *3 ¼* **Tuscania**[21] 4066 5-9-10 81........................ DanielTudhope 1 87
(Lucy Wadham) *mid-div: hdwy to trck ldrs 3f out: nt clr run and swtchd rt over 1f out: styd on to take 2nd last 100yds: rdr dropped whip: no imp* **6/1**[3]
5541 **3** *1 ½* **Nemushka**[21] 4066 4-9-5 76........................ PaulHanagan 5 79
(Richard Fahey) *hld up in rr: hdwy 4f out: trcking ldrs 3f out: hung lft: kpt on to take 3rd clsng stages* **7/1**
2-01 **4** *1 ½* **Northern Star (IRE)**[57] 2827 3-9-2 83........................ RichardKingscote 2 83
(Tom Dascombe) *trckd ldrs: effrt over 4f out: led 2f out: sn hdd: edgd lft: one pce* **10/1**
2310 **5** *2 ¾* **Maven**[15] 4264 5-10-0 85........................ DavidAllan 6 80
(Tim Easterby) *trckd ldr: led over 3f out: hdd 2f out: wkng whn hmpd ins fnl f* **15/2**
1145 **6** *2* **Christmas Light**[15] 4264 6-9-2 80........................ JacobButterfield(7) 7 71
(Brian Ellison) *in rr-div: drvn over 3f out: nvr a factor* **10/1**
1-54 **7** *2* **Mystery Bet (IRE)**[50] 3048 3-8-12 79........................[1] TonyHamilton 4 66
(Richard Fahey) *led: hdd 2f out: sn lost pl* **11/1**
1 **8** *17* **Velvety (USA)**[19] 4125 3-9-1 82........................ FrederikTylicki 8 37
(Charlie Appleby) *stdd s: hld up in last: effrt outside 3f out: nvr a factor: lost pl over 1f out: eased clsng stages* **4/1**[2]

2m 9.42s (-3.08) **Going Correction** -0.225s/f (Firm)
WFA 3 from 4yo+ 10lb 8 Ran SP% **111.7**
Speed ratings (Par 104): **103,100,99,98,95 94,92,79**
toteswingers 1&2 £5.10, 1&3 £3.80, 2&3 £5.00 CSF £18.48 CT £100.53 TOTE £3.60: £1.70, £2.00, £2.00; EX 19.40 Trifecta £72.50 Pool: £1,144.01 - 11.82 winning units..
Owner A E Oppenheimer **Bred** Hascombe And Valiant Studs **Trained** Newmarket, Suffolk

FOCUS
Rail on home bend from 1m1f to entrance to home straight moved onto fresh ground reducing distances of 1m and beyond by 20yds. A fairly useful fillies' handicap which went the way of a progressive sort. The gallop was just a modest one until the top of the straight. The form is rated around the second.

4778 SKY BET HOME OF THE PRICE BOOST H'CAP 7f
2:20 (2:21) (Class 2) (0-105,104) 3-Y-0+ **£16,172** (£4,812; £2,405; £1,202) **Stalls** Low

Form RPR
-040 **1** **Sirius Prospect (USA)**[35] 3557 5-9-12 102........................ RobertWinston 6 112
(Dean Ivory) *hld up towards rr: hdwy 3f out: led jst ins fnl f: styd on wl towards fin* **11/2**[2]
0102 **2** *1 ¼* **Smarty Socks (IRE)**[14] 4308 9-9-8 98........................ DanielTudhope 3 105
(David O'Meara) *dwlt: hld up in rr: smooth hdwy over 2f out: chal jst ins fnl f: nk down whn rdr dropped whip 100yds out: kpt on same pce last 50yds* **5/2**[1]
6213 **3** *3* **Al Khan (IRE)**[6] 4560 4-8-2 85........................ OisinMurphy(7) 2 84
(Violet M Jordan) *sn trcking ldrs: upsides over 1f out: kpt on same pce* **15/2**
0011 **4** *¾* **Dark Castle**[18] 4138 4-8-9 85 oh1........................ MichaelO'Connell 4 82
(Micky Hammond) *chsd ldrs: upsides 1f out: kpt on same pce* **8/1**
0020 **5** *½* **Nameitwhatyoulike**[14] 4308 4-8-13 89........................ PhillipMakin 5 85
(Michael Easterby) *led: hdd jst ins fnl f: no ex* **10/1**
-226 **6** *nse* **Les Troyens**[21] 4062 5-9-6 96........................ FrederikTylicki 11 91
(Saeed bin Suroor) *hld up towards rr: effrt over 2f out: edgd lft and kpt on same pce fnl f* **7/1**[3]
00 **7** *½* **Mehdi (IRE)**[14] 4285 4-8-12 88........................(t) TonyHamilton 10 82
(David Nicholls) *mid-div: drvn over 2f out: one pce* **12/1**
-000 **8** *¾* **Webbow (IRE)**[21] 4062 11-8-9 92........................ JacobButterfield(7) 12 84
(Julie Camacho) *sn chsng ldrs: drvn over 2f out: one pce over 1f out* **16/1**
4061 **9** *1 ½* **Verse Of Love**[15] 4245 4-8-9 85 oh2........................ DavidAllan 9 73
(David Evans) *sn drvn along: sn chsng ldrs: wknd over 1f out* **20/1**
-010 **10** *nse* **Garde Cotiere (USA)**[14] 4310 5-9-0 90........................ PaulHanagan 7 78
(Richard Fahey) *hld up in rr: effrt 3f out: nvr a threat* **9/1**

1m 22.83s (-2.47) **Going Correction** -0.125s/f (Firm) 10 Ran SP% **116.8**
Speed ratings (Par 109): **109,107,104,103,102 102,102,101,99,99**
toteswingers 1&2 £2.80, 1&3 £11.00, 2&3 £5.20 CSF £19.64 CT £104.65 TOTE £6.40: £2.40, £1.20, £3.20; EX 15.80 Trifecta £131.90 Pool: £1,828.68 - 10.39 winning units..
Owner Miss N Yarrow **Bred** Brookdale And Dr Ted Folkerth **Trained** Radlett, Herts
■ Stewards' Enquiry : Oisin Murphy two-day ban: used whip above permitted level (Aug 10-11)

FOCUS
A useful handicap which was soundly run. The winner rates back to last autumn's form.

4779 SKY BET YORK STKS (GROUP 2) 1m 2f 88y
2:55 (2:55) (Class 1) 3-Y-0+
£56,710 (£21,500; £10,760; £5,360; £2,690; £1,350) **Stalls** Low

Form RPR
-123 **1** **Mukhadram**[21] 4082 4-9-2 125........................ PaulHanagan 5 117
(William Haggas) *mde all: hung rt bnd over 6f out: increased pce 4f out: drvn over 1f out: edgd rt and styd on* **4/9**[1]
12-4 **2** *¾* **Grandeur (IRE)**[16] 4213 4-9-5 115........................ FrankieDettori 1 118
(Jeremy Noseda) *trckd wnr: t.k.h: stdd after 2f: hdwy over 3f out: drvn to chse wnr appr fnl f: kpt on same pce last 100yds* **6/1**[2]
-035 **3** *4* **Wigmore Hall (IRE)**[16] 4213 6-9-2 113........................ WilliamTwiston-Davies 3 107
(Michael Bell) *dwlt: hld up in rr: hdwy on ins 4f out: chsng wnr over 1f out: hung rt and kpt on one pce* **20/1**
122 **4** *nk* **The Apache (SAF)**[119] 1267 6-9-5 115........................ PatCosgrave 4 110
(M F De Kock, South Africa) *sn chsng ldrs: effrt over 2f out: kpt on one pce over 1f out* **8/1**[3]
0-00 **5** *6* **Sri Putra**[22] 4027 7-9-2 114........................(b) RobertWinston 2 95
(Roger Varian) *chsd ldrs: drvn over 3f out: lost pl over 1f out* **18/1**
2112 **6** *3 ¼* **King George River (IRE)**[101] 1623 3-8-6 103........................ FrederikTylicki 6 89
(Alan Bailey) *stdd s: hld up in rr: hdwy to trck ldrs 7f out: chsng wnr over 2f out: wknd over 1f out* **16/1**

2m 7.18s (-5.32) **Going Correction** -0.225s/f (Firm)
WFA 3 from 4yo+ 10lb 6 Ran SP% **110.6**
Speed ratings (Par 115): **112,111,108,107,103 100**
toteswingers 1&2 £1.50, 1&3 £4.90, 2&3 £8.80 CSF £3.43 TOTE £1.30: £1.10, £2.70; EX 3.60 Trifecta £29.30 Pool: £5,104.06 - 130.51 winning units..
Owner Hamdan Al Maktoum **Bred** Wardall Bloodstock **Trained** Newmarket, Suffolk

FOCUS
A good renewal of this Group 2. The winner was able to dictate what was no more than a modest gallop, the tempo not really increasing until the final 4f. Mukhadram didn't need to match his G1 form.

4780 SKY BET DASH (H'CAP) 6f
3:30 (3:31) (Class 2) (0-105,100) 3-Y-0+
£31,125 (£9,320; £4,660; £2,330; £1,165; £585) **Stalls** Centre

Form RPR
0121 **1** **Tropics (USA)**[28] 3840 5-9-10 100........................ RobertWinston 12 111+
(Dean Ivory) *mid-div: hdwy to chse ldrs over 2f out: led jst ins fnl f: edgd lft: all out* **9/2**[1]
1004 **2** *shd* **Summerinthecity (IRE)**[14] 4285 6-8-12 88........................ MichaelO'Connell 10 98
(David Nicholls) *w ldrs: wnt 2nd jst ins fnl f: carried lft and bmpd twice: jst hld* **40/1**
0614 **3** *1 ¾* **Khubala (IRE)**[35] 3558 4-9-8 98........................(b) FrankieDettori 17 102+
(Hugo Palmer) *towards rr: hdwy whn sltly hmpd over 1f out: styd on wl to take 3rd nr fin* **6/1**[2]
3200 **4** *¾* **Prodigality**[28] 3846 5-9-10 100........................ FrederikTylicki 3 102
(Ronald Harris) *w ldrs: led 2f out: hdd jst ins fnl f: kpt on same pce* **20/1**
0050 **5** *½* **Tarooq (USA)**[1] 4730 7-8-1 80........................(t) JulieBurke(3) 6 80
(Stuart Williams) *halaf rrd s: sn prom: outpcd over 2f out: kpt on fnl f* **14/1**

0-10 **6** *hd* **Baccarat (IRE)**[36] 3527 4-9-4 **94** PaulHanagan 5 98+
(Richard Fahey) *half-rrd s: in rr: sme hdwy whn bdly hmpd over 1f out: styd on wl ins fnl f: nt rch ldrs* **9/2**[1]
0124 **7** *1* **Dick Bos**[6] 4569 4-9-1 **91** DanielTudhope 8 88
(David O'Meara) *chsd ldrs: edgd rt and kpt on same pce over 1f out* **11/1**[3]
3013 **8** *½* **Rasaman (IRE)**[8] 4472 9-8-6 **82** AndrewElliott 18 77
(Jim Goldie) *mid-div: keeping on whn n.m.r 1f out: styng on at fin* **33/1**
6631 **9** *½* **Rodrigo De Torres**[8] 4472 6-9-5 **95** TonyHamilton 15 88
(David Nicholls) *chsd ldrs: one pce whn n.m.r over 1f out* **20/1**
-040 **10** *hd* **Gramercy (IRE)**[14] 4297 6-9-0 **90** PatCosgrave 16 83
(David Simcock) *in rr-div: hdwy over 2f out: nvr a factor* **20/1**
1650 **11** *hd* **Regal Parade**[35] 3558 9-9-5 **100** (t) MatthewLawson(5) 19 92
(Milton Bradley) *s.i.s: hld up in rr: kpt on fnl 2f: nvr a factor* **50/1**
2202 **12** *¾* **Fast Shot**[8] 4472 5-8-13 **89** DavidAllan 1 79
(Tim Easterby) *w ldrs far side: edgd lft and fdd over 1f out* **16/1**
0314 **13** *nk* **Al's Memory (IRE)**[8] 4472 4-8-10 **91** DeclanBates(5) 11 80
(David Evans) *mid-div: effrt over 2f out: nvr trbld ldrs* **22/1**
-005 **14** *¾* **Farlow (IRE)**[73] 2366 5-8-3 **86** SamanthaBell(7) 13 72
(Richard Fahey) *in rr: no threat whn n.m.r 1f out* **25/1**
145 **15** *½* **Line Of Reason (IRE)**[19] 4117 3-8-7 **88** RoystonFfrench 14 73
(Paul Midgley) *dwlt: swtchd lft after s: sme hdwy over 2f out: sn wknd* **33/1**
4401 **16** *nse* **Fitz Flyer (IRE)**[5] 4579 7-8-6 **89** 6ex (v) JordanNason(7) 4 74
(David Nicholls) *chsd ldrs far side: hung lft and wknd over 1f out* **25/1**
0006 **17** *1* **Ahern**[15] 4255 3-8-13 **94** (b) PhillipMakin 9 75
(David Barron) *s.i.s: a in rr* **25/1**
6000 **18** *¾* **Secret Witness**[28] 3848 7-9-5 **98** (b) WilliamTwiston-Davies(3) 20 77
(Ronald Harris) *a towards rr* **20/1**
265 **19** *5* **Mississippi**[8] 4472 4-8-12 **88** PaulMulrennan 2 51
(David Barron) *chsd ldrs far side: lost pl wl over 1f out: heavily easeed clsng stages* **12/1**
3000 **U** **Bogart**[63] 2669 4-9-7 **97** AmyRyan 7
(Kevin Ryan) *led centre: sddle slipped and hdd 2f out: hdd and uns rdr over 1f out* **16/1**

1m 9.89s (-2.01) **Going Correction** -0.10s/f (Good)
WFA 3 from 4yo+ 5lb **20** Ran SP% **130.3**
Speed ratings (Par 109): **109,108,106,105,104 104,103,102,101,101 101,100,100,99,98 98,96,95,89,**
toteswingers 1&2 £198.90, 1&3 £9.00, 2&3 £61.30 CSF £206.88 CT £1158.28 TOTE £4.60: £1.70, £10.30, £2.00, £6.50; EX 256.40 Trifecta £3303.20 Pool: £47,642.50 - 10.81 winning units..
Owner Dean Ivory **Bred** D Konecny, S Branch & A Branch **Trained** Radlett, Herts

FOCUS
A useful sprint, though not that many ever really got into it, which is not unusual for here. The winner's performance is perhaps worth marking up slightly as he was able to get there from off the pace. The runner-up is the key to the level.

4781 READ RICHARD FAHEY ON SPORTINGLIFE.COM MEDIAN AUCTION MAIDEN STKS 6f
4:05 (4:06) (Class 4) 2-Y-O **£6,469** (£1,925; £962; £481) **Stalls** Centre

Form RPR
1 **Hot Streak (IRE)** 2-9-5 0 PhillipMakin 7 80+
(Kevin Ryan) *hld up in rr: smooth hdwy to trck ldr over 2f out: shkn up to ld 1f out: drvn out* **7/4**[1]
30 **2** *2¼* **Pensax Lad (IRE)**[40] 3413 2-9-5 0 RobertWinston 5 70
(Ronald Harris) *led: hdd 1f out: kpt on same pce* **16/1**
02 **3** *1¼* **Kickboxer (IRE)**[10] 4412 2-9-5 0 SamHitchcott 2 66
(Mick Channon) *w ldr: drvn over 2f out: one pce* **4/1**[3]
0 **4** *hd* **Lazy Sioux**[34] 3605 2-9-0 0 RobbieFitzpatrick 6 60
(Richard Guest) *chsd ldrs: kpt on one pce fnl 2f* **33/1**
0 **5** *½* **The Grumpy Gnome (IRE)**[14] 4312 2-9-5 0 PaulHanagan 8 64+
(Richard Fahey) *chsd ldrs: drvn over 2f out: n.m.r over 1f out: hung lft and kpt on towards fin* **5/2**[2]
00 **6** *½* **Petergate**[42] 3350 2-9-5 0 PaulMulrennan 4 62
(Brian Rothwell) *dwlt: in rr: effrt over 2f out: nvr trbld ldrs* **25/1**
7 *8* **Dandys Perier (IRE)** 2-9-5 0 FrederikTylicki 3 37
(Ronald Harris) *n.m.r sn after s: in rr: bhd fnl 2f* **14/1**
8 *2¼* **First Commandment** 2-9-5 0 DavidAllan 9 29
(Tim Easterby) *edgy in stalls: dwlt: in rr: drvn and hdwy over 2f out: sn lost pl* **6/1**

1m 12.68s (0.78) **Going Correction** -0.10s/f (Good) **8** Ran SP% **118.6**
Speed ratings (Par 96): **90,87,85,85,84 83,73,70**
toteswingers 1&2 £6.30, 1&3 £1.30, 2&3 £4.30 CSF £33.71 TOTE £2.60: £1.30, £2.90, £1.50; EX 22.50 Trifecta £52.00 Pool: £1,976.79 - 28.50 winning units..
Owner Qatar Racing Limited **Bred** Barry Noonan **Trained** Hambleton, N Yorks

FOCUS
Not a strong maiden for the course by any means and the bare form is ordinary, but the winner was impressive.

4782 SKYVEGAS.COM H'CAP 2m 88y
4:40 (4:41) (Class 3) (0-90,90) 4-Y-O+ **£8,409** (£2,502; £1,250; £625) **Stalls** Low

Form RPR
3042 **1** **Flashman**[35] 3587 4-8-6 **75** PaulHanagan 8 84+
(Richard Fahey) *mid-div: puhsed along 5f out: styd on to ld over 2f out: edgd rt ins fnl f: drvn rt out* **7/2**[1]
0166 **2** *½* **Rocktherunway (IRE)**[29] 3765 4-8-5 **79** (p) ConnorBeasley(5) 1 87
(Michael Dods) *hld up in last: hdwy on ins over 3f out: styd on to take 2nd nr fin* **14/1**
/056 **3** *nk* **All The Aces (IRE)**[14] 4313 8-9-4 **87** FrederikTylicki 11 95
(Nicky Henderson) *drvn early to chse ldrs: upsides over 3f out: outpcd over 1f out: rallied jst ins fnl f: styd on same pce* **10/1**
5-42 **4** *3½* **Teak (IRE)**[10] 4407 6-8-7 **76** TonyHamilton 12 80
(Ian Williams) *swtchd lft after s: chsd ldrs: narrow ld over 3f out: hdd over 2f out: one pce* **13/2**[2]
6411 **5** *1½* **Dr Irv**[17] 4159 4-8-1 **73** DeclanCannon(3) 5 75
(Philip Kirby) *upset in stalls: hood removed late and s.s: hdwy into midfield after 4f: trcking ldrs over 3f out: chal over 2f out: edgd lft and fdd fnl 150yds* **9/1**
2026 **6** *3¾* **Moidore**[28] 3824 4-9-7 **90** MichaelO'Connell 9 88
(John Quinn) *sn chsng ldrs: drvn over 4f out: one pce* **7/1**[3]
-400 **7** *¾* **Dazinski**[49] 3099 7-9-0 **83** PhillipMakin 3 80
(Mark H Tompkins) *hld up in rr: sme hdwy over 2f out: nvr a factor* **10/1**
5340 **8** *hd* **Come Here Yew (IRE)**[30] 3726 5-8-0 **72** JulieBurke(3) 10 68
(Declan Carroll) *mid-div: shkn up 7f out: drvn 4f out: one pce* **12/1**
0330 **9** *4½* **Art History (IRE)**[14] 4313 5-9-0 **83** DanielTudhope 6 74
(David O'Meara) *led: hdd over 3f out: wknd fnl 2f* **11/1**
4232 **10** *7* **Aleksandar**[17] 4159 4-8-4 **73** AndrewElliott 13 56
(Jim Goldie) *swtchd lft after s: chsd ldr: lost pl over 2f out* **16/1**
0000 **11** *¾* **Crackentorp**[28] 3824 8-9-7 **90** DavidAllan 4 72
(Tim Easterby) *in rr: drvn 7f out: brief effrt on wd outside 4f out: sn wknd* **10/1**
414 **12** *7* **Mister Pagan**[30] 3726 5-8-0 **76** JordanNason(7) 2 49
(Jim Goldie) *chsd ldrs: lost pl over 2f out: sn bhd* **8/1**

3m 30.01s (-4.49) **Going Correction** -0.225s/f (Firm) course record **12** Ran SP% **125.0**
Speed ratings (Par 107): **102,101,101,99,99 97,96,96,94,91 90,87**
toteswingers 1&2 £11.50, 1&3 £13.50, 2&3 £28.00 CSF £59.35 CT £468.48 TOTE £4.20: £1.90, £4.30, £3.30; EX 59.00 Trifecta £634.60 Pool: £3,205.08 - 3.78 winning units..
Owner The G-Guck Group **Bred** Avenue Farm Stud **Trained** Musley Bank, N Yorks

FOCUS
A fairly useful staying event. It was run at no more than a fair gallop but the form is sound.

4783 SKY BET NURSERY H'CAP 5f
5:15 (5:17) (Class 3) 2-Y-O **£7,762** (£2,310; £1,154; £577) **Stalls** Centre

Form RPR
3132 **1** **Innocently (IRE)**[7] 4511 2-9-4 **75** DanielTudhope 4 77
(David O'Meara) *led travelling strly: shkn up over 1f out: drvn and edgd lft: hld on towards fin* **3/1**[2]
6514 **2** *nk* **Mr Dandy Man (IRE)**[42] 3311 2-9-2 **73** RobertWinston 1 74
(Ronald Harris) *w wnr: kpt on wl fnl f: no ex clsng stages* **12/1**
0314 **3** *1* **Hello Beautiful (IRE)**[15] 4261 2-8-12 **69** PJMcDonald 7 66
(Ann Duffield) *chsd ldrs: outpcd over 1f out: styd on fnl f* **5/1**
1022 **4** *1¼* **Baytown Kestrel**[15] 4261 2-9-3 **74**[1] PhillipMakin 6 67
(Phil McEntee) *stdd s: trckd ldrs: effrt and hung lft over 1f out: kpt on ins fnl f* **6/1**
422 **5** *½* **Simply Black (IRE)**[14] 4289 2-9-2 **78** JustinNewman(5) 3 69
(Bryan Smart) *s.i.s: edgd lft and chsd ldrs over 3f out: one pce over 1f out* **4/1**[3]
0442 **6** *nk* **M'Selle (IRE)**[15] 4239 2-8-13 **70** FrederikTylicki 5 60
(Ronald Harris) *in rr: hdwy to chse ldrs over 2f out: one pce over 1f out* **14/1**
0105 **7** *½* **Neighbother**[14] 4314 2-9-4 **75** PaulHanagan 2 63
(Richard Fahey) *chsd ldrs: rdn and outpcd over 1f out* **11/4**[1]

59.53s (0.23) **Going Correction** -0.10s/f (Good) **7** Ran SP% **117.0**
Speed ratings (Par 98): **94,93,91,89,89 88,87**
toteswingers 1&2 £10.20, 1&3 £2.90, 2&3 £11.10 CSF £38.54 TOTE £4.10: £2.20, £4.20; EX 36.60 Trifecta £130.30 Pool: £2,509.64 - 14.44 winning units..
Owner Hollowdean **Bred** Longfort Stud **Trained** Nawton, N Yorks

FOCUS
A fair nursery. The leading pair dominated throughout and the form is rated around the second and third.
T/Plt: £15.80 to a £1 stake. Pool: £165,354.01 - 7,627.60 winning units T/Qpdt: £6.40 to a £1 stake. Pool £6,382.40 - 736.80 winning units WG

4784 - 4791a (Foreign Racing) - See Raceform Interactive

4043 DEAUVILLE (R-H)
Saturday, July 27

OFFICIAL GOING: Turf: good to soft: fibresand: standard (abandoned after race 5 due to electrical storms)

4792a PRIX DE PSYCHE (GROUP 3) (3YO FILLIES) (TURF) 1m 2f
4:30 (12:00) 3-Y-O **£32,520** (£13,008; £9,756; £6,504; £3,252)

RPR
1 **Tasaday (USA)**[41] 3385 3-8-11 0 Pierre-CharlesBoudot 3 113
(A Fabre, France) *mde all: shkn up whn pressed 2f out: qckned clr under hands and heels ent fnl f: pushed out: comf* **4/5**[1]
2 *2½* **Sparkling Beam (IRE)**[27] 3877 3-9-2 0 ThierryJarnet 2 113
(J E Pease, France) *prom on inner: shuffled bk and 4th 2f out: swtchd out and rdn over 1f out: r.o and wnt 2nd cl home: no ch w wnr* **5/2**[2]
3 *½* **Alumna (USA)**[27] 3877 3-8-11 0 MaximeGuyon 6 107
(A Fabre, France) *trckd ldr in 2nd on outer: rdn to chal 2f out: outpcd by wnr ent fnl f: kpt on but dropped to 3rd cl home* **5/1**[3]
4 *1¼* **Melodique (FR)**[52] 3008 3-8-11 0 FlavienPrat 1 104
(C Laffon-Parias, France) *hld up in last: rdn 2f out: outpcd in rr ent fnl f: styd on u.p and tk n.d 4th fnl strides* **27/1**
5 *snk* **Aquatinta (GER)**[90] 1869 3-8-11 0 IoritzMendizabal 4 104
(Clive Cox) *t.k.h: midfield in tch: hdwy on outer to chal 2f out: sn rdn: outpcd by wnr ent fnl f: no ex: dropped to 5th fnl strides* **16/1**
6 *2½* **Piana (FR)**[52] 3008 3-8-11 0 ThierryThulliez 5 99
(A Bonin, France) *hld up in tch in last pair: rdn 2f out: sn outpcd and btn: dropped to last ins fnl f: nvr threatened* **10/1**

2m 9.07s (-1.13) **6** Ran SP% **119.3**
WIN (incl. 1 euro stake): 1.80. PLACES: 1.20, 1.50. SF: 2.80.
Owner Godolphin SNC **Bred** Darley Stud Management Co Ltd **Trained** Chantilly, France

4793 - 4794a (Foreign Racing) - See Raceform Interactive

4742 ASCOT (R-H)
Sunday, July 28

OFFICIAL GOING: Good changing to good to firm (good in places) after race 1 (2.30)
Wind: Moderate, half against Weather: Fine,. warm

4795 ANDERS FOUNDATION EBF CROCKER BULTEEL MAIDEN STKS 6f
2:30 (2:32) (Class 2) 2-Y-O **£12,938** (£3,850; £1,924; £962) **Stalls** Centre

Form RPR
1 **Piping Rock** 2-9-0 0 RyanMoore 2 87+
(Richard Hannon) *mde virtually all: rdn 2f out: hung lft fnl f but r.o wl* **7/2**[2]
2 *1¼* **Makhfar (IRE)** 2-9-0 0 FrankieDettori 7 83+
(John Gosden) *hld up in last: rdn and gd prog over 1f out to chse wnr fnl f: r.o but hld nr fin* **6/1**
3 *5* **Dutch Art Dealer** 2-9-0 0 JimCrowley 6 67
(Paul Cole) *trckd ldrs: gng wl 1/2-way: rdn and nt qckn 2f out: kpt on to take 3rd ins fnl f* **5/2**[1]
4 *2* **Supersta** 2-9-0 0 LukeMorris 4 61
(Ronald Harris) *prom: w wnr over 2f out: rdn and outpcd fnl 2f* **10/1**
5 *½* **Reaffirmed (IRE)** 2-9-0 0 JimmyFortune 1 59
(Ed Vaughan) *dwlt: in tch: prog to join wnr 2f out to over 1f out: rn green and wknd qckly* **8/1**

The Form Book Flat, Raceform Ltd, Compton, RG20 6NL.

6 2 **Knockroon** 2-9-0 0 DavidProbert 3 53
(Andrew Balding) *dwlt: trckd ldrs: pushed along 2f out: steadily wknd* **25/1**

7 ½ **Etaad (USA)** 2-9-0 0 DaneO'Neill 5 51
(J W Hills) *trckd ldrs: lost pl and pushed along over 2f out: steadily wknd after* **4/1**[3]

8 6 **Beatabout The Bush (IRE)** 2-9-0 0 SteveDrowne 8 32
(Charles Hills) *dwlt: sn rcvrd and w wnr to over 2f out: wknd rapidly* **16/1**

1m 17.21s (2.71) **Going Correction** +0.075s/f (Good) **8 Ran SP% 115.0**
Speed ratings (Par 100): **84,82,75,73,72 69,69,61**
Tote Swingers: 1&2 £3.20, 1&3 £2.90, 2&3 £4.30 CSF £24.92 TOTE £3.90: £1.10, £1.90, £1.60; EX 20.60 Trifecta £63.70 Pool: £2,864.81 - 34.04 winning units..
Owner R J McCreery & Pall Mall Partners **Bred** Stowell Hill Ltd **Trained** East Everleigh, Wilts

FOCUS
No previous form to go on here, but it looks a fair maiden with the front pair coming clear.

4796 GL EVENTS OWEN BROWN H'CAP (THE SUNDAY £5K BONUS RACE) 1m 4f
3:05 (3:05) (Class 2) (0-105,104) 3-Y-0+

£12,450 (£3,728; £1,864; £932; £466; £234) **Stalls** Low

Form RPR

1-43 1 **Bishop Roko**[25] 3960 4-9-3 **93** JamesDoyle 6 100
(Roger Charlton) *trckd ldng pair: squeezed between them to ld 1f out: drvn and jst hld on* **5/2**[1]

-320 2 hd **Genzy (FR)**[37] 3525 5-9-8 **98** JimCrowley 3 105
(Ian Williams) *t.k.h: hld up in last pair: nt clr run fr jst over 2f out tl 1f out: r.o whn in the clr fnl f: tk 2nd nr fin: jst failed* **12/1**

-301 3 nk **Rawaki (IRE)**[29] 3838 5-9-4 **97** ThomasBrown(3) 8 103
(Andrew Balding) *trckd ldrs on outer: moved up to chal 2f out: on terms ins fnl f: wnt 2nd briefly but nt qckn last 75yds* **7/2**[3]

434- 4 1 **Barbican**[371] 4363 5-10-0 **104** SebSanders 5 108
(Alan Bailey) *t.k.h: hld up in midfield: waiting for a gap fr 2f out: swtchd ins and drvn 1f out: styd on but nt pce to chal* **16/1**

131- 5 hd **Saytara (IRE)**[302] 6677 4-9-4 **94** MickaelBarzalona 4 98
(Saeed bin Suroor) *trckd ldr: rdn to ld over 1f out: hdd 1f out: fdd nr fin* **3/1**[2]

1030 6 ¾ **Itlaaq**[15] 4313 7-9-1 **91** (t) FrankieDettori 9 93
(Michael Easterby) *hld up in last trio: rdn and sme prog on outer 2f out: nt qckn 1f out: one pce after* **20/1**

3350 7 3 ¼ **Scatter Dice (IRE)**[22] 4060 4-9-1 **91** JoeFanning 11 88
(Mark Johnston) *led and crossed fr wd draw: rdn and hdd over 1f out: wknd fnl f* **7/1**

3-00 8 ½ **Viking Storm**[71] 2443 5-9-12 **102** [1] JimmyFortune 2 98
(Harry Dunlop) *hld up in last pair: rdn and no prog jst over 2f out: btn after* **16/1**

2400 9 16 **Buckland (IRE)**[36] 3559 5-9-10 **100** GeorgeBaker 1 71
(Hans Adielsson) *hld up in midfield: effrt on inner over 2f out: wknd rapidly wl over 1f out: t.o* **25/1**

2m 31.07s (-1.43) **Going Correction** +0.075s/f (Good) **9 Ran SP% 116.4**
Speed ratings (Par 109): **107,106,106,106,105 105,103,102,92**
Tote Swingers: 1&2 £5.00, 1&3 £3.10, 2&3 £8.30 CSF £34.25 CT £106.30 TOTE £3.60: £1.40, £3.20, £1.80; EX 30.00 Trifecta £118.30 Pool: £3,168.55 - 20.08 winning units..
Owner Michael Pescod **Bred** P T Tellwright **Trained** Beckhampton, Wilts

FOCUS
They went a solid pace in this decent handicap and the form may well have bearing on the prestigious Ebor Handicap at York in August.

4797 MILWARD PRINTING H'CAP 6f
3:40 (3:40) (Class 4) (0-85,85) 3-Y-0 **£6,469** (£1,925; £962; £481) **Stalls** Centre

Form RPR

2433 1 **Red Refraction (IRE)**[15] 4283 3-9-1 **79** RyanMoore 2 87
(Richard Hannon) *hld up in last: rdn and gng nowhere 2f out: picked up over 1f out: clsng whn impeded ins fnl f and swtchd rt: drvn and r.o to ld last 50yds* **4/1**[2]

2410 2 ¾ **Can You Conga**[51] 3066 3-9-4 **82** JoeFanning 9 87
(Kevin Ryan) *disp ld 2f: styd prom: led again 2f out: drvn fnl f: hdd last 50yds: styd on* **6/1**

3620 3 ¾ **Purcell (IRE)**[16] 4255 3-9-7 **85** JimmyFortune 8 88
(Andrew Balding) *trckd ldrs: rdn to chal over 1f out: hung bdly lft jst ins fnl f and forfeited ch: styd on nr fin* **7/2**[1]

3211 4 3 **Grand Denial (IRE)**[48] 3159 3-9-0 **78** (b) SteveDrowne 6 71
(Clive Cox) *trckd ldrs: chal and upsides 2f out: wknd tamely fnl f* **4/1**[2]

045 5 ½ **Khefyn (IRE)**[16] 4244 3-8-2 **66** LukeMorris 3 58
(Ronald Harris) *hld up in 7th: rdn 2f out: sme prog over 1f out: outpcd fnl f* **25/1**

-064 6 1 ¼ **Alcando (IRE)**[12] 4367 3-8-13 **77** ShaneKelly 10 65
(Denis Coakley) *disp ld 2f: lost pl and rdn jst over 2f out: steadily fdd* **33/1**

3024 7 shd **Ceelo**[15] 4303 3-8-10 **74** (p) PatDobbs 1 61
(Sylvester Kirk) *dwlt: hld up in 8th: drvn 2f out: no real prog* **10/1**

4005 8 9 **Equitania**[30] 3786 3-8-11 **82** TimClark(7) 5 41
(Alan Bailey) *awkward s: rcvrd to ld after 2f: drvn and hdd 2f out: wknd rapidly jst over 1f out: t.o* **14/1**

0301 9 20 **Tartary (IRE)**[12] 4367 3-8-13 **77** JamesDoyle 4
(Roger Charlton) *trckd ldrs: rdn and wknd rapidly over 1f out: eased w rdr looking down: wl t.o* **5/1**[3]

1m 13.74s (-0.76) **Going Correction** +0.075s/f (Good) **9 Ran SP% 115.7**
Speed ratings (Par 102): **108,107,106,102,101 99,99,87,60**
Tote Swingers: 1&2 £5.00, 1&3 £3.70, 2&3 £5.30 CSF £28.32 CT £92.25 TOTE £4.60: £1.40, £2.10, £1.60; EX 26.30 Trifecta £166.60 Pool: £2,340.84 - 10.53 winning units..
Owner Middleham Park Racing IV & James Pak **Bred** Tally-Ho Stud **Trained** East Everleigh, Wilts

FOCUS
A fair 3-y-o sprint handicap in which the main action developed near the stands' side.

4798 MITIE EVENTS & LEISURE H'CAP 1m 2f
4:15 (4:15) (Class 3) (0-95,90) 3-Y-0+

£8,092 (£2,423; £1,211; £605; £302; £152) **Stalls** Low

Form RPR

/10- 1 **Charles Camoin (IRE)**[448] 1882 5-10-0 **90** LiamKeniry 5 98
(Sylvester Kirk) *t.k.h: hld up in 5th: nt clr run briefly jst over 2f out: prog between rivals to go 2nd jst over 1f out: pushed along firmly and r.o to ld last 100yds: readily* **20/1**

3140 2 nk **Haylaman (IRE)**[22] 4060 5-10-0 **90** JimCrowley 8 97
(David Simcock) *trckd ldr: drvn ahd 2f out: styd on wl but hdd and hld last 100yds* **11/4**[2]

6512 3 2 ¼ **Love Marmalade (IRE)**[10] 4441 3-8-11 **83** JoeFanning 3 86
(Mark Johnston) *trckd ldng pair: shkn up to dispute 2nd over 1f out: rdn and styd on one pce fnl f* **9/4**[1]

3200 4 3 ½ **Forgotten Hero (IRE)**[15] 4310 4-9-13 **89** SteveDrowne 1 87
(Charles Hills) *hld up in 6th: hanging but making prog on inner whn nowhere to go and snatched up over 1f out: no ch after: kpt on to take 4th nr fin* **8/1**

0213 5 ¾ **Cashpoint**[23] 4028 8-9-5 **81** JamesDoyle 9 75
(Ian Williams) *trckd ldng trio: rdn and cl up on outer wl over 1f out: wknd fnl f* **9/2**[3]

2111 6 nk **Hydrant**[24] 3996 7-9-0 **81** ConnorBeasley(5) 6 74
(Richard Guest) *led: rdn and hdd 2f out: wknd fnl f* **10/1**

1661 7 nk **Take Two**[22] 4075 4-9-8 **84** RyanMoore 4 77
(Alex Hales) *dwlt: mostly in last and detached at various stages: rdn 3f out: nvr a factor but kpt on ins fnl f* **7/1**

-600 8 2 ½ **Johnno**[44] 3293 4-9-4 **80** (t) SebSanders 7 68
(J W Hills) *hld up in 7th: rdn wl over 2f out: sn struggling: wknd over 1f out* **20/1**

2m 7.3s (-0.10) **Going Correction** +0.075s/f (Good)
WFA 3 from 4yo+ 10lb **8 Ran SP% 117.8**
Speed ratings (Par 107): **103,102,100,98,97 97,97,95**
Tote Swingers: 1&2 £11.90, 1&3 £10.20, 2&3 £2.80 CSF £77.10 CT £176.94 TOTE £18.00: £4.30, £1.50, £1.10; EX 123.20 Trifecta £718.80 Pool: £3,625.17 - 3.78 winning units..
Owner Chris Wright & The Hon Mrs J M Corbett **Bred** Pat Grogan **Trained** Upper Lambourn, Berks

FOCUS
A fair handicap, run at an average pace and the principals forged clear.

4799 ASCOT LAWYERS MAIDEN FILLIES' STKS 1m (S)
4:50 (4:51) (Class 4) 3-Y-O **£5,175** (£1,540; £769; £384) **Stalls** Centre

Form RPR

1 **Expressly (IRE)** 3-9-0 0 [1] MickaelBarzalona 1 89
(Charlie Appleby) *dwlt: hld up in last trio: smooth prog over 2f out: led wl over 1f out: pushed clr: comf* **7/2**[3]

0 2 4 ½ **Mu'Ajiza**[12] 4382 3-9-0 0 JoeFanning 3 79
(Mark Johnston) *trckd ldrs: shkn up 2f out: chsd clr wnr jst over 1f out: no imp* **12/1**

6 3 nk **Snow Powder (IRE)**[20] 4125 3-9-0 0 NickyMackay 8 78
(John Gosden) *led: shkn up and hdd wl over 1f out: kpt on same pce after* **14/1**

352 4 1 **International Love (IRE)**[34] 3619 3-9-0 75 [1] DavidProbert 5 76
(Andrew Balding) *hld up in last trio: prog to trck ldrs 3f out: rdn and fnd nil 2f out: one pce after* **2/1**[1]

4 5 hd **Princess Loulou (IRE)**[30] 3759 3-9-0 0 DaneO'Neill 7 76
(Roger Varian) *trckd ldrs: shkn up and lost pl over 2f out: n.d after: kpt on again fnl f* **11/2**

-02 6 7 **Candy Kitten**[32] 3696 3-9-0 0 LukeMorris 6 59
(Alastair Lidderdale) *trckd ldng pair: rdn over 2f out: sn wknd* **12/1**

65 7 2 ¼ **Stockhill Diva**[42] 3372 3-9-0 0 PatDobbs 2 54
(Brendan Powell) *s.s: a in last trio: shkn up and wknd 2f out* **33/1**

43- 8 2 ¼ **Syrenka**[291] 6978 3-9-0 0 RyanMoore 9 49
(Marcus Tregoning) *pressed ldr to 3f out: edgd lft and sn wknd* **10/3**[2]

1m 40.98s (0.18) **Going Correction** +0.075s/f (Good) **8 Ran SP% 119.0**
Speed ratings (Par 99): **102,97,97,96,96 89,86,84**
Tote Swingers: 1&2 £4.80, 1&3 £8.80, 2&3 £9.10 CSF £46.04 TOTE £5.60: £1.80, £3.40, £2.80; EX 63.80 Trifecta £590.50 Pool: £4,329.72 - 5.49 winning units..
Owner Godolphin **Bred** Darley **Trained** Newmarket, Suffolk

■ Charlie Appleby's first winner. He was previously assistant to Mahmood Al Zarooni.

FOCUS
Probably an above-average fillies' maiden and a promising winner.

4800 SIS LIVE H'CAP 5f
5:20 (5:22) (Class 2) 3-Y-0+

£28,012 (£8,388; £4,194; £2,097; £1,048; £526) **Stalls** Centre

Form RPR

6300 1 **Barnet Fair**[9] 4472 5-8-9 **90** ConnorBeasley(5) 5 103
(Richard Guest) *taken down early: impeded s: hld up in last of gp towards far side: swtchd wdst of all and gd prog to ld 1f out: r.o wl* **10/1**[3]

1430 2 1 **Steps (IRE)**[15] 4275 5-9-6 **96** (b) DaneO'Neill 19 106+
(Roger Varian) *racd towards nr side tl trckd only rival against rail after 2f: drvn to ld the pair 1f out: r.o wl: jst hld* **7/1**[1]

4310 3 1 **Lupo D'Oro (IRE)**[23] 4024 4-8-9 **85** SteveDrowne 10 91
(John Best) *hld up in last pair in gp towards far side: rdn and prog over 1f out: styd on to take 3rd nr fin* **25/1**

3-65 4 nk **Ahtoug**[15] 4275 5-9-6 **96** MickaelBarzalona 3 101
(Charlie Appleby) *hld up in gp towards far side: prog to trck ldrs 2f out: rdn and styd on fnl f: nt pce to chal* **12/1**

3006 5 ½ **Judge 'n Jury**[29] 3848 9-9-5 **98** (t) ThomasBrown(3) 2 101
(Ronald Harris) *racd freely: w overall ldr towards far side: led 2f out: hdd and no ex 1f out* **12/1**

0600 6 shd **Face The Problem (IRE)**[15] 4275 5-9-9 **99** JamesDoyle 6 102
(Jamie Osborne) *wnt rt s: hld up in far side gp: rdn and prog over 1f out: styd on fnl f: unable to chal* **14/1**

-003 7 ¾ **Zero Money (IRE)**[15] 4275 7-8-13 **96** (b) NoelGarbutt(7) 1 96
(Hugo Palmer) *led gp towards far side and sn overall ldr: hdd u.p 2f out: one pce* **12/1**

6131 8 hd **Blanc De Chine (IRE)**[20] 4123 4-8-13 **89** JimmyFortune 22 88
(Peter Makin) *led gp towards nr side: edgd rt to join other gp 1/2-way and nt on terms w ldrs: one pce over 1f out* **12/1**

0410 9 shd **Storm Moon (USA)**[9] 4472 3-8-9 **89** JoeFanning 11 87
(Mark Johnston) *prom in gp towards nr side: brought to rail after 2f w one rival chsng: overtaken and one pce fnl f* **20/1**

3020 10 nse **Joe Packet**[15] 4275 6-9-2 **92** JimCrowley 16 91
(Jonathan Portman) *hld up in tch in gp towards nr side: drifted towards centre 1/2-way: rdn over 1f out: one pce and nvr able to threaten* **8/1**[2]

0000 11 hd **Cheviot (USA)**[16] 4263 7-9-3 **93** (p) FrankieDettori 21 91
(Ian Semple) *chsd ldr of gp towards nr side: edgd to centre 1/2-way: nt on terms w ldrs over 1f out: one pce* **12/1**

-044 12 ½ **Long Awaited (IRE)**[15] 4275 5-9-4 **94** (b) ShaneKelly 17 90
(David Barron) *wnt lft s: hld up in rr nr side gp: rdn fnl f: one pce and n.d* **7/1**[1]

-600 13 shd **Swan Song**[51] 3046 4-9-3 **93** DavidProbert 9 89
(Andrew Balding) *prom in gp towards far side: fdd fnl f* **20/1**

2614 14 ½ **Rebecca Romero**[17] 4217 6-8-6 **82** JohnFahy 18 76
(Denis Coakley) *squeezed out s: mostly in last of gp towards nr side: sme prog fnl f: styng on but no ch whn short of room nr fin* **25/1**

5050 **15** *nk* **Taajub (IRE)**[15] 4275 6-9-3 **93** SebSanders 7 86
(Peter Crate) *prom in gp towards far side: fdd over 1f out* **8/1**[2]
3051 **16** *shd* **Another Wise Kid (IRE)**[9] 4507 5-9-0 **90** MickyFenton 12 83
(Paul Midgley) *chsd ldrs in nr side gp: drifted to centre 1/2-way: wl in rr over 1f out: kpt on* **20/1**
0143 **17** *3/4* **Sandfrankskipsgo**[3] 4675 4-8-6 **82** JimmyQuinn 4 72
(Peter Crate) *taken down early: awkward s: sn chsd ldrs towards far side: wknd over 1f out* **25/1**
4/00 **18** *8* **Evens And Odds (IRE)**[29] 3846 9-8-8 **89** SladeO'Hara(5) 20 50
(Peter Grayson) *nvr on terms: t.o fnl 2f* **50/1**

59.71s (-0.79) **Going Correction** +0.075s/f (Good)
WFA 3 from 4yo+ 4lb **18** Ran SP% **129.2**
Speed ratings (Par 109): **109,107,105,105,104 104,103,102,102,102 102,101,101,100,100 99,98,85**
Tote Swingers 1&2 £29.00, 2&3 £59.70, 1&3 £42.60 CSF £74.20 CT £1801.17 TOTE £11.50: £2.60, £1.80, £6.60, £3.40; EX 93.70 Trifecta £3393.50 Pool: £4,977.23 - 1.10 winning units..
Owner Donald Wheatley **Bred** Mrs J M Russell **Trained** Wetherby, W Yorks

FOCUS
A good-quality sprint handicap. The runners fanned across the track with the first and second nearest to either side at the finish.
T/Jkpt: Not won. T/Plt: £46.00 to a £1 stake. Pool: £151,104.22 - 2,395.09 winning tickets. T/Qpdt: £26.00 to a £1 stake. Pool: £8,888.94 - 252.20 winning tickets. JN

4051 CARLISLE (R-H)
Sunday, July 28

OFFICIAL GOING: Soft (7.3)
Wind: Breezy, half against Weather: Overcast

4801 LLOYD MINI CARLISLE MAIDEN AUCTION STKS 5f 193y
2:10 (2:12) (Class 5) 2-Y-O £3,234 (£962; £481; £240) **Stalls** Low

Form RPR
652 **1** **Soul Instinct**[10] 4443 2-8-2 68 KevinStott(7) 3 70
(Kevin Ryan) *mde all: rdn and edgd lft over 1f out: kpt on fnl f: jst hld on* **7/4**[1]
2 *nse* **Ribbleton** 2-8-9 0 TonyHamilton 8 70+
(Richard Fahey) *s.i.s: rn green in rr: hdwy over 1f out: chsd wnr last 100yds: kpt on wl: jst hld* **9/2**[3]
0 **3** *1 1/2* **Kenny The Captain (IRE)**[22] 4053 2-8-12 0 DuranFentiman 6 68
(Tim Easterby) *in tch: rdn and outpcd after 2f: rallied to chse wnr briefly ins fnl f: one pce nr fin* **18/1**
05 **4** *2 1/4* **Camatini (IRE)**[22] 4053 2-8-7 0 TomEaves 7 57
(Michael Dods) *in tch: rdn and outpcd 1/2-way: rallied and edgd rt 1f out: no imp* **7/1**
40 **5** *7* **Shamardyh (IRE)**[17] 4215 2-8-10 0 PaulMulrennan 5 39
(James Tate) *dwlt: t.k.h and sn chsd ldrs: wnt 2nd 1/2-way: effrt over 1f out: wknd ent fnl f* **11/4**[2]
6 *5* **Samhain** 2-8-12 0 SeanLevey 4 26
(Ed McMahon) *chsd wnr to 1/2-way: sn rdn: wknd over 1f out* **8/1**

1m 15.48s (1.78) **Going Correction** +0.25s/f (Good) **6** Ran SP% **110.1**
Speed ratings (Par 94): **98,97,95,92,83 76**
Tote Swingers: 1&2 £2.30, 1&3 £4.80, 2&3 £4.70 CSF £9.54 TOTE £2.20: £1.70, £2.30; EX 10.30 Trifecta £76.00 Pool: £1,421.02 - 14.01 winning units..
Owner Dominic Cork **Bred** Rosyground Stud **Trained** Hambleton, N Yorks

FOCUS
Rail moved from innermost configuration, adding 9yds to 7f & 1m races and 11yds to 1m1f & 1m4f races. The ground had eased following overnight rain. The time for this modest maiden was around 3secs outside standard, suggesting conditions weren't too slow.

4802 WINDERMERE NURSERY H'CAP 5f
2:45 (2:45) (Class 4) 2-Y-O £6,469 (£1,925; £962; £481) **Stalls** Low

Form RPR
653 **1** **De Repente (IRE)**[9] 4477 2-8-8 **64** FrannyNorton 7 69
(Paul Green) *t.k.h: w ldr: led after 2f: edgd rt and rdn clr over 1f out: kpt on wl fnl f* **5/2**[2]
552 **2** *1 3/4* **Our Gabrial (IRE)**[15] 4282 2-9-5 **75** BarryMcHugh 6 73
(Richard Fahey) *prom: rdn and outpcd 1/2-way: rallied and edgd rt over 1f out: kpt on fnl f: tk 2nd cl home* **5/2**[2]
022 **3** *shd* **Broadcaster (IRE)**[13] 4337 2-9-7 **77** SeanLevey 1 75
(Ed McMahon) *trckd ldrs: effrt and chsd wnr over 1f out: sn rdn and edgd rt: one pce ins fnl f: lost 2nd cl home* **9/4**[1]
310 **4** *10* **Secret Applause**[23] 4019 2-8-10 **66** PaulMulrennan 2 28
(Michael Dods) *led 2f: sn drvn along: lost 2nd and wknd over 1f out* **10/3**[3]

1m 2.64s (1.84) **Going Correction** +0.25s/f (Good) **4** Ran SP% **111.0**
Speed ratings (Par 96): **95,92,92,76**
CSF £9.08 TOTE £5.90; EX 14.00 Trifecta £23.30 Pool: £649.23 - 20.81 winning units..
Owner Mike Nolan **Bred** O Bourke **Trained** Lydiate, Merseyside

FOCUS
An ordinary little nursery.

4803 NOMINATION CLAIMING STKS 7f 200y
3:20 (3:21) (Class 5) 3-Y-O+ £3,234 (£962; £481; £240) **Stalls** Low

Form RPR
3202 **1** **Extraterrestrial**[23] 4012 9-9-2 75 TonyHamilton 9 79
(Richard Fahey) *hld up in tch: stdy hdwy over 2f out: effrt and hung rt over 1f out: styd on wl to ld towards fin* **7/2**[2]
5030 **2** *nk* **Toto Skyllachy**[15] 4310 8-9-12 94 DavidNolan 1 88
(David O'Meara) *led: rdn 2f out: kpt on fnl f: hdd towards fin* **7/2**[2]
045- **3** *2 1/2* **Kimbali (IRE)**[225] 8133 4-9-5 75 BarryMcHugh 8 75
(Richard Fahey) *trckd ldrs: hdwy on outside over 3f out: rdn and edgd rt 2f out: kpt on same pce fnl f* **14/1**
5330 **4** *2 3/4* **Beacon Lodge (IRE)**[22] 4062 8-9-12 93 FrannyNorton 5 76
(David Nicholls) *plld hrd: trckd ldrs: effrt and drvn whn hung rt over 1f out: wknd ins fnl f* **6/4**[1]
5214 **5** *1 1/2* **Krupskaya (FR)**[31] 3718 3-8-3 73 JoeyHaynes(7) 4 62
(Mrs K Burke) *trckd ldr: rdn 3f out: wknd appr fnl f* **9/2**[3]
000- **6** *5* **Ravi River (IRE)**[54] 7968 9-9-7 61 PJMcDonald 7 56
(Alistair Whillans) *hld up: struggling over 3f out: sn btn* **80/1**

1m 42.62s (2.62) **Going Correction** +0.30s/f (Good)
WFA 3 from 4yo+ 8lb **6** Ran SP% **110.5**
Speed ratings (Par 103): **98,97,95,92,90 85**
Tote Swingers: 1&2 £1.90, 1&3 £5.00, 2&3 £10.10 CSF £15.49 TOTE £4.10: £2.30, £2.20; EX 15.10 Trifecta £83.70 Pool: £1,678.95 - 15.04 winning units..
Owner G J Paver **Bred** Lostford Manor Stud **Trained** Musley Bank, N Yorks

FOCUS
A decent race of its type, but as with most claimers there are doubts over the form's reliability.

4804 WELCOME MYRA HOLLINWORTH TO CARLISLE H'CAP 1m 3f 107y
3:55 (3:55) (Class 4) (0-85,84) 3-Y-O+ £6,469 (£1,925; £962; £481) **Stalls** High

Form RPR
-334 **1** **Wadaa (USA)**[27] 3891 3-8-8 **75** ow1 PaulMulrennan 4 85
(James Tate) *trckd ldrs: pushed along 3f out: rallied: led wl ins fnl f: drvn out* **5/1**[3]
0020 **2** *1* **Choisan (IRE)**[15] 4313 4-9-4 **74** DuranFentiman 8 82
(Tim Easterby) *chsd ldr: led over 2f out: rdn over 1f out: hdd wl ins fnl f: kpt on same pce* **20/1**
0505 **3** *1* **Party Line**[16] 4234 4-10-0 **84** FrannyNorton 10 90
(Mark Johnston) *midfield on outside: hdwy and cl up 3f out: sn rdn: kpt on same pce last 100yds* **3/1**[2]
2240 **4** *1/2* **Allnecessaryforce (FR)**[57] 2879 3-8-11 **78** BarryMcHugh 9 83
(Richard Fahey) *hld up: n.m.r and pushed along over 3f out: no imp tl styd on strly fnl f* **5/2**[1]
0653 **5** *1/2* **Prophesy (IRE)**[16] 4264 4-9-4 **77** NeilFarley(3) 6 82
(Declan Carroll) *prom: rdn over 2f out: one pce appr fnl f* **5/1**[3]
-363 **6** *1/2* **Almagest**[4] 4626 5-9-7 **82** (b) DavidBergin(5) 5 86
(David O'Meara) *towards rr: effrt and rdn over 2f out: no imp appr fnl f* **7/1**
0104 **7** *11* **Cosmic Sun**[20] 4110 7-9-3 **73** (t) TonyHamilton 2 58
(Richard Fahey) *hld up towards rr: struggling over 2f out: sn btn* **12/1**
140 **8** *13* **Mohawk Ridge**[31] 3726 7-9-6 **76** TomEaves 1 39
(Michael Dods) *led to over 2f out: rdn and wknd wl over 1f out* **22/1**
430/ **9** *25* **Non Dom (IRE)**[441] 1367 7-8-6 **65** JulieBurke(3) 3
(Wilf Storey) *bhd: struggling 5f out: sn btn: t.o* **66/1**

2m 26.03s (2.93) **Going Correction** +0.30s/f (Good)
WFA 3 from 4yo+ 11lb **9** Ran SP% **117.7**
Speed ratings (Par 105): **101,100,99,99,98 98,90,81,62**
Tote Swingers: 1&2 £10.50, 1&3 £3.60, 2&3 £7.50 CSF £98.75 CT £353.42 TOTE £4.90: £2.00, £4.50, £1.60; EX 105.30 Trifecta £1202.40 Pool: £2,042.81 - 1.27 winning units..
Owner Saeed Manana **Bred** Rabbah Bloodstock Llc **Trained** Newmarket, Suffolk

FOCUS
A fair handicap.

4805 SUPPORT RACING WELFARE MAIDEN STKS 1m 1f 61y
4:30 (4:31) (Class 5) 3-Y-O+ £3,234 (£962; £481; £240) **Stalls** Low

Form RPR
2- **1** **I Say (IRE)**[274] 7403 3-9-0 0 PhillipMakin 3 68
(William Haggas) *prom: effrt over 2f out: drifted to stands' side over 1f out: led ins fnl f: styd on wl* **4/11**[1]
05 **2** *1* **Magic Skyline (IRE)**[18] 4157 3-9-0 0 DaleSwift 9 66
(Brian Ellison) *chsd ldr: effrt and c to stands' side 3f out: led over 1f out to ins fnl f: kpt on: hld nr fin* **25/1**
2 **3** *nk* **Saffron Town (IRE)**[18] 4157 4-10-0 0 (t) TomEaves 6 71
(Alan Swinbank) *dwlt: hld up: hdwy and styd far side over 2f out: drvn and ch over 1f out: kpt on ins fnl f* **8/1**[3]
5- **4** *3 1/4* **Frank's Folly (IRE)**[311] 6409 4-10-0 0 DuranFentiman 4 64
(Tim Walford) *hld up: hdwy on outside over 3f out: drifted to stands' side 2f out: kpt on same pce fnl f* **14/1**
5 *1 1/2* **Advisory** 3-9-5 0 FrannyNorton 10 60
(Mark Johnston) *chsd ldrs: effrt and styd far side over 2f out: outpcd fr over 1f out* **6/1**[2]
6 **6** *4 1/2* **Henpecked**[30] 3774 3-9-0 0 PaulMulrennan 7 45
(Alistair Whillans) *hld up: styd far side and outpcd over 2f out: sn n.d* **33/1**
2-06 **7** *1 3/4* **Loch Moy**[41] 3398 3-9-5 70 (v1) TonyHamilton 5 46
(Richard Fahey) *led: styd far side over 2f out: hdd over 1f out: sn wknd* **8/1**[3]
0- **8** *68* **Toepaz**[345] 5316 4-9-7 0 LouisSteward(7) 1
(Alan Kirtley) *chsd ldrs: lost pl 1/2-way: styd far side and lost tch fr 3f out* **150/1**

2m 0.15s (2.55) **Going Correction** +0.30s/f (Good)
WFA 3 from 4yo 9lb **8** Ran SP% **123.9**
Speed ratings (Par 103): **100,99,98,95,94 90,89,28**
Tote Swingers: 1&2 £5.00, 1&3 £2.60, 2&3 £12.00 CSF £18.94 TOTE £1.40: £1.10, £7.00, £3.10; EX 16.10 Trifecta £72.80 Pool: £4,151.26 - 42.74 winning units..
Owner Raymond Tooth **Bred** Old Carhue Stud **Trained** Newmarket, Suffolk

FOCUS
A maiden lacking depth. The first two, and the fourth, came over to the stands' side in the straight.

4806 ULTIMATE LADIES NIGHT ON AUGUST 5TH H'CAP 1m 1f 61y
5:00 (5:00) (Class 5) (0-70,68) 3-Y-O £3,234 (£962; £481; £240) **Stalls** Low

Form RPR
0064 **1** **Fraserburgh (IRE)**[8] 4515 3-9-5 **66** FrannyNorton 5 76
(Mark Johnston) *trckd ldr: led stands' rail over 2f out: pushed clr fnl f* **7/2**[2]
2226 **2** *2* **Polar Forest**[10] 4449 3-8-5 **57** PhilipPrince(5) 8 63
(Richard Guest) *hld up and bhd: styd hdwy over 2f out: effrt and swtchd rt over 1f out: chsd (clr) wnr last 100yds: kpt on* **15/2**
3431 **3** *2 1/4* **Baltic Prince (IRE)**[15] 4288 3-9-6 **67** TonyHamilton 3 68
(Paul Green) *led: rdn and hdd over 2f out: rallied: kpt on same pce fnl f* **11/2**[3]
0300 **4** *2* **Ella Motiva (IRE)**[12] 4391 3-8-2 **49** oh4 PaulQuinn 2 46
(Mark Brisbourne) *hld up: rdn 3f out: styd on fnl f: nvr able to chal* **16/1**
4542 **5** *nk* **Gabrial The Thug (FR)**[8] 4515 3-9-7 **68** (t) BarryMcHugh 7 64
(Richard Fahey) *prom: effrt and drvn over 2f out: wknd appr fnl f* **3/1**[1]
-464 **6** *1 1/2* **Kolonel Kirkup**[19] 4140 3-9-6 **67** (b1) PaulMulrennan 6 60
(Michael Dods) *in tch: effrt and rdn over 2f out: wknd appr fnl f* **15/2**
0-40 **7** *4* **Multifact**[87] 1967 3-8-7 **54** [1] PJMcDonald 1 38
(Michael Dods) *hld up in tch: rdn wl over 2f out: wknd over 1f out* **12/1**
402 **8** *9* **Bitusa (USA)**[71] 2464 3-9-2 **63** TomEaves 4 27
(Alan Swinbank) *chsd ldrs: drvn over 3f out: wknd fr 2f out* **7/1**

2m 0.13s (2.53) **Going Correction** +0.30s/f (Good) **8** Ran SP% **112.2**
Speed ratings (Par 100): **100,98,96,94,94 92,89,81**
Tote Swingers 1&2 £5.90, 2&3 £4.50, 1&3 £5.10 CSF £28.52 CT £138.94 TOTE £4.20: £1.80, £1.70, £2.00; EX 28.10 Trifecta £332.30 Pool: £1,771.43 - 3.99 winning units..
Owner Sheikh Hamdan Bin Mohammed Al Maktoum **Bred** L Dettori **Trained** Middleham Moor, N Yorks

■ Stewards' Enquiry : Paul Quinn one-day ban: careless riding (Aug 11)

FOCUS
An ordinary handicap run in an almost identical time to the preceding maiden. The whole field tacked over in the straight.

4807 RONAN KEATING LIVE ON AUGUST 5TH H'CAP 6f 192y
5:30 (5:30) (Class 5) (0-75,75) 3-Y-0+ £3,234 (£962; £481; £240) Stalls Low

Form				RPR
2006	1		**Dream Walker (FR)**[43] 3329 4-8-9 56 DaleSwift 6 (Brian Ellison) t.k.h early: cl up: drvn 3f out: led over 1f out: kpt on wl towards fin 6/4[1]	68+
6511	2	½	**Silver Rime (FR)**[15] 4294 8-9-11 72 PhillipMakin 9 (Linda Perratt) hld up: hdwy 2f out: chsd wnr ent fnl f: r.o: hld towards fin 12/1	83
210	3	¾	**Ted's Brother (IRE)**[22] 4055 5-9-1 67 (e) PhilipPrince(5) 10 (Richard Guest) hld up: hdwy on outside 2f out: kpt on same pce ins fnl f 3/1[2]	76
1016	4	3½	**Jebel Tara**[13] 4341 8-9-7 75 (bt) KevinStott(7) 11 (Alan Brown) prom: effrt and rdn over 2f out: outpcd fnl f 10/1	75
06/6	5	6	**Beau Amadeus (IRE)**[108] 1507 4-9-12 73 FrannyNorton 8 (David Nicholls) led: rdn and hdd over 1f out: wknd fnl f 7/1[3]	57
64-0	6	shd	**Nezami (IRE)**[16] 4250 8-9-8 69 (b) RussKennemore 4 (Patrick Clinton) hld up towards rr: rdn over 2f out: sn no imp 40/1	53
0331	7	nse	**Ferdy (IRE)**[16] 4250 4-9-5 71 DavidBergin(5) 2 (Paul Green) cl up: drvn over 2f out: wknd over 1f out 10/1	55
-000	8	16	**First Class Favour (IRE)**[24] 3983 5-8-13 60 DuranFentiman 5 (Tim Easterby) midfield: drvn over 2f out: sn wknd: t.o 12/1	
0-00	9	17	**Starbotton**[30] 3762 3-8-4 58 AndrewElliott 1 (James Bethell) towards rr: struggling over 3f out: sn wknd: t.o 28/1	

1m 28.33s (1.23) **Going Correction** +0.30s/f (Good)
WFA 3 from 4yo+ 7lb 9 Ran SP% 117.0
Speed ratings (Par 103): **104,103,102,98,91 91,91,73,53**
Tote Swingers: 1&2 £5.50, 2&3 £6.60, 1&3 £1.90 CSF £22.16 CT £50.65 TOTE £2.40: £1.40, £2.20, £1.40; EX 27.80 Trifecta £83.90 Pool: £1,404.79 - 12.55 winning units..
Owner Keith Brown **Bred** John Berry **Trained** Norton, N Yorks
FOCUS
Sound form to this handicap, in which they again came stands' side.
T/Plt: £182.00 to a £1 stake. Pool: £87,115.39 - 349.26 winning tickets. T/Qpdt: £19.30 to a £1 stake. Pool: £4,800.37 - 183.29 winning tickets. RY

4505 PONTEFRACT (L-H)
Sunday, July 28

OFFICIAL GOING: Good (7.2) changing to good to soft after race 2 (2.55)
Wind: moderate 1/2 behind Weather: changeable, showers

4808 YOUR GUIDE TO PONTEFRACT AT PONTEFRACTRACECOURSETIPS.CO.UK MAIDEN STKS (SUNDAY £5K BONUS RACE) 5f
2:20 (2:22) (Class 4) 2-Y-0 £6,469 (£1,925; £962; £481) Stalls Low

Form				RPR
02	1		**Back Lane**[12] 4370 2-9-5 0 PaulHanagan 8 (Richard Fahey) awkward s: mde all: styd on wl 8/1[2]	81
3	2	2¼	**Northern Water**[8] 4539 2-9-5 0 NeilCallan 4 (Mrs K Burke) chsd ldrs: 2nd over 1f out: kpt on: no imp 7/4[1]	73
3302	3	½	**Captain Midnight (IRE)**[20] 4107 2-9-5 71 GrahamLee 3 (David Brown) chsd ldrs: 3rd over 1f out: kpt on same pce 12/1[3]	71
05	4	¾	**Lincoln (IRE)**[16] 4231 2-9-5 0 SamHitchcott 1 (Mick Channon) mid-div: hdwy over 2f out: 4th over 1f out: kpt on same pce 7/4[1]	68
	5	2	**Shared Equity** 2-9-5 0 JamesSullivan 2 (Jedd O'Keeffe) s.s: in rr: t.k.h: kpt on fnl 2f: nvr nr ldrs 66/1	61+
0	6	7	**Snugfit Sam**[22] 4046 2-9-5 0 MichaelO'Connell 7 (John Quinn) prom: drvn over 2f out: lost pl over 1f out 66/1	36
0	7	1	**Lucky Surprise**[17] 4215 2-9-0 0 JackMitchell 9 (Gay Kelleway) towards rr: nvr a factor 20/1	27
6	8	6	**Gulland Rock**[13] 4346 2-9-5 0 MartinDwyer 10 (William Muir) dwlt: swtchd lft after s: in rr: n.m.r ins over 1f out: sn lost pl and bhd 25/1	11
30	9	2	**Abisko (IRE)**[72] 2426 2-8-11 0 PaulPickard(3) 5 (Brian Ellison) s.v.s and wnt lft: a in rr 33/1	+
3332	10	11	**Bounty Girl (IRE)**[16] 4259 2-9-0 71 DavidAllan 6 (Tim Easterby) chsd ldrs: lost pl wl over 1f out: eased whn bhd 14/1	
55	11	dist	**Offshore Bond**[15] 4282 2-9-5 0 LeeTopliss 11 (Jedd O'Keeffe) swvd rt s: sn chsng ldrs on outer: hung bdly lft and lost pl over 2f out: eased over 1f out: virtually p.u 50/1	

1m 4.3s (1.00) **Going Correction** +0.075s/f (Good) 11 Ran SP% 114.7
Speed ratings (Par 96): **95,91,90,89,86 75,73,63,60,43**
Tote Swingers: 1&2 £3.50, 1&3 £4.40, 2&3 £5.10 CSF £20.73 TOTE £7.60: £2.60, £1.10, £3.10; EX 22.20 Trifecta £2.20 Pool: £1,354.70 - 5.47 winning units..
Owner David W Armstrong **Bred** Highfield Farm Llp **Trained** Musley Bank, N Yorks
FOCUS
False rail removed and a 15ft strip of fresh ground provided over last 6f. Almost certainly a modest event, but it was competitive all the same.

4809 MOOR TOP FARM SHOP HEMSWORTH H'CAP 1m 4f 8y
2:55 (2:56) (Class 5) (0-70,70) 3-Y-0+ £4,528 (£1,347; £673; £336) Stalls Low

Form				RPR
3160	1		**Darakti (IRE)**[29] 3809 3-8-4 58 ow1 (b¹) MartinDwyer 3 (Alan McCabe) s.i.s: in rr: hdwy over 3f out: swtchd rt over 1f out: led and hung lft 1f out: drvn out 28/1	66
03	2	2½	**Bavarian Nordic (USA)**[33] 3652 8-9-1 57 (v) RobertWinston 1 (Richard Whitaker) hld up in mid-div: t.k.h: nt clr run over 2f out tl edgd rt jst ins fnl f: styd on to go 2nd clsng stages 8/1	61+
5321	3	nk	**Madrasa (IRE)**[7] 4563 5-9-2 65 (bt) JacobButterfield(7) 8 (Keith Reveley) trckd ldrs: t.k.h: nt clr run over 2f out tl swtchd rt 1f out: rdr dropped whip: styd on to take 3rd nr line 7/2[2]	70+
60	4	nk	**Princeofthedesert**[57] 2860 7-8-11 53 GrahamLee 6 (Garry Woodward) chsd ldrs: drvn over 2f out: styd on fnl f 40/1	56
011-	5	1	**Gosforth Park**[304] 6608 7-9-13 69 DavidAllan 12 (Mel Brittain) w ldr: led after 2f: hdd 1f out: wknd towards fin 16/1	70
1045	6	2½	**Exning Halt**[31] 3729 4-10-0 70 MichaelO'Connell 9 (John Quinn) hld up in rr: hdwy 4f out: nt clr run over 2f out: kpt on one pce over 1f out 20/1	67
-426	7	4	**Badea**[23] 4016 4-9-12 68 PaulHanagan 4 (Richard Fahey) in rr: drvn 7f out: hung lft and hdwy over 2f out: nvr a factor 6/1[3]	59
-010	8	3	**Grammar**[11] 4403 4-8-7 52 (e) RaulDaSilva(3) 2 (David Thompson) chsd ldrs: drvn over 2f out: crowded 3f out: lost pl over 1f out: eased nr fin 28/1	38
3320	9	6	**Blue Top**[11] 4403 4-8-8 55 (p) JasonHart(5) 11 (Tim Walford) in rr: hdwy to chse ldrs after 2f: drvn 4f out: lost pl over 1f out: eased clsng stages 7/1	32
30-4	10	8	**Fleeting Fashion**[10] 4455 4-8-11 53 AndrewMullen 7 (Michael Appleby) trckd ldrs: upsides 3f out: lost pl over 1f out: heavily eased clsng stages 25/1	17
1303	11	5	**Wyldfire (IRE)**[30] 3756 3-9-1 69 LeeTopliss 5 (Richard Fahey) in tch: chsd ldrs 4f out: sn drvn and edgd lft: lost pl over 1f out: eased clsng stages 5/2[1]	25
3260	12	2¾	**Niknad**[33] 3653 3-8-0 54 oh3 (p) PatrickMathers 10 (Brian Ellison) in rr: drvn 4f out: bhd fnl 2f: eased ins fnl f 22/1	5

2m 42.09s (1.29) **Going Correction** +0.075s/f (Good)
WFA 3 from 4yo+ 12lb 12 Ran SP% 116.9
Speed ratings (Par 103): **98,96,96,95,95 93,90,88,84,79 76,74**
Tote Swingers: 1&2 £42.80, 1&3 £38.60, 2&3 £4.30 CSF £218.08 CT £993.87 TOTE £42.60: £9.20, £2.10, £1.80; EX 232.40 Trifecta £706.80 Part won. Pool: £942.51 - 0.25 winning units..
Owner Mrs D E Sharp **Bred** Mrs Mary Coonan **Trained** Averham Park, Notts
FOCUS
Not a strong contest and a messy finish.

4810 GRAHAM ROCK MEMORIAL H'CAP 1m 2f 6y
3:30 (3:30) (Class 4) (0-80,80) 3-Y-0+ £7,115 (£2,117; £1,058; £529) Stalls Low

Form				RPR
0445	1		**Arc Light (IRE)**[8] 4542 5-9-4 70 DavidAllan 2 (Tim Easterby) t.k.h in midfield: hdwy over 3f out: chsng wnr over 2f out: styd on to ld towards fin 4/1[1]	81
2252	2	nk	**Muharrer**[20] 4110 4-10-0 80 (p) LeeTopliss 3 (Michael Dods) drvn to ld: hdd after 2f: led over 2f out: hdd and no ex wl ins fnl f 5/1[3]	90
0-44	3	4	**Obboorr**[20] 4118 4-8-12 64 JamesSullivan 1 (Brian Rothwell) chsd ldrs: 3rd over 2f out: hung lft and one pce fnl f 22/1	66
0502	4	½	**Barren Brook**[16] 4264 6-9-13 79 GrahamLee 9 (Michael Easterby) dwlt: t.k.h in rr: hdwy on ins 3f out: 4th 2f out: kpt on same pce appr fnl f 8/1	80
0034	5	9	**Flying Applause**[9] 4502 8-8-13 68 (b) MarkCoumbe(3) 4 (Roy Bowring) w ldr: led after 2f: clr 8f out: hdd over 2f out: wknd over 1f out 20/1	51
3020	6	1¾	**Gran Maestro (USA)**[8] 4543 4-9-6 75 (b) LMcNiff(3) 5 (Ruth Carr) hld up towards rr: sme hdwy over 2f out: nvr nr ldrs 16/1	55
55	7	5	**Jordaura**[5] 4609 7-9-0 66 RobertWinston 8 (Alan Berry) in rr: sme hdwy over 2f out: nvr a factor 28/1	36
3200	8	18	**Jacobs Son**[72] 2418 5-9-6 72 AndrewMullen 7 (Michael Appleby) in rr: rdn 4f out: sn bhd 20/1	
-316	9	3¼	**Tuscan Fun**[18] 4167 3-9-0 76 NeilCallan 11 (Roger Varian) mid-div: effrt 3f out: sn btn 9/2[2]	
-414	10	19	**Carthaginian (IRE)**[35] 3607 4-9-9 75 PaulHanagan 12 (Richard Fahey) chsd ldrs on outer: drvn 4f out: lost pl over 2f out: eased whn bhd: t.o 5/1[3]	
0400	11	10	**Carragold**[16] 4264 7-9-4 70 PatCosgrave 6 (Mel Brittain) chsd ldrs: reminders 4f out: lost pl over 2f out: sn bhd: t.o 22/1	
0-06	12	4½	**Handsome Ransom**[55] 2923 4-9-8 74 KierenFallon 10 (David O'Meara) hld up in rr: effrt on outer 4f out: sn lost pl and bhd: t.o 16/1	

2m 12.72s (-0.98) **Going Correction** +0.075s/f (Good)
WFA 3 from 4yo+ 10lb 12 Ran SP% 116.1
Speed ratings (Par 105): **106,105,102,102,94 93,89,75,72,57 49,45**
Tote Swingers: 1&2 £5.70, 1&3 £19.60, 2&3 £24.90 CSF £20.94 CT £390.10 TOTE £4.80: £1.70, £2.20, £6.40; EX 26.70 Trifecta £1041.30 Part won. Pool: £1,388.51 - 0.52 winning units..
Owner J Beamson **Bred** Monsieurs D Blot & Christian De Asis Trem **Trained** Great Habton, N Yorks
■ Stewards' Enquiry : Neil Callan one-day ban: careless riding (Aug 11)
FOCUS
The going was changed to Good to Soft prior to this race. Flying Applause went off at a good gallop but his rivals ignored him early.

4811 SKYBET SUPPORTING THE YORKSHIRE RACING SUMMER FESTIVAL POMFRET STKS (LISTED RACE) 1m 4y
4:05 (4:05) (Class 1) 3-Y-0+
£25,519 (£9,675; £4,842; £2,412; £1,210; £607) Stalls Low

Form				RPR
-503	1		**Fire Ship**[27] 3913 4-9-1 97 NeilCallan 3 (William Knight) trckd ldrs: led over 1f out: edgd rt then lft: styd on wl 11/2[3]	110
3305	2	2¼	**Gabrial (IRE)**[15] 4276 4-9-5 110 PaulHanagan 2 (Richard Fahey) dwlt: in rr: hdwy over 2f out: chsd wnr jst ins fnl f: kpt on same pce 4/1[2]	109
4000	3	3¼	**Aesop's Fables (USA)**[15] 4276 4-9-1 110 (p) KierenFallon 4 (Saeed bin Suroor) hld up in rr: hdwy over 2f out: chsng ldrs whn carried wd wl over 1f out: kpt on to take 3rd last 75yds 7/2[1]	97
0032	4	3	**Arsaadi (IRE)**[8] 4525 4-8-10 99 (b) LiamJones 9 (William Haggas) w ldr: led after 2f: hdd over 1f out: wknd jst ins fnl f 11/2[3]	85
46-0	5	shd	**Trade Commissioner (IRE)**[39] 3458 5-9-1 104 RobertHavlin 6 (John Gosden) dwlt: sn trcking ldrs: drvn over 2f out: carried wd wl over 1f out: kpt on towards fin 7/2[1]	90
6101	6	2¼	**Mont Ras (IRE)**[24] 3984 6-9-1 98 GrahamLee 5 (David O'Meara) t.k.h: led 2f: hdd and hmpd after 2f: w ldr: hung rt wl over 1f out: racd stands' side and wknd over 1f out 8/1	85
-051	7	17	**Storm King**[29] 3812 4-9-1 94 (p) PatCosgrave 7 (Jane Chapple-Hyam) hld up towards rr: effrt over 2f out: lost pl over 1f out: sn bhd and eased 12/1	57

1m 44.73s (-1.17) **Going Correction** +0.075s/f (Good)
WFA 3 from 4yo+ 8lb 7 Ran SP% 114.0
Speed ratings (Par 111): **108,105,102,99,99 97,80**
Tote Swingers: 1&2 £3.70, 1&3 £5.50, 2&3 £2.40 CSF £27.42 TOTE £7.70: £3.10, £2.90; EX 27.00 Trifecta £219.00 Pool: £1,481.82 - 5.07 winning units..
Owner IGP Partnership & P Winkworth **Bred** Yorton Farm **Trained** Patching, W Sussex
■ Stewards' Enquiry : Liam Jones caution: careless riding.

FOCUS
A decent field for the level but an unsatisfactory finish.

4812 INFINITY ECOMAX TYRES H'CAP — 6f
4:40 (4:41) (Class 3) (0-90,89) 3-Y-0+
£9,337 (£2,796; £1,398; £699; £349; £175) **Stalls** Low

Form				RPR
0006	1		**Colonel Mak**[71] 2460 6-9-9 **86** PaulHanagan 4 (David Barron) *mde all: drvn clr over 1f out: styd on strly: unchal* **10/3**[1]	104
3140	2	4	**My Kingdom (IRE)**[22] 4067 7-9-0 **77** (t) NeilCallan 3 (Stuart Williams) *chsd ldrs: styd on to chse wnr jst ins fnl f* **7/2**[2]	82
4010	3	2 ½	**Half A Billion (IRE)**[40] 3441 4-9-5 **82** LeeTopliss 2 (Michael Dods) *trckd wnr: t.k.h: kpt on same pce fnl 2f* **7/1**[3]	79
2505	4	hd	**Barkston Ash**[7] 4560 5-8-10 **78** (p) JasonHart(5) 6 (Eric Alston) *s.i.s: in rr: hdwy 2f out: kpt on ins fnl f* **12/1**	74
2260	5	1 ½	**Orbit The Moon (IRE)**[7] 4560 5-9-1 **78** (tp) GrahamLee 1 (Michael Dods) *s.i.s: hdwy over 2f out: kpt on: nvr nr ldrs* **14/1**	70
1550	6	6	**Johnny Cavagin**[43] 3351 4-9-2 **79** (t) RobertWinston 7 (Richard Guest) *s.s: in rr: sme hdwy and hung lft over 1f out: nvr on terms* **7/1**[3]	51
1205	7	1 ¼	**Capo Rosso (IRE)**[22] 4062 3-9-6 **88** StephenCraine 5 (Tom Dascombe) *chsd ldrs: drvn over 2f out: lost pl wl over 1f out* **8/1**	55
1510	8	7	**Lucky Numbers (IRE)**[30] 3776 7-9-12 **89** KierenFallon 8 (David O'Meara) *chsd ldrs on outer: rdn 2f out: sn lost pl* **11/1**	35
01-0	9	4 ½	**Magic Secret**[29] 3840 5-9-10 **87** MartinDwyer 9 (William Muir) *in rr on outer: bhd fnl 2f* **8/1**	19

1m 15.87s (-1.03) **Going Correction** +0.075s/f (Good)
WFA 3 from 4yo+ 5lb — **9** Ran SP% **115.2**
Speed ratings (Par 107): **109,103,100,100,98 90,88,79,73**
Tote Swingers: 1&2 £3.70, 1&3 £4.40, 2&3 £5.30 CSF £15.11 CT £75.69 TOTE £3.80: £1.40, £1.70, £2.50; EX 20.00 Trifecta £76.80 Pool: £2,438.24 - 23.79 winning units..
Owner Norton Common Farm Racing,O'Kane,Murphy **Bred** Peter Baldwin **Trained** Maunby, N Yorks

FOCUS
Little got into this.

4813 STEVE "TAT" TAYLOR'S 40TH BIRTHDAY MAIDEN STKS — 1m 4y
5:10 (5:14) (Class 5) 3-4-Y-0
£3,881 (£1,155; £577; £288) **Stalls** Low

Form				RPR
0-33	1		**Inaad (IRE)**[19] 4151 3-9-3 69 PaulHanagan 2 (Saeed bin Suroor) *led after 1f: clr over 2f out: drvn out* **13/8**[1]	81
23-0	2	13	**Be My Rock**[40] 3434 4-9-6 73 StevieDonohoe 6 (Rae Guest) *chsd ldrs: drvn over 2f out: kpt on to take 2nd nr fin* **2/1**[2]	48
000-	3	nk	**Be Royale**[305] 6571 3-8-12 45 AndrewMullen 5 (Michael Appleby) *mid-div: effrt wnt 3rd and edgd rt over 2f out: chsd clr wnr over 1f out: kpt on same pce* **50/1**	45
	4	4 ½	**Bordah (USA)** 3-9-3 DominicFox 4 (Roger Varian) *dwlt: in rr: hdwy over 3f out: tk modest 4th last 100yds* **5/1**[3]	40
-6	5	2 ½	**Rosy Ryan (IRE)**[30] 3759 3-8-12 0 JamesSullivan 1 (Tina Jackson) *t.k.h: sn trcking ldrs: 2nd over 2f out: wknd fnl f* **100/1**	29
0	6	5	**Young Jay**[20] 4118 3-9-3 0 NeilCallan 3 (Mark Johnston) *led 1f: chsd ldrs: pushed wd bnd over 1f out: hung lft and lost pl over 1f out* **17/2**	23
5	7	17	**Pearl Queen (USA)**[20] 4125 3-8-12 0 HarryBentley 7 (Chris Wall) *in rr: sn pushed along: hdwy 4f out: lost pl wl over 1f out* **12/1**	
55	8	10	**Brother Duke**[13] 4356 3-8-12 0 JustinNewman(5) 8 (Garry Moss) *chsd ldrs: drvn over 3f out: lost pl over 2f out: sn bhd* **50/1**	
	9	20	**Lady Dapper** 3-8-9 0 RaulDaSilva(3) 9 (David Thompson) *s.i.s: sn detached in last: t.o over 2f out* **100/1**	
	U		**Top Line Banker** 3-9-0 0 PaulPickard(3) 10 (Brian Ellison) *uns rdr and rn loose gng to s: rrd s, swvd rt and sn uns rdr* **33/1**	

1m 45.69s (-0.21) **Going Correction** +0.075s/f (Good)
WFA 3 from 4yo 8lb — **10** Ran SP% **115.2**
Speed ratings (Par 103): **104,91,90,86,83 78,61,51,31,**
Tote Swingers 1&2 £2.00, 2&3 £18.30, 1&3 £17.90 CSF £4.86 TOTE £2.30: £1.30, £1.20, £7.70; EX 5.20 Trifecta £128.00 Pool: £3,709.15 - 21.71 winning units..
Owner Godolphin **Bred** Shadwell Estate Company Limited **Trained** Newmarket, Suffolk

FOCUS
Not a race that took a great deal of winning.

4814 FESTIVAL FINALE H'CAP — 5f
5:40 (5:41) (Class 5) (0-70,69) 3-Y-0+
£3,881 (£1,155; £577; £288) **Stalls** Low

Form				RPR
5044	1		**Amenable (IRE)**[10] 4448 6-8-6 **56** (p) OisinMurphy(7) 10 (Violet M Jordan) *led 1f: w ldr: led 1f out: rdr sn dropped whip: idled and drvn rt out* **9/1**	67
0016	2	hd	**Majestic Manannan (IRE)**[22] 4074 4-9-10 **67** AndrewMullen 1 (David Nicholls) *led after 1f: hdd 1f out: rallied and kpt on towards fin* **11/4**[1]	77
4533	3	2 ½	**Script**[6] 4582 4-9-2 **59** PaddyAspell 2 (Alan Berry) *chsd ldrs: effrt 2f out: kpt on one pce* **5/1**[3]	60
-100	4	2 ½	**China Excels**[22] 4047 6-9-0 **62** GeorgeDowning(5) 3 (Sue Smith) *sn in rr: hdwy on inner over 2f out: nvr rchd ldrs* **9/1**	54
344	5	½	**Captain Scooby**[2] 4728 7-9-7 **69** JustinNewman(5) 4 (Richard Guest) *in rr and sn drvn along: hdwy on outer over 1f out: styng on at fin* **4/1**[2]	59
4045	6	1 ¼	**Commanche Raider (IRE)**[22] 4051 6-9-10 **67** (b) LeeTopliss 11 (Michael Dods) *trckd ldrs: rdn 2f out: fdd fnl f* **20/1**	53
0012	7	6	**Sir Geoffrey (IRE)**[12] 4377 7-9-1 **58** (p) JamesSullivan 6 (Scott Dixon) *mid-div: effrt and chsd ldrs over 2f out: lost pl over 1f out* **9/1**	22
255	8	8	**Baron Run**[46] 3212 3-9-6 **67** [1] FrederikTylicki 7 (Mrs K Burke) *in rr: sme hdwy over 2f out: sn lost pl* **8/1**	
-000	9	7	**El McGlynn (IRE)**[68] 2550 4-9-6 **68** JasonHart(5) 9 (Eric Alston) *t.k.h: chsd ldrs on outer: lost pl over 2f out: sn bhd* **14/1**	

1m 4.1s (0.80) **Going Correction** +0.075s/f (Good)
WFA 3 from 4yo+ 4lb — **9** Ran SP% **115.9**
Speed ratings (Par 103): **96,95,91,87,86 84,75,62,51**
Tote Swingers 1&2 £6.20, 2&3 £3.10, 1&3 £7.60 CSF £34.14 CT £141.33 TOTE £10.90: £3.20, £1.50, £1.60; EX 43.30 Trifecta £228.70 Pool: £3,308.90 - 10.84 winning units..
Owner Rakebackmypoker.com **Bred** Michael Downey & Roalso Ltd **Trained** Moreton Morrell, Warwicks

FOCUS
A modest sprint in which it paid to race handy.

T/Plt: £34.50 to a £1 stake. Pool: £91,324.08 - 1,931.88 winning tickets. T/Qpdt: £15.10 to a £1 stake. Pool: £4,630.70 - 225.75 winning tickets. WG

4791 DEAUVILLE (R-H)
Sunday, July 28

OFFICIAL GOING: Turf: good to soft changing to soft after race 9 (14:08); fibresand: standard.

4815a PRIX DE PONT AUDEMER (CONDITIONS) (3YO) (TURF) — 1m 4f 110y
12:30 (12:00) 3-Y-O **£13,821** (£5,528; £4,146; £2,764; £1,382)

			RPR
1		**Penglai Pavilion (USA)**[22] 3-9-0 0 MaximeGuyon 1 (A Fabre, France) *mde all: set mod gallop: qckmd pce 3f out: shkn up and wnt clr appr fnl f: won easing down* **2/5**[1]	97
2	1 ¼	**Aristoteles (FR)**[37] 3-9-0 0 UmbertoRispoli 4 (M Delzangles, France) **10/1**	95
3	1	**Nearly Caught (IRE)**[104] 1584 3-9-0 0 IoritzMendizabal 2 (Hughie Morrison) *trckd ldr: rdn to chse ldr whn pce qcknd 3f out: outpcd 2f out: styd on u.p appr fnl f: kpt on wout having pce to chal* **7/1**[3]	94
4	½	**Ketchikan (IRE)**[80] 2203 3-9-0 0 RonanThomas 5 (J-P Carvalho, France) **17/1**	93
5	½	**Paris Snow**[47] 3-9-0 0 ThierryJarnet 3 (F Head, France) **33/10**[2]	92

2m 50.67s (4.27) — **5** Ran SP% **121.8**
WIN (incl. 1 euro stake): 1.40. PLACES: 1.10, 1.70. SF: 6.20.
Owner Godolphin SNC **Bred** Darley Stud Management **Trained** Chantilly, France

4816a PRIX DE CABOURG JOCKEY CLUB DE TURQUIE (GROUP 3) (2YO) (TURF) — 6f
1:30 (12:00) 2-Y-O **£32,520** (£13,008; £9,756; £6,504; £3,252)

			RPR
1		**My Catch (IRE)**[4] 4651 2-8-11 0 JamieSpencer 2 (David Brown) *sweated up: mde all: broke wl and led on rail: shkn up under 2f out: rdn and hung rt 1 1/2f out: edgd rt but r.o u.p ins fnl f: hld on gamely* **11/4**[1]	103
2	hd	**Al Muthana (FR)**[21] 2-8-11 0 Christophe-PatriceLemaire 7 (F-H Graffard, France) *trckd ldr on outer: shkn up under 2f out: rdn and chal ldr 1f out: r.o u.p fnl f: a jst hld* **10/1**	102
3	snk	**Jally (IRE)**[24] 2-8-11 0 ChristopheSoumillon 5 (J-C Rouget, France) *awkward leaving stalls: settled 5th but wl in tch: swtchd outside and styd on appr fnl f: hrd rdn and r.o ins fnl f: nvr quite getting there* **3/1**[2]	102
4	1 ¼	**Whaleweigh Station**[17] 4212 2-8-11 0 WilliamBuick 4 (Tom Dascombe) *rrd in stalls: towards rr but in tch on inner: rdn and no imp over 1 1/2f out: styd on u.p fnl f: nt pce to chal* **7/1**	98
5	snk	**Empreinte (USA)**[28] 3875 2-8-8 0 FlavienPrat 1 (C Laffon-Parias, France) *trckd ldr taking a t.k.h on rail: rdn and outpcd over 1 1/2f out: kpt on ins fnl f but nt pce to chal* **11/2**	95
6	1	**Make It Reel (FR)**[31] 3752 2-8-11 0 ThierryThulliez 3 (P Bary, France) *trckd ldrs taking a t.k.h: rdn and nt qckn 1 1/2f out: one pce fnl f* **9/2**[3]	94
7	snk	**Vintage Red (FR)**[26] 2-8-8 0 MaximeGuyon 6 (C Baillet, France) *awkward leaving stalls and wnt rt: in rr but in tch: rdn and no imp fr 2f out: styd on u.p appr fnl f: run sn flattened out and one pce last 150yds* **8/1**	91

1m 10.1s (-0.90) **Going Correction** -0.35s/f (Firm) — **7** Ran SP% **117.9**
Speed ratings: **92,91,91,89,89 88,88**
WIN (incl. 1 euro stake): 3.40. PLACES: 2.80, 9.30. SF: 62.50.
Owner Qatar Racing Limited **Bred** D Noonan & Loughphilip Bloodstock **Trained** Averham Park, Notts

4817a PRIX ROTHSCHILD (GROUP 1) (3YO+ FILLIES & MARES) (TURF) — 1m (R)
2:40 (12:00) 3-Y-O+ **£139,365** (£55,756; £27,878; £13,926; £6,975)

			RPR
1		**Elusive Kate (USA)**[16] 4254 4-9-2 0 WilliamBuick 8 (John Gosden) *w ldr: led over 2f out: rdn and swtchd lft to rail once clr: r.o strly and asserted: pushed out: comf* **5/2**[1]	118
2	2 ½	**Duntle (IRE)**[39] 3456 4-9-2 0 WayneLordan 10 (David Wachman, Ire) *trckd ldrs: rdn to chal over 2f out: outpcd by wnr ent fnl f: kpt on and jst hld on for 2nd* **5/1**[2]	112
3	shd	**Kenhope (FR)**[37] 3524 3-8-8 0 ThierryJarnet 4 (H-A Pantall, France) *t.k.h: midfield in tch: rdn over 2f out: wnt 3rd ent fnl f: r.o and jst denied 2nd: no ch w wnr* **11/1**	110
4	¾	**Topaze Blanche (IRE)**[56] 2906 3-8-8 0 Christophe-PatriceLemaire 11 (C Laffon-Parias, France) *t.k.h: midfield on outer: rdn 2f out: r.o to take 4th ins fnl f: no ch w wnr* **12/1**	108
5	nk	**Peace Burg (FR)**[56] 2906 3-8-8 0 IoritzMendizabal 9 (J-C Rouget, France) *stmbld s: midfield in tch: rdn 2f out: r.o but n.d to wnr* **10/1**	107
6	nk	**Grace Lady (FR)**[65] 2644 4-9-2 0 AntoineHamelin 12 (Mlle T Puitg, France) *midfield on outer early: prom after 3f: rdn and outpcd by ldrs 2f out: no ex and fdd* **16/1**	109
7	shd	**Maureen (IRE)**[37] 3524 3-8-8 0 JamieSpencer 6 (Richard Hannon) *hld up in rr on inner: swtchd rt and rdn 2f out: r.o but n.d* **16/1**	106
8	shd	**Laygirl (FR)**[42] 3387 5-9-2 0 UmbertoRispoli 7 (J-M Capitte, France) *restrained and hld up in rr: rdn over 2f out: kpt on wout threatening* **50/1**	108
9	nse	**Chigun**[39] 3456 4-9-2 0 TomQueally 3 (Lady Cecil) *led on rail: rdn and hdd over 2f out: sn outpcd by wnr: no ex ins fnl f: fdd* **8/1**	108
10	3	**Mayyadah (IRE)**[21] 4105 3-8-8 0 MaximeGuyon 5 (F Head, France) *hld up towards rr: rdn and hdwy into midfield 2f out: no ex ent fnl f: fdd and eased towards fin* **11/1**	99
11	18	**Poupee Flash (USA)**[21] 4104 4-9-2 0 StephanePasquier 2 (P Bary, France) *dwlt: sn rcvrd and racd in midfield in tch: rdn 3f out: lost pl and btn 2f out: sn eased and t.o* **50/1**	60

12 1 3/4 **Giofra**[16] 4254 5-9-2 0..(p) ChristopheSoumillon 1 56
(A De Royer-Dupre, France) *midfield in tch on inner: rdn 3f out: lost pl and btn 2f out: sn eased and dropped to last: t.o* **11/2**[3]

1m 35.2s (-5.60) **Going Correction** -0.35s/f (Firm)
WFA 3 from 4yo+ 8lb **12** Ran SP% **120.9**
Speed ratings: **114,111,111,110,110 110,109,109,109,106 88,87**
WIN (incl. 1 euro stake): 2.90. PLACES: 1.50, 2.40, 2.30. DF: 9.10. SF: 14.10.
Owner Teruya Yoshida **Bred** Clovelly Farms **Trained** Newmarket, Suffolk

FOCUS
The great Goldikova made this race her own, winning it four times between 2008 and 2011, and this year's winner was repeating her success from 12 months earlier. The pace held up well and the first two have been rated to their best.

4818 - (Foreign Racing) - See Raceform Interactive

2696 MUNICH (L-H)
Sunday, July 28

OFFICIAL GOING: Turf: good

4819a GROSSER DALLMAYR-PREIS - BAYERISCHES ZUCHTRENNEN (GROUP 1) (3YO+) (TURF) 1m 2f
4:05 (12:00) 3-Y-O+ **£81,300** (£24,390; £12,195; £5,691; £2,439)

RPR

1 **Neatico (GER)**[23] 4042 6-9-6 0.. AStarke 4 113+
(P Schiergen, Germany) *midfield: rdn and hdwy 2f out: 3rd ent fnl f: styd on to ld cl home and won gng away* **7/2**[3]

2 1 1/4 **Opposite (IRE)**[24] 4-9-6 0.. OlivierPeslier 1 111+
(A Fabre, France) *led: rdn and hdd 2f out: styd on u.p and battled bk to regain advantage fr eventual 3rd 100yds out: hdd cl home and no ex* **5/2**[2]

3 1 **Hunter's Light (IRE)**[70] 2494 5-9-6 0....................... SilvestreDeSousa 3 109
(Saeed bin Suroor) *trckd ldr on inner: swtchd out and smooth hdwy to ld 2f out: sn rdn: styd on but hdd by original ldr 100yds out: no ex and dropped to 3rd* **2/1**[1]

4 3 **Kitco (GER)**[64] 4-9-6 0.. EddyHardouin 6 103
(A Kleinkorres, Germany) *hld up in last pair on inner: rdn in 4th 2f out: styd on steadily but nt pce to chal* **25/1**

5 13 **Global Bang (GER)**[21] 4103 3-8-10 0.............................. AndreaAtzeni 5 77
(Mario Hofer, Germany) *dwlt: hld up in last pair on outer: rdn and outpcd by ldrs 2f out: sn bhd and btn: nvr a factor* **5/1**

6 1/2 **Baschar**[28] 3879 6-9-6 0..(b) FilipMinarik 7 76
(M G Mintchev, Germany) *trckd ldr on outer: rdn and lost pl 3f out: last and btn 2f out: wknd and sn bhd* **16/1**

2m 4.07s (-4.90)
WFA 3 from 4yo+ 10lb **6** Ran SP% **110.5**
WIN (incl. 10 euro stake): 46. PLACES: 17, 16. SF: 86.
Owner Gestut Ittlingen **Bred** Gestut Hof Ittlingen **Trained** Germany

FOCUS
This was run at a strong pace, the second and third duelling some way out.

4576 AYR (L-H)
Monday, July 29

OFFICIAL GOING: Soft (heavy in places; 8.4)
Wind: Light, half against Weather: Overcast, showers

4820 BET & WATCH WITH RACINGUK'S APP MEDIAN AUCTION MAIDEN STKS 6f
2:00 (2:01) (Class 5) 2-Y-O **£2,587** (£770; £384; £192) **Stalls** Low

Form RPR

1 **Les Gar Gan (IRE)** 2-9-0 0.. PaulMulrennan 6 72+
(Keith Dalgleish) *dwlt: sn in tch and swtchd to far rail: smooth hdwy to ld over 1f out: pushed out fnl f: comf* **13/8**[1]

0 2 1 1/4 **Toboggan Star**[23] 4053 2-9-5 0...................................... PJMcDonald 1 70
(Ann Duffield) *led tl rdn and hdd over 1f out: rallied: kpt on same pce ins fnl f* **12/1**

3 3 **Missouri Spirit** 2-9-5 0.. GrahamLee 2 61
(Kevin Ryan) *cl up: effrt and ev ch over 2f out: edgd rt wl over 1f out: sn outpcd by first two* **7/2**[3]

525 4 2 1/4 **The Dukkerer (IRE)**[21] 4115 2-9-0 63............................ KierenFallon 3 49
(David O'Meara) *prom: rdn along and outpcd over 2f out: edgd lft over 1f out: sn no imp* **11/4**[2]

5 5 **Maid In Rio (IRE)** 2-9-0 0.. JoeFanning 4 34
(Mark Johnston) *dwlt: rn green in rr: hdwy 1/2-way: effrt and hung lft over 1f out: sn btn* **6/1**

0 6 5 **Geniusinrhyme**[105] 1565 2-9-5 0...................................... TonyHamilton 5 24
(Nigel Tinkler) *t.k.h: chsd ldrs: drvn over 2f out: sn wknd* **66/1**

1m 15.62s (3.22) **Going Correction** +0.325s/f (Good) **6** Ran SP% **110.5**
Speed ratings (Par 94): **91,89,85,82,75 69**
toteswingers 1&2 £4.80, 1&3 £1.70, 2&3 £4.80 CSF £21.04 TOTE £2.40: £1.40, £4.20; EX 18.40 Trifecta £57.40 Pool: £1828.56 - 23.86 winning units..
Owner Middleham Park Racing XLIII **Bred** Sean O'Sullivan **Trained** Carluke, S Lanarks

FOCUS
Home turn bend out 4m adding approx. 12yds to race distances over 7f plus. The opener was a modest juvenile maiden in which they went an even, sensible gallop on ground officially described as soft, heavy in places. The level is fluid with the fourth rated a few pounds off his previously consistent form.

4821 DOWNLOAD THE FREE RACING UK APP H'CAP (QUALIFIER FOR THE £15,000 BETFAIR SCOTTISH SPRINT SERIES) 5f
2:30 (2:32) (Class 5) (0-75,74) 3-Y-O+ **£2,587** (£770; £384; £192) **Stalls** Low

Form RPR

6224 1 **Jinky**[14] 4340 5-9-11 73.. TomEaves 5 82
(Linda Perratt) *prom: effrt and drvn over 1f out: styd on u.p fnl f: led cl home* **8/1**

-115 2 shd **Gowanharry (IRE)**[51] 3078 4-9-7 74........................ ConnorBeasley(5) 8 83
(Michael Dods) *t.k.h: led: rdn and qcknd over 1f out: kpt on fnl f: hdd cl home* **7/2**[2]

0300 3 1 1/4 **Crimson Knot (IRE)**[6] 4613 5-9-12 74............................ JoeFanning 1 78
(Alan Berry) *hld up in tch: effrt and hdwy over 1f out: keeping on whn n.m.r towards fin* **9/2**[3]

1315 4 2 **Black Annis Bower**[23] 4074 5-9-5 67............................. JamesSullivan 6 64
(Michael Easterby) *pressed ldr: rdn over 2f out: kpt on same pce fnl f* **12/1**

032 5 nse **Findog**[6] 4613 3-9-3 69... PaulMulrennan 3 66
(Linda Perratt) *hld up: pushed along and hdwy over 1f out: edgd lft: kpt on fnl f: nrst fin* **5/2**[1]

-061 6 1 1/2 **Alexandrakollontai (IRE)**[73] 2409 3-8-8 63...............(b) JulieBurke(3) 4 54
(Alistair Whillans) *chsd ldrs: rdn over 2f out: outpcd fnl f* **10/1**

00 7 nk **Breezolini**[31] 3778 5-9-5 67... DuranFentiman 7 57
(Geoffrey Harker) *dwlt: bhd and pushed along: sme late hdwy: nvr on terms* **6/1**

4005 8 2 **Compton Heights**[7] 4582 4-8-12 60................................ GrahamLee 9 43
(Jim Goldie) *hld up: rdn over 2f out: nvr able to chal* **16/1**

6000 9 3 **Distant Sun (USA)**[11] 4448 9-8-7 55 oh3.....................(p) PJMcDonald 2 27
(Linda Perratt) *hld up in tch: rdn over 2f out: wknd wl over 1f out* **50/1**

1m 0.41s (1.01) **Going Correction** +0.325s/f (Good)
WFA 3 from 4yo+ 4lb **9** Ran SP% **119.0**
Speed ratings (Par 103): **104,103,101,98,98 96,95,92,87**
toteswingers 1&2 £5.10, 1&3 £7.40, 2&3 £4.30 CSF £37.33 CT £145.88 TOTE £8.90: £3.30, £2.00, £1.50; EX 35.70 Trifecta £165.10 Pool: £1801.11 - 8.18 winning units..
Owner John Murphy **Bred** J Breslin **Trained** East Kilbride, S Lanarks

FOCUS
A fair sprint handicap in which the gallop looked particularly solid. The runner-up sets the level.

4822 RACING UK YOUR RACING HOME FROM HOME H'CAP (QUALIFIER FOR THE £15,000 BETFAIR SCOTTISH STAYERS') 1m 5f 13y
3:00 (3:00) (Class 5) (0-75,74) 3-Y-O+ **£2,587** (£770; £384; £192) **Stalls** Low

Form RPR

0-26 1 **Beat The Tide**[24] 4023 3-8-11 70.................................... PaulMulrennan 2 80
(Michael Dods) *led 1f: trckd ldr: led gng wl over 2f out: qcknd over 1f out: hld on wl fnl f* **15/8**[1]

0161 2 1/2 **A Southside Boy (GER)**[32] 3709 5-9-3 63........................ GrahamLee 3 69
(Jim Goldie) *t.k.h: in tch: rdn and outpcd over 2f out: rallied to chse wnr ins fnl f: kpt on* **3/1**[2]

60-6 3 1 1/4 **Embsay Crag**[13] 4376 7-9-0 63................................... DeclanCannon(3) 5 67
(Philip Kirby) *hld up: rdn and hdwy wl over 1f out: kpt on fnl f: nt gng pce to chal* **14/1**

-606 4 1 1/4 **My Destination (IRE)**[35] 3627 4-9-0 63........................ NeilFarley(3) 6 65
(Declan Carroll) *prom: rdn over 2f out: kpt on same pce appr fnl f* **8/1**

0552 5 2 1/4 **Activate**[8] 4559 6-9-11 71.. JoeFanning 7 70
(Keith Dalgleish) *t.k.h: hld up in tch: stdy hdwy over 3f out: chsd wnr over 1f out to ins fnl f: sn btn* **7/2**[3]

2242 6 1 3/4 **Schmooze (IRE)**[7] 4578 4-9-1 66............................... ConnorBeasley(5) 1 62
(Linda Perratt) *hld up: rdn over 2f out: edgd lft and no imp fr over 1f out* **6/1**

0000 7 3/4 **Roc Fort**[8] 4562 4-8-9 55 oh10.......................................(p) PaddyAspell 9 50
(James Moffatt) *led after 1f: rdn and hdd over 2f out: wknd fnl f* **100/1**

61/0 8 10 **High On A Hill (IRE)**[9] 4543 6-9-5 70..................... GarryWhillans(5) 8 50
(Iain Jardine) *hld up in tch: rdn on outside 3f out: sn wknd* **33/1**

3m 3.23s (9.23) **Going Correction** +0.10s/f (Good)
WFA 3 from 4yo+ 13lb **8** Ran SP% **118.0**
Speed ratings (Par 103): **75,74,73,73,71 70,70,64**
toteswingers 1&2 £1.80, 1&3 £5.30, 2&3 £11.50 CSF £7.98 CT £60.01 TOTE £3.40: £1.10, £1.80, £3.60; EX 10.20 Trifecta £150.20 Pool: £1804.06 - 9.00 winning units..
Owner J A Wynn-Williams & D Neale **Bred** C E Stedman **Trained** Denton, Co Durham

FOCUS
An ordinary staying handicap in which they went a sensible gallop on soft ground. The third is rated to his late 2012 form and sets the level.

4823 WATCH RACING UK ON SKY 432 H'CAP 7f 50y
3:30 (3:31) (Class 6) (0-65,64) 3-Y-O+ **£2,045** (£603; £302) **Stalls** High

Form RPR

-034 1 **Monel**[27] 3934 5-9-0 52.. GrahamLee 1 60
(Jim Goldie) *dwlt: t.k.h and sn trckd ldrs: effrt and swtiched rt 2f out: styd on u.p fnl f to ld nr fin* **7/1**

0143 2 nk **Jessie's Spirit (IRE)**[24] 4005 4-9-10 62.......................... PJMcDonald 11 69
(Ann Duffield) *t.k.h: trckd ldr: disp ld over 2f out: sn rdn: kpt on fnl f: jst hld* **10/3**[2]

2024 3 shd **Alluring Star**[33] 3686 5-9-12 64.................................... JamesSullivan 2 71
(Michael Easterby) *led at stdy pce: rdn over 1f out: kpt on fnl f: hdd nr fin* **6/1**

0250 4 2 3/4 **Icy Blue**[21] 4119 5-9-3 55..(p) TonyHamilton 8 55
(Richard Whitaker) *hld up: rdn along 3f out: kpt on fnl f: nvr able to chal* **5/2**[1]

6053 5 1/2 **Berbice (IRE)**[6] 4615 8-8-4 45....................................... JulieBurke(3) 10 44
(Linda Perratt) *dwlt: hld up in tch: stdy hdwy to chse ldrs over 1f out: rdn and outpcd fnl f* **12/1**

2100 6 nse **Ptolemy**[18] 4198 4-9-5 60... LMcNiff(3) 9 58
(David Barron) *hld up towards rr: drvn over 2f out: no imp fr over 1f out* **20/1**

3426 7 3 3/4 **Joshua The First**[22] 4100 4-9-11 63..............................(t) JoeFanning 4 52
(Keith Dalgleish) *prom: rdn over 2f out: hung lft and wknd wl over 1f out* **4/1**[3]

1m 35.16s (1.76) **Going Correction** +0.10s/f (Good) **7** Ran SP% **110.9**
Speed ratings (Par 101): **93,92,92,89,88 88,84**
toteswingers 1&2 £4.80, 1&3 £3.90, 2&3 £3.00 CSF £28.60 CT £141.86 TOTE £8.00: £2.80, £2.50; EX 32.60 Trifecta £257.70 Pool: £2034.23 - 5.91 winning units..
Owner J S Goldie **Bred** Frank Brady And Brian Scanlon **Trained** Uplawmoor, E Renfrews

FOCUS
A modest handicap in which they went a sensible gallop on testing ground. The winner is rated to last year's form with the placed horses slightly up on this year's marks.

4824 READ HAYLEY TURNER EVERY FRIDAY RACINGUK.COM H'CAP 1m 1f 20y
4:00 (4:00) (Class 6) (0-65,65) 3-Y-O+ **£2,045** (£603; £302) **Stalls** Low

Form RPR

0002 1 **Save The Bees**[14] 4357 5-9-4 60..................................... JasonHart(5) 9 72
(Declan Carroll) *mde all: rdn and hrd pressed over 2f out to over 1f out: kpt on strly fnl f* **3/1**[2]

0245 2 3 3/4 **Eilean Mor**[10] 4469 5-8-3 47.. NoelGarbutt(7) 4 51
(R Mike Smith) *trckd ldrs: wnt 2nd and clr of rest over 3f out: ev ch over 2f out to over 1f out: one pce fnl f* **12/1**

50-4 3 2 3/4 **Captain Baldwin**[15] 3285 4-8-9 46 oh1.........................(v) AndrewElliott 2 47
(Jim Goldie) *hld up on ins: hdwy whn nt clr run over 2f out to over 1f out: kpt on strly fnl f: no ch w first two* **33/1**

0204 4 2 3/4 **Flipping**[21] 4109 6-9-3 54... GrahamLee 10 46
(Nicky Richards) *midfield: hdwy to chse clr ldng pair over 2f out: rdn and no further imp fr over 1f out* **4/1**[3]

61 **5** *6* **Snap Music (USA)**[12] 4400 3-9-2 **62**.................................. JoeFanning 5 39
(Mark Johnston) *prom: drvn and outpcd over 3f out: rallied over 2f out: sn no imp and btn over 1f out* **15/8**[1]

0424 **6** *5* **Look On By**[24] 4008 3-8-7 **53**.................................. JamesSullivan 1 19
(Ruth Carr) *t.k.h: in tch: drvn over 2f out: btn over 1f out* **11/2**

0020 **7** *1 ½* **District Attorney (IRE)**[21] 4119 4-9-1 **52**.................... DuranFentiman 8 16
(Chris Fairhurst) *hld up: rdn and shortlived effrt on outside 3f out: sn wknd* **16/1**

5006 **8** *3* **Hayley**[10] 4474 3-7-8 **47** oh1 ow1.......................... SophieRobertson(7) 11 4
(Jim Goldie) *s.v.s: hdwy to join main gp after 2f: rdn and struggling 3f out: sn btn* **66/1**

0 **9** *23* **Musical Express (IRE)**[113] 1414 10-8-11 **48**.................... KierenFallon 7
(W A Murphy, Ire) *pressed ldr to over 3f out: sn struggling: eased whn no ch fnl 2f* **28/1**

1m 59.99s (2.49) **Going Correction** +0.10s/f (Good)
WFA 3 from 4yo+ 9lb **9** Ran SP% **116.6**
Speed ratings (Par 101): **92,88,86,83,78 74,72,70,49**
toteswingers 1&2 £5.10, 1&3 £13.50, 2&3 £19.90 CSF £38.04 CT £995.60 TOTE £4.30: £1.10, £3.20, £6.00; EX 32.50 Trifecta £488.20 Pool: £3213.48 - 4.93 winning units..
Owner Steve Ryan **Bred** S P Ryan **Trained** Sledmere, E Yorks

FOCUS
The theme of prominent runners proving hard to peg back on the round course off a sedate tempo continued in this modest handicap. The form is weak and it is hard to be too positive about the form.

4825 33 RACECOURSES LIVE ON SKY 432 H'CAP 1m
4:30 (4:30) (Class 3) (0-95,95) 3-Y-0+ **£7,762** (£2,310; £1,154; £577) **Stalls** Low

Form RPR

-244 **1** **Le Chat D'Or**[37] 3570 5-8-9 **76**....................................(bt) PaulMulrennan 2 87
(Michael Dods) *t.k.h early: hld up in tch: hdwy against far rail to ld over 1f out: rdn and r.o strly fnl f* **7/2**[1]

-163 **2** *2 ¾* **Suits Me**[14] 4342 10-9-12 **93**.................................. PhillipMakin 3 98
(David Barron) *led: rdn over 2f out: hdd over 1f out: kpt on fnl f: no ch w wnr* **13/2**

2300 **3** *1* **Fort Belvedere**[32] 3725 5-9-7 **88**.................................. GrahamLee 6 90
(Keith Dalgleish) *hld up: hdwy and prom over 1f out: kpt on same pce ins fnl f* **10/1**

140 **4** *1 ¾* **Sound Advice**[55] 2964 4-8-11 **78**.................................. TomEaves 1 76
(Keith Dalgleish) *chsd ldr 1f: cl up: effrt and rdn over 2f out: outpcd appr fnl f* **10/1**

2546 **5** *hd* **Dubai Dynamo**[2] 4758 8-9-8 **89**.................................. JamesSullivan 4 87
(Ruth Carr) *hld up: rdn over 2f out: hdwy over 1f out: kpt on fnl f: nvr able to chal* **7/1**

40-3 **6** *8* **Balducci**[32] 3725 6-10-0 **95**.................................. KierenFallon 5 74
(David O'Meara) *prom tl rdn and wknd fr 2f out* **5/1**[3]

1450 **7** *4* **Invincible Hero (IRE)**[30] 3812 6-8-10 **80**.......................... NeilFarley(3) 7 50
(Declan Carroll) *s.i.s: sn pushed along to chse ldr after 1f: rdn and hung rt over 2f out: wknd over 1f out* **9/2**[2]

5600 **8** *6* **Steer By The Stars (IRE)**[14] 4342 3-8-5 **80**.......................... JoeFanning 8 36
(Mark Johnston) *hld up in tch: rdn and struggling over 2f out: sn btn* **5/1**[3]

1m 42.94s (-0.86) **Going Correction** +0.10s/f (Good)
WFA 3 from 4yo+ 8lb **8** Ran SP% **117.8**
Speed ratings (Par 107): **108,105,104,102,102 94,90,84**
toteswingers 1&2 £3.10, 1&3 £5.20, 2&3 £5.50 CSF £27.46 CT £211.50 TOTE £5.10: £1.60, £2.10, £3.60; EX 18.30 Trifecta £258.90 Pool: £3156.91 - 9.14 winning units..
Owner Dr Anne J F Gillespie **Bred** Dr A Gillespie **Trained** Denton, Co Durham

FOCUS
The seven different trainers in this good quality handicap were responsible for no less than 52 winners between them in the previous fortnight, and there was a contested, strong gallop. A personal-best from the winner with the second in line with recent form.

4826 RACING REPLAY, ALL TODAY'S RACING SKY 432 APPRENTICE H'CAP 1m
5:00 (5:00) (Class 6) (0-60,62) 3-Y-0+ **£2,045** (£603; £302) **Stalls** Low

Form RPR

0061 **1** **Dream Walker (FR)**[1] 4807 4-10-2 **62** 6ex.................. JacobButterfield 8 77+
(Brian Ellison) *prom on outside: pushed along briefly over 3f out: hdwy to ld over 2f out: clr whn drifted lft over 1f out: kpt on strly fnl f* **10/11**[1]

4-00 **2** *7* **Blackamoor Harry**[69] 2536 4-9-0 **46** oh1.......................(t) NoelGarbutt 3 45
(Richard Ford) *sn niggled towards rr: smooth hdwy and in tch over 3f out: effrt and chsd wnr 2f out: sn edgd lft: kpt on: no imp* **33/1**

4033 **3** *5* **Remember Rocky**[10] 4469 4-9-3 **49**.......................(v) DavidBergin 5 37
(Lucy Normile) *cl up: hdwy and ev ch over 3f out: sn drvn along: kpt on same pce fr 2f out* **4/1**[2]

-606 **4** *½* **Baraboy (IRE)**[31] 3772 3-8-10 **53**.......................... KevinStott(3) 7 39
(Barry Murtagh) *prom: effrt and drvn over 2f out: one pce wl over 1f out* **20/1**

0004 **5** *2 ¾* **Cufflink**[8] 4559 4-9-3 **54**....................................(b) RowanScott(5) 2 34
(Iain Jardine) *hld up in tch: stdy hdwy whn n.m.r briefly over 3f out: sn drvn and outpcd: no imp fnl 2f* **20/1**

4-55 **6** *1* **Lucy Bee**[45] 3281 3-8-13 **60**.......................... GeorginaBaxter(7) 6 38
(Keith Dalgleish) *w ldrs: led over 3f out to over 2f out: rdn and outpcd wl over 1f out* **12/1**

1/0- **7** *6* **Funky Munky**[112] 1052 8-9-3 **54**.......................... PaulMcGiff(5) 4 18
(Alistair Whillans) *bhd: pushed along after 2f: hdwy over 3f out: rdn and wknd over 2f out* **25/1**

-605 **8** *2* **Fine Altomis**[22] 4100 4-9-12 **58**.......................(b) ConnorBeasley 1 17
(Michael Dods) *led to over 3f out: sn rdn and wknd* **9/2**[3]

/0 **9** *3 ½* **Ros Cuire (IRE)**[136] 1020 8-8-9 **46** oh1.....................(t) JordanHibberd(5) 9
(W A Murphy, Ire) *s.v.s: a wl bhd* **66/1**

1m 45.0s (1.20) **Going Correction** +0.10s/f (Good)
WFA 3 from 4yo+ 8lb **9** Ran SP% **116.1**
Speed ratings (Par 101): **98,91,86,85,82 81,75,73,70**
toteswingers 1&2 £14.30, 1&3 £2.10, 2&3 £25.70 CSF £47.97 CT £93.62 TOTE £2.00: £1.30, £7.10, £1.80; EX 67.50 Trifecta £314.70 Pool: £3413.74 - 8.13 winning units..
Owner Keith Brown **Bred** John Berry **Trained** Norton, N Yorks

FOCUS
The concluding handicap for apprentice riders was a moderate affair. The winner seemed suited by the softer conditions.
T/Plt: £192.90 to a £1 stake. Pool: £66688.89 - 252.31 winning tickets T/Qpdt: £27.70 to a £1 stake. Pool: £5541.13 - 147.75 winning tickets RY

4589 WINDSOR (R-H)
Monday, July 29

OFFICIAL GOING: Good to firm (8.9)
Wind: Fresh, behind Weather: Cloudy, shower race 5; warm

4827 RICE 10TH ANNIVERSARY MAIDEN STKS 6f
6:00 (6:01) (Class 5) 2-Y-0 **£2,587** (£770; £384; £192) **Stalls** Low

Form RPR

52 **1** **Classic Pursuit**[14] 4347 2-9-5 0.................................. GeorgeBaker 10 75
(Ronald Harris) *pressed ldng pair on outer: shkn up to ld over 1f out: kpt on wl fnl f and a holding rivals* **10/1**[3]

6 **2** *½* **Bold Spirit**[17] 4231 2-9-5 0.................................. RyanMoore 5 73
(Richard Hannon) *pressed ldr: drvn and upsides over 1f out: nt qckn and hld ins fnl f* **5/6**[1]

25 **3** *hd* **Meeting Waters**[33] 3694 2-9-0 0.................................. LiamJones 4 69
(William Haggas) *taken down early: trckd ldng trio: rdn and cl up 2f out: eased to outside 1f out: drvn and styd on to press runner-up nr fin* **4/1**[2]

46 **4** *1 ¾* **Autopilot**[14] 4351 2-9-5 0..(b[1]) NeilCallan 2 67
(Brian Meehan) *mde most against nr side rail to over 1f out: fdd fnl f* **12/1**

5 *2 ¼* **Naughty Spice** 2-9-0 0.................................. AndreaAtzeni 12 55
(Rod Millman) *pushed along in 7th after 2f and nt on terms: outpcd after: tk modest 5th fnl f* **33/1**

6 *6* **Katja** 2-9-0 0.................................. SteveDrowne 7 36+
(J W Hills) *chsd ldrs: pushed along 1/2-way: wknd jst over 2f out* **33/1**

7 *2 ½* **Silvercombe** 2-9-5 0.................................. MartinDwyer 3 33
(Sylvester Kirk) *sed slowest of all: wl bhd: pushed along and sme modest late prog* **33/1**

6 **8** *½* **Man Of Law (USA)**[16] 4304 2-9-5 0.................................. JimCrowley 14 31+
(Ralph Beckett) *trckd ldrs: wl in tch tl reminder and wknd jst over 2f out: eased over 1f out* **20/1**

9 *4 ½* **King Calypso** 2-9-5 0.................................. CathyGannon 11 17
(Denis Coakley) *s.s: rn green and a bhd* **50/1**

10 *15* **Ignight** 2-9-5 0.................................. DavidProbert 9
(Mark Usher) *s.v.s: a wl bhd: t.o* **33/1**

P **Generous Heart** 2-9-0 0.................................. MartinLane 6
(Harry Dunlop) *sn struggling: lost action and p.u sn after 1/2-way: dismntd* **25/1**

1m 11.69s (-1.31) **Going Correction** -0.225s/f (Firm) **11** Ran SP% **113.7**
Speed ratings (Par 94): **99,98,98,95,92 84,81,80,74,54**
toteswingers 1&2 £2.10, 1&3 £4.80, 2&3 £1.60 CSF £16.32 TOTE £9.20: £2.40, £1.10, £1.60; EX 19.20 Trifecta £45.90 Pool: £1235.76 - 20.18 winning units..
Owner David & Gwyn Joseph **Bred** B & B Equine Limited **Trained** Earlswood, Monmouths

FOCUS
Inner of straight dolled out 11yds at 6f and 6yds at the winning post. Top bend dolled out 5yds from normal inner configuration, adding 22yds to race distances of 1m and over. Few got into what was an ordinary maiden, with the third back to her debut effort.

4828 ISLA CECIL BRIGHTER FUTURE MAIDEN FILLIES' STKS 5f 10y
6:30 (6:33) (Class 5) 2-Y-0 **£2,587** (£770; £384; £192) **Stalls** Low

Form RPR

2303 **1** **Oriel**[18] 4215 2-9-0 85..(p) RyanMoore 9 80
(Richard Hannon) *put into stalls wout jockey: wnt lft s: sn chsd ldrs: rdn on outer bef 1/2-way: clsd over 1f out: drvn ahd ins fnl f: all out* **4/6**[1]

34 **2** *nk* **Trinity River**[17] 4259 2-8-11 0.................................. ThomasBrown(3) 2 79
(Daniel Kubler) *led: rdn over 1f out: hdd ins fnl f: kpt on wl: jst hld* **25/1**

0 **3** *nk* **Simple Magic (IRE)**[80] 2204 2-9-0 0.................................. RobertHavlin 5 78
(John Gosden) *hld up bhd ldrs: gng wl 2f out: swtchd to rail and shkn up over 1f out: styd on to take 3rd last 100yds: jst unable to chal* **4/1**[2]

533 **4** *1 ¼* **State Anthem**[18] 4191 2-9-0 70.................................. SamHitchcott 6 73
(Mick Channon) *pressed ldrs: rdn over 2f out: stl wl there 1f out: one pce* **33/1**

2220 **5** *¾* **Go Glamorous (IRE)**[40] 3459 2-9-0 80.................................. SteveDrowne 1 70
(Ronald Harris) *pressed ldr: rdn and upsides jst over 1f out: fdd ins fnl f* **12/1**

02 **6** *1* **Gentle Breeze (IRE)**[12] 4409 2-9-0 0.................................. MickaelBarzalona 8 67
(Charlie Appleby) *chsd ldrs: rdn over 2f out: nt qckn over 1f out: fdd ins fnl f* **9/2**[3]

7 *6* **Roman Royal** 2-9-0 0..(e[1]) KieranO'Neill 7 45
(Richard Hannon) *walked to post by jockey: sn outpcd in last: rdn 1/2-way: nvr on terms* **33/1**

0 **8** *4 ½* **Picanight**[13] 4379 2-9-0 0.................................. JohnFahy 3 29
(Eve Johnson Houghton) *a in rr: lost tch u.p sn after 1/2-way* **66/1**

0 **9** *1 ¾* **Zaftual**[18] 4215 2-9-0 0.................................. JimmyQuinn 4 23
(K F Clutterbuck) *in tch 2f: sn struggling* **100/1**

59.5s (-0.80) **Going Correction** -0.225s/f (Firm) **9** Ran SP% **118.1**
Speed ratings (Par 91): **97,96,96,94,92 91,81,74,71**
toteswingers 1&2 £6.30, 1&3 £1.50, 2&3 £11.00 CSF £27.84 TOTE £1.60: £1.02, £4.40, £1.80; EX 24.20 Trifecta £100.40 Pool: £2140.54 - 15.98 winning units..
Owner Highclere Thoroughbred Racing -Petrushka **Bred** M Kerr-Dineen **Trained** East Everleigh, Wilts

FOCUS
A fair fillies' maiden but tricky to rate with steps up from the runner-up and fourth.

4829 BOODLES DIAMOND H'CAP 1m 67y
7:00 (7:00) (Class 5) (0-70,70) 3-Y-0 **£2,587** (£770; £384; £192) **Stalls** Low

Form RPR

-405 **1** **Soaring Spirits (IRE)**[19] 4168 3-9-7 **70**.......................(b) AndreaAtzeni 3 77
(Roger Varian) *pressed ldr: u.p bef 1/2-way: responded to driving to maintain press: drvn ahd ins fnl f: hld on* **3/1**[2]

4-00 **2** *hd* **Rioja Day (IRE)**[9] 4521 3-8-11 **60**.......................(b[1]) MartinLane 5 66
(J W Hills) *led at gd pce: had several of rivals hrd at work 3f out: drvn jst over 2f out: kpt on but hdd ins fnl f: tried to rally: jst hld* **25/1**

1-00 **3** *1 ¾* **Makin (IRE)**[73] 2420 3-9-5 **68**.......................(t) NeilCallan 2 70
(Marco Botti) *trckd ldng pair: rdn 2f out: nt clrest of runs over 1f out: nt qckn sn after: one pce* **12/1**

-605 **4** *2* **Admirals Walk (IRE)**[10] 4503 3-8-11 **60**.......................(tp) LiamKeniry 8 57
(Sylvester Kirk) *trckd ldng trio: rdn and nt qckn 2f out: one pce and no imp after* **16/1**

6-10 **5** *¾* **Blackball (USA)**[38] 3546 3-9-4 **67**.......................(b) TedDurcan 4 62
(David Lanigan) *chsd ldrs: rdn fr 1/2-way: tried to cl over 1f out: no hdwy fnl f* **11/2**[3]

1216 **6** ½ **The Scuttler (IRE)**[17] 4241 3-9-0 **66**.......................... CharlesBishop(3) 1 60
(Mick Channon) *chsd ldrs: rdn 3f out: tried to cl over 1f out: no imp fnl f* **6/1**

0433 **7** 1¾ **Admirable Art (IRE)**[35] 3621 3-9-2 **65**.......................... RyanMoore 7 58
(Tony Carroll) *sn off the pce in last trio: taken to outer and hrd rdn 2f out: threatened to cl over 1f out: sn no hdwy* **11/4**[1]

0-65 **8** 1¾ **Estibdaad (IRE)**[9] 4521 3-9-1 **64**.......................... SteveDrowne 6 50
(Anthony Honeyball) *a in last trio and off the pce: pushed along and no prog fr 1/2-way* **20/1**

0004 **9** 1½ **Santo Prince (USA)**[30] 3818 3-9-4 **67**.......................... JimCrowley 9 50
(Michael Bell) *stdd s: hld up in last and wl off the pce: single reminder 2f out: nvr remotely involved* **8/1**

1m 41.69s (-3.01) **Going Correction** -0.375s/f (Firm) **9** Ran SP% **114.6**
Speed ratings (Par 100): **100,99,98,96,95 94,93,91,89**
toteswingers 1&2 £26.40, 1&3 £12.20, 2&3 £54.10 CSF £72.06 CT £788.68 TOTE £3.50: £1.70, £3.90, £3.70; EX 115.50 Trifecta £657.50 Pool: £1290.43 - 1.47 winning units..
Owner J Collins, N Horsfall & N O'Sullivan **Bred** Kevin & Meta Cullen **Trained** Newmarket, Suffolk

FOCUS
Modest handicap form. They went off at a good gallop, the field soon being strung out, but the leaders held their positions. The first two are rated pretty much to their marks.

4830 CORAL.CO.UK FILLIES' H'CAP 6f
7:30 (7:30) (Class 4) (0-80,78) 3-Y-0+ **£4,851** (£1,443; £721; £360) **Stalls** Low

Form RPR

2321 **1** **Royal Guinevere**[4] 4670 3-9-5 **74** 6ex.......................... JimmyQuinn 5 82
(Dean Ivory) *taken down early and quite free to post: chsd ldrs: rdn over 2f out: prog over 1f out but drifted lft: wnt 2nd ins fnl f: hrd drvn and styd on to ld nr fin* **7/4**[1]

1102 **2** ½ **Maria Montez**[13] 4368 4-8-9 **66**.......................... ShelleyBirkett(7) 6 73
(J W Hills) *led and racd against nr side rail: 2 l clr fr 1/2-way: rdn over 1f out: kpt on but hdd nr fin* **8/1**

124- **3** 1¼ **Diamond Belle**[314] 6331 4-10-0 **78**.......................... PatCosgrave 7 81
(Noel Quinlan) *prom: rdn to chse ldr over 2f out: one pce and no imp over 1f out: lost 2nd ins fnl f* **16/1**

0301 **4** 1¼ **Ginzan**[13] 4368 5-9-6 **77**.......................... RyanWhile(7) 3 76
(Malcolm Saunders) *chsd ldr to over 2f out: drvn and stl in tch but no imp over 1f out: fdd* **7/1**[3]

4302 **5** 2¼ **Gift Of Music (IRE)**[24] 4033 3-8-12 **67**.......................... CathyGannon 4 58
(James Eustace) *chsd ldrs: rdn and struggling over 2f out: tried to rally over 1f out: wknd fnl f* **8/1**

66-6 **6** 3 **Lucilla**[203] 90 3-8-6 **61**.......................... AndreaAtzeni 2 42
(Stuart Williams) *mostly in last: shkn up and no prog sn after 1/2-way: nvr on terms* **20/1**

13 **7** 1¼ **Maria Lombardi**[30] 3818 3-8-11 **66**..........................(t) RyanMoore 11 49
(Jeremy Noseda) *dwlt: prog fr rr on outer 1/2-way: rdn over 2f out: wknd over 1f out: eased* **9/4**[2]

5546 **8** 3¼ **Night Trade (IRE)**[13] 4368 6-8-13 **68**..........................(p) PhilipPrince(5) 8 36
(Ronald Harris) *a towards rr: struggling on outer over 2f out: wknd over 1f out* **33/1**

1m 10.8s (-2.20) **Going Correction** -0.225s/f (Firm)
WFA 3 from 4yo+ 5lb **8** Ran SP% **115.4**
Speed ratings (Par 102): **105,104,102,101,98 94,92,88**
toteswingers 1&2 £4.80, 1&3 £6.50, 2&3 £10.10 CSF £16.96 CT £169.60 TOTE £2.40: £1.20, £2.20, £2.90; EX 18.60 Trifecta £97.00 Pool: £1038.29 - 8.02 winning units..
Owner M J Yarrow **Bred** Plantation Stud **Trained** Radlett, Herts

FOCUS
An average sprint rated through the runner-up.

4831 DOWNLOAD CORAL MOBILE FROM THE APP STORE H'CAP 1m 2f 7y
8:00 (8:01) (Class 5) (0-75,74) 3-Y-0+ **£2,587** (£770; £384; £192) **Stalls** Centre

Form RPR

6126 **1** **Breaking The Bank**[21] 4126 4-9-10 **70**.......................... MartinDwyer 5 80
(William Muir) *mde virtually all: upped the pce fr 4f out: rdn over 2f out: kpt on wl: nvr seriously threatened* **9/2**[3]

0-04 **2** 1¾ **Bobbyscot (IRE)**[19] 4167 6-9-13 **73**.......................... RyanMoore 2 79
(Gary Moore) *chsd wnr: shkn up over 3f out: nt qckn and lost 2nd over 2f out: kpt on to chse wnr again nr fin* **7/4**[1]

-314 **3** ½ **Hector's Chance**[29] 3854 4-9-2 **62**.......................... AndreaAtzeni 8 67
(Heather Main) *hld up in last pair: prog 1/2-way and sn prom: rdn to chse wnr over 2f out: no imp: lost 2nd nr fin* **12/1**

3051 **4** 1½ **Significant Move**[21] 4126 6-9-9 **74**..........................(b) MichaelJMMurphy(5) 7 76
(Stuart Kittow) *in tch: rdn 3f out: clsd on ldrs 2f out: one pce fr over 1f out* **11/4**[2]

0050 **5** 3½ **Poetic Lord**[2] 4771 4-9-10 **70**.......................... LiamKeniry 3 65
(Sylvester Kirk) *trckd ldrs: rdn over 3f out: no prog and wl hld fnl 2f* **20/1**

/0-2 **6** 1¾ **Ze King**[179] 450 4-9-7 **67**.......................... GeorgeBaker 1 59
(Chris Wall) *hld up: a in last pair: jst pushed along fr 3f out: nvr involved* **6/1**

6000 **7** 24 **Ajeeb (USA)**[25] 3976 5-9-5 **65**.......................... NeilCallan 4
(Michael Scudamore) *trckd ldrs: rdn over 3f out: wknd rapidly 2f out: t.o* **33/1**

2m 6.16s (-2.54) **Going Correction** -0.375s/f (Firm) **7** Ran SP% **110.9**
Speed ratings (Par 103): **95,93,93,92,89 87,68**
toteswingers 1&2 £3.00, 1&3 £6.00, 2&3 £2.30 CSF £12.01 CT £81.06 TOTE £7.30: £2.60, £1.70; EX 13.60 Trifecta £87.80 Pool: £1043.95 - 8.90 winning units..
Owner R W Devlin **Bred** Cheveley Park Stud Ltd **Trained** Lambourn, Berks

FOCUS
They went no great gallop but the form looks reasonable and is taken at face value through the runner-up.

4832 CITY AIR EXPRESS H'CAP 1m 3f 135y
8:30 (8:31) (Class 5) (0-75,75) 4-Y-0+ **£2,587** (£770; £384; £192) **Stalls** Centre

Form RPR

515 **1** **Poyle Thomas**[16] 4301 4-9-7 **75**.......................... JimCrowley 8 82
(Ralph Beckett) *hld up in tch: rdn and prog over 2f out: clsd on outer to ld ins fnl f: styd on* **11/10**[1]

4142 **2** ½ **Kittens**[5] 4626 4-8-13 **67**.......................... MartinDwyer 4 73
(William Muir) *hld up in tch: prog on wd outside over 2f out: clsd to chal and w wnr ins fnl f: nt qckn nr fin* **6/1**[3]

106- **3** ¾ **Swift Blade (IRE)**[92] 7744 5-9-0 **68**.......................... SebSanders 6 73
(Lady Herries) *hld up: last and shoved along 3f out: prog 2f out: styd on fnl f to take 3rd last strides* **20/1**

0055 **4** ½ **Aldwick Bay (IRE)**[5] 4638 5-9-7 **75**.......................... RyanMoore 9 79
(Richard Hannon) *chsd ldr to 1/2-way: rdn to go 2nd again 3f out: clsd to chal 1f out: no ex last 150yds* **9/2**[2]

4021 **5** 2½ **Shirataki (IRE)**[10] 4489 5-8-8 **69**.......................... EoinWalsh(7) 2 69
(Peter Hiatt) *dwlt: hld up tl rapid prog arnd field bnd 6f out to ld 5f out: rdn 2f out: hdd & wknd ins fnl f* **8/1**

04-3 **6** 1½ **Ice Nelly (IRE)**[29] 3854 5-8-6 **60**.......................... MartinLane 3 57
(Stuart Kittow) *awkward s: rousted along to go prom after 1f: rdn 3f out: wknd 2f out* **8/1**

1046 **7** nk **Highlife Dancer**[25] 3985 5-8-13 **67**.......................... SamHitchcott 7 64
(Mick Channon) *led to 5f out: chsd ldr to 3f out: wknd over 1f out* **33/1**

0200 **8** 9 **Gold Mine**[18] 4208 5-9-2 **70**..........................[1] DavidProbert 1 51
(Andrew Balding) *hld up in tch: rdn 3f out: wknd rapidly 2f out: t.o* **14/1**

2m 27.43s (-2.07) **Going Correction** -0.375s/f (Firm) **8** Ran SP% **116.7**
Speed ratings (Par 103): **91,90,90,89,88 87,86,80**
toteswingers 1&2 £3.50, 1&3 £11.00, 2&3 £14.60 CSF £8.45 CT £85.75 TOTE £2.30: £1.10, £1.90, £5.20; EX 7.90 Trifecta £126.20 Pool: £1655.20 - 9.82 winning units..
Owner Cecil And Miss Alison Wiggins **Bred** Miss Alison Wiggins **Trained** Kimpton, Hants

FOCUS
This looked a good opportunity for the unexposed Poyle Thomas and he just did enough. The runner-up to her latest mark sets the level.
T/Plt: £28.70 to a £1 stake. Pool: £121954.62 - 3100.41 winning tickets T/Qpdt: £23.10 to a £1 stake. Pool: £7039.23 - 225.36 winning tickets JN

4351 WOLVERHAMPTON (A.W) (L-H)
Monday, July 29

OFFICIAL GOING: Standard
Wind: Fresh behind Weather: Sunshine and showers

4833 BETVICTOR GLORIOUS GOODWOOD MONEY BACK OFFER NOVICE MEDIAN AUCTION STKS 7f 32y(P)
2:15 (2:17) (Class 5) 2-Y-0 **£2,749** (£818; £408; £204) **Stalls** High

Form RPR

0215 **1** **Al Baz**[16] 4300 2-9-5 **83**.......................... NeilCallan 1 81
(James Tate) *mde all: shkn up over 2f out: styd on* **85/40**[2]

0251 **2** 1¼ **Zain Zone (IRE)**[25] 3972 2-9-2 **77**..........................(p) DaneO'Neill 6 75
(Gerard Butler) *chsd wnr: pushed along over 2f out: rdn over 1f out: edgd lft: styd on same pce ins fnl f* **10/11**[1]

456 **3** 10 **Severnwind (IRE)**[47] 3211 2-9-0 **62**.......................... FrederikTylicki 4 46
(Ronald Harris) *chsd ldrs: pushed along 4f out: sn outpcd* **28/1**

0 **4** ¾ **Aspenbreeze**[51] 3112 2-8-7 **0**.......................... TimClark(7) 5 44
(Alan Bailey) *sn pushed along in rr: bhd fnl 5f* **50/1**

5 23 **Our Old Fella** 2-9-0 **0**.......................... ShaneKelly 3
(Daniel Mark Loughnane) *s.s: hdwy over 5f out: wknd 4f out* **80/1**

6 4 **Hot Reply** 2-8-4 **0**.......................... RosieJessop(5) 2
(Sir Mark Prescott Bt) *sn outpcd* **5/1**[3]

1m 28.47s (-1.13) **Going Correction** -0.25s/f (Stan) **6** Ran SP% **107.7**
Speed ratings (Par 94): **96,94,83,82,56 51**
toteswingers 1&2 £1.10, 1&3 £3.80, 2&3 £3.30 CSF £4.02 TOTE £3.80: £2.50, £1.10; EX 4.20 Trifecta £13.80 Pool: £2711.41 - 146.86 winning units..
Owner Saif Ali **Bred** Norman Court Stud **Trained** Newmarket, Suffolk

FOCUS
This only ever concerned the two market leaders and the form is rated around the pair.

4834 BETVICTOR 2 GOOD AT GLORIOUS GOODWOOD H'CAP 7f 32y(P)
2:45 (2:45) (Class 6) (0-55,55) 3-Y-0+ **£1,940** (£577; £288; £144) **Stalls** High

Form RPR

15-0 **1** **Angel Cake (IRE)**[23] 4070 4-9-5 **53**.......................... AndrewMullen 10 69
(Michael Appleby) *chsd ldr: led over 1f out: rdn clr ins fnl f* **14/1**

5556 **2** 3¾ **Arabian Flight**[14] 4357 4-9-6 **54**.......................... NeilCallan 2 60
(Michael Appleby) *a.p: rdn over 2f out: styd on to go 2nd wl ins fnl f: no ch w wnr* **7/2**[2]

0040 **3** ½ **Spinning Ridge (IRE)**[20] 4153 8-9-7 **55**..........................(b) FrederikTylicki 12 60+
(Ronald Harris) *s.i.s: hld up: r.o ins fnl f: nrst fin* **16/1**

0040 **4** 2¼ **Marshall Art**[35] 3643 4-9-6 **54**..........................(tp) JackMitchell 6 52
(Ken Wingrove) *led: rdn over 2f out: hdd over 1f out: wknd ins fnl f* **50/1**

2004 **5** ½ **Kielty's Folly**[35] 3644 9-9-7 **55**.......................... KierenFox 9 52
(Brian Baugh) *prom: racd keenly: rdn over 1f out: wknd ins fnl f* **20/1**

0/60 **6** nk **Bond Artist (IRE)**[35] 3644 4-9-2 **50**.......................... MickyFenton 11 46
(Geoffrey Oldroyd) *s.i.s: hld up: r.o ins fnl f: nvr nrr* **33/1**

2060 **7** ¾ **Bertie Blu Boy**[35] 3643 5-9-4 **52**..........................(v) RoystonFfrench 3 46
(Lisa Williamson) *chsd ldrs: rdn over 2f out: wknd ins fnl f* **33/1**

4412 **8** nk **Very First Blade**[35] 3644 4-8-12 **53**..........................(p) MatthewHopkins(7) 4 46
(Mark Brisbourne) *trckd ldrs: plld hrd: rdn over 2f out: wknd ins fnl f* **14/1**

2253 **9** hd **Moss Hill**[44] 3326 4-9-5 **53**.......................... RobertWinston 8 46
(Charles Hills) *hld up: rdn over 1f out: n.d* **11/10**[1]

2406 **10** shd **Blue Noodles**[13] 4377 7-9-0 **53**..........................(v) AdamCarter(5) 1 46
(Neville Bycroft) *hld up: hdwy 2f out: sn rdn: wknd fnl f* **12/1**[3]

140 **11** ½ **Just Five (IRE)**[35] 3642 7-8-11 **52**..........................(v) JoeyHaynes(7) 5 43
(John Weymes) *hld up: rdn over 1f out: nvr on terms* **14/1**

000- **12** 4½ **Odd Ball (IRE)**[266] 7593 6-9-2 **53**.......................... MarkCoumbe(3) 7 32
(Lisa Williamson) *hmpd s: in rr and n.m.r 6f out: nvr on terms* **40/1**

1m 28.84s (-0.76) **Going Correction** -0.25s/f (Stan) **12** Ran SP% **118.5**
Speed ratings (Par 101): **94,89,89,86,86 85,84,84,84,84 83,78**
toteswingers 1&2 £7.90, 1&3 £24.80, 2&3 £11.20 CSF £59.83 CT £829.76 TOTE £19.80: £3.40, £1.40, £5.20; EX 78.30 Trifecta £464.80 Pool: £2951.73 - 4.76 winning units..
Owner W Sewell **Bred** Stephanie Hanly **Trained** Danethorpe, Notts

FOCUS
A moderate handicap and there wasn't much pace on early, causing a few to take a grip. It resulted in a 1-2 for trainer Michael Appleby. The form is muddling.

4835 BETVICTOR 2 GOOD MONEY BACK AT GOODWOOD H'CAP 1m 4f 50y(P)
3:15 (3:15) (Class 6) (0-60,60) 3-Y-0+ **£1,940** (£577; £288; £144) **Stalls** Low

Form RPR

0/6- **1** **Weybridge Light**[25] 4941 8-8-11 **46**..........................(b) RaulDaSilva(3) 5 58
(David Thompson) *hld up: hdwy over 2f out: led wl over 1f out: rdn out* **16/1**

/043 **2** 3¾ **Waahej**[9] 4522 7-9-9 **60**.......................... ThomasGarner(5) 9 66
(Peter Hiatt) *hld up: hdwy over 3f out: ev ch over 1f out: sn rdn: styd on same pce ins fnl f* **9/1**

0-06 **3** 3¾ **Souter Point (USA)**[20] 4147 7-9-6 **52**.......................... AdamBeschizza 3 52
(William Kinsey) *hld up: hdwy 4f out: rdn over 1f out: wknd ins fnl f* **20/1**

3-63 **4** 6 **Finch Flyer (IRE)**[12] 4036 6-8-9 **48**..........................(p) EoinWalsh(7) 1 38
(Aytach Sadik) *mid-div: hdwy and hmpd over 2f out: wknd over 1f out* **25/1**

6-00 **5** *1 ½* **Korngold**[32] 3727 5-9-9 **55** ShaneKelly 10 43
(Ollie Pears) *led over 10f out: pushed along over 5f out: rdn and hdd wl over 2f out: wknd over 1f out* **4/1**[2]

500- **6** *½* **So Cheeky**[60] 6210 4-9-0 **46** RobbieFitzpatrick 7 33
(Richard Guest) *s.i.s: hld up: rdn over 1f out: nvr nrr* **40/1**

4533 **7** *2 ¾* **Torero**[24] 4010 4-9-9 **55** (v) NeilCallan 6 38
(Kevin Ryan) *sn pushed along to ld: hdd over 10f out: chsd ldr: rdn to ld 2f out: sn hdd & wknd* **9/2**[3]

000 **8** *14* **Pure Mischief (IRE)**[40] 3469 3-9-1 **59** TedDurcan 8 19
(David Lanigan) *chsd ldrs: pushed along over 4f out: led wl over 2f out: sn rdn: hdd & wknd 2f out: eased* **2/1**[1]

5603 **9** *2 ½* **Excellent News (IRE)**[14] 4355 4-8-12 **51** OisinMurphy(7) 11 7
(Tony Forbes) *prom: rdn over 2f out: wknd over 1f out* **16/1**

0-00 **10** *3* **Phantom Ranch**[40] 3473 4-8-10 **47** (b[1]) MichaelJMMurphy(5) 4
(Alastair Lidderdale) *sn pushed along in rr: bhd fnl 5f* **33/1**

60-5 **11** *28* **Art Thief**[14] 4355 5-9-4 **50** (p) AndrewMullen 2
(Michael Appleby) *prom: pushed along 1/2-way: wknd over 3f out: eased* **14/1**

/35- **12** *80* **Tropical Bachelor (IRE)**[441] 2134 7-10-0 **60** FrederikTylicki 12
(John Stimpson) *hld up: bhd fnl 6f* **16/1**

2m 36.66s (-4.44) **Going Correction** -0.25s/f (Stan)
WFA 3 from 4yo+ 12lb 12 Ran SP% **119.8**
Speed ratings (Par 101): **104,101,99,95,94 93,91,82,80,78 60,6**
toteswingers 1&2 £26.40, 1&3 £22.80, 2&3 £24.20 CSF £148.04 CT £2902.36 TOTE £32.60: £6.10, £2.60, £4.20; EX 160.70 Trifecta £2118.90 Part won. Pool: £2825.32 - 0.51 winning units..
Owner J A Moore **Bred** Hascombe And Valiant Studs **Trained** Bolam, Co Durham

FOCUS
A moderate handicap full of horses who find winning difficult. It was run in a monsoon. The pace was decent, but the fancied pair Korngold and Torero almost certainly did too much early and set it up for the closers. There is nothing solid about the form with most of these on the downgrade.

4836 BETVICTOR.COM FOR GLORIOUS GOODWOOD BETTING H'CAP (DIV I) 5f 216y(P)
3:45 (3:46) (Class 6) (0-60,60) 3-Y-O+ **£1,940** (£577; £288; £144) **Stalls** Low

Form RPR

6664 **1** **Reginald Claude**[30] 3841 5-9-3 **56** SilvestreDeSousa 5 67
(Mark Usher) *hld up: hdwy over 1f out: shkn up to ld wl ins fnl f: edgd lft: r.o* **5/2**[1]

0505 **2** *½* **Powerful Pierre**[11] 4456 6-9-6 **59** (b) ShaneKelly 3 68
(Ollie Pears) *hld up: hdwy over 1f out: rdn ins fnl f: r.o wl* **10/3**[2]

0001 **3** *2 ¼* **Almaty Express**[5] 4621 11-8-13 **59** 6ex (b) JoeyHaynes(7) 13 61
(John Weymes) *chsd ldrs: led over 2f out: hdd and no ex wl ins fnl f* **12/1**

0005 **4** *1 ¼* **Hinton Admiral**[35] 3643 9-8-6 **50** RobertTart(5) 1 48
(Pat Eddery) *hld up: hdwy u.p over 1f out: nt rch ldrs* **11/1**

00 **5** *½* **Gracie's Games**[19] 4163 7-8-7 **46** oh1 (b[1]) NickyMackay 11 43
(John Spearing) *chsd ldr tl rdn 1/2-way: styd on same pce fnl f* **33/1**

3300 **6** *1 ¼* **Flow Chart (IRE)**[68] 2582 6-8-9 **53** ow2 SladeO'Hara(5) 8 46
(Peter Grayson) *sn outpcd: hdwy u.p over 1f out: edgd lft ins fnl f: nt rch ldrs* **14/1**

4000 **7** *1 ½* **Ishetoo**[5] 4635 9-8-7 **46** oh1 (b) PatrickMathers 2 34
(Peter Grayson) *sn pushed along and prom: drvn along 1/2-way: no ex fnl f* **50/1**

0640 **8** *2 ¾* **Katy Spirit (IRE)**[55] 2951 3-9-2 **60** LiamKeniry 9 38
(Michael Blanshard) *prom: rdn over 2f out: wknd fnl f* **20/1**

0302 **9** *1* **Winnie Perry**[12] 4410 3-9-0 **58** DaneO'Neill 6 33
(Rod Millman) *prom: rdn over 2f out: wknd fnl f* **7/2**[3]

/066 **10** *nk* **Mr Man In The Moon (IRE)**[44] 3317 5-9-5 **58** TomMcLaughlin 10 33
(Mandy Rowland) *led: rdn and hdd over 2f out: wknd ins fnl f* **18/1**

000- **11** *nk* **Monty Fay (IRE)**[221] 8184 4-8-4 **46** RyanPowell(3) 4 20
(Derek Haydn Jones) *prom tl rdn and wknd over 2f out* **33/1**

6004 **12** *25* **Copper Leyf**[12] 4410 3-7-13 **46** (t) SimonPearce(3) 7
(Jeremy Gask) *unruly to post: awkward leaving stalls and reluctant: a bhd* **25/1**

1m 13.48s (-1.52) **Going Correction** -0.25s/f (Stan)
WFA 3 from 4yo+ 5lb 12 Ran SP% **118.3**
Speed ratings (Par 101): **100,99,96,94,94 92,90,86,85,84 84,51**
toteswingers 1&2 £2.50, 1&3 £8.20, 2&3 £8.70 CSF £9.86 CT £85.67 TOTE £3.50: £1.10, £1.60, £2.00; EX 12.30 Trifecta £73.90 Pool: £3680.05 - 37.33 winning units..
Owner High Five Racing **Bred** Whitsbury Manor Stud **Trained** Upper Lambourn, Berks

FOCUS
A moderate sprint handicap The runner-up sets the standard backed up by the third..

4837 BETVICTOR GLORIOUS GOODWOOD 2 GOOD OFFER H'CAP 5f 216y(P)
4:15 (4:15) (Class 5) (0-75,75) 3-Y-O+ **£3,234** (£962; £481; £240) **Stalls** Low

Form RPR

-002 **1** **Fathsta (IRE)**[12] 4398 8-9-12 **75** SilvestreDeSousa 4 85
(Ian Williams) *chsd ldrs: rdn to ld wl ins fnl f: r.o* **4/1**[2]

1510 **2** *½* **Point North (IRE)**[30] 3811 6-9-9 **72** (b) RobertWinston 2 80
(John Balding) *a.p: shkn up over 1f out: rdn and ev ch wl ins fnl f: r.o* **9/2**[3]

1-30 **3** *1 ¼* **Going French (IRE)**[65] 2664 6-9-5 **68** DaneO'Neill 6 72
(Dai Burchell) *led: rdn and hdd wl ins fnl f: styd on same pce* **20/1**

0040 **4** *hd* **Fayr Fall (IRE)**[26] 3945 4-9-8 **71** (v) DavidAllan 9 75
(Tim Easterby) *hld up: hdwy over 1f out: sn rdn: r.o* **10/3**[1]

0004 **5** *nk* **Avonvalley**[5] 4636 6-8-10 **64** SladeO'Hara(5) 10 67
(Peter Grayson) *hld up: rdn and r.o ins fnl f: nt rch ldrs* **16/1**

3320 **6** *hd* **Emiratesdotcom**[39] 3511 7-9-1 **71** (p) WillPettis(7) 1 73
(Milton Bradley) *chsd ldrs: rdn over 1f out: styd on* **20/1**

00-2 **7** *1 ¼* **Dominium (USA)**[203] 95 6-9-4 **70** RyanClark(3) 3 68
(Jeremy Gask) *s.i.s: hld up: r.o ins fnl f: nt rch ldrs* **9/1**

0021 **8** *nse* **Diamondhead (IRE)**[14] 4338 4-9-12 **75** LiamKeniry 11 73
(Ed de Giles) *prom: chsd ldr over 4f out: rdn over 1f out: styd on same pce ins fnl f* **9/2**[3]

0326 **9** *2* **Storm Lightning**[10] 4487 4-9-9 **72** (p) TomMcLaughlin 5 64
(Mark Brisbourne) *chsd ldrs: rdn over 2f out: no ex ins fnl f* **16/1**

4000 **10** *7* **Colourbearer (IRE)**[26] 3949 6-9-9 **72** (t) SebSanders 8 41
(Milton Bradley) *hld up: rdn over 1f out: wknd fnl f* **33/1**

0000 **11** *5* **Pick A Little**[16] 4303 5-9-10 **73** JackMitchell 7 26
(Michael Blake) *mid-div: drvn along and lost pl over 3f out: sn wknd* **40/1**

1m 13.22s (-1.78) **Going Correction** -0.25s/f (Stan) 11 Ran SP% **116.1**
Speed ratings (Par 103): **101,100,98,98,98 97,96,96,93,84 77**
toteswingers 1&2 £4.50, 1&3 £12.80, 2&3 £11.40 CSF £20.92 CT £320.45 TOTE £5.30: £1.80, £1.80, £3.90; EX 22.60 Trifecta £238.10 Pool: £3136.32 - 9.87 winning units..
Owner Dr Marwan Koukash **Bred** Brian Miller **Trained** Portway, Worcs

FOCUS
A slightly better sprint handicap and a tight finish. This rated the winner's best effort in the past year with the second t this year's form.

4838 £25 FREE BET AT BETVICTOR.COM H'CAP 1m 5f 194y(P)
4:45 (4:45) (Class 5) (0-70,70) 4-Y-O+ **£2,587** (£770; £384; £192) **Stalls** Low

Form RPR

1033 **1** **Nolecce**[32] 3719 6-8-0 **56** ow3 OisinMurphy(7) 6 66
(Tony Forbes) *chsd ldrs: led over 2f out: rdn and edgd lft ins fnl f: jst hld on* **16/1**

4002 **2** *nk* **Toughness Danon**[40] 3473 7-8-13 **62** (t) SilvestreDeSousa 9 71
(Ian Williams) *broke wl: rel to r and given reminders: sn bhd: tk cl order 8f out: hdwy over 2f out: chsd wnr over 1f out: rdn and r.o wl: nt quite get there* **11/8**[1]

3-64 **3** *8* **Sedgwick**[30] 3808 11-8-6 **62** GaryMahon(7) 8 59
(Shaun Harris) *hld up: hdwy u.p over 1f out: hung lft fnl f: nt trble ldrs* **16/1**

-443 **4** *2 ¾* **Abbraccio**[20] 4153 5-9-3 **66** (t) AidanColeman 5 60
(Fergal O'Brien) *hld up: hdwy over 2f out: rdn and wknd over 1f out* **8/1**

4445 **5** *½* **Hallstatt (IRE)**[9] 4512 7-9-3 **66** (t) FrannyNorton 3 59
(John Mackie) *chsd ldrs: shkn up and nt clr run over 2f out: wknd over 1f out* **6/1**[3]

0254 **6** *6* **Rowlestone Lad**[28] 3884 6-8-0 **56** DanielMuscutt(7) 4 40
(John Flint) *led: rdn and hdd over 2f out: wknd over 1f out* **15/2**

3504 **7** *2 ¾* **Between The Lines (IRE)**[13] 4380 4-8-5 **57** (t) SimonPearce(3) 1 38
(Anthony Middleton) *hld up: rdn over 2f out: wknd over 1f out* **12/1**

4020 **8** *7* **Blazing Desert**[46] 3231 9-8-10 **64** RobertTart(5) 7 35
(William Kinsey) *prom: chsd ldr over 8f out tl rdn over 2f out: wknd over 1f out* **5/1**[2]

2m 59.65s (-6.35) **Going Correction** -0.25s/f (Stan) 8 Ran SP% **115.4**
Speed ratings (Par 103): **108,107,103,101,101 97,96,92**
toteswingers 1&2 £5.90, 1&3 £13.30, 2&3 £8.00 CSF £39.03 CT £380.05 TOTE £16.60: £4.20, £1.10, £5.40; EX 56.60 Trifecta £386.70 Pool: £3043.02 - 5.90 winning units..
Owner Tony Forbes **Bred** Hedsor Stud **Trained** Stramshall, Staffs

FOCUS
An ordinary staying handicap. The runner-up is rated close to his winter form.

4839 MIKE LANGLEY HALF CENTURY CELEBRATION MAIDEN STKS 5f 20y(P)
5:15 (5:16) (Class 5) 3-Y-O+ **£2,587** (£770; £384; £192) **Stalls** Low

Form RPR

4 **1** **Josefa Goya**[48] 3170 3-9-0 0 SilvestreDeSousa 10 67
(Hughie Morrison) *trckd ldrs: plld hrd: r.o u.p to ld wl ins fnl f* **11/2**[3]

23 **2** *½* **Hi Filwah (USA)**[31] 3759 3-9-5 0 (v[1]) SebSanders 12 70
(Jeremy Noseda) *chsd ldrs: rdn to ld 1f out: hdd wl ins fnl f* **10/11**[1]

06 **3** *2 ¼* **Sabrina's Secret**[18] 4200 3-9-0 0 MickyFenton 8 57
(Tom Tate) *hld up: plld hrd: r.o ins fnl f: nt trble ldrs* **28/1**

50 **4** *1 ¼* **Time For Crabbies (IRE)**[27] 3932 3-9-2 0 MarkCoumbe(3) 1 57
(Lisa Williamson) *led: rdn and hdd 1f out: styd on same pce* **66/1**

0 **5** *1 ¼* **Never A Quarrel (IRE)**[90] 1896 3-8-11 0 [1] RyanClark(3) 9 48
(Jeremy Gask) *w ldr tl rdn over 1f out: no ex ins fnl f* **50/1**

6-2 **6** *½* **Timeless Appeal (IRE)**[69] 2556 3-9-0 0 FrannyNorton 3 46
(Peter Chapple-Hyam) *mid-div: hdwy 2f out: rdn over 1f out: no ex fnl f* **9/2**[2]

3-6 **7** *½* **Lars Krister (IRE)**[19] 4176 3-9-0 0 NicoleNordblad(5) 7 49
(Hans Adielsson) *in rr: sme hdwy over 1f out: n.d* **14/1**

8 *½* **Alberto** 3-9-0 0 ThomasGarner(5) 4 47
(Matthew Salaman) *s.s: outpcd* **33/1**

06 **9** *1 ¼* **Dropping Zone**[70] 2499 3-9-5 0 ShaneKelly 11 43
(Des Donovan) *s.s: outpcd* **80/1**

5 **10** *nse* **Lady Rain**[5] 4627 4-8-11 0 WillPettis(7) 2 39
(Milton Bradley) *chsd ldrs: pushed along 1/2-way: wknd over 1f out* **150/1**

11 *1 ½* **Kindlelight Storm (USA)** 3-9-5 0 TomMcLaughlin 5 37
(Nick Littmoden) *s.s: outpcd* **8/1**

0/6 **12** *2 ¼* **Lady Cricketer**[14] 4353 4-9-4 0 (b) AdamBeschizza 6 25
(Michael Squance) *sn outpcd* **150/1**

1m 1.22s (-1.08) **Going Correction** -0.25s/f (Stan)
WFA 3 from 4yo 4lb 12 Ran SP% **116.1**
Speed ratings (Par 103): **98,97,93,91,89 88,88,87,85,85 82,79**
toteswingers 1&2 £1.90, 1&3 £12.90, 2&3 £9.90 CSF £10.41 TOTE £7.50: £2.20, £1.10, £8.50; EX 13.30 Trifecta £157.30 Pool: £2724.25 - 12.98 winning units..
Owner Lord Margadale **Bred** Fonthill Stud **Trained** East Ilsley, Berks

FOCUS
A modest 3yo sprint maiden, but a couple of these can make their mark in ordinary handicaps. The winner is rated close to her debut effort.

4840 BETVICTOR.COM FOR GLORIOUS GOODWOOD BETTING H'CAP (DIV II) 5f 216y(P)
5:45 (5:45) (Class 6) (0-60,60) 3-Y-O+ **£1,940** (£577; £288; £144) **Stalls** Low

Form RPR

0420 **1** **Burren View Lady (IRE)**[56] 2916 3-8-11 **55** (v) DavidAllan 3 63+
(Tim Easterby) *s.i.s: hld up: hdwy over 1f out: r.o to ld towards fin* **8/1**

0214 **2** *¾* **Whipphound**[20] 4148 5-9-7 **60** TomMcLaughlin 4 67
(Mark Brisbourne) *chsd ldrs: led ins fnl f: rdn and hdd towards fin* **5/1**[3]

0350 **3** *2* **Chester Deelyte (IRE)**[13] 4371 5-8-5 **47** ow1 (v) MarkCoumbe(3) 7 48
(Lisa Williamson) *chsd ldrs: led 2f out: sn rdn: hdd and unable qck ins fnl f* **22/1**

0000 **4** *¾* **Direct Trade**[6] 4607 3-7-9 **46** oh1 JoeyHaynes(7) 12 43
(Mark Usher) *hld up: rdn and r.o ins fnl f: nt rch ldrs* **50/1**

25 **5** *½* **Phils Wish (IRE)**[20] 4155 4-8-13 **57** RobertTart(5) 1 58+
(John C McConnell, Ire) *chsd ldrs: cl up whn nt clr run ins fnl f: nt rcvr* **7/2**[1]

4135 **6** *nse* **Hamis Al Bin (IRE)**[9] 4517 4-9-7 **60** LiamTreadwell 6 56
(Milton Bradley) *prom: racd keenly: stmbld and lost pl over 5f out: hdwy over 1f out: styd on* **4/1**[2]

4550 **7** *3 ¼* **Dingaan (IRE)**[135] 1042 10-8-7 **46** oh1 PatrickMathers 10 32
(Peter Grayson) *hld up: styd on ins fnl f: nvr nrr* **28/1**

500 **8** *1 ¾* **Novalist**[35] 3630 5-9-1 **54** RobertWinston 11 34
(Robin Bastiman) *led to 1/2-way: rdn and wknd over 1f out* **11/2**

3026 **9** *shd* **Penbryn (USA)**[20] 4155 6-9-6 **59** SebSanders 8 39
(Nick Littmoden) *hld up: pushed along over 2f out: n.d* **13/2**

-605 **10** *hd* **Mystical Witch**[13] 4388 4-8-0 **46** oh1 (v) OisinMurphy(7) 2 25
(Christine Dunnett) *chsd ldr tl led 1/2-way: rdn and hdd 2f out: wknd fnl f* **50/1**

The Form Book Flat, Raceform Ltd, Compton, RG20 6NL.

530 **11** *1* **Lord Buffhead**[22] 4102 4-8-12 **51**............................(v) RobbieFitzpatrick 9 27
(Richard Guest) *chsd ldrs tl rdn and wknd over 1f out* **14/1**

1m 13.79s (-1.21) **Going Correction** -0.25s/f (Stan)
WFA 3 from 4yo+ 5lb **11** Ran SP% **117.1**
Speed ratings (Par 101): **98,97,94,93,92 92,88,85,85,85 84**
toteswingers 1&2 £11.40, 1&3 £29.70, 2&3 £16.90 CSF £46.05 CT £848.43 TOTE £10.90: £3.50, £1.80, £5.60; EX 81.20 Trifecta £1289.00 Part won. Pool: £1718.68 - 0.90 winning units..
Owner Habton Farms **Bred** L Mulryan **Trained** Great Habton, N Yorks

FOCUS
The early pace didn't look strong and the winning time was 0.31sec slower than division one. The winner looks on the upgrade.
T/Jkpt: Not won. T/Plt: £147.00 to a £1 stake. Pool: £103620.35 - 514.44 winning tickets T/Qpdt: £31.00 to a £1 stake. Pool: £7571.20 - 180.30 winning tickets CR

1738 LES LANDES
Sunday, July 28

OFFICIAL GOING: Turf: firm

4846a BLOODSTOCK ADVISORY SERVICES H'CAP 1m 6f
4:50 (4:50) (0-55,) 3-Y-0+ **£1,460** (£525; £315)

RPR

1 **River Du Nord (FR)**[335] 6-8-5 .... JemmaMarshall 3
(Susan Gardner) **7/2**

2 *5* **Garden Party**[14] 9-10-12 ....(b) AntonyProcter 2
(T J Bougourd, Guernsey) **5/4**[1]

3 *5* **Lady Petrus**[14] 8-8-13 .... MrPCollington 4
(S Arthur, Jersey) **3/1**[3]

4 *2* **Nordic Affair**[14] 9-9-5 .... MattieBatchelor 1
(S Arthur, Jersey) **9/4**[2]

5 *3 1/2* **Toggle**[14] 9-9-1 ....(p) JoshBaudains 6
(Mrs A Corson, Jersey) **10/1**

6 *10* **Robbmaa (FR)**[42] 8-9-3 ow3........................(b) ThomasGarner 5
(Mrs J L Le Brocq, Jersey) **4/1**

3m 18.0s (198.00) **6** Ran SP% **151.5**
Owner J Mercier & Miss J Edgar **Bred** Mrs Jane Edgar & John Mercier **Trained** Longdown, Devon

4583 BEVERLEY (R-H)
Tuesday, July 30

OFFICIAL GOING: Good to firm (good in places; 8.2)
Wind: Light half against Weather: Cloudy with sunny periods

4847 BEVERLEY ANNUAL BADGEHOLDERS MAIDEN AUCTION FILLIES' STKS 5f
2:20 (2:28) (Class 5) 2-Y-0 **£3,234** (£962; £481; £240) **Stalls** Low

Form RPR

60 **1** **Local Flier**[45] 3324 2-8-4 0........................ BarryMcHugh 6 64
(Brian Ellison) *trckd ldrs on inner: swtchd lft and hdwy 2f out: sn chal: rdn and slt ld jst ins fnl f: drvn and kpt on wl towards fin* **12/1**

2 *3/4* **Omaha Gold (IRE)** 2-8-7 0........................ RoystonFfrench 1 65
(Bryan Smart) *slt ld: rdn over 1f out: drvn and hdd jst ins fnl f: kpt on wl u.p* **5/1**[3]

5 **3** *1* **Baileys Forever**[52] 3084 2-8-11 0........................ DaleSwift 4 65
(James Given) *in tch on inner: pushed along: green and sltly outpcd 1/2-way: hdwy wl over 1f out: swtchd lft and rdn appr fnl f: kpt on same pce* **22/1**

005 **4** *nk* **Princess Myla (IRE)**[19] 4199 2-8-1 0........................ DeclanCannon(3) 5 57
(Paul Midgley) *dwlt and towards rr: hdwy 1/2-way: effrt to chse ldrs and n.m.r over 1f out: sn rdn and kpt on fnl f: nrst fin* **20/1**

0033 **5** *hd* **Fredricka**[12] 4431 2-8-5 64 ow1........................ PJMcDonald 8 57
(Garry Moss) *midfield: hdwy to chse ldrs 2f out: sn rdn and kpt on fnl f: nrst fin* **11/4**[2]

6 **6** *4 1/2* **Ladies In Waiting**[22] 4115 2-8-4 0........................ PatrickMathers 11 40
(Richard Fahey) *wnt rt s and towards rr: hdwy on outer 2f out: sn rdn and edgd rt: kpt on fnl f* **10/1**

3522 **7** *4* **Hatti (IRE)**[12] 4422 2-8-4 65........................(p) LiamJones 9 26
(John Ryan) *chsd ldrs: rdn along 2f out: drvn and wknd over 1f out* **7/4**[1]

0042 **8** *1 1/4* **Elualla (IRE)**[10] 4538 2-8-8 58 ow1........................ TomEaves 2 25
(Nigel Tinkler) *cl up: rdn along 1/2-way: wknd wl over 1f out* **20/1**

604 **9** *nse* **Red Tiger Lily**[8] 4583 2-8-0 0........................ DanielleMooney(7) 10 24
(Nigel Tinkler) *a in rr* **66/1**

10 *2 1/4* **Little Briar Rose** 2-8-4 0........................ ChrisCatlin 3 13
(John Spearing) *dwlt and wnt rt s: a in rr* **33/1**

0240 **11** *8* **Midnight Muscida (IRE)**[21] 4134 2-8-7 62........................(b[1]) DuranFentiman 7
(Tim Easterby) *a in rr* **16/1**

1m 4.69s (1.19) **Going Correction** -0.025s/f (Good) **11** Ran SP% **120.7**
Speed ratings (Par 91): **89,87,86,85,85 78,71,69,69,66 53**
toteswingers 1&2 £27.50, 2&3 £11.30, 1&3 £47.30 CSF £68.19 TOTE £18.10; EX 129.50 Trifecta £1254.10 Part won. Pool: £1672.21 - 0.26 winning units..
Owner Keith Brown **Bred** West Dereham Abbey Stud **Trained** Norton, N Yorks

FOCUS
Bottom bend moved in adding 12yds to races beyond 5f. A weak 2-y-o maiden auction fillies' race.

4848 EBF HOLDERNESS PONY CLUB MAIDEN STKS 7f 100y
2:50 (2:54) (Class 5) 2-Y-0 **£3,234** (£962; £481; £240) **Stalls** Low

Form RPR

4233 **1** **Ocean Storm (IRE)**[29] 3905 2-9-5 74........................ PaulMulrennan 3 76
(James Tate) *mde all: rdn clr wl over 1f out: readily* **1/2**[1]

0 **2** *4* **Shirocco Passion**[12] 4432 2-9-0 0........................ BarryMcHugh 2 59
(Tony Coyle) *chsd ldng pair: rdn along wl over 2f out: styd on to chse wnr fr 1 1/2f out: drvn and no imp fnl f* **33/1**

3 *5* **Zal Zilhom (IRE)** 2-9-5 0........................ TomEaves 4 52+
(Kevin Ryan) *chsd wnr: green and hung lft home turn: rdn over 2f out: wknd wl over 1f out* **6/1**[3]

00 **4** *1 1/4* **Slinky McVelvet**[47] 3245 2-9-0 0........................ PJMcDonald 6 43
(Garry Moss) *chsd ldrs: rdn along over 2f out: sn one pce* **66/1**

5 *3 3/4* **Zumurudah (FR)** 2-9-0 0........................ LiamJones 1 34+
(Mark Johnston) *wnt lft s and s.i.s: green and a in rr* **3/1**[2]

6 *59* **L'Es Fremantle (FR)** 2-8-12 0........................ DanielleMooney(7) 5
(Michael Chapman) *wnt lft s and s.i.s: green: a outpcd and bhd* **66/1**

1m 35.17s (1.37) **Going Correction** -0.025s/f (Good) **6** Ran SP% **111.9**
Speed ratings (Par 94): **91,86,80,79,75 7**
toteswingers 1&2 £2.60, 2&3 £4.20, 1&3 £1.10 CSF £21.01 TOTE £1.60: £1.02, £9.90; EX 11.30 Trifecta £28.80 Pool: £2401.88 - 62.39 winning units..
Owner Saeed Manana **Bred** Epona Bloodstock Ltd And P A Byrne **Trained** Newmarket, Suffolk

FOCUS
The market suggested that this would prove plain sailing for the 74-rated favourite and so it proved.

4849 RACING UK ON SKY 432 (S) H'CAP 1m 4f 16y
3:25 (3:25) (Class 6) (0-65,51) 3-Y-0 **£2,264** (£673; £336; £168) **Stalls** Low

Form RPR

-642 **1** **Jebulani**[8] 4587 3-9-2 **46**........................ DanielTudhope 5 56
(David O'Meara) *mde all: stdd pce 7f out: pushed along and qcknd 3f out: rdn clr wl over 1f out: kpt on u.p fnl f* **11/10**[1]

0500 **2** *1 1/2* **Ground Ginger**[25] 4008 3-9-1 **45**........................ PJMcDonald 1 50
(James Bethell) *hld up in rr: hdwy 3f out: rdn to chse ldrs wl over 1f out: drvn and edgd rt ent fnl f: kpt on: no ch w wnr* **25/1**

0454 **3** *3* **Duchess Of Dreams**[11] 4474 3-8-10 **45**........................ PhilipPrince(5) 3 45
(Richard Guest) *hld up in rr: hdwy over 3f out: rdn 2f out: styng on whn n.m.r ent fnl f: sn swtchd lft and kpt on towards fin* **12/1**

3340 **4** *3/4* **Halfwaytocootehill (IRE)**[29] 3893 3-9-7 **51**........................(t) TomEaves 2 50
(Ollie Pears) *trckd ldrs: hdwy over 4f out: chsd wnr over 2f out: rdn wl over 1f out: drvn and wknd appr fnl f* **2/1**[2]

-000 **5** *8* **Threepence**[21] 4140 3-9-1 **45**........................(p) PaulQuinn 4 31
(Richard Whitaker) *chsd ldng pair on inner: pushed along after 4f: rdn 5f out: wknd over 3f out* **66/1**

6-66 **6** *1/2* **Santa Fe Stinger**[8] 4587 3-9-1 **45**........................(b[1]) DavidAllan 7 30
(Tim Easterby) *awkward and wnt lft s: sn chsng ldrs: rdn along over 5f out: drvn along 3f out: sn wknd* **11/1**

0365 **7** *7* **Jomari (IRE)**[8] 4587 3-8-8 **45**........................ LukeLeadbitter(7) 6 19
(Declan Carroll) *chsd wnr: cl up 1/2-way: rdn along 3f out: wknd 2f out* **8/1**[3]

2m 40.68s (0.88) **Going Correction** -0.025s/f (Good) **7** Ran SP% **113.4**
Speed ratings (Par 98): **96,95,93,92,87 86,82**
toteswingers 1&2 £3.60, 2&3 £29.00, 1&3 £6.20 CSF £31.13 TOTE £1.70: £1.30, £6.70; EX 21.50 Trifecta £110.90 Pool: £1754.74 - 11.86 winning units..There was no bid for the winner.
Owner Mrs Claire Hollowood **Bred** Mrs C Hollowood **Trained** Nawton, N Yorks

FOCUS
The seven runners were 0-57 ahead of this rock-bottom 3yo selling handicap.

4850 WILFORD WATTS MEMORIAL H'CAP 1m 100y
4:00 (4:01) (Class 4) (0-85,83) 3-Y-0+ **£6,469** (£1,925; £962; £481) **Stalls** Low

Form RPR

2251 **1** **Robert The Painter (IRE)**[14] 4373 5-9-8 **77**........................(v) DanielTudhope 3 96
(David O'Meara) *hld ldng pair on inner: smooth hdwy 3f out: sn chsng ldr: chal 2f out: led over 1f out: rdn clr fnl f: styd on strly* **7/4**[1]

5403 **2** *7* **Fame Again**[14] 4375 5-9-1 **70**........................ PaulMulrennan 4 73
(Michael Easterby) *cl up: led after 1f: rdn along and jnd 2f out: drvn and hdd over 1f out: plugged on: no ch w wnr* **5/1**[3]

5333 **3** *1* **Nimiety**[23] 4100 4-9-1 **70**........................ LiamJones 6 71
(Mark Johnston) *hld up in rr: hdwy on inner over 2f out: rdn along wl over 1f out: styd on fnl f: nrst fin* **13/2**

1116 **4** *3/4* **Talent Scout (IRE)**[17] 4308 7-9-7 **83**........................(p) GemmaTutty(7) 5 82
(Karen Tutty) *led 1f: cl up: rdn along over 2f out: grad wknd* **9/2**[2]

22-3 **5** *1 3/4* **Multi Bene**[22] 4124 4-9-11 **80**........................ RoystonFfrench 8 75
(Ed McMahon) *t.k.h: chsd ldrs: rdn along 3f out: drvn wl over 1f out: sn wknd* **5/1**[3]

6-55 **6** *1* **Change The Subject (USA)**[11] 4475 5-8-11 **71**........................ PhilipPrince(5) 2 64
(Richard Guest) *pushed along and wnt rt s: trck ldrs on inner: hdwy 3f out: rdn over 2f out: sn drvn and wknd wl over 1f out* **20/1**

2405 **7** *2* **Shadowtime**[14] 4373 8-9-7 **76**........................ BarryMcHugh 7 64
(Tracy Waggott) *hld up: effrt 3f out: rdn along over 2f out: n.d* **11/1**

1m 46.09s (-1.51) **Going Correction** -0.025s/f (Good) **7** Ran SP% **114.3**
Speed ratings (Par 105): **106,99,98,97,95 94,92**
toteswingers 1&2 £2.70, 2&3 £4.60, 1&3 £1.80 CSF £10.81 CT £45.23 TOTE £2.30: £1.50, £5.60; EX 10.50 Trifecta £45.00 Pool: £1967.25 - 32.77 winning units..
Owner Stephen Humphreys **Bred** Ballylinch Stud **Trained** Nawton, N Yorks

FOCUS
A decent and open looking 0-83 extended mile handicap and a very ready, bang in-form winner.

4851 BEVERLEY MIDDLE DISTANCE SERIES H'CAP 1m 4f 16y
4:35 (4:35) (Class 5) (0-75,75) 3-Y-0+ **£3,234** (£962; £481; £240) **Stalls** Low

Form RPR

6431 **1** **Brigadoon**[7] 4612 6-10-0 **75** 6ex........................ MichaelO'Connell 7 82
(Philip Kirby) *trckd ldrs: smooth hdwy 3f out: led 1 1/2f out: sn clr: styd on strly* **1/1**[1]

0033 **2** *3 1/2* **Strike Force**[8] 4584 9-8-11 **63**........................(t) TobyAtkinson(5) 3 64
(Alison Hutchinson) *hld up in rr: hdwy over 2f out: rdn wl over 1f out: styd on to chse wnr ins fnl f: no imp* **18/1**

0040 **3** *2* **Valentine's Gift**[14] 4376 5-8-9 **56** oh10........................(p) AndrewElliott 1 54
(Neville Bycroft) *t.k.h early: trckd ldrs on inner: effrt and nt clr run over 1f out: sn swtchd lft and hmpd ent fnl f: rdn and styd on to take 3rd nr line* **66/1**

1336 **4** *shd* **Bright Applause**[10] 4543 5-9-11 **72**........................ BarryMcHugh 5 70
(Tracy Waggott) *trckd ldr: cl up 4f out: rdn and ev ch 2f out: drvn and one pce fr over 1f out* **11/2**[3]

5-4 **5** *1/2* **Time Of My Life (IRE)**[33] 3729 4-9-10 **71**........................(t) DuranFentiman 6 68
(Patrick Holmes) *hld up in tch: effrt on outer 3f out: rdn along over 2f out: sn no imp* **12/1**

3-23 **6** *2 1/2* **Gods Gift (IRE)**[137] 1009 3-8-11 **70**........................ ChrisCatlin 4 63
(Rae Guest) *led: hung lft bnd after 2f: pushed along over 3f out: rdn over 2f out: hdd 1 1/2f out: sn drvn and wknd* **2/1**[2]

2m 39.0s (-0.80) **Going Correction** -0.025s/f (Good)
WFA 3 from 4yo+ 12lb **6** Ran SP% **113.2**
Speed ratings (Par 103): **101,98,97,97,96 95**
toteswingers 1&2 £3.50, 2&3 £13.80, 1&3 £9.20 CSF £21.11 TOTE £1.60: £1.10, £8.10; EX 15.60 Trifecta £130.70 Pool: £3528.68 - 20.24 winning units..
Owner Robin Oliver **Bred** Biddestone Stud **Trained** Middleham, N Yorks

FOCUS
A modest middle-distance handicap.

4852 NEWCOMERS RACEDAY H'CAP 5f
5:10 (5:10) (Class 5) (0-75,75) 3-Y-O+ £3,234 (£962; £481; £240) Stalls Far side

Form RPR
1313 1 **Bondi Beach Boy**[4] 4728 4-9-3 66 PJMcDonald 1 76
(James Turner) *qckly away: mde all: clr 2f out: rdn over 1f out: drvn fnl f: jst hld on* **5/4**[1]
0035 2 nk **Indian Trail**[4] 4728 13-8-13 69 (b) OisinMurphy(7) 4 78
(David Nicholls) *in tch: hdwy wl over 1f out: swtchd rt and rdn ent fnl f: styd on strly: jst failed* **12/1**
4420 3 1 3/4 **Mercers Row**[19] 4203 6-9-8 71 DanielTudhope 2 74
(Karen Tutty) *trckd ldrs: swtchd lft and hdwy over 1f out: rdn and one pce ins fnl f* **7/1**[3]
4436 4 1 3/4 **Phoenix Clubs (IRE)**[25] 4017 4-9-7 70 BarryMcHugh 12 66
(Paul Midgley) *towards rr: hdwy wl over 1f out: sn rdn and styd on fnl f: nrst fin* **20/1**
0600 5 1/2 **Elusive Bonus (IRE)**[4] 4728 4-9-1 69 (v[1]) DavidBergin(5) 10 64
(David O'Meara) *trckd ldrs: hdwy 2f out: sn chsng wnr: rdn and hung rt over 1f out: one pce after* **25/1**
4226 6 2 **Holy Angel (IRE)**[4] 4728 4-9-0 70 (e) RachelRichardson(7) 8 57
(Tim Easterby) *towards rr: hdwy on inner whn nt clr run and hmpd over 1f out: kpt on fnl f: nrst fin* **7/2**[2]
0050 7 nk **Tyfos**[11] 4479 8-9-7 75 MatthewLawson(5) 13 61
(Brian Baugh) *chsd ldrs: rdn 2f out: grad wknd* **20/1**
0204 8 1 **Steelcut**[29] 3904 9-8-12 61 (p) LiamJones 5 44
(Mark Buckley) *nvr bttr then midfield* **40/1**
0600 9 2 1/2 **Caranbola**[4] 4730 7-9-4 74 RobertDodsworth(7) 14 48
(Mel Brittain) *wnt lft s: swtchd to r alone nr stands' rail: a towards rr* **16/1**
0502 10 2 1/2 **Mey Blossom**[8] 4588 8-8-13 62 (p) TomEaves 9 27
(Richard Whitaker) *a towards rr* **10/1**
4000 11 nk **Master Rooney (IRE)**[8] 4588 7-9-12 75 RoystonFfrench 3 39
(Geoffrey Harker) *chsd wnr: rdn 2f out: sn drvn and wknd over 1f out* **20/1**

1m 2.77s (-0.73) **Going Correction** -0.025s/f (Good) **11** Ran SP% **122.4**
Speed ratings (Par 103): **104,103,100,97,97 93,93,91,87,83 83**
toteswingers 1&2 £3.30, 2&3 £9.70, 1&3 £3.10 CSF £17.65 CT £85.53 TOTE £2.10: £1.70, £2.70, £1.30; EX 18.60 Trifecta £68.20 Pool: £2391.84 - 26.28 winning units..
Owner G R Turner & H Turner **Bred** G R & H Turner **Trained** Norton-le-Clay, N Yorks

FOCUS
A modest sprint handicap with the first three starting from inside stalls.

4853 LADY JANE BETHELL MEMORIAL LADY RIDERS' H'CAP (FOR LADY AMATEUR RIDERS) 1m 1f 207y
5:45 (5:56) (Class 6) (0-65,65) 3-Y-O+ £2,305 (£709; £354) Stalls Low

Form RPR
5522 1 **Hernando Torres**[14] 4376 5-9-13 59 (p) AnnaHesketh(5) 2 69
(Michael Easterby) *in tch on inner: hdwy to chse ldrs 2f out: chsd ldr whn swtchd lft and rdn ent fnl f: styd on to ld last 75yds* **11/2**[2]
2026 2 1 1/2 **Politbureau**[35] 3652 6-9-5 49 MissJoannaMason(3) 10 56
(Michael Easterby) *hld up in rr: stdy hdwy wl over 2f out: rdn to chse ldrs over 1f out: kpt on wl fnl f* **14/1**
4303 3 1/2 **Rockweiller**[24] 4071 6-10-0 55 (v) MissJCoward 12 61
(Steve Gollings) *led: rdn along 2f out: edgd rt ent fnl f: sn drvn: hdd and no ex last 75yds* **8/1**
0620 4 1 1/2 **Miss Ella Jade**[39] 3543 4-9-9 53 MissJRRichards(3) 7 56
(Richard Whitaker) *trckd ldrs: hdwy over 4f out: rdn to chse ldrs wl over 1f out: kpt on same pce fnl f* **9/1**
6001 5 4 1/2 **Bahamamay**[14] 4374 3-9-12 63 MissADeniel 6 57
(Richard Fahey) *trckd ldrs: hdwy over 3f out: chsd ldr 2f out and sn ev ch tl rdn and wknd appr fnl f* **6/1**[3]
6145 6 1 3/4 **Pertuis (IRE)**[10] 4543 7-10-10 65 MissSBrotherton 14 56
(Micky Hammond) *hld up and bhd: stdy hdwy 3f out: rdn to chse ldrs over 1f out: no imp* **8/1**
0614 7 1 1/4 **Flag Of Glory**[13] 4403 6-10-4 64 MissMEdden(5) 4 52
(Peter Hiatt) *hld up in rr: sme hdwy 3f out: sn rdn: n.d* **12/1**
2401 8 3 **Outlaw Torn (IRE)**[3] 4763 4-9-11 57 (e) MissKMargarson(5) 9 39
(Richard Guest) *trckd ldng pair: effrt 4f out: rdn along wl over 2f out: sn wknd* **3/1**[1]
4306 9 1 3/4 **Tinseltown**[16] 3808 7-10-7 65 (p) MissHBethell(3) 15 44
(Brian Rothwell) *prom: cl up 1/2-way: rdn along over 3f out: sn wknd* **14/1**
5024 10 1/2 **Meglio Ancora**[14] 4376 6-9-11 55 MissBAndrews(3) 3 33
(Richard Ford) *in tch: hdwy on outer over 3f out: rdn along over 2f out: sn wknd* **25/1**
00-4 U **Voice From Above (IRE)**[26] 3977 4-10-2 64 MissAChadwick(7) 1
(Patrick Holmes) *in rr whn hmpd and uns rdr after 1f* **12/1**

2m 7.63s (0.63) **Going Correction** -0.025s/f (Good)
WFA 3 from 4yo+ 10lb **11** Ran SP% **119.5**
Speed ratings (Par 101): **96,94,94,93,89 88,87,84,83,83**
toteswingers 1&2 £7.40, 2&3 £16.10, 1&3 £7.40 CSF £81.20 CT £621.69 TOTE £4.80: £1.90, £4.50, £2.50; EX 61.20 Trifecta £1242.30 Part won. Pool: £1656.43 - 0.93 winning units..
Owner R F H Partnership 1 **Bred** Mrs J A Chapman & Mrs Shelley Dwyer **Trained** Sheriff Hutton, N Yorks
■ Stewards' Enquiry : Miss J Coward seven-day ban: careless riding (tbn)

FOCUS
A modest lady amateurs' event.
T/Plt: £154.10 to a £1 stake. Pool of £47684.77 - 225.78 winning tickets. T/Qpdt: £4.50 to a £1 stake. Pool of £3412.50 - 551.70 winning tickets. JR

3528 GOODWOOD (R-H)
Tuesday, July 30

OFFICIAL GOING: Good to soft (6.8)
Wind: medium, gusty, against Weather: drizzly rain and misty after a wet morning

4854 BET365.COM STKS (H'CAP) 1m 1f 192y
1:55 (1:55) (Class 2) 4-Y-O+
£31,125 (£9,320; £4,660; £2,330; £1,165; £585) Stalls Low

Form RPR
1-43 1 **Viewpoint (IRE)**[4] 4706 4-9-2 91 RichardHughes 13 102
(Richard Hannon) *stdd s: hld up in tch in last trio: stl plenty to do whn swtchd lft and effrt wdst over 1f out: qcknd and str run to ld wl ins fnl f: sn in command* **16/1**
-321 2 1 **Nabucco**[31] 3832 4-9-9 98 WilliamBuick 17 107
(John Gosden) *dwlt: pushed along and steadily rcvrd to chse ldrs 1/2-way: drvn and effrt to ld over 1f out: hdd and outpcd wl ins fnl f: battled on to hold 2nd* **8/1**[3]
10-0 3 nk **Labarinto**[39] 3525 5-9-10 99 RyanMoore 15 107
(Sir Michael Stoute) *t.k.h: hld up in tch towards rr: swtchd lft and effrt 2f out: hdwy u.p over 1f out and ev ch ins fnl f: one pce fnl 100yds* **12/1**
6102 4 1/2 **Spirit Of The Law (IRE)**[31] 3827 4-8-5 85 GeorgeChaloner(5) 14 92
(Richard Fahey) *on toes: hld up in tch in last quartet: nt clr run and forced to switch lft and effrt over 1f out: hdwy u.p 1f out: styd on wl ins fnl f* **16/1**
1303 5 3/4 **Fennell Bay (IRE)**[11] 4501 4-9-0 89 JoeFanning 5 95
(Mark Johnston) *lw: chsd ldrs tl rdn to ld over 2f out: drvn and hdd over 1f out: no ex fnl 150yds* **11/1**
0020 6 1 1/4 **Strictly Silver (IRE)**[24] 4060 4-9-4 98 RobertTart(5) 18 101
(Alan Bailey) *in tch in midfield on outer: rdn and effrt ent fnl 2f: kpt on fnl f but nvr gng pce to threaten ldrs* **14/1**
2512 7 nk **Reset City**[5] 4663 7-8-4 79 FrannyNorton 9 82
(Mark Johnston) *dwlt: hld up in rr: swtchd rt and effrt on inner 2f out: swtchd lft and hdwy between horses 1f out: styd on wl: nvr trbld ldrs* **20/1**
0-40 8 nse **Blue Surf**[38] 3559 4-9-8 97 PatDobbs 6 100
(Amanda Perrett) *chsd ldrs: drvn and unable qck over 1f out: wknd ins fnl f* **13/2**[1]
2046 9 nk **Hi There (IRE)**[15] 4342 4-8-11 86 LeeTopliss 10 88
(Richard Fahey) *lw: t.k.h: hld up in tch towards rr: rdn and sme hdwy whn edgd rt over 1f out: kpt on wl ins fnl f but no threat to ldrs* **33/1**
111- 10 1/2 **Fast Or Free**[404] 3294 4-9-7 96 PaulHanagan 11 97
(William Haggas) *hld up in tch in midfield: effrt to chse ldng pair wl over 1f out: no ex u.p ent fnl f: wknd fnl 150yds* **13/2**[1]
0/0- 11 1 **Heddwyn (IRE)**[465] 1510 6-8-11 86 MartinDwyer 4 85
(Marcus Tregoning) *stdd s: t.k.h: hld up in tch in midfield: hdwy on inner over 2f out: nt clr run and swtchd lft over 1f out: drvn and no ex 1f out: wknd ins fnl f* **50/1**
-115 12 3 1/2 **Clon Brulee (IRE)**[17] 4310 4-9-4 93 PhillipMakin 8 85
(David Barron) *hld up in tch in midfield: rdn and unable qck ent fnl 2f: dropping towards rr whn squeezed for room over 1f out: n.d after* **7/1**[2]
1611 13 3 **Whispering Warrior (IRE)**[31] 3827 4-9-4 93 JimCrowley 7 79
(David Simcock) *lw: hld up in tch in last quartet: stl travelling wl but nowhere to go over 2f out: swtchd rt 2f out: rdn and no hdwy over 1f out: eased ins fnl f* **7/1**[2]
2362 14 1 **Tepmokea (IRE)**[24] 4060 7-9-3 92 ShaneKelly 16 76
(Mrs K Burke) *chsd ldr: rdn and ev ch over 2f out: struggling u.p wl over 1f out: wkng whn squeezed for room jst over 1f out* **20/1**
0340 15 1 1/4 **Calaf**[34] 3685 5-8-8 83 HarryBentley 1 65
(Brian Ellison) *led tl rdn and hdd over 2f out: wkng whn squeezed for room jst over 1f out: eased ins fnl f* **20/1**
4-10 16 4 1/2 **Expert Fighter (USA)**[17] 4310 4-9-5 94 SilvestreDeSousa 2 67
(Saeed bin Suroor) *in tch in midfield: rdn and losing pl whn squeezed for room 2f out: sn wknd: bhd and eased ins fnl f* **16/1**

2m 7.71s (-0.39) **Going Correction** +0.025s/f (Good) **16** Ran SP% **122.3**
Speed ratings (Par 109): **102,101,100,100,99 98,98,98,98,98 97,94,92,91,90 86**
toteswingers 1&2 £22.30, 2&3 £13.50, 1&3 £36.80 CSF £129.70 CT £1617.40 TOTE £19.30: £3.80, £2.40, £3.40, £5.00; EX 182.00 Trifecta £1783.50 Pool: £4215.74 - 1.77 winning units..
Owner The Heffer Syndicate **Bred** F Dunne **Trained** East Everleigh, Wilts

FOCUS
Top bend dolled out 3yds, lower bend out 5yds. Straight dolled out 5yds increasing distances on Round course by about 10yds. After persistent morning rain the going was changed from Good (Good to Firm in places) to Good to Soft. The jockeys confirmed it was riding on the slow side of good. A highly competitive handicap to start the meeting with the time indicating the ground matched the official description. The winner came from off the pace and the first four were drawn 13, 17, 15, 14.

4855 BET365 MOLECOMB STKS (GROUP 3) 5f
2:30 (2:30) (Class 1) 2-Y-O
£28,355 (£10,750; £5,380; £2,680; £1,345; £675) Stalls High

Form RPR
210 1 **Brown Sugar (IRE)**[19] 4212 2-9-0 0 PatDobbs 1 107
(Richard Hannon) *lw: taken down early: hld up in tch in last trio: clsd 1/2-way: trckd ldrs gng wl over 1f out: rdn to chal ins fnl f: drvn to ld fnl 75yds: wnt lft u.p towards fin: a jst holding on* **8/1**
1135 2 nk **Anticipated (IRE)**[9] 4572 2-9-0 103 RichardHughes 5 106
(Richard Hannon) *stdd leaving stalls but sn pushed along: in tch in rr and bk on bridle 3f out: effrt and n.m.r over 1f out: swtchd lft and str run ins fnl f: wnt 2nd towards fin: nvr quite getting to wnr* **7/2**[2]
1416 3 1 1/4 **Ambiance (IRE)**[9] 4572 2-9-0 104 MartinHarley 8 102
(Mick Channon) *hld up in tch in midfield and travelled wl: swtchd rt and chal ent fnl f: drvn to ld fnl 150yds: hdd fnl 75yds: no ex and hld whn sltly hmpd towards fin* **8/1**
410 4 hd **Sleeper King (IRE)**[42] 3424 2-9-0 97 PhillipMakin 6 101
(Kevin Ryan) *racd keenly: chsd ldr tl rdn to ld wl over 1f out: hdd jst ins fnl f: no ex and one pce fnl 100yds* **8/1**
132 5 shd **Supplicant**[42] 3424 2-9-0 103 RyanMoore 3 100+
(Richard Fahey) *in tch towards rr: sltly outpcd and rdn ent fnl 2f: hdwy whn nt clr run and swtchd rt jst ins fnl f: nt clr run again and forced to switch further rt fnl 100yds: r.o* **11/4**[1]
15 6 5 **Reroute (IRE)**[41] 3459 2-8-11 0 WilliamBuick 2 79
(Ed Walker) *b.hind: t.k.h: hld up wl in tch in midfield: rdn and effrt over 1f out: no ex and btn 1f out: sn wknd* **4/1**[3]
0213 7 nk **Majestic Alexander (IRE)**[25] 4025 2-8-11 95 NeilCallan 7 78
(David Evans) *led: rdn and hdd wl over 1f out: drvn and btn 1f out: wknd fnl f* **16/1**
1210 8 7 **Meritocracy (IRE)**[10] 4528 2-9-0 90 (b[1]) JamieSpencer 4 56
(Paul Cole) *on toes: pressed ldrs: rdn and no ex 2f out: wknd over 1f out: bhd fnl f* **20/1**

59.3s (-0.90) **Going Correction** -0.20s/f (Firm) **8** Ran SP% **112.9**
Speed ratings (Par 104): **99,98,96,96,96 88,87,76**
toteswingers 1&2 £6.90, 2&3 £4.30, 1&3 £7.90 CSF £35.18 TOTE £10.30: £3.50, £1.70, £3.20; EX 48.60 Trifecta £190.10 Pool: £7082.98 - 27.93 winning units..
Owner De La Warr Racing **Bred** Ballylinch Stud **Trained** East Everleigh, Wilts
■ Stewards' Enquiry : Pat Dobbs one-day ban: careless riding (Aug 13)

FOCUS
Not a particularly strong-looking Molecomb and the leaders were picked off after going a bit quick. They raced middle-to-stands' side with there no obvious track bias. A one-two for Richard Hannon, who was winning this race for the third time in the last five years.

4856 BET365 LENNOX STKS (GROUP 2) 7f
3:05 (3:05) (Class 1) 3-Y-O+

£85,065 (£32,250; £16,140; £8,040; £4,035; £2,025) **Stalls** Low

Form RPR

-104 **1** **Garswood**^{41} 3455 3-8-9 111 .... RyanMoore 7 109
(Richard Fahey) *lw: short of room leaving stalls: hld up in tch in last trio: rdn and effrt 2f out: str run u.p on outer fnl f: led and edging rt fnl 75yds: r.o wl: drvn out* **9/4**^{1}

654- **2** *nk* **Caspar Netscher**^{317} 6296 4-9-2 116 .... ShaneKelly 3 112
(David Simcock) *lw: t.k.h: hld up wl in tch in midfield: shuffled bk and nt clr run over 1f out: swtchd lft and rdn 1f out: str run to chal fnl 75yds: r.o wl but jst hld* **10/1**

3-45 **3** *1* **Boom And Bust (IRE)**^{90} 1919 6-9-2 106 .... GeorgeBaker 1 109
(Marcus Tregoning) *led and set stdy gallop: gng wl 2f out: rdn over 1f out: hdd and one pce u.p fnl 75yds* **20/1**

0460 **4** *nk* **Libranno**^{31} 3831 5-9-2 111 .... PatCosgrave 12 108
(Richard Hannon) *chsd ldr tl wl over 1f out: sn drvn and pressing ldr again 1f out: one pce fnl 100yds* **20/1**

5605 **5** *nse* **Monsieur Chevalier (IRE)**^{31} 3840 6-9-2 99 .... JamieSpencer 10 108?
(P J O'Gorman) *hld up in tch in rr: clsd and wl in tch but nowhere to go wl over 1f out: stl waiting and switching lft ins fnl f: fnlly in the clr and r.o fnl 100yds* **66/1**

4-16 **6** *3/4* **Fencing (USA)**^{73} 2446 4-9-2 114 .... WilliamBuick 5 106
(John Gosden) *chsd ldrs: rdn and chsd ldr wl over 1f out tl 1f out: styd on same pce fnl 150yds* **5/1**^{3}

4111 **7** *1/2* **Professor**^{44} 3373 3-8-9 110 .... TomQueally 2 102
(Richard Hannon) *swtg: chsd ldrs: n.m.r wl over 1f out: rdn and rallied against far rail to chse ldrs 1f out: one pce fnl f* **7/1**

4230 **8** *shd* **Pastoral Player**^{17} 4276 6-9-2 111 .... GrahamLee 9 106
(Hughie Morrison) *taken down early: t.k.h: hld up in tch in last trio: clsd but stuck bhd horses wl over 1f out: pushed along but stl bhd horses 1f out: nt clr run again ins fnl f: nvr able to mount a chal* **20/1**

2333 **9** *8* **Krypton Factor**^{10} 4527 5-9-2 115 ....(b) KierenFallon 11 88
(Fawzi Abdulla Nass, Bahrain) *t.k.h: hld up wl in tch in midfield: rdn and unable qck 2f out: wknd ent fnl f: eased ins fnl f* **8/1**

0141 **10** *3/4* **Producer**^{31} 3831 4-9-2 111 .... RichardHughes 6 89
(Richard Hannon) *t.k.h: in tch in midfield: effrt on inner to chse ldrs 2f out: rdn and unable qck and lost pl whn n.m.r jst over 1f out: wknd 1f out: eased ins fnl f* **4/1**^{2}

1m 27.3s (0.30) **Going Correction** +0.025s/f (Good)
WFA 3 from 4yo+ 7lb **10** Ran SP% **115.9**
Speed ratings (Par 115): **99,98,97,97,97 96,95,95,86,85**
toteswingers 1&2 £5.40, 2&3 £9.20, 1&3 £12.60 CSF £24.46 TOTE £3.20: £1.80, £3.40, £4.50; EX 30.10 Trifecta £529.40 Pool: £7516.77 - 10.64 winning units..
Owner D W Armstrong & Cheveley Park Stud **Bred** Cheveley Park Stud Ltd **Trained** Musley Bank, N Yorks

FOCUS
A messy race with Boom And Bust setting what looked a steady early pace (slow time), resulting in a bunch finish and some these finding trouble.

4857 BET365 SUMMER STKS (H'CAP) 1m 6f
3:40 (3:40) (Class 2) 3-Y-O+

£46,687 (£13,980; £6,990; £3,495; £1,747; £877) **Stalls** Low

Form RPR

3-23 **1** **Harris Tweed**^{31} 3830 6-9-7 **105** ....(p) GeorgeBaker 12 118
(William Haggas) *lw: mde all: stdd gallop 6f out: rdn and readily asserted wl over 1f out: clr and r.o wl after: easily* **14/1**

025- **2** *6* **Camborne**^{276} 7405 5-9-10 **108** ....(p) WilliamBuick 14 113
(John Gosden) *stdd s: hld up off the pce in last pair: clsd 6f out: rdn and hdwy but hanging rt over 1f out: no ch w wnr but kpt on to go 2nd fnl 100yds* **8/1**

3-00 **3** *1 1/2* **Suraj**^{42} 3423 4-8-9 **93** .... TomQueally 10 96
(Michael Bell) *s.i.s: rn in snatches in rr: rdn over 3f out: styd on past btn horses fnl f to snatch 3rd on post: nvr trbld ldrs* **14/1**

4001 **4** *nse* **Silver Lime (USA)**^{18} 4233 4-9-0 **98** .... RyanMoore 9 100
(Roger Charlton) *lw: hld up off the pce in last quartet: clsd 6f out: rdn and effrt over 2f out: hdwy u.p to chse clr wnr ent fnl f* **11/2**^{2}

221 **5** *3/4* **Duke Of Clarence (IRE)**^{39} 3531 4-8-12 **96** .... RichardHughes 5 97
(Richard Hannon) *hld up in tch in midfield: nt clr run and swtchd lft 2f out: stl nt clr run: no ch w wnr whn swtchd bk rt jst over 1f out: barging match w rival ent fnl f: styd on same pce* **8/1**

1-13 **6** *1* **Clowance Estate (IRE)**^{31} 3838 4-8-9 **93** .... GrahamLee 3 93
(Roger Charlton) *b: in tch in midfield: pushed along along 8f out: rdn and unable qck ent fnl 2f: keeping on same pce and wl hld whn edgd rt and barging match w rival ent fnl f* **5/1**^{1}

-604 **7** *nk* **Guarantee**^{17} 4309 4-9-3 **101** .... PhillipMakin 4 101
(William Haggas) *hld up in midfield: rdn and unable qck over 2f out: outpcd and no ch w wnr over 1f out: plugged on* **8/1**

0600 **8** *nse* **Sir Graham Wade (IRE)**^{17} 4309 4-9-3 **101** ....(b^{1}) FrannyNorton 6 100
(Mark Johnston) *t.k.h: chsd wnr: rdn over 2f out: outpcd and btn over 1f out: lost 2nd and pushed rt ent fnl f: wknd* **8/1**

/550 **9** *1* **Saptapadi (IRE)**^{17} 4310 7-8-10 **94** .... DaneO'Neill 8 92
(Brian Ellison) *stdd s: hld up off the pce in rr: clsd 6f out: effrt on inner whn nt clr run 2f out: lost any ch: swtchd lft over 1f out: kpt on but n.d* **25/1**

6202 **10** *5* **Oriental Fox (GER)**^{31} 3824 5-9-1 **99** .... JoeFanning 2 90
(Mark Johnston) *lw: t.k.h: chsd ldrs: rdn and unable qck over 2f out: outpcd and btn over 1f out: fdd fnl f* **6/1**^{3}

23-4 **11** *3 1/2* **Cavaleiro (IRE)**^{111} 1484 4-8-13 **97** .... ShaneKelly 1 83
(Marcus Tregoning) *chsd ldrs: lost pl u.p ent fnl 2f: wknd over 1f out* **20/1**

1-10 **12** *6* **Ardlui (IRE)**^{31} 3824 5-8-12 **96** .... NeilCallan 11 74
(Alan King) *chsd ldrs: hdwy to chse ldng pair 5f out: lost pl u.p over 2f out: wknd over 1f out: bhd and eased ins fnl f* **16/1**

3m 2.69s (-0.91) **Going Correction** +0.025s/f (Good) **12** Ran SP% **118.6**
Speed ratings (Par 109): **103,99,98,98,98 97,97,97,96,94 92,88**
toteswingers 1&2 £19.00, 2&3 £22.90, 1&3 £35.00 CSF £121.77 CT £1612.38 TOTE £17.30: £3.90, £2.70, £4.10; EX 167.50 Trifecta £1120.80 Pool: £5282.58 - 3.53 winning units..
Owner B Haggas **Bred** J B Haggas **Trained** Newmarket, Suffolk

FOCUS
Another hot handicap in which a high draw has been important in recent years and that proved the case again, with the first three drawn 12, 14, and 10.

4858 CASINO AT BET365 EBF MAIDEN STKS 6f
4:15 (4:15) (Class 2) 2-Y-O **£12,938** (£3,850; £1,924; £962) **Stalls** High

Form RPR

22 **1** **Brazos (IRE)**^{17} 4312 2-9-0 0 .... RyanMoore 13 87+
(Clive Brittain) *t.k.h early: hld up in tch in midfield: switching rt and effrt over 1f out: swtchd rt again and hdwy 1f out: rdn to ld wl ins fnl f: edging rt but r.o wl* **3/1**^{2}

42 **2** *nk* **Lyn Valley**^{23} 4096 2-9-0 0 .... JoeFanning 12 86+
(Mark Johnston) *w'like: str: chsd ldr: rdn to ld over 1f out: kpt on wl u.p tl hdd wl ins fnl f: kpt on gamely but unable qck cl home* **8/1**^{3}

3 **3** *nk* **Mystique Rider**^{68} 2595 2-9-0 0 .... HarryBentley 4 85
(Olly Stevens) *cmpt: chsd ldrs: effrt and carried rt briefly ent fnl 2f: upsides ldr and rdn over 1f out: drvn and ev ch thrght fnl f: no ex cl home* **8/1**^{3}

32 **4** *2* **Munfallet (IRE)**^{48} 3211 2-9-0 0 .... PaulHanagan 9 79
(Richard Hannon) *led: rdn and hdd over 1f out: outpcd u.p 1f out: switching rt and kpt on same pce ins fnl f* **10/1**

2262 **5** *nk* **Sacha Park (IRE)**^{17} 4299 2-9-0 97 .... RichardHughes 11 78
(Richard Hannon) *t.k.h: hld up in tch in midfield: effrt and rdn to chse ldrs ent fnl f: sn drvn and no ex: wknd towards fin* **9/4**^{1}

30 **6** *1 1/2* **Fiftyshadesofgrey (IRE)**^{42} 3424 2-9-0 0 .... PatCosgrave 8 73
(George Baker) *on toes: hld up in tch towards rr: stmbld after 1f: switching rt and hdwy u.p over 1f out: kpt on same pce ins fnl f* **16/1**

6 **7** *nk* **Blurred Vision**^{54} 3017 2-9-0 0 .... WilliamBuick 2 75+
(William Jarvis) *in tch in midfield: hdwy to press ldrs over 1f out: rdn and hung rt 1f out: kpt gng rt and sn btn: wknd fnl 100yds* **20/1**

8 *nk* **Muir Lodge** 2-9-0 0 .... JimCrowley 1 71+
(Andrew Balding) *w'like: dwlt and swtchd lft after s: rn green but in tch in last trio: hdwy into midfield over 2f out: rdn and no ex over 1f out: wknd ins fnl f* **33/1**

9 *1/2* **Upholland** 2-9-0 0 .... LeeTopliss 10 69+
(Richard Fahey) *w'like: str: dwlt and swtchd lft after s: in tch towards rr: rdn and outpcd wl over 1f out: no threat to ldrs but kpt on ins fnl f* **25/1**

10 *4* **Fyrecracker (IRE)** 2-9-0 0 .... ShaneKelly 5 57
(Marcus Tregoning) *athletic: in tch in midfield: hdwy and chsd ldrs ent fnl 2f: rdn and no ex over 1f out: wknd fnl f* **50/1**

11 *1/2* **Morally Bankrupt** 2-9-0 0 .... PatDobbs 6 55
(Richard Hannon) *w'like: sltly hmpd s: rn green: in tch in rr: rdn and struggling over 2f out: wknd 2f out* **20/1**

3 **12** *7* **Retrofit**^{15} 4347 2-9-0 0 .... MartinDwyer 7 33
(William Muir) *str: racd freely: chsd ldrs tl rdn: hung rt and lost pl ent fnl 2f: bhd 1f out* **16/1**

13 *1/2* **Under The Moon (IRE)** 2-9-0 0 .... JamieSpencer 3 31
(Charles Hills) *w'like: rn green: in tch in rr: rdn over 2f out: wknd over 1f out: bhd fnl f* **33/1**

1m 12.59s (0.39) **Going Correction** -0.20s/f (Firm) **13** Ran SP% **120.1**
Speed ratings (Par 100): **89,88,88,85,85 83,82,82,81,76 75,66,65**
toteswingers 1&2 £6.30, 2&3 £10.00, 1&3 £4.50 CSF £24.74 TOTE £5.30: £2.50, £2.00, £2.90; EX 34.90 Trifecta £219.30 Pool: £5895.96 - 20.16 winning units..
Owner Saeed Manana **Bred** John O'Kelly Bloodstock Services **Trained** Newmarket, Suffolk

FOCUS
A decent maiden, but dominated by those with experience. They raced middle-to-stands' side and the first two emerged from the top two boxes.

4859 POKER AT BET365 STKS (H'CAP) 1m
4:50 (4:50) (Class 3) (0-90,90) 3-Y-O+ **£9,703** (£2,887; £1,443; £721) **Stalls** Low

Form RPR

-626 **1** **Ascription (IRE)**^{74} 2424 4-9-7 **83** ....(t) WilliamBuick 1 99
(Hugo Palmer) *t.k.h: chsd ldrs: swtchd out lft ent fnl 2f: rdn to ld over 1f out and sn qcknd clr: r.o wl: readily* **7/1**^{1}

-506 **2** *4 1/2* **Jack's Revenge (IRE)**^{11} 4488 5-10-0 **90** ....(bt) PatCosgrave 16 96
(George Baker) *stdd s: t.k.h: hld up in tch in rr: hdwy u.p on outer over 1f out: chsd clr wnr ins fnl f: kpt on but nvr a threat* **8/1**^{3}

0252 **3** *3/4* **Albaqaa**^{13} 4415 8-9-2 **83** .... RobertTart$^{(5)}$ 5 87
(P J O'Gorman) *t.k.h: chsd ldr tl led 4f out: rdn ent fnl 2f: hdd over 1f out and immediately by wnr: lost 2nd ins fnl f* **16/1**

3220 **4** *nk* **Democretes**^{39} 3527 4-10-0 **90** .... RichardHughes 3 93
(Richard Hannon) *lw: t.k.h: hld up in tch towards rr: nt clr run and swtchd rt 2f: hdwy whn swtchd lft jst ins fnl f: awkward hd carriage but kpt on u.p fnl 150yds* **7/1**^{1}

121- **5** *1 3/4* **Juvenal (IRE)**^{332} 5837 4-9-8 **84** .... RyanMoore 15 83
(Richard Hannon) *lw: stdd s: hld up in tch in rr: rdn and effrt over 1f out: kpt on u.p fnl f: no ch w wnr* **16/1**

21 **6** *hd* **Desert Revolution**^{11} 4481 3-8-13 **83** .... JoeFanning 11 80
(Mark Johnston) *lw: chsd ldrs on outer: rdn and unable qck 2f out: outpcd and no ch w wnr over 1f out: plugged on u.p* **10/1**

0402 **7** *shd* **Uppercut**^{19} 4207 5-9-7 **83** ....(v) NeilCallan 19 82
(Stuart Kittow) *hld up in tch in midfield: rdn and outpcd 3f out: styd on u.p fnl f: no ch w wnr* **16/1**

00-0 **8** *shd* **Kyllachy Star**^{18} 4245 7-8-12 **74** .... JamieSpencer 4 72
(Richard Fahey) *hld up in tch in midfield: rdn and effrt 2f out: outpcd and no threat to wnr over 1f out: styng on same pce whn pushed lft jst ins fnl f* **12/1**

0140 **9** *1* **Head Of Steam (USA)**^{3} 4744 6-10-0 **90** .... PatDobbs 13 86
(Amanda Perrett) *s.i.s: hld up in tch in last trio: effrt over 2f out: n.m.r and no imp wl over 1f out: swtchd lft and kpt on ins fnl f: nvr trbld ldrs* **16/1**

4534 **10** *1/2* **Country Western**^{38} 3563 3-9-4 **88** .... SteveDrowne 14 81
(Charles Hills) *t.k.h: hld up in tch in midfield: nt clr run 2f out: rdn and keeping on same pce whn pushed lft jst ins fnl f: wl hld and eased towards fin* **16/1**

1520 **11** *1 1/4* **Snooky**^{17} 4308 4-9-3 **79** .... PaulHanagan 2 71
(Richard Fahey) *lw: sn led: hdd 4f out but styd upsides ldr tl outpcd u.p over 1f out: wknd fnl f* **8/1**^{3}

-00 **12** *2* **Dellbuoy**^{27} 3961 4-8-13 **75** .... FergusSweeney 6 62
(Pat Phelan) *in tch in midfield: rdn and unable qck ent fnl 2f: wknd over 1f out* **40/1**

5421 **13** *2* **Copperwood**^{19} 4207 8-9-2 **78** .... FrannyNorton 7 61
(Mark Johnston) *s.i.s: rcvrd to chse ldrs over 6f out: rdn and unable qck ent fnl 2f: wkng and wl hld whn squeezed for room jst ins fnl f* **14/1**

5421 **14** *3/4* **Silverheels (IRE)**^{10} 4540 4-9-9 **88** .... AshleyMorgan$^{(3)}$ 9 69
(Paul Cole) *on toes: hld up in tch in midfield: lost pl and towards rr whn rdn 3f out: wknd wl over 1f out: eased towards fin* **16/1**

0100 **15** ¾ **Capaill Liath (IRE)**[3] 4746 5-10-0 **90**............................(p) GrahamLee 17 69
(Kevin Ryan) *hld up in tch in rr: struggling 2f out: wl btn whn hmpd and swtchd rt over 1f out* **33/1**

312- **16** *nk* **Captain Cat (IRE)**[298] 6831 4-10-0 **90**.........................[1] GeorgeBaker 18 69
(Roger Charlton) *on toes: t.k.h: hld up in tch in midfield: rdn and fnd little over 1f out: wl btn whn hmpd jst ins fnl f: eased towards fin* **15/2**[2]

17 *9* **Bronze Prince**[68] 2585 6-10-0 **90**.................................. RobertHavlin 20 48
(Michael Attwater) *on toes: hood removed fractionally late and wnt lft s: t.k.h: hld up towards rr on outer: rdn and no hdwy 2f out: sn wknd* **40/1**

1m 38.53s (-1.37) **Going Correction** +0.025s/f (Good)
WFA 3 from 4yo+ 8lb 17 Ran SP% **125.6**
Speed ratings (Par 107): **107,102,101,101,99 99,99,99,98,97 96,94,92,91,91 90,81**
toteswingers 1&2 £13.20, 2&3 £50.40, 1&3 £25.10 CSF £61.39 CT £912.62 TOTE £7.20: £2.20, £2.20, £3.80, £2.20; EX 60.50 Trifecta £1229.40 Pool: £6361.77 - 3.88 winning units..
Owner V I Araci **Bred** Haras De Manneville **Trained** Newmarket, Suffolk

FOCUS
Another decent, competitive handicap in which six of the runners shared top weight.

4860 MOBILE AT BET365 STKS (H'CAP) 5f
5:25 (5:29) (Class 3) (0-90,90) 4-Y-0+ **£9,703** (£2,887; £1,443; £721) **Stalls** High

Form RPR

0012 **1** **Tidal's Baby**[19] 4220 4-7-13 **71** oh3............................ RaulDaSilva(3) 9 83
(Tony Carroll) *bhd: rdn along over 3f out: gd hdwy nrest far rail jst over 1f out: str run to ld and hung lft wl ins fnl f: gng away at fin* **25/1**

4205 **2** 1 ¾ **Six Wives**[8] 4588 6-8-2 **71**...(p) PaoloSirigu 7 77
(Scott Dixon) *broke fast: led and crossed towards stands' rail: rdn and clr w rival over 1f out: hdd wl ins fnl f: no ex* **20/1**

4632 **3** *shd* **Cruise Tothelimit (IRE)**[4] 4728 5-8-3 **75**.................... RyanPowell(3) 19 80
(Ian Williams) *chsd ldr tl 1/2-way: sltly outpcd u.p over 1f out: swtchd rt and styd on again ins fnl f* **7/1**[1]

6464 **4** ½ **Waseem Faris (IRE)**[14] 4364 4-8-4 **73**........................... JoeFanning 15 77
(Mick Channon) *swtchd lft sn after s: hld up in midfield: clsd over 1f out: rdn ins fnl f: kpt on fnl 100yds* **16/1**

0146 **5** *hd* **Arctic Feeling (IRE)**[18] 4263 5-9-3 **86**........................ PaulHanagan 6 89
(Richard Fahey) *in tch in midfield: hdwy u.p over 1f out: chsng ldrs and keeping on same pce whn sltly hmpd towards fin* **10/1**[3]

2246 **6** 1 ½ **Titus Gent**[26] 3973 8-8-13 **85**... RyanClark(3) 22 82
(Jeremy Gask) *bhd: rdn over 2f out: r.o wl u.p ins fnl f: nt rch ldrs* **33/1**

4340 **7** *nk* **Fair Value (IRE)**[17] 4275 5-9-7 **90**................................ KierenFallon 20 86
(Simon Dow) *chsd ldrs tl wnt 2nd 1/2-way: rdn and clr w wnr over 1f out: no ex ins fnl f: wknd qckly wl ins fnl f: eased cl home* **16/1**

2526 **8** *nse* **Whitecrest**[4] 4707 5-8-10 **79**... DaneO'Neill 26 75
(John Spearing) *bhd: rdn wl over 1f out: r.o wl u.p ins fnl f: nt rch ldrs* **33/1**

250 **9** ½ **Cadeaux Pearl**[9] 4569 5-8-9 **78**....................................(p) TomQueally 23 72
(Scott Dixon) *in tch in midfield: lost pl and rdn 1/2-way: rallied and styd on u.p ins fnl f: no threat to ldrs* **33/1**

0000 **10** *hd* **Mister Manannan (IRE)**[32] 3776 6-9-2 **85**...................(p) PhillipMakin 8 79
(David Nicholls) *chsd ldrs: rdn and unable qck over 1f out: wknd ins fnl f: n.m.r towards fin* **16/1**

1400 **11** *nk* **Mata Hari Blue**[10] 4536 7-8-11 **80**..............................(t) AndrewMullen 18 73
(Michael Appleby) *dwlt: sn rcvrd to chse ldrs: rdn and nt qckn over 1f out: wknd ins fnl f* **20/1**

1401 **12** ¾ **Lost In Paris (IRE)**[6] 4620 7-8-11 **80** 6ex......................(p) RyanMoore 11 70
(Tim Easterby) *bhd: rdn and hdwy ent fnl f: nt clr run and swtchd lft ins fnl f: kpt on: nvr trbld ldrs* **9/1**[2]

0-00 **13** *nse* **Edge Closer**[25] 4024 9-9-7 **90**... PatDobbs 1 80
(Tony Carroll) *hld up towards rr: rdn and effrt over 1f out: kpt on ins fnl f: nvr trbld ldrs* **33/1**

4011 **14** ½ **Hamoody (USA)**[6] 4619 9-9-1 **84** 6ex.............................. FrannyNorton 25 72
(David Nicholls) *bhd: rdn 2f out: nt clr run ent fnl f: kpt on wl ins fnl f: nt rch ldrs* **12/1**

006 **15** *nk* **Dorback**[5] 4675 6-9-0 **83**...(t) MartinHarley 21 70
(Violet M Jordan) *chsd ldrs: rdn and unable qck wl over 1f out: wknd ins fnl f* **33/1**

0565 **16** *nk* **Alpha Delta Whisky**[4] 4712 5-8-3 **72** oh3 ow1..........(v[1]) MartinDwyer 12 58
(John Gallagher) *in tch in midfield: rdn and unable qck wl over 1f out: wknd ins fnl f* **50/1**

4405 **17** *nse* **Putin (IRE)**[5] 4675 5-7-11 **71** oh7.............................(bt) NathanAlison(5) 16 57
(Phil McEntee) *chsd ldrs: rdn and struggling 2f out: wknd fnl f* **66/1**

3101 **18** 3 ¾ **Hopes N Dreams (IRE)**[12] 4444 5-8-10 **79**...................... NeilCallan 13 51
(Kevin Ryan) *in tch in midfield: rdn and no rspnse over 2f out: wknd over 1f out* **16/1**

-000 **19** ½ **Tioman Legend**[31] 3840 4-9-4 **87**.................................(b[1]) GeorgeBaker 3 57
(Roger Charlton) *stdd s: hld up towards rr: rdn and effrt over 1f out: no imp and btn ins fnl f: wl hld and eased towards fin* **9/1**[2]

22 **20** 1 ¾ **Jedward (IRE)**[38] 3561 6-9-3 **86**..................................(p) JamieSpencer 24 50
(Kevin Ryan) *towards rr: rdn over 2f out: hrd drvn and no hdwy over 1f out: wknd fnl f* **7/1**[1]

58.31s (-1.89) **Going Correction** -0.20s/f (Firm) 20 Ran SP% **116.8**
Speed ratings (Par 107): **107,104,104,103,102 100,100,99,99,98 98,97,97,96,95 95,95,89,88,85**
toteswingers 1&2 £99.50, 2&3 £15.50, 1&3 £18.40 CSF £397.40 CT £3400.16 TOTE £26.80: £5.90, £6.50, £2.10, £3.80; EX 698.50 TRIFECTA Not won..
Owner Mrs Bernadette Quinn **Bred** Mr & Mrs J Quinn **Trained** Cropthorne, Worcs

FOCUS
A number of non-runners, including Rusty Rocket, who had to be withdrawn after being unruly in the stalls, and Valmina, who wouldn't enter the gates, but 20 of them still lined up. They raced middle-to-stands' side through the opening stages, and all the early pace was in the near-side group, but they were spread out across the track late on.
T/Jkpt: Not won. T/Plt: £867.40 to a £1 stake. Pool of £356445.58 - 299.96 winning tickets. T/Qpdt: £154.10 to a £1 stake. Pool of £21662.11 - 103.96 winning tickets. SP

4686 YARMOUTH (L-H)
Tuesday, July 30

OFFICIAL GOING: Good to firm changing to good after race 5 (5.00)
Wind: light breeze Weather: overcast with showers; 19 degrees

4861 GREENE KING EASTERN FESTIVAL 17TH-19TH SEPTEMBER MAIDEN AUCTION STKS 7f 3y
2:10 (2:10) (Class 6) 2-Y-0 **£1,940** (£577; £288; £144) **Stalls** Centre

Form RPR

4332 **1** **Lucky Visione**[21] 4154 2-8-12 74.. LukeMorris 2 69
(Gay Kelleway) *mde all: v modest pce tl 1/2-way: hrd rdn over 1f out: fnlly gained upper hand wl ins fnl f* **6/5**[1]

3655 **2** 1 ¼ **Evacusafe Lady**[12] 4431 2-8-4 59..............................(p) KirstyMilczarek 1 58
(John Ryan) *stdd s: effrt to chse wnr wl over 2f out: sn drvn: ev ch 1f out: outpcd wl ins fnl f* **16/1**

6 **3** *1* **Hulcolt (IRE)**[35] 3648 2-8-7 0.................................... ConnorBeasley(5) 5 63
(Garry Moss) *pressed ldrs: rdn over 2f out: plugged on same pce fnl f* **6/1**[3]

54 **4** 2 ¾ **Sleeping Venus (IRE)**[36] 3631 2-8-7 0............................ TedDurcan 4 51
(George Baker) *stdd s: bhd: drvn over 3f out: fnd little and wl hld over 1f out* **6/4**[2]

0 **5** 1 ½ **Bushy Glade (IRE)**[75] 2382 2-8-7 0.......................... AdamBeschizza 3 47
(Julia Feilden) *pressed ldr: rdn over 3f out: racd awkwardly whn wkng fnl 2f* **66/1**

1m 28.87s (2.27) **Going Correction** -0.30s/f (Firm) 5 Ran SP% **107.1**
Speed ratings (Par 92): **75,73,72,69,67**
CSF £17.75 TOTE £1.50: £1.40, £2.60; EX 11.70 Trifecta £37.20 Pool: £2590.75 - 52.21 winning units..
Owner Hodson, Tyler, Bartram & McLean **Bred** Redmyre Bloodstock Ltd **Trained** Exning, Suffolk

FOCUS
Back straight and bottom bend doled out 3m. It had been raining for at least an hour before racing, but it hadn't really got into the ground, with Connor Beasley describing it as "lovely". Moderate maiden form.

4862 LION CLUB CHARITY COLLECTION (S) STKS 6f 3y
2:40 (2:40) (Class 6) 2-Y-0 **£1,940** (£577; £288; £144) **Stalls** Centre

Form RPR

533 **1** **Music Stop**[5] 4676 2-8-6 0...(bt) CathyGannon 2 55
(Phil McEntee) *led at brisk pce: 5 l clr 1/2-way: drvn over 1f out: hld on wl cl home: all out* **6/1**[3]

403 **2** *nk* **Red Dakota (IRE)**[14] 4387 2-8-6 56.................................. LukeMorris 5 54
(Alan McCabe) *taken down early: 3rd tl chsd wnr over 2f out: hrd drvn over 1f out: tried to chal ins fnl f: ev ch tl no imp fnl 75yds* **6/5**[1]

65 **3** 3 ½ **Chanceuse**[12] 4422 2-7-13 0.................................... ShelleyBirkett(7) 4 43
(Gay Kelleway) *chsd wnr who was clr: drvn 1/2-way: 3rd fr over 2f out: easily hld over 1f out* **16/1**

4602 **4** 1 ¼ **My Little Friend**[26] 3992 2-8-11 59.........................(b) RobertWinston 3 44
(Mark H Tompkins) *racd in 4th: drvn and wl outpcd and nt looking keen fr 1/2-way* **2/1**[2]

5 *4* **Tolly McGuiness** 2-8-11 0.. AdamBeschizza 1 31
(Julia Feilden) *lost abt 10 l at s and maintained this disadvantage thrght: v green* **10/1**

1m 14.94s (0.54) **Going Correction** -0.30s/f (Firm) 5 Ran SP% **108.0**
Speed ratings (Par 92): **84,83,78,77,71**
CSF £13.30 TOTE £6.30: £1.80, £1.60; EX 10.40 Trifecta £59.80 Pool: £2398.89 - 30.06 winning units..There was no bid for the winner. Red Dakota was claimed by C Bjorling for £5000.
Owner Steve Jakes **Bred** Compagnia Generale S R L **Trained** Newmarket, Suffolk

FOCUS
The front pair had it to themselves from quite a way out in what was a weak seller.

4863 MARTIN FOULGER MEMORIAL H'CAP 6f 3y
3:15 (3:18) (Class 4) (0-85,83) 3-Y-0+ **£4,690** (£1,395; £697; £348) **Stalls** Centre

Form RPR

0014 **1** **Lionheart**[15] 4354 3-8-13 **75**... KirstyMilczarek 1 89
(Luca Cumani) *cl up: led 2f out: rdn clr 1f out: comf* **2/1**[2]

1130 **2** 3 ¾ **Commanche**[11] 4494 4-9-3 **74**.. CathyGannon 4 77
(Chris Dwyer) *taken down early: t.k.h and prom: rdn and outpcd by wnr over 1f out: 5th 100yds out: edgd lft but kpt on and snatched modest 2nd* **9/2**[3]

64 **3** *shd* **Maglietta Fina (IRE)**[14] 4389 4-9-12 **83**..................... FrederikTylicki 3 86
(Robert Cowell) *led: rdn and hdd 2f out: nt qckn 1f out: ev ch of wl hld 2nd tl fnl strides* **25/1**

2505 **4** *shd* **Piazza San Pietro**[14] 4389 7-9-8 **79**........................(p) RobertWinston 2 82
(Zoe Davison) *chsd ldrs: rdn 1/2-way: clsd to go 2nd over 1f out: sn no ch w wnr but jst pipped in r for 2nd* **20/1**

4-03 **5** *nk* **Signor Sassi**[18] 4235 4-9-12 **83**.. LukeMorris 6 85
(William Knight) *uns gng to s and awkward to load: lost 5 l s and bustled along: drvn and effrt but nt gng wl enough over 1f out: disp 2nd briefly wl ins fnl f: no ex* **15/8**[1]

0054 **6** 3 ¼ **Lenny Bee**[11] 4507 7-9-1 **77**...................................(t) ConnorBeasley(5) 5 68
(Garry Moss) *t.k.h: chsd ldrs: rdn 2f out: struggling over 1f out* **6/1**

1m 11.6s (-2.80) **Going Correction** -0.30s/f (Firm)
WFA 3 from 4yo+ 5lb 6 Ran SP% **109.2**
Speed ratings (Par 105): **106,101,100,100,100 96**
toteswingers 1&2 £2.10, 2&3 £6.30, 1&3 £5.40 CSF £10.67 TOTE £3.60: £1.50, £4.00; EX 9.90 Trifecta £74.60 Pool: £3634.43 - 36.50 winning units..
Owner Fittocks Stud & Andrew Bengough **Bred** Fittocks Stud **Trained** Newmarket, Suffolk

FOCUS
Only two or three could be given a serious chance in this.

4864 SHIRLEY GILL MEMORIAL H'CAP 7f 3y
3:50 (3:50) (Class 4) (0-80,80) 3-Y-0+ **£4,690** (£1,395; £697; £348) **Stalls** Centre

Form RPR

4254 **1** **Excuse To Linger**[17] 4288 3-9-7 **80**..............................(v[1]) TedDurcan 4 89
(Jeremy Noseda) *t.k.h and pressed ldrs: led 2f out: rdn 3 l clr 1f out: nt in danger after* **4/1**[2]

-010 **2** *2* **Fantasy Gladiator**[18] 4237 7-9-3 **69**..............................(p) JimmyQuinn 5 76
(John Quinn) *taken down early: settled in rr: gd prog 2f out: rdn and chsd wnr vainly fnl f: nt finding much for driving* **11/1**

4102 **3** *nk* **Whipper Snapper (IRE)**[11] 4494 3-9-5 **78**...................... LukeMorris 3 81
(William Knight) *chsd ldrs: rdn over 2f out: sn outpcd and swtchd rt: rallied u.p and kpt on stoutly ins fnl f: too much to do* **9/4**[1]

62 **4** 1¾ **Azrael**[24] 4067 5-9-7 **80** .... AaronJones(7) 1 81
(Alan McCabe) *led tl pushed along and hdd 2f out: kpt on same pce fnl f* **13/2**

4003 **5** 1½ **Comrade Bond**[33] 3741 5-9-9 **75** .... RobertWinston 7 72
(Mark H Tompkins) *pressed ldr tl rdn 2f out: btn over 1f out* **7/1**

000 **6** 1½ **Greensward**[45] 3322 7-9-3 **72** .... ThomasBrown(3) 6 65
(Mike Murphy) *lost 6 l s: pushed along and nvr travelling in rr: wl btn 2f out* **16/1**

1525 **7** ¾ **Darnathean**[18] 4237 4-9-7 **73** ....(p) FrederikTylicki 2 64
(Paul D'Arcy) *taken down v early: cl up tl drvn and lost pl over 2f out* **5/1**[3]

1450 **8** 13 **Olney Lass**[33] 3741 6-8-6 **61** .... SimonPearce(3) 8 17
(Lydia Pearce) *midfield tl rdn 1/2-way: t.o over 1f out* **20/1**

1m 24.43s (-2.17) **Going Correction** -0.30s/f (Firm)
WFA 3 from 4yo+ 7lb **8** Ran SP% **112.2**
Speed ratings (Par 105): **100,97,97,95,93 91,91,76**
toteswingers 1&2 £5.20, 2&3 £4.00, 1&3 £2.70 CSF £44.64 CT £119.77 TOTE £7.20: £3.30, £4.00, £1.10; EX 51.60 Trifecta £155.40 Pool: £2686.55 - 12.96 winning units..
Owner A Ferguson **Bred** Mrs J Kersey **Trained** Newmarket, Suffolk

FOCUS
An ordinary handicap and no surprise to see it go to one of the 3-y-os.

4865 ONLINE DISCOUNTED TICKETS @GREATYARMOUTH-RACECOURSE.CO.UK H'CAP 1m 3y
4:25 (4:25) (Class 5) (0-75,72) 3-Y-0+ **£2,587** (£770; £384; £192) **Stalls** Centre

Form RPR

266 **1** **Saigon City**[20] 4182 3-9-1 **70** ....(b) PatrickHills(3) 6 78
(Luca Cumani) *chsd ldrs: pushed along over 3f out: 4th and rdn 2f out: clsd 1f out to ld fnl 100yds: edgd rt and nt looking easy but sn in command* **6/1**[3]

-015 **2** 1¼ **Qanan**[32] 3780 4-10-0 **72** ....[1] TedDurcan 7 79+
(Chris Wall) *swtchd rt to r alone stands' side: rdn and effrt wl over 1f out: wnt 2nd fnl 100yds: nt rch wnr* **7/4**[1]

6203 **3** ¾ **Magical Rose (IRE)**[12] 4453 3-9-6 **72** ....(p) FrederikTylicki 2 75
(Paul D'Arcy) *prom: gng wl 3f out: led 2f out: drvn over 1f out: hdd 100yds out: nt qckn* **11/4**[2]

6130 **4** 3 **Jonnie Skull (IRE)**[11] 4496 7-9-8 **66** ....(vt) LukeMorris 4 64
(Phil McEntee) *led: rdn 3f out: hdd 1f out: one pce and sn btn* **9/1**

4-45 **5** nk **Rock Anthem (IRE)**[92] 1873 9-9-0 **58** .... KieranO'Neill 8 56
(Mike Murphy) *dropped out last: rdn over 2f out: nvr trbld ldrs* **12/1**

2605 **6** 8 **Rough Rock (IRE)**[20] 4183 8-9-5 **63** .... CathyGannon 3 42
(Chris Dwyer) *stdd s: bhd: rdn and racing awkwardly and btn over 2f out* **10/1**

2055 **7** 1¾ **Three Choirs (IRE)**[13] 4416 3-9-5 **71** ....(tp) WilliamCarson 5 44
(William Stone) *pressed ldr tl hrd drvn 1/2-way: wknd over 2f out* **10/1**

1m 37.19s (-3.41) **Going Correction** -0.30s/f (Firm)
WFA 3 from 4yo+ 8lb **7** Ran SP% **113.2**
Speed ratings (Par 103): **105,103,103,100,99 91,89**
toteswingers 1&2 £2.20, 2&3 £2.40, 1&3 £2.40 CSF £16.62 CT £34.85 TOTE £6.40: £3.50, £1.50; EX 19.40 Trifecta £46.90 Pool: £2656.48 - 42.42 winning units..
Owner Leonidas Marinopoulos **Bred** Martin Percival **Trained** Newmarket, Suffolk

FOCUS
Ordinary handicap form, but at least the right horses came to the fore.

4866 YOUR WEDDING AT GREAT YARMOUTH RACECOURSE H'CAP 5f 43y
5:00 (5:00) (Class 5) (0-70,70) 3-Y-0+ **£2,587** (£770; £384; £192) **Stalls** Centre

Form RPR

1520 **1** **Smokethatthunders (IRE)**[27] 3956 3-9-8 **70** .... LukeMorris 4 78
(James Toller) *2nd in main far side bunch: drvn to join ldr 2f out: asserted fnl 100yds* **3/1**[2]

0240 **2** ¾ **Welease Bwian (IRE)**[22] 4120 4-9-1 **59** .... AdamBeschizza 7 65
(Stuart Williams) *swtchd rt to r on stands' rail: pressed ldrs: drvn over 1f out: chal ins fnl f: no imp fnl 100yds* **7/2**[3]

1114 **3** 1½ **Nafa (IRE)**[9] 4569 5-9-9 **70** .... ThomasBrown(3) 6 71
(Daniel Mark Loughnane) *trckd ldrs: wnt 2nd and looked to be gng wl 2f out: w wnr tl rdn and no ex ins fnl f* **6/5**[1]

0650 **4** 7 **Danzoe (IRE)**[15] 4344 6-9-12 **70** .... TomMcLaughlin 5 46
(Christine Dunnett) *t.k.h and chsd ldrs: drvn and outpcd over 2f out: wl btn over 1f out* **18/1**

3235 **5** 5 **Love You Louis**[45] 3317 7-9-9 **67** ....(v) FrederikTylicki 3 25
(J R Jenkins) *led: drvn and hdd 2f out: dropped out rapidly* **14/1**

60-0 **6** 4½ **Laura's Bairn**[147] 885 4-9-5 **68** ....(v) DannyBrock(5) 2 10
(J R Jenkins) *bhd: hrd drvn and struggling bdly over 2f out: t.o* **50/1**

650 **7** 1 **Marmalade Moon**[26] 3994 4-8-7 **51** oh1 .... CathyGannon 1
(Robert Cowell) *awkward leaving stalls: swtchd fr far side to stands' side after 2f but a struggling in rr: t.o* **25/1**

1m 1.19s (-1.51) **Going Correction** -0.30s/f (Firm)
WFA 3 from 4yo+ 4lb **7** Ran SP% **110.4**
Speed ratings (Par 103): **100,98,96,85,77 70,68**
toteswingers 1&2 £2.00, 2&3 £1.50, 1&3 £1.80 CSF £12.90 TOTE £4.60: £3.40, £3.50; EX 16.00 Trifecta £41.10 Pool: £3599.11 - 65.56 winning units..
Owner M E Wates **Bred** P Doyle Bloodstock & J K Thoroughbred **Trained** Newmarket, Suffolk

FOCUS
The market leaders dominated this sprint.

4867 ARENA RACING COMPANY H'CAP 2m
5:35 (5:35) (Class 6) (0-65,67) 4-Y-0+ **£1,940** (£577; £288; £144) **Stalls** Centre

Form RPR

4512 **1** **Baan (USA)**[20] 4173 10-8-6 **55** .... RosieJessop(5) 3 64
(James Eustace) *hld up last tl 1/2-way: clsd gng wl 4f out: led 3f out: pushed along after: kpt on v gamely fnl f* **4/1**[3]

0563 **2** 1½ **Capriska**[26] 3997 4-7-9 **46** oh1 .... JoeyHaynes(7) 1 53
(Willie Musson) *cl up: rdn 4f out: wnt 2nd over 2f out: nvr making any imp on wnr after* **2/1**[1]

0422 **3** 6 **Outback (IRE)**[5] 4692 4-9-7 **65** ....(v) MartinLane 5 65
(Neil King) *pressed ldr: hrd drvn over 4f out: lost tch w ldng pair over 2f out: fin tamely* **11/2**

1541 **4** nk **Underwritten**[5] 4692 4-9-4 **67** 6ex ....(b) ConnorBeasley(5) 2 67
(John Weymes) *led at str pce: shkn up 6f out: hrd drvn over 4f out: hdd 3f out: btn over 2f out: lost 3rd nr fin* **9/4**[2]

0133 **5** 5 **Dr Finley (IRE)**[14] 4392 6-9-3 **64** ....(v) SimonPearce(3) 4 58
(Lydia Pearce) *a same pl: rdn and lost tch 6f out: plodded on* **8/1**

00-0 **6** 99 **Thecornishwren (IRE)**[29] 3907 4-8-0 **47** oh1 ow1 .... ShelleyBirkett(7) 6
(John Ryan) *dropped bk last u.p at 1/2-way: sn hopelessly t.o* **66/1**

3m 32.72s (0.32) **Going Correction** +0.075s/f (Good) **6** Ran SP% **112.1**
Speed ratings (Par 101): **102,101,98,98,95 46**
toteswingers 1&2 £2.20, 2&3 £2.60, 1&3 £3.40 CSF £12.42 TOTE £4.30: £2.20, £1.80; EX 26.60 Trifecta £71.20 Pool: £2320.38 - 24.41 winning units..
Owner Mrs James Eustace **Bred** Shadwell Farm Inc **Trained** Newmarket, Suffolk

FOCUS
This was run at a good gallop and it provided a thorough test at the distance, with the front pair drawing clear.
T/Plt: £82.60 to a £1 stake. Pool of £47651.67 - 420.99 winning tickets. T/Qpdt: £34.10 to a £1 stake. Pool of £3444.45 - 74.70 winning tickets. IM

4868 - (Foreign Racing) - See Raceform Interactive

4841 GALWAY (R-H)
Tuesday, July 30

OFFICIAL GOING: Flat - yielding; nh - good

4869a TOPAZ MILE H'CAP 1m 100y
6:45 (6:45) 3-Y-0+
£56,097 (£17,764; £8,414; £2,804; £1,869; £934)

RPR

1 **Brendan Brackan (IRE)**[31] 3844 4-9-6 **104** .... ColinKeane(5) 10 114
(G M Lyons, Ire) *chsd ldrs: prog in 3rd under 3f out: travelled wl into 2nd under 2f out: sn led and drvn clr appr fnl f: styd on strly to extend advantage* **10/1**

2 8½ **Brog Deas (IRE)**[12] 4465 4-9-1 **94** ....(v) DannyGrant 6 85
(Patrick J Flynn, Ire) *racd in mid-div tl tk clsr order in 4th under 2f out: drvn to chse wnr appr fnl f but nvr on terms: kpt on same pce* **12/1**

3 1¾ **Vastonea (IRE)**[12] 4465 5-9-0 **96** .... SamJames(3) 16 83
(Kevin Prendergast, Ire) *chsd ldrs: prog u.p in 3rd under 2f out: nt qckn appr fnl f: kpt on same pce* **20/1**

4 2 **Seanie (IRE)**[17] 4316 4-8-11 **90** .... GaryCarroll 4 73
(David Marnane, Ire) *chsd ldrs on inner tl lost grnd whn short of room over 2f out: wnt 7th 1f out: kpt on wl into 4th cl home* **14/1**

5 ½ **Pintura**[45] 3347 6-9-7 **105** .... ConnorKing(5) 9 87
(Kevin Ryan) *racd in mid-div: pushed along and nt qckn under 2f out: 8th appr fnl f: kpt on into 5th in clsng stages* **9/1**[3]

6 nk **Fortify (IRE)**[6] 4648 3-9-13 **114** 5ex ....(v) JosephO'Brien 7 93
(A P O'Brien, Ire) *racd in mid-div: kpt on fr over 1f out: nvr on terms* **8/1**[2]

7 hd **Salam Alaykum (IRE)**[30] 3872 5-8-11 **90** .... JFEgan 18 71
(John Francis Egan, Ire) *hld up in rr: reminders after 1/2-way: prog u.p on inner home turn: kpt on: nvr nrr* **33/1**

8 hd **Tandem**[12] 4465 4-9-10 **103** ....(v) PatSmullen 8 83
(D K Weld, Ire) *racd in mid-div tl tk clsr order u.p in 5th under 2f out: no imp and wknd ins fnl f* **11/4**[1]

9 1½ **Campanology**[39] 3527 4-8-13 **92** ....(t) NGMcCullagh 3 69
(J P Murtagh, Ire) *w.w: sme prog under 2f out: nvr on terms* **10/1**

10 1½ **Global Village (IRE)**[101] 1675 8-9-4 **97** .... ChrisHayes 13 71
(Brian Ellison) *hld up towards rr: sme hdwy 2f out: sn no imp* **9/1**[3]

11 2½ **Captain Joy (IRE)**[31] 3844 4-9-12 **108** .... RonanWhelan(3) 5 76
(Tracey Collins, Ire) *chsd ldrs on inner tl wknd under 2f out* **14/1**

12 nk **Beyond Thankful (IRE)**[58] 2907 3-8-11 **98** ....(p) KevinManning 14 64
(J S Bolger, Ire) *racd in cl 2nd: pressed ldr 1/2-way and led over 2f out: hdd sn after: wknd in st* **20/1**

13 1¼ **Captain Cullen (IRE)**[19] 4226 4-8-1 **83** oh1 .... IJBrennan(3) 11 48
(Gerard Keane, Ire) *nvr bttr than mid-div: no imp 2f out* **16/1**

14 7½ **Strait Of Zanzibar (USA)**[10] 4548 4-8-1 **83** .... ConorHoban(3) 15 31
(K J Condon, Ire) *a towards rr: no threat 3f out* **40/1**

15 1¼ **Swiftly Done (IRE)**[30] 3869 6-8-8 **90** ....(v) NeilFarley(3) 1 36
(Declan Carroll) *slowly away and a in rr: nvr a threat* **9/1**[3]

16 4¼ **Golden Shoe (IRE)**[27] 3966 5-8-4 **83** oh2 .... WayneLordan 2 19
(J T Gorman, Ire) *sn led: hdd and sltly hmpd over 2f out: wknd qckly* **22/1**

17 23 **Ansgar (IRE)**[30] 3869 5-9-12 **105** ....(t) RoryCleary 12
(Sabrina J Harty, Ire) *sn trckd ldrs in 4th: pushed along and wknd over 3f out: eased in st: t.o* **16/1**

18 31 **Billyford (IRE)**[14] 4394 8-8-12 **91** .... FMBerry 17
(Liam Roche, Ire) *nvr bttr than mid-div: no threat 3f out and eased bef home turn: t.o* **40/1**

1m 48.71s (-1.49)
WFA 3 from 4yo+ 8lb **18** Ran SP% **140.4**
CSF £131.65 CT £2429.17 TOTE £11.90: £3.00, £2.90, £6.20, £3.10; DF 140.40.
Owner Anamoine Limited **Bred** Anamoine Ltd **Trained** Dunsany, Co. Meath

FOCUS
Fiercely competitive, as you would expect for the lucrative pot on offer. The early gallop was more than generous and they were well strung out coming down the hill. But what transpired from there was not what you would expect from a big-field handicap, not least around here. The winner has been rated 8lb higher than his previous best.

4854 GOODWOOD (R-H)
Wednesday, July 31

OFFICIAL GOING: Good to soft (7.2)
Wind: medium, against Weather: overcast, dry

4873 UBS GOODWOOD STKS (H'CAP) 2m 5f
1:55 (1:56) (Class 2) (0-95,94) 3-Y-0+
£24,900 (£7,456; £3,728; £1,864; £932; £468)

Form RPR

3521 **1** **Broxbourne (IRE)**[5] 4704 4-9-0 **84** 3ex .... JoeFanning 2 93
(Mark Johnston) *hld up in midfield: shuffled bk 7f out: plenty to do and rdn whn pushed lft and hmpd over 3f out: gd hdwy over 1f out: styd on relentlessly to ld fnl 100yds: r.o wl* **7/1**[2]

-213 **2** ½ **Lieutenant Miller**[43] 3423 7-9-4 **88** .... TomQueally 1 96
(Nicky Henderson) *lw: chsd ldrs: wnt 2nd 3f out: rdn and upsides ldrs wl over 1f out: hrd drvn and led narrowly ins fnl f: hdd and styd on same pce fnl 100yds* **6/1**[1]

-143 **3** 1 **Seaside Sizzler**[39] 3560 6-9-2 **86** ....(vt) JimCrowley 17 93
(Ralph Beckett) *lw: hld up in midfield: effrt and swtchd sharply lft over 3f out: swtchd further lft and hdwy over 2f out: styd on u.p to press ldrs ins fnl f: one pce fnl 100yds* **11/1**

2133 **4** ¾ **Beyond Conceit (IRE)**[53] 3099 4-9-8 **92** .... JamieSpencer 18 98
(Andrew Balding) *chsd ldr tl after 4f: rdn and clr w rival 2f out: hdd ins fnl f: no ex and one pce fnl 150yds* **8/1**[3]

0343 **5** 1½ **Brockwell**[32] 3824 4-9-8 **92** .... RichardKingscote 16 97
(Tom Dascombe) *hld up off the pce in midfield: effrt but stl plenty to do 3f out: kpt on wl u.p fnl f: nt rch ldrs* **12/1**

0204 **6** *nk* **High Office**[19] 4262 7-8-9 **79** PaulHanagan 19 83
(Richard Fahey) *chsd ldrs: 4th and rdn over 2f out: unable qck u.p and plugged on same pce fnl f* **25/1**

0021 **7** *1 1/4* **Sula Two**[11] 4530 6-8-8 **83** PhilipPrince(5) 4 86
(Ron Hodges) *hld up towards rr: effrt on outer but stl plenty to do over 2f out: kpt on wl u.p: nvr trbld ldrs* **33/1**

6001 **8** *4 1/2* **Mexicali (IRE)**[21] 4166 5-8-10 **80** DavidProbert 7 79
(Dean Ivory) *t.k.h: chsd ldng pair: rdn and unable qck over 2f out: btn over 1f out: wknd fnl f* **16/1**

4544 **9** *3* **First Avenue**[14] 4407 8-9-1 **85** JackMitchell 8 81
(Laura Mongan) *hld up off the pce towards rr: plenty to do and effrt 3f out: plugged on fr over 1f out: nvr trbld ldrs* **25/1**

0-55 **10** *1 1/2* **Cloudy Spirit**[39] 3560 8-8-10 **80** JimmyQuinn 5 74
(Andrew Hollinshead) *hld up in midfield: n.m.r over 2f out: sn rdn and unable qck: wknd over 1f out* **10/1**

-312 **11** *2 1/4* **Italian Riviera**[41] 3512 4-8-10 **80** LukeMorris 15 72
(Sir Mark Prescott Bt) *t.k.h: chsd ldrs: drvn 4f out: outpcd and btn over 2f out: sn wknd* **12/1**

2-50 **12** *1 3/4* **Sohar**[39] 3560 5-8-13 **83** FrankieDettori 6 73
(James Toller) *v s.i.s: wl detached in rr: clsd to bk of field 12f out: rdn 3f out: sn btn and wknd* **8/1**[3]

6050 **13** *4* **Good Morning Star (IRE)**[32] 3824 4-9-7 **91** FrannyNorton 12 77
(Mark Johnston) *hld up in midfield: rdn and no prog 3f out: sn wknd: wl bhd fnl f* **25/1**

0-00 **14** *10* **The Betchworth Kid**[67] 2654 8-9-1 **85** WilliamBuick 20 61
(Michael Bell) *s.i.s: wl bhd: clsd to bk of field 12f out: rdn and outpcd 3f out: sn bhd: t.o* **33/1**

0-00 **15** *4 1/2* **Ermyn Lodge**[28] 3959 7-8-9 **79** (v) FergusSweeney 10 51
(Pat Phelan) *lw: v s.i.s and pushed along early: a in rr: clsd to bk of field 12f out: rdn and btn over 3f out: sn bhd: t.o* **66/1**

-010 **16** *7* **Herostatus**[18] 4313 6-9-4 **88** KierenFallon 13 53
(Jason Ward) *v rel to r: wl off the pce in rr: clsd to bk of field 12f out: rdn over 3f out: sn btn and bhd: t.o* **33/1**

40-1 **17** *1 1/4* **Beyond (IRE)**[31] 3856 6-9-3 **90** (tp) ThomasBrown(3) 9 53
(David Pipe) *led for 4f: chsd ldr tl rdn and struggling 4f out: sn dropped out: t.o* **12/1**

111 **18** *155* **Kazbow (IRE)**[100] 1721 7-8-12 **82** (t) GrahamLee 14
(Richard Ford) *hld up in midfield: rdn and btn 4f out: sn lost tch: wl t.o and virtually p.u fnl 2f* **12/1**

4m 32.96s (1.96) **Going Correction** +0.10s/f (Good) **18** Ran SP% **124.9**
Speed ratings (Par 109): **100,99,99,99,98 98,97,96,95,94 93,93,91,87,85 83,82,**
toteswingers 1&2 £4.20, 1&3 £21.70, 2&3 £12.60 CSF £45.55 CT £474.10 TOTE £7.10: £2.10, £2.00, £2.40, £2.70; EX 27.80 Trifecta £329.60 Pool: £6145.71 - 13.98 winning units..
Owner Ready To Run Partnership **Bred** Mount Coote Stud And M Johnston **Trained** Middleham Moor, N Yorks

FOCUS
Despite a small amount of rain in the morning, the going remained Good to soft (Goingstick 7.2) and the jockeys in the opener were in agreement. The top bend was out 3yds and the lower bend out 5yds. The straight was dolled out 5yds, increasing race distances by about 10yds. With no stalls for this marathon handicap, the actual starting positions for the majority of the runners had only a spiritual connection with those published. Four of them basically blew their chances as soon as the tape went across, with Sohar, Herostatus and Ermyn Lodge proving reluctant to jump off and The Betchworth Kid giving his rivals a start. The pace was an even one.

4874 NEPTUNE INVESTMENT MANAGEMENT GORDON STKS (GROUP 3) 1m 4f
2:30 (2:31) (Class 1) 3-Y-O

£42,532 (£16,125; £8,070; £4,020; £2,017; £1,012) **Stalls** High

Form RPR

-344 **1** **Cap O'Rushes**[32] 3849 3-9-0 110 MickaelBarzalona 4 108
(Charlie Appleby) *t.k.h: chsd ldrs: rdn to chal ent fnl 2f: ev ch after tl lft in ld fnl 100yds: hrd pressed cl home: jst lasted: all out* **9/2**[3]

20-3 **2** *hd* **Excess Knowledge**[26] 4027 3-9-0 106 WilliamBuick 5 107
(John Gosden) *hld up wl in tch: effrt and short of room ent fnl 2f: rallying whn rdr dropped rein 1f out: hmpd again ins fnl f: bk on an even keel and str run u.p fnl 100yds: jst hld* **7/4**[1]

1130 **3** *3/4* **Spillway**[41] 3486 3-9-0 88 TomQueally 3 106
(Eve Johnson Houghton) *hld up in tch in rr: hdwy u.p over 1f out: led and wnt rt u.p 1f out: wnt sharply lft u.p and hdd fnl 100yds: one pce after and hld whn squeezed for room nr fin* **33/1**

614 **4** *3/4* **Testudo (IRE)**[20] 4211 3-9-0 99 KierenFallon 6 105
(Brian Meehan) *led and set stdy gallop: rdn and qcknd over 3f out: kpt on u.p tl hdd 1f out: no ex and one pce fnl 100yds* **16/1**

1364 **5** *hd* **Secret Number**[41] 3485 3-9-0 106 SilvestreDeSousa 2 107
(Saeed bin Suroor) *t.k.h: chsd ldrs: stl gng wl and nt clr run 2f out: rdn and effrt jst over 1f out: running on again whn nt clr run and hmpd ins fnl f: nt rcvr* **4/1**[2]

-115 **6** *2 1/4* **Elkaayed (USA)**[41] 3485 3-9-0 106 PaulHanagan 1 101
(Roger Varian) *lw: hld up wl in tch in last trio: nowhere to go on inner over 2f out: rdn and no hdwy over 1f out: nvr gng pce to threaten ldrs* **9/2**[3]

4353 **7** *3* **Havana Beat (IRE)**[20] 4211 3-9-0 100 DavidProbert 7 96
(Andrew Balding) *lw: chsd ldr tl lost pl and squeezed for room ent fnl 2f: bhd after: wknd over 1f out* **8/1**

2m 39.13s (0.73) **Going Correction** +0.10s/f (Good) **7** Ran SP% **112.7**
Speed ratings (Par 110): **101,100,100,99,99 98,96**
toteswingers 1&2 £2.50, 1&3 £14.00, 2&3 £17.40 CSF £12.43 TOTE £3.40: £1.80, £1.50; EX 8.90 Trifecta £111.90 Pool: £17,249.52 - 115.59 winning units..
Owner Godolphin **Bred** Darley **Trained** Newmarket, Suffolk
■ Stewards' Enquiry : Tom Queally one-day ban: careless riding (Aug 14)

FOCUS
Traditionally a significant trial for the St Leger, Encke didn't prove good enough to beat Noble Mission in this last year but went on to Classic success. Third that day was Michelangelo, who filled the same position at Doncaster. Arctic Cosmos was third here in 2010 and went on to land the St Leger, as did winners Conduit (2008) and Sixties Icon (2006). Plenty of other hugely talented individuals have emerged from the contest - Fiorente, Hunter's Light, Well Sharp, Dandino and Harbinger among others - so it's worth noting down plenty of these for the future. The early pace was far from frenetic and one got the feeling it turned into a dash to the line, producing an unsatisfactory finish.

4875 QIPCO SUSSEX STKS (BRITISH CHAMPIONS SERIES) (GROUP 1) 1m
3:05 (3:06) (Class 1) 3-Y-O+

£170,130 (£64,500; £32,280; £16,080; £8,070; £4,050) **Stalls** Low

Form RPR

-142 **1** **Toronado (IRE)**[43] 3421 3-8-13 123 RichardHughes 7 129
(Richard Hannon) *lw: stdd and dropped in after s: hld up in last pair: clsd smoothly to trck ldrs 2f out: swtchd lft and effrt jst over 1f out: str run u.p fnl f to ld wl ins fnl f: pushed out towards fin* **11/4**[2]

-101 **2** *1/2* **Dawn Approach (IRE)**[43] 3421 3-8-13 124 KevinManning 4 128
(J S Bolger, Ire) *broke wl and led early: sn stdd bk into 3rd: rdn and effrt to chse ldr over 2f out: drvn to ld wl over 1f out: r.o gamely u.p tl hdd and no ex wl ins fnl f* **10/11**[1]

1512 **3** *2 1/2* **Declaration Of War (USA)**[25] 4082 4-9-7 121 JosephO'Brien 5 123
(A P O'Brien, Ire) *stdd s: hld up in midfield: clsd to trck ldrs and gng wl over 2f out: rdn to chse ldr over 1f out: sn drvn and unable qck: one pce and edgd rt ins fnl f* **7/2**[3]

1454 **4** *5* **Trade Storm**[18] 4276 5-9-7 115 JamieSpencer 6 112
(David Simcock) *stdd and dropped in bhd after s: hld up in rr: rdn and effrt over 2f out: outpcd and wl btn over 1f out: plugged on to go modest 4th wl ins fnl f* **33/1**

-213 **5** *1 1/2* **Gregorian (IRE)**[43] 3419 4-9-7 115 WilliamBuick 3 108
(John Gosden) *hld up in midfield: clsd and trcking ldrs over 2f out: n.m.r 2f out: sn rdn and unable qck: wknd ent fnl f* **18/1**

0103 **6** *4* **Leitir Mor (IRE)**[11] 4549 3-8-13 109 (tp) RonanWhelan 1 98
(J S Bolger, Ire) *swtg: s.i.s: sn rdn along and rcvrd to ld after 1f: clr 6f out: rdn and hdd wl over 1f out: sn btn and dropped out* **200/1**

2500 **7** *16* **Reply (IRE)**[32] 3846 4-9-7 106 (v) SeamieHeffernan 2 62
(A P O'Brien, Ire) *chsd ldr after 1f: rdn and struggling 3f out: dropped to rr 2f out: lost tch over 1f out* **200/1**

1m 36.29s (-3.61) **Going Correction** +0.10s/f (Good)
WFA 3 from 4yo+ 8lb **7** Ran SP% **110.5**
Speed ratings (Par 117): **122,121,119,114,112 108,92**
toteswingers 1&2 £1.10, 1&3 £1.30, 2&3 £1.10 CSF £5.21 TOTE £3.20: £1.80, £1.40; EX 6.80 Trifecta £15.10 Pool: £30,968.66 - 1535.73 winning units..
Owner HE Sh Joaan Bin Hamad Al Thani **Bred** Paul Nataf **Trained** East Everleigh, Wilts
■ Stewards' Enquiry : Kevin Manning four-day ban: used whip above the permitted level (Aug 14-17)

FOCUS
Although there were only three that could seriously be fancied once likely pacemakers and horses that had a bit to find on official figures were discounted, this was a truly fascinating contest. It featured two top-class 3-y-os, including a 2000 Guineas/Royal Ascot winner, taking on a highly regarded 4-y-o, arguably back down to his optimum distance. Leitir Mor and Reply, both 200-1 shots, ensured the pace was strong and even throughout. As they faded, the big players started to move into contention and the race started to take shape.

4876 VEUVE CLICQUOT VINTAGE STKS (GROUP 2) 7f
3:40 (3:41) (Class 1) 2-Y-O

£42,532 (£16,125; £8,070; £4,020; £2,017; £1,012) **Stalls** Low

Form RPR

1 **1** **Toormore (IRE)**[64] 2741 2-9-0 0 RichardHughes 1 109+
(Richard Hannon) *tall: str: hld up in midfield: effrt and pushed lft over 1f out: drvn and chsd wnr ins fnl f: qcknd u.p to ld cl home: immediately eased* **5/4**[1]

1 **2** *nk* **Outstrip**[39] 3581 2-9-0 0 MickaelBarzalona 2 108+
(Charlie Appleby) *w'like: leggy: hld up in tch in midfield: rdn and qcknd to ld over 1f out: r.o u.p fnl f tl hdd and no ex cl home* **5/1**[3]

12 **3** *1 1/2* **Parbold (IRE)**[43] 3422 2-9-0 0 PaulHanagan 4 104+
(Richard Fahey) *in tch in last pair: niggled along 5f out: drvn over 1f out: swtchd lft and str run 1f out: wnt 3rd ins fnl f: gng on at fin* **11/4**[2]

1052 **4** *2 3/4* **Rosso Corsa**[11] 4524 2-9-0 90 MartinHarley 6 97
(Mick Channon) *t.k.h: w ldrs tl led 5f out: rdn and hdd over 1f out: no ex u.p: wknd ins fnl f* **50/1**

421 **5** *1* **Expert (IRE)**[4] 4764 2-9-0 0 PatDobbs 3 94
(Richard Hannon) *led tl 5f out: swtchd lft and effrt over 1f out: sn drvn and unable qck: wknd ins fnl f* **16/1**

1021 **6** *2 1/4* **Lanark (IRE)**[11] 4524 2-9-0 97 SilvestreDeSousa 5 88
(Mark Johnston) *t.k.h: w ldrs: wnt 2nd 4f out: rdn over 2f out: lost 2nd over 1f out and sn struggling: wknd 1f out* **7/1**

10 **7** *1/2* **Recanted (USA)**[18] 4296 2-9-0 0 FrankieDettori 7 87
(Brian Meehan) *hld up in last pair: effrt ent fnl 2f: drvn and btn over 1f out: wknd fnl f* **25/1**

1m 27.57s (0.57) **Going Correction** +0.10s/f (Good) **7** Ran SP% **112.0**
Speed ratings (Par 106): **100,99,97,94,93 91,90**
toteswingers 1&2 £1.50, 1&3 £1.60, 2&3 £2.40 CSF £7.65 TOTE £2.90: £1.70, £2.40; EX 10.60 Trifecta £25.20 Pool: £13907.97 - 412.73 winning units..
Owner Middleham Park Racing IX & James Pak **Bred** BEC Bloodstock **Trained** East Everleigh, Wilts

FOCUS
A race that has been won by some top-class colts over the years, such as the subsequent classic winners Troy, Don't Forget Me, Dr Devious, Mister Baileys and Sir Percy, while last year's winner Olympic Glory went on to Group 1 success. The form looks solid with a couple of once-raced colts fighting out the finish and Richard Hannon was winning the race for the fourth successive year.

4877 MARKEL INSURANCE MAIDEN FILLIES' STKS 6f
4:15 (4:15) (Class 2) 2-Y-O **£12,938** (£3,850; £1,924; £962) **Stalls** High

Form RPR

2 **1** **Valonia**[20] 4215 2-9-0 0 DaneO'Neill 13 89
(Henry Candy) *lw: led for 1f: styd w ldr tl shkn up to ld and hung rt wl over 1f out: kpt gng rt but qcknd clr 1f out: stl gng rt but in command fnl f: eased towards fin* **3/1**[2]

2 *1 1/2* **Stars Above Me** 2-9-0 0 JamesDoyle 8 84+
(Roger Charlton) *w'like: rn green: t.k.h: hld up in tch in midfield: effrt u.p over 1f out: wnt 3rd and swtchd lft ins fnl f: sn chsng wnr: kpt on* **16/1**

3 hd **Coral Mist** 2-9-0 0 .... RichardKingscote 12 84
(Charles Hills) *leggy: in tch towards rr: dropped to last and pushed along over 2f out: str run against stands' rail fnl f: almost snatched 2nd* **33/1**

22 4 ½ **Autumn Sunrise (IRE)**[12] 4484 2-9-0 0 .... RichardHughes 14 82
(Richard Hannon) *lw: hld up in tch towards rr: rdn and effrt wl over 1f out: swtchd rt and hdwy u.p 1f out: kpt on same pce fnl 100yds* **5/1**[3]

5 1 **Valen (IRE)** 2-9-0 0 .... JamieSpencer 3 79
(Michael Bell) *leggy: dwlt: in tch in rr: swtchd lft to stands' rail over 4f out: switching rt and nt clr run over 1f out: hdwy ins fnl f: styd on wl: no threat to wnr* **25/1**

0 6 ½ **Kanz**[12] 4484 2-9-0 0 .... MartinHarley 4 77
(Mick Channon) *wl in tch in midfield: effrt and rdn wl over 1f out: edgd lft and no ex u.p 1f out: one pce fnl f* **16/1**

32 7 1½ **Aqlaam Vision**[60] 2869 2-9-0 0 .... KierenFallon 11 72
(Clive Brittain) *athletic: w ldrs for 2f: lost pl and rdn ent fnl 2f: stuck bhd rival over 1f out: swtchd rt and no imp fnl f* **14/1**

4 8 ¾ **Flycatcher (IRE)**[27] 3978 2-9-0 0 .... PaulHanagan 7 70
(Richard Fahey) *w'like: w ldrs: rdn and unable qck wl over 1f out: btn ent fnl f: wknd fnl 150yds* **8/1**

2 9 hd **Much Promise**[14] 4408 2-9-0 0 .... WilliamBuick 10 69
(John Gosden) *leggy: on toes: t.k.h: chsd ldrs tl hdwy to ld after 1f: hdd and hung rt whn rdn wl over 1f out: btn and lost 2nd ins fnl f: fdd and eased towards fin* **11/4**[1]

10 1 **Arranger (IRE)** 2-9-0 0 .... PatDobbs 5 66
(Richard Hannon) *w'like: dwlt: in tch towards rr: effrt u.p 2f out: no imp and btn 1f out: wknd ins fnl f* **33/1**

11 1 **Fashion Fund** 2-9-0 0 .... FrankieDettori 1 63
(Brian Meehan) *lengthy: str: dwlt: t.k.h and racd nrest centre: hdwy after 2f: chsd ldrs and rdn over 1f out: no ex and btn 1f out: wknd and eased wl ins fnl f* **12/1**

4 12 nk **Merry Me (IRE)**[35] 3690 2-9-0 0 .... DavidProbert 6 62
(Andrew Balding) *w'like: t.k.h: chsd ldrs: rdn and unable qck wl over 1f out: drvn: edgd rt and btn ent fnl f: wknd* **20/1**

0 13 7 **Emerald Breeze (IRE)**[12] 4484 2-9-0 0 .... SteveDrowne 2 40
(Charles Hills) *chsd ldrs: rdn and btn over 1f out: fdd ins fnl f* **66/1**

1m 12.22s (0.02) **Going Correction** -0.075s/f (Good) **13** Ran SP% **121.6**
Speed ratings (Par 97): **96,94,93,93,91 91,89,88,87,86 85,84,75**
toteswingers 1&2 £14.00, 1&3 £28.20, 2&3 £99.30 CSF £48.16 TOTE £5.00: £2.20, £4.40, £10.40; EX 56.60 Trifecta £976.60 Pool: £8597.23 - 6.60 winning units..
Owner Henry Candy **Bred** Tibthorpe Stud **Trained** Kingston Warren, Oxon

FOCUS
This looked a decent fillies' maiden, with several already having shown a decent level of ability lining up against some interesting debutantes.

4878 BRITISH STALLION STUDS TURF CLUB EBF FILLIES' STKS (H'CAP) 1m 1f

4:50 (4:53) (Class 3) (0-95,95) 3-Y-0+
£10,893 (£3,262; £1,631; £815; £407; £204) **Stalls** Low

Form RPR

1-11 1 **Ribbons**[39] 3583 3-8-10 **86** .... JamesDoyle 13 99
(James Fanshawe) *b. hind: hld up towards rr early: gd hdwy to chse ldrs 4f out: rdn to ld 2f out: clr whn wnt lft u.p jst ins fnl f: r.o strly: readily* **7/2**[2]

-010 2 2¾ **Rhagori**[44] 3409 4-9-4 **85** .... JimCrowley 14 93
(Ralph Beckett) *hld up in tch towards rr: hdwy u.p to chse clr wnr jst over 1f out: kpt on but no imp ins fnl f* **33/1**

0203 3 ¾ **Forgive**[11] 4525 4-9-9 **90** .... RichardHughes 5 96
(Richard Hannon) *hld up in tch in midfield: shuffled bk and n.m.r jst over 2f out: hdwy u.p over 1f out: wnt 3rd ins fnl f: one pce fnl 100yds* **20/1**

1-13 4 2¾ **Jabhaat (USA)**[18] 4278 3-8-9 **85** .... PaulHanagan 1 84
(Ed Dunlop) *in tch in midfield: rdn and effrt over 1f out: 4th and styd on same pce ins fnl f* **7/1**[3]

5112 5 ½ **Saucy Minx (IRE)**[18] 4307 3-8-7 **83** ....(b) PatDobbs 11 81
(Amanda Perrett) *dwlt: pushed along and sn rcvrd to chse ldrs and t.k.h: nt clr run and shuffled bk wl over 1f out: sn swtchd lft and drvn: kpt on but n.d* **7/1**[3]

-031 6 hd **A Star In My Eye (IRE)**[49] 3201 3-8-3 **79** .... FrannyNorton 15 77
(Kevin Ryan) *lengthy: t.k.h: chsd ldr tl jst over 2f out: unable qck u.p and btn ent fnl f: plugged on* **14/1**

-231 7 1¼ **Close At Hand**[31] 3860 3-8-0 **76** .... NickyMackay 3 71
(John Gosden) *t.k.h: chsd ldrs: effrt u.pr ent fnl 2f: drvn and outpcd over 1f out: wknd ins fnl f* **9/1**

1-21 8 nk **Great Timing (USA)**[32] 3835 3-9-5 **95** ....[1] MickaelBarzalona 7 89
(Charlie Appleby) *t.k.h: hld up in tch in midfield on outer: n.m.r over 3f out: rdn whn bdly hmpd and dropped to rr jst over 2f out: one pce and wl hld after* **3/1**[1]

1202 9 1¼ **Opera Box**[12] 4488 5-9-4 **85** .... FrankieDettori 6 78
(Marcus Tregoning) *sn led and set stdy gallop: rdn and qcknd 3f out: hdd and no ex 2f out: lost 2nd and btn jst over 1f out: wknd fnl f* **12/1**

300- 10 ½ **Creme Anglaise**[308] 6595 5-9-10 **91** .... LukeMorris 2 83
(Michael Bell) *bit bkwd: t.k.h: hld up in tch towards rr: effrt u.p 2f out: no imp over 1f out: n.d* **66/1**

4214 11 1 **Invincible Cara (IRE)**[12] 4485 3-8-1 **77** .... SilvestreDeSousa 12 65
(Ed Dunlop) *s.i.s: t.k.h: hld up in tch in rr: hdwy and hmpd 4f out: drvn and no hdwy ent fnl 2f: wknd over 1f out* **20/1**

1534 12 nk **Eastern Destiny**[33] 3775 4-9-3 **89** .... GeorgeChaloner[(5)] 9 78
(Richard Fahey) *dwlt: sn pushed along: in tch towards rr: rdn and no hdwy 2f out: nvr trbld ldrs* **16/1**

-214 13 shd **Iffraaj Pink (IRE)**[50] 3177 3-8-6 **82** ....(b[1]) AndreaAtzeni 16 69
(Roger Varian) *t.k.h: chsd ldrs on outer: rdn and losing pl whn hmpd jst over 2f out: rdn and no hdwy 2f out: wknd fnl f* **14/1**

1m 55.37s (-0.93) **Going Correction** +0.10s/f (Good)
WFA 3 from 4yo+ 9lb **13** Ran SP% **123.1**
Speed ratings (Par 104): **108,105,104,102,102 101,100,100,99,98 98,97,97**
toteswingers 1&2 £25.60, 1&3 £17.00, 2&3 £66.50 CSF £127.29 CT £2147.76 TOTE £4.20: £2.00, £9.40, £4.50; EX 123.80 Trifecta £3437.90 Pool: £7379.91 - 1.60 winning units..
Owner Elite Racing Club **Bred** Elite Racing Club **Trained** Newmarket, Suffolk

FOCUS
With plenty of in-form fillies taking their chance, this looked a strong contest.

4879 HARWOODS RACING CLUB H'CAP (SPONSORED BY HARWOODS GROUP) 7f

5:25 (5:26) (Class 3) (0-90,90) 3-Y-0+ **£11,320** (£3,368; £1,683; £841) **Stalls** Low

Form RPR

6131 1 **Magic City (IRE)**[13] 4440 4-9-12 **90** .... RichardHughes 18 101
(Richard Hannon) *hld up in tch towards rr: swtchd lft 2f out: rdn and gd hdwy over 1f out: str run to ld fnl 100yds: sn in command and eased cl home* **5/1**[1]

2041 2 1 **Alejandro (IRE)**[16] 4340 4-9-7 **85** .... PaulHanagan 7 93
(Richard Fahey) *lw: led: brought field towards centre st: drvn and battled on gamely fr 2f out: hdd fnl 100yds: no ex* **12/1**

0005 3 ¾ **Accession (IRE)**[25] 4067 4-9-0 **78** ....(b) SteveDrowne 17 84
(Clive Cox) *hld up wl in tch: hmpd and lost pl 5f out: towards rr after tl rdn and hdwy over 1f out: nt clr run and swtchd lft 1f out: kpt on wl u.p ins fnl f* **9/1**

1143 4 1¼ **Ancient Greece**[47] 2380 6-8-10 **77** ....(t) ThomasBrown[(3)] 13 80
(George Baker) *towards rr: c nrest stands' rail st: stl bhd whn hdwy u.p ent fnl f: styd on strly: no threat to wnr* **33/1**

6111 5 hd **Nenge Mboko**[9] 4592 3-9-1 **86** 6ex ....(v) PatCosgrave 8 85
(George Baker) *hld up wl in tch in midfield: rdn and effrt wl over 1f out: pressed ldrs 1f out: no ex and wknd fnl 100yds* **16/1**

11 6 1¼ **Askaud (IRE)**[25] 4067 5-9-8 **86** ....(p) FrederikTylicki 12 85
(Scott Dixon) *lw: chsd ldr: rdn 3f out: outpcd u.p and swtchd rt over 1f out: plugged on same pce ins fnl f* **11/1**

3216 7 nse **Good Authority (IRE)**[25] 4067 6-9-10 **88** .... LukeMorris 4 87
(Karen George) *in tch in midfield: barging match w rival 5f out: hdwy u.p to chse ldrs over 1f out: no ex 1f out: wknd ins fnl f* **8/1**

0035 8 ½ **Spirit Of Sharjah (IRE)**[13] 4440 8-9-4 **82** ....(p) FrankieDettori 11 79
(Julia Feilden) *stdd and hmpd s: hld up in tch in rr: swtchd rt and effrt jst over 1f out: kpt on fnl f: nvr trbld ldrs* **20/1**

-132 9 ½ **Tidentime (USA)**[18] 4281 4-9-2 **80** .... MartinHarley 16 76
(Mick Channon) *wl in tch in midfield: outpcd u.p over 1f out: kpt on same pce fnl f* **11/1**

1402 10 nk **My Kingdom (IRE)**[3] 4812 7-8-13 **77** ....(t) MickaelBarzalona 6 72
(Stuart Williams) *chsd ldrs: rdn and press ldrs 2f out: no ex u.p 1f out: wknd fnl 100yds* **6/1**[2]

0006 11 ½ **Johannes (IRE)**[12] 4472 10-8-13 **82** .... GeorgeChaloner[(5)] 14 76
(Richard Fahey) *in tch in midfield: lost pl and drvn wl over 2f out: swtchd rt 1f out: n.d but plugged on fnl f* **20/1**

2000 12 ¾ **Discression**[11] 4540 4-9-2 **80** .... NeilCallan 9 72
(Kevin Ryan) *lengthy: chsd ldrs: rdn and struggling 2f out: sn lost pl: wknd fnl f* **12/1**

60 13 hd **Noble Citizen (USA)**[46] 3339 8-9-5 **83** ....(b) MartinLane 15 74
(David Simcock) *s.i.s: bhd: rdn 3f out: sme hdwy but stl plenty to do whn nt clr run and swtchd rt over 1f out: sn hung rt and plugged on same pce fnl f* **14/1**

-003 14 1½ **Johnny Castle**[39] 3586 5-9-5 **83** .... PatDobbs 1 70
(Amanda Perrett) *hld up towards rr: hdwy to trck ldrs and gng wl 2f out: rdn and fnd nil over 1f out: fdd fnl f* **13/2**[3]

4010 15 8 **Unknown Villain (IRE)**[32] 3828 3-8-12 **83** .... RichardKingscote 2 45
(Tom Dascombe) *chsd ldrs: rdn and btn over 1f out: fdd fnl f* **25/1**

0-00 16 52 **Esprit De Midas**[40] 3538 7-9-7 **85** .... SebSanders 3
(Dean Ivory) *in tch in midfield: hmpd and lost pl 5f out: rdn and btn over 2f out: virtually p.u fnl f: t.o* **20/1**

1m 26.38s (-0.62) **Going Correction** +0.10s/f (Good)
WFA 3 from 4yo+ 7lb **16** Ran SP% **131.1**
Speed ratings (Par 107): **107,105,105,103,103 101,101,101,100,100 99,98,98,97,87 28**
toteswingers 1&2 £13.20, 1&3 £15.60, 2&3 £12.40 CSF £64.80 CT £572.41 TOTE £5.50: £1.90, £3.70, £2.90, £7.90; EX 67.30 Trifecta £718.20 Pool: £6869.16 - 7.17 winning units..
Owner Barker, Ferguson, Mason, Hassiakos, Done **Bred** Miss Annmarie Burke **Trained** East Everleigh, Wilts

FOCUS
A competitive handicap, but with the field coming centre-to-stands' side up the home straight the usual bias towards those drawn low was turned on its head.
T/Jkpt: £8660.90. Pool of £286,664.97 - 23.50 winning units. T/Plt: £40.90. Pool of £351,100.12 - 6252.90 winning units. T/Qpdt: £18.30. Pool of £13,763.62 - 556.25 winning units. SP

4623 LEICESTER (R-H)

Wednesday, July 31

OFFICIAL GOING: Soft (good to soft in places; 7.0)
Wind: Light behind Weather: Light rain

4880 BRITISH STALLION STUDS EBF MEDIAN AUCTION MAIDEN FILLIES' STKS 5f 218y

6:00 (6:01) (Class 5) 2-Y-O **£3,557** (£1,058; £529; £264) **Stalls** Centre

Form RPR

40 1 **Value (IRE)**[27] 3986 2-9-0 0 .... SeanLevey 10 74
(Richard Hannon) *chsd ldrs: led 2f out: rdn and edgd lft over 1f out: styd on* **7/1**

0 2 1 **Nimble Kimble**[36] 3663 2-8-9 0 .... RyanTate[(5)] 11 71
(James Eustace) *hld up: hdwy over 3f out: outpcd over 2f out: rallied over 1f out: r.o* **10/1**

00 3 1¼ **Island Remede**[14] 4409 2-9-0 0 .... JimmyQuinn 4 67+
(Ed Dunlop) *chsd ldrs: rdn over 2f out: styd on* **40/1**

4 nk **Serata Di Gala (FR)** 2-9-0 0 .... PaoloSirigu 12 66+
(Marco Botti) *s.i.s: hdwy 1/2-way: rdn over 1f out: edgd rt ins fnl f: styd on* **18/1**

22 5 ½ **Secret Kode (IRE)**[18] 4302 2-9-0 0 .... WilliamCarson 2 65
(Brendan Powell) *sn led: hdd over 3f out: rdn and ev ch over 1f out: sn hung rt: no ex ins fnl f* **3/1**[1]

6 2¾ **Lady Stella** 2-9-0 0 .... ChrisCatlin 5 57+
(Rae Guest) *mid-div: hdwy over 1f out: edgd lft and no ex ins fnl f* **40/1**

7 2½ **Enharmonic (USA)** 2-9-0 0 .... RobertHavlin 6 49
(John Gosden) *s.i.s: hld up: shkn up over 2f out: nt trble ldrs* **11/2**

8 2¾ **Monarch Maid** 2-9-0 0 .... AdamBeschizza 1 41
(Peter Hiatt) *s.i.s: sn prom: rdn and wknd over 1f out* **125/1**

02 9 ½ **Where The Boys Are (IRE)**[23] 4115 2-9-0 0 .... RoystonFfrench 9 39
(Ed McMahon) *plld hrd and prom: rdn over 1f out: wknd fnl f* **5/1**[3]

10 1½ **Keep To The Beat** 2-9-0 0 .... GrahamLee 8 38+
(Kevin Ryan) *s.i.s: rn green and a in rr* **4/1**[2]

00 **11** *9* **Crazy Brenda (IRE)**22 4154 2-9-0 0 LiamKeniry 7 8
(Sylvester Kirk) *chsd ldrs: led over 3f out: rdn and hdd 2f out: sn wknd* **80/1**

0 **12** *2 3/4* **Star Anise (FR)**28 3958 2-9-0 0 TedDurcan 3
(Harry Dunlop) *chsd ldrs: pushed along and lost pl over 3f out: sn bhd* **20/1**

1m 15.06s (2.06) **Going Correction** +0.175s/f (Good) **12** Ran SP% **115.6**
Speed ratings (Par 91): **93,91,90,89,88 85,81,78,77,75 63,59**
toteswingers 1&2 £14.70, 1&3 £38.60, 2&3 £40.90 CSF £70.06 TOTE £11.50: £3.80, £2.70, £13.50; EX 73.70 Trifecta £728.50 Part won. Pool: £971.34 - 0.27 winning units..
Owner Mrs J Wood **Bred** Michael O'Dwyer & Knockainey Stud **Trained** East Everleigh, Wilts

FOCUS
A probably a fair fillies' maiden.

4881 ROTHLEY (S) STKS — 7f 9y
6:30 (6:31) (Class 6) 3-Y-O **£1,940** (£577; £288; £144) **Stalls** Centre

Form				RPR
0236	**1**		**Avatar Star (IRE)**15 4383 3-8-9 65 (tp) NataliaGemelova(3) 4 (Marco Botti) *a.p: chsd ldr 3f out: led over 1f out: edgd rt and sn pushed clr* **11/8**1	67
	2	*2*	**Well Owd Mon** 3-8-12 0 JimmyQuinn 7 (Andrew Hollinshead) *sn pushed along in rr: hdwy u.p over 1f out: r.o to go 2nd ins fnl f: no ch w wnr* **50/1**	62
2604	**3**	*7*	**Tiger's Home**34 3740 3-8-7 55 AdamBeschizza 2 (Julia Feilden) *sn led: rdn and hdd over 1f out: wknd ins fnl f* **22/1**	39
-304	**4**	*1*	**Baltic Gin (IRE)**19 4240 3-8-7 59 CathyGannon 8 (Malcolm Saunders) *chsd ldrs: rdn over 2f out: wknd fnl f* **9/2**3	36
0640	**5**	*1*	**East Texas Red (IRE)**5 4721 3-8-12 58 (v1) PaoloSirigu 6 (Mick Quinn) *chsd ldrs: rdn over 2f out: wknd over 1f out* **7/1**	38
-006	**6**	*1 1/4*	**Cio Cio San (IRE)**11 4521 3-8-0 55 (b1) NoelGarbutt(7) 1 (Bill Turner) *chsd ldrs: rdn 1/2-way: wknd over 1f out* **20/1**	30
4-5	**7**	*6*	**Paddy Burke**28 3950 3-8-12 0 ShaneKelly 3 (Stuart Kittow) *sn outpcd* **16/1**	20
2014	**8**	*39*	**Roland**26 4033 3-9-3 71 (p) GrahamLee 5 (Kevin Ryan) *chsd ldrs: rdn over 4f out: wknd 1/2-way* **7/2**2	

1m 28.22s (2.02) **Going Correction** +0.175s/f (Good) **8** Ran SP% **112.0**
Speed ratings (Par 98): **95,92,84,83,82 81,74,29**
toteswingers 1&2 £9.80, 1&3 £8.30, 2&3 £12.90 CSF £92.69 TOTE £2.30: £1.10, £19.10, £7.70; EX 70.50 Trifecta £281.10 Pool: £1503.90 - 4.01 winning units..There was no bid for the winner.
Owner Mrs Lucie Botti **Bred** Acorn Stud **Trained** Newmarket, Suffolk

FOCUS
A weak 3yo seller.

4882 BOSWORTH FIELD H'CAP — 1m 1f 218y
7:05 (7:05) (Class 4) (0-80,78) 3-Y-O+ **£4,851** (£1,443; £721; £360) **Stalls** Low

Form				RPR
4-30	**1**		**Thomas Hobson**55 3021 3-9-1 75 RobertHavlin 9 (John Gosden) *a.p: led over 2f out: rdn clr fnl f* **9/2**2	93
5031	**2**	*3 3/4*	**Break Rank (USA)**27 3971 4-10-0 78 LiamKeniry 8 (Ed de Giles) *a.p: rdn to chse wnr over 1f out: edgd rt: styd on same pce fnl f* **10/1**	88
0243	**3**	*4*	**Ivanhoe**37 3636 3-8-8 68 JimmyQuinn 1 (Michael Blanshard) *hld up: hdwy and nt clr run over 2f out: rdn over 1f out: styd on same pce fnl f: wnt 3rd nr fin* **8/1**	70
-664	**4**	*1/2*	**Perfect Delight**43 3427 4-9-3 72 RyanTate(5) 2 (Clive Cox) *chsd ldrs: rdn and ev ch over 2f out: no ex fnl f* **14/1**	73
10-	**5**	*1*	**Authorship (IRE)**307 6597 3-9-2 76 GrahamLee 6 (Charlie Appleby) *hld up: hmpd 8f out: sn pushed along and nvr gng wl afterwards: rdn: hdwy and swtchd rt over 1f out: nt clr run ins fnl f: n.d* **11/10**1	81+
00/5	**6**	*16*	**Mister Carter (IRE)**41 3512 6-9-6 70 (p) AidanColeman 5 (Ian Williams) *chsd ldr: rdn over 3f out: wknd over 1f out* **40/1**	37
0-02	**7**	*shd*	**Snow Hill**27 3977 5-9-11 75 TedDurcan 7 (Chris Wall) *sn pushed along in rr: hdwy u.p over 2f out: wknd over 1f out: eased* **11/2**3	53
-643	**8**	*nk*	**Astrosapphire**57 2967 3-8-9 69 ChrisCatlin 4 (Mark H Tompkins) *led: rdn and hdd over 2f out: wknd over 1f out* **33/1**	35

2m 10.21s (2.31) **Going Correction** +0.375s/f (Good)
WFA 3 from 4yo+ 10lb **8** Ran SP% **113.4**
Speed ratings (Par 105): **105,102,98,98,97 84,84,84**
toteswingers 1&2 £4.70, 1&3 £6.20, 2&3 £9.10 CSF £47.14 CT £346.84 TOTE £4.20: £1.40, £4.40, £2.60; EX 68.10 Trifecta £246.10 Pool: £1412.58 - 4.30 winning units..
Owner Bailey, Hall & Hood **Bred** Mount Coote Stud And M H Dixon **Trained** Newmarket, Suffolk

FOCUS
A modest handicap.

4883 BRITISH STALLION STUDS EBF MAIDEN STKS — 5f 218y
7:40 (7:40) (Class 4) 2-Y-O **£4,528** (£1,347; £673; £336) **Stalls** Centre

Form				RPR
	1		**Boadicee** 2-9-0 0 ChrisCatlin 7 (Rae Guest) *s.i.s: rn green in rr: hdwy over 2f out: rdn to ld wl ins fnl f: sn clr: readily* **6/1**3	78
0	**2**	*2*	**Nova Champ (IRE)**58 2925 2-9-5 0 HarryBentley 4 (Stuart Williams) *trckd ldr: led over 2f out: rdn: hdd and no ex ins fnl f* **2/1**2	77
	3	*3 1/2*	**Rostrum Farewell** 2-9-5 0 SeanLevey 5 (David Brown) *chsd ldrs: rdn over 1f out: no ex ins fnl f* **6/1**3	67
	4	*3 3/4*	**Biotic** 2-9-5 0 WilliamCarson 1 (Rod Millman) *prom: rdn over 2f out: hung rt over 1f out: wknd fnl f* **20/1**	55
	5	*1*	**Marengo** 2-9-5 0 LiamKeniry 6 (Ed de Giles) *s.i.s: outpcd* **33/1**	52
00	**6**	*3*	**Nip A Bear**12 4505 2-9-5 0 GrahamLee 2 (John Holt) *led 1f: chsd ldrs: rdn and wknd over 2f out* **40/1**	43
4	**7**	*3/4*	**Tez**20 4199 2-9-5 0 PaoloSirigu 3 (Marco Botti) *led 5f out: hdd over 2f out: rdn and wknd over 1f out* **13/8**1	41

1m 15.7s (2.70) **Going Correction** +0.175s/f (Good) **7** Ran SP% **110.1**
Speed ratings (Par 96): **89,86,81,76,75 71,70**
toteswingers 1&2 £2.00, 1&3 £4.70, 2&3 £1.30 CSF £17.04 TOTE £14.50: £5.50, £1.10; EX 18.90 Trifecta £118.20 Pool: £1306.59 - 8.28 winning units..
Owner C J Murfitt **Bred** Pantile Stud **Trained** Newmarket, Suffolk

FOCUS
An ordinary juvenile maiden.

4884 ROTHLEY H'CAP — 5f 218y
8:10 (8:11) (Class 5) (0-70,76) 3-Y-O+ **£2,587** (£770; £384; £192) **Stalls** Centre

Form				RPR
-342	**1**		**Bajan Bear**18 4303 5-9-9 70 WilliamTwiston-Davies(3) 14 (Michael Blanshard) *racd stands' side: hld up in tch: rdn over 1f out: r.o to ld overall wl ins fnl f* **14/1**	81
1301	**2**	*1 1/2*	**Clubland (IRE)**6 4669 4-10-2 74 6ex JimmyQuinn 8 (Roy Bowring) *racd stands' side: chsd ldrs: rdn to ld that gp over 1f out: edgd rt: hdd wl ins fnl f: styd 2nd of 6 in gp* **3/1**1	81
2242	**3**	*nk*	**Fenella Fudge**6 4669 5-8-12 63 (v) AdamMcLean(7) 13 (Derek Shaw) *racd stands' side: s.i.s: hld up: hdwy over 1f out: sn rdn and edgd rt: styd on: 3rd of 6 in gp* **6/1**2	69
5540	**4**	*hd*	**George Fenton**89 1994 4-8-8 59 (p) NoelGarbutt(7) 6 (Richard Guest) *racd centre: chsd ldrs: rdn over 2f out: led overall over 1f out: hdd and no ex wl ins fnl f: 1st of 7 in gp* **22/1**	64
6010	**5**	*3*	**The Strig**12 4494 6-9-5 63 J-PGuillambert 10 (Stuart Williams) *racd stands' side: led that gp tl rdn and hdd over 1f out: styd on same pce: 4th of 6 in gp* **16/1**	59
5631	**6**	*1/2*	**Key Ambition**48 3247 4-9-4 67 (vt) JustinNewman(5) 3 (Garry Moss) *racd centre: s.i.s: hdwy 1/2-way: rdn over 1f out: styd on same pce ins fnl f: 2nd of 7 in gp* **9/1**	62
3445	**7**	*2 1/2*	**Captain Scooby**3 4814 7-9-11 69 (p) GrahamLee 5 (Richard Guest) *racd centre: chsd ldrs: rdn over 1f out: wknd ins fnl f: 3rd of 7 in gp* **6/1**2	56
5460	**8**	*nse*	**Night Trade (IRE)**2 4830 6-9-3 68 (p) EoinWalsh(7) 12 (Ronald Harris) *racd stands' side: hld up: hdwy over 3f out: rdn and ev ch over 1f out: wknd ins fnl f: 5th of 6 in gp* **33/1**	55
30-3	**9**	*2 1/2*	**Ambitious Boy**34 3733 4-9-12 70 ShaneKelly 1 (Andrew Hollinshead) *racd centre: hld up: hdwy over 2f out: rdn over 1f out: wknd fnl f: 4th of 7 in gp* **6/1**2	49
0050	**10**	*2*	**Barons Spy (IRE)**44 3411 12-9-5 70 DanielMuscutt(7) 7 (Richard Price) *racd centre: in rr: pushed along 1/2-way: n.d: 5th of 7 in gp* **33/1**	43
0026	**11**	*1 3/4*	**We Have A Dream**20 4220 8-9-10 68 MartinDwyer 9 (William Muir) *overall ldr centre over 3f: wknd ins fnl f: 6th of 7 in gp* **8/1**3	36
000	**12**	*2 1/2*	**Ficelle (IRE)**58 2918 4-8-11 55 WilliamCarson 11 (Ronald Harris) *racd stands' side: chsd ldrs: rdn over 2f out: wknd over 1f out: eased: last of 6 in gp* **20/1**	16
062-	**13**	*1*	**Beachwood Bay**373 4406 5-8-11 55 (p) CathyGannon 2 (Jo Hughes) *racd centre: chsd ldrs: led over 2f out: rdn and hdd over 1f out: wknd fnl f: last of 7 in gp* **40/1**	13

1m 13.49s (0.49) **Going Correction** +0.175s/f (Good) **13** Ran SP% **118.9**
Speed ratings (Par 103): **103,101,100,100,96 95,92,92,88,86 83,80,79**
toteswingers 1&2 £12.30, 1&3 £14.80, 2&3 £3.60 CSF £52.36 CT £300.86 TOTE £10.50: £4.70, £1.10, £3.30; EX 65.20 Trifecta £519.40 Pool: £781.14 - 1.12 winning units..
Owner C McKenna **Bred** Mr And Mrs C McKenna **Trained** Upper Lambourn, Berks

FOCUS
A moderate sprint handicap.

4885 SHANGTON H'CAP — 1m 60y
8:45 (8:46) (Class 6) (0-65,65) 3-Y-O **£1,940** (£577; £288; £144) **Stalls** Low

Form				RPR
0463	**1**		**Calm Attitude (IRE)**45 3376 3-8-11 55 ChrisCatlin 4 (Rae Guest) *chsd ldrs: rdn over 1f out: r.o to ld wl ins fnl f* **5/1**2	62
660	**2**	*1 1/2*	**Emperatriz**36 3649 3-9-5 63 RobertHavlin 14 (John Holt) *trckd ldr: rdn and ev ch fr over 1f out: styd on same pce towards fin* **11/2**3	67
2000	**3**	*1/2*	**Nelson Quay (IRE)**15 4383 3-9-3 61 (p) GeorgeBaker 9 (Jeremy Gask) *led: rdn over 2f out: hdd and no ex wl ins fnl f* **9/2**1	64
6353	**4**	*1/2*	**Red Tulip**41 3495 3-8-13 57 ShaneKelly 8 (James Fanshawe) *hld up in tch: shkn up over 1f out: styd on same pce ins fnl f* **11/2**3	59
0-42	**5**	*2 3/4*	**Pour La Victoire (IRE)**79 2330 3-8-5 49 JimmyQuinn 2 (Tony Carroll) *chsd ldrs: rdn over 2f out: no ex ins fnl f* **5/1**2	44
0556	**6**	*1/2*	**Haatefina**12 4485 3-8-11 62 (v) DanielMuscutt(7) 13 (Mark Usher) *s.i.s: hld up: hdwy over 2f out: sn rdn: no ex fnl f* **8/1**	56
2563	**7**	*3 3/4*	**Fair Comment**31 3859 3-8-11 58 WilliamTwiston-Davies(3) 12 (Michael Blanshard) *hld up: rdn over 2f out: nt trble ldrs* **8/1**	44
2515	**8**	*2*	**Black Truffle (FR)**44 3405 3-8-10 54 (v) LiamKeniry 5 (Mark Usher) *hld up: plld hrd: rdn over 2f out: wknd over 1f out* **12/1**	35
0-00	**9**	*1 1/4*	**My Renaissance**39 3585 3-9-0 58 TedDurcan 6 (Ben Case) *hld up: rdn over 2f out: wknd over 1f out* **40/1**	36

1m 51.78s (6.68) **Going Correction** +0.375s/f (Good) **9** Ran SP% **114.6**
Speed ratings (Par 98): **81,79,79,78,75 75,71,69,68**
toteswingers 1&2 £5.30, 1&3 £6.90, 2&3 £6.60 CSF £32.36 CT £132.75 TOTE £4.90: £1.10, £3.10, £3.30; EX 45.40 Trifecta £197.80 Pool: £595.46 - 2.25 winning units..
Owner The Calm Again Partnership **Bred** R N Auld **Trained** Newmarket, Suffolk

FOCUS
A weak handicap, run at a steady pace.
T/Plt: £318.00. Pool of £86,101.14 - 197.61 winning units. T/Qpdt: £45.70. Pool of £7783.76 - 125.95 winning units. CR

4556 REDCAR (L-H)
Wednesday, July 31

OFFICIAL GOING: Good (good to firm in places; 8.4)
Wind: moderate 1/2 behind Weather: fine and sunny. becoming overcast, light showers race 5 onwards

4886 BRITISH STALLION STUDS EBF MAIDEN STKS — 6f
2:05 (2:07) (Class 5) 2-Y-O **£3,067** (£905; £453) **Stalls** Centre

Form				RPR
2	**1**		**Smart Salute**23 4121 2-9-5 0 GeorgeBaker 10 (Ed Walker) *chsd ldrs: drvn over 1f out: styd on to ld clsng stages* **1/1**1	77+
	2	*1/2*	**Dutch Breeze** 2-9-5 0 DavidAllan 2 (Tim Easterby) *w ldrs: led after 1f: edgd rt 1f out: hdd and no ex clsng stages* **16/1**	75+
	3	*1/2*	**Roachdale House (IRE)** 2-9-5 0 TonyHamilton 9 (Richard Fahey) *dwlt: in rr: edgd rt over 2f out: hdwy over 1f out: styd on wl towards fin: will improve* **9/1**3	74+
25	**4**	*1 3/4*	**Thornaby Nash**65 2701 2-9-5 0 DanielTudhope 4 (David O'Meara) *w ldrs: kpt on same pce fnl f* **12/1**	68

The Form Book Flat, Raceform Ltd, Compton, RG20 6NL.

320 **5** 2 1/4 **Morning Post**[11] 4528 2-8-12 84 KevinStott(7) 5 61
(Kevin Ryan) *led 1f: chsd ldrs: rdn 2f out: one pce* **9/4**[2]
6 *nse* **Secret Oasis** 2-9-0 0 TomEaves 6 56
(Bryan Smart) *dwlt: sn chsng ldrs: outpcd over 2f out: styd on ins fnl f* **33/1**
000 **7** 3 1/4 **Fuel Injection**[15] 4370 2-9-5 57 LeeTopliss 3 50
(Paul Midgley) *w ldrs: t.k.h: hmpd and swtchd lft 1f out: sn wknd* **66/1**
8 2 1/4 **Victory Danz (IRE)** 2-9-5 0 DavidNolan 1 43
(David O'Meara) *sn chsng ldrs on outside: sn drvn along: lost pl over 2f out* **40/1**
06 **9** 1 3/4 **Reale Silenzio**[10] 4556 2-9-0 0 JamesSullivan 7 33
(John Weymes) *chsd ldrs: lost pl after 2f* **100/1**
10 5 **Jaeger Connoisseur (IRE)** 2-9-0 0 RobertWinston 8 17
(Mrs K Burke) *chsd ldrs: lost pl after 2f* **25/1**
11 28 **Thisonesmine (IRE)** 2-9-2 0 (b1) LMcNiff(3) 11
(David C Griffiths) *s.v.s: detached in last: t.o fnl 2f* **50/1**

1m 11.49s (-0.31) **Going Correction** -0.20s/f (Firm) **11** Ran SP% **118.0**
Speed ratings (Par 94): **94,93,92,90,87 87,82,79,77,70 33**
toteswingers 1&2 £3.90, 1&3 £4.00, 2&3 £8.30 CSF £19.47 TOTE £1.80: £2.00, £7.30, £5.10; EX 19.80 Trifecta £144.80 Pool: £2684.31 - 13.90 winning units..
Owner Brandon T C Liu **Bred** Bumble Bs, D F Powell & S Nicholls **Trained** Newmarket, Suffolk

FOCUS
Jimmy Sullivan described the ground as "good, with plenty of juice in it", while David Allan felt it was "just on the quick side of good".

4887 READ HAYLEY TURNER EVERY FRIDAY RACINGUK.COM MAIDEN STKS 7f
2:40 (2:40) (Class 5) 3-Y-0+ **£2,726** (£805; £402) **Stalls** Centre

Form RPR
-320 **1** **You're The Boss**[74] 2448 3-9-5 80 GeorgeBaker 4 70
(Ed Walker) *s.i.s: hld up in rr: hdwy and nt clr run over 2f out: sn trcking ldrs: led jst ins fnl f: sn rdn and hung lft: drvn rt out* **8/13**[1]
00- **2** 1/2 **Messageinabottle (USA)**[274] 7460 3-9-0 0 PJMcDonald 8 64
(James Bethell) *trckd ldrs: upsides 1f out: carried lft and crowded: kpt on to take 2nd clsng stages* **33/1**
4-44 **3** 1 **Mishaal (IRE)**[14] 4400 3-9-5 67 DaleSwift 2 66
(Michael Herrington) *t.k.h: led: hdd jst ins fnl f: no ex* **14/1**[3]
0- **4** 5 **Kalithea**[287] 7159 3-9-0 0 (e1) PaulMulrennan 1 48
(Julie Camacho) *dwlt: hld up in rr: hdwy on outer over 2f out: hung rt and kpt on fnl f: tk modest 4th nr fin* **16/1**
4 **5** 1/2 **Thorntoun Lady (USA)**[26] 4013 3-9-0 0 DanielTudhope 6 46
(Jim Goldie) *sn trcking ldrs: effrt over 1f out: one pce* **7/2**[2]
05 **6** 1 1/2 **Manatee Bay**[33] 3759 3-9-5 0 PaulQuinn 7 47
(David Nicholls) *mid-div: effrt over 2f out: one pce whn hung rt ins fnl f* **50/1**
3645 **7** 1 1/2 **Midnight Warrior**[13] 4436 3-9-0 62 ConnorBeasley(5) 3 43
(Ron Barr) *mid-div: drvn over 2f out: one pce whn hung rt fnl f* **14/1**[3]
56 **8** 2 1/2 **Latin Rebel (IRE)**[26] 4012 6-9-12 0 AndrewElliott 15 39
(Jim Goldie) *mid-div: drvn over 2f out: nvr a factor* **25/1**
9 4 **Cape Rosa** 3-9-0 0 PaddyAspell 9 21
(James Moffatt) *s.i.s: reminders after 2f: a in rr* **66/1**
65 **10** 2 1/4 **True That (IRE)**[29] 3932 3-9-5 0 TonyHamilton 10 19
(David Nicholls) *trckd ldrs: hung lft and lost pl over 1f out* **33/1**
0050 **11** 2 1/2 **Miss Bossy Boots**[68] 2613 4-9-7 35 BarryMcHugh 13 11
(Tracy Waggott) *trckd ldrs: drvn 3f out: sn lost pl* **100/1**
0 **12** 8 **Nos Da**[87] 2041 3-9-0 0 (t) TomEaves 14
(Bryan Smart) *sn bhd and drvn along* **20/1**
00 **13** 1 1/4 **Babushka's Girl**[15] 4381 4-9-4 0 MarkCoumbe(3) 5
(Lisa Williamson) *w ldr: rdn 3f out: sn lost pl and bhd* **100/1**

1m 23.6s (-0.90) **Going Correction** -0.20s/f (Firm)
WFA 3 from 4yo+ 7lb **13** Ran SP% **123.3**
Speed ratings (Par 103): **97,96,95,89,89 87,85,82,78,75 72,63,62**
toteswingers 1&2 £11.40, 1&3 £4.00, 2&3 £58.30 CSF £40.82 TOTE £1.50: £1.02, £13.70, £3.10; EX 40.70 Trifecta £345.20 Pool: £2815.06 - 6.11 winning units..
Owner Laurence A Bellman **Bred** Mrs Fiona Denniff **Trained** Newmarket, Suffolk

FOCUS
A modest maiden.

4888 DOWNLOAD THE FREE RACING UK APP (S) STKS 1m 2f
3:15 (3:16) (Class 6) 3-Y-0+ **£2,045** (£603; £302) **Stalls** Low

Form RPR
06-0 **1** **Full Toss**[24] 4098 7-9-6 78 DanielTudhope 3 72
(Jim Goldie) *trckd ldrs: effrt and swtchd rt 3f out: swtchd lft and styd on to ld over 1f out: drvn out* **6/4**[2]
5301 **2** 1 1/4 **Demolition**[10] 4559 9-9-4 81 JoeyHaynes(7) 5 75
(Noel Wilson) *led 1f: chsd ldr: led over 2f out: edgd rt and hdd over 1f out: kpt on same pce* **11/8**[1]
50-0 **3** 3 1/4 **Auto Mac**[64] 2752 5-9-1 56 AdamCarter(5) 4 63
(Neville Bycroft) *mid-div: hdwy to chse ldrs over 2f out: one pce over 1f out* **50/1**
0024 **4** 4 1/2 **Betty Boo (IRE)**[22] 4143 3-8-0 35 [1] ConnorBeasley(5) 2 49
(Shaun Harris) *mid-div: effrt over 3f out: kpt on fnl 2f: tk 4th nr fin* **66/1**
0553 **5** 1/2 **Valantino Oyster (IRE)**[11] 4543 6-9-11 58 (p) DaleSwift 10 58
(Tracy Waggott) *drvn: swtchd lft and led after 1f: hdd over 2f out: wknd fnl f* **8/1**[3]
00-0 **6** 6 **City Of The Kings (IRE)**[105] 1603 8-9-6 58 BarryMcHugh 9 41
(Tracy Waggott) *hld up in rr: effrt over 3f out: lost pl over 1f out: b.b.v* **25/1**
5400 **7** 6 **Eijaaz (IRE)**[28] 3947 12-9-6 53 (p) DuranFentiman 1 29
(Geoffrey Harker) *hld up in rr: sme hdwy on outer over 3f out: lost pl over 1f out* **25/1**
/16- **8** 7 **Bollin Dolly**[11] 6229 10-9-1 71 PaddyAspell 7 10
(James Moffatt) *chsd ldrs: drvn over 4f out: lost pl over 2f out* **8/1**[3]
40/ **9** 38 **Chippy**[22] 3080 5-9-6 0 (tp) TomEaves 8
(John Holt) *t.k.h: trckd ldrs: lost pl over 3f out: sn wl bhd: virtually p.u: hopelessly t.o* **100/1**
5 **10** 14 **Redwood Blade**[42] 3465 4-9-1 0 AndrewElliott 6
(Jim Goldie) *in rr and sn drvn along: detached 5f out: sn t.o: virtually p.u* **66/1**

2m 4.77s (-2.33) **Going Correction** -0.20s/f (Firm)
WFA 3 from 4yo+ 10lb **10** Ran SP% **118.0**
Speed ratings (Par 101): **101,100,97,93,93 88,83,78,47,36**
toteswingers 1&2 £1.50, 1&3 £12.40, 2&3 £10.10 CSF £3.79 TOTE £2.70: £1.50, £1.02, £6.10; EX 5.00 Trifecta £47.90 Pool: £4328.64 - 67.73 winning units..The winner was bought in for £3,500
Owner Johnnie Delta Racing **Bred** The Queen **Trained** Uplawmoor, E Renfrews

FOCUS
This claimer looked a match beforehand and the big two in the market came clear.

4889 MARKET CROSS JEWELLERS H'CAP 1m 2f
3:50 (3:53) (Class 5) (0-75,74) 3-Y-0+ **£2,587** (£770; £384; £192) **Stalls** Low

Form RPR
5025 **1** **Morocco**[26] 4016 4-9-6 66 DanielTudhope 5 80+
(David O'Meara) *hld up in rr: hdwy to trck ldrs 7f out: nt clr run over 3f out: swtchd rt over 2f out: led on bit wl over 1f out: shkn up and wnt clr: eased clsng stages* **9/2**[3]
-000 **2** 3 1/2 **Jonny Lesters Hair (IRE)**[64] 2753 8-9-3 63 DavidAllan 2 66
(Tim Easterby) *led: hdd wl over 1f out: kpt on to take 2nd 1f out: no ch w wnr* **12/1**
365 **3** 1/2 **Discay**[13] 4435 4-9-7 67 LiamJones 1 69
(Mark Johnston) *sn chsng ldrs: drvn over 4f out: hung lft and outpcd over 2f out: kpt on to take 3rd nr fin* **9/2**[3]
5-00 **4** 3/4 **Buster Brown (IRE)**[60] 2886 4-9-7 67 DaleSwift 6 68
(James Given) *hld up detached in last: drvn 4f out: hdwy over 2f out: kpt on one pce* **7/2**[1]
0-03 **5** 1 **Rock Supreme (IRE)**[34] 3729 4-10-0 74 PaulMulrennan 8 73
(Michael Dods) *trckd ldr: drvn over 2f out: hdd wl over 1f out: one pce* **4/1**[2]
1/26 **6** 1 3/4 **Spes Nostra**[60] 2881 5-9-11 71 RobertWinston 10 67
(David Barron) *trckd ldrs on outside: t.k.h: lost pl over 2f out* **15/2**
0034 **7** *hd* **Gold Show**[15] 4373 4-9-8 68 TomEaves 4 63
(Edwin Tuer) *sn chsng ldrs: drvn 4f out: lost pl 2f out* **6/1**

2m 3.93s (-3.17) **Going Correction** -0.20s/f (Firm)
WFA 3 from 4yo+ 10lb **7** Ran SP% **112.3**
Speed ratings (Par 103): **104,101,100,100,99 98,97**
toteswingers 1&2 £8.50, 1&3 £4.30, 2&3 £6.30 CSF £52.22 CT £253.46 TOTE £6.60: £3.20, £4.80; EX 51.90 Trifecta £350.90 Pool: £3637.89 - 7.77 winning units..
Owner Equality Racing **Bred** Cheveley Park Stud Ltd **Trained** Nawton, N Yorks

FOCUS
They appeared to go a decent gallop in this modest handicap and it produced a ready winner.

4890 WATCH RACING UK ON SKY 432 H'CAP (STRAIGHT-MILE CHAMPIONSHIP QUALIFIER) 1m
4:25 (4:28) (Class 4) (0-85,83) 3-Y-0 **£6,469** (£1,925; £962; £481) **Stalls** Centre

Form RPR
4113 **1** **Woody Bay**[25] 4077 3-8-11 73 DaleSwift 7 83
(James Given) *hmpd s: chsd ldrs: led over 2f out: edgd lft and forged clr appr fnl f* **15/2**
5112 **2** 4 **Aeronwyn Bryn (IRE)**[9] 4581 3-9-1 82 ConnorBeasley(5) 10 83
(Michael Dods) *hld up towards rr: hdwy over 2f out: chsd wnr over 1f out: no imp* **9/2**[2]
6442 **3** 2 1/4 **Strong Conviction**[18] 4306 3-8-13 75 SamHitchcott 8 71
(Mick Channon) *trckd ldrs: effrt over 2f out: kpt on same pce over 1f out* **8/1**
1213 **4** 1/2 **Black Rider (IRE)**[18] 4288 3-8-10 72 PaulMulrennan 6 67
(Julie Camacho) *in rr: hdwy 4f out: outpcd over 2f out: styd on fnl f* **7/1**
300 **5** 3/4 **Old Man Clegg**[25] 4048 3-8-11 73 ow1 PhillipMakin 1 66
(Michael Easterby) *sn chsng ldrs: rdn over 2f out: one pce* **14/1**
5505 **6** 1 3/4 **Steelriver (IRE)**[18] 4295 3-9-7 83 PJMcDonald 3 72
(James Bethell) *mid-div: effrt 3f out: sn rdn: hung lft over 1f out: nvr a threat* **4/1**[1]
4363 **7** 5 **Light Rose (IRE)**[12] 4502 3-9-0 76 LiamJones 9 53
(Mark Johnston) *led: hdd over 2f out: sn lost pl* **14/1**
1-02 **8** 5 **Polar Chief**[39] 3571 3-9-5 81 JamesSullivan 4 47
(Kristin Stubbs) *swvd rt s: chsd ldrs: lost pl over 1f out: bhd whn carried rt over 1f out* **9/2**[2]
1250 **P** **Darkside**[20] 4198 3-8-2 64 oh2 PaulQuinn 2
(Tracy Waggott) *chsd ldrs: sn hung rt: drvn and lost pl over 3f out: bhd whn broke down over 1f out: fatally injured* **6/1**[3]

1m 36.23s (-0.37) **Going Correction** -0.20s/f (Firm) **9** Ran SP% **119.4**
Speed ratings (Par 102): **112,108,105,105,104 102,97,92,**
toteswingers 1&2 £4.70, 1&3 £9.70, 2&3 £5.60 CSF £42.66 CT £283.80 TOTE £8.50: £3.30, £1.02, £3.80; EX 37.00 Trifecta £259.00 Pool: £4300.51 - 12.45 winning units..
Owner J Barson **Bred** Cheveley Park Stud Ltd **Trained** Willoughton, Lincs

FOCUS
No hanging around here and the front pair drew clear in what was a fair race.

4891 RACING REPLAY, ALL TODAY'S RACING SKY 432 H'CAP (DIV I) 6f
5:00 (5:02) (Class 6) (0-65,65) 3-Y-0+ **£1,940** (£577; £288; £144) **Stalls** Centre

Form RPR
-062 **1** **Scentpastparadise**[29] 3929 3-9-7 65 PJMcDonald 8 75
(Ann Duffield) *trckd ldr: led over 2f out: jnd 1f out: hld on gamely* **11/1**
65-6 **2** *nk* **Sir Nod**[202] 143 11-9-5 58 PaulMulrennan 6 68
(Julie Camacho) *hld up in rr: hdwy over 2f out: upsides 1f out: no ex clsng stages* **22/1**
0035 **3** 2 **Karate Queen**[5] 4727 8-8-3 47 (p) ConnorBeasley(5) 2 51
(Ron Barr) *in rr: drvn and outpcd over 2f out: hdwy on outer over 1f out: styd on to take 3rd last 30yds* **16/1**
6004 **4** 1/2 **Black Douglas**[9] 4582 4-8-11 50 AndrewElliott 1 52
(Jim Goldie) *chsd ldrs on outer: outpeced over 2f out: hdwy over 1f out: kpt on to take 4th nr fin* **7/1**[3]
010 **5** 1 **Choc'A'Moca (IRE)**[13] 4448 6-9-11 64 (v) MickyFenton 11 63
(Paul Midgley) *anticipated s: best away: led: hdd over 2f out: kpt on same pce fnl f* **22/1**
3342 **6** *hd* **Perfect Words (IRE)**[21] 4162 3-9-3 64 (p) RaulDaSilva(3) 3 61
(Marjorie Fife) *chsd ldrs: n.m.r over 1f out: kpt on same pce* **7/2**[2]
0646 **7** 1 1/2 **Queens Revenge**[8] 4609 4-9-7 60 (b1) DavidAllan 9 53
(Tim Easterby) *s.i.s: hdwy over 3f out: kpt on one pce over 1f out* **9/1**
2030 **8** 1 **Lees Anthem**[8] 4615 6-8-12 51 DaleSwift 7 41
(Michael Smith) *mid-div: drvn and outpcd over 2f out: no threat after* **20/1**
5423 **9** 4 1/2 **Legal Bond**[28] 3946 4-9-10 63 (p) DanielTudhope 5 39
(David O'Meara) *chsd ldrs: drvn 2f out: n.m.r and wknd over 1f out* **9/4**[1]
-044 **10** 3 **Logans Legend (IRE)**[21] 4160 5-9-2 55 (p) RobertWinston 12 21
(Lawrence Mullaney) *rrd s: s.i.s: sme hdwy over 2f out: hung lft and lost pl over 1f out* **11/1**
2000 **11** 1 3/4 **Lady Kildare (IRE)**[7] 4621 5-9-1 54 TomEaves 10 15
(Jedd O'Keeffe) *chsd ldrs: lost pl over 1f out* **20/1**

20U0 12 7 **Lucy Minaj**[11] 4544 3-8-6 **50** DuranFentiman 4
(Bryan Smart) *s.i.s: chsd ldrs on outer over 3f out: lost pl wl over 1f out: sn bhd* **40/1**

1m 10.32s (-1.48) **Going Correction** -0.20s/f (Firm)
WFA 3 from 4yo+ 5lb **12** Ran SP% **118.7**
Speed ratings (Par 101): **101,100,97,97,95 95,93,92,86,82 80,70**
toteswingers 1&2 £23.30, 1&3 £25.10, 2&3 £51.50 CSF £235.25 CT £3879.38 TOTE £11.50: £2.60, £6.80, £4.90; EX 177.70 Trifecta £1676.80 Part won. Pool: £2235.78 - 0.29 winning units..
Owner Easton Park Stud **Bred** Brookridge Timber Ltd **Trained** Constable Burton, N Yorks

FOCUS
The front pair drew clear in division one of what was a low-grade sprint.

4892 RACING REPLAY, ALL TODAY'S RACING SKY 432 H'CAP (DIV II) 6f
5:35 (5:35) (Class 6) (0-65,65) 3-Y-0+ **£1,940** (£577; £288; £144) **Stalls** Centre

Form RPR
6502 1 **Little Jimmy Odsox (IRE)**[22] 4148 5-9-9 **62** (b) DuranFentiman 8 71
(Tim Easterby) *led: rdn and hung rt 2f out: hrd rdn and kpt on stands' side to assert towards fin* **5/1**[3]
0644 2 ½ **Layla's Hero (IRE)**[7] 4621 6-9-5 **58** (v) TonyHamilton 11 65
(David Nicholls) *dwlt: hdwy over 2f out: chsng ldrs over 1f out: upsides ins fnl f: no ex towards fin* **7/2**[1]
6-P4 3 ½ **Copper To Gold**[25] 4050 4-8-0 **46** GaryMahon(7) 5 51
(Robin Bastiman) *s.i.s: in rr: hdwy over 1f out: styd on wl to take cl 3rd towards fin* **14/1**
4600 4 nk **Amadeus Denton (IRE)**[13] 4430 4-9-1 **59** (p) ConnorBeasley(5) 2 63
(Michael Dods) *chsd ldrs: rdn 2f out: kpt on ins fnl f* **7/1**
062 5 ¾ **Tongalooma**[12] 4471 7-9-4 **57** PaddyAspell 4 59
(James Moffatt) *w ldrs: upsides 1f out: hung rt and kpt on one pce* **8/1**
0520 6 1¾ **Ryedane (IRE)**[13] 4430 11-9-3 **63** (b) RachelRichardson(7) 7 59
(Tim Easterby) *in rr: hdwy over 1f out: styd on towards fin* **16/1**
5-03 7 nk **Emily Hall**[15] 4377 4-8-11 **50** PaulMulrennan 9 45
(Bryan Smart) *s.i.s: t.k.h in rr: hdwy 2f out: n.m.r and swtchd lft over 1f out: hung rt and one pce* **4/1**[2]
30-0 8 2½ **Baybshambles (IRE)**[7] 4621 9-9-1 **54** TomEaves 10 41
(Tina Jackson) *chsd ldrs: rdn 2f out: wknd fnl f* **33/1**
-626 9 ¾ **Constant Dream**[56] 2996 3-9-2 **60** JamesSullivan 6 44
(James Given) *w ldrs: drvn over 2f out: wknd jst ins fnl f* **20/1**
0/00 10 1¾ **Storey Hill (USA)**[49] 3196 8-8-9 **48** (b[1]) RobbieFitzpatrick 12 27
(Charles Smith) *chsd ldrs: wknd appr fnl f* **66/1**
2510 11 12 **A J Cook (IRE)**[23] 4114 3-9-4 **65** (bt) LMcNiff(3) 1 5
(David Barron) *chsd ldrs: drvn over 2f out: lost pl over 1f out: sn bhd and eased* **7/1**

1m 11.0s (-0.80) **Going Correction** -0.20s/f (Firm)
WFA 3 from 4yo+ 5lb **11** Ran SP% **116.7**
Speed ratings (Par 101): **97,96,95,95,94 91,91,88,87,84 68**
toteswingers 1&2 £6.50, 1&3 £15.20, 2&3 £11.60 CSF £22.25 CT £235.13 TOTE £5.60: £2.20, £1.80, £3.20; EX 34.20 Trifecta £420.30 Pool: £1943.54 - 3.46 winning units..
Owner Reality Partnerships III **Bred** Dr D Crone & P Lafarge & P Johnston **Trained** Great Habton, N Yorks
■ Stewards' Enquiry : Duran Fentiman two-day ban: used whip above permitted level (Aug 14-15)

FOCUS
Probably the stronger of the two divisions.

4893 BETFAIR NOVICE FLAT AMATEUR RIDERS' H'CAP (FOR NOVICE AMATEUR RIDERS) 1m
6:10 (6:14) (Class 6) (0-65,65) 4-Y-0+ **£1,871** (£580; £290; £145) **Stalls** Centre

Form RPR
6024 1 **Eeny Mac (IRE)**[15] 4375 6-11-3 **61** (p) MrSebSpencer 1 72
(Neville Bycroft) *trckd ldrs: chal 1f out: led post* **10/1**
6402 2 shd **Rio Cobolo (IRE)**[7] 4623 7-10-8 **55** MrDPCostello(3) 4 66
(David Nicholls) *led: jnd 1f out: hdd last stride* **9/2**[1]
0345 3 3¼ **Shamrocked (IRE)**[26] 4005 4-11-1 **62** MrKWood(3) 6 66
(Ollie Pears) *trckd ldrs far side: effrt over 2f out: kpt on same pce fnl f* **8/1**[3]
5261 4 nk **Boy The Bell**[7] 4623 6-10-13 **57** 6ex (be) MissHDukes 20 60
(Ollie Pears) *chsd ldrs: t.k.h: kpt on ins fnl f* **12/1**
6-33 5 ¾ **Dhaular Dhar (IRE)**[13] 4446 11-11-0 **61** MrsICGoldie(3) 14 62
(Jim Goldie) *hld up in rr: stdy hdwy towards stands' side 2f out: styd on clsng stages* **7/1**[2]
3054 6 1½ **The Blue Banana (IRE)**[23] 4119 4-10-5 **52** MrPDennis(3) 19 50
(Edwin Tuer) *chsd ldrs stands' side: drvn and outpcd 2f out: kpt on ins fnl f* **8/1**[3]
5253 7 1 **Maggie Mey (IRE)**[10] 4562 5-10-8 **52** MissKMargarson 11 47
(Lawrence Mullaney) *w ldrs: one pce appr fnl f* **14/1**
-506 8 hd **Liliargh (IRE)**[56] 2974 4-11-7 **65** MrAlexFerguson 3 60
(Ben Haslam) *in rr: hdwy 2f out: kpt on: nvr nr ldrs* **16/1**
5-00 9 1 **Gadobout Dancer**[32] 3814 6-10-7 **51** MissLWilson 5 44
(Julie Camacho) *rrd s: in rr: hdwy 2f out: nvr a factor* **33/1**
0560 10 1 **Sir George (IRE)**[53] 3081 8-10-4 **48** MrAaronJames 2 38
(Suzzanne France) *in rr: sme hdwy over 1f out: nvr a factor* **20/1**
2010 11 ½ **Rasselas (IRE)**[21] 4160 6-11-4 **62** (p) AnnaHesketh 10 51
(David Nicholls) *hld up towards rr: sme hdwy over 1f out: nvr a factor* **12/1**
5066 12 1¾ **Nonaynever**[12] 4509 5-10-2 **46** oh1 (b) MrRColley 15 31
(Ruth Carr) *stmbld sn after s: sn chsng ldrs: drvn over 2f out: wknd over 1f out* **16/1**
0500 13 ½ **Bachelor Knight (IRE)**[26] 4005 5-9-13 **46** oh1 (e[1]) MrJPearce(3) 9 30
(Suzzanne France) *hood removed late: s.s: in rr: sme hdwy 2f out: nvr on terms* **33/1**
0306 14 10 **Cross The Boss (IRE)**[10] 4562 6-10-10 **57** MissRHeptonstall(3) 18 18
(David O'Meara) *dwlt: in rr: rdn over 2f out: sn bhd: eased clsng stages* **14/1**
345 15 ¾ **Munro Bagger (IRE)**[61] 2831 4-10-8 **55** (p) MrOJPimlott(3) 12 14
(John Quinn) *chsd ldrs: lost pl over 2f out: sn bhd* **25/1**
4006 16 nk **Medam**[34] 3738 4-10-0 **47** (t) MrJAMcEntee(3) 8 6
(Shaun Harris) *mid-div: drvn 3f out: sn lost pl and bhd* **33/1**
0010 17 7 **Lady Del Sol**[18] 4292 5-11-2 **60** MrJamesHughes 13 2
(Jo Hughes) *chsd ldrs centre: edgd lft and lost pl 2f out: eased whn bhd clsng stages* **20/1**

1m 38.45s (1.85) **Going Correction** -0.20s/f (Firm) **17** Ran SP% **124.7**
Speed ratings (Par 101): **101,100,97,97,96 95,94,93,92,91 91,89,89,79,78 78,71**
toteswingers 1&2 £10.70, 1&3 £19.30, 2&3 £7.70 CSF £50.35 CT £299.83 TOTE £11.80: £6.10, £1.30, £1.30, £4.90; EX 52.90 Trifecta £182.00 Pool: £1227.63 - 5.05 winning units..
Owner Mrs J Dickinson **Bred** Kenneth Heelan **Trained** Brandsby, N Yorks

FOCUS
Few got into this weak amateur riders' handicap, with the main action unfolding centre-to-far side.

T/Plt: £485.20. Pool of £58,862.14 - 88.55 winning units. T/Qpdt: £105.30. Pool of £3858.92 - 27.10 winning units. WG

4680 SANDOWN (R-H)
Wednesday, July 31

OFFICIAL GOING: Good (good to soft in places; 7.8)
Wind: Moderate, half against Weather: Cloudy, humid

4894 HAAGEN-DAZS APPRENTICE H'CAP 1m 14y
5:50 (5:50) (Class 5) (0-70,70) 4-Y-0+ **£3,234** (£962; £481; £240) **Stalls** Low

Form RPR
1062 1 **Ishikawa (IRE)**[7] 4638 5-9-5 **70** RobJFitzpatrick(7) 10 79
(Mrs K Burke) *trckd ldng pair after 3f and sn clr of rest: clsd to ld over 2f out: rdn and kpt on wl fnl 2f* **5/2**[1]
5334 2 1½ **Lutine Charlie (IRE)**[20] 4194 6-9-0 **61** RobertTart(3) 9 67
(Pat Eddery) *pressed ldr: led over 3f out to over 2f out: clr of rest after but nt qckn and hld fr over 1f out* **8/1**
6302 3 5 **Silvas Romana (IRE)**[12] 4482 4-9-7 **70** JackDuern(5) 2 65
(Mark Brisbourne) *w ldng pair 2f: dropped off ldrs in 4th by 1/2-way: wandered u.p over 2f out: tk modest 3rd again jst over 1f out* **7/2**[2]
0206 4 1 **Saint Irene**[29] 3926 4-8-12 **61** OisinMurphy(5) 5 53
(Michael Blanshard) *hld up in midfeld: lost tch w ldrs 1/2-way: rdn over 2f out: plugged on and no threat* **15/2**
14-0 5 2 **Silver Lace (IRE)**[15] 4385 4-9-7 **65** AshleyMorgan 7 53
(Chris Wall) *hld up in rr: lost tch w ldrs by 1/2-way: v modest late prog u.p* **10/1**
0500 6 1½ **Warbond**[39] 3575 5-8-4 **51** oh4 PhilipPrince(3) 8 35
(Michael Madgwick) *hld up in last pair: lost tch w ldrs by 1/2-way: nvr on terms after* **33/1**
0003 7 1¾ **Siouxperhero (IRE)**[9] 4593 4-9-0 **63** (b) ThomasGarner(5) 6 43
(William Muir) *s.s: hld up in last pair: lost tch w ldrs by 1/2-way: nvr on terms after* **7/1**[3]
0625 8 1½ **Balady (IRE)**[20] 4208 4-9-3 **66** JoshBaudains(5) 4 43
(Dominic Ffrench Davis) *led to over 3f out: wknd qckly fnl 2f* **10/1**
5000 9 8 **Lily Edge**[4] 4755 4-8-13 **60** MichaelJMMurphy(3) 3 18
(John Bridger) *sn pushed along in midfield: lost tch w ldrs 1/2-way: wknd over 2f out: t.o* **12/1**

1m 44.53s (1.23) **Going Correction** +0.25s/f (Good) **9** Ran SP% **115.0**
Speed ratings (Par 103): **103,101,96,95,93 92,90,88,80**
toteswingers 1&2 £9.00, 1&3 £2.00, 2&3 £6.50 CSF £23.10 CT £70.11 TOTE £2.90: £1.40, £3.20, £1.20; EX 18.50 Trifecta £119.90 Pool: £1070.25 - 6.69 winning units..
Owner Tim Dykes **Bred** Ken Carroll **Trained** Middleham Moor, N Yorks
■ Stewards' Enquiry : Philip Prince four-day ban: careless riding (Aug 14-17)

FOCUS
Round course rail moved 6yds out from 7f to winning post increasing distances by about 21yds. After 4mm of rain the previous afternoon, the going remained good, good to soft in places with a GoingStick reading of 7.5. Overcast, humid conditions met the runners for this ordinary apprentices' handicap, which was run at a decent pace. Few got into it.

4895 STUBHUB TICKETS CLAIMING STKS 1m 14y
6:20 (6:20) (Class 5) 4-Y-0+ **£3,234** (£962; £481; £240) **Stalls** Low

Form RPR
5000 1 **Brae Hill (IRE)**[18] 4297 7-9-7 92 JamieSpencer 3 97
(Richard Fahey) *mde all and sn set fair pce: gng far bttr than rest over 2f out: rdn out fnl f* **7/4**[1]
2106 2 2¾ **Classic Colori (IRE)**[32] 3812 6-9-1 86 (v) WilliamBuick 2 85
(David O'Meara) *hld up in last and sn detached: pushed along 1/2-way: kpt on u.p fr 2f out to take 2nd nr fin: no ch w wnr* **7/4**[1]
3416 3 ¾ **Balty Boys (IRE)**[18] 4281 4-9-7 89 (b) AdamKirby 4 89
(Jamie Osborne) *disp 2nd tl rdn to chse wnr over 2f out: hd to one side and no imp: lost 2nd nr fin* **9/4**[2]
3500 4 22 **Lowther**[27] 3974 8-9-7 83 (b) KierenFox 1 38
(Lee Carter) *blindfold stl on as stalls opened but lost no grnd: disp 2nd to over 2f out: wknd qckly: t.o* **25/1**[3]

1m 43.45s (0.15) **Going Correction** +0.25s/f (Good) **4** Ran SP% **107.3**
Speed ratings (Par 103): **109,106,105,83**
CSF £5.07 TOTE £2.50; EX 4.60 Trifecta £6.30 Pool: £499.27 - 58.56 winning units..There were no claims.
Owner Dr Marwan Koukash **Bred** James Doyle **Trained** Musley Bank, N Yorks

FOCUS
A paucity of runners, though a relatively competitive claimer run at a fair pace.

4896 BRITISH STALLION STUDS EBF MAIDEN STKS 7f 16y
6:55 (6:55) (Class 5) 2-Y-O **£3,881** (£1,155; £577; £288) **Stalls** Low

Form RPR
3 1 **Voice Of A Leader (IRE)**[19] 4256 2-9-5 0 JamieSpencer 2 89
(Peter Chapple-Hyam) *mde all: gng easily over 2f out: pushed along and in n.d fnl f: unchal* **4/7**[1]
2 4½ **Tornesel** 2-9-5 0 WilliamBuick 5 77
(John Gosden) *chsd ldng pair: pushed into 2nd 2f out: kpt on steadily but no ch w wnr* **4/1**[2]
3 2¼ **Top Tug (IRE)** 2-9-5 0 KierenFallon 4 71+
(Sir Michael Stoute) *chsd ldrs in 5th: pushed along over 2f out: kpt on to take 3rd jst over 1f out: n.d* **8/1**[3]
4 2¼ **Liberty Red (GER)** 2-9-5 0 AndreaAtzeni 9 65
(Ed Dunlop) *dwlt: mostly in 6th: pushed along 3f out: kpt on to take 4th ins fnl f: no ch* **16/1**
5 1¾ **Mishko (IRE)** 2-9-5 0 AdamKirby 7 60
(Clive Cox) *dwlt: chsd ldrs on outer: no imp over 2f out: fdd fnl f* **25/1**
6 5 **Gavlar** 2-9-5 0 JamesDoyle 3 46
(William Knight) *dwlt: rn v green and sn shoved along in detached last: nvr on terms but lost no further grnd fr 1/2-way* **33/1**
0 7 shd **Gloss (IRE)**[19] 4231 2-9-5 0 RichardHughes 1 46
(Richard Hannon) *chsd wnr to 2f out: sn wknd: eased ins fnl f* **10/1**
8 nk **Storm Force Ten** 2-9-5 0 DavidProbert 6 45
(Andrew Balding) *s.s: a in last pair: no prog over 2f out* **20/1**

1m 30.92s (1.42) **Going Correction** +0.25s/f (Good) **8** Ran SP% **121.3**
Speed ratings (Par 94): **101,95,93,90,88 83,82,82**
toteswingers 1&2 £1.50, 1&3 £2.20, 2&3 £5.10 CSF £3.39 TOTE £1.20: £1.02, £1.40, £2.60; EX 4.80 Trifecta £16.00 Pool: £1996.42 - 93.44 winning units..
Owner Mrs Hay,Michael Tabor & Mrs John Magnier **Bred** Lynch Bages Ltd **Trained** Newmarket, Suffolk

The Form Book Flat, Raceform Ltd, Compton, RG20 6NL.

FOCUS
A truly-run race for this juvenile maiden, in which there were some representatives from powerful yards among some modest performers. They finished strung out.

4897 PREMIER LEAGUE CREATING CHANCES H'CAP 1m 14y
7:30 (7:40) (Class 3) (0-90,90) 3-Y-O **£7,439** (£2,213; £1,106; £553) **Stalls Low**

Form RPR

4225 **1** **George Cinq**[37] [3633] 3-9-1 **84**.................................. JamieSpencer 7 92
(Michael Bell) *restrained after s and hld up in last: prog on outer 2f out: str run fnl f to ld last 75yds: hung rt after* **14/1**

1100 **2** *nk* **Sea Shanty (USA)**[20] [4214] 3-9-7 **90**.........................(p) RichardHughes 3 97
(Richard Hannon) *sn led: urged along and narrowly hdd jst over 2f out: rallied on inner and drvn ahd 100yds out: sn hdd: styd on* **6/1**[3]

-010 **3** *1 ½* **So Beloved**[41] [3484] 3-9-7 **90**.................................. JamesDoyle 6 95
(Roger Charlton) *trckd ldrs on outer: moved up to chal 2f out: pushed into ld 1f out: sn rdn and edgd lft then rt: hdd last 100yds: hld whn squeezed out nr fin* **9/2**[2]

6211 **4** *1* **Morpheus**[19] [4236] 3-9-2 **85**.................................. TomQueally 1 88
(Lady Cecil) *t.k.h: hld up in midfield on inner: looking for room over 2f out: eased out wl over 1f out: keeping on but no ch whn nt clr run ins fnl f* **1/1**[1]

1P15 **5** *nse* **Ogbourne Downs**[18] [4280] 3-8-13 **82**.......................... SteveDrowne 10 83
(Charles Hills) *sn trckd ldr: shkn up to ld narrowly jst over 2f out: hdd 1f out: fdd last 100yds* **10/1**

3043 **6** *1 ¼* **Flashlight (IRE)**[11] [4540] 3-9-0 **83**.......................... JoeFanning 2 81
(Mark Johnston) *cl up bhd ldr: rdn 2f out: nt qckn and lost pl over 1f out: one pce whn n.m.r ins fnl f* **16/1**

-404 **7** *3* **Lizzie Tudor**[19] [4252] 3-9-3 **86**.......................... DavidProbert 5 77
(Andrew Balding) *mostly in midfield: rdn and nt qckn over 2f out: nvr on terms after: one pce* **16/1**

53-3 **8** *2* **Beedee**[14] [4415] 3-9-4 **87**.................................. PatDobbs 4 74
(Richard Hannon) *a in rr: last and detached over 2f out: no ch after* **28/1**

2-14 **9** *9* **Granell (IRE)**[53] [3117] 3-9-4 **87**.........................(b[1]) KierenFallon 8 53
(Brian Meehan) *a towards rr: pushed along 1/2-way: wknd over 2f out: t.o* **12/1**

1m 45.29s (1.99) **Going Correction** +0.25s/f (Good) **9** Ran SP% **121.1**
Speed ratings (Par 104): **100,99,98,97,97 95,92,90,81**
toteswingers 1&2 £11.40, 1&3 £15.00, 2&3 £2.10 CSF £99.89 CT £452.72 TOTE £20.00: £3.40, £2.20, £1.20; EX 94.90 Trifecta £502.60 Pool: £2305.46 - 3.43 winning units..
Owner Tamdown Group Limited **Bred** Oakhill Stud **Trained** Newmarket, Suffolk
■ Stewards' Enquiry : Jamie Spencer three-day ban: careless riding (Aug 14-16)

FOCUS
An eventful handicap run at an indifferent pace and it provided something of a shock winner, completing a treble on the night for his rider.

4898 HURST PARK FILLIES' H'CAP 1m 1f
8:00 (8:02) (Class 5) (0-75,75) 3-Y-O+ **£3,881** (£1,155; £577; £288) **Stalls Low**

Form RPR

61-1 **1** **Willow Beck**[27] [3996] 4-9-11 **72**.................................. WilliamBuick 6 81
(John Gosden) *trckd ldrs: rdn over 2f out: making heavy weather of it tl picked up wl to go 2nd ins fnl f: sn clsd and led last 100yds: wl on top at fin* **11/8**[1]

5320 **2** *1* **Running Deer (IRE)**[33] [3765] 4-9-11 **72**.......................... TomQueally 13 79
(Lady Cecil) *dwlt: rapid prog on outer to press ldr after 2f: rdn over 2f out: drvn ahd jst over 1f out: hdd and hld last 100yds* **7/1**[3]

3224 **3** *½* **Tilstarr (IRE)**[32] [3842] 3-8-9 **70**.......................... RobertTart[(5)] 3 75
(Roger Teal) *in tch in midfield: rdn over 2f out: styd on fr over 1f out: maintained effrt to take 3rd nr fin* **16/1**

3-31 **4** *1* **Capella's Song (IRE)**[16] [4356] 3-9-2 **72**.......................... AdamKirby 15 75
(Michael Bell) *mde most: kicked on over 2f out: drvn and hdd jst over 1f out: one pce* **12/1**

605 **5** *shd* **Lybica (IRE)**[61] [2850] 3-8-8 **64**.......................... AndreaAtzeni 14 66
(Gary Moore) *w.w towards rr: rdn and prog on outer 2f out: edgd rt over 1f out: styd on fnl f: nrst fin* **25/1**

-431 **6** *shd* **Familliarity**[14] [4404] 3-9-4 **74**.......................... DaneO'Neill 11 76
(Roger Varian) *trckd ldrs: rdn over 2f out: tried to cl over 1f out but kpt on at same pce* **6/1**[2]

4-60 **7** *2 ¼* **Pearl Street (USA)**[27] [3975] 3-9-0 **70**.......................... JamieSpencer 4 67
(Henry Candy) *stdd s: hld up in last: stl there 3f out: prog on outer 2f out: kpt on but no hope of troubling ldrs* **12/1**

-632 **8** *1 ½* **Mesmerized (IRE)**[11] [4523] 3-8-11 **67**.......................... MartinHarley 5 61
(Marco Botti) *t.k.h: pressed ldrs: rdn over 2f out: stl cl up over 1f out: fdd* **14/1**

0615 **9** *½* **Simply Elegant (IRE)**[47] [3292] 3-9-0 **70**.......................... JimCrowley 7 63
(Amanda Perrett) *trckd ldrs: rdn over 2f out: edgd lft over 1f out: fdd* **16/1**

5304 **10** *5* **Everleigh**[36] [3666] 3-9-4 **74**.........................(b[1]) RichardHughes 12 56
(Richard Hannon) *hld up wl in rr: rdn wl over 2f out: no real prog over 1f out: wknd* **20/1**

5211 **11** *1* **Travelling**[146] [919] 4-9-9 **75**.......................... GeorgeDowning[(5)] 8 56
(Tony Carroll) *towards rr: pushed along 3f out: no prog u.p 2f out: sn wknd* **25/1**

2-62 **12** *½* **Princess Icicle**[84] [2155] 5-9-6 **67**.......................... FergusSweeney 10 47
(Jo Crowley) *in tch in midfield: rdn over 2f out: making no prog whn squeezed out over 1f out: wknd* **50/1**

00-0 **13** *4* **Downhill Dancer (IRE)**[48] [3241] 3-8-2 **58**.......................... MartinLane 9 28
(Brian Meehan) *ponied to post: a wl in rr: pushed along 4f out: no prog* **40/1**

2-12 **14** *44* **Easter Diva (IRE)**[16] [4348] 4-10-0 **75**.......................... JamesDoyle 1
(Gerard Butler) *in tch in midfield tl wknd rapidly over 2f out: eased and wl t.o* **12/1**

1m 57.27s (1.57) **Going Correction** +0.25s/f (Good)
WFA 3 from 4yo+ 9lb **14** Ran SP% **127.3**
Speed ratings (Par 100): **103,102,101,100,100 100,98,97,96,92 91,91,87,48**
toteswingers 1&2 £4.70, 1&3 £8.20, 2&3 £25.10 CSF £10.83 CT £125.72 TOTE £2.10: £1.10, £2.80, £7.10; EX 17.80 Trifecta £247.00 Pool: £2003.78 - 6.08 winning units..
Owner HRH Princess Haya Of Jordan **Bred** Worksop Manor Stud **Trained** Newmarket, Suffolk

FOCUS
A competitive fillies' handicap run at a fair pace for the easy surface. The form looks solid.

4899 HERSHAM H'CAP 1m 6f
8:35 (8:36) (Class 4) (0-80,76) 3-Y-O **£4,851** (£1,443; £721; £360) **Stalls Low**

Form RPR

1-42 **1** **Alwilda**[30] [3908] 3-9-5 **74**.................................. LukeMorris 2 83
(Sir Mark Prescott Bt) *settled in 5th: rdn over 2f out: prog to ld jst over 1f out: sn jnd: battled on wl u.str.p* **15/8**[1]

4222 **2** *½* **Astrum**[7] [4634] 3-9-1 **70**.................................. AndreAtzeni 3 78
(Rod Millman) *sn tucked in bhd ldng pair: rdn over 2f out: clsd to take 2nd 1f out and upsides wnr ins fnl f: jst hld nr fin* **8/1**

5521 **3** *1 ¾* **Sunblazer (IRE)**[16] [4349] 3-9-0 **69**.......................... RichardHughes 1 75
(William Muir) *hld up in last: rdn 4f out: sed to make prog 2f out: kpt on after to take 3rd wl ins fnl f* **7/1**

5231 **4** *1 ¼* **Nateeja (IRE)**[16] [4352] 3-9-5 **74**.......................... PaulHanagan 4 78
(J W Hills) *sn won battle for ld at frntic early pce: set more relaxed gallop after 4f: rdn and hdd 3f out: fought bk tl no ex fnl f* **5/2**[2]

-422 **5** *2 ½* **Thorpe (IRE)**[22] [4150] 3-9-7 **76**.......................... JimCrowley 6 76
(Ralph Beckett) *hld up in 6th: rdn over 2f out: sn nt qckn and no imp on ldrs: n.d after* **5/1**[3]

004 **6** *½* **Rock God (IRE)**[30] [3907] 3-9-4 **73**.......................... JohnFahy 7 73
(Eve Johnson Houghton) *tried to ld but forced to trck ldr after 2f: rdn to ld 3f out: hdd & wknd jst over 1f out* **16/1**

355 **7** *3* **Nellie Forbush**[44] [3402] 3-9-1 **70**.........................(v[1]) DavidProbert 5 65
(Andrew Balding) *sn hld up bhd ldng trio: rdn over 2f out: steadily wknd* **16/1**

3m 8.21s (3.71) **Going Correction** +0.25s/f (Good) **7** Ran SP% **115.4**
Speed ratings (Par 102): **99,98,97,97,95 95,93**
toteswingers 1&2 £1.60, 1&3 £4.70, 2&3 £10.30 CSF £18.06 TOTE £2.70: £1.80, £2.90; EX 17.80 Trifecta £51.90 Pool: £1512.86 - 21.84 winning units..
Owner Miss K Rausing **Bred** Miss K Rausing **Trained** Newmarket, Suffolk

FOCUS
The pace was weak for this competitive 3-y-o handicap but the market proved correct.
T/Plt: £95.40. Pool of £63,487.86 - 485.43 winning units. T/Qpdt: £25.50. Pool of £5790.63 - 167.52 winning units. JN

4900 - 4903a (Foreign Racing) - See Raceform Interactive

[4674]EPSOM (L-H)
Thursday, August 1

OFFICIAL GOING: Good to firm (8.6)
Wind: Strong, across (towards stands) Weather: Fine, hot

4904 RUBBING HOUSE APPRENTICE H'CAP 1m 2f 18y
5:55 (5:56) (Class 5) (0-70,70) 4-Y-O+ **£3,234** (£962; £481; £240) **Stalls Low**

Form RPR

-510 **1** **Attraction Ticket**[57] [2982] 4-9-4 **69**.......................... GeorgeBuckell[(7)] 6 74
(David Simcock) *hld up in last: stdy prog fr 3f out to chse ldr over 1f out: clsd and rdn to ld fnl 100yds: fnd jst enough to hold on* **9/4**[2]

4000 **2** *hd* **Blue Deer (IRE)**[14] [4423] 5-8-9 **53**.........................(p) AshleyMorgan 3 58
(Lee Carter) *led at mod pce: kicked on over 3f out: rdn wl over 1f out: hdd last 100yds: kpt on wl: jst hld* **33/1**

0200 **3** *1* **Market Puzzle (IRE)**[26] [4071] 6-8-0 **51** oh3.................(p) GaryMahon[(7)] 2 54
(Mark Brisbourne) *mostly chsd ldr: edgd rt fr 2f out: lost 2nd over 1f out: stl cl enough ins fnl f: nt qckn* **12/1**

1111 **4** *7* **Green Earth (IRE)**[37] [3656] 6-8-11 **62**.......................... SophieRalston[(7)] 8 51
(Pat Phelan) *prom: cl 4th st: nt qckn over 2f out: short of room briefly sn after: fdd over 1f out* **7/4**[1]

6616 **5** *9* **Silkee Supreme**[157] [789] 4-8-8 **59**.........................(b) StephenKing[(7)] 4 30
(Richard Hannon) *slowly away: racd wd thrght: sn prom: cl 5th st: wknd 2f out* **4/1**[3]

3640 **6** *2 ½* **Honey Of A Kitten (USA)**[13] [4475] 5-9-5 **70**.................(v) EoinWalsh[(7)] 7 36
(David Evans) *restless stalls: prom: disp 2nd st: sn wknd and bhd* **11/2**

2m 12.14s (2.44) **Going Correction** -0.25s/f (Firm) **6** Ran SP% **113.2**
Speed ratings (Par 103): **80,79,79,73,66 64**
toteswingers 1&2 £4.80, 2&3 £11.20, 1&3 £9.50 CSF £57.02 CT £732.35 TOTE £5.60: £2.40, £6.00; EX 102.60 Trifecta £385.70 Pool: £1726.74 - 3.35 winning units..
Owner Oliver Brendon **Bred** The Kathryn Stud Ltd **Trained** Newmarket, Suffolk
■ George Buckell's first winner in Britain, to go with five in Bahrain.

FOCUS
All rail at inner configuration and distances as advertised. A weak apprentice handicap to start and there was little pace early, arguably too much mid-race and, aside from the front three, they finished strung out. They fanned out from the far rail to the centre of the track from 4f out. The form is rated negatively.

4905 HEADLEY H'CAP 6f
6:25 (6:28) (Class 4) (0-85,81) 3-Y-O **£4,690** (£1,395; £697; £348) **Stalls High**

Form RPR

5024 **1** **Fortinbrass (IRE)**[13] [4478] 3-9-7 **81**.......................... RichardKingscote 3 89
(Ralph Beckett) *mde all: rdn and drifted rt over 1f out: styd on wl and in command after* **3/1**[3]

0235 **2** *2 ¼* **Al Udeid (IRE)**[26] [4056] 3-9-3 **77**.........................(p) RichardHughes 4 78
(Kevin Ryan) *trckd wnr over 4f out: shkn up and edgd rt over 2f out: nt qckn after and wl hld fnl f* **7/4**[1]

6-21 **3** *½* **Strictly Silca**[43] [3479] 3-9-6 **80**.........................(v) MartinHarley 2 79
(Mick Channon) *trckd wnr to over 4f out: rdn to dispute 2nd 2f out: nt qckn over 1f out: wl hld after* **2/1**[2]

2221 **4** *18* **Lager Time (IRE)**[6] [4712] 3-8-7 **72** 6ex.......................... DeclanBates[(5)] 1 14
(David Evans) *a in last: nt handle downhill and detached: t.o* **13/2**

1m 8.09s (-1.31) **Going Correction** -0.25s/f (Firm) **4** Ran SP% **108.0**
Speed ratings (Par 102): **98,95,94,70**
CSF £8.54 TOTE £5.30; EX 14.10 Trifecta £23.30 Pool: £1402.28 - 44.97 winning units..
Owner Hillier, Lawrence, Turney & Goddard **Bred** Tom Wallace **Trained** Kimpton, Hants

FOCUS
An competitive handicap run at a decent pace for such a small field. It proved wholly uneventful and produced an all-the-way winner. The winner was back to his penultimate Leicester form.

4906 BRITISH STALLION STUDS EBF MAIDEN STKS 7f
6:55 (6:56) (Class 5) 2-Y-O **£3,881** (£1,155; £577; £288) **Stalls Low**

Form RPR

36 **1** **Grevillea (IRE)**[21] [4215] 2-9-0 0.......................... MartinHarley 1 78
(Mick Channon) *trckd ldng pair: rdn and prog to ld over 1f out: styd on wl* **4/1**[3]

0 **2** *1 ¼* **If (GER)**[20] [4231] 2-9-5 0.......................... LiamKeniry 2 80
(Andrew Balding) *led: drvn and hdd over 1f out: flashed tail once: one pce* **33/1**

62 **3** *3 ¼* **Blue Atlantic (USA)**[11] [4556] 2-9-5 0.......................... SilvestreDeSousa 3 71
(Mark Johnston) *chsd ldr to jst over 2f out: nt qckn u.p: fdd fnl f* **11/4**[2]

42 **4** *4 ½* **Sebs Sensei (IRE)**[38] [3631] 2-9-5 0.......................... RichardHughes 6 60
(Richard Hannon) *trckd ldng trio: rdn ent st: sn struggling: hung rt fr over 2f out: and wl btn after* **5/6**[1]

5 *¾* **Daisy Boy (IRE)** 2-9-5 0.......................... KieranO'Neill 4 58
(Stuart Williams) *dwlt: hld up: 5th st: pushed along and one pce fnl 2f: no imp* **25/1**

06 **6** *1* **Almost Famous (IRE)**[14] 4439 2-9-5 0........................ FergusSweeney 5 55
(Jamie Osborne) *hld up: last st: shkn up briefly over 2f out: no prog* **50/1**
1m 23.22s (-0.08) **Going Correction** -0.25s/f (Firm) **6** Ran SP% **110.0**
Speed ratings (Par 94): **90,88,84,79,78 77**
toteswingers 1&2 £6.20, 2&3 £7.10, 1&3 £1.50 CSF £87.10 TOTE £3.60: £1.30, £5.30; EX 80.70 Trifecta £261.80 Pool: £1799.99 - 5.15 winning units..
Owner N J Hitchins **Bred** Mr & Mrs Nick Hitchins **Trained** West Ilsley, Berks
FOCUS
A reasonable maiden for paucity of runners. They went a fair pace and another hot-pot was turned over. The form makes sense.

4907 TOTEPOOL.COM CONDITIONS STKS 1m 2f 18y
7:30 (7:30) (Class 3) 3-Y-0+ **£7,158** (£2,143; £1,071; £535) **Stalls** Low

Form RPR
4-44 **1** **Cameron Highland (IRE)**[33] 3830 4-9-0 105..............(p[1]) AndreaAtzeni 4 104
(Roger Varian) *mde all stretched clr jst over 2f out: shkn up over 1f out: unchal* **11/4**[2]
14-2 **2** *8* **Ashdan**[21] 4216 3-8-6 107 ow1.. WilliamBuick 2 90
(John Gosden) *cl up: chsd wnr 3f out: sn rdn and fnd nil: no ch over 1f out* **30/100**[1]
4205 **3** *4 1/2* **Cayuga**[48] 3293 4-9-0 80.. KieranO'Neill 3 80
(Brett Johnson) *hld up in last: detached 4f out: clsd over 2f out: shkn up to take 3rd over 1f out: no hdwy after* **33/1**[3]
60-0 **4** *3* **Freddy Q (IRE)**[36] 3692 4-8-7 79.................................. OisinMurphy(7) 1 74?
(Roger Teal) *chsd wnr to 3f out: fdd fnl 2f* **66/1**
2m 4.74s (-4.96) **Going Correction** -0.25s/f (Firm)
WFA 3 from 4yo 9lb **4** Ran SP% **108.0**
Speed ratings (Par 107): **109,102,99,96**
CSF £4.03 TOTE £3.50; EX 3.80 Trifecta £7.70 Pool: £1051.46 - 101.47 winning units..
Owner H R H Sultan Ahmad Shah **Bred** Epona Bloodstock Ltd **Trained** Newmarket, Suffolk
FOCUS
The market was dominated by two of the quartet for this decent conditions event which proved a tactical affair with no great pace. A similar effort from the winner as to when winning this last year.

4908 CHALK LANE H'CAP 1m 114y
8:00 (8:02) (Class 4) (0-80,80) 3-Y-0+ **£4,690** (£1,395; £697; £348) **Stalls** Low

Form RPR
20-0 **1** **Young Dottie**[65] 2745 7-8-9 64.................................. JemmaMarshall(3) 5 73
(Pat Phelan) *trckd ldrs: 5th st: clsd over 2f out: shkn up to ld jst over 1f out: styd on* **50/1**
5413 **2** *1 3/4* **Croquembouche (IRE)**[16] 4366 4-9-7 73.......................... LiamKeniry 4 78
(Ed de Giles) *led: rdn 2f out: hdd and one pce jst over 1f out* **8/1**
3000 **3** *1/2* **Hipster**[24] 4124 3-9-3 77..............................(v) RichardKingscote 8 81
(Ralph Beckett) *trckd ldr: rdn to chal 2f out: nrly upsides jst over 1f out: one pce after* **14/1**
3162 **4** *3/4* **Frozen Over**[28] 3976 5-9-8 74.. AndreaAtzeni 1 76
(Stuart Kittow) *hld up: 7th st: sme prog over 2f out: drvn and kpt on same pce to press for 3rd nr fin* **7/2**[1]
01-3 **5** *3/4* **Intrepid (IRE)**[57] 2984 3-9-4 78... WilliamBuick 2 78+
(Jeremy Noseda) *trckd ldng pair: swtchd lft and tried to cl over 2f out: nt qckn wl over 1f out: one pce after* **7/2**[1]
6310 **6** *1 3/4* **Hunting Rights (USA)**[5] 4769 3-9-4 78.................. SilvestreDeSousa 3 74+
(Mark Johnston) *hld up: in last st: drvn on outer wl over 2f out: hanging but sme prog after: nvr rchd ldrs* **9/2**[2]
1053 **7** *3 1/2* **Elusive Hawk (IRE)**[8] 4628 9-9-2 73............................ DeclanBates(5) 9 61
(David Evans) *hld up: 10th st: jst pushed along on inner and mod prog over 2f out: nvr involved* **20/1**
-310 **8** *3 1/4* **Ghost Runner (IRE)**[54] 3117 3-9-6 80........................... TomQueally 11 61
(Lady Cecil) *hld up: 9th: st: shkn up and tried to make prog over 2f out: sn no hdwy and btn* **10/1**
2055 **9** *5* **Starwatch**[21] 4207 6-9-12 78.................................(v) RichardHughes 10 47
(John Bridger) *chsd ldrs: 6th and rdn st: sn lost pl and btn: eased over 1f out* **11/1**
0544 **10** *7* **Yojimbo (IRE)**[21] 4207 5-9-11 77.. MartinHarley 7 30
(Mick Channon) *towards rr: 8th st: sn struggling and dropped to last pair over 2f out* **7/1**[3]
6010 **11** *1 3/4* **Halling Dancer**[28] 3974 4-9-7 73.. KierenFox 6 22
(Lee Carter) *chsd ldrs: 4th and drvn st: sn wknd qckly* **33/1**
1m 42.58s (-3.52) **Going Correction** -0.25s/f (Firm)
WFA 3 from 4yo+ 8lb **11** Ran SP% **120.0**
Speed ratings (Par 105): **105,103,103,102,101 100,97,94,89,83 81**
toteswingers 1&2 £32.90, 2&3 £26.60, 1&3 £110.90 CSF £414.53 CT £5857.51 TOTE £24.10: £5.00, £2.60, £3.00; EX 211.70 Trifecta £1070.10 Part won..
Owner Chelgate Public Relations Ltd **Bred** Tony J Smith **Trained** Epsom, Surrey
FOCUS
Up front was where it paid to race in this competitive handicap which was run at an average pace. Very few got into it. A surprise winner but the form is taken at face value with the second to form.

4909 BRIDGET FILLIES' H'CAP 7f
8:30 (8:31) (Class 5) (0-75,74) 3-Y-0+ **£3,234** (£962; £481; £240) **Stalls** Low

Form RPR
3122 **1** **Sarangoo**[20] 4243 5-10-0 74.. RichardHughes 2 83
(Malcolm Saunders) *mde all: kicked clr 2f out: in n.d after: pushed out* **8/13**[1]
0-04 **2** *1 1/2* **Batgirl**[7] 4671 6-9-7 67.. KierenFox 1 72
(Martin Smith) *hld up: 4th st: rdn 2f out: prog to take 2nd ins fnl f: styd on but unable to chal* **13/2**[3]
4002 **3** *1 3/4* **Welsh Inlet (IRE)**[22] 4163 5-9-0 60................................... KieranO'Neill 5 60
(John Bridger) *chsd ldng pair: rdn 2f out: sn outpcd: kpt on fnl f* **14/1**
2605 **4** *1 1/4* **Baby Dottie**[29] 3955 6-8-8 57.................................(t) JemmaMarshall(3) 8 54
(Pat Phelan) *pressed wnr: nt qckn wl over 1f out: hld after: wknd ins fnl f* **16/1**
3514 **5** *nse* **Renoir's Lady**[14] 4424 5-8-9 55 oh1.................................... AndreaAtzeni 4 52
(Simon Dow) *stdd s: hld up in last: shuffled along 2f out: styd on ins fnl f: nvr involved* **4/1**[2]
0-00 **6** *13* **Silvee**[19] 4303 6-8-6 55 oh5... SimonPearce(3) 7 17
(John Bridger) *chsd ldng trio to 4f out: sn struggling: t.o* **28/1**
1m 22.62s (-0.68) **Going Correction** -0.25s/f (Firm)
WFA 3 from 5yo+ 6lb **6** Ran SP% **111.3**
Speed ratings (Par 100): **93,91,89,87,87 72**
toteswingers 1&2 £1.50, 2&3 £3.20, 1&3 £2.10 CSF £5.14 CT £25.55 TOTE £1.30: £1.10, £2.90; EX 5.10 Trifecta £16.60 Pool: £1210.48 - 54.36 winning units..
Owner Lockstone Business Services Ltd **Bred** M S Saunders And Chris Scott **Trained** Green Ore, Somerset
FOCUS
A pretty weak fillies' handicap which shaped to be a tactical affair on paper, and so it proved. The winner is rated to her Chepstow latest.

T/Plt: £6,607.50 to a £1 stake. Pool of £50235.80 - 5.55 winning tickets. T/Qpdt: £288.30 to a £1 stake. Pool of £4753.88 - 12.20 winning tickets. JN

4602 FFOS LAS (L-H)
Thursday, August 1
OFFICIAL GOING: Good (good to soft in places; 7.6)
Wind: moderate against Weather: sunny spells

4910 RAY GRAVELL AND FRIENDS CHARITABLE TRUST NURSERY H'CAP 5f
5:40 (5:41) (Class 5) (0-75,70) 2-Y-0 **£2,587** (£770; £384; £192) **Stalls** Centre

Form RPR
4426 **1** **M'Selle (IRE)**[5] 4783 2-9-7 70.. SteveDrowne 3 75
(Ronald Harris) *cl up: pushed along over 2f out: chal 1f out: sn led: drvn to assert fnl 50yds* **5/2**[2]
0054 **2** *3/4* **Outback Lover (IRE)**[8] 4639 2-8-9 65......................(b) JoeyHaynes(7) 6 67
(J S Moore) *led: rdn 2f out: jnd 1f out: sn hdd: no ex fnl 50yds* **5/1**[3]
5543 **3** *1 3/4* **Resist**[16] 4363 2-8-12 61.. MartinLane 2 57
(Tobias B P Coles) *hld up: rdn over 2f out: sn chsng ldrs: unable qck fnl f* **2/1**[1]
3556 **4** *shd* **Narborough**[16] 4363 2-8-13 62.. SamHitchcott 4 57
(Mick Channon) *hld up in rr: clsd after 2f: sn rdn: kpt on one pce* **7/1**
4065 **5** *1 3/4* **Paradise Child**[22] 4174 2-7-12 54...............................(b[1]) NoelGarbutt(7) 5 43
(Bill Turner) *racd keenly: hld up bhd ldrs: rdn 2f out: sn one pce and no imp* **8/1**
0505 **6** *2 3/4* **Chilly In Rio (IRE)**[23] 4141 2-8-2 51...............................(p) CathyGannon 1 30
(William Muir) *prom early: outpcd and dropped to rr after 2f: edgd lft u.p over 1f out: sn wknd* **12/1**
1m 0.86s (2.56) **Going Correction** +0.075s/f (Good) **6** Ran SP% **109.9**
Speed ratings (Par 94): **82,80,78,77,75 70**
toteswingers 1&2 £3.50, 2&3 £3.20, 1&3 £1.30 CSF £14.48 TOTE £2.70: £1.60, £4.90; EX 20.90 Trifecta £43.50 Pool: £1669.10 - 28.74 winning units..
Owner Robert & Nina Bailey **Bred** Kilshannig Stud **Trained** Earlswood, Monmouths
FOCUS
A routine sprint nursery. The winner is rated back towards her early form.

4911 BRITISH STALLION STUDS EBF MAIDEN STKS 6f
6:15 (6:15) (Class 5) 3-Y-0 **£3,881** (£1,155; £577; £288) **Stalls** Centre

Form RPR
3225 **1** **The Dark Wizard (IRE)**[19] 4303 3-9-5 70........................(p) MartinLane 3 74
(Roger Charlton) *chsd ldrs: wnt 2nd 3f out: rdn to ld 1f out: a holding runner-up* **4/6**[1]
223 **2** *3/4* **Hand Grenade (IRE)**[8] 4627 3-9-0 0...................................... JohnFahy 2 67
(Eve Johnson Houghton) *reacked keenly: trckd ldr tl led over 3f out: rdn over 1f out: sn hdd: kpt on but a being hld* **9/1**[3]
3 *3* **Enfijaar (IRE)** 3-9-0 0.. DaneO'Neill 4 59
(William Haggas) *s.i.s: hld up in last: hdwy to trck ldrs over 2f out: effrt over 1f out: sn hld by ldng pair: eased ins fnl f* **7/4**[2]
-404 **4** *29* **Rectory Lane**[55] 3036 3-9-0 50.....................................(b) SteveDrowne 1
(Eve Johnson Houghton) *led over 2f: qckly dropped to rr: reminders 2f out: wknd bdly: t.o* **50/1**
1m 11.79s (1.79) **Going Correction** +0.075s/f (Good) **4** Ran SP% **108.3**
Speed ratings (Par 100): **91,90,86,47**
CSF £7.07 TOTE £1.60; EX 5.20 Trifecta £6.20 Pool: £417.67 - 50.47 winning units..
Owner P Inglett & D Carter **Bred** Rossenarra Bloodstock Limited **Trained** Beckhampton, Wilts
FOCUS
A weak sprint maiden. The 1-2 are rated to their turf bests, although the time was slow.

4912 BULMERS CIDER/BRITISH STALLION STUDS EBF MAIDEN STKS 5f
6:45 (6:45) (Class 5) 2-Y-0 **£2,911** (£866; £432; £216) **Stalls** Centre

Form RPR
023 **1** **Kickboxer (IRE)**[5] 4781 2-9-5 0.. SamHitchcott 1 74
(Mick Channon) *chsd ldr: rdn over 2f out: r.o u.p to ld last strides* **8/1**[3]
3200 **2** *hd* **Urban Dreamer (IRE)**[12] 4528 2-8-12 75......................... PatMillman(7) 4 73
(Rod Millman) *led: rdn 2 l clr over 2f out: kpt on u.p: hdd last strides* **4/1**[2]
0 **3** *1* **Amnesia (IRE)**[21] 4215 2-9-0 0.. DaneO'Neill 2 64
(William Haggas) *chsd ldng pair: rdn over 1f out: kpt on same pce* **1/2**[1]
4 *1/2* **High On Life** 2-9-5 0.. MartinLane 3 69+
(Jamie Osborne) *s.s: in rr: shkn up over 1f out: 3rd and running on whn n.m.r and briefly eased ins fnl f* **20/1**
4 **5** *4* **Drive On (IRE)**[7] 4680 2-9-5 0.. JohnFahy 5 53
(Eve Johnson Houghton) *racd in 4th: pushed along over 2f out: no imp on ldrs: hung lft and wknd ins fnl f* **16/1**
59.1s (0.80) **Going Correction** +0.075s/f (Good) **5** Ran SP% **108.4**
Speed ratings (Par 94): **96,95,94,93,86**
CSF £36.85 TOTE £6.30: £1.80, £1.70; EX 15.20 Trifecta £31.10 Pool: £1101.82 - 26.53 winning units..
Owner Mrs T Burns **Bred** Rathasker Stud **Trained** West Ilsley, Berks
FOCUS
A modest little maiden. The form is rated around the second and third.

4913 RED LION AT LLANDYFAELOG H'CAP 2m (R)
7:15 (7:16) (Class 4) (0-80,79) 4-Y-0+ **£4,690** (£1,395; £697; £348) **Stalls** Low

Form RPR
642 **1** **Eshtyaaq**[9] 4606 6-8-7 65.. CathyGannon 1 74
(David Evans) *hld up in rr: racd keenly: rapid hdwy to ld after 6f: qcknd over 3f out: styd on strly fnl 2f* **16/1**
612 **2** *2 3/4* **Presto Volante (IRE)**[29] 3959 5-9-7 79..............................(p) DaneO'Neill 3 85
(Amanda Perrett) *in tch: rdn over 2f out: r.o to take 2nd nr fin* **9/2**[2]
-162 **3** *1/2* **Filatore (IRE)**[29] 3952 4-8-8 73..............................(p) DanielMuscutt(7) 4 78
(Bernard Llewellyn) *prom: chsd wnr over 3f out: sn rdn and no imp: lost 2nd nr fin* **12/1**
0433 **4** *3 1/4* **Montaff**[15] 4407 7-9-5 77.. SamHitchcott 7 78
(Mick Channon) *s.i.s: hld up in rr: hdwy on ins to chse ldrs over 3f out: wknd fnl f* **16/1**
-104 **5** *2* **Sign Manual**[34] 3765 4-9-7 79.. JohnFahy 2 78
(Michael Bell) *hld up towards rr: rdn over 2f out: styd on: nvr trbld ldrs* **7/2**[1]
2323 **6** *nk* **Gabrial's King (IRE)**[19] 4313 4-9-6 78............................ KirstyMilczarek 9 76
(David Simcock) *towards rr: sme hdwy on ins 3f out: nvr trbld ldrs* **9/2**[2]
0-55 **7** *2 1/4* **L Frank Baum (IRE)**[9] 4606 6-8-13 78............................... JoeyHaynes(7) 5 74
(Bernard Llewellyn) *led 6f: styd prom: lost 2nd over 3f out: one pce fnl 2f* **20/1**

The Form Book Flat, Raceform Ltd, Compton, RG20 6NL.

-125 **8** 3 3/4 **Zarosa (IRE)**[38] 3627 4-7-11 **62** NoelGarbutt(7) 11 53
(John Berry) *chsd ldrs: pushed along over 4f out: wknd over 1f out* **12/1**
565 **9** 2 3/4 **Gabrial's Star**[34] 3765 4-9-7 **79** (p) SteveDrowne 6 67
(Ian Williams) *a towards rr: rdn over 2f out: no imp* **8/1**
3010 **10** 2 1/2 **Riptide**[40] 3560 7-9-4 **76** RussKennemore 8 61
(Michael Scudamore) *prom: rdn 4f out: wknd over 2f out* **25/1**
6111 **11** 1 1/4 **Kashgar**[33] 3807 4-9-4 **76** MartinLane 10 59
(Bernard Llewellyn) *mid-div: outpcd and rdn over 3f out: wknd over 2f out* **7/1**[3]

3m 31.79s (1.79) **Going Correction** +0.075s/f (Good) **11** Ran SP% **118.0**
Speed ratings (Par 105): **98,96,96,94,93 93,92,90,89,87 87**
toteswingers 1&2 £12.10, 2&3 £6.80, 1&3 £16.50 CSF £86.94 CT £915.64 TOTE £16.90: £3.40, £1.40, £4.10; EX 114.70 Trifecta £609.90 Part won..
Owner Trevor Gallienne **Bred** P T Tellwright **Trained** Pandy, Monmouths

FOCUS
A modest staying handicap in which the winner made all. Ordinary, slightly muddling form.

4914 EP INDUSTRIES H'CAP 1m 4f (R)
7:45 (7:46) (Class 3) (0-90,89) 3-Y-0+ **£7,439** (£2,213; £1,106; £553) **Stalls** Low

Form RPR
2-14 **1** **Astra Hall**[59] 2923 4-8-10 **71** JohnFahy 4 80
(Ralph Beckett) *hld up in 6th: hdwy to chse clr ldng pair wl over 2f out: r.o to ld fnl 100yds: rdn clr* **14/1**
2-31 **2** 1 3/4 **Stock Hill Fair**[62] 2849 5-9-5 **85** MatthewLawson(5) 7 91
(Brendan Powell) *chsd ldrs: wnt 2nd 6f out: tk narrow ld 4f out: duelled w 3rd tl hdd and one pce fnl 100yds* **17/2**
6/10 **3** nk **Sir Bedivere (IRE)**[77] 2385 4-9-7 **82** (t) NickyMackay 5 87
(Brian Meehan) *led: narrowly hdd 4f out: rdn over 2f out: stl ev ch 1f out tl no ex fnl 100yds* **14/1**
1213 **4** 1 **Edwyn Ralph**[20] 4249 3-8-4 **76** MartinLane 2 80
(David Simcock) *in tch: outpcd by ldng pair 4f out: rdn and briefly in 3rd 3f out: styd on towards fin* **3/1**[2]
-135 **5** 2 3/4 **Mama Quilla (USA)**[33] 3834 4-9-1 **76** DaneO'Neill 6 76
(William Haggas) *a same pl: rdn over 3f out: one pce over 1f out* **9/2**[3]
1436 **6** 7 **Poetic Verse**[20] 4234 3-8-4 **76** CathyGannon 1 64
(Rod Millman) *hld up in last: rdn over 3f out: no hdwy fnl 2f* **16/1**
6/62 **7** 1 1/2 **Sadler's Risk (IRE)**[6] 4720 5-10-0 **89** ConorO'Farrell 8 75
(Mark Johnston) *trckd ldr 6f: styd prom: rdn over 3f out: wknd 2f out* **13/8**[1]
1-6 **8** 3/4 **Kayalar (IRE)**[24] 1973 5-8-11 **72** KirstyMilczarek 3 57
(Evan Williams) *wnt lft s: a in rr* **40/1**

2m 37.69s (0.29) **Going Correction** +0.075s/f (Good)
WFA 3 from 4yo+ 11lb **8** Ran SP% **113.5**
Speed ratings (Par 107): **102,100,100,99,98 93,92,91**
toteswingers 1&2 £17.40, 2&3 £8.50, 1&3 £8.10 CSF £123.09 CT £1694.07 TOTE £10.40: £3.50, £2.30, £4.40; EX 101.40 Trifecta £723.00 Part won..
Owner G B Balding **Bred** Miss B Swire **Trained** Kimpton, Hants

FOCUS
A steadily run handicap until the second and third kicked on early in the straight. The winner still has a bit of potential in her.

4915 RAY GRAVELL AND FRIENDS CHARITABLE TRUST H'CAP 1m 4f (R)
8:15 (8:16) (Class 5) (0-70,71) 4-Y-0+ **£2,587** (£770; £384; £192) **Stalls** Low

Form RPR
00-1 **1** **Bohemian Rhapsody (IRE)**[6] 4714 4-9-13 **71** 6ex ConorO'Farrell 2 85+
(Seamus Durack) *in tch in 5th: clsd 5f out: nt clr run and swtchd rt over 2f out: chsd ldr over 1f out: led ins fnl f: readily* **10/11**[1]
04-4 **2** 1 **Mister Fizz**[13] 4489 5-8-12 **63** DanielCremin(7) 5 72
(Miss Imogen Pickard) *trckd ldr tl led over 4f out: rdn over 1f out: hdd ins fnl f: unable qck* **18/1**
360 **3** 8 **James Pollard (IRE)**[6] 4714 8-9-6 **64** (t) MartinLane 3 60
(Bernard Llewellyn) *hld up towards rr: hdwy over 3f out: disp 2nd 2f out: sn one pce* **20/1**
0012 **4** 2 3/4 **Stag Hill (IRE)**[9] 4604 4-8-8 **59** JoeyHaynes(7) 4 51
(Bernard Llewellyn) *in tch: chsd ldr 3f out tl over 1f out: wknd* **5/1**[3]
0-21 **5** 1 1/2 **On Stage**[27] 4036 4-9-3 **61** CathyGannon 1 50
(Stuart Kittow) *in rr: hdwy over 3f out: rdn over 2f out: wknd over 1f out* **9/2**[2]
5236 **6** 3 3/4 **Taste The Wine (IRE)**[6] 4714 7-8-13 **64** DanielMuscutt(7) 7 47
(Bernard Llewellyn) *in tch: rdn to chse ldr 4f out: lost 2nd 3f out: wknd 2f out* **9/1**
330- **7** 29 **Bazart**[267] 6232 11-8-6 **57** (b) LouisSteward(7) 6
(Bernard Llewellyn) *led tl over 4f out: sn wknd: t.o fnl 2f* **33/1**

2m 37.37s (-0.03) **Going Correction** +0.075s/f (Good) **7** Ran SP% **110.2**
Speed ratings (Par 103): **103,102,97,95,94 91,72**
toteswingers 1&2 £5.10, 2&3 £6.30, 1&3 £5.00 CSF £18.46 TOTE £1.90: £1.20, £5.50; EX 19.20 Trifecta £126.10 Pool: £1136.97 - 6.75 winning units..
Owner A A Byrne **Bred** Sweetmans Bloodstock **Trained** Baydon, Wilts

FOCUS
An ordinary handicap. The winner built on his Chepstow win, with the form rated around the runner-up.

4916 WRW GROUP H'CAP 6f
8:50 (8:51) (Class 6) (0-60,58) 3-Y-0 **£1,940** (£577; £288; £144) **Stalls** Centre

Form RPR
4602 **1** **Angels Calling**[6] 4722 3-8-10 **54** JoeyHaynes(7) 3 64
(Mrs K Burke) *chsd ldr: rdn to ld ins fnl f: r.o wl to draw clr fnl 100yds* **11/8**[1]
-060 **2** 3 **Dee Aitch Dove**[36] 3679 3-9-6 **57** DaneO'Neill 2 57
(George Baker) *racd in centre: led: rdn 2f out: sn edgd rt: hdd ins fnl f: no ex fnl 100yds* **10/1**
0335 **3** 1 1/4 **Tregereth (IRE)**[16] 4368 3-9-1 **57** MatthewLawson(5) 6 53
(Jonathan Portman) *chsd ldrs: rdn over 2f out: kpt on same pce* **3/1**[2]
-563 **4** 2 **New Rich**[7] 4654 3-9-6 **57** JohnFahy 5 47
(Eve Johnson Houghton) *hld up in tch: effrt over 2f out: sn edgd lft and no imp on ldrs* **5/1**[3]
2624 **5** 1 1/4 **Imperial Spirit**[9] 4607 3-9-2 **53** SamHitchcott 4 39
(Mick Channon) *prom: rdn over 1f out: sn one pce* **6/1**
4-5 **6** 7 **Frosted Off**[38] 3621 3-9-7 **58** CathyGannon 1 21
(John Spearing) *wnt to post early: racd keenly: hld up in tch: hdwy over 2f out: sn ev ch: wknd appr fnl f* **14/1**

1m 12.3s (2.30) **Going Correction** +0.075s/f (Good) **6** Ran SP% **113.8**
Speed ratings (Par 98): **87,83,81,78,77 67**
toteswingers 1&2 £6.20, 2&3 £2.70, 1&3 £1.90 CSF £16.54 TOTE £2.30: £1.60, £2.70; EX 16.40 Trifecta £60.20 Pool: £1704.59 - 21.21 winning units..
Owner Ontoawinner & Mrs E Burke **Bred** Kb Spigot Ltd **Trained** Middleham Moor, N Yorks

FOCUS
A weak sprint handicap. The winner built on her previous winning form, which came over C&D.
T/Plt: £373.10 to a £1 stake. Pool of £51334.22 -100.43 winning tickets. T/Qpdt: £50.30 to a £1 stake.Pool of £5977.12 - 87.90 winning tickets. RL

4873 GOODWOOD (R-H)
Thursday, August 1

OFFICIAL GOING: Good (good to soft in a few places) changing to good after race 1 (2.15)
Wind: light to medium, half behind Weather: sunny and warm

4917 GORDON'S STKS (H'CAP) 1m 1f 192y
2:15 (2:15) (Class 2) 3-Y-O
£31,125 (£6,990; £6,990; £2,330; £1,165; £585) **Stalls** Low

Form RPR
2126 **1** **Broughton (GER)**[19] 4279 3-8-1 **86** FrannyNorton 10 95+
(Mark Johnston) *chsd ldr tl squeezed for room and hmpd ent fnl 3f: chsd ldrs after: swtchd lft and hdwy ent fnl f: r.o wl to ld fnl 50yds: rdn out* **8/1**
0012 **2** 3/4 **Red Avenger (USA)**[21] 4214 3-8-10 **95** RyanMoore 7 102
(Ed Dunlop) *chsd ldrs: wnt 2nd 3f out: drvn to chal over 2f out: forged ahd gamely over 1f out: hdd and no ex fnl 50yds* **11/2**[3]
0126 **2** dht **Aussie Reigns (IRE)**[19] 4295 3-8-1 **86** ow1 (v) AndreaAtzeni 1 93
(William Knight) *hld up in tch in midfield: rdn and effrt on inner 2f out: hdwy ent fnl f: swtchd lft ins fnl f: kpt on wl towards fin* **25/1**
-161 **4** 1 1/4 **Noble Gift**[22] 4168 3-8-0 **85** oh3 JimmyQuinn 8 90+
(William Knight) *s.i.s: hld up in rr: stuck bhd horses on inner over 2f out: switching lft over 1f out then bk rt and hdwy 1f out: n.m.r but running on whn forced to switch lft again fnl 75yds: r.o: nt rch ldrs* **14/1**
-401 **5** nk **Code Of Honor**[27] 4028 3-8-11 **96** JamesDoyle 9 100
(Henry Candy) *in tch in midfield: effrt u.p pce over 2f out: chsd ldrs but unable qck 1f out: styd on same pce after* **4/1**[1]
1321 **6** 1 **Mushaakis (IRE)**[12] 4542 3-8-1 **86** PaulHanagan 5 88
(Mark Johnston) *led: rdn wl over 2f out: jnd and duelled w rival over 2f out tl hdd over 1f out: wknd wl ins fnl f* **10/1**
2104 **7** shd **Cruck Realta**[13] 4473 3-8-10 **95** MartinHarley 4 97
(Mick Channon) *chsd ldrs: edgd rt u.p and unable qck over 1f out: kpt on same pce fnl f* **20/1**
-362 **8** hd **Buckstay (IRE)**[66] 2717 3-8-0 **85** oh9 KieranO'Neill 2 86
(Peter Chapple-Hyam) *t.k.h: hld up in tch towards rr: rdn and effrt ent fnl 2f: edging out lft over 1f out: kpt on fnl f: nvr gng pce to rch ldrs* **50/1**
6112 **9** shd **Double Discount (IRE)**[20] 4251 3-8-5 **90** JoeFanning 6 91
(Tom Dascombe) *lw: dwlt: sn rcvrd and in tch in midfield: rdn and unable qck over 2f out: outpcd over 1f out: one pce after* **12/1**
-361 **10** 1 1/2 **Ajmany (IRE)**[13] 4502 3-8-8 **93** ow1 (b) RichardHughes 13 91
(Luca Cumani) *stdd s: hld up in last pair: stuck bhd horses 2f out: rdn and sme hdwy ent fnl f: no imp ins fnl f* **8/1**
-201 **11** 1/2 **Tha'ir (IRE)**[12] 4537 3-9-7 **106** SilvestreDeSousa 12 103
(Saeed bin Suroor) *lw: in tch in midfield on outer: rdn and no rspnse over 2f out: one pce and btn over 1f out* **9/2**[2]
0002 **12** 3 1/4 **Mundahesh (IRE)**[26] 4084 3-8-0 **85** oh1 DavidProbert 11 76
(William Haggas) *b.hind: hld up in tch towards rr: n.m.r and shuffled bk over 2f out: n.d after* **20/1**
1126 **13** 2 1/2 **King George River (IRE)**[5] 4779 3-9-4 **103** KierenFallon 3 89
(Alan Bailey) *t.k.h: hld up in tch in last trio: shkn up 2f out: rdn and no hdwy over 1f out: wknd ins fnl f* **12/1**

2m 5.81s (-2.29) **Going Correction** -0.15s/f (Firm) **13** Ran SP% **122.3**
Speed ratings (Par 106): **103,102,102,101,101 100,100,100,100,98 98,95,93**PL: Red Avenger £2.00, Aussie Reigns £6.60 EX: Broughton/RA £29.90 B/AR £183.70 CSF: B/RA £25.21 B/AR £101.21 TRICAST: B/RA/AR £538.87 B/AR/RA £603.44 toteswingers: RA&1 £10.70, RA&AR £34.50, 1&AR £63.90 CSF £101.21 CT £603.44 TOTE £8.90: £3.00; EX 183.70 TRIFECT27 Owner.

FOCUS
Fresh ground provided on last 3.5f from lower bend to Winning Post. Top bend dolled out 3yds, lower bend out 5yds, increasing distances on Round course by about 10yds.Drying ground all the time on what was a hot, sunny day, and following feedback from those who rode in the opener, the ground was changed to good. Times suggested it was drying throughout the afternoon. A good, competitive 3yo handicap, run at a fair gallop, and the form looks rock-solid. The winner may prove better than a handicapper. The runners stayed on the inside in the straight.

4918 AUDI RICHMOND STKS (GROUP 2) (C&G) 6f
2:45 (2:45) (Class 1) 2-Y-O
£42,532 (£16,125; £8,070; £4,020; £2,017; £1,012) **Stalls** High

Form RPR
110 **1** **Saayerr**[42] 3481 2-9-0 94 RyanMoore 1 108
(William Haggas) *wnt rt s: t.k.h and sn chsng ldrs: rdn to chse ldr ent fnl 2f: drvn and chal over 1f out: led fnl 100yds: r.o gamely* **5/1**[2]
41 **2** nk **Cable Bay (IRE)**[59] 2925 2-9-0 0 JamieSpencer 10 107
(Charles Hills) *w'like: stdd s: hld up in rr: switching rt and hdwy u.p over 1f out: str chal and edgd rt fnl 100yds: kpt on but hld cl home* **20/1**
1145 **3** 2 1/4 **Thunder Strike**[13] 4486 2-9-0 101 RichardHughes 3 100
(Richard Hannon) *led: rdn and qcknd 2f out: sustained duel w wnr tl hdd fnl 100yds: wknd towards fin* **7/1**
12 **4** 1/2 **Figure Of Speech (IRE)**[21] 4212 2-9-0 0 MickaelBarzalona 5 99
(Charlie Appleby) *awkward as stall opened and dwlt: t.k.h: sn rcvrd and hld up in tch: travelling wl and nt clr run over 1f out tl ent fnl f: drvn and kpt on same pce fnl f* **2/1**[1]
1534 **5** shd **Jallota**[12] 4547 2-9-0 103 MartinHarley 8 98
(Mick Channon) *lw: hld up in tch towards rr: nt clr run and swtchd rt jst over 1f out: hrd drvn and kpt on fnl f: nvr gng pce to chal* **8/1**
410 **6** hd **Ben Hall (IRE)**[44] 3424 2-9-0 97 WilliamBuick 2 98
(John Gosden) *wl in tch in midfield on outer: rdn and struggling to qckn whn pushed rt over 1f out: sn outpcd and btn fnl 150yds* **6/1**[3]
3121 **7** nk **Salford Red Devil**[20] 4248 2-9-0 90 JimCrowley 4 97
(Richard Fahey) *on toes: chsd ldrs: rdn ent fnl 2f: drvn and no ex 1f out: sn outpcd and no ex ins fnl f* **16/1**
1201 **8** 1/2 **Andhesontherun (IRE)**[14] 4434 2-9-0 93 AndreaAtzeni 6 95
(Roger Varian) *chsd ldr tl unable qck u.p ent fnl 2f: btn 1f out: wknd ins fnl f* **9/1**
4111 **9** 1 1/4 **Miracle Of Medinah**[13] 4486 2-9-0 99 LiamKeniry 11 91
(Mark Usher) *in tch towards rr: rdn and no imp ent fnl 2f: edgd rt and btn 1f out* **8/1**

6310 **10** *nk* **Bahamian Heights**[21] 4212 2-9-0 88.................... JamesDoyle 7 91
(Clive Brittain) *in tch in midfield: effrt but no imp over 1f out: wknd ins fnl f* **50/1**

1m 10.14s (-2.06) **Going Correction** -0.325s/f (Firm) **10** Ran SP% **121.6**
Speed ratings (Par 106): **100,99,96,95,95 95,95,94,92,92**
toteswingers 1&2 £15.70, 2&3 £17.60, 1&3 £4.30 CSF £102.96 TOTE £6.00: £2.00, £5.40, £2.10; EX 138.20 Trifecta £735.30 Pool: £6821.51 - 6.95 winning units..
Owner Sheikh Ahmed Al Maktoum **Bred** Cheveley Park Stud Ltd **Trained** Newmarket, Suffolk

FOCUS
Probably only fair form for the grade, with it being a bit of a messy contest, and the main action unfolded down the centre of the track. The first two improved but it was an ordinary renewal.

4919 ARTEMIS GOODWOOD CUP (BRITISH CHAMPIONS SERIES) (GROUP 2) 2m
3:15 (3:15) (Class 1) 3-Y-0+

£56,710 (£21,500; £10,760; £5,360; £2,690; £1,350) **Stalls** Low

Form RPR
30-1 **1** **Brown Panther**[39] 3608 5-9-7 113.................... RichardKingscote 2 117
(Tom Dascombe) *lw: chsd ldr tl 7f out: chsd ldng pair after: rdn and chal between horses whn edgd lft 2f: sn led: clr 1f out: r.o strly: readily* **13/2**[3]

2122 **2** *3 ½* **Ahzeemah (IRE)**[21] 4213 4-9-7 111....................(p) KierenFallon 4 113
(Saeed bin Suroor) *lw: in tch in midfield: 6th and rdn whn galloped qcknd over 4f out: swtchd lft 2f out: styng on whn swtchd lft again over 1f out: chsd clr wnr 1f out: kpt on but no imp* **12/1**

2-15 **3** *¾* **Altano (GER)**[42] 3483 7-9-7 112....................(t) EPedroza 9 112+
(A Wohler, Germany) *hld up in last quintet: clsd over 7f out: outpcd whn galloped qcknd 4f out: rdn and plenty to do over 3f out: hdwy over 1f out: styd on wl to go 3rd fnl 100yds: nvr trbld ldrs* **8/1**

4203 **4** *1 ¼* **Number Theory**[19] 4309 5-9-7 107.................... FrannyNorton 6 110
(John Holt) *lw: chsd ldrs: rdn over 3f out: effrt to ld whn edgd rt and jostled rival 2f out: sn hdd and unable qck: kpt on same pce after* **33/1**

-136 **5** *nk* **No Heretic**[40] 3560 5-9-7 95.................... JimCrowley 14 110
(David Simcock) *led: stdd gallop 7f out: qcknd gallop again over 4f out: rdn and hdd 2f out: styd on same pce after* **50/1**

3153 **6** *1* **Cavalryman**[21] 4213 7-9-7 114.................... MickaelBarzalona 5 109
(Saeed bin Suroor) *hld up off the pce in midfield: clsd 7f out: outpcd whn galloped qcknd over 4f out: rdn 3f out: hdwy over 1f out: kpt on steadily ins fnl f: nvr trbld ldrs* **14/1**

0-04 **7** *1* **Colour Vision (FR)**[42] 3483 5-9-7 113....................(v) SilvestreDeSousa 13 108
(Saeed bin Suroor) *s.i.s: t.k.h and sn in tch in midfield: 8th and outpcd whn galloped qcknd over 4f out: styd on steadily fr over 1f out: nvr threatened ldrs* **8/1**

0-15 **8** *1* **Mount Athos (IRE)**[40] 3556 6-9-7 117.................... JamieSpencer 12 106
(Luca Cumani) *hld up in rr: clsd 7f out: outpcd and bhd again whn gallop qcknd over 4f out: plenty to do and effrt on outer over 2f out: awkward hd carriage but plugged on ins fnl f: nvr trbld ldrs* **3/1**[1]

1-21 **9** *1 ¼* **Caucus**[26] 4083 6-9-7 110.................... WilliamBuick 1 105
(John Gosden) *t.k.h: hld up towards rr: clsd 7f out: outpcd whn gallop qcknd over 4f out: rdn and effrt 3f out: kpt edging rt and nvr much room fr over 1f out: plugged on: nvr trbld ldrs* **5/1**[2]

3-00 **10** *1 ½* **Askar Tau (FR)**[63] 2810 8-9-7 105....................(v) GeorgeBaker 7 103
(Marcus Tregoning) *dwlt: hld up in rr: clsd 7f out: outpcd and bhd whn gallop qcknd over 4f out: rdn over 3f out: sme hdwy on inner over 1f out: nvr trbld ldrs* **33/1**

2443 **11** *1 ¾* **Mister Impatience**[13] 4473 3-8-6 97.................... JoeFanning 11 101
(Mark Johnston) *chsd ldrs tl wnt 2nd 7f out: rdn and struggling to qckn whn jostled 2f out: sn btn and wknd over 1f out* **25/1**

-500 **12** *¾* **Saddler's Rock (IRE)**[42] 3483 5-9-7 112....................(t) DeclanMcDonogh 8 100
(John M Oxx, Ire) *racd in midfield: 5th and rdn over 4f out: no imp u.p over 2f out: wknd over 1f out* **10/1**

4-15 **13** *12* **Glen's Diamond**[32] 3873 5-9-7 113.................... TonyHamilton 10 86
(Richard Fahey) *hld up in midfield: rdn whn gallop qcknd over 4f out: lost pl and bhd whn edgd over 1f out: eased ins fnl f* **33/1**

6-04 **14** *18* **Repeater**[26] 4083 4-9-7 102....................(p) RichardHughes 3 76
(Sir Mark Prescott Bt) *stdd s: hld up in rr: clsd 7f out: outpcd whn gallop qcknd over 4f out: rdn no hdwy 3f out: bhd and swtchd rt over 2f out: sn eased: t.o* **25/1**

3m 22.79s (-6.21) **Going Correction** -0.15s/f (Firm)
WFA 3 from 4yo+ 15lb **14** Ran SP% **119.1**
Speed ratings (Par 115): **109,107,106,106,106 105,105,104,103,103 102,101,95,86**
toteswingers 1&2 £51.30, 2&3 £20.20, 1&3 £8.40 CSF £74.89 TOTE £6.90: £2.20, £3.40, £3.20; EX 119.90 Trifecta £576.00 Pool: £3364.07 - 4.38 winning units..
Owner A Black & Owen Promotions Limited **Bred** Owen Promotions Ltd **Trained** Malpas, Cheshire
■ Stewards' Enquiry : E Pedroza one-day ban: careless riding (Aug 15)

FOCUS
A competitive renewal and, while it was clearly an advantage to race up with the pace, little should be taken away from the winner's performance. The gallop steadied mid-race before the leader quickened things up turning down the hill, and this caused the pack to fracture. An up-to-scratch renewal, Brown Panther entitled to win this with the favourite disappointing.

4920 BLACKROCK FILLIES' STKS (REGISTERED AS THE LILLIE LANGTRY STAKES) (GROUP 3) (F&M) 1m 6f
3:45 (3:45) (Class 1) 3-Y-0+

£34,026 (£12,900; £6,456; £3,216; £1,614; £810) **Stalls** Low

Form RPR
/11- **1** **Wild Coco (GER)**[322] 6163 5-9-5 113.................... TomQueally 6 109+
(Lady Cecil) *lw: travelled wl thrght: hld up in midfield: clsd and jnd ldr on bit ent fnl 2f: rdn and qcknd to ld jst over 1f out: clr and r.o wl fnl f: comf* **5/6**[1]

2413 **2** *2 ½* **Elik (IRE)**[42] 3482 3-8-6 105.................... RyanMoore 3 105
(Sir Michael Stoute) *hld up in tch in rr: effrt to chse ldrs over 1f out: chsd clr wnr ins fnl f: kpt on but no imp* **3/1**[2]

1022 **3** *1 ¾* **Alta Lilea (IRE)**[13] 4473 3-8-6 95.................... FrannyNorton 7 103
(Mark Johnston) *swtg: chsd ldr tl led over 3f out: rdn and jnd ent fnl 2f: hdd over 1f out and unable qck: 3rd and one pce fnl f* **12/1**

342 **4** *2 ½* **Souviens Toi**[39] 3608 4-9-5 102.................... AndreaAtzeni 8 100
(Marco Botti) *t.k.h: chsd ldrs: effrt u.p over 2f out: no ex and btn over 1f out: wknd fnl f* **7/1**[3]

4342 **5** *2* **Jathabah (IRE)**[21] 4211 3-8-7 97 ow1.................... JamesDoyle 1 98
(Clive Brittain) *chsd ldrs: cl up whn stmbld over 3f out: rdn and no ex over 1f out: wknd ent fnl f* **16/1**

-230 **6** *8* **Jehannedarc (IRE)**[54] 3100 5-9-5 100.................... RichardHughes 2 86
(Ed Dunlop) *hld up in tch in last trio: rdn and shortlived effrt over 2f out: wknd wl over 1f out: bhd fnl f* **12/1**

2342 **7** *shd* **Miss Cap Estel**[20] 4234 4-9-5 83.................... DavidProbert 5 85
(Andrew Balding) *hld up in tch in last trio: rdn and effrt over 2f out: sn outpcd and btn: wknd wl over 1f out: bhd fnl f* **33/1**

204- **8** *18* **Suzi's A Class Act**[290] 7109 5-9-5 81....................(p) MartinHarley 9 60
(Paul D'Arcy) *led tl over 3f out: sn dropped out: bhd fnl 2f* **33/1**

2m 59.0s (-4.60) **Going Correction** -0.15s/f (Firm)
WFA 3 from 4yo+ 13lb **8** Ran SP% **119.2**
Speed ratings (Par 110): **107,105,104,103,102 97,97,87**
toteswingers 1&2 £1.60, 2&3 £4.90, 1&3 £3.20 CSF £3.68 TOTE £1.90: £1.10, £1.10, £4.00; EX 4.00 Trifecta £32.40 Pool: £9083.23 - 209.99 winning units..
Owner K I Farm Corporation **Bred** Gestut Rottgen **Trained** Newmarket, Suffolk

FOCUS
This looked a great opportunity for the winner and so it proved. She's rated similar to her reappearance last year. Sound form.

4921 EBF BRITISH STALLION STUDS NEW HAM MAIDEN FILLIES' STKS 7f
4:20 (4:23) (Class 2) 2-Y-0 **£12,938** (£3,850; £1,924; £962) **Stalls** Low

Form RPR
03 **1** **Amazing Maria (IRE)**[13] 4484 2-9-0 0.................... FrankieDettori 1 92+
(Ed Dunlop) *str: scope: lw: chsd ldrs tl led on bit 3f out: rdn and qcknd wl over 1f out: in n.d after: eased towards fin* **7/2**[1]

2 *6* **Inchila** 2-9-0 0.................... JamieSpencer 2 76+
(Peter Chapple-Hyam) *leggy: t.k.h: hld up in midfield: n.m.r and hmpd over 5f out: hdwy on inner over 2f out: pressing for placings whn nt clr run over 1f out: pushed along and wnt 2nd ins fnl f: r.o: no ch w wnr* **16/1**

4 **3** *2 ½* **Jersey Brown (IRE)**[19] 4302 2-9-0 0.................... MartinHarley 4 70
(Mick Channon) *chsd ldrs: swtchd lft and rdn to chse wnr ent fnl 2f: sn outpcd and btn over 1f out: lost 2nd ins fnl f* **20/1**

4 *½* **Angleterre (FR)** 2-9-0 0.................... PatDobbs 8 69+
(Richard Hannon) *rn green: t.k.h: hld up in tch: squeezed for room and stmbld after 1f out: outpcd and swtchd lft over 2f out: sn hung lft: styd on wl under hands and heels fnl f: nvr trbld ldrs* **14/1**

5 *hd* **Radiator** 2-9-0 0.................... RyanMoore 7 68+
(Sir Michael Stoute) *w'like: str: in tch in midfield: outpcd and swtchd lft over 2f out: styd on wl under hands and heels fnl f: nvr trbld ldrs* **7/2**[1]

0 **6** *3* **Bajan Beauty (IRE)**[17] 4347 2-9-0 0.................... WilliamBuick 13 60
(Charles Hills) *leggy: chsd ldng trio: rdn and unable qck over 2f out: 4th and wl hld over 1f out: wknd ins fnl f* **20/1**

0 **7** *½* **Nakuti (IRE)**[28] 3986 2-9-0 0.................... LiamKeniry 17 59+
(Sylvester Kirk) *athletic: hld up towards rr: swtchd to inner and hdwy wl over 1f out: pushed along after and no imp fnl f* **100/1**

8 *1* **Regardez** 2-9-0 0.................... JimCrowley 18 56+
(Ralph Beckett) *w'like: bit bkwd: rn green: hld up in midfield on outer: lost pl over 3f out: trying to rally whn pushed lft over 2f out: pushed along and kpt on steadily fnl f: nvr trbld ldrs* **20/1**

9 *1* **Tender Emotion** 2-9-0 0.................... MickaelBarzalona 11 54
(Charlie Appleby) *lengthy: lean: edgy: rn green: t.k.h: hld up towards rr: wl off the pce and rdn 3f out: modest hdwy fnl f: nvr trbld ldrs* **10/1**

10 *½* **Remember** 2-9-0 0.................... RichardHughes 5 52
(Richard Hannon) *athletic: rn green: wnt sharply lft s: t.k.h and sn rcvrd to chse ldrs: rdn and unable qck ent fnl 2f: wknd over 1f out: wl hld and eased wl ins fnl f* **5/1**[2]

11 *nk* **Cayman Cry (USA)** 2-9-0 0.................... KierenFallon 15 52
(Brian Meehan) *w'like: chsd ldng trio: rdn and unable qck over 2f out: outpcd and wl btn over 1f out: fdd ins fnl f* **20/1**

12 *1 ¼* **Dream And Hope** 2-9-0 0.................... JoeFanning 16 48
(Clive Brittain) *w'like: leggy: rn green: s.i.s: in rr: sme hdwy past btn horses ent fnl f: n.d* **33/1**

6 **13** *¾* **Ejadah (IRE)**[13] 4491 2-9-0 0....................[1] PaulHanagan 3 47
(Roger Varian) *led: hdd 3f out: rdn and struggling 2f out: sn btn: fdd fnl f* **7/1**[3]

14 *6* **Isabella Liberty (FR)** 2-9-0 0.................... AndreaAtzeni 20 31
(Robert Eddery) *w'like: tall: stdd and swtchd rt after s: a bhd: lost tch 2f out* **66/1**

15 *nk* **All Yours (IRE)** 2-9-0 0.................... NeilCallan 19 30
(William Knight) *w'like: bit bkwd: towards rr: rdn and struggling 1/2-way: bhd fnl 2f* **50/1**

16 *nk* **Satin Waters** 2-9-0 0.................... TomQueally 14 29
(Eve Johnson Houghton) *w'like: tall: a towards rr: bhd fnl 2f* **50/1**

17 *2* **Tiptree Lace** 2-9-0 0.................... JamesDoyle 6 24
(William Knight) *w'like: str: bit bkwd: s.i.s: bhd: sme hdwy on inner over 2f out: swtchd lft over 1f out: midfield and wl hld 1f out: heavily eased wl ins fnl f* **50/1**

1m 26.03s (-0.97) **Going Correction** -0.15s/f (Firm) **17** Ran SP% **125.6**
Speed ratings (Par 97): **99,92,89,88,88 85,84,83,82,81 81,79,79,72,71 71,69**
toteswingers 1&2 £16.00, 2&3 £30.70, 1&3 £10.80 CSF £58.39 TOTE £5.00: £1.90, £5.70, £5.60; EX 68.00 Trifecta £1247.90 Pool: £3577.56 - 2.15 winning units..
Owner Sir Robert Ogden **Bred** Sir Robert Ogden **Trained** Newmarket, Suffolk

FOCUS
This proved very straightforward for the winner, who stepped up on her previous effort. She's rated the best winner of this race for a few years.

4922 TATLER STKS (H'CAP) 7f
4:50 (4:54) (Class 2) (0-105,98) 3-Y-0

£15,562 (£4,660; £2,330; £1,165; £582; £292) **Stalls** Low

Form RPR
3311 **1** **Majestic Moon (IRE)**[13] 4492 3-8-9 **86**.................... PaulHanagan 7 97
(Richard Fahey) *swtg: mde all: rdn and wnt clr over 1f out: drvn ins fnl f: jst hld on: all out* **7/1**[3]

1143 **2** *nse* **Pythagorean**[26] 4078 3-9-1 **92**.................... JamesDoyle 8 102+
(Roger Charlton) *t.k.h: hld up in midfield: n.m.r ent fnl 2f: hdwy u.p to chse ldng trio 1f out: chsd wnr ins fnl f: r.o strly: jst failed* **7/2**[1]

-250 **3** *2* **Regal Dan (IRE)**[20] 4255 3-8-10 **87**.................... RyanMoore 11 92+
(Charles Hills) *hld up in last trio: effrt and carried lft wl over 1f out: hdwy u.p 1f out: r.o strly to snatch 3rd on post* **12/1**

3105 **4** *nse* **Kyllachy Rise**[26] 4078 3-8-5 **82**.................... JimmyQuinn 3 87
(Richard Hannon) *t.k.h: hld up in midfield: nt clr run on inner 2f out tl rdn and hdwy over 1f out: chsd ldng pair ins fnl f: kpt on: lost 3rd on post* **12/1**

2341 **5** *1 ½* **Yourartisonfire**[8] 4641 3-8-10 **87** 6ex....................(v[1]) JimCrowley 1 88
(Mrs K Burke) *chsd ldr tl 5f out and again 2f: unable qck w wnr over 1f out: lost 2nd ins fnl f: wknd towards fin* **8/1**

-135 **6** *2 ¾* **Melvin The Grate (IRE)**[72] 2554 3-8-5 **82**....................[1] DavidProbert 13 75
(Andrew Balding) *in tch in midfield: n.m.r 2f: carried rt over 1f out: kpt on u.p ins fnl f: no threat to ldrs* **25/1**

1453 **7** 1/2 **Firmdecisions (IRE)**[15] 4413 3-8-2 **79** oh3 FrannyNorton 2 71
(Brett Johnson) *b: t.k.h: chsd ldrs: hmpd bnd over 4f out: rdn and unable qck 2f out: wknd ins fnl f* **33/1**

-536 **8** 1 1/2 **Burning Blaze**[5] 4767 3-8-12 **89** JamieSpencer 16 77+
(Kevin Ryan) *hld up in last trio: trying to switch lft but hanging rt over 2f out: swtchd lft wl over 1f out: kpt on fnl f: no threat to ldrs* **12/1**

2110 **9** hd **Equity Risk (USA)**[20] 4255 3-8-13 **90** NeilCallan 15 77+
(Kevin Ryan) *hld up towards rr: switching to inner and effrt jst over 2f out: nvr much room fr over 1f out: kpt on ins fnl f: nvr trbld ldrs* **20/1**

12 **10** shd **Homage (IRE)**[56] 3020 3-8-13 **90** WilliamBuick 14 77
(Jeremy Noseda) *stdd s: hld up in rr: swtchd lft and effrt jst over 2f out: no imp tl styd on ins fnl f: nvr trbld ldrs* **6/1**[2]

3050 **11** 1/2 **Chilworth Icon**[20] 4255 3-9-4 **98** WilliamTwiston-Davies(3) 12 84
(Mick Channon) *hld up towards rr: nt clr run and switching to inner over 1f out: pushed along and sme hdwy on inner ins fnl f: nvr trbld ldrs* **50/1**

1-32 **12** nk **Muharrib (IRE)**[19] 4295 3-9-3 **94** SilvestreDeSousa 5 79
(Saeed bin Suroor) *short of room leaving stalls: sn pushed up to rcvr: chsd wnr 5f out tl 2f out: no ex u.p over 1f out: wknd ins fnl f* **8/1**

0614 **13** nk **Correspondent**[19] 4284 3-9-7 **98** TomQueally 10 82
(Brian Meehan) *swtg: hld up in midfield: shkn up and wanting to edge rt over 1f out: no prog after* **20/1**

4101 **14** 2 1/4 **Shafaani**[7] 4690 3-8-12 **89** 6ex (t) KierenFallon 6 67
(Clive Brittain) *chsd ldrs: rdn over 2f out: unable qck and edging rt u.p over 1f out: wknd ins fnl f* **33/1**

513 **15** 3/4 **Czech It Out (IRE)**[56] 3020 3-8-6 **83** JoeFanning 4 59
(Amanda Perrett) *lw: in tch in midfield: n.m.r and shuffled bk wl over 1f out: nvr enough room after: nvr able to chal* **10/1**

1-06 **16** 2 1/4 **Chelwood Gate (IRE)**[33] 3803 3-8-13 **90** (p) AndreaAtzeni 9 60
(Roger Varian) *in tch in midfield: rdn and unable qck over 2f out: wknd over 1f out* **33/1**

1m 25.0s (-2.00) **Going Correction** -0.15s/f (Firm) **16** Ran SP% **127.6**
Speed ratings (Par 106): **105,104,102,102,100 97,97,95,95,95 94,94,93,91,90 87**
toteswingers 1&2 £15.90, 2&3 £6.80, 1&3 £43.60 CSF £30.47 CT £306.82 TOTE £9.40: £2.10, £1.70, £2.90, £3.10; EX 43.10 Trifecta £812.30 Pool: £3736.71 - 3.45 winning units..
Owner James Gaffney **Bred** Tony Cosgrave **Trained** Musley Bank, N Yorks
■ Stewards' Enquiry : James Doyle two-day ban: used whip above permitted level (Aug 15-16)

FOCUS
Like in the previous maiden the winner stuck to the inside rail. He has improved since front running. The second ran a personal best.

4923 QIPCO FUTURE STARS APPRENTICE STKS (H'CAP) 1m 1f
5:25 (5:26) (Class 3) (0-90,90) 4-Y-0+ **£9,703** (£2,887; £1,443; £721) **Stalls** Low

Form RPR

2253 **1** **Highland Duke (IRE)**[21] 4207 4-8-12 **79** RyanTate(3) 14 95
(Clive Cox) *hld up in midfield: clsng whn n.m.r over 2f out: hdwy over 1f out: led ins fnl f: r.o strly: readily* **16/1**

1002 **2** 4 **Sir Mike**[6] 4718 4-8-11 **75** RyanClark 13 82
(Amanda Perrett) *lw: in tch in midfield on outer: rdn and effrt to press ldr over 2f out: led 1f out: sn hdd and outpcd by wnr: hld on for 2nd* **11/1**

3412 **3** shd **Ree's Rascal (IRE)**[32] 3864 5-9-4 **85** NathanAlison(3) 16 92
(Jim Boyle) *hld up in rr: rdn and hdwy on outer 2f out: drvn and pressing ldrs ent fnl f: outpcd by wnr but kpt on fnl f* **8/1**[3]

0555 **4** 1/2 **Benzanno (IRE)**[27] 4028 4-9-9 **87** ThomasBrown 18 93
(Andrew Balding) *stdd after s: hld up in last quartet: clsng but forced to swtchd lft over 2f out: styd on wl fnl f: nvr trbld ldrs* **8/1**[3]

05/0 **5** 1 3/4 **Zafisio (IRE)**[47] 3339 7-8-11 **82** HarryBurns(7) 12 84
(Jo Hughes) *hld up towards rr: swtchd lft and hdwy over 2f out: rdn to chse ldrs over 1f out: no ex 1f out* **40/1**

3236 **6** 1/2 **Sheila's Buddy**[66] 2728 4-8-9 **76** TobyAtkinson(3) 8 77
(J S Moore) *in tch in midfield: effrt on inner to ld over 2f out: drvn and hdd 1f out: wknd fnl 75yds* **22/1**

4345 **7** 3 3/4 **Lord Ofthe Shadows (IRE)**[13] 4488 4-9-7 **85** WilliamTwiston-Davies 17 77
(Richard Hannon) *hld up towards rr: rdn and hdwy on outer over 2f out: no imp over 1f out* **10/1**

4141 **8** 1/2 **Silver Alliance**[50] 3218 5-8-6 **75** (p) ShelleyBirkett(5) 10 66
(Julia Feilden) *hld up in tch in midfield: clsd to press ldrs and pushed rt over 2f out: chsd ldrs and unable qck u.p over 1f out: n.m.r ent fnl f: wknd ins fnl f* **16/1**

3411 **9** nse **Xinbama (IRE)**[14] 4441 4-8-11 **78** (t) NicoleNordblad(3) 1 69+
(J W Hills) *s.i.s: bhd: hdwy on inner over 2f out: chsng ldrs whn pushed against rail and bdly hmpd 2f out: lost all ch and swtchd lft over 1f out: kpt on* **12/1**

0654 **10** 1/2 **Commend**[19] 4280 4-8-13 **80** (tp) RobertTart(3) 4 70
(Sir Michael Stoute) *lw: t.k.h: hld up wl in tch in midfield: clsd to press ldrs whn jostled and pushed rt over 2f out: no ex u.p over 1f out: wknd fnl f* **15/2**[2]

3400 **11** 3/4 **Calaf**[2] 4854 5-9-2 **83** GeorgeChaloner(3) 5 72
(Brian Ellison) *chsd ldrs: stl handy whn pushed rt and hmpd over 2f out: swtchd rt2f out: no ex u.p: wknd 1f out* **25/1**

1300 **12** 5 **Maverik**[41] 3527 5-9-12 **90** PatrickHills 3 68
(William Knight) *led tl rdn and hdd over 1f out: btn over 1f out: fdd fnl f* **20/1**

4210 **13** 2 1/4 **Copperwood**[2] 4859 8-8-11 **78** MichaelJMMurphy(3) 7 51
(Mark Johnston) *in tch in midfield: rdn and effrt to press ldrs whn edgd rt over 2f out: switching lft 2f out: wknd u.p over 1f out* **12/1**

2114 **14** 3/4 **Laughing Jack**[24] 4126 5-8-10 **77** GeorgeDowning(3) 11 48+
(Tony Carroll) *lw: chsd ldrs: rdn to press ldrs 4f out: rdn and losing pl whn bdly hmpd over 2f out: n.d after: eased wl ins fnl f* **12/1**

1-23 **15** 23 **Mean It (IRE)**[72] 2539 4-8-7 **78** [1] SiobhanMiller(7) 15
(David Simcock) *a bhd and nvr travelling: rdn and lost tch over 2f out: t.o* **7/2**[1]

0400 **16** 3/4 **Right Step**[33] 3827 6-8-8 **79** (v) DavidParkes(7) 2
(Alan Jarvis) *chsd ldrs: rdn whn pushed rt and bdly hmpd 2f out: dropped to rr and sn eased: t.o* **33/1**

-600 **17** 4 **Jake's Destiny (IRE)**[13] 4488 4-9-4 **87** (t) ThomasGarner(5) 9
(George Baker) *w ldr: rdn and losing pl whn bdly hmpd over 2f out: bhd after: eased fnl f: t.o* **20/1**

1m 53.36s (-2.94) **Going Correction** -0.15s/f (Firm) **17** Ran SP% **131.6**
Speed ratings (Par 107): **107,103,103,102,101 100,97,97,97,96 95,91,89,88,68 67,64**
toteswingers 1&2 £15.90, 2&3 £6.80, 1&3 £43.60 CSF £178.51 CT £992.04 TOTE £17.80: £4.00, £2.60, £2.70, £2.70; EX 243.30 Trifecta £2636.30 Part won..
Owner Highland Thoroughbred Ltd **Bred** Philip Brady **Trained** Lambourn, Berks
■ Stewards' Enquiry : George Chaloner three-day ban: careless riding (Aug 15-17)

FOCUS
Not form to put much faith in going forward, with them going too hard up front early, and the race set up perfectly for the closers. The winner won on merit though, and the form is taken at face value.
T/Jkpt: Not won. T/Plt: £262.90 to a £1 stake. Pool of £352381.15 - 978.24 winning tickets.
T/Qpdt: £22.50 to a £1 stake. Pool of £17595.45 - 577.53 winning tickets. SP

4497 NOTTINGHAM (L-H)
Thursday, August 1

OFFICIAL GOING: Good to soft (soft in places) changing to good to soft after race 3 (3.25)
Wind: Light across Weather: Sunny periods

4924 BRITISH STALLION STUDS EBF MAIDEN FILLIES' STKS 6f 15y
2:25 (2:25) (Class 5) 2-Y-O **£3,234** (£962; £481; £240) **Stalls** High

Form RPR

4 **1** **Dorothy B (IRE)**[15] 4409 2-9-0 0 RobertHavlin 4 86+
(John Gosden) *trckd ldrs: hdwy 2f out: led wl over 1f out: pushed clr fnl f: kpt on* **2/1**[1]

3200 **2** 2 1/4 **Hoku (IRE)**[15] 4408 2-9-0 82 HarryBentley 9 79+
(Olly Stevens) *trckd ldrs on inner: effrt and nt clr run 2f out and again over 1f out: sn swtchd lft and rdn ent fnl f: kpt on: nt rch wnr* **3/1**[2]

3 3/4 **Online Alexander (IRE)** 2-9-0 0 PhillipMakin 5 77+
(Kevin Ryan) *trckd ldrs: hdwy 2f out: rdn to chse wnr 1f out: sn no imp* **8/1**

4 **4** 3 1/2 **Starlit Cantata**[22] 4164 2-9-0 0 ShaneKelly 8 66
(Eve Johnson Houghton) *slt ld: hdd over 3f out: cl up: rdn along 2f out: grad wknd* **25/1**

5 **5** 1 1/4 **More Aspen (USA)**[22] 4164 2-9-0 0 LukeMorris 3 63
(Marco Botti) *chsd ldrs: rdn along wl over 2f out: drvn and one pce fr wl over 1f out* **5/1**[3]

6 1 **Miss Buckshot (IRE)** 2-9-0 0 ChrisCatlin 6 60
(Rae Guest) *in tch on outer: pushed along to chse ldrs over 2f out: sn rdn and one pce* **25/1**

0 **7** 3 **Spirit Of Alsace (IRE)**[21] 4215 2-9-0 0 SeanLevey 2 51
(Roger Varian) *cl up: led over 2f out: rdn along 2f out: sn hdd & wknd* **6/1**

8 3 **Dutch Lady** 2-9-0 0 TomEaves 7 42
(John Holt) *s.i.s: a in rr* **100/1**

9 16 **Genax (IRE)** 2-9-0 0 DanielTudhope 1
(Mrs K Burke) *wnt lft s and slowly away: a in rr: bhd fnl 2f* **40/1**

1m 14.9s (0.20) **Going Correction** -0.05s/f (Good) **9** Ran SP% **111.5**
Speed ratings (Par 91): **96,93,92,87,85 84,80,76,55**
toteswingers 1&2 £1.30, 2&3 £7.30, 1&3 £3.50 CSF £7.40 TOTE £2.30: £1.20, £1.50, £3.00; EX 8.60 Trifecta £44.80 Pool: £1791.55 - 29.93 winning units..
Owner R J H Geffen **Bred** Slow Sand Syndicate **Trained** Newmarket, Suffolk

FOCUS
Outer track used. Home bend rail moved 2m out from inside line increasing distances by about 6yds on Round course. A moderate maiden for juvenile fillies, run at a steady pace. The winner can probably prove better than this.

4925 BREEDERS BACKING RACING EBF MAIDEN STKS (DIV I) 1m 75y
2:55 (2:57) (Class 5) 2-Y-O **£3,234** (£962; £481; £240) **Stalls** Centre

Form RPR

1 **Stagemanship (USA)** 2-9-5 0 AhmedAjtebi 6 73+
(Charlie Appleby) *chsd ldng pair: hdwy to chse ldr over 4f out and sn rn green: effrt over 2f out: sn rdn and ev ch: green and drvn ent fnl f: styd on wl to ld nr fin* **13/8**[1]

2 nk **Hunters Creek (IRE)** 2-9-5 0 RobertHavlin 4 73+
(John Gosden) *trckd ldrs: hdwy on wd outside over 3f out and sn cl up: led 2f out: rdn over 1f out: drvn and edgd lft last 100yds: hdd and no ex nr fin* **3/1**[2]

3 3/4 **Power Up** 2-9-0 0 LiamJones 5 66+
(Mark Johnston) *led: pushed salong over 3f out: rdn and hdd 2f out: drvn and ev ch over 1f out: kpt on fnl f* **14/1**

4 1 **Oasis Fantasy (IRE)** 2-9-5 0 PaulMulrennan 3 68
(Ed Dunlop) *trckd ldrs: hdwy on inner over 3f out: rdn and ev ch 2f out: drvn and one pce appr fnl f* **7/1**

5 nk **Nakeeta** 2-9-5 0 TomEaves 8 68+
(Mick Channon) *s.i.s and bhd: hdwy over 3f out: rdn to chse ldrs wl over 1f out: kpt on fnl f: nrst fin* **18/1**

00 **6** 6 **Arrowzone**[13] 4505 2-9-0 0 JustinNewman(5) 7 54
(Garry Moss) *towards rr: hdwy and in tch 1/2-way: rdn along 3f out: sn wknd* **100/1**

00 **7** nk **Bentons Lad**[57] 2985 2-9-5 0 PJMcDonald 10 53
(George Moore) *in tch: rdn along over 3f out: sn wknd* **200/1**

8 nk **Aldreth** 2-9-5 0 PhillipMakin 2 53
(Michael Easterby) *dwlt: a towards rr* **33/1**

50 **9** nse **Hostile Takeover (IRE)**[8] 4631 2-9-2 0 (t) CharlesBishop(3) 1 53
(Olly Stevens) *chsd ldr: rdn along 1/2-way: drvn 3f out: grad wknd* **40/1**

2 **10** 21 **Craggaknock**[33] 3810 2-9-5 0 DuranFentiman 9
(Tim Walford) *s.i.s: a in rr: bhd fnl 3f* **7/2**[3]

1m 48.56s (-0.44) **Going Correction** -0.225s/f (Firm) **10** Ran SP% **116.6**
Speed ratings (Par 94): **93,92,91,90,90 84,84,84,84,63**
toteswingers 1&2 £1.30, 2&3 £7.30, 1&3 £3.50 CSF £6.48 TOTE £2.10: £1.10, £3.00, £2.90; EX 9.80 Trifecta £76.50 Pool: £2176.37 - 21.32 winning units..
Owner Godolphin **Bred** S Kelly, J Kelly & H C Alexander **Trained** Newmarket, Suffolk

FOCUS
Quite a test for 2yos over an extended mile on easy ground. The was time was slow and they finished relatively compressed, and the bare form is only fair.

4926 BREEDERS BACKING RACING EBF MAIDEN STKS (DIV II) 1m 75y
3:25 (3:25) (Class 5) 2-Y-O **£3,234** (£962; £481; £240) **Stalls** Centre

Form RPR

1 **Rising Breeze (FR)** 2-9-5 0 DanielTudhope 7 80+
(Mrs K Burke) *in tch: hdwy to trck ldrs 1/2-way: effrt to chse ldr 2f out: rdn to chal over 1f out: led ins fnl f: styd on strly* **7/2**[2]

552 **2** 2 **Floating Ballerino (IRE)**[8] 4631 2-9-5 0 HarryBentley 2 75
(Olly Stevens) *trckd ldrs: smooth hdwy over 3f out: led wl over 2f out: rdn over 1f out: hdd ins fnl f: kpt on same pce* **7/2**[2]

3 4 **Astrowolf** 2-9-5 0 RobertWinston 4 66
(Mark H Tompkins) *towards rr: hdwy over 3f out: swtchd rt and rdn 2f out: chsd ldng pair over 1f out: no imp fnl f* **33/1**

4 1½ **Devilment** 2-9-5 0 ... AhmedAjtebi 5 66+
(Charlie Appleby) *dwlt and stmbld s: t.k.h and bhd: swtchd rt to outer and hdwy 3f out: rdn to chse ldrs 2f out: sn no imp* **4/1**[3]

06 **5** 7 **Sirpertan**[73] 2502 2-9-5 0 ...(p) DuranFentiman 9 46
(Tim Walford) *cl up: rdn along 3f out: drvn and grad wknd fnl 2f* **50/1**

3 **6** 7 **Art Wave (IRE)**[16] 4386 2-9-5 0 ... LukeMorris 3 30
(Marco Botti) *trckd ldng pair on inner: pushed along over 3f out: sn rdn and wknd* **9/4**[1]

0 **7** 1½ **That Be Grand**[14] 4432 2-8-11 0 ... NeilFarley(3) 1 22
(Shaun Harris) *chsd ldrs: rdn along 1/2-way: sn outpcd* **200/1**

8 2 **Mukhtazel (IRE)** 2-9-5 0 ... LiamJones 8 22
(Mark Johnston) *led: rdn along over 3f out: hdd wl over 2f out: sn drvn and wknd* **8/1**

9 1¾ **Kaizen Factor** 2-9-5 0 ... WilliamCarson 6 18
(Rod Millman) *dwlt and a in rr* **25/1**

1m 47.54s (-1.46) **Going Correction** -0.225s/f (Firm) 9 Ran SP% **115.6**
Speed ratings (Par 94): **98,96,92,90,83 76,75,73,71**
toteswingers 1&2 £5.20, 2&3 £0.00, 1&3 £0.00 CSF £15.86 TOTE £7.70: £1.30, £1.70, £6.70; EX 31.00 Trifecta £521.70 Pool: £953.02 - 1.37 winning units..
Owner Market Avenue Racing Club Ltd **Bred** Gerard Belloir **Trained** Middleham Moor, N Yorks

FOCUS
Not quite so many interesting newcomers in this juvenile contest, but a couple of runners with fair form already in the book. The winner looks sure to do better from here.

4927 EAT IN OUR ROOFTOP RESTAURANT MEDIAN AUCTION MAIDEN STKS 1m 75y
3:55 (3:57) (Class 6) 3-4-Y-0 **£2,587** (£770; £384; £192) **Stalls** Centre

Form RPR
6646 **1** **Loved One**[27] 4013 3-9-0 72 ... ShaneKelly 8 78+
(James Fanshawe) *trckd ldrs: hdwy over 3f out: chsd ldr 2f out: sn cl up: rdn to ld last 75yds: readily* **10/3**[2]

2 **2** ¾ **Blighty (IRE)**[44] 3435 3-9-5 0 ... MartinDwyer 9 81+
(Lady Cecil) *t.k.h: sn chsng ldr: led over 3f out: jnd and rdn wl over 1f out: drvn ins fnl f: hdd and no ex last 75yds* **5/2**[1]

44 **3** 2½ **Ruffled**[16] 4381 3-9-0 0 ... RobertHavlin 1 71+
(John Gosden) *in tch: pushed along and sltly outpcd over 3f out: hdwy whn swtchd rt and rdn wl over 1f out: kpt on fnl f: nrst fin* **5/2**[1]

4-00 **4** 1¼ **Ningbo Express (IRE)**[54] 3116 3-9-0 67 ... J-PGuillambert 4 68
(Rae Guest) *plld hrd: chsd ldrs: hdwy 3f out: rdn and edgd lft wl over 1f out: sn drvn and one pce* **17/2**[3]

5-4 **5** 3 **Frank's Folly (IRE)**[4] 4805 4-9-12 0 ... DuranFentiman 3 67
(Tim Walford) *t.k.h: chsd ldrs: rdn along over 2f out: grad wknd* **10/1**

6 4½ **Pretty Bubbles** 4-9-7 0 ... DanielTudhope 11 51
(J R Jenkins) *towards rr: hdwy 3f out: swtchd lft and rdn over 2f out: n.d* **66/1**

05 **7** 2¼ **Cherokee Princess (IRE)**[13] 4500 3-9-0 0 ... WilliamCarson 6 45
(Tim Pitt) *s.i.s: a towards rr* **40/1**

5-5 **8** ¾ **Shenval**[189] 350 3-9-5 0 ... PatCosgrave 5 49
(Noel Quinlan) *hld up: hdwy on wd outside over 3f out: rdn to chse ldrs over 2f out: sn wknd* **66/1**

9 ¾ **Rowlestone Lass** 3-9-0 0 ... DaleSwift 10 42
(Richard Price) *s.i.s: a in rr* **100/1**

5 **10** 2 **Heroes Welcome (IRE)**[211] 14 3-9-0 0 ... PaulMulrennan 7 37
(Deborah Sanderson) *a towards rr* **100/1**

00- **11** ½ **Razzle Dazzle 'Em**[451] 1923 4-9-9 0 ... NeilFarley(3) 2 42
(Shaun Harris) *a towards rr* **200/1**

46- **12** nk **Shagwa (IRE)**[293] 7020 3-9-0 0 ... LiamJones 12 35
(Mark Johnston) *led: rdn along and hdd over 3f out: sn drvn and wknd* **16/1**

1m 47.66s (-1.34) **Going Correction** -0.225s/f (Firm)
WFA 3 from 4yo 7lb 12 Ran SP% **113.6**
Speed ratings (Par 101): **97,96,93,92,89 85,82,82,81,79 78,78**
toteswingers 1&2 £1.20, 2&3 £1.50, 1&3 £1.60 CSF £11.44 TOTE £4.70: £1.30, £1.40, £1.10; EX 11.00 Trifecta £26.80 Pool: £884.84 - 24.68 winning units..
Owner Cheveley Park Stud **Bred** Cheveley Park Stud Ltd **Trained** Newmarket, Suffolk

FOCUS
Just a handful seemed to have realistic chances in this moderate maiden. The winner is rated back to her penultimate form over C&D.

4928 ENJOY AFTERNOON TEA IN FRANKIES BISTRO H'CAP 1m 75y
4:30 (4:30) (Class 5) (0-75,74) 3-Y-0+ **£3,234** (£962; £481; £240) **Stalls** Centre

Form RPR
2333 **1** **Knight Owl**[26] 4068 3-9-1 68 ... LukeMorris 10 78+
(James Fanshawe) *hld up in tch: hdwy on outer 3f out: chsd ldrs 2f out: sn chal: rdn to ld ent fnl f: edgd lft and styd on strly* **7/2**[1]

0504 **2** 1½ **Master Of Song**[26] 4070 6-8-4 55 ...(p) PhilipPrince(5) 9 62
(Roy Bowring) *chsd ldr: led after 2f and sn clr: pushed along over 3f out: rdn over 2f out: drvn and hdd ent fnl f: kpt on same pce* **14/1**

205 **3** ½ **Imaginary World (IRE)**[33] 3814 5-9-1 61 ...(p) DanielTudhope 1 67
(John Balding) *chsd ldng pair: tk clsr order 3f out: rdn 2f out: drvn and kpt on same pce fnl f* **8/1**[3]

2206 **4** 2½ **Skyfire**[40] 3573 6-9-5 65 ... MichaelStainton 2 65
(Nick Kent) *led 2f: chsd clr ldr: rdn along wl over 2f out: drvn wl over 1f out: sn one pce* **12/1**

3212 **5** nk **Fluctuation (IRE)**[117] 1402 5-8-13 64 ...(v) ConnorBeasley(5) 6 64
(Ian Williams) *hld up: hdwy on inner 3f out: chsd ldrs 2f out: sn rdn and no imp appr fnl f* **10/1**

4641 **6** 1¾ **West End Lad**[13] 4503 10-9-9 72 ...(b) MarkCoumbe(3) 4 68
(Roy Bowring) *dwlt and bhd tl styd on fnl 2f: n.d* **8/1**[3]

3201 **7** 1¼ **Not Rigg (USA)**[26] 4077 3-9-7 74 ...(t) ShaneKelly 3 66
(Gary Harrison) *chsd ldrs: rdn along 3f out: wknd over 2f out* **11/2**[2]

100 **8** 1¼ **Testa Rossa (IRE)**[49] 3241 3-8-9 62 ... MartinDwyer 5 51
(J W Hills) *chsd ldrs: pushed along 3f out: rdn over 2f out: sn drvn and wknd* **11/2**[2]

5060 **9** 7 **Aerodynamic (IRE)**[38] 3628 6-9-7 67 ... PaulMulrennan 7 41
(Michael Easterby) *s.i.s: a bhd* **11/2**[2]

1m 46.24s (-2.76) **Going Correction** -0.225s/f (Firm)
WFA 3 from 5yo+ 7lb 9 Ran SP% **114.0**
Speed ratings (Par 103): **104,102,102,99,99 97,96,94,87**
toteswingers 1&2 £0.00, 2&3 £0.00, 1&3 £0.00 CSF £53.84 CT £366.79 TOTE £6.30: £2.00, £7.20, £2.40; EX 89.10 Trifecta £280.20 Pool: £1472.45 - 3.94 winning units..
Owner Miss Annabelle Condon **Bred** Car Colston Hall Stud **Trained** Newmarket, Suffolk

FOCUS
A modest handicap, but competitive on paper. It was 20lb faster than the preceding maiden and the form makes sense.

4929 SPONSOR A RACE AT NOTTINGHAM RACECOURSE H'CAP 1m 2f 50y
5:00 (5:00) (Class 4) (0-85,83) 3-Y-0+ **£6,469** (£1,925; £962; £481) **Stalls** Low

Form RPR
-223 **1** **Elhaame (IRE)**[28] 3995 3-9-4 82 ... LukeMorris 12 92+
(Luca Cumani) *towards rr: pushed along over 5f out: hdwy 3f out: rdn to chal wl over 1f out: drvn ins fnl f: kpt on gamely to ld last 50yds* **5/1**[2]

0-01 **2** ½ **Missed Call (IRE)**[34] 3764 3-9-1 79 ... MartinDwyer 6 88+
(Lady Cecil) *towards rr: pushed along and hdwy 3f out: rdn to chse ldrs 2f out: sn n.m.r and swtchd rt over 1f out: drvn and styd onl fnl f* **2/1**[1]

2412 **3** shd **Stellar Express (IRE)**[13] 4502 4-9-13 82 ... AndrewMullen 10 91
(Michael Appleby) *sn led and set str pce: pushed along over 2f out: rdn along wl over 1f out: drvn ins fnl f: hdd and no ex last 50yds* **17/2**

3465 **4** 2¼ **Gala Casino Star (IRE)**[37] 3651 8-9-0 76 ...(v) JordanNason(7) 3 81
(Geoffrey Harker) *trckd ldr: cl up over 2f out: rdn and ev ch whn edgd lft over 1f out: drvn and one pce ins fnl f* **15/2**[3]

0030 **5** nk **War Poet**[36] 3685 6-10-0 83 ...(v) DanielTudhope 4 87
(David O'Meara) *dwlt and towards rr: stdy hdwy on inner 3f out: trckd ldrs whn nt clr run and hmpd over 1f out: rdn and n.m.r ins fnl f: kpt on* **12/1**

0020 **6** 3¼ **Getabuzz**[61] 2855 5-9-12 81 ... DuranFentiman 2 79
(Tim Easterby) *t.k.h early: chsd ldrs: hdwy 3f out: rdn along 2f out: drvn and one pce appr fnl f* **22/1**

6005 **7** shd **Mr Red Clubs (IRE)**[27] 4012 4-9-11 80 ... ShaneKelly 7 78
(Tim Pitt) *stdd s and hld up in rr: hdwy 3f out: rdn 2f out: kpt on fnl f: nrst fin* **33/1**

1052 **8** 4½ **Lamusawama**[16] 4384 3-9-2 80 ... PaulMulrennan 11 69
(Ed Dunlop) *midfield: hdwy to chse ldrs over 4f out: rdn along 3f out: sn wknd* **9/1**

1216 **9** 1¼ **Never Forever**[43] 3477 4-9-3 72 ... PJMcDonald 9 59
(George Moore) *a towards rr* **8/1**

0345 **10** 3 **Flying Applause**[4] 4810 8-8-10 68 ...(b) MarkCoumbe(3) 5 49
(Roy Bowring) *dwlt: rapid hdwy to chse ldr after 2f: rdn along 4f out: sn wknd* **20/1**

1032 **11** 27 **Rosie's Lady (IRE)**[167] 675 4-8-8 66 ... RaulDaSilva(3) 8
(Paul Green) *t.k.h: chsd ldrs: rdn along 4f out: sn wknd and bhd whn eased wl over 1f out* **33/1**

2m 11.08s (-3.22) **Going Correction** -0.225s/f (Firm)
WFA 3 from 4yo+ 9lb 11 Ran SP% **116.1**
Speed ratings (Par 105): **103,102,102,100,100 97,97,94,93,90 69**
toteswingers 1&2 £1.60, 2&3 £10.40, 1&3 £5.10 CSF £14.39 CT £81.36 TOTE £4.10: £2.70, £2.10, £1.50; EX 20.20 Trifecta £256.40 Pool: £2482.74 - 7.26 winning units..
Owner Sheikh Mohammed Obaid Al Maktoum **Bred** W Maxwell Ervine **Trained** Newmarket, Suffolk

FOCUS
Plenty could be fancied in this fair middle-distance handicap but the first two were the most interesting in terms of potential. The third ran as well as ever.

4930 FIND NOTTINGHAM RACECOURSE ON FACEBOOK H'CAP 5f 13y
5:30 (5:32) (Class 5) (0-75,75) 3-Y-0+ **£2,587** (£770; £384; £192) **Stalls** High

Form RPR
-013 **1** **Steel Rain**[31] 3888 5-8-13 62 ... RobertWinston 8 71
(Nikki Evans) *sltly hmpd s: sn trcking ldrs: hdwy 2f out: led over 1f out: rdn ent fnl f: sn drvn and hld on gamely nr fin* **8/1**[3]

2133 **2** nse **Haajes**[34] 3769 9-9-12 75 ...(v) MickyFenton 4 84
(Paul Midgley) *midfield: hdwy to chse ldrs 2f out: rdn to chal ent fnl f: ev ch tl drvn and no ex nr line* **16/1**

5060 **3** 2¼ **Quality Art (USA)**[35] 3716 5-8-2 56 ... ConnorBeasley(5) 1 57
(Richard Guest) *in tch: hdwy 2f out: rdn over 1f out: ch ins fnl f: sn drvn and nt qckn* **16/1**

0-0U **4** nk **Master Bond**[65] 2755 4-9-6 74 ...(t) JustinNewman(5) 13 74
(Bryan Smart) *hld up: hdwy 2f out: rdn over 1f out: kpt on wl fnl f: nrst fin* **12/1**

-540 **5** hd **Eland Ally**[21] 4203 5-9-10 73 ...(p) PhillipMakin 5 72
(Tom Tate) *prom: rdn along 2f out: drvn over 1f out: kpt on same pce fnl f* **12/1**

6514 **6** hd **Monsieur Jamie**[47] 3341 5-9-8 71 ...(v) DanielTudhope 9 69
(J R Jenkins) *dwlt and hmpd s: hdwy after 2f: rdn to chse ldrs wl over 1f out: drvn and no imp fnl f* **7/1**[2]

6006 **7** ¾ **Beau Mistral (IRE)**[13] 4479 4-9-0 66 ... RaulDaSilva(3) 2 62
(Paul Green) *in tch: hdwy on wd outside 2f out: rdn to chse ldrs over 1f out: one pce ins fnl f* **9/1**

454 **8** ½ **Ambitious Icarus**[35] 3738 4-8-12 61 ...(e) RobbieFitzpatrick 11 55
(Richard Guest) *towards rr: hdwy 2f out: rdn over 1f out: no imp fnl f* **12/1**

61-1 **9** 3 **Rock On Candy**[61] 2870 4-9-4 67 ... ChrisCatlin 3 50
(John Spearing) *prom: rdn along 2f out: sn wknd* **7/2**[1]

3540 **10** ½ **Royal Bajan (USA)**[6] 4728 5-9-5 68 ...(b) DaleSwift 12 49
(James Given) *racd nr stands' rail: led: rdn along 2f out: hdd over 1f out and sn wknd* **10/1**

43-0 **11** ½ **Therapeutic**[49] 3247 3-8-7 59 ...(p) MartinDwyer 6 37
(Scott Dixon) *prom: rdn along over 2f out: drvn over 1f out: wknd ent fnl f* **20/1**

1420 **12** 2½ **Monnoyer**[62] 2832 4-9-5 68 ...(be) LukeMorris 10 38
(Scott Dixon) *wnt lft s: chsd ldrs: rdn along over 2f out: sn wknd* **8/1**[3]

1m 0.65s (-0.85) **Going Correction** -0.05s/f (Good)
WFA 3 from 4yo+ 3lb 12 Ran SP% **115.6**
Speed ratings (Par 103): **104,103,100,99,99 99,98,97,92,91 90,86**
toteswingers 1&2 £4.40, 2&3 £0.00, 1&3 £0.00 CSF £125.74 CT £2013.93 TOTE £7.70: £2.30, £2.50, £7.70; EX 56.20 TRIFECTA Not won..
Owner John Berry (Gwent) **Bred** L T Roberts **Trained** Pandy, Monmouths

FOCUS
A modest sprint handicap, weakened by the late defection of likely favourite Oil Strike. Ordinary form, the first two towards the rail.

4931 IRISH NIGHT ON TUESDAY 13TH AUGUST H'CAP 2m 9y
6:00 (6:01) (Class 6) (0-65,65) 3-Y-0 **£1,940** (£577; £288; £144) **Stalls** Low

Form RPR
-564 **1** **Pearl Spice (IRE)**[21] 4222 3-9-7 65 ...(b) WilliamCarson 1 83+
(Tim Pitt) *set str pce: pushed clr 5f out: rdn and wl clr over 2f out: styd on strly unchal* **20/1**

0000 **2** 11 **Fitzwilly**[12] 2599 3-8-2 46 ... DuranFentiman 10 51
(Mick Channon) *trckd ldrs: hdwy 5f out: rdn to go 12 l 2nd 3f out: drvn 2f out: no imp* **16/1**

-4V4 **3** *17* **Honey Haven (IRE)**[17] 4352 3-7-13 **46** oh1 NeilFarley(3) 8 31
(Mark Brisbourne) *bhd: hdwy over 4f out: rdn along over 3f out: plugged on to take remote 3rd 2f out* **50/1**

0-00 **4** *15* **Dusky Lark**[70] 2599 3-9-4 **62** RobertHavlin 7 29
(Hughie Morrison) *hld up towards rr: pushed along and hdwy 4f out: rdn 3f out: plugged on fnl 2f for remote 4th* **20/1**

4660 **5** *9* **Dawn Beat**[21] 4222 3-8-8 **52** ShaneKelly 12 8
(Jonathan Portman) *midfield: hdwy to chse ldng pair after 6f: rdn along to chse wnr 5f out: drvn over 3f out: sn wknd* **20/1**

-000 **6** *1 1/4* **Erica Starprincess**[49] 3232 3-7-13 **46** oh1 DeclanCannon(3) 15
(George Moore) *a in rr: nvr a factor* **66/1**

006 **7** *5* **Snow Train**[22] 4157 3-8-2 **46** oh1 AndrewMullen 4
(James Given) *towards rr: hdwy and in tch 7f out: rdn along to chse ldrs 5f out: drvn and wknd over 3f out: sn bhd* **33/1**

0-01 **8** *11* **Rancher (IRE)**[65] 2748 3-8-9 **53** PatCosgrave 3
(Tony Carroll) *midfield: effrt and sme hdwy 7f out: sn rdn along and nvr a factor: t.o fnl 3f* **10/1**

0-53 **9** *13* **Frederick Alfred**[45] 3403 3-8-5 **49** ChrisCatlin 6
(Mark H Tompkins) *chsd ldrs: rdn along over 5f out: rn v wd home turn and sn bhd: t.o* **12/1**

5-06 **10** *3 3/4* **Rocky Two (IRE)**[45] 3394 3-9-7 **65** TomEaves 9
(Michael Dods) *a towards rr: t.o fnl 4f* **16/1**

-051 **11** *1 1/4* **Tobacco**[21] 4222 3-8-10 **54** PaulQuinn 14
(Tim Easterby) *hld up: a bhd: t.o fnl 4f* **6/1**[2]

0-61 **12** *4 1/2* **Man From Seville**[66] 2716 3-9-3 **61** LukeMorris 11
(Sir Mark Prescott Bt) *prom: chsd wnr after 4f: pushed along 7f out: rdn over 5f out: drvn and wknd 4f out: sn bhd and t.o fnl 3f* **5/4**[1]

0504 **13** *48* **Moaning Butcher**[10] 4587 3-8-11 **55** LiamJones 2
(Mark Johnston) *chsd ldrs: rdn along bef 1/2-way: sn lost pl and bhd: t.o fnl 4f* **9/1**[3]

5000 **14** *1 1/2* **Pursivere**[38] 3636 3-9-2 **60** (b[1]) SeanLevey 13
(Hughie Morrison) *in tch: rdn along 6f out: sn wknd and t.o fnl 3f* **28/1**

3m 30.85s (-3.65) **Going Correction** -0.225s/f (Firm) course record **14** Ran SP% **121.4**
Speed ratings (Par 98): **100,94,86,78,74 73,70,65,58,57 56,54,30,29**
toteswingers 1&2 £0.00, 2&3 £0.00, 1&3 £0.00 CSF £291.17 CT £14684.31 TOTE £12.50: £5.10, £8.80, £16.50; EX 184.00 TRIFECTA Not won..
Owner Decadent Racing **Bred** Airlie Stud **Trained** Newmarket, Suffolk

FOCUS
A low-grade finale, in which the joint-top-weights were rated 65 and the favourite was disappointing. A good time fore the grade from the winer, and they were strung out behind him. This was a big step up from him.
T/Plt: £45.80 to a £1 stake. Pool of £48496.15 - 771.38 winning tickets. T/Qpdt: £13.80 to a £1 stake. Pool of £2726.20 - 146.10 winning tickets. JR

4932 - 4934a (Foreign Racing) - See Raceform Interactive

4815 DEAUVILLE (R-H)
Thursday, August 1
OFFICIAL GOING: Turf: soft; fibresand: standard

4935a PRIX DU CERCLE (LISTED RACE) (3YO+) (TURF) 5f
1:20 (12:00) 3-Y-O+ **£21,138** (£8,455; £6,341; £4,227; £2,113)

RPR

1 **Riskit Fora Biskit (IRE)**[20] 4247 3-8-8 0 IoritzMendizabal 2 98
(Michael Bell) *racd in trio against nr side rail: in midfield overall: rdn over 1f out: r.o strly to ld cl home: drvn out* **131/10**

2 *3/4* **Gammarth (FR)**[40] 3557 5-9-7 0 FabriceVeron 14 106
(H-A Pantall, France) **33/10**[2]

3 *nse* **Stepper Point**[13] 4493 4-9-1 0 (p) ChristopheSoumillon 6 100
(William Muir) *racd in centre: w ldrs: rdn to ld over 1f out: r.o but hdd cl home and dropped to 3rd post* **3/1**[1]

4 *snk* **A Huge Dream (IRE)**[14] 4-8-11 0 StephanePasquier 15 95
(F Rohaut, France) **10/1**

5 *hd* **Mirza**[33] 3822 6-9-5 0 (p) ThierryJarnet 3 103
(Rae Guest) *racd in trio against nr side rail: in midfield overall: upsides eventual wnr ent fnl f: r.o and wnt 5th cl home: nt quite pce to chal* **12/1**

6 *hd* **Caspian Prince (IRE)**[14] 4-9-1 0 MaximeGuyon 1 98?
(E J O'Neill, France) **18/1**

7 *3/4* **Morning Frost (IRE)**[25] 4105 3-8-13 0 JulienAuge 11 95
(C Ferland, France) **12/1**

8 *nk* **Vital Spirit (FR)**[25] 4-9-1 0 UmbertoRispoli 9 94
(E J O'Neill, France) **18/1**

9 *nk* **Blue Soave (FR)**[26] 4093 5-9-1 0 ThierryThulliez 8 93
(F Chappet, France) **18/1**

10 *snk* **Mister Ryan (FR)**[25] 4-9-1 0 OlivierPeslier 13 92
(H-A Pantall, France) **83/10**[3]

0 **Ruby's Day**[18] 4-8-11 0 (b[1]) GregoryBenoist 10
(E J O'Neill, France) **45/1**

0 **Matchday**[25] 4-8-11 0 EddyHardouin 4
(Frau E Mader, Germany) **102/1**

0 **Faithfilly (IRE)**[51] 3186 3-8-8 0 (p) Francois-XavierBertras 5
(F Rohaut, France) **20/1**

0 **Via Garibaldi (ITY)**[74] 2491 4-9-1 0 CristianDemuro 12
(L Riccardi, Italy) **42/1**

56.09s (-1.41)
WFA 3 from 4yo+ 3lb **14** Ran SP% **116.6**
WIN (incl. 1 euro stake): 14.10. PLACES: 3.50, 1.80, 1.80. DF: 30.90. SF: 97.50.
Owner Chris Wright & The Hon Mrs J M Corbett **Bred** Edmond Kent **Trained** Newmarket, Suffolk

4095 OVREVOLL (R-H)
Thursday, August 1
OFFICIAL GOING: Turf: good

4936a POLAR CUP (GROUP 3) (3YO+) (TURF) 6f 187y
7:15 (12:00) 3-Y-O+ **£33,185** (£11,061; £5,530; £3,318; £2,212)

RPR

1 **Ragazzo (NOR)**[54] 4-9-4 0 EspenSki 3 102
(Annike Bye Hansen, Norway) *chsd ldr tl led after 1f: mde rest: forged clr over 1 1/2f out: r.o wl under hands and heels fnl f: a holding runner-up* **49/10**[3]

2 *1/2* **Giant Sandman (IRE)**[26] 6-9-4 0 LennartHammer-Hansen 5 101
(Rune Haugen, Norway) *trckd ldrs: shkn up to chse ldr 2 1/2f out: briefly outpcd over 2f out: styd on u.p to chse wnr over 1f out: kpt on ins fnl f but a hld by wnr* **1/2**[1]

3 *1* **Govinda (USA)**[29] 3970 6-9-8 0 OliverWilson 2 102
(Vanja Sandrup, Sweden) *towards rr but wl in tch: hdwy into 4th and gng wl 2 1/2f out: rdn and outpcd over 2f out: styd on appr 1f out: kpt on wl u.p fnl f: nt pce to chal* **9/1**

4 *2 1/2* **Coprah**[23] 5-9-4 0 ElioneChaves 4 90
(Cathrine Erichsen, Norway) *hld up in rr: hdwy on inner 2 1/2f out: pressed ldr ent fnl 2f: rdn and no ex appr 1f out: one pce fnl f* **171/10**

5 *1* **Hansinger (IRE)**[51] 8-9-4 0 RafaelSchistl 1 88
(Cathrine Erichsen, Norway) *broke wl and led: hdd after 1f: remained prom tl rdn and lost pl over 3f out: kpt on again fr over 1f out: no threat to ldrs* **141/10**

6 *1 1/2* **Nova Valorem (IRE)**[23] 5-9-4 0 MRobaldo 6 83
(Bent Olsen, Denmark) *towards rr: last at 1/2-way: nvr threatened ldrs* **213/10**

7 *3* **Silver Ocean (USA)**[23] 5-9-8 0 FJohansson 7 78
(Niels Petersen, Norway) *prom on outer: rdn and lost pl over 2f out: wknd fnl f* **43/10**[2]

1m 20.7s (80.70) **7** Ran SP% **129.1**
PARI-MUTUEL (all including 1krone stakes): WIN 5.92; PLACE 1.36, 1.20, 1.50; DF 19.75.
Owner Stall Trotting **Bred** Johan C Loken **Trained** Norway

4653 BATH (L-H)
Friday, August 2
OFFICIAL GOING: Firm (good to firm in places; 9.4)
Wind: Moderate across Weather: Sunny spells

4937 ALIDE HIRE MAIDEN AUCTION STKS 5f 161y
5:30 (5:32) (Class 5) 2-Y-O **£2,587** (£770; £384; £192) **Stalls** Centre

Form RPR

43 **1** **Douneedahand**[6] 4749 2-8-4 0 FrankieMcDonald 8 63
(Seamus Mullins) *mde all: rdn 2f out: edging lft u.p ins fnl f: hld on wl* **12/1**

2 *1/2* **Jacob Black** 2-8-6 0 RyanTate(5) 5 68
(Clive Cox) *broke wl: sn drvn and outpcd: hdwy ins fnl 2f: kpt on wl fnl f to take 2nd clsng stages: nt rch wnr* **7/2**[2]

23 **3** *3/4* **Flicksta (USA)**[23] 4175 2-8-13 0 LukeMorris 1 68
(Ronald Harris) *s.i.s: sn in tch: rdn 1/2-way: styd on u.p to chse wnr ins fnl f: no imp and one pce into 3rd clsng stages* **11/10**[1]

4 *2* **Penny's Boy** 2-8-11 0 JackMitchell 2 59
(Sylvester Kirk) *in rr: drvn and hdwy fr 2f out: styd on fnl f but nvr gng pce to chal* **25/1**

5 *3/4* **Monte Viso** 2-8-11 0 MartinDwyer 6 57
(Stuart Kittow) *t.k.h: in rr: haedway over 2f out: nvr seeing much daylight but kpt on clsng stages* **16/1**

50 **6** *hd* **Good Morning Lady**[14] 4505 2-7-13 0 DanielCremin(7) 9 51
(Mick Channon) *in rr: drvn and hdwy on outer fr 2f out: nvr quite gng pce to press ldrs and styd on one pce fnl f* **10/1**

00 **7** *hd* **Monsieur Blanc (IRE)**[48] 3310 2-8-11 0 (v[1]) CathyGannon 4 55
(Denis Coakley) *chsd ldrs: rdn over 2f out: wknd fnl f* **25/1**

8 *1 1/2* **Lovely Lily** 2-8-1 0 RyanWhile(7) 3 48
(Bill Turner) *chsd ldrs: rdn over 2f out: wknd over 1f out* **16/1**

60 **9** *3/4* **Notnow Penny**[31] 3914 2-7-11 0 ShelleyBirkett(7) 10 41
(Milton Bradley) *chsd ldr to 1/2-way: wknd ins fnl 2f* **100/1**

10 *8* **Kopenhagen (IRE)** 2-8-13 0 RyanPowell(3) 7 27
(Ed de Giles) *s.i.s: hmpd after 1f: a outpcd* **8/1**[3]

1m 11.17s (-0.03) **Going Correction** -0.20s/f (Firm) **10** Ran SP% **118.2**
Speed ratings (Par 94): **92,91,90,87,86 86,86,84,83,72**
toteswingers 1&2 £5.60, 1&3 £2.80, 2&3 £2.50 CSF £53.89 TOTE £12.20: £2.80, £1.50, £1.10; EX 60.80 Trifecta £157.40 Pool: £1642.96 - 7.82 winning units..
Owner Caloona Racing **Bred** New England, Myriad B/S And Barton Stud **Trained** Wilsford-Cum-Lake, Wilts

FOCUS
There was an all-the-way winner in this maiden and the clear market leader was a bit laboured. The third and sixth set an ordinary level.

4938 SYMONDS FOUNDERS RESERVE CIDER H'CAP 2m 1f 34y
6:00 (6:00) (Class 5) (0-70,71) 4-Y-O+ **£2,587** (£770; £384; £192) **Stalls** Low

Form RPR

3123 **1** **Hi Note**[13] 4530 5-9-2 **70** HarryPoulton(5) 9 78
(Sheena West) *sn chsng ldr: dropped to cl 3rd 5f out: chsd ldr again over 2f out: drvn to ld appr fnl f: kpt on wl* **2/1**[2]

26/6 **2** *2 1/4* **Dark Spirit (IRE)**[32] 3882 5-8-13 **62** MartinDwyer 5 68
(Evan Williams) *led: rdn 2f out: hdd and edgd rt over 1f out: styd on same pce* **10/3**[3]

5331 **3** *8* **Candelita**[8] 4655 6-9-2 **65** 6ex CathyGannon 6 62
(Jo Hughes) *trckd ldrs: wnt 2nd 5f out: rdn and no imp over 3f out: dropped to 3rd over 2f out: wknd fnl f* **5/4**[1]

4250 **4** *38* **Fuzzy Logic (IRE)**[32] 3884 4-8-2 **51** oh5 LukeMorris 2
(Bernard Llewellyn) *pushed along 13f out: rdn over 7f out: wknd 3f out* **10/1**

3m 46.04s (-5.86) **Going Correction** -0.25s/f (Firm) **4** Ran SP% **109.9**
Speed ratings (Par 103): **103,101,98,80**
CSF £8.73 TOTE £3.00; EX 11.00 Trifecta £13.20 Pool: £585.28 - 33.02 winning units..
Owner Gerald West **Bred** J A And Mrs Duffy **Trained** Falmer, E Sussex

FOCUS
The in-form winner scored in decent style from off the stop-start pace in this staying handicap, but the race was weakened by several withdrawals.

4939 BULMERS CIDER H'CAP 1m 3f 144y
6:35 (6:37) (Class 6) (0-60,64) 3-Y-O **£1,940** (£577; £288; £144) **Stalls** Low

Form RPR

0-46 **1** **First Secretary**[33] 3860 3-9-7 **60** MartinDwyer 2 74+
(Roger Charlton) *towards rr but in tch: hdwy 4f out: chsd ldrs over 2f out: led over 1f out: shkn up and edgd lft ins fnl f: styd on wl* **11/4**[2]

3041 **2** *2 1/2* **See And Be Seen**[8] 4664 3-8-12 **51** 6ex RenatoSouza 3 60
(Sylvester Kirk) *in rr: hdwy over 2f out: sn hrd drvn: kpt on fnl f to take 2nd last strides but no ch w wnr* **12/1**

64-1 **3** *nk* **Alzavola**[8] 4657 3-9-11 **64** 6ex LukeMorris 6 72
(Sir Mark Prescott Bt) *led: rdn over 3f out: hdd over 1f out: one pce fnl f and sn outpcd by wnr: lost 2nd clsng stages* **11/10**[1]

-635 **4** *5* **Uncle Bernie (IRE)**[16] 4405 3-9-3 **56** JohnFahy 7 56
(Andrew Hollinshead) *chsd ldrs: rdn to 2nd over 2f out: wknd over 1f out* **7/1**[3]

605 **5** *2 ¾* **Hattie Jacques**[16] 4404 3-9-3 **59** CharlesBishop(3) 5 54
(Mick Channon) *in rr: sme hdwy over 2f out: nvr rchd ldrs and wknd wl over 1f out* **7/1**[3]

-000 **6** *4 ½* **Secretori**[56] 3040 3-9-1 **54** CathyGannon 4 42
(Jo Hughes) *chsd ldrs: ridedn over 3f out: wknd over 2f out* **25/1**

000 **7** *11* **Eleanor Roosevelt (IRE)**[88] 2093 3-9-5 **58** GeorgeBaker 8 27
(Jamie Osborne) *chsd ldr tl wknd qckly over 2f out* **16/1**

2m 29.71s (-0.89) **Going Correction** -0.25s/f (Firm) 7 Ran SP% **116.7**
Speed ratings (Par 98): **92,90,90,86,84 81,74**
toteswingers 1&2 £3.60, 1&3 £2.20, 2&3 £2.80 CSF £35.50 CT £55.72 TOTE £3.80: £2.00, £3.20; EX 39.30 Trifecta £71.50 Pool: £1803.75 - 18.90 winning units..
Owner Lady Rothschild **Bred** Kincorth Investments Inc **Trained** Beckhampton, Wilts

FOCUS
An unexposed filly scored in good style in this minor handicap and the form looks strong for the grade.

4940 LA CLARK H'CAP — 1m 2f 46y
7:10 (7:10) (Class 4) (0-80,78) 3-Y-O — **£5,175** (£1,540; £769) **Stalls** Low

Form RPR

1553 **1** **Aneedh**[8] 4672 3-9-1 **72** (p) GeorgeBaker 4 76
(William Haggas) *trckd ldr: chal and hung lft 2f out and sn led: hung lft again appr fnl f: pushed out and a doing enough clsng stages* **4/11**[1]

6-05 **2** *¾* **Happy Families**[22] 4223 3-8-6 **70** OisinMurphy(7) 2 72
(Heather Main) *led: jnd 2f out: edgd rt u.p and sn hdd: styd pressing wnr: edgd rt and bmpd again appr fnl f: nt qckn fnl 110yds* **8/1**[3]

2166 **3** *6* **The Scuttler (IRE)**[4] 4829 3-8-2 **66** DanielCremin(7) 5 56
(Mick Channon) *trckd ldrs in 3rd: hdwy to chal between horses 2f out and sn bmpd on either side: styd chalng tl hmpd again appr fnl f: sn wknd* **3/1**[2]

2m 10.98s (-0.02) **Going Correction** -0.25s/f (Firm) 3 Ran SP% **109.4**
Speed ratings (Par 102): **90,89,84**
CSF £3.70 TOTE £1.30; EX 2.50 Trifecta £4.70 Pool: £729.48 - 114.32 winning units..
Owner Mohammed Jaber **Bred** Rabbah Bloodstock Limited **Trained** Newmarket, Suffolk
■ Stewards' Enquiry : George Baker one-day ban: careless riding (Aug 16)

FOCUS
There were only three runners but this was a rough race and the third was hampered a couple of times.

4941 REDLEISURE.CO.UK FILLIES' H'CAP — 1m 5y
7:40 (7:41) (Class 4) (0-80,78) 3-Y-O+ — **£5,175** (£1,540; £769; £384) **Stalls** Low

Form RPR

3134 **1** **Oratorio's Joy (IRE)**[18] 4348 3-9-0 **71** JamesDoyle 7 75
(Jamie Osborne) *chsd ldrs: rdn and outpcd over 2f out: rallied u.p fnl f: led last strides* **5/1**[3]

531 **2** *hd* **Starlight Symphony (IRE)**[18] 4348 3-9-3 **74** (b) JohnFahy 1 78
(Eve Johnson Houghton) *hld up in rr: gd hdwy fr 3f out to chal 2f out and sn led: hung lft u.p 1f out: hung bdly rt u.p sn after: hdd last strides* **3/1**[1]

4424 **3** *1 ¾* **Society Pearl (IRE)**[23] 4157 3-8-13 **70** LukeMorris 2 73+
(Charles Hills) *in rr: drvn and hdwy over 1f out: styng on to cl and ev ch whn bdly hmpd and nt rcvr fnl 50yds* **9/2**[2]

201- **4** *½* **Sugar House (USA)**[380] 4217 3-8-12 **76** AhmadAlSubousi(7) 6 77+
(Charlie Appleby) *slowly away: sn rcvrd but sddle slipped: led 5f out and racd wd: rdn and jnd over 2f out: hdd over 1f out: styd wl there and stl a ch whn bdly hmpd fnl 100yds* **5/1**[3]

51-5 **5** *2 ¼* **Snow Rose (USA)**[41] 3583 3-9-7 **78** AhmedAjtebi 8 72
(Charlie Appleby) *sn led: hdd 5f out but styd pressing ldr: rdn 2f out: nt clr run 1f out: wknd ins fnl f* **3/1**[1]

20-3 **6** *3 ½* **Madame Elizabeth**[13] 4515 3-8-13 **70** ShaneKelly 3 56
(Andrew Hollinshead) *chsd ldrs: rdn over 2f out: wkng whn hmpd jst ins fnl f* **17/2**

1m 42.33s (1.53) **Going Correction** -0.25s/f (Firm) 6 Ran SP% **112.0**
Speed ratings (Par 102): **82,81,80,79,77 73**
toteswingers 1&2 £3.30, 1&3 £2.50, 2&3 £1.50 CSF £20.16 CT £70.56 TOTE £8.10: £3.00, £2.50; EX 27.20 Trifecta £64.40 Pool: £649.38 - 7.55 winning units..
Owner Dominic Christian **Bred** R Mahon & J Reilly **Trained** Upper Lambourn, Berks
■ Stewards' Enquiry : John Fahy (1st incident) three-day ban: careless riding (Aug 16-18); (2nd) one-day ban: careless riding (Aug 19)

FOCUS
They went a steady pace in this handicap and it was a messy race.

4942 STRONGBOW CIDER H'CAP — 5f 11y
8:10 (8:10) (Class 5) (0-75,74) 3-Y-O — **£2,587** (£770; £384; £192) **Stalls** Centre

Form RPR

0505 **1** **Secret Missile**[74] 2521 3-9-7 **74** MartinDwyer 3 79
(William Muir) *chsd ldrs: outpcd and drvn 2f out: rallied u.p fnl f: led clsng stages: readily* **5/4**[1]

3401 **2** *1* **Edged Out**[8] 4654 3-8-12 **72** 6ex OisinMurphy(7) 1 73
(Christopher Mason) *led 1f: styd pressing ldr: led wl over 1f out: rdn fnl f: hdd and outpcd clsng stages* **7/2**[3]

2- **3** *½* **Truly Madly (IRE)**[25] 4129 3-8-7 **65** RyanTate(5) 4 65
(Hans Adielsson) *in tch: outpcd over 2f out: hdwy over 1f out: styd on to take 3rd fnl 50yds: nt trble ldng duo* **14/1**

510- **4** *¾* **Somoud (IRE)**[296] 6984 3-9-6 **73** ShaneKelly 2 70
(J R Jenkins) *in rr but in tch: hdwy to cl on ldrs ins fnl 2f: no ex u.p fnl f: wknd clsng stages* **12/1**

4062 **5** *1 ¼* **Small Fury (IRE)**[6] 4772 3-9-7 **74** CathyGannon 6 66
(Jo Hughes) *led after 1f but hrd pressed tl hdd wl over 1f out: hld whn hmpd fnl 30yds* **9/4**[2]

1m 1.33s (-1.17) **Going Correction** -0.20s/f (Firm) 5 Ran SP% **111.8**
Speed ratings (Par 100): **101,99,98,97,95**
CSF £6.14 TOTE £2.40: £1.40, £1.60; EX 8.70 TRIFECTA Pool: £615.11 - 13.55 winning units..
Owner Muir Racing Partnership - Manchester **Bred** Whitsbury Manor Stud **Trained** Lambourn, Berks

FOCUS
They finished in a bunch in this sprint handicap and the revitalised winner swooped late.

4943 BUBBLECHRISTMASPARTIES.CO.UK H'CAP — 5f 11y
8:40 (8:40) (Class 6) (0-60,60) 4-Y-O+ — **£1,940** (£577; £288; £144) **Stalls** Centre

Form RPR

0324 **1** **Arch Walker (IRE)**[6] 4761 6-9-0 **53** (b) KieranO'Neill 8 62
(John Weymes) *chsd ldrs: led 2f out: sn rdn: edgd lft u.p clsng stages: hld on wl* **2/1**[1]

0662 **2** *1 ¼* **Chester'Slittlegem (IRE)**[8] 4660 4-8-8 **47** CathyGannon 2 52
(Jo Hughes) *chsd ldrs: rdn over 2f out: styd on to chse wnr fnl f: one pce whn pushed lft clsng stages* **5/1**

4524 **3** *¾* **Johnny Splash (IRE)**[15] 4427 4-8-6 **52** OisinMurphy(7) 6 54
(Roger Teal) *in rr: hdwy over 2f out: styd on fnl f: nt rch ldng duo* **4/1**[3]

0635 **4** *1 ¾* **Ingleby Star (IRE)**[10] 4608 8-9-7 **60** (p) ShaneKelly 4 56
(Daniel Mark Loughnane) *towards rr: hdwy fr 2f out: styd on to chse ldrs fnl f and ev ch: n.m.r on rails and eased cl home* **10/1**

4350 **5** *1 ½* **Volcanic Dust (IRE)**[15] 4427 5-8-8 **54** (t) WillPettis(7) 5 44
(Milton Bradley) *in tch: chsd ldrs and rdn 2f out: no ex fnl f* **20/1**

0656 **6** *hd* **Brandywell Boy (IRE)**[8] 4659 10-8-0 **46** oh1 NoraLooby(7) 3 35
(Dominic Ffrench Davis) *in rr: sme hdwy over 1f out: nvr gng pce to trble ldrs* **20/1**

5-00 **7** *3 ¾* **Too Ambitious**[8] 4659 4-8-7 **46** (p) MartinDwyer 9 22
(Andrew Hollinshead) *led: hdd 2f out: wknd over 1f out* **20/1**

60U1 **8** *3* **Spic 'n Span**[10] 4608 8-9-3 **56** 6ex (b) LukeMorris 11 21
(Ronald Harris) *chsd ldrs: chal 2f out: wknd over 1f out* **8/1**

5001 **9** *11* **Brown Volcano (IRE)**[8] 4659 4-9-2 **58** 6ex ThomasBrown(3) 1
(John O'Shea) *slowly away: nt rcvr and a wl behid* **5/2**[2]

1m 1.74s (-0.76) **Going Correction** -0.20s/f (Firm) 9 Ran SP% **133.1**
Speed ratings (Par 101): **98,96,94,92,89 89,83,78,60**
toteswingers 1&2 £7.10, 1&3 £5.30, 2&3 £7.90 CSF £14.66 TOTE £4.50: £1.70, £2.50, £1.90; EX 28.60 Trifecta £71.30 Pool: £832.54 - 8.75 winning units..
Owner High Moor & Thoroughbred Partners **Bred** T Hirschfeld **Trained** Middleham Moor, N Yorks

FOCUS
The went a decent pace in this sprint handicap and the favourite put in a gutsy display under a prominent ride.
T/Plt: £93.60 to a £1 stake. Pool: £47523.34 - 370.61 winning tickets T/Qpdt: £28.70 to a £1 stake. Pool: £3219.15 - 82.80 winning tickets ST

4917 GOODWOOD (R-H)
Friday, August 2

OFFICIAL GOING: Good (good to firm in places; 8.0)
Wind: Medium to fresh, against Weather: Overcast, brightening up

4944 COUTTS GLORIOUS STKS (GROUP 3) — 1m 4f
1:55 (1:55) (Class 1) 4-Y-O+
£34,026 (£12,900; £6,456; £3,216; £1,614; £810) **Stalls** High

Form RPR

50/1 **1** **Forgotten Voice (IRE)**[42] 3525 8-9-0 **110** JohnnyMurtagh 1 114
(Nicky Henderson) *stdd s: t.k.h: hld up off the pce in last pair: clsd over 2f out: rdn and effrt over 1f out: r.o wl to ld fnl 75yds: rdn out* **3/1**[2]

35-1 **2** *½* **Lost In The Moment (IRE)**[34] 3830 6-9-0 **110** (p) SilvestreDeSousa 3 113
(Saeed bin Suroor) *lw: chsd clr ldng pair: drvn and effrt 3f out: clsd u.p to ld over 1f out: edgd rt 1f out: hdd fnl 75yds: kpt on but a hld* **10/3**[3]

1212 **3** *1 ½* **Sheikhzayedroad**[42] 3525 4-9-0 **104** MartinLane 6 112+
(David Simcock) *lw: stdd s: hld up off the pce in rr: effrt and hung rt on to rail over 2f out: hdwy to chse ldrs and swtchd lft 1f out: pressing ldrs whn hmpd ins fnl f: nt rcvrd and one pce after* **5/1**

15 **4** *3* **Montaser (IRE)**[20] 4309 4-9-0 **101** JimCrowley 4 107+
(David Simcock) *chsd ldr and clr of rivals: clsd to join ldr over 3f out: rdn to ld over 2f out: hdd over 1f out: stl pressing ldr but looking btn whn hmpd twice ins fnl f: wknd fnl 75yds* **14/1**

213- **5** *2 ¾* **Masterstroke (USA)**[299] 6912 4-9-0 **114** MickaelBarzalona 7 102
(Charlie Appleby) *str: t.k.h: hld up off the pce in 4th: rdn and effrt over 2f out: sme hdwy wl over 1f out: btn ent fnl f: wknd* **5/2**[1]

2-10 **6** *6* **Mijhaar**[33] 3873 5-9-0 **109** AndreaAtzeni 5 92
(Roger Varian) *swtg: led and clr w a rival: rdn and hdd over 2f out: 3rd and unable qck 2f out: wknd over 1f out* **8/1**

2m 36.95s (-1.45) **Going Correction** -0.10s/f (Good) 6 Ran SP% **111.1**
Speed ratings (Par 113): **100,99,98,96,94 90**
toteswingers 1&2 £3.00, 1&3 £2.40, 2&3 £2.60 CSF £13.05 TOTE £3.60: £1.60, £2.10; EX 13.60 Trifecta £58.50 Pool: £3141.67 - 40.25 winning units..
Owner Mrs Susan Roy **Bred** Swettenham Stud And Ben Sangster **Trained** Upper Lambourn, Berks
■ Stewards' Enquiry : Silvestre De Sousa two-day ban: careless riding (Aug 16-17)

FOCUS
Top bend dolled out increasing distances by about 8yds. This Group 3 prize was weakened by the withdrawal of Aiken, but it was still a tight affair and they went a solid pace with the two early leaders going clear.

4945 BONHAMS THOROUGHBRED STKS (GROUP 3) — 1m
2:30 (2:30) (Class 1) 3-Y-O
£34,026 (£12,900; £6,456; £3,216; £1,614; £810) **Stalls** Low

Form RPR

3121 **1** **Montiridge (IRE)**[22] 4216 3-9-0 **113** RichardHughes 2 117+
(Richard Hannon) *lw: stdd s: hld up in tch in last trio: swtchd out and trckd rival jst over 1f out: rdn and qcknd to ld fnl 100yds: pushed out: comf* **5/6**[1]

-433 **2** *1 ¼* **Tawhid**[44] 3455 3-9-0 **111** SilvestreDeSousa 4 114
(Saeed bin Suroor) *chsd ldng pair: rdn to chal and pushed lft over 2f out: drvn to ld over 1f out: edgd rt u.p 1f out: hdd fnl 100yds: nt pce of wnr: kpt on* **6/1**[3]

2341 **3** *2 ¼* **Snowboarder (USA)**[13] 4531 3-9-0 **107** MickaelBarzalona 1 111+
(Charlie Appleby) *lw: hld up in tch in midfield: trcking ldrs and travelling wl whn swtchd rt 2f out: pressing ldrs whn squeezed and bdly hmpd 1f out: kpt on same pce after* **10/1**

-325 **4** *1 ¼* **Glory Awaits (IRE)**[45] 3421 3-9-0 **114** (p) JamieSpencer 8 106
(Kevin Ryan) *lw: led: rdn wl over 2f out: hdd over 1f out: stl ev ch but struggling to qckn whn pushed rt and bdly hmpd 1f out: wl hld and one pce after* **7/1**

010- **5** *1 ½* **Whipper's Boy (IRE)**[366] 4698 3-9-0 **100** KierenFallon 6 103
(Brian Meehan) *stdd s: t.k.h: hld up in rr: pushed along and effrt on inner 2f out: sltly hmpd 1f out: kpt on fnl f: eased cl home* **33/1**

0410 **6** 3/4 **Well Acquainted (IRE)**[44] 3455 3-9-0 107 JamesDoyle 5 101
(Clive Cox) *chsd ldr: rdn to chal whn hit by rival jockey's whip and jinked lft over 2f out: no ex over 1f out: wknd ins fnl f* **25/1**

1321 **7** nse **Baltic Knight (IRE)**[48] 3347 3-9-0 111 RyanMoore 3 101
(Richard Hannon) *lw: in tch in last trio: rdn and effrt over 2f out: no prog over 1f out: wknd ins fnl f* **9/2**[2]

1m 37.37s (-2.53) **Going Correction** -0.10s/f (Good) 7 Ran SP% **115.4**
Speed ratings (Par 110): **108,106,104,103,101 101,100**
toteswingers 1&2 £2.30, 1&3 £2.40, 2&3 £5.40 CSF £6.63 TOTE £1.70: £1.10, £3.50; EX 7.50 Trifecta £35.90 Pool: £5476.75 - 114.24 winning units..
Owner M Clarke,J Jeffries,R Ambrose,B Reilly **Bred** Century Bloodstock **Trained** East Everleigh, Wilts
■ Stewards' Enquiry : Silvestre De Sousa four-day ban: careless riding (Aug 18-20,24)

FOCUS
Only the second year since this race was upgraded from Listed status and it went to a potentially high-class colt in the shape of the improving Montiridge.

4946 BETFRED MILE (HERITAGE H'CAP) 1m
3:05 (3:07) (Class 2) 3-Y-0+

£80,925 (£24,232; £12,116; £6,058; £3,029; £1,521) **Stalls** Low

Form RPR

-343 **1** **Wentworth (IRE)**[27] 4080 3-8-10 **99** RichardHughes 13 110+
(Richard Hannon) *lw: hld up wl in tch in midfield: swtchd lft and squeezed between rivals ent fnl f: rdn and qcknd to ld fnl 100yds: eased last strides* **6/1**[2]

115 **2** 3/4 **Cape Peron**[43] 3484 3-8-12 **101** DaneO'Neill 5 110+
(Henry Candy) *lw: t.k.h: hld up chsng ldrs: stl travelling wl whn swtchd rt and then bk lft over 1f out: drvn and gd hdwy to chal fnl 100yds: styd on same pce towards fin* **5/1**[1]

0200 **3** hd **Sandagiyr (FR)**[44] 3458 5-9-6 **102** MickaelBarzalona 8 112
(Saeed bin Suroor) *stdd and awkward leaving stalls: hld up towards rr: clsng on inner whn nt clr run and hmpd 2f out: swtchd lft and the bk rt and gd hdwy u.p over 1f out: r.o wl ins fnl f* **25/1**

0011 **4** 3/4 **Galician**[6] 4744 4-9-2 **98** 6ex JoeFanning 14 106
(Mark Johnston) *chsd ldrs: rdn and effrt ent fnl 2f: keeping on whn pushed lft jst over 1f out: kpt on u.p ins fnl f* **11/1**

5031 **5** hd **Fire Ship**[5] 4811 4-9-4 **100** 3ex NeilCallan 7 108
(William Knight) *lw: chsd ldrs: rdn and effrt ent fnl 2f: drvn to ld over 1f out: hdd and no ex fnl 100yds: lost 2 pls wl ins fnl f* **10/1**

2230 **6** 1 3/4 **Es Que Love (IRE)**[6] 4744 4-9-5 **101** JohnnyMurtagh 22 105
(Mark Johnston) *swtg: hld up in tch in midfield: nt clr run 2f out and switching rt and lft over 1f out: hdwy whn gap opened 1f out: r.o: nvr able to chal* **16/1**

1560 **7** 1 3/4 **Windhoek**[27] 4080 3-9-1 **104** FrannyNorton 3 103
(Mark Johnston) *led: rdn over 2f out: kpt on gamely u.p tl hdd and no ex over 1f out: wknd ins fnl f* **10/1**

3406 **8** 1/2 **Two For Two (IRE)**[42] 3525 5-9-4 **100** DanielTudhope 15 99
(David O'Meara) *hld up in tch: rdn and effrt jst over 2f out: hdwy u.p over 1f out: styd on f: nvr threatened ldrs* **33/1**

0615 **9** shd **Field Of Dream**[6] 4744 6-9-5 **101** 3ex (b) WilliamBuick 17 99
(Jamie Osborne) *mounted on crse and taken down early: s.i.s: bhd: rdn and effrt on outer over 2f out: kpt on ins fnl f: nvr trbld ldrs* **20/1**

0064 **10** 1/2 **Dance And Dance (IRE)**[20] 4297 7-8-12 **94** (b) RyanMoore 1 91
(Ed Vaughan) *hld up in tch in midfield: swtchd lft over 2f out: rdn and effrt whn short of room wl over 1f out: one pce and hld 1f out* **15/2**[3]

0401 **11** 3/4 **Sirius Prospect (USA)**[6] 4778 5-9-9 **105** 3ex JimCrowley 21 101
(Dean Ivory) *lw: hld up off the pce in last pair: swtchd to outer and effrt over 2f out: kpt on steadily fr over 1f out: nvr trbld ldrs* **25/1**

13-1 **12** shd **Haafaguinea**[98] 1809 3-8-9 **98** JohnFahy 16 92
(Clive Cox) *swtg: dwlt: hld up towards rr: rdn and 2f out: sn switching lft: no real imp and n.m.r 1f out: kpt on but nvr a threat* **20/1**

4-61 **13** 1 1/4 **Brendan Brackan (IRE)**[3] 4869 4-9-6 **107** 3ex ColinKeane(5) 12 99
(G M Lyons, Ire) *tall: chsd ldrs: rdn and unable qck over 2f out: losing pl whn n.m.r 2f out: n.d after* **6/1**[2]

-552 **14** 3/4 **Dream Tune**[42] 3527 4-8-13 **95** JamesDoyle 18 86
(Clive Cox) *hld up in tch towards rr: rdn and sme hdwy u.p on outer wl over 1f out: wknd ins fnl f* **16/1**

0451 **15** 3/4 **Set The Trend**[13] 4514 7-9-5 **101** 3ex KierenFallon 20 90
(David O'Meara) *chsd ldrs: rdn and effrt over 2f out: unable qck wl over 1f out: wknd ent fnl f* **50/1**

0010 **16** 1 3/4 **Captain Bertie (IRE)**[44] 3458 5-8-13 **95** FrankieDettori 9 80
(Jane Chapple-Hyam) *chsd ldrs: rdn and struggling to qckn whn n.m.r and lost pl 2f out: wknd over 1f out* **25/1**

0600 **17** 9 **St Moritz (IRE)**[20] 4308 7-8-9 **91** PaulHanagan 6 55
(David O'Meara) *pressed ldr: rdn and no ex wl over 1f out: btn ent fnl f: wknd* **40/1**

-015 **18** 12 **Asatir (USA)**[27] 4080 4-8-13 **95** (v) SilvestreDeSousa 11 32
(Saeed bin Suroor) *in tch in midfield: rdn and fnd little over 2f out: sn lost pl: bhd and eased ins fnl f* **20/1**

1m 36.71s (-3.19) **Going Correction** -0.10s/f (Good)
WFA 3 from 4yo+ 7lb 18 Ran SP% **128.4**
Speed ratings (Par 109): **111,110,110,109,109 107,105,105,105,104 103,103,102,101,100 99,90,78**
toteswingers 1&2 £7.60, 1&3 £106.20, 2&3 £65.10 CSF £32.33 CT £754.36 TOTE £6.50: £1.90, £2.10, £8.60, £2.40; EX 34.00 Trifecta £3317.90 Pool: £53087.73 - 12.00 winning units..
Owner Mrs John Magnier & Michael Tabor & Derrick Smith **Bred** Denis McDonnell **Trained** East Everleigh, Wilts
■ Stewards' Enquiry : Dane O'Neill one-day ban: careless riding (Aug 16)

FOCUS
This is traditionally one of the biggest betting handicaps of the season in which a low draw is often crucial, with just one winner defying a double-figure stall in the past decade. However, that tally was doubled this time around as a well-handicapped 3yo landed a gamble from stall 13. The form looks rock-solid.

4947 BETFRED KING GEORGE STKS (GROUP 2) 5f
3:40 (3:43) (Class 1) 3-Y-0+

£56,710 (£21,500; £10,760; £5,360; £2,690; £1,350) **Stalls** High

Form RPR

1122 **1** **Moviesta (USA)**[21] 4255 3-8-12 104 PaulMulrennan 5 115
(Bryan Smart) *stdd s: sn in tch in midfield: rdn and hdwy over 1f out: swtchd lft and squeezed between horses 1f out: drvn to ld ins fnl f: hung lft but in command after* **5/1**[2]

-020 **2** 1 1/2 **Swiss Spirit**[45] 3420 4-9-1 111 WilliamBuick 17 114+
(John Gosden) *towards rr: hdwy u.p but hanging rt fr over 1f out: chsd wnr wl ins fnl f: carried lft and no imp after* **6/1**[3]

3251 **3** hd **Justineo**[14] 4493 4-9-1 105 (b) AndreaAtzeni 3 110
(Roger Varian) *taken down early: led: rdn over 1f out: hdd ins fnl f: styd on same pce towards fin* **40/1**

0625 **4** nse **Glass Office**[41] 3558 3-8-12 108 JimCrowley 10 109
(David Simcock) *towards rr: swtchd rt and effrt nrest far rail jst over 1f out: r.o wl u.p ins fnl f* **25/1**

1051 **5** 1 **Ladies Are Forever**[21] 4260 5-8-12 105 (b) PaulHanagan 8 104
(Geoffrey Oldroyd) *lw: hld up in midfield: clsd and nt clr run whn swtchd lft ent fnl f: hdwy and swtchd lft again ins fnl f: r.o: nt rch ldrs* **14/1**

5100 **6** shd **Spirit Quartz (IRE)**[27] 4079 5-9-5 110 (p) JamieSpencer 12 110
(Robert Cowell) *chsd ldrs: rdn and pressing ldrs over 1f out: styng on same pce whn carried lft and hmpd wl ins fnl f* **33/1**

1051 **7** 1 1/4 **Tickled Pink (IRE)**[27] 4079 4-8-12 109 TomQueally 1 99+
(Lady Cecil) *chsd ldrs: rdn and effrt over 1f out: pressing ldrs whn squeezed and bdly hmpd 1f out: unable to rcvr and styd on same pce u.p after* **3/1**[1]

2021 **8** 1/2 **Masamah (IRE)**[20] 4275 7-9-1 107 (p) NeilCallan 4 100+
(Marco Botti) *pressed ldr: rdn over 1f out: stl pressing ldrs but struggling to qckn whn bdly hmpd ins fnl f: nt rcvr and eased wl ins fnl f* **10/1**

0105 **9** hd **Medicean Man**[34] 3848 7-9-1 109 (b) JamesDoyle 11 99
(Jeremy Gask) *dwlt: bhd: rdn 1/2-way: hdwy u.p and swtchd lft 1f out: styd on ins fnl f: nvr trbld ldrs* **25/1**

5106 **10** hd **Duke Of Firenze**[27] 4079 4-9-1 101 RyanMoore 7 98
(Sir Michael Stoute) *in tch in midfield: effrt u.p over 1f out: keeping on whn short of room 1f out: no hdwy after* **9/1**

00-6 **11** 1/2 **Borderlescott**[20] 4311 11-9-1 108 SilvestreDeSousa 14 97
(Robin Bastiman) *in tch in midfield: rdn 1/2-way: carried rt and hmpd 1f out: kpt on but no threat to ldrs fnl f* **40/1**

6440 **12** 1 1/4 **Elusivity (IRE)**[41] 3558 5-9-1 103 KierenFallon 2 92+
(David O'Meara) *in tch in midfield: effrt over 1f out: nt clr run and hmpd 1f out: nvr enough room after and lost any ch: eased wl ins fnl f* **20/1**

4004 **12** dht **Bungle Inthejungle**[27] 4079 3-8-12 102 MartinHarley 15 91
(Mick Channon) *taken down early: racd nrest stands' rail: chsd ldrs: rdn and lost pl over 1f out: hld and plugged on same pce fnl f* **20/1**

-144 **14** 1/2 **Bettolle (ITY)**[13] 4527 4-8-12 102 FrankieDettori 16 87
(Marco Botti) *towards rr: rdn 1/2-way: plugged on fnl f: nvr trbld ldrs* **50/1**

2102 **15** shd **Kingsgate Native (IRE)**[27] 4079 8-9-5 112 ShaneKelly 9 94
(Robert Cowell) *lw: hld up in midfield: effrt whn nt clr run jst ins fnl f: n.d* **14/1**

2312 **16** 1 3/4 **Smoothtalkinrascal (IRE)**[62] 2865 3-8-12 106 DanielTudhope 18 83
(David O'Meara) *lw: a in rr: n.d* **8/1**

0221 **17** 1 **Jwala**[20] 4311 4-8-12 103 SteveDrowne 6 77
(Robert Cowell) *awkward leaving stalls: sn chsng ldrs: rdn and struggling over 1f out: fdd ins fnl f* **20/1**

56.72s (-3.48) **Going Correction** -0.35s/f (Firm)
WFA 3 from 4yo+ 3lb 17 Ran SP% **131.2**
Speed ratings (Par 115): **113,110,110,110,108 108,106,105,105,105 104,102,102,101,101 98,96**
toteswingers 1&2 £8.80, 1&3 £47.30, 2&3 £59.70 CSF £32.98 TOTE £5.70: £2.30, £2.80, £11.90; EX 50.50 Trifecta £2147.20 Pool: £9600.51 - 3.35 winning units..
Owner Redknapp, Salthouse & Fiddes **Bred** John D Gunther **Trained** Hambleton, N Yorks
■ Stewards' Enquiry : Paul Mulrennan six-day ban: careless riding (Aug 16-21)

FOCUS
A competitive running of this Group 2 sprint. They split into two groups early, but soon merged and much of the action unfolded middle-to-far side.

4948 GOLF AT GOODWOOD NURSERY H'CAP 6f
4:15 (4:17) (Class 2) 2-Y-0 **£12,938** (£3,850; £1,924; £962) **Stalls** High

Form RPR

324 **1** **Flying Bear (IRE)**[32] 3883 2-8-5 **72** AndreaAtzeni 4 76
(Jeremy Gask) *lw: t.k.h: hld up towards rr: rdn and hdwy over 1f out: chal ins fnl f: edgd lft but led wl ins fnl f: r.o wl* **25/1**

2231 **2** 1/2 **Tanseeb**[14] 4498 2-9-6 **87** PaulHanagan 3 90
(Mark Johnston) *chsd ldrs: rdn over 1f out: ev ch ins fnl f: kpt on wl but no ex cl home* **7/1**[3]

5620 **3** hd **Jazz (IRE)**[45] 3424 2-9-2 **83** SteveDrowne 10 85
(Charles Hills) *hld up in midfield: hdwy and swtchd rt over 1f out: kpt on wl u.p ins fnl f: nt quite rch ldrs* **25/1**

0023 **4** hd **Deeds Not Words (IRE)**[21] 4259 2-8-2 **72** RaulDaSilva(3) 6 73
(Mick Channon) *lw: towards rr: short of room and swtchd rt 2f out: hdwy u.p 1f out: styd on wl fnl 100yds: nt quite rch ldrs* **10/1**

1403 **5** hd **Ifwecan**[21] 4248 2-9-6 **87** JoeFanning 13 88
(Mark Johnston) *led: rdn over 1f out: kpt on gamely u.p tl hdd wl ins fnl f: lost 3 pls cl home* **14/1**

120 **6** shd **Suite (IRE)**[42] 3522 2-9-7 **88** PatDobbs 21 88+
(Richard Hannon) *in tch in midfield: rdn and effrt over 1f out: swtchd lft jst ins fnl f: styd on strly fnl 100yds: nt rch ldrs* **33/1**

3434 **7** hd **Ixelles Diamond (IRE)**[27] 4053 2-8-2 **69** SilvestreDeSousa 14 69
(Richard Fahey) *chsd ldrs: sltly outpcd over 1f out: trying to rally but hanging rt ins fnl f: kpt on wl towards fin* **40/1**

333 **8** hd **Major Crispies**[29] 3991 2-8-12 **79** MartinHarley 1 78
(James Eustace) *hld up towards rr: hdwy 2f out: rdn and ev ch ins fnl f: nt qckn fnl 100yds: one pce towards fin* **11/2**[2]

2221 **9** 1 3/4 **Speed The Plough**[18] 4346 2-8-10 **77** RichardHughes 9 71
(Richard Hannon) *stdd s: hld up in rr: hdwy and carried rt over 1f out: gd hdwy u.p 1f out: chsd ldrs ins fnl f: no ex fnl 100yds: eased towards fin* **15/2**

12 **10** 3/4 **Grecian (IRE)**[21] 4232 2-9-2 **83** JimCrowley 17 75
(Paul Cole) *lw: in tch in midfield: drvn and unable qck over 1f out: carried rt and no imp ins fnl f* **4/1**[1]

2601 **11** 1/2 **Primitorio (IRE)**[13] 4519 2-8-2 **69** (b) MartinLane 16 59
(Ralph Beckett) *dwlt: sn rcvrd to chse ldrs after 1f: ev ch and rdn 2f out: no ex jst ins fnl f: wknd ins fnl f* **25/1**

5323 **12** shd **Royal Connection**[20] 4277 2-8-3 **70** KieranO'Neill 5 60
(Richard Hannon) *in tch in midfield: rdn and unable qck ent fnl f: hld whn nt clr run and swtchd rt fnl 100yds* **25/1**

51 **13** nk **Oyster (IRE)**[25] 4115 2-8-0 **67** JimmyQuinn 15 56
(Gary Harrison) *lw: s.i.s: bhd: nt clr run 2f out: swtchd rt and hdwy 1f out: styd on wl ins fnl f: nvr trbld ldrs* **28/1**

054 **14** 1/2 **Shepherd Gate (USA)**[13] 4524 2-8-12 **79** (b[1]) KierenFallon 2 69
(J S Moore) *dwlt: towards rr: rdn and hdwy 2f out: no imp jst ins fnl f: hld and eased towards fin* **33/1**

0261 **15** 1/2 **Porteous**[17] 4387 2-8-0 **67** oh1 NickyMackay 11 53
(Mick Channon) *stdd s and hld up in rr: plenty to do and effrt nrest stands' rail over 1f out: kpt on: nvr trbld ldrs* **50/1**

043 **16** *4* **Debt Settler (IRE)**[23] 4177 2-7-7 **67** oh5........................ JackGarritty(7) 7 41
(Luke Dace) *chsd ldrs tl 2f out: sn outpcd: wknd u.p over 1f out* **66/1**

410 **17** *1* **Yorkshire Relish (IRE)**[13] 4528 2-8-13 **80**................ JamieSpencer 19 51+
(Kevin Ryan) *swtg: midfield: lost pl 1/2-way: switching rt and no hdwy over 1f out: bhd ins fnl f* **7/1**[3]

1 **18** *½* **Belayer (IRE)**[17] 4370 2-8-8 **75**.................................... PaulMulrennan 20 45+
(Kevin Ryan) *w'like: hung rt thrght: in tch in midfield: wnt bdly rt and lost pl ent fnl f: eased ins fnl f* **12/1**

504 **19** *1¼* **Double Czech (IRE)**[15] 4439 2-8-3 **70**......................(p) FrannyNorton 22 36
(Amanda Perrett) *lw: chsd ldrs tl 1/2-way: sn struggling: bhd over 1f out* **20/1**

512 **20** *63* **Regiment**[16] 4399 2-9-3 **84**.. RyanMoore 8
(Richard Fahey) *in tch in midfield tl lost pl 2f out: sn eased and virtually p.u ins fnl f: t.o* **12/1**

1m 12.23s (0.03) **Going Correction** -0.35s/f (Firm) **20** Ran SP% **138.7**
Speed ratings (Par 100): **85,84,84,83,83 83,83,82,80,79 78,78,78,77,77 71,70,69,68,**
toteswingers 1&2 £37.60, 1&3 Not won, 2&3 £75.30 CSF £193.68 CT £4588.09 TOTE £45.30: £6.70, £2.40, £6.80, £3.50; EX 445.60 Trifecta £2013.50 Part won. Pool: £2684.71 - 0.10 winning units..
Owner Flying Bear Partnership **Bred** Joseph Flanagan & Jarlath Fahey **Trained** Sutton Veny, Wilts

FOCUS
Loads of runners in this competitive nursery and the race developed middle-to-stands' side. The winner is rated to his pre-race mark and the second is progressing well.

4949 BETFRED TV OAK TREE STKS (GROUP 3) (F&M) 7f
4:50 (4:51) (Class 1) 3-Y-O+

£34,026 (£12,900; £6,456; £3,216; £1,614; £810) **Stalls** Low

Form RPR

6114 **1** **Annecdote**[7] 4705 3-8-10 **97**.................................... RichardKingscote 10 107
(Jonathan Portman) *lw: wnt rt s: hld up in tch in midfield: hdwy on inner 2f out: swtchd lft 1f out: qcknd to ld fnl 75yds: r.o wl: pushed out* **14/1**

-341 **2** *¾* **Winning Express (IRE)**[36] 3734 3-8-10 **107**.................. FrannyNorton 5 105
(Ed McMahon) *chsd ldrs: rdn and effrt 2f out: led over 1f out: hdd and styd same pce fnl 75yds* **2/1**[1]

50-6 **3** *½* **Instance**[34] 3831 5-9-2 **93**...(p) FrankieDettori 12 106
(Jeremy Noseda) *stdd s: t.k.h: hld up in last pair: rdn and hdwy on inner over 1f out: styd on wl ins fnl f* **40/1**

-001 **4** *¾* **The Gold Cheongsam (IRE)**[13] 4529 3-8-10 **102**.......(t) PaulHanagan 7 102
(Jeremy Noseda) *hld up in tch in midfield: effrt u.p wl over 1f out: str chal ent fnl f: no ex fnl 150yds: wknd towards fin* **8/1**

110 **5** *hd* **Pavlosk (USA)**[42] 3524 3-8-10 **103**................................... RyanMoore 11 101+
(Sir Michael Stoute) *lw: hld up in last trio: rdn and no imp over 1f out: hdwy and swtchd lft 1f out: styd on strly: nt rch ldrs* **11/2**[2]

-001 **6** *¾* **Ladyship**[20] 4284 4-9-2 **94**.. KierenFallon 1 101
(Sir Michael Stoute) *in tch in midfield: rdn and swtchd lft over 1f out: styd on same pce u.p ins fnl f: eased cl home* **14/1**

2210 **7** *¾* **Shuruq (USA)**[125] 1264 3-8-13 **112**........................(p) SilvestreDeSousa 4 100
(Saeed bin Suroor) *chsd ldr: rdn to ld wl over 1f out: sn hdd and unable qck: wknd ins fnl f* **16/1**

-005 **8** *2* **Ollie Olga (USA)**[27] 4081 3-8-10 **100**............................ MartinHarley 8 92
(Mick Channon) *hld up in tch in midfield: n.m.r over 2f out: sn rdn: unable qck over 1f out: wknd ins fnl f* **14/1**

-040 **9** *nk* **Nargys (IRE)**[27] 4081 3-8-10 **107**................................ JamieSpencer 9 91
(Luca Cumani) *lw: s.i.s: hld up in last pair: rdn and fnd little over 1f out: no imp after: nvr trbld ldrs* **15/2**[3]

-200 **10** *1* **Agent Allison**[42] 3524 3-8-10 **103**.................................... JimCrowley 2 88
(Peter Chapple-Hyam) *in tch in midfield: drvn over 2f out: keeping on same pce and n.m.r over 1f out: wknd ins fnl f* **14/1**

3136 **11** *hd* **Woodland Aria**[27] 4081 3-8-10 **98**................................ WilliamBuick 6 88
(John Gosden) *lw: in tch in midfield: n.m.r and shuffled bk 2f out: rdn and no hdwy over 1f out: nvr trbld ldrs* **20/1**

-105 **12** *1* **How's Life**[36] 3734 3-8-10 **92**.................................... PaulMulrennan 3 85
(Kevin Ryan) *led tl rdn and hdd wl over 1f out: sn struggling and btn 1f out: wknd fnl f* **66/1**

-221 **13** *5* **Indignant**[21] 4252 3-8-10 **96**.. RichardHughes 13 78
(Richard Hannon) *in tch in midfield: rdn and no hdwy over 1f out: btn 1f out: wknd and heavily eased towards fin* **10/1**

6423 **13** *dht* **Victrix Ludorum (IRE)**[36] 3734 3-8-10 **95**........................ PatDobbs 14 71
(Richard Hannon) *in tch in midfield: rdn and no ex 2f out: lost pl and bhd 1f out: wknd fnl f* **50/1**

1m 25.33s (-1.67) **Going Correction** -0.10s/f (Good)
WFA 3 from 4yo+ 6lb **14** Ran SP% **123.9**
Speed ratings (Par 113): **105,104,103,102,102 101,100,98,98,97 96,95,89,89**
toteswingers 1&2 £9.90, 1&3 £66.20, 2&3 £27.30 CSF £42.30 TOTE £23.70: £7.10, £1.40, £11.90; EX 66.00 Trifecta £2473.20 Pool: £7199.50 - 2.18 winning units..
Owner Tom Edwards & Partners **Bred** The Hon Mrs R Pease **Trained** Upper Lambourn, Berks

FOCUS
Last year this fillies and mares' contest was one of the meeting's weaker Group races, but it was a much stronger running again this season and all bar two represented the Classic crop. They went a sound pace and those running towards the inside were at an advantage.

4950 BETFRED MOBILE LOTTO STKS (H'CAP) 1m 3f
5:25 (5:25) (Class 3) (0-90,90) 3-Y-O

£9,337 (£2,796; £1,398; £699; £349; £175) **Stalls** Low

Form RPR

01 **1** **Retirement Plan**[47] 3364 3-9-5 **88**.................................... TomQueally 14 103+
(Lady Cecil) *lw: sn bustled along to chse ldrs: rdn to chse ldr over 3f out: led 2f out: pressed but fnd ex over 1f out: styd on strly to go clr ins fnl f* **4/1**[2]

414 **2** *3* **Goodwood Mirage (IRE)**[22] 4214 3-9-6 **89**.................. FrankieDettori 15 98
(William Knight) *lw: stdd s: t.k.h: hld up in rr: rdn and hdwy 2f out: edgd rt but clsd to chse ldng pair over 1f out: nt pce of wnr but wnt 2nd ins fnl f: kpt on* **3/1**[1]

1351 **3** *½* **Silver Dixie (USA)**[14] 4490 3-8-7 **76** ow1.................. JamieSpencer 10 84
(Jeremy Noseda) *stdd s: hld up in rr: clsng and nt clr run over 2f out: swtchd lft and hdwy over 1f out: chsd ldrs 1f out: kpt on but no ch w wnr* **9/2**[3]

5322 **4** *nk* **Ambleside**[14] 4480 3-8-3 **72**.. FrannyNorton 4 80+
(Mark Johnston) *lw: t.k.h: hld up towards rr: rdn and n.m.r ent fnl 2f: plenty to do and hdwy 1f out: styd on wl ins fnl f: no threat to wnr* **14/1**

21 **5** *1¾* **Statutory (IRE)**[15] 4445 3-9-5 **88**.................................... JoeFanning 12 92
(Mark Johnston) *chsd ldrs: rdn and unable qck whn carried rt over 1f out: styd on same pce fnl f* **8/1**

3621 **6** *½* **Bee Jay Kay**[14] 4474 3-8-3 **72**.. NickyMackay 8 76
(Mick Channon) *in tch in midfield on outer: pushed along briefly 1/2-way: rdn and outpcd 2f out: rallied and kpt on ins fnl f: no threat to wnr* **25/1**

41 **7** *½* **Northern Meeting (IRE)**[23] 4157 3-8-8 **77**.................. RyanMoore 7 80
(Sir Michael Stoute) *lw: hld up in tch in midfield: swtchd lft and effrt 2f out: edging rt but hdwy to chal over 1f out: no ex jst ins fnl f: wknd fnl 100yds* **11/2**

-021 **8** *1¼* **Teolagi (IRE)**[12] 4575 3-8-4 **73** 6ex.. AndreaAtzeni 1 73
(J S Moore) *bustled along leaving stalls: hmpd on inner bnd 10f out: rdn and hdwy on inner 2f out: no imp whn hmpd over 1f out: n.d after* **50/1**

-631 **9** *1¼* **Shamaheart (IRE)**[22] 4209 3-8-8 **80**........... WilliamTwiston-Davies(3) 11 78
(Richard Hannon) *chsd ldrs: rdn ent fnl 2f: unable qck and looking btn whn squeezed for room and hmpd over 1f out: wknd fnl f* **40/1**

0365 **10** *1½* **King Muro**[32] 3908 3-8-6 **75**.. DavidProbert 6 70
(Andrew Balding) *led: clr 8f out tl rdn and hdd over 2f out: btn over 1f out: wknd fnl f* **25/1**

41-0 **11** *8* **Empiricist (IRE)**[49] 3276 3-8-10 **79**............................ PatDobbs 3 60
(Amanda Perrett) *chsd ldrs: rdn and no ex over 2f out: lost pl 2f out: wknd and bhd ent fnl f* **33/1**

4211 **12** *4½* **Couloir Extreme (IRE)**[39] 3636 3-8-11 **80**.................. DaneO'Neill 9 53
(Gary Moore) *hld up in tch in midfield: rdn 2f out: sn btn and wknd: bhd and eased wl fnl f* **20/1**

6051 **13** *72* **Nile Knight**[8] 4679 3-8-2 **71** 6ex..................................(b) JimmyQuinn 13
(Marcus Tregoning) *in tch in midfield: lost pl and rdn 3f out: sn lost tch and eased fnl 2f: t.o* **20/1**

2m 23.73s (-2.77) **Going Correction** -0.10s/f (Good) **13** Ran SP% **120.9**
Speed ratings (Par 104): **106,103,103,103,101 101,101,100,99,98 92,89,36**
toteswingers 1&2 £5.30, 1&3 £6.90, 2&3 £4.90 CSF £15.09 CT £57.62 TOTE £4.60: £2.10, £1.70, £2.00; EX 14.80 Trifecta £85.60 Pool: £5492.81 - 48.10 winning units..
Owner K Abdullah **Bred** Juddmonte Farms Ltd **Trained** Newmarket, Suffolk

FOCUS
A decent 3-y-o handicap featuring several progressive middle-distance performers. The pace set by King Muro was solid.
T/Jkpt: Not won. T/Plt: £265.00 to a £1 stake. Pool: £331267.97 - 912.48 winning tickets T/Qpdt: £85.20 to a £1 stake. Pool: £22800.57 - 198.00 winning tickets SP

4609 MUSSELBURGH (R-H)
Friday, August 2

OFFICIAL GOING: Good (7.8)
Wind: Moderate acrosws Weather: Sunny periods

4951 CASHINO.COM - GREAT ONLINE GAMING AMATEUR RIDERS' H'CAP 1m 5f
6:10 (6:11) (Class 5) (0-70,67) 4-Y-O+ **£3,119** (£967; £483; £242) **Stalls** Low

Form RPR

5641 **1** **Gucci D'Oro (USA)**[16] 4403 4-10-3 **61**.................... MrAlexFerguson(5) 9 72
(David Simcock) *trckd ldrs: pushed along and sltly outpcd over 2f out: rdn over 1f out: styd on wl to ld last 50yds* **7/2**[2]

-033 **2** *1* **Golden Future**[12] 4563 10-9-11 **53**............................ MrJHamilton(3) 8 62
(Peter Niven) *led 2f: cl up: led again 4f out: rdn along 2f out and sn jnd: drvn and hdd ins fnl f: rallied towards fin* **12/1**

0632 **3** *½* **Volcanic Jack (IRE)**[9] 4622 5-10-4 **57**............................ MikeyEnnis 5 65
(Philip Kirby) *in tch: hdwy to trck ldrs after 4f: effrt to chse ldr 3f out: rdn along on inner to chal wl over 1f out: drvn and slt ld ins fnl f: hdd and no ex last 50yds* **9/4**[1]

0056 **4** *10* **Frosty Berry**[70] 2630 4-9-12 **58**.................................... MrAFrench(7) 7 51
(Neville Bycroft) *in rr: hdwy over 4f out: rdn along 3f out: plugged on fnl 2f: nvr nr ldrs* **25/1**

6063 **5** *nk* **Brunello**[30] 3947 5-10-4 **60**...(p) MissHBethell(3) 1 53
(Philip Kirby) *a towards rr* **10/1**

00-0 **6** *5* **Inniscastle Boy**[36] 3727 4-9-12 **51**............................ MissCWalton 6 36
(Jim Goldie) *a towards rr* **6/1**[3]

3004 **7** *2¼* **Al Furat (USA)**[12] 4563 5-9-13 **57**................................(p) MrsVDavies(5) 2 39
(Ron Barr) *t.k.h: chsd ldrs tl led after 2f: pushed along over 5f out: hdd 4f out: rdn over 3f out and sn wknd* **12/1**

-101 **8** *nk* **City Ground (USA)**[17] 4376 6-11-0 **67**.................... MissSBrotherton 4 48
(Michael Easterby) *in tch: pushed along and lost pl over 5f out: sn bhd* **12/1**

0502 **9** *10* **Altnaharra**[18] 4343 4-9-10 **49**...(v) MrsCBartley 3 15
(Jim Goldie) *chsd ldng pair: rdn along over 4f out: sn wknd* **12/1**

2m 52.45s (0.45) **Going Correction** -0.025s/f (Good) **9** Ran SP% **111.0**
Speed ratings (Par 103): **97,96,96,89,89 86,85,85,78**
toteswingers 1&2 £3.10, 1&3 £3.30, 2&3 £3.10 CSF £41.96 CT £108.04 TOTE £3.90: £1.10, £2.90, £1.50; EX 27.40 Trifecta £132.10 Pool: £1985.43 - 11.26 winning units..
Owner Mrs John Ferguson **Bred** Donna Tullner & Stephen Glessner **Trained** Newmarket, Suffolk
■ Stewards' Enquiry : Mr J Hamilton two-day ban: careless riding (Aug 16,25)

FOCUS
Bottom bend moved out 2m. Bottom bend moved out 2m. The going had dried out to good all round (GoingStick 7.8). They went pretty steady early on in this amateur riders' event, but the pace really picked up down the back and by the time they made the turn out of the back straight four horses had broken clear.

4952 WILKINSON & ASSOCIATES NURSERY H'CAP 5f
6:45 (6:46) (Class 6) (0-65,64) 2-Y-O **£1,940** (£577; £288; £144) **Stalls** High

Form RPR

6001 **1** **Touch The Clouds**[15] 4450 2-8-10 **60**............................ KevinStott(7) 6 67+
(Kevin Ryan) *mde all: rdn clr ent fnl f: styd on strly* **9/4**[2]

250 **2** *3¼* **Kirtling Belle**[49] 3280 2-9-4 **61**.................................... RussKennemore 2 56
(Keith Dalgleish) *chsd ldng pair: effrt on inner 2f out: rdn to chse wnr ins fnl f: no imp* **3/1**[3]

0234 **3** *4½* **Stoney Quine (IRE)**[16] 4399 2-9-7 **64**............................ TomEaves 1 43
(Keith Dalgleish) *cl up: effrt over 2f out: sn rdn: drvn and one pce appr fnl f* **2/1**[1]

0400 **4** *12* **Countess Lupus (IRE)**[46] 3391 2-8-5 **49** ow2........... MarkCoumbe(3) 5
(Lisa Williamson) *dwlt: hdwy on outer 1/2-way: rdn along 2f out: sn edgd lft and wknd* **12/1**

1m 0.21s (-0.19) **Going Correction** -0.025s/f (Good) **4** Ran SP% **96.8**
Speed ratings (Par 92): **100,94,87,68**
CSF £7.00 TOTE £3.40; EX 6.00 Trifecta £10.00 Pool: £345.29 - 25.71 winning units..
Owner Matt & Lauren Morgan 1 **Bred** Stuart McPhee Bloodstock Ltd **Trained** Hambleton, N Yorks

FOCUS
A weak nursery with little depth. The winner is progressing with racing.

4953 PDM LTD AND FP MCCANN H'CAP 1m 1f
7:20 (7:20) (Class 5) (0-70,68) 3-Y-0+ £3,234 (£962; £481; £240) Stalls Low

Form RPR
2644 1 **Manchester**[27] 4076 3-9-6 **68** TonyHamilton 8 78+
(Richard Fahey) *trckd ldng pair: hdwy 3f out: cl up 2f out: rdn to ld ent fnl f: kpt on strly towards fin* **5/1**[1]
5322 2 ½ **Push Me (IRE)**[114] 1480 6-9-8 **67** GarryWhillans(5) 2 76
(Iain Jardine) *dwlt and hld up in rr: hdwy 2f out: n.m.r over 1f out: sn swtchd lft and rdn: styd on to chal ins fnl f: no ex towards fin* **10/1**
1214 3 2 **Lord Franklin**[15] 4446 4-9-9 **66** NeilFarley(3) 9 71
(Eric Alston) *led: rdn along 3f out: drvn 2f out: sn hdd and kpt on same pce appr fnl f* **5/1**[1]
4010 4 ½ **Outlaw Torn (IRE)**[3] 4853 4-9-3 **57** (e) LeeTopliss 6 61
(Richard Guest) *trckd ldrs: hdwy 3f out: rdn to ld wl over 1f out: drvn: edgd rt and hdd ent fnl f: kpt on same pce* **13/2**[2]
0002 5 1 ½ **Jonny Lesters Hair (IRE)**[2] 4889 8-9-9 **63** DavidAllan 4 63
(Tim Easterby) *chsd ldr: cl up over 3f out: rdn 2f out: sn drvn and grad wknd* **5/1**[1]
334 6 14 **Dandarrell**[23] 4169 6-9-9 **63** MickyFenton 5 32
(Julie Camacho) *trckd ldrs: pushed along and lost pl 1/2-way: sn bhd* **7/1**[3]
-262 7 3 ½ **Chloe's Image**[27] 4049 3-8-4 **55** DeclanCannon(3) 7 17
(Philip Kirby) *a towards rr* **5/1**[1]
3653 8 3 **Music Festival (USA)**[25] 4109 6-9-0 **54** AndrewElliott 1 9
(Jim Goldie) *dwlt and in rr: hdwy and in tch over 4f out: rdn along 3f out: sn wknd* **12/1**
2134 9 1 ¼ **Tectonic (IRE)**[10] 4609 4-9-11 **65** (p) TomEaves 3 17
(Keith Dalgleish) *in tch: rdn along over 4f out: sn btn* **10/1**

1m 53.01s (-0.89) **Going Correction** -0.025s/f (Good)
WFA 3 from 4yo+ 8lb 9 Ran SP% **118.4**
Speed ratings (Par 103): **102,101,99,99,98 85,82,79,78**
toteswingers 1&2 £13.30, 1&3 £7.30, 2&3 £9.60 CSF £56.98 CT £267.53 TOTE £4.30: £2.10, £2.40, £1.90; EX 27.50 Trifecta £179.60 Pool: £790.22 - 3.29 winning units..
Owner Mr & Mrs G Calder **Bred** Mr & Mrs G Calder **Trained** Musley Bank, N Yorks

FOCUS
Modest handicap form.

4954 CASHINO GAMING - THE WAY TO WIN@MUSSELBURGH H'CAP 5f
7:50 (7:50) (Class 3) (0-90,89) 3-Y-0+ £7,762 (£2,310; £1,154; £577) Stalls High

Form RPR
0100 1 **Noodles Blue Boy**[14] 4507 7-8-11 **76** (p) TomEaves 9 87
(Ollie Pears) *chsd ldrs: rdn along wl over 1f out: styd on u.p ent fnl f to ld last 75yds* **40/1**
0330 2 ¾ **Moorhouse Lad**[78] 2388 10-8-13 **83** JustinNewman(5) 4 91
(Garry Moss) *chsd ldrs: hdwy 2f out: rdn to chal over 1f: led ins fnl f: drvn: hdd and no ex last 75yds* **22/1**
3144 3 ¾ **Midnight Dynamo**[11] 4579 6-8-13 **78** AndrewElliott 2 83
(Jim Goldie) *sltly hmpd shortly after s and towards rr: swtchd rt to outer and gd hdwy over 1f out: rdn and styd on strly fnl f* **25/1**
1213 4 nk **Avon Breeze**[22] 4217 4-8-13 **83** GeorgeChaloner(5) 3 87+
(Richard Whitaker) *swtchd rt to outer shortly after s: trckd ldrs: hdwy 2f out: rdn to cfhallenge over 1f out: ev ch tl drvn and one pce wl ins fnl f* **7/2**[2]
3003 5 1 **Crimson Knot (IRE)**[4] 4821 5-8-6 **74** MarkCoumbe(3) 1 75
(Alan Berry) *towards rr: hdwy 1/2-way: rdn to chse ldrs wl over 1f out: drvn and one pce fnl f* **20/1**
1465 6 ¾ **The Nifty Fox**[10] 4613 9-8-12 **77** (p) MickyFenton 12 75
(Tim Easterby) *towards rr: rdn along 2f out: styd on fnl f: nrst fin* **20/1**
0011 7 1 ½ **Oil Strike**[7] 4728 6-8-9 **74** 6ex (b) DuranFentiman 8 67+
(Michael Easterby) *hmpd s and bhd: swtchd rt and hdwy wl over 1f out: sn rdn: no imp fnl f* **11/2**[3]
5003 8 nk **Oldjoesaid**[14] 4507 9-8-13 **78** RussKennemore 5 69
(Paul Midgley) *in tch: rdn along and hdwy 2f out: styd on fnl f: n.d* **14/1**
220 9 ½ **Jedward (IRE)**[3] 4860 6-9-0 **86** (v[1]) KevinStott(7) 7 76
(Kevin Ryan) *prom: hdwy to ld wl over 1f out: rdn ent fnl f: sn hdd & wknd* **8/1**
0-05 10 ½ **Mayoman (IRE)**[35] 3776 8-9-7 **86** (v) DavidNolan 6 74
(David O'Meara) *wnt lft s: a towards rr* **15/2**
0000 11 3 ¼ **Captain Dunne (IRE)**[14] 4507 8-9-10 **89** [1] DavidAllan 10 65
(Tim Easterby) *led: rdn 2f out: sn hdd & wknd appr fnl f* **10/1**
1101 12 1 **Red Baron (IRE)**[10] 4613 4-9-0 **82** 6ex NeilFarley(3) 11 55
(Eric Alston) *cl up: rdn along over 2f out: sn drvn and wknd* **10/3**[1]
0000 13 5 **Rothesay Chancer**[14] 4472 5-8-12 **77** LeeTopliss 13 32
(Jim Goldie) *a in rr* **20/1**

59.35s (-1.05) **Going Correction** -0.025s/f (Good) 13 Ran SP% **124.2**
Speed ratings (Par 107): **107,105,104,104,102 101,98,98,97,96 91,90,82**
toteswingers 1&2 £72.90, 1&3 £91.90, 2&3 £17.00 CSF £719.50 CT £20800.26 TOTE £48.00: £11.50, £6.60, £8.60; EX 1548.40 Trifecta £476.40 Part won. Pool: £635.29 - 0.02 winning units..
Owner Keith Taylor & Keith West **Bred** Fifehead Farms M C Denning **Trained** Norton, N Yorks

FOCUS
Plenty could be given a chance here and as it turned out there was a shock result.

4955 WILKINSON & ASSOCIATES H'CAP 1m
8:20 (8:20) (Class 6) (0-65,65) 3-Y-0 £1,940 (£577; £288; £144) Stalls Low

Form RPR
1055 1 **Lexington Blue**[15] 4449 3-8-13 **57** (v[1]) DavidNolan 3 71
(David O'Meara) *trckd ldng pair: hdwy 4f out: rdn to chal 2f out: sn led and drvn clr: readily* **3/1**[2]
013 2 6 **Bousatet (FR)**[46] 3396 3-9-7 **65** TomEaves 2 65
(Kevin Ryan) *trckd ldr: cl up 4f out: led on bit 3f out: jnd 2f out and sn hdd: rdn and one pce fr over 1f out* **11/10**[1]
5003 3 10 **Inovate (IRE)**[14] 4509 3-8-3 **47** (b) DuranFentiman 6 24
(Tim Easterby) *s.i.s and bhd: hdwy 4f out: rdn over 2f out: plugged on: n.d* **9/2**
0020 4 4 ½ **Birdy Boy (USA)**[23] 4160 3-9-1 **59** AdrianNicholls 4 26
(Mark Johnston) *led: rdn along 4f out: hdd 3f out: sn wknd* **4/1**[3]

1m 40.57s (-0.63) **Going Correction** -0.025s/f (Good) 4 Ran SP% **110.8**
Speed ratings (Par 98): **102,96,86,81**
CSF £6.96 TOTE £4.70; EX 8.10 Trifecta £11.50 Pool: £314.03 - 20.37 winning units..
Owner Middleham Park Racing XLIX & Partners **Bred** The National Stud Blakeney Club **Trained** Nawton, N Yorks

FOCUS
This proved very straightforward for the winner.

4956 CASHINO - THE WAY TO WIN H'CAP (QUALIFIER FOR THE BETFAIR SCOTTISH MILE SERIES FINAL) 7f 30y
8:50 (8:50) (Class 5) (0-75,74) 3-Y-0+ £3,234 (£962; £481; £240) Stalls Low

Form RPR
1115 1 **Just Paul (IRE)**[23] 4158 3-8-7 **64** DeclanCannon(3) 5 74+
(Philip Kirby) *hld up in tch: hdwy wl over 2f out: rdn to chse ldrs over 1f out: swtchd rt and led ent fnl f: sn drvn and kpt on wl* **3/1**[1]
-602 2 1 ½ **Jeannie Galloway (IRE)**[26] 4097 6-9-10 **72** DavidNolan 4 78
(Keith Dalgleish) *hld up in rr: hdwy 3f out: rdn to chse wnr over 1f out: swtchd lft and drvn ins fnl f: kpt on* **11/2**[3]
2450 3 2 ¾ **Mowhoob**[18] 4340 3-9-2 **70** LeeTopliss 9 67
(Jim Goldie) *hld up in rr: hdwy over 2f out: rdn over 1f out: swtchd rt to inner ins fnl f: styd on wl towards fin* **12/1**
0-14 4 hd **Cara's Request (AUS)**[83] 2280 8-8-12 **60** TomEaves 6 58+
(Michael Dods) *led: rdn along over 2f out: drvn and edgd lft over 1f out: hdd ent fnl f: one pce* **13/2**
560 5 3 ¾ **Imperator Augustus (IRE)**[22] 4198 5-9-8 **70** RussKennemore 8 59
(Patrick Holmes) *chsd ldrs: hdwy on outer 3f out: rdn and ch 2f out: sn drvn and wknd appr fnl f* **11/1**
0000 6 3 **Henry Bee**[39] 3628 4-9-3 **65** (b) TonyHamilton 3 46
(Richard Fahey) *trckd ldr: effrt 3f out: rdn along 2f out: drvn and wknd appr fnl f* **16/1**
50-2 7 5 **Dumbarton Rock**[9] 4624 3-8-13 **67** MickyFenton 2 33
(William Jarvis) *trckd ldrs: hdwy on inner 1/2-way: chsd ldr 3f out: sn rdn and wknd 2f out* **9/2**[2]
5026 8 2 ¾ **Majestic Dream (IRE)**[27] 4051 5-9-4 **73** (b) MatthewHopkins(7) 1 34
(Michael Easterby) *t.k.h: in tch on inner: hdwy 3f out: sn rdn and wknd* **10/1**
2266 U **Llewellyn**[30] 3945 5-9-12 **74** PaulQuinn 7
(David Nicholls) *rrd and uns rdr stalls at s* **9/2**[2]

1m 29.62s (0.62) **Going Correction** -0.025s/f (Good)
WFA 3 from 4yo+ 6lb 9 Ran SP% **121.1**
Speed ratings (Par 103): **95,93,90,89,85 82,76,73,**
toteswingers 1&2 £3.00, 1&3 £17.10, 2&3 £16.40 CSF £20.80 TOTE £4.20: £2.10, £2.00, £4.70; EX 30.20 Trifecta £375.10 Pool: £762.38 - 1.52 winning units..
Owner Mr and Mrs Paul Chapman **Bred** Oghill House Stud **Trained** Middleham, N Yorks

FOCUS
They went a decent pace here.
T/Plt: £4,426.60 to a £1 stake. Pool: £50026.99 - 8.25 winning tickets T/Qpdt: £1,428.70 to a £1 stake. Pool: £4633.70 - 2.40 winning tickets JR

4764 NEWMARKET (R-H)
Friday, August 2

OFFICIAL GOING: Good (7.5)
Wind: Light across Weather: Fine

4957 BRISTOL STREET MOTORS H'CAP 1m
5:50 (5:50) (Class 4) (0-80,80) 3-Y-0+ £5,175 (£1,540; £769; £384) Stalls High

Form RPR
513- 1 **Brownsea Brink**[219] 8240 3-9-4 **77** SeanLevey 4 86
(Richard Hannon) *mde all: set stdy pce tl qcknd over 2f out: rdn over 1f out: edgd lft ins fnl f: r.o* **5/1**[2]
001 2 1 ¼ **Investment Expert (IRE)**[14] 4495 3-9-1 **74** SebSanders 8 80+
(Jeremy Noseda) *s.i.s: hld up: hdwy u.p over 1f out: styd on* **7/2**[1]
4524 3 1 ¼ **Kickingthelilly**[44] 3477 4-9-12 **78** ChrisCatlin 7 82
(Rae Guest) *a.p: chsd wnr over 3f out: rdn and ev ch over 1f out: styd on same pce ins fnl f* **8/1**
210 4 ½ **Ocean Applause**[17] 4383 3-9-7 **80** (tp) KirstyMilczarek 9 82
(John Ryan) *prom: rdn over 1f out: styd on same pce fnl f* **7/1**[3]
634 5 1 ¾ **Mandy's Boy (IRE)**[41] 3571 3-8-11 **70** RoystonFfrench 5 68
(Ian Williams) *chsd wnr over 4f: rdn over 1f out: no ex fnl f* **7/1**[3]
3404 6 2 ¼ **Chapter And Verse (IRE)**[47] 3368 7-9-10 **76** TedDurcan 6 70
(Mike Murphy) *trckd ldrs: rdn over 1f out: wknd fnl f* **8/1**
1040 7 2 **Perfect Haven**[14] 4485 3-9-4 **77** LiamKeniry 1 65
(Ralph Beckett) *hld up: hdwy over 2f out: rdn and wknd over 1f out* **12/1**
0446 8 10 **Flash Crash**[29] 3997 4-8-9 **61** WilliamCarson 3 27
(Anthony Carson) *hld up: rdn over 2f out: wknd over 1f out* **33/1**
-663 9 shd **Barwick**[57] 3019 5-9-7 **76** AshleyMorgan(3) 2 42
(Mark H Tompkins) *s.i.s: hld up: rdn over 2f out: hung lft and wknd over 1f out* **5/1**[2]

1m 43.61s (3.61) **Going Correction** +0.225s/f (Good)
WFA 3 from 4yo+ 7lb 9 Ran SP% **113.4**
Speed ratings (Par 105): **90,88,87,87,85 83,81,71,70**
toteswingers 1&2 £1.80, 1&3 £10.20, 2&3 £1.40 CSF £22.40 CT £137.01 TOTE £8.10: £2.70, £1.60, £1.80; EX 20.80 Trifecta £132.50 Pool: £696.50 - 3.94 winning units..
Owner The Heffer Syndicate **Bred** Carmel Stud **Trained** East Everleigh, Wilts

FOCUS
Stands' side track used. Stalls far side except 1m2f & 1m4f: centre. A repeat of the meeting seven days previously, with the ground officially good. The GoingStick read 7.5. Older horses were in the minority in this fair handicap, in which they appeared to be making quite a print. The finish was fought out by two 3-y-os with few miles on the clock.

4958 HYPHEN BLOODSTOCK EBF MAIDEN STKS 6f
6:25 (6:26) (Class 4) 2-Y-0 £4,528 (£1,347; £673; £336) Stalls High

Form RPR
2 1 **Music Theory (IRE)**[14] 4497 2-9-5 0 MickaelBarzalona 8 93+
(Charlie Appleby) *a.p: swtchd lft over 2f out: chsd ldr over 1f out: rdn to ld wl ins fnl f: r.o* **5/2**[2]
3 2 2 **Toofi (FR)**[21] 4231 2-9-5 0 WilliamBuick 1 87+
(Roger Varian) *chsd ldrs: led 2f out: rdn: edgd lft and hdd wl ins fnl f: styd on same pce* **7/4**[1]
3 5 **Dandana (IRE)** 2-9-5 0 SebSanders 5 72+
(Clive Brittain) *hld up: pushed along 1/2-way: r.o ins fnl f: wnt 3rd post: nt trble ldrs* **25/1**
4 nse **Greeb** 2-9-5 0 PaulHanagan 12 72+
(Charles Hills) *prom: rdn over 1f out: wknd ins fnl f* **16/1**
5 3 **Sahra Al Khadra** 2-9-2 0 PatrickHills(3) 10 63
(Charles Hills) *hld up: pushed along and hdwy over 2f out: rdn over 1f out: wknd fnl f* **50/1**
0 6 shd **Lawyer (IRE)**[21] 4231 2-9-5 0 KirstyMilczarek 6 63
(Luca Cumani) *chsd ldrs: rdn over 1f out: wknd fnl f* **20/1**

6 **7** 3/4 **Mathematics**[29] 3991 2-9-5 0 .... SilvestreDeSousa 2 60
(Charlie Appleby) *edgd lft s: sn led: rdn and hdd 2f out: wknd fnl f* **12/1**

0 **8** 4 **Alaskan (IRE)**[77] 2411 2-9-5 0 .... SeanLevey 4 48+
(Richard Hannon) *prom: rdn over 2f out: wknd over 1f out* **20/1**

33 **9** 7 **Showpiece**[41] 3581 2-9-5 0 .... RichardHughes 3 27
(Richard Hannon) *s.i.s and hmpd s: hld up: effrt over 2f out: hung lft and wknd 1f out: eased* **10/3**[3]

0 **10** 1/2 **Spreadable (IRE)**[7] 4716 2-9-5 0 .... J-PGuillambert 11 26
(Nick Littmoden) *chsd ldrs: rdn over 2f out: wknd over 1f out* **100/1**

11 7 **Sexy Secret** 2-9-5 0 .... ChrisCatlin 9
(Noel Quinlan) *sn outpcd* **33/1**

12 3 **Plough Boy (IRE)** 2-9-5 0 .... TedDurcan 7
(Willie Musson) *s.i.s: outpcd* **100/1**

1m 13.43s (0.93) **Going Correction** +0.225s/f (Good) **12** Ran SP% **121.8**
Speed ratings (Par 96): **102,99,92,92,88 88,87,82,72,72 62,58**
toteswingers 1&2 £1.60, 1&3 £26.70, 2&3 £14.50 CSF £6.98 TOTE £3.70: £1.50, £1.30, £6.90; EX 6.40 Trifecta £313.80 Pool: £1607.51 - 3.84 winning units..
Owner Godolphin **Bred** Forenaghts Stud **Trained** Newmarket, Suffolk

FOCUS
A few smart types have taken this maiden in the last decade, most notably subsequent 2000 Guineas and Champion Stakes hero Haafhd. The winner built on a good debut and the second shaped with a lot of promise.

4959 CANTAB CAPITAL NOVICE STKS 7f
6:55 (6:55) (Class 4) 2-Y-O **£4,528** (£1,347; £673; £336) **Stalls** High

Form RPR

1 **1** **Shifting Power**[16] 4414 2-9-2 0 .... RichardHughes 6 104+
(Richard Hannon) *chsd ldrs: shkn up to ld and edgd rt 1f out: rdn clr: eased nr fin* **5/2**[2]

021 **2** 6 **Treaty Of Paris (IRE)**[14] 4505 2-9-5 90 .... FergusSweeney 1 91
(Henry Candy) *chsd ldrs: rdn to ld over 1f out: sn hdd: wknd wl ins fnl f* **13/2**

1 **3** 2 1/4 **Snow Squall**[28] 4021 2-9-5 0 .... MickaelBarzalona 2 85
(Charlie Appleby) *hld up: hdwy u.p 1f out: wknd ins fnl f* **7/1**

6411 **4** nk **Fire Fighting (IRE)**[15] 4439 2-9-5 88 .... NeilCallan 4 84
(Mark Johnston) *edgd rt s: led: rdn and hdd over 1f out: hmpd sn after: wknd ins fnl f* **4/1**[3]

1 **5** 2 3/4 **Emirates Galloper (IRE)**[28] 4026 2-9-5 0 .... SilvestreDeSousa 3 77
(Saeed bin Suroor) *s.i.s: sn pushed along in rr: hdwy 1/2-way: rdn and wknd over 1f out* **7/4**[1]

6 24 **Shaheen Shah (GER)** 2-9-0 0 .... SebSanders 5 10
(Conrad Allen) *chsd ldrs 4f: sn wknd* **66/1**

1m 26.17s (0.47) **Going Correction** +0.225s/f (Good) **6** Ran SP% **112.3**
Speed ratings (Par 96): **106,99,96,96,93 65**
toteswingers 1&2 £3.10, 1&3 £3.60, 2&3 £4.60 CSF £18.58 TOTE £3.40: £1.80, £3.00; EX 18.30 Trifecta £83.60 Pool: £944.76 - 8.47 winning units..
Owner Ms Elaine Chivers & Potensis Ltd **Bred** John And Susan Davis **Trained** East Everleigh, Wilts

FOCUS
A strong novice contest with all bar the debutant Shaheen Shah arriving here on the back of a victory. The winner impressed and is up to winning at Listed level.

4960 FIRESTONE BUILDING PRODUCTS H'CAP 7f
7:30 (7:30) (Class 4) (0-85,85) 4-Y-0+ **£5,175** (£1,540; £769; £384) **Stalls** High

Form RPR

-553 **1** **Angelic Upstart (IRE)**[21] 4243 5-8-7 71 ow1 .... LiamKeniry 5 79
(Andrew Balding) *chsd ldrs: rdn and hung lft ins fnl f: r.o to ld nr fin* **10/1**

033 **2** nse **Ocean Tempest**[37] 3693 4-9-5 83 .... (p) KirstyMilczarek 1 91
(John Ryan) *chsd ldr tl led over 4f out: rdn over 1f out: edgd lft and hdd nr fin* **6/1**[3]

-111 **3** hd **Levi Draper**[29] 3993 4-8-12 76 .... RichardHughes 9 83+
(James Fanshawe) *hld up: hdwy over 1f out: sn rdn: hmpd wl ins fnl f: r.o* **11/4**[1]

2523 **4** 1/2 **Albaqaa**[3] 4859 8-9-0 83 .... RobertTart(5) 2 89
(P J O'Gorman) *chsd ldrs: rdn over 1f out: r.o* **5/1**[2]

3422 **5** 2 3/4 **Kakatosi**[34] 3812 6-9-6 84 .... TomQueally 3 83
(Mike Murphy) *s.i.s: hdwy u.p over 1f out: styd on same pce ins fnl f* **7/1**

0360 **6** 1/2 **Jungle Bay**[20] 4281 6-8-10 74 .... (b) MickaelBarzalona 6 71
(Jane Chapple-Hyam) *chsd ldrs: rdn over 2f out: no ex ins fnl f* **16/1**

0321 **7** 1 3/4 **Bravo Echo**[30] 3969 7-9-4 82 .... SebSanders 10 74
(Michael Attwater) *racd alone and led over 2f: remained w ldrs: jnd main gp 1/2-way: rdn over 1f out: eased whn btn ins fnl f* **6/1**[3]

-116 **8** 16 **Bassara (IRE)**[21] 4258 4-9-7 85 .... TedDurcan 7 34
(Chris Wall) *hld up: effrt over 2f out: wknd over 1f out* **5/1**[2]

1m 26.17s (0.47) **Going Correction** +0.225s/f (Good) **8** Ran SP% **116.0**
Speed ratings (Par 105): **106,105,105,105,102 101,99,99**
toteswingers 1&2 £9.60, 1&3 £5.80, 2&3 £4.40 CSF £69.25 CT £213.23 TOTE £11.10: £2.10, £2.50, £1.60; EX 84.40 Trifecta £354.80 Pool: £1211.51 - 2.56 winning units..
Owner Barry Burdett **Bred** Swordlestown Stud **Trained** Kingsclere, Hants
■ Stewards' Enquiry : Liam Keniry two-day ban: careless riding (Aug 16-17)

FOCUS
A fair handicap with few looking anything more than fairly treated.

4961 PIPER-HEIDSIECK H'CAP 1m 4f
8:00 (8:02) (Class 5) (0-70,70) 3-Y-O **£3,234** (£962; £481; £240) **Stalls** Centre

Form RPR

-411 **1** **Duchess Of Gazeley (IRE)**[9] 4634 3-9-7 70 6ex .... J-PGuillambert 5 80+
(Gary Harrison) *hld up: hdwy over 2f out: rdn and n.m.r over 1f out: styd on to ld wl ins fnl f* **6/1**[3]

0650 **2** 1 **Faustinatheyounger (IRE)**[14] 4500 3-8-5 54 .... AdamBeschizza 4 62
(David Elsworth) *a.p: racd keenly: rdn over 1f out: ev ch ins fnl f: styd on same pce* **25/1**

0-36 **3** hd **Gamble**[22] 4223 3-9-7 70 .... TomQueally 9 78
(Michael Bell) *led: hdd over 10f out: chsd ldr: rdn over 2f out: led ins fnl f: sn hdd and unable qck* **10/1**

1043 **4** 3 1/2 **Getaway Car**[32] 3908 3-9-2 65 .... (b) NeilCallan 2 67
(Gerard Butler) *mid-div: nt clr run and lost pl over 4f out: swtchd rt and hdwy over 2f out: rdn and nt clr run over 1f out: styd on same pce* **8/1**

040 **5** 1 1/4 **Perfect Spell**[22] 4223 3-9-6 69 .... LiamKeniry 7 69
(Andrew Balding) *mid-div: hdwy over 3f out: rdn over 1f out: styd on same pce* **20/1**

2612 **6** nk **Gabrial The Duke (IRE)**[7] 4714 3-9-4 67 .... WilliamBuick 10 67
(David Simcock) *chsd ldrs: rdn over 2f out: no ex fnl f* **15/8**[1]

3440 **7** 5 **Bursledon (IRE)**[16] 4417 3-9-7 70 .... RichardHughes 11 62
(Richard Hannon) *prom: led over 10f out: rdn and hung lft over 1f out: hdd and rdr dropped rein ins fnl f: sn wknd* **15/2**

-606 **8** 13 **The Ginger Berry**[17] 4391 3-8-3 52 .... WilliamCarson 6 23
(Dr Jon Scargill) *hld up: plld hrd: rdn over 3f out: wknd over 2f out* **25/1**

-050 **9** 15 **Vanvitelli**[70] 2628 3-9-5 68 .... (t) SilvestreDeSousa 1 15
(James Fanshawe) *chsd ldrs: rdn over 3f out: wknd over 2f out* **9/2**[2]

0064 **10** hd **Cherry Princess**[8] 4679 3-8-2 51 oh6 .... MartinLane 3
(Stuart Williams) *hld up: rdn and wknd over 2f out* **33/1**

066 **11** 4 1/2 **Hallingham**[29] 3989 3-9-0 68 .... MatthewLawson(5) 8 7
(Jonathan Portman) *s.i.s: hld up: hdwy over 5f out: rdn over 3f out: wknd sn after* **20/1**

2m 32.17s (-0.73) **Going Correction** +0.225s/f (Good) **11** Ran SP% **119.4**
Speed ratings (Par 100): **111,110,110,107,107 106,103,94,84,84 81**
toteswingers 1&2 £17.40, 1&3 £4.40, 2&3 £11.50 CSF £152.17 CT £1484.50 TOTE £6.20: £2.30, £7.90, £2.70; EX 207.50 Trifecta £1050.60 Part won. Pool: £1400.81 - 0.20 winning units..
Owner Franconson Partners **Bred** Overbury Stallions Ltd And D Boocock **Trained** Newmarket, Suffolk

FOCUS
Modest handicap form.

4962 PIPER-HEIDSIECK ROSE SAUVAGE H'CAP 6f
8:30 (8:30) (Class 5) (0-75,75) 3-Y-O **£3,234** (£962; £481; £240) **Stalls** High

Form RPR

4-00 **1** **Aye Aye Skipper (IRE)**[35] 3782 3-9-5 73 .... MartinLane 7 82
(Dean Ivory) *mde all: rdn and hung rt fr over 1f out: r.o* **16/1**

012 **2** 2 1/4 **Jubilant Queen**[34] 3841 3-9-3 71 .... RichardHughes 6 73+
(Clive Cox) *s.i.s: hld up: hdwy 2f out: rdn to chse wnr ins fnl f: no imp* **15/8**[1]

3213 **3** 1 1/2 **Realize**[11] 4592 3-9-7 75 .... SilvestreDeSousa 2 72
(Hughie Morrison) *edgd lft s: a.p: chsd wnr over 2f out: rdn over 1f out: edgd lft and styd on same pce ins fnl f* **5/2**[2]

-655 **4** 2 1/4 **True Spirit**[36] 3740 3-8-9 63 .... LiamKeniry 4 53
(Paul D'Arcy) *chsd ldrs: rdn over 1f out: styd on same pce* **20/1**

2215 **5** 1/2 **Gold Beau (FR)**[22] 4198 3-8-12 66 .... (p) TedDurcan 3 54
(Kristin Stubbs) *hmpd s: hld up: pushed along 1/2-way: rdn over 1f out: styd on same pce* **7/1**

0-51 **6** 1 3/4 **Tychaios**[33] 3866 3-8-6 60 .... ChrisCatlin 1 43
(Stuart Williams) *in rr: hdwy over 2f out: wknd over 1f out* **5/1**[3]

0-32 **7** nk **Sakhee's Rose**[27] 4064 3-8-11 65 .... RoystonFfrench 8 47
(Ed McMahon) *prom tl rdn and wknd over 1f out* **10/1**

1440 **8** 1 1/4 **Star Of Rohm**[20] 4303 3-9-4 72 .... TomQueally 5 50
(Michael Bell) *chsd wnr over 3f: rdn and hung lft over 1f out: wknd ins fnl f* **8/1**

1m 13.95s (1.45) **Going Correction** +0.225s/f (Good) **8** Ran SP% **123.4**
Speed ratings (Par 100): **99,96,94,91,90 88,87,85**
toteswingers 1&2 £4.50, 1&3 £10.50, 2&3 £2.10 CSF £50.23 TOTE £15.40: £3.40, £1.30, £1.40; EX 78.80 Trifecta £302.40 Pool: £1927.02 - 4.77 winning units..
Owner Heather Yarrow & Lesley Ivory **Bred** Ballyhane Stud **Trained** Radlett, Herts

FOCUS
An ordinary sprint for 3-y-os to close the card.
T/Plt: £51.50 to a £1 stake. Pool: £61374.42 - 869.56 winning tickets T/Qpdt: £18.70 to a £1 stake. Pool: £4659.82 - 184.27 winning tickets CR

4722 THIRSK (L-H)
Friday, August 2

OFFICIAL GOING: Good (good to firm in places; 8.2)
Wind: Light 1/2 behind Weather: Fine and sunny, warm

4963 BRITISH STALLION STUDS SUPPORTING BRITISH RACING EBF MAIDEN STKS 5f
2:20 (2:22) (Class 4) 2-Y-O **£4,075** (£1,212; £606; £303) **Stalls** High

Form RPR

4 **1** **Lucy Parsons (IRE)**[13] 4539 2-9-0 0 .... AndrewMullen 10 73+
(David Barron) *mde all: drvn clr fnl f* **5/2**[2]

4 **2** 2 3/4 **Kano's Ghirl (IRE)**[25] 4107 2-9-0 0 .... TomEaves 13 63
(Keith Dalgleish) *chsd ldrs: styd on to take 2nd last 100yds: no imp* **16/1**

43 **3** nk **Steele Ranger**[17] 4379 2-9-5 0 .... RobertWinston 5 69+
(Peter Chapple-Hyam) *mid-div: hdwy and edgd rt over 2f out: nt clr run over 1f out: styd on to take 3rd nr fin* **9/4**[1]

4 **4** 3/4 **Elite Freedom (IRE)**[18] 4346 2-9-0 0 .... PJMcDonald 11 59
(Jo Hughes) *chsd wnr: clr 2nd over 1f out: hung lft and kpt on same pce* **8/1**

5 **5** 7 **The Hooded Claw (IRE)**[84] 2238 2-9-5 0 .... DuranFentiman 12 39
(Tim Easterby) *in rr: hmpd on ins over 2f out: kpt on fnl f* **20/1**

542 **6** 2 1/4 **Heroique (IRE)**[14] 4505 2-9-0 73 .... DavidAllan 2 26
(Tim Easterby) *chsd ldrs: wknd over 1f out* **7/1**

7 1 1/2 **Precariously Good** 2-9-0 0 .... HarryBentley 9 21
(David Barron) *mid-div: carried rt over 2f out: nvr a factor* **6/1**[3]

06 **8** 1 1/2 **Absconder (IRE)**[20] 4289 2-9-5 0 .... LiamJones 8 20
(Mark Johnston) *chsd ldrs: lost pl over 1f out* **50/1**

40 **9** 1 1/4 **Alaskan Night (IRE)**[13] 4539 2-9-5 0 .... PhillipMakin 6 16
(Kevin Ryan) *chsd ldrs: hung lft and wknd over 1f out* **40/1**

4 **10** 1 1/4 **Bob Masnicken**[10] 4602 2-9-5 0 .... MichaelO'Connell 1 11
(Scott Dixon) *led to s: in tch on outside: lost pl over 2f out* **33/1**

4 **11** 1 1/4 **Argent Touch**[29] 3979 2-9-5 0 .... PatrickMathers 4 7
(Derek Shaw) *sn drvn along in rr: swtchd lft over 1f out: nvr on terms* **100/1**

12 2 **Mavree (IRE)** 2-8-9 0 .... DarylByrne(5) 3
(Tim Easterby) *sn outpcd and bhd: hung lft over 2f out* **66/1**

58.81s (-0.79) **Going Correction** -0.25s/f (Firm) **12** Ran SP% **117.7**
Speed ratings (Par 96): **96,91,91,89,78 75,72,70,68,66 64,61**
toteswingers 1&2 £10.10, 1&3 £2.30, 2&3 £7.80 CSF £38.58 TOTE £3.90: £1.50, £4.10, £1.40; EX 38.10 Trifecta £125.80 Pool: £2253.41 - 13.43 winning units..
Owner Norton Common Farm Racing **Bred** Brian Miller **Trained** Maunby, N Yorks

FOCUS
Both bends moved off inner line which added 10yds to races of 7f & 1m and 15yds to 1m4f and 2m races. An ordinary juvenile maiden in which the winner made all at a decent tempo up the stands' rail. The first four were clear and the form is worth at least this much.

4964 WATCH RACING UK ON SKY 432 CLAIMING STKS 7f
2:55 (2:55) (Class 5) 2-Y-O **£3,234** (£962; £481; £240) **Stalls** Low

Form RPR

503 **1** **Witchy Woman**[13] 4538 2-7-12 53 .... JoeyHaynes(7) 2 56
(Mrs K Burke) *mde all: sent 3 l clr over 2f out: drvn rt out* **4/1**[3]

043 **2** *1* **Tunnel Tiger (IRE)**[27] 4065 2-8-7 58 .... LiamJones 3 55
(J S Moore) *chsd ldrs: 2nd appr fnl f: edgd lft ins fnl f: kpt on same pce* **5/1**

4014 **3** *nk* **Ding Ding**[66] 2759 2-8-4 58 .... SamHitchcott 1 51
(Mick Channon) *dwlt: mid-div: hdwy over 1f out: swtchd rt ins fnl f: styng on at fin* **9/1**

0 **4** *2 1/4* **Escarlata Rossa**[24] 4154 2-8-2 0 .... NeilFarley(3) 8 46
(J S Moore) *chsd wnr: hung lft and one pce over 1f out* **40/1**

3321 **5** *2 1/4* **Lady Captain (IRE)**[13] 4538 2-8-9 61 .... PJMcDonald 5 45
(Kevin Ryan) *s.i.s: in rr: drvn 3f out: hung lft: nvr a threat* **9/4**[1]

5420 **6** *shd* **Jaga Time**[49] 3298 2-8-9 58 .... BarryMcHugh 4 44
(Richard Fahey) *mid-div: chsng ldrs over 2f out: one pce* **12/1**

065 **7** *1* **Mount Cheiron (USA)**[9] 4631 2-9-0 0 .... (b[1]) PhillipMakin 9 47
(Brian Meehan) *hld up in rr: effrt over 2f out: nvr a factor* **3/1**[2]

000 **8** *45* **Spirit O Goodchild**[24] 4142 2-8-10 0 .... (b[1]) AndrewMullen 7
(Alan McCabe) *chsd ldrs on outer: hung rt and lost pl bnd over 3f out: bhd over 2f out: eased over 1f out: virtually p.u: hopelessly t.o* **100/1**

1m 28.75s (1.55) **Going Correction** +0.125s/f (Good) **8** Ran SP% **113.6**
Speed ratings (Par 94): **96,94,94,91,89 89,88,36**
toteswingers 1&2 £4.40, 1&3 £5.80, 2&3 £4.20 CSF £23.91 TOTE £5.20: £1.40, £2.20, £2.10; EX 30.80 Trifecta £179.60 Pool: £2093.03 - 8.73 winning units..Tunnel Tiger was claimed by Mr P. W. Chapple-Hyam for £8,000.

Owner Mrs Melba Bryce **Bred** Laundry Cottage Stud Farm **Trained** Middleham Moor, N Yorks

FOCUS
A modest juvenile claimer. The winner showed slightly improved form.

4965 WEATHERBYS BANK FOREIGN EXCHANGE FILLIES' NURSERY H'CAP 5f
3:30 (3:32) (Class 4) (0-85,79) 2-Y-O **£3,881** (£1,155; £577; £288) **Stalls** High

Form RPR

321 **1** **Hay Chewed (IRE)**[23] 4177 2-9-7 **79** .... RobertWinston 6 95+
(Peter Chapple-Hyam) *mde all: hung lft and drvn clr fnl f: v readily* **10/3**[3]

10 **2** *3 3/4* **Race Hunter (USA)**[42] 3522 2-9-6 **78** .... HarryBentley 3 80+
(David Barron) *chsd wnr: upsides over 1f out: hung lft and kpt on same pce fnl f* **2/1**[1]

4103 **3** *2 1/2* **Sandsman's Girl (IRE)**[24] 4141 2-9-2 **74** .... JamesSullivan 5 67
(James Given) *towards rr: hdwy over 2f out: edgd lft 1f out: kpt on to take 3rd towards fin* **33/1**

454 **4** *nk* **She Can Jig**[24] 4142 2-8-1 **59** .... AndrewMullen 8 51
(Kevin Ryan) *sn outpcd and in rr: styd on fnl f* **11/1**

5130 **5** *1 1/2* **Lorimer's Lot (IRE)**[44] 3459 2-9-0 **77** .... JasonHart(5) 9 64
(Tim Walford) *chsd ldrs: kpt on same pce fnl 2f* **3/1**[2]

036 **6** *3/4* **Another Royal**[13] 4539 2-8-4 **62** .... (b[1]) DuranFentiman 4 46
(Tim Easterby) *in rr: hdwy 2f out: one pce* **14/1**

216 **7** *4* **Classical Diva**[21] 4261 2-9-3 **78** .... NeilFarley(3) 7 47
(Declan Carroll) *dwlt: reminders after 1f: sn swtchd outside: chsd ldrs over 3f out: lost pl over 1f out* **11/1**

1 **8** *1 1/2* **Madagascar Moll (IRE)**[30] 3942 2-8-11 **72** .... JulieBurke(3) 1 36
(David O'Meara) *chsd ldrs: lost pl over 1f out* **12/1**

5350 **9** *4* **Marilyn Marquessa**[55] 3092 2-8-8 **66** .... LiamJones 2 16
(Jo Hughes) *dwlt: sn chsng ldrs: wknd 2f out* **50/1**

58.26s (-1.34) **Going Correction** -0.25s/f (Firm) **9** Ran SP% **117.3**
Speed ratings (Par 93): **100,94,90,89,87 85,79,77,70**
toteswingers 1&2 £3.10, 1&3 £25.80, 2&3 £21.00 CSF £10.60 CT £184.27 TOTE £3.60: £1.40, £1.50, £6.30; EX 14.30 Trifecta £215.50 Pool: £4242.36 - 14.76 winning units..

Owner John C Davies **Bred** Newlands House Stud **Trained** Newmarket, Suffolk

FOCUS
A fairly good fillies' nursery in which they went a decent tempo throughout. The winner is likely to remain well treated when reassessed.

4966 MARKET CROSS JEWELLERS H'CAP (DIV I) 7f
4:05 (4:05) (Class 5) (0-70,70) 3-Y-0+ **£2,587** (£770; £384; £96; £96) **Stalls** Low

Form RPR

0620 **1** **Glenridding**[18] 4357 9-9-2 **58** .... (p) DaleSwift 8 66
(James Given) *chsd ldrs on outer: drvn and lost pl bnd over 4f out: hdwy on outside over 2f out: led last 50yds: jst hld on* **14/1**

0223 **2** *nse* **My New Angel (IRE)**[12] 4557 4-9-4 **60** .... PJMcDonald 12 68
(Jason Ward) *chsd ldrs on outer: lost pl after 1f: hdwy whn nt clr run and swtchd outside over 2f out: styd on wl ins fnl f: jst failed* **17/2**

2142 **3** *1 1/4* **Whipphound**[4] 4840 5-9-4 **60** .... TomMcLaughlin 10 65
(Mark Brisbourne) *trckd ldrs travelling strly: led wl over 1f out: hdd and no ex last 50yds* **8/1**

0013 **4** *3/4* **No Quarter (IRE)**[63] 2837 6-9-6 **62** .... BarryMcHugh 5 65
(Tracy Waggott) *trckd ldrs: upsides 1f out: styd on same pce* **9/1**

1422 **4** *dht* **Jontleman (IRE)**[6] 4751 3-9-8 **70** .... SamHitchcott 4 71
(Mick Channon) *mid-div: whn nt clr run over 2f out and over 1f out: swtchd rt to chse ldrs: kpt on same pce to dead-heat for 4th* **5/2**[1]

2250 **6** *1/2* **Bunce (IRE)**[25] 4119 5-9-7 **68** .... DavidBergin(5) 2 69
(David O'Meara) *s.i.s: in rr: hdwy over 2f out: chsng ldrs 1f out: kpt on same pce* **5/1**[3]

065 **7** *2 1/4* **Eium Mac**[25] 4118 4-8-11 **58** .... AdamCarter(5) 6 53
(Neville Bycroft) *s.i.s: in rr: hdwy over 2f out: chsng ldrs over 1f out: one pce* **28/1**

0-0 **8** *3 3/4* **Ursus**[39] 3630 8-8-10 **52** .... (p) PaddyAspell 3 37
(Christopher Wilson) *w ldrs: led over 4f out: hdd wl over 1f out: sn wknd* **80/1**

3600 **9** *20* **Sardanapalus**[21] 4245 4-10-0 **70** .... (p) PhillipMakin 1
(Kevin Ryan) *dwlt: sn chsng ldrs: drvn over 3f out: lost pl and heavily eased over 1f out: virtually p.u: t.o* **4/1**[2]

3220 **10** *5* **Dhhamaan (IRE)**[18] 4339 8-8-13 **55** .... (b) JamesSullivan 7
(Ruth Carr) *drvn to ld: hdd over 4f out: lost pl over 2f out: sn bhd and eased: virtually p.u: t.o* **14/1**

1m 27.67s (0.47) **Going Correction** +0.125s/f (Good)
WFA 3 from 4yo+ 6lb **10** Ran SP% **114.9**
Speed ratings (Par 103): **102,101,100,99,99 99,96,92,69,63**
toteswingers 1&2 £16.90, 1&3 £18.10, 2&3 £7.20 CSF £125.57 CT £731.00 TOTE £24.10: £5.20, £2.40, £2.10; EX 188.80 Trifecta £875.50 Pool: £4064.96 - 3.48 winning units..

Owner Tremousser Partnership **Bred** Bolton Grange **Trained** Willoughton, Lincs

FOCUS
A modest handicap in which they went a contested gallop, to the benefit of those who came from towards the rear.

4967 MARKET CROSS JEWELLERS H'CAP (DIV II) 7f
4:40 (4:40) (Class 5) (0-70,69) 3-Y-0+ **£2,587** (£770; £384; £192) **Stalls** Low

Form RPR

0506 **1** **Destination Aim**[17] 4375 6-9-2 **63** .... JasonHart(5) 8 72
(Frederick Watson) *mde all: drvn over 2f out: kpt on wl* **25/1**

3635 **2** *1 1/4* **Hazza The Jazza**[14] 4499 3-8-6 **59** .... (b) ConnorBeasley(5) 6 63
(Richard Guest) *tk keem hold: chsd ldrs: styd on to take 2nd ins fnl f: kpt on same pce* **9/2**[2]

4-00 **3** *nk* **Evanescent (IRE)**[17] 4375 4-9-6 **69** .... JoeDoyle(7) 12 74
(John Quinn) *t.k.h: trckd wnr: kpt on same pce fnl f* **25/1**

-000 **4** *1 1/2* **Clumber Place**[22] 4198 7-9-3 **59** .... DaleSwift 3 60
(James Given) *chsd ldrs: kpt on same pce over 1f out* **16/1**

0660 **5** *1/2* **Nonaynever**[2] 4893 5-8-9 **51** oh6 .... (b) JamesSullivan 7 50
(Ruth Carr) *chsd ldrs: drvn over 2f out: one pce over 1f out: edgd lft ins fnl f* **33/1**

5102 **6** *1/2* **Blue Maisey**[17] 4375 5-9-4 **65** .... DavidBergin(5) 11 63
(Edwin Tuer) *in rr-div: hdwy and hung lft over 2f out: one pce over 1f out* **7/2**[1]

5005 **7** *nk* **Summer Dancer (IRE)**[17] 4375 9-9-4 **60** .... PhillipMakin 2 57
(Paul Midgley) *s.s: in rr: hdwy on outside over 2f out: styd on fnl f* **9/2**[2]

3235 **8** *1/2* **Hoppy's Flyer (FR)**[7] 4709 5-9-4 **60** .... TomMcLaughlin 1 59+
(Mark Brisbourne) *t.k.h in mid-div: effrt and nt clr run over 2f out: keeping on whn nt clr run clsng stages* **11/2**[3]

40-0 **9** *1/2* **Tamara Bay**[98] 1800 5-9-2 **58** .... PJMcDonald 9 53+
(John Davies) *hld up towards rr: effrt 2f out: nvr a factor* **17/2**

0200 **10** *shd* **Dream Scenario**[7] 4725 3-9-7 **69** .... PatCosgrave 4 65+
(Mel Brittain) *s.i.s: hdwy whn nt clr run over 2f out: keeping on whn nt clr run wl ins fnl f* **12/1**

0000 **11** *3* **Mujaadel (USA)**[17] 4375 8-9-10 **66** .... (p) BarryMcHugh 5 52
(David Nicholls) *mid-div: effrt over 2f out: n.m.r over 1f out: nvr a threat* **14/1**

0000 **12** *18* **Thrust Control (IRE)**[23] 4160 6-8-13 **55** .... (v) RobertWinston 10
(Tracy Waggott) *chsd ldrs: lost pl 2f out: heavily eased fnl f: t.o* **33/1**

1m 27.44s (0.24) **Going Correction** +0.125s/f (Good)
WFA 3 from 4yo+ 6lb **12** Ran SP% **118.3**
Speed ratings (Par 103): **103,101,101,99,98 98,98,97,96,96 93,72**
toteswingers 1&2 £19.40, 1&3 £45.50, 2&3 £14.60 CSF £130.28 CT £2905.82 TOTE £41.60: £7.80, £1.90, £5.50; EX 174.10 Trifecta £1402.50 Pool: £3828.58 - 2.04 winning units..

Owner F Watson **Bred** Darley **Trained** Sedgefield, Co Durham

■ Fred Watson's first winner for more than ten years.

FOCUS
The second division of this modest handicap.

4968 WEATHERBYS HAMILTON INSURANCE MAIDEN STKS 1m
5:10 (5:12) (Class 4) 3-Y-0+ **£4,851** (£1,443; £721; £360) **Stalls** High

Form RPR

4 **1** **Alegra**[17] 4382 3-9-0 0 .... PatCosgrave 1 79+
(Lady Cecil) *chsd ldrs: drvn and outpcd over 3f out: styd on to chse ldrs over 1f out: led jst ins fnl f: forged clr* **7/4**[1]

2 **2** *3 1/4* **Iptisam**[25] 4118 4-9-12 0 .... HarryBentley 8 78
(James Tate) *t.k.h: trckd ldrs: led 3f out: hung lft and hdd jst ins fnl f: styd on same pce* **3/1**[3]

33 **3** *1 1/2* **Dual Mac**[41] 3592 6-9-12 0 .... DaleSwift 5 75
(Neville Bycroft) *t.k.h: led after 1f: hdd over 3f out: kpt on same pce fnl f* **20/1**

02 **4** *nse* **Mu'Ajiza**[5] 4799 3-9-0 0 .... LiamJones 2 68
(Mark Johnston) *led 1f: chsd ldrs: led briefly over 3f out: kpt on one pce over 1f out* **11/4**[2]

0 **5** *14* **Red Warrior (IRE)**[41] 3585 3-9-5 0 .... RobertWinston 6 41
(Ismail Mohammed) *chsd ldrs: wknd and eased over 2f out* **25/1**

6 *1 3/4* **Cottam Maybel** 4-9-7 0 .... PJMcDonald 7 33
(Mel Brittain) *s.i.s: sn detached in last: nvr on terms* **66/1**

3 **7** *3* **For Posterity**[14] 4495 3-9-5 0 .... RobertHavlin 3 30
(Charlie Appleby) *dwlt: in tch: drvn and lost pl over 3f out: sn bhd* **5/1**

60 **8** *13* **Gregori (IRE)**[17] 4382 3-9-5 0 .... PhillipMakin 9
(Brian Meehan) *t.k.h on outside: trckd ldrs: lost pl bnd over 4f out: bhd 3f out: eased clsng stages* **25/1**

1m 39.77s (-0.33) **Going Correction** +0.125s/f (Good)
WFA 3 from 4yo+ 7lb **8** Ran SP% **118.6**
Speed ratings (Par 105): **106,102,101,101,87 85,82,69**
toteswingers 1&2 £2.70, 1&3 £5.10, 2&3 £5.70 CSF £7.31 TOTE £2.70: £1.10, £2.30, £3.80; EX 11.30 Trifecta £63.20 Pool: £2857.91 - 33.90 winning units..

Owner Sir Robert Ogden **Bred** Miss K Rausing **Trained** Newmarket, Suffolk

FOCUS
A fair maiden in which historically the Classic generation have a good record.

4969 DAVID HIGGS RACECOURSE ELECTRICIAN 50 YEARS H'CAP 2m
5:45 (5:46) (Class 5) (0-75,70) 4-Y-0+ **£2,587** (£770; £384; £192) **Stalls** High

Form RPR

0-06 **1** **Hawk Mountain (UAE)**[55] 3085 8-9-7 **70** .... MichaelO'Connell 5 79
(John Quinn) *chsd ldrs: edgd lft and led over 3f out: kpt on fnl f: hld on towards fin* **10/1**

6064 **2** *1/2* **My Destination (IRE)**[4] 4822 4-8-9 **63** .... JasonHart(5) 8 71
(Declan Carroll) *hld up in rr: hdwy to chse ldrs over 3f out: 2nd over 2f out: kpt on: no ex towards fin* **5/1**[3]

1262 **3** *3 1/4* **Petella**[6] 4759 7-8-9 **58** .... (p) PJMcDonald 6 62
(George Moore) *mid-div: drvn over 5f out: chsng ldrs over 3f out: 3rd over 2f out: one pce over 1f out* **9/1**

4642 **4** *4* **Beat The Shower**[39] 3627 7-8-11 **60** .... RobertWinston 7 59
(Peter Niven) *hld up in rr: hdwy to chse ldrs over 4f out: 4th over 2f out: one pce over 1f out* **4/1**[2]

3213 **5** *1/2* **Madrasa (IRE)**[5] 4809 5-8-9 **65** .... (bt) JacobButterfield(7) 3 64
(Keith Reveley) *hld up in mid-div: effrt on ins 3f out: kpt on one pce: nvr a threat* **6/4**[1]

0-60 **6** *16* **Authentication**[39] 3627 4-8-13 **62** .... PatCosgrave 1 42
(Mel Brittain) *chsd ldrs: rdn over 3f out: sn lost pl* **40/1**

6000 **7** *hd* **Patavium (IRE)**[12] 4563 10-8-11 **60** .... JamesSullivan 9 39
(Edwin Tuer) *hld up in rr: hdwy to chse ldrs over 3f out: lost pl over 2f out* **40/1**

0-02 **8** *hd* **Joyful Motive**[22] 4204 4-8-2 **51** oh1 .... AndrewMullen 4 30
(Tom Tate) *led: wd bnd after 6f: sn drvn: hdd over 3f out: lost pl over 2f out* **12/1**

4-00 **9** ¾ **Jawaab (IRE)**[13] 4512 9-9-7 **70**..(p) PhillipMakin 2 48
(Philip Kirby) *trckd ldrs: t.k.h: reminders over 6f out: lost pl over 3f out* **16/1**

0606 **10** 3¾ **Bijou Dan**[30] 3944 12-7-13 **51** oh5.. JulieBurke(3) 11 25
(George Moore) *sn w ldr: carried wd bnd after 6f: drvn 4f out: lost pl over 2f out* **40/1**

3m 29.83s (1.53) **Going Correction** +0.125s/f (Good) **10** Ran SP% **116.6**
Speed ratings (Par 103): **101,100,99,97,96 88,88,88,88,86**
toteswingers 1&2 £5.40, 1&3 £8.40, 2&3 £7.20 CSF £58.78 CT £466.13 TOTE £12.30: £3.30, £1.30, £2.00; EX 59.00 Trifecta £652.50 Pool: £1547.68 - 1.77 winning units..
Owner N E F Luck **Bred** Darley **Trained** Settrington, N Yorks

FOCUS
A modest staying handicap in which they went just a respectable gallop.

4970 GO RACING IN YORKSHIRE FUTURE STARS APPRENTICE H'CAP (APPRENTICE SERIES) 6f
6:20 (6:22) (Class 5) (0-70,70) 3-Y-O+ **£2,587** (£770; £384; £192) **Stalls** Low

Form RPR

0-15 **1** **Gran Canaria Queen**[6] 4762 4-8-12 **56**.......................... GaryMahon(2) 11 73
(Tim Easterby) *dwlt and wnt rt s: in rr: gd hdwy stands' side over 2f out: led wl over 1f out: wnt clr ins fnl f: v readily* **3/1**[1]

4643 **2** 4½ **Keep It Dark**[8] 4669 4-9-8 **64**.. JacobButterfield 3 67
(Tony Coyle) *s.i.s: hdwy on outer 2f out: hung rt and tk 2nd last 100yds* **9/2**[2]

4015 **3** ½ **Mandalay King (IRE)**[20] 4291 8-9-13 **69**....................(p) LouisSteward 9 70
(Marjorie Fife) *towards rr and sn pushed along: hdwy 2f out: styd on to take 3rd last 100yds* **14/1**

3662 **4** 2¼ **Celtic Sixpence (IRE)**[65] 2780 5-9-12 **68**........................ DavidBergin 2 62
(Nick Kent) *chsd ldrs on outer: one pce over 1f out* **9/1**

0030 **5** 3 **Lucky Lodge**[45] 3446 3-8-12 **60**............................ RobertDodsworth(2) 6 44
(Mel Brittain) *chsd ldrs: one pce fnl 2f* **40/1**

5206 **6** 1 **Ryedane (IRE)**[2] 4892 11-9-5 **63**........................(b) RachelRichardson(2) 8 44
(Tim Easterby) *sn outpcd and in rr: hung rt and kpt on fnl f* **20/1**

1513 **7** 1 **Red Cape (FR)**[9] 4619 10-9-11 **67**..................................(b) GemmaTutty 4 45
(Ruth Carr) *t.k.h: led tl wl over 1f out: sn fdd* **16/1**

0006 **8** 4 **Partner (IRE)**[18] 4338 7-10-0 **70**.....................................(b) JoeyHaynes 10 35
(Noel Wilson) *chsd ldrs: wknd over 1f out* **7/1**[3]

4204 **9** 3½ **Paradise Spectre**[32] 3897 6-9-12 **70**......................... RobJFitzpatrick(2) 5 24
(Mrs K Burke) *chsd ldrs: rdn over 2f out: lost pl over 1f out* **28/1**

1450 **10** ¾ **Secret City (IRE)**[14] 4510 7-10-0 **70**..........................(b) LukeLeadbitter 12 22
(Robin Bastiman) *chsd ldrs: sn drvn along: lost pl over 1f out* **8/1**

6442 **11** 8 **Layla's Hero (IRE)**[2] 4892 6-9-2 **58**.................................(b[1]) JordanNason 1
(David Nicholls) *restless in stalls: virtually ref to r: a detached in last* **9/2**[2]

1m 10.63s (-2.07) **Going Correction** -0.25s/f (Firm)
WFA 3 from 4yo+ 4lb **11** Ran SP% **118.2**
Speed ratings (Par 103): **103,97,96,93,89 88,86,81,76,75 65**
toteswingers 1&2 £5.10, 1&3 £12.00, 2&3 £14.30 CSF £15.77 CT £167.03 TOTE £6.70: £2.00, £3.40, £4.30; EX 23.10 Trifecta £267.80 Pool: £963.17 - 2.69 winning units..
Owner M Gillies **Bred** H Moszkowicz And Whitsbury Manor Stud **Trained** Great Habton, N Yorks

FOCUS
A modest sprint handicap for apprentice riders in which there was a strong, contested pace.
T/Plt: £399.80 to a £1 stake. Pool: £61968.56 - 113.12 winning tickets T/Qpdt: £73.90 to a £1 stake. Pool: £4199.70 - 42.00 winning tickets WG

4971 - 4975a (Foreign Racing) - See Raceform Interactive

[4667] DONCASTER (L-H)
Saturday, August 3

OFFICIAL GOING: Good (good to firm in places; 8.8)
Wind: Moderate; across Weather: Cloudy with sunny periods

4976 UNISON YOUR FRIENDS AT WORK H'CAP 5f
2:25 (2:28) (Class 5) (0-70,69) 3-Y-O **£2,911** (£866; £432; £216) **Stalls** High

Form RPR

0412 **1** **Green Monkey**[18] 4390 3-9-2 **64**.. ShaneKelly 9 75+
(James Fanshawe) *trckd ldrs: hdwy wl over 1f out: chal ent fnl f: qcknd to ld last 100yds: pushed out* **4/1**[2]

1 **2** nk **Friendship Is Love**[152] 876 3-8-8 **56**.................................. LiamKeniry 11 66
(David Elsworth) *trckd ldrs on outer: hdwy 2f out: led over 1f out: sn jnd and rdn: hdd and nt qckn last 100yds* **12/1**

0605 **3** 2½ **Layla's Oasis**[21] 4283 3-9-4 **66**.................................. PatrickMathers 1 67
(Richard Fahey) *hld up towards rr: hdwy on outer over 2f out: rdn to chse ldrs over 1f out: kpt on same pce* **12/1**

6066 **4** ½ **Mysterious Wonder**[7] 4762 3-8-0 **55**.............................. EvaMoscrop(7) 4 54
(Philip Kirby) *towards rr: rdn along over 2f out: styd on appr fnl f: nrst fin* **25/1**

1621 **5** ½ **Secret Advice**[11] 4611 3-9-7 **69**..................................... RichardMullen 8 66
(Keith Dalgleish) *cl up: led 1/2-way: rdn 2f out: hdd over 1f out: wknd ent fnl f* **4/1**[2]

-160 **6** 5 **Different**[63] 2888 3-9-6 **68**... TomEaves 3 47
(Bryan Smart) *trckd ldrs: rdn along over 2f out: sn wknd* **11/4**[1]

-60 **7** 1¼ **Partner's Gold (IRE)**[45] 3479 3-8-2 **50** oh5.......................... AndrewMullen 12 25
(Alan Berry) *dwlt: a in rr* **66/1**

-060 **8** ½ **Red Cobra (IRE)**[36] 3758 3-9-0 **62**..................................... TedDurcan 10 35
(Tim Easterby) *prom: rdn along over 2f out: sn wknd* **8/1**[3]

-344 **9** nse **Shillito**[10] 4624 3-9-5 **67**... MichaelO'Connell 5 40
(Tony Coyle) *led: pushed along and hdd 1/2-way: sn wknd* **12/1**

0004 **10** 3 **Fidget**[16] 4430 3-7-13 **50**.. RaulDaSilva(3) 7 12
(David Brown) *chsd ldrs: rdn along 1/2-way: sn wknd* **9/1**

1m 0.65s (0.15) **Going Correction** 0.0s/f (Good) **10** Ran SP% **116.2**
Speed ratings (Par 100): **98,97,93,92,91 83,81,81,81,76**
toteswingers 1&2 £3.50, 1&3 £14.70, 2&3 £46.90 CSF £51.03 CT £544.93 TOTE £3.40: £1.70, £2.50, £2.90; EX 24.70 Trifecta £187.70 Pool: £852.66 - 3.40 winning units..
Owner Mr & Mrs P Hopper, Mr & Mrs M Morris **Bred** Jan & Peter Hopper **Trained** Newmarket, Suffolk

FOCUS
Round course railed out from 1m2f to where it joins straight. Only 1mm of rain over the previous 24 hours meant the going was given as good, good to firm in places (GoingStick 8.8). Two came clear in this sprint handicap and the winner is progressing nicely.

4977 UNISON SPEAKING UP FOR PUBLIC SERVICES MAIDEN AUCTION STKS 7f
3:00 (3:01) (Class 5) 2-Y-O **£2,911** (£866; £432; £216) **Stalls** High

Form RPR

1 **Evening Attire** 2-8-13 0.. SeanLevey 2 80+
(David Brown) *trckd ldrs: hdwy 2f out: n.m.r wl over 1f out: swtchd rt and rdn to chal whn sltly hmpd ins fnl f: led last 100yds: kpt on wl* **4/1**[3]

0 **2** ¾ **Roseburg (IRE)**[15] 4477 2-9-2 0.. AndreaAtzeni 7 81
(Luca Cumani) *trckd ldrs: hdwy on outer 1/2-way: chal over 2f out: led jst over 1f out: rdn and hung bdly rt ins fnl f: hdd last 100yds: sn edgd lft and no ex* **5/1**

62 **3** 5 **Ellalan**[17] 4414 2-8-11 0.. RichardMullen 4 66
(David Simcock) *led: jnd 2f out: sn rdn hdd jst 1f out: cl up whn bdly hmpd ins fnl f: one pce after* **7/4**[1]

4 3 **Makin The Rules (IRE)** 2-8-13 0.............................. MichaelO'Connell 5 57
(John Quinn) *cl up: rdn along 2f out: sn drvn and wknd* **14/1**

5 2¼ **Prostate Awareness (IRE)** 2-8-9 0.............................. AndrewElliott 11 47
(Patrick Holmes) *dwlt and towards rr: hdwy over 2f out: sn rdn and kpt on appr fnl f: n.d* **33/1**

4 **6** ½ **Stella Clavisque (IRE)**[18] 4379 2-8-11 0.............................. TedDurcan 8 48
(Brian Meehan) *in tch: rdn along over 2f out: n.d* **7/2**[2]

00 **7** 4 **Casper Lee (IRE)**[21] 4312 2-8-6 0................................ DeclanCannon(3) 9 36
(Nigel Tinkler) *prom: rdn along wl over 2f out: sn wknd* **66/1**

0 **8** nk **Syrian Pearl**[24] 4175 2-8-7 0 ow1.. RobertHavlin 1 33
(Chris Wall) *prom: cl up 1/2-way: rdn along over 2f out: sn wknd* **16/1**

9 ½ **Roving Bunny** 2-8-4 0... AndrewMullen 6 29
(James Given) *dwlt: green and a in rr* **20/1**

05 **10** 2¾ **Bertha Burnett (IRE)**[39] 3648 2-7-11 0................................ JoeyHaynes(7) 10 21
(Brian Rothwell) *in tch: pushed along 1/2-way: rdn along 3f out: sn wknd* **20/1**

1m 29.01s (2.71) **Going Correction** 0.0s/f (Good) **10** Ran SP% **121.8**
Speed ratings (Par 94): **84,83,77,74,71 70,66,65,65,62**
toteswingers 1&2 £24.50, 1&3 £3.00, 2&3 £4.30 CSF £24.47 TOTE £5.60: £2.10, £1.90, £1.20; EX 35.80 Trifecta £98.40 Pool: £761.03 - 5.79 winning units..
Owner J C Fretwell **Bred** Howard Barton Stud **Trained** Averham Park, Notts

FOCUS
They didn't go much of a pace early on in this maiden. The first two came clear and the form could possibly be rated a bit better.

4978 UNISON AND UIA HOME INSURANCE MAIDEN STKS 1m 2f 60y
3:35 (3:39) (Class 5) 3-4-Y-O **£2,911** (£866; £432; £216) **Stalls** Low

Form RPR

1 **Groundbreaking** 3-9-3 0.. RobertHavlin 5 92+
(Charlie Appleby) *trckd ldrs: hdwy on outer 3f out: rdn to chse ldr over 1f out: styd on strly to ld last 100yds: sn clr* **6/1**[3]

4 **2** 4 **Cosmic Curious (GER)**[23] 4223 3-9-3 0.............................. RichardMullen 7 85
(Lady Cecil) *trckd ldng pair: hdwy 3f out: rdn wl over 1f out: drvn ins fnl f: sn edgd lft and no imp* **5/2**[1]

3 hd **Desert Wings (IRE)** 3-9-3 0... AhmedAjtebi 9 84+
(Charlie Appleby) *trckd ldr: hdwy to ld 2f out: sn rdn clr: drvn ent fnl f: hdd & wknd last 100yds* **14/1**

5-3 **4** ¾ **Deserted**[29] 4013 3-8-12 0.. KirstyMilczarek 11 78
(Luca Cumani) *hld up in towards rr: hdwy on outer 3f out: rdn wl over 1f out: styd on fnl f: nrst fin* **4/1**[2]

5 ½ **Martian (IRE)** 3-9-3 0... ShaneKelly 4 82+
(William Haggas) *hld up in midfield: hdwy over 3f out: pushed along over 2f out: styd on fnl f: nrst fin* **11/1**

6 4 **Jeeraan (USA)** 3-9-3 0... SeanLevey 3 74
(Ed Dunlop) *trckd ldrs: hdwy 4f out: rdn along wl over 2f out: sn drvn and one pce* **33/1**

00 **7** 7 **Filia Regina**[10] 4632 3-8-12 0.. TedDurcan 8 56
(Ed Dunlop) *hld up: a towards rr* **33/1**

2 **8** ¾ **China Creek (IRE)**[9] 4667 3-8-12 0.................................. MichaelStainton 2 55
(Mark Johnston) *led: rdn along 3f out: hdd 2f out and sn wknd* **5/2**[1]

9 5 **Eco Warrior** 3-9-3 0.. LiamKeniry 10 50
(J W Hills) *a towards rr* **33/1**

00 **10** 2¼ **A Good Year (IRE)**[51] 3237 3-8-9 0.................................. RyanClark(3) 1 41
(J W Hills) *in tch: rdn along on inner over 3f out: sn wknd* **33/1**

11 30 **Sinister (IRE)** 3-9-3 0.. AndreaAtzeni 6
(Roger Varian) *dwlt: a in rr* **11/1**

2m 10.46s (1.06) **Going Correction** -0.15s/f (Firm) **11** Ran SP% **126.5**
Speed ratings (Par 103): **89,85,85,85,84 81,75,75,71,69 45**
toteswingers 1&2 £6.10, 1&3 £7.50, 2&3 £7.60 CSF £22.53 TOTE £8.10: £2.80, £1.60, £3.50; EX 27.50 Trifecta £224.90 Pool: £1,452.32 - 4.84 winning units..
Owner Godolphin **Bred** Highclere Stud **Trained** Newmarket, Suffolk

FOCUS
This good maiden was dominated by the Charlie Appleby-trained Godolphin pair. The form is rated around the race averages.

4979 UNISON ESSENTIAL COVER WHEREVER YOU WORK H'CAP 1m 2f 60y
4:10 (4:13) (Class 2) (0-100,99) 3-Y-O+
£12,450 (£3,728; £1,864; £932; £466; £234) **Stalls** Low

Form RPR

40-1 **1** **Winterlude (IRE)**[25] 4151 3-8-12 **92**................................ AhmedAjtebi 6 100+
(Charlie Appleby) *trckd ldrs: hdwy wl over 2f out: rdn to ld jst over 1f out: sn drvn and hld on gamely towards fin* **9/2**[2]

2252 **2** ½ **Come On Blue Chip (IRE)**[21] 4280 4-9-3 **88**..............(p) LiamKeniry 11 95
(Paul D'Arcy) *hld up: stdy hdwy on outer over 3f out: rdn to chse ldrs wl over 1f out: rdn to chal ins fnl f: ev ch tl no ex nr fin* **20/1**

3043 **3** ½ **Ruscello (IRE)**[15] 4488 4-9-5 **90**..................................... TomMcLaughlin 2 96
(Ed Walker) *trckd ldrs: hdwy over 2f out: n.m.r and swtchd rt over 1f out: sn rdn and ev ch ins fnl f: drvn and kpt on towards fin* **8/1**

3035 **4** hd **Fennell Bay (IRE)**[4] 4854 4-9-4 **89**.............................. MichaelStainton 3 95
(Mark Johnston) *led: rdn along 3f out: drvn 2f out: hdd appr fnl f: kpt on gamely u.p tl no ex last 75yds* **12/1**

-025 **5** 2¾ **Lahaag**[42] 3559 4-10-0 **99**.. RobertHavlin 1 99
(John Gosden) *prom: trckd ldng pair: hdwy to chse ldr 2f out: sn rdn and ch tl drvn and one pce ent fnl f* **2/1**[1]

03 **6** 1/2 **Centurius**16 4452 3-9-3 **97** .... AndreaAtzeni 7 96
(Marco Botti) *hld up in tch: hdwy wl over 2f out: rdn wl over 1f out: drvn and no imp fnl f* **16/1**

0034 **7** 1 1/4 **Be Perfect (USA)**85 2240 4-9-2 **87** .... PaulQuinn 10 84
(David Nicholls) *hld up towards rr: hdwy 3f out: rdn along 2f out: nvr nrr* **33/1**

3134 **8** *shd* **Awake My Soul (IRE)**21 4310 4-9-6 **96** .... DavidBergin(5) 4 93
(David O'Meara) *hld up towards rr: hdwy on inner 3f out: rdn to chse ldrs whn swtchd rt over 1f out: sn drvn and no imp* **11/2**3

0000 **9** *1* **Memory Cloth**35 3825 6-8-12 **83** .... SeanLevey 5 78
(Brian Ellison) *in tch: pushed along over 3f out: rdn wl over 2f out: sn wknd* **33/1**

0021 **10** *3* **Silvery Moon (IRE)**38 3684 6-9-4 **89** .... TedDurcan 9 78
(Tim Easterby) *sn trcking ldr: effrt 3f out: rdn along over 2f out: drvn wl over 1f out: sn edgd lft and wknd* **12/1**

66-0 **11** *5* **World Domination (USA)**29 4027 5-9-8 **93** .... RichardMullen 8 73
(Lady Cecil) *dwlt: hld up: a in rr* **16/1**

3055 **12** 2 3/4 **Art Scholar (IRE)**15 4501 6-9-7 **92** .... AndrewMullen 12 67
(Michael Appleby) *hld up and bhd: sme hdwy on inner over 3f out: sn rdn and wknd* **20/1**

2m 10.14s (0.74) **Going Correction** -0.15s/f (Firm)
WFA 3 from 4yo+ 9lb **12** Ran SP% **120.6**
Speed ratings (Par 109): **91,90,90,90,87 87,86,86,85,83 79,76**
toteswingers 1&2 £19.40, 1&3 £9.10, 2&3 £38.60 CSF £97.45 CT £705.31 TOTE £5.50: £2.20, £5.00, £1.80; EX 68.30 Trifecta £1168.80 Part won. Pool: £1,558.48 - 0.02 winning units..
Owner Godolphin **Bred** Darley **Trained** Newmarket, Suffolk

FOCUS
This looked a competitive handicap but the early pace wasn't particularly strong. That counted against the likes of World Domination, Awake My Soul and Memory Cloth, who didn't settle that well towards the rear of the field. The fourth sets the standard. The winner can't go up much for this.

4980 UNISON EVERYONE DESERVES A LIVING WAGE H'CAP 1m 4f
4:45 (4:46) (Class 4) (0-85,85) 3-Y-O **£5,175** (£1,540; £769; £384) **Stalls** Low

Form RPR

3413 **1** **Emerging**50 3294 3-9-2 **80** .... (p) LiamKeniry 4 90
(David Elsworth) *trckd ldrs: smooth hdwy on outer over 3f out: slt ld wl over 2f out and sn rdn: drvn over 1f out: hld on gamely towards fin* **7/1**

2212 **2** 1/2 **Duke Of Perth**15 4476 3-9-2 **80** .... KirstyMilczarek 5 89
(Luca Cumani) *hld up in rr: gd hdwy 3f out and sn cl up: rdn to dispute ld 2f out and ev ch tl drvn ent fnl f: no ex towards fin* **4/1**2

1-2 **3** 1/2 **Wadi Al Hattawi (IRE)**23 4202 3-9-7 **85** .... (v1) TedDurcan 3 93
(Saeed bin Suroor) *hld up in rr: hdwy on inner 3f out: rdn and outpcd over 2f out: swtchd rt to wd outside and hdwy to chse ldng pair ins fnl f: sn drvn: edgd lft and kpt on towards fin* **10/11**1

-322 **4** *5* **Autun (USA)**24 4167 3-9-7 **85** .... RichardMullen 1 85
(Lady Cecil) *trckd ldng pair: hdwy on inner and cl up 3f out: sn disp ld: rdn 2f out: ev ch tl drvn and wknd ent fnl f* **5/1**3

2152 **5** *8* **Interior Minister**16 4447 3-9-6 **84** .... ShaneKelly 2 71
(Jo Hughes) *led: rdn along over 3f out: drvn and hdd wl over 2f out: sn wknd* **14/1**

6100 **6** *7* **Federal Blue (USA)**21 4279 3-9-5 **83** .... RobertHavlin 6 59
(Mark Johnston) *trckd ldr: rdn along over 3f out: sn drvn and wknd wl over 2f out* **16/1**

2m 31.98s (-2.92) **Going Correction** -0.15s/f (Firm) **6** Ran SP% **114.1**
Speed ratings (Par 102): **103,102,102,99,93 89**
toteswingers 1&2 £3.30, 1&3 £2.10, 2&3 £2.40 CSF £35.23 TOTE £8.10: £3.30, £2.70; EX 30.40 Trifecta £79.50 Pool: £1,801.78 - 16.99 winning units..
Owner Ben CM Wong **Bred** D R Tucker **Trained** Newmarket, Suffolk
■ Stewards' Enquiry : Kirsty Milczarek six-day ban: used whip above permitted level down shoulder in the forehand (Aug 17-22)

FOCUS
They went a fair gallop here and the first three raced in the last three places for most of the race. Each of them looks ahead of their marks, with the winner improving on his Sandown run.

4981 TRADE UNION UNISON AND THOMPSONS SOLICITORS CONDITIONS STKS 6f
5:20 (5:21) (Class 3) 3-Y-O+
£8,092 (£2,423; £1,211; £605; £302; £152) **Stalls** High

Form RPR

133- **1** **Taayel (IRE)**280 7400 3-8-9 108 .... RobertHavlin 7 102+
(John Gosden) *racd wd: trckd ldrs: hdwy over 1f out: effrt ent fnl f: sn shkn up and qcknd to ld last 100yds: readily* **11/4**2

060- **2** 3/4 **Valbchek (IRE)**301 6867 4-8-13 102 .... RichardMullen 3 101
(Jeremy Noseda) *trckd ldrs: hdwy wl over 2f out: cl up wl over 1f out: rdn to ld jst ins fnl f: sn drvn and hdd last 100yds: kpt on* **8/1**

0-20 **3** 3/4 **Royal Rock**42 3558 9-8-13 100 .... TedDurcan 4 99
(Chris Wall) *hld up in rr: hdwy wl over 2f out: rdn to chse ldng pair over 1f out: drvn and kpt on fnl f* **5/1**

3030 **4** 3/4 **Dubawi Sound**7 4744 5-8-13 100 .... (t) SeanLevey 2 96
(David Brown) *led: rdn wl over 1f out: drvn and hdd jst ins fnl f: kpt on same pce* **3/1**3

335 **5** 1 1/4 **Superboot (IRE)**28 4058 3-8-9 80 .... ShaneKelly 6 91
(Michael Wigham) *hld up in rr: hdwy 3f out: chsd ldrs wl over 1f out: sn rdn and kpt on same pce appr fnl f* **33/1**

0-34 **6** *6* **Restiadargent (FR)**22 4260 4-8-8 104 .... AndreaAtzeni 5 68
(William Haggas) *chsd ldrs: rdn along 3f out: sn wknd* **15/8**1

400 **7** *1* **Seachantach (USA)**35 3840 7-8-13 102 .... (t) PaoloSirigu 1 70
(Marco Botti) *racd wd: prom: rdn along 3f out: wknd over 2f out* **20/1**

1m 11.84s (-1.76) **Going Correction** 0.0s/f (Good)
WFA 3 from 4yo+ 4lb **7** Ran SP% **114.4**
Speed ratings (Par 107): **111,110,109,108,106 98,97**
toteswingers 1&2 £3.60, 1&3 £4.50, 2&3 £7.10 CSF £24.60 TOTE £4.30: £2.70, £4.00; EX 19.40 Trifecta £135.20 Pool: £1,963.57 - 10.88 winning units..
Owner Hamdan Al Maktoum **Bred** Corrin Stud **Trained** Newmarket, Suffolk

FOCUS
One or two of these had questions to answer, including the winner, but he did it well and has the potential to rate higher. The race is rated cautiously given the grade.

4982 UNISON AND LV=FRIZZELL CAR INSURANCE FILLIES' H'CAP 6f
5:50 (5:51) (Class 5) (0-70,69) 3-Y-O+ **£2,911** (£866; £432; £216) **Stalls** High

Form RPR

-410 **1** **Queen Hermione (IRE)**25 4148 5-8-12 **55** .... (vt) SeanLevey 6 69
(Derek Shaw) *hld up: hdwy over 2f out: swtchd lft to outer over 1f out: rdn and str run ent fnl f: led last 75yds: sn clr* **16/1**

523 **2** 2 1/4 **Lulu The Zulu (IRE)**23 4200 5-9-7 **64** .... AndrewMullen 3 71
(Michael Appleby) *trckd ldrs: smooth hdwy and cl up over 2f out: led wl over 1f out: rdn and edgd lft ins fnl f: hdd and one pce last 75yds* **11/8**1

3233 **3** *2* **Busy Bimbo (IRE)**7 4761 4-8-7 **50** oh1 .... PaulQuinn 8 51
(Alan Berry) *in tch: hdwy over 2f out: rdn to chse ldrs over 1f out: ch ent fnl f: sn drvn and one pce* **10/1**

2143 **4** *nk* **Big Wave (IRE)**9 4690 5-9-12 **69** .... RobertHavlin 9 69
(Alison Hutchinson) *cl up: led 1/2-way: rdn and hdd wl over 1f out: drvn and wknd fnl f* **7/1**3

0342 **5** 2 3/4 **See Clearly**8 4727 4-9-10 **67** .... (p) TedDurcan 4 58
(Tim Easterby) *chsd ldrs: hdwy 2f out: sn rdn and wknd appr fnl f* **4/1**2

0060 **6** 1 1/4 **Medam**3 4893 4-8-7 **50** oh3 .... (t) KirstyMilczarek 2 37
(Shaun Harris) *dwlt: hdwy 1/2-way: chsd ldrs 2f out: sn rdn and wknd over 1f out* **25/1**

-653 **7** *1* **Somethingboutmary**9 4674 3-8-9 **56** .... (b) AndreaAtzeni 7 39
(Tim Pitt) *a towards rr* **12/1**

-500 **8** 1/2 **El Molino Blanco**18 4374 3-8-6 **53** .... (b1) AndrewElliott 1 34
(Michael Easterby) *dwlt: a towards rr* **20/1**

0-04 **9** 3 3/4 **Secret Lodge**15 4504 5-8-4 **50** oh5 .... RyanPowell(3) 5 20
(Garry Woodward) *chsd ldrs: pushed along after 2f: sn lost pl and bhd* **33/1**

1661 **10** 2 3/4 **Charlemagne Diva**8 4727 3-8-9 **63** .... (t) NoelGarbutt(7) 10 23
(Richard Guest) *led: hdd 1/2-way: sn rdn along and wknd* **7/1**3

1m 13.54s (-0.06) **Going Correction** 0.0s/f (Good)
WFA 3 from 4yo+ 4lb **10** Ran SP% **121.3**
Speed ratings (Par 100): **100,97,94,93,90 88,87,86,81,77**
toteswingers 1&2 £9.10, 1&3 £15.60, 2&3 £2.30 CSF £39.30 CT £259.69 TOTE £19.10: £4.50, £1.30, £1.80; EX 62.20 Trifecta £357.00 Pool: £1,686.16 - 3.54 winning units..
Owner Dr David Chapman-Jones **Bred** Knocklong House Stud **Trained** Sproxton, Leics

FOCUS
A gamble on handicap debutante Lulu The Zulu was foiled here. The winner built on her weak Chepstow win.
T/Plt: £412.10 to a £1 stake. Pool: £64,219.94 - 113.75 winning units T/Qpdt: £69.80 to a £1 stake. Pool: £3,791.70 - 40.15 winning units JR

4944 GOODWOOD (R-H)
Saturday, August 3

OFFICIAL GOING: Good (7.6)
Wind: Strong; against Weather: Breezy, bright spells

4983 ROBINS FARM RACING STEWARDS' SPRINT STKS (H'CAP) 6f
2:05 (2:09) (Class 2) 3-Y-O+
£21,787 (£6,524; £3,262; £1,631; £815; £409) **Stalls** High

Form RPR

4133 **1** **Seeking Magic**63 2868 5-9-5 **93** .... (t) RyanTate(5) 27 104
(Clive Cox) *chsd ldrs: str chal and edging rt jst ins fnl f: r.o u.p to ld on post* **16/1**

602- **2** *nse* **Take Cover**262 7716 6-9-6 **89** .... DavidProbert 24 99
(David C Griffiths) *taken down early and led to s: led: rdn and hung rt fr over 1f out: battled on gamely u.p fnl f: hdd on post* **50/1**

0200 **3** 3/4 **Chooseday (IRE)**35 3802 4-9-2 **85** .... (p) GrahamLee 21 93
(Kevin Ryan) *hld up in midfield: sltly outpcd and lost pl 2f: rallied and swtchd lft ins fnl f: r.o strly fnl 100yds* **25/1**

3-11 **4** *shd* **Above Standard (IRE)**50 3299 5-9-5 **88** .... (t) DanielTudhope 18 96
(Michael Easterby) *hld up in bhd ldrs and travelled wl: rdn and str chal jst ins fnl f: no ex fnl 75yds* **12/1**

-130 **5** 1 1/2 **Out Do**15 4472 4-9-8 **91** .... KierenFallon 9 94+
(Luca Cumani) *in tch in midfield: swtchd rt and effrt over 1f out: wnt lft u.p jst ins fnl f: styd on same pce fnl 100yds* **14/1**

1000 **6** 1/2 **Yeeoow (IRE)**15 4472 4-9-10 **93** .... MartinHarley 1 94
(Mrs K Burke) *in tch: rdn and effrt over 1f out: styd on same pce u.p ins fnl f* **20/1**

202 **7** *hd* **El Viento (FR)**21 4285 5-9-4 **92** .... (p) GeorgeChaloner(5) 11 93
(Richard Fahey) *in tch in midfield: rdn and effrt over 1f out: edgd rt 1f out: styd on fnl 100yds: nvr threatened ldrs* **14/1**

41 **8** *hd* **Baby Strange**35 3823 9-8-11 **87** .... AdamMcLean(7) 6 87
(Derek Shaw) *stdd after s: hld up towards rr: rdn and effrt over 1f out: swtchd rt jst ins fnl f: styd on towards fin: nt rch ldrs* **20/1**

-120 **9** *nk* **Enrol**43 3527 4-9-10 **93** .... RyanMoore 20 92+
(Sir Michael Stoute) *in tch in midfield: n.m.r and shuffled bk over 1f out: sn swtchd lft and drvn: styd on wl fnl 100yds: nt rch ldrs* **5/1**1

0140 **10** *nse* **Best Trip (IRE)**38 3684 6-9-0 **83** .... SilvestreDeSousa 15 82+
(Brian Ellison) *hld up in midfield: nt clr run over 1f out tl ins fnl f: r.o fnl 75yds: nvr trbld ldrs* **25/1**

3211 **11** *hd* **Picture Dealer**8 4730 4-9-2 **85** 6ex .... JamesDoyle 10 83+
(Gary Moore) *rrd as stalls opened and v.s.a: clsd on to bk of field 1/2-way: rdn and hdwy over 1f out: no imp ins fnl f* **6/1**2

6103 **12** *hd* **Noverre To Go (IRE)**15 4494 7-8-10 **79** .... (p) CathyGannon 2 77
(Ronald Harris) *chsd ldrs: rdn and ev ch ent fnl f: no ex and btn jst ins fnl f: wknd fnl 100yds* **25/1**

5603 **13** 1 1/2 **Nassau Storm**18 4389 4-9-7 **90** .... NeilCallan 23 83
(William Knight) *racd in midfield: rdn and no imp over 1f out: styd on same pce ins fnl f* **33/1**

1010 **14** 1/2 **Milly's Gift**22 4252 3-8-12 **85** .... WilliamBuick 5 75
(Clive Cox) *chsd ldrs: rdn and effrt 2f out: no ex ent fnl f and btn whn sltly hmpd jst ins fnl f: wknd* **20/1**

1465 **15** 3/4 **Arctic Feeling (IRE)**4 4860 5-9-3 **86** .... TonyHamilton 13 75
(Richard Fahey) *racd in midfield: rdn over 2f out and sn lost pl and bhd whn hung rt over 1f out: no threat to ldrs but plugged on ins fnl f* **25/1**

0142 **16** *1* **Tax Free (IRE)**14 4536 11-9-0 **90** .... OisinMurphy(7) 12 76
(David Nicholls) *chsd ldr tl carried rt and hmpd over 1f out: sn lost pl and btn 1f out: wknd ins fnl f* **14/1**

0264 **17** *2* **Goldream**14 4536 4-9-10 **93** .... JimCrowley 14 72
(Robert Cowell) *in tch in midfield: rdn and no imp 2f out: btn ent fnl f: wknd* **20/1**

1-00 **18** 2 1/4 **Sacrosanctus**7 4744 5-9-7 **90** .... TomQueally 25 62
(Scott Dixon) *racd keenly: chsd ldrs: rdn and struggling over 2f out: wkng whn n.m.r jst over 1f out* **50/1**

2306 **19** 1/2 **Alnoomaas (IRE)**22 4235 4-8-7 **76** .... JimmyQuinn 8 46
(Luke Dace) *in tch in midfield: rdn and struggling over 2f out: wknd over 1f out* **50/1**

0106 **20** 3/4 **Piscean (USA)**48 3367 8-9-4 **87** .... RoystonFfrench 22 55
(Tom Keddy) *s.i.s: a bhd: rdn and no hdwy ent fnl 2f: n.d* **33/1**

0122 **21** *2* **Links Drive Lady**[14] 4534 5-9-2 **85** JoeFanning 17 47
(Dean Ivory) *s.i.s: a bhd: rdn and no hdwy 2f out: n.d* **9/1**[3]

0343 **22** *5* **Apollo D'Negro (IRE)**[7] 4746 5-8-11 **80** (v) SteveDrowne 7 26
(Clive Cox) *a bhd: rdn 1/2-way: wknd wl over 1f out: wl bhd and eased towards fin* **33/1**

556 **23** *nk* **Dominate**[42] 3584 3-9-2 **89** RichardHughes 4 33
(Richard Hannon) *hld up towards rr: swtchd lft 2f out: no imp and wknd over 1f out: wl bhd and eased towards fin* **14/1**

-150 **24** *1 ¾* **Personal Touch**[50] 3300 4-8-12 **81** PaulHanagan 3 20
(Richard Fahey) *in tch in midfield: losing pl and pushed along over 2f out: bhd over 1f out: wl bhd and eased towards fin* **16/1**

1m 10.79s (-1.41) **Going Correction** -0.025s/f (Good)
WFA 3 from 4yo+ 4lb **24** Ran SP% **136.2**
Speed ratings (Par 109): **108,107,106,106,104 104,103,103,103,103 102,102,100,99,98 97,94,91,91,90 87,80,80,78**
toteswingers 1&2 not won, 1&3 £47.40, 2&3 not won CSF £683.10 CT £8809.84 TOTE £19.30: £4.60, £22.80, £8.50, £3.70; EX 1810.60 TRIFECTA Not won..
Owner The Seekers **Bred** R, J D & M R Bromley Gardner **Trained** Lambourn, Berks

FOCUS
All distances as advertised. The consolation race for those who didn't make it into the Stewards' Cup, but despite the view that the far rail might be the faster strip, the field raced centre-to-nearside early and it was only due to the principals hanging that they ended up towards the far rail late on. The first four came from stalls 27, 24, 21 and 18. The first four all recorded personal bests.

4984 RAC STKS (H'CAP) 1m 4f
2:40 (2:40) (Class 2) (0-105,99) 3-Y-O

£31,125 (£9,320; £4,660; £2,330; £1,165; £585) **Stalls** Low

Form RPR

1202 **1** **Pether's Moon (IRE)**[21] 4301 3-9-3 **95** RichardHughes 6 106
(Richard Hannon) *broke wl: t.k.h and stdd towards rr after 4f: stdy hdwy over 2f out: trckd ldr 1f out: qcknd to ld fnl 110yds and shkn up: readily* **4/1**[2]

6521 **2** *1 ¼* **Salutation (IRE)**[14] 4541 3-8-12 **90** SilvestreDeSousa 8 99
(Mark Johnston) *trckd ldr: chal 3f out: led 2f out and sn rdn: hdd u.p fnl 110yds: kpt on: nt pce of wnr* **16/1**

2-11 **3** *½* **Havana Cooler (IRE)**[21] 4301 3-8-13 **91** KierenFallon 7 99+
(Luca Cumani) *in rr: pushed along 4f out: hdwy over 2f out: kpt on u.p fnl f to take 3rd clsng stages: fin wl* **4/1**[2]

4213 **4** *1 ½* **Van Percy**[63] 2879 3-8-8 **86** CathyGannon 11 92
(Andrew Balding) *t.k.h: chsd ldrs: rdn over 2f out: tk 3rd over 1f out: styd on same pce ins fnl f: dropped to 4th clsng stages* **8/1**

3221 **5** *½* **Elidor**[44] 3486 3-9-1 **93** MartinHarley 3 98
(Mick Channon) *in tch: drvn and hdwy to chse ldrs fr 3f out: kpt on same pce fnl f* **8/1**

2110 **6** *5* **Royal Skies (IRE)**[43] 3526 3-9-3 **95** JoeFanning 10 92
(Mark Johnston) *led: jnd 3f out: sn rdn: hdd 2f out: wknd appr fnl f* **5/1**[3]

1131 **7** *3 ½* **Bold Sniper**[21] 4279 3-9-7 **99** RyanMoore 1 97
(Sir Michael Stoute) *hld up in rr: drvn and sme hdwy whn hung rt fr over 2f out: fnd little and nvr on terms: eased whn no ch fnl f* **3/1**[1]

2312 **8** *18* **Royal Signaller**[38] 3698 3-8-4 **82** (p) MartinDwyer 9 45
(Amanda Perrett) *chsd ldrs: rdn 3f out: btn whn n.m.r on rails 2f out* **16/1**

124 **9** *5* **Pitchoun (IRE)**[15] 4501 3-8-12 **90** WilliamBuick 2 45
(Mark Johnston) *rdn over 2f out: a bhd* **25/1**

2m 37.23s (-1.17) **Going Correction** +0.075s/f (Good) **9** Ran SP% **119.5**
Speed ratings (Par 106): **106,105,104,103,103 100,97,85,82**
toteswingers 1&2 £11.50, 1&3 £4.50, 2&3 £8.80 CSF £67.36 CT £276.94 TOTE £5.20: £1.90, £3.80, £1.80; EX 80.50 Trifecta £697.00 Pool: £4,995.99 - 5.37 winning units..
Owner John Manley **Bred** Michael G Daly **Trained** East Everleigh, Wilts
■ Stewards' Enquiry : Richard Hughes (1st incident), two-day ban: careless riding (Aug 17-18); (2nd) caution: careless riding.

FOCUS
This is strong handicap form. A couple of the Mark Johnston runners raced clear of the others, with Royal Skies setting what seemed a fair gallop while being closely followed by Salutation. The winner reversed Newmarket latest with the third.

4985 MARKEL INSURANCE NASSAU STKS (BRITISH CHAMPIONS SERIES) (GROUP 1) (F&M) 1m 1f 192y
3:15 (3:17) (Class 1) 3-Y-O+

£113,420 (£43,000; £21,520; £10,720; £5,380; £2,700) **Stalls** Low

Form RPR

2-14 **1** **Winsili**[44] 3482 3-8-11 103 WilliamBuick 15 116
(John Gosden) *stdd after s: t.k.h: hld up in last quintet: swtchd lft and effrt ent fnl 2f: str run to chal: edgd rt and bmpd ent fnl f: led ins fnl f: hld on wl fnl 100yds: rdn out* **20/1**

-310 **2** *nk* **Thistle Bird**[45] 3456 5-9-6 108 JamesDoyle 14 115
(Roger Charlton) *taken down early: stdd after s: t.k.h: hld up in rr: swtchd lft and effrt 2f out: str run to chal ins fnl f: r.o wl but hld fnl 75yds* **33/1**

1-10 **3** *2* **Hot Snap**[90] 2047 3-8-11 113 TomQueally 5 111+
(Lady Cecil) *hld up in tch in midfield: lost pl and nt clr run 3f out: swtchd lft over 2f out: stl plenty to do but hdwy ent fnl f: r.o wl to go 3rd towards fin: no threat to ldrs* **5/1**[3]

1114 **4** *½* **Sajjhaa**[97] 1872 6-9-6 115 SilvestreDeSousa 4 110
(Saeed bin Suroor) *hld up wl in tch in midfield: rdn to chse ldr 2f out: sn chalng: wnt lft u.p and bmpd rival ent fnl f: sn led: hdd and no ex ins fnl f: wknd towards fin* **8/1**

2112 **5** *1 ¾* **Sky Lantern (IRE)**[22] 4254 3-8-11 119 RichardHughes 13 107+
(Richard Hannon) *hld up in tch in midfield: clsd to trck ldrs and travelling wl but nowhere to go over 1f out: hmpd 1f out: bdly hmpd again sn after: sme room and pushed along ins fnl f: no hdwy and nt given a hrd time after* **7/4**[1]

1323 **6** *hd* **Just Pretending (USA)**[14] 4550 3-8-11 114 SeamieHeffernan 11 106
(A P O'Brien, Ire) *led: almost tk wrong crse 1/2-way: rdn over 2f out: hdd jst over 1f out: wknd ins fnl f* **20/1**

11 **7** *¾* **Integral**[28] 4081 3-8-11 104 RyanMoore 1 105+
(Sir Michael Stoute) *hld up in tch in midfield: stuck in bhd ldrs and no where to go over 1f out: swtchd lft and effrt ent fnl f: kpt on but no threat to ldrs* **8/1**

1-26 **8** *¾* **Magical Dream (IRE)**[14] 4550 3-8-11 105 MichaelHussey 12 103
(A P O'Brien, Ire) *hld up in tch in last quintet: travelling wl enough but stuck bhd horses on inner fr over 2f out: swtchd lft and effrt ent fnl f: plugged on: nvr trbld ldrs* **50/1**

-231 **9** *2* **Ambivalent (IRE)**[34] 3870 4-9-6 110 JohnnyMurtagh 7 102+
(Roger Varian) *t.k.h: hld up in tch in midfield: hdwy to chse ldrs 5f out: wnt 2nd jst over 3f out tl wl over 1f out: wknd ent fnl f* **16/1**

1312 **10** *2 ¾* **Moment In Time (IRE)**[28] 4059 4-9-6 108 MartinHarley 2 97+
(David Simcock) *t.k.h: chsd ldrs: effrt on inner to press ldrs over 2f out: no ex and struggling whn hmpd over 1f out: wknd fnl f* **25/1**

-000 **11** *¾* **Semayyel (IRE)**[25] 4137 4-9-6 95 NeilCallan 6 92
(Clive Brittain) *chsd ldrs: rdn and lost pl whn n.m.r ent fnl 2f: wknd over 1f out* **100/1**

-213 **12** *7* **Just The Judge (IRE)**[43] 3524 3-8-11 110 JamieSpencer 10 78
(Charles Hills) *stdd sharply after s: hld up in last pair: swtchd lft and no hdwy over 2f out: wl bhd and eased ins fnl f* **9/2**[2]

2-04 **13** *¾* **Beatrice Aurore (IRE)**[45] 3456 5-9-6 106 [1] OlivierPeslier 8 77
(Ed Dunlop) *hmpd and dropped to rr sn after s: hld up in tch in last quintet: hdwy but nt clr run over 2f out: rdn and wknd over 1f out* **33/1**

1105 **14** *18* **Banoffee (IRE)**[28] 4059 3-8-11 103 KierenFallon 3 41
(Hughie Morrison) *chsd ldr tl jst over 3f out: sn lost pl: bhd 2f out: eased ins fnl f: t.o* **25/1**

2m 6.19s (-1.91) **Going Correction** +0.075s/f (Good)
WFA 3 from 4yo+ 9lb **14** Ran SP% **125.4**
Speed ratings (Par 117): **110,109,108,107,106 106,105,105,103,101 100,95,94,80**
toteswingers 1&2 £132.10, 1&3 £31.10, 2&3 £83.00 CSF £544.00 TOTE £31.00: £5.90, £13.30, £2.20; EX 1191.30 Trifecta £7660.40 Part won. Pool: £10,213.96 - 0.49 winning units..
Owner K Abdullah **Bred** Juddmonte Farms Ltd **Trained** Newmarket, Suffolk
■ Stewards' Enquiry : James Doyle four-day ban: used whip above permitted level (Aug 17-20)
William Buick two-day ban: used whip above permitted level (Aug 17-18)

FOCUS
Plenty of runners, but not a great deal between a whole host of them and, with several still competitive late on, a few found trouble. The early gallop seemed reasonable enough, but this was quite a messy race and the form shouldn't be taken too literally. There were a couple of superb rides on the first pair, who were drawn in the top two boxes, but were soon tucked in well off the pace before being produced with sustained challenges out wide. Winsili is rated up there with Talent among the leading middle-distance British fillies. Sky Lantern was the chief sufferer of the interference.

4986 ROBINS FARM RACING STEWARDS' CUP (HERITAGE H'CAP) 6f
3:50 (3:53) (Class 2) 3-Y-O+

£62,250 (£18,640; £9,320; £4,660; £2,330; £1,170) **Stalls** High

Form RPR

262 **1** **Rex Imperator**[35] 3840 4-9-4 **104** (p) NeilCallan 26 116
(William Haggas) *hld up and travelled wl in midfield: clsd to trck ldrs over 1f out: swtchd lft and qcknd to ld ins fnl f: r.o strly: readily* **12/1**

-100 **2** *2 ¼* **Ajjaadd (USA)**[21] 4275 7-8-9 **98** WilliamTwiston-Davies[(3)] 25 103
(Ted Powell) *chsd ldrs: led travelling strly ent fnl 2f: rdn ent fnl f: hdd and nt pce of wnr ins fnl f: kpt on to hold 2nd* **66/1**

3600 **3** *½* **Burwaaz**[21] 4297 4-8-11 **97** (b[1]) PaulHanagan 28 100
(Ed Dunlop) *racd against stands' rail thrght: chsd ldrs: ev ch u.p over 1f out: styd on same pce ins fnl f* **25/1**

1202 **4** *½* **Racy**[21] 4275 6-8-9 **95** HarryBentley 7 97+
(Brian Ellison) *chsd ldrs: rdn and ev ch over 1f out: kpt on same pce u.p fnl 150yds* **16/1**

1304 **5** *hd* **Ninjago**[22] 4255 3-8-13 **103** RichardHughes 17 103+
(Richard Hannon) *hld up wl bhd: hdwy and swtchd rt ent fnl f: swtchd lft and r.o wl fnl 100yds: no threat to wnr* **8/1**[2]

1211 **6** *nk* **Tropics (USA)**[7] 4780 5-9-6 **106** 6ex JimCrowley 6 106+
(Dean Ivory) *hld up towards rr: gd hdwy ent fnl 2f: swtchd rt and rdn chal 1f out: hung lft and no ex ins fnl f* **9/2**[1]

-601 **7** *nk* **Louis The Pious**[28] 4058 5-9-0 **100** DanielTudhope 27 99
(David O'Meara) *hld up in tch in midfield: rdn and effrt over 1f out: r.o ins fnl f: no threat to wnr* **16/1**

4650 **8** *nk* **Hawkeyethenoo (IRE)**[7] 4744 7-9-8 **108** GrahamLee 5 106
(Jim Goldie) *hld up in midfield: effrt and nt clr run over 1f out: r.o ins fnl f: no threat to wnr* **14/1**

0000 **9** *½* **Secret Witness**[7] 4780 7-8-12 **98** (b) MartinHarley 13 94
(Ronald Harris) *chsd ldrs: drvn 2f out: keeping on same pce and hld whn edgd rt u.p ins fnl f* **50/1**

-033 **10** *shd* **Dinkum Diamond (IRE)**[42] 3558 5-9-3 **103** CathyGannon 16 99
(Henry Candy) *wnt rt s: hld up in tch in midfield: effrt u.p to chse ldrs over 1f out: keeping on same pce and hld whn pushed rt and hmpd ins fnl f: nt clr run and eased towards fin* **16/1**

1141 **11** *nse* **Heaven's Guest (IRE)**[22] 4255 3-8-10 **100** 6ex TonyHamilton 22 95
(Richard Fahey) *in tch in midfield: niggled along over 3f out: rdn and chsd ldrs 2f out: no ex u.p 1f out: wknd fnl 100yds* **10/1**[3]

3001 **12** *nk* **Barnet Fair**[6] 4800 5-8-11 **97** 6ex DavidProbert 10 92
(Richard Guest) *t.k.h: hld up towards rr: hdwy over 2f out: chsd ldrs and rdn over 1f out: no ex ins fnl f: wknd towards fin* **28/1**

2004 **13** *1* **Prodigality**[7] 4780 5-9-0 **100** TomQueally 9 92
(Ronald Harris) *in tch in midfield and travelled wl: rdn and effrt whn edgd rt jst over 1f out: no ex and btn whn pushed rt and hmpd ins fnl f: wknd towards fin* **16/1**

4242 **14** *hd* **Shropshire (IRE)**[42] 3558 5-9-3 **103** RyanMoore 21 94
(Charles Hills) *bhd: rdn and effrt over 1f out: kpt on ins fnl f: nvr trbld ldrs* **8/1**[2]

55-0 **15** *½* **Hoof It**[21] 4311 6-9-12 **112** KierenFallon 19 102
(Michael Easterby) *in tch in midfield: pushed along 1/2-way: keeping on but no threat to ldrs whn nt clr run ins fnl f: eased towards fin* **14/1**

1153 **16** *1 ¾* **Dr Red Eye**[21] 4284 5-8-9 **95** (p) SilvestreDeSousa 3 79
(Scott Dixon) *chsd ldrs: rdn and no ex over 1f out: btn whn pushed rt and hmpd ins fnl f: eased after* **33/1**

6500 **17** *½* **Regal Parade**[7] 4780 9-8-9 **100** (t) MatthewLawson[(5)] 11 82
(Milton Bradley) *towards rr: rdn over 1f out: nt clr run and swtchd lft ins fnl f: styd on fnl 100yds n.d* **66/1**

-060 **18** *nk* **Free Zone**[35] 3822 4-8-12 **98** RoystonFfrench 20 79+
(Bryan Smart) *chsd ldrs: ev ch and drvn over 1f out: btn jst ins fnl f: wkng whn pushed rt and hmpd sn after* **66/1**

204 **19** *nk* **Humidor (IRE)**[53] 3187 6-9-4 **104** (t) PatCosgrave 8 84
(George Baker) *hld up towards rr: rdn and effrt jst over 1f out: keeping on but no ch whn nt clr run and hmpd ins fnl f* **25/1**

1421 **20** *2* **York Glory (USA)**[42] 3558 5-9-9 **109** (b) JamieSpencer 4 83
(Kevin Ryan) *awkward and stdd s: hld up wl in rr: effrt over 1f out: swtchd rt and rdn 1f out: no real imp and nvr a threat: eased towards fin* **8/1**[2]

0-00 **21** *1 ¼* **Blaine**[45] 3455 3-9-0 **104** JoeFanning 15 73
(Kevin Ryan) *sltly hmpd s and slowly away: a bhd: no ch whn swtchd rt jst ins fnl f* **33/1**

1140 **22** *nk* **Polski Max**[49] 3348 3-8-5 **100** GeorgeChaloner[(5)] 1 68
(Richard Fahey) *chsd ldrs: drvn ent fnl 2f: no ex and btn 1f out: fdd ins fnl f* **66/1**

05-0 **23** *½* **Mac's Power (IRE)**[35] 3840 7-8-9 **95** (t) WilliamBuick 24 63
(Willie Musson) *sn bhd: rdn and no rspnse over 1f out: n.d* **40/1**

 The Form Book Flat, Raceform Ltd, Compton, RG20 6NL.

6412 **24** *hd* **Whozthecat (IRE)**[13] 4569 6-8-8 **101** 6ex.............(v) LukeLeadbitter(7) 23 68
(Declan Carroll) *led tl drvn and hdd ent fnl 2f: sn struggling: wknd over 1f out* **33/1**

6006 **25** *1 1/4* **Face The Problem (IRE)**[6] 4800 5-9-1 **101**...................... JamesDoyle 2 64
(Jamie Osborne) *t.k.h: swtchd lft sn after s: hld up in midfield: rdn and fnd nil 2f out: btn 1f out: heavily eased fnl 100yds* **25/1**

3005 **26** *3/4* **Pabusar**[14] 4536 5-8-9 **95**.. MartinDwyer 12 55
(Jamie Osborne) *chsd ldrs: rdn and struggling 2f out: btn over 1f out: fdd ins fnl f* **33/1**

-000 **27** *3 1/2* **Tiddliwinks**[70] 2676 7-9-7 **107**... BrianHughes 18 56
(Kevin Ryan) *in tch in midfield tl rdn and wknd over 2f out: bhd 1f out* **50/1**

1m 10.35s (-1.85) **Going Correction** -0.025s/f (Good)
WFA 3 from 4yo+ 4lb **27** Ran SP% **144.2**
Speed ratings (Par 109): **111,108,107,106,106 106,105,105,104,104 104,103,102,102,101 99,98,98,97,95 93,93,92,92,90 89,**
toteswingers 1&2 £381.30, 1&3 £68.80, 2&3 £381.30 CSF £709.16 CT £8910.35 TOTE £13.60: £3.20, £26.60, £8.00, £4.90; EX 1635.90 Trifecta £8414.00 Part won. Pool: £11,218.77 - 0.81 winning units..
Owner George Turner **Bred** Christopher J Mason **Trained** Newmarket, Suffolk

FOCUS
The last two winners of the Stewards' Cup were back for another try and eight of these had contested last month's Wokingham, including the first three at Ascot. As in the opener, they raced centre-to-stands' side early and again those drawn high were favoured, with the first four coming from stalls 26, 25, 28 and 7. The winning time was nearly half a second quicker than the consolation race. The winner had looked capable of this sort of form in the past and has Group-race potential, while the runner-up helps sets the standard.

4987 NATWEST AHEAD FOR BUSINESS EBF MAIDEN STKS 7f

4:25 (4:28) (Class 2) 2-Y-O **£12,938** (£3,850; £1,924; £962) **Stalls** Low

Form RPR

3 **1** **Snow Trouble (USA)**[38] 3689 2-9-0 0......................... JohnnyMurtagh 9 83
(Marcus Tregoning) *wnt lft s: trckd ldrs: chal fr 2f out tl slt ld appr fnl f but remained hrd pressed: hld on gamely clsng stages* **3/1**[2]

2 *nk* **Master The World (IRE)** 2-9-0 0.................................... JamesDoyle 3 82+
(Gerard Butler) *chsd ldrs: drvn to chal fr 1f out and remained upsides thrght fnl f: no ex last strides* **40/1**

3 *1 1/4* **Tahadee (IRE)** 2-9-0 0... MartinHarley 8 79+
(Mick Channon) *chsd ldrs: styd on u.p to take 3rd fnl 110yds: no imp on ldng duo* **16/1**

4 *1 3/4* **Golden Town (IRE)** 2-9-0 0.................................. SilvestreDeSousa 12 74+
(Saeed bin Suroor) *s.i.s: in rr and stl plenty to do fr 3f out: hdwy on outside fr 2f out: styd on wl thrght fnl f: gng on cl home* **8/1**

33 **5** *2* **Mime Dance**[16] 4439 2-9-0 0.. DavidProbert 18 69
(Andrew Balding) *sn led: drvn appr fnl 2f: sn hdd: wknd ins fnl f* **25/1**

0 **6** *1/2* **Under My Wing (IRE)**[70] 2653 2-9-0 0........................... PaulHanagan 2 68
(Richard Hannon) *s.i.s: sn rcvrd and in tch: rdn and one pce over 2f out: kpt on again fnl f* **50/1**

7 *1 1/4* **Sellingallthetime (IRE)** 2-9-0 0.................................... SteveDrowne 5 65
(Charles Hills) *slowly away: sn rcvrd: in tch over 3f out and n.m.r on inner: rdn 2f out: styd on same pce* **50/1**

8 *1* **Glasgow Central** 2-9-0 0.. TomQueally 6 62
(Charles Hills) *chsd ldrs: rdn 2f out: wknd fnl f* **25/1**

9 *1 3/4* **War Spirit** 2-9-0 0.. RichardHughes 1 58+
(Richard Hannon) *trckd ldrs: drvn to chal between horses whn nt clr run ins 2f out: btn sn after: eased ins fnl f* **5/2**[1]

10 *shd* **Beach Bar (IRE)** 2-9-0 0.. NeilCallan 10 57
(William Knight) *hmpd s and slowly away: sme hdwy over 2f out: sn rdn: kpt on same pce* **33/1**

11 *1* **Gamesome (FR)** 2-9-0 0... JamieSpencer 15 55
(Olly Stevens) *in rr: sme hdwy towards outside and green over 2f out: no further prog* **14/1**

12 *2 1/2* **Pack Leader (IRE)** 2-9-0 0.. KierenFallon 11 48
(Amanda Perrett) *in rr: drvn and hdwy 3f out: nvr rchd ldrs: wknd 2f out* **20/1**

0 **13** *1 3/4* **Filosofo (IRE)**[15] 4483 2-9-0 0......................... WilliamTwiston-Davies 14 44
(Richard Hannon) *outpcd most of way* **66/1**

14 *1* **Sir Charlie Kunz** 2-9-0 0.. JoeFanning 4 41
(Mark Johnston) *chsd ldrs: rdn 2f out: wknd over 1f out* **16/1**

15 *1 1/2* **Allergic Reaction (IRE)** 2-9-0 0.................................... JimCrowley 16 37
(William Knight) *slowly away: rdn: green and veered lft sn after s: a towards rr* **33/1**

2 **16** *1 3/4* **After The Goldrush**[7] 4773 2-9-0 0................................. RyanMoore 17 33
(Richard Hannon) *mid-div: sme prog 3f out: sn wknd* **6/1**[3]

302 **17** *2 1/2* **Oriental Relation (IRE)**[31] 3943 2-9-0 80....................... GrahamLee 19 26
(James Given) *towards rr most of way* **20/1**

1m 28.17s (1.17) **Going Correction** -0.05s/f (Good) **17** Ran SP% **128.4**
Speed ratings (Par 100): **91,90,89,87,84 84,82,81,79,79 78,75,73,72,70 68,65**
toteswingers 1&2 £53.40, 1&3 £14.80, 2&3 £148.50 CSF £134.59 TOTE £4.10: £1.80, £8.80, £4.60; EX 286.30 Trifecta £4005.00 Pool: £6,191.70 - 1.15 winning units..
Owner Guy Brook **Bred** Brushwood Stable **Trained** Whitsbury, Hants

FOCUS
Sometimes a good maiden, last year's race was won by Steeler, who later landed a Listed contest and the Royal Lodge, and back in sixth was Wentworth, who won this season's Betfred Mile. It was quite a rough race and the form matches the race averages.

4988 FAIRMONT NURSERY H'CAP 7f

5:00 (5:01) (Class 2) 2-Y-O **£12,938** (£3,850; £1,924; £962) **Stalls** Low

Form RPR

2421 **1** **Art Official (IRE)**[9] 4676 2-9-5 **84**................................ RichardHughes 4 88
(Richard Hannon) *t.k.h: mde all: rdn and qcknd clr over 1f out: kpt on fnl f: a holding on* **11/4**[1]

221 **2** *nk* **Shot In The Sun (IRE)**[28] 4044 2-7-13 **71**................. SamanthaBell(7) 2 74
(Richard Fahey) *in tch in midfield: rdn and nt much roo over 1f out: gap opened and hdwy 1f out: wnt 3rd but stl plenty to do jst ins fnl f: r.o strly: wnt 2nd fnl 75yds: nvr quite getting to wnr* **25/1**

12 **3** *1 1/4* **Homestretch**[26] 4108 2-9-0 **79**...................................... MartinHarley 1 79
(Mick Channon) *t.k.h early: chsd ldrs: rdn and chsd wnr over 1f out: kpt on same pce and lost 2nd fnl 75yds* **10/1**

0211 **4** *hd* **Our Queenie (IRE)**[21] 4302 2-9-7 **86**.............................. RyanMoore 9 85
(Richard Hannon) *racd in last pair: swtchd lft 2f out: no imp u.p tl r.o strly ins fnl f: nt rch ldrs* **7/1**

01 **5** *2 1/2* **Mezel**[23] 4199 2-8-12 **77**.. PaulHanagan 8 70
(Sir Michael Stoute) *t.k.h: hld up in tch in midfield: effrt and hmpd 2f out: swtchd lft over bt outpcd over 1f out: edging rt and sme hdwy 1f out: kpt on but no threat to ldrs* **9/2**[2]

434 **6** *1 3/4* **Munjally**[29] 4026 2-9-3 **82**.. GrahamLee 10 70
(Richard Hannon) *hld up in tch in last trio: lost pl and n.m.r 2f out: drvn and no imp over 1f out: kpt on but wl hld fnl f* **7/1**

3214 **7** *shd* **Rizal Park (IRE)**[8] 4703 2-8-12 **77**................................. DavidProbert 5 65
(Andrew Balding) *t.k.h: hld up in tch in midfield: rdn and unable qck 2f out: outpcd over 1f out: one pce and wl hld after* **12/1**

6431 **8** *hd* **Latenightrequest**[26] 4108 2-8-6 **71**.......................... SilvestreDeSousa 7 59
(Richard Fahey) *wl in tch in midfield: rdn over 2f out: no ex u.p over 1f out: wknd ent fnl f* **20/1**

1 **9** *3/4* **Mr Carbonfootprint**[76] 2474 2-9-0 **79**............................ TonyHamilton 3 65
(Richard Fahey) *t.k.h and racd awkwardly: hld up in tch: rdn and no rspnse 2f out: wknd over 1f out* **14/1**

201 **10** *1 1/2* **Bureau (IRE)**[18] 4386 2-8-10 **75**.. JoeFanning 14 57
(Mark Johnston) *chsd ldr: rdn ent fnl 2f: unable qck and lost 2nd over 1f out: wknd fnl f* **5/1**[3]

003 **11** *6* **Bowsers Bold**[26] 4121 2-8-4 **69**.. JimmyQuinn 12 35
(Marcus Tregoning) *stdd and dropped in bhd after s: hld up in rr: rdn 2f out: sn wknd* **20/1**

1m 27.31s (0.31) **Going Correction** -0.05s/f (Good) **11** Ran SP% **123.3**
Speed ratings (Par 100): **96,95,94,94,91 89,89,88,87,86 79**
toteswingers 1&2 £16.80, 1&3 £6.00, 2&3 £20.40 CSF £87.06 CT £512.57 TOTE £3.10: £1.50, £5.70, £3.70; EX 114.50 Trifecta £789.60 Pool: £5,077.25 - 4.82 winning units..
Owner Chris Giles,Potensis Ltd,J Palmer-Brown **Bred** Lisieux Stud **Trained** East Everleigh, Wilts

FOCUS
Possibly not that strong a nursery for the level but another improved effort from the winner, who got a fairly easy time on the lead.

4989 TELEGRAPH STKS (H'CAP) 5f

5:35 (5:35) (Class 3) (0-95,92) 3-Y-O

£9,337 (£2,796; £1,398; £699; £349; £175) **Stalls** High

Form RPR

-435 **1** **Pal Of The Cat**[15] 4487 3-8-2 **73** oh5..............................(tp) JimmyQuinn 2 82
(Brian Gubby) *mde all: rdn over 1f out: hrd pressed 1f out: sustained duel w runner-up fnl f: r.o wl: all out* **20/1**

5620 **2** *shd* **Jillnextdoor (IRE)**[8] 4734 3-9-2 **87**........................... SilvestreDeSousa 1 96
(Mick Channon) *stdd s: hld up towards rr: swtchd rt and effrt over 1f out: drvn and str chal 1f out: sustained duel w wnr fnl f: r.o: jst hld* **16/1**

1112 **3** *1* **Lexington Place**[9] 4674 3-8-11 **82**............................. DanielTudhope 10 87
(David O'Meara) *stdd s: t.k.h: hld up in rr: clsd and travelling wl 2f out: chsd ldrs and rdn 1f out: drvn and styd on same pce fnl 100yds* **8/1**

2121 **4** *nk* **Holley Shiftwell**[9] 4674 3-8-7 **78**................................. PaulHanagan 5 82
(Stuart Williams) *in tch in midfield: n.m.r over 1f out: swtchd rt and effrt 1f out: drvn and styd on same pce ins fnl f* **7/2**[1]

1643 **5** *1* **Normal Equilibrium**[26] 4112 3-9-7 **92**......................... JamieSpencer 4 93
(Robert Cowell) *stdd s: hld up in tch in rr: clsd 2f out: swtchd rt and effrt u.p ent fnl f: no ex ins fnl f: wknd towards fin* **14/1**

2121 **6** *1 1/2* **Extrasolar**[50] 3279 3-9-0 **85**...(t) JamesDoyle 9 80
(Amanda Perrett) *in tch in midfield: effrt u.p 2f out: chsd wnr over 1f out tl 1f out: wknd ins fnl f* **4/1**[2]

0334 **7** *nse* **Miss Diva**[17] 4413 3-8-10 **81**.. RyanMoore 8 76
(Richard Hannon) *in tch towards rr: dropped to rr 2f: rdn over 1f out: modest late hdwy: nvr trbld ldrs* **12/1**

1241 **8** *1 1/2* **Shore Step (IRE)**[56] 3104 3-9-0 **85**............................. MartinHarley 6 75
(Mick Channon) *chsd wnr tl wl over 2f out: rdn and struggling over 1f out: drvn and wknd ins fnl f* **5/1**[3]

1253 **9** *nk* **The Art Of Racing (IRE)**[18] 4367 3-9-0 **85**..................(t) HarryBentley 7 74
(Olly Stevens) *chsd ldrs: wnt 2nd over 2f out tl rdn and fnd little over 1f out: sn btn: wknd fnl f* **14/1**

6-20 **10** *1 1/4* **Vincentti (IRE)**[49] 3348 3-9-6 **91**.................................... TomQueally 3 75
(Ronald Harris) *chsd ldrs: rdn 2f out: unable qck and struggling over 1f out: wknd fnl f* **12/1**

0662 **11** *2* **Jadanna (IRE)**[26] 4117 3-9-3 **88**....................................... GrahamLee 11 65
(James Given) *in tch in midfield tl pushed along and lost pl after 2f: n.d after* **12/1**

2141 **12** *8* **Pixilated**[17] 4413 3-8-10 **81**...................................... RichardHughes 12 29
(Gay Kelleway) *chsd ldrs: struggling and edgd rt 2f out: sn lost pl and bhd: eased wl ins fnl f* **11/1**

58.15s (-2.05) **Going Correction** -0.30s/f (Firm) **12** Ran SP% **125.4**
Speed ratings (Par 104): **104,103,102,101,100 97,97,95,94,92 89,76**
toteswingers 1&2 £43.10, 1&3 £35.60, 2&3 £36.30 CSF £323.10 CT £2828.84 TOTE £22.80: £5.00, £5.00, £2.60; EX 360.60 Trifecta £2525.70 Part won. Pool: £3,367.70 - 0.15 winning units..
Owner Brian Gubby **Bred** B Gubby **Trained** Bagshot, Surrey

FOCUS
Stall 2 beat stall 1 in this fair 3yo handicap, which seemed at odds with the two sprints earlier on the card, but this was a much smaller field and the first two merely raced up the centre. However, with that pair having a combined record of 1-30 coming into this, it would not have been the easiest result to predict. The form is rated around the third and fourth.
T/Jkpt: Not won. T/Plt: £6,553.60 to a £1 stake. Pool: £262,439.59 - 29.23 winning units T/Qpdt: £415.10 to a £1 stake. Pool: £17,496.45 - 31.19 winning units SP

4469 HAMILTON (R-H)

Saturday, August 3

OFFICIAL GOING: Good (good to soft in places; 7.7)
Wind: Fairly strong; half behind Weather: Cloudy; bright

4990 AVIA SIGNS NURSERY H'CAP 6f 5y

6:15 (6:16) (Class 6) (0-65,64) 2-Y-O **£2,587** (£770; £384; £192) **Stalls** High

Form RPR

05 **1** **It's All A Game**[26] 4108 2-8-0 **48**.................................(v[1]) PhilipPrince(5) 5 57+
(Richard Guest) *mde all centre: rdn 2f out: drew clr fnl f* **5/1**

4404 **2** *3 1/4* **Bandolier**[36] 3767 2-9-7 **64**... LeeTopliss 1 63
(Richard Fahey) *chsd ldrs centre: rdn over 2f out: rallied to chse (clr) wnr ins fnl f: kpt on* **8/1**

500 **3** *3 1/2* **Claudia Octavia**[94] 1930 2-7-13 **45**................................ NeilFarley(3) 3 34
(Brian Ellison) *n.m.r sn after s: in tch centre: rdn and chsd wnr over 1f out to ins fnl f: sn outpcd* **20/1**

505 **4** *1 1/4* **May Whi (IRE)**[33] 3905 2-9-3 **60**.................................. StephenCraine 9 45
(Tom Dascombe) *cl up stands' rail: rdn over 2f out: one pce fr over 1f out* **9/2**[3]

604 **5** *nk* **Please Let Me Go**[35] 3826 2-9-3 **60**............................... PaddyAspell 7 44
(Kevin Ryan) *prom towards centre: effrt and rdn 2f out: outpcd whn edgd rt ins fnl f* **10/3**[2]

2044 **6** 2 ½ **Dotesy (IRE)**[28] 4054 2-8-6 **56**..........(p) JoeDoyle[(7)] 8 33
(John Quinn) *chsd ldrs towards stands' side: rdn over 2f out: wknd over 1f out* **12/1**

400 **7** hd **Tricksome (IRE)**[31] 3943 2-8-4 **54**.......... RowanScott[(7)] 2 30
(Ann Duffield) *cl up centre tl rdn and wknd over 1f out* **20/1**

600 **8** 4 ½ **Sassy Brown (IRE)**[15] 4505 2-8-10 **58** ow1..........(b[1]) SladeO'Hara[(5)] 4 21
(Tim Easterby) *prom centre: rdn over 2f out: wknd fnl f* **16/1**

545 **9** 7 **Tamayuz Dream (IRE)**[30] 3972 2-9-7 **64**.......... J-PGuillambert 6 6
(Mark Johnston) *dwlt: sn drvn along in rr: nvr on terms: eased whn no ch fnl f* **3/1**[1]

1m 12.81s (0.61) **Going Correction** -0.10s/f (Good) 9 Ran SP% **117.1**
Speed ratings (Par 92): **91,86,82,80,79 76,76,70,61**
toteswingers 1&2 £6.90, 1&3 £14.00, 2&3 £22.30 CSF £45.17 CT £729.91 TOTE £6.10: £2.10, £1.90, £6.70; EX 39.20 Trifecta £289.40 Pool: £979.53- 2.53 winning units..
Owner Viscount Environmental Ltd **Bred** Mrs G Sainty **Trained** Wetherby, W Yorks
■ Stewards' Enquiry : Philip Prince two-day ban: careless riding (Aug 18-19)

FOCUS
All distances as advertised but ground saved on far side of home straight. A weak nursery with those that raced mid-race dominant. They may well rate higher again.

4991 MCGUIRE ON FIRE MAIDEN STKS 6f 5y
6:45 (6:47) (Class 5) 3-Y-O+ **£2,911** (£866; £432; £216) **Stalls** High

Form RPR

0050 **1** **Stoneacre Oskar**[73] 2576 4-8-13 39.......... SladeO'Hara[(5)] 1 62
(Peter Grayson) *dwlt: bhd: gd hdwy over 1f out: kpt on wl to ld cl home* **80/1**

44 **2** hd **Pilates (IRE)**[14] 4535 3-9-0 0.......... J-PGuillambert 5 60
(Mark Johnston) *cl up: rdn over 2f out: led ent fnl f: kpt on: hdd cl home* **9/2**[3]

3 ¾ **Yarn** 3-9-0 0.......... PhillipMakin 7 58
(William Haggas) *cl up: led gng wl over 2f out: rdn and hdd ent fnl f: kpt on same pce* **11/8**[1]

3-0 **4** ¾ **Hanalei Bay (IRE)**[23] 4200 3-8-12 0.......... GeorginaBaxter[(7)] 3 61
(Keith Dalgleish) *midfield on outside: pushed along over 2f out: kpt on ins fnl f* **16/1**

30-2 **5** ¾ **Meeting In Paris (IRE)**[28] 4050 3-9-0 60.......... LeeTopliss 2 53
(Richard Fahey) *chsd ldrs: effrt and rdn over 2f out: no ex ins fnl f* **7/4**[2]

0520 **6** 2 ¾ **Royal Duchess**[16] 4448 3-8-11 47.......... NeilFarley[(3)] 10 44
(Lucy Normile) *led to over 2f out: sn rdn: wknd fnl f* **16/1**

3365 **7** 1 ½ **Lady Calantha**[11] 4611 3-9-0 44.......... PaddyAspell 6 40
(Alan Berry) *in tch: rdn over 2f out: edgd rt and wknd over 1f out* **66/1**

2504 **8** 3 **Pastoral Prey**[21] 4290 3-9-0 54..........(p) PhilipPrince[(5)] 4 35
(Ian Semple) *dwlt: sn pushed along towards rr: no imp fr 2f out* **18/1**

-060 **9** 14 **Cara's Delight (AUS)**[12] 4582 6-9-4 34..........(vt[1]) DuranFentiman 9
(Frederick Watson) *in tch tl rdn and wknd over 2f out* **100/1**

000 **10** 4 ½ **Princess Cayan (IRE)**[12] 4582 3-8-7 28..........(v[1]) RossSmith[(7)] 8
(Linda Perratt) *missed break: bhd and rdn: hung rt and wknd fr 1/2-way* **100/1**

1m 12.16s (-0.04) **Going Correction** -0.10s/f (Good)
WFA 3 from 4yo+ 4lb 10 Ran SP% **118.4**
Speed ratings (Par 103): **96,95,94,93,92 89,87,83,64,58**
toteswingers 1&2 £39.80, 1&3 £25.40, 2&3 £2.10 CSF £421.35 TOTE £58.90: £20.90, £2.10, £1.10; EX 973.30 Trifecta £1041.70 Part won. Pool: £1,389.05 - 0.04 winning units..
Owner Richard Teatum **Bred** Clover Lea Bloodstock **Trained** Formby, Lancs

FOCUS
Very little depth to this maiden which produced a shock result. The fancied horses probably underperformed a bit and the bare form is limited.

4992 FREE BETS @FREEBETS.CO.UK H'CAP 5f 4y
7:15 (7:25) (Class 5) (0-75,75) 3-Y-O+ **£3,234** (£962; £481; £240) **Stalls** Centre

Form RPR

0335 **1** **Perfect Pasture**[14] 4544 3-8-5 **57**..........(v[1]) DuranFentiman 11 74
(Michael Easterby) *dwlt: sn cl up and racd alone stands' side: overall ldr over 2f out: drvn and styd on strly fnl f* **6/1**[1]

400 **2** 3 ½ **Tom Sawyer**[42] 3569 5-8-9 **63**..........(b) ConnorBeasley[(5)] 9 68
(Julie Camacho) *prom centre: hdwy to chse stands' side wnr over 1f out: kpt on fnl f: no imp* **8/1**[3]

6-02 **3** 2 ¼ **Da'Quonde (IRE)**[124] 1278 5-9-7 **75**.......... JustinNewman[(5)] 7 72
(Bryan Smart) *cl up centre: checked over 4f out and sn pushed along: ev ch 2f out: kpt on same pce appr fnl f* **7/1**[2]

5333 **4** ¾ **Script**[6] 4814 4-8-10 **59**.......... PaddyAspell 5 53
(Alan Berry) *prom centre: checked wl over 3f out: effrt 2f out: sn one pce* **7/1**[2]

-150 **5** ½ **Colbyor**[19] 4338 4-9-4 **67**.......... LeeTopliss 4 59
(Richard Fahey) *chsd ldrs: blkd after 2f: rdn and effrt in centre 2f out: kpt on same pce* **7/1**[2]

5046 **6** ½ **Rock Canyon (IRE)**[16] 4448 4-8-0 **56** oh7..........(p) JoeDoyle[(7)] 3 47
(Linda Perratt) *cl up far side: effrt and drvn over 2f out: outpcd appr fnl f* **20/1**

-046 **7** 1 ½ **Fol Hollow (IRE)**[37] 3714 8-8-6 **62**.......... RowanScott[(7)] 1 47
(Stuart Coltherd) *cl up far side tl rdn and wknd over 1f out* **22/1**

-006 **8** 1 **Foxy Music**[29] 4018 9-9-6 **72**.......... NeilFarley[(3)] 8 54
(Eric Alston) *led: hung rt thrght and ended up towards far side over 3f out: hdd over 2f out: wknd over 1f out* **16/1**

5-05 **9** 15 **Princess In Exile**[40] 3626 3-7-13 **56**.......... PhilipPrince[(5)] 6
(Ian Semple) *bhd centre: struggling 1/2-way: nvr on terms* **40/1**

59.14s (-0.86) **Going Correction** -0.10s/f (Good)
WFA 3 from 4yo+ 3lb 9 Ran SP% **80.3**
Speed ratings (Par 103): **102,96,92,91,90 90,87,86,62**
toteswingers 1&2 £9.60, 1&3 £2.70, 2&3 £7.20 CSF £22.05 TOTE £3.40: £1.70, £2.60, £1.80; EX 32.60 Trifecta £73.80 Pool: £154.37 - 1.56 winning units..
Owner Mrs Jean Turpin **Bred** Mrs Jean Turpin **Trained** Sheriff Hutton, N Yorks
■ Chasing Dreams (4-1, ref to ent stalls) & Findog (uns rdr & bolted bef s) were withdrawn. Deduct 40p in the £ under R4.

FOCUS
A moderate sprint handicap. The winner raced solo up the rail and it's hard to know how literally to take the form.

4993 TBA BRITISH STALLION STUDS EBF FILLIES' H'CAP 6f 5y
7:45 (7:48) (Class 3) (0-90,88) 3-Y-O+ **£9,703** (£2,887; £1,443; £721) **Stalls** High

Form RPR

1010 **1** **Hopes N Dreams (IRE)**[4] 4860 5-9-3 **79**.......... PhillipMakin 3 97
(Kevin Ryan) *mde all: pushed along over 1f out: drew clr fnl f: readily* **14/5**[1]

0013 **2** 4 ½ **Dartrix**[8] 4727 4-8-3 **70**.......... ConnorBeasley[(5)] 5 74
(Michael Dods) *dwlt: bhd: rdn and effrt on outside over 2f out: chsd wnr 1f out: kpt on: nt pce to chal* **3/1**[2]

6603 **3** 2 ¾ **Dream Maker (IRE)**[7] 4757 3-9-5 **85**.......... DuranFentiman 2 79
(Tim Easterby) *chsd wnr: rdn over 2f out: lost 2nd and outpcd 1f out* **13/2**

5324 **4** ½ **Economic Crisis (IRE)**[10] 4620 4-8-8 **70**.......... PaddyAspell 8 63
(Alan Berry) *prom: drvn along 2f out: kpt on same pce fnl f* **12/1**

1000 **5** 1 ¼ **Meandmyshadow**[8] 4730 5-9-3 **79**.......... DaleSwift 7 68
(Alan Brown) *chsd ldrs: sn pushed along: outpcd and edgd rt 2f out: no imp fnl f* **4/1**[3]

000 **6** 1 **Breezolini**[5] 4821 5-8-0 **69** oh2..........(b[1]) JordanNason[(7)] 1 55
(Geoffrey Harker) *bhd: rdn along 1/2-way: kpt on fnl f: nvr able to chal* **11/1**

-060 **7** ½ **Strange Magic (IRE)**[42] 3562 3-9-8 **88**.......... LeeTopliss 6 71
(Richard Fahey) *in tch on outside: effrt and drvn over 2f out: wknd appr fnl f* **16/1**

154 **8** 1 ¼ **Black Annis Bower**[5] 4821 5-8-4 **69** oh2.......... NeilFarley[(3)] 9 49
(Michael Easterby) *t.k.h: prom: rdn and edgd rt over 2f out: wknd over 1f out* **10/1**

1m 11.04s (-1.16) **Going Correction** -0.10s/f (Good)
WFA 3 from 4yo+ 4lb 8 Ran SP% **115.6**
Speed ratings (Par 104): **103,97,93,92,91 89,89,87**
toteswingers 1&2 £2.50, 1&3 £3.10, 2&3 £4.50 CSF £11.60 TOTE £3.20: £1.20, £1.50, £2.40; EX 10.90 Trifecta £78.20 Pool: £774.76 - 7.42 winning units..
Owner JCG Chua & CK Ong **Bred** J & Mrs Brennan & Edward & Mrs O'Regan **Trained** Hambleton, N Yorks

FOCUS
Not the strongest Class 3 handicap for fillies' but the speedy winner made all against the rail. It has to rate a personal best.

4994 IHE STAINLESS LTD H'CAP (A QUALIFIER FOR £15000 BETFAIR SCOTTISH MILE SERIES FINAL) 1m 65y
8:15 (8:16) (Class 5) (0-75,75) 3-Y-O+ **£3,234** (£962; £481; £240) **Stalls** Low

Form RPR

2103 **1** **Ted's Brother (IRE)**[6] 4807 5-9-1 **67**..........(e) PhilipPrince[(5)] 4 77
(Richard Guest) *stmbld s: t.k.h and hld up towards rr: hdwy to ld over 1f out: sn rdn: hld on wl fnl f* **11/4**[1]

5400 **2** nk **Satanic Beat (IRE)**[52] 3204 4-9-13 **74**.......... PhillipMakin 3 83
(Jedd O'Keeffe) *trckd ldr: led and rdn over 2f out: hdd over 1f out: rallied and ev ch fnl f: hld nr fin* **8/1**

0566 **3** 2 ¼ **High Resolution**[15] 4475 6-9-2 **68**.......... ConnorBeasley[(5)] 5 72
(Linda Perratt) *s.i.s: hld up: hdwy on ins 2f out: kpt on fnl f: nrst fin* **16/1**

0164 **4** 1 ½ **Jebel Tara**[6] 4807 8-9-7 **75**..........(bt) KevinStott[(7)] 11 76
(Alan Brown) *led tl rdn and hdd over 2f out: edgd lft and outpcd over 1f out* **18/1**

0330 **5** nk **Dark Ocean (IRE)**[18] 4384 3-9-0 **68**.......... MichaelO'Connell 6 67
(Jedd O'Keeffe) *hld up towards rr: effrt and pushed along over 2f out: kpt on fnl f: nvr able to chal* **20/1**

-060 **6** ¾ **Pivotman**[37] 3729 5-9-4 **65**..........(t) GrahamGibbons 10 63
(Michael Easterby) *in tch: effrt and rdn over 2f out: no imp appr fnl f* **7/1**

6642 **7** 4 **Spavento (IRE)**[13] 4561 7-9-6 **72**.......... JasonHart[(5)] 1 61
(Eric Alston) *in tch: drvn and outpcd over 3f out: rallying whn n.m.r over 1f out: sn btn* **12/1**

1336 **8** hd **Ingleby Symphony (IRE)**[41] 3610 3-9-2 **70**.......... LeeTopliss 7 58
(Richard Fahey) *in tch on outside: effrt and drvn 3f out: wknd over 1f out* **8/1**

1122 **9** 7 **Argaki (IRE)**[16] 4446 3-9-7 **75**.......... TomEaves 9 47
(Keith Dalgleish) *hld up towards rr: rdn and effrt on outside over 2f out: sn wknd* **6/1**[3]

0105 **10** 3 ¼ **Dubious Escapade (IRE)**[21] 4294 4-9-7 **68**..........(p) PJMcDonald 8 33
(Ann Duffield) *trckd ldrs: rdn and outpcd over 2f out: sn btn* **25/1**

3341 **11** 11 **Wellingrove (IRE)**[15] 4475 3-9-3 **71**.......... J-PGuillambert 2 10
(Mark Johnston) *prom tl rdn and wknd 2f out* **9/2**[2]

1m 46.64s (-1.76) **Going Correction** -0.10s/f (Good)
WFA 3 from 4yo+ 7lb 11 Ran SP% **121.3**
Speed ratings (Par 103): **104,103,101,99,99 98,94,94,87,84 73**
toteswingers 1&2 £4.00, 1&3 £24.30, 2&3 £16.20 CSF £26.23 TOTE £3.60: £1.30, £4.50, £4.80; EX 34.40 Trifecta £575.50 Pool: £844.92 - 1.10 winning units..
Owner Ontoawinner & Bob McCoy **Bred** T Counihan **Trained** Wetherby, W Yorks

FOCUS
A competitive if ordinary handicap, which looked sound run. The winner's latest run had been franked by the winner there.

4995 MARGARET SMITH MEMORIAL H'CAP (QUALIFIER FOR £15000 BETFAIR SCOTTISH STAYERS' SERIES FINAL) 1m 3f 16y
8:45 (8:47) (Class 5) (0-75,75) 3-Y-O+ **£3,881** (£1,155; £577; £288) **Stalls** High

Form RPR

1225 **1** **Corton Lad**[16] 4446 3-9-2 **73**..........(tp) TomEaves 9 82
(Keith Dalgleish) *in tch: hdwy wl over 1f out: led ins fnl f: hld on wl u.p* **14/1**

1052 **2** nk **Cosmic Halo**[12] 4584 4-9-11 **72**.......... LeeTopliss 5 80
(Richard Fahey) *hld up: rdn and hdwy over 2f out: chsd wnr ins fnl f: kpt on: hld cl home* **7/1**[3]

6055 **3** 2 **Woodstock (IRE)**[8] 4729 3-8-6 **63**.......... DuranFentiman 7 67
(Brian Ellison) *hld up: hdwy over 2f out: edgd lft and styd on strly fnl f: nt rch first two* **14/1**

6051 **4** 2 ¼ **King Kurt (IRE)**[30] 3977 5-9-13 **74**.......... PhillipMakin 6 74
(Kevin Ryan) *led after 2f and set stdy pce: rdn 2f out: hdd ins fnl f: sn hung lft and no ex* **10/1**

0135 **5** 2 ½ **King Of Paradise (IRE)**[11] 4612 4-9-2 **68**.......... JasonHart[(5)] 4 64
(Eric Alston) *t.k.h: cl up: effrt and ev ch over 2f out: sn rdn: wknd fnl f* **9/2**[2]

133- **6** 1 ½ **Calculated Risk**[98] 7108 4-9-6 **67**.......... MichaelO'Connell 3 60
(John Quinn) *hld up: rdn over 2f out: no imp fr over 1f out* **5/4**[1]

313- **7** ¾ **Pertemps Networks**[224] 7980 9-10-0 **75**.......... GrahamGibbons 8 67
(Michael Easterby) *led 2f: chsd ldr: rdn over 2f out: wknd over 1f out* **20/1**

556 **8** hd **Swift Encounter (IRE)**[29] 4010 4-8-9 **56**.......... PJMcDonald 2 47
(Ann Duffield) *in tch: rdn over 3f out: wknd 2f out* **16/1**

3551 **9** 1 ¾ **First Sargeant**[26] 4122 3-8-1 **65**.......... JordanNason[(7)] 10 53
(Geoffrey Harker) *in tch on outside: drvn over 2f out: wandered and wknd wl over 1f out* **7/1**[3]

2m 25.6s **Going Correction** -0.10s/f (Good)
WFA 3 from 4yo+ 10lb 9 Ran SP% **120.7**
Speed ratings (Par 103): **96,95,94,92,90 89,89,89,87**
toteswingers 1&2 £21.10, 1&3 £18.50, 2&3 £18.90 CSF £112.70 CT £1420.88 TOTE £18.30: £3.80, £2.90, £2.80; EX 131.50 Trifecta £645.90 Part won. Pool: £861.33 - 0.45 winning units..
Owner J Hutton **Bred** Frank Brady And Brian Scanlon **Trained** Carluke, S Lanarks

The Form Book Flat, Raceform Ltd, Compton, RG20 6NL.

FOCUS
Not a bad handicap for the class, run at a fairly steady pace. The winner is rated in line with his penultimate effort.
T/Plt: £127.90 to a £1 stake. Pool: £71,901.75 - 410.35 winning units T/Qpdt: £24.80 to a £1 stake. Pool: £6,415.50 - 191.30 winning units RY

4749 LINGFIELD (L-H)
Saturday, August 3

OFFICIAL GOING: Turf course - good to firm (8.7); all-weather course - standard
Wind: Moderate; half behind Weather: Fine; warm

4996 VINES BMW APPRENTICE H'CAP — 7f 140y
5:30 (5:31) (Class 6) (0-65,63) 3-Y-0+ **£2,045** (£603; £302) **Stalls** Centre

Form RPR
1405 **1** **The Mongoose**22 4250 5-9-12 **61**....(t) EoinWalsh 3 69
(David Evans) *trckd ldng pair against rail: gap appeared fr 2f out: drvn to ld over 1f out: jst hld on* **8/1**
3352 **2** *nk* **South Cape**24 4169 10-9-10 **63**.... HectorCrouch(4) 5 70
(Gary Moore) *towards rr: rdn 3f out: plenty to do 2f out: styd on after: tk 2nd and clsd on wnr fin* **6/1**2
0530 **3** *3/4* **Remix (IRE)**56 3098 4-9-3 **56**.... LouisSteward(4) 2 61
(Ian Williams) *trckd ldrs: cl up and rdn 2f out: kpt on same pce fr over 1f out: a hld* **14/1**
1-11 **4** *2 1/4* **Resonare**49 3326 4-9-5 **58**.... JeanVanOvermeire(4) 8 58
(Stuart Williams) *disp ld against nr side rail: edgd lft fr over 2f out: hdd over 1f out: continued to edge lft and no ex* **6/4**1
3234 **5** *1/2* **Takitwo**7 4771 10-9-5 **58**.... CharlieBennett(4) 4 57
(Geoffrey Deacon) *wl in rr: rdn 3f out: stl wl adrift over 1f out: styd on fnl f: nrst fin* **7/1**3
5423 **6** *1/2* **Proper Charlie**14 4520 5-8-10 **47**.... DanielCremin(2) 6 44
(Lee Carter) *disp ld: carried lft and hdd over 1f out: fdd* **7/1**3
0000 **7** *1/2* **Bajan Story**26 4126 4-8-13 **52**....(b1) JackGarritty(4) 1 48
(Michael Blanshard) *wnt lft s: chsd ldrs: u.p and outpcd 3f out: hanging but styd on again fr over 1f out* **16/1**
6300 **8** *1* **Byrd In Hand (IRE)**7 4752 6-9-4 **53**.... PatMillman 10 47
(John Bridger) *chsd ldrs in 5th: rdn and no imp over 2f out: fdd fnl f* **20/1**
/005 **9** *7* **Mr Mallo**39 3657 4-8-6 **45**.... AaronFallon(4) 7 21
(John Stimpson) *a wl in rr: bhd fr over 2f out* **33/1**
00- **10** *19* **River Pageant**383 4144 4-9-7 **60**.... DavidParkes(4) 11
(Brendan Powell) *a bhd: t.o* **20/1**
00-5 **U** **Copper Rag**16 4423 3-8-0 **46**.... CharlotteJenner(4) 9
(J S Moore) *t.k.h: trckd ldrs tl hit rail and uns rdr 5f out* **33/1**

1m 30.2s (-2.10) **Going Correction** -0.20s/f (Firm)
WFA 3 from 4yo+ 7lb — 11 Ran SP% **118.4**
Speed ratings (Par 101): **102,101,100,98,98 97,97,96,89,70**
toteswingers 1&2 £11.40, 1&3 £18.40, 2&3 £16.10 CSF £53.03 CT £664.24 TOTE £9.80: £2.80, £2.30, £3.80; EX 48.60 Trifecta £767.60 Part won. Pool: £1,023.57 - 0.43 winning units..
Owner G Evans & P D Evans **Bred** Kincorth Investments Inc **Trained** Pandy, Monmouths

FOCUS
With well-backed Resonare proving an awkward ride, this doesn't look very strong form, even for this grade, with a few of the others ideally needing further.

4997 DANNY AND PIP'S 30TH ANNIVERSARY MEDIAN AUCTION MAIDEN STKS — 7f 140y
6:00 (6:02) (Class 6) 2-Y-0 **£2,045** (£603; £302) **Stalls** Centre

Form RPR
6 **1** **Never To Be (USA)**7 4764 2-9-5 0....(t) WilliamBuick 5 72+
(John Gosden) *trckd ldrs on outer: clsd to chal 2f out: rdn to ld jst over 1f out: drvn and jst hld on nr fin* **7/4**1
55 **2** *shd* **Mawzoona**16 4439 2-8-11 0.... CharlesBishop(3) 3 67
(Mick Channon) *led against nr side rail: edgd lft and hdd jst over 1f out: rallied wl nr fin: jst failed* **14/1**
3 *2 3/4* **Jelly Fish** 2-9-5 0.... SteveDrowne 9 65+
(Amanda Perrett) *trckd ldrs: gng wl 3f out: rdn and tried to chal wl over 1f out: one pce after* **7/2**2
0 **4** *3/4* **Photography (IRE)**17 4414 2-9-5 0.... MartinDwyer 4 64
(Hugo Palmer) *trckd ldrs: cl enough towards outer over 1f out: one pce after* **7/1**
530 **5** *2* **Khee Society**42 3555 2-9-0 **70**.... DeclanBates(5) 2 59
(David Evans) *chsd ldr to 2f out: steadily wknd* **5/1**3
6 *1* **Nova Princesse (GER)** 2-9-0 0.... LukeMorris 11 51
(Marco Botti) *trckd ldrs against nr side rail: plld out and drvn to chal wl over 1f out: sn wknd* **7/1**
06 **7** *15* **Society Diva (IRE)**24 4175 2-9-0 0.... PatCosgrave 7 15
(George Baker) *a in same pl and nvr on terms w ldrs: t.o* **33/1**
8 *4* **Lingfield Lupus (IRE)** 2-9-5 0.... KieranO'Neill 8 11
(John Best) *dwlt: rn green and a wl off the pce in last trio: t.o* **33/1**
9 *1 1/4* **The Champagne Boy** 2-9-0 0.... NathanAlison(5) 6 8
(Jim Boyle) *dwlt: a wl off the pce in last trio: t.o* **33/1**
10 *1 1/2* **No Second Thoughts (IRE)** 2-8-11 0..... WilliamTwiston-Davies(3) 10
(Michael Blanshard) *a last and wl bhd: t.o* **20/1**

1m 31.07s (-1.23) **Going Correction** -0.20s/f (Firm) — 10 Ran SP% **120.5**
Speed ratings (Par 92): **98,97,95,94,92 91,76,72,71,69**
toteswingers 1&2 £6.60, 1&3 £2.90, 2&3 £8.10 CSF £29.25 TOTE £2.70: £1.30, £2.50, £2.40; EX 26.50 Trifecta £119.00 Pool: £1,418.05 - 8.93 winning units..
Owner M Al-Qatami, K Al-Mudhaf & Mrs G Voute **Bred** John Griggs & Linda Griggs **Trained** Newmarket, Suffolk

FOCUS
Probably no more than an ordinary maiden, but a good effort from the winner having raced well away from stands rail.

4998 LINGFIELD PARK OWNERS GROUP H'CAP — 7f
6:30 (6:30) (Class 5) (0-75,73) 3-Y-0+ **£2,726** (£805; £402) **Stalls** High

Form RPR
3311 **1** **My Own Way Home**11 4603 5-8-12 **62**.... DeclanBates(5) 2 72
(David Evans) *mde all and racd against nr side rail: sn at least 4 l clr: hld together tl rdn jst over 1f out: styd on wl* **4/1**3
6451 **2** *2 1/4* **Countryman**8 4710 3-9-0 **72**.... CharlieBennett(7) 1 74+
(Hughie Morrison) *chsd wnr but sn at least 4 l down: pushed along to cl 2f out: no imp fnl f* **6/4**1
0500 **3** *4* **Golden Desert (IRE)**10 4637 9-9-12 **71**.... LukeMorris 7 65+
(Simon Dow) *hmpd by loose horse after 150yds: hld up disputing 3rd: shkn up and tried to cl 2f out: no imp fnl f* **10/1**
-050 **4** *shd* **Rondeau (GR)**30 3974 8-9-7 **73**.... OisinMurphy(7) 5 66+
(Patrick Chamings) *hmpd by loose horse after 150yds: t.k.h after and hld up off the pce: shkn up and tried to cl 2f out: no imp fnl f* **8/1**
-010 **5** *1 1/4* **Relentless Harry (IRE)**63 2884 4-10-0 **73**....(t) PatCosgrave 3 63
(George Baker) *hld up in last and wl off the pce: sltly clsr 2f out: nt shkn up tl jst over 1f out on outer: no prog after* **3/1**2
100- **6** *18* **Torres Del Paine**248 7902 6-9-9 **68**.... KieranO'Neill 6 11
(Brett Johnson) *hld up disputing 3rd: rdn over 2f out: wknd over 1f out: eased and t.o* **16/1**
206 **U** **Kamchatka**15 4492 3-9-3 **68**.... SteveDrowne 4
(Philip Hide) *restless stalls: awkward s and uns rdr* **12/1**

1m 22.65s (-0.65) **Going Correction** -0.20s/f (Firm)
WFA 3 from 4yo+ 6lb — 7 Ran SP% **118.8**
Speed ratings (Par 103): **95,92,87,87,86 65,**
toteswingers 1&2 £1.30, 1&3 £4.10, 2&3 £3.50 CSF £11.06 CT £56.58 TOTE £3.30: £1.90, £1.50; EX 9.40 Trifecta £38.00 Pool: £1,120.29 - 22.06 winning units..
Owner Trevor Gallienne **Bred** Theresa Fitsall **Trained** Pandy, Monmouths

FOCUS
This turned out to be quite uncompetitive.

4999 FREDDIE PARKER WINNING FASHION H'CAP — 6f
7:00 (7:01) (Class 6) (0-65,64) 3-Y-0+ **£2,045** (£603; £302) **Stalls** High

Form RPR
4040 **1** **Commandingpresence (USA)**18 4385 7-9-12 **64**....... KieranO'Neill 10 73
(John Bridger) *mde all and racd against nr side rail: drvn 2f out: edgd lft and kpt on u.p* **7/1**
0004 **2** *2* **Multitask**7 4751 3-9-1 **57**.... LukeMorris 3 59
(Michael Madgwick) *trckd ldng trio against rail: prog to chse wnr wl over 1f out: sn rdn and nt qckn: one pce after* **14/1**
5243 **3** *hd* **Rambo Will**9 4691 5-9-7 **59**.... DavidProbert 2 61+
(J R Jenkins) *racd on outer in cl 3rd: rdn to chse wnr over 2f out to wl over 1f out: kpt on to press runner-up nr fin* **9/2**2
2400 **4** *3/4* **Spellmaker**46 3433 4-8-13 **51**....(e1) PatCosgrave 6 51
(Tony Newcombe) *hld up towards rr against rail: rdn over 2f out: sme prog over 1f out: kpt on same pce fnl f* **10/1**
5 *1 3/4* **Amy Farah Fowler (IRE)**314 6521 4-8-5 **46** ow1....... MarkCoumbe(3) 8 40
(Ian Williams) *s.i.s: detached in last and pushed along: no prog tl wl over 1f out: styd on fnl f* **6/1**
2326 **6** *hd* **Wishformore (IRE)**7 4752 6-9-2 **54**....(p) RichardThomas 7 47
(Zoe Davison) *hld up in 8th and off the pce against rail: rdn over 2f out: sme late prog: nvr a threat* **5/1**3
2560 **7** *2 1/2* **Aaranyow (IRE)**15 4496 5-8-9 **52**.... NathanAlison(5) 9 37
(Clifford Lines) *pressed wnr to over 2f out: wknd over 1f out* **9/4**1
3051 **8** *1 3/4* **Little China**19 4353 4-9-0 **52**....(b) MartinDwyer 4 32
(William Muir) *racd on outer: nvr beyond midfield: struggling fr 2f out: fdd* **16/1**
6-53 **9** *15* **Birdie Queen**56 3091 3-9-3 **59**.... SteveDrowne 5
(John Best) *mounted on crse abt a f of way to post and then v keen: stdd s: hld up in rr: wknd 2f out: eased: t.o* **16/1**

1m 10.0s (-1.20) **Going Correction** -0.20s/f (Firm)
WFA 3 from 4yo+ 4lb — 9 Ran SP% **119.9**
Speed ratings (Par 101): **100,97,97,96,93 93,90,87,67**
toteswingers 1&2 £25.10, 1&3 £4.70, 2&3 £12.50 CSF £102.25 CT £497.83 TOTE £7.20: £2.30, £4.30, £1.30; EX 119.40 Trifecta £509.40 Pool: £758.82 - 1.11 winning units..
Owner T Wallace & J J Bridger **Bred** Lazy Lane Farms Inc **Trained** Liphook, Hants
■ Stewards' Enquiry : David Probert one-day ban: failed to ride to draw (Aug 17)

FOCUS
A weak handicap and, as is often the cases here, the stands' rail proved crucial.

5000 BRITISH STALLION STUDS SUPPORTING BRITISH RACING EBF MAIDEN STKS — 5f (P)
7:30 (7:31) (Class 5) 2-Y-0 **£2,911** (£866; £432; £216) **Stalls** High

Form RPR
03 **1** **Fine Art Fair (IRE)**16 4422 2-9-5 0.... GeorgeBaker 4 70
(Gary Moore) *led 1f: pressed ldr to 2f out: styd on terms: drvn to ld ins fnl f: styd on* **12/1**
2 *1/2* **Travis Bickle (IRE)** 2-9-5 0.... KieranO'Neill 3 68
(Sylvester Kirk) *dwlt: pushed along in 6th: prog jst over 1f out: styd on wl fnl f to snatch 2nd last strides* **25/1**
6 **3** *hd* **Our Sherona**63 2869 2-8-7 0.... OisinMurphy(7) 1 62
(Gary Harrison) *prom: wnt 2nd 2f out: rdn to ld over 1f out: hdd and nt qckn ins fnl f: lost 2nd last strides* **8/1**
65 **4** *1/2* **Aya's Gift**18 4379 2-8-12 0.... BradleyBosley(7) 5 66+
(Ed Walker) *dwlt: hld up in last pair and sn wl off the pce: stl only 8th over 1f out: urged along and r.o wl fnl f: too much to do* **10/1**
03 **5** *2 1/2* **Grass Green**9 4680 2-9-0 0....(p) JimCrowley 10 52
(William Haggas) *chsd ldrs: rdn 2f out: nt qckn over 1f out: no imp after* **4/1**2
6 *1/2* **Rebel Code (USA)** 2-9-5 0.... GrahamLee 8 55
(James Given) *rn green towards rr and sn pushed along: nvr on terms: wl btn over 1f out* **6/1**3
26 **7** *nk* **Krackerjill (IRE)**8 4708 2-8-7 0.... DanielMuscutt(7) 2 49
(Mark Usher) *led after 1f to over 1f out: wknd fnl f* **8/1**
43 **8** *1* **Boston Alex (IRE)**25 4142 2-8-9 0.... RyanTate(5) 7 45
(Conor Dore) *pressed ldrs: rdn jst over 2f out: wknd on inner over 1f out* **7/2**1
9 *14* **Risk 'N' Reward (IRE)** 2-9-5 0.... AdamKirby 6
(Amy Weaver) *dwlt: rn green in last pair and sn wl off the pce: t.o* **7/2**1

1m 0.12s (1.32) **Going Correction** +0.125s/f (Slow) — 9 Ran SP% **121.6**
Speed ratings (Par 94): **94,93,92,92,88 87,86,85,62**
toteswingers 1&2 £25.60, 1&3 £17.70, 2&3 £24.40 CSF £274.26 TOTE £13.90: £3.70, £5.90, £2.70; EX 330.00 Trifecta £424.70 Part won. Pool: £566.36 - 0.23 winning units..
Owner R A Green **Bred** Tally-Ho Stud **Trained** Lower Beeding, W Sussex

FOCUS
Not form to get excited about, but the winner was an improver.

5001 HAVE A GREAT WEEKEND CARLEY ROBERTS H'CAP — 1m 4f (P)
8:00 (8:00) (Class 5) (0-70,69) 3-Y-0+ **£3,067** (£905; £453) **Stalls** Low

Form RPR
0-54 **1** **Slip Of The Tongue**10 4634 3-8-7 **59**.... LukeMorris 7 74+
(Sir Mark Prescott Bt) *led after 150yds: mde rest: set mod pce tl dashed for home over 2f out: clr w jockey looking rnd over 1f out: unchal* **9/4**2

4035 **2** *4* **Sweet Martoni**[25] 4150 3-9-3 **69** .... JimCrowley 6 74
(William Knight) *led 150yds: chsd wnr tl outpcd and lost 2nd 2f out: kpt on to take 2nd again ins fnl f* **8/1**

6-06 **3** *¾* **Don Padeja**[25] 4152 3-9-2 **68** .... DavidProbert 4 72
(Luca Cumani) *hld up in last pair: wnr already gone for home whn sing to make prog over 2f out: rdn over 1f out: styd on to take 3rd nr fin: no ch* **5/1**[3]

231 **4** *nk* **Kastini**[17] 4405 3-8-13 **65** .... JimmyQuinn 1 68
(Denis Coakley) *trckd ldrs: chsd wnr 2f out but already outpcd: rdn over 1f out: no imp: lost 2 pls ins fnl f* **5/4**[1]

3243 **5** *7* **Danisa**[29] 4035 4-9-7 **65** .... (t) WilliamTwiston-Davies(3) 2 57
(David Bridgwater) *hld up in tch: rdn and outpcd over 2f out: no ch after* **14/1**

0343 **6** *1¼* **Chrissycross (IRE)**[14] 4523 4-9-12 **67** .... (p) AdamKirby 3 57
(Roger Teal) *hld up in last pair: rdn over 3f out: sn outpcd and btn* **14/1**

1540 **7** *1¾* **Emman Bee (IRE)**[22] 4234 4-9-13 **68** .... LiamTreadwell 5 55
(Luke Dace) *trckd ldrs on outer: rdn 3f out: wknd over 2f out* **20/1**

2m 33.43s (0.43) **Going Correction** +0.125s/f (Slow)
WFA 3 from 4yo 11lb 7 Ran SP% **121.1**
Speed ratings (Par 103): **103,100,99,99,94 94,92**
toteswingers 1&2 £4.00, 1&3 £3.00, 2&3 £10.20 CSF £22.21 TOTE £4.00: £1.10, £5.50; EX 31.30 Trifecta £117.90 Pool: £770.76 - 4.89 winning units..
Owner J Fishpool - Osborne House **Bred** Miss K Rausing **Trained** Newmarket, Suffolk

FOCUS
They went very steady early and the winner had the run of things. He was value for extra, though.

5002 LINGFIELD PARK SUPPORTS YOUNG EPILEPSY H'CAP — 1m 2f (P)
8:30 (8:31) (Class 6) (0-60,60) 3-Y-O+ — **£2,045** (£603; £302) **Stalls** Low

Form — RPR

04-5 **1** **Santadelacruze**[23] 4195 4-9-7 **55** .... (b[1]) GeorgeBaker 13 66
(Gary Moore) *trckd ldng trio: moved into 2nd 2f out: led over 1f out: drvn and r.o wl* **12/1**

1441 **2** *1* **Precision Five**[17] 4411 4-9-11 **59** .... (p) JimCrowley 3 68
(Jeremy Gask) *trckd ldrs in 6th: gng strly over 2f out: prog over 1f out: drvn to chse wnr ins fnl f: no imp last 75yds* **5/2**[1]

6650 **3** *1¾* **Delightful Sleep**[19] 4357 5-9-10 **58** .... AdamKirby 10 64+
(David Evans) *hld up towards rr: prog on outer over 2f out: rdn over 1f out: r.o to take 3rd ins fnl f: no imp after: only one of principals to have racd in the rr* **16/1**

540/ **4** *2¼* **Emerald Glade (IRE)**[25] 1577 6-9-10 **58** .... GrahamLee 4 59
(Jim Best) *led at mod pce: hdd over 1f out: outpcd* **11/4**[2]

4034 **5** *½* **Sutton Sid**[9] 4664 3-8-12 **55** .... (p) PatCosgrave 1 55
(Chris Gordon) *trckd ldng pair: rdn over 2f out: outpcd fr over 1f out* **20/1**

0005 **6** *nk* **Norwegian Reward (IRE)**[19] 4357 5-9-5 **53** .... DavidProbert 8 52
(Michael Wigham) *wl in tch in 7th: rdn and cl up 2f out: outpcd fr over 1f out* **7/1**[3]

2110 **7** *nk* **Young Jackie**[28] 4071 5-9-8 **56** .... (b) KieranO'Neill 5 55
(George Margarson) *trckd ldrs in 5th: n.m.r on inner over 2f out: nt qckn over 1f out: outpcd after* **7/1**[3]

0164 **8** *nse* **Hawaiian Freeze**[23] 4195 4-8-12 **46** .... (p) JimmyQuinn 9 45
(John Stimpson) *hld up in midfield: rdn 2f out: nt qckn over 1f out: no prog after* **33/1**

0430 **9** *2¼* **Dolly Colman (IRE)**[19] 4350 5-8-12 **46** .... (p) LukeMorris 12 40
(Zoe Davison) *t.k.h: racd wd: hld up in last trio: shkn up 2f out: no real prog after* **20/1**

5-00 **10** *nk* **Rhossili Bay**[65] 2801 4-8-13 **47** .... SteveDrowne 6 41
(Alastair Lidderdale) *reluctant to go to post: s.s: a in rr: shkn up and no prog over 1f out* **33/1**

500- **11** *¾* **Ryedale Lass**[286] 7270 5-9-5 **58** .... DeclanBates(5) 14 50
(Geoffrey Deacon) *awkward s: hld up in last trio: rdn and no prog over 2f out* **33/1**

4256 **12** *¾* **Cane Cat (IRE)**[19] 4350 6-9-4 **57** .... (t) GeorgeDowning(5) 11 48
(Tony Carroll) *s.s: hld up in last trio: rdn and no prog over 2f out: no ch after* **20/1**

0/06 **13** *nk* **King Of Forces**[4] 712 4-9-6 **54** .... (p) SaleemGolam 7 44
(Denis Quinn) *pressed ldr to 2f out: wknd qckly* **40/1**

-00 **14** *1½* **Addikt (IRE)**[59] 2982 8-9-9 **60** .... WilliamTwiston-Davies(3) 2 47
(Michael Scudamore) *s.s: sn in midfield: lost pl and btn over 2f out: fdd* **8/1**

2m 7.94s (1.34) **Going Correction** +0.125s/f (Slow)
WFA 3 from 4yo+ 9lb 14 Ran SP% **130.5**
Speed ratings (Par 101): **99,98,96,95,94 94,94,94,92,92 91,90,90,89**
toteswingers 1&2 £10.30, 1&3 £52.10, 2&3 £11.60 CSF £42.30 CT £524.37 TOTE £15.10: £3.50, £1.60, £6.30; EX 71.30 Trifecta £820.30 Part won. Pool: £1,093.76 - 0.20 winning units..
Owner D M & Mrs M A Newland **Bred** Mrs M Newland **Trained** Lower Beeding, W Sussex

FOCUS
Low-grade fare and a steady gallop, with the first two always prominent. The winner had slipped to a good mark.
T/Plt: £733.60 to a £1 stake. Pool £54,473.75 - 54.20 winning units T/Qpdt: £153.90 to a £1 stake. Pool: £6,143.84 - 29.54 winning units JN

4957 NEWMARKET (R-H)
Saturday, August 3

OFFICIAL GOING: Good (7.6)
Wind: Light; across Weather: Cloudy with sunny spells, turning showery after Race 5

5003 32RED CASINO EBF MAIDEN FILLIES' STKS — 7f
1:45 (1:46) (Class 4) 2-Y-O — **£4,528** (£1,347; £673; £336) **Stalls** Low

Form — RPR

1 **Sound Reflection (USA)** 2-9-0 0 .... MickaelBarzalona 4 92+
(Charlie Appleby) *racd stands' side: chsd ldrs: led overall over 1f out: rdn clr* **5/2**[1]

2 *3½* **Night Party (IRE)** 2-9-0 0 .... ChrisCatlin 13 83+
(Saeed bin Suroor) *racd centre: chsd ldrs: pushed along over 2f out: rdn to ld centre and chsd wnr 1f out: styd on same pce ins fnl f: 1st of 10 in gp* **17/2**

3 **3** *3¾* **Halljoy (IRE)**[16] 4432 2-9-0 0 .... SebSanders 2 73
(Clive Brittain) *overall ldr on stands' side: rdn and hdd over 1f out: styd on same pce fnl f: 2nd of 4 in gp* **5/1**[3]

5 **4** *1½* **Redinha**[39] 3664 2-9-0 0 .... AdamKirby 12 69
(Clive Cox) *led centre: rdn: hung rt and ev ch over 1f out: hdd that gp 1f out: no ex fnl f: 2nd of 10 in gp* **8/1**

3 **5** *nk* **Makruma**[15] 4491 2-9-0 0 .... DaneO'Neill 3 68
(J W Hills) *racd stands' side: chsd ldr: rdn over 1f out: no ex fnl f: 3rd of 4 in gp* **11/4**[2]

6 *1* **Rosehill Artist (IRE)** 2-9-0 0 .... RichardKingscote 9 66+
(Charles Hills) *racd centre: hld up: pushed along 1/2-way: r.o ins fnl f: nvr nrr: 3rd of 10 in gp* **33/1**

7 *½* **Rawoof (IRE)** 2-9-0 0 .... MartinLane 7 65
(Ed Dunlop) *racd centre: chsd ldrs: rdn over 2f out: wknd fnl f: 4th of 10 in gp* **25/1**

8 *3¼* **Sighora (IRE)** 2-9-0 0 .... PatDobbs 5 56
(Richard Hannon) *racd centre: s.i.s: outpcd: styd on ins fnl f: nvr nrr: 5th of 10 in gp* **20/1**

9 *¾* **Heavenly** 2-9-0 0 .... FrankieDettori 14 54
(Jeremy Noseda) *racd centre: mid-div: hdwy 1/2-way: wknd over 1f out: 6th of 10 in gp* **12/1**

33 **10** *1* **Jersey Cream (IRE)**[23] 4206 2-9-0 0 .... FergusSweeney 11 52
(Gary Moore) *racd centre: plld hrd and prom: lost pl 1/2-way: wknd over 1f out: 7th of 10 in gp* **33/1**

11 *2* **Earthflight** 2-9-0 0 .... WilliamCarson 6 46
(Philip McBride) *racd centre: in rr: pushed along 1/2-way: n.d: 8th of 10 in gp* **50/1**

00 **12** *shd* **Saffire Song**[23] 4215 2-8-7 0 .... TimClark(7) 8 46
(Alan Bailey) *racd centre: prom: rdn over 2f out: wknd over 1f out: 9th of 10 in gp* **150/1**

0 **13** *2¾* **Tempelfeuer (GER)**[78] 2419 2-9-0 0 .... FrannyNorton 10 39
(Conrad Allen) *racd centre: chsd ldrs: pushed along 1/2-way: wknd over 2f out: last of 10 in gp* **100/1**

14 *12* **La Faisan Blanche (USA)** 2-8-11 0 .... PatrickHills(3) 1
(Luca Cumani) *racd stands' side: hld up: pushed along 1/2-way: sn wknd: last of 4 in gp* **50/1**

1m 25.66s (-0.04) **Going Correction** +0.05s/f (Good) 14 Ran SP% **121.3**
Speed ratings (Par 93): **102,98,93,92,91 90,89,86,85,84 81,81,78,64**
toteswingers 1&2 £3.60, 1&3 £3.40, 2&3 £6.50 CSF £23.04 TOTE £3.70: £1.70, £3.20, £2.20; EX 31.60 Trifecta £235.00 Pool: £852.46 - 2.72 winning units..
Owner Godolphin **Bred** Darley **Trained** Newmarket, Suffolk

FOCUS
Stands' side track used with stalls on stands' side except 1mf & 1m4: centre. The going was good after rain the previous day and the jockeys confirmed that description. A fillies' maiden whose best recent winner was the subsequent Coronation Stakes heroine Fallen For You. The field raced in two groups early, but they all ended up towards the stands' rail. The third and fourth set the standard and the winner looks a potential 100+ filly.

5004 32RED.COM H'CAP — 7f
2:20 (2:20) (Class 3) (0-90,87) 3-Y-O — **£12,938** (£3,850; £1,924; £962) **Stalls** Low

Form — RPR

0404 **1** **Bluegrass Blues (IRE)**[23] 4274 3-9-3 **83** .... LukeMorris 3 91
(Paul Cole) *chsd ldrs: rdn to ld and edgd rt over 1f out: styd on u.p* **10/1**

-241 **2** *nk* **Mazaaher**[8] 4721 3-8-9 **75** .... DaneO'Neill 7 82+
(J W Hills) *hld up: pushed along over 2f out: hdwy u.p over 1f out: edgd rt: r.o* **4/1**[2]

1453 **3** *½* **Lord Ashley (IRE)**[22] 4265 3-9-2 **82** .... RichardKingscote 5 88
(Tom Dascombe) *chsd ldrs: rdn over 1f out: r.o* **7/2**[1]

-100 **4** *nk* **Lancelot Du Lac (ITY)**[49] 3342 3-9-7 **87** .... MartinLane 2 92
(Dean Ivory) *hld up: hdwy 1/2-way: rdn and ev ch over 1f out: styd on same pce towards fin* **10/1**

0521 **5** *3½* **Front Page News**[30] 3988 3-8-1 **72** .... RobertTart(5) 6 67+
(Robert Eddery) *hood removed late: dwlt: outpcd: rdn and r.o ins fnl f: nvr nrr* **5/1**

3602 **6** *½* **Lady Of The House (IRE)**[23] 4201 3-9-5 **85** .... (p) FergusSweeney 4 79
(Kevin Ryan) *w ldrs: rdn and ev ch over 1f out: no ex wl ins fnl f* **25/1**

1010 **7** *1¾* **Skytrain**[10] 4628 3-8-13 **79** .... FrannyNorton 8 68
(Mark Johnston) *led: hdd over 5f out: pushed along 1/2-way: wknd over 1f out* **13/2**

5312 **8** *hd* **Harry Bosch**[40] 3633 3-8-11 **77** .... (b) FrankieDettori 1 66
(Brian Meehan) *w ldrs: led over 5f out: rdn and hdd over 1f out: wknd ins fnl f* **9/2**[3]

1-00 **9** *½* **Tommy's Secret**[58] 3020 3-9-5 **85** .... PatDobbs 9 72
(Jane Chapple-Hyam) *s.i.s: hld up: pushed along 1/2-way: n.d* **33/1**

1m 25.4s (-0.30) **Going Correction** +0.05s/f (Good) 9 Ran SP% **115.4**
Speed ratings (Par 104): **103,102,102,101,97 97,95,94,94**
toteswingers 1&2 £10.20, 1&3 £3.90, 2&3 £3.40 CSF £49.77 CT £171.51 TOTE £12.30: £3.50, £1.90, £1.50; EX 51.60 Trifecta £288.20 Pool: £1,746.13 - 4.54 winning units..
Owner Mrs Fitri Hay **Bred** Yeomanstown Stud **Trained** Whatcombe, Oxon
■ Stewards' Enquiry : Dane O'Neill seven-day ban: used whip above permitted level (Aug 17-23)

FOCUS
A decent handicap in which a low draw has proved to be an asset in recent seasons. That was the case again, although the time was just 0.26sec faster than the opening juvenile maiden. The three early pacemakers, Lady Of The House, Skytrain and the second favourite Harry Bosch, took each other on and all were done with in the Dip. The first two and fourth all challenged towards the stands' side. The winner is rated up a length on previous 6f form.

5005 32RED FILLIES' NURSERY H'CAP — 6f
2:55 (2:56) (Class 2) 2-Y-O — **£25,876** (£7,700; £3,848; £1,924) **Stalls** Low

Form — RPR

1 **1** **J Wonder (USA)**[15] 4484 2-8-13 **79** .... MartinLane 6 95+
(Brian Meehan) *racd centre: stdd s: hld up: smooth hdwy 2 out: led over 1f out: shkn up and r.o: readily* **5/4**[1]

2103 **2** *¾* **Midnite Angel (IRE)**[34] 3857 2-9-5 **85** .... FrankieDettori 13 96
(Richard Hannon) *racd centre: hld up: hdwy over 2f out: rdn and ev ch fr over 1f out: r.o: 2nd of 12 in gp* **12/1**

224 **3** *4* **Dancealot**[15] 4491 2-8-9 **75** .... LukeMorris 8 74
(Clive Brittain) *racd centre: chsd ldrs: pushed along over 2f out: rdn over 1f out: styd on same pce: 3rd of 12 in gp* **20/1**

5232 **4** *1* **Princess Rose**[16] 4431 2-8-10 **76** .... (p) LiamJones 14 72
(William Haggas) *racd centre: chsd ldrs: rdn over 2f out: no ex ins fnl f: 4th of 12 in gp* **22/1**

541 **5** *½* **Inspiriter**[17] 4409 2-8-12 **78** .... MickaelBarzalona 11 73
(Charlie Appleby) *racd centre: chsd ldrs: rdn over 1f out: no ex fnl f: 5th of 12 in gp* **20/1**

0024 **6** *hd* **Lady Frances**[21] 4277 2-9-2 **82** .... SebSanders 3 76
(Mark Johnston) *racd stands' side: led that trio: hung lft almost thrght: rdn over 1f out: styd on same pce: 1st of 3 in gp* **40/1**

5211 **7** *nk* **Azagal (IRE)**[8] 4726 2-9-7 **87** .... DavidAllan 4 80
(Tim Easterby) *racd centre: hld up: hdwy over 2f out: rdn over 1f out: styd on same pce: 6th of 12 in gp* **6/1**[2]

The Form Book Flat, Raceform Ltd, Compton, RG20 6NL.

521 **8** ½ **Musicora**[24] 4164 2-9-2 **82** DaneO'Neill 15 74
(Richard Hannon) *overall ldr centre tl rdn and hdd over 1f out: wknd ins fnl f: 7th of 12 in gp* **10/1**[3]

5221 **9** 2¾ **Augusta Ada**[10] 4616 2-9-7 **87** GeorgeBaker 2 70
(Ollie Pears) *racd stands' side: chsd ldrs: rdn over 1f out: wknd ins fnl f: 2nd of 3 in gp* **33/1**

044 **10** 1½ **Dry Your Eyes (IRE)**[15] 4505 2-8-9 **75** FrannyNorton 9 54
(Mark Johnston) *racd centre: chsd ldrs tl rdn and wknd over 1f out: 8th of 12 in gp* **25/1**

211 **11** 1 **Excel's Beauty**[16] 4451 2-9-2 **82** AdamKirby 5 58
(James Tate) *racd centre: hld up: rdn over 2f out: wknd over 1f out: 9th of 12 in gp* **10/1**[3]

131 **12** ¾ **One Penny Piece**[25] 4134 2-8-10 **76** WilliamCarson 7 50
(Philip McBride) *racd centre: mid-div: rdn over 2f out: wknd over 1f out: 10th of 12 in gp* **28/1**

0153 **13** 1¼ **Jive**[15] 4498 2-8-1 **67** KieranO'Neill 10 37
(Richard Hannon) *racd centre: chsd ldrs tl rdn and wknd over 1f out: 11th of 12 in gp* **50/1**

01 **14** nk **Chutney (IRE)**[38] 3694 2-8-12 **78** PatDobbs 12 47
(Richard Hannon) *racd centre: sn outpcd: last of 12 in gp* **14/1**

0114 **15** ¾ **Diamond Lady**[8] 4726 2-9-7 **87** JohnFahy 1 54
(Jo Hughes) *racd stands' side: sn chsng ldr: rdn over 2f out: wknd over 1f out: last of 3 in gp* **25/1**

1m 12.08s (-0.42) **Going Correction** +0.05s/f (Good) **15** Ran SP% **123.6**
Speed ratings (Par 97): **104,103,97,96,95 95,95,94,90,88 87,86,84,84,83**
toteswingers 1&2 £5.90, 1&3 £11.40, 2&3 £60.00 CSF £14.63 TOTE £2.20: £1.10, £4.10, £5.40; EX 20.40 Trifecta £219.10 Pool: £1,715.62 - 5.87 winning units..
Owner Andrew Rosen **Bred** Canterbury Lace Syndicate **Trained** Manton, Wilts

FOCUS
A valuable and competitive fillies' nursery that has thrown up horses capable of competing at pattern level. This year's winner has the potential to be another. The first two were clear and the runner-up also has stakes race possibilities.

5006 NEWMARKET EQUINE HOSPITAL H'CAP 1m 2f
3:30 (3:30) (Class 3) (0-90,90) 3-Y-O+ **£12,938** (£3,850; £1,924; £962) **Stalls** Centre

Form RPR

1 **1** **Urban Dance (IRE)**[22] 4257 3-9-5 **90** MickaelBarzalona 9 103+
(Charlie Appleby) *hld up: hdwy u.p and nt clr run over 1f out: led ins fnl f: r.o wl* **5/2**[3]

512 **2** 3¼ **Velox**[29] 4023 3-9-3 **88** AdamKirby 8 94+
(Luca Cumani) *hld up: hdwy 1/2-way: rdn to ld over 1f out: sn hung rt: hung lft and hdd ins fnl f: styd on same pce* **2/1**[1]

0-05 **3** 1½ **Commissar**[31] 3961 4-8-11 **73** RichardKingscote 7 76
(Ian Williams) *chsd ldrs: rdn over 1f out: styd on same pce fnl f* **33/1**

1402 **4** hd **It's My Time**[14] 4542 4-8-9 **71** oh5 LukeMorris 2 74
(Richard Fahey) *chsd ldrs: led over 2f out: rdn and hdd over 1f out: styd on same pce fnl f* **22/1**

5123 **5** 2 **Love Marmalade (IRE)**[6] 4798 3-8-12 **83** FrannyNorton 6 82
(Mark Johnston) *led over 7f: sn rdn: no ex fnl f* **9/4**[2]

1255 **6** ½ **Dandy (GER)**[16] 4441 4-8-7 **76** (p) DanielMuscutt[(7)] 1 74
(Andrew Balding) *chsd ldr: rdn over 2f out: no fr over 1f out* **33/1**

-006 **7** 1¼ **Ed De Gas**[41] 3608 4-9-11 **87** SebSanders 4 83
(Rae Guest) *hld up: hdwy over 1f out: sn rdn: wknd ins fnl f* **20/1**

4-30 **8** ½ **Lucanin**[38] 3692 4-9-0 **76** PatDobbs 5 71
(Sir Michael Stoute) *hld up: rdn over 2f out: wknd over 1f out* **16/1**

0-40 **9** 10 **Cocozza (USA)**[35] 3831 5-9-11 **87** (p) DougieCostello 3 62
(K F Clutterbuck) *prom: rdn over 2f out: wknd over 1f out* **66/1**

2m 4.17s (-1.33) **Going Correction** +0.05s/f (Good)
WFA 3 from 4yo+ 9lb **9** Ran SP% **115.0**
Speed ratings (Par 107): **107,104,103,103,101 101,100,99,91**
toteswingers 1&2 £1.10, 1&3 £9.90, 2&3 £19.00 CSF £7.38 CT £123.90 TOTE £3.60: £1.70, £1.10, £6.00; EX 7.60 Trifecta £115.80 Pool: £2,687.93 - 17.40 winning units..
Owner Godolphin **Bred** Darley **Trained** Newmarket, Suffolk

FOCUS
A good handicap in which the interest centred around the trio of 3-y-os taking on their elders, and two of them dominated the finish. The winner looks smart and the level of this form is limited to some extent by the fourth.

5007 WT'S SNOOKER AND SPORTING CLUB EBF CONDITIONS STKS 1m
4:05 (4:05) (Class 2) 4-Y-O+ **£12,450** (£3,728; £1,864; £932; £466) **Stalls** Low

Form RPR

6020 **1** **Premio Loco (USA)**[21] 4276 9-9-6 **111** GeorgeBaker 6 113
(Chris Wall) *led: shkn up and hdd 1f out: rallied to ld wl ins fnl f: r.o* **3/1**[2]

2200 **2** nk **Sovereign Debt (IRE)**[21] 4298 4-8-9 **112** LukeMorris 5 101
(Michael Bell) *trckd wnr: rdn to ld 1f out: edgd rt: hdd and unable qck wl ins fnl f* **4/7**[1]

106 **3** 3 **Bancnuanaheireann (IRE)**[38] 3697 6-8-10 **90** ow1 DaneO'Neill 1 95
(Michael Appleby) *hld up: hdwy over 2f out: rdn over 1f out: styd on same pce fnl f* **14/1**

5346 **4** 4 **Proud Chieftain**[35] 3832 5-9-0 **96** AdamKirby 4 90
(Clifford Lines) *chsd ldrs: pushed along over 3f out: styd on same pce fr over 1f out* **10/1**[3]

-500 **5** 11 **Mister Music**[64] 2841 4-8-9 **93** PatDobbs 3 60
(Richard Hannon) *chsd ldrs: rdn over 2f out: wknd over 1f out* **14/1**

1m 39.05s (-0.95) **Going Correction** +0.05s/f (Good) **5** Ran SP% **111.1**
Speed ratings (Par 109): **106,105,102,98,87**
CSF £5.19 TOTE £3.40: £1.20, £1.30; EX 7.50 Trifecta £24.40 Pool: £2,520.30 - 77.17 winning units..
Owner Bernard Westley **Bred** Kidder, Cole & Griggs **Trained** Newmarket, Suffolk
■ Stewards' Enquiry : Luke Morris one-day ban: careless riding (Aug 17)

FOCUS
Two stood out on official ratings in this conditions stakes and they fought out an exciting finish. Rather muddling form, with the winner had been below form the last twice.

5008 MICKEY FLYNN'S AMERICAN POOL HALL H'CAP 1m 4f
4:40 (4:40) (Class 4) (0-85,85) 4-Y-O+ **£5,175** (£1,540; £769; £384) **Stalls** Centre

Form RPR

043 **1** **Miss Dashwood**[53] 3177 4-9-1 **79** PatDobbs 8 89
(James Fanshawe) *hld up: wnt centre turning for home: hdwy over 3f out: hmpd wl over 1f out: sn chsng ldr: rdn to ld ins fnl f: styd on* **14/1**

1234 **2** 1¼ **Reve De Nuit (USA)**[23] 4202 7-9-3 **81** FrannyNorton 1 89
(Mrs K Burke) *chsd ldrs: wnt centre turning for home: rdn and ev ch 1f out: styd on same pce ins fnl f* **7/2**[2]

4100 **3** 4 **Harry Buckle**[21] 4301 4-9-7 **85** WilliamCarson 2 87
(Philip McBride) *chsd ldr: styd stands' side turning for home tl jnd centre gp over 6f out: led over 5f out: rdn and hung lft fr over 2f out: hdd ins fnl f: wknd towards fin* **12/1**

42-3 **4** 2¼ **Spiritoftomintoul**[48] 3364 4-9-2 **80** FrankieDettori 7 78
(Lady Cecil) *s.i.s: hld up: wnt centre turning for home: rdn over 3f out* **7/4**[1]

00L4 **5** 5 **Halfsin (IRE)**[16] 4435 5-9-7 **85** AdamKirby 5 75
(Marco Botti) *prom: wnt centre turning for home: rdn to chse ldr over 3f out: hung lft wl over 1f out: wknd ins fnl f* **14/1**

211 **6** 2 **Nave (USA)**[23] 4208 6-9-3 **81** MartinLane 9 68
(David Simcock) *hld up: wnt centre turning for home: hdwy over 3f out: rdn and wknd over 1f out* **5/1**[3]

1524 **7** 22 **Paloma's Prince (IRE)**[23] 4208 4-8-12 **76** (p) SebSanders 6 28
(Jim Boyle) *chsd ldrs: wnt centre turning for home: rdn over 2f out: sn hung lft and wknd* **16/1**

4655 **8** 23 **The Bull Hayes (IRE)**[49] 3344 7-9-4 **82** DaneO'Neill 4
(Michael Appleby) *chsd ldrs: wnt centre turning for home: led that gp and overall ldr 7f out: hdd over 5f out: wknd over 3f out* **10/1**

63-6 **9** 24 **Valid Reason**[190] 378 6-9-0 **78** LiamJones 3
(Dean Ivory) *led: styd stands' side tuning for home: hdd 7f out: sn hung lft: wknd 4f out* **16/1**

2m 31.62s (-1.28) **Going Correction** +0.05s/f (Good) **9** Ran SP% **117.1**
Speed ratings (Par 105): **106,105,102,101,97 96,81,66,50**
toteswingers 1&2 £8.90, 1&3 £13.50, 2&3 £6.10 CSF £63.58 TOTE £13.80: £2.90, £1.40, £3.00; EX 81.50 Trifecta £691.60 Pool: £3,643.26 - 3.95 winning units..
Owner Helena Springfield Ltd **Bred** Meon Valley Stud **Trained** Newmarket, Suffolk

FOCUS
There was a thunderstorm in the lead-up to this race. They went a steady pace early and was dominated by horses best known for their AW exploits. The winner has a generally progressive profile.

5009 AUDIOLINK RADIO COMMUNICATIONS H'CAP 6f
5:15 (5:16) (Class 3) (0-90,92) 3-Y-O+ **£12,938** (£3,850; £1,924; £962) **Stalls** Low

Form RPR

5403 **1** **Secret Look**[35] 3802 3-9-5 **87** FrannyNorton 6 98
(Ed McMahon) *racd centre: mid-div: hdwy over 2f out: rdn and hung lft ins fnl f: r.o to ld nr fin* **14/1**

0061 **2** ½ **Colonel Mak**[6] 4812 6-10-0 **92** 6ex DavidAllan 11 102
(David Barron) *racd centre: chsd ldrs: rdn and ev ch fr over 1f out: r.o: 2nd of 13 in gp* **7/2**[1]

-120 **3** nse **Mayaasem**[57] 3066 3-8-13 **81** DaneO'Neill 13 90
(Charles Hills) *s.i.s: racd centre: hld up: hdwy over 2f out: rdn to ld ins fnl f: hdd nr fin: 3rd of 13 in gp* **12/1**

3112 **4** ½ **Clear Spring (IRE)**[18] 4389 5-9-8 **86** NickyMackay 8 96+
(John Spearing) *racd centre: hld up: hdwy over 1f out: rdn and hmpd ins fnl f: r.o: 4th of 13 in gp* **10/1**

-006 **5** nk **L'Ami Louis (IRE)**[37] 3720 5-9-5 **83** FergusSweeney 10 90
(Henry Candy) *racd centre: chsd ldrs: led 1/2-way: rdn over 1f out: hdd ins fnl f: kpt on: 5th of 13 in gp* **10/1**

3231 **6** 1 **Head Space (IRE)**[13] 4560 5-9-6 **84** (p) JamesSullivan 4 88+
(Ruth Carr) *racd centre: hld up: hdwy over 1f out: rdn and r.o ins fnl f: nt rch ldrs: 6th of 13 in gp* **16/1**

31-0 **7** 1 **Midnight Rider (IRE)**[23] 4217 5-9-7 **85** GeorgeBaker 12 86
(Chris Wall) *hld up: hdwy over 1f out: shkn up and running on whn hmpd ins fnl f: nvr able to chal: 7th of 13 in gp* **25/1**

3400 **8** 1¼ **Fratellino**[15] 4507 6-9-8 **86** (tp) FrankieDettori 9 83
(Alan McCabe) *racd centre: overall ldr to 1/2-way: rdn over 1f out: styng on same pce whn hmpd and eased ins fnl f: 8th of 13 in gp* **33/1**

462- **9** ¾ **Milika**[274] 7521 4-9-5 **83** ChrisCatlin 17 78
(Rae Guest) *racd centre: prom: rdn over 1f out: no ex ins fnl f: 9th of 13 in gp* **16/1**

-113 **10** 4½ **If So**[45] 3472 4-9-0 **78** PatDobbs 7 58
(James Fanshawe) *racd centre: hld up: hdwy 1/2-way: rdn over 1f out: wknd fnl f: 10th of 13 in gp* **11/2**[2]

6000 **11** nk **Baddilini**[23] 4217 3-8-12 **85** RobertTart[(5)] 15 63
(Alan Bailey) *racd centre: prom: rdn over 2f out: wknd over 1f out: 11th of 13 in gp* **33/1**

0-00 **12** shd **West Leake Diman (IRE)**[21] 4285 4-9-9 **90** PatrickHills[(3)] 16 69
(Charles Hills) *racd centre: chsd ldrs: rdn over 1f out: wknd fnl f: 12th of 13 in gp* **40/1**

-155 **13** 1¼ **Trojan Rocket (IRE)**[35] 3823 5-9-3 **81** MickaelBarzalona 2 56
(Michael Wigham) *racd stands' side: chsd ldr tl rdn to ld that pair 2f out: sn hung lft and wknd: 1st of 2 that side* **6/1**[3]

P/2- **14** 2 **Slip Sliding Away (IRE)**[448] 2070 6-9-2 **80** JohnFahy 5 49
(Peter Hedger) *racd centre: outpcd: last of 13 in gp* **40/1**

0-00 **15** 1 **Top Offer**[38] 3697 4-9-9 **87** AdamKirby 1 52
(Roger Charlton) *led stands' side pair tl rdn and hdd 2f out: sn hung lft and wknd: last of 2 that side* **8/1**

1m 13.39s (0.89) **Going Correction** +0.05s/f (Good)
WFA 3 from 4yo+ 4lb **15** Ran SP% **121.9**
Speed ratings (Par 107): **96,95,95,94,94 92,91,89,88,82 82,82,80,78,76**
toteswingers 1&2 £16.80, 1&3 £39.60, 2&3 £12.40 CSF £60.11 CT £641.48 TOTE £18.20: £4.10, £2.00, £4.50; EX 90.00 Trifecta £2373.70 Part won. Pool: £3,164.95 - 0.73 winning units..

Owner S L Edwards **Bred** S L Edwards **Trained** Lichfield, Staffs
■ Stewards' Enquiry : Franny Norton two-day ban: careless riding (Aug 17-18)

FOCUS
A field of mainly battle-hardened sprinters in this handicap, but there was a fair bit of scrimmaging in the closing stages and the time was 1.31secs slower than the earlier fillies' nursery. The form reads well enough with the well treated runner-up splitting a 3yo pair.

T/Plt: £39.40 to a £1 stake. Pool: £86,611.33 - 1,603.19 winning units T/Qpdt: £12.40 to a £1 stake. Pool: £4,791.49 - 285.30 winning units CR

[4963]THIRSK (L-H)

Saturday, August 3

OFFICIAL GOING: Good (good to firm in places; 8.2)

Wind: Fresh; half behind Weather: Fine and sunny; very breezy

5010 YORKSHIRE OUTDOORS ADVENTURE EXPERIENCES MAIDEN (S) STKS 1m 4f

1:55 (1:55) (Class 5) 3-Y-O **£2,587** (£770; £384; £192) **Stalls** Low

Form RPR

0020 **1** **Harbinger Lass**[24] 4157 3-8-7 70 SamHitchcott 4 57
(Mick Channon) *hld up: hdwy to trck ldrs 7f out: chal over 2f out: edgd lft and led over 1f out: styd on clsng stages* **13/8**[2]

0200 **2** *1 ¼* **Star Of Namibia (IRE)**[7] 4753 3-8-9 61 (b) ThomasBrown(3) 1 60
(J S Moore) *trckd ldrs: drvn 4f out: led over 2f out: hdd over 1f out: kpt on same pce last 75yds* **11/8**[1]

0005 **3** *8* **Threepence**[4] 4849 3-8-12 40 (p) PaulQuinn 6 47
(Richard Whitaker) *rrd s: t.k.h: chsd ldr after 1f: drvn over 5f out: one pce whn hmpd and swtchd rt over 1f out* **40/1**

60 **4** *8* **Hollow Beat**[105] 1684 3-8-4 0 NeilFarley(3) 5 29
(Tim Walford) *in rr: drvn over 4f out: outpcd and lost pl over 3f out: tk poor 4th nr fin* **16/1**

5253 **5** *¾* **Attansky (IRE)**[12] 4587 3-8-12 57 (b[1]) DuranFentiman 2 33
(Tim Easterby) *t.k.h: led: drvn 3f out: sn hdd: wknd 2f out* **7/2**[3]

2m 37.21s (1.01) **Going Correction** +0.05s/f (Good) **5** Ran SP% **110.7**

Speed ratings (Par 100): **98,97,91,86,86**

CSF £4.27 TOTE £2.30: £1.50, £1.30; EX 4.40 Trifecta £19.90 Pool: £1,056.10 - 39.64 winning units..The winner was bought in £10,000.

Owner Mrs T Burns **Bred** Grovewood Stud **Trained** West Ilsley, Berks

FOCUS

Both bends moved off inner line which added 10yds to races of 7f & 1m and 15yds to 1m4f and 2m races. No hanging around here and the two with the best chance at the weights pulled clear.

5011 PETER BELL MEMORIAL H'CAP 6f

2:30 (2:31) (Class 4) (0-85,85) 3-Y-O+ **£4,851** (£1,443; £721; £360) **Stalls** High

Form RPR

4142 **1** **Sunrise Dance**[10] 4620 4-8-7 71 ConnorBeasley(5) 2 83
(Robert Johnson) *swtchd rt after s: mde all: styd on strly* **8/1**

6000 **2** *2 ¼* **Caranbola**[4] 4852 7-8-12 71 PaulMulrennan 10 75
(Mel Brittain) *chsd ldrs: 2nd over 1f out: kpt on: no imp* **20/1**

5560 **3** *¾* **Roker Park (IRE)**[30] 3981 8-9-2 75 (v) DavidNolan 12 77
(David O'Meara) *in tch: edgd rt over 2f out: styd on over 1f out: tk 3rd nr fin* **12/1**

1235 **4** *nk* **Mutafaakir (IRE)**[15] 4510 4-8-13 72 (p) PJMcDonald 7 73
(Ruth Carr) *in tch: hdwy to chse ldrs over 1f out: kpt on same pce* **9/2**[1]

0410 **5** *2* **Indego Blues**[31] 3945 4-8-12 71 PaulQuinn 6 66
(David Nicholls) *mid-div: hdwy over 2f out: kpt on same pce over 1f out* **14/1**

4304 **6** *½* **Cocktail Charlie**[13] 4560 5-9-1 74 (p) DuranFentiman 13 67
(Tim Easterby) *in rr: hdwy 2f out: styng on at fin* **6/1**[2]

1053 **7** *nk* **Khelman (IRE)**[33] 3894 3-8-10 73 BarryMcHugh 5 64
(Richard Fahey) *chsd ldrs: wknd appr fnl f* **12/1**

0025 **8** *2 ¼* **Chiswick Bey (IRE)**[15] 4482 5-9-1 74 (p) PhillipMakin 9 59
(Philip Kirby) *towards rr: drvn over 2f out: chsng ldrs over 1f out: wknd clsng stages* **7/1**[3]

0111 **9** *2 ¼* **Nasharra (IRE)**[30] 3980 5-9-4 84 (tp) KevinStott(7) 3 62
(Kevin Ryan) *mid-div on outer: drvn over 2f out: no threat* **8/1**

400 **10** *shd* **Tango Sky (IRE)**[10] 4620 4-9-2 75 AdrianNicholls 11 52
(David Nicholls) *in rr: reminders over 3f out: nvr a factor* **20/1**

0000 **11** *2* **Hazelrigg (IRE)**[22] 4263 8-9-6 79 (be) RobertWinston 8 50
(Tim Easterby) *dwlt: in rr: edgd rt over 1f out* **20/1**

0000 **12** *4* **Kuanyao (IRE)**[40] 3628 7-8-8 67 SamHitchcott 14 25
(David Nicholls) *in rr: nt clr run on ins over 2f out: nvr a factor* **14/1**

00-6 **13** *14* **Marine Commando**[107] 1646 5-9-0 73 MickyFenton 15
(Ruth Carr) *chsd ldrs: n.m.r: hung lft and lost pl over 2f out: n.m.r and eased over 1f out: t.o* **14/1**

00/5 **14** *18* **Enderby Spirit (GR)**[48] 3367 7-9-7 85 (t) JustinNewman(5) 4
(Bryan Smart) *s.i.s: sme hdwy on outer over 2f out: sn lost pl: bhd whn eased: t.o* **10/1**

1m 9.7s (-3.00) **Going Correction** -0.35s/f (Firm)

WFA 3 from 4yo+ 4lb **14** Ran SP% **126.0**

Speed ratings (Par 105): **106,103,102,101,98 98,97,94,91,91 89,83,65,41**

toteswingers 1&2 £39.20, 1&3 £39.20, 2&3 £39.20 CSF £167.40 CT £1950.97 TOTE £9.00: £3.10, £7.00, £4.80; EX 257.90 Trifecta £257.80 Part won. Pool: £343.73 - 0.01 winning units..

Owner M Saunders **Bred** Mrs Ann Jarvis **Trained** Newburn, Tyne & Wear

FOCUS

Few got into this ordinary sprint handicap.

5012 CONSTANT SECURITY NURSERY H'CAP 5f

3:05 (3:06) (Class 3) (0-95,88) 2-Y-O **£6,469** (£1,925; £962; £481) **Stalls** High

Form RPR

41 **1** **Fast Track**[35] 3826 2-9-2 83 GrahamGibbons 3 85
(David Barron) *half-rrd s: swtchd stands' side rail over 3f out: upsides over 2f out: hung lft and led over 1f out: kpt on wl towards fin* **4/5**[1]

2210 **2** *nk* **Memory Styx**[14] 4528 2-8-11 78 SamHitchcott 2 79
(Mick Channon) *sn drvn along and outpcd: hdwy over 1f out: hung lft and upsides ins fnl f: no ex towards fin* **14/1**

51 **3** *2 ½* **Straits Of Malacca**[26] 4107 2-8-7 74 PJMcDonald 1 66
(Kevin Ryan) *chsd ldrs: hung lft and outpcd over 3f out: hdwy over 1f out: styd on to take 3rd line* **7/1**

2604 **4** *nse* **Blithe Spirit**[22] 4248 2-8-7 79 JasonHart(5) 6 71
(Eric Alston) *led: hung lft and hdd over 1f out: wknd fnl 75yds* **4/1**[2]

4011 **5** *2 ¾* **Zalzilah**[14] 4511 2-9-7 88 (p) PaulMulrennan 5 70
(James Tate) *w ldr: rdn over 2f out: wknd 1f out: eased towards fin* **5/1**[3]

58.18s (-1.42) **Going Correction** -0.35s/f (Firm) **5** Ran SP% **111.4**

Speed ratings (Par 98): **97,96,92,92,88**

CSF £13.07 TOTE £1.70: £1.10, £3.00; EX 9.80 Trifecta £24.70 Pool: £1,179.89 - 35.79 winning units..

Owner Raymond Miquel **Bred** Jnp Bloodstock Ltd **Trained** Maunby, N Yorks

5013 BREEDERS BACKING RACING EBF CONDITIONS STKS 7f

3:40 (3:43) (Class 3) 3-Y-O+ **£9,703** (£2,887; £1,443; £721) **Stalls** Low

Form RPR

4043 **1** **Lockwood**[35] 3839 4-9-4 105 FrederikTylicki 5 111
(Saeed bin Suroor) *trckd ldrs: effrt over 3f out: led narrowly over 1f out: hld on towards fin* **9/4**[2]

-311 **2** *¾* **Diescentric (USA)**[35] 3825 6-9-4 106 PaulMulrennan 2 109
(Julie Camacho) *hld up in last: pushed along and hdwy on outside 3f out: upsides over 1f out: no ex last 50yds* **5/6**[1]

5-00 **3** *3 ¼* **The Cheka (IRE)**[80] 2368 7-9-4 104 (p) RobertWinston 3 100
(Eve Johnson Houghton) *trckd ldrs: upsides over 5f out: drvn over 3f out: kpt on same pce appr fnl f* **6/1**[3]

0-03 **4** *2 ½* **Bannock (IRE)**[14] 4514 4-8-11 103 AhmadAlSubousi(7) 1 93
(Charlie Appleby) *fast away: led: racd wd: qcknd pce over 3f out: hdd over 1f out: sn wknd* **11/1**

1m 25.56s (-1.64) **Going Correction** +0.05s/f (Good) **4** Ran SP% **107.9**

Speed ratings (Par 107): **111,110,106,103**

CSF £4.54 TOTE £4.00; EX 4.80 Trifecta £11.10 Pool: £727.64 - 48.88 winning units..

Owner Godolphin **Bred** Darley **Trained** Newmarket, Suffolk

FOCUS

The big two in the market pulled clear late on.

5014 TOTEPOOL.COM THIRSK SUMMER CUP (H'CAP) 1m

4:15 (4:17) (Class 3) (0-90,95) 3-Y-O+ **£19,407** (£5,775; £2,886; £1,443) **Stalls** Low

Form RPR

1060 **1** **Norse Blues**[21] 4308 5-9-7 90 LMcNiff(3) 7 101
(David Barron) *s.i.s: sn mid-div: hdwy over 2f out: styd on to ld ins fnl f: styd on wl* **10/1**

1202 **2** *1 ¾* **Karaka Jack**[7] 4746 6-9-2 82 AdrianNicholls 17 89
(David Nicholls) *in rr: effrt and swtchd rt over 2f out: styd on wl to take 2nd fnl strides* **8/1**[3]

4362 **3** *hd* **Trail Blaze (IRE)**[7] 4744 4-9-8 95 (b) KevinStott(7) 5 102
(Kevin Ryan) *trckd ldrs: t.k.h: effrt over 2f out: edgd rt 1f out: kpt on wl* **5/1**[1]

4500 **4** *2 ½* **Invincible Hero (IRE)**[5] 4825 6-8-9 80 JasonHart(5) 6 81
(Declan Carroll) *chsd ldrs: drvn 3f out: hung rt and kpt on one pce over 1f out* **16/1**

0232 **5** *hd* **Our Boy Jack (IRE)**[19] 4340 4-8-12 78 BarryMcHugh 15 78
(Richard Fahey) *trckd ldr: led over 2f out: hdd ins fnl f: fdd* **8/1**[3]

1304 **6** *nse* **Ingleby Angel (IRE)**[14] 4540 4-9-4 84 DavidNolan 3 84
(David O'Meara) *in rr-div: hdwy over 2f out: kpt on wl fnl f* **10/1**

6054 **7** *1* **No Poppy (IRE)**[8] 4733 5-8-8 79 AdamCarter(5) 18 77
(Tim Easterby) *mid-div: hdwy on outer over 2f out: kpt on: nvr rchd ldrs* **22/1**

0225 **8** *3 ¾* **Savanna Days (IRE)**[21] 4278 4-8-12 78 (v) SamHitchcott 1 67
(Mick Channon) *hld up in mid-div: hdwy to chse ldrs over 2f out: wknd over 1f out* **25/1**

0030 **9** *2 ½* **Fieldgunner Kirkup (GER)**[19] 4340 5-9-4 84 GrahamGibbons 13 68
(David Barron) *s.i.s: hld up in rr: kpt on fnl 2f: nvr a factor* **22/1**

226- **10** *1 ¼* **Subtle Knife**[283] 7334 4-9-0 83 ThomasBrown(3) 2 64
(Giles Bravery) *in rr: kpt on fnl 2f: nvr a factor* **16/1**

3116 **11** *½* **Oddysey (IRE)**[14] 4525 4-9-8 88 PaulMulrennan 10 67
(Michael Dods) *chsd ldrs: effrt over 2f out: wknd over 1f out* **18/1**

1201 **12** *½* **Snow Bay**[36] 3757 7-9-6 86 MickyFenton 9 64
(Paul Midgley) *led tl over 2f out: wknd over 1f out* **16/1**

6542 **13** *nk* **Osteopathic Remedy (IRE)**[27] 4101 9-9-10 90 TomEaves 11 68
(Michael Dods) *prom: effrt over 2f out: wknd wl over 1f out* **14/1**

4000 **14** *4* **Sam Nombulist**[50] 3300 5-9-3 83 (v) RobertWinston 14 51
(Richard Whitaker) *t.k.h towards rr: brief effrt on outer over 2f out: sn wknd* **33/1**

2100 **15** *¾* **Copperwood**[2] 4923 8-8-12 78 FrederikTylicki 8 45
(Mark Johnston) *in tch: effrt over 2f out: wknd and eased fnl f* **25/1**

0053 **16** *15* **Al Muheer (IRE)**[21] 4308 8-9-7 87 (b) PJMcDonald 4 19
(Ruth Carr) *chsd ldrs: lost pl over 2f out: bhd whn eased 1f out: t.o* **13/2**[2]

1m 38.72s (-1.38) **Going Correction** +0.05s/f (Good)

WFA 3 from 4yo+ 7lb **16** Ran SP% **119.3**

Speed ratings (Par 107): **108,106,106,103,103 103,102,98,96,94 94,93,93,89,88 73**

toteswingers 1&2 £26.10, 1&3 £10.80, 2&3 £8.30 CSF £79.39 TOTE £11.90: £3.20, £2.30, £1.60, £4.00; EX 126.00 Trifecta £757.20 Pool: £2,076.94 - 2.05 winning units..

Owner J Bollington & Partners **Bred** Littleton Stud **Trained** Maunby, N Yorks

FOCUS

No hanging around in this competitive handicap and the closers eventually came through.

5015 SHIRLEY ANNE FAILL MEMORIAL FILLIES' H'CAP 1m 4f

4:50 (4:50) (Class 4) (0-85,84) 3-Y-O+ **£4,851** (£1,443; £721; £360) **Stalls** Low

Form RPR

11 **1** **Court Pastoral**[30] 3976 3-9-2 83 GrahamGibbons 5 95+
(Lady Cecil) *mde all: qcknd pce over 3f out: jnd and rdn over 2f out: edgd rt: styd on strly to forge clr fnl f: readily* **4/5**[1]

2241 **2** *4* **Bantam (IRE)**[12] 4594 3-8-12 79 PaulMulrennan 7 85
(Ed Dunlop) *swtchd lft s: hld up: hdwy 5f out: trcking wnr over 3f out: chal over 2f out: styd on same pce appr fnl f* **2/1**[2]

541 **3** *4* **Pernica**[16] 4454 3-8-11 78 FrederikTylicki 1 78
(Lucy Wadham) *trckd wnr: drvn over 4f out: wd bnd over 3f out: one pce fnl 2f* **11/2**[3]

2343 **4** *7* **Maybeagrey**[7] 4760 4-8-12 68 RobertWinston 2 60
(Tim Easterby) *hld up: hdwy to trck ldrs 7f out: drvn over 3f out: wknd over 1f out: eased clsng stages* **14/1**

2m 35.53s (-0.67) **Going Correction** +0.05s/f (Good)

WFA 3 from 4yo 11lb **4** Ran SP% **110.9**

Speed ratings (Par 102): **104,101,98,94**

CSF £2.77 TOTE £1.40; EX 2.50 Trifecta £2.90 Pool: £900.31 - 232.01 winning units..

Owner J Shack **Bred** Newsells Park Stud **Trained** Newmarket, Suffolk

FOCUS

A fair fillies' handicap.

5016 READ HAYLEY TURNER EVERY FRIDAY RACINGUK.COM H'CAP 1m

5:25 (5:27) (Class 5) (0-70,70) 3-Y-O **£2,587** (£770; £384; £192) **Stalls** Low

Form RPR

4246 **1** **Look On By**[5] 4824 3-8-1 53 RaulDaSilva(3) 17 63
(Ruth Carr) *mde all: kpt on wl fnl f* **8/1**

4455 **2** *1* **Megamunch (IRE)**[19] 4354 3-8-11 67 (p) JacobButterfield(7) 6 74
(Kristin Stubbs) *chsd ldrs: wnt 2nd appr fnl f: kpt on same pce* **7/1**[3]

6112 **3** 1 ½ **Rocket Ronnie (IRE)**[18] 4374 3-9-5 **68**........................ AdrianNicholls 15 72+
(David Nicholls) *in tch: hdwy over 2f out: 3rd appr fnl f: kpt on same pce* **9/2**[1]
1035 **4** 2 ½ **War Lord (IRE)**[25] 4140 3-9-0 **63**....................................(v[1]) DavidNolan 4 61
(David O'Meara) *trckd ldrs: 2nd over 3f out: one pce over 1f out* **5/1**[2]
4646 **5** 1 ¾ **Kolonel Kirkup**[6] 4806 3-9-4 **67**................................(b) PaulMulrennan 11 61
(Michael Dods) *swtchd lft after s: in rr: hdwy on ins over 2f out: kpt on ins fnl f* **9/1**
000 **6** ½ **Taxiformissbyron**[28] 4045 3-8-7 **56**.............................. BarryMcHugh 10 49
(Michael Herrington) *prom: effrt over 2f out: one pce* **28/1**
522 **7** 1 ¾ **Special Report (IRE)**[9] 4657 3-7-11 **53** oh4 ow2....... ShelleyBirkett[(7)] 9 42
(Peter Hiatt) *in tch: effrt over 2f out: one pce* **25/1**
020 **8** 1 **Bitusa (USA)**[6] 4806 3-9-0 **63**...................................... RobertWinston 5 50
(Alan Swinbank) *in tch: effrt over 2f out: edgd rt over 1f out: one pce* **20/1**
2100 **9** shd **Iggy**[8] 4725 3-8-8 **64**..(t) MatthewHopkins[(7)] 16 51
(Michael Easterby) *in rr: c wd over 3f out: kpt on fnl 2f: nvr on terms* **25/1**
0530 **10** 4 ½ **Multisure**[8] 4722 3-7-13 **51** oh3.. JulieBurke[(3)] 8 27
(Ruth Carr) *chsd ldrs: edgd rt and wknd over 1f out* **28/1**
233 **11** 7 **Aglaophonos**[32] 3927 3-9-5 **68**................................(b[1]) FrederikTylicki 12 28
(Roger Varian) *in rr: c wd over 3f out: nvr on terms* **9/2**[1]
564 **12** nk **Sakhees Romance**[36] 3772 3-7-13 **51** oh1.............. DeclanCannon[(3)] 1 10
(Noel Wilson) *gave problems s: chsd ldrs: rdn and outpcd over 2f out: sn lost pl* **20/1**
340 **13** 2 **Echo Of Lightning**[17] 4400 3-7-11 **53**........................... JoeyHaynes[(7)] 3 8
(Noel Wilson) *in rr: c wd over 3f out: nvr on terms* **25/1**
0-66 **14** 4 **Finn Mac**[76] 2480 3-8-4 **58**... TobyAtkinson[(5)] 2 4
(John Norton) *in rr: bhd fnl 2f* **50/1**
0205 **15** 5 **Laudation**[40] 3634 3-9-3 **66**.. MickyFenton 7
(Danielle McCormick) *t.k.h in rr: c wd over 3f out: sn lost pl* **28/1**
0226 **U** **Jullundar (IRE)**[14] 4515 3-9-4 **67**................................. SamHitchcott 14
(Mick Channon) *prom: rdn over 2f out: wl hld whn uns rdr 100yds out* **20/1**

1m 39.85s (-0.25) **Going Correction** +0.05s/f (Good) **16** Ran SP% **124.8**
Speed ratings (Par 100): **103,102,100,98,96 95,94,93,92,88 81,81,79,75,70**
toteswingers 1&2 £13.40, 1&3 £7.30, 2&3 £6.00 CSF £55.25 CT £302.00 TOTE £11.40: £2.60, £2.40, £1.30, £1.60; EX 102.70 Trifecta £786.80 Pool: £1,646.31 - 1.56 winning units..
Owner J A Swinburne **Bred** S L Edwards **Trained** Huby, N Yorks

FOCUS
Little got into this.
T/Plt: £173.40 to a £1 stake. Pool: £53,389.56 - 224.74 winning units T/Qpdt: £24.30 to a £1 stake. Pool: £2,774.40 - 84.35 winning units WG

5017 - 5018a (Foreign Racing) - See Raceform Interactive

4971 GALWAY (R-H)

Saturday, August 3

OFFICIAL GOING: Soft

5019a IRISH STALLION FARMS EUROPEAN BREEDERS FUND "AHONOORA" H'CAP (PREMIER HANDICAP) 7f

3:10 (3:10) 3-Y-0+
£48,780 (£15,447; £7,317; £2,439; £1,626; £813)

RPR
1 **Northern Rocked (IRE)**[38] 3707 7-8-3 **85**..................(v) LeighRoche[(3)] 5 91
(D K Weld, Ire) *prom early: settled bhd ldrs: 3rd 1/2-way: pushed along fr 2f out and rdn into st on outer: clsd to ld fnl 100yds and kpt on wl* **6/1**[3]
2 ½ **Pintura**[4] 4869 6-9-12 **105**......................................(b[1]) DeclanMcDonogh 4 110
(Kevin Ryan) *hld up: 8th 1/2-way: hdwy over 2f out: rdn in 5th over 1f out and clsd wl u.p between horses into 2nd ins fnl 50yds: hld* **6/1**[3]
3 nk **Stuccodor (IRE)**[94] 1937 4-9-9 **102**.............................(v) PatSmullen 9 106
(D K Weld, Ire) *hld up in rr of mid-div: 9th 1/2-way: rdn into st and clsd u.p into 3rd ins fnl f: kpt on wl: hld* **4/1**[1]
4 1 ¼ **An Saighdiur (IRE)**[13] 4569 6-8-12 **91**.................................... WJLee 11 92
(Andrew Slattery, Ire) *sn led: narrow advantage 1/2-way: strly pressed into st and hdd ins fnl f: no ex u.p* **25/1**
5 nse **Al Khan (IRE)**[7] 4778 4-8-2 **86**....................................... ConnorKing[(5)] 3 86
(Violet M Jordan) *chsd ldrs: 5th 1/2-way: rdn and kpt on same pce ins fnl f wout threatening principals* **10/1**
6 1 ½ **Captain Cullen (IRE)**[4] 4869 4-8-4 **83** oh1......................... BenCurtis 10 79
(Gerard Keane, Ire) *dwlt sltly and racd towards rr: t.k.h: tk clsr order in 7th fr 2f out: sn no ex u.p: kpt on same pce* **25/1**
7 shd **Cash Or Casualty (IRE)**[29] 4039 5-8-10 **89**.......................(t) RoryCleary 8 85
(Damian Joseph English, Ire) *rrd s and racd in mid-div: 7th 1/2-way: rdn into st and sn n.m.r bhd horses: kpt on towards fin* **16/1**
8 shd **Boots And Spurs**[7] 4744 4-9-0 **93**..................................(v) ChrisHayes 2 89
(Mrs K Burke) *prom: sn trckd ldr in 2nd: rdn into st and sn short of room: no ex: wknd* **5/1**[2]
9 hd **Bubbly Bellini (IRE)**[13] 4569 6-9-0 **96**............................(p) IJBrennan[(3)] 6 91
(Adrian McGuinness, Ire) *towards rr: pushed along fr 3f out: no imp into st: kpt on same pce* **14/1**
10 4 ¼ **Seanie (IRE)**[4] 4869 4-8-11 **90**.. FergalLynch 1 74
(David Marnane, Ire) *prom early: settled bhd ldrs: 4th 1/2-way: rdn into st and n.m.r ins fnl f: sn wknd* **6/1**[3]
11 ½ **Legal Lyric (IRE)**[10] 4647 4-8-4 **83** oh2......................... WayneLordan 12 66
(W P Mullins, Ire) *hld up in rr of mid-div: pushed along over 2f out and sn no imp on principals: kpt on same pce* **10/1**
12 3 ½ **Battleroftheboyne (IRE)**[35] 3846 4-8-4 **86**.................... ConorHoban[(3)] 13 59
(Michael Mulvany, Ire) *s.i.s and racd in rr: rdn into st and no imp: one pce fnl f* **20/1**
13 14 **Ask Dad**[14] 4548 3-8-5 **90**...(p) NGMcCullagh 7 23
(J P Murtagh, Ire) *chsd ldrs: 6th 1/2-way: rdn and lost pl bef st: hmpd 2f out: no ex: eased fnl f* **14/1**

1m 30.13s (-1.47)
WFA 3 from 4yo+ 6lb **13** Ran SP% **129.4**
CSF £44.57 CT £167.59 TOTE £9.30: £2.90, £2.30, £2.20; DF 53.80.
Owner G Olivero **Bred** Moyglare Stud Farm Ltd **Trained** The Curragh, Co Kildare

FOCUS
Despite being off the bridle at a relatively early stage, it was a good tough performance from Northern Rocked to win this competitive and hard-fought contest. He had slipped to a good mark, while the second has been rated as running a fair personal best and the third has been rated to his best.

5021a LADBROKES FEELING LUCKY H'CAP 1m 4f

4:55 (4:56) (50-80,80) 3-Y-O+ **£7,573** (£1,756; £768; £439)

RPR
1 **Tin Town Boy (IRE)**[73] 2144 12-8-4 **56** oh4...................(t) ChrisHayes 17 60
(H Rogers, Ire) *settled in rr of mid-div: hdwy in 12th fr over 4f out into cl 4th 2f out: clsd on outer to ld ent fnl f and sn clr: styd on wl* **12/1**
2 3 **Quick Jack (IRE)**[125] 8089 4-8-12 **64**..................................... FMBerry 9 63
(A J Martin, Ire) *hld up towards rr: prog fr over 3f out to chse ldrs in 5th into st: qcknd into 2nd ins fnl f and kpt on wl: nt trble wnr* **6/1**[3]
3 1 **Benash (IRE)**[12] 4595 9-9-8 **79**....................................... ColinKeane[(5)] 8 76
(John G Carr, Ire) *w.w in rr of mid-div: hdwy fr over 3f out to chse ldrs into st: kpt on wl ins fnl f wout threatening wnr* **18/1**
4 ½ **Phangio (USA)**[7] 4787 4-9-3 **69**.. WJLee 11 66
(P J Rothwell, Ire) *chsd ldrs: cl 5th 1/2-way: rdn and no imp on ldrs fr 2f out: kpt on same pce fnl f* **12/1**
5 1 **Skimming Stone (IRE)**[29] 4040 3-7-13 **67** oh13............... ShaneGray[(5)] 62?
(John Joseph Murphy, Ire) *chsd ldrs: cl 4th 1/2-way: rdn and no imp on ldrs fr over 1f out: kpt on same pce* **16/1**
6 1 ¼ **Time To Work (IRE)**[21] 2201 5-10-0 **80**....................(b) DavyCondon 10 73
(Gordon Elliott, Ire) *racd in mid-div: no imp on ldrs appr st: kpt on ins fnl f* **10/1**
7 nse **Apisata (GER)**[307] 4-8-8 **60**.. DannyGrant 12 53
(Mervyn Torrens, Ire) *racd in mid-div: tk clsr order fr 1/2-way: rdn and no imp fr 2f out* **20/1**
8 1 ¾ **Carinya (IRE)**[81] 2349 5-9-2 **73**................................... ConnorKing[(5)] 18 63
(Amy Weaver) *sltly awkward s: settled in rr of mid-div: prog fr 4f out and rdn in 2nd into st: sn no ex: wknd fnl f* **20/1**
9 1 ¾ **Dundrum (IRE)**[753] 3971 9-9-5 **71**..............................(t) KevinManning 5 58
(Mrs John Harrington, Ire) *racd in mid-div: pushed along in 11th fr 4f out and sn no ex: kpt on one pce* **16/1**
10 ½ **Diamond Pro (IRE)**[265] 5929 4-8-4 **56**......................... NGMcCullagh 14 43
(John Joseph Murphy, Ire) *in rr of mid-div: rdn and no imp fr 2f out* **25/1**
11 1 ½ **Magnolia Ridge (IRE)**[21] 4321 3-9-3 **80**........................(b) PatSmullen 3 64
(D K Weld, Ire) *prom: settled bhd ldr: cl 2nd 1/2-way: led gng wl bef 2f out: sn rdn and hdd ent fnl f: no ex: wknd* **10/3**[1]
12 3 ¾ **Tohugo (IRE)**[7] 4789 4-8-4 **56** oh2...........................(p) TadhgO'Shea 6 34
(Michael Mulvany, Ire) *s.i.s: sn chsd ldrs: rdn and wknd fr over 2f out* **20/1**
13 5 ½ **Badger Or Bust (IRE)**[34] 3871 8-8-4 **56** oh5..................... BenCurtis 16 25
(Stephen Michael Cox, Ire) *prom: settled bhd ldrs: rdn and wknd fr 2f out: eased nr fin* **33/1**
14 7 ½ **Face Value**[4] 4872 5-9-4 **73**....................................(p) IJBrennan[(3)] 15 30
(Adrian McGuinness, Ire) *a bhd: rdn and no imp fr 3f out: eased st* **7/2**[2]
15 3 ½ **Plastiki**[16] 4457 4-9-2 **68**.. WayneLordan 1 20
(T J O'Mara, Ire) *chsd ldrs: cl 5th 1/2-way: rdn and wknd fr 2f out* **25/1**
16 3 ¾ **Johann Bach (IRE)**[51] 3265 4-9-12 **78**.......................... JosephO'Brien 4 24
(Patrick G Harney, Ire) *sn led: pushed along fr 3f out and sn hdd: wknd into st: eased fnl f* **9/1**
17 33 **Beau Michael**[4] 4872 9-9-7 **76**..............................(tp) RonanWhelan[(3)] 13
(Adrian McGuinness, Ire) *towards rr thrght: niggled along bef 1/2-way: sn detached: eased: t.o* **12/1**

2m 47.77s (4.67)
WFA 3 from 4yo+ 11lb **17** Ran SP% **143.7**
CSF £88.36 CT £1375.06 TOTE £16.20: £2.70, £2.00, £4.20, £3.00; DF 76.50.
Owner L P McCormack **Bred** Miss C Oliver & F J Oliver **Trained** Ardee, Co. Louth

FOCUS
Five years have gone by since the veteran Tin Town Boy last won at Galway and he turned back the years. The runner-up, third and fourth help set the standard.

5020 - 5024a (Foreign Racing) - See Raceform Interactive

4282 CHESTER (L-H)

Sunday, August 4

OFFICIAL GOING: Good (7.4)
Wind: Light; half behind Weather: Overcast and showers

5025 BRITISH STALLION STUDS EBF MAIDEN STKS 7f 2y

2:00 (2:01) (Class 4) 2-Y-O **£6,469** (£1,925; £962; £481) **Stalls** Low

Form RPR
2 **1** **Gallic Breeze (FR)**[12] 4610 2-9-5 0.......................... MichaelO'Connell 2 80+
(John Quinn) *chsd ldrs: faltered wl over 1f out: squeezed through on inner to ld jst ins fnl f: sn edgd rt: r.o wl* **6/4**[1]
63 **2** 1 ½ **Emaad (USA)**[16] 4470 2-9-5 0...................................... PaulHanagan 5 76
(Mark Johnston) *led: rdn over 1f out: hdd and bmpd jst ins fnl f: outpcd by wnr towards fin* **10/1**
033 **3** 2 ¼ **Solo Hunter**[22] 4304 2-9-5 68... NeilCallan 6 70
(David Evans) *s.i.s: midfield: hdwy 2f out: rdn to chse ldrs ent fnl f: styd on same pce and no imp fnl 100yds* **11/2**[3]
2 **4** 4 ½ **Blue Bounty**[45] 3493 2-9-5 0.. RobertWinston 7 59
(Mark H Tompkins) *chsd ldr tl rdn and hung lft over 1f out: sn unable qck: wknd ins fnl f* **10/1**
056 **5** 2 ½ **Mfiftythreedotcom (IRE)**[29] 4046 2-9-5 70.................. TonyHamilton 9 52
(Richard Fahey) *hld up: rdn over 1f out: no imp: one pce ins fnl f* **16/1**
05 **6** 5 **Rockie Road (IRE)**[15] 4513 2-9-5 0.............................. FrannyNorton 8 39
(Paul Green) *chsd ldrs tl rdn and wknd over 1f out* **25/1**
0 **7** 2 ¼ **Dalaki (IRE)**[68] 2741 2-9-5 0.. KierenFallon 3 33
(Clive Brittain) *sn towards rr: pushed along over 4f out: outpcd 2f out: nvr a threat* **7/2**[2]
00 **8** 1 ¾ **Cabaan (IRE)**[16] 4483 2-9-5 0...................................... PaulMulrennan 10 29+
(Brian Meehan) *hld up: niggled along over 2f out: wl adrift over 1f out: nvr on terms* **16/1**
9 3 ½ **Suni Dancer** 2-8-11 0.. RaulDaSilva[(3)] 1 15
(Paul Green) *dwlt: in rr: effrt on outer into midfield over 2f out: no imp on ldrs: hung bdly rt and lost pl ent st wl over 1f out: bhd after* **33/1**

1m 30.62s (4.12) **Going Correction** +0.50s/f (Yiel) **9** Ran SP% **114.3**
Speed ratings (Par 96): **96,94,91,86,83 78,75,73,69**
toteswingers 1&2 £4.30, 1&3 £3.00, 2&3 £5.80 CSF £17.86 TOTE £2.10: £1.20, £2.40, £1.60; EX 13.80 Trifecta £38.20 Pool: £3,570.50 - 70.05 winning units.
Owner Seamus Burns **Bred** Michel Monfort **Trained** Settrington, N Yorks

FOCUS
Rail realignment increased distance of races 1, 2, 3, 4 & 5 by 37yds, race 6 by 41yds and race 7 by 60yds. An ordinary maiden, but proven form came to the fore with the front quartet all having previously been placed. The third helps set the level.

5026 HALLIWELL JONES BMW MILE (H'CAP) 7f 122y
2:30 (2:32) (Class 3) (0-95,95) 3-Y-O+ **£7,762** (£2,310; £1,154; £577) **Stalls** Low

Form RPR

/600 **1** **Tellovoi (IRE)**[57] 3096 5-8-10 **80**..........(v[1]) RyanPowell(3) 7 89
(Ian Williams) *hld up in midfield: hdwy over 1f out: rdn and r.o ins fnl f: led fnl 50yds* **28/1**

2005 **2** ½ **Chosen Character (IRE)**[31] 3984 5-9-5 **91**..........(vt) NatashaEaton(5) 8 99
(Tom Dascombe) *chsd ldr: rdn to ld over 1f out: hdd fnl 50yds* **16/1**

0400 **3** 2¼ **Gramercy (IRE)**[8] 4780 6-9-7 **88**.......... KierenFallon 3 90
(David Simcock) *midfield early: chsd ldrs on inner 4f out: rdn over 1f out: chal ins fnl f: styd on same pce fnl 50yds* **4/1**[2]

1034 **4** 2¼ **Shebebi (USA)**[15] 4531 3-9-6 **94**.......... PaulHanagan 6 90
(Mark Johnston) *led: rdn and hdd over 1f out: stl wl there ins fnl f: no ex fnl 75yds* **5/2**[1]

0610 **5** 1 **Verse Of Love**[8] 4778 4-9-2 **83**.......... NeilCallan 5 77
(David Evans) *hmpd s: towards rr: n.m.r and lost grnd over 3f out: rdn over 1f out: styd on ins fnl f: nvr able to rch ldrs* **14/1**

0014 **6** hd **Ortac Rock (IRE)**[8] 4758 4-8-10 **77**..........(t) TonyHamilton 9 71
(Richard Fahey) *chsd ldrs: pushed along over 2f out: one pce fnl f* **25/1**

0161 **7** 1½ **Lord Of The Dance (IRE)**[8] 4746 7-9-5 **93**.......... JoeyHaynes(7) 2 83
(Michael Mullineaux) *towards rr: sn niggled along: hrd at work over 1f out: kpt on u.p ins fnl f: nvr able to trble ldrs* **17/2**

5145 **8** ¾ **Day Of The Eagle (IRE)**[39] 3683 7-8-9 **76**..........(v[1]) GrahamGibbons 4 64
(Michael Easterby) *bmpd s: midfield: rdn over 1f out: no imp: wl btn wl ins fnl f* **9/2**[3]

0002 **9** 1¾ **One Scoop Or Two**[23] 4250 7-8-9 **76** oh2..........(v) RichardKingscote 1 60
(Andrew Hollinshead) *chsd ldrs: rdn over 2f out: wknd ins fnl f* **10/1**

0610 **10** ½ **Green Park (IRE)**[23] 4250 10-8-6 **76**..........(b) NeilFarley(3) 11 58
(Declan Carroll) *in rr: pushed along 2f out: nvr able to get on terms* **33/1**

6122 **11** 93 **Able Master (IRE)**[8] 4758 7-10-0 **95**.......... DanielTudhope 12
(David O'Meara) *restless in stalls: in tch on outer: pushed along and lost pl over 4f out: sn wl bhd: t.o* **12/1**

1m 36.11s (2.31) **Going Correction** +0.50s/f (Yiel)
WFA 3 from 4yo+ 7lb **11 Ran SP% 116.8**
Speed ratings (Par 107): **108,107,105,103,102 101,100,99,97,97 4**
toteswingers 1&2 £58.00, 1&3 £26.20, 2&3 £13.00 CSF £408.47 CT £2221.61 TOTE £41.30: £10.80, £5.20, £1.80; EX 425.10 Trifecta £2221.90 Pool: £3,642.67 - 1.22 winning units.
Owner Global Commodity Imports Ltd **Bred** Whisperview Trading Ltd **Trained** Portway, Worcs

FOCUS
A decent handicap and, with a few in here that like to force it, a good pace was always likely.

5027 WINTER WONDERLAND QUEENSFERRY STKS (LISTED RACE) 6f 18y
3:05 (3:05) (Class 1) 3-Y-O+
£20,982 (£7,955; £3,981; £1,983; £995; £499) **Stalls** Low

Form RPR

3010 **1** **Hitchens (IRE)**[43] 3558 8-9-7 108.......... GrahamGibbons 5 113
(David Barron) *hld up: hdwy 3f out: sn trckd ldrs: swtchd lft to chal over 1f out: rdn and r.o ins fnl f: led fnl 75yds* **17/2**

2663 **2** ½ **Intransigent**[22] 4285 4-9-0 90.......... FrannyNorton 4 104
(Andrew Balding) *chsd ldr: rdn to ld 1f out: hdd fnl 75yds: hld cl home* **8/1**

2010 **3** 1 **Ballista (IRE)**[71] 2662 5-9-4 110.......... RichardKingscote 2 105
(Tom Dascombe) *led: rdn over 1f out: sn hdd: stl chalng ins fnl f: no ex towards fin* **9/4**[1]

6143 **4** 2¼ **Khubala (IRE)**[8] 4780 4-9-0 99..........(b) MartinDwyer 8 94+
(Hugo Palmer) *hmpd s: bhd: hdwy on inner over 2f out: rdn to chse ldrs over 1f out: kpt on and wanted to hang lft ins fnl f: unable to chal* **7/2**[2]

02-0 **5** 9 **Soul (AUS)**[43] 3557 6-9-0 113.......... KierenFallon 12 65+
(Saeed bin Suroor) *dwlt: impr to chse ldrs after 1f: rdn and unable to go w ldrs over 1f out: wknd ins fnl f* **11/2**[3]

0315 **6** 2¼ **Sylvia Pankhurst (IRE)**[10] 4670 3-8-5 78..........(p) HarryBentley 3 52
(David C Griffiths) *prom: lost pl 3f out: outpcd after* **40/1**

0563 **7** nk **Perfect Blossom**[13] 4580 6-8-9 80.......... PaulMulrennan 1 52
(Alan Berry) *chsd ldrs: pushed along over 2f out: wknd over 1f out* **66/1**

3140 **8** 5 **Al's Memory (IRE)**[8] 4780 4-9-0 90.......... NeilCallan 9 41
(David Evans) *hld up: pushed along in midfield 3f out: wknd over 1f out* **25/1**

0111 **9** 8 **Cincinnati Kit**[15] 4536 4-8-9 81..........(t) AndrewMullen 6 10
(Stuart Williams) *in tch: pushed along and lost pl over 3f out: in rr after and n.d* **25/1**

0-2 **10** 2¾ **Intibaah**[95] 1921 3-8-10 101.......... PaulHanagan 7
(Brian Meehan) *hmpd s: hld up: pushed along over 2f out: nvr on terms: eased whn wl btn ins fnl f* **6/1**

1m 16.2s (2.40) **Going Correction** +0.55s/f (Yiel)
WFA 3 from 4yo+ 4lb **10 Ran SP% 115.9**
Speed ratings (Par 111): **106,105,104,101,89 86,85,78,68,64**
toteswingers 1&2 £11.00, 1&3 £6.10, 2&3 £5.70 CSF £71.07 TOTE £11.10: £2.90, £2.20, £1.60; EX 73.90 Trifecta £253.80 Pool: £3,845.27 - 11.35 winning units.
Owner Laurence O'Kane & Paul Murphy **Bred** Curragh Bloodstock Agency Ltd **Trained** Maunby, N Yorks

FOCUS
An interesting Listed sprint, run at a strong pace, but some of these faced a tall order on these terms and few ever got into it.

5028 BREEDERS BACKING RACING EBF CONDITIONS STKS 6f 18y
3:40 (3:41) (Class 2) 2-Y-O **£12,602** (£3,772; £1,886; £944; £470) **Stalls** Low

Form RPR

12 **1** **Zaraee (IRE)**[17] 4434 2-9-1 0.......... PaulHanagan 1 87
(William Haggas) *mde all: rdn and edgd rt over 1f out: kpt on wl towards fin* **5/4**[1]

1U0 **2** ¾ **Intermath (IRE)**[24] 4212 2-9-1 82.......... NeilCallan 2 85
(David Evans) *chsd ldrs: rdn to take 2nd over 1f out: styd on and tried to chal wl ins fnl f: hld towards fin* **13/2**[3]

1514 **3** 1¼ **Cool Bahamian (IRE)**[16] 4486 2-9-8 88.......... JohnFahy 5 88
(Eve Johnson Houghton) *dwlt: hld up in rr: effrt over 1f out: styd on whn chsng ldrs ins fnl f: one pce towards fin* **10/1**

5421 **4** 1¼ **Bounty Hunter (IRE)**[12] 4602 2-9-1 77..........(p) RichardKingscote 4 77
(Tom Dascombe) *chsd wnr: pushed along 2f out: rdn and lost 2nd over 1f out: one pce and btn ins fnl f* **8/1**

631 **5** 6 **Hatha Hooh**[58] 3035 2-9-1 86.......... KierenFallon 3 61
(Richard Hannon) *chsd ldrs: niggled along fr 4f out: outpcd over 1f out: eased whn btn ins fnl f* **2/1**[2]

1m 17.75s (3.95) **Going Correction** +0.55s/f (Yiel) **5 Ran SP% 111.3**
Speed ratings (Par 100): **95,94,92,90,82**
CSF £9.92 TOTE £2.20: £1.50, £3.40; EX 9.30 Trifecta £41.40 Pool: £2,750.54 - 49.76 winning units.
Owner Hamdan Al Maktoum **Bred** London Thoroughbred Services Ltd **Trained** Newmarket, Suffolk

FOCUS
A decent little conditions event in which the runners spurned the inside rail up the home straight and came up the middle. The winner can do better again.

5029 RACING UK NURSERY H'CAP (THE SUNDAY £5K BONUS RACE) 6f 18y
4:15 (4:15) (Class 4) (0-85,83) 2-Y-O **£6,469** (£1,925; £962; £481) **Stalls** Low

Form RPR

3342 **1** **Party Ruler (IRE)**[23] 4246 2-9-0 **76**.......... RichardKingscote 4 80
(Tom Dascombe) *led: hdd narrowly over 2f out: rdn to regain ld 1f out: r.o and in control towards fin* **4/1**[2]

0343 **2** 1½ **Emily Davison (IRE)**[15] 4511 2-8-0 **62**.......... AndrewMullen 8 62
(David C Griffiths) *w ldr: led narrowly over 2f out: rdn and hdd 1f out: stl chal ins fnl f: no ex towards fin* **33/1**

21 **3** ½ **Tobougg Happy**[17] 4422 2-9-7 **83**.......... NeilCallan 3 81
(James Tate) *chsd ldrs: rdn and nt qckn over 1f out: styd on and clsd towards fin* **7/4**[1]

4005 **4** ½ **Intense Feeling (IRE)**[15] 4519 2-8-10 **72**.......... JohnFahy 1 69
(David Evans) *chsd ldrs: rdn over 2f out: nt qckn over 1f out: styd on and clsd towards fin* **11/1**

4430 **5** 2¾ **Orton Park (IRE)**[15] 4528 2-9-4 **80**.......... HarryBentley 2 68
(Tobias B P Coles) *hld up in tch: rdn and nt qckn over 1f out: one pce fnl 150yds* **6/1**

6105 **6** 2 **Know Your Name**[23] 4246 2-8-13 **75**.......... FrannyNorton 7 57
(David Evans) *squeezed out s and s.i.s: in rr and nudged along: rdn over 1f out: nvr a threat: eased whn btn fnl 100yds* **7/1**

45 **7** 2¼ **Red Forever**[15] 4511 2-8-0 **62** oh7.......... PaulQuinn 6 38
(Alan Berry) *hld up: rdn over 1f out: nvr on terms* **33/1**

431 **8** 22 **Boogangoo (IRE)**[17] 4443 2-8-10 **72**.......... PaulMulrennan 5
(Keith Dalgleish) *chsd ldrs: pushed along and wknd over 2f out: bhd over 1f out* **11/2**[3]

1m 18.75s (4.95) **Going Correction** +0.60s/f (Yiel) **8 Ran SP% 112.7**
Speed ratings (Par 96): **91,89,88,87,84 81,78,49**
toteswingers 1&2 £9.70, 1&3 £2.70, 2&3 £8.30 CSF £110.19 CT £307.91 TOTE £4.40: £1.40, £4.00, £1.40; EX 49.60 Trifecta £148.50 Pool: £3,113.98 - 15.72 winning units.
Owner Attenborough Bellman Ingram Lowe **Bred** John Quigley **Trained** Malpas, Cheshire

FOCUS
A fair nursery, but the front two dominated from the start. Straightforward form.

5030 PERRIER JOUET H'CAP 1m 2f 75y
4:45 (4:47) (Class 4) (0-80,78) 3-Y-O **£6,469** (£1,925; £962; £481) **Stalls** High

Form RPR

-521 **1** **Topamichi**[66] 2802 3-8-13 **70**.......... RobertWinston 2 82+
(Mark H Tompkins) *hld up: hdwy 2f out: rdn to chal strly ins fnl f: led fnl 75yds: r.o u.p* **11/2**[3]

1-31 **2** ½ **Rhombus (IRE)**[44] 3528 3-9-7 **78**.......... NeilCallan 5 89
(Ismail Mohammed) *trckd ldrs: effrt 3 wd 2f out: rdn to ld over 1f out: pressed ins fnl f: hdd fnl 75yds: r.o u.p* **10/1**

0-35 **3** 5 **Are You Mine (IRE)**[11] 4633 3-9-1 **72**.......... RichardKingscote 4 74
(Ralph Beckett) *led: rdn and hdd over 1f out: no ex ins fnl f* **14/1**

3321 **4** nk **Evangelist**[34] 3899 3-9-7 **78**..........(v[1]) KierenFallon 1 79+
(Sir Michael Stoute) *trckd ldrs: rdn and nt qckn over 1f out: sn outpcd: styd on towards fin* **6/4**[1]

4323 **5** nse **Eric The Grey (IRE)**[22] 4293 3-9-1 **72**.......... PaulHanagan 3 73+
(Richard Fahey) *completely missed break: wl bhd: styd on fr over 1f out: nrst fin* **4/1**[2]

16 **6** 4½ **Thistleandtworoses (USA)**[113] 1543 3-9-6 **77**..........[1] FrannyNorton 8 69
(Andrew Balding) *racd keenly: hld up: rdn 3f out: outpcd 2f out: nvr able to trble ldrs* **7/1**

055 **7** 1¾ **Konzert (ITY)**[58] 3047 3-8-9 **69**.......... RyanPowell(3) 7 58
(Ian Williams) *racd keenly: w ldr: rdn to chal 2f out: wknd ins fnl f* **25/1**

545 **8** 30 **Red Red Wine**[41] 3632 3-8-8 **65**..........(b[1]) MartinDwyer 6
(Hugo Palmer) *trckd ldrs: rdn over 3f out: wknd over 2f out: t.o* **16/1**

2m 16.12s (4.92) **Going Correction** +0.60s/f (Yiel) **8 Ran SP% 113.4**
Speed ratings (Par 102): **104,103,99,99,99 95,94,70**
toteswingers 1&2 £6.50, 1&3 £11.60, 2&3 £10.40 CSF £57.04 CT £724.67 TOTE £6.80: £2.10, £1.80, £3.40; EX 37.50 Trifecta £642.30 Pool: £3,115.54 - 3.63 winning units.
Owner Roalco Limited **Bred** Dullingham Park Stud & M P Bowring **Trained** Newmarket, Suffolk

FOCUS
A fair handicap, but despite a disputed lead a few of these were inclined to pull, including the winner.

5031 RACING WELFARE H'CAP 1m 4f 66y
5:15 (5:18) (Class 4) (0-85,83) 3-Y-O+ **£6,469** (£1,925; £962; £481) **Stalls** Low

Form RPR

4221 **1** **Zenafire**[15] 4512 4-9-1 **70**..........(p) PaulQuinn 1 82+
(Andrew Hollinshead) *hld up: hdwy 2f out: r.o to ld narrowly fnl 150yds: in control towards fin* **3/1**[2]

2 ½ **Kashmir Peak (IRE)**[142] 5957 4-9-9 **78**.......... MichaelO'Connell 5 89
(John Quinn) *chsd ldrs: rdn to ld wl over 1f out: hdd narrowly fnl 150yds: r.o u.p: hld towards fin* **7/4**[1]

-130 **3** 5 **Next Edition (IRE)**[26] 3345 5-9-5 **81**.......... EvaMoscrop(7) 4 84
(Philip Kirby) *hld up: outpcd over 2f out: rdn over 1f out: styd on ins fnl f: tk 3rd fnl 75yds: nt trble front two* **14/1**

2122 **4** 1¾ **El Bravo**[22] 4287 7-8-12 **70**.......... NeilFarley(3) 8 70
(Shaun Harris) *broke wl: chsd ldrs: rdn over 3f out: chal fr 2f out to 1f out: no ex fnl 100yds* **20/1**

52 **5** 1 **Villa Royale**[37] 3791 4-10-0 **83**..........(v[1]) DanielTudhope 9 81
(David O'Meara) *in tch: rdn over 1f out: sn hung lft and outpcd: n.d after* **7/1**[3]

5-44 **6** nk **Watts Up Son**[36] 3804 5-9-4 **78**..........(v) JasonHart(5) 3 76
(Declan Carroll) *bustled along to ld: clr after 4f: reduced advantage 3f out: rdn and hdd wl over 1f out: no ex ins fnl f* **7/1**[3]

0120 **7** 3½ **Sir Boss (IRE)**[24] 4202 8-9-6 **82**.......... JoeyHaynes(7) 2 74
(Michael Mullineaux) *trckd ldrs: tried to chal 2f out: rdn over 1f out: wknd ins fnl f* **16/1**

/5-5 **8** *31* **Secret Dancer (IRE)**66 2348 8-9-1 **70**............................ FrannyNorton 6 13
(Alan Jones) *in rr: pushed along 4f out: wl bhd over 2f out: t.o* **17/2**
2m 44.31s (5.81) **Going Correction** +0.65s/f (Yiel) **8** Ran SP% **114.2**
Speed ratings (Par 105): **106,105,102,101,100 100,97,77**
toteswingers 1&2 £2.70, 1&3 £8.60, 2&3 £6.20 CSF £8.62 CT £59.62 TOTE £4.10: £1.70, £1.10, £3.30; EX 11.80 Trifecta £105.00 Pool: £2,757.81 - 19.69 winning units.
Owner E Coquelin R Moseley **Bred** R J R Moseley & Mrs E Coquelin **Trained** Upper Longdon, Staffs
FOCUS
A fair middle-distance handicap and, with the pace a decent one, the form looks solid.
T/Plt: £74.00 to a £1 stake. Pool: £88,695.03 - 874.08 winning units T/Qpdt: £13.90 to a £1 stake. Pool: £5,456.48 - 289.30 winning units DO

4524 NEWBURY (L-H)
Sunday, August 4
OFFICIAL GOING: Good (good to firm in places)
Wind: Moderate; across Weather: Cloudy but humid

5032 JRL GROUP GENTLEMAN AMATEUR RIDERS' H'CAP 1m 2f 6y
2:10 (2:10) (Class 5) (0-70,70) 3-Y-O+ **£2,495** (£774; £386; £193) **Stalls** Centre

Form RPR
0160 **1** **Shahrazad (IRE)**39 3700 4-9-9 **50**..............................(t) JackGilligan(7) 8 61
(Patrick Gilligan) *led 7f out: hrd pressed 3f out tl narrowly hdd 1f out: styd chalng and slt ld agian fnl 75yds: hld on all out* **33/1**
0-26 **2** *shd* **Herod The Great**50 3343 3-10-8 **70**.................. MrJoshuaNewman(5) 7 81
(Alan King) *chsd ldrs: hdwy 3f out: wnt 2nd ins fnl 2f: slt ld 1f out but styd hrd pressed: narrowly hdd fnl 75yds: kpt on but no ex last strides* **9/2**3
0551 **3** *5* **Minority Interest**20 4350 4-10-10 **58**............................(b) MrSWalker 11 59
(Brett Johnson) *led 3f: styd chsng wnr: chal 3f out: sn rdn: wknd appr fnl f* **4/1**2
3134 **4** *5* **Khelac**17 4442 3-10-9 **69**...(b) MrFMitchell(3) 3 60
(Philip Hide) *in tch: drvn to chse ldrs 3f out: wknd ins fnl 2f* **9/1**
003 **5** *5* **Samoan (IRE)**35 3858 4-11-0 **69**...............................(b1) MrORJSangster(7) 1 50
(Brian Meehan) *in rr: pushed along 3f out: nvr gng pce to rch ldrs* **9/1**
6214 **6** *3* **Automotive**34 3882 5-10-8 **56**....................................... MrRossBirkett 4 31
(Julia Feilden) *in rr: drvn and hdwy over 2f out: nvr rchd ldrs* **11/4**1
-003 **7** *1 ¼* **Bountiful Girl**8 4771 4-10-9 **64**................................. MrAFrench(7) 2 36
(Neville Bycroft) *in tch: chsd ldrs 4f out: wknd 3f out* **7/1**
5-53 **8** *3 ½* **Cuckoo Rock (IRE)**48 3406 6-10-4 **57**..................(p) MrJHarding(5) 5 22
(Jonathan Portman) *wl bhd: rdn fr 5f out: mod hdwy fnl f* **8/1**
3600 **9** *1 ¼* **Justcallmehandsome**101 1797 11-9-11 **50** oh5 MrBenFfrenchDavis(5) 9 13
(Dominic Ffrench Davis) *a in rr* **40/1**
3000 **10** *1 ¼* **Rapid Water**24 4195 7-9-11 **50** oh2......................... MrAlexFerguson(5) 10 10
(Pat Eddery) *sn chsng ldrs: wknd 3f out* **40/1**
2m 7.62s (-1.18) **Going Correction** -0.20s/f (Firm)
WFA 3 from 4yo+ 9lb **10** Ran SP% **116.3**
Speed ratings (Par 103): **96,95,91,87,83 81,80,77,76,75**
toteswingers 1&2 £28.20, 1&3 £18.60, 2&3 £4.00 CSF £174.30 CT £739.84 TOTE £41.60: £8.70, £2.20, £1.80; EX 271.10 Trifecta £1911.80 Part won. Pool: £2,549.13 - 0.72 winning units..
Owner Linton Doolan **Bred** Shadwell Estate Company Limited **Trained** Newmarket, Suffolk
FOCUS
Rail between 1m1f and 5f moved out increasing distances on Round course by about 22m. It proved hard to make up significant ground in this modest amateur riders' contest.

5033 ACADEMY INSURANCE EBF MAIDEN STKS 6f 8y
2:40 (2:41) (Class 4) 2-Y-O **£4,075** (£1,212; £606; £303) **Stalls** High

Form RPR
1 **First Flight (IRE)** 2-9-5 0.............................. SilvestreDeSousa 9 85+
(Saeed bin Suroor) *s.i.s and green in rr: hdwy over 2f out: styd on strly to ld over 1f out: c clr: comf* **5/2**2
302 **2** *3* **Ice Slice (IRE)**9 4716 2-9-5 73.................................... PatDobbs 11 76
(Richard Hannon) *led: rdn 2f out: hdd over 1f out: sn no ch w wnr but kpt on wl for 2nd* **7/1**3
0 **3** *4* **Sandy Cove**20 4347 2-9-5 0.. JamesDoyle 3 64+
(Roger Charlton) *in rr: drvn and hdwy over 1f out: styd on to take 3rd ins fnl f: no imp on ldng duo* **8/1**
4 *¾* **Yaakooum (IRE)** 2-9-5 0.. RichardHughes 14 62+
(Richard Hannon) *chsd ldrs: rdn over 2f and no prog: outpcd fnl f* **7/4**1
5 *2 ¾* **Decimus Maximus** 2-9-5 0.. SeanLevey 5 54
(Richard Hannon) *chsd ldrs: rdn over 2f out: wknd appr fnl f* **20/1**
6 *nse* **Charles Molson** 2-9-5 0... DaneO'Neill 2 53
(Henry Candy) *chsd ldrs: rdn 2f out: wknd fnl f* **12/1**
60 **7** *1* **Mister Mayday (IRE)**52 3238 2-9-5 0................................ PatCosgrave 7 50
(George Baker) *in rr: pushed along 2f out: kpt on ins fnl f* **40/1**
8 *hd* **Telegraph (IRE)** 2-9-5 0.. DavidProbert 10 50
(Andrew Balding) *in rr: hdwy over 2f out: kpt on fnl f: nvr gng pce to get into contention* **25/1**
9 *hd* **Heska (IRE)** 2-9-5 0.. MartinHarley 15 49
(Mick Channon) *s.i.s: in rr: hdwy over 1f out: styd on but nvr gng pce to rch ldrs* **50/1**
10 *½* **Faure Island** 2-9-5 0... FergusSweeney 13 48
(Henry Candy) *broke wl: sn outpcd towards rr: styd on again clsng stages* **22/1**
11 *½* **Clodoaldo (IRE)** 2-9-5 0... FrankieDettori 8 46
(Brian Meehan) *chsd ldrs 4f* **25/1**
12 *8* **Groundworker (IRE)** 2-9-5 0... LiamKeniry 6 22
(Sylvester Kirk) *chsd ldrs 4f* **66/1**
1m 13.78s (0.78) **Going Correction** +0.15s/f (Good) **12** Ran SP% **118.9**
Speed ratings (Par 96): **100,96,90,89,86 85,84,84,84,83 82,72**
toteswingers 1&2 £4.20, 1&3 £5.80, 2&3 £7.30 CSF £18.66 TOTE £3.30: £1.40, £2.20, £3.20; EX 18.50 Trifecta £78.40 Pool: £2,957.09 - 28.27 winning units.
Owner Godolphin **Bred** Darley **Trained** Newmarket, Suffolk
FOCUS
Perhaps not that strong a maiden with the runner-up setting only a fair standard, but there was a smart-looking winner with the potential to do a good bit better.

5034 GRUNDON RECYCLE NURSERY H'CAP 7f (S)
3:15 (3:17) (Class 4) (0-85,82) 2-Y-O **£3,881** (£1,155; £577; £288) **Stalls** High

Form RPR
1 **1** **Cricklewood Green (USA)**35 3853 2-9-2 **77**........................ PatDobbs 4 85+
(Richard Hannon) *led 1f: styd trcking ldrs: led again over 2f out: rdn and hdd over 1f out: rallied fnl f and styd on gamely to ld on line* **2/1**2
1 **2** *nse* **Nezar (IRE)**27 4121 2-9-1 **76**... WilliamBuick 1 84+
(William Haggas) *in tch: hdwy to trck ldrs 3f out: led over 1f out and sn drvn: kpt on whn chal ins fnl f: hdd last stride* **7/4**1
0053 **3** *3 ½* **Sleepy Joe (IRE)**17 4451 2-7-11 **61** oh1..................... SimonPearce(3) 5 60
(Mick Channon) *in tch: hdwy over 2f out: styd on to take 3rd ins fnl f: no ch w ldng duo* **33/1**
000 **4** *2 ¼* **Mildenhall**40 3663 2-8-0 **61** oh1... JimmyQuinn 2 54+
(Richard Hannon) *in rr but in tch: hdwy over 2f out: styd on same pce fr over 1f out* **50/1**
0563 **5** *nse* **Dovil's Duel (IRE)**15 4519 2-8-0 **61** oh1.......................(p) KieranO'Neill 6 54
(Rod Millman) *t.k.h: chsd ldrs: hung rt to stands' rails ins fnl 2f: one pce fnl f* **10/1**
054 **6** *1 ½* **Aristocracy**15 4513 2-8-0 **61**... CathyGannon 8 50
(Mick Channon) *broke wl: sn outpcd: rdn over 2f out: kpt on fnl f but nvr any ch* **16/1**
503 **7** *3 ½* **Chance Of Romance (IRE)**43 3574 2-8-2 **63**.................. LukeMorris 7 43
(Clive Cox) *led after 1f: hdd over 2f out: sn btn* **20/1**
0666 **8** *2* **Jana**48 3414 2-7-7 **61** oh3.. CameronHardie(7) 9 36
(Sylvester Kirk) *chsd ldrs: wknd ins fnl 2f* **66/1**
31 **9** *5* **Downturn**51 3291 2-9-7 **82**... RichardHughes 3 44
(Richard Hannon) *chsd ldrs: rdn over 2f out: wknd qckly 2f out* **4/1**3
1m 26.97s (1.27) **Going Correction** +0.15s/f (Good) **9** Ran SP% **115.8**
Speed ratings (Par 96): **98,97,93,91,91 89,85,83,77**
toteswingers 1&2 £1.90, 1&3 £13.10, 2&3 £9.60 CSF £5.71 CT £80.08 TOTE £3.10: £1.30, £1.30, £4.10; EX 7.90 Trifecta £143.40 Pool: £4,520.01 - 23.62 winning units.
Owner Chris Wright & Andy MacDonald **Bred** Stratford Place Stud **Trained** East Everleigh, Wilts
FOCUS
Probably decent enough form with a couple of once-raced winners from good stables pulling clear to fight out the finish, albeit they're both already gelded.

5035 BRITISH STALLION STUDS EBF CHALICE STKS (LISTED RACE) 1m 4f 5y
3:50 (3:50) (Class 1) 3-Y-O+
£22,684 (£8,600; £4,304; £2,144; £1,076; £540) **Stalls** Centre

Form RPR
21-1 **1** **Seal Of Approval**32 3960 4-9-3 95.................................. GeorgeBaker 8 102+
(James Fanshawe) *trckd ldrs 7f out: lost position 3f out: nt clr run 2f out: drvn between horses over 1f out: squeezed through fnl 100yds to ld cl home* **7/2**2
11 **2** *nk* **Songbird (IRE)**52 3258 4-9-3 103................................ FrankieDettori 5 101
(Lady Cecil) *hld up in rr: hdwy on outer over 2f out chal 1f out: sn led but hrd pressed: hdd cl home* **15/8**1
-521 **3** *hd* **Cushion**52 3239 3-8-6 80.. WilliamBuick 10 101
(John Gosden) *hld up in rr: hdwy on outside over 2f out: styd on u.p to chal fnl f: kpt on: no ex last strides* **10/1**
0-55 **4** *nk* **Savanna La Mar (USA)**17 4468 3-8-6 96........................ LukeMorris 6 100
(Sir Mark Prescott Bt) *chsd ldrs: drvn along fr over 3f out: led u.p wl over 1f out: narrowly hdd ins fnl f but styd on wl: outpcd clsng stages* **16/1**
-121 **5** *3 ½* **Kikonga**23 4234 3-8-6 93... KirstyMilczarek 7 95
(Luca Cumani) *chsd ldrs: n.m.r over 2f out: wknd appr fnl f* **4/1**3
2124 **6** *¾* **Danat Al Atheer**15 4537 3-8-6 89....................................(b) ChrisCatlin 1 93
(William Haggas) *s.i.s: in rr: hdwy over 2f out: styd on same pce over 1f out* **33/1**
2312 **7** *nk* **Spicy Dal**52 3240 3-8-6 92.. SilvestreDeSousa 3 93
(Hughie Morrison) *chsd ldrs: led over 2f out: hdd wl over 1f out: wknd fnl f* **10/1**
4335 **8** *6* **Whippy Cream (IRE)**15 4532 3-8-6 102.......................(p) JimmyQuinn 4 83
(Marco Botti) *led main gp tl overall ldr wl over 3f out: hdd over 2f out: sn btn* **22/1**
-426 **9** *11* **Bite Of The Cherry**29 4083 4-9-3 97.............................. RichardHughes 9 74
(Michael Bell) *racd wd and led tl hdd wl over 3f out: sn btn: eased fnl f* **10/1**
2m 30.89s (-4.61) **Going Correction** -0.20s/f (Firm)
WFA 3 from 4yo 11lb **9** Ran SP% **117.4**
Speed ratings (Par 111): **107,106,106,106,104 103,103,99,92**
toteswingers 1&2 £2.90, 1&3 £6.90, 2&3 £6.10 CSF £10.66 TOTE £5.40: £1.90, £1.10, £3.30; EX 13.50 Trifecta £115.00 Pool: £3,905.22 - 25.45 winning units.
Owner T R G Vestey **Bred** T R G Vestey **Trained** Newmarket, Suffolk
FOCUS
There was a bunch finish, but this looked a decent enough fillies' Listed contest.

5036 BATHWICK TYRES H'CAP 5f 34y
4:25 (4:26) (Class 4) (0-85,88) 3-Y-O+ **£4,851** (£1,443; £721; £360) **Stalls** High

Form RPR
222 **1** **Swendab (IRE)**16 4487 5-9-1 **74**...................................(v) FrankieDettori 5 86
(John O'Shea) *pressed ldrs: led over 1f out: drvn out* **10/3**2
-026 **2** *¾* **Angel Way (IRE)**19 4389 4-8-11 **70**..................................... PatDobbs 3 79
(Mike Murphy) *chsd ldr: led 1/2-way: hdd over 1f out: styd on but nver quite gng pce of wnr* **10/1**
0632 **3** *1 ¼* **Tagula Night (IRE)**25 4165 7-9-6 **79**............................(bt) GeorgeBaker 8 84
(Dean Ivory) *in rr: stl last and pushed along fnl 120yds: fin strly clsng stages to take 3rd: nt rch ldng duo* **9/2**3
0202 **4** *hd* **Gladiatrix**9 4707 4-9-10 **88**.................................. MichaelJMMurphy(5) 1 92
(Rod Millman) *led to 1/2-way: styd on same pce fnl f* **2/1**1
6022 **5** *1* **Howyadoingnotsobad (IRE)**10 4675 5-8-7 **73**............ RyanWhile(7) 7 73
(Karen George) *in rr: rdn 1/2-way: styd on fnl f but nvr nr ldrs* **10/1**
0330 **6** *½* **West Coast Dream**27 4123 6-9-3 **79**..........................1 MarkCoumbe(3) 6 77
(Roy Brotherton) *chsd ldrs: wknd fnl 110yds* **16/1**
5400 **7** *nse* **First In Command (IRE)**14 4569 8-9-4 **77**....................(t) ShaneKelly 2 75
(Daniel Mark Loughnane) *s.i.s in rr: drvn 2f out: kpt on fnl f but nvr any ch w ldrs* **10/1**
0224 **8** *1 ½* **Griffin Point (IRE)**20 4344 6-8-7 **66** oh7...............(b) SilvestreDeSousa 4 59
(William Muir) *wnt lft s: chsd ldrs: rdn 1/2-way: wknd ins fnl 2f* **14/1**
1m 1.43s (0.03) **Going Correction** +0.15s/f (Good) **8** Ran SP% **114.4**
Speed ratings (Par 105): **105,103,101,101,99 99,99,96**
toteswingers 1&2 £5.70, 1&3 £2.70, 2&3 £7.20 CSF £36.11 CT £151.52 TOTE £2.90: £1.70, £2.90, £1.70; EX 39.00 Trifecta £200.90 Pool: £3,725.26 - 13.90 winning units.
Owner The Cross Racing Club & Patrick Brady **Bred** P Brady **Trained** Elton, Gloucs
FOCUS
A fair sprint handicap.

5037 AJC PREMIER FILLIES' H'CAP 1m 2f 6y
4:55 (4:58) (Class 5) (0-75,75) 3-Y-O **£2,587** (£770; £384; £192) **Stalls** Centre

Form RPR
5-34 **1** **Raskova (USA)**16 4500 3-9-1 **69**................................. FrankieDettori 10 76
(William Jarvis) *hld up in rr: gd hdwy on outside fr over 2f out: chal ins fnl f: drvn to ld fnl 50yds* **14/1**

5-44 **2** ½ **Fatima's Gift**[31] 3975 3-9-2 70 MartinHarley 1 76
(David Simcock) *chsd ldrs: rdn 2f out: wnt 2nd over 1f out styng on to chal whn bmpd ins fnl f: rallied to re-take 2nd clsng stages but nt pce of wnr* **11/2**[3]

5213 **3** ¾ **Serenity Spa**[20] 4348 3-9-7 75 JamesDoyle 3 80
(Roger Charlton) *led: rdn 2f out: hrd pressed and edgd rt ins fnl f: hdd fnl 50yds: lost 2nd cl home* **11/4**[2]

-500 **4** 1½ **Point Of Control**[36] 3820 3-8-6 60 LukeMorris 8 62
(Michael Bell) *in rr: hdwy and rdn over 3f out: styd on fnl f: nt rch ldrs* **25/1**

5-16 **5** ¾ **Russian Royale**[54] 3179 3-9-3 71 ShaneKelly 5 71
(Stuart Kittow) *chsd ldrs: rdn over 2f out: styd on same pce* **22/1**

-3U5 **6** ½ **Martinas Delight (USA)**[16] 4485 3-9-1 74 MichaelJMMurphy(5) 6 75
(Alan Jarvis) *sn chsng ldr: rdn and one pce whn hmpd ins fnl f* **16/1**

-213 **7** 4 **Rosie Rebel**[51] 3276 3-9-5 73 ChrisCatlin 7 64
(Rae Guest) *in rr: rdn on ins fr 3f out: mod prog 2f out but nvr on terms and sn wknd* **2/1**[1]

1446 **8** 1¼ **Movementneverlies**[15] 4523 3-9-5 73 WilliamBuick 4 62
(Charles Hills) *in rr: sme hdwy on outer 3f out: sn wknd* **14/1**

3031 **9** ½ **Equitissa (IRE)**[23] 4240 3-9-3 71 RichardHughes 2 59
(Richard Hannon) *chsd ldr: tl wknd wl over 1f out* **8/1**

2m 8.5s (-0.30) **Going Correction** -0.20s/f (Firm) 9 Ran SP% **113.9**
Speed ratings (Par 97): **93,92,92,90,90 89,86,85,85**
toteswingers 1&2 £8.00, 1&3 £8.10, 2&3 £4.50 CSF £87.69 CT £277.34 TOTE £11.80: £2.50, £2.30, £1.40; EX 63.30 Trifecta £314.80 Pool: £3,173.24 - 7.55 winning units.
Owner Kevin Hickman **Bred** Dean Fleming **Trained** Newmarket, Suffolk
■ Stewards' Enquiry : James Doyle two-day ban: careless riding (Aug 24-25)

FOCUS
An ordinary fillies' handicap.

5038 INTERACTIVE MAIDEN FILLIES' STKS 1m 3f 5y
5:25 (5:29) (Class 5) 3-Y-0+ **£3,234** (£962; £481; £240) **Stalls** Centre

Form RPR

505 **1** **Phaenomena (IRE)**[23] 4257 3-9-0 80 RichardHughes 5 87+
(Lady Cecil) *trckd ldrs: chsd ldr and rdn over 1f out: led jst ins fnl f: drvn out* **11/4**[2]

32 **2** ¾ **Saddaqa (USA)**[11] 4633 3-9-0 0 SilvestreDeSousa 8 86
(Saeed bin Suroor) *sn chsng ldr: led ins fnl 3f: rdn 2f out: hdd jst ins fnl f: styd on same pce u.p* **1/1**[1]

4/- **3** ½ **Aquilla (IRE)**[641] 7232 4-9-10 0 WilliamBuick 10 85
(David Simcock) *hld up in rr: hdwy ins fnl 2f: styd on fnl f: kpt on cl home but nt rch ldng duo* **16/1**

3 **4** 4½ **Annawi**[16] 4500 3-9-0 0 DaneO'Neill 6 77
(Henry Candy) *chsd ldrs: rdn to go 2nd 2f out but no imp: wknd fnl f* **4/1**[3]

5 8 **Invincible Magic (IRE)** 3-9-0 0 JamesDoyle 3 63
(Charlie Appleby) *chsd ldrs: rdn and btn 2f out* **10/1**

00 **6** 3½ **Mystery Drama**[11] 4632 3-9-0 0 FergusSweeney 7 56
(Alan King) *in tch: sme hdwy on outside over 2f out: nvr rchd ldrs and sn wknd* **66/1**

55- **7** 6 **Zaminate**[227] 8187 4-9-10 0 DavidProbert 9 46
(Patrick Chamings) *in rr: hdwy 3f out: nvr rchd ldrs and wknd over 2f out* **50/1**

50 **8** 27 **Palkin**[16] 4500 3-9-0 0 FrankieDettori 2 49
(William Haggas) *led: rdn and hdd ins fnl 3f: eased whn no ch over 1f out* **20/1**

2m 20.21s (-0.99) **Going Correction** -0.20s/f (Firm)
WFA 3 from 4yo 10lb 8 Ran SP% **119.9**
Speed ratings (Par 100): **95,94,94,90,85 82,78,58**
toteswingers 1&2 £1.40, 1&3 £5.30, 2&3 £3.60 CSF £6.13 TOTE £3.70: £1.10, £1.10, £3.60; EX 7.40 Trifecta £53.50 Pool: £3,993.78 - 55.97 winning units.
Owner Niarchos Family **Bred** Mrs C L Weld **Trained** Newmarket, Suffolk

FOCUS
Not a bad maiden.
T/Jkpt: Not won. T/Plt: £38.80 to a £1 stake. Pool: £97,830.75 - 1,839.56 winning units T/Qpdt: £7.50 to a £1 stake. Pool £7,490.88 - 738.19 winning units ST

4935 DEAUVILLE (R-H)
Sunday, August 4

OFFICIAL GOING: Turf: good to soft; fibresand: standard

5039a PRIX DE L'HIPPODROME ARGENTINO DE PALERMO (CONDITIONS) (2YO COLTS & GELDINGS) (TURF) 7f 110y
1:00 (12:00) 2-Y-0 **£13,821** (£5,528; £4,146; £2,764; £1,382)

RPR

1 **Double Point (IRE)**[43] 3574 2-9-0 0 OlivierPeslier 2 87
(Paul Cole) *chsd clr ldr: clsd over 2f out: rdn to ld over 1f out: jnd ent fnl and sustained duel w eventual runner-up: r.o strly: drvn and edgd ahd cl home* **57/10**[3]

2 hd **Honeymoon Cocktail (FR)**[28] 2-9-0 0 ChristopheSoumillon 5 87
(J-C Rouget, France) **3/1**[2]

3 2 **Rogue Agent (IRE)**[27] 2-9-0 0 MaximeGuyon 1 82
(A Fabre, France) **2/5**[1]

4 1 **Master's Spirit (IRE)** 2-8-10 0 StephanePasquier 3 76
(P Demercastel, France) **21/1**

5 18 **Picador (IRE)** 2-9-0 0 (p) FredericSpanu 4 37
(Carmen Bocskai, Switzerland) **16/1**

1m 32.72s (4.32) 5 Ran SP% **121.8**
WIN (incl. 1 euro stake): 6.70. PLACES: 3.50, 2.70. SF: 20.60.
Owner Black Run Racing **Bred** Victor Stud Bloodstock Ltd **Trained** Whatcombe, Oxon

5040a LARC PRIX MAURICE DE GHEEST (GROUP 1) (3YO+) (TURF) 6f 110y(S)
2:08 (12:00) 3-Y-0+ **£162,593** (£65,048; £32,524; £16,247; £8,138)

RPR

1 **Moonlight Cloud**[29] 4093 5-8-13 0 ThierryJarnet 11 122
(F Head, France) *settled in midfield on outer: shkn up and hdwy 2f out: rdn to ld ent fnl f and qcknd clr: pushed out cl home: impressive* **5/4**[1]

2 1¾ **Lethal Force (IRE)**[22] 4298 4-9-2 0 AdamKirby 9 120
(Clive Cox) *sn led and crossed to rail: rdn over 2f out: hung rt u.p: hdd ent fnl f and readily outpcd by wnr: kpt on wl for 2nd* **5/2**[2]

3 ¾ **Gordon Lord Byron (IRE)**[15] 4549 5-9-2 0 JohnnyMurtagh 1 118
(T Hogan, Ire) *midfield in tch on inner: rdn over 2f out: edgd rt u.p but r.o to take 3rd cl home: nt pce of front pair* **8/1**[3]

4 1¼ **Tulips (IRE)**[36] 3851 4-8-13 0 MaximeGuyon 10 111
(A Fabre, France) *stdd and hld up in midfield: rdn 3f out: r.o but nt pce to chal* **25/1**

5 shd **American Devil (FR)**[36] 3851 4-9-2 0 UmbertoRispoli 13 114
(J Van Handenhove, France) *hld up towards rr on outer: hdwy 2f out: rdn over 1f out: r.o but nt pce to chal* **50/1**

6 hd **Silas Marner (FR)**[29] 4093 6-9-2 0 ChristopheSoumillon 5 113
(J-C Rouget, France) *hld up towards rr: rdn 2f out: r.o but nt pce to chal* **25/1**

7 2½ **Abu Sidra (FR)**[36] 3851 4-9-2 0 OlivierPeslier 7 106
(J-F Bernard, France) *prom: swtchd rt over 4f out: rdn and ev ch 2f out: nt qckn over 1f out: steadily fdd* **20/1**

8 hd **Catcall (FR)**[63] 2909 4-9-2 0 Francois-XavierBertras 4 105
(P Sogorb, France) *midfield: rdn 2f out: outpcd by ldrs ent fnl f: kpt on but n.d* **20/1**

9 4½ **Don Bosco (FR)**[28] 4104 6-9-2 0 GregoryBenoist 12 92
(D Smaga, France) *t.k.h early: prom: rdn over 2f out: sn outpcd and btn: fdd and eased towards fin* **33/1**

10 2 **Us Law (IRE)**[35] 3876 3-8-11 0 (b[1]) Christophe-PatriceLemaire 2 86
(P Bary, France) *hld up in midfield on inner: rdn 2f out: sn outpcd and btn: nvr a factor* **25/1**

11 nk **Gale Force Ten**[22] 4298 3-8-11 0 (b) RyanMoore 3 85
(A P O'Brien, Ire) *sn prom on inner: rdn over 2f out: no ex and btn 1f out: fdd and eased ins fnl f* **10/1**

12 8 **Indian Sly (FR)**[15] 4555 8-9-2 0 JimmyTastayre 6 63
(P Capelle, France) *a in rr: rdn and btn 2f out: nvr a factor* **250/1**

13 1¾ **Nova Neyev (FR)**[15] 4555 5-9-2 0 AlexisBadel 14 57
(P Capelle, France) *dwlt: dropped in fr wdst draw and hld up in last: nvr put under serious press but btn 2f out: nvr a factor* **250/1**

14 snk **Princedargent (FR)**[36] 3851 3-8-11 0 FabriceVeron 8 56
(H-A Pantall, France) *led early: sn restrained and trckd ldr: rdn and wknd qckly 2f out: wl bhd and eased ins fnl f: relegated to last fnl strides* **25/1**

1m 14.33s (-2.87) **Going Correction** +0.025s/f (Good)
WFA 3 from 4yo+ 4lb 14 Ran SP% **123.8**
Speed ratings: **117,115,114,112,112 112,109,109,104,101 101,92,90,90**
WIN (incl. 1 euro stake): 2.20. PLACES: 1.30, 1.60, 2.20. DF: 3.60. SF: 3.80.
Owner George Strawbridge **Bred** George Strawbridge **Trained** France

FOCUS
This Group 1 looked a two-horse race beforehand and that is how it turned out. The form is rated around the third, fourth and sixth.

5041a OSAF PRIX DE REUX (GROUP 3) (3YO+) (TURF) 1m 4f 110y
2:40 (12:00) 3-Y-0+ **£32,520** (£13,008; £9,756; £6,504; £3,252)

RPR

1 **Tres Blue (IRE)**[28] 4103 3-8-11 0 FabriceVeron 3 117+
(H-A Pantall, France) *midfield in tch on outer: rdn 2f out: styd on to chal ins fnl f: led cl home and readily asserted: shade cosily* **3/1**[3]

2 ¾ **Montclair (IRE)**[70] 2692 3-8-7 0 (b) MaximeGuyon 1 112
(A Fabre, France) *midfield in tch on inner: rdn over 2f out: styd on against rail to chal ins fnl f: wnt 2nd cl home but readily hld by wnr* **8/1**

3 snk **First Mohican**[81] 2365 5-9-5 0 TomQueally 2 112
(Lady Cecil) *led: rdn and strly pressed fr 2f out: styd on and kpt finding u.p but hdd cl home and dropped to 3rd* **5/2**[1]

4 2 **Slow Pace (USA)**[55] 3165 5-9-10 0 OlivierPeslier 5 114
(F Head, France) *trckd ldr on outer: rdn to chal 2f out: nt qckn ins fnl f: fdd and dropped to 4th* **11/2**

5 shd **Au Revoir (IRE)**[22] 4325 3-8-7 0 CoreyBrown 6 109+
(A Fabre, France) *hld up in tch in last pair on outer: rdn 2f out: outpcd in last ent fnl f: styd on and wnt 5th ins fnl 100yds: clsng towards fin but nvr threatened ldrs* **11/4**[2]

6 1 **Victorinna (FR)**[14] 4574 5-9-2 0 ChristopheSoumillon 4 104
(C Laffon-Parias, France) *hld up in tch in last pair on inner: rdn 2f out: styd on but nt pce to chal and dropped to last ins fnl 100yds* **10/1**

2m 40.14s (-6.26)
WFA 3 from 5yo 11lb 6 Ran SP% **115.8**
WIN (incl. 1 euro stake): 3.60. PLACES: 1.90, 2.70. SF: 26.20.
Owner Horst Rapp **Bred** Chevotel De La Hauquerie **Trained** France

5042a PRIX DE L'HIPPODROME DE SAN ISIDRO (CLAIMER) (4YO+) (LADY RIDERS) (FIBRESAND) 1m 1f 110y
3:40 (12:00) 4-Y-0+ **£6,504** (£2,601; £1,951; £1,300; £650)

RPR

1 **Primera Vista**[17] 4467 7-9-6 0 (b) DelphineSantiago 15 81
(Mario Hofer, Germany) **93/10**

2 snk **Got Slick (FR)**[99] 6-9-7 0 MlleNathalieDesoutter 14 82
(P Monfort, France) **63/10**[2]

3 ½ **Glamour Star (GER)**[17] 4467 4-8-10 0 MlleZoePfeil(6) 9 76
(W Mongil, Germany) **33/10**[1]

4 ½ **Caroz (FR)**[32] 6-8-6 0 (p) LauraGrosso(6) 8 71
(J-P Gauvin, France) **12/1**

5 nk **Lone Rider (FR)**[32] 7-8-10 0 (b) MllePaulineDominois(6) 7 74
(S Cerulis, France) **7/1**[3]

6 snk **Atomic Waves**[104] 4-9-2 0 PaulineProd'homme 2 74
(P Bary, France) **10/1**

7 hd **Special Request (FR)**[90] 6-9-2 0 ManonScandella-Lacaille 4 73
(M Gentile, France) **63/10**[2]

8 1¼ **Mont Athos (FR)**[64] 4-8-8 0 MlleAmelieFoulon(3) 5 66
(R Chotard, France) **41/1**

9 ¾ **Fille D'Avril (FR)**[32] 5-8-13 0 NadegeOuakli 11 66
(E Leenders, France) **52/1**

10 ½ **Doctor Sim (IRE)**[183] 498 4-8-6 0 MlleMarie-AnneBernadet(5) 3 63
(D De Waele, France) **39/1**

11 2½ **Kadison (GER)**[49] 5-9-2 0 (p) CelineLaunay 12 63
(H Blume, Germany) **55/1**

12 1½ **Conducting**[20] 4350 5-9-2 0 CarlaO'Halloran 6 60
(Gay Kelleway) *prom: rdn over 2f out: lost pl over 1f out: sn no ex and btn: fdd and eased ins fnl f* **15/1**

13 shd **Winning Dream (FR)**[63] 4-8-0 0 MlleSarahLeger(8) 10 52
(J-P Carvalho, France) **117/1**

14 1¾ **Arluno (FR)**[17] 4467 4-8-6 0 MlleJeanneCotta(5) 13 51
(J-Y Artu, France) **92/1**

15 2½ **Mano Diao**[90] 4-8-11 0 StefanieHofer 1 46
(Mario Hofer, Germany) **9/1**

The Form Book Flat, Raceform Ltd, Compton, RG20 6NL.

16 *dist* **Pianoro (FR)**[442] 4-8-11 0.................................. MlleGwladysFradelin 16
(F Pedrono, France) **132/1**
2m 1.77s (121.77) **16** Ran SP% **117.1**
WIN (incl. 1 euro stake): 10.30. PLACES: 3.10, 2.00, 1.80. DF: 22.70. SF: 62.40.
Owner Guido-Werner-Hermann-Schmitt **Bred** Meon Valley Stud **Trained** Germany

5043 - (Foreign Racing) - See Raceform Interactive

3604 DUSSELDORF (R-H)

Sunday, August 4

OFFICIAL GOING: Turf: good

5044a HENKEL-PREIS DER DIANA - DEUTSCHES STUTEN-DERBY (GROUP 1) (3YO FILLIES) (TURF) 1m 3f

4:05 (4:11) 3-Y-O **£186,991** (£73,170; £36,585; £20,325; £8,130)

RPR

1 **Penelopa**[43] 3604 3-9-2 0.. EPedroza 2 102+
(M G Mintchev, Germany) *settled in rr: hdwy into midfield 1/2-way: in tch but short of room 3f out: rdn and prog whn briefly short of room 2f out: chal between horses 1 1/2f out: 3rd and styd on u.p appr fnl f: led fnl 100yds* **16/1**

2 ¾ **Secret Gesture**[65] 2842 3-9-2 0.................................... JamieSpencer 5 101+
(Ralph Beckett) *scrubbed along early to chse ldrs: settled in 5th: tk clsr order on outer 3f out: shkn up to chal fr 2f out: hrd rdn and tk narrow ld over 1f out: edgd rt and r.o u.p ins fnl f: hdd fnl 100yds* **5/4**[1]

3 *nk* **Adoya (GER)**[22] 4323 3-9-2 0.. FabienLefebvre 14 100
(Andreas Lowe, Germany) *in rr: rdn and prog on inner over 2f out: styd on to chse ldng trio 1 1/2f out: hrd rdn appr 1f out: kpt on u.p fnl f but nvr quite on terms* **50/1**

4 *shd* **Red Lips (GER)**[36] 3852 3-9-2 0... DPorcu 3 100
(Andreas Lowe, Germany) *midfield on inner: prog to chse ldrs 2 1/2f out: short of room and hmpd sn after: styng on whn clipped ldr's heels and stmbld 2f out: nt rcvr immediately: styd on wl u.p ins fnl f: gng on at fin* **50/1**

5 *nk* **Quilita (GER)**[29] 4092 3-9-2 0.. AStarke 12 100
(P Schiergen, Germany) *midfield: rdn and prog over 2f out: chsd ldrs fr 1 1/2f out: kpt on ins fnl f: nt pce to chal* **14/1**

6 2 ½ **Viletta (GER)**[43] 3604 3-9-2 0.. KClijmans 10 95
(J Hirschberger, Germany) *towards rr: hdwy ins fnl 2f: styd on strly u.p ins fnl f: nrest at fin* **40/1**

7 *shd* **Calyxa**[36] 3852 3-9-2 0... RobertHavlin 4 95
(Ferdinand J Leve, Germany) *chsd ldng trio: hrd rdn to ld over 1 1/2f out: sn strly pressed by eventual runner-up: hdd over 1f out: rallied u.p ins fnl f: wknd last 100yds* **25/1**

8 7 **Orion Love**[42] 3614 3-9-2 0.. ASuborics 8 82
(H-A Pantall, France) *towards rr: prog on outer 3f out: hrd rdn to chse ldrs 2f out: wknd u.p fr over 1f out: eased last 100yds* **6/1**[3]

9 3 ½ **Oriental Lady (GER)**[29] 4092 3-9-2 0..................................... FilipMinarik 15 76
(J Hirschberger, Germany) *midfield on outer: rdn and no imp over 2f out: eased whn btn ins fnl f* **25/1**

10 2 ½ **Wild Silva**[29] 4092 3-9-2 0... FrederikTylicki 11 72
(Markus Klug, Germany) *towards rr: sme prog u.p 1 1/2f out: nvr in contention* **25/1**

11 *nk* **Lady Liberty (IRE)**[29] 4092 3-9-2 0............................. CristianDemuro 7 71
(Andreas Lowe, Germany) *in fnl 3rd on inner: rdn and hdwy on inner over 2f out: short of room and wknd 1 1/2f out* **33/1**

12 2 **Thunderstruck (GER)**[29] 4092 3-9-2 0................................... APietsch 6 68
(R Dzubasz, Germany) *in fnl 3rd on outer: nvr in contention* **66/1**

13 5 **Ars Nova (GER)**[29] 4092 3-9-2 0....................................... AndreaAtzeni 1 59
(W Figge, Germany) *led: hdd after 5f and trckd ldr: rallied and pressed ldr over 2 1/2f out: regained ld over 2f out: sn hrd rdn and hdd over 1 1/2f out: sn wknd* **16/1**

14 2 ½ **Daytona Bay**[29] 4092 3-9-2 0......................... LennartHammer-Hansen 16 54
(Ferdinand J Leve, Germany) *settled in 6th: hrd rdn to hold pl 2 1/2f out: wknd ins fnl 2f: wl bhd fnl f* **4/1**[2]

15 3 **Miss You Too**[17] 4468 3-9-2 0.. MartinLane 9 49
(David Simcock) *chsd ldr racing freely between horses: squeezed out and slipped rnding first bnd: rdn and chsd ldrs fr 2 1/2f out: looked hld whn short of room on rail and lost pl 1 1/2f out: sn wknd* **14/1**

16 8 **Next Green (GER)**[42] 3612 3-9-2 0........................ MrDennisSchiergen 13 34
(P Schiergen, Germany) *pressed ldr: led after 5f: hdd over 2f out: remained prom tl wknd u.p fr 1 1/2f out: wl bhd fnl f* **33/1**

2m 13.53s (133.53) **16** Ran SP% **129.1**
WIN (incl. 10 euro stake): 160. PLACES: 36, 23, 60. SF: 810.
Owner Litex Commerce Ad **Bred** Litex Commerce **Trained** Germany

FOCUS
They were bunched turning in before seven pulled clear.

KLAMPENBORG

Sunday, August 4

OFFICIAL GOING: Turf: good to soft

5045a LANWADES STUD SCANDINAVIAN OPEN CHAMPIONSHIP (GROUP 3) (3YO+) (TURF) 1m 4f

3:05 (12:00) 3-Y-O+ **£32,644** (£10,881; £5,440; £3,264; £2,176)

RPR

1 **Bank Of Burden (USA)**[29] 4095 6-9-4 0.............. Per-AndersGraberg 1 104
(Niels Petersen, Norway) **10/9**[1]

2 1 ½ **Berling (IRE)**[29] 4095 6-9-2 0.. ManuelMartinez 5 99
(Jessica Long, Sweden) **37/10**[3]

3 2 **Touch Of Hawk (FR)**[29] 4095 7-9-2 0.................................... EspenSki 2 96
(Wido Neuroth, Norway) **14/5**[2]

4 1 ½ **Jubilance (IRE)**[35] 4-9-2 0.. JacobJohansen 6 94
(Bent Olsen, Denmark) **7/1**

5 2 **Bomar (IRE)**[29] 4095 4-9-2 0... FJohansson 7 90
(Wido Neuroth, Norway) **73/10**

6 3 **East Meets West (IRE)**[35] 4-9-2 0...................................... OliverWilson 8 86
(Bent Olsen, Denmark) **15/1**

2m 23.6s (143.60) **6** Ran SP% **125.8**
PARI-MUTUEL (all including 1krone stakes): WIN 2.11; PLACE 1.21, 1.32, 1.32; SF 9.01.
Owner Stall Trick Or Treat Ab **Bred** Bjarne Minde **Trained** Norway

4801 CARLISLE (R-H)

Monday, August 5

OFFICIAL GOING: Good to soft (soft in places down the hill)
Wind: Almost nil Weather: Overcast

5047 LANES H'CAP (PRO-AM LADY RIDERS' RACE) 5f

6:15 (6:16) (Class 6) (0-65,65) 4-Y-O+ **£3,234** (£962; £481; £240) **Stalls** Low

Form RPR

0441 1 **Amenable (IRE)**[8] 4814 6-10-4 **62** 6ex.........................(p) LucyAlexander 4 75
(Violet M Jordan) *mde virtually all: rdn 2f out: kpt on wl fnl f* **7/2**[1]

2333 2 2 ¾ **Busy Bimbo (IRE)**[2] 4982 4-9-5 **49**.................................. MissJRRichards 2 52
(Alan Berry) *prom centre: effrt and ev ch over 1f out: sn chsng wnr: kpt on fnl f* **10/1**

0466 3 *hd* **Rock Canyon (IRE)**[2] 4992 4-9-5 **49**...........................(p) SamanthaBell 5 51
(Linda Perratt) *prom: effrt and pushed along over 1f out: kpt on ins fnl f* **14/1**

3416 4 ½ **Foreign Rhythm (IRE)**[15] 4560 8-10-1 **64**..................... MrsVDavies(5) 7 64
(Ron Barr) *taken early to post: chsd ldng gp: effrt and hdwy over 1f out: r.o ins fnl f* **7/1**[3]

6403 5 1 **Wicked Wilma (IRE)**[9] 4762 9-9-3 **47**........................ MissHayleyMoore 6 44
(Alan Berry) *in tch: effrt and edgd rt over 1f out: no imp fnl f* **7/1**[3]

0066 5 *dht* **Rutterkin (USA)**[31] 4034 5-9-4 **48**..................................... CathyGannon 10 45
(James Moffatt) *t.k.h early: in tch: effrt over 1f out: one pce fnl f* **11/2**[2]

3303 7 *hd* **Silly Billy (IRE)**[11] 4660 5-8-11 **46**.................................. MissNHayes(5) 1 42
(Brian Ellison) *in tch: pushed along centre over 2f out: no imp fr over 1f out* **7/2**[1]

0460 8 *nk* **Fol Hollow (IRE)**[2] 4992 8-10-4 **62**................................ KirstyMilczarek 9 57
(Stuart Coltherd) *cl up tl rdn and wknd appr fnl f* **8/1**

2500 9 *nk* **M J Woodward**[103] 1758 4-10-2 **65**....................... MissAimeeMKing(5) 3 59
(Paul Green) *dwlt: hdwy to dispute ld centre after 2f: effrt over 1f out: sn outpcd* **25/1**

0005 10 3 ½ **Ivestar (IRE)**[12] 4619 8-9-10 **54**.........................(vt) MissJoannaMason 11 35
(Michael Easterby) *s.i.s: bhd and outpcd: no ch fr 1/2-way* **20/1**

1m 2.59s (1.79) **Going Correction** +0.425s/f (Yiel) **10** Ran SP% **120.3**
Speed ratings (Par 101): **102,97,97,96,94 94,94,94,93,88**
toteswingers 1&2 £2.90, 1&3 £12.80, 2&3 £10.30 CSF £41.59 CT £446.97 TOTE £4.00: £2.00, £2.60, £4.70; EX 26.50 Trifecta £201.70 Pool: £926.13 - 3.44 winning units.
Owner Rakebackmypoker.com **Bred** Michael Downey & Roalso Ltd **Trained** Moreton Morrell, Warwicks
■ Stewards' Enquiry : Lucy Alexander one-day ban: careless riding (19 Aug)

FOCUS
All rails on inside. Carlisle's unique all-female jockeys' meeting. The wet weather resulted in the going being changed to mainly good to soft. The jockeys reported it was riding as described. A moderate sprint handicap in which they came stands' side and finished in something of a heap. The winner found his form after a big slide in the weights in the past year.

5048 BOOKMAKERS.CO.UK H'CAP (PRO-AM LADY RIDERS' RACE) 2m 1f 52y

6:45 (6:47) (Class 5) (0-70,70) 4-Y-O+ **£3,234** (£962; £481; £240) **Stalls** Low

Form RPR

3400 1 **Come Here Yew (IRE)**[9] 4782 5-10-7 **70**..................... KirstyMilczarek 3 79
(Declan Carroll) *chsd ldrs: rdn over 3f out: rallied over 2f out: led ins fnl f: styd on wl* **5/2**[1]

5-00 2 1 ¾ **Danceintothelight**[43] 2120 6-9-1 **55**........................ MissBeckySmith(5) 9 62
(Micky Hammond) *in tch: stdy hdwy over 3f out: kpt on fnl f: tk 2nd cl home* **20/1**

0152 3 *nk* **Bygones For Coins (IRE)**[9] 4760 5-9-10 **59**................ MrsCBartley 14 66
(Robert Johnson) *led and clr: rdn 2f out: hdd ins fnl f: kpt on: hdd nr fin* **14/1**

-540 4 6 **Uncut Stone (IRE)**[27] 3595 5-9-2 **51** oh1................(p) MissSBrotherton 1 51
(Peter Niven) *midfield: lost pl 1/2-way: styd on fr 2f out: nrst fin* **14/1**

14 5 ¾ **Miss Macnamara (IRE)**[16] 3944 4-10-0 **63**............... LucyAlexander 13 62
(Martin Todhunter) *hld up: effrt and c stands' side over 2f out: kpt on fnl f: nt rch far side ldrs* **12/1**

05/2 6 7 **Sergeant Pink (IRE)**[5] 2630 7-9-5 **54**........................... MissHCuthbert 5 46
(Dianne Sayer) *chsd clr ldr to 3f out: sn rdn and outpcd fr 2f out* **10/1**

0-04 7 1 ½ **Bandanaman (IRE)**[38] 3771 7-9-8 **57**............................ RachaelGreen 6 47
(Alan Swinbank) *hld up: rdn over 3f out: sn no imp* **3/1**[2]

5206 8 6 **Teenage Idol (IRE)**[28] 4110 9-9-8 **62**................. MissEButterworth(5) 10 45
(Dianne Sayer) *hld up: rdn and c stands' side over 3f out: sn n.d* **12/1**

1000 9 3 ¼ **Dubara Reef (IRE)**[35] 3910 6-8-11 **51** oh5.........(p) MissAimeeMKing(5) 7 31
(Paul Green) *midfield: pushed along and outpcd over 3f out: sn wknd* **40/1**

11-0 10 1 **Ministerofinterior**[76] 2545 8-10-5 **68**..........................(tp) CathyGannon 8 47
(Richard Ford) *in tch: rdn and outpcd over 4f out: n.d after* **7/1**[3]

-000 11 12 **Queen's Estate (GER)**[27] 4135 4-9-11 **65**...............(p) MissJoeyEllis(5) 2 30
(Patrick Gilligan) *chsd ldrs: outpcd whn c stands' side over 2f out: sn btn* **25/1**

3645 12 ½ **Jan Smuts (IRE)**[33] 3944 5-9-8 **62**......................(tp) MissSMDoolan(5) 11 27
(Wilf Storey) *hld up: rdn over 3f out: c stands' side over 2f out: sn n.d* **20/1**

44-0 13 27 **Terenzium (IRE)**[84] 2313 11-9-4 **53** oh4 ow2.............(p) MissCWalton 12
(Micky Hammond) *bhd: struggling over 4f out: sn lost tch: t.o* **33/1**

3m 54.33s (1.33) **Going Correction** +0.175s/f (Good) **13** Ran SP% **122.6**
Speed ratings (Par 103): **103,102,102,99,98 95,94,92,90,90 84,84,71**
toteswingers 1&2 £11.40, 1&3 £8.80, 2&3 £30.90 CSF £62.32 CT £614.21 TOTE £3.70: £1.60, £5.70, £4.20; EX 65.50 Trifecta £663.30 Part won. Pool: £884.48 - 0.29 winning units..
Owner K MacKay & L Ibbotson **Bred** Norelands Bloodstock **Trained** Sledmere, E Yorks

FOCUS
This ordinary staying handicap was run in a moderate time and the first three were up with the pace throughout. The first two returned to form.

5049 SYSTEM PEOPLE'S ROUND ROBIN H'CAP (PRO-AM LADY RIDERS' RACE) 5f 193y

7:15 (7:19) (Class 5) (0-75,72) 4-Y-O+ **£3,234** (£962; £481; £240) **Stalls** Low

Form RPR

5010 1 **Just The Tonic**[20] 4375 6-9-11 **67**.................................. MissNHayes(5) 10 78
(Marjorie Fife) *s.i.s: hld up: hdwy against stands' rail over 2f out: led ins fnl f: kpt on wl* **8/1**

5406 2 1 ¾ **Rigolleto (IRE)**[12] 4636 5-10-0 **65**.............................. MissJoannaMason 9 70
(Anabel K Murphy) *cl up: led 2f out to ins fnl f: kpt on same pce towards fin* **11/2**[3]

3024 **3** 2¼ **Beckermet (IRE)**[14] 4577 11-10-2 **67**.......................... MissSBrotherton 7 65
(Ruth Carr) *missed break: hld up: hdwy and prom 1/2-way: effrt over 1f out: one pce fnl f* **11/4**[2]

6004 **4** ¾ **Spread Boy (IRE)**[18] 4444 6-9-2 **53** oh8.................... MissJRRichards 8 49
(Alan Berry) *chsd ldrs: outpcd over 2f out: kpt on fnl f: no imp* **22/1**

3560 **5** nk **Methaaly (IRE)**[24] 4245 10-9-6 **57**........................(be) MissMMullineaux 1 52
(Michael Mullineaux) *s.i.s: hld up: effrt on outside 2f out: edgd rt: no imp fnl f* **11/1**

0012 **6** 1 **Planetex (IRE)**[30] 4072 4-10-2 **67**.................. LucyAlexander 3 59
(John Quinn) *t.k.h: chsd ldrs: outpcd and edgd lft wl over 1f out: no imp fnl f* **5/2**[1]

6 **7** 2¼ **Red Roar (IRE)**[83] 2343 6-9-6 **57**.................................... CathyGannon 5 41
(Alan Berry) *t.k.h early: led to 2f out: wknd fnl f* **6/1**

0040 **8** 5 **Lucky Dan (IRE)**[24] 4245 7-10-2 **72**...................... MissAimeeMKing(5) 4 40
(Paul Green) *prom tl hung rt and wknd fr 2f out* **16/1**

1m 16.23s (2.53) **Going Correction** +0.425s/f (Yiel) **8** Ran SP% **114.6**
Speed ratings (Par 103): **100,97,94,93,93 91,88,82**
toteswingers 1&2 £7.00, 1&3 £6.60, 2&3 £5.00 CSF £51.34 CT £152.22 TOTE £8.70: £3.20, £2.80, £1.02; EX 51.50 Trifecta £188.00 Pool: £949.88 - 3.78 winning units.

Owner R W Fife **Bred** West Dereham Abbey Stud **Trained** Stillington, N Yorks
■ The first winner for Natasha Hayes.

FOCUS
Quite a competitive-looking sprint and again they came stands' side. A personal best from the winner, with the second to this year's form.

5050 DEBENHAMS CLAIMING STKS (PRO-AM LADY RIDERS' RACE) 1m 1f 61y
7:45 (7:45) (Class 5) 4-Y-O+ **£3,234** (£962; £481; £240) **Stalls** Low

Form RPR

6210 **1** **Seattle Drive (IRE)**[9] 4746 5-10-2 78.............................. CathyGannon 2 73
(Brian Ellison) *hld up: pushed along and outpcd over 3f out: rallied over 1f out: rdn and ev ch last 100yds: led cl home* **2/1**[1]

2021 **2** shd **Extraterrestrial**[8] 4803 9-9-13 75.. LauraBarry 7 70
(Richard Fahey) *hld up: pushed along 3f out: hdwy to chse clr ldr over 1f out: hung rt: led ins fnl f: hdd cl home* **11/4**[2]

-000 **3** 1¼ **Kathlatino**[37] 3814 6-9-5 50... MissCWalton 4 59
(Micky Hammond) *prom: pushed along and effrt over 2f out: kpt on ins fnl f* **33/1**

550 **4** nk **Jordaura**[8] 4810 7-9-13 65... MissJRRichards 9 66
(Alan Berry) *hld up: rdn over 3f out: hdwy over 1f out: edgd rt and one pce fnl f* **20/1**

0302 **5** 4½ **Toto Skyllachy**[8] 4803 8-10-2 94.................................. MissJGillam(5) 5 64
(David O'Meara) *led and clr after 2f: rdn over 1f out: hdd ins fnl f: sn btn* **7/2**[3]

14-0 **6** 8 **My Mate Jake (IRE)**[51] 3349 5-10-7 77..................(b) MissSBrotherton 8 47
(James Given) *chsd ldng pair: pushed along over 3f out: wknd wl over 1f out* **7/1**

0240 **7** 3¼ **Sunnybridge Boy (IRE)**[51] 3349 4-10-7 73............ MissHayleyMoore 6 40
(Mrs K Burke) *chsd clr ldr tl hung rt and wknd wl over 1f out* **7/1**

0000 **8** 1½ **Landesherr (GER)**[20] 4376 6-9-11 43......................... MissHCuthbert 1 26
(Thomas Cuthbert) *hld up in tch: outpcd over 3f out: sn btn* **50/1**

1m 59.53s (1.93) **Going Correction** +0.175s/f (Good) **8** Ran SP% **116.9**
Speed ratings (Par 103): **98,97,96,96,92 85,82,81**
toteswingers 1&2 £1.90, 1&3 £15.40, 2&3 £32.70 CSF £7.75 TOTE £3.50: £1.60, £1.50, £5.90; EX 10.40 Trifecta £426.90 Pool: £848.36 - 1.49 winning units.There were no claims.

Owner Steve May **Bred** Littleton Stud **Trained** Norton, N Yorks
■ Stewards' Enquiry : Laura Barry four-day ban: use of whip

FOCUS
Some fair performers in this claimer, but the form horses weren't at their best.

5051 ULTIMATE LADIES' NIGHT H'CAP (PRO-AM LADY RIDERS' RACE) 7f 200y
8:15 (8:16) (Class 4) (0-85,82) 4-Y-O+ **£6,469** (£1,925; £962; £481) **Stalls** Low

Form RPR

2246 **1** **Hot Rod Mamma (IRE)**[30] 4055 6-9-11 **72**................... LucyAlexander 3 86
(Dianne Sayer) *hld up and bhd: hdwy and weaved through fr 2f out: rdn to ld ins fnl f: sn clr* **4/1**[2]

6200 **2** 5 **Chookie Royale**[21] 4342 5-10-7 **82**.................................(p) LauraBarry 4 84
(Keith Dalgleish) *in tch: hdwy to ld over 1f out: hdd ins fnl f: kpt on: no ch w wnr* **10/1**

-534 **3** 1¼ **Lisiere (IRE)**[32] 3988 4-10-3 **78**.............................(p) MissHayleyMoore 7 77
(Mrs K Burke) *t.k.h: cl up: led over 2f out to over 1f out: kpt on same pce fnl f* **6/1**[3]

6043 **4** 1 **Chookie Avon**[14] 4577 6-9-4 **70**............................(p) GeorginaBaxter(5) 10 67
(Keith Dalgleish) *midfield: pushed along over 2f out: kpt on fnl f: nrst fin* **20/1**

6100 **5** 1¼ **Green Park (IRE)**[1] 5026 10-9-10 **76**...............(b) RachelRichardson(5) 5 70
(Declan Carroll) *t.k.h: chsd ldrs: ev ch 2f out: outpcd fnl f* **25/1**

5663 **6** nk **High Resolution**[2] 4994 6-9-7 **68**.................................... SamanthaBell 1 61
(Linda Perratt) *hld up: pushed along over 2f out: no imp fr over 1f out* **16/1**

0-02 **7** shd **Lady Chaparral**[30] 4055 6-10-7 **82**............................ KirstyMilczarek 13 75
(Michael Dods) *unruly in preliminaries: midfield: hdwy to chse ldrs 2f out: rdn and outpcd appr fnl f* **2/1**[1]

-506 **8** 3¼ **Edas**[49] 3397 11-9-2 **63** oh7.. MissHCuthbert 12 49
(Thomas Cuthbert) *in tch tl edgd rt and wknd fr 2f out* **33/1**

1506 **9** 2¾ **It's A Mans World**[38] 3777 7-10-1 **76**.............................. CathyGannon 8 55
(Brian Ellison) *hld up: rdn over 2f out: no imp fr over 1f out* **10/1**

1055 **10** 5 **Space War**[9] 4746 6-9-3 **69**..(t) AnnaHesketh(5) 2 37
(Michael Easterby) *s.v.s: hdwy into midfield after 3f: rdn and wknd over 2f out* **25/1**

-235 **11** 5 **Regal Swain (IRE)**[112] 1568 5-9-11 **72**......................... RachaelGreen 6 28
(Alan Swinbank) *hld up: rdn and struggling over 2f out: sn btn* **7/1**

-006 **12** 8 **I'll Be Good**[13] 4613 4-9-2 **63**... MrsCBartley 11
(Robert Johnson) *led to over 2f out: rdn and sn wknd* **33/1**

1m 40.81s (0.81) **Going Correction** +0.175s/f (Good) **12** Ran SP% **122.5**
Speed ratings (Par 105): **102,97,95,94,93 93,93,89,87,82 77,69**
toteswingers 1&2 £10.10, 1&3 £7.40, 2&3 £19.30 CSF £41.94 CT £242.39 TOTE £5.00: £1.60, £4.00, £2.60; EX 56.40 Trifecta £567.80 Pool: £769.78 - 1.01 winning units.

Owner A Slack **Bred** Philip Hore Jnr **Trained** Hackthorpe, Cumbria

FOCUS
The feature race of the night and, helped by a good early pace, the best comparative time. The winner's best form since her second in this race last year.

5052 RONAN KEATING LIVE AFTER RACING TONIGHT H'CAP (PRO-AM LADY RIDERS' RACE) 1m 3f 107y
8:45 (8:45) (Class 5) (0-70,70) 4-Y-O+ **£3,234** (£962; £481; £240) **Stalls** High

Form RPR

40-0 **1** **Spin Cast**[65] 2886 5-10-6 **69**.. MissHBethell 1 77
(Philip Kirby) *chsd clr ldr: hdwy to ld over 2f out: drifted lft ins fnl f: pushed out towards fin* **8/1**

0250 **2** ¾ **Rayadour (IRE)**[46] 3504 4-9-9 **63**..........................(t) MissBeckySmith(5) 8 70
(Micky Hammond) *chsd ldrs: effrt over 2f out: wnt 2nd ins fnl f: kpt on: hld nr fin* **9/1**

5315 **3** 1 **Ebony Express**[23] 4293 4-10-4 **67**.................................. RachaelGreen 6 72
(Alan Swinbank) *prom: hdwy to chse wnr over 2f out to ins fnl f: kpt on same pce towards fin* **3/1**[2]

6353 **4** 3½ **Call Of Duty (IRE)**[30] 4052 8-9-6 **60**..................... MissEButterworth(5) 4 59
(Dianne Sayer) *t.k.h: hld up: pushed along and hdwy 2f out: kpt on fnl f: nrst fin* **6/1**[3]

0430 **5** 8 **Royal Sea (IRE)**[9] 4755 4-9-8 **57**........................(be) MissMMullineaux 11 42
(Michael Mullineaux) *hld up in midfield on outside: rdn over 3f out: no imp fnl 2f* **12/1**

0-00 **6** 1 **Grethel (IRE)**[14] 4376 9-9-2 **51** oh6.............................. MissJRRichards 9 35
(Alan Berry) *s.i.s: hld up: rdn over 3f out: nvr rchd ldrs* **50/1**

1-00 **7** ¾ **Adili (IRE)**[52] 3301 4-9-13 **62**... KirstyMilczarek 5 45
(Brian Ellison) *prom: rdn and outpcd over 2f out: n.d after* **6/1**[3]

0 **8** ¾ **Sendiym (FR)**[14] 4110 6-9-13 **62**.........................(p) MissJoannaMason 7 43
(Dianne Sayer) *hld up: rdn and outpcd over 3f out: no imp fnl 2f* **25/1**

-003 **9** 7 **Rosselli (IRE)**[74] 2594 4-10-1 **64**.............................. MissHayleyMoore 3 33
(Mrs K Burke) *led and sn clr: rdn and hdd over 2f out: wknd over 1f out* **11/4**[1]

6044 **10** ½ **The Lodge Road (IRE)**[19] 4016 5-9-6 **55**...................... LucyAlexander 2 23
(Martin Todhunter) *hld up: struggling wl over 3f out: sn btn* **14/1**

2m 29.44s (6.34) **Going Correction** +0.175s/f (Good) **10** Ran SP% **121.5**
Speed ratings (Par 103): **83,82,81,79,73 72,72,71,66,66**
toteswingers 1&2 £18.10, 1&3 £9.70, 2&3 £9.20 CSF £81.13 CT £269.98 TOTE £12.10: £3.60, £3.00, £1.60; EX 80.60 Trifecta £426.80 Pool: £703.75 - 1.23 winning units.

Owner W A Bethell **Bred** P W Harris **Trained** Middleham, N Yorks

FOCUS
A modest middle-distance handicap but, as with the earlier stayers' race, it paid to race prominently, with the first three always in the first four. The form is rated around the runner-up to this year's form.

T/Plt: £172.50 to a £1 stake. Pool: £69,252.83 - 292.91 winning units T/Qpdt: £16.20 to a £1 stake. Pool: £6927.40 - 314.95 winning units RY

4538 RIPON (R-H)
Monday, August 5

OFFICIAL GOING: Good to soft (8.2)
Wind: Virtually nil Weather: Heavy cloud and showers

5053 BRITISH STALLION STUDS EBF MAIDEN FILLIES' STKS 6f
2:15 (2:17) (Class 5) 2-Y-O **£3,881** (£1,155; £577; £288) **Stalls** High

Form RPR

250 **1** **Khalice**[16] 4528 2-9-0 71.. TonyHamilton 4 75+
(Richard Fahey) *sn led stands' side gp: effrt 2f out: rdn over 1f out: edgd rt and drvn to ld overall ins fnl f: kpt on wl* **3/1**[1]

6666 **2** 1¼ **Rough Courte (IRE)**[9] 4747 2-9-0 81................................ SamHitchcott 8 71
(Mick Channon) *in tch stands' side: hdwy over 2f out: sn rdn and styd on fnl f: 2nd of 10 in gp* **4/1**[2]

2 **3** 1 **Margrets Gift**[47] 3476 2-9-0 0...................................... DavidAllan 3 68
(Tim Easterby) *trckd ldr far side: led that gp and overall ldr over 2f out: rdn over 1f out: hdd and one pce ins fnl f* **9/2**[3]

662 **4** 7 **Omanome (IRE)**[17] 4470 2-9-0 67................................... DanielTudhope 1 47
(David O'Meara) *overall ldr far side: rdn along and hdd over 2f out: grad wknd: 2nd of 3 in gp* **7/1**

02 **5** 6 **Sukari Gold (IRE)**[12] 4616 2-9-0 0................................ GrahamLee 12 29
(Kevin Ryan) *prom stands' side: rdn along wl over 2f out: sn one pce: 3rd of 10 in gp* **10/1**

6 2¾ **Lady Dancer (IRE)** 2-9-0 0.. AndrewElliott 11 21
(George Moore) *towards rr stands' side: sme hdwy 2f out: n.d: 4th of 10 in gp* **40/1**

7 2½ **Tell Me When** 2-9-0 0... MickyFenton 2 13
(Brian Rothwell) *chsd ldng pair far side: rdn along 1/2-way: sn outpcd and bhd: 3rd of 3 in gp* **66/1**

56 **8** ½ **Ivy Trump**[17] 4497 2-9-0 0....................................... AndrewMullen 10 12
(Michael Appleby) *prom stands' side: rdn along over 2f out: sn wknd: 5th of 10 in gp* **10/1**

66 **9** ½ **Moving Waves (IRE)**[17] 4505 2-9-0 0........................... RobertWinston 6 10
(Ollie Pears) *dwlt and a in rr stands' side: 6th of 10 in gp* **20/1**

10 1¼ **Madame Katie (IRE)** 2-8-11 0................................. DeclanCannon(3) 5 7
(Nigel Tinkler) *wnt lft s: a in rr stands' side: 7th of 10 in gp* **66/1**

00 **11** 2 **Hoof's So Lucky**[17] 4505 2-9-0 0.................................. GrahamGibbons 7 1
(Michael Easterby) *a towards rr stands' side: 8th of 10 in gp* **33/1**

12 ½ **Pacquita** 2-9-0 0.. FrannyNorton 13
(Mark Johnston) *dwlt: sn chsng ldrs stands' side: rdn along 1/2-way: sn wknd: 9th of 10 in gp* **6/1**

13 6 **Ponty Pursuit** 2-9-0 0.. DuranFentiman 9
(Tim Easterby) *dwlt: a in rr stands' side: 10th of 10 in gp* **33/1**

1m 13.8s (0.80) **Going Correction** -0.05s/f (Good) **13** Ran SP% **124.2**
Speed ratings (Par 91): **92,90,89,79,71 68,64,64,63,61 59,58,50**
toteswingers 1&2 £4.50, 1&3 £3.90, 2&3 £4.40 CSF £14.56 TOTE £2.80: £1.10, £1.60, £2.30; EX 19.30 Trifecta £102.00 Pool: £2743.05 - 20.15 winning units.

Owner The G-Guck Group **Bred** Limestone And Tara Studs **Trained** Musley Bank, N Yorks

FOCUS
Rail on bend from back straight to home straight moved out 3m adding about 7yds to races on Round course. After a wet morning, the ground was changed from good to good to soft, with a blustery wind helping runners down the home straight. Some fair form on offer for this fillies' maiden and with the yearling bonus on offer it was sure to be competitive. There was a difference of opinion between those at the head of the market with the winner (drawn in stall 4) coming across to the nearside, and the runner-up (stall 3) heading a group of three to race on the far side. Straightforward form.

5054 CHILDREN'S AIR AMBULANCE SERVICE (S) H'CAP 5f
2:45 (2:45) (Class 6) (0-65,60) 3-Y-O **£2,587** (£770; £384; £192) **Stalls** High

Form RPR
6004 **1** **Edith Anne**[20] 4377 3-9-5 **58**..[1] MickyFenton 11 64
(Paul Midgley) *cl up on inner: effrt 2f out: sn rdn: styd on to ld ins fnl f: sn drvn and edgd rt: kpt on wl towards fin* **4/1**[2]
4353 **2** ½ **Coconut Kisses**[21] 4353 3-9-0 **60**.................................... RyanWhile(7) 3 64
(Bill Turner) *cl up: led 1/2-way: rdn wl over 1f out: drvn and hdd ins fnl f: carried rt: kpt on* **6/1**[3]
3030 **3** ½ **Done Dreaming (IRE)**[20] 4371 3-9-3 **56**......................... TonyHamilton 7 58
(Richard Fahey) *chsd ldrs: rdn along over 2f out and sltly outpcd: styd on wl u.p fnl f: nrst fin* **7/1**
1-60 **4** 2 **Twilight Pearl**[42] 3638 3-9-7 **60**..(b) DavidAllan 2 55
(Tim Easterby) *sn led: hdd 1/2-way and sn pushed along: rdn wl over 1f out: sn one pce* **6/1**[3]
0660 **5** nse **Moss The Boss (IRE)**[18] 4430 3-8-1 **45**............... ShirleyTeasdale(5) 10 40
(Paul Midgley) *towards rr: hdwy on inner 2f out: sn rdn and kpt on fnl f: nrst fin* **20/1**
2032 **6** ½ **Chloe's Dream (IRE)**[18] 4448 3-9-0 **60**......................... RowanScott(7) 9 53
(Ann Duffield) *chsd ldrs: swtchd rt to outer 2f out: sn rdn and one pce* **9/4**[1]
5050 **7** 10 **Poppy Bond**[23] 4290 3-8-11 **50**...................................... PaulMulrennan 8 7
(Chris Fairhurst) *a outpcd in rr* **14/1**
0-06 **8** 5 **Swift Code (IRE)**[12] 4627 3-8-3 **45**............................ DeclanCannon(3) 4
(Nigel Tinkler) *a outpcd in rr* **66/1**
3025 **9** 76 **Queen Flush (IRE)**[15] 4558 3-9-2 **55**..........................(b) AdrianNicholls 6
(David Nicholls) *chsd ldrs: rdn along 1/2-way: drvn whn lost action wl over 1f out and sn heavily eased* **13/2**

59.79s (-0.21) **Going Correction** -0.05s/f (Good) **9** Ran SP% **118.1**
Speed ratings (Par 98): **99,98,97,94,94 93,77,69,**
toteswingers 1&2 £5.60, 1&3 £5.30, 2&3 £4.80 CSF £28.99 CT £165.73 TOTE £3.80: £1.70, £2.00, £2.10; EX 29.30 Trifecta £180.80 Pool: £2387.34 - 9.90 winning units.There were no bids for the winner.
Owner David Mann **Bred** M Kerr-Dineen **Trained** Westow, N Yorks
■ Stewards' Enquiry : Rowan Scott two-day ban: failed to ride out four fourth (19-20 Aug)

FOCUS
A weak selling handicap for 3yos.

5055 RIPONBET PLACE6 H'CAP 1m 1f 170y
3:15 (3:15) (Class 4) (0-85,83) 3-Y-O+ **£4,725** (£1,414; £707; £354; £176) **Stalls** Low

Form RPR
5233 **1** **Triple Eight (IRE)**[16] 4542 5-9-0 **69**.........................(b) MichaelO'Connell 4 82+
(Philip Kirby) *trckd ldrs on inner: pushed along wl over 2f out: effrt and n.m.r wl over 1f out: sn swtchd lft to outer and rdn: styd on to ld ent fnl f: sn clr* **17/2**
-531 **2** 5 **Dame Nellie Melba**[12] 4629 3-8-9 **73**............................. FrannyNorton 2 76
(Mark Johnston) *trckd ldr: hdwy and cl up over 3f out: led wl over 2f out: rdn wl over 1f out: hdd ent fnl f: kpt on same pce* **10/11**[1]
1064 **3** 1 ¾ **San Cassiano (IRE)**[16] 4542 6-9-12 **81**......................... JamesSullivan 3 80
(Ruth Carr) *led: rdn along 3f out: sn hdd and cl up: drvn and rallied to have ev ch over 1f out: one pce ins fnl f* **8/1**
0-00 **4** nk **Persian Peril**[76] 2552 9-9-7 **76**.................................... RobertWinston 5 75
(Alan Swinbank) *hld up in rr: hdwy over 3f out: rdn to chal on outer over 2f out: drvn wl over 1f out and sn one pce* **25/1**
5554 **5** 12 **Patently (IRE)**[10] 4721 3-8-5 **69**..(t) LiamJones 8 43
(Brian Meehan) *chsd ldng pair: cl up on outer 1/2-way: rdn along 3f out: sn wknd* **7/1**[3]
501- **6** 8 **Braveheart Move (IRE)**[366] 4823 7-10-0 **83**.................. PaulMulrennan 1 41
(Geoffrey Harker) *stdd s: hld up: a in rr: bhd fnl 2f* **25/1**
6306 **7** 22 **Amaze**[78] 2478 5-10-0 **83**... DaleSwift 7
(Brian Ellison) *chsd ldrs: rdn along after 3f: rn in snatches: drvn 3f out: sn wknd and bhd* **4/1**[2]

2m 5.11s (-0.29) **Going Correction** +0.125s/f (Good)
WFA 3 from 5yo+ 9lb **7** Ran SP% **114.2**
Speed ratings (Par 105): **106,102,100,100,90 84,66**
toteswingers 1&2 £2.50, 1&3 £2.60, 2&3 £2.50 CSF £16.73 CT £64.81 TOTE £8.60: £2.50, £1.90; EX 19.40 Trifecta £75.60 Pool: £2787.99 - 27.63 winning units.
Owner The Well Oiled Partnership **Bred** Moyglare Stud Farm Ltd **Trained** Middleham, N Yorks

FOCUS
An interesting 1m2f handicap with an in-form 3yo filly taking on some older geldings who have been around the block.

5056 ARMSTRONG MEMORIAL H'CAP 6f
3:45 (3:49) (Class 3) (0-95,95) 3-Y-O **£7,561** (£2,263; £1,131; £566; £282) **Stalls** High

Form RPR
2010 **1** **Spinatrix**[37] 3823 5-9-7 **95**..................................(p) ConnorBeasley(5) 10 107
(Michael Dods) *chsd ldr whn sltly hmpd after 1f: trckd ldrs: rdn along wl over 1f out: swtchd rt and hdwy to chal over 1f out: rdn to ld jst ins fnl f: drvn out* **4/1**[3]
-066 **2** ½ **Pearl Ice**[37] 3823 5-9-5 **88**.. GrahamGibbons 1 98
(David Barron) *prom: swtchd lft to join ldr after 1f: cl up: rdn to ld briefly ent fnl f: sn hdd and edgd rt: drvn: kpt on* **3/1**[2]
0205 **3** nk **Nameitwhatyoulike**[9] 4778 4-9-5 **88**.............................. PaulMulrennan 4 97
(Michael Easterby) *qckly away and sn swtchd lft to stands' rail: led: rdn along wl over 1f out: drvn: hdd and edgd rt ent fnl f: kpt on same pce* **9/1**
1036 **4** 2 ¼ **Right Touch**[44] 3566 3-8-4 **77**... BarryMcHugh 9 78
(Richard Fahey) *trckd ldrs: effrt 2f out: sn rdn and kpt on same pce ent fnl f* **12/1**
4020 **5** nk **Misplaced Fortune**[17] 4472 8-9-6 **89**.................................(v) DaleSwift 6 90
(Nigel Tinkler) *towards rr: rdn along and hdwy on inner over 1f out: kpt on fnl f: nrst fin* **10/1**
4010 **6** ½ **Fitz Flyer (IRE)**[9] 4780 7-9-5 **88**................................(v) TonyHamilton 12 88
(David Nicholls) *chsd ldrs on inner: rdn along 2f out: sn drvn and no imp* **20/1**
-400 **7** 1 ¼ **Emilio Largo**[23] 4297 5-9-11 **94**...............................(t) FrederikTylicki 3 90
(James Fanshawe) *towards rr: rdn along and sme hdwy on outer 1/2-way: sn drvn and n.d* **11/4**[1]
0000 **8** 1 ½ **Mister Manannan (IRE)**[6] 4860 6-9-2 **85**..................(p) AdrianNicholls 2 76
(David Nicholls) *a towards rr* **25/1**
6040 **9** 1 ¼ **Bachotheque (IRE)**[30] 4056 3-8-6 **79**.......................... DuranFentiman 5 65
(Tim Easterby) *in tch: hdwy to chse ldrs over 2f out: sn rdn and wknd over 1f out* **20/1**
0000 **10** 1 ¾ **Klynch**[27] 4138 7-9-2 **85**...(b) JamesSullivan 8 66
(Ruth Carr) *trckd ldrs: effrt 2f out: sn rdn and wknd over 1f out* **20/1**

1m 11.5s (-1.50) **Going Correction** -0.05s/f (Good)
WFA 3 from 4yo+ 4lb **10** Ran SP% **116.6**
Speed ratings (Par 107): **108,107,106,103,103 102,101,99,97,95**
toteswingers 1&2 £3.40, 1&3 £6.30, 2&3 £5.50 CSF £15.34 CT £103.69 TOTE £4.10: £1.50, £1.60, £2.70; EX 20.60 Trifecta £122.30 Pool: £2747.63 - 16.83 winning units.
Owner Mrs J W Hutchinson & Mrs P A Knox **Bred** T K & Mrs P A Knox **Trained** Denton, Co Durham
■ Stewards' Enquiry : Connor Beasley trainer said, regarding the apparent improvement of form, that the mare benefitted from a short break and runs well at Ripon

FOCUS
The feature on the card was an ultra-competitive sprint handicap with plenty of the runners having already recorded successes at the track. Bedloe's Island refused to go in the stalls.

5057 RIPONBET BET PLACE ONLY H'CAP 5f
4:15 (4:16) (Class 4) (0-85,85) 3-Y-O **£4,851** (£1,443; £721; £360) **Stalls** High

Form RPR
1134 **1** **Bondesire**[9] 4757 3-9-2 **80**.. DanielTudhope 6 91+
(David O'Meara) *led: rdn along and hdd 2f out: sn n.m.r and swtchd rt: drvn to chal ent fnl f: styd on to ld last 75yds* **3/1**[2]
2113 **2** ½ **Jofranka**[10] 4734 3-8-9 **73**... GrahamGibbons 1 82
(David Barron) *cl up: rdn to ld 2f out and sn edgd lft: jnd and drvn ent fnl f: hdd and no ex last 75yds* **6/4**[1]
3602 **3** 3 ½ **Angus Og**[28] 4112 3-9-4 **82**.. RobertWinston 7 78
(Mrs K Burke) *in tch: hdwy 1/2-way: rdn wl over 1f out and ev ch tl drvn and one pce ent fnl f* **5/1**[3]
3042 **4** 2 ¾ **Rhagori Aur**[17] 4478 3-8-13 **77**...................................(b) PaulMulrennan 4 64
(Bryan Smart) *chsd ldrs: rdn along and outpcd 2f out: kpt on fnl f: n.d* **8/1**
4000 **5** nk **Lady Ibrox**[37] 3802 3-9-7 **85**.. DaleSwift 2 70
(Alan Brown) *chsd ldrs: hdwy 2f out: sn rdn and wknd appr fnl f* **8/1**
0250 **6** 8 **Bapak Sayang (USA)**[10] 4734 3-9-2 **80**.......................... GrahamLee 5 37
(Kevin Ryan) *stmbld s: in rr and rdn along 1/2-way: sn outpcd* **11/1**

58.95s (-1.05) **Going Correction** -0.05s/f (Good) **6** Ran SP% **112.2**
Speed ratings (Par 102): **106,105,99,95,94 81**
toteswingers 1&2 £2.40, 1&3 £2.10, 2&3 £1.70 CSF £7.93 TOTE £2.80: £1.10, £2.10; EX 8.80 Trifecta £30.30 Pool: £3074.72 - 75.93 winning units.
Owner Geoff & Sandra Turnbull **Bred** A C M Spalding **Trained** Nawton, N Yorks

FOCUS
Some in-form 3yos lined up for this handicap run over the minimum trip.

5058 SIS LIVE MAIDEN STKS 1m 4f 10y
4:45 (4:46) (Class 5) 3-Y-O+ **£3,234** (£962; £481; £240) **Stalls** Low

Form RPR
524 **1** **Battalion (IRE)**[32] 3989 3-9-3 79................................ GrahamGibbons 2 88+
(William Haggas) *trckd ldng pair: swtchd lft and hdwy to ld 3f out: rdn clr wl over 1f out: kpt on* **5/6**[1]
4 **2** 4 ½ **Certification (IRE)**[12] 4633 3-9-3 0................................ FrannyNorton 1 79+
(Mark Johnston) *t.k.h early: hld up in rr: hdwy 4f out: chsd wnr 2f out: rdn, rn green and hung rt wl over 1f out: sn no imp* **6/1**[3]
0 **3** 10 **Aryizad (IRE)**[86] 2279 4-9-9 0..................................... RobertWinston 3 58
(Alan Swinbank) *trckd ldng pair: hdwy to trck ldr after 2f: cl up 3f out: sn rdn and wknd 2f out* **50/1**
2323 **4** ½ **The Welsh Wizard (IRE)**[43] 3606 3-9-3 78........................ GrahamLee 5 62
(Charles Hills) *led: pushed along 4f out: rdn and hdd 3f out: sn drvn and hdwy* **6/4**[2]

2m 37.83s (1.13) **Going Correction** +0.125s/f (Good)
WFA 3 from 4yo+ 11lb **4** Ran SP% **110.8**
Speed ratings (Par 103): **101,98,91,91**
CSF £6.39 TOTE £6.20; EX 4.90 Trifecta £18.90 Pool: £3020.87 - 119.74 winning units.
Owner Sheikh Juma Dalmook Al Maktoum **Bred** Kildaragh Stud **Trained** Newmarket, Suffolk

FOCUS
Just the four runners in this middle-distance maiden, but a couple of them had shown themselves capable of winning a race like this.

5059 THEAKSTON TERRACE BAR H'CAP 1m 4f 10y
5:15 (5:15) (Class 5) (0-75,74) 3-Y-O+ **£3,234** (£962; £481; £240) **Stalls** Low

Form RPR
0202 **1** **Choisan (IRE)**[8] 4804 4-10-0 **74**.................................... DuranFentiman 4 82
(Tim Easterby) *led 3f: chsd ldr tl led again 4f out: rdn over 2f out: drvn over 1f out: kpt on gamely u.p towards fin* **7/2**[1]
3101 **2** nk **Maybeme**[14] 4584 7-9-3 **63**......................................(p) AndrewElliott 2 71
(Neville Bycroft) *hld up: hdwy 4f out: chsd ldrs 3f out: rdn over 1f out: drvn to chse wnr ins fnl f: ev ch tl edgd rt and no ex towards fin* **5/1**[2]
032 **3** 3 ½ **Bavarian Nordic (USA)**[8] 4809 8-8-11 **57**..........(v) FrannyNorton 10 59
(Richard Whitaker) *trckd ldrs: hdwy 4f out: cl up 3f out: rdn to chal wl over 1f out and ev ch tl drvn and one pce ent fnl f* **7/2**[1]
3364 **4** ¾ **Bright Applause**[6] 4851 5-9-12 **72**.................................. BarryMcHugh 3 73
(Tracy Waggott) *trckd ldrs: hdwy 3f out: n.m.r 2f out: sn rdn: drvn and one pce appr fnl f* **7/1**[3]
11-5 **5** 1 ½ **Gosforth Park**[8] 4809 7-9-9 **69**.. DavidAllan 9 67
(Mel Brittain) *chsd ldr: led after 3f: rdn along and hdd 4f out: drvn along on inner 3f out: grad wknd* **7/2**[1]
4260 **6** 5 **Badea**[8] 4809 4-9-8 **68**...(b) TonyHamilton 6 58
(Richard Fahey) *dwlt and in rr tl sme hdwy fnl 2f: nvr a factor* **12/1**
3060 **7** nse **Tinseltown**[6] 4853 7-9-5 **65**.......................................(p) MickyFenton 8 55
(Brian Rothwell) *t.k.h: trckd ldrs: hdwy and cl up 1/2-way: rdn along 3f out: sn drvn and wknd* **20/1**
3210 **8** 1 ½ **Honoured (IRE)**[41] 3651 6-9-7 **67**................................(t) AndrewMullen 5 55
(Michael Appleby) *hld up towards rr: effrt 4f out: sn rdn along and no hdwy* **10/1**
20-0 **9** 1 ¾ **Ay Tay Tate (IRE)**[18] 4435 7-8-9 **62**.....................(p) RobJFitzpatrick(7) 1 47
(Noel Wilson) *trckd ldrs on inner: pushed along 4f out: rdn 3f out and sn wknd* **25/1**

2m 40.11s (3.41) **Going Correction** +0.125s/f (Good) **9** Ran SP% **121.2**
Speed ratings (Par 103): **93,92,90,89,88 85,85,84,83**
CSF £22.41 CT £67.38 TOTE £4.10: £1.90, £1.70, £1.30; EX 18.00 Trifecta £45.40 Pool: £2342.80 - 38.63 winning units.
Owner Croft, Taylor & Hebdon **Bred** David A Cahill **Trained** Great Habton, N Yorks

FOCUS
There was an exciting finish to this ordinary handicap and, not for the first time on the card, a course specialist proved successful.

T/Plt: £31.30 to a £1 stake. Pool: £72,199.57 - 1680.17 winning units T/Qpdt: £6.30 to a £1 stake. Pool: £4276.62 - 499.70 winning units JR

4827 WINDSOR (R-H)

Monday, August 5

OFFICIAL GOING: Good to soft changing to soft after race 1 (6.00)

Wind: Light, behind Weather: Heavy rain from 4.00 until just before racing; stopped after race 2

5060 CORAL.CO.UK H'CAP — 5f 10y

6:00 (6:00) (Class 5) (0-70,70) 3-Y-O+ — **£2,587** (£770; £384; £192) **Stalls** Low

Form — RPR

05-4 **1** **Ladweb**[46] 3509 3-8-11 **60** .... ChrisCatlin 9 — 71
(John Gallagher) *racd in centre and on terms: drifted to far side 1/2-way: overall ldr over 1f out: drvn and styd on wl* **25/1**

5504 **2** 2 ¾ **Macdillon**[17] 4487 7-9-2 **67** .... (t) MichaelJMMurphy(5) 1 — 69
(Stuart Kittow) *sn pushed along to chse ldrs nr side: swtchd to centre after 2f: styd on u.p to take 2nd ins fnl f: no imp on wnr* **9/4**[1]

5444 **3** 1 ¼ **Pharoh Jake**[12] 4635 5-8-5 **51** oh1 .... WilliamCarson 6 — 49
(John Bridger) *overall ldr nr side: styd alone nr side as rest swtchd: stl probable ldr 2f out: sn hdd: edgd lft and one pce jst over 1f out* **25/1**

-050 **4** ¾ **Royal Award**[28] 4123 4-9-4 **69** .... MatthewLawson(5) 5 — 64
(Jonathan Portman) *wl in rr: swtchd to centre after 2f: drvn and kpt on same pce fr over 1f out: n.d* **20/1**

2402 **5** 1 ½ **Welease Bwian (IRE)**[6] 4866 4-8-13 **59** .... (b[1]) AndreaAtzeni 11 — 49
(Stuart Williams) *immediately taken to far side and nt on terms: clsd against far rail 2f out: fdd fnl f* **10/3**[3]

6031 **6** 2 ¼ **Dangerous Age**[12] 4635 3-8-13 **62** .... RyanMoore 10 — 42
(J W Hills) *racd in centre and on terms w ldrs: drifted across to far side 1/2-way: wknd wl over 1f out* **3/1**[2]

0531 **7** 1 ¾ **Dreams Of Glory**[20] 4369 5-9-6 **66** .... DavidProbert 7 — 41
(Ron Hodges) *pressed ldr nr side: swtchd to centre after 2f: on terms 2f out: wknd over 1f out* **8/1**

6556 **8** 1 ¾ **Jarrow (IRE)**[10] 4712 6-8-13 **66** ....[1] WillPettis(7) 2 — 35
(Milton Bradley) *blindfold off late and slowly away: a wl in rr: swtchd to centre 1/2-way: no prog* **14/1**

-145 **9** 3 ¾ **Ada Lovelace**[152] 894 3-9-7 **70** .... JimmyQuinn 4 — 24
(Dean Ivory) *towards rr: swtchd fr nr to far side 1/2-way: toiling after* **20/1**

1m 1.05s (0.75) **Going Correction** +0.175s/f (Good)
WFA 3 from 4yo+ 3lb — **9** Ran SP% **113.8**
Speed ratings (Par 103): **101,96,94,93,91 87,84,81,75**
toteswingers 1&2 £19.40, 1&3 £18.70, 2&3 £13.00 CSF £76.85 CT £1474.27 TOTE £29.60: £6.20, £1.40, £3.90; EX 123.90 Trifecta £1008.10 Pool: £1401.05 - 1.04 winning units.
Owner Adweb Ltd **Bred** Adweb Ltd **Trained** Chastleton, Oxon

FOCUS
Inner of straight dolled out 11yds at 6f and 6yds at winning post. Top bend dolled out 5yds from normal inner configuration, adding 22yds to races of 1m and beyond. The rain began bucketing down a few hours before racing with around 5-6mm falling on already watered ground, resulting in two going changes. The ground was expected to ride on the soft side of good and it was no surprise the far-side route was explored in the opening sprint handicap. That proved the place to be in a muddling affair and they got sorted out inside the final 2f. Hard to know how literally to take this form.

5061 BRITISH STALLION STUDS EBF MAIDEN FILLIES' STKS — 6f

6:30 (6:32) (Class 5) 2-Y-O — **£2,911** (£866; £432; £216) **Stalls** Low

Form — RPR

2002 **1** **Hoku (IRE)**[4] 4924 2-9-0 83 .... HarryBentley 11 — 83
(Olly Stevens) *pressed ldr: led 1/2-way: shkn up and drew rt away fr 2f out* **11/10**[1]

2 7 **Laurelita (IRE)** 2-9-0 0 .... PatCosgrave 14 — 62+
(George Baker) *prom: rdn 2f out: no ch w wnr but kpt on to take 2nd ins fnl f* **40/1**

3 1 ¼ **Perfect Alchemy (IRE)** 2-9-0 0 .... JimCrowley 3 — 58+
(Ralph Beckett) *hld up in tch: gd prog fr 1/2-way to chse wnr 2f out: rn green and no imp: lost 2nd ins fnl f* **5/1**[2]

4 nk **Veiled Intrigue** 2-8-9 0 .... AmyScott(5) 4 — 57+
(Henry Candy) *hld up at rr of ldng gp: pushed along 1/2-way: styd on wl fr jst over 1f out: gng on at fin* **16/1**

05 **5** 2 **Pink Mirage (IRE)**[14] 4589 2-8-9 0 .... MatthewLawson(5) 5 — 51
(Jonathan Portman) *wl in rr: gd prog jst over 2f out to chse ldrs over 1f out: hanging and no imp after: fdd* **16/1**

6 ¾ **Yeah Baby (IRE)** 2-9-0 0 ....[1] WilliamCarson 7 — 49
(Charles Hills) *slowly away: wl off the pce in last: nudged along and kpt on steadily fr over 2f out: nt disgracd* **25/1**

7 1 ¾ **Abatis (USA)** 2-9-0 0 .... SteveDrowne 12 — 44
(Charles Hills) *slowly away: off the pce in last pair: pushed along 1/2-way: late prog fr over 1f out* **8/1**[3]

00 **8** 1 ¼ **My Secret Dream (FR)**[36] 3853 2-9-0 0 .... DavidProbert 6 — 40
(Ron Hodges) *led: tk field along in centre: hdd 1/2-way: chsd wnr to 2f out: wknd* **100/1**

0 **9** 1 ½ **Rosina Jay (IRE)**[19] 4408 2-9-0 0 .... JamesDoyle 8 — 36
(Clive Cox) *prom tl wknd jst over 2f out* **10/1**

10 shd **Goodwood Storm** 2-9-0 0 .... RichardHughes 1 — 35
(William Knight) *chsd ldrs: shkn up over 2f out: wknd wl over 1f out* **14/1**

0 **11** nk **Joybringer (IRE)**[52] 3288 2-9-0 0 .... RyanMoore 15 — 34
(Richard Hannon) *s.i.s: rcvrd to chse ldrs: shkn up 1/2-way: wknd 2f out* **10/1**

0 **12** 6 **Trinity Lorraine (IRE)**[17] 4491 2-9-0 0 .... LiamKeniry 10 — 16
(Alan Bailey) *nvr bttr than midfield: wknd 2f out* **50/1**

6000 **13** 10 **Movie Magic**[23] 4304 2-9-0 40 .... ChrisCatlin 2
(John Bridger) *a in rr: t.o* **100/1**

1m 13.08s (0.08) **Going Correction** +0.175s/f (Good) — **13** Ran SP% **122.2**
Speed ratings (Par 91): **106,96,95,94,91 90,88,86,84,84 84,76,63**
toteswingers 1&2 £13.90, 1&3 £3.40, 2&3 £29.30 CSF £73.36 TOTE £2.10: £1.10, £8.70, £2.30; EX 71.60 Trifecta £439.20 Pool: £1408.45 - 2.40 winning units.
Owner Sheikh Suhaim Al Thani **Bred** Mark Hanly **Trained** Chiddingfold, Surrey

FOCUS
Little strength in depth to this fillies' maiden, in which the entire field went far side, and the winner routed them. She's rated back to her best, but this could underestimate her.

5062 RITTAL RIMATRIXS H'CAP — 6f

7:00 (7:01) (Class 4) (0-85,85) 3-Y-O+ — **£4,851** (£1,443; £721; £360) **Stalls** Low

Form — RPR

5332 **1** **Kinglami**[24] 4237 4-8-12 **74** .... (p) ThomasBrown(3) 5 — 84
(Brian Gubby) *pressed ldr: led over 2f out: drvn over 1f out: styd on wl and in command fnl f* **11/4**[1]

3266 **2** 2 ¼ **Ashpan Sam**[26] 4165 4-9-5 **78** .... JamesDoyle 8 — 81
(John Spearing) *t.k.h: hld up bhd ldrs: rdn to go 2nd wl over 1f out: cl enough sn after: no imp fnl f* **8/1**

3421 **3** 1 ½ **Bajan Bear**[5] 4884 5-9-3 **76** 6ex .... LiamKeniry 4 — 74
(Michael Blanshard) *hld up in tch: prog 2f out: rdn to chse ldng pair over 1f out: sn outpcd* **3/1**[2]

2550 **4** 2 **Ocean Legend (IRE)**[11] 4685 8-8-9 **68** .... JimmyQuinn 1 — 60
(Tony Carroll) *cl up: drvn 2f out: steadily wknd over 1f out* **25/1**

1401 **5** 3 ½ **School Fees**[25] 4210 4-9-10 **83** .... RyanMoore 10 — 64
(Olly Stevens) *s.i.s: sn rcvrd to press ldrs: wknd 2f out* **11/4**[1]

000- **6** 4 ½ **R Woody**[264] 7716 6-9-7 **80** .... SteveDrowne 7 — 46
(Robert Cowell) *restrained into last sn after s: shkn up and wknd over 1f out: sn eased* **25/1**

5012 **7** 2 ½ **Arctic Lynx (IRE)**[11] 4690 6-9-9 **82** .... JimCrowley 6 — 40
(Robert Cowell) *led to over 2f out: wknd qckly wl over 1f out: eased fnl f* **6/1**[3]

1m 13.06s (0.06) **Going Correction** +0.175s/f (Good)
WFA 3 from 4yo+ 4lb — **7** Ran SP% **111.4**
Speed ratings (Par 105): **106,103,101,98,93 87,84**
toteswingers 1&2 £3.40, 1&3 £2.50, 2&3 £4.40 CSF £23.63 CT £66.82 TOTE £3.20: £1.90, £3.70; EX 20.60 Trifecta £81.20 Pool: £1169.84 - 10.79 winning units.
Owner Brian Gubby **Bred** Cheveley Park Stud Ltd **Trained** Bagshot, Surrey

FOCUS
A modest sprint handicap. They went an ordinary early pace and they finished fairly strung out. This rates a personal best from the winner.

5063 DOWNLOAD CORAL MOBILE FROM THE APP STORE H'CAP — 1m 67y

7:30 (7:30) (Class 4) (0-85,84) 3-Y-O+ — **£4,851** (£1,443; £721; £360) **Stalls** Low

Form — RPR

000- **1** **Bay Knight (IRE)**[275] 7559 7-9-10 **80** .... JamesDoyle 4 — 88
(Sean Curran) *mde virtually all: rdn jst over 2f out: edgd lft wl over 1f out: asserted fnl f* **20/1**

-025 **2** 1 ¼ **Jack Who's He (IRE)**[14] 4593 4-9-5 **75** .... JimCrowley 7 — 80
(William Muir) *pressed wnr: rdn whn tighened up wl over 1f out: kpt on same pce fnl f and readily hld* **10/1**

6251 **3** ½ **Choral Festival**[35] 3900 7-9-6 **76** .... RyanMoore 6 — 80
(John Bridger) *broke wl but stdd into last pair: cl up: nt clr run against far rail over 1f out: kpt on same pce fnl f* **4/1**[2]

000 **4** 2 **Uncle Dermot (IRE)**[9] 4755 5-8-12 **68** .... WilliamCarson 5 — 67
(Brendan Powell) *hld up in last pair: cl enough whn nt clr run wl over 1f out: no prog after: fdd fnl f* **6/1**[3]

21-5 **5** 1 **Juvenal (IRE)**[6] 4859 4-10-0 **84** .... (p) RichardHughes 1 — 81
(Richard Hannon) *trckd ldng pair: pushed along over 2f out: rdn and nt qckn over 1f out: wknd and eased fnl f* **4/6**[1]

1m 45.07s (0.37) **Going Correction** +0.175s/f (Good)
WFA 3 from 4yo+ 7lb — **5** Ran SP% **108.1**
Speed ratings (Par 105): **105,103,103,101,100**
CSF £162.44 TOTE £22.60: £6.40, £4.10; EX 124.00 Trifecta £362.10 Pool: £921.43 - 1.90 winning units.
Owner Scuderia Vita Bella **Bred** Pat Roach **Trained** Hatford, Oxon

FOCUS
This was weakened by the three defections and it proved tactical. The field were closely grouped until the pace got serious at the top of the home straight. The form is rated around the second and third.

5064 GOOD LUCK ALEX MAIDEN STKS — 1m 2f 7y

8:00 (8:02) (Class 5) 3-4-Y-O — **£2,726** (£805; £402) **Stalls** Centre

Form — RPR

3-02 **1** **Zipp (IRE)**[49] 3417 3-8-13 78 .... JamesDoyle 7 — 82
(Charles Hills) *pressed ldr: taken to far rail over 2f out: rdn to ld wl over 1f out: r.o wl to draw clr fnl f* **9/2**[2]

0 **2** 3 ¼ **Sharareh**[58] 3116 3-8-13 0 .... RichardHughes 2 — 75
(Luca Cumani) *trckd ldng pair: rdn over 2f out: chal wl over 1f out: outpcd fnl f* **8/1**[3]

003 **3** 1 ¼ **Bohemian Dance (IRE)**[53] 3237 3-8-13 79 .... RyanMoore 10 — 73
(Sir Michael Stoute) *trckd ldrs: rdn in centre over 2f out: nt qckn and hld wl over 1f out: kpt on to take 3rd nr fin* **7/4**[1]

03 **4** ¾ **Calling**[36] 3860 3-8-13 0 .... FrankieDettori 3 — 71
(Brian Meehan) *mde most to wl over 1f out: steadily wknd* **20/1**

2 **5** 3 **Apparently**[34] 3923 3-9-4 0 .... MickaelBarzalona 4 — 70
(Charlie Appleby) *hld up in rr: shoved along over 4f out: no imp on ldrs 3f out: plugged on fnl 2f* **7/4**[1]

50 **6** ½ **Rocky Ride (IRE)**[20] 4381 3-8-6 0 .... DanielMuscutt(7) 8 — 64
(Andrew Balding) *in tch in midfield: pushed along and outpcd fr over 2f out: one pce after* **40/1**

500- **7** 3 **Cape Samba**[399] 3711 4-9-10 68 .... ThomasBrown(3) 5 — 63
(Ismail Mohammed) *hld up in rr: shkn up over 3f out: sn outpcd: one pce and nvr on terms after* **33/1**

50 **8** nk **Calon Lad (IRE)**[14] 4590 3-9-4 0 .... PatCosgrave 9 — 62
(George Baker) *hld up in last trio: shuffled along and outpcd by ldrs 3f out: nvr on terms after* **66/1**

9 1 ¾ **Gentlemax (FR)** 3-8-13 0 .... MichaelJMMurphy(5) 6 — 59
(Alan Jarvis) *hld up in last: pushed along over 4f out and rn green: nvr on terms but kpt on fnl 2f* **50/1**

0 **10** 18 **Moreamore (IRE)**[38] 3764 3-8-13 0 .... JimCrowley 1 — 18
(Alan Jarvis) *chsd ldrs to over 4f out: sn wknd qckly: t.o* **66/1**

0 **11** 1 ½ **Aster's Approval**[19] 4404 3-9-4 0 .... DougieCostello 11 — 20
(Tim Vaughan) *prom tl wknd rapidly and hung bdly lft fr 3f out: t.o* **100/1**

2m 10.0s (1.30) **Going Correction** +0.175s/f (Good)
WFA 3 from 4yo 9lb — **11** Ran SP% **118.1**
Speed ratings (Par 103): **101,98,97,96,94 94,91,91,89,75 74**
toteswingers 1&2 £6.70, 1&3 £1.50, 2&3 £2.70 CSF £37.91 TOTE £4.60: £1.40, £2.40, £1.20; EX 35.20 Trifecta £147.60 Pool: £1820.74 - 9.25 winning units.
Owner Richard Morecombe & S E Sangster **Bred** Lynch Bages Ltd & Samac Ltd **Trained** Lambourn, Berks

FOCUS
Little strength in depth and underfoot conditions looked to find out the majority. A fair maiden although not up to the race's last two runnings.

5065 ANTHONY TAYLOR 50TH BIRTHDAY AMATEUR RIDERS' H'CAP 1m 3f 135y
8:30 (8:30) (Class 5) (0-75,75) 3-Y-O+ £2,495 (£774; £386; £193) Stalls Centre

Form RPR
-164 1 **Chocolate Block (IRE)**[30] 4049 3-8-9 56 oh1........... MissAliceMills(3) 6 68
(Pat Phelan) *trckd clr ldrs: clsd 4f out: led briefly 3f out: sn taken to far side: rdn to press ldr fr 2f out: led ins fnl f: hld on wl* **16/1**
653 2 *nk* **Luggers Hall (IRE)**[66] 2849 5-10-8 72.......................... MrChrisMartin(3) 8 83
(Tony Carroll) *hld up off the pce: clsd fr 5f out: taken to far side 3f out: overall ldr jst over 2f out: drvn and hdd ins fnl f: styd on: jst hld* **3/1**[1]
5353 3 4 1/2 **No Such Number**[18] 4437 5-10-11 72.........................(p) MrRossBirkett 5 76
(Julia Feilden) *trckd clr ldng pair: clsd 4f out: initially taken towards centre then bk to nr side 3f out: led gp 1f out: kpt on but no ch w pair on far side* **14/1**
6020 4 2 1/4 **Capitol Gain (IRE)**[18] 4440 4-9-13 67...................... MrORJSangster(7) 9 67
(Brian Meehan) *hld up: chsd clr ldng trio 7f out: taken to far side in st: cl up jst over 2f out: wknd over 1f out* **12/1**
145- 5 1/2 **Hyperlink (IRE)**[43] 6608 4-10-4 70.......................... MrAlexFerguson(5) 1 69
(Michael Bell) *t.k.h: trckd ldr at quick pce and clr of rest: styd nr side in st and led gp over 2f out to 1f out: fdd* **11/2**[2]
2432 6 2 1/2 **Royal Etiquette (IRE)**[36] 3865 6-10-0 61................(v) MissGAndrews 10 56
(Lawney Hill) *hld up in last pair early: prog 6f out: on terms and taken to far rail 3f out: wknd 2f out* **3/1**[1]
0040 7 1 3/4 **Missionaire (USA)**[43] 3169 6-9-6 58 ow1...................... MrDLevey(5) 14 51
(Tony Carroll) *hld up: clsd 4f out: on terms and taken to far side 3f out: wknd 2f out* **25/1**
4- 8 3/4 **Estinaad (USA)**[34] 3941 3-9-5 70.............................. MissJLambert(7) 12 61
(Brian Ellison) *a in rr: lost tch over 4f out: styd nr side in st: plugged on* **6/1**[3]
-310 9 3/4 **Teide Peak (IRE)**[46] 3504 4-9-13 65.......................... MrsRWilson(5) 13 55
(Paul D'Arcy) *hld up: clsd fr 4f out: taken to far side 3f out: sn wknd* **11/1**
0/0- 10 2 1/2 **Park Lane**[218] 2694 7-10-1 69.............................. MissMBishop-Peck(7) 7 55
(Noel Quinlan) *hld up: lost tch 5f out: wl bhd 4f out: styd nr side st: plugged on* **33/1**
50-0 11 31 **Urban Space**[14] 4591 7-10-0 66................................ MrGeorgeCrate(5) 3
(Tony Carroll) *led at str pce and spreadeagled field early: hdd & wknd rapidly 3f out: t.o* **20/1**

2m 31.57s (2.07) **Going Correction** +0.175s/f (Good)
WFA 3 from 4yo+ 11lb 11 Ran SP% 119.8
Speed ratings (Par 103): **100,99,96,95,94 93,92,91,91,89 68**
toteswingers 1&2 £16.10, 1&3 £12.90, 2&3 £8.90 CSF £63.62 CT £717.75 TOTE £12.50: £3.30, £1.50, £3.40; EX 79.90 Trifecta £550.70 Pool: £1043.60 - 1.42 winning units.
Owner Wood Hall Stud Limited **Bred** Wood Hall Stud Limited **Trained** Epsom, Surrey

FOCUS
A moderate handicap for amateur riders. There was a very strong early pace on and, despite split opinion in the home straight, it was again the far side that proved to be the best ground. A clear personal best from the winner.
T/Jkpt: Not won. T/Plt: £328.50 to a £1 stake. Pool: £114,479.70 - 254.35 winning units T/Qpdt: £84.10 to a £1 stake. Pool: £9151.38 - 80.50 winning units JN

4833 WOLVERHAMPTON (A.W) (L-H)
Monday, August 5

OFFICIAL GOING: Standard
Wind: Fresh behind Weather: Raining

5066 THE BLACK COUNTRY'S ONLY RACECOURSE NURSERY H'CAP 5f 20y(P)
2:30 (2:32) (Class 6) (0-60,60) 2-Y-O £1,940 (£577; £288; £144) Stalls Low

Form RPR
2051 1 **Lilo Lil**[9] 4749 2-9-7 60..(p) DavidProbert 5 66
(David C Griffiths) *chsd ldr: rdn to ld ins fnl f: r.o* **5/2**[1]
5042 2 1 3/4 **Anfield**[18] 4451 2-8-12 51.. PaoloSirigu 3 51
(Mick Quinn) *sn led: rdn over 1f out: hdd and unable qck ins fnl f* **10/1**
0655 3 2 **Paradise Child**[4] 4910 2-9-1 54.................................... LukeMorris 4 47
(Bill Turner) *sn pushed along and prom: rdn over 1f out: rdr dropped whip jst ins fnl f: styd on same pce* **9/1**
4005 4 2 **Maximilianthefirst**[19] 4412 2-8-4 48........................... RobertTart(5) 10 34
(P J O'Gorman) *mid-div: pushed along 1/2-way: hdwy over 1f out: styd on same pce fnl f* **16/1**
0400 5 *shd* **Patisserie**[16] 4538 2-9-1 54..(b[1]) TomEaves 9 39
(Ann Duffield) *sn pushed along in rr: rdn over 1f out: r.o ins fnl f: nvr nrr* **25/1**
0550 6 *nk* **Zac's Princess**[34] 3914 2-8-0 46..............................(t) ShelleyBirkett(7) 11 30
(Milton Bradley) *prom: rdn over 1f out: edgd lft and no ex fnl f* **66/1**
335 7 1 1/4 **Yellow Lady (IRE)**[27] 4142 2-9-3 56..........................(t) HarryBentley 12 36
(Olly Stevens) *hld up: shkn up over 1f out: kpt on ins fnl f: nvr on terms* **9/2**[2]
500 8 *nse* **John Lea (IRE)**[27] 4142 2-8-13 52.............................. MartinDwyer 1 31
(Derek Shaw) *chsd ldrs: rdn 1/2-way: wknd ins fnl f* **40/1**
005 9 1/2 **Kopkap**[40] 3681 2-9-2 55.. RoystonFfrench 8 33
(Ed McMahon) *chsd ldrs: rdn and nt clr run over 1f out: wknd ins fnl f* **8/1**
500 10 3 **Dawnfromthepast (IRE)**[41] 3659 2-8-8 47................. FergusSweeney 6 14
(Jamie Osborne) *s.i.s: a in rr* **14/1**
030 11 3 **Tinsill**[10] 4724 2-9-0 53...(v) SilvestreDeSousa 7 9
(Nigel Tinkler) *mid-div: sn drvn along: wknd over 1f out* **11/2**[3]
0644 12 1 3/4 **Faye Belle**[27] 4141 2-8-9 48.. JoeFanning 2
(Derek Shaw) *sn pushed along and a in rr* **14/1**
5400 13 1/2 **Brockholes Flyer (IRE)**[75] 2562 2-9-6 59................... SebSanders 13 7
(Brendan Powell) *s.i.s: drvn along 1/2-way: wknd over 1f out* **40/1**

1m 1.78s (-0.52) **Going Correction** -0.225s/f (Stan) 13 Ran SP% 121.8
Speed ratings (Par 92): **95,92,89,85,85 85,83,83,82,77 72,69,69**
toteswingers 1&2 £8.40, 1&3 £8.40, 2&3 £17.10 CSF £28.75 CT £179.29 TOTE £3.10: £2.30, £2.30, £3.40; EX 18.80 Trifecta £154.20 Pool: £27121.94 - 13.19 winning units.
Owner Mickley Stud,D C Griffiths & D Clarke **Bred** S And R Ewart **Trained** Bawtry, S Yorks

FOCUS
A very moderate nursery in which they went a decent gallop. The winner is rated back to her early-season mark.

5067 LIKE US ON FACEBOOK WOLVERHAMPTON RACECOURSE H'CAP 5f 20y(P)
3:00 (3:00) (Class 6) (0-65,65) 3-Y-O £1,940 (£577; £288; £144) Stalls Low

Form RPR
3100 1 **Little Eli**[28] 4114 3-8-6 55.. JasonHart(5) 1 63
(Eric Alston) *mde all: shkn up over 1f out: rdn out* **5/1**[3]
-503 2 1 1/4 **Compton Albion (IRE)**[13] 4607 3-8-4 53 ow2.............(p) RobertTart(5) 5 57+
(Jeremy Gask) *hld up: pushed along 1/2-way: hdwy u.p 1f out: sn hung lft: r.o: nt rch wnr* **9/2**[2]
2003 3 *shd* **Megaleka**[13] 4611 3-8-7 51.. JoeFanning 6 54
(Alan Bailey) *chsd wnr: rdn over 1f out: styd on same pce towards fin* **14/1**
-064 4 *shd* **Mandy Lexi (IRE)**[10] 4712 3-9-0 58.......................... SilvestreDeSousa 7 61
(Ian Williams) *chsd ldrs: n.m.r over 3f out: rdn over 1f out: r.o* **7/2**[1]
5045 5 1 3/4 **Cymeriad**[10] 4722 3-8-3 47..(b[1]) LukeMorris 8 44
(Michael Easterby) *chsd ldrs: edgd lft over 3f out: rdn over 1f out: styd on same pce ins fnl f* **10/1**
524 6 *hd* **Borough Boy (IRE)**[45] 3540 3-8-12 56........................(v) MartinDwyer 2 52
(Derek Shaw) *hld up: hdwy over 1f out: rdn whn hmpd ins fnl f: nt trble ldrs* **8/1**
-405 7 3/4 **Southern Sapphire**[102] 1771 3-7-13 50 ow2................ OisinMurphy(7) 3 43
(Kristin Stubbs) *sn pushed along in rr: kpt on ins fnl f: nvr nrr* **33/1**
4-00 8 *hd* **Shatin Secret**[60] 3025 3-8-13 60.............................. NeilFarley(3) 9 53
(Noel Wilson) *sn pushed along in rr: rdn 1/2-way: nvr trbld ldrs* **25/1**
0366 9 1/2 **Outbid**[40] 3679 3-9-2 60.. FergusSweeney 10 51
(Jamie Osborne) *prom: effrt over 1f out: hmpd ins fnl f: no ex* **33/1**
4466 10 25 **Hardy Blue (IRE)**[11] 4670 3-9-7 65............................. TomQueally 4
(Danielle McCormick) *sn outpcd* **7/2**[1]

1m 1.18s (-1.12) **Going Correction** -0.225s/f (Stan) 10 Ran SP% 115.9
Speed ratings (Par 98): **99,97,96,96,93 93,92,92,91,51**
toteswingers 1&2 £7.70, 1&3 £16.50, 2&3 £11.60 CSF £27.06 CT £298.25 TOTE £8.00: £2.00, £3.10, £3.10; EX 54.10 Trifecta £601.80 Pool: £1855.19 - 2.31 winning units.
Owner Whittle Racing Partnership **Bred** J E Jackson **Trained** Longton, Lancs

FOCUS
A modest 3yo sprint handicap in which they went a good clip.

5068 DOWNLOAD OUR IPHONE APP NURSERY H'CAP 7f 32y(P)
3:30 (3:31) (Class 5) (0-70,70) 2-Y-O £2,911 (£866; £432; £216) Stalls High

Form RPR
640 1 **Lady Marl**[41] 3663 2-8-10 59...[1] ShaneKelly 5 61
(Gary Moore) *hld up: nt clr run over 2f out: hdwy over 1f out: rdn and r.o wl to ld post* **12/1**
603 2 *shd* **Quincel**[44] 3568 2-9-1 64.. RichardKingscote 3 66
(Tom Dascombe) *sn led: rdn over 1f out: hdd post* **2/1**[1]
000 3 3/4 **Basil Berry**[25] 4218 2-8-13 62.................................... SaleemGolam 2 62
(Chris Dwyer) *awkward leaving stalls: sn prom: chsd wnr over 1f out: sn rdn: r.o* **33/1**
004 4 1/2 **Jazri**[31] 4031 2-8-1 50.. LukeMorris 11 49
(Milton Bradley) *mid-div: pushed along 1/2-way: hdwy over 2f out: rdn and edgd lft ins fnl f: styd on* **40/1**
3044 5 2 3/4 **Tyrsal (IRE)**[16] 4519 2-8-8 57.................................(p) NickyMackay 4 49
(Robert Eddery) *prom: rdn over 1f out: styd on same pce fnl f* **8/1**
025 6 1 1/2 **Taleteller (USA)**[18] 4432 2-9-5 68........................... MickaelBarzalona 7 57
(Charlie Appleby) *chsd ldrs: rdn over 2f out: wknd ins fnl f* **5/2**[2]
3453 7 1 1/2 **Dancing Sal (IRE)**[24] 4246 2-9-1 64............................. TomQueally 1 49
(David Evans) *hld up: rdn over 2f out: wknd over 1f out* **9/1**
0250 8 1/2 **Kraka Gym (IRE)**[12] 4618 2-8-11 60................................ TomEaves 6 44
(Michael Easterby) *chsd ldr tl rdn wl over 1f out: wknd ins fnl f* **22/1**
000 9 2 1/4 **Volodina (IRE)**[32] 3978 2-7-11 49 oh3...................... NataliaGemelova(3) 9 27
(Alan McCabe) *s.i.s: a in rr* **40/1**
054 10 52 **Centrality**[17] 4497 2-9-5 68.. JoeFanning 8
(Mark Johnston) *hld up: pushed along 3f out: sn wknd* **6/1**[3]

1m 28.64s (-0.96) **Going Correction** -0.225s/f (Stan) 10 Ran SP% 117.2
Speed ratings (Par 94): **96,95,95,94,91 89,87,87,84,25**
toteswingers 1&2 £7.40, 1&3 £42.90, 2&3 £18.70 CSF £35.57 CT £792.47 TOTE £16.90: £3.50, £1.20, £10.00; EX 56.00 Trifecta £1895.00 Pool: £2964.05 - 1.17 winning units.
Owner Sir Eric Parker **Bred** Sir Eric Parker **Trained** Lower Beeding, W Sussex

FOCUS
A modest nursery in which they went an even gallop. The winner should remain competitive in low-grade nurseries.

5069 HOTEL & CONFERENCING AT WOLVERHAMPTON MAIDEN STKS 7f 32y(P)
4:00 (4:02) (Class 5) 3-Y-O £2,911 (£866; £432; £216) Stalls High

Form RPR
52 1 **Satwa Story**[16] 4535 3-9-5 0.................................... MickaelBarzalona 11 88+
(Charlie Appleby) *a.p: chsd ldr over 5f out: led over 4f out: rdn clr fr over 1f out* **8/13**[1]
4455 2 6 **Living Desert**[33] 3961 3-9-5 75.................................... SebSanders 12 72
(James Toller) *a.p: chsd wnr 4f out: rdn over 2f out: hung lft and outpcd fr over 1f out* **4/1**[2]
00 3 1 1/2 **Sleek**[20] 4382 3-9-0 0... MartinHarley 9 63
(Marco Botti) *led: hdd over 4f out: rdn over 2f out: wknd over 1f out* **33/1**
0- 4 5 **Lawmans Thunder**[409] 3346 3-9-5 0.........................(t) SilvestreDeSousa 5 54+
(Charlie Appleby) *s.i.s: hld up: styd on ins fnl f: nvr nrr* **9/2**[3]
5 *shd* **Shotgun Start** 3-9-5 0.. SeanLevey 6 54
(Michael Wigham) *plld hrd and prom: lost pl over 4f out: n.d after: hung lft fr over 1f out* **20/1**
6 1/2 **Princess Bounty** 3-9-0 0.. LukeMorris 3 48
(Phil McEntee) *hld up: rdn over 2f out: n.d* **100/1**
7 2 **Stanlow** 3-9-5 0.. ShaneKelly 10 47
(Daniel Mark Loughnane) *s.i.s: a in rr* **40/1**
0- 8 1 **Zed Candy Girl**[268] 7686 3-9-0 0................................ TomMcLaughlin 2 40
(John Stimpson) *chsd ldrs: rdn over 2f out: sn wknd: carried lft ins fnl f* **66/1**
04 9 6 **Eaton Oak**[33] 3950 3-9-5 0.. TomEaves 7 29
(Lisa Williamson) *hld up: hdwy over 4f out: rdn and wknd over 2f out* **100/1**
10 *nk* **Vol Freak** 3-9-5 0.. SaleemGolam 8 28
(Willie Musson) *s.i.s: hld up: a in rr* **66/1**
11 *nk* **Polvere D'Oro** 3-9-0 0.. SladeO'Hara(5) 1 27
(Michael Mullineaux) *hld up: rdn 1/2-way: a in rr* **100/1**

0 12 18 **Valley Fire**31 4013 3-9-0 0 RoystonFfrench 4
(Ed McMahon) *prom: pushed along over 2f out: sn wknd* **80/1**
1m 28.13s (-1.47) **Going Correction** -0.225s/f (Stan) 12 Ran SP% **117.4**
Speed ratings (Par 100): **99,92,90,84,84 84,81,80,73,73 73,52**
toteswingers 1&2 £1.60, 1&3 £4.40, 2&3 £5.90 CSF £3.05 TOTE £1.50: £1.10, £1.10, £5.10; EX 3.00 Trifecta £29.60 Pool: £4871.31 - 123.36 winning units.
Owner Godolphin **Bred** Darley **Trained** Newmarket, Suffolk
FOCUS
A fair 3yo maiden in which there was a muddling early gallop.

5070 WOLVERHAMPTON-RACECOURSE.CO.UK H'CAP 1m 141y(P)
4:30 (4:30) (Class 5) (0-75,75) 3-Y-0+ £3,234 (£962; £481; £240) Stalls Low

Form RPR
3050 1 **High Time Too (IRE)**17 4509 3-9-0 **69** MartinDwyer 3 76
(Hugo Palmer) *a.p: chsd ldr over 2f out: rdn to ld and hung lft over 1f out: r.o* **16/1**
6011 2 1 1/2 **Pelmanism**21 4357 6-10-0 **75** AidanColeman 1 79
(Brian Ellison) *a.p: rdn over 2f out: r.o to go 2nd towards fin: nt rch wnr* **5/1**3
1403 3 hd **Prime Exhibit**35 3886 8-10-0 **75** (t) ShaneKelly 8 79
(Daniel Mark Loughnane) *a.p: rdn over 2f out: r.o* **16/1**
0004 4 3/4 **Berlusca (IRE)**17 4482 4-9-6 **72** DavidBergin(5) 2 74
(David O'Meara) *chsd ldr tl rdn over 2f out: cl up whn hmpd over 1f out: styd on* **6/1**
-003 5 1/2 **Makin (IRE)**7 4829 3-9-4 **73** (t) NeilCallan 5 74
(Marco Botti) *led at stdy pce tl qcknd over 2f out: rdn: hdd and hmpd over 1f out: no ex wl ins fnl f* **9/2**2
5561 6 2 1/2 **Spirit Rider (USA)**27 4152 3-9-6 **75** (b1) WilliamBuick 4 70
(John Gosden) *pushed along in rr early: hld up: rdn over 2f out: nvr on terms* **11/8**1
3563 7 3/4 **Madeira Girl (IRE)**27 4145 4-9-3 **64** GeorgeBaker 7 57
(Jonjo O'Neill) *hld up: rdn over 1f out: nvr on terms* **14/1**
4434 8 6 **Abbraccio**7 4838 5-9-2 **66** (t) WilliamTwiston-Davies(3) 6 45
(Fergal O'Brien) *s.i.s: a in rr* **16/1**
1m 48.78s (-1.72) **Going Correction** -0.225s/f (Stan)
WFA 3 from 4yo+ 8lb 8 Ran SP% **115.6**
Speed ratings (Par 103): **98,96,96,95,95 93,92,87**
toteswingers 1&2 £14.50, 1&3 £22.10, 2&3 £9.00 CSF £94.48 CT £1335.31 TOTE £35.00: £5.70, £1.20, £3.70; EX 120.40 Trifecta £1878.00 Pool: £3208.85 - 1.28 winning units.
Owner Mrs Sophie Magnier **Bred** Christopher Maye **Trained** Newmarket, Suffolk
FOCUS
A fair handicap in which they went quite steady early.

5071 SPONSOR A RACE BY CALLING 01902 390000 MAIDEN FILLIES' STKS 1m 141y(P)
5:00 (5:02) (Class 5) 3-Y-0+ £2,587 (£770; £384; £192) Stalls Low

Form RPR
5 1 **Quantify (USA)**40 3696 3-8-12 0 SilvestreDeSousa 8 72+
(Luca Cumani) *mde all: set stdy pce tl qcknd over 2f out: rdn out* **4/1**3
0- 2 1 **Conserve (IRE)**300 6966 3-8-12 0 TomQueally 4 70+
(Lady Cecil) *chsd wnr over 2f: remained handy: wnt 2nd again over 1f out: rdn and ev ch ins fnl f: unable qck towards fin* **11/10**1
3 1 1/4 **Duchess Of Seville** 3-8-12 0 NeilCallan 12 67+
(Marco Botti) *a.p: rdn over 2f out: hung lft ins fnl f: styd on same pce* **7/1**
4 4 1/2 **Sagesse** 3-8-12 0 LukeMorris 1 56+
(Sir Mark Prescott Bt) *chsd ldrs: rdn over 2f out: styd on same pce fr over 1f out* **11/4**2
5 5 3/4 **Meet Marhaba (IRE)**17 4495 3-8-12 0 DaneO'Neill 9 55
(J W Hills) *prom: chsd wnr 6f out tl rdn over 1f out: wknd ins fnl f* **20/1**
6 nk **Millies Quest** 4-8-13 0 JordanVaughan(7) 11 54
(Martin Smith) *hld up: hdwy over 5f out: rdn over 1f out: wknd ins fnl f* **50/1**
0 7 2 **Goldie Horn**32 3989 5-9-6 0 (t) SeanLevey 5 49
(Nigel Twiston-Davies) *hld up: rdn over 2f out: n.d* **50/1**
0 8 hd **Shelling Peas**69 2746 4-8-13 0 AdamMcLean(7) 7 49
(Derek Shaw) *mid-div: hdwy over 3f out: rdn over 2f out: sn wknd* **100/1**
9 4 **Raafa's Jigsaw** 4-9-1 0 TobyAtkinson(5) 6 40
(Michael Appleby) *stareted slowly: hld up: shkn up over 2f out: n.d* **50/1**
10 6 **Nautical Twilight** 3-8-7 0 GeorgeChaloner(5) 10 26
(Malcolm Jefferson) *s.i.s: hld up and a in rr: lost tch over 3f out* **50/1**
11 14 **Anne's Valentino** 3-8-12 0 TomEaves 3
(Malcolm Jefferson) *s.s: a in rr: lost tch over 3f out* **50/1**
1m 51.08s (0.58) **Going Correction** -0.225s/f (Stan)
WFA 3 from 4yo+ 8lb 11 Ran SP% **122.3**
Speed ratings (Par 100): **88,87,86,82,81 81,79,79,75,70 57**
toteswingers 1&2 £1.70, 1&3 £4.80, 2&3 £3.00 CSF £8.91 TOTE £5.40: £1.30, £1.20, £2.70; EX 11.60 Trifecta £40.30 Pool: £4171.53 - 77.54 winning units.
Owner Michael Tabor, John Magnier & Derrick Smith **Bred** Tower Bloodstock **Trained** Newmarket, Suffolk
FOCUS
A modest fillies' maiden in which they went a steady gallop in producing the worst comparative time on the card so far.

5072 HOLIDAY INN WOLVERHAMPTON H'CAP (DIV I) 1m 141y(P)
5:30 (5:31) (Class 6) (0-60,63) 3-Y-0+ £1,940 (£577; £288; £72; £72) Stalls Low

Form RPR
5-01 1 **Angel Cake (IRE)**7 4834 4-9-6 **59** 6ex TobyAtkinson(5) 7 72
(Michael Appleby) *chsd ldrs: led 1f out: rdn out* **4/1**2
0551 2 3 **Lexington Blue**3 4955 3-9-7 **63** 6ex (v) DavidNolan 13 69
(David O'Meara) *hld up: hdwy over 3f out: rdn and edgd lft over 1f out: styd on to go 2nd nr fin* **2/1**1
0004 3 1/2 **Bang Tidy (IRE)**27 4155 4-9-10 **58** (t) AidanColeman 8 63
(Brian Ellison) *hld up: hdwy over 3f out: rdn over 1f out: no ex ins fnl f* **6/1**3
4-35 4 1 1/4 **Giantstepsahead (IRE)**105 1735 4-9-12 **60** TomMcLaughlin 6 62
(Michael Wigham) *mid-div: lost pl 4f out: hdwy and swtchd rt over 1f out: r.o* **12/1**
040- 4 dht **Ana Shababiya (IRE)**340 5763 3-8-9 **51** SeanLevey 12 53
(Ismail Mohammed) *hld up: hdwy on outer over 2f out: styd on same pce fnl f* **33/1**
0333 6 nk **Handsome Stranger (IRE)**19 4405 3-8-10 **59** TimClark(7) 5 60
(Alan Bailey) *chsd ldrs: rdn over 2f out: styd on u.p ins fnl f* **20/1**
065 7 2 **Lexi's Dancer**10 4715 3-8-11 **53** (v1) SilvestreDeSousa 2 50
(Ian Williams) *led: hdd over 6f out: chsd ldr: led again wl over 1f out: rdn and hdd 1f out: wknd ins fnl f* **7/1**
264 8 3/4 **Is This Love (IRE)**60 3016 3-9-3 **59** FergusSweeney 4 54
(Jamie Osborne) *s.i.s: hld up: rdn over 3f out: n.d* **16/1**
-446 9 1 **Piccolo Express**175 617 7-9-9 **57** ShaneKelly 9 50
(Brian Baugh) *chsd ldrs: rdn over 2f out: wknd fnl f* **33/1**
4412 10 5 **Crucis Abbey (IRE)**11 4658 5-9-2 **50** (p) RobbieFitzpatrick 3 31
(Mark Brisbourne) *hld up: rdn over 1f out: n.d* **10/1**
00-0 11 7 **Odd Ball (IRE)**7 4834 6-9-2 **53** MarkCoumbe(3) 11 18
(Lisa Williamson) *a in rr: bhd fnl 5f* **50/1**
0000 12 3 3/4 **Forever Janey**26 4160 4-8-9 **46** oh1 RaulDaSilva(3) 10 3
(Paul Green) *chsd ldr: led over 6f out: rdn and hdd wl over 1f out: hmpd sn after and wknd* **66/1**
65/0 13 6 **Edin Burgher (FR)**11 4691 12-8-5 **46** oh1 JordanVaughan(7) 1
(Michael Murphy) *chsd ldrs: rdn over 3f out: wknd over 2f out* **66/1**
1m 48.22s (-2.28) **Going Correction** -0.225s/f (Stan)
WFA 3 from 4yo+ 8lb 13 Ran SP% **118.4**
Speed ratings (Par 101): **101,98,97,96,96 96,94,94,93,88 82,79,73**
toteswingers 1&2 £3.20, 1&3 £8.40, 2&3 £6.30 CSF £11.53 CT £49.03 TOTE £5.30: £1.90, £1.50, £2.60; EX 15.30 Trifecta £84.30 Pool: £2240.71 - 19.91 winning units.
Owner W Sewell **Bred** Stephanie Hanly **Trained** Danethorpe, Notts
FOCUS
A moderate handicap in which they went a decent gallop.

5073 HOLIDAY INN WOLVERHAMPTON H'CAP (DIV II) 1m 141y(P)
6:05 (6:05) (Class 6) (0-60,60) 3-Y-0+ £1,940 (£577; £288; £144) Stalls Low

Form RPR
0003 1 **Warden Bond**21 4357 5-9-12 **60** (p) NeilCallan 7 69
(William Stone) *a.p: chsd ldr 3f out: shkn up to ld over 1f out: rdn and edgd lft ins fnl f: jst hld on* **6/1**2
0065 2 nk **Tatting**34 3924 4-9-3 **51** LukeMorris 6 59+
(Chris Dwyer) *hld up: hdwy over 2f out: rdn over 1f out: r.o wl* **7/1**
-000 3 2 1/4 **Aureolin Gulf**17 4503 4-8-7 **46** oh1 JackDuern(5) 9 49
(Andrew Hollinshead) *led: rdn and hdd over 1f out: styd on same pce ins fnl f* **66/1**
-151 4 hd **Winslow Arizona (IRE)**41 3665 3-9-3 **59** JamieSpencer 11 62+
(Michael Bell) *hld up: hdwy over 1f out: r.o u.p: nt rch ldrs* **11/10**1
2563 5 1 1/4 **Buaiteoir (FR)**35 3910 7-9-3 **58** OisinMurphy(7) 5 58
(Nikki Evans) *chsd ldrs: rdn over 1f out: no ex ins fnl f* **9/1**
6516 6 7 **Safwaan**9 4755 6-9-11 **59** J-PGuillambert 8 43
(Gary Harrison) *hld up: hdwy u.p over 2f out: wknd over 1f out* **13/2**3
0005 7 1/2 **Switcharooney (IRE)**16 4515 3-9-4 **60** (vt1) RichardKingscote 4 43
(Tom Dascombe) *chsd ldr tl pushed along 3f out: rdn and wknd over 1f out* **8/1**
0000 8 4 **Miss Chardonay**17 4504 6-8-12 **46** oh1 (t) SaleemGolam 13 19
(Mandy Rowland) *prom: rdn over 2f out: wknd over 1f out* **80/1**
0 9 1 1/2 **Refuse Colette (IRE)**26 4161 4-8-9 **46** oh1 (b) RaulDaSilva(3) 12 16
(Paul Green) *hld up and a in rr* **40/1**
0-64 10 99 **Land Hawk (IRE)**32 3996 7-9-5 **56** SimonPearce(3) 1
(Lydia Pearce) *hld up: rdn over 2f out: sn wknd and eased* **40/1**
0-00 U **Buds Bruvver**34 3919 4-8-12 **46** oh1 ShaneKelly 2
(Brian Baugh) *unruly sn after leaving stalls and uns rdr* **100/1**
1m 48.53s (-1.97) **Going Correction** -0.225s/f (Stan)
WFA 3 from 4yo+ 8lb 11 Ran SP% **117.4**
Speed ratings (Par 101): **99,98,96,96,95 89,88,85,83,**
toteswingers 1&2 £4.40, 1&3 £34.80, 2&3 £46.90 CSF £46.50 CT £2515.45 TOTE £5.20: £1.60, £2.60, £7.30; EX 50.80 Trifecta £1226.10 Part won. Pool: £1634.87 - 0.82 winning units..
Owner J A Ross & Miss C Scott **Bred** Park Farm Racing **Trained** West Wickham, Cambs
FOCUS
The second division of a moderate handicap in which they went an honest gallop, and the winning time was only marginally slower than the first division.
T/Plt: £67.70 to a £1 stake. Pool: £68,024.73 - 733.37 winning units T/Qpdt: £10.20 to a £1 stake. Pool: £5910.89 - 425.20 winning units CR

5074 - 5081a (Foreign Racing) - See Raceform Interactive

LA TESTE DE BUCH (R-H)
Monday, August 5
OFFICIAL GOING: Turf: good

5082a CRITERIUM DU BEQUET - VENTES OSARUS (LISTED RACE) (2YO) (TURF) 6f
4:40 (12:00) 2-Y-0 £22,357 (£8,943; £6,707; £4,471; £2,235)

RPR
1 **Noozhoh Canarias (SPA)**36 2-9-2 0 J-LMartinez 6 114
(E Leon Penate, Spain) **128/10**
2 3 **Elusive Pearl (FR)**25 2-8-13 0 FranckBlondel 7 100
(F Rossi, France) **4/5**1
3 3 1/2 **Another Party (FR)**15 4572 2-9-2 0 MickaelForest 5 93
(Matthieu Palussiere, France) **8/1**3
4 nse **Salai (FR)**34 2-9-2 0 Jean-BernardEyquem 4 92
(J-C Rouget, France) **23/10**2
5 4 **La Cumbia (IRE)**34 2-8-13 0 JimmyMartin 2 77
(X Thomas-Demeaulte, France) **20/1**
6 snk **Skiperia (FR)**13 2-8-13 0 FabriceVeron 1 77
(H-A Pantall, France) **11/1**
7 1 1/2 **Hopefilly (IRE)**16 4528 2-8-13 0 ThomasHenderson 3 72
(Ed Walker) *broke wl and led: hdd by eventual wnr after 1 1/2f: trckd ldr: 2nd and pushed along 2f out: rdn and hung lft over 1 1/2f out: wknd u.p fnl f*
1m 13.28s (73.28) 7 Ran SP% **117.3**
WIN (incl. 1 euro stake): 13.80. PLACES: 3.60, 1.50. SF: 33.80.
Owner J C Bolanos Marrero **Bred** Grupo Bolanos Gran Canaria **Trained** Spain

The Form Book Flat, Raceform Ltd, Compton, RG20 6NL.

4616 CATTERICK (L-H)

Tuesday, August 6

OFFICIAL GOING: Soft (good to soft in places; 7.4)

Wind: light 1/2 against Weather: fine

5083 BRITISH STALLION STUDS EBF MAIDEN STKS 7f

2:15 (2:16) (Class 5) 2-Y-O £2,911 (£866; £432; £216) Stalls Centre

Form RPR

3 1 **Braidley (IRE)**[18] 4505 2-9-5 0 GrahamLee 4 73+
(James Bethell) *in rr: chsd ldrs over 4f out: effrt 3f out: styd on to ld over 1f out: drvn out* 3/1[2]

03 2 2 1/4 **El Beau (IRE)**[10] 4756 2-9-5 0 MichaelO'Connell 1 67
(John Quinn) *s.i.s: hdwy to chse ldrs 3f out: kpt on to take 2nd jst ins fnl f: no imp* 8/1[3]

4 3 3/4 **Chookie's Lass**[18] 4470 2-9-0 0 TomEaves 3 60
(Keith Dalgleish) *chsd ldrs: drvn and outpcd over 3f out: kpt on to take 3rd last 100yds* 25/1

420 4 2 1/2 **Ahoy There (IRE)**[24] 4312 2-9-5 72 MickyFenton 2 59
(Tom Tate) *led hdd over 2f out: swtchd rt ins fnl f: tk 4th nr line* 9/1

5646 5 1/2 **Crowdmania**[13] 4618 2-9-5 79 FrannyNorton 5 57
(Mark Johnston) *w ldrs: led over 2f out: hdd over 1f out: wknd fnl f* 4/5[1]

0 6 3 3/4 **Mister Uno (IRE)**[31] 4053 2-9-5 0 PaulMulrennan 6 48
(Ann Duffield) *swtchd lft and lost pl over 4f out: wknd over 1f out* 50/1

35 7 8 **Kirkstall Abbey (IRE)**[50] 3391 2-9-0 0 BarryMcHugh 7 22
(Tony Coyle) *trckd ldrs: drvn over 3f out: lost pl over 2f out: sn bhd* 12/1

0 8 37 **Poco Piccolo**[31] 4046 2-9-5 0 PatrickMathers 8
(Deborah Sanderson) *wnt rt s: t.k.h: w ldrs on outside: lost pl 3f out: sn bhd: t.o whn eased ins fnl f* 80/1

1m 30.3s (3.30) **Going Correction** +0.45s/f (Yiel) 8 Ran SP% **116.4**

Speed ratings (Par 94): **99,96,95,92,92 87,78,36**

Tote Swingers: 1&2 £3.00, 1&3 £6.70, 2&3 £8.30 CSF £27.00 TOTE £3.90: £1.30, £2.10, £4.00; EX 23.20 Trifecta £173.90 Pool: £3,750.15 - 16.16 winning units..

Owner Clarendon Thoroughbred Racing **Bred** A Pettinari **Trained** Middleham Moor, N Yorks

FOCUS

Bend into home straight and home straight moved out 3m, adding 12yds to races of 6f and over and 24yds to 2m race. The going was soft, good to soft in places. Little strength to this maiden, which was run at a fair pace. The form has a straightforward feel.

5084 WATCH RACING UK ON SKY 432 (S) STKS 1m 7f 177y

2:45 (2:45) (Class 6) 3-5-Y-O £2,385 (£704; £352) Stalls Centre

Form RPR

5330 1 **Torero**[8] 4835 4-9-8 55 (p) BrianHughes 3 55
(Kevin Ryan) *hld up: trckd ldrs 7f out: wnt cl 2nd 3f out: led 2f out: drvn out* 11/1[3]

6421 2 1 **Jebulani**[7] 4849 3-8-13 49 DanielTudhope 6 60
(David O'Meara) *led: hung rt: reminders and hdd bnd 8f out: drvn over 4f out: outpcd 3f out: swtchd rt 2f out: chsng wnr 1f out: kpt on same pce* 11/8[1]

0-55 3 2 3/4 **Queen Of Epirus**[28] 4010 5-9-3 53 MickyFenton 1 45
(Brian Rothwell) *dwlt: sn trcking ldrs: drvn over 4f out: swtchd rt over 2f out: one pce* 16/1

4543 4 4 1/2 **Duchess Of Dreams**[7] 4849 3-7-11 45 PhilipPrince(5) 2 40
(Richard Guest) *stdd s: t.k.h in rr: drvn over 4f out: sn outpcd: sme hdwy 2f out: nvr a threat* 12/1

-034 5 12 **Eanans Bay (IRE)**[40] 3744 4-9-8 45 (b) RobertWinston 5 32
(Mark H Tompkins) *trckd ldrs: led 8f out: qcknd pce 6f out: hdd 2f out: sn wknd: heavily eased ins fnl f* 20/1

3531 6 1 1/2 **Star Alliance (IRE)**[21] 4380 5-10-0 62 (b) GrahamLee 7 33
(Ian Williams) *trckd ldrs: drvn 6f out: sn lost pl and bhd* 15/8[2]

1200 7 7 **Kingarrick**[22] 4343 5-9-7 58 RobJFitzpatrick(7) 4 24
(Noel Wilson) *hld up in rr: t.k.h: reminders and lost pl over 4f out: sn bhd* 11/1[3]

3m 41.56s (9.56) **Going Correction** +0.45s/f (Yiel)

WFA 3 from 4yo+ 15lb 7 Ran SP% **111.9**

Speed ratings (Par 101): **94,93,92,89,83 83,79**

Tote Swingers: 1&2 £2.80, 1&3 £16.00, 2&3 £6.20 CSF £25.58 TOTE £10.50: £4.70, £1.60; EX 27.50 Trifecta £277.50 Pool: £3,060.76 - 8.27 winning units..There was no bid for the winner. Jebulani bought by Mr F. P. Murtagh £5,000.

Owner Exors of The Late Guy Reed **Bred** G Reed **Trained** Hambleton, N Yorks

■ Brian Hughes's first Flat winner since his apprentice days.

FOCUS

The pace was steady for this poor seller. The runner-up is the best guide.

5085 SSAFA H'CAP 5f

3:15 (3:16) (Class 6) (0-60,60) 3-Y-O+ £2,385 (£704; £352) Stalls Low

Form RPR

0000 1 **Sophie's Beau (USA)**[19] 4456 6-8-4 **50** (bt) DanielleMooney(7) 2 57
(Michael Chapman) *chsd ldrs: sn drvn along: styd on ins fnl f: led post* 33/1

2506 2 nse **Prigsnov Dancer (IRE)**[55] 3196 8-8-0 **46** oh1 (p) JordanNason(7) 1 53
(Deborah Sanderson) *chsd ldrs on inner: n.m.r 1f out: squeezed through to ld briefly wl ins fnl f: hdd last stride* 12/1

00-3 3 1 1/4 **Gottcher**[14] 4613 5-9-7 **60** JoeFanning 3 62
(Keith Dalgleish) *led: rdn and edgd lft 1f out: hdd and no ex last 30yds* 4/1[2]

0120 4 1 1/2 **Sir Geoffrey (IRE)**[9] 4814 7-9-5 **58** (p) GrahamLee 8 55
(Scott Dixon) *mid-div: rdn and outpcd over 2f out: kpt on fnl f* 7/1[3]

-000 5 hd **Piste**[10] 4761 7-8-7 **46** (e) JamesSullivan 10 42
(Tina Jackson) *chsd ldrs: drvn over 2f out: kpt on same pce over 1f out* 14/1

5050 6 1/2 **One Kool Dude**[32] 4009 4-9-1 **54** (b[1]) AndrewElliott 9 48
(Neville Bycroft) *sn outpcd and in rr: styd on fnl f: nt rch ldrs* 14/1

0603 7 1 **Quality Art (USA)**[5] 4930 5-8-12 **56** ConnorBeasley(5) 6 47
(Richard Guest) *mid-div: drvn over 2f out: nvr a threat* 5/2[1]

4035 8 nk **Wicked Wilma (IRE)**[1] 5047 9-8-1 **47** (p) JordanHibberd(7) 11 37+
(Alan Berry) *stmbld s: in rr: hdwy over 1f out: one pce whn swtchd lft ins fnl f* 15/2

0600 9 2 **Robyn**[33] 3994 3-8-4 **46** (p) PaoloSirigu 4 28
(Scott Dixon) *dwlt: swtchd lft s: in rr: sme hdwy 2f out: nvr a factor* 25/1

6050 10 hd **Mystical Witch**[8] 4840 4-8-7 **46** oh1 (v) FrannyNorton 5 28
(Christine Dunnett) *in rr: nvr a factor* 33/1

3-00 11 3/4 **Sharp Shoes**[74] 2611 6-8-10 **49** PaddyAspell 13 28
(Christopher Wilson) *chsd ldrs: lost pl over 1f out* 22/1

6020 12 1/2 **Pavers Star**[10] 4762 4-9-6 **59** RobertWinston 7 36
(Noel Wilson) *w ldrs: wknd and eased 1f out* 8/1

0006 13 18 **Bird Dog**[74] 2643 7-8-2 **46** oh1 (v) DannyBrock(5) 12
(Phil McEntee) *in rr: bhd whn heavily eased appr fnl f* 66/1

1m 1.5s (1.70) **Going Correction** +0.375s/f (Good)

WFA 3 from 4yo+ 3lb 13 Ran SP% **120.5**

Speed ratings (Par 101): **101,100,98,96,96 95,93,93,90,89 88,87,59**

Tote Swingers: 1&2 £62.50, 1&3 £26.20, 2&3 £13.00 CSF £375.89 CT £1399.30 TOTE £42.90: £7.40, £3.60, £1.50; EX 625.90 Trifecta £3023.30 Part won. Pool: £4,031.18 - 0.44 winning units..

Owner Mrs M Chapman **Bred** Steve C Snowden & Doug Wilson **Trained** Market Rasen, Lincs

FOCUS

A weak handicap run at a fair pace with the three inside stalls filling the first three places. It paid to race prominently and the first two are rated to their 2012 bests.

5086 ABF SOLDIER'S CHARITY H'CAP 1m 5f 175y

3:45 (3:46) (Class 4) (0-85,84) 3-Y-O+ £6,469 (£1,925; £962; £481) Stalls Low

Form RPR

2152 1 **Platinum (IRE)**[21] 4372 6-9-9 **79** (p) RussKennemore 2 89
(Philip Kirby) *trckd ldrs: n.m.r and swtchd rt over 2f out: chal over 1f out: led jst ins fnl f: pushed out* 7/2[3]

6620 2 1/2 **Linguine (FR)**[24] 4279 3-9-0 **83** MickyFenton 6 92
(Seamus Durack) *drvn early to chse ldr: led over 2f out: hdd jst ins fnl f: no ex* 11/4[2]

5053 3 nk **Party Line**[9] 4804 4-10-0 **84** FrannyNorton 4 93+
(Mark Johnston) *trckd ldrs: lost pl after 5f: hdwy 5f out: sn chsng ldrs: outpcd over 2f out: rallied and 3rd 1f out: kpt on same pce* 15/8[1]

0364 4 4 1/2 **Dark Dune (IRE)**[17] 4543 5-9-2 **72** DavidAllan 8 74
(Tim Easterby) *rrd s: hld up in rr: hdwy over 3f out: chsng ldrs whn hmpd over 2f out: wknd fnl f* 12/1

0355 5 11 **Moccasin (FR)**[48] 3477 4-9-12 **82** (p) GrahamLee 3 67
(Geoffrey Harker) *hld up towards rr: hdwy after 5f: effrt over 4f out: lost pl over 1f out* 9/1

1-00 6 12 **Narcissist (IRE)**[81] 2431 4-9-6 **76** GrahamGibbons 5 43
(Michael Easterby) *led: drvn over 4f out: wknd and eased over 1f out* 20/1

0064 7 10 **Alsahil (USA)**[48] 3480 7-8-10 **66** (p) JoeFanning 7 18
(Alan Swinbank) *chsd ldrs: drvn over 3f out: lost pl over 2f out: sn bhd* 16/1

3m 7.5s (3.90) **Going Correction** +0.45s/f (Yiel)

WFA 3 from 4yo+ 13lb 7 Ran SP% **112.0**

Speed ratings (Par 105): **106,105,105,102,96 89,84**

Tote Swingers: 1&2 £2.60, 1&3 £2.30, 2&3 £2.10 CSF £12.97 CT £21.91 TOTE £3.60: £1.60, £2.60; EX 12.90 Trifecta £38.20 Pool: £3,537.63 - 69.28 winning units..

Owner Mrs Philippa Kirby **Bred** Lodge Park Stud **Trained** Middleham, N Yorks

■ Stewards' Enquiry : Russ Kennemore one-day ban: careless riding (Aug 20)

FOCUS

This fair handicap was run at an honest pace. Straightforward form.

5087 CATTERICKBRIDGE.CO.UK CLASSIFIED CLAIMING STKS (QUALIFIER FOR 2013 CATTERICK 12F SERIES) 1m 3f 214y

4:15 (4:17) (Class 6) 3-Y-O+ £3,408 (£1,006; £503) Stalls Low

Form RPR

00-0 1 **Yasir (USA)**[17] 4521 5-9-4 75 (p) GrahamLee 6 76
(Conor Dore) *stdd s: hld up in rr: hdwy over 6f out: sn trcking ldrs: 2nd 4f out: led 2f out: kpt on fnl f: all out* 5/1

0206 2 shd **Gran Maestro (USA)**[9] 4810 4-9-3 75 (b) LMcNiff(3) 1 78
(Ruth Carr) *trckd ldrs: 2nd 2f out: sn upsides: hrd rdn ins fnl f jst hld* 9/4[1]

0006 3 15 **Indepub**[24] 4293 4-9-6 65 (p) PaulMulrennan 3 54
(Kevin Ryan) *sn drvn along: chsd ldrs: led after 2f: reminders over 7f out: hdd over 2f out: wknd fnl f* 7/2[3]

-215 4 1/2 **Just Lille (IRE)**[59] 3085 10-8-13 73 (p) RowanScott(7) 2 53
(Ann Duffield) *led 2f: pushed along 7f out: outpcd over 4f out: kpt on fnl 2f: no threat: poor 4th 1f out* 3/1[2]

3231 5 2 1/4 **Town Mouse**[17] 3319 3-8-11 69 MartinLane 4 51+
(Neil King) *bolted full circ bef s: stdd s: t.k.h in rr: effrt and modest 4th 3f out: wknd over 1f out* 6/1

16-0 6 10 **Bollin Dolly**[6] 4888 10-9-1 71 (b[1]) PaddyAspell 5 28
(James Moffatt) *w ldrs: t.k.h: lost pl 3f out: sn bhd* 20/1

2m 42.29s (3.39) **Going Correction** +0.45s/f (Yiel)

WFA 3 from 4yo+ 11lb 6 Ran SP% **113.7**

Speed ratings (Par 101): **106,105,95,95,94 87**

Tote Swingers: 1&2 £2.50, 1&3 £4.10, 2&3 £2.60 CSF £17.03 TOTE £6.20: £3.50, £1.90; EX 15.20 Trifecta £55.20 Pool: £3,753.12 - 50.91 winning units..

Owner Mrs Louise Marsh **Bred** Shadwell Farm LLC **Trained** Hubbert's Bridge, Lincs

■ Stewards' Enquiry : L McNiff four-day ban: used whip above permitted level (Aug 20,24-26)

FOCUS

A tight claimer. The pace was sound with the front two finishing a long way clear. Only they gave their running.

5088 AUGUST 16TH IS LADIES' EVENING H'CAP 5f 212y

4:45 (4:45) (Class 5) (0-75,75) 3-Y-O+ £2,911 (£866; £432; £216) Stalls Low

Form RPR

3400 1 **Solar Spirit (IRE)**[28] 4138 8-9-11 **75** BarryMcHugh 10 82+
(Tracy Waggott) *trckd ldrs on outer: led over 1f out: r.o* 16/1

0000 2 3/4 **Towbee**[13] 4620 4-9-11 **75** (v[1]) GrahamGibbons 8 80+
(Michael Easterby) *trckd ldrs: nt clr run and swtchd rt over 1f out: chsd wnr last 75yds: hung rt and kpt on* 20/1

2142 3 3/4 **Tajneed (IRE)**[47] 3501 10-9-7 **71** AdrianNicholls 2 74
(David Nicholls) *mid-div: drvn and lost pl over 3f out: hdwy and c wd appr fnl f: edgd lft ins fnl f: styd on wl to take 3rd nr line* 8/1

5603 4 nk **Roker Park (IRE)**[3] 5011 8-9-11 **75** (v) DanielTudhope 1 77
(David O'Meara) *drvn early: in rr: hdwy over 1f out: styd on wl to take 4th towards fin* 11/4[1]

2354 5 nk **Mutafaakir (IRE)**[3] 5011 4-9-8 **72** (p) JamesSullivan 6 73
(Ruth Carr) *mid-div on inner: nt clr run and swtchd rt over 1f out: styd on to take 5th nr fin* 3/1[2]

1425 6 2 1/4 **Hit The Lights (IRE)**[46] 3540 3-9-3 **71** RobertWinston 7 64
(Ollie Pears) *led 1f: w ldrs: upsides over 1f out: fdd and eased last 100yds* 9/1

3603 7 1 **Art Dzeko**[28] 4146 4-9-2 **66** DavidAllan 4 57
(Tim Easterby) *mid-div: drvn 3f out: nvr a threat* 20/1

0162 8 nk **Majestic Manannan (IRE)**[9] 4814 4-9-3 **67** FrannyNorton 5 57
(David Nicholls) *led after 1f: hdd over 1f out: sn wknd* 13/2[3]

30-0 9 1/2 **Fama Mac**[79] 2479 6-9-5 **69** AndrewElliott 3 58
(Neville Bycroft) *s.i.s: sme hdwy whn sltly hmpd 1f out: nvr on terms* 16/1

0060 **10** ½ **Partner (IRE)**[4] 4970 7-9-6 70....(t) PaulMulrennan 12 57
(Noel Wilson) *s.i.s: swtchd lft after s: in rr: sme hdwy over 2f out: nvr a factor* **25/1**

6002 **11** ½ **Lexi's Hero (IRE)**[13] 4619 5-9-10 74....(p) JoeFanning 9 60
(David Nicholls) *chsd ldrs on outer: wknd over 1f out: eased clsng stages* **10/1**

1m 16.13s (2.53) **Going Correction** +0.45s/f (Yiel)
WFA 3 from 4yo+ 4lb **11** Ran SP% **120.3**
Speed ratings (Par 103): **101,100,99,98,98 95,93,93,92,92 91**
Tote Swingers: 1&2 £27.20, 1&3 £20.00, 2&3 £27.40 CSF £304.37 CT £2803.98 TOTE £16.60: £4.90, £5.50, £2.30; EX 186.80 Trifecta £906.10 Pool: £4,046.71 - 3.34 winning units..
Owner Christopher James Allan **Bred** Paul Hensey **Trained** Spennymoor, Co Durham
■ Stewards' Enquiry : Adrian Nicholls caution: careless riding.

FOCUS
An open handicap run at a decent pace. Solid form.

5089 YORKSHIRE-OUTDOORS.CO.UK H'CAP 7f
5:15 (5:15) (Class 6) (0-65,65) 3-Y-O **£2,385** (£704; £352) **Stalls** Centre

Form RPR

352 **1** **Dennis**[20] 4400 3-9-2 65....DarylByrne(5) 4 71
(Tim Easterby) *trckd ldr: led over 2f out: idled and drvn out* **9/4**[2]

5001 **2** *nk* **Absolute Diamond**[27] 4158 3-8-11 58....RaulDaSilva(3) 10 63
(John Quinn) *hld up in rr: effrt and swtchd rt over 2f out: hung lft: styd on to take 2nd ins fnl f: no real imp* **2/1**[1]

3650 **3** 1¾ **Lady Calantha**[3] 4991 3-8-2 46 oh1....PaulQuinn 5 46
(Alan Berry) *dwlt: mid-div: drvn 3f out: swtchd rt over 1f out: styd on to take 3rd last 50yds* **20/1**

4005 **4** 1¼ **Senora Lobo (IRE)**[14] 4607 3-8-7 51....(p) RoystonFfrench 7 48
(Lisa Williamson) *t.k.h: trckd ldrs: drvn over 3f out: chsd wnr over 1f out: wknd ins fnl f* **20/1**

S000 **5** 2¾ **Elle Rebelle**[29] 4113 3-9-0 58....RobertWinston 6 48
(Mark Brisbourne) *hld up in mid-div: hdwy over 3f out: sn chsng ldrs: hung lft and wknd over 1f out* **5/1**[3]

5060 **6** 1½ **Rose Of May (IRE)**[13] 4621 3-8-3 47....MartinLane 3 33
(David O'Meara) *hld up in rr: drvn 3f out: wknd over 1f out* **11/2**

-604 **7** 3½ **Unassailable**[63] 2950 3-8-10 54....(b) TomEaves 9 31
(Kevin Ryan) *led: hdd over 2f out: lost pl over 1f out* **9/1**

1m 31.0s (4.00) **Going Correction** +0.45s/f (Yiel) **7** Ran SP% **115.7**
Speed ratings (Par 98): **95,94,92,91,88 86,82**
Tote Swingers: 1&2 £1.80, 1&3 £7.80, 2&3 £6.90 CSF £7.38 CT £63.50 TOTE £2.60: £2.00, £1.80; EX 7.90 Trifecta £76.30 Pool: £2,538.08 - 24.94 winning units..
Owner Habton Farms **Bred** Miss S L Shaw **Trained** Great Habton, N Yorks

FOCUS
This pace was fair for this modest contest. The front two are going the right way.
T/Plt: £1,047.90 to a £1 stake. Pool: £62,937.00 - 43.84 winning tickets. T/Qpdt: £147.80 to a £1 stake. Pool: £5,714.00 - 28.60 winning tickets. WG

4910 FFOS LAS (L-H)
Tuesday, August 6

OFFICIAL GOING: Soft (5.7)
Wind: virtually nil Weather: dry, bright spells

5090 TIP TOP TOILETS/BRITISH STALLION STUDS EBF MEDIAN AUCTION MAIDEN FILLIES' STKS 6f
2:00 (2:02) (Class 5) 2-Y-O **£2,911** (£866; £432) **Stalls** Centre

Form RPR

6022 **1** **Sefaat**[13] 4639 2-9-0 73....DaneO'Neill 1 71
(Brian Meehan) *mde all: rdn over 1f out: kpt on and a doing enough: rdn out* **1/3**[1]

2 ¾ **Flashy Queen (IRE)** 2-9-0 0....LiamKeniry 6 69+
(Joseph Tuite) *hld up in tch in 3rd: rdn and effrt 2f out: kpt on and chsd wnr fnl 100yds: r.o towards fin* **14/1**[3]

4 **3** 1¾ **Alfie Lunete (IRE)**[15] 4589 2-9-0 0....JohnFahy 3 64
(J S Moore) *chsd wnr: rdn and effrt 2f out: edgd lft and unable qck 1f out: lost 2nd and one pce fnl 100yds* **11/4**[2]

1m 14.31s (4.31) **Going Correction** +0.70s/f (Yiel) **3** Ran SP% **108.4**
Speed ratings (Par 91): **99,98,95**
CSF £4.99 TOTE £1.30; EX 3.50 Trifecta £5.50 Pool: £1,277.05 - 171.93 winning units..
Owner Hamdan Al Maktoum **Bred** Shadwell Estate Company Limited **Trained** Manton, Wilts

FOCUS
A dry day, but the course had seen four inches of rain in the preceding week and the ground was demanding. They went a sound enough pace in this moderate little fillies' maiden. Seemingly straightforward form, with the winner just to her mark.

5091 OWEN FUELS OJ WILLIAMS PREMIER FUEL DISTRIBUTORS H'CAP (DIV I) 1m (R)
2:30 (2:31) (Class 6) (0-55,55) 3-Y-0+ **£1,940** (£577; £288; £144) **Stalls** Low

Form RPR

0304 **1** **Guest Book (IRE)**[91] 2126 6-9-5 53....CathyGannon 10 69
(Alan Jones) *s.i.s: hld up in tch in last pair: hdwy on outer to ld jst over 1f out: r.o wl and a holding rival ins fnl f: rdn out* **6/1**

P006 **2** ½ **Mr Fickle (IRE)**[20] 4411 4-9-7 55....(b) RichardHughes 12 70
(Gary Moore) *hld up in tch towards rr: hdwy on outer over 2f out: rdn to ld over 1f out: sn hdd buit stl ev ch after: r.o u.p but a hld by wnr ins fnl f* **9/2**[3]

4314 **3** 6 **Greyemkay**[14] 4604 5-8-10 51....DanielMuscutt(7) 7 52
(Richard Price) *in tch towards rr: rdn and hdwy over 3f out: led over 2f out tl hdd and unable qck over 1f out: outpcd by ldng pair but plugged on to hold 3rd fnl f* **5/2**[1]

-000 **4** 2 **Operettist**[56] 3169 4-8-11 50....GeorgeDowning(5) 2 46
(Tony Carroll) *hld up in last pair: rdn and effrt over 3f out: hdwy 2f out: 4th and no imp whn hung rt fnl f* **20/1**

5-00 **5** 1 **Lordship (IRE)**[13] 4623 9-8-7 46....JakePayne(5) 5 40
(Tom Gretton) *t.k.h: chsd ldrs: rdn over 2f out: unable qck and btn over 1f out: wl hld whn carried rt fnl f* **14/1**

0054 **6** 2¾ **Vermeyen**[17] 4522 4-8-7 46 oh1....DeclanBates(5) 6 34
(Geoffrey Deacon) *t.k.h: hld up in tch in midfield: lost pl 3f out: rallied and sme hdwy on inner over 1f out: plugged on but no ch w ldrs fnl f* **25/1**

0403 **7** 2 **Spinning Ridge (IRE)**[8] 4834 8-9-7 55....(b) SteveDrowne 1 38
(Ronald Harris) *t.k.h: hld up in tch on inner: effrt u.p over 2f out: no ex and btn over 1f out: wknd fnl f* **10/1**

0640 **8** *nk* **Blue Clumber**[17] 4008 3-8-2 48....(b[1]) MichaelJMMurphy(5) 4 30
(Shaun Harris) *led tl 6f out: styd chsng ldrs tl struggling over 2f out: wknd over 1f out* **33/1**

00-3 **9** 1¼ **Be Royale**[9] 4813 3-8-5 46 oh1....AndrewMullen 8 25
(Michael Appleby) *hld up in tch towards rr: hdwy on outer and rdn to chse ldr briefly 2f out: btn over 1f out: wknd fnl f* **7/2**[2]

0520 **10** *nse* **On The Cusp (IRE)**[27] 2514 6-9-2 50....(p) MartinHarley 3 30
(Violet M Jordan) *rdn along leaving stalls: chsd ldr tl led after 2f: hdd over 2f out: wknd u.p over 1f out* **16/1**

1m 46.46s (5.46) **Going Correction** +0.70s/f (Yiel)
WFA 3 from 4yo+ 7lb **10** Ran SP% **116.5**
Speed ratings (Par 101): **100,99,93,91,90 87,85,85,84,84**
Tote Swingers: 1&2 £5.00, 1&3 £3.80, 2&3 £5.40 CSF £32.30 CT £85.24 TOTE £5.40: £1.60, £1.80, £1.50; EX 38.30 Trifecta £171.20 Pool: £1,749.17 - 7.66 winning units..
Owner T S M S Riley-Smith **Bred** Darley **Trained** Bickham, Somerset

FOCUS
A weak handicap, run at a fair pace and two came well clear. The winner was very well treated on last season's form. A slightly positive view has been taken of the race.

5092 OWEN FUELS OJ WILLIAMS PREMIER FUEL DISTRIBUTORS H'CAP (DIV II) 1m (R)
3:00 (3:00) (Class 6) (0-55,61) 3-Y-0+ **£1,940** (£577; £288; £144) **Stalls** Low

Form RPR

4631 **1** **Calm Attitude (IRE)**[6] 4885 3-9-6 61 6ex....ChrisCatlin 4 67+
(Rae Guest) *t.k.h: in tch in midfield: hdwy to ld 2f out: c clr w runner-up 1f out: edging lft but a jst doing enough ins fnl f: rdn out* **1/1**[1]

-053 **2** *hd* **Sudden Wish (IRE)**[193] 375 4-9-4 52....RichardHughes 11 58
(Gary Moore) *chsd ldrs on outer: upsides wnr and travelling wl 2f out: ev ch and r.o u.p fnl f: a jst hld* **3/1**[2]

-002 **3** 4½ **Blackamoor Harry**[8] 4826 4-8-5 46 oh1....(t) NoelGarbutt(7) 10 41
(Richard Ford) *hld up in tch towards rr: pushed along and hdwy to chse ldrs 3f out: 3rd and unable qck ent fnl f and outpcd by ldng pair fnl f: plugged on* **8/1**[3]

0600 **4** 1¼ **Penang Power**[37] 3859 3-8-11 52....JohnFahy 6 43
(Michael Bell) *dwlt and pushed along leaving stalls: hdwy to chse ldrs after 2f: rdn and pressing ldrs 2f out: unable qck over 1f out: hld and plugged on same pce fnl f* **16/1**

645 **5** 2½ **Cheers Big Ears (IRE)**[31] 4077 7-8-6 47....DanielMuscutt(7) 8 34
(Richard Price) *hld up in tch towards rr: effrt whn hmpd and forced to switch lft wl over 1f out: sn drvn and no imp: wknd fnl f* **8/1**[3]

0000 **6** ½ **Ficelle (IRE)**[6] 4884 4-9-0 55....OisinMurphy(7) 7 40
(Ronald Harris) *detached in last: c wdst st: effrt 2f out: no imp and btn over 1f out: wknd* **12/1**

4-00 **7** 18 **Shes Ellie**[41] 3679 3-8-13 54....(b[1]) CathyGannon 2
(Jo Hughes) *racd keenly: led for 1f: chsd ldr tl led again 3f out: rdn and hdd 2f out: sn dropped out: fdd fnl f* **25/1**

00 **8** 12 **Idolise (IRE)**[52] 3319 4-8-12 46 oh1....(b[1]) SamHitchcott 1
(John Spearing) *led after 1f: rdn and hdd 3f out: sn dropped out and bhd: t.o over 1f out* **50/1**

1m 46.16s (5.16) **Going Correction** +0.70s/f (Yiel)
WFA 3 from 4yo+ 7lb **8** Ran SP% **116.6**
Speed ratings (Par 101): **102,101,97,96,93 93,75,63**
Tote Swingers: 1&2 £1.80, 1&3 £5.00, 2&3 £3.80 CSF £4.16 CT £14.73 TOTE £1.90: £1.10, £1.30, £1.60; EX 5.30 Trifecta £19.80 Pool: £1,944.28 - 73.43 winning units..
Owner The Calm Again Partnership **Bred** R N Auld **Trained** Newmarket, Suffolk

FOCUS
The field shunned the far rail off the home turn and it was another race where the first pair pulled well clear. The winner is thriving and the second looked to have least matched her recent AW figures.

5093 CASTELL HOWELL FOODS H'CAP 1m 6f (R)
3:30 (3:30) (Class 6) (0-60,60) 4-Y-0+ **£1,940** (£577; £288; £144) **Stalls** Low

Form RPR

3422 **1** **Arch Event**[11] 4713 8-8-4 50....(p) DanielMuscutt(7) 10 57
(Bernard Llewellyn) *chsd ldrs: c to stands' rail st: rdn to ld 2f out: asserting whn hung lft 1f out: in command after: kpt on* **3/1**[2]

422 **2** 2 **Steely**[21] 4380 5-9-7 60....RichardHughes 2 64
(Gary Moore) *chsd ldr tl led 5f out: c to stands' rail st: rdn and hdd 2f out: hung rt and nt qckn 1f out: hld but kpt on again ins fnl f* **2/1**[1]

3-00 **3** 3¼ **Camelopardalis**[36] 3907 4-8-11 57....NoelGarbutt(7) 3 57
(Tobias B P Coles) *chsd ldrs: styd towards centre and racing alone in st: no ex u.p over 1f out: plugged on same pce fnl f* **14/1**

5004 **4** 1½ **Richo**[14] 4429 7-8-2 46 oh1....MichaelJMMurphy(5) 4 44
(Shaun Harris) *in tch towards rr: rdn 4f out: 6th and styng on u.p 2f out: kpt on u.p fnl f* **33/1**

5065 **5** ¾ **Reach The Beach**[40] 3744 4-8-11 50....JackMitchell 6 47
(Brendan Powell) *chsd ldrs: jnd ldrs 5f out and c stands' side st: no ex u.p over 1f out: wknd fnl f* **6/1**[3]

4000 **6** ½ **Waving**[15] 4591 4-9-3 59....(t) MarkCoumbe(3) 1 55
(Tony Carroll) *dwlt and pushed along leaving stalls: in tch in midfield: effrt u.p 4f out: 7th and no imp over 1f out: plugged on but no threat to ldrs* **25/1**

600/ **7** 17 **Sure Fire (GER)**[686] 6240 8-8-4 50....EoinWalsh(7) 7 24
(David Evans) *led: hdd and rdn 5f out: wknd wl over 2f out: bhd over 1f out* **16/1**

50 **8** 15 **Sunday Meadow (IRE)**[13] 4633 4-9-7 60....CathyGannon 12 15
(William Knight) *taken down early: t.k.h: hld up in tch rdn and effrt 4f out: no hdwy and wl btn 2f out: eased over 1f out: t.o* **16/1**

00/3 **9** 4½ **Cabuchon (GER)**[14] 4605 6-8-4 48....(t) DeclanBates(5) 11
(David Evans) *in tch in midfield: rdn and struggling 4f out: wl bhd over 2f out: t.o and eased over 1f out* **8/1**

5600 **10** 7 **Kristallo (GER)**[11] 4714 8-8-8 47....SamHitchcott 5
(Dai Burchell) *hld up towards rr: rdn 7f out: lost tch over 4f out: t.o and eased over 2f out* **16/1**

46 **11** 16 **The Yank**[69] 2777 4-9-1 54....(t) JimmyQuinn 9
(Tony Carroll) *in tch towards rr: rdn and no hdwy 5f out: sn bhd: t.o and eased over 2f out* **10/1**

3m 13.79s (9.99) **Going Correction** +0.70s/f (Yiel) **11** Ran SP% **123.9**
Speed ratings (Par 101): **99,97,96,95,94 94,84,76,73,69 60**
Tote Swingers: 1&2 £2.50, 1&3 £12.60, 2&3 £10.90 CSF £9.99 CT £76.03 TOTE £3.50: £1.90, £1.10, £4.50; EX 12.20 Trifecta £215.20 Pool: £1,706.27 - 5.94 winning units..
Owner David Maddocks **Bred** P And Mrs Wafford **Trained** Fochriw, Caerphilly

FOCUS
A moderate staying handicap that served up a real test. The main action came stands' side late on. The third and fourth give perspective.

5094 KNOWLEDGE CENTRE FILLIES' H'CAP 5f
4:00 (4:01) (Class 5) (0-75,67) 3-Y-O+ **£2,587** (£770; £384; £192) **Stalls** Centre

Form RPR
1-10 **1** **Rock On Candy**[5] 4930 4-9-10 **67** ChrisCatlin 4 77+
(John Spearing) *upsides ldr tl led 1/2-way: rdn jst over 1f out: r.o wl ins fnl f* **7/4**[1]
1632 **2** 1 ½ **Shirley's Pride**[26] 4221 3-9-7 **67** (t) RichardHughes 2 71
(Michael Appleby) *taken down early: hld up trcking ldrs: swtchd rt 1f out: sn rdn and effrt to chse wnr: r.o but no imp fnl 100yds* **9/4**[2]
2240 **3** 3 ½ **Griffin Point (IRE)**[2] 5036 6-9-2 **59** (b) SteveDrowne 3 51
(William Muir) *led tl 1/2-way: styd pressing ldr: unable qck over 1f out: wknd fnl 100yds* **9/2**[3]
500 **4** 2 ¼ **Danziger (IRE)**[18] 4487 4-9-2 **64** (v[1]) DeclanBates(5) 1 48
(David Evans) *chsd ldrs: rdn and unable qck over 1f out: wknd ins fnl f: eased cl home* **20/1**
-004 **5** 1 ¼ **Madame Kintyre**[14] 4603 5-8-9 **52** (b) CathyGannon 6 31+
(Rod Millman) *plunged forward jst bef stalls opened and slowly away: swtchd to r against stands' rail sn after s: clsd to chse ldrs 3f out: wknd u.p ent fnl f* **10/1**
2000 **6** 5 **Superior Edge**[42] 3667 6-8-10 **60** (p) OisinMurphy(7) 5 21+
(Christopher Mason) *rrd as stalls opened and v.s.a: nvr able to rcvr: n.d* **6/1**

1m 1.42s (3.12) **Going Correction** +0.70s/f (Yiel)
WFA 3 from 4yo+ 3lb **6** Ran SP% **113.5**
Speed ratings (Par 100): **103,100,95,91,89 81**
Tote Swingers: 1&2 £1.10, 1&3 £1.90, 2&3 £1.70 CSF £6.07 TOTE £2.50: £2.10, £1.20; EX 7.50 Trifecta £24.90 Pool: £3,534.59 - 106.36 winning units..
Owner Tom Hayes **Bred** T M Hayes **Trained** Kinnersley, Worcs

FOCUS
An ordinary sprint handicap for fillies. The fornt pair were clear and the form has been rated slightly positively.

5095 TBA/BRITISH STALLION STUDS EBF FILLIES' H'CAP 1m 4f (R)
4:30 (4:30) (Class 3) (0-95,84) 3-Y-O+ **£9,703** (£2,887; £1,443) **Stalls** Low

Form RPR
0232 **1** **Divergence (IRE)**[10] 4770 3-8-5 **79** LouisSteward(7) 3 87
(Michael Bell) *stdd s: t.k.h: led after 1f: mde rest: rdn and qcknd over 2f out: r.o wl ins fnl f* **5/1**[3]
-334 **2** 1 ½ **Princess Caetani (IRE)**[38] 3834 4-10-0 **84** MartinHarley 2 90
(David Simcock) *hld up in 3rd: clsd to chse ldr 3f out: rdn whn gallop qcknd over 2f out: flashed tail and nt qckn u.p 1f out: btn fnl 100yds* **13/8**[2]
-421 **3** 28 **Soryah (IRE)**[12] 4678 3-9-3 **84** RichardHughes 1 60
(Luca Cumani) *led for 1f: chsd wnr: rdn 5f out: drvn and dropped to 3rd 3f out: btn 2f out: sn eased: t.o* **5/6**[1]

2m 46.24s (8.84) **Going Correction** +0.70s/f (Yiel)
WFA 3 from 4yo 11lb **3** Ran SP% **109.3**
Speed ratings (Par 104): **98,97,78**
CSF £12.32 TOTE £4.00; EX 9.00 Trifecta £9.40 Pool: £1,877.03 - 149.65 winning units..
Owner Lawrie Inman **Bred** L K I Bloodstock Ltd **Trained** Newmarket, Suffolk

FOCUS
A disappointing turnout for a decent prize. It effectively turned into a match, but the form has been taken at face value.

5096 WALK ON WALES H'CAP 1m (R)
5:00 (5:00) (Class 5) (0-75,74) 3-Y-O **£2,587** (£770; £384; £192) **Stalls** Low

Form RPR
4212 **1** **Combustible (IRE)**[28] 4145 3-9-7 **74** RichardHughes 5 81
(Daniel Mark Loughnane) *t.k.h: stdd and dropped in bhd after s: hld up in tch: clsd and n.m.r 2f out: rdn to ld over 1f out: looked in command fnl 100yds: rdn hands and heels towards fin: jst hld on* **11/4**[2]
40-0 **2** nse **Unison (IRE)**[21] 4383 3-8-7 **65** DeclanBates(5) 2 72
(Peter Makin) *in tch in last pair: rdn and effrt 2f out: n.m.r over 1f out: hdwy u.p fnl 150yds: str chal towards fin: jst failed* **6/1**
5140 **3** 1 ¼ **Callmeakhab (IRE)**[63] 2951 3-9-2 **69** SteveDrowne 1 73
(Charles Hills) *chsd ldr: rdn 2f out: pressing wnr u.p 1f out: styd on same pce fnl 100yds* **7/2**[3]
04-3 **4** 4 ½ **Tammuz (IRE)**[47] 3508 3-8-2 **60** MichaelJMMurphy(5) 3 54
(Tony Carroll) *t.k.h: chsd ldrs: rdn and effrt ent fnl 2f: unable qck over 1f out: wknd ins fnl f* **10/1**
5311 **5** 1 ½ **Harbour Captain (IRE)**[10] 4771 3-9-4 **71** CathyGannon 4 61
(Jo Hughes) *taken down early: racd keenly: led tl rdn: edgd lft and hdd over 1f out: wknd ins fnl f* **6/4**[1]

1m 47.24s (6.24) **Going Correction** +0.70s/f (Yiel) **5** Ran SP% **112.3**
Speed ratings (Par 100): **96,95,94,90,88**
CSF £18.67 TOTE £3.20: £1.40, £3.20; EX 23.10 Trifecta £67.80 Pool: £2,635.27 - 29.14 winning units..
Owner Mrs C Loughnane **Bred** Minch Bloodstock **Trained** Baldwin's Gate, Staffs

FOCUS
They went a fair pace in this ordinary handicap. The winner seemingly ran to a similar level to her AW form.

5097 CBI INTERIORS SUPPORTS RYAN JONES H'CAP 6f
5:30 (5:31) (Class 6) (0-65,68) 3-Y-O+ **£1,940** (£577; £288; £144) **Stalls** Centre

Form RPR
4345 **1** **Fairy Wing (IRE)**[28] 4146 6-9-12 **63** (b) MartinHarley 2 71
(Violet M Jordan) *taken down early: led: rdn and jnd over 1f out: hdd jst ins fnl f: battled on wl to ld again fnl 50yds* **12/1**
0131 **2** nk **Steel Rain**[5] 4930 5-9-10 **68** 6ex OisinMurphy(7) 8 75
(Nikki Evans) *chsd ldr: rdn and ev ch over 1f out: drvn to ld jst ins fnl f: hdd and no ex fnl 50yds* **7/4**[1]
0122 **3** 1 ¾ **Verus Delicia (IRE)**[14] 4603 4-9-9 **60** RichardHughes 1 62
(Daniel Mark Loughnane) *in tch: clsd and rdn to chse ldrs 2f out: styd on same pce u.p fnl f* **3/1**[2]
005 **4** nk **Gracie's Games**[8] 4836 7-8-13 **50** (b) ChrisCatlin 6 51
(John Spearing) *in tch: effrt to chse ldrs and drvn over 1f out: styd on same pce ins fnl f* **12/1**
0-00 **5** 2 **All Right Now**[28] 4155 6-8-4 **46** MichaelJMMurphy(5) 13 41
(Tony Newcombe) *in tch in midfield: effrt u.p 2f out: no imp ent fnl f: one pce fnl f* **12/1**
0500 **6** hd **Diamond Vine (IRE)**[28] 4148 5-9-4 **55** (p) CathyGannon 12 50
(Ronald Harris) *in tch in midfield: rdn and no imp 2f out: outpcd over 1f out: no threat to ldrs but kpt on again ins fnl f* **20/1**
3004 **7** 1 ¾ **Depden (IRE)**[12] 4691 5-8-1 **45** LouisSteward(7) 9 34
(Richard Price) *chsd ldrs: rdn 2f out: wknd and edgd lft ent fnl f* **16/1**
02-0 **8** ½ **Giorgio's Dragon (IRE)**[39] 3788 4-9-12 **63** AdamBeschizza 5 51
(Robert Stephens) *squeezed for room leaving stalls: bhd: rdn and sme hdwy over 1f out: no imp fnl f: nvr trbld ldrs* **20/1**
0020 **9** ¾ **Mistress Shy**[28] 4146 6-8-10 **47** (t) AndrewMullen 3 33
(Michael Appleby) *wnt rt s: chsd ldrs: rdn and struggling over 2f out: wknd over 1f out* **33/1**
-000 **10** shd **Cristaliyev**[54] 3246 5-8-6 **48** (p) DeclanBates(5) 11 33
(David Evans) *bhd: rdn and no hdwy 2f out: nvr trbld ldrs* **7/1**[3]
0540 **11** 7 **Lady Mango (IRE)**[187] 449 5-9-1 **52** SteveDrowne 7 16
(Ronald Harris) *a towards rr: rdn and no hdwy 2f out: lost tch over 1f out* **20/1**

1m 14.85s (4.85) **Going Correction** +0.70s/f (Yiel) **11** Ran SP% **120.0**
Speed ratings (Par 101): **95,94,92,91,89 88,86,85,84,84 75**
Tote Swingers: 1&2 £4.90, 1&3 £10.00, 2&3 £1.90 CSF £32.34 CT £86.45 TOTE £16.70: £3.50, £1.20, £1.60; EX 47.90 Trifecta £126.80 Pool: £1,801.69 - 10.65 winning units..
Owner Rakebackmypoker.com **Bred** H Fitzpatrick **Trained** Moreton Morrell, Warwicks

FOCUS
Sound form for the class with the pace holding up well. The winner bounced back towards the level of this year's Fibresand form.
T/Plt: £16.70 to a £1 stake. Pool: £64,264.00 - 2,795.51 winning tickets. T/Qpdt: £9.00 to a £1 stake. Pool: £4,315.00 - 354.65 winning tickets. SP

4378 KEMPTON (A.W) (R-H)
Tuesday, August 6

OFFICIAL GOING: Standard
Wind: Virtually nil Weather: Sunny spells early

5098 CONOR MAYNARD LIVE AT KEMPTON 14.09.13 CLASSIFIED STKS 1m (P)
6:00 (6:00) (Class 6) 3-Y-O+ **£1,940** (£577; £288; £144) **Stalls** Low

Form RPR
40/0 **1** **Barnmore**[27] 4169 5-9-1 60 CharlesBishop(3) 1 71
(Peter Hedger) *in rr: hdwy fr 2f out: led ins fnl f: drvn out* **33/1**
-421 **2** 1 ¾ **Bertie Moon**[47] 3495 3-8-11 64 JamesDoyle 8 66
(Geoffrey Deacon) *chsd ldrs: rdn to take slt ld 2f out: hdd ins fnl f: styd on same pce* **4/1**[2]
-363 **3** ½ **My Gigi**[28] 4144 3-8-11 63 (be) RyanMoore 9 65
(Gary Moore) *sn led: narrowly hdd 2f out: stl ev ch u.p 1f out: styd on same pce fnl f* **9/2**[3]
3330 **4** ¾ **Peter's Friend**[18] 4509 4-9-4 63 PatDobbs 7 64
(Michael Herrington) *chsd ldrs: rdn over 1f out: styd on same pce* **6/1**
0503 **5** ¾ **Knight Charm**[12] 4661 3-8-4 65 (p) CharlieBennett(7) 6 61
(Eve Johnson Houghton) *in rr: impr 4f out: pushed along fr over 1f out and kpt on but nt rch ldrs* **20/1**
5-43 **6** ½ **Perpetual Ambition**[40] 3739 3-8-11 65 (p) FrederikTylicki 2 60
(Paul D'Arcy) *chsd ldrs: rdn over 2f out: styd on same pce* **7/2**[1]
-040 **7** 1 **Eton Rambler (USA)**[51] 3376 3-8-11 60 (b) PatCosgrave 3 58
(George Baker) *in rr: drvn over 2f out: mod hdwy fnl f* **10/1**
0000 **8** 1 ¼ **Confirmed**[42] 3657 4-9-4 45 (t[1]) SilvestreDeSousa 10 56
(Sean Curran) *stdd s: pushed along over 2f out: nvr gng pce to get into contention* **33/1**
-650 **9** 3 **Cherry Tiger**[21] 4383 3-8-11 63 KirstyMilczarek 4 48
(James Toller) *a towards rr* **9/2**[3]
-000 **10** 23 **Red Eight (USA)**[17] 2949 3-8-11 62 (p) TomQueally 5
(John Butler) *chsd ldrs 4f: sn wknd u.p* **25/1**

1m 39.88s (0.08) **Going Correction** +0.05s/f (Slow)
WFA 3 from 4yo+ 7lb **10** Ran SP% **116.5**
Speed ratings (Par 101): **101,99,98,98,97 96,95,94,91,68**
Tote Swingers: 1&2 £37.60, 1&3 £24.40, 2&3 £4.10 CSF £155.72 TOTE £48.40: £7.80, £2.50, £1.50; EX 500.60 Trifecta £1274.50 Part won. Pool: £1,699.41 - 0.49 winning units..
Owner P C F Racing Ltd **Bred** J J Whelan **Trained** Dogmersfield, Hampshire

FOCUS
A modest classified event in which the gallop was no more than fair. The winner came raced against the inside rail throughout. Straightforward form, the winner returning to his best.

5099 BETVICTOR CASINO ON YOUR MOBILE H'CAP 1m 4f (P)
6:30 (6:32) (Class 6) (0-65,65) 3-Y-O+ **£1,940** (£577; £288; £144) **Stalls** Centre

Form RPR
0643 **1** **Dukes Delight (IRE)**[10] 4755 3-9-2 **64** TedDurcan 5 73+
(David Lanigan) *trckd ldrs: led 2f out: drvn fr over 1f out: kpt on clsng stages and a jst doing enough* **11/4**[1]
-444 **2** shd **Opera Buff**[10] 4755 4-10-0 **65** (p) SilvestreDeSousa 11 73
(Sean Curran) *chsd ldr: drvn 3f out: styd on to chse wnr fr 2f out: kpt on wl to cl u.p thrght fnl f: jst failed* **7/1**[3]
-560 **3** 1 ¾ **Mick Duggan**[21] 4383 3-9-3 **65** DavidProbert 6 70+
(Simon Hodgson) *s.i.s: in rr: rapid hdwy over 2f out: kpt on to take 3rd fnl 110yds but no imp on ldng duo* **13/2**[2]
00-0 **4** 1 **My Manekineko**[20] 4411 4-9-4 **55** AidanColeman 2 58
(J R Jenkins) *in tch: hdwy u.p 2f out: chsd ldrs 1f out: one pce clsng stages* **33/1**
0430 **5** 1 **Muskat Link**[13] 4633 3-8-10 **63** AmyScott(5) 14 65
(Henry Candy) *chsd ldrs: drvn and styd on fr 2f out: nt qckn ins fnl f* **16/1**
3131 **6** 1 ¾ **Golden Jubilee (USA)**[14] 4604 4-9-9 **63** WilliamTwiston-Davies(3) 12 62
(Nigel Twiston-Davies) *in tch: hdwy fr 4f out: rdn over 2f out: styd on same pce fr over 1f out* **8/1**
100- **7** ½ **Maoi Chinn Tire (IRE)**[17] 6981 6-10-0 **65** (p) TomQueally 9 63
(Jennie Candlish) *in rr: hdwy u.p over 1f out: styd on clsng stages* **33/1**
0023 **8** shd **Bold And Free**[21] 4374 3-9-3 **65** (p) WilliamCarson 7 63
(David Elsworth) *chsd ldrs: rdn over 2f out: wknd ins fnl f* **10/1**
0446 **9** ¾ **Rodrigo De Freitas (IRE)**[87] 2284 6-9-3 **54** (v) PatCosgrave 8 51
(Jim Boyle) *in rr: pushed along over 2f out: sme hdwy fnl f* **25/1**
6-52 **10** 1 **Lombok**[41] 3688 7-10-0 **65** (v) RyanMoore 13 60
(Gary Moore) *in rr: sme hdwy on outside over 3f out: shkn up and nvr rchd ldrs over 2f out* **10/1**
0234 **11** 1 ¾ **Hermosa Vaquera (IRE)**[12] 4688 3-8-13 **61** JamieSpencer 1 53
(Peter Chapple-Hyam) *led at modest pce: drvn ins fnl 3f: hdd 2f out: wknd qckly over 1f out* **10/1**
0465 **12** 1 ½ **Marlborough House**[13] 4629 3-8-10 **58** MartinDwyer 4 48
(James Given) *in rr: sme hdwy 4f out: rdn and no prog over 2f out* **15/2**

545 **13** *4* **Standing Strong (IRE)**[26] 4205 5-9-11 **62**....................(p) LiamKeniry 10 46
(Zoe Davison) *s.i.s: bhd most of way* **50/1**

0462 **14** *13* **Tartan Trip**[17] 4522 6-10-0 **65**.............................. SeanLevey 3 28
(Luke Dace) *in tch: hdwy 3f out: wknd over 2f out* **33/1**

2m 36.56s (2.06) **Going Correction** +0.05s/f (Slow)
WFA 3 from 4yo+ 11lb **14** Ran SP% **123.2**
Speed ratings (Par 101): **95,94,93,93,92 91,90,90,90,89 88,87,84,76**
Tote Swingers: 1&2 £7.30, 1&3 £15.10, 2&3 £14.60 CSF £20.70 CT £120.17 TOTE £3.30: £1.30, £2.60, £3.00; EX 26.70 Trifecta £379.80 Pool: £1,336.31 - 2.63 winning units..
Owner B E Nielsen **Bred** Bjorn Nielsen **Trained** Upper Lambourn, Berks

FOCUS
A couple of unexposed sorts in a modest handicap. The steady gallop suited the prominent racers and the winner came down the centre in the straight. Straightforward form behind the lightly raced winner.

5100 BOOK NOW FOR LADIES DAY 07.09.13 MEDIAN AUCTION MAIDEN STKS 1m 3f (P)
7:00 (7:15) (Class 6) 3-5-Y-O **£1,940** (£577; £288; £144) **Stalls** Low

Form RPR

33 **1** **I'm Fraam Govan**[21] 4382 5-9-13 0..............................(t) PatCosgrave 12 84+
(George Baker) *trckd ldrs: led 2f out: c clr over 1f out: comf* **4/1**[2]

2 *2 ¼* **Mahdiyah** 3-8-12 0.............................. DaneO'Neill 7 75+
(Saeed bin Suroor) *in rr but in tch: hdwy and wnt sharply lft over 2f out: styd on fr over 1f out to chse wnr ins fnl f but no imp* **7/2**[1]

2 **3** *4 ½* **Le Grande Cheval (IRE)**[22] 4356 3-9-3 0.............................. JamesDoyle 6 71
(Harry Dunlop) *led: rdn ins fnl 3f: hdd 2f out: styd on same pce and lost 2nd ins fnl f* **7/1**

6 **4** *½* **Perfect Summer (IRE)**[28] 4151 3-8-12 0.............................. TomQueally 9 65+
(Lady Cecil) *in rr: rdn over 3f out: styng on towards outside whn bmpd and hmpd over 2f out: kpt on again fr over 1f out: gng on clsng stages* **10/1**

5 **5** *2* **Ocean Secret (IRE)**[36] 3907 3-9-3 0.............................. RyanMoore 4 67
(Jeremy Noseda) *chsd ldrs: rdn over 2f out: wknd over 1f out* **11/2**[3]

4 **6** *2* **Rancho Montoya (IRE)**[48] 3469 3-8-12 0.............................. LiamKeniry 5 59
(Andrew Balding) *in rr: rdn 4f out: hdwy towards outside whn hmpd over 2f out: styd on again fnl f* **6/1**

63 **7** *3 ¾* **Aiyana**[36] 3907 3-8-12 0.............................. SeanLevey 2 53
(Hughie Morrison) *chsd ldrs: disp 2nd and u.p over 2f out: wknd sn after* **14/1**

66 **8** *7* **Dumbfounded (FR)**[13] 4633 5-9-13 0.............................. TedDurcan 10 50
(Lady Herries) *in tch: chsd ldrs 4f out and stl in tch whn hmpd over 2f out: no ch after* **25/1**

00 **9** *½* **Holli Deya**[13] 4632 3-8-7 0.............................. RobertTart(5) 14 41
(Andi Brown) *chsd ldr: rdn and edgd lft over 2f out: sn btn* **100/1**

0- **10** *1 ¾* **Perforce**[293] 7174 4-9-13 0..............................(p) DougieCostello 3 43
(Lucy Wadham) *towards rr most of way* **25/1**

40 **11** *hd* **Tee It Up Tommo (IRE)**[13] 4632 4-9-13 0.............................. GeorgeBaker 11 43
(Michael Wigham) *loose for 15 minutes bef s: mid-div tl wknd 4f out* **33/1**

12 *½* **First Warning** 3-9-3 0.............................. PatDobbs 8 42
(Amanda Perrett) *s.i.s: rdn over 4f out: a towards rr* **16/1**

13 *99* **Invincibull (IRE)** 3-9-3 0.............................. RobertHavlin 1
(Linda Jewell) *t.o fr 1/2-way* **100/1**

2m 20.67s (-1.23) **Going Correction** +0.05s/f (Slow)
WFA 3 from 4yo+ 10lb **13** Ran SP% **118.6**
Speed ratings (Par 101): **106,104,101,100,99 97,95,90,89,88 88,87,15**
Tote Swingers: 1&2 £4.70, 1&3 £7.50, 2&3 £5.20 CSF £17.50 TOTE £5.00: £1.80, £1.60, £2.00; EX 19.90 Trifecta £126.80 Pool: £1,279.71 - 7.56 winning units..
Owner Sir Alex Ferguson **Bred** M Kehoe **Trained** Manton, Wilts
■ Stewards' Enquiry : Dane O'Neill three-day ban: careless riding (Aug 24-26)

FOCUS
A delay of 15 minutes preceded the start of this fair maiden. The gallop was fair and the winner came down the centre in the straight. He more than confirmed his earlier turf form.

5101 BETVICTOR.COM/BRITISH STALLION STUDS EBF MAIDEN STKS 7f (P)
7:30 (7:46) (Class 5) 2-Y-O **£2,911** (£866; £432; £216) **Stalls** Low

Form RPR

4 **1** **Festival Theatre (IRE)**[24] 4304 2-9-5 0.............................. RyanMoore 3 81+
(Sir Michael Stoute) *in rr but in tch: drvn over 2f out: str run over 1f out to chse ldr fnl f: chal fnl 110yds: on top clsng stages whn bmpd nr line* **7/4**[1]

2 *nk* **Intermedium** 2-9-5 0.............................. MickaelBarzalona 11 80+
(Charlie Appleby) *s.i.s: rapid hdwy to chse ldr after 2f: led 2f out: rdn over 1f out: hung lft u.p fnl f: jnd fnl 110yds: hdd clsng stages: no ex whn wnt lft again nr line* **9/4**[2]

0 **3** *8* **Punk**[25] 4256 2-9-5 0.............................. FrederikTylicki 8 59
(Fawzi Abdulla Nass, Bahrain) *chsd ldrs: rdn over 2f out: styd on same pce for wl-hld 3rd fnl f* **25/1**

53 **4** *1 ½* **Diplomatic Force (USA)**[32] 4021 2-9-5 0.............................. SilvestreDeSousa 9 56
(Charlie Appleby) *in rr: rdn 3f out: sme hdwy 2f out: nvr rchd ldrs and styd on same pce* **3/1**[3]

4 **5** *nk* **Officer Drivel (IRE)**[27] 4175 2-9-5 0.............................. FergusSweeney 2 55
(Luke Dace) *t.k.h: chsd ldrs: outpcd fr over 2f out* **16/1**

0 **6** *hd* **Zambeasy**[45] 3574 2-9-5 0.............................. GeorgeBaker 10 54
(Philip Hide) *sn led: hdd 2f out: wknd over 1f out* **50/1**

7 *3 ½* **Buy Out Boy** 2-9-5 0.............................. DaneO'Neill 6 45
(Jo Hughes) *s.i.s: in rr: mod prog fnl f* **33/1**

0 **8** *1 ¾* **Dizzy Miss Lizzy (IRE)**[41] 3694 2-9-0 0.............................. SeanLevey 7 36
(Richard Hannon) *chsd ldrs: rdn 3f out: wknd over 2f out* **20/1**

04 **9** *½* **Aspenbreeze**[8] 4833 2-8-12 0.............................. TimClark(7) 1 39
(Alan Bailey) *chsd ldrs over 4f* **33/1**

1m 27.02s (1.02) **Going Correction** +0.05s/f (Slow) **9** Ran SP% **114.5**
Speed ratings (Par 94): **96,95,86,84,84 84,80,78,77**
Tote Swingers: 1&2 £1.60, 1&3 £8.60, 2&3 £11.00 CSF £5.42 TOTE £2.80: £1.10, £1.10, £8.90; EX 6.20 Trifecta £63.40 Pool: £1,177.47 - 13.92 winning units..
Owner Ballymacoll Stud **Bred** Ballymacoll Stud Farm Ltd **Trained** Newmarket, Suffolk

FOCUS
Not much strength in depth but a race in which the two market leaders pulled clear. The gallop was an ordinary one and the winner came down the centre in the straight.

5102 FOLLOW US ON TWITTER @BETVICTOR H'CAP 2m (P)
8:00 (8:10) (Class 5) (0-75,75) 3-Y-O **£2,587** (£770; £384; £192) **Stalls** Low

Form RPR

5641 **1** **Pearl Spice (IRE)**[5] 4931 3-9-3 **71** 6ex.......................(b) WilliamCarson 3 81
(Tim Pitt) *drvn fr stalls to ld after 2f: shkn up 7f out: hrd drvn over 2f out and sn edgd lft: hung rt u.p fnl f: rdn out* **13/8**[1]

0-33 **2** *1 ½* **Ballinderry Boy**[75] 2602 3-9-0 **68**.............................. DavidProbert 6 76
(Andrew Balding) *in tch: hdwy and rdn 3f out: chsd wnr wl over 1f out: styd on u.p fnl f but no imp fnl 110yds* **7/2**[3]

2-51 **3** *2 ¾* **Chocala (IRE)**[69] 2784 3-9-7 **75**.............................. FergusSweeney 2 80
(Alan King) *chsd ldrs in 3rd: rdn and styd on same pce fr over 1f out* **11/4**[2]

0211 **4** *1* **Miss Tiger Lily**[10] 4753 3-9-6 **74**.............................. JamesDoyle 5 78
(Harry Dunlop) *led 2f: styd chsng wnr: rdn and styd on same pce fr over 2f out* **6/1**

53-1 **5** *2* **Afro**[68] 2800 3-8-11 **65**.............................. JimmyQuinn 1 66
(Peter Hedger) *in rr but in tch: rdn and outpcd over 3f out: styd on again over 1f out but nver any ch* **16/1**

0545 **6** *43* **Mighty Thor**[120] 1425 3-8-3 **57**.............................. SilvestreDeSousa 4 7
(Lydia Richards) *in rr: t.k.h: hdwy 7f out: wknd qckly over 3f out* **16/1**

3m 32.45s (2.35) **Going Correction** +0.05s/f (Slow) **6** Ran SP% **113.0**
Speed ratings (Par 100): **96,95,93,93,92 70**
Tote Swingers: 1&2 £1.60, 2&3 £2.80 CSF £7.77 TOTE £4.50: £3.00, £2.70; EX 8.70 Trifecta £26.70 Pool: £909.33 - 25.51 winning units..
Owner Decadent Racing **Bred** Airlie Stud **Trained** Newmarket, Suffolk

FOCUS
Four last-time-out winners in a fair handicap. The gallop was no more than fair and the winner ended up towards the far side in the closing stages. The third and fourth set the level.

5103 DOWNLOAD THE BETVICTOR MOBILE APP H'CAP 6f (P)
8:30 (8:35) (Class 4) (0-85,85) 3-Y-O **£4,690** (£1,395; £697; £348) **Stalls** Low

Form RPR

-001 **1** **Badr Al Badoor (IRE)**[41] 3691 3-9-7 **85**.......................(v) JamesDoyle 7 91+
(James Fanshawe) *stdd s: hld up in rr but in tch: drvn to chse ldrs whn pushed lft appr fnl f: styd on u.p to ld fnl 75yds: won gng away* **2/1**[2]

25-0 **2** *1 ½* **Rio's Pearl**[53] 3279 3-9-0 **78**.............................. JamieSpencer 2 80
(Ralph Beckett) *chsd ldr: drvn 2f out: slt ld fr 1f out: hdd fnl 75yds: outpcd clsng stages* **13/2**

0050 **3** *nk* **Equitania**[9] 4797 3-9-0 **85**.............................. TimClark(7) 4 86
(Alan Bailey) *led: hrd pressed over 1f out: narrowly hdd sn after: kpt on pressing for 2nd but no ch w wnr fnl 50yds* **14/1**

2-03 **4** *1 ¾* **Agerzam**[48] 3474 3-9-7 **85**.............................. WilliamBuick 1 80
(Roger Varian) *chsd ldrs: rdn to chal whn edgd lft appr fnl f: sn btn* **13/8**[1]

421- **5** *4 ½* **Ferjaan**[299] 7006 3-9-1 **79**.............................. DaneO'Neill 6 61
(John Gosden) *stdd s: in rr but in tch: sme hdwy over 2f out: sn rdn: nvr rchd ldrs and wknd over 1f out* **4/1**[3]

1m 12.74s (-0.36) **Going Correction** +0.05s/f (Slow) **5** Ran SP% **111.4**
Speed ratings (Par 102): **104,102,101,99,93**
CSF £14.69 TOTE £2.90: £2.00, £2.50; EX 10.00 Trifecta £82.00 Pool: £507.10 - 4.63 winning units..
Owner Mohamed Obaida **Bred** Con Harrington **Trained** Newmarket, Suffolk

FOCUS
A useful handicap in which the gallop was just an ordinary one to the home turn. The winner came centre to stands' side in the straight and is going the right way.

5104 £25 FREE BET AT BETVICTOR.COM FILLIES' H'CAP 6f (P)
9:00 (9:00) (Class 5) (0-70,70) 3-Y-O+ **£2,587** (£770; £384; £192) **Stalls** Low

Form RPR

2-3 **1** **Truly Madly (IRE)**[4] 4942 3-9-2 **65**.............................. JamesDoyle 7 70
(Hans Adielsson) *in rr: hrd drvn and hdwy over 1f out: styd on u.p fnl f to ld clsng stages: all out* **8/1**[3]

321 **2** *nk* **Dodina (IRE)**[12] 4687 3-9-7 **70**.............................. JamieSpencer 4 74
(Peter Chapple-Hyam) *chsd ldrs: wnt 2nd over 1f out: str chal fnl 110yds tl outpcd by wnr clsng stages* **11/10**[1]

6602 **3** *½* **Elusive Gold (IRE)**[21] 4378 3-9-2 **65**.............................. DaneO'Neill 1 68
(J W Hills) *chsd ldrs: led wl over 1f out: jnd fnl 110yds: outpcd into 3rd clsng stages* **9/1**

4050 **4** *1 ¼* **Amber Heights**[18] 4487 5-9-0 **64**.............................. AmyScott(5) 6 64
(Henry Candy) *in rr: hdwy over 1f out: styd on clsng stages: nt rch ldrs* **20/1**

5634 **5** *nk* **Glastonberry**[21] 4385 5-9-10 **69**.............................. GeorgeBaker 8 68
(Geoffrey Deacon) *chsd ldrs: rdn and outpcd over 1f out: kpt on again clsng stages* **4/1**[2]

-305 **6** *1 ¼* **Camache Queen (IRE)**[78] 2513 5-9-6 **65**.......................(t) LiamKeniry 2 60
(Joseph Tuite) *chsd ldrs: rdn and outpcd over 1f out* **14/1**

0401 **7** *shd* **Commandingpresence (USA)**[3] 4999 7-9-5 **64** 6ex......... KieranO'Neill 3 59
(John Bridger) *led: rdn over 2f out: hdd wl over 1f out: wknd fnl f* **12/1**

6033 **8** *½* **Catalinas Diamond (IRE)**[12] 4659 5-9-7 **66**............(t) FergusSweeney 5 59
(Pat Murphy) *in tch: chsd ldrs over 2f out: wknd over 1f out* **8/1**[3]

1m 13.49s (0.39) **Going Correction** +0.05s/f (Slow)
WFA 3 from 5yo+ 4lb **8** Ran SP% **119.0**
Speed ratings (Par 100): **99,98,97,96,95 94,94,93**
Tote Swingers: 1&2 £3.70, 1&3 £4.00, 2&3 £4.80 CSF £18.02 CT £87.85 TOTE £18.60: £4.90, £2.00, £5.50; EX 29.40 Trifecta £185.60 Pool: £944.12 - 3.81 winning units..
Owner Hans Adielsson A B **Bred** Laundry Cottage Stud Farm **Trained** Kingston Lisle, Oxon

FOCUS
A modest fillies' handicap run at an ordinary gallop and a race in which the whole field finished in a bit of a heap. The winner raced down the centre in the straight. Ordinary form as befits the grade.
T/Jkpt: £100,695.80 to a £1 stake. Pool: £992,775.85 - 7.00 winning tickets. T/Plt: £71.40 to a £1 stake. Pool: £92,089.22 - 940.80 winning tickets. T/Qpdt: £15.60 to a £1 stake. Pool: £6,257.08 - 295.51 winning tickets. ST

5053 RIPON (R-H)
Tuesday, August 6

OFFICIAL GOING: Good (good to soft in places; 8.2)
Wind: Virtually nil Weather: Cloudy with sunny periods

5105 SILKS AND SADDLES BAR MAIDEN STKS 6f
6:10 (6:10) (Class 5) 2-Y-O **£3,234** (£962; £481; £240) **Stalls** High

Form RPR

3 **1** **Ventura Quest (USA)**[24] 4312 2-9-5 0.............................. TonyHamilton 7 80+
(Richard Fahey) *slt ld: rdn along 2f out: hdd jst over 1f out: drvn and rallied to ld again ins fnl f: edgd rt and kpt on* **2/5**[1]

03 **2** *2* **Kenny The Captain (IRE)**[9] 4801 2-9-5 0.............................. DuranFentiman 2 73+
(Tim Easterby) *trckd ldrs: hdwy 2f out: rdn over 1f out: styd on fnl f* **8/1**[3]

5 **3** *3* **See The Sun**[17] 4539 2-9-5 0.............................. DavidAllan 4 64
(Tim Easterby) *cl up: rdn wl over 1f out: slt ld appr fnl f: sn drvn: hdd ins fnl f: wknd* **9/2**[2]

The Form Book Flat, Raceform Ltd, Compton, RG20 6NL.

4 1/2 **An Chulainn (IRE)** 2-9-0 0 .... FrannyNorton 1 61+
(Mark Johnston) *wnt rt and s.i.s: green and bhd: pushed along and hdwy 1/2-way: rdn and rn green 2f out: styd on fnl f: nrst fin* **9/1**

00 **5** 3 3/4 **Rokeby**[97] 1930 2-9-5 0 .... AndrewElliott 3 51
(George Moore) *towards rr: pushed along and sme hdwy 2f out: n.d* **80/1**

05 **6** 2 **Freddie Kilroy**[11] 4716 2-9-5 0 .... GrahamLee 5 45
(Ed Dunlop) *hld up in rr: pushed along wl over 2f out: swtchd rt to outer and rdn wl over 1f out: n.d* **14/1**

0 **7** 5 **Bashiba (IRE)**[11] 4724 2-9-5 0 .... PaulMulrennan 9 30
(Nigel Tinkler) *chsd ldrs: rdn along over 2f out: sn wknd* **20/1**

0 **8** nk **Nu Form Fire (IRE)**[17] 4539 2-9-2 0 .... DeclanCannon(3) 8 29
(Nigel Tinkler) *trckd ldrs: pushed along wl over 2f out: rdn and wknd wl over 1f out* **100/1**

1m 13.23s (0.23) **Going Correction** 0.0s/f (Good) **8** Ran SP% **124.4**
Speed ratings (Par 94): **98,95,91,90,85 83,76,75**
Tote Swingers: 1&2 £2.80, 1&3 £1.10, 2&3 £3.30 CSF £5.55 TOTE £1.40: £1.02, £1.40, £1.80; EX 6.10 Trifecta £15.30 Pool: £1,253.34 - 61.18 winning units..
Owner Middleham Park Racing LXIX **Bred** James T Gottwald **Trained** Musley Bank, N Yorks

FOCUS
Rail on bend from back straight to home straight moved out 3m, adding about 7yds to races on Round course. A moderate 2yo maiden. The winner was fully entitled to win this well as the odds suggested. The bare form is perhaps a bit better than rated.

5106 CONSTANT SECURITY SERVICES NURSERY H'CAP 5f
6:40 (6:40) (Class 5) (0-75,73) 2-Y-O **£3,234** (£962; £481; £240) **Stalls** High

Form RPR

0000 **1** **Fuel Injection**[6] 4886 2-8-2 **54** .... JamesSullivan 1 63
(Paul Midgley) *chsd ldrs and swtchd lft towards stands' rail: chsd ldr after 2f: rdn to ld 1 1/2f out: styd on strly* **3/1**[2]

032 **2** 3 1/2 **Anytimeatall (IRE)**[28] 4142 2-8-6 **63** .... NatashaEaton(5) 4 59
(Alan Bailey) *sn led: rdn along and hdd 1 1/2f out: sn drvn and one pce* **5/2**[1]

3104 **3** 3/4 **Secret Applause**[9] 4802 2-8-9 **66** .... ConnorBeasley(5) 6 59
(Michael Dods) *prom early: sn rdn along and outpcd in rr: hdwy wl over 1f out: styd on fnl f to take 3rd nr fin* **4/1**[3]

24F2 **4** 3/4 **Cheeky Peta'S**[22] 4351 2-9-3 **69** .... GrahamLee 3 60
(James Given) *in tch: hdwy to chse ldng pair wl over 2f out: rdn wl over 1f out: sn no imp* **9/1**

6265 **5** 12 **Song Of Rowland (IRE)**[13] 4616 2-9-4 **70** ....(v[1]) DanielTudhope 5 17
(David O'Meara) *chsd ldng pair: rdn along bef 1/2-way: sn wknd and eased whn bhd fr wl over 1f out* **5/2**[1]

1m 0.3s (0.30) **Going Correction** 0.0s/f (Good) **5** Ran SP% **112.1**
Speed ratings (Par 94): **97,91,90,89,69**
CSF £11.07 TOTE £3.20: £3.10, £1.30; EX 15.30 Trifecta £55.00 Pool: £647.81 - 8.82 winning units..
Owner Mrs Mandy Verity **Bred** Whitsbury Manor Stud & Pigeon House Stud **Trained** Westow, N Yorks

FOCUS
Not many got into this modest nursery, which had little depth to it.

5107 WASHROOM COMPANY H'CAP 1m 4f 10y
7:10 (7:11) (Class 4) (0-80,78) 3-Y-O **£4,851** (£1,443; £721; £360) **Stalls** Low

Form RPR

323 **1** **Bushel (USA)**[19] 4454 3-9-7 **78** .... FrannyNorton 4 85
(Mark Johnston) *set stdy pce: pushed along and qcknd 3f out: rdn 2f out: drvn ent fnl f and hld on gamely* **11/4**[2]

5514 **2** 1/2 **Esteaming**[66] 2879 3-9-7 **78** .... PhillipMakin 3 84
(David Barron) *trckd ldrs: hdwy on outer 3f out: cl up 2f out: rdn to chal wl over 1f out and ev ch tl drvn and no ex wl ins fnl f* **8/11**[1]

154 **3** 1 3/4 **Nonotnow**[12] 4672 3-8-10 **67** .... DavidAllan 1 70
(Tim Easterby) *trckd ldrs on inner: pushed along and sltly outpcd 3f out: hdwy 2f out: swtchd lft and rdn ins fnl f: styd on wl to take 3rd nr fin* **5/1**[3]

4030 **4** nse **Precision Strike**[12] 4688 3-7-12 **60** oh3 ow1 ....(v) PhilipPrince(5) 5 63?
(Richard Guest) *prom: cl up on outer 1/2-way: pushed along 3f out: rdn 2f out and ev ch tl drvn and one pce ins fnl f* **25/1**

20-0 **5** 15 **Vicky Valentine**[64] 2915 3-8-5 **62** .... MartinLane 2 43
(Alistair Whillans) *hld up in rr: hdwy and tk clsr order 4f out: rdn along 3f out: sn drvn and wknd* **16/1**

2m 39.97s (3.27) **Going Correction** +0.15s/f (Good) **5** Ran SP% **111.0**
Speed ratings (Par 102): **95,94,93,93,83**
CSF £5.22 TOTE £2.30: £2.10, £1.02; EX 6.80 Trifecta £9.80 Pool: £450.45 - 34.15 winning units..
Owner Sheikh Hamdan Bin Mohammed Al Maktoum **Bred** Darley **Trained** Middleham Moor, N Yorks

FOCUS
A modest 3-y-o handicap in which the winner dictated. He probably showed improved form but the slow time and prominence of the fourth raise doubts.

5108 DAVID CHAPMAN MEMORIAL H'CAP 5f
7:40 (7:41) (Class 3) (0-95,93) 3-Y-O- **£7,561** (£2,263; £1,131; £566; £282) **Stalls** High

Form RPR

0000 **1** **Cheviot (USA)**[9] 4800 7-9-5 **93** ....(p) JasonHart(5) 2 101
(Ian Semple) *racd alone centre and cl up: rdn and edgd lft to join main gp 2f out: rdn to ld over 1f out: drvn ins fnl f: jst hld on* **11/1**

1061 **2** nse **Adam's Ale**[18] 4510 4-8-0 **74** oh1 .... ShirleyTeasdale(5) 1 82
(Paul Midgley) *cl up far side: led that gp over 1f out and ev ch: drvn ins fnl f: jst failed: 1st of 2 in gp* **10/1**

0205 **3** nk **Rylee Mooch**[11] 4707 5-8-5 **79** ....(e) ConnorBeasley(5) 3 86
(Richard Guest) *led far side gp and cl up: rdn 2f out: drvn and hdd over 1f out: kpt on wl u.p fnl f: 2nd of 2 in gp* **10/1**

4644 **4** 1/2 **Waseem Faris (IRE)**[7] 4860 4-8-5 **74** oh1 .... FrannyNorton 13 79
(Mick Channon) *chsd ldrs on stands' rail: hdwy and n.m.r wl over 1f out: sn swtchd rt and rdn: fin strly: 2nd of 13 in gp* **13/2**[2]

0053 **5** 1 1/4 **Silvanus (IRE)**[13] 4620 8-8-11 **80** .... PaulMulrennan 6 81
(Paul Midgley) *in tch stands' side: hdwy to chse ldrs 2f out: sn rdn and kpt on same pce fnl f: 3rd of 13 in gp* **14/1**

-502 **6** hd **Singeur (IRE)**[18] 4507 6-9-7 **90** .... RobertWinston 11 90
(Robin Bastiman) *in rr stands' side: hdwy wl over 1f out: hmpd and swtchd rt ent fnl f: rdn and styd on wl towards fin: 4th of 13 in gp* **6/1**[1]

5100 **7** hd **Lucky Numbers (IRE)**[9] 4812 7-9-6 **89** .... DanielTudhope 5 88
(David O'Meara) *wnt lft and n.m.r s: in tch stands' side: hdwy wl over 1f out: rdn and kpt on fnl f: 5th of 13 in gp* **20/1**

3046 **8** shd **Cocktail Charlie**[3] 5011 5-8-5 **74** ....(b) DuranFentiman 9 73
(Tim Easterby) *sn led stands' side gp and overall ldr: rdn 2f out: drvn and hdd over 1f out: grad wknd: 6th of 13 in gp* **14/1**

0030 **9** 1 1/4 **Oldjoesaid**[4] 4954 9-8-4 **78** .... GeorgeChaloner(5) 10 72
(Paul Midgley) *chsd ldrs stands' side: rdn along wl over 1f out: grad wknd: 7th of 13 in gp* **12/1**

0510 **10** 1/2 **Another Wise Kid (IRE)**[9] 4800 5-9-7 **90** .... MickyFenton 14 87
(Paul Midgley) *in tch stands' side: hdwy whn nt clr run over 1f out: one pce after: 8th of 13 in gp* **12/1**

500 **11** nse **Cadeaux Pearl**[7] 4860 5-8-7 **76** ....(b) LukeMorris 15 68
(Scott Dixon) *prom stands' side: rdn 2f out: sn drvn and wknd over 1f out: 9th of 13 in gp* **16/1**

-413 **12** nk **Jack Luey**[39] 3776 6-9-3 **86** .... TomEaves 8 77
(Lawrence Mullaney) *hmpd s: a in rr stands' side: 10th of 13 in gp* **7/1**[3]

0000 **13** 2 **Hazelrigg (IRE)**[3] 5011 8-8-10 **79** .... DavidAllan 12 63
(Tim Easterby) *prom stands' side: rdn 2f out: sn wknd: 11th of 13 in gp* **25/1**

1506 **14** 1 1/2 **Chunky Diamond (IRE)**[13] 4620 4-8-6 **75** ....(t) JamesSullivan 7 54
(Ruth Carr) *hmpd s: a in rr stands' side: 12th of 13 in gp* **22/1**

4100 **15** 3 **Storm Moon (USA)**[9] 4800 3-9-3 **89** .... JoeFanning 4 56
(Mark Johnston) *midfield: stands' side: rdn along bef 1/2-way: sn wknd: last of 13 in gp* **10/1**

58.97s (-1.03) **Going Correction** 0.0s/f (Good)
WFA 3 from 4yo+ 3lb **15** Ran SP% **123.3**
Speed ratings (Par 107): **108,107,107,106,104 104,104,103,101,101 100,100,97,94,90**
Tote Swingers: 1&2 £59.10, 1&3 £19.10, 2&3 £58.60 CSF £115.54 CT £768.91 TOTE £11.70: £3.20, £6.70, £3.00; EX 256.30 Trifecta £439.40 Part won. Pool: £585.93 - 0.41 winning units..
Owner Mrs J Penman, G Robertson, W Robinson **Bred** Darley **Trained** Carluke, S Lanarks
■ Stewards' Enquiry : Shirley Teasdale two-day ban: careless riding (Aug 20,24)

FOCUS
A fair sprint. The winner ran all over the place, but the majority kept stands' side. The winner was well in on his form from last year.

5109 RIPONBET OUR PROFITS STAY IN RACING H'CAP 2m
8:10 (8:15) (Class 4) (0-85,82) 3-Y-O+ **£4,851** (£1,443; £721; £360) **Stalls** High

Form RPR

3636 **1** **Almagest**[9] 4804 5-9-12 **80** .... DanielTudhope 6 88
(David O'Meara) *trckd ldrs: effrt and nt clr run 2f out: swtchd lft and rdn over 1f out: drvn ins fnl f: styd on to ld nr fin* **8/1**[3]

0-60 **2** hd **Rosairlie (IRE)**[88] 2242 5-9-1 **69** .... FrannyNorton 8 77
(Micky Hammond) *trckd ldrs: hdwy over 3f out: rdn to chal wl over 1f out: led ent fnl f: sn drvn: hdd and no ex nr fin* **25/1**

421 **3** 1 **Alwilda**[6] 4899 3-8-11 **80** 6ex .... LukeMorris 7 87
(Sir Mark Prescott Bt) *trckd ldng pair: hdwy 3f out: cl up over 2f out: rdn to ld over 1f out: drvn: edgd lft and hdd ent fnl f: kpt on same pce towards fin* **4/5**[1]

2262 **4** 1 1/4 **Brasingaman Eric**[40] 3726 6-8-13 **67** .... AndrewElliott 4 72
(George Moore) *led: pushed along over 3f out: rdn wl over 2f out: drvn and hdd over 1f out: kpt on u.p fnl f* **16/1**

3-55 **5** 3/4 **Mojolika**[21] 4372 5-9-5 **73** .... GrahamGibbons 1 77
(Tim Easterby) *trckd ldrs on inner: hdwy 3f out: rdn along and n.m.r 2f out: sn drvn and kpt on same pce appr fnl f* **10/1**

0001 **6** 1 1/2 **Man Of Plenty**[54] 3248 4-9-10 **78** ....(p) GrahamLee 3 80
(Ed Dunlop) *hld up towards rr: effrt and hdwy 3f out: rdn along over 2f out: sn drvn and no imp* **5/1**[2]

3014 **7** 5 **Tartan Jura**[21] 4372 5-9-6 **74** ....(p) JoeFanning 5 70
(Mark Johnston) *trckd ldr: cl up 5f out: rdn along over 3f out: drvn and wknd over 2f out* **14/1**

1662 **8** nk **Rocktherunway (IRE)**[10] 4782 4-10-0 **82** ....(p) TomEaves 9 78
(Michael Dods) *hld up in rr: swtchd to outer and sme hdwy 3f out: sn rdn and btn* **10/1**

3m 31.62s (-0.18) **Going Correction** +0.15s/f (Good)
WFA 3 from 4yo+ 15lb **8** Ran SP% **117.9**
Speed ratings (Par 105): **106,105,105,104,104 103,101,101**
Tote Swingers: 1&2 £35.60, 1&3 £1.70, 2&3 £9.60 CSF £177.82 CT £332.85 TOTE £10.10: £2.50, £7.40, £1.10; EX 191.50 Trifecta £459.40 Part won. Pool: £612.59 - 0.32 winning units..
Owner The Marooned Crew **Bred** Juddmonte Farms Ltd **Trained** Nawton, N Yorks

FOCUS
A fair staying handicap and the winner is one to follow. The second and fourth set the level.

5110 SIS LIVE MAIDEN STKS 1m 1f 170y
8:40 (8:41) (Class 5) 3-4-Y-O **£3,234** (£962; £481; £240) **Stalls** Low

Form RPR

4-5 **1** **Spirit Of Rio (IRE)**[12] 4667 3-9-3 0 .... GrahamGibbons 10 79+
(David Barron) *trckd ldrs: hdwy on outer 3f out: cl up 2f out: rdn to ld and edgd rt 1 1/2f out: drvn clr ent fnl f: kpt on strly* **7/2**[2]

2332 **2** 3 1/4 **Response**[20] 4404 3-9-3 75 ....(p) LiamJones 2 73
(William Haggas) *led: pushed along 3f out: jnd and rdn 2f out: hdd whn n.m.r and sltly hmpd 1 1/2f out: sn drvn and kpt on same pce* **11/8**[1]

66 **3** 4 1/2 **Henpecked**[9] 4805 3-8-12 0 .... MichaelO'Connell 4 59
(Alistair Whillans) *chsd ldrs: rdn along and sltly outpcd 3f out: styd on u.p fr over 1f out: nrst fin* **50/1**

54 **4** 3/4 **Duke Of Grazeon (IRE)**[18] 4481 3-9-3 0 ....(b[1]) RoystonFfrench 1 63
(Mrs Ilka Gansera-Leveque) *trckd ldrs on inner: effrt 3f out and sn pushed along: rdn 2f out: one pce u.p fnl f* **66/1**

06 **5** 3/4 **Young Jay**[9] 4813 3-9-3 0 .... FrannyNorton 5 62
(Mark Johnston) *in tch: effrt 3f out: rdn along over 2f out: sn no imp* **33/1**

6 2 **Bold Citizen (IRE)** 3-9-3 0 .... GrahamLee 9 58
(Ed Dunlop) *dwlt and outpcd in rr: hdwy and in tch 1/2-way: rdn along over 2f out: sn one pce* **8/1**[3]

4-4 **7** nk **Bourbon (IRE)**[46] 3539 3-9-3 0 .... JoeFanning 3 57
(Mark Johnston) *trckd ldrs: swtchd to outer and hdwy over 3f out: rdn to chal over 2f out: drvn and wknd wl over 1f out* **7/2**[2]

8 13 **Roycano** 3-9-3 0 .... JamesSullivan 7 33
(Michael Easterby) *hld up: a in rr* **33/1**

4 **9** 42 **Bordah (USA)**[9] 4813 3-9-3 0 .... AndreaAtzeni 8
(Roger Varian) *chsd ldr: rdn along over 3f out: sn wknd: lost action and eased wl over 1f out: virtually p.u fnl f* **8/1**[3]

2m 5.38s (-0.02) **Going Correction** +0.15s/f (Good) **9** Ran SP% **118.1**
Speed ratings (Par 103): **106,103,99,99,98 97,96,86,52**
Tote Swingers: 1&2 £2.50, 1&3 £20.00, 2&3 £25.20 CSF £8.79 TOTE £4.60: £2.00, £1.10, £12.60; EX 14.50 Trifecta £458.60 Pool: £821.40 - 1.34 winning units..
Owner Billy & Debbie Glover **Bred** Kilnamoragh Stud **Trained** Maunby, N Yorks

FOCUS
An interesting maiden. The winner did it quite well but caution has been taken when rating the race.
T/Plt: £43.00 to a £1 stake. Pool: £63,915.30 - 1,084.10 winning tickets. T/Qpdt: £18.40 to a £1 stake. Pool: £5,122.29 - 205.29 winning tickets. JR

5111 - 5114a (Foreign Racing) - See Raceform Interactive

3377 CORK (R-H)

Tuesday, August 6

OFFICIAL GOING: Good (good to yielding in places)

5115a IRISH STALLION FARMS EUROPEAN BREEDERS FUND GIVE THANKS STKS (GROUP 3) (FILLIES) 1m 4f

7:05 (7:05) 3-Y-0+ **£40,955** (£11,971; £5,670; £1,890)

RPR

1 **Venus De Milo (IRE)**[17] 4550 3-8-13 114 ow1 JosephO'Brien 4 105+
(A P O'Brien, Ire) *sn led: 3 l clr 1/2-way: pushed along whn pressed for ld over 2f out: rdn over 1f out and stretched clr wl ins fnl f* **1/4**[1]

2 3 ½ **Bunairgead (IRE)**[19] 4465 3-8-12 101 (b) KevinManning 2 96+
(J S Bolger, Ire) *broke wl: restrained and sn trckd ldr in 2nd: rdn to chal 2f out: kpt on wl u.p but no imp on wnr wl ins fnl f* **7/1**[2]

3 nk **Midnight Soprano (IRE)**[31] 4059 6-9-12 105 MarcMonaghan 1 99
(P D Deegan, Ire) *broke wl and led: sn restrained and chsd ldrs in 3rd: rdn over 3f out and relegated to 4th: responded to press to chal over 1f out and wnt 3rd: kpt on but sn no ch w wnr* **7/1**[2]

4 ½ **Kiss Goodnight (IRE)**[20] 4419 3-8-12 85 WJLee 3 95
(John Joseph Murphy, Ire) *chsd ldrs: 4th 1/2-way: wnt 3rd over 3f out: sn rdn and r.o same pce: 4th and no imp on wnr ins fnl f* **33/1**

5 ¾ **Beach Of Falesa (IRE)**[37] 3871 4-9-9 93 SeamieHeffernan 5 94
(A P O'Brien, Ire) *settled towards rr: 5th 1/2-way: rdn over 2f out and no ex: styd on same pce ins fnl f* **16/1**[3]

6 1 ¾ **Sleeping Beauty (IRE)**[41] 3704 3-8-12 89 PatSmullen 6 91
(D K Weld, Ire) *settled in rr: 6th 1/2-way: rdn over 2f out and no ex: styd on same pce* **16/1**[3]

2m 39.88s (-8.02)
WFA 3 from 4yo+ 11lb **6** Ran SP% **119.7**
CSF £3.37 TOTE £1.10: £1.02, £2.00; DF 3.80.
Owner Mrs John Magnier & Michael Tabor & Derrick Smith **Bred** Tullpark Ltd **Trained** Ballydoyle, Co Tipperary

FOCUS
For the second year in succession, a long odds-on favourite. Given the vast amount of talented females at his disposal over the last decade, it's hard to believe Aidan O'Brien had only won this race twice in that time. The winner didn't need to match her best.

5116 - 5118a (Foreign Racing) - See Raceform Interactive

5039 DEAUVILLE (R-H)

Tuesday, August 6

OFFICIAL GOING: Turf: good; fibresand: standard

5119a PRIX DE COURBEPINE (MAIDEN) (3YO FILLIES) (FIBRESAND) 1m 1f 110y

1:50 (1:50) 3-Y-0 **£10,162** (£4,065; £3,048; £2,032; £1,016)

RPR

1 **Grandezza (GER)**[19] 3-9-0 0 MaximeGuyon 5 82
(W Mongil, Germany) **18/1**

2 ¾ **Sinnderelle (FR)**[61] 3-9-0 0 AlexisBadel 10 80
(Mme M Bollack-Badel, France) **9/1**[3]

3 1 ¼ **Udana (IRE)** 3-9-0 0 UmbertoRispoli 2 78
(M Delzangles, France) **17/1**

4 1 ½ **Elwaaryaa**[67] 3-9-0 0 (b[1]) OlivierPeslier 8 75
(F Head, France) **13/2**[2]

5 ¾ **Cortogna (USA)**[51] 3-9-0 0 ThierryThulliez 3 73
(N Clement, France) **15/1**

6 nk **Blue Shining (USA)**[26] 3-9-0 0 FlavienPrat 11 73
(T Clout, France) **12/1**

7 2 ½ **Monsoon (IRE)**[66] 3-9-0 0 ChristopheSoumillon 6 68
(P Bary, France) **4/5**[1]

8 hd **Polar Legend (FR)** 3-9-0 0 FLenclud 7 67
(L A Urbano-Grajales, France) **77/1**

9 1 ½ **Corniche (FR)** 3-9-0 0 TheoBachelot 4 64
(David Elsworth) *dwlt: settled in midfield on inner: rdn and no imp fr over 2f out: nvr in contention* **23/1**

10 shd **Gut Instinct (FR)**[19] 3-9-0 0 StephaneBreux 9 64
(Mme R-W Allen, France) **42/1**

11 20 **Cesta Punta (FR)**[26] 3-9-0 0 StephanePasquier 1 23
(Mlle V Dissaux, France) **17/1**

2m 3.82s (123.82) **11** Ran SP% **117.0**
WIN (incl. 1 euro stake): 19.40. PLACES: 4.50, 2.50, 5.30. DF: 40.30. SF: 138.30.
Owner Rennstall Gestut Hachtsee **Bred** Gestut Hachtsee **Trained** Germany

5120a PRIX DE TOURGEVILLE (LISTED RACE) (3YO COLTS & GELDINGS) (TURF) 1m (R)

2:20 (2:20) 3-Y-0 **£22,357** (£8,943; £6,707; £4,471; £2,235)

RPR

1 **Mshawish (USA)**[49] 3421 3-9-2 0 FrankieDettori 6 117
(M Delzangles, France) **9/10**[1]

2 nk **Market Share**[40] 3-8-11 0 ThierryThulliez 1 111
(P Bary, France) **17/2**

3 3 **Five Avenue (IRE)**[40] 3-8-11 0 ChristopheSoumillon 5 104
(J-C Rouget, France) **9/2**[2]

4 1 ¼ **Kapstadt (FR)**[32] 4043 3-8-11 0 (p) IoritzMendizabal 4 101
(F Doumen, France) **19/1**

5 ¾ **Pont Neuilly (FR)**[32] 4043 3-8-11 0 Pierre-CharlesBoudot 8 100
(Y De Nicolay, France) **14/1**

6 1 ¼ **Mondialiste (IRE)**[37] 3876 3-9-2 0 OlivierPeslier 7 102
(F Head, France) **15/2**[3]

7 hd **Alhebayeb (IRE)**[26] 4216 3-8-11 0 PaulHanagan 2 96
(Richard Hannon) *towards rr on inner: tk clsr order over 2f out: sn rdn and no imp: kpt on at one pce fnl f: nvr trbld ldrs* **15/1**

1m 39.47s (-1.33) **7** Ran SP% **111.0**
WIN (incl. 1 euro stake): 1.90. PLACES: 1.20, 1.50, 1.30. DF: 9.40. SF: 8.50.
Owner HE Sh Joaan Bin Hamad Al Thani **Bred** OTIF 2007 **Trained** France

4660 BRIGHTON (L-H)

Wednesday, August 7

OFFICIAL GOING: Good to firm (good in places; 7.5)
Wind: medium, half behind, Weather: overcast, dry

5121 LEXI BOO STRICKLAND NURSERY H'CAP 5f 59y

2:20 (2:21) (Class 5) (0-75,75) 2-Y-0 **£2,587** (£770; £384; £192) **Stalls** Low

Form RPR

412 1 **Umneyati**[28] 4174 2-9-3 71 NeilCallan 3 75+
(James Tate) *t.k.h: chsd ldr tl rdn to ld over 1f out: rdn out hands and heels fnl 100yds: comf* **9/4**[1]

3410 2 1 **Weisse Socken (IRE)**[18] 4528 2-9-4 72 (p) JimCrowley 4 71
(Ralph Beckett) *t.k.h: hld up in tch: trcking ldng pair whn gap clsd and forced to switch rt jst over 1f out: rallied to chse wnr wl ins fnl f: r.o* **11/4**[2]

5142 3 ½ **Mr Dandy Man (IRE)**[11] 4783 2-9-7 75 MartinHarley 1 73
(Ronald Harris) *broke fast: led: edgd lft and hit rail over 2f out: rdn and hdd over 1f out: styd on same pce after: lost 2nd wl ins fnl f* **4/1**

0602 4 2 **Limegrove**[14] 4630 2-9-2 70 TomQueally 6 60
(David Evans) *mounted on crse: in tch in rr: rdn and effrt wl over 2f out: 4th and styd on same pce fnl f* **12/1**

4432 5 7 **Prisca**[37] 3896 2-9-4 72 RichardHughes 7 37
(Richard Hannon) *in tch: rdn and effrt 2f out: no ex and btn ent fnl f: eased ins fnl f* **3/1**[3]

1m 2.2s (-0.10) **Going Correction** -0.15s/f (Firm) **5** Ran SP% **110.1**
Speed ratings (Par 94): **94,92,91,88,77**
CSF £8.71 TOTE £3.30: £1.20, £1.60; EX 8.90 Trifecta £29.10 Pool: £ 3302.49 - 84.91 winning units..
Owner Sheikh Rashid Dalmook Al Maktoum **Bred** Mrs Hugh Maitland-Jones **Trained** Newmarket, Suffolk

FOCUS
Rail dolled out from 6f to 3.5f increasing distances by about 13yds. Good to firm ground and a breezy day so drying all the time, indeed the course was riding much quicker than many expected. All five runners seemed ill-at-ease in the conditions and this isn't form to take too literally.

5122 SOUTH EAST LEISURE GROUP / BRITISH STALLION STUDS EBF MAIDEN STKS 6f 209y

2:50 (2:50) (Class 5) 2-Y-0 **£2,911** (£866; £432; £216) **Stalls** Low

Form RPR

02 1 **Anglophile**[13] 4662 2-9-5 0 MickaelBarzalona 1 76+
(Charlie Appleby) *chsd ldr: rdn and qcknd to ld wl over 1f out: clr and edgd lft ins fnl f: r.o wl: comf* **8/11**[1]

0 2 2 ¼ **Opera Fan (FR)**[20] 4432 2-9-0 0 SilvestreDeSousa 5 65
(Mark Johnston) *led: rdn and hdd wl over 1f out: no ex and btn whn sltly hmpd ins fnl f: one pce after* **8/1**[3]

4 3 nk **Supersta**[10] 4795 2-9-5 0 MartinHarley 2 69
(Ronald Harris) *in tch in last pair: rdn and unable qck 2f out: no threat to wnr but kpt on u.p fnl 100yds* **11/4**[2]

4 4 1 ¾ **Master Dancer**[34] 3972 2-9-5 0 SteveDrowne 3 64
(Philip Hide) *chsd ldng pair: rdn and unable qck whn edgd lft over 1f out: hld and one pce fnl f* **12/1**

0 5 13 **Habdab**[35] 3958 2-9-0 0 RichardHughes 6 24
(Richard Hannon) *stdd s: hld up in tch in rr: effrt and no hdwy 2f out: btn over 1f out: eased ins fnl f* **20/1**

1m 22.45s (-0.65) **Going Correction** -0.15s/f (Firm) **5** Ran SP% **108.1**
Speed ratings (Par 94): **97,94,94,92,77**
CSF £6.95 TOTE £1.50: £1.10, £4.00; EX 7.00 Trifecta £13.70 Pool: £4493.28 - 244.49 winning units..
Owner Godolphin **Bred** Darley **Trained** Newmarket, Suffolk

FOCUS
A modest maiden.

5123 LA CORSA DI CAVALLI BIRRA MORETTI (S) H'CAP 1m 3f 196y

3:20 (3:20) (Class 6) (0-55,55) 3-Y-0+ **£1,940** (£577; £288; £144) **Stalls** High

Form RPR

-425 1 **Anginola (IRE)**[21] 4411 4-9-10 55 NeilCallan 2 64
(John Ryan) *chsd ldng pair and a travelling strly: led over 1f out: sn rdn clr: r.o wl: easily* **7/2**[2]

600- 2 3 ¼ **Orla's Rainbow (IRE)**[236] 8112 3-8-6 48 (b) SamHitchcott 10 52
(Gary Moore) *hld up in tch in midfield: rdn and effrt over 4f out: racing awkwardly u.p over 1f out: chsd wnr fnl 150yds: no imp* **10/3**[1]

0640 3 1 ¾ **Mariet**[33] 4035 4-9-6 51 [1] CathyGannon 8 52
(Suzy Smith) *stdd s: hld up wl bhd: pushed along and stl plenty to do wl over 3f out: kpt on ins fnl f to snatch 3rd last stride: nvr trbld ldrs* **6/1**[3]

0-50 4 shd **Art Thief**[9] 4835 5-9-5 50 AndrewMullen 5 51
(Michael Appleby) *t.k.h: chsd ldr: rdn over 4f out: drvn and styd on same pce fr over 2f out* **20/1**

025 5 1 ¼ **Hilden**[23] 4345 4-9-10 55 (b) MartinDwyer 1 54
(William Muir) *led: rdn and hung rt over 2f out: hdd over 1f out and sn brushed aside by wnr: lost 2nd fnl 150yds: wknd* **17/2**

0052 6 6 **Omega Omega**[28] 4178 4-9-1 46 oh1 (b) AdamBeschizza 7 35
(Julia Feilden) *chsd ldng trio: rdn and outpcd 3f out: no ch w wnr but battling for placings over 1f out: fdd fnl f* **10/1**

4460 7 6 **Midnight Sequel**[22] 4380 4-9-7 52 MartinLane 9 32
(Michael Blake) *hld up in tch in midfield: rdn and 4f out: outpcd and btn over 2f out: wknd and wl btn whn eased ins fnl f* **8/1**

0306 8 6 **Ermyntrude**[27] 4205 6-9-8 53 (v) FergusSweeney 6 23
(Pat Phelan) *hld up in last trio: rdn and no hdwy 4f out: wl bhd over 1f out* **8/1**

5200 9 18 **Mcconnell (USA)**[42] 3687 8-9-1 46 oh1 (p) MartinHarley 4
(Violet M Jordan) *taken down early: t.k.h: hld up in last trio: rdn and no hdwy over 3f out: t.o and eased fnl f* **16/1**

000- 10 43 **Pearl Frost**[334] 5989 4-9-1 46 oh1 JimCrowley 3
(Laura Mongan) *hld up in last trio: rdn and lost tch over 4f out: wl t.o over 2f out* **33/1**

2m 34.39s (1.69) **Going Correction** -0.15s/f (Firm)
WFA 3 from 4yo+ 11lb **10** Ran SP% **115.0**
Speed ratings (Par 101): **88,85,84,84,83 79,75,71,59,31**
toteswingers 1&2 £3.10, 2&3 £4.60, 1&3 £4.50 CSF £15.36 CT £66.74 TOTE £4.40: £1.40, £1.50, £3.40; EX 20.70 Trifecta £108.20 Pool: £2425.03 - 16.80 winning units..There was no bid for the winner.
Owner John Ryan Racing Partnership **Bred** T C Clarke **Trained** Newmarket, Suffolk

FOCUS
A poor race run in a slow time. The winner is rated back to her 2yo best.

5124 JOHN SMITH'S BRIGHTON MILE CHALLENGE TROPHY (H'CAP) 7f 214y
3:50 (3:52) (Class 4) (0-80,80) 3-Y-0+
£12,450 (£3,728; £1,864; £932; £466; £234) Stalls Centre

Form RPR
2603 1 **Party Royal**[16] 4581 3-9-3 **80** SilvestreDeSousa 4 89
(Mark Johnston) *chsd ldr: rdn and effrt to chal 2f out: drvn to ld ent fnl f: hld on towards fin* **11/2**[1]
-334 2 nk **Bank On Me**[11] 4765 4-9-6 **76** WilliamCarson 15 85
(Philip McBride) *in tch in midfield: effrt to chse ldrs 2f out: drvn to chse wnr ins fnl f: r.o but nvr quite getting to wnr* **11/2**[1]
0112 3 1 3/4 **Aqua Ardens (GER)**[20] 4426 5-9-1 **71** (t) PatCosgrave 8 76
(George Baker) *hld up in tch in midfield: rdn and effrt over 1f out: r.o u.p ins fnl f to go 3rd wl ins fnl f* **16/1**
0051 4 1/2 **Lunar Deity**[20] 4426 4-9-7 **77** NeilCallan 2 81
(Eve Johnson Houghton) *led: rdn ent fnl 2f: hdd and unable qck ent fnl f: styd on same pce and lost 2 pls after* **14/1**
36 5 nk **Toga Tiger (IRE)**[14] 4642 6-9-9 **79** FergusSweeney 12 82
(Jeremy Gask) *hld up in tch in midfield: swtchd lft and effrt 2f out: chsd ldrs but unable qck 1f out: styd on same pce ins fnl f* **7/1**[2]
5312 6 hd **Enriching (USA)**[11] 4752 5-9-0 **70** (t) AndreaAtzeni 7 73
(Gary Harrison) *chsd ldrs: rdn over 2f out: outpcd and drvn over 1f out: styd on same pce ins fnl f* **15/2**[3]
1033 7 3 1/2 **Raging Bear (USA)**[20] 4438 3-8-13 **76** (p) RichardHughes 6 70
(Richard Hannon) *in tch in midfield: rdn and effrt towards inner jst over 2f out: no ex ent fnl f: wknd fnl 150yds* **9/1**
0001 8 1 3/4 **Brocklebank (IRE)**[26] 4237 4-9-7 **77** TomQueally 3 68
(Simon Dow) *hld up in tch towards rr: rdn 3f out: no hdwy u.p over 1f out: nvr threatened ldrs* **14/1**
4110 9 nk **Hill Of Dreams (IRE)**[35] 3961 4-9-8 **78** (b) JimCrowley 1 68
(Dean Ivory) *dwlt: sn rcvrd and in tch in midfield: effrt and hdwy on inner to chse ldrs 2f out: btn over 1f out: wknd fnl f* **16/1**
41-5 10 1/2 **The Cayterers**[26] 4242 11-9-3 **80** OisinMurphy(7) 10 69
(Ronald Harris) *hld up in tch towards rr: rdn ent fnl 2f: sn outpcd: no threat to ldrs but plugged on ins fnl f* **40/1**
0- 11 hd **Slim Chance (IRE)**[23] 4359 4-8-12 **68** CathyGannon 13 57
(Simon West) *t.k.h: hld up towards rr: hdwy into midfield 3f out: rdn and no hdwy ent fnl 2f: nvr trbld ldrs* **12/1**
0653 12 1/2 **Brown Pete (IRE)**[20] 4441 5-8-12 **68** MartinHarley 9 55
(Violet M Jordan) *hld up in tch towards rr: rdn and no hdwy ent fnl 2f: nvr trbld ldrs* **20/1**
0550 13 3/4 **Starwatch**[6] 4908 6-9-8 **78** KieranO'Neill 16 64
(John Bridger) *t.k.h: hld up in tch in last quartet: rdn over 2f out: no prog 2f out: nvr trbld ldrs* **33/1**
300- 14 3 **Jubilee Brig**[319] 6487 3-9-3 **80** SeanLevey 11 58
(Gary Moore) *t.k.h: hld up in rr: rdn and no hdwy over 2f out: n.d* **20/1**
2302 15 nk **Exceedexpectations (IRE)**[36] 3926 4-9-2 **72** LiamKeniry 14 50
(Conor Dore) *t.k.h: hld up in tch in midfield: rdn and no hdwy over 2f out: wknd over 1f out: wl btn and eased wl ins fnl f* **14/1**

1m 33.41s (-2.59) **Going Correction** -0.15s/f (Firm)
WFA 3 from 4yo+ 7lb 15 Ran SP% **119.4**
Speed ratings (Par 105): **106,105,103,103,103 102,99,97,97,96 96,96,95,92,92**
toteswingers 1&2 £6.80, 2&3 £22.50, 1&3 £19.30 CSF £31.34 CT £472.45 TOTE £5.60: £1.90, £2.50, £5.00; EX 32.80 Trifecta £815.30 Pool: £4832.91- 4.44 winning units..
Owner D & G Mercer 1 **Bred** Old Mill Stud & S Williams & J Parry **Trained** Middleham Moor, N Yorks

FOCUS
A good prize on offer and a typically competitive event, although neither of the first two had won a handicap before. It seemed to pay to be near the speed. The winner rates back to his best.

5125 EBF STALLIONS / LAINES BEST FILLIES' H'CAP 6f 209y
4:20 (4:21) (Class 4) (0-85,84) 3-Y-0+ £6,469 (£1,925; £962; £481) Stalls Low

Form RPR
2121 1 **Floating Along (IRE)**[27] 4219 3-9-0 **78** RichardHughes 8 88+
(William Haggas) *mde all: rdn and wnt clr w rival wl over 1f out: asserted 1f out: pressed wl ins fnl f: edgd lft but hld on cl home* **11/4**[1]
1023 2 hd **Maid A Million**[19] 4492 3-9-6 **84** WilliamCarson 4 93
(David Elsworth) *chsd ldng trio: drvn to chse ldng pair but sltly outpcd over 1f out: rallied to chse wnr ins fnl f: pressing wnr fnl 50yds: r.o but hld cl home* **9/2**[2]
0253 3 2 3/4 **New Falcon (IRE)**[20] 4442 3-8-9 **73** (v[1]) NeilCallan 5 75
(James Tate) *hld up in last trio: rdn and effrt over 2f out: styd on wl ins fnl f: wnt 3rd wl ins fnl f: no threat to ldng pair* **11/1**[3]
320 4 1 **Queen Aggie (IRE)**[20] 4453 3-9-3 **81** TomQueally 2 80
(David Evans) *stdd s: hld up in rr: effrt but stl plenty to do whn nt clr run and swtchd lft over 1f out: styd on fnl f: no threat to ldng pair* **16/1**
00-0 5 hd **Rayaheen**[62] 3020 3-9-4 **82** PaulHanagan 1 80
(Richard Hannon) *awkward leaving stalls: sn rcvrd and in tch in midfield: drvn and unable qck wl over 1f out: kpt on same pce fnl f* **14/1**
3104 6 hd **Finesse**[27] 4219 4-9-2 **74** JimCrowley 10 74
(Ralph Beckett) *chsd wnr: rdn and wnt clr w wnr over 1f out: no ex 1f out: wknd fnl 100yds* **12/1**
-132 7 1 3/4 **Al Manaal**[27] 4219 3-9-2 **80** (t) SilvestreDeSousa 9 73
(Saeed bin Suroor) *t.k.h: hld up in tch in midfield on outer: rdn and no hdwy over 1f out: plugged on same pce after and wl hld whn nt clr run and eased wl ins fnl f* **11/4**[1]
0420 8 3 **Fulney**[14] 4642 4-9-3 **78** RosieJessop(3) 3 65
(James Eustace) *in tch in midfield: rdn and no hdwy whn edgd lft over 1f out: wknd ins fnl f* **16/1**
-356 9 1 **Fanzine**[39] 3842 3-8-7 **71** AndreaAtzeni 7 53
(Hughie Morrison) *short of room sn after s: hdwy into midfield 4f out: rdn and lost pl 2f out: n.d after* **12/1**
4235 10 1/2 **Strictly Ballroom (IRE)**[16] 4577 3-8-10 **74** MartinLane 6 55
(Mark Johnston) *chsd ldrs tl rdn and unable qck 2f out: lost pl over 1f out: wknd 1f out* **25/1**

1m 21.0s (-2.10) **Going Correction** -0.15s/f (Firm)
WFA 3 from 4yo 6lb 10 Ran SP% **117.5**
Speed ratings (Par 102): **106,105,102,101,101 101,99,95,94,93**
toteswingers 1&2 £3.80, 2&3 £11.60, 1&3 £7.10 CSF £15.08 CT £118.27 TOTE £3.00: £1.20, £2.10, £2.30; EX 13.60 Trifecta £139.30 Pool: £4611.94 - 24.82 winning units..
Owner Lael Stable **Bred** Wentworth Racing **Trained** Newmarket, Suffolk
■ Stewards' Enquiry : Richard Hughes one-day ban: failed to ride to draw (Aug 24)

FOCUS
A competitive and decent fillies' handicap, run at a sound gallop, but once again it proved hard for anything to make an impact from off the pace. The winner has more to offer.

5126 STAR GREAT PUBS & BARS H'CAP (DIV I) 1m 1f 209y
4:50 (4:53) (Class 6) (0-55,55) 3-Y-0+ £1,940 (£577; £288; £144) Stalls High

Form RPR
063 1 **Dawn Rock**[28] 4170 3-8-3 **46** SilvestreDeSousa 3 55
(Simon Dow) *mde all: rdn over 2f out: clr w rival over 1f out: edgd lft 1f out: lft in command fnl 75yds: eased cl home* **9/2**[3]
3004 2 2 **Ella Motiva (IRE)**[10] 4806 3-7-10 **46** oh1 NoelGarbutt(7) 4 51
(Mark Brisbourne) *chsd ldrs: rdn ent fnl 2f: outpcd by ldng pair over 1f out: kpt on same pce ins fnl f: lft 2nd fnl 75yds: no imp* **6/1**
-044 3 3/4 **Another Squeeze**[12] 4711 5-9-0 **48** CathyGannon 1 55+
(Peter Hiatt) *t.k.h: chsd ldrs: effrt on inner to chse wnr over 2f out: awkward hd carriage but ev ch over 1f out: stl pressing wnr whn squeezed against rail and bdly hmpd fnl 75yds: nt rcvr and lost 2nd sn after* **4/1**[2]
02U3 4 3/4 **Lady Barastar (IRE)**[36] 3924 5-9-4 **52** (b) RichardHughes 5 54
(Amanda Perrett) *hld up in tch in midfield: drvn and no imp over 2f out: swtchd lft and hdwy to chse ldrs over 1f out: styd on same pce and swtchd rt ins fnl f* **11/4**[1]
0400 5 4 **Culture Trip**[36] 3918 3-8-3 **46** oh1 (v[1]) WilliamCarson 9 40
(Gary Moore) *t.k.h: hld up wl in tch in midfield: rdn and unable qck 2f out: wknd ent fnl f* **11/1**
0-16 6 1 1/4 **Entrance**[28] 4180 5-8-9 **50** ShelleyBirkett(7) 10 42
(Julia Feilden) *dwlt: hld up in last trio: hdwy into midfield 1/2-way: rdn and no hdwy over 2f out: wknd over 1f out* **6/1**
0-03 7 2 1/2 **Novel Dancer**[20] 4429 5-8-12 **46** (t) SteveDrowne 2 33
(Lydia Richards) *chsd wnr tl over 2f out: sn lost pl u.p: wknd over 1f out* **16/1**
-630 8 1 **World Freight Girl**[160] 824 3-8-8 **51** MartinLane 6 36
(Dean Ivory) *hld up in tch towards rr: rdn and no hdwy wl over 2f out: wl btn over 1f out* **20/1**
0060 9 3/4 **Daniel Thomas (IRE)**[17] 4562 11-9-7 **55** (tp) MartinHarley 8 38
(Violet M Jordan) *stdd s: hld up in tch in last trio: rdn and no hdwy wl over 2f out: bhd over 1f out* **25/1**
0600 10 nk **Keyhole Kate**[13] 4658 4-8-12 **46** oh1 LiamKeniry 7 28
(Polly Gundry) *hld up in last trio: rdn and struggling 3f out: bhd over 1f out* **50/1**

2m 3.35s (-0.25) **Going Correction** -0.15s/f (Firm)
WFA 3 from 4yo+ 9lb 10 Ran SP% **118.2**
Speed ratings (Par 101): **95,93,92,92,89 88,86,85,84,84**
toteswingers 1&2 £6.20, 2&3 £5.60, 1&3 £3.40 CSF £31.45 CT £118.10 TOTE £5.90: £2.40, £1.90, £1.90; EX 43.30 Trifecta £223.50 Pool: £3101.80 - 10.40 winning units..
Owner Malcolm & Alicia Aldis **Bred** Mr & Mrs R & P Scott **Trained** Epsom, Surrey

FOCUS
Weak handicap form and yet again the winner raced close to the speed. Slower than the first division, but the better form.

5127 STAR GREAT PUBS & BARS H'CAP (DIV II) 1m 1f 209y
5:25 (5:25) (Class 6) (0-55,55) 3-Y-0+ £1,940 (£577; £288; £144) Stalls High

Form RPR
4/60 1 **Thewinningmachine**[23] 4357 4-9-5 **53** PatCosgrave 8 59
(Jo Hughes) *chsd ldr tl rdn to ld wl over 1f out: edgd lft ent fnl f: tiring fnl 50yds: jst hld on* **8/1**
5052 2 nse **Petersboden**[22] 4365 4-8-12 **46** oh1 FergusSweeney 7 52
(Michael Blanshard) *in tch in midfield: rdn and effrt towards centre 2f out: chsd ldrs 1f out: kpt on u.p fnl 100yds: jst failed* **8/1**
2003 3 shd **Market Puzzle (IRE)**[6] 4904 6-8-7 **48** (p) NoelGarbutt(7) 1 54
(Mark Brisbourne) *chsd ldrs: rdn and effrt ent fnl 2f: chsd wnr wl over 1f out: no imp tl styd on fnl 50yds: nt quite rch wnr* **4/1**[2]
6062 4 1/2 **Chasin' Rainbows**[15] 4605 5-9-3 **51** LiamKeniry 3 56
(Sylvester Kirk) *in tch in midfield: clsd ent fnl 2f: swtchd lft and effrt on inner over 1f out: gap clsd and forced to swtchd rt jst ins fnl f: sn drvn and no imp tl kpt on fnl 50yds* **2/1**[1]
5406 5 9 **Jd Rockefeller**[18] 2743 3-8-4 **47** WilliamCarson 4 34
(Paul D'Arcy) *hld up in last pair: rdn and racd awkwardly on downhill run over 2f out: sme hdwy u.p whn bdly hmpd over 1f out: n.d after and swtchd rt jst ins fnl f* **14/1**
300- 6 1 3/4 **Kapunda**[377] 4495 5-8-12 **46** oh1 DougieCostello 6 29
(Sean Curran) *chsd ldrs: rdn and struggling ent fnl 2f: wknd u.p over 1f out* **5/1**[3]
0-03 7 13 **Soubrette**[13] 4657 3-8-3 **46** oh1 KieranO'Neill 2 3
(George Margarson) *led: clr 7f out tl rdn and hdd wl over 1f out: sn btn and hung lft: fdd fnl f* **25/1**
040 8 7 **One Dark Night**[105] 1769 3-8-3 **46** CathyGannon 9
(Gary Moore) *stdd s: t.k.h: hld up in rr: rdn and no hdwy 3f out: wl bhd 1f out: t.o* **6/1**

2m 1.97s (-1.63) **Going Correction** -0.15s/f (Firm)
WFA 3 from 4yo+ 9lb 8 Ran SP% **117.0**
Speed ratings (Par 101): **100,99,99,99,92 90,80,74**
toteswingers 1&2 £9.30, 2&3 £5.20, 1&3 £6.90 CSF £70.94 CT £296.61 TOTE £11.30: £2.60, £2.50, £1.70; EX 71.00 Trifecta £528.60 Pool: £1514.67 - 2.14 winning units..
Owner J A Rattigan **Bred** Genesis Green Stud Ltd **Trained** Lambourn, Berks
■ Stewards' Enquiry : Fergus Sweeney two-day ban: used whip above permitted level (Aug 24-25)

FOCUS
More weak form, but the pace was strong thanks to Soubrett, who went tearing off, and the time was quicker than the first division.

5128 MAISON MAURICE H'CAP 5f 213y
5:55 (5:56) (Class 6) (0-55,55) 3-Y-0 £1,940 (£577; £288; £144) Stalls Low

Form RPR
0333 1 **Koharu**[20] 4424 3-9-2 **55** (t) DeclanBates(5) 10 63
(Peter Makin) *racd off the pce in last quartet: rdn 3f out: stl plenty to do whn hdwy u.p over 1f out: r.o wl to ld fnl 75yds: rdn out* **4/1**[2]
504 2 3/4 **High Tone**[28] 4176 3-8-13 **47** MartinLane 1 53
(Dean Ivory) *chsd ldrs: rdn to ld 2f out: clr and edgd lft jst ins fnl f: hdd and no ex fnl 75yds* **9/1**
00R6 3 3 1/2 **Sakhee's Alround**[18] 4535 3-8-12 **46** oh1 (p) AdamBeschizza 9 40
(K F Clutterbuck) *taken down early: sn outpcd and pushed along in rr: hung rt and drvn over 2f out: stl last 2f out: r.o wl past btn horses ins fnl f: no threat to ldrs* **50/1**

0355 **4** *nk* **Royal Caper**[12] 4721 3-9-6 **54**........................(v) CathyGannon 7 47
(John Ryan) *racd off the pce in last quartet: rdn over 2f out: hdwy u.p over 1f out: styd on to go 3rd wl ins fnl f: no threat to ldrs and lost 3rd last strides* **6/1**[3]

5500 **5** *2 ¼* **Chelsea Grey (IRE)**[42] 3679 3-8-12 **46**.....................(b) MartinHarley 13 32
(Ronald Harris) *rdn leaving stalls to ld fr outside draw: rdn and hdd 2f out: btn ent fnl f: wknd and lost 2 pls wl ins fnl f* **33/1**

4464 **6** *1 ¾* **Princess Cammie (IRE)**[13] 4666 3-9-6 **54**..................(p) KieranO'Neill 4 35
(John Bridger) *chsd ldr tl rdn and unable qck 2f out: btn ent fnl f: wl hld whn sddle slipped and eased wl ins fnl f* **14/1**

-025 **7** *¾* **Our Three Graces (IRE)**[20] 4424 3-9-7 **55**.....................(b[1]) SeanLevey 6 33
(Gary Moore) *in tch in midfield: rdn and racd awkwardly 2f out: fnd nil and wknd ent fnl f* **9/1**

106 **8** *2 ¼* **Lincolnrose (IRE)**[53] 3316 3-9-4 **52**............................ AndrewMullen 2 23
(Michael Appleby) *rdn along leaving stalls: chsd ldrs: unable qck and drvn 2f out: wknd ent fnl f: fdd* **10/1**

2246 **9** *1 ½* **Foie Gras**[15] 4607 3-9-3 **51**..(p) MartinDwyer 8 17
(William Muir) *a outpcd in last pair and sn rdn along: n.d* **8/1**

0031 **10** *2 ¾* **Sweet Talking Guy (IRE)**[22] 4388 3-9-4 **55**............(t) SimonPearce(3) 3 12
(Lydia Pearce) *chsd ldrs: rdn and unable qck ent fnl 2f: wknd over 1f out: bhd and eased wl ins fnl f* **11/4**[1]

0000 **11** *6* **Bheleyf (IRE)**[22] 4369 3-9-7 **55**...................................(bt[1]) LiamKeniry 12
(Joseph Tuite) *in tch in midfield: rdn and lost pl ent fnl 2f: bhd fnl f* **25/1**

1m 9.36s (-0.84) **Going Correction** -0.15s/f (Firm) **11** Ran SP% **116.6**
Speed ratings (Par 98): **99,98,93,92,89 87,86,83,81,77 69**
toteswingers 1&2 £17.30, 2&3 £50.10, 1&3 £41.20 CSF £38.85 CT £1586.98 TOTE £3.80: £1.30, £3.30, £13.60; EX 67.40 Trifecta £996.60 Part won. Pool: £1328.83 - 0.27 winning units..
Owner Keith And Brian Brackpool **Bred** N E and Mrs Poole and Trickledown Stud **Trained** Ogbourne Maisey, Wilts
■ Stewards' Enquiry : Adam Beschizza two-day ban: used whip above permitted level (Aug 24-25)

FOCUS
Again not great form, but a solid-enough gallop and a likeable performance.
T/Jkpt: £5,071.40 to a £1 stake. Pool of £25000.0 - 3.50 winning tickets. T/Plt: £43.70 to a £1 stake. Pool of £80773.93- 1347.69 winning tickets. T/Qpdt: £23.80 to a £1 stake. Pool of £5801.84 - 180.03 winning tickets. SP

5098 KEMPTON (A.W) (R-H)
Wednesday, August 7

OFFICIAL GOING: Standard
Wind: Virtually nil Weather: Sunny early

5129 WINNERS ARE WELCOME AT BETDAQ APPRENTICE H'CAP (LONDON MIDDLE DISTANCE SERIES QUALIFIER) 1m 3f (P)
6:00 (6:00) (Class 4) (0-85,83) 4-Y-0+ **£4,690** (£1,395; £697; £348) **Stalls** Low

Form RPR

0006 **1** **Shavansky**[19] 4502 9-9-7 **83**... PatMillman(5) 1 93
(Rod Millman) *s.i.s: and hld up in rr tl stdy hdwy over 3f out: chal 2f out: sn led: pushed out fnl f* **8/1**

0604 **2** *¾* **Takeitfromalady (IRE)**[42] 3692 4-9-5 **79**.................(b) OisinMurphy(3) 7 88
(Lee Carter) *chsd ldrs: drvn to chal 2f out: chsd wnr sn after: kpt on fnl f but a hld* **11/2**[3]

654 **3** *2* **Layline (IRE)**[40] 3791 6-9-3 **77**....................................... DanielMuscutt(3) 3 82
(Gay Kelleway) *in rr: hdwy over 3f out: styd on fr 2f out to chse ldrs over 1f out: nt qckn fnl f* **10/1**

1220 **4** *8* **King Olav (UAE)**[28] 4167 8-9-3 **74**..................................... GeorgeDowning 4 65
(Tony Carroll) *chsd ldr: rdn ins fnl 4f: chal u.p 2f out: wknd qckly over 1f out* **5/1**[2]

1200 **5** *1* **Sir Boss (IRE)**[3] 5031 8-9-8 **82**....................................... JackDuern(3) 6 71
(Michael Mullineaux) *chsd ldrs: rdn over 2f out: wknd wl over 1f out* **15/2**

3212 **6** *1 ¾* **Manomine**[20] 4435 4-8-7 **69**...(b) LaurenHaigh(5) 8 55
(Clive Brittain) *t.k.h: sn led and wl clr wknd fr 3f out: jnd 2f out: sn hdd & wknd* **5/1**[2]

1115 **7** *¾* **Standpoint**[38] 3854 7-9-7 **78**... CharlesBishop 2 63
(Conor Dore) *rdn over 3f out: towards rr most of way* **10/1**

040 **8** *33* **English Summer**[14] 4643 6-9-3 **79**......................................(t) LewisWalsh(5) 5
(David Simcock) *chsd ldrs tl wknd rapidly wl over 3f out* **7/2**[1]

2m 20.5s (-1.40) **Going Correction** -0.025s/f (Stan) **8** Ran SP% **112.0**
Speed ratings (Par 105): **104,103,102,96,95 94,93,69**
toteswingers 1&2 £3.40, 2&3 £23.00, 1&3 £13.00 CSF £49.09 CT £441.75 TOTE £9.80: £2.80, £1.90, £2.40; EX 84.80 Trifecta £401.00 Pool: £554.06 - 1.03 winning units..
Owner The Links Partnership **Bred** George Strawbridge **Trained** Kentisbeare, Devon

FOCUS
A fair apprentice event. Clear leader Manomine was ignored by the rest for a long way, but the overall pace was soon still sound enough, the field finishing well strung out behind the first three. A number of these, including the winner, were on good marks on old form.

5130 BETDAQ 1ST UK RACE COMMISSION FREE FILLIES' H'CAP 1m 4f (P)
6:30 (6:30) (Class 5) (0-70,70) 3-Y-0+ **£2,587** (£770; £384; £192) **Stalls** Centre

Form RPR

4031 **1** **Prospera (IRE)**[20] 4436 3-9-1 **68**......................................(b) JimCrowley 2 82
(Ralph Beckett) *chsd ldrs: chal 2f out: sn led: pushed clr fnl f* **3/1**[1]

3434 **2** *4* **Magika**[21] 4417 3-9-1 **68**...(t) AndreaAtzeni 5 76
(Marco Botti) *chsd ldr: led 7f out: jnd 2f out: sn hdd: styd chsng wnr but no ch fnl f* **5/1**[3]

6150 **3** *2 ¼* **Simply Elegant (IRE)**[7] 4898 3-9-3 **70**.............................. NeilCallan 8 74
(Amanda Perrett) *in tch: hdwy 4f out: wnt 3rd over 2f out: kpt on but no ch w ldng duo* **8/1**

3-13 **4** *6* **Decana**[91] 2174 5-9-11 **67**.. PatDobbs 7 62
(Hughie Morrison) *in tch: drvn to chse ldrs 3f out: wknd over 2f out* **8/1**

0-24 **5** *1 ½* **Lily Potts**[11] 4775 4-9-4 **60**... AidanColeman 6 52
(Chris Down) *in rr: rdn and sme hdwy 4f out: wknd wl over 2f out* **25/1**

-223 **6** *6* **Spieta (IRE)**[36] 3925 3-9-2 **69**.. KierenFallon 4 52
(Luca Cumani) *chsd ldr 4f: rdn 5f out: wknd 3f out* **4/1**[2]

240 **7** *10* **Saint Helena (IRE)**[26] 4234 5-9-13 **69**............................ JamesDoyle 3 36
(Harry Dunlop) *s.i.s: a bhd* **10/1**

4435 **8** *2 ¼* **Sultanah Heyam**[14] 4634 3-8-13 **66**................................... PaulHanagan 1 29
(William Haggas) *led tl hdd 7f out: rdn over 3f out: wknd sn after* **4/1**[2]

2m 33.25s (-1.25) **Going Correction** -0.025s/f (Stan)
WFA 3 from 4yo+ 11lb **8** Ran SP% **116.8**
Speed ratings (Par 100): **103,100,98,94,93 89,83,81**
toteswingers 1&2 £4.70, 2&3 £6.60, 1&3 £7.30 CSF £18.73 CT £109.19 TOTE £6.30: £2.50, £1.10, £4.30; EX 26.30 Trifecta £177.10 Pool: £1071.34 - 4.53 winning units..
Owner The Millennium Madness Partnership **Bred** Mount Coote Stud **Trained** Kimpton, Hants

FOCUS
Another handicap in which the field finished well strung out, clearly quite a few running well below form. The pace picked up once the runner-up went to the front around halfway. The form is rated around the second and third.

5131 BRITISH STALLION STUDS EBF MAIDEN FILLIES' STKS 7f (P)
7:00 (7:01) (Class 5) 2-Y-0 **£2,911** (£866; £432; £216) **Stalls** Low

Form RPR

0 **1** **Turin (IRE)**[19] 4491 2-9-0 0.. SilvestreDeSousa 5 79+
(Charlie Appleby) *in tch: gd hdwy over 2f out: led appr fnl f: drvn and styd on strly* **7/1**

52 **2** *1 ½* **Miss Lillie**[61] 3049 2-9-0 0... KierenFallon 12 74
(Roger Teal) *sn chsng ldr: led 2f out: sn drvn: hdd appr fnl f: kpt on: nt gng pce of wnr but hld on wl for 2nd* **11/2**[3]

3 *shd* **Tears Of The Sun** 2-9-0 0.. JamieSpencer 9 74+
(Roger Varian) *chsd ldrs: drvn and outpcd on outside over 2f out: styd on wl fnl f and fin strly to press for 2nd but no imp on wnr* **10/1**

5 **4** *2 ¾* **Crown Pleasure (IRE)**[27] 4215 2-9-0 0.............................. JamesDoyle 1 66
(Clive Brittain) *chsd ldrs: rdn over 2f out: no ex fnl f* **5/2**[1]

5 *nk* **Arabian Comet (IRE)** 2-9-0 0... MickaelBarzalona 6 67+
(Charlie Appleby) *in tch: rdn and outpcd over 2f out: styd on again ins fnl f* **3/1**[2]

53 **6** *1 ½* **Touch Paper (IRE)**[93] 2082 2-9-0 0................................... RichardHughes 8 61
(Richard Hannon) *led 1f: styd trcking ldrs: shkn up and fdd fnl f* **12/1**

0 **7** *½* **Assoluta (IRE)**[60] 3107 2-9-0 0.. AndreaAtzeni 14 60
(Sylvester Kirk) *stdd s and swtchd rt: in rr: drvn and hdwy fr 2f out: kpt on ins fnl f: nt rch ldrs* **100/1**

8 *½* **Rehanaat (USA)** 2-9-0 0.. PaulHanagan 7 59
(Ed Dunlop) *in tch: hdwy over 2f out: styd on fnl f* **14/1**

9 *2* **Encore Encore (FR)** 2-9-0 0... JimCrowley 10 53
(Harry Dunlop) *s.i.s: in rr: pushed over 2f out: late prog fnl f* **33/1**

0 **10** *1* **Lady Emmuska**[19] 4484 2-9-0 0... PatDobbs 13 51
(Richard Hannon) *led after 1f: hdd 2f out: wknd over 1f out* **25/1**

0 **11** *¾* **Cueca (FR)**[60] 3107 2-9-0 0.. RichardKingscote 11 49
(Jonathan Portman) *chsd ldrs: wknd over 2f out* **50/1**

12 *1 ¼* **Fraygrance (IRE)** 2-9-0 0... TomQueally 2 45
(Paul Cole) *a towards rr* **33/1**

00 **13** *2 ¾* **Soiree D'Ete**[35] 3958 2-8-11 0.. RosieJessop(3) 3 38
(Sir Mark Prescott Bt) *a towards rr* **50/1**

14 *2 ¼* **Snow Conditions** 2-9-0 0.. SteveDrowne 4 32
(Philip Hide) *slowly away: a in rr* **66/1**

1m 27.2s (1.20) **Going Correction** -0.025s/f (Stan) **14** Ran SP% **121.0**
Speed ratings (Par 91): **92,90,90,87,86 84,84,83,81,80 79,78,74,72**
toteswingers 1&2 £9.00, 2&3 £15.50, 1&3 £5.80 CSF £43.73 TOTE £8.40: £3.30, £2.00, £2.90; EX 50.50 Trifecta £730.00 Pool: £1181.07 - 1.21 winning units..
Owner Godolphin **Bred** Airlie Stud **Trained** Newmarket, Suffolk

FOCUS
Plenty have the scope for further progress, but the time was slow so the bare form is limited.

5132 £200 FREE BETS AT BETDAQ H'CAP (LONDON MIDDLE DISTANCE SERIES QUALIFIER) 1m 3f (P)
7:30 (7:32) (Class 4) (0-80,76) 3-Y-0 **£4,690** (£1,395; £697; £348) **Stalls** Low

Form RPR

13 **1** **Nearly Caught (IRE)**[10] 4815 3-9-7 **78**.............................. JimCrowley 3 92+
(Hughie Morrison) *chsd ldrs: led appr fnl 2f: drvn and jnd fnl f: styd on gamely: hld on all out* **5/2**[1]

6131 **2** *shd* **Fast Pace**[18] 4523 3-9-7 **78**... RobertHavlin 6 91
(Amanda Perrett) *in rr but in tch: hdwy over 2f out: chsd wnr over 1f out: str chal fnl f: nt quite get up* **5/1**[3]

6-43 **3** *2 ½* **Candoluminescence**[28] 4172 3-8-13 **70**.......................... JamesDoyle 8 78
(Roger Charlton) *hld up in rr: hdwy on outside 3f out: rdn over 2f out: styd on to disput 3rd fnl f: chsd ldng duo in clsng stages but no imp* **10/1**

3552 **4** *hd* **Jazz Master**[19] 4490 3-8-13 **70**......................................(b[1]) KierenFallon 4 78
(Luca Cumani) *chsd ldrs: rdn and effrt over 2f out: disputed 3rd fr over 1f out: no imp on ldng duo fnl f: dropped to 4th in clsng stages* **13/2**

0300 **5** *6* **Strawberry Jam**[61] 3067 3-8-10 **67**.................................... TomQueally 1 64
(Paul Cole) *led: rdn 3f out: hdd appr fnl 2f: wknd qckly appr fnl f* **20/1**

60-6 **6** *½* **Red Pilgrim (IRE)**[22] 4382 3-8-8 **65**.............................. KirstyMilczarek 7 61
(James Toller) *s.i.s: in rr: rdn over 2f out: nvr nr ldrs* **7/1**

200 **7** *1 ¼* **Gold Medal (IRE)**[26] 4257 3-9-1 **72**..................................... PatDobbs 5 66
(Richard Hannon) *in rr: pushed along and no prog over 2f out* **12/1**

-521 **8** *13* **Stiff Upper Lip (IRE)**[16] 4591 3-9-4 **75**.......................... RichardHughes 2 46
(Richard Hannon) *chsd ldrs: wknd qckly over 2f out* **4/1**[2]

2136 **9** *25* **Back On The Trail**[68] 2827 3-9-3 **74**................................ PaulHanagan 9
(Michael Blake) *sn chsng ldr: rdn over 4f out: wknd 3f out: t.o* **25/1**

2m 20.25s (-1.65) **Going Correction** -0.025s/f (Stan) **9** Ran SP% **116.5**
Speed ratings (Par 102): **105,104,103,102,98 98,97,87,69**
toteswingers 1&2 £3.80, 2&3 £8.70, 1&3 £7.00 CSF £15.22 CT £106.58 TOTE £3.70: £1.40, £2.20, £2.40; EX 16.20 Trifecta £59.20 Pool: £1390.72 - 17.60 winning units..
Owner A N Solomons **Bred** Irish National Stud **Trained** East Ilsley, Berks

FOCUS
This is form to view in a positive light, the first four home all essentially progressive coming into the race, and the field finished well strung out off the back of a sound pace. The winner looked well in on his French run.

5133 CONOR MAYNARD LIVE AT KEMPTON 14.09.13 MAIDEN STKS 1m (P)
8:00 (8:04) (Class 5) 3-Y-0+ **£2,587** (£770; £384; £192) **Stalls** Low

Form RPR

32 **1** **Don't Stare**[22] 4381 3-9-5 0.. FrederikTylicki 8 85
(James Fanshawe) *chsd ldrs: led 2f out: drvn fnl f: hrd pressed in clsng stages but a holding on* **2/1**[1]

2 *hd* **Ennobled Friend (USA)** 3-9-5 0.................................... MickaelBarzalona 10 84
(Charlie Appleby) *chsd ldrs: rdn over 2f out: chsd wnr 1f out: styd on wl u.p in clsng stages but a jst hld* **11/4**[2]

40 **3** *4 ½* **Legends (IRE)**[61] 3059 3-9-5 0... KierenFallon 6 74
(Sir Michael Stoute) *chsd ldrs: rdn 2f out: effrt to cl on ldrs over 1f out: sn outpcd* **8/1**

2 **4** *5* **Bejeweled (IRE)**[28] 4182 3-9-0 0.. TomQueally 13 58+
(Lady Cecil) *in tch: rdn and outpcd over 2f out: styd on again fr over 1f out* **8/1**

5 *shd* **Speedy Writer** 3-9-5 0.. FergusSweeney 5 62+
(Henry Candy) *in rr: pushed along over 2f out: styd on wl fnl f but nvr any threat* **33/1**

34 **6** *½* **Munhamer (IRE)**[128] 1291 3-9-5 0.. PaulHanagan 1 61
(John Gosden) *led: rdn and hdd 2f out: sn btn* **6/1**[3]

The Form Book Flat, Raceform Ltd, Compton, RG20 6NL.

4 **7** *3* **Primo D'Oro (USA)**[13] 4684 3-9-5 0 RichardHughes 2 54
(Richard Hannon) *chsd ldrs: drvn to chal 2f out: wknd and eased 1f out* **20/1**

2-6 **8** *½* **Catch The Cider**[22] 4381 3-9-0 0 NicoleNordblad(5) 12 53
(Hans Adielsson) *s.i.s: in rr: styd on fnl f* **12/1**

8 *dht* **Tingle Tangle (USA)**[69] 3-9-5 0 KirstyMilczarek 11 53
(Tony Carroll) *in rr: styd hdwy and nt clr run fnl f: kpt on in clsng stages* **66/1**

3 **10** *½* **Scarlette D'Or**[187] 479 4-9-7 0 RichardKingscote 3 48
(Alastair Lidderdale) *chsd ldrs: rdn over 3f out and sn btn* **66/1**

- **11** *1* **Flying Giant (IRE)** 3-9-5 0[1] CathyGannon 4 50
(Jo Hughes) *chsd ldr: chal 3f out: wknd ins fnl 2f* **50/1**

0 **12** *shd* **Vol Freak**[2] 5069 3-9-5 0 SaleemGolam 7 49
(Willie Musson) *in tch: rdn and wknd ins fnl 3f* **100/1**

13 *6* **Majnon Fajer (IRE)** 3-9-5 0 RobertHavlin 14 36
(Roger Ingram) *s.i.s: a in rr* **100/1**

14 *3¾* **Spiritofsixtynine (IRE)** 5-9-7 0 HarryPoulton(5) 9 28
(Jamie Poulton) *mid-div: wknd fr 4f out* **100/1**

1m 39.62s (-0.18) **Going Correction** -0.025s/f (Stan)
WFA 3 from 4yo+ 7lb 14 Ran SP% **119.8**
Speed ratings (Par 103): **99,98,94,89,89 89,86,85,85,85 84,84,78,77**
toteswingers 1&2 £4.50, 2&3 £11.00, 1&3 £6.60 CSF £6.95 TOTE £3.00: £1.20, £1.90, £3.10; EX 13.00 Trifecta £73.20 Pool: £1551.67 - 15.89 winning units..
Owner Guy A A C Gredley **Bred** Denford Stud Ltd **Trained** Newmarket, Suffolk
■ Stewards' Enquiry : Mickael Barzalona two-day ban: used whip above permitted level (Aug 24-25)

FOCUS
Useful efforts from the leading pair, who came nicely clear. The form makes sense around the race averages.

5134 COMMISSION FREE 1ST MONTH AT BETDAQ H'CAP (LONDON MILE SERIES QUALIFIER) 1m (P)
8:30 (8:31) (Class 4) (0-85,84) 3-Y-0 **£4,690** (£1,395; £697; £348) **Stalls** Low

Form RPR

2102 **1** **Bartack (IRE)**[20] 4425 3-9-2 **79** (b) KierenFallon 5 84
(Luca Cumani) *trckd ldr: led over 4f out: drvn along fr 2f out: styd on wl fnl f* **6/1**

1555 **2** *½* **Dark Emerald (IRE)**[11] 4769 3-9-7 **84** (v[1]) RichardHughes 4 88
(Brendan Powell) *chsd wnr ins fnl 4f: chal fnl f: no ex in clsng stages* **8/1**

3 *½* **Big Whiskey (IRE)**[34] 4001 3-9-0 **77** RichardKingscote 6 80
(Edward Creighton) *in rr: drvn and hdwy over 1f out: styd on between horses ins fnl f to take 3rd fnl 50yds: nt gng pce of ldng duo* **20/1**

-210 **4** *1* **Stresa**[49] 3460 3-9-5 **82** WilliamBuick 7 83+
(John Gosden) *led tl hdd over 4f out: styd chsng ldrs: rdn over 2f out: kpt on u.p fnl f but no imp in clsng stages* **5/2**[1]

61 **5** *hd* **African Oil (FR)**[22] 4366 3-9-5 **82** SteveDrowne 3 82
(Charles Hills) *chsd ldrs: rdn over 2f out: outpcd fnl f* **9/2**[3]

5415 **6** *nk* **Fiducia**[22] 4385 3-8-5 **68** AndreaAtzeni 2 67
(Simon Dow) *s.i.s: in rr: rdn and hdwy over 1f out: kpt on in clsng stages* **8/1**

4-41 **7** *shd* **Quest For More (IRE)**[16] 4593 3-8-9 **72** JamesDoyle 1 71+
(Roger Charlton) *in rr: rdn and hdwy over 2f out: sn one pce: styd on again ins fnl f* **3/1**[2]

1m 38.43s (-1.37) **Going Correction** -0.025s/f (Stan) 7 Ran SP% **113.0**
Speed ratings (Par 102): **105,104,104,103,102 102,102**
toteswingers 1&2 £10.00, 2&3 £19.00, 1&3 £8.90 CSF £50.28 TOTE £7.00: £2.20, £3.60; EX 43.20 Trifecta £584.50 Pool: £1502.03 - 1.92 winning units..
Owner Bruce Corman **Bred** Alberto Panetta **Trained** Newmarket, Suffolk

FOCUS
For the first time on the evening, they finished in a bit if a heap here, suggesting none of these are well ahead of their marks. Doubts over the bare form.

5135 LADIES DAY AT KEMPTON 07.09.13 H'CAP 1m (P)
9:00 (9:02) (Class 6) (0-65,65) 3-Y-0+ **£1,940** (£577; £288; £144) **Stalls** Low

Form RPR

0000 **1** **Tevez**[41] 3719 8-9-7 **65** (p) OisinMurphy(7) 4 72
(Des Donovan) *s.i.s: in rr: hdwy on ins over 2f out: sn rdn: led ins fnl f: hld on all out* **9/2**[1]

300- **2** *nk* **Cool Hand Jake**[380] 4411 7-10-0 **65** JamesDoyle 10 71
(Ben De Haan) *in rr: rdn along 4f out: hdwy on ins fr 2f out: styd on u.p fnl f to take 2nd in clsng stages: nt quite rch wnr* **14/1**

0050 **3** *shd* **Princess Spirit**[23] 4350 4-8-5 **49** (p) JenniferFerguson(7) 8 55
(Edward Creighton) *in rr: stl plenty to do and nt clr run over 1f out: squeezed through horses ins fnl f and fin wl: nt quite get up* **25/1**

2030 **4** *nk* **Solvanna**[61] 3040 3-9-4 **62** AndreaAtzeni 6 66
(Heather Main) *chsd ldrs: rdn over 2f out: styd on wl fnl f: kpt on cl home* **10/1**

4526 **5** *nk* **Piccolo Mondo**[32] 4070 7-9-2 **60** (p) ShelleyBirkett(7) 5 65
(Philip Hide) *chsd ldr: led ins fnl 3f: hdd ins fnl f: styd on same pce in clsng stages* **8/1**

1600 **6** *nk* **Tagalaka (IRE)**[28] 4168 3-9-4 **62**[1] TomQueally 12 65
(Eve Johnson Houghton) *in rr: hdwy over 1f out: styd on wl fnl f: kpt on in clsng stages* **7/1**[3]

500 **7** *1* **Diplomatic (IRE)**[34] 3993 8-9-9 **65** (p) HarryPoulton(5) 2 67
(Michael Squance) *chsd ldrs: rdn over 2f out: wknd ins fnl f* **20/1**

-505 **8** *½* **Bladewood Girl**[28] 4169 5-9-8 **59** RichardHughes 11 59
(J R Jenkins) *in rr: hdwy over 1f out: styd on same pce ins fnl f* **7/1**[3]

2550 **9** *nse* **Hierarch (IRE)**[47] 3534 6-9-8 **64** LauraPike(5) 13 64
(David Simcock) *in rr: pushed along 2f out: styd on fnl f: kpt on in clsng stages* **8/1**

456 **10** *1¾* **Viennese Verse**[39] 3821 3-8-12 **56** (v[1]) FergusSweeney 1 51
(Henry Candy) *chsd ldrs: rdn over 2f out: wknd fnl f* **5/1**[2]

-203 **11** *2¼* **Exopuntia**[154] 907 7-8-13 **50** AdamBeschizza 14 41
(Julia Feilden) *in tch: rdn and hd high fr over 2f out: wknd over 1f out* **20/1**

3246 **12** *17* **Hawaiian Dream (IRE)**[20] 4442 3-9-2 **60** KierenFallon 7 11
(Roger Teal) *chsd ldrs: wknd ins fnl 3f* **12/1**

5650 **13** *11* **Bankroll**[16] 4593 6-9-12 **63** (t) DougieCostello 3
(Jonjo O'Neill) *sn led: hdd ins fnl 3f: wknd sn after* **16/1**

1m 39.46s (-0.34) **Going Correction** -0.025s/f (Stan)
WFA 3 from 4yo+ 7lb 13 Ran SP% **124.8**
Speed ratings (Par 101): **100,99,99,99,99 98,97,97,97,95 93,76,65**
toteswingers 1&2 £19.50, 2&3 £111.90, 1&3 £53.30 CSF £69.47 CT £1457.23 TOTE £6.40: £2.60, £4.40, £6.80; EX 76.10 Trifecta £1850.60 Part won. Pool: £2467.54 - 0.71 winning units..
Owner River Racing **Bred** P A And Mrs D G Sakal **Trained** Exning, Suffolk
■ Stewards' Enquiry : Oisin Murphy two-day ban: used whip above permitted level (Aug 24-25)

FOCUS
A modest handicap. They went a good gallop and the first three home came from well off the pace. The winner was still 10lb off his form of this time last year.
T/Plt: £550.50 to a £1 stake. Pool of £63754.34 - 84.54 winning tickets. T/Qpdt: £45.00 to a £1 stake. Pool of £7418.75 - 121.94 winning tickets. ST

4756 NEWCASTLE (L-H)
Wednesday, August 7

OFFICIAL GOING: Soft (good to soft in places) changing to good to soft (soft in places) after race 1 (2.10)
Wind: Slight, half behind Weather: Cloudy, warm

5136 WEATHERBYS HAMILTON INSURANCE NURSERY H'CAP 7f
2:10 (2:10) (Class 4) (0-85,80) 2-Y-0 **£3,752** (£1,116; £557; £278) **Stalls** Centre

Form RPR

2512 **1** **Lily Rules (IRE)**[32] 4061 2-9-7 **80** BarryMcHugh 2 84
(Tony Coyle) *prom: effrt and rdn over 1f out: edgd rt and led ins fnl f: styd on strly* **9/2**[2]

0414 **2** *1* **Heskin (IRE)**[26] 4246 2-8-12 **71** (p) TonyHamilton 3 72
(Richard Fahey) *w ldrs: led 1/2-way to over 1f out: rallied to chse wnr wl ins fnl f: r.o* **3/1**[1]

2613 **3** *1¼* **Atlantic Affair (IRE)**[30] 4108 2-9-4 **77** JoeFanning 1 75
(Mark Johnston) *t.k.h: w ldrs: led and rdn over 1f out: hdd ins fnl f: kpt on same pce* **11/2**[3]

354 **4** *¾* **Irondale Express**[40] 3761 2-8-11 **70** MickyFenton 5 66
(Tony Coyle) *dwlt: hld up bhd ldng gp: effrt on outside over 2f out: kpt on ins fnl f* **16/1**

0330 **5** *½* **Street Boss (IRE)**[14] 4618 2-8-6 **65** (t) DuranFentiman 6 60
(Tim Easterby) *prom: effrt over 2f out: kpt on same pce ins fnl f* **14/1**

0503 **6** *1¼* **Baltic Fire (IRE)**[14] 4618 2-7-7 **59** (b) JoeyHaynes(7) 7 51
(Mrs K Burke) *chsd ldrs: rdn and outpcd over 2f out: kpt on ins fnl f: no imp* **7/1**

14 **7** *2* **Angel Rosa**[30] 4108 2-8-7 **66** TomEaves 8 53
(Keith Dalgleish) *dwlt: t.k.h and sn cl up: rdn over 2f out: wknd over 1f out* **10/1**

6432 **8** *¾* **Sakhalin Star (IRE)**[14] 4618 2-7-12 **64** JoeDoyle(7) 4 49
(John Quinn) *slt ld to 1/2-way: rdn and wknd fr 2f out* **9/2**[2]

1m 27.32s (-0.48) **Going Correction** -0.225s/f (Firm) 8 Ran SP% **110.9**
Speed ratings (Par 96): **93,91,90,89,89 87,85,84**
toteswingers 1&2 £2.60, 2&3 £3.00, 1&3 £3.20 CSF £17.24 CT £69.96 TOTE £4.40: £1.60, £1.20, £1.40; EX 12.50 Trifecta £33.30 Pool: £2598.17 - 58.44 winning units..
Owner C E Whiteley **Bred** Lynn Lodge Stud **Trained** Norton, N Yorks

FOCUS
Home straight bend moved in 2m as at meeting on July 27th. General opinion amongst the riders was that the ground was just on the easy side of good. A fair nursery that saw those at the head of the weights come to the fore. They raced centre-field. Straightforward form.

5137 STRAIGHTLINE CONSTRUCTION H'CAP 1m 6f 97y
2:40 (2:40) (Class 5) (0-70,69) 3-Y-0+ **£2,587** (£770; £384; £192) **Stalls** Centre

Form RPR

0/55 **1** **Lochiel**[36] 3930 9-8-11 **52** PaulMulrennan 1 61+
(Ian Semple) *in tch: smooth hdwy to ld over 2f out: clr whn edgd lft over 1f out: kpt on strly* **10/1**

3431 **2** *3¼* **Attention Seaker**[16] 4587 3-9-1 **69** DuranFentiman 10 73+
(Tim Easterby) *t.k.h: hld up in tch: hdwy to chse (clr) wnr over 1f out: kpt on fnl f: no imp* **5/2**[1]

0-06 **3** *2¼* **Cowslip**[35] 3947 4-8-8 **52** oh7 RaulDaSilva(3) 9 53
(George Moore) *hld up: rdn and effrt over 2f out: kpt on fnl f: nvr able to chal* **66/1**

0400 **4** *½* **Shirls Son Sam**[27] 4204 5-8-11 **52** oh7 MichaelStainton 8 52
(Chris Fairhurst) *plld hrd: hld up on outside: hdwy to chse ldr 1/2-way: led over 4f out to over 2f out: one pce over 1f out* **28/1**

4-00 **5** *2¼* **Key Gold**[67] 2860 4-9-7 **67** GeorgeChaloner(5) 7 64
(Richard Fahey) *t.k.h: prom: effrt and rdn over 2f out: one pce fr over 1f out* **3/1**[2]

20-0 **6** *¾* **Generous Dream**[123] 1390 5-9-6 **61** DavidAllan 6 57
(Mel Brittain) *chsd ldr to 1/2-way: effrt and ev ch over 2f out: rdn and outpcd fnl f* **7/1**

01-3 **7** *½* **Tobrata**[63] 2991 7-8-12 **60** RobertDodsworth(7) 2 55
(Mel Brittain) *t.k.h: led to over 4f out: rdn and wknd wl over 1f out* **14/1**

00-2 **8** *½* **Harvey's Hope**[128] 1279 7-9-8 **63** (t) TomEaves 4 58
(Keith Reveley) *dwlt: hld up: effrt an pushed along 3f out: no imp fr 2f out* **5/1**[3]

6433 **9** *shd* **Moheebb (IRE)**[11] 4759 9-8-13 **61** (p) JackGarritty(7) 3 55
(Robert Johnson) *s.i.s: hld up: struggling over 2f out: n.d after* **9/1**

003 **U** **Miss Mohawk (IRE)**[29] 4147 4-8-4 **52** oh7 (b[1]) KevinStott(7) 5
(Alan Brown) *stmbld and uns rdr leaving stalls* **40/1**

3m 11.6s (0.30) **Going Correction** +0.10s/f (Good)
WFA 3 from 4yo+ 13lb 10 Ran SP% **115.9**
Speed ratings (Par 103): **103,101,99,99,98 97,97,97,97,**
toteswingers 1&2 £5.80, 2&3 £24.90, 1&3 £41.50 CSF £34.72 CT £1594.69 TOTE £12.90: £4.50, £1.20, £9.80; EX 61.20 Trifecta £1581.70 Pool: £2818.82 - 1.33 winning units..
Owner Oatridge Ltd **Bred** D W Barker **Trained** Carluke, S Lanarks

FOCUS
A moderate staying handicap run at just an average gallop. The form is rather shaky with the third and fourth out of the handicap.

5138 BOOKER CASH & CARRY H'CAP 7f
3:10 (3:13) (Class 5) (0-75,74) 3-Y-0+ **£2,587** (£770; £384; £192) **Stalls** Centre

Form RPR

0611 **1** **Dream Walker (FR)**[9] 4826 4-8-7 **62** 6ex JacobButterfield(7) 6 82
(Brian Ellison) *checked s: sn pushed along in tch: gd hdwy to ld over 1f out: pushed clr* **4/6**[1]

0121 **2** *7* **Strong Man**[20] 4456 5-9-11 **73** (b) GrahamGibbons 2 75
(Michael Easterby) *t.k.h: led to over 1f out: kpt on same pce fnl f* **20/1**

-444 **3** *nse* **Broctune Papa Gio**[14] 4628 6-9-8 **70** TomEaves 5 72
(Keith Reveley) *checked s: hld up: rdn over 2f out: kpt on fnl f: no imp* **25/1**

266U **4** *3* **Llewellyn**[5] 4956 5-9-12 **74** AdrianNicholls 11 68
(David Nicholls) *in tch: rdn over 2f out: one pce fr over 1f out* **12/1**[3]

5422 **5** *¾* **My Single Malt (IRE)**[14] 4628 5-9-10 **72** (p) PaulMulrennan 9 64
(Julie Camacho) *hld up in midfield: pushed along 2f out: kpt on fnl f: nvr able to chal* **11/2**[2]

0434 **6** 2 **Chookie Avon**[2] 5051 6-9-8 **70**....(p) JoeFanning 4 57
(Keith Dalgleish) *checked s: hld up towards rr: effrt over 2f out: edgd lft and wknd 1f out* **14/1**

0655 **7** hd **Orpsie Boy (IRE)**[23] 4340 10-9-1 **66**.... JulieBurke(3) 8 52
(Ruth Carr) *hld up: rdn over 2f out: nvr on terms* **25/1**

140 **8** 1 3/4 **King Pin**[67] 2884 8-9-5 **67**.... BarryMcHugh 7 49
(Tracy Waggott) *hmpd s: bhd: drvn and effrt over 2f out: sn btn* **22/1**

0060 **9** 4 **I'll Be Good**[2] 5051 4-8-8 **63**.... JackGarritty(7) 1 34
(Robert Johnson) *chsd ldrs tl rdn and wknd over 1f out* **40/1**

005 **10** 2 3/4 **Pivotal Prospect**[78] 2542 5-9-1 **63**.... RoystonFfrench 10 27
(Tracy Waggott) *cl up tl rdn and wknd wl over 1f out* **25/1**

04-0 **11** 10 **Polish World (USA)**[33] 4007 9-9-11 **73**.... MickyFenton 3 11
(Paul Midgley) *wnt rt s: t.k.h: chsd ldrs to 3f out: sn wknd* **25/1**

1m 25.42s (-2.38) **Going Correction** -0.225s/f (Firm) 11 Ran SP% **116.7**
Speed ratings (Par 103): **104,96,95,92,91 89,89,87,82,79 68**
toteswingers 1&2 £3.90, 2&3 £14.50, 1&3 £6.50 CSF £20.44 CT £196.59 TOTE £1.60: £1.10, £2.10, £5.10; EX 11.50 Trifecta £83.50 Pool: £5507.82 - 49.46 winning units..
Owner Keith Brown **Bred** John Berry **Trained** Norton, N Yorks

FOCUS
A race that centred around Dream Walker and he duly won with ease. His new mark will not necessarily be beyond him.

5139 R F HENDERSON LTD H'CAP 6f
3:40 (3:41) (Class 6) (0-65,65) 3-Y-O+ **£1,940** (£577; £288; £144) **Stalls** Centre

Form RPR

4 **1** **Monakova (IRE)**[18] 4544 3-9-8 **65**.... DanielTudhope 11 83
(David O'Meara) *midfield: smooth hdwy to ld over 1f out: rdn clr fnl f* **8/1**

0243 **2** 3 3/4 **Alluring Star**[9] 4823 5-9-11 **64**....(b1) GrahamGibbons 8 71
(Michael Easterby) *led tl rdn and hdd over 1f out: kpt on fnl f: nt gng pce of wnr* **7/1**3

0/00 **3** 1/2 **Durham Express (IRE)**[28] 4160 6-8-10 **49** oh1 ow3(p) PaulMulrennan 15 54
(Tina Jackson) *cl up: effrt and ev ch over 1f out: kpt on ins fnl f* **25/1**

4201 **4** 1 **Burren View Lady (IRE)**[9] 4840 3-9-4 **61** 6ex....(v) DavidAllan 1 62
(Tim Easterby) *dwlt: hld up: smooth hdwy to chse ldrs over 2f out: rdn and one pce ins fnl f* **12/1**

0-00 **5** 1/2 **Imperial Bond**[11] 4762 4-8-7 **46** oh1.... TomEaves 3 47
(Jason Ward) *hld up: effrt on outside over 2f out: sn outpcd: kpt on ins fnl f: no imp* **66/1**

6432 **6** hd **Keep It Dark**[5] 4970 4-9-4 **64**.... JacobButterfield(7) 10 64
(Tony Coyle) *dwlt: bhd: rdn and effrt 2f out: kpt on fnl f: nrst fin* **11/4**1

0234 **7** 1/2 **Graceful Act**[17] 4561 5-9-0 **53**.... DuranFentiman 7 51
(Ron Barr) *midfield: rdn along over 2f out: no imp fr over 1f out* **18/1**

5404 **8** nk **George Fenton**[7] 4884 4-9-1 **59**....(p) ConnorBeasley(5) 16 56
(Richard Guest) *hld up: rdn over 2f out: kpt on fnl f: nt gng pce to chal* **7/2**2

2446 **9** 3/4 **Headstight (IRE)**[22] 4371 4-8-12 **51**....(p) MickyFenton 5 46
(Paul Midgley) *in tch: effrt over 2f out: edgd lft over 1f out: wknd ins fnl f* **25/1**

4230 **10** 1 3/4 **Legal Bond**[7] 4891 4-9-5 **63**....(v) DavidBergin(5) 4 52
(David O'Meara) *cl up: rdn over 2f out: wknd fnl f* **12/1**

0-40 **11** 1/2 **Deliberation (IRE)**[50] 3445 5-9-2 **55**....(p) MichaelO'Connell 6 43
(John Quinn) *chsd ldrs: rdn over 2f out: wknd over 1f out* **14/1**

2546 **12** 2 1/4 **Hab Reeh**[16] 4582 5-9-3 **56**....(t) PJMcDonald 9 37
(Ruth Carr) *midfield: rdn over 2f out: wknd over 1f out* **22/1**

0041 **13** 1 **Captain Royale (IRE)**[11] 4761 8-9-8 **61**....(p) BarryMcHugh 12 38
(Tracy Waggott) *dwlt: bhd: rdn 1/2-way: nvr on terms* **20/1**

0000 **14** 7 **Riponian**[22] 4374 3-8-0 **46** oh1.... DeclanCannon(3) 2
(Susan Corbett) *in tch on outside 2f: sn drvn and outpcd: no ch fnl 2f* **66/1**

30 **15** 2 **Isle Of Ellis (IRE)**[22] 4377 6-8-2 **46** oh1....(v) ShirleyTeasdale(5) 13
(Ron Barr) *hld up towards nr side: rdn over 2f out: sn wknd* **66/1**

1m 13.0s (-1.60) **Going Correction** -0.225s/f (Firm)
WFA 3 from 4yo+ 4lb 15 Ran SP% **121.1**
Speed ratings (Par 101): **101,96,95,94,93 93,92,92,91,88 88,85,83,74,71**
toteswingers 1&2 £11.30, 2&3 £33.80, 1&3 £55.70 CSF £58.69 CT £1380.08 TOTE £9.40: £3.50, £2.60, £10.60; EX 64.70 Trifecta £2744.60 Part won. Pool: £3659.53 - 0.61 winning units..
Owner Dundalk Racing Club **Bred** Thomas Jones **Trained** Nawton, N Yorks

FOCUS
What had looked an open sprint was won in dominant fashion. The form makes plenty of sense.

5140 F1 SIGNS MEDIAN AUCTION MAIDEN STKS 6f
4:10 (4:12) (Class 6) 2-Y-O **£1,940** (£577; £288; £144) **Stalls** Centre

Form RPR

30 **1** **Foxy Clarets (IRE)**[18] 4528 2-9-5 0.... TonyHamilton 4 74
(Richard Fahey) *t.k.h: w ldr: led over 2f out: rdn and hung rt over 1f out: hrd pressed ins fnl f: kpt on wl towards fin* **10/11**1

2 hd **No Leaf Clover (IRE)** 2-9-5 0.... RobertWinston 6 73
(Ollie Pears) *dwlt: hld up in tch: effrt and edgd lft over 2f out: carried sltly lft over 1f out: ev ch ins fnl f: kpt on: jst hld* **4/1**2

5 **3** 4 1/2 **The Doyle Machine (IRE)**[53] 3310 2-9-5 0.... PJMcDonald 5 60
(Noel Quinlan) *led to over 2f out: edgd lft and outpcd over 1f out: kpt on fnl f: no ch w first two* **16/1**

4 nk **Ainmire** 2-9-5 0.... MichaelO'Connell 2 59+
(John Quinn) *prom: rn green and outpcd over 2f out: styd on wl fnl f: no imp* **20/1**

04 **5** 2 1/4 **Shyron**[12] 4716 2-9-5 0.... BarryMcHugh 1 52
(George Margarson) *cl up: effrt and ev ch whn edgd lft over 1f out: wknd ins fnl f* **25/1**

3 **6** 1 **Thornaby Princess**[12] 4724 2-9-0 0.... DanielTudhope 7 44
(Marjorie Fife) *t.k.h: cl up: effrt over 2f out: wknd fnl f* **6/1**3

7 5 **Bonnie Fairy** 2-9-0 0.... JoeFanning 3 29
(Keith Dalgleish) *dwlt: bhd and sn outpcd: no ch fr 1/2-way* **10/1**

1m 14.77s (0.17) **Going Correction** -0.225s/f (Firm) 7 Ran SP% **110.3**
Speed ratings (Par 92): **89,88,82,82,79 78,71**
toteswingers 1&2 £1.40, 2&3 £7.10, 1&3 £3.90 CSF £4.29 TOTE £1.60: £1.10, £1.50; EX 6.00 Trifecta £34.70 Pool: £4233.90 - 91.41 winning units..
Owner Hazel Tattersall & G Hyde **Bred** Simon Holt David Thorpe & R J Beggan **Trained** Musley Bank, N Yorks

FOCUS
The front pair drew clear in what was an ordinary juvenile maiden. The winner basically ran to his previous form.

5141 WEATHERBYS BANK H'CAP 5f
4:40 (4:41) (Class 5) (0-75,74) 3-Y-O **£2,587** (£770; £384; £192) **Stalls** Centre

Form RPR

5-50 **1** **Exotic Guest**[26] 4258 3-9-1 **68**.... BarryMcHugh 3 77
(George Margarson) *bhd and outpcd after 2f: gd hdwy over 1f out: led ins fnl f: r.o wl* **10/1**

0621 **2** 1 1/4 **Scentpastparadise**[7] 4891 3-9-4 **71** 6ex.... PJMcDonald 4 75
(Ann Duffield) *prom: hdwy to chse ldr over 1f out: sn rdn: ev ch ins fnl f: kpt on* **2/1**1

0004 **3** nk **Balinka**[12] 4727 3-8-7 **60**....(v) DavidAllan 5 63
(Mel Brittain) *led at decent gallop: rdn 2f out: edgd rt and hdd ins fnl f: one pce* **5/1**

3105 **4** 1 1/2 **Ichimoku**[25] 4290 3-8-5 **58**....(t) RoystonFfrench 6 56
(Bryan Smart) *chsd ldrs: drvn 2f out: kpt on same pce ins fnl f* **4/1**3

-05 **5** 1 3/4 **Dark Opal (IRE)**[67] 2888 3-9-3 **70**.... DuranFentiman 7 61
(John Weymes) *sn chsng ldrs: effrt over 2f out: wknd fnl f* **7/2**2

6000 **6** 1 1/4 **Bogsnog (IRE)**[12] 4734 3-9-7 **74**.... TomEaves 1 61
(Kristin Stubbs) *sn pushed along bhd ldng gp: sme late hdwy: nvr on terms* **8/1**

1m 0.41s (-0.69) **Going Correction** -0.225s/f (Firm) 6 Ran SP% **112.4**
Speed ratings (Par 100): **96,94,93,91,88 86**
toteswingers 1&2 £3.10, 2&3 £2.70, 1&3 £6.40 CSF £30.55 TOTE £12.20: £4.00, £1.70; EX 37.70 Trifecta £219.30 Pool: £2567.35 - 8.77 winning units..
Owner John Guest Racing **Bred** D Cantillon And E Cantillon **Trained** Newmarket, Suffolk

FOCUS
They went a fast gallop in this 3yo sprint, with the field soon being quite well strung out. The winner was among the better treated of these on 2yo form.

5142 NORTH SEA LOGISTICS APPRENTICE H'CAP (DIV I) 1m 2f 32y
5:10 (5:10) (Class 6) (0-60,66) 3-Y-O+ **£1,940** (£577; £288; £144) **Stalls** Centre

Form RPR

0021 **1** **Save The Bees**[9] 4824 5-10-1 **66** 6ex.... LukeLeadbitter(5) 2 76+
(Declan Carroll) *trckd ldrs: led over 2f out: rdn and hld on wl fnl f* **2/1**1

0504 **2** 3/4 **Euston Square**[19] 4475 7-9-6 **52**.... ConnorBeasley 3 61
(Alistair Whillans) *hld up in tch: hdwy over 2f out: chsd wnr fnl f: edgd lft: kpt on: hld nr fin* **9/2**2

6064 **3** 3 **Baraboy (IRE)**[9] 4826 3-8-9 **53**.... KevinStott(3) 1 56
(Barry Murtagh) *prom: effrt and chsd wnr briefly over 1f out: kpt on same pce fnl f* **11/1**

3410 **4** 6 **Amazing Blue Sky**[31] 4099 7-9-13 **59**.... GemmaTutty 6 51
(Ruth Carr) *t.k.h early: led at stdy pce: rdn and hdd over 2f out: outpcd over 1f out* **5/1**3

0-02 **5** 1 1/4 **Ptolomeos**[55] 3252 10-8-9 **46**.... JackGarritty(5) 10 35
(Sean Regan) *s.i.s: hld up: hdwy on ins over 2f out: rdn and no imp over 1f out* **8/1**

0555 **6** 5 **Mishhar (IRE)**[17] 4557 4-9-8 **54**....(v) LauraBarry 8 34
(Tony Coyle) *chsd ldr: effrt and ev ch over 2f out: wknd over 1f out* **8/1**

60-4 **7** 3 1/4 **Bollin Billy**[22] 4374 3-8-0 **46** oh1.... RachelRichardson(5) 5 20
(Tim Easterby) *hld up in tch: drvn and outpcd over 3f out: n.d after* **11/1**

0666 **8** 2 1/2 **West Beat**[14] 4629 3-8-9 **50**.... DavidBergin 4 19
(David O'Meara) *t.k.h: chsd ldrs tl wknd over 2f out* **28/1**

060/ **9** 8 **Bollin Freddie**[846] 1324 9-9-1 **52**.... EireannCagney(5) 9 6
(Alan Lockwood) *hld up: rdn over 3f out: wknd over 2f out* **40/1**

2m 12.01s (0.11) **Going Correction** +0.10s/f (Good)
WFA 3 from 4yo+ 9lb 9 Ran SP% **113.0**
Speed ratings (Par 101): **103,102,100,95,94 90,87,85,79**
toteswingers 1&2 £4.30, 2&3 £9.50, 1&3 £4.90 CSF £10.48 CT £75.90 TOTE £2.20: £1.50, £1.90, £1.60; EX 13.40 Trifecta £75.70 Pool: £1995.71 - 19.76 winning units..
Owner Steve Ryan **Bred** S P Ryan **Trained** Sledmere, E Yorks

FOCUS
The first division of this moderate apprentice handicap was run at a steady gallop and that worked ideally in the favour of the winner. He built on his Ayr win.

5143 NORTH SEA LOGISTICS APPRENTICE H'CAP (DIV II) 1m 2f 32y
5:35 (5:35) (Class 6) (0-60,59) 3-Y-O+ **£1,940** (£577; £288; £144) **Stalls** Centre

Form RPR

0-00 **1** **Szabo's Art**[22] 4382 3-8-11 **51**.... TimClark 1 58+
(Sir Mark Prescott Bt) *t.k.h: cl up: led over 3f out: clr over 1f out: hld on wl towards fin* **3/1**2

-043 **2** 1 **Diddy Eric**[20] 4449 3-8-2 **47**.... RobJFitzpatrick(5) 8 53
(Micky Hammond) *hld up: hdwy over 2f out: chsd wnr last 100yds: kpt on but a hld* **11/1**

0263 **3** nk **Elizabeth Coffee (IRE)**[13] 4673 5-9-7 **52**.... JoeyHaynes 3 57
(John Weymes) *chsd ldrs: rdn and chsd (clr) wnr over 1f out to last 100yds: one pce* **12/1**

366- **4** 1 1/4 **Spanish Legacy**[323] 6341 4-9-5 **50**.... JacobButterfield 2 53
(Julie Camacho) *prom: effrt and rdn over 2f out: kpt on same pce fnl f* **20/1**

0564 **5** 3/4 **Echo Of Footsteps**[23] 4355 4-9-5 **53**....1 KevinStott(3) 7 54
(Michael Herrington) *prom: effrt over 2f out: kpt on same pce fnl f* **7/1**3

-060 **6** 1/2 **Hurricane John (IRE)**[43] 3653 3-8-5 **45**.... JordanNason 6 45
(David Nicholls) *led at stdy pce: hdd over 3f out: rallied: outpcd fnl f* **12/1**

0-43 **7** 3/4 **Captain Baldwin**[9] 4824 4-8-9 **45**....(v) SophieRobertson(5) 9 44
(Jim Goldie) *t.k.h: cl up: effrt 3f out: outpcd fr over 1f out* **14/1**

6050 **8** 1 **Fine Altomis**[9] 4826 4-9-13 **58**.... ConnorBeasley 4 55
(Michael Dods) *plld hrd: hld up: shortlived effrt over 2f out: btn over 1f out* **8/1**

/0-0 **9** 3 1/4 **Funky Munky**[9] 4826 8-9-4 **54**.... RowanScott(5) 10 45
(Alistair Whillans) *t.k.h: midfield on outside: struggling wl over 2f out: sn btn* **40/1**

1523 **10** 4 1/2 **Bygones For Coins (IRE)**[2] 5048 5-9-9 **59**.... JackGarritty(5) 5 41
(Robert Johnson) *plld hrd: hld up: hdwy over 3f out: wknd over 2f out* **9/4**1

2m 15.1s (3.20) **Going Correction** +0.10s/f (Good)
WFA 3 from 4yo+ 9lb 10 Ran SP% **117.0**
Speed ratings (Par 101): **91,90,89,88,88 87,87,86,83,80**
toteswingers 1&2 £7.70, 2&3 £5.80, 1&3 £3.40 CSF £36.33 CT £350.34 TOTE £4.00: £1.20, £2.70, £2.80; EX 41.70 Trifecta £242.50 Pool: £2626.68 - 8.11 winning units..
Owner C G Rowles Nicholson **Bred** Limestone Stud **Trained** Newmarket, Suffolk

FOCUS
Quite a messy race, with them going a steady gallop, and a couple of the runners, including favourite Bygones For Coins, pulled hard towards the rear. Muddling form, probably not up to much.

T/Plt: £32.70 to a £1 stake. Pool of £63306.70 - 1410.20 winning tickets. T/Qpdt: £12.80 to a £1 stake. Pool of £4625.40 - 267.40 winning tickets. RY

4808 PONTEFRACT (L-H)

Wednesday, August 7

OFFICIAL GOING: Good (7.4)

Wind: light 1/2 against Weather: fine

5144 FAMILY DAY ON 18TH AUGUST H'CAP (FOR GENTLEMAN AMATEUR RIDERS) 1m 2f 6y

2:00 (2:01) (Class 5) (0-75,71) 3-Y-O+ **£3,119** (£967; £483; £242) **Stalls** Low

Form RPR

0606 **1** **Pivotman**[4] 4994 5-10-10 **65** MrHAABannister(5) 6 76
(Michael Easterby) *sn chsng ldr: led wl over 1f out: drvn out* **8/1**

-631 **2** *1¾* **Sehnsucht (IRE)**[72] 2710 4-11-0 **71** (p) MrKWood(7) 1 79+
(John Quinn) *in rr: gd hdwy 2f out: hung lft and 3rd 1f out: styd on strly to take 2nd in clsng stages* **7/2**[1]

1456 **3** *1¾* **Pertuis (IRE)**[8] 4853 7-11-1 **65** (p) MrWHogg 2 69
(Micky Hammond) *hld up in rr: hdwy to chse ldrs over 2f out: 2nd over 1f out: kpt on same pce* **14/1**

2064 **4** *8* **Skyfire**[6] 4928 6-11-1 **65** MrSWalker 7 53
(Nick Kent) *mid-div: hdwy to chse ldrs over 2f out: wknd fnl f* **7/1**

0351 **5** *½* **The Ducking Stool**[34] 3997 6-11-3 **67** MrRossBirkett 4 54
(Julia Feilden) *in rr: drvn and hdwy over 4f out: wknd fnl f* **5/1**[2]

0025 **6** *1¾* **Jonny Lesters Hair (IRE)**[5] 4953 8-10-8 **63** MrWEasterby(5) 5 47
(Tim Easterby) *swtchd lft after s: led: clr after 2f: hdd wl over 1f out: rdr dropped whip and sn wknd* **13/2**

460 **7** *11* **Zainda (IRE)**[70] 2765 3-9-3 **55** MrAFrench(7) 3 17
(Neville Bycroft) *mid-div: wknd over 2f out* **20/1**

6204 **8** *23* **Miss Ella Jade**[8] 4853 4-10-0 **53** MrJHamilton(3) 9
(Richard Whitaker) *mid-div: lost pl over 3f out: sn bhd: t.o* **15/2**

0612 **9** *25* **Taro Tywod (IRE)**[17] 4562 4-10-12 **62** MrPCollington 8
(Mark Brisbourne) *sn drvn along in mid-div: lost pl over 2f out: sn wl bhd: virtually p.u: hopelessly t.o* **11/2**[3]

2m 14.42s (0.72) **Going Correction** +0.05s/f (Good)
WFA 3 from 4yo+ 9lb **9** Ran SP% **114.4**
Speed ratings (Par 103): **99,97,96,89,89 88,79,60,40**
toteswingers 1&2 £7.20, 2&3 £9.10, 1&3 £22.10 CSF £35.81 CT £388.14 TOTE £13.50: £3.50, £1.10, £3.50; EX 50.50 Trifecta £515.00 Pool: £3222.87 - 4.69 winning units..
Owner Mrs Jean Turpin **Bred** Cheveley Park Stud Ltd **Trained** Sheriff Hutton, N Yorks

FOCUS
A competitive handicap for the class, confined to gentleman amateur riders. There was a sound pace on early and the principals were clear at the finish. The winner's best form for his current yard.

5145 FAMILY AND FRIENDS OF FRANCIS HAMILTON MEMORIAL EBF MAIDEN STKS 6f

2:30 (2:33) (Class 4) 2-Y-O **£4,528** (£1,347; £673; £336) **Stalls** Low

Form RPR

65 **1** **New Bidder**[74] 2670 2-9-5 0 RussKennemore 4 79
(Jedd O'Keeffe) *trckd ldrs: n.m.r over 4f out: chal over 1f out: led 1f out: drvn out* **6/1**[3]

023 **2** *1½* **Captain Midnight (IRE)**[10] 4808 2-9-5 71 GrahamLee 11 74
(David Brown) *w ldrs on outer: edgd lft over 4f out: led over 1f out: sn hdd: kpt on same pce* **8/1**

6 **3** *3* **Tancred (IRE)**[74] 2670 2-9-5 0 DaneO'Neill 5 65
(Peter Chapple-Hyam) *chsd ldrs: hmpd over 4f out: kpt on fnl f: tk 3rd nr fin* **5/2**[1]

0 **4** *nk* **Bow Creek (IRE)**[60] 3112 2-9-5 0 FrannyNorton 6 64
(Mark Johnston) *led: hdd over 1f out: wknd last 100yds* **7/2**[2]

60 **5** *3* **Desert Colours**[12] 4724 2-9-5 0 DavidNolan 3 55
(Kevin Ryan) *chsd ldrs: rdn and outpcd over 2f out: kpt on fnl f* **50/1**

6 *¾* **Paddy's Rock (IRE)** 2-9-5 0 DaleSwift 1 53+
(Ann Duffield) *dwlt: in rr: hdwy over 1f out: swtchd lft ins fnl f: styd on wl: will improve* **25/1**

7 *nk* **Abbey Village (IRE)** 2-9-5 0 LeeTopliss 2 52+
(Richard Fahey) *sn drvn along in rr: hdwy 2f out: kpt on fnl f* **15/2**

3 **8** *16* **Souville**[34] 3978 2-9-0 0 SebSanders 9
(Chris Wall) *trckd ldrs on outside: t.k.h: hung bdly rt: stmbld and lost pl bnd over 2f out: sn bhd and eased* **6/1**[3]

0 **9** *hd* **Silvercombe**[9] 4827 2-9-5 0 LiamJones 10
(Sylvester Kirk) *prom: hmpd over 4f out: lost pl wl over 2f out: sn bhd: t.o* **40/1**

6 **10** *shd* **Celtic Ice (IRE)**[59] 3132 2-9-2 0 DarrenEgan(3) 7
(Alan McCabe) *sn wl outpcd and bhd: t.o 2f out* **66/1**

11 *18* **Oriental Dream (IRE)** 2-9-5 0 PhillipMakin 8
(Nigel Tinkler) *hmpd sn after s: chsd ldrs: bdly hmpd over 4f out: lost pl 3f out: sn bhd: t.o* **25/1**

1m 19.09s (2.19) **Going Correction** +0.05s/f (Good) **11** Ran SP% **115.8**
Speed ratings (Par 96): **87,85,81,80,76 75,75,53,53,53 29**
toteswingers 1&2 £6.20, 2&3 £5.60, 1&3 £4.40 CSF £49.59 TOTE £7.10: £1.80, £2.50, £1.30; EX 33.20 Trifecta £167.30 Pool: £4234.73 - 18.97 winning units..
Owner Highbeck Racing **Bred** West Is Best Syndicate **Trained** Middleham Moor, N Yorks
■ Stewards' Enquiry : Graham Lee two-day ban: careless riding (Aug 24-25)

FOCUS
A modest 2yo maiden which proved a messy race through the early parts. The winner is progressing with racing, and the runner-up is consistent.

5146 BIG FELLAS NIGHTCLUB H'CAP 1m 2f 6y

3:00 (3:01) (Class 4) (0-85,82) 3-Y-O **£4,690** (£1,395; £697) **Stalls** Low

Form RPR

3524 **1** **Correggio**[19] 4508 3-8-6 **67** FrannyNorton 2 78
(Micky Hammond) *stdd s: hld up in last: niglled along 7f out: drvn over 3f: swtchd rt and wnt 2nd wl over 1f out: led appr fnl f: edgd lft: drvn clr* **12/1**[3]

1 **2** *5* **Buchanan**[14] 4632 3-9-7 **82** DaneO'Neill 3 84
(Henry Candy) *trckd ldr: drvn to chal over 2f out: led wl over 1f out: hdd appr fnl f: kpt on same pce* **5/4**[2]

-432 **3** *17* **Leitrim Pass (USA)**[21] 4416 3-9-1 **76** PhillipMakin 1 62
(William Haggas) *led: drvn over 2f out: hdd wl over 1f out: sn wknd: eased in clsng stages* **4/5**[1]

2m 13.69s (-0.01) **Going Correction** +0.05s/f (Good) **3** Ran SP% **107.7**
Speed ratings (Par 102): **102,98,84**
CSF £25.34 TOTE £5.50; EX 8.20 Trifecta £9.70 Pool: £1673.87 - 129.39 winning units..
Owner Forty Forty Twenty **Bred** Christopher & Annabelle Mason **Trained** Middleham Moor, N Yorks

FOCUS
A disappointing turnout and the two market leaders were both disappointing. Thankfully there was a strong early pace on.

5147 BEST DRESSED LADY AT PONTEFRACT H'CAP 1m 4f 8y

3:30 (3:30) (Class 3) (0-95,92) 3-Y-O+ **£9,337** (£2,796; £1,398; £699; £349; £175) **Stalls** Low

Form RPR

5063 **1** **Kiama Bay (IRE)**[18] 4512 7-9-1 **79** FrannyNorton 7 88
(Richard Fahey) *hld up in rr: hdwy 2f out: swtchd ins 1f out: squeezed through to ld last 50yds: kpt on wl* **6/1**[3]

0054 **2** *¾* **Rio's Rosanna (IRE)**[53] 3345 6-9-7 **85** RussKennemore 3 93
(Richard Whitaker) *dwlt: t.k.h in rr: hdwy 9f out: nt clr run and swtchd rt over 1f out: upsides ins fnl f: kpt on to take 2nd nr fin* **7/1**

-304 **3** *¾* **Beaufort Twelve**[25] 4301 4-9-9 **87** GrahamLee 2 94
(William Jarvis) *t.k.h: trckd ldrs: wnt cl 2nd 2f out: led jst ins fnl f: hdd and no ex last 50yds* **3/1**[1]

2522 **4** *1* **Muharrer**[10] 4810 4-9-2 **80** (p) LeeTopliss 5 85
(Michael Dods) *trckd ldrs: upsides 8f out: drvn to ld over 2f out: hdd jst ins fnl f: kpt on same pce* **3/1**[1]

0100 **5** *1¾* **Sirvino**[53] 3345 8-9-8 **89** LMcNiff(3) 6 91
(David Barron) *trckd ldrs effrt over 2f out: sltly hmpd over 1f out: one pce* **12/1**

1023 **6** *5* **Noble Silk**[26] 4233 4-9-11 **92** (p) DarrenEgan(3) 8 86
(Lucy Wadham) *hld up in rr: effrt over 2f out: hung lft and lost pl over 1f out* **4/1**[2]

210- **7** *¾* **Stormy Weather (FR)**[151] 7051 7-9-9 **87** (p) DaleSwift 1 80
(Brian Ellison) *drvn to sn ld: hung rt thrght: stepped up gallop 3f out: hdd over 2f out: wknd appr fnl f* **20/1**

2240 **8** *10* **Northside Prince (IRE)**[42] 3685 7-9-5 **83** DaneO'Neill 4 60
(Alan Swinbank) *led early: trckd ldrs: drvn over 2f out: sn wknd: bhd whn eased in clsng stages* **16/1**

2m 42.51s (1.71) **Going Correction** +0.05s/f (Good) **8** Ran SP% **115.1**
Speed ratings (Par 107): **96,95,95,94,93 89,89,82**
toteswingers 1&2 £8.40, 2&3 £6.50, 1&3 £5.10 CSF £47.42 CT £150.48 TOTE £6.80: £2.00, £2.00, £1.50; EX 36.20 Trifecta £262.80 Pool: £3116.65 - 8.89 winning units..
Owner Dr Marwan Koukash **Bred** Tipper House Stud **Trained** Musley Bank, N Yorks
■ Stewards' Enquiry : Russ Kennemore one-day ban: careless riding (Aug 24)

FOCUS
This fair handicap was contested at an uneven tempo, which resulted in a tight finish. There's every chance the winner can do better.

5148 CHAPLINS CLUB H'CAP 5f

4:00 (4:00) (Class 5) (0-75,75) 3-Y-O+ **£3,234** (£962; £481; £240) **Stalls** Low

Form RPR

0200 **1** **Chosen One (IRE)**[19] 4479 8-8-12 **63** JamesSullivan 1 71
(Ruth Carr) *fast away: led early: trckd ldrs: 2nd over 1f out: styd on to ld last 50yds: hld on nr fin* **8/1**

4364 **2** *½* **Phoenix Clubs (IRE)**[8] 4852 4-9-5 **70** GrahamLee 4 76
(Paul Midgley) *trckd ldrs: wnt handy 3rd over 1f out: hung lft and styd on ins fnl f: tk 2nd nr fin* **10/3**[2]

0004 **3** *½* **Come On Dave (IRE)**[16] 4588 4-9-8 **73** [1] FrannyNorton 5 77
(David Nicholls) *gave problems gng to s: sn led: wnt clr 2f out: edgd rt and hdd wl ins fnl f: no ex* **9/2**[3]

0126 **4** *2½* **Planetex (IRE)**[2] 5049 4-8-13 **67** DarrenEgan(3) 2 62
(John Quinn) *sn outpcd in rr: hdwy over 12f out: kpt on fnl f: nvr a threat* **2/1**[1]

0214 **5** *5* **Comptonspirit**[22] 4369 9-9-0 **70** MatthewLawson(5) 3 47
(Brian Baugh) *in rr: drvn over 2f out: kpt on fnl f: nvr nr ldrs* **9/1**

126 **6** *6* **Mr Mo Jo**[75] 2614 5-9-5 **70** DaneO'Neill 8 26
(Lawrence Mullaney) *chsd ldrs: drvn over 2f out: lost pl over 1f out* **9/2**[3]

1m 2.97s (-0.33) **Going Correction** +0.05s/f (Good) **6** Ran SP% **113.9**
Speed ratings (Par 103): **104,103,102,98,90 80**
toteswingers 1&2 £4.90, 2&3 £2.30, 1&3 £5.10 CSF £35.15 CT £135.41 TOTE £9.00: £3.70, £1.70; EX 36.50 Trifecta £125.90 Pool: £2420.47 - 14.41 winning units..
Owner Bridget Houlston, Chris Jeffery & Co **Bred** Carl Holt **Trained** Huby, N Yorks

FOCUS
A modest little sprint handicap and predictably there was no hanging about. The winner bounced back.

5149 MATTY BOWN VETERANS H'CAP 1m 4y

4:30 (4:30) (Class 4) (0-80,80) 6-Y-O+ **£5,175** (£1,540; £769; £384) **Stalls** Low

Form RPR

-500 **1** **Fazza**[18] 4540 6-8-9 **68** JamesSullivan 6 78
(Edwin Tuer) *dwlt: in rr: hdwy 2f out: sn trcking ldrs on inner: styd on to ld last 100yds: jst hld on* **16/1**

000- **2** *shd* **Junket**[265] 7722 6-8-12 **74** (t) DarrenEgan(3) 2 84
(Dr Jon Scargill) *s.i.s: in rr: hdwy on outside over 2f out: tk 2nd last 75yds: styd on: jst failed* **11/2**[2]

1316 **3** *2¼* **Dolphin Rock**[25] 4287 6-9-6 **79** DaleSwift 8 84
(Brian Ellison) *w ldrs: led after 2f: hdd and no ex last 100yds* **10/3**[1]

0-06 **4** *1¼* **Tiger Reigns**[39] 3827 7-9-5 **78** (t) PhillipMakin 10 80
(Michael Dods) *dwlt: in rr: hdwy over 2f out: styd on fnl f: tk 4th nr fin* **18/1**

545 **5** *1½* **Steel Stockholder**[12] 4733 7-9-3 **76** FrannyNorton 4 75
(Mel Brittain) *led 2f: chsd ldrs: one pce over 1f out* **8/1**

0-00 **6** *1* **Venutius**[20] 4435 6-9-0 **80** EvaMoscrop(7) 3 76
(Philip Kirby) *chsd ldrs: one pce over 1f out* **17/2**

4160 **7** *1* **The Osteopath (IRE)**[46] 3570 10-9-2 **75** SebSanders 9 74+
(John Davies) *stdd s: hld up in rr: hdwy over 4f out: nt clr run over 2f out: nt clr run and snatched up over 1f out: nt rcvr* **14/1**

3543 **8** *1¼* **Paramour**[23] 4341 6-8-4 **70** JoshDoyle(7) 1 61
(David O'Meara) *trckd ldrs on inner: nt clr run over 2f out: fdd fnl f* **10/3**[1]

0 **9** *7* **Kay Gee Be (IRE)**[31] 4101 9-9-2 **75** PaddyAspell 7 50
(Alan Berry) *chsd ldrs on outer: drvn over 2f out: lost pl over 1f out: eased in clsng stages* **25/1**

0-15 **10** *2½* **Staff Sergeant**[72] 2705 6-9-3 **76** GrahamLee 11 45
(Iain Jardine) *trckd ldrs: t.k.h: lost pl over 1f out: bhd whn eased in clsng stages* **7/1**[3]

1m 45.26s (-0.64) **Going Correction** +0.05s/f (Good) **10** Ran SP% **117.3**
Speed ratings: **105,104,102,101,99 98,97,96,89,87**
toteswingers 1&2 £17.00, 2&3 £5.30, 1&3 £12.20 CSF £102.24 CT £378.46 TOTE £17.90: £4.20, £2.70, £1.60; EX 171.50 Trifecta £993.70 Pool: £2664.00 - 2.01 winning units..
Owner E Tuer **Bred** D R Tucker **Trained** Birkby, N Yorks

FOCUS
They went a fair pace in this handicap for veterans and the first pair, who came clear late on, were both closers. The second is rated to her AW form.

5150 KEITH HAMMILL MEMORIAL H'CAP 6f
5:00 (5:01) (Class 5) (0-75,74) 3-Y-O **£3,234** (£962; £481; £240) **Stalls** Low

Form RPR
6-14 **1** **Rocksilla**[48] 3489 3-9-7 **74** SebSanders 3 84
(Chris Wall) *sn drvn along towards rr: hdwy on ins over 2f out: styd on to ld last 100yds: kpt on* **7/1**[3]
6352 **2** ½ **Hazza The Jazza**[5] 4967 3-8-1 **59** (b) PhilipPrince(5) 5 67
(Richard Guest) *dwlt: bhd and sn drvn along: hdwy whn sltly hmpd 1f out: styd on to take 2nd last 50yds* **7/2**[1]
1534 **3** 1 ¼ **Silkelly**[16] 4586 3-9-7 **74** (t) LeeTopliss 4 78
(David O'Meara) *led: hdd ins fnl f: no ex* **14/1**
0050 **4** 1 ¼ **Delores Rocket**[12] 4725 3-9-3 **70** (b) DavidNolan 7 70
(Kevin Ryan) *chsd ldrs: rdn 2f out: edgd lft 1f out: kpt on same pce* **12/1**
2-40 **5** 3 ½ **Millkwood**[62] 3025 3-9-1 **68** PhillipMakin 2 57
(John Davies) *t.k.h in mid-div: swtchd rt over 1f out: hung lft and wknd jst ins fnl f* **8/1**
1113 **6** ¾ **Cara Gina**[27] 4221 3-9-5 **72** (b) LiamJones 1 58
(William Haggas) *trckd ldrs: t.k.h: drvn 2f out: edgd rt 1f out: wknd ins fnl f* **11/2**[2]
00-4 **7** ¾ **Bond Club**[71] 2756 3-9-3 **70** GrahamLee 6 54
(Geoffrey Oldroyd) *in rr on outer: sme hdwy over 1f out: nvr a threat* **8/1**
1335 **8** 4 **Teetotal (IRE)**[19] 4478 3-8-13 **71** JasonHart(5) 9 42
(Nigel Tinkler) *in tch on outer: rdn and lost pl 2f out* **14/1**
0123 **9** 2 **Ayasha**[19] 4510 3-9-0 **70** LMcNiff(3) 10 35
(Bryan Smart) *mid-div on outer: rdn and chsng ldrs over 2f out: wknd over 1f out* **10/1**
2211 **10** 3 **Bosham**[13] 4661 3-8-13 **69** DarrenEgan(3) 8 24
(William Jarvis) *chsd ldrs: drvn over 2f out: wknd over 1f out: eased in clsng stages* **11/2**[2]

1m 17.71s (0.81) **Going Correction** +0.05s/f (Good) **10 Ran SP% 117.8**
Speed ratings (Par 100): **96,95,93,92,87 86,85,80,77,73**
toteswingers 1&2 £7.40, 2&3 £12.40, 1&3 £17.70 CSF £32.09 CT £340.03 TOTE £8.80: £2.80, £2.20, £6.30; EX 42.60 Trifecta £712.30 Pool: £2377.67 - 2.50 winning units..
Owner Moyns Park Stud **Bred** Moyns Park Estate And Stud Ltd **Trained** Newmarket, Suffolk

FOCUS
This looked wide-open, but few got seriously involved and again it saw a winner negating the inside passage. The winner built on her maiden win.
T/Plt: £670.40 to a £1 stake. Pool of £51527.22 - 56.10 winning tickets. T/Qpdt: £120.20 to a £1 stake. Pool of £3152.40 - 19.40 winning tickets. WG

4861 YARMOUTH (L-H)
Wednesday, August 7

OFFICIAL GOING: Good to firm (7.7)
Wind: Fresh behind Weather: Sunny spells

5151 GEORGE DARLING MEMORIAL MAIDEN AUCTION STKS 7f 3y
5:20 (5:21) (Class 6) 2-Y-O **£1,940** (£577; £288; £144) **Stalls** Centre

Form RPR
4 **1** **Born To Fly (IRE)**[22] 4370 2-8-5 0 JimmyQuinn 6 65+
(Gary Harrison) *trckd ldrs: wnt 2nd 4f out: shkn up to ld over 1f out: rdn and r.o wl* **15/8**[1]
2 2 ½ **Water For Life** 2-8-5 0 LukeMorris 5 58+
(Dave Morris) *hld up: hdwy 1/2-way: rdn to chse wnr fnl f: styd on same pce ins fnl f* **3/1**[3]
00 **3** 1 ¼ **Ohio (IRE)**[19] 4491 2-8-3 0 RyanPowell(3) 7 56
(Gary Harrison) *sn led: hdd over 1f out: styd on same pce ins fnl f* **25/1**
0 **4** 1 **Polar Express**[21] 4414 2-8-11 0 TedDurcan 2 58
(Jonathan Portman) *prom: rdn over 2f out: styd on same pce fr over 1f out* **5/2**[2]
5 3 ¾ **Solent Lad (USA)** 2-8-10 0 NickyMackay 4 47
(Robert Eddery) *in rr: rdn over 2f out: nvr on terms* **9/1**
6 15 **Dubai Gold** 2-8-4 0 PaoloSirigu 1
(John Best) *sn pushed along in rr: hdwy 1/2-way: rdn and wknd wl over 1f out* **12/1**
500 **7** 12 **Mystic Angellina**[37] 3896 2-7-12 45 DanielleMooney(7) 3
(Michael Chapman) *plld hrd: trckd ldr 3f: sn pushed along: wknd over 2f out* **150/1**

1m 24.3s (-2.30) **Going Correction** -0.55s/f (Hard) **7 Ran SP% 110.6**
Speed ratings (Par 92): **91,88,86,85,81 64,50**
toteswingers 1&2 £2.10, 2&3 £14.50, 1&3 £6.30 CSF £7.22 TOTE £2.40: £1.50, £1.70; EX 9.50 Trifecta £60.70 Pool: £2352.53 - 29.03 winning units..
Owner Franconson Partners **Bred** Tally-Ho Stud **Trained** Newmarket, Suffolk

FOCUS
Back straight and bottom bend dolled out 3m. With dry weather leading up to the meeting the going was Good to firm and there was a breeze mainly behind the runners in the straight. The jockeys reported it was riding "beautiful" and "fast but safe" A moderate-looking maiden. The third and the time guide the lowly level.

5152 MOULTON NURSERIES FILLIES' H'CAP 7f 3y
5:50 (5:50) (Class 5) (0-75,75) 3-Y-O+ **£2,587** (£770; £384; £192) **Stalls** Centre

Form RPR
2-32 **1** **Trucanini**[34] 3983 3-9-6 **75** GeorgeBaker 9 84+
(Chris Wall) *racd stands' side: led that trio: rdn clr of those over 1f out: r.o to ld post* **11/8**[1]
3414 **2** *shd* **Lovesome**[20] 4453 3-8-10 **72** LouisSteward(7) 5 81
(Michael Bell) *racd centre: overall ldr: rdn and edgd rt ins fnl f: hdd post: 1st of 5 in gp* **4/1**[2]
-042 **3** 1 ½ **Batgirl**[6] 4909 6-8-11 **67** GeorgeBuckell(7) 6 74
(Martin Smith) *racd centre: a.p: rdn to chse ldr over 1f out: styd on same pce ins fnl f: 2nd of 5 in gp* **8/1**
1201 **4** 2 ¾ **Bright Glow**[11] 4751 3-9-5 **74** (p) TedDurcan 1 72
(David Lanigan) *racd centre: hld up: hdwy over 1f out: sn rdn: nt trble ldrs: 3rd of 5 in gp* **13/2**[3]
1-60 **5** 1 ¼ **Keep The Secret**[22] 4383 3-9-1 **70** [1] LukeMorris 2 64
(William Knight) *s.i.s: racd centre: in rr: hdwy u.p over 1f out: styd on same pce ins fnl f: 4th of 5 in gp* **11/1**
004- **6** 3 **Fever Few**[280] 7484 4-9-0 **70** IanBurns(7) 4 58
(Jane Chapple-Hyam) *racd centre: chsd ldr tl rdn over 1f out: wknd fnl f: last of 5 in gp* **28/1**
4616 **7** 5 **Napinda**[16] 4585 3-8-1 **56** (v) NickyMackay 8 29
(Philip McBride) *racd stands' side: prom: chsd wnr over 4f out: rdn over 2f out: wknd over 1f out: 2nd of 3 in gp* **20/1**
454- **8** 1 **Amulet**[287] 7329 3-8-9 **64** JohnFahy 7 34
(Eve Johnson Houghton) *racd stands' side: chsd wnr tl over 4f out: rdn over 2f out: wknd over 1f out: last of 3 in gp* **12/1**
1000 **9** 6 **Alice Rose (IRE)**[19] 4496 4-9-1 **64** (p) JimmyQuinn 3 20
(Rae Guest) *racd alone towards far side: w ldrs tl; pushed along over 2f out: wknd over 1f out* **20/1**

1m 22.57s (-4.03) **Going Correction** -0.55s/f (Hard)
WFA 3 from 4yo+ 6lb **9 Ran SP% 115.5**
Speed ratings (Par 100): **101,100,99,96,94 91,85,84,77**
toteswingers 1&2 £2.70, 2&3 £6.60, 1&3 £2.30 CSF £6.48 CT £31.58 TOTE £1.90: £1.10, £1.80, £2.30; EX 9.40 Trifecta £39.70 Pool: £1593.63 - 30.10 winning units..
Owner Dolly's Dream Syndicate **Bred** The National Stud Never Say Die Club Ltd **Trained** Newmarket, Suffolk

FOCUS
This fair fillies' handicap was run much faster than the opening maiden. There was a difference of opinion between the jockeys and the runners were spread all over the track. The winner was perhaps a bit better than the bare form.

5153 CONFERENCES AT GREAT YARMOUTH RACECOURSE H'CAP 1m 3y
6:20 (6:20) (Class 5) (0-75,70) 4-Y-O+ **£2,587** (£770; £384; £192) **Stalls** Centre

Form RPR
1304 **1** **Jonnie Skull (IRE)**[8] 4865 7-9-3 **66** (vt) LukeMorris 1 74
(Phil McEntee) *mde all: shkn up over 2f out: rdn over 1f out: styd on wl* **9/1**
4020 **2** 2 ¼ **Greyfriarschorista**[12] 4718 6-9-7 **70** GeorgeBaker 2 73
(Tom Keddy) *chsd wnr 2f: remained handy: wnt 2nd again 2f out: sn rdn: styd on same pce ins fnl f* **9/2**
-411 **3** *shd* **Absent Amy (IRE)**[48] 3496 4-9-6 **69** (t) JamieMackay 6 72
(Amy Weaver) *hld up: racd keenly: rdn over 1f out: styd on ins fnl f: nvr nrr* **3/1**[3]
4424 **4** *nk* **Four Winds**[14] 4638 7-9-0 **66** WilliamTwiston-Davies(3) 5 68
(Robert Cowell) *a.p: chsd wnr 6f out tl rdn 2f out: sn edgd lft: styd on same pce ins fnl f* **11/4**[2]
0102 **5** 4 ½ **Fantasy Gladiator**[8] 4864 7-9-6 **69** (p) JimmyQuinn 3 61
(John Quinn) *hld up: pushed along over 2f out: wknd ins fnl f* **5/2**[1]

1m 36.24s (-4.36) **Going Correction** -0.55s/f (Hard) **5 Ran SP% 108.4**
Speed ratings (Par 103): **99,96,96,96,91**
CSF £44.73 TOTE £9.30: £2.90, £2.50; EX 37.80 Trifecta £73.00 Pool: £964.98 - 9.91 winning units..
Owner Eventmaker Racehorses **Bred** Canice Farrell Jnr **Trained** Newmarket, Suffolk

FOCUS
A tight little handicap with just 4lb covering the depleted field. The winner seemed to take his form to a modest new high.

5154 CUSTOM KITCHENS, BEDROOM OR BATHROOMS TOO H'CAP 6f 3y
6:50 (6:50) (Class 5) (0-70,70) 3-Y-O+ **£2,587** (£770; £384; £192) **Stalls** Centre

Form RPR
1434 **1** **Big Wave (IRE)**[4] 4982 5-9-6 **69** (t) TobyAtkinson(5) 2 78
(Alison Hutchinson) *overal ldr centre 5f out: rdn over 1f out: r.o: hung lft towards fin* **5/2**[2]
6056 **2** 1 ¾ **Rough Rock (IRE)**[8] 4865 8-9-0 **63** (v[1]) RobertTart(5) 4 66
(Chris Dwyer) *racd centre: chsd wnr 5f 5f out: rdn over 2f out: r.o: 2nd of 4 in gp* **7/1**
-040 **3** 1 ½ **Oh So Spicy**[30] 4120 6-9-12 **70** (t[1]) GeorgeBaker 9 69
(Chris Wall) *racd stands' side: overall ldr 1f: stl led that gp: rdn and hung lft fr over 1f out: styd on same pce ins fnl f: 1st of 3 that side* **13/8**[1]
2654 **4** *nk* **Ryan Style (IRE)**[15] 4608 7-9-7 **65** (b[1]) FrankieDettori 5 63
(Lisa Williamson) *led centre tl swtchd stands' side 5f out: sn swtchd centre again: chsd ldrs: rdn over 1f out: no ex ins fnl f: 3rd of 4 in gp* **7/1**
0010 **5** 1 **Brown Volcano (IRE)**[5] 4943 4-8-13 **57** LukeMorris 7 51
(John O'Shea) *racd stands' side: prom: rdn and hung lft fr over 1f out: styd on same pce fnl f: 2nd of 3 in gp* **13/2**[3]
4000 **6** 10 **Lewamy (IRE)**[23] 4354 3-9-8 **70** TedDurcan 3 31
(John Best) *racd centre: hld up: rdn over 2f out: wknd over 1f out: last of 4 in gp* **16/1**
000- **7** 3 ¾ **Red Bay**[336] 5942 4-9-3 **68** IanBurns(7) 8 18
(Jane Chapple-Hyam) *racd stands' side: chsd ldr tl pushed along 1/2-way: sn hung lft and wknd: last of 3 in gp* **28/1**

1m 10.56s (-3.84) **Going Correction** -0.55s/f (Hard)
WFA 3 from 4yo+ 4lb **7 Ran SP% 114.3**
Speed ratings (Par 103): **103,100,98,98,96 83,78**
toteswingers 1&2 £5.30, 2&3 £1.20, 1&3 £2.40 CSF £20.18 CT £35.32 TOTE £2.80: £1.80, £2.50; EX 23.50 Trifecta £37.40 Pool: £813.28 - 16.27 winning units..
Owner Miss A L Hutchinson **Bred** P De Vere Hunt **Trained** Exning, Suffolk

FOCUS
Again there was difference of opinion amongst the jockeys and this time the centre group prevailed. Another front-running here, who rates a small personal best under the claimer.

5155 BANHAM POULTRY H'CAP 5f 43y
7:20 (7:21) (Class 4) (0-80,80) 3-Y-O+ **£4,690** (£1,395; £697; £348) **Stalls** Centre

Form RPR
221 **1** **Swendab (IRE)**[3] 5036 5-9-12 **80** 6ex (v) FrankieDettori 6 92
(John O'Shea) *sn pushed along to ld: shkn up and edgd lft fr over 1f out: r.o wl: comf* **5/6**[1]
0111 **2** 2 ¼ **Sleepy Blue Ocean**[19] 4479 7-9-5 **78** (p) MichaelJMMurphy(5) 5 82
(John Balding) *sn pushod along to chse ldrs: rdn to go 2nd over 1f out: no imp ins fnl f* **9/4**[2]
265 **3** 2 ¼ **Beauty Pageant (IRE)**[92] 2132 6-8-7 **61** JimmyQuinn 2 57
(David Brown) *led early: chsd wnr tl rdn over 1f out: styd on same pce fnl f* **13/2**[3]
6504 **4** 2 ¼ **Danzoe (IRE)**[8] 4866 6-9-2 **70** (v) TomMcLaughlin 1 58
(Christine Dunnett) *sn pushed along and prom: rdn over 1f out: no ex fnl f* **16/1**
3 **5** 4 **Battibecco (IRE)**[37] 3897 4-9-7 **75** GeorgeBaker 4 48
(Robert Cowell) *in rr: pushed along 1/2-way: rdn over 1f out: n.d* **20/1**

1m 0.57s (-2.13) **Going Correction** -0.55s/f (Hard) **5 Ran SP% 109.3**
Speed ratings (Par 105): **95,91,87,84,77**
CSF £2.86 TOTE £1.50: £1.10, £1.60; EX 3.10 Trifecta £5.50 Pool: £1103.54 - 150.39 winning units..
Owner The Cross Racing Club & Patrick Brady **Bred** P Brady **Trained** Elton, Gloucs

The Form Book Flat, Raceform Ltd, Compton, RG20 6NL.

FOCUS
The feature race of the night and featuring a couple of in-form sprinters. The first two look sound enough.

5156 GREENE KING EASTERN FESTIVAL 17TH-19TH SEPTEMBER H'CAP 5f 43y
7:50 (7:52) (Class 6) (0-60,60) 3-Y-O £1,940 (£577; £288; £144) **Stalls** Centre

Form RPR
0002 **1** **Welsh Moonlight**[40] [3789] 3-9-7 **60** .... GeorgeBaker 2 67+
(Stuart Williams) *mde all: shkn up over 1f out: r.o* **10/11**[1]
0040 **2** *nk* **Fidget**[4] [4976] 3-8-4 **50** .... ClaireMurray(7) 4 56
(David Brown) *w wnr: rdn over 1f out: r.o* **7/2**[3]
006 **3** *3¾* **Lily The Dragon (IRE)**[48] [3494] 3-8-3 **47** oh1 ow1 .... RobertTart(5) 7 39
(Mick Quinn) *chsd ldrs: rdn 1/2-way: no ex fnl f* **22/1**
060 **4** *nk* **Two No Bids (IRE)**[12] [4721] 3-9-2 **55** ....(p) LukeMorris 1 46
(Phil McEntee) *chsd ldrs: rdn and hung lft over 1f out: styd on same pce fnl f* **11/4**[2]
6055 **5** *1¾* **Marvelous Miss (IRE)**[22] [4390] 3-8-7 **46** oh1 .... JimmyQuinn 3 31
(Christine Dunnett) *s.i.s: sn prom: rdn over 1f out: no ex fnl f* **25/1**
0000 **6** *6* **Grapes Hill**[22] [4391] 3-8-3 **47** ....(b) TobyAtkinson(5) 5 10
(Mark Rimmer) *prom: pushed along 1/2-way: rdn and wknd over 1f out* **16/1**

1m 1.63s (-1.07) **Going Correction** -0.55s/f (Hard) **6** Ran SP% **115.3**
Speed ratings (Par 98): **86,85,79,79,76 66**
toteswingers 1&2 £1.10, 2&3 £9.50, 1&3 £5.60 CSF £4.71 TOTE £1.70: £1.20, £2.10; EX 6.30 Trifecta £26.60 Pool: £1264.40 - 35.53 winning units..
Owner Seize The Day Racing Partnership **Bred** Mrs F Midwood & P Sells **Trained** Newmarket, Suffolk

FOCUS
This moderate 3yo handicap was run 1.06secs slower than the preceding handicap for older horses, but the two leaders came clear, confirming a pace bias that had been evident throughout the evening. The winner is rated in line with her latest effort.

5157 GREATYARMOUTH-RACECOURSE.CO.UK H'CAP 1m 6f 17y
8:20 (8:20) (Class 5) (0-75,74) 3-Y-O+ £2,587 (£770; £384) **Stalls** High

Form RPR
13-5 **1** **Bridgehampton**[14] [4643] 4-9-11 **74** .... WilliamTwiston-Davies(3) 1 81+
(Michael Bell) *trckd ldr: led over 1f out: sn rdn: jst hld on* **6/4**[2]
2-24 **2** *nse* **Khotan**[63] [2971] 3-8-12 **71** .... LukeMorris 3 78+
(Sir Mark Prescott Bt) *led: rdn and hdd over 1f out: r.o u.p* **6/5**[1]
0141 **3** *1½* **Choral Prince (IRE)**[22] [4392] 3-8-8 **72** .... MichaelJMurphy(5) 5 77
(Mike Murphy) *hld up: pushed along over 3f out: rdn over 1f out: r.o: nvr able to chal* **9/2**[3]

3m 4.61s (-2.99) **Going Correction** -0.55s/f (Hard)
WFA 3 from 4yo+ 13lb **3** Ran SP% **103.6**
Speed ratings (Par 103): **104,103,103**
CSF £3.46 TOTE £2.60; EX 3.00 Trifecta £2.90 Pool: £283.70 - 71.81 winning units..
Owner M B Hawtin **Bred** The Kingwood Partnership **Trained** Newmarket, Suffolk

FOCUS
An already small field was reduced to just three following morning withdrawals, but the longest race of the day produced the closest finish. The form makes enough sense.
T/Plt: £47.10 to a £1 stake. Pool of £52966.15 - 820.32 winning tickets. T/Qpdt: £23.50 to a £1 stake.Pool of £4493.89 - 141.20 winning tickets CR

5158 - 5164a (Foreign Racing) - See Raceform Interactive

5121 BRIGHTON (L-H)
Thursday, August 8

OFFICIAL GOING: Good to firm (7.4)
Wind: light, across Weather: bright and sunny

5165 BETVICTOR.COM H'CAP 5f 59y
2:20 (2:20) (Class 5) (0-75,74) 4-Y-O+ £2,587 (£770; £384; £192) **Stalls** Centre

Form RPR
4411 **1** **Amenable (IRE)**[3] [5047] 6-9-1 **68** 12ex ....(p) MartinHarley 2 78
(Violet M Jordan) *chsd ldrs: rdn and effrt to chse ldr over 1f out: r.o to ld fnl 75yds: r.o wl* **5/2**[2]
0335 **2** *¾* **Volito**[14] [4659] 7-8-2 **55** .... PaulQuinn 3 62
(Anabel K Murphy) *s.i.s: bhd: rdn and effrt over 1f out: r.o wl fnl 100yds: snatched 2nd last stride* **16/1**
1022 **3** *shd* **Maria Montez**[10] [4830] 4-8-13 **66** .... SebSanders 4 73
(J W Hills) *led: rdn over 1f out: drvn ent fnl f: hdd and one pce fnl 75yds* **7/4**[1]
0105 **4** *shd* **The Strig**[8] [4884] 6-8-10 **63** ....(v) J-PGuillambert 6 69
(Stuart Williams) *in tch: rdn and effrt between horses over 1f out: kpt on u.p fnl 100yds* **7/2**[3]
4056 **5** *2¾* **Drawnfromthepast (IRE)**[24] [4344] 8-9-7 **74** .... AdamKirby 1 71
(Jamie Osborne) *chsd ldr tl over 1f out: sn drvn and unable qck: wknd fnl 75yds* **8/1**
1630 **6** *hd* **Above The Stars**[15] [4636] 5-9-7 **74** .... LiamKeniry 5 70
(Conor Dore) *in tch: rdn and effrt over 1f out: keeping on same pce whn squeezed for room and hmpd 1f out: n.d and one pce after* **14/1**

1m 2.97s (0.67) **Going Correction** +0.05s/f (Good) **6** Ran SP% **110.8**
Speed ratings (Par 103): **96,94,94,94,90 89**
toteswingers 1&2 £4.70, 2&3 £4.50, 1&3 £1.60 CSF £36.19 TOTE £3.20: £2.30, £4.40; EX 30.60 Trifecta £60.30 Pool: £2357.92 - 29.32 winning units..
Owner Rakebackmypoker.com **Bred** Michael Downey & Roalso Ltd **Trained** Moreton Morrell, Warwicks

FOCUS
Rail dolled out from 6f to 3.5f, increasing distances by about 13yds. A fair sprint handicap for the grade. The winner continued his revival and the second is rated to form.

5166 BRIGHTON BOAT SALES AND SEA RAY (S) H'CAP 6f 209y
2:50 (2:50) (Class 6) (0-60,58) 3-Y-O+ £1,940 (£577; £288; £144) **Stalls** Centre

Form RPR
0223 **1** **For Shia And Lula (IRE)**[19] [4521] 4-9-7 **58**(p) WilliamTwiston-Davies(3) 9 66
(Daniel Mark Loughnane) *chsd ldrs: rdn to ld over 1f out: pressed wl ins fnl f: rn and wl and holding runner-up towards fin* **3/1**[2]
5064 **2** *nk* **Dancing Welcome**[13] [4709] 7-9-1 **49** ....(bt) AdamKirby 4 56
(Milton Bradley) *hld up in tch in midfield: swtchd lft and effrt u.p over 1f out: chsd wnr 1f out: ev ch fnl 100yds: r.o but hld towards fin* **9/2**[3]
4560 **3** *¾* **Thomasina**[39] [3859] 3-8-2 **45** .... DarrenEgan(3) 2 48
(Denis Coakley) *in tch in midfield: rdn and effrt over 1f out: styd on wl u.p fnl 100yds: nvr quite getting to ldrs* **9/1**
3561 **4** *3¼* **Surrey Dream (IRE)**[14] [4660] 4-9-0 **48** ....(tp) KieranO'Neill 5 44
(John Bridger) *stdd after s: bhd and rn in snatches: rdn and sme hdwy 1/2-way: kpt on u.p fnl f: nvr trbld ldrs* **9/2**[3]
-456 **5** *¾* **Katy's Secret**[35] [3993] 6-9-1 **52** .... ThomasBrown(3) 7 46
(William Jarvis) *hld up in tch in midfield: hdwy over 2f out: rdn to chse wnr over 1f out tl 1f out: wknd ins fnl f* **11/4**[1]
6-06 **6** *3¼* **Lady Valtas**[14] [4660] 5-8-11 **45** ....(vt) MartinHarley 6 30
(Martin Bosley) *racd in last pair: rdn over 2f out: no imp 2f out: plugged on but wl hld after* **66/1**
0005 **7** *1* **Courageous (IRE)**[14] [4660] 7-8-10 **51** .... WillPettis(7) 8 34
(Milton Bradley) *led: rdn and hdd over 1f out: sn btn and fdd ins fnl f* **16/1**
3635 **8** *3¼* **Rooknrasbryripple**[33] [4072] 4-8-7 **46** .... RyanTate(5) 10 20
(Ralph Smith) *taken down early: chsd ldr tl over 1f out: sn btn and fdd fnl f* **20/1**
5060 **9** *7* **Mayforde Jack**[120] [1474] 4-8-11 **45** .... WilliamCarson 3
(Simon Hodgson) *t.k.h: hld up in midfield: rdn and lost pl over 2f out: bhd fnl f* **25/1**
500/ **10** *11* **Musical Strike**[623] [7530] 4-8-11 **45** .... PatCosgrave 1
(Shaun Harris) *chsd ldrs tl lost pl u.p 2f out: wl bhd and eased wl ins fnl f: t.o* **33/1**

1m 24.21s (1.11) **Going Correction** +0.05s/f (Good)
WFA 3 from 4yo+ 6lb **10** Ran SP% **117.0**
Speed ratings (Par 101): **95,94,93,90,89 85,84,80,72,60**
toteswingers 1&2 £3.90, 2&3 £8.40, 1&3 £6.80 CSF £16.31 CT £111.38 TOTE £3.20: £1.30, £1.50, £3.00; EX 17.90 Trifecta £165.10 Pool: £2480.82 - 11.26 winning units..There was no bid for the winner.
Owner Loughnane,Fletcher,Ward & Ebanks-Blake **Bred** A M F Persse **Trained** Baldwin's Gate, Staffs

FOCUS
This was not a strong contest. The pace was honest with the field finishing well strung out. This rates a turf best from the winner.

5167 SQUAREONEFINANCIAL.CO.UK WEALTHBUILDER MAIDEN AUCTION STKS 7f 214y
3:20 (3:20) (Class 5) 2-Y-O £2,587 (£770; £384; £192) **Stalls** Centre

Form RPR
02 **1** **If (GER)**[7] [4906] 2-8-13 0 .... LiamKeniry 4 77+
(Andrew Balding) *chsd ldrs: wnt 2nd 5f out: shkn up to ld 2f out: hung lft but wnt clr 1f out: in command fnl 150yds: comfortaby* **8/13**[1]
2 *3¼* **Giant's Legend (USA)** 2-9-0 0 .... AdamKirby 2 70+
(J S Moore) *rn green: s.i.s: in tch in rr: effrt to chse ldng pair and rdn wl over 1f out: no ex 1f out: swtchd rt and pushed along to go 2nd fnl 75yds: no threat to wnr* **16/1**
0 **3** *¾* **Nice Arty (IRE)**[22] [4414] 2-8-11 0 .... RyanMoore 1 65
(Jamie Osborne) *chsd ldr tl led after 1f: rdn and hdd 2f out: styd pressing ldr tl ent fnl f: struggling whn sltly hmpd jst ins fnl f: sn btn: wknd and lost 2nd fnl 75yds* **9/4**[2]
0 **4** *7* **Black Sceptre (IRE)**[29] [4175] 2-8-3 0 .... JenniferFerguson(7) 3 48
(Edward Creighton) *t.k.h: led for 1f: chsd ldrs tl dropped into last pair but stl wl in tch over 4f out: rdn 2f out: sn wknd* **66/1**
6552 **5** *11* **Evacusafe Lady**[9] [4861] 2-8-5 59 ....(p) FrannyNorton 5 17
(John Ryan) *in tch: chsd ldng pair over 5f out tl wl over 1f out: sn btn: fdd ent fnl f* **10/1**[3]

1m 38.15s (2.15) **Going Correction** +0.05s/f (Good) **5** Ran SP% **109.2**
Speed ratings (Par 94): **91,87,87,80,69**
CSF £11.76 TOTE £3.60: £1.10, £5.90; EX 7.50 Trifecta £17.30 Pool: £2064.45 - 89.33 winning units..
Owner N Botica, Rex & Mrs Wendy Gorell **Bred** Gestut Am Schlossgarten Gbr **Trained** Kingsclere, Hants

FOCUS
Not much pace on for this uncompetitive maiden.

5168 FROSTS4CARS.CO.UK BRIGHTON CHALLENGE CUP (H'CAP) 1m 3f 196y
3:50 (3:53) (Class 4) (0-80,80) 3-Y-O+
£12,450 (£3,728; £1,864; £932; £466; £234) **Stalls** High

Form RPR
1221 **1** **Beacon Lady**[14] [4663] 4-8-5 **64** .... DarrenEgan(3) 6 77
(William Knight) *hld up wl off the pce in last trio: c wdst whn rdn and effrt over 2f out: str run over 1f out to ld fnl 150yds: edging lft but sn clr: r.o strly: readily* **9/1**
3213 **2** *3½* **St Ignatius**[16] [4612] 6-8-0 **61** ....(v[1]) NatashaEaton(5) 12 68
(Alan Bailey) *chsd ldr and clr of field tl led 9f out: rdn and clr over 2f out: hdd fnl 150yds and sn outpcd by wnr: kpt on for clr 2nd* **25/1**
2134 **3** *1¼* **Edwyn Ralph**[7] [4914] 3-8-9 **76** .... RyanMoore 1 81
(David Simcock) *chsd ldrs: rdn wl over 2f out: kpt on u.p to chse ldrs over 1f out: outpcd by wnr and kpt on same pce ins fnl f* **13/8**[1]
6136 **4** *nk* **Presburg (IRE)**[55] [3293] 4-9-9 **79** .... LiamKeniry 13 84+
(Joseph Tuite) *stdd s: t.k.h and sn in midfield: effrt to chse ldrs and rdn ent fnl 2f: kpt on same pce ins fnl f* **8/1**[3]
5042 **5** *1½* **Rossetti**[14] [4679] 5-9-2 **72** .... GeorgeBaker 2 74
(Gary Moore) *led for 3f: chsd ldr and clr of field after: hung lft and no ex u.p over 1f out: wknd ins fnl f* **9/1**
4314 **6** *1¼* **The Holyman (IRE)**[39] [3856] 5-9-5 **75** .... PatCosgrave 14 75
(Jo Crowley) *chsd ldr: drvn and unable qck over 2f out: outpcd over 1f out: hld and plugged on same pce fnl f* **16/1**
1114 **7** *1¾* **Green Earth (IRE)**[7] [4904] 6-8-6 **62** .... FrannyNorton 11 59
(Pat Phelan) *hld up in tch in midfield: rdn and unable qck over 2f out: no threat to ldrs and plugged on same pce u.p fr over 1f out* **16/1**
-320 **8** *4½* **Ethics Girl (IRE)**[43] [3685] 7-9-10 **80** ....(t) AdamKirby 7 70
(John Berry) *in tch in midfield: rdn and lost pl over 2f out: no threat to ldrs fnl 2f: plugged on past btn horses over 1f out* **6/1**[2]
0204 **9** *½* **Laser Blazer**[14] [4673] 5-9-0 **70** ....(p) JimCrowley 4 59
(Jeremy Gask) *s.i.s: detached in last early: hdwy into midfield 6f out: rdn and outpcd over 2f out: wknd and wl hld over 1f out* **20/1**
400- **10** *7* **Tri Nations (UAE)**[5] [8020] 8-8-1 **64** ....(vt) NoelGarbutt(7) 10 42
(Anthony Middleton) *in tch in midfield: sme hdwy and rdn 3f out: wknd u.p over 1f out* **50/1**
0215 **11** *1* **Shirataki (IRE)**[10] [4832] 5-8-13 **69** .... WilliamCarson 5 46
(Peter Hiatt) *s.i.s: hld up in last trio: rdn and no hdwy over 2f out: wknd wl over 1f out: n.d* **33/1**
020- **12** *7* **Filun**[321] [6441] 8-8-4 **65** .... RyanTate(5) 9 30
(Anthony Middleton) *hld up towards rr: dropped to rr and rdn 3f out: lost tch wl over 1f out* **66/1**
5/0- **13** *1* **Bollin Judith**[22] [3661] 7-9-10 **80** ....(t) DougieCostello 3 44
(Jim Best) *a towards rr: rdn and struggling in last 4f out: lost tch wl over 1f out: eased wl ins fnl f* **40/1**

/520 **14** *6* **Dr Livingstone (IRE)**[101] 1884 8-9-4 **77**....... WilliamTwiston-Davies(3) 8 31
(Charles Egerton) *in tch in midfield: lost pl and rdn 4f out: lost tch wl over 1f out: eased ins fnl f: t.o* **16/1**

2m 31.65s (-1.05) **Going Correction** +0.05s/f (Good)
WFA 3 from 4yo+ 11lb **14** Ran SP% **118.6**
Speed ratings (Par 105): **105,102,101,101,100 99,98,95,95,90 89,85,84,80**
toteswingers 1&2 £19.10, 2&3 £13.40, 1&3 £3.20 CSF £224.53 CT £550.96 TOTE £7.60: £2.30, £7.00, £1.40; EX 145.30 Trifecta £1031.30 Pool: £4497.79 - 3.27 winning units..
Owner The Pro-Claimers **Bred** Ashley House Stud **Trained** Patching, W Sussex

FOCUS
A decent prize on offer and the sponsors where rewarded with a competitive contest. It was run at a sound pace, with the winner the only runner able to close from behind. The form makes sense.

5169 OVER 300 USED CARS AT FROSTS FILLIES' H'CAP 1m 1f 209y
4:20 (4:23) (Class 4) (0-85,83) 3-Y-0+ **£4,690** (£1,395; £697; £348) **Stalls** High

Form RPR
4213 **1** **Curly Come Home**[20] 4489 4-9-6 **75**.............................(t) GeorgeBaker 4 84+
(Chris Wall) *stdd s: hld up in tch in last pair: clsd to loin ldrs and gng best over 2f out: rdn to ld jst over 1f out: clr ins fnl f: r.o wl: readily* **4/1**[3]

-254 **2** *2 ¾* **Love Magic**[26] 4278 3-9-4 **82**.............................. RyanMoore 1 85
(Sir Michael Stoute) *chsd ldr tl 6f out: rdn and ev ch jst over 2f out: outpcd by wnr jst ins fnl f: wnt 2nd and styd on same pce fnl 100yds* **11/8**[1]

44-6 **3** *¾* **Penny Rose**[131] 1250 3-9-5 **83**.............................. FrannyNorton 3 85
(Mark Johnston) *led: rdn and jnd jst over 2f out: hdd jst over 1f out and outpcd by wnr jst ins fnl f: one pce after and lost 2nd fnl 100yds* **5/2**[2]

415 **4** *½* **Ardingly (IRE)**[33] 4066 3-8-11 **75**..............................[1] JimCrowley 2 76
(Roger Varian) *stdd s: t.k.h: hld up in last pair: effrt on inner and rdn to press ldrs 2f out: kpt on same pce ins fnl f* **11/1**

1265 **5** *1* **Of Course Darling**[46] 3610 3-9-2 **80**.............................. SebSanders 5 79
(Ed Dunlop) *taken down early: chsd ldrs tl wnt 2nd 6f out: rdn and ev ch jst over 2f out: outpcd by wnr jst ins fnl f: wknd towards fin* **10/1**

2m 5.04s (1.44) **Going Correction** +0.05s/f (Good)
WFA 3 from 4yo 9lb **5** Ran SP% **108.1**
Speed ratings (Par 102): **96,93,93,92,92**
CSF £9.62 TOTE £4.20: £1.70, £1.40; EX 6.50 Trifecta £12.80 Pool: £2733.82 - 159.11 winning units..
Owner The Hut Partnership & Partner **Bred** Farmers Hill Stud **Trained** Newmarket, Suffolk

FOCUS
Not a bad fillies' handicap, despite the small field size. The pace was steady with five virtually in a line at the furlong pole. The form makes sense.

5170 HARRINGTONS LETTINGS H'CAP 7f 214y
4:50 (4:50) (Class 6) (0-60,60) 3-Y-0+ **£1,940** (£577; £288; £144) **Stalls** Centre

Form RPR
-425 **1** **Pour La Victoire (IRE)**[8] 4885 3-8-3 **49**.............................. RobertTart(5) 5 54
(Tony Carroll) *chsd ldrs tl jnd ldr 3f out: rdn to ld over 1f out: kpt on u.p to assert jst ins fnl f: pushed along and holding rivals towards fin* **3/1**[2]

5630 **2** *½* **Fair Comment**[8] 4885 3-9-3 **58**.............................. LiamKeniry 2 62
(Michael Blanshard) *wl in tch in midfield: rdn and effrt whn edgd lft over 1f out: chsd wnr fnl 100yds: styd on but a hld by wnr* **12/1**

0616 **3** *nk* **Lightning Spirit**[37] 3924 5-9-8 **56**..............................(p) GeorgeBaker 9 60
(Gary Moore) *stdd s: hld up in tch in rr: effrt on outer 2f out: rdn and hdwy to chse ldrs ins fnl f: kpt on fnl 100yds but hld by wnr towards fin* **5/2**[1]

0056 **4** *3 ¼* **Norwegian Reward (IRE)**[5] 5002 5-9-5 **53**.................. FrannyNorton 4 50
(Michael Wigham) *dwlt and pushed along leaving stalls: hdwy to chse ldr over 4f out tl 3f out: rdn and pressing wnr over 1f out: no ex and wknd fnl 100yds* **3/1**[2]

5244 **5** *1 ¼* **Fairy Mist (IRE)**[19] 4517 6-8-12 **46** oh1.................. KieranO'Neill 3 40
(John Bridger) *t.k.h: led: jnd 3f out: rdn over 2f out: hdd and no ex over 1f out: wknd fnl f* **14/1**

5006 **6** *1 ¼* **Warbond**[8] 4894 5-8-13 **47**..............................(v) WilliamCarson 8 38
(Michael Madgwick) *in tch in last pair but nvr looked happy: rdn and no hdwy 2f out: wl hld fnl f* **20/1**

4422 **7** *hd* **Azelle**[24] 4345 3-9-2 **60**.............................. ThomasBrown(3) 1 49
(Brendan Powell) *chsd ldr tl over 4f out: lost pl and rdn over 2f out: wknd u.p ent fnl f* **11/2**[3]

1m 36.58s (0.58) **Going Correction** +0.05s/f (Good)
WFA 3 from 4yo+ 7lb **7** Ran SP% **113.1**
Speed ratings (Par 101): **99,98,98,94,93 92,92**
toteswingers 1&2 £5.80, 2&3 £5.80, 1&3 £3.00 CSF £36.22 CT £100.75 TOTE £4.20: £2.30, £5.30; EX 45.30 Trifecta £215.70 Pool: £2578.24 - 8.96 winning units..
Owner Curry House Corner **Bred** L Fox **Trained** Cropthorne, Worcs

FOCUS
A weak contest run at a steady pace. The winner was close to his early 2yo form.

5171 FROSTS CHEVROLET LADY AMATEUR RIDERS' H'CAP 1m 1f 209y
5:20 (5:21) (Class 5) (0-70,64) 3-Y-0+ **£2,495** (£774; £386; £193) **Stalls** High

Form RPR
3322 **1** **Whinging Willie (IRE)**[44] 3656 4-10-5 **62**........... MissHayleyMoore(3) 1 69
(Gary Moore) *stdd s: hld up in tch towards rr: rdn and hdwy to chal whn hung rt over 1f out: led over 1f out: a jst doing enough ins fnl f: rdn out* **5/4**[1]

6140 **2** *hd* **Flag Of Glory**[9] 4853 6-10-5 **64**.............................. MissMEdden(5) 8 70
(Peter Hiatt) *led: rdn over 1f out: hdd 1f out: kpt on and pressed wnr thrght fnl f: a jst hld* **4/1**[2]

/06- **3** *2 ¼* **It's A Girl Thing (IRE)**[441] 2425 4-10-4 **63**.............. MissKMargarson(5) 6 65
(Gary Moore) *stdd s: hld up in tch in rr: hdwy on outer and rdn to chse ldrs over 1f out: no ex and one pce fnl 100yds* **14/1**

0240 **4** *1* **Benandonner (USA)**[15] 4623 10-9-7 **52** ow2...........(p) MissMBryant(5) 7 52
(Paddy Butler) *t.k.h: hld up in tch in midfield: hdwy to chse ldrs 4f out: rdn and unable qck whn n.m.r 1f out: kpt on same pce fnl f* **14/1**

3603 **5** *¾* **James Pollard (IRE)**[7] 4915 8-10-1 **62**................(t) MissBHampson(7) 2 60
(Bernard Llewellyn) *hld up in tch in midfield: effrt to chse ldrs and rdn over 1f out: no ex and one pce fnl f* **8/1**

/300 **6** *5* **Walter De La Mare (IRE)**[32] 3169 6-9-2 **45**.........(v[1]) MissAliceMills(3) 9 33
(Anabel K Murphy) *chsd ldr tl rdn and nt qckn 2f out: lost pl and btn over 1f out: wknd fnl f* **20/1**

P00- **7** *nk* **Royal Alcor (IRE)**[423] 2984 6-9-13 **60**.(t[1]) MissAnne-SophieCrombez(7) 5 48
(Gay Kelleway) *chsd ldrs: shuffled bk towards rr but stl wl in tch 3f out: rdn and chsd ldrs again over 1f out: btn 1f out: wknd ins fnl f* **25/1**

06/0 **8** *2 ¾* **Appyjack**[24] 4350 5-9-12 **55**.............................. MissJRRichards(3) 4 37
(Tony Carroll) *chsd ldrs: rdn and effrt 2f out: no ex and btn over 1f out: wknd ins fnl f* **7/1**[3]

0006 **9** *6* **Tartaria**[93] 2130 7-9-1 **46**.............................. AnnaHesketh(5) 3 16
(Edward Creighton) *t.k.h: hld up in tch towards rr: rdn and no hdwy 2f out: wknd and hung lft ent fnl f* **16/1**

2m 5.84s (2.24) **Going Correction** +0.05s/f (Good) **9** Ran SP% **115.9**
Speed ratings (Par 103): **93,92,91,90,89 85,85,83,78**
toteswingers 1&2 £1.70, 1&3 £5.10, 2&3 £6.30 CSF £6.14 CT £46.17 TOTE £2.10: £1.10, £1.60, £3.70; EX 7.40 Trifecta £36.50 Pool: £1253.57 - 25.75 winning units..
Owner P B Moorhead **Bred** Joe Rogers **Trained** Lower Beeding, W Sussex

FOCUS
This weak handicap, confined to lady amateur riders, was run at a fair pace. The form is rated on the negative side.
T/Plt: £80.10 to a £1 stake. Pool of £69187.36 - 630.22 winning tickets. T/Qpdt: £13.90 to a £1 stake. Pool of £4038.59 - 214.46 winning tickets. SP

4708 CHEPSTOW (L-H)
Thursday, August 8

OFFICIAL GOING: Good (7.5)
Wind: Moderate across Weather: Sunny spells early

5172 PETESMITHCARSALES.CO.UK & JOHNOSHEARACING.CO.UK H'CAP (FOR LADY AMATEUR RIDERS) 1m 14y
5:15 (5:19) (Class 5) (0-70,70) 3-Y-0+ **£2,495** (£774; £386; £193) **Stalls** Centre

Form RPR
0-50 **1** **Tanforan**[33] 4070 11-9-5 **52**.............................. MissSBrotherton 7 60
(Brian Baugh) *mde virtually all: drvn over 1f out: kpt on wl u.p fnl f* **7/1**

6503 **2** *½* **Delightful Sleep**[5] 5002 5-9-6 **58**.............................. MissHDoyle(5) 3 65
(David Evans) *in tch: hdwy to chse wnr fr 3f out: rdn 2f out: kpt on ins fnl f but a hld* **6/1**

0313 **3** *1 ¾* **Supa Seeker (USA)**[43] 3700 7-9-2 **52**............... MissJoannaMason(3) 8 55
(Tony Carroll) *in rr: hdwy 2f out: wnt 3rd u.p over 1f out: kpt on same pce fnl f* **9/2**[3]

552 **4** *1* **Peak Storm**[13] 4711 4-10-0 **66**.............................. MissSMDoolan(5) 5 67
(John O'Shea) *in rr: drvn and hdwy 2f out: nvr rchd ldrs and styd on same pce fnl f* **11/4**[1]

0000 **5** *1 ¾* **Rapid Water**[4] 5032 7-9-4 **51** oh3.............................. MissRachelKing 6 48
(Pat Eddery) *hld up in rr: hrd rdn over 1f out: styd on fnl f but nvr gng pce to rch ldrs* **25/1**

3023 **6** *6* **Silvas Romana (IRE)**[8] 4894 4-10-6 **70**......... MissBeckyBrisbourne(3) 1 53
(Mark Brisbourne) *chsd ldrs: wknd over 2f out* **4/1**[2]

000- **7** *½* **Marvo**[245] 8010 9-8-11 **51** oh1.............................. MissSLewis(7) 2 33
(Dai Burchell) *chsd ldrs: wknd 2f out* **16/1**

5046 **8** *1 ¼* **Shomberg**[30] 4153 4-9-4 **51** oh1..............................(p) MrsAlexDunn 4 30
(Dai Burchell) *chsd ldrs over 5f* **8/1**

1m 35.68s (-0.52) **Going Correction** 0.0s/f (Good) **8** Ran SP% **112.5**
Speed ratings (Par 103): **102,101,99,98,97 91,90,89**
toteswingers 1&2 £8.60, 2&3 £3.70, 1&3 £5.80 CSF £46.61 CT £210.45 TOTE £9.10: £2.20, £2.10, £1.70; EX 82.00 Trifecta £268.40 Pool: £1243.70 - 3.47 winning units..
Owner Miss S M Potts **Bred** Bearstone Stud **Trained** Audley, Staffs

FOCUS
After a dry night the going was changed to good. The pace was not very strong in this handicap and a veteran made all. He showed similar form to this race last year.

5173 REDLEISURE.CO.UK FILLIES' H'CAP 1m 14y
5:50 (5:50) (Class 5) (0-75,73) 3-Y-0+ **£2,587** (£770; £384) **Stalls** Centre

Form RPR
431 **1** **Narmin (IRE)**[19] 4535 3-9-7 **73**.............................. DaneO'Neill 2 85
(John Gosden) *hld up and sn trcking ldrs: drvn to go 2nd 2f out: led appr fnl f: readily* **1/2**[1]

0565 **2** *2 ¾* **Mystical Moment**[40] 3817 3-9-5 **71**.............................. RichardHughes 5 77
(Richard Hannon) *sn led: hdd after 2f: drvn to ld again over 2f out: hdd appr fnl f: sn outpcd but kpt on wl for clr 2nd* **9/4**[2]

0-30 **3** *10* **Black Eyed Girl (IRE)**[22] 4410 3-8-3 **55** ow1.................. LiamJones 3 38
(J S Moore) *led after 2f: hdd over 2f out: wknd qckly over 1f out* **33/1**

00-3 **4** *12* **Three Crowns**[35] 3988 3-8-13 **70**.............................. MatthewLawson(5) 4 25
(Jonathan Portman) *in rr: rdn 3f out: sn btn* **10/1**[3]

1m 34.94s (-1.26) **Going Correction** 0.0s/f (Good)
WFA 3 from 4yo 7lb **4** Ran SP% **109.5**
Speed ratings (Par 100): **106,103,93,81**
CSF £1.92 TOTE £1.20; EX 2.00 Trifecta £8.00 Pool: £943.91 - 88.44 winning units..
Owner Hamdan Al Maktoum **Bred** Shadwell Estate Company Limited **Trained** Newmarket, Suffolk

FOCUS
The hot favourite had to work quite hard but scored with something in hand in this small-field handicap and the first two pulled a long way clear. No depth to this and the winner stood out on recent form. She's likely to get hit for this.

5174 £32 FREE AT 32RED.COM MAIDEN FILLIES' STKS 5f 16y
6:20 (6:22) (Class 5) 2-Y-0 **£2,587** (£770; £384; £192) **Stalls** Centre

Form RPR
00 **1** **Heavens Edge**[83] 2411 2-9-0 0.............................. DavidProbert 6 80
(Christopher Mason) *chsd ldr: rdn over 2f out: led 1f out: styd on wl u.p* **12/1**

06 **2** *2 ½* **Kanz**[8] 4877 2-9-0 0.............................. RichardHughes 4 71
(Mick Channon) *led: rdn over 2f out: hdd 1f out: styd on same pce* **4/6**[1]

00 **3** *1* **Raajis (IRE)**[13] 4702 2-9-0 0.............................. DaneO'Neill 3 67
(Richard Hannon) *chsd ldrs: rdn 3f out: styd on same pce fnl 2f* **9/4**[2]

65 **4** *7* **Rosita**[13] 4708 2-8-9 0..............................(b) AmyScott(5) 2 42
(Henry Candy) *unruly s: a outpcd* **10/1**[3]

5 *3 ½* **Clapperboard** 2-9-0 0.............................. LiamJones 5 30
(Paul Fitzsimons) *a outpcd* **33/1**

59.56s (0.26) **Going Correction** 0.0s/f (Good) **5** Ran SP% **110.5**
Speed ratings (Par 91): **97,93,91,80,74**
CSF £21.20 TOTE £14.00: £5.40, £1.10; EX 25.50 Trifecta £72.50 Pool: £911.24 - 9.42 winning units..
Owner Christopher & Annabelle Mason **Bred** Christopher & Annabelle Mason **Trained** Caewent, Monmouthshire

FOCUS
The hot favourite was turned over in this maiden.

5175 32RED.COM NURSERY H'CAP 6f 16y
6:50 (6:51) (Class 5) (0-75,72) 2-Y-0 **£2,587** (£770; £384; £192) **Stalls** Centre

Form RPR
061 **1** **Threetimesalady**[13] 4708 2-9-2 **70**.............................. RosieJessop(3) 3 76+
(Sir Mark Prescott Bt) *trckd ldrs: led wl over 1f out: pushed along ins fnl f: styd on strly clsng stages* **6/1**

The Form Book Flat, Raceform Ltd, Compton, RG20 6NL.

4646 **2** *1* **Handwoven (IRE)**[13] 4703 2-9-2 **67** LiamJones 6 68
(Mark Johnston) *chsd ldrs: rdn to ld over 2f out: hdd wl over 1f out: styd on u.p fnl f but a hld by wnr: jst kpt 2nd last strides* **5/1**[3]

51 **3** *nse* **It's All A Game**[5] 4990 2-7-12 **54** 6ex (v) PhilipPrince(5) 2 55
(Richard Guest) *led after 2f: hdd over 2f out: sn rdn and one pce: rallied u.p fnl f to chal for 2nd last stride but no imp on wnr* **4/1**[2]

4253 **4** *1 3/4* **Queen Of The Tarts**[29] 4174 2-8-10 **64** CharlesBishop(3) 1 60
(Olly Stevens) *in tch: drioven to chse ldrs 2f out: styd on same pce fnl f* **6/1**

10 **5** *3 3/4* **Bird Of Light (IRE)**[19] 4528 2-9-7 **72** RichardHughes 5 59+
(Richard Hannon) *in rr: pushed along over 2f out: outpcd* **9/4**[1]

000 **6** *3/4* **Hickster (IRE)**[34] 4021 2-8-5 **56** CathyGannon 7 38
(Tom Dascombe) *led 2f: rdn 3f out: wknd fr 2f out* **7/1**

310 **7** *18* **Sakuramachi**[19] 4519 2-8-7 **65** EoinWalsh(7) 4
(Nikki Evans) *s.i.s: a outpcd* **16/1**

1m 11.95s (-0.05) **Going Correction** 0.0s/f (Good) **7** Ran SP% **114.4**
Speed ratings (Par 94): **100,98,98,96,91 90,66**
toteswingers 1&2 £7.50, 2&3 £4.50, 1&3 £5.50 CSF £35.60 TOTE £6.80: £4.80, £4.90; EX 31.90 Trifecta £260.10 Pool: £998.99 - 2.88 winning units..
Owner Bluehills Racing Limited **Bred** Bluehills Racing Limited **Trained** Newmarket, Suffolk

FOCUS
The winner completed a double in good style in this nursery. The second and third help with the level.

5176 32RED MAIDEN STKS — 7f 16y
7:25 (7:29) (Class 5) 3-Y-0+ **£2,587** (£770; £384; £192) **Stalls** Centre

Form RPR

1 **Spin Artist (USA)** 3-9-5 0 LiamJones 6 83+
(Mark Johnston) *chsd ldrs: wnt 2nd over 1f out: styd on u.p to ld fnl 150yds: won gng away* **8/1**[3]

324 **2** *2* **Disco Inferno (IRE)**[14] 4667 3-9-5 79 (t) RichardHughes 5 78
(Brian Meehan) *led 1f: styd trcking ldr: led appr fnl 2f: hdd u.p fnl 150yds: sn no ex* **7/4**[2]

0- **3** *9* **Mukhabarat (IRE)**[322] 6411 3-9-5 0 DaneO'Neill 4 54+
(Saeed bin Suroor) *led after 1f: hdd and rdn appr fnl 2f: wknd qckly fnl f* **10/11**[1]

4 *5* **Ninepointsixthree** 3-9-5 0 AidanColeman 1 40+
(John O'Shea) *in rr: green and bdly outpcd in rr 1/2-way: drvn over 2f out: kpt on ins fnl f but stl wl bhd ldng trio* **33/1**

0 **5** *hd* **Cadeaux Royale**[58] 3176 5-8-13 0 [1] JoshBaudains(7) 9 37
(Dominic Ffrench Davis) *in rr: outpcd and off pce over 2f out: kpt on fnl f to cl for wl hld 4th* **100/1**

6 *1/2* **Foiled** 3-9-5 0 SeanLevey 3 38
(Richard Hannon) *chsd ldrs: rdn 3f out: wknd 2f out* **8/1**[3]

0-0 **7** *1 3/4* **Nandura**[66] 2938 3-9-0 0 CathyGannon 10 29
(Harry Dunlop) *in rr: drvn and in tch wl over 2f out: sn wknd* **50/1**

0- **8** *1/2* **Call Me Marilyn (USA)**[279] 7525 3-8-11 0 (t) AshleyMorgan(3) 2 27
(Paul Cole) *chsd ldrs over 4f* **25/1**

1m 23.53s (0.33) **Going Correction** 0.0s/f (Good)
WFA 3 from 5yo 6lb **8** Ran SP% **120.7**
Speed ratings (Par 103): **98,95,85,79,79 78,76,76**
toteswingers 1&2 £2.30, 2&3 £1.02, 1&3 £2.70 CSF £23.55 TOTE £13.30: £3.80, £1.10, £1.10; EX 21.50 Trifecta £47.70 Pool: £792.54 - 12.45 winning units..
Owner Sheikh Hamdan Bin Mohammed Al Maktoum **Bred** Respite Farm Inc **Trained** Middleham Moor, N Yorks

FOCUS
A newcomer overhauled the leading form contender in this maiden and they finished well strung out. Little depth but the winner looks above average.

5177 32RED CASINO H'CAP — 7f 16y
8:00 (8:04) (Class 6) (0-65,62) 3-Y-0+ **£1,940** (£577; £288; £144) **Stalls** Centre

Form RPR

4051 **1** **The Mongoose**[5] 4996 5-9-4 **61** (t) EoinWalsh(7) 14 75
(David Evans) *racd alone on stands' side and w ldrs tl slt ld after 3f: rdn 2f out: styd on wl u.p fnl f* **9/2**[2]

6020 **2** *2 3/4* **Tenbridge**[71] 2773 4-9-4 **57** (b) RosieJessop(3) 10 64
(Derek Haydn Jones) *chsd ldrs: wnt 2nd over 3f out: rdn and styd on fnl 2f but no imp on wnr fnl f* **16/1**

2233 **3** *2 1/2* **Offbeat Safaris (IRE)**[13] 4711 5-9-3 **58** EDLinehan(5) 2 59
(Ronald Harris) *in tch: drvn to chse ldrs fr over 2f out: one pce into 3rd fnl 2f* **5/1**[3]

-203 **4** *3/4* **Cape Crossing**[13] 4709 4-9-0 **50** (t) RichardHughes 11 49
(Andrew Balding) *chsd ldrs: rdn over 3f out: styd on same pce fnl 2f* **7/2**[1]

0016 **5** *2* **Loyal N Trusted**[12] 4771 5-9-10 **60** (p) AidanColeman 13 53
(Richard Price) *in tch: hdwy to chse ldrs fr 3f out: btn 2f out* **14/1**

-345 **6** *1/2* **Assertive Agent**[63] 3016 3-9-1 **62** GeorgeDowning(5) 9 52
(Tony Carroll) *in tch: drvn and hdwy to cl on ldrs 3f out: btn fr 2f out* **16/1**

3045 **7** *3/4* **Katmai River (IRE)**[38] 3909 6-8-11 **47** (v) DaneO'Neill 4 37
(Mark Usher) *in rr: rdn over 2f out: kpt on fnl f but nvr any ch* **8/1**

0000 **8** *1* **Kept**[66] 2920 4-9-0 **55** PhilipPrince(5) 5 43
(Ronald Harris) *chsd ldrs: rdn 3f out: no ch fr over 2f out* **14/1**

0320 **9** *1/2* **Stonecrabstomorrow (IRE)**[13] 4712 10-9-9 **62** AshleyMorgan(3) 6 51
(Roy Brotherton) *in rr: mod hdwy fr 3f out: nvr rchd ldrs: eased whn no ch fnl f* **25/1**

362 **10** *2 1/4* **Tooley Woods (IRE)**[13] 4709 4-9-5 **55** SeanLevey 7 42
(Tony Carroll) *sn led: hdd after 3f: wknd 2f out* **6/1**

4021 **11** *1* **Hawk Moth (IRE)**[12] 4752 5-9-11 **61** (b) CathyGannon 12 39
(John Spearing) *in rr: rdn and mod prog 3f out: wknd 2f out* **14/1**

0006 **12** *7* **The Bendy Fella (IRE)**[21] 4456 5-8-9 **45** (p) SamHitchcott 8
(Mark Usher) *chsd ldrs: rdn 4f out: sn btn* **33/1**

0000 **13** *4* **Quan (IRE)**[45] 3623 4-8-9 **45** [1] LiamJones 3
(Milton Bradley) *chsd ldrs: wknd over 3f out* **33/1**

0000 **14** *19* **Memphis Man**[13] 4712 10-8-7 **48** (p) DeclanBates(5) 1
(Milton Bradley) *nvr travelling sn wl bhd* **20/1**

1m 23.0s (-0.20) **Going Correction** 0.0s/f (Good)
WFA 3 from 4yo+ 6lb **14** Ran SP% **128.7**
Speed ratings (Par 101): **101,97,95,94,91 91,90,89,88,86 85,77,72,50**
toteswingers 1&2 £28.90, 2&3 £26.30, 1&3 £6.70 CSF £76.92 TOTE £4.80: £1.80, £4.30, £2.10; EX 105.30 Trifecta £863.60 Part won. Pool: £1151.59 - 0.65 winning units..
Owner G Evans & P D Evans **Bred** Kincorth Investments Inc **Trained** Pandy, Monmouths
■ Stewards' Enquiry : Eoin Walsh two-day ban: used whip above permitted level (Aug 24-25)

FOCUS
The winner raced alone against the stands' rail in this big field handicap and not many got involved. The form makes sense.

5178 32REDBINGO.COM H'CAP — 1m 4f 23y
8:35 (8:35) (Class 6) (0-60,60) 3-Y-0 **£1,940** (£577; £288; £144) **Stalls** Low

Form RPR

0640 **1** **Jacobella**[40] 3820 3-9-2 **60** MatthewLawson(5) 7 66
(Jonathan Portman) *towards rr: hdwy fr 3f out: chal ins fnl 2f: led wl over 1f out: drvn out* **3/1**[2]

0-00 **2** *1* **Ocean Power (IRE)**[33] 4070 3-8-8 **47** SeanLevey 4 51
(Richard Phillips) *in tch: hdwy 3f out: chal ins fnl 2f: chsd wnr fr over 1f out: styd on same pce* **20/1**

2262 **3** *1/2* **Polar Forest**[11] 4806 3-8-13 **57** PhilipPrince(5) 1 61
(Richard Guest) *hld up in rr: rdn: swtchd rt and hdwy over 2f out: styd on to take 3rd ins fnl f: kpt on clsng stages* **7/4**[1]

0246 **4** *1 1/2* **Aphrodite Spirit (IRE)**[24] 4352 3-8-7 **46** oh1 LiamJones 3 47
(Pat Eddery) *led: hdd over 4f out: rdn 3f out: styd on same pce u.p fr over 1f out* **7/1**

0-00 **5** *hd* **Downhill Dancer (IRE)**[8] 4898 3-9-5 **58** DaneO'Neill 6 59
(Brian Meehan) *chsd ldrs: rdn and outpcd fr 3f out: swtchd rt and styd on again fnl f* **4/1**[3]

0-15 **6** *2 1/2* **Instinctual**[52] 3403 3-8-12 **51** (b) CathyGannon 5 48
(Brendan Powell) *t.k.h: chsd ldr: led over 4f out: rdn 3f out: jnd ins fnl 2f: sn hdd: wknd fnl f* **5/1**

2m 42.24s (3.24) **Going Correction** +0.225s/f (Good) **6** Ran SP% **115.3**
Speed ratings (Par 98): **98,97,97,96,95 94**
toteswingers 1&2 £13.90, 2&3 £4.70, 1&3 £3.00 CSF £52.98 TOTE £4.40: £2.40, £15.50; EX 51.60 Trifecta £140.70 Pool: £514.51 - 2.74winning units..
Owner Stuart McPhee & Mike Webley **Bred** Mike Webley & Stuart McPhee **Trained** Upper Lambourn, Berks

FOCUS
A low-grade handicap. The pace was fair but they finished in a bunch. The winner is rated to form.
T/Plt: £45.10 to £1 stake. Pool of £47011.71 - 760.10 winning tickets. T/Qpdt: £9.00 to a £1 stake. Pool of £4760.0 - 390.40 winning tickets. ST

4511 HAYDOCK (L-H)
Thursday, August 8

OFFICIAL GOING: Good (8.1)
Wind: Light, hafl against Weather: Fine

5179 SAM AINSCOUGH SNR. H'CAP (JOCKEY CLUB GRASSROOTS MIDDLE DISTANCE SERIES QUALIFIER) — 1m 2f 95y
2:10 (2:10) (Class 5) (0-70,72) 3-Y-0+ **£2,587** (£770; £384; £192) **Stalls** Centre

Form RPR

0251 **1** **Morocco**[8] 4889 4-10-2 **72** 6ex DanielTudhope 8 88+
(David O'Meara) *hld up: hdwy over 2f out: rdn to ld jst over 1f out: kpt on gamely whn pressed ins fnl 100yds* **11/8**[1]

5042 **2** *1/2* **Euston Square**[1] 5142 7-8-10 **52** JoeFanning 2 67
(Alistair Whillans) *midfield: hdwy 3f out: rdn to chal jst over 1f out: continued press wnr ins fnl 100yds: hld fnl strides* **4/1**[2]

3453 **3** *5* **Spanish Plume**[14] 4655 5-8-13 **60** (e) JackDuern(5) 10 66
(Andrew Hollinshead) *led: abt 4 l clr over 4f out: rdn 2f out: hdd jst over 1f out: no ex ins fnl 100yds* **9/1**

0-00 **4** *6* **Judicious**[48] 3545 6-10-0 **70** RobertWinston 5 64
(Geoffrey Harker) *hld up in rr: pushed along over 2f out: sme hdwy over 1f out: kpt on ins fnl f but no imp on ldrs* **11/1**

-004 **5** *hd* **Buster Brown (IRE)**[8] 4889 4-9-11 **67** GrahamLee 9 61
(James Given) *midfield: rdn 2f out: sme hdwy over 1f out: kpt on fnl f but no imp on ldrs* **9/2**[3]

-024 **6** *nk* **Opus Maximus (IRE)**[38] 3909 8-8-9 **51** oh1 (p) PaulMulrennan 6 44
(Jennie Candlish) *hld up: rdn 2f out: kpt on fnl f but no imp on ldrs* **10/1**

6163 **7** *14* **Smirfy's Silver**[126] 1342 9-8-8 **55** SladeO'Hara(5) 4 22
(Michael Mullineaux) *handy: chsd ldr 6f out: pushed along 3f out: rdn and wknd wl over 1f out* **25/1**

0-4U **8** *10* **Voice From Above (IRE)**[9] 4853 4-9-8 **64** DuranFentiman 7 12
(Patrick Holmes) *chsd ldr to 6f out: pushed along over 4f out: rdn over 3f out: wknd over 2f out* **33/1**

2m 10.4s (-5.10) **Going Correction** -0.425s/f (Firm)
WFA 3 from 4yo+ 9lb **8** Ran SP% **114.5**
Speed ratings (Par 103): **103,102,98,93,93 93,82,74**
toteswingers 1&2 £3.90, 2&3 £7.10, 1&3 £2.30 CSF £6.93 CT £34.35 TOTE £2.40: £1.50, £1.10, £1.50; EX 8.30 Trifecta £43.70 Pool: £1953.12 - 33.51 winning units..
Owner Equality Racing **Bred** Cheveley Park Stud Ltd **Trained** Nawton, N Yorks

FOCUS
An ordinary middle-distance handicap, though the pace was honest and few got involved. The first two were both well in on their previous starts.

5180 GRUNDY MAIDEN STKS — 1m
2:40 (2:43) (Class 5) 2-Y-0 **£2,587** (£770; £384; £192) **Stalls** Low

Form RPR

34 **1** **Top Of The Glas (IRE)**[22] 4414 2-9-0 0 MichaelJMMurphy(5) 6 80+
(Alan Jarvis) *in tch: effrt 2f out: rdn to ld over 1f out: r.o ins fnl f: in command towards fin* **7/2**[2]

2 *1 1/4* **Hymenaios (IRE)** 2-9-5 0 SeanLevey 8 77+
(Richard Hannon) *s.i.s: hld up: smooth hdwy over 3f out: rdn to chse wnr ins fnl f: styd on and edgd lft: hld towards fin* **10/3**[1]

3 *3 1/2* **Major Surprise (USA)** 2-9-5 0 DanielTudhope 7 69
(Mrs K Burke) *racd keenly: prom: lft in ld on bnd wl over 4f out: rdn and hdd over 1f out: no ex fnl 100yds* **5/1**[3]

4 *3 1/4* **Year Of Glory (IRE)** 2-9-5 0 AndreaAtzeni 5 62
(Marco Botti) *niggled along in rr: effrt 2f out: rdn and kpt on fr over 1f out: nt gng pce to trble ldrs* **12/1**

3 **5** *3 3/4* **Newgate Queen**[18] 4556 2-9-0 0 StephenCraine 1 48
(Tony Coyle) *trckd ldrs: rdn over 2f out: wknd over 1f out* **25/1**

4 **6** *2* **Damaah (USA)**[16] 4610 2-9-0 0 JoeFanning 9 43+
(Mark Johnston) *prom: carried wd on bnd fr over 5f out: bk on crse over 4f out: chal 2f out: rdn and wknd over 1f out* **8/1**

02 **7** *11* **Shirocco Passion**[9] 4848 2-9-0 0 BarryMcHugh 3 18+
(Tony Coyle) *led: rn wd on bnd fr over 5f out: hdd wl over 4f out: bk on crse sn after and ev ch: pushed along and wknd ent fnl 2f: sn eased whn wl btn* **14/1**

8 8 **Rising Rainbow** 2-9-5 0 ....(b[1]) DavidAllan 2
(Mel Brittain) *s.i.s: hld up: pushed along and outpcd over 3f out: lft bhd over 2f out: eased whn wl btn fnl f* **66/1**

1m 41.99s (-1.71) **Going Correction** -0.425s/f (Firm) 8 Ran SP% **92.8**
Speed ratings (Par 94): **91,89,86,83,79 77,66,58**
toteswingers 1&2 £2.80, 2&3 £5.30, 1&3 £2.40 CSF £10.10 TOTE £2.90: £1.10, £1.70, £1.90; EX 10.20 Trifecta £31.90 Pool: £1085.37 - 25.50 winning units..
Owner Market Avenue Racing Club Ltd **Bred** Seamus McConnon **Trained** Twyford, Bucks

FOCUS
This maiden was weakened by the fancied Godolphin newcomer Napoleon's Comet refusing to enter the stalls (7-2, deduct 20p in the £ under R4).

5181 ROSE BLOSSOM TRUST FILLIES' H'CAP — 1m
3:10 (3:18) (Class 5) (0-75,75) 3-Y-0+ £2,587 (£770; £384; £192) Stalls Low

Form RPR

3223 1 **Visit Copenhagen (USA)**[18] 4561 3-9-4 **72**............ DanielTudhope 8 78
(Mrs K Burke) *mde all: rdn 2f out: hrd pressed ins fnl f: all out and hld on grimley* **9/2[3]**

0-36 2 *nse* **Madame Elizabeth**[6] 4941 3-8-11 **70**............ JackDuern[(5)] 2 76
(Andrew Hollinshead) *hld up: hdwy 2f out: nt qckn and carried hd sltly high over 1f out: r.o and fin strly: jst failed* **20/1**

114 3 *nse* **Drahem**[29] 4180 3-9-2 **70**............ FrederikTylicki 3 76
(James Fanshawe) *broke loose and uns rdr bef r: hld up: rdn and hdwy over 1f out: r.o to chal wl ins fnl f: jst denied* **4/1[2]**

1033 4 ½ **Azenzar**[23] 4385 3-9-2 **70**............ AndreaAtzeni 9 75
(Roger Varian) *racd keenly: chsd wnr: rdn to chal over 1f out: kpt on ins fnl f: hld fnl stride* **10/3[1]**

156 5 2½ **Whispering Lady (IRE)**[76] 2622 3-9-4 **72**............ PhillipMakin 5 71
(David Simcock) *hld up in rr: rdn 2f out: kpt on ins fnl f: nvr able to chal* **13/2**

4560 6 ½ **Authoritarian**[13] 4718 4-9-8 **69**............ SeanLevey 4 67
(Richard Hannon) *in tch: effrt 3f out: sn chsd ldrs: no ex ins fnl f* **14/1**

2-04 7 9 **Signature Dish (IRE)**[19] 4523 3-8-6 **67**............ OisinMurphy[(7)] 7 44
(Andrew Balding) *in tch: lost pl over 4f out: lft bhd 2f out: edgd lft whn wl btn over 1f out* **8/1**

131 8 1¼ **Mandy The Nag (USA)**[13] 4711 3-9-7 **75**............ GrahamLee 6 49
(Ian Williams) *trckd ldrs: pushed along 3f out: wknd over 1f out* **11/2**

1m 39.84s (-3.86) **Going Correction** -0.425s/f (Firm)
WFA 3 from 4yo 7lb 8 Ran SP% **112.5**
Speed ratings (Par 100): **102,101,101,101,98 98,89,88**
toteswingers 1&2 £10.40, 2&3 £8.90, 1&3 £4.20 CSF £82.30 CT £387.93 TOTE £5.90: £2.00, £4.70, £2.00; EX 63.90 Trifecta £1540.40 Pool: £2491.38 - 1.21 winning units..
Owner Kentaur A/S **Bred** Ceka Ireland Ltd Et Al **Trained** Middleham Moor, N Yorks
■ Stewards' Enquiry : Daniel Tudhope two-day ban: used whip above permitted level (Aug 24-25)

FOCUS
There was a bunch finish to this fillies' handicap and it saw a game front-running success by the winner. The form seems ordinary.

5182 PICKAVANCE H'CAP — 1m
3:40 (3:42) (Class 3) (0-95,95) 3-Y-O £8,086 (£2,406; £1,202; £601) Stalls Low

Form RPR

6143 1 **Hay Dude**[47] 3563 3-9-7 **95**............ DanielTudhope 1 105
(Mrs K Burke) *hld up: nt clr run over 2f out: hdwy and swtchd rt over 1f out: r.o to ld fnl 150yds: pushed out towards fin* **5/2[1]**

2-30 2 ¾ **Yarroom (IRE)**[12] 4743 3-9-2 **90**............(p) AndreaAtzeni 8 98
(Roger Varian) *a.p: led over 1f out: sn rdn: hdd fnl 150yds: unable to go w wnr towards fin* **7/2[3]**

3504 3 *nse* **Gabrial's Kaka (IRE)**[12] 4769 3-8-12 **86**............ JoeFanning 2 95+
(Richard Fahey) *a handy: denied clr run fr 2f out: pushed along over 1f out: squeezed through gap ins fnl 150yds: r.o towards fin* **11/1**

-201 4 2 **Gworn**[49] 3492 3-8-13 **87**............ GrahamLee 6 91
(Ed Dunlop) *s.i.s: in rr: struggling to go pce 2f out: styd on ins fnl f: unable to rch ldrs* **11/4[2]**

1131 5 1¼ **Woody Bay**[8] 4890 3-8-5 **79** 6ex............ JamesSullivan 7 80
(James Given) *hld up: hdwy 3f out: chal 2f out: sn rdn: no ex fnl 150yds* **11/2**

531 6 *nk* **Cupertino**[31] 4118 3-8-3 **77**............ DuranFentiman 3 77
(Kevin Ryan) *led: rdn and hdd over 1f out: stl ev ch ins fnl f: fdd fnl 100yds* **16/1**

35-0 7 6 **Fat Gary**[91] 2188 3-8-9 **83**............ RichardKingscote 5 69
(Tom Dascombe) *chsd ldrs: niggled along 5f out: rdn 2f out: wknd over 1f out* **20/1**

1m 39.12s (-4.58) **Going Correction** -0.425s/f (Firm) 7 Ran SP% **111.8**
Speed ratings (Par 104): **105,104,104,102,100 100,94**
toteswingers 1&2 £3.10, 2&3 £7.60, 1&3 £5.20 CSF £11.03 CT £76.41 TOTE £3.80: £2.00, £2.20; EX 12.40 Trifecta £60.90 Pool: £1552.38 - 19.11 winning units..
Owner Ray Bailey **Bred** Ray Bailey **Trained** Middleham Moor, N Yorks

FOCUS
A well-run 3yo handicap with the time 0.72sec quicker than the earlier fillies' handicap. The winner's Ayr form reads well and he progressed again.

5183 DAVID SMITH TRAVEL H'CAP — 6f
4:10 (4:10) (Class 4) (0-85,84) 3-Y-0+ £5,175 (£1,540; £769; £384) Stalls Centre

Form RPR

2235 1 **Diman Waters (IRE)**[13] 4730 6-9-1 **78**............ JasonHart[(5)] 9 87
(Eric Alston) *mde all: rdn over 1f out: pressed ins fnl f: hld on wl fnl strides* **11/1**

0050 2 *hd* **Decision By One**[29] 4165 4-9-4 **76**............(t) RichardKingscote 10 84
(Tom Dascombe) *racd keenly: chsd ldrs: rdn over 1f out: wnt 2nd ins fnl f: r.o and str chal cl home* **10/1**

-004 3 *hd* **Bop It**[13] 4730 4-9-6 **78**............ DanielTudhope 14 86
(David O'Meara) *midfield: rdn 2f out: hdwy and edgd lft over 1f out: r.o ins fnl f: gng on cl home* **11/4[1]**

-056 4 ¾ **Hadaj**[13] 4730 4-9-5 **77**............ JamesSullivan 1 82
(Ruth Carr) *a.p: rdn and ev ch fr over 1f out: no ex cl home* **15/2**

161- 5 ½ **Fairway To Heaven (IRE)**[460] 1862 4-9-12 **84**............ FrankieDettori 13 88+
(Michael Wigham) *dwlt: hld up: hdwy nr side to chse ldrs over 1f out: kpt on same pce fnl 75yds* **3/1[2]**

020 6 2 **Italian Tom (IRE)**[54] 3315 6-8-11 **76**............ OisinMurphy[(7)] 7 73
(Ronald Harris) *chsd ldrs: rdn over 1f out: one pce ins fnl f* **16/1**

0010 7 *shd* **Pea Shooter**[13] 4730 4-9-7 **79**............(p) GrahamLee 8 76
(Kevin Ryan) *hld up: hdwy and pushed along over 1f out: nvr able to chal* **7/1[3]**

0010 8 2 **Mount Hollow**[13] 4730 8-9-2 **79**............(p) JackDuern[(5)] 3 70
(Andrew Hollinshead) *in tch: rdn 2f out: nt qckn over 1f out: one pce ins fnl f* **33/1**

0000 9 ¾ **Trade Secret**[13] 4730 6-9-3 **75**............ DavidAllan 5 63
(Mel Brittain) *s.i.s: rdn along thrght: outpcd: plugged on ins fnl f: nvr on terms* **25/1**

6040 10 *shd* **Sound Amigo (IRE)**[13] 4730 5-9-3 **78**............ NeilFarley[(3)] 6 66
(Declan Carroll) *midfield: pushed along and outpcd over 2f out: n.d after* **16/1**

3310 11 3¾ **Ferdy (IRE)**[11] 4807 4-8-13 **71**............ PaulMulrennan 4 47
(Paul Green) *midfield tl rdn and wknd over 1f out* **33/1**

0020 12 17 **Lexi's Hero (IRE)**[2] 5088 5-9-2 **74**............(p) JoeFanning 2
(David Nicholls) *prom: lost pl 2f out: u.p and n.d after: eased whn wl btn ins fnl f* **16/1**

1m 12.7s (-1.10) **Going Correction** -0.025s/f (Good) 12 Ran SP% **120.7**
Speed ratings (Par 105): **106,105,105,104,103 101,101,98,97,97 92,69**
toteswingers 1&2 £25.90, 2&3 £7.60, 1&3 £5.70 CSF £116.33 CT £332.84 TOTE £15.20: £2.70, £3.90, £1.60; EX 231.50 Trifecta £562.20 Pool: £2067.72 - 2.75 winning units..
Owner Paul Buist & John Thompson **Bred** Mrs Chris Harrington **Trained** Longton, Lancs

FOCUS
A competitive sprint handicap in which seven of the 12 runners had run in the same race at York 13 days earlier, including today's winner, third and fourth. Few got involved here and the winner rates pretty much back to his best.

5184 SAINTS FOUNDATION H'CAP (JOCKEY CLUB GRASSROOTS SPRINT SERIES QUALIFIER) — 6f
4:40 (4:42) (Class 5) (0-70,69) 3-Y-O £2,587 (£770; £384; £192) Stalls Centre

Form RPR

2621 1 **Bapak Muda (USA)**[23] 4378 3-9-6 **68**............ PaulMulrennan 3 75
(Kevin Ryan) *mde all: rdn ins fnl f: kpt on wl fnl f* **4/1[2]**

0521 2 1 **Abraham Monro**[19] 4544 3-8-7 **55**............ JamesSullivan 9 59
(Ruth Carr) *hld up: rdn 2f out: hdwy over 1f out: wnt 2nd ins fnl f: styd on: nt quite gng pce to get to wnr* **3/1[1]**

2121 3 *nk* **Someone's Darling**[17] 4580 3-9-7 **69**............ GrahamLee 7 72
(Jim Goldie) *hld up: rdn over 1f out whn nt quite clr run: prog ins fnl f: gng on at fin* **3/1[1]**

2000 4 *shd* **Dream Scenario**[6] 4967 3-9-5 **67**............ DavidAllan 4 70
(Mel Brittain) *missed break: in rr: pushed along 4f out: rdn and hdwy over 1f out: styd on ins fnl f: one pce fnl strides* **9/1**

550 5 ½ **Baron Run**[11] 4814 3-8-12 **67**............ JoeyHaynes[(7)] 8 68
(Mrs K Burke) *prom: rdn over 1f out: styd on same pce ins fnl f* **16/1**

4053 6 3¼ **Starlight Angel (IRE)**[27] 4244 3-8-10 **65**............ OisinMurphy[(7)] 5 56
(Ronald Harris) *chsd ldrs: rdn 2f out: nt qckn ins fnl f: fdd fnl 100yds* **8/1[3]**

4063 7 1¼ **Ishi Honest**[15] 4624 3-8-6 **61**............ DanielMuscutt[(7)] 6 48
(Mark Usher) *in tch: rdn 2f out: stl wl there chsng ldrs over 1f out: wknd fnl 100yds* **12/1**

6053 8 ¾ **Layla's Oasis**[5] 4976 3-9-4 **66**............(p) JoeFanning 2 50
(Richard Fahey) *prom: rdn over 1f out: wknd ins fnl f* **9/1**

664- 9 *shd* **Angel Grigio**[261] 7797 3-8-2 **50** oh1............(e[1]) PatrickMathers 1 34
(Geoffrey Oldroyd) *hld up: pushed along 2f out: bhd fnl f* **33/1**

1m 13.52s (-0.28) **Going Correction** -0.025s/f (Good) 9 Ran SP% **117.6**
Speed ratings (Par 100): **100,98,98,98,97 93,91,90,90**
toteswingers 1&2 £3.00, 2&3 £3.20, 1&3 £3.10 CSF £16.79 CT £41.17 TOTE £5.30: £1.20, £1.60, £1.60; EX 16.70 Trifecta £50.20 Pool: £3532.43 - 52.74 winning units..
Owner T A Rahman **Bred** Flaxman Holdings Limited **Trained** Hambleton, N Yorks

FOCUS
A modest 3yo sprint handicap and another all-the-way winner. The runner-up is rated back to his 2yo form.

5185 WALTER GOTT MEMORIAL H'CAP — 1m 6f
5:10 (5:10) (Class 4) (0-80,85) 4-Y-0+ £5,175 (£1,540; £769; £384) Stalls Low

Form RPR

3041 1 **Silver Samba**[27] 4238 4-8-7 **73**............ OisinMurphy[(7)] 4 87
(Andrew Balding) *racd in midfield in chsng gp: hdwy on inner to ld jst over 3f out: rdn clr 1f out: styd on wl fnl f* **11/4[2]**

0212 2 6 **Merchant Of Dubai**[19] 4512 8-9-3 **76**............ GrahamLee 6 81
(Jim Goldie) *handy in chsng gp: hdwy 6f out: wnt 2nd over 2f out: no imp on wnr over 1f out: kpt on u.p fnl f: no ch* **5/2[1]**

0-33 3 *hd* **Diamond Penny (IRE)**[29] 4167 5-8-13 **72**............(p) SteveDrowne 7 77
(Seamus Durack) *midfield in chsng gp: hdwy over 3f out: rdn and no imp on wnr over 1f out: kpt on whn chalng for 2nd fnl f* **5/1[3]**

0254 4 ¾ **Spice Fair**[15] 4643 6-9-2 **80**............ ThomasGarner[(5)] 8 84
(Mark Usher) *dwlt: hld up: hdwy on inner 3f out: sn chsd ldrs: rdn over 1f out: sn one pce* **8/1**

-110 5 9 **Albonny (IRE)**[34] 4029 4-8-9 **73**............ MichaelJMMurphy[(5)] 9 64
(Alan Jarvis) *towards rr: pushed along over 3f out: rdn over 2f out: plugged on: nvr a threat* **13/2**

5-45 6 3¼ **Time Of My Life (IRE)**[9] 4851 4-8-12 **71**............(t) RussKennemore 5 58
(Patrick Holmes) *chsd clr ldrs: clsd 6f out: led 4f out: hdd jst over 3f out: rdn over 2f out: wknd over 1f out* **22/1**

4155 7 22 **Tetbury (USA)**[21] 4447 4-9-3 **76**............(v) DanielTudhope 1 32
(David O'Meara) *set str pce and clr w rival tl 6f out: hdd 4f out: sn wknd: eased whn wl btn fnl f* **7/1**

-606 8 17 **Authentication**[6] 4969 4-8-3 **62**............ DuranFentiman 3
(Mel Brittain) *w ldr and helped set str pce: clr of others tl 6f out: rdn and wknd over 3f out: bhd fnl 3f: eased whn wl btn fnl f* **40/1**

2m 56.01s (-5.99) **Going Correction** -0.425s/f (Firm) 8 Ran SP% **115.6**
Speed ratings (Par 105): **100,96,96,96,90 89,76,66**
toteswingers 1&2 £1.70, 2&3 £4.70, 1&3 £4.90 CSF £10.22 CT £31.64 TOTE £3.00: £1.50, £1.10, £1.70; EX 8.00 Trifecta £56.20 Pool: £2330.86 - 31.08 winning units..
Owner BA Racing **Bred** Ptarmigan Bloodstock Ltd **Trained** Kingsclere, Hants

FOCUS
A fair staying handicap, run at a decent pace, with Tetbury and Authentication taking each other on early and not doing each other any favours. The form makes sense with the winner improving again.

T/Jkpt: Not won. T/Plt: £16.00 to a £1 stake. Pool of £85344.45 - 3882.46 winning tickets. T/Qpdt: £9.90 to a £1 stake. Pool of £4586.80 - 342.80 winning tickets. DO

[4894]SANDOWN (R-H)

Thursday, August 8

OFFICIAL GOING: Good (good to firm in places; 8.4)
Wind: Light, against Weather: Fine, warm

5186 BRITISH STALLION STUDS EBF MAIDEN STKS 5f 6y
5:40 (5:40) (Class 5) 2-Y-O **£3,881** (£1,155; £577; £288) **Stalls** Low

Form RPR
1 **Outer Space** 2-9-5 0 PatDobbs 7 89+
(Richard Hannon) *w'like: close coupled: dwlt: chsd ldng pair: quick move on outer to ld over 1f out: sn clr: pushed out* **8/1**[3]
2 2 ¾ **Jacob's Pillow** 2-9-5 0 RyanMoore 1 77+
(William Haggas) *str: lw: dwlt and s.i.s: racd in last pair: pushed along 2f out: plld out and styd on fr over 1f out to take 2nd ins fnl f: no ch w wnr* **4/5**[1]
3 2 **Pool House** 2-9-5 0 JamieSpencer 6 70
(Andrew Balding) *str: b.bkwd: dwlt: settled in last pair: pushed along over 1f out: no ch but kpt on fnl f to take 3rd last stride* **20/1**
222 4 hd **Exceeder**[23] 4379 2-9-5 75 AdamKirby 2 69
(Marco Botti) *lw: led against far rail: rdn and hdd over 1f out: no ch w wnr: one pce fnl f* **5/2**[2]
302 5 hd **Pensax Lad (IRE)**[12] 4781 2-9-5 71 JamesDoyle 4 68
(Ronald Harris) *leggy: pressed ldr: rdn to chal over 1f out: wnr sn swept by and outpcd after* **25/1**
2420 6 1 **Finflash (IRE)**[51] 3424 2-9-5 80 MartinHarley 5 72
(Mick Channon) *trckd ldng pair against far rail: waiting for a gap fr 2f to the fin out that nvr appeared: lost pl fnl f* **12/1**

1m 1.44s (-0.16) **Going Correction** -0.125s/f (Firm) 6 Ran SP% 111.5
Speed ratings (Par 94): **96,91,88,88,87 86**
toteswingers 1&2 £2.00, 2&3 £4.80, 1&3 £16.00 CSF £14.85 TOTE £11.30: £4.10, £2.00; EX 21.00 Trifecta £223.80 Pool: £1526.25 - 5.11 winning units..
Owner Derrick Smith & Mrs John Magnier & Michael Tabor **Bred** Catridge Farm Stud & B & H Jellett **Trained** East Everleigh, Wilts

FOCUS
Round course rail moved 7yds out from 7f to winning post, increasing distances by about 22yds. An ordinary juvenile sprint maiden and no surprise to see it go to one of the newcomers, although it wasn't the one the market suggested it would be.

5187 IMBER COURT H'CAP 7f 16y
6:10 (6:13) (Class 4) (0-85,85) 3-Y-O+ **£5,175** (£1,540; £769; £384) **Stalls** Low

Form RPR
3442 1 **Gracious George (IRE)**[12] 4776 3-8-7 72 RoystonFfrench 6 82
(Jimmy Fox) *hld up in last pair: shkn up over 2f out: prog on outer wl over 1f out to chse ldr fnl f: styd on wl to ld last strides* **10/1**
2212 2 hd **Future Reference (IRE)**[13] 4729 3-8-13 78 (t) SilvestreDeSousa 5 87
(Saeed bin Suroor) *lw: trckd ldr: led over 2f out: kicked 2 l clr over 1f out: drvn fnl f: hdd last strides* **6/4**[1]
0203 3 2 ½ **Top Cop**[14] 4677 4-9-8 81 (p) RyanMoore 4 86
(Andrew Balding) *lw: hld up in 5th: shkn up over 2f out: hdwy to chse wnr briefly jst over 1f out: one pce after* **6/1**[3]
0011 4 nk **Dashing David (IRE)**[12] 4776 3-9-6 85 PatDobbs 3 87
(Richard Hannon) *hld up in last pair: pushed along over 2f out: stl last 1f out: shkn up and styd on after: nrst fin* **7/1**
3210 5 1 **Bravo Echo**[6] 4960 7-9-9 82 SebSanders 2 83
(Michael Attwater) *lw: led: rdn and hdd over 2f out: steadily wknd over 1f out* **7/1**
325 6 ½ **Entwined (IRE)**[56] 3242 3-8-1 71 RyanTate(5) 1 69+
(Clive Cox) *trckd ldng trio: cl up on inner whn nowhere to go 2f out to 1f out: no hdwy fnl f* **9/2**[2]
4241 7 3 ¼ **Kakapuka**[14] 4677 6-9-1 74 MartinHarley 7 65
(Anabel K Murphy) *racd on outer: pressed ldng pair to over 1f out: wknd qckly* **12/1**

1m 29.94s (0.44) **Going Correction** +0.225s/f (Good)
WFA 3 from 4yo+ 6lb 7 Ran SP% 114.3
Speed ratings (Par 105): **106,105,102,102,101 100,97**
toteswingers 1&2 £3.20, 2&3 £2.60, 1&3 £9.90 CSF £25.53 TOTE £11.30: £4.40, £1.10; EX 18.90 Trifecta £114.50 Pool: £1411.60 - 9.24 winning units..
Owner Mrs Barbara Fuller **Bred** D Fuller **Trained** Collingbourne Ducis, Wilts

FOCUS
The front pair drew clear in what was just a fair handicap.

5188 BREEDERS BACK RACING EBF MAIDEN STKS 1m 14y
6:40 (6:42) (Class 5) 2-Y-O **£3,881** (£1,155; £577; £288) **Stalls** Low

Form RPR
1 **Chief Barker (IRE)** 2-9-5 0 PatDobbs 9 77+
(Richard Hannon) *str: lengthy: scope: lw: hld up in midfield: pushed along and no prog over 2f out: stl pushed along whn clsd on ldrs over 1f out: shkn up and r.o fnl f to ld last 50yds* **13/2**[3]
0 2 ½ **All Talk N No Do (IRE)**[15] 4640 2-9-5 0 MickyFenton 2 76
(Seamus Durack) *leggy: led: hrd pressed by variety of chalrs fr over 2f out: edgd lft fr over 1f out but fought on wl: hdd last 50yds* **66/1**
0 3 hd **Ghaawy**[20] 4483 2-9-5 0 PaulHanagan 8 75
(Sir Michael Stoute) *str: lengthy: lw: trckd ldng trio: shkn up over 2f out: clsd to chal and upsides over 1f out: nt qckn ins fnl f* **9/2**[2]
6 4 1 **Adventure Seeker (IRE)**[43] 3689 2-9-5 0 AdamKirby 4 73
(Ed Vaughan) *leggy: dwlt: hld up in last trio: prog and swtchd towards inner fr 2f out: kpt on to press ldrs fnl f: one pce last 100yds* **8/1**
5 2 ¾ **Early Morning (IRE)** 2-9-5 0 JamesDoyle 6 67
(Harry Dunlop) *w'like: b.bkwd: dwlt: hld up towards rr: prog fr 3f out: rdn to chal wl over 1f out: losing pl whn short of room ins fnl f* **25/1**
0 6 1 ¼ **Morally Bankrupt**[9] 4858 2-9-5 0 RyanMoore 7 64
(Richard Hannon) *trckd ldr: chal over 2f out tl fdd wl over 1f out* **9/2**[2]
7 ¾ **Gold Trail (IRE)** 2-9-5 0 SilvestreDeSousa 5 62
(Charlie Appleby) *athletic: v.s.a: detached in last early: rdn 3f out: sme prog on outer 2f out: fdd fnl f* **5/2**[1]
0 8 8 **Iconic Artist (USA)**[47] 3581 2-9-5 0 JamieSpencer 1 44
(Andrew Balding) *w'like@ str: b.bkwd: dwlt: hld up in last trio: hanging and green wl over 2f out: sn wknd* **7/1**
6 9 1 ¼ **Son Of Feyan (IRE)**[15] 4640 2-9-5 0 JimCrowley 3 41
(Roger Teal) *w'like: chsd ldng pair to 3f out: sn wknd* **10/1**

1m 45.9s (2.60) **Going Correction** +0.225s/f (Good) 9 Ran SP% 116.3
Speed ratings (Par 94): **96,95,95,94,91 90,89,81,80**
toteswingers 1&2 £94.10, 2&3 £70.70, 1&3 £6.70 CSF £308.82 TOTE £9.60: £3.40, £10.10, £1.40; EX 243.10 Trifecta £591.80 Part won. Pool: £789.11 -0.04 winning units..
Owner Middleham Park Racing Xxiii **Bred** Eimear Mulhern **Trained** East Everleigh, Wilts

FOCUS
Probably just an ordinary juvenile maiden by course standards, run at just a steady gallop, and the runners bunched up late on.

5189 CHELSEA FC FOUNDATION H'CAP 1m 2f 7y
7:15 (7:15) (Class 3) (0-90,87) 3-Y-O **£7,439** (£2,213; £1,106; £553) **Stalls** Low

Form RPR
16-5 1 **Pearl Castle (IRE)**[108] 1725 3-8-13 79 JamieSpencer 1 90
(Andrew Balding) *mde all: skipped clr wl over 2f out: rdn over 1f out: styd on: unchal* **11/2**
1142 2 2 ½ **Tajheez (IRE)**[19] 4516 3-9-2 82 PaulHanagan 3 88+
(Roger Varian) *snatched up sn after s and dropped to last: rdn and prog on outer jst over 2f out: tk 2nd over 1f out: styd on but no threat to wnr* **4/1**[3]
4361 3 1 ¾ **Arlecchino (IRE)**[20] 4509 3-8-9 75 (b) RoystonFfrench 4 78
(Ed McMahon) *trckd ldrs: shkn up over 2f out: sn outpcd: styd on same pce fr over 1f out* **20/1**
3100 4 3 ½ **Pasaka Boy**[28] 4214 3-9-7 87 JamesDoyle 6 83
(Jonathan Portman) *lw: mostly chsd wnr: rdn and outpcd over 2f out: lost 2nd and wknd over 1f out* **9/2**
0-13 5 3 ¼ **Vital Evidence (USA)**[20] 4476 3-9-3 83 (v[1]) RyanMoore 5 72
(Sir Michael Stoute) *slowly away: settled in 5th: rdn 3f out: struggling whn hmpd wl over 1f out: wknd* **9/4**[1]
6-01 6 1 ¾ **Ikhtisas (USA)**[14] 4672 3-8-12 78 SilvestreDeSousa 2 64
(Saeed bin Suroor) *t.k.h: cl up: rdn and wknd over 2f out* **7/2**[2]

2m 10.74s (0.24) **Going Correction** +0.225s/f (Good) 6 Ran SP% 111.3
Speed ratings (Par 104): **108,106,104,101,99 97**
toteswingers 1&2 £4.60, 2&3 £4.40, 1&3 £15.90 CSF £26.78 TOTE £7.00: £3.20, £2.70; EX 32.30 Trifecta £112.70 Pool: £750.56 -4.99 winning units..
Owner Qatar Racing Limited **Bred** Mogeely Stud **Trained** Kingsclere, Hants

FOCUS
There's a slight question as to the merit of this form, with the winner being able to dictate off the front and at least two of the key players failing to give their running.

5190 VICTORIAN CHRISTMAS PARTIES AT SANDOWN PARK H'CAP 1m 2f 7y
7:50 (7:50) (Class 4) (0-80,80) 3-Y-O+ **£4,690** (£1,395; £697; £348) **Stalls** Low

Form RPR
1-11 1 **Regal Hawk**[66] 2915 3-9-2 79 RyanMoore 8 88+
(James Tate) *lw: trckd ldr: shkn up to chal over 2f out: led over 1f out: rdn and steadily asserted fnl f* **10/11**[1]
0044 2 1 ¾ **Scottish Star**[14] 4683 5-9-5 78 RyanTate(5) 7 83
(James Eustace) *led: rdn and pressed over 2f out: hdd over 1f out: kpt on same pce after* **8/1**
2513 3 ¾ **Choral Festival**[3] 5063 7-9-8 76 KieranO'Neill 3 80
(John Bridger) *trckd ldng pair: waiting for a gap over 2f out to over 1f out: rdn and styd on same pce fnl f* **14/1**
2-42 4 ¾ **Hassle (IRE)**[17] 4590 4-9-11 79 AdamKirby 5 81
(Clive Cox) *lw: hld up in 6th: rdn and prog on outer over 2f out: no imp on ldrs over 1f out: one pce* **6/1**[2]
4533 5 1 **Jewelled**[31] 4126 7-9-5 73 (v) SebSanders 1 73
(Lady Herries) *t.k.h: hld up in 5th: shkn up over 2f out: no imp on ldrs over 1f out: one pce after* **14/1**
5342 6 4 ½ **Forceful Appeal (USA)**[14] 4677 5-9-12 80 PaulHanagan 4 71
(Simon Dow) *hld up in last: reminder 2f out: nvr involved* **12/1**
2053 7 4 ½ **Cayuga**[7] 4907 4-9-12 80 JamesDoyle 6 62
(Brett Johnson) *chsd ldng trio to 2f out: sn wknd qckly* **7/1**[3]

2m 12.01s (1.51) **Going Correction** +0.225s/f (Good)
WFA 3 from 4yo+ 9lb 7 Ran SP% 111.3
Speed ratings (Par 105): **102,100,100,99,98 95,91**
toteswingers 1&2 £4.70, 2&3 £23.50, 1&3 £3.50 CSF £8.33 CT £57.51 TOTE £1.60: £1.40, £3.00; EX 8.60 Trifecta £62.50 Pool: £655.61 -7.85 winning units..
Owner Saeed Manana **Bred** Hesmonds Stud Ltd **Trained** Newmarket, Suffolk

FOCUS
Little got into this, with the pace just a steady one.

5191 BETFRED SUMMER RACEDAY 31ST AUGUST H'CAP 1m 14y
8:25 (8:25) (Class 5) (0-75,75) 3-Y-O+ **£3,234** (£962; £481; £240) **Stalls** Low

Form RPR
0022 1 **Sir Mike**[7] 4923 4-10-0 75 PatDobbs 6 84
(Amanda Perrett) *mde all: hrd pressed fr 2f out: drvn and styd on wl fnl f* **11/4**[2]
0621 2 1 ¼ **Ishikawa (IRE)**[8] 4894 5-9-3 71 RobJFitzpatrick(7) 5 77
(Mrs K Burke) *trckd ldng trio: moved up to take 2nd and chal over 2f out: upsides over 1f out: nt qckn after* **2/1**[1]
-362 3 2 **Take A Note**[23] 4366 4-10-0 75 JimCrowley 3 77
(Patrick Chamings) *hld up in 5th: shkn up over 2f out: outpcd by ldng pair but kpt on to take 3rd ins fnl f* **6/1**[3]
0644 4 shd **Evervescent (IRE)**[23] 4366 4-9-8 69 (b) JamieSpencer 8 70
(J S Moore) *stdd s: hld up in last: pushed along over 2f out: sme prog over 1f out: drvn and styd on to press for 3rd nr fin: no ch* **16/1**
0/11 5 1 **Two Minds (FR)**[29] 4169 6-9-2 63 WilliamCarson 2 62
(Eugene Stanford) *trckd ldng pair: rdn 3f out: lost pl and struggling sn after: rallied over 1f out: one pce fnl f* **8/1**
4036 6 4 **Red To Amber (IRE)**[56] 3241 3-9-2 70 (b) AdamKirby 7 60
(Clive Cox) *chsd ldr to over 2f out: wandered u.str.p in 3rd pl tl wknd fnl f* **13/2**
2064 7 1 ¾ **Saint Irene**[8] 4894 4-8-11 61 ThomasBrown(3) 4 47
(Michael Blanshard) *hld up in last trio: brief prog on outer over 2f out: wknd over 1f out* **20/1**
550- 8 1 **Newtown Cross (IRE)**[321] 6443 3-8-7 61 KieranO'Neill 1 44
(Jimmy Fox) *a in rr: shkn up and no prog over 2f out* **16/1**

1m 45.44s (2.14) **Going Correction** +0.225s/f (Good)
WFA 3 from 4yo+ 7lb 8 Ran SP% 115.3
Speed ratings (Par 103): **98,96,94,94,93 89,87,86**
toteswingers 1&2 £1.30, 2&3 £2.00, 1&3 £4.90 CSF £8.76 TOTE £3.00: £1.10, £1.20, £2.30; EX 7.60 Trifecta £35.20 Pool: £941.76 - 20.02 winning units..
Owner M H and Mrs G Tourle **Bred** M H And Mrs G Tourle **Trained** Pulborough, W Sussex

FOCUS
Solid form for the level, with the to at the head of the market having it to themselves from 2f out.
T/Plt: £47.90 to a £1 stake. Pool of £42008.28 - 639.96 winning tickets. T/Qpdt: £11.80 to a £1 stake. Pool of £4414.51 - 275.20 winning tickets. JN

4141 SOUTHWELL (L-H)

Thursday, August 8

OFFICIAL GOING: Standard

Wind: Moderate across Weather: Cloudy with sunny periods

5192 EVANS HALSHAW PEUGEOT MANSFIELD FILLIES' H'CAP — 7f (F)

4:55 (4:55) (Class 5) (0-70,67) 3-Y-0+ — **£2,726** (£805; £402) **Stalls** Low

Form — RPR

053 **1** **Imaginary World (IRE)**[7] 4928 5-9-3 **61**............(p) LMcNiff(3) 9 71
(John Balding) *hld up towards rr: smooth hdwy over 2f out: chsd ldrs over 1f out: rdn to chse ldr ins fnl f: styd on wl to ld last 75yds* **11/2**[3]

6602 **2** ¾ **Emperatriz**[8] 4885 3-9-2 **63**............ RobertHavlin 8 69
(John Holt) *chsd ldrs on outer: wd st: rdn 2f out: chsd ldr appr fnl f: sn drvn and kpt on to take 2nd nr line* **10/1**

6320 **3** *shd* **Mesmerized (IRE)**[8] 4898 3-9-6 **67**............ NeilCallan 1 73
(Marco Botti) *slt ld: rdn clr wl over 1f out: drvn ent fnl f: hdd and no ex last 75yds* **5/2**[1]

2232 **4** 5 **My New Angel (IRE)**[6] 4966 4-9-4 **59**............ PJMcDonald 4 54
(Jason Ward) *in rr and pushed along after 2f out: rdn along wl over 2f out: hdwy over 1f out: kpt on u.p fnl f: nrst fin* **11/4**[2]

0650 **5** 2 ¾ **Marina Ballerina**[42] 3721 5-8-7 **48** oh3............(p) JimmyQuinn 6 36
(Roy Bowring) *dwlt and towards rr whn hung bdly rt bnd after 2f: rdn along over 3f out: styd on fnl 2f: n.d* **20/1**

2346 **6** ½ **Ishiamiracle**[15] 4623 4-8-7 **48** oh3............(p) LukeMorris 2 34
(Phil McEntee) *chsd ldrs: hdwy over 2f out: rdn wl over 1f out: grad wknd* **10/1**

345 **7** *shd* **Una Bella Cosa**[14] 4689 3-8-0 **50**............(b[1]) NataliaGemelova(3) 7 36
(Alan McCabe) *chsd ldrs: rdn along over 2f out: grad wknd* **12/1**

-600 **8** 1 ½ **Kwanto**[20] 4499 3-8-3 **50**............ AndrewMullen 3 32
(Michael Appleby) *cl up: effrt 3f out: rdn over 2f out: drvn wl over 1f out: sn wknd* **8/1**

0/00 **9** 14 **Enchanted Dream**[13] 4727 5-8-10 **51**............(tp) MartinDwyer 5
(David C Griffiths) *chsd ldrs: rdn along 1/2-way: sn wknd* **16/1**

1m 29.06s (-1.24) **Going Correction** -0.10s/f (Stan)
WFA 3 from 4yo+ 6lb — **9** Ran SP% **118.3**
Speed ratings (Par 100): **103,102,102,96,93 92,92,90,74**
toteswingers 1&2 £10.40, 1&3 £4.40, 2&3 £8.80 CSF £60.34 CT £173.45 TOTE £5.70: £3.20, £2.90, £1.10; EX 96.80 Trifecta £320.60 Pool: £1338.33 - 3.13 winning units..
Owner Hairy Gorrilaz **Bred** Denis McDonnell **Trained** Scrooby, Notts

FOCUS
Modest form.

5193 TESCO'S FINEST MEDIAN AUCTION MAIDEN STKS — 7f (F)

5:25 (5:25) (Class 6) 2-Y-0 — **£2,045** (£603; £302) **Stalls** Low

Form — RPR

02 **1** **Toboggan Star**[10] 4820 2-9-5 0............ PJMcDonald 1 60
(Ann Duffield) *led 2f: trckd ldng pair: hdwy to chal 2f out: sn rdn: led jst over 1f out: drvn ins fnl f and kpt on wl* **11/10**[1]

0000 **2** 1 ¼ **Volodina (IRE)**[3] 5068 2-9-0 46............(b[1]) AndrewMullen 3 52
(Alan McCabe) *dwlt and in rr: sn swtchd wd: hdwy whn hung rt and rn v wd home turn: rdn and gd hdwy wl over 1f out: styd on strly fnl f: nrst fin* **20/1**

0 **3** 1 ¾ **Black Vale (IRE)**[24] 4351 2-9-5 0............(p) NeilCallan 8 52
(James Tate) *t.k.h: cl up: led 3f out: rdn 2f out: drvn: edgd rt and hdd appr fnl f: kpt on same pce* **11/4**[2]

6 **4** 1 ¾ **Shaheen Shah (GER)**[6] 4959 2-9-5 0............ MartinDwyer 7 48
(Conrad Allen) *prom: led after 2f: pushed along and hdd 3f out: rdn 2f out: drvn and wknd appr fnl f* **4/1**[3]

5 15 **Nahthen Alice** 2-8-9 0............ ConnorBeasley(5) 4 4
(Shaun Harris) *chsd ldrs: rdn along over 3f out: sn outpcd* **25/1**

6 **6** 25 **Hot Reply**[10] 4833 2-9-0 0............ LukeMorris 5
(Sir Mark Prescott Bt) *dwlt: sn swtchd to wd outside and rdn along: sn bhd and t.o fnl 3f* **15/2**

1m 32.22s (1.92) **Going Correction** -0.10s/f (Stan) — **6** Ran SP% **114.7**
Speed ratings (Par 92): **85,83,81,79,62 33**
toteswingers 1&2 £4.80, 1&3 £1.50, 2&3 £6.30 CSF £25.80 TOTE £1.30: £1.10, £9.70; EX 12.50 Trifecta £54.50 Pool: £1008.01 - 13.85 winning units..
Owner T P McMahon and D McMahon **Bred** D McMahon **Trained** Constable Burton, N Yorks

FOCUS
An uncompetitive two-year-old median auction maiden.

5194 SPORTS MEDIA PROMOTIONS MAIDEN STKS — 6f (F)

6:00 (6:00) (Class 5) 2-Y-0 — **£2,587** (£770; £384; £192) **Stalls** Low

Form — RPR

33 **1** **Yajamila**[13] 4708 2-9-0 0............ NeilCallan 5 73
(James Tate) *trckd ldrs on outer: hdwy and cl up 1/2-way: chal on outer 2f out: rdn to ld ent fnl f: sn drvn and edgd lft: styd on strly towards fin* **3/1**[3]

5 **2** 2 ¼ **Pennine Warrior**[115] 1580 2-9-5 0............ LukeMorris 3 72
(Scott Dixon) *slt ld: rdn 2f out: drvn over 1f out: hdd ent fnl f: ev ch whn sltly hmpd ins fnl f: kpt on same pce* **5/2**[2]

233 **3** 4 ½ **Bewitchment**[17] 4589 2-9-0 70............ GrahamGibbons 4 53
(Sir Mark Prescott Bt) *cl up: effrt 3f out: rdn 2f out and ev ch tl drvn and one pce appr fnl f* **2/1**[1]

40 **4** 3 **Tez**[8] 4883 2-9-0 0............ TobyAtkinson(5) 6 49
(Marco Botti) *t.k.h: chsd ldrs on outer: hdwy wl over 2f out: rdn along wl over 1f out: sn edgd lft and wknd* **6/1**

635 **5** 8 **Nelson's Pride**[33] 4046 2-9-0 67............ RobertWinston 2 23
(Kevin Ryan) *trckd ldrs: hdwy 3f out: rdn over 2f out: sn drvn and wknd* **10/1**

0 **6** 16 **Solicitation (IRE)**[13] 4708 2-9-2 0............(p) RaulDaSilva(3) 1
(Ralph Beckett) *awkward s: chsd ldrs on inner: rdn along wl over 2f out: sn drvn and wknd* **22/1**

1m 16.46s (-0.04) **Going Correction** -0.10s/f (Stan) — **6** Ran SP% **114.6**
Speed ratings (Par 94): **96,93,87,83,72 51**
toteswingers 1&2 £2.40, 1&3 £1.10, 2&3 £1.80 CSF £11.29 TOTE £6.00: £2.10, £1.80; EX 12.30 Trifecta £34.70 Pool: £1376.11 - 29.71 winning units..
Owner Sheikh Rashid Dalmook Al Maktoum **Bred** Wood Hall Stud Limited **Trained** Newmarket, Suffolk

FOCUS
An interesting maiden.

5195 FRANKE SISSONS H'CAP — 1m (F)

6:30 (6:31) (Class 4) (0-85,85) 3-Y-0+ — **£4,690** (£1,395; £697; £348) **Stalls** Low

Form — RPR

1110 **1** **Sofias Number One (USA)**[66] 2929 5-8-12 **72**......(b) SimonPearce(3) 6 88
(Roy Bowring) *rdn along s and sn lost pl: in rr and swtchd wd after 1f: rdn and bhd 1/2-way: gd hdwy over 2f out: chsd ldrs over 1f out: styd on strly to ld ins fnl f: sn clr and kpt on strly* **20/1**

0505 **2** 3 ¾ **Mingun Bell (USA)**[20] 4502 6-9-3 **77**............(p) MarkCoumbe(3) 11 84
(Ed de Giles) *trckd ldrs: hdwy over 3f out: effrt to chse ldr wl over 1f out: drvn and ch ent fnl f: kpt on same pce* **10/1**

4553 **3** *nk* **Light Burst (USA)**[29] 4181 4-9-11 **82**............ RobertWinston 8 88
(Ismail Mohammed) *trckd ldrs: smooth hdwy to ld wl over 3f out: clr 2f out: rdn over 1f out: drvn and hdd ins fnl f: one pce* **11/2**[3]

0120 **4** 6 **The Lock Master (IRE)**[55] 3293 6-9-9 **85**............ TobyAtkinson(5) 10 78
(Michael Appleby) *trckd ldrs: hdwy over 3f out: rdn to chse ldr 2f out: drvn wl over 1f out: sn one pce* **11/1**

4002 **5** 5 **Satanic Beat (IRE)**[5] 4994 4-9-3 **74**............ PhillipMakin 5 55
(Jedd O'Keeffe) *prom: rdn along and outpcd on inner over 3f out: plugged on u.p fnl 2f: n.d* **9/2**[2]

0006 **6** ½ **Hit The Jackpot (IRE)**[21] 4435 4-9-5 **81**............(v[1]) DavidBergin(5) 7 61
(David O'Meara) *trckd ldrs: hdwy to chse ldr 3f out: rdn over 2f out: sn drvn and wknd wl over 1f out* **12/1**

3030 **7** *nk* **Flying Pickets (IRE)**[30] 4146 4-8-10 **67**............(be) MartinDwyer 13 46
(Alan McCabe) *s.i.s and in rr: wd st: sme hdwy 2f out: sn rdn and n.d* **33/1**

0-65 **8** 2 ¾ **Winged Icarus (USA)**[40] 3828 3-8-8 **72**............(p) DaleSwift 2 45
(Brian Ellison) *prom on inner: rdn along over 3f out: sn wknd* **3/1**[1]

6-60 **9** 1 ½ **Hidden Talent**[47] 3582 3-9-2 **80**............(p) PJMcDonald 12 49
(David Brown) *cl up on outer: rdn along over 3f out: drvn and wknd over 2f out* **33/1**

1350 **10** *nk* **Grilletto (USA)**[64] 2984 3-9-0 **78**............(b) NeilCallan 4 47
(James Tate) *dwlt: in rr and swtchd rt to wd outside after 1f: a bhd* **6/1**

2113 **11** 5 **Royal Holiday (IRE)**[52] 3395 6-8-10 **70**............(p) RaulDaSilva(3) 9 27
(Marjorie Fife) *sn led: rdn along and hdd wl over 3f out: wknd over 2f out* **7/1**

6230 **12** 7 **Ewell Place (IRE)**[26] 4287 4-9-6 **77**............ AndrewMullen 3 18
(David Nicholls) *chsd ldrs: rdn along over 3f out: sn wknd* **20/1**

1m 41.28s (-2.42) **Going Correction** -0.10s/f (Stan)
WFA 3 from 4yo+ 7lb — **12** Ran SP% **125.9**
Speed ratings (Par 105): **108,104,103,97,92 92,92,89,87,87 82,75**
toteswingers 1&2 £33.70, 1&3 £12.30, 2&3 £15.90 CSF £210.93 CT £1288.97 TOTE £16.70: £5.50, £4.70, £2.30; EX 121.30 Trifecta £592.70 Pool: £1075.15 - 1.36 winning units..
Owner S R Bowring **Bred** Rosecrest Farm Llc **Trained** Edwinstowe, Notts
■ Stewards' Enquiry : Raul Da Silva two-day ban: careless riding (Aug 24-25)

FOCUS
A competitive mile handicap and the pace was strong. The complexion changed dramatically late on.

5196 MANSFIELD TOWN FOOTBALL CLUB H'CAP — 1m 4f (F)

7:05 (7:05) (Class 6) (0-70,70) 3-Y-0+ — **£2,726** (£805; £402) **Stalls** Low

Form — RPR

4-65 **1** **Picalily**[36] 3953 4-8-13 **55**............ LukeMorris 9 71
(Brendan Powell) *trckd ldrs: hdwy over 4f out: cl up 3f out: led wl over 2f out: rdn clr over 1f out: styd on strly: v easily* **8/1**

0450 **2** 9 **Light The City (IRE)**[22] 4403 6-8-9 **51** oh5............ PJMcDonald 7 53
(Ruth Carr) *trckd ldr: cl up 1/2-way: led over 3f out: sn rdn and hdd wl over 2f out: drvn and one pce fr over 1f out* **6/1**[3]

4046 **3** 6 **Hell Hath No Fury**[69] 2828 4-8-9 **51** oh2............ AndrewMullen 4 43
(Michael Appleby) *trckd ldng pair: effrt over 4f out: rdn along over 3f out: drvn over 2f out and plugged on same pce* **3/1**[2]

-236 **4** 10 **Gods Gift (IRE)**[9] 4851 3-9-3 **70**............ NeilCallan 2 46
(Rae Guest) *led: rdn along over 4f out: hdd and drvn over 3f out: sn wknd* **5/4**[1]

503/ **5** 9 **Ocean Club**[25] 3724 6-8-11 **53**............ TomEaves 3 15
(Brian Ellison) *s.i.s: a in rr* **8/1**

00-6 **6** 12 **So Cheeky**[10] 4835 4-8-9 **51** oh5............(e[1]) MartinDwyer 8
(Richard Guest) *chsd ldrs on outer: rdn along 5f out: sn outpcd and bhd* **20/1**

50-0 **7** 21 **Run Of The Day**[80] 2511 4-8-9 **51**............(b[1]) JimmyQuinn 5
(Eve Johnson Houghton) *chsd ldrs: rdn along over 5f out: sn outpcd and bhd* **11/1**

2m 39.04s (-1.96) **Going Correction** -0.10s/f (Stan)
WFA 3 from 4yo+ 11lb — **7** Ran SP% **119.0**
Speed ratings (Par 101): **102,96,92,85,79 71,57**
toteswingers 1&2 £5.70, 1&3 £3.40, 2&3 £3.30 CSF £57.11 CT £179.63 TOTE £8.30: £2.60, £6.20; EX 52.70 Trifecta £288.60 Pool: £855.46 - 2.22 winning units..
Owner W A Harrison-Allan **Bred** W A Harrison-Allan **Trained** Upper Lambourn, Berks

FOCUS
A weak 1m4f handicap.

5197 BRIAN APPLEYARD REMEMBRANCE H'CAP — 1m 6f (F)

7:40 (7:41) (Class 6) (0-60,65) 3-Y-0 — **£1,940** (£577; £288; £144) **Stalls** Low

Form — RPR

-541 **1** **Slip Of The Tongue**[5] 5001 3-9-13 **65** 6ex............ LukeMorris 4 83+
(Sir Mark Prescott Bt) *mde all: rdn wl over 2f out: kpt on strly appr fnl f* **1/4**[1]

0-06 **2** 3 ½ **Katie Gale**[12] 4753 3-8-9 **47**............(b[1]) JimmyQuinn 6 54
(Tim Pitt) *trckd wnr to 1/2-way: chsd ldng pair: rdn to chse wnr wl over 2f out: drvn wl over 1f out: no imp fnl f* **8/1**[3]

1601 **3** 18 **Darakti (IRE)**[11] 4809 3-9-11 **63** 6ex............(b) MartinDwyer 2 45
(Alan McCabe) *trckd ldrs: hdwy and cl up 1/2-way: rdn along over 3f out: drvn over 2f out and plugged on one pce* **6/1**[2]

0000 **4** 17 **Pure Flight (IRE)**[22] 4405 3-8-9 **50**............ RachaelGreen(3) 3 8
(Anthony Honeyball) *trckd ldrs: sme hdwy 1/2-way: rdn along over 4f out: sn wknd and bhd fr 3f out* **20/1**

0244 **5** 88 **Betty Boo (IRE)**[8] 4888 3-8-2 **45**............ ConnorBeasley(5) 1
(Shaun Harris) *prom: rdn along 1/2-way: lost pl 5f out: sn bhd and t.o* **20/1**

3m 7.93s (-0.37) **Going Correction** -0.10s/f (Stan) — **5** Ran SP% **114.9**
Speed ratings (Par 98): **97,95,84,75,24**
CSF £3.46 TOTE £7.10: £1.10, £2.90; EX 3.50 Trifecta £6.90 Pool: £912.74 - 97.99 winning units..
Owner J Fishpool - Osborne House **Bred** Miss K Rausing **Trained** Newmarket, Suffolk

The Form Book Flat, Raceform Ltd, Compton, RG20 6NL.

FOCUS
An uncompetitive, one-sided stayers' handicap. The winner was value for considerably more than the winning margin and has plenty more improvement in him.

5198 DADDY MAC H'CAP 7f (F)
8:10 (8:10) (Class 6) (0-55,55) 3-Y-O+ £1,940 (£577; £288; £144) Stalls Low

Form RPR
6605 1 **Nonaynever**[6] 4967 5-8-12 **46** oh1 (b) JamesSullivan 14 58
(Ruth Carr) *in tch: hdwy to chse ldrs 3f out: rdn to ld wl over 1f out: drvn and kpt on wl fnl f* **12/1**
5042 2 1 ½ **Master Of Song**[7] 4928 6-9-4 **55** (p) MarkCoumbe(3) 11 63+
(Roy Bowring) *s.i.s and bhd: wd st: gd hdwy over 2f out: rdn over 1f out: styd on to chse ldr ent fnl f: sn drvn and no imp towards fin* **11/4**[1]
2004 3 2 ¾ **Koo And The Gang (IRE)**[42] 3728 6-9-3 **51** (p) DaleSwift 5 52
(Brian Ellison) *rdn along s and sn chsng ldrs: hdwy 3f out: chal 2f out: sn rdn and ev ch tl drvn and one pce appr fnl f* **7/2**[2]
2530 4 1 ½ **Maggie Mey (IRE)**[8] 4893 5-9-3 **51** GrahamGibbons 2 48
(Lawrence Mullaney) *cl up on inner: disp ld 3f out: sn rdn: drvn and one pce fr wl over 1f out* **14/1**
0050 5 ¾ **Loukoumi**[65] 2956 5-8-13 **47** (b) DavidAllan 9 42
(Tim Easterby) *bhd: rdn along over 3f out: swtchd rt to outer and drvn over 2f out: styd on appr fnl f: nrst fin* **9/1**
3500 6 ½ **Elusive Warrior (USA)**[78] 2575 10-8-6 **47** (p) AaronJones(7) 3 41
(Alan McCabe) *chsd ldrs: rdn along wl over 2f out: drvn wl over 1f out: sn one pce* **25/1**
4120 7 ¾ **Very First Blade**[10] 4834 4-8-12 **53** (p) MatthewHopkins(7) 8 45
(Mark Brisbourne) *in tch on inner: hdwy 3f out: prom 2f out: sn rdn and ch tl drvn and wknd appr fnl f* **12/1**
-030 8 3 ¼ **Maisie's Moon (USA)**[38] 3885 3-9-1 **55** (p) NeilCallan 10 38
(Hughie Morrison) *chsd ldrs on outer: rdn along 3f out: drvn and wknd 2f out* **11/2**[3]
3006 9 2 ½ **Flow Chart (IRE)**[10] 4836 6-8-12 **51** SladeO'Hara(5) 12 28
(Peter Grayson) *swtchd lft to inner s: a towards rr* **20/1**
3340 10 shd **Glan Lady (IRE)**[30] 4145 7-8-12 **46** (v[1]) AndrewMullen 4 23
(Michael Appleby) *a towards rr* **20/1**
1034 11 nk **Tony Hollis**[18] 4557 5-8-12 **53** GemmaTutty(7) 6 29
(Karen Tutty) *led: rdn along wl over 2f out: drvn and hdd wl over 1f out: sn wknd* **25/1**
0066 12 2 ½ **Toffee Shot**[39] 3859 3-8-12 **52** LukeMorris 7 21
(J W Hills) *s.i.s: a in rr* **16/1**
-634 13 6 **Poetic Belle**[49] 3494 3-8-10 **55** MichaelJMMurphy(5) 13 9
(Shaun Harris) *cl up: rdn along over 3f out: sn wknd* **20/1**
1450 14 2 ½ **Ace Of Spies (IRE)**[78] 2578 8-9-6 **54** JimmyQuinn 1
(Mandy Rowland) *a towards rr* **20/1**

1m 29.76s (-0.54) **Going Correction** -0.10s/f (Stan)
WFA 3 from 4yo+ 6lb **14** Ran SP% **128.9**
Speed ratings (Par 101): **99,97,94,92,91 91,90,86,83,83 83,80,73,70**
toteswingers 1&2 £10.30, 1&3 £9.60, 2&3 £3.80 CSF £43.27 CT £152.54 TOTE £13.70: £4.70, £1.40, £1.40; EX 55.70 Trifecta £355.10 Pool: £910.60 - 1.92 winning units..
Owner Grange Park Racing, S Doyle, R Carr **Bred** Dr Ornella Cozzi Carlini **Trained** Huby, N Yorks

FOCUS
A low-grade handicap but not many got into it from halfway.
T/Plt: £300.50 to a £1 stake. Pool of £42425.34 - 103.03 winning tickets. T/Qpdt: £63.60 to a £1 stake. Pool of £3349.07 - 38.95 winning tickets. JR

5151 YARMOUTH (L-H)
Thursday, August 8

OFFICIAL GOING: Good to firm
Wind: Light half-behind Weather: Cloudy with sunny spells

5199 BRITISH STALLION STUDS EBF MAIDEN STKS 6f 3y
2:30 (2:31) (Class 5) 2-Y-O £3,072 (£914; £456; £228) Stalls Centre

Form RPR
2 1 **Strategical (USA)**[20] 4477 2-9-5 0 MickaelBarzalona 9 83+
(Charlie Appleby) *sn led: rdn over 1f out: edgd lft ins fnl f: styd on* **1/4**[1]
60 2 1 ½ **Blurred Vision**[9] 4858 2-9-5 0 WilliamBuick 2 78+
(William Jarvis) *a.p: chsd wnr over 3f out: rdn over 1f out: styd on* **7/1**[2]
0 3 4 **Pyjama Day**[62] 3064 2-9-0 0 (b[1]) MartinLane 4 60
(Hugo Palmer) *s.i.s: hdwy over 4f out: outpcd over 2f out: edgd rt wl over 1f out: styd on ins fnl f* **50/1**
4 3 ¼ **Stormardal (IRE)** 2-9-5 0 TedDurcan 1 55+
(Ismail Mohammed) *sn outpcd: nt clr run wl over 1f out: nvr on terms* **33/1**
2 5 1 **Bush Beauty (IRE)**[93] 2131 2-9-0 0 KierenFallon 6 47
(Clive Brittain) *chsd ldrs: sn pushed along: wknd over 1f out* **8/1**[3]
6 12 **Alisios (GR)** 2-9-2 0 PatrickHills(3) 10 13
(Luca Cumani) *sn outpcd* **33/1**
00 7 6 **Ellingham (IRE)**[52] 3413 2-9-0 0 TomMcLaughlin 3
(Christine Dunnett) *led early: chsd wnr tl over 3f out: rdn and wknd over 2f out* **200/1**

1m 12.82s (-1.58) **Going Correction** -0.20s/f (Firm) **7** Ran SP% **112.0**
Speed ratings (Par 94): **102,100,94,90,89 73,65**
toteswingers 1&2 £1.60, 2&3 £11.10, 1&3 £3.50 CSF £2.37 TOTE £1.30: £1.10, £2.00; EX 2.40 Trifecta £26.70 Pool: £2389.60 - 67.11 winning units..
Owner Godolphin **Bred** Daniel J Burke **Trained** Newmarket, Suffolk

FOCUS
Back straight and bottom bend dolled out 3m. Dry overnight and the jockeys confirmed the ground to be on the quick side. An uncompetitive maiden run at a reasonable gallop.

5200 HOOFBEATS TOURS MAIDEN H'CAP 6f 3y
3:00 (3:00) (Class 6) (0-65,65) 3-Y-O+ £1,940 (£577; £288; £144) Stalls Centre

Form RPR
035 1 **Assembly**[79] 2535 3-9-3 **60** (b[1]) WilliamBuick 3 73
(William Haggas) *led 5f out: rdn over 1f out: r.o: comf* **9/4**[2]
-500 2 4 **Marsh Dragon**[72] 2763 3-9-1 **58** TedDurcan 5 59
(Mark H Tompkins) *sn pushed along in rr: hdwy u.p over 1f out: styd on to go 2nd nr fin: no ch w wnr* **5/1**
36 3 ½ **Whatwehavewehold**[22] 4410 3-8-13 **56** KierenFallon 2 55
(Alan McCabe) *a.p: chsd wnr 1/2-way: rdn over 1f out: styd on same pce ins fnl f: lost 2nd nr fin* **9/2**[3]
-423 4 ½ **Honeymoon Express (IRE)**[23] 4390 3-9-1 **65** ShelleyBirkett(7) 1 62
(Julia Feilden) *chsd ldrs: pushed along over 2f out: styd on same pce ins fnl f* **2/1**[1]
0000 5 1 ½ **Firefly**[45] 3642 4-8-7 **46** oh1 (be) MartinLane 6 39
(John Weymes) *sn pushed along in rr: rdn over 2f out: kpt on ins fnl f: nvr on terms* **25/1**
6350 6 1 ¾ **Give Us A Belle (IRE)**[45] 3644 4-8-7 **46** oh1 (vt) AdamBeschizza 8 33
(Christine Dunnett) *prom: pushed along 1/2-way: wknd fnl f* **20/1**
2000 7 5 **Imtithal (IRE)**[38] 3910 4-8-10 **49** (b) RichardMullen 7 20
(John Weymes) *led 1f: chsd wnr to 1/2-way: sn rdn: wknd over 1f out* **16/1**

1m 12.77s (-1.63) **Going Correction** -0.20s/f (Firm)
WFA 3 from 4yo 4lb **7** Ran SP% **113.4**
Speed ratings (Par 101): **102,96,96,95,93 91,84**
toteswingers 1&2 £3.10, 2&3 £3.60, 1&3 £2.10 CSF £13.73 CT £45.47 TOTE £2.80: £1.40, £2.70; EX 15.90 Trifecta £42.50 Pool: £2586.33 - 45.60 winning units..
Owner Highclere Thoroughbred Racing - Coventry **Bred** Cheveley Park Stud Ltd **Trained** Newmarket, Suffolk

FOCUS
A modest handicap in which the gallop appeared reasonable.

5201 FOLLOW US ON TWITTER AT GREAT YARMOUTH RACECOURSE (S) STKS 1m 3y
3:30 (3:30) (Class 6) 3-Y-O £1,940 (£577; £288) Stalls Centre

Form RPR
5641 1 **Scala Romana (IRE)**[15] 4625 3-9-0 62 RyanPowell(3) 1 65
(Sir Mark Prescott Bt) *mde all: set stdy pce tl qcknd 2f out: pushed clr fnl f: eased nr fin* **4/6**[1]
5-00 2 8 **Cardmaster (IRE)**[19] 4515 3-9-3 65 (b[1]) JohnFahy 3 47
(Eve Johnson Houghton) *chsd wnr: pushed along 1/2-way: rdn over 2f out: wknd ins fnl f* **5/1**[3]
0 3 2 ½ **Sun Valley**[72] 2746 3-8-12 0 MartinLane 2 36
(Anthony Carson) *chsd ldrs: rdn over 2f out: wknd fnl f* **9/4**[2]

1m 41.41s (0.81) **Going Correction** -0.20s/f (Firm) **3** Ran SP% **107.4**
Speed ratings (Par 98): **87,79,76**
CSF £3.98 TOTE £1.50; EX 3.20 Trifecta £2.90 Pool: £2004.44 - 503.13 winning units..The winner was bought by A Darton for 7600gns.
Owner Mr & Mrs John Kelsey-Fry **Bred** John Kelsey-Fry **Trained** Newmarket, Suffolk

FOCUS
A modest and uncompetitive seller in which the gallop was on the steady side.

5202 BBC RADIO NORFOLK FILLIES' H'CAP 1m 3y
4:00 (4:00) (Class 4) (0-85,85) 3-Y-O £4,690 (£1,395; £697; £348) Stalls Centre

Form RPR
0-11 1 **Estiqaama (USA)**[55] 3292 3-9-7 **85** KierenFallon 1 103
(William Haggas) *led 7f out: shkn up over 3f out: pushed clr over 1f out: rdn and r.o wl* **6/4**[1]
130 2 8 **Dream Wild**[27] 4252 3-9-0 **78** WilliamBuick 3 78
(Sir Michael Stoute) *prom: racd keenly: rdn to chse wnr over 1f out: styd on same pce* **7/2**[2]
5060 3 2 ¼ **Califante**[12] 4766 3-9-7 **85** HarryBentley 4 79
(William Muir) *hld up: hdwy u.p over 1f out: wknd ins fnl f* **14/1**
10 4 3 ¾ **Velvety (USA)**[12] 4777 3-9-2 **80** MickaelBarzalona 5 66
(Charlie Appleby) *led 1f: chsd wnr: rdn over 2f out: wknd over 1f out* **10/1**
5312 5 1 ½ **Starlight Symphony (IRE)**[6] 4941 3-8-10 **74** (b) JohnFahy 6 56
(Eve Johnson Houghton) *hld up: hdwy over 2f out: rdn and wknd wl over 1f out* **6/1**
4143 6 2 ¼ **Sharqawiyah**[20] 4485 3-9-6 **84** KirstyMilczarek 2 61
(Luca Cumani) *trckd ldrs: racd keenly: rdn over 2f out: wknd wl over 1f out* **9/2**[3]

1m 37.8s (-2.80) **Going Correction** -0.20s/f (Firm) **6** Ran SP% **110.4**
Speed ratings (Par 99): **106,98,95,92,90 88**
toteswingers 1&2 £1.60, 2&3 £13.10, 1&3 £8.60 CSF £6.65 TOTE £1.70: £1.10, £2.40; EX 6.30 Trifecta £38.30 Pool: £2054.08 - 40.19 winning units..
Owner Hamdan Al Maktoum **Bred** Shadwell Farm LLC **Trained** Newmarket, Suffolk

FOCUS
A useful fillies' handicap run at a reasonable gallop.

5203 JENNINGSBET.COM H'CAP 1m 3f 101y
4:30 (4:30) (Class 5) (0-75,74) 3-Y-O £2,587 (£770; £384; £192) Stalls Centre

Form RPR
605 1 **Dambuster (IRE)**[23] 4381 3-9-7 **74** WilliamBuick 4 83+
(Sir Michael Stoute) *s.i.s: hld up: hdwy over 2f out: rdn to ld ins fnl f: styd on* **5/6**[1]
5-33 2 nk **Runninglikethewind (IRE)**[21] 4436 3-8-10 **63** TedDurcan 1 71
(Chris Wall) *led: rdn and n.m.r fr over 2f out tl hdd ins fnl f: styd on gamely* **5/2**[2]
0-54 3 4 **Inherited**[49] 3497 3-8-4 **60** RyanPowell(3) 3 62
(Sir Mark Prescott Bt) *chsd ldr after 1f: rdn and edgd lft fr over 3f out: sn ev ch tl no ex ins fnl f* **4/1**[3]
6430 4 31 **Astrosapphire**[8] 4882 3-9-2 **69** KierenFallon 2 18
(Mark H Tompkins) *racd keenly: trckd ldr 1f: remained handy tl pushed along over 3f out: wknd and eased over 2f out* **12/1**

2m 25.0s (-3.70) **Going Correction** -0.20s/f (Firm) **4** Ran SP% **110.8**
Speed ratings (Par 100): **105,104,101,79**
CSF £3.31 TOTE £3.90; EX 2.40 Trifecta £5.20 Pool: £1893.60 - 271.35 winning units..
Owner Philip Newton **Bred** Philip Newton **Trained** Newmarket, Suffolk

FOCUS
An uncompetitive handicap in which the gallop was on the steady side and this bare form may not be reliable.

5204 HOOFBEATS RACING CLUB H'CAP 1m 1f
5:00 (5:00) (Class 6) (0-65,65) 3-Y-O+ £1,940 (£577; £288; £144) Stalls Centre

Form RPR
-551 1 **Marju's Quest (IRE)**[14] 4665 3-9-5 **64** MartinLane 6 79+
(David Simcock) *hld up: racd keenly: hdwy over 3f out: led over 1f out: pushed out: comf* **9/2**[2]
3653 2 2 ½ **North Pole**[12] 4751 3-9-1 **63** (p) RyanPowell(3) 3 70
(Sir Mark Prescott Bt) *chsd ldrs: rdn over 1f out: hung lft ins fnl f: styd on to go 2nd post* **7/1**
0441 3 shd **Sonnetation (IRE)**[14] 4658 3-8-7 **52** MickaelBarzalona 8 59
(Jim Boyle) *chsd ldr 4f: remained handy: led again over 2f out: sn rdn: hdd over 1f out: styd on same pce ins fnl f: lost 2nd post* **9/2**[2]
640 4 1 ½ **Magic Lando (FR)**[56] 3250 3-9-5 **64** TedDurcan 5 67
(Ismail Mohammed) *prom: lost pl 4f out: rallied over 1f out: styd on same pce ins fnl f* **6/1**
0551 5 1 ¼ **Diletta Tommasa (IRE)**[12] 4755 3-9-4 **63** WilliamBuick 9 64
(John Stimpson) *hld up: hdwy over 2f out: no ex ins fnl f* **16/1**

/461 **6** 2 3/4 **Hamble**48 3534 4-9-0 **58** ShelleyBirkett(7) 7 53
(Julia Feilden) *prom: trckd ldr over 5f out: rdn and ev ch over 2f out: wknd ins fnl f* **5/1**3

505 **7** 1/2 **Hail Promenader (IRE)**15 4623 7-9-6 **57** (p) SaleemGolam 2 51
(Anthony Carson) *s.i.s and sn pushed along in rr: rdn over 2f out: n.d* **14/1**

00-0 **8** 8 **Oriental Cavalier**35 3977 7-9-4 **55** (b1) RichardMullen 1 31
(Mark Buckley) *pushed along in rr early: hld up: hdwy over 3f out: rdn and wknd over 1f out* **33/1**

-436 **9** nk **Perpetual Ambition**2 5098 3-9-6 **65** (p) KierenFallon 4 40
(Paul D'Arcy) *sn pushed along to ld: rdn and hdd over 2f out: wknd over 1f out* **4/1**1

1m 54.47s (-1.33) **Going Correction** -0.20s/f (Firm)
WFA 3 from 4yo+ 8lb **9** Ran SP% **115.3**
Speed ratings (Par 101): **97,94,94,93,92 89,89,82,81**
toteswingers 1&2 £10.10, 2&3 £8.70, 1&3 £4.70 CSF £35.88 CT £150.68 TOTE £5.00: £1.50, £3.00, £1.90; EX 24.50 Trifecta £115.20 Pool: £1438.98 - 9.36 winning units..
Owner Favourites Racing **Bred** Derrinstown Stud Ltd **Trained** Newmarket, Suffolk
FOCUS
A modest handicap run at just an ordinary gallop to the home straight.

5205 GREENE KING FESTIVAL 17TH-19TH SEPTEMBER APPRENTICE H'CAP 7f 3y
5:30 (5:30) (Class 5) (0-70,71) 4-Y-0+ **£2,587** (£770; £384; £192) **Stalls** Centre

Form RPR

0001 **1** **Tevez**1 5135 8-9-6 **71** 6ex (p) LouisSteward(5) 5 81
(Des Donovan) *s.i.s: bhd and pushed along 4f out: hdwy over 2f out: shkn up to ld over 1f out: edgd lft ins fnl f: styd on* **3/1**3

0650 **2** 1 1/2 **Emkanaat**12 4746 5-9-7 **70** AnaO'Brien(3) 7 76
(Amy Weaver) *chsd ldrs: rdn and ev ch over 1f out: hung lft ins fnl f: styd on* **11/4**2

0502 **3** 2 **Mishrif (USA)**22 4411 7-9-3 **63** (v) GeorgeBuckell 3 64
(J R Jenkins) *prom: outpcd 4f out: rdn over 1f out: styd on ins fnl f* **9/1**

P110 **4** 1 3/4 **Amosite**35 3988 7-9-5 **70** (p) JackGarritty(5) 6 66
(J R Jenkins) *led: edgd rt over 2f out: rdn and hdd over 1f out: no ex ins fnl f* **13/2**

4226 **5** 6 **Duke Of Destiny (IRE)**36 3946 4-8-11 **64** BradleyBosley(7) 4 44
(Ed Walker) *s.i.s: hdwy over 5f out: rdn and nt clr run over 2f out: swtchd lft: wknd over 1f out* **2/1**1

-306 **6** 6 **Mudhish (IRE)**105 1783 8-8-6 **57** (b) LaurenHaigh(5) 2 20
(Clive Brittain) *prom: rdn over 2f out: sn wknd* **20/1**

1m 26.62s (0.02) **Going Correction** -0.20s/f (Firm) **6** Ran SP% **113.1**
Speed ratings (Par 103): **91,89,87,85,78 71**
toteswingers 1&2 £2.80, 2&3 £3.70, 1&3 £4.00 CSF £11.85 TOTE £4.70: £2.60, £1.40; EX 12.70 Trifecta £95.30 Pool: £1340.73 - 95.30 winning units..
Owner River Racing **Bred** P A And Mrs D G Sakal **Trained** Exning, Suffolk
FOCUS
A modest handicap in which the early gallop was on the steady side.
T/Plt: £18.30 to a £1 stake. Pool of £49,742.86 - 1980.62 winning tickets. T/Qpdt: £8.80 to a £1 stake. Pool of £2371.30 - 198.25 winning tickets. CR

5206 - 5208a (Foreign Racing) - See Raceform Interactive

4693 LEOPARDSTOWN (L-H)
Thursday, August 8

OFFICIAL GOING: Good to firm

5209a BALLYROAN STKS (GROUP 3) 1m 4f
6:45 (6:45) 3-Y-0+ **£31,707** (£9,268; £4,390; £1,463)

RPR

1 **Ernest Hemingway (IRE)**39 3873 4-9-12 115 JosephO'Brien 4 116+
(A P O'Brien, Ire) *w.w in rr of quartet: tk clsr order in 3rd 4f out: pushed along in 3rd over 2f out and rdn to chal ent fnl f: clsd wl u.p to ld narrowly fnl 100yds: styd on wl* **11/8**1

2 1/2 **Royal Diamond (IRE)**21 4463 7-9-9 112 JohnnyMurtagh 1 112
(J P Murtagh, Ire) *attempted to make all: sn clr: reduced advantage and 3 l clr 1/2-way: stl gng wl into st: rdn 1 1/2f out and sn pressed: jnd ins fnl f and hdd narrowly fnl 100yds: kpt on wl: nt match wnr* **9/4**3

3 1/2 **Scintillula (IRE)**14 4696 3-8-12 115 (t) KevinManning 3 111+
(J S Bolger, Ire) *trckd ldr in 2nd: 3 l bhd at 1/2-way: rdn into st and clsd u.p between horses to chal ins fnl f: sn no ex u.p in 3rd ins fnl 100yds: kpt on* **2/1**2

4 3 1/4 **St Jean (IRE)**29 4190 3-8-12 94 (t) ChrisHayes 2 106
(Kevin Prendergast, Ire) *hld up bhd ldrs in 3rd: dropped to 4th but stl in tch 4f out: sn pushed along and no imp on ldrs under 2f out: kpt on same pce* **33/1**

2m 32.04s (-3.26) **Going Correction** -0.025s/f (Good)
WFA 3 from 4yo+ 11lb **4** Ran SP% **109.1**
Speed ratings: **109,108,108,106**
CSF £4.83 TOTE £2.00; DF 4.70.
Owner Mrs John Magnier & Michael Tabor & Derrick Smith **Bred** Barronstown Stud **Trained** Ballydoyle, Co Tipperary
FOCUS
This was only Aidan O'Brien's second win in this event - his previous success was in 1999. The fourth limits the form a little.

5210 - 5212a (Foreign Racing) - See Raceform Interactive

CLAIREFONTAINE (R-H)
Thursday, August 8

OFFICIAL GOING: Turf: soft

5213a PRIX DE LA VILLE DE SAINT-GATIEN DES BOIS (CLAIMER) (FILLIES) (APPRENTICES & YOUNG JOCKEYS) (TURF) 7f
3:40 (12:00) 2-Y-0 **£7,723** (£3,089; £2,317; £1,544; £772)

RPR

1 **Sweet Alibi (IRE)**26 4277 2-8-13 0 SoufyaneMoulin(3) 15 62
(J S Moore) *broke wl and jnd ldrs fr wdst draw: a.p on outer: shkn up 2f out: edgd rt 1 1/2f out: r.o u.p to ld narrowly ent fnl f: edgd rt again and hrd pressed all way to line: hld on gamely* **63/10**3

2 nse **Haswell (SPA)**79 2558 2-8-4 0 AllanMonnier(5) 4 55
(M Delcher Sanchez, France) **17/2**

3 1 1/2 **Besnardine (FR)**34 2-8-7 0 (b1) ValentinSeguy(6) 10 55
(J Merienne, France) **11/2**2

4 1 3/4 **Infolinia (USA)** 2-8-7 0 Georges-AntoineAnselin(6) 1 50
(C Lerner, France) **23/1**

5 1 1/4 **Good Things (FR)** 2-8-9 0 CesarPasserat(4) 3 47
(N Bertran De Balanda, France) **24/1**

6 snk **Mamy Way (FR)** 2-8-5 0 MedhiChouit(8) 2 46
(J Heloury, France) **56/1**

7 1/2 **Dolce La Hulpe**29 2-8-4 0 (b) ValentinGambart(5) 6 41
(C Boutin, France) **25/1**

8 1 **Eba Chope (FR)**29 2-8-10 0 (p) AntoineCoutier(6) 14 45
(F Chappet, France) **5/1**1

9 shd **Secret Run (FR)**69 2-8-4 0 MlleZoePfeil(5) 11 38
(V Luka Jr, Czech Republic) **18/1**

10 nk **Larra Chope (FR)**6 2-8-7 0 (p) JimmyTastayre(6) 9 41
(C Boutin, France) **17/1**

11 1/2 **Mindsforgemanacles (IRE)**6 2-8-13 0 (p) AntoineWerle(3) 8 43
(C Boutin, France) **15/2**

12 hd **Pleats (FR)** 2-8-5 0 SoufianeSaadi(8) 12 39
(J-C Rouget, France) **17/2**

13 hd **Doshermanas (FR)**6 2-8-13 0 StevanBourgois(3) 5 42
(C Boutin, France) **34/1**

14 2 1/2 **Diamond Dust (FR)**16 2-8-7 0 ThibaultSpeicher(6) 13 32
(Mario Hofer, Germany) **7/1**

1m 25.2s (85.20) **14** Ran SP% **118.5**
WIN (incl. 1 euro stake): 7.30. PLACES: 2.70, 2.60, 2.50. DF: 32.90. SF: 130.40.
Owner G V March & J S Moore **Bred** Patrick F Kelly And M J Foley **Trained** Upper Lambourn, Berks

5214a PRIX FROMAGERIE GRAINDORGE (CLAIMER) (2YO COLTS & GELDINGS) (APPRENTICES & YOUNG JOCKEYS) (TURF) 7f
4:10 (12:00) 2-Y-0 **£7,723** (£3,089; £2,317; £1,544; £772)

RPR

1 **Cockney Bob**17 4599 2-8-13 0 SoufyaneMoulin(3) 6 76
(J S Moore) *sn prom in main gp bhd clr ldr: 3rd and rdn whn sltly hmpd 2f out: slowly cut deficit to ldr on run to 1f out: r.o wl u.p fnl f to ld 25yds out: won gng away* **9/10**1

2 1 1/4 **Twombly (SPA)**29 2-8-4 0 (b) JimmyTastayre(5) 5 66
(C Boutin, France) **15/1**

3 nk **L'Ami Fernand (FR)** 2-8-13 0 (b) AntoineCoutier(3) 4 72
(D De Waele, France) **12/1**

4 1 **Molesne Chop (FR)**16 2-8-7 0 (b) AllanMonnier(6) 7 66
(Mlle C Cardenne, France) **83/10**3

5 1/2 **Vim (FR)**6 2-8-13 0 (p) AntoineWerle(3) 9 68
(C Boutin, France) **9/1**

6 1 **Schiaman Force (ITY)** 2-8-8 0 AlexandreChampenois(6) 8 63
(G Botti, France) **68/10**2

7 snk **My Dear Watson**15 4651 2-8-7 0 (b1) SoufianeSaadi(6) 10 62
(Matthieu Palussiere, France) **12/1**

8 3/4 **Rouge Sang (FR)**6 2-8-9 0 (b) CesarPasserat(4) 2 60
(J Bertran De Balanda, France) **38/1**

9 7 **One Lord (FR)**6 2-8-7 0 ThibaultSpeicher(6) 3 42
(T Castanheira, France) **31/1**

10 1 3/4 **College Succes (FR)**6 2-9-0 0 (b) StevanBourgois(3) 1 41
(Robert Collet, France) **24/1**

1m 24.4s (84.40) **10** Ran SP% **117.5**
WIN (incl. 1 euro stake): 1.90. PLACES: 1.40, 3.10, 3.00. DF: 13.30. SF: 17.00.
Owner Miss D L Wisbey, R Viney & J S Moore **Bred** Miss Deborah Wisbey **Trained** Upper Lambourn, Berks

5165 BRIGHTON (L-H)
Friday, August 9

OFFICIAL GOING: Good (7.5)
Wind: light, across changing to moderate to fresh, half-against Weather: mainly sunny

5215 EBF/SD2 BRIGHTON'S BIGGEST NEW FESTIVAL SD2FESTIVAL.CO.UK MAIDEN STKS 5f 213y
2:10 (2:10) (Class 5) 2-Y-0 **£2,911** (£866; £432; £216) **Stalls** Centre

Form RPR

6432 **1** **Minley**21 4498 2-9-5 71 SebSanders 2 78+
(Rae Guest) *chsd ldng pair: rdn to ld over 1f out: edgd lft but drew clr 1f out: eased cl home: comf* **4/9**1

643 **2** 6 **Le Laitier (FR)**21 4497 2-9-5 72 JamesDoyle 1 58
(Scott Dixon) *led: rdn over 2f out: hdd over 1f out and btn ent fnl f: wl btn but plugged on for clr 2nd* **3/1**2

353 **3** 2 1/4 **Goadby**16 4616 2-9-0 68 RobertHavlin 4 46
(John Holt) *t.k.h: chsd ldrs: rdn and effrt 2f out: 3rd and btn 1f out: wknd ins fnl f* **8/1**3

0 **4** 13 **Walta (IRE)**16 4631 2-9-5 0 SteveDrowne 3 9
(Ronald Harris) *s.i.s: rn green and detached in last thrght: hit rail over 4f out: eased ins fnl f* **33/1**

1m 13.58s (3.38) **Going Correction** +0.30s/f (Good) **4** Ran SP% **108.3**
Speed ratings (Par 94): **89,81,78,60**
CSF £2.06 TOTE £1.30; EX 2.50 Trifecta £3.20 Pool: £2744.46 - 640.69 winning units..
Owner C J Mills **Bred** C J Mills **Trained** Newmarket, Suffolk
FOCUS
Rail dolled out from 6f to 3.5f, increasing distances by about 13yds. (As on Thursday but slightly wider on apex of bend). Following 5mm of morning rain the ground had eased to good all round. Seb Sanders said: "It is still riding on the quick side and is beautiful ground." The horses faced a headwind through the card and they stayed on the far side all day. A weakly contested maiden.

5216 PAPA JOHN'S PIZZA H'CAP 1m 3f 196y
2:40 (2:40) (Class 6) (0-65,70) 3-Y-0+ **£1,940** (£577; £288; £144) **Stalls** Low

Form RPR

2211 **1** **Beacon Lady**1 5168 4-9-13 **70** 6ex OisinMurphy(7) 8 82
(William Knight) *taken down early: s.i.s: hld up in rr: hdwy 3f out: shkn up to ld over 1f out: sn clr: in command and idling fnl f: pushed out: easily* **11/8**1

1665 **2** 3 1/4 **Jan De Heem**14 4714 3-9-1 **62** (b) JimCrowley 1 69
(Ralph Beckett) *chsd ldr tl rdn to ld ent fnl 2f: drvn and hdd over 1f out: no ch w wnr but kpt on to hold 2nd fnl f* **9/2**2

0005 **3** *1 3/4* **Baltic Blade (IRE)**[13] 4755 3-9-1 **62** LiamKeniry 10 66
(Gary Moore) *in tch in midfield: rdn and effrt over 2f out: no ch w wnr but plugged on to go 3rd wl ins fnl f* **8/1**[3]

2340 **4** *1/2* **Hermosa Vaquera (IRE)**[3] 5099 3-9-0 **61** RobertHavlin 9 64
(Peter Chapple-Hyam) *t.k.h: hld up in tch towards rr: hdwy into midfield: rdn and chsd ldrs 2f out: outpcd and edgd lft 1f out: plugged on same pce fnl f* **9/2**[2]

-000 **5** *2 1/2* **The Wonga Coup (IRE)**[18] 4591 6-9-5 **55** FergusSweeney 3 54
(Pat Phelan) *hld up in tch: rdn and effrt over 2f out: no imp and one pce fr over 1f out* **25/1**

2030 **6** *4 1/2* **Vertueux (FR)**[40] 3271 8-9-3 **53** HarryBentley 2 45
(Tony Carroll) *dwlt: sn rcvrd and in tch in midfield: rdn and struggling over 2f out: wknd over 1f out* **33/1**

0031 **7** *10* **Frosty Secret**[42] 3792 4-9-2 **52** (b) LiamJones 7 28
(Jane Chapple-Hyam) *led tl rdn and hdd ent fnl f: sn btn: fdd fnl f* **8/1**[3]

3030 **8** *2 1/2* **Highly Likely (IRE)**[44] 3688 4-9-6 **56** (t) JamesDoyle 5 28
(Steve Woodman) *in tch in midfield: lost pl 6f out: last and rdn 3f out: no hdwy: wknd 2f out* **20/1**

0000 **9** *nk* **Burnbrake**[86] 2159 8-8-9 **45** KirstyMilczarek 6 17
(Richard Rowe) *chsd ldrs: rdn and lost pl 3f out: bhd over 1f out* **80/1**

2m 36.02s (3.32) **Going Correction** +0.30s/f (Good)
WFA 3 from 4yo+ 11lb **9** Ran SP% **113.5**
Speed ratings (Par 101): **100,97,96,96,94 91,85,83,83**
toteswingers 1&2 £2.70, 2&3 £6.20, 1&3 £3.60 CSF £7.10 CT £34.65 TOTE £2.20: £1.40, £1.60, £2.00; EX 10.90 Trifecta £48.10 Pool: £5621.31 - 87.49 winning units..
Owner The Pro-Claimers **Bred** Ashley House Stud **Trained** Patching, W Sussex

FOCUS
A moderate handicap.

5217 BRIGHTONCARBOOTSALE.CO.UK H'CAP 1m 1f 209y
3:10 (3:10) (Class 6) (0-60,60) 3-Y-O **£1,940** (£577; £288; £144) **Stalls** Low

Form RPR

0400 **1** **Eton Rambler (USA)**[3] 5098 3-9-7 **60** (p) PatCosgrave 8 71
(George Baker) *chsd ldng pair: chsd ldr and effrt on inner ent fnl 2f: led over 1f out: in command and idling ins fnl f: pushed out* **9/4**[1]

5220 **2** *3 3/4* **Special Report (IRE)**[6] 5016 3-8-1 **47** ShelleyBirkett(7) 3 51
(Peter Hiatt) *chsd ldr tl led over 2f out: rdn clr w wnr and hdd over 1f out: wl hld but plugged on ins fnl f* **9/2**

6054 **3** *6* **Admirals Walk (IRE)**[11] 4829 3-9-7 **60** (tp) LiamKeniry 7 52
(Sylvester Kirk) *t.k.h: hld up in tch in midfield: rdn and effrt over 2f out: outpcd and wnt modest 3rd ent fnl f: no imp* **4/1**[3]

4065 **4** *shd* **Jd Rockefeller**[2] 5127 3-8-3 **47** MichaelJMMurphy(5) 4 39
(Paul D'Arcy) *hld up in tch: rdn: hld hd high and outpcd over 1f out: wl hld and swtchd rt 1f out: no ch but battling for modest 3rd wl ins fnl f* **6/1**

6526 **5** *3* **Lucky Mountain**[14] 4722 3-8-9 **48** JamesDoyle 1 35
(Scott Dixon) *led: rdn and hdd over 2f out: 3rd and outpcd wl over 1f out: wknd fnl f* **10/3**[2]

6400 **6** *28* **Mastered (IRE)**[52] 3432 3-8-9 **48** FrederikTylicki 6
(John Best) *s.i.s: a detached in last and nvr travelling wl: pushed along and sme hdwy 4f out: wl btn and hung lft 2f out: heavily eased ins fnl f: t.o* **20/1**

2m 7.06s (3.46) **Going Correction** +0.30s/f (Good) **6** Ran SP% **111.1**
Speed ratings (Par 98): **98,95,90,90,87 65**
toteswingers 1&2 £2.40, 2&3 £2.50, 1&3 £2.30 CSF £12.38 CT £35.25 TOTE £3.10: £2.90, £2.50; EX 12.60 Trifecta £46.10 Pool: £3003.66 - 48.80 winning units..
Owner The Eton Ramblers **Bred** Darley, Bengal B'Stock Llc, J D Vice,Dvm **Trained** Manton, Wilts

FOCUS
A maiden handicap in all but name, and not form to get excited about. The time was 1.5sec slower than the following 61-80 handicap.

5218 HARRY BLOOM MEMORIAL H'CAP 1m 1f 209y
3:40 (3:40) (Class 4) (0-80,80) 3-Y-O **£6,301** (£1,886; £943; £472; £235) **Stalls** Low

Form RPR

4543 **1** **Swift Bounty**[23] 4416 3-8-12 **76** MichaelJMMurphy(5) 5 83+
(Alan Jarvis) *chsd ldng pair tl rdn to ld over 2f out: drvn clr and in command fr over 1f out: pushed out ins fnl f* **9/4**[1]

2362 **2** *1 1/2* **Mizyen (IRE)**[15] 4665 3-8-9 **68** JamesDoyle 2 72
(James Tate) *chsd ldr tl over 2f out: chsd clr wnr u.p wl over 1f out: kpt on u.p but no threat to wnr* **5/2**[2]

104 **3** *nk* **Ocean Applause**[7] 4957 3-9-7 **80** (tp) SebSanders 1 84
(John Ryan) *stdd after s: hld up in tch in rr: hdwy and rdn over 2f out: battling for 2nd but kpt wanting to edge lft fr over 1f out: kpt on: no threat to wnr* **8/1**[3]

5423 **4** *6* **Sacred Square (GER)**[28] 4241 3-8-9 **68** (v) FrederikTylicki 3 60
(William Haggas) *hld up in tch in last pair: dropped to last and drvn over 3f out: outpcd and wl btn over 1f out* **5/2**[2]

3014 **5** *4 1/2* **Saint Jerome (IRE)**[14] 4729 3-9-7 **80** FergusSweeney 4 64
(Jamie Osborne) *sn led: rdn and hdd over 2f out: wknd over 1f out: fdd ins fnl f* **8/1**[3]

2m 5.56s (1.96) **Going Correction** +0.30s/f (Good) **5** Ran SP% **110.1**
Speed ratings (Par 102): **104,102,102,97,94**
CSF £8.19 TOTE £3.40: £1.60, £1.10; EX 9.80 Trifecta £48.50 Pool: £3206.06 - 49.56 winning units..
Owner T&J Partnership **Bred** Ermyn Lodge Stud Limited **Trained** Twyford, Bucks

FOCUS
A fair handicap run at a reasonable gallop, resulting in a time 1.5sec quicker than the preceding 46-60 handicap.

5219 DOWNLOAD THE BETVICTOR APP BRIGHTON BULLET H'CAP 5f 213y
4:10 (4:10) (Class 4) (0-80,81) 3-Y-O **£7,561** (£2,263; £1,131; £566; £282) **Stalls** Centre

Form RPR

1030 **1** **Noverre To Go (IRE)**[6] 4983 7-9-12 **79** (p) SteveDrowne 8 88
(Ronald Harris) *s.i.s: bhd: stl last whn swtchd rt over 1f out: str run u.p on outer fnl f to ld last strides* **12/1**

6323 **2** *nk* **Cruise Tothelimit (IRE)**[10] 4860 5-9-7 **77** RyanPowell(3) 5 85
(Ian Williams) *led: rdn ent fnl f: hrd fr over 1f out: battled on v gamely tl hdd and no ex last strides* **8/1**

1302 **3** *hd* **Commanche**[10] 4863 4-9-2 **74** RobertTart(5) 11 82
(Chris Dwyer) *taken down early: in tch in midfield: effrt u.p ent fnl 2f: pressed ldr 1f out: chsd wnr and ev ch wl ins fnl f: no ex cl home* **10/1**

3014 **4** *1 1/4* **Ginzan**[11] 4830 5-9-10 **77** TomMcLaughlin 1 81
(Malcolm Saunders) *chsd ldrs: rdn and effrt towards inner 2f out: chsd ldr 1f out tl no ex wl ins fnl f: wknd towards fin* **20/1**

0054 **5** *3/4* **Another Try (IRE)**[22] 4440 8-9-1 **73** MichaelJMMurphy(5) 9 75
(Alan Jarvis) *in tch in midfield: effrt u.p over 2f out: kpt on u.p ins fnl f: nvr quite gng pce to chal* **20/1**

0-01 **6** *shd* **Desert Command**[16] 4636 3-9-2 **73** LiamKeniry 10 73
(Andrew Balding) *taken down early: racd keenly: chsd ldr: rdn 2f out: unable qck and lost 2nd 1f out: wknd wl ins fnl f* **10/1**

3130 **7** *hd* **Langley Vale**[14] 4707 4-9-10 **77** SebSanders 2 78
(Roger Teal) *hld up in tch in midfield: rdn and effrt 2f out: styng on whn swtchd lft and drvn ins fnl f: kpt on same pce after* **6/1**[3]

0563 **8** *nk* **Corporal Maddox**[14] 4730 6-9-3 **77** OisinMurphy(7) 3 77
(Ronald Harris) *s.i.s: hld up towards rr: hdwy u.p on inner 2f out: no ex 1f out: wknd wl ins fnl f* **11/2**[2]

5054 **9** *2* **Piazza San Pietro**[10] 4863 7-9-12 **79** (p) JamesDoyle 7 73
(Zoe Davison) *in tch towards rr: effrt u.p over 2f out: no imp: nvr trbld ldrs* **25/1**

1356 **10** *shd* **Aye Aye Digby (IRE)**[29] 4210 8-9-8 **75** FergusSweeney 6 68
(Patrick Chamings) *chsd ldrs: rdn ent fnl f: losing pl whn n.m.r ent fnl f: wknd ins fnl f* **33/1**

0141 **11** *2 1/4* **Lionheart**[10] 4863 3-9-10 **81** 6ex KirstyMilczarek 4 67
(Luca Cumani) *in tch in midfield: rdn over 2f out: outpcd over 1f out: wknd fnl f* **6/4**[1]

1m 11.14s (0.94) **Going Correction** +0.30s/f (Good)
WFA 3 from 4yo+ 4lb **11** Ran SP% **123.0**
Speed ratings (Par 105): **105,104,104,102,101 101,101,100,98,98 95**
toteswingers 1&2 £13.70, 2&3 £9.90, 1&3 £18.10 CSF £103.54 CT £1030.79 TOTE £16.90: £4.40, £2.60, £3.00; EX 85.10 Trifecta £641.30 Pool: £3616.47 - 4.22 winning units..
Owner Robert & Nina Bailey **Bred** Gestut Gorlsdorf **Trained** Earlswood, Monmouths
■ Stewards' Enquiry : Ryan Powell four-day ban: used whip above permitted level (Aug 24-27)

FOCUS
A competitive sprint handicap.

5220 £25 FREE BET AT BETVICTOR.COM MAIDEN H'CAP 5f 213y
4:40 (4:41) (Class 6) (0-65,62) 3-Y-O+ **£1,940** (£577; £288; £144) **Stalls** Centre

Form RPR

2-52 **1** **Pastureyes**[46] 3626 3-9-2 **62** RobertTart(5) 4 69
(Scott Dixon) *chsd ldr: rdn and ev ch 2f out: led over 1f out: edgd rt u.p but forged ahd fnl 100yds: styd on* **4/1**[3]

0203 **2** *3/4* **Sally Bruce**[94] 2123 3-8-4 **52** JenniferFerguson(7) 3 56
(Edward Creighton) *stdd s: hld up in rr: clsd 1/2-way: swtchd rt 2f out: swtchd bk lft and hdwy over 1f out: str chal 1f out: no ex and one pce fnl 75yds* **20/1**

-502 **3** *3/4* **Speedfit Boy (IRE)**[15] 4666 3-9-7 **62** JamesDoyle 5 64
(George Margarson) *racd in last pair: niggled along after 1f and nvr travelling wl after: clsd 1/2-way: drvn over 2f out: no real imp tl styd on to go 3rd wl ins fnl f: nvr threatened ldrs* **5/4**[1]

25/5 **4** *3/4* **Royal Trix**[13] 4774 4-9-6 **62** MichaelJMMurphy(5) 2 63
(Marcus Tregoning) *led: rdn 2f out: hdd over 1f out: no ex u.p and edgd lft 1f out: wknd wl ins fnl f* **3/1**[2]

340 **5** *3/4* **Compton Prince**[37] 3949 4-9-2 **60** (b) WillPettis(7) 7 59
(Milton Bradley) *chsd ldng pair: ev ch whn wandered u.p 2f out: nt qckn and outpcd over 1f out: btn and one pce fnl f* **6/1**

56-0 **6** *nk* **Birdie King**[52] 3438 3-9-5 **60** PaoloSirigu 6 60
(John Best) *t.k.h early: hld up in midfield: effrt on inner jst over 2f out: chsng ldrs and keeping on whn nt clr run and hmpd jst ins fnl f: nt rcvr and one pce after* **14/1**

1m 13.51s (3.31) **Going Correction** +0.30s/f (Good)
WFA 3 from 4yo 4lb **6** Ran SP% **115.2**
Speed ratings (Par 101): **89,88,87,86,85 84**
toteswingers 1&2 £3.60, 2&3 £3.90, 1&3 £1.80 CSF £68.33 CT £153.19 TOTE £4.60: £1.70, £3.60; EX 34.50 Trifecta £87.90 Pool: £3843.89 - 32.76 winning units..
Owner Paul J Dixon & Mrs Jayne Jackson **Bred** Mrs Yvette Dixon **Trained** Babworth, Notts

FOCUS
A low-grade handicap.

5221 HILTON BRIGHTON METROPOLE H'CAP 5f 59y
5:10 (5:10) (Class 6) (0-60,60) 3-Y-O+ **£1,940** (£577; £288; £144) **Stalls** Centre

Form RPR

-021 **1** **Excellent Aim**[22] 4427 6-9-4 **60** RyanPowell(3) 4 74+
(George Margarson) *chsd ldng pair: wnt 2nd wl over 2f out: rdn and qcknd to ld jst over 1f out: sn clr: pushed out: easily* **11/8**[2]

4025 **2** *5* **Welease Bwian (IRE)**[4] 5060 4-9-6 **59** JamesDoyle 1 52
(Stuart Williams) *hld up in last pair: clsd to trck ldrs 2f out: swtchd rt and effrt u.p over 1f out: chsd clr wnr and edgd lft 1f out: no hdwy and sn wl btn: plugged on* **5/4**[1]

0004 **3** *1/2* **Flaxen Lake**[15] 4660 6-8-0 **46** oh1 (p) ShelleyBirkett(7) 2 37
(Milton Bradley) *dwlt: hld up in last pair: clsd 1/2-way: rdn and effrt 2f out: no ch w wnr but plugged on to go 3rd wl ins fnl f* **33/1**

0000 **4** *2 1/2* **Roy's Legacy**[13] 4761 4-8-9 **53** (t) MichaelJMMurphy(5) 3 35
(Shaun Harris) *chsd ldr tl wl over 2f out: styd handy: rdn and unable qck over 1f out: wknd ins fnl f* **14/1**

0050 **5** *3 1/4* **Courageous (IRE)**[1] 5166 7-8-12 **51** LiamKeniry 6 22
(Milton Bradley) *racd freely: led tl 3f out: styd chsng ldrs tl rdn and wknd over 1f out: fdd ins fnl f* **14/1**

1643 **6** *1* **Burnt Cream**[22] 4427 6-8-7 **49** (t) CharlesBishop(3) 5 16
(Martin Bosley) *stdd s: t.k.h: in tch in midfield: hdwy to ld 3f out: rdn wl over 1f out: hdd and wandered jst over 1f out: sn btn: fdd ins fnl f* **10/1**[3]

1m 4.52s (2.22) **Going Correction** +0.30s/f (Good) **6** Ran SP% **111.9**
Speed ratings (Par 101): **94,86,85,81,76 74**
toteswingers 1&2 £1.50, 2&3 £7.80, 1&3 £6.60 CSF £3.40 TOTE £2.00: £1.10, £1.50; EX 4.50 Trifecta £29.00 Pool: £2279.78 - 58.91 winning units..
Owner Graham Lodge Partnership **Bred** Norcroft Park Stud **Trained** Newmarket, Suffolk

FOCUS
A very modest handicap which lacked depth.
T/Plt: £133.30 to a £1 stake. Pool of £64596.23 - 353.68 winning tickets. T/Qpdt: £33.50 to a £1 stake. Pool of £4251.72 - 93.78 winning tickets. SP

5179 HAYDOCK (L-H)

Friday, August 9

OFFICIAL GOING: Good (8.4)

Wind: Light, against Weather: Fine

5222 BETDAQ HAYDOCK PARK APPRENTICE TRAINING SERIES H'CAP (PART OF THE RACING EXCELLENCE INITIATIVE) 1m 3f 200y

5:50 (5:50) (Class 5) (0-75,74) 4-Y-0+ £2,587 (£770; £384; £192) Stalls Centre

Form RPR

4305 1 **Royal Sea (IRE)**4 5052 4-8-6 57 (be) TimClark(3) 5 64
(Michael Mullineaux) *chsd ldrs: wnt 2nd 7f out: rdn to chal 2f out: r.o to ld wl ins fnl f* 10/1

1355 2 hd **King Of Paradise (IRE)**6 4995 4-9-6 68 JasonHart 2 75
(Eric Alston) *led: rdn whn pressed over 2f out: narrowly hdd wl ins fnl f* 11/4[1]

0404 3 3 **Silver Tigress**16 4622 5-8-7 58 ConnorBeasley(3) 4 60
(George Moore) *hld up: hdwy over 2f out: rdn and chal over 1f out: one pce fnl 100yds* 10/3[2]

0600 4 1 3/4 **Tinseltown**4 5059 7-9-3 65 ShirleyTeasdale 3 64
(Brian Rothwell) *chsd ldr tl 7f out: outpcd 3f out: kpt on but no imp ins fnl f* 9/1

0002 5 3 3/4 **Grandiloquent**22 4455 4-8-13 66 (b) KevinStott(5) 6 59
(Kevin Ryan) *missed break and lost abt 15 l: wl bhd tl in rr but in tch after 3f: effrt over 2f out: hung lft and no imp wl over 1f out: wl btn fnl f* 4/1

6066 6 1 1/2 **Dancing Primo**21 4489 7-9-5 70 JackDuern(3) 7 61
(Mark Brisbourne) *hld up: effrt 3f out: rdn and wknd over 1f out* 7/2[3]

2m 33.09s (-0.71) **Going Correction** -0.30s/f (Firm) 6 Ran SP% 111.1
Speed ratings (Par 103): **90,89,87,86,84 83**
toteswingers 1&2 £7.60, 1&3 £8.60, 2&3 £1.90 CSF £36.67 TOTE £14.90: £6.00, £1.90; EX 53.70 Trifecta £77.50 Pool: £1022.89 - 9.89 winning units..
Owner P Currey **Bred** Rabbah Bloodstock Limited **Trained** Alpraham, Cheshire

FOCUS
All races on Inner home straight and races on Round course reduced in distance by 5yds. A fairly uncompetitive contest, run at a steady early pace.

5223 KISS MIX H'CAP 1m 3f 200y

6:20 (6:20) (Class 4) (0-80,80) 3-Y-0 £5,303 (£1,668; £897) Stalls Centre

Form RPR

3224 1 **Ambleside**7 4950 3-8-13 72 FrannyNorton 4 81+
(Mark Johnston) *in rr: niggled along over 4f out: effrt 2f out: styd on to ld fnl 150yds: sn edgd lft: kpt on* 11/8[1]

1431 2 1/2 **Hawk High (IRE)**21 4480 3-9-7 80 DavidAllan 3 88
(Tim Easterby) *chsd ldr: led 2f out: sn rdn: edgd lft ins fnl f: hdd fnl 150yds: kpt on but hld after* 15/8[2]

2125 3 1 **Good Speech (IRE)**69 2878 3-8-11 70 MickyFenton 2 77
(Tom Tate) *led: rdn and hdd 2f out: stl ev ch u.p whn n.m.r and snatched up ins fnl f: sn swtchd rt: kpt on towards fin* 7/1

2404 P **Allnecessaryforce (FR)**12 4804 3-9-5 78 (v) LeeTopliss 1
(Richard Fahey) *veered across the crse and crashed into rail after abt 50yds: sn p.u* 9/2[3]

2m 29.41s (-4.39) **Going Correction** -0.30s/f (Firm) 4 Ran SP% 107.6
Speed ratings (Par 102): **102,101,101,**
CSF £4.19 TOTE £2.60; EX 4.10 Trifecta £5.70 Pool: £559.33 - 72.79 winning units..
Owner Sheikh Hamdan Bin Mohammed Al Maktoum **Bred** Mount Coote Partnership **Trained** Middleham Moor, N Yorks

FOCUS
This modest little handicap was run at a fair pace.

5224 BRITISH STALLION STUDS CHRIS FAYLE MEMORIAL EBF NOVICE STKS 7f

6:55 (6:57) (Class 4) 2-Y-0 £4,528 (£1,347; £673) Stalls Low

Form RPR

1 1 **Silent Bullet (IRE)**20 4513 2-9-4 0 SilvestreDeSousa 4 89+
(Saeed bin Suroor) *led: rdn and hdd narrowly jst over 1f out: rallied to regain ld fnl 50yds* 8/15[1]

215 2 1/2 **Safety Check (IRE)**13 4747 2-9-4 89 MickaelBarzalona 1 87
(Charlie Appleby) *hld up: plld off rail 2f out: led narrowly on bit jst over 1f out: rdn wl ins fnl f: hdd and no ex fnl 50yds* 13/8[2]

3 9 **Lady Yeats** 2-8-0 0 ConnorBeasley(5) 2 51
(George Moore) *sn chsd ldr: effrt to chal 3f out: dropped to rr 2f out: toiling fnl f* 33/1[3]

1m 32.9s (2.20) **Going Correction** -0.30s/f (Firm) 3 Ran SP% 106.3
Speed ratings (Par 96): **75,74,64**
CSF £1.65 TOTE £1.60; EX 1.40 Trifecta £1.40 Pool: £1083.18 - 560.88 winning units..
Owner Godolphin **Bred** Darley **Trained** Newmarket, Suffolk

FOCUS
Effectively a match and so it played out.

5225 HUNTER AND CO ACCOUNTANTS EBF MAIDEN STKS 6f

7:25 (7:27) (Class 5) 2-Y-0 £2,911 (£866; £432; £216) Stalls Centre

Form RPR

1 **We'Ll Shake Hands (FR)** 2-9-5 0 MartinHarley 6 74+
(Mrs K Burke) *hld up: hdwy to go prom 1/2-way: travelled wl: led over 1f out: sn rdn: r.o ins fnl f: in command towards fin* 6/5[1]

5 2 1 3/4 **Gold Club**25 4351 2-9-5 0 FrannyNorton 1 67
(Ed McMahon) *t.k.h: led: hdd after 2f: regained ld over 2f out: hdd over 1f out: rdn and edgd lft ins fnl f: no ex fnl 50yds* 9/2[3]

50 3 3/4 **Mimbleberry**30 4164 2-9-0 0 RichardKingscote 3 60+
(Tom Dascombe) *prom: lost pl after 2f: rdn and outpcd over 2f out: hdwy over 1f out: styd on ins fnl f: clsd towards fin* 7/2[2]

6236 4 7 **Evie Jay (IRE)**20 4511 2-9-0 70 SilvestreDeSousa 2 39
(Paul Green) *t.k.h: w ldr for 2f: stl in tch whn rdn over 2f out: wknd over 1f out* 7/2[2]

06 5 4 **Romantic Bliss (IRE)**16 4616 2-9-0 0 TomEaves 5 27
(Mrs K Burke) *hld up: pushed along 2f out: outpcd over 1f out* 20/1

000 6 24 **Paparima (IRE)**20 4513 2-9-0 20 PaulMulrennan 4
(Paul Green) *t.k.h: chsd ldrs: led after 2f and steadily edgd lft: rdn and hdd over 2f out: wknd wl over 1f out: sn eased whn wl btn* 66/1

1m 16.52s (2.72) **Going Correction** +0.10s/f (Good) 6 Ran SP% 114.3
Speed ratings (Par 94): **85,82,81,72,67 35**
toteswingers 1&2 £1.70, 1&3 £1.70, 2&3 £3.10 CSF £7.40 TOTE £2.40: £1.80, £2.50; EX 8.70 Trifecta £26.30 Pool: £1158.27 - 32.97 winning units..
Owner Market Avenue Racing Club & Mrs E Burke **Bred** Eric Puerari **Trained** Middleham Moor, N Yorks

FOCUS
An ordinary juvenile maiden.

5226 COUNTRYWIDE FREIGHT NURSERY H'CAP 6f

8:00 (8:00) (Class 4) (0-80,77) 2-Y-0 £4,528 (£1,347; £673; £336) Stalls Centre

Form RPR

21 1 **Free Code (IRE)**14 4724 2-9-7 77 PaulMulrennan 4 86+
(James Tate) *in rr: pushed along over 2f out: rdn and hdwy to chse ldr over 1f out: r.o to ld fnl 150yds: in command towards fin* 5/4[1]

021 2 1 **Ticking Katie (IRE)**25 4337 2-9-1 71 MartinHarley 5 77
(Mrs K Burke) *led: rdn over 1f out: hdd fnl 150yds: sn edgd lft: no ex towards fin* 7/4[2]

6531 3 10 **De Repente (IRE)**12 4802 2-9-0 70 6ex FrannyNorton 6 46
(Paul Green) *wnt rt s: in tch: rdn and outpcd ent fnl 2f: tk 3rd over 1f out: no ch w front two fnl f* 9/2[3]

626 4 4 1/2 **Bountiful Forest**41 3826 2-8-2 65 SamanthaBell(7) 1 28
(Richard Fahey) *prom tl rdn and wknd over 1f out* 16/1

50 5 1 1/4 **Red Forever**5 5029 2-8-0 56 oh1 PaulQuinn 3 15
(Alan Berry) *racd keenly: chsd ldrs: rdn 2f out: wknd over 1f out* 16/1

1m 14.62s (0.82) **Going Correction** +0.10s/f (Good) 5 Ran SP% 110.8
Speed ratings (Par 96): **98,96,83,77,75**
CSF £3.74 TOTE £2.10: £1.20, £1.50; EX 3.40 Trifecta £3.60 Pool: £801.48 - 165.21 winning units..
Owner Sheikh Rashid Dalmook Al Maktoum **Bred** Rory O'Brien **Trained** Newmarket, Suffolk

FOCUS
A modest nursery.

5227 SUPPLY UK FILLIES' H'CAP 5f

8:30 (8:31) (Class 5) (0-70,70) 3-Y-0+ £2,587 (£770; £384; £192) Stalls Centre

Form RPR

-151 1 **Gran Canaria Queen**7 4970 4-8-10 56 DavidAllan 3 70+
(Tim Easterby) *a.p: led 1f out: r.o ins fnl f: pushed out* 11/10[1]

0060 2 1 1/2 **Beau Mistral (IRE)**8 4930 4-9-6 66 SilvestreDeSousa 9 75+
(Paul Green) *in tch: pushed along whn nt clr run and snatched up 2f out: sn swtchd lft: rdn and r.o to take 2nd wl ins fnl f: nt rch wnr* 11/2[2]

3334 3 1 3/4 **Script**6 4992 4-8-13 59 PaddyAspell 10 61
(Alan Berry) *towards rr: hdwy 2f out: sn rdn: kpt on ins fnl f: nt pce to chal ldrs* 10/1

5400 4 1/2 **Passionada**35 4017 4-9-6 66 FrannyNorton 7 67
(Ed McMahon) *prom: rdn over 1f out: styd on same pce ins fnl f* 7/1[3]

01-2 5 1/2 **Ballarina**64 3024 7-8-11 62 JasonHart(5) 11 61
(Eric Alston) *led: rdn and hung lft over 1f out: sn hdd: no ex fnl 75yds* 9/1

0021 6 nk **Song Of Parkes**20 4520 6-9-5 70 (b[1]) SladeO'Hara(5) 8 68
(Peter Grayson) *in tch: pushed along and lost pl 2f out: kpt on u.p ins fnl f but unable to chal* 16/1

5000 7 1/2 **Scarlet Strand**24 4371 3-8-2 51 oh6 PaulQuinn 6 47
(Andrew Hollinshead) *s.i.s: in rr: rdn 2f out: kpt on and edgd lft ins fnl f: no imp on ldrs* 50/1

2360 8 6 **Miss Bunter**14 4728 4-9-4 69 DavidBergin(5) 1 43
(David O'Meara) *in tch: rdn wl over 1f out: sn wknd* 20/1

0000 9 1 3/4 **El McGlynn (IRE)**12 4814 4-9-1 68 (p) LukeLeadbitter(7) 5 36
(Eric Alston) *prom tl rdn and wknd wl over 1f out* 25/1

2002 10 1 3/4 **Baby Queen (IRE)**14 4712 7-9-4 69 MatthewLawson(5) 2 31
(Brian Baugh) *towards rr: rdn 2f out: nvr on terms* 20/1

-000 11 4 **Too Ambitious**7 4943 4-8-0 51 oh5 (p) ShirleyTeasdale(5) 4
(Andrew Hollinshead) *n.m.r sn after s: midfield: pushed along over 2f out: wknd over 1f out* 50/1

1m 0.92s (0.12) **Going Correction** +0.10s/f (Good)
WFA 3 from 4yo+ 3lb 11 Ran SP% 117.8
Speed ratings (Par 100): **103,100,97,97,96 95,94,85,82,79 73**
toteswingers 1&2 £2.50, 1&3 £3.50, 2&3 £10.60 CSF £6.50 CT £40.87 TOTE £2.10: £1.30, £1.90, £2.90; EX 10.20 Trifecta £58.60 Pool: £1423.27 - 18.21 winning units..
Owner M Gillies **Bred** H Moszkowicz And Whitsbury Manor Stud **Trained** Great Habton, N Yorks

FOCUS
A weak fillies' handicap.
T/Plt: £25.70 to a £1 stake. Pool: £53680.29 - 1524.71 winning tickets T/Qpdt: £3.90 to a £1 stake. Pool: £5102.04 - 950.59 winning tickets DO

4996 LINGFIELD (L-H)

Friday, August 9

OFFICIAL GOING: Standard

Wind: Light, half against Weather: Fine but cloudy, warm

5228 LADBROKES NOVICE STKS 5f (P)

2:20 (2:21) (Class 5) 2-Y-0 £2,726 (£805; £402) Stalls High

Form RPR

4103 1 **Green Door (IRE)**27 4299 2-9-5 93 (b[1]) JamieSpencer 4 91
(Olly Stevens) *edgy in stalls: booted out of them and mde all: hrd rdn and hung rt fr over 1f out: hld on* 8/13[1]

112 2 nk **Scruffy Tramp (IRE)**15 4653 2-9-4 83 SeanLevey 2 89
(Michael Wigham) *chsd wnr: rdn 2f out: chal on outer over 1f out: carried rt and drifted rt of own volition: clsd nr fin: a hld* 5/1[3]

13 3 2 1/4 **Blue Mood (IRE)**15 4653 2-9-0 0 [1] AhmedAjtebi 5 77
(Charlie Appleby) *edgy stalls: chsd ldng pair: rdn and nt qckn 2f out: styd on inner in st: kpt on but nvr able to chal* 11/4[2]

4 14 **Dynamo Walt (IRE)** 2-9-0 0 MartinDwyer 1 26
(Derek Shaw) *s.v.s: outpcd and a wl bhd* 33/1

59.23s (0.43) **Going Correction** +0.10s/f (Slow) 4 Ran SP% 108.2
Speed ratings (Par 94): **100,99,95,73**
CSF £4.12 TOTE £1.40; EX 4.00 Trifecta £2.90 Pool: £1942.82 - 491.08 winning units..
Owner D Redvers & Michael H Watt **Bred** Mrs Sue Lenehan **Trained** Chiddingfold, Surrey
■ Stewards' Enquiry : Jamie Spencer one-day ban: careless riding (Aug 24)

FOCUS
An interesting little novice event. Straightforward form, rated around the front two.

5229 LADBROKES FILLIES' (S) STKS 6f (P)

2:50 (2:52) (Class 6) 2-Y-0 £2,045 (£603; £302) Stalls Low

Form RPR

653 1 **Chanceuse**10 4862 2-8-5 0 DanielMuscutt(7) 3 50+
(Gay Kelleway) *pressed ldr: led over 2f out: shkn up and kpt on one pce fr over 1f out* 14/1

4004 **2** 2 3/4 **Countess Lupus (IRE)**[7] 4952 2-8-9 49..................(v[1]) MarkCoumbe(3) 5 42
(Lisa Williamson) *rousted early then snatched up whn keen after 1f: rousted again and prog on outer to ld 1/2-way: awkward and hdd over 2f out: fnd nil in pursuit of wnr after* **20/1**

3 **3** *nk* **Hannah Louise (IRE)**[16] 4630 2-8-7 0......................(t) NathanAlison(5) 2 41
(Olivia Maylam) *taken down early: chsd ldrs: outpcd and rdn 1/2-way: kpt on over 1f out to take 3rd ins fnl f: pressed runner-up nr fin* **5/1**[3]

0 **4** 2 1/4 **Flair For Fashion (IRE)**[37] 3942 2-8-12 0.......................... SeanLevey 6 34
(Ed McMahon) *chsd ldrs: rdn and nt qckn wl over 2f out: no imp after: lost 3rd ins fnl f* **5/6**[1]

5 *10* **Brean Splash Susie** 2-8-7 0.. JakePayne(5) 4 4
(Bill Turner) *taken down early: a in rr: outpcd and rdn bef 1/2-way: sn bhd* **10/1**

6 *13* **Lucarvey** 2-8-12 0.. SaleemGolam 7
(Chris Dwyer) *fractious bef gng in stalls: hung rt and struggling bnd after 2f: sn bhd: t.o* **33/1**

5331 **7** *15* **Music Stop**[10] 4862 2-9-3 58..(bt) AdamKirby 1
(Phil McEntee) *led to 1/2-way: wknd rapidly: virtually p.u fnl f* **4/1**[2]

1m 15.04s (3.14) **Going Correction** +0.10s/f (Slow) **7** Ran SP% **114.7**
Speed ratings (Par 89): **83,79,78,75,62 45,25**
toteswingers 1&2 £14.00, 2&3 £12.40, 1&3 £2.80 CSF £232.83 TOTE £10.60: £4.10, £13.10; EX 84.80 Trifecta £721.50 Pool: £4860.23 - 5.05 winning units..There was no bid for the winner.
Owner Ben Parish & Gay Kelleway **Bred** Gracelands Stud **Trained** Exning, Suffolk

FOCUS
This looked a really weak seller beforehand and, with the front two in the market running below expectations, the form is desperate.

5230 LADBROKES H'CAP — 6f (P)
3:20 (3:20) (Class 6) (0-60,62) 3-Y-O+ **£2,045** (£603; £302) **Stalls** Low

Form RPR

-112 **1** **Victorian Number (FR)**[52] 3433 5-9-10 60...................... GeorgeBaker 9 67+
(Geoffrey Deacon) *pressed ldng pair on outer: pushed along 1/2-way: drvn over 1f out: clsd to ld last 150yds: hld on* **6/4**[1]

0054 **2** 1/2 **Hinton Admiral**[11] 4836 9-8-11 50.............................. DarrenEgan(3) 3 54
(Pat Eddery) *hld up in 6th: plenty to do whn prog jst over 2f out: hrd rdn and r.o to take 2nd last 75yds: nt rch wnr* **7/1**

6000 **3** 1 1/4 **Sarah Berry**[13] 4752 4-9-5 55......................................(v[1]) SaleemGolam 8 55
(Chris Dwyer) *pressed ldr: drvn upsides 2f out: stl upsides but nt qckn 1f out: one pce after* **20/1**

0406 **4** *nk* **Beach Rhythm (USA)**[16] 4635 6-8-5 46 oh1...........(b[1]) DeclanBates(5) 4 45
(Jim Allen) *led: rdn and jnd 2f out: styd on inner in st: hdd and no ex last 150yds* **16/1**

3503 **5** *nk* **Chester Deelyte (IRE)**[11] 4840 5-8-7 46.................(v) MarkCoumbe(3) 7 44
(Lisa Williamson) *t.k.h: chsd ldrs: rdn in 4th over 2f out: no imp over 1f out: one pce* **14/1**

0040 **6** 1 1/2 **Copper Leyf**[11] 4836 3-8-6 46..................................(t) FrankieMcDonald 6 39
(Jeremy Gask) *t.k.h: hld up in last pair: lot to do whn rdn and sme prog over 1f out: no real hdwy fnl f* **33/1**

6641 **7** *hd* **Reginald Claude**[11] 4836 5-9-5 62 6ex...................... DanielMuscutt(7) 1 55
(Mark Usher) *hld up in rr: shuffled along on inner fr 2f out: kpt on but nvr involved* **11/4**[2]

0064 **8** *9* **South Kenter (USA)**[37] 3955 4-8-5 46...........................(p) RyanTate(5) 5 10
(Heather Main) *chsd ldrs to 1/2-way: wknd u.p: t.o* **6/1**[3]

600 **9** *4* **Purford Green**[112] 1660 4-8-3 46 oh1..........................(p) PaigeBolton(7) 2
(Michael Attwater) *s.i.s: hld up in last pair: wknd over 2f out: t.o* **50/1**

1m 12.87s (0.97) **Going Correction** +0.10s/f (Slow)
WFA 3 from 4yo+ 4lb **9** Ran SP% **115.7**
Speed ratings (Par 101): **97,96,94,94,93 91,91,79,74**
toteswingers 1&2 £3.00, 2&3 £15.10, 1&3 CSF £12.60 CT £150.54 TOTE £2.40: £1.30, £2.70, £5.80; EX 11.40 Trifecta £142.50 Pool: £4209.11 - 22.14 winning units..
Owner Andy Pittman **Bred** Charles Barel **Trained** Compton, Berks
■ Stewards' Enquiry : Saleem Golam two-day ban: careless riding (Aug 24-25)

FOCUS
A moderate handicap.

5231 DOWNLOAD THE LADBROKES APP H'CAP — 2m (P)
3:50 (3:52) (Class 5) (0-75,74) 4-Y-O+ **£3,408** (£1,006; £503) **Stalls** Low

Form RPR

1031 **1** **Meetings Man (IRE)**[30] 4179 6-9-4 71..............................(p) AdamKirby 8 82
(Ali Brewer) *hld up in midfield: trckd ldrs after 7f: prog to ld over 2f out: sn rdn clr: drew rt away fnl f* **6/1**[3]

0350 **2** *8* **Beat Route**[37] 3959 6-9-7 74.. RobertHavlin 10 75
(Michael Attwater) *hld up in rr: prog over 4f out: last of six w a ch over 3f out: styd on over 2f out: tk 2nd nr fin: no ch w wnr* **7/1**

136- **3** *1* **Alfraamsey**[306] 4606 5-9-0 72.. HarryPoulton(5) 4 72
(Sheena West) *pressed ldr: led 4f out: drvn and hdd over 2f out: no ch w wnr: lost 2nd nr fin* **20/1**

020 **4** *2* **Priors Gold**[35] 4029 6-9-5 72.. JackMitchell 7 70
(Laura Mongan) *trckd ldrs: wnt 3rd over 2f out to wl over 1f out: fdd* **12/1**

5642 **5** *7* **Tingo In The Tale (IRE)**[29] 4208 4-9-2 72... WilliamTwiston-Davies(3) 6 61
(David Arbuthnot) *trckd ldrs: cl up 3f out: wknd over 2f out* **6/1**[3]

6621 **6** 3 3/4 **Comedy House**[13] 4754 5-8-7 65................................ PhilipPrince(5) 11 50
(Michael Madgwick) *drvn in rr 7f out: plld out wd 5f out: lost tch w ldrs over 3f out: no ch after* **12/1**

1032 **7** 3 1/4 **Honourable Knight (IRE)**[13] 4754 5-9-2 69.................... WilliamBuick 9 50
(Mark Usher) *trckd ldrs early: lost pl and nt gng wl in rr 1/2-way: lost tch 4f out: no ch after* **5/1**[2]

03-4 **8** 1 1/4 **Ascalon**[30] 4166 9-8-12 68.. DarrenEgan(3) 3 48
(Pat Eddery) *led to 4f out: wknd 3f out* **4/1**[1]

1122 **9** *6* **Our Folly**[20] 4530 5-9-7 74...(t) MartinDwyer 2 46
(Stuart Kittow) *mostly in last and nvr appeared to be gng wl: lost tch over 4f out: no ch after* **6/1**[3]

/0-3 **10** 3 1/4 **Ibn Hiyyan (USA)**[15] 4692 6-8-2 55.......................... FrankieMcDonald 12 23
(Conor Dore) *trckd ldrs: reminder 1/2-way: drvn and wknd over 4f out* **40/1**

1515 **11** *36* **Irene Kennet**[52] 3437 6-9-1 68.. JimmyQuinn 5
(Paul Burgoyne) *a in rr: wknd 4f out: wl t.o* **10/1**

3m 23.32s (-2.38) **Going Correction** +0.10s/f (Slow) **11** Ran SP% **123.7**
Speed ratings (Par 103): **109,105,104,103,100 98,96,95,92,91 73**
toteswingers 1&2 £2.10, 2&3 £4.20, 1&3 £3.90 CSF £50.39 CT £811.90 TOTE £10.00: £2.90, £2.70, £4.50; EX 72.40 Trifecta £1530.40 Pool: £4066.63 - 1.99 winning units..
Owner Mrs Bettine Evans **Bred** Hakan Keles **Trained** Eastbury, Berks
■ Squad was withdrawn on vet's advice (14-1, deduct 15p in the £ under R4)

FOCUS
This looked a fair race for the grade beforehand.

5232 LADBROKES FOLLOW US ON TWITTER H'CAP — 7f (P)
4:20 (4:23) (Class 6) (0-60,60) 3-Y-O+ **£2,045** (£603; £302) **Stalls** Low

Form RPR

3156 **1** **The Great Gabrial**[20] 4520 4-9-7 60..............................(b) JimCrowley 11 75
(Ian Williams) *pressed ldng pair: wnt 2nd 3f out: led 2f out: drvn clr 1f out: in n.d after* **7/2**[1]

5150 **2** 3 1/4 **Black Truffle (FR)**[9] 4885 3-9-0 59..............................(e[1]) WilliamBuick 5 63
(Mark Usher) *slowly away: hld up in 11th: great deal to do 2f out: rapid prog on outer jst over 1f out: r.o to take 2nd last 100yds: no ch to threaten wnr* **5/1**[2]

5065 **3** *2* **Nordikhab (IRE)**[16] 4625 3-9-1 60.............................. JimmyQuinn 9 59
(Kevin Ryan) *chsd ldrs: rdn 3f out: wnt 3rd wl over 1f out but nt on terms: one pce after* **8/1**[3]

1-54 **4** 3/4 **Patavium Prince (IRE)**[135] 1194 10-9-7 60...................... AdamKirby 12 59
(Jo Crowley) *hld up in rr: trying to make prog but n.d whn nt clr run 1f out: kpt on fnl f* **8/1**[3]

06-5 **5** *nse* **Saint Boniface**[55] 3326 4-8-13 52......................................(e) SeanLevey 2 51
(Peter Makin) *trckd ldrs: gng wl enough over 2f out though outpcd: rdn and nt qckn over 1f out: one pce after* **10/1**

2530 **6** 3/4 **Moss Hill**[11] 4834 4-8-10 52.......................... WilliamTwiston-Davies(3) 10 49
(Charles Hills) *mde most to 2f out: lost 2nd and wknd ins fnl f* **5/1**[2]

600 **7** 1 3/4 **Bertie Blu Boy**[11] 4834 5-8-10 52.............................(b) MarkCoumbe(3) 8 44
(Lisa Williamson) *dwlt: rcvrd to chse ldrs: drvn to go 3rd wl over 2f out to wl over 1f out: wknd* **16/1**

4025 **8** 1 1/4 **Amis Reunis**[15] 4691 4-9-6 59......................................(p) WilliamCarson 4 48
(Anthony Carson) *wl in tch: rdn over 2f out: sn outpcd: no hdwy fnl f* **14/1**

0045 **9** *hd* **Kielty's Folly**[11] 4834 9-9-2 55.. KierenFox 7 44
(Brian Baugh) *hld up in rr: rdn 2f out: no prog over 1f out* **33/1**

0164 **10** *5* **Cuthbert (IRE)**[55] 3329 6-8-4 50..............................(b) PaigeBolton(7) 3 26
(Michael Attwater) *a in rr: pushed along and struggling over 2f out* **20/1**

0154 **11** 1 3/4 **Chandrayaan**[98] 1981 6-8-13 52..............................(v) RichardThomas 1 23
(John E Long) *mostly in last and wl off the pce: nvr a factor* **25/1**

6650 **12** 1 3/4 **King Vahe (IRE)**[91] 2234 4-9-7 60..............................(t) GeorgeBaker 6 27
(Olivia Maylam) *taken steadily to post: w ldr to jst over 3f out: wknd rapidly and eased* **10/1**

1m 24.64s (-0.16) **Going Correction** +0.10s/f (Slow)
WFA 3 from 4yo+ 6lb **12** Ran SP% **120.1**
Speed ratings (Par 101): **104,100,98,97,97 96,94,92,92,86 84,82**
toteswingers 1&2 £4.30, 2&3 £12.80, 1&3 £8.20 CSF £19.99 CT £135.49 TOTE £4.60: £1.90, £2.50, £3.50; EX 26.60 Trifecta £191.90 Pool: £3771.88 - 14.74 winning units..
Owner Dr Marwan Koukash **Bred** Juddmonte Farms Ltd **Trained** Portway, Worcs

FOCUS
Quite a strong race for the grade. The surface may be important for the winner.

5233 LADBROKES MAIDEN STKS — 1m 5f (P)
4:50 (4:50) (Class 5) 3-Y-O+ **£2,726** (£805; £402) **Stalls** Low

Form RPR

56 **1** **Phiz (GER)**[37] 3957 3-8-10 0.. WilliamBuick 2 75+
(John Gosden) *trckd ldr 2f: styd cl up: drvn and 3 l bhd ldng pair wl over 1f out: r.o fnl f to ld last strides* **3/1**[3]

322 **2** 1/2 **Story Writer**[30] 4166 4-9-13 71.. AdamKirby 3 79
(William Knight) *prom: trckd ldr 7f out: drvn to ld narrowly wl over 1f out: kpt on u.p: hdd last strides* **11/4**[2]

3 **3** 1 1/4 **Al Arish (IRE)**[18] 4590 3-9-1 0.. GeorgeBaker 7 77
(Lady Cecil) *led at mod pce: gng bttr than most 3f out: drvn and hdd narrowly wl over 1f out: nt qckn after* **3/1**[3]

32 **4** *2* **Astorgs Galaxy**[47] 3606 3-8-10 0.. JimCrowley 1 69
(Sir Michael Stoute) *trckd ldrs: cl up 3f out: rdn and nt qckn over 2f out: one pce after* **5/2**[1]

00- **5** *15* **Prairie Prince (IRE)**[280] 7517 3-8-8 0.......................... DanielMuscutt(7) 8 52
(Gay Kelleway) *hld up in rr: prog to chse ldrs and wl in tch fr 4f out tl wknd qckly over 2f out* **33/1**

0060 **6** *10* **Parsons Green**[16] 4632 4-9-8 40.. JimmyQuinn 4 32
(Michael Attwater) *in tch tl lft bhd by ldng quintet fr 4f out* **100/1**

0 **7** *12* **Storm Quest**[16] 4632 6-9-5 0.......................... WilliamTwiston-Davies(3) 9 14
(Robin Dickin) *s.s: in tch in rr to over 4f out: sn wknd: t.o* **100/1**

0-0 **8** *23* **Sings Poet**[198] 333 3-9-1 0.. WilliamCarson 5
(Peter Hiatt) *squeezed out s: in tch in rr to over 4f out: wknd qckly: t.o* **100/1**

0 **9** *92* **Just Gets Better (IRE)**[18] 4590 4-9-13 0.......................... AidanColeman 6
(Sean Curran) *wore net muzzle: trckd ldr after 2f to 7f out: wknd rapidly over 4f out: wl t.o* **66/1**

2m 47.19s (1.19) **Going Correction** +0.10s/f (Slow)
WFA 3 from 4yo+ 12lb **9** Ran SP% **112.6**
Speed ratings (Par 103): **100,99,98,97,88 82,74,60,4**
toteswingers 1&2 £2.40, 2&3 £2.70, 1&3 £3.00 CSF £11.26 TOTE £3.30: £1.02, £1.50, £4.00; EX 13.00 Trifecta £47.60 Pool: £3899.34 - 61.33 winning units..
Owner R J H Geffen **Bred** Gestut Etzean **Trained** Newmarket, Suffolk

FOCUS
Just an ordinary maiden. The form makes sense with the runner-up a good guide.

5234 BET ON YOUR MOBILE WITH LADBROKES H'CAP — 1m 2f (P)
5:20 (5:23) (Class 6) (0-65,65) 3-Y-O+ **£2,045** (£603; £302) **Stalls** Low

Form RPR

-400 **1** **Posh Boy (IRE)**[13] 4755 3-9-2 62.. GeorgeBaker 2 67
(Chris Wall) *trckd ldr 2f: styd cl up: wnt 2nd again jst over 2f out: rdn to ld wl over 1f out: edgd rt but hld on wl* **5/1**[2]

4061 **2** 3/4 **Exclusion (USA)**[31] 4144 3-9-1 61 ow1..............................(b) AdamKirby 4 65
(Noel Quinlan) *hld up in rr: prog on outer jst over 2f out: drvn and r.o to take 2nd nr fin: clsd on wnr but hld* **10/1**

0644 **3** 1/2 **Catchanova (IRE)**[44] 3687 6-9-6 57.. JohnFahy 6 60
(Eve Johnson Houghton) *hld up and sn towards rr: stdy prog on inner fr over 3f out gng easily: rdn and nt qckn over 1f out: kpt on same pce fnl f* **12/1**

-006 **4** *1* **Claude Monet (BRZ)**[22] 4441 4-9-13 65.............................. SeanLevey 9 65
(Simon Dow) *trckd ldr after 2f: gng strly whn led 4f out: rdn and hdd wl over 1f out: nt qckn* **25/1**

3005 **5** 1/2 **Scamperdale**[48] 3580 11-9-12 63.. KierenFox 12 63
(Brian Baugh) *dwlt: hld up in last: prog on outer fr 3f out: clsd on wnr and looked a threat jst over 1f out: effrt petered out fnl f* **14/1**

-434 **6** 1 1/4 **Lisa's Legacy**[21] 4503 3-9-5 65.. WilliamBuick 7 63
(Daniel Kubler) *prom early: lost pl after 4f: wl in rr over 2f out: rdn on outer over 1f out: styd on fnl f* **9/2**[1]

3-06 **7** *2* **Geeaitch**[18] 4591 4-10-0 **65** .... WilliamCarson 10 59
(Anthony Carson) *stdd s: hld up in last: stl in last whn snatched up over 2f out: rdn and passed wkng rivals fr over 1f out: no ch* **6/1**[3]

3/5- **8** *hd* **Red Willow**[344] 5771 7-9-5 **56** .... RichardThomas 14 50
(John E Long) *mde most to 4f out: stl cl up 2f out: wknd over 1f out* **50/1**

443- **9** *5* **Two Sugars**[310] 6774 5-9-5 **56** .... PatCosgrave 11 40
(Laura Mongan) *trckd ldrs: drvn over 4f out: sn lost pl and btn* **20/1**

2000 **10** *1 3/4* **El Massivo (IRE)**[13] 4753 3-9-5 **65** .... SteveDrowne 8 46
(William Jarvis) *hld up in midfield: in tch 3f out: shkn up and wknd over 2f out* **5/1**[2]

55-0 **11** *1 1/2* **Yajber (USA)**[71] 2807 4-9-8 **64** .... HarryPoulton(5) 3 42
(Jamie Poulton) *hld up in rr: lost tch w ldrs over 3f out: sn bhd* **33/1**

0002 **12** *2 1/4* **Blue Deer (IRE)**[8] 4904 5-8-13 **53** ....(p) AshleyMorgan(3) 1 27
(Lee Carter) *dwlt: a in rr: lost tch w ldrs over 3f out: sn bhd* **20/1**

5-60 **13** *3/4* **Common Courtesy**[31] 4152 3-9-1 **61** .... JimmyQuinn 5 33
(John Butler) *chsd ldrs: wknd rapidly 3f out: sn bhd* **50/1**

2m 7.72s (1.12) **Going Correction** +0.10s/f (Slow)
WFA 3 from 4yo+ 9lb **13** Ran SP% **109.5**
Speed ratings (Par 101): **99,98,98,97,96 95,94,94,90,88 87,85,85**
toteswingers 1&2 £7.20, 2&3 £26.60, 1&3 £13.80 CSF £38.29 CT £359.15 TOTE £6.70: £2.50, £3.50, £3.50; EX 59.40 Trifecta £578.30 Pool: £2727.41 - 3.53 winning units..
Owner Des Thurlby **Bred** Deerfield Farm **Trained** Newmarket, Suffolk
■ Motion Lass was withdrawn on vet's advice (9-2, deduct 15p in the £ under R4).
FOCUS
They didn't go much of a pace, resulting in something of a bunch finish, and four of the first five traded at 2.1 or shorter in running on Betfair. Very ordinary form.
T/Plt: £500.40 to a £1 stake. Pool of £64490.98 - 94.07 winning tickets. T/Qpdt: £27.30 to a £1 stake. Pool of £7444.75 - 201.62 winning tickets. JN

4951 MUSSELBURGH (R-H)
Friday, August 9

OFFICIAL GOING: Good (good to firm in places;7.9)
Wind: Light against Weather: Cloudy with sunny periods

5235 WATERMANS PERSONAL INJURY SOLICITORS NURSERY H'CAP 7f 30y
2:00 (2:00) (Class 3) (0-95,78) 2-Y-O **£7,762** (£2,310; £1,154; £577) **Stalls** Low

Form RPR

1033 **1** **Sandsman's Girl (IRE)**[7] 4965 2-9-3 **74** .... GrahamLee 3 77+
(James Given) *t.k.h early: hld up: hdwy to trck ldrs wl over 2f out: effrt and n.m.r wl over 1f out: swtchd lft and hdwy to chal over 1f out: rdn and qcknd to ld ins fnl f* **9/2**[3]

3233 **2** *2* **Split Rock**[35] 4006 2-9-7 **78** .... JoeFanning 4 76
(Mark Johnston) *led: pushed along over 2f out: rdn over 1f out: drvn and hdd ins fnl f: kpt on same pce* **15/8**[1]

140 **3** *3/4* **Angel Rosa**[2] 5136 2-8-9 **66** .... PJMcDonald 2 62
(Keith Dalgleish) *trckd ldng pair on inner: effrt and cl up 3f out: sn rdn along and sltly outpcd 2f out: kpt on u.p fnl f* **7/1**

6410 **4** *nk* **Atheera (IRE)**[28] 4246 2-8-13 **70** .... PaulMulrennan 5 65
(Mark Johnston) *trckd ldr: effrt 3f out and sn cl up: rdn along over 2f out: drvn and edgd lft over 1f out: sn one pce* **7/1**

0033 **5** *3/4* **Imshivalla (IRE)**[14] 4726 2-8-9 **66** .... TonyHamilton 1 59
(Richard Fahey) *dwlt and in rr: hdwy over 2f out: sn rdn: kpt on fnl f: nrst fin* **11/4**[2]

15 **6** *1* **Cascadia (IRE)**[31] 4134 2-8-2 **62** .... RaulDaSilva(3) 6 53
(Mrs K Burke) *trckd ldrs on outer: hdwy over 3f out: rdn and ch over 2f out: drvn over 1f out and grad wknd* **16/1**

1m 31.7s (2.70) **Going Correction** +0.025s/f (Good) **6** Ran SP% **110.5**
Speed ratings (Par 98): **85,82,81,81,80 79**
toteswingers 1&2 £1.40, 2&3 £2.50, 1&3 £4.10 CSF £12.97 TOTE £2.60: £1.10, £2.10; EX 13.10 Trifecta £73.60 Pool: £2839.81 - 28.91 winning units..
Owner Peter Swann **Bred** Pat Todd **Trained** Willoughton, Lincs
FOCUS
Bottom bend moved out 2m. A modest nursery run at a steady gallop until the pace quickened once in the straight. The second and third help with the level.

5236 BRITISH STALLION STUDS EBF CONDITIONS STKS 5f
2:30 (2:31) (Class 3) 2-Y-O **£8,086** (£2,406; £1,202; £601) **Stalls** High

Form RPR

0411 **1** **Viva Verglas (IRE)**[28] 4261 2-9-2 91 .... GrahamGibbons 3 92+
(David Barron) *wnt rt s: trckd ldr: smooth hdwy and cl up 2f out: shkn up jst over 1f out: rdn to ld ins fnl f: sn edgd lft and kpt on strly* **7/4**[2]

021 **2** *2 3/4* **Back Lane**[12] 4808 2-9-2 0 .... TonyHamilton 4 82
(Richard Fahey) *led: pushed along 2f out: sn jnd and rdn over 1f out: drvn ent fnl f: sn hdd and kpt on same pce* **3/1**[3]

6 **3** *9* **Rebel Code (USA)**[6] 5000 2-8-13 0 .... GrahamLee 5 47
(James Given) *chsd ldng pair: rdn along 1/2-way: sn outpcd* **16/1**

11 **4** *4 1/2* **Mick's Yer Man**[132] 1247 2-9-0 0 ....(p) RyanWhile(7) 2 39
(Bill Turner) *dwlt: sn rdn along in rr: a outpcd* **6/4**[1]

1m 2.15s (1.75) **Going Correction** +0.30s/f (Good) **4** Ran SP% **107.2**
Speed ratings (Par 98): **98,93,79,72**
CSF £7.03 TOTE £1.90; EX 5.60 Trifecta £26.70 Pool: £3522.58 - 98.71 winning units..
Owner Raymond Miquel **Bred** Mrs Mary Coonan **Trained** Maunby, N Yorks
FOCUS
An interesting conditions event for 2yos which was weakened by the disappointing run of the favourite. The winner face a routine task otherwise.

5237 ARCHERFIELD CUP (H'CAP) 1m 6f
3:00 (3:00) (Class 2) (0-100,97) 3-Y-O+ **£16,172** (£4,812; £2,405; £1,202) **Stalls** Centre

Form RPR

0533 **1** **Party Line**[3] 5086 4-9-1 **84** ....(v[1]) JoeFanning 4 93
(Mark Johnston) *trckd ldng pair: hdwy to chse ldr 3f out: led over 2f out: rdn clr appr fnl f: kpt on* **9/2**[2]

632- **2** *2 1/2* **Tropical Beat**[335] 6031 5-10-0 **97** .... DanielTudhope 5 103
(David O'Meara) *hld up towards rr: hdwy over 2f out: rdn over 1f out: styd on to chse wnr ins fnl f: no imp towards fin* **5/1**[3]

1-20 **3** *2 1/4* **Noble Alan (GER)**[41] 3824 10-9-6 **89** .... PaulMulrennan 8 92
(Nicky Richards) *sn trcking ldr: cl up 4f out: led over 3f out: jnd and rdn over 2f out: sn hdd: drvn and kpt on same pce appr fnl f* **9/2**[2]

-130 **4** *4 1/2* **Jonny Delta**[27] 4313 6-8-11 **80** .... PhillipMakin 2 77
(Jim Goldie) *hld up towards rr: hdwy wl over 2f out: rdn wl over 1f out: kpt on fnl f: n.d* **8/1**

6211 **5** *1 1/2* **Hawdyerwheesht**[22] 4447 5-8-10 **79** .... GrahamLee 3 73
(Jim Goldie) *chsd ldrs: rdn along 3f out: sn wknd* **12/1**

0-11 **6** *4* **O Ma Lad (IRE)**[96] 2040 5-9-8 **91** ....(p) MichaelO'Connell 7 80
(John Quinn) *in tch: effrt and sme hdwy 3f out: rdn along over 2f out: sn btn* **7/1**

334 **7** *1 1/2* **Between Us**[20] 4532 4-9-2 **85** .... TonyHamilton 1 72
(Sir Mark Prescott Bt) *led: rdn along and hdd over 3f out: sn wknd* **7/2**[1]

-053 **8** *1/2* **Incendo**[38] 2590 7-8-13 **83** ....(t) GeorgeChaloner(5) 6 69
(Ian Williams) *a towards rr* **25/1**

3m 2.46s (-2.84) **Going Correction** +0.025s/f (Good) **8** Ran SP% **110.4**
Speed ratings (Par 109): **109,107,106,103,102 100,99,99**
toteswingers 1&2 £3.40, 2&3 £4.30, 1&3 £4.20 CSF £25.22 CT £99.35 TOTE £5.50: £1.60, £1.30, £1.80; EX 27.40 Trifecta £87.50 Pool: £5326.94 - 45.63 winning units..
Owner S R Counsell **Bred** Highclere Stud And Balmerino Bloodstock **Trained** Middleham Moor, N Yorks
FOCUS
Not the stongest Class 2 handicap, but it was competitive. Straightforward form, the third giving perspective.

5238 NAIRNS OATCAKES H'CAP 7f 30y
3:30 (3:30) (Class 3) (0-95,92) 3-Y-O+ **£7,762** (£2,310; £1,154; £577) **Stalls** Low

Form RPR

0412 **1** **Alejandro (IRE)**[9] 4879 4-9-0 **85** .... GeorgeChaloner(5) 6 96
(Richard Fahey) *trckd ldr: smooth hdwy to ld 2 1/2f out: rdn over 1f out: kpt on* **11/4**[2]

6231 **2** *1 1/2* **Frog Hollow**[14] 4733 4-9-9 **89** .... DanielTudhope 9 96+
(David O'Meara) *hld up towards rr: hdwy 3f out: swtchd lft and rdn wl over 1f out: styd on fnl f* **13/8**[1]

5112 **3** *nk* **Silver Rime (FR)**[12] 4807 8-8-7 **73** oh1 .... PJMcDonald 1 79
(Linda Perratt) *trckd ldrs: hdwy wl over 2f out: rdn to chse wnr over 1f out: sn drvn and kpt on same pce* **12/1**

1000 **4** *2* **Powerful Presence (IRE)**[28] 4235 7-9-9 **89** .... DavidNolan 7 90
(David O'Meara) *led: rdn along 3f out: hdd 2 1/2f out: drvn and one pce fr wl over 1f out* **22/1**

3003 **5** *3/4* **Laffan (IRE)**[13] 4758 4-9-6 **86** .... DuranFentiman 2 85
(Tim Easterby) *t.k.h: hld up in tch: effrt over 2f out: n.m.r wl over 1f out and again appr fnl f: sn rdn and kpt on towards fin* **9/1**[3]

4451 **6** *shd* **Wannabe King**[48] 3590 7-9-5 **92** ....(v) JordanNason(7) 8 90
(Geoffrey Harker) *hld up: hdwy 1/2-way: rdn to chse ldrs over 2f out: sn drvn and one pce* **14/1**

0130 **7** *1 1/2* **Rasaman (IRE)**[13] 4780 9-9-1 **81** .... GrahamLee 3 75
(Jim Goldie) *hld up: a towards rr* **10/1**

-001 **8** *1/2* **King Torus (IRE)**[20] 4521 5-9-5 **85** ....(b) DaleSwift 5 78+
(Ruth Carr) *a in rr* **25/1**

4002 **9** *4 1/2* **Kung Hei Fat Choy (USA)**[37] 3945 4-8-9 **75** ....(b) JamesSullivan 4 56
(James Given) *chsd ldrs: rdn along 3f out: drvn and wknd over 2f out* **18/1**

1m 28.54s (-0.46) **Going Correction** +0.025s/f (Good) **9** Ran SP% **111.7**
Speed ratings (Par 107): **103,101,100,98,97 97,95,95,90**
toteswingers 1&2 £2.10, 2&3 £4.20, 1&3 £3.90 CSF £7.18 CT £40.79 TOTE £2.80: £1.10, £1.40, £2.40; EX 9.00 Trifecta £52.40 Pool: £6005.23 - 85.88 winning units..
Owner F L F S Ltd **Bred** Yeomanstown Stud **Trained** Musley Bank, N Yorks
FOCUS
The pace was sensible in this competitive handicap and the form should work out. The winner is rated at least to his previous level.

5239 ARTHRITIS RESEARCH UK H'CAP 1m
4:00 (4:01) (Class 5) (0-70,68) 4-Y-O+ **£3,234** (£962; £481; £240) **Stalls** Low

Form RPR

-030 **1** **Ralphy Boy (IRE)**[22] 4446 4-8-13 **60** .... MichaelO'Connell 8 69
(Alistair Whillans) *led: pushed along and jnd over 3f out: rdn and hdd 2f out: cl up: drvn and rallied to ld again ins fnl f: kpt on gamely* **8/1**

4410 **2** *nk* **Border Bandit (USA)**[19] 4557 5-8-11 **58** .... BarryMcHugh 2 66
(Tracy Waggott) *trckd wnr: cl up over 3f out: slt ld 2f out: shkn up over 1f out and sn rdn: drvn and hdd ins fnl f: no ex* **9/2**[3]

2506 **3** *4* **Bunce (IRE)**[7] 4966 5-9-7 **68** .... DanielTudhope 7 67
(David O'Meara) *trckd ldrs on inner: hdwy 3f out: rdn over 2f out: drvn and kpt on same pce fr over 1f out* **3/1**[2]

0535 **4** *1 3/4* **Berbice (IRE)**[11] 4823 8-7-13 **49** oh4 .... JulieBurke(3) 4 44
(Linda Perratt) *in tch on inner: hdwy to chse ldrs wl over 2f out: rdn wl over 1f out: no imp fnl f* **25/1**

2342 **5** *hd* **Royal Straight**[17] 4609 8-9-6 **67** ....(t) PhillipMakin 5 62
(Linda Perratt) *in tch: hdwy over 2f out: sn rdn and no imp fr over 1f out* **8/1**

2044 **6** *1 1/4* **Flipping**[11] 4824 6-8-7 **54** .... RoystonFfrench 3 46
(Nicky Richards) *in rr: effrt and sme hdwy over 2f out: sn rdn along and n.d* **9/1**

3222 **7** *5* **Push Me (IRE)**[7] 4953 6-9-1 **67** .... GarryWhillans(5) 6 47
(Iain Jardine) *rrd stalls and v s.i.s: bhd tl hdwy 1/2-way: effrt on outer 3f out: rdn along over 2f out: sn wknd* **5/2**[1]

00-3 **8** *13* **Doyouknowwhoiam**[180] 600 4-7-13 **49** oh2 .... RaulDaSilva(3) 9
(John Quinn) *chsd ldng pair: rdn along wl over 2f out: sn wknd* **16/1**

1m 42.02s (0.82) **Going Correction** +0.025s/f (Good) **8** Ran SP% **113.7**
Speed ratings (Par 103): **96,95,91,89,89 88,83,70**
toteswingers 1&2 £6.00, 2&3 £3.30, 1&3 £4.90 CSF £43.24 CT £133.88 TOTE £5.60: £1.10, £2.50, £1.10; EX 47.60 Trifecta £252.40 Pool: £5758.71 - 17.10 winning units..
Owner Frank Lowe **Bred** Frank Lowe **Trained** Newmill-On-Slitrig, Borders
FOCUS
A modest handicap in which the pace was steady and the front two were always in the right position. The bare form is perhaps worth a little more.

5240 DAIKIN CLIMATE CONTROL H'CAP 1m 4f 100y
4:30 (4:30) (Class 6) (0-65,77) 3-Y-O+ **£2,587** (£770; £384; £192) **Stalls** Low

Form RPR

6654 **1** **Vittachi**[17] 4614 6-8-11 **48** .... MichaelO'Connell 2 56
(Alistair Whillans) *in tch: hdwy over 3f out: rdn to chal over 1f out and ev ch: sn drvn: styd on wl fnl f to ld on line* **8/1**

3535 **2** *nse* **Geanie Mac (IRE)**[17] 4614 4-8-9 **46** ....(v) PJMcDonald 5 54
(Linda Perratt) *sn led and swtchd rt to inner rail: hdd after 1 1/2f: prom: shkn up to ld 3f out: rdn wl over 1f out: drvn ins fnl f: hdd on line* **7/1**

1411 **3** *3/4* **Grand Diamond (IRE)**[18] 4578 9-8-13 **57** ....(p) JordanNason(7) 6 64
(Jim Goldie) *hld up towards rr: hdwy to trck ldng pair after 4f: effrt on inner and cl up 3f out: rdn along 2f out: swtchd lft and drvn over 1f out: kpt on fnl f* **7/2**[2]

6411 **4** *1/2* **Pearl Spice (IRE)**[3] 5102 3-10-1 **77** 12ex ....(b) DougieCostello 8 83+
(Tim Pitt) *rdn along after s to chse ldrs and cl up after 2f: disp ld over 7f out: rdn and lost pl over 2f out: drvn and n.m.r over 1f out: swtchd rt ent fnl and kpt on towards fin* **5/2**[1]

/6-1 **5** *1* **Weybridge Light**[11] 4835 8-8-12 **52** 6ex......................(b) RaulDaSilva(3) 4 57
(David Thompson) *in rr: hdwy on wd outside over 2f out: sn rdn and kpt on fnl f: nrst fin* **6/1**[3]

0403 **6** *1 1/4* **Valentine's Gift**[10] 4851 5-8-9 **46**..............................(p) AndrewElliott 3 49
(Neville Bycroft) *cl up whn hmpd and swtchd lft after 1f: sn led: rdn along 4f out: hdd 3f out and sn n.m.r: hmpd and lost pl wl over 2f out: styd on u.p to chse ldrs over 1f out: kpt on same pce fnl f* **12/1**

0-40 **7** *1* **Bollin Billy**[2] 5142 3-8-0 **48** oh3.................................. DuranFentiman 7 49
(Tim Easterby) *prom: pushed along and lost pl bef 1/2-way: towards rr and rdn along over 3f out: plugged on one pce u.p fnl 2f* **20/1**

03-0 **8** *78* **Foolbythepool**[25] 4339 3-9-0 **62**.................................. GrahamLee 1
(Keith Dalgleish) *a in rr: outpcd 4f out: sn wl bhd and eased: t.o* **13/2**

2m 45.24s (3.24) **Going Correction** +0.025s/f (Good)
WFA 3 from 4yo+ 11lb **8** Ran SP% **114.5**
Speed ratings (Par 101): **90,89,89,89,88 87,86,34**
toteswingers 1&2 £9.10, 2&3 £4.80, 1&3 £4.80 CSF £62.25 CT £232.03 TOTE £9.70: £2.50, £2.00, £1.20; EX 68.70 Trifecta £771.70 Pool: £3096.08 - 3.00 winning units..
Owner Sutherland Five **Bred** London Thoroughbred Services Ltd **Trained** Newmill-On-Slitrig, Borders
■ Stewards' Enquiry : P J McDonald one-day ban: careless riding (Aug 24)

FOCUS
A moderate handicap with a tight finish, but straightforward form.

5241 THOMSON TRAVEL SHOP AMATEUR RIDERS' H'CAP (QUALIFIER FOR THE BETFAIR SCOTTISH STAYERS' SERIES) 2m
5:00 (5:00) (Class 5) (0-70,67) 4-Y-0+ **£3,119** (£967; £483; £242) **Stalls** High

Form RPR

0332 **1** **Golden Future**[7] 4951 10-9-11 **53**.................................. MrJHamilton(3) 3 65
(Peter Niven) *set stdy pce: qcknd over 6f out: pushed along over 2f out: rdn clr over 1f out: styd on strly* **11/4**[2]

6411 **2** *6* **Gucci D'Oro (USA)**[7] 4951 4-10-9 **67** 6ex.............. MrAlexFerguson(5) 6 73
(David Simcock) *hld up: hung lft and rn wd bnd 9f out: hdwy to chse ldng pair over 3f out: rdn 2f out: keeping on whn swtchd to inner and hmpd ent fnl f: sn swtchd lft and drvn: no imp* **8/11**[1]

0061 **3** *hd* **La Bacouetteuse (FR)**[17] 4614 8-11-0 **67**......................(b) MikeyEnnis 4 72
(Iain Jardine) *trckd ldng pair: hdwy and cl up 1/2-way: effrt and rdn along 3f out: drvn and hld whn hung rt ent fnl f: sn wknd* **6/1**[3]

053 **4** *32* **Bollin Bob**[21] 4481 4-10-5 **63**.................................. MrWEasterby(5) 1 29
(Tim Easterby) *prom: pushed along 1/2-way: rdn along over 4f out: sn outpcd* **9/1**

3m 39.02s (5.52) **Going Correction** +0.025s/f (Good) **4** Ran SP% **108.9**
Speed ratings (Par 103): **87,84,83,83**
CSF £5.27 TOTE £3.80; EX 6.30 Trifecta £8.70 Pool: £2054.94 - 176.08 winning units..
Owner The Little Ice Club **Bred** Larksborough Stud Limited **Trained** Barton-le-Street, N Yorks

FOCUS
The pace was steady in this four-runner handicap and the winner made all. The form is taken at face value.
T/Plt: £104.90 to a £1 stake.Pool of £62216.43 -432.72 winning tickets. T/Qpdt: £23.70 to a £1 stake. Pool of £5607.40 - 175.05 winning tickets. JR

5003 NEWMARKET (R-H)
Friday, August 9

OFFICIAL GOING: Good (good to firm in places) changing to good to firm after race 2 (6:10)
Wind: Light behind Weather: Cloudy

5242 TURFTV NURSERY H'CAP 7f
5:40 (5:40) (Class 4) (0-85,78) 2-Y-0 **£3,881** (£1,155; £577; £288) **Stalls** High

Form RPR

0621 **1** **Chinese Jade**[15] 4662 2-9-3 **74**.................................. LukeMorris 2 78+
(Sir Mark Prescott Bt) *s.i.s: rcvrd to ld 6f out: shkn up over 2f out: rdn over 1f out: styd on u.p* **11/4**[2]

31 **2** *1 1/4* **Sea The Skies**[16] 4640 2-9-7 **78**.................................. NeilCallan 4 79
(Gerard Butler) *edgd rt s: plld hrd and prom: trckd wnr over 5f out: rdn over 2f out: styd on* **4/6**[1]

3230 **3** *nk* **Royal Connection**[7] 4948 2-8-13 **70**.................................. RichardHughes 5 70
(Richard Hannon) *led 1f: trckd ldrs: rdn over 1f out: styd on* **6/1**[3]

3624 **4** *1* **Senorita Guest (IRE)**[16] 4618 2-8-8 **68**.................................. SimonPearce(3) 1 66
(Mick Channon) *hld up: racd keenly: rdn over 1f out: styd on: nt trble ldrs* **16/1**

1m 26.58s (0.88) **Going Correction** -0.10s/f (Good) **4** Ran SP% **106.8**
Speed ratings (Par 96): **90,88,88,87**
CSF £4.97 TOTE £2.50; EX 4.80 Trifecta £8.40 Pool: £960.97 - 85.31 winning units..
Owner Lady O'Reilly **Bred** Castlemartin Sky & Skymarc Farm **Trained** Newmarket, Suffolk

FOCUS
Far side track used. Stalls far side except 1m2f: centre. Repositioning of bend into home straight added 18m to 1m2f race. Four went to post for the opening nursery, in which the well-touted favourite was turned over.

5243 JULY COURSE (S) STKS 7f
6:10 (6:10) (Class 5) 2-Y-0 **£3,234** (£962; £481; £240) **Stalls** High

Form RPR

5220 **1** **Hatti (IRE)**[10] 4847 2-8-8 65..................................(p) DavidProbert 9 57+
(John Ryan) *hld up: hdwy and nt clr run over 2f out: r.o u.p to ld wl ins fnl f: sn clr* **7/4**[1]

0533 **2** *1 3/4* **Sleepy Joe (IRE)**[5] 5034 2-9-1 60.................................. SimonPearce(3) 4 62
(Mick Channon) *hld up: hdwy over 2f out: rdn whn edgd lft: hdd and unable qck wl ins fnl f* **2/1**[2]

0 **3** *1 1/2* **Secret Ocean (IRE)**[31] 4154 2-8-13 0..........................(b[1]) SamHitchcott 2 53
(J S Moore) *awkward leaving stalls: rcvrd to chse ldr 6f out: led over 4f out: rdn and hdd over 1f out: styd on same pce ins fnl f* **20/1**

04 **4** *hd* **Escarlata Rossa**[7] 4964 2-8-8 0.................................. LukeMorris 6 48
(J S Moore) *chsd ldr 1f: remained han dy: pushed along 4f out: rdn over 1f out: styd on u.p* **12/1**

002 **5** *3* **Mr Childrey (IRE)**[16] 4617 2-8-13 49..........................(b) AndreaAtzeni 8 45
(J S Moore) *led: hdd over 4f out: chsd ldr: rdn and ev ch over 1f out: wknd ins fnl f* **16/1**

6024 **6** *1 1/2* **My Little Friend**[10] 4862 2-8-13 59..........................(p) NeilCallan 3 41
(Mark H Tompkins) *chsd ldrs: rdn over 1f out: wknd ins fnl f* **20/1**

0 **7** *10* **Plough Boy (IRE)**[7] 4958 2-8-13 0.................................. TedDurcan 1 14
(Willie Musson) *sn pushed along in rr: wknd over 1f out* **20/1**

8 *2 3/4* **Four Maries (FR)** 2-8-3 0 ow2.................................. RobJFitzpatrick(7) 5 3
(Mrs K Burke) *in rr: pushed along 1/2-way: rdn and wknd over 2f out* **13/2**[3]

1m 26.09s (0.39) **Going Correction** -0.10s/f (Good) **8** Ran SP% **110.9**
Speed ratings (Par 94): **93,91,89,89,85 83,72,69**
toteswingers 1&2 £1.30, 1&3 £10.50, 2&3 £9.00 CSF £4.96 TOTE £2.10: £1.10, £1.20, £4.90; EX 6.10 Trifecta £51.00 Pool: £2765.00 - 40.61 winning units..The winner was sold to Micky Hammond for 8,500gns.
Owner John Ryan Racing Partnership **Bred** Miss Imelda O'Shaughnessy **Trained** Newmarket, Suffolk

FOCUS
Previous renewals showed that any two-year-old capable of running to a mark in the low 60s would go close in this seller.

5244 NGK SPARK PLUGS MAIDEN STKS 7f
6:45 (6:46) (Class 4) 2-Y-0 **£3,881** (£1,155; £577; £288) **Stalls** High

Form RPR

1 **Almuheet** 2-9-5 0.................................. PaulHanagan 1 86+
(Sir Michael Stoute) *chsd ldrs: led over 1f out: pushed out* **7/2**[1]

2 *1* **Red Galileo** 2-9-5 0.................................. AndreaAtzeni 11 84+
(Ed Dunlop) *hld up: pushed along and nt clr run over 2f out: hdwy: nt clr run and swtchd rt over 1f out: rdn and r.o wl: nt rch wnr* **13/2**

3 *1* **Snow Sky** 2-9-5 0.................................. RyanMoore 6 81+
(Sir Michael Stoute) *chsd ldrs: shkn up over 1f out: r.o* **5/1**[3]

4 *1* **Sebastian Beach (IRE)** 2-9-5 0.................................. RichardHughes 8 78
(Richard Hannon) *led to 1/2-way: rdn over 1f out: styd on same pce ins fnl f* **5/1**[3]

5 *4* **Rasameel (USA)** 2-9-5 0.................................. DaneO'Neill 2 69+
(J W Hills) *hld up: hdwy over 2f out: rdn whn hmpd over 1f out: edgd rt and no ex* **33/1**

6 *1/2* **Juan Alonso (IRE)** 2-9-5 0.................................. PatDobbs 10 66
(Richard Hannon) *prom: pushed along 1/2-way: no ex fnl f* **16/1**

7 *shd* **Nashmi** 2-9-5 0.................................. DavidProbert 4 65
(Fawzi Abdulla Nass, Bahrain) *hld up: rdn and hmpd over 1f out: nt trble ldrs* **33/1**

8 *shd* **Prairie Prize** 2-9-5 0.................................. NeilCallan 3 67+
(David Elsworth) *hld up: hdwy over 2f out: rdn whn hmpd over 1f out: no ex* **12/1**

9 *1 1/4* **Al Khawaneej Star (USA)** 2-9-5 0.................................. HarryBentley 9 66+
(Michael Bell) *s.i.s: hld up: pushed along 3f out: r.o ins fnl f: nvr nrr* **20/1**

10 *shd* **Tolmias (GR)** 2-9-5 0.................................. KierenFallon 5 62+
(Luca Cumani) *chsd ldr tl led 1/2-way: rdn and hdd over 1f out: edgd rt: wknd ins fnl f* **20/1**

11 *3/4* **Ambria's Fury (IRE)** 2-9-5 0.................................. SamHitchcott 12 60
(Mick Channon) *s.i.s: sn pushed along and a in rr* **50/1**

12 *11* **State Law (IRE)** 2-9-5 0.................................. AhmedAjtebi 7 30
(Charlie Appleby) *hld up: pushed along whn hmpd 2f out: sn wknd* **4/1**[2]

1m 25.42s (-0.28) **Going Correction** -0.10s/f (Good) **12** Ran SP% **119.8**
Speed ratings (Par 96): **97,95,94,93,89 88,88,88,86,86 85,73**
toteswingers 1&2 £5.70, 1&3 £2.70, 2&3 £7.70 CSF £25.01 TOTE £4.90: £1.80, £2.20, £1.80; EX 34.00 Trifecta £138.10 Pool: £1742.73 - 9.46 winning units..
Owner Hamdan Al Maktoum **Bred** Shadwell Estate Company Limited **Trained** Newmarket, Suffolk

FOCUS
Twelve unraced juveniles went to post for this maiden, which has been the starting point for some smart types in recent years without producing a top-class performer. The form is rated in line with the race averages.

5245 ADNAMS NEWMARKET NIGHTS H'CAP 1m 2f
7:15 (7:17) (Class 5) (0-75,75) 3-Y-0+ **£3,234** (£962; £481; £240) **Stalls** Centre

Form RPR

3333 **1** **Nimiety**[10] 4850 4-9-9 **70**.................................. KierenFallon 6 83+
(Mark Johnston) *hld up: styd stands' side turning for home: hdwy to chse ldr over 3f out: shkn up to ld over 2f out: edgd rt: r.o: comf* **9/2**[2]

364 **2** *1 1/2* **Nautilus**[109] 1735 3-8-13 **69**..................................(p) RobertHavlin 4 77
(John Gosden) *a.p: racd keenly: trckd ldr in centre turning for home: rdn to ld that gp over 1f out: r.o: no ch w wnr: 1st of 7 in gp* **10/1**

4003 **3** *2 1/2* **Laconicos (IRE)**[21] 4490 11-8-9 **56** oh1..........................(t) LukeMorris 8 59
(William Stone) *racd keenly: trckd ldr tl led 8f out: styd stands' side turning for home and led overall: rdn and hdd over 2f out: no ex ins fnl f: 2nd of 3 in gp* **25/1**

4022 **4** *2 1/4* **Magique (IRE)**[14] 4721 3-9-4 **74**.................................. RyanMoore 3 73+
(Jeremy Noseda) *hld up: racd in centre turning for home: pushed along over 3f out: hdwy over 1f out: nt trble ldrs: 2nd of 7 in gp* **2/1**[1]

655 **5** *3/4* **Near Time**[47] 3606 3-9-5 **75**.................................. DavidProbert 7 72
(Andrew Balding) *hld up: racd in centre turning for home: hdwy over 2f out: sn rdn: styd on same pce fr over 1f out: 3rd of 7 in gp* **9/2**[2]

6243 **6** *1 3/4* **Wilfred Pickles (IRE)**[14] 4718 7-9-13 **74**.................... JamieSpencer 11 68
(Jo Crowley) *hld up: racd in centre turning for home: rdn over 2f out: swtchd rt over 1f out: n.d: 4th of 7 in gp* **12/1**

5000 **7** *nse* **Habeshia**[60] 3166 3-9-4 **74**..................................(v[1]) TedDurcan 2 67
(John Best) *prom: styd stands' side and chsd ldr turning for home: lost 2nd over 3f out: rdn and edgd lft over 1f out: no ex: last of 3 in gp* **33/1**

3000 **8** *9* **Merchant Of Medici**[24] 4376 6-9-1 **62**.................................. PaulHanagan 5 37
(Micky Hammond) *plld hrd and prom: racd in centre turning for home: rdn over 2f out: wknd over 1f out: 5th of 7 in gp* **12/1**

/0-0 **9** *hd* **Park Lane**[4] 5065 7-9-8 **69**.................................. AndreaAtzeni 10 44
(Noel Quinlan) *led 2f: wnt centre and led that gp turning for home: rdn: edgd rt and hdd over 2f out: sn wknd: 6th of 7 in gp* **33/1**

3042 **10** *9* **Whitby Jet (IRE)**[21] 4489 5-9-10 **71**.................................. RichardHughes 9 28
(Ed Vaughan) *s.i.s: hld up: wnt centre turning for home: rdn over 2f out: wknd over 1f out: last of 7 in gp* **6/1**[3]

2m 3.77s (-1.73) **Going Correction** -0.10s/f (Good)
WFA 3 from 4yo+ 9lb **10** Ran SP% **118.2**
Speed ratings (Par 103): **102,100,98,97,96 95,94,87,87,80**
toteswingers 1&2 £10.10, 1&3 £18.70, 2&3 £36.60 CSF £48.40 CT £1007.03 TOTE £6.00: £2.00, £3.40, £6.20; EX 51.60 Trifecta £1121.30 Part won. Pool: £1495.18 - 0.14 winning units..
Owner Miss K Rausing **Bred** Miss K Rausing **Trained** Middleham Moor, N Yorks

FOCUS
They split into two groups for this fair 1m2f handicap, with the three runners who stuck to the near rail filling out first and third positions.

5246 THOROUGHBRED BREEDERS' ASSOCIATION / EBF STALLIONS FILLIES' H'CAP 1m
7:50 (7:50) (Class 3) (0-95,95) 3-Y-O+ **£9,703** (£2,887; £1,443; £721) **Stalls** High

Form RPR
2033 **1** **Forgive**[9] 4878 4-9-9 **90**.................. RichardHughes 1 99
(Richard Hannon) *mde all: rdn and qcknd over 2f out: r.o: eased nr fin* **8/1**
4211 **2** *1* **Magic Of Reality (FR)**[27] 4307 3-9-1 **89**.................. TomQueally 7 96
(Lady Cecil) *chsd wnr: shkn up over 2f out: rdn over 1f out: styd on* **7/4**[2]
-210 **3** *1 1/4* **Great Timing (USA)**[9] 4878 3-9-7 **95**.................. RyanMoore 5 99
(Charlie Appleby) *chsd ldrs: rdn over 2f out: styd on* **6/4**[1]
-512 **4** *1 1/4* **Magic Destiny**[20] 4514 4-9-7 **88**.................. NeilCallan 2 89
(Mrs K Burke) *prom: racd keenly: rdn over 2f out: styd on same pce fnl f* **10/1**
0302 **5** *21* **Princess Of Orange**[27] 4278 4-9-8 **89**.................. JamieSpencer 3 42
(Rae Guest) *s.i.s: hld up: rdn over 2f out: wknd over 1f out* **7/1**[3]

1m 37.32s (-2.68) **Going Correction** -0.10s/f (Good)
WFA 3 from 4yo+ 7lb **5** Ran SP% **109.1**
Speed ratings (Par 104): **109,108,106,105,84**
CSF £22.06 TOTE £6.80: £2.80, £1.70; EX 17.20 Trifecta £27.90 Pool: £1336.14 - 35.87 winning units..
Owner Highclere Thoroughbred Racing-Spearmint **Bred** The Athenians And Cheveley Park Stud Ltd **Trained** East Everleigh, Wilts

FOCUS
A decent field of fillies went to post for this 1m handicap.

5247 RACING UK H'CAP 6f
8:20 (8:20) (Class 3) (0-95,95) 3-Y-O+ **£7,439** (£2,213; £1,106; £553) **Stalls** High

Form RPR
0023 **1** **Elusive Flame**[20] 4534 4-9-6 **89**.................. RyanMoore 1 98
(David Elsworth) *racd stands' side: mde all: rdn over 1f out: r.o u.p* **6/1**[2]
0000 **2** *nk* **Secret Witness**[6] 4986 7-9-12 **95**..................(b) LukeMorris 2 103
(Ronald Harris) *racd stands' side: chsd wnr: rdn over 1f out: edgd lft and ev ch ins fnl f: r.o: 2nd of 4 in gp* **12/1**
0114 **3** *1 1/4* **Dark Castle**[13] 4778 4-9-1 **84**.................. FrankieDettori 10 88
(Micky Hammond) *racd far side: hld up in tch: rdn over 1f out: edgd rt: r.o to ld that gp wl ins fnl f: no ch w stands' side gp: 1st of 9 in gp* **11/2**[1]
0200 **4** *3/4* **Joe Packet**[12] 4800 6-9-9 **92**.................. TomQueally 8 94
(Jonathan Portman) *racd far side: trckd ldrs: rdn and ev ch that side over 1f out: styd on: 2nd of 9 in gp* **9/1**
5000 **5** *nk* **Palace Moon**[13] 4744 8-9-7 **90**..................(t) NeilCallan 9 91
(William Knight) *racd far side: trckd ldr: rdn to ld that gp over 1f out: edgd rt: hdd and unable qck wl ins fnl f: 3rd of 9 in gp* **16/1**
2232 **6** *1/2* **Nardin**[13] 4757 3-8-12 **85**..................(p) PaulHanagan 12 84
(Ed Dunlop) *racd far side: hld up: hdwy over 1f out: sn rdn: r.o: nt trble ldrs: 4th of 9 in gp* **6/1**[2]
4015 **7** *1/2* **School Fees**[4] 5062 4-9-0 **83**.................. JamieSpencer 4 80
(Olly Stevens) *racd stands' side: hld up: hdwy and edgd lft over 1f out: rdn and edgd rt ins fnl f: styd on same pce: 3rd of 4 in gp* **14/1**
4000 **8** *1 1/4* **Fratellino**[6] 5009 6-9-3 **86**..................(tp) MartinDwyer 11 79
(Alan McCabe) *racd far side: led far side: rdn over 2f out: hdd over 1f out: no ex ins fnl f: 5th of 9 in gp* **25/1**
4124 **9** *nk* **Red Explorer (USA)**[18] 4592 3-8-12 **85**.................. TedDurcan 3 78
(Charles Hills) *racd stands' side: chsd ldrs: rdn and hung lft over 2f out: no ex fnl f: last of 4 in gp* **12/1**
4020 **10** *1 1/2* **My Kingdom (IRE)**[9] 4879 7-8-3 **77**..................(t) RyanTate(5) 5 65
(Stuart Williams) *racd far side: hld up in tch: rdn over 2f out: outpcd fr over 1f out: 6th of 9 in gp* **14/1**
2540 **11** *1/2* **Kyleakin Lass**[35] 4024 4-9-10 **93**.................. RichardHughes 6 79
(Jonathan Portman) *racd far side: hld up: effrt over 1f out: no ex ins fnl f: 7th of 9 in gp* **20/1**
0300 **12** *1/2* **Mezzotint (IRE)**[27] 4297 4-9-9 **92**.................. RobertHavlin 7 77
(Marco Botti) *racd far side: s.s: nvr on terms: 8th of 9 in gp* **15/2**[3]
3520 **13** *1 1/2* **King Of Jazz (IRE)**[48] 3590 5-9-4 **87**.................. KierenFallon 13 67
(Peter Bowen) *racd far side: hld up: rdn over 2f out: n.d: in last of 9 in gp* **8/1**

1m 10.59s (-1.91) **Going Correction** -0.10s/f (Good)
WFA 3 from 4yo+ 4lb **13** Ran SP% **120.0**
Speed ratings (Par 107): **108,107,105,104,104 103,103,101,101,99 98,97,95**
toteswingers 1&2 £14.80, 1&3 £2.60, 2&3 £10.10 CSF £76.63 CT £438.25 TOTE £6.10: £1.80, £4.20, £2.40; EX 80.00 Trifecta £1936.50 Part won. Pool: £2582.06 - 0.33 winning units..
Owner J C Smith **Bred** Littleton Stud **Trained** Newmarket, Suffolk

FOCUS
A fiercely competitive sprint handicap to close the card.
T/Jkpt: Not won. T/Plt: £255.70 to a £1 stake. Pool: £80498.75 - 229.77 winning tickets T/Qpdt: £71.10 to a £1 stake. Pool: £7742.40 - 80.50 winning tickets CR

5248 - 5254a (Foreign Racing) - See Raceform Interactive

4795 ASCOT (R-H)
Saturday, August 10

OFFICIAL GOING: Good (good to firm in places; straight 8.0, round 8.0)
Wind: Virtually nil Weather: Sunny spells

5255 LES AMBASSADEURS CASINO SHERGAR CUP MILE (H'CAP) 1m (R)
12:55 (12:58) (Class 2) (0-100,99) 4-Y-O+
£14,754 (£5,166; £2,361; £1,842; £1,623; £1,182) **Stalls** Low

Form RPR
21-0 **1** **Nine Realms**[28] 4308 4-9-8 **93**.................. JamesDoyle 9 103+
(William Haggas) *mde all: rdn and jnd appr fnl f: styd on wl u.p in clsng stages* **9/2**[2]
2-20 **2** *3/4* **Famous Poet (IRE)**[28] 4276 4-9-9 **94**.................. JoaoMoreira 10 102
(Saeed bin Suroor) *chsd ldrs: drvn and styng on strly whn edgd lft u.p ins fnl f: rdr dropped reins and lost momentum in clsng stages: rallied last strides to take 2nd: nt rch wnr* **11/2**[3]
5062 **3** *shd* **Jack's Revenge (IRE)**[11] 4859 5-9-6 **91**..................(bt) GeraldMosse 2 99
(George Baker) *chsd ldrs: wnt 2nd ins fnl 2f: str chal u.p appr fnl f tl no ex in clsng stages: lost 2nd last strides* **10/3**[1]
3003 **4** *3* **Redact (IRE)**[37] 3987 4-9-7 **92**.................. RosieNapravnik 7 93
(Richard Hannon) *sn in tch: hdwy and wd into st ins fnl 3f: kpt on fnl f but nt gng pce of ldng trio* **25/1**
6110 **5** *1 1/4* **Roserrow**[35] 4080 4-9-10 **95**.................. GaryStevens 12 93
(Andrew Balding) *chsd ldr: rdn over 2f out: sn lost 2nd: wknd fnl f* **6/1**
-312 **6** *shd* **Sam Sharp (USA)**[21] 4531 7-9-8 **93**.................. CathyGannon 4 91
(Ian Williams) *s.i.s: in rr: drvn and styd on fr over 1f out: nt rch ldrs* **11/2**[3]
1100 **7** *1 1/4* **Directorship**[35] 4080 7-10-0 **99**.................. IoritzMendizabal 11 94
(Patrick Chamings) *in rr: drvn over 2f out: mod hdwy fnl f* **9/1**
0620 **8** *1* **Sweetnessandlight**[15] 4705 4-9-7 **92**.................. YasunariIwata 3 85
(Jason Ward) *in rr: pushed along over 2f out: mod prog fnl f* **16/1**
1-00 **9** *hd* **Jacob Cats**[45] 3697 4-9-9 **94**.................. LisaAllpress 1 86
(Olly Stevens) *in tch: chsd ldrs and rdn over 2f out: btn appr fnl f* **20/1**
1650 **10** *28* **Boonga Roogeta**[71] 2839 4-9-8 **93**.................. KevinManning 8 21
(Peter Charalambous) *charged stalls: slowly away: bhd: lost tch over 2f out: eased whn no ch* **20/1**

1m 40.69s (-0.01) **Going Correction** +0.125s/f (Good) **10** Ran SP% **115.6**
Speed ratings (Par 109): **105,104,104,101,99 99,98,97,97,69**
toteswingers 1&2 £6.40, 1&3 £3.90, 2&3 £4.90 CSF £28.25 CT £94.26 TOTE £5.20: £2.10, £2.20, £1.80; EX 33.30 Trifecta £200.00 Pool: £1695.12 - 6.35 winning units..
Owner Mr & Mrs D Hearson **Bred** Granham Farm Partnership **Trained** Newmarket, Suffolk

FOCUS
Rail realignment added 8yds to Old (Round Mile) and 12yds to 1m4f & 2m races. As always with this novelty meeting, the form should be treated with a degree of caution. It was dry overnight and the opening time certainly pointed to it being quick ground. A cutaway had been provided on turning into the straight. Little got into this, with the first three home sitting in front four throughout, and jockeyship very much decided the outcome, with James Doyle excelling aboard the winner. The second and third set the standard.

5256 REDCENTRIC SHERGAR CUP STAYERS (H'CAP) 2m
1:30 (1:31) (Class 2) (0-100,99) 4-Y-O+
£14,754 (£5,166; £2,361; £1,842; £1,623; £1,182) **Stalls** Low

Form RPR
5102 **1** **Homeric (IRE)**[15] 4704 4-9-3 **90**.................. KierenFallon 4 96
(Ed Dunlop) *in rr whn slipped bnd after 3f: hdwy to trck ldrs 1/2-way: drvn on outside over 2f out: styd on wl u.p to ld nr fimish* **9/2**[1]
2341 **2** *nk* **Mutual Regard (IRE)**[18] 4606 4-9-6 **93**..................(p) GeraldMosse 6 99
(Sir Mark Prescott Bt) *chsd ldrs: drvn over 2f out: disp 2nd u.p fnl f: ev ch in clsng stages: no ex last strides* **9/2**[1]
2020 **3** *hd* **Oriental Fox (GER)**[11] 4857 5-9-12 **99**.................. IoritzMendizabal 10 105+
(Mark Johnston) *sn chsng ldr: styng on whn hmpd on rails over 1f out: swtchd lft and rallied ins fnl f: kpt on cl home: fin 4th: plcd 3rd* **17/2**
1043 **4** *shd* **Highland Castle**[15] 4704 5-9-6 **93**.................. CathyGannon 7 98
(David Elsworth) *t.k.h: led: rdn over 2f out: hung rt u.p over 1f out: kpt slt ld u.p ins fnl f tl hdd and no ex nr fin: fin 3rd, nk, sh: disqualified and plcd 4th* **7/1**[3]
3013 **5** *hd* **Rawaki (IRE)**[13] 4796 5-9-11 **98**.................. JamesDoyle 5 103
(Andrew Balding) *in tch whn awkward bnd after 3f and dropped towards rr: hdwy fr 3f out: pressed ldrs u.p over 1f out tl nt qckn in clsng stages* **8/1**
5211 **6** *1 3/4* **Broxbourne (IRE)**[10] 4873 4-9-2 **89**.................. LisaAllpress 9 92+
(Mark Johnston) *slipped bnd after 3f and bhd: stl plenty to do on ins fr 2f out: gd hdwy fnl f: fin wl* **5/1**[2]
3435 **7** *1 1/2* **Brockwell**[10] 4873 4-9-5 **92**.................. YasunariIwata 1 93
(Tom Dascombe) *in tch: lost position 5f out: drvn over 2f out: kpt on again fnl f* **7/1**[3]
5500 **8** *3* **Saptapadi (IRE)**[11] 4857 7-9-6 **93**.................. JoaoMoreira 8 91
(Brian Ellison) *in rr: rdn over 2f out and sme hdwy: no prog fr over 1f out* **11/1**
-005 **9** *1/2* **Softsong (FR)**[29] 4233 5-9-3 **90**.................. RosieNapravnik 2 87
(Philip Hobbs) *t.k.h in rr: hdwy on outside to chse ldrs over 3f out: wknd fr 2f out* **20/1**
0500 **10** *1 1/4* **Good Morning Star (IRE)**[10] 4873 4-9-2 **89**.................. AStarke 3 84
(Mark Johnston) *chsd ldrs: rdn 3f out: wknd fr 2f out* **20/1**

3m 30.27s (1.27) **Going Correction** +0.125s/f (Good) **10** Ran SP% **117.5**
Speed ratings (Par 109): **101,100,100,100,100 99,98,97,97,96**
toteswingers 1&2 £2.50, 1&3 £7.30, 2&3 £13.90 CSF £24.73 CT £137.46 TOTE £3.80: £1.70, £1.90, £3.90; EX 19.30 Trifecta £351.60 Pool: £2334.38 - 4.97 winning units..
Owner Highclere Thoroughbred Racing - Jackson **Bred** Lynch Bages Ltd **Trained** Newmarket, Suffolk

■ Stewards' Enquiry : Cathy Gannon four-day ban: careless riding (Aug 24-27)
Lisa Allpress seven-day ban: used whip above permitted level without giving filly time to respond (Aug 24-30)

FOCUS
A messy race, with them going a steady gallop and first five being separated by little at the line. There looked to be a couple of hard-luck stories in behind. The winner only needed to run to her latest C&D form. The third sets the standard.

5257 BARCLAYS SHERGAR CUP DASH (H'CAP) 5f
2:05 (2:07) (Class 2) (0-105,103) 3-Y-O+
£14,754 (£5,166; £2,361; £1,842; £1,623; £1,182) **Stalls** High

Form RPR
-654 **1** **Ahtoug**[13] 4800 5-9-6 **95**.................. JoaoMoreira 1 104
(Charlie Appleby) *chsd ldrs: led and hung lft over 1f out: drvn out fnl f* **11/2**[2]
4302 **2** *3/4* **Steps (IRE)**[13] 4800 5-9-10 **99**..................(b) JamesDoyle 10 105
(Roger Varian) *in rr: drvn and hdwy over 1f out: chsd wnr fnl 110yds but no imp* **11/4**[1]
6000 **3** *1* **Swan Song**[13] 4800 4-9-2 **91**.................. LisaAllpress 2 94
(Andrew Balding) *led: rdn 2f out: hdd over 1f out whn nt clr run and swtchd rt: styd on same pce fr 3rd ins fnl f* **16/1**
0030 **4** *3/4* **Zero Money (IRE)**[13] 4800 7-9-6 **95**..................(b) IoritzMendizabal 5 95
(Hugo Palmer) *broke wl: outpcd 1/2-way: drvn and rallied over 1f out: styd on same pce u.p ins fnl f* **8/1**[3]
2024 **5** *shd* **Racy**[7] 4986 6-9-10 **99**.................. AStarke 12 99
(Brian Ellison) *chsd ldrs: rdn over 1f out: styd on same pce ins fnl f* **11/4**[1]
4005 **6** *nk* **Pandar**[22] 4493 4-9-6 **95**.................. KierenFallon 4 94
(Robert Cowell) *towards rr: hdwy over 1f out and sn u.p: nt qckn ins fnl f* **20/1**
012 **7** *2 3/4* **Doctor Parkes**[30] 4217 7-9-3 **92**.................. GaryStevens 7 81
(Stuart Williams) *chsd ldrs: rdn 1/2-way: wknd over 1f out* **10/1**
0065 **8** *1 3/4* **Judge 'n Jury**[13] 4800 9-9-8 **97**..................(t) RosieNapravnik 11 79
(Ronald Harris) *chsd ldrs: rdn 2f out: wknd over 1f out* **9/1**
4655 **9** *nk* **Bear Behind (IRE)**[73] 2768 4-10-0 **103**.................. KevinManning 6 84
(Tom Dascombe) *rdn 2f out: a outpcd* **9/1**

1m 0.29s (-0.21) **Going Correction** +0.225s/f (Good) **9** Ran SP% **119.6**
Speed ratings (Par 109): **110,108,107,106,105 105,100,98,97**
toteswingers 1&2 £2.10, 1&3 £30.80, 2&3 £42.30 CSF £21.84 CT £234.95 TOTE £7.20: £1.80, £1.60, £4.80; EX 19.00 Trifecta £455.60 Pool: £3199.59 - 5.26 winning units..

 The Form Book Flat, Raceform Ltd, Compton, RG20 6NL.

Owner Godolphin **Bred** Darley **Trained** Newmarket, Suffolk
■ The first British winner for top Brazilian rider Joao Moreira, who is based in Singapore.
■ Stewards' Enquiry : Joao Moreira one-day ban: careless riding (Aug 24)

FOCUS
A good-quality sprint, and with there being plenty of front-runners, the early speed was quite well spread. Sound form, the winner close to his mark in this last year.

5258 KELTBRAY SHERGAR CUP CLASSIC (H'CAP) 1m 4f
2:40 (2:40) (Class 3) (0-95,94) 3-Y-O
£14,754 (£5,166; £2,361; £1,842; £1,623; £1,182) **Stalls** Low

Form RPR
1106 **1** **Royal Skies (IRE)**[7] 4984 3-10-0 **94** GeraldMosse 7 104
(Mark Johnston) *mde all: drvn ins fnl 2f: styd on strly fnl f and a jst doing enough* **7/1**
3231 **2** *½* **Bushel (USA)**[4] 5107 3-9-1 **81** 3ex KierenFallon 10 90
(Mark Johnston) *sn chsng ldrs: rdn 3f out: wnt 2nd over 1f out: styd on wl u.p but a jst hld* **15/2**
215 **3** *1* **Statutory (IRE)**[8] 4950 3-9-8 **88** AStarke 9 96+
(Mark Johnston) *in rr: drvn and hdwy over 2f out: tk 3rd fnl 110yds but nt rch ldng duo* **12/1**
-214 **4** *1 ¾* **Prairie Ranger**[28] 4279 3-9-10 **90** LisaAllpress 8 95
(Andrew Balding) *plld hrd: sn chsng wnr: rdn over 2f out: lost 2nd over 1f out: sn outpcd* **11/2**[2]
2316 **5** *nk* **Ducab (IRE)**[16] 4683 3-9-4 **84** JamesDoyle 4 88
(Roger Varian) *in tch: rdn and hdwy fr 2f out: swtchd lft over 1f out: styd on one pce* **14/1**
1261 **6** *¾* **Broughton (GER)**[9] 4917 3-9-12 **92** GaryStevens 1 95
(Mark Johnston) *in rr: hdwy over 2f out: styd on fnl f but nvr gng pce to rch ldrs* **7/1**
1006 **7** *¾* **Federal Blue (USA)**[7] 4980 3-9-0 **80** JoaoMoreira 6 82
(Mark Johnston) *t.k.h: towards rr tl hdwy 5f out: rdn 2f out: sn outpcd* **33/1**
1-23 **8** *2 ¼* **Wadi Al Hattawi (IRE)**[7] 4980 3-9-9 **89** (v) Yasunarilwata 2 87
(Saeed bin Suroor) *a towards rr* **6/1**[3]
9 *shd* **Cardinal Palace (IRE)**[35] 4090 3-10-0 **94** CathyGannon 3 92
(John Joseph Murphy, Ire) *chsd ldrs: rdn and wknd 2f out* **14/1**
1-31 **10** *hd* **Chesterfield (IRE)**[37] 3990 3-9-9 **89** KevinManning 5 87
(Charlie Appleby) *in rr: rdn and hdwy into mid-div on outer 4f out: nvr rchd ldrs: wknd over 2f out* **11/4**[1]

2m 33.15s (0.65) **Going Correction** +0.125s/f (Good) **10** Ran SP% **117.1**
Speed ratings (Par 104): **102,101,101,99,99 99,98,97,97,96**
toteswingers 1&2 £12.80, 1&3 £21.20, 2&3 £14.30 CSF £58.83 CT £624.29 TOTE £8.70: £2.60, £1.90, £4.00; EX 65.40 Trifecta £417.50 Pool: £2209.72 - 3.96 winning units..
Owner Sheikh Hamdan Bin Mohammed Al Maktoum **Bred** P Moen **Trained** Middleham Moor, N Yorks
■ Stewards' Enquiry : Kieren Fallon four-day ban: used whip above permitted level (Aug 24-27)

FOCUS
This was run at stop-start gallop and once again very little got into it from off the pace. Mark Johnston, who provided half of the field, trained the first three home. The winner is rated back to his early wins.

5259 PAGEGROUP SHERGAR CUP CHALLENGE (H'CAP) 1m 4f
3:15 (3:15) (Class 3) (0-95,94) 4-Y-O+
£14,754 (£5,166; £2,361; £1,842; £1,623; £1,182) **Stalls** Low

Form RPR
210 **1** **Star Lahib (IRE)**[28] 4310 4-9-11 **92** IoritzMendizabal 5 103
(Mark Johnston) *in tch: hdwy 3f out: drvn to ld 2f out: drvn clr fnl f* **5/1**[3]
/620 **2** *4 ½* **Sadler's Risk (IRE)**[9] 4914 5-9-12 **93** GeraldMosse 9 97
(Mark Johnston) *in rr: drvn and hdwy over 2f out: chsd wnr appr fnl f but nvr any ch* **10/1**
4200 **3** *1 ¼* **Icebuster**[22] 4488 5-9-5 **86** AStarke 2 88
(Rod Millman) *s.i.s: in rr: hdwy fr 2f out: styd on to take 3rd fnl 110yds: kpt on same pce* **16/1**
3-06 **4** *¾* **Willie Wag Tail (USA)**[28] 4301 4-9-7 **88** KierenFallon 1 89
(Ed Walker) *in tch: chsd ldrs in 3rd over 3f out: styd on same pce fnl 2f and dropped to 4th fnl 110yds* **3/1**[1]
1402 **5** *1 ¼* **Haylaman (IRE)**[13] 4798 5-9-13 **94** CathyGannon 3 93
(David Simcock) *in rr: hdwy over 2f out: rdn and styd on over 1f out but nvr a threat* **9/1**
-135 **6** *3 ¾* **Ustura (USA)**[38] 3960 4-9-12 **93** (t) Yasunarilwata 7 86
(Saeed bin Suroor) *chsd ldrs: wknd 2f out* **4/1**[2]
3500 **7** *1 ¾* **Scatter Dice (IRE)**[13] 4796 4-9-8 **89** LisaAllpress 4 79
(Mark Johnston) *chsd ldrs: led over 3f out: hdd 2f out: wknd appr fnl f* **14/1**
-116 **8** *½* **Jupiter Storm**[42] 3838 4-9-5 **86** RosieNapravnik 10 75
(Gary Moore) *chsd ldrs: chal over 4f out and upsides tl 2f out: wknd over 1f out* **12/1**
3043 **9** *18* **Beaufort Twelve**[3] 5147 4-9-6 **87** KevinManning 11 47
(William Jarvis) *in tch: hdwy on outside to chse ldrs fr 4f out: wknd qckly over 2f out: eased whn no ch* **11/2**
0-00 **10** *12* **Cry Fury**[42] 3832 5-9-7 **88** GaryStevens 8 29
(Gary Moore) *sn led: hdd over 3f out: sn btn: eased whn no ch* **16/1**

2m 31.34s (-1.16) **Going Correction** +0.125s/f (Good) **10** Ran SP% **122.3**
Speed ratings (Par 107): **108,105,104,103,102 100,99,98,86,78**
toteswingers 1&2 £10.00, 1&3 £17.10, 2&3 £25.90 CSF £56.99 CT £762.26 TOTE £5.20: £1.90, £3.70, £5.20; EX 48.50 Trifecta £975.40 Pool: £2346.56 - 1.80 winning units..
Owner Jaber Abdullah **Bred** Piercetown Stud **Trained** Middleham Moor, N Yorks

FOCUS
More pace on here than in earlier races and those coming from off the speed were favoured this time. A clear personal best from the winner.

5260 DUBAI DUTY FREE SHERGAR CUP SPRINT (H'CAP) 6f
3:50 (3:52) (Class 2) (0-100,96) 3-Y-O
£14,754 (£5,166; £2,361; £1,842; £1,623; £1,182) **Stalls** High

Form RPR
1064 **1** **Annunciation**[35] 4058 3-9-13 **96** GaryStevens 7 103
(Richard Hannon) *in rr: outpcd and detached 1/2-way: hdwy over 1f out: str run ins fnl f to ld last stride* **8/1**[3]
2141 **2** *shd* **Noble Deed**[14] 4757 3-9-5 **88** RosieNapravnik 8 94+
(William Haggas) *chsd ldr: led: rdn and edgd lft over 1f out: kpt on fnl f: hdd last stride* **3/1**[1]
3300 **3** *¾* **Barracuda Boy (IRE)**[29] 4255 3-9-9 **92** IoritzMendizabal 12 96
(Tom Dascombe) *s.i.s: sn rcvrd to chse ldrs: rdn 2f out: styd on ins fnl f: kpt on cl home but nt quite pce of ldng duo* **9/2**[2]
0500 **4** *shd* **Chilworth Icon**[9] 4922 3-9-12 **95** CathyGannon 1 99
(Mick Channon) *chsd ldrs: chal appr fnl f: no ex u.p and outpcd into 4th in clsng stages* **10/1**
0000 **5** *nk* **Heavy Metal**[14] 4767 3-9-5 **88** JoaoMoreira 6 91
(Mark Johnston) *towards rr 1/2-way: hdwy 2f out: styd on fnl f but nt rch ldrs* **14/1**
1000 **6** *4 ½* **Storm Moon (USA)**[4] 5108 3-9-5 **88** Yasunarilwata 4 76
(Mark Johnston) *led: hdd over 1f out: wknd ins fnl f* **20/1**
4052 **7** *2 ½* **Shahdaroba (IRE)**[29] 4242 3-9-11 **94** KierenFallon 2 74
(Rod Millman) *chsd ldrs: rdn 3f out: wknd over 1f out* **9/2**[2]
6455 **8** *¾* **Tassel**[21] 4534 3-9-5 **88** AStarke 5 66
(Richard Hannon) *in tch: rdn and effrt 2f out: wknd appr fnl f* **12/1**
6620 **9** *3 ¼* **Jadanna (IRE)**[7] 4989 3-9-5 **88** JamesDoyle 9 56
(James Given) *chsd ldrs: rdn over 2f out: sn btn* **9/1**
-200 **10** *3 ¼* **Vincentti (IRE)**[7] 4989 3-9-6 **89** KevinManning 11 46
(Ronald Harris) *chsd ldrs: hung rt and btn 1/2-way* **11/1**

1m 14.55s (0.05) **Going Correction** +0.225s/f (Good) **10** Ran SP% **119.0**
Speed ratings (Par 106): **108,107,106,106,106 100,97,96,91,87**
toteswingers 1&2 £7.40, 1&3 £4.60, 2&3 £3.00 CSF £32.95 CT £125.00 TOTE £9.00: £2.80, £1.80, £1.80; EX 34.20 Trifecta £151.10 Pool: £4065.31 - 20.17 winning units..
Owner Middleham Park Racing XXXIX & James Pak **Bred** Abingdon & Witney College **Trained** East Everleigh, Wilts
■ The European riders' team won the Shergar Cup, with Gerald Mosse the leading jockey.

FOCUS
They went hard enough up front early on but the time wasn't great. The winner was on a fair mark on a best view of his form and the second continues on the up.
T/Plt: £213.00 to a £1 stake. Pool of £169,500.22 - 580.86 winning units T/Qpdt: £49.50 to a £1 stake. Pool of £10,950.61 - 163.53 winning units ST

4820 AYR (L-H)
Saturday, August 10

OFFICIAL GOING: Good (8.9)
Wind: Light, half behind Weather: Overcast

5261 JOCKEYJAN.CO.UK JAN WILSON MEMORIAL APPRENTICE H'CAP 1m
5:35 (5:35) (Class 6) (0-65,63) 3-Y-O+ **£2,045** (£603; £302) **Stalls** High

Form RPR
-430 **1** **Captain Baldwin**[3] 5143 4-8-10 **45** (v) JordanNason 1 55
(Jim Goldie) *trckd ldrs: rdn to ld over 1f out: pushed out fnl f* **11/1**
2452 **2** *2 ½* **Eilean Mor**[12] 4824 5-8-7 **47** DanielleMooney[(5)] 3 51
(R Mike Smith) *t.k.h: w ldr: led over 3f out to over 1f out: kpt on same pce fnl f* **4/1**[2]
63-0 **3** *1 ½* **Sir Bruno (FR)**[26] 96 6-10-0 **63** (p) DanielMuscutt 6 64
(Tim Vaughan) *prom: effrt over 2f out: edgd lft over 1f out: kpt on same pce fnl f* **5/2**[1]
5354 **4** *2 ¼* **Berbice (IRE)**[1] 5239 8-8-10 **45** SamanthaBell 2 40
(Linda Perratt) *s.i.s: in tch: stdy hdwy over 2f out: rdn over 1f out: sn no ex* **17/2**[3]
0104 **5** *nk* **Outlaw Torn (IRE)**[8] 4953 4-9-11 **60** (e) ConnorBeasley 4 55
(Richard Guest) *taken early to post: slt ld to over 3f out: rallied: wknd over 1f out* **5/2**[1]
000- **6** *1* **Windsor Secret**[314] 6708 3-7-11 **46** ow1 GeorginaBaxter[(7)] 8 38
(Keith Dalgleish) *hld up: pushed along and outpcd over 2f out: styd on fnl f: no imp* **33/1**
60-0 **7** *½* **Hills Of Dakota**[19] 4582 5-9-13 **62** LauraBarry 7 53
(Keith Dalgleish) *hld up: pushed along over 2f out: no imp fr over 1f out* **16/1**
0044 **8** *nk* **Spread Boy (IRE)**[5] 5049 6-8-5 **45** JordanHibberd[(5)] 5 35
(Alan Berry) *in tch: rdn and outpcd over 2f out: n.d after* **16/1**

1m 42.06s (-1.74) **Going Correction** -0.175s/f (Firm)
WFA 3 from 4yo+ 7lb **8** Ran SP% **110.7**
Speed ratings (Par 101): **101,98,97,94,94 93,92,92**
toteswingers 1&2 £4.60, 1&3 £2.60, 2&3 £3.20 CSF £51.12 CT £140.81 TOTE £8.80: £1.30, £1.80, £1.50; EX 32.70 Trifecta £198.70 Pool: £666.97 - 2.51 winning units..
Owner Johnnie Delta Racing **Bred** W G H Barrons **Trained** Uplawmoor, E Renfrews

FOCUS
Home bend moved out 6m, adding about 18yds to races on Round course. Home bend moved out 6m adding about 18yds to races on Round course. A modest, but tight handicap. The ground was described as good, and the forecast showers had not yet materialised. The gallop was just medium. Weak form with the winner reversing course form with the runner-up.

5262 EBF/QUALITY LINK RECRUITMENT MAIDEN STKS 7f 50y
6:05 (6:07) (Class 5) 2-Y-O **£3,234** (£962; £481; £240) **Stalls** High

Form RPR
3 **1** **Bremner**[15] 4731 2-9-5 0 GrahamLee 1 83+
(Kevin Ryan) *mde virtually all: rdn over 2f out: styd on wl appr fnl f* **30/100**[1]
6 **2** *6* **Porthos Du Vallon**[57] 3282 2-9-5 0 TomEaves 4 67
(Keith Dalgleish) *t.k.h: w wnr: rdn over 2f out: no ex over 1f out* **14/1**[3]
6 **3** *17* **Strassman**[21] 4513 2-9-5 0 PhillipMakin 5 23
(Mark Johnston) *chsd clr ldrs: hung rt and outpcd over 2f out: sn btn: eased whn no ch fnl f* **4/1**[2]
4 *22* **Raise A Billion** 2-9-2 0 MarkCoumbe[(3)] 3
(Alan Berry) *s.i.s: bhd and a outpcd* **33/1**

1m 32.6s (-0.80) **Going Correction** -0.175s/f (Firm) **4** Ran SP% **106.5**
Speed ratings (Par 94): **97,90,70,45**
CSF £5.17 TOTE £1.10; EX 5.00 Trifecta £7.30 Pool: £842.09 - 85.66 winning units..
Owner Highbank Stud **Bred** Highbank Stud **Trained** Hambleton, N Yorks

FOCUS
The gallop was strong early, but the winning time was four seconds above standard. The more experienced riders confirmed the views of the first-race riders that the ground was good.

5263 UNISON SUPPORTING ST. VINCENT'S HOSPICE 25TH YEAR H'CAP (QUALIFIER BETFAIR SCOTTISH MILE SERIES) 7f 50y
6:35 (6:36) (Class 5) (0-70,73) 3-Y-O+ **£2,587** (£770; £384; £192) **Stalls** High

Form RPR
3314 **1** **Circuitous**[26] 4338 5-9-12 **70** (v) TomEaves 4 79
(Keith Dalgleish) *mde all at stdy pce: rdn and qcknd over 2f out: kpt on strly fnl f: unchal* **8/1**
1222 **2** *1 ¼* **Ifan (IRE)**[26] 3676 5-9-1 **66** DanielMuscutt[(7)] 8 72
(Tim Vaughan) *trckd wnr thrght: rdn over 2f out: edgd lft over 1f out: kpt on same pce fnl f* **4/1**[3]

0004 **3** 3 **Clumber Place**[8] 4967 7-9-0 **58**........ PhillipMakin 2 56
(James Given) *t.k.h early: trckd ldrs: rdn over 2f out: one pce fr over 1f out* **16/1**

0616 **4** ½ **Alexandrakollontai (IRE)**[12] 4821 3-8-9 **62**........(b) JulieBurke(3) 7 59+
(Alistair Whillans) *s.i.s: sn pushed along in rr: hdwy over 1f out: kpt on: nvr able to chal* **12/1**

1432 **5** 3¾ **Jessie's Spirit (IRE)**[12] 4823 4-9-4 **62**........ PJMcDonald 3 49
(Ann Duffield) *t.k.h: chsd ldrs: rdn over 2f out: wknd over 1f out* **11/4**[1]

1031 **6** 2 **Ted's Brother (IRE)**[7] 4994 5-9-10 **73**........(e) PhilipPrince(5) 5 55
(Richard Guest) *plld hrd early: in tch: rdn over 2f out: wknd over 1f out* **3/1**[2]

0341 **7** 4½ **Monel**[12] 4823 5-8-10 **54**........ GrahamLee 6 24
(Jim Goldie) *dwlt: sn pushed along and in tch: struggling over 2f out: btn over 1f out* **5/1**

1m 31.44s (-1.96) **Going Correction** -0.175s/f (Firm)
WFA 3 from 4yo+ 6lb **7** Ran SP% **113.0**
Speed ratings (Par 103): **104,102,99,98,94 92,86**
toteswingers 1&2 £5.50, 1&3 £7.00, 2&3 £5.90 CSF £38.76 CT £498.96 TOTE £9.30: £4.00, £1.50; EX 40.20 Trifecta £356.50 Pool: £1,712.31 - 3.60 winning units..
Owner Alison Walker Sarah Cousins **Bred** Deepwood Farm Stud **Trained** Carluke, S Lanarks

FOCUS
A modest handicap in which the first three were always prominent. A length personal best from the winner.

5264 UNISON'S AYRSHIRE & ARRAN HEALTH BRANCH H'CAP 1m 2f
7:05 (7:05) (Class 5) (0-75,71) 3-Y-0+ **£2,587** (£770; £384; £192) **Stalls** High

Form RPR

0653 **1** **Woodacre**[46] 3651 6-9-2 **59**........ RussKennemore 4 67
(Richard Whitaker) *pressed ldr: led over 2f out: sn rdn: hdd appr fnl f: edgd rt and rallied to regain ld ins fnl f: hld on gamely* **15/8**[1]

130 **2** *hd* **Day Of Destiny (IRE)**[49] 3573 8-9-11 **68**........ GrahamLee 2 76
(James Given) *trckd ldrs: rdn and hdwy to ld appr fnl f: hdd wl ins fnl f: hld whn blkd cl home* **11/4**[2]

233 **3** 2½ **Arr' Kid (USA)**[32] 4139 3-9-5 **71**........(b[1]) TomEaves 6 74
(Keith Dalgleish) *t.k.h: led at stdy pce to over 2f out: sn rdn: rallied over 1f out: kpt on fnl f: no imp* **6/1**[3]

560 **4** 3½ **Latin Rebel (IRE)**[10] 4887 6-8-9 **52**........ AndrewElliott 1 48
(Jim Goldie) *hld up in tch: rdn and outpcd 2f out: no imp fnl f* **9/1**

-110 **5** 9 **Coral Sands (IRE)**[75] 2705 5-9-9 **66**........ MartinLane 5 44
(Alan Swinbank) *in tch: drvn over 2f out: wknd wl over 1f out* **7/1**

-556 **6** 27 **Change The Subject (USA)**[11] 4850 5-9-6 **68**........(t) PhilipPrince(5) 3
(Richard Guest) *s.v.s: bhd: rdn and no ch fr 3f out* **15/2**

2m 9.16s (-2.84) **Going Correction** -0.175s/f (Firm)
WFA 3 from 5yo+ 9lb **6** Ran SP% **110.0**
Speed ratings (Par 103): **104,103,101,99,91 70**
toteswingers 1&2 £1.60, 1&3 £3.00, 2&3 £2.50 CSF £6.87 TOTE £2.50: £1.20, £2.80; EX 9.30 Trifecta £29.30 Pool: £969.28 - 24.73 winning units..
Owner Mrs R M Whitaker **Bred** Hellwood Stud Farm **Trained** Scarcroft, W Yorks
■ Stewards' Enquiry : Russ Kennemore four-day ban: used whip above permitted level down the shoulder in the forehand (Aug 24-27)

FOCUS
A competitive race for the grade and sound run for the small field. The first three are rated up slightly.

5265 BELLA MANI SALONS H'CAP 5f
7:35 (7:36) (Class 6) (0-65,65) 3-Y-0 **£2,045** (£603; £302) **Stalls** High

Form RPR

0025 **1** **Amelia Jay**[66] 2998 3-8-4 **48** oh1 ow2........ AndrewElliott 8 55
(Danielle McCormick) *hld up in tch: nt clr run over 1f out: qcknd against stands' rail to ld last 100yds: kpt on wl* **16/1**

60-0 **2** ¾ **Baker's Pursuit**[57] 3283 3-8-8 **52** ow1........ TomEaves 6 56+
(Jim Goldie) *swtchd rt sn after s: hld up: nt clr run over 1f out to ins fnl f: weaved through to chse wnr last 75yds: kpt on* **25/1**

0 **3** 1¼ **Modern Lady**[71] 2832 3-9-2 **65**........ PhilipPrince(5) 5 65
(Richard Guest) *led tl rdn and hdd ins fnl f: kpt on same pce towards fin* **7/1**[3]

630 **4** *shd* **Cracking Choice (IRE)**[21] 4544 3-8-9 **58**........(tp) ConnorBeasley(5) 6 57
(Michael Dods) *trckd ldrs: effrt and ev ch over 1f out: kpt on same pce ins fnl f* **9/4**[1]

0-66 **5** 3 **Lichen Angel**[17] 4619 3-8-4 **48**........ MartinLane 4 37
(Richard Whitaker) *prom: effrt and rdn 2f out: outpcd fnl f* **10/1**

6260 **6** 1½ **Constant Dream**[10] 4892 3-8-13 **57**........ GrahamLee 3 40
(James Given) *prom: rdn along whn flashed tail and edgd lft over 1f out: sn btn* **7/1**[3]

0062 **7** 3¾ **Rat Catcher (IRE)**[17] 4621 3-8-10 **57**........(b) DeclanCannon(3) 2 27
(Andrew Crook) *prom on outside: rdn 2f out: wknd appr fnl f* **5/2**[2]

0-40 **8** 2¾ **Ridgeblade**[108] 1762 3-8-0 **47**........ JulieBurke(3) 7
(Noel Wilson) *trckd ldrs: pushed along whn n.m.r over 1f out: sn wknd* **10/1**

59.96s (0.56) **Going Correction** +0.125s/f (Good) **8** Ran SP% **112.3**
Speed ratings (Par 98): **100,98,96,96,91 89,83,79**
toteswingers 1&2 £36.60, 1&3 £11.30, 2&3 £15.10 CSF £317.60 CT £3037.76 TOTE £13.70: £3.90, £4.10, £1.90; EX 388.40 Trifecta £553.00 Pool: £809.60 - 1.09 winning units..
Owner M R Johnson **Bred** Exors Of The Late T E Pocock **Trained** Westhead, Lancs

FOCUS
A competitive, low-grade sprint handicap, that was run at a good gallop. The winner is rated to her best.

5266 QTS H'CAP 5f
8:05 (8:08) (Class 4) (0-85,79) 3-Y-0+ **£5,175** (£1,540; £769; £384) **Stalls** High

Form RPR

144 **1** **Algar Lad**[49] 3566 3-9-0 **72**........ GrahamLee 5 81
(Jim Goldie) *dwlt: in tch: hdwy stands' rail over 1f out: rdn and styd on wl fnl f to ld cl home* **9/2**[2]

2053 **2** ½ **Rylee Mooch**[4] 5108 5-9-5 **79**........(e) PhilipPrince(5) 2 86
(Richard Guest) *pressed ldr: rdn over 1f out: led ins fnl f: hdd and no ex towards fin* **3/1**[1]

4656 **3** ¾ **The Nifty Fox**[8] 4954 9-9-7 **76**........(p) PhillipMakin 4 80
(Tim Easterby) *in tch: effrt over 1f out: nt clr run ins fnl f: kpt on towards fin* **14/1**

0035 **4** *nse* **Crimson Knot (IRE)**[8] 4954 5-9-1 **73**........ MarkCoumbe(3) 6 77
(Alan Berry) *prom: effrt and edgd lft appr fnl f: kpt on same pce ins fnl f* **8/1**[3]

1152 **5** ¾ **Gowanharry (IRE)**[12] 4821 4-9-3 **77**........ ConnorBeasley(5) 3 78
(Michael Dods) *led: rdn 2f out: hung lft and hdd ins fnl f: sn outpcd* **3/1**[1]

2241 **6** 2 **Jinky**[12] 4821 5-9-8 **77**........ TomEaves 1 71
(Linda Perratt) *trckd ldrs on outside: rdn and outpcd over 1f out: no imp whn edgd rt ins fnl f* **8/1**[3]

59.29s (-0.11) **Going Correction** +0.125s/f (Good)
WFA 3 from 4yo+ 3lb **6** Ran SP% **97.1**
Speed ratings (Par 105): **105,104,103,102,101 98**
toteswingers 1&2 £4.10, 1&3 £8.00, 2&3 £8.90 CSF £13.50 TOTE £4.40: £1.90, £1.50; EX 16.50 Trifecta £131.30 Pool: £770.41 - 4.40 winning units..
Owner Great Northern Partnership **Bred** Highclere Stud **Trained** Uplawmoor, E Renfrews

FOCUS
A small field but a competitive affair with recent C&D form being put to the test. The pace wasn't breakneck, but unsurprisingly was quicker than the previous race over C&D. The winner built on his debut promise.

5267 THOMSON REMOVALS AND SELF STORAGE H'CAP (QUALIFIER FOR £15,000 BETFAIR SCOTTISH STAYERS' SERIES) 1m 7f
8:35 (8:35) (Class 6) (0-65,65) 4-Y-0+ **£1,940** (£577; £288; £144) **Stalls** Low

Form RPR

3142 **1** **Goldan Jess (IRE)**[18] 4614 9-8-12 **56**........ RussKennemore 4 74+
(Philip Kirby) *mde virtually all: clr w one other over 6f out: drew clr fr 3 out: eased ins fnl f* **7/2**[3]

0630 **2** 8 **Sohcahtoa (IRE)**[20] 4563 7-9-2 **63**........ LMcNiff(3) 5 68
(Andrew Crook) *hld up: rdn and hdwy over 2f out: chsd (clr) wnr ent fnl f: r.o* **10/1**

0/2- **3** 2¼ **Viva Diva**[36] 4040 5-9-2 **65**........ ConnorBeasley(5) 7 67
(John C McConnell, Ire) *hld up in tch: hdwy to chse (clr) wnr over 2f out to ent fnl f: sn outpcd* **2/1**[1]

4133 **4** 7 **Forrest Flyer (IRE)**[19] 4578 9-9-7 **65**........ GrahamLee 6 58
(Jim Goldie) *w wnr: clr of rest over 6f out: rdn over 4f out: outpcd fnl 2f* **3/1**[2]

5020 **5** 1¼ **Altnaharra**[8] 4951 4-7-11 **48**........(v) SophieRobertson(7) 3 39
(Jim Goldie) *in tch: drvn and outpcd over 4f out: n.d after* **16/1**

5352 **6** 6 **Geanie Mac (IRE)**[1] 5240 4-7-9 **46**........(v) SamanthaBell(7) 1 30
(Linda Perratt) *hld up in tch: struggling over 4f out: sn btn* **9/2**

0-00 **7** 41 **Rare Coincidence**[19] 4343 12-7-9 **46** oh1........(tp) JordanHibberd(7) 2
(Alan Berry) *awkward s: sn chsng ldrs: struggling over 4f out: sn lost tch* **33/1**

3m 21.33s (0.93) **Going Correction** -0.175s/f (Firm) **7** Ran SP% **116.7**
Speed ratings (Par 101): **90,85,84,80,80 76,55**
toteswingers 1&2 £4.20, 1&3 £3.00, 2&3 £6.30 CSF £38.25 TOTE £4.10: £1.20, £4.60; EX 46.30 Trifecta £238.90 Pool: £956.14 - 3.00 winning units..
Owner The Jessies,Colin Fletcher,Philip Kirby **Bred** Bendis Partnership **Trained** Middleham, N Yorks

FOCUS
The forecast rain arrived and this low-grade handicap was run during a heavy shower. The pace looked decent and the winner is worth a personal best.
T/Plt: £179.80 to a £1 stake. Pool: £53,533.85 - 217.31 winning units T/Qpdt: £83.90 to a £1 stake. Pool: £4,265.92 - 37.60 winning units RY

5222 HAYDOCK (L-H)
Saturday, August 10

OFFICIAL GOING: Good to firm (good in places; 8.7)
Wind: Light, half against Weather: Sunny

5268 BETFRED MOBILE SPORTS H'CAP (LONDON MILE SERIES QUALIFIER) 1m
1:45 (1:45) (Class 3) (0-95,95) 3-Y-0+ **£8,086** (£2,406; £1,202; £601) **Stalls** Low

Form RPR

0434 **1** **Graphic (IRE)**[14] 4746 4-9-1 **82**........ JosephO'Brien 6 97
(William Haggas) *a.p: led briefly wl over 2f out: rdn whn gamely regained ld 1f out: r.o and drew away fnl 50yds* **7/1**[3]

261 **2** 2 **Ascription (IRE)**[11] 4859 4-9-13 **94**........(t) RyanMoore 8 104
(Hugo Palmer) *trckd ldrs: led over 2f out: rdn whn hdd 1f out: stl ev ch ins fnl f: no ex fnl 50yds* **2/1**[1]

5004 **3** 2½ **Invincible Hero (IRE)**[7] 5014 6-8-9 **79**........ JasonHart(3) 2 84
(Declan Carroll) *s.i.s: bustled along and sn rcvrd to ld: rdn and hdd wl over 2f out: outpcd by ldrs over 1f out: kpt on ins fnl f but no imp* **16/1**

3101 **4** ¾ **Postscript (IRE)**[29] 4242 5-9-10 **91**........ JimCrowley 4 94
(David Simcock) *trckd ldrs: rdn 2f out: plld out over 1f out: styd on same pce and no imp on front two fnl f* **9/1**

0510 **5** *hd* **Storm King**[13] 4811 4-9-13 **94**........(p) AdamKirby 1 96
(Jane Chapple-Hyam) *broke wl: sn dropped into midfield: rdn over 2f out: kpt on ins fnl f: nvr able to chal* **14/1**

4533 **6** ½ **Lord Ashley (IRE)**[7] 5004 3-8-8 **82**........ RichardKingscote 11 83
(Tom Dascombe) *cl up on outer: rdn over 2f out: btn over 1f out: one pce fnl f* **9/2**[2]

0050 **7** 1¾ **Swiftly Done (IRE)**[11] 4869 6-9-4 **88**........(v) NeilFarley(3) 5 85
(Declan Carroll) *midfield: rdn 3f out: sn outpcd: plugged on but n.d fnl f* **25/1**

0530 **8** 3 **Al Muheer (IRE)**[7] 5014 8-9-6 **87**........(b) PJMcDonald 3 77
(Ruth Carr) *hld up: rdn over 2f out: nvr a threat* **33/1**

4114 **9** 1¾ **Swift Cedar (IRE)**[17] 4641 3-8-2 **81**........ MichaelJMMurphy(5) 9 67
(Alan Jarvis) *midfield: rdn 3f out: wknd over 2f out* **20/1**

0052 **10** 2¾ **Chosen Character (IRE)**[6] 5026 5-9-5 **91**........(vt) NatashaEaton(5) 7 71
(Tom Dascombe) *s.i.s: hld up: rdn over 2f out: nvr a threat* **7/1**[3]

2266 **11** 1¾ **Les Troyens**[14] 4778 5-10-0 **95**........ SilvestreDeSousa 10 71
(Saeed bin Suroor) *in rr: pushed along over 2f out: nvr threatened* **16/1**

1m 42.36s (-1.34) **Going Correction** -0.20s/f (Firm)
WFA 3 from 4yo+ 7lb **11** Ran SP% **116.5**
Speed ratings (Par 107): **98,96,93,92,92 92,90,87,85,82 81**
toteswingers 1&2 £3.70, 1&3 £23.50, 2&3 £8.20 CSF £20.58 CT £224.47 TOTE £8.20: £2.40, £1.30, £5.80; EX 23.60 Trifecta £546.40 Pool: £1913.79 - 2.62 winning units..
Owner The Royal Ascot Racing Club **Bred** Kevin & Meta Cullen **Trained** Newmarket, Suffolk

FOCUS
All races on outer home straight and races on Round course increased in distance by 55yds. A decent handicap run over the actual distance of 1m55yds. It proved advantageous to race up with the pace, with nothing getting involved from the rear. The winner is rated back to his best.

5269 BETFRED "BETTER PRICES ON GOALS GALORE" H'CAP 1m 2f 95y
2:20 (2:21) (Class 2) (0-105,104) 3-Y-0+**£32,345** (£9,625; £4,810; £2,405) **Stalls** Centre

Form RPR

1124 **1** **Robin Hoods Bay**[133] 1241 5-9-11 **101**........ LukeMorris 7 112
(Ed Vaughan) *midfield: rdn and hdwy over 2f out: wnt 2nd over 1f out: r.o to ld fnl 150yds: in command towards fin* **25/1**

1121 **2** 1 ½ **Sennockian Star**[15] 4706 3-8-12 **97**.....(v) JoeFanning 6 105
(Mark Johnston) *trckd ldrs: rdn over 2f out: hdd fnl 150yds: hld by wnr towards fin* **9/2**[1]

0100 **3** 1 ½ **Educate**[28] 4310 4-9-9 **99**..... JohnnyMurtagh 9 106+
(Ismail Mohammed) *hld up: hdwy 2f out: nt clr run on heels of ldrs whn stmbld over 1f out: under hands ride after tl swtchd rt ins fnl 100yds: r.o and fin wl* **8/1**[3]

3421 **4** nk **Gabrial The Great (IRE)**[22] 4488 4-9-6 **96**..... AdamKirby 2 101
(Luca Cumani) *hld up: rdn and hdwy over 2f out: hung lft whn chsng ldrs over 1f out: kpt on ins fnl f: one pce and no imp fnl 100yds* **8/1**[3]

5212 **5** ¾ **Vasily**[15] 4706 5-9-0 **97**..... KevinStott[(7)] 5 100
(Robert Eddery) *led: rdn and hdd over 2f out: stl ev ch wl over 1f out: styd on same pce ins fnl f* **14/1**

/-55 **6** nse **Tahaamah**[75] 2718 5-9-1 **91**.....(t) SilvestreDeSousa 3 94
(Saeed bin Suroor) *midfield: hdwy 3f out: effrt on inner over 2f out: chal over 1f out: nt qckn ins fnl f: styd on same pce* **12/1**

3620 **7** 1 **Tepmokea (IRE)**[11] 4854 7-9-2 **92**..... RichardKingscote 15 93
(Mrs K Burke) *prom: rdn whn n.m.r 2f out: one pce fnl f* **33/1**

-110 **8** 2 ¼ **Niceofyoutotellme**[28] 4310 4-9-2 **92**.....[1] JimCrowley 16 89
(Ralph Beckett) *in rr: rdn over 2f out: plugged on fnl f: nvr trbld ldrs* **9/1**

3105 **9** 1 ¼ **Maven**[14] 4777 5-8-9 **85** oh1..... DuranFentiman 12 80
(Tim Easterby) *midfield: pushed along over 3f out: no imp* **50/1**

3011 **10** ¾ **Chancery (USA)**[29] 4264 5-9-5 **95**..... DavidNolan 4 88
(David O'Meara) *hld up: rdn over 3f out: nvr able to get on terms w ldrs* **13/2**[2]

0-03 **11** 1 ¾ **Labarinto**[11] 4854 5-9-10 **100**..... RyanMoore 8 90
(Sir Michael Stoute) *midfield: rdn over 1f out: no imp over 1f out: wknd ins fnl f: eased whn btn fnl 100yds* **8/1**[3]

-105 **12** 4 ½ **Navajo Chief**[28] 4284 6-9-9 **104**..... MichaelJMMurphy[(5)] 10 85
(Alan Jarvis) *hld up: pushed along over 4f out: nvr on terms* **50/1**

2261 **13** 3 **Danchai**[28] 4310 4-9-9 **99**.....(p) JosephO'Brien 11 75
(William Haggas) *trckd ldrs: pushed along struggling to hold pl and hld whn n.m.r and hmpd over 1f out: sn eased* **13/2**[2]

1340 **14** 3 ½ **Awake My Soul (IRE)**[7] 4979 4-9-5 **95**.....[1] PatSmullen 14 64
(David O'Meara) *in tch: pushed along and lost pl 3f out: bhd fnl 2f* **22/1**

2m 10.82s (-4.68) **Going Correction** -0.20s/f (Firm)
WFA 3 from 4yo+ 9lb **14** Ran SP% **117.6**
Speed ratings (Par 109): **110,108,107,107,106 106,105,104,103,102 101,97,95,92**
toteswingers 1&2 £26.60, 1&3 £94.70, 2&3 £14.20 CSF £126.96 CT £1003.02 TOTE £25.80: £5.60, £1.60, £3.40; EX 152.60 Trifecta £2249.50 Pool: £116,445.51 - 38.82 winning units..
Owner A M Pickering **Bred** Palm Tree Thoroughbreds **Trained** Newmarket, Suffolk

FOCUS
The race's actual distance was 1m2f150yds. This handicap was worth considerably more than it had been a year ago, and it attracted a strong field. The pace was brisk. The winner rates better than ever and the third was arguably unlucky.

5270 BETFRED ROSE OF LANCASTER STKS (GROUP 3) 1m 2f 95y

2:55 (2:56) (Class 1) 3-Y-0+

£34,026 (£12,900; £6,456; £3,216; £1,614; £810) **Stalls** Centre

Form RPR

-054 **1** **David Livingston (IRE)**[36] 4027 4-9-3 106..... JohnnyMurtagh 8 115
(M F De Kock, South Africa) *chsd ldr: rdn to ld 2f out: r.o ins fnl f: in command towards fin* **15/2**[3]

21-1 **2** 1 **Telescope (IRE)**[23] 4452 3-8-8 114..... RyanMoore 7 113
(Sir Michael Stoute) *racd keenly: trckd ldrs: chal fr 2f out: rdn over 1f out: one pce and hld towards fin* **4/9**[1]

3414 **3** hd **Noble Mission**[49] 3556 4-9-3 111..... TomQueally 5 113
(Lady Cecil) *bustled along whn s.i.s: hld up: hdwy over 2f out: rdn whn swtchd lft to chse ldrs over 1f out: kpt on ins fnl f* **6/1**[2]

4210 **4** 4 **Area Fifty One**[28] 4310 5-9-3 105..... PatSmullen 9 105
(Richard Fahey) *led: rdn and hdd 2f out: stl ch over 1f out: one pce fnl 150yds* **25/1**

-005 **5** 1 ½ **Sri Putra**[14] 4779 7-9-3 110.....(b) JosephO'Brien 6 102
(Roger Varian) *stdd s: hld up: pushed along and struggling over 3f out: kpt on ins fnl f but n.d* **20/1**

-236 **6** nk **City Style (USA)**[133] 1267 7-9-3 115..... MickaelBarzalona 1 102
(Charlie Appleby) *hld up: effrt to chse ldrs 2f out: no imp 1f out: no ex fnl 150yds* **10/1**

1221 **7** 2 ¼ **Quick Wit**[23] 4433 6-9-3 109.....(p) SilvestreDeSousa 2 97
(Saeed bin Suroor) *trckd ldrs: rdn 3f out: sn lost pl: no imp after* **14/1**

0-04 **8** 5 **Black Spirit (USA)**[21] 4526 6-9-3 106.....(t) AdamKirby 3 88
(Clive Cox) *midfield: rdn over 2f out: wknd over 1f out* **33/1**

2m 11.83s (-3.67) **Going Correction** -0.20s/f (Firm)
WFA 3 from 4yo+ 9lb **8** Ran SP% **122.6**
Speed ratings (Par 113): **106,105,105,101,100 100,98,94**
toteswingers 1&2 £2.30, 1&3 £4.90, 2&3 £1.90 CSF £11.95 TOTE £9.40: £1.90, £1.02, £1.90; EX 14.50 Trifecta £54.70 Pool: £5978.35 - 81.95 winning units..
Owner Dr Cyrus Poonawalla **Bred** Rhinestone Bloodstock & Lynch-Bages Ltd **Trained** South Africa

FOCUS
Actual race distance 1m2f150yds. This ordinary Group 3 was run at a fairly steady pace, in a time a second slower than the preceding handicap. David Livingston rates back to his old best with Telescope disappointing.

5271 BETFRED/EBF STALLIONS DICK HERN FILLIES' STKS (LISTED RACE) 1m

3:25 (3:28) (Class 1) 3-Y-0+

£26,653 (£10,105; £5,057; £2,519; £1,264; £634) **Stalls** Low

Form RPR

533- **1** **Amazonas (IRE)**[316] 6635 3-8-7 102..... PatSmullen 2 102
(Ed Dunlop) *trckd ldrs: led 1f out: sn rdn: edgd rt wl ins fnl f: kpt on wl and a doing enough cl home* **10/1**

4-60 **2** nk **Reyaadah**[94] 2148 3-8-7 94.....[1] JoeFanning 4 102
(Charles Hills) *t.k.h: trckd ldrs: travelled strly bef chal 1f out: kpt on ins fnl f: hld cl home* **20/1**

5432 **3** ¾ **Ultrasonic (USA)**[15] 4705 4-9-0 101..... RyanMoore 3 100
(Sir Michael Stoute) *led: rdn over 1f out: sn hdd: stl ev ch ins fnl f: one pce cl home* **11/8**[1]

-466 **4** 1 ¾ **Falls Of Lora (IRE)**[15] 4705 4-9-0 96..... SilvestreDeSousa 5 96
(Charlie Appleby) *hld up: nt clr run whn plld out and hdwy over 1f out: kpt on ins fnl f: nvr able to chal ldrs* **6/1**[3]

-300 **5** nk **Melbourne Memories**[69] 2910 3-8-7 100..... LukeMorris 9 95
(Clive Cox) *broke wl: a.p: nudged along 3f out: chal fr 2f out: nt qckn ins fnl f: no ex fnl 75yds* **7/1**

1 **6** 1 ¾ **Expressly (IRE)**[13] 4799 3-8-7 88..... MickaelBarzalona 8 91
(Charlie Appleby) *in rr: rdn 2f out: effrt to chse ldrs over 1f out: sn no imp: btn ins fnl f* **11/4**[2]

05 **7** nse **Spellwork (USA)**[170] 743 4-9-0 100.....[1] AhmedAjtebi 6 91
(Saeed bin Suroor) *hld up: rdn whn n.m.r and hmpd over 1f out: sn lost grnd: edgd lft wl ins fnl f whn n.d* **16/1**

1m 44.09s (0.39) **Going Correction** -0.20s/f (Firm)
WFA 3 from 4yo+ 7lb **7** Ran SP% **115.3**
Speed ratings (Par 108): **90,89,88,87,86 85,85**
toteswingers 1&2 £10.50, 1&3 £2.90, 2&3 £4.70 CSF £171.89 TOTE £10.00: £3.40, £6.60; EX 238.30 Trifecta £369.50 Pool: £2948.80 - 5.98 winning units..
Owner Sir Robert Ogden **Bred** Sir Robert Ogden **Trained** Newmarket, Suffolk

FOCUS
Actual race distance 1m55yds. The third running of this event at Haydock, and not an especially strong race for the grade. The pace was only ordinary and the time slow compared with the opening handicap. The form is rated a bit cautiously.

5272 BETFRED "DOUBLE DELIGHT" NURSERY H'CAP 5f

4:00 (4:02) (Class 2) 2-Y-0 **£9,703** (£2,887; £1,443; £721) **Stalls** Centre

Form RPR

0011 **1** **Touch The Clouds**[8] 4952 2-8-4 **69**..... SilvestreDeSousa 6 74+
(Kevin Ryan) *chsd ldrs: led wl over 1f out: sn rdn and hung lft: pressed after: kpt on and in control cl home* **9/2**

1451 **2** ½ **Suzi's Connoisseur**[42] 3801 2-9-7 **86**..... FrannyNorton 1 89+
(Mark Johnston) *hld up: hdwy 2f out: str chal and upsides wnr over 1f out: rdn ins fnl f: no ex cl home* **3/1**[2]

1321 **3** 6 **Innocently (IRE)**[14] 4783 2-8-13 **78**..... JimCrowley 3 59
(David O'Meara) *chsd ldr: rdn and ev ch over 1f out: one pce and unable to go w front pair ins fnl f* **10/3**[3]

610 **4** 2 ¾ **Mahlah (IRE)**[14] 4742 2-9-5 **84**..... RyanMoore 5 56
(Richard Hannon) *dwlt: hld up: pushed along over 1f out: no imp: eased whn wl btn wl ins fnl f* **2/1**[1]

012 **5** 4 ½ **Tweety Pie (IRE)**[15] 4726 2-8-6 **74**..... NeilFarley[(3)] 4 29
(Declan Carroll) *wnt rt s: led: rdn 2f out: sn hdd: wknd over 1f out* **8/1**

1m 0.79s (-0.01) **Going Correction** 0.0s/f (Good) **5** Ran SP% **110.7**
Speed ratings (Par 100): **100,99,89,85,78**
CSF £18.10 TOTE £6.60: £2.40, £2.10; EX 18.70 Trifecta £60.10 Pool: £1781.57 - 22.23 winning units..
Owner Matt & Lauren Morgan 1 **Bred** Stuart McPhee Bloodstock Ltd **Trained** Hambleton, N Yorks

FOCUS
Quite a valuable nursery, and a strong pace considering the small field. The first two pulled clear.

5273 BETFRED DUKE OF LANCASTER'S OWN YEOMANRY H'CAP 6f

4:30 (4:31) (Class 5) (0-70,74) 3-Y-0+ **£5,175** (£1,540; £769; £384) **Stalls** Centre

Form RPR

0-30 **1** **Ambitious Boy**[10] 4884 4-9-12 **70**..... TomQueally 5 81
(Andrew Hollinshead) *towards rr: hdwy over 1f out: led wl ins fnl f: r.o* **7/1**

0350 **2** ¾ **Rich Again (IRE)**[20] 4560 4-9-5 **63**..... RyanMoore 6 72
(James Bethell) *midfield: hdwy 1/2-way: led 1f out: hdd wl ins fnl f: unable to go w wnr cl home* **5/1**[2]

2266 **3** 1 **Holy Angel (IRE)**[11] 4852 4-9-12 **70**.....(be) RobertWinston 2 76
(Tim Easterby) *hld up: smooth hdwy over 1f out: effrt ins fnl f: styd on towards fin* **10/1**

3231 **4** ¾ **Pull The Pin (IRE)**[32] 4146 4-8-8 **52**..... FrannyNorton 12 55
(Paul Green) *prom: rdn and ev ch over 1f out: nt qckn ins fnl f: styd on same pce towards fin* **8/1**

5504 **5** 1 ¾ **Admiralofthesea (USA)**[16] 4670 3-9-4 **66**..... NickyMackay 3 64
(Robert Eddery) *midfield: effrt to chse ldrs over 1f out: one pce ins fnl f* **25/1**

1423 **6** 1 ¼ **Whipphound**[8] 4966 5-9-4 **62**..... TomMcLaughlin 7 56
(Mark Brisbourne) *trckd ldrs: rdn 2f out: led over 1f out: sn hdd: fdd fnl 100yds* **14/1**

5605 **7** 1 ½ **Methaaly (IRE)**[5] 5049 10-8-8 **57**.....(be) NatashaEaton[(5)] 9 46
(Michael Mullineaux) *late removal of blindfold and s.i.s: in rr: rdn and edgd lft over 1f out: kpt on fnl f: nvr able to trble ldrs* **33/1**

0021 **8** 1 ¾ **Fathsta (IRE)**[12] 4837 8-10-2 **74**..... SilvestreDeSousa 11 57
(Ian Williams) *prom: rdn over 2f out: wknd over 1f out* **6/1**[3]

1350 **9** nk **Gabrial's Gift (IRE)**[29] 4250 4-9-12 **70**..... AdamKirby 14 52
(David Simcock) *awkward s: racd on stands' rail: midfield: rdn over 1f out: wknd ent fnl f* **3/1**[1]

0501 **10** nk **Stoneacre Oskar**[7] 4991 4-8-12 **61**..... SladeO'Hara[(5)] 13 42
(Peter Grayson) *bhd: outpcd 1/2-way: nvr on terms* **25/1**

605 **11** 1 ¼ **Imperator Augustus (IRE)**[8] 4956 5-9-10 **68**.....(b[1]) DuranFentiman 8 45
(Patrick Holmes) *led: rdn and hdd over 1f out: wknd ins fnl f* **25/1**

4313 **12** 6 **Baltic Prince (IRE)**[13] 4806 3-9-2 **67**..... RaulDaSilva[(3)] 4 25
(Paul Green) *chsd ldrs: rdn over 2f out: wknd over 1f out* **14/1**

3332 **13** 3 **Busy Bimbo (IRE)**[5] 5047 4-8-7 **51** oh2..... JoeFanning 1
(Alan Berry) *prom: rdn over 2f out: wknd over 1f out* **18/1**

5500 **14** 12 **Dingaan (IRE)**[12] 4840 10-8-7 **51** oh6.....(p) PatrickMathers 10
(Peter Grayson) *stmbld s: towards rr: pujshed along and outpcd 1/2-way: nvr on terms* **66/1**

1m 13.11s (-0.69) **Going Correction** 0.0s/f (Good)
WFA 3 from 4yo+ 4lb **14** Ran SP% **123.2**
Speed ratings (Par 103): **104,103,101,100,98 96,94,92,91,91 89,81,77,61**
toteswingers 1&2 £6.30, 1&3 £12.50, 2&3 £12.70 CSF £40.67 CT £361.58 TOTE £8.10: £2.70, £2.40, £3.70; EX 48.70 Trifecta £336.60 Pool: £3855.93 - 8.59 winning units..
Owner C W Wardle & Mrs J E Wardle **Bred** Cecil W Wardle & Mrs Janet E Wardle **Trained** Upper Longdon, Staffs

FOCUS
An ordinary sprint handicap. They all came down the centre except for Gabrial's Gift. Quite solid form.

5274 BETFRED "HAT TRICK HEAVEN" LEVY BOARD H'CAP 1m 3f 200y

5:05 (5:07) (Class 2) 3-Y-0

£31,125 (£9,320; £4,660; £2,330; £1,165; £585) **Stalls** Centre

Form RPR

6322 **1** **Glenard**[14] 4748 3-8-6 **85**..... MickaelBarzalona 6 95
(Charles Hills) *racd keenly: hld up: hdwy over 2f out: rdn to ld over 1f out: styd on ins fnl f: strly pressed towards fin: hld on gamely on the nod* **11/1**

121 **2** shd **Renew (IRE)**[30] 4202 3-9-0 **93**..... RyanMoore 7 103
(Marco Botti) *chsd ldrs: pushed along and outpcd over 3f out: rallied u.p over 1f out: wnt 2nd wl ins fnl f: styd on to chal strly towards fin: jst denied on the nod* **4/1**[3]

5212 **3** 3 ¼ **Salutation (IRE)**[7] 4984 3-9-0 **93** .... JoeFanning 5 98
(Mark Johnston) *led: hdd over 9f out: remained prom: regained ld 2f out: rdn and hdd over 1f out: styd on same pce and unable to go w front two fnl 100yds* **9/2**

-215 **4** ¾ **Dare To Achieve**[30] 4211 3-9-3 **96** .... JosephO'Brien 8 100
(William Haggas) *hld up in tch: effrt to chal fr 2f out: nt qckn u.p ent fnl f: one pce fnl 150yds* **11/4**[1]

2111 **5** nk **Big Thunder**[14] 4748 3-9-1 **94** .... LukeMorris 4 97
(Sir Mark Prescott Bt) *bustled along early: prom: led over 9f out: hdd 2f out: stl chalng for press over 1f out: no ex fnl 150yds* **7/2**[2]

-013 **6** 2 ¾ **Shrewd**[21] 4541 3-9-0 **93** .... TomQueally 2 92
(Michael Bell) *in rr: pushed along over 3f out: rdn and hdwy 2f out: chsd ldrs and ch over 1f out: lugged lft u.p and no ex ins fnl f* **10/1**

4131 **7** 11 **Emerging**[7] 4980 3-8-7 **86** ....(p) LiamKeniry 9 67
(David Elsworth) *prom: pushed along 3f out: rdn and lost pl over 2f out: wknd over 1f out: eased whn btn wl ins fnl f* **15/2**

2m 30.2s (-3.60) **Going Correction** -0.20s/f (Firm) **7** Ran SP% **116.3**
Speed ratings (Par 106): **104,103,101,101,101 99,91**
toteswingers 1&2 £7.80, 1&3 £8.20, 2&3 £3.70 CSF £55.81 CT £231.50 TOTE £12.90: £4.90, £3.40; EX 77.60 Trifecta £165.60 Pool: £3567.42 - 16.15 winning units..
Owner Highclere T'Bred Racing & John C Grant **Bred** Denford Stud Ltd **Trained** Lambourn, Berks

FOCUS
Actual race distance 1m4f35yds. The second running of this valuable handicap was contested by some progressive 3yos. Sound form.
T/Plt: £1,004.20 to a £1 stake. Pool of £129173.88 - 93.90 winning tickets. T/Qpdt: £163.00 to a £1 stake. Pool of £7412.78 - 33.65 winning tickets. DO

5228 LINGFIELD (L-H)
Saturday, August 10

OFFICIAL GOING: Turf course - firm (good to firm in places; 9.2); all-weather course - standard
Wind: Light, behind Weather: Fine but cloudy

5275 LADBROKES H'CAP — 7f 140y
5:15 (5:16) (Class 6) (0-60,60) 3-Y-O — **£2,045** (£603; £302) **Stalls** Centre

Form RPR

1001 **1** **Little Indian**[44] 3739 3-9-1 **59** .... DannyBrock(5) 5 66
(J R Jenkins) *stdd s: racd wdst of all: hld up in last trio: stdy prog fr 3f out: drvn to ld 1f out: hld on* **5/1**[2]

066- **2** ¾ **Sword Of The Lord**[277] 7598 3-9-5 **58** .... StevieDonohoe 8 63
(Michael Bell) *dwlt but rousted to press ldr and racd against rail: led 4f out: drvn over 1f out: hdd and nt qckn w hd high 1f out: styd on again nr fin* **3/1**[1]

4220 **3** ½ **Azelle**[2] 5170 3-9-4 **60** .... ThomasBrown(3) 3 63
(Brendan Powell) *chsd ldrs in 6th: pushed along 1/2-way: rdn and prog over 2f out: wnt 2nd and chal over 1f out: one pce fnl f* **8/1**

003 **4** 1 ¾ **Polish Rider**[16] 4684 3-8-7 **46** oh1 .... HarryBentley 9 45
(Richard Hannon) *chsd ldrs against rail: rdn 4f out: nt qckn 2f out: kpt on again ins fnl f* **6/1**[3]

0060 **5** ½ **Otto The First**[16] 4658 3-8-4 **48** .... RyanTate(5) 1 46
(John Best) *stdd s: hld up in last pair: taken to outer fr 3f out: rdn over 1f out: sme prog but nvr cl enough to threaten* **33/1**

3554 **6** 4 ½ **Royal Caper**[3] 5128 3-9-1 **54** ....(v) FergusSweeney 4 41
(John Ryan) *hld up in last pair: taken to outer fr 3f out: rdn and no prog wl over 1f out* **3/1**[1]

2653 **7** shd **Ishisoba**[29] 4240 3-9-2 **55** .... SteveDrowne 7 41
(Alastair Lidderdale) *narrow ld to 4f out: pressed ldr to wl over 1f out: wknd* **8/1**

0655 **8** ¾ **Smart Alice**[25] 4391 3-8-7 **46** oh1 .... ChrisCatlin 2 30
(Chris Wall) *chsd ldng pair to jst over 2f out: sn wknd* **14/1**

556 **9** 1 **Father Fred**[32] 4143 3-8-8 **50** ....(p) RyanClark(3) 6 32
(Chris Dwyer) *dwlt: t.k.h: trckd ldrs to over 2f out: wknd* **16/1**

1m 29.67s (-2.63) **Going Correction** -0.40s/f (Firm) **9** Ran SP% **118.7**
Speed ratings (Par 98): **97,96,95,94,93 89,88,88,87**
toteswingers 1&2 £1.70, 1&3 £3.80, 2&3 £7.80 CSF £21.03 CT £121.22 TOTE £4.50: £2.40, £1.10, £1.80; EX 19.40 Trifecta £69.00 Pool: £1,856.45 - 20.15 winning units..
Owner Two Little Indians **Bred** D R Tucker **Trained** Royston, Herts

FOCUS
The form of this moderate handicap is limited but should work out. The winner built on his Yarmouth victory.

5276 BET ON YOUR MOBILE WITH LADBROKES NURSERY H'CAP — 6f
5:45 (5:45) (Class 6) (0-60,59) 2-Y-O — **£2,045** (£603; £302) **Stalls** High

Form RPR

5054 **1** **Oxlip**[25] 4363 2-8-12 **53** .... WilliamTwiston-Davies(3) 7 58+
(Richard Hannon) *trckd ldr: led jst over 2f out: drvn and pressed ins fnl f: hld on* **11/4**[2]

600 **2** ½ **Choral Clan (IRE)**[24] 4414 2-9-3 **55** .... JackMitchell 5 58
(Philip Mitchell) *hld up in last pair against nr side rail: prog 2f out: hrd rdn fr over 1f out: wnt 2nd ins fnl f and pressed wnr: jst hld* **5/2**[1]

0430 **3** 2 ½ **Debt Settler (IRE)**[8] 4948 2-9-0 **59** .... JackGarritty(7) 3 54
(Luke Dace) *stdd s: plld hrd in last pair: prog on outer over 2f out: wnt 2nd jst over 1f out and looked a threat: shkn up and fnd nil ins fnl f* **9/2**[3]

0054 **4** 6 **Maximilianthefirst**[5] 5066 2-8-10 **48** .... HarryBentley 4 24
(P J O'Gorman) *t.k.h: cl up on outer: pressed wnr 2f out to jst over 1f out: wknd qckly* **8/1**

006 **5** 7 **Bold Jack Donahue (IRE)**[14] 4773 2-9-6 **58** ....(b[1]) JamesDoyle 6 12
(Ralph Beckett) *led against nr side rail: hdd jst over 2f out: wknd rapidly: t.o* **5/2**[1]

1m 10.47s (-0.73) **Going Correction** -0.40s/f (Firm) **5** Ran SP% **113.1**
Speed ratings (Par 92): **88,87,84,76,66**
CSF £10.30 TOTE £3.40: £1.80, £1.50; EX 9.90 Trifecta £31.80 Pool: £1,356.85 - 31.90 winning units..
Owner Rockcliffe Stud **Bred** Rockcliffe Stud **Trained** East Everleigh, Wilts
■ Stewards' Enquiry : Jack Mitchell four-day ban: used whip above permitted level (Aug 24-27)

FOCUS
A weak nursery.

5277 LADBROKES MAIDEN STKS — 6f
6:15 (6:17) (Class 5) 3-Y-O+ — **£2,726** (£805; £402) **Stalls** High

Form RPR

232 **1** **Secret Beau**[15] 4710 3-9-5 75 ....(v) JamesDoyle 9 63+
(Ralph Beckett) *restless in stalls: trckd ldrs: clsd to chal 2f out: hrd rdn to ld jst ins fnl f: edgd lft but styd on* **2/7**[1]

2 ¾ **Pearl Angel (IRE)** 3-9-0 0 .... HarryBentley 4 56+
(Olly Stevens) *s.s: rcvrd and in tch in rr: prog over 2f out: clsd on ldrs 1f out: pressed wnr last 100yds: hld nr fin* **5/1**[2]

04 **3** 1 ¼ **Nifty Kier**[36] 4032 4-9-4 0 .... ThomasGarner(5) 2 57
(Martin Bosley) *w ldrs: led over 3f out: rdn over 1f out: hdd jst ins fnl f: one pce* **66/1**

00 **4** 2 ¼ **One In A Thousand (IRE)**[17] 4625 3-9-0 0 ....(p[1]) SaleemGolam 3 45
(Chris Dwyer) *chsd ldrs in 5th: rdn 2f out: tk 4th over 1f out: nt pce to threaten* **100/1**

0 **5** 3 ¼ **Presumido (IRE)**[25] 4382 3-9-5 0 .... AmirQuinn 8 39
(Simon Dow) *hld up in rr: pushed along over 2f out: no imp on ldrs after* **33/1**

6 **6** shd **Princess Bounty**[5] 5069 3-8-9 0 .... NathanAlison(5) 5 34
(Phil McEntee) *w ldrs: rdn over 2f out: wknd over 1f out* **20/1**

43 **7** 1 ½ **Mcdelta**[36] 4032 3-9-5 0 .... SebSanders 7 34
(Geoffrey Deacon) *hld up in rr: shuffled along fr over 2f out: no prog and nvr involved* **12/1**[3]

33 **8** 12 **Copper Trade**[14] 4774 3-9-5 0 .... JohnFahy 6
(Eve Johnson Houghton) *led against nr side rail to over 3f out: nt run on over 2f out and sn dropped out: t.o* **5/1**[2]

9 ½ **Be Gifted** 3-8-11 0 .... NataliaGemelova(3) 1
(John E Long) *rn v green and sn t.o* **33/1**

1m 10.17s (-1.03) **Going Correction** -0.40s/f (Firm)
WFA 3 from 4yo 4lb **9** Ran SP% **131.9**
Speed ratings (Par 103): **90,89,87,84,80 79,77,61,61**
toteswingers 1&2 £1.70, 1&3 £14.80, 2&3 £31.10 CSF £3.03 TOTE £1.40: £1.02, £1.70, £21.70; EX 3.90 Trifecta £91.50 Pool: £2,000.17 - 16.37 winning units..
Owner Mrs M E Slade **Bred** Mrs M E Slade **Trained** Kimpton, Hants

FOCUS
A weak maiden run in a slow time. There's some doubt as to what the form is worth.

5278 DOWNLOAD THE LADBROKES APP H'CAP — 6f
6:45 (6:45) (Class 5) (0-75,73) 3-Y-O+ — **£2,726** (£805; £402) **Stalls** High

Form RPR

6340 **1** **Clear Praise (USA)**[28] 4303 6-9-8 **71** .... SebSanders 4 83
(Simon Dow) *taken down early: mde all against nr side rail: 5 l clr over 4f out: ld eroded 2f out: urged along and drew away again over 1f out* **4/1**[3]

1100 **2** 2 ¾ **Panther Patrol (IRE)**[93] 2190 3-9-6 **73** .... FrankieDettori 6 76
(Eve Johnson Houghton) *chsd wnr and 5 l down over 4f out: clsd and in tch 2f out: drvn and lft bhd again over 1f out* **3/1**[2]

054 **3** 2 ¾ **Gung Ho Jack**[33] 4120 4-9-2 **65** .... JamesDoyle 8 59
(John Best) *chsd ldng pair: rdn 2f out: no imp after* **2/1**[1]

560 **4** 2 ¾ **Frognal (IRE)**[42] 3841 7-9-2 **68** ....(bt) CharlesBishop(3) 5 54
(Paddy Butler) *s.i.s: hld up and off the pce: no imp on ldrs in 4th fr 2f out* **8/1**

2443 **5** 3 ¼ **Belle Bayardo (IRE)**[15] 4712 5-9-5 **68** .... SteveDrowne 1 43
(Ronald Harris) *hld up and off the pce: shkn up and no prog over 2f out: fdd* **6/1**

6060 **6** 2 ½ **Blazing Knight (IRE)**[59] 3212 3-9-5 **72** .... JohnFahy 3 39
(Ralph Beckett) *a off the pce in rr: rdn and struggling over 2f out* **8/1**

1m 8.13s (-3.07) **Going Correction** -0.40s/f (Firm) course record
WFA 3 from 4yo+ 4lb **6** Ran SP% **114.8**
Speed ratings (Par 103): **104,100,96,93,88 85**
toteswingers 1&2 £3.60, 1&3 £2.90, 2&3 £2.10 CSF £16.87 CT £30.13 TOTE £5.10: £2.70, £1.10; EX 21.10 Trifecta £35.00 Pool: £894.22 - 19.14 winning units..
Owner Racing Clear Partnership **Bred** Juddmonte Farms Inc **Trained** Epsom, Surrey
■ Clear Praise broke the course record set back in 1986.

FOCUS
An ordinary sprint handicap. The winner got a soft lead but is rated to his turf best.

5279 LADBROKES / BRITISH STALLION STUDS EBF MAIDEN STKS — 1m (P)
7:15 (7:16) (Class 5) 2-Y-O — **£2,911** (£866; £432; £216) **Stalls** High

Form RPR

2 **1** **Hunters Creek (IRE)**[9] 4925 2-9-5 0 .... RobertHavlin 4 80
(John Gosden) *mde all: shkn up to assert over 1f out: rdn fnl f: ld dwindling nr fin* **4/6**[1]

36 **2** ½ **Art Wave (IRE)**[9] 4926 2-9-5 0 .... PaoloSirigu 7 79
(Marco Botti) *chsd wnr: rdn and no imp 2f out: styd on ins fnl f: clsng at fin* **12/1**

0 **3** 1 **Anipa**[22] 4491 2-9-0 0 .... FrankieDettori 5 72
(Ed Dunlop) *s.i.s: towards rr but in tch: rdn and prog 2f out: wnt 3rd fnl f: styd on but nvr able to chal* **6/1**[3]

4 7 **Sullivan Street (IRE)** 2-9-5 0 .... JamesDoyle 1 60
(Charlie Appleby) *trckd ldrs: shkn up over 2f out: pressed runner-up on inner over 1f out: wknd sn after* **6/1**[3]

05 **5** 4 **Jeremos (IRE)**[22] 4483 2-9-5 0 .... RichardHughes 9 51
(Richard Hannon) *racd wd: trckd ldrs: rdn over 2f out: lost grnd bnd sn after: wknd and eased* **5/1**[2]

00 **6** 13 **Stalactite (IRE)**[14] 4764 2-9-5 0 .... KierenFallon 2 21
(Charlie Appleby) *pushed along to chse ldrs: lost pl over 2f out: wd bnd sn after: eased and t.o* **16/1**

0 **7** 3 ¾ **Jarlath**[77] 2653 2-9-5 0 .... SteveDrowne 6 13
(Seamus Mullins) *sn struggling: t.o fr 1/2-way* **50/1**

8 6 **Lady Tee** 2-8-7 0 .... RyanWhile(7) 8
(Bill Turner) *v fractious bef s: in tch for 3f: sn t.o* **33/1**

1m 39.39s (1.19) **Going Correction** +0.05s/f (Slow) **8** Ran SP% **123.7**
Speed ratings (Par 94): **96,95,94,87,83 70,66,60**
toteswingers 1&2 £3.80, 1&3 £3.30, 2&3 £4.80 CSF £12.43 TOTE £1.70: £1.02, £3.70, £1.50; EX 11.90 Trifecta £43.40 Pool: £1,245.71 - 21.52 winning units..
Owner HRH Princess Haya Of Jordan **Bred** Airlie Stud **Trained** Newmarket, Suffolk

FOCUS
Not a bad 2yo maiden and the form looks sound.

5280 LADBROKES FOLLOW US ON TWITTER H'CAP — 7f (P)
7:45 (7:45) (Class 5) (0-70,75) 3-Y-O — **£2,726** (£805; £402) **Stalls** Low

Form RPR

1-40 **1** **Pivotal Movement**[52] 3472 3-9-7 **75** .... RichardHughes 6 85+
(Richard Hannon) *mde all: dictated mod pce but untrbld: kicked clr 2f out: drvn fnl f: a holding on* **7/4**[1]

13-4 **2** 1 **Broughtons Charm (IRE)**[38] 3956 3-9-5 **73** .... KierenFallon 8 77
(Willie Musson) *t.k.h early: a in 2nd: outpcd by wnr 2f out: styd on to cl gap fnl f: nvr able to chal* **7/2**[2]

0543 **3** ½ **Lucky Di**[38] 3956 3-9-2 **73** .... CharlesBishop(3) 4 76
(Peter Hedger) *hld up in last trio: nt clr run briefly on inner 2f out as wnr wnt clr: prog over 1f out: styd on fnl f: nvr able to chal* **8/1**

2665 4 ½ **Keene's Pointe**[28] 4288 3-9-5 **73**........................ SebSanders 2 75
(J W Hills) *t.k.h: hld up in tch: rdn 2f out: hanging and nt qckn over 1f out: styd on again ins fnl f* **6/1**

-416 5 1 ¾ **Oasis Spirit**[23] 4453 3-9-1 **72**........................ ThomasBrown(3) 7 69
(Andrew Balding) *hld up in last trio: wd bnd 2f out and rdn: nvr any ch after: kpt on* **7/1**

0242 6 ½ **Club House (IRE)**[22] 4504 3-9-2 **70**........................ JamesDoyle 5 66
(Robert Mills) *dwlt: hld up in last trio: pushed along and prog over 1f out: rdn and fnd nil fnl f* **5/1**[3]

06U 7 5 **Kamchatka**[7] 4998 3-9-0 **68**........................(t) FergusSweeney 3 50
(Philip Hide) *chsd ldrs: drvn over 2f out: sn wknd* **25/1**

15-6 8 2 ¾ **Bobby Two Shoes**[19] 4592 3-9-1 **72**............ WilliamTwiston-Davies(3) 1 47
(Brett Johnson) *chsd ldrs: rdn over 2f out: wknd qckly over 1f out* **25/1**

1m 26.65s (1.85) **Going Correction** +0.05s/f (Slow) **8** Ran SP% **120.8**
Speed ratings (Par 100): **91,89,89,88,86 86,80,77**
toteswingers 1&2 £1.80, 1&3 £4.50, 2&3 £4.90 CSF £8.56 CT £38.63 TOTE £2.10: £1.02, £1.80, £3.40; EX 11.40 Trifecta £43.30 Pool: £1,012.71 - 17.52 winning units..
Owner Sir A Ferguson,G Mason,R Wood & P Done **Bred** W And R Barnett Ltd **Trained** East Everleigh, Wilts

FOCUS
A steadily run 3-y-o handicap. The winner rates better than the bare form, with the third a good guide.

5281 DOWNLOAD THE LADBROKES APP MEDIAN AUCTION MAIDEN STKS 1m 2f (P)

8:15 (8:16) (Class 6) 3-4-Y-O **£2,045** (£603; £302) **Stalls** Low

Form RPR

2333 1 **Playbill**[22] 4506 3-8-12 74........................ RichardHughes 1 73
(Sir Michael Stoute) *led 3f: pressed ldr: led again over 3f out: shkn up and drew clr fr 2f out: eased last 50yds* **4/5**[1]

4 2 4 ½ **Al Guwair (IRE)**[42] 3821 3-9-3 0........................ FrankieDettori 10 69
(Lady Cecil) *led after 3f to over 3f out: rdn and outpcd by wnr 2f out: styd on to keep 2nd pl* **7/4**[2]

06 3 hd **The Wizard Of Aus (IRE)**[19] 4590 3-9-0 0.............. ThomasBrown(3) 4 69
(Andrew Balding) *trckd ldrs: gng bttr than most 3f out: rdn and effrt 2f out: pressed for 2nd fnl f: styd on* **7/1**[3]

0 4 7 **Rainbows And Roses**[82] 2519 3-8-12 0........................ TedDurcan 5 50
(Chris Wall) *chsd ldrs: pushed along over 4f out: cl enough 3f out: wknd 2f out* **10/1**

0 5 1 ¼ **Eco Warrior**[7] 4978 3-9-3 0........................ SebSanders 9 52
(J W Hills) *trckd ldrs on outer: rdn and cl enough 3f out: wknd 2f out* **33/1**

00 6 2 ½ **Le Tigre De Bronze**[38] 3957 3-9-3 0........................ DougieCostello 3 47
(Hughie Morrison) *settled towards rr: pushed along and outpcd in 6th over 3f out: nvr on terms after* **33/1**

7 4 ½ **Maygo's Joy** 3-9-3 0........................ RobertHavlin 8 38
(Jamie Poulton) *a in rr: struggling in last trio 4f out* **50/1**

0 8 3 **Karitza (FR)**[32] 4152 3-8-12 0........................ JamesDoyle 2 27
(Jeremy Gask) *a towards rr: rdn 5f out: struggling in last trio 4f out* **66/1**

0 9 1 **Tarmo (IRE)**[17] 4632 3-9-3 0........................ PaoloSirigu 7 30
(Marco Botti) *rrd s and v.s.a: a bhd* **50/1**

2m 6.73s (0.13) **Going Correction** +0.05s/f (Slow)
WFA 3 from 4yo 9lb **9** Ran SP% **124.8**
Speed ratings (Par 101): **101,97,97,91,90 88,85,82,81**
toteswingers 1&2 £1.02, 1&3 £2.70, 2&3 £4.00 CSF £2.63 TOTE £1.60: £1.02, £1.20, £1.50; EX 2.70 Trifecta £8.40 Pool: £986.49 - 87.50 winning units..
Owner Lady Rothschild **Bred** Carwell Equities Ltd **Trained** Newmarket, Suffolk

FOCUS
Straightforward enough maiden form, although a race with little depth.
T/Plt: £13.30 to a £1 stake. Pool: £59,473.71 - 3,263.79 winning units T/Qpdt: £4.30 to a £1 stake. Pool: £6,474.33 - 1,106.19 winning units JN

5242 NEWMARKET (R-H)

Saturday, August 10

OFFICIAL GOING: Good to firm (watered; 7.8)
Wind: Light; half-behind Weather: Overcast

5282 BBAG-SALES.DE-THE GERMAN BLOODSTOCK SALES MAIDEN FILLIES' STKS 7f

2:25 (2:25) (Class 4) 2-Y-O **£3,881** (£1,155; £577; £288) **Stalls** Low

Form RPR

1 **Night Song** 2-9-0 0........................ WilliamBuick 5 79+
(John Gosden) *s.i.s and rn green in rr: pushed along over 2f out: swtchd rt and hdwy over 1f out: r.o to ld wl ins fnl f: edgd lft: readily* **9/2**[2]

2 ¾ **Casual Smile** 2-9-0 0........................ DavidProbert 8 77+
(Andrew Balding) *mid-div: hdwy over 2f out: rdn over 1f out: r.o* **10/1**

3 1 **Dime Dancer (IRE)** 2-9-0 0........................ RichardHughes 3 74
(Richard Hannon) *a.p: rdn over 1f out: styd on* **6/1**[3]

4 1 **My Painter (IRE)** 2-9-0 0........................ FrankieDettori 13 72
(Charles Hills) *chsd ldrs: rdn to ld over 1f out: edgd lft: hdd and unable qck wl ins fnl f* **20/1**

5 ¾ **Wahgah (USA)** 2-9-0 0........................ PaulHanagan 12 70+
(Saeed bin Suroor) *hld up: hdwy u.p and hung lft over 1f out: styd on: nt trble ldrs* **10/11**[1]

6 ½ **Christmas Wish** 2-9-0 0........................ MartinHarley 10 68
(Mick Channon) *chsd ldrs: swished tail sn after s: rdn over 2f out: ev ch over 1f out: styd on same pce ins fnl f* **40/1**

7 ¾ **Wedding Wish (IRE)** 2-9-0 0........................ JamieSpencer 7 66
(Michael Bell) *led: rdn and hdd over 1f out: no ex ins fnl f* **14/1**

8 ¾ **Great Wave (IRE)** 2-9-0 0........................ RichardMullen 11 64
(David Simcock) *prom: rdn over 2f out: no ex ins fnl f* **50/1**

9 1 ¼ **Ghinia (IRE)** 2-9-0 0........................ FergusSweeney 9 61
(Pam Sly) *dwlt: hld up: hdwy over 2f out: sn rdn: styd on same pce fr over 1f out* **66/1**

10 ½ **Bella Varenna (IRE)** 2-9-0 0........................ NeilCallan 14 59
(Marco Botti) *edgd rt s: chsd ldrs: rdn over 2f out: styd on same pce appr fnl f* **33/1**

11 ¾ **Three Heart's** 2-9-0 0........................ MartinDwyer 6 57+
(Hugo Palmer) *hld up: pushed along 1/2-way: n.d* **66/1**

12 ¾ **Step Away** 2-9-0 0........................ SteveDrowne 1 55
(Charles Hills) *hld up: rdn over 2f out: n.d* **33/1**

13 2 ½ **Thatchereen (IRE)** 2-9-0 0........................ JohnFahy 2 49
(Michael Bell) *s.i.s: a in rr* **100/1**

14 1 ¾ **Poetic Choice** 2-9-0 0........................ J-PGuillambert 4 44
(Nick Littmoden) *hld up: rdn over 2f out: wknd over 1f out* **40/1**

1m 26.67s (0.97) **Going Correction** -0.12s/f (Firm) **14** Ran SP% **122.1**
Speed ratings (Par 93): **89,88,87,85,85 84,83,82,81,80 79,79,76,74**
toteswingers 1&2 £6.70, 1&3 £3.20, 2&3 £4.90 CSF £45.50 TOTE £5.80: £1.60, £2.60, £2.10; EX 41.90 Trifecta £207.70 Pool: £1,371.98 - 4.95 winning units..
Owner Lady Bamford & Alice Bamford **Bred** New England Stud And Partners **Trained** Newmarket, Suffolk

FOCUS
Far side track used with stalls on far side except 1m2f, 1m4f & 2m: centre. Repositioning of the bend into the home straight increased distances of races at 1m2f-plus by 18 metres. This maiden for unraced fillies' has gone to subsequent Group 1 winners twice in the past decade, namely Passage Of Time (2006), who won the Criterium de Saint-Cloud, and last season Winsili, who recently landed the Nassau. The visual impression of this year's race was they went steady early (plenty were keen, time 2.6secs slower than Sweet Solera), but started 'racing' quite a way out.

5283 RACEBETS.COM - THE BIGGEST RACING OFFER WORLDWIDE H'CAP 1m 2f

3:00 (3:01) (Class 2) (0-100,97) 3-Y-O+ **£12,938** (£3,850; £1,924; £962) **Stalls** Centre

Form RPR

0206 1 **Strictly Silver (IRE)**[11] 4854 4-9-9 **97**........................(p) RobertTart(5) 7 106
(Alan Bailey) *a.p: jnd ldrs over 3f out: led over 2f out: rdn and edgd lft fr over 1f out: styd on* **8/1**

5151 2 ¾ **Ningara**[16] 4683 3-8-5 **83**........................ DavidProbert 6 91+
(Andrew Balding) *hld up: hdwy and nt clr run over 2f out: rdn to chse wnr fnl f: r.o* **5/2**[1]

2601 3 2 **Clayton**[14] 4765 4-9-13 **96**........................ FrankieDettori 5 100
(Kevin Ryan) *chsd ldr tl pushed along over 3f out: rdn over 1f out: styd on same pce ins fnl f* **7/1**

3464 4 hd **Proud Chieftain**[7] 5007 5-9-12 **95**........................(b[1]) PaulHanagan 4 98
(Clifford Lines) *hld up: hdwy 1/2-way: rdn and outpcd over 1f out: rallied ins fnl f: r.o* **14/1**

1/2- 5 1 **Conduct (IRE)**[371] 4795 6-10-0 **97**........................ RichardHughes 9 98
(William Haggas) *chsd ldrs: led wl over 2f out: sn hdd: rdn over 1f out: edgd lft and no ex ins fnl f* **13/2**[3]

21-0 6 1 ¼ **True To Form (IRE)**[42] 3812 6-9-1 **84**........................ MartinDwyer 3 83
(Alan McCabe) *s.i.s: hld up: rdn over 2f out: styd on ins fnl f: nvr nrr* **28/1**

00-0 7 1 ¼ **Creme Anglaise**[10] 4878 5-9-6 **89**........................ JamieSpencer 10 85
(Michael Bell) *s.i.s: hld up: pushed along over 3f out: nvr nrr* **33/1**

/14- 8 ¾ **Anomaly**[415] 3296 4-9-12 **95**........................ WilliamBuick 1 90
(Charlie Appleby) *stmbld s: sn prom: rdn and ev ch over 2f out: wknd fnl f* **9/2**[2]

2000 9 1 **Beaumont's Party (IRE)**[28] 4310 6-9-11 **94**........................ DaleSwift 2 87
(Brian Ellison) *hld up: racd keenly: hdwy over 4f out: rdn over 2f out: wknd over 1f out* **10/1**

0354 10 ½ **Fennell Bay (IRE)**[7] 4979 4-9-6 **89**........................ NeilCallan 8 81
(Mark Johnston) *led: rdn and hdd wl over 2f out: wknd over 1f out* **8/1**

2m 4.09s (-1.41) **Going Correction** -0.125s/f (Firm)
WFA 3 from 4yo+ 9lb **10** Ran SP% **117.0**
Speed ratings (Par 109): **100,99,97,97,96 95,94,94,93,93**
toteswingers 1&2 £7.20, 1&3 £5.90, 2&3 £6.50 CSF £28.38 CT £150.61 TOTE £10.60: £2.50, £1.30, £2.30; EX 41.30 Trifecta £443.80 Pool: £1,784.68 - 3.01 winning units..
Owner A J H **Bred** Langton Stud **Trained** Newmarket, Suffolk

FOCUS
A decent enough handicap if most of them were fairly exposed. The winner rates a length personal best.

5284 GERMAN-THOROUGHBRED.COM SWEET SOLERA STKS (GROUP 3) (FILLIES) 7f

3:35 (3:35) (Class 1) 2-Y-O

£28,355 (£10,750; £5,380; £2,680; £1,345; £675) **Stalls** Low

Form RPR

223 1 **Ihtimal (IRE)**[49] 3555 2-8-12 94........................ WilliamBuick 7 104+
(Saeed bin Suroor) *chsd ldrs: shkn up over 2f out: led over 1f out: rdn and r.o wl* **11/4**[1]

1032 2 2 ¾ **Midnite Angel (IRE)**[7] 5005 2-8-12 90........................ FrankieDettori 6 97
(Richard Hannon) *dwlt: hld up: hdwy over 1f out: rdn to chse wnr fnl f: styd on same pce* **3/1**[2]

15 3 ½ **Wedding Ring (IRE)**[50] 3522 2-8-12 0........................ JamieSpencer 8 96+
(Charlie Appleby) *hld up: hdwy 2f out: rdn over 1f out: styd on same pce ins fnl f* **7/2**[3]

021 4 1 ¾ **Adhwaa**[23] 4432 2-8-12 85........................ PaulHanagan 9 91
(J W Hills) *led: rdn and hdd over 1f out: no ex ins fnl f* **16/1**

362 5 2 ¾ **Tinga (IRE)**[23] 4432 2-8-12 84........................ MartinHarley 3 84
(Mick Channon) *stmbld s: sn chsng ldr: rdn over 2f out: wknd fnl f* **16/1**

513 6 ¾ **Lamar (IRE)**[16] 4682 2-8-12 89........................ NeilCallan 4 82
(James Tate) *prom: chsd ldr 1/2-way: rdn over 1f out: wknd fnl f* **12/1**

4021 7 5 **Clever Miss**[32] 4154 2-8-12 79........................ MartinDwyer 2 69
(Alan McCabe) *hld up: racd keenly: rdn over 2f out: wknd over 1f out* **66/1**

1 8 5 **Baby Bush (IRE)**[37] 3986 2-8-12 0........................ RichardHughes 1 56
(Richard Hannon) *hld up: pushed along over 2f out: rdn and wknd over 1f out* **5/1**

1m 24.07s (-1.63) **Going Correction** -0.125s/f (Firm) **8** Ran SP% **111.5**
Speed ratings (Par 101): **104,100,100,98,95 94,88,82**
toteswingers 1&2 £2.40, 1&3 £2.60, 2&3 £1.40 CSF £10.62 TOTE £3.80: £1.50, £1.40, £1.70; EX 11.20 Trifecta £43.50 Pool: £2,852.98 - 49.15 winning units..
Owner Godolphin **Bred** Darley **Trained** Newmarket, Suffolk

FOCUS
This is usually a good, informative contest and has been won subsequent top-level winners such as Maids Causeway (Coronation Stakes), Rainbow View (Fillies' Mile, Matron Stakes), White Moonstone (Fillies' Mile) and, just last year, Certify (Fillies' Mile), who was followed home by Sky Lantern (Moyglare Stud Stakes, 1000 Guineas, Coronation Stakes). It's hard to get too excited by the form of this year's edition.

5285 BREED GERMAN-BUY GERMAN-WIN GERMAN H'CAP 7f

4:10 (4:10) (Class 2) (0-105,99) 3-Y-O+

£12,450 (£3,728; £1,864; £932; £466; £234) **Stalls** Low

Form RPR

-200 1 **Gabriel's Lad (IRE)**[42] 3846 4-9-8 **95**........................ PaulHanagan 13 106
(Denis Coakley) *hld up: hdwy over 2f out: shkn up to ld over 1f out: rdn out* **9/2**[2]

2204 2 nk **Democretes**[11] 4859 4-9-3 **90**........................(p) RichardHughes 9 100+
(Richard Hannon) *prom: nt clr run and lost pl over 2f out: hdwy u.p and hung lft over 1f out: r.o* **9/2**[2]

0106 **3** 1 1/4 **Highland Colori (IRE)**[28] 4297 5-9-12 **99**.................... DavidProbert 12 106
(Andrew Balding) *led: hdd over 5f out: chsd ldr: rdn and ev ch over 1f out: styd on* **7/2**[1]

1400 **4** *nk* **Head Of Steam (USA)**[11] 4859 6-9-2 **89**.................... PatDobbs 8 95
(Amanda Perrett) *hld up: hdwy over 1f out: sn rdn: r.o: nt rch ldrs* **12/1**

5234 **5** 2 1/4 **Albaqaa**[8] 4960 8-8-10 **83**.................... WilliamCarson 5 83
(P J O'Gorman) *a.p: rdn over 1f out: styd on same pce fnl f* **12/1**

6330 **6** 2 1/2 **I'm So Glad**[21] 4534 4-9-2 **92**.................... CharlesBishop(3) 4 85
(Mick Channon) *chsd ldrs: led over 5f out: rdn and hdd over 1f out: wknd ins fnl f* **14/1**

4440 **7** 1/2 **Ducal**[14] 4744 5-9-0 **87**.................... TedDurcan 11 79
(Mike Murphy) *hld up: effrt over 1f out: nvr on terms* **16/1**

1000 **8** 1/2 **Capaill Liath (IRE)**[11] 4859 5-9-1 **88**....................(b) NeilCallan 14 78
(Kevin Ryan) *chsd ldrs: rdn over 1f out: wknd fnl f* **33/1**

0600 **9** 1 **Common Touch (IRE)**[14] 4744 5-9-0 **87**....................(b) WilliamBuick 6 75
(Willie Musson) *rrd s: hld up: rdn over 1f out: a in rr* **7/1**[3]

621 **10** 3/4 **Shamdarley (IRE)**[38] 3961 5-9-2 **89**....................(p) MartinHarley 2 75
(Marco Botti) *prom: rdn over 2f out: wknd ins fnl f* **7/1**[3]

00-0 **11** 8 **Arabian Star (IRE)**[28] 4308 5-8-12 **85**.................... MartinDwyer 1 49
(Alan McCabe) *hld up: effrt over 2f out: hung lft and wknd over 1f out* **50/1**

1m 23.18s (-2.52) **Going Correction** -0.125s/f (Firm) **11** Ran SP% **116.4**
Speed ratings (Par 109): **109,108,107,106,104 101,100,100,99,98 89**
toteswingers 1&2 £6.80, 1&3 £4.40, 2&3 £3.90 CSF £24.80 CT £78.97 TOTE £6.10: £2.20, £1.40, £1.80; EX 26.60 Trifecta £101.80 Pool: £2,653.08 - 19.54 winning units..
Owner Killoran Ennis Conway **Bred** Yeomanstown Stud **Trained** West Ilsley, Berks

FOCUS
A good, competitive handicap, which was sound run. The winner belatedly built on his 3yo form.

5286 POPPY MAIDEN STKS 1m 4f
4:45 (4:45) (Class 5) 3-Y-0+ **£3,234** (£962; £481; £240) **Stalls** Centre

Form RPR

4444 **1** **She's Late**[38] 3957 3-9-1 76....................(p) WilliamBuick 4 92
(John Gosden) *trckd ldr: racd keenly: rdn over 2f out: edgd rt over 1f out: styd on to ld nr fin* **10/1**[3]

32 **2** 3/4 **Bostonian**[15] 4719 3-9-1 0.................... NeilCallan 6 91+
(Mark Johnston) *led at stdy pce tl qckng 3f out: rdn and hung lft over 1f out: hdd nr fin* **9/4**[2]

2 **3** 1 **Refectory (IRE)**[29] 4257 3-9-1 0.................... RichardHughes 5 89+
(Andrew Balding) *s.i.s: hld up: hdwy 1/2-way: rdn over 3f out: sn outpcd: rallied u.p fnl f: r.o* **8/11**[1]

4 4 **Ridgeway Storm (IRE)** 3-9-1 0.................... PatCosgrave 7 83
(Lady Cecil) *hld up: pushed along 4f out: outpcd over 2f out: styd on ins fnl f* **14/1**

06 **5** 4 1/2 **Markttag**[54] 3417 3-8-12 0.................... PatrickHills(3) 1 76+
(Luca Cumani) *prom: rdn over 3f out: wknd over 1f out* **33/1**

2465 **6** 9 **Enaitch (IRE)**[24] 4417 3-8-10 72.................... MartinHarley 9 56
(Mick Channon) *chsd ldrs: rdn over 3f out: wknd over 2f out* **20/1**

2m 32.65s (-0.25) **Going Correction** -0.125s/f (Firm)
WFA 3 from 4yo+ 11lb **6** Ran SP% **112.1**
Speed ratings (Par 103): **95,94,93,91,88 82**
toteswingers 1&2 £2.20, 1&3 £2.40, 2&3 £1.30 CSF £32.74 TOTE £7.10: £2.30, £1.80; EX 20.70 Trifecta £46.20 Pool: £3,866.14 - 62.68 winning units..
Owner Martin Hughes & Michael Kerr-Dineen **Bred** Cheveley Park Stud Ltd **Trained** Newmarket, Suffolk

FOCUS
Not a bad maiden, but rather muddling. The winner took advantage of the favourite running below form and the runner-up hanging.

5287 ROYAL BRITISH LEGION H'CAP 1m
5:20 (5:21) (Class 2) (0-100,98) 3-Y-0 **£12,938** (£3,850; £1,924; £962) **Stalls** Low

Form RPR

53-1 **1** **Breden (IRE)**[25] 4382 3-8-6 **83** ow1.................... WilliamBuick 4 91+
(John Gosden) *hld up: rdn: swtchd lft and hdwy over 1f out: r.o u.p to ld nr fin* **11/4**[1]

5431 **2** *shd* **Top Notch Tonto (IRE)**[14] 4769 3-9-1 **92**.................... DaleSwift 7 99
(Brian Ellison) *sn chsng ldrs: rdn to ld over 1f out: r.o u.p: hdd nr fin* **8/1**

1-22 **3** 3/4 **Veeraya**[22] 4492 3-8-8 **85**....................(p) NeilCallan 5 90
(William Haggas) *hld up: hdwy u.p over 1f out: r.o: nt rch ldrs* **5/1**

5231 **4** *nk* **Bold Prediction (IRE)**[19] 4581 3-8-4 **81**.................... MartinDwyer 8 86
(Mrs K Burke) *led: hdd over 6f out: chsd ldr tl led again 2f out: sn rdn: edgd rt and hdd: styd on same pce ins fnl f* **20/1**

660 **5** 2 3/4 **Ayaar (IRE)**[51] 3484 3-9-7 **98**.................... MartinHarley 2 96
(Mick Channon) *hld up: rdn over 2f out: nt trble ldrs* **20/1**

-061 **6** *hd* **Azrur (IRE)**[49] 3582 3-8-11 **88**.................... JamieSpencer 3 86
(Michael Bell) *chsd ldrs: led over 6f out: rdn and hdd 2f out: edgd rt: no ex ins fnl f* **12/1**

0213 **7** 2 1/2 **Intrigo**[14] 4743 3-9-5 **96**.................... RichardHughes 6 88
(Richard Hannon) *chsd ldrs: rdn over 2f out: no ex fnl f: eased towards fin* **7/2**[2]

-412 **8** 20 **Altharoos (IRE)**[15] 4733 3-8-10 **87**.................... PaulHanagan 1 65
(Sir Michael Stoute) *hld up: rdn over 2f out: wknd and eased over 1f out* **4/1**[3]

1m 37.75s (-2.25) **Going Correction** -0.125s/f (Firm) **8** Ran SP% **113.9**
Speed ratings (Par 106): **106,105,105,104,102 101,99,79**
toteswingers 1&2 £4.00, 1&3 £7.40, 2&3 £7.30 CSF £25.22 CT £102.21 TOTE £4.20: £1.90, £3.10, £1.40; EX 30.40 Trifecta £121.30 Pool: £2,745.96 - 16.97 winning units..
Owner Lady Rothschild **Bred** Mrs C L Weld **Trained** Newmarket, Suffolk

FOCUS
A couple of the fancied runners bombed out, but the form still looks pretty good. The winner could do better.

5288 ALZHEIMER'S RESEARCH UK H'CAP (IN MEMORY OF REG DAY) 2m 24y
5:55 (5:58) (Class 3) (0-90,90) 3-Y-0+ **£9,056** (£2,695; £1,346; £673) **Stalls** Centre

Form RPR

2241 **1** **Argent Knight**[24] 4417 3-8-4 **81**....................(v) PaulHanagan 1 93
(William Jarvis) *hld up in tch: chsd ldr over 3f out: shkn up to ld over 2f out: rdn over 1f out: edgd lft ins fnl f: styd on* **11/4**[1]

5-03 **2** 1 1/2 **Waterclock (IRE)**[18] 4606 4-9-7 **83**.................... GeorgeBaker 12 93
(Roger Charlton) *hld up: hdwy over 2f out: sn rdn: chsd wnr over 1f out: swtchd lft ins fnl f: unable qck towards fin* **14/1**

0641 **3** 3 3/4 **Eagle Rock (IRE)**[28] 4313 5-9-3 **79**....................(p) MickyFenton 5 85
(Tom Tate) *chsd ldrs: rdn and ev ch over 2f out: styd on same pce fnl f* **10/1**

-110 **4** 3/4 **Arch Villain (IRE)**[42] 3824 4-10-0 **90**.................... PatDobbs 10 95
(Amanda Perrett) *hld up: hdwy over 4f out: rdn over 1f out: styd on same pce fnl f* **15/2**

4113 **5** 2 1/4 **Good Evans**[28] 4286 3-8-1 **78**.................... KieranO'Neill 6 80
(Tom Dascombe) *chsd ldr: led over 12f out tl over 10f out: led again over 4f out: rdn and hdd over 2f out: wknd ins fnl f* **5/1**[2]

003 **6** 13 **Cosimo de Medici**[17] 4643 6-9-2 **78**.................... WilliamBuick 8 64
(Hughie Morrison) *free to post: hld up: bhd 12f out: hdwy over 4f out: rdn and wknd over 2f out* **12/1**

12-0 **7** 6 **Courtesy Call (IRE)**[49] 3560 4-9-10 **86**.................... NeilCallan 4 65
(Nicky Henderson) *prom: rdn over 2f out: wknd over 1f out* **6/1**[3]

0114 **8** 4 **Big Time Billy (IRE)**[28] 4313 7-8-13 **75**....................(v) DougieCostello 15 49
(Peter Bowen) *sn prom: rdn over 4f out: wknd over 2f out* **6/1**[3]

0-04 **9** 8 **Sergeant Ablett (IRE)**[36] 4029 5-9-2 **78**....................(p) AidanColeman 3 43
(Luke Dace) *prom: rdn over 3f out: wknd over 2f out* **40/1**

-403 **10** 10 **Danvilla**[64] 3065 6-9-4 **80**.................... WilliamCarson 2 33
(Paul Webber) *led: hdd over 12f out: led again over 10f out: hdd over 4f out: wknd and eased over 2f out* **16/1**

04-0 **11** 25 **Suzi's A Class Act**[9] 4920 5-9-5 **81**....................(p) FrederikTylicki 9
(Paul D'Arcy) *hld up: rdn over 4f out: sn wknd and eased* **28/1**

50-0 **12** 30 **Bernie The Bolt (IRE)**[84] 2451 7-9-4 **80**....................[1] DavidProbert 11
(Andrew Balding) *s.i.s: hld up: in rr and pushed along 1/2-way: wknd over 5f out: eased* **20/1**

3m 23.03s (-3.97) **Going Correction** -0.125s/f (Firm)
WFA 3 from 4yo+ 15lb **12** Ran SP% **123.7**
Speed ratings (Par 107): **104,103,101,101,99 93,90,88,84,79 66,51**
toteswingers 1&2 £10.30, 1&3 £10.20, 2&3 £18.40 CSF £46.21 CT £353.97 TOTE £4.10: £1.60, £3.70, £3.20; EX 48.60 Trifecta £706.00 Pool: £3,683.39 - 3.91 winning units..
Owner Dr J Walker **Bred** Mr & Mrs A E Pakenham **Trained** Newmarket, Suffolk

FOCUS
A good staying handicap for the grade. Personal bests from the 1-2.
T/Jkpt: Not won. T/Plt: £76.50 to a £1 stake. Pool: £98,203.44 - 936.36 winning units T/Qpdt: £15.20 to a £1 stake. Pool: £5,996.60 - 291.90 winning units CR

4886 REDCAR (L-H)
Saturday, August 10

OFFICIAL GOING: Good to firm (firm in places; watered; 9.1)
Wind: Moderate; half against Weather: Overcast

5289 RACING UK ICARD FOR TODAY'S RACECARDS (S) STKS 6f
2:00 (2:00) (Class 6) 2-Y-O **£2,045** (£603; £302) **Stalls** Centre

Form RPR

3215 **1** **Lady Captain (IRE)**[8] 4964 2-8-12 61....................(p) PaulMulrennan 3 61
(Kevin Ryan) *mde virtually all: jnd and drvn over 2f out: carried hd high: kpt on towards fin* **6/4**[1]

2400 **2** 1 3/4 **Midnight Muscida (IRE)**[11] 4847 2-8-7 58 ow1....................(b) DavidAllan 5 49
(Tim Easterby) *trckd ldrs: effrt over 2f out: wnt 2nd 1f out: kpt on same pce last 50yds* **7/2**[3]

004 **3** 3 1/4 **Highland Princess (IRE)**[21] 4538 2-8-1 43.................... ShirleyTeasdale(5) 7 38
(Paul Midgley) *w wnr: drvn over 2f out: fdd fnl f* **16/1**

4206 **4** 1 1/4 **Jaga Time**[8] 4964 2-8-11 55....................(b[1]) TonyHamilton 2 39
(Richard Fahey) *wnt lft s: sn chsng ldrs: drvn and outpcd over 2f out: chsd ldrs over 1f out: sn wknd* **7/4**[2]

00 **5** 10 **Elsie Bond**[21] 4538 2-8-6 0....................(b) JamesSullivan 1 2
(Tim Easterby) *hmpd and wnt lft s: sn chsng ldrs: drvn 3f out: sn lost pl and bhd* **33/1**

1m 13.2s (1.40) **Going Correction** -0.325s/f (Firm) **5** Ran SP% **107.4**
Speed ratings (Par 92): **77,74,70,68,55**
CSF £6.72 TOTE £1.70: £1.70, £1.10; EX 5.90 Trifecta £23.60 Pool: £818.15 - 25.93 winning units..There was no bid for the winner.
Owner Mrs J Ryan **Bred** Noel O'Callaghan **Trained** Hambleton, N Yorks

FOCUS
A moderate seller got proceedings underway in which there was a contested pace.

5290 FOLLOW REDCARRACING ON FACEBOOK & TWITTER MEDIAN AUCTION MAIDEN STKS 7f
2:35 (2:35) (Class 5) 3-4-Y-O **£2,587** (£770; £384; £192) **Stalls** Centre

Form RPR

0400 **1** **Fab Lolly (IRE)**[38] 3946 3-8-12 60.................... JamesSullivan 7 58
(James Bethell) *hld up: hdwy over 3f out: rdn to chse wnr 1f out: edgd lft and kpt on to ld last 30yds* **9/1**

-443 **2** *nk* **Mishaal (IRE)**[10] 4887 3-9-3 67.................... BarryMcHugh 5 62
(Michael Herrington) *bmpd s: t.k.h: led: hdd and no ex wl ins fnl f* **15/8**[2]

3 4 1/2 **Discussiontofollow (IRE)** 3-9-3 0.................... PaulMulrennan 1 50+
(Geoffrey Harker) *dwlt: t.k.h: sn trcking ldrs: drvn 2f out: sn w ldrs: rdn and wknd 1f out* **5/4**[1]

00 **4** 1 **Maillot Jaune (IRE)**[36] 4013 3-8-7 0.................... DeclanBates(5) 8 42
(Patrick Holmes) *in rr: outpcd and lost pl 3f out: hdwy over 1f out: keeping on at fin* **80/1**

000 **5** *nk* **Medecis Mountain**[74] 2757 4-9-9 41....................(p) GrahamGibbons 3 48
(Neville Bycroft) *wnt rt s: sn upsides ldr: wknd appr fnl f* **40/1**

4- **6** 3/4 **Mon Chic**[311] 6781 3-8-12 0.................... RoystonFfrench 4 39
(Geoffrey Oldroyd) *wnt rt s: chsd ldrs: drvn over 2f out: wknd over 1f out* **33/1**

7 9 **Spring Bird** 4-9-4 0.................... PaulQuinn 2 17
(David Nicholls) *hmpd s: t.k.h in rr: hdwy to chse ldrs over 4f out: drvn over 3f out: sn lost pl and bhd* **25/1**

0 **8** 1 1/2 **St Elmo's Fire**[49] 3585 3-9-3 0.................... LiamJones 6 16
(Peter Chapple-Hyam) *drvn to chse ldrs: lost pl wl over 1f out: sn bhd* **9/2**[3]

1m 24.45s (-0.05) **Going Correction** -0.325s/f (Firm)
WFA 3 from 4yo 6lb **8** Ran SP% **117.9**
Speed ratings (Par 103): **87,86,81,80,80 79,68,67**
toteswingers 1&2 £2.20, 1&3 £2.90, 2&3 £1.90 CSF £26.78 TOTE £10.20: £2.50, £1.10, £1.10; EX 23.70 Trifecta £63.40 Pool: £1,390.76 - 16.45 winning units..
Owner James Lambert **Bred** James F Hanly **Trained** Middleham Moor, N Yorks

FOCUS
A weak maiden in which the runner-up set an honest gallop. The form is rated cautiously.

5291 DOWNLOAD THE FREE RACING UK APP H'CAP (QUALIFIER FOR STRAIGHT-MILE CHAMPIONSHIP) 1m
3:10 (3:10) (Class 4) 3-Y-0+ **£6,469** (£1,925; £962; £481) **Stalls** Centre

Form RPR

3046 **1** **Ingleby Angel (IRE)**[7] 5014 4-9-11 **83**.................... GrahamGibbons 6 92
(David O'Meara) *trckd ldrs: drvn to chse ldr 1f out: styd on to ld nr fin* **10/3**[2]

3020 **2** *nk* **Kiwi Bay**[35] 4055 8-9-3 **75**.. PaulMulrennan 3 83
(Michael Dods) *led: qcknd pce 3f out: no ex and hdd clsng stages* **9/2**[3]
5106 **3** *1 ½* **Hakuna Matata**[21] 4540 6-9-6 **78**..(b) LeeTopliss 9 83
(Michael Dods) *wnt rt s: hld up in rr: hdwy over 2f out: drvn and chsng ldrs over 1f out: styd on same pce ins fnl f* **11/1**
2022 **4** *3* **Karaka Jack**[7] 5014 6-9-10 **82**.. AdrianNicholls 4 80
(David Nicholls) *hld up towards rr: effrt and swtchd lft over 2f out: chsng ldrs over 1f out: wknd jst ins fnl f* **5/2**[1]
3631 **5** *3 ¾* **Declamation (IRE)**[19] 4586 3-8-9 **74**.. LiamJones 5 62
(Mark Johnston) *wnt rt after s: chsd ldr: drvn over 2f out: wknd appr fnl f* **9/2**[3]
0241 **6** *¾* **Eeny Mac (IRE)**[10] 4893 6-8-10 **68** ow1..................(p) MichaelO'Connell 2 56
(Neville Bycroft) *chsd ldrs: drvn and outpcd over 2f out: wknd over 1f out* **16/1**
103 **7** *2* **Jo'Burg (USA)**[15] 4733 9-9-7 **84**.. DavidBergin(5) 8 67
(David O'Meara) *dwlt: hld up in rr: hdwy over 4f out: drvn and outpcd over 2f out: edgd lft and wknd over 1f out* **10/1**
1m 36.56s (-0.04) **Going Correction** -0.325s/f (Firm)
WFA 3 from 4yo+ 7lb **7** Ran SP% **111.3**
Speed ratings (Par 105): **106,105,104,101,97 96,94**
toteswingers 1&2 £3.00, 1&3 £11.40, 2&3 £6.30 CSF £17.59 CT £140.03 TOTE £4.40: £1.50, £2.00; EX 22.10 Trifecta £114.80 Pool: £1,133.09 - 7.39 winning units..
Owner Dave Scott **Bred** Dave Scott **Trained** Nawton, N Yorks
■ Stewards' Enquiry : Graham Gibbons two-day ban: used whip above permitted level (Aug 24-25)
FOCUS
A decent handicap in which they went a good, even pace. Pretty straightforward form.

5292 ALEC & MARY GOLDEN WEDDING ANNIVERSARY H'CAP 7f
3:45 (3:46) (Class 4) (0-85,85) 3-Y-0+ **£6,469** (£1,925; £962; £481) **Stalls** Centre

Form RPR
6-31 **1** **Big Johnny D (IRE)**[117] 1570 4-9-2 **75**.. GrahamGibbons 8 93
(David Barron) *led after 1f: shkn up over 1f out: wnt clr: v readily* **15/8**[1]
00 **2** *4 ½* **Mehdi (IRE)**[14] 4778 4-9-12 **85**..(t) AdrianNicholls 10 91
(David Nicholls) *w ldrs: 2nd 2f out: sn rdn: kpt on: no imp* **7/1**
4064 **3** *1 ¼* **Who's Shirl**[22] 4510 7-8-10 **69**.. MichaelStainton 1 72
(Chris Fairhurst) *in rr: hdwy on outer over 2f out: edgd lft over 1f out: styd on same pce* **25/1**
0610 **4** *hd* **Victoire De Lyphar (IRE)**[14] 4758 6-9-7 **80**..............(e) JamesSullivan 9 83
(Ruth Carr) *chsd ldrs: rdn and outpcd over 2f out: edgd lft and hdwy over 1f out: kpt on same pce* **10/1**
0140 **5** *¾* **Shrimper Roo**[15] 4734 3-9-4 **83**..(b) TonyHamilton 11 82
(Tim Easterby) *hld up in mid-div: effrt over 2f out: kpt on same pce over 1f out* **22/1**
5112 **6** *5* **West Leake Hare (IRE)**[19] 4577 4-9-5 **78**.. PaulQuinn 6 66
(David Nicholls) *in rr: drvn over 2f out: no threat* **11/2**[3]
4211 **7** *1 ¼* **Illustrious Prince (IRE)**[17] 4628 6-8-8 **74**................ LukeLeadbitter(7) 7 58
(Declan Carroll) *chsd ldrs: drvn 3f out: wknd over 1f out* **11/1**
2111 **8** *½* **Relight My Fire**[19] 4585 3-8-10 **75**..(b) DavidAllan 2 56
(Tim Easterby) *w ldrs: drvn over 2f out: lost pl over 1f out* **9/2**[2]
5054 **9** *2 ¼* **Barkston Ash**[13] 4812 5-9-3 **76**.. PaddyAspell 3 53
(Eric Alston) *chsd ldrs: lost pl over 2f out* **20/1**
2605 **10** *14* **Orbit The Moon (IRE)**[13] 4812 5-9-3 **76**..................(tp) PaulMulrennan 5 17
(Michael Dods) *s.i.s: sn detached in last: reminders over 3f out: eased ins fnl f* **20/1**
1m 22.55s (-1.95) **Going Correction** -0.325s/f (Firm)
WFA 3 from 4yo+ 6lb **10** Ran SP% **116.0**
Speed ratings (Par 105): **98,92,91,91,90 84,83,82,80,64**
toteswingers 1&2 £4.10, 1&3 £35.90, 2&3 £16.70 CSF £14.17 CT £253.47 TOTE £2.50: £1.50, £1.40, £7.40; EX 19.60 Trifecta £353.70 Pool: £1,492.03 - 3.16 winning units..
Owner Clive Washbourn **Bred** David McGuinness **Trained** Maunby, N Yorks
FOCUS
A good handicap run in a decent time. The form could be rated a bit higher.

5293 MARKET CROSS JEWELLERS CLAIMING STKS 1m
4:20 (4:20) (Class 6) 3-Y-0 **£2,045** (£603; £302) **Stalls** Centre

Form RPR
45 **1** **Mandy's Boy (IRE)**[8] 4957 3-8-11 68.. PaulMulrennan 6 73
(Ian Williams) *w ldr: led 4f out: sn stepped up pce: pushed clr fnl f* **11/10**[1]
-05 **2** *4 ½* **Jubilee Games**[49] 3571 3-9-9 76.. TonyHamilton 2 75
(Richard Fahey) *fly-jmpd s: sn trcking ldrs: cl 3rd over 2f out: rdn over 1f out: kpt on to take modest 2nd nr fin* **4/1**[3]
2036 **3** *¾* **Shearian**[22] 4508 3-8-13 63.. BarryMcHugh 7 63
(Tracy Waggott) *led 4f: swtchd lft over 1f out: kpt on same pce* **8/1**
6000 **4** *5* **Tinctoria**[40] 3893 3-8-3 53..(b[1]) PaulMcGiff(7) 1 49
(Kevin Ryan) *wnt lft s: chsd ldrs 5f out: drvn over 3f out: wl outpcd and hung rt over 1f out* **25/1**
2145 **5** *28* **Krupskaya (FR)**[13] 4803 3-8-10 72.. GrahamGibbons 3
(Mrs K Burke) *chsd ldrs: drvn over 3f out: lost pl over 2f out: bhd whn eased over 1f out: virtually p.u: hopelessly t.o* **5/2**[2]
1m 37.28s (0.68) **Going Correction** -0.325s/f (Firm) **5** Ran SP% **111.1**
Speed ratings (Par 98): **102,97,96,91,63**
CSF £6.00 TOTE £1.50: £1.10, £2.60; EX 6.00 Trifecta £17.40 Pool: £1,551.76 - 66.59 winning units..Mandy's Boy was subject to a friendly claim by Mr Ian Williams for £8,000
Owner Dr Marwan Koukash **Bred** John Doyle **Trained** Portway, Worcs
FOCUS
A fair claimer in which they went an even gallop. The form makes sense bar the fifth.

5294 WIN A VIP DAY OUT AT REDCARRACING.CO.UK H'CAP 6f
4:55 (4:55) (Class 4) (0-85,85) 3-Y-0+ **£4,690** (£1,395; £697; £348) **Stalls** Centre

Form RPR
2316 **1** **Head Space (IRE)**[7] 5009 5-9-11 **84**..(p) JamesSullivan 13 96
(Ruth Carr) *hld up in rr: hdwy stands' side over 2f out: chsng ldng pair 1f out: edgd lft and styd on to ld nr fin* **9/2**[2]
0002 **2** *hd* **Carambola**[7] 5011 7-8-12 **71**.. DavidAllan 7 82
(Mel Brittain) *chsd ldrs: led over 1f out: idled and edgd lft ins fnl f: hdd clsng stages* **16/1**
0043 **3** *1* **Bop It**[2] 5183 4-9-0 **78**.. DavidBergin(5) 9 86
(David O'Meara) *mid-div: hdwy to chse ldr over 1f out: kpt on same pce last 75yds* **2/1**[1]
0153 **4** *3 ¼* **Mandalay King (IRE)**[8] 4970 8-8-4 **68**..............(b[1]) ShirleyTeasdale(5) 3 66
(Marjorie Fife) *mid-div: hdwy over 2f out: one pce and edgd lft over 1f out* **22/1**
2102 **5** *½* **Dancheur (IRE)**[19] 4580 4-9-6 **79**.. GrahamGibbons 11 75
(Mrs K Burke) *led tl over 2f out: fdd appr fnl f* **8/1**
5440 **6** *nk* **Bonnie Charlie**[15] 4730 7-9-3 **76**..(p) PaulQuinn 2 71
(David Nicholls) *in rr: hdwy over 1f out: nvr nr ldrs* **10/1**
3515 **7** *½* **Deepest Blue**[17] 4624 3-8-6 **69**..(b[1]) BarryMcHugh 12 63
(Declan Carroll) *s.s: in rr: styd on fnl 2f: nvr a factor* **33/1**
010 **8** *nse* **Burning Thread (IRE)**[18] 4613 6-9-12 **85**..............(b) AdamBeschizza 10 78
(Tim Etherington) *w ldr: led over 2f out: edgd rt and hdd over 1f out: hrd rdn and edgd rt: fdd* **33/1**
1421 **9** *3* **Sunrise Dance**[7] 5011 4-8-11 **77**.. JacobButterfield(7) 6 61
(Robert Johnson) *w ldrs: drvn over 2f out: lost pl over 1f out* **11/2**[3]
0000 **10** *¾* **Escape To Glory (USA)**[20] 4560 5-9-7 **80**................(t) PaulMulrennan 4 61
(Michael Dods) *dwlt: a in rr* **9/1**
1000 **11** *¾* **Mission Impossible**[43] 3778 8-8-11 **70**.. RoystonFfrench 5 49
(Tracy Waggott) *chsd ldrs: drvn 2f out: hung rt and sn wknd* **33/1**
0620 **12** *3 ½* **Another Citizen (IRE)**[22] 4479 5-8-11 **75**....................(b) DarylByrne(5) 8 43
(Tim Easterby) *mid-div: drvn over 2f out: lost pl over 1f out* **33/1**
1m 10.43s (-1.37) **Going Correction** -0.325s/f (Firm)
WFA 3 from 4yo+ 4lb **12** Ran SP% **119.1**
Speed ratings (Par 105): **96,95,94,90,89 89,88,88,84,83 82,77**
toteswingers 1&2 £11.40, 1&3 £3.10, 2&3 £8.50 CSF £68.82 CT £187.43 TOTE £4.80: £1.20, £5.70, £1.90; EX 86.70 Trifecta £247.50 Pool: £2,451.12 - 7.42 winning units..
Owner The Bottom Liners & Mrs R Carr **Bred** Castlemartin Stud And Skymarc Farm **Trained** Huby, N Yorks
FOCUS
A decent sprint handicap in which there was a three-way contested gallop. The form is rated around the third.

5295 LADIES' & GENTS' EVENING 24TH AUGUST H'CAP 1m 6f 19y
5:30 (5:31) (Class 6) (0-65,65) 3-Y-0+ **£1,940** (£577; £288; £144) **Stalls** Low

Form RPR
6145 **1** **Spats Colombo**[22] 4474 3-8-3 **53**.. JamesSullivan 3 62
(Micky Hammond) *mid-div: pushed along 5f out: hdwy and swtchd rt 3f out: chsd ldr jst ins fnl f: styd on to ld towards fin* **5/2**[2]
3152 **2** *¾* **Sally Friday (IRE)**[20] 4563 5-9-2 **60**..(p) KevinStott(7) 4 68+
(Edwin Tuer) *trckd ldrs: swtchd rt over 3f out: led over 2f out: edgd lft and hdd wl ins fnl f* **13/8**[1]
5100 **3** *2 ¼* **Spiekeroog**[20] 4563 7-9-9 **65**.. DavidBergin(5) 2 70
(David O'Meara) *hld up in rr: hdwy over 2f out: kpt on to take 3rd last 100yds* **7/1**
2535 **4** *2 ½* **Attansky (IRE)**[7] 5010 3-8-7 **57**..(p) DavidAllan 9 58
(Tim Easterby) *sn chsng ldr: drvn over 5f out: led over 3f out: hdd over 2f out: kpt on one pce* **11/2**[3]
0002 **5** *½* **Dean Iarracht (IRE)**[14] 4763 7-8-9 **46** oh1..............(p) RoystonFfrench 7 47
(Tracy Waggott) *trckd ldrs: wnt handy 3rd 3f out: one pce* **12/1**
/55- **6** *11* **Word Of Warning**[56] 4431 9-8-13 **50**.. LeeTopliss 6 35
(Martin Todhunter) *hld up in rr: drvn over 4f out: sn bhd* **25/1**
00-0 **7** *1* **Speedy Star (IRE)**[58] 3252 4-8-10 **47** oh1 ow1.........(p) PaulMulrennan 8 31
(Tina Jackson) *dwlt: swtchd lft after s: in rr: drvn 4f out: hung lft: nvr on terms* **50/1**
604 **8** *nse* **Yourholidayisover (IRE)**[23] 4445 6-8-13 **55**................ DeclanBates(5) 5 39
(Patrick Holmes) *mid-div: drvn and outpcd over 4f out: sn bhd* **18/1**
0000 **9** *4* **Roc Fort**[12] 4822 4-8-11 **48**..(p) PaddyAspell 1 26
(James Moffatt) *led: hdd over 3f out: lost pl over 2f out: sn bhd* **50/1**
3m 1.03s (-3.67) **Going Correction** -0.325s/f (Firm)
WFA 3 from 4yo+ 13lb **9** Ran SP% **115.3**
Speed ratings (Par 101): **97,96,95,93,93 87,86,86,84**
toteswingers 1&2 £2.20, 1&3 £4.40, 2&3 £3.90 CSF £6.82 CT £22.63 TOTE £3.50: £1.30, £1.10, £1.90; EX 10.00 Trifecta £47.10 Pool: £1,779.28 - 28.29 winning units..
Owner M H O G **Bred** Peter J Davies **Trained** Middleham Moor, N Yorks
FOCUS
A modest staying handicap in which they went a good, even gallop. The form is rated around the third and fourth.
T/Plt: £22.10 to a £1 stake. Pool: £65,784.75 - 2,166.04 winning units T/Qpdt: £15.00 to a £1 stake. Pool: £2,920.00 - 144.00 winning units WG

5362 DEAUVILLE (R-H)
Saturday, August 10
OFFICIAL GOING: Turf: good; fibresand: standard.

5296a FIRST EUROPEAN YOUNG BREEDERS RACE (PRIX DE COLLEVILLE) (CONDITIONS) (2YO) (FIBRESAND) 6f 110y
12:00 (12:00) 2-Y-0 **£11,788** (£4,715; £3,536; £2,357; £1,178)

RPR
1 **Tchekhov (FR)** 2-8-13 0.. ChristopheSoumillon 2 80
(J-C Rouget, France) **13/10**[1]
2 *2* **Stella Clavisque (IRE)**[7] 4977 2-8-9 0.. MaximeGuyon 3 70
(Brian Meehan) *midfield in tch on inner: rdn and hdwy on turn into st: wnt 2nd 2f out: r.o but readily outpcd by wnr ins fnl f: jst hld on for 2nd* **44/5**
3 *hd* **Fairwater (USA)**[44] 3752 2-8-6 0.. StephanePasquier 8 66
(Mme C Head-Maarek, France) **9/5**[2]
4 *2* **Mitlaa (FR)** 2-8-0 0..(p) AllanMonnier(6) 6 61
(F Rohaut, France) **6/1**[3]
5 *¾* **Princess Kiara (FR)**[6] 2-8-4 0.. ValentinSeguy(5) 1 62
(N Caullery, France) **20/1**
6 *hd* **Rajang (FR)** 2-8-7 0.. AntoineCoutier(6) 5 65
(F Chappet, France) **15/1**
7 *1 ½* **Espoir En Tete (FR)**[20] 2-8-9 0.. RonanThomas 7 57
(P Adda, France) **49/1**
1m 21.96s (81.96) **7** Ran SP% **116.7**
WIN (incl. 1 euro stake): 2.30. PLACES: 1.10, 1.60, 1.20. DF: 7.80. SF: 9.10.
Owner E Pokrovsky & Cuadra Montalban **Bred** Ecurie La Vallee Martigny Earl **Trained** Pau, France

5297a PRIX DE POMONE (GROUP 2) (3YO+ FILLIES & MARES) (TURF) 1m 4f 110y
1:30 (12:00) 3-Y-0+ **£60,243** (£23,252; £11,097; £7,398; £3,699)

RPR
1 **La Pomme D'Amour**[28] 4324 5-9-4 0.. FlavienPrat 1 111
(A Fabre, France) *trckd ldr on inner: rdn 2f out: angled off rail and styd on to chal ent fnl f: led ins fnl 150yds and asserted* **9/2**[3]
2 *¾* **Chalnetta (FR)**[48] 3614 3-8-6 0.. JulienAuge 7 110
(C Ferland, France) *led: shkn up 2f out: rdn and strly pressed ent fnl f: hdd ins fnl 100yds: styd on but hld* **10/1**

3 ½ **Emirates Queen**[35] 4059 4-9-8 0 AndreaAtzeni 3 113+
(Luca Cumani) *midfield on inner: rdn 2f out: wnt 3rd ent fnl f: styd on wl and clsng on ldng pair at fin but nvr able to chal* **68/10**

4 1 ½ **Lucky Look (FR)**[28] 4323 3-8-6 0 GregoryBenoist 9 107
(D Smaga, France) *prom on outer: rdn over 2f out: styd on but nt pce of ldng trio* **14/1**

5 shd **Pirika (IRE)**[48] 3615 5-9-4 0 Pierre-CharlesBoudot 4 106+
(A Fabre, France) *stdd and hld up in last: swtchd to wd outside and rdn over 1f out: styd on and tk n.d 5th cl home: nrest at fin* **3/1**[1]

6 1 ¼ **Ferevia (IRE)**[48] 3614 3-8-6 0 ThierryThulliez 8 104
(C Laffon-Parias, France) *midfield on outer: rdn over 2f out: outpcd by ldrs over 1f out: styd on and wnt 6th cl home* **9/1**

7 snk **Galvaun (IRE)**[61] 3165 4-9-4 0 MaximeGuyon 2 104
(A Fabre, France) *hld up towards rr on outer: rdn over 2f out: styd on and wnt 7th post but n.d* **4/1**[2]

8 nse **Quiz Mistress**[63] 3100 5-9-4 0 UmbertoRispoli 5 104
(Hughie Morrison) *slow to stride and hld up towards rr on inner: checked whn ct on heels on bnd after 4f: rdn over 2f out: sn outpcd by ldrs: styd on but dropped to 8th post* **40/1**

9 1 **Loredana (FR)**[28] 4323 3-8-6 0 (p) Christophe-PatriceLemaire 10 103
(M Delzangles, France) *got across fr wdst draw and trckd ldr on outer: rdn in cl 2nd 2f out: lost pl over 1f out: sn btn and fdd* **73/10**

10 2 ½ **Regina Mundi (IRE)**[48] 6-9-4 0 CristianDemuro 6 99?
(Ottavio Di Paolo, Italy) *hld up in last pair on inner: rdn over 2f out: outpcd in last ent fnl f: plugged on but nvr a factor* **75/1**

2m 42.45s (-3.95)
WFA 3 from 4yo+ 11lb **10** Ran SP% **117.6**
WIN (incl. 1 euro stake): 5.50. PLACES: 2.00, 3.00, 2.50. DF: 29.50. SF: 52.40.
Owner Exors of The Late Guy Reed **Bred** G Reed **Trained** Chantilly, France

5298a PRIX GONTAUT-BIRON HONG KONG JOCKEY CLUB (GROUP 3) (4YO+) (TURF) 1m 2f

2:40 (12:00) 4-Y-0+ **£32,520** (£13,008; £9,756; £6,504; £3,252)

RPR

1 **Petit Chevalier (FR)**[36] 4042 5-8-11 0 MaximeGuyon 3 111
(W Mongil, Germany) *trckd ldr on outer: clsd to chal 2f out: rdn to ld over 1f out: strly pressed thrght fnl f but styd on strly and a holding runner-up* **83/10**

2 hd **Cirrus Des Aigles (FR)**[14] 4745 7-8-10 0 ow1 OlivierPeslier 7 110+
(Mme C Barande-Barbe, France) *midfield in tch on outer: shkn up 2f out: r.o and wnt 2nd ins fnl 150yds: rdn and pressed wnr all the way to fin but a being hld* **9/10**[1]

3 1 ¼ **Smoking Sun (USA)**[61] 3165 4-8-11 0 StephanePasquier 2 109+
(P Bary, France) *midfield in tch on inner: cl 3rd 3f out: rdn over 1f out: nt clr run and swtchd rt ins fnl f: r.o and jst hld on for 3rd: shade unlucky* **11/2**[3]

4 hd **Mandour (USA)**[36] 4027 4-8-11 0 Christophe-PatriceLemaire 6 109+
(A De Royer-Dupre, France) *hld up in last: rdn 2f out: stl last ent fnl f: styd on down wd outside and tk 4th cl home: almost snatched 3rd post: nrst fin* **23/10**[2]

5 1 **Starboard**[161] 873 4-8-9 0 FlavienPrat 1 104
(T Clout, France) *led: rdn and strly pressed fr 2f out: hdd over 1f out: styd on and kpt pressing eventual wnr tl no ex ins fnl f: fdd and dropped to 5th cl home* **34/1**

6 nk **Pagera (FR)**[20] 4574 5-8-6 0 (p) FabriceVeron 4 100
(H-A Pantall, France) *hld up in last trio on outer: rdn over 2f out: nt qckn over 1f out: styd on but nvr threatened* **30/1**

7 1 ½ **Gold For Tina (FR)**[20] 4574 4-8-6 0 (p) UmbertoRispoli 5 97
(J Van Handenhove, France) *slow to stride and hld up in last trio on inner: rdn 2f out: nt qckn over 1f out: styd on but dropped to last ins fnl f: eased cl home whn hld* **47/1**

2m 8.0s (-2.20) **7** Ran SP% **117.2**
WIN (incl. 1 euro stake): 9.30. PLACES: 2.70, 1.40. DF: 30.80. SF: 111.20.
Owner Rennstall Gestut Hachtsee **Bred** Gestut Hachtsee **Trained** Germany

4880 LEICESTER (R-H)

Sunday, August 11

OFFICIAL GOING: Good to firm (good in places; 8.6)
Wind: Light; half-against Weather: Overcast

5299 BRITISH STALLION STUDS EBF MAIDEN STKS 7f 9y

2:25 (2:26) (Class 4) 2-Y-0 **£5,175** (£1,540; £769; £384) **Stalls** Centre

Form RPR

3 1 **Day Of Conquest**[38] 3979 2-9-5 0 JimCrowley 5 82+
(Richard Hannon) *a.p: chsd ldr 1/2-way: rdn to ld and hung lft over 1f out: styd on: wnt rt nr fin* **25/1**

2 2 ¼ **Shafrah (IRE)** 2-9-5 0 SeanLevey 8 76+
(Richard Hannon) *hld up: hdwy 1/2-way: rdn over 1f out: styd on same pce ins fnl f* **5/1**[3]

2 3 nk **Torrid**[23] 4483 2-9-5 0 PatDobbs 3 75
(Amanda Perrett) *led: rdn and hdd over 1f out: styd on same pce ins fnl f* **7/4**[1]

32 4 1 ¾ **Istimraar (IRE)**[29] 4304 2-9-5 0 SilvestreDeSousa 4 70
(Saeed bin Suroor) *a.p: rdn over 2f out: styd on same pce fnl f* **5/2**[2]

5 2 **Toast Of New York (USA)** 2-9-5 0 JamesDoyle 9 65+
(Jamie Osborne) *hld up: rdn over 2f out: r.o ins fnl f: nvr nrr* **66/1**

5 6 3 ¾ **Charlie Wells (IRE)**[56] 3374 2-9-5 0 NeilCallan 2 55
(Eve Johnson Houghton) *prom: rdn over 2f out: wknd fnl f* **15/2**

7 1 ½ **Flying Cape (IRE)** 2-9-5 0 GrahamLee 10 51
(Andrew Hollinshead) *chsd ldr to 1/2-way: rdn and wknd wl over 1f out* **50/1**

8 1 ¼ **Desert Skywalker (IRE)** 2-9-5 0 MickaelBarzalona 7 47
(Charlie Appleby) *s.i.s: hdwy over 5f out: rdn 1/2-way: wknd 2f out* **9/1**

0 9 18 **Suni Dancer**[7] 5025 2-8-11 0 RaulDaSilva(3) 6
(Paul Green) *hld up: rdn over 2f out: wknd wl over 1f out* **100/1**

5 10 1 ¼ **Nabstarlini**[26] 4386 2-9-5 0 (b[1]) JimmyQuinn 1
(Ed Vaughan) *s.i.s: outpcd* **100/1**

1m 24.05s (-2.15) **Going Correction** -0.225s/f (Firm) **10** Ran SP% **112.6**
Speed ratings (Par 96): **103,100,100,98,95 91,89,88,67,66**
toteswingers 1&2 £12.70, 1&3 £5.50, 2&3 £2.60 CSF £139.23 TOTE £17.20: £4.20, £1.70, £1.20; EX 101.60 Trifecta £603.70 Pool: £4512.15 - 5.60 winning units..
Owner Mohammed Sultan **Bred** Bearstone Stud **Trained** East Everleigh, Wilts

FOCUS
The ground looked to be riding as advertised. This maiden has been won by useful types in Tamayuz Star and Stipulate in the last couple of seasons, and winners should come out of this edition.

5300 JAMES GRAHAM H'CAP 5f 218y

2:55 (2:55) (Class 5) (0-70,74) 3-Y-0 **£3,881** (£1,155; £577; £288) **Stalls** Centre

Form RPR

2456 1 **Clock Opera (IRE)**[51] 3540 3-8-8 **57** KirstyMilczarek 5 65
(William Stone) *plld hrd: led 5f out: rdn over 1f out: edgd rt fnl f: styd on* **20/1**

6211 2 ¾ **Bapak Muda (USA)**[3] 5184 3-9-4 **74** 6ex KevinStott(7) 1 80
(Kevin Ryan) *prom: pushed along 4f out: rdn over 2f out: chsd wnr over 1f out: edgd rt: styd on* **11/8**[1]

-612 3 1 ¾ **Perfect Venture**[18] 4636 3-9-6 **69** AdamKirby 4 69
(Clive Cox) *s.i.s: sn pushed along in rr: hdwy u.p over 1f out: styd on same pce ins fnl f* **9/2**[3]

0215 4 1 ¼ **Laughing Rock (IRE)**[24] 4453 3-8-9 **63** TobyAtkinson(5) 6 59
(Michael Appleby) *chsd ldrs: hung rt almost thrght: rdn 1/2-way: styd on same pce fr over 1f out* **7/2**[2]

2015 5 6 **Alhaarth Beauty (IRE)**[46] 3678 3-9-6 **69** NeilCallan 7 46
(Ismail Mohammed) *racd keenly: led 1f: chsd ldr tl rdn over 1f out: wknd fnl f* **8/1**

455 6 12 **Khefyn (IRE)**[14] 4797 3-9-1 **64** JamesDoyle 8
(Ronald Harris) *hld up: rdn over 2f out: sn wknd and eased* **6/1**

1m 11.75s (-1.25) **Going Correction** -0.225s/f (Firm) **6** Ran SP% **112.7**
Speed ratings (Par 100): **99,98,95,94,86 70**
toteswingers 1&2 £5.80, 1&3 £7.10, 2&3 £1.90 CSF £48.83 CT £153.38 TOTE £19.20: £9.80, £1.50; EX 49.90 Trifecta £117.00 Pool: £2482.54 - 15.90 winning units..
Owner Caroline Scott & Shane Fairweather **Bred** Ms H W Topping **Trained** West Wickham, Cambs

FOCUS
A modest handicap and a rather messy race.

5301 RUTLAND (S) STKS 7f 9y

3:25 (3:25) (Class 6) 3-4-Y-0 **£2,264** (£673; £336; £168) **Stalls** Centre

Form RPR

0-60 1 **Red Art (IRE)**[44] 3757 4-9-2 80 JamesDoyle 2 78
(Charles Hills) *led 1f: chsd ldrs: wnt 2nd over 2f out: rdn to ld over 1f out: styd on* **6/4**[1]

0114 2 1 ¾ **All Or Nothin (IRE)**[37] 4012 4-9-0 75 JoeDoyle(7) 1 78
(John Quinn) *plld hrd: led 6f out: rdn and hdd over 1f out: sn hung rt: styd on same pce ins fnl f* **11/4**[2]

2 3 7 **Well Owd Mon**[11] 4881 3-8-5 0 JackDuern(5) 6 53
(Andrew Hollinshead) *prom: pushed along 1/2-way: rdn over 1f out: styd on same pce* **10/1**

3453 4 nk **Shamrocked (IRE)**[11] 4893 4-8-9 62 JacobButterfield(7) 4 54
(Ollie Pears) *chsd ldr tl rdn over 2f out: styd on same pce fr over 1f out* **4/1**[3]

3620 5 11 **Tooley Woods (IRE)**[3] 5177 4-9-2 55 SeanLevey 5 26
(Tony Carroll) *prom: rdn over 2f out: wknd over 1f out: eased* **7/1**

6 35 **Come On Flo** 3-7-12 0 JoeyHaynes(7) 3
(Michael Mullineaux) *s.i.s: outpcd* **25/1**

1m 23.49s (-2.71) **Going Correction** -0.225s/f (Firm)
WFA 3 from 4yo 6lb **6** Ran SP% **112.1**
Speed ratings (Par 101): **106,104,96,95,83 43**
toteswingers 1&2 £1.70, 1&3 £3.00, 2&3 £3.40 CSF £5.81 TOTE £2.40: £1.40, £2.20; EX 7.70 Trifecta £33.40 Pool: £2933.71 - 65.86 winning units..Red Art was bought in for 7000gns; All Or Nothin was bought by Miss M Bryant for £6,000
Owner Des Anderson & The Hon R J Arculli **Bred** H Q Spooner **Trained** Lambourn, Berks

FOCUS
They came down the centre in this seller, in which the first two came clear.

5302 BJORN AGAIN H'CAP 1m 1f 218y

3:55 (3:55) (Class 4) (0-85,86) 3-Y-0+ **£6,469** (£1,925; £962; £481) **Stalls** Low

Form RPR

2231 1 **Elhaame (IRE)**[10] 4929 3-9-6 **86** JamesDoyle 4 99
(Luca Cumani) *a.p: chsd ldr over 3f out: led 2f out: sn shkn up and edgd rt: styd on wl: comf* **11/10**[1]

0621 2 2 ¾ **Aquilonius (IRE)**[25] 4407 4-9-6 **77** (t) NeilCallan 2 84
(Stuart Williams) *led: t.k.h: rdn and hdd 2f out: styd on same pce ins fnl f* **3/1**[2]

3514 3 2 ¼ **Now My Sun**[35] 4098 4-9-7 **78** PhillipMakin 3 81
(Mrs K Burke) *hld up: hdwy over 2f out: rdn and edgd rt over 1f out: no ex ins fnl f* **5/1**[3]

6043 4 9 **Karam Albaari (IRE)**[24] 4435 5-10-0 **85** FrederikTylicki 5 70
(J R Jenkins) *chsd ldr tl rdn over 3f out: hung rt and wknd over 1f out* **11/2**

0660 5 1 ¾ **Carazam (IRE)**[37] 4028 6-9-0 **71** MartinLane 1 52
(Bernard Llewellyn) *prom: rdn over 4f out: wknd 2f out* **20/1**

2m 5.32s (-2.58) **Going Correction** -0.15s/f (Firm)
WFA 3 from 4yo+ 9lb **5** Ran SP% **109.4**
Speed ratings (Par 105): **104,101,100,92,91**
CSF £4.56 TOTE £2.10: £1.30, £1.90; EX 5.30 Trifecta £8.20 Pool: £1820.33 - 165.51 winning units..
Owner Sheikh Mohammed Obaid Al Maktoum **Bred** W Maxwell Ervine **Trained** Newmarket, Suffolk

FOCUS
They went just an average pace in this fair handicap.

5303 PETER ANDRE H'CAP 5f 218y

4:25 (4:25) (Class 3) (0-90,87) 3-Y-0 **£9,451** (£2,829; £1,414; £708; £352) **Stalls** Centre

Form RPR

0315 1 **Brazen**[30] 4247 3-9-7 **87** (be) NeilCallan 6 97
(David Simcock) *mde all: rdn and hung lft fr over 1f out: styd on* **8/1**

3-22 2 1 ¼ **Gravitational (IRE)**[80] 2593 3-8-13 **79** SebSanders 10 85
(Chris Wall) *hld up: swtchd rt sn after s: hdwy over 2f out: rdn to chse wnr over 1f out: r.o* **3/1**[2]

1216 3 ½ **Extrasolar**[8] 4989 3-9-5 **85** (t) PatDobbs 9 89
(Amanda Perrett) *hld up: rdn over 2f out: hdwy over 1f out: r.o* **9/1**

221 4 nk **Port Alfred**[18] 4627 3-9-3 **83** MickaelBarzalona 2 86
(Charlie Appleby) *trckd ldrs: plld hrd: rdn over 1f out: styd on* **11/4**[1]

4331 5 nk **Red Refraction (IRE)**[14] 4797 3-9-1 **84** WilliamTwiston-Davies(3) 7 86
(Richard Hannon) *hld up in tch: pushed along over 2f out: rdn over 1f out: styd on* **12/1**

0241 6 4 ½ **Fortinbrass (IRE)**[10] 4905 3-9-5 **85** JimCrowley 4 73
(Ralph Beckett) *chsd wnr tl rdn over 1f out: wknd ins fnl f* **15/2**

122 7 2 ¾ **Freddy With A Y (IRE)**31 4210 3-9-7 **87** JamesDoyle 3 66
(Gary Moore) *hld up: hdwy u.p 2f out: wknd over 1f out* **5/1**3
2566 8 nk **Sewn Up**95 2158 3-8-8 **74** (p) JimmyQuinn 8 52
(Andrew Hollinshead) *hld up: rdn over 2f out: wknd over 1f out* **40/1**
16-0 9 4 ½ **Jamesbo's Girl**99 2022 3-9-7 **87** (t) SeanLevey 5 51
(Alan Berry) *chsd ldrs: rdn 1/2-way: wknd over 1f out* **18/1**
1m 10.96s (-2.04) **Going Correction** -0.225s/f (Firm) **9** Ran SP% **116.6**
Speed ratings (Par 104): **104,102,101,101,100 94,91,90,84**
toteswingers 1&2 £5.50, 1&3 £10.20, 2&3 £5.70 CSF £32.60 CT £225.49 TOTE £12.50: £3.60, £1.60, £2.10; EX 45.50 Trifecta £430.40 Pool: £3589.83 - 6.25 winning units..
Owner Al Asayl Bloodstock Ltd **Bred** Lostford Manor Stud Ltd **Trained** Newmarket, Suffolk
FOCUS
A decent sprint handicap, run in a time just inside the standard. They came down the centre, although the winner hung to the rail.

5304 BOOK YOUR CHRISTMAS PARTY AT LEICESTER H'CAP (THE SUNDAY £5K BONUS RACE) 1m 60y
4:55 (4:57) (Class 5) (0-75,75) 3-Y-0+ **£3,881** (£1,155; £577; £288) **Stalls** Low

Form RPR
0030 1 **Siouxperhero (IRE)**11 4894 4-9-2 **63** (p) JimCrowley 6 73
(William Muir) *chsd ldrs: rdn over 1f out: styd on u.p to ld post* **20/1**
2143 2 shd **Lord Franklin**9 4953 4-9-1 **65** JasonHart(3) 4 75
(Eric Alston) *chsd ldr tl rdn to ld over 2f out: hrd pressed fnl f: hdd post* **7/2**1
025 3 2 ¼ **Oratory (IRE)**22 4540 7-9-6 **67** PhillipMakin 13 72
(Mrs K Burke) *a.p: rdn over 2f out: styd on same pce ins fnl f* **6/1**2
63P5 4 3 ½ **Breccbennach**51 3528 3-9-5 **73** (t) MickyFenton 9 69
(Seamus Durack) *plld hrd and prom: rdn over 2f out: hung rt over 1f out: styd on same pce ins fnl f* **20/1**
6530 5 ½ **Brown Pete (IRE)**4 5124 5-9-7 **68** NeilCallan 1 63
(Violet M Jordan) *hld up: hdwy 1/2-way: rdn over 2f out: edgd rt over 1f out: styd on same pce ins fnl f* **9/1**
-006 6 3 **Woolston Ferry (IRE)**20 4593 7-9-9 **70** FergusSweeney 8 58
(Henry Candy) *hld up: rdn over 2f out: styd on ins fnl f: nvr nrr* **14/1**
3052 7 2 **No Dominion (IRE)**22 4540 4-10-0 **75** GrahamLee 5 59
(James Given) *s.i.s: hld up: rdn over 2f kpt on ins fnl f: nvr on terms* **7/1**3
4-06 8 ¾ **Nezami (IRE)**14 4807 8-9-0 **66** JackDuern(5) 3 48
(Patrick Clinton) *chsd ldrs: rdn over 3f out: wknd over 1f out* **25/1**
0500 9 2 ½ **Barons Spy (IRE)**11 4884 12-9-4 **65** AidanColeman 12 41
(Richard Price) *hld up: rdn over 2f out: wknd over 1f out* **40/1**
1013 10 1 **Zaitsev (IRE)**20 4586 3-9-0 **75** JacobButterfield(7) 10 48
(Ollie Pears) *led: rdn and hdd over 2f out: wknd fnl f* **10/1**
1341 11 5 **Oratorio's Joy (IRE)**9 4941 3-9-4 **72** JamesDoyle 7 34
(Jamie Osborne) *hld up: hdwy u.p over 2f out: wknd over 1f out: eased* **8/1**
3323 12 2 ¾ **Lean On Pete (IRE)**108 1796 4-9-5 **66** TomEaves 2 22
(Ollie Pears) *hld up: a in rr: rdn over 2f out: wknd over 1f out* **17/2**
0135 13 4 ½ **Typhon (USA)**17 4672 3-9-4 **72** TedDurcan 11 17
(David Lanigan) *hld up: rdn over 2f out: sn edgd rt and wknd: eased over 1f out* **11/1**
1m 42.91s (-2.19) **Going Correction** -0.15s/f (Firm)
WFA 3 from 4yo+ 7lb **13** Ran SP% **120.5**
Speed ratings (Par 103): **104,103,101,98,97 94,92,91,89,88 83,80,76**
toteswingers 1&2 £19.50, 1&3 £28.10, 2&3 £4.40 CSF £86.35 TOTE £21.90: £3.60, £1.70, £3.10; EX 123.80 Trifecta £761.80 Pool: £2460.91 - 2.42 winning units..
Owner Muir Racing Partnership - Bath **Bred** J & J Waldron **Trained** Lambourn, Berks
■ Stewards' Enquiry : Phillip Makin two-day ban: used whip in incorrect place (Aug 25-26)
FOCUS
Quite a competitive race for the grade on paper, but few got into it with the first three always to the fore.

5305 SMOOTH RADIO H'CAP 5f 2y
5:25 (5:25) (Class 6) (0-65,62) 3-Y-0+ **£2,587** (£770; £384; £192) **Stalls** Centre

Form RPR
6030 1 **Quality Art (USA)**5 5085 5-8-13 **56** ConnorBeasley(5) 7 68
(Richard Guest) *hld up: hdwy 2f out: led over 1f out: sn rdn and edgd rt: r.o wl* **11/2**3
2314 2 2 ½ **Pull The Pin (IRE)**1 5273 4-8-11 **52** RaulDaSilva(3) 2 55
(Paul Green) *chsd ldrs: pushed along 1/2-way: rdn and ev ch over 1f out: styd on same pce ins fnl f* **15/8**1
0566 3 1 ½ **Lady Royale**16 4727 5-9-9 **61** (p) GrahamLee 1 59
(Geoffrey Oldroyd) *chsd ldrs: rdn and ev ch over 1f out: no ex ins fnl f* **10/1**
246 4 2 ½ **Borough Boy (IRE)**6 5067 3-9-1 **56** (v) MartinDwyer 4 44
(Derek Shaw) *hld up: rdn over 1f out: nt trble ldrs* **8/1**
0-32 5 6 **Maltease Ah**18 4635 4-9-7 **59** JimCrowley 6 26
(Andrew Reid) *w ldr tl rdn 1/2-way: wknd over 1f out* **7/2**2
1-25 6 11 **Ballarina**2 5227 7-9-7 **62** JasonHart(3) 3
(Eric Alston) *led: rdn and hdd over 1f out: sn wknd* **7/2**2
59.58s (-0.42) **Going Correction** -0.225s/f (Firm)
WFA 3 from 4yo+ 3lb **6** Ran SP% **114.8**
Speed ratings (Par 101): **94,90,87,83,74 56**
toteswingers 1&2 £2.50, 1&3 £7.7, 2&3 £3.80 CSF £16.82 TOTE £5.90: £2.30, £1.80; EX 14.70 Trifecta £124.50 Pool: £1872.48 - 11.27 winning units..
Owner Mrs Alison Guest **Bred** Farfellow Farms & Darley Stud Management **Trained** Wetherby, W Yorks
FOCUS
A weak handicap run at a good clip.
T/Jkpt: Not won. T/Plt: £46.40 to a £1 stake. Pool: £116,665.92 - 1833.99 winning tickets.
T/Qpdt: £14.90 to a £1 stake. Pool: £7583.00 - 375.14 winning tickets. CR

5060 WINDSOR (R-H)
Sunday, August 11

OFFICIAL GOING: Good to firm (8.8)
Wind: Fresh, half behind Weather: Fine, warm

5306 MACDONALD HOTEL WINDSOR NOVICE AUCTION STKS (THE SUNDAY £5K BONUS RACE) 5f 10y
2:10 (2:10) (Class 5) 2-Y-0 **£2,587** (£770; £384) **Stalls** Low

Form RPR
1212 1 **Lilbourne Lass**22 4528 2-9-0 **93** RichardHughes 1 93+
(Richard Hannon) *mde virtually all: pushed along to assert wl over 1f out: comf* **1/16**1
2102 2 3 **Memory Styx**8 5012 2-8-8 **80** MartinHarley 3 76
(Mick Channon) *broke wl but trckd wnr: shkn up to try to chal 2f out: one pce over 1f out* **10/1**2
3 3 ¾ **Orlando Star (CAN)** 2-8-7 0 RobertTart(5) 2 67
(Roger Teal) *s.s: sn in tch in last: shkn up 2f out: rn green and lft bhd over 1f out* **33/1**3
1m 0.5s (0.20) **Going Correction** -0.35s/f (Firm) **3** Ran SP% **106.1**
Speed ratings (Par 94): **84,79,73**
CSF £1.28 TOTE £1.10; EX 1.10 Trifecta £1.30 Pool: £1750.35 - 956.53 winning units..
Owner Hon Mrs Sarah Ensor **Bred** Alvediston Stud **Trained** East Everleigh, Wilts
FOCUS
Inner of straight dolled out 16ds at 6f and 9yds at winning post. Top bend dolled out 8yds from normal inner configuration, adding 34yds to races of 1m and beyond. Straightforward form.

5307 JOIN YOUNG HOOVES KIDS CLUB TODAY MAIDEN AUCTION STKS 6f
2:40 (2:41) (Class 5) 2-Y-0 **£2,587** (£770; £384; £192) **Stalls** Low

Form RPR
224 1 **Autumn Sunrise (IRE)**11 4877 2-8-10 **80** RichardHughes 5 82+
(Richard Hannon) *mde all: pushed along and wl in command over 1f out: comf* **2/5**1
2 1 ½ **Shilla (IRE)** 2-8-4 0 CathyGannon 3 68+
(Henry Candy) *t.k.h early: cl up: shkn up to chse wnr over 1f out: styd on but unable to pose a threat* **20/1**
50 3 1 ¼ **Craftsmanship (FR)**25 4414 2-8-11 0 NickyMackay 2 71
(Robert Eddery) *trckd ldrs: shkn up and clsd 2f out: wnt 3rd jst over 1f out: kpt on same pce* **33/1**
4 2 ½ **Go For Broke** 2-8-11 0 KieranO'Neill 12 63+
(Richard Hannon) *hld up in tch: outpcd and pushed along 1/2-way: kpt on to take 4th ins fnl f: n.d* **16/1**
04 5 1 ¼ **Photography (IRE)**8 4997 2-9-0 0 PatCosgrave 1 62
(Hugo Palmer) *hld up towards rr: outpcd fr 1/2-way: reminder 2f out: styd on fnl f: n.d* **12/1**3
00 6 ½ **Blunos (IRE)**29 4304 2-8-9 0 RobertHavlin 8 56
(Rod Millman) *mostly chsd wnr to over 1f out: wknd* **33/1**
7 shd **You're Fired (IRE)** 2-8-7 0 MichaelJMMurphy(5) 6 61+
(Alan Jarvis) *dropped to rr and urged along over 4f out: no ch after but styd on quite takingly last 150yds* **25/1**
0 8 1 ¾ **Little Briar Rose**12 4847 2-8-2 0 ow1 SimonPearce(3) 9 46
(John Spearing) *mostly chsd ldng pair to over 1f out: wkng whn n.m.r sn after* **33/1**
0 9 7 **King Calypso**13 4827 2-8-10 0 MartinHarley 4 28
(Denis Coakley) *snatched up sn after s: a in rr after: bhd fnl 2f* **33/1**
2 10 3 ¾ **Jacob Black**9 4937 2-8-6 0 RyanTate(5) 14 17
(Clive Cox) *hld up in midfield on outer: struggling over 2f out: sn bhd* **6/1**2
11 1 ¼ **Sydney James (IRE)** 2-8-13 0 LiamKeniry 10 15
(Richard Hannon) *slowly away: a in last pair: nvr a factor* **20/1**
0 12 ½ **Yankee Red**45 3752 2-8-12 0 PaoloSirigu 13 13
(John Best) *sn outpcd and rdn in last pair: nvr a factor* **25/1**
1m 11.7s (-1.30) **Going Correction** -0.35s/f (Firm) **12** Ran SP% **128.3**
Speed ratings (Par 94): **94,92,90,87,85 84,84,82,72,67 66,65**
toteswingers 1&2 £4.60, 1&3 £8.80, 2&3 £73.10 CSF £17.29 TOTE £1.30: £1.02, £5.70, £7.90; EX 15.00 Trifecta £322.80 Pool: £3460.57 - 8.04 winning units..
Owner Michael Daniels **Bred** B Kennedy **Trained** East Everleigh, Wilts
FOCUS
An uncompetitive 2-y-o maiden and few got in a blow.

5308 CORAL FILLIES' H'CAP 6f
3:10 (3:10) (Class 4) (0-85,84) 3-Y-0+ **£4,851** (£1,443; £721; £360) **Stalls** Low

Form RPR
122 1 **Jubilant Queen**9 4962 3-8-9 **71** RichardHughes 5 80
(Clive Cox) *hld up in rr: prog 2f out: sn rdn: led 1f out: styd on wl* **11/4**1
62-0 2 1 ¼ **Miliika**8 5009 4-9-10 **82** ChrisCatlin 1 88
(Rae Guest) *trckd ldrs: rdn over 2f out: clsd to chal 1f out: styd on same pce after* **3/1**2
0144 3 hd **Ginzan**2 5219 5-9-5 **77** TomMcLaughlin 2 82
(Malcolm Saunders) *trckd ldrs: prog 2f out: tried to chal jst over 1f out: styd on same pce* **5/1**
5260 4 1 **Whitecrest**12 4860 5-8-13 **78** EoinWalsh(7) 8 80
(John Spearing) *prom on outer: led 2f out: hdd and fdd 1f out* **12/1**
-213 5 ½ **Strictly Silca**10 4905 3-9-4 **80** (v) MartinHarley 4 80
(Mick Channon) *hld up in midfield: gng strly over 2f out: rdn and nt qckn over 1f out: kpt on ins fnl f* **7/2**3
1035 6 ¾ **Red Larkspur (IRE)**46 3691 4-9-5 **77** (p1) LiamKeniry 7 75
(Roger Teal) *hld up towards rr: rdn over 1f out: one pce and nvr threatened* **25/1**
1460 7 7 **Fanrouge (IRE)**15 4746 4-9-5 **84** PatMillman(7) 6 60
(Rod Millman) *snatched up sn after s: a in last pair: bhd fnl 2f* **10/1**
1/04 8 5 **Appointee (IRE)**17 4677 4-8-12 **75** (p) RyanTate(5) 3 35
(Robert Cowell) *mde most to 2f out: wknd rapidly* **25/1**
1m 10.4s (-2.60) **Going Correction** -0.35s/f (Firm)
WFA 3 from 4yo+ 4lb **8** Ran SP% **115.0**
Speed ratings (Par 102): **103,101,101,99,99 98,88,82**
toteswingers 1&2 £2.50, 1&3 £3.40, 2&3 £3.00 CSF £11.34 CT £37.36 TOTE £3.00: £1.10, £1.60, £2.10; EX 12.00 Trifecta £53.80 Pool: £3557.15 - 49.54 winning units..
Owner Doreen Swinburn & Pierpont Scott **Bred** Genesis Green Stud & P Scott **Trained** Lambourn, Berks
FOCUS
A modest sprint handicap for fillies, run at a solid pace.

5309 OSSIE & HUTCH MEMORIAL MAIDEN STKS 1m 67y
3:40 (3:40) (Class 5) 2-Y-0 **£2,587** (£770; £384; £192) **Stalls** Low

Form RPR
53 1 **The Alamo (IRE)**38 3972 2-9-5 0 RichardHughes 2 74+
(Richard Hannon) *mde all: rdn wl over 1f out: hrd pressed and drvn out fnl f: a holding on* **2/1**1
056 2 ¾ **Calrissian (IRE)**23 4483 2-9-0 **78** MichaelJMMurphy(5) 4 72
(Alan Jarvis) *mostly chsd wnr: rdn over 2f out: tried to chal over 1f out: kpt on but a hld* **4/1**3
2 3 shd **Rudi Five One (FR)**22 4533 2-9-0 0 RobertTart(5) 7 72
(Robert Eddery) *hld up in last: brought wdst of all and prog over 2f out: drvn to dispute 2nd ins fnl f: kpt on but a hld* **33/1**
00 4 1 ¾ **Dalaki (IRE)**7 5025 2-9-5 0 (b1) WilliamCarson 3 68
(Clive Brittain) *t.k.h: pressed ldrs: awkward briefly bnd over 5f out: rdn 3f out: nt qckn 2f out: one pce after* **20/1**

5 **5** ½ **Nakeeta**[10] 4925 2-9-5 0 .... MartinHarley 5 67
(Mick Channon) *t.k.h: hld up in midfield: cl enough over 2f out: drvn and one pce over 1f out* **4/1**[3]

63 **6** *nk* **Newmarket Warrior (IRE)**[15] 4764 2-9-5 0 .... LiamKeniry 9 66
(Michael Bell) *hld up in tch: taken wd and sme prog 2f out: one pce and no hdwy jst over 1f out* **11/4**[2]

7 *1* **Thunder Pass (IRE)** 2-9-5 0 .... RobertHavlin 6 64+
(Hughie Morrison) *hld up in rr: pushed along over 2f out: one pce and no imp on ldrs 1f out: eased nr fin* **14/1**

0 **8** *16* **Kaizen Factor**[10] 4926 2-8-12 0 .... PatMillman[(7)] 8 27
(Rod Millman) *pressed ldrs tl wknd rapidly 3f out: t.o* **33/1**

1m 44.19s (-0.51) **Going Correction** -0.45s/f (Firm) **8** Ran SP% **117.3**
Speed ratings (Par 94): **84,83,83,81,80 80,79,63**
toteswingers 1&2 £2.20, 1&3 £6.70, 2&3 £17.20 CSF £10.50 TOTE £2.80: £1.40, £1.40, £3.60; EX 12.00 Trifecta £103.30 Pool: £3930.88 - 28.51 winning units..
Owner Ivory, Woodcock, Bull, Hannon **Bred** Tommy James **Trained** East Everleigh, Wilts

FOCUS
A fair juvenile maiden, run at a sound pace.

5310 DOWNLOAD CORAL MOBILE FROM THE APP STORE H'CAP — 1m 67y
4:10 (4:10) (Class 4) (0-80,82) 3-Y-O+ **£4,851** (£1,443; £721; £360) **Stalls** Low

Form RPR

2025 **1** **Storming (IRE)**[26] 4383 3-8-12 **71** ....(p) CathyGannon 7 80
(Andrew Balding) *trckd ldng trio: rdn 2f out: sn chsd ldr: clsd to ld 1f out: drvn out and styd on wl* **11/4**[1]

1214 **2** ¾ **Cruiser**[25] 4415 5-9-12 **78** ....(p) DougieCostello 4 86
(William Muir) *trckd ldr after 1f: led 3f out: drvn 2f out: hdd 1f out: styd on but hld ins fnl f* **9/2**[2]

5440 **3** 1 ¾ **Yojimbo (IRE)**[10] 4908 5-9-6 **75** ....(v) CharlesBishop[(3)] 3 79
(Mick Channon) *trckd ldr 1f: cl up in 3rd after: rdn and nt qckn jst over 2f out: kpt on same pce after* **7/1**

0046 **4** 1 ¾ **Fabled City (USA)**[16] 4718 4-9-1 **72** ....(t) RyanTate[(5)] 6 72
(Clive Cox) *hld up in 5th: rdn over 2f out: clsd on ldrs over 1f out: wknd last 100yds* **8/1**

2550 **5** *6* **Flamborough Breeze**[22] 4523 4-9-8 **74** ....(t) MartinHarley 2 60
(Ed Vaughan) *stdd s: hld up in 6th: pushed along over 2f out: clsd sltly over 1f out but sn no imp: wknd and eased fnl f* **10/1**

1434 **6** *6* **Ancient Greece**[11] 4879 6-9-11 **77** ....(t) PatCosgrave 9 50
(George Baker) *hld up in last pair: rdn and no prog 3f out: wl btn fnl 2f* **5/1**[3]

32-0 **7** 2 ¾ **Rugosa**[218] 79 4-9-10 **76** .... SteveDrowne 10 42
(Charles Hills) *led at gd pce: hdd 3f out: hanging lft and wknd rapidly over 1f out* **10/1**

5310 **8** *nse* **Macchiara**[18] 4642 4-9-12 **78** .... ChrisCatlin 1 44
(Rae Guest) *dwlt: t.k.h in last pair: rdn 3f out: no prog and wl btn 2f out* **8/1**

1m 39.96s (-4.74) **Going Correction** -0.45s/f (Firm)
WFA 3 from 4yo+ 7lb **8** Ran SP% **114.4**
Speed ratings (Par 105): **105,104,102,100,94 88,86,85**
toteswingers 1&2 £3.50, 1&3 £4.80, 2&3 £5.70 CSF £15.06 CT £76.93 TOTE £3.60: £1.50, £1.40, £3.00; EX 18.20 Trifecta £90.40 Pool: £3276.43 - 27.17 winning units..
Owner CJJR Partnership **Bred** Jim McCormack **Trained** Kingsclere, Hants

FOCUS
A modest handicap. They went an even pace and the first two dominated inside the final furlong.

5311 ICE CREAM FESTIVAL MONDAY AUGUST 19TH H'CAP — 1m 2f 7y
4:40 (4:40) (Class 5) (0-70,70) 3-Y-O+ **£2,587** (£770; £384; £192) **Stalls** Centre

Form RPR

0003 **1** **Sinaadi (IRE)**[17] 4689 3-9-1 **66** .... RichardHughes 3 78
(Clive Brittain) *chsd clr ldng pair: pushed along over 3f out: clsd over 2f out: drvn to ld over 1f out: styd on wl* **6/5**[1]

1601 **2** 3 ½ **Shahrazad (IRE)**[7] 5032 4-8-7 **56** 6ex ....(t) ShelleyBirkett[(7)] 7 61
(Patrick Gilligan) *alternated ld w one rival and clr of rest: shkn up 3f out: hdd and one pce over 1f out* **5/2**[2]

6235 **3** *2* **Gaelic Ice**[19] 4605 4-8-12 **54** .... RobertHavlin 6 55
(Rod Millman) *racd off the pce in 5th: rdn 3f out: no prog 2f out: kpt on to take 3rd ins fnl f* **7/1**

5614 **4** 1 ¼ **Understory (USA)**[57] 3330 6-9-6 **67** .... RobertTart[(5)] 8 66
(Tim McCarthy) *alternated ld w one rival and clr of rest: drvn 3f out: hdd & wknd wl over 1f out* **5/1**[3]

4300 **5** *4* **Dolly Colman (IRE)**[8] 5002 5-8-9 **51** oh6 ....(p) CathyGannon 4 42
(Zoe Davison) *rrd s: wl off the pce in last: pushed along 5f out: brief prog over 2f out: no hdwy after* **33/1**

0136 **6** *15* **Tawseef (IRE)**[58] 3273 5-9-11 **70** .... MarkCoumbe[(3)] 1 31
(Roy Brotherton) *dwlt: chsd clr ldng pair: rdn over 3f out: wknd rapidly over 2f out: eased w rdr looking down* **12/1**

2m 5.53s (-3.17) **Going Correction** -0.45s/f (Firm)
WFA 3 from 4yo+ 9lb **6** Ran SP% **113.8**
Speed ratings (Par 103): **94,91,89,88,85 73**
toteswingers 1&2 £1.40, 1&3 £2.40, 2&3 £2.70 CSF £4.53 CT £12.94 TOTE £2.30: £1.90, £1.70; EX 6.40 Trifecta £20.10 Pool: £3130.67 - 116.52 winning units..
Owner Saeed Manana **Bred** Shortgrove Manor Stud **Trained** Newmarket, Suffolk

FOCUS
They took off after 2f in this moderate handicap. The runner-up sets the level.

5312 NEW MG3 FROM SMC H'CAP — 1m 3f 135y
5:10 (5:10) (Class 5) (0-70,70) 4-Y-O+ **£2,587** (£770; £384; £192) **Stalls** Centre

Form RPR

0512 **1** **Certavi (IRE)**[27] 4350 4-9-2 **65** .... LiamKeniry 10 73
(Brendan Powell) *hld up in last trio: stdy prog fr 3f out: clsd on ldrs over 1f out: shkn up to ld ins fnl f: styd on* **3/1**[2]

2 *1* **Mont Blanc**[84] 2487 4-9-7 **70** ....(p) RichardHughes 2 76
(Jane Chapple-Hyam) *trckd ldr 2f and again over 3f out: rdn to ld over 2f out: hdd over 1f out: kpt on ins fnl f* **5/2**[1]

0-04 **3** ½ **My Manekineko**[5] 5099 4-8-6 **55** .... WilliamCarson 1 60
(J R Jenkins) *t.k.h for much of r: hld up in midfield: clsd on ldrs 3f out: rdn to ld over 1f out: hdd and no ex ins fnl f* **16/1**

4-42 **4** *1* **Mister Fizz**[10] 4915 5-8-9 **65** .... DanielCremin[(7)] 9 69
(Miss Imogen Pickard) *trckd ldr after 2f to over 3f out: rdn and nt qckn over 2f out: kpt on same pce after* **7/2**[3]

366- **5** *3* **Not Til Monday (IRE)**[59] 7377 7-9-3 **66** .... DougieCostello 5 65
(J R Jenkins) *hld up in last pair: pushed along 5f out: stl pushed along and in last pair 2f out: styd on fnl f: nvr involved* **33/1**

2014 **6** ½ **Bold Cross (IRE)**[16] 4714 10-8-12 **64** .... ThomasBrown[(3)] 4 62
(Edward Bevan) *hld up in last trio: tried to cl on ldrs over 2f out: rdn and no imp wl over 1f out* **12/1**

0460 **7** *4* **Highlife Dancer**[13] 4832 5-8-13 **65** ....(v) CharlesBishop[(3)] 7 56
(Mick Channon) *led and sn clr: hdd & wknd over 2f out* **20/1**

0204 **8** 4 ½ **The Quarterjack**[16] 4720 4-9-2 **70** .... PhilipPrince[(5)] 8 53
(Ron Hodges) *chsd ldrs: drvn over 2f out: no imp over 1f out: sn wknd: heavily eased last 100yds* **9/2**

2624 **9** ½ **Norfolk Sky**[31] 4205 4-9-6 **69** .... JackMitchell 3 52
(Laura Mongan) *in tch: rdn 4f out: hmpd jst over 3f out: sn struggling in last pair* **16/1**

2m 26.08s (-3.42) **Going Correction** -0.45s/f (Firm) **9** Ran SP% **121.1**
Speed ratings (Par 103): **93,92,92,91,89 89,86,83,83**
toteswingers 1&2 £4.20, 1&3 £9.90, 2&3 £9.10 CSF £11.60 CT £105.32 TOTE £4.40: £1.40, £1.60, £4.80; EX 15.10 Trifecta £211.50 Pool: £2807.01 - 9.94 winning units..
Owner Nigel M Davies **Bred** Anthony Jones **Trained** Upper Lambourn, Berks
■ Stewards' Enquiry : Liam Keniry caution: careless riding.

FOCUS
An ordinary handicap, run at a sound pace.
T/Plt: £5.20 to a £1 stake. Pool: £98,884.52 - 13,843.55 winning tickets. T/Qpdt: £4.10 to a £1 stake. Pool: £6144.67 - 1100.55 winning tickets. JN

5296 DEAUVILLE (R-H)
Sunday, August 11

OFFICIAL GOING: Turf: good; fibresand: standard

5313a PRIX FRANCOIS BOUTIN (LISTED RACE) (2YO) (TURF) — 7f
1:00 (12:00) 2-Y-0 **£22,357** (£8,943; £6,707; £4,471; £2,235)

RPR

1 **Bunker (IRE)**[50] 3555 2-9-2 0 .... FrankieDettori 3 105+
(Richard Hannon) *led: shkn up to extend advantage 3f out: rdn and clsd down fr 2f out: strly pressed and hdd ent fnl f: drew clr w eventual runner-up: battled bk gamely u.p and got bk up cl home* **1/1**[1]

2 *shd* **Karakontie (JPN)**[41] 2-9-2 0 .... StephanePasquier 5 105+
(J E Pease, France) **48/10**[3]

3 *4* **Coulsty (IRE)**[15] 4768 2-9-2 0 .... RyanMoore 1 94
(Richard Hannon) *t.k.h early: trckd ldr: rdn 2f out: sn outpcd by front pair: swtchd rt ins fnl f and r.o: jst prevailed for 3rd* **12/1**

4 *shd* **Stormy Paradise (IRE)**[16] 4703 2-9-2 0 .... DaneO'Neill 4 94
(Brian Meehan) *dwlt sltly: hld up in last pair but wl in tch: rdn 2f out: sn outpcd by front pair: r.o but jst denied 3rd* **22/1**

5 1 ¼ **Apache Spirit**[35] 2-9-2 0 .... MaximeGuyon 2 90
(A Fabre, France) **6/4**[2]

1m 22.64s (-5.66) **Going Correction** -0.75s/f (Hard) **5** Ran SP% **119.3**
Speed ratings: **102,101,97,97,95**
WIN (incl. 1 euro stake): 2.00. PLACES: 1.40, 2.00. SF: 7.90.
Owner ShJoaan Al Thani MorecombeAndersonHughes **Bred** Lynn Lodge Stud **Trained** East Everleigh, Wilts

5314a PRIX DU HARAS DE FRESNAY-LE-BUFFARD - JACQUES LE MAROIS (GROUP 1) (3YO+) (TURF) — 1m (R)
2:45 (12:00) 3-Y-0+ **£278,731** (£111,512; £55,756; £27,853; £13,951)

RPR

1 **Moonlight Cloud**[7] 5040 5-9-1 0 .... ThierryJarnet 11 125
(F Head, France) *midfield: smooth hdwy to chal 2f out: shkn up and led over 1f out: qcknd clr ent fnl f and looked in full control 100yds out: rapidly diminishing advantage cl home: jst hld on* **11/4**[3]

2 *shd* **Olympic Glory (IRE)**[91] 2298 3-8-11 0 .... FrankieDettori 7 127+
(Richard Hannon) *hld up in rr: stdy hdwy fr 3f out: rdn 2f out: nt clr run briefly and swtchd rt over 1f out: r.o and wnt 2nd 100yds out: clsng rapidly on wnr towards fin: jst failed* **18/1**

3 1 ¾ **Intello (GER)**[35] 4104 3-8-11 0 .... OlivierPeslier 5 122
(A Fabre, France) *midfield in tch: rdn over 2f out: wnt 2nd ent fnl f: chsd wnr but no imp and dropped to 3rd 100yds out: kpt on* **5/2**[2]

4 *hd* **Declaration Of War (USA)**[11] 4875 4-9-4 0 .... RyanMoore 2 123
(A P O'Brien, Ire) *hld up in rr: rdn over 2f out: hdwy fr over 1f out: wnt 4th 100yds out: r.o wl and pressed for 3rd cl home but nt pce of front pair* **11/1**

5 *6* **Dawn Approach (IRE)**[11] 4875 3-8-11 0 .... KevinManning 6 108
(J S Bolger, Ire) *t.k.h under restraint early: prom: rdn to chal over 2f out: readily outpcd by eventual wnr ent fnl f: sn no ex and btn: fdd and dropped to 5th* **2/1**[1]

6 *snk* **Leitir Mor (IRE)**[11] 4875 3-8-11 0 .... RonanWhelan 4 108
(J S Bolger, Ire) *led on rail: rdn over 2f out: strly pressed and hdd over 1f out: no ex and btn: fdd but rdn out and got bk up for 6th cl home* **150/1**

7 1 ½ **Elusive Kate (USA)**[14] 4817 4-9-1 0 .... WilliamBuick 1 102
(John Gosden) *trckd ldrs: rdn to chal 2f out: outpcd by wnr over 1f out: no ex and btn ins fnl f: fdd: eased and lost 6th cl home* **10/1**

8 *8* **Aljamaaheer (IRE)**[29] 4276 4-9-4 0 .... PaulHanagan 13 87
(Roger Varian) *midfield in tch on outer: travelling strly and prom 3f out: shkn up to chal 2f out: sn rdn and readily outpcd by wnr: no ex and btn over 1f out: fdd* **20/1**

9 2 ½ **Peace At Last (IRE)**[42] 3876 3-8-11 0 .... FabriceVeron 12 80
(H-A Pantall, France) *t.k.h: midfield in tch: rdn 3f out: outpcd and btn over 1f out: fdd and eased ins fnl f* **66/1**

10 *12* **Nova Neyev (FR)**[7] 5040 5-9-4 0 .... DelphineSantiago 8 54
(P Capelle, France) *awkward s and wnt rt: a towards rr: pushed along over 2f out and sn btn: eased ins fnl f and t.o: nvr a factor* **500/1**

11 *3* **Burwaaz**[8] 4986 4-9-4 0 .... DaneO'Neill 10 47
(Ed Dunlop) *prom: rdn 3f out: no ex and lost pl 2f out: fdd: eased ent fnl f and t.o* **150/1**

12 *4* **Prince D'Alienor (IRE)**[35] 4104 5-9-4 0 ....(p) FlavienPrat 3 38
(A Fabre, France) *slow to stride and rousted along to go forward early: sn pressing ldr on outer: no ex 3f out: dropped to rr qckly and eased: t.o* **150/1**

13 1 ½ **Indian Sly (FR)**[7] 5040 8-9-4 0 .... JimmyTastayre 9 34
(P Capelle, France) *bmpd s: a in rr: rdn 3f out: last and btn 2f out: eased and t.o: nvr a factor* **500/1**

1m 33.39s (-7.41) **Going Correction** -0.50s/f (Hard)
WFA 3 from 4yo+ 7lb **13** Ran SP% **119.9**
Speed ratings: **117,116,115,114,108 108,107,99,96,84 81,77,76**
WIN (incl. 1 euro stake): 3.20. PLACES: 1.30, 2.50, 1.20. DF: 28.20. SF: 39.10.
Owner George Strawbridge **Bred** George Strawbridge **Trained** France

FOCUS
A truly top-class field and one of the races of the current campaign. Moonlight Cloud is rated to her best course form, with Olympic Glory a shade unlucky.

5315a PRIX MINERVE (GROUP 3) (3YO FILLIES) (TURF) 1m 4f 110y
3:20 (12:00) 3-Y-O **£32,520** (£13,008; £9,756; £6,504; £3,252)

RPR

1 **Pomology (USA)**26 4384 3-8-9 0 WilliamBuick 1 108+
(John Gosden) *trckd ldr on inner: swtchd out and smooth hdwy to chal on turn into st: rdn to ld over 1f out: styd on strly u.p and asserted: diminishing advantage towards fin but nvr in any danger* **7/2**3

2 ½ **Artiste Divine**29 4323 3-8-9 0 MaximeGuyon 4 107+
(A Fabre, France) *midfield in tch: rdn over 1f out: wnt 2nd ins fnl f: styd on and chsd wnr: clsd towards fin but no real danger* **10/3**2

3 3 **Gosh (IRE)**37 3-8-9 0 AntoineHamelin 2 103
(Mme Pia Brandt, France) *dwlt sltly: midfield on inner: rdn over 2f out: styd on and wnt 3rd cl home: nt pce of front pair* **8/1**

4 1 **Mila (FR)**29 4323 3-8-9 0 Christophe-PatriceLemaire 5 101
(A De Royer-Dupre, France) *led: strly pressed on turn into st: rdn and hdd over 1f out: kpt on tl no ex ins fnl f: fdd and dropped to 4th* **9/4**1

5 ½ **Commute**31 3-8-9 0 GregoryBenoist 3 100
(D Smaga, France) *restless stalls: dwlt sltly: restrained and hld up in last pair on inner: rdn over 2f out: rn green u.p and nt clr run ins fnl f but styd on under hands and heels to take n.d 5th cl home: do bttr* **6/1**

6 snk **Oriental Wind**28 3-8-10 0 ow1 ChristopheSoumillon 6 101
(Rod Collet, France) *midfield on outer: clsd 5f out: rdn and ev ch 2f out: outpcd by ldrs ent fnl f: styd on but dropped to 6th cl home* **12/1**

7 4 **Tunkwa (FR)**41 3912 3-8-9 0 TheoBachelot 8 94
(D Sepulchre, France) *dwlt sltly: dropped in fr wdst draw and hld up in last: rdn over 2f out: plugged on u.p but sn outpcd and btn: eased towards fin* **16/1**

8 8 **Daksha (FR)**36 4092 3-8-9 0 FranckBlondel 7 82
(W Hickst, Germany) *trckd ldr on outer: rdn and brief effrt to chal on turn into st: no ex and btn over 1f out: fdd and dropped to last: eased ent fnl f* **20/1**

2m 41.8s (-4.60) **Going Correction** -0.175s/f (Firm) 8 Ran SP% **119.8**
Speed ratings: **107,106,104,104,103 103,101,96**
WIN (incl. 1 euro stake): 4.80. PLACES: 2.30, 1.80, 2.00. DF: 12.80. SF: 29.30.
Owner HRH Princess Haya Of Jordan **Bred** Dr John A Chandler **Trained** Newmarket, Suffolk
FOCUS
Pomology did this with a bit to spare.

4564 CURRAGH (R-H)
Sunday, August 11

OFFICIAL GOING: Round course - good to firm; straight course - good (good to firm in places)

5317a BET ONLINE AT THETOTE.COM ROYAL WHIP STKS (GROUP 3) 1m 2f
2:45 (2:45) 3-Y-0+ **£31,707** (£9,268; £4,390; £1,463)

RPR

1 **Maputo**23 4473 3-9-0 JoeFanning 1 116
(Mark Johnston) *prom early: sn settled bhd ldr in 2nd: tk clsr order fr 4f out and clsd gng wl to ld 2f out: sn pushed 1 l clr: rdn ins fnl f and styd on wl* **5/4**1

2 1 **Caponata (USA)**21 4567 4-9-6 108 PatSmullen 2 111
(D K Weld, Ire) *hld up bhd ldrs: 4th 1/2-way: tk clsr order fr 4f out: hdwy between horses fr 2f out into 2nd ent fnl f: rdn and sn no imp on wnr: kpt on wl towards fin* **9/2**3

3 2 ¼ **Fortify (IRE)**12 4869 3-9-0 109 (v) JosephO'Brien 4 110
(A P O'Brien, Ire) *trckd ldrs: 3rd 1/2-way: prog on outer into st: rdn 2f out and sn no imp on wnr u.p: kpt on same pce in 3rd ins fnl f* **5/1**

4 1 ¾ **Scintillula (IRE)**3 5209 3-9-0 115 (t) RoryCleary 5 106
(J S Bolger, Ire) *sn led: 2 l clr 1/2-way: pushed along into st and hdd narrowly 2f out: rdn and sn no ex u.p: dropped to 4th ins fnl f and kpt on same pce* **11/4**2

5 4 ½ **Qewy (IRE)**34 4132 3-9-0 98 DeclanMcDonogh 3 97
(John M Oxx, Ire) *racd in rr of quintet thrght: rdn and no imp on ldrs over 2f out: kpt on same pce ins fnl f* **16/1**

2m 8.13s (-1.17) **Going Correction** -0.275s/f (Firm)
WFA 3 from 4yo 9lb 5 Ran SP% **111.8**
Speed ratings: **113,112,110,109,105**
CSF £7.44 TOTE £1.40: £1.02, £2.80; DF 4.10.
Owner Sheikh Hamdan Bin Mohammed Al Maktoum **Bred** Darley **Trained** Middleham Moor, N Yorks
FOCUS
Only a couple of runs after winning in handicap company Maputo took the step up in grade in his stride. The second and fifth help wiith the standard.

5318a FRIARSTOWN STUD DEBUTANTE STKS (FILLIES) (GROUP 2) 7f
3:15 (3:17) 2-Y-O **£52,845** (£15,447; £7,317; £2,439)

RPR

1 **Tapestry (IRE)**21 4566 2-9-0 JosephO'Brien 4 109+
(A P O'Brien, Ire) *chsd ldrs: 3rd 1/2-way: hdwy fr 2f out on outer to chal 1f out: rdn to ld ins fnl 150yds and drvn clr* **4/5**1

2 1 ¾ **Perhaps (IRE)**24 4462 2-9-0 101 (p) SeamieHeffernan 6 104
(A P O'Brien, Ire) *sn led: 3 l clr 1/2-way: reduced advantage fr 2f out and sn rdn: chal 1f out and hdd ins fnl 150yds: kpt on wl towards fin: match wnr* **11/4**2

3 ½ **Avenue Gabriel**24 4462 2-9-0 100 ChrisHayes 5 103
(P D Deegan, Ire) *trckd ldr in 2nd: rdn fr 2f out and clsd u.p to chal briefly ins fnl f: sn no ex in 3rd: kpt on same pce* **8/1**3

4 5 ½ **Minorette (USA)**32 4185 2-9-0 MichaelHussey 1 88
(A P O'Brien, Ire) *w.w towards rr: 5th 1/2-way: tk clsr order into st: pushed along in mod 4th 2f out and no imp on ldrs: kpt on one pce* **12/1**

5 2 ½ **Sacred Aspect (IRE)**29 4318 2-9-0 93 (t) JohnnyMurtagh 2 81
(K J Condon, Ire) *hld up: tk clsr order in 4th after 1/2-way: sn rdn and no imp on principals: kpt on one pce* **10/1**

6 4 ¾ **Glassatura (IRE)**69 2944 2-9-0 ShaneFoley 7 68
(M Halford, Ire) *on toes befhand: hld up in tch: received slt bump bef 1/2-way: sn niggled along in rr and no imp on principals: one pce fnl 2f* **14/1**

1m 22.89s (-7.91) **Going Correction** -0.85s/f (Hard) 6 Ran SP% **116.8**
Speed ratings: **111,109,108,102,99 93**
CSF £3.44 TOTE £1.60: £1.02, £2.10; DF 3.50.
Owner Mrs J Magnier & M Tabor & D Smith & Flaxman Stable **Bred** Orpendale And The Niarchos Family **Trained** Ballydoyle, Co Tipperary
■ Stewards' Enquiry : Seamie Heffernan four-day ban: excessive use and frequency of the whip without giving filly time to respond (Aug 27-29,31)
FOCUS
There wasn't a bad filly among the six of these and this was a hot contest. No prisoners were taken with the gallop that was set.

5319a KEENELAND PHOENIX STKS (C&F) (GROUP 1) 6f
3:45 (3:45) 2-Y-O **£94,308** (£30,894; £14,634; £4,878; £3,252)

RPR

1 **Sudirman (USA)**43 3847 2-9-3 110 WayneLordan 4 114
(David Wachman, Ire) *prom: settled bhd ldrs: 3rd 1/2-way: hdwy over 2f out to chal 1 1/2f out: rdn to ld ent fnl f and kpt on wl u.p towards fin: all out* **4/1**2

2 ½ **Big Time (IRE)**43 3847 2-9-3 108 PatSmullen 5 112
(John Joseph Murphy, Ire) *prom: settled bhd ldr in 2nd: 2 l bhd at 1/2-way: tk clsr order 2f out: rdn between horses to chal and edgd sltly lft over 1f out: kpt on wl towards fin: hld* **7/1**3

3 ½ **War Command (USA)**54 3422 2-9-3 119 JosephO'Brien 3 111
(A P O'Brien, Ire) *w.w: niggled along in 4th 1/2-way: rdn fr 2f out on outer and wnt 3rd u.p ent fnl f: sn no imp on wnr and kpt on same pce* **2/5**1

4 3 ½ **Ambiance (IRE)**12 4855 2-9-3 (v1) JohnnyMurtagh 1 100
(Mick Channon) *tacked over to nr side to ld early: over 2 l clr 1/2-way: reduced advantage and pushed along over 2f out: sn jnd and hdd over 1f out: short of room on inner and swtchd rt: kpt on same pce in 4th towards fin* **14/1**

5 2 **Sniper**13 4841 2-9-3 (b1) JamieSpencer 6 94
(G M Lyons, Ire) *hld up in rr: rdn over 2f out and sn no imp on principals: kpt on one pce* **40/1**

1m 9.35s (-6.15) **Going Correction** -0.80s/f (Hard) 5 Ran SP% **113.0**
Speed ratings: **109,108,107,103,100**
CSF £29.57 TOTE £7.10: £15.20, £15.10; DF 30.50.
Owner Mrs Fitri Hay/Mrs John Magnier **Bred** Kathryn Nikkel & Jeanne Canty **Trained** Goolds Cross, Co Tipperary
FOCUS
The first and second from the Railway Stakes ran more or less the same race once more, and the form makes sense with the front pair both showing improvement in keeping with what would be expected. War Command was the best part of two lengths below his Coventry win, but the form of that race is working out well overall. This was run in a record time for juveniles.

5320a PAYPAL SUPPORTING IRISH AUTISM ACTION PHOENIX SPRINT STKS (GROUP 3) 6f
4:15 (4:15) 3-Y-O+ **£31,707** (£9,268; £4,390; £1,463)

RPR

1 **Slade Power (IRE)**29 4298 4-9-10 115 WayneLordan 4 117+
(Edward Lynam, Ire) *a.p: cl 2nd 1/2-way: hdwy gng best to dispute 2f out: pushed out to ld over 1f out: styd on wl* **2/1**2

2 1 ½ **Hamza (IRE)**22 4527 4-9-7 (b) PatSmullen 9 109
(Kevin Ryan) *led: narrow advantage 1/2-way: sn pushed along and jnd 2f out: hdd u.p over 1f out and sn no imp on wnr in 2nd: kpt on same pce* **11/2**3

3 1 ½ **Sea Siren (AUS)**28 4328 5-9-4 113 (b) JosephO'Brien 6 101
(A P O'Brien, Ire) *prom: cl 3rd 1/2-way: rdn under 2f out and sn no ex u.p in 3rd: kpt on same pce* **1/1**1

4 1 **Dandy Boy (ITY)**50 3557 7-9-7 106 (t) FergalLynch 3 101
(David Marnane, Ire) *hood fr rival landed on rdrs hd briefly leaving stalls: racd in rr: pushed along over 2f out and sn swtchd rt: rdn in 5th 1 1/2f out and prog u.p into nvr threatening 4th ins fnl 150yds: kpt on same pce* **16/1**

5 1 ¾ **Mass Rally (IRE)**43 3822 6-9-7 (b) PaulMulrennan 2 96
(Michael Dods) *trckd ldrs: 5th 1/2-way: rdn and no imp on ldrs in 4th 1 1/2f out: kpt on same pce ins fnl f* **14/1**

6 11 **In Salutem**6 5077 3-9-3 89 JohnnyMurtagh 7 59
(K J Condon, Ire) *trckd ldrs: 4th 1/2-way: sn pushed along and no ex: dropped towards rr ent fnl f: eased* **33/1**

7 nk **Sendmylovetorose**10 4933 3-9-0 102 ChrisHayes 10 55
(A Oliver, Ire) *w.w towards rr: niggled along in 6th 1/2-way and sn no imp: eased ins fnl f* **25/1**

1m 9.33s (-6.17) **Going Correction** -0.80s/f (Hard)
WFA 3 from 4yo+ 4lb 7 Ran SP% **118.1**
Speed ratings: **109,107,105,103,101 86,86**
CSF £14.28 TOTE £3.00: £1.60, £3.80; DF 10.50.
Owner Mrs S Power **Bred** Mrs S Power **Trained** Dunshaughlin, Co Meath
FOCUS
The rise up the sprinting ranks of Slade Power needed a performance like this to give it that bit more credence and he delivered like a good horse. He confirmed his Group 1 personal best latest.

LE LION-D'ANGERS (R-H)
Sunday, August 11

OFFICIAL GOING: Turf: good to soft

5323a PRIX DE LA VEZ (MAIDEN) (2YO) (TURF) 7f
10:15 (12:00) 2-Y-O **£5,691** (£2,276; £1,707; £1,138; £569)

RPR

1 **Artiste Celebre (FR)**118 2-8-13 0 AlexandreRoussel 5 77
(W Menuet, France) **174/10**

2 nk **Race For Fame (IRE)**21 2-9-2 0 FabriceVeron 6 79
(H-A Pantall, France) **6/4**1

3 1 ½ **Solonder (FR)** 2-8-8 0 MlleZoePfeil(8) 10 75
(M Le Forestier, France) **9/1**

4 2 ½ **Lacalifornie (FR)** 2-8-13 0 GeraldAvranche 8 66
(E Leenders, France) **36/1**

5 nk **Khabi** 2-8-11 0 AdrienFouassier 11 63
(E J O'Neill, France) **22/1**

6 ¾ **Speedy Glaz (FR)** 2-9-2 0 (p) AnthonyClement 4 66
(A Clement, France) **44/5**3

7 2 ½ **Sarina (GER)** 2-8-9 0 ow1 ThomasHenderson 1 52
(J-P Carvalho, France) **22/1**

8 3 **Kerstenia (FR)** 2-8-13 0 AnthonyCrastus 2 49
(D Sepulchre, France) **9/5**2

9 *8* **Mizzeni (FR)** 2-8-11 0 MickaelForest 9 26
(Gay Kelleway) *stood stl whn stalls opened: slow to stride and wl adrift in last: on terms in rr after 2f: rdn and no imp over 2f out: nvr in contention: eased fnl f* **41/1**
10 *10* **Valcy Great (FR)** 2-8-11 0 ArnaudBourgeais 3
(E Lecoiffier, France) **77/1**
11 *20* **Royal Derby (FR)** 2-8-10 0 (b) StephaneLaurent(6) 7
(C Plisson, France) **39/1**
1m 27.76s (87.76) **11** Ran SP% **118.9**
WIN (incl. 11 euro stake): 18.40. PLACES: 3.60, 1.50, 2.50. DF: 21.20. SF: 51.70.
Owner Ecurie Armand Israel **Bred** Haras De Bernesq & Jean Zorbibe **Trained** France

4819 MUNICH (L-H)

Sunday, August 11

OFFICIAL GOING: Turf: good

5324a GROSSER PREIS VON BAYERN (FORMERLY RHEINLAND-POKAL) (GROUP 1) (3YO+) (TURF) 1m 4f

4:20 (12:00) 3-Y-0+ **£81,300** (£24,390; £12,195; £5,691; £2,439)

RPR
1 **Seismos (IRE)**[42] 3879 5-9-6 0 AndreaAtzeni 6 112+
(A Wohler, Germany) *led after 2f and mde rest: rdn on turn into st: styd on strly and forged clr: coasted home fnl 75yds: v readily* **124/10**
2 *4* **Empoli (GER)**[35] 4103 3-8-9 0 AStarke 3 106
(P Schiergen, Germany) *midfield in tch on outer: rdn over 2f out: wnt 2nd over 1f out: styd on but no real imp on ready wnr* **27/10[2]**
3 *3/4* **Girolamo (GER)**[21] 4571 4-9-6 0 DPorcu 1 104
(P Schiergen, Germany) *hld up in tch on inner: last whn rdn over 2f out: wnt 3rd over 1f out: styd on but no real imp on ready wnr* **89/10**
4 *5* **Feuerblitz (GER)**[245] 8043 4-9-6 0 MircoDemuro 4 96
(M Figge, Germany) *hld up in sltly detached last: clsd on outer 4f out: rdn over 2f out: sn outpcd by wnr: plugged on for mod 4th* **48/10[3]**
5 *3* **Temida (IRE)**[21] 4571 5-9-3 0 FilipMinarik 5 89
(M G Mintchev, Germany) *trckd ldr on outer: rdn to try and chal on turn into st: sn readily outpcd by wnr: no ex and btn over 1f out: fdd* **4/5[1]**
6 *6* **Quidamo**[28] 6-9-6 0 ASuborics 2 82
(Frau J Mayer, Germany) *led 2f: trckd ldr on inner whn hdd: rdn over 2f out: sn readily outpcd by wnr: no ex and btn over 1f out: fdd and dropped to last* **104/10**
2m 33.2s (153.20)
WFA 3 from 4yo+ 11lb **6** Ran SP% **126.2**
WIN (incl. 10 euro stake): 134. PLACES: 30, 28. SF: 591.
Owner Gestut Karlshof **Bred** Gestt Karlshof **Trained** Germany

2145 JAGERSRO (R-H)

Sunday, August 11

OFFICIAL GOING: Dirt: standard

5325a ZAWAWI CUP (GROUP 3) (3YO+) (DIRT) 6f (D)

3:45 (12:00) 3-Y-0+ **£28,382** (£14,191; £6,811; £4,541; £2,838)

RPR
1 **Verde-Mar (BRZ)**[350] 5647 6-9-6 0 ValmirDeAzeredo 9 106
(Fabricio Borges, Sweden) *smartly away: trckd ldng trio: hdwy on outside over 2f out: hrd rdn and r.o to ld 110yds out: hld on gamely u.p* **5/4[1]**
2 *nk* **Ragazzo (NOR)**[10] 4936 4-9-6 0 EspenSki 3 105
(Annike Bye Hansen, Norway) *slow to stride and in rr: shkn up and hdwy 1/2-way: 5th and styng on over 2f out: r.o wl u.p fnl f: clsd on wnr all way to line but nvr quite getting there* **16/5[2]**
3 *1 3/4* **Beat Baby (IRE)**[36] 6-9-6 0 Per-AndersGraberg 6 99
(Niels Petersen, Norway) *broke wl and led: rdn over 1 1/2f out: r.o gamely: hdd 110yds out: wknd cl home* **69/10[3]**
4 *1/2* **Govinda (USA)**[10] 4936 6-9-6 0 OliverWilson 4 98
(Vanja Sandrup, Sweden) *chsd ldr on outer: rdn and outpcd over 1 1/2f out: kpt on ins fnl f* **218/10**
5 *nk* **Alcohuaz (CHI)**[61] 8-9-6 0 ElioneChaves 7 97
(Lennart Reuterskiold Jr, Sweden) *towards rr: rdn and hdwy over 2f out: styd on u.p fnl f: nvr on terms* **71/10**
6 *3* **Match Point (FR)**[36] 7-9-3 0 LennartHammer-Hansen 10 84
(Niels Petersen, Norway) *towards rr: hdwy 2f out: kpt on at same pce fnl f: nvr in contention* **225/10**
7 *5* **Let'sgoforit (IRE)**[61] 5-9-6 0 FJohansson 1 71
(Bodil Hallencreutz, Sweden) *chsd ldrs: rdn and outpcd over 2f out: wknd fnl f* **207/10**
8 *1 3/4* **Timeless Stride (IRE)**[96] 2145 6-9-6 0 MadeleineSmith 8 66
(Madeleine Smith, Sweden) *towards rr: rdn and no imp fr 2f out: sn wknd* **221/10**
9 *hd* **Cave Man (NOR)** 4-9-6 0 RafaelSchistl 5 65
(Are Hyldmo, Norway) *midfield: rdn and outpcd over 2f out: sn wknd* **167/10**
10 *dist* **Secret Asset (IRE)**[30] 4263 8-9-6 0 (p) MichaelO'Connell 2
(Jane Chapple-Hyam) *chsd ldng gp: 5th and scrubbed along 1/2-way: sn outpcd and wl bhd fnl 2f* **102/10**
1m 11.6s (71.60) **10** Ran SP% **125.4**
PARI-MUTUEL (all including 1sek stake): WIN 2.24; PLACE 1.32, 1.64, 1.66; SF 9.80.
Owner Energi Dupla Racing AB **Bred** Haras Santa Rita Da Serra **Trained** Sweden

5326a LAND ROVER SVENSKT DERBY (LISTED RACE) (3YO) (DIRT) 1m 4f

4:15 (12:00) 3-Y-0
£83,065 (£38,210; £16,613; £11,629; £8,306; £4,983)

RPR
1 **Hurricane Red (IRE)** 3-9-4 0 ElioneChaves 4 97
(Lennart Reuterskiold Jr, Sweden) **37/20[1]**
2 *3* **London Citizen (USA)**[22] 4541 3-9-4 0 ManuelSantos 2 92
(Mrs K Burke) *led: sn 3 l clr: 1 l ld and rdn 2f out: edgd rt 1 1/2f out: hdd ins fnl f: no ex* **158/10**
3 *3/4* **Be My Award (SWE)** 3-9-4 0 JacobJohansen 6 91
(Lennart Reuterskiold Jr, Sweden) **106/10**
4 *6* **Giftorm (USA)** 3-9-4 0 GeorgeBaker 1 81
(Fredrik Reuterskiold, Sweden) **183/10**
5 *1 1/4* **Over The Ocean (USA)**[64] 3-9-4 0 RafaelSchistl 14 79
(Niels Petersen, Norway) **89/10**
6 *6* **Whistler (DEN)**[42] 3-9-1 0 ShaneKarlsson 7 67
(Niels Petersen, Norway) **26/1**
7 *3* **Ikc Dragon Heart (USA)** 3-9-4 0 OliverWilson 5 65
(Johan Reuterskiold, Sweden) **68/1**
8 *nk* **Quite A Mission (SWE)**[42] 3-9-4 0 (p) Per-AndersGraberg 9 64
(Niels Petersen, Norway) **81/10**
9 *1 1/2* **Mr Edge (USA)** 3-9-4 0 (b) ManuelMartinez 12 62
(Lennart Reuterskiold Jr, Sweden) **33/1**
10 *4* **Mill Marin (IRE)**[52] 3-9-1 0 LennartHammer-Hansen 10 53
(Wido Neuroth, Norway) **45/1**
11 *1/2* **Diamant (GER)**[92] 3-9-4 0 Jan-ErikNeuroth 11 55
(Wido Neuroth, Norway) **56/10[3]**
12 *hd* **Desert Dawn (SWE)** 3-9-4 0 EspenSki 8 54
(Roy Arne Kvisla, Sweden) **35/1**
13 *dist* **Alcaeus**[15] 4770 3-9-4 0 LukeMorris 3
(Sir Mark Prescott Bt) *dwlt and outpcd early: scrubbed along to chse ldng gp: pushed along to hold pl 1/2-way: wknd qckly over 3 1/2f out: eased whn wl bhd fnl 2 1/2f* **51/10[2]**
14 *dist* **Twistedlittlestar (IRE)** 3-9-1 0 FJohansson 13
(Niels Petersen, Norway) **192/10**
2m 32.4s (152.40) **14** Ran SP% **125.5**
PARI-MUTUEL (all including 1sek stake): WIN 2.84; PLACE 1.80, 4.07, 2.29; SF 43.53.
Owner Stall Zada **Bred** Grangemore Stud **Trained** Sweden

4846 LES LANDES

Sunday, August 11

OFFICIAL GOING: Good

5327a LADBROKES ODDS ON! BIG THREE COUPON H'CAP 7f

3:05 (3:06) 3-Y-0+ **£1,460** (£525; £315)

RPR
1 **Pas D'Action**[14] 5-9-1 LauraPike 6
(Mrs A Malzard, Jersey) **6/4[1]**
2 *3* **Spanish Bounty**[28] 8-10-12 MattieBatchelor 4
(Mrs A Malzard, Jersey) **3/1[3]**
3 *3* **First Cat**[14] 6-10-1 AntonyProcter 2
(S Arthur, Jersey) **7/2**
4 *nk* **Aciano (IRE)**[54] 3429 5-9-13 (tp) JoshBaudains 1
(Brendan Powell) **2/1[2]**
5 *2 1/2* **Mr Opulence**[14] 4-9-8 TimClark 5
(T Le Brocq, Jersey) **12/1**
6 *12* **Lively Little Lady**[44] 3789 3-8-11 ow6 MatthewLawson 7
(Mrs A Corson, Jersey) **12/1**
7 *1 1/2* **Country Blue (FR)**[14] 4-9-9 (p) ThomasGarner 3
(Mrs A Malzard, Jersey) **3/1[3]**
1m 31.0s (1.00)
WFA 3 from 4yo+ 6lb **7** Ran SP% **160.9**

Owner J Jamouneau **Bred** Jenny Hall Bloodstock Ltd **Trained** St Ouen, Jersey

5328a COUTTS & CO CHANNEL ISLANDS H'CAP 1m 100y

3:40 (3:39) (0-55,) 3-Y-0+ **£1,790** (£660; £400)

RPR
1 **Jackpot**[17] 4666 3-9-3 MissJenniferPowell 1
(Brendan Powell) **3/1[3]**
2 *3 1/2* **Fast Freddie**[14] 9-10-12 (p) JoshBaudains 2
(Mrs A Corson, Jersey) **9/2**
3 *4* **Vamos (IRE)**[14] 7-9-2 (b) ThomasGarner 5
(Mrs A Malzard, Jersey) **6/1**
4 *7* **Lady Petrus**[14] 4846 8-8-10 TimClark 4
(S Arthur, Jersey) **10/1**
5 *3 1/2* **Rebel Woman**[14] 7-10-4 MatthewLawson 7
(Mrs A Corson, Jersey) **5/4[1]**
6 *7* **Lucifers Shadow (IRE)**[14] 4-10-11 AntonyProcter 3
(Mrs C Gilbert, Jersey) **15/8[2]**
7 *1 1/2* **La Verte Rue (USA)**[14] 7-10-1 MattieBatchelor 6
(Mrs A Malzard, Jersey) **5/1**
1m 52.0s (112.00)
WFA 3 from 4yo+ 7lb **7** Ran SP% **162.5**

Owner Philip Banfield **Bred** P Banfield **Trained** Upper Lambourn, Berks

5329a LADBROKES "THE ODDSFATHER" H'CAP 1m 4f

4:50 (4:54) (0-60,) 3-Y-0+ **£1,460** (£525; £315)

RPR
1 **Garden Party**[14] 4846 9-10-4 (b) AntonyProcter 8
(T J Bougourd, Guernsey) **10/3[3]**
2 *nk* **I'm Harry**[19] 4605 4-10-12 (vt) MattieBatchelor 2
(George Baker) **5/4[1]**
3 *5* **River Du Nord (FR)**[14] 4846 6-8-5 TimClark 7
(Susan Gardner) **15/8[2]**
4 *6* **Sissi Guihen (FR)**[28] 7-10-5 ThomasGarner 1
(Mrs A Malzard, Jersey) **5/1**
5 *7* **King Kenny**[14] 8-10-6 MatthewLawson 3
(Mrs A Corson, Jersey) **4/1**
6 *1 1/2* **Toggle**[14] 4846 9-8-12 ow7 (v) JoshBaudains 5
(Mrs A Corson, Jersey) **12/1**
7 *1/2* **Bollin Fergus**[14] 9-9-1 MrPCollington 4
(Mrs J L Le Brocq, Jersey) **9/2**
8 *1/2* **Rocquaine (IRE)**[28] 4-9-2 LauraPike 9
(Mrs A Malzard, Jersey) **10/1**
9 *hd* **Robbmaa (FR)**[14] 4846 8-8-13 ow8 (b) MissKMargarson 6
(Mrs J L Le Brocq, Jersey) **15/2**
2m 49.0s (-1.00) **9** Ran SP% **185.7**

Owner T J Bougourd **Bred** The Queen **Trained** Guernsey

The Form Book Flat, Raceform Ltd, Compton, RG20 6NL.

[5261] AYR (L-H)

Monday, August 12

OFFICIAL GOING: Good (good to firm in places; 9.0)

Wind: Fresh, half against Weather: Overcast

5330 EBF/TENNENT'S LAGER MAIDEN FILLIES' STKS 7f 50y

2:30 (2:30) (Class 4) 2-Y-O **£4,204** (£1,251; £625; £312) **Stalls** High

Form RPR

0 **1** **Hala Hala (IRE)**[48] 3664 2-8-11 0................. WilliamTwiston-Davies(3) 1 73
(Michael Bell) *hld up in tch: hdwy over 2f out: rdn to ld ins fnl f: kpt on wl* **16/1**

44 **2** *1* **Charlotte's Day**[17] 4723 2-9-0 0.. LukeMorris 7 71
(Sir Mark Prescott Bt) *chsd ldr: led and hung lft over 1f out: hdd ins fnl f: kpt on same pce* **7/2**[2]

3 *nk* **Vivere (IRE)** 2-9-0 0.. PhillipMakin 3 70+
(David O'Meara) *in tch: n.m.r briefly and outpcd over 2f out: rallied over 1f out: kpt on wl fnl f* **14/1**

6 **4** *3/4* **Lovelocks (IRE)**[17] 4702 2-9-0 0..................................... SteveDrowne 8 68
(Charles Hills) *dwlt and wnt rt s: bhd: effrt over 2f out: swtchd rt over 1f out: kpt on fnl f: nt pce to chal* **6/4**[1]

5 *1* **Scots Law (IRE)** 2-9-0 0... TomEaves 4 65
(Keith Dalgleish) *dwlt: hld up in tch: n.m.r briefly over 2f out: sn rdn: kpt on fnl f: no imp* **50/1**

3 **6** *3/4* **Power Up**[11] 4925 2-9-0 0.. JoeFanning 5 64
(Mark Johnston) *led: rdn and hdd over 1f out: sn outpcd* **4/1**[3]

0 **7** *hd* **Western Sands (IRE)**[45] 3760 2-9-0 0.............................. LeeTopliss 6 63
(Richard Fahey) *hld up in tch on outside: rdn and effrt over 2f out: edgd lft and outpcd over 1f out* **10/1**

8 *1 1/4* **Light Weight (IRE)** 2-9-0 0.. GrahamLee 2 60
(Kevin Ryan) *trckd ldrs: rdn over 2f out: wknd over 1f out* **11/1**

1m 33.53s (0.13) **Going Correction** -0.10s/f (Good) **8** Ran SP% **114.2**

Speed ratings (Par 93): **95,93,93,92,91 90,90,89**

toteswingers 1&2 £12.60, 1&3 £26.60, 2&3 £8.30 CSF £71.13 TOTE £17.90: £3.60, £1.20, £4.50; EX 105.70 Trifecta £885.30 Pool: £2284.07 - 1.93 winning units..

Owner Sultan Ali **Bred** Forenaghts Stud Farm Ltd **Trained** Newmarket, Suffolk

FOCUS

Home bend moved out 8m adding about 24yds to races on Round course The going had dried out a little, so that there were good to firm patches. The jockeys said it was "lovely ground." An ordinary looking fillies' maiden run in a moderate time, but some powerful yards were represented. Tricky to pin this form down, but the front pair improved.

5331 JEREMIAH WEED H'CAP 7f 50y

3:00 (3:00) (Class 6) (0-60,58) 3-Y-O+ **£2,045** (£603; £302) **Stalls** High

Form RPR

-556 **1** **Lucy Bee**[14] 4826 3-9-3 **57**.. TomEaves 14 65
(Keith Dalgleish) *in tch: hdwy on outside to ld over 2f out: sn hrd pressed: hld on wl u.p fnl f* **18/1**

2043 **2** *nk* **Lil Sophella (IRE)**[19] 4623 4-9-1 **49**........................... RussKennemore 3 58
(Patrick Holmes) *dwlt: hld up on ins: hdwy whn nt clr run briefly over 2f out: rdn and styd on wl fnl f: jst hld* **9/2**[2]

50-6 **3** *1 1/2* **Carrie's Magic**[24] 4471 6-8-12 **46**............................ MichaelO'Connell 12 51
(Alistair Whillans) *trckd ldrs: ev ch over 2f out to ins fnl f: drvn and one pce towards fin* **25/1**

3544 **4** *1 1/2* **Berbice (IRE)**[2] 5261 8-8-8 **45**... JulieBurke(3) 4 46
(Linda Perratt) *s.i.s: hld up: stdy hdwy whn nt clr run briefly over 2f out: shkn up over 1f out: one pce ins fnl f* **12/1**

5-32 **5** *1/2* **Burnwynd Boy**[20] 4615 8-9-8 **56**.. JoeFanning 13 56
(Keith Dalgleish) *in tch: effrt and swtchd rt wl over 1f out: kpt on same pce fnl f* **3/1**[1]

24-2 **6** *1 1/4* **Last Minute Lisa (IRE)**[7] 5078 3-8-12 **55**......................... IJBrennan(3) 6 50
(S Donohoe, Ire) *in tch: pushed along and outpcd 2f out: n.d after* **28/1**

0-00 **7** *nse* **Tamara Bay**[10] 4967 5-9-8 **56**...(p) LukeMorris 11 53
(John Davies) *missed break: bhd: effrt and drvn over 2f out: no imp fr over 1f out* **9/1**

-040 **8** *3/4* **Fife Jo**[56] 3392 3-8-12 **52**.. PJMcDonald 10 45
(Jim Goldie) *midfield: drvn along over 2f out: no imp fr over 1f out* **25/1**

-P43 **9** *shd* **Copper To Gold**[12] 4892 4-8-7 **48**................................... GaryMahon(7) 5 43
(Robin Bastiman) *midfield: hdwy and swtchd sharply rt 2f out: sn no imp* **8/1**

0441 **10** *5* **Goninodaethat**[28] 4339 5-9-9 **57**....................................... GrahamLee 9 39
(Jim Goldie) *chsd ldr: rdn and ev ch over 2f out: wknd over 1f out* **11/2**[3]

0043 **11** *2 1/2* **Clumber Place**[2] 5263 7-9-10 **58**..................................... PhillipMakin 8 33
(James Given) *led to over 2f out: rdn and wknd over 1f out* **8/1**

1m 32.29s (-1.11) **Going Correction** -0.10s/f (Good)

WFA 3 from 4yo+ 6lb **11** Ran SP% **114.9**

Speed ratings (Par 101): **102,101,99,98,97 96,96,95,95,89 86**

toteswingers 1&2 £15.40, 1&3 £61.40, 2&3 £25.70 CSF £93.08 CT £2080.77 TOTE £19.90: £6.30, £1.30, £8.00; EX 161.50 Trifecta £1462.20 Part won. Pool: £1949.66 - 0.17 winning units..

Owner Mrs Lucille Bone **Bred** Sandy Bone **Trained** Carluke, S Lanarks

FOCUS

A moderate handicap but sound enough form.

5332 COURVOISIER H'CAP (QUALIFIER FOR THE £15,000 BETFAIR SCOTTISH MILE SERIES FINAL) 1m

3:30 (3:30) (Class 5) (0-75,75) 3-Y-O+ **£2,587** (£770; £384; £192) **Stalls** High

Form RPR

1123 **1** **Silver Rime (FR)**[3] 5238 8-10-0 **75**.................................... PhillipMakin 1 85+
(Linda Perratt) *hld up in tch: gd hdwy to ld over 1f out: rdn out fnl f* **7/2**[1]

10-0 **2** *1 3/4* **Star Links (USA)**[7] 5080 7-9-11 **72**........................(b) RobertWinston 4 78
(S Donohoe, Ire) *hld up in tch: hdwy to ld over 2f out: hdd over 1f out: kpt on same pce ins fnl f* **40/1**

024 **3** *hd* **Mu'Ajiza**[10] 4968 3-9-6 **74**.. JoeFanning 10 79+
(Mark Johnston) *in tch on outside: effrt and pushed along 2f out: kpt on ins fnl f* **9/2**[3]

6430 **4** *1* **Another For Joe**[16] 4746 5-9-12 **73**...................................... GrahamLee 8 76
(Jim Goldie) *hld up on outside: effrt and rdn 2f out: kpt on ins fnl f* **13/2**

1340 **5** *nk* **Tectonic (IRE)**[10] 4953 4-9-1 **62**.......................................(p) TomEaves 6 66
(Keith Dalgleish) *trckd ldrs: pushed along 2f out: kpt on same pce fnl f* **10/1**

000- **6** *shd* **Toufan Express**[9] 5020 11-9-2 **66**................................(b) IJBrennan(3) 5 68
(Adrian McGuinness, Ire) *hld up: rdn and hdwy over 1f out: kpt on fnl f: nt pce to chal* **12/1**

-035 **7** *1 1/2* **Rock Supreme (IRE)**[12] 4889 4-9-7 **73**........................ ConnorBeasley(5) 2 72
(Michael Dods) *hld up: stdy hdwy over 2f out: rdn over 1f out: sn n.d* **4/1**[2]

0211 **8** *2* **Cono Zur (FR)**[20] 4609 6-9-9 **70**..................................... JamesSullivan 3 64
(Ruth Carr) *led to over 2f out: rdn and wknd over 1f out* **5/1**

465 **9** *4 1/2* **Adorable Choice (IRE)**[28] 4341 5-8-9 **56** oh2............(vt) SteveDrowne 9 40
(Tom Dascombe) *sn pushed along to chse ldr: rdn over 2f out: sn wknd* **20/1**

1m 42.01s (-1.79) **Going Correction** -0.10s/f (Good)

WFA 3 from 4yo+ 7lb **9** Ran SP% **114.4**

Speed ratings (Par 103): **104,102,102,101,100 100,99,97,92**

toteswingers 1&2 £18.90, 1&3 £3.40, 2&3 £24.20 CSF £132.51 CT £642.03 TOTE £3.90: £1.70, £10.00, £2.90; EX 119.70 Trifecta £760.70 Pool: £1621.22 - 1.59 winning units..

Owner Ken McGarrity **Bred** Jean-Philippe Dubois **Trained** East Kilbride, S Lanarks

FOCUS

A fair but competitive handicap rated around the placed horses.

5333 WOODFORD RESERVE H'CAP (QUALIFIER FOR THE £15,000 BETFAIR SCOTTISH SPRINT SERIES FINAL) 6f

4:00 (4:01) (Class 5) (0-75,74) 3-Y-O+ **£2,587** (£770; £384; £192) **Stalls** High

Form RPR

2064 **1** **Flighty Clarets (IRE)**[35] 4114 3-8-11 **63**........................... LeeTopliss 11 71+
(Richard Fahey) *trckd ldrs: nt clr run fr 1/2-way to ent fnl f: styd on strly to ld cl home* **10/1**[3]

6034 **2** *nk* **Roker Park (IRE)**[6] 5088 8-9-9 **74**...............................(v) JulieBurke(3) 2 81
(David O'Meara) *cl up on outside: rdn over 2f out: led over 1f out: kpt on fnl f: hdd cl home* **6/1**[2]

6212 **3** *1/2* **Salvatore Fury (IRE)**[20] 4611 3-9-3 **69**..........................(p) JoeFanning 4 74
(Keith Dalgleish) *hld up in tch: hdwy on outside over 1f out: ev ch and rdn ins fnl f: hld towards fin* **3/1**[1]

5021 **4** *1/2* **Little Jimmy Odsox (IRE)**[12] 4892 5-9-4 **66**..........(b) DuranFentiman 10 70
(Tim Easterby) *led against stands' rail: rdn and hdd over 1f out: rallied ins fnl f: kpt on: hld towards fin* **6/1**[2]

000- **5** *1 1/2* **Boris Grigoriev (IRE)**[286] 7452 4-9-6 **68**...................(b) JamesSullivan 7 67
(Michael Easterby) *sn trcking ldrs: rdn over 2f out: edgd lft ent fnl f: kpt on same pce* **3/1**[1]

6 *nk* **Go Go Green (IRE)**[93] 2276 7-9-9 **71**................................. GrahamLee 8 69
(Jim Goldie) *dwlt and wnt rt s: hld up: nt clr run over 2f out to over 1f out: kpt on fnl f: no imp* **12/1**

6050 **7** *1* **Opt Out**[28] 4338 3-9-1 **67**... PJMcDonald 6 62
(Alistair Whillans) *hld up bhd ldng gp: n.m.r over 2f out to over 1f out: no imp fnl f* **14/1**

3244 **8** *1 1/4* **Economic Crisis (IRE)**[9] 4993 4-9-7 **69**............................ PaddyAspell 9 60
(Alan Berry) *w ldr: rdn over 2f out: hung lft and wknd ins fnl f* **11/1**

/4 **9** *3 1/2* **Pitt Rivers**[99] 2038 4-9-0 **67**...................................... ConnorBeasley(5) 3 47
(Linda Perratt) *hld up on outside: rdn over 2f out: hung rt and wknd over 1f out* **50/1**

1m 12.1s (-0.30) **Going Correction** +0.05s/f (Good)

WFA 3 from 4yo+ 4lb **9** Ran SP% **112.3**

Speed ratings (Par 103): **104,103,102,102,100 99,98,96,92**

toteswingers 1&2 £10.00, 1&3 £8.00, 2&3 £3.70 CSF £66.33 CT £225.42 TOTE £14.50: £3.60, £2.20, £1.60; EX 76.90 Trifecta £355.20 Pool: £3792.10 - 8.00 winning units..

Owner The Matthewman One Partnership **Bred** R A Fahey **Trained** Musley Bank, N Yorks

FOCUS

A modest sprint handicap and a close finish. The form looks straightforward rated around the placed horses.

5334 COCA-COLA H'CAP 1m 2f

4:30 (4:31) (Class 6) (0-60,60) 3-Y-O **£2,045** (£603; £302) **Stalls** High

Form RPR

-001 **1** **Artful Prince**[27] 4391 3-9-0 **53**..(b) GrahamLee 8 74+
(James Given) *mde all: rdn over 2f out: styd on strly fnl f: eased nr fin* **7/1**

-133 **2** *4* **Mash Potato (IRE)**[56] 3418 3-9-2 **60**.....................(p) ConnorBeasley(5) 3 72
(Michael Dods) *trckd ldrs: effrt and wnt 2nd 3f out: sn rdn: kpt on same pce appr fnl f* **5/1**[2]

00- **3** *12* **Las Encinas**[5] 5163 3-8-6 **48**... IJBrennan(3) 11 36
(Adrian McGuinness, Ire) *s.s: bhd tl styd on fr 2f out: kpt on: no ch w first two* **14/1**

6304 **4** *hd* **Hello Gorgeous**[25] 4449 3-8-10 **49**.................................... JoeFanning 6 37
(Keith Dalgleish) *prom: rdn and outpcd over 2f out: plugged on fnl f: no imp* **14/1**

006 **5** *shd* **Taxiformissbyron**[9] 5016 3-9-0 **53**................................... PhillipMakin 12 40
(Michael Herrington) *hld up: rdn 3f out: styd on fnl f: nvr on terms* **16/1**

5300 **6** *1/2* **Multisure**[9] 5016 3-8-8 **47**... JamesSullivan 2 33
(Ruth Carr) *midfield: hdwy and prom over 3f out: rdn and outpcd fr 2f out* **33/1**

0643 **7** *3 1/4* **Baraboy (IRE)**[5] 5142 3-8-4 **50**.. KevinStott(7) 7 30
(Barry Murtagh) *hld up in tch: effrt and pushed along over 2f out: hung lft and wknd over 1f out* **13/2**[3]

-001 **8** *6* **Szabo's Art**[5] 5143 3-8-12 **51**.. LukeMorris 10 19
(Sir Mark Prescott Bt) *trckd ldr: rdn over 3f out: wknd over 1f out* **1/1**[1]

-600 **9** *9* **Denton Skyline (IRE)**[54] 3463 3-8-9 **48**..........................(p) TomEaves 4
(Michael Dods) *hld up: rdn over 4f out: nvr on terms* **50/1**

0-50 **10** *1 1/4* **Smooth Handle**[18] 4672 3-8-7 **46**................................. DuranFentiman 9
(Danielle McCormick) *hld up: struggling over 4f out: btn over 2f out* **100/1**

0060 **11** *1 3/4* **Hayley**[14] 4824 3-8-7 **46** oh1.. PJMcDonald 1
(Jim Goldie) *missed break: bhd: struggling over 4f out: sn btn* **100/1**

2m 7.76s (-4.24) **Going Correction** -0.10s/f (Good) **11** Ran SP% **118.6**

Speed ratings (Par 98): **112,108,99,99,98 98,95,91,83,82 81**

toteswingers 1&2 £5.70, 1&3 £13.80, 2&3 £10.60 CSF £41.95 CT £482.94 TOTE £8.20: £2.00, £1.60, £2.70; EX 31.20 Trifecta £428.00 Pool: £4211.61 - 7.37 winning units..

Owner Ingram Racing **Bred** Graham Wilson **Trained** Willoughton, Lincs

FOCUS

A moderate 3-y-o handicap that was turned into a procession. The pace appeared to be steady before quickening at the end of the back straight. The winner recorded a personal best and the time was very good.

5335 CALEDONIA BEST H'CAP 1m 2f

5:00 (5:00) (Class 3) (0-95,95) 3-Y-O+ **£7,762** (£2,310; £1,154; £577) **Stalls** High

Form RPR

1024 **1** **Spirit Of The Law (IRE)**[13] 4854 4-8-13 **85**........... GeorgeChaloner(5) 1 93+
(Richard Fahey) *trckd ldrs: effrt whn nt clr run 2f out: swtchd rt and qckned to ld ins fnl f: kpt on strly* **7/2**[3]

3003 **2** *3/4* **Fort Belvedere**[14] 4825 5-9-6 **87**.................................. WilsonRenwick 4 93
(Keith Dalgleish) *hld up in tch: hdwy on outside to ld over 1f out: sn rdn: hdd ins fnl f: kpt on* **9/1**

2 **3** *hd* **Kashmir Peak (IRE)**[8] 5031 4-8-11 **78**.................... MichaelO'Connell 7 84
(John Quinn) *pressed ldr: disp ld over 2f out to over 1f out: kpt on ins fnl f* **15/8**[1]

216 **4** *1 ¼* **Desert Revolution**[13] 4859 3-8-7 **83**.................................. JoeFanning 8 86
(Mark Johnston) *mde most tl rdn and hdd over 1f out: kpt on same pce ins fnl f* **5/2**[2]

6-01 **5** *4* **Full Toss**[12] 4888 7-8-10 **77**.. GrahamLee 9 72
(Jim Goldie) *hld up in tch: rdn and outpcd over 2f out: no imp fr over 1f out* **16/1**

5415 **6** *1 ¾* **Ginger Jack**[28] 4342 6-9-8 **89**.. PJMcDonald 3 81
(Geoffrey Harker) *in tch: drvn and outpcd over 2f out: sn btn* **11/1**

2m 10.46s (-1.54) **Going Correction** -0.10s/f (Good)
WFA 3 from 4yo+ 9lb **6** Ran SP% **109.8**
Speed ratings (Par 107): **102,101,101,100,97 95**
toteswingers 1&2 £4.80, 1&3 £2.10, 2&3 £3.50 CSF £31.21 CT £68.67 TOTE £4.40: £1.90, £3.20; EX 33.40 Trifecta £100.10 Pool: £2639.67 - 19.76 winning units..
Owner The Matthewman One Partnership **Bred** Georgestown Stud **Trained** Musley Bank, N Yorks

FOCUS
The feature event of the afternoon but the time was 2.7secs slower than the preceding event. This rates a personal best for the winner with the runner-up to form.

5336 KOPPARBERG CIDER H'CAP 5f
5:30 (5:31) (Class 6) (0-65,65) 3-Y-O+ **£2,045** (£603; £302) **Stalls** High

Form RPR

5400 **1** **Royal Bajan (USA)**[11] 4930 5-9-10 **65**......................(p) JamesSullivan 10 78
(James Given) *mde all against stands' rail: clr over 1f out: rdn out* **10/1**

3132 **2** *2 ½* **Saxonette**[21] 4582 5-8-13 **54**.. PJMcDonald 8 58
(Linda Perratt) *midfield: effrt and pushed along 2f out: chsd wnr ins fnl f: r.o* **7/2**[1]

0-00 **3** *½* **Lizzy's Dream**[53] 3505 5-9-6 **61**.. RobertWinston 3 63+
(Robin Bastiman) *missed break: hld up: rdn and hdwy over 1f out: kpt on fnl f: nvr able to chal* **4/1**[2]

0350 **4** *shd* **Wicked Wilma (IRE)**[6] 5085 9-8-6 **47**....................(p) PatrickMathers 12 49
(Alan Berry) *chsd ldr: rdn 2f out: kpt on same pce fnl f* **10/1**

4663 **5** *nk* **Rock Canyon (IRE)**[7] 5047 4-8-1 **49**......................(p) SamanthaBell(7) 7 50
(Linda Perratt) *chsd ldrs: rdn over 2f out: kpt on same pce fnl f* **12/1**

5066 **6** *1 ½* **Here Now And Why (IRE)**[16] 4761 6-9-1 **56**.......(p) MichaelO'Connell 5 51
(Iain Jardine) *in tch on outside: drvn 2f out: btn ins fnl f* **12/1**

0050 **7** *nse* **Compton Heights**[14] 4821 4-9-2 **57**.. GrahamLee 11 52
(Jim Goldie) *dwlt: hld up: rdn and hdwy over 1f out: kpt on fnl f: no imp* **14/1**

0000 **8** *1* **Distant Sun (USA)**[14] 4821 9-8-10 **51**................................(p) TomEaves 1 43
(Linda Perratt) *stdd s: hld up: rdn over 1f out: nvr rchd ldrs* **25/1**

0251 **9** *2 ¾* **Amelia Jay**[2] 5265 3-8-7 **51** 6ex.. DuranFentiman 2 33
(Danielle McCormick) *midfield on outside: rdn and struggling wl over 1f out: sn btn* **6/1**[3]

4600 **10** *2* **Fol Hollow (IRE)**[7] 5047 8-8-11 **59**................................(v[1]) BTTreanor(7) 4 33
(Stuart Coltherd) *midfield on outside: struggling 2f out: sn btn* **20/1**

-004 **11** *2 ¼* **Quaroma**[80] 2632 8-9-10 **65**.. LeeTopliss 6 31
(Paul Midgley) *hld up towards rr: rdn whn edgd lft over 1f out: sn wknd* **9/1**

5040 **12** *2 ½* **Pastoral Prey**[9] 4991 3-8-10 **54**.......................................(b) LukeMorris 9 11
(Ian Semple) *chsd ldrs tl rdn and wknd fr 2f out* **20/1**

59.14s (-0.26) **Going Correction** -0.10s/f (Good)
WFA 3 from 4yo+ 3lb **12** Ran SP% **118.2**
Speed ratings (Par 101): **98,94,93,93,92 90,90,88,84,80 77,73**
toteswingers 1&2 £8.50, 1&3 £9.20, 2&3 £4.30 CSF £43.76 CT £170.38 TOTE £10.40: £3.80, £1.50, £1.80; EX 52.30 Trifecta £267.50 Pool: £1270.52 - 3.56 winning units..
Owner The Cool Silk Partnership **Bred** West Wind Farm **Trained** Willoughton, Lincs

FOCUS
An ordinary sprint handicap best rated through the runner-up.
T/Plt: £1447.40 to a £1 stake. Pool: £90,117.81 - 45.45 winning tickets. T/Qpdt: £36.80 to a £1 stake. Pool: £7839.69 - 157.40 winning tickets. RY

5010 THIRSK (L-H)
Monday, August 12

OFFICIAL GOING: Good changing to good to soft after race 2 (6.00)
Wind: fresh 1/2 against Weather: changeable, heavy showers

5337 BETFAIR NOVICE-FLAT-AMATEUR H'CAP (FOR NOVICE-AMATEUR RIDERS) 2m
5:25 (5:26) (Class 6) (0-65,65) 4-Y-O+ **£1,871** (£580; £290; £145) **Stalls** Low

Form RPR

-033 **1** **Strikemaster (IRE)**[19] 4622 7-10-6 **50**.........................(t) MrAaronJames 1 60
(Lee James) *in rr: hdwy on outer over 3f out: kpt on to ld last 100yds* **10/1**

564 **2** *2 ¾* **Frosty Berry**[10] 4951 4-10-10 **57**.. MrAFrench(3) 7 64
(Neville Bycroft) *s.i.s: hdwy over 2f out: edgd lft and 2nd over 1f out: kpt on to chse wnr towards fin* **11/1**

0/56 **3** *1 ¼* **Mister Carter (IRE)**[12] 4882 6-11-7 **65**.............................(v[1]) MrPJohn 3 70
(Ian Williams) *trckd ldrs: led 4f out: wnt clr over 2f out: wknd and hdd ins fnl f* **10/1**

-020 **4** *8* **Joyful Motive**[10] 4969 4-10-3 **50**............................ MissEmilyBullock(3) 2 45
(Tom Tate) *chsd ldrs: outpcd and lost pl after 5f: hdwy over 4f out: sn chsng ldrs: wknd over 1f out* **8/1**

-046 **5** *5* **Ferney Boy**[57] 3363 7-9-13 **46** oh1.. MrDPCostello(3) 5 35
(Chris Fairhurst) *trckd ldrs: t.k.h: effrt over 3f out: wknd over 1f out* **22/1**

0540 **6** *1* **Raleigh Quay (IRE)**[20] 4614 6-10-12 **56**.................(v[1]) MissBeckySmith 11 44
(Micky Hammond) *trckd ldrs: drvn 4f out: one pce* **8/1**

1012 **7** *5* **Maybeme**[7] 5059 7-11-7 **65**...(p) MrSebSpencer 8 47
(Neville Bycroft) *trckd ldrs: t.k.h: effrt over 2f out: wknd over 1f out* **9/2**[2]

046- **8** *9* **Haymarket**[248] 3722 4-11-7 **65**.. MrAlexFerguson 6 36
(Michael Bell) *led: t.k.h: hdd 4f out: lost pl over 2f out* **10/3**[1]

225/ **9** *16* **Sea The Flames (IRE)**[697] 6087 5-10-3 **50**........................ MrSMurray(3) 10
(David O'Meara) *s.i.s: hld up in rr: lost pl over 3f out: sn wl bhd* **6/1**[3]

0660 **10** *5* **Inffiraaj (IRE)**[16] 4754 4-10-4 **51**.. MissEllaSmith(3) 9
(Mick Channon) *rrd s: hdwy after 3f: w ldr after 5f: rn wd bnd after 6f: upsides 8f out: lost pl over 3f out* **25/1**

30/0 **11** *8* **Non Dom (IRE)**[15] 4804 7-11-2 **60**......................................(e[1]) MrRSmith 4
(Wilf Storey) *in rr: detached last and drvn 6f out* **50/1**

3m 39.58s (11.28) **Going Correction** +0.425s/f (Yiel) **11** Ran SP% **114.4**
Speed ratings (Par 101): **88,86,86,82,79 79,76,72,64,61 57**
toteswingers 1&2 £17.10, 1&3 £9.40, 2&3 £19.40 CSF £109.15 CT £1127.52 TOTE £8.50: £2.70, £3.30, £2.70; EX 136.20 Trifecta £602.30 Part won. Pool: £803.13 - 0.19 winning units..
Owner Mrs Carol Lloyd-James **Bred** Dr Peter Harms **Trained** Norton, N Yorks

FOCUS
The course had received 6mm of rain between 2-5pm and a further heavy downpour after the opener would have seen the ground riding on the easy side. They got racing quite a way out in this novice amateur riders' handicap and it was no surprise to see the closers get on top late on. The winner is rated close to last year's form.

5338 WATCH RACING UK ON FREEVIEW 231 MAIDEN AUCTION STKS 7f
6:00 (6:03) (Class 5) 2-Y-O **£2,587** (£770; £384; £192) **Stalls** Low

Form RPR

53 **1** **Baileys Forever**[13] 4847 2-8-7 0.. FrederikTylicki 1 70
(James Given) *awkward to load: chsd ldr: edgd lft and led over 1f out: hld on nr fin* **17/2**[3]

6 **2** *½* **Eddiemaurice (IRE)**[17] 4724 2-8-9 0.......................... RobbieFitzpatrick 7 71
(Richard Guest) *s.i.s: in rr: hdwy over 2f out: styd on wl to take 2nd wl ins fnl f: r.o* **16/1**

2 **3** *nk* **Ribbleton**[15] 4801 2-8-9 0.. TonyHamilton 14 70
(Richard Fahey) *chsd ldrs: effrt whn hmpd and struck over hd by rival's whip over 1f out: styd on ins fnl f: tk 3rd nr fin* **5/4**[1]

63 **4** *nk* **Hulcolt (IRE)**[13] 4861 2-8-9 0.. JasonHart(3) 5 72
(Garry Moss) *chsd ldrs: led wl over 1f out: sn hdd: kpt on same pce ins fnl f* **25/1**

5 *3* **Ice Mayden** 2-8-4 0.. RoystonFfrench 15 56
(Bryan Smart) *dwlt: sn drvn in mid-div: styd on fnl 2f* **40/1**

6 *2 ¼* **Gold Class** 2-8-9 0.. SeanLevey 6 55
(Ed McMahon) *mid-div and sn drvn along: styd on fnl 2f: nt rch ldrs* **14/1**

0 **7** *¾* **Blue Talisman (IRE)**[68] 2985 2-8-12 0.................................. DavidAllan 11 57
(Tim Easterby) *racd wd: mid-div: hdwy over 2f out: kpt on fnl f* **50/1**

4 **8** *¾* **Singapore Secret (IRE)**[18] 4668 2-8-1 0.......................... NeilFarley(3) 13 47
(James Given) *set str pce: hdd wl over 1f out: sn wknd* **13/2**[2]

0 **9** *6* **Miss Sophisticated**[18] 4668 2-8-9 0 ow2.................. GrahamGibbons 2 36
(David Barron) *s.i.s: hdwy into mid-div over 4f out: wknd over 1f out* **12/1**

0 **10** *1 ½* **Running Wolf (IRE)**[49] 3624 2-8-2 0.......................... JoeyHaynes(7) 4 32
(Michael Dods) *in rr: sme hdwy 2f out: nvr on terms* **40/1**

36 **11** *¾* **Darling Boyz**[57] 3366 2-8-9 0.. MickyFenton 8 30
(John Quinn) *mid-div: lost pl over 4f out* **9/1**

0 **12** *1* **Roving Bunny**[9] 4977 2-8-4 0.. BarryMcHugh 16 23
(James Given) *swtchd lft after 1f: mid-div: sme hdwy 4f out: wknd over 1f out* **100/1**

0 **13** *2 ½* **Trinity Star (IRE)**[56] 3391 2-8-12 0.................................. PaulMulrennan 3 24
(Michael Dods) *sn bhd: sme hdwy on inner over 2f out: sn wknd* **28/1**

00 **14** *1* **Jacbequick**[24] 4505 2-8-9 0.. AndrewElliott 10 18
(Karen Tutty) *sn bhd* **150/1**

15 *14* **False Witness (IRE)** 2-8-12 0.. AdrianNicholls 9
(David Nicholls) *s.s: racd wd: detached last and reminder after 1f: sn bhd: eased clsng stages* **33/1**

1m 30.48s (3.28) **Going Correction** +0.425s/f (Yiel) **15** Ran SP% **117.3**
Speed ratings (Par 94): **98,97,97,96,93 90,89,89,82,80 79,78,75,74,58**
toteswingers 1&2 £13.60, 1&3 £3.60, 2&3 £8.20 CSF £123.46 TOTE £11.00: £2.00, £6.20, £1.10; EX 145.00 Trifecta £497.80 Pool: £1748.65 - 2.63 winning units..
Owner G R Bailey Ltd (Baileys Horse Feeds) **Bred** P And Mrs A G Venner **Trained** Willoughton, Lincs

FOCUS
The ground was changed to good to soft following this contest. An ordinary juvenile maiden that was run at a furious gallop. The form is rated around the race averages.

5339 BRITISH STALLION STUDS EBF MAIDEN STKS 5f
6:30 (6:32) (Class 4) 2-Y-O **£4,204** (£1,251; £625; £312) **Stalls** High

Form RPR

1 **Racing Mate (IRE)** 2-9-5 0.. FrederikTylicki 8 84+
(Paul D'Arcy) *dwlt: sn chsng ldrs: swtchd lft appr fnl f: styd on wl to ld last 75yds* **14/1**

2 **2** *1 ½* **Dutch Breeze**[12] 4886 2-9-5 0.. DavidAllan 4 79
(Tim Easterby) *w ldr: led over 1f out: hdd and no ex last 75yds* **6/4**[1]

542 **3** *3* **Wickhambrook (IRE)**[49] 3640 2-9-5 **77**.................... MickaelBarzalona 6 68
(Charlie Appleby) *led: t.k.h: hdd over 1f out: wknd last 100yds* **7/4**[2]

4 *2* **Rock N Rouge (IRE)** 2-9-0 0.. JimCrowley 3 56
(David Brown) *dwlt and wnt lft s: t.k.h: hdwy on outside over 2f out: sn trcking ldrs: wknd fnl f* **8/1**

04 **5** *2 ½* **Lazy Sioux**[16] 4781 2-9-0 0.. RobbieFitzpatrick 7 47
(Richard Guest) *dwlt: sn chsng ldrs: outpcd over 2f out: kpt on fnl f* **25/1**

05 **6** *1 ¾* **The Grumpy Gnome (IRE)**[16] 4781 2-9-5 0.................. TonyHamilton 9 45
(Richard Fahey) *unruly s: chsd ldrs: drvn and lost pl over 2f out: hung lft over 1f out* **6/1**[3]

6 **7** *6* **Lady Dancer (IRE)**[7] 5053 2-9-0 0.. AndrewElliott 1 19
(George Moore) *chsd ldrs: drvn over 2f out: hung lft and lost pl over 1f out: sn bhd* **100/1**

1m 0.54s (0.94) **Going Correction** +0.175s/f (Good) **7** Ran SP% **113.3**
Speed ratings (Par 96): **99,96,91,88,84 81,72**
toteswingers 1&2 £4.70, 1&3 £5.90, 2&3 £1.10 CSF £34.97 TOTE £22.00: £8.90, £1.10; EX 52.60 Trifecta £117.70 Pool: £1508.48 - 9.61 winning units..
Owner Champion Bloodstock Ltd **Bred** W Kane **Trained** Newmarket, Suffolk

FOCUS
An ordinary maiden but the winner was quite impressive.

5340 MARKET CROSS JEWELLERS H'CAP 5f
7:00 (7:00) (Class 4) (0-85,85) 3-Y-O **£4,851** (£1,443; £721; £360) **Stalls** High

Form RPR

6023 **1** **Angus Og**[7] 5057 3-8-10 **81**.. JoeyHaynes(7) 8 89
(Mrs K Burke) *mde all stands' side rail: drvn over 1f out: hld on nr fin* **4/1**[3]

0310 **2** *hd* **Sharaarah (IRE)**[22] 4569 3-9-2 **80**.................................. TonyHamilton 4 87
(David O'Meara) *s.i.s: swtchd rt after s: hdwy 2f out: styd on in outer fnl f: tk 2nd nr fin: jst hld* **12/1**

6042 **3** *½* **Huntsmans Close**[18] 4670 3-8-12 **83**.......................... LouisSteward(7) 6 88
(Michael Bell) *dwlt: sn chsng ldrs: upsides over 1f out: no ex last 50yds* **11/4**[2]

4232 **4** *1* **Dusty Storm (IRE)**[17] 4734 3-9-1 **79**.. SeanLevey 9 81+
(Ed McMahon) *t.k.h in mid-div: smooth hdwy 2f out: nt clr run and swtchd wd jst ins fnl f: kpt on same pce towards fin* **9/4**[1]

0500 **5** *2* **Mayfield Girl (IRE)**[17] 4734 3-9-4 **82**.. DavidAllan 5 76
(Mel Brittain) *w wnr: wknd last 150yds* **12/1**

13 **6** *4 ½* **Trinityelitedotcom (IRE)**[24] 4487 3-8-8 **77**.......................... JackDuern(5) 2 55
(Tom Dascombe) *dwlt: sn w ldrs on outside: wknd fnl f* **9/2**

1m 0.07s (0.47) **Going Correction** +0.175s/f (Good) **6** Ran SP% **111.0**
Speed ratings (Par 102): **103,102,101,100,97 89**
toteswingers 1&2 £6.60, 1&3 £2.70, 2&3 £6.00 CSF £44.96 CT £145.95 TOTE £5.00: £2.10, £3.60; EX 52.80 Trifecta £101.30 Pool: £712.18 - 5.27 winning units..
Owner D Simpson & Mrs E Burke **Bred** Shane O'Sullivan **Trained** Middleham Moor, N Yorks

FOCUS
Quite a good handicap, and the form makes sense.

5341 READ HAYLEY TURNER EVERY FRIDAY RACINGUK.COM (S) H'CAP 1m

7:30 (7:31) (Class 6) (0-65,65) 3-Y-0+ **£2,587** (£770; £384; £192) **Stalls Low**

Form RPR

066 **1** **Throwing Roses**[38] 4005 3-7-13 **46** oh1 RaulDaSilva(3) 16 55
(Lawrence Mullaney) *chsd ldrs: upsides over 1f out: led last 100yds: hld on towards fin* **16/1**

5105 **2** *nk* **Jupiter Fidius**[33] 4160 6-9-2 **60** GemmaTutty(7) 12 69
(Karen Tutty) *hld up in rr: hdwy on outside over 2f out: led over 1f out: hdd ins fnl f: no ex towards fin* **15/2**

0050 **3** *4* **Summer Dancer (IRE)**[10] 4967 9-9-7 **58** MickyFenton 11 58
(Paul Midgley) *stdd to rr sn after s: hdwy over 2f out: chsng ldrs over 1f out: kpt on to take 3rd nr fin* **8/1**

2504 **4** *½* **Icy Blue**[14] 4823 5-9-3 **54** (p) TonyHamilton 13 53
(Richard Whitaker) *mid-div: hdwy over 2f out: edgd rt: chsng ldrs over 1f out: kpt on same pce* **5/1**[1]

-402 **5** *1 ¾* **Lothair (IRE)**[30] 4292 4-8-13 **50** PaulMulrennan 4 45
(Alan Swinbank) *trckd ldr: t.k.h: led 2f out: sn hdd: wknd last 50yds* **8/1**

6555 **6** *hd* **Monsieur Pontaven**[35] 4109 6-8-7 **47** (b) JasonHart(3) 18 41
(Robin Bastiman) *s.s: bhd: hdwy on outside over 2f out: chsng ldrs over 1f out: one pce* **11/2**[2]

0-03 **7** *1 ¼* **Auto Mac**[12] 4888 5-9-4 **60** (p) AdamCarter(5) 8 51
(Neville Bycroft) *chsd ldrs: drvn over 2f out: one pce* **12/1**

0000 **8** *1 ¼* **Mujaadel (USA)**[10] 4967 8-9-13 **64** (p) FrannyNorton 14 52
(David Nicholls) *s.i.s: hdwy on inner over 2f out: chsng ldrs over 1f out: wknd ins fnl f* **13/2**[3]

0100 **9** *4* **Rasselas (IRE)**[12] 4893 6-9-11 **62** (p) AdrianNicholls 17 41
(David Nicholls) *sn drvn along: chsd ldrs on outer: edgd lft 2f out: sn lost pl* **18/1**

1440 **10** *2* **Whispered Times (USA)**[20] 4615 6-9-12 **63** (p) BarryMcHugh 2 38
(Tracy Waggott) *trckd ldrs: effrt over 2f out: wknd over 1f out* **20/1**

0000 **11** *1 ¾* **Thrust Control (IRE)**[10] 4967 6-9-1 **52** FrederikTylicki 5 23
(Tracy Waggott) *led: hdd 2f out: sn wknd* **20/1**

-550 **12** *9* **Jack Barker**[46] 3738 4-8-12 **49** J-PGuillambert 9
(Robin Bastiman) *chsd ldrs: wkng whn hmpd and lost pl 2f out: sn bhd: eased* **33/1**

1m 43.6s (3.50) **Going Correction** +0.425s/f (Yiel)
WFA 3 from 4yo+ 7lb **12** Ran SP% **117.0**
Speed ratings (Par 101): **99,98,94,94,92 92,91,89,85,83 82,73**
toteswingers 1&2 £33.00, 1&3 £21.50, 2&3 £14.20 CSF £129.64 CT £1044.04 TOTE £22.60: £5.40, £2.90, £3.20; EX 150.80 Trifecta £580.00 Part won. Pool: £773.44 - 0.05 winning units..There was no bid for the winner
Owner Wildcard Racing Syndicate X1 **Bred** Catridge Farm & Mrs Hamilton Fairley **Trained** Great Habton, N Yorks

FOCUS
In all truth this was quite a poor handicap. The front two pulled a few lengths clear and it was a simple case of switch the jockeys, change the result. The winner's best run since her early 2yo days.

5342 CALVERTS CARPETS H'CAP 1m

8:00 (8:01) (Class 5) (0-75,75) 3-Y-0 **£3,234** (£962; £481; £240) **Stalls Low**

Form RPR

1123 **1** **Rocket Ronnie (IRE)**[9] 5016 3-9-0 **68** AdrianNicholls 3 76
(David Nicholls) *trckd ldrs on outer: t.k.h: led 2f out: sn jnd: fnd ex clsng stages* **5/1**[3]

5633 **2** *nk* **Confusing**[49] 3629 3-8-12 **66** JimCrowley 5 73
(David O'Meara) *hld up in mid-div: hdwy over 2f out: chal over 1f out: no ex clsng stages* **6/1**

0446 **3** *1* **Medici Dancer**[57] 3365 3-8-9 **68** DarylByrne(5) 8 73
(Tim Easterby) *lost pl and in rr after 1f: hdwy over 2f out: swtchd lft over 1f out: styd on to take 3rd last 50yds* **16/1**

615 **4** *¾* **Snap Music (USA)**[14] 4824 3-8-8 **62** FrannyNorton 6 65+
(Mark Johnston) *s.i.s: in rr and drvn along: hdwy 2f out: styd on to take 4th nr fin* **15/2**

4552 **5** *nk* **Megamunch (IRE)**[9] 5016 3-8-9 **70** (p) JacobButterfield(7) 7 73
(Kristin Stubbs) *chsd ldrs: swtchd rt 2f out: kpt on one pce* **4/1**[1]

6450 **6** *4 ½* **Midnight Warrior**[12] 4887 3-8-1 **60** ShirleyTeasdale(5) 2 52
(Ron Barr) *chsd ldrs: edgd rt over 1f out: sn fdd* **25/1**

6465 **7** *10* **Kolonel Kirkup**[9] 5016 3-8-10 **64** (b) PaulMulrennan 4 33
(Michael Dods) *mid-div: chsng ldrs 4f out: wknd over 1f out: bhd whn eased clsng stages* **8/1**

4301 **8** *½* **Mister Marcasite**[83] 2549 3-9-7 **75** DavidAllan 10 43
(Mel Brittain) *racd wd: led: hdd 5f out: lost pl over 1f out: bhd whn eased clsng stages* **13/2**

005 **9** *2 ½* **Old Man Clegg**[12] 4890 3-9-3 **71** GrahamGibbons 1 33
(Michael Easterby) *chsd ldr: led 5f out: hdd 2f out: sn lost pl: bhd whn eased clsng stages* **9/2**[2]

1m 43.25s (3.15) **Going Correction** +0.425s/f (Yiel) **9** Ran SP% **115.1**
Speed ratings (Par 100): **101,100,99,98,98 94,84,83,81**
toteswingers 1&2 £8.70, 1&3 £10.90, 2&3 £17.70 CSF £34.88 CT £448.11 TOTE £3.60: £2.20, £2.00, £3.90; EX 17.60 Trifecta £806.50 Part won. Pool: £1075.40 - 0.85 winning units..
Owner Mills, Fallon, Purchase & Love **Bred** Sandra Russell **Trained** Sessay, N Yorks
■ Stewards' Enquiry : Adrian Nicholls two-day ban: used whip down shoulder in the forehand (Aug 26-27)

FOCUS
The early pace appeared quite steady in what was a modest handicap. A slightly positive view has been taken of the form.

5343 DOWNLOAD THE FREE RACING UK APP H'CAP 1m 4f

8:30 (8:30) (Class 5) (0-70,74) 3-Y-0 **£3,234** (£962; £481; £240) **Stalls High**

Form RPR

0432 **1** **Bayan Kasirga (IRE)**[26] 4401 3-8-13 **60** TonyHamilton 3 69
(Richard Fahey) *stdd into last after 3f: swtchd to r alone on ins 3f out: led over 1f out: edgd rt and kpt on ins fnl f* **9/1**

4212 **2** *2 ¼* **Jebulani**[6] 5084 3-7-13 **49** RaulDaSilva(3) 5 54
(Barry Murtagh) *led after 1f: c wd over 3f out: hdd over 1f out: edgd lft and kpt on same pce ins fnl f* **2/1**[1]

0432 **3** *2* **Diddy Eric**[5] 5143 3-8-2 **49** oh2 FrannyNorton 2 51
(Micky Hammond) *t.k.h: led 1f: upsides over 8f out: drvn 4f out: edgd rt over 2f out: kpt on to take 3rd nr fin* **9/2**

4214 **4** *nk* **Duke Of Yorkshire**[16] 4770 3-9-2 **66** NeilFarley(3) 1 68
(Declan Carroll) *chsd ldrs after 3f: shkn up over 5f out: kpt on same pce over 1f out* **3/1**[2]

3002 **5** *26* **Grayswood**[16] 4753 3-9-6 **67** PaulMulrennan 6 27
(William Muir) *sn trcking ldrs: lost pl 2f out: sn bhd and eased: t.o* **7/2**[3]

2m 44.36s (8.16) **Going Correction** +0.425s/f (Yiel) **5** Ran SP% **108.7**
Speed ratings (Par 100): **89,87,86,85,68**
CSF £26.62 TOTE £6.50: £2.40, £1.10; EX 32.00 Trifecta £41.40 Pool: £540.52 - 9.78 winning units..
Owner Stephen Humphreys **Bred** Lynn Lodge Stud **Trained** Musley Bank, N Yorks

FOCUS
A couple of these failed to give their running and the form looks a bit suspect. The winner is rated back to her 2yo best.
T/Jkpt: Not won. T/Plt: £3517.40 to a £1 stake. Pool: £83,117.87 - 17.25 winning tickets. T/Qpdt: £417.70 to a £1 stake. Pool: £6210.37 - 11.00 winning tickets. WG

5306 WINDSOR (R-H)

Monday, August 12

OFFICIAL GOING: Good to firm (watered; 8.7)
Wind: Moderate, half behind Weather: Fine but cloudy

5344 TRAILFINDERS, THE WORLDWIDE FLIGHT SPECIALISTS MAIDEN STKS 6f

5:40 (5:40) (Class 5) 2-Y-0 **£2,587** (£770; £384; £192) **Stalls Low**

Form RPR

4 **1** **Zampa Manos (USA)**[47] 3695 2-9-2 0 ThomasBrown(3) 3 80+
(Andrew Balding) *trckd ldrs: rdn to ld over 1f out: drvn and kpt on wl fnl f* **8/1**[3]

6 **2** *½* **Zawiyah**[21] 4589 2-9-0 0 AndreaAtzeni 10 73
(Luca Cumani) *s.i.s: prog fr rr on outer 1/2-way: rdn over 1f out: styd on to take 2nd last 50yds: a hld* **3/1**[2]

3 *¾* **Qatar Princess (IRE)** 2-9-0 0 HarryBentley 7 71
(Olly Stevens) *prom: rdn to chal over 1f out: stl chalng 100yds out: one pce nr fin* **33/1**

6 **4** *½* **Merletta**[45] 3760 2-9-0 0 RyanMoore 5 72+
(Jeremy Noseda) *pressed ldr against rail: shkn up whn n.m.r and swtchd lft wl over 1f out: drvn and kpt on one pce fnl f* **1/1**[1]

5 *4 ½* **Master Of Alkmaar** 2-9-2 0 DarrenEgan(3) 4 60
(Roger Varian) *s.i.s: mostly in last pair but in tch: outpcd and pushed along over 2f out: sme late prog* **33/1**

00 **6** *½* **Exceed And Exceed**[66] 3044 2-9-5 0 RichardHughes 6 58
(Richard Hannon) *mde most to over 1f out: wknd and eased* **8/1**[3]

7 *hd* **Presidente** 2-9-5 0 TomMcLaughlin 8 57
(Ed Walker) *sn in rr: pushed along and outpcd over 2f out: no imp on ldrs after* **33/1**

8 *½* **Excellent Royale (IRE)** 2-9-5 0 JamesDoyle 9 56
(Charles Hills) *s.i.s: in tch in rr: pushed along and outpcd over 2f out: one pce and no imp on ldrs after* **16/1**

9 *2 ¾* **Crystalized (IRE)** 2-9-0 0 PatDobbs 1 42
(Richard Hannon) *s.i.s: towards rr: pushed along and outpcd over 2f out: nt on terms after* **33/1**

10 *6* **Classic Mission** 2-9-0 0 MatthewLawson(5) 11 28
(Jonathan Portman) *slowly away: rcvrd on wd outside and prom after 2f: wknd qckly over 2f out* **66/1**

1m 11.66s (-1.34) **Going Correction** -0.20s/f (Firm) **10** Ran SP% **116.4**
Speed ratings (Par 94): **100,99,98,97,91 91,90,90,86,78**
toteswingers 1&2 £2.80, 1&3 £12.60, 2&3 £56.80 CSF £31.05 TOTE £9.00: £2.90, £1.50, £10.10; EX 32.90 Trifecta £1260.00 Part won. Pool: £1680.13 - 0.47 winning units..
Owner N M Watts **Bred** Hunter Valley Farm Et Al **Trained** Kingsclere, Hants

FOCUS
Inner of straight dolled out 16yds at 6f and 9yds at Winning Post. Top bend dolled out 8 yds from normal inner configuration, adding 34yds to races of 1m and beyond. This looked a decent maiden, with a number of big stables involved.

5345 TRAILFINDERS THE TRAVEL EXPERTS MAIDEN STKS 5f 10y

6:10 (6:11) (Class 5) 3-4-Y-0 **£2,587** (£770; £384; £192) **Stalls Low**

Form RPR

4 **1** **Emjayem**[122] 1519 3-9-5 0 JamesDoyle 1 71
(Ed McMahon) *trckd ldrs: rdn over 1f out: chal ins fnl f: drvn to ld nr fin* **25/1**

232 **2** *shd* **Hi Filwah (USA)**[14] 4839 3-9-5 70 (v) RyanMoore 7 70
(Jeremy Noseda) *pressed ldng pair: rdn 1/2-way: drvn ahd over 1f out: kpt on same pce fnl f: hdd nr fin* **8/11**[1]

05 **3** *1 ¼* **Never A Quarrel (IRE)**[14] 4839 3-8-11 0 RyanClark(3) 4 61
(Jeremy Gask) *w ldr: upsides over 1f out: edgd rt jst ins fnl f: nt qckn* **33/1**

0 **4** *¾* **Joyous**[44] 3837 3-9-0 0 LiamKeniry 5 58
(Dean Ivory) *slowly away: hld up in tch: gng wl enough 2f out: clsd on ldrs over 1f out but hanging lft: one pce fnl f* **25/1**

3-35 **5** *1 ¼* **Sky Garden**[37] 4068 3-9-0 68 (b) LiamJones 8 53
(William Haggas) *chsd ldrs: rdn 1/2-way: nt qckn 2f out: one pce after* **5/2**[2]

0 **6** *12* **Alberto**[14] 4839 3-9-0 0 ThomasGarner(5) 3 15
(Paul Fitzsimons) *slowly away: a in last pair: lost tch sn after 1/2-way: t.o* **50/1**

02 **7** *1 ½* **Trisara**[42] 3898 3-9-0 0 RichardHughes 2 48+
(Harry Dunlop) *mde most against rail to over 1f out: sing to lose pl whn hmpd jst ins fnl f: nrly fell and eased* **6/1**[3]

59.11s (-1.19) **Going Correction** -0.20s/f (Firm) **7** Ran SP% **113.4**
Speed ratings (Par 103): **101,100,98,97,95 76,74**
toteswingers 1&2 £3.60, 1&3 £14.40, 2&3 £9.70 CSF £43.87 TOTE £16.70: £5.10, £1.10; EX 35.00 Trifecta £344.80 Pool: £1904.76 - 4.14 winning units..
Owner Mrs J McMahon **Bred** Mrs J McMahon **Trained** Lichfield, Staffs

FOCUS
This was contested by lightly raced 3yos, many of whom will improve a bit at a sensible level. However there are enough doubts to be cautious about this form.

5346 LOVE TRAVEL, LOVE TRAILFINDERS H'CAP 1m 67y

6:40 (6:40) (Class 5) (0-70,68) 3-Y-0+ **£2,587** (£770; £384; £192) **Stalls Low**

Form RPR

0562 **1** **Wordismybond**[16] 4771 4-9-1 **57** RichardHughes 3 67
(Peter Makin) *trckd ldr: pushed into ld over 1f out: drvn and pressed ins fnl f: hld on* **7/4**[1]

346 **2** *nk* **Lady Sylvia**[47] 3676 4-9-5 **61** PatDobbs 2 70
(Joseph Tuite) *hld up in midfield: prog 2f out: rdn to chse wnr fnl f: str chal last 75yds: jst hld* **10/1**

-441 3 2 3/4 **Jay Bee Blue**[44] 3841 4-9-11 67 (bt) JamesDoyle 9 70
(Sean Curran) *dwlt: hld up in rr: prog over 2f out: styd on to take 3rd wl ins fnl f: unable to threaten* 4/1[2]
-002 4 nk **Rioja Day (IRE)**[14] 4829 3-9-0 63 (b) MartinLane 10 64
(J W Hills) *led to over 1f out: fdd ins fnl f* 7/1[3]
3260 5 1 1/2 **Shifting Star (IRE)**[19] 4637 8-9-12 68 (t[1]) SamHitchcott 5 67
(John Bridger) *hld up towards rr: drvn wl over 2f out: sme modest late prog but nvr a threat* 12/1
05-0 6 hd **Norphin**[21] 4591 3-8-13 62 PatCosgrave 8 59
(Denis Coakley) *a abt same pl: rdn whn n.m.r 2f out: no prog after* 12/1
050 7 3/4 **Royal Marskell**[34] 4151 4-9-7 68 LauraPike(5) 4 64
(K F Clutterbuck) *dwlt: detached in 9th early: ct up after 3f then sed pulling hrd: rdn and struggling in last 3f out: nvr on terms after* 14/1
4640 8 2 1/2 **Our Golden Girl**[41] 3919 3-8-2 51 CathyGannon 1 41
(Shaun Lycett) *chsd ldrs: drvn 3f out: wknd fr 2f out* 33/1
-455 9 1/2 **Rock Anthem (IRE)**[13] 4865 9-9-1 57 KieranO'Neill 7 46
(Mike Murphy) *s.v.s: wl bhd early: ct up at bk of field 5f out: stl at bk whn nt clr run 2f out to over 1f out: no prog after* 14/1
0/40 10 9 **Kilburn**[68] 2981 9-9-9 65 LiamKeniry 6 42
(Alastair Lidderdale) *trckd ldrs: rdn 3f out: sn wknd: eased over 1f out: t.o* 20/1

1m 42.33s (-2.37) **Going Correction** -0.20s/f (Firm)
WFA 3 from 4yo+ 7lb 10 Ran SP% **114.4**
Speed ratings (Par 103): **103,102,99,99,98 97,97,94,94,85**
toteswingers 1&2 £7.80, 1&3 £1.60, 2&3 £6.70 CSF £20.03 CT £63.37 TOTE £2.60: £1.20, £3.50, £2.10; EX 22.20 Trifecta £91.00 Pool: £1082.33 - 8.91 winning units..
Owner T W Wellard & Partners **Bred** Henry And Mrs Rosemary Moszkowicz **Trained** Ogbourne Maisey, Wilts

FOCUS
Few of these were in great form beforehand, so this has a modest look to it.

5347 CORAL.CO.UK NURSERY H'CAP 1m 67y
7:10 (7:10) (Class 4) (0-80,74) 2-Y-O **£4,851** (£1,443; £721; £360) **Stalls** Low

Form RPR
5522 1 **Floating Ballerino (IRE)**[11] 4926 2-9-3 70 HarryBentley 6 75
(Olly Stevens) *trckd ldrs: clsd 2f out: shkn up to ld over 1f out: edgd rt but wl in command fnl f* 7/4[2]
006 2 1 1/2 **Rising Dawn (IRE)**[26] 4414 2-8-8 61 RichardHughes 2 64
(Richard Hannon) *led or disp: pushed along over 3f out: hdd u.p over 1f out: swtchd lft ins fnl f: kpt on but no imp* 5/4[1]
1433 3 2 3/4 **Left Defender (IRE)**[17] 4717 2-9-5 72 RyanMoore 3 67
(Jo Hughes) *hld up in last pair: pushed along 1/2-way: drvn and swtchd lft 2f out: kpt on to take 3rd nr fin* 7/1[3]
0143 4 1/2 **Ding Ding**[10] 4964 2-8-0 56 SimonPearce(3) 4 50
(Mick Channon) *w ldr: upsides and rdn over 2f out: wknd over 1f out* 25/1
0004 5 3 1/4 **Mildenhall**[8] 5034 2-8-7 60 JimmyQuinn 7 47
(Richard Hannon) *hld up in last: pushed along 1/2-way: reminders wl over 1f out: no real prog* 25/1
5305 6 1 1/2 **Khee Society**[9] 4997 2-9-0 67 JamesDoyle 1 50
(David Evans) *trckd ldng pair: rdn 3f out: wknd 2f out: eased fnl f* 10/1

1m 44.09s (-0.61) **Going Correction** -0.20s/f (Firm) 6 Ran SP% **110.1**
Speed ratings (Par 96): **95,93,90,90,87 85**
toteswingers 1&2 £1.10, 1&3 £2.50, 2&3 £1.80 CSF £4.09 TOTE £2.40: £1.30, £1.20; EX 5.40 Trifecta £13.00 Pool: £1596.63 - 91.93 winning units..
Owner Qatar Racing Limited **Bred** Camogue Stud Ltd **Trained** Chiddingfold, Surrey

FOCUS
A fair nursery in which the first two have potential to rate higher. The winner is rated to his mark here.

5348 DOWNLOAD CORAL MOBILE FROM THE APP STORE H'CAP 1m 2f 7y
7:40 (7:40) (Class 3) (0-90,88) 3-Y-O+ **£7,439** (£2,213; £1,106; £553) **Stalls** Centre

Form RPR
4132 1 **Croquembouche (IRE)**[11] 4908 4-9-0 74 LiamKeniry 8 86
(Ed de Giles) *mde all: kicked on over 3f out: nrly jnd and rdn over 1f out: styd on wl fnl f* 8/1[3]
-201 2 1 3/4 **Regal Silk**[21] 4590 3-8-10 79 RyanMoore 5 88
(Jeremy Noseda) *trckd ldng pair: wnt 2nd over 2f out: drvn to chal over 1f out: nt qckn fnl f* 5/6[1]
6105 3 1 3/4 **Verse Of Love**[8] 5026 4-9-9 83 PatCosgrave 4 88
(David Evans) *trckd wnr to over 2f out: n.m.r sn after: one pce fr over 1f out* 20/1
3204 4 1 1/2 **Purple 'n Gold (IRE)**[26] 4075 4-9-2 76 (v) JamesDoyle 7 78
(David Pipe) *hld up in last: in trble once pce lifted over 3f out: kpt on u.p fnl 2f: did best of those fr off the pce* 12/1
0306 5 hd **Mawaakef (IRE)**[30] 4280 5-9-13 87 RichardHughes 3 89
(J R Jenkins) *trckd ldng trio: shkn up and nt qckn 3f out: pushed along and one pce after* 14/1
-241 6 2 1/2 **Lucky Henry**[77] 2728 4-9-11 85 AdamKirby 6 82
(Clive Cox) *hld up in 5th: in trble once pce lifted over 3f out: no hdwy and wl btn 2f out* 4/1[2]
2366 7 1 1/4 **Sheila's Buddy**[11] 4923 4-9-1 75 LiamJones 9 69
(J S Moore) *dwlt: t.k.h and hld up in 6th: rdn once pce lifted 3f out: no prog and wl btn 2f out* 10/1
5004 8 hd **Lowther**[12] 4895 8-9-6 80 (v) KierenFox 2 74
(Lee Carter) *hld up in 7th: outpcd and shkn up 3f out: nudged along and no hdwy after* 50/1

2m 4.93s (-3.77) **Going Correction** -0.20s/f (Firm)
WFA 3 from 4yo+ 9lb 8 Ran SP% **115.8**
Speed ratings (Par 107): **107,105,104,103,102 100,99,99**
toteswingers 1&2 £2.60, 1&3 £10.50, 2&3 £7.50 CSF £15.33 CT £135.65 TOTE £10.30: £2.60, £1.10, £4.20; EX 24.80 Trifecta £323.40 Pool: £1344.44 - 3.11 winning units..
Owner John Manser **Bred** Ballymacoll Stud Farm Ltd **Trained** Ledbury, H'fords

FOCUS
This was a decent handicap in which the front-running winner slackened the pace around the turn after a good early gallop, allowing him to find extra when challenged.

5349 SCOUTING FOR GIRLS SATURDAY 24TH AUGUST H'CAP 6f
8:10 (8:13) (Class 5) (0-70,70) 3-Y-O+ **£2,587** (£770; £384; £192) **Stalls** Low

Form RPR
060- 1 **Jinker Noble**[312] 6811 4-9-12 70 LiamKeniry 2 82
(Ed de Giles) *trckd ldrs gng strly: plld out over 1f out: drvn to chse ldr fnl f: r.o to ld last strides* 16/1
3546 2 hd **Generalyse**[18] 4669 4-9-11 69 (b) AdamKirby 11 80
(Ben De Haan) *trckd ldrs: clsd 2f out: drvn to ld jst over 1f out: edgd rt but styd on: hdd last strides* 6/1[3]
1213 3 3 1/4 **Fossa**[19] 4636 3-9-6 68 SebSanders 4 69+
(Dean Ivory) *wl in rr: rdn and prog jst over 2f out: kpt on fnl f to take 3rd nr fin* 5/1[2]
3642 4 1/2 **Little Choosey**[18] 4654 3-8-13 66 (p) RyanTate(5) 8 65
(Clive Cox) *led: drvn and hdd jst over 1f out: fdd* 16/1
2600 5 3/4 **Divine Call**[49] 3622 6-9-10 68 LiamTreadwell 9 65
(Milton Bradley) *trckd ldr: chal and stl gng wl enough over 1f out: nt qckn then fdd fnl f* 16/1
-046 6 1/2 **The Wee Chief (IRE)**[30] 4303 7-9-8 66 KieranO'Neill 3 61
(Jimmy Fox) *sn in last: rdn and sme prog on outer fr over 2f out: no hdwy fnl f* 7/1
0023 7 3 1/4 **Welsh Inlet (IRE)**[11] 4909 5-9-1 59 RichardHughes 7 44
(John Bridger) *a towards rr: rdn and no real prog 2f out* 8/1
0301 8 6 **Idle Curiosity (IRE)**[20] 4607 3-8-12 60 PatCosgrave 10 26
(Jim Boyle) *prom to 2f out: wknd and eased* 14/1
3056 9 nk **Camache Queen (IRE)**[6] 5104 5-9-7 65 (t) CathyGannon 1 30
(Joseph Tuite) *stmbld bdly after 100yds: a wl in rr after* 20/1
6413 10 1 **Sole Danser (IRE)**[30] 4303 5-9-12 70 (p) RyanMoore 5 32
(Milton Bradley) *s.i.s: a wl in rr: no prog 2f out: eased fnl f* 3/1[1]
1000 R **Black Cadillac (IRE)**[24] 4487 5-9-4 69 (p) DanielMuscutt(7) 12
(Andrew Balding) *reluctant to go to post: ref to r* 16/1
0050 P **Bussa**[20] 4608 5-9-6 67 (t) DeclanBates(3) 6
(David Evans) *wl in tch in midfield: nt qckn 2f out: lost action over 1f out: p.u and dismntd* 12/1

1m 11.25s (-1.75) **Going Correction** -0.20s/f (Firm)
WFA 3 from 4yo+ 4lb 12 Ran SP% **122.2**
Speed ratings (Par 103): **103,102,98,97,96 96,91,83,83,82 ,**
toteswingers 1&2 £27.00, 1&3 £27.50, 2&3 £4.80 CSF £112.52 CT £574.42 TOTE £21.00: £5.10, £2.80, £1.80; EX 189.10 Trifecta £958.30 Part won. Pool: £1277.79 - 0.06 winning units..
Owner Alexander Ridgers **Bred** A S Reid **Trained** Ledbury, H'fords
■ Stewards' Enquiry : Ryan Tate six-day ban: careless riding (Aug 26-31)

FOCUS
Many of these weren't in top form, and the winner was making his seasonal debut, so there isn't much depth to the result.
T/Plt: £51.90 to a £1 stake. Pool: £90,403.23 - 1269.85 winning tickets. T/Qpdt: £4.90 to a £1 stake. Pool: £9643.63 - 1429.65 winning tickets. JN

5066 WOLVERHAMPTON (A.W) (L-H)
Monday, August 12

OFFICIAL GOING: Standard
Wind: Fresh behind Weather: Cloudy with sunny spells

5350 DOWNLOAD OUR IPHONE APP MEDIAN AUCTION MAIDEN STKS 5f 20y(P)
2:15 (2:18) (Class 6) 2-Y-O **£1,940** (£577; £288; £144) **Stalls** Low

Form RPR
342 1 **Trinity River**[14] 4828 2-9-0 78 SilvestreDeSousa 10 77
(Daniel Kubler) *mde all: clr 1/2-way: shkn up over 1f out: easily* 4/9[1]
2 4 **Amadaffair** 2-9-0 0 StephenCraine 6 63+
(Tom Dascombe) *a.p: pushed along 1/2-way: rdn to go 2nd over 1f out: no ch w wnr* 7/1[3]
3 1 3/4 **Captain Myles (IRE)** 2-9-5 0 StevieDonohoe 1 61+
(Nicky Vaughan) *dwlt: sn pushed along in rr: hung rt 2f out: r.o wl ins fnl f: wnt 3rd nr fin: nt trble ldrs* 16/1
4 nk **By Rights** 2-9-0 0 AdamKirby 7 55
(Tony Carroll) *hld up: hdwy 1/2-way: rdn over 1f out: styd on* 14/1
54 5 5 **Chuckamental**[17] 4724 2-9-5 0 (t) RoystonFfrench 3 42
(Bryan Smart) *chsd wnr: rdn 1/2-way: lost 2nd over 1f out: wknd fnl f* 4/1[2]
0 6 3/4 **Liefie**[112] 1724 2-8-7 0 HarryBurns(7) 4 35
(Jo Hughes) *s.i.s: sn outpcd: styd on ins fnl f: nvr nrr* 50/1
503 7 2 **Oakley Dancer**[62] 3167 2-9-0 46 JimmyQuinn 2 27
(Tony Carroll) *prom: pushed along 1/2-way: wknd over 1f out* 25/1
000 8 12 **Crazy Brenda (IRE)**[12] 4880 2-9-0 25 LiamKeniry 5
(Sylvester Kirk) *sn pushed along towards rr: wknd 1/2-way* 66/1

1m 1.92s (-0.38) **Going Correction** -0.20s/f (Stan) 8 Ran SP% **121.6**
Speed ratings (Par 92): **95,88,85,85,77 76,72,53**
toteswingers 1&2 £3.60, 1&3 £2.00, 2&3 £8.90 CSF £4.96 TOTE £1.30: £1.02, £1.80, £4.50; EX 5.70 Trifecta £35.90 Pool: £3957.93 - 82.56 winning units..
Owner Patrick Whitten **Bred** P Whitten **Trained** Whitsbury, Hants

FOCUS
An uncompetitive maiden and all very straightforward for the favourite. Modest form.

5351 BOOK HOSPITALITY AT WOLVERHAMPTON RACECOURSE CLAIMING STKS 5f 20y(P)
2:45 (2:45) (Class 6) 2-Y-O **£1,940** (£577; £288; £144) **Stalls** Low

Form RPR
0224 1 **Baytown Kestrel**[16] 4783 2-9-5 80 AdamKirby 3 70
(Phil McEntee) *mde all: shkn up and edgd rt over 1f out: r.o* 11/8[1]
331 2 2 **Black Treacle (IRE)**[21] 4583 2-9-6 69 (p) SilvestreDeSousa 6 64
(Keith Dalgleish) *chsd wnr tl pushed along 3f out: remained handy: styd on u.p to go 2nd again wl ins fnl f* 9/4[2]
3500 3 1 1/4 **Marilyn Marquessa**[10] 4965 2-8-1 62 (b[1]) CathyGannon 7 40
(Jo Hughes) *s.i.s: hdwy to chse wnr 3f out: rdn over 1f out: no ex wl ins fnl f* 8/1
66 4 1 1/4 **Danetimeranger (IRE)**[91] 2327 2-8-2 0 PhilipPrince(5) 5 42+
(Ronald Harris) *s.i.s: in rr: drvn along 1/2-way: r.o ins fnl f: nvr nrr* 80/1
6440 5 1 1/4 **Faye Belle**[7] 5066 2-8-0 45 (v[1]) AdamMcLean(7) 2 37
(Derek Shaw) *chsd ldrs: rdn 1/2-way: sn outpcd* 80/1
6024 6 4 1/2 **Limegrove**[5] 5121 2-8-8 70 DeclanBates(3) 4 25
(David Evans) *s.i.s: outpcd* 4/1[3]
0 7 7 **Lovely Lily**[10] 4937 2-8-8 0 RyanWhile(7) 1 4
(Bill Turner) *sn pushed along and prom: rdn 1/2-way: sn wknd* 33/1

1m 1.83s (-0.47) **Going Correction** -0.20s/f (Stan) 7 Ran SP% **109.4**
Speed ratings (Par 92): **95,91,89,87,85 78,67**
toteswingers 1&2 £1.60, 1&3 £2.60, 2&3 £3.00 CSF £4.20 TOTE £2.40: £1.50, £1.70; EX 5.10 Trifecta £15.00 Pool: £3581.70 - 178.51 winning units..Baytown Kestrel was claimed by Mr B Ellison for £12,000
Owner Mrs Rebecca McEntee **Bred** R F And S D Knipe **Trained** Newmarket, Suffolk

FOCUS
A modest juvenile claimer and another all-the-way winner. The winning time was 0.09 seconds quicker than the preceding maiden and the fourth and fifth offer perspective.

5352 BRITISH STALLION STUDS EBF MAIDEN FILLIES' STKS 5f 216y(P)
3:15 (3:16) (Class 5) 2-Y-O **£2,911** (£866; £432; £216) **Stalls** Low

Form RPR
03 **1** **Simple Magic (IRE)**[14] 4828 2-9-0 0 WilliamBuick 4 85+
(John Gosden) *mde all: shkn up and qcknd clr over 1f out: easily* **4/5**[1]
60 **2** *8* **Palace Princess (FR)**[17] 4702 2-9-0 0 AdamKirby 8 61
(Ed Dunlop) *broke wl: sn stdd and lost pl: hdwy over 2f out: styd on to go 2nd wl ins fnl f: nt trble wnr* **10/1**
3 *shd* **Rocksee (IRE)** 2-9-0 0 StephenCraine 6 61
(Tom Dascombe) *chsd ldrs: rdn over 1f out: styd on same pce* **28/1**
5 **4** *nk* **Exceed Areeda (IRE)**[24] 4497 2-9-0 0 NeilCallan 5 60
(James Tate) *chsd wnr: rdn over 1f out: sn outpcd* **12/1**
6 **5** *2 3/4* **Alquimia (IRE)**[52] 3536 2-9-0 0 SilvestreDeSousa 7 52+
(Ed Dunlop) *s.i.s: hld up: shkn up over 1f out: nvr nrr* **5/1**[2]
44 **6** *1* **Elite Freedom (IRE)**[10] 4963 2-9-0 0 CathyGannon 2 49
(Jo Hughes) *chsd ldrs: rdn over 2f out: wknd fnl f* **8/1**[3]
0 **7** *hd* **Division Belle**[17] 4702 2-9-0 0 MartinDwyer 3 48
(William Muir) *prom: pushed along over 2f out: wknd over 1f out* **80/1**
8 *1 1/2* **Whispering Star (USA)** 2-9-0 0 MartinLane 10 43
(David Simcock) *sn bhd: nvr on terms* **14/1**
06 **9** *1/2* **Maysville (IRE)**[33] 4164 2-9-0 0 FrannyNorton 9 42
(Charles Hills) *hld up: pushed along over 2f out: sn wknd* **28/1**
00 **10** *4* **Shamouti (IRE)**[66] 3064 2-9-0 0 JamieSpencer 1 30
(Kevin Ryan) *hld up: racd keenly: hdwy over 2f out: wknd over 1f out* **33/1**
00 **11** *13* **Emerald Breeze (IRE)**[12] 4877 2-9-0 0 WilliamCarson 12
(Charles Hills) *stdd s: sn outpcd* **66/1**

1m 13.6s (-1.40) **Going Correction** -0.20s/f (Stan) **11** Ran SP% **119.3**
Speed ratings (Par 91): **101,90,90,89,86 84,84,82,81,76 59**
toteswingers 1&2 £3.10, 1&3 £14.30, 2&3 £21.70 CSF £9.73 TOTE £1.60: £1.10, £2.80, £8.40; EX 8.20 Trifecta £208.30 Pool: £3960.42 - 14.25 winning units..
Owner Prince A A Faisal **Bred** Nawara Stud Co Ltd **Trained** Newmarket, Suffolk

FOCUS
Another uncompetitive maiden and the third winner on the day to do it from the front. The easy winner held a solid pre-race edge.

5353 CORE ASSETS FOSTERING FILLIES' H'CAP 7f 32y(P)
3:45 (3:46) (Class 5) (0-75,74) 3-Y-0+ **£2,587** (£770; £384; £192) **Stalls** High

Form RPR
2422 **1** **Al Freej (IRE)**[114] 1686 4-9-12 **74** DaleSwift 1 82
(Brian Ellison) *hld up: plld hrd: hdwy 4f out: pushed along over 2f out: r.o u.p to ld and edgd lft wl ins fnl f* **7/1**
-125 **2** *1/2* **Miss Avonbridge (IRE)**[34] 4145 3-9-6 **74** StephenCraine 3 78
(Tom Dascombe) *led: rdn over 1f out: hdd wl ins fnl f* **5/1**[3]
5023 **3** *shd* **Summer Dream (IRE)**[28] 4354 3-9-6 **74** (b) AdamKirby 2 78
(Marco Botti) *chsd ldrs: rdn and ev ch ins fnl f: styd on* **5/2**[2]
4322 **4** *2 1/2* **Amethyst Dawn (IRE)**[19] 4637 7-9-7 **69** MartinDwyer 7 68
(Alan McCabe) *chsd ldr: ev ch fr over 2f out tl rdn over 1f out: no ex ins fnl f* **10/1**
-321 **5** *1/2* **Clear Pearl (USA)**[18] 4689 3-9-5 **73** JamieSpencer 5 69
(Ed Vaughan) *hld up: rdn over 1f out: styd on same pce ins fnl f* **9/4**[1]
5343 **6** *4* **Silkelly**[5] 5150 3-9-1 **74** (t) DavidBergin(5) 6 59
(David O'Meara) *s.i.s: sn chsng ldrs: rdn and hung rt wl over 1f out: wknd fnl f* **7/1**
0365 **7** *1* **Loulou Vuitton**[37] 4064 3-8-1 **55** oh1 (b[1]) JimmyQuinn 8 37
(Frank Sheridan) *s.i.s: hld up: hdwy over 1f out: wknd fnl f* **25/1**

1m 28.52s (-1.08) **Going Correction** -0.20s/f (Stan)
WFA 3 from 4yo+ 6lb **7** Ran SP% **113.9**
Speed ratings (Par 100): **98,97,97,94,93 89,88**
toteswingers 1&2 £4.70, 1&3 £4.10, 2&3 £4.00 CSF £41.00 CT £111.25 TOTE £6.40: £4.00, £4.40; EX 32.00 Trifecta £113.60 Pool: £3959.83 - 26.12 winning units..
Owner Kevin Corcoran Aaron Pierce Chris Weare **Bred** Mrs Sandra McCarthy **Trained** Norton, N Yorks

FOCUS
An ordinary fillies' handicap, but a stirring finish.

5354 BOOK HORIZONS RESTAURANT AT WOLVERHAMPTON H'CAP 7f 32y(P)
4:15 (4:15) (Class 6) (0-65,66) 3-Y-0+ **£1,940** (£577; £288; £144) **Stalls** High

Form RPR
0443 **1** **Excellent Jem**[33] 4163 4-9-12 **65** (b[1]) MartinDwyer 2 74
(Jane Chapple-Hyam) *mde all: rdn over 1f out: edgd rt ins fnl f: styd on* **5/2**[2]
4460 **2** *3/4* **Piccolo Express**[7] 5072 7-9-4 **57** JackMitchell 3 64
(Brian Baugh) *mid-div: hdwy over 2f out: rdn and r.o to go 2nd ins fnl f: nt rch wnr* **14/1**
6201 **3** *1 3/4* **Glenridding**[10] 4966 9-9-11 **64** (p) DaleSwift 1 66
(James Given) *chsd ldrs: pushed along 1/2-way: rdn to chse wnr over 1f out tl ins fnl f: styd on same pce* **10/1**
5052 **4** *1/2* **Powerful Pierre**[14] 4836 6-9-9 **62** (b) JimmyQuinn 8 63
(Ollie Pears) *s.i.s: hld up: hdwy over 1f out: sn rdn: styd on: nt trble ldrs* **5/1**[3]
-011 **5** *3* **Angel Cake (IRE)**[7] 5072 4-9-8 **66** 6ex TobyAtkinson(5) 9 59
(Michael Appleby) *prom: rdn over 2f out: styd on same pce fnl f* **7/4**[1]
300 **6** *1/2* **Time To Begin (IRE)**[111] 1742 3-8-13 **58** (p) NeilCallan 4 49
(Alan McCabe) *wnt rt s: trckd wnr tl rdn over 1f out: wknd ins fnl f* **9/1**
0004 **7** *8* **Direct Trade**[14] 4840 3-7-12 **46** oh1 RyanPowell(3) 6 16
(Mark Usher) *s.i.s: rdn over 2f out: a in rr* **16/1**
0000 **8** *shd* **Forever Janey**[7] 5072 4-8-4 **46** oh1 RaulDaSilva(3) 10 16
(Paul Green) *hld up: plld hrd: hdwy u.p over 2f out: wknd over 1f out* **50/1**
000 **9** *9* **Babushka's Girl**[12] 4887 4-8-6 **48** oh1 ow2 MarkCoumbe(3) 5
(Lisa Williamson) *s.i.s: a in rr: rdn and wknd over 2f out* **100/1**

1m 28.49s (-1.11) **Going Correction** -0.20s/f (Stan)
WFA 3 from 4yo+ 6lb **9** Ran SP% **116.2**
Speed ratings (Par 101): **98,97,95,94,91 90,81,81,71**
toteswingers 1&2 £5.80, 1&3 £5.20, 2&3 £8.80 CSF £37.59 CT £261.29 TOTE £3.60: £1.60, £3.60, £1.80; EX 40.10 Trifecta £270.60 Pool: £3874.42 - 10.73 winning units..
Owner Chris Fahy **Bred** Norcroft Park Stud **Trained** Dalham, Suffolk

FOCUS
A moderate handicap and normal service was resumed with the winner again making all.

5355 NEW CAPTUR NOW AT RENAULT WOLVERHAMPTON H'CAP 1m 141y(P)
4:45 (4:45) (Class 4) (0-85,85) 3-Y-0+ **£4,690** (£1,395; £697; £348) **Stalls** Low

Form RPR
4-16 **1** **Mount Tiger**[26] 4416 3-8-13 **78** NeilCallan 8 89+
(James Tate) *trckd ldrs: rdn to ld ins fnl f: r.o* **11/8**[1]
332 **2** *1* **Ocean Tempest**[10] 4960 4-9-13 **84** (p) AdamKirby 5 93
(John Ryan) *led over 3f: chsd ldr tl rdn to ld again over 2f out: rdr dropped whip 1f out: sn hdd: unable qck towards fin* **11/4**[2]
-004 **3** *nk* **Invisible Hunter (USA)**[53] 3503 4-9-4 **82** (v[1]) AhmadAlSubousi(7) 7 90
(Saeed bin Suroor) *hld up: plld hrd: hdwy and racd wd fr over 6f out: led 5f out: rdn and hdd over 2f out: hung lft and ev ch ins fnl f: no ex towards fin* **9/1**
3132 **4** *1 3/4* **Mon Brav**[17] 4730 6-9-6 **77** AidanColeman 1 81
(Brian Ellison) *prom: rdn over 1f out: styd on* **14/1**
0641 **5** *1 1/4* **Fraserburgh (IRE)**[15] 4806 3-8-6 **71** SilvestreDeSousa 6 72
(Mark Johnston) *chsd ldr 3f: remained handy: rdn over 2f out: styd on same pce ins fnl f* **6/1**[3]
1062 **6** *12* **Classic Colori (IRE)**[12] 4895 6-9-9 **85** (v) DavidBergin(5) 2 59
(David O'Meara) *prom: pushed along 4f out: rdn and wknd over 2f out* **16/1**
-400 **7** *1* **Cocozza (USA)**[9] 5006 5-9-9 **80** (p) JimmyQuinn 4 52
(K F Clutterbuck) *s.i.s: racd keenly and sn prom: lost pl over 6f out: rdn and wknd over 2f out* **40/1**
6636 **8** *1* **Assizes**[39] 3976 4-9-6 **77** DaleSwift 3 46
(Ruth Carr) *s.i.s: a in rr: rdn and wknd over 2f out* **18/1**

1m 48.35s (-2.15) **Going Correction** -0.20s/f (Stan)
WFA 3 from 4yo+ 8lb **8** Ran SP% **113.3**
Speed ratings (Par 105): **101,100,99,98,97 86,85,84**
toteswingers 1&2 £1.80, 1&3 £4.10, 2&3 £4.70 CSF £5.04 CT £22.00 TOTE £2.30: £1.10, £2.00, £3.10; EX 6.80 Trifecta £42.80 Pool: £3559.69 - 62.34 winning units..
Owner Saif Ali **Bred** Rabbah Bloodstock Limited **Trained** Newmarket, Suffolk

FOCUS
The best race on the card and a bit of a mess, but it was truly run and stamina won the day.

5356 FIND US ON FACEBOOK WOLVERHAMPTON RACECOURSE H'CAP 1m 4f 50y(P)
5:20 (5:20) (Class 5) (0-75,74) 3-Y-0+ **£2,587** (£770; £384; £192) **Stalls** Low

Form RPR
-540 **1** **Mallory Heights (IRE)**[60] 3243 3-8-11 **68** SilvestreDeSousa 1 81+
(Luca Cumani) *trckd ldrs: led 4f out: rdn clr fnl f* **15/8**[1]
411- **2** *4 1/2* **Ty Gwr**[270] 7718 4-9-10 **70** DaleSwift 3 74+
(Brian Ellison) *hld up: plld hrd: hdwy over 2f out: rdn to chse wnr over 1f out: styd on same pce fnl f* **7/1**[3]
-020 **3** *nk* **Snow Hill**[12] 4882 5-10-0 **74** (b[1]) SebSanders 2 78
(Chris Wall) *trckd ldrs: nt clr run over 2f out: rdn over 1f out: styd on same pce fnl f* **15/2**
0432 **4** *1 3/4* **Waahej**[14] 4835 7-9-2 **62** WilliamCarson 10 63+
(Peter Hiatt) *sn led: hdd over 4f out: remained handy tl nt clr run and lost pl over 2f out: rallied over 1f out: styd on* **17/2**
34-2 **5** *1/2* **Gravitate**[41] 1653 4-9-10 **70** (t) MartinDwyer 8 70
(Paul Webber) *chsd ldrs: rdn over 1f out: styd on same pce* **12/1**
2-36 **6** *shd* **Squeeze My Brain (IRE)**[48] 3666 3-9-2 **73** (t[1]) JamieSpencer 4 73
(Ralph Beckett) *hld up: hdwy over 1f out: nvr rchd ldrs* **6/1**[2]
0331 **7** *1 1/4* **Nolecce**[14] 4838 6-8-10 **63** MatthewHopkins(7) 6 61
(Tony Forbes) *hld up: nt clr run over 2f out: r.o ins fnl f: nvr trbld ldrs* **16/1**
050 **8** *8* **Bravestar (IRE)**[56] 3417 3-9-1 **72** TedDurcan 9 57
(David Lanigan) *hld up: hdwy over 3f out: rdn and wknd over 1f out* **15/2**
-215 **9** *9* **Renegotiate**[22] 167 4-9-11 **71** ChrisCatlin 5 42
(Dr Richard Newland) *sn pushed along in rr: drvn along 1/2-way: wknd 3f out* **14/1**
305/ **10** *25* **Cool Strike (UAE)**[613] 6202 7-9-13 **73** (v) NeilCallan 7
(Alex Hales) *prom: led over 10f out: hdd 4f out: rdn over 3f out: wknd 2f out* **40/1**

2m 38.7s (-2.40) **Going Correction** -0.20s/f (Stan)
WFA 3 from 4yo+ 11lb **10** Ran SP% **118.3**
Speed ratings (Par 103): **100,97,96,95,95 95,94,89,83,66**
toteswingers 1&2 £4.10, 1&3 £3.60, 2&3 £9.40 CSF £15.50 CT £82.84 TOTE £2.30: £1.30, £2.60, £2.40; EX 14.80 Trifecta £85.00 Pool: £2263.64 - 19.97 winning units..
Owner Merry Fox Stud Limited **Bred** Merry Fox Stud Limited **Trained** Newmarket, Suffolk

FOCUS
A modest middle-distance handicap.
T/Plt: £23.40 to a £1 stake. Pool: £80,012.43 - 2494.39 winning tickets. T/Qpdt: £12.80 to a £1 stake. Pool: £5664.50 - 325.96 winning tickets. CR

5357 - 5359a (Foreign Racing) - See Raceform Interactive

5213 CLAIREFONTAINE (R-H)
Monday, August 12

OFFICIAL GOING: Turf: soft

5360a PRIX RADIO BALANCES (PRIX LUTH ENCHANTEE) (LISTED RACE) (4YO+ FILLIES & MARES) (TURF) 1m 1f
1:50 (12:00) 4-Y-0+ **£19,512** (£7,804; £5,853; £3,902; £1,951)

RPR
1 **Shanjia (GER)**[23] 4-8-11 0 IoritzMendizabal 8 101
(Frau C Brandstatter, Germany) **26/1**
2 *1/2* **Keegsquaw (IRE)**[23] 4555 4-8-11 0 Pierre-CharlesBoudot 1 100
(Mme A Fabre, France) **20/1**
3 *nk* **Foreign Tune**[23] 4555 4-8-11 0 OlivierPeslier 9 99
(C Laffon-Parias, France) **33/10**[2]
4 *hd* **Endellion (USA)**[18] 4-8-11 0 MaximeGuyon 4 99
(A Fabre, France) *led: c stands' side st: hrd pressed fr 2f out but r.o u.p: hdd and no ex 50yds out: dropped to 4th cl home* **13/2**
5 *snk* **Hippy (FR)**[43] 5-8-11 0 UmbertoRispoli 7 99
(E Libaud, France) **4/1**[3]
6 *2* **Queen Bubble (IRE)**[22] 4574 4-8-11 0 (p) AntoineHamelin 5 94
(Y De Nicolay, France) **37/1**
7 *hd* **Dutchessa**[12] 4-8-11 0 StephanePasquier 6 94
(C Ferland, France) **15/2**
8 *3* **Baino Rock (FR)**[100] 4-8-11 0 ChristopheSoumillon 2 88
(J-C Rouget, France) **3/1**[1]

9 2 ½ **Yojojo (IRE)**[55] 3427 4-8-11 0............ ThierryJarnet 3 82
(Gay Kelleway) *trckd ldr on inner: rdn and nt qckn under 2f out: wknd u.p fnl f* **15/2**
1m 50.3s (110.30) 9 Ran SP% **116.2**
WIN (incl. 1 euro stake): 27.50. PLACES: 5.60, 4.30, 2.10. DF: 92.80. SF: 333.30.
Owner Stall Carneval **Bred** H Hasler **Trained** Germany

[5323]LE LION-D'ANGERS (R-H)
Monday, August 12
OFFICIAL GOING: Turf: good to soft

5361a PRIX ROBERT DE CHOLET (GRAND PRIX DU LION-D'ANGERS) (LISTED RACE) (3YO) (TURF) 1m 2f
5:15 (12:00) 3-Y-O **£22,357** (£8,943; £6,707; £4,471; £2,235)

RPR
1 **Vanishing Cupid (SWI)**[49] 3645 3-8-11 0............(p) FabriceVeron 7 107
(H-A Pantall, France) **14/5**[1]
2 2 ½ **Royal Law (IRE)**[42] 3912 3-8-11 0............ AdrienFouassier 12 102
(A Couetil, France) **12/1**
3 4 **Kenbella (FR)**[52] 3-8-8 0............ FlavienPrat 11 91
(H-A Pantall, France) **19/1**
4 1 **Himalaya Dream (FR)**[21] 4600 3-8-11 0............ GeraldAvranche 6 92
(E Libaud, France) **38/1**
5 hd **Nausica Time (GER)** 3-8-8 0............ NRichter 8 89
(S Smrczek, Germany) **31/1**
6 hd **Sempre Medici (FR)**[21] 4600 3-8-11 0............ AlexisBadel 13 91
(Mme M Bollack-Badel, France) **73/10**
7 2 **Mutabaser**[59] 3309 3-8-11 0............ FranckBlondel 10 87
(F Rohaut, France) **10/1**
8 hd **Chika Dream (FR)**[36] 3-8-11 0............ AlexandreRoussel 9 87
(Y Barberot, France) **34/1**
9 2 ½ **Odyssee (FR)**[37] 3-8-8 0............ MarcLerner 2 79
(C Lerner, France) **28/1**
10 1 **Amarysia (FR)**[25] 4468 3-8-8 0............ AnthonyCrastus 5 77
(C Laffon-Parias, France) **15/1**
11 20 **Wall Of Sound**[24] 4485 3-8-8 0............ RichardKingscote 1 37
(Tom Dascombe) *led: hdd after 3 1/2f: pressed ldr on inner: disp ld 4f out: sn rdn and outpcd: lost pl fr 2 1/2f out: wknd and eased ins fnl f* **10/1**
12 1 **Frankyfourfingers (FR)**[43] 3-8-11 0............ Jean-BernardEyquem 3 38
(C Delcher-Sanchez, Spain) **13/2**[3]
13 5 **Zerdabi (FR)**[21] 3-8-11 0............ Christophe-PatriceLemaire 4 28
(A De Royer-Dupre, France) **48/10**[2]
2m 8.65s (128.65) 13 Ran SP% **118.1**
WIN (incl. 1 euro stake): 3.80. PLACES: 1.80, 3.40, 6.10. DF: 18.50. SF: 43.50.
Owner Mme Sibylle Egloff **Bred** Gestut Sohrenhof **Trained** France

[5119]DEAUVILLE (R-H)
Friday, August 9
OFFICIAL GOING: Turf: good; fibresand: standard

5362a PRIX DE BAVENT (CLAIMER) (2YO COLTS & GELDINGS) (TURF) 6f
1:50 (12:00) 2-Y-O **£10,975** (£4,390; £3,292; £2,195; £1,097)

RPR
1 **Talksalot (IRE)**[27] 4302 2-9-0 0............ IoritzMendizabal 7 80
(J S Moore) *wnt rt s: mde virtually all: gng best 2f out: rdn over 1f out: jinked lft u.p ent fnl f but r.o strly and asserted: drvn clr* **11/5**[1]
2 2 **Shepherd Gate (USA)**[7] 4948 2-8-9 0............(b) ThierryJarnet 2 69
(J S Moore) *midfield in tch: rdn 2f out: r.o u.p and wnt 2nd fnl strides: no imp on wnr* **9/1**
3 hd **Oromo (FR)** 2-8-13 0............ ChristopheSoumillon 8 72
(J Heloury, France) **18/5**[3]
4 1 ¼ **Color Code (FR)**[65] 2-8-9 0............ TheoBachelot 3 65
(K Borgel, France) **11/1**
5 1 **Always The Gent**[15] 2-8-9 0............ TonyPiccone 9 62
(Matthieu Palussiere, France) **35/1**
6 snk **Boogy Man (ITY)**[61] 2-9-0 0............ UmbertoRispoli 6 66
(G Botti, France) **17/5**[2]
7 5 **Ponthieu (FR)**[15] 2-8-9 0............(b) AntoineHamelin 1 46
(Matthieu Palussiere, France) **9/1**
8 12 **Duc De Formigny (FR)**[7] 2-8-9 0............(p) ThierryThulliez 5 10
(C Boutin, France) **19/1**
9 dist **Simply Ozzy (IRE)** 2-9-0 0............ PetrForet 4
(V Luka Jr, Czech Republic) **13/1**
1m 10.6s (-0.40) 9 Ran SP% **119.0**
WIN (incl. 1 euro stake): 3.20. PLACES: 1.50, 2.40, 1.80. DF: 16.70. SF: 23.20.
Owner J Bond-Smith & J S Moore **Bred** C Kelly **Trained** Upper Lambourn, Berks

5363a PRIX D'HEROUVILLE (CLAIMER) (2YO FILLIES) (TURF) 6f
2:20 (12:00) 2-Y-O **£10,975** (£4,390; £3,292; £2,195; £1,097)

RPR
1 **Blu Axara (ITY)**[18] 4599 2-8-9 0............ UmbertoRispoli 8 71
(F Chappet, France) **114/10**
2 nk **Galinea (IRE)**[15] 2-8-13 0............ OlivierPeslier 2 74
(C Laffon-Parias, France) **11/2**[2]
3 nk **Atlantic City (FR)**[15] 2-8-13 0............ MatthiasLauron(5) 5 78
(X Nakkachdji, France) **8/1**
4 snk **Maremmadiavola (IRE)**[24] 4397 2-9-7 0............ IoritzMendizabal 12 81
(J Heloury, France) **9/1**
5 1 ¾ **Vodka Chaser (IRE)**[13] 4749 2-8-9 0............ ThierryJarnet 3 64
(J S Moore) *t.k.h early: trckd ldr: rdn and ev ch 1f out: nt qckn ins fnl f: kpt on* **15/2**
6 snk **Stella Indiana (FR)**[17] 2-9-0 0............ CristianDemuro 10 68
(J Heloury, France) **31/1**
7 hd **Victorianvalentine (FR)**[17] 2-9-0 0............ AntoineHamelin 7 67
(Matthieu Palussiere, France) **15/1**
8 1 ½ **Ascot Memory (IRE)** 2-8-13 0............ TheoBachelot 11 62
(S Wattel, France) **13/2**[3]
9 hd **Stone Me (FR)** 2-8-13 0............ ChristopheSoumillon 4 61
(J-C Rouget, France) **14/5**[1]
10 5 **Stake Winning (FR)**[127] 2-8-9 0............ CesarPasserat(4) 1 46
(S Wattel, France) **24/1**
11 1 ½ **La Goutte D'Or (FR)**[10] 2-8-2 0............(p) ValentinGambart(7) 6 38
(M Boutin, France) **12/1**
1m 11.13s (0.13) 11 Ran SP% **117.0**
WIN (incl. 1 euro stake): 12.40. PLACES: 4.30, 2.10, 2.80. DF: 39.30. SF: 74.70.
Owner Fabrice Chappet **Bred** Azienda Agricola Luciani Loreto **Trained** France

[5047]CARLISLE (R-H)
Tuesday, August 13
OFFICIAL GOING: Good to firm (7.7)
Weather: Overcast

5364 RUGBY LEAGUE WORLD CUP 2013 MEDIAN AUCTION MAIDEN STKS 5f 193y
2:15 (2:17) (Class 5) 2-Y-O **£2,911** (£866; £432; £216) **Stalls Low**

Form RPR
4 1 **Makin The Rules (IRE)**[10] 4977 2-9-5 0............ MichaelO'Connell 11 73
(John Quinn) *towards rr: rdn along 1/2-way: gd hdwy over 1f out: styd on wl to ld towards fin* **14/1**
2 2 ¾ **Omaha Gold (IRE)**[14] 4847 2-9-0 0............ RoystonFfrench 4 66
(Bryan Smart) *t.k.h: led: rdn clr wl over 1f out: edgd lft ins fnl f: hdd towards fin* **5/1**
043 3 nse **Beltor**[36] 4107 2-9-5 70............ TomEaves 10 70
(Michael Dods) *t.k.h: hld up: swtchd lft and hdwy over 1f out: styd on strly fnl f: nrst fin* **4/1**[2]
4 1 ¼ **Lexington Abbey** 2-9-5 0............ PhillipMakin 1 66
(Kevin Ryan) *prom: effrt and chsd ldr over 1f out to ins fnl f: kpt on same pce* **9/2**[3]
3 5 ½ **Nowinaminute (IRE)**[22] 4583 2-9-0 0............ GrahamLee 8 60
(James Given) *midfield: pushed along over 2f out: rallied over 1f out: kpt on same pce fnl f* **16/1**
5 6 2 **Neuf Des Coeurs**[43] 3896 2-9-0 0............ PaulMulrennan 6 53+
(Keith Dalgleish) *bhd: pushed along 1/2-way: hdwy over 1f out: styd on fnl f: nrst fin* **16/1**
40 7 ¾ **Gym Shoes**[24] 4528 2-9-5 0............ TonyHamilton 5 56
(Richard Fahey) *chsd ldr to over 1f out: sn rdn: wknd ent fnl f* **13/2**
00 8 2 ¼ **Suni Dancer**[2] 5299 2-9-0 0............ PJMcDonald 7 44
(Paul Green) *midfield: drvn over 2f out: btn fnl f* **50/1**
24 9 7 **Blue Bounty**[9] 5025 2-9-5 0............ RobertWinston 2 26
(Mark H Tompkins) *cl up: rdn over 2f out: wknd fnl f* **11/4**[1]
10 14 **Nam Ma Prow** 2-9-5 0............ AndrewElliott 3
(Simon West) *s.i.s: bhd and outpcd: no ch fr 1/2-way: t.o* **125/1**
11 17 **Lunesdale Buddy** 2-9-5 0............ PaddyAspell 9
(Alan Berry) *s.i.s: bhd and drvn along: lost tch fr 1/2-way: t.o* **150/1**
1m 12.96s (-0.74) **Going Correction** -0.10s/f (Good) 11 Ran SP% **116.7**
Speed ratings (Par 94): **100,99,98,97,96 93,92,89,80,61 39**
toteswingers 1&2 £11.30, 2&3 £3.50, 1&3 £14.00 CSF £82.14 TOTE £19.40: £4.20, £1.50, £1.90; EX 115.20 Trifecta £515.10 Pool: £2749.02 - 4.00 winning units..
Owner C W Makin **Bred** Godfrey Moylan **Trained** Settrington, N Yorks

FOCUS
Rail at inner configuration and all distances as advertised. An ordinary maiden, but the winning time was only around half a second outside the 2yo course record, suggesting quick ground. The second and third help with the level.

5365 AUSSIE PUB GROUP H'CAP 5f 193y
2:45 (2:46) (Class 6) (0-65,69) 3-Y-O+ **£2,587** (£770; £384; £192) **Stalls Low**

Form RPR
4606 1 **Diamond Blue**[25] 4510 5-9-10 **63**............(p) PhillipMakin 10 71
(Richard Whitaker) *hld up: hdwy on outside over 1f out: led ins fnl f: drvn out* **10/1**
6000 2 ½ **Cheyenne Red (IRE)**[68] 3024 7-8-4 **46** oh1............ JasonHart(3) 9 52
(Michael Herrington) *chsd ldrs: hdwy to ld over 1f out: hdd ins fnl f: kpt on same pce towards fin* **66/1**
6-00 3 nk **Bapak Pesta (IRE)**[36] 4114 3-8-9 **59**............ KevinStott(7) 5 63
(Kevin Ryan) *in tch: effrt whn nt clr run briefly over 1f out: swtchd rt and styd on fnl f: nrst fin* **15/2**
0410 4 1 ¾ **Captain Royale (IRE)**[6] 5139 8-9-8 **61**............(p) BarryMcHugh 13 61
(Tracy Waggott) *in tch on outside: effrt over 2f out: hung rt and ev ch over 1f out: one pce ins fnl f* **16/1**
5450 5 1 **Blue Shoes (IRE)**[18] 4727 4-9-8 **61**............(b[1]) DavidAllan 11 58
(Tim Easterby) *chsd ldr: rdn to ld briefly over 1f out: outpcd ins fnl f* **5/1**[2]
-030 6 1 ¼ **Emily Hall**[13] 4892 4-8-10 **49**............ RoystonFfrench 8 42
(Bryan Smart) *taken early to post: sn drvn and in tch: effrt and drvn whn n.m.r briefly over 1f out: sn one pce* **12/1**
3506 7 nk **Seamster**[50] 3643 6-9-4 **57**............(vt) PJMcDonald 4 49
(Richard Ford) *upset in stalls: bhd: rdn and hdwy whn nt clr run over 1f out: edgd rt and styd on fnl f: n.d* **16/1**
5000 8 1 **M J Woodward**[8] 5047 4-9-12 **65**............ PaulMulrennan 14 53
(Paul Green) *hld up on outside: rdn over 2f out: outpcd over 1f out* **18/1**
0625 9 ½ **Tongalooma**[13] 4892 7-9-4 **57**............ GrahamLee 12 44
(James Moffatt) *chsd ldrs: rdn over 2f out: wknd ent fnl f* **11/2**[3]
0P0- 10 hd **Gambino (IRE)**[315] 6753 3-7-10 **46** oh1............ JordanHibberd(7) 2 31+
(Alan Berry) *hld up on ins: rdn and outpcd 1/2-way: sme late hdwy: n.d* **200/1**
01 11 2 ¼ **Natures Law (IRE)**[103] 1962 3-9-5 **62**............ TomEaves 7 40
(Keith Dalgleish) *taken early to post: towards rr: rdn over 2f out: no imp fr over 1f out* **10/3**[1]
1004 12 3 **China Excels**[16] 4814 6-9-7 **60**............ RussKennemore 3 29
(Sue Smith) *led tl rdn and hdd over 1f out: sn wknd* **17/2**
0006 13 3 **Henry Bee**[11] 4956 4-9-7 **60**............(b) TonyHamilton 6 20
(Richard Fahey) *bhd: struggling after 2f: nvr on terms* **16/1**
1m 12.67s (-1.03) **Going Correction** -0.10s/f (Good)
WFA 3 from 4yo+ 4lb 13 Ran SP% **119.1**
Speed ratings (Par 101): **102,101,100,98,97 95,95,93,93,92 89,85,81**
toteswingers 1&2 £43.00, 2&3 £75.00, 1&3 £18.60 CSF £518.20 CT £5141.04 TOTE £13.20: £4.10, £11.00, £4.30; EX 614.10 Trifecta £1988.40 Part won. Pool: £2651.27 - 0.26 winning units..
Owner Mrs Jane Newett **Bred** Hellwood Stud Farm **Trained** Scarcroft, W Yorks

FOCUS
A moderate sprint handicap. Straightforward form.

5366 BOOKMAKERS.CO.UK NURSERY H'CAP 5f
3:15 (3:16) (Class 5) (0-75,76) 2-Y-O £4,528 (£1,347; £673; £336) Stalls Low

Form RPR
1 1 Pull The Plug (IRE)29 4351 2-9-4 72 NeilFarley(3) 1 81+
(Declan Carroll) chsd ldrs: effrt and drvn over 1f out: led ins fnl f: kpt on strly 11/2³
5313 2 2 ¼ De Repente (IRE)4 5226 2-9-3 68 PaulMulrennan 6 69
(Paul Green) led: rdn over 1f out: hdd ins fnl f: kpt on same pce 7/1
0611 3 nk Threetimesalady5 5175 2-9-8 76 6ex RosieJessop(3) 5 76
(Sir Mark Prescott Bt) dwlt: outpcd in rr: plenty to do 1/2-way: hdwy on wd outside over 1f out: edgd lft: kpt on wl fnl f: nrst fin 15/8¹
0054 4 3 Princess Myla (IRE)14 4847 2-8-8 59 MickyFenton 4 48
(Paul Midgley) dwlt: in tch: drvn along 2f out: no imp appr fnl f 16/1
266 5 1 Bajan Rebel28 4370 2-8-9 60 (b¹) GrahamGibbons 2 46
(Michael Easterby) cl up: rdn and hung rt wl over 1f out: outpcd fnl f 9/1
6521 6 1 ¼ Soul Instinct16 4801 2-8-13 71 KevinStott(7) 3 52
(Kevin Ryan) in tch: hung lft to 2f out: rdn and edgd rt over 1f out: wknd 5/2²
2064 7 2 ¼ Jaga Time3 5289 2-8-4 55 BarryMcHugh 8 28
(Richard Fahey) sn drvn along in rr: struggling fr over 2f out 33/1
1m 0.56s (-0.24) **Going Correction** -0.10s/f (Good) 7 Ran SP% 110.1
Speed ratings (Par 94): **97,93,92,88,86 84,80**
toteswingers 1&2 £7.00, 2&3 £2.90, 1&3 £1.10 CSF £39.39 CT £91.10 TOTE £8.10: £3.00, £2.60; EX 40.10 Trifecta £166.10 Pool: £3053.15 - 13.78 winning units..
Owner C Harding **Bred** Peter Molony **Trained** Sledmere, E Yorks

FOCUS
They went a decent gallop in this ordinary nursery, but on this occasion the pace held up. The form is taken at face value.

5367 IAN'S RETIREMENT PARTY CLAIMING STKS 1m 1f 61y
3:45 (3:45) (Class 5) 3-Y-O+ £2,911 (£866; £432; £216) Stalls Low

Form RPR
3025 1 Toto Skyllachy8 5050 8-10-0 91 GrahamGibbons 5 88
(David O'Meara) mde all: rdn and qcknd clr wl over 1f out: kpt on strly fnl f: unchal 4/1
2062 2 2 ¼ Gran Maestro (USA)7 5087 4-9-6 74 (b) LMcNiff(3) 8 78
(Ruth Carr) hld up in tch: rdn and outpcd over 2f out: rallied and hung rt over 1f out: styd on to chse wnr towards fin 7/2³
3012 3 ½ Demolition13 4888 9-8-12 79 JoeyHaynes(7) 6 73
(Noel Wilson) in tch: drvn over 3f out: rallied over 1f out: wnt 2nd briefly wl ins fnl f: one pce 5/2¹
3246 4 ½ Bling King78 2705 4-9-2 76 JordanNason(7) 3 76
(Geoffrey Harker) dwlt: hld up: hdwy on outside to chse (clr) wnr over 1f out: no ex wl ins fnl f 17/2
0000 5 3 ¾ Memory Cloth10 4979 6-9-7 80 JacobButterfield(7) 2 74
(Brian Ellison) trckd ldrs: effrt and wnt 2nd over 3f out to over 1f out: sn btn 11/4²
40 6 29 Croftamie50 3625 4-9-2 52 (p) MichaelO'Connell 7
(Tracy Waggott) chsd wnr to over 3f out: sn struggling: t.o 66/1
1m 54.68s (-2.92) **Going Correction** -0.10s/f (Good) 6 Ran SP% 109.5
Speed ratings (Par 103): **108,106,105,105,101 76**
toteswingers 1&2 £2.80, 2&3 £2.80, 1&3 £2.10 CSF £17.26 TOTE £3.70: £1.90, £3.30; EX 15.70 Trifecta £46.80 Pool: £2824.29 - 45.21 winning units..
Owner Richard Walker **Bred** Mrs G Slater **Trained** Nawton, N Yorks

FOCUS
Despite this being the claimer, these were the classiest horses on the card and the pace was solid. The winner enjoyed an easy lead and the form is rated a few pounds below where it could have been.

5368 PREMIER SPORTS NO 1 FOR RUGBY LEAGUE H'CAP 1m 1f 61y
4:15 (4:15) (Class 5) (0-70,69) 3-Y-O+ £2,911 (£866; £432; £216) Stalls Low

Form RPR
0211 1 Save The Bees6 5142 5-9-8 66 JasonHart(3) 5 75
(Declan Carroll) mde all: rdn over 2f out: styd on strly fnl f 5/2¹
0422 2 1 Euston Square5 5179 7-8-11 52 DaleSwift 7 59
(Alistair Whillans) dwlt: sn pushed along to chse ldrs: wnt 2nd over 4f out: ev ch and rdn 2f out: edgd rt: kpt on fnl f 3/1²
2502 3 nse Mixed Message (IRE)35 4143 3-9-5 68 GrahamLee 6 75
(Brian Ellison) prom: drvn and outpcd over 2f out: rallied over 1f out: kpt on fnl f 9/2³
-443 4 ¾ Obboorr16 4810 4-9-9 64 MickyFenton 8 69
(Brian Rothwell) dwlt: t.k.h: hld up: effrt on outside over 2f out: r.o ins fnl f 8/1
3030 5 ½ Wyldfire (IRE)16 4809 3-9-4 67 LeeTopliss 1 71
(Richard Fahey) taken early to post: t.k.h: chsd ldrs: rdn and outpcd 3f out: rallied over 1f out: kpt on same pce ins fnl f 11/2
4260 6 2 ¼ Joshua The First15 4823 4-9-6 61 (b¹) TomEaves 2 61
(Keith Dalgleish) t.k.h: chsd wnr to over 4f out: rdn and outpcd fr over 1f out 25/1
421- 7 15 Dark Ruler (IRE)317 6711 4-10-0 69 RobertWinston 4 39
(Alan Swinbank) hld up: rdn and outpcd over 3f out: btn fr 2f out: t.o 14/1
1m 57.34s (-0.26) **Going Correction** -0.10s/f (Good)
WFA 3 from 4yo+ 8lb 7 Ran SP% 108.8
Speed ratings (Par 103): **97,96,96,95,94 92,79**
toteswingers 1&2 £1.90, 2&3 £3.10, 1&3 £2.50 CSF £9.10 CT £26.38 TOTE £3.40: £2.30, £1.80; EX 8.40 Trifecta £20.80 Pool: £2396.93 - 86.17 winning units..
Owner Steve Ryan **Bred** S P Ryan **Trained** Sledmere, E Yorks

FOCUS
They only went a steady gallop in this handicap, which suited those that raced up with the pace. The winning time was 2.66 seconds slower than the claimer and the form is rated around the first four..

5369 GRAFIX SIGNS H'CAP 7f 200y
4:45 (4:46) (Class 5) (0-70,69) 3-Y-O+ £2,911 (£866; £432; £216) Stalls Low

Form RPR
5113 1 True Pleasure (IRE)21 4609 6-9-3 58 PJMcDonald 8 67+
(James Bethell) hld up: hdwy on outside to ld 2f out: sn rdn and edgd rt: hld on wl fnl f 3/1²
3006 2 nk Moral Issue53 3546 5-9-1 56 RobertWinston 1 64
(Alan Swinbank) hld up: rdn and hdwy over 2f out: chsd wnr ins fnl f: kpt on: hld cl home 12/1
063 3 ¾ Dance For Georgie49 3649 4-9-8 63 GrahamLee 2 70
(Ben Haslam) cl up: led over 3f out to 2f out: rallied: kpt on fnl f: hld nr fin 11/4¹
643- 4 3 ½ Cheers Buddy (IRE)319 6646 5-8-11 52 TomEaves 6 51
(Keith Dalgleish) in tch: hdwy to chse ldrs over 2f out: sn rdn and edgd rt: outpcd fnl f 7/1
0-00 5 2 Tukitinyasok (IRE)84 2537 6-8-11 52 MichaelO'Connell 3 46
(Clive Mulhall) chsd ldrs: drvn over 2f out: wknd appr fnl f 40/1
3402 6 1 ½ Secret Empress22 4585 3-8-2 50 oh1 DuranFentiman 7 41
(Bryan Smart) in tch: drvn along over 4f out: no imp fr 2f out 12/1
130- 7 nse Indian Giver335 6131 5-9-5 63 PaulPickard(3) 4 53
(Alan Berry) s.i.s: hld up: hdwy and swtchd lft over 2f out: no imp over 1f out 20/1
0204 8 23 Birdy Boy (USA)11 4955 3-8-9 57 PaulMulrennan 5
(Mark Johnston) led to over 3f out: rdn and wknd 2f out: t.o 14/1
0044 9 6 Berlusca (IRE)8 5070 4-10-0 69 GrahamGibbons 9
(David O'Meara) t.k.h: cl up on outside tl rdn and wknd 2f out: t.o 7/2³
1m 38.43s (-1.57) **Going Correction** -0.10s/f (Good)
WFA 3 from 4yo+ 7lb 9 Ran SP% 115.6
Speed ratings (Par 103): **103,102,101,98,96 94,94,71,65**
toteswingers 1&2 £6.80, 2&3 £7.70, 1&3 £3.00 CSF £38.75 CT £110.02 TOTE £3.80: £1.60, £3.00, £1.90; EX 51.50 Trifecta £168.00 Pool: £3286.06 - 14.66 winning units..
Owner Clarendon Thoroughbred Racing **Bred** Michael O'Mahony **Trained** Middleham Moor, N Yorks

FOCUS
An ordinary handicap, but they went a decent pace thanks to a contested lead. Straightforward form.

5370 WHITEHAVEN RLFC AND MAIN SPONSOR NMP H'CAP 1m 3f 107y
5:15 (5:16) (Class 6) (0-60,59) 3-Y-O+ £2,587 (£770; £384; £192) Stalls High

Form RPR
4340 1 Ailsa Craig (IRE)24 4543 7-9-5 59 (p) KevinStott(7) 2 67
(Edwin Tuer) blindfold slow to remove and s.s: sn rcvrd and hld up: smooth hdwy on outside 3f out: led over 1f out: drvn out 7/2¹
00-6 2 ¾ Ravi River (IRE)16 4803 9-9-7 59 GarryWhillans(5) 11 66
(Alistair Whillans) midfield: rdn and hdwy to ld over 2f out: hdd over 1f out: rallied: kpt on towards fin 14/1
6-15 3 ¾ Weybridge Light4 5240 8-9-3 53 (b) RaulDaSilva(3) 7 59
(David Thompson) hld up: hdwy far rail 2f out: rdn and styd on fnl f: nrst fin 7/2¹
00-4 4 nk Like Clockwork81 2642 4-9-6 53 RobertWinston 8 59
(Mark H Tompkins) prom: effrt and edgd lft 2f out: rallied: kpt on same pce ins fnl f 5/1³
005 5 2 ¾ Korngold15 4835 5-9-4 51 BarryMcHugh 13 52
(Tracy Waggott) hld up: hdwy and cl up on outside over 2f out: no ex appr fnl f 4/1²
55 6 9 My Mum Mo53 3542 5-9-4 51 PaddyAspell 5 38
(Simon West) s.i.s: hld up: effrt whn n.m.r briefly 2f out: sn outpcd 10/1
0034 7 7 Captain Rhyric37 4099 4-9-2 49 PhillipMakin 9 25
(James Moffatt) t.k.h: led: rdn and hdd over 2f out: wknd over 1f out 8/1
00-0 8 6 Idarose (IRE)223 28 4-8-5 45 (p) VictorSantos(7) 12 11
(Alan Berry) in tch on outside: stdy hdwy over 4f out: wknd over 2f out 100/1
535- 9 5 Wind Shuffle (GER)377 3577 10-9-6 53 GrahamLee 10 11
(Lucinda Russell) t.k.h: cl up to 3f out: sn rdn and wknd 16/1
2m 25.25s (2.15) **Going Correction** -0.10s/f (Good) 9 Ran SP% 114.9
Speed ratings (Par 101): **88,87,86,86,84 78,73,68,65**
toteswingers 1&2 £10.10, 2&3 £9.10, 1&3 £3.30 CSF £52.99 CT £183.25 TOTE £4.20: £1.80, £2.50, £1.30; EX 44.40 Trifecta £357.50 Pool: £1989.31 - 4.17 winning units..
Owner Ontoawinner **Bred** P J B O'Callaghan **Trained** Birkby, N Yorks

FOCUS
A moderate handicap and despite the early pace looking modest, it favoured those that came from behind. Low-grade, straightforward form.
T/Jkpt: £266,438.90 to a £1 stake. Pool of £750532.22 - 2.0 winning tickets. T/Plt: £1,425.70 to a £1 stake. Pool of £96382.82 - 49.35 winning tickets. T/Qpdt: £20.30 to a £1 stake. Pool of £6494.70 - 235.60 winning tickets. RY

4924 NOTTINGHAM (L-H)
Tuesday, August 13

OFFICIAL GOING: Good (good to firm in places; 8.7)
Wind: Light half against Weather: Cloudy with showers and sunny periods

5371 SCL BLOCKFOIL NURSERY H'CAP 6f 15y
5:00 (5:01) (Class 5) (0-75,75) 2-Y-O £3,234 (£962; £481; £240) Stalls High

Form RPR
335 1 Meaning Of Life (IRE)40 3991 2-9-0 73 (t) TobyAtkinson(5) 1 79
(Marco Botti) wnt lft s: sn cl up: chal 2f out: sn led: rdn ent fnl f: edgd lft and kpt on 12/1
5635 2 1 ¼ Dovil's Duel (IRE)9 5034 2-8-6 60 AndreaAtzeni 5 62
(Rod Millman) dwlt and towards rr: pushed along and outpcd over 3f out: gd hdwy wl over 1f out: swtchd rt and rdn to chse wnr ins fnl f: no imp towards fin 9/2
1 3 1 ¼ Chess Valley47 3717 2-9-7 75 TomQueally 7 73
(Rae Guest) dwlt and wnt lft s: towards rr: hdwy after 1f: trckd ldrs 4f out: rdn to chse wnr over 1f out: sn edgd lft and one pce fnl f 4/1³
000 4 3 Two Shades Of Grey (IRE)24 4539 2-8-9 68 GeorgeChaloner(5) 3 57
(Richard Fahey) chsd ldrs: rdn along 2f out: sn one pce 8/1
521 5 shd Classic Pursuit15 4827 2-9-7 75 SteveDrowne 8 64
(Ronald Harris) trckd ldng pair: effrt 2f out: sn rdn and wknd over 1f out 3/1¹
066 6 7 Dont Have It Then28 4379 2-8-11 65 KierenFallon 9 33
(Willie Musson) led: pushed along 1/2-way: rdn 2f out: sn hdd & wknd 7/2²
0050 7 6 Caledonia Laird18 4703 2-8-9 63 SilvestreDeSousa 2 13
(Jo Hughes) a towards rr: outpcd and bhd fnl 2f 12/1
1m 13.64s (-1.06) **Going Correction** -0.275s/f (Firm) 7 Ran SP% 111.9
Speed ratings (Par 94): **96,94,92,88,88 79,71**
toteswingers 1&2 £5.10, 2&3 £4.20, 1&3 £5.00 CSF £61.71 CT £255.04 TOTE £14.10: £6.80, £1.70; EX 80.40 Trifecta £318.20 Pool: £2385.60 - 5.62 winning units..
Owner Scuderia Effevi SRL **Bred** Darley **Trained** Newmarket, Suffolk

FOCUS
Outer track used and home bend moved out 5m from inner line increasing distances on Round course by about 11yds. There was a ten-minute downpour an hour before racing which produced 3mm, but the track took it well and the ground was still on the quick side. A competitive nursery rated around the second and third.

5372 EBF SIMPLY CARTONS LTD NOVICE STKS 6f 15y
5:35 (5:36) (Class 4) 2-Y-O £5,175 (£1,540; £769; £384) Stalls High

Form RPR
31 1 **Brave Boy (IRE)**25 4497 2-9-5 0 SilvestreDeSousa 4 99+
(Saeed bin Suroor) *t.k.h and edgd lft early: mde all: shkn up and qcknd clr over 1f out: readily* 1/1[1]
10 2 3 **Wee Jean**17 4742 2-9-0 0 MartinHarley 5 85+
(Mick Channon) *hld up: hdwy over 2f out: chsd wnr wl over 1f out: sn rdn and no imp* 2/1[2]
114 3 10 **Mick's Yer Man**4 5236 2-9-3 0 (b[1]) RyanWhile(7) 2 63
(Bill Turner) *cl up: rdn along wl over 2f out: sn wandered and wknd wl over 1f out* 25/1
21 4 8 **Harwoods Volante (IRE)**17 4773 2-9-5 0 JimCrowley 3 34+
(Amanda Perrett) *awkward s: chsd ldng pair on outer: rdn along wl over 2f out: sn wknd and eased* 7/2[3]
1m 12.73s (-1.97) **Going Correction** -0.275s/f (Firm) 4 Ran SP% 109.4
Speed ratings (Par 96): **102,98,84,74**
CSF £3.34 TOTE £1.30; EX 3.00 Trifecta £16.30 Pool: £1741.61 - 79.81 winning units..
Owner Godolphin **Bred** Darley **Trained** Newmarket, Suffolk

FOCUS
A one-sided 2yo novice event.

5373 SCL STEHLIN HOSTAG H'CAP 6f 15y
6:05 (6:06) (Class 6) (0-60,63) 3-Y-0+ £1,940 (£577; £288; £144) Stalls High

Form RPR
540 1 **Ambitious Icarus**12 4930 4-9-9 59 (e) RobbieFitzpatrick 3 68
(Richard Guest) *in tch on wd outside: stdy hdwy over 2f out: rdn to chse ldr ent fnl f: drvn and kpt on wl to ld nr fin* 10/1
0340 2 nk **Ace Master**39 4009 5-9-1 54 (b) MarkCoumbe(3) 7 62
(Roy Bowring) *qckly away and sn clr: pushed along wl over 1f out: rdn ent fnl f: hdd and no ex nr fin* 12/1
442 3 2 3/4 **Pilates (IRE)**10 4991 3-9-6 60 JoeFanning 10 59
(Mark Johnston) *prom: hdwy to chse clr ldr 1/2-way: rdn along wl over 1f out: drvn and no imp fnl f* 3/1[1]
3140 4 3 3/4 **My Sweet Lord**27 4410 3-9-6 60 (p) DaneO'Neill 4 48
(Mark Usher) *towards rr: pushed along 1/2-way: rdn and hdwy wl over 1f out: kpt on fnl f: nrst fin* 10/1
0604 5 1/2 **Two No Bids (IRE)**6 5156 3-9-1 55 (be[1]) FrederikTylicki 12 41
(Phil McEntee) *racd nr stands' rail: chsd clr ldr: rdn along wl over 2f out: grad wknd* 16/1
0305 6 2 **Errigal Lad**19 4669 8-8-11 47 KirstyMilczarek 5 28
(Garry Woodward) *towards rr: hdwy over 2f out: swtchd rt and rdn wl over 1f out: styd on fnl f: nrst fin* 8/1
6020 7 nk **Kings 'n Dreams**45 3841 6-9-6 56 (b) KierenFallon 14 36
(Dean Ivory) *racd nr stands' rail: in tch: rdn along 2f out: sn no hdwy* 5/1[2]
0400 8 2 1/2 **Aussie Blue (IRE)**25 4504 9-9-7 57 (b) MichaelStainton 2 30
(Charles Pogson) *prom: rdn along 2f out: sn wknd* 25/1
000- 9 3/4 **Royal Intruder**530 744 8-9-3 53 MartinHarley 1 23
(Violet M Jordan) *chsd ldrs on outer: rdn along 2f out: sn drvn and wknd* 7/1[3]
1356 10 2 1/2 **Hamis Al Bin (IRE)**15 4840 4-9-3 60 WillPettis(7) 6 23
(Milton Bradley) *hmpd sn after s: a in rr* 16/1
0-02 11 3 3/4 **Our Sweet Art**21 4607 3-9-2 56 WilliamBuick 9 7
(John Best) *wnt lft sn after s: a towards rr* 7/1[3]
0/60 12 1 **Lady Cricketer**15 4839 4-8-11 47 (b) AdamBeschizza 8
(Michael Squance) *towards rr whn hmpd after s: bhd after* 50/1
1m 12.71s (-1.99) **Going Correction** -0.275s/f (Firm)
WFA 3 from 4yo+ 4lb 12 Ran SP% 121.2
Speed ratings (Par 101): **102,101,97,92,92 89,89,85,84,81 76,75**
toteswingers 1&2 £19.70, 2&3 £8.80, 1&3 £9.80 CSF £127.12 CT £460.02 TOTE £14.60: £5.10, £3.80, £1.60; EX 156.30 Trifecta £616.60 Pool: £1521.93 - 1.85 winning units..
Owner ABS Metals & Waste **Bred** L T Roberts **Trained** Wetherby, W Yorks

FOCUS
A low grade sprint handicap. They raced in one group middle to stands' side and very few got into it. The winner is rated a fraction up on this year's form

5374 SIMPLY CARTONS OPERATIONS H'CAP 1m 6f 15y
6:35 (6:35) (Class 3) (0-90,90) 3-Y-0+ £7,470 (£2,236; £1,118; £559) Stalls Low

Form RPR
0221 1 **Fledged**20 4633 3-9-1 90 WilliamBuick 4 101+
(John Gosden) *chsd ldr: cl up 1/2-way: led wl over 2f out: rdn clr over 1f out: kpt on strly* 8/13[1]
5-00 2 4 1/2 **Muntasir (IRE)**66 3099 4-9-9 85 SilvestreDeSousa 5 88
(Saeed bin Suroor) *trckd ldng pair: tk clsr order over 4f out: rdn to chse wnr 2f out: edgd lft and drvn ent fnl f: no imp* 5/1[3]
-000 3 1 1/2 **The Betchworth Kid**13 4873 8-9-6 82 TomQueally 6 83
(Michael Bell) *hld up in rr: hdwy over 4f out: rdn and hung lft 2f out: sn drvn and edgd rt: one pce* 14/1
3042 4 1/2 **Montjess (IRE)**27 4417 3-8-0 75 oh1 (v) KieranO'Neill 2 75
(Tom Dascombe) *led: jnd 1/2-way: pushed along over 4f out: rdn 3f out and sn hdd: drvn and one pce fnl 2f* 7/2[2]
3m 0.06s (-6.94) **Going Correction** -0.45s/f (Firm)
WFA 3 from 4yo+ 13lb 4 Ran SP% 107.5
Speed ratings (Par 107): **101,98,97,97**
CSF £4.00 TOTE £1.20; EX 3.90 Trifecta £13.90 Pool: £925.99 - 49.85 winning units..
Owner K Abdullah **Bred** Juddmonte Farms Ltd **Trained** Newmarket, Suffolk

FOCUS
Quite a valuable prize but only four faced the starter. Little depth but the winner can do better still.

5375 SIMPLY CARTONS LTD CONDITIONS STKS 5f 13y
7:05 (7:06) (Class 3) 3-Y-0+
£8,715 (£2,609; £1,304; £652; £326; £163) Stalls High

Form RPR
0033 1 **Stepper Point**12 4935 4-8-11 100 (p) MartinDwyer 6 106
(William Muir) *cl up: rdn over 1f out: styd on ins fnl f to ld last 100yds: sn edgd lft and kpt on* 7/2[2]
4600 2 1 1/4 **Inxile (IRE)**76 2768 8-8-11 102 (p) AdrianNicholls 2 102
(David Nicholls) *chsd ldng pair: hdwy and cl up 2f out: rdn over 1f out: drvn and ev ch ins fnl f tl no ex last 100yds* 14/1
-500 3 1/2 **Prohibit**31 4275 8-8-11 99 (p) JimCrowley 8 100
(Robert Cowell) *racd towards stands' rail: trckd ldrs: effrt over 1f out: swtchd lft and rdn whn n.m.r ins fnl f: kpt on towards fin* 8/1
0064 4 nk **Addictive Dream (IRE)**25 4493 6-8-11 98 KierenFallon 4 99
(David Nicholls) *slt ld: rdn wl over 1f out: drvn and hdd ins fnl f: sn edgd lft and wknd last 100yds* 10/1
5-05 5 1 1/4 **Pearl Acclaim (IRE)**66 3103 3-8-11 95 JamieSpencer 5 96
(Robert Cowell) *trckd ldrs: swtchd lft to outer and hdwy wl over 1f out: rdn and ev ch ent fnl f: sn drvn and one pce* 7/1[3]
4400 6 hd **Elusivity (IRE)**11 4947 5-8-11 102 TomQueally 1 93
(David O'Meara) *chsd ldng pair on outer: hdwy 2f out: sn rdn and ev ch tl drvn and wknd jst ins fnl f* 7/4[1]
0600 7 1/2 **Free Zone**10 4986 4-8-11 96 RoystonFfrench 3 92
(Bryan Smart) *a towards rr* 7/1[3]
59.0s (-2.50) **Going Correction** -0.275s/f (Firm) course record
WFA 3 from 4yo+ 3lb 7 Ran SP% 110.5
Speed ratings (Par 107): **109,107,106,105,103 103,102**
toteswingers 1&2 £7.10, 2&3 £16.20, 1&3 £4.90 CSF £45.09 TOTE £5.90: £3.10, £6.90; EX 44.60 Trifecta £223.00 Pool: £1207.56 - 4.05 winning units..
Owner C L A Edginton **Bred** Whitsbury Manor Stud **Trained** Lambourn, Berks

FOCUS
A Class 3 sprint with the majority having something to prove at present. All but one were in with a chance entering the final furlong. Straightforward form at this level.

5376 SIMPLY CARTONS PRODUCTION H'CAP 5f 13y
7:35 (7:35) (Class 5) (0-70,75) 3-Y-0+ £3,234 (£962; £481; £240) Stalls High

Form RPR
0602 1 **Beau Mistral (IRE)**4 5227 4-9-4 64 TomQueally 8 75+
(Paul Green) *mde all: rdn over 1f out: drvn and edgd lft ins fnl f: kpt on strly* 6/4[1]
0533 2 2 **Best Be Careful (IRE)**18 4707 5-9-9 69 DaneO'Neill 6 73
(Mark Usher) *trckd ldrs: swtchd lft and effrt over 1f out: rdn and n.m.r jst ins fnl f: sn drvn and kpt on same pce* 4/1[3]
4111 3 nk **Amenable (IRE)**5 5165 6-10-1 75 12ex (p) MartinHarley 5 78
(Violet M Jordan) *cl up: chal wl over 1f out: sn rdn and ev ch tl drvn: edgd rt and no ex wl ins fnl f* 3/1[2]
5560 4 3 1/4 **Jarrow (IRE)**8 5060 6-9-6 66 (p) JoeFanning 2 57
(Milton Bradley) *dwlt: chsd ldrs: rdn along 2f out: sn no imp* 16/1
6543 5 3/4 **Mossgo (IRE)**21 4608 3-8-12 61 (t) SilvestreDeSousa 4 48
(John Best) *dwlt: chsd ldrs: hdwy 1/2-way: rdn over 1f out: wknd ent fnl f* 12/1
0-60 6 13 **Marine Commando**10 5011 5-9-10 70 JamesSullivan 3 12
(Ruth Carr) *cl up on outer: pushed along 1/2-way: rdn 2f out: sn edgd lft and wknd* 6/1
59.58s (-1.92) **Going Correction** -0.275s/f (Firm)
WFA 3 from 4yo+ 3lb 6 Ran SP% 112.9
Speed ratings (Par 103): **104,100,100,95,93 73**
toteswingers 1&2 £1.90, 2&3 £2.20, 1&3 £2.40 CSF £7.95 CT £15.12 TOTE £1.90: £1.10, £2.20; EX 6.60 Trifecta £17.50 Pool: £977.74 - 41.70 winning units..
Owner The Winsor Not Group **Bred** John McEnery **Trained** Lydiate, Merseyside

FOCUS
An ordinary sprint handicap. The winner confirmed her return to form and the race could be rated 3lb better.

5377 SIMPLY CARTONS COMMERCIAL APPRENTICE H'CAP 1m 2f 50y
8:05 (8:05) (Class 6) (0-60,60) 4-Y-0+ £1,940 (£577; £288; £144) Stalls Low

Form RPR
5513 1 **Minority Interest**9 5032 4-9-5 58 (b) OisinMurphy 8 69
(Brett Johnson) *mde all: rdn wl over 1f out: kpt on strly fnl f* 3/1[1]
-055 2 2 1/4 **Miss Blink**37 4099 6-9-1 59 GaryMahon(5) 3 65
(Robin Bastiman) *in tch hdwy 3f out: rdn 2f out: chsd wnr over 1f out: no imp ins fnl f* 9/2[3]
4460 3 1 1/4 **Flash Crash**11 4957 4-9-1 59 (t) LouisSteward(5) 12 63
(Anthony Carson) *in tch: hdwy wl over 2f out: rdn to chse ldrs over 1f out: kpt on same pce fnl f* 16/1
2040 4 3 1/2 **Iguacu**38 4071 9-8-11 50 (p) DanielMuscutt 11 47
(Richard Price) *in tch: hdwy 4f out: rdn to chse ldrs over 2f out: drvn and one pce fr over 1f out* 12/1
00-0 5 1 1/2 **Royal Alcor (IRE)**5 5171 6-9-0 60 (t) LaurenHunter(7) 5 55
(Gay Kelleway) *towards rr: hdwy on inner wl over 2f out: rdn to chse ldrs wl over 1f out: no imp fnl f* 20/1
0600 6 7 **Daniel Thomas (IRE)**6 5126 11-8-11 55 (tp) ClaireMurray(5) 7 36
(Violet M Jordan) *s.i.s and bhd: sme hdwy on wd outside over 2f out: n.d* 25/1
253 7 1 1/4 **Action Front (USA)**25 4504 5-8-10 52 (v) AdamMcLean(3) 1 31
(Derek Shaw) *nvr bttr then midfield* 7/2[2]
0033 8 3 **Market Puzzle (IRE)**6 5127 6-8-11 50 (p) NoelGarbutt 6 23
(Mark Brisbourne) *a towards rr* 7/1
6030 9 2 1/4 **Excellent News (IRE)**15 4835 4-8-2 46 oh1 (p) JackGarritty(5) 10 15
(Tony Forbes) *cl up: effrt over 3f out: sn rdn and wknd over 2f out* 10/1
0400 10 13 **Lady Tycoon**39 4036 4-8-7 46 oh1 JackDuern 2
(Mark Brisbourne) *chsd ldrs: rdn along over 3f out: sn wknd* 33/1
4002 11 1 1/4 **Lea Valley**181 641 4-8-7 46 oh1 ShelleyBirkett 4
(Julia Feilden) *chsd ldng pair: rdn along over 6f out: sn lost pl and bhd* 20/1
2m 9.38s (-4.92) **Going Correction** -0.45s/f (Firm) course record 11 Ran SP% 116.9
Speed ratings (Par 101): **101,99,98,95,94 88,87,85,83,73 72**
toteswingers 1&2 £4.30, 2&3 £16.70, 1&3 £10.70 CSF £15.40 CT £185.27 TOTE £2.50: £1.50, £1.90, £5.60; EX 15.00 Trifecta £209.20 Pool: £1106.36 - 3.96 winning units..
Owner G Gallagher **Bred** Juddmonte Farms Ltd **Trained** Epsom, Surrey

FOCUS
A low-grade apprentice handicap which very few got into, and the winner controlled things from the front. The form makes sense.

T/Plt: £249.20 to a £1 stake. Pool of £53074.46 - 155.46 winning tickets. T/Qpdt: £17.60 to a £1 stake. Pool of £5465.0 - 229.10 winning tickets. JR

4847 BEVERLEY (R-H)

Wednesday, August 14

OFFICIAL GOING: Good to firm (good in places; 8.6)

Wind: Light half against Weather: Cloudy with sunny periods

5378 JOURNAL CLASSIFIED CLAIMING STKS 7f 100y

2:10 (2:10) (Class 6) 3-Y-O+ £2,264 (£673; £336; £168) Stalls Low

Form RPR

0000 1 **Silverware (USA)**[23] 4577 5-9-10 69 GrahamGibbons 7 78
(Kristin Stubbs) *mde all: rdn wl over 1f out: drvn ins fnl f: hld on wl towards fin* **11/1**

0250 2 hd **Chiswick Bey (IRE)**[11] 5011 5-9-2 72 PhillipMakin 4 70
(Philip Kirby) *trckd ldng pair: effrt wl over 1f out and sn rdn: swtchd lft and drvn ent fnl f: kpt on wl: jst failed* **6/5**[1]

66U4 3 1 1/4 **Llewellyn**[7] 5138 5-9-10 74 AdrianNicholls 11 74
(David Nicholls) *cl up: effrt over 2f out: rdn wl over 1f out and ev ch tl drvn and one pce wl ins fnl f* **4/1**[2]

0600 4 4 1/2 **Partner (IRE)**[8] 5088 7-8-9 68 JoeyHaynes(7) 9 55
(Noel Wilson) *trckd ldrs: hdwy over 3f out: rdn wl over 1f out: sn one pce* **14/1**

45-3 5 2 3/4 **Kimbali (IRE)**[17] 4803 4-9-5 73 GeorgeChaloner(5) 8 56
(Richard Fahey) *trckd ldrs whn stmbld after 1f: effrt wl over 2f out: sn rdn and btn* **5/1**

6000 6 3 3/4 **Vogarth**[55] 3501 9-8-1 36 (b) EvaMoscrop(7) 5 31
(Michael Chapman) *a towards rr* **150/1**

6000 7 1 **Rolen Sly**[29] 4376 4-8-8 40 (p) AndrewMullen 10 28
(Brian Rothwell) *a towards rr* **100/1**

5430 8 4 1/2 **Paramour**[7] 5149 6-9-10 70 (b[1]) GrahamLee 6 33
(David O'Meara) *hld up towards rr: sme hdwy over 2f out: sn rdn and n.d* **9/2**[3]

1m 31.43s (-2.37) **Going Correction** -0.325s/f (Firm)
WFA 3 from 4yo+ 6lb 8 Ran SP% **117.0**
Speed ratings (Par 101): **100,99,98,93,90 85,84,79**
.Chiswick Bey was claimed by Leods Contracts Limited for £6000\n\x\x
Owner Paul & Linda Dixon **Bred** Alliand Equine **Trained** Norton, N Yorks

FOCUS
The rail around the bottom bend was back in its regular position and all race distances were as advertised. The first three finished a little way clear in what was a reasonable little claimer. Tricky to assess, the winner rated close to this year's AW form.

5379 HULL DAILY MAIL/BRITISH STALLION STUDS E B F MAIDEN STKS 7f 100y

2:40 (2:40) (Class 5) 2-Y-O £3,234 (£962; £481; £240) Stalls Low

Form RPR

05 1 **L'Artiste (IRE)**[20] 4668 2-9-0 0 MichaelO'Connell 4 70+
(John Quinn) *trckd ldrs: hdwy 3f out: rdn to ld wl over 1f out and sn edgd rt: drvn ins fnl f: kpt on wl towards fin* **12/1**

4 2 1 **Liberty Red (GER)**[14] 4896 2-9-5 0 GrahamLee 5 73+
(Ed Dunlop) *dwlt and in rr: green and hung lft bnd after 3f: hdwy to trck ldrs whn hung sharply rt wl over 1f out: sn rdn and green: styng on whn edgd lft ins fnl f: kpt on: nt rch wnr* **4/5**[1]

43 3 1 **Red Tide (IRE)**[46] 3810 2-9-5 0 AndrewMullen 7 70
(Alan McCabe) *towards rr: hdwy on outer over 2f out: rdn wl over 1f out: styd on fnl f* **6/1**[3]

4 3 **Innocent Touch (IRE)** 2-9-5 0 TonyHamilton 6 63+
(Richard Fahey) *in tch on inner whn n.m.r: hmpd and lost pl after 2f: hdwy 2f out: styd on fnl f: nrst fin* **5/1**[2]

06 5 6 **Mister Uno (IRE)**[8] 5083 2-9-5 0 PJMcDonald 1 49
(Ann Duffield) *trckd ldrs: hdwy whn bmpd wl over 1f out: sn rdn and no imp* **25/1**

06 6 shd **Leaderene**[46] 3810 2-9-0 0 JoeFanning 8 44
(Mark Johnston) *t.k.h: chsd ldrs on outer: hdwy 1/2-way: rdn along wl over 2f out: sn wknd* **14/1**

600 7 9 **Meconopsis**[21] 4616 2-9-5 42 DavidAllan 9 28
(Tim Easterby) *cl up: rdn to ld wl over 2f out: drvn and hdd wl over 1f out: sn n.m.r and wknd* **66/1**

60 8 hd **Celtic Ice (IRE)**[7] 5145 2-9-0 0 (p) ShirleyTeasdale(5) 2 27
(Alan McCabe) *slt ld: rdn along 3f out: sn hdd: wkng whn n.m.r on inner wl over 1f out* **50/1**

0 9 37 **Kashstaree**[19] 4723 2-9-0 0 GrahamGibbons 3
(David Barron) *hld up in rr whn hmpd after 2f: bhd and eased after* **11/1**

1m 33.66s (-0.14) **Going Correction** -0.325s/f (Firm) 9 Ran SP% **116.5**
Speed ratings (Par 94): **87,85,84,81,74 74,64,63,21**
toteswingers 1&2 £3.10, 2&3 £2.00, 1&3 £3.10 CSF £22.18 TOTE £13.90: £2.90, £1.10, £1.20; EX 33.00 Trifecta £114.20 Pool: £2,309.18 - 15.16 winning units..
Owner Mr & Mrs Paul Gaffney **Bred** T De La Heronniere, G Lugon & C Dem Sarl **Trained** Settrington, N Yorks

FOCUS
An average maiden in which the two at the head of the market saw their chances affected through the early stages of the race. The bare form is ordinary but the runner-up can do better.

5380 EAST RIDING MAIL MAIDEN AUCTION STKS 5f

3:10 (3:17) (Class 5) 2-Y-O £3,234 (£962; £481; £240) Stalls Low

Form RPR

32 1 **Northern Water**[17] 4808 2-8-10 0 JoeyHaynes(7) 11 84+
(Mrs K Burke) *cl up: rdn 2f out: led jst over 1f out: drvn and kpt on wl towards fin* **3/1**[1]

2 2 1 1/4 **City Zen (IRE)**[19] 4724 2-8-8 0 BarryMcHugh 12 71
(Tony Coyle) *wnt lft s and towards rr: swtchd lft and hdwy on outer wl over 1f out: rdn and str run ins fnl f: kpt on* **13/2**

3 1 **Alphabet Rap (IRE)** 2-9-3 0 GrahamGibbons 5 76
(David Barron) *wnt lft s: trckd ldrs: swtchd rt to inner and rdn over 1f out: styd on ins fnl f* **6/1**

232 4 1/2 **Captain Midnight (IRE)**[7] 5145 2-9-3 77 GrahamLee 8 74
(David Brown) *cl up: rdn along 2f out: drvn over 1f out and grad wknd* **5/1**[2]

230 5 1 1/4 **Jacquotte Delahaye**[53] 3565 2-8-10 79 TomEaves 3 63
(Bryan Smart) *led: rdn along 2f out: hdd appr fnl f: sn drvn and grad wknd* **5/1**[2]

23 6 4 **Margrets Gift**[9] 5053 2-8-7 0 ow1 DavidAllan 9 45
(Tim Easterby) *chsd ldrs: rdn along wl over 1f out: grad wknd* **11/2**[3]

00 7 3 1/4 **Nu Form Fire (IRE)**[8] 5105 2-9-0 0 DeclanCannon(3) 4 44
(Nigel Tinkler) *chsd ldrs: rdn along over 2f out: sn wknd* **66/1**

8 1 1/4 **Queen Of Arts** 2-8-6 0 PatrickMathers 6 28
(Richard Fahey) *hmpd s: a towards rr* **16/1**

300 9 1/2 **Abisko (IRE)**[17] 4808 2-8-3 0 (b[1]) RaulDaSilva(3) 7 26
(Brian Ellison) *sltly hmpd s: a towards rr* **20/1**

00 10 1/2 **Bridge Of Avon**[51] 3624 2-8-6 0 PJMcDonald 1 24
(Mel Brittain) *a towards rr* **66/1**

66 11 hd **Ladies In Waiting**[15] 4847 2-7-11 0 SamanthaBell(7) 2 22
(Richard Fahey) *bolted w rdr and galloped 6f bef s: chsd ldrs on inner: rdn along and lost pl 1/2-way: sn wknd* **33/1**

5 12 17 **Maid In Rio (IRE)**[16] 4820 2-8-8 0 JoeFanning 10
(Mark Johnston) *chsd ldrs: rdn along 1/2-way: sn wknd* **16/1**

1m 2.0s (-1.50) **Going Correction** -0.275s/f (Firm) 12 Ran SP% **123.8**
Speed ratings (Par 94): **101,99,97,96,94 88,83,81,80,79 79,51**
toteswingers 1&2 £5.90, 1&3 £5.20, 2&3 £10.60 CSF £23.35 TOTE £4.30: £1.50, £2.50, £2.50; EX 27.80 Trifecta £253.50 Pool: £3,916.83 - 11.58 winning units..
Owner Market Avenue Racing Club Ltd **Bred** M Humby & Dr J Leigh **Trained** Middleham Moor, N Yorks

FOCUS
A fair sprint maiden for the track. The third and the race averages offer perspective on the form.

5381 RAWFIELD AND PARAGON DATA H'CAP 5f

3:45 (3:45) (Class 5) (0-75,75) 3-Y-O+ £3,234 (£962; £481; £240) Stalls Low

Form RPR

3131 1 **Bondi Beach Boy**[15] 4852 4-9-6 **71** PJMcDonald 6 85
(James Turner) *trckd ldr: hdwy to ld over 1f out and sn rdn: drvn ins fnl f: hld on gamely towards fin* **9/2**[1]

31 2 hd **Ypres**[55] 3505 4-9-3 **68** TomEaves 1 81
(Jason Ward) *trckd ldrs: hdwy and n.m.r over 1f out: swtchd lft and rdn to chse wnr ent fnl f: sn drvn and jst hld* **7/1**[3]

0023 3 2 **Wild Sauce**[26] 4479 4-9-4 **74** (bt) JustinNewman(5) 3 80
(Bryan Smart) *sltly hmpd s and towards rr: hdwy on inner 1/2-way: n.m.r wl over 1f out: swtchd lft and rdn ent fnl f: kpt on: nrst fin* **7/1**[3]

0546 4 2 **Lenny Bee**[15] 4863 7-9-10 **75** (t) PhillipMakin 9 74
(Garry Moss) *cl up: rdn along wl over 2f out: wknd appr fnl f* **20/1**

0460 5 2 **Cocktail Charlie**[8] 5108 5-9-8 **73** (b) RobertWinston 5 65
(Tim Easterby) *in tch: hdwy wl over 1f out: sn rdn and kpt on fnl f: nt rch ldrs* **15/2**

2314 6 3/4 **Niceonemyson**[18] 4762 4-8-0 **58** KevinStott(7) 7 47
(Christopher Wilson) *chsd ldrs: rdn along wl over 1f out: grad wknd* **14/1**

2605 7 nk **Bronze Beau**[23] 4579 6-9-10 **75** (t) JamesSullivan 2 63
(Kristin Stubbs) *led: rdn along and hdd over 1f out: grad wknd* **16/1**

0612 8 hd **Adam's Ale**[8] 5108 4-9-8 **73** MickyFenton 8 60
(Paul Midgley) *in tch: rdn along 2f out: sn drvn and btn* **5/1**[2]

0352 9 4 1/2 **Indian Trail**[15] 4852 13-9-2 **72** (b) ShirleyTeasdale(5) 13 43
(David Nicholls) *hld up and sn swtchd rt: a towards rr* **20/1**

4203 10 shd **Mercers Row**[15] 4852 6-8-12 **70** (p) GemmaTutty(7) 4 41
(Karen Tutty) *sltly hmpd s: a towards rr* **12/1**

0022 11 7 **Caranbola**[4] 5294 7-9-6 **71** DavidAllan 10 16
(Mel Brittain) *in tch on outer: pushed along 2f out: sn rdn and outpcd: eased and bhd fnl f* **5/1**[2]

1m 1.55s (-1.95) **Going Correction** -0.275s/f (Firm) 11 Ran SP% **118.0**
Speed ratings (Par 103): **104,103,100,97,94 92,92,92,84,84 73**
toteswingers 1&2 £3.90, 1&3 £7.20, 2&3 £10.60 CSF £36.02 CT £219.23 TOTE £3.30: £1.30, £3.20, £2.80; EX 17.20 Trifecta £205.80 Pool: £2,204.33 - 8.03 winning units..
Owner G R Turner & H Turner **Bred** G R & H Turner **Trained** Norton-le-Clay, N Yorks

FOCUS
A competitive sprint and the form looks good, with two progressive types finishing clear. The form is rated around the third.

5382 WOLD CONSTRUCTION BRIAN AND IAN MEMORIAL H'CAP 1m 1f 207y

4:20 (4:20) (Class 4) (0-85,85) 3-Y-O+ £6,469 (£1,925; £962; £481) Stalls Low

Form RPR

1001 1 **Classic Punch (IRE)**[27] 4435 10-9-13 **84** GrahamLee 9 92
(Tim Etherington) *trckd ldr: hdwy and cl up 2f out: rdn over 1f out: drvn to ld ins fnl f: edgd rt and hld on wl towards fin* **12/1**

2331 2 nk **Triple Eight (IRE)**[9] 5055 5-9-4 **75** 6ex (b) MichaelO'Connell 1 82+
(Philip Kirby) *t.k.h early: trckd ldrs on inner: effrt and nt clr run over 1f out: rdn and squeezed through ins fnl f: sn ev ch: drvn and no ex nr fin* **11/4**[2]

116 3 1 1/4 **Hydrant**[17] 4798 7-9-5 **81** ConnorBeasley(5) 6 86
(Richard Guest) *set stdy pce: qckd 3f out: rdn 2f out: drvn and hdd ins fnl f: wknd towards fin* **9/2**[3]

2324 4 1 1/2 **Saint Thomas (IRE)**[23] 4584 6-9-0 **71** GrahamGibbons 7 73
(John Mackie) *trckd ldrs: hdwy on outer 2 1/2f out: rdn over 1f out: drvn and one pce fnl f* **7/1**

4451 5 1/2 **Arc Light (IRE)**[17] 4810 5-9-5 **76** DavidAllan 4 77+
(Tim Easterby) *t.k.h early: hld up towards rr: hdwy over 2f out: n.m.r over 1f out and again jst ins fnl f: sn rdn and kpt on: nrst fin* **5/2**[1]

0340 6 3 **Be Perfect (USA)**[11] 4979 4-10-0 **85** AdrianNicholls 8 80
(David Nicholls) *hld up: hdwy on outer over 2f out: rdn to chse ldrs over 1f out: one pce fnl f* **8/1**

1644 7 6 **Jebel Tara**[11] 4994 8-9-3 **74** (bt) PaulMulrennan 3 57
(Alan Brown) *t.k.h early: trckd ldrs: effrt wl over 2f out: rdn wl over 1f out: sn wknd* **25/1**

3555 8 nk **Moccasin (FR)**[8] 5086 4-9-4 **82** JordanNason(7) 5 64
(Geoffrey Harker) *hld up: a in rr* **12/1**

2m 5.56s (-1.44) **Going Correction** -0.325s/f (Firm) 8 Ran SP% **116.3**
Speed ratings (Par 105): **92,91,90,89,89 86,81,81**
toteswingers 1&2 £6.00, 1&3 £7.40, 2&3 £2.80 CSF £45.98 CT £176.29 TOTE £6.50: £2.30, £1.60, £1.90; EX 44.10 Trifecta £143.70 Pool: £2,939.64 - 15.33 winning units..
Owner Mrs Brown's Boys **Bred** Granham Farm **Trained** Norton, N Yorks

FOCUS
They appeared to go quite a steady gallop and little got into it from off the pace. The winner is rated back to last year's form.

5383 BEVERLEY ADVERTISER H'CAP 1m 1f 207y

4:50 (4:50) (Class 5) (0-70,70) 3-Y-O+ £3,234 (£962; £481; £240) Stalls Low

Form RPR

2416 1 **Eeny Mac (IRE)**[4] 5291 6-9-11 **67** AndrewElliott 5 76
(Neville Bycroft) *in rr: pushed along 1/2-way: hdwy wl over 2f out: rdn to chse ldrs over 1f out: drvn and styd on wl fnl f to ld nr fin* **12/1**

6061 2 3/4 **Pivotman**[7] 5144 5-9-13 **69** 6ex GrahamGibbons 3 77
(Michael Easterby) *trckd ldrs: hdwy 2f out: led over 1f out: rdn and edgd rt ent fnl f: sn drvn: hdd and no ex towards fin* **7/4**[1]

1045 3 1 1/2 **Outlaw Torn (IRE)**[4] 5261 4-8-13 **60** (e) ConnorBeasley(5) 7 65
(Richard Guest) *prom: cl up 3f out: led 1/2-way: rdn along 3f out: hdd over 1f out: drvn and kpt on same pce fnl f* **17/2**

3410 **4** *6* **Wellingrove (IRE)**[11] 4994 3-9-5 **70** JoeFanning 1 63
(Mark Johnston) *trckd ldng pair: hdwy to chse ldr over 3f out: rdn over 2f out: sn drvn and wknd over 1f out* **5/2**[2]

0231 **5** *14* **Mcmonagle (USA)**[24] 4557 5-9-0 **63** (tp) JacobButterfield(7) 4 28
(Alan Brown) *plld hrd: set str pce: hdd 1/2-way: rdn along 3f out: sn wknd* **5/1**[3]

6020 **6** *16* **Orions Hero (IRE)**[30] 4341 3-9-5 **70** TonyHamilton 2
(Richard Fahey) *in tch: pushed along 1/2-way: rdn 3f out: lost action and eased wl over 1f out* **6/1**

2m 2.85s (-4.15) **Going Correction** -0.325s/f (Firm)
WFA 3 from 4yo+ 9lb **6** Ran SP% **114.1**
Speed ratings (Par 103): **103,102,101,96,85 72**
toteswingers 1&2 £3.10, 1&3 £4.30, 2&3 £4.60 CSF £34.38 CT £194.33 TOTE £11.70: £4.20, £1.90; EX 40.10 Trifecta £220.10 Pool: £2,031.01 - 6.91 winning units..
Owner Mrs J Dickinson **Bred** Kenneth Heelan **Trained** Brandsby, N Yorks
■ Stewards' Enquiry : Andrew Elliott stewards noted trainer's explanation that gelding suited by drop in class and step up in trip.

FOCUS
They went a good gallop in this and the race set up nicely for the winner, who posted a personal best.

5384 PROPERTY GUIDE H'CAP (PART OF THE BEVERLEY MIDDLE DISTANCE SERIES) 1m 4f 16y
5:20 (5:21) (Class 5) (0-75,75) 3-Y-O+ **£3,234** (£962; £481; £240) **Stalls** Low

Form RPR
653 **1** **Discay**[14] 4889 4-9-5 **66** JoeFanning 4 73
(Mark Johnston) *trckd ldng pair: hdwy on outer over 2f out: rdn to chse ldr and edgd rt jst over 1f out: drvn and styd on wl to ld nr fin* **2/1**[1]

0514 **2** *½* **King Kurt (IRE)**[11] 4995 5-9-12 **73** BrianHughes 5 79
(Kevin Ryan) *trckd ldr: hdwy 3f out: led over 2f out: rdn wl over 1f out: drvn ins fnl f: hdd and no ex towards fin* **9/2**

0601 **3** *3 ¼* **Flying Power**[20] 4673 5-10-0 **75** PaddyAspell 3 76
(John Norton) *trckd ldrs on inner: hdwy over 2f out: effrt whn nt clr run and hmpd jst over 1f out: swtchd lft and rdn ent fnl f: no imp* **7/2**[2]

0025 **4** *½* **Grandiloquent**[5] 5222 4-9-5 **66** GrahamLee 6 66
(Kevin Ryan) *led: rdn along over 3f out: hdd over 2f out: drvn and hld whn hmpd on inner over 1f out* **4/1**[3]

4036 **5** *1 ½* **Valentine's Gift**[5] 5240 5-8-9 **56** oh3 (b[1]) AndrewElliott 2 54
(Neville Bycroft) *hld up in rr: hdwy 3f out: rdn along over 2f out: drvn and no imp over 1f out* **10/1**

0332 **6** *½* **Strike Force**[15] 4851 9-8-11 **63** (t) TobyAtkinson(5) 7 60
(Alison Hutchinson) *hld up in rr: hdwy 3f out: rdn along 2f out: sn drvn and no imp* **7/1**

2m 35.14s (-4.66) **Going Correction** -0.325s/f (Firm) **6** Ran SP% **115.3**
Speed ratings (Par 103): **102,101,99,99,98 97**
toteswingers 1&2 £2.10, 1&3 £2.50, 2&3 £2.00 CSF £11.82 CT £29.21 TOTE £2.30: £1.50, £2.40; EX 13.00 Trifecta £31.40 Pool: £2,021.99 - 48.20 winning units..
Owner C H Greensit & W A Greensit **Bred** C H And W A Greensit **Trained** Middleham Moor, N Yorks

FOCUS
Run at a true gallop, this proved a good test at the distance. The fifth puts the form into perspective.
T/Jkpt: Not won. T/Plt: £17.60 to a £1 stake. Pool of £73,866.97 - 3,050.55 winning tickets.
T/Qpdt: £9.00 to a £1 stake. Pool of £4,178.80 - 342.50 winning tickets. JR

5090 FFOS LAS (L-H)
Wednesday, August 14
OFFICIAL GOING: Good to soft changing to soft after race 2 (2.30)
Wind: slight across Weather: rain

5385 BRITISH STALLION STUDS E B F MAIDEN FILLIES' STKS 6f
2:00 (2:01) (Class 5) 2-Y-O **£2,911** (£866; £432; £216) **Stalls** Centre

Form RPR
5 **1** **Valen (IRE)**[14] 4877 2-8-11 0 WilliamTwiston-Davies(3) 1 86+
(Michael Bell) *hld up in tch: clsd over 2f out: led over 1f out: pushed out: comf* **7/4**[2]

2 *3* **Tides Reach (IRE)** 2-9-0 0 SteveDrowne 4 77+
(Roger Charlton) *s.i.s: towards rr: hdwy over 2f out: rdn over 1f out: r.o wl ins fnl f: tk 2nd last strides: will improve* **20/1**

2 **3** *nk* **Artistic Charm**[47] 3781 2-9-0 0 MartinLane 2 76
(David Simcock) *s.i.s: towards rr: clsd over 2f out: drvn over 1f out: chsd wnr ins fnl f: no imp and lost 2nd last strides* **5/6**[1]

5 **4** *2* **Alfaayza (IRE)**[89] 2419 2-9-0 0 DaneO'Neill 7 70
(Brian Meehan) *racd keenly early: cl up: led 3f out tl over 1f out: one pce and relegated 2 pls ins fnl f* **9/1**[3]

0 **5** *5* **Gower Princess**[26] 4491 2-9-0 0 LukeMorris 6 55
(Ronald Harris) *led 3f: sn rdn along: jinked rt over 1f out: wknd and edgd lft ins fnl f* **66/1**

0 **6** *2 ¾* **Golly Miss Molly**[28] 4409 2-9-0 0 FergusSweeney 3 47
(Jeremy Gask) *prom: rdn 2f out: wknd 1f out* **66/1**

4 **7** *1 ¾* **Ormer**[25] 4518 2-8-11 0 DeclanBates(3) 8 42
(David Evans) *chsd ldrs: pushed along and dropped in rr after 3f: lost tch 2f out* **100/1**

1m 15.39s (5.39) **Going Correction** +0.95s/f (Soft) **7** Ran SP% **109.7**
Speed ratings (Par 91): **102,98,97,94,88 84,82**
toteswingers 1&2 £3.50, 2&3 £2.70, 1&3 £1.40 CSF £28.16 TOTE £3.10: £1.80, £6.20; EX 25.30 Trifecta £67.70 Pool: £3,143.73 - 34.78 winning units..
Owner Mrs Melba Bryce **Bred** Scuderia San Pancrazio Sas **Trained** Newmarket, Suffolk

FOCUS
A decent juvenile fillies' maiden in which they went an even gallop on ground officially described as good to soft on a wet day. The winning time was nearly seven seconds slower than standard.

5386 LINDLEYGROUP.COM MEDIAN AUCTION MAIDEN STKS 1m (R)
2:30 (2:31) (Class 5) 3-5-Y-O **£2,587** (£770; £384; £192) **Stalls** Low

Form RPR
1 **Song Of Snowdon** 3-9-0 0 SteveDrowne 9 64
(William Muir) *s.s: in rr: rn green early and sn niggled along: hdwy over 2f out: rdn over 1f out: led ins fnl f: in command whn edgd rt nr fin* **16/1**

6532 **2** *¾* **North Pole**[6] 5204 3-9-5 **63** (p) LukeMorris 2 67
(Sir Mark Prescott Bt) *chsd ldrs: drvn over 1f out: sn ev ch: kpt on one pce u.p ins fnl f* **5/4**[1]

-004 **3** *shd* **Ningbo Express (IRE)**[13] 4927 3-9-0 **67** J-PGuillambert 7 62
(Rae Guest) *in tch: rdn along 3f out: sn outpcd by ldrs: styd on wl ins fnl f: tk 3rd nr fin* **5/2**[2]

54 **4** *½* **Landau (IRE)**[173] 748 3-9-5 0 LiamKeniry 3 66
(Sylvester Kirk) *trckd ldrs: led over 2f out: drvn and hdd ins fnl f: disputing 2nd and hld whn short of room nr fin* **10/1**

00 **5** *3 ¼* **Goldie Horn**[9] 5071 5-9-4 0 (t) WilliamTwiston-Davies(3) 8 53
(Nigel Twiston-Davies) *led: c down centre ent st 4f out and tk field w her: hdd over 2f out: grad wknd* **50/1**

0 **6** *1 ¼* **Crystal Tiger**[29] 4381 3-8-9 0 MichaelJMMurphy(5) 6 50
(Alan Jarvis) *towards rr: sltly hmpd after 2f: hdwy 3f out: sn chsng ldrs: one pce appr fnl f* **33/1**

7 *2 ½* **Defiant Spirit** 3-9-5 0 MartinLane 5 50
(Roger Charlton) *in rr: rdn 3f out: no imp: wknd over 1f out* **9/2**[3]

8 *2* **Summer In February** 3-8-7 0 OisinMurphy(7) 1 40
(Nikki Evans) *s.i.s: sn in tch: hdwy over 2f out: wknd over 1f out* **50/1**

0 **9** *7* **Rowlestone Lass**[13] 4927 3-9-0 0 FergusSweeney 4 24
(Richard Price) *trckd ldr tl rdn and wknd over 2f out* **80/1**

1m 48.16s (7.16) **Going Correction** +0.625s/f (Yiel)
WFA 3 from 5yo 7lb **9** Ran SP% **114.3**
Speed ratings (Par 103): **89,88,88,87,84 83,80,78,71**
toteswingers 1&2 £5.30, 1&3 £6.70, 2&3 £1.60 CSF £36.13 TOTE £25.80: £3.50, £1.40, £1.20; EX 48.00 Trifecta £241.60 Pool: £2,499.00 - 7.75 winning units..
Owner Usk Valley Stud 2 **Bred** Usk Valley Stud **Trained** Lambourn, Berks

FOCUS
A modest maiden. The ground description was changed to soft after the race.

5387 32RED H'CAP 1m (R)
3:00 (3:01) (Class 6) (0-65,69) 3-Y-O+ **£1,940** (£577; £288; £144) **Stalls** Low

Form RPR
2034 **1** **Cape Crossing**[6] 5177 4-8-6 **50** (t) OisinMurphy(7) 10 59+
(Andrew Balding) *prom: trckd wnr after 2f: led over 1f out: rdn and narrowly hdd ins fnl f: kpt on to ld again cl home* **9/4**[1]

3143 **2** *nk* **Greyemkay**[8] 5091 5-8-7 **51** DanielMuscutt(7) 5 59
(Richard Price) *chsd ldrs: rdn along over 2f out: tk narrow ld ins fnl f: hdd cl home* **6/1**[3]

4040 **3** *shd* **Mahadee (IRE)**[23] 4593 8-10-0 **65** (b) LiamTreadwell 7 73
(Ed de Giles) *towards rr: swtchd rt over 2f out: hdwy over 1f out: r.o u.p ins fnl f* **7/1**

4120 **4** *2* **Crucis Abbey (IRE)**[9] 5072 5-8-13 **50** (p) TomMcLaughlin 2 53
(Mark Brisbourne) *t.k.h: trckd ldrs: rdn 2f out: sn ev ch: one pce appr fnl f* **20/1**

-330 **5** *1 ¾* **Watcheroftheskies**[29] 4383 3-9-7 **65** MartinLane 9 64
(J W Hills) *hld up in tch: n.m.r after 2f: hdwy 3f out: drvn over 1f out: one pce fnl f* **12/1**

4212 **6** *nk* **Bertie Moon**[8] 5098 3-9-3 **64** DeclanBates(3) 14 62
(Geoffrey Deacon) *trckd ldr 2f: styd prom and t.k.h: drvn over 2f out: kpt on one pce* **10/1**

50-0 **7** *1 ¾* **Princess Gail**[37] 4109 5-8-2 **46** oh1 (t) NoelGarbutt(7) 4 40
(Mark Brisbourne) *s.s: in rr: clsd 3f out: rdn over 1f out: sn no imp on ldrs* **50/1**

0511 **8** *hd* **The Mongoose**[6] 5177 5-9-11 **69** 6ex (t) EoinWalsh(7) 6 63
(David Evans) *led: c over to stands' rail over 3f out and racd alone: sn drvn: hdd over 1f out: grad wknd* **6/1**[3]

2333 **9** *2 ¼* **Offbeat Safaris (IRE)**[6] 5177 5-9-7 **58** (p) LukeMorris 13 47
(Ronald Harris) *mid-div: hdwy 3f out: drvn 2f out: sn wknd* **5/1**[2]

0/01 **10** *11* **Barnmore**[8] 5098 5-9-12 **66** 6ex CharlesBishop(3) 3 29
(Peter Hedger) *s.s: in rr: wandered u.p over 2f out: no imp: eased over 1f out: t.o* **12/1**

1m 48.64s (7.64) **Going Correction** +0.625s/f (Yiel)
WFA 3 from 4yo+ 7lb **10** Ran SP% **119.7**
Speed ratings (Par 101): **86,85,85,83,81 81,79,79,77,66**
toteswingers 1&2 £3.80, 1&3 £6.60, 2&3 £8.70 CSF £16.31 CT £84.30 TOTE £4.30: £1.10, £1.70, £4.70; EX 22.10 Trifecta £101.90 Pool: £2,181.33 - 16.05 winning units..
Owner Mildmay Racing & D H Caslon **Bred** Jeremy Green & Sons & Brian McGrath **Trained** Kingsclere, Hants

FOCUS
A modest handicap.

5388 32RED.COM H'CAP 5f
3:35 (3:36) (Class 6) (0-65,65) 3-Y-O+ **£1,940** (£577; £288; £144) **Stalls** Centre

Form RPR
0024 **1** **Wooden King (IRE)**[20] 4659 8-9-10 **65** TomMcLaughlin 6 73
(Malcolm Saunders) *cl up on stands' side: rdn over 1f out: kpt on u.p to ld post* **4/1**[3]

004 **2** *nse* **Dark Lane**[26] 4471 7-9-3 **65** EoinWalsh(7) 1 73
(David Evans) *chsd one other down centre and towards rr overall: rdn, hdwy and edgd rt over 1f out: led narrowly ent fnl f and continued to hang rt: hdd post* **3/1**[2]

0045 **3** *1 ¾* **Madame Kintyre**[8] 5094 5-8-11 **52** MartinLane 4 54
(Rod Millman) *chsd ldrs stands' side: rdn over 2f out: kpt on same pce fnl f* **6/1**

3241 **4** *nk* **Arch Walker (IRE)**[12] 4943 6-9-3 **58** (b) DaneO'Neill 3 58
(John Weymes) *led pair racing down centre: in tch overall: rdn 2f out: sn carried rt: keeping on whn short of room early ins fnl f: unable qck after* **11/4**[1]

0U10 **5** *1 ¼* **Spic 'n Span**[12] 4943 8-9-0 **55** (b) LukeMorris 5 51
(Ronald Harris) *wnt to post early: racd stands' side: led: rdn over 1f out: hdd ent fnl f: one pce* **9/2**

020 **6** *7* **Green Millionaire**[117] 1660 3-9-4 **62** (p) FergusSweeney 2 33
(Jeremy Gask) *s.i.s: in rr stands' side: swtchd lft and effrt over 1f out: wknd fnl f* **14/1**

1m 2.99s (4.69) **Going Correction** +0.95s/f (Soft)
WFA 3 from 5yo+ 3lb **6** Ran SP% **110.8**
Speed ratings (Par 101): **100,99,97,96,94 83**
toteswingers 1&2 £1.80, 1&3 £5.50, 2&3 £4.20 CSF £15.87 TOTE £5.30: £2.20, £2.20; EX 15.00 Trifecta £76.20 Pool: £2,366.99 - 23.28 winning units..
Owner Pat Hancock **Bred** Terence E Connelly **Trained** Green Ore, Somerset
■ Stewards' Enquiry : Eoin Walsh three-day ban: careless riding (28-30 Aug)\n\x\x two-day ban: excessive use (31 Aug-01 Sep

FOCUS
A modest sprint handicap.

5389 £32 FREE AT 32RED.COM H'CAP 6f
4:10 (4:12) (Class 5) (0-75,78) 3-Y-O+ **£2,587** (£770; £384; £192) **Stalls** Centre

Form RPR
530 **1** **Elusive Hawk (IRE)**[13] 4908 9-9-5 **72** (v) DeclanBates(3) 3 84
(David Evans) *racd alone towards centre: mde all: pushed clr over 1f out: in full command whn rdr dropped whip 75yds out* **11/2**[3]

4435 **2** 2 3/4 **Belle Bayardo (IRE)**[4] 5278 5-9-4 **68**............................. CathyGannon 4 72
(Ronald Harris) *cl up: drvn over 2f out and sn outpcd by wnr: kpt on fnl f to hold 2nd* **14/1**

1312 **3** 3/4 **Steel Rain**[8] 5097 5-8-10 **67**... OisinMurphy(7) 9 69
(Nikki Evans) *racd in 4th: swtchd lft and rdn over 2f out: chal for 2nd fnl f but no ch w wnr* **11/10**[1]

3062 **4** 2 1/2 **Prince Of Burma (IRE)**[25] 4521 5-9-11 **78** ow3......... RichardEvans(3) 8 72
(David Evans) *s.i.s: in rr: rdn 3f out: wnt modest 4th ins fnl f: nvr threatened ldrs* **7/1**

2251 **5** 5 **The Dark Wizard (IRE)**[13] 4911 3-9-4 **72**.........................(p) MartinLane 6 51
(Roger Charlton) *chsd ldrs: rdn 2f out: wknd 1f out* **11/4**[2]

1m 15.04s (5.04) **Going Correction** +0.95s/f (Soft)
WFA 3 from 4yo+ 4lb **5** Ran SP% **108.8**
Speed ratings (Par 103): **104,100,99,96,89**
CSF £59.92 TOTE £6.30: £2.40, £3.40; EX 44.00 Trifecta £158.80 Pool: £2,405.18 - 11.35 winning units..
Owner Mrs I M Folkes **Bred** J Fike **Trained** Pandy, Monmouths

FOCUS
A fair sprint handicap.

5390 FUCHS LUBRICANTS H'CAP — 1m 4f (R)
4:40 (4:40) (Class 4) (0-80,79) 3-Y-O+ **£4,690** (£1,395; £697; £348) **Stalls** Low

Form RPR

0-11 **1** **Bohemian Rhapsody (IRE)**[13] 4915 4-10-0 **79**........... ConorO'Farrell 1 94+
(Seamus Durack) *in tch: hdwy 3f out: led 2f out: sn rdn clr: easily* **11/4**[2]

232 **2** 6 **White Month**[44] 3907 3-8-4 **73**.. OisinMurphy(7) 7 78
(Andrew Balding) *led: hdd 6f out: styd cl up: rdn 2f out: sn no ch w easy wnr: duelled for 2nd fnl f* **5/2**[1]

4225 **3** shd **Thorpe (IRE)**[14] 4899 3-9-0 **76**..(p) MartinLane 4 81
(Ralph Beckett) *cl up: led narrowly 6f out: rdn and hdd 2f out: duelled for 2nd fnl f but no ch w easy wnr* **13/2**

5213 **4** 6 **Sunblazer (IRE)**[14] 4899 3-8-8 **70**.................................... SteveDrowne 3 65
(William Muir) *hld up in tch: rdn along over 3f out: sn outpcd by ldng trio: kpt on ins fnl f* **7/2**[3]

6023 **5** 9 **May Be Some Time**[20] 4679 5-8-12 **68**.............(t) MichaelJMMurphy(5) 5 49
(Stuart Kittow) *in rr: rdn and wnt modest 5th 3f out: nvr threatened ldrs: wknd 2f out* **12/1**

-650 **6** 30 **Chief Executive (IRE)**[75] 2846 3-8-9 **71**......................... CathyGannon 6
(Jo Hughes) *t.k.h: sn trcking ldrs: rdn along over 3f out: sn wknd: t.o* **14/1**

225 **7** 6 **Pandorica**[41] 3985 5-8-10 **68**.......................................(p) DanielMuscutt(7) 2
(Bernard Llewellyn) *in tch: niggled along after 7f: dropped to rr 4f out: sn lost tch: t.o* **14/1**

2m 43.36s (5.96) **Going Correction** +0.625s/f (Yiel)
WFA 3 from 4yo+ 11lb **7** Ran SP% **111.8**
Speed ratings (Par 105): **105,101,100,96,90 70,66**
toteswingers 1&2 £2.30, 1&3 £2.40, 2&3 £2.50 CSF £9.59 TOTE £3.30: £1.50, £1.90; EX 8.40 Trifecta £52.60 Pool: £2,347.24 - 33.44 winning units..
Owner A A Byrne **Bred** Sweetmans Bloodstock **Trained** Baydon, Wilts

FOCUS
This fair middle-distance handicap was the feature race on the card, and understandably the winner recorded easily the best comparative time of the day.

5391 WALTERS UK H'CAP — 1m 2f (R)
5:10 (5:10) (Class 6) (0-65,65) 3-Y-O **£1,940** (£577; £288; £144) **Stalls** Low

Form RPR

0-02 **1** **Unison (IRE)**[8] 5096 3-9-7 **65**... SteveDrowne 3 76+
(Peter Makin) *t.k.h early: trckd ldrs: n.m.r 2f out: sn drvn: r.o to ld 50yds out: hld on wl* **7/2**[1]

03-3 **2** nk **Candyman Can (IRE)**[216] 141 3-9-7 **65**........................... LiamKeniry 9 75
(Dominic Ffrench Davis) *trckd ldr: led over 2f out: drvn ent fnl f: hdd 50yds out: kpt on* **14/1**

2243 **3** 1 3/4 **Whitefall (USA)**[26] 4474 3-8-8 **55**................................ DeclanBates(3) 11 62
(David Evans) *mid-div: hdwy 3f out: chal over 1f out: one pce ins fnl f* **9/2**[3]

0462 **4** 5 **Qibtee (FR)**[26] 4509 3-9-4 **62**.. SamHitchcott 1 60
(Mick Channon) *led: rdn 3f out: sn hdd: wknd fnl f* **8/1**

4630 **5** 9 **Star Of Mayfair (USA)**[50] 3665 3-9-1 **64**............ MichaelJMMurphy(5) 6 45
(Alan Jarvis) *towards rr: rdn over 3f out: modest late hdwy but nvr threatened ldrs* **11/2**

0005 **6** 2 1/4 **Elle Rebelle**[8] 5089 3-8-7 **58**.. EoinWalsh(7) 4 34
(Mark Brisbourne) *hld up in rr: rdn over 3f out: sn wknd* **28/1**

0042 **7** nse **Ella Motiva (IRE)**[7] 5126 3-7-9 **46** oh1.......................... NoelGarbutt(7) 2 22
(Mark Brisbourne) *mid-div: rdn 4f out: wknd 2f out* **10/1**

0003 **8** shd **Nelson Quay (IRE)**[14] 4885 3-9-2 **60**...............................(p) DaneO'Neill 8 36
(Jeremy Gask) *chsd ldrs: lost a cheekpiece 4f out: rdn 2f out: wknd fnl f* **4/1**[2]

0006 **9** 8 **Algorithmic (IRE)**[47] 3793 3-8-7 **54** ow1..(v[1]) WilliamTwiston-Davies(3) 7 15
(Michael Bell) *s.i.s: in rr: hdwy 5f out: drvn 3f out: sn wknd: t.o* **8/1**

2m 18.02s (8.62) **Going Correction** +0.625s/f (Yiel) **9** Ran SP% **117.2**
Speed ratings (Par 98): **90,89,88,84,77 75,75,75,68**
toteswingers 1&2 £6.00, 1&3 £4.10, 2&3 £7.40 CSF £53.99 CT £226.54 TOTE £3.90: £1.60, £3.20, £1.10; EX 57.20 Trifecta £156.40 Pool: £1,064.71 - 5.10 winning units..
Owner J P Carrington **Bred** Alan Dargan **Trained** Ogbourne Maisey, Wilts

FOCUS
A modest handicap in which they went a steady gallop on the soft ground, but the majority struggled in the conditions.
T/Plt: £176.20 to a £1 stake. Pool of £65,128.18 - 269.80 winning units. T/Qpdt: £77.10 to a £1 stake. Pool of £5,224.35 - 50.10 winning units. RL

5129 KEMPTON (A.W) (R-H)
Wednesday, August 14

OFFICIAL GOING: Standard
Wind: Moderate, across (away from stands) Weather: Raining until race 4; overcast after

5392 £200 FREE BETS AT BETDAQ APPRENTICE H'CAP (LONDON MIDDLE DISTANCE SERIES QUALIFIER) — 1m 3f (P)
6:15 (8:02) (Class 4) (0-80,76) 3-Y-O **£4,690** (£1,395; £697; £348) **Stalls** Low

Form RPR

3005 **1** **Strawberry Jam**[7] 5132 3-9-2 **67**...................................... NathanAlison 5 76
(Paul Cole) *hld up in midfield: rdn over 3f out: gng nowhere in 5th over 2f out: picked up over 1f out to chse clr ldr fnl f: styd on wl to ld last strides* **5/1**[3]

6024 **2** nk **Halling's Treasure**[32] 4305 3-9-3 **73**.............................. JackGarritty(5) 2 81+
(Andrew Balding) *trckd ldr: led 4f out: drew clr over 2f out: at least 4 l up 1f out: wilted and hdd last strides* **12/1**

5340 **3** 5 **Dragon City**[41] 3982 3-9-11 **76**.................................(p) MatthewLawson 6 75
(Harry Dunlop) *racd wd in last trio: drvn in last 3f out and looked to have no ch: styd on wl fr over 1f out to take 3rd nr fin* **5/1**[3]

624- **4** 2 **Lyric Piece**[252] 7989 3-9-4 **72**.. TimClark(3) 3 67
(Sir Mark Prescott Bt) *chsd ldng pair: awkward bnd after 2f and pushed along fr then on: rdn to chse ldr over 2f out: no imp: lost 2nd and wknd fnl f* **5/1**[3]

5525 **5** 2 1/4 **Gertrude Gray (IRE)**[41] 3975 3-9-4 **76**......................... AmeliaGreen(7) 4 67
(Lady Cecil) *led to 4f out: nt qckn over 2f out: steadily wknd fnl 2f* **6/1**

-243 **6** 2 **Neamour**[32] 4305 3-9-0 **70**... GeorgeBuckell(5) 7 58
(David Simcock) *t.k.h early: hld up in last: gng bttr than sme over 3f out: pushed along and no rspnse over 2f out* **9/2**[2]

055 **7** 2 1/2 **Midaz**[42] 3957 3-8-11 **67**... CharlieBennett(5) 1 50
(Hughie Morrison) *trckd ldrs: drvn and nt qckn over 2f out: wknd qckly over 1f out* **11/4**[1]

2m 20.98s (-0.92) **Going Correction** -0.05s/f (Stan) **7** Ran SP% **116.8**
Speed ratings (Par 102): **101,100,97,95,94 92,90**
toteswingers 1&2 £21.50, 2&3 £9.30, 1&3 £4.70 CSF £61.87 TOTE £10.50: £4.60, £6.60; EX 126.70 Trifecta £426.80 Pool: £1240.52 - 2.17 winning units..
Owner Ben & Sir Martyn Arbib **Bred** Arbib Bloodstock Partnership **Trained** Whatcombe, Oxon

FOCUS
A fair apprentice handicap in which none of the runners had previously won a race. An ordinary gallop only picked up around the home turn and the winner came down the centre in the straight. The first two pulled clear.

5393 LADIES DAY WITH TOBY ANSTIS 07.09.13 H'CAP — 7f (P)
6:45 (8:02) (Class 6) (0-65,65) 3-Y-O **£1,940** (£577; £288; £144) **Stalls** Low

Form RPR

2361 **1** **Avatar Star (IRE)**[14] 4881 3-9-7 **65**..............................(tp) MartinHarley 7 79
(Marco Botti) *sn trckd ldr: led over 2f out gng strly: drvn and hrd pressed fnl f: hld on wl* **7/4**[1]

0045 **2** nk **Marmalady (IRE)**[20] 4658 3-8-13 **57**.................................. RyanMoore 4 70
(Gary Moore) *t.k.h early: trckd ldng pair: rdn to go 2nd jst over 1f out and sn chalng: nt qckn nr fin* **5/1**[3]

2155 **3** 2 1/2 **Gold Beau (FR)**[12] 4962 3-9-7 **65**...................................(p) TedDurcan 5 71
(Kristin Stubbs) *led to over 2f out: chsd wnr to jst over 1f out: one pce* **8/1**

0633 **4** 2 1/2 **Poitin**[28] 4410 3-9-6 **64**... JimCrowley 2 64
(Harry Dunlop) *hld up in midfield: drvn in 4th 2f out: no imp on ldrs after: one pce* **12/1**

00-0 **5** 3 3/4 **Tracks Of My Tears**[20] 4691 3-7-13 **46** oh1.................. RyanPowell(3) 8 36
(Giles Bravery) *wl in rr: lft bhd fr 3f out: no ch after: kpt on fnl f* **50/1**

-006 **6** 1 1/2 **David's Secret**[21] 4637 3-9-6 **64**.................................. RichardHughes 3 50
(Hughie Morrison) *racd wd in midfield: drvn and no rspnse in 5th over 2f out: eased fnl f* **3/1**[2]

U6-5 **7** 2 **Fantasy Invader (IRE)**[55] 3509 3-8-11 **55**...................... WilliamBuick 9 35
(John Quinn) *awkward s: pushed along in last 4f out: lft bhd over 2f out* **10/1**

3-60 **8** 1 **Lars Krister (IRE)**[16] 4839 3-9-0 **63**...............................(b[1]) RyanTate(5) 6 40
(Hans Adielsson) *a in rr: lost tch over 2f out* **8/1**

005 **9** 18 **We'Re In The Red (IRE)**[60] 3327 3-8-3 **47**....................(t) KieranO'Neill 1
(Mark Hoad) *chsd ldrs: shoved along over 4f out: wknd rapidly 3f out: t.o* **66/1**

1m 26.43s (0.43) **Going Correction** -0.05s/f (Stan) **9** Ran SP% **120.5**
Speed ratings (Par 98): **95,94,91,88,84 82,80,79,58**
toteswingers 1&2 £3.70, 2&3 £4.40, 1&3 £4.20 CSF £11.57 CT £58.04 TOTE £2.60: £1.10, £3.10, £1.60; EX 13.10 Trifecta £42.90 Pool: £1411.01 - 24.65 winning units..
Owner Mrs Lucie Botti **Bred** Acorn Stud **Trained** Newmarket, Suffolk

FOCUS
A modest handicap run at an ordinary gallop to the two-furlong marker. The winner edged towards the far rail in the closing stages.

5394 BRITISH STALLION STUDS EBF MAIDEN FILLIES' STKS — 7f (P)
7:15 (8:02) (Class 5) 2-Y-O **£2,911** (£866; £432; £216) **Stalls** Low

Form RPR

0 **1** **Tender Emotion**[13] 4921 2-9-0 0............................ SilvestreDeSousa 12 75
(Charlie Appleby) *trckd ldng pair: clsd fr 2f out: drvn to ld last 150yds: styd on* **7/1**[3]

0 **2** 1/2 **Likelihood (USA)**[19] 4702 2-9-0 0...................................... WilliamBuick 6 74
(John Gosden) *trckd ldrs disputing 5th: rdn 2f out: stl green over 1f out: styd on to chse wnr nr fin: jst hld* **7/4**[1]

40 **3** 1/2 **Manderley (IRE)**[34] 4215 2-9-0 0.................................... RichardHughes 5 72
(Richard Hannon) *trckd ldng pair: wnt 2nd over 2f out: chal on inner over 1f out: nrly upsides fnl f: styd on same pce* **9/2**[2]

3 **4** nk **Gratzie**[19] 4702 2-9-0 0... MartinHarley 3 71
(Mick Channon) *chsd ldrs disputing 5th: shkn up 2f out: nt qckn over 1f out: styd on fnl f: nrst fin* **8/1**

00 **5** 1 **Queenie's Home**[74] 2856 2-9-0 0..................................... MartinDwyer 1 69
(James Given) *led: pressed fr 2f out: hdd & wknd last 150yds* **100/1**

30 **6** 1 1/2 **Full Day**[19] 4702 2-9-0 0.. JimCrowley 11 68+
(Ralph Beckett) *settled in 10th: pushed along 3f out: rdn and prog 2f out: styd on to take 6th fnl f: pushed along and no imp after* **8/1**

7 3/4 **Uchenna (IRE)** 2-9-0 0.. PatCosgrave 4 63+
(David Simcock) *dwlt: mostly in last trio tl rdn and prog over 2f out: styd on fnl f: gng on at fin* **50/1**

0 **8** 2 1/2 **Placidia (IRE)**[19] 4702 2-9-0 0... TedDurcan 7 56
(David Lanigan) *in tch disputing 7th: jst pushed along fr 2f out: no imp: nt disgracd* **50/1**

6 **9** 1 1/4 **Peacemaker (IRE)**[50] 3664 2-9-0 0...................................... JohnFahy 2 53
(Eve Johnson Houghton) *in tch disputing 7th: shkn up and reminder 2f out: one pce and no prog* **25/1**

10 1 1/4 **Mahatta (IRE)** 2-9-0 0... PaulHanagan 14 49
(Charles Hills) *dwlt: wl in rr: shkn up and no real prog over 2f out* **16/1**

11 3 1/2 **Adore** 2-9-0 0.. RyanMoore 13 40
(Sir Michael Stoute) *a wl in rr: pushed along 3f out: no prog* **10/1**

5 **12** 3/4 **Dance Bid**[49] 3689 2-9-0 0... FrederikTylicki 10 38
(Clive Brittain) *pressed ldr tl wknd rapidly over 2f out* **12/1**

0 **13** 1 1/2 **All Yours (IRE)**[13] 4921 2-9-0 0...................................... DavidProbert 9 34
(William Knight) *racd wd in midfield: lost pl bef 1/2-way: struggling in rr 3f out* **50/1**

14 *14* **Craftybird** 2-9-0 0.............(t) KieranO'Neill 8
(Brett Johnson) *dwlt: a in last pair: t.o* **100/1**
1m 26.22s (0.22) **Going Correction** -0.05s/f (Stan) **14 Ran SP% 123.6**
Speed ratings (Par 91): **96,95,94,94,93 91,90,87,86,85 81,80,78,62**
toteswingers 1&2 £5.30, 2&3 £4.10, 1&3 £7.80 CSF £19.63 TOTE £12.20: £3.70, £1.10, £2.10; EX 28.00 Trifecta £129.60 Pool: £1245.82 - 7.20 winning units..
Owner Godolphin **Bred** Darley **Trained** Newmarket, Suffolk

FOCUS
No more than a fair maiden and one in which several finished in a heap. An ordinary gallop suited the prominent racers and the winner came down the centre in the straight. The proximity of the fifth limits the form.

5395 COMMISSION FREE 1ST MONTH AT BETDAQ H'CAP (LONDON MILE SERIES QUALIFIER) 1m (P)
7:45 (7:46) (Class 5) (0-70,75) 3-Y-O **£2,587** (£770; £384; £192) **Stalls** Low

Form RPR
030 **1** **Gone Dutch**[64] 3176 3-9-6 **69**............. FrederikTylicki 9 77+
(James Fanshawe) *settled wl in rr: shkn up 3f out: prog on outer and drvn wl over 1f out: r.o wl to ld last 75yds* **3/1**[2]
0501 **2** *nk* **High Time Too (IRE)**[9] 5070 3-9-12 **75** 6ex............. MartinDwyer 1 82
(Hugo Palmer) *hld up in rr: smooth prog jst over 2f out to trck ldrs over 1f out: led jst ins fnl f: urged along after: hdd and nt qckn last 75yds* **14/1**
1410 **3** *1* **Moma Lee**[29] 4385 3-9-7 **70**............. WilliamBuick 5 75
(John Gosden) *settled in rr: pushed along 3f out: prog and drvn 2f out: clsd to chal 1f out: kpt on same pce after* **6/1**
1234 **4** *nk* **On With The Dance (IRE)**[29] 4383 3-9-7 **70**............. RyanMoore 7 74
(Ed Vaughan) *trckd ldr: drvn to ld wl over 1f out but others waiting to pounce: hdd and one pce jst ins fnl f* **11/4**[1]
-354 **5** *3* **Work Ethic (IRE)**[26] 4499 3-9-7 **70**............. LukeMorris 3 67
(Gerard Butler) *settled in last: rdn wl over 2f out: prog wl over 1f out but sn no imp on ldrs* **14/1**
3203 **6** *3/4* **Mesmerized (IRE)**[6] 5192 3-9-3 **66**.............(p) AdamKirby 2 61
(Marco Botti) *t.k.h: trckd ldr: hrd rdn and stl wl in tch 1f out: wknd* **7/2**[3]
5035 **7** *2* **Knight Charm**[8] 5098 3-8-9 **65**.............(p) CharlieBennett(7) 6 56
(Eve Johnson Houghton) *trckd ldrs on inner: rdn and in tch 2f out: wknd over 1f out* **33/1**
0300 **8** *4* **Maisie's Moon (USA)**[6] 5198 3-8-6 **55**.............(b[1]) SilvestreDeSousa 8 37
(Hughie Morrison) *led at decent pce: hdd & wknd wl over 1f out* **25/1**
1-00 **9** *6* **Shy Bride (IRE)**[83] 2593 3-9-7 **70**............. JimCrowley 10 38
(Alan Jarvis) *t.k.h: hld up bhd ldrs: wknd qckly 2f out* **14/1**
600 **10** *2 3/4* **Elusive Band (USA)**[62] 3250 3-9-6 **69**.............(b[1]) RichardHughes 4 30
(Brian Meehan) *nvr bttr than midfield: wknd over 2f out: eased* **14/1**
1m 39.44s (-0.36) **Going Correction** -0.05s/f (Stan) **10 Ran SP% 121.6**
Speed ratings (Par 100): **99,98,97,97,94 93,91,87,81,78**
toteswingers 1&2 £10.60, 2&3 £20.10, 1&3 £8.70 CSF £46.99 CT £251.19 TOTE £5.70: £1.80, £2.70, £1.70; EX 59.10 Trifecta £348.40 Pool: £1047.24 - 2.25 winning units..
Owner The Ice Syndicate **Bred** Cheveley Park Stud Ltd **Trained** Newmarket, Suffolk

FOCUS
A fair handicap run at just an ordinary gallop. The winner came down the centre in the straight.

5396 WINNERS ARE WELCOME AT BETDAQ NURSERY H'CAP 6f (P)
8:15 (8:15) (Class 3) (0-95,95) 2-Y-O **£6,225** (£1,864; £932) **Stalls** Low

Form RPR
0246 **1** **Lady Frances**[11] 5005 2-8-6 **80**............. SilvestreDeSousa 3 80+
(Mark Johnston) *mde virtually all at gd pce: shkn up whn pressed wl over 1f out: jnd fnl f but plld out more: on top nr fin* **2/1**[2]
2162 **2** *3/4* **Sunset Shore**[29] 4363 2-8-3 **77**............. LukeMorris 2 75
(Sir Mark Prescott Bt) *trckd wnr: rdn to chal 2f out: disp 1f out: r.o but hld last 100yds* **7/1**[3]
2110 **3** *8* **Legend Rising (IRE)**[55] 3481 2-9-7 **95**............. RichardHughes 1 69
(Richard Hannon) *restless stalls: hld up in last: shkn up and no rspnse over 2f out: no ch over 1f out: eased fnl f* **4/6**[1]
1m 12.08s (-1.02) **Going Correction** -0.05s/f (Stan) **3 Ran SP% 105.8**
Speed ratings (Par 98): **104,103,92**
CSF £9.91 TOTE £3.30; EX 6.50 Trifecta £29.10 Pool: £686.30 - 17.65 winning units..
Owner Sheikh Hamdan Bin Mohammed Al Maktoum **Bred** Darley **Trained** Middleham Moor, N Yorks

FOCUS
An uncompetitive nursery that turned into a match with the market leader running well below expectations. The gallop was a reasonable one and the winner came down the centre in the straight. The favourite failed to fire but the winner displayed a good attitude.

5397 KEMPTON.CO.UK H'CAP 6f (P)
8:45 (8:47) (Class 6) (0-65,65) 3-Y-O **£1,940** (£577; £288; £144) **Stalls** Low

Form RPR
6400 **1** **Katy Spirit (IRE)**[16] 4836 3-9-0 **58**............. LukeMorris 3 65
(Michael Blanshard) *trckd ldng pair: led 2f out: edgd lft over 1f out and drvn: hrd pressed fnl f: hld on wl* **8/1**
0032 **2** *hd* **Brynford**[44] 3903 3-8-13 **57**............. SaleemGolam 8 63
(Chris Dwyer) *racd wd: trckd ldrs: rdn 2f out: chsd wnr over 1f out: str chal last 100yds: jst hld* **11/4**[2]
3605 **3** *1 1/4* **Malaysian Boleh**[21] 4636 3-9-7 **65**............. RichardHughes 6 67
(Simon Dow) *hld up in 5th: clsd on ldrs 2f out: swtchd rt over 1f out: drvn to try to chal sn after: nt qckn and hld ins fnl f* **11/10**[1]
4646 **4** *3 1/2* **Princess Cammie (IRE)**[7] 5128 3-8-10 **54**.............(p) KieranO'Neill 7 45
(John Bridger) *chsd ldr to jst over 2f out: steadily wknd over 1f out* **14/1**
-000 **5** *2* **Shes Ellie**[8] 5092 3-8-10 **54**.............(b) SilvestreDeSousa 5 39
(Jo Hughes) *racd keenly early: led to 2f out: wknd over 1f out* **14/1**
2660 **6** *1 1/2* **Marmot Bay (IRE)**[116] 1695 3-8-8 **52**............. MartinLane 1 32
(David Flood) *awkward s: mostly in last: struggling to stay in tch 1/2-way: nvr a factor* **16/1**
643 **7** *1/2* **Mighty Mata**[44] 3898 3-9-2 **60**............. DavidProbert 2 38
(Mark Usher) *hld up in 6th: rdn and no prog over 2f out: eased whn btn fnl f* **7/1**[3]
1m 13.25s (0.15) **Going Correction** -0.05s/f (Stan) **7 Ran SP% 117.1**
Speed ratings (Par 98): **97,96,95,90,87 85,85**
toteswingers 1&2 £8.60, 2&3 £1.70, 1&3 £3.10 CSF £31.46 CT £43.45 TOTE £8.40: £2.50, £1.70; EX 36.30 Trifecta £55.50 Pool: £1072.91 - 14.47 winning units..
Owner A D Jones **Bred** Allevamento Pian Di Neve Srl **Trained** Upper Lambourn, Berks
■ Stewards' Enquiry : Saleem Golam four-day ban: excessive use (28-31 Aug)

FOCUS
A modest handicap run at a reasonable gallop. The winner came down the centre in the straight.

5398 BETDAQ 1ST UK COMMISSION FREE H'CAP 7f (P)
9:15 (9:16) (Class 5) (0-75,75) 3-Y-O+ **£2,587** (£770; £384; £192) **Stalls** Low

Form RPR
2655 **1** **Athletic**[21] 4637 4-8-13 **62**.............(v) DavidProbert 11 71
(Andrew Reid) *hld up disputing 8th: threaded way through between rivals fr 2f out: rdn to ld 150yds out: jst hld on* **20/1**
3060 **2** *hd* **Alnoomaas (IRE)**[11] 4983 4-9-11 **74**............. RichardHughes 10 82
(Luke Dace) *hld up in last trio: shkn up 2f out: gd prog on outer jst over 1f out: r.o to take 2nd last strides: jst failed* **8/1**
4016 **3** *hd* **Hidden Belief (IRE)**[20] 4671 3-9-4 **73**............. JimCrowley 3 78
(Ralph Beckett) *trckd ldng trio: clsd 2f out: drvn over 1f out: chsd wnr wl ins fnl f: styd on but lost 2nd last strides* **7/2**[2]
0446 **4** *1 1/2* **Rocky Reef**[27] 4440 4-9-7 **70**.............(v) PatDobbs 2 73
(Philip Hide) *trckd ldrs: drvn to cl 2f out: tried to chal 1f out: one pce after* **10/1**
3630 **5** *shd* **Light Rose (IRE)**[14] 4890 3-9-6 **75**............. SilvestreDeSousa 5 76
(Mark Johnston) *pressed ldr: drvn ahd over 1f out: hdd & wknd last 150yds* **12/1**
0002 **6** *1/2* **Charitable Act (FR)**[20] 4685 4-9-11 **74**............. RyanMoore 7 76
(Gary Moore) *hld up in midfield disputing 6th: rdn 2f out: nt qckn over 1f out: kpt on same pce after* **11/4**[1]
-043 **7** *1 3/4* **Eager To Bow (IRE)**[26] 4496 7-9-8 **71**............. GeorgeBaker 6 68
(Patrick Chamings) *hld up in midfield disputing 6th: tried to creep clsr over 1f out: sn rdn and nt qckn: fdd last 150yds* **5/1**[3]
0310 **8** *nk* **Sheikh The Reins (IRE)**[20] 4685 4-9-8 **71**.............(v) FrederikTylicki 1 67
(John Best) *led at gd pce: rdn and hdd over 1f out: wknd fnl f* **8/1**
6404 **9** *1 1/4* **Perfect Pastime**[21] 4637 5-9-5 **68**.............(v) PatCosgrave 9 61
(Jim Boyle) *awkward s: hld up disputing 8th: rdn on inner 2f out: no prog over 1f out: fdd* **25/1**
0440 **10** *1/2* **Piceno (IRE)**[114] 1723 5-9-5 **68**.............(p) LukeMorris 8 60
(Scott Dixon) *chsd ldng pair to 2f out: sn wknd* **20/1**
3502 **11** *1 1/2* **King Bertie (IRE)**[36] 4146 3-9-0 **69**............. SeanLevey 12 54
(Michael Wigham) *stdd s and swtchd to inner fr wd draw: hld up in last: shkn up and no prog 2f out* **12/1**
00-6 **12** *9* **Torres Del Paine**[11] 4998 6-9-10 **73**............. KieranO'Neill 4 36
(Brett Johnson) *a in last pair: wknd 2f out: t.o* **50/1**
1m 25.54s (-0.46) **Going Correction** -0.05s/f (Stan)
WFA 3 from 4yo+ 6lb **12 Ran SP% 127.6**
Speed ratings (Par 103): **100,99,99,97,97 97,95,94,93,92 91,80**
toteswingers 1&2 £20.50, 2&3 £11.00, 1&3 £13.30 CSF £177.71 CT £725.18 TOTE £12.90: £4.00, £3.90, £1.90; EX 115.40 Trifecta £704.70 Part won. Pool: £939.72 - 0.05 winning units..
Owner A S Reid **Bred** A S Reid **Trained** Mill Hill, London NW7

FOCUS
A fair handicap run at a reasonable gallop. The winner came down the centre in the straight.
T/Plt: £509.30 to a £1 stake. Pool of £64536.64 - 92.50 winning tickets. T/Qpdt: £29.10 to a £1 stake. Pool of £5907.67 - 149.90 winning tickets. JN

4771 SALISBURY (R-H)
Wednesday, August 14

OFFICIAL GOING: Good to firm (good in places last 4f; 9.0)
Wind: mild against Weather: some light rain, mainly overcast

5399 BRITISH STALLION STUDS E B F MOLSON COORS MAIDEN STKS 6f
2:20 (2:20) (Class 4) 2-Y-O **£4,204** (£1,251; £625; £312) **Stalls** Low

Form RPR
330 **1** **Showpiece**[12] 4958 2-9-5 79............. RyanMoore 11 83+
(Richard Hannon) *hld up: pushed along over 2f out: sn swtchd lft: hdwy in centre wl over 1f out: str run ent fnl f: led fnl 120yds: won gng away* **9/2**[3]
53 **2** *2 3/4* **Captain Bob (IRE)**[26] 4483 2-9-5 0............. FrankieDettori 9 75
(Charles Hills) *rn w 3 shoes after having one removed at s: towards rr: rdn over 2f out: stdy prog over 1f out: kpt on wl ins fnl f: wnt 2nd towards fin* **5/2**[1]
6 **3** *1/2* **Gamgoom**[42] 3948 2-9-5 0............. SilvestreDeSousa 7 73
(Harry Dunlop) *mid-div: hdwy over 2f out: rdn to dispute ld over 1f out: hdd whn nt gng pce of wnr fnl 120yds: lost disp 2nd nring fin* **22/1**
0234 **4** *nse* **Deeds Not Words (IRE)**[12] 4948 2-9-5 72............. MartinHarley 8 73
(Mick Channon) *trckd ldr: rdn to take narrow advantage over 2f out: jnd over 1f out: hdd fnl 120yds: nt gng pce of wnr: lost disp 2nd nring fin* **9/1**
0 **5** *nk* **Major Jack**[59] 3374 2-9-5 0............. JamesDoyle 1 72
(Roger Charlton) *wnt rt s: chsd ldrs: pushed along to hold pl over 3f out: rdn over 2f out: nt gng pce to chal but kpt on fnl f* **9/2**[3]
4 **6** *1* **Penny's Boy**[12] 4937 2-9-5 0............. JackMitchell 12 69
(Sylvester Kirk) *trckd ldrs: rdn and ev ch over 1f out: kpt on but no ex fnl f* **40/1**
7 *4* **Golden Journey (IRE)** 2-9-5 0............. AdamKirby 3 57
(Clive Cox) *mid-div: rdn wl over 2f out: nvr any imp: fdd fnl f* **16/1**
8 *2* **Illegal Action (USA)** 2-9-5 0.............(t) FrannyNorton 6 51
(Olly Stevens) *trckd ldr: rdn and ev ch over 2f out: wknd ent fnl f* **16/1**
9 *1/2* **Berrahri (IRE)** 2-9-5 0............. FrederikTylicki 5 50
(John Best) *mid-div: pushed along 3f out: sn wknd* **66/1**
5 **10** *3* **Decimus Maximus**[10] 5033 2-9-5 0............. RichardHughes 2 41
(Richard Hannon) *led tl rdn over 2f out: kpt chsng ldrs tl wknd over 1f out* **7/2**[2]
11 *2 1/4* **Coiste Bodhar (IRE)** 2-9-5 0.............[1] TedDurcan 10 34
(Joseph Tuite) *s.i.s: a in rr* **100/1**
0 **12** *1 3/4* **Shock**[18] 4773 2-9-5 0............. JohnFahy 4 29
(Daniel Kubler) *chsd ldrs: rdn over 2f out: wknd over 1f out* **100/1**
1m 14.52s (-0.28) **Going Correction** -0.175s/f (Firm) **12 Ran SP% 119.2**
Speed ratings (Par 96): **94,90,89,89,89 87,82,79,79,75 72,69**
toteswingers 1&2 £1.20, 2&3 £9.70, 1&3 £17.30 CSF £15.86 TOTE £5.20: £1.70, £1.60, £4.00; EX 21.30 Trifecta £380.30 Pool: £1,238.48 - 2.44 winning units..
Owner Cheveley Park Stud **Bred** Cheveley Park Stud Ltd **Trained** East Everleigh, Wilts
■ Stewards' Enquiry : John Fahy caution: entered wrong stall

FOCUS
Rail erected 20ft off far rail up straight. After light rain the going was changed to Good to firm, good in places in the last 4f. Richard Hughes reported it was riding "perfect". A fair maiden judged on those with official ratings and the first two came from well off the pace. The fourth helps set the level, with the runner-up a bit below previous form.

5400 STEVENS GARNIER LTD NURSERY H'CAP 1m
2:50 (2:50) (Class 3) (0-95,88) 2-Y-O **£7,115** (£2,117; £1,058; £529) **Stalls** Low

Form RPR
621 **1** **Truth Or Dare**[32] 4304 2-9-4 **85**........ RichardHughes 1 91+
(Richard Hannon) *slowly away: last: nudged along at times: moved clsr over 2f out: shkn up to ld ent fnl f: kpt up to work: readily* **4/5**[1]

0411 **2** *2 ¼* **Finn Class (IRE)**[19] 4717 2-8-6 **73**........ KieranO'Neill 5 73
(Michael Bell) *t.k.h early: trckd ldrs: pushed along whn nt clr run 2f out: sn swtchd lft and rdn: r.o ins fnl f: wnt 2nd nring fin: no ch w wnr* **13/2**[3]

4040 **3** *nk* **Street Force (USA)**[18] 4747 2-9-7 **88**........ JamesDoyle 2 87
(Clive Brittain) *trckd ldrs: chal over 2f out: rdn to ld over 1f out: hdd ent fnl f: nt pce of ready wnr: no ex whn lost 2nd towards fin* **9/1**

5214 **4** *4* **Culdaff (IRE)**[19] 4717 2-9-2 **83**........ FrankieDettori 3 73
(Charles Hills) *trckd ldrs: travelling wl whn ldng over 2f out: sn wandered and hdd whn u.p: fdd ins fnl f* **9/2**[2]

4205 **5** *3 ¼* **Brownsville (USA)**[26] 4477 2-8-4 **71**........ SilvestreDeSousa 4 53
(Mark Johnston) *led for 2f: outpcd in last 3f out: nvr bk on terms* **10/1**

552 **6** *7* **Mawzoona**[11] 4997 2-8-3 **70**........ FrannyNorton 6 36
(Mick Channon) *led after 2f: rdn and hdd over 2f out: wknd over 1f out* **16/1**

1m 42.19s (-1.31) **Going Correction** -0.175s/f (Firm) **6** Ran SP% **112.0**
Speed ratings (Par 98): **99,96,96,92,89 82**
toteswingers 1&2 £2.50, 1&3 £3.80, 2&3 £1.10 CSF £6.58 TOTE £1.60: £1.20, £2.50; EX 6.30 Trifecta £29.80 Pool: £1,464.88 - 36.79 winning units..
Owner Carmel Stud **Bred** D G Hardisty Bloodstock **Trained** East Everleigh, Wilts

FOCUS
A decent nursery, despite the small field, and a clear-cut winner. The winner impressed and the placed horses suggest the form is at least this good.

5401 GOLDRING SECURITY SERVICES PEMBROKE CUP (H'CAP) 1m
3:20 (3:21) (Class 4) (0-85,85) 3-Y-O **£6,469** (£1,925; £962; £481) **Stalls** Low

Form RPR
3-03 **1** **Russian Realm**[88] 2442 3-8-13 **77**........ RyanMoore 3 87
(Sir Michael Stoute) *in tch: nudged along over 3f out: rdn and hdwy 2f out: led ent fnl f: styd on wl and in control fnl 120yds* **5/2**[1]

3-30 **2** *¾* **Beedee**[14] 4897 3-9-6 **84**........ RichardHughes 7 92
(Richard Hannon) *trckd ldrs: rdn to chal 2f out: ev ch ent fnl f: kpt on but a being hld fnl 120yds* **18/1**

51- **3** *2 ¼* **Amralah (IRE)**[285] 7517 3-9-6 **84**........ MartinHarley 4 87
(Mick Channon) *in tch: effrt 2f out: ch ent fnl f: no ex fnl 120yds* **4/1**[2]

-411 **4** *2 ½* **Monsieur Rieussec**[32] 4306 3-9-4 **82**........ TedDurcan 6 79
(Jonathan Portman) *stdd s: in last trio: swtchd to centre over 2f out: sn rdn and drifted lft: styd on ins fnl f whn rching stands' side rails: wnt 4th towards fin: nvr threatening ldrs* **5/2**[1]

0022 **5** *½* **Related**[21] 4642 3-9-5 **83**........ AdamKirby 2 79
(Clive Cox) *trckd clr ldr after 1f: led over 2f out: sn rdn: hdd ent fnl f: no ex fnl 120yds* **6/1**[3]

2502 **6** *½* **Royal Prize**[18] 4769 3-9-7 **85**........ JimCrowley 5 80
(Ralph Beckett) *hld up in last trio but in tch: disp 5th over 3f out: swtchd lft whn rdn over 2f out: sn one pce* **9/1**

0056 **7** *3 ¾* **The Gatling Boy (IRE)**[51] 3633 3-8-13 **77**........ PatDobbs 8 63
(Richard Hannon) *led: sn 3 l clr: rdn and hdd over 2f out: wknd fnl f* **25/1**

-650 **8** *1 ¾* **Banovallum**[53] 3582 3-9-0 **78**........ JamesDoyle 1 60
(Sylvester Kirk) *hld up in last pair: rdn over 2f out: wknd ent fnl f* **20/1**

1m 41.43s (-2.07) **Going Correction** -0.175s/f (Firm) **8** Ran SP% **115.3**
Speed ratings (Par 102): **103,102,100,97,97 96,92,91**
toteswingers 1&2 £6.00, 1&3 £2.30, 2&3 £6.70 CSF £51.00 CT £177.93 TOTE £3.50: £1.60, £2.80, £1.60; EX 34.10 Trifecta £158.70 Pool: £1,119.75 - 5.28 winning units..
Owner Cheveley Park Stud **Bred** Cheveley Park Stud Ltd **Trained** Newmarket, Suffolk

FOCUS
A good, competitive handicap, but the first three came clear and the time was 0.76secs faster than the preceding nursery. The winner should go on from this.

5402 EUROPEAN BREEDERS' FUND UPAVON FILLIES' STKS (LISTED RACE) 1m 1f 198y
3:55 (3:57) (Class 1) 3-Y-O+
£24,101 (£9,137; £4,573; £2,278; £1,143; £573) **Stalls** Low

Form RPR
-120 **1** **Mango Diva**[56] 3460 3-8-5 94........ FrannyNorton 3 104
(Sir Michael Stoute) *v reluctant to load: trckd ldrs: travelling best whn pce increased over 3f out: waited for gap to appear which did wl over 1f out: sn rdn: led ent fnl f: picked up wl whn pressed fnl 100yds: drvn out* **5/1**[3]

-641 **2** *½* **Hippy Hippy Shake**[19] 4732 4-9-4 100........ RyanMoore 7 107+
(Luca Cumani) *hld up towards rr: swtchd to centre and rdn over 3f out: hdwy 2f out: styd on strly ent fnl f: wnt 2nd fnl 100yds: hld nring fin* **11/4**[1]

0311 **3** *1 ¼* **Rock Choir**[26] 4485 3-8-5 94........ AndreaAtzeni 10 101+
(William Haggas) *mid-div: rdn over 3f out: no imp tl hdwy over 1f out: styd on ins fnl f: wnt 3rd towards fin* **11/4**[1]

2062 **4** *½* **Gertrude Versed**[25] 4532 3-8-5 91........ NickyMackay 9 100
(John Gosden) *sn led: qcknd pce whn jnd wl over 3f out: kpt battling away: hdd ent fnl f: styd on same pce* **16/1**

-443 **5** *1 ¾* **Bana Wu**[54] 3525 4-9-0 102........ DavidProbert 1 96
(Andrew Balding) *little slowly away: towards rr: rdn whn pce qcknd over 3f out: hdwy over 1f out: chsd ldrs ent fnl f: styd on same pce* **9/2**[2]

0000 **6** *¾* **Semayyel (IRE)**[11] 4985 4-9-0 95........(p) FrederikTylicki 8 95
(Clive Brittain) *mid-div: rdn over 3f out: chsd ldrs jst over 1f out but hanging rt: no ex fnl 120yds* **33/1**

-313 **7** *7* **Rosaceous**[18] 4748 3-8-5 80........ JohnFahy 5 81
(Daniel Kubler) *wnt to s early: trckd ldr: rdn to press ldr over 3f out tl 2f out: sn wknd* **80/1**

0102 **8** *2 ½* **Rhagori**[14] 4878 4-9-0 88........ JimCrowley 4 76
(Ralph Beckett) *hld up towards rr: rdn wl over 3f out: nvr any imp: wknd ent fnl f* **25/1**

0620 **9** *2 ¼* **Light Up My Life (IRE)**[19] 4705 3-8-5 99........(p) PaulHanagan 2 71
(Richard Hannon) *wnt lft s: t.k.h: in tch whn sltly hmpd after 1f: rdn over 3f out: wknd over 1f out* **12/1**

6300 **10** *1* **Dark Orchid (USA)**[19] 4705 4-9-0 95........ SilvestreDeSousa 6 69
(Saeed bin Suroor) *trckd ldrs: sltly hmpd after 1f: rdn over 3f out: wknd over 1f out* **14/1**

2m 8.08s (-1.82) **Going Correction** -0.175s/f (Firm)
WFA 3 from 4yo 9lb **10** Ran SP% **116.4**
Speed ratings (Par 108): **100,99,98,98,96 96,90,88,86,86**
toteswingers 1&2 £4.10, 1&3 £3.80, 2&3 £2.10 CSF £18.86 TOTE £3.80: £1.10, £1.90, £1.20; EX 24.30 Trifecta £81.00 Pool: £2,706.01 - 25.05 winning units..
Owner Antoniades Family **Bred** A G Antoniades **Trained** Newmarket, Suffolk

FOCUS
Subsequent Group 1 winner Promising Lead and Grade 1 winner Ave were the best recent winners of this fillies' Listed race. This did not look the strongest renewal and it was run at a steady pace early. Improvement from the first three.

5403 CHAMPAGNE JOSEPH PERRIER H'CAP 1m 1f 198y
4:30 (4:30) (Class 5) (0-70,70) 3-Y-O+ **£2,911** (£866; £432; £216) **Stalls** Low

Form RPR
4346 **1** **Lisa's Legacy**[5] 5234 3-9-0 **65**........ JamesDoyle 5 75
(Daniel Kubler) *mde all: rdn whn pressed over 2f out: 2 l clr ent fnl f: enough in hand to hold on: rdn out* **7/2**[3]

3-43 **2** *¾* **Red Shuttle**[20] 4665 6-9-13 **69**........ AdamKirby 8 77
(Andi Brown) *wnt to s early: slowly away: last: pushed along early: in tch travelling best whn nt clr run fr over 2f out tl swtchd lft over 1f out: sn r.o u.p to chse wnr: clsng ins fnl f but a being hld* **15/2**

654 **3** *4* **Silk Route**[19] 4719 3-9-2 **67**........ RichardHughes 4 67
(Henry Candy) *trckd wnr: jnd wnr wl over 2f out: sn rdn: hld in disp 2nd over 1f out tl ent fnl f: kpt on same pce* **11/4**[2]

4243 **4** *nse* **Society Pearl (IRE)**[12] 4941 3-9-5 **70**........ HarryBentley 2 70
(Charles Hills) *hld up in tch: hdwy 3f out: rdn to dispute 2nd 2f out tl ent fnl f: kpt on same pce* **8/1**

63-5 **5** *6* **Superciliary**[20] 4679 4-9-4 **60**........ PatDobbs 1 48
(Chris Gordon) *trckd ldrs: rdn over 2f out: wknd over 1f out* **25/1**

0-44 **6** *2 ½* **Ingot Of Gold**[23] 4590 3-9-2 **67**........ JimCrowley 7 50
(Ralph Beckett) *trckd ldrs: chal gng wl over 2f out: sn rdn: fnd little: wknd over 1f out* **9/4**[1]

465- **7** *1* **Danehill Dante (IRE)**[10] 5507 5-9-10 **66**........ KierenFallon 6 47
(Alan King) *hld up in tch: nudged clsr over 3f out: sn rdn: nt pce to chal: wknd ent fnl f* **20/1**

2m 8.88s (-1.02) **Going Correction** -0.175s/f (Firm)
WFA 3 from 4yo+ 9lb **7** Ran SP% **111.1**
Speed ratings (Par 103): **97,96,93,93,88 86,85**
toteswingers 1&2 £4.20, 1&3 £3.40, 2&3 £4.60 CSF £27.55 CT £77.83 TOTE £5.20: £2.90, £2.60; EX 26.30 Trifecta £121.90 Pool: £2,599.33 - 15.98 winning units..
Owner Mrs P Wilson & C Wilson **Bred** Mrs Patricia Wilson **Trained** Whitsbury, Hants

FOCUS
A modest but competitive handicap run 0.8sec slower than the preceding Listed race.

5404 CGA RACING EXCELLENCE APPRENTICE H'CAP (WHIPS SHALL BE CARRIED BUT NOT USED) 6f 212y
5:00 (5:01) (Class 5) (0-70,70) 3-Y-O+ **£2,911** (£866; £432; £216) **Stalls** Low

Form RPR
6344 **1** **Perfect Mission**[124] 1514 5-9-11 **70**........(p) JonathanWilletts(3) 9 78
(Andrew Balding) *trckd ldrs: narrow ld wl over 1f out: sn jnd: hrd pressed thrght fnl f: kpt on: won on nod* **9/2**[2]

0400 **2** *shd* **Annes Rocket (IRE)**[20] 4685 8-9-11 **70**........ CameronHardie(3) 4 78
(Jimmy Fox) *hld up: t.k.h early: smooth hdwy 2f out: sn disp ld: kpt on thrght fnl f: lost on nod* **5/1**[3]

60-5 **3** *2 ¾* **Ivor's Princess**[22] 4603 4-9-11 **67**........(p) PatMillman 5 67
(Rod Millman) *hld up in tch: pushed along and prog fr over 2f out: chsd ldrs over 1f out: kpt on same pce* **8/1**

-006 **4** *½* **Silvee**[13] 4909 6-8-9 **51** oh1........ ShelleyBirkett 3 50
(John Bridger) *in tch: pushed along to chal 2f out: kpt on same pce fnl f* **18/1**

0405 **5** *½* **Danz Choice (IRE)**[19] 4710 3-9-4 **69**........ StephenKing(3) 6 65
(Richard Hannon) *hld up last: hdwy on far rails 2f out to chse ldrs: kpt on same pce fnl f* **3/1**[1]

5634 **6** *2 ¾* **New Rich**[13] 4916 3-8-4 **55**........ DavidParkes(3) 8 43
(Eve Johnson Houghton) *sn led: rdn whn pressed over 2f out: sn hdd: fdd ins fnl f* **7/1**

-040 **7** *hd* **Whitstable Native**[72] 2932 5-9-0 **56**........ NoraLooby 1 46
(Joseph Tuite) *in tch: pushed along over 2f out: wknd 1f out* **15/2**

4060 **8** *shd* **Pink Mischief**[27] 4424 3-8-0 **51** oh2........ DanielCremin(3) 2 38
(Harry Dunlop) *trckd ldrs: pushed along over 2f out: wknd ent fnl f* **14/1**

5250 **9** *shd* **The Name Is Frank**[20] 4659 8-8-10 **52**........(t) RyanWhile 7 41
(Mark Gillard) *s.i.s: sn trcking ldrs: rdn to chal over 2f out: wknd over 1f out* **10/1**

1m 28.93s (0.33) **Going Correction** -0.175s/f (Firm)
WFA 3 from 4yo+ 6lb **9** Ran SP% **116.2**
Speed ratings (Par 103): **91,90,87,87,86 83,83,83,83**
toteswingers 1&2 £4.80, 1&3 £4.00, 2&3 £12.20 CSF £27.49 CT £176.67 TOTE £4.50: £1.40, £2.30, £3.40; EX 27.49 Trifecta £102.40 Pool: £2,336.88 - 17.09 winning units..
Owner Mildmay Racing & D H Caslon **Bred** Mildmay Bloodstock Ltd **Trained** Kingsclere, Hants

FOCUS
An ordinary apprentice handicap with doubts over most. The winner is up slightly on this year's form.
T/Plt: £26.50 to a £1 stake. Pool of £67,868.80 - 1,866.15 winning units. T/Qpdt: £14.40 to a £1 stake. Pool of £3,992.68 - 203.87 winning tickets. TM

5199 YARMOUTH (L-H)
Wednesday, August 14

OFFICIAL GOING: Good to firm (7.6)
Wind: medium, against Weather: dry and sunny

5405 BRITISH STALLION STUDS EBF MAIDEN STKS 7f 3y
5:05 (5:05) (Class 5) 2-Y-O **£2,911** (£866; £432; £216) **Stalls** Centre

Form RPR
5 **1** **Postponed (IRE)**[33] 4256 2-9-5 0........ KirstyMilczarek 4 84+
(Luca Cumani) *t.k.h: chsd ldr: rn green and veered lft 5f out: led wl over 1f out: rdn clr over 1f out: styd on wl* **5/6**[1]

2 *2 ½* **Epic Voyage (USA)** 2-9-5 0........ RobertHavlin 3 77+
(John Gosden) *t.k.h: hld up wl in tch: effrt and rn green wl over 1f out: hung lft after: chsd clr wnr ins fnl f: kpt on but no imp* **6/1**[3]

3 *hd* **Mukaynis (IRE)** 2-9-5 0 TomQueally 6 77+
(Lady Cecil) *t.k.h: hld up chsng ldrs: rdn and effrt wl over 1f out: no threat to wnr but kpt on ins fnl f* **9/1**

4 *2 1/4* **Miner's Lamp (IRE)** 2-9-5 0 MickaelBarzalona 1 71
(Charlie Appleby) *dwlt: wl in tch in midfield: reminder 1/2-way: rdn 3f out: outpcd by wnr but pressing for 2nd over 1f out: no ex ins fnl f* **3/1**[2]

50 5 *4* **Holystones (IRE)**[26] 4497 2-9-0 0 RobertTart(5) 2 60
(Marco Botti) *led and set stdy gallop: rdn over 2f out: hdd wl over 1f out: outpcd over 1f out: lost 2nd and wknd ins fnl f* **50/1**

6 *6* **Byron Gala** 2-9-5 0 NeilCallan 5 44
(Marco Botti) *rn green: dwlt: hld up wl in tch in rr: rdn 2f out: sn struggling and wknd over 1f out* **16/1**

1m 28.41s (1.81) **Going Correction** +0.15s/f (Good) 6 Ran SP% **111.7**
Speed ratings (Par 94): **95,92,91,89,84 77**
toteswingers 1&2 £2.30, 2&3 £2.60, 1&3 £1.80 CSF £6.44 TOTE £1.70: £1.10, £2.20; EX 4.30 Trifecta £21.70 Pool: £1384.03 - 47.68 winning units..
Owner Sheikh Mohammed Obaid Al Maktoum **Bred** St Albans Bloodstock Llp **Trained** Newmarket, Suffolk

FOCUS
Back straight and bottom bend dolled out 3m. A nice little maiden to start proceedings and, although the pace was steady, the winner scored well from a couple of promising newcomers.

5406 GREAT YARMOUTH TOURIST AUTHORITY H'CAP 7f 3y
5:35 (5:35) (Class 5) (0-75,75) 3-Y-O+ **£2,587** (£770; £384; £192) **Stalls** Centre

Form RPR

2344 1 **Muftarres (IRE)**[20] 4685 8-9-0 68 (t) LauraPike(5) 6 80
(Frank Sheridan) *in tch in midfield: nt clr run and swtchd rt over 1f out: hdwy to chse ldrs and swtchd lft ent fnl f: led ins fnl f: sn qcknd clr: r.o wl* **8/1**

3041 2 *2 1/4* **Jonnie Skull (IRE)**[7] 5153 7-9-8 71 6ex (vt) TomQueally 2 77
(Phil McEntee) *led: rdn over 2f out: drvn and hdd ins fnl f: kpt on same pce after* **9/1**

2112 3 *3/4* **Cape Of Hope (IRE)**[20] 4661 3-9-6 75 RobertHavlin 4 79
(Peter Chapple-Hyam) *chsd ldr: rdn and effrt over 2f out: unable qck over 1f out: plugged on same pce ins fnl f* **5/2**[2]

006 4 *2 3/4* **Greensward**[15] 4864 7-9-7 70 (b[1]) RichardMullen 3 66
(Mike Murphy) *s.i.s: sn rcvrd and in tch in midfield: rdn and effrt over 2f out: pressing ldrs but nt qckn u.p over 1f out: wknd ins fnl f* **18/1**

1400 5 *1 1/2* **Valdaw**[26] 4496 5-9-2 65 NeilCallan 8 57
(Mike Murphy) *racd off the pce in last pair: clsng whn hmpd and snatched up over 1f out: n.d but kpt on ins fnl f* **16/1**

0005 6 *nk* **Kasbhom**[25] 4520 3-8-5 60 (t) WilliamCarson 7 52
(Anthony Carson) *s.i.s: hld up off the pce in rr: effrt and rdn over 2f out: clsng but stl plenty to do whn nt clr run and swtchd lft jst over 1f out: no imp fnl f* **25/1**

4142 7 *3 3/4* **Lovesome**[7] 5152 3-8-10 72 LouisSteward(7) 1 53
(Michael Bell) *chsd ldrs: rdn 1/2-way: no ex u.p over 1f out: wknd fnl f* **7/4**[1]

0562 8 *1* **Rough Rock (IRE)**[7] 5154 8-8-7 61 (v) RobertTart(5) 5 40
(Chris Dwyer) *in tch in midfield: rdn and effrt over 2f out: struggling whn squeezed for room and lost pl over 1f out: sn wknd* **7/1**[3]

1m 26.88s (0.28) **Going Correction** +0.15s/f (Good)
WFA 3 from 5yo+ 6lb 8 Ran SP% **113.5**
Speed ratings (Par 103): **104,101,100,97,95 95,91,89**
toteswingers 1&2 £6.00, 2&3 £3.20, 1&3 £4.30 CSF £75.20 CT £233.53 TOTE £7.30: £1.80, £3.00, £1.70; EX 74.40 Trifecta £267.40 Pool: £1792.38 - 5.02 winning units..
Owner Mark Andrew Smith **Bred** Shadwell Estate Company Limited **Trained** Wolverhampton, W Midlands
■ Stewards' Enquiry : Laura Pike two-day ban: careless riding (28-29 Aug)

FOCUS
This looked quite a tight little handicap on paper and the pace was sound thanks to the redoubtable Jonnie Skull, but the race was settled by a smart turn of foot from the winner. The runner-up is the best guide to the level.

5407 GREAT YARMOUTH RACECOURSE SUPPORTS CRY CHARITY H'CAP 7f 3y
6:05 (6:08) (Class 6) (0-55,55) 3-Y-O **£1,940** (£577; £288; £144) **Stalls** Centre

Form RPR

6523 1 **Sakash**[29] 4391 3-8-12 51 DannyBrock(5) 6 61
(J R Jenkins) *in tch in midfield: rdn and effrt to chal over 1f out: awkward hd carriage but led ins fnl f: forged ahd fnl 75yds: rdn out* **5/1**[2]

0R63 2 *3/4* **Sakhee's Alround**[7] 5128 3-8-12 46 oh1 (p) AdamBeschizza 5 54
(K F Clutterbuck) *taken down early: in tch in midfield: hdwy over 2f out: rdn to ld ent fnl 2f: clr w wnr 1f out: hdd and one pce fnl 75yds* **20/1**

006- 3 *2 3/4* **Lilly White (USA)**[244] 8093 3-9-4 52 MickaelBarzalona 8 53
(John Butler) *hld up in tch in last trio: swtchd rt and effrt 2f out: kpt on u.p to go 3rd wl ins fnl f: no threat to ldng pair* **10/1**

060 4 *1* **Dropping Zone**[16] 4839 3-9-3 51 DougieCostello 3 49
(Des Donovan) *taken down early and led to post: stdd s: t.k.h: hld up in tch in rr: hdwy and shkn up 2f out: drvn to chse ldng pair jst ins fnl f: no imp* **14/1**

5546 5 *3/4* **Royal Caper**[4] 5275 3-9-6 54 (p) RobertHavlin 2 50
(John Ryan) *in tch in midfield: effrt u.p over 2f out: chsd ldng pair but unable qck over 1f out: wknd ins fnl f* **6/1**[3]

3411 6 *2 3/4* **Just Isla**[20] 4666 3-9-7 55 (p) TomQueally 1 44
(Peter Makin) *restless in stalls: in tch in midfield: effrt u.p but little rspnse over 1f out: wknd fnl f* **11/4**[1]

-460 7 *nk* **Man In The Arena**[58] 3405 3-8-13 52 (b[1]) RobertTart(5) 11 40
(Dr Jon Scargill) *t.k.h: chsd ldrs: rdn over 2f out: no ex and outpcd over 1f out: wknd fnl f* **25/1**

5400 8 *6* **Whitford (IRE)**[55] 3495 3-9-4 55 DarrenEgan(3) 12 27
(Chris Dwyer) *in tch in midfield: lost pl and towards rr whn rdn over 2f out: hung lft and no imp over 1f out* **14/1**

6040 9 *1* **Unassailable**[8] 5089 3-9-6 54 (p) NeilCallan 4 23
(Kevin Ryan) *chsd ldrs: rdn and unable qck over 2f out: wknd over 1f out* **8/1**

0-44 10 *2 1/4* **Troy Boy**[23] 4585 3-8-9 46 (p) JasonHart(3) 7 9
(Robin Bastiman) *reminder leaving stall: sn led: rdn and hdd ent fnl 2f: wknd over 1f out* **6/1**[3]

006 11 *1 3/4* **Green And White (ITY)**[30] 4356 3-8-12 46 (bt[1]) MircoMimmocchi 10 4
(Frank Sheridan) *s.i.s: hld up in tch in last trio: rdn and short-lived effrt over 2f out: bhd over 1f out* **25/1**

0006 12 *112* **Grapes Hill**[7] 5156 3-8-13 47 (b) WilliamCarson 13
(Mark Rimmer) *racd alone against stands' rail: in tch in midfield: rdn 4f out: wknd over 2f out: t.o and virtually p.u fr over 1f out* **50/1**

1m 27.06s (0.46) **Going Correction** +0.15s/f (Good) 12 Ran SP% **119.9**
Speed ratings (Par 98): **103,102,99,97,97 93,93,86,85,82 80,**
toteswingers 1&2 £15.40, 2&3 £26.30, 1&3 £10.60 CSF £106.52 CT £975.66 TOTE £8.00: £1.60, £6.60, £2.70; EX 124.60 Trifecta £555.70 Pool: £1453.10 - 1.96 winning units..
Owner Mr & Mrs C Schwick **Bred** Mr & Mrs C Schwick **Trained** Royston, Herts

FOCUS
Most of these struggle to win, but the time was the fastest of the three over the trip and is rated slightly positively around the placed horses.

5408 NELSON MONUMENT H'CAP 5f 43y
6:35 (6:36) (Class 6) (0-55,55) 3-Y-O+ **£1,940** (£577; £288; £144) **Stalls** Centre

Form RPR

2236 1 **Imaginary Diva**[41] 3994 7-9-6 54 TomQueally 2 62
(George Margarson) *hld up in last pair: clsd to press ldrs gng wl over 1f out: rdn to ld ent fnl f: r.o wl and in command fnl 100yds: pushed out* **7/2**[2]

6436 2 *1 1/4* **Burnt Cream**[5] 5221 6-9-1 49 (t) RobertHavlin 4 53
(Martin Bosley) *dwlt: hld up in tch in midfield: clsd to press ldrs gng wl over 1f out: rdn and wnt clr w wnr 1f out: no ex and btn fnl 100yds* **5/1**[3]

0660 3 *3* **Mr Man In The Moon (IRE)**[16] 4836 5-9-7 55 JimmyQuinn 5 48
(Mandy Rowland) *racd keenly: sn led: drvn and hdd jst over 1f out: outpcd by ldng pair but hung on for 3rd ins fnl f* **6/1**

6006 4 *1/2* **Whiskey Junction**[20] 4691 9-8-13 47 WilliamCarson 7 38
(Mick Quinn) *racd alone nrest stands' rail: chsd ldrs: rdn 1/2-way: no threat to ldng pair and plugged on same pce fnl f* **7/1**

650/ 5 *hd* **Coalburn**[709] 5780 5-8-9 46 oh1 DarrenEgan(3) 3 36
(Gary Harrison) *in tch in midfield: effrt to chse ldrs and rdn 2f out: outpcd and btn 1f out: plugged on same pce fnl f* **10/1**

0000 6 *1 1/2* **Ishetoo**[16] 4836 9-8-9 48 oh1 ow2 (b) SladeO'Hara(5) 1 33
(Peter Grayson) *in tch in last pair: rdn 1/2-way: edgd lft and no imp over 1f out: nvr trbld ldrs* **16/1**

000 7 *1 1/4* **Novalist**[16] 4840 5-9-0 51 (b) JasonHart(3) 6 31
(Robin Bastiman) *w ldr: rdn and ev ch 2f out: no ex u.p over 1f out: wknd ins fnl f* **9/4**[1]

1m 3.35s (0.65) **Going Correction** +0.15s/f (Good) 7 Ran SP% **111.4**
Speed ratings (Par 101): **100,98,93,92,92 89,87**
totesingers 1&2 £1.50, 2&3 £6.00, 1&3 £3.60 CSF £20.05 TOTE £2.70: £1.40, £2.20; EX 13.30 Trifecta £72.20 Pool: £1324.30 - 13.75 winning units..
Owner Graham Lodge Partnership **Bred** Norcroft Park Stud **Trained** Newmarket, Suffolk

FOCUS
A solid gallop to this open-looking handicap. The form is not that solid though, even with the first two the best guides to the level.

5409 PERSIMMON HOMES ANGLIA H'CAP 2m
7:05 (7:05) (Class 5) (0-75,70) 4-Y-O+ **£2,587** (£770; £384; £192) **Stalls** Low

Form RPR

30-0 1 **Ampleforth**[18] 4754 5-9-2 65 (v) NeilCallan 4 75
(Ian Williams) *chsd ldng pair: rdn to chse ldr 4f out: no imp tl clsd and drvn to ld ent fnl f: styd on and drew clr fnl f* **7/4**[1]

3621 2 *4* **Green To Gold (IRE)**[25] 4204 8-9-7 70 (b) TomQueally 1 75
(Don Cantillon) *led: wnt clr 4f out: rdn over 1f out: sn hdd and btn 1f out: plugged on same pce after* **3/1**[3]

5121 3 *3 3/4* **Baan (USA)**[15] 4867 10-8-9 61 RosieJessop(3) 5 62
(James Eustace) *hld up in rr: clsd and in tch 6f out: outpcd and rdn 4f out: 4th and wl hld 2f out: wnt 3rd and plugged on fnl f* **9/4**[2]

06-4 4 *3 1/2* **Manshoor (IRE)**[38] 475 8-8-0 52 DarrenEgan(3) 2 48
(Lucy Wadham) *racd in 4th: clsd and in tch 5f out: rdn and outpcd 4f out: 3rd and wl hld 2f out: plugged on same pce: lost 3rd 1f out* **10/1**

0-30 5 *22* **Ibn Hiyyan (USA)**[5] 5231 6-8-6 55 JimmyQuinn 3 25
(Conor Dore) *pressed ldr tl over 4f out: lost 2nd 4f out and.sn btn: bhd fnl 2f: eased fnl f: t.o* **10/1**

3m 29.82s (-2.58) **Going Correction** -0.075s/f (Good) 5 Ran SP% **110.3**
Speed ratings (Par 103): **103,101,99,97,86**
CSF £7.34 TOTE £2.60: £1.50, £1.20; EX 8.30 Trifecta £15.90 Pool: £882.89 - 41.55 winning units..
Owner Macable Partnership **Bred** Plantation Stud **Trained** Portway, Worcs

FOCUS
The market got this race spot-on. The placed horses help set the level.

5410 PERSIMMON HOMES ANGLIA FILLIES' H'CAP 1m 1f
7:35 (7:35) (Class 4) (0-80,71) 3-Y-O+ **£4,690** (£1,395; £697) **Stalls** Low

Form RPR

0621 1 **Sureness (IRE)**[19] 4715 3-9-2 70 (t) NeilCallan 3 80
(Marco Botti) *t.k.h: mde all: readily wnt clr over 2f out: rdn over 1f out: in command but kpt up to work fnl f* **5/6**[1]

443 2 *1 3/4* **Ruffled**[13] 4927 3-9-3 71 RobertHavlin 2 77
(John Gosden) *stdd s: t.k.h: hld up in last: rdn and effrt 3f out: chsd clr wnr fnl 2f: kpt on but no real imp* **7/4**[2]

2520 3 *1 1/2* **Just Darcy**[25] 4523 3-8-11 70 (p) RobertTart(5) 1 73
(Sir Michael Stoute) *pressed wnr tl rdn over 3f out: 3rd and wl hld 2f out: plugged on but no threat* **5/1**[3]

1m 55.12s (-0.68) **Going Correction** -0.075s/f (Good) 3 Ran SP% **107.6**
Speed ratings (Par 102): **100,98,97**
CSF £2.58 TOTE £1.80; EX 1.90 Trifecta £1.90 Pool: £688.48 - 266.65 winning units..
Owner Augusto Cati **Bred** Alberto Panetta **Trained** Newmarket, Suffolk

FOCUS
An ordinary fillies' handicap. The winner is rated in line with her Donbcaster form.

5411 BOOK TRAFALGAR RESTAURANT H'CAP 1m 3f 101y
8:05 (8:05) (Class 5) (0-70,70) 3-Y-O **£2,587** (£770; £384) **Stalls** Low

Form RPR

5621 1 **Nullarbor Sky (IRE)**[20] 4688 3-8-11 63 (p) DarrenEgan(3) 3 71+
(Lucy Wadham) *mde all: set stdy gallop tl rdn and qcknd 2f out: r.o wl and in command ins fnl f* **5/4**[1]

-442 2 *2 1/2* **Fatima's Gift**[10] 5037 3-9-7 70 RichardMullen 5 73
(David Simcock) *hld up in 3rd: rdn and effrt nrest far rail 2f out: kpt on same pce ins fnl f: wnt 2nd wl ins fnl f* **6/4**[2]

5004 3 *shd* **Point Of Control**[10] 5037 3-8-11 60 TomQueally 1 63
(Michael Bell) *chsd wnr: rdn ent fnl 2f: styd on same pce ins fnl f: lost 2nd towards fin* **7/2**[3]

2m 39.56s (10.86) **Going Correction** -0.075s/f (Good) 3 Ran SP% **106.7**
Speed ratings (Par 100): **57,55,55**
CSF £3.37 TOTE £2.40; EX 4.30 Trifecta £2.30 Pool: £535.53 - 172.64 winning units..
Owner Tim Wood **Bred** Vincent Hannon **Trained** Newmarket, Suffolk

FOCUS
This looked quite a competitive little handicap despite there being only three runners. The winner recorded a personal-best.
T/Plt: £79.30 to a £1 stake. Pool of £53106.28 - 488.60 winning tickets. T/Qpdt: £14.20 to a £1 stake. Pool of £4841.89 - 251.79 winning tickets. SP

5412 - 5418a (Foreign Racing) - See Raceform Interactive

5360 CLAIREFONTAINE (R-H)
Wednesday, August 14

OFFICIAL GOING: Turf: soft

5419a PRIX THALASSO-SPA ALGOTHERM DE DEAUVILLE (PRIX DE VAUVILLE) (MAIDEN) (2YO FILLIES) (TURF) 7f
11:30 (12:00) 2-Y-O **£9,756** (£3,902; £2,926; £1,951; £975)

RPR
1 **Bird Flown**24 2-9-0 0 (b) Pierre-CharlesBoudot 1 79
(A Fabre, France) **6/4**1
2 hd **Margot Machance**17 2-9-0 0 ThierryJarnet 4 79
(F Doumen, France) **53/10**
3 1 3/4 **Mintaka (FR)** 2-9-0 0 Christophe-PatriceLemaire 7 74
(A De Royer-Dupre, France) **4/1**2
4 1 1/4 **Little Cupcake**29 4397 2-9-0 0 UmbertoRispoli 3 71
(E J O'Neill, France) **19/1**
5 hd **Owlam**54 2-9-0 0 AlexisBadel 6 71
(Mme M Bollack-Badel, France) **34/1**
6 1/2 **Kamellata (FR)**99 2-9-0 0 FabriceVeron 5 69
(H-A Pantall, France) **9/2**3
7 1 1/4 **Miss Acclaimed (IRE)**18 4756 2-9-0 0 OlivierPeslier 8 66
(Brian Ellison) *led: rdn and hdd 2f out: sn no ex: steadily fdd and dropped to last towards fin* **6/1**
1m 27.0s (87.00) **7** Ran SP% **116.2**
PARI-MUTUEL (all including 1 euro stakes): WIN 2.50; PLACE 1.20, 1.40, 1.60; DF 6.60; SF 8.30.
Owner K Abdullah **Bred** Juddmonte Farms Ltd **Trained** Chantilly, France

5378 BEVERLEY (R-H)
Thursday, August 15

OFFICIAL GOING: Good to firm (8.8)
Wind: Moderate; half against Weather: Cloudy with sunny periods

5420 DOWNLOAD THE FREE RACING UK APP (S) H'CAP 1m 4f 16y
2:00 (2:00) (Class 6) (0-60,60) 3-Y-O+ **£2,264** (£673; £336; £168) Stalls Low

Form RPR
5535 1 **Valantino Oyster (IRE)**15 4888 6-9-11 **57** (p) DaleSwift 9 65
(Tracy Waggott) *sn led: pushed along 2f out: rdn over 1f out: drvn and edgd sltly lft ins fnl f: hld on gamely* **15/2**
0025 2 nk **Dean Iarracht (IRE)**5 5295 7-9-0 **46** oh1 (p) FrannyNorton 5 53
(Tracy Waggott) *hld up in midfield: hdwy over 2f out: chsd ldrs over 1f out: sn swtchd lft and rdn to chal ins fnl f: drvn: edgd rt and no ex last 50yds* **7/1**3
0100 3 1 **Grammar**18 4809 4-9-2 **51** (e) RaulDaSilva(3) 6 56
(David Thompson) *trckd ldrs on inner: hdwy over 2f out: swtchd lft and effrt over 1f out: rdn ent fnl f: kpt on* **12/1**
6323 4 nk **Volcanic Jack (IRE)**13 4951 5-10-0 **60** RussKennemore 11 64
(Philip Kirby) *t.k.h: trckd ldrs: hdwy wl over 2f out: rdn to chal over 1f out: ev ch tl drvn and hld whn n.m.r and one pce last 100yds* **13/8**1
4502 5 6 **Light The City (IRE)**7 5196 6-9-3 **49** JamesSullivan 3 44
(Ruth Carr) *hld up in tch: hdwy over 2f out: rdn along wl over 1f out: no imp fnl f* **12/1**
406 6 hd **Croftamie**2 5367 4-9-6 **52** BarryMcHugh 7 47
(Tracy Waggott) *prom: rdn along on inner over 2f out: grad wknd* **50/1**
0365 7 1 3/4 **Valentine's Gift**1 5384 5-9-7 **53** (p) AndrewElliott 4 45
(Neville Bycroft) *t.k.h: trckd ldrs: hdwy and cl up over 5f out: rdn along over 3f out: sn wknd* **16/1**
-063 8 hd **Souter Point (USA)**17 4835 7-9-6 **52** AdamBeschizza 10 43
(William Kinsey) *hld up towards rr: sme hdwy wl over 2f out: sn rdn and n.d* **20/1**
0262 9 2 3/4 **Politbureau**16 4853 6-9-4 **50** PaulMulrennan 1 37
(Michael Easterby) *hld up: a in rr* **9/2**2
0-60 10 13 **Jeer (IRE)**43 3947 9-9-7 **60** MatthewHopkins(7) 2 26
(Michael Easterby) *hld up: a in rr* **33/1**
-553 11 1/2 **Queen Of Epirus**9 5084 5-9-7 **53** MickyFenton 8 18
(Brian Rothwell) *chsd ldrs on outer: rdn along over 3f out: wknd over 2f out* **25/1**
2m 38.26s (-1.54) **Going Correction** -0.25s/f (Firm) **11** Ran SP% **115.3**
Speed ratings (Par 101): **95,94,94,93,89 89,88,88,86,78 77**
toteswingers 1&2 £4.90, 1&3 £16.80, 2&3 £14.70 CSF £55.40 CT £625.15 TOTE £9.30: £2.50, £2.50, £3.50; EX 31.90 Trifecta £406.70 Pool: £1,793.34 - 3.30 winning units..There was no bid for the winner. Volcanic Jack was the subject of a friendly claim by Mr P. Kirby for £6,000.
Owner Steve Sawley **Bred** Des Vere Hunt Farm Co And Jack Ronan **Trained** Spennymoor, Co Durham
■ Stewards' Enquiry : Dale Swift caution: careless riding

FOCUS
Rail round bottom bend in original position and all distances as advertised. Four almost in a line inside the final furlong, but at the post a repeat of last year's finish. The first two are rated to the best of this year's form with the third to his July C&D mark.

5421 EBF WATCH RACING REPLAYS ON RACING UK MAIDEN FILLIES' STKS 5f
2:30 (2:30) (Class 5) 2-Y-O **£3,234** (£962; £481; £240) Stalls Low

Form RPR
3 1 **Online Alexander (IRE)**14 4924 2-9-0 0 PhillipMakin 10 84+
(Kevin Ryan) *wnt lft s: hld up towards rr: smooth hdwy on outer 2f out: rdn and qcknd to ld ent fnl f: sn clr: readily* **15/8**1
00 2 4 **Sleepy Sioux**55 3522 2-9-0 0 LukeMorris 1 66
(David Elsworth) *trckd ldrs: hdwy 2f out: nt clr run and hmpd over 1f out: sn swtchd lft and rdn: styd on wl fnl f: tk 2nd nr line* **5/2**2
45 3 shd **Skinny Love**31 4346 2-9-0 0 AdamBeschizza 7 66
(Robert Cowell) *trckd ldng pair: effrt 2f out: nt clr run and hmpd over 1f out: sn rdn and kpt on wl towards fin* **66/1**
4 4 shd **An Chulainn (IRE)**9 5105 2-9-0 0 FrannyNorton 9 65
(Mark Johnston) *dwlt and in rr: swtchd lft and hdwy over 2f out: effrt whn nt clr run and swtchd lft again over 1f out: rdn and green ent fnl f: styd on wl towards fin* **15/2**
026 5 4 **Gentle Breeze (IRE)**17 4828 2-9-0 74 GrahamLee 3 51
(Charlie Appleby) *cl up: led over 2f out: sn rdn: hdd & wknd over 1f out* **7/2**3
35 6 3/4 **Birkacre (IRE)**34 4259 2-9-0 0 TonyHamilton 4 48
(Richard Fahey) *chsd ldrs: rdn along wl over 1f out: sn btn* **16/1**
3432 7 3 1/4 **Emily Davison (IRE)**11 5029 2-9-0 62 (p) AndrewMullen 2 36
(David C Griffiths) *led: pushed along and hdd over 2f out: sn rdn and wknd over 1f out* **16/1**
1m 3.3s (-0.20) **Going Correction** -0.125s/f (Firm) **7** Ran SP% **110.6**
Speed ratings (Par 91): **96,89,89,89,82 81,76**
toteswingers 1&2 £1.90, 1&3 £10.80, 2&3 £18.20 CSF £6.26 TOTE £2.30: £1.60, £1.80; EX 7.00 Trifecta £142.20 Pool: £1,708.44 - 9.00 winning units..
Owner Noel O'Callaghan **Bred** Deer Forest Stud **Trained** Hambleton, N Yorks

FOCUS
Quite an interesting 2-y-o maiden fillies' race and an impressive winner. She can go on to better things but the race is rated on the negative side.

5422 RACING UK PROFITS ALL RETURNED TO RACING FILLIES' H'CAP 5f
3:05 (3:06) (Class 5) (0-70,69) 3-Y-O+ **£3,234** (£962; £481; £240) Stalls Low

Form RPR
2412 1 **Ingenti**19 4761 5-8-13 **65** KevinStott(7) 3 75
(Christopher Wilson) *trckd ldrs: hdwy wl over 1f out: swtchd lft and rdn to chse ldr whn rdr dropped whip ent fnl f: kpt on wl to ld last 50yds* **9/2**2
5020 2 1 **Mey Blossom**16 4852 8-9-4 **63** (p) RussKennemore 2 69
(Richard Whitaker) *trckd ldrs: hdwy on inner to chse ldr 1/2-way: rdn to ld wl over 1f out: drvn ins fnl f: hdd and no ex last 50yds* **12/1**
12 3 1/2 **Friendship Is Love**12 4976 3-8-13 **61** LukeMorris 7 65+
(David Elsworth) *dwlt and sltly hmpd s: towards rr: hdwy over 2f out: effrt whn nt clr run wl over 1f out: rdn and edgd rt ent fnl f: sn chsng ldng pair and swtchd lft: kpt on strly towards fin* **7/2**1
41 4 5 **Josefa Goya**17 4839 3-9-5 **67** GrahamLee 10 53+
(Hughie Morrison) *wnt sltly lft s and in rr: hdwy 2f out: swtchd lft and rdn over 1f out: styd on fnl f: nrst fin* **6/1**
4164 5 1/2 **Foreign Rhythm (IRE)**10 5047 8-9-0 **64** ShirleyTeasdale(5) 9 48
(Ron Barr) *chsd ldrs towards outer: rdn along wl over 1f out: sn one pce* **25/1**
3642 6 1/2 **Phoenix Clubs (IRE)**8 5148 4-9-10 **69** (p) BarryMcHugh 8 52
(Paul Midgley) *chsd ldrs: rdn wl over 1f out: drvn and one pce appr fnl f* **5/1**3
0040 7 nk **Rangooned**20 4734 3-9-6 **68** PJMcDonald 5 50
(Ann Duffield) *in tch: rdn along and sme hdwy over 2f out: sn drvn and no imp* **11/1**
6005 8 3 1/2 **Elusive Bonus (IRE)**16 4852 4-9-8 **67** (v) DavidNolan 1 36
(David O'Meara) *led: rdn along 2f out: sn hdd & wknd over 1f out* **7/1**
0000 9 6 **Lady Kildare (IRE)**15 4891 5-8-6 **51** JamesSullivan 4
(Jedd O'Keeffe) *chsd ldr: rdn along over 2f out: sn drvn and wknd* **14/1**
0043 10 5 **Balinka**8 5141 3-8-12 **60** (v) DavidAllan 6
(Mel Brittain) *wnt sltly lft s: prom: rdn along over 2f out: sn wknd* **12/1**
1m 2.81s (-0.69) **Going Correction** -0.125s/f (Firm)
WFA 3 from 4yo+ 3lb **10** Ran SP% **118.1**
Speed ratings (Par 100): **100,98,97,89,88 88,87,81,72,64**
toteswingers 1&2 £11.00, 1&3 £3.90, 2&3 £9.10 CSF £58.10 CT £216.56 TOTE £6.40: £1.80, £3.90, £2.40; EX 59.90 Trifecta £281.40 Pool: £2,753.05 - 7.33 winning units..
Owner David Bartlett **Bred** Mrs Andrea Bartlett **Trained** Manfield, N Yorks

FOCUS
A competitive sprint handicap in which the runner-up is the key.

5423 RACING UK ICARD FOR TODAY'S RACING H'CAP 2m 35y
3:35 (3:36) (Class 4) (0-85,85) 3-Y-O+ **£6,469** (£1,925; £962; £481) Stalls Low

Form RPR
6361 1 **Almagest**9 5109 5-10-4 **85** 6ex DavidNolan 5 93
(David O'Meara) *hld up in rr: hdwy over 3f out: chsd ldr over 1f out: sn rdn to chal: led appr fnl f: styd on* **13/2**
0140 2 1 1/4 **Tartan Jura**9 5109 5-9-7 **74** (p) FrannyNorton 1 80
(Mark Johnston) *led: pushed along after 3f: rn in snatches: hdd over 9f out: drvn and outpcd over 2f out: rallied u.p to chse wnr ins fnl f: kpt on* **9/1**
4233 3 6 **Nashville (IRE)**19 4754 4-9-2 **69** (p) TonyHamilton 3 68
(Richard Fahey) *chsd ldr 4f: pushed along over 6f out: sn rdn and outpcd 3f out: kpt on u.p fr over 1f out* **5/1**3
-555 4 hd **Mojolika**9 5109 5-9-6 **73** GrahamGibbons 6 72
(Tim Easterby) *trckd ldng pair: hdwy to chse ldr 6f out: rdn to ld over 2f out: drvn and hdd over 1f out: sn wknd* **9/2**2
3120 5 1/2 **Italian Riviera**15 4873 4-9-8 **75** LukeMorris 4 73
(Sir Mark Prescott Bt) *trckd ldng pair: hdwy to ld 9f out: rdn along over 2f out: sn hdd and drvn: one pce* **2/1**1
3m 33.11s (-6.69) **Going Correction** -0.25s/f (Firm) **5** Ran SP% **91.5**
Speed ratings (Par 105): **106,105,102,102,102**
CSF £34.90 TOTE £4.60: £2.30, £2.40; EX 27.80 Trifecta £69.40 Pool: £678.56 - 7.32 winning units..
Owner The Marooned Crew **Bred** Juddmonte Farms Ltd **Trained** Nawton, N Yorks

FOCUS
A messy stayers' handicap rated through the runner-up to his turf best.

5424 RACING REPLAY ALL TODAY'S RACING SKY432 NURSERY H'CAP 7f 100y
4:10 (4:12) (Class 5) (0-75,74) 2-Y-O **£3,234** (£962; £481; £240) Stalls Low

Form RPR
4161 1 **Flora Medici**22 4618 2-9-6 **73** LukeMorris 2 76
(Sir Mark Prescott Bt) *trckd ldng pair on inner: effrt and n.m.r over 1f out: swtchd lft and rdn to chal ent fnl f: sn drvn and kpt on wl to ld last 75yds* **11/2**2
2331 2 1 **Ocean Storm (IRE)**16 4848 2-9-7 **74** PaulMulrennan 1 75
(James Tate) *pushed along s and sn led: set gd pce: rdn along 2f out: drvn ent fnl f: hdd and no ex last 75yds* **6/5**1
5036 3 1/2 **Baltic Fire (IRE)**8 5136 2-7-13 **59** (b) JoeyHaynes(7) 8 59
(Mrs K Burke) *cl up: chal 2f out: sn rdn and ev ch tl drvn and kpt on same pce ins fnl f* **14/1**
504 4 3/4 **By The Light (IRE)**58 3426 2-8-11 **64** FrannyNorton 5 62+
(Mark Johnston) *towards rr: hdwy over 3f out: chsd ldrs on outer 2f out: sn rdn and kpt on fnl f* **10/1**

003 **5** 1 1/2 **Island Remede**[15] 4880 2-9-2 **69**.. GrahamLee 9 64
(Ed Dunlop) *towards rr: hdwy over 3f out: rdn to chse ldrs wl over 1f out: drvn and one pce fnl f* **15/2**[3]

006 **6** 1 1/4 **Petergate**[19] 4781 2-8-7 **65**.. ConnorBeasley(5) 3 57
(Brian Rothwell) *hld up in tch: pushed along and outpcd on inner over 3f out: rdn over 2f out: swtchd lft to outer and kpt on appr fnl f: n.d* **10/1**

513 **7** 1 **It's All A Game**[7] 5175 2-8-2 **58**..(v) RaulDaSilva(3) 10 47
(Richard Guest) *in rr: effrt: rdn along and sme hdwy 2f out: n.d* **9/1**

050 **8** hd **Fair Flutter (IRE)**[19] 4756 2-8-7 **60**.. TonyHamilton 7 49
(Richard Fahey) *chsd ldrs: rdn along over 2f out: drvn over 1f out and sn wknd* **12/1**

1m 32.4s (-1.40) **Going Correction** -0.25s/f (Firm) **8** Ran SP% **115.1**
Speed ratings (Par 94): **98,96,96,95,93 92,91,90**
toteswingers 1&2 £2.00, 1&3 £8.90, 2&3 £6.40 CSF £12.61 CT £88.22 TOTE £5.70: £1.30, £1.50, £3.80; EX 10.10 Trifecta £85.10 Pool: £2,953.86 - 26.01 winning units..
Owner Neil Greig **Bred** W N Greig **Trained** Newmarket, Suffolk

FOCUS
The first three home were in the first three throughout in this truly run nursery. The winner is rated to his C&D maiden form with the third pretty much to form.

5425 BET AND WATCH WITH RACINGUK'S APP H'CAP 1m 100y
4:40 (4:40) (Class 5) (0-70,74) 3-Y-O **£3,234** (£962; £481; £240) **Stalls** Low

Form RPR

1231 **1** **Rocket Ronnie (IRE)**[3] 5342 3-9-4 **74** 6ex.................. JordanNason(7) 2 88
(David Nicholls) *trckd ldng pair: smooth hdwy on inner to chal 2f out: sn led and pushed clr: kpt on strly* **6/4**[1]

0012 **2** 7 **Red Charmer (IRE)**[27] 4474 3-9-7 **70**.. PJMcDonald 4 68
(Ann Duffield) *trckd ldr: effrt over 2f out: sn rdn along to chse wnr: kpt on same pce: no ch w wnr* **7/2**[3]

6332 **3** 2 1/2 **Confusing**[3] 5342 3-9-3 **66**.. GrahamGibbons 6 58
(David O'Meara) *trckd ldrs: effrt over 2f out: rdn along wl over 1f out and sn no imp* **2/1**[2]

-400 **4** 1 3/4 **Rosie Hall (IRE)**[52] 3629 3-7-13 **51** oh1.. RaulDaSilva(3) 5 39
(Bryan Smart) *chsd ldrs: rdn along over 2f out: sn one pce* **33/1**

46-0 **5** 4 1/2 **Shagwa (IRE)**[14] 4927 3-8-9 **58**.. FrannyNorton 3 36
(Mark Johnston) *led: rdn along and edgd lft 2f out: sn hdd: drvn and wknd* **20/1**

0363 **6** 1 **Shearian**[5] 5293 3-9-0 **63**.. BarryMcHugh 1 38
(Tracy Waggott) *hld up in rr: hdwy on outer over 3f out: rdn along over 2f out: sn drvn and wknd* **10/1**

1m 45.29s (-2.31) **Going Correction** -0.25s/f (Firm) **6** Ran SP% **112.3**
Speed ratings (Par 100): **101,94,91,89,85 84**
toteswingers 1&2 £2.30, 1&3 £1.40, 2&3 £1.90 CSF £7.21 TOTE £2.50: £1.10, £2.00; EX 8.50 Trifecta £9.90 Pool: £2,745.04 - 207.48 winning units..
Owner Mills, Fallon, Purchase & Love **Bred** Sandra Russell **Trained** Sessay, N Yorks

FOCUS
Rocket Ronnie and Confusing, 1-2 on much softer ground at Thirsk three days earlier, renewed rivalry. Not form to take too literally with the winner taking a step forward.

5426 WHITE ROSE SADDLERY AMATEUR RIDERS' H'CAP (DIV I) 1m 100y
5:10 (5:11) (Class 6) (0-65,65) 4-Y-O+ **£2,183** (£677; £338; £169) **Stalls** Low

Form RPR

0600 **1** **Aerodynamic (IRE)**[14] 4928 6-10-9 **65**..............(b[1]) MrHAABannister(5) 5 76
(Michael Easterby) *in rr: pushed along over 3f out: swtchd to wd outside and hdwy 2f out: rdn to chal ent fnl f: sn led and kpt on* **6/1**

0000 **2** 1 1/4 **Violent Velocity (IRE)**[56] 3506 10-10-2 **60**........................ MrKWood(7) 7 68
(John Quinn) *hld up towards rr: stdy hdwy 3f out: rdn to chal over 1f out: led briefly ent fnl f: sn hdd: kpt on same pce* **5/1**[3]

0240 **3** 1 3/4 **Meglio Ancora**[16] 4853 6-9-8 **52**.. MrTGreenwood(7) 8 56+
(Richard Ford) *sn led: rdn along 2f out: drvn and hdd ent fnl f: one pce* **17/2**

4345 **4** 2 1/4 **Rub Of The Relic (IRE)**[29] 4403 8-10-3 **59**..............(v) MissHDukes(5) 1 58
(Paul Midgley) *hld up in tch on inner: effrt wl over 2f out: sn rdn along and plugged on one pce* **5/2**[1]

3400 **5** hd **Glan Lady (IRE)**[7] 5198 7-9-4 **48** ow2.. MrJLBaker(7) 3 46
(Michael Appleby) *trckd ldrs: pushed along wl over 2f out: rdn wl over 1f out: sn one pce* **16/1**

0505 **6** 3 1/4 **Loukoumi**[7] 5198 5-9-5 **47**..(b) MrWEasterby(5) 12 38
(Tim Easterby) *chsd ldrs: cl up whn rn wd bnd at 1/2-way: swtchd to inner and hdwy 2f out: rdn and hung lft over 1f out: sn wknd* **7/1**

5665 **7** 4 **Daneside (IRE)**[19] 4771 6-10-2 **60**..(v[1]) MrWDegnan(7) 9 42
(Gary Harrison) *t.k.h: chsd ldrs: cl up 1/2-way: rdn along over 2f out: sn wknd* **4/1**[2]

1400 **8** 1 **Just Five (IRE)**[17] 4834 7-9-9 **51**..(v) MissKBannon(5) 4 30
(John Weymes) *hld up in rr: effrt and sme hdwy wl over 2f out: sn rdn along and nvr a factor* **16/1**

1m 45.56s (-2.04) **Going Correction** -0.25s/f (Firm) **8** Ran SP% **114.3**
Speed ratings (Par 101): **100,98,97,94,94 91,87,86**
toteswingers 1&2 £5.70, 1&3 £9.90, 2&3 £8.30 CSF £35.88 CT £254.37 TOTE £6.60: £2.20, £2.10, £2.00; EX 35.70 Trifecta £134.50 Pool: £1,604.27 - 8.94 winning units..
Owner David Scott and Co (Pattern Makers) Ltd **Bred** Swettenham, Carradale, S Cosgrove & T Stack **Trained** Sheriff Hutton, N Yorks

FOCUS
The leader was hassled and they seemed to go a very good pace. The winner was last of all at halfway. The runner-up is rated to this year's form.

5427 WHITE ROSE SADDLERY AMATEUR RIDERS' H'CAP (DIV II) 1m 100y
5:40 (5:40) (Class 6) (0-65,64) 4-Y-O+ **£2,183** (£677; £338; £169) **Stalls** Low

Form RPR

3030 **1** **Silly Billy (IRE)**[10] 5047 5-9-5 **46**.. MissNHayes(5) 2 57
(Brian Ellison) *trckd ldrs on inner: smooth hdwy 2f out: effrt and squeezed through on inner ent fnl f: rdn to ld last 100yds: sn edgd lft and jst hld on* **11/2**[3]

0000 **2** shd **Unex Michelangelo (IRE)**[40] 4051 4-10-4 **59**....... MrHAABannister(5) 5 70
(Michael Easterby) *trckd ldrs: hdwy 2f out: rdn to chal ent fnl f: sn edgd rt and ev ch: drvn and sltly hmpd towards fin: jst failed* **9/2**[2]

3033 **3** 3 **Rockweiller**[16] 4853 6-10-5 **55**..(v) MikeyEnnis 1 59
(Steve Gollings) *led: pushed along 2f out: rdn over 1f out: drvn and edgd lft ent fnl f: hdd & wknd last 100yds* **3/1**[1]

0200 **4** 1 1/4 **District Attorney (IRE)**[17] 4824 4-10-1 **51**........................ MrWHogg 8 52
(Chris Fairhurst) *hld up: hdwy wl over 2f out: rdn along wl over 1f out: sn swtchd rt to inner and kpt on same pce fnl f* **14/1**

4022 **5** 3/4 **Rio Cobolo (IRE)**[15] 4893 7-10-3 **60**.. MrDPCostello(7) 6 59
(David Nicholls) *chsd ldr: effrt over 2f out: sn rdn along and wknd appr fnl f* **6/1**

2340 **6** 1 3/4 **Graceful Act**[8] 5139 5-9-12 **53**.. MrsVDavies(5) 10 48
(Ron Barr) *in tch: hdwy over 2f out: rdn along wl over 1f out: no imp* **14/1**

0006 **7** 4 1/2 **Hayek**[27] 4482 6-10-4 **59**..(b) MrWEasterby(5) 3 44
(Tim Easterby) *in tch: hdwy 3f out: rdn along wl over 1f out: sn wknd* **11/1**

0030 **8** 3 1/2 **Bountiful Girl**[11] 5032 4-10-7 **64**.. MrAFrench(7) 4 41
(Neville Bycroft) *dwlt: a in rr* **12/1**

0664 **9** nk **Cyflymder (IRE)**[23] 4615 7-10-12 **62**.. MissSBrotherton 11 38
(David C Griffiths) *racd wd: a in rr* **13/2**

1m 44.75s (-2.85) **Going Correction** -0.25s/f (Firm) **9** Ran SP% **115.5**
Speed ratings (Par 101): **104,103,100,99,98 97,92,89,88**
toteswingers 1&2 £6.40, 1&3 £2.80, 2&3 £4.30 CSF £30.48 CT £88.46 TOTE £6.70: £3.00, £2.90, £1.60; EX 35.20 Trifecta £158.60 Pool: £1,400.65 - 6.61 winning units..
Owner L S Keys **Bred** Sir E J Loder **Trained** Norton, N Yorks
■ Stewards' Enquiry : Miss N Hayes caution: careless riding.

FOCUS
Part two and again the gallop was sound. The winner took advantage of a lower turf mark.
T/Jkpt: Not won. T/Plt: £112.90 to a £1 stake. Pool: £56,139.97 - 362.90 winning units T/Qpdt: £13.80 to a £1 stake. Pool: £4,833.40 - 258.40 winning units JR

5172 CHEPSTOW (L-H)
Thursday, August 15

OFFICIAL GOING: Soft (6.9)
Wind: Virtually nil Weather: Overcast

5428 32RED CASINO EBF MAIDEN STKS 5f 16y
5:15 (5:15) (Class 5) 2-Y-O **£2,911** (£866; £432; £216) **Stalls** Centre

Form RPR

4206 **1** **Finflash (IRE)**[7] 5186 2-9-5 80.. RichardHughes 4 80
(Mick Channon) *mde all: pushed along over 1f out: rdn ins fnl f and r.o strly* **7/4**[2]

02 **2** 2 1/4 **Nova Champ (IRE)**[15] 4883 2-9-5 0.. HarryBentley 1 72
(Stuart Williams) *chsd wnr 2f and again fr 2f out: sn rdn: nt qckn fnl f* **11/10**[1]

2002 **3** 1 1/4 **Urban Dreamer (IRE)**[14] 4912 2-8-12 72........................ PatMillman(7) 3 67
(Rod Millman) *s.i.s: sn rcvrd and chsd wnr after 2f: drvn and dropped to 3rd 2f out: kpt on same pce fnl f* **7/2**[3]

4 5 **Captain Devious** 2-9-2 0.. DeclanBates(3) 5 49
(David Evans) *chsd ldrs: drvn along 2f out: wknd over 1f out* **25/1**

1m 1.56s (2.26) **Going Correction** +0.175s/f (Good) **4** Ran SP% **110.1**
Speed ratings (Par 94): **88,84,82,74**
CSF £4.16 TOTE £2.50; EX 5.00 Trifecta £5.70 Pool: £856.27 - 111.14 winning units..
Owner Insignia Racing (Coronet) **Bred** Rathasker Stud **Trained** West Ilsley, Berks

FOCUS
12mm of rain on run up to meeting on top of watered ground saw the ground change to soft. Richard Hughes said: " The ground is good to soft. They have left a good cover of grass and that helped." An uncompetitive maiden run at an ordinary gallop with the winner rated back to early season form.

5429 £32 FREE AT 32RED.COM H'CAP 1m 14y
5:45 (5:46) (Class 6) (0-55,58) 3-Y-O+ **£1,940** (£577; £288; £144) **Stalls** Centre

Form RPR

0062 **1** **Mr Fickle (IRE)**[9] 5091 4-9-7 **55**..(b) RichardHughes 3 65
(Gary Moore) *in tch and rdn 1/2-way: drvn again over 2f out and styd on to chse ldr over 1f out: kpt on u.p to ld fnl 150yds: in command clsng stages* **2/1**[1]

-501 **2** 3/4 **Tanforan**[7] 5172 11-9-3 **58** 6ex.. ShelleyBirkett(7) 12 66
(Brian Baugh) *chsd ldrs: led appr fnl 2f: rdn appr fnl f: hdd fnl 150yds: no ex* **4/1**[2]

-003 **3** 1 **Compton Bird**[50] 3687 4-8-13 **52**.. RyanTate(5) 6 58
(Hans Adielsson) *mid-div: hdwy and rdn over 2f out: tk 3rd appr fnl f and styd on clsng stages but no imp on ldng duo* **10/1**

0660 **4** 2 1/4 **Tweedle Dee**[49] 3727 4-9-0 **48**.. JohnFahy 7 49
(Noel Quinlan) *in rr: hdwy 3f out: sn rdn: tk one pce 3rd fnl f* **7/1**[3]

0600 **5** 2 **Lambert Pen (USA)**[36] 4170 3-8-7 **55**........................ DanielCremin(7) 16 50
(Mick Channon) *in rr: drvn over 3f out: styd on fnl 2f: nt rch ldrs* **14/1**

040 **6** nk **Roxy Lane**[24] 4590 4-9-4 **52**.. JimmyQuinn 1 47
(Peter Hiatt) *chsd ldrs: chal over 2f out: wknd over 1f out* **14/1**

0003 **7** 6 **Aureolin Gulf**[10] 5073 4-8-7 **46** oh1.. JackDuern(5) 2 27
(Andrew Hollinshead) *led: jnd after 2f but kpt ld tl hdd ins fnl 3f: wknd 2f out* **16/1**

0-60 **8** 3/4 **My Stroppy Poppy**[85] 2578 4-8-9 **46** oh1.................. DeclanBates(3) 14 26
(David Evans) *in rr: hdwy to chse ldrs fr 1/2-way: rdn 3f out: wknd 2f out* **25/1**

0214 **9** 1 1/2 **Devon Diva**[21] 4658 7-8-10 **49**.. MichaelJMMurphy(5) 4 25
(John Gallagher) *chsd ldrs: rdn 3f out: wknd over 2f out* **8/1**

006- **10** 3 1/2 **Gifted Heir (IRE)**[388] 4405 9-8-7 **46** oh1........................ NatashaEaton(5) 15 14
(Ray Peacock) *pressed ldr after 2f tl wknd over 3f out* **66/1**

00-0 **11** 3 1/4 **Komreyev Star**[56] 3513 11-8-5 **46** oh1........................ LouisSteward(7) 10 7
(Ray Peacock) *a in rr* **66/1**

4030 **12** nk **Spinning Ridge (IRE)**[9] 5091 8-9-2 **55**........................(b) EDLinehan(5) 5 15
(Ronald Harris) *chsd ldrs: led ins fnl 3f: hdd appr fnl 2f: sn wknd* **25/1**

050 **13** 43 **American Kiss (SWE)**[107] 1611 4-8-9 **46** oh1(b[1]) WilliamTwiston-Davies(3) 9
(Robin Dickin) *s.i.s: a bhd: eased whn no ch* **50/1**

46-5 **14** nse **Just River**[152] 1035 4-8-13 **47**.. LiamKeniry 13
(Seamus Mullins) *prom to 1/2-way: wknd qckly: eased whn no ch fnl f* **20/1**

1m 37.36s (1.16) **Going Correction** +0.175s/f (Good)
WFA 3 from 4yo+ 7lb **14** Ran SP% **122.7**
Speed ratings (Par 101): **101,100,99,97,95 94,88,87,86,82 79,79,36,36**
toteswingers 1&2 £2.90, 1&3 £4.60, 2&3 £6.80 CSF £8.76 CT £68.47 TOTE £2.60: £1.20, £2.70, £3.60; EX 10.20 Trifecta £38.90 Pool: £948.70 - 18.26 winning units..
Owner Tony Perkins **Bred** M Duffy **Trained** Lower Beeding, W Sussex

FOCUS
A moderate handicap run at a reasonable gallop. The winner was well in and the runner-up has run his best races here at this time of year and is rated in line with those marks.

5430 PREMIER AND NORBORD 20TH YEAR ANNIVERSARY FILLIES' H'CAP 1m 14y
6:15 (6:18) (Class 5) (0-75,74) 3-Y-O+ **£2,587** (£770; £384; £192) **Stalls** Centre

Form RPR

0202 **1** **Tenbridge**[7] 5177 4-8-8 **57**..(v[1]) RosieJessop(3) 3 66
(Derek Haydn Jones) *t.k.h: chsd ldr tl led over 4f out: pushed along 2f out: kpt on wl: drvn and kpt on wl fnl f* **11/4**[3]

The Form Book Flat, Raceform Ltd, Compton, RG20 6NL.

0236 **2** *1 3/4* **Silvas Romana (IRE)**[7] 5172 4-9-5 **70**.......... JackDuern(5) 1 75
(Mark Brisbourne) *chsd ldrs: wnt 2nd 3f out: rdn over 2f out: kpt on same pce fr over 1f out* **12/1**

2-31 **3** *7* **Truly Madly (IRE)**[9] 5104 3-8-13 **71** 6ex.......... RyanTate(5) 2 59
(Hans Adielsson) *chsd ldrs: rdn and outpcd 3f out: styd on to take mod 3rd ins fnl f* **12/1**

6212 **4** *3 1/4* **Lady Bayside**[52] 3617 5-10-0 **74**.......... RichardHughes 4 55
(Malcolm Saunders) *in rr but in tch: drvn along 4f out: hdwy to dispute 2nd over 2f out but no imp on wnr: wknd over 1f out and lost 3rd ins fnl f* **6/4**[1]

2042 **5** *19* **Oilinda**[34] 4240 3-8-10 **70**.......... LouisSteward(7) 5 7
(Michael Bell) *walked to post: sn led: hdd over 4f out: wknd qckly ins fnl 3f* **5/2**[2]

1m 37.72s (1.52) **Going Correction** +0.175s/f (Good)
WFA 3 from 4yo+ 7lb **5** Ran SP% **110.6**
Speed ratings (Par 100): **99,97,90,87,68**
CSF £29.80 TOTE £3.40: £1.70, £3.20; EX 26.40 Trifecta £64.00 Pool: £808.56 - 9.46 winning units..
Owner Mrs E M Haydn Jones **Bred** Mrs M L Parry **Trained** Efail Isaf, Rhondda C Taff

FOCUS
A fair handicap run at a reasonable pace. The form is rated around the first two to recent form.

5431 32RED MAIDEN H'CAP 6f 16y
6:45 (6:46) (Class 6) (0-65,65) 3-Y-0 **£1,940** (£577; £288; £144) **Stalls** Centre

Form RPR

6400 **1** **Blue Clumber**[9] 5091 3-8-4 **48**.......... (be) JimmyQuinn 7 55
(Shaun Harris) *sn led: hdd over 4f out: rdn over 2f out: styd on appr fnl f: led fnl 110yds: pushed out* **25/1**

4042 **2** *1 3/4* **Roanne (USA)**[21] 4659 3-9-1 **64**.......... (bt) RyanTate(5) 4 66
(Clive Cox) *in tch but rdn 3f out: hdwy 2f out and led over 1f out: sn edgd lft u.p: hdd and fnd no ex fnl 110yds* **5/4**[1]

6245 **3** *2 1/2* **Imperial Spirit**[14] 4916 3-8-4 **51**.......... (v) SimonPearce(3) 2 46
(Mick Channon) *chsd ldrs: rdn over 2f out: styd on for wl-hld 3rd ins fnl f* **8/1**

600 **4** *3 3/4* **Gregori (IRE)**[13] 4968 3-9-2 **60**.......... RichardHughes 1 43
(Brian Meehan) *led over 4f out: rdn ins fnl 2f: hdd over 1f out: edgd lft: btn ins fnl f* **7/4**[2]

3044 **5** *1 1/2* **Baltic Gin (IRE)**[15] 4881 3-8-6 **57**.......... RyanWhile(7) 6 36
(Malcolm Saunders) *a in rr: pushed along and bdly outpcd fr 1/2-way: modest prog fnl f* **5/1**[3]

1m 14.05s (2.05) **Going Correction** +0.175s/f (Good) **5** Ran SP% **112.4**
Speed ratings (Par 98): **93,90,87,82,80**
CSF £58.75 TOTE £26.80: £9.40, £1.50; EX 35.70 Trifecta £105.70 Pool: £558.32 - 3.95 winning units..
Owner Miss H Ward **Bred** Worksop Manor Stud **Trained** Carburton, Notts

FOCUS
A modest maiden handicap in which the gallop seemed sound. The runner-up to her latest mark sets the level.

5432 32RED.COM MAIDEN H'CAP 2m 2f
7:15 (7:17) (Class 6) (0-65,65) 3-Y-0+ **£1,940** (£577; £288; £144) **Stalls** Low

Form RPR

/00- **1** **Princesse Fleur**[37] 6821 5-8-11 **51** oh1.......... WilliamTwiston-Davies(3) 2 56
(Michael Scudamore) *hld up towards rr: hdwy 1/2-way: trckd ldrs 4f out: wnt 2nd over 3f out: pushed along to ld over 1f out: drvn ins fnl f: kpt on wl* **7/1**

4V43 **2** *2* **Honey Haven (IRE)**[14] 4931 3-7-7 **55** oh10.......... NoelGarbutt(7) 4 58
(Mark Brisbourne) *in rr: drvn and hdwy over 3f out: styd on u.p fnl 2f to chse ldrs fnl f: tk 2nd clsng stages but no ch w wnr* **20/1**

0002 **3** *nse* **Fitzwilly**[14] 4931 3-7-11 **55** oh5.......... SimonPearce(3) 1 58
(Mick Channon) *led 2f: styd chsng ldrs to 10f out: wnt: chal over 4f out and sn led: drvn to assert 3f out but hdd over 1f out: styd on same pce and dropped to 3rd clsng stages* **7/4**[1]

4-00 **4** *hd* **Captain Oats (IRE)**[59] 3406 10-9-0 **51** oh3.......... RichardHughes 8 54
(Pam Ford) *towards rr: hdwy over 3f out: chsd ldrs 2f out and sn rdn: styd on same pce for 4th fnl f* **14/1**

3550 **5** *11* **Nellie Forbush**[15] 4899 3-8-10 **65**.......... (v) DavidProbert 7 55
(Andrew Balding) *t.k.h: in tch: chsd ldrs and disp 2nd over 3f out: wknd 2f out* **9/2**[2]

6600 **6** *8* **Lacey**[31] 4355 4-8-10 **52**.......... (p) JackDuern(5) 3 34
(Andrew Hollinshead) *t.k.h: chsd ldrs: rdn 3f out: sn btn* **20/1**

-004 **7** *3 1/4* **Dusky Lark**[14] 4931 3-8-7 **62** ow2.......... RobertHavlin 13 40
(Hughie Morrison) *chsd ldrs: wnt 2nd 10f out: led ins fnl 5f: jnd over 4f out and sn hdd: wknd fr 3f* **11/2**[3]

0-43 **8** *1 1/2* **Nicky Nutjob (GER)**[13] 4365 7-9-0 **51** oh6.......... (p) JimmyQuinn 9 27
(John O'Shea) *rdn 4f out: a towards rr* **8/1**

5434 **9** *40* **Duchess Of Dreams**[9] 5084 3-8-0 **55** oh10.......... (e1) JamieMackay 5
(Richard Guest) *t.k.h: sme prog 6f out: rdn 4f out: sn btn* **25/1**

-000 **10** *18* **Falcun**[41] 4035 6-8-9 **51** oh6.......... (bp1) RyanTate(5) 14
(Nikki Evans) *led after 2f: hrd pressed and rdn 6f out: hdd ins fnl 5f: wknd qckly: t.o* **25/1**

4m 5.7s (2.10) **Going Correction** +0.175s/f (Good)
WFA 3 from 4yo+ 18lb **10** Ran SP% **117.4**
Speed ratings (Par 101): **102,101,101,101,96 92,91,90,72,64**
toteswingers 1&2 £25.90, 1&3 £3.70, 2&3 £8.30 CSF £139.20 CT £348.30 TOTE £7.10: £1.90, £6.00, £1.40; EX 183.50 Trifecta £426.50 Part won. Pool: £568.75 - 0.17 winning units..
Owner The Honfleur Syndicate **Bred** Baker And Readings Partnership **Trained** Bromsash, H'fords
■ Stewards' Enquiry : Simon Pearce two-day ban: used whip above permitted level (Aug 29-30)

FOCUS
A modest handicap in which all bar three of the runners raced from out of the handicap. The gallop was reasonable and this was a fair test in the conditions. The winner is rated close to her old Flat form.

5433 CENTURION VAT NIFTY AT FIFTY H'CAP 1m 4f 23y
7:45 (7:45) (Class 6) (0-60,60) 3-Y-0+ **£1,940** (£577; £288; £144) **Stalls** Low

Form RPR

4221 **1** **Arch Event**[9] 5093 8-9-3 **56** 6ex.......... (p) DanielMuscutt(7) 10 65+
(Bernard Llewellyn) *in tch: hdwy 4f out: chsd ldr 2f out: led sn after: edgd lft over 1f out: pushed along fnl f: clr whn idled fnl 110yds: comf* **4/1**[3]

222 **2** *3/4* **Steely**[9] 5093 5-10-0 **60**.......... (v1) RichardHughes 8 66
(Gary Moore) *led: drvn and qcknd over 3f out: hdd ins fnl 2f: swtchd rt and hld whn crossed over 1f out: but styd on to cl on idling wnr fnl 110yds* **3/1**[2]

3425 **3** *5* **Glens Wobbly**[30] 4365 5-8-9 **46**.......... RyanTate(5) 6 44
(Jonathan Geake) *chsd ldrs: wnt 2nd 4f out: rdn and no imp over 3f out: wknd over 1f out* **14/1**

0304 **4** *6* **Precision Strike**[9] 5107 3-8-6 **56**.......... (v) NoelGarbutt(7) 11 44
(Richard Guest) *slowly away: in rr: rdn over 5f out: hdwy over 2f out: nvr rchd ldrs and styd on for one pce 4th* **7/1**

4366 **5** *1 3/4* **Red Current**[23] 4605 9-8-11 **46**.......... WilliamTwiston-Davies(3) 9 32
(Michael Scudamore) *rrd stalls and slowly away: hdwy 4f out: nvr rchd ldrs: wknd fnl 2f* **16/1**

03 **6** *2 3/4* **Rock Peak (IRE)**[45] 3884 8-9-0 **46**.......... (b) MartinLane 2 27
(Bernard Llewellyn) *chsd ldrs: rdn 5f out: wknd wl over 3f out* **12/1**

0044 **7** *1 1/4* **Richo**[9] 5093 7-8-9 **46** oh1.......... MichaelJMMurphy(5) 3 25
(Shaun Harris) *slowly away: in rr: effrt u.p 4f out: nvr rchd ldrs and sn wknd* **25/1**

6502 **8** *16* **Faustinatheyounger (IRE)**[13] 4961 3-9-0 **57**.......... LiamKeniry 1 11
(David Elsworth) *chsd ldrs: rdn 4f out: sn btn* **9/4**[1]

5 **9** *10* **Up In Flames (IRE)**[41] 4036 4-9-4 **57**.......... (b) OllieGarner(7) 4
(Martin Keighley) *chsd ldr to 4f out: wknd qckly wl over 3f out* **33/1**

-000 **10** *62* **Endura**[35] 4195 3-8-3 **46** oh1.......... (b1) JimmyQuinn 7
(Harry Dunlop) *in rr: t.o fnl 5f* **33/1**

2m 41.19s (2.19) **Going Correction** +0.175s/f (Good)
WFA 3 from 4yo+ 11lb **10** Ran SP% **118.2**
Speed ratings (Par 101): **99,98,95,91,90 88,87,76,70,28**
toteswingers 1&2 £3.50, 1&3 £7.00, 2&3 £7.10 CSF £16.38 CT £151.11 TOTE £6.30: £1.90, £1.10, £4.00; EX 17.30 Trifecta £55.00 Pool: £611.28 - 8.32 winning units..
Owner David Maddocks **Bred** P And Mrs Wafford **Trained** Fochriw, Caerphilly

FOCUS
A moderate handicap run at a reasonable gallop. The form is rated around the first two.

5434 32REDBINGO.COM H'CAP 1m 2f 36y
8:15 (8:15) (Class 6) (0-65,65) 3-Y-0+ **£1,940** (£577; £288; £144) **Stalls** Low

Form RPR

2433 **1** **Whitefall (USA)**[1] 5391 3-8-9 **55**.......... JimmyQuinn 3 63
(David Evans) *trckd ldrs: wnt 2nd over 3f out: chal 2f out tl led wl over 1f out: drvn and styd on wl fnl 110yds* **11/4**[1]

603 **2** *1 1/4* **Belle Park**[43] 3954 6-9-1 **52**.......... RichardHughes 1 58
(Karen George) *in tch: rdn and hdwy 3f out: swtchd lft and chsd wnr ins fnl f: kpt on but a readily hld* **9/2**[3]

0443 **3** *1 3/4* **Another Squeeze**[8] 5126 5-8-11 **48**.......... CathyGannon 10 50
(Peter Hiatt) *sn led: jnd and rdn 2f out: hdd wl over 1f out: one pce into 3rd fnl f* **4/1**[2]

0-50 **4** *1 1/2* **Present Day**[63] 3252 4-8-12 **49**.......... (b) JohnFahy 7 48
(Clive Cox) *chsd ldr: t.k.h: rdn over 2f out: sn btn* **14/1**

6035 **5** *4* **James Pollard (IRE)**[7] 5171 8-9-6 **62**.......... (t) RobertWilliams(5) 6 54
(Bernard Llewellyn) *chsd ldrs: rdn over 2f out: sn btn* **8/1**

-000 **6** *2* **Euroquip Boy (IRE)**[20] 4714 6-8-10 **47**.......... LiamKeniry 4 35
(Michael Scudamore) *t.k.h in tch: rdn 3f out: mod prog fnl f* **20/1**

/005 **7** *1/2* **Ernest Speak (IRE)**[20] 4711 4-8-6 **46** oh1.......... (t) DeclanBates(3) 2 33
(David Evans) *in rr: rdn 4f out: mod prog fnl f* **50/1**

650 **8** *2* **La Rosiere (USA)**[36] 4167 4-9-9 **60**.......... JackMitchell 9 43
(Pat Murphy) *towards rr: pushed along and sme hdwy 4f out: nvr rchd ldrs and sn btn* **33/1**

04-0 **9** *5* **Pearla**[27] 4500 3-8-12 **65**.......... DanielMuscutt(7) 11 39
(Robert Stephens) *s.i.s: t.k.h: towards rr most of way* **25/1**

00/4 **10** *3/4* **Global Recovery (IRE)**[79] 2764 6-8-2 **46** oh1.......... EoinWalsh(7) 8 18
(David Evans) *bhd most of way* **20/1**

0061 **11** *14* **Bondi Mist (IRE)**[43] 3953 4-9-5 **61**.......... (v) RyanTate(5) 5
(Jonathan Geake) *rdn over 5f out: a in rr* **5/1**

2m 12.66s (2.06) **Going Correction** +0.175s/f (Good)
WFA 3 from 4yo+ 9lb **11** Ran SP% **117.6**
Speed ratings (Par 101): **98,97,95,94,91 89,89,87,83,83 71**
toteswingers 1&2 £2.80, 1&3 £2.70, 2&3 £5.90 CSF £13.90 CT £49.31 TOTE £4.10: £1.10, £2.00, £2.10; EX 21.30 Trifecta £162.90 Pool: £518.55 - 2.38 winning units..
Owner Mrs E Evans **Bred** Darley **Trained** Pandy, Monmouths

FOCUS
A modest handicap in which the gallop was fair. The runner-up is rated pretty much to form and sets the level.
T/Plt: £174.60 to a £1 stake. Pool: £51,818.60 - 216.58 winning units T/Qpdt: £30.80 to a £1 stake. Pool: £5,548.82 - 133.10 winning units ST

5282 NEWMARKET (R-H)
Thursday, August 15

OFFICIAL GOING: Good to firm (watered; 7.7)
Wind: Light to medium; half behind Weather: Overcast; dry and muggy

5435 BRIAN LIVERSAGE MEMORIAL MEDIAN AUCTION MAIDEN FILLIES' STKS 6f
2:10 (2:10) (Class 5) 2-Y-0 **£3,234** (£962; £481; £240) **Stalls** High

Form RPR

0 **1** **Remember**[14] 4921 2-9-0 0.......... RyanMoore 2 82+
(Richard Hannon) *racd in centre: in tch: rdn and effrt to ld over 1f out: styd on strly and drew clr fnl f: rdn out: comf* **6/4**[1]

3 **2** *3 3/4* **Perfect Alchemy (IRE)**[10] 5061 2-9-0 0.......... SebSanders 5 70
(Ralph Beckett) *racd in centre: chsd ldrs: effrt u.p to press ldrs 2f out: unable qck w wnr jst over 1f out: wnt 2nd but no imp ins fnl f* **3/1**[2]

3 *3/4* **Elsie Partridge (IRE)** 2-9-0 0.......... PatCosgrave 4 68
(Noel Quinlan) *racd in centre: chsd overall ldr: ev ch 2f out: rdn: rn green and wandered over 1f out: outpcd by wnr jst over 1f out: lost 2nd and plugged on same pce fnl f* **33/1**

06 **4** *1 1/4* **River Goddess (IRE)**[29] 4409 2-9-0 0.......... WilliamCarson 7 64
(Charles Hills) *racd against far rail thrght: overall ldr tl rdn and hdd over 1f out: no ex and btn 1f out: plugged on same pce after* **25/1**

43 **5** *3/4* **Lady Tiana**[29] 4409 2-9-0 0.......... FrederikTylicki 8 61
(Lucy Wadham) *racd towards far rail thrght: plld hrd: hld up wl in tch: effrt and rdn to chse ldrs 2f out: no ex and btn ent fnl f: plugged on* **7/2**[3]

40 **6** *5* **Relation Alexander (IRE)**[48] 3781 2-9-0 0.......... RobertWinston 10 45
(Paul D'Arcy) *racd against far rail thrght: in tch in midfield: rdn and effrt jst over 2f out: no ex and btn over 1f out: sn wknd* **20/1**

05 **7** *1 1/4* **Green Music**[42] 3986 2-9-0 0.......... [1] AdamKirby 6 41
(James Eustace) *racd in centre: hld up in tch: rdn and effrt wl over 2f out: sn struggling: wknd over 1f out: bhd fnl f* **12/1**

06 **8** *nk* **Musalaha (IRE)**[20] 4723 2-9-0 0.......... PaulHanagan 1 40+
(Ed Dunlop) *racd in centre: wnt rt s: in tch in rr: rdn and outpcd over 2f out: bhd over 1f out* **25/1**

0 **9** *1/2* **Penara**[47] 3836 2-9-0 0.......... SamHitchcott 3 39
(Philip Hide) *racd in centre: in tch in midfield: rdn 1/2-way: struggling ent fnl 2f: sn wknd* **150/1**

10 10 **Al Ghashamiya (IRE)** 2-9-0 0 NeilCallan 9 7
(Marco Botti) *racd against far rail thrght: a in rr: lost tch wl over 1f out* **20/1**

1m 12.34s (-0.16) **Going Correction** +0.10s/f (Good) **10 Ran SP% 115.7**
Speed ratings (Par 91): **105,100,99,97,96 89,88,87,86,73**
toteswingers 1&2 £2.80, 1&3 £16.60, 2&3 £26.20 CSF £5.35 TOTE £2.30: £1.40, £1.30, £4.60; EX 7.00 Trifecta £152.30 Pool: £1,848.71 - 9.09 winning units..
Owner Saeed Manana **Bred** Fittocks Stud **Trained** East Everleigh, Wilts

FOCUS
Far side track used. Stalls far side except 1m2f: centre. Repositioning of bend into home straight added 16m to 1m2f race. Little depth to this fillies' maiden, although the winner was quite impressive. The race is rated in line with the two previous renewals.

5436 LYNDSAY WICKS BIRTHDAY CELEBRATION H'CAP (JOCKEY CLUB GRASSROOTS MIDDLE DISTANCE SERIES QUALIFIER) 1m 2f
2:40 (2:40) (Class 4) (0-85,85) 3-Y-0+ **£4,851** (£1,443; £721; £360) **Stalls** Centre

1-11 1 **Willow Beck**[15] 4898 4-9-4 77 WilliamBuick 7 90+
(John Gosden) *chsd ldr: rdn and effrt to ld over 1f out: styd on wl and drew clr ins fnl f: readily* **15/8**[1]

6231 2 2 3/4 **Livia's Dream (IRE)**[19] 4760 4-9-8 81 TomMcLaughlin 8 88
(Ed Walker) *sn led: rdn ent fnl 2f: hdd over 1f out: no ex and styd on same pce fnl f* **12/1**

421- 3 3 1/2 **Flow (USA)**[329] 6412 3-9-2 84 TomQueally 1 84
(Lady Cecil) *stdd s: t.k.h: hld up in rr: effrt to chse ldrs against stands' rail 2f out: drvn and btn 1f out: edgd lft and wknd ins fnl f* **7/2**[3]

1130 4 1/2 **Theodore Gericault (IRE)**[61] 3338 3-9-3 85 RyanMoore 2 84
(Sir Michael Stoute) *chsd ldrs: rdn and effrt 2f out: 4th and no ex u.p ent fnl f: carried lft and wknd ins fnl f* **9/4**[2]

1-55 5 6 **Juvenal (IRE)**[10] 5063 4-9-11 84 (p) SeanLevey 3 71
(Richard Hannon) *stdd s: hld up in tch in last pair: hdwy 3f out: rdn and btn over 1f out: fdd fnl f* **18/1**

3052 6 1 1/4 **Greylami (IRE)**[38] 4126 8-9-3 76 AdamKirby 6 61
(Clive Cox) *in tch in midfield: rdn and effrt over 2f out: wknd and bhd over 1f out* **12/1**

2m 4.97s (-0.53) **Going Correction** +0.10s/f (Good)
WFA 3 from 4yo+ 9lb **6 Ran SP% 108.4**
Speed ratings (Par 105): **106,103,101,100,95 94**
toteswingers 1&2 £1.80, 1&3 £2.80, 2&3 £4.50 CSF £22.21 CT £63.02 TOTE £2.60: £1.20, £4.20; EX 18.50 Trifecta £56.90 Pool: £1,902.78 - 25.04 winning units..
Owner HRH Princess Haya Of Jordan **Bred** Worksop Manor Stud **Trained** Newmarket, Suffolk

FOCUS
A decent handicap, won by a filly very much on the upgrade. The runner-up sets the standard.

5437 NEWMARKETRACECOURSES.CO.UK H'CAP 7f
3:15 (3:15) (Class 4) (0-85,85) 3-Y-0+ **£4,851** (£1,443; £721; £360) **Stalls** High

Form RPR

0100 1 **Skytrain**[12] 5004 3-8-13 78 NeilCallan 2 85
(Mark Johnston) *racd centre to stands' side: chsd ldrs: rdn to ld 2f out: hung lft after and racing nr far rail ins fnl f: kpt on wl u.p* **10/1**

0050 2 nk **Farlow (IRE)**[19] 4780 5-9-10 83 PaulHanagan 4 91
(Richard Fahey) *racd centre to stands' side: in tch in midfield: hdwy u.p and hung lft 1f out: styd on to chse wnr towards fin: nvr quite getting to wnr* **6/1**[3]

3115 3 1/2 **Consign**[22] 4642 3-9-3 82 (v) WilliamBuick 1 87
(Jeremy Noseda) *racd centre to stands' side: hld up in rr: rdn 2f out: hdwy and carried lft 1f out: stl carried lft but kpt on wl ins fnl f: wnt 3rd cl home* **7/2**[1]

5215 4 1/2 **Front Page News**[12] 5004 3-8-0 72 OisinMurphy(7) 5 75
(Robert Eddery) *racd centre to stands' side: hld up in tch: effrt to chse wnr and carried lft fr wl over 1f out: racing nr far rail and no ex wl ins fnl f: lost 2 pls towards fin* **4/1**[2]

6-45 5 3/4 **Piddie's Power**[21] 4671 6-9-8 81 RoystonFfrench 10 84
(Ed McMahon) *taken down early: racd towards far side: chsd ldr tl 2f out: rdn and hmpd over 1f out: kpt on same pce ins fnl f* **16/1**

4143 6 1 1/2 **Benoni**[33] 4281 3-8-7 72 TedDurcan 7 71
(Henry Candy) *racd towards far side: t.k.h: hld up in tch in midfield: rdn and effrt 2f out: 3rd and keeping on one pce whn hmpd ins fnl f* **6/1**[3]

624 7 1 3/4 **Azrael**[16] 4864 5-9-7 80 SeanLevey 8 75
(Alan McCabe) *racd towards far side: overall ldr tl rdn and hdd 2f out: sn struggling and hmpd whn btn over 1f out: wknd fnl f* **25/1**

0425 8 2 **Amadeus Wolfe Tone (IRE)**[21] 4677 4-9-12 85 (b) AdamKirby 9 74
(Jamie Osborne) *racd towards far side: hld up in rr: swtchd rt and effrt wl over 1f out: hrd drvn and no hdwy ent fnl f: wknd fnl 150yds* **16/1**

1-51 9 nk **Balti's Sister (IRE)**[203] 358 4-9-1 74 RobertWinston 3 62
(Martin Smith) *racd centre to stands' side: hld up in tch in rr: rdn and effrt 2f out: no hdwy u.p 1f out: nvr trbld ldrs* **12/1**

3120 10 3 3/4 **Poisson D'Or**[19] 4766 4-9-6 79 TomQueally 6 57
(Rae Guest) *racd centre to stands' side: in tch in midfield: rdn and effrt 2f out: lost pl and bhd 1f out: wknd* **8/1**

1m 25.22s (-0.48) **Going Correction** +0.10s/f (Good)
WFA 3 from 4yo+ 6lb **10 Ran SP% 114.3**
Speed ratings (Par 105): **106,105,105,104,103 101,99,97,97,93**
toteswingers 1&2 £9.30, 1&3 £7.00, 2&3 £3.80 CSF £67.47 CT £220.63 TOTE £10.20: £3.10, £2.50, £1.10; EX 82.00 Trifecta £148.90 Pool: £2,375.40 - 11.96 winning units..
Owner A D Spence **Bred** Brook Stud Bloodstock Ltd **Trained** Middleham Moor, N Yorks
■ Stewards' Enquiry : Neil Callan three-day ban: careless riding (Aug 29-31)

FOCUS
A competitive handicap, but it was a messy race. The third is rated to form backed up by the fourth and fifth.

5438 NEWMARKETEXPERIENCE.CO.UK CONDITIONS STKS 7f
3:45 (3:45) (Class 2) 2-Y-0 **£9,056** (£2,695; £1,346; £673) **Stalls** High

Form RPR

21 1 **Music Theory (IRE)**[13] 4958 2-9-0 0 WilliamBuick 1 100+
(Charlie Appleby) *mde all: gng clr on bit over 1f out: rdn and qcknd wl clr 1f out: heavily eased towards fin: nt extended* **1/5**[1]

6315 2 9 **Hatha Hooh**[11] 5028 2-9-0 85 RyanMoore 2 76
(Richard Hannon) *t.k.h: w wnr: rdn over 2f out: no ex and btn whn lost 2nd over 1f out: wnt modest 2nd again and plugged on ins fnl f* **5/1**[2]

0 3 4 **Chainsaw**[68] 3112 2-9-0 0 NeilCallan 4 65+
(Stuart Williams) *stdd and dropped in bhd after s: t.k.h: wnt 3rd 1/2-way: rdn to chse clr wnr over 1f out: no imp: lost 2nd and fdd ins fnl f* **66/1**

4 1 3/4 **Samtu (IRE)** 2-8-12 0 TomQueally 3 58
(Clive Brittain) *rn green: pushed along in 3rd tl dropped to last and rdn 1/2-way: lost tch 2f out: plugged on fnl f* **20/1**[3]

1m 26.64s (0.94) **Going Correction** +0.10s/f (Good) **4 Ran SP% 106.3**
Speed ratings (Par 100): **98,87,83,81**
CSF £1.47 TOTE £1.10; EX 1.20 Trifecta £11.30 Pool: £2,457.05 - 162.82 winning units..
Owner Godolphin **Bred** Forenaghts Stud **Trained** Newmarket, Suffolk

FOCUS
An uncompetitive 2-y-o conditions event. The form is taken at close to face value.

5439 JULY COURSE H'CAP 7f
4:20 (4:20) (Class 2) (0-100,97) 3-Y-O **£12,291** (£3,657; £1,827; £913) **Stalls** High

Form RPR

12- 1 **Seek Again (USA)**[303] 7125 3-9-0 90 WilliamBuick 4 99+
(John Gosden) *hld up wl in tch in midfield: swtchd rt and effrt wl over 1f out: rdn and hdwy 1f out: led fnl 75yds: pushed out hands and heels towards fin* **3/1**[2]

0232 2 1/2 **Maid A Million**[8] 5125 3-8-8 84 WilliamCarson 1 92
(David Elsworth) *chsd ldrs: rdn and ev ch 2f out: drvn to ld ent fnl f: hdd fnl 75yds: r.o but a hld after* **9/1**

1144 3 hd **Secret Art (IRE)**[19] 4743 3-8-9 85 NeilCallan 6 92
(Ralph Beckett) *t.k.h: w ldr: rdn to ld ent fnl 2f: hdd but stl ev ch whn edgd lft ent fnl f: r.o but no ex fnl 50yds* **4/1**[3]

2010 4 3/4 **Tamayuz Star (IRE)**[19] 4743 3-9-7 97 RyanMoore 5 102
(Richard Hannon) *hld up wl in tch in rr: rdn and effrt over 1f out: switching rt ins fnl f: styd on fnl 100yds: nvr able to chal* **17/2**

3-14 5 3/4 **Gold Hunter (IRE)**[19] 4767 3-9-2 92 PaulHanagan 7 95
(Saeed bin Suroor) *stdd s: hld up wl in tch in midfield: rdn and effrt 2f out: chsd ldrs and carried lft 1f out: btn fnl 100yds: wknd towards fin* **5/2**[1]

3022 6 nse **Fils Anges (IRE)**[34] 4258 3-9-0 90 TomQueally 2 93
(Michael Bell) *hld up wl in tch in last pair: effrt over 1f out: drvn and kpt on same pce ins fnl f* **8/1**

0436 7 6 **Flashlight (IRE)**[15] 4897 3-8-6 82 JoeFanning 3 69
(Mark Johnston) *led and set stdy gallop: qcknd over 2f out but sn rdn and hdd: lost pl and bhd 1f out: wl hld and eased wl ins fnl f* **16/1**

1m 25.74s (0.04) **Going Correction** +0.10s/f (Good) **7 Ran SP% 111.1**
Speed ratings (Par 106): **103,102,102,101,100 100,93**
toteswingers 1&2 £3.80, 1&3 £3.70, 2&3 £7.80 CSF £27.58 TOTE £3.40: £2.20, £3.80; EX 32.90 Trifecta £110.40 Pool: £2,272.94 - 15.43 winning units..
Owner K Abdullah **Bred** Juddmonte Farms Inc **Trained** Newmarket, Suffolk

FOCUS
A decent 3-y-o handicap that developed into a dash from 2f out. The form looks muddling but is taken at face value through the runner-up, with the third and fourth close to their respective bests.

5440 ADNAMS NEWMARKET NIGHTS H'CAP 1m
4:50 (4:50) (Class 4) (0-85,85) 3-Y-O **£4,851** (£1,443; £721; £360) **Stalls** High

Form RPR

2114 1 **Morpheus**[15] 4897 3-9-7 85 TomQueally 4 94+
(Lady Cecil) *travelled wl: chsd ldr: rdn ent fnl 2f: ev ch and drvn over 1f out: led fnl 100yds: kpt on wl* **11/8**[1]

3513 2 hd **Silver Dixie (USA)**[13] 4950 3-8-13 77 RyanMoore 3 86+
(Jeremy Noseda) *dwlt: sn rcvrd and ld and c to stands' rail: rdn over 2f out: hrd pressed but battled on wl fr over 1f out tl hdd fnl 100yds: kpt on but a jst hld after* **2/1**[2]

313 3 3/4 **Broadway Duchess (IRE)**[55] 3532 3-9-2 80 SeanLevey 2 87
(Richard Hannon) *hld up in tch in rr: rdn and effrt over 2f out: hdwy to chse ldrs and swtchd lft ins fnl f: kpt on towards fin* **10/1**[3]

043 4 1 3/4 **Ocean Applause**[6] 5218 3-9-1 79 (tp) AdamKirby 7 82
(John Ryan) *hld up in tch in midfield: hdwy u.p to chse ldrs over 1f out: no ex and one pce ins fnl f* **14/1**

0435 5 3 3/4 **George Rooke (IRE)**[34] 4265 3-9-4 82 NeilCallan 6 76
(Kevin Ryan) *racd in centre: in tch in midfield: effrt to chse ldrs and merged w nr side gp over 2f out: no ex 1f out: wknd ins fnl f* **10/1**[3]

4423 6 6 **Strong Conviction**[15] 4890 3-8-11 75 SamHitchcott 5 55
(Mick Channon) *racd in centre: chsd ldrs: rdn and merged w nr side gp over 2f out: wknd over 1f out* **25/1**

3106 7 8 **Hunting Rights (USA)**[14] 4908 3-8-13 77 (b[1]) JoeFanning 8 39
(Mark Johnston) *restless in stalls: in tch in midfield: rdn and struggling whn hmpd jst over 2f out: bhd over 1f out: eased wl ins fnl f* **20/1**

2544 8 3 1/4 **Punditry**[44] 3923 3-8-4 73 RobertTart(5) 1 27
(James Toller) *s.i.s: a bhd: rdn 3f out: lost tch wl over 1f out* **33/1**

1m 38.7s (-1.30) **Going Correction** +0.10s/f (Good) **8 Ran SP% 111.8**
Speed ratings (Par 102): **110,109,109,107,103 97,89,86**
toteswingers 1&2 £1.50, 1&3 £3.70, 2&3 £3.50 CSF £3.94 CT £15.83 TOTE £2.30: £1.30, £1.20, £2.00; EX 5.20 Trifecta £19.10 Pool: £3,033.09 - 118.51 winning units..
Owner K Abdullah **Bred** Juddmonte Farms Ltd **Trained** Newmarket, Suffolk

FOCUS
A fair 3-y-o handicap, run at a sound pace. The fourth to this season's C&D handicap form sets the level.

5441 TURFTV H'CAP 5f
5:25 (5:25) (Class 4) (0-85,84) 3-Y-0+ **£4,851** (£1,443; £721; £360) **Stalls** High

Form RPR

0262 1 **Angel Way (IRE)**[11] 5036 4-8-10 70 RyanMoore 2 80+
(Mike Murphy) *chsd ldrs tl led 1/2-way: rdn wl over 1f out: fnd ex and r.o wl ins fnl f* **15/8**[1]

2466 2 1 1/4 **Titus Gent**[16] 4860 8-9-7 84 RyanClark(3) 3 90
(Jeremy Gask) *in tch in midfield: rdn and effrt 2f out: chalng over 1f out: kpt on same pce ins fnl f* **11/1**

5042 3 hd **Macdillon**[10] 5060 7-8-0 67 (t) OisinMurphy(7) 4 72
(Stuart Kittow) *chsd ldr tl 1/2-way: styd prom: rdn and pressed wnr over 1f out: no ex ins fnl f* **7/2**[3]

0520 4 3/4 **Flash City (ITY)**[27] 4507 5-9-1 80 (vt) JustinNewman(5) 7 82
(Bryan Smart) *stdd s: t.k.h: hld up in tch in rr: rdn and hdwy to press ldrs 1f out: no ex and btn ins fnl f* **12/1**

5201 5 1 **Smokethatthunders (IRE)**[16] 4866 3-8-6 74 RobertTart(5) 1 71
(James Toller) *in tch in last pair: effrt u.p over 1f out: no imp fnl f* **5/2**[2]

13-U 6 4 1/2 **Ziggy's Secret**[41] 4033 3-8-12 75 FrederikTylicki 5 56
(Lucy Wadham) *led tl 1/2-way: rdn ent fnl 2f: wknd 1f out: fdd ins fnl f* **8/1**

59.05s (-0.05) **Going Correction** +0.10s/f (Good)
WFA 3 from 4yo+ 3lb **6 Ran SP% 112.7**
Speed ratings (Par 105): **104,102,101,100,98 91**
toteswingers 1&2 £4.40, 1&3 £1.90, 2&3 £5.30 CSF £22.74 CT £66.27 TOTE £2.70: £1.80, £3.00; EX 13.90 Trifecta £74.60 Pool: £1,526.37 - 15.32 winning units..
Owner D J Ellis **Bred** Rathasker Stud **Trained** Westoning, Beds

The Form Book Flat, Raceform Ltd, Compton, RG20 6NL.

FOCUS
A fair sprint handicap which went to an improving filly. The runner-up is rated to his best excluding his Epsom figure.
T/Plt: £24.70 to a £1 stake. Pool: £53,553.04 - 1,580.22 winning units T/Qpdt: £8.20 to a £1 stake. Pool: £3,512.18 - 313.60 winning units SP

5399 SALISBURY (R-H)

Thursday, August 15

OFFICIAL GOING: Good (good to firm in places; 8.8)
Wind: Fresh; against Weather: Sunny periods

5442 TOTESUPERSCOOP6 AVAILABLE AT THE EBOR FESTIVAL MAIDEN AUCTION STKS (DIV I) 6f 212y
1:50 (1:52) (Class 5) 2-Y-O **£3,234** (£962; £481; £240) **Stalls** Centre

Form RPR

2 **1** **Starlight Serenade**[65] 3175 2-8-4 0 MartinLane 4 66
(Ralph Beckett) *w'like: trckd ldrs: chal over 2f out sn rdn: led narrowly jst over 1f out tl ins fnl f: battled bk to ld fnl stride* **5/2**[1]

0333 **2** *nse* **Solo Hunter**[11] 5025 2-8-11 68 CathyGannon 12 73
(David Evans) *sn led: rdn whn jnd 2f out: narrowly hdd jst over 1f out: rallied gamely to regain advantage ins fnl f: hdd fnl stride* **9/2**[3]

6 **3** *1 ½* **Juan Alonso (IRE)**[6] 5244 2-9-2 0 PatDobbs 7 74
(Richard Hannon) *str: trckd ldrs: rdn over 2f out: nt quite pce to chal: kpt on ins fnl f* **9/2**[3]

03 **4** *hd* **Tubeanie (IRE)**[49] 3717 2-8-8 0 SteveDrowne 6 66
(Clive Cox) *prom tl rdn to chse ldng pair 2f out: nt quite pce to get bk upsides but kpt on ins fnl f* **16/1**

5 *1 ¼* **Crystal Nymph (IRE)** 2-8-11 0 RichardHughes 8 65+
(Richard Hannon) *athletic: hld up towards rr: rdn over 2f out: stdy prog fr over 1f out: styd on ins fnl f but nvr gng pce to rch ldrs* **7/2**[2]

0 **6** *4* **Stagewise (IRE)**[24] 4589 2-8-6 0 AndreaAtzeni 9 50
(Jonathan Portman) *leggy: s.i.s: mid-div: rdn 3f out: nvr any real imp: kpt on same pce* **100/1**

7 *2 ¼* **Black Label** 2-8-11 0 JimCrowley 2 49
(Harry Dunlop) *lengthy: mid-div: rdn over 2f out: wknd fnl f* **25/1**

0 **8** *¾* **Khloe**[42] 3986 2-8-6 0 KirstyMilczarek 11 42
(Michael Blanshard) *neat: wnt rt s: t.k.h in midfield: hdwy 3f out: rdn whn swtchd rt to chse ldrs 2f out: sn hung rt: wknd ent fnl f* **66/1**

0 **9** *2 ½* **Benoordenhout (IRE)**[29] 4414 2-8-9 0 JohnFahy 5 40
(Jonathan Portman) *w'like: in tch: rdn to chse ldrs over 2f out: wknd fnl f* **66/1**

10 *7* **Company Secretary (USA)** 2-8-11 0 SilvestreDeSousa 10 22
(Jo Hughes) *unf: scope: s.i.s: struggling 1/2-way: a towards rr* **9/1**

11 *3* **Dream Impossible (IRE)** 2-8-6 0 KieranO'Neill 1 10
(Peter Makin) *lenghty: mid-div: rdn over 3f out: wknd 2f out* **33/1**

55 **12** *11* **Unfashionable (IRE)**[35] 4206 2-8-6 0 ChrisCatlin 3
(Stuart Kittow) *leggy: a towards rr: wknd wl over 1f out* **100/1**

1m 29.12s (0.52) **Going Correction** -0.225s/f (Firm) 12 Ran SP% **114.8**
Speed ratings (Par 94): **88,87,86,86,84 80,77,76,73,65 62,49**
toteswingers 1&2 £2.80, 1&3 £5.10, 2&3 £2.80 CSF £12.90 TOTE £2.70: £1.10, £2.10, £2.00; EX 13.90 Trifecta £34.70 Pool: £928.04 - 20.01 winning units..
Owner Melody Racing **Bred** Melody Bloodstock **Trained** Kimpton, Hants

FOCUS
There had been a small amount of rain overnight and prior to racing, although general consensus among those who rode in the opener was that it was 'good' ground. Little got into the first division of what was an ordinary maiden, the time of which was 0.33secs slower than the following contest. The form is routine and towards the lower end of race averages.

5443 TOTESUPERSCOOP6 AVAILABLE AT THE EBOR FESTIVAL MAIDEN AUCTION STKS (DIV II) 6f 212y
2:20 (2:23) (Class 5) 2-Y-O **£3,234** (£962; £481; £240) **Stalls** Centre

Form RPR

0 **1** **Bright Cecily (IRE)**[20] 4702 2-8-11 0 SteveDrowne 1 76+
(Clive Cox) *str: stmbld bdly leaving stalls: towards rr: rdn and stdy prog fr 2f out: swtchd lft jst ins fnl f: str run fnl 120yds: led fnl strides* **9/2**[3]

00 **2** *hd* **Nakuti (IRE)**[14] 4921 2-8-8 0 LiamKeniry 10 72
(Sylvester Kirk) *lw: in tch: cruised upsides ldr jst over 2f out: rdn wl over 1f out: led fnl 120yds: collared fnl strides* **11/1**

4 **3** *1 ¼* **Warrendale**[51] 3663 2-8-6 0 CathyGannon 12 67
(Henry Candy) *athletic: prom: led over 3f out: rdn whn strly pressed fr jst over 2f out: kpt battling tl hdd fnl 120yds: no ex* **4/1**[2]

5 **4** *½* **Ninety Minutes (IRE)**[29] 4414 2-8-11 0 RichardHughes 2 71
(John Best) *w'like: lw: cl up: rdn 2f out: kpt on but nt pce to mount chal* **10/3**[1]

5340 **5** *1* **Seaham**[20] 4708 2-8-13 73 AndreaAtzeni 3 70
(Rod Millman) *trckd ldrs: rdn 2f out: kpt on but nt pce to mount chal* **15/2**

43 **6** *7* **Jersey Brown (IRE)**[14] 4921 2-8-5 0 SimonPearce(3) 6 47
(Mick Channon) *in tch: rdn to dispute 3rd over 2f out: wknd ent fnl f* **9/2**[3]

7 *10* **Our Duchess (IRE)** 2-8-6 0 KieranO'Neill 11 19
(Richard Hannon) *leggy: s.i.s: sn in tch: rdn 3f out: wknd 2f out* **10/1**

0 **8** *5* **No Second Thoughts (IRE)**[12] 4997 2-8-6 0 KirstyMilczarek 4 6
(Michael Blanshard) *w'like: sn struggling in rr: nvr a factor* **100/1**

9 *2* **Holy Water (IRE)** 2-8-6 0 MatthewLawson(5) 7 6
(Jonathan Portman) *w'like: sn outpcd and green: a in rr* **40/1**

10 *½* **Cadmium** 2-8-4 0 MartinLane 9
(Harry Dunlop) *str: mid-div: pushed along over 4f out: sn bhd* **50/1**

0 **11** *1 ¼* **Commanding Force**[22] 4631 2-8-9 0 ChrisCatlin 8
(John Bridger) *w'like: led tl over 3f out: sn wknd* **200/1**

1m 28.79s (0.19) **Going Correction** -0.225s/f (Firm) 11 Ran SP% **114.5**
Speed ratings (Par 94): **89,88,87,86,85 77,66,60,58,57 56**
toteswingers 1&2 £25.90, 1&3 £3.30, 2&3 £8.50 CSF £50.94 TOTE £3.80: £1.40, £4.10, £1.50; EX 59.70 Trifecta £252.10 Pool: £905.18 - 2.69 winning units..
Owner Old Peartree Stud **Bred** J Stan Cosgrove **Trained** Lambourn, Berks

FOCUS
The first five finished in a heap, but it's a race that should still produce winners. The time was 0.33secs quicker than division one. Race averages and the fifth offer perspective.

5444 MARY WORT MEMORIAL MAIDEN STKS 6f 212y
2:50 (2:54) (Class 5) 3-4-Y-O **£3,234** (£962; £481; £240) **Stalls** Centre

Form RPR

32 **1** **Paradise Watch**[41] 4011 3-9-5 0 KierenFallon 5 85+
(Luca Cumani) *str: lw: trckd ldr: pushed into ld over 2f out: in command fnl f: kpt on wl* **8/11**[1]

3225 **2** *2* **It's Taboo**[21] 4685 3-9-0 71 DavidProbert 7 74
(Mark Usher) *trckd ldrs: rdn to chse wnr wl over 1f out: kpt on but a being hld fnl f* **4/1**[2]

3 *8* **Caerwyn** 3-9-5 0 MartinDwyer 10 57+
(Marcus Tregoning) *athletic: slowly away: towards rr: outpcd over 3f out: hdwy 2f out: styd on to go 3rd jst ins fnl f: no ch w front pair* **14/1**

30 **4** *1* **Moortahan**[107] 1908 3-9-5 0 PatDobbs 3 55
(Richard Hannon) *led: rdn and hdd over 2f out: kpt on tl no ex ent fnl f* **10/1**

2 **5** *shd* **Perfect Muse**[218] 123 3-9-0 0 RichardHughes 9 49
(Clive Cox) *str: trckd ldrs: rdn over 2f out: fdd fnl f* **9/2**[3]

6 *2* **Cataria Girl (USA)** 4-9-6 0 (t) GeorgeBaker 2 46
(Marcus Tregoning) *athletic: hld up bhd: sme hdwy 2f out: sn shkn up: nvr rchd ldrs: fdd fnl f* **20/1**

7 *8* **Lagan Honey** 3-8-7 0 RyanWhile(7) 1 22
(Bill Turner) *w'like: mid-div: rdn over 2f out: wknd over 1f out* **50/1**

6 **8** *1 ¾* **Dreaming Again**[19] 4774 3-9-5 0 KieranO'Neill 4 23
(Jimmy Fox) *unf: mid-div tl outpcd over 3f out* **66/1**

9 *12* **Graceful Willow** 3-9-0 0 KirstyMilczarek 8
(John E Long) *w'like: reminders sn after s: a struggling and green in rr* **66/1**

1m 28.37s (-0.23) **Going Correction** -0.225s/f (Firm)
WFA 3 from 4yo 6lb 9 Ran SP% **121.6**
Speed ratings (Par 103): **92,89,80,79,79 77,67,65,52**
toteswingers 1&2 £1.10, 1&3 £5.30, 2&3 £10.80 CSF £4.18 TOTE £1.60: £1.02, £1.70, £3.30; EX 5.00 Trifecta £28.50 Pool: £1,312.17 - 34.46 winning units..
Owner Leonidas Marinopoulos **Bred** Miss J Chaplin **Trained** Newmarket, Suffolk

FOCUS
An uncompetitive maiden and the two who stood out on form drew clear. The bare form looks modest though.

5445 TOTEPOOL HOME OF KING SIZE POOLS EBF FILLIES' H'CAP 1m 4f
3:25 (3:25) (Class 4) (0-80,80) 3-Y-O+ **£6,469** (£1,925; £962; £481) **Stalls** High

Form RPR

2412 **1** **Bantam (IRE)**[12] 5015 3-9-3 **80** AndreaAtzeni 1 89+
(Ed Dunlop) *lw: hld up in tch: pushed along over 3f out: rdn over 2f out: swtchd lft: styd on ent fnl f to ld fnl 40yds: rdn out* **4/1**[3]

12 **2** *½* **Java Rose**[27] 4506 4-9-5 **71** FergusSweeney 2 79
(Henry Candy) *lw: squeezed up s: trckd ldrs tl moved upsides over 3f out: rdn to dispute fr over 2f out: ev ch on the nod thrght fnl f tl hdd fnl 40yds* **6/1**

222 **3** *hd* **Shalwa**[24] 4594 3-9-1 **78** (p) SilvestreDeSousa 5 86
(Marco Botti) *led: rdn whn jnd fr wl over 2f out: kpt battling away most courageously: ev ch on nod thrght fnl f tl hdd fnl 40yds* **3/1**[2]

0311 **4** *3 ¼* **Prospera (IRE)**[8] 5130 3-8-11 **74** 6ex (b) JimCrowley 3 76
(Ralph Beckett) *swtg: trckd ldrs: rdn wl to chse ldng pair over 2f out but unable to mount challnge: edgd rt and hld ent fnl f* **6/1**

535- **5** *4 ½* **Infinite Hope (USA)**[280] 7655 4-10-0 **80** KirstyMilczarek 6 75
(Luca Cumani) *w ldr: sltly hmpd on bnd over 5f out: short of room over 3f out: sn rdn: kpt chsng ldrs tl fdd ent fnl f* **10/1**

5133 **6** *10* **Choral Festival**[7] 5190 7-9-10 **76** KieranO'Neill 7 55
(John Bridger) *hld up last but in tch: rdn over 3f out: nvr any imp* **28/1**

0113 **7** *27* **Pivotal Silence**[19] 4770 3-8-8 **71** RichardHughes 4 57
(Amanda Perrett) *hld up in tch: pushed along and hdwy over 3f out: sn rdn: wknd 2f out: virtually p.u fnl f* **11/4**[1]

2m 34.65s (-3.35) **Going Correction** -0.225s/f (Firm)
WFA 3 from 4yo+ 11lb 7 Ran SP% **112.8**
Speed ratings (Par 102): **102,101,101,99,96 89,71**
toteswingers 1&2 £2.30, 1&3 £2.70, 2&3 £1.90 CSF £26.99 TOTE £5.20: £2.40, £2.70; EX 23.10 Trifecta £79.50 Pool: £1,066.60 - 10.05 winning units..
Owner Brooke Kelly Partnership **Bred** Airlie Stud And Sir Thomas Pilkington **Trained** Newmarket, Suffolk

■ Stewards' Enquiry : Fergus Sweeney two-day ban: used whip above permitted level (Aug 29-30)

FOCUS
A good fillies' handicap for the grade, with some progressive types dominating the finish. The runner-up is rated to his latest Pontefract form.

5446 TOTEPOOL.COM SOVEREIGN STKS (GROUP 3) (C&G) 1m
3:55 (3:55) (Class 1) 3-Y-O+
£42,532 (£16,125; £8,070; £4,020; £2,017; £1,012) **Stalls** Low

Form RPR

2-02 **1** **Afsare**[41] 4027 6-9-0 115 AndreaAtzeni 2 121
(Luca Cumani) *lw: trckd ldrs: cruised upsides 2f out: led jst over 1f out: qcknd clr: impressive* **9/4**[1]

53 **2** *6* **Boom And Bust (IRE)**[16] 4856 6-9-0 108 GeorgeBaker 4 107
(Marcus Tregoning) *led: rdn over 2f out: hdd jst over 1f out: sn outpcd by wnr: edgd rt: jst hld on for 2nd* **8/1**

1110 **3** *shd* **Professor**[16] 4856 3-8-7 110 RichardHughes 1 106
(Richard Hannon) *hld up 6th: rdn into 3rd 2f out: kpt on same pce fr over 1f out: nrly got up for 2nd fnl stride* **3/1**[2]

-522 **4** *6* **Highland Knight (IRE)**[98] 2186 6-9-0 111 (t) DavidProbert 6 93
(Andrew Balding) *w ldr tl rdn over 2f out: kpt chsng ldrs tl fdd ins fnl f* **6/1**[3]

2303 **5** *1 ¼* **Fulbright**[28] 4433 4-9-0 110 (t) AhmedAjtebi 3 90
(Charlie Appleby) *trckd ldrs: rdn over 2f out: wknd fnl f* **16/1**

3413 **6** *8* **Snowboarder (USA)**[13] 4945 3-8-7 107 SilvestreDeSousa 5 78
(Charlie Appleby) *hld up 5th: effrt over 2f out: nvr threatened ldng pair: wknd over 1f out* **3/1**[2]

1m 39.28s (-4.22) **Going Correction** -0.225s/f (Firm)
WFA 3 from 4yo+ 7lb 6 Ran SP% **112.0**
Speed ratings (Par 113): **112,106,105,99,98 90**
toteswingers 1&2 £4.40, 1&3 £6.60, 2&3 £2.40 CSF £20.34 TOTE £3.10: £1.80, £4.10; EX 22.30 Trifecta £86.50 Pool: £1,783.20 - 15.45 winning units..
Owner Sheikh Mohammed Obaid Al Maktoum **Bred** Darley **Trained** Newmarket, Suffolk

FOCUS
A couple of the key players failed to give their running, but it was nonetheless an impressive performance by Afsare. He is rated a marginal improver and could be underrated.

5447 BILL GARNETT MEMORIAL FILLIES' H'CAP 6f
4:30 (4:30) (Class 5) (0-70,69) 3-Y-O+ **£2,911** (£866; £432; £216) **Stalls** Low

Form RPR

3353 **1** **Tregereth (IRE)**[14] 4916 3-8-5 57 ow1 MatthewLawson(5) 3 65
(Jonathan Portman) *trckd ldrs: rdn over 2f out: chal ent fnl f: sn leaned upon: led fnl 120yds: kpt on wl: rdn out* **7/1**

5145 **2** *1* **Renoir's Lady**[14] 4909 5-8-11 **54**........................ AndreaAtzeni 7 60
(Simon Dow) *hld up: tk clsr order but nt clr run over 2f out tl swtchd rt over 1f out: rdn to take narrow ld ent fnl f: edgd rt: hdd fnl 120yds: kpt on* **11/4**[2]

111 **3** *2 ¼* **My Own Way Home**[12] 4998 5-9-10 **67**........................ CathyGannon 9 66
(David Evans) *trckd ldrs: rdn whn sltly outpcd over 2f out: kpt on ins fnl f: wnt 3rd towards fin* **9/4**[1]

0504 **4** *nk* **Amber Heights**[9] 5104 5-8-12 **60**........................ AmyScott(5) 8 58
(Henry Candy) *hld up: hdwy over 3f out: sn rdn: no further imp tl kpt on ins fnl f: wnt 4th towards fin* **6/1**[3]

0466 **5** *nk* **Talqaa**[55] 3533 3-9-1 **62**........................ SilvestreDeSousa 4 58
(Mick Channon) *w ldr: rdn and ev ch over 2f out tl jst ins fnl f: sn no ex* **8/1**

4010 **6** *¾* **Commandingpresence (USA)**[9] 5104 7-9-12 **69**......... KieranO'Neill 2 63
(John Bridger) *led: rdn over 2f out: hdd ent fnl f: no ex fnl 120yds* **12/1**

0330 **7** *½* **Catalinas Diamond (IRE)**[9] 5104 5-9-6 **63**.............(t) FergusSweeney 6 56
(Pat Murphy) *cl up: rdn over 2f out: kpt chsng ldrs tl no ex fnl 120yds* **17/2**

320- **8** *6* **Dawn Catcher**[344] 5940 3-9-5 **66**........................ GeorgeBaker 5 38
(Geoffrey Deacon) *stdd s: t.k.h: rdn to chse ldrs wl over 1f out: wknd ent fnl f* **25/1**

1m 14.9s (0.10) **Going Correction** -0.225s/f (Firm)
WFA 3 from 5yo+ 4lb **8** Ran SP% **117.4**
Speed ratings (Par 100): **90,88,85,85,84 83,83,75**
toteswingers 1&2 £3.60, 1&3 £3.20, 2&3 £2.20 CSF £27.39 CT £58.40 TOTE £6.50: £2.10, £1.60, £1.20; EX 28.00 Trifecta £76.50 Pool: £2,201.41 - 21.56 winning units..
Owner Prof C D Green **Bred** Prof C Green **Trained** Upper Lambourn, Berks

FOCUS
The front pair drew clear against the far rail late on in what was a modest fillies' handicap. A small personal-best from the winner with the runner-up close to form.

5448 KEVIN HALL & PAT BOAKES MEMORIAL H'CAP 1m 6f 21y
5:00 (5:00) (Class 4) (0-85,84) 3-Y-O **£4,851** (£1,443; £721; £360)

Form RPR

4304 **1** **Sizzler**[21] 4681 3-9-1 **78**........................ JimCrowley 3 93
(Ralph Beckett) *mde all: rdn 3 l clr ent fnl f: styd on strly* **5/1**

3110 **2** *7* **Lion Beacon**[42] 3982 3-9-6 **83**........................ PatDobbs 1 89
(Amanda Perrett) *lw: hld up bhd ldrs: tk clsr order 4f out: sn rdn: wnt 3rd over 2f out: styd on to go 2nd jst ins fnl f: no ch w wnr* **10/3**[3]

-111 **3** *2 ½* **Portrait**[21] 4656 3-9-4 **81**........................ ChrisCatlin 2 84
(Sir Mark Prescott Bt) *trckd wnr: rdn over 3f out: hld over 1f out: no ex whn lost 2nd jst ins fnl f* **11/4**[2]

6216 **4** *2 ¼* **Bee Jay Kay**[13] 4950 3-8-9 **72**........................ AndreaAtzeni 6 72
(Mick Channon) *trckd ldrs: rdn over 3f out: one pce fnl 2f* **7/1**

3522 **5** *6* **Lady Pimpernel**[21] 4681 3-9-3 **80**........................ FergusSweeney 4 72
(Henry Candy) *trckd ldrs: rdn over 3f out: hld 2f out: sn wknd* **5/2**[1]

1525 **6** *6* **Interior Minister**[12] 4980 3-9-7 **84**........................ CathyGannon 5 68
(Jo Hughes) *swtg: trckd ldrs: rdn 3f out: wknd 2f out* **20/1**

3m 2.7s (-4.70) **Going Correction** -0.225s/f (Firm) **6** Ran SP% **112.2**
Speed ratings (Par 102): **104,100,98,97,93 90**
toteswingers 1&2 £2.20, 1&3 £3.50, 2&3 £1.70 CSF £21.79 TOTE £6.80: £2.90, £2.70; EX 24.30 Trifecta £129.30 Pool: £1,885.01 - 10.93 winning units..
Owner Heseltine, Henley & Jones **Bred** Newsells Park Stud **Trained** Kimpton, Hants

FOCUS
A decent staying handicap for 3-y-os. The winner is rated in line with his previous form but could be worth more at face value.
T/Plt: £28.00 to a £1 stake. Pool: £49,921.85 - 1,298.79 winning units T/Qpdt: £10.40 to a £1 stake. Pool: £3,452.27 - 245.54 winning units TM

5449 - 5452a (Foreign Racing) - See Raceform Interactive

5206 LEOPARDSTOWN (L-H)
Thursday, August 15

OFFICIAL GOING: Good (good to firm in places) changing to good after race 2 (5.50) changing to good (good to yielding in places) after race 3 (6.20)

5453a DESMOND STKS (GROUP 3) 1m
7:25 (7:25) 3-Y-O+ **£31,707** (£9,268; £4,390; £1,463)

RPR

1 **Gordon Lord Byron (IRE)**[11] 5040 5-9-9 114............ JohnnyMurtagh 2 108+
(T Hogan, Ire) *hld up towards rr: tk clsr order in 5th 1/2-way: nt clr run bhd horses into st: sn rdn in 4th between horses and clsd u.p ins fnl f to ld fnl strides* **4/9**[1]

2 *nk* **Ansgar (IRE)**[16] 4869 5-9-9 105........................(t) RoryCleary 1 107
(Sabrina J Harty, Ire) *prom: pushed along on inner to sn ld: over 1 l clr 1/2-way: rdn fr over 2f out and sn strly pressed: jnd wl ins fnl f and hdd fnl strides* **25/1**

3 *shd* **Leitir Mor (IRE)**[4] 5314 3-9-5 109........................(t) RonanWhelan 3 109+
(J S Bolger, Ire) *w.w: cl 6th 1/2-way: pushed along on outer into st and clsd to chal ins fnl f: ev ch on terms fnl 100yds: hdd cl home* **7/1**[2]

4 *2 ¾* **Custom Cut (IRE)**[9] 5114 4-9-12 109........................(p) DannyGrant 5 103
(George J Kent, Ire) *chsd ldrs: cl 3rd 1/2-way: rdn 2f out and sn no imp on ldrs: no ex over 1f out* **14/1**

5 *1 ½* **Dont Bother Me (IRE)**[57] 3455 3-9-2 102........................ ShaneFoley 9 96
(Niall Moran, Ire) *led early tl settled bhd ldr in 2nd: rdn into st and sn no imp: dropped to 5th jst ins fnl f: one pce towards fin* **11/1**[3]

6 *¾* **One Spirit (IRE)**[340] 6079 5-9-6 103........................ NGMcCullagh 6 92
(F Dunne, Ire) *chsd ldrs: cl 4th 1/2-way: rdn over 2f out and sn no ex u.p: dropped to 6th ent fnl f: kpt on one pce* **7/1**[2]

7 *2 ½* **Royal Blue Star (IRE)**[9] 5114 5-9-6 97........................(b) ConnorKing 7 87
(Mrs John Harrington, Ire) *s.i.s and racd in rr: rdn and no imp fr 3f out: one pce fnl 2f* **12/1**

1m 38.74s (-2.46) **Going Correction** -0.025s/f (Good)
WFA 3 from 4yo+ 7lb **7** Ran SP% **120.8**
Speed ratings: **111,110,110,107,106 105,103**
CSF £17.92 TOTE £1.50: £1.50, £8.10; DF 35.10.
Owner Dr Cyrus Poonawalla & Morgan J Cahalan **Bred** Roland H Alder **Trained** Nenagh, Co Tipperary
■ Stewards' Enquiry : Rory Cleary three-day ban: used whip with excessive frequency (Aug 29,31,Sep 2)

FOCUS
The standard for this Group 3 is set through the second and third.

5454 - 5459a (Foreign Racing) - See Raceform Interactive

5313 DEAUVILLE (R-H)
Thursday, August 15

OFFICIAL GOING: Turf: good; fibresand: standard

5460a PRIX DE LA VALLEE D'AUGE (LISTED RACE) (2YO) (TURF) 5f
1:50 (1:52) 2-Y-O **£22,357** (£8,943; £6,707; £4,471; £2,235)

RPR

1 **Shamshon (IRE)**[21] 4680 2-9-0 0........................ FrankieDettori 8 102
(Richard Hannon) *dwlt: towards rr on outer early: stdy hdwy fr over 3f out: rdn to chal over 1f out: drvn to ld ins fnl 100yds and asserted: pushed out towards fin* **9/5**[1]

2 *¾* **Aventure Love (FR)**[30] 4397 2-8-10 0........................(p) ThierryJarnet 9 95
(M Gentile, France) **12/1**

3 *nk* **Muharaaj (IRE)**[25] 4572 2-9-0 0........................ AntoineHamelin 3 98
(Matthieu Palussiere, France) **7/2**[3]

4 *½* **Here's Johnny (USA)** 2-9-0 0........................(b) DFlores 10 96
(Wesley A Ward, U.S.A) **5/2**[2]

5 *2 ½* **Quiz Evolution (ITY)**[46] 3880 2-9-0 0........................ DarioVargiu 5 87
(B Grizzetti, Italy) **30/1**

6 *¾* **Winshine (FR)**[30] 4397 2-8-10 0........................ Pierre-CharlesBoudot 2 81
(J-M Capitte, France) **30/1**

7 *¾* **Quatuor (IRE)**[34] 4248 2-8-10 0........................ RichardKingscote 7 78
(Tom Dascombe) *pressed ldr on outer: rdn 2f out: lost pl over 1f out: sn no ex and btn: fdd* **33/1**

8 *8* **Easy Risk (FR)**[37] 2-8-10 0........................ ChristopheSoumillon 4 49
(F Chappet, France) **9/1**

9 *¾* **Stay Tuned (ITY)** 2-8-10 0........................ UmbertoRispoli 6 47
(Jessica Lari, Italy) **28/1**

57.75s (0.25) **9** Ran SP% **117.0**
WIN (incl. 1 euro stake): 2.80. PLACES: 1.50, 2.00, 1.50. DF: 18.00. SF: 20.80.
Owner HE Sh Joaan Bin Hamad Al Thani **Bred** Stonethorn Stud Farms Ltd **Trained** East Everleigh, Wilts

5461a PRIX DE LIEUREY (GROUP 3) (3YO FILLIES) (TURF) 1m (R)
2:20 (2:21) 3-Y-O **£32,520** (£13,008; £9,756; £6,504; £3,252)

RPR

1 **Zibelina (IRE)**[20] 4705 3-8-11 0........................ MickaelBarzalona 10 107
(Charlie Appleby) *t.k.h: prom on outer: rdn 2f out: led over 1f out: r.o: drvn out and a doing enough* **3/1**[2]

2 *nk* **Table Ronde (IRE)**[46] 3877 3-8-11 0........................ ChristopheSoumillon 9 106
(J-C Rouget, France) *t.k.h: midfield on outer: rdn over 1f out: r.o and wnt 2nd ins fnl 100yds: clsng on wnr at fin* **6/1**[3]

3 *1 ¼* **Siyenica (FR)**[21] 4700 3-8-11 0........................ Christophe-PatriceLemaire 11 103
(A De Royer-Dupre, France) *stdd and hld up towards rr on outer: rdn over 1f out: r.o and wnt 3rd cl home: nrst fin* **11/4**[1]

4 *½* **Belonging**[46] 3877 3-8-11 0........................ MaximeGuyon 12 102
(A Fabre, France) *hld up in last pair: rdn 2f out: swtchd lft over 1f out: r.o to go 4th cl home: nrst fin* **12/1**

5 *snk* **Mayyadah (IRE)**[18] 4817 3-8-11 0........................ ThierryJarnet 7 102
(F Head, France) *stdd and hld up in last: rdn over 1f out: r.o down wd outside and wnt 5th fnl strides: nrst fin* **8/1**

6 *snk* **What A Name (IRE)**[74] 2906 3-9-2 0........................ UmbertoRispoli 4 106
(M Delzangles, France) *midfield in tch on outer: rdn 2f out: r.o but dropped to 6th fnl strides* **6/1**[3]

7 *nk* **More Than Sotka (FR)**[21] 4700 3-8-11 0........................ FrankieDettori 2 101?
(Matthieu Palussiere, France) *trckd ldr: rdn to cl over 2f out: 2nd and ev ch ent fnl f: kpt on tl no ex ins fnl 100yds: fdd and dropped to 7th* **25/1**

8 *1 ¼* **Spinacre (IRE)**[39] 4105 3-8-11 0........................ GeraldMosse 3 98
(P Bary, France) *midfield in tch on inner: rdn 2f out: kpt on same pce and nvr threatened* **16/1**

9 *¾* **Baie D'Honneur (FR)**[71] 3008 3-8-11 0........................ IoritzMendizabal 6 96
(D De Watrigant, France) *midfield on inner: rdn 2f out: kpt on steadily but nvr threatened* **25/1**

10 *3 ½* **Indigo (FR)**[56] 3521 3-8-11 0........................(b) OlivierPeslier 8 88
(C Ferland, France) *hld up towards rr on inner: rdn 2f out: sn outpcd and btn: nvr a factor* **12/1**

11 *1 ½* **Askania Nova (IRE)**[28] 3-8-11 0........................ AntoineHamelin 1 84
(A De Royer-Dupre, France) *prom on inner: rdn 2f out: sn no ex and btn: steadily fdd and dropped to rr* **25/1**

12 *3 ½* **Shenliyka (FR)**[21] 4700 3-8-11 0........................ NJeanpierre 5 76
(A De Royer-Dupre, France) *led: 4 l ahd 3f out: rdn and clsd down fr 2f out: hdd over 1f out: qckly btn and eased: fdd and dropped to last* **66/1**

1m 40.91s (0.11) **12** Ran SP% **125.6**
WIN (incl. 1 euro stake): 3.60. PLACES: 1.60, 1.50, 1.30. DF: 9.60. SF: 22.70.
Owner Godolphin **Bred** Darley **Trained** Newmarket, Suffolk

5462a PRIX GUILLAUME D'ORNANO HARAS DU LOGIS SAINT-GERMAIN (GROUP 2) (3YO) (TURF) 1m 2f
2:55 (2:56) 3-Y-O **£185,365** (£71,544; £34,146; £22,764; £11,382)

RPR

1 **Vancouverite**[24] 4600 3-9-2 0........................ Pierre-CharlesBoudot 4 118+
(A Fabre, France) *prom on inner: swtchd lft and rdn over 1f out: r.o to chal ent fnl f: sn led and qckd clr: pushed out towards fin: readily* **5/1**[3]

2 *1 ¼* **Pilote (IRE)**[25] 4573 3-9-2 0........................ FlavienPrat 8 115+
(A Fabre, France) *hld up in last trio on inner: rdn 2f out: swtchd lft and nt clr run over 1f out: swtchd bk ins and r.o to take 2nd ins fnl 100yds: no real imp on wnr* **18/1**

3 *½* **Zhiyi (USA)**[41] 4043 3-9-2 0........................ ThierryThulliez 1 114+
(P Bary, France) *dwlt: qckly rcvrd and settled in midfield on inner: looking for room 2f out: swtchd lft and rdn over 1f out: hanging u.p but sn stened out and r.o to take 3rd cl home* **12/1**

4 *nk* **Silasol (IRE)**[60] 3385 3-8-13 0........................ OlivierPeslier 9 110+
(C Laffon-Parias, France) *hld up in last: rdn 2f out: styd on down wd outside and wnt 4th cl home: nvr nrr* **11/2**

5 *½* **Havana Gold (IRE)**[46] 3876 3-9-2 0........................ MickaelBarzalona 3 112+
(Richard Hannon) *prom on outer: rdn over 2f out: cl 3rd and ev ch ent fnl f: sn outpcd by wnr: kpt on tl no ex towards fin and dropped to 5th* **11/4**[2]

6 *½* **Buckwheat**[25] 4573 3-9-2 0........................ MaximeGuyon 6 111+
(A Fabre, France) *hld up in last trio on outer: rdn over 2f out: styd on steadily and wnt 6th post but nvr threatened* **16/1**

The Form Book Flat, Raceform Ltd, Compton, RG20 6NL.

7 hd **Morandi (FR)**74 2907 3-9-2 0 ChristopheSoumillon 5 111+
(J-C Rouget, France) *chsd clr ldr: clsd 2f out: rdn to ld over 1f out: strly pressed ent fnl f and sn hdd: kpt on tl no ex ins fnl 100yds: fdd and dropped to 7th post* **6/4**1

8 4 **Superplex (FR)**45 3911 3-9-2 0 FrankieDettori 2 103+
(M Figge, Germany) *midfield on outer: rdn over 2f out: kpt on tl no ex and btn ent fnl f: fdd* **16/1**

9 6 **Plaine Monceau (FR)**10 3-8-13 0 AntoineCoutier 7 88?
(D Henderson, France) *led and sn clr: 10 l ahd 5f out: steadily diminishing advantage fr 4f out: rdn and hdd over 1f out: no ex and btn: fdd and dropped to last ins fnl f: eased* **100/1**

2m 4.22s (-5.98) **9** Ran SP% **124.4**
WIN (incl. 1 euro stake): 4.50 (Vancouverite coupled with Buckwheat). PLACES: 2.30, 4.20, 3.50. DF: 35.90. SF: 66.70.
Owner Godolphin SNC **Bred** Darley Stud Management Co Ltd **Trained** Chantilly, France

5463a PRIX MICHEL HOUYVET (LISTED RACE) (3YO) (TURF) 1m 7f
3:25 (3:25) 3-Y-0 **£22,357** (£8,943; £6,707; £4,471; £2,235)

RPR

1 **Destruct**64 3-8-11 0 MaximeGuyon 5 110
(A Fabre, France) **8/5**1

2 1 1/2 **Mohicane (FR)**31 3-8-8 0 MickaelForest 2 105
(W Walton, France) **39/1**

3 3 **Green Byron (FR)**60 3386 3-8-11 0 IoritzMendizabal 7 104
(J-M Lefebvre, France) **19/1**

4 nk **London Bridge (USA)**33 4279 3-8-11 0 GeraldMosse 4 104
(Jo Hughes) *led: jnd 3f out: rdn 2f out: hdd over 1f out: sn no ex: fdd and dropped to 4th ins fnl f* **7/1**

5 nk **Golden Bowl (FR)**60 3386 3-8-11 0 ThierryJarnet 1 103
(J Bertran De Balanda, France) **18/1**

6 1 1/4 **Park Reel (FR)**33 4325 3-8-11 0 GregoryBenoist 3 102
(E Lellouche, France) **3/1**2

7 1/2 **Ruggero**89 3-8-11 0 Pierre-CharlesBoudot 8 101
(A Fabre, France) *dropped in fr wdst draw and hld up in last pair on outer: pushed along 5f out: rdn in last 2f out: plugged on but nvr a factor* **25/1**

8 1 1/2 **Gianni (FR)**36 3-8-11 0 (b) OlivierPeslier 6 99
(C Ferland, France) **33/10**3

3m 9.17s (-9.93) **8** Ran SP% **115.8**
WIN (incl. 1 euro stake): 2.60. PLACES: 1.70, 5.00, 3.70. DF: 31.40. SF: 41.70.
Owner K Abdullah **Bred** Juddmonte Farms Ltd **Trained** Chantilly, France

POMPADOUR (L-H)
Thursday, August 15
OFFICIAL GOING: Turf: good

5464a PRIX MARQUISE DE POMPADOUR (CONDITIONS) (4YO+) (LADY AMATEURS) (TURF) 1m 3f 110y
2:30 (12:00) 4-Y-0+ **£2,845** (£1,138; £853; £569; £284)

RPR

1 **Sundream (GER)**51 5-9-4 0 MlleBarbaraGuenet 5 67
(G Macaire, France) **6/4**1

2 nk **Thomaraz (FR)**194 498 6-9-13 0 (b) MlleMarie-PierreGuy 9 75
(P Sogorb, France)

3 12 **Mezzotinto (FR)**42 6-9-2 0 (p) MlleLinePayet-Burin(4) 3 49
(P Le Gal, France)

4 2 **Irons On Fire (USA)**28 4467 5-9-6 0 ow6 (p) MlleCharleyLauffer(4) 1 50
(Gay Kelleway)

5 6 **Adena (FR)**243 6-9-7 0 MlleJustineMercier 4 37
(T Mercier, France)

6 3 **Portland Stone**1525 9-9-0 0 (b) MlleAnnabelleFreby(4) 2 30
(O Auchere, France)

7 6 **Demon Express (FR)**1117 6-9-4 0 MmeMartineDefontaine 8 20
(Mme A-L Guildoux, France)

8 dist **Voix Des Aigles (FR)**465 5-9-4 0 (p) MlleIngridGrard 7
(E Daure, France)

9 4 **Dreamlim (FR)** 4-9-0 0 (p) MmePaulineAntoine(4) 6
(Mme A-L Guildoux, France)

2m 30.72s (150.72) **9** Ran SP% **40.0**
WIN (incl. 1 euro stake): 2.50. PLACES: 1.20, 1.30, 1.90..
Owner Bernd Glutsch **Bred** Gestut Graditz **Trained** Les Mathes, France

SAN SEBASTIAN (R-H)
Thursday, August 15
OFFICIAL GOING: Turf: good

5465a PREMIO COPA DE ORO DE SAN SEBASTIAN (LISTED RACE) (3YO+) (TURF) 1m 4f
5:30 (12:00) 3-Y-0+ **£32,520** (£13,008; £6,504; £3,252)

RPR

1 **Abdel (FR)**300 7234 5-9-4 0 VJanacek 8 100
(J-M Osorio, Spain) **76/10**

2 1 1/4 **Celtic Rock** 4-9-4 0 J-LMartinez 4 98
(J C Fernandez, Spain) **6/4**1

3 1 3/4 **Avante**46 4-9-4 0 JeremyCrocquevieille 5 95
(J-M Osorio, Spain) **13/1**

4 2 1/4 **Esles (FR)**24 4601 5-9-4 0 AnthonyCrastus 9 91
(C Laffon-Parias, France) **3/1**2

5 3 3/4 **Australia Day (IRE)**26 4029 10-9-4 0 OscarUrbina 2 85
(Paul Webber) **37/1**

6 1 **Pepito Grillo**165 5-9-4 0 (b) Francois-XavierBertras 7 84
(L A Urbano-Grajales, France) **43/10**3

7 6 1/4 **Phuket (SPA)**365 5252 4-9-4 0 JHorcajada 1 74
(A Remolina Diaz, Spain) **34/1**

8 7 **Sleeping Wan**298 3-8-8 0 MlleGloriaMaderoParayre 3 64
(Mlle A Imaz-Ceca, France) **11/1**

9 13 **Roatan**154 8-9-4 0 IBorrego 6 42
(Mlle A Imaz-Ceca, France) **55/1**

2m 25.95s (145.95)
WFA 3 from 4yo+ 11lb **9** Ran SP% **118.2**
DIVIDENDS (all including 1 euro stakes): WIN 8.60; PLACE 1.70, 1.10, 1.90; DF 10.30; SF 30.90.
Owner Duke Of Alburquerque **Bred** Duc D'Alburquerque **Trained** Spain

5083 CATTERICK (L-H)
Friday, August 16
OFFICIAL GOING: Good (good to firm in places; 8.2)
Wind: moderate 1/2 against Weather: fine

5466 PIN POINT RECRUITMENT AMATEUR RIDERS' H'CAP 1m 3f 214y
5:40 (5:40) (Class 5) (0-75,74) 3-Y-0+ **£2,807** (£870; £435; £217) **Stalls** Centre

Form RPR

6004 1 **Tinseltown**7 5222 7-10-4 **64** MissADeniel 1 71
(Brian Rothwell) *mde all: jnd over 1f out: kpt on wl* **16/1**

0040 2 1 **Al Furat (USA)**14 4951 5-9-5 **56** 1 MrsVDavies(5) 5 61
(Ron Barr) *trckd ldrs: t.k.h: 2nd over 2f out: upsides over 1f out: kpt on same pce last 50yds* **22/1**

0622 3 1/2 **Gran Maestro (USA)**3 5367 4-11-0 **74** (b) MissSBrotherton 8 79+
(Ruth Carr) *hld up in mid-div: hdwy and swtchd rt 2f out: styd on wl ins fnl f* **11/4**1

0635 4 nk **Brunello**14 4951 5-9-13 **59** (p) MissHBethell 4 63
(Philip Kirby) *chsd ldrs: rdn and edgd rt over 1f out: kpt on ins fnl f* **15/2**

45-5 5 nk **Hyperlink (IRE)**11 5065 4-10-5 **70** MrAlexFerguson(5) 10 74+
(Michael Bell) *stdd s: hld up in rr: detached last over 3f out: hdwy on ins over 2f out: styd on same pce ins fnl f* **8/1**

1400 6 1 1/4 **Mohawk Ridge**19 4804 7-10-7 **74** MrPDennis(7) 7 76
(Michael Dods) *in rr: hdwy on outer over 3f out: chsng ldrs over 2f out: one pce* **20/1**

3644 7 1 1/2 **Dark Dune (IRE)**10 5086 5-10-7 **72** MrWEasterby(5) 2 71
(Tim Easterby) *hld up in mid-div: hdwy over 2f out: one pce: sddle slipped* **9/2**2

3534 8 2 1/2 **Call Of Duty (IRE)**11 5052 8-9-9 **60** MissEButterworth(5) 9 55
(Dianne Sayer) *mid-div: hdwy on outside over 4f out: 3rd over 2f out: wknd fnl f* **18/1**

3051 9 1 1/4 **Royal Sea (IRE)**7 5222 4-9-8 **57** (be) MissMMullineaux(3) 6 50
(Michael Mullineaux) *s.i.s: sme hdwy on inner over 2f out: wknd over 1f out* **10/1**

4563 10 1/2 **Pertuis (IRE)**9 5144 7-9-13 **64** (v1) MissBeckySmith(5) 11 56
(Micky Hammond) *hld up in rr: effrt over 2f out: wknd appr fnl f* **7/1**3

3524 11 16 **Keep It Cool (IRE)**20 4759 9-10-5 **72** MrSMurray(7) 3 39
(David O'Meara) *chsd wnr: lost pl over 2f out: sn bhd: t.o* **16/1**

2m 40.47s (1.57) **Going Correction** +0.10s/f (Good) **11** Ran SP% **115.5**
Speed ratings (Par 103): **98,97,97,96,96 95,94,93,92,91 81**
toteswingers 1&2 £39.10, 1&3 £12.80, 2&3 £20.30 CSF £316.63 CT £1261.95 TOTE £27.30: £5.70, £6.60, £2.50; EX 401.50 Trifecta £801.10 Part won. Pool: £1068.21 - 0.11 winning units..
Owner Tony Arnott **Bred** Biddestone Stud **Trained** Norton, N Yorks

FOCUS
Races on Round course increased in distance by 12yds. The pace wasn't great, which helped the front-running winner, and the first five were covered by barely two lengths. The runner-up is rated to his recent best, backed up by the fourth.

5467 OOPS A DAISY FLORISTS (S) STKS 7f
6:10 (6:11) (Class 6) 2-Y-0 **£2,385** (£704; £352) **Stalls** Centre

Form RPR

0650 1 **Mount Cheiron (USA)**14 4964 2-8-11 63 GrahamLee 5 60
(Alan Berry) *in rr: hdwy on ins over 2f out: swtchd rt 1f out: led last 100yds: hld on toward fin* **14/1**

5056 2 1 **Chilly In Rio (IRE)**15 4910 2-8-6 45 PatrickMathers 3 52
(William Muir) *led early: chsd ldrs: cl 2nd 100yds out: no ex* **40/1**

1434 3 nk **Ding Ding**4 5347 2-8-3 56 RaulDaSilva(3) 4 51
(Mick Channon) *sn drvn along and outpcd in rr: hung rt bnd 3f out: hdwy on outside over 1f out: styd on wl towards fin* **11/4**2

4002 4 hd **Midnight Muscida (IRE)**6 5289 2-8-6 58 (b) DavidAllan 6 51
(Tim Easterby) *sn led: hdd 3f out: kpt on same pce ins fnl f* **9/1**

4320 5 1 1/2 **Sakhalin Star (IRE)**9 5136 2-8-11 64 MichaelO'Connell 2 52
(John Quinn) *w ldrs: led 3f out: hdd ins fnl f: wknd nr fin* **13/8**1

4005 6 17 **Patisserie**11 5066 2-8-6 54 (b) PJMcDonald 8 1
(Ann Duffield) *mid-div: sme hdwy over 2f out: sn hung rt and lost pl* **16/1**

03 7 8 **Artistic Acclaim (IRE)**23 4617 2-8-6 0 DuranFentiman 7
(John Weymes) *dwlt: sn chsng ldrs: lost pl over 3f out: sn bhd* **66/1**

156 U **Cascadia (IRE)**7 5235 2-8-0 62 ow1 RobJFitzpatrick(7) 1
(Mrs K Burke) *rdr lost iron s: sn stmbld and uns rdr* **7/2**3

1m 28.43s (1.43) **Going Correction** +0.10s/f (Good) **8** Ran SP% **113.5**
Speed ratings (Par 92): **95,93,93,93,91 72,63,**
.Mount Cheiron was bought by Mr Arthur Slack for £4,500\n\x\x Sakhalin Star was claimed by Mr Richard Guest for £5,000
Owner A B Parr **Bred** Swettenham Stud **Trained** Cockerham, Lancs

FOCUS
A few of these had some reasonable form to their name, but the first two home hadn't done much beforehand. The form is modest but probably par for the grade.

5468 ROCKLIFFE HALL HOTEL AND SPA NURSERY H'CAP 5f 212y
6:40 (6:40) (Class 4) (0-85,81) 2-Y-0 **£5,175** (£1,540; £769; £384) **Stalls** Low

Form RPR

5220 1 **Blockade (IRE)**27 4528 2-9-7 **81** GrahamLee 5 92
(James Tate) *trckd ldrs: led 2f out: styd on strly to forge clr fnl f* **9/2**2

0231 2 3 1/4 **Kickboxer (IRE)**15 4912 2-8-13 **73** GrahamGibbons 6 74
(Mick Channon) *chsd ldrs: upsides 2f out: styd on same pce fnl f* **9/2**2

601 3 1 1/2 **Local Flier**17 4847 2-8-2 **65** RaulDaSilva(3) 8 61
(Brian Ellison) *led: hdd over 4f out: styd on same pce over 1f out* **8/1**3

3143 4 3/4 **Hello Beautiful (IRE)**20 4783 2-8-9 **69** PJMcDonald 3 63
(Ann Duffield) *chsd ldrs: hmpd bnd over 4f out: kpt on same pce over 1f out* **8/1**3

1651 5 1 3/4 **Money Team (IRE)**37 4156 2-9-6 **80** AdamBeschizza 4 68
(Philip Kirby) *chsd ldrs: drvn over 2f out: one pce over 1f out* **7/2**1

4340 6 1 3/4 **Ixelles Diamond (IRE)**14 4948 2-8-8 **68** PatrickMathers 7 51
(Richard Fahey) *s.i.s: hung rt and reminders bnd over 4f out: sme hdwy over 2f out: hung lft over 1f out: nvr a threat* **10/1**

0514 **7** *hd* **Overstep (IRE)**[20] 4768 2-9-6 **80** .... JoeFanning 9 62
(Mark Johnston) *wnt rt s: sn w ldrs: led over 4f out: hdd 2f out: wknd fnl f* **12/1**

1305 **8** *6* **Lorimer's Lot (IRE)**[14] 4965 2-9-1 **75** .... DuranFentiman 1 38
(Tim Walford) *mid-div: n.m.r and lost pl bnd over 4f out: rdn over 2f out: bhd over 1f out* **8/1**[3]

0004 **9** *1 1/2* **Lady Liz**[53] 3624 2-7-13 **62** .... DeclanCannon(3) 2 20
(George Moore) *sn drvn along in rr: lost pl over 3f out: sn bhd* **16/1**

1m 13.85s (0.25) **Going Correction** +0.10s/f (Good) **9** Ran SP% **114.6**
Speed ratings (Par 96): **102,97,95,94,92 90,89,81,79**
toteswingers 1&2 £4.20, 1&3 £4.40, 2&3 £10.90 CSF £24.86 CT £156.28 TOTE £4.00: £1.50, £2.50, £2.20; EX 24.20 Trifecta £127.50 Pool: £997.54 - 5.86 winning units..
Owner Saeed Manana **Bred** Patrick A Cassidy **Trained** Newmarket, Suffolk
■ Stewards' Enquiry : Raul Da Silva two-day ban: careless riding (Aug 30-31)

FOCUS
This was a decent nursery, in which the winner looked particularly useful. The form should prove reasonable.

5469 DAWN CAROLINE PHOTOGRAPHY MAIDEN STKS — 1m 3f 214y
7:10 (7:11) (Class 5) 3-Y-O+ **£2,911** (£866; £432; £216) **Stalls** Centre

Form — RPR

2 **1** **Commissioned (IRE)**[46] 3902 3-9-2 0 .... JoeFanning 9 99+
(Mark Johnston) *trckd ldrs: 2nd over 3f out: pushed into ld over 2f out: wl clr over 1f out: heavily eased* **10/11**[1]

3-3 **2** *11* **Omnipresent**[74] 2938 3-9-2 0 .... GrahamLee 6 78
(Sir Michael Stoute) *trckd ldrs after 1f: led over 3f out: rdn and hdd over 2f out: no ch w wnr* **7/4**[2]

23 **3** *14* **Saffron Town (IRE)**[19] 4805 4-9-12 0 ....(t) RussKennemore 3 56
(Alan Swinbank) *hld up in rr: hdwy 7f out: 4th and wl outpcd over 3f out: one pce 3rd over 2f out* **4/1**[3]

4 *3 1/4* **Razera (IRE)** 3-9-2 0 .... MichaelO'Connell 8 51
(John Quinn) *dwlt: t.k.h in rr: 5th and wl outpcd over 3f out: one pce and modest 4th over 1f out* **16/1**

00/5 **5** *10* **Eila Wheeler**[29] 4445 6-9-0 42 .... DavidParkes(7) 1 30
(Maurice Barnes) *mid-div: hopelessly outpcd and lost pl 5f out* **100/1**

0 **6** *4* **Roycano**[10] 5110 3-9-2 0 .... GrahamGibbons 10 28
(Michael Easterby) *led: drvn and hdd over 3f out: wknd over 2f out* **33/1**

0/00 **7** *24* **Regy From Sedgy**[56] 3542 6-9-9 30 ....(p) NeilFarley(3) 7
(Frederick Watson) *in rr: drvn over 5f out: sn lost pl and bhd: t.o 2f out* **100/1**

00 **8** *3/4* **Jimsneverright**[22] 4667 5-9-5 0 .... JordanNason(7) 2
(Geoffrey Harker) *t.k.h in rr: stmbld bnd after 3f: lost pl over 4f out: sn wl bhd: t.o whn eased over 1f out* **100/1**

9 *14* **Zorro's Blade**[69] 5-9-7 0 ....(p) SladeO'Hara(5) 5
(Michael Mullineaux) *dwlt: in rr: reminders and lost pl 8f out: sn bhd: t.o 5f out* **66/1**

0-0 **10** *95* **Toepaz**[19] 4805 4-9-9 0 .... DeclanCannon(3) 4
(Alan Kirtley) *t.k.h: trckd ldrs: lost pl 5f out: sn t.o: virtually p.u: eventually completed* **100/1**

2m 37.31s (-1.59) **Going Correction** +0.10s/f (Good)
WFA 3 from 4yo+ 10lb **10** Ran SP% **123.0**
Speed ratings (Par 103): **109,101,92,90,83 80,64,64,55,**
toteswingers 1&2 £1.10, 1&3 £1.50, 2&3 £2.00 CSF £2.96 TOTE £1.40: £1.10, £1.10, £1.20; EX 4.70 Trifecta £9.80 Pool: £1797.12 - 136.33 winning units..
Owner Sheikh Hamdan Bin Mohammed Al Maktoum **Bred** Kilfrush Stud **Trained** Middleham Moor, N Yorks
■ Stewards' Enquiry : David Parkes two-day ban: careless riding (Aug 30-31)

FOCUS
The first three were strung out like steeplechasers and the others were all big prices, so the race has a hollow look to it. The winner impressed in what has been a reasonable maiden in earlier years, so with the time good he could prove a useful handicapper at least.

5470 YORKSHIRE-OUTDOORS.CO.UK H'CAP — 5f
7:45 (7:45) (Class 6) (0-65,71) 3-Y-O+ **£2,385** (£704; £352) **Stalls** Low

Form — RPR

300 **1** **Lord Buffhead**[18] 4840 4-8-12 **53** ....(v) RobbieFitzpatrick 2 62
(Richard Guest) *chsd ldrs: led over 1f out: hld on towards fin* **16/1**

0456 **2** *nk* **Commanche Raider (IRE)**[19] 4814 6-9-10 **65** .... GrahamLee 8 73
(Michael Dods) *in rr: hdwy far side 2f out: drvn to chse ldrs 1f out: styd on to take 2nd towards fin* **12/1**

5062 **3** *3/4* **Prigsnov Dancer (IRE)**[10] 5085 8-8-0 **48** oh1 ow2.(p) JordanNason(7) 7 53
(Deborah Sanderson) *chsd ldrs: upsides over 1f out: kpt on same pce last 50yds* **8/1**

6656 **4** *3/4* **Lady Poppy**[26] 4558 3-9-5 **62** .... PJMcDonald 1 65
(George Moore) *w ldrs: kpt on same pce last 150yds* **15/2**[3]

4121 **5** *3/4* **Ingenti**[1] 5422 5-9-9 **71** 6ex .... KevinStott(7) 5 71
(Christopher Wilson) *chsd ldrs: drvn over 2f out: kpt on same pce fnl f* **2/1**[1]

0665 **6** *nk* **Rutterkin (USA)**[11] 5047 5-8-4 **48** .... JulieBurke(3) 10 47
(James Moffatt) *mid-div: hdwy 2f out: one pce fnl f* **18/1**

0450 **7** *nk* **Windforpower (IRE)**[23] 4621 3-8-9 **52** ....(p) JoeFanning 12 50
(Tracy Waggott) *hld up in rr: edgd lft over 2f out: hdwy on inner over 1f out: sn chsng ldrs: n.m.r and eased clsng stages* **16/1**

3426 **8** *1/2* **Perfect Words (IRE)**[16] 4891 3-9-2 **64** ....(p) ShirleyTeasdale(5) 9 60
(Marjorie Fife) *chsd ldrs: fdd fnl 150yds* **10/1**

0005 **9** *3/4* **Piste**[10] 5085 7-8-5 **46** ....(e) JamesSullivan 13 39
(Tina Jackson) *outpcd and in rr on outer over 3f out: hdwy over 1f out: keeping on at fin* **28/1**

0050 **10** *1 3/4* **Ivestar (IRE)**[11] 5047 8-8-13 **54** ....(v) GrahamGibbons 14 41
(Michael Easterby) *towards rr on outer: nvr a factor* **33/1**

105 **11** *hd* **Choc'A'Moca (IRE)**[16] 4891 6-9-8 **63** ....(v) MickyFenton 15 49
(Paul Midgley) *in rr on outer: sme hdwy 2f out: nvr a factor* **20/1**

3504 **12** *nk* **Wicked Wilma (IRE)**[4] 5336 9-7-13 **47** .... JordanHibberd(7) 3 32
(Alan Berry) *w ldrs: led over 2f out: hdd over 1f out: wknd jst ins fnl f* **10/1**

3146 **13** *2* **Niceonemyson**[2] 5381 4-9-3 **58** .... TomEaves 6 36
(Christopher Wilson) *led tl over 3f out: lost pl 2f out* **7/1**[2]

1m 0.25s (0.45) **Going Correction** +0.175s/f (Good)
WFA 3 from 4yo+ 2lb **13** Ran SP% **122.8**
Speed ratings (Par 101): **103,102,101,100,98 98,97,97,95,93 92,92,89**
toteswingers 1&2 £20.30, 1&3 £26.20, 2&3 £26.90 CSF £196.46 CT £1670.50 TOTE £23.40: £3.80, £4.40, £2.80; EX 284.60 Trifecta £656.10 Part won. Pool: £874.88 - 0.01 winning units..
Owner Mrs Alison Guest **Bred** T K & Mrs P A Knox **Trained** Wetherby, W Yorks

FOCUS
This attracted a line-up with horses rated from 45 to 71 (including a penalty), but it was competitive. The first nine were well bunched at the finish. The form looks straightforward rated around the first three.

5471 RACING AGAIN ON 28TH AUGUST H'CAP — 7f
8:15 (8:17) (Class 6) (0-60,63) 3-Y-O+ **£2,385** (£704; £352) **Stalls** Centre

Form — RPR

2200 **1** **Dhhamaan (IRE)**[14] 4966 8-9-4 **54** ....(b) JamesSullivan 6 63
(Ruth Carr) *mde all: 2 1/2 l clr over 2f out: drvn rt out: hld on towards fin* **22/1**

0004 **2** *1/2* **Thatcherite (IRE)**[26] 4562 5-9-5 **55** ....(t) StephenCraine 5 63+
(Tony Coyle) *hld up in rr: hdwy over 2f out: swtchd ins over 1f out: styd on to take 2 1/2 l 2nd last 100yds: nt quite rch wnr* **8/1**

2350 **3** *1 1/4* **Hoppy's Flyer (FR)**[14] 4967 5-9-9 **59** .... MickyFenton 14 63
(Mark Brisbourne) *swtchd lft after s: mid-div: hdwy on outer over 2f out: edgd lft and tk 3rd last 50yds* **16/1**

0040 **4** *1 1/2* **Star City (IRE)**[32] 4357 4-9-6 **56** ....(p) TomEaves 10 56
(Michael Dods) *chsd wnr: 2nd over 1f out: kpt on same pce* **20/1**

0340 **5** *2 1/2* **Tony Hollis**[8] 5198 5-9-0 **53** .... LMcNiff(3) 3 46
(Karen Tutty) *chsd ldrs: one pce fnl 2f* **33/1**

1000 **6** *nk* **Iggy**[13] 5016 3-9-5 **60** ....(bt[1]) GrahamLee 1 53
(Michael Easterby) *mid-div: hdwy on ins over 2f out: one pce appr fnl f* **9/2**[2]

6460 **7** *nk* **Queens Revenge**[16] 4891 4-9-7 **57** ....(p) DavidAllan 11 49
(Tim Easterby) *s.i.s: in rr: styd on fnl 2f: nt rch ldrs* **14/1**

6550 **8** *1* **Viking Warrior (IRE)**[63] 3286 6-9-4 **59** ....(p) ConnorBeasley(5) 12 48
(Michael Dods) *prom on outer: effrt over 2f out: wknd over 1f out* **16/1**

0440 **9** *1 1/2* **Logans Legend (IRE)**[16] 4891 5-8-13 **54** ....(p) DarylByrne(5) 9 39
(Lawrence Mullaney) *chsd ldrs: wknd over 1f out* **28/1**

1052 **10** *1 1/2* **Jupiter Fidius**[4] 5341 6-9-3 **60** .... GemmaTutty(7) 15 41
(Karen Tutty) *s.i.s: swtchd lft after s: in rr: stl last over 1f out: sme late hdwy on outside: nvr a factor* **6/1**[3]

1006 **11** *2 1/4* **Ptolemy**[18] 4823 4-9-9 **59** .... GrahamGibbons 2 34
(David Barron) *chsd ldrs: drvn over 3f out: wknd over 2f out* **10/1**

1561 **12** *1 3/4* **The Great Gabrial**[7] 5232 4-9-8 **63** 6ex ....(b) GeorgeDowning(5) 8 33
(Ian Williams) *hld up in mid-div: effrt over 2f out: sn wknd* **15/2**

0012 **13** *3/4* **Absolute Diamond**[10] 5089 3-9-3 **58** ....(p) MichaelO'Connell 7 26
(John Quinn) *s.i.s: in rr: lost pl bnd over 4f out: sme hdwy over 2f out: sn wknd* **3/1**[1]

0-4 **14** *3 3/4* **Drive Home (USA)**[114] 1757 6-9-6 **59** .... NeilFarley(3) 4 17
(Noel Wilson) *mid-div: drvn over 3f out: sn lost pl and bhd* **12/1**

1m 27.46s (0.46) **Going Correction** +0.10s/f (Good)
WFA 3 from 4yo+ 5lb **14** Ran SP% **131.1**
Speed ratings (Par 101): **101,100,99,97,94 94,93,92,90,89 86,84,83,79**
toteswingers 1&2 £89.70, 1&3 £74.70, 2&3 £38.30 CSF £197.65 CT £3026.97 TOTE £18.20: £6.00, £6.20, £4.50; EX 384.00 Trifecta £583.70 Part won. Pool: £778.28 - 0.01 winning units..
Owner S B Clark **Bred** D Veitch And Musagd Abo Salim **Trained** Huby, N Yorks

FOCUS
This was a modest handicap, with few of the runners in great form beforehand. The winner is the best guide, rated to this year's form.
T/Plt: £1604.50 to a £1 stake. Pool: £50,774.91 - 23.10 winning units T/Qpdt: £125.20 to a £1 stake. Pool: £5500.97 - 32.50 winning units WG

5032 NEWBURY (L-H)
Friday, August 16

OFFICIAL GOING: Good (6.7)
Wind: Moderate across Weather: White cloud

5472 DON DEADMAN MEMORIAL EUROPEAN BREEDERS' FUND MAIDEN STKS (DIV I) — 7f (S)
1:50 (1:50) (Class 4) 2-Y-O **£4,075** (£1,212; £606; £303) **Stalls** Centre

Form — RPR

1 **God Willing** 2-9-5 0 .... HarryBentley 11 82+
(Ed Dunlop) *str: scope: unrly stalls: sn chasinjg ldrs: wnt 2nd appr fnl f: pushed along to ld finnal 110yds: a doing enough* **6/1**

4 **2** *nk* **Raise Your Gaze**[23] 4640 2-9-5 0 .... AdamKirby 10 81
(Clive Cox) *w'like: led but jnd tl shaklen up and qcknd over 1f out: styd on tl hdd fnl 110yds: nt pce of wnr cl home* **9/2**[3]

0 **3** *3/4* **What About Carlo (FR)**[28] 4483 2-9-5 0 .... TomQueally 7 79
(Eve Johnson Houghton) *unf: swtg: hld up in tch: hdwy over 2f out: styd on to take 3rd fnl 150yds but a hld by ldng duo* **6/1**

4 *1 1/4* **Ehtifaal (IRE)** 2-9-5 0 .... PaulHanagan 9 76+
(William Haggas) *athletic: s.i.s: in rr: drvn 2f out: hdwy fnl f and styd on clsng stages: nt rch ldrs* **8/1**

5 *1 1/2* **Signposted (IRE)** 2-9-5 0 .... DavidProbert 12 72+
(Andrew Balding) *unf: in tch: drvn along over 2f out: styd on again ins fnl f* **25/1**

6 *1* **Alketios (GR)** 2-9-5 0 .... AndreaAtzeni 4 69
(Luca Cumani) *w'like: str: bit bkwd: sn pressing ldr: rdn 2f out: wknd ins fnl f* **25/1**

7 *3/4* **Template (IRE)** 2-9-5 0 .... SeanLevey 2 69+
(Richard Hannon) *str: scope: s.i.s: in rr: rdn over 2f out: styd on ins fnl f* **18/1**

8 *nk* **Eye Contact** 2-9-5 0 .... RyanMoore 8 67+
(Sir Michael Stoute) *w'like: scope: chsd ldrs: rdn 2f out: wknd appr fnl f* **4/1**[2]

065 **9** *1* **Loving Your Work**[20] 4773 2-9-5 0 .... JackMitchell 1 64
(George Baker) *s.i.s: racd w hd high and sme hdwy 2f out: sn drvn and wandered: didn't look keen* **100/1**

10 *3/4* **Pupil (IRE)** 2-9-5 0 .... RichardHughes 6 62
(Richard Hannon) *str: in rr: drvn over 2f out and no imp* **7/2**[1]

11 *shd* **Allegation (FR)** 2-9-0 0 .... TedDurcan 3 57
(David Lanigan) *w'like: strong: pushed along over 2f out: a towards rr* **33/1**

0 **12** *nk* **Ambria's Fury (IRE)**[7] 5244 2-9-5 0 .... CathyGannon 5 61
(Mick Channon) *leggy: chsd ldrs 4f* **100/1**

1m 29.77s (4.07) **Going Correction** +0.10s/f (Good) **12** Ran SP% **118.0**
Speed ratings (Par 96): **80,79,78,77,75 74,73,73,72,71 71,70**
toteswingers 1&2 £9.80, 1&3 £16.00, 2&3 £9.20 CSF £31.76 TOTE £7.50: £2.70, £1.80, £2.10; EX 39.30 Trifecta £123.30 Pool: £801.72 - 4.87 winning units..
Owner Qatar Racing & Essafinaat **Bred** Highbank Stud **Trained** Newmarket, Suffolk

The Form Book Flat, Raceform Ltd, Compton, RG20 6NL.

FOCUS
Races on Round course increased in distance by 8m. This maiden always seems to throw up a newcomer with Group aspirations and this year's first division looks bound to throw up future winners.

5473 DON DEADMAN MEMORIAL EUROPEAN BREEDERS' FUND MAIDEN STKS (DIV II) 7f (S)
2:20 (2:21) (Class 4) 2-Y-O **£4,075** (£1,212; £606; £303) **Stalls** Centre

Form RPR
1 **Barley Mow (IRE)** 2-9-5 0 RichardHughes 4 92+
(Richard Hannon) *str: scope: broke wl: stdd towards rr: hdwy over 2f out: chsd ldr 1f out: drvn and qcknd ins fnl f to ld last strides* **6/4**[1]
2 *nk* **Yuften** 2-9-5 0 KierenFallon 11 91+
(William Haggas) *leggy: athletic: s.i.s: sn in tch: hdwy 3f out: chal 2f out: sn led: kpt on wl fnl f: hdd last strides* **14/1**
3 *4 1/2* **Emef Diamond** 2-9-5 0 TedDurcan 5 78+
(Mick Channon) *w'like: lw: chsd ldrs: drvn and ev ch fr over 2f out: outpcd by ldng duo fnl f* **66/1**
4 *2 1/4* **Marmoom** 2-9-5 0 PatSmullen 6 72+
(Charles Hills) *w'like: str: bit bkwd: s.i.s: in rr: hdwy 2f out: drvn and kpt on fnl f but nvr a threat* **14/1**
3 5 *2* **Glebe Spirit (IRE)**[20] 4773 2-9-5 0 RyanMoore 10 66
(Richard Hannon) *unf: chsd ldrs: drvn and ev ch over 2f out: wknd fnl f* **6/1**[3]
6 *hd* **Zerfaal** 2-9-5 0 PaulHanagan 2 66
(John Gosden) *w'like: str: awkward stalls: in rr: drvn and hdwy over 2f out: sn outpcd* **2/1**[2]
0 7 *1* **Winter Spice (IRE)**[30] 4414 2-9-5 0 AdamKirby 3 63+
(Clive Cox) *w'like: in rr: hdwy over 2f out: wknd over 1f out* **14/1**
8 *2 1/4* **Roskilly (IRE)** 2-9-5 0 DavidProbert 1 58
(Andrew Balding) *w'like: in rr: drvn over 2f out: one pce* **25/1**
00 9 *1/2* **Fiftyshadesfreed (IRE)**[31] 4379 2-9-5 0 SeanLevey 9 56
(George Baker) *w'like: led: jnd over 2f out: hdd sn after and wknd* **100/1**
10 *16* **Cameley Dawn** 2-8-9 0 MatthewLawson[(5)] 7 10
(Malcolm Saunders) *leggy: chsd ldrs: rdn 3f out: wknd qckly over 2f out* **100/1**
11 *3 1/2* **Bold Runner** 2-9-5 0 DougieCostello 8
(Sean Curran) *str: chsd ldrs to 1/2-way* **100/1**

1m 26.71s (1.01) **Going Correction** +0.10s/f (Good) **11** Ran SP% **115.9**
Speed ratings (Par 96): **98,97,92,89,87 87,86,83,83,64 60**
toteswingers 1&2 £6.20, 1&3 £30.20, 2&3 £30.20 CSF £24.03 TOTE £2.60: £1.30, £3.50, £7.70; EX 27.10 Trifecta £1026.40 Part won. Pool: £1368.56 - 0.64 winning units..
Owner Lady Rothschild **Bred** The Rt Hon Lord Rothschild **Trained** East Everleigh, Wilts

FOCUS
The second division of the 2-y-o maiden. They went quicker early in this edition and it too should prove a fruitful source of winners.

5474 CHRISTOPHER SMITH ASSOCIATES CLAIMING STKS 7f (S)
2:50 (2:52) (Class 5) 3-Y-O+ **£2,587** (£770; £384; £192) **Stalls** Centre

Form RPR
6124 1 **Tatlisu (IRE)**[21] 4725 3-9-9 80 RyanMoore 2 89
(Richard Fahey) *lw: broke wl: stdd towards rr but in tch: hdwy 3f out: chsd ldr ins fnl 2f: rdn to ld over 1f out: hld on all out* **7/1**
4163 2 *nk* **Balty Boys (IRE)**[16] 4895 4-9-12 88 (b) RichardHughes 1 88
(Jamie Osborne) *led: rdn and hdd over 1f out: rallied u.p fnl f: kpt on but a jst hld* **9/4**[1]
5502 3 *3 1/4* **Mabait**[41] 4062 7-9-11 88 DarrenEgan[(3)] 7 81
(David Simcock) *hld up in rr: stdy hdwy over 2f out: drvn to chse ldrs over 1f out: no imp and kpt on same pce* **7/2**[2]
-000 4 *shd* **Sword In Hand**[83] 2659 4-9-4 73 (t) MichaelJMMurphy[(5)] 3 76
(Alan Jarvis) *swtg: chsd ldrs: rdn over 2f out: outpcd wl over 1f out but kpt on to press for wl-hld 3rd cl home* **20/1**
0-36 5 *5* **Balducci**[18] 4825 6-9-12 94 KierenFallon 5 66
(David O'Meara) *chsd ldrs: rdn ins fnl 3f: wknd ins fnl 2f* **7/2**[2]
2042 6 *5* **Polar Kite (IRE)**[29] 4438 5-9-8 82 AdamKirby 4 48
(Sean Curran) *in rr but in tch: rdn and effrt 3f out: wknd fr 2f out* **11/2**[3]
0504 6 *dht* **Rondeau (GR)**[13] 4998 8-8-8 71 OisinMurphy[(7)] 6 41
(Patrick Chamings) *s.i.s: sn chsng ldrs: wknd 2f out* **20/1**

1m 26.21s (0.51) **Going Correction** +0.10s/f (Good)
WFA 3 from 4yo+ 5lb **7** Ran SP% **112.6**
Speed ratings (Par 103): **101,100,96,96,91 85,85**
toteswingers 1&2 £1.30, 1&3 £5.00, 2&3 £3.10 CSF £22.46 TOTE £6.10: £2.30, £1.80; EX 21.90 Trifecta £90.30 Pool: £1997.47 - 16.58 winning units..
Owner Middleham Park Racing LIV **Bred** J C And Rocal Bloodstock **Trained** Musley Bank, N Yorks

FOCUS
An above-average claimer. They went a sound pace down the centre, with the first pair coming clear.

5475 PUNTER SOUTHALL TRANSACTION SERVICES H'CAP 1m 5f 61y
3:20 (3:21) (Class 3) (0-90,90) 3-Y-O+ **£7,439** (£2,213; £1,106; £553) **Stalls** Centre

Form RPR
5151 1 **Poyle Thomas**[18] 4832 4-9-3 79 JimCrowley 4 87+
(Ralph Beckett) *chsd ldrs: drvn to chal over 1f out: sn led: hdd ins fnl f: rallied u.p to ld again last strides* **11/2**
2112 2 *nk* **Continuum**[42] 4020 4-10-0 90 TomQueally 5 98+
(Lady Cecil) *s.i.s: hld up in rr: haeadway on outside 3f out: pushed rt wl over 2f out: str chal fr over 1f out: styd on u.p clsng stages: jst failed* **3/1**[2]
/103 3 *shd* **Sir Bedivere (IRE)**[15] 4914 4-9-6 82 (t) RyanMoore 7 89+
(Brian Meehan) *lw: trckd ldr: led over 3f out: jnd over 1f out: briefly hdd: sn led again: remained hrd pressed: hdd last strides* **17/2**
2153 4 *2 1/4* **Statutory (IRE)**[6] 5258 3-9-1 88 KierenFallon 2 92
(Mark Johnston) *in tch: drvn to chse ldrs and edgd rt wl over 2f out: chal 2f out tl wknd fnl 110yds* **2/1**[1]
1311 5 *6* **Sunny Future (IRE)**[20] 4775 7-9-0 76 RichardHughes 6 72
(Malcolm Saunders) *led: hdd over 3f out: wknd 2f out* **10/1**
010- 6 *3 1/2* **Uriah Heep (FR)**[153] 6848 4-9-9 85 AdamKirby 1 76
(Alan King) *chsd ldrs: rdn 3f out: wknd over 2f out* **33/1**
1233 7 *38* **Masquerading (IRE)**[36] 4202 3-9-1 88 TedDurcan 3 26
(David Lanigan) *hld up in rr: hdwy fr 3f out: rdn 2f out: wknd over 1f out: eased fnl f* **5/1**[3]

2m 53.15s (1.15) **Going Correction** +0.10s/f (Good)
WFA 3 from 4yo+ 11lb **7** Ran SP% **112.9**
Speed ratings (Par 107): **100,99,99,98,94 92,69**
toteswingers 1&2 £4.50, 1&3 £9.40, 2&3 £5.90 CSF £21.77 TOTE £5.30: £3.30, £2.30; EX 22.70 Trifecta £181.40 Pool: £1365.02 - 5.64 winning units..
Owner Cecil And Miss Alison Wiggins **Bred** Miss Alison Wiggins **Trained** Kimpton, Hants

FOCUS
A fair staying handicap. They didn't go that quickly so it wasn't surprising to see a tight finish play out.

5476 BATHWICK TYRES ST HUGH'S STKS (LISTED RACE) 5f 34y
3:55 (3:55) (Class 1) 2-Y-O
£14,461 (£5,482; £2,743; £1,366; £685; £344) **Stalls** Centre

Form RPR
4135 1 **Wind Fire (USA)**[20] 4742 2-8-12 101 RyanMoore 6 102
(David Brown) *lw: hld up in rr: drvn and str hdwy over 1f out: qcknd fnl f to ld clsng stages: won gng away* **7/4**[2]
2110 2 *1* **Excel's Beauty**[13] 5005 2-8-12 82 (b[1]) JimCrowley 4 98
(James Tate) *led: rdn and 4 l clr jst ins fnl f: kpt on u.p tl hdd and outpcd by wnr clsng stages* **25/1**
2121 3 *1 1/2* **Lilbourne Lass**[5] 5306 2-8-12 93 RichardHughes 5 93
(Richard Hannon) *lw: broke wl: stdd towards rr but in tch: hdwy fr 2f out: drvn to take 3rd fnl f: kpt on but no imp on ldng duo clsng stages* **5/4**[1]
100 4 *4 1/2* **Lady Chantilly (IRE)**[26] 4572 2-8-12 0 CathyGannon 3 77
(Jo Hughes) *sn chsng ldrs: rdn 2f out: wknd over 1f out* **25/1**
01 5 *3 3/4* **Autumns Blush (IRE)**[101] 2131 2-8-12 84 KierenFallon 2 63
(Jeremy Noseda) *s.i.s: in rr: drvn and hdwy to dispute 2nd 2f out: wknd fnl f* **16/1**
3 6 *1 1/4* **Abbakova (IRE)**[34] 4318 2-8-12 0 PatSmullen 9 59
(W McCreery, Ire) *chsd ldrs: disp 2nd 2f out: wknd appr fnl f* **6/1**[3]
3421 7 *1* **Trinity River**[4] 5350 2-8-12 78 ThomasBrown 1 55
(Daniel Kubler) *chsd ldrs: rdn 1/2-way: wknd ins fnl 2f* **33/1**
2130 8 *8* **Majestic Alexander (IRE)**[17] 4855 2-8-12 95 TomQueally 8 26
(David Evans) *sn chsng ldrs: rdn appr fnl 2f: sn btn* **16/1**

1m 1.67s (0.27) **Going Correction** +0.10s/f (Good) **8** Ran SP% **117.5**
Speed ratings (Par 102): **101,99,97,89,83 81,80,67**
toteswingers 1&2 £7.00, 1&3 £1.60, 2&3 £4.00 CSF £47.76 TOTE £2.90: £1.10, £5.00, £1.10; EX 44.80 Trifecta £135.90 Pool: £3643.61 - 20.09 winning units..
Owner Qatar Racing Limited **Bred** Kinsman Farm **Trained** Averham Park, Notts

FOCUS
A fair bunch of 2-y-o fillies. There was a solid pace on and few got in a serious blow as the principals were clear. The form looks sound with the first three clear.

5477 INSPIRATION INC H'CAP 6f 8y
4:30 (4:30) (Class 4) (0-80,79) 3-Y-O **£4,851** (£1,443; £721; £360) **Stalls** Centre

Form RPR
4224 1 **Jontleman (IRE)**[14] 4966 3-8-12 73 CharlesBishop[(3)] 5 83
(Mick Channon) *in rr but in tch: hdwy fr 2f out: drvn to ld appr fnl f: styd on strly clsng stages* **8/1**
1002 2 *1 3/4* **Panther Patrol (IRE)**[6] 5278 3-9-1 73 RyanMoore 3 78
(Eve Johnson Houghton) *lw: in rr: hdwy ins fnl 2f: chsd wnr ins fnl f: kpt on wl u.p but a readily hld* **9/2**[3]
2114 3 *2 1/2* **Grand Denial (IRE)**[19] 4797 3-9-6 78 (b) AdamKirby 1 75
(Clive Cox) *in rr: drvn and hdwy over 1f out: tk 3rd u.p ins fnl f: kpt on one pce* **3/1**[1]
-001 4 *6* **Aye Aye Skipper (IRE)**[14] 4962 3-9-7 79 RobertWinston 8 58
(Dean Ivory) *chsd ldr to 1/2-way and styd disputing 2nd to 2f out: wknd over 1f out* **7/1**
0135 5 *5* **Hartwright**[27] 4529 3-8-13 78 LouisSteward[(7)] 4 42
(Michael Bell) *chsd ldrs: disp 2nd over 2f out: wknd wl over 1f out* **11/1**
0232 6 *nk* **Exzachary**[32] 4354 3-8-13 78 JosephineGordon[(7)] 10 41
(Jo Hughes) *led: sn clr c over to stands' rail over 1f out and sn hdd: wknd qckly* **20/1**
2214 7 *2 3/4* **Lager Time (IRE)**[15] 4905 3-8-12 70 TomQueally 2 25
(David Evans) *chsd ldrs: disp 2nd u.p 2f out: wknd wl over 1f out* **16/1**
5051 8 *1/2* **Secret Missile**[14] 4942 3-9-6 78 MartinDwyer 11 32
(William Muir) *rdn 1/2-way: a outpcd* **7/1**
4350 9 *9* **Overrider**[21] 4707 3-8-12 70 (t) JamieMackay 9
(Alastair Lidderdale) *slowly away: a in rr* **66/1**
0351 10 *3 1/2* **Assembly**[8] 5200 3-8-8 66 6ex (b) KierenFallon 7
(William Haggas) *chsd ldrs: wknd qckly over 2f out* **4/1**[2]

1m 13.05s (0.05) **Going Correction** +0.10s/f (Good) **10** Ran SP% **119.8**
Speed ratings (Par 102): **103,100,97,89,82 82,78,77,65,61**
toteswingers 1&2 £8.60, 1&3 £7.50, 2&3 £4.10 CSF £45.18 CT £135.63 TOTE £10.30: £2.70, £2.30, £1.40; EX 41.30 Trifecta £199.20 Pool: £2482.98 - 9.34 winning units..
Owner Paul Corbett **Bred** Old Carhue & Graeng Bloodstock **Trained** West Ilsley, Berks

FOCUS
A modest 3-y-o sprint handicap and, run at a strong pace, it was another race in which the principals finished clear of the rest.

5478 KKA - HIGHPOINT MAIDEN FILLIES' STKS 1m 2f 6y
5:00 (5:04) (Class 5) 3-Y-O+ **£2,587** (£770; £384; £192) **Stalls** Centre

Form RPR
42 1 **Bonanza Creek (IRE)**[28] 4500 3-8-13 0 RyanMoore 12 84+
(Luca Cumani) *lw: trckd ldr: led 3f out: drvn 2f out: styd on wl u.p fnl f* **6/4**[1]
322 2 *1 3/4* **Saddaqa (USA)**[12] 5038 3-8-13 84 (p) KierenFallon 6 81
(Saeed bin Suroor) *swtg: chsd ldrs: wnt 2nd 3f out: styd on u.p fnl 2f but no imp thrght fnl f* **5/2**[2]
63 3 *1/2* **Snow Powder (IRE)**[19] 4799 3-8-13 0 RichardHughes 11 80
(John Gosden) *towards rr on outside: hdwy fr 4f out: rdn and edgd lft 2f out: kpt on same pce ins fnl f* **8/1**
4 *nk* **Wizara (IRE)** 3-8-13 0 RobertWinston 3 79
(Saeed bin Suroor) *w'like: in rr: hdwy 3f out: chsd ldrs fr 2f out: edgd lft over 1f out: kpt on same pce fnl f* **25/1**
23 5 *2 3/4* **Archive**[56] 3530 3-8-13 0 TomQueally 5 74+
(Lady Cecil) *t.k.h towards rr: hdwy 3f out: pushed along and kpt on same pce fr over 1f out* **6/1**[3]
6 *6* **Pim Street (USA)**[45] 3940 3-8-13 57 PatSmullen 10 63
(W McCreery, Ire) *in tch: chsd ldrs 3f out: rdn 2f out: hld whn hmpd on rails wl over 1f out* **25/1**
7 *4 1/2* **Lady Theodora** 3-8-8 0 MichaelJMMurphy[(5)] 9 54
(Alan Jarvis) *w'like: str: s.i.s: sn drvn along: a towards rr* **100/1**
6-4 8 *5* **Everlasting Light**[29] 4454 3-8-13 0 MartinDwyer 4 44
(Luca Cumani) *pushed along 3f out: towards rr most of way* **20/1**
6 9 *12* **Fossola (USA)**[28] 4500 3-8-13 0 JimCrowley 8 22
(Charlie Appleby) *str: lengthy: a in rr* **12/1**

6-0 **10** *2 ½* **Vega Dance (IRE)**[98] 2231 3-8-8 0 RyanTate(5) 2 17
(Clive Cox) *led: clr fr 6f out: hdd 3f out: sn wknd* **40/1**

2m 7.64s (-1.16) **Going Correction** +0.10s/f (Good)
WFA 3 from 5yo 8lb **10** Ran SP% **117.5**
Speed ratings (Par 100): **108,106,106,105,103 98,95,91,81,79**
toteswingers 1&2 £1.90, 1&3 £3.90, 2&3 £3.90 CSF £4.95 TOTE £2.50: £1.40, £1.10, £2.40; EX 7.30 Trifecta £44.20 Pool: £3310.44 - 56.10 winning units..
Owner Wildenstein Stables Limited **Bred** Dayton Investments Ltd **Trained** Newmarket, Suffolk

FOCUS
A fair fillies' maiden, run at a strong pace.

5479 ROBIN J.W. HALL 60TH BIRTHDAY APPRENTICE H'CAP 1m 1f
5:30 (5:31) (Class 5) (0-70,70) 4-Y-O+ **£2,587** (£770; £384; £192) **Stalls** Centre

Form RPR
3143 **1** **Hector's Chance**[18] 4831 4-9-3 **61** RyanTate 2 70
(Heather Main) *swtg: hld up in rr: hdwy over 2f out: drvn and r.o wl to ld fnl 130yds: readily* **5/1[2]**

5-30 **2** *1 ¼* **Elsie Bay**[163] 896 4-8-13 **62** CharlotteJenner(5) 1 69
(J S Moore) *in rr: hdwy over 2f out: styd on wl fnl f to chal fnl 130yds: outpcd by wnr clsng stages* **25/1**

3110 **3** *2* **Balmoral Castle**[64] 3244 4-9-10 **68** MatthewLawson 5 71
(Jonathan Portman) *in tch on outside: led 3f out: sn rdn: kpt on tl hdd and no ex fnl 130yds* **5/1[2]**

0-23 **4** *1 ½* **Malih**[25] 4591 4-9-10 **68** MichaelJMMurphy 8 68
(Jamie Osborne) *s.i.s: sn chsng ldr: chal 3f out: no ex fnl 110yds* **7/2[1]**

6120 **5** *1* **Taro Tywod (IRE)**[9] 5144 4-9-1 **62** JackDuern(3) 9 60
(Mark Brisbourne) *chsd ldrs: rdn 3f out: wknd over 1f out* **9/1**

4250 **6** *1* **April Ciel**[45] 3917 4-9-6 **67** OisinMurphy(3) 3 63
(Ronald Harris) *led: hdd 3f out: wknd over 1f out* **5/1[2]**

2125 **7** *2 ½* **Fluctuation (IRE)**[15] 4928 5-9-4 **62** (v) DannyBrock 6 53
(Ian Williams) *lw: towards rr: hdwy on ins to chse ldrs 3f out: sn rdn: wknd over 1f out* **14/1**

0505 **8** *4* **Poetic Lord**[18] 4831 4-9-6 **67** JoshBaudains(3) 7 50
(Sylvester Kirk) *racd on outer: rdn and sme hdwy fr 3f out: nvr rchd ldrs and wknd fr 2f out* **16/1**

-421 **9** *½* **Fly Haaf (IRE)**[48] 3821 4-9-6 **67** (t) ThomasGarner(3) 4 49
(George Baker) *sn chsng ldrs: rdn 3f out: wknd ins fnl 3f* **7/1[3]**

030 **10** *¾* **Dimitar (USA)**[53] 3617 4-9-9 **70** EDLinehan(3) 10 50
(Brendan Powell) *racd on outer towards rr: rdn 3f out: brief effrt: sn wknd* **16/1**

1m 55.72s (0.22) **Going Correction** +0.10s/f (Good) **10** Ran SP% **117.0**
Speed ratings (Par 103): **103,101,100,98,97 97,94,91,90,90**
toteswingers 1&2 £21.30, 1&3 £8.50, 2&3 £20.80 CSF £119.69 CT £660.20 TOTE £5.80: £2.00, £5.90, £2.10; EX 106.80 Trifecta £681.00 Pool: £1718.68 - 1.89 winning units..
Owner M Scott Russell **Bred** Wickham Stud **Trained** Kingston Lisle, Oxon
■ Stewards' Enquiry : Jack Duern 18-day ban (six days deferred until Oct 22): used whip above shoulder height, fifth suspension within six months (Aug 30-Sep 10)

FOCUS
A moderate handicap, confined to apprentice rider.
T/Plt: £104.00 to a £1 stake. Pool: £61,240.50 - 429.85 winning units T/Qpdt: £16.20 to a £1 stake. Pool: £5017.76 - 228.32 winning units ST

5136 NEWCASTLE (L-H)
Friday, August 16

OFFICIAL GOING: Good to soft (6.3)
Wind: Breezy, half against Weather: Cloudy, bright

5480 MALONE & SONS NURSERY H'CAP 5f
2:10 (2:10) (Class 6) (0-60,60) 2-Y-O **£1,940** (£577; £288; £144) **Stalls** Centre

Form RPR
4544 **1** **She Can Jig**[14] 4965 2-8-10 **56** KevinStott(7) 4 61+
(Kevin Ryan) *prom: hdwy to ld appr fnl f: pushed out last 100yds* **9/2[3]**

0335 **2** *½* **Fredricka**[17] 4847 2-9-2 **60** JustinNewman(5) 3 61
(Garry Moss) *disp ld to ins fnl f: kpt on: hld nr fin* **5/1**

060 **3** *2 ¼* **Reale Silenzio**[16] 4886 2-8-6 **45** JamesSullivan 1 38
(John Weymes) *in tch: outpcd over 2f out: rallied over 1f out: kpt on towards fin* **50/1**

000 **4** *½* **Scarborough (IRE)**[62] 3350 2-8-13 **52** GrahamLee 5 43
(Paul Midgley) *t.k.h: led to appr fnl f: outpcd last 100yds* **5/4[1]**

052 **5** *1* **Autumn Tide (IRE)**[29] 4450 2-8-6 **52** (p) JoeDoyle(7) 7 40
(John Quinn) *in tch: hdwy and cl up 2f out: sn rdn: outpcd fnl f* **10/1**

035 **6** *2 ¼* **Grass Green**[13] 5000 2-8-5 **49** NathanAlison(5) 2 29
(William Haggas) *cl up tl rdn and wknd appr fnl f* **4/1[2]**

1m 3.64s (2.54) **Going Correction** +0.225s/f (Good) **6** Ran SP% **110.3**
Speed ratings (Par 92): **88,87,83,82,81 77**
toteswingers 1&2 £2.90, 1&3 £6.30, 2&3 £11.00 CSF £25.57 TOTE £5.70: £2.90, £2.90; EX 15.00 Trifecta £348.00 Pool: £2349.83 - 5.06 winning units..
Owner Cockrill Emmerson & Woodley **Bred** Guy Stephenson **Trained** Hambleton, N Yorks
■ Stewards' Enquiry : Justin Newman two-day ban: excessive use (30-31 Aug)

FOCUS
Course same as last meeting on August 7th. Just a modest nursery run on ground which had eased after overnight rain.

5481 HENRY THOMAS CRAIB 1ST BIRTHDAY H'CAP 7f
2:40 (2:40) (Class 4) (0-85,85) 3-Y-O+ **£4,690** (£1,395; £697; £348) **Stalls** Centre

Form RPR
0000 **1** **Green Howard**[21] 4733 5-9-2 **78** JasonHart(3) 9 87
(Robin Bastiman) *missed break: bhd: rdn over 2f out: hdwy and bk on bridle to ld over 1f out: rdn out fnl f* **5/1[3]**

6104 **2** *1 ¼* **Victoire De Lyphar (IRE)**[6] 5292 6-9-7 **80** (e) PJMcDonald 7 86
(Ruth Carr) *taken early to post: cl up: led over 3f out to over 1f out: edgd lft: kpt on ins fnl f* **13/2**

0000 **3** *shd* **King Of Eden (IRE)**[41] 4067 7-9-12 **85** (b) DavidAllan 3 90
(Eric Alston) *dwlt: bhd: gd hdwy over 1f out: kpt on wl fnl f: nrst fin* **12/1**

0531 **4** *shd* **Barney McGrew (IRE)**[25] 4577 10-9-5 **78** PhillipMakin 1 83
(Michael Dods) *taken early to post: hld up in tch: effrt and rdn over 1f out: flashed tail ins fnl f: one pce nr fin* **12/1**

0000 **5** *1 ¾* **Discression**[16] 4879 4-9-5 **78** (p) GrahamLee 8 79
(Kevin Ryan) *t.k.h: trckd ldrs: effrt and rdn 2f out: kpt on same pce fnl f* **3/1[1]**

0300 **6** *¾* **Fieldgunner Kirkup (GER)**[13] 5014 5-9-10 **83** GrahamGibbons 4 82
(David Barron) *in tch: effrt and rdn over 1f out: outpcd fnl f* **15/2**

2325 **7** *¾* **Our Boy Jack (IRE)**[13] 5014 4-9-5 **78** TonyHamilton 6 75
(Richard Fahey) *led to over 3f out: rallied: rdn and wknd over 1f out* **7/2[2]**

1005 **8** *1 ¾* **Green Park (IRE)**[11] 5051 10-9-0 **76** (b) NeilFarley(3) 2 68
(Declan Carroll) *prom: rdn over 2f out: one pce fr over 1f out* **28/1**

5455 **9** *3 ½* **Steel Stockholder**[9] 5149 7-9-3 **76** DuranFentiman 5 59
(Mel Brittain) *w ldrs: rdn over 2f out: wknd wl over 1f out* **20/1**

0260 **10** *1 ¾* **Majestic Dream (IRE)**[14] 4956 5-8-13 **72** (b) JamesSullivan 10 51
(Michael Easterby) *hld up: rdn and outpcd over 2f out: sn btn* **28/1**

1m 28.45s (0.65) **Going Correction** +0.225s/f (Good) **10** Ran SP% **116.0**
Speed ratings (Par 105): **105,103,103,103,101 100,99,97,93,91**
toteswingers 1&2 £7.50, 1&3 £17.00, 2&3 £13.80 CSF £36.27 CT £373.83 TOTE £9.20: £2.20, £2.10, £4.20; EX 55.50 Trifecta £662.20 Pool: £2664.98 - 3.01 winning units..
Owner Ms M Austerfield **Bred** Miss A J Rawding & P M Crane **Trained** Cowthorpe, N Yorks

FOCUS
A fairly useful handicap which was soundly run with three of the first four coming from off the pace.

5482 HAPPY 40TH BIRTHDAY MARK DRUMMOND / E B F MAIDEN STKS 7f
3:10 (3:16) (Class 5) 2-Y-O **£2,911** (£866; £432; £216) **Stalls** Centre

Form RPR
32 **1** **Longton**[25] 4576 2-9-5 0 TonyHamilton 1 74+
(Richard Fahey) *cl up: led over 2f out: rdn and edgd rt ins fnl f: kpt on wl* **15/8[1]**

006 **2** *1 ½* **Arrowzone**[15] 4925 2-9-2 55 (p) JasonHart(3) 9 70
(Garry Moss) *led to over 2f out: sn rdn and rallied: hld last 100yds* **16/1**

3 *3 ½* **Ralphy Lad (IRE)** 2-9-5 0 RussKennemore 3 61
(Alan Swinbank) *hld up in midfeld: hdwy to chse ldrs 2f out: kpt on same pce ins fnl f* **14/1**

6 **4** *1 ½* **Paddy's Rock (IRE)**[9] 5145 2-9-5 0 PJMcDonald 13 57
(Ann Duffield) *midfield: effrt whn nt clr run over 2f out: hdwy over 1f out: kpt on fnl f* **3/1[2]**

5 *½* **Sketch Map (IRE)** 2-9-5 0 MichaelO'Connell 7 56+
(Jedd O'Keeffe) *dwlt: bhd: hdwy 2f out: kpt on fnl f: nvr able to chal* **33/1**

6 *1 ¾* **Outback Warrior (IRE)** 2-9-5 0 GrahamLee 11 51
(Kevin Ryan) *prom: effrt and ev ch over 2f out: outpcd over 1f out* **6/1[3]**

7 *hd* **Miss Lucy Jane** 2-9-0 0 LeeTopliss 10 46
(Richard Fahey) *dwlt: rn green and sn pushed along in rr: hdwy over 1f out: n.d* **15/2**

0 **8** *¾* **Aldreth**[15] 4925 2-9-5 0 JamesSullivan 2 49
(Michael Easterby) *dwlt: bhd: struggling over 3f out: hdwy over 1f out: kpt on fnl f: nvr rchd ldrs* **33/1**

5 **9** *2 ½* **Prostate Awareness (IRE)**[13] 4977 2-9-5 0 AndrewElliott 12 42
(Patrick Holmes) *midfield: outpcd over 2f out: n.d after* **11/1**

60 **10** *½* **Wolfwood**[72] 2985 2-9-5 0 PhillipMakin 8 41
(John Davies) *t.k.h: in tch: n.m.r briefly over 2f out: rdn and edgd lft over 1f out: sn wknd* **100/1**

06 **11** *1 ¾* **Boy Ranger (IRE)**[27] 4538 2-8-12 0 RowanScott(7) 14 36
(Ann Duffield) *bhd: drvn along over 2f out: nvr on terms* **100/1**

12 *10* **Application** 2-9-5 0 RoystonFfrench 5 10
(Bryan Smart) *bhd: rdn over 3f out: btn fnl 2f* **22/1**

1m 30.33s (2.53) **Going Correction** +0.225s/f (Good) **12** Ran SP% **118.9**
Speed ratings (Par 94): **94,92,88,86,86 84,83,82,80,79 77,66**
toteswingers 1&2 £7.90, 1&3 £7.00, 2&3 £24.40 CSF £34.30 TOTE £2.70: £1.10, £3.90, £5.10; EX 34.90 Trifecta £548.40 Pool: £3661.74 - 5.00 winning units..
Owner David W Armstrong **Bred** Toby Barker **Trained** Musley Bank, N Yorks

FOCUS
A modest contest.

5483 CATALYST4SOCCER H'CAP 1m 2f 32y
3:45 (3:45) (Class 5) (0-75,75) 3-Y-O **£2,587** (£770; £384; £192) **Stalls** Centre

Form RPR
1332 **1** **Mash Potato (IRE)**[4] 5334 3-8-6 **60** (p) PJMcDonald 3 73+
(Michael Dods) *t.k.h early: trckd ldrs: n.m.r fr over 2f out: squeezed through to ld ins fnl f: edgd rt nr fin: jst hld on* **11/4[1]**

10-5 **2** *nse* **Authorship (IRE)**[16] 4882 3-9-6 **74** AhmedAjtebi 1 87+
(Charlie Appleby) *hld up: stdy hdwy against far rail whn no room over 1f out: angled out and styd on strly fnl f: jst hld* **11/4[1]**

0013 **3** *1 ¾* **Naaz (IRE)**[66] 3173 3-9-5 **73** (b) PhillipMakin 7 81
(Ed Dunlop) *t.k.h early: hld up in tch: hdwy to ld over 1f out: hdd ins fnl f: one pce* **9/2[2]**

0015 **4** *3* **Bahamamay**[17] 4853 3-8-9 **63** LeeTopliss 6 65
(Richard Fahey) *trckd ldrs: drvn over 2f out: outpcd appr fnl f* **25/1**

6351 **5** *hd* **The Codger**[106] 1967 3-8-10 **64** TonyHamilton 8 66+
(David O'Meara) *hld up: rdn along over 2f out: styd on fnl f: nvr able to chal* **12/1**

4115 **6** *shd* **Al Thumama**[30] 4401 3-9-1 **69** (p) GrahamLee 5 70
(Kevin Ryan) *pressed ldr: drvn and ev ch over 2f out to over 1f out: outpcd fnl f* **20/1**

2352 **7** *2* **Gioia Di Vita**[22] 4672 3-9-7 **75** AdrianNicholls 2 73
(David Nicholls) *t.k.h early: in tch: no room fr over 2f out to ent fnl f: nt rcvr* **7/1**

2213 **8** *2 ½* **Sunbula (USA)**[23] 4634 3-9-6 **74** GrahamGibbons 4 72
(Charles Hills) *led: rdn and hdd over 1f out: outpcd whn hmpd ins fnl f: sn btn* **13/2[3]**

2m 12.73s (0.83) **Going Correction** +0.125s/f (Good) **8** Ran SP% **113.6**
Speed ratings (Par 100): **101,100,99,97,97 96,95,93**
toteswingers 1&2 £3.10, 1&3 £4.10, 2&3 £5.30 CSF £9.96 CT £31.41 TOTE £3.30: £1.20, £1.60, £1.70; EX 10.50 Trifecta £62.70 Pool: £2637.49 - 31.54 winning units..
Owner Bennett Potatoes & Banister **Bred** David Barry **Trained** Denton, Co Durham

FOCUS
Form to view positively from the leading pair, who quickened nicely clear in the end, the performance of the runner-up particularly eye-catching.

5484 PARKLANDSGOLF.CO.UK MAIDEN STKS 1m 2f 32y
4:20 (4:21) (Class 5) 3-Y-O+ **£2,587** (£770; £384; £192) **Stalls** Centre

Form RPR
6 **1** **Jeeraan (USA)**[13] 4978 3-9-5 0 PhillipMakin 5 86+
(Ed Dunlop) *hld up in midfield: gd hdwy 2f out: led ins fnl f: kpt on strly* **12/1**

23/ **2** *2 ½* **Llanarmon Lad (IRE)**[728] 5254 4-9-13 0 BarryMcHugh 3 80+
(Brian Ellison) *trckd ldrs: effrt whn nt clr run over 1f out to ent fnl f: chsd wnr last 75yds: r.o* **5/1[2]**

/ **3** *1 ½* **Stereotypical**[167] 4-9-13 0 SebSanders 1 75
(Ralph Beckett) *led: rdn over 2f out: hdd ins fnl f: kpt on same pce* **13/2**

45 **4** *½* **Mutanaweb (IRE)**[90] 2456 3-9-5 0 NickyMackay 14 74+
(John Gosden) *hld up: drvn on outside over 2f out: styd on wl fnl f: nrst fin* **8/1**

20 **5** *2 1/4* **China Creek (IRE)**[13] 4978 3-9-0 0 .... JoeFanning 7 65
(Mark Johnston) *t.k.h early: cl up: ev ch over 2f out to over 1f out: wknd ins fnl f* **8/1**

25 **6** *nk* **Apparently**[11] 5064 3-9-5 0 .... GrahamLee 10 70
(Charlie Appleby) *hld up in tch: effrt and rdn over 2f out: no imp fr over 1f out* **6/1**[3]

3 **7** *3 3/4* **Desert Wings (IRE)**[13] 4978 3-9-5 0 .... AhmedAjtebi 2 62
(Charlie Appleby) *plld hrd early: trckd ldrs: rdn over 2f out: wknd over 1f out: eased whn btn ins fnl f* **2/1**[1]

8 *14* **Glasgon** 3-9-2 0 .... NeilFarley(3) 8 36
(Declan Carroll) *midfield: lost pl after 3f: sn rdn: n.d after* **66/1**

0 **9** *10* **Anne's Valentino**[11] 5071 3-9-0 0 .... TomEaves 11 12
(Malcolm Jefferson) *s.i.s: bhd: drvn over 4f out: sn btn* **200/1**

6 **10** *2 1/4* **Slip Of A Girl (IRE)**[39] 4118 3-9-0 0 .... RussKennemore 13 8
(Patrick Holmes) *hld up: rdn over 3f out: wknd wl over 2f out* **100/1**

43 **11** *1 1/2* **Caledonia**[72] 2971 6-9-10 0 .... LucyAlexander(3) 12 10
(Jim Goldie) *rrd as stalls opened and s.v.s: bhd and detached: nvr on terms* **18/1**

0 **12** *1/2* **Nautical Twilight**[11] 5071 3-9-0 0 .... LeeTopliss 6
(Malcolm Jefferson) *hld up: rdn and struggling over 3f out: sn btn* **200/1**

2m 11.12s (-0.78) **Going Correction** +0.125s/f (Good)
WFA 3 from 4yo+ 8lb **12** Ran SP% **116.3**
Speed ratings (Par 103): **108,106,104,104,102 102,99,88,80,78 77,76**
toteswingers 1&2 £12.70, 1&3 £13.10, 2&3 £8.60 CSF £70.20 TOTE £16.30: £3.60, £1.90, £2.60; EX 124.30 Trifecta £636.50 Pool: £3173.57 - 3.73 winning units..
Owner Hamdan Al Maktoum **Bred** Shadwell Farm LLC **Trained** Newmarket, Suffolk

FOCUS
Fair form in a maiden which was run at a sound pace.

5485 APEX RADIO H'CAP 5f
4:50 (4:51) (Class 5) (0-70,70) 3-Y-O £2,587 (£770; £384; £192) **Stalls** Centre

Form RPR

0305 **1** **Lucky Lodge**[14] 4970 3-8-10 59 .... (b[1]) AndrewElliott 4 64
(Mel Brittain) *prom: rdn over 2f out: hdwy over 1f out: led ins fnl f: hld on wl* **14/1**

-405 **2** *nk* **Millkwood**[9] 5150 3-9-5 68 .... (p) PhillipMakin 5 72
(John Davies) *hld up in tch: rdn and hdwy 2f out: disp ld ins fnl f: kpt on: hld nr fin* **7/2**[1]

304 **3** *1 1/4* **Cracking Choice (IRE)**[6] 5265 3-8-9 58 .... (b) TomEaves 8 58
(Michael Dods) *led at decent gallop: rdn over 1f out: hdd ins fnl f: kpt on same pce towards fin* **11/2**

-055 **4** *shd* **Dark Opal (IRE)**[9] 5141 3-9-7 70 .... JamesSullivan 6 69
(John Weymes) *hld up: rdn and hdwy over 1f out: kpt on ins fnl f: nt pce to chal* **5/1**[3]

0303 **5** *nk* **Done Dreaming (IRE)**[11] 5054 3-8-0 56 .... SamanthaBell(7) 7 54
(Richard Fahey) *bhd: pushed along 1/2-way: hdwy over 1f out: kpt on fnl f: no imp* **7/1**

3-04 **6** *1 1/4* **Mandy Layla (IRE)**[26] 4558 3-9-3 66 .... RoystonFfrench 2 60
(Bryan Smart) *disp ld 2f: cl up tl rdn and no ex fnl f* **15/2**

1001 **7** *1 1/4* **Little Eli**[11] 5067 3-8-9 61 6ex .... JasonHart(3) 1 50
(Eric Alston) *trckd ldrs: rdn and edgd lft over 1f out: wknd ins fnl f* **7/1**

063 **8** *7* **Sabrina's Secret**[18] 4839 3-8-13 62 .... MickyFenton 9 26
(Tom Tate) *taken early to post: s.i.s: sn in tch: rdn and hung lft over 2f out: sn wknd* **9/2**[2]

-050 **9** *13* **Princess In Exile**[13] 4992 3-8-1 53 .... NeilFarley(3) 3
(Ian Semple) *chsd ldrs tl rdn and wknd wl over 2f out: t.o* **50/1**

1m 2.05s (0.95) **Going Correction** +0.225s/f (Good) **9** Ran SP% **117.8**
Speed ratings (Par 100): **101,100,98,98,97 95,93,82,61**
totesSwingers 1&2 £9.20, 1&3 £13.10, 2&3 £5.00 CSF £63.97 CT £314.12 TOTE £15.00: £4.50, £1.10, £2.60; EX 49.00 Trifecta £353.00 Pool: £3784.54 - 8.04 winning units..
Owner Mel Brittain **Bred** Mel Brittain **Trained** Warthill, N Yorks
■ Stewards' Enquiry : Andrew Elliott two-day ban: used whip above permitted level (Aug 30-31)

FOCUS
A modest sprint which was run at a good pace from the off.

5486 MTREC RECRUITMENT/TRAINING H'CAP (DIV I) 6f
5:20 (5:20) (Class 6) (0-65,71) 3-Y-O+ £1,940 (£577; £288; £144) **Stalls** Centre

Form RPR

41 **1** **Monakova (IRE)**[9] 5139 3-10-1 71 6ex .... DavidNolan 4 80+
(David O'Meara) *prom: hdwy to ld over 1f out: rdn out fnl f* **8/11**[1]

0-25 **2** *1 1/4* **Meeting In Paris (IRE)**[13] 4991 3-9-1 57 .... TonyHamilton 5 60
(Richard Fahey) *dwlt: bhd: rdn over 2f out: hdwy to chse (clr) wnr ins fnl f: r.o* **5/1**[2]

3320 **3** *1/2* **Busy Bimbo (IRE)**[6] 5273 4-8-11 50 ow1 .... RussKennemore 9 52
(Alan Berry) *hld up: rdn and hdwy over 1f out: disp 2nd pl ins fnl f: kpt on: hld towards fin* **16/1**

4040 **4** *3/4* **George Fenton**[9] 5139 4-9-6 59 .... (v) RobbieFitzpatrick 3 59
(Richard Guest) *hld up in tch: rdn and hdwy over 1f out: kpt on same pce ins fnl f* **13/2**[3]

056 **5** *2* **Manatee Bay**[16] 4887 3-8-11 53 .... AdrianNicholls 2 47
(David Nicholls) *chsd ldrs: ev ch and hung lft over 1f out: sn chsng wnr: lost 2nd and wknd ins fnl f* **12/1**

0050 **6** *3/4* **Baltic Bomber (IRE)**[20] 4761 4-9-1 54 .... BarryMcHugh 7 45
(John Quinn) *hld up in tch: drvn over 2f out: no imp fr over 1f out* **20/1**

5316 **7** *nk* **Romanticize**[109] 1886 7-9-5 58 .... TomEaves 8 48
(Jason Ward) *chsd ldr to over 1f out: sn rdn and wknd* **14/1**

2600 **8** *9* **Code Six (IRE)**[38] 4148 4-8-13 52 .... (p) RoystonFfrench 1 15
(Bryan Smart) *led to over 1f out: sn rdn and wknd* **33/1**

1m 15.09s (0.49) **Going Correction** +0.225s/f (Good)
WFA 3 from 4yo+ 3lb **8** Ran SP% **115.8**
Speed ratings (Par 101): **105,103,102,101,99 98,97,85**
toteswingers 1&2 £2.50, 1&3 £4.00, 2&3 £4.10 CSF £4.77 CT £31.93 TOTE £1.50: £1.02, £1.50, £3.60; EX 5.70 Trifecta £43.80 Pool: £2396.02 - 40.97 winning units..
Owner Dundalk Racing Club **Bred** Thomas Jones **Trained** Nawton, N Yorks

FOCUS
Another run-of-the-mill sprint.

5487 MTREC RECRUITMENT/TRAINING H'CAP (DIV II) 6f
5:55 (5:55) (Class 6) (0-65,65) 3-Y-O+ £1,940 (£577; £288; £144) **Stalls** Centre

Form RPR

0044 **1** **Black Douglas**[16] 4891 4-8-10 49 .... TomEaves 7 56
(Jim Goldie) *prom: niggled over 2f out: hdwy and swtchd rt over 1f out: styd on wl fnl f to ld towards fin* **9/2**[3]

0506 **2** *nk* **One Kool Dude**[10] 5085 4-9-1 54 .... (b) AndrewElliott 5 60
(Neville Bycroft) *t.k.h early: cl up: led 1/2-way: rdn and edgd lft over 1f out: styd on fnl f: hdd towards fin* **16/1**

3522 **3** *1 3/4* **Hazza The Jazza**[9] 5150 3-9-1 60 .... (b) JasonHart(3) 2 61
(Richard Guest) *dwlt: hld up in tch: pushed along over 2f out: hdwy over 1f out: kpt on same pce wl ins fnl f* **6/4**[1]

5212 **4** *3* **Abraham Monro**[8] 5184 3-8-13 55 .... JamesSullivan 8 47
(Ruth Carr) *led to 1/2-way: sn rdn and rallied: edgd rt over 1f out: outpcd fnl f* **2/1**[2]

-300 **5** *3/4* **Belinsky (IRE)**[22] 4669 6-9-6 59 .... [1] BarryMcHugh 6 49
(Julie Camacho) *trckd ldrs: effrt and rdn over 2f out: edgd rt over 1f out: wknd ins fnl f* **14/1**

3000 **6** *3/4* **Dr Victoria**[80] 2757 4-8-9 48 oh1 ow2 .... PaddyAspell 3 35
(John Norton) *hld up bhd ldng gp: effrt 2f out: no imp fnl f* **66/1**

450 **7** *4* **Star Up In The Sky (USA)**[22] 4670 3-9-9 65 .... BrianHughes 9 40
(Kevin Ryan) *taken early to post: trckd ldrs tl rdn and wknd appr 2f out* **12/1**

1m 15.86s (1.26) **Going Correction** +0.225s/f (Good)
WFA 3 from 4yo+ 3lb **7** Ran SP% **113.2**
Speed ratings (Par 101): **100,99,97,93,92 91,85**
toteswingers 1&2 £3.30, 1&3 £2.10, 2&3 £6.70 CSF £66.65 CT £154.47 TOTE £6.00: £2.30, £3.10; EX 34.60 Trifecta £134.00 Pool: £1511.51 - 8.45 winning units..
Owner Dr J Walker **Bred** D P And Mrs J A Martin **Trained** Uplawmoor, E Renfrews

FOCUS
The second division of this low-grade sprint.
T/Plt: £398.30 to a £1 stake. Pool: £61,200.49 - 112.15 winning units T/Qpdt: £19.20 to a £1 stake. Pool: £6055.15 - 232.55 winning units RY

5435 NEWMARKET (R-H)
Friday, August 16

OFFICIAL GOING: Good to firm changing to good (good to firm in places) after race 1 (5.25)
Wind: Light to medium; half behind Weather: Showers and bright spells

5488 TURFTV MEDIAN AUCTION MAIDEN STKS 7f
5:25 (5:26) (Class 5) 2-Y-O £3,234 (£962; £481; £240) **Stalls** High

Form RPR

1 **Hors De Combat** 2-9-5 0 .... FrederikTylicki 10 87+
(James Fanshawe) *trckd ldrs and a travelling wl: gng best and nt clr run 2f out: swtchd rt over 1f out and qcknd to ld ent fnl f: r.o strly: readily* **12/1**

6 **2** *1 3/4* **Rosehill Artist (IRE)**[13] 5003 2-9-0 0 .... AndreaAtzeni 9 77
(Charles Hills) *chsd ldrs: effrt u.p to chal over 1f out: chsd wnr fnl f: r.o but a hld* **5/1**[3]

2 **3** *3 1/2* **Inchila**[15] 4921 2-9-0 0 .... RobertHavlin 11 68
(Peter Chapple-Hyam) *pressed ldr: rdn and ev ch 2f out: no ex and btn fnl 150yds: wknd towards fin* **5/4**[1]

6 **4** *4* **Moonspring (IRE)**[23] 4631 2-9-0 0 .... MartinLane 6 58
(Tobias B P Coles) *rn green: in tch in midfield: rdn and outpcd 2f out: modest 5th over 1f out: no threat but kpt on steadily fnl f* **50/1**

5 *1* **Interconnection** 2-9-5 0 .... LukeMorris 7 60
(Ed Vaughan) *towards rr: rdn and sme hdwy over 2f out: 6th and no imp whn rn green and edgd lft over 1f out: wl hld but kpt on steadily ins fnl f* **33/1**

0 **6** *1* **Nashmi**[7] 5244 2-9-5 0 .... KirstyMilczarek 1 58
(Fawzi Abdulla Nass, Bahrain) *t.k.h: led: rdn wl over 1f out: hdd 1f out: sn btn: fdd qckly ins fnl f* **16/1**

0 **7** *2 1/2* **Earthflight**[13] 5003 2-9-0 0 .... WilliamCarson 5 46
(Philip McBride) *in tch towards rr: rdn and struggling 3f out: wknd ent fnl 2f: wl btn and swtchd rt over 1f out* **50/1**

8 *1* **Irish Tears** 2-9-5 0 .... WilliamBuick 3 49
(John Gosden) *rn green: s.i.s: a in rr: rdn and struggling 3f out: bhd over 1f out* **9/2**[2]

9 *3* **Magnus Romeo** 2-9-5 0 .... NeilCallan 8 41
(Marco Botti) *s.i.s: sn in tch in midfield: rdn and struggling over 2f out: wknd qckly wl over 1f out* **13/2**

00 **10** *3* **Spreadable (IRE)**[14] 4958 2-9-5 0 .... J-PGuillambert 2 33
(Nick Littmoden) *t.k.h: chsd ldrs tl rdn and lost pl over 2f out: fdd over 1f out* **100/1**

0 **11** *2 1/4* **Sexy Secret**[14] 4958 2-9-5 0 .... SaleemGolam 4 27
(Noel Quinlan) *stdd s: a in rr: lost tch over 2f out* **50/1**

1m 26.2s (0.50) **Going Correction** 0.0s/f (Good) **11** Ran SP% **116.0**
Speed ratings (Par 94): **97,95,91,86,85 84,81,80,76,73 70**
toteswingers 1&2 £4.40, 1&3 £4.00, 2&3 £2.60 CSF £68.56 TOTE £16.50: £3.40, £1.60, £1.10; EX 84.50 Trifecta £395.00 Pool: £2108.93 - 4.00 winning units..
Owner Chris Van Hoorn **Bred** Newsells Park Stud **Trained** Newmarket, Suffolk

FOCUS
Far side track used. Stalls far side except 1m2f: centre. Repositioning of bend into home straight added 16m to 1m2f race. They raced against the far rail in this maiden. The leading form contender was a bit disappointing but a newcomer scored in good style and they finished quite well strung out. The form is fluid but fits in with the lower end of race averages.

5489 TALK NIGHT CLUB SOUTHEND H'CAP (JOCKEY CLUB GRASSROOTS SPRINT SERIES QUALIFIER) 6f
6:00 (6:01) (Class 4) (0-85,85) 3-Y-O+ £4,851 (£1,443; £721; £360) **Stalls** High

Form RPR

0564 **1** **Hadaj**[8] 5183 4-9-4 77 .... FrederikTylicki 8 89
(Ruth Carr) *led tl over 3f out: styd pressing ldr tl rdn to ld again over 1f out: styd on wl fnl f: rdn out* **7/2**[1]

1-00 **2** *1 1/2* **Midnight Rider (IRE)**[13] 5009 5-9-11 84 .... GeorgeBaker 2 91
(Chris Wall) *hld up in tch in last pair: rdn and hdwy whn swtchd rt jst over 1f out: styd on wl ins fnl f: snatched 2nd last stride* **13/2**

3023 **3** *shd* **Commanche**[7] 5219 4-8-10 74 .... RobertTart(5) 9 81
(Chris Dwyer) *taken down early: chsd ldrs: drvn to chse wnr jst over 1f out: styd on same pce ins fnl f: lost 2nd last stride* **17/2**

0065 **4** *1/2* **L'Ami Louis (IRE)**[13] 5009 5-9-10 83 .... FergusSweeney 5 88
(Henry Candy) *t.k.h: chsd ldr tl led over 3f out: rdn and hdd over 1f out: styd on same pce ins fnl f* **6/1**[3]

0540 **5** *1 1/2* **Piazza San Pietro**[7] 5219 7-9-6 79 .... (b[1]) NeilCallan 6 79
(Zoe Davison) *awkward leaving stalls: sn in tch in midfield: rdn and sltly outpcd 2f out: kpt on but no threat to ldrs fnl f* **33/1**

0004 **6** *2 1/2* **Living Leader**[21] 4718 4-9-0 73 .... (v) TomMcLaughlin 3 65
(Nick Littmoden) *taken down early: chsd ldrs: rdn and unable qck ent fnl 2f: outpcd over 1f out: one pce after* **20/1**

1550 **7** *1/2* **Trojan Rocket (IRE)**[13] 5009 5-9-7 80 .... ChrisCatlin 4 71
(Michael Wigham) *s.i.s: sn pushed along in rr: drvn and no real imp wl over 1f out: kpt on past btn horses ins fnl f: n.d* **8/1**

4213 8 hd **Bajan Bear**11 5062 5-9-2 75 LukeMorris 1 65
(Michael Blanshard) *in tch in midfield: effrt u.p but no imp over 1f out: wl hld and one pce fnl f* **9/1**

2424 9 2 3/4 **Peace Seeker**28 4494 5-9-5 78 WilliamCarson 10 59
(Anthony Carson) *in tch in midfield: u.p and nt qckning 2f out: btn over 1f out: wknd fnl f* **10/1**

0013 10 3 1/4 **Jack My Boy (IRE)**46 3887 6-9-1 77 (b) DeclanBates(3) 11 48
(David Evans) *chsd ldrs: lost pl and rdn 1/2-way: bhd and eased wl ins fnl f* **20/1**

2541 11 1 **Excuse To Linger**17 4864 3-9-9 85 (v) WilliamBuick 7 53
(Jeremy Noseda) *rrd as stalls opened and slowly away: plld hrd and hld up in tch in rr: hdwy over 2f out: no imp and edgd lft 1f out: sn wknd and eased wl ins fnl f* **11/2**2

1m 12.71s (0.21) **Going Correction** 0.0s/f (Good)
WFA 3 from 4yo+ 3lb 11 Ran SP% **118.4**
Speed ratings (Par 105): **98,96,95,95,93 89,89,88,85,80 79**
toteswingers 1&2 £7.70, 1&3 £7.90, 2&3 £5.30 CSF £25.43 CT £185.27 TOTE £4.20: £1.60, £2.50, £3.00; EX 28.60 Trifecta £232.80 Pool: £1407.43 - 4.53 winning units..
Owner Sprint Thoroughbred Racing **Bred** Rabbah Bloodstock Limited **Trained** Huby, N Yorks

FOCUS
They raced up the centre of the track in this fair handicap. The pace was not very strong and the favourite scored under a prominent ride. The winner might be able to do better with the placed horses setting the level.

5490 HONEY TRAP AT TALK NIGHT CLUB EBF MAIDEN STKS 1m
6:30 (6:33) (Class 4) 2-Y-O **£4,528** (£1,347; £673; £336) **Stalls** High

Form RPR

1 **Pinzolo** 2-9-5 0 MartinLane 4 83+
(Charlie Appleby) *hld up in tch in midfield: rdn and effrt 2f out: chal over 1f out: led ins fnl f: rn green and hung rt in front: r.o wl* **10/1**

4 2 1 1/2 **Sudden Wonder (IRE)**55 3581 2-9-5 0 MickaelBarzalona 2 80
(Charlie Appleby) *niggled along in midfield: hdwy to chse ldrs and travelling bttr over 3f out: wnt 2nd jst over 2f out: drvn and ev ch over 1f out: chsd wnr and kpt on same pce ins fnl f* **9/4**2

3 3/4 **Munjaz** 2-9-5 0 PaulHanagan 1 78+
(John Gosden) *rn green: dwlt: in tch in rr: hdwy and rdn to chse ldrs over 1f out: kpt on same pce and wnt 3rd wl ins fnl f* **13/8**1

4 4 1 3/4 **Rock 'N' Roll Star**35 4256 2-9-5 0 GeorgeBaker 9 74
(Charles Hills) *led: wnt rt after 1f: rdn wl over 1f out: drvn and hrd pressed over 1f out: hdd ins fnl f: sn btn wknd towards fin* **3/1**3

5 8 **Almerzem (USA)** 2-9-5 0 ChrisCatlin 10 56
(Saeed bin Suroor) *chsd ldr tl jst over 2f out: sn outpcd and btn: wknd over 1f out* **12/1**

0 6 2 3/4 **Frederic Chopin**20 4764 2-9-5 0 AndreaAtzeni 7 50
(Stuart Williams) *chsd ldrs: rdn over 1f out: sn struggling: wknd over 1f out* **66/1**

7 24 **Black Tie Dancer (IRE)** 2-9-5 0 LukeMorris 6
(Gay Kelleway) *t.k.h: chsd ldrs tl lost pl and bhd 1/2-way: lost tch 2f out: t.o* **25/1**

6 8 1/2 **Lucarvey**7 5229 2-9-0 0 1 SaleemGolam 3
(Chris Dwyer) *taken down early: t.k.h: hld up in rr: rdn and struggling 3f out: sn lost tch: t.o* **100/1**

1m 41.63s (1.63) **Going Correction** 0.0s/f (Good) 8 Ran SP% **117.0**
Speed ratings (Par 96): **91,89,88,87,79 76,52,51**
toteswingers 1&2 £4.00, 1&3 £3.90, 2&3 £1.50 CSF £33.56 TOTE £15.10: £2.40, £1.10, £1.20; EX 40.70 Trifecta £165.70 Pool: £2396.25 - 10.83 winning units..
Owner Godolphin **Bred** Fittocks Stud **Trained** Newmarket, Suffolk

FOCUS
This is usually a hot maiden. It was won by the mighty Frankel in 2010 and subsequent Derby hero Motivator landed the race in 2004. The pace was not very strong in this interesting renewal and a 10-1 winner beat his stablemate in a fairly tight four-way finish. The level is fluid but the form could work out well.

5491 MARITIME CARGO SERVICES H'CAP 1m
7:00 (7:01) (Class 5) (0-75,75) 3-Y-O+ **£3,234** (£962; £481; £240) **Stalls** High

Form RPR

6103 1 **Azma (USA)**21 4721 3-9-4 73 PaulHanagan 8 83
(Conrad Allen) *mde all: rdn 2f out: hrd pressed and battled on gamely u.p fnl f: all out* **7/2**2

00-2 2 1/2 **Junket**9 5149 6-9-8 74 (t) DarrenEgan(3) 9 84+
(Dr Jon Scargill) *hld up in tch towards rr: hdwy u.p over 1f out: ev ch ins fnl f: kpt on same pce fnl 50yds: wnt 2nd last stride* **5/1**3

6000 3 nse **Sardanapalus**14 4966 4-9-4 67 (p) NeilCallan 2 77
(Kevin Ryan) *in tch in midfield: effrt u.p over 1f out: swtchd lft and str chal ent fnl f: no ex and one pce fnl 50yds: lost 2nd last stride* **12/1**

-314 4 2 1/2 **Capella's Song (IRE)**16 4898 3-9-3 72 WilliamBuick 6 75
(Michael Bell) *in tch in midfield: shuffled bk 2f out: rdn and rallied over 1f out: chsd ldng trio jst ins fnl f: one pce and no imp after* **3/1**1

3126 5 1 3/4 **Enriching (USA)**9 5124 5-9-2 70 RobertTart(5) 5 70
(Gary Harrison) *chsd ldrs: rdn 3f out: drvn and outpcd wl over 1f out: rallied and kpt on ins fnl f: no threat to ldrs* **6/1**

2010 6 3 1/2 **Poor Duke (IRE)**25 4593 3-9-3 72 (p) FergusSweeney 7 63
(Jamie Osborne) *chsd ldrs: drvn and no ex over 1f out: btn and edgd rt 1f out: wknd ins fnl f* **10/1**

0344 7 1/2 **Thecornishcowboy**28 4490 4-9-8 71 (t) KirstyMilczarek 11 62
(John Ryan) *chsd ldrs: rdn over 2f out: drvn and outpcd over 1f out: wknd fnl f* **14/1**

4-05 8 1/2 **Silver Lace (IRE)**16 4894 4-9-0 63 TedDurcan 4 53
(Chris Wall) *hld up in tch in rr: effrt u.p wl over 1f out: no real hdwy and btn 1f out: wknd fnl f* **14/1**

2110 9 5 **Travelling**16 4898 4-9-12 75 SeanLevey 1 53
(Tony Carroll) *hld up in tch towards rr: drvn and no hdwy wl over 1f out: wknd ent fnl f* **16/1**

0045 10 1 1/2 **Beau Select (IRE)**22 4665 3-8-6 61 AndreaAtzeni 12 35
(Robert Eddery) *in tch in midfield: rdn and unable qck over 2f out: wknd u.p over 1f out* **25/1**

0550 11 22 **Three Choirs (IRE)**17 4865 3-8-8 68 (tp) LauraPike(5) 3
(William Stone) *dwlt: nvr gng wl in rr: rdn and struggling 1/2-way: lost tch 2f out: t.o* **33/1**

1m 39.18s (-0.82) **Going Correction** 0.0s/f (Good)
WFA 3 from 4yo+ 6lb 11 Ran SP% **121.0**
Speed ratings (Par 103): **104,103,103,100,99 95,95,94,89,88 66**
toteswingers 1&2 £5.50, 1&3 £11.00, 2&3 £20.10 CSF £22.20 CT £198.20 TOTE £4.20: £1.70, £2.30, £4.90; EX 23.50 Trifecta £574.20 Pool: £1074.73 - 1.40 winning units..
Owner A Al Hajri **Bred** Robert Raphaelson **Trained** Newmarket, Suffolk

FOCUS
There was a tight three-way finish in this competitive handicap. The runner-up sets the level rated to her latest Pontefract mark.

5492 PIPER-HEIDSIECK H'CAP 1m 2f
7:35 (7:37) (Class 5) (0-70,70) 3-Y-O+ **£3,234** (£962; £481; £240) **Stalls** Centre

Form RPR

3642 1 **Nautilus**7 5245 3-9-5 69 WilliamBuick 4 92+
(John Gosden) *t.k.h: led for over 1f: chsd ldr after tl rdn to ld ent fnl 2f: drew clr u.p over 1f out: eased towards fin* **11/8**1

0033 2 15 **Laconicos (IRE)**7 5245 11-8-13 55 (t) LukeMorris 8 49
(William Stone) *taken down early: in tch in midfield: rdn and lost pl over 3f out: wl btn over 1f out: plugged on past btn horses ins fnl f: wnt 2nd nr fin: no ch w wnr* **10/1**

-354 3 1/2 **Giantstepsahead (IRE)**11 5072 4-9-4 60 TedDurcan 6 53
(Michael Wigham) *t.k.h: chsd ldrs: rdn and struggling 3f out: outpcd and wl btn over 1f out: plugged on fnl 100yds to snatch 3rd last strides* **10/1**

0000 4 hd **Ela Goog La Mou**57 3496 4-8-6 51 oh6 RosieJessop(3) 3 44
(Peter Charalambous) *t.k.h: sn chsng ldr tl led over 8f out: racd along towards stands' rail in st: rdn and hdd ent fnl 2f: no ch w wnr over 1f out: tired but battled on gamely fnl f: lost 2 pls nr fin* **66/1**

4423 5 nk **Kingston Eucalypt**22 4656 3-9-4 68 AndreaAtzeni 5 60
(Ed Vaughan) *chsd ldrs: rdn and effrt over 2f out: outpcd and wl btn over 1f out: plugged on same pce fnl f* **12/1**

0543 6 1 1/2 **Petrify**23 4629 3-8-9 59 KirstyMilczarek 7 48
(Luca Cumani) *t.k.h: hld up in tch in midfield: rdn and effrt over 2f out: no ch w wnr but pressing for pls over 1f out: plugged on same pce* **7/2**2

0210 7 1/2 **Super Cookie**28 4508 3-9-2 66 WilliamCarson 1 54
(Philip McBride) *in tch in midfield: rdn and effrt to chse ldrs over 2f out: btn but ev ch of 2nd over 1f out: wknd ins fnl f* **5/1**3

3365 8 3 3/4 **Mcbirney (USA)**28 4490 6-10-0 70 FrederikTylicki 10 51
(Paul D'Arcy) *hld up in tch in last pair: hdwy to chse ldrs and rdn 3f out: outpcd and wl btn over 1f out: wknd ins fnl f* **20/1**

0-60 9 91 **Masters Blazing**137 1290 4-9-11 67 ChrisCatlin 9
(John Ryan) *hld up in last pair: lost tch 4f out: t.o and virtually p.u fnl 2f* **33/1**

2m 5.84s (0.34) **Going Correction** 0.0s/f (Good)
WFA 3 from 4yo+ 8lb 9 Ran SP% **116.1**
Speed ratings (Par 103): **98,86,85,85,85 84,83,80,7**
toteswingers 1&2 £3.70, 1&3 £2.60, 2&3 £15.70 CSF £16.62 CT £102.32 TOTE £2.10: £1.20, £2.40, £2.00; EX 16.40 Trifecta £124.90 Pool: £1608.03 - 9.64 winning units..
Owner Abdulla Al Khalifa **Bred** Sheikh Abdulla Bin Isa Al Khalifa **Trained** Newmarket, Suffolk

FOCUS
A highly progressive 3-y-o absolutely hammered his rivals in this handicap. The form could be rated higher through the runner-up but is treated cautiously with doubts about the third and fourth.

5493 PIPER-HEIDSIECK FILLIES' H'CAP 7f
8:05 (8:07) (Class 3) (0-95,86) 3-Y-O+ **£7,439** (£2,213; £1,106; £553) **Stalls** High

Form RPR

116 1 **Askaud (IRE)**16 4879 5-9-12 86 (p) FrederikTylicki 3 95
(Scott Dixon) *mde all: rdn 2f out: fnd ex and drew clr w rival jst ins fnl f: styd on gamely: all out* **7/2**2

3-13 2 1 **Ghanaian (FR)**48 3835 3-9-7 86 MickaelBarzalona 8 90
(Charlie Appleby) *hld up in tch in midfield: clsd 2f out: rdn and qcknd to chal over 1f out: ev ch and clr w wnr ins fnl f: no ex fnl 50yds* **7/4**1

1511 3 4 1/2 **Malekat Jamal (IRE)**20 4766 4-9-3 80 DarrenEgan(3) 4 74
(David Simcock) *hld up in tch in rr: hdwy 3f out: rdn to chse ldrs over 1f out: no ex u.p 1f out: wknd ins fnl f* **4/1**3

0400 4 4 **Perfect Haven**14 4957 3-8-9 74 PaulHanagan 5 55
(Ralph Beckett) *chsd ldrs: rdn and effrt over 2f out: chsd wnr briefly 2f out: 4th and btn over 1f out: wknd fnl f* **12/1**

3634 5 1 1/4 **Alice's Dancer (IRE)**27 4525 4-9-6 80 DougieCostello 7 60
(William Muir) *plld hrd: hld up in tch in rr: hdwy 3f out: rdn and no hdwy over 1f out: 5th and wknd fnl f* **10/1**

24-3 6 15 **Diamond Belle**18 4830 4-9-4 78 PatCosgrave 2 17
(Noel Quinlan) *t.k.h: chsd ldrs: rdn and unable qck ent fnl 2f: wknd qckly over 1f out* **9/1**

-554 7 nk **Tipping Over (IRE)**20 4766 3-8-12 84 NoelGarbutt(7) 1 21
(Hugo Palmer) *chsd ldrs: wnt 2nd over 4f out tl 2f out: sn btn and wknd* **8/1**

0-06 8 18 **Thecornishwren (IRE)**17 4867 4-8-2 67 oh22 (b1) NatashaEaton(5) 6
(John Ryan) *chsd wnr tl over 4f out: sn lost pl and bhd fnl 2f: t.o* **100/1**

1m 25.78s (0.08) **Going Correction** 0.0s/f (Good)
WFA 3 from 4yo+ 5lb 8 Ran SP% **117.5**
Speed ratings (Par 104): **99,97,92,88,86 69,69,48**
toteswingers 1&2 £2.40, 1&3 £2.20, 2&3 £1.80 CSF £10.37 CT £25.31 TOTE £6.60: £1.50, £1.20, £1.70; EX 12.10 Trifecta £27.20 Pool: £2546.86 - 70.18 winning units..
Owner Paul J Dixon **Bred** John P Jones **Trained** Babworth, Notts

FOCUS
They went a steady pace up the centre of the track in this handicap but the two market leaders pulled clear and the form looks solid.
T/Jkpt: Not won. T/Plt: £12.40 to a £1 stake. Pool: £63,565.58 - 3726.98 winning units T/Qpdt: £3.80 to a £1 stake. Pool: £5452.90 - 1048.79 winning units SP

5371 NOTTINGHAM (L-H)
Friday, August 16

OFFICIAL GOING: Good to soft (good in places; 7.5)
Wind: Light half against Weather: Cloudy with sunny periods

5494 BREEDERS BACKING RACING E B F MAIDEN STKS 6f 15y
2:00 (2:01) (Class 5) 2-Y-O **£3,234** (£962; £481; £240) **Stalls** Centre

Form RPR

0 1 **Gamesome (FR)**13 4987 2-9-5 0 MickaelBarzalona 10 95+
(Olly Stevens) *hld up in tch: smooth hdwy 1/2-way: trckd ldr wl over 1f out: rdn to ld ins fnl f: edgd lft and sn clr* **6/1**3

04 2 3 **Speedfiend**43 3991 2-9-5 0 PatCosgrave 6 86
(Noel Quinlan) *led: rdn along wl over 1f out: hdd ins fnl f: kpt on same pce* **5/1**2

2 3 7 **Makhfar (IRE)**19 4795 2-9-5 0 WilliamBuick 3 64
(John Gosden) *trckd ldrs: pushed along 1/2-way: rdn and outpcd over 2f out: kpt on same pce appr fnl f* **1/2**1

4 1 1/2 **Look Here's Al** 2-9-5 0 FrannyNorton 11 60+
(Ed McMahon) *hld up towards rr: pushed along over 2f out: styd on fr over 1f out: nrst fin* **16/1**

5 2 **Oak Bluffs (IRE)** 2-8-12 0 .... JoshQuinn(7) 8 54
(Richard Fahey) *towards rr tl sme late hdwy* **50/1**

5 6 *nk* **Sahra Al Khadra**[14] 4958 2-9-2 0 .... PatrickHills(3) 1 53
(Charles Hills) *in tch: hdwy on wd outside to chse ldrs 1/2-way: rdn along over 2f out: wkng whn bmpd and carried lft wl over 1f out* **12/1**

7 *1/2* **Misu's Maite** 2-8-11 0 .... MarkCoumbe(3) 4 46
(Roy Bowring) *prom: rdn along over 2f out: sn hung lft and wknd wl over 1f out* **66/1**

0544 8 *4* **Maximilianthefirst**[6] 5276 2-9-5 48 .... (t) J-PGuillambert 7 39
(P J O'Gorman) *chsd ldr: rdn along 1/2-way: sn wknd* **200/1**

9 *3 1/4* **Injaz** 2-9-5 0 .... StephenCraine 9 29
(Kevin Ryan) *wnt lft s: green and a in rr* **33/1**

10 *37* **Vadara** 2-9-5 0 .... SamHitchcott 5
(Michael Easterby) *s.i.s: green and a in rr: outpcd and bhd fr 1/2-way* **100/1**

1m 14.87s (0.17) **Going Correction** -0.05s/f (Good) **10** Ran SP% **119.1**
Speed ratings (Par 94): **96,92,82,80,78 77,76,71,67,17**
toteswingers 1&2 £6.20, 1&3 £3.60, 2&3 £1.40 CSF £36.29 TOTE £10.30: £2.10, £1.30, £1.02; EX 37.00 Trifecta £108.40 Pool: £1504.97 - 10.40 winning units..

Owner Qatar Racing & Essafinaat **Bred** Jean-Pierre Deroubaix **Trained** Chiddingfold, Surrey

FOCUS
Outer track used and home bend moved out 5m from inner line, increasing distances on Round course by about 11yds. No great depth to this maiden and, with the red-hot favourite running poorly, it would be unwise to get carried away with the form.

5495 YOUR EXPERT GUIDE TO NOTTINGHAM NOTTINGHAMRACECOURSETIPS.CO.UK MAIDEN STKS 1m 75y

2:30 (2:32) (Class 5) 3-Y-0 **£3,234** (£962; £481; £240) **Stalls** Centre

Form RPR

2222 1 **Thouwra (IRE)**[29] 4454 3-9-5 82 .... (p) MickaelBarzalona 2 84+
(Saeed bin Suroor) *trckd ldrs: hdwy over 3f out: chsd ldr over 2f out: led wl over 1f out: sn rdn clr* **4/6**[1]

05 2 *2 3/4* **Red Warrior (IRE)**[14] 4968 3-9-5 0 .... PatCosgrave 7 78+
(Ismail Mohammed) *sn led: pushed clr 3f out: rdn 2f out: hdd and drvn over 1f out: kpt on same pce* **40/1**

5 3 *2 3/4* **Angus Glens**[25] 4590 3-9-5 0 .... SteveDrowne 1 72+
(Ali Brewer) *trckd ldr: pushed along over 3f out: rdn over 2f out: kpt on same pce* **9/1**[3]

0 4 *2* **Evermore (IRE)**[31] 4381 3-9-0 0 .... FrannyNorton 3 62
(Mark Johnston) *trckd ldrs: hdwy to chse ldr after 3f: rdn along 3f out: grad wknd fnl 2f* **10/1**

5 *1* **Empress Adelaide** 3-9-0 0 .... LiamJones 11 62+
(William Haggas) *towards rr: hdwy over 3f out: rdn along 2f out: sn no imp* **12/1**

6 *1 3/4* **Cornrow** 3-9-5 0 .... [1] WilliamBuick 9 61
(John Gosden) *t.k.h in rr: swtchd rt and hdwy wl over 2f out: kpt on appr fnl f: n.d* **7/2**[2]

5-50 7 *3 3/4* **Shenval**[15] 4927 3-9-5 0 .... StevieDonohoe 6 52
(Noel Quinlan) *in tch: rdn along 3f out: sn outpcd* **66/1**

06 8 *5* **Hispania (IRE)**[30] 4404 3-8-7 0 .... ThomasHemsley(7) 12 36
(Michael Bell) *a towards rr* **80/1**

0-0 9 *1 1/2* **Zarla**[98] 2215 3-9-0 0 .... JimmyQuinn 8 32
(Tom Dascombe) *chsd ldrs: rdn along over 3f out: sn wknd* **50/1**

0-0 10 *1 3/4* **Captain Caroline**[38] 4151 3-9-0 0 .... PatDobbs 13 28
(Mike Murphy) *a towards rr* **80/1**

0 11 *5* **Up Tipp**[31] 4381 3-9-5 0 .... KieranO'Neill 5 22
(Mike Murphy) *a towards rr* **100/1**

12 *28* **Spurned Girl** 3-9-0 0 .... AndrewMullen 10
(Michael Appleby) *v.s.a and green: a wl bhd* **80/1**

1m 46.45s (-2.55) **Going Correction** -0.25s/f (Firm) **12** Ran SP% **119.6**
Speed ratings (Par 100): **102,99,96,94,93 91,88,83,81,79 74,46**
toteswingers 1&2 £26.00, 1&3 £3.50, 2&3 £27.30 CSF £47.22 TOTE £1.80: £1.02, £9.70, £2.40; EX 28.50 Trifecta £182.70 Pool: £1688.80 - 6.93 winning units..

Owner Godolphin **Bred** Darley **Trained** Newmarket, Suffolk

FOCUS
This was all about the previously frustrating odds-on winner.

5496 THOROUGHBRED BREEDERS' ASSOCIATION FILLIES' H'CAP 1m 2f 50y

3:00 (3:01) (Class 3) (0-95,84) 3-Y-0 **£9,703** (£2,887; £1,443; £721) **Stalls** Low

Form RPR

412 1 **Odeliz (IRE)**[43] 3995 3-8-12 82 .... JoeyHaynes(7) 3 95+
(Mrs K Burke) *trckd ldng pair: effrt and nt clr run 2f out and again over 1f out: squeezed through to chal 1f out: rdn and qcknd to ld ins fnl f: styd on wl* **11/4**[2]

-012 2 *1 1/4* **Missed Call (IRE)**[15] 4929 3-9-6 83 .... MickaelBarzalona 4 91
(Lady Cecil) *trckd ldrs: hdwy 3f out: led over 2f out: rdn over 1f out: drvn and hdd ins fnl f: kpt on same pce* **85/40**[1]

4-63 3 *4 1/2* **Penny Rose**[8] 5169 3-9-6 83 .... FrannyNorton 8 82
(Mark Johnston) *cl up: effrt to dispute ld 3f out: cl up and rdn 2f out: drvn and wknd over 1f out* **12/1**

410 4 *2 1/2* **Northern Meeting (IRE)**[14] 4950 3-9-0 77 .... PatDobbs 7 71
(Sir Michael Stoute) *hld up in tch: hdwy 3f out: rdn and cl up 2f out: ev ch whn drvn over 1f out and sn wknd* **11/2**[3]

1122 5 *1* **Aeronwyn Bryn (IRE)**[16] 4890 3-9-0 82 .... ConnorBeasley(5) 6 74
(Michael Dods) *hld up in rr: hdwy on wd outside 3f out: rdn and ch wl over 1f out: sn drvn and wknd* **12/1**

1024 6 *3 1/4* **Fersah (USA)**[27] 4541 3-9-7 84 .... (p) PatCosgrave 2 70
(William Haggas) *led: rdn along 3f out: hdd over 2f out: sn drvn and wknd* **7/1**

0316 7 *2 3/4* **A Star In My Eye (IRE)**[16] 4878 3-9-1 78 .... JimmyQuinn 1 59
(Kevin Ryan) *chsd ldrs: sn rdn along: rn in snatches: lost pl 1/2-way: sn in rr* **8/1**

2m 11.38s (-2.92) **Going Correction** -0.25s/f (Firm) **7** Ran SP% **113.0**
Speed ratings (Par 101): **101,100,96,94,93 91,88**
toteswingers 1&2 £2.10, 1&3 £17.70, 2&3 £8.00 CSF £8.81 CT £55.99 TOTE £2.90: £1.90, £1.40; EX 8.30 Trifecta £47.70 Pool: £1069.81 - 16.80 winning units..

Owner McMahon Thoroughbreds Ltd & Mrs E Burke **Bred** Aleyrion Bloodstock Ltd **Trained** Middleham Moor, N Yorks

FOCUS
A good fillies' handicap, albeit one that was run at just a steady gallop, and the front pair drew clear.

5497 FREEBETS.CO.UK FREE BETS H'CAP 1m 2f 50y

3:35 (3:35) (Class 6) (0-65,65) 3-Y-0 **£2,045** (£603; £302) **Stalls** Low

Form RPR

0011 1 **Artful Prince**[4] 5334 3-9-1 59 6ex .... (b) DaleSwift 4 66
(James Given) *trckd ldrs: hdwy 3f out: chsd ldr 2f out: rdn and edgd lft over 1f out: drvn to chal and edgd lft ins fnl f: styd on wl u.p to ld nr fin* **8/11**[1]

5634 2 *hd* **Sixties Queen**[22] 4689 3-8-2 53 .... TimClark(7) 7 60
(Alan Bailey) *hld up in tch: smooth hdwy to ld wl over 2f out: rdn clr over 1f out: edgd lft ins fnl f: hdd and no ex nr line* **14/1**

0354 3 *3* **War Lord (IRE)**[13] 5016 3-9-4 62 .... (v) FrannyNorton 8 64
(David O'Meara) *led: rdn along over 3f out: hdd wl over 2f out: drvn wl over 1f out: kpt on same pce* **4/1**[2]

5-04 4 *6* **Lucky Black Star (IRE)**[23] 4629 3-9-2 60 .... PatCosgrave 9 50
(George Baker) *hld up in rr: hdwy 3f out: rdn along over 2f out: no imp* **25/1**

004- 5 *1 1/4* **Likelikelikelikeit**[330] 6413 3-8-10 57 .... SimonPearce(3) 6 44
(Mark H Tompkins) *in rr: rdn and sme hdwy over 2f out: n.d* **40/1**

3323 6 *10* **Zhuba (IRE)**[22] 4688 3-9-7 65 .... (p) SteveDrowne 5 33
(John Best) *chsd ldr: rdn along over 3f out: sn wknd* **15/2**[3]

-060 7 *shd* **Rocky Two (IRE)**[15] 4931 3-8-11 60 .... (p) ConnorBeasley(5) 3 28
(Michael Dods) *trckd ldng pair: hdwy to chse ldr 3f out: rdn over 2f out and sn wknd* **9/1**

2m 13.13s (-1.17) **Going Correction** -0.25s/f (Firm) **7** Ran SP% **112.6**
Speed ratings (Par 98): **94,93,91,86,85 77,77**
toteswingers 1&2 £19.90, 1&3 £1.10, 2&3 £5.90 CSF £12.60 CT £26.86 TOTE £1.50: £1.10, £7.80; EX 16.80 Trifecta £60.70 Pool: £1926.17 - 23.79 winning units..

Owner Ingram Racing **Bred** Graham Wilson **Trained** Willoughton, Lincs

FOCUS
Moderate handicap form.

5498 BONUS.CO.UK GET YOUR CASINO BONUS FILLIES' H'CAP (JOCKEY CLUB GRASSROOTS SPRINT SERIES QUALIFIER) 6f 15y

4:10 (4:11) (Class 3) (0-80,79) 3-Y-0+ **£6,469** (£1,925; £962; £481) **Stalls** Centre

Form RPR

5232 1 **Lulu The Zulu (IRE)**[13] 4982 5-8-13 66 .... AndrewMullen 8 76+
(Michael Appleby) *trckd ldrs: hdwy over 2f out: chsd ldr over 1f out: rdn to ld and edgd lft ins fnl f: sn drvn and hung lft: styd on wl towards fin* **11/4**[1]

4341 2 *1* **Big Wave (IRE)**[9] 5154 5-9-2 74 6ex .... (t) TobyAtkinson(5) 4 80+
(Alison Hutchinson) *rrd and wnt rt s: sn chsng ldrs: led 1/2-way: clr wl over 1f out: rdn and hdd ins fnl f: sn carried lft and hmpd: no ex towards fin* **10/1**

0005 3 *2 3/4* **Meandmyshadow**[13] 4993 5-9-11 78 .... DaleSwift 6 76
(Alan Brown) *led to 1/2-way: cl up: rdn along over 2f out: grad wknd* **15/2**

0340 4 *nse* **Ray Of Joy**[46] 3892 7-9-3 70 .... FrannyNorton 5 68
(J R Jenkins) *hmpd s: trckd ldrs: hdwy over 2f out: rdn wl over 1f out: kpt on same pce appr fnl f* **20/1**

0220 5 *3 1/4* **Caranbola**[2] 5381 7-9-4 71 .... JimmyQuinn 7 59
(Mel Brittain) *trckd ldrs: rdn along 2f out: grad wknd* **13/2**[3]

4101 6 *1* **Queen Hermione (IRE)**[13] 4982 5-8-2 62 .... (vt) AdamMcLean(7) 10 47
(Derek Shaw) *a towards rr* **4/1**[2]

0216 7 *3 3/4* **Song Of Parkes**[7] 5227 6-8-12 70 .... (b) SladeO'Hara(5) 11 44
(Peter Grayson) *a towards rr* **16/1**

2604 8 *1 3/4* **Whitecrest**[5] 5308 5-9-11 78 .... SamHitchcott 9 46
(John Spearing) *prom: rdn along bef 1/2-way: sn wknd* **8/1**

2043 9 *2* **Elnadwa (USA)**[20] 4776 3-9-6 76 .... (b[1]) PatDobbs 2 38
(Saeed bin Suroor) *chsd ldrs on outer: rdn along wl over 2f out: sn wknd* **8/1**

1m 14.75s (0.05) **Going Correction** -0.05s/f (Good)
WFA 3 from 4yo+ 3lb **9** Ran SP% **113.7**
Speed ratings (Par 104): **97,95,92,91,87 86,81,78,76**
toteswingers 1&2 £8.80, 1&3 £10.30, 2&3 £16.80 CSF £30.73 CT £185.35 TOTE £3.10: £1.40, £3.30, £2.70; EX 29.30 Trifecta £130.90 Pool: £1643.96 - 9.41 winning units..

Owner The Ab Kettlebys **Bred** Hong Kong Breeders Club **Trained** Danethorpe, Notts

■ Stewards' Enquiry : Andrew Mullen caution: careless riding.

FOCUS
The front pair drew clear late on.

5499 FREEBETS.CO.UK DOWNLOAD OUR FREE BETS APP H'CAP 5f 13y

4:40 (4:40) (Class 6) (0-60,66) 3-Y-0+ **£1,940** (£577; £288; £144) **Stalls** Centre

Form RPR

033 1 **Megaleka**[11] 5067 3-8-3 51 .... TimClark(7) 12 64+
(Alan Bailey) *towards rr: gd hdwy 2f out: str run whn edgd lft appr fnl f: sn rdn to ld and hung bdly lft ins fnl f: kpt on* **8/1**[3]

054 2 *2 3/4* **Gracie's Games**[10] 5097 7-8-11 50 .... (b) LiamJones 2 53
(John Spearing) *sltly hmpd s: trckd ldrs: hdwy on wd outside 2f out: rdn to chal over 1f out: ev ch whn hmpd ins fnl f: kpt on* **9/1**

0301 3 *1 1/2* **Quality Art (USA)**[5] 5305 5-9-4 62 6ex .... ConnorBeasley(5) 5 60
(Richard Guest) *trckd ldrs: cl up 1/2-way: led over 2f out: rdn and hdd whn hmpd jst ins fnl f: one pce after* **2/1**[1]

5-41 4 *2 3/4* **Ladweb**[11] 5060 3-9-8 66 6ex .... WilliamTwiston-Davies(3) 13 54
(John Gallagher) *in tch: hdwy 2f out: rdn over 1f out: sn no imp* **3/1**[2]

1204 5 *1/2* **Sir Geoffrey (IRE)**[10] 5085 7-9-4 57 .... (p) PaoloSirigu 9 43
(Scott Dixon) *prom: cl up 1/2-way: rdn along 2f out: drvn whn hmpd appr fnl f: one pce after* **10/1**

363 6 *1 1/4* **Whatwehavewehold**[8] 5200 3-9-1 56 .... (p) PatDobbs 3 38
(Alan McCabe) *led: rdn along 1/2-way: hdd over 2f out and grad wknd* **12/1**

000- 7 *1/2* **College Doll**[250] 8045 4-8-4 46 .... RyanPowell(3) 10 26
(Christine Dunnett) *a towards rr* **33/1**

3506 8 *1 1/4* **Give Us A Belle (IRE)**[8] 5200 4-8-7 46 oh1 .... (vt) SamHitchcott 8 22
(Christine Dunnett) *in tch: hdwy wl over 1f out: rdn and hld whn hmpd appr fnl f* **50/1**

4-56 9 *6* **Frosted Off**[15] 4916 3-9-0 55 .... FrannyNorton 14 9
(John Spearing) *a towards rr* **20/1**

0500 10 *3 3/4* **Mystical Witch**[10] 5085 4-8-4 46 oh1 .... (p) SimonPearce(3) 1
(Christine Dunnett) *chsd ldrs: rdn along 1/2-way: sn wknd* **50/1**

0602 11 6 **Dee Aitch Dove**[15] 4916 3-9-2 **57** PatCosgrave 11
(George Baker) *a in rr* **8/1**[3]

1m 1.01s (-0.49) **Going Correction** -0.05s/f (Good)
WFA 3 from 4yo+ 2lb **11 Ran SP% 119.0**
Speed ratings (Par 101): **101,96,94,89,89 87,86,84,74,68 59**
toteswingers 1&2 £8.10, 1&3 £3.70, 2&3 £6.50 CSF £202.70 TOTE £6.80: £1.60, £2.40, £2.20; EX 62.90 Trifecta £377.60 Pool: £2444.45 - 4.85 winning units..
Owner North Cheshire Trading & Storage Ltd **Bred** North Cheshire Trading And Storage Ltd **Trained** Newmarket, Suffolk

FOCUS
What had looked quite a competitive sprint was won in dominant fashion.

5500 FREEBETS.CO.UK PREMIERSHIP FOOTBALL BETTING H'CAP 1m 6f 15y
5:10 (5:10) (Class 6) (0-65,58) 3-Y-O **£1,940** (£577; £288; £144) **Stalls** Low

Form RPR

6055 1 **Hattie Jacques**[14] 4939 3-9-7 **58** SamHitchcott 4 66
(Mick Channon) *hld up in rr: hdwy on inner 3f out: rdn to chse ldrs 2f out: swtchd rt and drvn ins fnl f: styd on wl to ld nr fin* **9/1**

-004 2 hd **Mr Vendman (IRE)**[59] 3432 3-8-5 **45** (v[1]) RyanPowell(3) 3 52
(Ian Williams) *chsd ldr: hdwy to ld over 2f out: rdn: hung rt and hdd over 1f out: drvn and rallied to ld again ins fnl f: hdd and no ex nr fin* **12/1**

4521 3 1 **Noor Al Haya (IRE)**[21] 4713 3-9-3 **54** KieranO'Neill 5 59
(Mark Usher) *hld up in tch: hdwy on inner over 3f out: cl up over 2f out: rdn to ld over 1f out: drvn and hdd ins fnl f: no ex last 75yds* **3/1**[1]

0262 4 ½ **Uganda Glory (USA)**[22] 4664 3-9-6 **57** (p) PatCosgrave 6 62
(George Baker) *trckd ldrs: hdwy over 3f out: rdn along 2f out: drvn to chse ldrs ent fnl f: kpt on* **6/1**

0536 5 2¾ **Halling's Wish**[30] 4417 3-9-2 **53** SteveDrowne 1 54
(John Best) *led: rdn along 3f out: hdd over 2f out: sn drvn and wknd over 1f out* **8/1**

0000 6 4 **Brave Helios**[21] 4714 3-9-7 **58** (p) StevieDonohoe 8 54
(Jonathan Portman) *chsd ldng pair: rdn along 4f out: drvn 3f out and plugged on one pce* **8/1**

5002 7 ½ **Ground Ginger**[17] 4849 3-8-8 **45** JimmyQuinn 2 40
(James Bethell) *trckd ldng pair: hdwy over 3f out: rdn over 2f out: drvn and wknd over 1f out* **11/2**[3]

2623 8 ½ **Polar Forest**[6] 5178 3-9-2 **58** ConnorBeasley(5) 7 53
(Richard Guest) *hld up in rr: hdwy on wd outside over 3f out: chsd ldrs wl over 2f out: sn rdn and wknd wl over 1f out* **4/1**[2]

3m 8.06s (1.06) **Going Correction** -0.25s/f (Firm) **8 Ran SP% 114.6**
Speed ratings (Par 98): **86,85,85,85,83 81,80,80**
toteswingers 1&2 £9.20, 1&3 £8.20, 2&3 £8.90 CSF £108.29 CT £400.76 TOTE £11.70: £2.90, £1.40, £1.60; EX 113.70 Trifecta £833.30 Pool: £2012.39 - 1.81 winning units..
Owner Norman Court Stud **Bred** Norman Court Stud **Trained** West Ilsley, Berks
■ Stewards' Enquiry : Kieran O'Neill two-day ban: used whip above permitted level (Aug 30-31)

FOCUS
A moderate staying event for 3yos, but it's probably sound enough form for the grade.
T/Plt: £6.60 to a £1 stake. Pool: £48,777.87 - 53601.79 winning units T/Qpdt: £5.60 to a £1 stake. Pool: £2869.60 - 376.30 winning units JR

5501 - 5507a (Foreign Racing) - See Raceform Interactive

5025 CHESTER (L-H)
Saturday, August 17

OFFICIAL GOING: Good (6.8) changing to good to soft after race 1 (2.00)
Wind: Overcast and breezy; rain Race 3 and Race 5 onwards Weather: Blustery; half behind

5508 HEMINGWAY MAIDEN AUCTION STKS 7f 2y
2:00 (2:00) (Class 4) 2-Y-O **£6,469** (£1,925; £962; £481) **Stalls** Low

Form RPR

4 1 **Master Of Finance (IRE)**[22] 4731 2-9-1 0 JoeFanning 3 83+
(Mark Johnston) *mde all: styd on strly: readily* **5/1**[3]

054 2 1½ **Lincoln (IRE)**[20] 4808 2-9-0 76 SamHitchcott 2 78
(Mick Channon) *trckd ldrs: t.k.h: chsd wnr over 1f out: styd on: no real imp* **3/1**[2]

5402 3 3¼ **Shepherd Gate (USA)**[8] 5362 2-8-6 74 (b) JoeyHaynes(7) 8 69
(J S Moore) *chsd ldrs: kpt on same pce fnl 2f* **25/1**

4 hd **Wealth (IRE)** 2-9-1 0 JimmyQuinn 6 70+
(Richard Fahey) *dwlt: in rr: hdwy 2f out: r.o ins fnl f: will improve* **16/1**

6 5 nk **Penhill**[21] 4756 2-9-0 0 GrahamLee 1 68
(James Bethell) *mid-div: hdwy on ins over 1f out: kpt on same pce* **8/1**

22 6 ¾ **Gown (IRE)**[51] 3710 2-8-6 0 DavidProbert 10 58
(Charles Hills) *chsd ldrs on outer: drvn over 2f out: one pce* **10/1**

2324 7 1¼ **Princess Rose**[14] 5005 2-8-10 75 (p) LiamJones 4 59
(William Haggas) *chsd wnr: drvn over 2f out: fdd over 1f out* **11/4**[1]

032 8 1½ **El Beau (IRE)**[11] 5083 2-8-10 73 MichaelO'Connell 5 55
(John Quinn) *mid-div: effrt over 2f out: nvr a threat* **12/1**

032 9 4½ **Kenny The Captain (IRE)**[11] 5105 2-8-7 74 DarylByrne(5) 9 45
(Tim Easterby) *in rr: sme hdwy on outside 3f out: sn lost pl* **14/1**

0 10 ½ **Emerahldz (IRE)**[21] 4756 2-8-4 0 NeilFarley(3) 7 39
(Richard Fahey) *sn drvn along in rr: nvr on terms* **40/1**

1m 28.05s (1.55) **Going Correction** +0.075s/f (Good) **10 Ran SP% 115.1**
Speed ratings (Par 96): **94,92,88,88,88 87,85,84,78,78**
toteswingers 1&2 £3.20, 1&3 £23.40, 2&3 £23.40 CSF £20.06 TOTE £8.80: £3.20, £1.10, £7.60; EX 38.30 Trifecta £472.80 Part won. Pool: £630.53 - 0.55 winning units..
Owner J David Abell & Markus Graff **Bred** Maddenstown Equine Enterprise Ltd **Trained** Middleham Moor, N Yorks

FOCUS
Track at inner configuration and all distances as advertised. A fair maiden in which the placed horses give the form perspective.

5509 LA DOLCEVITA NURSERY H'CAP 5f 16y
2:35 (2:35) (Class 3) (0-95,88) 2-Y-O **£7,762** (£2,310; £1,154; £577) **Stalls** Low

Form RPR

6044 1 **Blithe Spirit**[14] 5012 2-8-8 **78** NeilFarley(3) 1 81
(Eric Alston) *led: drvn over 1f out: jst hld on* **4/1**[2]

311 2 nse **Bushcraft (IRE)**[24] 4639 2-9-7 **88** GeorgeBaker 3 91+
(Ed Walker) *bmpd s: sn chsng ldrs: effrt 2f out: styd on to chse wnr last 100yds: kpt on wl towards fin: jst failed* **5/6**[1]

0511 3 1¼ **Lilo Lil**[12] 5066 2-8-1 **68** oh1 ow1 (p) DavidProbert 2 66
(David C Griffiths) *wnt rt s: chsd wnr: kpt on same pce fnl f* **7/1**[3]

4102 4 1¾ **Weisse Socken (IRE)**[10] 5121 2-8-5 **72** (p) JimmyQuinn 6 64
(Ralph Beckett) *carried rt s: hld up in last: hdwy over 1f out: nvr trbld ldrs* **7/1**[3]

425 5 7 **Dodger Marley (IRE)**[33] 4347 2-8-0 **67** PaoloSirigu 4 34
(Stuart Williams) *carried rt s: sn chsng ldrs: effrt over 2f out: lost pl over 1f out* **7/1**[3]

1m 0.78s (-0.22) **Going Correction** +0.075s/f (Good) **5 Ran SP% 112.1**
Speed ratings (Par 98): **104,103,101,99,87**
CSF £8.02 TOTE £7.90: £2.40, £1.40; EX 16.60 Trifecta £38.50 Pool: £854.15 - 16.61 winning units..
Owner Liam & Tony Ferguson **Bred** Liam & Tony Ferguson **Trained** Longton, Lancs

FOCUS
The ground was changed to good to soft after the opener. Not a bad nursery, run at a sound pace and a marginal personal-best from the winner.

5510 ARCHERY H'CAP 7f 122y
3:10 (3:12) (Class 2) (0-105,97) 3-Y-O **£29,110** (£8,662; £4,329; £2,164) **Stalls** Low

Form RPR

6140 1 **Correspondent**[16] 4922 3-9-7 **97** NGMcCullagh 4 106
(Brian Meehan) *chsd ldr: led jst ins fnl f: styd on wl* **8/1**

3235 2 1¼ **Rene Mathis (GER)**[21] 4767 3-8-7 **86** NeilFarley(3) 8 92
(Richard Fahey) *led: hdd jst ins fnl f: styd on same pce* **11/2**[3]

605 3 1½ **Ayaar (IRE)**[7] 5287 3-9-5 **95** (v[1]) SamHitchcott 3 97
(Mick Channon) *mid-div: hdwy over 2f out: chsd ldng pair over 1f out: kpt on same pce to take 3rd ins fnl f* **12/1**

3415 4 3¼ **Yourartisonfire**[16] 4922 3-8-3 **86** JoeyHaynes(7) 1 80
(Mrs K Burke) *chsd ldrs: drvn over 3f out: one pce fnl 2f* **10/3**[1]

1423 5 2 **Penny Garcia**[22] 4725 3-8-4 **80** JimmyQuinn 2 69
(Tim Easterby) *trckd ldrs: effrt over 2f out: one pce* **17/2**

0005 6 4 **Heavy Metal**[7] 5260 3-8-12 **88** JoeFanning 7 67
(Mark Johnston) *in rr: drvn over 3f out: sme hdwy over 1f out: nvr a factor* **10/1**

110 7 ½ **Ajraam (USA)**[59] 3455 3-9-5 **95** GrahamLee 9 73
(Charles Hills) *in rr: drvn over 2f out: nvr on terms* **8/1**

-223 8 1 **Veeraya**[7] 5287 3-8-10 **86** (t) LiamJones 5 61
(William Haggas) *mid-div: drvn over 2f out: sn wknd* **4/1**[2]

2050 9 2 **Capo Rosso (IRE)**[20] 4812 3-8-11 **87** StephenCraine 6 57
(Tom Dascombe) *a in rr* **16/1**

6606 10 shd **Operation Chariot (IRE)**[42] 4078 3-8-7 **83** DavidProbert 10 53
(Andrew Balding) *chsd ldrs: lost pl over 2f out* **25/1**

1m 33.16s (-0.64) **Going Correction** +0.075s/f (Good) **10 Ran SP% 117.7**
Speed ratings (Par 106): **106,104,103,100,98 94,93,92,90,90**
toteswingers 1&2 £18.60, 1&3 £26.80, 2&3 £26.30 CSF £52.12 CT £544.77 TOTE £9.40: £1.90, £3.60, £2.70; EX 64.70 Trifecta £294.70 Pool: £962.75 - 2.44 winning units..
Owner Mrs P Good **Bred** Mrs P Good **Trained** Manton, Wilts

FOCUS
A good-quality 3-y-o handicap. It was another race where it paid to race handily. The first two ran close to their previous course meeting.

5511 BRYDEN H'CAP 6f 18y
3:45 (3:45) (Class 3) (0-90,85) 3-Y-O **£10,350** (£3,080; £1,539; £769) **Stalls** Low

Form RPR

6203 1 **Purcell (IRE)**[20] 4797 3-9-7 **85** DavidProbert 4 91+
(Andrew Balding) *trckd ldrs: nt clr run over 2f out: chsd ldr jst ins fnl f: led towards fin: all out* **2/1**[1]

5-06 2 hd **Lastchancelucas**[71] 3066 3-9-2 **83** NeilFarley(3) 1 88
(Declan Carroll) *broke smartly: led over 1f: chsd ldr: rallied ins fnl f: tk 2nd and jst hld nr fin* **4/1**[2]

3213 3 nk **Smart Daisy K**[36] 4247 3-9-2 **85** JackDuern(5) 2 89+
(Andrew Hollinshead) *trckd ldr: led over 4f out: edgd rt fnl f: hdd nr fin* **4/1**[2]

6033 4 11 **Dream Maker (IRE)**[14] 4993 3-9-6 **84** GrahamLee 3 53
(Tim Easterby) *chsd ldrs: wknd over 1f out* **6/1**[3]

5660 5 5 **Sewn Up**[6] 5303 3-8-10 **74** (p) LiamJones 5 27
(Andrew Hollinshead) *sn detached in rr: nvr on terms* **25/1**

3156 6 4½ **Sylvia Pankhurst (IRE)**[13] 5027 3-8-6 **77** (p) JoeyHaynes(7) 7 15
(David C Griffiths) *sn chsng ldrs on outer: lost pl 2f out* **10/1**

4502 7 1 **Surge Ahead (IRE)**[45] 3956 3-8-9 **73** JimmyQuinn 6 8
(Ed Walker) *sn chsng ldrs on outer: lost pl 2f out* **8/1**

1m 13.99s (0.19) **Going Correction** +0.075s/f (Good) **7 Ran SP% 111.7**
Speed ratings (Par 104): **101,100,100,85,79 73,71**
toteswingers 1&2 £4.00, 1&3 £1.10, 2&3 £2.00 CSF £9.59 TOTE £2.00: £1.20, £5.10; EX 13.50 Trifecta £31.80 Pool: £707.27 - 16.68 winning units..
Owner Highclere Thoroughbred Racing-JohnPorter **Bred** Rathbarry Stud **Trained** Kingsclere, Hants

FOCUS
A fair 3-y-o sprint handicap in which the runner-up was the key to the form.

5512 ZNAP MAIDEN STKS 7f 2y
4:20 (4:21) (Class 4) 3-Y-O+ **£6,469** (£1,925; £962; £481) **Stalls** Low

Form RPR

22 1 **Iptisam**[15] 4968 4-9-8 0 GrahamLee 6 82+
(James Tate) *t.k.h: mde all: increased pce over 2f out: styd on strly* **7/4**[1]

5353 2 2½ **Rufoof**[28] 4544 3-8-12 70 JoeFanning 5 66
(Charles Hills) *sn trcking wnr: drvn 2f out: styd on same pce* **3/1**[2]

30 3 3 **Natalia**[78] 2824 4-8-12 0 JackDuern(5) 7 60
(Andrew Hollinshead) *in rr: drvn over 4f out: hdwy over 2f out: kpt on to take modest 3rd ins fnl f* **20/1**

4-22 4 3¼ **Martial Art (IRE)**[45] 3950 3-9-3 73 DavidProbert 4 54
(Andrew Balding) *chsd ldrs: drvn over 2f out: wknd over 1f out* **4/1**

-600 5 ¾ **Annie Besant**[58] 3509 3-8-7 49 [1] SladeO'Hara(5) 1 47
(Michael Mullineaux) *chsd ldrs: drvn and outpcd over 2f out: sn wknd* **33/1**

3242 6 10 **Disco Inferno (IRE)**[9] 5176 3-9-3 77 (t) NGMcCullagh 8 25
(Brian Meehan) *trckd ldrs on outer: effrt 3f out: sn lost pl: eased whn bhd clsng stages* **7/2**[3]

1m 28.01s (1.51) **Going Correction** +0.075s/f (Good)
WFA 3 from 4yo 5lb **6 Ran SP% 111.3**
Speed ratings (Par 105): **94,91,87,84,83 71**
toteswingers 1&2 £2.00, 1&3 £3.80, 2&3 £3.80 CSF £7.13 TOTE £2.20: £1.70, £2.20; EX 10.60 Trifecta £81.10 Pool: £488.26 - 4.51 winning units..
Owner Saeed Manana **Bred** Darley **Trained** Newmarket, Suffolk

FOCUS
A modest maiden in which the winner made a small step up, although the proximity of the fifth raises doubts about the form.

5513 FITZROY H'CAP 1m 4f 66y
4:50 (4:50) (Class 2) (0-105,94) 3-Y-0+ **£12,938** (£3,850; £1,924; £962) **Stalls** Low

Form RPR
0631 **1** **Kiama Bay (IRE)**[10] 5147 7-9-3 **83**.................... GrahamLee 2 93
(Richard Fahey) *hld up in rr: hdwy over 4f out: drvn to chse ldrs over 2f out: styd on to ld clsng stages* **11/4**[2]
5000 **2** ¾ **Scatter Dice (IRE)**[7] 5259 4-9-7 **87**.................... SamHitchcott 6 96
(Mark Johnston) *led: drvn over 2f out: hdd and no ex fnl 50yds* **14/1**
2342 **3** 2½ **Reve De Nuit (USA)**[14] 5008 7-8-12 **85**.................... JoeyHaynes(7) 4 90
(Mrs K Burke) *trckd ldr: chal 5f out: kpt on same pce appr fnl f* **6/1**
-300 **4** 1¾ **Communicator**[42] 4060 5-10-0 **94**....................[1] DavidProbert 3 96
(Andrew Balding) *s.i.s: in rr: drvn 4f out: sn outpcd: kpt on fnl f: tk 4th nr fin: no threat* **4/1**[3]
2123 **5** ½ **Salutation (IRE)**[7] 5274 3-9-3 **93**.................... JoeFanning 5 94
(Mark Johnston) *hld up in rr: effrt over 3f out: kpt on one pce fnl 2f* **9/4**[1]
5213 **6** 2¾ **Burnham**[35] 4280 4-9-0 **80**....................(p) LiamJones 1 77
(Hughie Morrison) *chsd ldrs: sn pushed along: outpcd over 3f out: lost pl 2f out* **11/2**

2m 39.81s (1.31) **Going Correction** +0.075s/f (Good)
WFA 3 from 4yo+ 10lb **6** Ran SP% **113.8**
Speed ratings (Par 109): **98,97,95,94,94 92**
toteswingers 1&2 £4.10, 1&3 £3.90, 2&3 £5.30 CSF £37.39 TOTE £3.10: £2.60, £8.90; EX 38.70 Trifecta £71.90 Pool: £732.90 - 7.64 winning units..
Owner Dr Marwan Koukash **Bred** Tipper House Stud **Trained** Musley Bank, N Yorks
FOCUS
A decent handicap that looks sound enough rated around the placed horses.

5514 TIFFANY H'CAP 1m 5f 89y
5:25 (5:28) (Class 4) (0-80,80) 3-Y-0+ **£7,762** (£2,310; £1,154; £577) **Stalls** Low

Form RPR
0231 **1** **Lemon Pearl**[29] 4500 3-9-0 **77**.................... GrahamLee 3 87
(Ralph Beckett) *mde all: drvn 4f out: styd on wl fnl f: won gng away* **10/3**[2]
2644 **2** 2½ **Gabrial The Master (IRE)**[35] 4286 3-8-8 **71**.................... SamHitchcott 7 76
(Richard Fahey) *chsd wnr: chal over 2f out: kpt on to regain 2nd nr fin* **8/1**
013 **3** shd **Madame Vestris (IRE)**[31] 4417 3-8-13 **76**.................... JimmyQuinn 8 81+
(Sir Michael Stoute) *hld up in rr on outer: hdwy over 5f out: trcking ldrs over 3f out: chal and 2nd 2f out: kpt on same pce fnl f* **3/1**[1]
0-10 **4** 3 **Swinging Hawk (GER)**[36] 4233 7-9-8 **74**.................... LiamJones 10 74
(Ian Williams) *s.i.s: in rr: drvn 6f out: kpt on fnl 3f: tk modest 4th fnl f* **11/2**
3143 **5** 6 **Tenhoo**[30] 4447 7-9-3 **72**.................... NeilFarley(3) 4 63
(Eric Alston) *mid-div: drvn over 3f out: sn outpcd: wknd fnl f* **16/1**
0642 **6** 2½ **My Destination (IRE)**[15] 4969 4-8-8 **67**.................... LukeLeadbitter(7) 6 55
(Declan Carroll) *mid-div: pushed along over 7f out: sn lost pl: reminders over 5f out: no threat after* **10/1**
3200 **7** ½ **Ethics Girl (IRE)**[9] 5168 7-9-11 **77**....................(t) StephenCraine 11 64
(John Berry) *drvn to chse ldrs: lost pl over 2f out* **10/1**
0242 **8** 17 **Halling's Treasure**[3] 5392 3-8-10 **73**....................(p) DavidProbert 1 34
(Andrew Balding) *chsd ldrs: drvn over 3f out: sn lost pl and bhd: t.o* **9/2**[3]
0320 **9** 52 **Rosie's Lady (IRE)**[16] 4929 4-8-13 **65**.................... JoeFanning 5
(Paul Green) *t.k.h in rr: effrt 4f out: sn lost pl and bhd: t.o whn virtually p.u: eventually completed* **20/1**

2m 57.52s (4.82) **Going Correction** +0.075s/f (Good)
WFA 3 from 4yo+ 11lb **9** Ran SP% **121.6**
Speed ratings (Par 105): **88,86,86,84,80 79,79,68,36**
toteswingers 1&2 £3.70, 1&3 £2.20, 2&3 £1.70 CSF £32.08 CT £90.82 TOTE £4.00: £1.40, £2.50, £1.50; EX 33.40 Trifecta £76.40 Pool: £489.58 - 4.80 winning units..
Owner Pearl Bloodstock Ltd & N H Wrigley **Bred** Baron F Von Oppenheim **Trained** Kimpton, Hants
FOCUS
This was competitive for the class and it proved a decent test. A personal-best from the winner with the second setting the standard.
T/Plt: £145.50 to a £1 stake. Pool: £44,880.08 - 225.14 winning units T/Qpdt: £26.20 to a £1 stake. Pool: £2,302.20 - 64.90 winning units WG

4976 DONCASTER (L-H)
Saturday, August 17

OFFICIAL GOING: Good to firm (good in places; 9.0)
Wind: Fresh against Weather: Cloudy

5515 CROWN HOTEL BAWTRY LEGER PREVIEW DINNER H'CAP 7f
1:55 (1:56) (Class 5) (0-70,70) 3-Y-0+ **£2,911** (£866; £432; £216) **Stalls** High

Form RPR
5345 **1** **Red Paladin (IRE)**[24] 4628 3-9-2 **65**....................(p) FMBerry 4 73+
(Kevin Ryan) *dwlt and hmpd s: sn bhd and rdn along: detached 1/2-way: hdwy over 1f out: swtchd lft and drvn ent fnl f: styd on strly to ld nr fin* **4/1**[1]
0531 **2** ½ **Imaginary World (IRE)**[9] 5192 5-9-2 **63**....................(p) LMcNiff(3) 9 71
(John Balding) *trckd ldrs: hdwy over 2f out: cl up wl over 1f out: rdn to ld jst over 1f out: edgd rt and drvn ins fnl f: hdd and no ex nr fin* **13/2**[2]
3133 **3** 1½ **Shaolin (IRE)**[53] 3665 3-9-6 **69**.................... ConorO'Farrell 12 73+
(Seamus Durack) *trckd ldrs: smooth hdwy 2f out: chal on bit over 1f out: rdn ent fnl f and ev ch tl drvn and one pce last 100yds* **4/1**[1]
6530 **4** 1¼ **Music Festival (USA)**[15] 4953 6-8-2 **53**.................... JordanNason(7) 7 54
(Jim Goldie) *hld up: hdwy wl over 2f out: chsd ldrs over 1f out: drvn and one pce fnl f* **7/1**[3]
5010 **5** nk **Stoneacre Oskar**[7] 5273 4-8-11 **60**.................... SladeO'Hara(5) 8 60
(Peter Grayson) *towards rr: hdwy 3f out: rdn to chse ldrs over 1f out: kpt on same pce fnl f* **33/1**
0000 **6** 2 **Miss Matiz**[27] 4557 6-8-4 **51** oh6.................... DeclanCannon(3) 13 46
(Alan Kirtley) *in tch: hdwy to chse ldrs over 2f out: sn rdn along and one pce* **100/1**
00-6 **7** 5 **First Glance**[29] 4504 4-8-7 **51** oh3....................(p) AndrewMullen 2 32
(Michael Appleby) *hld up towards rr: hdwy over 2f out: rdn along wl over 1f out: sn no imp* **28/1**
40-0 **8** ¾ **Pearl War (USA)**[176] 758 4-9-0 **58**.................... PaddyAspell 10 37
(John Mackie) *prom: led after 2f: rdn along 2f out: hdd jst over 1f out: sn wknd* **25/1**
0461 **9** 4 **Dancing Maite**[75] 2932 8-9-0 **61**....................(b) MarkCoumbe(3) 1 29
(Roy Bowring) *s.i.s and bhd: hdwy on outer to chse ldrs wl over 2f out: sn rdn and wknd* **17/2**
4245 **10** 3¾ **Arbeel**[21] 4751 3-9-5 **68**....................[1] DuranFentiman 11 26
(Peter Chapple-Hyam) *led 2f: cl up: rdn along wl over 2f out: sn wknd* **14/1**
/0-0 **11** 5 **Electrickery**[66] 3223 4-8-7 **51**.................... AdamBeschizza 3
(Mark Buckley) *a towards rr* **66/1**
-660 **12** 15 **Finn Mac**[14] 5016 3-8-2 **54**.................... JulieBurke(3) 14
(John Norton) *prom: rdn along 1/2-way: sn wknd* **50/1**
000- **13** 7 **Nakuru Breeze (IRE)**[386] 4549 4-8-11 **55**.................... AndrewElliott 6
(Suzzanne France) *midfield: hdwy on outer and in tch 3f out: rdn along wl over 2f out: sn lost pl and bhd* **100/1**

1m 27.15s (0.85) **Going Correction** -0.025s/f (Good)
WFA 3 from 4yo+ 5lb **13** Ran SP% **98.7**
Speed ratings (Par 103): **94,93,91,90,89 87,81,81,76,72 66,49,41**
Tote Swingers 1&2 £4.70, 2&3 £4.00, 1&3 £4.30 CSF £18.49 CT £59.76 TOTE £4.50: £1.40, £2.10, £1.80; EX 25.80 Trifecta £135.30 Pool: £1,320.50 - 7.31 winning tickets..
Owner Hambleton Racing Ltd XXII **Bred** Noel O'Callaghan **Trained** Hambleton, N Yorks
FOCUS
Rail out from 1m2f to where round course joins straight. A sound gallop to an otherwise ordinary looking handicap which threw up quite an extraordinary performance from the winner who got miles behind appeared to have little chance of placing let alone winning. The winner is rated to May C&D form with the runner-up to his latest AW mark.

5516 S SMITH T/A PRO-PAVE LTD EBF MAIDEN FILLIES' STKS 1m (S)
2:30 (2:30) (Class 5) 2-Y-0 **£2,911** (£866; £432; £216) **Stalls** High

Form RPR
0 **1** **Mutatis Mutandis (IRE)**[22] 4702 2-9-0 0.................... TomMcLaughlin 5 77+
(Ed Walker) *set stdy pce: qcknd 3f out: rdn and qcknd wl over 1f out: drvn and edgd lft ins fnl f: hld on wl* **6/1**
0 **2** ¾ **Rawoof (IRE)**[14] 5003 2-9-0 0.................... FrederikTylicki 7 75
(Ed Dunlop) *trckd ldrs on inner: swtchd lft and hdwy over 3f out: chal 2f out: rdr over 1f out: ev ch ins fnl f tl drvn and no ex towards fin* **5/2**[1]
0 **3** 3½ **Spring Carnival (USA)**[53] 3664 2-8-7 0.................... AhmadAlSubousi(7) 1 67
(Charlie Appleby) *hld up towards rr: stdy hdwy on outer 1/2-way: effrt and ev ch wl over 1f out: rdn ent fnl f and kpt on same pce* **15/2**
4 7 **Psiloveyou** 2-9-0 0.................... SebSanders 3 52+
(John Gosden) *s.i.s and bhd: clsd up after 2f: pushed along wl over 2f out: rdn and kpt on appr fnl f: nvr nr ldrs* **11/4**[2]
5 1¾ **Dangerous Flower (USA)** 2-8-11 0.................... CharlesBishop(3) 6 46
(Mick Channon) *trckd ldr: rdn along wl over 2f out: wknd wl over 1f out* **20/1**
6 ½ **Heartily (IRE)** 2-9-0 0.................... AhmedAjtebi 2 45
(Charlie Appleby) *trckd ldng pair: effrt 3f out: rdn along over 2f out: sn wknd* **9/2**[3]
7 5 **Hasta La Vista** 2-9-0 0.................... FMBerry 4 33
(Mark Johnston) *trckd ldrs: pushed along 1/2-way: rdn wl over 2f out: sn wknd* **12/1**

1m 41.74s (2.44) **Going Correction** -0.025s/f (Good) **7** Ran SP% **111.9**
Speed ratings (Par 91): **86,85,81,74,73 72,67**
Tote Swingers 1&2 £5.30, 2&3 £3.30, 1&3 £9.40 CSF £20.47 TOTE £9.50: £4.10, £1.50; EX 32.50 Trifecta £199.90 Pool: £2,485.52 - 9.32 winning tickets..
Owner Chasemore Farm **Bred** Kildaragh Stud **Trained** Newmarket, Suffolk
FOCUS
Some nicely bred fillies on show, but they dawdled through the first half of the race and this turned into a sprint, so this isn't form to hang your hat on and will take time to settle.

5517 BEAUTY AT DONCASTER MAIDEN STKS 6f
3:05 (3:05) (Class 5) 3-4-Y-0 **£2,911** (£866; £432; £216) **Stalls** High

Form RPR
0-3 **1** **Mukhabarat (IRE)**[9] 5176 3-9-5 0....................[1] AhmedAjtebi 6 73+
(Saeed bin Suroor) *trckd ldrs: cl up 1/2-way: led over 2f out: edgd rt ent fnl f: rdn out* **3/1**[2]
45 **2** ¾ **Thorntoun Lady (USA)**[17] 4887 3-9-0 0.................... AndrewElliott 9 66
(Jim Goldie) *hld up: hdwy wl over 2f out: n.m.r and swtchd lft over 1f out: rdn ent fnl f: styd on wl towards fin* **8/1**
000- **3** 3 **Ri Na Si**[257] 7963 3-9-5 45.................... AndrewMullen 8 61
(Michael Appleby) *in tch: hdwy to chse ldrs over 2f out: rdn to chse wnr ent fnl f: sn drvn and kpt on same pce* **50/1**
0- **4** 1 **Smart Eighteen**[365] 5325 3-9-5 0.................... FrederikTylicki 5 58+
(Paul D'Arcy) *hld up: hdwy to chse ldrs over 2f out: rdn along wl over 1f out: swtchd rt and kpt on fnl f: nrst fin* **7/2**[3]
00-2 **5** ½ **Messageinabottle (USA)**[17] 4887 3-9-0 64.................... SebSanders 4 51
(James Bethell) *trckd ldrs: cl up on outer 1/2-way: rdn along 2f out: drvn and wknd over 1f out* **9/4**[1]
6 1 **Pearl Style (FR)** 3-9-2 0.................... CharlesBishop(3) 1 53+
(Olly Stevens) *dwlt and in rr tl styd on fr wl over 1f out: nrst fin* **8/1**
600 **7** nk **Partner's Gold (IRE)**[14] 4976 3-9-5 31.................... PaddyAspell 13 52
(Alan Berry) *slt ld: rdn along 1/2-way: hdd over 2f out: grad wknd* **150/1**
0-0 **8** ½ **Zed Candy Girl**[12] 5069 3-9-0 0.................... StevieDonohoe 2 46
(John Stimpson) *in tch: rdn along over 2f out: grad wknd* **33/1**
U **9** 1 **Top Line Banker**[20] 4813 3-9-5 0....................[1] ConorO'Farrell 10 47
(Brian Ellison) *dwlt: a towards rr* **25/1**
50- **10** 9 **Chorister Choir (IRE)**[366] 5267 3-9-0 0.................... DuranFentiman 14 14
(Tim Easterby) *cl up: rdn along wl over 2f out: sn wknd* **12/1**
5- **11** 16 **Classy Anne**[443] 2614 3-8-7 0.................... JordanNason(7) 7
(Jim Goldie) *t.k.h: trckd ldrs: pushed along 1/2-way: sn wknd* **16/1**

1m 14.23s (0.63) **Going Correction** -0.025s/f (Good) **11** Ran SP% **123.2**
Speed ratings (Par 103): **94,93,89,87,87 85,85,84,83,71 49**
Tote Swingers 1&2 £4.50, 2&3 £39.30, 1&3 £24.00 CSF £28.29 TOTE £2.90: £1.40, £2.20, £15.60; EX 24.30 Trifecta £567.80 Pool: £2,170.66 - 2.86 winning tickets..
Owner Godolphin **Bred** Darley **Trained** Newmarket, Suffolk
FOCUS
This doesn't look very strong maiden form, but the front two came clear and look reasonable prospects. The runner-up sets the level but the form is fluid.

5518 PC EXCAVATIONS LTD H'CAP 7f
3:40 (3:40) (Class 2) (0-105,99) 3-Y-0+ **£12,938** (£3,850; £1,924; £962) **Stalls** High

Form RPR
0344 **1** **Shebebi (USA)**[13] 5026 3-9-1 **93**....................(b1) FMBerry 10 106
(Mark Johnston) *trckd ldrs: hdwy over 2f out: led wl over 1f out: rdn clr ent fnl f: readily* **9/4**[1]
000 **2** 3¼ **Pied A Terre (AUS)**[42] 4062 5-9-12 **99**.................... AhmedAjtebi 11 105
(Saeed bin Suroor) *trckd ldrs: hdwy 2f out: rdn over 1f out: kpt on to chse wnr ins fnl f: no imp* **12/1**
5-50 **3** nk **Spiritual Star (IRE)**[62] 3373 4-9-12 **99**.................... SaleemGolam 8 104
(Anthony Carson) *hld up towards rr: hdwy wl over 2f out: rdn over 1f out: styd on fnl f: nrst fin* **40/1**

2010 **4** *1* **Snow Bay**[14] 5014 7-8-8 **86** ShirleyTeasdale(5) 6 88
(Paul Midgley) *sn led: pushed along over 2f out: rdn wl over 1f out: sn hdd and drvn: wknd fnl f* **15/2**

1022 **5** *2 1/4* **Smarty Socks (IRE)**[21] 4778 9-9-8 **98** JulieBurke(3) 3 94+
(David O'Meara) *dwlt and in rr: effrt on outer over 2f out and sn rdn along: styd on appr fnl f: n.d* **3/1**[2]

6633 **6** *1/2* **Lutine Bell**[24] 4642 6-8-9 **82** (b) MickyFenton 9 77
(Mike Murphy) *dwlt and towards rr: hdwy 3f out: chsd ldr over 2f out: rdn along wl over 1f out: grad wknd* **7/2**[3]

1500 **7** *nk* **Yair Hill (IRE)**[21] 4758 5-9-2 **89** FrederikTylicki 4 83
(Noel Wilson) *trckd ldrs: rdn along wl over 2f out: sn wknd* **16/1**

6-00 **8** *6* **Jamesbo's Girl**[6] 5303 3-8-9 **87** AdamBeschizza 1 63
(Alan Berry) *cl up: rdn along wl over 2f out: sn wknd* **20/1**

0- **9** *25* **Chellalla**[461] 4-9-1 **88** StevieDonohoe 7
(Ian Williams) *prom: rdn along 1/2-way: sn wknd: bhd and eased wl over 1f out* **16/1**

1m 26.08s (-0.22) **Going Correction** -0.025s/f (Good)
WFA 3 from 4yo+ 5lb **9** Ran SP% **116.4**
Speed ratings (Par 109): **100,96,95,94,92 91,91,84,55**
Tote Swingers 1&2 £4.80, 2&3 £33.80, 1&3 £16.20 CSF £31.44 CT £850.62 TOTE £3.30: £1.40, £3.20, £7.40; EX 30.30 Trifecta £322.10 Pool: £2,040.27 - 4.74 winning tickets..
Owner Hamdan Al Maktoum **Bred** Shadwell Farm LLC **Trained** Middleham Moor, N Yorks

FOCUS
A quality race although a little surprising to see the top weights rated 6lb below the ceiling rating for the grade, suggesting this wasn't as competitive as it could have been. With that in mind, plus one of the major contenders Smarty Socks never getting competitive and the placed horses having been out of form previously, it is probably unwise to get too carried away with the form.

5519 JOC MURRAY MEMORIAL H'CAP 5f
4:15 (4:18) (Class 3) (0-95,95) 3-Y-O+ **£8,409** (£2,502; £1,250; £625) **Stalls** High

Form RPR

120 **1** **Doctor Parkes**[7] 5257 7-9-7 **92** J-PGuillambert 8 102
(Stuart Williams) *towards rr: pushed along and hdwy wl over 1f out: rdn and str run appr fnl f: led last 110yds: kpt on* **16/1**

100 **2** *3/4* **Burning Thread (IRE)**[7] 5294 6-8-13 **84** (b) AdamBeschizza 10 91
(Tim Etherington) *in tch: hdwy over 1f out: str run to ld briefly ent fnl f: sn hdd and drvn: one pce last 100yds* **22/1**

1112 **3** *1/2* **Sleepy Blue Ocean**[10] 5155 7-8-7 **78** (p) AndrewMullen 17 84
(John Balding) *in tch: hdwy 2f out: rdn to chse ldrs over 1f out: drvn and kpt on wl fnl f* **6/1**[3]

0000 **4** *1* **Threes Grand**[27] 4569 3-8-5 **78** JamieMackay 6 80
(Scott Dixon) *hld up: hdwy wl over 1f out: rdn and styd on wl fnl f: nrst fin* **16/1**

3302 **5** *hd* **Moorhouse Lad**[15] 4954 10-9-0 **85** AndrewElliott 12 86
(Garry Moss) *led: hdd 1/2-way: cl up: rdn and ev ch over 1f out tl drvn and wknd ins fnl f* **16/1**

1001 **6** *1/2* **Noodles Blue Boy**[15] 4954 7-8-10 **81** (p) PaddyAspell 13 80
(Ollie Pears) *trckd ldrs: effrt over 1f out: sn rdn: kpt on same pce fnl f* **20/1**

1310 **7** *hd* **Blanc De Chine (IRE)**[20] 4800 4-9-1 **89** DeclanBates(3) 4 88
(Peter Makin) *cl up: led 1/2-way: rdn along wl over 1f out: drvn appr fnl f: sn hdd and grad wknd* **8/1**

0425 **8** *nse* **Sir Maximilian (IRE)**[35] 4285 4-9-4 **89** StevieDonohoe 7 87
(Nicky Vaughan) *in tch: pushed along 2f out: sn rdn: kpt on fnl f: nrst fin* **11/2**[2]

-006 **9** *shd* **Dungannon**[43] 4024 6-8-13 **87** (p) ThomasBrown(3) 5 85
(Andrew Balding) *trckd ldrs: pushed along and sltly outpcd 2f out: sn rdn: styd on fnl f* **3/1**[1]

600 **10** *5* **Stone Of Folca**[36] 4263 5-9-7 **92** FrederikTylicki 9 72
(John Best) *prom: rdn 2f out: sn drvn and wknd* **14/1**

5100 **11** *1* **Another Wise Kid (IRE)**[11] 5108 5-9-4 **89** MickyFenton 2 66
(Paul Midgley) *midfield: swtchd lft and hdwy 2f out: rdn wl over 1f out: sn wknd* **16/1**

1420 **12** *3/4* **Tax Free (IRE)**[14] 4983 11-9-8 **93** FMBerry 1 67
(David Nicholls) *a towards rr* **10/1**

0000 **13** *2 1/4* **Captain Dunne (IRE)**[15] 4954 8-9-1 **86** DuranFentiman 3 52
(Tim Easterby) *prom: rdn along wl over 1f out: sn wknd* **20/1**

1/00 **14** *3/4* **Captain Carey**[105] 2014 7-9-4 **89** TomMcLaughlin 15 52
(Malcolm Saunders) *a in rr* **33/1**

510/ **15** *3* **Your Gifted (IRE)**[714] 5706 6-8-7 **81** MarkCoumbe(3) 16 33
(Lisa Williamson) *a in rr* **33/1**

59.3s (-1.20) **Going Correction** -0.025s/f (Good)
WFA 3 from 4yo+ 2lb **15** Ran SP% **124.8**
Speed ratings (Par 107): **108,106,106,104,104 103,102,102,102,94 93,91,88,87,82**
Tote Swingers 1&2 £68.00, 2&3 £30.90, 1&3 £13.30 CSF £343.00 CT £2405.35 TOTE £18.10: £4.80, £10.10, £2.10; EX 351.70 Trifecta £1652.80 Part won. Pool: £2,203.83 - 0.65 winning tickets..
Owner Mrs S Mason & Partners **Bred** Joseph Heler **Trained** Newmarket, Suffolk

FOCUS
A wide open sprint handicap and they appeared to go quite hard from the outset. That helped set things up for the closers. The form looks straightforward rated around the first three.

5520 EXPERT GUIDE TO DONCASTER AT DONCASTERRACECOURSETIPS.CO.UK H'CAP 1m 6f 132y
4:45 (4:45) (Class 4) (0-85,84) 3-Y-O+ **£5,175** (£1,540; £769; £384) **Stalls** Low

Form RPR

3323 **1** **Shwaiman (IRE)**[45] 3957 3-8-13 **82** FrederikTylicki 4 99+
(James Fanshawe) *hld up in rr: smooth hdwy on outer wl over 2f out: led wl over 1f out: rdn clr appr fnl f: readily* **5/4**[1]

4311 **2** *7* **Brigadoon**[18] 4851 6-9-13 **83** MichaelO'Connell 9 87
(Philip Kirby) *hld up in rr: hdwy wl over 2f out: rdn to chse ldrs over 1f out: drvn and styd on ins fnl f: tk 2nd nr line: no ch w wnr* **3/1**[2]

3-51 **3** *shd* **Bridgehampton**[10] 5157 4-9-3 **76** WilliamTwiston-Davies(3) 2 80
(Michael Bell) *trckd ldng pair: hdwy 3f out: cl up 2f out: sn rdn and ev ch: drvn: edgd rt and one pce ent fnl f: lost 2nd nr line* **8/1**

21 **4** *1/2* **Eshtyaaq**[16] 4913 6-8-10 **69** DeclanBates(3) 1 72
(David Evans) *trckd ldng pair on inner: hdwy over 3f out: led briefly jst over 2f out: hdd and drvn wl over 1f out: one pce* **16/1**

3511 **5** *4* **Porcini**[24] 4643 4-9-11 **84** (p) ThomasBrown(3) 6 82
(Philip McBride) *led: rdn along 3f out: hdd jst over 2f out and sn wknd* **9/2**[3]

4334 **6** *8* **Montaff**[16] 4913 7-9-6 **76** ConorO'Farrell 5 64
(Mick Channon) *trckd ldrs: hdwy 3f out: rdn along over 2f out: sn drvn and wknd* **16/1**

3-60 **7** *8* **Valid Reason**[14] 5008 6-9-5 **75** TomMcLaughlin 8 52
(Dean Ivory) *cl up: rdn along 4f out: wknd over 3f out* **33/1**

3m 9.82s (2.42) **Going Correction** +0.325s/f (Good)
WFA 3 from 4yo+ 13lb **7** Ran SP% **113.4**
Speed ratings (Par 105): **106,102,102,101,99 95,91**
Tote Swingers 1&2 £1.90, 2&3 £4.60, 1&3 £3.30 CSF £5.03 CT £19.11 TOTE £2.00: £1.50, £2.10; EX 5.60 Trifecta £26.70 Pool: £2,145.05 - 60.12 winning tickets..
Owner Mohamed Obaida **Bred** Rabbah Bloodstock Limited **Trained** Newmarket, Suffolk

FOCUS
This looked fairly open on paper but it proved anything but in the race itself. The winner took a step forward on his handicap debut but the form behind is not solid, although it is given a chance.

5521 FOOTBALL BETTING IS BACK FREEBETS.CO.UK APPRENTICE H'CAP 1m 2f 60y
5:20 (5:20) (Class 5) (0-75,75) 4-Y-O+ **£2,911** (£866; £432; £216) **Stalls** Low

Form RPR

5303 **1** **Remix (IRE)**[14] 4996 4-8-7 **56** DannyBrock 3 66
(Ian Williams) *hld up towards rr: stdy hdwy on outer 3f out: chsd ldrs 2f out: rdn to ld over 1f out: edgd lft ins fnl f: kpt on* **14/1**

23-1 **2** *1 1/2* **Bishop's Castle (USA)**[161] 950 4-9-9 **75** OisinMurphy(3) 9 82
(Brian Ellison) *trckd ldng pair: hdwy over 2f out: rdn to ld wl over 1f out: edgd rt and hdd over 1f out: drvn and kpt on fnl f* **6/4**[1]

4330 **3** *hd* **Cabal**[29] 4469 6-8-2 **56** oh2 (b) GaryMahon(5) 7 63
(Andrew Crook) *in tch: hdwy to trck ldrs 5f out: effrt over 2f out: rdn and ev ch whn n.m.r appr fnl f: sn drvn and kpt on same pce* **25/1**

456 **4** *4* **Exning Halt**[20] 4809 4-9-1 **69** JoeDoyle(5) 1 68
(John Quinn) *hld up: hdwy over 3f out: rdn to chse ldrs 2f out: kpt on same pce fnl f* **7/1**

-060 **5** *1 3/4* **Nezami (IRE)**[6] 5304 8-8-12 **66** MatthewHopkins(5) 4 62
(Patrick Clinton) *t.k.h: trckd ldng pair: led after 3f: rdn along 3f out: hdd jst over 2f out: sn drvn and grad wknd* **33/1**

4654 **6** *nk* **Gala Casino Star (IRE)**[16] 4929 8-9-9 **75** (v) JordanNason(3) 8 70
(Geoffrey Harker) *t.k.h: set stdy pce: hdd after 3f: trckd ldr: effrt to ld again on inner briefly 2f out: sn rdn and hdd: wknd over 1f out* **11/2**[2]

-4U0 **7** *1/2* **Voice From Above (IRE)**[9] 5179 4-8-11 **60** DeclanBates 11 54
(Patrick Holmes) *a towards rr* **28/1**

3121 **8** *5* **Breakheart (IRE)**[24] 4638 6-9-5 **75** (v) RobHornby(7) 10 60
(Andrew Balding) *hld up: a in rr* **11/2**[2]

0522 **9** *3/4* **Cosmic Halo**[14] 4995 4-9-5 **75** JoshQuinn(7) 6 58
(Richard Fahey) *hld up: a towards rr* **6/1**[3]

000- **10** *1 3/4* **Stadium Of Light (IRE)**[57] 6361 6-8-7 **56** oh11 ShirleyTeasdale 2 36
(Shaun Harris) *chsd ldrs: rdn along on inner 4f out: sn wknd* **50/1**

2m 11.73s (2.33) **Going Correction** +0.325s/f (Good) **10** Ran SP% **116.4**
Speed ratings (Par 103): **103,101,101,98,97 96,96,92,91,90**
Tote Swingers 1&2 £4.30, 2&3 £9.10, 1&3 £19.70 CSF £34.50 CT £549.72 TOTE £14.70: £3.70, £1.10, £6.40; EX 51.80 Trifecta £722.30 Pool: £1,561.89 - 1.62 winning tickets..
Owner Global Commodity Imports Ltd **Bred** Dr Dean Harron **Trained** Portway, Worcs
■ Stewards' Enquiry : Danny Brock one-day ban: careless riding (Aug 31)
Joe Doyle seven-day ban: used whip above permitted level (Aug 31,Sep 1-6)

FOCUS
They went steady early on and quite a few of these were keen. The placed horses set the level with the second to his maiden form and the third to last year's turf best.
T/Plt: £182.80 to a £1 stake. Pool: £59,667.78 - 238.20 winning units T/Qpdt: £28.80 to a £1 stake. Pool: £3,350.64 - 85.96 winning units JR

5275 LINGFIELD (L-H)
Saturday, August 17

OFFICIAL GOING: Turf course - good to firm (firm in places; 9.3); all-weather course - standard
Wind: Fresh, behind Weather: Cloudy; light rain from Race six

5522 CAUSEWAY STEEL 10TH ANNIVERSARY APPRENTICE TRAINING SERIES H'CAP (RACING EXCELLENCE INITIATIVE) 6f
5:00 (5:00) (Class 5) (0-70,70) 4-Y-O+ **£2,726** (£805; £402) **Stalls** High

Form RPR

-613 **1** **Pucon**[24] 4635 4-8-13 **64** SineadAlderman(5) 10 73
(Roger Teal) *mde all: clr 1/2-way: pushed along over 1f out: comf* **14/1**

4050 **2** *1 3/4* **Putin (IRE)**[18] 4860 5-8-13 **64** (bt) LouisSteward(5) 5 67
(Phil McEntee) *chsd wnr: drvn along 2f out: styd on same pce* **6/1**[3]

3206 **3** *1/2* **Emiratesdotcom**[19] 4837 7-9-1 **66** (p) WillPettis(5) 11 68
(Milton Bradley) *prom: hrd rdn 2f out: kpt on fnl f* **8/1**

634- **4** *1/2* **Game All (IRE)**[281] 7668 4-8-12 **58** NoelGarbutt 9 58
(Hugo Palmer) *mainly 5th tl rdn and styd on fnl 2f: nvr able to chal* **7/1**

4443 **5** *1 3/4* **Pharoh Jake**[12] 5060 5-8-5 **51** oh1 ShelleyBirkett 1 46
(John Bridger) *chsd ldrs: outpcd 1/2-way: rdn and no ex fnl 2f* **16/1**

543 **6** *1/2* **Gung Ho Jack**[7] 5278 4-9-4 **64** TimClark 2 57
(John Best) *dwlt: towards rr: hrd rdn over 1f out: nvr rchd ldrs* **9/2**[2]

3352 **7** *1* **Volito**[9] 5165 7-8-10 **56** IanBurns 8 46
(Anabel K Murphy) *outpcd towards rr: nvr trbld ldrs* **12/1**

335 **8** *6* **Purley Queen (IRE)**[128] 1503 4-9-1 **61** JoshBaudains 6 32
(Sylvester Kirk) *outpcd: a bhd* **20/1**

1U0 **9** *4* **Midnight Feast**[35] 4281 5-9-9 **69** (v) DanielMuscutt 12 27
(Lee Carter) *awkward leaving stalls and s.s: a wl bhd* **4/1**[1]

6502 **U** **Emkanaat**[9] 5205 5-9-7 **70** (p) JoshCrane(3) 3
(Amy Weaver) *dipped and uns rdr as stalls opened* **9/2**[2]

1m 8.93s (-2.27) **Going Correction** -0.30s/f (Firm) **10** Ran SP% **119.3**
Speed ratings (Par 103): **103,100,100,99,97 96,95,87,81,**
toteswingers 1&2 £12.60, 1&3 £11.70, 2&3 £18.20 CSF £97.82 CT £746.25 TOTE £17.50: £3.50, £2.40, £3.20; EX 91.30 Trifecta £601.70 Part won. Pool: £802.36 - 0.18 winning units..
Owner J A Redmond **Bred** J Redmond **Trained** Ashtead, Surrey
■ Stewards' Enquiry : Noel Garbutt two-day ban: used whip above permitted level (Aug 31-Sep 1)

FOCUS
A mixed meeting on a damp evening with conditions standard for the final three races on the all-weather and good to firm, firm in places for the first four on the turf. A competitive apprentice sprint handicap on paper but with Emkanaat virtually falling out of the stalls and unseating his rider, along with Gung Ho Jack and Midnight Feast completely missing the break, it proved straightforward for the winner. The winner recorded a personal-best with the placed horses a little off recent form.

5523 BIRTH OF AIBEN SMITH-ANTHONY (S) STKS 6f
5:30 (5:30) (Class 6) 3-Y-O+ **£2,045** (£603; £302) **Stalls** High

Form RPR
0260 **1** **We Have A Dream**[17] 4884 8-9-1 65..............................(p) MartinDwyer 8 74
(William Muir) *mde all against stands' rail: clr fnl f: comf* **9/4**[2]
0210 **2** *4 ½* **Fathsta (IRE)**[7] 5273 8-9-1 72.................................. GeorgeDowning(5) 6 65
(Ian Williams) *cl up: rdn to chse wnr over 1f out: unable qck* **2/1**[1]
606 **3** *nk* **Whisky Bravo**[39] 4146 4-9-6 66.. ChrisCatlin 3 64
(David Brown) *towards rr in centre: effrt over 2f out: styd on same pce* **10/1**
040 **4** *nk* **Paradise Spectre**[15] 4970 6-8-8 68.......................(p) RobJFitzpatrick(7) 5 58
(Mrs K Burke) *dwlt and rdn s: drvn along and sme hdwy 2f out: no imp fnl f* **8/1**
1113 **5** *5* **Amenable (IRE)**[4] 5376 6-9-6 72..................................(p) KieranO'Neill 1 47
(Violet M Jordan) *mainly in rr: nvr able to chal* **4/1**[3]
6500 **6** *1 ½* **King Vahe (IRE)**[8] 5232 4-8-10 57.................................(v) LauraPike(5) 4 37
(Olivia Maylam) *prom over 4f* **25/1**
00-0 **7** *1* **Ansells Pride (IRE)**[28] 4520 10-8-10 60.......................(tp) JakePayne(5) 7 34
(Bill Turner) *chsd wnr tl wknd over 1f out* **16/1**
1m 9.08s (-2.12) **Going Correction** -0.30s/f (Firm) **7** Ran SP% **114.0**
Speed ratings (Par 101): **102,96,95,95,88 86,85**
toteswingers 1&2 £2.20, 1&3 £3.30, 2&3 £4.10 CSF £7.14 TOTE £3.20: £1.80, £1.70; EX 6.80 Trifecta £41.90 Pool: £1,383.74 - 24.74 winning units..There was no bid for the winner.
Owner The Dreaming Squires **Bred** Whitsbury Manor Stud **Trained** Lambourn, Berks
FOCUS
A modest sprint best rated through the winner.

5524 FREDDIE PARKER WINNING FASHION/BRITISH STALLION STUDS EBF NOVICE STKS 7f
6:00 (6:00) (Class 5) 2-Y-O **£3,067** (£905; £453) **Stalls** High

Form RPR
1 **1** **Hiking (USA)**[54] 3631 2-8-11 0... ChrisCatlin 5 80+
(Roger Charlton) *prom: effrt towards centre 2f out: led ins fnl f: drvn out* **10/11**[1]
13 **2** *1* **Snow Squall**[15] 4959 2-9-5 0.. AdamKirby 4 85
(Charlie Appleby) *trckd ldrs: gap opened on stands' rail over 1f out: wnt 2nd ins fnl f: unable qck* **6/4**[2]
1U02 **3** *½* **Intermath (IRE)**[13] 5028 2-9-5 83.................................... CathyGannon 1 84
(David Evans) *led and sn got across to stands' rail: edgd lft over 1f out: hdd and one pce ins fnl f* **10/1**
031 **4** *3* **Faintly (USA)**[28] 4518 2-9-5 0... MartinDwyer 2 76
(Amanda Perrett) *chsd ldr: swtchd lft over 4f out: edgd lft over 1f out: sn wknd* **8/1**[3]
04 **5** *6* **M'Lady Ermyn**[24] 4630 2-8-9 0.................................. FrankieMcDonald 3 50
(Pat Phelan) *outpcd: nvr trbld ldrs* **100/1**
60 **6** *19* **Flying Author (IRE)**[77] 2863 2-8-9 0............................ NathanAlison(5) 6 3
(Phil McEntee) *outpcd in centre: no ch fnl 2f* **100/1**
1m 20.55s (-2.75) **Going Correction** -0.30s/f (Firm) 2y crse rec **6** Ran SP% **114.6**
Speed ratings (Par 94): **103,101,101,97,91 69**
toteswingers 1&2 £1.10, 1&3 £1.50, 2&3 £1.70 CSF £2.61 TOTE £1.80: £1.10, £1.60; EX 3.60 Trifecta £8.70 Pool: £1,659.73 - 141.47 winning units..
Owner K Abdullah **Bred** Juddmonte Farms Inc **Trained** Beckhampton, Wilts
FOCUS
The previous two runnings of this novices' stakes has produced some Group performers including Ayaar, a Group 3 winner in Germany last year, who dead-heated in a match for this contest with the useful Snowboarder last year. A decent pace for an interesting contest which saw the 7f course record for juveniles being broken. The third and fifth are the best guides to the form.

5525 SANDRA HARMAN BIRTHDAY H'CAP 7f 140y
6:30 (6:30) (Class 6) (0-60,58) 3-Y-O+ **£2,045** (£603; £302) **Stalls** Centre

Form RPR
3500 **1** **King Of Wing (IRE)**[24] 4623 4-9-0 **48**.........................(be) CathyGannon 8 56
(Phil McEntee) *prom: pressed ldr fr 4f out: str chal on stands' rail over 1f out: drvn to ld ins fnl f* **7/1**
0543 **2** *¾* **Admirals Walk (IRE)**[8] 5217 3-9-4 **58**................................(tp) PatDobbs 2 63
(Sylvester Kirk) *prom: slt ld 4f out: hrd rdn and hdd ins fnl f: kpt on* **3/1**[1]
2345 **3** *6* **Takitwo**[14] 4996 10-9-10 **58**.. MartinDwyer 1 49
(Geoffrey Deacon) *bhd: rdn over 3f out: sme hdwy 2f out: styd on to take 3rd nr fin* **3/1**[1]
0-26 **4** *nk* **Squirrel Wood (IRE)**[23] 4658 5-9-9 **57**......................... DougieCostello 9 47
(Mary Hambro) *s.i.s: sn rdn to ld on stands' rail: hdd 4f out: edgd lft and no ex 2f out* **4/1**[2]
004 **5** *2 ¾* **Jackie Love (IRE)**[60] 3430 5-8-11 **50**..........................(v) NathanAlison(5) 3 33
(Olivia Maylam) *chsd ldrs in centre: hrd rdn over 2f out: wknd wl over 1f out* **25/1**
5614 **6** *6* **Surrey Dream (IRE)**[9] 5166 4-9-0 **48**..............................(t) KieranO'Neill 4 16
(John Bridger) *in tch in centre tl wknd over 2f out* **6/1**[3]
1540 **7** *2* **Chandrayaan**[8] 5232 6-9-3 **51**...................................(v) RichardThomas 5 14
(John E Long) *hld up in 6th: drvn along over 3f out: sn wknd* **12/1**
0000 **8** *19* **Yalding Dancer**[114] 1781 4-8-11 **45**.. ChrisCatlin 7
(John Best) *sn bhd: no ch fnl 3f* **33/1**
1m 29.36s (-2.94) **Going Correction** -0.30s/f (Firm)
WFA 3 from 4yo+ 6lb **8** Ran SP% **118.5**
Speed ratings (Par 101): **102,101,95,94,92 86,84,65**
toteswingers 1&2 £3.30, 1&3 £6.80, 2&3 £1.90 CSF £29.45 CT £78.67 TOTE £10.40: £2.20, £1.50, £1.90; EX 44.70 Trifecta £269.00 Pool: £1,187.72 - 3.31 winning units..
Owner Mrs Rebecca McEntee **Bred** Anthony Hanahoe **Trained** Newmarket, Suffolk
FOCUS
A low-grade handicap and not that solid, so rated cautiously around the first two.

5526 BOB MALTS HORSES WITH JOHN BEST H'CAP 1m 4f (P)
7:00 (7:00) (Class 5) (0-70,75) 3-Y-O+ **£3,067** (£905; £453) **Stalls** Low

Form RPR
5411 **1** **Slip Of The Tongue**[9] 5197 3-9-9 **75**................................... LukeMorris 1 85+
(Sir Mark Prescott Bt) *mde all: rdn over 2f out: hld on u.p fnl f* **1/4**[1]
1564 **2** *1* **Knight's Parade (IRE)**[21] 4748 3-9-2 **68**................................ PatDobbs 4 76
(Amanda Perrett) *trckd ldr: hrd rdn over 1f out: pressed wnr and kpt on wl fnl f: a jst hld* **5/1**[2]
00-0 **3** *2 ¼* **Crystal Monarch (IRE)**[45] 3953 4-8-13 **55**......................... ChrisCatlin 2 59
(Lady Cecil) *dwlt: sn rdn into 3rd: outpcd and lost tch w ldng pair 5f out: styd on again fr over 1f out* **12/1**[3]
03-0 **4** *40* **No Compromise**[40] 4126 4-10-0 **70**.............................. DougieCostello 3 10
(Richard Phillips) *a last: rdn and outpcd 7f out: bhd fnl 5f* **20/1**
2m 31.43s (-1.57) **Going Correction** -0.025s/f (Stan)
WFA 3 from 4yo+ 10lb **4** Ran SP% **109.1**
Speed ratings (Par 103): **104,103,101,75**
CSF £1.95 TOTE £1.02; EX 1.40 Trifecta £2.50 Pool: £558.68 - 167.20 winning units..
Owner J Fishpool - Osborne House **Bred** Miss K Rausing **Trained** Newmarket, Suffolk
FOCUS
An uncompetitive contest with the third to his maiden form the best guide.

5527 BIG THANK YOU TO CAUSEWAY STEEL EMPLOYEES CLAIMING STKS 1m (P)
7:30 (7:31) (Class 6) 3-Y-O **£2,045** (£603; £302) **Stalls** High

Form RPR
4660 **1** **Zero Game (IRE)**[22] 4721 3-8-1 66..............................(e) LouisSteward(7) 4 68
(Michael Bell) *mde all: rdn and qcknd clr 2f out: in n.d after: easily* **3/1**[2]
063 **2** *6* **Gabrial The Boss (USA)**[22] 4710 3-9-0 74.................(t) DarrenEgan(3) 9 63
(David Simcock) *hld up in rr: rdn and hdwy over 1f out: r.o to take 2nd ins fnl f: nvr nr wnr* **2/1**[1]
6160 **3** *¾* **Napinda**[10] 5152 3-8-2 55.. WilliamCarson 2 46
(Philip McBride) *chsd ldrs: drvn along and outpcd 3f out: styd on fnl f* **10/1**
050 **4** *1* **Marguerite St Just**[21] 4752 3-7-13 47 ow2.................. NathanAlison(5) 1 44
(Olivia Maylam) *prom: rdn and outpcd 3f out: kpt on fnl f* **33/1**
5545 **5** *nk* **Patently (IRE)**[12] 5055 3-9-7 68...................................(bt[1]) MartinDwyer 3 62
(Brian Meehan) *sn prom: chsd wnr after 2f: faltered and wknd over 1f out: lost 2nd ins fnl f* **3/1**[2]
5043 **6** *¾* **Tornado Battle**[21] 4750 3-8-11 51...................................... CathyGannon 6 51
(Phil McEntee) *hld up in rr: rdn over 2f out: sme late hdwy* **16/1**
-600 **7** *3 ½* **Hidden Talent**[9] 5195 3-8-13 75.. LukeMorris 7 45
(David Brown) *hld up in 6th: rdn over 3f out: sn outpcd* **5/1**[3]
8 *6* **You're A Rich Girl** 3-8-6 0... KieranO'Neill 5 24
(Dr Jon Scargill) *stdd s: t.k.h and hld up in 5th: rdn 3f out: sn wknd* **25/1**
1m 38.23s (0.03) **Going Correction** -0.025s/f (Stan) **8** Ran SP% **121.8**
Speed ratings (Par 98): **98,92,91,90,89 89,85,79**
toteswingers 1&2 £2.70, 1&3 £7.60, 2&3 £2.30 CSF £10.18 TOTE £4.90: £1.40, £1.10, £3.80; EX 10.70 Trifecta £108.10 Pool: £1,251.18 - 8.67 winning units..Zero Game was claimed by Miss Amy Weaver for £8,000
Owner Edward J Ware **Bred** Islanmore Stud **Trained** Newmarket, Suffolk
■ Stewards' Enquiry : Nathan Alison three-day ban: weighed-in 2lb heavy (Aug 31,Sep 1-2)
FOCUS
With Scala Romana defecting many of the runners in this claimer came here with questions to answer and very few got involved after a fine piece of riding by the winning jockey. The winner is rated back to form with the second below his best.

5528 LAUREN THEA BIRTHDAY H'CAP 1m 2f (P)
8:00 (8:00) (Class 6) (0-60,60) 3-Y-O+ **£2,045** (£603; £302) **Stalls** Low

Form RPR
-000 **1** **Exclusive Waters (IRE)**[49] 3820 3-8-13 **58**................. DarrenEgan(3) 11 71
(William Knight) *s.i.s: bhd tl gd hdwy to join ldrs 6f out: rdn over 3f out: led over 2f out: clr 1f out: comf* **5/2**[2]
020 **2** *3* **Aminah**[61] 3418 3-9-4 **60**... PatDobbs 10 67
(Robert Cowell) *chsd ldrs: effrt 2f out: wnt 2nd 1f out: kpt on u.p: no ch w wnr* **7/1**[3]
041 **3** *2 ¼* **Archelao (IRE)**[129] 1473 5-9-9 **57**...................................(t) LukeMorris 5 60
(Richard Rowe) *in tch: effrt over 2f out: styd on same pce* **8/1**
1050 **4** *shd* **Entrapping**[23] 4688 3-8-12 **54**... CathyGannon 8 56
(John E Long) *hld up in last pl: rdn and hdwy over 1f out: styd on to dispute 3rd ins fnl f* **14/1**
00-0 **5** *5* **Ryedale Lass**[14] 5002 5-9-8 **56**...................................... MartinDwyer 12 48
(Geoffrey Deacon) *prom: led and gng wl 3f out: hdd over 2f out: wknd over 1f out* **16/1**
2234 **6** *4 ½* **Megalala (IRE)**[23] 4665 12-9-10 **58**..............................(p) KieranO'Neill 7 41
(John Bridger) *sn led: rdn 4f out: hdd and btn 3f out* **14/1**
2550 **7** *1 ½* **Queenie's Star (IRE)**[61] 3399 6-8-12 **46** oh1.................(t) RobertHavlin 9 26
(Michael Attwater) *towards rr: rdn and nt trble ldrs fnl 3f* **20/1**
0006 **8** *3 ¼* **Sporting Club Girl**[23] 4664 3-8-4 **46** oh1....................(v) WilliamCarson 3 20
(William Knight) *towards rr: rdn over 4f out: n.d after* **50/1**
-000 **9** *3 ½* **Waspy**[33] 4350 4-8-12 **53**......................................(tp) LouisSteward(7) 13 20
(Dr Jeremy Naylor) *a towards rr* **33/1**
/5-0 **10** *6* **Red Willow**[8] 5234 7-9-7 **55**... RichardThomas 14 10
(John E Long) *chsd ldrs tl hrd rdn and wknd over 3f out* **25/1**
-366 **11** *28* **Bell'Arte (IRE)**[89] 2508 3-9-1 **57**.. JackMitchell 2
(Laura Mongan) *mid-div: rdn 4f out: sn bhd* **25/1**
4-51 **P** **Santadelacruze**[14] 5002 4-9-11 **59**................................(b) GeorgeBaker 1
(Gary Moore) *broke wl: trckd ldrs: sing to lose pl whn p.u 2f out: dismntd* **7/4**[1]
2m 6.36s (-0.24) **Going Correction** -0.025s/f (Stan)
WFA 3 from 4yo+ 8lb **12** Ran SP% **125.1**
Speed ratings (Par 101): **99,96,94,94,90 87,85,83,80,75 53,**
toteswingers 1&2 £4.90, 1&3 £5.20, 2&3 £12.10 CSF £20.48 CT £130.56 TOTE £3.70: £1.40, £3.30, £3.40; EX 18.50 Trifecta £266.50 Pool: £1,535.09 - 4.31 winning units..
Owner The Old Brokers **Bred** M M Sammon **Trained** Patching, W Sussex
FOCUS
A low-grade handicap with plenty of early pace. The runner-up is rated to her best with the third to his winter form.
T/Plt: £33.30 to a £1 stake. Pool: £39,718.64 - 870.12 winning units T/Qpdt: £2.60 to a £1 stake. Pool: £5,015.70 - 1,405.84 winning units LM

5472 NEWBURY (L-H)
Saturday, August 17

OFFICIAL GOING: Good (7.2)
Wind: Moderate across Weather: White cloud

5529 BETFRED BETTER ODDS ON GOALS GALORE EBF MAIDEN FILLIES' STKS 6f 8y
1:35 (1:37) (Class 4) 2-Y-O **£4,528** (£1,347; £673; £336) **Stalls** Centre

Form RPR
1 **Lightning Thunder** 2-9-0 0.. HarryBentley 13 85+
(Olly Stevens) *hld up in rr: gd hdwy over 2f out: qcknd to ld appr fnl f: comf* **7/1**[3]

4 **2** 1 ½ **Tea In Transvaal (IRE)**[22] 4702 2-9-0 0 PatDobbs 7 80
(Richard Hannon) *sn led: rdn along ins fnl 2f: hdd appr fnl f: kpt on but nt pce of wnr* **5/2**[1]
0 **3** 1 ¼ **Fashion Fund**[17] 4877 2-9-0 0 PaulHanagan 8 76
(Brian Meehan) *chsd ldr: rdn ins fnl 2f: styd on same pce ins fnl f* **11/4**[2]
4 *shd* **Sound Of Summer (IRE)** 2-9-0 0 JohnnyMurtagh 9 76
(Charles Hills) *chsd ldrs: pushed along 2f out: styd on same pce ins fnl f* **15/2**
5 ½ **Country Drive (USA)** 2-9-0 0 PatSmullen 2 74
(Ed Dunlop) *towards rr: hdwy fr 2f out: pushed along and kpt on fnl f: nvr gng pce to trble ldrs* **20/1**
6 *1* **Pretty Flemingo (IRE)** 2-9-0 0 GeraldMosse 12 71+
(Richard Hannon) *s.i.s: in rr: hdwy over 2f out: pushed along and one pce fnl f* **10/1**
7 *5* **China In My Hands** 2-9-0 0 CathyGannon 15 56+
(Mick Channon) *slowly away and green in rr: drvn over 2f out: hdwy over 1f out: kpt on wl fnl 110yds* **14/1**
0 **8** *nk* **Clear Focus (IRE)**[47] 3896 2-9-0 0 JackMitchell 4 56
(Brendan Powell) *chsd ldrs: rdn over 2f out: wknd wl over 1f out* **100/1**
0 **9** 1 ½ **Black Rodded**[29] 4484 2-9-0 0 RobertHavlin 5 51
(Hughie Morrison) *chsd ldrs: rdn 2f out: sn btn* **33/1**
10 *2* **Kinloss** 2-9-0 0 TedDurcan 6 45
(Richard Hannon) *chsd ldrs 4f* **16/1**
11 *nk* **Prim And Proper** 2-8-9 0 RyanTate(5) 10 44
(Brendan Powell) *in rr: sme hdwy to cl on ldrs over 2f out: wknd sn after* **100/1**
12 *4* **Highland Stardust** 2-9-0 0 AdamKirby 3 32
(Clive Cox) *spd 3f* **33/1**
13 1 ¼ **Arabian Sunset (IRE)** 2-9-0 0 KierenFallon 11 28
(Brendan Powell) *s.i.s: sn chsng ldrs: wknd ins fnl 2f* **20/1**
14 *8* **Mini Light** 2-8-7 0 DanielCremin(7) 1
(Mick Channon) *rdn 1/2-way: a bhd* **66/1**

1m 14.62s (1.62) **Going Correction** +0.15s/f (Good) **14** Ran SP% **120.0**
Speed ratings (Par 93): **95,93,91,91,90 89,82,82,80,77 77,71,70,59**
Tote Swingers 1&2 £4.80, 2&3 £2.50, 1&3 £5.00 CSF £23.32 TOTE £9.20: £2.70, £1.50, £1.60; EX 35.20 Trifecta £110.00 Pool: £4,323.78 - 29.46 winning tickets..
Owner Mohd Al Kubasi & Pearl Bloodstock Ltd **Bred** S A Douch **Trained** Chiddingfold, Surrey

FOCUS
Races on Round course increased in distance by 8m. This looked an interesting fillies' maiden and it should produce winners, with the runner-up setting the level for now.

5530 DENFORD STUD STKS (REGISTERED AS THE WASHINGTON SINGER STAKES) (LISTED RACE) 7f (S)
2:05 (2:07) (Class 1) 2-Y-O
£14,461 (£5,482; £2,743; £1,366; £685; £344) **Stalls** Centre

Form RPR
142 **1** **Somewhat (USA)**[35] 4296 2-9-0 102 GeraldMosse 2 110+
(Mark Johnston) *mde all: shkn up wl over 1f out: pushed along and qcknd ins fnl f: wnt clr fnl 110yds: easily* **11/8**[1]
2 4 ½ **Be Ready (IRE)** 2-8-11 0 KierenFallon 7 95+
(Saeed bin Suroor) *hld up towards rr: hdwy 3f out: trckd wnr over 2f out: pushed along and effrt 1f out and sn swtchd lft: sn outpcd but kpt on wl for clr 2nd* **5/2**[2]
61 **3** 3 ¼ **Speedy Approach**[49] 3810 2-9-0 0 JohnnyMurtagh 6 90
(Michael Bell) *in rr: pushed along and hdwy over 2f out: rdn and kpt on to take wl-hld 3rd fnl 110yds* **11/2**[3]
4215 **4** 1 ½ **Expert (IRE)**[17] 4876 2-9-0 95 PatDobbs 1 86
(Richard Hannon) *chsd ldrs in 3rd: rdn over 1f out: sn outpcd: dropped to wl-hld 4th fnl 110yds* **8/1**
10 **5** *2* **Noble Metal**[35] 4296 2-9-0 0 ShaneKelly 4 81
(Peter Chapple-Hyam) *chsd wnr tl over 2f out: sn rdn: wknd wl over 1f out* **28/1**
153 **6** *7* **Lone Warrior (IRE)**[21] 4747 2-9-0 99 AdamKirby 5 63
(David Evans) *chsd ldrs: rdn 3f out: btn sn after* **9/1**
361 **7** *26* **Grevillea (IRE)**[16] 4906 2-8-9 78 TedDurcan 3
(Mick Channon) *rdn over 3f out: a in rr: lost tch over 2f out* **33/1**

1m 25.57s (-0.13) **Going Correction** +0.15s/f (Good) **7** Ran SP% **113.6**
Speed ratings (Par 102): **106,100,97,95,93 85,55**
Tote Swingers 1&2 £1.40, 2&3 £2.40, 1&3 £2.00 CSF £4.87 TOTE £2.10: £1.10, £2.10; EX 5.10 Trifecta £13.80 Pool: £4205.00 - 228.36 winning tickets..
Owner Sheikh Majid Bin Mohammed al Maktoum **Bred** B P Walden Jr, P W Madden Et Al **Trained** Middleham Moor, N Yorks

FOCUS
This race has been won by some top-class horses over the years, such as Rodrigo de Triano, Lammtarra and Haafhd, while the Irish 1000 Guineas winner Just The Judge took it last year. They seemed to go just a sensible pace, but even so they finished very well spread out and the winner was impressive.

5531 BETFRED TV GEOFFREY FREER STKS (GROUP 3) 1m 5f 61y
2:40 (2:40) (Class 1) 3-Y-O+
£34,026 (£12,900; £6,456; £3,216; £1,614; £810) **Stalls** Centre

Form RPR
2201 **1** **Royal Empire (IRE)**[28] 4526 4-9-4 112 KierenFallon 2 113+
(Saeed bin Suroor) *in rr: pushed along 4f out: hdwy 3f out: led 2f out: drvn over 1f out: styd on strly ins fnl f* **8/1**
3006 **2** 1 ½ **Red Cadeaux**[21] 4745 7-9-10 115 GeraldMosse 7 117
(Ed Dunlop) *in rr: hdwy fr 3f out: styd on wl fr 2f out to chse wnr fnl f: no imp* **13/2**
5-12 **3** ½ **Lost In The Moment (IRE)**[15] 4944 6-9-4 108 (p) PatSmullen 9 111+
(Saeed bin Suroor) *in rr: hdwy to cl on ldrs 2f out: rdn and one pce over 1f out: styd on wl again ins fnl f to take 3rd fnl 110yds* **6/1**[3]
3202 **4** 1 ¼ **Genzy (FR)**[20] 4796 5-9-4 100 PatDobbs 3 108
(Ian Williams) *in rr: drvn and hdwy over 2f out: styd on fnl f to take 4th last strides: nt trble ldrs* **25/1**
4-62 **5** *hd* **I'm Your Man (FR)**[49] 3830 4-9-4 109 AntoineHamelin 4 108
(A De Royer-Dupre, France) *chsd ldrs: wnt 2nd 7f out: rdn to take slt ld appr fnl 2f: sn hdd: wknd ins fnl f* **5/1**[2]
442- **6** 1 ½ **Aiken**[301] 7235 5-9-4 112 RobertHavlin 8 106
(John Gosden) *in tch: hdwy to cl on ldrs 5f out: pushed along 3f out: drvn and outpcd 2f out: kpt on again clsng stages* **3/1**[1]
1-42 **7** 1 ¼ **Biographer**[42] 4083 4-9-4 109 TedDurcan 6 104
(David Lanigan) *in rr: rdn and sme hdwy 3f out: nvr rchd ldrs: one pce fnl 2f* **5/1**[2]
6144 **8** *nk* **Testudo (IRE)**[17] 4874 3-8-7 105 PaulHanagan 10 104
(Brian Meehan) *sn led: rdn over 2f out: hdd appr fnl 2f: wknd fnl f* **16/1**
4305 **9** ¾ **Model Pupil**[42] 4083 4-9-4 108 JohnnyMurtagh 5 102
(Charles Hills) *trckd ldrs drvn over 3f out: wknd 2f out* **12/1**
100 **10** ¾ **Ralston Road (IRE)**[49] 3849 3-8-7 98 (b) TadhgO'Shea 1 101
(John Patrick Shanahan, Ire) *chsd ldrs: rdn 3f out: wknd 2f out* **33/1**

2m 50.43s (-1.57) **Going Correction** +0.15s/f (Good)
WFA 3 from 4yo+ 11lb **10** Ran SP% **117.4**
Speed ratings (Par 113): **110,109,108,108,107 106,106,106,105,105**
Tote Swingers 1&2 £8.70, 2&3 £9.40, 1&3 £7.80 CSF £59.62 TOTE £7.70: £2.60, £1.80, £2.90; EX 66.00 Trifecta £600.10 Pool: £5,762.47 - 7.20 winning tickets..
Owner Godolphin **Bred** Twelve Oaks Stud **Trained** Newmarket, Suffolk

FOCUS
Formerly a Group 2, the Geoffrey Freer has been a Group 3 since 2006 and has been won by some high-class middle-distances performers/stayers over the years including Charlottown, Levmoss, Ile de Bourbon, Ardross (twice) and Drum Taps. The subsequent St Leger winner Ridge Wood won the inaugural running, while Moon Madness, Silver Patriarch and Sixties Icon all won this after they had taken the final Classic. This year's renewal was notable for a lack of pace and there wasn't that much covering the ten runners at the line, suggesting the form may not be totally reliable. The runners came down the centre of the track in the straight and the form looks sound enough, rated around the first three.

5532 BETFRED HUNGERFORD STKS (GROUP 2) 7f (S)
3:15 (3:15) (Class 1) 3-Y-O+ **£56,710** (£21,500; £10,760; £5,360; £2,690) **Stalls** Centre

Form RPR
2135 **1** **Gregorian (IRE)**[17] 4875 4-9-3 115 RobertHavlin 5 118
(John Gosden) *trckd ldrs: drvn 2f out: hdwy sn after and led ins fnl f: rdn out* **3/1**[3]
111 **2** 1 ½ **Soft Falling Rain (SAF)**[140] 1262 4-9-5 115 PaulHanagan 4 116
(M F De Kock, South Africa) *led: pushed along and qcknd 2f out: rdn over 1f out whn hrd pressed: hdd ins fnl f: outpcd by wnr but kpt on wl for 2nd* **9/4**[1]
4332 **3** 1 ¼ **Tawhid**[15] 4945 3-8-12 111 JohnnyMurtagh 3 109
(Saeed bin Suroor) *chsd ldr: drvn to chal wl over 1f out: wknd into 3rd ins fnl f* **5/2**[2]
54-2 **4** 4 ½ **Caspar Netscher**[18] 4856 4-9-3 114 ShaneKelly 1 98
(David Simcock) *broke wl: stdd in bhd ldrs and t.k.h: hdwy 2f out: nvr quite on terms and wknd appr fnl f* **7/2**
4604 **5** 1 ¼ **Libranno**[18] 4856 5-9-3 109 KierenFallon 2 95
(Richard Hannon) *hld up in rr: pushed along and sme hdwy over 3f out: wl in tch w ldrs 2f out: sn wknd* **12/1**

1m 25.84s (0.14) **Going Correction** +0.15s/f (Good)
WFA 3 from 4yo+ 5lb **5** Ran SP% **114.3**
Speed ratings (Par 115): **105,103,101,96,95**
CSF £10.58 TOTE £5.80: £2.00, £1.10; EX 16.10 Trifecta £47.80 Pool: £19,095.67 - 299.27 winning tickets..
Owner HRH Princess Haya Of Jordan **Bred** Rathasker Stud **Trained** Newmarket, Suffolk

FOCUS
Promoted to Group 2 status in 2006, within the last 20 years the Hungerford Stakes has been won by the likes of the 1,000 Guineas winner Harayir, Chic, Paco Boy and Excelebration, while this season's dual Group 1 winner Lethal Force took it last year. The 3yo generation had won four of the previous five runnings. This year's renewal was something off a messy affair, with the favourite looking a reluctant leader, and it developing into something of a sprint. The winner looks the best guide to the form, with the second rated to the best of his Dubai form.

5533 BETFRED MOBILE SPORTS LADIES DAY H'CAP 7f (S)
3:50 (3:50) (Class 3) (0-95,95) 3-Y-O+
£12,450 (£3,728; £1,864; £932; £466; £234) **Stalls** Centre

Form RPR
0414 **1** **Glen Moss (IRE)**[21] 4744 4-9-7 **90** JohnnyMurtagh 1 105+
(Charles Hills) *disp ld towards centre tl overall ldr 2f out: c clr fnl f: easily* **5/2**[1]
0640 **2** *3* **Dance And Dance (IRE)**[15] 4946 7-9-11 **94** (b) KierenFallon 13 100+
(Ed Vaughan) *s.i.s: in rr: hdwy over 1f out: str run ins fnl f to take 2nd last strides but no ch w easy wnr* **7/1**[2]
64-6 **3** *nk* **Axiom**[71] 3060 9-8-9 **85** (p) BradleyBosley(7) 2 90
(Ed Walker) *chsd wnr towards centre: easily outpcd fnl f: lost 2nd last strides* **25/1**
-060 **4** *1* **Born To Surprise**[71] 3060 4-9-10 **93** PaulHanagan 7 95
(Michael Bell) *chsd ldrs: rdn 2f out: styd on same pce fnl f* **10/1**
6030 **5** ½ **Nassau Storm**[14] 4983 4-9-6 **89** ShaneKelly 3 90
(William Knight) *chsd ldrs towards centre: rdn 2f out: outpcd fnl f* **25/1**
-206 **6** 1 ¾ **Poetic Dancer**[28] 4534 4-9-4 **87** AdamKirby 12 83
(Clive Cox) *disp ld on stands' side tl hdd by wnr 2f out: wknd fnl f* **12/1**
3103 **7** 1 ¾ **Lupo D'Oro (IRE)**[20] 4800 4-9-2 **85** TedDurcan 9 77
(John Best) *in rr: hdwy 2f out: kpt on fnl f: nt trble ldrs* **20/1**
3310 **8** *nk* **The Confessor**[21] 4744 6-9-9 **92** CathyGannon 14 83
(Henry Candy) *chsd ldrs: rdn 2f out: sn btn* **16/1**
5-5 **9** 2 ½ **Tariq Too**[85] 2621 6-9-12 **95** DougieCostello 11 79
(Amy Weaver) *in tch: rdn over 2f out: no ch after* **20/1**
1060 **10** *shd* **Piscean (USA)**[14] 4983 8-9-3 **86** HarryBentley 5 70
(Tom Keddy) *chsd ldrs towards centre: wknd 2f out* **28/1**
2042 **11** 1 ½ **Democretes**[7] 5285 4-9-3 **93** CameronHardie(7) 10 73
(Richard Hannon) *in rr: sme hdwy over 2f out: nvr rchd ldrs and sn wknd* **8/1**[3]
312- **12** ½ **Janoub Nibras (IRE)**[321] 6700 3-9-4 **92** PatDobbs 6 70
(Richard Hannon) *in tch: rdn and sme hdwy over 2f out: nvr rchd ldrs and wknd wl over 1f out* **10/1**
6000 **13** *2* **Common Touch (IRE)**[7] 5285 5-9-2 **85** (b) JackMitchell 4 58
(Willie Musson) *in rr: sme prog 3f out: sn bhd* **16/1**
-120 **14** 2 ¾ **Secret Talent**[58] 3484 3-9-2 **90** PatSmullen 16 55
(Hughie Morrison) *chsd ldrs over 4f* **7/1**[2]

1m 25.28s (-0.42) **Going Correction** +0.15s/f (Good)
WFA 3 from 4yo+ 5lb **14** Ran SP% **123.0**
Speed ratings (Par 107): **108,104,104,103,102 100,98,98,95,95 93,92,90,87**
Tote Swingers 1&2 £4.10, 2&3 £55.90, 1&3 £20.40 CSF £17.67 CT £380.89 TOTE £3.00: £1.60, £2.20, £10.70; EX 19.20 Trifecta £746.40 Pool: £50,511.14 - 50.75 winning tickets..
Owner John C Grant **Bred** Rathbarry Stud **Trained** Lambourn, Berks

The Form Book Flat, Raceform Ltd, Compton, RG20 6NL.

FOCUS
A decent handicap in which they soon split into two, with ten horses racing nearside and four coming up the centre. The smaller group provided the winner, third and fifth. The winner was impressive, recording a personal-best, and this was the third's best effort since last summer.

5534 BETFRED WATCH FRED'S PUSHES ON BETFRED TV H'CAP 1m 2f 6y
4:25 (4:25) (Class 4) (0-85,85) 3-Y-O **£4,851** (£1,443; £721; £360) **Stalls** Centre

Form RPR
301 **1** **Thomas Hobson**[17] 4882 3-9-6 **84** RobertHavlin 4 91+
(John Gosden) *chsd ldr: rdn over 2f out and styd pressing ldrs: rallied u.p to ld fnl 100yds: gamely* **9/4**[1]
-134 **2** ½ **Jabhaat (USA)**[17] 4878 3-9-6 **84** [1] PaulHanagan 5 90
(Ed Dunlop) *chsd ldrs: drvn and styd on fr over 2f out to take slt ld appr fnl f: hdd and no ex fnl 100yds* **3/1**[2]
3620 **3** 1 ¼ **Buckstay (IRE)**[16] 4917 3-9-5 **83** ShaneKelly 3 86
(Peter Chapple-Hyam) *in rr: hdwy over 2f out: drvn to chal over 1f out: outpcd fnl 100yds* **8/1**
1600 **4** ¾ **Le Deluge (FR)**[37] 4214 3-9-5 **83** TedDurcan 2 85
(John Best) *led: rdn over 2f out: hdd over 1f out: wknd fnl 120yds* **33/1**
-600 **5** 3 ¾ **Pearl Street (USA)**[17] 4898 3-8-5 **69** HarryBentley 6 63
(Henry Candy) *in rr: hdwy 3f out: chsd ldrs 2f out but nvr on terms: wknd fnl f* **8/1**
-550 **6** 2 **Ronaldinho (IRE)**[64] 3276 3-9-7 **85** PatDobbs 7 75
(Richard Hannon) *in rr: rdn over 2f out: nvr rchd ldrs* **20/1**
5431 **7** shd **Swift Bounty**[8] 5218 3-8-13 **82** MichaelJMMurphy(5) 8 72
(Alan Jarvis) *chsd ldrs: rdn 3f out: wknd over 2f out* **4/1**[3]
5552 **8** 7 **Dark Emerald (IRE)**[10] 5134 3-9-7 **85** (v) KierenFallon 1 61
(Brendan Powell) *chsd ldrs: wknd ins fnl 3f* **8/1**

2m 8.56s (-0.24) **Going Correction** +0.15s/f (Good) **8 Ran SP% 116.8**
Speed ratings (Par 102): **106,105,104,104,101 99,99,93**
Tote Swingers 1&2 £2.50, 2&3 £5.10, 1&3 £4.50 CSF £9.37 CT £45.03 TOTE £3.10: £1.30, £1.60, £2.50; EX 10.70 Trifecta £64.10 Pool: £2,833.47 - 33.11 winning tickets..
Owner Bailey, Hall & Hood **Bred** Mount Coote Stud And M H Dixon **Trained** Newmarket, Suffolk

FOCUS
The pace didn't look that strong in this fair handicap and, unlike in the only previous race on the round course, the runners stayed more towards the inside in the straight. The form is a bit muddling with the fourth the key to the level.

5535 BETFRED "TREBLE ODDS ON LUCKY 15'S" LADIES DERBY (H'CAP) (FOR LADY AMATEUR RIDERS) 1m 4f 5y
4:55 (4:55) (Class 4) (0-80,77) 3-Y-O+ **£4,679** (£1,451; £725; £363) **Stalls** Centre

Form RPR
1231 **1** **Hi Note**[15] 4938 5-9-13 **73** MissSMDoolan(5) 3 88
(Sheena West) *mde all: forged clr over 1f out: unchal* **7/2**[2]
325 **2** 7 **Jezza**[45] 3952 7-9-6 **64** (bt) MissCBoxall(3) 9 68
(Karen George) *in rr: hdwy over 2f out: styd on wl fnl f to take 2nd fnl 30yds but no ch w wnr* **13/2**[3]
400 **3** 1 ¼ **Saint Helena (IRE)**[10] 5130 5-10-3 **77** AnnaHesketh(5) 4 79
(Harry Dunlop) *in rr: hdwy on outside fr 3f out: styd on to chse wnr over 1f out but no imp: one pce and lost 2nd fnl 30yds* **8/1**
5200 **4** 4 **Dr Livingstone (IRE)**[9] 5168 8-10-3 **75** MissHayleyMoore(3) 7 70
(Charles Egerton) *chsd ldrs: wnt 2nd 2f out but no imp on wnr u.p: wknd ins fnl f* **11/1**
1641 **5** 1 ¼ **Chocolate Block (IRE)**[12] 5065 3-8-9 **63** MissAliceMills(3) 8 56
(Pat Phelan) *chsd ldr: rdn over 2f out: btn sn after* **3/1**[1]
0554 **6** 1 ¼ **Aldwick Bay (IRE)**[19] 4832 5-10-6 **75** MissEJJones 5 66
(Richard Hannon) *chsd ldrs: rdn 3f out: wknd over 1f out* **4/1**[3]
0-60 **7** 4 ½ **Shades Of Grey**[85] 2619 6-10-6 **75** MissRachelKing 1 59
(Clive Cox) *in rr: sme hdwy 4f out: sn btn* **7/2**[2]

2m 38.19s (2.69) **Going Correction** +0.15s/f (Good)
WFA 3 from 4yo+ 10lb **7 Ran SP% 113.3**
Speed ratings (Par 105): **97,92,91,88,88 87,84**
Tote Swingers 1&2 £3.20, 2&3 £5.10, 1&3 £7.50 CSF £25.60 CT £167.49 TOTE £4.20: £2.10, £2.70; EX 22.40 Trifecta £154.60 Pool: £2,229.37 - 10.80 winning tickets..
Owner Gerald West **Bred** J A And Mrs Duffy **Trained** Falmer, E Sussex
■ Stewards' Enquiry : Anna Hesketh one-day ban: careless riding (Sep 2)

FOCUS
A fair race of its type with the runner-up close to recent turf marks.
T/Plt: £30.50 to a £1 stake. Pool: £97,534.65 - 2,330.59 winning units T/Qpdt: £15.00 to a £1 stake. Pool: £4,479.75 - 219.54 winning units ST

5488 NEWMARKET (R-H)
Saturday, August 17
OFFICIAL GOING: Good (good to firm in places; 7.6)
Wind: fresh to strong, behind Weather: dry, breezy

5536 LANWADES STUD FILLIES' NURSERY H'CAP 7f
1:50 (1:51) (Class 2) 2-Y-O **£12,938** (£3,850; £1,924; £962) **Stalls** Low

Form RPR
2243 **1** **Dancealot**[14] 5005 2-8-1 **73** LukeMorris 2 81
(Clive Brittain) *racd nr stands' rail thrght: chsd ldr tl rdn to ld over 1f out: styd on wl u.p fnl f* **7/1**[2]
5121 **2** 1 ¼ **Lily Rules (IRE)**[10] 5136 2-8-13 **85** BarryMcHugh 8 90
(Tony Coyle) *bmpd s: in tch in rr: hdwy 1/2-way: rdn and effrt 2f out: chsd wnr 1f out: styd on but no imp fnl 100yds* **11/1**
4142 **3** ¾ **Heskin (IRE)**[10] 5136 2-8-1 **73** (p) PatrickMathers 4 76
(Richard Fahey) *chsd ldrs: rdn and effrt to chse ldrs over 1f out: kpt on same pce u.p ins fnl f* **16/1**
633 **4** 1 **Gender Agenda**[31] 4408 2-8-0 **75** DarrenEgan(3) 12 75+
(Michael Bell) *t.k.h: chsd ldrs: effrt u.p 2f out: chsd wnr over 1f out tl 1f out: one pce fnl f* **10/1**
612 **5** ½ **Cornish Path**[22] 4717 2-8-5 **77** NickyMackay 15 76+
(Henry Candy) *towards rr: hdwy over 2f out: rdn and chsd ldrs over 1f out: styd on same pce ins fnl f* **15/2**[3]
212 **6** nk **Shot In The Sun (IRE)**[14] 4988 2-7-10 **75** SamanthaBell(7) 6 73
(Richard Fahey) *hld up in tch towards rr: rdn and hdwy over 1f out: styd on fnl f: nvr trbld ldrs* **10/1**
651 **7** nk **Lady In Blue (IRE)**[23] 4686 2-7-9 **72** NathanAlison(5) 13 69+
(William Haggas) *hld up in tch towards rr: rdn and hdwy to chse ldrs over 1f out: no ex 1f out: one pce after* **12/1**
1310 **8** 1 ¾ **One Penny Piece**[14] 5005 2-8-3 **75** WilliamCarson 1 68
(Philip McBride) *racd against stands' rail: led: rdn and hdd over 1f out: wknd ins fnl f* **33/1**
3031 **9** 4 **Oriel**[19] 4828 2-8-13 **85** (p) SeanLevey 5 67
(Richard Hannon) *stdd s: t.k.h: hld up in tch towards rr: hdwy into midfield 3f out: rdn and effrt 2f out: drvn and btn over 1f out: wknd: wl btn and eased towards fin* **10/1**
0331 **10** 2 ¾ **Sandsman's Girl (IRE)**[8] 5235 2-8-7 **79** AndreaAtzeni 9 54
(James Given) *awkward leaving stalls: sn rcvrd and in tch in midfield: rdn and unable qck 2f out: wknd u.p over 1f out* **16/1**
101 **11** ½ **Autumn Lily (USA)**[35] 4277 2-9-7 **93** NeilCallan 11 67
(Charlie Appleby) *t.k.h: chsd ldrs: rdn 2f out: chsd wnr briefly wl over 1f out: btn 1f out: fdd fnl f* **4/1**[1]
510 **12** 4 ½ **Oyster (IRE)**[15] 4948 2-7-10 **73** oh8 ow1 NatashaEaton(5) 14 35
(Gary Harrison) *hld up in tch towards rr: rdn and no hdwy over 2f out: bhd fnl f* **40/1**
5334 **13** 2 ¼ **State Anthem**[19] 4828 2-8-1 **73** MartinLane 10 29
(Mick Channon) *chsd ldrs: rdn and struggling jst over 2f out: wknd over 1f out: wl btn and heavily eased towards fin* **20/1**
413 **14** 7 **Gold Top (IRE)**[28] 4524 2-8-12 **84** JimCrowley 7 22
(Richard Hannon) *chsd ldrs: losing pl and towards rr whn hmpd wl over 1f out: sn bhd: heavily eased ins fnl f* **9/1**

1m 26.0s (0.30) **Going Correction** +0.05s/f (Good) **14 Ran SP% 119.5**
Speed ratings (Par 97): **100,98,97,96,96 95,95,93,88,85 85,79,77,69**
Tote Swingers 1&2 £2.20, 2&3 £42.80, 1&3 £18.50 CSF £79.61 CT £1199.72 TOTE £7.60: £2.60, £3.10, £6.20; EX 91.60 Trifecta £976.00 Part won. Pool: £1301.45 - 0.14 winning tickets..
Owner Saeed Manana **Bred** Mr & Mrs G Middlebrook **Trained** Newmarket, Suffolk

FOCUS
Far side track used with stalls on stands' side, except 1m2f, 1m4f: centre. Repositioning of bend into home straight added 16m to 1m2f & 1m4f races. Subsequent Listed winner Pimpernel won this fillies nursery in 2010 and Light Up My Life went close in a Group 3 after landing this race last year. Five last-time-out winners lined up in this hot renewal and they raced centre to stands' side. The pace was not very strong and the favourite was disappointing, but one her main market rivals scored in decent style. The runner-up continues her progression.

5537 32RED.COM SUPPORTS RACING WELFARE GREY HORSE H'CAP (FOR GREY HORSES ONLY) 6f
2:20 (2:21) (Class 4) (0-85,85) 3-Y-O+
£12,450 (£3,728; £1,864; £932; £466; £234) **Stalls** Low

Form RPR
2305 **1** **Crew Cut (IRE)**[36] 4235 5-9-4 **84** (b) RobertTart(5) 7 92
(Jeremy Gask) *in tch in midfield: hdwy u.p over 1f out: ev ch ins fnl f: r.o wl to ld last strides* **8/1**[2]
0031 **2** hd **Light From Mars**[47] 3906 8-9-6 **81** (p) JimCrowley 10 88
(Tom Dascombe) *in tch in midfield: effrt u.p over 1f out: drvn to ld fnl 150yds: r.o u.p: hdd and no ex last strides* **20/1**
410 **3** shd **Baby Strange**[14] 4983 9-9-3 **85** AdamMcLean(7) 13 92+
(Derek Shaw) *stdd s: hld up in tch in rr: hdwy and nt clr run over 1f out: hdwy between horses ent fnl f: r.o u.p and ev ch wl ins fnl f: nt quite rch ldng pair* **7/1**[1]
0532 **4** ¾ **Rylee Mooch**[7] 5266 5-9-6 **81** (e) MartinDwyer 4 86
(Richard Guest) *led: rdn over 1f out: hdd fnl 150yds: no ex and styd on same pce fnl 75yds* **12/1**
3500 **5** 1 ¼ **Gabrial's Gift (IRE)**[7] 5273 4-8-5 **69** DarrenEgan(3) 8 70
(David Simcock) *fly-jmpd leaving stalls: hld up in tch in midfield: hdwy u.p over 1f out: chsd ldr and styd on same pce fnl 100yds* **7/1**[1]
0/50 **6** nk **Enderby Spirit (GR)**[14] 5011 7-9-9 **84** (t) RoystonFfrench 2 84
(Bryan Smart) *hld towards rr: rdn and effrt over 1f out: styd on wl fnl 100yds: nt rch ldrs* **33/1**
540 **7** 1 ½ **Black Annis Bower**[14] 4993 5-8-5 **66** (b) LukeMorris 3 61
(Michael Easterby) *t.k.h: chsd ldrs: wnt 2nd 1/2-way tl drvn and no ex jst over 1f out: wknd ins fnl f* **25/1**
-000 **8** hd **Tommy's Secret**[14] 5004 3-8-9 **80** IanBurns(7) 6 74
(Jane Chapple-Hyam) *in tch towards rr: effrt u.p 2f out: styd on steadily ins fnl f: nvr trbld ldrs* **20/1**
531 **9** 1 ¼ **Majesty (IRE)**[43] 4032 3-9-6 **84** SeanLevey 12 74
(Richard Hannon) *chsd ldrs: rdn and unable qck 2f out: drvn and btn ent fnl f: wknd fnl 100yds* **8/1**[2]
4003 **10** nse **Dream Catcher (FR)**[30] 4440 5-8-4 **70** AmyScott(5) 5 60
(Henry Candy) *chsd ldr tl 1/2-way: lost pl and bhd whn n.m.r over 1f out: plugged on but no threat to ldrs fnl f* **7/1**[1]
2352 **11** ½ **Al Udeid (IRE)**[16] 4905 3-8-13 **77** (p) NeilCallan 11 65
(Kevin Ryan) *chsd ldrs: rdn and effrt 2f out: unable qck whn edgd lft and bmpd rival jst over 1f out: wknd ins fnl f* **7/1**[1]
643 **12** 2 **Maglietta Fina (IRE)**[18] 4863 4-9-8 **83** AndreaAtzeni 15 65
(Robert Cowell) *stdd s: t.k.h: hld up in tch in midfield: rdn and no rspnse 2f out: wknd ent fnl f* **20/1**
0020 **13** shd **Medici Time**[22] 4730 8-9-0 **75** (v) RobertWinston 9 57
(Tim Easterby) *stdd s: swtchd rt to r against stands' rail sn after s: hld up in rr: rdn and effrt ent fnl f: no hdwy: n.d* **10/1**[3]
14 **14** 5 **Bilash**[29] 4479 6-8-7 **68** MartinLane 1 34
(Andrew Hollinshead) *in tch in midfield: rdn and unable qck 2f out: btn over 1f out: sn wknd* **12/1**

1m 12.74s (0.24) **Going Correction** +0.05s/f (Good)
WFA 3 from 4yo+ 3lb **14 Ran SP% 117.8**
Speed ratings (Par 105): **100,99,99,98,96 96,94,94,92,92 91,89,89,82**
Tote Swingers 1&2 £13.40, 2&3 £13.70, 1&3 £6.50 CSF £163.01 CT £1209.97 TOTE £8.40: £2.80, £5.50, £2.70; EX 188.20 Trifecta £398.40 Pool: £1,299.34 - 2.44 winning tickets..
Owner Coral Champions Club **Bred** Rathbarry Stud **Trained** Sutton Veny, Wilts
■ Stewards' Enquiry : Darren Egan two-day ban: used whip above permitted level (Aug 31-Sep 1)

FOCUS
There was a big field for this annual sprint confined to greys. The runners were spread across the track and there was a very tight three-way finish. The runner-up is rated a length off his AW best with the third and fourth fitting in.

5538 32RED SUPPORTS RACING WELFARE STKS (H'CAP) 6f
2:55 (2:55) (Class 2) (0-105,105) 3-Y-O
£31,125 (£9,320; £4,660; £2,330; £1,165; £585) **Stalls** Low

Form RPR
4102 **1** **Can You Conga**[20] 4797 3-7-11 **84** RaulDaSilva(3) 3 93
(Kevin Ryan) *racd towards stands' rail: chsd ldr: rdn and ev ch whn carried lft over 1f out: led ent fnl f: battled on v gamely and hld on fnl 100yds: all out* **12/1**
1053 **2** nk **Secretinthepark**[21] 4767 3-8-8 **92** ow1 RobertWinston 7 100
(Ed McMahon) *racd towards stands' side: hld up in tch in midfield: rdn and effrt over 1f out: hdwy and str chal fnl 150yds: r.o wl u.p but a jst hld* **13/2**[3]

2322 **3** *shd* **Maid A Million**[2] 5439 3-8-3 **87**.......................... RoystonFfrench 4 95+
(David Elsworth) *racd towards stands' rail: t.k.h: hld up in tch in midfield: swtchd rt and effrt over 1f out: r.o strly u.p fnl 150yds: nt quite rch ldrs* **8/1**

112 **4** *2* **Midnight Flower (IRE)**[21] 4767 3-8-8 **95**.................. DarrenEgan(3) 2 97+
(David Simcock) *racd towards stands' side: stdd: wnt rt and bmpd rival s: hld up in tch in rr: rdn and hdwy jst over 1f out: kpt on fnl f: nvr trbld ldrs* **4/1**[1]

2401 **5** *nse* **Lucky Beggar (IRE)**[21] 4767 3-9-5 **103**..................... WilliamCarson 5 104
(Charles Hills) *racd against stands' rail: led: rdn and hung lft over 1f out: hdd ent fnl f: no ex and btn fnl 100yds* **14/1**

5004 **6** *nk* **Chilworth Icon**[7] 5260 3-8-12 **96**.......................... MartinDwyer 6 96
(Mick Channon) *racd towards stands' side: chsd ldrs: rdn ent fnl 2f: drvn and carried lft over 1f out: btn and styd on same pce fnl f* **20/1**

3045 **7** *1 ½* **Ninjago**[14] 4986 3-9-5 **103**.................................... SeanLevey 12 99
(Richard Hannon) *racd in centre: hld up in tch towards rr: rdn and effrt 2f out: hrd drvn and sme hdwy ent fnl f: styd on same pce fnl 150yds* **9/2**[2]

120- **8** *½* **Rocky Ground (IRE)**[359] 5515 3-9-0 **98**..................... AndreaAtzeni 10 92
(Roger Varian) *racd in centre: t.k.h: chsd ldrs: rdn and effrt 2f out: no ex and outpcd ent fnl f: wknd fnl 150yds* **14/1**

3136 **9** *¾* **Hasopop (IRE)**[63] 3348 3-9-7 **105**............................ NeilCallan 1 97
(Marco Botti) *racd nr stands' rail: bmpd s: hld up in rr: hdwy 1/2-way: rdn and no hdwy wl over 1f out: plugged on same pce and wl hld fnl f* **17/2**

1010 **10** *3* **Shafaani**[16] 4922 3-8-3 **87**..............................(t) LukeMorris 9 69
(Clive Brittain) *racd in centre: chsd ldrs: rdn and struggling ent fnl 2f: wknd u.p jst over 1f out* **20/1**

0006 **11** *hd* **Storm Moon (USA)**[7] 5260 3-8-3 **87**........................ MartinLane 13 68
(Mark Johnston) *racd in centre: t.k.h: hld up wl in tch: rdn and unable qck ent fnl 2f: wknd jst over 1f out* **33/1**

0060 **12** *½* **Ahern**[21] 4780 3-8-9 **93** ow1...................................... JimCrowley 8 73
(David Barron) *racd in centre: s.i.s and bustled along early: in tch in rr: rdn and little rspnse 2f out: wknd ent fnl f* **12/1**

2163 **13** *1 ¼* **Extrasolar**[6] 5303 3-8-1 **85**............................(t) NickyMackay 11 61
(Amanda Perrett) *racd in centre: hld up in rr: effrt and hung lft wl over 1f out: no real hdwy and btn over 1f out: wknd ent fnl f* **14/1**

1m 11.73s (-0.77) **Going Correction** +0.05s/f (Good) **13** Ran SP% **121.0**
Speed ratings (Par 106): **107,106,106,103,103 103,101,100,99,95 95,94,93**
Tote Swingers 1&2 £13.60, 2&3 £13.30, 1&3 £10.00 CSF £86.93 CT £676.89 TOTE £10.10: £3.20, £2.50, £2.80; EX 132.40 Trifecta £1176.80 Part won. Pool: £1,569.00 - 0.47 winning tickets..
Owner Guy Reed Racing **Bred** G Reed **Trained** Hambleton, N Yorks

FOCUS
Subsequent Group 1 winner King's Apostle scored in this hot sprint handicap in 2007 and last year's winner Hamza has finished runner-up in Group 3 events this season. The pace was not very strong in this renewal and there was a tight finish between three runners who raced towards the stands' side for most of the way. The form looks solid enough, rated around the placed horses.

5539 CHEVELEY PARK STUD EBF MAIDEN STKS — 6f
3:25 (3:26) (Class 4) 2-Y-O **£4,528** (£1,347; £673; £336) **Stalls** Low

Form RPR

422 **1** **Lyn Valley**[18] 4858 2-9-5 90.................................... NeilCallan 1 86+
(Mark Johnston) *mde all: rdn and hung lft 2f out: kpt wanting to hang lft after: forged ahd ins fnl f: styd on wl and gng away at fin* **2/5**[1]

042 **2** *2 ½* **Greed Is Good**[24] 4640 2-9-5 73............................... LukeMorris 7 78
(Mrs K Burke) *t.k.h: upsides wnr: bmpd and rdn 2f out: ev ch and carried lft over 1f out: no ex and btn ins fnl f: plugged on* **8/1**[3]

3 *1 ¼* **Amood (IRE)** 2-9-5 0.. JimCrowley 4 74+
(Charles Hills) *rn green: s.i.s: in tch in rr: pushed along over 2f out: outpcd and modest 4th over 1f out: kpt on steadily and swtchd rt ins fnl f* **5/1**[2]

03 **4** *2 ¾* **Punk**[11] 5101 2-9-5 0.. AndreaAtzeni 5 66
(Fawzi Abdulla Nass, Bahrain) *t.k.h: chsd ldrs: rdn 2f out: 3rd and outpcd over 1f out: wknd ins fnl f* **25/1**

4 **5** *6* **Shrewd Bob (IRE)**[21] 4749 2-9-5 0............................ NickyMackay 2 48
(Robert Eddery) *in tch in midfield: rdn and outpcd ent fnl 2f: wknd over 1f out* **40/1**

00 **6** *7* **Pay The Greek**[22] 4716 2-9-5 0................................ PatCosgrave 6 27
(Noel Quinlan) *in tch in midfield: shkn up and hung lft 2f out: sn wl btn* **66/1**

0 **7** *5* **Ultimate Warrior (IRE)**[64] 3275 2-9-5 0...................... SeanLevey 3 12
(Richard Hannon) *dwlt and reminders sn after s: a in rr: rdn and struggling 1/2-way: wl bhd fnl 2f* **14/1**

1m 14.09s (1.59) **Going Correction** +0.05s/f (Good) **7** Ran SP% **113.7**
Speed ratings (Par 96): **91,87,86,82,74 65,58**
Tote Swingers 1&2 £1.70, 2&3 £2.70, 1&3 £1.30 CSF £4.33 TOTE £1.30: £1.10, £3.60; EX 3.60 Trifecta £8.70 Pool: £2,285.60 - 195.31 winning tickets..
Owner J Barson **Bred** Highclere Stud And Floors Farming **Trained** Middleham Moor, N Yorks

FOCUS
There was not much in strength in depth in this maiden, but the hot favourite beat his main form rival and there was promise from a well-related newcomer in third. The winner is rated below his Goodwood mark.

5540 THAMES MATERIALS LTD CONDITIONS STKS — 1m 2f
4:00 (4:00) (Class 2) 3-Y-O+ **£12,450** (£3,728; £1,864; £932; £466) **Stalls** Centre

Form RPR

1120 **1** **Kassiano (GER)**[140] 1269 4-9-4 113............................ NeilCallan 5 107+
(Saeed bin Suroor) *trckd ldng pair tl led on bit over 1f out: shkn up and readily qcknd clr jst ins fnl f: v easily* **4/5**[1]

6-05 **2** *3 ½* **Trade Commissioner (IRE)**[20] 4811 5-9-1 104............ NickyMackay 4 92
(John Gosden) *led and set stdy gallop: rdn and qcknd 2f out: hdd and brushed aside by wnr over 1f out: kpt on to hold 2nd fnl f* **3/1**[2]

-431 **3** *nk* **Viewpoint (IRE)**[18] 4854 4-9-1 96............................ SeanLevey 2 91
(Richard Hannon) *stdd s: hld up in tch in rr: rdn and effrt 2f out: no ch w wnr but battling for 2nd fnl f: kpt on* **8/1**

434 **4** *3 ½* **Ocean Applause**[2] 5440 3-8-7 79.......................(tp) DarrenEgan 1 84?
(John Ryan) *wl in tch in 4th: rdn and unable qck 2f out: 4th and wl hld fnl f: plugged on* **66/1**

51-2 **5** *1* **Mujazif (IRE)**[113] 1812 3-8-7 91............................(t) MartinLane 3 82
(Brian Meehan) *chsd ldr tl over 1f out: outpcd and dropped to last whn edgd lft 1f out: plugged on* **11/2**[3]

2m 12.58s (7.08) **Going Correction** +0.05s/f (Good)
WFA 3 from 4yo+ 8lb **5** Ran SP% **108.5**
Speed ratings (Par 109): **73,70,69,67,66**
CSF £3.32 TOTE £1.70: £1.10, £1.40; EX 2.90 Trifecta £8.00 Pool: £2,099.45 - 196.80 winning tickets..
Owner Godolphin **Bred** Gestut Rottgen **Trained** Newmarket, Suffolk

FOCUS
They went a steady pace in this tactical conditions event but the hot favourite scored in impressive style and his main form rival finished second. The form is muddling though and limited by the proximity of the fourth.

5541 MARY LOBECK 90TH BIRTHDAY H'CAP — 7f
4:30 (4:30) (Class 4) (0-80,80) 3-Y-O **£5,175** (£1,540; £769; £384) **Stalls** Low

Form RPR

4131 **1** **Tight Fit**[23] 4685 3-9-1 74.................................... FergusSweeney 10 89+
(Henry Candy) *stdd and dropped in bhd after s: hld up in tch in rr: clsd to chse ldrs and travelling strly 2f out: shkn up and qcknd to ld over 1f out: drew wl clr fnl f: v easily* **6/1**[3]

0411 **2** *6* **Shady McCoy (USA)**[22] 4725 3-9-7 80......................... RobertWinston 6 82+
(David Barron) *t.k.h: hld up wl in tch in midfield: nt clr run and hmpd 2f out: gap opened and effrt over 1f out: kpt on to go 2nd cl home: no ch w wnr* **5/4**[1]

2624 **3** *nse* **Dance With Dragons (IRE)**[29] 4492 3-9-4 80..........(p) RaulDaSilva(3) 2 79
(William Stone) *led: rdn ent fnl 2f: hdd over 1f out and immediately brushed aside by wnr: wl hld and edging lft fnl f: lost 2nd cl home* **7/1**

3 **4** *3 ½* **Big Whiskey (IRE)**[10] 5134 3-9-4 77.......................... AndreaAtzeni 8 67
(Edward Creighton) *chsd ldrs: rdn and effrt 2f out: outpcd and btn over 1f out: plugged on to go modest 4th ins fnl f* **14/1**

0646 **5** *¾* **Alcando (IRE)**[20] 4797 3-9-1 74................................ NeilCallan 1 62
(Denis Coakley) *t.k.h: chsd ldr: rdn 2f out: outpcd and wl btn 4th over 1f out: wl btn but plugged on fnl f* **20/1**

314- **6** *3 ½* **Cut No Ice (IRE)**[304] 7164 3-9-4 77.......................... LukeMorris 5 56
(Paul Cole) *hld up in tch towards rr: drvn and effrt wl over 1f out: no hdwy and sn outpcd: wknd over 1f out* **20/1**

7 *¾* **Marciano (IRE)**[54] 3-9-3 76..................................(b) SeanLevey 4 53
(Alan Brown) *t.k.h: hld up in tch towards rr: rdn and no hdwy wl over 1f out: sn wknd* **20/1**

05-0 **8** *7* **Carlarajah**[24] 4637 3-8-5 67................................ DarrenEgan(3) 7 26
(Michael Bell) *hld up in tch in midfield: shuffled bk and nt clr run 2f out: rdn and no hdwy wl over 1f out: sn wknd* **25/1**

60-5 **9** *3* **All On Red (IRE)**[80] 2783 3-9-7 80..........................(t) PatCosgrave 9 31
(George Baker) *in tch in midfield: rdn over 2f out: sn struggling: wknd over 1f out: wl bhd fnl f* **33/1**

1023 **10** *5* **Whipper Snapper (IRE)**[18] 4864 3-9-5 78..................(v¹) JimCrowley 3 16
(William Knight) *stdd s: hld up in rr: rdn and no hdwy over 2f out: wl bhd and eased ins fnl f* **9/2**[2]

1m 25.45s (-0.25) **Going Correction** +0.05s/f (Good) **10** Ran SP% **117.2**
Speed ratings (Par 102): **103,96,96,92,91 87,86,78,74,69**
Tote Swingers 1&2 £4.00, 2&3 £3.00, 1&3 £3.60 CSF £12.88 CT £56.88 TOTE £5.40: £1.70, £1.10, £2.20; EX 11.80 Trifecta £66.80 Pool: £1,597.49 - 17.91 winning tickets..
Owner W M Lidsey & H Candy **Bred** W M Lidsey **Trained** Kingston Warren, Oxon

FOCUS
They went a steady pace in this handicap and the clear favourite ran into some trouble, but the winner powered clear to improve her record to 3-9. This was a clear personal-best, and could be worth more at face value through the placed horses.

5542 DOUBLE O SEVEN H'CAP — 1m 4f
5:05 (5:05) (Class 4) (0-85,85) 3-Y-O+ **£6,469** (£1,925; £962; £481) **Stalls** Centre

Form RPR

-025 **1** **Royal Dutch**[22] 4720 4-9-2 73................................ PatCosgrave 4 81
(Denis Coakley) *chsd ldr: rdn to chal 2f out: ev ch and drifted lft 1f out: led ins fnl f: wnt lft again fnl 100yds: hrd pressed towards fin: a jst lasting home* **7/2**[2]

-313 **2** *nk* **Hold On Tight (IRE)**[26] 4594 3-8-12 79........................ JimCrowley 1 87+
(Ralph Beckett) *trckd ldrs: rdn and effrt 2f out: edging lft and no imp: swtchd rt and hdwy ins fnl f: chsd wnr and hung lft wl ins fnl f: clsng qckly towards fin but nvr quite getting up* **5/6**[1]

5-00 **3** *1* **Toptempo**[73] 2990 4-8-11 68................................ RobertWinston 5 74
(Mark H Tompkins) *in tch: hdwy to chse ldr 3f out: pressing ldrs and carried lft 1f out: wnt 2nd and pressing wnr whn hmpd fnl 100yds: one pce after* **8/1**

1003 **4** *2 ½* **Harry Buckle**[14] 5008 4-10-0 85.............................. WilliamCarson 3 87
(Philip McBride) *led: rdn ent fnl 2f: drvn and hrd pressed whn edgd lft over 1f out: hdd ins fnl f: no ex and wknd fnl 75yds* **11/2**[3]

5 *28* **Cropley (IRE)**[231] 3800 4-9-0 74............................ RaulDaSilva(3) 2 31
(Tony Carroll) *plld hrd: hld up in tch in rr: rdn 3f out: lost tch 2f out: eased fnl f: t.o* **10/1**

2m 36.03s (3.13) **Going Correction** +0.05s/f (Good)
WFA 3 from 4yo 10lb **5** Ran SP% **112.4**
Speed ratings (Par 105): **91,90,90,88,69**
CSF £7.07 TOTE £3.70: £1.30, £1.30; EX 8.50 Trifecta £29.70 Pool: £1,832.72 - 46.25 winning tickets..
Owner Chris Van Hoorn **Bred** Sir Eric Parker **Trained** West Ilsley, Berks
■ Stewards' Enquiry : Pat Cosgrave caution: careless riding.

FOCUS
They went a steady pace in this small-field handicap and there was a tight finish. The form is muddling and best rated around the winner and fourth.
T/Jkpt: £15,765.90 to a £1 stake. Pool: £55,513.98 - 2.50 winning units T/Plt: £83.00 to a £1 stake. Pool: £92,337.54 - 811.78 winning units T/Qpdt: £6.70 to a £1 stake. Pool: £4,087.95 - 445.50 winning units SP

5105 RIPON (R-H)
Saturday, August 17

OFFICIAL GOING: Good (8.4)
Wind: Fresh; behind Weather: Cloudy; drizzle on and off before more persistent rain after 5th

5543 WOOLTEX UK MAIDEN AUCTION STKS — 6f
2:15 (2:16) (Class 5) 2-Y-O **£4,528** (£1,347; £673; £336) **Stalls** High

Form RPR

025 **1** **Pensax Lad (IRE)**[9] 5186 2-9-3 71.............................. SteveDrowne 1 71
(Ronald Harris) *chsd ldrs towards outer: rdn over 2f out: led appr fnl f: kpt on* **9/2**

3 **2** *¾* **Zal Zilhom (IRE)**[18] 4848 2-9-1 0............................ PhillipMakin 8 67
(Kevin Ryan) *w ldr: rdn over 2f out: kpt on but a hld by wnr fnl f* **7/2**[2]

5426 **3** *½* **Heroique (IRE)**[15] 4963 2-8-10 73.............................. DavidAllan 6 60
(Tim Easterby) *led narrowly: rdn over 2f out: hdd appr fnl f: one pce* **4/1**[3]

0 **4** *1* **Tell Me When**[12] 5053 2-7-13 0.......................... ConnorBeasley(5) 7 51
(Brian Rothwell) *sn outpcd towards rr: bhd tl kpt on fr over 1f out: nrst fin* **66/1**

4F24 **5** ½ **Cheeky Peta'S**11 5106 2-8-6 67 JamesSullivan 4 52
(James Given) *in tch: rdn over 2f out: sn one pce and no imp on ldrs* **8/1**

4204 **6** shd **Ahoy There (IRE)**11 5083 2-8-11 69 MickyFenton 5 56
(Tom Tate) *chsd ldrs: sn pushed along: rdn 1/2-way: one pce and no imp on ldrs* **9/4**1

0 **7** ½ **Sandfield (IRE)**22 4731 2-8-9 0 LeeTopliss 2 53
(Paul Midgley) *dwlt: hld up: pushed along 1/2-way: nvr threatened* **20/1**

8 3½ **Maidana (IRE)** 2-7-11 0 GaryMahon(7) 3 37+
(Tim Easterby) *slowly away: a bhd* **20/1**

1m 12.84s (-0.16) **Going Correction** -0.25s/f (Firm) **8** Ran SP% **113.3**
Speed ratings (Par 94): **91,90,89,88,87 87,86,81**
toteswingers 1&2 £4.00, 1&3 £2.90, 2&3 £5.20 CSF £19.91 TOTE £4.90: £1.40, £1.80, £1.60; EX 29.80 Trifecta £109.30 Pool: £1,068.34 - 7.32 winning units..
Owner S & A Mares **Bred** Seamus And James McMullan **Trained** Earlswood, Monmouths

FOCUS
Rail at innermost configuration and all distances as advertised. A fair event in theory using official figures, but the form looks ordinary with the winner to his mark.

5544 WILLIAM HILL SILVER TROPHY (H'CAP) (CONSOLATION FOR THE WILLIAM HILL GREAT ST WILFRID STKS) 6f

2:50 (2:51) (Class 2) 3-Y-O+

£12,450 (£3,728; £1,864; £932; £466; £234) **Stalls** High

Form RPR

1124 **1** **Clear Spring (IRE)**14 5009 5-9-7 87 TomEaves 13 100
(John Spearing) *prom stands' side: rdn over 2f out: led wl over 1f out: kpt on wl* **16/1**

002 **2** 1¼ **Mehdi (IRE)**7 5292 4-9-4 84 (t) AdrianNicholls 17 93
(David Nicholls) *chsd ldrs stands' side: rdn over 2f out: wnt 2nd over 1f out: kpt on but a hld by wnr* **8/1**3

2134 **3** 1½ **Avon Breeze**15 4954 4-9-3 83 RussKennemore 2 87+
(Richard Whitaker) *chsd ldrs far side: rdn over 2f out: kpt on: wnt 3rd post: 1st of 9 in gp* **16/1**

2003 **4** hd **Chooseday (IRE)**14 4983 4-9-7 87 (p) PJMcDonald 1 91+
(Kevin Ryan) *w ldr far side: rdn over 2f out: led gp and 3rd overall appr fnl f: kpt on: lost 3rd post: 2nd of 9 in gp* **6/1**1

1400 **5** 1½ **Best Trip (IRE)**14 4983 6-9-3 83 DaleSwift 3 82
(Brian Ellison) *led narrowly on far side: rdn over 2f out: hdd appr fnl f: no ex ins fnl f: 3rd of 9 in gp* **7/1**2

5026 **6** ¾ **Singeur (IRE)**11 5108 6-9-7 90 JasonHart(3) 15 86
(Robin Bastiman) *racd stands' side: sn pushed along in midfield: kpt on fr over 1f out: 3rd of 11 in gp* **12/1**

3161 **7** nse **Head Space (IRE)**7 5294 5-9-10 90 (p) JamesSullivan 5 86
(Ruth Carr) *midfield far side: rdn over 2f out: kpt on one pce: 4th of 9 in gp* **14/1**

2020 **8** ½ **Fast Shot**21 4780 5-9-8 88 DavidAllan 4 83
(Tim Easterby) *midfield far side: rdn over 2f out: kpt on one pce: 5th of 9 in gp* **9/1**

0301 **9** 1¾ **Noverre To Go (IRE)**8 5219 7-9-3 83 (p) SteveDrowne 16 72
(Ronald Harris) *hld up stands' side: rdn 1/2-way: sme late hdwy but nvr threatened: 4th of 11 in gp* **25/1**

0004 **10** shd **Powerful Presence (IRE)**8 5238 7-9-8 88 DavidNolan 7 77
(David O'Meara) *dwlt: hld up in midfield far side: rdn over 2f out: nvr threatened: 6th of 9 in gp* **33/1**

2053 **11** nse **Nameitwhatyoulike**12 5056 4-9-10 90 GrahamGibbons 18 79
(Michael Easterby) *racd stands' side: overall ldr: rdn whn hdd wl over 1f out: sn wknd: 5th of 11 in gp* **10/1**

3012 **12** ½ **Love Island**36 4263 4-9-10 90 (p) PaulQuinn 8 77
(Richard Whitaker) *hld up far side: rdn over 2f out: nvr threatened: 7th of 9 in gp* **12/1**

0101 **13** 4½ **Hopes N Dreams (IRE)**14 4993 5-9-8 88 PhillipMakin 14 61
(Kevin Ryan) *prom stands' side: rdn over 2f out: wknd over 1f out: 6th of 11 in gp* **16/1**

/0-0 **14** hd **Tarrsille (IRE)**34 4329 7-9-2 82 LeeTopliss 6 54
(Paul Midgley) *s.i.s: a bhd far side: 8th of 9 in gp* **100/1**

0000 **15** ½ **Gouray Girl (IRE)**52 3684 6-8-11 82 ConnorBeasley(5) 9 52
(Brian Ellison) *slowly away: a towards rr far side: last of 9 in gp* **28/1**

-550 **16** ¾ **Bajan Tryst (USA)**49 3846 7-9-3 90 KevinStott(7) 11 58
(Kevin Ryan) *midfield towards outer stands' side: rdn 1/2-way: wknd over 1f out: 7th of 11 in gp* **22/1**

4650 **17** hd **Arctic Feeling (IRE)**14 4983 5-9-5 85 TonyHamilton 10 52
(Richard Fahey) *dwlt: swtchd lft to r stands' side: a bhd: 8th of 11 in gp* **22/1**

0060 **18** ½ **Dorback**18 4860 6-8-9 82 (t) OisinMurphy(7) 20 48
(Tony Newcombe) *chsd ldrs stands' side: rdn over 2f out: wknd over 1f out: 9th of 11 in gp* **33/1**

1110 **19** 5 **Nasharra (IRE)**14 5011 5-8-11 84 (tp) PaulMcGiff(7) 19 34
(Kevin Ryan) *dwlt: a towards rr stands' side: 10th of 11 in gp* **40/1**

0621 **20** nse **Gabbiano**22 4707 4-9-9 89 (p) ShaneFoley 12 38
(Jeremy Gask) *hld up stands' side: rdn 1/2-way: sn btn* **12/1**

1m 10.12s (-2.88) **Going Correction** -0.25s/f (Firm) **20** Ran SP% **129.7**
Speed ratings (Par 109): **109,107,105,105,103 102,102,101,99,98 98,98,92,91,91 90,89,89,82,82**
toteswingers 1&2 £19.80, 1&3 £25.30, 2&3 £31.00 CSF £132.11 CT £2170.97 TOTE £14.60: £3.20, £3.00, £6.30, £1.90; EX 316.50 Trifecta £1001.20 Part won. Pool: £1,334.97 - 0.01 winning units..
Owner H James **Bred** Rocal Bloodstock **Trained** Kinnersley, Worcs

FOCUS
The second running of the consolation race for the Great St Wilfrid was predictably strong, with only 8lb separating the top and bottom weight on ratings, and there didn't seem too many bad luck stories in behind. The winner continues to progress while the second built slightly on his previous effort. The next two home ran well on the less favoured side.

5545 WILLIAM HILL GREAT ST WILFRID STKS (H'CAP) 6f

3:30 (3:31) (Class 2) 3-Y-O+

£43,575 (£13,048; £6,524; £3,262; £1,631; £819) **Stalls** High

Form RPR

-106 **1** **Baccarat (IRE)**21 4780 4-8-9 94 TonyHamilton 9 105
(Richard Fahey) *trckd ldrs far side: pushed along and hdwy over 1f out: drvn jst ins fnl f: kpt on to ld towards fin* **9/2**1

0101 **2** nk **Spinatrix**12 5056 5-8-10 100 (p) ConnorBeasley(5) 1 110
(Michael Dods) *racd far side: overall ldr: rdn over 2f out: kpt on wl: hdd towards fin: 2nd of 12 in gp* **9/1**3

6310 **3** 3¼ **Rodrigo De Torres**21 4780 6-8-4 94 TobyAtkinson(5) 7 94
(David Nicholls) *prom far side: rdn over 2f out: one pce and no ch w ldng pair ins fnl f: 3rd of 12 in gp* **33/1**

5000 **4** ½ **Regal Parade**14 4986 9-8-7 97 (t) MatthewLawson(5) 6 95
(Milton Bradley) *s.i.s: hld up far side: swtchd to centre and hdwy 2f out: kpt on: 4th of 12 in gp* **40/1**

0042 **5** 1 **Summerinthecity (IRE)**21 4780 6-8-8 93 AdrianNicholls 18 88
(David Nicholls) *dwlt: hld up stands' side: swtchd rt to outer of gp 3f out: hdwy 1/2-way: rdn to ld gp appr fnl f: sn edgd rt: one pce fnl 100yds: 1st of 8 in gp* **12/1**

0000 **6** 1 **Thunderball**57 3527 7-8-6 91 (p) JamesSullivan 17 83
(Scott Dixon) *chsd ldr stands' side: rdn over 2f out: kpt on: edgd rt ins fnl f: 2nd of 8 in gp* **50/1**

0-60 **7** nk **Borderlescott**15 4947 11-9-2 104 JasonHart(3) 2 95
(Robin Bastiman) *chsd ldrs far side: rdn over 2f out: grad wknd fnl f: 5th of 12 in gp* **33/1**

1530 **8** nk **Dr Red Eye**14 4986 5-8-10 95 (p) RussKennemore 15 85
(Scott Dixon) *led stands' side: rdn whn hdd in gp appr fnl f: no ex: 3rd of 8 in gp* **40/1**

1400 **9** shd **Polski Max**14 4986 3-8-10 98 LeeTopliss 5 87
(Richard Fahey) *hld up far side: sn pushed along: sme late hdwy: nvr threatened: 6th of 12 in gp* **40/1**

0040 **10** nk **Prodigality**14 4986 5-8-7 99 OisinMurphy(7) 13 87
(Ronald Harris) *dwlt: swtchd rt to r far side after 100yds: midfield: sme hdwy 2f out: wknd ins fnl f: 7th of 12 in gp* **9/1**3

0662 **11** shd **Pearl Ice**12 5056 5-8-3 91 (p) ConorHoban(3) 3 79
(David Barron) *midfield far side: rdn over 2f out: no imp: 8th of 12 in gp* **9/1**3

6010 **12** nse **Louis The Pious**14 4986 5-9-1 100 DavidNolan 4 88
(David O'Meara) *midfield far side: rdn 1/2-way: nvr threatened: 9th of 12 in gp* **8/1**2

5-00 **13** 1 **Hoof It**14 4986 6-9-10 109 1 GrahamGibbons 16 94
(Michael Easterby) *hld up stands' side: nvr threatened: edgd rt ins fnl f: 4th of 8 in gp* **12/1**

0026 **14** ½ **Captain Ramius (IRE)**121 1637 7-9-8 107 PhillipMakin 8 90
(Kevin Ryan) *hld up far side: sn pushed along: minor late hdwy whn short of room fnl 100yds: 10th of 12 in gp* **22/1**

020 **15** shd **El Viento (FR)**14 4983 5-8-8 93 (p) DaleSwift 19 76
(Richard Fahey) *hld up stands' side: nvr threatened: 5th of 8 in gp* **11/1**

1240 **16** 1¾ **Dick Bos**21 4780 4-8-6 91 ShaneFoley 11 73
(David O'Meara) *wnt rt s: midfield far side: rdn over 2f out: sn no imp: eased ins fnl f: 11th of 12 in gp* **10/1**

6000 **17** 1¼ **Confessional**50 3776 6-8-11 96 (e) DavidAllan 12 69
(Tim Easterby) *chsd ldr stands' side: wknd over 1f out: 6th of 8 in gp* **33/1**

6323 **18** nk **Zacynthus (IRE)**57 3538 5-8-6 91 PJMcDonald 14 63
(Kevin Ryan) *midfield stands' side: rdn over 2f out: wknd over 1f out: 7th of 8 in gp* **16/1**

0002 **19** 1¾ **Secret Witness**8 5247 7-8-13 98 (b) SteveDrowne 20 65
(Ronald Harris) *a bhd stands' side: last of 8 in gp* **20/1**

-000 **20** 2¾ **Blaine**14 4986 3-8-12 100 TomEaves 10 58
(Kevin Ryan) *chsd ldrs far side tl wknd over 2f out* **40/1**

1m 9.72s (-3.28) **Going Correction** -0.25s/f (Firm) course record
WFA 3 from 4yo+ 3lb **20** Ran SP% **127.6**
Speed ratings (Par 109): **111,110,106,105,104 102,102,102,102,101 101,101,100,99,99 96,95,94,92,88**
toteswingers 1&2 £6.20, 1&3 £31.50, 2&3 £131.80 CSF £39.19 CT £1266.38 TOTE £5.30: £1.70, £2.80, £6.80, £11.00; EX 45.10 Trifecta £2381.00 Pool: £5,647.42 - 1.77 winning units..
Owner Sir Robert Ogden **Bred** Twelve Oaks Stud **Trained** Musley Bank, N Yorks
■ Stewards' Enquiry : Connor Beasley seven-day ban: used whip above permitted level (Aug 31,Sep 1-6)

FOCUS
A hugely competitive handicap as one would imagine for the money on offer, and the winner lowered a course record set by two horses previously, Quoit in 1966 and Tadeo in 1997. The draw appeared to have a strong influence on the final outcome, with those racing close to the inside rail holding an advantage, although that group did have leading fancies in it. The runner-up loves it around here and recorded another personal-best.

5546 VW VAN CENTRE (WEST YORKSHIRE) H'CAP 1m

4:05 (4:07) (Class 3) (0-90,90) 3-Y-O-£9,451 (£2,829; £1,414; £708; £352) **Stalls** Low

Form RPR

2511 **1** **Robert The Painter (IRE)**18 4850 5-9-13 89 (v) GrahamGibbons 17 102
(David O'Meara) *swtchd rt fr outside stall to ld on rail: mde all: rdn over 2f out: strly pressed over 1f out: kpt on wl: asserted towards fin* **14/1**

0540 **2** ½ **No Poppy (IRE)**14 5014 5-8-11 78 AdamCarter(5) 1 90
(Tim Easterby) *trckd wnr: rdn over 2f out: upsides over 1f out: kpt on: hld towards fin* **6/1**2

2540 **3** 3¾ **Lord Aeryn (IRE)**22 4733 6-9-11 87 TonyHamilton 6 90
(Richard Fahey) *in tch on inner: rdn over 2f out: kpt on: wnt 3rd fnl 50yds* **8/1**

0243 **4** nk **Mu'Ajiza**5 5332 3-8-6 74 AdrianNicholls 14 77
(Mark Johnston) *trckd wnr: rdn over 2f out: no ex fnl f: lost 3rd fnl 50yds* **12/1**

1063 **5** 1½ **Hakuna Matata**7 5291 6-8-11 78 (b) ConnorBeasley(5) 5 77+
(Michael Dods) *hld up in midfield: rdn over 3f out: no imp initially and stl plenty to do over 1f out: r.o strly ins fnl f* **5/1**1

0212 **6** 1 **Extraterrestrial**12 5050 9-8-13 75 LeeTopliss 7 72
(Richard Fahey) *dwlt: hld up in midfield: rdn over 2f out: kpt on: nvr threatened ldrs* **14/1**

5465 **7** nk **Dubai Dynamo**19 4825 8-9-11 87 PJMcDonald 8 83
(Ruth Carr) *hld up in midfield: rdn 3f out: kpt on one pce: nvr threatened ldrs* **7/1**3

1-00 **8** 1 **Anton Chigurh**49 3825 4-10-0 90 SteveDrowne 9 84
(Tom Dascombe) *slowly away: sn midfield on inner: rdn over 2f out: sn no imp* **22/1**

0-00 **9** 1 **Desert Creek (IRE)**112 1840 7-9-1 77 (p) PaulQuinn 3 68
(David Nicholls) *dwlt: racd keenly in midfield on inner: rdn over 2f out: nvr threatened* **25/1**

-40 **10** ½ **Stevie Thunder**77 2858 8-9-6 85 RyanPowell(3) 10 75
(Ian Williams) *midfield: rdn and sme hdwy on outer 3f out: wknd over 1f out* **17/2**

2030 **11** ½ **Eutropius (IRE)**35 4308 4-8-13 75 RussKennemore 4 64
(Alan Swinbank) *trckd ldrs: t.k.h early: rdn 3f out: wknd over 1f out* **25/1**

5024 **12** 1¼ **Barren Brook**20 4810 6-9-3 79 PhillipMakin 13 65
(Michael Easterby) *s.i.s: hld up in rr: sme late hdwy whn short of room ins fnl f: nvr threatened* **10/1**

0500 **13** 1 **Swiftly Done (IRE)**7 5268 6-9-7 86 (v) JasonHart(3) 11 85+
(Declan Carroll) *hld up in rr: pushed along over 2f out: sme hdwy whn hmpd ins fnl f: eased* **12/1**

2000 **14** *10* **Xilerator (IRE)**63 3335 6-9-5 **86** TobyAtkinson(5) 15 47
(David Nicholls) *dwlt: midfield: rdn 3f out: wknd over 1f out* **40/1**
0010 **15** *nk* **King Torus (IRE)**8 5238 5-9-9 **85** (b) DaleSwift 16 45
(Ruth Carr) *hld up: a towards rr* **33/1**
2441 **16** *3/4* **Le Chat D'Or**19 4825 5-9-6 **82** (bt) TomEaves 12 41
(Michael Dods) *t.k.h in midfield: rdn over 2f out: sn wknd* **12/1**

1m 37.93s (-3.47) **Going Correction** -0.25s/f (Firm)
WFA 3 from 4yo+ 6lb **16** Ran SP% **128.0**
Speed ratings (Par 107): **107,106,102,102,100 99,99,98,97,97 96,95,94,84,84 83**
toteswingers 1&2 £5.80, 1&3 £7.00, 2&3 £10.70 CSF £94.92 CT £775.19 TOTE £9.30: £2.20, £2.70, £2.30, £4.10; EX 87.70 Trifecta £641.80 Part won. Pool: £855.80 - 0.03 winning units..
Owner Stephen Humphreys **Bred** Ballylinch Stud **Trained** Nawton, N Yorks

FOCUS
A right mix of ages and abilities on show for this handicap, but it paid to race handily. The runner-up is rated to his best 1m form away from soft ground.

5547 FREEBETS.CO.UK RIPON HORN BLOWER CONDITIONS STKS 6f
4:35 (4:35) (Class 3) 2-Y-O **£9,451** (£2,829) **Stalls** High

Form RPR
1325 **1** **Supplicant**18 4855 2-9-5 103 TonyHamilton 2 94+
(Richard Fahey) *mde all: pushed out fr over 1f out: firmly in command fnl 100yds* **1/20**1
1325 **2** *2 1/4* **Milly's Secret (IRE)**24 4618 2-8-12 79 PJMcDonald 1 76
(Ann Duffield) *trckd wnr: rdn appr fnl f: one pce and sn no ch w wnr* **11/1**2

1m 14.1s (1.10) **Going Correction** -0.25s/f (Firm) **2** Ran SP% **103.6**
Speed ratings (Par 98): **82,79**
TOTE £1.02.
Owner Cheveley Park Stud **Bred** Cheveley Park Stud Ltd **Trained** Musley Bank, N Yorks

FOCUS
A match that the long odds-on winner made a meal of winning.

5548 BRITISH STALLION STUDS EBF FILLIES' H'CAP 1m 1f 170y
5:10 (5:10) (Class 4) (0-80,80) 3-Y-O+ **£6,301** (£1,886; £943; £472; £235) **Stalls** Low

Form RPR
5413 **1** **Nemushka**21 4777 4-9-10 **76** TonyHamilton 1 82
(Richard Fahey) *in tch on inner: led gng wl 2f out: pushed along to assert over 1f out: rdn out fnl 100yds* **3/1**2
2461 **2** *1/2* **Hot Rod Mamma (IRE)**12 5051 6-10-0 **80** PJMcDonald 3 85
(Dianne Sayer) *s.i.s: hld up in tch on inner: rdn and hdwy over 1f out: kpt on: wnt 2nd post* **7/2**3
-353 **3** *nse* **Are You Mine (IRE)**13 5030 3-8-11 **71** GrahamGibbons 5 76
(Ralph Beckett) *led for 1f: trckd ldr: rdn over 2f out: kpt on: lost 2nd post* **5/1**
2-1 **4** *3* **I Say (IRE)**20 4805 3-9-5 **79** PhillipMakin 4 78
(William Haggas) *in tch: drvn 2f out: sn one pce: wknd ins fnl f* **5/2**1
4300 **5** *3* **Tussie Mussie**23 4671 3-8-11 **71** AdrianNicholls 6 64
(Mark Johnston) *led after 1f: set stdy pce: rdn whn hdd 2f out: sn wknd* **12/1**
3434 **6** *1* **Maybeagrey**14 5015 4-8-13 **65** DavidAllan 2 56
(Tim Easterby) *midfield: pushed along over 3f out: sn btn* **9/1**
2655 **7** *8* **Of Course Darling**9 5169 3-9-3 **77** (b1) SteveDrowne 7 51
(Ed Dunlop) *s.i.s: hld up: a towards rr* **14/1**

2m 3.12s (-2.28) **Going Correction** -0.25s/f (Firm)
WFA 3 from 4yo+ 8lb **7** Ran SP% **116.8**
Speed ratings (Par 102): **99,98,98,96,93 92,86**
toteswingers 1&2 £1.50, 1&3 £7.30, 2&3 £7.30 CSF £14.51 TOTE £6.80: £3.30, £2.10; EX 22.90 Trifecta £114.50 Pool: £835.53 - 5.47 winning units..
Owner The G-Guck Group **Bred** Avenue Farm Stud **Trained** Musley Bank, N Yorks

FOCUS
The early pace didn't look quick in this, and one felt it turned into a bit of a sprint down the home straight. The form was bit muddling, but the winner is rated to his Leicester mark with the runner-up to his best in the last year.

5549 SIS LIVE H'CAP 1m 4f 10y
5:45 (5:45) (Class 5) (0-75,74) 3-Y-O **£4,528** (£1,347; £673; £336) **Stalls** Low

Form RPR
2241 **1** **Ambleside**8 5223 3-9-7 **74** AdrianNicholls 2 85
(Mark Johnston) *s.i.s: hld up: wnt in snatches: rdn over 3f out: hdwy to chal over 1f out: led narrowly ins fnl f: edgd lft: jst hld on* **15/8**1
1253 **2** *hd* **Good Speech (IRE)**8 5223 3-9-2 **69** MickyFenton 3 80
(Tom Tate) *led: rdn over 3f out: jnd over 1f out: hdd ins fnl f: kpt on: jst hld* **9/4**2
-261 **3** *9* **Beat The Tide**19 4822 3-9-6 **73** TomEaves 1 71
(Michael Dods) *trckd ldr: rdn over 3f out: wknd over 1f out* **6/1**
2144 **4** *3 1/2* **Duke Of Yorkshire**5 5343 3-8-10 **66** JasonHart(3) 4 58
(Declan Carroll) *trckd ldr: rdn over 3f out: wknd over 1f out* **5/2**3

2m 35.4s (-1.30) **Going Correction** -0.25s/f (Firm) **4** Ran SP% **108.4**
Speed ratings (Par 100): **94,93,87,85**
CSF £6.34 TOTE £2.40; EX 4.30 Trifecta £11.90 Pool: £569.58 - 35.68 winning units..
Owner Sheikh Hamdan Bin Mohammed Al Maktoum **Bred** Mount Coote Partnership **Trained** Middleham Moor, N Yorks
■ Stewards' Enquiry : Adrian Nicholls caution: careless riding.

FOCUS
Despite there only being a small field, this was run at a solid gallop. The winner confirmed his Haydock form with the runner-up.
T/Plt: £108.30 to a £1 stake. Pool: £65,157.85 - 438.93 winning units T/Qpdt: £14.60 to a £1 stake. Pool: £3,725.79 - 187.56 winning units AS

ARLINGTON PARK (L-H)
Saturday, August 17

OFFICIAL GOING: Turf: firm

5550a AMERICAN ST. LEGER STKS (CONDITIONS) (3YO+) (TURF) 1m 5f 110y
9:52 (10:01) 3-Y-O+
£145,766 (£48,588; £24,294; £12,147; £7,288; £4,858)

RPR
1 **Dandino**56 3556 6-8-7 0 RyanMoore 4 105
(Marco Botti) *midfield on inner: clsd 3f out: rdn 2f out: nt clr run and swtchd rt ent fnl f: styd on strly to ld cl home: punched out w firm hands and heels* **4/5**1
2 *1/2* **Suntracer (USA)**35 5-8-7 0 ECastro 5 104
(Chris Block, U.S.A) *hld up in last pair on inner: clsd 3f out: rdn and swtchd rt over 1f out: styd on to go 2nd cl home: nt quite pce of wnr* **84/10**
3 *3/4* **Najjaar (USA)**35 4-8-7 0 JamesGraham 7 103
(Daniel Peitz, U.S.A) *midfield on outer: clsd 3f out: rdn over 2f out: styd on to chal over 1f out: w ldr and ev ch tl front pair wnt by cl home: tk 3rd fnl strides* **54/10**3
4 *hd* **Code Of Conduct (USA)**28 5-8-7 0 (b) FGeroux 3 103
(Wayne Catalano, U.S.A) *trckd ldr on inner: chsd clr ldng pair after 4f: clsd 3f out: rdn to chal 2f out and sn led: jnd ins fnl f: styd on but hdd cl home and dropped to 4th fnl strides* **161/10**
5 *3 3/4* **Wigmore Hall (IRE)**21 4779 6-8-7 0 JamieSpencer 8 97
(Michael Bell) *dwlt: hld up in last pair on outer: clsd 3f out: rdn 2f out: plugged on but outpcd by ldrs ins fnl f and nvr threatened* **39/10**2
6 *5 1/4* **Ioya Bigtime (USA)**35 6-8-7 0 FTorres 6 89
(Chris Block, U.S.A) *trckd ldr on outer: jnd ldr after 4f and wnt clr of remainder: led 4f out: clsd down 3f out: rdn and strly pressed 2f out: sn hdd and no ex: fdd* **102/10**
7 *dist* **Ojos De Hielo (USA)**42 4-8-7 0 JASanchez 2
(Larry Rivelli, U.S.A) *led: jnd after 4f and wnt clr of remainder: rdn and hdd 4f out: qckly btn and wknd: eased and dropped to last: tailed rt off* **204/10**

2m 50.78s (170.78) **7** Ran SP% **121.7**
PARI-MUTUEL (all including $2 stakes): WIN 3.60; PLACE (1-2) 3.00, 5.40; SHOW (1-2-3) 2.40, 4.60, 3.60; SF 21.00.
Owner Australian Thoroughbred Bloodstock **Bred** Elite Racing Club **Trained** Newmarket, Suffolk

5551a SECRETARIAT STKS (GRADE 1) (3YO) (TURF) 1m 2f
10:23 (12:00) 3-Y-O
£171,165 (£57,055; £28,527; £14,263; £8,558; £5,705)

RPR
1 **Admiral Kitten (USA)**35 3-8-7 0 (b) RosieNapravnik 5 112
(Michael J Maker, U.S.A) *hld up towards rr: rdn and hdwy fr 3f out: styd on steadily in st and reeled in ldr: led ins fnl 150yds and qckly asserted: readily* **26/5**3
2 *1 1/4* **Stormy Len (USA)**35 3-8-7 0 ASolis 10 110
(David Donk, U.S.A) *prom on outer: jnd ldr 3f out: led 2f out: crossed to rail and rdn clr: steadily reeled in and hdd ins fnl 150yds: no ex* **146/10**
3 *1 1/4* **Jack Milton (USA)**34 3-8-9 0 JRosario 9 109
(Todd Pletcher, U.S.A) *sn settled in midfield on outer: hdwy fr 3f out: rdn 2f out: styd on but nt pce of front pair* **12/5**1
4 *4 1/4* **Draw Two (USA)**34 3-8-7 0 GaryStevens 12 99
(Michelle Nihei, U.S.A) *hld up in last pair: rdn to improve 3f out: styd on and tk mod 4th cl home: nvr nrr* **103/10**
5 *3/4* **Visiyani (FR)**41 3-8-7 0 Christophe-PatriceLemaire 2 97
(A De Royer-Dupre, France) *prom on inner: rdn and ev ch 2f out: readily outpcd by ldrs ins fnl f: fdd and dropped to 5th cl home* **43/5**
6 *3/4* **Amen Kitten (USA)**35 3-8-7 0 EBaird 11 96
(Wesley A Ward, U.S.A) *hld up in last: rdn 2f out: styd on for n.d 6th* **57/1**
7 *1 1/4* **Balthazar (USA)**21 3-8-7 0 RAlbarado 8 93
(Dale Romans, U.S.A) *hld up in midfield: rdn over 2f out: outpcd by ldrs over 1f out: plugged on* **37/1**
8 *1* **First Cornerstone (IRE)**76 2907 3-8-7 0 ChrisHayes 4 91
(A Oliver, Ire) *midfield in tch on outer: rdn and lost pl rapidly 3f out: n.d after* **141/10**
9 *1* **Tattenham (USA)**42 3-8-7 0 KDesormeaux 13 89
(William Mott, U.S.A) *midfield: clsd 3f out: lost pl on turn into st: sn no ex and btn* **102/10**
10 *hd* **Yeager (USA)**21 4743 3-8-7 0 RyanMoore 7 89
(Jeremy Noseda) *midfield on inner: clsng and stl ev ch whn hmpd on rail 3f out: sn lost pl and rdn: styd on again in st but nt rcvr* **89/10**
11 *1 1/2* **Rydilluc (USA)**34 3-8-11 0 EPrado 3 90
(Gary Contessa, U.S.A) *trckd ldr: led 3f out and immediately jnd: rdn and hdd 2f out: sn no ex and btn: fdd* **9/2**2
12 *1 3/4* **Golden Jason (USA)**10 3-8-7 0 (b1) JEFelix 1 82
(Gennadi Dorochenko, U.S.A) *led: rdn and hdd 3f out: no ex and btn: steadily fdd* **98/1**
13 *1/2* **Bethel (USA)**34 3-8-7 0 FGeroux 6 81
(Gennadi Dorochenko, U.S.A) *a towards rr: nvr a factor* **122/1**

2m 2.17s (0.53) **13** Ran SP% **121.2**
PARI-MUTUEL (all including $2 stakes): WIN 12.40; PLACE (1-2) 5.00, 14.40; SHOW (1-2-3) 3.20, 6.80, 3.00; SF 155.60.
Owner Kenneth L & Sarah K Ramsey **Bred** Kenneth L & Sarah K Ramsey **Trained** USA

5552a BEVERLY D. STKS (GRADE 1) (3YO+ FILLIES & MARES) (TURF) 1m 1f 110y
11:02 (12:00) 3-Y-O+
£267,791 (£89,263; £44,631; £22,315; £13,389; £8,926)

RPR
1 **Dank**27 4567 4-8-11 0 RyanMoore 4 116+
(Sir Michael Stoute) *hld up in tch: rdn and hdwy on outer 2f out: r.o to ld ins fnl f and stormed clr: v impressive* **16/5**2
2 *4 1/4* **Gifted Girl (IRE)**39 4137 4-8-11 0 TomQueally 5 107
(Paul Cole) *hld up in last trio on inner: rdn 2f out: swtchd rt ent fnl f and r.o to go 2nd ins fnl 100yds: no ch w v impressive wnr* **119/10**
3 *1 1/2* **Ausus (USA)**35 4-8-11 0 JamesGraham 9 104
(Daniel Peitz, U.S.A) *hld up in last: rdn and hdwy fr 2f out: styd on against rail in st and wnt 3rd post: nvr nrr* **208/10**
4 *nse* **Marketing Mix (CAN)**34 5-8-11 0 GaryStevens 6 104
(Thomas F Proctor, U.S.A) *prom: rdn over 2f out: readily outpcd by wnr ins fnl f: kpt on* **11/10**1
5 *hd* **La Tia (USA)**35 4-8-11 0 KDesormeaux 1 104
(Armando de la Cerda, U.S.A) *led: rdn over 1f out: hdd ins fnl f and readily outpcd by wnr: no ex* **31/1**
6 *nk* **Solid Appeal (USA)**41 4-8-11 0 (b) JRosario 3 103
(Reade Baker, Canada) *trckd ldr on outer: rdn to chal over 1f out: readily outpcd by wnr ins fnl f: no ex* **77/10**
7 *2* **Duntle (IRE)**20 4817 4-8-11 0 WayneLordan 2 99
(David Wachman, Ire) *midfield in tch on inner: rdn 2f out: no ex and fdd ins fnl f* **66/10**3
8 *4 3/4* **Artemus Kitten (USA)**35 5-8-11 0 RosieNapravnik 8 89
(Michael J Maker, U.S.A) *hld up in last trio on outer: rdn over 3f out: sn outpcd: plugged on in st but nvr a factor* **36/1**

9 13 **Starformer (USA)**[49] 5-8-11 0 EPrado 7 63
(William Mott, U.S.A) *midfield in tch on outer: rdn and lost pl over 2f out: sn in rr and btn: t.o* **107/10**

1m 53.38s (-2.09) 9 Ran SP% **122.8**
PARI-MUTUEL (all including $2 stakes): WIN 8.40; PLACE (1-2) 5.60, 13.40; SHOW (1-2-3) 4.20, 8.20, 8.00; SF 88.60.
Owner James Wigan **Bred** London Thoroughbred Services Ltd **Trained** Newmarket, Suffolk

5553a ARLINGTON MILLION STKS (GRADE 1) (3YO+) (TURF) 1m 2f

11:44 (12:00) 3-Y-0+

£342,331 (£114,110; £57,055; £28,527; £17,116; £11,411)

RPR

1 *hd* **Real Solution (USA)**[70] 3126 4-9-0 0 AGarcia 1 114+
(Chad C Brown, U.S.A) *midfield: 9th and pushed along over 2 1/2f out: rdn and prog 1 1/2f out: 5th and styng on 1f out: r.o wl to join ldr 100yds out: bmpd and carried rt fnl 50yds: fin 2nd: awrdd the r* **84/10**

2 **The Apache (SAF)**[21] 4779 6-9-0 0 ChristopheSoumillon 10 114
(M F De Kock, South Africa) *midfield: gng wl 3f out: rdn to ld over 1f out: edgd lft and sltly hmpd two rivals: r.o u.p but edgd rt under a lft-hand drive: bmpd and carried rival rt fnl 50yds: fin 1st: disqualified and plcd 2nd* **66/10**

3 *2* **Side Glance**[59] 3457 6-9-0 0 JamieSpencer 6 110
(Andrew Balding) *a.p: cl 4th and travelling wl 3f out: hemmed in on rail fr over 2f out tl gap c ins fnl f: r.o wl but first two had already flown* **244/10**

4 *½* **Finnegans Wake (USA)**[35] 4334 4-9-0 0 RAlbarado 2 109
(Dale Romans, U.S.A) *towards rr: hdwy over 2 1/2f out: forced wd fnl bnd: styd on u.p fr 1 1/2f out: nt pce to chal* **28/1**

5 *1 ¼* **Temeraine (USA)**[35] 4-9-0 0 ECastro 5 106
(Thomas F Proctor, U.S.A) *dwlt: w.w towards rr on inner: styd on u.p fr 1 1/2f out: sltly hmpd and swtchd outside 1f out: r.o fnl f: nvr on terms* **61/1**

6 *nk* **Little Mike (USA)**[42] 4094 6-9-0 0 JRosario 11 106
(Dale Romans, U.S.A) *broke wl and led: hdd over 4f out: trckd ldr tl led again 3f out: rdn under 2f out: hdd appr fnl f: one pce fnl f* **23/5**[3]

7 *½* **Grandeur (IRE)**[21] 4779 4-9-0 0 WilliamBuick 13 105+
(Jeremy Noseda) *towards rr on outer: rdn and effrt 2f out: pushed v wd fnl bnd: styd on ins fnl f: nvr on terms* **39/10**[2]

8 *½* **Mull Of Killough (IRE)**[35] 4276 7-9-0 0 JosephO'Brien 8 104
(Jane Chapple-Hyam) *trckd ldr on outer: led over 4f out: hdd over 3f out: prom and hrd rdn 1 1/2f out: sltly hmpd by ldr 1f out: fdd ins fnl f* **203/10**

9 *¾* **Guest Of Honour (IRE)**[35] 4276 4-9-0 0 (p) MartinHarley 9 102
(Marco Botti) *w.w towards rr on outer: rdn and no real imp fnl 2f: nvr in contention* **26/1**

10 *nk* **Hunter's Light (IRE)**[20] 4819 5-9-0 0 RyanMoore 3 112+
(Saeed bin Suroor) *midfield: 5th and travelling wl 1 1/2f out: sn short of room and hmpd: stmbld over 1f out: nt rcvr* **93/10**

11 *6 ¼* **Rahystrada (USA)**[35] 9-9-0 0 RosieNapravnik 12 89
(Byron G Hughes, U.S.A) *prom: bmpd 2f out: sn rdn and wknd* **26/1**

12 *6 ¾* **Nates Mineshaft (USA)**[21] 6-9-0 0 EBaird 4 75
(Anne P Smith, U.S.A) *chsd ldrs on inner: lost pl 1/2-way: wl btn fr over 2f out* **41/1**

13 *6 ¼* **Indy Point (ARG)**[23] 4-9-0 0 GaryStevens 7 63
(Richard E Mandella, U.S.A) *towards rr thrght: lost tch over 2f out* **14/5**[1]

2m 0.99s (-0.65) 13 Ran SP% **121.6**
PARI-MUTUEL (all including $2 stakes): WIN 18.80; PLACE (1-2) 8.60, 7.80; SHOW (1-2-3) 6.20, 5.60, 12.20; SF 153.80.
Owner Kenneth L & Sarah K Ramsey **Bred** Kenneth L Ramsey & Sarah K Ramsey **Trained** USA

5460 DEAUVILLE (R-H)

Saturday, August 17

OFFICIAL GOING: Turf: good; fibresand: standard

5555a PMU PRIX DU CALVADOS (GROUP 3) (2YO FILLIES) (TURF) 7f

1:30 (12:00) 2-Y-0

£32,520 (£13,008; £9,756; £6,504; £1,626; £1,626)

RPR

1 **Sandiva (IRE)**[57] 3522 2-8-11 0 FrankieDettori 11 106+
(Richard Fahey) *midfield on outer: stdy hdwy 3f out: rdn to ld 2f out: hung lft to rail u.p but qcknd clr and asserted: r.o strly ins fnl f: readily* **13/5**[1]

2 *1 ½* **Straight Thinking (USA)**[23] 2-8-11 0 MaximeGuyon 5 102
(A Fabre, France) *short of room early stages: hld up: rdn over 2f out: wnt 2nd ent fnl f: qcknd clr of remainder and chsd wnr but no real imp* **4/1**[3]

3 *4 ½* **Stormyra (FR)**[21] 4791 2-8-11 0 ThierryJarnet 7 90
(J-P Gallorini, France) *midfield: rdn 2f out: r.o u.p and wnt 3rd cl home: nt pce of front pair* **22/1**

4 *½* **Richies Party Girl (USA)**[44] 2-8-11 0 (b) DFlores 10 89
(Wesley A Ward, U.S.A) *led: rdn and hdd 2f out: qckly outpcd by wnr: kpt on steadily u.p* **20/1**

5 *snk* **Malka (FR)**[23] 4701 2-8-11 0 EddyHardouin 6 88
(Matthieu Palussiere, France) *hld up in last pair: pushed along whn nt clr run 3f out: rdn over 2f out: swtchd rt ins fnl f and r.o to dead-heat for 5th post: nvr nrr* **42/1**

5 *dht* **Caja (FR)**[28] 2-8-11 0 FabriceVeron 8 88
(H-A Pantall, France) *trckd ldr on outer: rdn to chal and ev ch 2f out: qckly outpcd by wnr: kpt on u.p: jnd for 5th post* **13/1**

7 *snk* **Feedyah (USA)**[23] 4682 2-8-11 0 MickaelBarzalona 2 88
(Charlie Appleby) *midfield on inner: rdn over 2f out: kpt on same pce but nvr threatened* **21/1**

8 *hd* **Hot Coffee (IRE)**[44] 3978 2-8-11 0 RichardKingscote 4 87
(Tom Dascombe) *hld up in last pair on inner: rdn and outpcd in last 2f: kpt on u.p and sme late hdwy but nvr a factor* **11/1**

9 *1 ¼* **Chriselliam (IRE)**[37] 4218 2-8-11 0 OlivierPeslier 1 84
(Charles Hills) *trckd ldr on inner: rdn and brief effrt to chal 2f out: sn outpcd by wnr: no ex and fdd* **12/1**

10 *4* **Macau (FR)**[10] 2-8-11 0 TonyPiccone 9 73
(Matthieu Palussiere, France) *a towards rr: rdn over 2f out: outpcd and btn over 1f out: eased ins fnl f* **88/1**

11 *5* **Ice Love (FR)**[16] 2-8-11 0 UmbertoRispoli 3 59
(T Castanheira, France) *plld hrd: trckd ldr in centre: rdn and lost pl 2f out: sn no ex and btn: eased 1f out: fdd and dropped to last* **25/1**

U **Lacarolina (FR)**[21] 4791 2-8-11 0 GregoryBenoist 12
(J-C Rouget, France) *jinked leaving stalls and uns rdr* **3/1**[2]

1m 22.27s (-6.03) 12 Ran SP% **116.9**
WIN (incl. 1 euro stake): 3.60. PLACES: 1.70, 2.00, 3.20. DF: 7.50. SF: 13.50.
Owner HE Sh Joaan Bin Hamad Al Thani **Bred** Denis McDonnell **Trained** Musley Bank, N Yorks

5556 - 5557a (Foreign Racing) - See Raceform Interactive

5144 PONTEFRACT (L-H)

Sunday, August 18

OFFICIAL GOING: Good to firm (good in places; 7.5)

Wind: fresh half behind Weather: Sunny

5558 BRITISH STALLION STUDS EBF TREVOR WOODS MEMORIAL MAIDEN STKS 5f

2:15 (2:17) (Class 4) 2-Y-0 **£5,175** (£1,540; £769; £384) **Stalls** Low

Form RPR

53 1 **See The Sun**[12] 5105 2-9-5 0 DavidAllan 1 82+
(Tim Easterby) *mde all: rdn over 1f out: kpt on wl* **8/1**

0 2 *3* **Muir Lodge**[19] 4858 2-9-5 0 JimCrowley 3 71
(Andrew Balding) *trckd ldrs: rdn over 1f out: kpt on to go 2nd fnl 100yds: no threat wnr* **6/4**[1]

0023 3 *½* **Urban Dreamer (IRE)**[3] 5428 2-8-12 72 PatMillman(7) 2 69
(Rod Millman) *hld up in tch: rdn over 2f out: kpt on to go 3rd fnl 50yds* **11/2**[3]

4 4 *½* **Chorlton Manor (IRE)**[34] 4351 2-9-5 0 StevieDonohoe 4 68
(Nicky Vaughan) *prom: rdn over 2f out: no ex and lost 2 pls fnl 100yds* **25/1**

25 5 *5* **Bahamian C**[36] 4312 2-9-5 0 PaulHanagan 6 50
(Richard Fahey) *sn pushed along in rr: drvn over 1f out: hung lft: nvr threatened* **9/4**[2]

3 6 *¾* **Rostrum Farewell**[18] 4883 2-9-5 0 SeanLevey 7 47
(David Brown) *hld up in tch: rdn over 2f out: sn btn* **20/1**

7 *6* **Penny Pursuits** 2-9-0 0 PaddyAspell 5 20
(Alan Berry) *slowly away: a towards rr* **100/1**

0 8 *1 ½* **The Boss Of Me**[72] 3044 2-9-5 0 GrahamLee 8 20
(Kevin Ryan) *chsd ldrs towards outer: wknd fnl 2f* **14/1**

1m 3.47s (0.17) **Going Correction** 0.0s/f (Good) 8 Ran SP% **113.5**
Speed ratings (Par 96): **98,93,92,91,83 82,72,70**
Tote Swingers: 1&2 £3.10, 1&3 £2.80, 2&3 £2.50 CSF £20.07 TOTE £9.90: £2.30, £1.10, £1.50; EX 26.40 Trifecta £129.60 Pool: £2,636.71 - 15.25 winning units..
Owner Habton Farms **Bred** R C Dollar **Trained** Great Habton, N Yorks

FOCUS
Following only a small amount of rain the going remained Good to firm, good in places (GoingStick 7.5). This looked just an ordinary maiden and not many got into it. The winner was quite impressive and the third gives the form solid perspective.

5559 TOTEPOOL HOME OF KING SIZE POOLS H'CAP (THE SUNDAY £5K BONUS RACE) 1m 4f 8y

2:45 (2:45) (Class 3) (0-90,88) 3-Y-0 **£9,337** (£2,796; £1,398; £699; £349) **Stalls** Low

Form RPR

3540 1 **Fennell Bay (IRE)**[8] 5283 4-9-11 **88** JoeFanning 5 95
(Mark Johnston) *mde all: set stdy pce: rdn over 1f out: kpt on and a holding runner-up* **11/10**[1]

4000 2 *¾* **Calaf**[17] 4923 5-9-4 **81** DaleSwift 1 87
(Brian Ellison) *racd keenly: trckd ldr: rdn over 2f out: kpt on but a hld by wnr fnl f* **3/1**[2]

0206 3 *7* **Getabuzz**[17] 4929 5-9-2 **79** DavidAllan 6 74
(Tim Easterby) *trckd ldr: rdn over 2f out: briefly pressed wnr: wknd over 1f out* **4/1**[3]

01-6 4 *8* **Braveheart Move (IRE)**[13] 5055 7-9-6 **83** PJMcDonald 4 65
(Geoffrey Harker) *dwlt: hld up: rdn over 3f out: sn btn* **10/1**

1204 5 *11* **The Lock Master (IRE)**[10] 5195 6-9-0 **82** TobyAtkinson(5) 3 46
(Michael Appleby) *in tch: rdn over 4f out: wknd over 2f out* **14/1**

2m 41.72s (0.92) **Going Correction** 0.0s/f (Good) 5 Ran SP% **108.4**
Speed ratings (Par 107): **96,95,90,85,78**
CSF £4.44 TOTE £2.00: £1.20, £1.50; EX 3.90 Trifecta £10.20 Pool: £1,696.47 - 124.03 winning units..
Owner Sheikh Hamdan Bin Mohammed Al Maktoum **Bred** J R Wills **Trained** Middleham Moor, N Yorks

FOCUS
This decent handicap was almost won in the first furlong. The winner is rated to this year's best with the runner-up to form.

5560 ST. JOHN AMBULANCE H'CAP 2m 1f 22y

3:15 (3:15) (Class 5) (0-70,74) 3-Y-0+ **£3,881** (£1,155; £577; £288) **Stalls** Low

Form RPR

0-63 1 **Embsay Crag**[20] 4822 7-9-4 **63** DeclanCannon(3) 7 79
(Philip Kirby) *midfield: smooth hdwy 4f out: led on bit over 1f out: rdn clr: easily* **8/1**[3]

0-20 2 *10* **Harvey's Hope**[11] 5137 7-9-6 **62** (t) TomEaves 4 67
(Keith Reveley) *midfield: rdn over 3f out: styd on: wnt 2nd fnl 100yds: no ch w wnr* **10/1**

4001 3 *1 ¼* **Come Here Yew (IRE)**[13] 5048 5-10-1 **74** NeilFarley(3) 11 78
(Declan Carroll) *trckd ldr: led 4f out: sn rdn: jnd 3f out: hdd over 1f out: grad wknd* **4/1**[1]

5040 4 *hd* **Moaning Butcher**[17] 4931 3-8-1 **57** (v[1]) JoeFanning 10 60
(Mark Johnston) *in tch: hdwy 4f out: rdn to press ldr 3f out: grad wknd over 1f out* **8/1**[3]

5404 5 *9* **Uncut Stone (IRE)**[13] 5048 5-8-9 **51** oh1 (p) JamesSullivan 15 45
(Peter Niven) *hld up: rdn over 3f out: minor late hdwy: nvr threatened ldrs* **16/1**

0000 6 *¾* **Mr Crystal (FR)**[22] 4759 9-9-4 **60** (p) GrahamLee 9 53
(Micky Hammond) *hld up in rr: rdn over 3f out: nvr threatened ldrs* **14/1**

0654 7 *½* **Blackstone Vegas**[44] 4035 7-8-13 **55** (v) SeanLevey 16 47
(Derek Shaw) *hld up in midfield: rdn over 3f out: nvr threatened ldrs* **7/1**[2]

2623 8 *14* **Petella**[16] 4969 7-9-4 **60** (p) PJMcDonald 2 37
(George Moore) *hld up in midfield: reminders 1/2-way: wknd over 3f out* **4/1**[1]

4004 9 *2* **Shirls Son Sam**[11] 5137 5-8-9 **51** oh1 MichaelStainton 3 26
(Chris Fairhurst) *trckd ldr: led 5f out: hdd 4f out: sn wknd* **25/1**

2000 10 *10* **Jacobs Son**[21] 4810 5-9-13 **69** AndrewMullen 6 33
(Michael Appleby) *midfield: rdn over 3f out: wknd over 2f out* **16/1**

003U 11 *2 ¾* **Miss Mohawk (IRE)**[11] 5137 4-8-9 **51** oh6 (b) HarryBentley 5 12
(Alan Brown) *hld up: nvr threatened* **66/1**

1335 **12** *9* **Dr Finley (IRE)**[19] 4867 6-9-4 **63**.................... SimonPearce(3) 14 14
(Lydia Pearce) *midfield: rdn over 3f out: sn wknd* **18/1**
2060 **13** *40* **Teenage Idol (IRE)**[13] 5048 9-9-1 **60**.................. LucyAlexander(3) 12
(Dianne Sayer) *hld up: a towards rr* **33/1**
5414 **14** *21* **Underwritten**[19] 4867 4-10-0 **70**..........................(b) LukeMorris 1
(John Weymes) *led: rdn whn hdd 5f out: sn wknd: eased* **16/1**
3m 47.52s (2.92) **Going Correction** 0.0s/f (Good)
WFA 3 from 4yo+ 14lb **14** Ran SP% **121.7**
Speed ratings (Par 103): **93,88,87,87,83 83,82,76,75,70 69,65,46,36**
Tote Swingers: 1&2 £19.20, 1&3 £9.80, 2&3 £13.30 CSF £85.49 CT £374.54 TOTE £11.00: £3.60, £3.10, £2.00; EX 116.90 Trifecta £557.40 Pool: £1,305.90 - 1.75 winning units..
Owner Grange Park Racing IV & Partner **Bred** Mrs Glenda Swinglehurst **Trained** Middleham, N Yorks

FOCUS
A modest staying handicap, but there was no hiding place with three soon scampering into a clear lead. The winner is rated to somewhere near last year's form, with the placed horses helping to set the level.

5561 EBF HIGHFIELD FARM FLYING FILLIES' STKS (LISTED RACE) 6f
3:45 (3:46) (Class 1) 3-Y-O+

£28,355 (£10,750; £5,380; £2,680; £1,345; £675) **Stalls** Low

Form RPR
26-1 **1** **Artistic Jewel (IRE)**[71] 3102 4-9-4 105.......................... GrahamLee 7 110
(Ed McMahon) *prom: rdn over 1f out: led ent fnl f: kpt on wl* **8/1**
1212 **2** *1 ¼* **Minalisa**[25] 4647 4-9-0 101.......................... SebSanders 2 102
(Rae Guest) *trckd ldng pair on inner: rdn and ev ch ent fnl f: kpt on: hld fnl 100yds* **9/2**[3]
1200 **3** *2 ¾* **Enrol**[15] 4983 4-9-0 93..........................(v[1]) ShaneKelly 1 93
(Sir Michael Stoute) *stdd s: hld up towards inner: hdwy over 2f out: rdn to chse ldrs over 1f out: kpt on: wnt 3rd fnl 50yds* **5/1**
2304 **4** *1* **Pearl Sea (IRE)**[29] 4529 3-8-11 92.......................... HarryBentley 8 90
(David Brown) *led: rdn over 2f out: hdd ent fnl f: wknd* **33/1**
0114 **5** *1 ¾* **Galician**[16] 4946 4-9-0 101.......................... JoeFanning 3 84+
(Mark Johnston) *hld up: rdn over 2f out: kpt on: nvr threatened ldrs* **10/3**[1]
2010 **6** *3 ¼* **City Girl (IRE)**[37] 4260 3-8-11 101.......................... JimCrowley 4 74
(Ralph Beckett) *midfield: rdn over 2f out: sn no imp* **14/1**
-123 **7** *shd* **March**[37] 4260 3-8-11 100.......................... LukeMorris 5 74
(Marco Botti) *s.i.s: hld up: rdn over 2f out: nvr threatened* **4/1**[2]
0231 **8** *nse* **Elusive Flame**[9] 5247 4-9-0 93.......................... WilliamCarson 11 74
(David Elsworth) *chsd ldrs: rdn over 2f out: wknd over 1f out* **25/1**
0400 **9** *5* **Nargys (IRE)**[16] 4949 3-8-11 106..........................(v[1]) AndreaAtzeni 10 58
(Luca Cumani) *hld up: rdn over 2f out: nvr threatened* **10/1**
5630 **10** *5* **Perfect Blossom**[14] 5027 6-9-0 79.......................... PaddyAspell 6 42
(Alan Berry) *midfield: wknd over 1f out* **150/1**
1050 **11** *4* **How's Life**[16] 4949 3-8-11 90.......................... TomEaves 9 29
(Kevin Ryan) *chsd ldrs: wknd fnl 2f* **50/1**
2024 **12** *1* **Gladiatrix**[14] 5036 4-9-0 88.......................... PaulHanagan 12 26
(Rod Millman) *midfield towards outer: rdn 1/2-way: wknd over 1f out* **33/1**
1m 15.66s (-1.24) **Going Correction** 0.0s/f (Good)
WFA 3 from 4yo+ 3lb **12** Ran SP% **117.1**
Speed ratings (Par 108): **108,106,102,101,99 94,94,94,87,81 75,74**
Tote Swingers: 1&2 £5.20, 1&3 £8.00, 2&3 £4.50 CSF £41.87 TOTE £10.90: £3.70, £1.90, £1.70; EX 59.50 Trifecta £346.80 Pool:£3,246.72 - 7.02 winning units..
Owner Exors of the Late R L Bedding **Bred** Jim McDonald **Trained** Lichfield, Staffs

FOCUS
Older fillies had dominated this Listed event for several years until the 3yo Mince won it last year, but normal service was resumed with only one from the Classic generation making the frame. It paid to race handily and few ever got into it. The runner-up looks the best guide to her Naas form, while those behind are rated 5lb or more off their best.

5562 CGC EVENTS FOR CONFERENCE & BANQUETING H'CAP 1m 4y
4:20 (4:21) (Class 3) (0-95,86) 3-Y-O **£12,450** (£3,728; £1,864; £932) **Stalls** Low

Form RPR
5043 **1** **Gabrial's Kaka (IRE)**[10] 5182 3-9-7 **86**.......................... TomEaves 4 98
(Richard Fahey) *trckd ldr: led over 2f out: sn rdn: kpt on wl* **7/1**
6441 **2** *3 ¼* **Manchestar**[16] 4953 3-8-7 **72**.......................... TonyHamilton 3 77
(Richard Fahey) *in tch: rdn over 2f out: kpt on to take 2nd ins fnl f: no ch w wnr* **6/1**[3]
316 **3** *6* **Magistral**[22] 4765 3-9-5 **84**.......................... RobertHavlin 5 75
(John Gosden) *dwlt: hld up in tch: rdn over 2f out: briefly chsd wnr over 1f out: wknd ins fnl f* **5/2**[2]
3216 **4** *3 ¾* **Mushaakis (IRE)**[17] 4917 3-9-7 **86**.......................... PaulHanagan 2 68
(Mark Johnston) *led: rdn whn hdd over 2f out: sn wknd* **11/8**[1]
1m 44.85s (-1.05) **Going Correction** 0.0s/f (Good) **4** Ran SP% **97.5**
Speed ratings (Par 104): **105,101,95,92**
CSF £31.33 TOTE £5.30; EX 18.80 Trifecta £70.00 Pool: £1,090.45 - 11.67 winning units..
Owner Dr Marwan Koukash **Bred** Dave Orme **Trained** Musley Bank, N Yorks

FOCUS
This valuable, if small-field 3yo handicap was weakened further when Bold Prediction was withdrawn after trying to get under her stall. The remaining quartet went a fair pace and it resulted in a 1-2 for trainer Richard Fahey. That pair are the best guides with the market leaders disappointing.

5563 TOTESUPERSCOOP6 AVAILABLE AT THE EBOR FESTIVAL MAIDEN STKS 1m 4y
4:50 (4:51) (Class 4) 3-Y-O+ **£5,175** (£1,540; £769; £384) **Stalls** Low

Form RPR
023 **1** **Cosseted**[24] 4667 3-9-0 74.......................... ShaneKelly 1 72+
(James Fanshawe) *trckd ldng pair: rdn over 1f out: led fnl 100yds: pushed out to hold on* **5/4**[1]
2 *nk* **Mahican (IRE)** 3-9-5 0.......................... JoeFanning 7 76
(Mark Johnston) *prom: rdn to press ldr 2f out: kpt on* **9/4**[2]
4 **3** *1* **Gaspard**[90] 2507 3-9-5 0.......................... DavidNolan 2 74
(David O'Meara) *led narrowly: rdn 2f out: hdd fnl 100yds: no ex* **6/1**
4 *nk* **Two Moons** 3-9-5 0.......................... BarryMcHugh 4 73
(Tony Coyle) *hld up in tch: rdn over 2f out: hdwy over 1f out: kpt on* **20/1**
32/ **5** *hd* **Montefeltro**[61] 6804 5-9-11 0.......................... DaleSwift 3 74
(Brian Ellison) *trckd ldr: rdn over 2f out: one pce: sltly short of room towards fin* **5/1**[3]
0 **6** *8* **Raafa's Jigsaw**[13] 5071 4-9-1 0.......................... TobyAtkinson(5) 5 50
(Michael Appleby) *racd keenly: hld up in rr: nvr threatened* **33/1**
0 **7** *18* **Spring Bird**[8] 5290 4-9-6 0.......................... PaulQuinn 8 9
(David Nicholls) *racd keenly: hld up in tch: pushed along 3f out: sn wknd* **33/1**
8 *2* **Moissanite** 4-9-3 0.......................... DeclanCannon(3) 6 4
(Sean Regan) *in tch on outer: rdn over 2f out: sn wknd* **50/1**
1m 46.95s (1.05) **Going Correction** 0.0s/f (Good)
WFA 3 from 4yo+ 6lb **8** Ran SP% **118.8**
Speed ratings (Par 105): **94,93,92,92,92 84,66,64**
Tote Swingers: 1&2 £1.10, 1&3 £2.20, 2&3 £2.90 CSF £4.30 TOTE £2.00: £1.02, £1.70, £2.00; EX 5.60 Trifecta £13.80 Pool: £1,985.19 - 107.33 winning units..
Owner Cheveley Park Stud **Bred** Cheveley Park Stud Ltd **Trained** Newmarket, Suffolk

FOCUS
A modest older-horse maiden. The winning time was more than two seconds slower than the preceding handicap and the first five finished in a heap, suggesting the form is ordinary and somewhat fluid, with the winner and fifth the best guides for now.

5564 NOVA DISPLAY H'CAP 6f
5:20 (5:21) (Class 5) (0-75,80) 3-Y-O+ **£3,881** (£1,155; £577; £288) **Stalls** Low

Form RPR
0400 **1** **Showboating (IRE)**[44] 4014 5-9-9 **72**..........................(tp) SeanLevey 6 83
(Alan McCabe) *midfield: rdn over 2f out: hdwy over 1f out: r.o to ld towards fin* **8/1**
2110 **2** *¾* **Illustrious Prince (IRE)**[8] 5292 6-9-8 **74**.......................... JasonHart(3) 4 83
(Declan Carroll) *chsd ldrs: rdn 1/2-way: led over 1f out: kpt on: hdd towards fin* **5/1**[2]
4-00 **3** *4* **Polish World (USA)**[11] 5138 9-9-9 **72**.......................... MickyFenton 3 68
(Paul Midgley) *led: rdn over 2f out: hdd over 1f out: grad wknd fnl f* **12/1**
6624 **4** *hd* **Celtic Sixpence (IRE)**[16] 4970 5-9-5 **68**..........................(p) MichaelStainton 5 63
(Nick Kent) *trckd ldrs: rdn over 2f out: grad wknd fnl f* **7/1**
4326 **5** *3* **Keep It Dark**[11] 5139 4-9-0 **63**.......................... GrahamLee 7 49
(Tony Coyle) *s.i.s: hld up: hdwy into midfield 1/2-way: rdn 2f out: carried hd high and no imp on ldrs* **9/2**[1]
6061 **6** *½* **Diamond Blue**[5] 5365 5-9-6 **69** 6ex..........................(p) PhillipMakin 9 53
(Richard Whitaker) *hld up in midfield: rdn over 2f out: nvr threatened ldrs* **10/1**
-060 **7** *nk* **Loch Moy**[21] 4805 3-9-1 **67**..........................(v) PaulHanagan 2 50
(Richard Fahey) *midfield on inner: rdn over 2f out: no imp* **5/1**[2]
4001 **8** *nk* **Solar Spirit (IRE)**[12] 5088 8-10-3 **80**.......................... BarryMcHugh 1 62
(Tracy Waggott) *trckd ldrs: rdn and ev ch over 1f out: wknd fnl f* **6/1**[3]
30/4 **9** *5* **Dazeen**[76] 2911 6-9-10 **73**.......................... JoeFanning 10 39
(Richard Ford) *hld up: rdn over 2f out: nvr threatened* **18/1**
3343 **10** *½* **Script**[9] 5227 4-8-1 **57**.......................... JordanHibberd(7) 13 29
(Alan Berry) *hld up: a towards rr* **16/1**
0006 **11** *29* **Lewamy (IRE)**[11] 5154 3-8-13 **65**..........................(v[1]) FrederikTylicki 12
(John Best) *prom tl wknd qckly 3f out: eased* **33/1**
1m 17.23s (0.33) **Going Correction** 0.0s/f (Good)
WFA 3 from 4yo+ 3lb **11** Ran SP% **120.3**
Speed ratings (Par 103): **97,96,90,90,86 85,85,84,78,77 38**
Tote Swingers: 1&2 £8.50, 1&3 £18.10, 2&3 £14.30 CSF £48.92 CT £488.99 TOTE £9.80: £2.30, £2.10, £4.00; EX 58.80 Trifecta £1062.70 Pool: £2,487.06 - 1.75 winning units..
Owner Mr & Mrs L Cooke A Pierce A McCabe **Bred** Crone Stud Farms Ltd **Trained** Averham Park, Notts

FOCUS
A modest sprint handicap with the winner rated to this year's form but not that solid in behind.
T/Jkpt: Not won. T/Plt: £93.20 to a £1 stake. Pool: £91,153.08 - 713.31 winning tickets. T/Qpdt: £39.40 to a £1 stake. Pool: £5,239.97 - 98.20 winning tickets. AS

5565 - 5572a (Foreign Racing) - See Raceform Interactive

5555 DEAUVILLE (R-H)
Sunday, August 18

OFFICIAL GOING: Turf: good to soft; fibresand: standard

5573a DARLEY PRIX MORNY (GROUP 1) (2YO COLTS & FILLIES) (TURF) 6f
1:30 (12:00) 2-Y-O **£162,593** (£65,048; £32,524; £16,247; £8,138)

RPR
1 **No Nay Never (USA)**[59] 3481 2-9-0 0..........................(b) DFlores 8 117+
(Wesley A Ward, U.S.A) *t.k.h early: disp ld on outer: led over 2f out: rdn and qcknd clr ent fnl f: r.o strly and asserted: readily* **7/4**[2]
2 *1* **Vorda (FR)**[28] 4572 2-8-10 0.......................... GregoryBenoist 5 110+
(P Sogorb, France) *hld up in tch: rdn and hdwy fr 2f out: r.o and wnt 2nd ins fnl 75yds: no real imp on wnr* **13/8**[1]
3 *¾* **Rizeena (IRE)**[37] 4253 2-8-10 0.......................... RyanMoore 1 108+
(Clive Brittain) *hld up in rr on inner: rdn 2f out: str run ins fnl f and snatched 3rd fnl strides: nrst fin* **6/1**[3]
4 *nk* **Jallota**[17] 4918 2-9-0 0.......................... SamHitchcott 9 111
(Mick Channon) *sn prom on outer: rdn 2f out: 2nd but outpcd by wnr ent fnl f: kpt on but dropped to 4th fnl strides* **40/1**
5 *1* **Brown Sugar (IRE)**[19] 4855 2-9-0 0.......................... PatDobbs 6 108
(Richard Hannon) *hld up in rr: rdn over 2f out: swtchd to wd outside and r.o: nt pce to chal* **14/1**
6 *3* **Muharaaj (IRE)**[3] 5460 2-9-0 0.......................... AntoineHamelin 2 99
(Matthieu Palussiere, France) *disp ld on inner: rdn and hdd over 2f out: sn outpcd and btn: fdd* **40/1**
7 *2* **Al Muthana (FR)**[21] 4816 2-9-0 0.......................... Christophe-PatriceLemaire 3 93
(F-H Graffard, France) *hld up in midfield: rdn over 2f out: sn outpcd in rr: kpt on u.p and wnt 7th cl home but nvr threatened* **33/1**
8 *snk* **Figure Of Speech (IRE)**[17] 4918 2-9-0 0..........................(p) MickaelBarzalona 7 92
(Charlie Appleby) *midfield in tch on outer: rdn over 2f out: kpt on tl no ex and btn ins fnl f: fdd and dropped to 8th cl home* **12/1**
9 *2* **Anticipated (IRE)**[19] 4855 2-9-0 0.......................... ChristopheSoumillon 4 86
(Richard Hannon) *midfield in tch: rdn over 2f out: outpcd whn briefly short of room over 1f out: sn no ex and btn: coasted home fnl 100yds* **20/1**
10 *1* **Vedeux (IRE)**[28] 4572 2-9-0 0.......................... MarcLerner 11 83
(C Lerner, France) *trckd ldrs: rdn 2f out: lost pl and btn over 1f out: fdd and dropped to last ins fnl f* **16/1**
1m 9.82s (-1.18) **Going Correction** +0.025s/f (Good) **10** Ran SP% **121.6**
Speed ratings: **108,106,105,105,103 99,97,97,94,93**
WIN (incl. 1 euro stake): 3.20. PLACES: 1.30, 1.10, 1.40. DF: 3.80. SF: 7.10.
Owner Mrs John Magnier & Michael Tabor & Derrick Smith e **Bred** Jayne Doi Johnson & David Sparrow **Trained** North America

FOCUS
Bad horses don't win this Group 1, with such superstars like Arazi and Zafonic gracing the roll of honour down the years among other top-class 2yos, and although it's unclear how much we'll see him, No Nay Never is clearly an extremely good sprinter. However, given the way the race unfolded, he couldn't have had things more his own way.

5574a DARLEY PRIX JEAN ROMANET (GROUP 1) (4YO+ FILLIES & MARES) (TURF) 1m 2f
2:40 (12:00) 4-Y-O+ **£116,138** (£46,463; £23,231; £11,605; £5,813)

RPR

1 **Romantica**[86] 2644 4-9-0 0 MaximeGuyon 3 114+
(A Fabre, France) *trckd ldr on outer: rdn and jnd ldr whn carried wd on turn into st: led over 1f out: styd on strly and asserted: pushed out: comf* **2/1**[1]

2 1 ¼ **Sarkiyla (FR)**[60] 3456 4-9-0 0 Christophe-PatriceLemaire 4 111+
(A De Royer-Dupre, France) *midfield in tch on outer: rdn over 2f out: styd on and wnt 2nd towards fin: nt pce of wnr* **9/2**

3 1 **Dalkala (USA)**[56] 3615 4-9-0 0 ChristopheSoumillon 5 109
(A De Royer-Dupre, France) *led: rdn and jnd whn c wd on turn into st: hdd over 1f out: styd on but dropped to 3rd towards fin* **11/4**[2]

4 1 ¼ **Harem Lady (FR)**[32] 4421 4-9-0 0 GregoryBenoist 2 107
(D Smaga, France) *midfield in tch on inner: rdn over 2f out: styd on but nt pce to chal* **20/1**

5 shd **Vally Jem (FR)**[32] 4421 4-9-0 0 (p) ArnaudBourgeais 6 106
(D Sepulchre, France) *hld up in last pair on outer: rdn over 2f out: styd on u.p but nvr threatened* **20/1**

6 2 **Grace Lady (FR)**[21] 4817 4-9-0 0 GeraldMosse 1 102
(Mlle T Puitg, France) *hld up in last pair on inner: rdn over 2f out: outpcd in last ent fnl f: kpt on tl eased whn btn cl home: nvr a factor* **3/1**[3]

2m 10.72s (0.52) **Going Correction** +0.425s/f (Yiel) **6** Ran SP% **112.7**
Speed ratings: **114,113,112,111,111 109**
WIN (incl. 1 euro stake): 2.40. PLACES: 1.50, 2.10. SF: 7.30.
Owner K Abdullah **Bred** Juddmonte Farms Ltd **Trained** Chantilly, France

FOCUS
They went a steady pace here, but the winner, who raced in around third early, did it well in the end.

5575a DARLEY PRIX KERGORLAY (GROUP 2) (3YO+) (TURF) 1m 7f
3:15 (12:00) 3-Y-O+
£60,243 (£23,252; £11,097; £7,398; £1,849; £1,849)

RPR

1 **Verema (FR)**[36] 4324 4-9-3 0 Christophe-PatriceLemaire 5 110+
(A De Royer-Dupre, France) *midfield: 5th and shkn up on outside 1 1/2f out: hrd rdn appr 1f out: r.o wl ins fnl f: led 50yds out: readily* **11/4**[1]

2 ½ **Joshua Tree (IRE)**[56] 3615 6-9-8 0 RyanMoore 9 114
(Ed Dunlop) *led: set stdy gallop: qcknd tempo over 2 1/2f out: rallied gamely whn pressed on both sides 1 1/2f out: r.o u.p fnl f: hdd 50yds out: no ex* **10/1**[3]

3 snk **Dance Moves**[35] 4336 5-9-4 0 MaximeGuyon 4 110+
(A Fabre, France) *midfield: towards rr 2 1/2f out: rdn and briefly short of room over 1 1/2f out: styd on wl u.p fnl f: wnt 3rd cl home: jst missed 2nd* **5/1**[2]

4 shd **Gloomy Sunday (FR)**[80] 2810 4-9-1 0 OlivierPeslier 8 107
(C Ferland, France) *trckd ldr on outer: rdn to chal for ld 1 1/2f out: cl 3rd and styng on ent fnl f: kpt on u.p wout qckning: lost 3rd cl home* **5/1**[2]

5 nse **Hammerfest**[25] 4652 6-9-4 0 FabienLefebvre 3 110
(J E Hammond, France) *midfield: 4th on inner 1 1/2f out: shkn up and short of room bhd three ldrs over 1f out: swtchd ins and styd on fnl 100yds to share 5th on line* **139/10**

5 dht **Top Trip**[59] 3483 4-9-4 0 MickaelBarzalona 7 110
(F Doumen, France) *trckd ldr on inner: rdn to chal on ins 1 1/2f out: nt qckn appr fnl f: one pce u.p fr 1f out: jnd for 5th on line* **11/4**[1]

7 ½ **Goldtara (FR)**[36] 4324 5-9-1 0 ThierryJarnet 1 106
(A Lyon, France) *dwlt: towards rr: 6th and pushed along 2f out: styd on u.p ins fnl f: nt pce to chal* **12/1**

8 1 ½ **Trip To Rhodos (FR)**[42] 4-9-4 0 AntoineHamelin 6 107
(Pavel Tuma, Czech Republic) *in rr: tk clsr order on outside over 2f out: rdn and no imp 1 1/2f out: kpt on at one pce fnl f* **20/1**

9 20 **Only A Pleasure (IRE)**[77] 2908 4-9-4 0 Pierre-CharlesBoudot 2 83
(A Fabre, France) *a towards rr: rdn and no imp fr 2 1/2f out: wl bhd fnl 2f* **12/1**

3m 22.09s (2.99) **Going Correction** +0.425s/f (Yiel) **9** Ran SP% **122.6**
Speed ratings: **109,108,108,108,108 108,108,107,96**
WIN (incl. 1 euro stake): 3.80. PLACES: 1.60, 2.50, 2.20. DF: 16.50. SF: 26.30.
Owner H H Aga Khan **Bred** The Aga Khan's Studs Sc **Trained** Chantilly, France

FOCUS
A slow gallop followed by a sprint in what was not a test at the trip.

HANOVER (L-H)
Sunday, August 18
OFFICIAL GOING: Turf: good

5576a GROSSER PREIS DES AUDI ZENTRUMS HANNOVER (GROUP 3) (3YO) (TURF) 1m 2f
4:05 (12:00) 3-Y-O
£26,016 (£8,943; £4,471; £2,439; £1,626; £1,219)

RPR

1 **Limario (GER)**[42] 4103 3-9-2 0 TedDurcan 7 104
(R Dzubasz, Germany) *trckd ldr: rdn to ld on stands' side rail 1 1/2f out: drvn ent fnl f and r.o: in control last 100yds* **17/5**[3]

2 1 ¼ **Dubday**[21] 3-8-11 0 ADeVries 1 96
(A Trybuhl, Germany) *towards rr on inner: tk clsr order over 2f out: rdn to chal ent fnl f: kpt on u.p but a hld by wnr* **31/10**[2]

3 1 ½ **Bermuda Reef (IRE)**[42] 4103 3-8-11 0 AStarke 5 93
(P Schiergen, Germany) *w.w in tch bhd ldrs: rdn over 1 1/2f out: rallied and chsd ldr appr fnl f: sn short of room and swtchd outside: one pce u.p last 150yds* **23/5**

4 2 **Vif Monsieur (GER)**[14] 3-9-2 0 KClijmans 2 94
(J Hirschberger, Germany) *led: c stands' side fnl bnd into st: rdn and hdd 1 1/2f out: grad dropped away fr 1f out* **17/5**[3]

5 shd **Nicolosio (IRE)**[42] 4103 3-9-0 0 APietsch 9 92
(W Hickst, Germany) *towards rr on outer: rdn and styd on fr 2f out: kpt on u.p fnl f: nt pce to chal* **21/10**[1]

6 2 ½ **Windsor (GER)** 3-8-11 0 AHelfenbein 3 84
(Markus Klug, Germany) *chsd ldng pair: rdn and outpcd over 2f out: fdd ins fnl f* **102/10**

7 4 ½ **Bathyrhon (GER)**[56] 3-8-11 0 VSchulepov 6 75
(S Arslangirej, Czech Republic) *in rr: isolated in centre of crse ent st: nvr in contention* **214/10**

1m 57.99s (117.99) **7** Ran SP% **133.4**
WIN (incl. 10 euro stake): 44. PLACES: 21, 20. SF: 198.
Owner Frau Marlene Haller **Bred** Frau Martha Niebuhr **Trained** Germany

5337 THIRSK (L-H)
Monday, August 19
OFFICIAL GOING: Good (good to soft in places; 7.9)
Wind: moderate 1/2 against Weather: fine but breezy

5577 BRITISH STALLION STUDS EBF MAIDEN STKS 6f
2:00 (2:00) (Class 4) 2-Y-O **£4,204** (£1,251; £625; £312) **Stalls** High

Form RPR

532 1 **Inyordreams**[24] 4723 2-9-0 74 DaleSwift 3 76
(James Given) *swtchd rt after s: w ldrs: led over 1f out: styd on wl* **7/4**[1]

55 2 2 ¼ **The Hooded Claw (IRE)**[17] 4963 2-9-5 0 DavidAllan 5 72
(Tim Easterby) *swtchd rt after s: led: hdd over 1f out: styd on same pce* **50/1**

52 3 3 ½ **Pennine Warrior**[11] 5194 2-9-5 0 FrederikTylicki 12 62
(Scott Dixon) *chsd ldrs: kpt on same pce appr fnl f* **9/2**[3]

0 4 1 **Johara (IRE)**[40] 4164 2-9-0 0 TedDurcan 13 54
(Chris Wall) *chsd ldrs: swtchd lft over 2f out: styd on ins fnl f* **8/1**

3 5 1 ¾ **Missouri Spirit**[21] 4820 2-9-5 0 GrahamLee 4 54+
(Kevin Ryan) *chsd ldrs: one pce over 1f out* **10/1**

0 6 shd **Modify**[24] 4723 2-9-0 0 RoystonFfrench 11 48
(Bryan Smart) *dwlt: sn chsng ldrs: drvn 3f out: hung rt and one pce over 1f out* **20/1**

7 nk **Pure Impressions** 2-9-5 0 MichaelO'Connell 6 55+
(Mrs K Burke) *s.i.s: in rr: hdwy 2f out: swtchd lft and kpt on ins fnl f* **22/1**

8 1 ½ **Soul Artist (IRE)** 2-9-0 0 DuranFentiman 9 43
(Tim Easterby) *s.i.s: bhd: hdwy over 1f out: nvr a factor* **50/1**

00 9 6 **Barbara Elizabeth**[73] 3064 2-9-0 0 BarryMcHugh 1 25+
(Tony Coyle) *wnt rt s: a bhd* **150/1**

005 10 ¾ **Rokeby**[13] 5105 2-9-5 55 AndrewElliott 10 28
(George Moore) *mid-div: drvn over 2f out: sn lost pl* **80/1**

11 ¾ **Bretherton** 2-9-5 0 TonyHamilton 2 25+
(Richard Fahey) *s.i.s: sn chsng ldrs on outside: effrt over 2f out: lost pl over 1f out* **3/1**[2]

0 12 nse **Halloween Moon**[53] 3724 2-9-5 0 PJMcDonald 8 25
(James Bethell) *half-rrd s: a bhd* **100/1**

13 ¾ **Sleeping Star** 2-9-0 0 TomEaves 7 18+
(Mel Brittain) *chsd ldrs: wknd 2f out* **100/1**

1m 12.36s (-0.34) **Going Correction** -0.025s/f (Good) **13** Ran SP% **116.7**
Speed ratings (Par 96): **101,98,93,92,89 89,89,87,79,78 77,77,76**
Tote Swingers 1&2 £11.40, 2&3 £20.60, 1&3 £3.30 CSF £119.74 TOTE £2.50: £1.30, £6.20, £1.80; EX 52.50 Trifecta £298.80 Pool: £2,366.70 - 5.94 winning tickets..
Owner Bolton Grange **Bred** Exors Of The Late J Ellis **Trained** Willoughton, Lincs

FOCUS
A modest 2-y-o maiden with a comfortable winner. Improved form from the runner-up.

5578 DOWNLOAD THE FREE RACING UK APP CLAIMING STKS 5f
2:30 (2:32) (Class 4) 2-Y-O **£3,881** (£1,155; £577; £288) **Stalls** High

Form RPR

6264 1 **Bountiful Forest**[10] 5226 2-7-13 62 SamanthaBell(7) 4 57
(Richard Fahey) *w ldrs: led over 2f out: hdd over 1f out: rallied to ld nr fin* **10/3**[2]

5 2 1 **Baltic Spirit (IRE)**[51] 3826 2-8-10 0 JoeFanning 2 57+
(Keith Dalgleish) *w ldrs on outside: led over 1f out: edgd rt: hdd and no ex towards fin* **4/6**[1]

0 3 3 ½ **Madame Katie (IRE)**[14] 5053 2-8-4 0 DeclanCannon(3) 6 42+
(Nigel Tinkler) *fly-jmpd s: sn chsng ldrs: hung lft over 3f out: swtchd lft over 1f out: kpt on one pce* **50/1**

54 4 1 ¾ **Straight Gin**[35] 4337 2-8-13 0 TomEaves 7 42
(Alan Berry) *chsd ldrs: outpcd over 2f out: hdwy over 1f out: one pce* **14/1**

040 5 1 **Red Tiger Lily**[20] 4847 2-8-0 40 DanielleMooney(7) 3 32
(Nigel Tinkler) *led tl over 2f out: wknd last 75yds* **100/1**

6 9 **Hillbilly Girl** 2-8-3 0 RyanWhile(7) 5 3
(Bill Turner) *s.i.s: sn outpcd and detached in last* **5/1**[3]

59.96s (0.36) **Going Correction** -0.025s/f (Good) **6** Ran SP% **109.4**
Speed ratings (Par 96): **96,94,88,86,84 70**
Tote Swingers 1&2 £1.30, 2&3 £5.90, 1&3 £9.90 CSF £5.60 TOTE £4.10: £1.40, £1.10; EX 5.90 Trifecta £39.20 Pool: £2,789.87 - 53.31 winning tickets.The winner was claimed by Noel Wilson for £5,000.
Owner J Miller **Bred** Genesis Green Stud Ltd **Trained** Musley Bank, N Yorks

FOCUS
A weak juvenile claimer and routine form. The winner had the rail in the last furlong.

5579 BET & WATCH WITH RACINGUK'S APP H'CAP 5f
3:00 (3:00) (Class 4) (0-80,79) 4-Y-O+ **£4,851** (£1,443; £721; £360) **Stalls** High

Form RPR

1311 1 **Bondi Beach Boy**[5] 5381 4-9-5 77 6ex PJMcDonald 8 88
(James Turner) *chsd ldrs: swtchd rt over 1f out: led last 50yds: r.o* **3/1**[1]

-023 2 1 **Da'Quonde (IRE)**[16] 4992 5-9-2 74 RoystonFfrench 12 81
(Bryan Smart) *chsd ldrs: styd on wl clsng stages: tk 2nd nr fin* **5/1**

0043 3 hd **Come On Dave (IRE)**[12] 5148 4-9-2 74 AdrianNicholls 1 80
(David Nicholls) *wnt lft s: swtchd rt after s: led: edgd lft over 1f out: hdd wl ins fnl f: no ex* **12/1**

6444 4 shd **Waseem Faris (IRE)**[13] 5108 4-9-2 74 FrannyNorton 6 80
(Mick Channon) *mid-div: hdwy over 1f out: edgd lft and styd on ins fnl f* **4/1**[2]

5060 5 1 ½ **Chunky Diamond (IRE)**[13] 5108 4-8-12 73 (t) LMcNiff(3) 9 74
(Ruth Carr) *towards rr: hdwy over 1f out: nvr rchd ldrs* **33/1**

6 6 ½ **Go Go Green (IRE)**[7] 5333 7-8-13 71 GrahamLee 11 70
(Jim Goldie) *s.s: nt clr run 2f out: hdwy over 1f out: styng on at fin* **11/1**

5405 **7** *shd* **Eland Ally**[18] 4930 5-9-0 **72**.....................(p) MickyFenton 4 70
(Tom Tate) *chsd ldrs: hung lft and one pce over 1f out* **20/1**

0354 **8** *shd* **Crimson Knot (IRE)**[9] 5266 5-8-12 **73**..................... MarkCoumbe(3) 7 71
(Alan Berry) *mid-div: hdwy over 1f out: kpt on: nvr a threat* **16/1**

2503 **9** *1* **Waking Warrior**[44] 4047 5-8-11 **76**.....................(tp) KevinStott(7) 2 70
(Kevin Ryan) *a towards rr: nvr a factor* **9/2**[3]

2001 **10** *2 ¼* **Chosen One (IRE)**[12] 5148 8-8-9 **67**..................... JamesSullivan 10 53
(Ruth Carr) *in rr: sme hdwy 2f out: sn wknd* **25/1**

100- **11** *7* **Kyzer Chief**[364] 5412 8-8-0 **61** ow1..................... NeilFarley(3) 3 22
(Tina Jackson) *hood removed after s: hdwy on outside to chse ldrs over 3f out: lost pl over 1f out* **80/1**

58.75s (-0.85) **Going Correction** -0.025s/f (Good) **11** Ran SP% **114.5**
Speed ratings (Par 105): **105,103,103,102,100 99,99,99,97,94 83**
Tote Swingers 1&2 £6.20, 2&3 £12.40, 1&3 £5.20 CSF £16.66 CT £158.56 TOTE £3.50: £1.90, £2.00, £3.10; EX 20.50 Trifecta £254.70 Pool: £2,939.91 - 8.65 winning tickets..
Owner G R Turner & H Turner **Bred** G R & H Turner **Trained** Norton-le-Clay, N Yorks

FOCUS
This was decent sprint form for the class. The winner recorded another personal-best and the second is rated close to form and sets the level.

5580 JAMES HERRIOT APP H'CAP 1m
3:30 (3:32) (Class 4) (0-80,80) 3-Y-0+ **£4,851** (£1,443; £721; £360) **Stalls** Low

Form RPR

404 **1** **Sound Advice**[21] 4825 4-9-11 **77**..................... TomEaves 10 87
(Keith Dalgleish) *trckd ldrs: led over 1f out: kpt on wl* **14/1**

1600 **2** *1 ½* **The Osteopath (IRE)**[12] 5149 10-9-9 **75**..................... DuranFentiman 4 82
(John Davies) *in rr: hdwy on wd outside over 3f out: chsng ldrs over 1f out: kpt on to take 2nd nr fin* **28/1**

4434 **3** *½* **Obboorr**[6] 5368 4-8-12 **64**..................... MickyFenton 12 69
(Brian Rothwell) *mid-div: hdwy over 2f out: chsng ldrs over 1f out: kpt on to take 3rd clsng stages* **6/1**[2]

3305 **4** *¾* **Dark Ocean (IRE)**[16] 4994 3-8-9 **67**..................... MichaelO'Connell 7 71
(Jedd O'Keeffe) *chsd ldrs: n.m.r 1f out: kpt on same pce fnl f* **16/1**

4400 **5** *½* **Piceno (IRE)**[5] 5398 5-9-2 **68**.....................(p) FrederikTylicki 16 71
(Scott Dixon) *swtchd lft after s and led 1f: trckd ldrs: led over 2f out: hdd and edgd lft over 1f out: kpt on same pce* **40/1**

0043 **6** *hd* **Invincible Hero (IRE)**[9] 5268 6-9-10 **79**..................... JasonHart(3) 5 83+
(Declan Carroll) *trckd ldrs: effrt on ins over 2f out: nt clr run and swtchd rt over 1f out: hung rt and kpt on* **5/1**[1]

5001 **7** *½* **Fazza**[12] 5149 6-9-6 **72**..................... JamesSullivan 11 77+
(Edwin Tuer) *hld up in rr: hdwy on ins over 2f out: nvr saw daylight: eased clsng stages* **8/1**[3]

365 **8** *1 ½* **Toga Tiger (IRE)**[12] 5124 6-9-12 **78**..................... RobertWinston 1 75
(Jeremy Gask) *s.i.s: in rr and sn drvn along: hdwy over 2f out: one pce and hung rt* **6/1**[2]

20 **9** *1 ½* **Kuwait Star**[47] 3945 4-9-6 **72**..................... JoeFanning 2 66
(Jason Ward) *mid-div: effrt over 2f out: n.m.r: fdd over 1f out* **12/1**

-064 **10** *nk* **Tiger Reigns**[12] 5149 7-9-10 **76**.....................(t) PhillipMakin 6 69
(Michael Dods) *in tch: effrt over 2f out: one pce: fdd last 75yds* **10/1**

5060 **11** *1 ¼* **It's A Mans World**[14] 5051 7-9-5 **74**..................... PaulPickard(3) 9 64
(Brian Ellison) *in rr: effrt over 2f out: nvr on terms* **10/1**

0-00 **12** *1 ¾* **Rustic Deacon**[37] 4281 6-10-0 **80**..................... GrahamLee 8 66
(Willie Musson) *s.i.s: in rr: hdwy over 2f out: n.m.r over 1f out: sn wknd* **25/1**

0066 **13** *5* **Hit The Jackpot (IRE)**[11] 5195 4-9-8 **79**.....................(v) DavidBergin(5) 3 54
(David O'Meara) *mid-div: effrt over 2f out: sn lost pl* **20/1**

-300 **14** *3 ¾* **Meshardal (GER)**[46] 3977 3-8-7 **65**..................... PJMcDonald 15 31
(Ruth Carr) *swtchd lft after s: led after 1f: hdd over 2f out: lost pl over 1f out* **28/1**

1450 **15** *1 ¾* **Day Of The Eagle (IRE)**[15] 5026 7-9-9 **75**..................... GrahamGibbons 13 37
(Michael Easterby) *mid-div: slipped bnd over 4f out: drvn over 3f out: lost pl over 2f out* **10/1**

1m 40.83s (0.73) **Going Correction** +0.225s/f (Good)
WFA 3 from 4yo+ 6lb **15** Ran SP% **121.8**
Speed ratings (Par 105): **105,103,103,102,101 101,101,99,98,97 96,94,89,86,84**
Tote Swingers 1&2 £76.10, 2&3 £58.10, 1&3 £28.70 CSF £372.28 CT £2656.93 TOTE £14.40: £4.50, £6.90, £2.50; EX 330.30 Trifecta £2009.40 Part won. Pool: £2,679.24 - 0.06 winning tickets..
Owner G L S Partnership **Bred** G L S Partnership **Trained** Carluke, S Lanarks

FOCUS
A strongly run handicap and fair form, which looks sound enough.

5581 GBI RACING WELCOMES NICOSIA RACE CLUB H'CAP 7f
4:00 (4:02) (Class 5) (0-75,74) 3-Y-0 **£3,234** (£962; £481; £240) **Stalls** Low

Form RPR

1213 **1** **Someone's Darling**[11] 5184 3-9-3 **70**..................... GrahamLee 4 77+
(Jim Goldie) *trckd ldrs: 2nd over 3f out: led 1f out: jst hld on* **7/2**[2]

132 **2** *hd* **Bousatet (FR)**[17] 4955 3-8-5 **65**..................... KevinStott(7) 8 71+
(Kevin Ryan) *edgd lft after s: trckd ldrs: effrt on ins 3f out: styd on wl towards fin: jst hld* **11/4**[1]

3021 **3** *½* **Marcus Caesar (IRE)**[24] 4722 3-8-11 **64**..................... JamesSullivan 3 69
(Ruth Carr) *led: edgd rt and hdd 1f out: no ex clsng stages* **13/2**

0004 **4** *2 ½* **Dream Scenario**[11] 5184 3-9-0 **67**..................... DavidAllan 1 65
(Mel Brittain) *s.i.s: sn chsng ldrs: drvn and lost pl over 4f out: styd on and swtchd rt over 1f out: one pce* **8/1**

3-04 **5** *hd* **Hanalei Bay (IRE)**[16] 4991 3-9-2 **69**..................... JoeFanning 6 67
(Keith Dalgleish) *chsd ldrs on outer: edgd rt over 1f out: wknd last 100yds* **14/1**

4650 **6** *10* **Kolonel Kirkup**[7] 5342 3-8-11 **64**.....................(p) TomEaves 5 35
(Michael Dods) *hmpd s: mid-div: drvn over 3f out: lost pl over 2f out* **14/1**

3521 **7** *½* **Dennis**[13] 5089 3-8-9 **67**..................... DarylByrne(5) 2 36
(Tim Easterby) *dwlt: in rr: drvn and wandered 3f out: sn lost pl and bhd* **11/2**[3]

1m 27.81s (0.61) **Going Correction** +0.225s/f (Good) **7** Ran SP% **102.1**
Speed ratings (Par 100): **105,104,104,101,101 89,89**
Tote Swingers 1&2 £2.60, 2&3 £3.00, 1&3 £2.70 CSF £10.71 CT £39.69 TOTE £4.00: £1.80, £2.20; EX 11.80 Trifecta £47.30 Pool: £2,929.86 - 46.42 winning tickets..
Owner The McMaster Springford Partnership **Bred** W G H Barrons **Trained** Uplawmoor, E Renfrews

■ Jubilee Games was withdrawn (15-2, ref to ent stalls). Deduct 10p in the £ under R4.
■ Stewards' Enquiry : Kevin Stott two-day ban: careless riding (2-3 Sep)

FOCUS
A a fair 3-y-o handicap for the class, run at a solid pace. The winner stepped up on recent 6f form and the third is rated to his latest C&D form.

5582 WATCH RACING UK ON SKY 432 H'CAP 1m 4f
4:30 (4:30) (Class 4) (0-85,80) 3-Y-0 **£4,851** (£1,443; £721; £360) **Stalls** High

Form RPR

5142 **1** **Esteaming**[13] 5107 3-9-7 **80**..................... GrahamGibbons 2 91+
(David Barron) *w ldr: led after 1f: drvn over 3f out: styd on strly: eased clsng stages* **4/7**[1]

404P **2** *2 ½* **Allnecessaryforce (FR)**[10] 5223 3-9-5 **78**.....................(p) TonyHamilton 5 83
(Richard Fahey) *s.i.s: chsd ldrs over 8f out: drvn and outpcd over 3f out: styd on to chse wnr over 1f out: no imp* **6/1**[3]

3110 **3** *5* **Chant (IRE)**[32] 4447 3-8-13 **72**..................... PJMcDonald 3 69
(Ann Duffield) *chsd ldr: chal over 3f out: wknd over 1f out* **17/2**

00-0 **4** *19* **Grey Blue (IRE)**[110] 1934 3-8-13 **72**..................... FrannyNorton 1 39
(Mark Johnston) *led 1f: drvn over 4f out: lost pl over 3f out: bhd whn eased ins fnl f* **4/1**[2]

2m 37.87s (1.67) **Going Correction** +0.225s/f (Good) **4** Ran SP% **108.5**
Speed ratings (Par 102): **103,101,98,85**
CSF £4.41 TOTE £1.60; EX 4.10 Trifecta £6.60 Pool: £2,629.15 - 295.51 winning tickets..
Owner D E Cook **Bred** Mr & Mrs A E Pakenham & Daniel James **Trained** Maunby, N Yorks

FOCUS
A modest 3-y-o handicap, run at a fair pace. Another step forward from the winner with the runner-up rated to his sound Carlisle form.

5583 READ HAYLEY TURNER EVERY FRIDAY RACINGUK.COM LADY AMATEUR RIDERS' H'CAP 6f
5:00 (5:02) (Class 5) (0-70,68) 3-Y-0+ **£2,495** (£774; £386; £193) **Stalls** High

Form RPR

0404 **1** **George Fenton**[3] 5486 4-9-6 **58**.....................(p) AnnaHesketh(5) 12 68+
(Richard Guest) *dwlt: in rr: hdwy 2f out: nt clr run on ins 1f out: styd on wl to ld fnl stride* **4/1**[2]

4062 **2** *shd* **Rigolleto (IRE)**[14] 5049 5-10-5 **66**..................... MrsCBartley 8 74
(Anabel K Murphy) *trckd ldrs: 2nd over 2f out: led last 100yds: hdd post* **16/1**

312 **3** *¾* **Ypres**[5] 5381 4-10-7 **68**..................... MissSBrotherton 2 74+
(Jason Ward) *hld up in mid-div: hdwy over 2f out: edgd rt appr fnl f: upsides ins fnl f: no ex nr fin* **9/4**[1]

0000 **4** *1 ¼* **El McGlynn (IRE)**[10] 5227 4-10-3 **64**..................... MissCWalton 4 66
(Eric Alston) *swtchd rt after s: led: hdd ins fnl f: wknd nr fin* **40/1**

5-62 **5** *1 ¾* **Sir Nod**[19] 4891 11-9-10 **62**..................... MissLWilson(5) 6 58
(Julie Camacho) *s.i.s: hdwy over 2f out: n.m.r appr fnl f: kpt on same pce* **16/1**

6610 **6** *1* **Charlemagne Diva**[16] 4982 3-9-8 **63**.....................(t) MissBeckySmith(5) 9 56
(Richard Guest) *chsd ldrs: outpcd over 2f out: n.m.r 1f out: kpt on same pce* **11/1**[3]

5460 **7** *2 ¼* **Hab Reeh**[12] 5139 5-9-7 **54**.....................(t) MissADeniel 3 40
(Ruth Carr) *s.i.s: in rr: hdwy over 2f out: nvr nr ldrs* **16/1**

002 **8** *nk* **Triskaidekaphobia**[31] 4469 10-8-11 **49** oh4.....................(t) MissHDoyle(5) 7 34
(Wilf Storey) *chsd ldr: wkng whn hmpd appr fnl f* **50/1**

3425 **9** *hd* **See Clearly**[16] 4982 4-10-6 **67**.....................(p) MissHBethell 10 51
(Tim Easterby) *in rr: drvn over 2f out: sme hdwy and edgd rt over 1f out: nvr a factor* **4/1**[2]

5130 **10** *7* **Red Cape (FR)**[17] 4970 10-10-0 **66**.....................(b) MissSMDoolan(5) 11 28
(Ruth Carr) *mid-div: drvn and outpcd over 2f out: lost pl over 1f out* **12/1**

010 **11** *¾* **Mitchum**[30] 4540 4-10-1 **67**.....................(p) MrsVDavies(5) 1 26
(Ron Barr) *rrd s: sme hdwy on outer over 3f out: lost pl 2f out* **14/1**

1m 12.39s (-0.31) **Going Correction** -0.025s/f (Good)
WFA 3 from 4yo+ 3lb **11** Ran SP% **115.5**
Speed ratings (Par 103): **101,100,99,98,95 94,91,91,90,81 80**
Tote Swingers 1&2 £9.60, 2&3 £7.50, 1&3 £3.20 CSF £65.08 CT £179.54 TOTE £4.40: £1.60, £3.40, £1.40; EX 84.40 Trifecta £248.70 Pool: £3,623.66 - 10.92 winning tickets..
Owner Mrs Alison Guest **Bred** R P Williams **Trained** Wetherby, W Yorks

FOCUS
An ordinary sprint handicap, confined to lady amateur riders and once again the stands' side was the place to be. The winner is rated close to his AW best.
T/Jkpt: £1,576.80 to a £1 stake. Pool: £35,533.76 - 16.00 winning tickets. T/Plt: £71.90 to a £1 stake. Pool: £86,088.88 - 873.33 winning tickets. T/Qpdt: £34.00 to a £1 stake. Pool: £5,455.65 - 118.7 winning tickets. WG

5344 WINDSOR (R-H)
Monday, August 19

OFFICIAL GOING: Good to firm (watered; 8.7)
Wind: Moderate, behind Weather: Fine, warm

5584 ROYAL BERKSHIRE ODDFELLOWS/EBF MAIDEN STKS 6f
5:30 (5:33) (Class 5) 2-Y-0 **£2,911** (£866; £432; £216) **Stalls** Low

Form RPR

3 **1** **Dutch Art Dealer**[22] 4795 2-9-5 0..................... JimCrowley 4 74+
(Paul Cole) *chsd ldng quartet: rdn over 1f out: r.o to ld last 100yds: sn in command* **2/1**[1]

2 *1 ½* **Mocacha (IRE)** 2-9-5 0..................... RyanMoore 7 70+
(William Haggas) *difficult to load into stalls: s.i.s: sn in midfield: urged along and prog over 2f out: clsd 1f out: styd on same pce last 100yds* **6/1**

0 **3** *shd* **Monarch Maid**[19] 4880 2-9-0 0..................... WilliamCarson 12 64
(Peter Hiatt) *pressed ldr: led after 2f: rdn against nr side rail over 1f out: hdd and one pce last 100yds* **66/1**

0 **4** *3* **Heska (IRE)**[15] 5033 2-9-5 0..................... SamHitchcott 2 60
(Mick Channon) *sn pushed along in midfield: kpt on one pce fr 2f out to take 4th ins fnl f* **25/1**

0 **5** *1 ¼* **Beatabout The Bush (IRE)**[22] 4795 2-9-5 0..................... JamieSpencer 3 56
(Charles Hills) *slowly away: wl off the pce in last quartet: shkn up over 2f out: taken to outer and sme prog over 1f out: nvr on terms* **12/1**

03 **6** *1* **Sandy Cove**[15] 5033 2-9-5 0..................... GeorgeBaker 9 53
(Roger Charlton) *led 2f: styd prom tl wknd over 1f out* **4/1**[2]

4 **7** *3 ¼* **Biotic**[19] 4883 2-9-5 0..................... AndreaAtzeni 1 44
(Rod Millman) *pressed ldrs to 2f out: wknd and racd awkwardly fr over 1f out* **20/1**

8 *½* **Midnight Rambler (IRE)** 2-9-5 0..................... RichardHughes 5 42
(Richard Hannon) *slowly away: rn green: wl in rr and reminder over 4f out: nvr on terms* **9/2**[3]

The Form Book Flat, Raceform Ltd, Compton, RG20 6NL.

40 **9** *8* **Redlorryellowlorry (IRE)**[82] 2778 2-9-5 0 PatCosgrave 8 18
(George Baker) *s.i.s: a towards rr: hanging bdly lft fr 1/2-way: bhd after* **100/1**

10 *1 ½* **Babyfact** 2-9-0 0 SeanLevey 11 9
(Malcolm Saunders) *slowly away: sn last and rn green: nvr a factor* **25/1**

63 **11** *1 ¾* **Our Sherona**[16] 5000 2-8-7 0 OisinMurphy(7) 6
(Gary Harrison) *pressed ldrs over 3f: wknd rapidly* **16/1**

1m 12.21s (-0.79) **Going Correction** -0.15s/f (Firm) **11** Ran SP% **114.3**
Speed ratings (Par 94): **99,97,96,92,91 89,85,84,74,72 69**
Tote Swingers 1&2 £3.90, 2&3 £68.80, 1&3 £26.50 CSF £12.95 TOTE £2.60: £1.30, £1.60, £10.40; EX 17.50 Trifecta £400.70 Pool: £2,057.69 - 3.85 winning tickets..

Owner R A Green **Bred** Raymond Clive Tooth **Trained** Whatcombe, Oxon

FOCUS
Inner of straight dolled out 8yds at 6f and 5yds at Winning Post. Top bend dolled out 8 yds from normal inner configuration adding 30yds to races of 1m and beyond. Not a strong maiden but the first two can both do better.

5585 WIN £1 MILLION ON CORAL'S "FOOTBALL JACKPOT" H'CAP 5f 10y
6:00 (6:01) (Class 4) (0-85,83) 3-Y-O **£4,851** (£1,443; £721; £360) **Stalls** Low

Form RPR
0-10 **1** **Reqaaba**[93] 2449 3-9-2 **78** [1] PatCosgrave 4 88
(Robert Cowell) *taken down early: trckd ldr: shkn up to ld over 1f out: r.o wl fnl f: readily* **16/1**

2214 **2** *2* **Port Alfred**[8] 5303 3-9-7 **83** RichardHughes 2 86
(Charlie Appleby) *hld up in 4th: clsd 2f out: rdn to chse wnr fnl f: one pce and no imp* **8/11**[1]

401- **3** *1 ¾* **Greenery (IRE)**[262] 7930 3-8-9 **71** RyanMoore 1 68
(Roger Charlton) *difficult to load into stalls: t.k.h early: trckd ldng pair: nt qckn jst over 1f out: one pce after* **5/1**[3]

10-4 **4** *shd* **Somoud (IRE)**[17] 4942 3-8-10 **72** AndreaAtzeni 3 68
(J R Jenkins) *free to post: led: rdn and hdd over 1f out: no rspnse and sn btn* **25/1**

615 **5** *1* **Exotic Isle**[28] 4592 3-9-4 **80** JamieSpencer 5 73
(Ralph Beckett) *awkward s: hld up in last: effrt over 1f out: sn shkn up and nt qckn* **3/1**[2]

59.08s (-1.22) **Going Correction** -0.15s/f (Firm) **5** Ran SP% **109.3**
Speed ratings (Par 102): **103,99,97,96,95**
CSF £28.60 TOTE £19.30: £6.40, £1.10; EX 36.90 Trifecta £124.70 Pool: £1,859.24 - 11.17 winning tickets..

Owner HOH Stable **Bred** Manor Farm Stud (rutland) **Trained** Six Mile Bottom, Cambs

FOCUS
Quite a useful small-field contest. The early gallop wasn't that strong for a sprint. The runner-up is rated to his latest handicap form.

5586 WIN £1 MILLION ON CORAL'S "FOOTBALL JACKPOT" (S) STKS 1m 3f 135y
6:30 (6:33) (Class 6) 3-Y-O+ **£1,940** (£577; £288; £144) **Stalls** Low

Form RPR
030/ **1** **Mungo Park**[18] 6988 5-9-10 72 (t) SaleemGolam 7 70
(Sophie Leech) *in tch: pushed along firmly to chse ldng quartet over 3f out: wnt 2nd 2f out: rdn to ld over 1f out: wandered but clr ins fnl f: kpt on* **33/1**

/0-0 **2** *1 ¼* **While You Wait (IRE)**[209] 318 4-9-10 72 RyanMoore 15 68
(Gary Moore) *hld up in last trio: prog jst over 3f out: swtchd and shkn up wl over 1f out: r.o to take 2nd ins fnl f: clsd on wnr but too much to do* **5/1**[3]

0-00 **3** *4 ½* **Urban Space**[14] 5065 7-9-10 61 AdamKirby 11 60
(Tony Carroll) *towards rr: prog on outer fr 1/2-way to ld over 3f out: drvn and hdd over 1f out: fdd fnl f* **12/1**

0030 **4** *5* **Silver Marizah (IRE)**[44] 4071 4-9-5 43 RobertHavlin 14 47
(Roger Ingram) *pressed ldr: chal over 3f out: nt qckn over 2f out: steadily fdd* **100/1**

3452 **5** *2 ¾* **Into The Wind**[26] 4643 6-8-12 67 PatMillman(7) 3 42
(Rod Millman) *hld up early: trckd ldrs on inner 5f out: chal 3f out: chsd ldr over 2f out briefly: wknd tamely* **7/4**[1]

00-0 **6** *1 ¼* **Zinnobar**[59] 3530 3-8-9 38 WilliamCarson 4 40
(Jonathan Portman) *mde most to over 3f out: steadily wknd fr over 2f out* **100/1**

-300 **7** *1 ¼* **Isola Bella**[137] 908 4-8-12 40 DavidCoyle(7) 2 38
(Jonathan Portman) *pressed ldrs tl wknd over 3f out* **66/1**

8 *9* **God's County (FR)**[33] 8-9-10 80 (vt[1]) SeanLevey 6 35
(Sophie Leech) *hld up towards rr: nudged along and no imp on ldng gp over 3f out: wknd and eased 2f out* **16/1**

4210 **9** *1* **Fly Haaf (IRE)**[3] 5479 4-10-1 67 (t) RichardHughes 5 43
(George Baker) *hld up in midfield: rdn to chse ldrs over 3f out: hanging and wknd over 2f out: heavily eased over 1f out* **9/2**[2]

0000 **10** *8* **Burnbrake**[10] 5216 8-9-10 38 ChrisCatlin 12 12
(Richard Rowe) *mostly in last trio: no prog 4f out: bhd over 2f out* **100/1**

0 **11** *2 ¾* **Scala Santa**[39] 4223 4-9-0 0 ThomasGarner(5) 8
(Martin Bosley) *prom tl drvn and wknd jst over 4f out: sn bhd* **100/1**

00-0 **12** *1 ¼* **Pearl Frost**[12] 5123 4-9-10 43 (v) JackMitchell 13
(Laura Mongan) *chsd ldrs tl wknd 4f out: sn wl bhd* **100/1**

5 **13** *3 ¾* **Lenderking (IRE)**[77] 2926 5-9-3 0 OllieGarner(7) 10
(Michael Chapman) *prom tl wknd rapidly over 3f out: sn wl bhd* **100/1**

0 **U** **Spiritofsixtynine (IRE)**[12] 5133 5-9-5 0 HarryPoulton(5) 1
(Jamie Poulton) *a in last trio: no ch whn stmbld and uns rdr over 2f out* **100/1**

2m 27.5s (-2.00) **Going Correction** -0.30s/f (Firm)
WFA 3 from 4yo+ 10lb **14** Ran SP% **96.2**
Speed ratings (Par 101): **94,93,90,86,85 84,83,77,76,71 69,68,66,**
Tote Swingers 1&2 £14.40, 2&3 £5.00, 1&3 £34.00 CSF £114.65 TOTE £22.00: £4.10, £1.50, £3.00; EX 137.10 Trifecta £914.70 Part won. Pool: £1,219.63 - 0.03 winning tickets..There was no bid for the winner. Into The Wind was claimed by Jim Best for £5,000. While You Wait was subject to a friendly claim for £5,000.

Owner C J Leech **Bred** Newsells Park Stud **Trained** Elton, Gloucs
■ Saleem Golam's first winner of the season, and Sophie Leech's first ever on the Flat.

FOCUS
Piers Galveston was withdrawn on vet's advice (3-1, deduct 25p in the £ under R4). Fair efforts from the leading pair, who pulled a long way clear in this seller. The form is not solid with the fourth and sixth the keys.

5587 WIN £1 MILLION ON CORAL'S "FOOTBALL JACKPOT" APPRENTICE H'CAP 1m 2f 7y
7:00 (7:00) (Class 5) (0-75,75) 4-Y-O+ **£2,587** (£770; £384; £192) **Stalls** Centre

Form RPR
1261 **1** **Breaking The Bank**[21] 4831 4-9-1 **73** ThomasGarner(5) 5 84
(William Muir) *mde all: drew clr over 3f out: rdn but in n.d over 1f out: eased last 75yds* **9/4**[1]

0-01 **2** *5* **Young Dottie**[18] 4908 7-8-9 **69** SophieRalston(7) 2 71
(Pat Phelan) *t.k.h: cl up: chsd wnr 1/2-way: outpcd over 3f out: no imp after* **7/1**

5500 **3** *1 ¾* **Starwatch**[12] 5124 6-9-5 **75** MichaelJMMurphy(3) 4 73
(John Bridger) *sn in 5th: pushed along over 4f out: outpcd over 3f out: plugged on to take 3rd last 100yds* **12/1**

6644 **4** *¾* **Perfect Delight**[19] 4882 4-9-0 **70** RyanTate(3) 3 67
(Clive Cox) *chsd wnr to 1/2-way: pushed along and outpcd over 3f out: n.d after: wknd fnl f* **11/4**[2]

5101 **5** *7* **Attraction Ticket**[18] 4904 4-8-12 **70** GeorgeBuckell(5) 6 53
(David Simcock) *hld up in last: effrt 3f out: sn rdn and no prog: wknd wl over 1f out* **5/1**

1410 **6** *1 ¾* **Silver Alliance**[18] 4923 5-9-2 **74** (p) ShelleyBirkett(5) 1 54
(Julia Feilden) *sn in 4th: rdn and outpcd over 3f out: n.d after: wknd over 1f out* **9/2**[3]

2m 4.67s (-4.03) **Going Correction** -0.30s/f (Firm) **6** Ran SP% **112.5**
Speed ratings (Par 103): **104,100,98,98,92 91**
Tote Swingers 1&2 £3.70, 2&3 £14.70, 1&3 £3.20 CSF £18.24 TOTE £2.90: £1.90, £2.70; EX 15.00 Trifecta £206.70 Pool: £1,506.10 - 5.46 winning tickets..

Owner R W Devlin **Bred** Cheveley Park Stud Ltd **Trained** Lambourn, Berks

FOCUS
A one-sided apprentice handicap. The winner stepped up on recent C&D form with the runner-up to last year's turf form.

5588 CSP MAIDEN STKS 1m 67y
7:30 (7:32) (Class 5) 3-4-Y-O **£2,587** (£770; £384; £192) **Stalls** Low

Form RPR
1 **Talented Kid**[78] 4-9-11 0 AdamKirby 9 93+
(Mark Johnston) *trckd ldrs in 5th: smooth prog over 3f out to ld wl over 2f out: shkn up over 1f out: wl in command after* **7/1**[3]

2-64 **2** *3* **Vanity Rules**[66] 3292 3-9-0 82 RichardHughes 12 80
(John Gosden) *led at gd pce: shkn up and hdd wl over 2f out: kpt on but no ch w wnr fr over 1f out* **8/11**[1]

3 *2 ½* **Proximate** 3-9-5 0 RyanMoore 4 79+
(Sir Michael Stoute) *towards rr and off the pce: pushed along and prog fr 1/2-way: styd on fnl 2f to take 3rd ins fnl f* **5/1**[2]

5 **4** *½* **Speedy Writer**[12] 5133 3-9-0 0 AmyScott(5) 6 78
(Henry Candy) *trckd ldr to over 3f out: reminders and one pce after: nt disgracd* **8/1**

50 **5** *9* **Pearl Queen (USA)**[22] 4813 3-9-0 0 HarryBentley 11 52
(Chris Wall) *prom: chsd ldr briefly over 3f out: wknd qckly fnl 2f* **50/1**

04 **6** *½* **Beep**[91] 2519 3-9-0 0 [1] PatCosgrave 7 51
(Lydia Richards) *chsd ldng trio: rdn sn after 1/2-way: wknd over 2f out* **20/1**

40 **7** *3 ¼* **Primo D'Oro (USA)**[12] 5133 3-9-5 0 PatDobbs 3 49
(Richard Hannon) *dwlt: off the pce towards rr: shkn up and struggling sn after 1/2-way* **50/1**

8 *½* **Camisole (IRE)** 3-9-0 0 SteveDrowne 10 42+
(Charles Hills) *dwlt: rn green in last pair and sn off the pce: no ch whn nt clr run over 2f out: pushed along and no real hdwy after* **20/1**

9 *1 ½* **Admirer (IRE)** 3-9-5 0 MartinLane 5 44
(David Simcock) *dwlt: rn green and sn wl off the pce in last pair: shkn up and v modest hdwy 3f out: sn no hdwy* **14/1**

30 **10** *4* **Scarlette D'Or**[12] 5133 4-8-13 0 ShelleyBirkett(7) 8 31
(Alastair Lidderdale) *a off the pce towards rr: rdn sn after 1/2-way: sn no ch* **100/1**

0 **11** *¾* **Majnon Fajer (IRE)**[12] 5133 3-9-5 0 RobertHavlin 2 33
(Roger Ingram) *chsd ldng quintet but nt on terms: rdn and struggling sn after 1/2-way: wknd* **100/1**

6 **12** *50* **Foiled**[11] 5176 3-9-5 0 SeanLevey 13
(Richard Hannon) *a towards rr: wknd 4f out: t.o and virtually p.u fnl 2f* **33/1**

1m 40.52s (-4.18) **Going Correction** -0.30s/f (Firm)
WFA 3 from 4yo 6lb **12** Ran SP% **123.2**
Speed ratings (Par 103): **108,105,102,102,93 92,89,88,87,83 82,32**
Tote Swingers 1&2 £2.30, 2&3 £1.90, 1&3 £6.70 CSF £12.41 TOTE £9.70: £1.90, £1.10, £2.30; EX 19.60 Trifecta £60.40 Pool: £2,384.19 - 29.59 winning tickets..

Owner Sheikh Hamdan Bin Mohammed Al Maktoum **Bred** Whitsbury Manor Stud And Mrs M E Slade **Trained** Middleham Moor, N Yorks

FOCUS
A range of abilities in this maiden and they were quite well strung out from an early stage. The winner is rated to his latest handicap mark.

5589 ZUMTOBEL LIGHTING FILLIES' H'CAP 1m 67y
8:00 (8:00) (Class 4) (0-85,82) 3-Y-O+ **£4,851** (£1,443; £721; £360) **Stalls** Low

Form RPR
1-6 **1** **Al Jamal**[106] 2054 3-9-1 **76** HarryBentley 1 88
(Saeed bin Suroor) *hld up in 4th: pushed along and nt seemingly gng wl 1/2-way: clsd on outer over 2f out: shkn up to ld over 1f out: r.o wl and clr fnl f* **3/1**[2]

3331 **2** *2 ¾* **Playbill**[9] 5281 3-8-13 **74** RyanMoore 3 80
(Sir Michael Stoute) *trckd ldng pair: pushed along 3f out: trying to cl but hld whn tightened up wl over 1f out: rdn and styd on to take 2nd ins fnl f* **9/4**[1]

1221 **3** *2 ½* **Sarangoo**[18] 4909 5-9-9 **78** RichardHughes 2 79
(Malcolm Saunders) *led 1f: trckd ldr: chal and upsides fr 1/2-way to over 1f out: fdd* **5/1**[3]

1125 **4** *nk* **Saucy Minx (IRE)**[19] 4878 3-9-7 **82** (b) PatDobbs 4 82
(Amanda Perrett) *led after 1f: jnd 1/2-way: drvn and hdd over 1f out: fdd* **9/4**[1]

1100 **5** *8* **Hill Of Dreams (IRE)**[12] 5124 4-9-6 **75**.........................(b) JimCrowley 5 57
(Dean Ivory) *hld up in last: shkn up wl over 2f out: no prog and btn over 1f out: eased* **16/1**

1m 41.58s (-3.12) **Going Correction** -0.30s/f (Firm)
WFA 3 from 4yo+ 6lb **5** Ran SP% **109.1**
Speed ratings (Par 102): **103,100,97,97,89**
CSF £9.93 TOTE £4.10: £2.40, £1.40; EX 9.30 Trifecta £34.00 Pool: £1,205.02 - 26.53 winning tickets..
Owner Godolphin **Bred** Darley **Trained** Newmarket, Suffolk

FOCUS
A fair fillies' handicap rated through the solid runner-up.
T/Plt: £239.00 to a £1 stake. Pool: £92,037.51 - 281.10 winning tickets. T/Qpdt: £52.60 to a £1 stake. Pool: £5,999.30 - 84.32 winning tickets. JN

[5350] WOLVERHAMPTON (A.W) (L-H)
Monday, August 19

OFFICIAL GOING: Standard
Wind: Light half-behind Weather: Overcast early giving way to sunny periods

5590 LIKE US ON FACEBOOK WOLVERHAMPTON RACECOURSE NOVICE STKS 5f 20y(P)
5:50 (5:50) (Class 5) 2-Y-O **£3,234** (£962; £481; £240) **Stalls** Low

Form RPR
21 **1** **Strategical (USA)**[11] 5199 2-9-5 85.........................MickaelBarzalona 3 90
(Charlie Appleby) *sn trcking ldr: led 1/2-way: pushed clr fr over 1f out: easily* **1/20**[1]
4 **2** *11* **Dynamo Walt (IRE)**[10] 5228 2-9-0 0.........................MartinDwyer 5 43
(Derek Shaw) *chsd ldrs: shkn up to go 2nd 1f out: no ch w wnr* **100/1**
63 **3** *nk* **Rebel Code (USA)**[10] 5236 2-9-0 0.........................DaleSwift 4 42
(James Given) *sn pushed along to ld: rdn and hdd 1/2-way: outpcd fr over 1f out* **14/1**[2]
60 **4** *3 3/4* **Sing Out Sister**[28] 4589 2-8-9 0.........................MartinHarley 2 24
(Mick Channon) *hld up: rdn 1/2-way: a in rr* **40/1**[3]
5 *1 1/4* **Royal Bushida** 2-9-0 0.........................PatrickMathers 1 24
(Derek Shaw) *sn pushed along and a in rr* **100/1**

1m 1.21s (-1.09) **Going Correction** -0.175s/f (Stan) **5** Ran SP% **106.3**
Speed ratings (Par 94): **101,83,82,76,74**
CSF £14.45 TOTE £1.10: £1.02, £11.10; EX 7.30 Trifecta £12.30 Pool: £1,871.81 - 113.38 winning tickets..
Owner Godolphin **Bred** Daniel J Burke **Trained** Newmarket, Suffolk

FOCUS
A straightforward task for the long odds-on winner, who was value for a bit extra.

5591 BOOK HOSPITALITY AT WOLVERHAMPTON RACECOURSE CLAIMING STKS 5f 216y(P)
6:20 (6:20) (Class 6) 2-Y-O **£1,940** (£577; £288; £144) **Stalls** Low

Form RPR
0246 **1** **Limegrove**[7] 5351 2-7-12 67.........................NoelGarbutt(7) 8 62
(David Evans) *s.i.s: outpcd: hdwy over 2f out: rdn to ld ins fnl f: r.o* **10/1**
2151 **2** *1 1/4* **Lady Captain (IRE)**[9] 5289 2-8-11 62.........................NeilCallan 9 64
(Kevin Ryan) *chsd ldrs: rdn over 1f out: ev ch ins fnl f: styd on same pce* **7/1**
0542 **3** *1 1/2* **Outback Lover (IRE)**[18] 4910 2-8-4 67.........................(b) JoeyHaynes(7) 4 59
(J S Moore) *sn led: rdn over 1f out: hdd and unable qck ins fnl f* **11/2**[3]
3312 **4** *1 1/4* **Black Treacle (IRE)**[7] 5351 2-9-4 69.........................(p) LukeMorris 6 62
(Keith Dalgleish) *chsd ldrs: rdn 1/2-way: nt clr run over 1f out: styd on same pce ins fnl f* **2/1**[1]
5003 **5** *1 3/4* **Marilyn Marquessa**[7] 5351 2-8-1 62.........................(b) CathyGannon 3 40
(Jo Hughes) *chsd ldr: rdn over 2f out: hung lft over 1f out: no ex ins fnl f* **15/2**
5332 **6** *3 3/4* **Sleepy Joe (IRE)**[10] 5243 2-9-6 64.........................MartinHarley 5 47
(Mick Channon) *chsd ldrs: pushed along over 2f out: rdn over 1f out: wknd ins fnl f* **7/2**[2]
664 **7** *4 1/2* **Danetimeranger (IRE)**[7] 5351 2-9-1 0.........................DavidProbert 7 27
(Ronald Harris) *sn pushed along in rr: rdn and wknd over 1f out* **40/1**
8 *2 3/4* **Mrs Sands** 2-8-7 0.........................LiamJones 2 10
(J S Moore) *s.s: outpcd* **16/1**
00 **9** *1/2* **Phoenix Angel**[41] 4142 2-9-2 0.........................MartinDwyer 1 18
(Derek Shaw) *s.i.s: outpcd* **80/1**

1m 14.96s (-0.04) **Going Correction** -0.175s/f (Stan) **9** Ran SP% **113.9**
Speed ratings (Par 92): **93,91,89,87,85 80,74,70,70**
Tote Swingers 1&2 £7.60, 2&3 £4.00, 1&3 £8.50 CSF £76.72 TOTE £11.90: £2.30, £1.40, £1.20; EX 73.50 Trifecta £714.20 Part won. Pool: £952.37 - 0.54 winning tickets..
Owner J E Abbey **Bred** Mark Windsor **Trained** Pandy, Monmouths

FOCUS
A strong gallop in this nursery and most of these were flat to the boards by the two-pole. The winner was still below her early-season form.

5592 FOLLOW US ON TWITTER @WOLVESRACES H'CAP 1m 5f 194y(P)
6:50 (6:51) (Class 6) (0-60,60) 3-Y-O+ **£2,102** (£625; £312; £156) **Stalls** Low

Form RPR
/551 **1** **Lochiel**[12] 5137 9-9-13 **59**.........................NeilCallan 9 64
(Ian Semple) *trckd ldrs: shkn up to ld over 1f out: rdn out* **7/4**[1]
6354 **2** *nk* **Uncle Bernie (IRE)**[17] 4939 3-8-11 **55**.........................ShaneKelly 1 60
(Andrew Hollinshead) *a.p: racd keenly: nt clr run over 2f out: rdn ins fnl f: r.o wl: nt quite rch wnr* **3/1**[2]
00/0 **3** *1 3/4* **Sure Fire (GER)**[13] 5093 8-8-11 **46** oh1.........................DeclanBates(3) 3 49
(David Evans) *chsd ldr tl led over 1f out: rdn and hdd over 1f out: styd on same pce ins fnl f* **40/1**
35-6 **4** *3* **Eightfold**[78] 1948 4-10-0 **60**.........................(t) ConorO'Farrell 5 58
(Seamus Durack) *hld up: rdn over 1f out: r.o ins fnl f: nvr nrr* **10/1**
0630 **5** *1 1/4* **Souter Point (USA)**[4] 5420 7-9-1 **52**.........................ConnorBeasley(5) 7 49
(William Kinsey) *hld up: hdwy over 2f out: rdn over 1f out: styd on same pce* **13/2**[3]
0000 **6** *3/4* **Dubara Reef (IRE)**[14] 5048 6-9-0 **46**.........................(p) LukeMorris 2 42
(Paul Green) *led at stdy pce tl qcknd 5f out: pushed along over 3f out: hdd over 2f out: wknd ins fnl f* **20/1**
000 **7** *2* **A Good Year (IRE)**[16] 4978 3-8-5 **52**.........................RyanClark(3) 6 45
(J W Hills) *hld up: hdwy on outer over 2f out: sn rdn: wknd fnl f* **12/1**
00 **8** *hd* **Rajeh (IRE)**[181] 714 10-8-11 **48**.........................SladeO'Hara(5) 8 40
(Peter Grayson) *hld up: rdn over 1f out: n.d* **20/1**
5645 **9** *10* **Echo Of Footsteps**[12] 5143 4-9-2 **51**.........................WilliamTwiston-Davies(3) 4 45
(Michael Herrington) *chsd ldrs: nt clr run over 2f out: sn rdn: wknd fnl f: fin lame* **9/1**

3m 10.18s (4.18) **Going Correction** -0.175s/f (Stan)
WFA 3 from 4yo+ 12lb **9** Ran SP% **113.4**
Speed ratings (Par 101): **81,80,79,78,77 76,75,75,70**
Tote Swingers 1&2 £1.40, 2&3 £17.90, 1&3 £15.20 CSF £6.50 CT £140.63 TOTE £2.30: £1.30, £1.90, £11.80; EX 7.50 Trifecta £195.70 Pool: £993.89 - 3.80 winning tickets..
Owner Oatridge Ltd **Bred** D W Barker **Trained** Carluke, S Lanarks

FOCUS
An uncompetitive handicap which was run at a dawdle and turned into a sprint from the home turn. All in all, not great form even for this grade. The winner is rated in line with his maiden form.

5593 THE BLACK COUNTRY'S ONLY RACECOURSE MAIDEN AUCTION FILLIES' STKS 5f 216y(P)
7:20 (7:21) (Class 5) 2-Y-O **£2,587** (£770; £384; £192) **Stalls** Low

Form RPR
03 **1** **Pyjama Day**[11] 5199 2-8-7 0.........................(b) MartinDwyer 8 72
(Hugo Palmer) *hld up: hdwy to join ldr over 3f out: led over 1f out: rdn out* **7/1**[3]
02 **2** *1* **Nimble Kimble**[19] 4880 2-8-7 0.........................LukeMorris 10 69
(James Eustace) *chsd ldrs: pushed along 1/2-way: rdn over 1f out: r.o* **4/1**[2]
00 **3** *1 1/4* **Sheacheval (IRE)**[50] 3857 2-8-7 0.........................LiamJones 2 65+
(J S Moore) *hld up: pushed along 1/2-way: hdwy u.p over 1f out: edgd rt towards fin: r.o* **14/1**
2 **4** *nk* **Amadaffair**[7] 5350 2-8-4 0.........................KieranO'Neill 6 61
(Tom Dascombe) *chsd ldrs: pushed along over 2f out: rdn over 1f out: r.o* **4/1**[2]
43 **5** *hd* **Alfie Lunete (IRE)**[13] 5090 2-7-11 0.........................JoeyHaynes(7) 5 60
(J S Moore) *chsd ldrs: rdn over 1f out: r.o* **7/2**[1]
2 **6** *2 1/4* **Flashy Queen (IRE)**[13] 5090 2-8-13 0.........................LiamKeniry 4 62
(Joseph Tuite) *led: rdn and hdd over 1f out: wknd wl ins fnl f* **7/2**[1]
00 **7** *nk* **Syrian Pearl**[16] 4977 2-8-10 0.........................AshleyMorgan(3) 9 61
(Chris Wall) *s.i.s: outpcd: hdwy on outer over 2f out: wknd fnl f* **33/1**
4 **8** *1 1/4* **By Rights**[7] 5350 2-8-4 0.........................JimmyQuinn 1 48
(Tony Carroll) *plld hrd and prom: nt clr run over 2f out: sn rdn: wknd ins fnl f* **11/1**

1m 15.05s (0.05) **Going Correction** -0.175s/f (Stan) **8** Ran SP% **114.9**
Speed ratings (Par 91): **92,90,89,88,88 85,84,83**
Tote Swingers 1&2 £4.80, 2&3 £3.70, 1&3 £15.70 CSF £35.27 TOTE £9.50: £2.80, £2.20, £5.70; EX 52.40 Trifecta £598.00 Pool: £940.37 - 1.17 winning tickets..
Owner Anglia Bloodstock Syndicate III **Bred** Miss Otis Partnership **Trained** Newmarket, Suffolk

FOCUS
Some unexposed and potentially useful fillies on show but the pace was very steady and the bare form is only modest.

5594 BOOK HORIZONS RESTAURANT H'CAP 7f 32y(P)
7:50 (7:51) (Class 6) (0-60,63) 3-Y-O+ **£1,940** (£577; £288; £144) **Stalls** High

Form RPR
0653 **1** **Nordikhab (IRE)**[10] 5232 3-9-2 **58**.........................(p) NeilCallan 1 72
(Kevin Ryan) *mde all: rdn over 1f out: r.o wl* **10/3**[1]
0653 **2** *4 1/2* **Moe's Place (IRE)**[24] 4722 3-8-11 **60**.........................JacobButterfield(7) 5 62
(Kristin Stubbs) *a.p: chsd wnr 3f out: rdn and hung lft over 1f out: styd on same pce fnl f* **7/1**
1502 **3** *2 1/4* **Black Truffle (FR)**[10] 5232 3-9-4 **60**.........................(e) LiamKeniry 7 56+
(Mark Usher) *hld up: hdwy 2f out: rdn: edgd lft and wnt 3rd wl ins fnl f: nt trble ldrs* **8/1**
0165 **4** *3/4* **Loyal N Trusted**[11] 5177 5-9-8 **59**.........................(p) RussKennemore 3 55
(Richard Price) *hld up in tch: pushed along over 2f out: styd on same pce fnl f* **17/2**
5265 **5** *1/2* **Piccolo Mondo**[12] 5135 7-9-6 **60**.........................(p) WilliamTwiston-Davies(3) 4 55
(Philip Hide) *chsd ldrs: rdn over 2f out: wknd ins fnl f* **9/2**[3]
0642 **6** *2 3/4* **Dancing Welcome**[11] 5166 7-9-8 **59**.........................(bt) LukeMorris 6 46
(Milton Bradley) *hld up: drvn along 1/2-way: n.d* **20/1**
5300 **7** *9* **High On The Hog (IRE)**[35] 4357 5-9-5 **56**.........................(p) TomMcLaughlin 12 19
(Mark Brisbourne) *s.i.s: hld up: nvr trbld ldrs* **33/1**
0043 **8** *1 3/4* **Bang Tidy (IRE)**[14] 5072 4-9-7 **58**.........................(t) DaleSwift 8 16
(Brian Ellison) *prom: rdn over 2f out: wknd over 1f out* **4/1**[2]
0404 **9** *1/2* **Marshall Art**[21] 4834 4-8-13 **53**.........................(tp) MarkCoumbe(3) 2 10
(Ken Wingrove) *s.i.s: a in rr* **28/1**
5561 **10** *2 1/4* **Lucy Bee**[7] 5331 3-9-7 **63** 6ex.........................AndrewMullen 10 14
(Keith Dalgleish) *prom: rdn 1/2-way: wknd over 2f out* **12/1**
0000 **11** *6* **Time Medicean**[26] 4635 7-9-6 **57**.........................RobertWinston 9
(Tony Carroll) *chsd ldr tl pushed along 3f out: wknd over 1f out* **25/1**

1m 27.72s (-1.88) **Going Correction** -0.175s/f (Stan)
WFA 3 from 4yo+ 5lb **11** Ran SP% **118.1**
Speed ratings (Par 101): **103,97,95,94,93 90,80,78,77,75 68**
Tote Swingers 1&2 £5.90, 2&3 £5.70, 1&3 £3.90 CSF £25.73 CT £178.15 TOTE £4.60: £2.00, £2.20, £2.70; EX 33.90 Trifecta £359.70 Pool: £637.71 - 1.32 winning tickets..
Owner Hambleton Racing Ltd XXIII **Bred** John Quinn **Trained** Hambleton, N Yorks

FOCUS
Not many got into this. The runner-up looks the best guide to the level.

5595 DOWNLOAD OUR IPHONE APP NURSERY H'CAP 5f 20y(P)
8:20 (8:20) (Class 5) (0-70,67) 2-Y-O **£3,234** (£962; £481; £240) **Stalls** Low

Form RPR
031 **1** **Fine Art Fair (IRE)**[16] 5000 2-9-7 **67**.........................GeorgeBaker 4 72
(Gary Moore) *led 2f: chsd ldr: r.o u.p to ld wl ins fnl f* **5/4**[1]
431 **2** *nk* **Douneedahand**[17] 4937 2-9-2 **62**.........................KieranO'Neill 6 66
(Seamus Mullins) *w ldr tl led 3f out: rdn over 1f out: hdd wl ins fnl f* **14/1**
4303 **3** *1 1/4* **Debt Settler (IRE)**[9] 5276 2-8-11 **57**.........................JimmyQuinn 2 56
(Luke Dace) *chsd ldrs: rdn over 1f out: styd on* **6/1**[3]
3313 **4** *1 1/2* **Captain Ryan**[26] 4639 2-9-4 **67**.........................[1] DeclanBates(3) 1 61
(Peter Makin) *a.p: rdn 1/2-way: styd on* **8/1**
004 **5** *1 1/2* **Little Big Man**[33] 4412 2-8-2 **48**.........................CathyGannon 8 37
(Sylvester Kirk) *trckd ldrs: edgd lft and bmpd over 3f out: rdn over 1f out: styd on same pce* **16/1**
4504 **6** *1 1/4* **Shelley's Choice (IRE)**[30] 4511 2-9-2 **62**.........................RichardKingscote 10 46
(Tom Dascombe) *swtchd lft sn after s: in rr: rdn over 1f out: nvr trbld ldrs* **9/1**
0322 **7** *5* **Anytimeatall (IRE)**[13] 5106 2-9-2 **62**.........................ShaneKelly 5 28
(Alan Bailey) *plld hrd and prom: hmpd over 3f out: rdn and wknd over 1f out* **5/1**[2]

The Form Book Flat, Raceform Ltd, Compton, RG20 6NL.

3354 8 3 1/4 **Loma Mor**[31] 4498 2-9-2 65........................(p) WilliamTwiston-Davies(3) 3 19
(Alan McCabe) *hmpd sn after s: a in rr: rdn and wknd over 1f out* **25/1**
1m 2.38s (0.08) **Going Correction** -0.175s/f (Stan) **8** Ran SP% **112.9**
Speed ratings (Par 94): **92,91,89,87,84 82,74,69**
Tote Swingers 1&2 £4.40, 2&3 £13.60, 1&3 £2.90 CSF £20.55 CT £79.54 TOTE £1.60: £1.10, £2.30, £1.70; EX 17.80 Trifecta £127.40 Pool: £932.60 - 5.48 winning tickets..
Owner R A Green **Bred** Tally-Ho Stud **Trained** Lower Beeding, W Sussex
FOCUS
Again it proved very difficult to make an impact from off the pace and the front two filled those positions throughout. The bare form has an ordinary feel.

5596 WOLVERHAMPTON-RACECOURSE.CO.UK H'CAP 1m 141y(P)
8:50 (8:50) (Class 6) (0-60,60) 3-Y-O+ **£1,940** (£577; £288; £144) **Stalls** Low

Form RPR
0002 1 **Unex Michelangelo (IRE)**[4] 5427 4-9-11 59................ JamesSullivan 7 78
(Michael Easterby) *a.p: chsd ldr 3f out: led 2f out: rdn clr fnl f* **11/10**[1]
0652 2 5 **Tatting**[14] 5073 4-9-5 53.. LukeMorris 2 60
(Chris Dwyer) *a.p: rdn to chse wnr over 1f out: edgd lft fnl f: styd on same pce* **9/2**[2]
0000 3 2 3/4 **Bajan Story**[16] 4996 4-9-9 57.. LiamKeniry 9 58
(Michael Blanshard) *hld up: rdn over 1f out: r.o ins fnl f: wnt 3rd nr fin* **20/1**
625 4 1/2 **Loraine**[40] 4170 3-9-5 60.. FergusSweeney 1 60
(Jamie Osborne) *hld up: hdwy u.p over 1f out: nvr rchd ldrs* **14/1**
400- 5 shd **De Lesseps (USA)**[370] 5185 5-8-11 52........................ VictorSantos(7) 8 51
(James Moffatt) *sn led: rdn and hdd 2f out: wknd ins fnl f* **50/1**
5032 6 nk **Delightful Sleep**[11] 5172 5-9-5 60................................ EoinWalsh(7) 11 59
(David Evans) *hld up: racd keenly: hdwy over 2f out: rdn over 1f out: no ex fnl f* **17/2**
0246 7 1 **Opus Maximus (IRE)**[11] 5179 8-9-2 50..................(p) StephenCraine 13 46
(Jennie Candlish) *dwlt: hld up: styd on fr over 1f out: nvr nrr* **16/1**
5562 8 3/4 **Arabian Flight**[21] 4834 4-9-6 54.. AndrewMullen 6 49
(Michael Appleby) *prom: rdn over 1f out: wknd fnl f* **7/1**[3]
0450 9 3/4 **Kielty's Folly**[10] 5232 9-9-5 53.. KierenFox 5 46
(Brian Baugh) *hld up: racd keenly: rdn over 1f out: n.d* **33/1**
/601 10 1 3/4 **Thewinningmachine**[12] 5127 4-9-7 55........................ CathyGannon 4 44
(Jo Hughes) *chsd ldr over 5f: sn rdn: wknd fnl f* **12/1**
0-00 11 14 **Odd Ball (IRE)**[14] 5072 6-9-0 51..............................(p) MarkCoumbe(3) 10
(Lisa Williamson) *s.i.s: a in rr: rdn over 3f out: sn lost tch* **50/1**
1m 49.1s (-1.40) **Going Correction** -0.175s/f (Stan)
WFA 3 from 4yo+ 7lb **11** Ran SP% **120.7**
Speed ratings (Par 101): **99,94,92,91,91 91,90,89,89,87 75**
Tote Swingers 1&2 £2.40, 2&3 £12.00, 1&3 £9.00 CSF £5.92 CT £66.28 TOTE £2.40: £1.10, £2.00, £7.20; EX 7.40 Trifecta £88.40 Pool: £1,389.22 - 11.77 winning tickets..
Owner Mrs Jean Turpin **Bred** Chenchikova Syndicate **Trained** Sheriff Hutton, N Yorks
■ Stewards' Enquiry : Victor Santos four-day ban: use of whip (2-5 sept)
FOCUS
A modest handicap in which the winner built on his recent effort and the second is rated close to his latest form.
T/Plt: £29.30 to a £1 stake. Pool: £78,116.69 - 1944.79 winning tickets. T/Qpdt: £9.80 to a £1 stake. Pool: £6,257.90 - 468.7 winning tickets. CR

5597 - 5600a (Foreign Racing) - See Raceform Interactive

5419 CLAIREFONTAINE (R-H)
Monday, August 19

OFFICIAL GOING: Turf: soft

5601a PRIX ASSOCIATION CONDUIRE POUR LA VIE (CLAIMER) (4YO+) (TURF) 1m 3f
3:10 (12:00) 4-Y-O+
£6,504 (£2,601; £1,951; £1,300; £325; £325)

RPR
1 **Uphold**[91] 6-9-11 0..(b) MaximeGuyon 5 81
(Gay Kelleway) *trckd ldr: led on inner over 4f out: 2 l clr and qcknd as c stands' side st: drvn clr ent fnl f: sn in control: comf* **48/10**[1]
2 3 **Diyalani (FR)**[80] 5-9-2 0..(b) EddyHardouin 3 67
(W Mongil, Germany) **83/10**
3 1/2 **Schachspieler (GER)**[443] 7-8-11 0............................ ThierryThulliez 11 61
(W Figge, Germany) **15/1**
4 snk **Dynamis (FR)**[333] 5-8-8 0...................................... StephaneLaurent(8) 14 66
(Mlle B Renk, France) **48/1**
5 3/4 **Chock Dee (FR)**[32] 4467 8-9-2 0..............................(p) GregoryBenoist 4 64
(Y Barberot, France) **16/1**
5 dht **Talusstern (GER)**[124] 4-9-6 0....................................(p) BriceRaballand 9 68
(P Sogorb, France) **53/10**[2]
7 6 **Glamour Star (GER)**[15] 5042 4-9-2 0........................ AntoineHamelin 1 54
(Mme P Butel, France) **11/1**
8 2 1/2 **Sisyphe (FR)**[91] 4-8-13 0.. AntoineCoutier(3) 15 49
(P Demercastel, France) **48/1**
9 3/4 **Alpe Doloise (FR)**[93] 9-8-5 0............................ MlleAmelieFoulon(3) 17 40
(J Phelippon, France) **33/1**
10 3/4 **Jigsaw (FR)**[25] 4-8-11 0.. TheoBachelot 8 41
(S Wattel, France) **15/1**
11 nk **Wolverine (FR)**[93] 6-9-2 0..(p) OlivierPeslier 7 46
(H Billot, France) **25/1**
12 nse **Eleven Park (FR)**[18] 4-9-2 0.. IoritzMendizabal 12 46
(N Bertran De Balanda, France) **13/1**
13 1/2 **Roxy De Vindecy (FR)**[104] 8-9-2 0.................................. RonanThomas 10 45
(J Phelippon, France) **12/1**
14 1 1/2 **Got Slick (FR)**[15] 5042 6-9-7 0.. FabriceVeron 13 47
(P Monfort, France) **13/2**[3]
15 3/4 **Gold Save The King (IRE)**[22] 6-9-2 0........................(p) GeraldMosse 2 41
(F Doumen, France) **22/1**
16 1 1/4 **Rouge Carmen (FR)**[111] 4-8-6 0 ow1........................ CesarPasserat(3) 6 32
(D Allard, France) **99/1**
17 1 1/2 **Aerobic (GER)** 4-8-8 0.. CristianDemuro 16 28
(M Schwinn, Germany) **32/1**
2m 18.5s (138.50) **17** Ran SP% **118.0**
WIN (incl. 1 euro stake): 5.80. PLACES: 2.90, 3.20, 4.70. DF: 43.80. SF: 70.20.
Owner Miss Gay Kelleway **Bred** Juddmonte Farms Ltd **Trained** Exning, Suffolk

5215 BRIGHTON (L-H)
Tuesday, August 20

OFFICIAL GOING: Good to firm (firm in places) changing to firm (good to firm in places) after race 5 (4.15)
Wind: light to medium, against Weather: dry and sunny

5602 LOTHBURY PENDIL FINANCIAL SERVICES H'CAP 5f 213y
2:15 (2:15) (Class 6) (0-60,60) 3-Y-O+ **£1,940** (£577; £288; £144) **Stalls** Low

Form RPR
4310 1 **Artful Lady (IRE)**[69] 3223 4-9-5 58.. NeilCallan 1 68+
(George Margarson) *in tch in midfield: effrt on inner 2f out: led 1f out: r.o strly: readily* **7/2**[2]
3010 2 1 3/4 **Idle Curiosity (IRE)**[8] 5349 3-9-4 60........................ WilliamCarson 6 64
(Jim Boyle) *sn led: rdn ent fnl 2f: hdd 1f out: kpt on same pce ins fnl f* **8/1**
-400 3 3/4 **Deliberation (IRE)**[13] 5139 5-8-11 53............................ DarrenEgan(3) 5 55
(John Quinn) *chsd ldr: rdn and effrt 2f out: drvn and unable qck over 1f out: styd on same pce fnl f* **9/4**[1]
2032 4 1/2 **Sally Bruce**[11] 5220 3-8-5 54.................................. JenniferFerguson(7) 2 54
(Edward Creighton) *hld up in tch in last trio: rdn and effrt 2f out: no imp on and wnr and styd on same pce ins fnl f* **12/1**
2440 5 nk **Ridgeway Sapphire**[26] 4659 6-8-0 46....................(p) DanielMuscutt(7) 7 45
(Mark Usher) *hld up in tch in last pair: rdn and effrt over 2f out: swtchd rt 1f out: kpt on steadily ins fnl f: no ch w wnr* **5/1**
400 6 1/2 **Trending (IRE)**[35] 4377 4-9-3 56..(b) MartinLane 3 54
(Jeremy Gask) *dwlt: sn in midfield and t.k.h: rdn and no imp 2f out: no threat to wnr and styd on same pce fnl f* **9/2**[3]
-065 7 7 **Elounta**[26] 4654 3-8-4 46 oh1.. LukeMorris 8 21
(John Best) *taken down early: chsd ldrs: rdn over 2f out: wknd over 1f out: wl btn and eased wl ins fnl f* **25/1**
6-06 8 6 **Birdie King**[11] 5220 3-9-3 59.. PaoloSirigu 9 15
(John Best) *a in rr: rdn 1/2-way: wknd 2f out: wl bhd fnl f* **20/1**
1m 10.38s (0.18) **Going Correction** -0.15s/f (Firm)
WFA 3 from 4yo+ 3lb **8** Ran SP% **115.3**
Speed ratings (Par 101): **97,94,93,93,92 91,82,74**
Tote Swingers: 1&2 £4.50, 1&3 £2.70, 2&3 £5.40 CSF £31.65 CT £76.26 TOTE £4.20: £1.20, £2.30, £1.60; EX 20.00 Trifecta £89.30 Pool: £2,544.45 - 21.35 winning units..
Owner Graham Lodge Partnership **Bred** Michael Begley **Trained** Newmarket, Suffolk
FOCUS
Rail at inner configuration and all distances as advertised.A modest sprint handicap. The winner was value for a shade extra.

5603 EBF STALLIONS / JOHN HEAL 70TH BIRTHDAY CELEBRATION MEDIAN AUCTION MAIDEN STKS 6f 209y
2:45 (2:45) (Class 5) 2-Y-O **£2,911** (£866; £432; £216) **Stalls** Low

Form RPR
6 1 **Lady Stella**[20] 4880 2-9-0 0.. LukeMorris 3 72+
(Rae Guest) *racd keenly: sn led: rdn and readily asserted over 1f out: in command and r.o wl fnl f: comf* **10/3**[2]
225 2 3 1/4 **Secret Kode (IRE)**[20] 4880 2-9-0 74................................ KierenFallon 5 63
(Brendan Powell) *chsd ldrs: rdn and effrt to chse wnr over 2f out: drvn and outpcd over 1f out: wl hld but kpt on to hold 2nd fnl f* **4/9**[1]
00 3 1 1/4 **Acquaint (IRE)**[29] 4589 2-9-0 0.. PatDobbs 2 60+
(Richard Hannon) *in tch in last pair: rdn 3f out: n.m.r ent fnl 2f: no threat to wnr and kpt on same pce ins fnl f* **12/1**[3]
4 3/4 **Winter Picnic (IRE)** 2-9-0 0.. MartinLane 4 58
(Tobias B P Coles) *chsd ldr tl over 2f out: outpcd u.p and btn over 1f out: 4th and plugged on same pce ins fnl f* **20/1**
66 5 6 **Speed Society**[67] 3275 2-9-5 0.. WilliamCarson 1 47
(Jim Boyle) *stdd s: hld up in tch in rr: rdn and effrt over 2f out: no prog: wknd 1f out* **33/1**
1m 25.01s (1.91) **Going Correction** -0.15s/f (Firm) **5** Ran SP% **107.7**
Speed ratings (Par 94): **83,79,77,77,70**
CSF £4.99 TOTE £3.80: £1.60, £1.10; EX 5.30 Trifecta £11.30 Pool: £2,327.43 - 153.81 winning units..
Owner Can Artam **Bred** C Artam **Trained** Newmarket, Suffolk
FOCUS
An ordinary maiden. The winner showed improved form but enjoyed a soft lead.

5604 JOHN "JACK" BRODRICK MEMORIAL H'CAP 7f 214y
3:15 (3:15) (Class 6) (0-65,64) 3-Y-O **£1,940** (£577; £288; £144) **Stalls** Low

Form RPR
5322 1 **North Pole**[6] 5386 3-9-6 63..(p) LukeMorris 5 74
(Sir Mark Prescott Bt) *dwlt: sn rcvrd to chse ldng trio: rdn and effrt over 2f out: hrd drvn to chse ldr over 1f out: styd on to chal fnl 100yds: led fnl 50yds: gng away at fin* **2/1**[1]
4251 2 1/2 **Pour La Victoire (IRE)**[12] 5170 3-8-1 51........................ OisinMurphy(7) 3 60
(Tony Carroll) *chsd ldng pair: rdn to ld over 2f out: clr and idling over 1f out: hrd pressed fnl 100yds: hdd and no ex fnl 50yds* **2/1**[1]
5023 3 3 1/2 **Speedfit Boy (IRE)**[11] 5220 3-9-5 62.................................... NeilCallan 8 63
(George Margarson) *in tch in midfield: effrt u.p over 2f out: no threat to ldng pair but kpt on fnl f: wnt 3rd cl home* **17/2**[3]
3513 4 nk **Sovereign Power**[40] 4196 3-9-4 61.. MartinLane 1 61
(Paul Cole) *led: rdn and hdd over 2f out: 3rd and outpcd over 1f out: plugged on same pce fnl f: lost 3rd cl home* **7/1**[2]
5603 5 hd **Thomasina**[12] 5166 3-8-1 47.. DarrenEgan(3) 4 46
(Denis Coakley) *hld up in last pair: rdn and effrt wl over 1f out: no real imp tl styd on ins fnl f: nvr trbld ldrs* **16/1**
2426 6 6 **Club House (IRE)**[10] 5280 3-9-7 64.................................... KierenFox 6 49
(Robert Mills) *stdd s: hld up in tch in rr: rdn and effrt wl over 2f out: no prog: wknd over 1f out* **14/1**
6302 7 2 1/4 **Fair Comment**[12] 5170 3-9-2 59.. LiamKeniry 7 39
(Michael Blanshard) *chsd ldr tl rdn and unable qck over 2f out: wknd over 1f out: wl btn and hung lft 1f out* **10/1**
-000 8 2 **Terpsichore**[51] 3859 3-8-2 45.. FrankieMcDonald 2 20
(Sylvester Kirk) *in tch in midfield: pushed along 5f out: rdn and btn over 2f out: bhd over 1f out* **66/1**
1m 36.11s (0.11) **Going Correction** -0.15s/f (Firm) **8** Ran SP% **112.8**
Speed ratings (Par 98): **93,92,89,88,88 82,80,78**
Tote Swingers: 1&2 £1.50, 1&3 £3.60, 2&3 £3.90 CSF £5.49 CT £24.89 TOTE £3.00: £1.40, £1.10, £2.50; EX 7.30 Trifecta £23.80 Pool: £3,401.15 - 106.78 winning units..
Owner Lady Fairhaven & The Hon C & H Broughton **Bred** Lady Fairhaven **Trained** Newmarket, Suffolk

FOCUS
A modest handicap, but the first two pulled clear and the form has been given a slight chance.

5605 F10 EVENTS H'CAP 1m 1f 209y
3:45 (3:45) (Class 5) (0-70,70) 3-Y-O+ £2,587 (£770; £384; £192) Stalls High

Form RPR
5335 **1** **Jewelled**[12] 5190 7-10-0 **70**..........(v) MartinLane 5 78
(Lady Herries) *in tch in midfield: rdn and effrt to chal 2f out: led over 1f out: drvn and clr ins fnl f: r.o wl* **9/2**[3]

4442 **2** 2 ¼ **Banreenahreenkah (IRE)**[26] 4656 3-9-1 **65**.......... KierenFallon 1 71
(Denis Coakley) *t.k.h: hld up in tch in last pair: hdwy to press ldr whn squeezed for room over 5f out: rdn and effrt over 2f out: wnt 2nd and hung lft jst ins fnl f: one pce after* **2/1**[2]

5305 **3** 3 **Brown Pete (IRE)**[9] 5304 5-9-4 **67**.......... OisinMurphy(7) 4 65
(Violet M Jordan) *t.k.h: hld up in tch in last pair: rdn and effrt wl over 2f out: unable qck over 1f out: 4th and btn 1f out: wnt 3rd ins fnl f* **9/1**

650 **4** 3 **Lexi's Dancer**[15] 5072 3-7-13 **52**..........[1] RyanPowell(3) 6 45
(Ian Williams) *t.k.h: chsd ldr tl rdn to ld 3f out: hdd and no ex over 1f out: 3rd and btn whn hmpd ins fnl f: wknd and eased towards fin* **16/1**

4-13 **5** 1 ¾ **Alzavola**[18] 4939 3-9-1 **65**.......... LukeMorris 3 54
(Sir Mark Prescott Bt) *led: rdn along whn pressed on inner over 5f out: drvn and hdd 3f out: plugging on same pce and btn whn n.m.r ins fnl f: wknd* **15/8**[1]

06-3 **6** 8 **It's A Girl Thing (IRE)**[12] 5171 4-9-7 **63**.......... GeorgeBaker 2 37
(Gary Moore) *chsd ldrs tl dropped to rr over 4f out: rdn and no hdwy over 2f out: wknd over 1f out* **10/1**

2m 3.23s (-0.37) **Going Correction** -0.15s/f (Firm)
WFA 3 from 4yo+ 8lb 6 Ran SP% **111.3**
Speed ratings (Par 103): **95,93,90,88,87 80**
Tote Swingers: 1&2 £2.40, 1&3 £5.70, 2&3 £3.80 CSF £13.70 TOTE £6.60: £3.10, £1.70; EX 16.40 Trifecta £125.80 Pool: £2,760.34 - winning units..
Owner Angmering Park **Bred** Wyck Hall Stud Ltd **Trained** Patching, W Sussex
■ The first winner of the season for Lady Herries.

FOCUS
A fair handicap, but it was a messy race and the winner made her challenge widest of all. She is rated back to form.

5606 ABF THE SOLDIERS' CHARITY H'CAP 1m 3f 196y
4:15 (4:15) (Class 5) (0-70,70) 3-Y-O £2,587 (£770; £384; £192) Stalls High

Form RPR
5511 **1** **Marju's Quest (IRE)**[12] 5204 3-9-7 **70**.......... MartinLane 4 81+
(David Simcock) *stdd s: hld up in last pair: clsd 5f out: wl in tch and gng strly 3f out: led on bit wl over 1f out: sn rdn and qcknd clr: in command fnl f: eased towards fin* **3/1**[2]

3622 **2** 2 ¼ **Mizyen (IRE)**[11] 5218 3-9-5 **68**.......... NeilCallan 5 73
(James Tate) *chsd ldrs: clsd 5f out: rdn and ev ch 2f out: 2nd but outpcd by wnr over 1f out: kpt on same pce u.p fnl f* **3/1**[2]

0510 **3** 1 **Nile Knight**[18] 4950 3-9-2 **70**..........(b) MichaelJMMurphy(5) 2 74
(Marcus Tregoning) *hld up in last pair: clsd 5f out: rdn and chsd ldrs over 2f out: 3rd and keeping on same pce whn swtchd rt ins fnl f* **17/2**

-332 **4** 6 **Runninglikethewind (IRE)**[17] 5203 3-9-2 **65**.......... GeorgeBaker 6 59
(Chris Wall) *chsd ldr tl led 3f out: sn rdn: hdd wl over 1f out: sn btn: wknd ent fnl f* **5/2**[1]

5642 **5** 4 ½ **Knight's Parade (IRE)**[3] 5526 3-9-5 **68**.......... PatDobbs 3 55
(Amanda Perrett) *in tch in midfield: rdn and effrt over 2f out: 5th and btn over 1f out: sn wknd* **6/1**[3]

-052 **6** 43 **Happy Families**[18] 4940 3-9-6 **69**.......... JimCrowley 1
(Heather Main) *led tl rdn and hdd 3f out: sn btn and dropped out: t.o and virtually p.u over 1f out* **10/1**

2m 29.94s (-2.76) **Going Correction** -0.15s/f (Firm) 6 Ran SP% **112.5**
Speed ratings (Par 100): **103,101,100,96,93 65**
Tote Swingers: 1&2 £1.60, 1&3 £5.10, 2&3 £3.90 CSF £12.45 TOTE £3.40: £2.30, £1.20; EX 8.80 Trifecta £77.40 Pool: £2,922.28 - 28.29 winning units..
Owner Favourites Racing **Bred** Derrinstown Stud Ltd **Trained** Newmarket, Suffolk

FOCUS
This looked a competitive handicap on paper, but the winner was in control from some way out. The pace was sound and there's a straightforward feel to the form.

5607 CREATIVEFOODCOURTS.CO.UK H'CAP 6f 209y
4:45 (4:45) (Class 5) (0-70,70) 3-Y-O+ £2,587 (£770; £384; £192) Stalls Low

Form RPR
06U0 **1** **Kamchatka**[10] 5280 3-9-2 **65**..........(bt) LiamKeniry 1 76
(Philip Hide) *mde all: sn clr: rdn and in command over 1f out: rdn out hands and heels fnl f: unchal* **14/1**

3441 **2** 2 ½ **Perfect Mission**[6] 5404 5-9-5 **70**..........(p) DanielMuscutt(7) 4 76
(Andrew Balding) *chsd inner thrght: rdn wl over 1f out: kpt on for clr 2nd but no imp on wnr* **5/2**[2]

-544 **3** 3 ½ **Patavium Prince (IRE)**[11] 5232 10-9-11 **69**.......... KierenFallon 5 66
(Jo Crowley) *racd in midfield: effrt u.p over 2f out: no imp: wnt 3rd 1f out: no threat to wnr* **6/1**[3]

0210 **4** 1 ¾ **Hawk Moth (IRE)**[12] 5177 5-9-3 **61**..........(b) LukeMorris 7 53
(John Spearing) *sn pushed along in rr: n.m.r briefly over 2f out: sn drvn: kpt on same pce fnl and no threat to wnr 2f* **10/1**

3331 **5** hd **Koharu**[13] 5128 3-8-9 **61**..........(t) DeclanBates(3) 2 50
(Peter Makin) *hld up in last pair: rdn and effrt on inner over 2f out: no ch w wnr but battling for 3rd 1f out: wknd fnl 75yds* **9/4**[1]

0030 **6** 2 ¾ **Uprise**[26] 4669 4-9-7 **65**.......... NeilCallan 3 49
(George Margarson) *chsd ldng pair: rdn over 3f out: hrd drvn and no hdwy 2f out: wl btn and lost 3rd 1f out: wknd* **6/1**[3]

0020 **7** 27 **Flavius Victor (IRE)**[31] 4517 4-9-7 **65**..........[1] GeorgeBaker 6
(Patrick Chamings) *hld up in last trio: rdn and no rspnse over 2f out: sn btn: t.o and eased fnl f* **11/1**

1m 21.68s (-1.42) **Going Correction** -0.15s/f (Firm)
WFA 3 from 4yo+ 5lb 7 Ran SP% **112.0**
Speed ratings (Par 103): **102,99,95,93,92 89,58**
Tote Swingers: 1&2 £7.20, 1&3 £11.80, 2&3 £2.90 CSF £47.14 TOTE £23.20: £8.30, £1.60; EX 61.60 Trifecta £397.20 Pool: £3,303.66 - 6.23 winning units..
Owner S P C Woods **Bred** Whitsbury Manor Stud **Trained** Findon, W Sussex

FOCUS
A modest handicap in which the winner got a soft lead. He's rated back towards his best 2yo form.

5608 TRAVEL & TEACH, TEACH EFL AT ISEHOVE.COM H'CAP 5f 59y
5:15 (5:15) (Class 6) (0-65,71) 3-Y-O+ £1,940 (£577; £288; £144) Stalls Low

Form RPR
4001 **1** **Royal Bajan (USA)**[8] 5336 5-10-2 **71** 6ex..........(p) JimCrowley 5 80
(James Given) *taken down early: mde all: hrd pressed and rdn over 1f out: sustained duel w runner-up fnl f: hld on wl: all out* **9/4**[1]

1054 **2** hd **The Strig**[12] 5165 6-9-9 **64**..........(v) J-PGuillambert 1 72
(Stuart Williams) *wl in tch in midfield: effrt to chal on inner over 1f out: sustained duel fnl f: r.o but jst hld* **4/1**[2]

3520 **3** 2 ½ **Volito**[3] 5522 7-9-1 **56**.......... GeorgeBaker 2 55
(Anabel K Murphy) *s.i.s: bhd: hdwy whn nt clr run and swtchd rt 2f out: edging lft over 1f out: styd on to go 3rd fnl 100yds: nvr trbld ldng pair* **4/1**[2]

5243 **4** 2 **Johnny Splash (IRE)**[18] 4943 4-8-4 **52**..........(v) OisinMurphy(7) 3 44
(Roger Teal) *wl in tch in midfield: rdn and chsd ldng pair 2f out: no imp over 1f out: lost 3rd and wknd fnl 100yds* **9/2**[3]

5/54 **5** 11 **Royal Trix**[11] 5220 4-9-1 **61**..........[1] MichaelJMMurphy(5) 4 13
(Marcus Tregoning) *chsd wnr tl over 2f out: sn struggling u.p wknd over 1f out: bhd fnl f* **10/1**

2361 **6** hd **Imaginary Diva**[6] 5408 7-9-2 **60** 6ex.......... RyanPowell(3) 6 12
(George Margarson) *chsd ldrs tl rdn and unable qck over 2f out: wknd over 1f out: sn bhd* **13/2**

1m 2.5s (0.20) **Going Correction** -0.15s/f (Firm) 6 Ran SP% **111.4**
Speed ratings (Par 101): **92,91,87,84,66 66**
Tote Swingers: 1&2 £2.80, 1&3 £3.20, 2&3 £3.30 CSF £11.23 TOTE £3.20: £1.60, £2.40; EX 13.50 Trifecta £39.50 Pool: £1,304.54 - 24.73 winning units..
Owner The Cool Silk Partnership **Bred** West Wind Farm **Trained** Willoughton, Lincs

FOCUS
A modest but competitive handicap which featured a couple of last-time-out winners. Straightforward form.
T/Plt: £22.00 to a £1 stake. Pool: £79,991.19 - 2,644.06 winning tickets. T/Qpdt: £11.50 to a £1 stake. Pool: £4,862.29 - 312.20 winning tickets. SP

5299 LEICESTER (R-H)
Tuesday, August 20

OFFICIAL GOING: Good to firm (good in places)
Wind: Almost nil Weather: Cloudy with sunny spells

5609 WIDMERPOOL MAIDEN AUCTION FILLIES' STKS 5f 2y
5:00 (5:01) (Class 5) 2-Y-O £2,587 (£770; £384; £192) Stalls Centre

Form RPR
062 **1** **Kanz**[12] 5174 2-8-8 75.......... MartinHarley 7 77
(Mick Channon) *trckd ldrs: rdn and edgd rt ins fnl f: r.o to ld nr fin* **9/4**[2]

2 **2** shd **Shilla (IRE)**[9] 5307 2-8-4 0.......... CathyGannon 2 73
(Henry Candy) *trckd ldr: shkn up to ld over 1f out: rdn: edgd lft and hdd nr fin* **11/10**[1]

3 1 ½ **Kuala Queen (IRE)** 2-8-6 0.......... JohnFahy 5 69
(Denis Coakley) *s.i.s: hdwy over 1f out: r.o: n.m.r towards fin* **50/1**

00 **4** 2 **Lucky Surprise**[23] 4808 2-8-1 0.......... RaulDaSilva(3) 8 60
(Gay Kelleway) *sn pushed along in rr: r.o ins fnl f: nvr nrr* **6/1**[3]

020 **5** 1 ¾ **Where The Boys Are (IRE)**[20] 4880 2-8-9 68 ow1.......... GrahamLee 3 59
(Ed McMahon) *led: racd keenly: rdn and hdd over 1f out: wknd ins fnl f* **14/1**

6 1 ½ **Artemis (IRE)** 2-8-4 0.......... AndreaAtzeni 1 48
(Conrad Allen) *s.i.s: hdwy over 3f out: rdn over 1f out: wknd ins fnl f* **33/1**

7 ½ **Mossy Lea** 2-8-4 0.......... BarryMcHugh 6 47
(Richard Fahey) *mid-div: pushed along 1/2-way: outpcd fnl 2f* **12/1**

00 **8** 10 **Biscuiteer**[45] 4073 2-8-4 0..........(e[1]) JamieMackay 4 11
(Scott Dixon) *chsd ldrs: pushed along 1/2-way: rdn: hung rt and wknd over 1f out* **100/1**

9 4 **Miss Lawlass (IRE)** 2-8-4 0.......... JamesSullivan 9
(James Given) *sn outpcd* **50/1**

59.56s (-0.44) **Going Correction** -0.275s/f (Firm) 9 Ran SP% **114.9**
Speed ratings (Par 91): **92,91,89,86,83 81,80,64,57**
Tote Swingers: 1&2 £1.50, 1&3 £11.10, 2&3 £9.60 CSF £4.95 TOTE £2.70: £1.10, £1.10, £10.30; EX 6.80 Trifecta £43.30 Pool: £3,372.40 - 58.32 winning units..
Owner M Al-Qatami & K M Al-Mudhaf **Bred** Broughton Bloodstock **Trained** West Ilsley, Berks

FOCUS
After a dry spell the ground had quickened up and was generally described as very much on the fast side of good. A modest maiden auction 2-y-o fillies' race and the two market leaders fought out the finish. The winner is rated to her mark.

5610 KINOULTON NURSERY H'CAP 5f 218y
5:30 (5:33) (Class 6) (0-65,65) 2-Y-O £1,940 (£577; £288; £144) Stalls Centre

Form RPR
6352 **1** **Dovil's Duel (IRE)**[7] 5371 2-9-2 **60**.......... AndreaAtzeni 16 67
(Rod Millman) *trckd ldrs: shkn up over 1f out: rdn and r.o to ld wl ins fnl f* **9/4**[1]

5564 **2** 1 ½ **Narborough**[19] 4910 2-8-13 **60**.......... CharlesBishop(3) 8 62
(Mick Channon) *hld up: hdwy 1/2-way: rdn to ld over 1f out: hdd and unable qck wl ins fnl f* **20/1**

6545 **3** ½ **Noble Reach**[48] 3942 2-8-2 **53**.......... JordanNason(7) 5 53
(Geoffrey Harker) *trckd ldrs: rdn and ev ch over 1f out: styd on same pce ins fnl f* **33/1**

0541 **4** 1 ¾ **Oxlip**[10] 5276 2-8-10 **57**.......... WilliamTwiston-Davies(3) 7 52
(Richard Hannon) *chsd ldrs: rdn over 2f out: styd on same pce fnl f* **8/1**[3]

056 **5** ½ **Rockie Road (IRE)**[16] 5025 2-8-9 **53**.......... FrannyNorton 9 46
(Paul Green) *hld up: drvn along over 2f out: hdwy over 1f out: styd on same pce ins fnl f* **8/1**[3]

000 **6** 1 ½ **Saffire Song**[17] 5003 2-8-11 **60**.......... RobertTart(5) 11 49
(Alan Bailey) *hld up: rdn over 2f out: styd on ins fnl f: nt trble ldrs* **20/1**

605 **7** nse **Desert Colours**[13] 5145 2-9-5 **63**.......... GrahamLee 6 52
(Kevin Ryan) *led: hdd over 3f out: rdn and ev ch over 1f out: no ex ins fnl f* **8/1**[3]

4000 **8** 1 ¼ **Brockholes Flyer (IRE)**[15] 5066 2-8-11 **55**.......... JackMitchell 1 40
(Brendan Powell) *chsd ldrs: rdn over 2f out: wknd ins fnl f* **100/1**

260 **9** ¾ **Krackerjill (IRE)**[17] 5000 2-8-4 **55**.......... JoeyHaynes(7) 15 37
(Mark Usher) *chsd ldrs: rdn over 2f out: wknd ins fnl f* **14/1**

066 **10** 1 ¼ **Almost Famous (IRE)**[19] 4906 2-9-1 **59**..........(b[1]) FergusSweeney 2 38+
(Jamie Osborne) *s.i.s: hdwy over 4f out: led over 3f out: rdn and hdd over 1f out: wknd ins fnl f* **16/1**

The Form Book Flat, Raceform Ltd, Compton, RG20 6NL.

600 **11** *1 1/4* **Mister Mayday (IRE)**[16] 5033 2-9-7 **65**.......................... PatCosgrave 13 40
(George Baker) *hld up: hdwy over 2f out: sn rdn: eased whn btn ins fnl f* **5/1**[2]

5030 **12** *2* **Chance Of Romance (IRE)**[16] 5034 2-8-11 **60**................ RyanTate(5) 3 29
(Clive Cox) *chsd ldrs: rdn over 2f out: wknd fnl f* **14/1**

4405 **13** *3 3/4* **Faye Belle**[8] 5351 2-7-12 **45**..(v) RaulDaSilva(3) 10
(Derek Shaw) *prom: lost pl over 4f out: sn bhd* **33/1**

560 **14** *5* **Silver Starlet (IRE)**[41] 4164 2-8-5 **52**..........................[1] SimonPearce(3) 4
(Alastair Lidderdale) *sn pushed along in rr: bhd fnl 4f* **50/1**

1m 12.08s (-0.92) **Going Correction** -0.275s/f (Firm) **14** Ran SP% **118.3**
Speed ratings (Par 92): **95,93,92,90,89 87,87,85,84,82 81,78,73,66**
Tote Swingers: 1&2 £4.10, 1&3 £16.00, 2&3 £43.90 CSF £56.94 CT £1227.76 TOTE £3.00: £1.10, £5.50, £13.50; EX 55.00 Trifecta £459.00 Pool: £2,597.89 - 4.24 winning units..
Owner Always Hopeful Partnership **Bred** David Allan **Trained** Kentisbeare, Devon

FOCUS
Only one previous winner and eight 2-y-os making their handicap debuts. Straightforward form but a lack of depth to the race.

5611 SIS LIVE H'CAP 5f 218y
6:00 (6:00) (Class 4) (0-80,79) 3-Y-O **£4,851** (£1,443; £721; £360) **Stalls** Centre

Form RPR

-066 **1** **Joey's Destiny (IRE)**[38] 4283 3-8-11 **72**.................... ThomasBrown(3) 3 83+
(George Baker) *hld up: hdwy over 2f out: rdn to ld over 1f out: edgd lft ins fnl f: r.o* **10/1**[3]

0006 **2** *1 1/2* **Bogsnog (IRE)**[13] 5141 3-9-0 **72**.. TomEaves 4 75
(Kristin Stubbs) *led: rdn and hdd over 1f out: nt clr run ins fnl f: styd on same pce* **25/1**

2154 **3** *1* **Laughing Rock (IRE)**[9] 5300 3-8-5 **63**............................ AndrewMullen 7 63
(Michael Appleby) *chsd ldrs: rdn over 2f out: styd on same pce ins fnl f* **12/1**

-111 **4** *1/2* **Jubilee Dancer**[30] 4558 3-9-4 **76**.. GrahamLee 5 75
(Geoffrey Oldroyd) *awkward leaving stalls: trckd ldr: rdn and ev ch over 1f out: no ex ins fnl f* **9/4**[2]

0021 **5** *2 1/4* **Welsh Moonlight**[13] 5156 3-8-7 **65**................................. AndreaAtzeni 6 57
(Stuart Williams) *chsd ldrs: rdn over 2f out: no ex fnl f* **20/1**

-222 **6** *nk* **Gravitational (IRE)**[9] 5303 3-9-7 **79**................................ SebSanders 1 70
(Chris Wall) *hld up: rdn over 2f out: nvr trbld ldrs* **10/11**[1]

1m 10.22s (-2.78) **Going Correction** -0.275s/f (Firm) **6** Ran SP% **108.5**
Speed ratings (Par 102): **107,105,103,103,100 99**
Tote Swingers: 1&2 £19.60, 1&3 £4.70, 2&3 £12.60 CSF £167.65 CT £2697.67 TOTE £14.10: £7.30, £13.20; EX 140.70 Trifecta £610.30 Pool: £2,459.10 - 3.02 winning units..
Owner Delancey **Bred** Brian Wallace **Trained** Manton, Wilts
■ Stewards' Enquiry : Thomas Brown caution: careless riding.

FOCUS
A competitive 3-y-o sprint but a surprise outcome. The winner was value for extra and the form could be rated up to 3lb higher.

5612 SHELDUCK H'CAP 1m 3f 183y
6:30 (6:30) (Class 5) (0-75,75) 3-Y-O+ **£2,587** (£770; £384; £192) **Stalls** Low

Form RPR

-063 **1** **Don Padeja**[17] 5001 3-8-11 **68**.. AndreaAtzeni 5 79+
(Luca Cumani) *hld up: hdwy over 2f out: led over 1f out: shkn up and r.o wl* **11/10**[1]

6535 **2** *2 1/2* **Prophesy (IRE)**[23] 4804 4-10-0 **75**.............................. GrahamGibbons 7 80
(Declan Carroll) *chsd ldrs: led over 2f out: rdn and hdd over 1f out: edgd rt and styd on same pce ins fnl f* **5/1**[3]

600- **3** *1/2* **Hot Spice**[63] 6933 5-9-10 **71**.. JamesSullivan 9 75
(Michael Easterby) *hld up: racd keenly: pushed along over 5f out: hdwy over 2f out: shkn up over 1f out: styd on same pce ins fnl f* **20/1**

-405 **4** *3 1/4* **Forget Me Not Lane (IRE)**[46] 4020 4-10-0 **75**.................. GrahamLee 1 74
(Kevin Ryan) *led: hdd over 8f out: chsd ldr tl led again over 3f out: rdn and hdd over 2f out: no ex fnl f* **9/2**[2]

2433 **5** *hd* **Ivanhoe**[20] 4882 3-8-10 **67**... FergusSweeney 3 66
(Michael Blanshard) *prom: pushed along over 3f out: no ex fnl f* **11/2**

065 **6** *14* **Young Jay**[14] 5110 3-8-8 **65**.. JoeFanning 11 41
(Mark Johnston) *chsd ldrs: rdn over 2f out: wknd over 1f out* **12/1**

3450 **7** *7* **Flying Applause**[19] 4929 8-9-2 **66**...........................(b) MarkCoumbe(3) 8 31
(Roy Bowring) *hld up: hdwy to ld over 8f out: clr over 6f out: rdn and hdd over 3f out: wknd over 2f out* **50/1**

2m 29.96s (-3.94) **Going Correction** -0.275s/f (Firm)
WFA 3 from 4yo+ 10lb **7** Ran SP% **112.3**
Speed ratings (Par 103): **102,100,100,97,97 88,83**
Tote Swingers: 1&2 £1.60, 1&3 £6.00, 2&3 £12.60 CSF £6.70 CT £65.11 TOTE £1.90: £1.40, £2.90; EX 7.50 Trifecta £81.80 Pool: £1,905.44 - 17.46 winning units..
Owner Bartisan Racing Ltd **Bred** Tsega Mares Sarl **Trained** Newmarket, Suffolk

FOCUS
They went a sound gallop here and the unexposed, lightly raced winner will go on to better things. He was value for extra, with the next two helping with the level.

5613 WYSALL H'CAP 1m 60y
7:00 (7:00) (Class 4) (0-85,85) 3-Y-O+ **£4,851** (£1,443; £721; £360) **Stalls** Low

Form RPR

2345 **1** **Albaqaa**[10] 5285 8-9-6 **82**.. RobertTart(5) 6 90
(P J O'Gorman) *a.p: chsd ldr 5f out: rdn to ld over 1f out: r.o* **4/1**[2]

4403 **2** *1 1/4* **Yojimbo (IRE)**[9] 5310 5-9-1 **75**.............................(v) CharlesBishop(3) 5 81
(Mick Channon) *chsd ldr 3f: remained handy: nt clr run over 1f out: swtchd lft ins fnl f: r.o to go 2nd nr fin: nt rch wnr* **4/1**[2]

0-00 **3** *1/2* **Arabian Star (IRE)**[10] 5285 5-9-8 **82**............ WilliamTwiston-Davies(3) 2 86
(Alan McCabe) *led: rdn and hdd over 1f out: styd on same pce ins fnl f* **25/1**

6301 **4** *1/2* **Goldstorm**[47] 3983 5-9-11 **82**.. GrahamLee 7 86
(Brian Baugh) *s.i.s: hld up: pushed along over 2f out: hdwy and nt clr run fr over 1f out tl wl ins fnl f: r.o: nt rch ldrs* **5/2**[1]

1000 **5** *1 3/4* **Copperwood**[17] 5014 8-9-6 **77**... JoeFanning 4 76
(Mark Johnston) *chsd ldrs: rdn over 1f out: styd on same pce ins fnl f* **6/1**[3]

5300 **6** *1/2* **Al Muheer (IRE)**[10] 5268 8-10-0 **85**.............................(b) JamesSullivan 8 83
(Ruth Carr) *hld up: rdn and hung rt 1f out: nvr on terms* **16/1**

3100 **7** *nk* **Ferdy (IRE)**[12] 5183 4-8-10 **70**.. RaulDaSilva(3) 3 67
(Paul Green) *hld up in tch: racd keenly: rdn over 2f out: styd on same pce fnl f* **20/1**

0-0 **8** *1* **Alakhan (IRE)**[122] 1673 7-9-7 **78**................................... FrannyNorton 9 73
(Ian Williams) *hld up: racd keenly: hdwy over 3f out: rdn over 2f out: no ex fnl f* **8/1**

2045 **9** *16* **The Lock Master (IRE)**[2] 5559 6-9-6 **82**..................... TobyAtkinson(5) 1 40+
(Michael Appleby) *s.i.s: hmpd sn after s and nvr really travelling: rdn 1/2-way: wknd wl over 2f out* **16/1**

1m 42.52s (-2.58) **Going Correction** -0.275s/f (Firm) **9** Ran SP% **114.3**
Speed ratings (Par 105): **101,99,99,98,97 96,96,95,79**
Tote Swingers: 1&2 £3.40, 1&3 £22.40, 2&3 £26.40 CSF £20.18 CT £351.09 TOTE £4.60: £1.80, £2.30, £9.10; EX 24.40 Trifecta £457.10 Pool: £1,616.40 - 2.65 winning units..
Owner Racing To The Max **Bred** C Eddington And Partners **Trained** Newmarket, Suffolk

FOCUS
A fair handicap, rated around the winner's more recent form.

5614 GILMORTON H'CAP 7f 9y
7:30 (7:35) (Class 6) (0-65,65) 3-Y-O+ **£2,264** (£505; £505; £168) **Stalls** Centre

Form RPR

6050 **1** **Imperator Augustus (IRE)**[10] 5273 5-9-6 **64**............. JackGarritty(7) 16 73+
(Patrick Holmes) *hld up: hdwy over 2f out: led over 1f out: edgd rt: r.o* **8/1**

5306 **2** *2* **Minty Jones**[53] 3754 4-8-4 **46** oh1..................................(v) RobertTart(5) 9 50
(Michael Mullineaux) *led: racd freely: rdn and hdd over 1f out: styd on same pce ins fnl f* **66/1**

0432 **2** *dht* **Lil Sophella (IRE)**[8] 5331 4-8-12 **49**......................... RussKennemore 14 53
(Patrick Holmes) *hld up: hdwy u.p over 1f out: edgd rt: r.o* **5/1**[2]

2432 **4** *3 3/4* **Alluring Star**[13] 5139 5-9-13 **64**...................................... JamesSullivan 6 58
(Michael Easterby) *a.p: chsd ldr 1/2-way: rdn over 1f out: no ex ins fnl f* **6/1**[3]

0422 **5** *1/2* **Master Of Song**[12] 5198 6-9-6 **57**...................................(p) JimmyQuinn 5 50
(Roy Bowring) *s.i.s: sn pushed along in rr: hdwy u.p over 1f out: styd on same pce ins fnl f* **4/1**[1]

3224 **6** *2 3/4* **Amethyst Dawn (IRE)**[8] 5353 7-9-11 **65**..(t) WilliamTwiston-Davies(3) 12 51
(Alan McCabe) *hld up: drvn along 1/2-way: r.o ins fnl f: nvr nrr* **8/1**

4534 **7** *1/2* **Shamrocked (IRE)**[9] 5301 4-9-11 **62**...............................(v[1]) TomEaves 7 47
(Ollie Pears) *prom: racd keenly: rdn over 2f out: wknd fnl f* **12/1**

0106 **8** *1* **Kingscombe (USA)**[66] 3326 4-9-0 **51**............................ RobertHavlin 11 33
(Linda Jewell) *prom: rdn over 2f out: wknd over 1f out* **33/1**

2614 **9** *3/4* **Boy The Bell**[20] 4893 6-8-11 **55**..........................(be) JacobButterfield(7) 3 35
(Ollie Pears) *sn pushed along to chse ldrs: rdn over 2f out: wknd over 1f out* **7/1**

455 **10** *1 1/4* **Cheers Big Ears (IRE)**[14] 5092 7-8-6 **46**.................... RaulDaSilva(3) 15 23
(Richard Price) *mid-div: drvn along over 2f out: sn wknd* **16/1**

-043 **11** *hd* **Chez Vrony**[90] 2575 7-8-9 **46** oh1...................................(p) JoeFanning 1 22
(Dave Morris) *hld up: rdn over 2f out: n.d* **20/1**

600 **12** *2 1/2* **Lady Cricketer**[7] 5373 4-8-10 **47**................................(b) CathyGannon 10 17
(Michael Squance) *hld up: stmbld 4f out: rdn over 2f out: sn wknd* **100/1**

0400 **13** *3 1/4* **Whitstable Native**[6] 5404 5-9-5 **56**................................. GrahamLee 2 17
(Joseph Tuite) *hld up: rdn 1/2-way: wknd 2f out* **25/1**

0-00 **14** *6* **Branston Jubilee**[110] 1961 3-8-4 **46** oh1......................... FrannyNorton 8
(Geoffrey Harker) *hld up: racd keenly: rdn over 2f out: sn wknd: eased over 1f out* **50/1**

0060 **15** *23* **Mr Snooks**[54] 3739 3-8-6 **48** ow1.................................(p) AdrianNicholls 4
(David Nicholls) *trckd ldrs: rdn over 2f out: wknd wl over 1f out: eased* **33/1**

00-0 **16** *9* **Toothache**[104] 2170 5-8-10 **47** oh1 ow1.......................... MickyFenton 13
(Garry Woodward) *s.i.s: sn outpcd* **66/1**

1m 23.87s (-2.33) **Going Correction** -0.275s/f (Firm)
WFA 3 from 4yo+ 5lb **16** Ran SP% **119.7**
Speed ratings (Par 101): **102,99,99,95,94 91,91,90,89,87 87,84,80,74,47 37**PL: Lil Sophella £1.50, Minty Jones £8.30, Alluring Star £1.70. Exacta: Imperator Augustus,LS £33.80, IA,MJ £330.50 CSF: IA,LS £21.84, IA,MJ £237.66 Tricast: IA,LS,MJ £1,289.11, IA,MJ,LS £1,499.18. Tote Swingers: 1&LS £12.60, 1&MJ £157.80, 2&2 £51.20. CSF £0.027 CT £Owner TOTE £Foulrice Park Racing Limited: £Bred, £Western Bloodstock, £Trained, £Middleham, N Yorks .

FOCUS
A modest 7f handicap and not many entered the argument. The winner travelled well and returned to form.

5615 LOWESBY H'CAP 1m 1f 218y
8:00 (8:01) (Class 6) (0-60,64) 3-Y-O+ **£1,940** (£577; £288; £144) **Stalls** Low

Form RPR

40-4 **1** **Ana Shababiya (IRE)**[15] 5072 3-8-7 **52** ow2........... ThomasBrown(3) 13 60
(Ismail Mohammed) *racd keenly: led over 8f out: rdn over 1f out: edgd lft ins fnl f: styd on gamely* **10/1**[3]

4U00 **2** *1/2* **Voice From Above (IRE)**[3] 5521 4-9-12 **60**............ RussKennemore 10 67
(Patrick Holmes) *hld up: hdwy over 2f out: rdn over 1f out: r.o* **25/1**

6342 **3** *1* **Sixties Queen**[4] 5497 3-8-6 **53**.................................... RobertTart(5) 8 58
(Alan Bailey) *trckd ldrs: racd keenly: rdn and ev ch ins fnl f: unable qck towards fin* **11/4**[1]

-043 **4** *3/4* **My Manekineko**[9] 5312 4-9-7 **55**............................... DougieCostello 7 59
(J R Jenkins) *a.p: racd keenly: rdn and ev ch fr over 1f out tl no ex wl ins fnl f* **12/1**

6443 **5** *3/4* **Catchanova (IRE)**[11] 5234 6-9-9 **57**.................................... JohnFahy 6 59
(Eve Johnson Houghton) *mid-div: hdwy over 2f out: rdn over 1f out: styd on u.p* **12/1**

0522 **6** *nk* **Petersboden**[13] 5127 4-8-13 **47**................................ FergusSweeney 12 49
(Michael Blanshard) *mid-div: hdwy over 3f out: rdn over 1f out: styd on same pce ins fnl f* **14/1**

0001 **7** *1* **Exclusive Waters (IRE)**[3] 5528 3-9-5 **64** 6ex................ DarrenEgan(3) 3 64+
(William Knight) *hld up: plld hrd: rdn over 1f out: r.o ins fnl f: nvr nrr* **11/4**[1]

0050 **8** *4 1/2* **Mr Mallo**[17] 4996 4-8-12 **46** oh1.. AndreaAtzeni 11 37
(John Stimpson) *hld up: rdn over 3f out: nvr on terms* **50/1**

1630 **9** *3/4* **Smirfy's Silver**[12] 5179 9-8-11 **50**................................. SladeO'Hara(5) 9 40+
(Michael Mullineaux) *s.i.s: hdwy over 6f out: rdn over 3f out: wknd fnl f* **33/1**

1101 **10** *hd* **Sofias Number One (USA)**[12] 5195 5-9-9 **60**......(b) MarkCoumbe(3) 16 49
(Roy Bowring) *in rr: bhd 6f out: rdn over 2f out: n.d* **7/1**[2]

0150 **11** *3* **Double Star**[41] 4170 3-8-10 **52**.. CathyGannon 2 36
(Jonathan Portman) *chsd ldrs: rdn over 2f out: wknd fnl f* **20/1**

0034 **12** *9* **Polish Rider**[10] 5275 3-8-4 **46** oh1................................. KieranO'Neill 1 13
(Richard Hannon) *led: hdd over 8f out: chsd ldrs: rdn over 2f out: wknd over 1f out* **12/1**

00 **13** *2* **Refuse Colette (IRE)**[15] 5073 4-8-12 **46** oh1...........(v[1]) FrannyNorton 15 9
(Paul Green) *s.i.s: hld up: a in rr: wknd over 2f out* **50/1**

2m 6.97s (-0.93) **Going Correction** -0.275s/f (Firm)
WFA 3 from 4yo+ 8lb **13** Ran SP% **120.1**
Speed ratings (Par 101): **92,91,90,89 89,88,84,84,84 81,74,73**
Tote Swingers 1&2 £49.90, 2&3 £29.80, 1&3 £6.50 CSF £245.64 CT £878.58 TOTE £9.00: £3.00, £6.10, £1.70; EX 212.70 Trifecta £200.00 Pool: £819.93 - 3.07 winning units..
Owner Ahmad Abdulla Al Shaikh **Bred** Thomas Hassett **Trained** Newmarket, Suffolk

FOCUS
A low-grade handicap and all-the-way winner off a steady pace. Straightforward form.

T/Jkpt: Not won. T/Plt: £655.80 to a £1 stake. Pool: £90,430.86 - 100.65 winning tickets. T/Qpdt: £223.60 to a £1 stake. Pool: £6,801.54 - 22.50 winning tickets. CR

[5405]YARMOUTH (L-H)

Tuesday, August 20

OFFICIAL GOING: Good to firm (7.5)
Wind: almost nil Weather: sunny and bright; 22 degrees

5616 GREENE KING FESTIVAL 17TH-19TH SEPTEMBER MEDIAN AUCTION MAIDEN STKS 6f 3y
2:00 (2:02) (Class 6) 3-Y-O **£1,940** (£577; £288; £144) **Stalls** Centre

Form RPR
4234 **1** **Honeymoon Express (IRE)**[12] 5200 3-8-7 65........(p) ShelleyBirkett[(7)] 1 66
(Julia Feilden) *broke smartly and mde all: rdn over 2f out: edgd rt over 1f out: styd on gamely* **10/1**[3]
6323 **2** ¾ **Rock Up (IRE)**[32] 4499 3-9-5 66........(b) RyanMoore 3 69
(David Elsworth) *pressed wnr: rdn and impeded over 1f out: no imp fnl 100yds* **3/1**[2]
3355 **3** hd **Superboot (IRE)**[17] 4981 3-9-5 92........ShaneKelly 4 68
(Michael Wigham) *stdd in last: drvn and effrt over 1f out: fnd nthing ins fnl f and nvr looked like winning: lost duel for 2nd nr fin: fin lame* **1/3**[1]
004 **4** 8 **One In A Thousand (IRE)**[10] 5277 3-9-0 51........(p) SaleemGolam 2 37
(Chris Dwyer) *chsd ldrs: drvn wl over 2f out: no rspnse and sn btn* **66/1**
66 **5** 1¾ **Princess Bounty**[10] 5277 3-8-9 0........NathanAlison[(5)] 5 32
(Phil McEntee) *plld hrd in rr: drvn 1/2-way: btn and hanging bdly lft 2f out* **100/1**

1m 14.25s (-0.15) **Going Correction** 0.0s/f (Good) **5 Ran SP% 111.6**
Speed ratings (Par 98): **101,100,99,89,86**
CSF £39.48 TOTE £10.00: £3.60, £1.30; EX 27.60 Trifecta £29.50 Pool: £3,040.91 - 77.24 winning units..
Owner Hoofbeats Ltd Racing Club **Bred** Stephanie Hanly **Trained** Exning, Suffolk

FOCUS
After a dry night, the going was officially Good to firm. The rails had been dolled out three metres on both bends and in the back straight. The odds-on favourite disappointed and the front two dictate the level.

5617 ROYAL MARINES ASSOCIATION - "SUPPORTING OUR WOUNDED" MAIDEN H'CAP 6f 3y
2:30 (2:30) (Class 5) (0-70,68) 3-Y-O+ **£2,587** (£770; £384; £192) **Stalls** Centre

Form RPR
2230 **1** **Gift Of Silence**[55] 3686 4-9-7 65........JamieSpencer 6 71
(John Berry) *settled last early: trckd ldrs: rdn over 2f out: drvn to ld over 1f out: clung on gamely fnl 100yds* **4/1**[2]
-540 **2** nk **Emerald Sea**[55] 3699 3-9-4 65........TedDurcan 5 70
(Chris Wall) *racd keenly and hld up: effrt 2f out: drvn to dispute ld briefly over 1f out: ev ch after tl no ex fnl 50yds* **6/1**
634 **3** 2¾ **Meddling**[55] 3696 3-9-5 66........RyanMoore 7 62
(Sir Michael Stoute) *cl up: led 2f out: sn rdn: drvn and hdd over 1f out: fading fnl 100yds* **5/4**[1]
6340 **4** ¾ **Poetic Belle**[12] 5198 3-8-2 54........(t) PhilipPrince[(5)] 4 48
(Shaun Harris) *slt ld tl rdn and hdd 2f out: lost tch w ldng pair over 1f out* **33/1**
0-20 **5** 8 **Dumbarton Rock**[18] 4956 3-9-7 68........(p) SteveDrowne 2 36
(William Jarvis) *prom: rdn 2f out: sn struggling: wl btn over 1f out* **9/2**[3]
636 **6** 8 **Whatwehavewehold**[4] 5499 3-8-8 55........(p) DavidProbert 3
(Alan McCabe) *plld v hrd: cl up tl drvn over 2f out: sn dropped rt out: t.o* **6/1**

1m 13.89s (-0.51) **Going Correction** 0.0s/f (Good)
WFA 3 from 4yo 3lb **6 Ran SP% 114.1**
Speed ratings (Par 103): **103,102,98,97,87 76**
Tote Swingers: 1&2 £4.40, 1&3 £1.20, 2&3 £2.60 CSF £27.85 TOTE £4.70: £2.60, £5.70; EX 39.20 Trifecta £88.30 Pool: £2,980.45 - 25.21 winning units..
Owner John Berry **Bred** Henry And Mrs Rosemary Moszkowicz **Trained** Newmarket, Suffolk

FOCUS
Just a very modest maiden handicap, but competitive on paper. Straightforward form.

5618 BBC RADIO NORFOLK MAIDEN STKS 7f 3y
3:00 (3:00) (Class 5) 3-Y-O+ **£2,587** (£770; £384) **Stalls** Centre

Form RPR
1 **Araqella (IRE)** 3-9-0 0........RyanMoore 1 73+
(William Haggas) *trckd ldr: pushed along to cl 2f out: led over 1f out: far more willing than rival and wl in control after* **11/10**[2]
2322 **2** 2 **Hi Filwah (USA)**[8] 5345 3-9-5 70........(v) SebSanders 3 67
(Jeremy Noseda) *plld hrd in last: urged along 2f out: forcefully rdn to go 2nd over 1f out but looking awkward after: outbattled fnl f* **8/11**[1]
-500 **3** 9 **Perseverent Pete (USA)**[84] 2762 3-8-12 48........EoinWalsh[(7)] 2 43
(Christine Dunnett) *led at decent pce and abt 3 l clr: rdn 2f out: hdd over 1f out: immediately outpcd* **50/1**[3]

1m 27.3s (0.70) **Going Correction** 0.0s/f (Good) **3 Ran SP% 107.5**
Speed ratings (Par 103): **96,93,83**
CSF £2.28 TOTE £1.90; EX 2.20 Trifecta £1.80 Pool: £1,855.85 - 733.61 winning units..
Owner Mr & Mrs D Hearson **Bred** Granham Farm Partnership **Trained** Newmarket, Suffolk

FOCUS
Only one runner with form of any consequence in this small-field maiden, but he found one too good again. The winner may do a lot better than this.

5619 YOUR WEDDING AT GREAT YARMOUTH RACECOURSE MAIDEN H'CAP 1m 6f 17y
3:30 (3:31) (Class 5) (0-70,70) 3-Y-O+ **£2,587** (£770; £384; £192) **Stalls** Low

Form RPR
4-65 **1** **Kelvingrove (IRE)**[89] 2589 3-9-2 70........FrederikTylicki 3 84+
(Ed Vaughan) *settled in 3rd: rdn 5f out: on and off bridle after: wnt 2nd 3f out: rdn to ld over 1f out and immediately surged wl clr* **8/11**[1]
5425 **2** 16 **Keep Kicking (IRE)**[75] 2749 6-9-11 67........JamieSpencer 1 60
(Simon Dow) *pushed into ld: rdn 5f out: hdd over 1f out and outpcd win a few strides* **9/4**[2]
4223 **3** 1 **Outback (IRE)**[21] 4867 4-9-8 64........(b) TomQueally 2 56
(Neil King) *settled in 2nd pl: rdn 5f out: lost 2nd 3f out and plodded on w no ch after* **5/1**[3]
0020 **4** 13 **Lea Valley**[7] 5377 4-8-3 52 oh7........(b) ShelleyBirkett[(7)] 4 27
(Julia Feilden) *a last: u.p 7f out: no rspnse: wl btn 4f out: t.o and eased* **40/1**

3m 6.21s (-1.39) **Going Correction** 0.0s/f (Good)
WFA 3 from 4yo+ 12lb **4 Ran SP% 107.8**
Speed ratings (Par 103): **103,93,93,85**
CSF £2.60 TOTE £2.00; EX 3.50 Trifecta £4.30 Pool: £2,343.02 - 404.62 winning units..
Owner The Kelvingrove Partnership **Bred** Mark Johnston Racing Ltd **Trained** Newmarket, Suffolk

FOCUS
Just three of the four participants had realistic claims in this weak maiden handicap. The easy winner showed useful form, with the rest below par.

5620 ONLINE DISCOUNTED TICKETS@GREATYARMOUTH-RACECOURSE.CO.UK H'CAP 5f 43y
4:00 (4:02) (Class 5) (0-75,74) 3-Y-O+ **£2,587** (£770; £384; £192) **Stalls** Centre

Form RPR
4121 **1** **Green Monkey**[17] 4976 3-9-3 71........ShaneKelly 3 83+
(James Fanshawe) *pressed ldrs: drvn to ld 1f out: sn asserted* **7/4**[1]
0510 **2** 1 **Irish Boy (IRE)**[25] 4707 5-8-9 68........(tp) EoinWalsh[(7)] 4 72
(Christine Dunnett) *cl up: drvn and outpcd 1/2-way: rallied to go 2nd 1f out: no ch w wnr* **12/1**
0211 **3** 1¾ **Excellent Aim**[11] 5221 6-9-2 68........TomQueally 2 66
(George Margarson) *prom: rdn and racing awkwardly 2f out: no ex fnl f* **7/4**[1]
4230 **4** hd **Indian Tinker**[26] 4675 4-9-2 68........JamieSpencer 1 65
(Robert Cowell) *led: rdn 1/2-way: hdd 1f out: kpt on same pce after* **5/1**[2]
/31- **5** 2¼ **Million Faces**[415] 3670 4-9-8 74........ChrisCatlin 5 65
(Rae Guest) *cl up: rdn wl over 1f out: eased whn btn ins fnl f* **6/1**[3]

1m 2.51s (-0.19) **Going Correction** 0.0s/f (Good)
WFA 3 from 4yo+ 2lb **5 Ran SP% 111.4**
Speed ratings (Par 103): **101,99,96,96,92**
CSF £22.41 TOTE £3.30: £1.10, £5.00; EX 22.00 Trifecta £41.20 Pool: £1,962.50 - 35.69 winning units..
Owner Mr & Mrs P Hopper, Mr & Mrs M Morris **Bred** Jan & Peter Hopper **Trained** Newmarket, Suffolk

FOCUS
Just a moderate contest, but none could be confidently discounted. The winner is thriving and the form is straightforward in behind.

5621 BBC NORFOLK H'CAP 7f 3y
4:30 (4:31) (Class 4) (0-80,80) 3-Y-O+ **£4,690** (£1,395; £697; £348) **Stalls** Centre

Form RPR
3441 **1** **Muftarres (IRE)**[6] 5406 8-9-0 74 6ex........(t) LauraPike[(5)] 6 82
(Frank Sheridan) *swtchd rt to trck ldng pair stands' side: rdn to ld over 1f out: jst hld on* **4/1**[2]
0010 **2** nk **Brocklebank (IRE)**[13] 5124 4-9-8 77........JamieSpencer 1 84
(Simon Dow) *wl outpcd in last of centre trio: v gd prog over 1f out: drvn and kpt on strly ins fnl f: jst failed* **8/1**
2410 **3** 3¼ **Kakapuka**[12] 5187 6-9-4 73........SamHitchcott 3 71
(Anabel K Murphy) *led trio who styd in centre of trck: w overall ldr: rdn and hdd over 1f out: nt qckn after* **20/1**
-353 **4** 2¼ **George Baker (IRE)**[26] 4685 6-9-5 74........RyanMoore 2 66
(George Baker) *2nd of three racing up centre: rdn over 1f out: sn btn* **7/4**[1]
0412 **5** 1¼ **Jonnie Skull (IRE)**[6] 5406 7-9-2 71........(vt) TomQueally 7 60
(Phil McEntee) *led stands' side quartet: rdn wl over 2f out: hdd over 1f out: nt qckn* **7/1**
240 **6** 1 **Azrael**[5] 5437 5-9-11 80........(p) DavidProbert 5 66
(Alan McCabe) *swtchd rt after 2f: sn chsd ldr stands' side: rdn over 2f out: no imp fnl f* **6/1**[3]
5250 **7** 6 **Darnathean**[21] 4864 4-9-2 71........FrederikTylicki 4 41
(Paul D'Arcy) *last of stands' quartet: nvr travelling and alwyays bdly outpcd* **7/1**

1m 26.56s (-0.04) **Going Correction** 0.0s/f (Good) **7 Ran SP% 111.5**
Speed ratings (Par 105): **100,99,95,93,91 90,83**
Tote Swingers: 1&2 £5.70, 2&3 £10.50 CSF £33.19 TOTE £4.80: £2.90, £4.10; EX 41.90 Trifecta £315.00 Pool: £4,369.49 - 10.40 winning units..
Owner Mark Andrew Smith **Bred** Shadwell Estate Company Limited **Trained** Wolverhampton, W Midlands

■ Stewards' Enquiry : Laura Pike four-day ban: used whip in incorrect place (Sep 3-6)

FOCUS
A decent handicap, with an 80-rated top weight. The field split on leaving the stalls. The winner's best run for a long time.

5622 ARENARACINGCOMPANY.CO.UK APPRENTICE TRAINING SERIES H'CAP (RACING EXCELLENCE INITIATIVE) 1m 3y
5:05 (5:05) (Class 6) (0-65,63) 4-Y-O+ **£1,940** (£577; £288; £144) **Stalls** Centre

Form RPR
2265 **1** **Duke Of Destiny (IRE)**[12] 5205 4-9-5 63........(p) BradleyBosley[(5)] 4 73
(Ed Walker) *chsd ldrs: effrt to ld over 2f out: pushed along and styd on wl fnl f: stylishly* **6/1**
5023 **2** 2¼ **Mishrif (USA)**[12] 5205 7-9-7 63........(v) GeorgeBuckell[(3)] 7 68
(J R Jenkins) *pressed ldr: rdn over 2f out: clr w wnr but no imp fnl f* **10/1**
4616 **3** 9 **Hamble**[12] 5204 4-9-4 57........(t) ShelleyBirkett 6 41
(Julia Feilden) *slt ld tl rdn and hdd over 2f out: plugged on steadily but no ch w ldng pair fnl f* **7/2**[1]
2030 **4** ¾ **Exopuntia**[13] 5135 7-8-12 50........AdamMcLean[(3)] 1 32
(Julia Feilden) *chsd ldr: pushed along over 2f out: nvr looked like chalng after* **16/1**
5001 **5** 3½ **King Of Wing (IRE)**[3] 5525 4-8-10 54 6ex........(be) LouisSteward[(5)] 5 28
(Phil McEntee) *chsd ldrs tl rdn wl over 2f out: sn lost tch w ldng pair: plugged on* **5/1**
3342 **6** nse **Lutine Charlie (IRE)**[20] 4894 6-9-5 63........DavidParkes[(5)] 3 37
(Pat Eddery) *chsd ldrs far side: rdn wl over 2f out: nvr making any imp* **9/2**[3]
10-0 **7** 2 **Percythepinto (IRE)**[223] 120 4-9-6 59........(t) ThomasGarner 2 29
(George Baker) *missed break: a struggling in rr* **12/1**
-060 **8** 9 **Thecornishwren (IRE)**[4] 5493 4-8-4 48 ow3........(b) JordonMcMurray[(5)] 8
(John Ryan) *chsd ldrs over 5f: sn dropped out: t.o* **100/1**
00/0 **9** 6 **Musical Strike**[12] 5166 4-8-1 45........JonathanWilletts[(5)] 10
(Shaun Harris) *nvr bttr than midfield: struggling fnl 3f: t.o* **100/1**
62 **10** 2¼ **Trulee Scrumptious**[25] 4715 4-8-13 52........(be) TimClark 9
(Peter Charalambous) *s.s: swtchd rt to r alone stands' side: wl bhd fr 1/2-way: t.o* **4/1**[2]

1m 41.02s (0.42) **Going Correction** 0.0s/f (Good) **10 Ran SP% 116.0**
Speed ratings (Par 101): **97,94,85,85,81 81,79,70,64,62**
Tote Swingers: 1&2 £4.50, 1&3 £2.70, 2&3 £5.40 CSF £64.11 CT £241.58 TOTE £5.60: £2.20, £3.70, £1.50; EX 87.00 Trifecta £415.10 Pool: £1,917.22 - 3.46 winning units..

Owner Dubai Thoroughbred Racing **Bred** John O'Connor **Trained** Newmarket, Suffolk
■ Bradley Bosley's first winner.
FOCUS
A low-grade finale, in which the top weight was rated just 63. The first two were clear but the form is only modest.
T/Plt: £1,383.40 to £1 stake. Pool: £50,619.89 - 26.71 winning tickets. T/Qpdt: £69.50 to £1 stake. Pool: £4,418.96 - 47.05 winning tickets. IM

5623 - 5627a (Foreign Racing) - See Raceform Interactive

5573 DEAUVILLE (R-H)
Tuesday, August 20
OFFICIAL GOING: Turf: good; fibresand: standard

5628a CRITERIUM DU FONDS EUROPEEN DE L'ELEVAGE (LISTED RACE) (2YO) (TURF) 1m (R)
1:50 (12:00) 2-Y-O **£49,593** (£19,837; £14,878; £9,918; £4,959)

RPR
1 **Ectot**22 2-8-11 0 GregoryBenoist 11 101
(E Lellouche, France) **47/10**3
2 snk **Baby Foot (IRE)**32 2-8-11 0 FranckBlondel 9 101
(F Rossi, France) **7/2**2
3 2 ½ **Elliptique (IRE)**24 2-8-11 0 MaximeGuyon 8 95
(A Fabre, France) **23/10**1
4 snk **Double Point (IRE)**16 5039 2-8-11 0 OlivierPeslier 10 95
(Paul Cole) *hld up towards rr on outer: pushed along and reminders over 3f out: rdn in last whn hmpd 2f out: hung rt u.p but r.o and wnt 4th ins fnl 100yds: nt pce to chal* **13/2**
5 2 **King Rubi** 2-8-11 0 AntoineHamelin 4 90
(Matthieu Palussiere, France) **26/1**
6 snk **Empreinte (USA)**23 4816 2-8-8 0 FlavienPrat 5 87
(C Laffon-Parias, France) **24/1**
7 1 ½ **Marie D'o (FR)**26 4701 2-8-8 0 NicolasPerret 3 83
(K Borgel, France) **31/1**
8 7 **Swinging Song**24 4791 2-8-8 0 UmbertoRispoli 6 67
(M Delzangles, France) **23/1**
9 snk **Battlefront (USA)**21 2-8-11 0 Christophe-PatriceLemaire 2 70
(J-C Rouget, France) **26/1**
10 10 **Zylpha (IRE)**24 4791 2-8-8 0 FabriceVeron 7 44
(H-A Pantall, France) **35/1**
11 1 ½ **Jally (IRE)**23 4816 2-8-11 0 (b1) IoritzMendizabal 1 43
(J-C Rouget, France) **73/10**
1m 41.84s (1.04) 11 Ran SP% **116.9**
WIN (incl. 1 euro stake): 5.70. PLACES: 1.70, 1.70, 1.50. DF: 7.90. SF: 13.40.
Owner G Augustin-Normand & Mme E Vidal **Bred** Ecurie Des Monceaux & Skymarc Farm **Trained** Lamorlaye, France

5629a PRIX DE LA NONETTE SHADWELL (GROUP 2) (3YO FILLIES) (TURF) 1m 2f
2:20 (12:00) 3-Y-O **£60,243** (£23,252; £11,097; £7,398; £3,699)

RPR
1 **Tasaday (USA)**24 4792 3-9-0 0 MaximeGuyon 5 116+
(A Fabre, France) *trckd ldr: clsd gng wl 3f out: shkn up to ld 2f out: rdn whn pressed over 1f out: styd on strly and forged clr ins fnl f: pushed out: v readily* **4/5**1
2 2 **Sparkling Beam (IRE)**24 4792 3-9-0 0 ThierryJarnet 4 112
(J E Pease, France) *midfield in tch on outer: rdn to chal 2f out: pressed wnr and ev ch tl outpcd ins fnl f: styd on wl for 2nd* **5/1**3
3 1 ¼ **Eleuthera (FR)**58 3614 3-9-0 0 Christophe-PatriceLemaire 6 110
(P Demercastel, France) *hld up in last pair on outer: rdn 2f out: styd on and wnt 3rd cl home: nt pce to chal* **16/1**
4 snk **Purr Along**39 4254 3-9-0 0 FrankieDettori 2 109
(William Muir) *racd a little keenly: midfield in tch on inner: angled out and rdn 2f out: outpcd by wnr ins fnl f: styd on but dropped to 4th cl home* **4/1**2
5 2 ½ **Siljan's Saga (FR)**33 4468 3-9-0 0 Pierre-CharlesBoudot 1 104
(J-P Gauvin, France) *led: rdn and hdd 2f out: sn no ex and btn: fdd but jst hld on for 5th* **8/1**
6 shd **Melodique (FR)**24 4792 3-9-0 0 OlivierPeslier 3 104
(C Laffon-Parias, France) *racd a little keenly: dwlt: hld up in last pair on inner: rdn in last 2f out: sn outpcd: styd on u.p but nvr threatened* **25/1**
2m 9.91s (-0.29) 6 Ran SP% **113.1**
WIN (incl. 1 euro stake): 1.50. PLACES: 1.10, 1.60. SF: 3.10.
Owner Godolphin SNC **Bred** Darley Stud Management Co Ltd **Trained** Chantilly, France
FOCUS
Thwey went a very slow pace.

5522 LINGFIELD (L-H)
Wednesday, August 21
OFFICIAL GOING: Turf - good to firm (firm in places; watered; 8.9); all-weather - standard
Wind: light, half behind Weather: sunny and warm

5630 BREATHE SPA AT LINGFIELD MARRIOTT H'CAP 2m
2:20 (2:20) (Class 6) (0-65,55) 3-Y-O **£2,045** (£603; £302) **Stalls** Low

Form RPR
0023 1 **Fitzwilly**6 5432 3-9-2 **50** SamHitchcott 6 58
(Mick Channon) *mde all: jnd and drvn ent fnl 2f: battled on u.str.p and forged ahd fnl 75yds: all out* **1/1**1
5213 2 ½ **Noor Al Haya (IRE)**5 5500 3-9-7 **55** KieranO'Neill 4 62
(Mark Usher) *stdd s: t.k.h: hld up in tch in rr: hdwy to trck ldrs 5f out: jnd wnr on bit 2f out: rdn and effrt over 1f out: fnd less than expected for press and btn fnl 50yds* **9/4**2
00-5 3 2 ¼ **Roy Rocket (FR)**27 4688 3-8-4 **45** NoelGarbutt(7) 3 50
(John Berry) *t.k.h: chsd ldrs tl wnt 2nd 12f out tl over 3f out: sltly outpcd and nt clr run whn swtchd rt over: kpt on same pce fnl 2f* **10/1**
050- 4 6 **Luckster**399 4222 3-8-8 **45** DeclanBates(3) 2 43
(David Evans) *chsd ldr tl 12f out: styd chsng ldrs tl dropped to 5th and rdn 5f out: outpcd and btn 3f out: plugged on again ins fnl f* **25/1**
00-2 5 3 ¼ **Orla's Rainbow (IRE)**14 5123 3-9-1 **49** (b) PatDobbs 7 43
(Gary Moore) *in tch in midfield: trckd ldrs 5f out: wnt 2nd over 3f out tl 2f out: sn rdn and btn: wknd over 1f out* **6/1**3
-040 6 7 **Paige Flyer**70 3219 3-8-11 **45** PaoloSirigu 1 30
(Mick Quinn) *in tch in last pair: pushed along 12f out: rdn and struggling in last 6f out: lost tch 4f out* **80/1**
3m 36.25s (1.45) **Going Correction** -0.25s/f (Firm) 6 Ran SP% **109.2**
Speed ratings (Par 98): **86,85,84,81,80 76**
toteswingers 1&2 £1.10, 1&3 £3.10, 2&3 £2.50 CSF £3.20 TOTE £1.90: £1.10, £1.50; EX 3.60 Trifecta £11.50 Pool: £2100.77 - 136.13 winning units..
Owner Peter Taplin **Bred** Imperial & Mike Channon Bloodstock Ltd **Trained** West Ilsley, Berks
FOCUS
A moderate staying handicap, run in blazing sunshine on quick ground. The form is not straightforward and is best assessed through the first two for now.

5631 EAST PARK RDA GROUP H'CAP 1m 2f
2:55 (2:55) (Class 6) (0-65,64) 4-Y-0+ **£2,045** (£603; £302) **Stalls** Low

Form RPR
3031 1 **Remix (IRE)**4 5521 4-8-9 **56** DannyBrock(5) 4 70
(Ian Williams) *stdd after s: hld up in rr: smooth hdwy to ld 2f out: sn rdn and qcknd clr: eased towards fin: easily* **8/15**1
0050 2 7 **The Guru Of Gloom (IRE)**42 4163 5-9-0 **61** (b) ThomasGarner(5) 1 61
(William Muir) *t.k.h: chsd ldrs tl led 7f out: rdn and hdd 2f out: sn outpcd and btn: kpt on for clr 2nd* **14/1**
0064 3 6 **Claude Monet (BRZ)**12 5234 4-9-7 **64** SeanLevey 2 51
(Simon Dow) *stdd s: t.k.h: hld up in tch: effrt on inner over 2f out: wnt modest 3rd wl over 1f out: no imp* **10/1**3
55-0 4 3 **Zaminate**17 5038 4-8-9 **51** DavidProbert 6 33
(Patrick Chamings) *hld up in tch: rdn and effrt 3f out: outpcd 2f out: sn wknd* **14/1**
0000 5 3 ½ **Ajeeb (USA)**23 4831 5-9-3 **62** WilliamTwiston-Davies(3) 3 37
(Michael Scudamore) *led tl 7f out: styd pressing ldr tl rdn and outpcd ent fnl 2f: sn wknd* **33/1**
413 6 ¾ **Archelao (IRE)**4 5528 5-8-12 **54** (t) LukeMorris 5 28
(Richard Rowe) *t.k.h: chsd ldr fr 3f out: styd chsng ldrs: rdn and unable qck over 2f out: wknd wl over 1f out* **9/2**2
2m 7.39s (-3.11) **Going Correction** -0.25s/f (Firm) 6 Ran SP% **108.8**
Speed ratings (Par 101): **102,96,91,89,86 85**
toteswingers 1&2 £3.20, 1&3 £2.30, 2&3 £5.70 CSF £8.75 TOTE £1.40: £1.40, £4.40; EX 8.80 Trifecta £31.50 Pool: £2385.93 - 56.64 winning units..
Owner Global Commodity Imports Ltd **Bred** Dr Dean Harron **Trained** Portway, Worcs
FOCUS
A weak handicap but the winner looks better than ever.

5632 ANTHONY MOORE DRY CLEANERS ELITE H'CAP 1m 2f
3:30 (3:30) (Class 5) (0-75,74) 3-Y-O **£2,726** (£805; £402) **Stalls** Low

Form RPR
-406 1 **Miss Marjurie (IRE)**25 4769 3-9-7 **74** PatCosgrave 6 84+
(Denis Coakley) *hld up wl in tch in midfield: rdn and effrt to chse ldrs over 2f out: led wl over 1f out: drew clr 1f out: in command and idling ins fnl f: comf* **4/1**3
1304 2 1 ¾ **Emulating (IRE)**30 4593 3-9-2 **72** WilliamTwiston-Davies(3) 2 77
(Richard Hannon) *chsd ldng pair: rdn and effrt over 2f out: shuffled bk and nt clr run over 1f out: sn swtchd rt: styd on fnl f to go 2nd towards fin* **4/1**3
51 3 ½ **Mandy's Boy (IRE)**11 5293 3-9-1 **68** JimCrowley 5 72
(Ian Williams) *taken down early: chsd ldrs: jnd ldr and travelling strly 3f out: rdn and nt pce of wnr wl over 1f out: kpt on same pce fnl f: lost 2nd towards fin* **9/4**1
0330 4 1 ½ **Raging Bear (USA)**14 5124 3-9-7 **74** (b1) PatDobbs 3 75
(Richard Hannon) *s.i.s: hld up in tch in rr: rdn and effrt over 2f out: kpt on same pce fr over 1f out* **10/1**
4051 5 ½ **Soaring Spirits (IRE)**23 4829 3-9-7 **74** (b) LukeMorris 1 74
(Roger Varian) *led: rdn ent fnl 2f: sn hdd and unable qck: no threat to wnr and plugged on same pce fnl f* **3/1**2
4030 6 16 **Sabre Rock**68 3294 3-9-6 **73** FrederikTylicki 4 41
(John Best) *hld up in tch in last pair: rdn and struggling over 2f out: sn btn: bhd and eased wl ins fnl f* **14/1**
2m 8.21s (-2.29) **Going Correction** -0.25s/f (Firm) 6 Ran SP% **111.5**
Speed ratings (Par 100): **99,97,97,96,95 82**
toteswingers 1&2 £2.90, 1&3 £3.30, 2&3 £1.70 CSF £19.79 TOTE £4.90: £2.80, £2.00; EX 16.80 Trifecta £78.10 Pool: £2691.14 - 25.84 winning units..
Owner Chris Van Hoorn **Bred** Coleman Bloodstock Limited **Trained** West Ilsley, Berks
FOCUS
Not the most competitive of races for the grade. The placed horses set the standard.

5633 LINGFIELD PARK OWNERS GROUP H'CAP 1m 3f 106y
4:05 (4:06) (Class 6) (0-55,55) 3-Y-0+ **£2,045** (£603; £302) **Stalls** High

Form RPR
60-5 1 **Spiritual Art**30 4591 7-9-6 **54** (v) SeanLevey 9 61
(Luke Dace) *hld up wl in tch in midfield: effrt and n.m.r whn barging match w rival over 2f out: rdn to chal 1f out: led fnl 75yds: r.o wl* **16/1**
0-05 2 1 **Royal Alcor (IRE)**8 5377 6-9-0 **55** (t) DanielMuscutt(7) 11 60
(Gay Kelleway) *hld up in tch in midfield: rdn and effrt over 2f out: led over 1f out: hdd and no ex fnl 75yds* **12/1**
4261 3 1 ¾ **Men Don't Cry (IRE)**29 4605 4-9-2 **53** (b) MarkCoumbe(3) 3 55
(Ed de Giles) *hld up in tch in midfield: effrt and barging match w rival over 2f out: chsd ldrs u.p on inner over 1f out: styd on same pce ins fnl f* **11/4**1
6324 4 1 ¼ **Dalliefour (IRE)**36 4391 3-8-9 **55** 1 WilliamTwiston-Davies(3) 4 55
(Michael Bell) *w ldr: rdn to ld over 2f out: hdd over 1f out: no ex and btn jst ins fnl f: wknd fnl 75yds* **11/4**1
1640 5 2 ¾ **Hawaiian Freeze**18 5002 4-8-12 **46** oh1 (p) ShaneKelly 6 42
(John Stimpson) *stdd after s: hld up in rr of main gp: effrt over 2f out: high hd carriage and no imp 2f out: coaxed along and kpt on ins fnl f: nvr trbld ldrs* **25/1**
43-0 6 3 ¾ **Two Sugars**12 5234 5-9-6 **54** 1 PatCosgrave 5 43
(Laura Mongan) *in tch in midfield: rdn 1/2-way: drvn and outpcd 3f out: plugged on but wl hld fnl 2f* **14/1**
4V12 7 nk **Helamis**27 4688 3-8-6 **54** TobyAtkinson(5) 10 43
(Alison Hutchinson) *chsd ldrs: rdn and effrt over 2f out: 5th and btn over 1f out: wknd fnl f* **9/2**2
3033 8 6 **Fushicho**17 4192 4-8-13 **47** (t) KierenFallon 2 25
(Brendan Powell) *taken down early: mde most tl rdn and hdd whn bmpd over 2f out: losing pl whn hmpd again 2f out: sn wknd* **10/1**3

000 9 *31* **Emerald Art (IRE)**[52] 3858 3-8-6 **52** ow2.......................... RyanClark(3) 7
(J W Hills) *in tch towards rr of main gp: rdn 5f out: lost tch over 3f out: t.o* **16/1**

360 10 *51* **Fire In Babylon (IRE)**[131] 1520 5-8-13 **47**.......................(t) ChrisCatlin 8
(Noel Quinlan) *s.i.s: sn detached in last: pushed along and nvr gng: t.o fnl 7f* **25/1**

2m 28.62s (-2.88) **Going Correction** -0.25s/f (Firm)
WFA 3 from 4yo+ 9lb **10** Ran SP% **114.4**
Speed ratings (Par 101): **100,99,98,97,95 92,92,87,65,28**
toteswingers 1&2 £20.40, 1&3 £9.10, 2&3 £7.70 CSF £189.64 CT £688.35 TOTE £22.40: £5.70, £5.60, £1.10; EX 248.30 Trifecta £999.90 Pool: £1624.34 - 1.21 winning units..
Owner Copped Hall Farm & Stud **Bred** R Haim **Trained** Five Oaks, W Sussex
■ Stewards' Enquiry : Mark Coumbe two-day ban: careless riding (Sep 4-5)

FOCUS
A weak middle-distance handicap, but it served up a good finish. The winner is rated to last year's turf best.

5634 VINES BMW NURSERY H'CAP 7f (P)
4:40 (4:40) (Class 5) (0-70,70) 2-Y-O **£2,726** (£805; £402) **Stalls** Low

Form RPR
1 1 **Cape Factor (IRE)**[42] 4175 2-9-0 **63**.................................. ChrisCatlin 6 68+
(Rae Guest) *chsd ldrs: rdn and qcknd to ld ent fnl f: pressed and r.o wl ins fnl f* **7/2**[1]

1530 2 *nk* **Jive**[18] 5005 2-9-2 **65**.. PatDobbs 10 69+
(Richard Hannon) *in tch in midfield: hdwy to chse ldng trio 2f out: drvn and chsd wnr 1f out: str chal ins fnl f: r.o but hld towards fin* **7/1**

534 3 *2* **Cockney Belle**[35] 4408 2-9-2 **70**.................................. TobyAtkinson(5) 7 69
(Marco Botti) *hld up in tch in midfield: swtchd rt and hdwy u.p over 1f out: chsd ldng pair 1f out: no ex and outpcd fnl 100yds* **6/1**

6244 4 *1 1/4* **Senorita Guest (IRE)**[12] 5242 2-9-0 **66**..................... SimonPearce(3) 8 62
(Mick Channon) *taken down early: stdd and swtchd lft after s: hld up in rr: stl travelling wl and looking for run over 2f out: nt clr run and swtchd rt over 1f out: r.o wl u.p fnl f: nt rch ldrs* **20/1**

0003 5 *1/2* **Basil Berry**[16] 5068 2-8-10 **64**.................................. RobertTart(5) 5 61
(Chris Dwyer) *in tch towards rr: hdwy but nt clr run 2f out: rdn and hdwy 1f out: styd on wl fnl f: nt rch ldrs* **5/1**[3]

330 6 *1* **Jersey Cream (IRE)**[18] 5003 2-9-2 **65**.......................... FergusSweeney 9 56
(Gary Moore) *stdd s: hld up towards rr: hdwy into midfield 3f out: n.m.r over 1f out: hdwy 1f out: styd on fnl f: nt rch ldrs* **12/1**

432 7 *2 3/4* **G Man (IRE)**[48] 3972 2-9-3 **69**.................................. CharlesBishop(3) 12 53
(Olly Stevens) *in tch in midfield on outer: rdn and effrt bnd wl over 1f out: sn drvn and outpcd: wl hld fnl f* **9/2**[2]

000 8 *1 3/4* **Baileys Celebrate**[32] 4539 2-8-0 **49** oh4.......................... LukeMorris 11 28
(Mark Johnston) *chsd ldr: rdn and ev ch 2f out tl over 1f out: btn 1f out: wknd ins fnl f* **25/1**

0445 9 *3* **Tyrsal (IRE)**[16] 5068 2-8-5 **54**... NickyMackay 2 25
(Robert Eddery) *led: rdn 2f out: drvn and hdd ent fnl f: sn btn and wknd* **16/1**

6500 10 *1 3/4* **Flying Kyte**[65] 3414 2-8-2 **51**.................................. FrankieMcDonald 13 17
(Pat Phelan) *s.i.s: sn pushed along in rr: n.d* **66/1**

000 11 *nk* **Cabaan (IRE)**[17] 5025 2-9-2 **65**.. KierenFallon 1 31
(Brian Meehan) *sn pushed along: chsd ldrs: rdn and losing pl 2f out: wknd and btn 1f out: no ch whn nt clr and run and eased ins fnl f* **8/1**

640 12 *24* **Black Geronimo**[37] 4351 2-9-2 **65**.................................. PatCosgrave 3
(David Evans) *sn rdn along in midfield: dropped to rr 2f out: bhd and eased over 1f out: t.o* **20/1**

1m 26.15s (1.35) **Going Correction** +0.075s/f (Slow) **12** Ran SP% **123.4**
Speed ratings (Par 94): **95,94,92,90,90 89,86,84,80,78 78,50**
toteswingers 1&2 £6.20, 1&3 £4.50, 2&3 £10.50 CSF £28.18 CT £148.40 TOTE £4.80: £2.00, £2.60, £2.50; EX 34.20 Trifecta £273.40 Pool: £2271.07 - 6.22 winning units..
Owner Derek J Willis **Bred** Nanallac Stud **Trained** Newmarket, Suffolk

5635 SURREY HILLS MAIDEN AUCTION STKS 6f (P)
5:15 (5:26) (Class 6) 2-Y-O **£2,045** (£603; £302) **Stalls** Low

Form RPR
1 **Tea Leaf (IRE)** 2-8-10 0.. JimCrowley 7 73+
(Ralph Beckett) *dwlt: bustled along early: hdwy into midfield after 1f: rdn and gd hdwy over 1f out: led ins fnl f: r.o wl* **3/1**[2]

45 2 *1/2* **Officer Drivel (IRE)**[15] 5101 2-8-11 0.......................... SeanLevey 6 72
(Luke Dace) *chsd ldrs: drvn and chsd ldr briefly over 1f out: kpt on to chse wnr wl ins fnl f: r.o but no imp cl home* **10/1**

66 3 *3/4* **Mendacious Harpy (IRE)**[33] 4484 2-8-8 0.................. PatCosgrave 1 67
(George Baker) *led: rdn wl over 1f out: hdd ins fnl f: no ex fnl 100yds* **7/4**[1]

3 4 *1* **Orlando Star (CAN)**[10] 5306 2-8-10 0.......................... RobertTart(5) 5 70
(Roger Teal) *chsd ldrs: effrt on inner to press ldrs 1f out: styd on same pce u.p fnl 150yds* **7/1**

004 5 *3 1/4* **Rural Affair**[28] 4631 2-8-5 54.................................. DavidProbert 8 50
(Harry Dunlop) *chsd ldrs: wnt 2nd over 3f out tl over 1f out: wknd ins fnl f* **25/1**

5 6 *1 1/4* **Pelagian (USA)**[56] 3690 2-8-12 0.................................. PatDobbs 10 53
(Dean Ivory) *s.i.s: in tch towards rr: sme hdwy into midfield over 2f out: 6th and outpcd wl over 1f out: no imp after* **40/1**

05 7 *6* **Soul Of Motion**[68] 3288 2-9-2 0.................................. LukeMorris 4 38
(Gay Kelleway) *s.i.s: in tch towards rr: rdn and reminders 4f out: rdn and no hdwy ent fnl 2f: wknd over 1f out* **9/2**[3]

8 *nk* **Fisher Lane** 2-8-10 0.. CharlesBishop(3) 11 34
(Olly Stevens) *s.i.s: detached in last and sn pushed along: bhd over 1f out* **12/1**

00 9 *5* **Yankee Red**[10] 5307 2-8-13 0.................................. FrederikTylicki 2 18
(John Best) *in tch in midfield: lost pl and rdn 3f out: bhd over 1f out* **50/1**

10 *2 3/4* **Lucky Dottie** 2-8-4 0.. FrankieMcDonald 3
(Pat Phelan) *uns rdr and loose bef s: chsd ldr tl over 3f out: steadily lost pl: bhd over 1f out* **50/1**

1m 13.43s (1.53) **Going Correction** +0.075s/f (Slow) **10** Ran SP% **119.0**
Speed ratings (Par 92): **92,91,90,89,84 83,75,74,67,64**
toteswingers 1&2 £5.90, 1&3 £2.90, 2&3 £4.30 CSF £32.66 TOTE £3.80: £1.10, £3.00, £1.60; EX 38.60 Trifecta £126.80 Pool: £2859.30 - 16.90 winning units..
Owner McCalmont and Drew **Bred** Barbara Prendergast **Trained** Kimpton, Hants

FOCUS
An informative, if probably only modest juvenile contest, won in likeable style. The favourite was disappointing.

5636 BHEST RACING TO SCHOOL H'CAP 6f (P)
5:50 (5:54) (Class 4) (0-80,79) 3-Y-O+ **£4,690** (£1,395; £697; £348) **Stalls** Low

Form RPR
1130 1 **If So**[18] 5009 4-9-9 **78**.. FrederikTylicki 4 93
(James Fanshawe) *trckd ldng pair and a gng wl: rdn and qcknd to ld 1f out: r.o strly: readily* **7/2**[2]

4011 2 *2 1/4* **Zhiggy's Stardust**[49] 3955 4-9-10 **79**.......................... FergusSweeney 6 87
(Henry Candy) *led: rdn wl over 1f out: hdd and nt gng pce of wnr 1f out: kpt on but no ch w wnr* **5/1**

-016 3 *1 1/4* **Desert Command**[12] 5219 3-9-1 **73**.......................... DavidProbert 8 77
(Andrew Balding) *taken down early: chsd ldr: rdn and effrt over 1f out: unable qck ent fnl f: styd on same pce after* **4/1**[3]

0602 4 *3* **Alnoomaas (IRE)**[7] 5398 4-9-5 **74**.......................... SeanLevey 7 68
(Luke Dace) *chsd ldng trio: rdn and effrt over 1f out: no imp and edgd lft 1f out: wknd ins fnl f* **7/1**

0-00 5 *1/2* **Novellen Lad (IRE)**[65] 3415 8-9-9 **78**.......................... ShaneKelly 1 71
(Willie Musson) *hld up in tch in midfield: rdn and effrt over 1f out: styd on same pce and no imp after* **33/1**

6664 6 *1/2* **Street Power (USA)**[82] 2825 8-9-5 **74**.......................... LukeMorris 5 65
(Jeremy Gask) *hld up wl off the pce in last trio: rdn and effrt but stl plenty to do wl over 1f out: plugged on: nvr trbld ldrs* **14/1**

1250 7 *3/4* **Polar Venture**[67] 3351 4-9-6 **75**.......................... JimCrowley 10 64
(William Haggas) *stdd and swtchd lft after s: hld up wl off the pce in last trio: rdn and effrt but stl plenty to do over 1f out: plugged on: nvr trbld ldrs* **5/2**[1]

/000 8 *1 1/4* **Evens And Odds (IRE)**[24] 4800 9-9-4 **78**.......................... SladeO'Hara(5) 9 63
(Peter Grayson) *racd off the pce in midfield: sme hdwy over 2f out: sn rdn: wknd over 1f out* **33/1**

/2-0 9 *1 3/4* **Slip Sliding Away (IRE)**[18] 5009 6-9-6 **78**.......................... RyanPowell(3) 3 57
(Peter Hedger) *s.i.s: hld up wl off the pce in last trio: stuck bhd horses and t.k.h over 3f out: n.d* **50/1**

000 10 *6* **Lastkingofscotland (IRE)**[70] 3215 7-9-4 **76**..........(b) SimonPearce(3) 2 36
(Conor Dore) *racd off the pce in last quartet: rdn and dropped to rr 2f out: wl bhd fnl f* **40/1**

1m 12.68s (0.78) **Going Correction** +0.075s/f (Slow)
WFA 3 from 4yo+ 3lb **10** Ran SP% **116.9**
Speed ratings (Par 105): **97,94,92,88,87 87,86,84,82,74**
toteswingers 1&2 £3.00, 1&3 £3.50, 2&3 £4.90 CSF £20.87 CT £72.95 TOTE £4.70: £1.60, £1.80, £1.70; EX 19.70 Trifecta £103.90 Pool: £2094.64 - 15.10 winning units..
Owner Hopper, Grundy, Handscombe **Bred** Mr & Mrs K W Grundy, Mr & Mrs P Hopper **Trained** Newmarket, Suffolk

FOCUS
A good turnout for the feature handicap and, with plenty of pace on throughout, the form looks rock solid rated around those in the frame behind the winner.
T/Plt: £23.80 to a £1 stake. Pool: £51098.27 - 1563.25 winning tickets T/Qpdt: £19.40 to a £1 stake. Pool: £3357.10 - 127.85 winning tickets SP

5235 MUSSELBURGH (R-H)
Wednesday, August 21

OFFICIAL GOING: Good (good to firm in places; 8.1)
Wind: Moderate against Weather: Cloudy with sunny periods

5637 TDC WASTE MANAGEMENT H'CAP (QUALIFIER FOR THE £15,000 BETFAIR SCOTTISH MILE SERIES FINAL) 1m
2:10 (2:10) (Class 5) (0-75,75) 4-Y-O+ **£3,234** (£962; £481; £240) **Stalls** Low

Form RPR
0002 1 **Violent Velocity (IRE)**[6] 5426 10-7-13 **60**.......................... JoeDoyle(7) 4 69
(John Quinn) *trckd ldrs: hdwy on outer over 2f out: rdn to chal wl over 1f out: styd on to ld last 150yds: edgd rt and kpt on* **16/1**

4102 2 *1 3/4* **Border Bandit (USA)**[12] 5239 5-8-7 **61**.......................... BarryMcHugh 2 66
(Tracy Waggott) *hld up in tch: hdwy to trck ldrs over 3f out: effrt and nt clr run over 1f out: swtchd lft and rdn ent fnl f: kpt on wl towards fin* **9/2**[2]

0301 3 *nse* **Ralphy Boy (IRE)**[12] 5239 4-8-11 **65**.......................... PJMcDonald 7 70
(Alistair Whillans) *trckd ldr: led 3f out: jnd and rdn 2f out: drvn ent fnl f: hdd and no ex last 150yds* **11/2**

33 4 *3/4* **Dance For Georgie**[8] 5369 4-8-11 **65** ow2.......................... PhillipMakin 5 68
(Ben Haslam) *trckd ldng pair: hdwy 3f out: chal 2f out: sn rdn and ev ch tl drvn and wknd last 150yds* **9/4**[1]

-335 5 *1 1/2* **Dhaular Dhar (IRE)**[21] 4893 11-8-0 **61** ow1.......................... JordanNason(7) 3 61
(Jim Goldie) *hld up in rr: hdwy wl over 2f out: rdn wl over 1f out: kpt on fnl f: nrst fin* **10/1**

2606 6 *2 1/4* **Joshua The First**[8] 5368 4-8-7 **61**..............................(b) TomEaves 1 56
(Keith Dalgleish) *s.i.s: a in rr* **20/1**

022 7 *1* **Jeannie Galloway (IRE)**[19] 4956 6-9-1 **72**.......................... JasonHart(3) 6 64
(Keith Dalgleish) *hld up towards rr: hdwy wl over 2f out: n.m.r and swtchd lft over 1f out: sn rdn and btn* **5/1**[3]

-150 8 *15* **Staff Sergeant**[14] 5149 6-9-7 **75**.......................... DavidAllan 8 33
(Iain Jardine) *set str pce: pushed along and hdd 3f out: sn rdn and wknd fnl 2f* **10/1**

1m 40.46s (-0.74) **Going Correction** +0.05s/f (Good) **8** Ran SP% **109.8**
Speed ratings (Par 103): **105,103,103,102,100 98,97,82**
toteswingers 1&2 £11.10, 1&3 £11.20, 2&3 £2.70 CSF £79.58 CT £427.16 TOTE £23.40: £5.80, £2.00, £2.70; EX 114.50 Trifecta £699.50 Pool: £1802.41 - 1.72 winning units..
Owner Mrs S Quinn **Bred** Miss Jill Finegan **Trained** Settrington, N Yorks

FOCUS
A modest handicap but it was open. They went a good pace courtesy of Staff Sergeant, who finished well beaten and has not built on his C&D win back in May. The placed horses are rated close to previous C&D form.

5638 BROWN SHIPLEY WEALTH WELL MANAGED MAIDEN AUCTION STKS 5f
2:45 (2:45) (Class 6) 2-Y-O **£1,940** (£577; £288; £144) **Stalls** High

Form RPR
23 1 **Jamboree Girl**[36] 4370 2-8-6 0.......................... DuranFentiman 2 75+
(Tim Easterby) *trckd ldng pair: swtchd rt and effrt over 1f out: rdn to ld ent fnl f: sn edgd lft: kpt on wl u.p towards fin* **3/1**[2]

2 *nk* **Sandra's Diamond (IRE)** 2-8-3 0.......................... JasonHart(3) 5 74+
(Keith Dalgleish) *green and outpcd in rr: hdwy 2f out: swtchd rt and rdn to chse ldrs over 1f out: styd on to chal wl ins fnl f: ev ch tl no ex nr fin* **10/1**

22 **3** *4* **Omaha Gold (IRE)**[8] 5364 2-8-6 0 RoystonFfrench 3 60
(Bryan Smart) *dwlt and wnt rt s: sn chsng ldrs: cl up and disputing ld after 1f: rdn to ld over 1f out: hdd and drvn ent fnl f: sn wknd* **11/10**[1]

4 *shd* **Annie's Rose** 2-8-4 0 JamesSullivan 4 57+
(Bryan Smart) *chsd ldrs: rdn along: green and outpcd 2f out: swtchd rt to outer over 1f out: styd on fnl f: nrst fin* **25/1**

42 **5** *2 1/2* **Kano's Ghirl (IRE)**[19] 4963 2-8-7 0 ow1 TomEaves 1 51
(Keith Dalgleish) *wnt rt s: sn led: jnd after 1f and slt ld: rdn along 2f out: hdd over 1f out: wknd fnl f* **4/1**[3]

4 **6** *6* **Raise A Billion**[11] 5262 2-8-9 0 PJMcDonald 6 32
(Alan Berry) *sn outpcd and a in rr* **100/1**

1m 0.87s (0.47) **Going Correction** +0.125s/f (Good) **6** Ran SP% **106.5**
Speed ratings (Par 92): **101,100,94,93,89 80**
toteswingers 1&2 £3.30, 1&3 £1.30, 2&3 £2.70 CSF £27.52 TOTE £3.80: £1.40, £3.50; EX 32.20 Trifecta £64.80 Pool: £2949.91 - 34.09 winning units..
Owner W T Whittle **Bred** Cheveley Park Stud Ltd **Trained** Great Habton, N Yorks

FOCUS
Half of this field had already demonstrated they had some ability on previous starts and it may have been a bit better than most Class 6 maidens. The principals are capable of better.

5639 ROBBIE HOWEY H'CAP 5f
3:20 (3:20) (Class 4) (0-80,80) 3-Y-O+ **£5,175** (£1,540; £769; £384) **Stalls** High

Form RPR

3102 **1** **Sharaarah (IRE)**[9] 5340 3-9-10 **80** DavidNolan 10 89
(David O'Meara) *trckd ldrs: hdwy 2f out: swtchd lft and rdn to chal ent fnl f: drvn and kpt on wl to ld last 50yds* **5/1**[2]

3 **2** *nk* **Modern Lady**[11] 5265 3-8-3 **64** PhilipPrince(5) 3 72
(Richard Guest) *cl up: led wl over 2f out: rdn ent fnl f: sn edgd rt: hdd and no ex last 50yds* **22/1**

5124 **3** *1 1/4* **Imperial Legend (IRE)**[29] 4613 4-9-5 **80** (p) JordanNason(7) 5 83
(David Nicholls) *hld up: hdwy 2f out: sn swtchd rt to outer and rdn to chal ent fnl f: ev ch tl drvn and one pce last 100yds* **9/2**[1]

0535 **4** *1/2* **Silvanus (IRE)**[15] 5108 8-9-11 **79** PJMcDonald 2 80
(Paul Midgley) *trckd ldrs: rdn along wl over 1f out: kpt on same pce fnl f* **5/1**[2]

4010 **5** *1/2* **Lost In Paris (IRE)**[22] 4860 7-9-12 **80** (p) DavidAllan 11 79
(Tim Easterby) *slt ld on stands' rail: rdn along 2f out: sn hdd: drvn and wknd ent fnl f* **11/2**[3]

-003 **6** *1 1/4* **Lizzy's Dream**[9] 5336 5-8-4 **61** JasonHart(3) 8 56
(Robin Bastiman) *in tch: rdn along and sme hdwy 2f out: sn drvn and no imp fnl f* **11/2**[3]

1443 **7** *3 3/4* **Midnight Dynamo**[19] 4954 6-9-10 **78** AndrewElliott 6 59
(Jim Goldie) *a in rr* **15/2**

110 **8** *nse* **Oil Strike**[19] 4954 6-9-11 **79** (b) JamesSullivan 1 60
(Michael Easterby) *prom on outer: pushed along 2f out: sn rdn and wknd* **9/1**

0000 **9** *7* **Rothesay Chancer**[19] 4954 5-9-0 **75** SophieRobertson(7) 9 31
(Jim Goldie) *in tch on inner: rdn along wl over 2f out: sn outpcd and bhd* **33/1**

1m 0.29s (-0.11) **Going Correction** +0.125s/f (Good)
WFA 3 from 4yo+ 2lb **9** Ran SP% **111.3**
Speed ratings (Par 105): **105,104,102,101,100 98,92,92,81**
toteswingers 1&2 £9.80, 1&3 £5.10, 2&3 £4.60 CSF £99.45 CT £517.14 TOTE £6.10: £2.80, £2.10, £2.00; EX 68.10 Trifecta £402.40 Pool: £2674.89 - 4.98 winning units..
Owner Middleham Park Racing XXXVII & C Tasker **Bred** Shadwell Estate Company Limited **Trained** Nawton, N Yorks

FOCUS
There was no hanging about in this fair sprint handicap and they went about half a second faster than the other two races ran over the same distance on the card. The third is close to form and sets the standard.

5640 RAY HAWTHORNE MEMORIAL H'CAP 2m
3:55 (3:55) (Class 4) (0-85,81) 4-Y-O+ **£6,469** (£1,925; £962; £481) **Stalls** High

Form RPR

1521 **1** **Platinum (IRE)**[15] 5086 6-9-7 **81** (p) RussKennemore 9 93+
(Philip Kirby) *in tch: hdwy to trck ldrs 6f out: led on bit 3f out: rdn clr over 1f out: styd on strly* **12/5**[1]

061 **2** *4 1/2* **Hawk Mountain (UAE)**[19] 4969 8-9-1 **75** TomEaves 5 80
(John Quinn) *trckd ldrs: hdwy over 2f out: swtchd rt and rdn wl over 1f out: sn chsng wnr: drvn and no imp fnl f* **10/1**

0613 **3** *1 3/4* **La Bacouetteuse (FR)**[12] 5241 8-8-7 **67** (b) DavidAllan 6 70
(Iain Jardine) *hld up and bhd: hdwy on outer 3f out: rdn to chse ldrs wl over 1f out: sn drvn and kpt on same pce fnl f* **25/1**

0005 **4** *3/4* **Harrison's Cave**[25] 4759 5-8-11 **74** JasonHart(3) 2 76
(Chris Grant) *t.k.h: hld up towards rr: rapid hdwy after 7f: led 1/2-way: rdn along 4f out: hdd 3f out: sn drvn and wknd wl over 1f out* **16/1**

2320 **5** *4* **Aleksandar**[25] 4782 4-8-5 **72** JordanNason(7) 7 69
(Jim Goldie) *prom: rdn along 3f out: drvn over 2f out and sn wknd* **4/1**[2]

2122 **6** *3/4* **Merchant Of Dubai**[13] 5185 8-9-3 **77** PhillipMakin 1 73
(Jim Goldie) *hld up in rr: hdwy 3f out: rdn wl over 1f out: n.d* **9/2**[3]

3300 **7** *7* **Art History (IRE)**[25] 4782 5-9-6 **80** (b) DavidNolan 4 68
(David O'Meara) *cl up: led after 3 1/2f: hdd 1/2-way: cl up tl rdn along over 3f out and grad wknd* **7/1**

0036 **8** *5* **Mason Hindmarsh**[25] 4759 6-8-7 **67** PJMcDonald 3 49
(Karen McLintock) *led 3 1/2f: prom tl pushed along and lost pl over 5f out: bhd after* **25/1**

3041 **9** *7* **Major Domo (FR)**[25] 4759 5-8-9 **69** AndrewElliott 8 43
(Alan Swinbank) *chsd ldrs: lost pl after 6f: bhd fnl 4f* **11/1**

3m 31.92s (-1.58) **Going Correction** +0.05s/f (Good) **9** Ran SP% **111.1**
Speed ratings (Par 105): **105,102,101,101,99 99,95,93,89**
toteswingers 1&2 £5.60, 1&3 £11.10, 2&3 £13.80 CSF £26.01 CT £455.18 TOTE £3.60: £1.20, £2.70, £4.90; EX 24.10 Trifecta £180.50 Pool: £3191.12 - 13.25 winning units..
Owner Mrs Philippa Kirby **Bred** Lodge Park Stud **Trained** Middleham, N Yorks

FOCUS
The feature race on the card was a decent staying handicap which included five previous course winners in the field. It was a true enough test and the form looks solid, rated around the first three.

5641 PARTNERSHIP CHALLENGE H'CAP (QUALIFIER FOR THE £15,000 BETFAIR SCOTTISH SPRINT SERIES FINAL) 5f
4:30 (4:30) (Class 6) (0-60,61) 3-Y-O+ **£1,940** (£577; £288; £144) **Stalls** High

Form RPR

0-33 **1** **Gottcher**[15] 5085 5-9-7 **60** TomEaves 3 78
(Keith Dalgleish) *cl up: led after 2f out: rdn clr over 1f out: kpt on strly* **11/4**[2]

0666 **2** *3 1/4* **Here Now And Why (IRE)**[9] 5336 6-9-3 **56** (p) DavidAllan 1 62
(Iain Jardine) *trckd ldrs: hdwy 2f out: rdn to chse wnr appr fnl f: sn drvn and no imp* **7/1**

-02 **3** *4* **Baker's Pursuit**[11] 5265 3-8-13 **54** AndrewElliott 6 46
(Jim Goldie) *sn rdn along and outpcd in rr: hdwy over 2f out: styd on u.p fnl f: tk modest 3rd nr line* **7/1**

3013 **4** *shd* **Quality Art (USA)**[5] 5499 5-9-3 **61** 6ex PhilipPrince(5) 7 53
(Richard Guest) *chsd ldrs on inner: swtchd rt and rdn to chal 2f out: drvn and one pce fnl f* **15/8**[1]

3203 **5** *2* **Busy Bimbo (IRE)**[5] 5486 4-8-12 **49** ow2 RussKennemore 2 35
(Alan Berry) *trckd ldrs: hdwy 2f out: rdn to chse ldng pair over 1f out: sn drvn and wknd* **4/1**[3]

0000 **6** *11* **Cayman Fox**[34] 4448 8-8-9 **48** (v) PJMcDonald 4
(Linda Perratt) *led 2f: sn rdn along and wknd 2f out* **18/1**

0500 **7** *2 3/4* **Miss Bossy Boots**[21] 4887 4-8-7 **46** oh1 BarryMcHugh 8
(Tracy Waggott) *cl up 1 1/2f: sn rdn along: lost pl and bhd* **66/1**

1m 0.94s (0.54) **Going Correction** +0.125s/f (Good)
WFA 3 from 4yo+ 2lb **7** Ran SP% **113.2**
Speed ratings (Par 101): **100,94,88,88,85 67,63**
toteswingers 1&2 £8.60, 1&3 £36.70, 2&3 £41.60 CSF £21.59 CT £119.95 TOTE £3.30: £2.10, £3.00; EX 24.10 Trifecta £100.00 Pool: £2253.75 - 16.90 winning units..
Owner The Wee Thackit Inn Synd & R Reid **Bred** Peter Webb **Trained** Carluke, S Lanarks

FOCUS
Moderate fare but the winner won well and is rated to his latter 3-y-o form.

5642 BLACKROCK H'CAP (QUALIFIER FOR THE £15,000 BETFAIR SCOTTISH MILE SERIES FINAL) 1m
5:05 (5:05) (Class 5) (0-75,75) 3-Y-O **£3,234** (£962; £481; £240) **Stalls** Low

Form RPR

1220 **1** **Argaki (IRE)**[18] 4994 3-9-3 **74** JasonHart(3) 6 84
(Keith Dalgleish) *chsd ldrs: rdn along to ld 2f out: drvn and kpt on wl fnl f* **10/1**

1151 **2** *2 1/2* **Just Paul (IRE)**[19] 4956 3-8-13 **70** DeclanCannon(3) 2 74
(Philip Kirby) *trckd ldrs on inner: smooth hdwy over 2f out: chsd wnr on bit wl over 1f out: sn shkn up: rdn and edgd lft ins fnl f: no imp* **11/4**[1]

200 **3** *3 1/2* **Bitusa (USA)**[18] 5016 3-8-6 **60** AndrewElliott 9 56
(Alan Swinbank) *hdwy on outer to chse ldng pair after 1f: cl up 3f out: rdn over 2f out: drvn over 1f out and kpt on same pce* **50/1**

5512 **4** *1* **Lexington Blue**[16] 5072 3-8-13 **67** (b[1]) DavidNolan 4 61
(David O'Meara) *towards rr: hdwy 1/2-way: rdn along to chse ldrs 2f out: swtchd rt and drvn over 1f out: sn one pce* **7/1**[3]

2461 **5** *3* **Look On By**[18] 5016 3-8-4 **58** JamesSullivan 5 45
(Ruth Carr) *led: pushed clr 4f out: rdn 3f out: hdd 2f out: sn drvn and wknd* **8/1**

4503 **6** *2 1/4* **Mowhoob**[19] 4956 3-8-8 **69** JordanNason(7) 1 51
(Jim Goldie) *trckd ldrs on inner: rdn along 3f out: wknd fnl 2f* **15/2**

6154 **7** *1* **Snap Music (USA)**[9] 5342 3-8-8 **62** RoystonFfrench 7 42
(Mark Johnston) *chsd ldrs on outer: rdn along wl over 2f out: sn wknd* **15/2**

010 **8** *2* **Natures Law (IRE)**[8] 5365 3-8-8 **62** TomEaves 8 37
(Keith Dalgleish) *t.k.h: hld up: a in rr* **14/1**

5316 **9** *nk* **Cupertino**[13] 5182 3-9-7 **75** PhillipMakin 3 49
(Kevin Ryan) *hld up: sme hdwy 1/2-way: rdn along and wknd 3f out* **7/2**[2]

1m 40.84s (-0.36) **Going Correction** +0.05s/f (Good) **9** Ran SP% **113.7**
Speed ratings (Par 100): **103,100,97,96,93 90,89,87,87**
CSF £37.15 CT £1327.56 TOTE £18.00: £3.60, £1.60, £9.30; EX 34.60 Trifecta £1372.10 Part won. Pool: £1829.47 - 0.38 winning units..
Owner D G Savala **Bred** A Christodoulou **Trained** Carluke, S Lanarks

FOCUS
A few progressive 3-y-os lined up for this handicap and the form looks solid enough.

5643 REDBUILD AMATEUR RIDERS' H'CAP 1m 6f
5:35 (5:35) (Class 6) (0-65,63) 4-Y-O+ **£1,871** (£580; £290; £145) **Stalls** Centre

Form RPR

0-03 **1** **Lady Gargoyle**[21] 4614 5-9-10 **45** MrsCBartley 4 52
(Jim Goldie) *led 3f: cl up tl led again wl over 2f out: rdn wl over 1f out: drvn and edgd lft ins fnl f: hld on gamely towards fin* **15/2**

3301 **2** *1* **Torero**[15] 5084 4-10-5 **54** (p) MrSWalker 5 60
(Kevin Ryan) *trckd ldrs: smooth hdwy over 3f out: trckd wnr 2f out: chal over 1f out: sn rdn and ev ch tl drvn and one pce wl ins fnl f* **7/4**[1]

3526 **3** *shd* **Geanie Mac (IRE)**[11] 5267 4-9-13 **48** (v) MrJHamilton 7 53
(Linda Perratt) *trckd ldng pair: hdwy 3f out: rdn wl over 1f out: swtchd rt and ev ch ent fnl f: sn drvn and kpt on same pce towards fin* **7/2**[2]

4113 **4** *hd* **Grand Diamond (IRE)**[12] 5240 9-10-2 **58** MrsICGoldie(7) 1 63+
(Jim Goldie) *hld up in rr: hdwy 3f out: chsd ldrs 2f out: rdn to chse wnr ent fnl f: sn drvn and ev ch: one pce last 100yds* **5/1**

6302 **5** *2* **Sohcahtoa (IRE)**[11] 5267 7-11-0 **63** MissSBrotherton 2 65
(Andrew Crook) *chsd ldrs: pushed along 5f out: effrt on outer 3f out: rdn over 2f out: drvn: edgd lft and no imp appr fnl f* **4/1**[3]

0/00 **6** *2* **Non Dom (IRE)**[9] 5337 7-10-8 **60** (v[1]) MissSMDoolan(3) 3 60?
(Wilf Storey) *trckd ldrs: hdwy to ld after 3f: rdn along over 3f out: hdd over 2f out: grad wknd* **50/1**

3m 12.51s (7.21) **Going Correction** +0.05s/f (Good) **6** Ran SP% **109.0**
Speed ratings (Par 101): **81,80,80,80,79 77**
toteswingers 1&2 £3.30, 1&3 £6.00, 2&3 £2.40 CSF £19.91 TOTE £11.40: £4.10, £1.10; EX 22.10 Trifecta £46.80 Pool: £1325.17 - 21.23 winning units..
Owner Johnnie Delta Racing **Bred** Jim Goldie **Trained** Uplawmoor, E Renfrews

FOCUS
There was little in the way of early pace in this weak amateurs' event. The first four ran close to their marks.
T/Plt: £175.80 to a £1 stake. Pool: £49099.54 - 203.85 winning tickets T/Qpdt: £37.80 to a £1 stake. Pool: £3948.40 - 77.10 winning tickets JR

4218 WARWICK (L-H)
Wednesday, August 21

OFFICIAL GOING: Good to firm (7.4)
Wind: Light behind Weather: Cloudy with sunny spells

5644 NEXUS CENTRAL MANAGEMENT SERVICES LTD APPRENTICE H'CAP 6f
5:00 (5:00) (Class 6) (0-65,65) 3-Y-O **£1,940** (£577; £288; £144) **Stalls** Low

Form RPR

4336 **1** **Eastern Dragon (IRE)**[27] 4685 3-9-11 **64** NoelGarbutt 10 72
(Michael Scudamore) *hld up: hdwy over 1f out: rdn to ld ins fnl f: r.o* **9/2**[3]

0536 **2** *1 ½* **Starlight Angel (IRE)**[13] 5184 3-9-12 **65**.......................... OisinMurphy 7 68
(Ronald Harris) *s.i.s: hld up: hdwy to ld over 1f out: rdn and hdd ins fnl f: styd on same pce* **7/1**

3020 **3** *1 ¾* **Winnie Perry**[23] 4836 3-9-2 **58**.......................... PatMillman(3) 3 55
(Rod Millman) *chsd ldrs: led wl over 1f out: sn rdn and hdd: styd on same pce ins fnl f* **12/1**

6023 **4** *½* **Elusive Gold (IRE)**[15] 5104 3-9-11 **64**.......................... ShelleyBirkett 1 60
(J W Hills) *chsd ldrs: rdn over 1f out: styd on same pce fnl f* **11/2**

0455 **5** *1 ¾* **Cymeriad**[16] 5067 3-8-7 **46**..........................(p) GemmaTutty 11 36
(Michael Easterby) *s.i.s and rdr lost iron leaving stalls: hdwy and rdr rcvrd iron over 2f out: rdn over 1f out: no ex fnl f* **20/1**

6021 **6** *1* **Angels Calling**[20] 4916 3-9-3 **61**.......................... RobJFitzpatrick(5) 2 48
(Mrs K Burke) *prom: rdn over 1f out: wknd ins fnl f* **4/1**[2]

4604 **7** *1 ¾* **Excellent Addition (IRE)**[26] 4722 3-9-5 **63**.......................... LukeLeadbitter(5) 6 44
(Declan Carroll) *led: rdn over 2f out: hdd wl over 1f out: wknd fnl f* **7/2**[1]

0402 **8** *2 ¾* **Fidget**[14] 5156 3-8-9 **53**.......................... ClaireMurray(5) 4 26
(David Brown) *chsd ldrs: rdn over 2f out: wknd over 1f out* **16/1**

3532 **9** *¾* **Coconut Kisses**[16] 5054 3-9-8 **61**.......................... RyanWhile 8 31
(Bill Turner) *racd keenly: w ldrs: rdn over 2f out: wknd over 1f out* **12/1**

1m 10.89s (-0.91) **Going Correction** -0.325s/f (Firm) 9 Ran SP% **114.3**
Speed ratings (Par 98): **93,91,88,88,85 84,82,78,77**
toteswingers 1&2 £5.10, 1&3 £11.80, 2&3 £11.40 CSF £35.54 CT £353.66 TOTE £5.30: £1.20, £3.40, £4.00; EX 43.00 Trifecta £967.00 Part won. Pool: £1289.34 - 0.60 winning units..
Owner JCG Chua & CK Ong **Bred** James Mahon **Trained** Bromsash, H'fords

FOCUS
A warm, dry day and the ground looked pretty quick. A low-grade apprentice riders' race to get things under way and the pace looked strong from the outset. The field were spread across the track as they straightened up for home but the first two home came from well off the pace and raced closest to the stands in the straight. The winner is rated in line with recent marks.

5645 ACORNS CHILDREN'S HOSPICE COVENTRY COMMITTEE (S) STKS 6f
5:30 (5:30) (Class 6) 3-Y-O+ **£1,940** (£577; £288; £144) **Stalls** Low

Form RPR

2102 **1** **Fathsta (IRE)**[4] 5523 8-9-5 72.......................... RichardKingscote 3 81
(Ian Williams) *chsd ldrs: shkn up to ld ins fnl f: r.o wl* **7/4**[1]

2601 **2** *3* **We Have A Dream**[4] 5523 8-9-5 65..........................(p) MartinDwyer 8 71
(William Muir) *chsd ldr: shkn up to ld and rdr dropped rein over 1f out: sn rdn and edgd lft: hdd and unable qck ins fnl f* **3/1**[2]

404 **3** *3* **Paradise Spectre**[4] 5523 6-8-13 68..........................(p) MartinHarley 4 56
(Mrs K Burke) *hld up: pushed along over 2f out: hdwy u.p over 1f out: wnt 3rd and hung lft ins fnl f: nt trble ldrs* **9/2**[3]

5604 **4** *2 ¾* **Jarrow (IRE)**[8] 5376 6-8-13 63..........................(p) SebSanders 2 47
(Milton Bradley) *prom: rdn and edgd rt over 1f out: wknd ins fnl f* **12/1**

0200 **5** *1 ¾* **Mistress Shy**[15] 5097 6-8-3 45..........................(t) ShirleyTeasdale(5) 5 36
(Michael Appleby) *sn nudged along towards rr: n.d* **66/1**

0565 **6** *1 ½* **Drawnfromthepast (IRE)**[13] 5165 8-9-5 72.......................... AdamKirby 1 43
(Jamie Osborne) *sn pushed along to ld: rdn and hdd over 1f out: hmpd sn after: wknd ins fnl f* **11/2**

0-03 **7** *1 ¾* **Albert Tatlock (IRE)**[46] 4072 4-8-13 65..........................(p) LiamKeniry 6 31
(John Butler) *prom: rdn over 2f out: hmpd and wknd over 1f out* **14/1**

05 **8** *5* **Cadeaux Royale**[13] 5176 5-8-8 0.......................... MartinLane 10 10
(Dominic Ffrench Davis) *s.i.s and wnt rt s: outpcd* **100/1**

600 **9** *10* **It Ain't To Grand**[209] 350 4-8-13 41.......................... RobertHavlin 9
(Roger Ingram) *s.i.s: a in rr: wknd over 2f out* **100/1**

1m 9.36s (-2.44) **Going Correction** -0.325s/f (Firm) course record
WFA 3 from 4yo+ 3lb 9 Ran SP% **112.8**
Speed ratings (Par 101): **103,99,95,91,89 87,84,78,64**
toteswingers 1&2 £2.30, 1&3 £2.50, 2&3 £4.80 CSF £6.80 TOTE £2.40: £1.20, £1.90, £1.60; EX 9.60 Trifecta £27.60 Pool: £1431.63 - 38.76 winning units..The winner was sold to Declan Carroll for 5,400gns. We Have A Dream was claimed by Mr S. Arnold for £6,000.
Owner Dr Marwan Koukash **Bred** Brian Miller **Trained** Portway, Worcs
■ Stewards' Enquiry : Martin Dwyer caution: careless riding

FOCUS
A few of these seemed to have solid claims on paper, but it proved a straightforward race for the winner. However, he is rated slightly off his best for now.

5646 BREEDERS BACKING RACING EBF MAIDEN STKS 6f
6:00 (6:02) (Class 5) 2-Y-O **£2,911** (£866; £432; £216) **Stalls** Low

Form RPR

4 **1** **Greeb**[19] 4958 2-9-5 0.......................... RichardKingscote 6 76+
(Charles Hills) *trckd ldr: rdn to ld 1f out: shkn up and r.o* **4/6**[1]

0 **2** *1 ¼* **Dandeena (IRE)**[90] 2601 2-9-0 0.......................... RobertWinston 2 67+
(Ronald Harris) *led: rdn and hung rt 2f out: hdd 1f out: styd on same pce ins fnl f* **33/1**

0 **3** *½* **Spiritual Flame**[35] 4409 2-9-0 0.......................... AndreaAtzeni 11 65
(William Haggas) *mid-div: hdwy u.p over 1f out: styd on* **16/1**

42 **4** *1 ½* **Golden Spear**[29] 4602 2-9-5 0..........................(b[1]) AdamKirby 4 66
(Noel Quinlan) *s.i.s: sn prom: rdn over 1f out: styd on same pce fnl f* **8/1**[3]

0 **5** *hd* **Stomp**[40] 4231 2-9-5 0.......................... GeorgeBaker 1 65
(Roger Charlton) *a.p: rdn and edgd lft over 1f out: styd on same pce* **7/1**[2]

4 **6** *1 ½* **High On Life**[20] 4912 2-9-5 0.......................... MartinLane 10 60
(Jamie Osborne) *hld up: hdwy: hung rt and nt clr run over 1f out: nt rch ldrs* **8/1**[3]

7 *¾* **Diffident Beats** 2-9-5 0.......................... MartinHarley 7 58
(Mick Channon) *s.i.s: sn pushed along in rr: n.d* **25/1**

8 *1 ½* **Dark Crystal** 2-8-9 0.......................... MichaelJMMurphy(5) 8 48
(John Gallagher) *s.i.s: a in rr* **50/1**

06 **9** *4* **Snugfit Sam**[24] 4808 2-9-5 0.......................... MichaelO'Connell 3 40
(John Quinn) *trckd ldrs: plld hrd: rdn and wknd over 1f out* **33/1**

10 *20* **Pacific Trip** 2-9-5 0.......................... LiamKeniry 5
(Andrew Balding) *s.s: rn green: outpcd* **25/1**

1m 10.7s (-1.10) **Going Correction** -0.325s/f (Firm) 2y crse rec 10 Ran SP% **116.1**
Speed ratings (Par 94): **94,92,91,89,89 87,86,84,79,52**
toteswingers 1&2 £13.40, 1&3 £3.60, 2&3 £31.10 CSF £38.80 TOTE £1.50: £1.10, £8.10, £3.40; EX 43.90 Trifecta £1054.00 Part won. Pool: £1405.33 - 0.84 winning units..
Owner Hamdan Al Maktoum **Bred** Shadwell Estate Company Limited **Trained** Lambourn, Berks

FOCUS
Not much depth to this maiden, with ordinary form in behind the winner.

5647 EBF STALLIONS / POWER OF BEE VENOM MAIDEN FILLIES' STKS 5f 110y
6:30 (6:30) (Class 5) 3-4-Y-O **£3,881** (£1,155; £577; £288) **Stalls** Low

Form RPR

2532 **1** **Marjong**[25] 4774 3-9-0 75.......................... SebSanders 6 72
(Simon Dow) *s.i.s: hld up: hdwy to ld over 1f out: rdn out* **6/4**[1]

2 **2** *1 ¾* **Teeline (IRE)**[27] 4687 3-9-0 0.......................... AhmedAjtebi 4 66
(Charlie Appleby) *racd keenly: w ldr tl lft in ld over 3f out: rdn and hdd over 1f out: styd on same pce ins fnl f* **11/4**[2]

2 **3** *½* **Pearl Angel (IRE)**[11] 5277 3-9-0 0.......................... HarryBentley 2 64
(Olly Stevens) *chsd ldrs: rdn over 2f out: styd on same pce ins fnl f* **3/1**[3]

04 **4** *1 ¾* **Joyous**[9] 5345 3-9-0 0.......................... LiamKeniry 1 58
(Dean Ivory) *w ldrs: hmpd over 3f out: rdn and ev ch over 1f out: no ex ins fnl f* **16/1**

232 **P** **Hand Grenade (IRE)**[20] 4911 3-9-0 65.......................... JohnFahy 3
(Eve Johnson Houghton) *led tl wnt wrong, hdd and p.u over 3f out: fatally injured* **8/1**

1m 4.52s (-1.38) **Going Correction** -0.325s/f (Firm) 5 Ran SP% **108.7**
Speed ratings (Par 100): **96,93,93,90,**
CSF £5.70 TOTE £2.00: £1.20, £1.60; EX 7.20 Trifecta £11.30 Pool: £1207.22 - 79.54 winning units..
Owner John Marsden **Bred** Newsells Park Stud & Cannon Bloodstock **Trained** Epsom, Surrey

FOCUS
An ordinary fillies' maiden which was marred by the death of Hand Grenade, who broke down in the early stages. The form is a bit fluid and is rated around the first three.

5648 MCLARENS LOSS ADJUSTERS NURSERY H'CAP 5f
7:00 (7:01) (Class 4) (0-85,76) 2-Y-O **£3,752** (£1,116; £557; £278) **Stalls** Low

Form RPR

4121 **1** **Umneyati**[14] 5121 2-9-7 **76**.......................... MartinHarley 2 89+
(James Tate) *s.i.s and hmpd s: hld up: hdwy to ld over 1f out: shkn up and r.o wl: comf* **5/4**[1]

2323 **2** *2 ½* **Stellarta**[37] 4346 2-9-0 **69**.......................... LiamKeniry 3 70
(Michael Blanshard) *a.p: rdn and ev ch over 1f out: styd on same pce ins fnl f* **9/2**[3]

0422 **3** *3* **Anfield**[16] 5066 2-8-0 **55** oh3.......................... PaoloSirigu 1 45
(Mick Quinn) *edgd rt s: led: rdn and hdd over 1f out: wknd ins fnl f* **12/1**

1423 **4** *3* **Mr Dandy Man (IRE)**[14] 5121 2-9-5 **74**.......................... RobertWinston 5 53
(Ronald Harris) *trckd ldrs: pushed along 1/2-way: rdn over 1f out: wknd fnl f* **11/4**[2]

2160 **5** *2* **Classical Diva**[19] 4965 2-9-0 **76**.......................... LukeLeadbitter(7) 4 48
(Declan Carroll) *sn pushed along to chse ldrs: rdn 1/2-way: wknd over 1f out* **8/1**

58.81s (-0.79) **Going Correction** -0.325s/f (Firm) 5 Ran SP% **108.1**
Speed ratings (Par 96): **93,89,84,79,76**
CSF £6.90 TOTE £1.50: £1.10, £2.50; EX 6.10 Trifecta £28.10 Pool: £1221.23 - 32.55 winning units..
Owner Sheikh Rashid Dalmook Al Maktoum **Bred** Mrs Hugh Maitland-Jones **Trained** Newmarket, Suffolk

FOCUS
Not a strong race for the grade with the top weight rated a full 9lb below the ceiling rating for the level. Straightforward form behind the easy winner.

5649 RSA SUMMER H'CAP 1m 2f 188y
7:30 (7:30) (Class 4) (0-85,80) 3-Y-O **£4,690** (£1,395; £697; £348) **Stalls** Low

Form RPR

3214 **1** **Evangelist**[17] 5030 3-9-4 **77**..........................(p) GeorgeBaker 3 91
(Sir Michael Stoute) *trckd ldr: rdn to ld over 1f out: r.o u.p* **5/2**[1]

-421 **2** *nk* **Qawaafy (USA)**[42] 4180 3-9-6 **79**.......................... AndreaAtzeni 2 92
(Roger Varian) *hld up: hdwy over 2f out: chsd wnr over 1f out: rdn and ev ch ins fnl f: r.o* **3/1**[2]

-223 **3** *6* **Legal Waves (IRE)**[86] 2717 3-9-7 **80**.......................... MartinLane 1 83
(Brian Meehan) *led at stdy pce tl qcknd over 2f out: rdn and hdd over 1f out: edgd lft and wknd ins fnl f* **3/1**[2]

5312 **4** *2 ½* **Dame Nellie Melba**[16] 5055 3-9-0 **73**.......................... FrannyNorton 4 71
(Mark Johnston) *chsd ldrs: rdn over 2f out: nt clr run and wknd ins fnl f* **5/2**[1]

2m 16.38s (-4.72) **Going Correction** -0.375s/f (Firm) 4 Ran SP% **107.1**
Speed ratings (Par 102): **102,101,97,95**
CSF £9.75 TOTE £3.30; EX 8.70 Trifecta £11.40 Pool: £408.94 - 26.71 winning units..
Owner Philip Newton **Bred** Philip Newton **Trained** Newmarket, Suffolk

FOCUS
An open race despite the small field and credit to the front two who left the other pair for dead in the final furlong. The form is slightly fluid but rated on the positive side.

5650 TRELAWNY SPT LTD H'CAP 1m 2f 188y
8:00 (8:00) (Class 6) (0-60,60) 3-Y-O+ **£1,940** (£577; £288; £144) **Stalls** Low

Form RPR

5131 **1** **Minority Interest**[8] 5377 4-9-3 **58**..........................(b) OisinMurphy(7) 1 65
(Brett Johnson) *mde all: rdn over 1f out: styd on wl* **5/6**[1]

3253 **2** *1 ¾* **Eyeline**[19] 3918 3-8-4 **52**..........................(p) JackDuern(5) 8 56
(Andrew Hollinshead) *trckd wnr: rdn and ev ch over 1f out: styd on same pce ins fnl f* **14/1**

3006 **3** *½* **Walter De La Mare (IRE)**[13] 5171 6-8-12 **46** oh1........(b) MartinHarley 9 49
(Anabel K Murphy) *s.i.s: hld up: hdwy u.p over 1f out: styd on: nt rch ldrs* **33/1**

3404 **4** *½* **Hermosa Vaquera (IRE)**[12] 5216 3-9-3 **60**..........................(p) RobertHavlin 2 62
(Peter Chapple-Hyam) *trckd ldrs: racd keenly: rdn over 1f out: styd on same pce ins fnl f* **8/1**[3]

6004 **5** *½* **Penang Power**[15] 5092 3-7-13 **49**.......................... LouisSteward(7) 6 50
(Michael Bell) *prom: rdn over 2f out: no ex ins fnl f* **16/1**

236 **6** *1* **Loucal**[26] 4721 3-9-3 **60**..........................(b) AdamKirby 7 60
(Noel Quinlan) *hld up: rdn over 2f out: no ex ins fnl f* **11/4**[2]

000- **7** *39* **Rocco Breeze (IRE)**[387] 4650 4-8-12 **46** oh1..........(p) RobertWinston 4
(James Unett) *hld up: rdn and wknd over 2f out* **33/1**

2m 19.21s (-1.89) **Going Correction** -0.375s/f (Firm)
WFA 3 from 4yo+ 9lb 7 Ran SP% **110.8**
Speed ratings (Par 101): **91,89,89,89,88 87,59**
toteswingers 1&2 £3.00, 1&3 £5.10, 2&3 £5.60 CSF £13.79 CT £205.16 TOTE £1.80: £1.30, £3.00; EX 14.90 Trifecta £156.80 Pool: £1223.03 - 5.84 winning units..
Owner G Gallagher **Bred** Juddmonte Farms Ltd **Trained** Epsom, Surrey

FOCUS
A weak handicap with the runner-up rated to form.
T/Plt: £36.00 to a £1 stake. Pool: £43717.20 - 885.56 winning tickets T/Qpdt: £8.00 to a £1 stake. Pool: £3633.57 - 332.10 winning tickets CR

4777 YORK (L-H)

Wednesday, August 21

OFFICIAL GOING: Good to firm (8.0)
Wind: fresh 1/2 behind Weather: fine

5651 SYMPHONY GROUP STKS (H'CAP) 5f 89y
1:55 (2:01) (Class 2) (0-105,100) 3-Y-O+
£31,125 (£9,320; £4,660; £2,330; £1,165; £585) **Stalls** Centre

Form RPR

000U **1** **Bogart**[25] 4780 4-9-7 **97** NeilCallan 15 109
(Kevin Ryan) *w ldrs stands' side: led overall over 1f out: hld on towards fin* **7/1**[2]

2640 **2** 3/4 **Goldream**[18] 4983 4-9-1 **91** (p) JamieSpencer 7 100
(Robert Cowell) *s.i.s: hdwy over 2f out: upsides 1f out: styd on same pce clsng stages* **9/1**

0060 **3** *hd* **Face The Problem (IRE)**[18] 4986 5-9-8 **98** JamesDoyle 10 106
(Jamie Osborne) *towards rr: hdwy 2f out: styd on wl ins fnl f: tk 3rd nr fin* **16/1**

-215 **4** 3/4 **Demora**[40] 4263 4-9-0 **90** AndrewMullen 5 96
(Michael Appleby) *overall ldr towards far side: hdd over 1f out: kpt on same pce last 50yds* **12/1**

0010 **5** *nk* **Barnet Fair**[18] 4986 5-9-1 **96** ConnorBeasley(5) 13 101
(Richard Guest) *stdd s: hld up in rr stands' side: hdwy over 1f out: styng on at fin* **9/1**

-114 **6** *nk* **Above Standard (IRE)**[18] 4983 5-9-0 **90** (t) GrahamGibbons 18 93
(Michael Easterby) *chsd ldrs stands' side: rdn over 1f out: kpt on same pce last 75yds* **4/1**[1]

201 **7** 3/4 **Doctor Parkes**[4] 5519 7-9-8 **98** 6ex AndreaAtzeni 17 99
(Stuart Williams) *towards rr stands' side: hdwy over 1f out: kpt on ins fnl f* **16/1**

0001 **8** 1/2 **Cheviot (USA)**[15] 5108 7-9-1 **96** (p) GeorgeChaloner(5) 14 95
(Ian Semple) *chsd ldrs: hung lft and kpt on same pce over 1f out* **25/1**

0016 **9** *nk* **Ladyship**[19] 4949 4-9-9 **99** RyanMoore 12 97
(Sir Michael Stoute) *hld up towards rr: hdwy over 2f out: kpt on fnl f: nt rch ldrs* **17/2**[3]

4120 **10** 1/2 **Whozthecat (IRE)**[18] 4986 6-9-3 **100** (v) LukeLeadbitter(7) 3 96
(Declan Carroll) *w ldrs far side: rdr lost whip appr fnl f: edgd lft and kpt on same pce* **20/1**

0040 **11** 3/4 **Angels Will Fall (IRE)**[64] 3420 4-9-8 **98** RobertWinston 9 93
(Charles Hills) *chsd ldrs: upsides over 1f out: one pce* **18/1**

3010 **12** 1 1/4 **Secret Asset (IRE)**[10] 5325 8-9-10 **100** (p) MichaelO'Connell 20 89
(Jane Chapple-Hyam) *chsd ldrs stands' side: wknd over 1f out* **20/1**

0020 **13** 1/2 **Ancient Cross**[39] 4275 9-9-8 **98** (t) GrahamLee 2 85
(Michael Easterby) *rr-div far side: sme hdwy over 2f out: lost pl over 1f out* **25/1**

6363 **14** 3/4 **Lady Gibraltar**[40] 4263 4-8-8 **89** MichaelJMMurphy(5) 11 73
(Alan Jarvis) *chsd ldrs: wknd fnl f* **14/1**

0304 **15** 3 1/4 **Zero Money (IRE)**[11] 5257 7-9-4 **94** (b) WilliamBuick 8 67
(Hugo Palmer) *chsd ldrs far side: wknd fnl f* **12/1**

4200 **16** 2 3/4 **Tax Free (IRE)**[4] 5519 11-9-3 **93** AdrianNicholls 19 56
(David Nicholls) *in rr stands' side: nvr on terms* **25/1**

2446 **17** 1/2 **Majestic Myles (IRE)**[39] 4284 5-9-10 **100** PaulHanagan 1 61
(Richard Fahey) *outpcd and in rr: bhd fnl 2f* **20/1**

1m 1.72s (-2.38) **Going Correction** -0.25s/f (Firm) course record **17** Ran SP% **127.9**
Speed ratings (Par 109): **109,107,107,106,105 105,104,103,102,102 100,98,98,96,91 87,86**
toteswingers 1&2 £13.70, 1&3 £33.30, 2&3 £30.20 CSF £63.80 CT £1017.25 TOTE £8.90: £2.70, £2.60, £6.00, £3.90; EX 92.20 Trifecta £1094.40 Pool: £8288.72 - 5.67 winning units..

Owner Mrs Angie Bailey **Bred** Toby Barker **Trained** Hambleton, N Yorks

FOCUS
Racing on traditional inside line around home bend and all distances as advertised. Punters could not have been handed a more difficult event to start off with, 17 fully primed and experienced sprinters hurtling down the straight course. The pace was sound and the track record was lowered, although the 5f 89yd distance is rarely used. The jockeys who rode in the opener all agreed it was quick ground. The runner-up is rated to his Dante meeting form with the third to his bes and the next two home close to their form.

5652 PINSENT MASONS LLP ACOMB STKS (GROUP 3) 7f
2:30 (2:33) (Class 1) 2-Y-O
£34,026 (£12,900; £6,456; £3,216; £1,614; £810) **Stalls** Low

Form RPR

0212 **1** **Treaty Of Paris (IRE)**[19] 4959 2-9-0 91 JamesDoyle 6 104
(Henry Candy) *led: qcknd pce over 3f out: edgd lft fnl f: hld on nr fin* **11/1**

1 **2** *nk* **The Grey Gatsby (IRE)**[39] 4312 2-9-0 0 GrahamLee 1 103+
(Kevin Ryan) *lw: trckd ldrs: drvn 3f out: outpcd over 1f out: edgd lft and styd on ins fnl f: jst hld* **5/4**[1]

61 **3** *1* **Il Paparazzi**[26] 4731 2-9-0 0 NeilCallan 4 100
(Daniel Kubler) *on toes: trckd ldrs: chal 2f out: styd on same pce fnl f* **7/1**

026 **4** 2 1/4 **Lady Lara (IRE)**[25] 4742 2-8-11 90 PaulHanagan 5 91
(Alan Jarvis) *hld up in rr: t.k.h: effrt over 2f out: one pce over 1f out* **20/1**

221 **5** *nk* **Brazos (IRE)**[22] 4858 2-9-0 91 RyanMoore 2 93
(Clive Brittain) *lw: trckd ldrs: t.k.h: effrt over 2f out: one pce over 1f out* **11/2**[3]

1 **6** *nk* **First Flight (IRE)**[17] 5033 2-9-0 0 SilvestreDeSousa 3 93
(Saeed bin Suroor) *dwlt: in rr: hdwy on ins over 3f out: chsng ldrs over 1f out: sn wknd* **3/1**[2]

1m 23.02s (-2.28) **Going Correction** -0.25s/f (Firm) **6** Ran SP% **110.4**
Speed ratings (Par 104): **103,102,101,98,98 98**
toteswingers 1&2 £3.30, 1&3 £3.70, 2&3 £2.80 CSF £24.66 TOTE £14.60: £5.30, £1.30; EX 35.90 Trifecta £209.00 Pool: £21722.93 - 77.94 winning units..

Owner One Too Many Partners **Bred** John Malone **Trained** Kingston Warren, Oxon

■ Stewards' Enquiry : James Doyle two-day ban: used whip in incorrect place (Sep 4-5)

FOCUS
The Acomb Stakes has produced some high-class types over the years, notably subsequent Classic winners King's Best (1999, following year's 2000 Guineas) and Rule Of Law (2003, following year's St Leger), and it was upgraded to Group 3 status in 2006. There have been some pretty ordinary runnings as well, though, and it's hard to take a positive view of this form with the winner, who hadn't looked anything out of the ordinary, allowed to dictate a modest pace. The fourth and fifth help with the level.

5653 NEPTUNE INVESTMENT MANAGEMENT GREAT VOLTIGEUR STKS (GROUP 2) (C&G) 1m 4f
3:05 (3:05) (Class 1) 3-Y-O
£85,065 (£32,250; £16,140; £8,040; £4,035; £2,025) **Stalls** Centre

Form RPR

1-12 **1** **Telescope (IRE)**[11] 5270 3-8-12 112 RyanMoore 2 116+
(Sir Michael Stoute) *lw: trckd ldrs: t.k.h: qcknd to ld over 2f out: edgd lft ins fnl f: drvn out* **5/4**[1]

2 1 1/4 **Foundry (IRE)**[290] 7579 3-8-12 0 SeamieHeffernan 1 113
(A P O'Brien, Ire) *w'like: str: hld up: hdwy 4f out: drvn 3f out: chsd wnr over 1f out: kpt on ins fnl f* **5/1**[2]

3645 **3** 1/2 **Secret Number**[21] 4874 3-8-12 106 SilvestreDeSousa 5 112
(Saeed bin Suroor) *swtg: trckd ldrs: drvn over 3f out: styd on to go 3rd jst ins fnl f: kpt on same pce* **5/1**[2]

1303 **4** 1 1/2 **Spillway**[21] 4874 3-8-12 106 TomQueally 4 110
(Eve Johnson Houghton) *hld up: effrt 3f out: edgd lft over 1f out: kpt on to take 4th last 150yds* **20/1**

2-46 **5** *6* **Willie The Whipper**[80] 2907 3-8-12 107 JamieSpencer 7 100
(Ann Duffield) *s.i.s: swtchd lft after s: hld up in last: drvn 3f out: no imp: tk modest 5th post* **10/1**

3441 **6** *nse* **Cap O'Rushes**[21] 4874 3-8-12 110 MickaelBarzalona 6 100
(Charlie Appleby) *trckd ldrs: chal 3f out: wknd fnl f* **8/1**[3]

-326 **7** *17* **Nichols Canyon**[61] 3526 3-8-12 97 (p) WilliamBuick 3 86
(John Gosden) *t.k.h: led: qcknd pce over 3f out: hdd over 2f out: sn lost pl: eased whn bhd* **8/1**[3]

2m 29.32s (-3.88) **Going Correction** -0.10s/f (Good) **7** Ran SP% **113.9**
Speed ratings (Par 112): **108,107,106,105,101 101,90**
toteswingers 1&2 £2.60, 1&3 £2.00, 2&3 £3.50 CSF £7.73 TOTE £2.00: £1.20, £3.00; EX 8.60 Trifecta £27.60 Pool: £17414.05 - 472.90 winning units..

Owner Highclere Thoroughbred Racing -Wavertree **Bred** Barronstown Stud **Trained** Newmarket, Suffolk

FOCUS
Since 1990, only Bob's Return (1993), Milan (2001), Rule Of Law (2004) and Lucarno (2007) have done the Great Voltigeur/St Leger double, although the Godolphin-owned pair Mastery and Encke were placed here before tasting Classic glory at Doncaster, as was Brian Boru in 2003 and Bollin Eric the year before. This renewal looked particularly strong, albeit with a couple of runners with something to prove, and plenty of subsequent winners should emerge from it. The third sets the standard.

5654 JUDDMONTE INTERNATIONAL STKS (BRITISH CHAMPIONS SERIES) (GROUP 1) 1m 2f 88y
3:40 (3:40) (Class 1) 3-Y-O+
£425,325 (£161,250; £80,700; £40,200; £20,175; £10,125) **Stalls** Low

Form RPR

1234 **1** **Declaration Of War (USA)**[10] 5314 4-9-5 120 JosephO'Brien 2 124
(A P O'Brien, Ire) *lw: trckd ldrs: effrt 3f out: r.o to ld jst ins fnl f: drvn out* **7/1**

3112 **2** 1 1/4 **Trading Leather (IRE)**[25] 4745 3-8-11 120 KevinManning 1 121
(J S Bolger, Ire) *led: drvn and increased pce over 3f out: hdd wl over 1f out: styd on to take 2nd last 100yds* **5/1**[3]

1111 **3** 1 1/2 **Al Kazeem**[46] 4082 5-9-5 124 JamesDoyle 3 118
(Roger Charlton) *trckd ldr: chal 3f out: led wl over 1f out: hdd jst ins fnl f: kpt on same pce* **11/8**[1]

2213 **4** 2 1/4 **Hillstar**[25] 4745 3-8-11 119 RyanMoore 6 114
(Sir Michael Stoute) *lw: t.k.h early: trckd ldrs: effrt over 3f out: one pce fnl 2f* **12/1**

-610 **5** 2 1/4 **Rewarded**[61] 3525 4-9-5 107 TomQueally 4 109
(James Toller) *settled detached in last: drvn 3f out: kpt on to take modest 5th over 1f out: nvr a factor* **100/1**

1421 **6** *15* **Toronado (IRE)**[21] 4875 3-8-11 126 RichardHughes 5 81
(Richard Hannon) *t.k.h early: settled in rr after 1f: drvn 3f out: nvr a threat: wknd and eased over 1f out: sn bhd* **9/4**[2]

2m 5.74s (-6.76) **Going Correction** -0.10s/f (Good)
WFA 3 from 4yo+ 8lb **6** Ran SP% **110.7**
Speed ratings (Par 117): **123,122,120,119,117 105**
toteswingers 1&2 £3.70, 1&3 £2.40, 2&3 £2.60 CSF £39.43 TOTE £9.90: £3.90, £3.30; EX 39.00 Trifecta £97.30 Pool: £20801.31 - 160.26 winning units..

Owner Mrs J Magnier & Michael Tabor & Derrick Smith & Jo **Bred** Joseph Allen **Trained** Ballydoyle, Co Tipperary

FOCUS
A disappointing turnout numerically and, with the 'big two' underperforming to varying degrees (Al Kazeem 7lb off his Eclipse defeat of Declaration Of War) the form isn't what it might have been. However, the winner and second, who both relish quick ground (in contrast to the third), are both high-class colts who posted personal bests, and this was still a good, interesting race with the fifth giving the race perspective.

5655 LANSTONE BUILDING CONSERVATION STKS (H'CAP) 2m 88y
4:20 (4:21) (Class 2) (0-100,96) 4-Y-O+ **£19,407** (£5,775; £2,886; £1,443) **Stalls** Low

Form RPR

2116 **1** **Broxbourne (IRE)**[11] 5256 4-9-0 **89** JoeFanning 13 98+
(Mark Johnston) *lw: mid-div: hdwy 7f out: styd on strly over 1f out: led towards fin* **6/1**[2]

6026 **2** *nk* **Mawaqeet (USA)**[26] 4704 4-9-1 **90** PaulHanagan 14 99
(Sir Michael Stoute) *hld up towards rr: hdwy 7f out: effrt over 2f out: styd on wl fnl f: tk 2nd nr fin* **16/1**

5331 **3** 1/2 **Party Line**[12] 5237 4-9-0 **89** (v) SilvestreDeSousa 16 97+
(Mark Johnston) *chsd ldrs: 3rd over 3f out: led over 2f out: drvn 3 l clr over 1f out: faltered and hdd towards fin* **12/1**

0563 **4** 1 3/4 **All The Aces (IRE)**[25] 4782 8-9-1 **90** NeilCallan 3 96
(Nicky Henderson) *lw: chsd ldrs: drvn over 3f out: kpt on same pce fnl f* **16/1**

6413 **5** 1 3/4 **Eagle Rock (IRE)**[11] 5288 5-8-5 **80** (p) FrannyNorton 4 84
(Tom Tate) *set stdy pce: qcknd gallop over 4f out: hdd over 2f out: one pce* **14/1**

4600 **6** *nk* **Blue Bajan (IRE)**[39] 4313 11-9-3 **92** (p) DanielTudhope 11 96
(David O'Meara) *warm: trckd ldrs: effrt over 2f out: kpt on one pce* **25/1**

0-46 **7** *nse* **Martin Chuzzlewit (IRE)**[68] 3297 4-8-11 **86**.................. WilliamBuick 10 90
(David Simcock) *mid-div: hdwy on outer over 2f out: kpt on fnl f* **16/1**

0421 **8** *1 ¼* **Flashman**[25] 4782 4-8-4 **79**.. JimmyQuinn 5 81
(Richard Fahey) *chsd ldrs: one pce fnl 2f* **8/1**[3]

-064 **9** *1 ¼* **Willie Wag Tail (USA)**[11] 5259 4-8-12 **87**..................(b[1]) JamieSpencer 9 88
(Ed Walker) *lw: s.i.s: hdwy to trck ldrs 10f out: 2nd over 5f out: chal 3f out: edgd lft and wknd appr fnl f: eased towards fin* **8/1**[3]

1021 **10** *¾* **Homeric (IRE)**[11] 5256 4-9-3 **92**.. RyanMoore 12 92+
(Ed Dunlop) *lw: hld up in rr: sme hdwy on outside over 2f out: nvr a factor* **9/2**[1]

-003 **11** *hd* **Suraj**[22] 4857 4-9-4 **93**.. TomQueally 7 93+
(Michael Bell) *s.i.s: in rr: sme hdwy over 2f out: nvr a factor* **12/1**

-000 **12** *1* **Viking Storm**[24] 4796 5-9-7 **96**.. JamesDoyle 2 94
(Harry Dunlop) *chsd ldrs: one pce whn hmpd and swtchd rt over 1f out* **25/1**

2046 **13** *nk* **High Office**[21] 4873 7-8-4 **79**.................................... PatrickMathers 8 77
(Richard Fahey) *hld up towards rr: nvr a factor* **25/1**

0236 **14** *¾* **Noble Silk**[14] 5147 4-9-0 **92**..(v[1]) DarrenEgan(3) 1 89
(Lucy Wadham) *a towards rr: nvr a factor* **16/1**

1304 **15** *1 ¾* **Jonny Delta**[12] 5237 6-8-1 **79**... NeilFarley(3) 6 74
(Jim Goldie) *chsd ldrs: lost pl over 2f out* **25/1**

0000 **16** *1 ½* **Crackentorp**[25] 4782 8-9-0 **89**.................................... GrahamGibbons 15 82
(Tim Easterby) *mid-div: hdwy 7f out: chsng ldrs over 3f out: lost pl over 1f out: eased clsng stages* **40/1**

6035 **17** *2 ¼* **Wyborne**[39] 4313 4-8-2 **80**... RaulDaSilva(3) 17 71
(Brian Ellison) *swtchd lft s: sn mid-div: effrt on inner 3f out: rdr lost whip over 2f out: lost pl over 1f out: eased clsng stages* **11/1**

3m 37.49s (2.99) **Going Correction** -0.10s/f (Good) **17** Ran SP% **126.4**
Speed ratings (Par 109): **88,87,87,86,85 85,85,85,84,84 83,83,83,82,82 81,80**
toteswingers 1&2 £27.20, 1&3 £14.10, 2&3 £27.30 CSF £95.12 CT £1146.78 TOTE £6.80: £2.10, £3.40, £3.40, £3.60; EX 131.10 Trifecta £1987.80 Pool: £7222.99 - 2.72 winning units..
Owner Ready To Run Partnership **Bred** Mount Coote Stud And M Johnston **Trained** Middleham Moor, N Yorks

FOCUS
A hugely competitive contest for stayers, which contained some already experienced over the distance and some having their first attempt at it. The early gallop was far from strong, and it saw the third hit 1.01 on Betfair in the win market for plenty and the winner matched for pennies at 1000. The fourth and fifth help set the level.

5656 BETVICTOR.COM STKS (NURSERY H'CAP) 6f
4:55 (4:56) (Class 2) 2-Y-O **£19,407** (£5,775; £2,886; £1,443) **Stalls** Centre

Form RPR

3100 **1** **Bahamian Heights**[20] 4918 2-9-4 **90**............................(b[1]) RyanMoore 10 97+
(Clive Brittain) *mde all: drvn and hung bdly lft fnl f: hld on nr fin* **12/1**

1023 **2** *½* **Coulsty (IRE)**[10] 5313 2-9-7 **93**.. RichardHughes 4 98
(Richard Hannon) *lw: w wnr on outer: edgd lft ins fnl f: styd on towards fin* **13/2**[2]

602 **3** *nk* **Blurred Vision**[13] 5199 2-8-7 **79**.................................. GrahamGibbons 1 83
(William Jarvis) *lw: trckd ldrs on outer: edgd rt over 2f out: styd on wl last 50yds* **8/1**

1 **4** *½* **Les Gar Gan (IRE)**[23] 4820 2-8-0 **72** oh2............................ JimmyQuinn 15 75+
(Keith Dalgleish) *leggy: in rr: hdwy stands' side over 1f out: kpt on wl towards fin* **12/1**

212 **5** *hd* **Banaadeer (IRE)**[26] 4703 2-8-8 **80**................................ PaulHanagan 17 82
(Richard Hannon) *lw: chsd ldrs: drvn over 2f out: styd on ins fnl f* **7/1**[3]

6203 **6** *½* **Jazz (IRE)**[19] 4948 2-8-11 **83**.. JamieSpencer 5 84+
(Charles Hills) *sn bhd: gd hdwy over 1f out: edgd lft: styd on clsng stages* **11/1**

4512 **7** *1* **Suzi's Connoisseur**[11] 5272 2-9-5 **91**.................... SilvestreDeSousa 9 88
(Mark Johnston) *mid-div: hdwy over 2f out: one pce over 1f out* **16/1**

3241 **8** *¾* **Flying Bear (IRE)**[19] 4948 2-8-0 **75**.............................. DarrenEgan(3) 14 70
(Jeremy Gask) *lw: chsd ldrs: wknd fnl 150yds* **14/1**

31 **9** *2 ½* **Ventura Quest (USA)**[15] 5105 2-8-8 **80**.......................... TonyHamilton 6 67
(Richard Fahey) *chsd ldrs on outer: hmpd over 2f out: drvn: hung lft over 1f out: sn wknd* **5/1**[1]

5231 **10** *2 ¼* **Instant Attraction (IRE)**[28] 4630 2-8-4 **79**.................... RaulDaSilva(3) 2 59
(Jedd O'Keeffe) *mid-div on outer: lost pl over 1f out* **40/1**

4035 **11** *nse* **Ifwecan**[19] 4948 2-9-1 **87**.. JoeFanning 7 67
(Mark Johnston) *chsd ldrs: drvn over 2f out: wknd fnl f* **7/1**[3]

2210 **12** *1 ¼* **Speed The Plough**[19] 4948 2-8-5 **77**...................... MickaelBarzalona 12 53
(Richard Hannon) *chsd ldrs: sn drvn along: lost pl 2f out* **16/1**

254 **13** *½* **Thornaby Nash**[21] 4886 2-7-12 **73**....................................... JulieBurke(3) 8 47
(David O'Meara) *s.i.s: a in rr* **33/1**

3031 **14** *5* **Tiger Twenty Two**[39] 4314 2-8-7 **84**.......................... GeorgeChaloner(5) 16 42
(Richard Fahey) *in rr and sn drvn along: bhd fnl 2f* **16/1**

1m 10.19s (-1.71) **Going Correction** -0.25s/f (Firm) **14** Ran SP% **119.5**
Speed ratings (Par 100): **101,100,99,99,99 98,97,96,92,89 89,87,87,80**
toteswingers 1&2 £15.20, 1&3 £17.90, 2&3 £10.90 CSF £87.34 CT £691.05 TOTE £14.80: £3.90, £2.80, £3.10; EX 92.80 Trifecta £860.90 Pool: £5880.43 - 5.12 winning units..
Owner Sheikh Juma Dalmook Al Maktoum **Bred** Pantile Stud **Trained** Newmarket, Suffolk

FOCUS
A decent nursery, but it proved hard to make up significant ground. The winner is rated in keeping with his Group form, and the form overall is up to the race's usual high standard.
T/Jkpt: Not won. T/Plt: £1,088.50 to a £1 stake. Pool: £303238.53 - 203.36 winning tickets
T/Qpdt: £265.70 to a £1 stake. Pool: £14636.30 - 40.75 winning tickets WG

5657 - 5664a (Foreign Racing) - See Raceform Interactive

4937 BATH (L-H)
Thursday, August 22

OFFICIAL GOING: Firm (9.1)
Wind: Moderate across Weather: Sunny

5665 BOB PARR'S HAPPY 80TH MEDIAN AUCTION MAIDEN STKS 5f 11y
2:20 (2:21) (Class 6) 2-Y-O **£1,940** (£577; £288; £144) **Stalls** Centre

Form RPR

1 **Secret Romance** 2-9-0 0.. StephenCraine 2 73+
(Tom Dascombe) *mde all: drvn and styd on strly fnl f* **11/4**[3]

2 *3* **Clumber Street** 2-9-5 0.. SeanLevey 4 67
(Ed McMahon) *chsd wnr: chal 3f out: drvn over 2f out: green and outpcd fnl f* **8/1**

524 **3** *3 ¾* **Costa Filey**[69] 3288 2-9-5 72.. LukeMorris 3 53+
(Ed Vaughan) *v unruly and rrng as stalls opened: chsd ldrs in 3rd and rdn 3f out: sn hanging lft: nt keen and no ch w ldng duo over 1f out* **2/1**[2]

4 *7* **Wadi Alamardi** 2-9-2 0.................................. WilliamTwiston-Davies(3) 1 27
(Michael Bell) *rdn after 2f: a outpcd* **7/4**[1]

1m 1.95s (-0.55) **Going Correction** -0.175s/f (Firm) **4** Ran SP% **107.5**
Speed ratings (Par 92): **97,92,86,75**
CSF £19.25 TOTE £3.30; EX 16.40 Trifecta £17.00 Pool: £1053.79 - 46.38 winning units..
Owner Hot To Trot Racing Club **Bred** Whitsbury Manor Stud & Pigeon House Stud **Trained** Malpas, Cheshire

FOCUS
Far side rail dolled out about 4yds from 5f to just beyond 3f to provide fresh line where sprint races meet main track and no change to advertised distances. An ordinary maiden lacking depth, but the winner could do a good bit better.

5666 LANSDOWN H'CAP 1m 5f 22y
2:55 (2:55) (Class 5) (0-70,66) 4-Y-O+ **£2,587** (£770; £384; £192) **Stalls** High

Form RPR

3512 **1** **Chapter Five**[26] 4775 6-8-12 **60**..................................(v[1]) RyanPowell(3) 2 68
(Ian Williams) *racd in cl 3rd: drvn to take narrow ld 2f out: hrd pressed fr over 1f out: styd on u.p fnl press: jst hld on* **15/8**[2]

4643 **2** *hd* **Hurakan (IRE)**[26] 4775 7-9-4 **66**................................ ThomasBrown(3) 4 73
(Richard Price) *racd in cl 4th: pushed along 3f out: rapid hdwy to chal 2f out and hung lft sn after: pressed wnr fr over 1f out: styd on in clsng stages: jst failed* **11/4**[3]

132 **3** *6* **St Ignatius**[14] 5168 6-8-13 **63**.....................................(v) NatashaEaton(5) 5 61
(Alan Bailey) *trckd ldr: rdn and one pce whn pushed lft ins fnl 2f: wknd over 1f out* **7/4**[1]

00-0 **4** *10* **Maoi Chinn Tire (IRE)**[16] 5099 6-9-5 **64**............................(p) JohnFahy 1 50
(Jennie Candlish) *led: rdn 3f out: hdd 2f out: wkng whn pushed lft sn after: wknd qckly over 1f out* **10/1**

2m 49.8s (-2.20) **Going Correction** -0.175s/f (Firm) **4** Ran SP% **106.9**
Speed ratings (Par 103): **99,98,95,89**
CSF £7.05 TOTE £2.80; EX 5.70 Trifecta £9.20 Pool: £1427.57 - 115.61 winning units..
Owner Mr & Mrs Hutton & Mrs Laing **Bred** Mrs Lesley A Hutton **Trained** Portway, Worcs
■ Stewards' Enquiry : Thomas Brown two-day ban: careless riding (Sep 5-6); two-day ban: used whip above permitted level (Sep 8-9)

FOCUS
The pace was honest for this tight handicap, with the front two fighting out an exciting finish. The first two are rated to their recent Salisbury form.

5667 BREEZE RADIO H'CAP 1m 2f 46y
3:30 (3:30) (Class 6) (0-60,57) 3-Y-O+ **£1,940** (£577; £288; £144) **Stalls** Low

Form RPR

4412 **1** **Precision Five**[19] 5002 4-9-7 **57**....................................(p) RobertTart(5) 9 72
(Jeremy Gask) *in rr: hdwy over 3f out: led wl over 1f out: drvn clr fnl f* **8/11**[1]

6-55 **2** *5* **Saint Boniface**[13] 5232 4-9-6 **51**.. SteveDrowne 4 56
(Peter Makin) *hld up in rr: hdwy on outside over 2f out: styd on fnl f to take 2nd last stride but no ch w wnr* **7/1**[3]

2202 **3** *hd* **Special Report (IRE)**[13] 5217 3-8-8 **47**........................ WilliamCarson 7 52
(Peter Hiatt) *chsd ldrs: rdn to ld over 2f out: hdd over 1f out: outpcd fnl f: lost 2nd last stride* **5/1**[2]

4060 **4** *3 ½* **Signora Frasi (IRE)**[36] 4411 8-9-5 **50**.................................. SeanLevey 8 48
(Tony Newcombe) *in rr: hdwy over 2f out: styd on same pce fr over 1f out* **8/1**

0050 **5** *4* **Ernest Speak (IRE)**[7] 5434 4-8-7 **45**..................................(t) EoinWalsh(7) 3 36
(David Evans) *in tch: rdn 3f out: wknd 2f out* **16/1**

0255 **6** *17* **Hilden**[15] 5123 4-9-8 **53**...(b) DougieCostello 1 11
(William Muir) *sn led: kpt slt ld tl hdd & wknd qckly over 2f out* **14/1**

-600 **7** *7* **My Stroppy Poppy**[7] 5429 4-8-7 **45**................................ NoelGarbutt(7) 6
(David Evans) *chsd ldr: racd wd: rdn over 3f out: wknd sn after* **20/1**

0600 **8** *13* **Mayforde Jack**[14] 5166 4-9-0 **45**.. LukeMorris 5
(Simon Hodgson) *chsd ldrs: wknd over 3f out* **50/1**

2m 8.91s (-2.09) **Going Correction** -0.175s/f (Firm)
WFA 3 from 4yo+ 8lb **8** Ran SP% **117.5**
Speed ratings (Par 101): **101,97,96,94,90 77,71,61**
toteswingers 1&2 £2.40, 2&3 £3.00, 1&3 £1.70 CSF £6.86 CT £16.84 TOTE £1.80: £1.10, £1.90, £1.20; EX 5.60 Trifecta £20.40 Pool: £2830.90 - 103.90 winning units..
Owner Calne Engineering Ltd **Bred** Edward J G Young **Trained** Sutton Veny, Wilts

FOCUS
A weak handicap but the time was reasonable and the winner proved she is as good on turf as on Polytrack.

5668 SATELLITE INFORMATION SERVICES H'CAP 1m 5y
4:05 (4:05) (Class 5) (0-70,69) 3-Y-O **£2,587** (£770; £384; £192) **Stalls** Low

Form RPR

4423 **1** **Pilates (IRE)**[9] 5373 3-8-12 **60**.. AdrianNicholls 3 70+
(Mark Johnston) *chsd ldr: rdn over 3f out: chal 2f out: slt ld u.p wl over 1f out: styd on wl in clsng stages* **4/1**[2]

3221 **2** *1 ¾* **North Pole**[2] 5604 3-9-7 **69** 6ex...(p) LukeMorris 1 76+
(Sir Mark Prescott Bt) *sn led: pushed along 3f out: jnd 2f out: narrowly hdd wl over 1f out: rallied u.p press ins fnl f: no ex in clsng stages* **4/6**[1]

1663 **3** *3 ¼* **The Scuttler (IRE)**[20] 4940 3-8-10 **65**............................ DanielCremin(7) 2 64
(Mick Channon) *chsd ldrs: rdn over 3f out: outpcd fnl 2f* **10/1**

0550 **4** *4 ½* **Konzert (ITY)**[18] 5030 3-8-13 **64**....................................... RyanPowell(3) 4 52
(Ian Williams) *t.k.h: trckd ldr: wd bnd 5f out: wknd over 2f out* **5/1**[3]

4055 **5** *5* **Danz Choice (IRE)**[8] 5404 3-9-4 **69**.........(b[1]) WilliamTwiston-Davies(3) 5 46
(Richard Hannon) *rdn over 3f out: a bhd* **20/1**

1m 39.11s (-1.69) **Going Correction** -0.175s/f (Firm) **5** Ran SP% **110.5**
Speed ratings (Par 100): **101,99,96,91,86**
CSF £7.21 TOTE £5.10: £1.20, £1.70; EX 8.10 Trifecta £27.70 Pool: £1963.51 - 53.06 winning units..
Owner Sheikh Hamdan Bin Mohammed Al Maktoum **Bred** Michael O'Mahony **Trained** Middleham Moor, N Yorks

FOCUS
An interesting 3-y-o handicap run at a sound pace. The third is rated to his recent form.

5669 MATTHEW CLARK H'CAP 5f 161y
4:40 (4:41) (Class 5) (0-75,75) 3-Y-O+ **£2,587** (£770; £384; £192) **Stalls** Centre

Form RPR

4000 **1** **Shamahan**[56] 3741 4-9-7 **72**... PatDobbs 2 83
(Gary Moore) *hld up in tch: hdwy 2f out: led 1f out: drvn and styd on strly* **7/4**[1]

5310 **2** *1 ¼* **Dreams Of Glory**[17] 5060 5-9-1 **66**................................ DavidProbert 3 73
(Ron Hodges) *chsd ldrs: led ins fnl 2f: edgd rt and hdd 1f out: kpt on but nt gng pce of wnr* **7/1**

0225 **3** *½* **Howyadoingnotsobad (IRE)**[18] 5036 5-9-0 **72**............. RyanWhile(7) 9 77
(Karen George) *chsd ldrs: rdn over 2f out: kpt on same pce fnl f* **8/1**

042 **4** *1* **Dark Lane**[8] 5388 7-8-7 **65** EoinWalsh(7) 5 67
(David Evans) *towards rr whn bmpd over 3f out: rdn and hdwy on outside over 1f out: kpt on: no imp on ldrs* **13/2**
4352 **5** *shd* **Belle Bayardo (IRE)**[8] 5389 5-9-2 **67** LukeMorris 4 69
(Ronald Harris) *in rr: drvn along 1/2-way: styd on fnl f: nvr gng pce to rch ldrs* **6/1**[3]
5210 **6** *½* **Mambo Spirit (IRE)**[26] 4746 9-9-3 **68** SeanLevey 8 68
(Tony Newcombe) *in rr and edgd lft over 3f out: drvn and hdwy to chse ldrs 1/2-way: styd on same pce* **9/2**[2]
0020 **7** *1* **Baby Queen (IRE)**[13] 5227 7-8-12 **68** MatthewLawson(5) 1 65
(Brian Baugh) *chsd ldrs: rdn over 2f out: wknd fnl 110yds* **20/1**
1035 **8** *8* **Powerful Wind (IRE)**[37] 4364 4-9-10 **75** SteveDrowne 7 45
(Ronald Harris) *led: hdd ins fnl 2f: wknd over 1f out* **16/1**

1m 9.46s (-1.74) **Going Correction** -0.175s/f (Firm) **8** Ran SP% **116.4**
Speed ratings (Par 103): **104,102,101,100,100 99,98,87**
toteswingers 1&2 £4.40, 2&3 £8.10, 1&3 £5.10 CSF £15.04 CT £79.52 TOTE £3.00: £1.10, £2.80, £2.80; EX 20.80 Trifecta £113.20 Pool: £2477.50 - 16.40 inning units..
Owner Heart Of The South Racing **Bred** Frank Brady **Trained** Lower Beeding, W Sussex
FOCUS
Plenty of pace on for this open handicap. The form is rated around the placed horses.

5670 WESTERN DAILY PRESS H'CAP 5f 11y
5:15 (5:15) (Class 6) (0-60,58) 4-Y-0+ **£1,940** (£577; £288; £144) **Stalls** Centre

Form RPR
2403 **1** **Griffin Point (IRE)**[16] 5094 6-9-7 **58** (b) WilliamCarson 2 68
(William Muir) *chsd ldrs: drvn along fr 3f out: styd on to ld fnl 110yds: rdn out* **4/1**[3]
6622 **2** *¾* **Chester'Slittlegem (IRE)**[20] 4943 4-8-4 **48** JosephineGordon(7) 1 55
(Jo Hughes) *led over 3f out: pushed along and hung rt fr ins fnl 2f: kpt on fnl f: hdd and outpcd fnl 110yds* **9/4**[1]
3505 **3** *1 ½* **Volcanic Dust (IRE)**[20] 4943 5-9-1 **52** (t) SebSanders 7 54
(Milton Bradley) *chsd ldrs: rdn over 2f out: ev ch 1f out: outpcd fnl 110yds* **14/1**
6566 **4** *1 ¼* **Brandywell Boy (IRE)**[20] 4943 10-8-5 **45** BillyCray(3) 5 42
(Dominic Ffrench Davis) *in rr: sn drvn along: hdwy over 1f out: styd on in clsng stages* **25/1**
2414 **5** *1 ¼* **Arch Walker (IRE)**[8] 5388 6-9-7 **58** (b) KieranO'Neill 6 51
(John Weymes) *chsd ldrs: rdn over 2f out: wknd fnl f* **3/1**[2]
0043 **6** *½* **Flaxen Lake**[13] 5221 6-8-1 **45** (p) ShelleyBirkett(7) 3 36
(Milton Bradley) *outpcd most of way: sme late prog* **16/1**
U105 **7** *nse* **Spic 'n Span**[8] 5388 8-9-4 **55** (b) LukeMorris 9 46
(Ronald Harris) *led tl hdd over 3f out: carried rt fr ins fnl 2f: wknd fnl f* **18/1**
0060 **8** *2* **Flow Chart (IRE)**[14] 5198 6-8-9 **51** ow2 SladeO'Hara(5) 8 34
(Peter Grayson) *outpcd* **14/1**
0453 **9** *¾* **Madame Kintyre**[8] 5388 5-8-13 **50** (b) DavidProbert 4 31
(Rod Millman) *outpcd* **15/2**

1m 1.33s (-1.17) **Going Correction** -0.175s/f (Firm) **9** Ran SP% **115.9**
Speed ratings (Par 101): **102,100,98,96,94 93,93,90,89**
toteswingers 1&2 £2.60, 2&3 £7.00, 1&3 £13.60 CSF £13.46 CT £113.95 TOTE £3.50: £1.10, £1.60, £5.20; EX 16.20 Trifecta £180.70 Pool: £1855.89 - 7.70 winning units..
Owner F Hope **Bred** Vincent Dunne **Trained** Lambourn, Berks
FOCUS
This was run at a fierce pace, which suited the closers. Modest form.

5671 WESTERN DAILY PRESS APPRENTICE H'CAP 1m 3f 144y
5:45 (5:45) (Class 6) (0-65,65) 4-Y-0+ **£1,940** (£577; £288; £144) **Stalls** Low

Form RPR
4533 **1** **Spanish Plume**[14] 5179 5-9-4 **60** (p1) JackDuern(3) 3 68
(Andrew Hollinshead) *trckd ldr: led 2f out: styd on wl* **7/4**[1]
0146 **2** *1 ½* **Bold Cross (IRE)**[11] 5312 10-9-8 **64** RyanWhile(3) 5 69
(Edward Bevan) *hld up in rr: hdwy 3f out: chsd wnr 2f out: no imp fnl f* **9/2**[3]
-634 **3** *6* **Finch Flyer (IRE)**[24] 4835 6-8-4 **48** (p) JackGarritty(5) 6 43
(Aytach Sadik) *chsd ldrs in 3rd thrght: outpcd fnl 2f* **8/1**
5 **4** *2 ½* **Shukhov (IRE)**[22] 4901 4-9-11 **64** ColinKeane 9 55
(J F Levins, Ire) *led: hdd 2f out: btn sn after* **10/1**
0124 **5** *1 ¼* **Stag Hill (IRE)**[21] 4915 4-9-7 **60** RobertWilliams 8 49
(Bernard Llewellyn) *in tch: rdn 3f out: btn 2f out* **11/4**[2]
0/40 **6** *2 ¾* **Global Recovery (IRE)**[7] 5434 6-8-4 **46** oh1 (p) EoinWalsh(3) 7 30
(David Evans) *in tch: bhd fnl 3f* **16/1**
6600 **7** *5* **Inffiraaj (IRE)**[10] 5337 4-8-7 **51** DanielCremin(5) 10 27
(Mick Channon) *rdn over 3f out: a in rr* **20/1**

2m 28.93s (-1.67) **Going Correction** -0.175s/f (Firm) **7** Ran SP% **112.1**
Speed ratings (Par 101): **98,97,93,91,90 88,85**
toteswingers 1&2 £2.80, 2&3 £3.40, 1&3 £2.80 CSF £9.55 CT £47.19 TOTE £2.70: £2.10, £4.00; EX 12.20 Trifecta £36.40 Pool: £1527.75 - 31.44 winning units..
Owner The Three R'S **Bred** Mrs J A Prescott **Trained** Upper Longdon, Staffs
FOCUS
This weak handicap confined to apprentice riders was run at a sound pace.
T/Plt: £51.50 to a £1stake. Pool of £46512.44 - 659.09 winning tickets. T/Qpdt: £4.00 to a £1 stake. Pool of £3430.80 - 629.70 winning tickets. ST

5590 WOLVERHAMPTON (A.W) (L-H)
Thursday, August 22

OFFICIAL GOING: Standard
Wind: Light behind Weather: Overcast

5672 HOLIDAY INN WOLVERHAMPTON AMATEUR RIDERS' H'CAP 1m 4f 50y(P)
5:50 (5:50) (Class 5) (0-70,70) 3-Y-0+ **£2,495** (£774; £386; £193) **Stalls** Low

Form RPR
103- **1** **Azrag (USA)**[296] 7455 5-11-0 **70** (p) MrSWalker 9 84
(Gerard Butler) *chsd ldrs: pushed along to go 2nd over 1f out: rdn to ld wl ins fnl f: r.o* **9/4**[1]
6012 **2** *1* **Shahrazad (IRE)**[11] 5311 4-9-13 **60** (t) JackGilligan(5) 8 72
(Patrick Gilligan) *led: pushed along over 1f out: rdn and hdd wl ins fnl f* **10/1**
0-00 **3** *6* **Park Lane**[13] 5245 7-10-1 **64** MissMBishop-Peck(7) 7 66
(Noel Quinlan) *chsd ldr tl rdn over 1f out: wknd ins fnl f* **40/1**
4324 **4** *3 ¼* **Waahej**[10] 5356 7-10-6 **62** MrPCollington 3 59
(Peter Hiatt) *hld up: hdwy over 2f out: rdn over 1f out: wknd fnl f* **9/2**[3]
4112 **5** *½* **Gucci D'Oro (USA)**[13] 5241 4-10-6 **67** MrAlexFerguson(5) 6 63
(David Simcock) *chsd ldrs: lost pl over 4f out: n.d after* **7/2**[2]

3100 **6** *1 ½* **Teide Peak (IRE)**[17] 5065 4-10-3 **64** MrsRWilson(5) 2 58
(Paul D'Arcy) *hld up: hdwy over 5f out: rdn and wknd over 1f out* **11/1**
0/03 **7** *½* **Sure Fire (GER)**[3] 5592 8-9-4 **51** oh6 MissHDoyle(5) 1 44
(David Evans) *hld up: swtchd rt over 2f out: nvr nr to chal* **18/1**
0513 **8** *4* **Dazzling Valentine**[28] 4663 5-10-13 **69** MissSBrotherton 5 56
(Alan Bailey) *hld up: hdwy over 4f out: rdn and wknd over 1f out* **8/1**
0-66 **9** *5* **Rocky Rebel**[30] 351 5-10-4 **63** (b) MissBAndrews(3) 4 42
(Michael Blake) *hld up: hdwy over 5f out: rdn over 2f out: sn wknd* **20/1**

2m 42.41s (1.31) **Going Correction** -0.15s/f (Stan) **9** Ran SP% **112.2**
Speed ratings (Par 103): **89,88,84,82,81 80,80,77,74**
toteswingers 1&2 £6.90, 2&3 £27.80, 1&3 £17.10 CSF £25.03 CT £684.07 TOTE £2.30: £1.10, £2.80, £12.00; EX 30.00 Trifecta £836.60 Part won. Pool: £1115.53 - 0.49 winning units..
Owner Beetle N Wedge Partnership **Bred** Aislabie Bloodstock **Trained** Newmarket, Suffolk
FOCUS
A pretty moderate amateurs' event, but a good effort from the winner.

5673 DOWNLOAD OUR IPHONE APP H'CAP 5f 20y(P)
6:20 (6:21) (Class 5) (0-75,75) 3-Y-0+ **£2,587** (£770; £384; £192) **Stalls** Low

Form RPR
3260 **1** **Storm Lightning**[24] 4837 4-9-4 **69** (b) TomMcLaughlin 7 80
(Mark Brisbourne) *a.p: shkn up to ld over 1f out: rdn out* **8/1**
6206 **2** *½* **Rocket Rob (IRE)**[42] 4217 7-9-10 **75** ShaneKelly 10 84
(Willie Musson) *hld up: hdwy over 1f out: rdn and r.o wl ins fnl f: nt quite rch wnr* **5/1**[2]
0316 **3** *1* **Dangerous Age**[17] 5060 3-9-3 **70** LiamKeniry 5 76
(J W Hills) *chsd ldrs: rdn and ev ch over 1f out: styd on* **5/1**[2]
0-00 **4** *1 ½* **Solemn**[77] 3018 8-9-10 **75** (b) AdamKirby 3 75
(Milton Bradley) *a.p: racd keenly: rdn and edgd lft over 1f out: styd on* **14/1**
5150 **5** *½* **Deepest Blue**[12] 5294 3-8-8 **68** LukeLeadbitter(7) 6 66
(Declan Carroll) *s.i.s: hdwy over 3f out: nt clr run 1/2-way: sn rdn: styd on u.p* **13/2**
0000 **6** *nse* **M J Woodward**[9] 5365 4-9-1 **69** RaulDaSilva(3) 2 67
(Paul Green) *w ldr: led over 3f out: rdn 1/2-way: hdd over 1f out: no ex ins fnl f* **16/1**
0340 **7** *2* **Boxing Shadows**[44] 4136 3-9-6 **73** RoystonFfrench 9 64
(Bryan Smart) *mid-div: drvn along over 3f out: n.d* **11/2**[3]
0203 **8** *3 ½* **Shawkantango**[86] 2736 6-8-12 **70** (v) AdamMcLean(7) 11 48
(Derek Shaw) *sn outpcd* **25/1**
0000 **9** *5* **Pick A Little**[24] 4837 5-9-5 **70** (p) JackMitchell 8 30
(Michael Blake) *sn pushed along in rr: bhd fnl 3f* **33/1**
014 **10** *1 ½* **Royal Acquisition**[42] 4221 3-9-7 **74** GeorgeBaker 4 29
(Robert Cowell) *led: hdd over 3f out: hung rt 1/2-way: sn rdn: wknd over 1f out: eased* **7/2**[1]

1m 1.66s (-0.64) **Going Correction** -0.15s/f (Stan)
WFA 3 from 4yo+ 2lb **10** Ran SP% **114.7**
Speed ratings (Par 103): **99,98,96,94,93 93,90,84,76,74**
toteswingers 1&2 £8.50, 2&3 £4.20, 1&3 £9.60 CSF £46.96 CT £226.81 TOTE £8.30: £2.50, £2.00, £2.20; EX 54.00 Trifecta £148.40 Pool: £1192.53 - 6.02 winning units..
Owner Law Abiding Citizens **Bred** New England Stud And Partners **Trained** Great Ness, Shropshire
FOCUS
Not as many got into this sprint as seemed likely turning for home.

5674 ENJOY THE PUNTERS PACKAGE GROUP OFFER H'CAP 5f 216y(P)
6:50 (6:50) (Class 6) (0-65,65) 3-Y-0+ **£1,940** (£577; £288; £144) **Stalls** Low

Form RPR
2014 **1** **Burren View Lady (IRE)**[15] 5139 3-9-2 **60** (v) DavidAllan 12 68+
(Tim Easterby) *s.i.s: sn pushed along in rr: hdwy u.p and flashed tail fr over 1f out: r.o to ld nr fin* **9/2**[3]
U304 **2** *hd* **Solarmaite**[44] 4144 4-9-0 **58** (b) MarkCoumbe(3) 13 65
(Roy Bowring) *a.p: edgd rt over 2f out: rdn over 1f out: edgd lft and ev ch wl ins fnl f: r.o* **25/1**
2040 **3** *¾* **Steelcut**[23] 4852 9-9-5 **60** (p) MartinDwyer 5 65
(Mark Buckley) *chsd ldrs: rdn to ld wl ins fnl f: hdd nr fin* **25/1**
3142 **4** *¾* **Pull The Pin (IRE)**[11] 5305 4-9-7 **65** RaulDaSilva(3) 9 68
(Paul Green) *led: pushed along and hdd over 2f out: sn rdn: styd on same pce ins fnl f* **11/1**
004 **5** *¾* **Gregori (IRE)**[7] 5431 3-9-2 **60** (t) MartinLane 3 60
(Brian Meehan) *chsd ldr tl pushed along to ld over 2f out: rdn over 1f out: hdd and no ex wl ins fnl f* **12/1**
003 **6** *½* **Sleek**[17] 5069 3-9-4 **62** (b1) AdamKirby 7 61
(Marco Botti) *chsd ldrs: rdn over 1f out: styd on same pce ins fnl f* **3/1**[1]
6410 **7** *shd* **Reginald Claude**[13] 5230 5-8-13 **61** JoeyHaynes(7) 2 59
(Mark Usher) *hld up: hdwy over 1f out: nt rch ldrs* **16/1**
0560 **8** *½* **Camache Queen (IRE)**[10] 5349 5-9-7 **62** (bt1) LiamKeniry 6 59
(Joseph Tuite) *chsd ldrs: rdn over 1f out: no ex ins fnl f* **16/1**
4236 **9** *3* **Whipphound**[12] 5273 5-9-6 **61** GeorgeBaker 1 48
(Mark Brisbourne) *mid-div: rdn over 1f out: nvr on terms* **10/3**[2]
0013 **10** *nse* **Almaty Express**[24] 4836 11-8-10 **56** (b) ConnorBeasley(5) 8 43
(John Weymes) *prom: rdn 1/2-way: wknd fnl f* **16/1**
6306 **11** *1 ¼* **Above The Stars**[14] 5165 5-9-6 **64** SimonPearce(3) 10 47
(Conor Dore) *hld up: rdn over 1f out: n.d* **33/1**
0000 **12** *12* **Prince James**[90] 2611 6-9-7 **62** JamesSullivan 4 6
(Michael Easterby) *s.s: outpcd* **25/1**
6030 **13** *1 ½* **Art Dzeko**[16] 5088 4-9-10 **65** DuranFentiman 11 5
(Brian Baugh) *hld up: rdn 1/2-way: sn wknd* **20/1**

1m 14.34s (-0.66) **Going Correction** -0.15s/f (Stan)
WFA 3 from 4yo+ 3lb **13** Ran SP% **119.2**
Speed ratings (Par 101): **98,97,96,95,94 94,93,93,89,89 87,71,69**
toteswingers 1&2 £30.30, 2&3 £27.90, 1&3 £31.60 CSF £120.70 CT £2625.67 TOTE £5.20: £1.90, £8.50, £7.90; EX 130.80 Trifecta £992.00 Part won. Pool: £1322.68 - 0.06 winning units..
Owner Habton Farms **Bred** L Mulryan **Trained** Great Habton, N Yorks
■ Stewards' Enquiry : Mark Coumbe two-day ban: used whip above permitted level (Sep 6,8)
FOCUS
A strange first-half to this race, with little pace on and plenty of riders looking around.

5675 GREAT OFFERS AT WOLVERHAMPTON-RACECOURSE.CO.UK MAIDEN AUCTION STKS 7f 32y(P)
7:20 (7:21) (Class 6) 2-Y-0 **£1,940** (£577; £288; £144) **Stalls** High

Form RPR
6 **1** **Andy Dandy (IRE)**[87] 2712 2-9-2 0 RichardKingscote 9 73+
(Tom Dascombe) *sn pushed along in rr: hdwy over 1f out: r.o to ld wl ins fnl f* **2/1**[1]
00 **2** *½* **Half Way**[42] 4218 2-8-6 0 AmyScott(5) 3 64
(Henry Candy) *a.p: rdn over 2f out: led and edgd lft ins fnl f: hdd wl ins fnl f* **14/1**

3 **1 ½** **Lightning Shower (USA)** 2-8-11 0 ... TobyAtkinson(5) 7 65
(Marco Botti) *s.i.s: in rr: rdn over 2f out: hdwy over 1f out: rinning on whn nt clr run wl ins fnl f* **12/1**

462 **4** *nk* **Stella Clavisque (IRE)**[12] 5296 2-9-2 0 ... (b[1]) JamieSpencer 2 65
(Brian Meehan) *chsd ldrs: rdn and ev ch 1f out: no ex towards fin* **2/1[1]**

5 *1 ¼* **Bousfield** 2-8-9 0 ... DavidAllan 6 55
(Declan Carroll) *sn pushed along to chse ldrs: shkn up and ev ch whn hung lft over 1f out: no ex ins fnl f* **15/2[3]**

40 **6** *3* **Singapore Secret (IRE)**[10] 5338 2-8-4 0 ... JamesSullivan 1 42
(James Given) *led: rdn over 1f out: hdd and no ex ins fnl f* **6/1[2]**

03 **7** *4 ½* **Nice Arty (IRE)**[14] 5167 2-9-0 0 ow1 ... AdamKirby 8 41
(Jamie Osborne) *chsd ldr: rdn and ev ch whn hmpd over 1f out: wknd ins fnl f* **12/1**

600 **8** *6* **Celtic Ice (IRE)**[8] 5379 2-8-11 0 ... (p) ShirleyTeasdale(5) 5 28
(Alan McCabe) *sn pushed along in rr: bhd fr 1/2-way* **100/1**

1m 29.91s (0.31) **Going Correction** -0.15s/f (Stan) **8 Ran SP% 115.8**
Speed ratings (Par 92): **92,91,89,89,87 84,79,72**
toteswingers 1&2 £5.40, 2&3 £11.50, 1&3 £6.50 CSF £34.93 TOTE £3.00: £1.20, £2.50, £3.60; EX 24.00 Trifecta £658.50 Part won. Pool: £878.08 - 0.98 winning units..
Owner Manor House Stables LLP **Bred** Geraldine Cosgrave **Trained** Malpas, Cheshire

FOCUS
Just routine form, but the winner was well backed and is likely to be well treated for nurseries.

5676 SUSAN BOX MEMORIAL H'CAP — 7f 32y(P)
7:50 (7:51) (Class 4) (0-80,80) 3-Y-O — **£4,690** (£1,395; £697; £348) **Stalls** High

Form — RPR

4415 **1** **Ziekhani**[34] 4492 3-9-7 **80** ... RobertHavlin 10 90+
(Hughie Morrison) *hld up: hdwy u.p over 1f out: r.o to post* **9/1**

3152 **2** *hd* **Ready (IRE)**[34] 4508 3-9-7 **80** ... (p) AdamKirby 3 89
(Garry Moss) *a.p: rdn over 2f out: styd on u.p to ld wl ins fnl f: sn hung lft: hdd post* **8/1[3]**

3421 **3** *1 ½* **Liberty Jack (IRE)**[26] 4750 3-9-4 **77** ... (p) GeorgeBaker 6 82
(Roger Charlton) *pushed along to chse ldr: led over 1f out: sn rdn: edgd lft ins fnl f: sn edgd rt and hdd: nt qckn* **13/8[1]**

-102 **4** *¾* **Burning Dawn (USA)**[35] 4453 3-9-0 **73** ... (t) JamieSpencer 9 76
(David Brown) *sn pushed along in rr: hrd rdn over 1f out: hung lft and r.o ins fnl f: nt rch ldrs* **3/1[2]**

4432 **5** *1 ½* **Mishaal (IRE)**[12] 5290 3-8-8 **67** ... TomEaves 2 66
(Michael Herrington) *led: rdn and hdd over 1f out: no ex ins fnl f* **25/1**

204 **6** *nk* **Queen Aggie (IRE)**[15] 5125 3-9-4 **80** ... DeclanBates(3) 4 78
(David Evans) *hld up: hdwy and nt clr run over 1f out: r.o: nt rch ldrs* **20/1**

3130 **7** *½* **Baltic Prince (IRE)**[12] 5273 3-8-4 **66** ... RaulDaSilva(3) 7 63
(Paul Green) *hld up: rdn over 1f out: r.o ins fnl f: nvr nrr* **20/1**

3500 **8** *1* **Grilletto (USA)**[14] 5195 3-9-5 **78** ... (b) LukeMorris 5 72
(James Tate) *mid-div: drvn along 1/2-way: n.d* **11/1**

1261 **9** *4 ½* **Yahilwa (USA)**[44] 4145 3-9-7 **80** ... JimCrowley 8 62
(James Tate) *chsd ldrs: rdn over 2f out: wknd fnl f* **14/1**

1540 **10** *16* **Street Battle (USA)**[126] 1647 3-8-13 **72** ... (t) BarryMcHugh 1 11
(Tony Coyle) *chsd ldrs: rdn over 2f out: wknd over 1f out* **33/1**

1m 27.45s (-2.15) **Going Correction** -0.15s/f (Stan) **10 Ran SP% 115.5**
Speed ratings (Par 102): **106,105,104,103,101 101,100,99,94,76**
toteswingers 1&2 £15.30, 2&3 £5.60, 1&3 £3.90 CSF £73.21 CT £181.68 TOTE £11.40: £2.90, £2.80, £1.10; EX 86.00 Trifecta £638.30 Part won. Pool: £851.10 - 0.89 winning units..
Owner The Fairy Story Partnership **Bred** Deepwood Farm Stud **Trained** East Ilsley, Berks

FOCUS
With the first four in the market clear of the remainder and a winning time 2.45 seconds quicker than that of the preceding C&D maiden, this form looks pretty satisfactory for the grade.

5677 THE BLACK COUNTRY'S ONLY RACECOURSE H'CAP — 7f 32y(P)
8:20 (8:21) (Class 6) (0-65,65) 3-Y-O+ — **£1,940** (£577; £288; £144) **Stalls** High

Form — RPR

055 **1** **Quintet (IRE)**[33] 4535 3-9-3 **63** ... JimCrowley 8 74
(Ralph Beckett) *chsd ldr 2f: remained handy: shkn up to ld over 1f out: edgd lft: rdn out* **11/1[3]**

0021 **2** *¾* **Unex Michelangelo (IRE)**[3] 5596 4-9-10 **65** 6ex ... JamesSullivan 1 76
(Michael Easterby) *sn pushed along to chse ldrs: lost pl over 4f out: hdwy over 2f out: rdn to chse wnr fnl f: styd on* **1/1[1]**

3304 **3** *2 ¾* **Peter's Friend**[16] 5098 4-9-7 **62** ... TomEaves 7 66
(Michael Herrington) *s.i.s: hdwy over 5f out: rdn over 2f out: styd on* **20/1**

6550 **4** *¾* **Orpsie Boy (IRE)**[15] 5138 10-9-6 **64** ... JulieBurke(3) 9 66
(Ruth Carr) *hld up: rdn over 1f out: r.o ins fnl f: nvr nrr* **22/1**

2350 **5** *¾* **Maakirr (IRE)**[47] 4070 4-9-4 **62** ... (p) MarkCoumbe(3) 11 62
(Roy Bowring) *prom: chsd ldr 5f out tl led 3f out: rdn and hdd over 1f out: no ex ins fnl f* **20/1**

-600 **6** *1 ¼* **Caramelita**[114] 1914 6-9-5 **65** ... (v) DannyBrock(5) 5 62
(J R Jenkins) *hld up: hdwy over 1f out: r.o: nt rch ldrs* **33/1**

7 *3 ¼* **Jumbo Steps (IRE)**[15] 5160 6-9-2 **57** ... JamieSpencer 3 45
(J F Levins, Ire) *led 4f: pushed along over 2f out: rdn and ev ch over 1f out: wknd ins fnl f* **2/1[2]**

0-34 **8** *2 ½* **Alfresco**[37] 4388 9-9-2 **57** ... (v) LukeMorris 6 38
(Martin Bosley) *hld up: rdn over 2f out: eased whn btn fnl f* **33/1**

6500 **9** *23* **Bankroll**[15] 5135 6-9-5 **60** ... (t) GeorgeBaker 10
(Jonjo O'Neill) *hld up: rdn over 2f out: sn wknd* **20/1**

-040 **10** *17* **Storma Norma**[43] 4162 3-9-5 **65** ... DuranFentiman 4
(Tim Easterby) *chsd ldrs: rdn 1/2-way: wknd over 2f out* **66/1**

1m 28.02s (-1.58) **Going Correction** -0.15s/f (Stan)
WFA 3 from 4yo+ 5lb **10 Ran SP% 117.7**
Speed ratings (Par 101): **103,102,99,98,97 95,92,89,63,43**
toteswingers 1&2 £4.50, 2&3 £5.00, 1&3 £17.60 CSF £21.15 CT £241.35 TOTE £15.40: £3.20, £1.02, £3.50; EX 33.00 Trifecta £221.80 Pool: £1200.40 - 4.05 winning units..
Owner Highclere Thoroughbred Racing - Party **Bred** Coleman Bloodstock Limited **Trained** Kimpton, Hants

FOCUS
They bet 11-1 bar two in a moderate handicap, won in a time nearly 0.6 seconds slower than the 0-80 immediately before it.

5678 SPONSOR A RACE BY CALLING 01902 390000 MAIDEN STKS — 1m 1f 103y(P)
8:50 (8:51) (Class 5) 3-Y-O+ — **£2,587** (£770; £384; £192) **Stalls** Low

Form — RPR

22- **1** **Ostaad (IRE)**[320] 6876 3-9-5 0 ... (v[1]) SilvestreDeSousa 12 85+
(Saeed bin Suroor) *dwlt: hdwy to ld 7f out: clr 6f out: rdn fnl f: all out* **4/6[1]**

0-2 **2** *2* **Conserve (IRE)**[17] 5071 3-9-0 0 ... TomQueally 10 76
(Lady Cecil) *chsd ldr 2f: remained handy: rdn to chse wnr who was clr 2f out: styd on wl: too much to do* **10/1**

3 **3** *4 ½* **Duchess Of Seville**[17] 5071 3-9-0 0 ... AdamKirby 3 67
(Marco Botti) *hld up: rdn over 3f out: styd on to go 3rd fnl f: nvr on terms* **10/1**

23 **4** *2 ¾* **Le Grande Cheval (IRE)**[16] 5100 3-9-5 0 ... JimCrowley 9 66
(Harry Dunlop) *led: hdd 7f out: chsd wnr who wnt clr fr 6f out tl lost 2nd 2f out: wknd over 1f out* **14/1**

3 **5** *1 ¼* **Exploratory (USA)**[29] 4632 3-9-5 0 ... AhmedAjtebi 2 63
(Charlie Appleby) *hld up: hdwy over 3f out: sn rdn: wknd over 1f out* **5/1[2]**

6 *13* **Wall Street Boss (USA)** 3-9-5 0 ...[1] FrederikTylicki 13 36
(James Fanshawe) *hld up: pushed along over 3f out: nvr on terms* **8/1[3]**

04 **7** *1* **Rainbows And Roses**[12] 5281 3-9-0 0 ... TedDurcan 6 29
(Chris Wall) *hld up: a in rr* **66/1**

8 *½* **Intrinsic** 3-9-5 0 ... (p) PatDobbs 7 33
(Sir Michael Stoute) *hld up: rdn over 3f out: n.d* **20/1**

9 *½* **Cardinal Pioneer (TUR)** 3-9-5 0 ... SebSanders 1 32
(J W Hills) *dwlt: hld up: nvr on terms* **25/1**

06 **10** *¾* **Roycano**[6] 5469 3-9-5 0 ... JamesSullivan 5 30
(Michael Easterby) *plld hrd and prom: wknd over 3f out* **100/1**

00 **11** *1 ½* **Shelling Peas**[17] 5071 4-9-0 0 ... AdamMcLean(7) 4 22
(Derek Shaw) *prom tl wknd over 2f out* **125/1**

6 **12** *8* **Bold Citizen (IRE)**[16] 5110 3-9-5 0 ... GeorgeBaker 8 10
(Ed Dunlop) *sn prom: pushed along over 3f out: sn wknd* **25/1**

1m 58.69s (-3.01) **Going Correction** -0.15s/f (Stan)
WFA 3 from 4yo 7lb **12 Ran SP% 128.3**
Speed ratings (Par 103): **107,105,101,98,97 86,85,84,84,83 82,75**
toteswingers 1&2 £2.30, 2&3 £5.90, 1&3 £3.70 CSF £9.34 TOTE £1.80: £1.10, £1.70, £3.80; EX 10.30 Trifecta £48.40 Pool: £1876.91 - 29.04 winning units..
Owner Godolphin **Bred** Shadwell Estate Company Limited **Trained** Newmarket, Suffolk

FOCUS
Modest form overall but the winner looks useful.
T/Plt: £122.20 to a £1 stake.Pool of £84769.05 - 506.12 winning tickets. T/Qpdt: £44.50 to a £1 stake. Pool of £6305.88 - 104.63 winning tickets. CR

5651 YORK (L-H)
Thursday, August 22

OFFICIAL GOING: Good to firm (7.7)
Wind: Virtually nil Weather: Sunny periods and warm

5679 DBS PREMIER YEARLING STKS — 6f
1:55 (1:56) (Class 2) 2-Y-O
£154,769 (£61,932; £30,966; £15,451; £7,741; £7,741) **Stalls** Centre

Form — RPR

3304 **1** **Haikbidiac (IRE)**[33] 4528 2-8-11 95 ... (p) LiamJones 17 101
(William Haggas) *prom nr stands' rail: cl up 1/2-way: rdn over 1f out: led jst ins fnl f: sn clr: styd on* **9/1**

1453 **2** *2* **Thunder Strike**[21] 4918 2-9-2 101 ... RichardHughes 2 100
(Richard Hannon) *racd towards far side: trckd ldrs: hdwy over 2f out: rdn to ld briefly ent fnl f: sn hdds and kpt on same pce towards fin* **7/1[2]**

12 **3** *hd* **Nezar (IRE)**[18] 5034 2-8-11 81 ... JohnnyMurtagh 7 94
(William Haggas) *lw: dwlt and bhd: gd hdwy 2f out: rdn over 1f out: styd on strly fnl f: nrst fin* **8/1[3]**

4104 **4** *nk* **Sleeper King (IRE)**[23] 4855 2-9-2 103 ... PhillipMakin 9 98+
(Kevin Ryan) *lw: hld up: hdwy over 2f out: rdn to chse ldrs over 1f out: edgd lft and kpt on wl fnl f* **8/1[3]**

13 **5** *1 ¼* **Rufford (IRE)**[52] 3890 2-8-11 0 ... PaulHanagan 16 89+
(Richard Fahey) *lw: chsd ldrs towards stands' rail: pushed along and outpcd over 2f out: sn rdn and styd on fnl f: nrst fin* **6/1[1]**

213 **6** *shd* **Tobougg Happy**[18] 5029 2-8-6 83 ... JoeFanning 10 84
(James Tate) *lw: in tch centre: hdwy to chse ldrs over 2f out: rdn wl over 1f out: kpt on same pce* **16/1**

1110 **7** *nk* **Miracle Of Medinah**[21] 4918 2-9-2 99 ... LiamKeniry 11 93
(Mark Usher) *chsd ldrs: rdn along 2f out: drvn and one pce appr fnl f* **14/1**

301 **8** *½* **Foxy Clarets (IRE)**[15] 5140 2-8-11 77 ... TonyHamilton 3 87?
(Richard Fahey) *racd towards far side: trckd ldrs: hdwy over 2f out: rdn wl over 1f out: drvn and no imp fnl f* **50/1**

4111 **9** *1 ½* **Viva Verglas (IRE)**[13] 5236 2-9-0 94 ... GrahamGibbons 5 85
(David Barron) *chsd ldrs towards centre: rdn along 2f out: sn one pce* **12/1**

3121 **10** *½* **Fair Ranger**[48] 4031 2-8-11 87 ... RyanMoore 6 80
(Richard Hannon) *dwlt: sn outpcd and detached at 1/2-way: hdwy wl over 1f out: kpt on fnl f: nrst fin* **14/1**

1031 **11** *¾* **Green Door (IRE)**[13] 5228 2-8-11 94 ... (b) JamieSpencer 4 78
(Olly Stevens) *overall ldr far side: qcknd clr wl over 1f out: sn rdn and edgd lft: hdd and drvn ent fnl f: sn wknd* **14/1**

1102 **12** *1* **Ventura Mist**[54] 3829 2-8-11 96 ... (p) DuranFentiman 18 75
(Tim Easterby) *chsd ldrs: rdn along 2f out: grad wknd* **12/1**

0111 **13** *1 ¼* **Touch The Clouds**[12] 5272 2-8-11 76 ... NeilCallan 20 71
(Kevin Ryan) *racd towards stands' rail: a towards rr* **50/1**

3205 **14** *hd* **Morning Post**[22] 4886 2-8-11 82 ... FrannyNorton 15 70
(Kevin Ryan) *chsd ldrs towards centre: rdn along over 2f out: grad wknd* **50/1**

613 **15** *nk* **Oasis Town**[33] 4528 2-8-6 89 ... SilvestreDeSousa 1 64
(Kevin Ryan) *racd towards far side: chsd ldrs: rdn along over 2f out: sn wknd* **10/1**

3421 **16** *¾* **Party Ruler (IRE)**[18] 5029 2-8-11 81 ... RichardKingscote 19 67
(Tom Dascombe) *qckly away and cl up stands' rail: pushed along bef 1/2-way: sn rdn and wknd over 2f out* **50/1**

4100 **17** *nk* **Yorkshire Relish (IRE)**[20] 4948 2-9-0 77 ... PaulMulrennan 14 69
(Kevin Ryan) *in tch centre: rdn along 1/2-way: sn wknd* **50/1**

22 **18** *1 ½* **Dutch Breeze**[10] 5339 2-8-11 0 ... DavidAllan 13 61
(Tim Easterby) *chsd ldrs centre: rdn along over 2f out: sn wknd* **33/1**

41 **19** *2 ½* **Xanthos**[26] 4756 2-8-11 0 ... TomMcLaughlin 8 53
(Ed Walker) *racd centre: prom: rdn along wl over 2f out: sn wknd* **20/1**

1m 10.55s (-1.35) **Going Correction** -0.20s/f (Firm) **19 Ran SP% 126.9**
Speed ratings (Par 100): **101,98,98,97,96 95,95,94,92,92 91,89,88,87,87 86,86,84,80**
toteswingers 1&2 £12.80, 2&3 £5.00, 1&3 £15.50 CSF £68.68 TOTE £9.90: £3.30, £2.60, £3.40; EX 79.20 Trifecta £698.80 Pool: £6865.53 - 7.36 winning units..
Owner Sheikh Juma Dalmook Al Maktoum **Bred** Silk Fan Syndicate **Trained** Newmarket, Suffolk

The Form Book Flat, Raceform Ltd, Compton, RG20 6NL.

FOCUS
Racing on traditional inside line around home bend and all distances as advertised. This ultra-valuable sales race has gone to some high-class juveniles in recent years, including subsequent Group 1 winners Dark Angel and Wootton Bassett. The field split into two early with the bulk of the field racing centre to stands' side, while four (including the runner-up) went far side. Those towards the head of the market dominated. This was far from a vintage renewal and the second and fourth help with the straightforward level of the form.

5680 CONNOLLY'S RED MILLS LOWTHER STKS (GROUP 2) (FILLIES) 6f
2:30 (2:31) (Class 1) 2-Y-O

£85,065 (£32,250; £16,140; £8,040; £4,035; £2,025) **Stalls** Centre

Form RPR
1161 **1** **Lucky Kristale**[41] 4253 2-9-1 107 .... TomQueally 9 110+
(George Margarson) *hld up: swtchd rt and hdwy 2f out: rdn and qckned to ld ent fnl f: kpt on: readily* **5/2**[1]

3132 **2** *1 ½* **Queen Catrine (IRE)**[26] 4742 2-8-12 100 .... JohnnyMurtagh 3 102
(Charles Hills) *warm: dwlt: sn cl up: led after 1f: pushed along 1/2-way: rdn and hdd 2f out: drvn over 1f out: kpt on wl u.p fnl f* **6/1**[3]

1351 **3** *hd* **Wind Fire (USA)**[6] 5476 2-8-12 101 .... JamieSpencer 5 102
(David Brown) *cl up: chal 2f out: rdn to ld over 1f out: drvn and hdd ent fnl f: kpt on same pce* **9/2**[2]

64 **4** *½* **Merletta**[10] 5344 2-8-12 0 .... RyanMoore 8 100
(Jeremy Noseda) *leggy: lw: trckd ldrs on outer: hdwy and cl up 1/2-way: rdn wl over 1f out: kpt on same pce fnl f* **25/1**

3105 **5** *nk* **Alutiq (IRE)**[33] 4528 2-8-12 92 .... HarryBentley 4 99
(Eve Johnson Houghton) *lw: hld up in tch: hdwy 2f out: sn rdn and kpt on same pce fnl f* **20/1**

2110 **6** *hd* **Azagal (IRE)**[19] 5005 2-8-12 85 .... DavidAllan 1 98
(Tim Easterby) *trckd ldrs: hdwy 2f out: rdn and ch whn n.m.r ent fnl f: sn edgd lft and kpt on same pce* **33/1**

11 **7** *½* **J Wonder (USA)**[19] 5005 2-8-12 0 .... MartinLane 7 97
(Brian Meehan) *t.k.h: trckd ldrs: effrt 2f out: sn rdn and no imp fnl f* **5/2**[1]

10 **8** *¾* **Kaiulani (IRE)**[64] 3459 2-8-12 0 .... MartinHarley 6 94
(Mick Channon) *hld up: a in rr* **16/1**

156 **9** *3 ¾* **Reroute (IRE)**[23] 4855 2-8-12 95 .... WilliamBuick 2 82
(Ed Walker) *lw: led 1f at stdy pce: cl up tl led again 2f out: sn rdn and hdd over 1f out: wknd fnl f* **11/1**

1m 10.58s (-1.32) **Going Correction** -0.20s/f (Firm) **9** Ran SP% **115.4**
Speed ratings (Par 103): **100,98,97,97,96 96,95,94,89**
toteswingers 1&2 £3.60, 2&3 £4.00, 1&3 £3.30 CSF £17.65 TOTE £2.90: £1.30, £1.60, £1.40; EX 16.90 Trifecta £40.00 Pool: £8724.39 - 163.53 winning units..
Owner Graham Lodge Partnership **Bred** Lilac Bloodstock & Redmyre Bloodstock **Trained** Newmarket, Suffolk

FOCUS
This didn't look an overly strong renewal of a major race for juvenile fillies considering one of the joint-favourites, albeit unbeaten, only had a maiden and nursery success to her name. The pace was decent and the filly with the best form won. Lucky Kristale is rated to her mark and the form is taken at face value despite a compressed finish in behind.

5681 CLIPPER LOGISTICS STKS (H'CAP) 1m
3:05 (3:06) (Class 2) 3-Y-O+

£46,687 (£13,980; £6,990; £3,495; £1,747; £877) **Stalls** Low

Form RPR
1016 **1** **Mont Ras (IRE)**[25] 4811 6-8-10 **98** .... DavidBergin(5) 13 107
(David O'Meara) *lw: mde all: rdn along 2f out: drvn ent fnl f: kpt on wl towards fin* **25/1**

5600 **2** *1* **Windhoek**[20] 4946 3-8-13 **102** .... JoeFanning 3 109
(Mark Johnston) *hld up in tch: hdwy 3f out: trckd ldrs 2f out: effrt to chse wnr ent fnl f: sn rdn and edgd lft: no imp towards fin* **5/1**[2]

\- **3** *½* **Hot Bed (IRE)**[29] 4648 4-9-4 **101** .... RyanMoore 15 107
(David Wachman, Ire) *w'like: dwlt and bhd: pushed along wl over 2f out: rdn and hdwy wl over 1f out: styd on wl fnl f: nrst fin* **9/1**

2312 **4** *hd* **Frog Hollow**[13] 5238 4-8-7 **90** .... TomEaves 9 96
(David O'Meara) *lw: dwlt and towards rr: hdwy over 3f out: rdn to chse ldrs wl over 1f out: drvn and edgd lft ent fnl f: kpt on same pce* **13/2**[3]

2306 **5** *nk* **Es Que Love (IRE)**[20] 4946 4-9-7 **104** .... FrankieDettori 11 109
(Mark Johnston) *trckd wnr: effrt 3f out: rdn 2f out: drvn ent fnl f and kpt on same pce* **12/1**

1330 **6** *nk* **Queensberry Rules (IRE)**[26] 4744 3-8-11 **100** .... JohnnyMurtagh 7 104
(William Haggas) *swtg: t.k.h: midfield: effrt 3f out: rdn to chse ldrs 2f out: drvn and kpt on same pce fnl f* **4/1**[1]

0601 **7** *1* **Norse Blues**[19] 5014 5-8-13 **96** .... GrahamGibbons 4 98
(David Barron) *lw: hld up towards rr: hdwy 3f out: rdn to chse ldrs 2f out: drvn and one pce appr fnl f* **14/1**

2300 **8** *½* **Anderiego (IRE)**[40] 4308 5-8-10 **93** .... TonyHamilton 10 94
(David O'Meara) *lw: t.k.h: chsd ldrs: rdn along over 2f out: drvn wl over 1f out: grad wknd* **20/1**

-620 **9** *shd* **Validus**[40] 4310 4-9-6 **103** .... KierenFallon 18 103
(Luca Cumani) *lw: hld up towards rr: hdwy on outer wl over 2f out: rdn and edgd lft over 1f out: kpt on fnl f: nrst fin* **16/1**

2003 **10** *1* **Sandagiyr (FR)**[20] 4946 5-9-10 **107** .... SilvestreDeSousa 17 105
(Saeed bin Suroor) *hld up towards rr: hdwy over 2f out: rdn wl over 1f out: drvn and no imp fnl f* **10/1**

1220 **11** *3* **Able Master (IRE)**[18] 5026 7-8-12 **95** .... DavidNolan 16 86
(David O'Meara) *prom: chsd wnr over 5f out: rdn along 3f out: drvn and wknd wl over 1f out* **50/1**

0225 **12** *nk* **Smarty Socks (IRE)**[5] 5518 9-9-1 **98** .... WilliamBuick 1 89
(David O'Meara) *in rr: swtchd rt to outer and rdn along wl over 2f out: n.d* **10/1**

2010 **13** *nk* **Prince Of Johanne (IRE)**[26] 4744 7-9-7 **104** ....(p) TomQueally 19 94
(Tom Tate) *midfield: rdn along on outer 3f out: wknd fnl 2f* **16/1**

1050 **14** *1 ½* **Navajo Chief**[12] 5269 6-9-1 **103** .... MichaelJMMurphy(5) 8 89
(Alan Jarvis) *chsd ldrs: rdn along over 3f out: sn wknd* **12/1**

1610 **15** *½* **Lord Of The Dance (IRE)**[18] 5026 7-8-7 **93** ow3........ RyanClark(3) 2 78
(Michael Mullineaux) *towards rr: sme hdwy on inner wl over 2f out: sn rdn and wknd* **33/1**

1052 **16** *7* **Pintura**[19] 5019 6-9-10 **107** ....(b) NeilCallan 5 76
(Kevin Ryan) *trckd ldrs on inner: rdn along 3f out: wknd 2f out* **25/1**

1m 36.55s (-2.45) **Going Correction** -0.05s/f (Good)
WFA 3 from 4yo+ 6lb **16** Ran SP% **129.4**
Speed ratings (Par 109): **110,109,108,108,108 107,106,106,106,105 102,102,101,100,99 92**
toteswingers 1&2 £45.80, 2&3 £13.00, 1&3 £47.10 CSF £147.62 CT £1313.33 TOTE £38.70: £7.70, £1.60, £2.30, £2.10; EX 330.40 Trifecta £4438.30 Pool: £7845.98 - 1.32 winning units..
Owner Colne Valley Racing **Bred** Patrick M Ryan **Trained** Nawton, N Yorks

FOCUS
A typically competitive handicap which had gone to a 3yo or 4yo in the previous nine runnings, but this was one for the older brigade. The early pace didn't look that strong and a couple of the fancied runners pulled hard, but things quickened up in the second-half of the contest. Solid form with the winner a length off his best.

5682 DARLEY YORKSHIRE OAKS (BRITISH CHAMPIONS SERIES) (GROUP 1) (F&M) 1m 4f
3:40 (3:40) (Class 1) 3-Y-O+

£200,895 (£76,163; £38,117; £18,987; £9,529; £4,782) **Stalls** Centre

Form RPR
3-30 **1** **The Fugue**[47] 4082 4-9-7 116 .... WilliamBuick 6 121
(John Gosden) *trckd ldrs: hdwy 3f out: cl up on bit 2f out: led appr fnl f: sn rdn clr: readily* **2/1**[1]

21 **2** *4* **Venus De Milo (IRE)**[16] 5115 3-8-11 114 .... RyanMoore 4 115
(A P O'Brien, Ire) *w'like: tall: chsd clr ldr: tk clsr order over 3f out: led over 2f out: sn jnd and rdn: drvn and hdd over 1f out: kpt on same pce* **9/4**[2]

-122 **3** *3 ¼* **Secret Gesture**[18] 5044 3-8-11 108 .... JamieSpencer 7 110
(Ralph Beckett) *hld up towards rr: hdwy over 3f out: rdn along 2f out: kpt on same pce appr fnl f* **6/1**

4134 **4** *3 ¾* **Scintillula (IRE)**[11] 5317 3-8-11 114 ....(t) KevinManning 2 104
(J S Bolger, Ire) *tall: lengthy: lw: led and clr: pushed along over 3f out: hdd over 2f out: sn drvn and wknd* **16/1**

2115 **5** *1 ¾* **Riposte**[33] 4550 3-8-11 112 .... TomQueally 8 101
(Lady Cecil) *hld up towards rr: hdwy over 3f out: rdn along over 2f out: drvn wl over 1f out and n.d* **5/1**[3]

3120 **6** *1 ½* **Moment In Time (IRE)**[19] 4985 4-9-7 108 .... JimCrowley 5 99
(David Simcock) *hld up: a towards rr* **28/1**

-613 **7** *4 ½* **Emirates Queen**[12] 5297 4-9-7 109 .... AndreaAtzeni 3 92
(Luca Cumani) *chsd ldng pair: rdn along over 3f out: sn wknd* **12/1**

2m 28.29s (-4.91) **Going Correction** -0.05s/f (Good)
WFA 3 from 4yo+ 10lb **7** Ran SP% **112.1**
Speed ratings (Par 117): **114,111,109,106,105 104,101**
toteswingers 1&2 £1.50, 2&3 £2.60, 1&3 £3.10 CSF £6.45 TOTE £3.40: £2.80, £1.60; EX 8.10 Trifecta £36.20 Pool: £11997.66 - 248.02 winning units..
Owner Lord Lloyd-Webber **Bred** Watership Down Stud **Trained** Newmarket, Suffolk

FOCUS
Even after the defection of Wild Coco due to the quick ground this was a competitive contest, but the winner, the only one of these to have previously taken a Group 1, proved much the best. The form is sure to be reliable. The Fugue rates a small personal best, with this slightly above the race standard, while Venus De Milo was up a length on her Irish Oaks form.

5683 "BREEDERS BACKING RACING" EBF GALTRES STKS (LISTED RACE) (F&M) 1m 4f
4:20 (4:20) (Class 1) 3-Y-O+

£28,355 (£10,750; £5,380; £2,680; £1,345; £675) **Stalls** Centre

Form RPR
61-1 **1** **Our Obsession (IRE)**[26] 4777 3-8-8 94 .... FrankieDettori 3 108
(William Haggas) *lw: t.k.h early: trckd ldng pair: swtchd rt and hdwy 3f out: cl up 2f out: rdn to ld jst over 1f out: jnd and drvn ins fnl f: kpt on wl towards fin* **3/1**[1]

0552 **2** *nk* **Say (IRE)**[8] 5415 3-8-8 110 .... RyanMoore 1 107
(A P O'Brien, Ire) *warm: hld up in tch: hdwy to trck ldrs over 4f out: effrt on outer over 2f out: rdn to chal over 1f out: drvn ins fnl f and ev ch tl no ex towards fin* **4/1**[3]

3425 **3** *1 ¾* **Jathabah (IRE)**[21] 4920 3-8-8 97 .... RichardHughes 9 104
(Clive Brittain) *led: pushed along wl over 3f out: jnd and rdn wl over 1f out: drvn and hdd appr fnl f: kpt on same pce* **18/1**

2101 **4** *¾* **Star Lahib (IRE)**[12] 5259 4-9-4 100 .... FrannyNorton 11 103
(Mark Johnston) *trckd ldr: hdwy 3f out: cl up 2f out: sn rdn and ev ch tl drvn and one pce ent fnl f* **7/2**[2]

0232 **5** *3 ¾* **Lady Nouf**[27] 4732 3-8-8 98 ....(p) AndreaAtzeni 5 97
(William Haggas) *hld up towards rr: hdwy 3f out: rdn along 2f out: sn drvn and no imp* **13/2**

0-60 **6** *1 ¼* **Coquet**[47] 4059 4-9-4 103 .... KierenFallon 8 95
(Hughie Morrison) *hld up towards rr: hdwy 3f out: rdn over 2f out: sn no imp* **20/1**

112 **7** *shd* **Songbird (IRE)**[18] 5035 4-9-4 98 .... TomQueally 4 95
(Lady Cecil) *swtg: trckd ldrs: rdn along over 2f out: sn drvn and wknd* **4/1**[3]

5340 **8** *8* **Eastern Destiny**[22] 4878 4-9-4 87 .... PaulHanagan 6 82
(Richard Fahey) *lw: a in rr* **50/1**

4260 **9** *1 ¼* **Bite Of The Cherry**[18] 5035 4-9-4 96 .... JohnnyMurtagh 12 80
(Michael Bell) *hld up: a in rr* **25/1**

2m 31.99s (-1.21) **Going Correction** -0.05s/f (Good)
WFA 3 from 4yo+ 10lb **9** Ran SP% **116.4**
Speed ratings (Par 111): **102,101,100,100,97 96,96,91,90**
toteswingers 1&2 £3.60, 2&3 £9.10, 1&3 £9.10 CSF £15.03 TOTE £3.10: £1.20, £1.80, £3.60; EX 12.20 Trifecta £99.90 Pool: £8512.39 - 63.86 winning units..
Owner A E Oppenheimer **Bred** Hascombe And Valiant Studs **Trained** Newmarket, Suffolk

FOCUS
This Listed race was run at an early dawdle and the winning time was 3.70sec slower than the Yorkshire Oaks. As a result those that raced up with the pace enjoyed a significant advantage. The 3yos had taken nine of the 12 runnings since 2000 and the Classic generation dominated again, filling the first three places. A rather muddling race but the progressive winner fits the race averages.

5684 EVENTMASTERS.CO.UK EBF FILLIES' STKS (H'CAP) 7f
4:55 (4:56) (Class 2) (0-100,96) 3-Y-O+ **£19,407** (£5,775; £2,886; £1,443) **Stalls** Low

Form RPR
0352 **1** **Dutch Rose (IRE)**[28] 4671 4-9-7 **91** .... KierenFallon 11 100
(David O'Meara) *lw: prom: cl up 2f out: sn rdn: led jst ins fnl f: kpt on gamely towards fin* **8/1**[3]

2210 **2** *nk* **Indignant**[20] 4949 3-9-7 **96** .... RichardHughes 2 102
(Richard Hannon) *lw: led: rdn wl over 1f out: drvn ent fnl f: sn hdd: ev ch tl no ex nr fin* **8/1**[3]

3112 **3** *½* **Ghasabah**[26] 4766 3-8-9 **84** .... PaulHanagan 4 93+
(William Haggas) *in tch: hdwy 2f out: nt clr run and hmpd over 1f out: swtchd lft to outer and rdn ins fnl f: squeezed through and fin strly* **4/1**[1]

6200 **4** *nk* **Sweetnessandlight**[12] 5255 4-9-1 **90** .... DavidBergin(5) 5 96
(Jason Ward) *in tch: hdwy over 2f out: rdn to chse ldrs over 1f out: drvn and kpt on fnl f* **14/1**

2211 **5** *nk* **Nurpur (IRE)**[27] 4729 3-8-10 **85** .... RyanMoore 15 88+
(David O'Meara) *hld up and bhd: swtchd to outer and rdn over 1f out: styd on strly fnl f: nrst fin* **6/1**[2]

2341 **6** *nk* **Shesastar**[28] 4671 5-8-9 **79** FrankieDettori 8 83
(David Barron) *hld up towards rr: hdwy 2f out: rdn over 1f out: drvn and kpt on fnl f: nrst fin* **8/1**[3]

2113 **7** *nse* **Elle Woods (IRE)**[28] 4671 3-8-12 **87** (p) PaulMulrennan 6 89
(Michael Dods) *trckd ldrs: effrt and nt clr run wl over 1f out and again 1f out: kpt on same pce fnl f* **12/1**

5124 **8** *1 1/4* **Magic Destiny**[13] 5246 4-9-4 **88** NeilCallan 10 89
(Mrs K Burke) *hld up in midfield: hdwy over 2f out: rdn to chse ldrs wl over 1f out: drvn and one pce fnl f* **16/1**

5113 **9** *1* **Malekat Jamal (IRE)**[6] 5493 4-8-7 **80** DarrenEgan(3) 7 78
(David Simcock) *lw: dwlt and bhd: hdwy wl over 1f out: rdn and styng on whn nt clr run ins fnl f: no ch after* **12/1**

5- **10** *nse* **Patrona Ciana (FR)**[83] 3-8-9 **84** WilliamBuick 12 80
(David O'Meara) *unf: hld up towards rr: hdwy over 2f out: rdn over 1f out: swtchd lft ins fnl f: no imp* **20/1**

5422 **11** *nk* **Dusky Queen (IRE)**[27] 4725 3-8-8 **83** TonyHamilton 14 78
(Richard Fahey) *in tch on outer: pushed along wl over 2f out: rdn wl over 1f out: drvn over 1f out and one pce* **9/1**

5343 **12** *3* **Lisiere (IRE)**[17] 5051 4-8-8 **78** (p) JoeFanning 16 67
(Mrs K Burke) *towards rr on outer: pushed along 1/2-way: n.d* **22/1**

6026 **13** *3 1/2* **Lady Of The House (IRE)**[19] 5004 3-8-9 **84** (p) FrannyNorton 9 62
(Kevin Ryan) *prom: cl up over 2f out: sn rdn and wknd over 1f out* **33/1**

6500 **14** *3/4* **Tartiflette**[26] 4766 4-9-6 **90** (b1) GrahamGibbons 13 68
(Ed McMahon) *in tch: hdwy to chse ldrs 1/2-way: rdn along wl over 2f out: wknd over 1f out* **11/1**

2-00 **15** *4* **Desert Image**[64] 3460 3-9-4 **93** JohnnyMurtagh 3 58
(Charles Hills) *trckd ldrs on inner: effrt over 2f out: rdn wl over 1f out: sn wknd* **20/1**

1m 22.96s (-2.34) **Going Correction** -0.20s/f (Firm)
WFA 3 from 4yo+ 5lb **15** Ran SP% **127.0**
Speed ratings (Par 96): **105,104,104,103,103 103,103,101,100,100 100,96,92,91,87**
toteswingers 1&2 £12.50, 2&3 £7.70, 1&3 £7.30 CSF £68.91 CT £308.16 TOTE £6.20: £2.20, £3.50, £1.80; EX 116.40 Trifecta £422.70 Pool: £7534.70 - 13.36 winning units..
Owner Favourites Racing XXIV **Bred** Joseph Kennedy **Trained** Nawton, N Yorks

FOCUS
A competitive contest but there was a messy finish and a few of those beaten appeared to have hard-luck stories. Good fillies' form, and sound enough.
T/Jkpt: Not won. T/Plt: £47.60 to a £1 stake. Pool of £376541.90 - 5773.96 winning tickets. T/Qpdt: £9.80 to a £1 stake. Pool of £17261.02 - 1296.06 winning tickets. JR

5685 - 5687a (Foreign Racing) - See Raceform Interactive

5248 TIPPERARY (L-H)
Thursday, August 22

OFFICIAL GOING: Good (good to firm in places)

5688a COOLMORE STUD FAIRY BRIDGE STKS (GROUP 3) (F&M) 7f 100y
6:40 (6:40) 3-Y-0+ **£33,028** (£9,654; £4,573; £1,524)

RPR

1 **Fiesolana (IRE)**[32] 4567 4-9-10 110 WJLee 1 110+
(W McCreery, Ire) *settled chsng ldrs: 3rd 1/2-way: rdn to chal between horses 2f out: kpt on strly to ld ent fnl f: r.o wl u.p cl home* **9/4**[2]

2 *1 1/4* **Sea Siren (AUS)**[11] 5320 5-9-5 113 (b) JosephO'Brien 2 102
(A P O'Brien, Ire) *sn settled in 5th: clsd up on outer 2f out: sn rdn to chal: chsd wnr ins fnl f: kpt on wl but hld cl home* **2/1**[1]

3 *1/2* **Rasmeyaa (IRE)**[109] 2047 3-9-0 98 PatSmullen 9 99+
(D K Weld, Ire) *settled in rr: rdn 2f out and styd on wl ins fnl f u.p to go nvr threatening 3rd cl home: nrst fin* **12/1**

4 *3/4* **Tobann (IRE)**[7] 5454 3-9-0 104 (t) RoryCleary 6 97
(J S Bolger, Ire) *settled in rr: n.m.r early in st: rdn over 2f out and kpt on same pce to go 4th cl home* **7/1**

5 *1/2* **Hanky Panky (IRE)**[8] 5415 3-9-0 98 (b1) SeamieHeffernan 7 96
(A P O'Brien, Ire) *mid-div: rdn over 2f out and styd on same pce u.p: nvr nr to chal* **16/1**

6 *3/4* **Bronte**[16] 5114 3-9-0 92 (p) WayneLordan 4 94
(David Wachman, Ire) *sn chsd ldrs: 4th 1/2-way: rdn in 3rd 2f out: sn no ex and wknd* **16/1**

7 *nk* **Hint Of A Tint (IRE)**[50] 3964 3-9-0 101 (p1) FMBerry 8 93
(David Wachman, Ire) *prom: narrow ldr 1/2-way: rdn over 2f out: hdd narrowly 2f out: no ex and styd on same pce* **6/1**[3]

8 *hd* **One Spirit (IRE)**[7] 5453 5-9-5 102 NGMcCullagh 10 94
(F Dunne, Ire) *sn led: hdd narrowly 1/2-way: styd 2nd: rdn to ld again 2f out: r.o wl but hdd ent fnl f: sn no ex* **14/1**

9 *1 3/4* **Ondeafears (IRE)**[21] 4933 6-9-5 96 ShaneFoley 3 90
(M Halford, Ire) *in rr: rdn over 2f out and no imp: nvr a factor* **33/1**

10 *1/2* **Precious Stone (IRE)**[63] 3517 4-9-5 91 (v1) DeclanMcDonogh 5 89
(David Wachman, Ire) *mid-div: 6th 1/2-way: rdn over 2f out and no ex: wknd ent fnl f* **33/1**

1m 32.35s (92.35)
WFA 3 from 4yo+ 5lb **10** Ran SP% **122.9**
CSF £7.65 TOTE £4.30: £1.60, £1.30, £2.60; DF 7.40.
Owner K Leavy/L Cribben/Mrs A McCreery **Bred** Robert De Vere Hunt **Trained** The Curragh, Co.Kildare

FOCUS
A red-hot running of this Group 3 contest. The early gallop was generous and there were no hard luck stories. The winner was best on the day and continued her superb summer. The likes of the third, fifth, sixth, ninth and tenth help with the standard, withe the winner rated close to her best.

5689 - 5691a (Foreign Racing) - See Raceform Interactive

5601 CLAIREFONTAINE (R-H)
Thursday, August 22

OFFICIAL GOING: Turf: very soft

5692a PRIX DE L'ASSOCIATION DES PROPRIETAIRES DU CENTRE-EST (PRIX DES AUBEPINES) (CLAIMER) (3YO) (TURF) 1m 6f 110y
1:20 (12:00) 3-Y-0 **£7,723** (£3,089; £2,317; £1,544; £772)

RPR

1 **Dalilar (USA)**[43] 3-9-1 0 (b) Christophe-PatriceLemaire 1 70
(A De Royer-Dupre, France) **58/10**

2 *2 1/2* **Churada (IRE)**[84] 3-8-8 0 JeromeClaudic 6 59
(C Laffon-Parias, France) **43/10**[2]

3 *1/2* **Star Of Namibia (IRE)**[19] 5010 3-9-1 0 (b) IoritzMendizabal 11 65
(J S Moore) *broke wl and trckd ldr: 3rd and outpcd 2 1/2f out: one of two to remain on ins turning into st: hrd rdn to chal over 1 1/2f out: one pce u.p fnl f* **10/1**

4 *snk* **Wingland (FR)**[20] 3-9-2 0 AlexisBadel 4 66
(Mme M Bollack-Badel, France) **11/2**[3]

5 *1 1/4* **Pixie Cut (IRE)**[26] 4753 3-8-13 0 SoufyaneMoulin(3) 3 64
(J S Moore) *tk a str hold: prom: 2nd and rdn over 2f out: sn outpcd by ldrs: kpt on at one pce u.p fnl f* **7/2**[1]

6 *1/2* **Spanish Art**[23] 3-8-11 0 (p) SylvainRuis 10 59
(Mlle M Henry, France) **38/1**

7 *2 1/2* **Almada (FR)** 3-8-11 0 NicolasPerret 7 55
(K Borgel, France) **78/10**

8 *8* **Feed Me Rainbow (FR)**[29] 3-8-11 0 (b) AnthonyCrastus 2 44
(R Pritchard-Gordon, France) **10/1**

9 *8* **Cadette D'Authie (FR)** 3-8-11 0 (p) TonyPiccone 8 33
(O Regley, France) **52/1**

10 *3* **Let It Song (FR)**[54] 3-9-1 0 MaximeGuyon 9 33
(E Libaud, France) **17/2**

3m 10.81s (190.81) **10** Ran SP% **115.7**
WIN (incl. 1 euro stake): 6.80. PLACES: 2.40, 2.10, 3.20. DF: 17.20. SF: 39.90.
Owner H H Aga Khan **Bred** His Highness The Aga Khan's Studs S C **Trained** Chantilly, France

5385 FFOS LAS (L-H)
Friday, August 23

OFFICIAL GOING: Good (7.7)
Wind: light, across Weather: dry, overcast, showers

5693 BET TOTEJACKPOT TEXT TOTE TO 89660 NURSERY H'CAP 6f
1:45 (1:47) (Class 4) (0-85,77) 2-Y-O **£3,752** (£1,116; £557; £278) **Stalls** Centre

Form RPR

0054 **1** **Intense Feeling (IRE)**[19] 5029 2-8-11 **70** DeclanBates(3) 2 73
(David Evans) *chsd ldrs: wnt 2nd over 2f out: drvn to chal over 1f out: led 1f out: kpt on wl fnl 100yds: hrd pressed cl home: all out* **18/1**

0221 **2** *hd* **Sefaat**[17] 5090 2-9-3 **73** ChrisCatlin 3 75
(Brian Meehan) *dwlt: hld up wl in tch in rr: clsd and gng wl whn nt clr run 2f out: swtchd rt and effrt over 1f out: chsd ldrs and swtchd lft ins fnl f: r.o wl and str chal cl home: jst hld* **7/1**

3022 **3** *1/2* **Ice Slice (IRE)**[19] 5033 2-9-2 **75** WilliamTwiston-Davies(3) 6 76
(Richard Hannon) *led: rdn ent fnl 2f: hdd 1f out: edgd lft u.p and one pce ins fnl f* **2/1**[1]

2312 **4** *nk* **Kickboxer (IRE)**[7] 5468 2-9-3 **73** SamHitchcott 1 73
(Mick Channon) *dwlt: hld up in tch in last pair: effrt and rdn 2f out: pressed ldng pair 1f out: no ex ins fnl f: wknd towards fin* **4/1**[3]

3332 **5** *7* **Solo Hunter**[8] 5442 2-8-12 **68** JimmyQuinn 7 47+
(David Evans) *chsd ldr tl over 3f out: rdn and lost pl over 2f out: wknd over 1f out* **9/4**[2]

0255 **6** *4 1/2* **Tautira (IRE)**[43] 4191 2-8-4 **67** OisinMurphy(7) 4 32
(Michael Bell) *chsd ldrs: wnt 2nd over 3f out tl over 2f out: sn struggling: wknd over 1f out: wl bhd fnl f* **10/1**

1m 12.54s (2.54) **Going Correction** +0.40s/f (Good) **6** Ran SP% **111.0**
Speed ratings (Par 96): **99,98,98,97,88 82**
toteswingers 1&2 £5.10, 1&3 £23.70, 2&3 £1.30 CSF £126.67 TOTE £13.00: £4.60, £3.50; EX 125.00 Trifecta £358.50 Pool: £1118.38 - 2.33 winning units..
Owner Mrs E Evans **Bred** R And Mrs R Hodgins **Trained** Pandy, Monmouths

FOCUS
Jockeys described the going to be on the easy side of good; stalls positioned in the centre for sprints. The top weight was 10lb below the ceiling rating for this race, so the form might not be that strong. Four finished clear and straightforward form rated around that quartet.

5694 YOUR FAVOURITE POOL BETS AT TOTEPOOL.COM H'CAP 1m 2f (R)
2:20 (2:22) (Class 5) (0-70,70) 3-Y-O+ **£2,587** (£770; £384; £192) **Stalls** Low

Form RPR

3500 **1** **Guilded Spirit**[38] 4384 3-8-10 **65** MichaelJMMurphy(5) 2 75+
(Stuart Kittow) *t.k.h: hld up in midfield: 2nd over 2f out: led wl over 1f out: sn clr r.o* **13/2**

1432 **2** *2 1/4* **Greyemkay**[9] 5387 5-8-2 **51** OisinMurphy(7) 5 56
(Richard Price) *hld up bhd: rdn and hdwy 3f out: chsd wnr over 1f: no imp* **3/1**[1]

0046 **3** *hd* **Batchelors Star (IRE)**[60] 3617 5-9-10 **66** (t) ConorO'Farrell 1 70
(Seamus Durack) *taken down early: hld up bhd: hdwy over 2f out: wnt 3rd 1f out: kpt on* **11/1**

3112 **4** *2 1/2* **Mr Lando**[67] 3410 4-9-8 **64** JimmyQuinn 8 64
(Tony Carroll) *prom main gp: 2nd 3f out tl over 2f: styd on same pce* **7/2**[2]

4400 **5** *6* **Bursledon (IRE)**[21] 4961 3-9-0 **67** (b1) WilliamTwiston-Davies(3) 9 55
(Richard Hannon) *s.i.s: hdwy to ld 8f out and sn clr: hdd wl over 1f out: wknd* **9/2**[3]

0201 **6** *6* **Harbinger Lass**[20] 5010 3-9-6 **70** SamHitchcott 3 47
(Mick Channon) *ld tl over 8f out: midfield: wknd over 2f out* **10/1**

4230 **7** *22* **Fearless Lad (IRE)**[37] 4416 3-8-10 **67** TimothyClark(7) 6 2
(John Best) *hld up in midfield: wknd 4f out: t.o* **16/1**

034 **8** *31* **Calling**[18] 5064 3-9-6 **70** NickyMackay 4
(Brian Meehan) *stdd s: hdwy to ld over 8f out: sn hdd and chsd clr ldr: lost 2nd 3f out: wl bhd and eased fnl 2f: t.o* **13/2**

2m 12.86s (3.46) **Going Correction** +0.40s/f (Good)
WFA 3 from 4yo+ 8lb **8** Ran SP% **115.4**
Speed ratings (Par 103): **102,100,100,98,93 88,70,46**
toteswingers 1&2 £13.50, 2&3 £7.60, 1&3 £25.20 CSF £26.61 CT £212.46 TOTE £9.70: £2.40, £1.40, £3.30; EX 48.60 Trifecta £864.90 Pool: £1153.30 - 0.93 winning units..
Owner The Racing Guild **Bred** R Phillips And Tweenhills Farm And Stud **Trained** Blackborough, Devon

FOCUS
After a jostle for the early lead, Bursledon went clear after a furlong, but was reeled in on the long run to home. The winner looks like fulfilling early promise and the form behind looks straightforward.

5695 BET TOTEQUADPOT TEXT TOTE TO 89660 MAIDEN FILLIES' STKS 1m (R)
2:55 (3:00) (Class 4) 3-Y-O+ **£4,690** (£1,395; £697; £348) **Stalls** Low

Form RPR

-023 **1** **Jadesnumberone (IRE)**[44] 4182 3-8-9 72 WilliamTwiston-Davies(3) 1 73
(Michael Bell) *chsd ldr tl led 2f out: in command fnl f: comf* **6/4**[1]

5 **2** 3 **Invincible Magic (IRE)**[19] 5038 3-8-5 .... AhmadAlSubousi(7) 3 66
(Charlie Appleby) *hld up in last pair: effrt over 2f out: chsd wnr over 1f out: no imp* **4/1**

056- **3** 2 ½ **Flemish School**[313] 7081 3-8-12 71................................ NickyMackay 4 60
(Gerard Butler) *ld tl rdn and hdd over 1f out: one pce after* **9/4**[2]

3 **4** ¾ **Sugarcraft (USA)**[56] 3774 3-8-12 .... JimmyQuinn 2 59
(Charlie Appleby) *t.k.h: hld up in last pair: swtchd rt and effrt over 2f out: styd on same pce after* **7/2**[3]

0 **5** nk **Finalee**[126] 1666 3-8-7 .... MichaelJMMurphy(5) 5 58?
(John Gallagher) *chsd ldrs tl lost pl 2f out: kpt on again ins fnl f* **28/1**

1m 47.58s (6.58) **Going Correction** +0.40s/f (Good) **5** Ran SP% **116.4**
Speed ratings (Par 102): **83,80,77,76,76**
CSF £8.54 TOTE £2.30: £1.60, £2.20; EX 8.10 Trifecta £19.40 Pool: £1833.79 - 70.76 winning units..
Owner Sir Alex Ferguson & Mike Dawson **Bred** Oak Lodge Bloodstock **Trained** Newmarket, Suffolk

FOCUS
The early pace was steady, but the form looks reliable with the two top-rated on RPRs finishing first and second. The form is rated at face value through the winner to her mark.

5696 KING SIZE POOLS AT TOTEPOOL.COM H'CAP 6f
3:30 (3:32) (Class 2) (0-100,99) 3-Y-£11,971 (£3,583; £1,791; £896; £446) **Stalls** Centre

Form RPR

4003 **1** **Gramercy (IRE)**[19] 5026 6-8-13 **88**................................(b[1]) ChrisCatlin 8 99
(David Simcock) *bhd: rdn and hdwy over 1f out: led fnl 100yds: r.o* **9/1**

0505 **2** 1 ¼ **Tarooq (USA)**[27] 4780 7-8-6 **81** oh1 ow1..................(t) AdamBeschizza 5 88
(Stuart Williams) *midfield: effrt 2f out: led 1f out: hdd fnl 100yds: r.o for clr 2nd* **11/2**[2]

1241 **3** 4 **Clear Spring (IRE)**[6] 5544 5-9-4 **93** 6ex......................... NickyMackay 2 88
(John Spearing) *hld up towards rr: effrt and nt clr run over 1f out: hdwy ins fnl f: wnt 3rd fnl 75yds: nvr trbld ldrs* **9/4**[1]

0005 **4** 1 **Palace Moon**[14] 5247 8-8-13 **88**.................................(t) JimmyQuinn 10 80
(William Knight) *midfield: effrt and swtchd rt 1f out: kpt on: nvr trbld ldrs* **16/1**

301 **5** ¾ **Elusive Hawk (IRE)**[9] 5389 9-8-0 **80** 6ex...................(v) NoelGarbutt(5) 9 70
(David Evans) *chsd ldrs: rdn to ld over 1f out: hdd 1f out: wknd ins fnl f* **20/1**

3040 **6** 1 ¾ **Our Jonathan**[62] 3558 6-9-10 **99**.................................... SamHitchcott 4 84
(David Simcock) *in tch: rdn 2f out: outpcd over 1f out: n.d after* **15/2**

2033 **7** ½ **Top Cop**[15] 5187 4-7-12 **80**.......................................(p) OisinMurphy(7) 12 63
(Andrew Balding) *racd towards nr side: midfield: edgd lft and no hdwy over 1f out: wknd fnl f* **6/1**[3]

5200 **8** 1 **King Of Jazz (IRE)**[14] 5247 5-8-11 **86**.....................(v) DougieCostello 7 66
(Peter Bowen) *chsd ldr tl over 1f out: wknd fnl f* **20/1**

211 **9** 3 ¼ **Swendab (IRE)**[16] 5155 5-8-9 **87**...............(v) WilliamTwiston-Davies(3) 6 58
(John O'Shea) *led tl 1f out: fdd fnl f* **10/1**

3232 **10** 8 **Cruise Tothelimit (IRE)**[14] 5219 5-8-2 **80**.................. RyanPowell(3) 13 27
(Ian Williams) *racd nr side: midfield: hung lft u.p and wknd over 1f out* **17/2**

1400 **11** 2 ¾ **Al's Memory (IRE)**[19] 5027 4-8-11 **89**......................... DeclanBates(3) 1 27
(David Evans) *midfield: lost pl 2f out: bhd fnl f* **20/1**

1m 11.03s (1.03) **Going Correction** +0.40s/f (Good) **11** Ran SP% **122.0**
Speed ratings (Par 109): **109,107,102,100,99 97,96,95,91,80 76**
toteswingers 1&2 £22.40, 2&3 £9.50, 1&3 £7.90 CSF £58.31 CT £151.10 TOTE £10.70: £2.60, £2.40, £1.80; EX 72.50 Trifecta £292.30 Pool: £1233.69 - 3.16 winning units..
Owner Dr Marwan Koukash **Bred** Michael Mullins **Trained** Newmarket, Suffolk

FOCUS
A competitive handicap. The field split into two groups with Top Cop and Cruise Tothelimit ploughing a fruitless furrow against the stands' rail. The form has a sound feel with the first pair clear.

4983 GOODWOOD (R-H)
Friday, August 23

OFFICIAL GOING: Good (7.5)
Wind: Almost nil Weather: Fine but cloudy, warm

5697 CHICHESTER OBSERVER APPRENTICE STKS (H'CAP) 6f
5:10 (5:10) (Class 5) (0-70,69) 3-Y-O+ **£3,234** (£962; £481; £240) **Stalls** High

Form RPR

5433 **1** **Lucky Di**[13] 5280 3-9-8 **68**.. CharlesBishop 6 78
(Peter Hedger) *in tch: rdn 2f out: prog over 1f out: r.o to ld ins fnl f: sn clr* **12/1**

0-20 **2** 2 **Dominium (USA)**[25] 4837 6-9-11 **68**.................................(b) RyanClark 3 72
(Jeremy Gask) *dwlt: in tch in last pair: prog 1/2-way: rdn 2f out: styd on fnl f to take 2nd last strides* **13/2**[2]

3220 **3** nse **Chevise (IRE)**[46] 4120 5-8-13 **59**...................................(p) RyanTate(3) 7 62
(Steve Woodman) *w ldr: led 1/2-way: hdd ins fnl f: tired and lost 2nd last strides* **16/1**

5462 **4** nk **Generalyse**[11] 5349 4-9-12 **69**.....................................(b) ThomasBrown 2 71
(Ben De Haan) *pressed ldrs: rdn to chal 2f out: nt qckn over 1f out: kpt on same pce fnl f* **7/4**[1]

412 **5** 3 ¾ **Jake The Snake (IRE)**[72] 3210 12-9-7 **67**............. GeorgeDowning(3) 1 57
(Tony Carroll) *sn in last: prog whn hung bdly rt fr over 2f out: ended up against far rail and no hdwy fnl f* **11/1**

6053 **6** ½ **Malaysian Boleh**[9] 5397 3-9-0 **65**................................ JackDuern(5) 9 54
(Simon Dow) *stdd s: hld up in tch: rdn and no prog 2f out: outpcd over 1f out* **16/1**

2063 **7** ¾ **Emiratesdotcom**[6] 5522 7-9-2 **66**...............................(p) WillPettis(7) 11 52
(Milton Bradley) *chsd ldrs and racd towards nr side: shkn up and no prog 2f out: fdd* **8/1**[3]

0223 **8** nse **Maria Montez**[15] 5165 4-9-7 **69**................................. ShelleyBirkett(5) 8 55
(J W Hills) *led to 1/2-way: wknd 2f out* **8/1**[3]

1300 **9** hd **Where's Reiley (USA)**[28] 4707 7-9-8 **65**.......................(v) DarrenEgan 5 51
(Michael Attwater) *in tch: rdn and no prog 2f out: fdd over 1f out* **16/1**

043 **10** 7 **Nifty Kier**[13] 5277 4-8-13 **61**... ThomasGarner(5) 10 24
(Martin Bosley) *chsd ldrs tl wknd jst over 2f out: t.o* **40/1**

01-0 **11** 1 ¾ **Take The Lead**[94] 2544 3-9-1 **68**............................ CameronHardie(7) 4 26
(Richard Hannon) *w ldrs: upsides jst over 2f out: wknd rapidly over 1f out: t.o* **14/1**

1m 10.99s (-1.21) **Going Correction** -0.275s/f (Firm)
WFA 3 from 4yo+ 3lb **11** Ran SP% **114.7**
Speed ratings (Par 103): **97,94,94,93,88 88,87,87,86,77 75**
toteswingers 1&2 £1.90, 1&3 £13.00, 2&3 £18.20 CSF £85.79 CT £1255.91 TOTE £12.60: £3.80, £2.50, £3.20; EX 94.10 Trifecta £794.10 Part won. Pool: £1058.86 - 0.08 winning units..
Owner P C F Racing Ltd **Bred** Cranford Stud **Trained** Dogmersfield, Hampshire

FOCUS
Lower bend dolled out 4yds increasing distances on that course by about 8yds. .A typically competitive contest for a race of this nature but it saw a comprehensive winner who is rated to his Polytrack form.

5698 REVIVAL MAIDEN STKS 1m
5:40 (5:41) (Class 4) 2-Y-O **£5,175** (£1,540; £769; £384) **Stalls** Low

Form RPR

2 **1** **Madeed**[27] 4764 2-9-5 0.. KierenFallon 6 82+
(Brian Meehan) *trckd ldng pair after 3f: quick move to ld 2f out: drvn to maintain narrow but decisive advantage fnl f* **2/1**[2]

0 **2** nk **Pack Leader (IRE)**[20] 4987 2-9-5 0........................... RichardKingscote 1 81
(Amanda Perrett) *disp ld: def advantage 3f out: hdd 2f out: fought on wl to press wnr after: hld last 100yds* **14/1**

2 **3** 1 **Hymenaios (IRE)**[15] 5180 2-9-5 0................................. RichardHughes 8 79+
(Richard Hannon) *hld up in midfield: prog 3f out: rdn to chse ldng pair wl over 1f out: tried to cl but edgd lft fnl f: styd on* **6/5**[1]

02 **4** 3 ¾ **All Talk N No Do (IRE)**[15] 5188 2-9-5 0.......................... MickyFenton 2 70
(Seamus Durack) *trckd ldrs: rdn over 2f out: nt qckn and outpcd fr wl over 1f out* **10/1**[3]

5 **5** 2 ½ **Mishko (IRE)**[23] 4896 2-9-5 0.. AdamKirby 12 65
(Clive Cox) *racd wd towards rr: outpcd over 2f out: edgd rt but kpt on fr over 1f out* **16/1**

6 ¾ **Act Of Charity (IRE)** 2-9-5 0... SaleemGolam 3 63
(Marco Botti) *s.v.s: sn in tch in last trio: pushed along 3f out: outpcd but kpt on fnl 2f* **40/1**

7 3 ¾ **Arantes** 2-9-5 0... TedDurcan 5 54
(Mick Channon) *dwlt: in tch in last trio: pushed along and modest prog over 2f out: fdd over 1f out* **25/1**

0 **8** 2 ¾ **Allergic Reaction (IRE)**[20] 4987 2-9-2 0....................... DarrenEgan(3) 4 48
(William Knight) *w ldr to 3f out: rn green and wknd qckly 2f out* **66/1**

9 2 ¼ **Libeccio (FR)** 2-9-5 0.. DavidProbert 9 43
(Andrew Balding) *in tch tl wknd over 2f out* **20/1**

0 **10** ½ **Thunder Pass (IRE)**[12] 5309 2-9-5 0................................ SebSanders 10 42+
(Hughie Morrison) *racd wd towards rr: shkn up and wknd wl over 2f out* **25/1**

11 39 **Spirited Silver** 2-9-0 0.. KieranO'Neill 7
(John Bridger) *dwlt: detached in last after 2f and rn green: t.o over 2f out* **200/1**

1m 38.26s (-1.64) **Going Correction** -0.275s/f (Firm) **11** Ran SP% **117.3**
Speed ratings (Par 96): **97,96,95,91,89 88,84,82,79,79 40**
toteswingers 1&2 £6.30, 1&3 £1.90, 2&3 £5.10 CSF £26.95 TOTE £3.50: £1.40, £4.80, £1.10; EX 40.30 Trifecta £76.10 Pool: £2204.55 - 21.69 winning units..
Owner Hamdan Al Maktoum **Bred** Watership Down Stud **Trained** Manton, Wilts

FOCUS
An informative juvenile event, the form of which looks solid with three horses coming clear. The third is the best guide.

5699 GORDON'S FILLIES' NURSERY STKS (H'CAP) 7f
6:15 (6:15) (Class 4) (0-85,83) 2-Y-O **£5,453** (£1,610; £805) **Stalls** Low

Form RPR

6334 **1** **Gender Agenda**[6] 5536 2-8-6 **75**................................ LouisSteward(7) 5 80+
(Michael Bell) *hld up in last pair: pushed along on inner 3f out: rdn and swtchd lft wl over 1f out: gd prog after to ld last 150yds: styd on wl* **7/2**[2]

105 **2** ¾ **Rasheeda**[29] 4682 2-9-6 **82**... AdamKirby 6 85
(Marco Botti) *hld up in tch: prog and squeezed through to ld over 1f out: hdd 150yds out: flashed tail but styd on: a hld* **7/1**[3]

41 **3** 4 ½ **Djinni (IRE)**[32] 4589 2-9-6 **82**...................................... RichardHughes 1 74
(Richard Hannon) *hld up in last: rdn and no prog over 2f out: btn after: plugged on to take 3rd ins fnl f* **11/10**[1]

1022 **4** ¾ **Memory Styx**[12] 5306 2-9-4 **80**.. TedDurcan 3 69
(Mick Channon) *hld up in tch: prog to chal 2f out: rdn and upsides over 1f out: wknd qckly fnl f* **16/1**

41 **5** ¾ **Born To Fly (IRE)**[16] 5151 2-8-5 **67**.............................. DavidProbert 2 54
(Gary Harrison) *mde most to over 1f out: wknd qckly* **9/1**

01 **6** 1 ½ **Turin (IRE)**[16] 5131 2-9-7 **83**... RichardMullen 7 67
(Charlie Appleby) *wnt lft s: chsd ldrs on outer: shkn up over 2f out: wknd wl over 1f out* **9/1**

536 **7** 4 **Touch Paper (IRE)**[16] 5131 2-8-6 **68**............................. KieranO'Neill 4 41
(Richard Hannon) *t.k.h: pressed ldr to over 2f out: wknd qckly* **33/1**

1m 26.5s (-0.50) **Going Correction** -0.275s/f (Firm) **7** Ran SP% **111.2**
Speed ratings (Par 93): **91,90,85,84,83 81,77**
toteswingers 1&2 £4.30, 1&3 £2.20, 2&3 £2.70 CSF £26.07 TOTE £5.40: £1.80, £3.40; EX 23.90 Trifecta £75.00 Pool: £2196.06 - 21.94 winning units..
Owner W J Gredley **Bred** Middle Park Stud Ltd **Trained** Newmarket, Suffolk

FOCUS
A fair contest, won in convincing fashion. The winner could do better while the runner-up's Listed form helps set the level.

5700 BRITISH STALLION STUDS EBF STKS (FILLIES' H'CAP) 6f
6:45 (6:45) (Class 3) (0-95,95) 3-Y-O+ **£9,056** (£2,695; £1,346; £673) **Stalls** High

Form RPR

2626 **1** **La Fortunata**[35] 4493 6-8-13 **89**.................................... RyanTate(5) 3 97
(Mike Murphy) *racd towards centre: mde all: drvn and styd on wl fnl f* **14/1**

1220 **2** 1 ¼ **Links Drive Lady**[20] 4983 5-9-3 **88**.. AdamKirby 2 92
(Dean Ivory) *dwlt: hld up in rr in centre: prog over 2f out: chsd wnr over 1f out and sn clsd: kpt on but no imp last 100yds* **13/2**

1124 **3** ¾ **Midnight Flower (IRE)**[6] 5538 3-9-4 **95**..................... DarrenEgan(3) 8 97
(David Simcock) *racd against rail: prom: rdn and disputing 2nd over 1f out: kpt on same pce* **9/4**[1]

2135 **4** hd **Strictly Silca**[12] 5308 3-8-6 **80**..(v) TedDurcan 1 81
(Mick Channon) *trckd wnr towards centre: rdn whn nt clr run briefly over 1f out: kpt on same pce fnl f* **14/1**

2326 **5** ¾ **Nardin**[14] 5247 3-8-10 **84**...................................(p) RichardKingscote 5 83
(Ed Dunlop) *dwlt: in tch: waiting for a gap 2f out: plld out over 1f out: rdn and kpt on same pce after* **7/2**[2]

0011 **6** ½ **Badr Al Badoor (IRE)**[17] 5103 3-9-3 **91**.....................(v) RichardMullen 7 88
(James Fanshawe) *in tch: rdn 2f out: hanging and nt qckn over 1f out: sn btn* **9/2**[3]

1025 **7** 1 ½ **Dancheur (IRE)**[13] 5294 4-8-8 **79**.................................... DavidProbert 6 71
(Mrs K Burke) *rrd as stalls opened and slowly away: t.k.h in last: pushed along 2f out: nvr on terms but kpt on* **16/1**

4550 8 12 **Tassel**[13] 5260 3-8-12 **86**........ RichardHughes 4 53
(Richard Hannon) *prom 4f: wknd qckly and eased: t.o* **14/1**

1m 10.39s (-1.81) **Going Correction** -0.275s/f (Firm)
WFA 3 from 4yo+ 3lb **8** Ran SP% **110.4**
Speed ratings (Par 104): **101,99,98,98,97 96,94,78**
toteswingers 1&2 £17.40, 2&3 £4.20, 1&3 £8.80 CSF £94.10 CT £271.34 TOTE £11.50: £2.60, £2.00, £1.20; EX 53.60 Trifecta £193.20 Pool: £1704.33 - 6.61 winning units..
Owner James Patton **Bred** James Patton **Trained** Westoning, Beds

FOCUS
A good turnout for the feature fillies' handicap and it saw a likeable performance. The first two were close to their marks.

5701 VETERANS STKS (H'CAP) 5f
7:20 (7:20) (Class 5) (0-75,74) 6-Y-0+ **£3,234** (£962; £481; £240) **Stalls** High

Form RPR
3560 1 **Aye Aye Digby (IRE)**[14] 5219 8-9-7 **74**........ RichardHughes 7 83
(Patrick Chamings) *racd against rail: led 1f: lost pl and rdn wl over 1f out: rallied fnl f: r.o to ld last strides* **4/1**[3]
2144 2 hd **Picansort**[93] 2561 6-8-9 **62**........(b) TedDurcan 4 70
(Peter Crate) *trckd ldrs: rdn to chal over 1f out: upsides ins fnl f: wandered and nt qckn: kpt on last strides* **11/2**
0542 3 shd **The Strig**[3] 5608 6-8-8 **64**........(v) DarrenEgan[(3)] 3 72
(Stuart Williams) *racd towards centre: in tch: prog 2f out: drvn to chal over 1f out: narrow ld ins fnl f: hdd last strides* **11/4**[1]
2052 4 2 ¼ **Six Wives**[24] 4860 6-9-5 **72**........(p) PaoloSirigu 6 72
(Scott Dixon) *led after 1f: drvn wl over 1f out: edgd lft and hdd ins fnl f: fdd* **3/1**[2]
2045 5 ½ **Sir Geoffrey (IRE)**[7] 5499 7-8-2 **58** ow1........(p) BillyCray[(3)] 2 56
(Scott Dixon) *racd towards centre: pressed ldrs: drvn and upsides over 1f out: fdd fnl f* **14/1**
6354 6 hd **Ingleby Star (IRE)**[21] 4943 8-8-6 **59**........(p) DavidProbert 5 56
(John Stimpson) *dwlt: mostly in last trio: rdn 2f out: tried to cl over 1f out: one pce fnl f* **14/1**
0106 7 nk **Commandingpresence (USA)**[8] 5447 7-9-2 **69**........ KieranO'Neill 1 65
(John Bridger) *fractious gng to post: mostly in last trio: rdn 2f out: tried to cl over 1f out: one pce after* **16/1**
1135 8 14 **Amenable (IRE)**[6] 5523 6-9-5 **72**........(p) SaleemGolam 8 18
(Violet M Jordan) *a in last trio: wknd 1/2-way: t.o* **12/1**

58.06s (-2.14) **Going Correction** -0.275s/f (Firm) **8** Ran SP% **114.0**
Speed ratings: **106,105,105,101,101 100,100,77**
toteswingers 1&2 £1.70, 2&3 £5.30, 1&3 £3.70 CSF £26.01 CT £69.69 TOTE £5.10: £1.20, £2.30, £1.60; EX 33.40 Trifecta £98.10 Pool: £930.38 - 7.10 winning units..
Owner Trolley Action **Bred** G J King **Trained** Baughurst, Hants

FOCUS
A strongly run handicap and a thrilling victory. The winner is rated back to his reappearance win.

5702 GOODWOOD HOME FARM STKS (H'CAP) 2m
7:50 (7:50) (Class 5) (0-70,69) 3-Y-0 **£3,234** (£962; £481; £240) **Stalls** Low

Form RPR
0640 1 **Cherry Princess**[21] 4961 3-8-3 **51** oh5 ow1........ DavidProbert 3 59
(Stuart Williams) *trckd ldr: clr of rest and clsd 3f out: led 2f out: urged along and kpt on wl fr over 1f out* **20/1**
0231 2 ½ **Fitzwilly**[2] 5630 3-8-5 **56** 6ex........ SimonPearce[(3)] 1 63
(Mick Channon) *led at gd pce: kicked for home over 3f out: drvn and hdd 2f out: kpt on wl to press wnr after: hld ins fnl f* **11/8**[1]
6120 3 9 **Flamingo Beat**[71] 3243 3-9-4 **66**........ RichardHughes 2 62
(Rae Guest) *hld up in 5th: prog to chse clr ldng pair 3f out: sn rdn: no imp after* **9/4**[2]
0412 4 3 ¼ **See And Be Seen**[21] 4939 3-8-5 **53** ow1........ RenatoSouza 6 45
(Sylvester Kirk) *chsd ldng pair: pushed along 4f out: no imp and lost 3rd 3f out: wl hld after* **8/1**
-052 5 ½ **Pencombe (FR)**[184] 731 3-9-4 **69**........ DarrenEgan[(3)] 5 61
(David Simcock) *reluctant to enter stalls: s.s: t.k.h in last: rdn over 3f out: racd awkwardly and n.d fnl 2f* **7/1**[3]
-005 6 4 **Downhill Dancer (IRE)**[15] 5178 3-8-9 **57**........ TedDurcan 4 44
(Brian Meehan) *chsd ldng pair: pushed along 4f out: struggling 3f out: fdd* **8/1**

3m 32.23s (3.23) **Going Correction** -0.275s/f (Firm) **6** Ran SP% **112.4**
Speed ratings (Par 100): **80,79,75,73,73 71**
toteswingers 1&2 £3.70, 2&3 £1.10, 1&3 £10.80 CSF £48.57 TOTE £17.50: £6.80, £1.40; EX 73.50 Trifecta £203.90 Pool: £964.08 - 3.54 winning units..
Owner B Piper & D Shekells **Bred** Old Mill Stud **Trained** Newmarket, Suffolk
■ Stewards' Enquiry : Simon Pearce four-day ban: used whip above permitted level (Sep 6,8-10)

FOCUS
A modest finale but much to like about the performances of the first two home, who pulled well clear of the remainder. The form is rated around the second, although there are some doubts.
T/Plt: £148.10 to a £1 stake. Pool: £65401.79 - 322.22 winning tickets T/Qpdt: £29.50 to a £1 stake. Pool: £5064.60 - 126.95 winning tickets JN

4990 HAMILTON (R-H)
Friday, August 23
OFFICIAL GOING: Good to firm (good in places; watered; 8.0)
Wind: Virtually nil Weather: Overcast, shower before 1st

5703 LADBROKES NURSERY H'CAP 6f 5y
5:30 (5:31) (Class 5) (0-75,75) 2-Y-0 **£3,234** (£962; £481; £240) **Stalls** High

Form RPR
6624 1 **Omanome (IRE)**[18] 5053 2-8-13 **67**........ DavidNolan 2 70
(David O'Meara) *in tch: rdn and hdwy 2f out: chal ins fnl f: kpt on to ld towards fin* **10/1**
6462 2 ½ **Handwoven (IRE)**[15] 5175 2-9-2 **70**........ JoeFanning 1 72
(Mark Johnston) *prom: led wl over 1f out: sn rdn: strly pressed ins fnl f: kpt on: hdd towards fin* **6/4**[1]
0366 3 1 ½ **Another Royal**[21] 4965 2-8-5 **59**........ DuranFentiman 3 56
(Tim Easterby) *trckd ldrs: rdn 2f out: kpt on ins fnl f* **11/2**[3]
4310 4 ½ **Boogangoo (IRE)**[19] 5029 2-9-4 **75**........ JulieBurke[(3)] 5 71
(Keith Dalgleish) *led narrowly: rdn whn hdd wl over 1f out: one pce* **8/1**
1403 5 2 **Angel Rosa**[14] 5235 2-8-7 **64**........ JasonHart[(3)] 6 54
(Keith Dalgleish) *sn pushed along in rr: outpcd 4f out: sme late hdwy: nvr threatened* **4/1**[2]
50 6 ¾ **Robynelle**[65] 3459 2-9-4 **72**........ TomEaves 4 59
(Keith Dalgleish) *in tch: rdn 2f out: wknd over 1f out* **11/2**[3]

1m 11.71s (-0.49) **Going Correction** -0.15s/f (Firm) **6** Ran SP% **111.0**
Speed ratings (Par 94): **97,96,94,93,91 90**
toteswingers 1&2 £2.60, 1&3 £6.70, 2&3 £2.90 CSF £25.06 TOTE £10.40: £5.10, £1.30; EX 35.00 Trifecta £260.90 Pool: £1227.22 - 3.52 winning units..
Owner John Patrick Halton **Bred** E Halton, J Halton & P Redmond **Trained** Nawton, N Yorks

FOCUS
A modest contest in which the winner improved just slightly on his previous best.

5704 VARIETY CLUB H'CAP 6f 5y
6:05 (6:05) (Class 6) (0-65,65) 3-Y-0 **£2,045** (£603; £302) **Stalls** Centre

Form RPR
1553 1 **Gold Beau (FR)**[9] 5393 3-9-0 **65**........(p) JacobButterfield[(7)] 6 73
(Kristin Stubbs) *chsd ldrs: rdn 2f out: led ent fnl f: edgd lft ins fnl f: kpt on* **3/1**[2]
P0-0 2 ¾ **Gambino (IRE)**[10] 5365 3-7-9 **46** oh1........ JordanHibberd[(7)] 2 52
(Alan Berry) *led narrowly: rdn whn hdd ent fnl f: sn edgd lft: sltly impeded by wnr 110yds out: kpt on* **80/1**
6164 3 nk **Alexandrakollontai (IRE)**[13] 5263 3-9-0 **61**........(b) JulieBurke[(3)] 10 66
(Alistair Whillans) *in tch: rdn to chse ldrs over 1f out: kpt on* **3/1**[2]
-003 4 1 ¼ **Bapak Pesta (IRE)**[10] 5365 3-8-8 **59**........ KevinStott[(7)] 5 60
(Kevin Ryan) *hld up: rdn and outpcd over 2f out: kpt on ins fnl f: nvr threatened ldrs* **9/4**[1]
4340 5 1 ¾ **Faither**[113] 1966 3-8-2 **46** oh1........ FrannyNorton 8 41
(Keith Dalgleish) *chsd ldrs: rdn over 2f out: sltly short of room 110yds out: wknd* **18/1**
6106 6 3 ¼ **Charlemagne Diva**[4] 5583 3-9-0 **63**........(t) PhilipPrince[(5)] 4 48
(Richard Guest) *w ldr: rdn over 2f out: wknd fnl f* **6/1**[3]
030 7 3 ¾ **Stand N Applaude**[60] 3629 3-8-5 **49**........ JoeFanning 3 22
(David Nicholls) *dwlt: hld up: rdn over 2f out: sn btn* **18/1**
0600 8 4 **Red Cobra (IRE)**[20] 4976 3-9-1 **59**........ DuranFentiman 1 19
(Tim Easterby) *chsd ldrs: wknd over 1f out* **16/1**
06-0 9 5 **Colours Of Nature**[34] 4544 3-8-12 **59**........ JasonHart[(3)] 9
(Eric Alston) *chsd ldrs tl wknd fnl 2f* **40/1**

1m 10.64s (-1.56) **Going Correction** -0.15s/f (Firm) **9** Ran SP% **115.1**
Speed ratings (Par 98): **104,103,102,100,98 94,89,83,77**
toteswingers 1&2 £32.80, 1&3 £3.00, 2&3 £44.00 CSF £179.50 CT £789.39 TOTE £3.90: £1.50, £13.00, £1.90; EX 165.80 Trifecta £730.20 Part won. Pool: £973.67 - 0.22 winning units..
Owner D Arundale **Bred** Haras Du Quesnay **Trained** Norton, N Yorks
■ Stewards' Enquiry : Jacob Butterfield two-day ban: careless riding (Sep 6,8)

FOCUS
A weak handicap, but the pace was strong from the outset, resulting in a much quicker time than the previous nursery. The form is taken at face value.

5705 DOWNLOAD THE LADBROKES APP H'CAP 6f 5y
6:35 (6:35) (Class 4) (0-85,83) 3-Y-0+ **£5,175** (£1,540; £769; £384) **Stalls** Centre

Form RPR
1 1 **Spin Artist (USA)**[15] 5176 3-9-6 **82**........ JoeFanning 8 92+
(Mark Johnston) *prom: pushed along to ld over 1f out: drvn ins fnl f: hld on towards fin* **4/1**[1]
0200 2 nk **Free Spin (IRE)**[55] 3811 4-9-9 **82**........ BenCurtis 2 91
(David Barron) *hld up: rdn and hdwy over 1f out: kpt on wl: jst hld* **4/1**[1]
2123 3 1 ¼ **Salvatore Fury (IRE)**[11] 5333 3-8-7 **69**........(p) TomEaves 9 74+
(Keith Dalgleish) *trckd ldrs: stl gng wl over 1f out: rdn ent fnl f: drvn and sn one pce ins fnl f* **6/1**[2]
4406 4 1 ¼ **Bonnie Charlie**[13] 5294 7-9-2 **75**........ FrannyNorton 1 76
(David Nicholls) *chsd ldrs: rdn 2f out: no ex fnl 100yds* **6/1**[2]
1420 5 shd **Sunraider (IRE)**[28] 4730 6-9-1 **79**........ ShirleyTeasdale[(5)] 3 80
(Paul Midgley) *hld up: rdn over 2f out: hdwy to chse ldrs over 1f out: one pce* **9/1**
0540 6 2 ½ **Barkston Ash**[13] 5292 5-8-12 **74**........(p) JasonHart[(3)] 10 67
(Eric Alston) *led: rdn whn hdd over 1f out: wknd* **4/1**[1]
2416 7 2 ½ **Jinky**[13] 5266 5-9-3 **76**........ DavidNolan 5 61
(Linda Perratt) *hld up: rdn over 2f out: wknd fnl f* **8/1**[3]
0 8 5 **Live Dangerously**[17] 5112 3-8-10 **72**........[1] DuranFentiman 4 41
(Keith Dalgleish) *s.i.s: sn pushed along towards rr: a bhd* **25/1**
/40 9 7 **Pitt Rivers**[11] 5333 4-8-2 **68** ow1........ KevinStott[(7)] 6 14
(Linda Perratt) *prom: rdn over 2f out: sn wknd* **66/1**

1m 10.45s (-1.75) **Going Correction** -0.15s/f (Firm)
WFA 3 from 4yo+ 3lb **9** Ran SP% **115.0**
Speed ratings (Par 105): **105,104,102,101,101 97,94,87,78**
toteswingers 1&2 £4.80, 2&3 £10.50, 1&3 £3.20 CSF £19.56 TOTE £4.70: £2.70, £1.70, £2.10; EX 23.30 Trifecta £86.70 Pool: £771.21 - 6.66 winning units..
Owner Sheikh Hamdan Bin Mohammed Al Maktoum **Bred** Respite Farm Inc **Trained** Middleham Moor, N Yorks

FOCUS
A competitive sprint handicap and plenty were in with a chance 2f out. A step up from the winner, who should do better again.

5706 LADBROKES LANARK SILVER BELL H'CAP 1m 4f 17y
7:05 (7:08) (Class 3) (0-90,89) 3-Y-0+ **£16,819** (£5,005; £2,501; £1,250) **Stalls** Low

Form RPR
2111 1 **Special Meaning**[35] 4506 3-8-10 **85**........ FrannyNorton 4 97+
(Mark Johnston) *mde all: rdn over 1f out: kpt on: comf* **7/4**[1]
3331 2 1 ¾ **Nimiety**[14] 5245 4-8-12 **77**........ JoeFanning 15 85
(Mark Johnston) *in tch: hdwy to chse wnr over 3f out: rdn over 2f out: kpt on but no ch w wnr* **11/2**[2]
1040 3 ¾ **Cosmic Sun**[26] 4804 7-8-7 **72**........(t) PatrickMathers 13 79
(Richard Fahey) *hld up: wnt midfield 1/2-way: rdn to 3rd over 2f out: kpt on one pce* **33/1**
5121 4 ½ **Certavi (IRE)**[12] 5312 4-8-1 **71** 6ex........ PhilipPrince[(5)] 9 77+
(Brendan Powell) *hld up: rdn over 3f out: kpt on fr over 1f out* **9/1**
0060 5 1 ¾ **Federal Blue (USA)**[13] 5258 3-8-0 **78**........ JulieBurke[(3)] 1 81
(Mark Johnston) *trckd ldr: rdn over 3f out: one pce* **10/1**
-203 6 ¾ **Noble Alan (GER)**[14] 5237 10-9-2 **88**........ KevinStott[(7)] 8 90
(Nicky Richards) *midfield: rdn over 3f out: one pce and nvr threatened ldrs* **13/2**[3]
1005 7 hd **Sirvino**[16] 5147 8-9-1 **87**........ GemmaTutty[(7)] 7 89
(David Barron) *hld up: rdn over 3f out: one pce and nvr threatened ldrs* **16/1**
0-20 8 4 ½ **Entihaa**[110] 2040 5-9-2 **81**........ BenCurtis 5 75
(Alan Swinbank) *hld up in rr: rdn and brief hdwy over 3f out: wknd fnl 2f* **33/1**
0032 9 hd **Fort Belvedere**[11] 5335 5-9-8 **87**........ WilsonRenwick 12 81
(Keith Dalgleish) *hld up: nvr threatened* **22/1**

5220 **10** ½ **Cosmic Halo**[6] 5521 4-8-5 **75** .... GeorgeChaloner(5) 3 68
(Richard Fahey) *s.i.s: sn in tch: rdn over 3f out: wknd over 1f out* **28/1**
1435 **11** *1* **Tenhoo**[6] 5514 7-8-4 **72** .... JasonHart(3) 2 64
(Eric Alston) *racd keenly: trckd ldr: rdn and lost pl over 3f out: btn whn short of room 2f out* **28/1**
-606 **12** *nk* **Perennial**[51] 3959 4-9-10 **89** .... DavidNolan 10 80
(David O'Meara) *midfield: rdn over 3f out: wknd fnl 2f* **10/1**
2021 **13** *4* **Choisan (IRE)**[18] 5059 4-9-1 **80** .... DuranFentiman 14 65
(Tim Easterby) *trckd ldr: rdn over 2f out: sn wknd* **28/1**
2115 **14** *6* **Hawdyerwheesht**[14] 5237 5-9-0 **79** .... TomEaves 11 54
(Jim Goldie) *hld up: rdn over 3f out: sn wknd* **20/1**

2m 33.67s (-4.93) **Going Correction** -0.225s/f (Firm)
WFA 3 from 4yo+ 10lb **14** Ran SP% **124.5**
Speed ratings (Par 107): **107,105,105,105,103 103,103,100,100,99 99,98,96,92**
toteswingers 1&2 £3.60, 1&3 £28.60, 2&3 £36.80 CSF £9.97 CT £244.38 TOTE £2.50: £1.40, £2.60, £11.40; EX 16.80 Trifecta £776.40 Part won. Pool: £1035.26 - 0.77 winning units..
Owner Newsells Park Stud **Bred** Newsells Park Stud **Trained** Middleham Moor, N Yorks
■ Stewards' Enquiry : Patrick Mathers two-day ban: used whip above permitted level (Sep 6,8)

FOCUS
A very competitive race but it was dominated by the most progressive horse. The form looks sound.

5707 ALWAYS TRYING OPEN MAIDEN STKS 1m 1f 36y
7:40 (7:40) (Class 5) 3-4-Y-O **£3,234** (£962; £481; £240) **Stalls** Low

Form RPR
1 **Nightster (IRE)** 3-9-5 0 .... JoeFanning 2 74+
(Mark Johnston) *in tch in 3rd: smooth hdwy 3f out: led 2f out: edgd rt: sn rdn 2 l clr: drvn and one pce fnl f: hld on all out* **3/1**[2]
03 **2** *nse* **Aryizad (IRE)**[18] 5058 4-9-7 0 .... BenCurtis 4 69
(Alan Swinbank) *hld up in 4th: rdn over 3f out: one pce and no imp initially: r.o strly ins fnl f: jst failed* **28/1**
052 **3** 1 ¾ **Magic Skyline (IRE)**[26] 4805 3-9-0 66 .... TomEaves 3 65
(Brian Ellison) *led: rdn whn hdd 2f out: kpt on one pce* **10/1**[3]
3-26 **4** 1 ½ **Heroine Required (FR)**[104] 2261 3-9-0 76 .... FrannyNorton 1 62
(William Haggas) *trckd ldr in 2nd: rdn over 2f out: one pce whn short of room over 1f out: dropped to 4th: drvn and no imp* **4/11**[1]

1m 58.89s (-0.81) **Going Correction** -0.225s/f (Firm)
WFA 3 from 4yo 7lb **4** Ran SP% **110.9**
Speed ratings (Par 103): **94,93,92,91**
CSF £37.50 TOTE £3.30; EX 38.30 Trifecta £85.90 Pool: £887.30 - 7.74 winning units..
Owner Sheikh Hamdan Bin Mohammed Al Maktoum **Bred** Darley **Trained** Middleham Moor, N Yorks
■ Stewards' Enquiry : Joe Fanning caution: careless riding.

FOCUS
The favourite was extremely disappointing and this is muddling form, rated around the third. The winner should improve on the bare form.

5708 AFM ELECTRICAL LTD H'CAP 5f 4y
8:10 (8:12) (Class 6) (0-60,66) 3-Y-0+ **£1,940** (£577; £288; £144) **Stalls** Centre

Form RPR
-331 **1** **Gottcher**[2] 5641 5-9-13 **66** 6ex .... TomEaves 10 79
(Keith Dalgleish) *mde all: rdn over 1f out: kpt on wl: comf* **6/5**[1]
6635 **2** 2 ¼ **Rock Canyon (IRE)**[11] 5336 4-8-10 **49** .... (p) JoeFanning 11 54
(Linda Perratt) *hld up: rdn 1/2-way: kpt on fr over 1f out: wnt 2nd nr fin: no ch w wnr* **12/1**
0-63 **3** *nk* **Carrie's Magic**[11] 5331 6-8-4 **46** .... JasonHart(3) 8 50
(Alistair Whillans) *awkward s: hld up: rdn 1/2-way: hdwy over 1f out: kpt on fnl f* **8/1**[3]
401 **4** ½ **Ambitious Icarus**[10] 5373 4-9-7 **65** 6ex .... (e) PhilipPrince(5) 2 67
(Richard Guest) *prom: rdn over 2f out: sn outpcd by wnr: plugged on ins fnl f* **17/2**
0000 **5** ¾ **Distant Sun (USA)**[11] 5336 9-8-7 **51** .... (p) GeorgeChaloner(5) 3 51
(Linda Perratt) *chsd ldrs: rdn 1/2-way: chsd wnr over 1f out: wknd fnl 100yds* **33/1**
1322 **6** *nse* **Saxonette**[11] 5336 5-8-8 **54** .... KevinStott(7) 7 53
(Linda Perratt) *s.i.s: sn outpcd in rr: kpt on fr over 1f out: nvr threatened* **4/1**[2]
2300 **7** 2 ½ **Magic Ice**[91] 2643 3-8-6 **54** .... JacobButterfield(7) 13 44
(Brian Ellison) *chsd ldrs: wknd over 1f out* **16/1**
0005 **8** *1* **Rio's Girl**[27] 4761 6-8-5 **49** .... ShirleyTeasdale(5) 9 36
(Tony Coyle) *prom: rdn 1/2-way: wknd over 1f out* **25/1**
5206 **9** ½ **Royal Duchess**[20] 4991 3-7-13 **47** .... GemmaTutty(7) 6 32
(Lucy Normile) *s.i.s: hld up: nvr threatened* **40/1**
5040 **10** *8* **Wicked Wilma (IRE)**[7] 5470 9-8-0 **46** .... JordanHibberd(7) 5 2
(Alan Berry) *chsd ldrs: wknd over 1f out* **16/1**
0004 **11** *10* **Roy's Legacy**[14] 5221 4-8-12 **51** .... (bt) DuranFentiman 1
(Shaun Harris) *racd alone far side: up w ldrs tl 1 1/2-way: wknd over 1f out* **33/1**

59.1s (-0.90) **Going Correction** -0.15s/f (Firm)
WFA 3 from 4yo+ 2lb **11** Ran SP% **118.7**
Speed ratings (Par 101): **101,97,96,96,94 94,90,89,88,75 59**
toteswingers 1&2 £4.70, 2&3 £9.50, 1&3 £4.50 CSF £17.18 CT £87.71 TOTE £2.10: £1.10, £2.60, £2.90; EX 24.40 Trifecta £92.50 Pool: £1097.13 - 8.88 winning units..
Owner The Wee Thackit Inn Synd & R Reid **Bred** Peter Webb **Trained** Carluke, S Lanarks

FOCUS
A weak race in which the winner edged closer to his 3yo form.

5480 NEWCASTLE (L-H)
Friday, August 23

OFFICIAL GOING: Good to firm (7.6)
Wind: moderate 1/2 behind Weather: overcast, rain last 2

5709 SPEEDFLEX (EUROPE) LTD "HANDS AND HEELS" APPRENTICE SERIES H'CAP (RACING EXCELLENCE) 6f
4:50 (4:50) (Class 6) (0-65,64) 3-Y-0+ **£1,940** (£577; £288; £144) **Stalls** Low

Form RPR
4230 **1** **John Coffey (IRE)**[38] 4377 4-9-6 **57** .... AliRawlinson(3) 2 71
(Michael Appleby) *hld up: hdwy whn nt clr run over 2f out tl over 1f out: led jst ins fnl f: styd on wl* **9/2**[3]
5062 **2** *3* **One Kool Dude**[7] 5487 4-9-2 **53** .... (b) LukeLeadbitter(3) 6 58
(Neville Bycroft) *reluctant to go to s: trckd ldrs: t.k.h: led 2f out: hdd jst ins fnl f: kpty on same pce* **7/2**[2]
0/30 **3** 1 ½ **Spirit Of Dixie**[160] 1042 6-8-8 **45** .... (p) AaronJones(3) 5 46
(Alan McCabe) *led: hdd 2f out: kpt on same pce fnl f* **50/1**
5056 **4** ¾ **Loukoumi**[8] 5426 5-8-9 **46** .... (b) RachelRichardson(3) 3 44
(Tim Easterby) *chsd ldr: kpt on one pce over 1f out* **5/1**
664 **5** *nk* **Mysterious Wonder**[20] 4976 3-9-3 **54** .... EvaMoscrop 10 51
(Philip Kirby) *hld up in rr: effrt over 2f out: kpt on one pce ins fnl f* **7/4**[1]
2035 **6** *2* **Busy Bimbo (IRE)**[2] 5641 4-8-10 **49** .... NicolaGrundy(5) 8 40
(Alan Berry) *reluctant to go to s: stdd s: hld up in rr: swtchd ins over 2f out: nt clr run over 1f out: wknd clsng stages* **13/2**
505 **7** ½ **Mousie**[38] 4377 4-8-8 **45** .... (t) JackGarritty(3) 9 35
(Alan McCabe) *unruly and uns rdr leaving paddock: rn loose to s: half rrd s: in rr: drvn over 3f out: nvr a factor* **20/1**

1m 12.86s (-1.74) **Going Correction** -0.425s/f (Firm)
WFA 3 from 4yo+ 3lb **7** Ran SP% **113.5**
Speed ratings (Par 101): **94,90,88,87,86 83,83**
toteswingers 1&2 £1.90, 2&3 £18.20, 1&3 £13.00 CSF £20.25 CT £680.99 TOTE £4.30: £1.70, £2.50; EX 16.30 Trifecta £285.30 Pool: £1434.28 - 3.77 winning units..
Owner Mick Appleby Racing **Bred** Mrs M McWey **Trained** Danethorpe, Notts
■ Stewards' Enquiry : Nicola Grundy three-day ban: struck filly whilst on the ground (Sep 6,8-9)

FOCUS
Rail moved 2m on Round course since meeting on August 16th. The forecast rain hadn't arrived. There were a number of non-runners throughout the card as the ground remained good to firm, good in places. An ordinary apprentice sprint handicap. The winner is rated up 8lb.

5710 PWC PRIVATE CLIENT NURSERY H'CAP 5f
5:25 (5:25) (Class 5) (0-75,75) 2-Y-0 **£2,587** (£770; £384; £192) **Stalls** Low

Form RPR
502 **1** **Kirtling Belle**[21] 4952 2-8-9 **63** .... PJMcDonald 6 66
(Keith Dalgleish) *chsd ldrs: styd on fnl f: led towards fin* **11/1**
0223 **2** ½ **Broadcaster (IRE)**[26] 4802 2-9-7 **75** .... SeanLevey 5 76
(Ed McMahon) *trckd ldrs: led jst ins fnl f: edgd lft and hdd towards fin* **15/8**[1]
6345 **3** *1* **Rosebay Coral (IRE)**[42] 4261 2-9-0 **68** .... BarryMcHugh 1 65
(Tony Coyle) *chsd ldrs far side: kpt on same pce ins fnl f: hld whn hmpd nr fin* **12/1**
4000 **4** *hd* **Tricksome (IRE)**[20] 4990 2-7-9 **56** oh3 ow2 .... (p) RowanScott(7) 8 53
(Ann Duffield) *sn towards rr: hdwy 2f out: styd on ins fnl f* **50/1**
155 **5** ½ **One Boy (IRE)**[28] 4726 2-8-12 **73** .... JoeyHaynes(7) 7 68
(Michael Dods) *t.k.h: led after 1f: hdd over 2f out: kpt on same pce over 1f out* **10/3**[2]
6013 **6** *shd* **Local Flier**[7] 5468 2-8-11 **65** .... DaleSwift 9 60
(Brian Ellison) *chsd ldrs: outpcd over 2f out: kpt on fnl f* **4/1**[3]
1043 **7** ¾ **Secret Applause**[17] 5106 2-8-4 **63** .... ConnorBeasley(5) 3 55
(Michael Dods) *led: 1f: w ldr: led over 2f out: hdd jst ins fnl f: wknd last 50yds* **11/1**
10 **8** *5* **Madagascar Moll (IRE)**[21] 4965 2-8-12 **71** .... DavidBergin(5) 2 45
(David O'Meara) *chsd ldrs: lost pl over 2f out* **7/1**

59.91s (-1.19) **Going Correction** -0.425s/f (Firm) **8** Ran SP% **116.7**
Speed ratings (Par 94): **92,91,89,89,88 88,87,79**
toteswingers 1&2 £5.80, 1&3 £7.50, 2&3 £5.40 CSF £32.79 CT £264.96 TOTE £8.80: £3.20, £1.50, £3.50; EX 39.00 Trifecta £241.80 Pool: £1230.15 - 3.81 winning units..
Owner Redgate Bloodstock **Bred** Redgate Bloodstock Ltd **Trained** Carluke, S Lanarks
■ Stewards' Enquiry : Sean Levey one-day ban: careless riding (Sep 6)

FOCUS
A competitive, if ordinary, nursery with a solid pace and plenty holding chances entering the final furlong. A step up from the winner.

5711 SIMP-LEE FITNESS H'CAP 7f
5:55 (5:55) (Class 5) (0-75,75) 3-Y-0+ **£2,587** (£770; £384; £192) **Stalls** Low

Form RPR
0643 **1** **Who's Shirl**[13] 5292 7-9-5 **68** .... AndrewElliott 11 77
(Chris Fairhurst) *sn in rr: outpcd over 3f out: hdwy stands' side over 1f out: edgd rt and led last 75yds: forged clr* **7/1**
3545 **2** *3* **Mutafaakir (IRE)**[17] 5088 4-9-7 **70** .... (p) PJMcDonald 10 69
(Ruth Carr) *led 5 other towards centrei: hdd and no ex last 75yds* **3/1**[1]
0000 **3** *1* **New Leyf (IRE)**[60] 3628 7-9-9 **72** .... AdrianNicholls 4 68
(David Nicholls) *swtchd rt after s: hld up in rr: hdwy over 2f out: kpt on fnl f to take 3rd last 30yds* **22/1**
6050 **4** *1* **Orbit The Moon (IRE)**[13] 5292 5-9-7 **75** .... (tp) ConnorBeasley(5) 8 68
(Michael Dods) *dwlt: sn chsng ldrs: outpcd over 2f out: kpt on fnl f* **14/1**
1102 **5** ½ **Illustrious Prince (IRE)**[5] 5564 6-9-8 **74** .... NeilFarley(3) 7 65
(Declan Carroll) *reminders after s: sn w ldr: kpt on same pce fnl f* **4/1**[2]
300- **6** ¾ **Andiamo Via**[440] 2924 6-8-13 **62** .... DaleSwift 5 51
(Brian Ellison) *swtchd lft s: led 3 others on far side: drvn 3f out: one pce fnl 2f*
0316 **7** *nk* **Ted's Brother (IRE)**[13] 5263 5-9-9 **72** .... (e) PhillipMakin 1 60
(Richard Guest) *t.k.h: trckd ldrs far side: one pce over 1f out* **15/2**
1212 **8** ¾ **Strong Man**[16] 5138 5-9-10 **73** .... (b) JamesSullivan 3 59
(Michael Easterby) *trckd ldrs far side: t.k.h: one pce over 1f out* **5/1**[3]
4400 **9** *nk* **Whispered Times (USA)**[11] 5341 6-9-0 **63** .... (p) MichaelO'Connell 6 48
(Tracy Waggott) *w ldrs: t.k.h: wknd fnl f* **28/1**
0101 **10** *2* **Just The Tonic**[18] 5049 6-9-6 **72** .... RaulDaSilva(3) 2 50
(Marjorie Fife) *trckd ldrs far side: lost pl over 1f out* **14/1**

1m 24.49s (-3.31) **Going Correction** -0.425s/f (Firm)
WFA 3 from 4yo+ 5lb **10** Ran SP% **116.2**
Speed ratings (Par 103): **101,97,96,95,94 93,93,92,92,90**
toteswingers 1&2 £4.90, 1&3 £38.40, 2&3 £12.10 CSF £28.16 CT £452.46 TOTE £9.50: £2.80, £1.30, £3.50; EX 31.30 Trifecta £253.20 Pool: £1076.63 -3.18 winning units..
Owner Mrs Shirley France **Bred** Mrs S France **Trained** Middleham Moor, N Yorks

FOCUS
Some winning and placed form but most of these came into this 56-75 handicap with questions to answer. A fair pace with the field splitting into two groups, with the group racing down the centre of the course always holding sway and producing the first five home. The winner is rated to her best form of the past year.

5712 "HAVE A HEART" TROPHY H'CAP 1m 4f 93y
6:25 (6:27) (Class 4) (0-80,80) 4-Y-0+ **£4,690** (£1,395; £697; £348) **Stalls** Low

Form RPR
-060 **1** **Handsome Ransom**[26] 4810 4-8-13 **72** .... PJMcDonald 4 88+
(David O'Meara) *hld up in rr: hdwy over 4f out: trcking ldrs and swtchd rt 2f out: 2nd 1f out: led last 75yds: styd on strly* **25/1**
53-6 **2** *1* **Cockney Sparrow**[100] 2369 4-9-5 **78** .... MichaelO'Connell 5 92
(John Quinn) *trckd ldrs: 2nd 3f out: led 2f out: hdd and no ex ins fnl f* **1/1**[1]
6531 **3** 3 ¾ **Discay**[9] 5384 4-8-12 **71** 6ex .... AdrianNicholls 3 79
(Mark Johnston) *awkward to load: trckd ldrs: t.k.h: drvn over 4f out: one pce and 3rd 1f out* **8/1**[3]

3153 **4** *5* **Ebony Express**[18] [5052] 4-8-8 **67** .... AndrewElliott 9 67
(Alan Swinbank) *swtchd lft after s: sn chsng ldrs: drvn and outpcd on outer over 3f out: edgd lft and kpt on ins fnl f: tk modest 4th nr fin* **9/1**
4556 **5** *½* **Royal Peculiar**[34] [4512] 5-9-2 **75** .... AndrewMullen 7 74
(Michael Appleby) *dwlt: sn mid-div: hdwy 6f out: effrt over 3f out: one pce fnl 2f* **8/1**[3]
1303 **6** *2 ¾* **Next Edition (IRE)**[19] [5031] 5-9-0 **80** .... EvaMoscrop(7) 1 75
(Philip Kirby) *t.k.h: led: hdd 2f out: sn wknd* **9/2**[2]
-000 **7** *6* **Jawaab (IRE)**[21] [4969] 9-8-5 **67** ....(p) DeclanCannon(3) 6 52
(Philip Kirby) *hld up in rr: drvn over 5f out: wl bhd fnl 3f* **18/1**
1/00 **8** *1* **High On A Hill (IRE)**[6] [4822] 6-8-6 **65** .... JamesSullivan 8 49
(Iain Jardine) *in rr: drvn over 5f out: wl bhd fnl 3f* **50/1**
2046 **9** *3 ¼* **Aegaeus**[56] [3791] 4-9-5 **78** ....(b[1]) PhillipMakin 2 56
(Ed Dunlop) *dwlt: t.k.h: sn trcking ldrs: led 4f out: hdd 2f out: sn lost pl* **12/1**

2m 38.73s (-6.87) **Going Correction** -0.425s/f (Firm) 9 Ran SP% **119.2**
Speed ratings (Par 105): **105,104,101,98,98 96,92,91,89**
toteswingers 1&2 £7.80, 2&3 £4.00, 1&3 £8.00 CSF £52.45 CT £248.08 TOTE £13.10: £3.40, £1.10, £2.00; EX 73.40 Trifecta £330.20 Pool: £1174.29 - 2.66 winning units..
Owner Normandie Stud Ltd **Bred** Normandie Stud Ltd **Trained** Nawton, N Yorks

FOCUS
An even gallop for a fair 1m4f handicap and the form should work out. The winner should improve again.

5713 LEE WESTWOOD GOLF AT CLOSE HOUSE H'CAP 1m 3y(S)
6:55 (6:57) (Class 5) (0-70,71) 3-Y-O+ **£2,587** (£770; £384; £192) **Stalls** Low

Form RPR
00-0 **1** **Cape Samba**[18] [5064] 4-9-8 **64** .... SeanLevey 5 75
(Ismail Mohammed) *chsd ldrs: styd on fnl f: led nr fin* **10/1**
0062 **2** *¾* **Moral Issue**[10] [5369] 5-9-0 **56** .... RobertWinston 11 65
(Alan Swinbank) *trckd ldrs: led over 1f out: hdd and no ex clsng stages* **3/1**[1]
6001 **3** *¾* **Aerodynamic (IRE)**[8] [5426] 6-10-1 **71** 6ex........(b) JamesSullivan 10 79
(Michael Easterby) *s.i.s: in rr: hdwy over 2f out: styd on to take 3rd clsng stages* **10/1**
-005 **4** *2* **Tukitinyasok (IRE)**[10] [5369] 6-8-10 **52** .... MichaelO'Connell 13 55
(Clive Mulhall) *w ldrs: led over 2f out: hdd over 1f out: kpt on same pce* **20/1**
3044 **5** *1 ¾* **Khajaaly (IRE)**[58] [3700] 6-8-10 **52** ....(t) AndrewMullen 7 51
(Michael Appleby) *hmpd s: mid-div: hdwy over 2f out: swtchd rt: one pce over 1f out* **10/1**
0042 **6** *nse* **Thatcherite (IRE)**[7] [5471] 5-8-13 **55** .... StephenCraine 14 54
(Tony Coyle) *hld up in rr: hdwy over 2f out: drvn over 1f out: one pce* **10/3**[2]
-006 **7** *3* **Monthly Medal**[48] [4052] 10-8-6 **55** ....(t) SamanthaBell(7) 16 47
(Wilf Storey) *t.k.h in mid-div: nt clr run and swtchd lft over 2f out: one pce* **12/1**
5063 **8** *shd* **Bunce (IRE)**[14] [5239] 5-9-6 **67** .... DavidBergin(5) 4 59
(David O'Meara) *hld up in rr: sme hdwy over 2f out: nvr a factor* **7/1**[3]
0440 **9** *4* **The Lodge Road (IRE)**[18] [5052] 5-8-6 **53** .... ConnorBeasley(5) 12 35
(Martin Todhunter) *in rr: effrt over 2f out: sn lost pl* **18/1**
5566 **10** *26* **Change The Subject (USA)**[13] [5264] 5-9-12 **68** ....(vt) LeeTopliss 15
(Richard Guest) *sn drvn along: sn chsng ldrs: led over 3f out: hung lft and hdd over 2f out: sn lost pl and hmpd: sn bhd: virtually p.u ins fnl f: t.o* **14/1**
/00- **11** *12* **Camerooney**[487] [1561] 10-9-6 **65** ....(p) PaulPickard(3) 6
(Marjorie Fife) *wnt rt s: led: drvn over 4f out: hdd over 3f out: sn lost pl: t.o whn eased ins fnl f: virtually p.u* **12/1**

1m 38.77s (-4.63) **Going Correction** -0.425s/f (Firm)
WFA 3 from 4yo+ 6lb 11 Ran SP% **119.9**
Speed ratings (Par 103): **106,105,104,102,100 100,97,97,93,67 55**
toteswingers 1&2 £5.50, 1&3 £9.50, 2&3 £2.60 CSF £40.89 CT £319.76 TOTE £8.60: £3.30, £1.70, £2.20; EX 30.10 Trifecta £320.80 Part won. Pool: £427.83 - 0.34 winning units..
Owner Ismail Mohammed **Bred** Jeremy Gompertz **Trained** Newmarket, Suffolk

FOCUS
Although five non-runners reduced the field to 11 it remained a competitive handicap over the straight mile. The pace was good and the form is sound.

5714 SPEEDFLEX FILLIES' H'CAP 6f
7:30 (7:30) (Class 5) (0-75,74) 3-Y-O+ **£2,587** (£770; £384; £192) **Stalls** Low

Form RPR
1511 **1** **Gran Canaria Queen**[14] [5227] 4-9-1 **65** .... DavidAllan 4 78
(Tim Easterby) *chsd ldr: drvn over 2f out: led over 1f out: styd on strly clsng stages: won gng away* **5/4**[1]
0132 **2** *1 ¾* **Dartrix**[20] [4993] 4-9-1 **70** .... ConnorBeasley(5) 2 77
(Michael Dods) *stdd s: shkn up over 3f out: hdwy over 2f out: upsides over 1f out: styd on same pce last 50yds* **13/8**[2]
3436 **3** *9* **Silkelly**[11] [5353] 3-9-7 **74** .... DanielTudhope 3 59
(David O'Meara) *led: shkn up over 2f out: hdd over 1f out: wknd and eased ins fnl f* **7/2**[3]
0045 **4** *5* **Star Request**[46] [4113] 3-8-1 **55** oh2 ow2........(p) NeilFarley(3) 6 20
(Frederick Watson) *sn chsng ldrs: drvn 3f out: carried hd high and hung lft: lost pl 2f out: sn bhd* **20/1**

1m 12.44s (-2.16) **Going Correction** -0.425s/f (Firm)
WFA 3 from 4yo+ 3lb 4 Ran SP% **109.5**
Speed ratings (Par 100): **97,94,82,76**
CSF £3.65 TOTE £2.00; EX 3.60 Trifecta £4.00 Pool: £394.08 - 72.93 winning units..
Owner M Gillies **Bred** H Moszkowicz And Whitsbury Manor Stud **Trained** Great Habton, N Yorks
■ Stewards' Enquiry : Neil Farley three-day ban: weighed in 2lb heavy (Sep 6,8-9)

FOCUS
The rain had started to fall. Only four runners remained from the seven declared but still an interesting fillies' sprint handicap. The first two improved to pull clear of the third.

5715 STAY AND PLAY GOLF AT CLOSE HOUSE MAIDEN STKS 7f
8:00 (8:00) (Class 5) 3-4-Y-O **£2,587** (£770; £384; £192) **Stalls** Low

Form RPR
0- **1** **Sherzam**[44] [4188] 3-9-0 76 .... PJMcDonald 5 67
(Michael Dods) *trckd ldrs: led travelling strly over 1f out: pushed out clsng stages* **7/4**[2]
0 **2** *1 ¼* **It Must Be Faith**[29] [4667] 3-9-5 0 .... AndrewMullen 2 69
(Michael Appleby) *t.k.h in rr: hdwy 3f out: chsng ldrs over 1f out: tk 2nd last 100yds: no real imp* **10/1**
3 **3** *¾* **Yarn**[20] [4991] 3-9-0 0 .... PhillipMakin 13 62
(William Haggas) *stdd s: t.k.h: sn trcking ldrs: kpt on same pce to take 3rd last 100yds* **13/8**[1]
0-4 **4** *hd* **Smart Eighteen**[6] [5517] 3-9-5 0 .... RobertWinston 3 66
(Paul D'Arcy) *hld up towards rr: hdwy 3f out: trcking ldrs 2f out: styd on same pce fnl f* **9/2**[3]
3-0 **5** *6* **Fleurtille**[186] [706] 4-9-5 0 .... LeeTopliss 7 47
(Robert Johnson) *w ldr: wknd appr fnl f* **33/1**
-65 **6** *2 ¼* **Rosy Ryan (IRE)**[26] [4813] 3-9-0 0 .... DaleSwift 11 39
(Tina Jackson) *led: hdd over 1f out: sn wknd* **50/1**
7 *3 ¼* **Perci French** 3-9-5 0 .... DanielTudhope 9 35
(David O'Meara) *t.k.h in rr: hdwy to trck ldrs after 2f: effrt over 2f out: sn wknd* **15/2**
0 **8** *1 ¼* **Cape Rosa**[23] [4887] 3-9-0 0 .... PaddyAspell 4 27
(James Moffatt) *in rr: drvn 3f out: sn lost pl* **50/1**
000- **9** *23* **High Meadow Prince**[429] [3289] 4-9-7 25 .... LMcNiff(3) 14
(Robert Johnson) *t.k.h in rr: drvn 4f out: lost pl over 2f out: sn bhd: t.o* **100/1**

1m 27.27s (-0.53) **Going Correction** -0.425s/f (Firm)
WFA 3 from 4yo 5lb 9 Ran SP% **121.3**
Speed ratings (Par 103): **86,84,83,83,76 74,70,68,42**
toteswingers 1&2 £6.30, 1&3 £1.10, 2&3 £5.90 CSF £20.54 TOTE £3.00: £1.10, £4.00, £1.10; EX 24.70 Trifecta £90.90 Pool: £537.81 - 4.43 winning units..
Owner Andrew Tinkler **Bred** Sir Eric Parker **Trained** Denton, Co Durham

FOCUS
With the form on offer this was just an ordinary maiden with a pace to match which resulted in a sprint to the finish. The winner didn't need to match her best Irish form.
T/Plt: £66.40 to £1 stake. Pool: £67499.46 - 741.95 winning tickets T/Qpdt: £9.90 to a £1 stake. Pool: £4388.66 - 326.78 winning tickets WG

5536 NEWMARKET (R-H)
Friday, August 23

OFFICIAL GOING: Good (good to firm in places; 7.2)
Wind: Light across Weather: Fine

5716 CHOOSE EBF NOMINATED MAIDEN FILLIES' STKS 7f
2:10 (2:10) (Class 4) 2-Y-O **£4,528** (£1,347; £673; £336) **Stalls** High

Form RPR
62 **1** **Enraptured (IRE)**[35] [4491] 2-9-0 0 .... RobertHavlin 5 81+
(John Gosden) *led 2f: remained w ldrs: led wl over 2f out: sn hdd: rdn to ld over 1f out: r.o wl* **12/1**
2 **2** *2 ¼* **Psychometry (FR)**[28] [4702] 2-9-0 0 .... KierenFallon 12 75
(Sir Michael Stoute) *chsd ldrs: rdn and ev ch fr over 1f out tl wl ins fnl f: styd on same pce* **5/2**[2]
3 *nk* **Volume** 2-9-0 0 .... KirstyMilczarek 7 74+
(Luca Cumani) *chsd ldrs: shkn up over 1f out: styd on wl* **66/1**
2 **4** *nse* **Night Party (IRE)**[20] [5003] 2-9-0 0 .... PaulHanagan 9 74
(Saeed bin Suroor) *w ldrs: led over 2f out: rdn and hdd over 1f out: styd on same pce wl ins fnl f* **15/8**[1]
4 **5** *½* **Angleterre (FR)**[22] [4921] 2-9-0 0 .... RichardHughes 6 73
(Richard Hannon) *chsd ldrs: led 5f out: hdd wl over 2f out: rdn over 1f out: styd on* **11/4**[3]
6 *½* **Dancing Sands (IRE)** 2-9-0 0 .... MickaelBarzalona 4 72+
(Charlie Appleby) *hld up: hdwy u.p and hung rt over 1f out: edgd lft ins fnl f: styd on* **7/1**
7 *1 ¼* **Tullia (IRE)** 2-9-0 0 .... LukeMorris 8 68
(William Knight) *s.i.s: in rr: pushed along 1/2-way: rdn and hung lft over 1f out: styd on: nt trble ldrs* **100/1**
0 **8** *1 ¾* **Mollasses**[28] [4702] 2-9-0 0 .... WilliamCarson 2 64
(Jonathan Portman) *prom: pushed along 1/2-way: no ex ins fnl f* **100/1**
9 *¾* **Percybelle** 2-9-0 0 .... HarryBentley 10 62
(William Knight) *hld up: effrt and hung lft over 1f out: no ex fnl f* **100/1**
44 **10** *1* **Starlit Cantata**[22] [4924] 2-9-0 0 .... JohnFahy 1 59
(Eve Johnson Houghton) *prom: rdn over 2f out: wknd over 1f out* **66/1**
11 *47* **Twenty Roses (IRE)** 2-9-0 0 .... TomMcLaughlin 3
(Ed Walker) *s.i.s: sn pushed along in rr: hung lft and lost tch 1/2-way* **66/1**

1m 28.0s (2.30) **Going Correction** +0.225s/f (Good) 11 Ran SP% **117.7**
Speed ratings (Par 93): **91,88,88,88,87 86,85,83,82,81 27**
toteswingers 1&2 £3.80, 2&3 £24.00, 1&3 £16.70 CSF £42.65 TOTE £7.50: £2.90, £1.20, £10.80; EX 20.80 Trifecta £433.20 Pool: £2469.96 - 4.27 winning units..
Owner Lady Bamford **Bred** Airlie Stud **Trained** Newmarket, Suffolk

FOCUS
Stands' side track used. Stalls Far side except 1m4f centre. They went a steady pace down the centre of the track in this useful fillies' maiden. The favourite came up a bit short but one of the other main form contenders scored in gritty style. The form is rated in line with the race averages.

5717 NEWMARKETEXPERIENCE.CO.UK NURSERY H'CAP 1m
2:45 (2:46) (Class 4) (0-80,77) 2-Y-O **£3,881** (£1,155; £577; £288) **Stalls** High

Form RPR
1 **1** **Chief Barker (IRE)**[15] [5188] 2-9-7 **77** .... RichardHughes 6 94+
(Richard Hannon) *hld up: pushed along over 3f out: nt clr run fr over 2f out tl swtchd rt over 1f out: sn chsng ldr: rdn: flashed tail but r.o to ld wl ins fnl f: readily* **5/4**[1]
01 **2** *½* **Trip To Paris (IRE)**[30] [4631] 2-9-6 **76** ....(b) JimCrowley 5 89
(Ed Dunlop) *chsd ldrs: pushed along over 2f out: led over 1f out: sn rdn: hdd wl ins fnl f* **12/1**
4112 **3** *8* **Finn Class (IRE)**[9] [5400] 2-9-3 **73** .... LukeMorris 2 68
(Michael Bell) *chsd ldrs: shake up to ld 2f out: sn rdn and hdd: wknd ins fnl f* **6/1**[3]
1 **4** *1 ½* **Stagemanship (USA)**[22] [4925] 2-9-7 **77** .... MickaelBarzalona 3 69
(Charlie Appleby) *led 1f: chsd ldr: rdn and ev ch over 1f out: wknd ins fnl f* **5/2**[2]
5221 **5** *12* **Floating Ballerino (IRE)**[11] [5347] 2-9-6 **76** 6ex........ HarryBentley 4 40
(Olly Stevens) *hld up: racd keenly: hdwy over 4f out: rdn and wknd over 1f out: eased* **17/2**
201 **6** *2 ¼* **Hatti (IRE)**[14] [5243] 2-8-9 **65** ....(p) MichaelStainton 1 24
(Micky Hammond) *led 7f out: rdn and hdd 2f out: sn wknd* **50/1**

1m 40.92s (0.92) **Going Correction** +0.225s/f (Good) 6 Ran SP% **107.5**
Speed ratings (Par 96): **104,103,95,94,82 79**
toteswingers 1&2 £1.90, 2&3 £10.50, 1&3 £1.50 CSF £15.63 TOTE £2.20: £1.90, £4.50; EX 16.90 Trifecta £66.60 Pool: £2573.16 - 28.96 winning units..
Owner Middleham Park Racing Xxiii **Bred** Eimear Mulhern **Trained** East Everleigh, Wilts

FOCUS
Five last-time-out winners lined-up in this nursery. They raced against the far side and the first two pulled clear. The runner-up will be the key to the form.

5718 BRITISH STALLION STUDS EBF MAIDEN STKS 7f
3:20 (3:21) (Class 4) 2-Y-O **£4,528** (£1,347; £673; £336) **Stalls** High

Form RPR
1 **Learaig (IRE)** 2-9-0 0 .... PatCosgrave 8 91+
(Lady Cecil) *hld up: hdwy over 2f out: led over 1f out: rdn ins fnl f: r.o* **33/1**
2 3/4 **Bon Voyage** 2-9-0 0 .... RichardHughes 11 89+
(Richard Hannon) *s.i.s: sn chsng ldrs: nt clr run over 1f out: rdn to chse wnr fnl f: r.o* **15/2[3]**
3 3 3/4 **Alex Vino (IRE)** 2-9-0 0 .... KierenFallon 1 79+
(Sir Michael Stoute) *hld up: shkn up over 2f out: hdwy and nt clr run over 1f out: styd on* **16/1**
4 1 **Hands Up (IRE)** 2-9-0 0 .... LukeMorris 6 77
(William Knight) *s.i.s: hld up: hdwy and nt clr run over 1f out: r.o: nt trble ldrs* **100/1**
5 hd **Istikshaf (IRE)** 2-9-0 0 .... RobertHavlin 2 76
(Saeed bin Suroor) *hld up: hdwy over 1f out: hung lft ins fnl f: r.o: nt trble ldrs* **20/1**
2 6 1 **Intermedium**[17] 5101 2-9-0 0 .... MickaelBarzalona 10 74
(Charlie Appleby) *w ldr tl led over 2f out: rdn and hdd over 1f out: edgd lft: wknd ins fnl f* **5/4[1]**
7 1 1/4 **Crafty Exit** 2-9-0 0 .... HarryBentley 9 70+
(William Knight) *hld up: effrt and nt clr run over 1f out: nvr able to chal* **50/1**
8 nse **Hanno (USA)** 2-9-0 0 .... JimCrowley 12 70+
(Ed Dunlop) *s.i.s: hdwy over 4f out: rdn whn n.m.r over 1f out: styd on same pce ins fnl f* **16/1**
0 9 1 1/2 **Prairie Prize**[14] 5244 2-9-0 0 .... WilliamCarson 7 67+
(David Elsworth) *prom: rdn over 2f out: wknd fnl f* **14/1**
10 1 1/2 **Almuhalab** 2-9-0 0 .... PaulHanagan 5 62
(Charles Hills) *w ldrs: rdn and ev ch over 1f out: wknd fnl f* **5/2[2]**
11 4 **Douman (USA)** 2-9-0 0 .... (t) FrederikTylicki 13 52
(Ed Dunlop) *awkward leaving stalls: sn led: rdn and hdd over 2f out: wkng whn hmpd over 1f out* **66/1**
12 8 **One Man Band (IRE)** 2-9-0 0 .... AhmedAjtebi 4 31
(Charlie Appleby) *s.i.s: hld up: plld hrd: rdn: hung rt and wknd over 2f out* **28/1**
13 3 3/4 **Rathealy (IRE)** 2-9-0 0 .... TomMcLaughlin 3 21
(Alan Bailey) *hld up in tch: hung lft fr over 4f out: wknd over 2f out* **66/1**

1m 28.17s (2.47) **Going Correction** +0.225s/f (Good) **13** Ran SP% **120.3**
Speed ratings (Par 96): **94,93,88,87,87 86,84,84,83,81 76,67,63**
toteswingers 1&2 £21.60, 2&3 £15.80, 1&3 £38.50 CSF £258.17 TOTE £37.90: £6.40, £3.00, £3.70; EX 226.70 Trifecta £1526.30 Pool: £2149.41 - 1.05 winning units..
Owner Mubarak Al Naemi **Bred** L Montgomery **Trained** Newmarket, Suffolk
FOCUS
They went a steady pace in this maiden. The two clear market leaders were both disappointing but a newcomer scored in good style and the first two pulled clear. The form matches the high average for this event.

5719 TURFTV H'CAP 1m 4f
3:55 (3:57) (Class 4) (0-85,85) 3-Y-O+ **£4,851** (£1,443; £721; £360) **Stalls** Centre

Form RPR
2 1 **Quick Jack (IRE)**[20] 5021 4-9-0 65 .... RichardHughes 2 76
(A J Martin, Ire) *chsd ldrs: pushed along over 3f out: rdn to ld 1f out: styd on* **7/1[3]**
6421 2 1/2 **Nautilus**[7] 5492 3-9-2 77 6ex .... RobertHavlin 4 87
(John Gosden) *led: rdn and hdd over 2f out: edgd lft: ev ch over 1f out: styd on u.p* **4/6[1]**
-111 3 2 3/4 **Bohemian Rhapsody (IRE)**[9] 5390 4-9-13 85 6ex... DanielMuscutt(7) 3 91
(Seamus Durack) *trckd ldr: pushed along over 3f out: led over 2f out: rdn and hdd 1f out: styd on same pce ins fnl f* **11/4[2]**
0051 4 27 **Strawberry Jam**[9] 5392 3-7-12 64 .... NathanAlison(5) 1 30
(Paul Cole) *hld up: racd keenly: hdwy 1/2-way: rdn and wknd over 2f out* **12/1**

2m 33.68s (0.78) **Going Correction** +0.225s/f (Good)
WFA 3 from 4yo 10lb **4** Ran SP% **106.8**
Speed ratings (Par 105): **106,105,103,85**
CSF £12.34 TOTE £5.80; EX 12.40 Trifecta £15.50 Pool: £2292.17 - 110.85 winning units..
Owner John Breslin **Bred** Newtown Anner Stud **Trained** Summerhill, Co. Meath
FOCUS
The three last-time-out winners in this race were all officially ahead of the handicapper but two of them got involved in a sustained duel and a maiden stayed on strongly to snatch the prize. The third is the best guide.

5720 NEWMARKETRACECOURSES.CO.UK MAIDEN STKS 1m
4:30 (4:30) (Class 5) 3-Y-O+ **£3,234** (£962; £481; £240) **Stalls** High

Form RPR
1 **Joe Sugden** 4-9-11 0 .... (t) MartinLane 7 82
(Mrs Ilka Gansera-Leveque) *chsd ldr: rdn to ld 1f out: styd on* **80/1**
3- 2 hd **Zurbriggen**[378] 5062 3-9-5 0 .... MickaelBarzalona 8 81+
(Charlie Appleby) *hld up: racd keenly: hdwy and hmpd over 1f out: sn rdn: ev ch ins fnl f: styd on* **4/5[1]**
5- 3 1 1/4 **Magic Hurricane (IRE)**[289] 7637 3-9-5 0 .... FrederikTylicki 1 78
(James Fanshawe) *hld up: hdwy u.p and edgd lft over 1f out: styd on same pce ins fnl f* **6/1[3]**
30 4 1 **For Posterity**[21] 4968 3-9-5 0 .... AhmedAjtebi 3 76
(Charlie Appleby) *led: rdn and hdd 1f out: styd on same pce ins fnl f: eased whn btn towards fin* **20/1**
2-25 5 1 **Nickels And Dimes (IRE)**[32] 4594 3-9-0 79 .... RobertHavlin 2 68
(John Gosden) *chsd ldrs: rdn over 2f out: edgd lft: styd on same pce fnl f* **7/2[2]**
6- 6 hd **The Best Doctor (IRE)**[303] 7330 3-9-5 0 .... PaulHanagan 6 73
(Jeremy Noseda) *hld up: effrt and edgd lft over 1f out: styd on same pce fnl f* **7/1**
6 7 3/4 **Millies Quest**[18] 5071 4-8-13 0 .... JordanVaughan(7) 5 67
(Martin Smith) *s.i.s: sn prom: rdn over 1f out: no ex ins fnl f* **66/1**

1m 42.09s (2.09) **Going Correction** +0.225s/f (Good)
WFA 3 from 4yo 6lb **7** Ran SP% **112.1**
Speed ratings (Par 103): **98,97,96,95,94 94,93**
toteswingers 1&2 £8.40, 2&3 £2.20, 1&3 £13.80 CSF £141.41 TOTE £49.60: £11.10, £1.20; EX 199.80 Trifecta £662.20 Pool: £4170.07 - 4.72 winning units..
Owner Brookside Breeders Club **Bred** Brookside Breeders Club **Trained** Newmarket, Suffolk

FOCUS
They finished in a bunch in this steadily-run maiden and there was an 80-1 winner. It might be dangerous to suspect this a fluke and the form could easily be rated 6lb better.

5721 RACING UK H'CAP 7f
5:05 (5:05) (Class 3) (0-90,90) 3-Y-O **£7,439** (£2,213; £1,106; £553) **Stalls** High

Form RPR
31 1 **Life Partner (IRE)**[29] 4667 3-9-7 90 .... MickaelBarzalona 1 96+
(Charlie Appleby) *hld up: swtchd lft sn after s: hdwy over 1f out: rdn to ld ins fnl f: r.o* **3/1[2]**
2154 2 1/2 **Front Page News**[8] 5437 3-8-3 72 .... LukeMorris 7 77
(Robert Eddery) *chsd ldrs: rdn and ev ch fr over 1f out: swvd rt wl ins fnl f: nt run on* **9/2[3]**
1630 3 3/4 **Extrasolar**[6] 5538 3-9-2 85 .... (t) RobertHavlin 3 88
(Amanda Perrett) *sn led: hdd over 5f out: led again 1/2-way: rdn and hdd ins fnl f: styd on* **12/1**
2142 4 shd **Stableford**[42] 4236 3-9-1 84 .... MartinLane 8 86
(Brian Meehan) *hld up: hdwy over 2f out: sn rdn: r.o* **9/4[1]**
-133 5 1 **Al Raqeeb (IRE)**[169] 920 3-8-9 78 .... J-PGuillambert 4 78
(Gary Harrison) *a.p: rdn over 1f out: styd on* **33/1**
12-0 6 2 1/4 **Tobacco Road (IRE)**[105] 2209 3-8-12 81 .... PatCosgrave 2 75
(Richard Hannon) *trckd ldrs: plld hrd: led over 5f out: hdd 1/2-way: rdn over 1f out: no ex fnl f* **9/1**
0114 7 1/2 **Dashing David (IRE)**[15] 5187 3-9-2 85 .... PatDobbs 6 78
(Richard Hannon) *hld up: hdwy over 2f out: sn rdn: no ex fnl f* **9/1**
1-00 8 5 **Kerbaaj (USA)**[97] 2438 3-8-9 78 .... PaulHanagan 5 58
(Charles Hills) *hld up: rdn over 1f out: sn wknd* **8/1**

1m 28.03s (2.33) **Going Correction** +0.225s/f (Good) **8** Ran SP% **115.7**
Speed ratings (Par 104): **95,94,93,93,92 89,89,83**
toteswingers 1&2 £4.60, 2&3 £10.70, 1&3 £7.10 CSF £17.21 CT £141.01 TOTE £3.40: £2.20, £2.80, £3.70; EX 22.40 Trifecta £159.80 Pool: £2493.42 - 11.70 winning units..
Owner Godolphin **Bred** Gigginstown House **Trained** Newmarket, Suffolk
FOCUS
They went a very steady gallop in this decent handicap but the well-backed winner scored from off the pace and the form looks solid enough, rated around the second and third.

5722 NEWMARKETRACECOURSES.CO.UK H'CAP (JOCKEY CLUB GRASSROOTS SPRINT SERIES QUALIFIER) 6f
5:35 (5:36) (Class 4) (0-85,83) 3-Y-O+ **£4,851** (£1,443; £721; £360) **Stalls** High

Form RPR
-623 1 **Saloomy**[83] 2871 4-9-8 82 .... MickaelBarzalona 6 91
(John Butler) *mde all: set stdy pce tl qcknd over 2f out: rdn over 1f out: r.o* **9/4[2]**
1203 2 3/4 **Mayaasem**[20] 5009 3-9-6 83 .... PaulHanagan 5 90
(Charles Hills) *trckd wnr: rdn over 1f out: r.o* **11/8[1]**
0200 3 1 **My Kingdom (IRE)**[14] 5247 7-9-2 76 .... (t) HarryBentley 1 80+
(Stuart Williams) *hld up: rdn over 1f out: r.o ins fnl f: nt rch ldrs* **8/1**
0030 4 1/2 **Johnny Castle**[23] 4879 5-9-8 82 .... PatDobbs 3 84
(Amanda Perrett) *chsd ldrs: rdn over 1f out: styd on* **9/2[3]**
5405 5 3/4 **Piazza San Pietro**[7] 5489 7-9-4 78 .... (b) LukeMorris 2 78
(Zoe Davison) *hld up in tch: rdn over 2f out: styd on same pce ins fnl f* **16/1**
04-6 6 hd **Billyrayvalentine (CAN)**[38] 4364 4-9-6 80 .... PatCosgrave 4 79
(George Baker) *rrd s: sn prom: rdn over 1f out: styd on same pce ins fnl f* **16/1**

1m 14.11s (1.61) **Going Correction** +0.225s/f (Good)
WFA 3 from 4yo+ 3lb **6** Ran SP% **113.9**
Speed ratings (Par 105): **98,97,95,95,94 93**
toteswingers 1&2 £1.20, 2&3 £2.10, 1&3 £3.60 CSF £5.89 TOTE £3.40: £1.60, £1.50; EX 6.10 Trifecta £22.60 Pool: £1571.93 - 52.11 winning units..
Owner Saleh Al Homaizi & Imad Al Sagar **Bred** D J And Mrs Deer **Trained** Newmarket, Suffolk
FOCUS
The two market leaders dominated this handicap and the hold-up performers couldn't get involved. The second more than confirmed his recent improvement.
T/Plt: £932.50 to a £1 stake. Pool of £58894.18 - 46.10 winning tickets. T/Qpdt: £274.10 to a £1 stake. Pool of £3112.0, 8.40 winning tickets. CR

5679 YORK (L-H)
Friday, August 23

OFFICIAL GOING: Good to soft (6.6; home straight: far side 6.3; centre 6.3; stands' side 6.1)
Wind: Fresh behind Weather: Cloudy

5723 SKY BET STKS (H'CAP) 1m 4f
1:55 (1:55) (Class 2) (0-100,98) 3-Y-O+
£31,125 (£9,320; £4,660; £2,330; £1,165; £585) **Stalls** Centre

Form RPR
0110 1 **Chancery (USA)**[13] 5269 5-9-7 91 .... DanielTudhope 10 102+
(David O'Meara) *trckd ldrs: smooth hdwy 3f out: led 2f out: rdn appr fnl f: kpt on strly* **7/1[2]**
542 2 1 1/4 **Rio's Rosanna (IRE)**[16] 5147 6-9-1 85 .... RussKennemore 2 93
(Richard Whitaker) *t.k.h early: trckd ldrs: hdwy 4f out: cl up 3f out: rdn 2f out and ev ch tl drvn and one pce fnl f* **9/1**
6311 3 nk **Kiama Bay (IRE)**[6] 5513 7-9-5 89 6ex .... GrahamLee 16 97
(Richard Fahey) *lw: hld up towards rr: hdwy on outer 3f out: rdn to chse ldrs wl over 1f out: sn drvn and kpt on fnl f: nrst fin* **8/1[3]**
412- 4 nk **White Nile (IRE)**[339] 6340 4-8-10 80 .... WilliamBuick 5 87+
(David Simcock) *lw: hld up: hdwy 3f out: swtchd to inner and rdn to chse ldrs wl over 1f out: drvn and one pce fnl f* **10/1**
0002 5 1 3/4 **Scatter Dice (IRE)**[6] 5513 4-9-3 87 .... FrannyNorton 7 91
(Mark Johnston) *cl up: led 3f out: sn rdn: hdd 2f out: sn drvn and kpt on same pce appr fnl f* **10/1**
-562 6 3 1/2 **Castilo Del Diablo (IRE)**[51] 3960 4-9-6 90 .... JamieSpencer 6 89
(David Simcock) *towards rr: pushed along 1/2-way: rdn 4f out: kpt on u.p fnl 2f: nrst fin* **8/1[3]**
110- 7 1/2 **Gospel Choir**[349] 6025 4-10-0 98 .... RyanMoore 4 96
(Sir Michael Stoute) *lw: t.k.h early: trckd ldrs on inner: hdwy over 4f out: rdn along wl over 2f out: drvn wl over 1f out and no imp* **7/2[1]**
2522 8 3 **Come On Blue Chip (IRE)**[20] 4979 4-9-5 89 .... (p) MartinHarley 14 82
(Paul D'Arcy) *hld up in midfield: hdwy 3f out: rdn along over 2f out: sn no imp* **22/1**
0306 9 3/4 **Itlaaq**[26] 4796 7-9-6 90 .... (t) GrahamGibbons 11 82
(Michael Easterby) *in tch: hdwy 3f out: rdn along over 2f out: sn btn* **25/1**

1364 **10** *8* **Presburg (IRE)**[15] 5168 4-8-9 **79**.. LiamKeniry 15 58
(Joseph Tuite) *warm: hld up in rr: sme hdwy on inner wl over 2f out: sn rdn and nvr a factor* **50/1**

6200 **11** *6* **Tepmokea (IRE)**[13] 5269 7-9-5 **89**.. ShaneKelly 3 58
(Mrs K Burke) *lw: led: rdn along and hdd 3f out: drvn over 2f out and sn wknd* **14/1**

0210 **12** *16* **Warlu Way**[42] 4262 6-9-5 **89**.. RobertWinston 9 33
(Michael Easterby) *v s.i.s: a bhd* **33/1**

4220 **13** *30* **Quixote**[48] 4060 4-9-6 **90**..(t) JamesDoyle 1
(Clive Brittain) *trckd ldng pair: rdn along wl over 3f out: sn wknd: bhd and eased fnl 2f* **25/1**

0-11 **14** *nk* **Winterlude (IRE)**[20] 4979 3-9-2 **96**.. SilvestreDeSousa 8
(Charlie Appleby) *chsd ldrs on outer: pushed along 1/2-way: rdn and lost pl over 5f out: bhd and eased fnl 2f* **7/1**[2]

2m 32.86s (-0.34) **Going Correction** +0.20s/f (Good)
WFA 3 from 4yo+ 10lb **14** Ran SP% **121.2**
Speed ratings (Par 109): **109,108,107,107,106 104,103,101,101,96 92,81,61,61**
toteswingers 1&2 £20.50, 2&3 £19.00, 1&3 £16.50 CSF £64.95 CT £524.71 TOTE £8.70: £3.00, £3.20, £3.00; EX 89.80 Trifecta £836.90 Pool: £4034.78 - 3.61 winning units..
Owner Hollowdean **Bred** Darley **Trained** Nawton, N Yorks

FOCUS
A thunderstorm deposited 20mm of rain overnight and that had quite a dramatic effect on the going, with the fast ground easing to good to soft (GoingStick 6.6, from 7.7 the previous day; home straight: far side 6.3; centre 6.3; stands' side 6.1). Jockeys reported it to be as described and the time of the opener was 3.56sec slower than standard. The rail in the back straight and on the home bend had been moved out 3m to create fresh ground, adding 7yds to distances of 1m and further. This looked competitive enough but the winner took it easily. The runner-up helps set a sound standard.

5724 WEATHERBYS HAMILTON INSURANCE LONSDALE CUP (BRITISH CHAMPIONS SERIES) (GROUP 2) 2m 88y
2:30 (2:30) (Class 1) 3-Y-O+

£85,065 (£32,250; £16,140; £8,040; £4,035; £2,025) **Stalls** Low

Form RPR
1222 **1** **Ahzeemah (IRE)**[22] 4919 4-9-3 111........................(p) SilvestreDeSousa 7 117
(Saeed bin Suroor) *lw: trckd ldr: hdwy and cl up over 2f out: rdn and edgd rt wl over 1f out: drvn to ld jst over 1f out: kpt on wl u.p towards fin* **4/1**[2]

5-42 **2** *hd* **Simenon (IRE)**[64] 3483 6-9-3 115.. JohnnyMurtagh 3 116
(W P Mullins, Ire) *led: pushed along and qcknd 5f out: c wd to stands' rail: rdn over 2f out: edgd lft over 1f out: sn hdd and drvn: ev ch tl no ex towards fin* **15/8**[1]

1-60 **3** *2 ¾* **Times Up**[64] 3483 7-9-3 113.. RyanMoore 1 114
(Ed Dunlop) *hld up in rr: hdwy 3f out: rdn to chse ldrs whn n.m.r over 1f out: kpt on same pce fnl f* **9/2**[3]

-210 **4** *1 ½* **Caucus**[22] 4919 6-9-3 110.. WilliamBuick 4 111
(John Gosden) *trckd ldng pair: pushed along 5f out: rdn wl over 2f out: drvn and n.m.r over 1f out: sn swtchd lft and one pce fnl f* **11/2**

-150 **5** *1* **Glen's Diamond**[22] 4919 5-9-3 112.. TonyHamilton 5 111
(Richard Fahey) *trckd ldrs: hdwy over 4f out: rdn along wl over 2f out: drvn and one pce fr wl over 1f out* **14/1**

-040 **6** *2 ½* **Colour Vision (FR)**[22] 4919 5-9-3 112.. JamesDoyle 2 108
(Saeed bin Suroor) *trckd ldrs: effrt 4f out: sn rdn along: drvn over 2f out and sn wknd* **8/1**

-000 **7** *29* **Askar Tau (FR)**[22] 4919 8-9-3 105..(vt) GeorgeBaker 6 72
(Marcus Tregoning) *hld up in rr: effrt over 3f out: sn rdn along and btn over 2f out* **25/1**

3m 34.75s (0.25) **Going Correction** +0.20s/f (Good) 7 Ran SP% **110.0**
Speed ratings (Par 115): **107,106,105,104,104 103,88**
toteswingers 1&2 £2.30, 2&3 £3.50, 1&3 £1.90 CSF £10.98 TOTE £4.30: £2.10, £1.70; EX 13.00 Trifecta £35.00 Pool: £5313.26 - 113.69 winning units..
Owner Godolphin **Bred** G O'Brien **Trained** Newmarket, Suffolk
■ Stewards' Enquiry : Silvestre De Sousa two-day ban: used whip above permitted level (Sep 6,8)

FOCUS
A race that has become part of the pattern for the top stayers in recent years. Last year's winner Times Up and the 2009 scorer Askar Tau were back for another go, plus the 2012 Gold Cup winner Colour Vision and this year's runner-up in that race Simenon were also in opposition. The pace was reasonable before picking up from the home turn - the first two held those positions throughout - but the time confirmed that the ground was only just on the soft side of good. This rates an ordinary renewal. Ahzzemah confirmed his Goodwood form with four of these and this rates a personal best.

5725 SKY BET STRENSALL STKS (GROUP 3) 1m 208y
3:05 (3:06) (Class 1) 3-Y-O+

£42,532 (£16,125; £8,070; £4,020; £2,017; £1,012) **Stalls** Low

Form RPR
2366 **1** **City Style (USA)**[13] 5270 7-9-5 113.. SilvestreDeSousa 2 114
(Charlie Appleby) *trckd ldng pair: hdwy 3f out: led 2f out: rdn clr over 1f out: drvn and edgd rt ins fnl f: hld on gamely towards fin* **9/1**

-156 **2** *nk* **Danadana (IRE)**[43] 4213 5-9-9 111.. AndreaAtzeni 4 117
(Luca Cumani) *trckd ldrs: hdwy over 2f out: rdn to chse wnr ent fnl f: sn drvn and edgd lft: styd on to chal last 75yds: ev ch tl edgd lft and no ex nr fin* **8/1**

3052 **3** *2 ¾* **Gabrial (IRE)**[26] 4811 4-9-5 110.. GrahamLee 6 107
(Richard Fahey) *t.k.h: hld up in rr: hdwy over 2f out: rdn and n.m.r whn edgd lft over 1f out: kpt on same pce fnl f* **9/1**

1105 **4** *1 ¾* **Pavlosk (USA)**[21] 4949 3-8-9 103.. RyanMoore 1 100
(Sir Michael Stoute) *lw: t.k.h: hld up: hdwy 4f out: rdn along wl over 2f out: drvn and no imp fr wl over 1f out* **6/4**[1]

0122 **5** *½* **Red Avenger (USA)**[22] 4917 3-8-12 98.. WilliamBuick 3 102
(Ed Dunlop) *chsd ldr: hdwy and cl up 3f out: rdn 2f out: wknd over 1f out* **9/1**

212- **6** *3 ¾* **Archbishop (USA)**[355] 5869 4-9-5 113.. FrankieDettori 5 94
(Brian Meehan) *warm: led: rdn along 3f out: hdd 2f out: sn wknd* **5/1**[2]

1241 **7** *32* **Robin Hoods Bay**[13] 5269 5-9-5 107.. JohnnyMurtagh 7 24
(Ed Vaughan) *trckd ldrs on outer: pushed along over 3f out: rdn wl over 2f out: sn outpcd and eased in rr* **6/1**[3]

1m 51.75s (-0.25) **Going Correction** +0.20s/f (Good)
WFA 3 from 4yo+ 7lb 7 Ran SP% **112.1**
Speed ratings (Par 113): **109,108,106,104,104 100,72**
toteswingers 1&2 £8.70, 2&3 £7.40, 1&3 £9.00 CSF £73.06 TOTE £11.90: £6.50, £5.80; EX 92.30 Trifecta £432.70 Pool: £5255.98 - 9.10 winning units..
Owner Godolphin **Bred** Stonerside Stable **Trained** Newmarket, Suffolk

FOCUS
This is a race that Godolphin have done well in over the years, sending out five of the previous nine winners. The winner was back to form if not quite at his best, with the runner-up the key.

5726 COOLMORE NUNTHORPE STKS (BRITISH CHAMPIONS SERIES) (GROUP 1) 5f
3:40 (3:43) (Class 1) 2-Y-O+

£154,534 (£58,587; £29,321; £14,606; £7,330; £3,678) **Stalls** Centre

Form RPR
2210 **1** **Jwala**[21] 4947 4-9-8 103.. SteveDrowne 8 115
(Robert Cowell) *wnt rt s: cl up: rdn over 1f out: led ent fnl f: drvn and hld on wl towards fin* **40/1**

1124 **2** *½* **Shea Shea (SAF)**[41] 4298 6-9-11 120.. FrankieDettori 5 116
(M F De Kock, South Africa) *lw: hld up in tch: hdwy whn edgd rt ent fnl f: sn rdn and fin wl* **3/1**[1]

1415 **3** *nse* **Sole Power**[41] 4298 6-9-11 117.. JohnnyMurtagh 2 116
(Edward Lynam, Ire) *hld up towards rr: swtchd rt 2f out: hdwy over 1f out: swtchd lft: rdn and styd on strly fnl f* **4/1**[2]

-560 **4** *½* **Hamish McGonagall**[69] 3334 8-9-11 109.. DavidAllan 11 114
(Tim Easterby) *slt ld: rdn wl over 1f out: hdd ent fnl f: sn drvn and kpt on same pce* **33/1**

1020 **5** *1* **Kingsgate Native (IRE)**[21] 4947 8-9-11 112........................[1] ShaneKelly 13 110
(Robert Cowell) *swtg: chsd ldrs: rdn over 1f out: drvn and one pce fnl f* **25/1**

0510 **6** *shd* **Tickled Pink (IRE)**[21] 4947 4-9-8 109.. TomQueally 16 107
(Lady Cecil) *racd nr stands' rail: prom: rdn along over 1f out: drvn and kpt on same pce fnl f* **16/1**

0515 **7** *¾* **Ladies Are Forever**[21] 4947 5-9-8 105..(b) GrahamLee 10 104
(Geoffrey Oldroyd) *chsd ldrs: rdn along wl over 1f out: kpt on same pce fnl f* **28/1**

4210 **8** *1 ¼* **York Glory (USA)**[20] 4986 5-9-11 109..(b) NeilCallan 12 103
(Kevin Ryan) *hld up towards rr: hdwy wl over 1f out: rdn and kpt on fnl f: nt rch ldrs* **25/1**

0000 **9** *½* **Tiddliwinks**[20] 4986 7-9-11 104.. JamesDoyle 14 101
(Kevin Ryan) *lw: in tch: hdwy wl over 1f out: sn rdn and no imp fnl f* **80/1**

0-30 **10** *½* **Caledonia Lady**[111] 2019 4-9-8 102.. DanielTudhope 15 96
(Jo Hughes) *racd towards stands' rail: hld up in rr: hdwy and nt clr run over 1f out: swtchd lft and rdn ent fnl f: kpt on: nrst fin* **66/1**

-450 **11** *½* **Rosdhu Queen (IRE)**[42] 4260 3-9-6 107..(p) RyanMoore 6 94
(William Haggas) *chsd ldrs: rdn wl over 1f out: grad wknd appr fnl f* **16/1**

0202 **12** *hd* **Swiss Spirit**[21] 4947 4-9-11 111.. WilliamBuick 7 97
(John Gosden) *a towards rr* **7/1**[3]

1006 **13** *nse* **Spirit Quartz (IRE)**[21] 4947 5-9-11 110..(p) JamieSpencer 20 97
(Robert Cowell) *racd nr stands' rail: cl up: rdn and ev ch over 1f out: wknd fnl f* **16/1**

0040 **14** *shd* **Bungle Inthejungle**[21] 4947 3-9-9 102.. MartinHarley 4 96
(Mick Channon) *lw: prom on outer: rdn along over 2f out: sn wknd* **66/1**

0131 **15** *1 ½* **Slade Power (IRE)**[12] 5320 4-9-11 116.. WayneLordan 9 91
(Edward Lynam, Ire) *dwlt and sltly hmpd s: a towards rr* **7/1**[3]

0330 **16** *nk* **Dinkum Diamond (IRE)**[20] 4986 5-9-11 102.. CathyGannon 1 90
(Henry Candy) *a towards rr* **40/1**

1221 **17** *nk* **Moviesta (USA)**[21] 4947 3-9-9 113.. PaulMulrennan 17 89
(Bryan Smart) *racd towards stands' rail: a towards rr* **7/1**[3]

57.34s (-1.96) **Going Correction** -0.025s/f (Good)
WFA 3 from 4yo+ 2lb **17** Ran SP% **123.3**
Speed ratings: **114,113,113,112,110 110,109,107,106,105 104,104,104,104,102 101,101**
toteswingers 1&2 £23.40, 2&3 £2.60, 1&3 £69.90 CSF £150.49 TOTE £84.20: £19.00, £1.10, £2.30; EX 437.60 Trifecta £2122.70 Pool: £13937.03 - 4.92 winning units..
Owner Manor Farm Stud & Miss S Hoare **Bred** Manor Farm Stud (rutland) **Trained** Six Mile Bottom, Cambs
■ Miss Lahar (66-1) was withdrawn after proving unruly in the stalls.
■ Stewards' Enquiry : Frankie Dettori two-day ban: used whip above permitted level (Sep 6,8)

FOCUS
One of the top 5f sprints of the European turf season. The durability of these sprinters was indicated by the presence in the big field of the 2007 winner Kingsgate Native and Sole Power, who triumphed in 2010, while dual winner Borderlescott was a late withdrawal. The field raced in two groups, five on the nearside and the remainder in the centre until they converged around 2f out, and it was those drawn in the larger group that came off best. This was rater out of line with Jwala's previous form, with the fourth the best guide, and it highlights the fluidity of the top 5f races.

5727 SKY BET MOBILE CONVIVIAL MAIDEN STKS 7f
4:20 (4:21) (Class 2) 2-Y-O **£19,407** (£5,775; £2,886; £1,443) **Stalls** Low

Form RPR
4 **1** **Golden Town (IRE)**[20] 4987 2-9-5 0..(t) SilvestreDeSousa 2 90+
(Saeed bin Suroor) *lw: chsd ldng pair: hdwy to ld 2f out: sn rdn clr: hung bdly rt to stands' rail ins fnl f: kpt on* **4/1**[3]

2 **2** *1 ½* **Red Galileo**[14] 5244 2-9-5 0.. AndreaAtzeni 10 86+
(Ed Dunlop) *trckd ldrs: hdwy over 2f out: rdn to chse wnr and swtchd lft ins fnl f: edgd lft and kpt on towards fin* **15/8**[1]

04 **3** *1 ½* **Bow Creek (IRE)**[16] 5145 2-9-5 0.. GrahamLee 13 81
(Mark Johnston) *sn led: rdn and hdd 2f out: drvn and one pce fnl f* **33/1**

3 **4** *1 ¾* **Tahadee (IRE)**[20] 4987 2-9-5 0.. MartinHarley 3 77
(Mick Channon) *warm: chsd ldrs: rdn along over 2f out: drvn and no imp appr fnl f* **10/1**

2 **5** *2 ½* **Master The World (IRE)**[20] 4987 2-9-5 0.. JamesDoyle 8 70+
(Gerard Butler) *trckd ldrs: effrt over 2f out: sn rdn and no imp* **9/1**

43 **6** *shd* **Supersta**[16] 5122 2-9-5 0.. PaulMulrennan 6 70
(Ronald Harris) *lw: hld up in rr: hdwy over 2f out: rdn and kpt on fnl f: nrst fin* **50/1**

7 *2* **Derbyshire (IRE)** 2-9-5 0.. NeilCallan 4 65+
(Kevin Ryan) *str: t.k.h early: hld up towards rr: effrt over 2f out: sn rdn and no hdwy* **3/1**[2]

8 *hd* **Maggie's Diamond** 2-9-0 0.. TonyHamilton 9 59
(Richard Fahey) *leggy: hld up in rr: sme hdwy whn n.m.r over 1f out: n.d* **33/1**

3 **9** *nk* **Dandana (IRE)**[21] 4958 2-9-5 0.. TomQueally 1 63
(Clive Brittain) *chsd ldrs: rdn along over 2f out: sn wknd* **16/1**

10 *2 ¾* **Lynngale** 2-9-0 0.. CathyGannon 5 51
(Jo Hughes) *w'like: a in rr* **100/1**

0 **11** *¾* **Sir Charlie Kunz**[20] 4987 2-9-5 0.. WilliamBuick 7 54
(Mark Johnston) *a in rr* **50/1**

02 **12** *8* **Rogue Wave (IRE)**[50] 3979 2-9-5 0 .... JohnnyMurtagh 12 33
(Alan Jarvis) *prom: rdn along over 2f out: sn wknd* **12/1**

1m 25.0s (-0.30) **Going Correction** -0.025s/f (Good) **12** Ran SP% **123.2**
Speed ratings (Par 100): **100,98,96,94,91 91,89,89,88,85 84,75**
toteswingers 1&2 £3.50, 2&3 £15.90, 1&3 £26.10 CSF £12.12 TOTE £5.10: £2.20, £1.40, £4.90; EX 15.50 Trifecta £319.40 Pool: £7885.33 - 18.51 winning units..
Owner Godolphin **Bred** Darley **Trained** Newmarket, Suffolk

FOCUS
Since this race was made a 7f contest three years ago each of the winners has gone on to be rated in three figures. This looked another strong edition with a time to back it up. The first two can both rate higher again.

5728 NATIONWIDE ACCIDENT REPAIR SERVICES STKS (H'CAP) 1m
4:55 (4:56) (Class 2) (0-100,100) 3-Y-O **£19,407** (£5,775; £2,886; £1,443) **Stalls** Low

Form RPR

2531 **1** **Short Squeeze (IRE)**[30] 4642 3-8-3 **82** .... MartinDwyer 5 100+
(Hugo Palmer) *hld up towards rr: hdwy 3f out: swtchd rt to outer 2f out: str run to ld appr fnl f: sn clr* **5/1**[2]

1100 **2** *3 ½* **Equity Risk (USA)**[22] 4922 3-8-9 **88** .... NeilCallan 1 98
(Kevin Ryan) *trckd ldrs: hdwy 3f out: led 2f out: sn rdn and hung rt: hdd jst over 1f out: drvn and one pce fnl f* **14/1**

1260 **3** *2* **King George River (IRE)**[22] 4917 3-9-2 **100** .... RobertTart(5) 17 105
(Alan Bailey) *hld up towards rr: hdwy over 2f out: rdn over 1f out: styd on fnl f: nrst fin* **20/1**

1443 **4** *1 ½* **Secret Art (IRE)**[8] 5439 3-8-6 **85** .... AndreaAtzeni 15 87
(Ralph Beckett) *lw: hld up and bhd: hdwy over 2f out: sn rdn and styd on fnl f: nrst fin* **7/1**[3]

1431 **5** *½* **Hay Dude**[15] 5182 3-9-6 **99** .... DanielTudhope 10 100
(Mrs K Burke) *lw: hld up in tch: smooth hdwy to trck ldrs 3f out: effrt whn n.m.r and sltly hmpd 2f out: sn rdn and one pce* **5/1**[2]

3111 **6** *½* **Majestic Moon (IRE)**[22] 4922 3-8-12 **91** .... TonyHamilton 2 91
(Richard Fahey) *sn led: rdn along 3f out: hdd 2f out: sn drvn and wknd over 1f out* **7/1**[3]

62 **7** *1* **Machete Mark (IRE)**[8] 5454 3-9-0 **93** .... GaryCarroll 3 90
(G M Lyons, Ire) *lw: chsd ldrs: rdn along 3f out: grad wknd fnl 2f* **4/1**[1]

-100 **8** *4 ½* **One Word More (IRE)**[65] 3455 3-9-4 **97** .... JamieSpencer 12 84
(Charles Hills) *chsd ldrs: rdn along over 2f out: sn wknd* **25/1**

0104 **9** *3 ¾* **Tamayuz Star (IRE)**[8] 5439 3-9-4 **97** .... WilliamBuick 16 75
(Richard Hannon) *a towards rr* **16/1**

6031 **10** *5* **Party Royal**[16] 5124 3-8-5 **84** .... LiamJones 4 51
(Mark Johnston) *chsd ldng pair: rdn along over 2f out: sn drvn and wknd* **25/1**

-130 **11** *¾* **Ebn Arab (USA)**[64] 3484 3-9-4 **97** .... FrankieDettori 7 71
(Charles Hills) *dwlt: a towards rr* **16/1**

0000 **12** *5* **Masarah (IRE)**[48] 4081 3-9-3 **96** .... JamesDoyle 13 50
(Clive Brittain) *prom: rdn along 4f out: sn wknd* **33/1**

1405 **13** *1 ¾* **Shrimper Roo**[13] 5292 3-8-3 **82** ....(b) CathyGannon 8 32
(Tim Easterby) *towards rr: rdn along over 3f out: bhd after* **50/1**

-320 **14** *6* **Muharrib (IRE)**[22] 4922 3-9-1 **94** .... SilvestreDeSousa 14 30
(Saeed bin Suroor) *nvr bttr than midfield* **10/1**

1m 37.58s (-1.42) **Going Correction** -0.025s/f (Good) **14** Ran SP% **123.2**
Speed ratings (Par 106): **106,102,100,99,98 98,97,92,88,83 83,78,76,70**
toteswingers 1&2 £13.00, 2&3 £36.90, 1&3 £25.50 CSF £70.08 CT £1347.37 TOTE £6.80: £2.50, £5.70, £5.80; EX 86.10 Trifecta £3165.60 Pool: £6085.62 - 1.44 winning units..
Owner W A L Duff Gordon **Bred** Des Swan **Trained** Newmarket, Suffolk

FOCUS
A decent, competitive mile handicap for 3yos with an impressive winner. They finished well strung out on the ground and the first two could still be ahead of their marks.
T/Jkpt: Not won. T/Plt: £509.60 to a £1 stake. Pool of £324930.14 - 465.43 winning tickets. T/Qpdt: £89.20 to a £1 stake. Pool of £17936.47 - 148.69 winning tickets. JR

5729 - 5734a (Foreign Racing) - See Raceform Interactive

5628 DEAUVILLE (R-H)
Friday, August 23
OFFICIAL GOING: Turf: good; fibresand: standard

5735a PRIX DE LA CORNICHE (CLAIMER) (4YO+) (FIBRESAND) 7f 110y
2:55 (12:00) 4-Y-O+ **£7,723** (£3,089; £2,317; £1,544; £772)

RPR

1 **Whip My Heart (IRE)**[26] 4-8-11 0 ....(b) AnthonyCrastus 13 83
(U Suter, France) **138/10**

2 *hd* **Montalban (FR)**[21] 6-9-3 0 ....(b) ThibaultSpeicher(5) 3 93
(D De Waele, France) **23/1**

3 *2* **High Star (FR)**[27] 6-9-1 0 .... SoufianeSaadi(7) 10 88
(J-C Rouget, France) **23/10**[1]

4 *1 ¼* **Larga Charla (IRE)**[26] 4-9-1 0 ....(b) UmbertoRispoli 1 78
(G Botti, France) **73/10**[3]

5 *1 ½* **Polarix**[21] 7-9-1 0 .... SebastienMartino(7) 16 81
(H-A Pantall, France) **11/1**

6 *1 ½* **Hi Ya Pal (USA)**[21] 4-9-4 0 .... ThierryThulliez 15 73
(N Clement, France) **15/1**

7 *4* **Kadou (FR)**[26] 5-9-1 0 .... MathieuAndrouin 8 60
(P Monfort, France) **48/1**

8 *¾* **Hearts And Minds (IRE)**[26] 4-8-6 0 ....(b) StephaneLaurent(5) 12 55
(Braem Horse Racing Sprl, Belgium) **92/1**

9 *shd* **Mister Six (FR)**[26] 4-8-11 0 ....(p) FlavienPrat 11 54
(A Lamotte D'Argy, France) **27/1**

10 *nk* **Full Pelt (USA)**[720] 5739 5-9-6 0 ....(b) DelphineSantiago 2 63
(Peggy Bastiaens-Vancauwenbergh, Belgium) **16/1**

11 *3* **Ertikaan**[43] 4207 6-8-11 0 ....(p) IoritzMendizabal 5 46
(Brendan Powell) *prom: rdn 2f out: outpcd and lost pl over 1f out: no ex and btn* **19/1**

12 *1 ½* **Evervescent (IRE)**[15] 5191 4-8-11 0 ....(b) SoufyaneMoulin(4) 7 46
(J S Moore) *t.k.h: pressed ldr on outer: rdn and ev ch 2f out: sn no ex and btn: fdd and eased* **25/1**

13 *½* **Anducas (FR)**[26] 4-8-11 0 ....(b) AntoineHamelin 6 41
(G Henrot, France) **41/1**

14 *6* **Blue Panis (FR)**[12] 6-9-3 0 .... AntoineCoutier(5) 9 37
(F Chappet, France) **48/10**[2]

15 *3 ½* **Wognan (IRE)**[75] 4-9-1 0 .... ThierryJarnet 14 21
(J Heloury, France) **11/1**

1m 30.42s (90.42) **15** Ran SP% **117.2**
WIN (incl. 1 euro stake): 14.80. PLACES: 3.70, 6.40, 1.80. DF: 197.50. SF: 333.30.
Owner Exors Of The Late Herman Stein **Bred** M O'Mahony **Trained** France

5736 - (Foreign Racing) - See Raceform Interactive

5697 GOODWOOD (R-H)
Saturday, August 24
OFFICIAL GOING: Good (7.5)
Wind: Light, half against Weather: Murky, drizzly

5737 WHITELEY CLINIC PRESTIGE STKS (GROUP 3) (FILLIES) 7f
2:20 (2:20) (Class 1) 2-Y-O
£22,684 (£8,600; £4,304; £2,144; £1,076; £540) **Stalls** Low

Form RPR

031 **1** **Amazing Maria (IRE)**[23] 4921 2-9-0 90 .... GeraldMosse 4 106+
(Ed Dunlop) *mde virtually all: stretched 3 l clr 2f out and had rest in trble: shkn up over 1f out: in n.d after: pushed out* **6/4**[1]

312 **2** *2 ½* **Qawaasem (IRE)**[30] 4682 2-9-0 94 .... PaulHanagan 1 100
(Charles Hills) *chsd wnr: rdn and outpcd over 2f out: styd on after but v little imp ins fnl f* **4/1**[3]

33 **3** *3 ¼* **Halljoy (IRE)**[21] 5003 2-9-0 0 .... JamesDoyle 6 91
(Clive Brittain) *hld up in 5th: rdn and dropped to last pair 2f out: kpt on fr over 1f out to take 3rd nr fin* **25/1**

0322 **4** *¾* **Midnite Angel (IRE)**[14] 5284 2-9-0 99 .... FrankieDettori 8 89
(Richard Hannon) *stdd s: hld up in last: prog over 2f out: chsd ldng pair over 1f out: no imp: lost 3rd nr fin* **11/4**[2]

102 **5** *¾* **Wee Jean**[11] 5372 2-9-0 90 .... SamHitchcott 3 87
(Mick Channon) *chsd ldng trio: rdn fr 1/2-way: lft bhd over 2f out* **14/1**

51 **6** *1 ½* **Valen (IRE)**[10] 5385 2-9-0 0 .... WilliamTwiston-Davies 2 85
(Michael Bell) *chsd ldng pair: rdn over 2f out: lost 3rd over 1f out: wl hld whn hmpd nr fin* **8/1**

522 **7** *½* **Miss Lillie**[17] 5131 2-9-0 79 .... AndreaAtzeni 7 82
(Roger Teal) *a in rr: rdn and no prog over 2f out* **33/1**

1m 26.13s (-0.87) **Going Correction** 0.0s/f (Good) **7** Ran SP% **111.2**
Speed ratings (Par 101): **104,101,97,96,95 94,93**
toteswingers 1&2 £2.10, 1&3 £6.50, 2&3 £13.00 CSF £7.35 TOTE £2.20: £1.30, £2.50; EX 6.20 Trifecta £54.90 Pool: £2091.83 - 28.54 winning units..
Owner Sir Robert Ogden **Bred** Sir Robert Ogden **Trained** Newmarket, Suffolk

FOCUS
Despite the ground being given as Good prior to the off and the going remaining unchanged for the card, the runners in the opener when making quite print in the ground. A few nice fillies have won this Group 3 down the years, Nannina in 2005 standing out as the best of them, but some big names have placed as well, including Guineas/Coronation Stakes winner Sky Lantern last season and Snow Fairy in 2009. This looked an average renewal and it's hard to rate the form much higher.

5738 BETFAIR CASH OUT STKS (HERITAGE H'CAP) 7f
2:55 (2:56) (Class 2) 3-Y-O+
£62,250 (£18,640; £9,320; £4,660; £2,330; £1,170) **Stalls** Low

Form RPR

1311 **1** **Magic City (IRE)**[24] 4879 4-8-13 **97** .... RichardHughes 7 107+
(Richard Hannon) *sweating: hld up in midfield disputing 9th: plld out 2f out: gd prog over 1f out: str run to ld last 75yds: readily* **13/2**[1]

6632 **2** *1* **Intransigent**[20] 5027 4-8-8 **99** .... DanielMuscutt(7) 8 106
(Andrew Balding) *t.k.h: trckd ldrs: pushed along and prog over 1f out: led briefly ins fnl f: outpcd last 50yds* **25/1**

000 **3** *shd* **Boots And Spurs**[21] 5019 4-8-6 **90** ....(v) ChrisCatlin 2 97
(Mrs K Burke) *led after 1f: kicked for home 2f out: hdd and outpcd ins fnl f* **33/1**

0623 **4** *½* **Jack's Revenge (IRE)**[14] 5255 5-8-9 **93** ....(bt) TedDurcan 6 99
(George Baker) *hld up wl in rr: pushed along and modest prog fr over 2f out: rchd midfield over 1f out: rdn and r.o strly last 150yds: too much to do* **9/1**

5023 **5** *nk* **Mabait**[8] 5474 7-7-11 **88** .... ShelleyBirkett(7) 19 93+
(David Simcock) *hld up wl in rr: stl in rr 2f out: swtchd ins and gd prog jst over 1f out: styd on fnl f: nrst fin* **50/1**

1432 **6** *1 ¾* **Pythagorean**[23] 4922 3-8-8 **97** ow1 .... JamesDoyle 18 95+
(Roger Charlton) *hld up wl in rr on outer: tried to make prog over 2f out but no real hdwy u.p: pushed along and styd on fnl f: n.d* **7/1**[2]

4141 **7** *¾* **Glen Moss (IRE)**[7] 5533 4-8-12 **96** 6ex .... FrankieDettori 12 94
(Charles Hills) *t.k.h: trckd ldrs: rdn and nt qckn over 1f out: one pce after* **15/2**[3]

1252 **8** *1* **Music Master**[35] 4529 3-9-0 **103** .... FergusSweeney 15 96
(Henry Candy) *led fr wd draw for 1f: chsd ldr after: gng strly 2f out: rdn and nt qckn over 1f out: wknd fnl f* **16/1**

35 **9** *½* **Al Khan (IRE)**[9] 5454 4-8-1 **85** .... KieranO'Neill 1 79
(Violet M Jordan) *chsd ldng trio: rdn and lost pl jst over 2f out: fdd fnl f* **66/1**

1145 **10** *½* **Galician**[6] 5561 4-9-3 **101** .... GeraldMosse 5 94
(Mark Johnston) *hld up wl in rr: pushed along and no real prog on inner 2f out: nt knocked abt but kpt on fr over 1f out* **8/1**

2063 **11** *hd* **Loving Spirit**[28] 4744 5-9-1 **99** ow1 .... GeorgeBaker 11 91
(James Toller) *hld up in rr on outer: tried to make prog over 2f out: no hdwy fr over 1f out* **15/2**[3]

3441 **12** *nk* **Shebebi (USA)**[7] 5518 3-8-10 **99** 6ex ....(b) PaulHanagan 3 88
(Mark Johnston) *chsd ldrs: rdn over 2f out: sn lost pl and btn over 1f out* **14/1**

4-63 **13** *1 ½* **Axiom**[7] 5533 9-7-8 **85** ....(p) BradleyBosley(7) 13 72
(Ed Walker) *dwlt: hld up in last: tried to make prog on inner fr over 2f out but only limited hdwy* **25/1**

1410 **14** *¾* **Heaven's Guest (IRE)**[21] 4986 3-8-12 **101** .... LeeTopliss 14 84
(Richard Fahey) *chsd ldrs in 8th: shkn up sn after 1/2-way: lost pl and struggling over 2f out* **16/1**

1000 **15** *1* **Excellent Guest**[28] 4744 6-8-13 **97** .... AndreaAtzeni 9 80
(George Margarson) *nvr bttr than midfield: lost pl and btn 2f out* **20/1**

4004 **16** *1* **Head Of Steam (USA)**[14] 5285 6-8-0 **89** .... RyanTate(5) 4 69
(Amanda Perrett) *a towards rr: shkn up and no prog over 2f out: wl btn after* **16/1**

0000 **17** *nse* **Webbow (IRE)**[28] 4778 11-8-6 **90** .... MartinDwyer 10 70
(Julie Camacho) *chsd ldng pair to 2f out: wknd qckly* **33/1**

6055 **18** *hd* **Monsieur Chevalier (IRE)**25 4856 6-9-2 **100**.............. HarryBentley 17 79
(P J O'Gorman) *s.s: a wl in rr: nvr a factor* **20/1**

1m 25.08s (-1.92) **Going Correction** 0.0s/f (Good)
WFA 3 from 4yo+ 5lb **18** Ran SP% **121.3**
Speed ratings (Par 109): **110,108,108,108,107 105,104,103,103,102 102,102,100,99,98 97,97,96**
toteswingers 1&2 £42.00, 1&3 £26.90, 2&3 £206.10 CSF £170.47 CT £4939.29 TOTE £5.20: £2.10, £7.90, £6.00, £2.70; EX 247.60 Trifecta £2337.50 Part won. Pool: £3116.76 - 0.66 winning units..
Owner Barker, Ferguson, Mason, Hassiakos, Done **Bred** Miss Annmarie Burke **Trained** East Everleigh, Wilts

FOCUS
A ridiculously hard race to fathom out, with the majority of the field having sound claims for victory. This is likely to be strong form, with the second and third setting the standard.

5739 BETFAIR CELEBRATION MILE (GROUP 2) 1m
3:30 (3:31) (Class 1) 3-Y-O+
£56,710 (£21,500; £10,760; £5,360; £2,690; £1,350) **Stalls** Low

Form RPR
021 **1** **Afsare**9 5446 6-9-1 116.......................... AndreaAtzeni 2 119+
(Luca Cumani) *reluctant to enter stalls: trckd ldrs: gap appeared on inner 2f out: pushed along and qcknd to ld over 1f out: rdn and r.o strly fnl f: impressive* **11/8**1

2323 **2** *2* **Stipulate**70 3347 4-9-1 109.......................... RichardHughes 3 114
(Lady Cecil) *hld up in rr: trying to cl on ldrs whn nt clr run over 1f out and snatched up: rallied and styd on wl fnl f to take 2nd nr fin* **15/2**3

4544 **3** *½* **Trade Storm**24 4875 5-9-4 115.......................... HarryBentley 4 116
(David Simcock) *stdd s: hld up in last: prog on outer over 2f out: edgd rt but led briefly wl over 1f out: no ch w wnr after: kpt on same pce after* **8/1**

0201 **4** *shd* **Premio Loco (USA)**21 5007 9-9-1 111.......................... GeorgeBaker 8 113
(Chris Wall) *led to over 6f out: chsd ldr to 2f out: sn rdn: outpcd over 1f out: kpt on to take 2nd again briefly ins fnl f* **12/1**

1003 **5** *1 ¾* **Educate**14 5269 4-9-1 100.......................... PaulHanagan 7 109+
(Ismail Mohammed) *t.k.h: racd wd in midfield: rdn whn squeezed out 2f out: no ch after: one pce* **9/1**

3102 **6** *nse* **Thistle Bird**21 4985 5-8-12 114.......................... JamesDoyle 5 105
(Roger Charlton) *trckd ldrs: rdn 2f out: nt qckn and sn lost pl: n.d after* **9/2**2

20-3 **7** *3 ½* **Shamalgan (FR)**38 4421 6-9-1 108........... Roberto-CarlosMontenegro 1 100
(X Thomas-Demeaulte, France) *t.k.h: hld up in rr: rdn on outer and no prog 2f out: sn wknd* **12/1**

0003 **8** *¾* **Aesop's Fables (USA)**27 4811 4-9-1 108....................(p) MartinDwyer 6 99
(Saeed bin Suroor) *plld way through to ld over 6f out: hdd wl over 1f out: wknd fnl f* **22/1**

1m 38.6s (-1.30) **Going Correction** 0.0s/f (Good) **8** Ran SP% **112.9**
Speed ratings (Par 115): **106,104,103,103,101 101,98,97**
toteswingers 1&2 £1.40, 1&3 £3.20, 2&3 £9.80 CSF £11.95 TOTE £2.20: £1.10, £1.80, £2.90; EX 10.80 Trifecta £69.80 Pool: £3222.84 - 34.62 winning units..
Owner Sheikh Mohammed Obaid Al Maktoum **Bred** Darley **Trained** Newmarket, Suffolk

FOCUS
Considering all the good racing that had been on over the previous few days at the York Ebor meeting, this wasn't a bad field quality wise. The runners raced as a pack in the easy-looking ground. The winner deserves his chance against the top milers and the second ran as well as ever.

5740 GREENE KING MAIDEN FILLIES' STKS 6f
4:05 (4:05) (Class 5) 2-Y-O **£5,175** (£1,540; £769; £384) **Stalls** High

Form RPR
4 **1** **Veiled Intrigue**19 5061 2-9-0 0.......................... FergusSweeney 4 79+
(Henry Candy) *w ldng pair: led over 1f out: shkn up and stl green but drew clr fnl f* **3/1**2

65 **2** *3 ½* **Alquimia (IRE)**12 5352 2-9-0 0.......................... GeraldMosse 7 69
(Ed Dunlop) *led against rail: shkn up and hdd over 1f out: outpcd but hld on for 2nd* **6/1**3

3 *nk* **Previous Acclaim (IRE)** 2-9-0 0.......................... RichardHughes 1 68+
(Richard Hannon) *carried rt s: trckd ldng trio: pushed along and effrt to dispute 2nd fnl f: no imp on wnr* **13/8**1

4 *hd* **Alys Love** 2-9-0 0.......................... MartinDwyer 3 67+
(William Muir) *wnt rt s: in tch in last pair: shkn up 2f out: no prog tl styd on ins fnl f* **7/1**

5 *1* **Serena Grae** 2-9-0 0.......................... HarryBentley 2 64
(Marcus Tregoning) *slowly away: in tch in last pair: pushed along and effrt on outer 2f out: one pce fr over 1f out* **14/1**

0 **6** *1* **Crystalized (IRE)**12 5344 2-9-0 0.......................... TedDurcan 5 61
(Richard Hannon) *trckd ldng trio: rdn over 1f out: sn fdd* **25/1**

0 **7** *nse* **China In My Hands**7 5529 2-9-0 0.......................... SamHitchcott 6 61
(Mick Channon) *w ldr: rdn jst over 2f out: nt qckn over 1f out: wknd fnl f* **8/1**

1m 14.37s (2.17) **Going Correction** 0.0s/f (Good) **7** Ran SP% **111.5**
Speed ratings (Par 91): **85,80,79,79,78 77,76**
toteswingers 1&2 £5.80, 1&3 £1.30, 2&3 £3.00 CSF £20.02 TOTE £4.10: £2.00, £2.80; EX 23.00 Trifecta £64.80 Pool: £1853.38 - 21.44 winning units..
Owner D B Clark/ J J Byrne **Bred** J Byrne And Partners **Trained** Kingston Warren, Oxon

FOCUS
Probably just an ordinary race in what looked testing enough conditions for juvenile fillies. The pre-race level looked pretty weak and the time was slow, but the winner did it quite well.

5741 MARCH STKS (LISTED RACE) 1m 6f
4:40 (4:40) (Class 1) 3-Y-O+
£22,684 (£8,600; £4,304; £2,144; £1,076; £540) **Stalls** Low

Form RPR
-231 **1** **Harris Tweed**25 4857 6-9-7 115....................(p) GeorgeBaker 7 116
(William Haggas) *mde all: shkn up and drew 2 l clr wl over 1f out: drvn fnl f: hld on gamely* **2/1**1

-150 **2** *hd* **Mount Athos (IRE)**23 4919 6-9-12 115.......................... RichardHughes 4 120
(Luca Cumani) *t.k.h: trckd wnr 2f then restrained into 3rd: tk 2nd again 3f out: drvn and outpcd wl over 1f out: clsd fnl f: jst failed* **2/1**1

160- **3** *6* **Tac De Boistron (FR)**291 7621 6-9-7 110.......................... FrankieDettori 5 107
(Marco Botti) *t.k.h: hld up in 4th: clsd to dispute 2nd 3f out to 2f out: sn lft bhd* **12/1**

25-2 **4** *4 ½* **Camborne**25 4857 5-9-7 108....................(p) NickyMackay 3 101
(John Gosden) *dwlt: hld up and mostly in last pair: pushed along over 4f out: laboured prog into 4th fnl f but no ch: gng v slowly at fin* **5/1**2

3050 **5** *½* **Model Pupil**7 5531 4-9-7 106.......................... JamesDoyle 6 100
(Charles Hills) *trckd wnr after 2f to 3f out: sn lost pl and btn* **16/1**

2306 **6** *½* **Jehannedarc (IRE)**23 4920 5-9-2 97....................(b1) GeraldMosse 2 94
(Ed Dunlop) *hld up and mostly in last trio: rdn over 3f out: wknd over 2f out* **40/1**

-162 **7** *4* **Songcraft (IRE)**42 4309 5-9-10 107....................(p) PaulHanagan 1 97
(Saeed bin Suroor) *hld up in last trio: effrt on outer over 3f out: pressed for a pl 2f out: wknd rapidly over 1f out* **15/2**3

3m 4.87s (1.27) **Going Correction** 0.0s/f (Good) **7** Ran SP% **111.1**
Speed ratings (Par 111): **98,97,94,91,91 91,89**
toteswingers 1&2 £1.40, 1&3 £4.50, 2&3 £3.70 CSF £5.46 TOTE £2.60: £1.90, £1.40; EX 6.30 Trifecta £37.50 Pool: £3771.81 - 75.33 winning units..
Owner B Haggas **Bred** J B Haggas **Trained** Newmarket, Suffolk

FOCUS
A cracking contest for the level and it produced a thrilling finish. The early fractions appeared far from strong. The winner was close to his C&D level with the second running as well as ever.

5742 CARLISLE SUPPORT SERVICES STKS (H'CAP) 1m 1f
5:15 (5:15) (Class 3) (0-90,90) 3-Y-O+
£9,337 (£2,796; £1,398; £699; £349; £175) **Stalls** Low

Form RPR
5005 **1** **Mister Music**21 5007 4-9-10 **89**.............(b1) WilliamTwiston-Davies(3) 10 103
(Richard Hannon) *trckd ldng pair: led wl over 2f out: drvn over 1f out: styd on wl fnl f* **25/1**

5542 **2** *2 ½* **Trader Jack**36 4501 4-10-0 **90**.......................... JamesDoyle 5 98
(Roger Charlton) *trckd ldng trio: prog to chse wnr wl over 1f out: hrd rdn fnl f: nt qckn and wl hld* **9/4**1

1614 **3** *2* **Noble Gift**23 4917 3-9-3 **86**.......................... GeorgeBaker 2 90+
(William Knight) *stdd s: hld up in last: stl plenty to do whn rdn over 2f out: no prog tl r.o fnl f to take 3rd last stride* **3/1**2

122 **4** *hd* **Tuscania**28 4777 5-9-7 **83**.......................... DougieCostello 13 86
(Lucy Wadham) *hld up in rr: shkn up over 2f out: prog over 1f out: styd on to chse ldng pair last 100yds: no imp and lost 3rd fnl stride* **20/1**

4020 **5** *1* **Uppercut**25 4859 5-9-6 **82**.......................... TedDurcan 12 83
(Stuart Kittow) *chsd ldrs in 5th: pushed along over 3f out: kpt on u.p to take 3rd briefly ins fnl f: one pce after* **12/1**

4123 **6** *1* **Ree's Rascal (IRE)**23 4923 5-9-4 **85**.......................... NathanAlison(5) 11 84
(Jim Boyle) *hld up in last trio: rdn on outer over 2f out: no real prog tl kpt on fnl f: n.d* **5/1**3

0221 **7** *¾* **Sir Mike**16 5191 4-9-3 **82**.......................... RyanClark(3) 3 79
(Amanda Perrett) *chsd clr ldr: clsd to ld over 3f out to wl over 2f out: lost 2nd wl over 1f out: wknd fnl f* **8/1**

-053 **8** *6* **Commissar**21 5006 4-8-9 **71**.......................... HarryBentley 1 55
(Ian Williams) *dwlt: hld up in midfield: rdn and struggling over 2f out: sn wknd* **11/1**

/0-0 **9** *½* **Heddwyn (IRE)**25 4854 6-9-7 **83**.......................... MartinDwyer 4 66
(Marcus Tregoning) *dwlt: t.k.h: hld up in midfield: reminders jst over 2f out and no hdwy: wknd and eased* **12/1**

0-0 **10** *37* **Chellalla**7 5518 4-9-6 **85**.......................... MarkCoumbe(3) 8
(Ian Williams) *led and sn clr: wknd and hdd over 3f out: t.o* **50/1**

1m 55.56s (-0.74) **Going Correction** 0.0s/f (Good)
WFA 3 from 4yo+ 7lb **10** Ran SP% **117.8**
Speed ratings (Par 107): **103,100,99,98,97 97,96,91,90,57**
toteswingers 1&2 £11.80, 1&3 £16.00, 2&3 £3.20 CSF £80.76 CT £236.59 TOTE £18.70: £4.10, £1.20, £1.50; EX 86.10 Trifecta £255.50 Pool: £1893.57 - 5.55 winning units..
Owner Longview Stud & Bloodstock Ltd **Bred** Longview Stud & Bloodstock Ltd **Trained** East Everleigh, Wilts

FOCUS
It's difficult to know what to make of this form, as the winner was bouncing back after some modest efforts. The pace held up and the second and third give the form a fairly solid look.

5743 CHICHESTER CITY STKS (H'CAP) 1m 4f
5:50 (5:50) (Class 4) (0-80,78) 3-Y-O **£6,469** (£1,925; £962; £481) **Stalls** High

Form RPR
1-2 **1** **Magog**105 2271 3-9-4 **75**.......................... JamesDoyle 1 96+
(Roger Charlton) *chsd ldr: shkn up over 2f out: clsd and rdn to ld over 1f out: forged clr* **11/8**1

5524 **2** *4* **Jazz Master**17 5132 3-8-13 **70**....................(b) HarryBentley 2 82
(Luca Cumani) *led: hld together over 2f out w rest of field being rdn: hdd and nt qckn over 1f out: no ch w wnr after* **4/1**2

4111 **3** *¾* **Duchess Of Gazeley (IRE)**22 4961 3-9-4 **75**............. J-PGuillambert 4 86
(Gary Harrison) *chsd ldng pair: pushed along 4f out: struggling and lost pl sltly over 2f out: kpt on wl again fr over 1f out* **9/2**3

041- **4** *2 ¼* **Sweet Deal (IRE)**332 6572 3-9-7 **78**.......................... GeorgeBaker 6 85
(Jeremy Noseda) *hld up in last trio: rdn 4f out: rdn to chse ldng pair over 2f out and cl enough: wknd and lost 3rd jst over 1f out* **7/1**

046 **5** *¾* **Rock God (IRE)**24 4899 3-8-13 **70**.......................... JohnFahy 5 76
(Eve Johnson Houghton) *trckd ldrs: disp 3rd 4f out to over 2f out: sn fdd* **16/1**

-341 **6** *hd* **Raskova (USA)**20 5037 3-9-2 **73**.......................... TedDurcan 9 79
(William Jarvis) *hld up in last trio: rdn 3f out: no imp on ldrs and sn btn* **14/1**

5413 **7** *10* **Pernica**21 5015 3-9-6 **77**.......................... DougieCostello 7 67
(Lucy Wadham) *in tch: shkn up 4f out: struggling and btn 3f out: wknd qckly* **18/1**

004- **8** *5* **Sweeping Rock (IRE)**302 7373 3-8-8 **65**.......................... MartinDwyer 3 47
(Marcus Tregoning) *t.k.h: hld up: lost tch 1/2-way and sn t.o: shkn up and lost little further grnd fnl 4f* **16/1**

2m 39.47s (1.07) **Going Correction** 0.0s/f (Good) **8** Ran SP% **116.5**
Speed ratings (Par 102): **96,93,92,91,90 90,84,80**
toteswingers 1&2 £2.30, 1&3 £1.90, 2&3 £3.30 CSF £7.11 CT £19.47 TOTE £2.10: £1.10, £1.90, £1.50; EX 8.70 Trifecta £27.20 Pool: £1385.30 - 38.16 winning units..
Owner Lady Rothschild **Bred** Carwell Equities Ltd **Trained** Beckhampton, Wilts

FOCUS
It paid to race handy as the first two home were in first and second throughout. The winner is capable of further improvement.

T/Plt: £21.80 to a £1 stake. Pool: £119792.40 - 3995.31 winning tickets T/Qpdt: £4.80 to a £1 stake. Pool: £4725.79 - 714.00 winning tickets JN

[5716]NEWMARKET (R-H)

Saturday, August 24

OFFICIAL GOING: Good to soft changing to good to soft (soft in places) after race 3 (3:20)

Wind: light, half behind Weather: rain

5744 STAY AT SOUTHEND AIRPORT HOLIDAY INN EBF MAIDEN STKS 6f

2:10 (2:10) (Class 4) 2-Y-O **£4,528** (£1,347; £673; £336) **Stalls** Low

Form RPR

1 **Ghazi (IRE)** 2-9-5 0 MickaelBarzalona 1 82+
(Saeed bin Suroor) *dwlt: rn green and pushed along towards rr early: hdwy into midfield 1/2-way: effrt u.p to chse ldrs 1f out: styd on wl to ld wl ins fnl f* **9/2[3]**

2 *1/2* **Moonfaarid** 2-9-5 0 PatCosgrave 6 78
(M F De Kock, South Africa) *chsd ldrs: rdn and ev ch whn edgd lft 1f out: drvn to ld ins fnl f: hdd and one pce wl ins fnl f* **9/2[3]**

3 **3** *1* **Pool House**[16] 5186 2-9-2 0 ThomasBrown(3) 4 75
(Andrew Balding) *led: rdn over 1f out: hdd ins fnl f: styd on same pce after* **3/1[1]**

4 *1 1/2* **Outback Traveller (IRE)** 2-9-5 0 GrahamLee 7 71
(Jeremy Noseda) *chsd ldrs: rdn and unable qck over 1f out: rn green and edgd lft 1f out: kpt on same pce fnl f* **16/1**

0 **5** *hd* **War Spirit**[21] 4987 2-9-5 0 SeanLevey 2 70
(Richard Hannon) *chsd ldng trio: effrt u.p over 1f out: hung lft 1f out: one pce fnl f* **7/2[2]**

0 **6** *3/4* **Faure Island**[20] 5033 2-9-5 0 AdamKirby 9 68
(Henry Candy) *t.k.h: hld up wl in tch in midfield: rdn and outpcd over 1f out: kpt on same pce ins fnl f* **9/1**

7 *1 1/2* **Silver Treasure (FR)** 2-9-5 0 RobertHavlin 12 63
(Amy Weaver) *s.i.s: hld up in tch in rr of main gp: swtchd rt and rdn 2f out: no imp and one pce fr over 1f out* **100/1**

06 **8** *1/2* **Lawyer (IRE)**[22] 4958 2-9-5 0 KirstyMilczarek 5 62
(Luca Cumani) *hld up in tch in midfield: rdn and effrt 2f out: outpcd over 1f out: one pce and no threat to ldrs after* **14/1**

9 *30* **Hurricane Harry** 2-9-5 0 (v[1]) WilliamBuick 3
(William Knight) *s.i.s: in rr: hung lft and lost tch over 2f out: t.o* **20/1**

10 *nk* **Dubawi's Thunder** 2-9-5 0 PatDobbs 8
(Richard Hannon) *a towards rr: dropped to last and lost tch 1/2-way: t.o* **16/1**

1m 14.77s (2.27) **Going Correction** +0.15s/f (Good) **10** Ran SP% **117.8**
Speed ratings (Par 96): **90,89,88,86,85 84,82,82,42,41**
toteswingers 1&2 £2.20, 2&3 £5.40, 1&3 £4.00 CSF £25.40 TOTE £4.80: £2.50, £1.80, £2.00; EX 28.30 Trifecta £94.70 Pool: £1057.38 - 8.37 winning units..
Owner Godolphin **Bred** Darley **Trained** Newmarket, Suffolk

FOCUS
Stands side track used with stalls on Stands side except 1m2f, 1m5f centre. Good to soft ground after overnight rain and a raft of non-runners through the card. Just an ordinary maiden by this track's standards and the finish was fought out by two newcomers. The bare form may not be up to the race average but this was a nice start by the winner.

5745 FLY AER LINGUS FROM LONDON SOUTHEND AIRPORT NURSERY H'CAP 7f

2:45 (2:45) (Class 3) (0-95,89) 2-Y-O **£7,762** (£2,310; £1,154; £577) **Stalls** Low

Form RPR

2152 **1** **Safety Check (IRE)**[15] 5224 2-9-7 **89** MickaelBarzalona 5 95+
(Charlie Appleby) *hld up wl in tch in last pair: rdn and effrt to chal over 1f out: led and hung lft 1f out: clr but stl gng lft ins fnl f: pushed out and a holding on fnl 75yds* **3/1[1]**

0212 **2** *nk* **Ticking Katie (IRE)**[15] 5226 2-8-7 **75** SeanLevey 2 80
(Mrs K Burke) *t.k.h: chsd ldr: rdn and ev ch wl over 1f out: hung lft u.p: chsd wnr 1f out: 2 l down ins fnl f: styd on but nvr quite getting to wnr* **10/3[2]**

2100 **3** *4* **Beau Nash (IRE)**[43] 4232 2-9-5 **87** PatDobbs 1 82
(Richard Hannon) *stdd s: hld up in tch in last pair: hdwy 1/2-way: rdn and outpcd over 1f out: 4th and wl hld 1f out: edgd lft and kpt on steadily ins fnl f* **11/1**

632 **4** *nk* **Emaad (USA)**[20] 5025 2-8-5 **73** FrannyNorton 3 68
(Mark Johnston) *led: rdn 2f out: hdd jst over 1f out: 3rd and btn fnl 150yds: wknd fnl 100yds* **3/1[1]**

41 **5** *2 1/2* **Zampa Manos (USA)**[12] 5344 2-8-10 **81** ThomasBrown(3) 4 69
(Andrew Balding) *in tch in midfield: lost pl and rdn 3f out: hung lft and outpcd 2f out: wknd over 1f out* **5/1[3]**

0403 **6** *3 3/4* **Street Force (USA)**[10] 5400 2-9-6 **88** (b[1]) GrahamLee 6 67
(Clive Brittain) *t.k.h: chsd ldrs: rdn and struggling over 2f out: wknd over 1f out* **7/1**

1m 26.85s (1.15) **Going Correction** +0.25s/f (Good) **6** Ran SP% **110.6**
Speed ratings (Par 98): **103,102,98,97,94 90**
Swingers 1&2 £1.30, 2&3 £5.70, 1&3 £5.50 CSF £12.81 TOTE £3.50: £2.10, £1.70; EX 11.90 Trifecta £39.70 Pool: £953.88 - 17.99 winning units..
Owner Godolphin **Bred** Malih Al Basti **Trained** Newmarket, Suffolk

FOCUS
A competitive little nursery in which the field clustered down the middle of the track. The winner showed useful, improved form.

5746 FLY EASYJET FROM LONDON SOUTHEND AIRPORT H'CAP 1m 5f

3:20 (3:22) (Class 2) (0-100,98) 3-Y-O+ **£25,876** (£7,700; £3,848; £1,924) **Stalls** Centre

Form RPR

2354 **1** **Mysterious Man (IRE)**[29] 4704 4-9-1 **88** [1] ThomasBrown(3) 9 99
(Andrew Balding) *chsd ldrs tl hdwy to ld 4f out: clr and rdn 3f out: hung lft but kpt on gamely fr over 1f out: all out* **8/1**

4204 **2** *3/4* **Suegioo (FR)**[43] 4233 4-9-4 **88** (p) PaoloSirigu 8 98
(Marco Botti) *hld up in last quartet: hdwy gng wl 3f out: rdn to chse clr wnr over 2f out: pressed wnr and edging lft fnl f: no ex fnl 75yds* **16/1**

-136 **3** *3 1/4* **Clowance Estate (IRE)**[25] 4857 4-9-9 **93** SeanLevey 7 98
(Roger Charlton) *chsd ldrs: chsd wnr wl over 3f out tl over 2f out: 3rd and styd on same pce fr over 1f out* **15/2[3]**

1356 **4** *nk* **Ustura (USA)**[14] 5259 4-9-8 **92** (t) MickaelBarzalona 6 97
(Saeed bin Suroor) *hld up in last quartet: hdwy gng wl 3f out: 4th and drvn wl over 1f out: plugged on same pce after* **8/1**

4323 **5** *2 1/4* **Villoresi (IRE)**[29] 4720 4-9-4 **88** FrederikTylicki 3 89
(James Fanshawe) *hld uip in last quartet: hdwy over 3f out: drvn and no imp 2f out: plugged on same pce after* **11/2[2]**

4110 **6** *2 1/4* **Eshtiaal (USA)**[65] 3486 3-8-13 **94** (t) RichardMullen 2 92
(Brian Meehan) *chsd ldrs: rdn 3f out: sn drvn and outpcd: plugged on but no threat to ldrs after* **11/2[2]**

2215 **7** *2* **Duke Of Clarence (IRE)**[25] 4857 4-9-12 **96** PatDobbs 11 91
(Richard Hannon) *hld up in midfield: rdn and effrt ent fnl 3f: outpcd and btn 2f out: 7th and no imp after* **14/1**

3240 **8** *6* **Abundantly**[50] 4029 4-8-9 **79** oh5 WilliamCarson 13 65
(Hughie Morrison) *hld up in midfield: rdn and effrt 3f out: sn wknd: wl btn over 1f out* **50/1**

2211 **9** *10* **Fledged**[11] 5374 3-9-3 **98** WilliamBuick 10 69
(John Gosden) *chsd ldrs: rdn over 3f out: sn struggling and wknd over 2f out: wl bhd fnl f* **7/2[1]**

10-5 **10** *hd* **Signed Up**[64] 3531 4-9-7 **91** RobertHavlin 14 62
(Amanda Perrett) *wl in tch in midfield: rdn over 3f out: sn struggling and btn wl over 1f out: wl bhd fnl f* **14/1**

6202 **11** *1 1/2* **Sadler's Risk (IRE)**[14] 5259 5-9-9 **93** FrannyNorton 5 61
(Mark Johnston) *led for 2f: chsd ldr tl 4f out: sn rdn and lost pl: wl bhd over 1f out* **16/1**

0-60 **12** *12* **Parlour Games**[56] 3838 5-9-10 **94** AhmedAjtebi 4 44
(Charlie Appleby) *hld up in last quartet: rdn over 3f out: sn lost tch: t.o* **16/1**

0-30 **13** *27* **Rockfella**[70] 3344 7-8-9 **79** oh1 PatCosgrave 15
(Denis Coakley) *dwlt: hdwy to ld after 2f: hdd 4f out: sn dropped out: t.o fnl 2f* **33/1**

2m 46.79s (2.79) **Going Correction** +0.25s/f (Good)
WFA 3 from 4yo+ 11lb **13** Ran SP% **122.9**
Speed ratings (Par 109): **101,100,98,98,96 95,94,90,84,84 83,76,59**
toteswingers 1&2 £32.30, 2&3 £30.10, 1&3 £8.90 CSF £133.17 CT £1014.41 TOTE £10.80: £3.10, £6.00, £3.10; EX 128.10 Trifecta £1191.00 Part won. Pool: £1588.10 - 0.66 winning units..
Owner Mr & Mrs R M Gorell **Bred** Barronstown Stud **Trained** Kingsclere, Hants

FOCUS
A really competitive staying handicap and the gallop looked sound from the off. Again the field congregated towards the centre of the track but it proved difficult for anything to make a serious impact from off the pace.

5747 STOBART MEMBERS CLUB HOPEFUL STKS (LISTED RACE) 6f

3:55 (3:57) (Class 1) 3-Y-O+

£22,684 (£8,600; £4,304; £2,144; £1,076; £540) **Stalls** Low

Form RPR

2116 **1** **Tropics (USA)**[21] 4986 5-9-0 106 JimCrowley 8 110
(Dean Ivory) *stdd s: hld up in tch in rr: smooth hdwy over 1f out: rdn and qcknd to ld ins fnl f: r.o wl* **2/1[1]**

1210 **2** *1* **Nocturn**[63] 3558 4-9-0 98 (p) MickaelBarzalona 10 107
(Jeremy Noseda) *racd alone towards centre: in tch in midfield: effrt u.p to chal over 1f out: chsd wnr and kpt on same pce ins fnl f* **7/1**

320- **3** *shd* **Master Of War**[315] 7049 3-8-11 108 SeanLevey 5 106
(Richard Hannon) *chsd ldr tl led ent fnl 2f: drvn over 1f out: hdd and unable qck ins fnl f: one pce after* **20/1**

60-2 **4** *hd* **Valbchek (IRE)**[21] 4981 4-9-0 102 (p) GrahamLee 3 106
(Jeremy Noseda) *hld up in tch in last pair: rdn and effrt over 1f out: kpt on u.p ins fnl f: no threat to wnr* **11/1**

1205 **5** *2* **Farmleigh House (IRE)**[6] 5567 6-9-0 108 NGMcCullagh 7 99
(W J Martin, Ire) *t.k.h: chsd ldrs: rdn and effrt over 1f out: outpcd ent fnl f: wknd fnl 100yds* **8/1**

0216 **6** *3/4* **Kavanagh (SAF)**[97] 2493 6-9-0 0 (t) PatCosgrave 9 97
(M F De Kock, South Africa) *t.k.h: hld up wl in tch in midfield: rdn and effrt 2f out: no ex ent fnl f: wknd ins fnl f* **11/2[3]**

33-1 **7** *7* **Taayel (IRE)**[21] 4981 3-8-11 108 WilliamBuick 1 75
(John Gosden) *led tl rdn and hdd ent fnl 2f: drvn and btn over 1f out: wknd fnl f* **5/2[2]**

1m 13.3s (0.80) **Going Correction** +0.35s/f (Good)
WFA 3 from 4yo+ 3lb **7** Ran SP% **114.0**
Speed ratings (Par 111): **108,106,106,106,103 102,93**
toteswingers 1&2 £3.60, 2&3 £19.80, 1&3 £7.30 CSF £16.52 TOTE £2.80: £1.70, £2.80; EX 14.80 Trifecta £82.90 Pool: £1123.87 - 10.16 winning units..
Owner Dean Ivory **Bred** D Konecny, S Branch & A Branch **Trained** Radlett, Herts

FOCUS
Many non-runners due to the ground and this wasn't as competitive as it looked overnight.

5748 FLY LONDON SOUTHEND AIRPORT TO TORONTO H'CAP 6f

4:30 (4:30) (Class 3) (0-90,89) 3-Y-O **£9,056** (£2,695; £1,346; £673) **Stalls** Low

Form RPR

1004 **1** **Lancelot Du Lac (ITY)**[21] 5004 3-9-4 **86** MickaelBarzalona 9 95
(Dean Ivory) *stdd s: t.k.h: hld up in tch in rr: hdwy 1/2-way: jnd ldr 2f out: rdn to ld ent fnl f: hld on wl: rdn out* **3/1[2]**

3040 **2** *1/2* **Kimberella**[51] 3974 3-8-12 **80** RobertHavlin 4 87
(Michael Attwater) *led: jnd 2f out: rdn and wnt clr w wnr over 1f out: hdd ent fnl f: kpt on gamely but a hld* **10/1**

3315 **3** *4 1/2* **Red Refraction (IRE)**[13] 5303 3-9-2 **84** SeanLevey 5 77
(Richard Hannon) *hld up in tch: shuffled bk 2f out: effrt over 1f out: swtchd lft 1f out: kpt on to go 3rd last strides: no threat to ldng pair* **9/1**

-210 **4** *nk* **Lewisham**[70] 3348 3-9-7 **89** JimCrowley 2 81
(Ralph Beckett) *chsd ldr tl 2f out: sn drvn: outpcd and btn whn edgd lft 1f out: plugged on but wl hld fnl f: lost 3rd last strides* **15/2**

421 **5** *hd* **Muthmir (IRE)**[44] 4200 3-9-5 **87** GrahamLee 8 78
(William Haggas) *t.k.h: chsd ldrs: rdn and effrt 2f out: outpcd and btn ent fnl f: battling for 3rd and one pce after* **7/4[1]**

2110 **6** *2 3/4* **Duke Cosimo**[56] 3803 3-8-13 **81** WilliamBuick 10 64
(Sir Michael Stoute) *hld up in tch in rr: rdn and effrt 2f out: drvn and no imp over 1f out: wknd ins fnl f* **4/1[3]**

1m 13.03s (0.53) **Going Correction** +0.35s/f (Good) **6** Ran SP% **112.2**
Speed ratings (Par 104): **110,109,103,102,102 99**
toteswingers 1&2 £5.80, 2&3 £6.30, 1&3 £5.30 CSF £30.68 CT £237.90 TOTE £4.20: £2.30, £3.60; EX 36.70 Trifecta £111.90 Pool: £2113.92 - 14.15 winning units..
Owner M J Yarrow **Bred** Elektra Di Fausto Martellozzo & C Sas **Trained** Radlett, Herts

FOCUS
This concerned only two horses from well over a furlong out.

5749 FLY LONDON SOUTHEND AIRPORT TO DUBLIN H'CAP 1m 2f

5:05 (5:05) (Class 3) (0-95,93) 3-Y-O+ **£9,056** (£2,695; £1,346; £673) **Stalls** Centre

Form RPR

10-2 **1** **Greek War (IRE)**[28] 4765 4-10-0 **93** MickaelBarzalona 4 104
(Charlie Appleby) *wl off the pce in rr: bustled along briefly sn after s: swtchd lft and rdn over 3f out: hdwy u.p to ld over 1f out: clr and hung rt ins fnl f: styd on: drvn out* **6/1[3]**

-111 2 2 **Willow Beck**[9] 5436 4-9-6 **85** WilliamBuick 6 92
(John Gosden) *hld up off the pce in midfield: clsd and rdn 3f out: 3rd and drvn over 1f out: plugged on same pce fnl f: wnt 2nd towards fin* **5/4**[1]

-556 3 ½ **Tahaamah**[14] 5269 5-9-11 **90** (t) FrederikTylicki 2 96
(Saeed bin Suroor) *hld up off the pce in midfield: rdn and effrt 3f out: led 2f out tl hung lft and hdd over 1f out: plugged on same pce fnl f: lost 2nd towards fin* **15/2**

1-06 4 2¾ **True To Form (IRE)**[14] 5283 6-9-2 **81** (p) JimCrowley 3 82
(Alan McCabe) *stdd s: t.k.h: hld up off the pce in last pair: clsd over 3f out: drvn and no imp 2f out: styd on ins fnl f: no threat to ldrs* **20/1**

1-43 5 ¾ **Cat O'Mountain (USA)**[42] 4301 3-9-3 **90** AhmedAjtebi 7 89
(Charlie Appleby) *chsd clr ldng pair: clsd over 3f out: rdn 3f out: outpcd and btn over 1f out: plugged on ins fnl f* **9/2**[2]

1235 6 4 **Salutation (IRE)**[7] 5513 3-9-6 **93** FrannyNorton 8 84
(Mark Johnston) *racd freely: sn clr w ldr: rdn and struggling over 3f out: lost pl 2f out: sn wknd* **7/1**

12-0 7 7 **Captain Cat (IRE)**[25] 4859 4-9-11 **90** (b[1]) SeanLevey 5 67
(Roger Charlton) *awkward leaving stalls: sn rcvrd to ld and clr w rival: drvn over 2f out: hdd 2f out: wknd over 1f out: bhd and eased ins fnl f* **12/1**

2m 7.82s (2.32) **Going Correction** +0.45s/f (Yiel)
WFA 3 from 4yo+ 8lb 7 Ran SP% **113.6**
Speed ratings (Par 107): **108,106,106,103,103 100,94**
toteswingers 1&2 £1.90, 2&3 £3.70, 1&3 £6.10 CSF £13.80 CT £56.54 TOTE £5.10: £2.60, £1.70; EX 10.10 Trifecta £89.20 Pool: £1300.72 - 10.93 winning units..
Owner Godolphin **Bred** Darley **Trained** Newmarket, Suffolk

FOCUS
They went a strong gallop as Captain Cat and Salutation took each other on at the head of affairs. That helped set things up for the hold-up horses.

5750 FLY LONDON SOUTHEND AIRPORT TO GENEVA H'CAP 5f
5:40 (5:41) (Class 4) (0-85,82) 3-Y-O+ **£5,175** (£1,540; £769; £384) **Stalls** Low

Form RPR
4240 1 **Peace Seeker**[8] 5489 5-9-2 **76** WilliamCarson 8 87
(Anthony Carson) *mde all: rdn over 1f out: styd on wl under hands and heels riding ins fnl f: gng away at fin* **2/1**[2]

6140 2 1½ **Rebecca Romero**[27] 4800 6-9-8 **82** PatCosgrave 4 88
(Denis Coakley) *stdd s: hld up in last: rdn and effrt over 1f out: drvn and hdwy to chse wnr ins fnl f: edgd lft and no ex fnl 50yds* **5/2**[3]

6323 3 1¾ **Tagula Night (IRE)**[20] 5036 7-9-5 **79** (bt) SeanLevey 3 78
(Dean Ivory) *chsd ldng pair: rdn 1/2-way: drvn and edging lft over 1f out: kpt on same pce ins fnl f* **6/4**[1]

2600 4 1½ **Red Aggressor (IRE)**[73] 3220 4-9-3 **77** (v[1]) FrannyNorton 5 71
(Clive Brittain) *chsd wnr: rdn and effrt wl over 1f out: no ex jst ins fnl f: wknd fnl 100yds* **7/1**

1m 0.33s (1.23) **Going Correction** +0.45s/f (Yiel) 4 Ran SP% **114.4**
Speed ratings (Par 105): **108,105,102,100**
CSF £7.68 TOTE £3.70; EX 8.70 Trifecta £11.10 Pool: £725.34 - 48.81 winning units..
Owner Hugh & Mindi Byrne **Bred** C J Mills **Trained** Newmarket, Suffolk

FOCUS
The rain totally changed the look and feel of this race, with four taken out.
T/Plt: £266.30 to a £1 stake. Pool of £77593.24 - 212.63 winning tickets. T/Qpdt: £92.40 to a £1 stake. Pool of £3886.70 - 31.10 winning tickets. SP

5289 REDCAR (L-H)
Saturday, August 24
5751 Meeting Abandoned - Waterlogged

5584 WINDSOR (R-H)
Saturday, August 24
OFFICIAL GOING: Good to soft changing to soft after race 1 (5:10)
Wind: Moderate across Weather: Rain

5757 BRAY MAIDEN STKS 6f
5:10 (5:10) (Class 5) 2-Y-O **£2,587** (£770; £384; £192) **Stalls** Low

Form RPR
0 1 **Musical Comedy**[77] 3112 2-9-5 0 LiamJones 8 81+
(Richard Hannon) *trckd ldrs: wnt 2nd 3f out: led 2f out: pushed clr appr fnl f: easily* **8/11**[1]

54 2 6 **Vallila**[68] 3414 2-9-0 0 ShaneKelly 6 55
(Roger Charlton) *chsd ldrs: drvn 1/2-way: styd on fnl f to take 2nd cl home but nvr any ch w wnr* **12/1**

3 ½ **Star Code (IRE)** 2-9-5 0 KieranO'Neill 2 59+
(Richard Hannon) *slowly away: t.k.h: hdwy and hung lft over 2f out: drvn to take narrow 2nd but no ch w wnr appr fnl f: no ex and dropped to 3rd cl home* **5/1**[3]

060 4 ½ **Society Diva (IRE)**[21] 4997 2-8-9 0 HyanTate(5) 7 52
(George Baker) *chsd ldr: rdn 2f out and sn no ch w wnr: lost 2nd 1f out but styd pressing for that position tl outpcd into 3rd clsng stages* **50/1**

5 12 **Android (IRE)** 2-9-5 0 (t) AdamKirby 3 21
(Clive Cox) *s.i.s: in rr: rdn and green: sme hdwy to cl on ldrs 1/2-way: green again and wknd 2f out* **7/2**[2]

06 6 ½ **Solicitation (IRE)**[16] 5194 2-9-5 0 (v[1]) ChrisCatlin 4 20
(Ralph Beckett) *led: sn 3 l clr: hdd 2f out and wknd rapidly* **20/1**

00 7 shd **King Calypso**[13] 5307 2-9-5 0 TadhgO'Shea 1 19
(Denis Coakley) *a outpcd* **33/1**

1m 14.59s (1.59) **Going Correction** +0.35s/f (Good) 7 Ran SP% **114.1**
Speed ratings (Par 94): **103,95,94,93,77 77,76**
toteswingers 1&2 £1.20, 1&3 £2.20, 2&3 £2.90 CSF £11.05 TOTE £1.80: £1.10, £3.30; EX 10.40 Trifecta £28.90 Pool: £1207.02 - 31.22 winning units..
Owner The Queen **Bred** The Queen **Trained** East Everleigh, Wilts

FOCUS
Inner of straight dolled out 2yds at 6f and tapered to normal width at Winning Post. Top bend dolled out 11 yds from normal inner configuration adding 38yds to races of 1m and beyond. Quite a weak juvenile contest, run on deteriorating ground, but it was won in grand style. The winner was value for at least an extra length but there was little depth in behind.

5758 GOODBYE MISS GARDNER, HELLO MRS COLES FILLIES' H'CAP 1m 67y
5:45 (5:45) (Class 5) (0-75,75) 3-Y-O+ **£2,587** (£770; £384; £192) **Stalls** Low

Form RPR
2 1 **Janna's Jingle (IRE)**[16] 5211 3-9-0 **69** TadhgO'Shea 7 78
(John Patrick Shanahan, Ire) *in rr: drvn and gd hdwy over 2f out: led 1f out: styd on wl u.p* **9/2**[3]

6461 2 ¾ **Loved One**[23] 4927 3-9-6 **75** ShaneKelly 2 82
(James Fanshawe) *in rr but in tch: hdwy over 3f out: drvn to chal appr fnl f: sn chsng wnr but a hld* **2/1**[1]

3144 3 2 **Capella's Song (IRE)**[8] 5491 3-9-3 **72** AdamKirby 12 74
(Michael Bell) *chsd ldrs: led 3f out and sn drvn: hdd 1f out: outpcd fnl f* **3/1**[2]

3-02 4 1 **Be My Rock**[27] 4813 4-9-4 **67** ChrisCatlin 3 68
(Rae Guest) *t.k.h: chsd ldrs: rdn and outpcd over 2f out: kpt on again ins fnl f but nvr a threat* **6/1**

0230 5 6 **Welsh Inlet (IRE)**[12] 5349 5-8-0 **56** ShelleyBirkett(7) 11 43
(John Bridger) *t.k.h: racd wd and led after 2f: hdd 3f out and styd alone in centre crse: no ch fr 2f out* **33/1**

3040 6 ½ **Everleigh**[24] 4898 3-9-3 **72** (v[1]) PatDobbs 5 57
(Richard Hannon) *led 2f: styd chsng ldr to 3f out: wknd 2f out* **11/1**

-510 7 6 **Balti's Sister (IRE)**[9] 5437 4-9-9 **72** LiamJones 8 44
(Martin Smith) *a in rr* **20/1**

51- 8 3¼ **Beam Of Light**[366] 5511 3-8-13 **73** ThomasGarner(5) 1 37
(Jamie Osborne) *t.k.h: chsd ldrs tl wknd 3f out* **25/1**

1m 46.04s (1.34) **Going Correction** +0.35s/f (Good)
WFA 3 from 4yo+ 6lb 8 Ran SP% **110.7**
Speed ratings (Par 100): **107,106,104,103,97 96,90,87**
CSF £12.93 CT £28.68 TOTE £5.40: £1.80, £1.20, £1.50; EX 12.00 Trifecta £40.20 Pool: £938.08 - 17.46 winning units..
Owner Thistle Bloodstock Limited **Bred** Thistle Bloodstock Ltd **Trained** Danesfort, Co. Kilkenny
■ Stewards' Enquiry : Tadhg O'Shea two-day ban: used whip above permitted level (Sep 8-9)

FOCUS
The official going was changed to soft from good to soft after the running of the opening juvenile maiden.

5759 HAPPY BIRTHDAY WENDY GILLINGS H'CAP 1m 67y
6:15 (6:15) (Class 4) (0-85,83) 3-Y-O+ **£4,851** (£1,443; £721; £360) **Stalls** Low

Form RPR
1-00 1 **Modern Tutor**[77] 3096 4-9-12 **83** AndreaAtzeni 1 97
(Sir Michael Stoute) *s.i.s: in rr: drvn over 2f out: styd on u.p to ld 1f out: r.o strly clsng stages* **5/1**[2]

1054 2 1¾ **Kyllachy Rise**[23] 4922 3-9-5 **82** RichardHughes 9 91
(Richard Hannon) *in tch: drvn over 2f out: kpt on u.p fnl f to take 2nd last strides but no ch w wnr* **11/10**[1]

0445 3 nk **First Post (IRE)**[38] 4415 6-8-10 **70** RosieJessop(3) 5 79
(Derek Haydn Jones) *trckd ldr: chal fr over 4f out and stl upsides appr fnl f: styd on same pce and lost 2nd last strides* **10/1**

00-1 4 1¼ **Bay Knight (IRE)**[19] 5063 7-9-12 **83** AdamKirby 11 89
(Sean Curran) *led: jnd 4f out: stl hrd pressed tl hdd 1f out: wknd ins fnl f* **10/1**

4- 5 3¾ **Calgacus (IRE)**[17] 5162 4-9-8 **79** TadhgO'Shea 3 77
(John Patrick Shanahan, Ire) *chsd ldrs: 3f out: rdn over 2f out and no ch after* **25/1**

-555 6 shd **Juvenal (IRE)**[9] 5436 4-9-8 **79** PatDobbs 2 77
(Richard Hannon) *s.i.s: pushed along 3f out: nvr gng pce to rch ldrs* **8/1**[3]

4122 7 2½ **Good Luck Charm**[47] 4124 4-9-12 **83** FergusSweeney 4 75
(Gary Moore) *in tch: rdn 3f out: wknd over 2f out* **5/1**[2]

1m 46.17s (1.47) **Going Correction** +0.35s/f (Good)
WFA 3 from 4yo+ 6lb 7 Ran SP% **114.1**
Speed ratings (Par 105): **106,104,103,102,98 98,96**
toteswingers 1&2 £3.60, 1&3 £3.20, 2&3 £3.10 CSF £10.89 CT £51.66 TOTE £5.20: £2.50, £1.50; EX 14.20 Trifecta £77.90 Pool: £1475.21 - 14.19 winning units..
Owner Lady Rothschild **Bred** Kincorth Investments Inc **Trained** Newmarket, Suffolk

FOCUS
A competitive race despite the quartet of withdrawals and it saw a thoroughly professional display.

5760 SHEILA MADDEN'S 60TH BIRTHDAY WINTER HILL STKS (GROUP 3) 1m 2f 7y
6:45 (6:45) (Class 1) 3-Y-O+ **£34,026** (£12,900; £6,456; £3,216; £1,614) **Stalls** Centre

Form RPR
-132 1 **Planteur (IRE)**[90] 2694 6-9-0 117 FrankieDettori 6 114
(Marco Botti) *t.k.h: led over 6f out and sn 4 l clr: stdd over 3f out: qcknd again wl over 2f out: drvn and edgd lft ins fnl f: kpt on wl* **1/2**[1]

-642 2 1¼ **Al Waab (IRE)**[35] 4526 3-8-6 108 AndreaAtzeni 7 111
(Lady Cecil) *chsd ldrs: wnt 2nd over 3f out: rdn over 2f out: styd on fr over 1f out: n.m.r on rail ins fnl f and readily hld fnl 100yds* **6/1**[3]

-340 3 ¾ **Chil The Kite**[67] 3419 4-9-0 108 RichardHughes 5 110
(Hughie Morrison) *hld up towards rr: hdwy to cl on ldrs 4f out: rdn in 3rd over 2f out: styd on fnl f but no imp on ldng duo* **4/1**[2]

2104 4 11 **Area Fifty One**[14] 5270 5-9-0 105 ShaneKelly 4 93
(Richard Fahey) *led: hdd over 6f out: rdn over 3f out: wknd fr 2f out* **12/1**

5 5 23 **Hold The Line (IRE)**[18] 5114 3-8-6 92 (t) TadhgO'Shea 2 42
(John Patrick Shanahan, Ire) *t.k.h: chsd ldrs: wknd qckly over 2f out* **50/1**

2m 8.0s (-0.70) **Going Correction** +0.35s/f (Good)
WFA 3 from 4yo+ 8lb 5 Ran SP% **110.6**
Speed ratings (Par 113): **116,115,114,105,87**
CSF £4.13 TOTE £1.50: £1.10, £2.10; EX 3.60 Trifecta £6.70 Pool: £1377.67 - 153.26 winning units..
Owner HE Sh Joaan Bin Hamad Al Thani **Bred** Dayton Investments Ltd **Trained** Newmarket, Suffolk

5761 EBF STALLIONS AUGUST STKS (LISTED RACE) 1m 3f 135y
7:15 (7:15) (Class 1) 3-Y-O+ **£22,684** (£8,600; £4,304; £2,144; £1,076) **Stalls** Centre

Form RPR
-441 1 **Cameron Highland (IRE)**[23] 4907 4-9-2 105 (p) AndreaAtzeni 2 108
(Roger Varian) *trckd ldrs in 3rd: drvn to chal 2f out: sn led: styd on strly appr fnl f: readily* **3/1**[2]

2-53 2 3 **Shirocco Star**[55] 3870 4-8-11 112 RichardHughes 5 98
(Hughie Morrison) *trckd ldr: chal 4f out: led ins fnl 3f: jnd 2f out and sn hdd: no ex u.p and btn ins fnl f* **10/11**[1]

3424 **3** 2 ½ **Souviens Toi**[23] 4920 4-9-2 102 FrankieDettori 3 99
(Marco Botti) *sn led: jnd 4f out: no ex u.p fnl 2f* **13/2**
643 **4** 1 ¾ **Saint Hilary**[43] 4234 4-8-11 87 FergusSweeney 4 91
(William Muir) *in tch: rdn over 2f out and sn btn* **33/1**
-450 **5** *nk* **Gallipot**[49] 4059 4-8-11 102 WilliamBuick 1 90
(John Gosden) *in tch: rdn over 2f out and sn btn* **6/1**[3]
2m 30.02s (0.52) **Going Correction** +0.35s/f (Good) **5** Ran SP% **107.9**
Speed ratings (Par 111): **112,110,108,107,106**
CSF £5.91 TOTE £3.60: £1.90, £1.10; EX 5.80 Trifecta £17.10 Pool: £1099.20 - 48.17 winning units..
Owner H R H Sultan Ahmad Shah **Bred** Epona Bloodstock Ltd **Trained** Newmarket, Suffolk
FOCUS
Some smart types on show in this Listed contest.

5762 SCOUTING FOR GIRLS H'CAP — 1m 3f 135y
7:45 (7:46) (Class 5) (0-70,70) 3-Y-O+ **£2,587** (£770; £384; £192) **Stalls** Centre

Form RPR
-014 **1** **Rutherglen**[69] 3365 3-9-4 **70** PatCosgrave 9 81
(George Baker) *in tch: hdwy 3f out: drvn to chse ldr appr fnl f: led fnl 100yds: kpt on wl* **6/1**
-461 **2** 1 ½ **First Secretary**[22] 4939 3-9-0 **66** FrankieDettori 5 74
(Roger Charlton) *in tch: hdwy over 3f out: led over 2f out: drvn over 1f out: one pce fnl f: hdd and no ex fnl 100yds* **7/4**[1]
0050 **3** 2 ½ **Hero's Story**[28] 4753 3-8-8 **60** (p) AndreaAtzeni 4 64
(Amanda Perrett) *in tch: hdwy 3f out: drvn and styd on to take 3rd ins fnl f: no imp on ldng duo* **20/1**
6250 **4** *nk* **Balady (IRE)**[24] 4894 4-9-9 **65** [1] AdamKirby 6 68
(Dominic Ffrench Davis) *chsd ldrs: slt ld 3f out: hdd over 2f out: wknd appr fnl f* **20/1**
0425 **5** *nk* **Rossetti**[16] 5168 5-10-0 **70** GeorgeBaker 2 73
(Gary Moore) *sn chsng ldr: drvn and outpcd over 2f out: kpt on again fnl f* **4/1**[2]
3065 **6** 2 ½ **If I Were A Boy (IRE)**[54] 3900 6-9-2 **65** (p) JoshBaudains[(7)] 1 64
(Dominic Ffrench Davis) *in rr: rdn 3f out: styd on fr over 1f out: nvr nr ldrs* **16/1**
630 **7** 1 ½ **Aiyana**[18] 5100 3-9-0 **66** WilliamBuick 11 62
(Hughie Morrison) *chsd ldrs: drvn along 6f out: styd on same pce fnl 3f* **14/1**
2346 **8** *nk* **Megalala (IRE)**[7] 5528 12-8-7 **56** ShelleyBirkett[(7)] 3 52
(John Bridger) *led: hdd 3f out: wknd over 2f out* **25/1**
50-0 **9** 2 ¼ **Newtown Cross (IRE)**[16] 5191 3-8-5 **57** KieranO'Neill 10 49
(Jimmy Fox) *rdn over 3f out: a in rr* **33/1**
-240 **10** 1 ½ **Pat's Legacy (USA)**[28] 4755 7-9-4 **63** JemmaMarshall[(3)] 8 52
(Pat Phelan) *s.i.s: rdn over 3f out: a towards rr* **20/1**
443 **11** 1 ¼ **Conquestadim**[67] 3435 3-9-4 **70** RichardHughes 7 57
(Hughie Morrison) *chsd ldrs: rdn over 3f out and sn btn* **5/1**[3]
2m 32.79s (3.29) **Going Correction** +0.35s/f (Good)
WFA 3 from 4yo+ 10lb **11** Ran SP% **120.9**
Speed ratings (Par 103): **103,102,100,100,99 98,97,97,95,94 93**
toteswingers 1&2 £6.20, 1&3 £36.90, 2&3 £12.40 CSF £16.03 CT £207.05 TOTE £7.00: £2.10, £1.10, £6.10; EX 22.60 Trifecta £222.70 Pool: £1914.03 - 6.44 winning units..
Owner Frank Brady **Bred** Frank Brady **Trained** Manton, Wilts
FOCUS
A competitive, if only moderate finale but it was run at a searching pace.
T/Plt: £3.00 to a £1 stake. Pool: £64820.90 - 15562.56 winning tickets T/Qpdt: £2.30 to a £1 stake. Pool: £7543.60 - 2409.71 winning tickets ST

5723 YORK (L-H)
Saturday, August 24

OFFICIAL GOING: Soft changing to soft (good to soft in places) after race 3 (3.15)
Wind: Moderate against Weather: Cloudy

5763 BETFRED CITY OF YORK STKS (LISTED RACE) — 7f
2:05 (2:05) (Class 1) 3-Y-O+ **£28,490** (£10,885; £5,515; £2,815; £1,480) **Stalls** Low

Form RPR
4010 **1** **Sirius Prospect (USA)**[22] 4946 5-9-0 105 RobertWinston 3 112
(Dean Ivory) *t.k.h: hld up in rr: hdwy on outer over 2f out: chal over 1f out: rdn to ld ins fnl f: kpt on* **5/2**[2]
2621 **2** *nk* **Rex Imperator**[21] 4986 4-9-0 110 (p) NeilCallan 8 111+
(William Haggas) *lw: t.k.h: trckd ldrs: hdwy to chse ldr 1/2-way: led wl over 2f out: jnd and rdn over 1f out: hdd ins fnl f: keeping on whn n.m.r last 75yds* **9/4**[1]
6 **3** 1 ¾ **Switcher (IRE)**[56] 3822 4-8-9 92 BarryMcHugh 7 102
(Richard Fahey) *t.k.h: chsd ldrs: rdn along 3f out: drvn 2f out: kpt on fnl f* **12/1**
4510 **4** 6 **Set The Trend**[22] 4946 7-9-0 104 (p) DanielTudhope 1 91
(David O'Meara) *trckd ldr to 1/2-way: sn pushed along: rdn wl over 2f out and sn one pce* **9/1**
0010 **5** 3 **Lightning Cloud (IRE)**[28] 4744 5-9-0 100 JamieSpencer 6 83
(Kevin Ryan) *t.k.h: set stdy pce: qcknd 1/2-way: rdn and hdd wl over 2f out: sn btn* **9/2**[3]
11-0 **U** **Fort Bastion (IRE)**[100] 2399 4-9-0 105 TonyHamilton 10
(Richard Fahey) *uns rdr s* **7/1**
1m 26.84s (1.54) **Going Correction** +0.525s/f (Yiel)
WFA 3 from 4yo+ 5lb **6** Ran SP% **107.7**
Speed ratings (Par 111): **112,111,109,102,99**
toteswingers 1&2 £1.20, 2&3 £3.80, 1&3 £4.90 CSF £7.79 TOTE £3.10: £2.00, £1.40; EX 7.30 Trifecta £41.70 Pool: £2999.94 - 53.90 winning units..
Owner Miss N Yarrow **Bred** Brookdale And Dr Ted Folkerth **Trained** Radlett, Herts

FOCUS
Races of one mile and beyond reduced in distance by about 24yds. Overnight rain resulted in the going being changed to soft, and as a result there were a number of non-runners on the card. Some of the interest from this race was lost when the two 3yos in the line-up were withdrawn, and it was made even less competitive when Fort Bastion unseated his rider leaving the stalls. The winner is rated to his latest C&D win, the second a length or so off his Stewards' Cup victory.

5764 BETFRED MELROSE STKS (H'CAP) — 1m 6f
2:40 (2:41) (Class 2) (0-105,98) 3-Y-O
£46,687 (£13,980; £6,990; £3,495; £1,747; £877) **Stalls** Low

Form RPR
1 **Dark Crusader (IRE)**[26] 4844 3-8-13 **90** FMBerry 16 101+
(A J Martin, Ire) *hld up in rr: smooth hdwy 3f out: trckd ldrs wl over 1f out: rdn to ld jst ins fnl f: rdn out* **8/1**
0106 **2** 1 ¼ **Dashing Star**[44] 4211 3-9-4 **95** LiamKeniry 13 104
(David Elsworth) *lw: racd wd early: chsd ldr tl led after 1f: hdd over 7f out: prom: rdn along over 2f out: ev ch whn sltly outpcd jst over 1f out: drvn and styd on wl towards fin* **16/1**
-113 **3** *nk* **Havana Cooler (IRE)**[21] 4984 3-9-2 **93** RyanMoore 10 102
(Luca Cumani) *lw: trckd ldng pair: hdwy 4f out: cl up over 2f out: rdn tgo dsipute ld and ev ch over 1f out: drvn and kpt on same pce ins fnl f* **11/4**[1]
2321 **4** 1 ¼ **Divergence (IRE)**[18] 5095 3-7-13 **83** LouisSteward[(7)] 2 90
(Michael Bell) *led 1f: cl up tl led again over 7f out: rdn along wl over 2f out: hdd wl over 1f out: sn drvn and one pce fnl f* **16/1**
2221 **5** ½ **Debdebdeb**[30] 4681 3-8-8 **85** DavidProbert 7 91
(Andrew Balding) *hld up: hdwy 3f out: rdn along 2f out: styd on u.p fnl f: nrst fin* **8/1**
2134 **6** *shd* **Van Percy**[21] 4984 3-8-2 **86** OisinMurphy[(7)] 11 92
(Andrew Balding) *hld up in tch: smooth hdwy on outer over 4f out: cl up 3f out: rdn to ld wl over 1f out: drvn and hdd jst ins fnl f: wknd* **7/1**[3]
4312 **7** 1 **Hawk High (IRE)**[15] 5223 3-8-3 **80** (p) DuranFentiman 12 85
(Tim Easterby) *hld up in rr: hdwy over 5f out: rdn to chse ldrs 3f out: drvn wl over 1f out and sn one pce* **10/1**
4430 **8** 2 ¾ **Mister Impatience**[23] 4919 3-9-6 **97** JoeFanning 3 98
(Mark Johnston) *chsd ldrs: rdn along over 3f out: drvn over 2f out and grad wknd* **6/1**[2]
3241 **9** 6 **Snowy Dawn**[42] 4286 3-8-3 **80** (p) JimmyQuinn 8 72
(Andrew Hollinshead) *hld up and bhd: sme hdwy on outer wl over 2f out: sn rdn along and n.d* **20/1**
2215 **10** ¾ **Elidor**[21] 4984 3-9-2 **93** MartinHarley 4 84
(Mick Channon) *trckd ldrs: hdwy over 4f out: rdn along 3f out: sn wknd* **14/1**
2411 **11** 1 ½ **Ambleside**[7] 5549 3-8-1 **78** MartinLane 6 67
(Mark Johnston) *dwlt: sn chsng ldr: rdn along over 4f out: sn wknd* **14/1**
2m 59.42s (-0.78) **Going Correction** +0.025s/f (Good) **11** Ran SP% **114.6**
Speed ratings (Par 106): **103,102,102,101,101 101,100,98,95,95 94**
Swingers 1&2 £16.70, 2&3 £7.40, 1&3 £4.20 CSF £124.94 CT £440.63 TOTE £8.30: £2.60, £5.00, £1.50; EX 120.30 Trifecta £225.40 Pool: £4620.93 - 15.37 winning units..
Owner Newtown Anner Stud Farm Ltd **Bred** Newtown Anner Stud **Trained** Summerhill, Co. Meath
FOCUS
The 3yos version of the Ebor handicap and a good race in its own right, having produced the subsequent Group 1 Caulfield Cup winner Tawqeet, plus other Group winners in Akmal, Mount Athos and Trick Or Treat in the last ten years. A number of withdrawals on account of the soft ground, but the pace was sound and the time suggested the ground was not that bad. The going description was changed to Soft, good to soft in places after this race. Siolid form, rated on the positive side.

5765 IRISH THOROUGHBRED MARKETING GIMCRACK STKS (GROUP 2) (C&G) — 6f
3:15 (3:16) (Class 1) 2-Y-O
£113,420 (£43,000; £21,520; £10,720; £5,380; £2,700) **Stalls** Centre

Form RPR
161 **1** **Astaire (IRE)**[28] 4768 2-8-12 104 NeilCallan 5 111
(Kevin Ryan) *wnt sltly rt s: sn led: rdn and qcknd 2f out: drvn and edgd lft ins fnl f: hld on wl towards fin* **5/1**[3]
01 **2** *nk* **Wilshire Boulevard (IRE)**[35] 4547 2-8-12 0 RyanMoore 6 110
(A P O'Brien, Ire) *leggy: angular: sltly hmpd s and in rr: niggled along 1/2-way: swtchd rt to outer and hdwy 2f out: rdn to chse wnr ins fnl f: sn drvn and edgd lft: no ex towards fin* **4/1**[2]
123 **3** *nk* **Parbold (IRE)**[24] 4876 2-8-12 106 TonyHamilton 3 109
(Richard Fahey) *cl up: effrt wl over 1f out: sn rdn and ev ch tl drvn and no ex towards fin* **11/4**[1]
412 **4** ½ **Cable Bay (IRE)**[23] 4918 2-8-12 107 RichardKingscote 4 108
(Charles Hills) *trckd ldrs: effrt 2f out: rdn over 1f out and ch tl drvn and one pce fnl f* **11/2**
2120 **5** 2 **Justice Day (IRE)**[67] 3424 2-8-12 95 LiamKeniry 1 102
(David Elsworth) *trckd ldrs: effrt 2f out: sn rdn and wknd over 1f out* **16/1**
1101 **6** 2 ¼ **Saayerr**[23] 4918 2-9-1 108 MartinHarley 7 98
(William Haggas) *lw: trckd ldrs: rdn along wl over 2f out: wknd wl over 1f out* **7/1**
2511 **7** 2 ¾ **My Catch (IRE)**[27] 4816 2-8-12 0 JamieSpencer 2 87
(David Brown) *lw: cl up on outer: rdn over 2f out: sn drvn and btn* **5/1**[3]
1m 13.72s (1.82) **Going Correction** +0.525s/f (Yiel) **7** Ran SP% **113.8**
Speed ratings (Par 106): **108,107,107,106,103 100,97**
toteswingers 1&2 £3.80, 2&3 £2.40, 1&3 £3.40 CSF £24.89 TOTE £5.90: £3.20, £2.30; EX 22.60 Trifecta £140.10 Pool: £3105.29 - 16.61 winning units..
Owner Mrs Angie Bailey **Bred** John O'Connor **Trained** Hambleton, N Yorks
■ Greatly enhanced prize money and a switch from the Friday for this historic race.
■ Stewards' Enquiry : Neil Callan four-day ban: used whip above permitted level (Sep 8-11)
FOCUS
As the betting suggested this was a tight race, although perhaps not the classiest running, despite the excellent prize-money on offer. Straightforward form, the fourth helping the level.

5766 BETFRED EBOR (HERITAGE H'CAP) — 1m 6f
3:50 (3:52) (Class 2) 3-Y-O+
£155,625 (£46,600; £23,300; £11,650; £5,825; £2,925) **Stalls** Low

Form RPR
2-12 **1** **Tiger Cliff (IRE)**[67] 3423 4-9-0 **98** TomQueally 18 106+
(Lady Cecil) *hld up in midfield: stdy hdwy over 3f out: trckd ldrs 2f out: rdn along over 1f out: drvn and styd on wl fnl f to ld nr fin* **5/1**[2]
2024 **2** ½ **Genzy (FR)**[7] 5531 5-9-0 **98** RichardKingscote 22 105
(Ian Williams) *lw: trckd ldrs: smooth hdwy 3f out: cl up 2f out: rdn to ld ent fnl f: drvn and edgd lft last 120yds: hdd and no ex nr fin* **11/1**

2034 **3** *1* **Number Theory**[23] 4919 5-9-9 **107** ... SebSanders 1 113
(John Holt) *prom: trckd ldr after 4f: effrt 3f out: rdn to ld 2f out: drvn and hdd ent fnl f: kpt on same pce towards fin* **16/1**

4 *1* **Ted Veale (IRE)**[3] 5664 6-8-13 **97** 4ex ... FMBerry 17 102+
(A J Martin, Ire) *lw: hld up and bhd: gd hdwy over 3f out: trckd ldrs whn n.m.r and swtchd rt over 1f out: sn rdn: styd on fnl f: nrst fin* **9/2**[1]

0204 **5** *½* **Oriental Fox (GER)**[14] 5256 5-9-1 **99** ... JoeFanning 4 103
(Mark Johnston) *trckd ldrs: hdwy over 3f out: rdn along 2f out: sn drvn and kpt on same pce* **16/1**

-400 **6** *¾* **Blue Surf**[25] 4854 4-8-13 **97** ... PaulMulrennan 10 100
(Amanda Perrett) *lw: trckd ldrs: hdwy over 3f out: cl up 2f out: sn rdn and ev ch tl drvn and one pce appr fnl f* **25/1**

6040 **7** *1 ½* **Guarantee**[25] 4857 4-9-3 **101** ...(p) PhillipMakin 19 102
(William Haggas) *hld up towards rr: hdwy 3f out: rdn to chse ldrs 2f out: kpt on u.p fnl f: nrst fin* **14/1**

5000 **8** *hd* **Saptapadi (IRE)**[14] 5256 7-8-10 **94** ... BarryMcHugh 9 94
(Brian Ellison) *hld up in midfield: hdwy on inner 3f out: rdn to chse ldrs 2f out: sn drvn and one pce appr fnl f* **25/1**

2123 **9** *nk* **Sheikhzayedroad**[22] 4944 4-9-6 **104** ... MartinLane 21 104
(David Simcock) *hld up and bhd: hdwy on wd outside wl over 2f out: rdn to chse ldrs over 1f out: no imp fnl f* **14/1**

-315 **10** *1 ½* **Opinion (IRE)**[49] 4060 4-9-5 **103** ...(t) RyanMoore 5 101
(Sir Michael Stoute) *v.s.a and lost many l s: sn w field: hdwy 4f out: rdn along 2f out: sn no imp* **5/1**[2]

-442 **11** *1* **Caravan Rolls On**[43] 4233 5-9-1 **99** ...(p) JamieSpencer 12 96
(Peter Chapple-Hyam) *lw: hld up: hdwy over 3f out: swtchd lft and rdn to chse ldrs wl over 1f out: sn drvn and wknd appr fnl f* **7/1**[3]

0200 **12** *2 ¼* **Hanoverian Baron**[49] 4060 8-8-4 **93** ... MichaelJMMurphy(5) 13 86
(Tony Newcombe) *trckd ldrs: effrt over 3f out: rdn along wl over 2f out: sn wknd* **28/1**

-431 **13** *shd* **Bishop Roko**[27] 4796 4-8-13 **97** 4ex ... MartinHarley 8 90
(Roger Charlton) *chsd ldng pair: rdn along over 3f out: sn wknd* **10/1**

0433 **14** *3* **Highland Castle**[14] 5256 5-8-9 **93** ... LiamKeniry 16 82
(David Elsworth) *set stdy pce: qcknd after 3f: rdn along and jnd 3f out: hdd 2f out and sn wknd* **22/1**

3m 3.36s (3.16) **Going Correction** +0.025s/f (Good) **14** Ran SP% **122.0**
Speed ratings (Par 109): **91,90,90,89,89 88,88,87,87,86 86,85,84,83**
toteswingers 1&2 £14.70, 2&3 £27.10, 1&3 £12.70 CSF £57.05 CT £837.10 TOTE £4.50: £2.00, £3.70, £4.30; EX 59.20 Trifecta £1304.50 Pool: £74508.00 - 42.83 winning units..
Owner W H Ponsonby **Bred** Mrs Clodagh McStay **Trained** Newmarket, Suffolk
■ Stewards' Enquiry : F M Berry two-day ban: careless riding (Sep 8-9)

FOCUS
The most valuable and one of the strongest handicaps for middle-distance/stayers of the season. The best recent winners were the subsequent multiple Group winner Sergeant Cecil, and Melbourne Cup runner-up Purple Moon. However, the rain resulted in so many withdrawals that the joint smallest field since 1947 lined up. The pace was steady early, the field came to race towards the stands' side in the straight and the time was 3.94secs slower than the earlier handicap for 3yos. Rather an ordinary Ebor, but there's every chance of more to come from the unexposed Tiger Cliff. The third and fifth set the standard.

5767 JULIA GRAVES ROSES STKS (LISTED RACE) 5f
4:25 (4:25) (Class 1) 2-Y-O
£28,355 (£10,750; £5,380; £2,680; £1,345; £675) **Stalls** Centre

Form RPR

1 **1** **Hot Streak (IRE)**[28] 4781 2-9-0 78 ... JamieSpencer 5 102+
(Kevin Ryan) *str: lw: hld up in tch: hdwy on outer 2f out: rdn to ld jst ins fnl f: kpt on strly* **3/1**[3]

411 **2** *1 ½* **Mecca's Angel (IRE)**[46] 4141 2-8-9 95 ... PaulMulrennan 6 92
(Michael Dods) *leggy: swtg: chsd ldrs: hdwy wl over 1f out: rdn and ev ch ins fnl f: drvn and one pce towards fin* **2/1**[1]

22 **3** *hd* **City Zen (IRE)**[10] 5380 2-8-9 0 ... BarryMcHugh 2 91
(Tony Coyle) *w'like: in rr: rdn along and outpcd 1/2-way: hdwy over 1f out: rdn and styd on wl fnl f: nrst fin* **14/1**

1102 **4** *1 ½* **Excel's Beauty**[8] 5476 2-8-9 100 ...(b) NeilCallan 8 86
(James Tate) *lw: plld hrd: set str pce: rdn and wandered over 1f out: hdd and drvn jst ins fnl f: wknd* **11/4**[2]

2241 **5** *3 ½* **Baytown Kestrel**[12] 5351 2-8-9 74 ... TomEaves 1 73
(Brian Ellison) *hld up in tch: hdwy to chse ldrs wl over 1f out: sn rdn and no imp* **20/1**

2214 **6** *18* **Disko (IRE)**[56] 3829 2-8-9 95 ... LukeMorris 7 8
(Daniel Kubler) *t.k.h: chsd ldr: rdn along over 2f out: sn wknd* **5/1**

1m 1.22s (1.92) **Going Correction** +0.525s/f (Yiel) **6** Ran SP% **113.1**
Speed ratings (Par 102): **105,102,102,99,94 65**
toteswingers 1&2 £1.90, 2&3 £6.20, 1&3 £4.10 CSF £9.60 TOTE £3.00: £2.00, £1.70; EX 9.30 Trifecta £63.50 Pool: £2194.18 - 25.88 winning units..
Owner Qatar Racing Limited **Bred** Barry Noonan **Trained** Hambleton, N Yorks

FOCUS
As expected this Listed contest was run at a strong pace thanks to Excel's Beauty, Mecca's Angel and Disko trapping from the gates, and it was rather set up for the winner, who sat in behind. The form looks well up to scratch for this race.

5768 BETFRED THE BONUS KING STKS (H'CAP) 1m 2f 88y
5:00 (5:01) (Class 2) (0-105,102) 3-Y-O+**£19,407** (£5,775; £2,886; £1,443) **Stalls** Low

Form RPR

3126 **1** **Sam Sharp (USA)**[14] 5255 7-9-5 **93** ... RichardKingscote 10 102
(Ian Williams) *dwlt and in rr: hdwy on outer over 2f out: rdn and edgd lft over 1f out: drvn to chal and edgd rt ins fnl f: styd on wl to ld last 75yds* **14/1**

1212 **2** *1* **Sennockian Star**[14] 5269 3-9-4 **100** ...(v) JoeFanning 5 107
(Mark Johnston) *trckd ldng pair: hdwy 3f out: chal 2f out and sn rdn: drvn to take slt ld ins fnl f: hdd and no ex last 75yds* **3/1**[1]

0460 **3** *hd* **Hi There (IRE)**[25] 4854 4-8-11 **85** ... BarryMcHugh 6 92
(Richard Fahey) *hld up towards rr: hdwy over 2f out: rdn and styd on ent fnl f: ev ch whn n.m.r and hit in face by wnrs whip fnl 50yds: no ex after* **16/1**

2061 **4** *½* **Strictly Silver (IRE)**[14] 5283 4-9-9 **102** ...(p) RobertTart(5) 13 108
(Alan Bailey) *b: sn trcking ldr: hdwy 3f out: slt ld over 2f out and sn rdn: drvn over 1f out: hdd ins fnl f: one pce towards fin* **10/1**

0241 **5** *2 ¼* **Spirit Of The Law (IRE)**[12] 5335 4-8-9 **88** ... GeorgeChaloner(5) 8 89
(Richard Fahey) *hld up towards rr: hdwy 3f out: effrt and n.m.r wl over 1f out: sn rdn to chse ldrs and n.m.r ent fnl f: kpt on: nrst fin* **13/2**[3]

2004 **6** *1 ¾* **Forgotten Hero (IRE)**[27] 4798 4-9-0 **88** ... JamieSpencer 11 86
(Charles Hills) *lw: hld up in rr: hdwy over 2f out: rdn over 1f out: no imp fnl f* **12/1**

0203 **7** *nk* **Rockalong (IRE)**[28] 4765 4-9-3 **91** ... RyanMoore 7 89
(Luca Cumani) *trckd ldrs: rdn over 2f out: drvn and wknd over 1f out* **9/2**[2]

10-1 **8** *¾* **Charles Camoin (IRE)**[27] 4798 5-9-7 **95** ... LiamKeniry 9 91
(Sylvester Kirk) *trckd ldrs on outer: hdwy 3f out: rdn 2f out: grad wknd* **10/1**

4060 **9** *2 ¼* **Two For Two (IRE)**[22] 4946 5-9-12 **100** ... DanielTudhope 12 92
(David O'Meara) *warm: trckd ldrs: hdwy over 3f out: effrt over 2f out: sn rdn and wknd over 1f out* **7/1**

1235 **10** *8* **Love Marmalade (IRE)**[21] 5006 3-8-1 **83** ... MartinLane 3 60
(Mark Johnston) *lw: led: rdn along and hdd over 2f out: sn wknd* **11/1**

0100 **11** *10* **Garde Cotiere (USA)**[28] 4778 5-9-0 **88** ...[1] DavidNolan 4 46
(Richard Fahey) *trckd ldrs: rdn along over 3f out: sn lost pl and bhd* **33/1**

2m 10.4s (-2.10) **Going Correction** +0.025s/f (Good)
WFA 3 from 4yo+ 8lb **11** Ran SP% **118.7**
Speed ratings (Par 109): **109,108,108,107,105 104,104,103,101,95 87**
toteswingers 1&2 £8.00, 2&3 £14.00, 1&3 £35.40 CSF £56.38 CT £703.90 TOTE £15.70: £4.20, £1.80, £3.90; EX 58.20 Trifecta £1155.50 Pool: £3749.15 - 2.43 winning units..
Owner N Martin **Bred** Michael Cahan Thoroughbreds **Trained** Portway, Worcs

FOCUS
Another strong handicap. The first and third came from the rear while the second and fourth were always in the leading group. Straightforward form.

5769 QIPCO FUTURE STARS APPRENTICE STKS (H'CAP) 5f
5:35 (5:36) (Class 2) (0-100,98) 3-Y-O **£19,407** (£5,775; £2,886; £1,443) **Stalls** Centre

Form RPR

0004 **1** **Threes Grand**[7] 5519 3-7-11 **79** oh1 ... TimClark(5) 4 91
(Scott Dixon) *towards rr: hdwy on wd outside wl over 1f out: rdn and styd on to chal ins fnl f: sn edgd rt: kpt on wl to ld last 100yds* **5/1**[1]

-115 **2** *1 ¼* **Hoofalong**[78] 3066 3-8-7 **84** ...(p) JasonHart 12 92+
(Michael Easterby) *rrd and wnt rt s: sn in tch: trckd ldrs over 2f out: hdwy to ld ent fnl f: sn rdn and edgd lft: hdd and one pce last 100yds* **5/1**[1]

6435 **3** *1 ½* **Normal Equilibrium**[21] 4989 3-9-0 **91** ... CharlesBishop 3 93
(Robert Cowell) *lw: chsd ldrs: hdwy 2f out: rdn and ev ch over 1f out: swtchd lft ins fnl f: kpt on* **11/2**[2]

1123 **4** *1 ¼* **Lexington Place**[21] 4989 3-8-5 **82** ... JulieBurke 9 80
(David O'Meara) *in tch: hdwy to chse ldrs over 1f out: sn swtchd lft and rdn: kpt on same pce fnl f* **9/1**

2205 **5** *¾* **Bispham Green**[71] 3299 3-8-0 **82** ... SamanthaBell(5) 5 77
(Richard Fahey) *cl up: rdn and ev ch over 1f out: drvn and one pce ent fnl f* **16/1**

6202 **6** *½* **Jillnextdoor (IRE)**[21] 4989 3-8-6 **90** ... DanielCremin(7) 8 83
(Mick Channon) *dwlt and in rr: hdwy wl over 1f out: rdn and kpt on fnl f: nrst fin* **12/1**

3034 **7** *hd* **Cosmic Chatter**[43] 4247 3-9-4 **98** ... RobertTart(3) 11 90
(David Barron) *a towards rr* **10/1**

0423 **8** *¾* **Huntsmans Close**[12] 5340 3-8-0 **84** ... LouisSteward(7) 7 74
(Michael Bell) *led: rdn along 2f out: hdd & wknd ent fnl f* **6/1**[3]

0334 **9** *1 ¼* **Dream Maker (IRE)**[7] 5511 3-7-12 **82** ... GaryMahon(7) 15 67
(Tim Easterby) *chsd ldrs on inner: cl up 1/2-way: sn rdn and wknd over 1f out* **20/1**

0503 **10** *hd* **Equitania**[18] 5103 3-7-12 **80** ... NoelGarbutt(5) 13 64
(Alan Bailey) *lw: cl up: rdn along 2f out: sn drvn and wknd over 1f out* **20/1**

3500 **11** *½* **Mary's Daughter**[43] 4255 3-8-5 **85** ... GeorgeChaloner(3) 1 68
(Richard Fahey) *chsd ldrs: hdwy 2f out: rdn over 1f out: sn drvn and wknd* **8/1**

0060 **12** *nk* **Storm Moon (USA)**[7] 5538 3-8-5 **85** ... MichaelJMMurphy(3) 10 67
(Mark Johnston) *a towards rr* **20/1**

5005 **13** *11* **Mayfield Girl (IRE)**[12] 5340 3-8-3 **80** ... NeilFarley 14 22
(Mel Brittain) *chsd ldrs whn hmpd and lost pl after 1 1/2f: sn bhd and eased wl over 1f out* **20/1**

1m 1.06s (1.76) **Going Correction** +0.525s/f (Yiel) **13** Ran SP% **125.8**
Speed ratings (Par 106): **106,104,101,99,98 97,97,96,94,93 92,92,74**
toteswingers 1&2 £7.00, 2&3 £6.60, 1&3 £8.50 CSF £29.10 CT £143.81 TOTE £7.20: £2.60, £2.00, £2.60; EX 42.40 Trifecta £245.90 Pool: £3579.39 - 10.91 winning units..
Owner Paul J Dixon & Mrs Jayne Jackson **Bred** Mrs Fiona Denniff **Trained** Babworth, Notts
■ Stewards' Enquiry : Tim Clark one-day ban: careless riding (Sep 8)

FOCUS
A good-quality handicap for apprentices. The winner is rated back to his best.
T/Jkpt: £119,133.10 to a £1 stake. Pool of £167,793.10 - 1.00 winning unit T/Plt: £58.00 to a £1 stake. Pool of £276893.04 - 3482.54 winning tickets. T/Qpdt: £33.70 to a £1 satke. Pool of £10008.87 - 219.51 winning tickets. JR

5316 CURRAGH (R-H)
Saturday, August 24

OFFICIAL GOING: Good

5771a IRISH FIELD CURRAGH STKS (LISTED RACE) 5f
2:35 (2:35) 2-Y-O **£21,138** (£6,178; £2,926; £975)

RPR

1 **Come To Heel (IRE)**[18] 5111 2-8-12 ... WayneLordan 4 100+
(David Wachman, Ire) *trckd ldrs in 5th tl swtchd rt appr fnl f: chsd ldr in 2nd ent fnl f: styd on wl to ld clsng stages: snug* **6/4**[1]

2 *½* **Hurryupharriet (IRE)**[15] 5248 2-8-12 87 ... PatSmullen 10 96
(W McCreery, Ire) *broke smartly and attempted to make all: pushed clr appr fnl f: hdd clsng stages and no ex w wnr* **9/1**

3 *1 ¾* **Boom The Groom (IRE)**[15] 5251 2-9-3 ... FergalLynch 7 95
(David Marnane, Ire) *w.w: pushed along to chse ldrs appr fnl f in 6th: styd on wl into 3rd fnl 100yds: nt trble principals* **12/1**

4 *nk* **Pleasant Bay (IRE)**[6] 5566 2-9-3 ... WJLee 8 94
(David Wachman, Ire) *trckd ldrs on stands' rails: nt qckn ent fnl f: kpt on same pce* **10/1**

5 *½* **Three D Alexander (IRE)**[9] 5449 2-8-12 ... DeclanMcDonogh 6 87
(David Wachman, Ire) *sn trckd ldr in 2nd: niggled along 2f out: no imp and wknd ins fnl f* **12/1**

6 *1* **Expedition (IRE)**[111] 2058 2-9-3 ...(b[1]) JosephO'Brien 9 88
(A P O'Brien, Ire) *hld up in rr: sltly checked early: pushed along and nt qckn 2f out: styd on wl ins fnl f under hands and heels* **4/1**[2]

7 *¾* **Candy Apples (IRE)**[3] 5661 2-8-12 86 ... ChrisHayes 2 81
(P J Prendergast, Ire) *trckd ldrs in 3rd tl nt qckn appr fnl f: one pce* **8/1**[3]

8 *2* **M'Selle (IRE)**[23] 4910 2-8-12 ... SeamieHeffernan 1 74
(Ronald Harris) *trckd ldrs in 4th far side tl wknd appr fnl f* **50/1**

9 *½* **Celtic Man (IRE)**[19] 5074 2-9-3 95 ... GaryCarroll 5 77
(David Marnane, Ire) *racd towards rr: nvr gng pce to get on terms: no imp over 1f out* **10/1**

10 *nk* **Intensical (IRE)** 2-9-3 .... KevinManning 3 76
(J S Bolger, Ire) *a towards rr: no imp 2f out* **12/1**
58.87s (-4.03) **Going Correction** -0.70s/f (Hard) **10** Ran SP% **124.3**
Speed ratings: **104,103,100,99,99 97,96,93,92,91**
CSF £17.79 TOTE £2.80: £1.30, £2.20, £4.50; DF 18.10.
Owner M Buckley, D Graham, Mrs P Shanahan **Bred** Lynn Lodge Stud **Trained** Goolds Cross, Co Tipperary
FOCUS
A nice contest, with David Wachman's hand especially strong. He won this last year with a colt. The winner was quite impressive but the field finished fairly comptessed, limiting confidence.

5772a FLYING FIVE STKS (GROUP 3) 5f
3:10 (3:10) 3-Y-O+ **£31,707** (£9,268; £4,390; £1,463)

RPR
1 **Dutch Masterpiece**[63] 3584 3-9-3 .... JosephO'Brien 13 113+
(Gary Moore) *chsd ldrs on stands' rails: 6th 1f out: qcknd wl between horses fnl 100yds to ld cl home* **4/1**[2]
2 *½* **Hamza (IRE)**[13] 5320 4-9-5 ....(b) PatSmullen 12 111
(Kevin Ryan) *broke wl and racd in cl 2nd tl led 2f out: strly pressed fnl 100yds: hdd cl home* **5/2**[1]
3 *nk* **Russian Soul (IRE)**[15] 5249 5-9-5 107..................(p) ShaneFoley 3 110
(M Halford, Ire) *w.w: pushed along to chse ldrs 1f out: styd on wl far side in 5th ent fnl f: kpt on wl into 3rd cl home* **6/1**[3]
4 *nk* **Kingsgate Choice (IRE)**[42] 4311 6-9-5 .... KevinManning 5 109
(Ed de Giles) *broke wl and sn settled jst off ldrs: strly rdn to press ldrs ent fnl f in 4th: no ex cl home* **6/1**[3]
5 *hd* **Abstraction (IRE)**[15] 5249 3-9-3 99.................. SeamieHeffernan 6 108
(Sarah Dawson, Ire) *sn trckd ldrs in 3rd: swtchd rt to press ldr in 2nd 1f out: no ex clsng stages and dropped to 5th* **20/1**
6 *½* **Scream Blue Murder (IRE)**[15] 5249 3-9-0 100.................. WayneLordan 9 103
(T Stack, Ire) *hld up towards stands' rails: prog to chse ldrs 1f out whn sltly short of room: styd on wl in clsng stages: nvr nrr* **20/1**
7 *1 ½* **My Propeller (IRE)**[42] 4311 4-9-2 .... DeclanMcDonogh 10 98
(Peter Chapple-Hyam) *chsd ldrs: prog to chal whn short of room and snatched up fnl 150yds: nt rcvr* **11/1**
8 *nk* **Nocturnal Affair (SAF)**[41] 4328 7-9-5 100..................(t) GaryCarroll 11 100
(David Marnane, Ire) *bit slowly away and racd in rr: last appr fnl f: styd on strly on stands' rails clsng stages: nrst fin* **28/1**
9 *nk* **Yulong Baoju (IRE)**[34] 4569 3-9-0 99..................(p) JohnnyMurtagh 4 96
(Edward Lynam, Ire) *hld up towards rr: prog and swtchd rt ent fnl f: sn no imp* **7/1**
10 *1 ¾* **Hoyam**[49] 4079 3-9-0 .... ChrisHayes 1 90
(Michael Bell) *w.w on far side: sme prog over 1f out: no imp whn carried rt ins fnl f* **20/1**
11 *¾* **Judge 'n Jury**[14] 5257 9-9-5 ....(t) RoryCleary 7 90
(Ronald Harris) *led tl hdd 2f out: wknd ins fnl f* **33/1**
12 *4 ¼* **Timeless Call (IRE)**[15] 5249 5-9-2 101.................. RonanWhelan 2 72
(Reginald Roberts, Ire) *waited towards far side: pushed along 2f out: no imp 1f out* **16/1**
58.0s (-4.90) **Going Correction** -0.70s/f (Hard)
WFA 3 from 4yo+ 2lb **12** Ran SP% **124.5**
Speed ratings: **111,110,109,109,108 108,105,105,104,101 100,93**
CSF £13.99 TOTE £4.80: £2.00, £1.20, £1.90; DF 14.50.
Owner R A Green **Bred** Bumble Bloodstock Ltd **Trained** Lower Beeding, W Sussex
FOCUS
There did not seem to be a great deal between these on paper and the race turned out to endorse that view. It was a race not devoid of bad-luck stories. The placed horses are the best guides to the level.

5773a TATTERSALLS IRELAND SUPER AUCTION SALE STKS 6f 63y
3:45 (3:47) 2-Y-O
£49,796 (£19,308; £12,536; £5,764; £2,369; £337)

RPR
1 **Vallado (IRE)**[9] 5449 2-8-10 .... PatSmullen 3 89+
(Edward Lynam, Ire) *chsd ldrs towards far side: prog under 2f out: led 1f out: pushed clr fnl 100yds* **7/4**[1]
2 *2 ½* **Atlantic Affair (IRE)**[17] 5136 2-8-8 .... JFEgan 1 80
(Mark Johnston) *sn trckd ldrs in 3rd: led under 2f out: strly pressed and hdd 1f out: no ex w wnr fnl 100yds* **14/1**
3 *nk* **An Chulainn (IRE)**[9] 5421 2-8-10 .... SeamieHeffernan 18 81
(Mark Johnston) *trckd ldrs on stands' side: sltly short of room under 2f out: styd on wl in 3rd ent fnl f: nt trble principals* **14/1**
4 *1 ¾* **Ava Star (IRE)**[10] 5413 2-8-7 79.................. DeclanMcDonogh 15 73
(David Wachman, Ire) *racd towards rr on stands' rails tl swtchd rt over 1f out in 6th: styd on wl ins fnl f* **16/1**
5 *2 ½* **Focussed (IRE)**[17] 5159 2-8-13 83..................(b) KevinManning 16 71
(Brendan W Duke, Ire) *trckd ldrs on stands' rails: clsd in 2nd 2f out: nt qckn appr fnl f: kpt on same pce* **13/2**[3]
6 *¾* **Pillow (IRE)**[41] 4326 2-8-8 .... FergalLynch 11 64
(J P Murtagh, Ire) *hld up: mid-div 1/2-way: prog whn swtchd rt over 1f out in 6th: kpt on same pce ins fnl f* **14/1**
7 *1 ¾* **De Repente (IRE)**[11] 5366 2-8-9 ow1.................. RonanWhelan 10 59
(Paul Green) *broke wl and led tl hdd under 2f out: wknd fnl f* **25/1**
8 *1 ½* **Evie Jay (IRE)**[15] 5225 2-8-6 .... ConnorKing 17 52
(Paul Green) *hld up towards rr on stands' rails: kpt on fr over 1f out: nvr on terms* **33/1**
9 *1 ½* **Pixie Hollow (IRE)**[17] 5158 2-8-10 .... ChrisHayes 13 51
(Kevin Prendergast, Ire) *racd in mid-div: pushed along and nt qckn under 2f out: kpt on one pce* **3/1**[2]
10 *hd* **Sandy Smile (IRE)**[6] 5566 2-8-6 .... ShaneFoley 4 47
(M Halford, Ire) *hld up towards rr: swtchd rt whn hmpd under 2f out: kpt on one pce* **12/1**
11 *½* **Princess Tamay (IRE)**[58] 3710 2-8-8 .... RoryCleary 6 47
(Mark Johnston) *trckd ldrs early: sn reminders in mid-div: no imp 2f out* **25/1**
12 *1 ¼* **Insight (IRE)** 2-8-10 ....(p) WayneLordan 5 46
(David Wachman, Ire) *nvr bttr than mid-div: no threat under 2f out* **14/1**
13 *hd* **Gwen Lady Byron (IRE)**[55] 3868 2-8-10 .... DannyGrant 9 45
(Michael Mulvany, Ire) *hld up towards rr: no imp 2f out* **25/1**
14 *6 ½* **Tom Dooley (IRE)**[3] 5657 2-8-11 65.................. GaryCarroll 2 26
(Michael Mulvany, Ire) *racd in mid-div tl wknd 2f out* **33/1**
15 *½* **Maid In Rio (IRE)**[10] 5380 2-8-6 .... BenCurtis 12 20
(Mark Johnston) *upset and uns rdr in stalls befhand: early spd: wknd fr 1/2-way* **33/1**
16 *3 ½* **Sweet Alibi (IRE)**[16] 5213 2-8-8 .... ConorHoban 14 11
(J S Moore) *trckd ldr in 2nd to beyond 1/2-way: sn wknd* **16/1**

17 *12* **Bearing Kisses (IRE)**[108] 2147 2-8-6 ....(v[1]) IJBrennan 7
(Shaun Harris) *nvr bttr than mid-div: wknd over 2f out* **50/1**
1m 14.82s (-4.28) **Going Correction** -0.70s/f (Hard) **17** Ran SP% **143.1**
Speed ratings: **100,96,96,93,90 89,87,85,83,83 82,80,80,71,71 66,50**
CSF £33.42 TOTE £2.70: £1.50, £4.20, £4.80; DF 39.00.
Owner Wood Hall Stud Limited **Bred** Rossenarra Bloodstock Limited **Trained** Dunshaughlin, Co Meath
FOCUS
This was an uncompetitive race considering the money on offer. There seemed to be no excuses. The fourth is the best guide to the level.

5774a GALILEO EUROPEAN BREEDERS FUND FUTURITY STKS (GROUP 2) 7f
4:20 (4:21) 2-Y-O **£48,780** (£15,447; £7,317; £2,439; £1,626)

RPR
1 **War Command (USA)**[13] 5319 2-9-6 119.................. JosephO'Brien 2 118+
(A P O'Brien, Ire) *settled in 4th towards far side: qcknd wl fr over 1f out: led ins fnl f and pushed clr: comf* **8/11**[1]
2 *3* **Mustajeeb**[26] 4841 2-9-3 .... PatSmullen 1 107
(D K Weld, Ire) *chsd clr ldr in 2nd tl pushed along to cl 2f out: dropped to 3rd 1f out where nt qckn w wnr: kpt on same pce into 2nd* **7/2**[2]
3 *hd* **Exogenesis (IRE)**[30] 4694 2-9-3 105.................. GaryCarroll 3 107
(G M Lyons, Ire) *t.k.h early in 3rd: sn settled: pushed along in 4th over 1f out: kpt on wl ins fnl f wout pce of wnr* **11/2**[3]
4 *2* **Friendship (IRE)**[2] 5687 2-9-3 97.................. SeamieHeffernan 4 101
(A P O'Brien, Ire) *sn led and clr 1/2-way: hdd ins fnl f: sn no ex* **7/1**
5 *16* **Freedom Square (IRE)**[63] 3555 2-9-3 90.................. KevinManning 5 60
(J S Bolger, Ire) *slowly away and a in rr: no imp under 2f out: sn adrift* **33/1**
1m 23.94s (-6.86) **Going Correction** -1.10s/f (Hard) **5** Ran SP% **111.0**
Speed ratings: **95,91,91,89,70**
CSF £3.63 TOTE £1.70: £1.02, £1.80; DF 3.60.
Owner J Allen/Mrs J Magnier/M Tabor/D Smith **Bred** Joseph Allen **Trained** Ballydoyle, Co Tipperary
FOCUS
Not a hugely competitive renewal but it was run at a scorching pace. The favourite was on a revival mission and did everything that could be asked of him. He can rate higher with the third the best guide to this for now.

5775a DUBLIN BAY CRUISES H'CAP 6f
4:55 (4:58) 3-Y-O+ **£7,292** (£1,691; £739; £422)

RPR
1 **Corporal Maddox**[15] 5219 6-9-2 77..................(p[1]) ChrisHayes 13 88+
(Ronald Harris) *racd towards rr: pushed along 1/2-way: swtchd rt under 2f out: stl plenty to do appr fnl f: qcknd wl to ld fnl 50yds* **10/1**[3]
2 *¾* **Sassaway (IRE)**[13] 5321 6-9-5 80.................. FergalLynch 12 89
(Eamonn O'Connell, Ire) *broke wl: disp after 2f: advantage under 2f out: kpt on wl: hdd fnl 50yds* **10/1**[3]
3 *nse* **Heuston (IRE)**[41] 4327 4-9-2 80..................[1] RonanWhelan(3) 1 89
(Reginald Roberts, Ire) *chsd ldrs on far side: gd prog in 5th 1f out: sn pressed ldr in 2nd: dropped to 3rd cl home* **11/1**
4 *hd* **Nero Emperor (IRE)**[15] 5250 4-10-0 89.................. WayneLordan 18 97+
(T Stack, Ire) *sn in rr: swtchd rt over 1f out whn hmpd: 10th ent fnl f: r.o strly clsng stages to go 4th cl home* **25/1**
5 *1* **Kiss The Stars (IRE)**[18] 5112 3-8-4 73.................. ConnorKing(5) 17 78
(T G McCourt, Ire) *racd in mid-div on stands' side: prog over 1f out: kpt on wl ins fnl f* **10/1**[3]
6 *nk* **Beau Mistral (IRE)**[11] 5376 4-8-10 71.................. SeamieHeffernan 2 75
(Paul Green) *chsd ldrs towards far side: prog into 3rd ent fnl f: no imp fnl 100yds* **16/1**
7 *1* **Ucanchoose (IRE)**[15] 5250 7-8-10 71..................(b) PatSmullen 14 72
(Andrew Slattery, Ire) *sn trckd ldrs: pushed along over 1f out: wknd wl ins fnl f* **16/1**
8 *shd* **Norville (IRE)**[17] 5160 6-9-3 78..................(b) GaryCarroll 5 78
(Lee Smyth, Ire) *racd in mid-div: reminders 1/2-way: kpt on wl fnl f wout getting on terms* **33/1**
9 *shd* **Toccata Blue (IRE)**[6] 5565 3-9-5 83.................. EmmetMcNamara 7 83
(G M Lyons, Ire) *chsd ldrs: pushed along 2f out: nvr on terms but kpt on ins fnl f* **14/1**
10 *hd* **Cash Or Casualty (IRE)**[6] 5567 5-9-12 87..................(t) RoryCleary 3 87
(Damian Joseph English, Ire) *racd in mid-div towards far side: no imp appr fnl f: kpt on same pce* **28/1**
11 *1 ¾* **Patrickswell (IRE)**[6] 5567 9-8-10 74.................. LeighRoche(3) 6 68
(Marcus Callaghan, Ire) *sn led: jnd after 2f and hdd under 2f out: wknd 1f out* **25/1**
12 *nk* **Speed Dream (IRE)**[6] 5565 9-8-13 81.................. DylanRobinson(7) 16 74
(James M Barrett, Ire) *hld up towards rr: no imp 2f out: kpt on ins fnl f* **12/1**
13 *nk* **Seal Rock**[17] 5160 5-9-13 88.................. JosephO'Brien 22 80
(A Oliver, Ire) *trckd ldrs on stands' side: pushed along in 4th 2f out: wknd appr fnl f* **8/1**[2]
14 *nk* **Lightnin Hopkins (IRE)**[6] 5567 3-9-6 89..................(b[1]) ColinKeane(5) 15 80
(G M Lyons, Ire) *chsd ldrs tl nt qckn over 1f out: sn one pce* **20/1**
15 *hd* **Ramone (IRE)**[16] 5206 3-9-2 80.................. JohnnyMurtagh 4 70
(W T Farrell, Ire) *uns rdr bef s: nvr bttr than mid-div: no imp under 2f out* **10/1**[3]
16 *1* **Foot Perfect (IRE)**[9] 5450 5-8-7 71..................(p) ConorHoban(3) 19 58
(M Halford, Ire) *hld up towards rr stands' side: no imp appr fnl f* **12/1**
17 *shd* **Enigma Code (UAE)**[6] 5570 8-8-3 69..................(t) ShaneGray(5) 9 56
(Damian Joseph English, Ire) *nvr bttr than mid-div: no imp 2f out* **33/1**
17 *shd* **Italian Tom (IRE)**[16] 5183 6-8-7 75.................. RossCoakley(7) 20 62
(Ronald Harris) *nvr bttr than mid-div: no imp 2f out* **16/1**
19 *nk* **Scatty Cat (IRE)**[49] 4089 3-8-11 75.................. MichaelHussey 10 61
(Peter McCreery, Ire) *a towards rr: nvr a factor* **25/1**
20 *1 ¾* **Regal Power**[71] 3305 4-9-5 80..................(p) DeclanMcDonogh 21 60
(Edward Lynam, Ire) *nvr bttr than mid-div: no imp 2f out* **6/1**[1]
21 *nk* **Susiescot (IRE)**[19] 5080 4-8-10 74.................. ShaneBKelly(3) 11 53
(W McCreery, Ire) *a towards rr: no threat over 2f out* **20/1**
22 *4* **Wandering Heart (IRE)**[735] 5294 5-8-7 68.................. BenCurtis 8 34
(Liam P Cusack, Ire) *a towards rr: nvr a factor* **33/1**
23 *3* **Man Of Erin (IRE)**[6] 5565 5-9-5 80..................(p) ShaneFoley 23 37
(W T Farrell, Ire) *trckd ldrs stands' side: pushed along 1/2-way: sn wknd* **16/1**
1m 11.85s (-3.65) **Going Correction** -0.70s/f (Hard)
WFA 3 from 4yo+ 3lb **23** Ran SP% **149.0**
Speed ratings: **96,95,94,94,93 92,91,91,91,91 88,88,87,87,87 85,85,85,85,82 82,77,73**
CSF £110.93 CT £1192.06 TOTE £21.60: £3.60, £1.40, £3.50, £8.80; DF 234.00.

Owner Robert & Nina Bailey **Bred** Theobalds Stud **Trained** Earlswood, Monmouths
FOCUS
Deeply competitive, without many of the runners seeming altogether well handicapped. A personal-best from teh runner-up with the sixth, seventh and ninth rated to their latest form.

5776a GAIN IRISH ST LEGER TRIAL STKS (GROUP 3) 1m 6f
5:25 (5:27) 3-Y-O+ £31,707 (£9,268; £4,390; £1,463)

RPR

1 **Royal Diamond (IRE)**16 5209 7-9-12 112.................... JohnnyMurtagh 2 115
(J P Murtagh, Ire) *sn led: strly pressed fr over 2f out: fnd plenty for press to reassert fnl 100yds* **7/2**2

2 ½ **Voleuse De Coeurs (IRE)**55 3873 4-9-9 108.................. PatSmullen 5 111
(D K Weld, Ire) *chsd ldr in 2nd: almost on terms over 2f out: kpt on wl tl no ex w wnr fnl 100yds* **9/2**3

3 5½ **Ernest Hemingway (IRE)**16 5209 4-9-12 116............. JosephO'Brien 1 107+
(A P O'Brien, Ire) *settled in 4th: niggled along in 3rd 3f out: no imp on ldrs under 2f out: kpt on one pce* **4/9**1

4 7½ **Sir Ector (USA)**29 4741 6-9-9 99.............................(b) ChrisHayes 4 93
(J J Lambe, Ire) *chsd ldrs in 3rd tl pushed along and dropped to 4th 3f out: sn no ex* **25/1**

5 9 **Shu Lewis (IRE)**29 4741 7-9-6 97..............................(t) ShaneGorey 3 78
(Ms M Dowdall Blake, Ire) *racd in rr: reminders and adrift under 4f out* **33/1**

2m 58.88s (-10.52) **Going Correction** -0.55s/f (Hard) **5 Ran SP% 116.4**
Speed ratings: **108,107,104,100,95**
CSF £19.81 TOTE £3.70: £1.70, £1.50; DF 11.30.
Owner Andrew Tinkler **Bred** Moyglare Stud Farm Ltd **Trained** Coolaghknock Glebe,Co Kildare
FOCUS
The first two ran to their marks, while the third underperformed.

5777 - (Foreign Racing) - See Raceform Interactive

2294 BADEN-BADEN (L-H)
Saturday, August 24

OFFICIAL GOING: Turf: good

5778a PREIS DER SPARKASSEN FINANZGRUPPE (GROUP 3) (4YO+) (TURF) 1m 2f
4:15 (12:00) 4-Y-0+
£26,016 (£8,943; £4,471; £2,439; £1,626; £1,219)

RPR

1 **Polish Vulcano (GER)**20 5-8-11 0.. WPanov 4 101+
(H J Groschel, Germany) *w.w in midfield: tk clsr order 2f out: rdn to chal appr 1f out: led ins fnl f: drvn out* **14/1**

2 ¾ **Earl Of Tinsdal (GER)**65 3483 5-9-0 0................................ EPedroza 7 102
(A Wohler, Germany) *trckd ldr: hrd rdn to chal 2f out: 2nd and ev ch over 1f out: one pce u.p fnl f* **23/5**3

3 hd **Petit Chevalier (FR)**14 5298 5-9-2 0.................................. ADeVries 2 104+
(W Mongil, Germany) *towards rr: last and rdn 1 1/2f out: styd on u.p fr over 1f out: short of room and swtchd outside ins fnl f: nt pce to chal* **5/2**2

4 hd **Andolini (GER)**34 4-9-2 0.. JBojko 6 104
(A Wohler, Germany) *hld up in rr: effrt on ins to chse ldrs 2f out: 3rd and ev ch over 1f out: one pce ins fnl f* **229/10**

5 nk **Quinindo (GER)**20 5-9-0 0.. SHellyn 5 101
(Elfie Schnakenberg, Germany) *led: shkn up and qcknd 2 1/2f out: pressed fr 2f out: hdd ins fnl f: no ex* **135/10**

6 hd **Neatico (GER)**27 4819 6-9-6 0.. AStarke 3 107
(P Schiergen, Germany) *hld up in midfield: rdn to chse ldrs over 1 1/2f out: nt qckn u.p 1f out: one pce fnl f* **7/10**1

7 13 **Wasimah (GER)**34 4-8-10 0.. FilipMinarik 1 71
(H J Groschel, Germany) *chsd ldrs on inner: rdn and outpcd 2 1/2f out: bhd fr under 1 1/2f out: eased ins fnl f* **19/2**

2m 3.75s (-1.24) **7 Ran SP% 132.5**
WIN (incl. 10 euro stake): 150. PLACES: 48, 34. SF: 589.
Owner Rennstall Darboven **Bred** Gestut Idee **Trained** Germany

5692 CLAIREFONTAINE (R-H)
Saturday, August 24

OFFICIAL GOING: Turf: soft

5779a PRIX BOURDIN AND CO - GRAND PRIX DE CLAIREFONTAINE (LISTED RACE) (3YO+) (TURF) 1m 4f
1:30 (12:00) 3-Y-O £22,357 (£8,943; £6,707; £4,471; £2,235)

RPR

1 **Au Revoir (IRE)**20 5041 3-9-2 0................................... MaximeGuyon 2 108+
(A Fabre, France) **7/5**1

2 snk **Prince Khurram**45 3-8-11 0............................... Pierre-CharlesBoudot 1 102+
(J-P Carvalho, France) **68/10**

3 1½ **Alta Lilea (IRE)**23 4920 3-8-8 0.................................. IoritzMendizabal 3 97
(Mark Johnston) *disp ld on outside of two rivals: led on rail after 1 1/2f: shkn up whn pressed 2 1/2f out: c stands' side st: hdd 1 1/2f out: rallied u.p but short of room between horses 1f out: one pce u.p fnl f* **4/1**3

4 hd **Notaire (IRE)**49 3-8-11 0.................................. ChristopheSoumillon 6 100+
(P Bary, France) **2/1**2

5 1 **Ketchikan (IRE)**27 4815 3-8-11 0....................................... RonanThomas 4 98
(J-P Carvalho, France) **23/1**

6 1¼ **Aylin (FR)**325 3-8-8 0... ThierryThulliez 5 93
(N Clement, France) **18/1**

3m 32.6s (54.70) **6 Ran SP% 117.3**
WIN (incl. 1 euro stake): 2.40. PLACES: 1.80, 2.70. SF: 11.90.
Owner OTI Management Pty Ltd **Bred** Bloomsbury Stud **Trained** Chantilly, France
FOCUS
Quite a slowly run race.

5420 BEVERLEY (R-H)
Sunday, August 25

OFFICIAL GOING: Good (good to firm in places; 8.8)
Wind: Moderate; half behind Weather: Cloudy with sunny periods

5783 JOHN JENKINS MEMORIAL CLAIMING STKS 7f 100y
2:20 (2:21) (Class 5) 3-Y-O+ £3,234 (£962; £481; £240) Stalls Low

Form RPR

1632 1 **Balty Boys (IRE)**9 5474 4-9-10 87...............................(b) JoeFanning 6 87
(Jamie Osborne) *mde all: rdn clr appr fnl f: kpt on strly* **7/4**1

6U43 2 7 **Llewellyn**11 5378 5-9-5 72.. AdrianNicholls 3 64
(David Nicholls) *trckd ldng pair: hdwy on inner to chse wnr 2f out: rdn over 1f out: drvn and wandered ins fnl f: one pce* **5/1**

0000 3 1 **Gouray Girl (IRE)**8 5544 6-9-0 80.................................(p) DaleSwift 2 57
(Brian Ellison) *hld up towards rr: hdwy over 2f out: sn rdn: kpt on u.p fnl f to take modest 3rd nr fin* **7/2**3

0251 4 ¾ **Toto Skyllachy**12 5367 8-9-10 90.................................... DavidNolan 4 65
(David O'Meara) *sn chsng wnr: rdn along wl over 2f out: drvn and wknd over 1f out* **5/2**2

5044 5 1¼ **Icy Blue**13 5341 5-8-7 52.................................(p) GeorgeChaloner(5) 5 50
(Richard Whitaker) *dwlt: t.k.h and towards rr: sme hdwy over 2f out: sn rdn and n.d* **14/1**

0456 6 ¾ **Conjuror's Bluff**34 4577 5-8-12 46..............................(p) JasonHart(3) 9 51
(Frederick Watson) *chsd ldrs: rdn along wl over 2f out: grad wknd* **80/1**

7 23 **Baby Mac** 5-9-2 0.. AdamCarter(5) 1
(Neville Bycroft) *s.i.s: a bhd* **33/1**

/000 8 3¼ **Regy From Sedgy**9 5469 6-8-11 30...............................(p) NeilFarley(3) 7
(Frederick Watson) *a towards rr: outpcd and bhd fnl 3f* **150/1**

1m 31.89s (-1.91) **Going Correction** +0.025s/f (Good) **8 Ran SP% 115.3**
Speed ratings (Par 103): **111,103,101,101,99 98,72,68**
toteswingers 1&2 £2.30, 1&3 £1.70, 2&3 £3.60 CSF £11.28 TOTE £2.50: £1.10, £1.80, £1.20; EX 11.00 Trifecta £29.80 Pool: £2,784.89 - 69.96 winning units..Balty Boys was claimed by Mr Brian Ellison for £15,000
Owner Dr Marwan Koukash **Bred** Lynn Lodge Stud **Trained** Upper Lambourn, Berks
FOCUS
The inside rail around bottom bend has been moved out to provide fresh ground increasing all races of 7f and beyond by 19yds. The track had largely missed the rain with just 6mm overnight but after winning the opener Joe Fanning reported it was riding "on the easy side of good". A good-class claimer and a very comfortable all-the-way winner.

5784 WOLD TOP BEER FESTIVAL HERE TODAY H'CAP 1m 100y
2:55 (2:55) (Class 4) (0-80,80) 3-Y-O £5,822 (£1,732; £865; £432) Stalls Low

Form RPR

020 1 **Polar Chief**25 4890 3-9-0 **80**.................................. JacobButterfield(7) 2 89
(Kristin Stubbs) *qckly away: mde all: rdn over 1f out: edgd lft ins fnl f: kpt on wl* **3/1**3

4233 2 2¼ **Simply Shining (IRE)**30 4729 3-9-2 **75**.......................(p) TonyHamilton 1 79
(Richard Fahey) *t.k.h: trckd ldrs on inner: hdwy 2f out: rdn over 1f out: drvn and kpt on fnl f* **11/4**2

1302 3 2¼ **Dream Wild**17 5202 3-9-5 **78**.. TomEaves 5 77
(Sir Michael Stoute) *trckd ldrs: effrt 2f out: sn rdn: drvn and kpt on same pce fnl f* **9/4**1

-300 4 2½ **Dutch Gal**73 3254 3-8-2 **61** oh3.. DuranFentiman 3 54
(John Holt) *hld up in rr: pushed along 3f out: swtchd lft to outer and rdn wl over 2f out: kpt on appr fnl f: nvr nr ldrs* **28/1**

1110 5 1¾ **Relight My Fire**15 5292 3-9-2 **75**......................................(b) DavidAllan 6 64
(Tim Easterby) *trckd ldrs: hdwy on outer to chse ldng pair 1/2-way: rdn wl over 1f out: edgd rt ent fnl f: wknd* **9/2**

050 6 4½ **Old Man Clegg**13 5342 3-8-9 **68**.................................(t) JamesSullivan 4 47
(Michael Easterby) *t.k.h: chsd wnr: hdwy and cl up 2f out: sn rdn: drvn and wknd over 1f out* **12/1**

2050 7 5 **Laudation**22 5016 3-8-5 **63** ow1.. AndrewElliott 8 31
(Danielle McCormick) *towards rr: effrt and sme hdwy wl over 2f out: sn rdn and wknd* **33/1**

1m 47.03s (-0.57) **Going Correction** +0.025s/f (Good) **7 Ran SP% 114.7**
Speed ratings (Par 102): **103,100,98,96,94 89,84**
toteswingers 1&2 £1.90, 1&3 £2.00, 2&3 £1.80 CSF £11.80 CT £20.95 TOTE £3.80: £1.50, £1.90; EX 14.30 Trifecta £28.40 Pool: £1,728.07 - 45.59 winning units..
Owner P & L Partners **Bred** J W Mitchell **Trained** Norton, N Yorks
FOCUS
Fair fillies' form.

5785 EBF OLD CROSSLEYANS RUGBY UNION FOOTBALL CLUB MEDIAN AUCTION MAIDEN STKS 1m 100y
3:30 (3:30) (Class 5) 2-Y-O £3,881 (£1,155; £577; £288) Stalls Low

Form RPR

3 1 **Jelly Fish**22 4997 2-9-5 0.. PaulMulrennan 3 77+
(Amanda Perrett) *prom: chsd ldr over 3f out: rdn to chal wl over 1f out: styd on to ld ins fnl f: drvn and kpt on strly towards fin* **2/1**2

55 2 1½ **Nakeeta**14 5309 2-9-5 0.. SamHitchcott 4 72
(Mick Channon) *t.k.h early: prom: led over 4f out: rdn wl over 1f out: drvn and hdd ins fnl f: no ex towards fin* **11/2**3

00 3 7 **Blue Talisman (IRE)**13 5338 2-9-5 0................................... DavidAllan 6 57
(Tim Easterby) *towards rr: pushed along 1/2-way: hdwy 2f out: sn rdn and styd on to take modest 3rd ins fnl f* **16/1**

4 1¼ **Mr Gallivanter (IRE)** 2-9-5 0...................................... MichaelO'Connell 1 55
(John Quinn) *towards rr: pushed along 1/2-way: rdn over 2f out: kpt on appr fnl f: n.d* **11/2**3

5 4½ **Galaxy (IRE)** 2-9-0 0.. ShirleyTeasdale(5) 7 45
(Alan McCabe) *s.i.s: a in rr* **20/1**

36 6 4 **Power Up**13 5330 2-9-0 0... JoeFanning 2 32
(Mark Johnston) *sn led: hdd over 4f out: rdn 3f out: sn drvn and wknd* **6/4**1

0 7 28 **Rising Rainbow**17 5180 2-9-5 0....................................... DuranFentiman 5
(Mel Brittain) *chsd ldrs: rdn along wl over 2f out: sn wknd* **66/1**

50 8 1¾ **Nabstarlini**14 5299 2-9-5 0...(b) PJMcDonald 8
(Ed Vaughan) *towards rr: rn wd bnd at 1/2-way: sn bhd* **66/1**

1m 47.37s (-0.23) **Going Correction** +0.025s/f (Good) **8 Ran SP% 117.7**
Speed ratings (Par 94): **102,100,93,92,87 83,55,54**
toteswingers 1&2 £2.90, 1&3 £4.40, 2&3 £7.80 CSF £13.84 TOTE £3.10: £1.50, £1.60, £3.70; EX 13.80 Trifecta £91.60 Pool: £2,279.52 - 18.64 winning units..
Owner K Abdullah **Bred** Millsec Limited **Trained** Pulborough, W Sussex

FOCUS
The first two finished clear in this extended one mile 2-y-o median auction maiden. The winner had a bit in hand with the runner-up rated a minor improver.

5786 BEVERLEY MIDDLE DISTANCE SERIES FINAL ROUND H'CAP 1m 4f 16y
4:05 (4:05) (Class 5) (0-75,75) 3-Y-0+ £5,175 (£1,540; £769; £384) Stalls Low

Form RPR
1550 1 **Tetbury (USA)**[17] 5185 4-10-0 75....(v) DavidNolan 1 86
(David O'Meara) *led 2f: cl up: led again 3f out: rdn clr wl over 1f out: styd on strly* 17/2
5142 2 4 ½ **King Kurt (IRE)**[11] 5384 5-9-7 75.... KevinStott(7) 4 79
(Kevin Ryan) *cl up: led after 2f: rdn along and hdd 3f out: drvn over 1f out: kpt on u.p fnl f: no ch w wnr* 5/1[2]
2510 3 1 ¼ **Danehill Flyer (IRE)**[47] 4135 3-9-1 72.... MichaelO'Connell 2 74
(Philip Kirby) *trckd ldrs on inner: hdwy wl over 2f out: rdn wl over 1f out: drvn and kpt on same pce appr fnl f* 9/4[1]
6013 4 hd **Flying Power**[11] 5384 5-10-0 75.... PaddyAspell 9 76
(John Norton) *trckd ldng pair: effrt wl over 2f out and sn rdn: drvn over 1f out: kpt on same pce* 14/1
3650 5 2 ½ **Valentine's Gift**[10] 5420 5-8-9 56 oh9.... DuranFentiman 8 53
(Neville Bycroft) *dwlt and in rr: hdwy on outer wl over 2f out: sn rdn: plugged on fnl 2f: nvr nr ldrs* 50/1
1-55 6 3 **Gosforth Park**[20] 5059 7-9-7 68.... DavidAllan 3 61
(Mel Brittain) *dwlt and towards rr: pushed along over 4f out: rdn 3f out: sme hdwy u.p fnl 2f: n.d* 13/2[3]
0120 7 4 ½ **Maybeme**[13] 5337 7-9-6 67....(p) AndrewElliott 7 52
(Neville Bycroft) *in tch: pushed along over 4f out: rdn 3f out: sn outpcd* 8/1
3321 8 7 **Golden Future**[16] 5241 10-8-7 59.... DavidBergin(5) 6 33
(Peter Niven) *in tch: rdn along over 3f out: sn wknd* 9/1
4-40 9 9 **Bourbon (IRE)**[19] 5110 3-9-4 75.... JoeFanning 5 35
(Mark Johnston) *chsd ldrs: rdn along over 4f out: wknd over 3f out* 5/1[2]
2m 38.86s (-0.94) **Going Correction** +0.025s/f (Good)
WFA 3 from 4yo+ 10lb 9 Ran SP% 117.7
Speed ratings (Par 103): **104,101,100,100,98 96,93,88,82**
toteswingers 1&2 £8.00, 1&3 £6.00, 2&3 £3.20 CSF £51.61 CT £129.66 TOTE £11.10: £3.30, £1.70, £1.20; EX 54.70 Trifecta £284.60 Pool: £2,212.26 - 5.82 winning units..
Owner Ebor Racing Club II **Bred** Juddmonte Farms Inc **Trained** Nawton, N Yorks

FOCUS
No hanging about here. The first two home were one-two throughout and the first four raced in the first four placings from start to finish.

5787 ANDREW LITTLE BUTCHERS OF HEDON NURSERY H'CAP (THE SUNDAY £5K BONUS RACE) 5f
4:40 (4:40) (Class 4) (0-85,83) 2-Y-0 £6,469 (£1,925; £962; £481) Stalls Low

Form RPR
324 1 **Captain Midnight (IRE)**[11] 5380 2-8-8 75.... ConnorBeasley(5) 2 81
(David Brown) *trckd ldng pair: hdwy 2f out: rdn to ld ent fnl f: styd on wl towards fin* 4/1[2]
321 2 2 ½ **Northern Water**[11] 5380 2-8-13 82.... JoeyHaynes(7) 7 79
(K R Burke) *hld up towards rr: hdwy on outer over 1f out: rdn and hung rt ent fnl f: kpt on same pce towards fin* 15/8[1]
6432 3 2 **Le Laitier (FR)**[16] 5215 2-8-7 69.... PJMcDonald 1 59
(Scott Dixon) *trckd ldrs on inner: hdwy over 1f out: sn rdn and kpt on same pce ins fnl f* 10/1
001 4 1 ¼ **Fuel Injection**[19] 5106 2-8-1 63.... JamesSullivan 4 48
(Paul Midgley) *qckly away and led: jnd 1/2-way: rdn wl over 1f out: drvn and hdd ent fnl f: sn wknd* 9/1
2210 5 ½ **Augusta Ada**[22] 5005 2-9-7 83.... PaulMulrennan 5 67
(Ollie Pears) *hld up in rr: hdwy 2f out: effrt and nt clr run over 1f out: swtchd lft and rdn whn n.m.r ent fnl f: one pce after* 11/2[3]
3213 6 3 ½ **Innocently (IRE)**[15] 5272 2-8-9 76.... DavidBergin(5) 6 47
(David O'Meara) *cl up: disp ld 1/2-way: rdn over 1f out: sn wknd* 7/1
5140 7 8 **Overstep (IRE)**[9] 5468 2-8-13 75.... JoeFanning 3 17
(Mark Johnston) *chsd ldrs: rdn 2f out: wknd over 1f out* 8/1
1m 2.5s (-1.00) **Going Correction** -0.275s/f (Firm) 7 Ran SP% 112.9
Speed ratings (Par 96): **97,93,89,87,87 81,68**
toteswingers 1&2 £2.00, 1&3 £7.90, 2&3 £4.40 CSF £11.62 TOTE £4.60: £2.20, £1.70; EX 12.30 Trifecta £95.60 Pool: £1,511.66 - 11.84 winning units..
Owner D A West **Bred** Tally-Ho Stud **Trained** Averham Park, Notts

FOCUS
The two leaders went off very fast in this quite valuable nursery. The winner improved and the second is rated to his recent course form.

5788 BEVERLEY LIONS H'CAP 5f
5:10 (5:10) (Class 6) (0-60,63) 3-Y-0 £2,385 (£704; £352) Stalls Low

Form RPR
0326 1 **Chloe's Dream (IRE)**[20] 5054 3-9-7 60.... PJMcDonald 8 68
(Ann Duffield) *t.k.h: cl up: led after 1 1/2f: rdn clr over 1f out: kpt on* 10/3[2]
3051 2 1 **Lucky Lodge**[9] 5485 3-9-10 63....(b) PaulMulrennan 3 67
(Mel Brittain) *towards rr: pushed along 1/2-way: swtchd rt and hdwy wl over 1f out: n.m.r and swtchd lft ent fnl f: rdn and kpt on towards fin* 3/1[1]
2-00 3 1 ¼ **Pearl Noir**[65] 3533 3-9-4 57....(t) TomEaves 4 57
(Scott Dixon) *led 1f: cl up: rdn along wl over 1f out: sn drvn and one pce fnl f* 11/2
4020 4 ½ **Fidget**[4] 5644 3-8-7 53....(b[1]) ClaireMurray(7) 5 51
(David Brown) *chsd ldrs: hdwy to chse wnr ent fnl f: sn hung rt: n.m.r and no ex towards fin* 8/1
6000 5 2 ½ **Robyn**[19] 5085 3-8-4 46 oh1....(p) BillyCray(3) 6 35
(Scott Dixon) *in tch: rdn to chse ldrs wl over 1f out: sn drvn and no imp* 14/1
2510 6 1 ¼ **Amelia Jay**[13] 5336 3-9-0 53.... AndrewElliott 2 38
(Danielle McCormick) *a towards rr* 4/1[3]
-000 7 2 ¼ **Shatin Secret**[20] 5067 3-9-1 57....(b[1]) JasonHart(3) 7 34
(Noel Wilson) *a towards rr* 12/1
504 8 2 ¾ **Time For Crabbies (IRE)**[27] 4839 3-9-2 58.... MarkCoumbe(3) 1 25
(Lisa Williamson) *chsd ldrs: rdn along over 2f out: sn wknd* 11/1
1m 3.28s (-0.22) **Going Correction** -0.275s/f (Firm) 8 Ran SP% 117.3
Speed ratings (Par 98): **90,88,86,85,81 79,76,71**
toteswingers 1&2 £3.70, 1&3 £3.20, 2&3 £3.10 CSF £14.22 CT £53.72 TOTE £4.10: £1.10, £1.60, £2.20; EX 15.70 Trifecta £84.50 Pool: £1,379.99 - 12.24 winning units..
Owner Middleham Park Racing XL **Bred** Maurice Burns **Trained** Constable Burton, N Yorks

5789 CONSTANT SECURITY H'CAP 1m 1f 207y
5:40 (5:40) (Class 6) (0-65,72) 3-Y-0 £2,264 (£673; £336; £168) Stalls Low

Form RPR
0553 1 **Woodstock (IRE)**[22] 4995 3-9-5 63.... DaleSwift 2 71
(Brian Ellison) *hld up in rr: hdwy on wd outside over 2f out: rdn to chse ldrs over 1f out: styd on to ld last 100yds: drvn out* 3/1[1]
0000 2 nk **Noosa Sound**[34] 4587 3-8-4 48 oh1 ow2....(t[1]) RoystonFfrench 9 55
(John Davies) *chsd ldrs: rdn along over 2f out: swtchd lft to outer and drvn over 1f out: styd on to chal ins fnl f: ev ch tl no ex nr fin* 50/1
3461 3 2 ½ **Lisa's Legacy**[11] 5403 3-10-0 72.... PaulMulrennan 1 74+
(Daniel Kubler) *sn led: rdn wl over 1f out: drvn ent fnl f: hdd and no ex last 100yds* 3/1[1]
4624 4 ¾ **Qibtee (FR)**[11] 5391 3-9-3 61.... SamHitchcott 8 62
(Mick Channon) *hld up towards rr: hdwy on inner 2f out: effrt and n.m.r over 1f out: rdn to chse ldrs ent fnl f: sn drvn and one pce* 17/2
3543 5 1 ¼ **War Lord (IRE)**[9] 5497 3-9-4 62.... DavidNolan 4 60
(David O'Meara) *trckd ldng pair on inner: hdwy over 2f out: swtchd lft and rdn to chse ldr over 1f out: drvn and wknd ent fnl f* 4/1[2]
233 6 9 **Primary Route (IRE)**[48] 4118 3-9-1 59.... AndrewMullen 3 39
(David Barron) *hld up in rr: hdwy wl over 2f out: rdn wl over 1f out: n.d* 5/1[3]
0033 7 1 ½ **Inovate (IRE)**[23] 4955 3-8-2 46....(bt) DuranFentiman 6 23
(Tim Easterby) *trckd ldrs: effrt over 2f out and sn rdn: drvn wl over 1f out: sn wknd* 18/1
56 8 15 **Continental Divide (IRE)**[59] 3735 3-9-7 65.... TonyHamilton 5 12
(Jamie Osborne) *cl up: rdn wl over 2f out: sn wknd* 14/1
6-05 9 18 **Shagwa (IRE)**[10] 5425 3-8-9 53.... JoeFanning 7
(Mark Johnston) *in tch: rdn along over 3f out: sn wknd* 12/1
2m 7.88s (0.88) **Going Correction** +0.025s/f (Good) 9 Ran SP% 118.8
Speed ratings (Par 98): **97,96,94,94,93 85,84,72,58**
toteswingers 1&2 £16.70, 1&3 £4.30, 2&3 £14.90 CSF £151.16 CT £497.18 TOTE £4.10: £1.40, £4.90, £1.40; EX 218.40 Trifecta £895.60 Pool: £1,194.16 - 0.91 winning units..
Owner Ian Hamilton **Bred** Butlersgrove Stud **Trained** Norton, N Yorks
■ Stewards' Enquiry : Royston Ffrench four-day ban: used whip above permitted level (Sep 8-11)

FOCUS
They went off very strong and the first two home both came wide from off the pace.
T/Plt: £23.30 to a £1 stake. Pool: £75,255.87 - 2,355.89 winning units T/Qpdt: £5.50 to a £1 stake. Pool: £4,451.40 - 594.70 winning units JR

5737 GOODWOOD (R-H)
Sunday, August 25

OFFICIAL GOING: Good (good to soft in places on straight course; 7.4)
Wind: Moderate; half behind Weather: Fine

5790 FAIRGROUND MAIDEN AUCTION STKS 1m
2:10 (2:10) (Class 5) 2-Y-0 £3,234 (£962; £481; £240) Stalls Low

Form RPR
03 1 **What About Carlo (FR)**[9] 5472 2-8-13 0.... WilliamBuick 7 83+
(Eve Johnson Houghton) *led 1f: trckd ldr: led again over 2f out: edgd rt but 2 l clr over 1f out: shkn up and styd on* 4/1[2]
63 2 1 ¼ **Juan Alonso (IRE)**[10] 5442 2-9-0 0.... RyanMoore 1 77
(Richard Hannon) *prom: shkn up to chse wnr wl over 1f out: styd on but no imp last 100yds* 4/1[2]
534 3 2 ¼ **Needless Shouting (IRE)**[29] 4756 2-8-9 67.... MartinHarley 10 67
(Mick Channon) *t.k.h: trckd ldrs: chsd ldng pair over 1f out: no imp* 8/1
4 ½ **Softly She Treads (IRE)** 2-8-3 0.... JemmaMarshall(3) 2 63+
(Pat Phelan) *dwlt: in tch towards rr: prog to chse ldrs 2f out: pushed along and kpt on one pce after* 50/1
5 hd **Castle Combe (IRE)** 2-8-12 0.... MartinDwyer 8 68+
(Marcus Tregoning) *dwlt: hld up in last pair: prog 2f out: pushed along over 1f out: kpt on but no imp fnl f: nt disgracd* 16/1
6 1 **Fun Mac (GER)** 2-8-13 0.... RobertHavlin 6 67
(Hughie Morrison) *dwlt: towards rr: pushed along over 2f out: prog over 1f out: one pce fnl f* 12/1
5 7 nk **Crystal Nymph (IRE)**[10] 5442 2-8-9 0.... RichardHughes 11 62+
(Richard Hannon) *hld up in last trio: asked for effrt 2f out: no hdwy tl styd on fnl f* 7/2[1]
8 1 ¼ **Skaters Waltz (IRE)** 2-8-10 0.... AshleyMorgan(3) 5 63
(Paul Cole) *slowly away and awkward s: mostly in last pair and rn green: sme hdwy 2f out: outpcd over 1f out* 18/1
9 ½ **Elysian Prince** 2-8-12 0.... DavidProbert 9 61
(Paul Cole) *in tch in midfield: pushed along over 2f out: lost pl sn after: one pce fnl f* 22/1
0 10 ¾ **Mariners Moon (IRE)**[45] 4218 2-9-0 0.... FrannyNorton 3 62
(Mark Johnston) *led after 1f to over 2f out: wknd qckly over 1f out* 11/2[3]
04 11 1 **Polar Express**[18] 5151 2-8-5 0.... MatthewLawson(5) 4 55
(Jonathan Portman) *t.k.h: trckd ldrs: rdn 2f out: sn wknd* 25/1
00 12 3 **Assoluta (IRE)**[18] 5131 2-8-8 0.... SeanLevey 12 46
(Sylvester Kirk) *nvr bttr than midfield: wknd over 2f out* 66/1
1m 40.69s (0.79) **Going Correction** -0.05s/f (Good) 12 Ran SP% 119.2
Speed ratings (Par 94): **94,92,90,90,89 88,88,87,86,86 85,82**
toteswingers 1&2 £3.10, 1&3 £6.40, 2&3 £5.50 CSF £19.84 TOTE £4.30: £1.70, £1.70, £2.90; EX 11.80 Trifecta £117.80 Pool: £2,785.36 - 17.72 winning units..
Owner Anthony Pye-Jeary & the late Mel Smith **Bred** Earl Haras Du Logis & J Ince **Trained** Blewbury, Oxon

FOCUS
Following rain overnight and a spot or two in the morning the ground was good, good to soft in places on the straight course (GoingStick 7.3) and good on the round course. There might not have been much strength in depth to this maiden, and few got into it. The third helps with the level.

5791 GOODWOOD REVIVAL (S) STKS 1m 3f
2:45 (2:45) (Class 4) 3-Y-0 £6,469 (£1,925; £962; £481) Stalls Low

Form RPR
2164 1 **Bee Jay Kay**[10] 5448 3-8-12 71.... MartinHarley 1 67+
(Mick Channon) *hld up in last pair: smooth prog 3f out: led over 1f out: clr whn shkn up briefly ins fnl f* 10/11[1]
4-0 2 3 ½ **Estinaad (USA)**[20] 5065 3-8-7 66.... SilvestreDeSousa 5 55
(Brian Ellison) *chsd ldr to 5f out: hrd rdn 3f out: kpt on one pce to take 2nd again last 100yds* 5/2[2]
4363 3 1 ¼ **Suspension**[32] 4625 3-8-7 51....(t) RobertHavlin 3 53
(Hughie Morrison) *racd freely: led and clr early: shkn up and hdd over 1f out: wknd fnl f* 16/1

0-06 **4** *2½* **Zinnobar**[6] 5586 3-8-7 38 RichardKingscote 2 49?
(Jonathan Portman) *cl up: chsd ldr 5f out to 3f out: fdd u.p* **33/1**

3055 **5** *46* **Yorkshireman (IRE)**[29] 4753 3-8-12 67 (p) RichardHughes 4
(David Brown) *hld up in last pair: rdn and wknd over 3f out: eased and t.o fnl 2f* **9/2**[3]

2m 26.68s (0.18) **Going Correction** -0.05s/f (Good) **5** Ran SP% **108.0**
Speed ratings (Par 102): **97,94,93,91,58**
CSF £3.23 TOTE £1.60: £1.10, £1.60; EX 3.00 Trifecta £10.60 Pool: £2,835.32 - 200.07 winning units..The winner was bought by Kristian Strangeway for 17,500gns
Owner M Channon **Bred** Mike Channon Bloodstock Ltd **Trained** West Ilsley, Berks

FOCUS
An uncompetitive seller.

5792 KATIE TAYLOR H'CAP 1m 1f 192y
3:20 (3:20) (Class 2) (0-100,96) 3-Y-O
£12,450 (£3,728; £1,864; £932; £466; £234) **Stalls** Low

Form RPR

3215 **1** **Circus Turn (USA)**[36] 4537 3-8-9 **84** RyanMoore 1 94
(Sir Michael Stoute) *mde all: hrd pressed fr 2f out: drvn and hld on wl fnl f* **11/1**

1262 **2** *hd* **Aussie Reigns (IRE)**[24] 4917 3-9-0 **89** (v) FrankieDettori 9 98
(William Knight) *hld up in last trio: stdy prog jst over 2f out: drvn and r.o fnl f: tk 2nd last strides: jst failed* **10/1**

4015 **3** *hd* **Code Of Honor**[24] 4917 3-9-7 **96** RichardHughes 8 105
(Henry Candy) *hld up in last trio: stdy prog jst over 2f out: chsd wnr jst over 1f out: chal fnl f: styd on but hld and lost 2nd last strides* **4/1**[2]

-312 **4** *1¾* **Rhombus (IRE)**[21] 5030 3-8-7 **82** NickyMackay 2 88
(Ismail Mohammed) *trckd ldng pair: pressed wnr over 2f out to jst over 1f out: fdd and hung lft ins fnl f* **15/2**

1 **5** *1½* **Groundbreaking**[22] 4978 3-9-0 **89** SilvestreDeSousa 10 92+
(Charlie Appleby) *t.k.h and trapped out wd early: restrained into last trio after 3f: pushed along and no prog in last 3f out: passed btn rivals fnl f* **11/4**[1]

2616 **6** *½* **Broughton (GER)**[15] 5258 3-9-3 **92** FrannyNorton 5 94
(Mark Johnston) *hld up in midfield: rdn and no prog jst over 2f out: fdd over 1f out* **9/2**[3]

5030 **7** *hd* **Fehaydi**[29] 4743 3-9-1 **90** (p) SteveDrowne 3 91
(William Haggas) *mostly chsd wnr to over 2f out: fdd over 1f out* **8/1**

1004 **8** *1¾* **Pasaka Boy**[17] 5189 3-8-10 **85** RichardKingscote 7 83
(Jonathan Portman) *chsd ldrs: shoved along 3f out: lost pl and btn 2f out* **16/1**

-362 **9** *hd* **Mr Fitzroy (IRE)**[46] 4168 3-8-2 **77** oh3 (p) DavidProbert 4 74
(Andrew Balding) *wl in tch: cl enough 2f out: sn rdn and wknd* **20/1**

2m 8.62s (0.52) **Going Correction** -0.05s/f (Good) **9** Ran SP% **115.8**
Speed ratings (Par 106): **95,94,94,93,92 91,91,90,89**
toteswingers 1&2 £7.40, 1&3 £8.00, 2&3 £8.10 CSF £114.92 CT £519.27 TOTE £10.50: £3.00, £2.10, £1.50; EX 112.80 Trifecta £711.80 Pool: £3,411.30 - 3.59 winning units..
Owner The Queen **Bred** Darley **Trained** Newmarket, Suffolk

FOCUS
This looked a decent, competitive handicap.

5793 GOODWOOD AMATEUR RIDER CHALLENGE H'CAP (IN MEMORY OF THE LATE GAY KINDERSLEY) 1m 1f
3:55 (3:56) (Class 5) (0-75,74) 4-Y-0+ **£6,239** (£1,935; £967; £484) **Stalls** Low

Form RPR

2146 **1** **Automotive**[21] 5032 5-10-6 **56** MrRossBirkett 2 69
(Julia Feilden) *prom: chsd ldr over 2f out: lft in ld over 1f out: pushed out: comf* **12/1**

1624 **2** *2½* **Frozen Over**[24] 4908 5-11-10 **74** MrMarioBaratti 12 81+
(Stuart Kittow) *hld up in rr and sn wl off the pce: gd prog wl over 2f out: chsd wnr over 1f out: styd on but no imp* **7/1**

1431 **3** *1¼* **Hector's Chance**[9] 5479 4-11-2 **66** MissSBrotherton 3 70
(Heather Main) *taken to post v early: s.s: rcvrd to chse ldrs: rdn 2f out: outpcd over 1f out: kpt on* **5/1**[1]

46-0 **4** *½* **Haymarket**[13] 5337 4-10-7 **62** MrAlexFerguson(5) 1 65
(Michael Bell) *prom: chsd ldr 1/2-way to over 2f out: outpcd after* **14/1**

4435 **5** *½* **Catchanova (IRE)**[5] 5615 6-10-2 **57** MrDLevey(5) 4 59
(Eve Johnson Houghton) *led: 2 l clr whn hung bdly lft jst over 2f out: hdd over 1f out: nt rcvr* **9/1**

0300 **6** *6* **Bountiful Girl**[10] 5427 4-10-6 **63** MrAFrench(7) 7 52
(Neville Bycroft) *t.k.h: trckd ldrs: rdn and lost tch fr 3f out* **40/1**

-302 **7** *¾* **Elsie Bay**[9] 5479 4-11-1 **65** MissEJJones 6 52
(J S Moore) *tried to chse ldrs but sn shoved along in 8th and nt on terms: nvr able to cl* **10/1**

0540 **8** *½* **Robin Hood (IRE)**[46] 4166 5-11-3 **70** MrFMitchell(3) 13 56
(Philip Mitchell) *hld up and sn wl off the pce in rr gp: rdn 4f out: nvr on terms* **13/2**[3]

1103 **9** *nse* **Balmoral Castle**[9] 5479 4-10-12 **67** MrJHarding(5) 8 53
(Jonathan Portman) *tried to chse ldrs but lost tch after 4f: struggling and nvr on terms after* **6/1**[2]

3462 **10** *2½* **Lady Sylvia**[13] 5346 4-10-12 **65** MrChrisMartin(3) 14 45
(Joseph Tuite) *sn wl off the pce in rr gp: nvr a factor* **16/1**

01 **11** *2¾* **Evergreen Forest (IRE)**[111] 2089 5-10-9 **66** (p) MrDPCostello(7) 10 40
(Natalie Lloyd-Beavis) *sn wl off the pce in rr gp: nvr a factor* **20/1**

1142 **12** *9* **All Or Nothin (IRE)**[14] 5301 4-11-5 **74** MissMBryant(5) 9 29
(Paddy Butler) *sn wl off the pce in rr gp: nvr a factor: t.o* **33/1**

4620 **13** *1½* **Tartan Trip**[19] 5099 6-10-12 **62** (p) MikeyEnnis 15 13
(Luke Dace) *chsd ldr to 1/2-way: wknd rapidly 3f out: t.o* **33/1**

3221 **14** *5* **Whinging Willie (IRE)**[17] 5171 4-11-1 **68** (v) MissHayleyMoore(3) 11 8
(Gary Moore) *restrained into last sn after s: sddle slipped bef 1/2-way and t.o after* **9/1**

1m 56.38s (0.08) **Going Correction** -0.05s/f (Good) **14** Ran SP% **119.2**
Speed ratings (Par 103): **97,94,93,93,92 87,86,86,86,84 81,73,72,67**
toteswingers 1&2 £15.40, 1&3 £14.00, 2&3 £7.90 CSF £89.37 CT £495.22 TOTE £15.40: £4.50, £2.40, £2.40; EX 152.90 Trifecta £855.30 Pool: £3,262.77 - 2.86 winning units..
Owner Stowstowquickquickstow Partnership **Bred** Juddmonte Farms Ltd **Trained** Exning, Suffolk

FOCUS
They went a decent gallop in this amateur riders' event.

5794 GREENE KING SUPREME STKS (GROUP 3) 7f
4:30 (4:32) (Class 1) 3-Y-O+
£34,026 (£12,900; £6,456; £3,216; £1,614; £810) **Stalls** Low

Form RPR

0431 **1** **Lockwood**[22] 5013 4-9-0 108 SilvestreDeSousa 1 113
(Saeed bin Suroor) *hld up in rr: prog on inner over 2f out: rdn to chse ldr over 1f out: clsd to ld last 100yds: styd on wl* **4/1**[2]

32 **2** *½* **Boom And Bust (IRE)**[10] 5446 6-9-0 108 MartinDwyer 4 111
(Marcus Tregoning) *trckd ldr: led wl over 2f out: drvn over 1f out: hdd last 100yds: styd on* **7/1**[3]

1103 **3** *nk* **Professor**[10] 5446 3-8-9 110 RichardHughes 2 108
(Richard Hannon) *hld up in last trio: prog on wd outside fr 2f out: drvn and r.o fnl f: gaining at fin* **11/4**[1]

2300 **4** *1¾* **Pastoral Player**[26] 4856 6-9-0 109 JimCrowley 9 105
(Hughie Morrison) *stdd s: hld up in last: prog 2f out: hrd rdn to chse ldrs 1f out: one pce after* **10/1**

4106 **5** *2¼* **Well Acquainted (IRE)**[23] 4945 3-8-9 106 SteveDrowne 5 97
(Clive Cox) *prom: chsd ldr 2f out to over 1f out: wknd ins fnl f* **20/1**

0020 **6** *2¾* **Penitent**[68] 3419 7-9-0 115 WilliamBuick 8 92
(David O'Meara) *in tch: rdn over 2f out: no prog wl over 1f out: fdd* **11/4**[1]

0 **7** *¾* **Bronze Prince**[26] 4859 6-9-0 89 RobertHavlin 3 90
(Michael Attwater) *led at gd pce: hdd wl over 2f out: short of room on inner 2f out: wknd* **100/1**

1264 **8** *1* **Custom Cut (IRE)**[10] 5453 4-9-4 108 (p) MartinHarley 7 91
(George J Kent, Ire) *prom: drvn to dispute 3rd 2f out: wknd over 1f out* **25/1**

6045 **9** *9* **Libranno**[8] 5532 5-9-0 107 RyanMoore 6 63
(Richard Hannon) *chsd ldrs: rdn over 2f out: wknd qckly over 1f out: t.o* **8/1**

1m 24.19s (-2.81) **Going Correction** -0.05s/f (Good)
WFA 3 from 4yo+ 5lb **9** Ran SP% **115.6**
Speed ratings (Par 113): **114,113,113,111,108 105,104,103,93**
toteswingers 1&2 £5.10, 1&3 £2.50, 2&3 £4.10 CSF £31.34 TOTE £4.80: £1.80, £1.80, £1.50; EX 33.90 Trifecta £132.00 Pool: £4,475.36 - 25.41 winning units..
Owner Godolphin **Bred** Darley **Trained** Newmarket, Suffolk

FOCUS
This looked a pretty competitive Group 3 and a contested lead led to three of the first four coming from well off the pace, including the winner.

5795 GREENE KING FILLIES' STKS (H'CAP) (THE SUNDAY £5K BONUS RACE) 1m 4f
5:00 (5:03) (Class 3) (0-90,89) 3-Y-O+
£9,337 (£2,796; £1,398; £699; £349; £175) **Stalls** High

Form RPR

431 **1** **Miss Dashwood**[22] 5008 4-9-10 **85** FrederikTylicki 12 97
(James Fanshawe) *hld up in last: lost tch and pushed along 5f out: sed to run on 3f out: relentless prog after: urged along and maintained effrt to ld last stride* **7/1**[3]

6-31 **2** *nk* **Astonishing (IRE)**[53] 3957 3-9-4 **89** RyanMoore 9 101
(Sir Michael Stoute) *trckd ldr: led over 8f out: rdn over 2f out: kpt on fr over 1f out: hdd last stride* **9/4**[1]

4121 **3** *1* **Bantam (IRE)**[10] 5445 3-8-13 **84** FrankieDettori 6 94
(Ed Dunlop) *trckd ldng trio: rdn to chse ldr over 2f out: kpt on but nvr quite able to chal: lost 2nd ins fnl f* **4/1**[2]

3342 **4** *3* **Princess Caetani (IRE)**[19] 5095 4-9-9 **84** SilvestreDeSousa 10 90
(David Simcock) *s.s: hld up in rr: rdn and prog over 2f out: disp 3rd briefly 1f out: wknd* **14/1**

0352 **5** *4½* **Sweet Martoni**[22] 5001 3-8-0 **71** oh2 NickyMackay 13 69
(William Knight) *chsd ldng pair: rdn 3f out: steadily wknd fr 2f out* **28/1**

122 **6** *6* **Java Rose**[10] 5445 4-8-12 **73** RichardHughes 3 62
(Henry Candy) *led to over 8f out: rdn and lost 2nd over 2f out: heavily eased whn btn fnl f: sddle slipped* **4/1**[2]

3420 **7** *½* **Miss Cap Estel**[24] 4920 4-9-8 **83** DavidProbert 7 71
(Andrew Balding) *hld up in midfield: rdn and no prog 3f out: wknd 2f out* **14/1**

141 **8** *3½* **Astra Hall**[24] 4914 4-9-4 **79** JimCrowley 5 61
(Ralph Beckett) *wl in tch: rdn and no prog 3f out: wknd 2f out* **10/1**

0-00 **9** *6* **Creme Anglaise**[15] 5283 5-9-6 **84** WilliamTwiston-Davies(3) 8 57
(Michael Bell) *chsd ldr tl wknd over 3f out: bhd over 1f out* **16/1**

2m 36.6s (-1.80) **Going Correction** -0.05s/f (Good)
WFA 3 from 4yo+ 10lb **9** Ran SP% **115.0**
Speed ratings (Par 104): **104,103,103,101,98 94,93,91,87**
toteswingers 1&2 £3.20, 1&3 £5.20, 2&3 £2.80 CSF £23.02 CT £72.27 TOTE £7.70: £2.30, £1.40, £1.50; EX 23.90 Trifecta £108.50 Pool: £3,435.54 - 23.74 winning units..
Owner Helena Springfield Ltd **Bred** Meon Valley Stud **Trained** Newmarket, Suffolk

FOCUS
For much of the way Ryan Moore once again looked to have judged things perfectly in front and saved enough to ensure that Astonishing won on her handicap debut, but she was grabbed close home.

5796 AUGUST BANK HOLIDAY STKS (H'CAP) 5f
5:30 (5:30) (Class 5) (0-70,69) 3-Y-O+ **£3,234** (£962; £481; £240) **Stalls** High

Form RPR

5650 **1** **Alpha Delta Whisky**[26] 4860 5-9-4 **66** (v) MichaelJMMurphy(5) 1 74
(John Gallagher) *mde virtually all: drvn and pressed fnl f: a looked like holding on but all out at fin* **7/2**[3]

0241 **2** *hd* **Wooden King (IRE)**[11] 5388 8-9-12 **69** TomMcLaughlin 5 76
(Malcolm Saunders) *prom: pressed wnr 1/2-way: rdn to chal fnl f: a looked hld but styd on nr fin: jst failed* **7/1**

3625 **3** *1* **Hot Secret**[50] 4069 3-9-10 **69** DavidProbert 3 72
(Andrew Balding) *hld up in tch: prog to chse ldng pair wl over 1f out: tried to chal fnl f: styd on but no imp last 100yds* **3/1**[2]

53 **4** *3* **Beauty Pageant (IRE)**[18] 5155 6-9-2 **59** RyanMoore 7 52
(David Brown) *pressed wnr to 1/2-way: sn rdn: wknd jst over 1f out* **11/4**[1]

6525 **5** *2¾* **Charming (IRE)**[32] 4635 4-9-5 **62** (e) SteveDrowne 6 45
(Olivia Maylam) *chsd ldrs: rdn to go 3rd briefly 2f out: wknd over 1f out* **11/1**

000 **6** *¾* **Purford Green**[16] 5230 4-8-7 **50** oh5 (v[1]) RobertHavlin 9 30
(Michael Attwater) *urged along leaving stalls and early reminder: chsd ldrs to 1/2-way: sn lost tch* **25/1**

The Form Book Flat, Raceform Ltd, Compton, RG20 6NL.

-104 7 2 1/4 **Spray Tan**[31] 4654 3-9-3 **62**........ SeanLevey 4 34
(Tony Carroll) *slowly away: a in last pair: rdn and no prog over 2f out* **6/1**

57.5s (-2.70) **Going Correction** -0.45s/f (Firm)
WFA 3 from 4yo+ 2lb 7 Ran SP% **112.9**
Speed ratings (Par 103): **103,102,101,96,91 90,87**
toteswingers 1&2 £5.00, 1&3 £2.70, 2&3 £2.10 CSF £26.92 CT £80.05 TOTE £4.20: £2.40, £2.10; EX 29.10 Trifecta £68.60 Pool: £2,684.65 - 29.32 winning units..
Owner double-r-racing.com **Bred** Kentford Farm Stud Ltd **Trained** Chastleton, Oxon

FOCUS
A modest sprint handicap.
T/Jkpt: Not won. T/Plt: £45.30 to a £1 stake. Pool: £114,693.26 - 1,846.47 winning units T/Qpdt: £18.00 to a £1 stake. Pool: £6,615.62 - 270.65 winning units JN

5616 YARMOUTH (L-H)

Sunday, August 25

OFFICIAL GOING: Good (good to firm in places; 7.1)
Wind: Light; across Weather: Dry; bright spells

5797 BRITISH STALLION STUDS EBF MAIDEN FILLIES' STKS 6f 3y

2:00 (2:03) (Class 5) 2-Y-O **£2,911** (£866; £432; £216) **Stalls** Centre

Form RPR

1 **Sweet Acclaim (IRE)** 2-9-0 0........ PatCosgrave 3 83+
(Noel Quinlan) *chsd ldrs: effrt 2f out: ev ch and rdn over 1f out: led and edgd lft fnl 75yds: in command and eased cl home* **40/1**

43 2 1/2 **Sunrise Star**[63] 3605 2-9-0 0........ PatDobbs 1 80
(Lady Cecil) *hld up wl in tch in midfield: effrt and rdn to chal 2f out: led jst ins fnl f: hdd and one pce fnl 75yds* **6/4**[1]

002 3 2 1/4 **Sleepy Sioux**[10] 5421 2-9-0 76........ SebSanders 7 73
(David Elsworth) *led: rdn ent fnl 2f: hdd jst ins fnl f: 3rd and keeping on same pce whn short of room wl ins fnl f: no ex* **8/1**[3]

4 3 1/2 **Stroll On (IRE)** 2-9-0 0........ LukeMorris 11 63
(Rae Guest) *t.k.h: chsd ldr tl 2f out: 4th and outpcd over 1f out: no threat to ldrs but hld on to 4th fnl f* **33/1**

55 5 1/2 **More Aspen (USA)**[24] 4924 2-9-0 0........ AdamKirby 12 61
(Marco Botti) *hld up in tch towards rr: pushed along and sme hdwy over 1f out: rdn and kpt on ins fnl f: nvr trbld ldrs* **25/1**

6 nk **Two Smart (IRE)** 2-9-0 0........ MartinLane 8 60
(K R Burke) *t.k.h: hld up wl in tch in midfield: rdn ent fnl 2f: outpcd over 1f out: no threat to ldrs and one pce fnl f* **3/1**[2]

7 1/2 **Oxsana** 2-9-0 0........ LiamJones 5 59
(William Haggas) *s.i.s: sn in tch in midfield: rdn and outpcd ent fnl f: kpt on but no threat to ldrs fnl f* **16/1**

8 1 1/2 **Laughing Dove (IRE)** 2-9-0 0........ PaulHanagan 13 54
(William Haggas) *wl in tch in midfield: rdn: lost pl and rn green over 2f out: n.d but plugged on fnl f* **10/1**

9 1 1/2 **Katawi** 2-9-0 0........ JamieSpencer 4 50+
(Peter Chapple-Hyam) *stdd after s: hld up in tch in last trio: effrt and hdwy over 2f out: no imp u.p 2f out: wknd over 1f out* **10/1**

00 10 3/4 **Earthflight**[9] 5488 2-9-0 0........ WilliamCarson 6 48
(Philip McBride) *in tch in midfield: rdn and effrt over 2f out: outpcd u.p 2f out: wknd over 1f out* **100/1**

3 11 1 3/4 **Pieman's Girl**[89] 2744 2-8-11 0........ ThomasBrown(3) 10 42
(Anthony Carson) *hld up in tch in rr: rdn and no hdwy over 2f out: bhd over 1f out* **16/1**

12 2 1/2 **Emporium** 2-9-0 0........ J-PGuillambert 9 35
(Gary Harrison) *s.i.s: hld up in rr: rn green and rdn over 2f out: sn btn: bhd over 1f out* **66/1**

1m 12.45s (-1.95) **Going Correction** -0.325s/f (Firm) 12 Ran SP% **117.8**
Speed ratings (Par 91): **100,99,96,91,91 90,89,87,85,84 82,79**
toteswingers 1&2 £14.10, 1&3 £21.70, 2&3 £3.80 CSF £98.35 TOTE £66.40: £6.90, £1.10, £2.00; EX 193.20 Trifecta £995.60 Part won. Pool: £1,327.59 - 0.17 winning units..
Owner Mrs C Cashman **Bred** Rathbarry Stud **Trained** Newmarket, Suffolk
■ Stewards' Enquiry : Pat Cosgrave caution: careless riding.

FOCUS
Both bends and back straight dolled out 3m. This looked an open contest but three came nicely clear. A decent race with the second and third helping with the level.

5798 PETER CLARINGBOLD 60TH BIRTHDAY H'CAP 6f 3y

2:30 (2:31) (Class 5) (0-75,77) 3-Y-O+ **£2,587** (£770; £384; £192) **Stalls** Centre

Form RPR

3606 1 **Jungle Bay**[23] 4960 6-9-7 **72**........(b) LiamJones 6 81
(Jane Chapple-Hyam) *chsd ldr: rdn ent fnl 2f: led 1f out: styd on wl: rdn out* **5/1**[2]

210 2 1 3/4 **Diamondhead (IRE)**[27] 4837 4-9-10 **75**........ JamieSpencer 4 78
(Ed de Giles) *chsd ldrs: rdn 1/2-way: kpt on same pce u.p fnl f: wnt 2nd on post* **5/4**[1]

1104 3 nse **Amosite**[17] 5205 7-9-4 **69**........(v) PatDobbs 7 72
(J R Jenkins) *led: rdn: over 1f out: hung rt and hdd 1f out: one pce fnl f: lost 2nd on post* **10/1**

5620 4 1 **Rough Rock (IRE)**[11] 5406 8-8-7 **63** ow2........(p) RobertTart(5) 5 63
(Chris Dwyer) *in tch in midfield: dropped to rr but stl in tch 4f out: effrt 2f out: drvn over 1f out: kpt on fnl 100yds: nt trble ldrs* **10/1**

5600 5 hd **Aaranyow (IRE)**[22] 4999 5-8-0 **56** oh4........(t) NathanAlison(5) 1 55
(Clifford Lines) *stdd after s: hld up in tch in last pair: rdn and effrt to chse ldrs 2f out: no ex u.p 1f out: one pce after* **16/1**

0502 6 1/2 **Putin (IRE)**[8] 5522 5-8-13 **64**........(bt) LukeMorris 2 62
(Phil McEntee) *in tch in midfield: effrt u.p over 2f out: drvn and unable qck over 1f out: btn and one pce fnl f* **6/1**[3]

3412 7 3 3/4 **Big Wave (IRE)**[9] 5498 5-9-7 **77**........(t) TobyAtkinson(5) 3 63
(Alison Hutchinson) *dwlt: rcvrd to chse ldrs after 2f: effrt u.p over 2f out: btn over 1f out: wknd fnl f* **5/1**[2]

1m 11.52s (-2.88) **Going Correction** -0.325s/f (Firm) 7 Ran SP% **116.1**
Speed ratings (Par 103): **106,103,103,102,102 101,96**
toteswingers 1&2 £2.10, 1&3 £8.20, 2&3 £4.80 CSF £12.07 TOTE £7.80: £4.20, £1.10; EX 17.80 Trifecta £143.10 Pool: £1,663.01 - 8.71 winning units..
Owner S Brewster & Essex Racing Club **Bred** Stowell Hill Ltd & Major & Mrs R B Kennard **Trained** Dalham, Suffolk

FOCUS
A fair-looking contest but under 4l separated the first six home.

5799 SEAFOOD RESTAURANT GREAT YARMOUTH H'CAP 7f 3y

3:05 (3:05) (Class 4) (0-85,83) 3-Y-O+ **£4,690** (£1,395; £697; £348) **Stalls** Centre

Form RPR

4125 1 **Jonnie Skull (IRE)**[5] 5621 7-9-0 **71**........(vt) LukeMorris 7 79
(Phil McEntee) *mde all and racd against stands' rail: rdn over 1f out: styd on wl and in command fnl f* **10/1**

1025 2 1 1/4 **Fantasy Gladiator**[18] 5153 7-8-12 **69**........(p) PatCosgrave 5 74
(John Quinn) *swtchd rt sn after s: in tch in midfield: effrt to chse clr wnr wl over 1f out: styd on same pce fnl f* **11/1**

600 3 1 **Noble Citizen (USA)**[25] 4879 8-9-9 **80**........(b) MartinLane 4 82
(David Simcock) *s.i.s: in tch in rr of main gp: rdn 1/2-way: hdwy u.p to go 3rd 1f out: styd on: nvr trbld wnr* **6/1**[3]

0011 4 4 1/2 **Tevez**[17] 5205 8-9-0 **76**........(p) DannyBrock(5) 3 66
(Des Donovan) *s.i.s: wl off the pce in rr: rdn 1/2-way: sme hdwy over 2f out: no imp over 1f out: wnt modest wnt modest 4th 1f out: no imp after: nvr trbld ldrs* **7/1**

2033 5 2 3/4 **Magical Rose (IRE)**[26] 4865 3-8-8 **70**........(p) JimmyQuinn 1 51
(Paul D'Arcy) *t.k.h: chsd wnr tl over 5f out: chsd ldrs after: rdn and struggling 2f out: outpcd and btn over 1f out: wknd fnl f* **4/1**[2]

521 6 5 **Satwa Story**[20] 5069 3-9-7 **83**........ AhmedAjtebi 6 57
(Charlie Appleby) *t.k.h: chsd ldrs: wnt 2nd over 5f out tl wl over 1f out: sn wl btn: wknd over 1f out* **13/8**[1]

242 7 1 1/4 **Mr David (USA)**[55] 3906 6-9-12 **83**........(b) AdamKirby 2 56
(Jamie Osborne) *in tch in midfield: rdn 1/2-way: struggling and lost pl whn n.m.r 2f out: wknd over 1f out: eased ins fnl f* **8/1**

1m 24.42s (-2.18) **Going Correction** -0.325s/f (Firm)
WFA 3 from 6yo+ 5lb 7 Ran SP% **113.4**
Speed ratings (Par 105): **99,97,96,91,88 82,81**
toteswingers 1&2 £11.90, 1&3 £7.70, 2&3 £9.00 CSF £106.22 TOTE £11.50: £4.80, £5.70; EX 125.20 Trifecta £801.50 Pool: £2,208.92 - 2.06 winning units..
Owner Eventmaker Racehorses **Bred** Canice Farrell Jnr **Trained** Newmarket, Suffolk

FOCUS
A fair handicap in which the favourite disappointed.

5800 HOOFBEAT TOURS FILLIES' H'CAP 5f 43y

3:40 (3:40) (Class 5) (0-70,71) 3-Y-O+ **£2,587** (£770; £384; £192) **Stalls** Centre

Form RPR

2341 1 **Honeymoon Express (IRE)**[5] 5616 3-9-2 **71** 6ex..(p) ShelleyBirkett(7) 1 78
(Julia Feilden) *mde all: rdn over 1f out: edgd lft but styd on wl ins fnl f: hld on cl home* **5/2**[2]

0331 2 nk **Megaleka**[9] 5499 3-8-6 **59**........[1] RobertTart(5) 4 65
(Alan Bailey) *t.k.h: hld up in 3rd: chsd wnr 2f out tl ins fnl f: hung lft but chsd wnr again wl ins fnl f: clsng towards fin: nvr quite getting to wnr* **3/1**[3]

-231 3 1 1/4 **Blessing Box**[40] 4390 3-9-8 **70**........ TedDurcan 5 71
(Chris Wall) *stdd s: hld up in rr: effrt and rdn over 1f out: chsd wnr 1f out: edgd lft and no ex fnl 100yds: lost 2nd and wknd wl ins fnl f* **1/1**[1]

6000 4 6 **Lady Cricketer**[5] 5614 4-8-2 **51** oh6........(b) RosieJessop(3) 2 30
(Michael Squance) *chsd wnr tl stmbld and rdn ent fnl 2f: sn dropped to last and struggling: wknd over 1f out* **25/1**

1m 1.63s (-1.07) **Going Correction** -0.325s/f (Firm)
WFA 3 from 4yo 2lb 4 Ran SP% **107.4**
Speed ratings (Par 100): **95,94,92,82**
CSF £9.76 TOTE £4.40; EX 9.80 Trifecta £12.90 Pool: £1,382.05 - 80.14 winning units..
Owner Hoofbeats Ltd Racing Club **Bred** Stephanie Hanly **Trained** Exning, Suffolk

FOCUS
Only three of these four made serious appeal.

5801 HAPPY 30TH BIRTHDAY MICHELLE STEVENS H'CAP 1m 6f 17y

4:15 (4:15) (Class 6) (0-60,59) 3-Y-O+ **£1,940** (£577; £288; £144) **Stalls** Centre

Form RPR

000 1 **Filia Regina**[22] 4978 3-9-2 **59**........ JamieSpencer 2 81+
(Ed Dunlop) *stdd s: hld up in tch in rr: clsd to trck ldrs on bit 4f out: led and cantering ent fnl 2f: readily stretched clr fnl f: v easily* **9/4**[2]

5632 2 8 **Capriska**[26] 4867 4-9-5 **50**........ AdamKirby 1 55
(Willie Musson) *chsd ldr for 2f: in tch in 4th after: rdn and effrt over 3f out: drvn and styd on to chse clr wnr 1f out: sn brushed aside: plugged on* **6/1**[3]

-543 3 1 1/2 **Inherited**[17] 5203 3-9-2 **59**........ LukeMorris 4 62
(Sir Mark Prescott Bt) *led for 2f: chsd ldr after: rdn and ev ch 4f out: 2nd but brushed aside by wnr over 1f out: 3rd and plugged on same pce fnl f* **11/10**[1]

600 4 9 **Kattaf (IRE)**[79] 3059 3-8-6 **54**........(b[1]) TobyAtkinson(5) 5 44
(Marco Botti) *chsd ldrs: led and rdn 4f out: hdd ent fnl 2f: 4th and btn over 1f out: fdd fnl f* **8/1**

0654 5 43 **Jd Rockefeller**[16] 5217 3-8-2 **45**........(b) JimmyQuinn 3
(Paul D'Arcy) *stdd after s: hld up in last pair: rapid hdwy to ld 12f out: rdn and hdd 4f out: sn dropped out: t.o over 2f out* **16/1**

3m 6.71s (-0.89) **Going Correction** -0.125s/f (Firm)
WFA 3 from 4yo 12lb 5 Ran SP% **109.7**
Speed ratings (Par 101): **97,92,91,86,61**
CSF £15.07 TOTE £3.30: £1.60, £1.60; EX 9.80 Trifecta £20.60 Pool: £2,113.97 - 76.60 winning units..
Owner Lord Derby **Bred** Stanley Estate And Stud Co **Trained** Newmarket, Suffolk

5802 HOOFBEATS RACING CLUB H'CAP 1m 2f 21y

4:50 (4:50) (Class 5) (0-75,75) 3-Y-O+ **£2,587** (£770; £384; £192) **Stalls** Low

Form RPR

5-34 1 **Deserted**[22] 4978 3-9-5 **74**........ KirstyMilczarek 9 80+
(Luca Cumani) *dwlt: sn rcvrd to chse ldrs and t.k.h: rdn and chal 2f out: sustained duel w rival after tl forged ahd wl ins fnl f: hld on cl home* **10/3**[2]

0152 2 hd **Qanan**[26] 4865 4-9-11 **72**........ TedDurcan 5 78
(Chris Wall) *chsd ldr tl 6f out: chsd ldrs tl sltly outpcd u.p over 2f out: swtchd rt and rallied u.p to chse ldrs 1f out: ev ch fnl 100yds: wnt 2nd towards fin: hld cl home* **9/2**[3]

0423 3 1/2 **Batgirl**[18] 5152 6-8-13 **67**........ GeorgeBuckell(7) 7 72
(Martin Smith) *stdd s: hld up in tch in rr: effrt on outer and hanging lft over 1f out: hdwy to chal fnl 100yds: no ex u.p and hld towards fin* **25/1**

3202 4 nk **Running Deer (IRE)**[25] 4898 4-10-0 **75**........ PatDobbs 10 79
(Lady Cecil) *styd wd tl crossed to inner rail over 6f out: led: rdn over 3f out: battled on u.p: hdd over 1f out: stl ev ch tl no ex wl ins fnl f: lost 2 pls nr fin* **5/2**[1]

3515 **5** *nk* **The Ducking Stool**[18] 5144 6-8-13 **67**........................ ShelleyBirkett(7) 1 71
(Julia Feilden) *hld up in tch in last trio: rdn 3f out: hdwy on far rail rail over 1f out: chsd ldrs and nt clr run ins fnl f: switching rt fnl 150yds: gap opened and styd on nr fin: nt quite rch ldrs* **9/1**

0000 **6** *1 ¼* **El Massivo (IRE)**[16] 5234 3-8-7 **62**..[1] JimmyQuinn 4 63
(William Jarvis) *t.k.h: hld up in tch in last trio: swtchd rt and effrt 2f out: no imp tl styd on fnl 100yds: nvr trbld ldrs* **20/1**

3326 **7** *1 ½* **Strike Force**[11] 5384 9-8-10 **62**..................................(t) TobyAtkinson(5) 2 60
(Alison Hutchinson) *in tch in midfield: rdn over 3f out: outpcd u.p 2f out: swtchd rt 1f out: kpt on fnl f but no threat to ldrs* **40/1**

5052 **8** *2* **Mingun Bell (USA)**[17] 5195 6-10-0 **75**........................(p) JamieSpencer 6 69
(Ed de Giles) *styd wd tl crossed to inner rail over 6f out: chsd ldrs: wnt 2nd 6f out tl over 2f out: unable qck 1f out: one pce and btn whn hmpd ins fnl f: eased after* **8/1**

2400 **9** *shd* **Sunnybridge Boy (IRE)**[20] 5050 4-9-9 **70**.................. LukeMorris 3 64
(K R Burke) *in tch in midfield: drvn and unable qck over 3f out: outpcd and btn wl over 1f out: plugged on same pce after* **18/1**

2104 **10** *2 ¼* **Excellent Puck (IRE)**[86] 2827 3-9-3 **72**............................ AdamKirby 8 62
(Jamie Osborne) *styd wd tl swtchd lft after 2f: in tch in midfield: effrt to chal over 2f out: drvn and unable qck whn hmpd over 1f out: btn 1f out and wknd fnl f* **11/1**

2m 8.23s (-2.27) **Going Correction** -0.125s/f (Firm)
WFA 3 from 4yo+ 8lb **10** Ran SP% **115.6**
Speed ratings (Par 103): **104,103,103,103,102 101,100,99,99,97**
toteswingers 1&2 £4.30, 1&3 £12.30, 2&3 £25.40 CSF £18.13 CT £318.56 TOTE £4.50: £1.50, £2.10, £4.30; EX 24.30 Trifecta £258.70 Pool: £2,727.89 - 7.90 winning units..
Owner Fittocks Stud **Bred** Fittocks Stud **Trained** Newmarket, Suffolk
FOCUS
A competitive contest that produced a messy finish.

5803 WEDDINGS AT GREAT YARMOUTH RACECOURSE APPRENTICE H'CAP 1m 2f 21y

5:20 (5:20) (Class 6) (0-60,58) 4-Y-0+ **£1,940** (£577; £288; £144) **Stalls** Low

Form RPR

4603 **1** **Flash Crash**[12] 5377 4-9-2 **58**..........................(t) LouisSteward(5) 7 71
(Anthony Carson) *hld up towards rr: hdwy into midfield 1/2-way: chsd ldr over 3f out: led over 2f out: clr and r.o wl fnl f* **7/2[1]**

2560 **2** *4* **Cane Cat (IRE)**[22] 5002 6-9-4 **55**.................................(t) JackDuern 8 60
(Tony Carroll) *hld up in last pair: hdwy over 3f out: wnt 3rd over 2f out: rdn to chse clr wnr wl over 1f out: no imp: plugged on same pce fnl f* **4/1[2]**

0004 **3** *7* **Ela Goog La Mou**[9] 5492 4-8-5 **45**............................ GeorgeBuckell(3) 1 37
(Peter Charalambous) *awkward leaving stalls: sn bustled along to chse ldrs: led 8f out: rdn over 3f out: hdd over 2f out: 3rd and btn over 1f out: wknd fnl f* **7/1**

4104 **4** *nse* **Corn Maiden**[82] 2968 4-9-2 **58**............................ LewisWalsh(5) 4 50
(Lydia Pearce) *led for 2f: chsd ldr: rdn 4f out: lost 2nd over 3f out: 4th and wl btn over 1f out: plugged on and battling for modest 3rd fnl 100yds* **11/2**

2633 **5** *4 ½* **Elizabeth Coffee (IRE)**[18] 5143 5-9-2 **53**.................... DanielMuscutt 6 36
(John Weymes) *chsd ldrs: rdn and effrt over 3f out: no ex and btn over 2f out: wknd and wl btn 5th over 1f out* **5/1[3]**

166 **6** *9* **Entrance**[18] 5126 5-8-12 **49**..(p) ShelleyBirkett 2 15
(Julia Feilden) *dwlt: pushed along in rr and nvr travelling wl: rdn and effrt 4f out: sn btn: wl bhd fnl 2f* **8/1**

0330 **7** *9* **Market Puzzle (IRE)**[12] 5377 6-8-12 **49**......................(p) NoelGarbutt 5
(Mark Brisbourne) *chsd ldrs: rdn and struggling 4f out: sn btn: wl btn and eased wl over 1f out: t.o* **13/2**

0600 **8** *34* **Thecornishwren (IRE)**[5] 5622 4-8-3 **45**................(p) BradleyBosley(5) 9
(John Ryan) *in tch in midfield: dropped to rr 5f out: sn lost tch: t.o fnl 3f* **33/1**

2m 8.22s (-2.28) **Going Correction** -0.125s/f (Firm) **8** Ran SP% **114.2**
Speed ratings (Par 101): **104,100,95,95,91 84,77,49**
toteswingers 1&2 £4.40, 1&3 £3.10, 2&3 £6.20 CSF £17.55 CT £91.32 TOTE £4.00: £1.20, £2.00, £3.10; EX 21.30 Trifecta £133.40 Pool: £2,211.91 - 12.43 winning units..
Owner David J Newman & Ross Bennett **Bred** J R Furlong **Trained** Newmarket, Suffolk
FOCUS
Nothing more than a modest event.
T/Plt: £980.70 to a £1 stake. Pool: £74,358.76 - 55.35 winning units T/Qpdt: £324.50 to a £1 stake. Pool: £3,947.45 - 9.00 winning units SP

5778 BADEN-BADEN (L-H)

Sunday, August 25

OFFICIAL GOING: Turf: good

5804a GOLDENE PEITSCHE - POWERED BY BURDA@TURF (GROUP 2) (3YO+) (TURF) 6f

3:35 (3:52) 3-Y-0+

£32,520 (£12,601; £5,284; £3,252; £2,032; £1,219)

RPR

1 **Giant Sandman (IRE)**[24] 4936 6-9-4 0.......... LennartHammer-Hansen 1 109
(Rune Haugen, Norway) *fly-jmpd leaving stalls: racd far side: w ldr: rdn to ld over 2f out: drifted rt and then lft u.p but r.o strly and asserted: readily* **43/5**

2 *3* **Gammarth (FR)**[24] 4935 5-9-4 0............................... FredericSpanu 8 99+
(H-A Pantall, France) *racd in centre: towards rr: rdn over 2f out: r.o and wnt 2nd fnl strides: no real imp on wnr* **9/2[2]**

3 *nk* **Namera (GER)**[14] 4-9-1 0.. MircoDemuro 3 95
(W Haustein, Germany) *racd far side: led: rdn and hdd over 2f out: sn outpcd by wnr: r.o but dropped to 3rd fnl strides* **33/1**

4 *shd* **Amarillo (IRE)**[50] 4093 4-9-4 0.. AStarke 9 98+
(P Schiergen, Germany) *racd nr side: in midfield: rdn 2f out: r.o and wnt 4th cl home: fin strly but no ch w wnr* **13/5[1]**

5 *1 ½* **Best Regards (IRE)**[14] 3-8-11 0.. EPedroza 5 89+
(P Harley, Germany) *racd in centre: prom: rdn over 1f out: r.o but nvr able to chal* **5/1[3]**

6 *¾* **Khubala (IRE)**[21] 5027 4-9-4 0..................................(b) GeorgeBaker 7 91+
(Hugo Palmer) *racd in centre: in midfield: rdn over 2f out: r.o but nvr able to chal* **9/1**

7 *shd* **Flavio Forte (GER)**[14] 4-9-4 0.. CristianDemuro 2 90+
(U Stoltefuss, Germany) *racd far side: in midfield: rdn over 2f out: r.o but nvr able to chal* **34/1**

8 *1 ¼* **Smooth Operator (GER)**[28] 7-9-4 0...............................(b) ADeVries 13 86+
(Mario Hofer, Germany) *racd nr side: prom: rdn 2f out: styd hrd against nr side rail in st: nt qckn ins fnl f: kpt on* **121/10**

9 *3* **Fortune Hunter (FR)**[57] 3851 4-9-1 0............ Francois-XavierBertras 11 74+
(F Rohaut, France) *racd nr side: towards rr: rdn over 2f out: sn outpcd: nvr threatened* **189/10**

10 *½* **Kolonel (GER)**[28] 4-9-4 0.. HarryBentley 12 75+
(Mario Hofer, Germany) *racd nr side: prom: rdn over 2f out: sn outpcd and btn: fdd* **105/10**

11 *1 ½* **Clever Man**[379] 5118 5-9-4 0.. FilipMinarik 4 70+
(P Vovcenko, Germany) *racd in centre: in midfield: rdn over 2f out: sn outpcd and btn: fdd* **222/10**

12 *nk* **Zanetto**[43] 4298 3-9-1 0.. LiamKeniry 6 69+
(Andrew Balding) *racd in centre: a towards rr: rdn over 2f out: sn outpcd and btn: nvr a factor* **73/10**

13 *2* **Ferro Sensation (GER)**[28] 7-9-4 0.. SHellyn 10 63+
(D Klomp, Holland) *racd nr side: a in rr: rdn over 2f out: sn outpcd in last and btn: eased towards fin: nvr a factor* **27/1**

1m 9.22s (-1.07)
WFA 3 from 4yo+ 3lb **13** Ran SP% **130.1**
WIN (incl. 10 euro stake): 96. PLACES: 29, 23, 81. SF: 539.
Owner Sandman Stables **Bred** Barronstown Stud **Trained** Norway
FOCUS
Those drawn low had an advantage here.

5735 DEAUVILLE (R-H)

Sunday, August 25

OFFICIAL GOING: Turf: good to soft; fibresand: standard

5805a PRIX CASINO BARRIERE TROUVILLE (CONDITIONS) (3YO) (FIBRESAND) 1m 1f 110y

12:30 (12:00) 3-Y-0 **£9,756** (£3,902; £2,926; £1,951; £975)

RPR

1 **Lictus (FR)**[62] 3-9-5 0.. AntoineCoutier(3) 5 84
(F Rohaut, France) **15/2**

2 *½* **Murillo (FR)**[45] 3-8-13 0............................ AlexandreChampenois(3) 7 77
(J-M Beguigne, France) **19/1**

3 *3* **Agy (IRE)** 3-9-6 0.. GregoryBenoist 1 75
(J-C Rouget, France) **9/5[1]**

4 *½* **Roccarina (FR)**[19] 3-9-5 0.. FabriceVeron 3 73
(H-A Pantall, France) **7/2[2]**

5 *¾* **Le Deluge (FR)**[8] 5534 3-9-6 0............................ Pierre-CharlesBoudot 8 72
(John Best) *led after 1f grad moving ins fr wd draw: qcknd 2f out: rdn 1 1/2f out: hdd ent fnl f: no ex u.p* **53/10[3]**

6 *1* **Hurrican Source (IRE)**[79] 3-8-13 0.. UmbertoRispoli 2 63
(M Delzangles, France) **53/10[3]**

7 *1 ½* **Medecriss (FR)** 3-9-1 0..................................(b) MatthiasLauron(5) 6 67
(Y Durepaire, France) **11/1**

8 *dist* **Pirate Du Bresil (FR)** 3-8-11 0.. AnthonyCrastus 4
(J Rossi, France) **31/1**

1m 58.15s (118.15) **8** Ran SP% **117.9**
WIN (incl. 1 euro stake: 8.50. PLACES: 2.30, 4.20, 1.50. DF: 60.30. SF: 93.50.
Owner Raphael Verspieren **Bred** Mme Rene Geffroy **Trained** Sauvagnon, France

5806a PRIX DE MEAUTRY LUCIEN BARRIERE (GROUP 3) (3YO+) (TURF) 6f

2:08 (12:00) 3-Y-0+ **£32,520** (£13,008; £9,756; £6,504; £3,252)

RPR

1 **Myasun (FR)**[57] 3851 6-9-1 0.. OlivierPeslier 14 113
(C Baillet, France) *towards rr on outside: hdwy on outer 2f out: r.o u.p to ld fnl 100yds: drvn out* **12/1**

2 *nk* **Tulips (IRE)**[21] 5040 4-8-11 0.. MaximeGuyon 13 108
(A Fabre, France) *midfield towards outside: rdn 2 1/2f out: prog to ld 1 1/2f out: r.o u.p ins fnl f: hdd 100yds out: rallied but a hld* **5/2[1]**

3 *snk* **Dibajj (FR)**[45] 4274 3-8-8 0............................ Christophe-PatriceLemaire 15 108
(A De Royer-Dupre, France) *midfield: rdn and hdwy on outer to chse ldr 1 1/2f out: 2nd and ev ch ent fnl f: kpt on u.p between horses: no ex fnl 50yds* **16/1**

4 *½* **Morning Frost (IRE)**[24] 4935 3-8-8 0.. JulienAuge 12 106
(C Ferland, France) *towards rr: tk clsr order 3f out: chsd ldrs 1 1/2f out and short of room: swtchd ins over 1f out: styd on u.p fnl 150yds: nt pce to chal* **33/1**

5 *4* **Abu Sidra (FR)**[21] 5040 4-9-5 0............................ ChristopheSoumillon 16 101
(J-F Bernard, France) *broke wl fr wd draw and trckd ldng gp: 5th and pushed along over 1 1/2f out: nt qckn w ldrs appr 1f out: one pce and wl hld fnl f* **7/1[2]**

6 *snk* **Wedge Trust (IRE)**[26] 3-8-8 0.. IoritzMendizabal 4 93
(J-C Rouget, France) *awkward leaving stalls: towards rr: pushed along but short of room fr 2f out: swtchd outside and styd on u.p fnl f: nvr on terms* **14/1**

7 *2 ½* **Fred Lalloupet**[100] 6-9-1 0.. GregoryBenoist 11 89
(D Smaga, France) *chsd ldr on outer: 2nd and ev ch 2f out: sn rdn and nt qckn over 1f out: grad dropped away fnl f* **20/1**

8 *2* **A Huge Dream (IRE)**[24] 4935 4-8-11 0.. ThierryThulliez 3 78
(F Rohaut, France) *broke wl: disp ld on inner: hdd 1 1/2f out: wknd fr 1f out* **25/1**

9 *1 ¼* **Place In My Heart**[44] 4260 4-8-11 0.. GeraldMosse 6 74
(Clive Cox) *trckd ldrs: rdn 2 1/2f out: struggling whn squeezed out between horses over 1f out: eased ins fnl f* **10/1[3]**

10 *1 ¼* **American Devil (FR)**[21] 5040 4-9-1 0.. UmbertoRispoli 1 74
(J Van Handenhove, France) *broke wl and chsd ldrs: rdn over 1 1/2f out: no imp: eased ins fnl f* **7/1[2]**

11 *shd* **Mazameer (IRE)**[84] 2909 3-8-11 0..................................(b) ThierryJarnet 9 73
(F Head, France) *disp ld on outer: rdn over 2f out: wknd fr over 1 1/2f out* **14/1**

12 *½* **Galateia (IRE)**[49] 4105 3-8-8 0.. AntoineHamelin 10 68
(A De Royer-Dupre, France) *chsd ldng gp: rdn and outpcd fr over 1 1/2f out: wknd and eased fnl f* **20/1**

13 *¾* **Morache Music**[57] 3851 5-9-1 0.. Pierre-CharlesBoudot 5 70
(Peter Makin) *midfield: chsd ldrs appr 1/2-way: rdn and nt qckn over 2f out: btn whn eased ins fnl f* **7/1[2]**

14 ½ **Princedargent (FR)**21 5040 3-8-11 0 FabriceVeron 8 67
(H-A Pantall, France) *tk a t.k.h in midfield: rdn and wknd qckly over 1 1/2f out* **11/1**

15 ¾ **Gordol Du Mes (USA)**77 3-8-11 0 GBietolini 2 65
(Gianluca Bietolini, Italy) *chsd ldrs: rdn and outpcd over 1 1/2f out: wl btn whn eased ins fnl f* **50/1**

16 20 **Thyan (FR)**34 6-9-1 0 JimmyTastayre 7
(P Capelle, France) *a bhd: lost tch fr 1/2-way: t.o* **50/1**

1m 10.14s (-0.86) **Going Correction** +0.20s/f (Good)
WFA 3 from 4yo+ 3lb **16** Ran SP% **130.6**
Speed ratings: **113,112,112,111,106 106,102,100,98,96 96,96,95,94,93 66**
WIN (incl. 1 euro stake): 14.40. PLACES: 3.90, 1.80, 4.50. DF: 26.60. SF: 61.20.
Owner Ecurie Jarlan **Bred** Sarl Ecurie Jarlan **Trained** France

FOCUS
Those racing widest of the rail were heavily favoured.

5807a LUCIEN BARRIERE GRAND PRIX DE DEAUVILLE (GROUP 2) (3YO+) (TURF) 1m 4f 110y
2:40 (12:00) 3-Y-O+ **£92,682** (£35,772; £17,073; £11,382; £5,691)

RPR

1 **Tres Blue (IRE)**21 5041 3-8-6 0 FabriceVeron 1 115
(H-A Pantall, France) *trckd ldrs on inner: rdn over 2f out: swtchd off rail over 1f out and styd on to chal wl ins fnl f: drvn to ld fnl strides: jst hld on* **11/1**

2 hd **Penglai Pavilion (USA)**28 4815 3-8-6 0 MaximeGuyon 9 115
(A Fabre, France) *stmbld s: trckd ldrs on outer: 4th whn rdn 3f out: styd on to chal wl ins fnl f: wnt 2nd fnl strides: pressed wnr: jst failed* **5/2**2

3 snk **Slow Pace (USA)**21 5041 5-9-3 0 OlivierPeslier 8 114
(F Head, France) *led: set stdy pce: rdn 2f out: qckned clr over 1f out: styd on but grad worn down and strly pressed wl ins fnl f: hdd and dropped to 3rd fnl strides* **20/1**

4 1¾ **Very Nice Name (FR)**29 4745 4-9-3 0 PierantonioConvertino 11 112+
(A De Mieulle, France) *dwlt: dropped in fr wdst draw and hld up in rr: rdn over 2f out: styd on down wd outside and wnt 4th fnl strides: nvr nrr* **16/1**

5 nk **Cirrus Des Aigles (FR)**15 5298 7-9-6 0 ChristopheSoumillon 2 114
(Mme C Barande-Barbe, France) *prom early: stdd and settled in midfield on outer: hdwy to press ldr 6f out: rdn to chal 2f out: no ex ent fnl f: fdd and dropped to 5th fnl strides* **2/1**1

6 2½ **Haya Landa (FR)**63 3615 5-9-0 0 FranckBlondel 3 104+
(Mme L Audon, France) *sltly slow to stride and pushed along early: midfield on inner: rdn 3f out: outpcd by ldrs over 1f out: styd on and wnt 6th towards fin* **12/1**

7 hd **Donn Halling (IRE)**35 4571 5-9-3 0 UmbertoRispoli 6 107+
(V Luka Jr, Czech Republic) *hld up towards rr on outer: hdwy into midfield 5f out: rdn 3f out: outpcd by ldrs over 1f out: styd on but dropped to 7th towards fin* **50/1**

8 1½ **First Mohican**21 5041 5-9-3 0 TomQueally 5 104+
(Lady Cecil) *dwlt and pushed along to rcvr: hld up towards rr on inner: rdn over 2f out: outpcd in st: plugged on u.p but nvr threatened* **12/1**

9 ¾ **Now We Can**84 2908 4-9-6 0 ThierryThulliez 10 106+
(N Clement, France) *hld up in rr: last 5f out: rdn over 2f out: sn outpcd: plugged on u.p but nvr a factor* **13/2**3

10 3½ **Singing (FR)**43 4325 3-8-6 0 FlavienPrat 7 98+
(C Laffon-Parias, France) *prom on outer: shuffled bk into midfield over 5f out: rdn over 2f out: outpcd and btn ent fnl f: fdd and eased towards fin* **11/1**

11 12 **Kapour (IRE)**41 4362 3-8-6 0 ThierryJarnet 4 78+
(F Rohaut, France) *t.k.h: hld up in tch: rdn and dropped to last over 2f out: sn bhd and btn: eased* **20/1**

2m 44.49s (-1.91) **Going Correction** +0.20s/f (Good)
WFA 3 from 4yo+ 10lb **11** Ran SP% **124.7**
Speed ratings: **113,112,112,111,111 109,109,108,108,106 98**
WIN (incl. 1 euro stake): 12.00. PLACES: 3.00, 1.70, 4.40. DF: 18.50. SF: 52.50.
Owner Horst Rapp **Bred** Chevotel De La Hauquerie **Trained** France

FOCUS
The first three and fifth were never far off the pace in a race not run at a strong gallop.

5808a PRIX QUINCEY LUCIEN BARRIERE (GROUP 3) (3YO+) (TURF) 1m (R)
3:10 (12:00) 3-Y-O+ **£32,520** (£13,008; £9,756; £6,504; £3,252)

RPR

1 **Fire Ship**23 4946 4-9-0 0 NeilCallan 8 107
(William Knight) *t.k.h under restraint early: w ldr: allowed to stride on and led after 2f: mde rest: rdn 2f out: strly pressed fr over 1f out: r.o strly: drvn out and jst hld on* **9/1**

2 snk **Belgian Bill**43 4297 5-9-0 0 (p) GeraldMosse 5 107+
(George Baker) *t.k.h: hld up in tch: rdn 2f out: r.o and wnt 2nd fnl strides: nt quite rch wnr* **12/1**

3 snk **Spoil The Fun (FR)**50 4093 4-9-0 0 JulienAuge 4 106
(C Ferland, France) *hld up in rr: hdwy into midfield over 3f out: rdn 2f out: r.o to chal and wnt 2nd ins fnl f: hld by wnr and dropped to 3rd fnl strides* **6/1**3

4 shd **Pinturicchio (IRE)**55 3913 5-9-0 0 AnthonyCrastus 2 106
(E Lellouche, France) *prom early: settled in midfield in tch: rdn 2f out: r.o: nrst fin* **14/1**

5 snk **High Spirit (IRE)**17 3-8-8 0 GregoryBenoist 1 105
(Mme Pia Brandt, France) *hld up in rr: rdn 2f out: r.o: nrst fin* **16/1**

6 ½ **Dragon Falls (IRE)**23 4-9-0 0 MaximeGuyon 6 105
(A Fabre, France) *plld hrd: trckd ldr: rdn 2f out: nt qckn: kpt on* **6/1**3

7 1¼ **Dastarhon (IRE)**84 2907 3-8-10 0 UmbertoRispoli 9 103
(Mme Pia Brandt, France) *dwlt sltly: hld up: rdn over 2f out: sn outpcd: kpt on and wnt 7th post but nvr threatened* **13/2**

8 hd **Silas Marner (FR)**21 5040 6-9-6 0 ChristopheSoumillon 3 107
(J-C Rouget, France) *t.k.h: led 2f: hdd and trckd ldr: rdn to chal over 1f out: ev ch tl no ex wl ins fnl f: fdd and lost multiple pls towards fin* **4/1**2

9 12 **Mainsail**49 4104 4-9-6 0 ThierryThulliez 7 80
(P Bary, France) *plld hrd: midfield in tch: hdwy to trck ldr 1/2-way: rdn over 2f out: no ex and btn over 1f out: fdd and dropped to last ins fnl f: eased and t.o* **9/4**1

1m 39.7s (-1.10) **Going Correction** +0.20s/f (Good)
WFA 3 from 4yo+ 6lb **9** Ran SP% **122.9**
Speed ratings: **113,112,112,112,112 111,110,110,98**
WIN (incl. 1 euro stake): 17.80. PLACES: 4.40, 6.60, 2.50. DF: 80.40. SF: 111.90.
Owner IGP Partnership & P Winkworth **Bred** Yorton Farm **Trained** Patching, W Sussex

FOCUS
The early pace was modest and there was a burn-up over the final 2f. There was hardly anything between the first five at the line.

4936 OVREVOLL (R-H)
Sunday, August 25

OFFICIAL GOING: Turf: good

5809a MARIT SVEAAS MINNELOP (GROUP 3) (3YO+) (TURF) 1m 1f
3:41 (12:00) 3-Y-O+ **£88,495** (£28,761; £13,274; £7,964; £5,309)

RPR

1 **Berling (IRE)**21 5045 6-9-4 0 ManuelMartinez 7 104
(Jessica Long, Sweden) *prom: lost pl over 3 1/2f out: rdn and hdwy on outside over 2f out: styd on wl u.p ins fnl f to ld last 50yds: drvn out* **197/10**

2 1 **Beatrice Aurore (IRE)**22 4985 5-9-1 0 AndreaAtzeni 1 99
(Ed Dunlop) *chsd ldng gp on inner: swtchd outside and hdwy over 1 1/2f out: rdn to ld fnl 100yds: hdd 50yds out: no ex* **7/1**

3 1 **Coprah**24 4936 5-9-4 0 ElioneChaves 11 100
(Cathrine Erichsen, Norway) *midfield: t.k.h: plld himself to join ldng quartet over 4f out: c v wd fnl bnd over 2 1/2f out: sn rejnd ldrs on ins: 4th and rdn 1 1/2f out: kpt on ins fnl f: no ex fnl 50yds* **225/10**

4 ½ **Bank Of Burden (USA)**21 5045 6-9-6 0 Per-AndersGraberg 4 101
(Niels Petersen, Norway) *midfield on inner: hdwy to press ldr 3 1/2f out: led over 2f out: hrd pressed and rallied gamely 1f out: hdd fnl 100yds: no ex* **11/5**1

5 1½ **Jubilance (IRE)**21 5045 4-9-4 0 ManuelSantos 9 96
(Bent Olsen, Denmark) *towards rr: rdn and styd on fr 1 1/2f out: nrest at fin: nt pce to chal* **34/1**

6 ½ **Touz Price (FR)**50 4095 5-9-6 0 JacobJohansen 2 97
(Rune Haugen, Norway) *led: hdd over 2f out: remained prom tl rdn and outpcd whn short of room 150yds out: sn wknd* **33/10**2

7 1½ **Without Fear (FR)**50 4095 5-9-6 0 FJohansson 6 93
(Niels Petersen, Norway) *trckd ldr: lost pl 3 1/2f out: styd on again fnl 1 1/2f: nt pce to chal* **68/10**3

8 5½ **Avon Pearl**47 4-9-4 0 (b) EspenSki 12 80
(Rune Haugen, Norway) *towards rr: effrt on outside 2 1/2f out: sn rdn: no imp fnl 1 1/2f* **44/5**

9 1½ **Manchester (FR)**56 5-9-4 0 OliverWilson 8 77
(Niels Petersen, Norway) *towards rr: sme mod prog 2f out: rdn and wknd fr 1 1/2f out* **228/10**

10 2½ **Touch Of Hawk (FR)**21 5045 7-9-4 0 Jan-ErikNeuroth 3 71
(Wido Neuroth, Norway) *chsd ldng gp: rdn and outpcd over 2f out: wknd fnl f* **73/10**

11 5 **Plantagenet (SPA)**50 4095 6-9-6 0 RafaelSchistl 5 63
(Niels Petersen, Norway) *towards rr: hdwy over 4f out: 3rd and styng on u.p 2 1/2f out: sn no further imp: wknd 1 1/2f out: eased ins fnl f* **114/10**

1m 46.9s (-3.00) **11** Ran SP% **126.3**
PARI-MUTUEL (all including 1krone stakes): WIN 20.71; PLACE 6.87, 6.31, 7.79; DF 270.55.
Owner Chess Racing Ab **Bred** Ballylinch Stud **Trained** Sweden

5810 - (Foreign Racing) - See Raceform Interactive

5428 CHEPSTOW (L-H)
Monday, August 26

OFFICIAL GOING: Good (good to firm in places; 8.2)
Wind: Nil Weather: Sunny

5811 GET FREE BETS AT THEBOOKIESOFFERS.CO.UK EBF MAIDEN STKS 1m 14y
2:05 (2:06) (Class 5) 2-Y-O **£2,911** (£866; £432; £216) **Stalls** Centre

Form RPR

03 1 **Ghaawy**18 5188 2-9-0 0 PaulHanagan 3 81+
(Sir Michael Stoute) *trckd ldr: chal over 2f out: led sn after: pushed clr fnl f: easily* **5/6**1

4 2 1¼ **Devilment**25 4926 2-9-0 0 MickaelBarzalona 2 78
(Charlie Appleby) *sn led: pushed along and jnd over 2f out: hdd sn after: kpt on but no ch w wnr* **5/2**2

3 1 **El Najmm (IRE)** 2-9-0 0 AndreaAtzeni 10 76+
(Roger Varian) *in tch: hdwy to chse ldrs fr 3f out: kpt on to cl on 2nd fnl f but nvr any ch w wnr* **7/1**3

56 4 7 **Charlie Wells (IRE)**15 5299 2-9-0 0 JohnFahy 9 60
(Eve Johnson Houghton) *in rr: pushed along 1/2-way: hdd over 2f out: styd on fnl f but nvr any ch w ldng trio* **12/1**

5 1¼ **Danz Star (IRE)** 2-8-9 0 PhilipPrince(5) 11 57+
(Malcolm Saunders) *s.i.s: green in rr: hdwy over 3f out: sn rdn: one pce fnl 2f* **50/1**

0 6 4½ **Dandys Perier (IRE)**30 4781 2-9-0 0 LukeMorris 6 47
(Ronald Harris) *chsd ldrs: rdn 3f out: wknd qckly fr 2f out* **50/1**

00 7 hd **Jarlath**16 5279 2-9-0 0 RobertHavlin 5 46
(Seamus Mullins) *in rr: shkn up over 2f out: sme prog ins fnl f* **100/1**

0 8 1½ **Lord Lexington**33 4640 2-9-0 0 RichardKingscote 1 43
(Richard Hannon) *s.i.s: sn chsng ldrs: wknd appr fnl 2f* **16/1**

04 9 nk **Heska (IRE)**7 5584 2-9-0 0 SamHitchcott 8 42
(Mick Channon) *s.i.s: outpcd* **20/1**

10 nk **Trigger Park (IRE)** 2-9-0 0 SteveDrowne 4 41
(Ronald Harris) *chsd ldrs 5f* **66/1**

1m 34.66s (-1.54) **Going Correction** -0.225s/f (Firm) **10** Ran SP% **120.4**
Speed ratings (Par 94): **98,96,95,88,87 83,82,81,81,80**
toteswingers 1&2 £1.50, 2&3 £3.40, 1&3 £2.60 CSF £3.02 TOTE £1.50: £1.10, £1.40, £2.10; EX 4.60 Trifecta £14.30 Pool: £1536.55 - 80.02 winning units..
Owner Hamdan Al Maktoum **Bred** Shadwell Estate Company Limited **Trained** Newmarket, Suffolk

FOCUS
Dry overnight and fast ground (GoingStick 7.5) but overcast and warm (23C). Probably an ordinary juvenile maiden despite some powerful yards represented and the market proved accurate. They went a modest pace early and it turned into something of a sprint from 3f out. The front three drew well clear, with the winner building on his pre-race form.

5812 BEST BOOKIES OFFERS FROM THEBOOKIESOFFERS.CO.UK EBF MEDIAN AUCTION MAIDEN FILLIES' STKS 1m 14y
2:40 (2:42) (Class 5) 2-Y-O **£2,911** (£866; £432; £216) **Stalls** Centre

Form RPR

02 1 **Likelihood (USA)**12 5394 2-9-0 0 RobertHavlin 5 80+
(John Gosden) *mde all: shkn up and c rt to r on stands' rail over 1f out: styd on strly fnl f: readily* **4/5**1

34 **2** 2 ¾ **Gratzie**[12] 5394 2-9-0 0 .... SamHitchcott 11 74
(Mick Channon) *in rr early: hdwy 1/2-way: drvn to chse wnr 2f out: sn hrd rdn: kpt on but readily outpcd fnl f* **9/2**[2]

05 **3** 2 ¼ **Habdab**[19] 5122 2-9-0 0 .... AndreaAtzeni 4 69
(Richard Hannon) *chsd ldrs: rdn 2f out: styd on same pce for 3rd fnl f* **25/1**

26 **4** 1 ¼ **Lady Red Oak**[46] 4218 2-9-0 0 .... RichardKingscote 10 66
(Tom Dascombe) *towards rr: hdwy over 2f out: nvr rchd ldrs and one pce fnl f* **9/2**[2]

0 **5** ½ **Cameley Dawn**[10] 5473 2-8-9 0 .... PhilipPrince(5) 6 64
(Malcolm Saunders) *chsd wnr to 2f out: sn btn* **100/1**

0 **6** 3 ¼ **Scottish Academy**[31] 4723 2-9-0 0 .... LiamJones 1 57
(Mark Johnston) *chsd ldrs: rdn 3f out: wknd fr 2f out* **14/1**

7 nk **Hallbeck** 2-9-0 0 .... LukeMorris 3 56+
(Henry Candy) *s.i.s: in rr: pushed along 3f out: sme late prog* **10/1**[3]

60 **8** 1 ¾ **Indie Star**[48] 4154 2-9-0 0 .... PaulHanagan 8 52
(Harry Dunlop) *chsd ldrs: pushed along over 2f out: sn btn* **33/1**

0 **9** 3 ½ **Satin Waters**[25] 4921 2-9-0 0 .... JohnFahy 2 44
(Eve Johnson Houghton) *outpcd* **33/1**

6 **10** 9 **Touche De Rouge (IRE)**[44] 4302 2-9-0 0 .... SteveDrowne 7 24
(Peter Makin) *in tch to 1/2-way* **50/1**

1m 35.03s (-1.17) **Going Correction** -0.225s/f (Firm) **10** Ran SP% **120.4**
Speed ratings (Par 91): **96,93,91,89,89 86,85,83,80,71**
toteswingers 1&2 £2.20, 2&3 £15.00, 1&3 £8.60 CSF £4.68 TOTE £1.90: £1.10, £1.50, £7.70; EX 5.10 Trifecta £57.10 Pool: £3136.31 -41.17 winning units..
Owner K Abdullah **Bred** Juddmonte Farms Inc **Trained** Newmarket, Suffolk

FOCUS
They went a decent pace for what looked an ordinary juvenile fillies' maiden, although the first two home look decent. The fifth may help with the long-term level of the form.

5813 FREE BETTING OFFERS AT THEBOOKIESOFFERS.CO.UK APPRENTICE (S) STKS 1m 2f 36y
3:15 (3:15) (Class 6) 3-4-Y-O **£1,940** (£577; £288; £144) **Stalls** Low

Form RPR

2353 **1** **Gaelic Ice**[15] 5311 4-8-10 53 .... (p[1]) PatMillman(5) 7 59
(Rod Millman) *chsd ldrs: hdwy over 3f out: chsd ldr over 2f out: led wl over 1f out: styd on wl* **9/4**[1]

1245 **2** 2 ¼ **Stag Hill (IRE)**[4] 5671 4-9-11 60 .... (tp) RobertWilliams 5 65
(Bernard Llewellyn) *in tch: hdwy over 3f out: drvn 2f out: styd on to take 2nd fnl 120yds but nvr any ch w wnr* **11/4**[2]

000 **3** 3 ¼ **Elusive Band (USA)**[12] 5395 3-8-12 64 .... (p) NathanAlison 2 54
(Brian Meehan) *t.k.h and sn ld: clr w 2nd 1/2-way: drvn over 3f out: hdd wl over 1f out: wknd into 3rd fnl 120yds* **6/1**

4 1 ¾ **Alpetetim**[54] 4-9-6 0 .... RobertTart 6 50
(Stuart Kittow) *in rr: hdwy 3f out: drvn 2f out: kpt on in clsng stages but nvr a threat* **16/1**

0- **5** 3 ½ **Hendry Trigger**[477] 1893 4-9-3 0 .... OisinMurphy(3) 1 44
(Bernard Llewellyn) *s.i.s: sn in tch: rdn and outpcd over 3f out: mod prog u.p fnl 2f* **33/1**

5040 **6** 2 ¼ **Drummond**[34] 4604 4-9-3 50 .... (tp) DanielMuscutt(3) 4 39
(Bernard Llewellyn) *chsd ldr and wl clr of 3rd after 3f: rdn 4f out: wknd over 2f out* **8/1**

010 **7** 2 ½ **Rancher (IRE)**[25] 4931 3-8-12 53 .... (b) GeorgeDowning 9 35
(Tony Carroll) *bhd fnl 4f* **9/2**[3]

8 32 **Mobley Chaos** 3-8-12 0 .... PhilipPrince 3
(Ronald Harris) *s.i.s: in tch 1/2-way: wknd ins fnl 4f: t.o* **20/1**

2m 10.49s (-0.11) **Going Correction** -0.225s/f (Firm)
WFA 3 from 4yo 8lb **8** Ran SP% **114.6**
Speed ratings (Par 101): **91,89,86,85,82 80,78,53**
toteswingers 1&2 £2.60, 2&3 £3.60, 1&3 £3.20 CSF £8.61 TOTE £2.90: £1.50, £1.10, £1.80; EX 7.20 Trifecta £34.10 Pool: £1862.03 - 40.88 winning units..
Owner The Jack High Racing Partnership **Bred** Berry Racing **Trained** Kentisbeare, Devon

FOCUS
A poor race and they finished well strung out. The first two were pretty much to their marks.

5814 WESSEX GARAGES HYUNDAI NURSERY H'CAP 5f 16y
3:50 (3:50) (Class 6) (0-65,65) 2-Y-O **£2,045** (£603; £302) **Stalls** Centre

Form RPR

600 **1** **Notnow Penny**[24] 4937 2-7-12 45 .... SimonPearce(3) 5 46
(Milton Bradley) *mde virtually all: strly chal both sides fr 2f out: jst lasted* **50/1**

0253 **2** nse **Zafraaj**[34] 4602 2-9-7 65 .... LukeMorris 7 66
(Ronald Harris) *in tch: rdn and hdwy over 1f out: str run fnl f to press wnr in clsng stages: nt quite get up* **7/1**[3]

5642 **3** nk **Narborough**[6] 5610 2-8-13 60 .... CharlesBishop(3) 3 60
(Mick Channon) *t.k.h: in tch: hdwy to chal fr 2f out and disp ld thrght fnl f: no ex last strides* **5/2**[2]

0050 **4** nk **Kopkap**[21] 5066 2-8-11 55 .... SteveDrowne 2 54
(Ed McMahon) *trckd wnr: chal fr 2f out: styd upsides thrght fnl f: no ex last strides* **12/1**

5506 **5** ½ **Zac's Princess**[21] 5066 2-7-12 45 .... (t) RosieJessop(3) 1 42
(Milton Bradley) *pressed ldrs: chal fr 2f out and stl upsides thrght fnl f tl fdd cl home* **16/1**

000 **6** 2 ¼ **Monsieur Blanc (IRE)**[24] 4937 2-8-13 57 .... (v) ShaneKelly 4 46
(Denis Coakley) *in tch: rdn over 1f out: wknd fnl f* **10/1**

062 **7** nse **Dream Sika (IRE)**[32] 4680 2-9-2 60 .... RichardHughes 6 49
(Clive Cox) *t.k.h: chsd ldrs 1/2-way: wknd fnl f* **1/1**[1]

59.86s (0.56) **Going Correction** -0.225s/f (Firm) **7** Ran SP% **115.7**
Speed ratings (Par 92): **86,85,85,84,84 80,80**
toteswingers 1&2 £16.70, 2&3 £1.60, 1&3 £23.20 CSF £363.03 TOTE £30.90: £15.60, £2.50; EX 223.30 Trifecta £1434.00 Pool: £2560.31 - 1.33 winning units..
Owner Evenco Gold Racing **Bred** Genesis Green Stud Ltd **Trained** Sedbury, Gloucs

FOCUS
They raced up the centre of the track. With six spread across the track with 1f to run, there was a blanket finish. Weak, selling-grade form.

5815 GLOUCESTERSHIRE COLLEGE, FOREST CAMPUS H'CAP 1m 14y
4:25 (4:27) (Class 5) (0-75,75) 3-Y-O+ **£2,587** (£770; £384; £192) **Stalls** Centre

Form RPR

4032 **1** **Yojimbo (IRE)**[6] 5613 5-9-8 74 .... (v) CharlesBishop(3) 5 82
(Mick Channon) *pressed ldr 3f: rdn and outpcd over 2f out: rallied fnl f: styd on u.p in clsng stages to ld nr fin* **9/4**[1]

-165 **2** nk **Russian Royale**[22] 5037 3-9-1 70 .... AndreaAtzeni 4 76
(Stuart Kittow) *in rr: rdn over 3f out: styd on u.p fnl f: fin wl to take 2nd last strides: nt rch wnr* **10/1**

3P54 **3** nk **Breccbennach**[15] 5304 3-9-1 70 .... (t) RichardHughes 11 75
(Seamus Durack) *led but hrd pressed for 3f: rdn over 2f out: hdd ins fnl f but styd chalng and kpt on wl in clsng stages: no ex last strides* **9/2**[2]

5110 **4** shd **The Mongoose**[12] 5387 5-8-12 68 .... (t) EoinWalsh(7) 2 74
(David Evans) *chsd ldrs: drvn to take slt ld ins fnl f: hdd and no ex nr fin* **10/1**

4464 **5** 1 ½ **Rocky Reef**[12] 5398 4-9-12 75 .... (v) RichardKingscote 1 78
(Philip Hide) *in rr: pushed along over 2f out: styd on fnl f but nvr gng pce to rch ldrs* **6/1**

4033 **6** 2 **Prime Exhibit**[21] 5070 8-9-12 75 .... (t) ShaneKelly 7 73
(John Stimpson) *in rr: hdwy 3f out: rdn over 2f out: kpt on ins fnl f: nvr gng pce to rch ldrs* **8/1**

6415 **7** 1 ½ **Fraserburgh (IRE)**[14] 5355 3-9-2 71 .... LiamJones 3 65
(Mark Johnston) *chsd ldrs and rdn 3f out: wknd over 1f out* **9/1**

0346 **8** 14 **Tawtheeq (IRE)**[33] 4628 3-9-6 75 .... PaulHanagan 9 36
(Richard Hannon) *in rr: hdwy to chse ldrs 3f out: wknd appr fnl 2f: eased whn no ch fnl f* **11/2**[3]

1m 33.49s (-2.71) **Going Correction** -0.225s/f (Firm)
WFA 3 from 4yo+ 6lb **8** Ran SP% **117.9**
Speed ratings (Par 103): **104,103,103,103,101 99,98,84**
toteswingers 1&2 £5.50, 2&3 £8.20, 1&3 £3.10 CSF £27.22 CT £97.03 TOTE £3.00: £1.50, £2.80, £1.90; EX 28.20 Trifecta £249.80 Pool: £2096.84 - 6.29 winning units..
Owner Jon and Julia Aisbitt **Bred** Peter Kelly And Ms Wendy Daly **Trained** West Ilsley, Berks

FOCUS
An ordinary if competitive handicap but the pace was true and the first four finished in a heap. Sound enough form.

5816 WESSEXGARAGES.COM H'CAP 7f 16y
5:00 (5:00) (Class 6) (0-65,65) 3-Y-O+ **£1,940** (£577; £288; £144) **Stalls** Centre

Form RPR

2021 **1** **Tenbridge**[11] 5430 4-9-5 61 .... (v) RosieJessop(3) 8 71
(Derek Haydn Jones) *sn in tch: hdwy 3f out: led 2f out: pushed along and styd on wl fnl f* **4/1**[2]

0630 **2** ½ **Emiratesdotcom**[3] 5697 7-9-12 65 .... (p) RichardKingscote 10 73
(Milton Bradley) *in rr: hdwy 2f out: drvn: swtchd lft and styd on ins fnl f: fin wl to go 2nd fnl strides but no imp on wnr* **7/1**

2512 **3** nk **Pour La Victoire (IRE)**[6] 5604 3-8-0 51 .... OisinMurphy(7) 12 56
(Tony Carroll) *chsd ldrs: wnt 2nd 2f out and sn rdn: styd chsng wnr but no imp ins fnl f: dropped to 3rd last strides* **5/2**[1]

0326 **4** ½ **Delightful Sleep**[7] 5596 5-9-0 60 .... EoinWalsh(7) 5 66
(David Evans) *in rr: hdwy 2f out: styd on u.p fnl f: no imp fnl 75yds* **12/1**

0-53 **5** 2 ½ **Ivor's Princess**[12] 5404 4-9-12 65 .... (p) AndreaAtzeni 1 64
(Rod Millman) *in rr: hdwy over 1f out: styd on u.p but nvr gng pce to rch ldrs* **10/1**

544 **6** ¾ **Landau (IRE)**[12] 5386 3-9-5 63 .... RichardHughes 3 58+
(Sylvester Kirk) *chsd ldrs: rdn over 1f out: one pce ins fnl f* **6/1**[3]

550 **7** ½ **Cheers Big Ears (IRE)**[6] 5614 7-8-0 46 .... (t) DanielMuscutt(7) 2 42
(Richard Price) *in rr: hdwy to chse ldrs over 3f out: wknd ins fnl f* **16/1**

-056 **8** nk **Schoolboy Champ**[187] 725 6-8-2 46 oh1 .... (tp) PhilipPrince(5) 13 41
(Lisa Williamson) *tk slt ld: narrowly hdd over 3f out: sn rdn: one pce and swtchd lft over 1f out* **33/1**

50 **9** ¾ **Up In Flames (IRE)**[11] 5433 4-8-6 52 .... (b) LouisSteward(7) 14 45
(Martin Keighley) *w ldr: slt advantage over 3f out: hdd 2f out: sn btn* **33/1**

3200 **10** 2 ¾ **Stonecrabstomorrow (IRE)**[18] 5177 10-9-5 61 .... MarkCoumbe(3) 6 47
(Roy Brotherton) *pressed ldrs: chal over 2f out: wknd over 1f out* **25/1**

0-00 **11** 2 ¼ **Nandura**[18] 5176 3-7-12 47 oh1 ow1 .... NathanAlison(5) 9 25
(Harry Dunlop) *chsd ldrs over 4f* **40/1**

3330 **12** ¾ **Offbeat Safaris (IRE)**[12] 5387 5-9-3 56 .... LukeMorris 4 34
(Ronald Harris) *in rr: sme hdwy 3f out: sn wknd* **10/1**

00-0 **13** 2 ¼ **Marvo**[18] 5172 9-8-7 46 oh1 .... (p) JohnFahy 15 17
(Dai Burchell) *s.i.s: towards rr most of way* **20/1**

2-00 **14** 8 **Giorgio's Dragon (IRE)**[20] 5097 4-9-8 61 .... LiamJones 7 11
(Robert Stephens) *chsd ldrs: rdn 3f out: sn btn* **25/1**

1m 21.93s (-1.27) **Going Correction** -0.225s/f (Firm)
WFA 3 from 4yo+ 5lb **14** Ran SP% **127.9**
Speed ratings (Par 101): **98,97,97,96,93 92,92,91,91,87 85,84,81,72**
toteswingers 1&2 £9.60, 2&3 £7.40, 1&3 £3.20 CSF £31.64 CT £88.07 TOTE £4.50: £1.50, £2.00, £1.80; EX 44.70 Trifecta £181.00 Pool: £2020.92 - 8.37 winning units..
Owner Mrs E M Haydn Jones **Bred** Mrs M L Parry **Trained** Efail Isaf, Rhondda C Taff

FOCUS
They went a decent pace for this poor handicap, initially splitting into two groups before coming together to race up the stands' side. The form looks fair for the grade with the runner-up helping with the standard.

5817 THEBOOKIESOFFERS.CO.UK H'CAP (DIV I) 6f 16y
5:35 (5:35) (Class 6) (0-55,55) 3-Y-O+ **£1,940** (£577; £288; £144) **Stalls** Centre

Form RPR

-005 **1** **All Right Now**[20] 5097 6-8-12 46 oh1 .... (p) RichardHughes 11 59
(Tony Newcombe) *trckd ldrs: drvn wl over 1f out: styd on u.p ins fnl f to ld cl home* **11/4**[1]

00-0 **2** nk **Monty Fay (IRE)**[28] 4836 4-8-9 46 oh1 .... RosieJessop(3) 1 58
(Derek Haydn Jones) *led: drvn fnl f: hrd pressed fnl 110yds: hdd cl home* **16/1**

2500 **3** 3 ½ **The Name Is Frank**[12] 5404 8-8-9 50 .... (t) OisinMurphy(7) 10 51
(Mark Gillard) *in tch: rdn over 2f out: styd on u.p fnl f to take 3rd last strides but no ch w ldng duo* **7/1**

5-00 **4** hd **Rosa Lockwood**[201] 530 4-8-12 46 oh1 .... ShaneKelly 8 46
(Ed McMahon) *n.m.r s and s.i.s: hdwy 2f out: styd on fnl f to take 3rd fnl 110yds: no imp on ldng duo and dropped to 4th last strides* **20/1**

045 **5** nk **Jackie Love (IRE)**[9] 5525 5-8-9 48 .... (v) LauraPike(5) 5 47
(Olivia Maylam) *sn chsng ldrs: rdn over 2f out: styd on same pce fnl f* **11/2**[2]

0000 **6** ½ **Colourbearer (IRE)**[28] 4837 6-9-2 50 .... (t) RichardKingscote 2 48
(Milton Bradley) *disp 2nd: rdn over 1f out: wknd fnl 110yds* **7/1**

0006 **7** ½ **Ficelle (IRE)**[20] 5092 4-9-4 52 .... LukeMorris 13 48
(Ronald Harris) *in rr: rdn 1/2-way: styd on u.p fnl f: nt rch ldrs* **7/1**

0445 **8** hd **Baltic Gin (IRE)**[11] 5431 3-8-10 54 .... (p) DanielMuscutt(7) 12 49
(Malcolm Saunders) *chsd ldrs: wknd fnl f* **8/1**

006 **9** 3 **Diamond Vine (IRE)**[20] 5097 5-9-0 53 .... (p) PhilipPrince(5) 6 39
(Ronald Harris) *outpcd most of way* **13/2**[3]

500- **10** 3 ½ **Valley Dreamer**[322] 6936 3-8-12 49 .... SteveDrowne 3 24
(Robert Stephens) *chsd ldrs: wknd qckly fr 2f out* **16/1**

1m 10.46s (-1.54) **Going Correction** -0.225s/f (Firm)
WFA 3 from 4yo+ 3lb **10** Ran SP% **120.5**
Speed ratings (Par 101): **101,100,95,95,95 94,93,93,89,85**
toteswingers 1&2 £14.10, 2&3 £26.00, 1&3 £7.40 CSF £53.50 CT £295.21 TOTE £3.70: £1.40, £5.60, £2.60; EX 59.20 Trifecta £154.60 Pool: £1215.54 - 5.89 winning units..

Owner Justin Hay **Bred** Rolyon Stud **Trained** Yarnscombe, Devon

FOCUS

Another tight finish for the first division of a weak sprint handicap, which was run at a fair pace and in a slightly faster time than the second division. They came up the middle of the track. The first two were both well treated on older form.

5818 THEBOOKIESOFFERS.CO.UK H'CAP (DIV II) 6f 16y

6:05 (6:10) (Class 6) (0-55,55) 3-Y-O+ **£1,940** (£577; £288; £144) **Stalls** Centre

Form RPR

6426 **1** **Dancing Welcome**[7] 5594 7-9-4 **52**....................(bt) RichardKingscote 12 63
(Milton Bradley) *mde all: hrd drvn fnl f: hld on all out* **6/1**[3]

0006 **2** *nk* **Euroquip Boy (IRE)**[11] 5434 6-8-12 **46** oh1....................... LiamJones 10 56
(Michael Scudamore) *chsd ldrs: rdn over 2f out: styd on wl fnl f: chsd wnr fnl 120yds: kpt on: nt quite get up* **10/1**

5035 **3** *2 ¾* **Chester Deelyte (IRE)**[17] 5230 5-8-9 **46**.................(v) MarkCoumbe(3) 6 47
(Lisa Williamson) *pressed ldrs: chsd wnr fr 2f out: no imp fnl f and outpcd into 3rd fnl 120yds* **25/1**

4003 **4** *2* **Deliberation (IRE)**[6] 5602 5-9-5 **53**................................ RichardHughes 3 48
(John Quinn) *chsd ldrs: rdn 2f out: wknd fnl f* **9/4**[1]

3650 **5** *1 ¼* **Loulou Vuitton**[14] 5353 3-8-10 **52**..................................(p) LauraPike(5) 1 43
(Frank Sheridan) *chsd ldrs: rdn over 2f out: wknd fnl f* **12/1**

0436 **6** *2* **Flaxen Lake**[4] 5670 6-8-9 **46** oh1...............................(p) DeclanBates(3) 11 30
(Milton Bradley) *in rr and rdn 1/2-way: styd on fnl f: nvr any ch* **20/1**

5400 **7** *¾* **Lady Mango (IRE)**[20] 5097 5-9-2 **50**................................ SteveDrowne 2 32
(Ronald Harris) *chsd ldrs: wknd 2f out* **16/1**

8 *1 ¼* **Manzanita (IRE)**[206] 485 3-8-4 **46** oh1.........................(t) RobertTart(5) 4 24
(D J Bunyan, Ire) *led to post: outpcd most of way* **4/1**[2]

3660 **9** *½* **Outbid**[21] 5067 3-8-13 **55**.. GeorgeDowning(5) 8 39
(Tony Carroll) *stmbld s: outpcd most of way* **20/1**

0000 **10** *½* **Cristaliyev**[20] 5097 5-8-12 **46**...(v) ShaneKelly 5 21
(David Evans) *outpcd most of way* **9/1**

06-0 **11** *¾* **Cashel's Missile (IRE)**[33] 4635 3-8-9 **53**.................... OisinMurphy(7) 13 25
(John Spearing) *chsd ldrs over 3f* **33/1**

1200 **12** *½* **Very First Blade**[18] 5198 4-8-10 **51**.............................(p) DanielMuscutt(7) 9 22
(Mark Brisbourne) *outpcd* **16/1**

50-0 **13** *16* **Fit For A King (IRE)**[32] 4691 3-8-11 **48**............................... LukeMorris 7
(John Best) *chsd ldrs 3f* **33/1**

1m 10.04s (-1.96) **Going Correction** -0.225s/f (Firm)
WFA 3 from 4yo+ 3lb **13** Ran SP% **122.9**
Speed ratings (Par 101): **104,103,99,97,95 92,91,90,89,88 87,87,65**
toteswingers 1&2 £11.10, 2&3 £38.80, 1&3 £12.50 CSF £61.67 CT £1447.25 TOTE £7.70: £2.30, £3.50, £3.10; EX 67.60 Trifecta £978.60 Pool: £1790.87 - 1.37 winning units..
Owner J M Bradley **Bred** The Hon Mrs E J Wills **Trained** Sedbury, Gloucs

FOCUS

The second division of the 6f sprint handicap was 0.42sec quicker than the first. The winner's best run since the AW in the winter.

T/Jkpt: Part won. £17750.00. Pool of £22893.96 - 0.50 winning units. T/Plt: £33.00 to a £1 stake.Pool of £69503.72 - 1536.44 winning tickets. T/Qpdt: £26.60 to a £1 stake. Pool of £3083.70 - 85.60 winning tickets. ST

4904 EPSOM (L-H)

Monday, August 26

OFFICIAL GOING: Good to soft (good in places on 5f course)

Rail dolled out up to 5yds from 1m to winning post, adding 10yds to races of 1m and over and 5yds to races of 6f & 7f.

Wind: Almost nil Weather: Sunny, very warm

5819 BRITISH STALLION STUDS EBF MEDIAN AUCTION MAIDEN STKS 7f

2:00 (2:01) (Class 5) 2-Y-O **£3,881** (£1,155; £577; £288) **Stalls** Low

Form RPR

5 **1** **Signposted (IRE)**[10] 5472 2-9-5 0..................................... DavidProbert 2 82+
(Andrew Balding) *hld up: 4th st: plld out and prog jst over 2f out: led 1f out: pushed clr: readily* **11/4**[2]

0542 **2** *3 ¼* **Lincoln (IRE)**[9] 5508 2-9-5 80... TedDurcan 7 76
(Mick Channon) *nt that wl away but sn led: shkn up 2f out: hdd and btn 1f out: fdd and eased nr fin* **2/1**[1]

0 **3** *1 ¼* **Speedbird One**[38] 4491 2-9-0 0.. WilliamBuick 3 66
(Peter Chapple-Hyam) *in tch: 5th st: outpcd 3f out: pushed along and kpt on again fr over 1f out: tk 3rd nr fin* **16/1**

06 **4** *½* **Morally Bankrupt**[18] 5188 2-9-5 0.................................... RyanMoore 5 69
(Richard Hannon) *prom: 3rd st: chsd ldr over 2f out to over 1f out: sn lft bhd: plugged on nr fin* **11/4**[2]

5 *6* **Avocadeau (IRE)** 2-9-5 0... MartinDwyer 1 54
(William Muir) *s.i.s: rn green and sn adrift in 6th: nvr on terms but kpt on fnl 2f* **25/1**

623 **6** *16* **Ellalan**[23] 4977 2-9-5 73.. MartinLane 4 12
(David Simcock) *mostly chsd ldr to over 2f out: wkng whn unbalanced jst over 1f out: heavily eased* **11/2**[3]

7 *35* **La Grassetta (GER)** 2-9-0 0...[1] ChrisCatlin 6
(Tobias B P Coles) *slowly away: sn hopelessly t.o* **50/1**

1m 26.0s (2.70) **Going Correction** +0.175s/f (Good) **7** Ran SP% **113.7**
Speed ratings (Par 94): **91,87,85,85,78 60,20**
toteswingers 1&2 £2.10, 2&3 £4.20, 1&3 £6.60 CSF £8.59 TOTE £3.70: £2.30, £1.30; EX 8.20 Trifecta £98.40 Pool: £1417.99 - 10.80 winning units..
Owner N Botica, Rex & Mrs Wendy Gorell **Bred** Tullamaine Castle Stud And Partners **Trained** Kingsclere, Hants

FOCUS

It's unlikely this juvenile contest took a great deal of winning but the winner could prove a good bit better than the bare form.

5820 BANSTEAD H'CAP 6f

2:30 (2:30) (Class 5) (0-75,75) 3-Y-O **£4,528** (£1,347; £673; £336) **Stalls** High

Form RPR

3520 **1** **Al Udeid (IRE)**[9] 5537 3-9-7 **75**................................. SilvestreDeSousa 2 82
(Kevin Ryan) *chsd ldng pair: pushed along 1/2-way: wnt 2nd jst over 2f out: rdn to chal over 1f out: persistent effrt and led last stride* **11/4**[1]

0163 **2** *shd* **Desert Command**[5] 5636 3-9-5 **73**................................... DavidProbert 6 80
(Andrew Balding) *led: pressed over 1f out: edgd rt u.p: kpt on wl but hdd last stride* **11/4**[1]

-313 **3** *2 ¼* **Truly Madly (IRE)**[11] 5430 3-9-1 **69**................................ JamesDoyle 4 69
(Hans Adielsson) *hld up in 5th: rdn 2f out: prog over 1f out: tk 3rd jst ins fnl f: styd on but no ch to chal* **8/1**

1504 **4** *2* **Indian Affair**[31] 4710 3-8-11 **72**................................... ShelleyBirkett(7) 3 65
(Milton Bradley) *chsd ldr to jst over 2f out: steadily wknd* **10/1**

-501 **5** *2 ½* **Exotic Guest**[19] 5141 3-9-5 **73**.. RyanMoore 1 58
(George Margarson) *chsd ldng trio: shkn up and no imp over 2f out: fdd fnl f* **5/1**[3]

3212 **6** *nse* **Dodina (IRE)**[20] 5104 3-9-5 **73**...................................... WilliamBuick 5 58
(Peter Chapple-Hyam) *hld up in last: shkn up over 2f out: nt qckn and no prog* **4/1**[2]

1m 11.17s (1.77) **Going Correction** +0.175s/f (Good) **6** Ran SP% **110.2**
Speed ratings (Par 100): **95,94,91,89,85 85**
toteswingers 1&2 £2.90, 2&3 £3.80, 1&3 £2.80 CSF £10.00 TOTE £3.70: £1.30, £3.40; EX 13.30 Trifecta £57.90 Pool: £1326.84 - 17.17 winning units..
Owner Mubarak Al Naemi **Bred** Messrs Mark Hanly & James Hanly **Trained** Hambleton, N Yorks
■ Stewards' Enquiry : Silvestre De Sousa two day ban: use of whip (9-10 Sep)

FOCUS

A fair sprint handicap, run at a strong pace. The winner was on a good mark and is rated to his best.

5821 GREAT SURREY H'CAP 5f

3:05 (3:05) (Class 2) (0-100,98) 3-Y-O+
£12,450 (£3,728; £1,864; £932; £466; £234) **Stalls** High

Form RPR

0003 **1** **Swan Song**[16] 5257 4-9-3 **91**.. DavidProbert 8 97
(Andrew Balding) *racd against nr side rail: disp ld thrght: hld together tl drvn to assert last 100yds* **7/2**[2]

6261 **2** *½* **La Fortunata**[3] 5700 6-9-2 **95** 6ex................................. DannyBrock(5) 2 99
(Mike Murphy) *pressed ldng pair and racd on outer of trio: rdn and nt qckn over 1f out: styd on again ins fnl f: tk 2nd post* **4/1**[3]

2200 **3** *shd* **Jedward (IRE)**[24] 4954 6-8-10 **84**..................................(b) RyanMoore 3 88
(Kevin Ryan) *w wnr: stl upsides and urged along ins fnl f: rdn and nt qckn last 100yds: lost 2nd post* **6/1**

3400 **4** *1 ¼* **Fair Value (IRE)**[27] 4860 5-9-1 **89**.................................... SebSanders 1 88
(Simon Dow) *hld up in tch: tried to cl on ldrs on outer fr 2f out: one pce fnl f* **11/4**[1]

1430 **5** *3 ¾* **Sandfrankskipsgo**[29] 4800 4-8-8 **82**................................ TedDurcan 7 68
(Peter Crate) *racd against rail: trckd ldrs: pushed along and outpcd 2f out: fdd* **12/1**

5500 **6** *3* **Jiroft (ITY)**[44] 4275 6-9-10 **98**... JamesDoyle 4 73
(Robert Cowell) *chsd ldrs: shkn up 1/2-way: wknd over 1f out* **4/1**[3]

54.94s (-0.76) **Going Correction** +0.05s/f (Good) **6** Ran SP% **110.9**
Speed ratings (Par 109): **108,107,107,105,99 94**
toteswingers 1&2 £2.30, 2&3 £4.10, 1&3 £4.00 CSF £17.19 CT £75.61 TOTE £3.80: £2.60, £1.80; EX 21.60 Trifecta £49.80 Pool: £1039.40 - 15.63 winning units..
Owner J C Smith **Bred** Littleton Stud **Trained** Kingsclere, Hants

FOCUS

Not the strongest of races for the lofty grade but it provided an exciting finish with fillies and mares dominating. A small step up from the winner.

5822 STANLEY WOOTTON CONDITIONS STKS 1m 2f 18y

3:40 (3:42) (Class 3) 3-Y-O+ **£7,470** (£2,236; £1,118; £559; £279) **Stalls** Low

Form RPR

2050 **1** **Fattsota**[66] 3525 5-9-2 102.. RyanMoore 5 107
(David O'Meara) *fast away: mde all and sn at least 6 l clr: breather and c bk to field 4f out: kicked on again 3f out: in command fnl f: rdn out* **11/4**[2]

2010 **2** *2 ½* **Tha'ir (IRE)**[25] 4917 3-8-8 105.................................... SilvestreDeSousa 1 102
(Saeed bin Suroor) *chsd wnr and sn least 6 l down: clsd 4f out: rdn and nt qckn wl over 2f out: no imp after* **5/4**[1]

130- **3** *shd* **Prince Alzain (USA)**[325] 6855 4-9-2 92............................ JamesDoyle 4 102
(Gerard Butler) *free to post: hld up: wnt 3rd 1/2-way: clsd and in tch st: rdn wl over 2f out: no imp on wnr but kpt on to press for 2nd fnl f* **16/1**

-304 **4** *6* **Questioning (IRE)**[58] 3839 5-9-2 103..............................[1] WilliamBuick 2 91
(John Gosden) *chsd clr ldng pair to 1/2-way: 4th st: rdn over 3f out: sn struggling* **9/2**[3]

10-5 **5** *7* **Whipper's Boy (IRE)**[24] 4945 3-8-8 100............................ MartinLane 6 77
(Brian Meehan) *awkward s: a in last: pushed along 4f out: no prog 3f out: sn wl btn* **6/1**

2m 8.76s (-0.94) **Going Correction** +0.175s/f (Good)
WFA 3 from 4yo+ 8lb **5** Ran SP% **109.5**
Speed ratings (Par 107): **110,108,107,103,97**
CSF £6.55 TOTE £3.20: £1.80, £1.40; EX 7.00 Trifecta £23.60 Pool: £1990.93 - 63.23 winning units..
Owner Middleham Park Racing XXVIII & Partner **Bred** Azienda Agricola Francesca **Trained** Nawton, N Yorks

FOCUS

An intriguing conditions event. The winner, given a good ride, needed only to run to this year's form, with the favourite below par.

5823 AMATEUR DERBY (H'CAP) (FOR GENTLEMAN AMATEUR RIDERS) 1m 4f 10y

4:15 (4:17) (Class 4) (0-85,83) 4-Y-O+ **£6,239** (£1,935; £967; £484) **Stalls** Centre

Form RPR

2111 **1** **Beacon Lady**[17] 5216 4-11-3 **79**.. MrPWMullins 6 93
(William Knight) *stdd s: hld up in last and detached early: clsd fr 1/2-way: 7th st: stdy prog after to chse ldr wl over 1f out: rdn to ld ins fnl f: r.o wl* **3/1**[2]

03-1 **2** *1 ¼* **Azrag (USA)**[4] 5672 5-11-0 **76** 6ex...................................(p) MrSWalker 8 88
(Gerard Butler) *trckd ldrs: clsd 5th st: pushed along and prog to ld 2f out: wandered both ways after: hdd ins fnl f: styd on wl but readily hld* **11/4**[1]

2063 **3** *14* **Getabuzz**[8] 5559 5-10-12 **79**... MrWEasterby(5) 9 69
(Tim Easterby) *hld up in last pair early: prog and cl 4th st: chsd ldr over 3f out to over 2f out: sn lft bhd by ldng pair* **13/2**

6223 **4** *1 ½* **Gran Maestro (USA)**[10] 5466 4-10-13 **75**.....................(b) MrJHamilton 7 62
(Ruth Carr) *trckd ldrs: led 4f out: drvn and hdd 2f out: sn wknd* **11/1**

3533 **5** *8* **No Such Number**[21] 5065 5-10-10 **72**..........................(p) MrRossBirkett 3 46
(Julia Feilden) *hld up in tch: cl 6th st: sn rdn and lft bhd by ldrs fr 2f out* **8/1**

5240 **6** *3 ¼* **Paloma's Prince (IRE)**[23] 5008 4-10-10 **75**............... MrChrisMartin(3) 5 44
(Jim Boyle) *chsd ldrs tl lost pl 5f out: 8th and nt on terms st: no ch after* **16/1**

2106 **7** *¾* **Admirable Duque (IRE)**[33] 4643 7-10-1 **68**.(b) MrBenFfrenchDavis(5) 10 36
(Dominic Ffrench Davis) *prom: cl 3rd st: wknd 3f out: sn bhd* **25/1**

1160 **8** *nse* **Jupiter Storm**[16] 5259 4-11-2 **83**.. MrDLevey(5) 1 51
(Gary Moore) *led 2f: led again 5f out to 4f out: wknd over 3f out: sn wl bhd* **5/1**[3]

0035 9 80 **Samoan (IRE)**22 5032 4-10-2 69 (b) MrORJSangster(5) 2
(Brian Meehan) *pushed up to ld after 2f: hdd 5f out: wknd rapidly: last and t.o st* 25/1
2m 43.12s (4.22) **Going Correction** +0.175s/f (Good) 9 Ran SP% 114.7
Speed ratings (Par 105): **92,91,81,80,75 73,72,72,19**
toteswingers 1&2 £2.70, 2&3 £5.30, 1&3 £6.10 CSF £11.60 CT £47.07 TOTE £3.60: £1.90, £1.10, £2.60; EX 9.50 Trifecta £44.70 Pool: £2737.58 - 45.87 winning units..
Owner The Pro-Claimers **Bred** Ashley House Stud **Trained** Patching, W Sussex

FOCUS
A strong renewal of this contest, the finish of which was fought out by two crack amateur riders, with Patrick Mullins getting the better of Simon Walker. The first two were clear and the winner improved again to beat the well treated runner-up.

5824 US OPEN TENNIS AT TOTEPOOL.COM H'CAP 1m 2f 18y
4:50 (4:51) (Class 3) (0-90,88) 3-Y-0+
£9,337 (£2,796; £1,398; £699; £349; £175) **Stalls** Low

Form RPR
0312 1 **Break Rank (USA)**26 4882 4-9-6 80 JamesDoyle 8 91
(Ed de Giles) *trckd ldng trio: smooth prog to ld 2f out: sn jnd and drvn: gd battle after: hld on wl* 7/1
5554 2 nk **Benzanno (IRE)**25 4923 4-9-13 87 DavidProbert 4 97
(Andrew Balding) *hld up: 5th st: smooth prog to chal 2f out: sustained battle w wnr after: nt qckn nr fin* 6/13
15-1 3 5 **Hilali (IRE)**166 810 4-9-7 81 TedDurcan 7 82
(Gary Brown) *hld up: 7th st: shoved along 3f out: prog 2f out: rdn and kpt on to take 3rd ins fnl f: no ch w ldng pair* 20/1
0005 4 2 1/4 **Discression**10 5481 4-9-3 77 SilvestreDeSousa 1 74
(Kevin Ryan) *hld up: 6th and pushed along st: trying to make prog whn carried lft 2f out: chsd clr ldng pair over 1f out to ins fnl f: fdd* 16/1
4110 5 3 **Xinbama (IRE)**25 4923 4-8-11 78 (t) ShelleyBirkett(7) 5 69
(J W Hills) *prom: 3rd st: rdn over 3f out: wknd 2f out* 14/1
2521 6 3/4 **Persepolis (IRE)**32 4684 3-9-6 88 RyanMoore 3 78
(Sir Michael Stoute) *dwlt: hld up in last: drvn over 3f out: no prog and wl btn 2f out* 7/41
2611 7 6 **Breaking The Bank**7 5587 4-8-13 73 MartinDwyer 9 51
(William Muir) *led after 2f: hung lft and hdd 2f out: sn wknd* 4/12
3165 8 8 **Ducab (IRE)**16 5258 3-9-2 84 (t) WilliamBuick 6 47
(Roger Varian) *led 2f: chsd ldr to over 2f out: sn wknd* 7/1
2m 10.24s (0.54) **Going Correction** +0.175s/f (Good)
WFA 3 from 4yo 8lb 8 Ran SP% 113.0
Speed ratings (Par 107): **104,103,99,97,95 94,90,83**
toteswingers 1&2 £2.70, 2&3 £5.30, 1&3 £6.10 CSF £47.03 CT £795.28 TOTE £8.90: £2.50, £1.70, £2.90; EX 55.30 Trifecta £733.50 Pool: £2562.50 - 2.62 winning units..
Owner T Gould **Bred** Millsec Ltd **Trained** Ledbury, H'fords

FOCUS
A competitive race on paper with five of the eight runners either having won last time or on their penultimate outings. Good efforts from the first two to pull clear.

5825 EWELL H'CAP 1m 114y
5:25 (5:26) (Class 4) (0-80,78) 3-Y-0+ **£6,469** (£1,925; £962; £481) **Stalls** Low

Form RPR
0514 1 **Lunar Deity**19 5124 4-9-13 77 RyanMoore 6 89
(Eve Johnson Houghton) *hld up in 5th: prog to chse ldr over 2f out: drvn to cl over 1f out: led ins fnl f: styd on* 5/1
5531 2 3/4 **Angelic Upstart (IRE)**24 4960 5-9-9 73 DavidProbert 4 83
(Andrew Balding) *trckd ldr 2f: 3rd st: led 3f out: hanging lft after: drvn and hdd ins fnl f: no ex nr fin* 4/13
5243 3 4 1/2 **Kickingthelilly**24 4957 4-10-0 78 ChrisCatlin 5 78+
(Rae Guest) *sn detached in 7th and pushed along: same pl st: prog u.p over 2f out: chsd ldng pair over 1f out: no imp and tired nr fin* 8/1
0252 4 1/2 **Jack Who's He (IRE)**21 5063 4-9-11 75 (p) MartinDwyer 7 74
(William Muir) *hld up in 6th and off the pce: prog to chse ldng pair 2f out but no imp: lost 3rd over 1f out: kpt on* 8/1
0420 5 nk **Whitby Jet (IRE)**17 5245 5-9-0 71 CameronHardie(7) 1 69
(Ed Vaughan) *s.i.s: wl off the pce in last: pushed along 3f out: styd on fr 2f out: nrst fin* 20/1
2133 6 6 **Serenity Spa**22 5037 3-9-6 77 (b1) JamesDoyle 10 61
(Roger Charlton) *trckd ldng trio: rdn 3f out: no prog and btn 2f out: wknd* 3/11
0100 7 20 **Halling Dancer**25 4908 4-9-8 72 KierenFox 2 10
(Lee Carter) *pushed up to ld and set str pce: hdd 3f out: wknd rapidly jst over 2f out: t.o* 25/1
0003 8 3 1/2 **Hipster**25 4908 3-9-6 77 (v) SebSanders 8 7
(Ralph Beckett) *trckd ldr after 2f to jst over 3f out: wknd qckly over 2f out: t.o* 7/22
1m 46.44s (0.34) **Going Correction** +0.175s/f (Good)
WFA 3 from 4yo+ 7lb 8 Ran SP% 114.7
Speed ratings (Par 105): **105,104,100,99,99 94,76,73**
toteswingers 1&2 £4.10, 2&3 £5.80, 1&3 £4.80 CSF £25.39 CT £156.93 TOTE £5.00: £1.40, £2.00, £2.10; EX 27.90 Trifecta £99.20 Pool: £2078.18 - 15.69 winning units..
Owner Eden Racing (III) **Bred** Hermes Services Ltd **Trained** Blewbury, Oxon

FOCUS
A strongly run finale. The winner's best figures since he was a 2yo have been here and at Brighton and he's rated to his best.
T/Plt: £70.30 to a £1 stake. Pool: £55161.83 - 572.37 winning tickets. T/Qpdt: £24.90 to a £1 stake. Pool: £2643.0 - 78.50 winning tickets. JN

5709 NEWCASTLE (L-H)
Monday, August 26
OFFICIAL GOING: Good to soft (soft in places; 6.5)
Wind: Breezy, half behind Weather: Hot, sunny

5826 CATCH FRED'S PUSHES ON BETFRED TV/EBF MAIDEN STKS (DIV I) 7f
2:15 (2:16) (Class 4) 2-Y-0 **£4,075** (£1,212; £606; £303) **Stalls** High

Form RPR
3 1 **Roachdale House (IRE)**26 4886 2-9-5 0 LeeTopliss 5 81+
(Richard Fahey) *missed break: hld up: n.m.r over 2f out: hdwy over 1f out: squeezed through to ld wl ins fnl f: r.o wl* 9/41
4 2 nk **Stormardal (IRE)**18 5199 2-9-5 0 RobertWinston 2 80
(Ismail Mohammed) *cl up: led over 2f out: rdn over 1f out: hdd wl ins fnl f: kpt on: hld cl home* 7/1
3 5 **Coin Broker (IRE)** 2-9-0 0 DanielTudhope 4 62+
(David O'Meara) *cl up: effrt and ev ch over 2f out: outpcd by first two ins fnl f* 5/22
3 4 2 1/4 **Archibald Thorburn (IRE)**37 4513 2-9-5 0 GrahamLee 8 61
(Ed McMahon) *colty and green thrght preliminaries: taken early to post: t.k.h: prom: rdn 2f out: wknd ins fnl f* 6/13
4 5 6 **Ainmire**19 5140 2-9-5 0 MichaelO'Connell 7 46
(John Quinn) *prom: rdn over 2f out: wknd over 1f out* 20/1
64 6 1 1/4 **Paddy's Rock (IRE)**10 5482 2-9-5 0 DaleSwift 6 43
(Ann Duffield) *prom: pushed along over 2f out: wknd over 1f out* 14/1
0 7 3/4 **Mukhtazel (IRE)**25 4926 2-9-5 0 JoeFanning 3 41
(Mark Johnston) *led to over 2f out: rdn and wknd over 1f out* 14/1
43 8 1 1/2 **Chookie's Lass**20 5083 2-9-0 0 TomEaves 1 32
(Keith Dalgleish) *wnt lft s: t.k.h: hld up in tch: rdn and wknd over 1f out* 12/1
9 22 **Take A Break** 2-9-0 0 JamesSullivan 10
(Robert Johnson) *dwlt: bhd: hung lft and struggling over 4f out: sn btn: t.o* 100/1
0 10 3 1/2 **Rocky Hill Ridge**48 4142 2-9-0 0 ShirleyTeasdale(5) 9
(Alan McCabe) *bhd and sn pushed along: lost tch 4f out: t.o* 100/1
1m 26.98s (-0.82) **Going Correction** -0.225s/f (Firm) 10 Ran SP% 113.9
Speed ratings (Par 96): **95,94,88,86,79 78,77,75,50,46**
toteswingers 1&2 £2.70, 1&3 £2.60, 2&3 £5.90 CSF £17.94 TOTE £3.40: £1.60, £3.20, £1.10; EX 19.40 Trifecta £94.40 Pool: £646.70 - 5.13 winning units..
Owner G Devlin **Bred** G Devlin **Trained** Musley Bank, N Yorks

FOCUS
An eight-race card got underway with the first division of a fair juvenile maiden in which they went a decent gallop. The winning time was under two seconds slower than standard, which is more conducive to good ground. The winner looks the type to rate higher again.

5827 CATCH FRED'S PUSHES ON BETFRED TV/EBF MAIDEN STKS (DIV II) 7f
2:50 (2:50) (Class 4) 2-Y-0 **£4,075** (£1,212; £606; £303) **Stalls** High

Form RPR
0 1 **Light Weight (IRE)**14 5330 2-9-0 0 JamieSpencer 5 77+
(Kevin Ryan) *chsd ldrs: led over 2f out: rdn out fnl f* 8/1
40 2 2 1/4 **Flycatcher (IRE)**26 4877 2-9-0 0 LeeTopliss 8 70
(Richard Fahey) *prom: rdn and outpcd over 2f out: rallied to chse wnr over 1f out: edgd both ways: kpt on same pce ins fnl f* 2/11
0433 3 1 1/4 **Beltor**13 5364 2-9-5 73 TomEaves 6 72
(Michael Dods) *in tch: outpcd and hung lft over 2f out: rallied over 1f out: kpt on ins fnl f* 11/42
50 4 1 3/4 **Prostate Awareness (IRE)**10 5482 2-9-5 0 AndrewElliott 2 67
(Patrick Holmes) *hld up in tch: hdwy over 2f out: rdn and one pce over 1f out* 40/1
5 5 3 3/4 **Scots Law (IRE)**14 5330 2-8-11 0 JasonHart(3) 9 52
(Keith Dalgleish) *cl up away fr main centre gp: ev ch over 2f out: wknd fnl f* 9/23
6 3/4 **Inevitable** 2-9-5 0 JoeFanning 1 56
(Mark Johnston) *towards rr and sn pushed along: shortlived effrt wl over 1f out: sn btn* 11/2
0 7 23 **Sleeping Star**7 5577 2-9-0 0 PaulMulrennan 7
(Mel Brittain) *t.k.h: led and sn hung lft: hdd over 2f out: wknd qckly over 1f out: t.o* 80/1
8 1 **Razin' Hell** 2-9-2 0 NataliaGemelova(3) 4
(Alan McCabe) *bhd and outpcd: no ch fr 1/2-way: t.o* 28/1
5 9 1 1/2 **Crazy Dancer**94 2612 2-9-0 0 RobbieFitzpatrick 3
(Richard Guest) *s.i.s: bhd and outpcd: no ch fr 1/2-way: t.o* 40/1
1m 26.67s (-1.13) **Going Correction** -0.225s/f (Firm) 9 Ran SP% 114.2
Speed ratings (Par 96): **97,94,93,91,86 85,59,58,56**
toteswingers 1&2 £3.30, 1&3 £4.10, 2&3 £1.80 CSF £23.78 TOTE £11.70: £2.40, £1.40, £1.70; EX 28.70 Trifecta £74.20 Pool: £847.86 - 8.55 winning units..
Owner Qatar Racing Limited **Bred** Cahermorris Stables Ltd **Trained** Hambleton, N Yorks

FOCUS
The second division of the juvenile maiden in which they went a decent gallop once again, and the field were spread out across the track, searching for better ground. The winning time was marginally better than the first division. The winner has the scope to do a good bit better.

5828 BETFRED GOALS GALORE CLAIMING STKS 1m 3y(S)
3:25 (3:25) (Class 6) 3-Y-0+ **£1,940** (£577; £288; £144) **Stalls** High

Form RPR
2126 1 **Extraterrestrial**9 5546 9-9-7 74 LeeTopliss 3 74
(Richard Fahey) *hld up: effrt and hdwy over 1f out: led wl ins fnl f: jst hld on* 5/21
00 2 shd **King Pin**19 5138 8-9-1 65 (p) DaleSwift 6 68
(Tracy Waggott) *hld up: rdn and hdwy over 1f out: ev ch wl ins fnl f: jst hld* 6/13
4000 3 1/2 **Whispered Times (USA)**3 5711 6-9-1 62 MichaelO'Connell 1 67
(Tracy Waggott) *led: rdn over 2f out: hdd wl ins fnl f: rallied: hld towards fin* 12/1
-004 4 nse **Plunder**90 2737 3-9-1 70 (p) JamieSpencer 7 72
(Kevin Ryan) *prom: hdwy and ev ch over 2f out: kpt on same pce wl ins fnl f* 9/22
030 5 9 **Jo'Burg (USA)**16 5291 9-9-13 84 DanielTudhope 9 58
(David O'Meara) *chsd one other stands' rail: effrt and rdn over 2f out: sn outpcd by centre gp* 5/21
5556 6 1 3/4 **Mishhar (IRE)**19 5142 4-8-6 50 (b1) BarryMcHugh 8 33
(Tony Coyle) *dwlt: sn prom: drvn over 2f out: wknd wl over 1f out* 18/1
4330 7 7 **Moheebb (IRE)**19 5137 9-9-3 60 (e) RobertWinston 4 28
(Robert Johnson) *in tch: drvn and outpcd 3f out: n.d after* 12/1
4300 8 1 1/4 **Paramour**12 5378 6-9-10 67 JulieBurke(3) 5 35
(David O'Meara) *racd w one other stands' rail: rdn over 3f out: sn outpcd by centre gp* 25/1
351/ 9 21 **Super Collider**9 136 6-9-10 75 JasonHart(3) 2
(Susan Corbett) *in tch: rdn over 3f out: sn btn: t.o* 50/1
1m 39.79s (-3.61) **Going Correction** -0.225s/f (Firm)
WFA 3 from 4yo+ 6lb 9 Ran SP% 116.1
Speed ratings (Par 101): **109,108,108,108,99 97,90,89,68**
toteswingers 1&2 £2.60, 1&3 £5.90, 2&3 £11.50 CSF £18.28 TOTE £3.20: £1.30, £2.20, £2.90; EX 20.90 Trifecta £116.90 Pool: £616.32 - 3.95 winning units..Plunder was claimed by Mr Richard Ford for £7,000.
Owner G J Paver **Bred** Lostford Manor Stud **Trained** Musley Bank, N Yorks
■ Stewards' Enquiry : Julie Burke one-day ban: did not keep straight from the stalls (9 Sep)

FOCUS
A fair claimer in which the majority of the field raced up the centre of the track, and that is where the action developed into a thrilling, four-way finish. The first two were a few pounds off their best.

5829 BETFRED MOBILE LOTTERY BLAYDON RACE (A NURSERY H'CAP) 1m 3y(S)
4:00 (4:00) (Class 2) 2-Y-O **£9,703** (£2,887; £1,443; £721) **Stalls** High

Form RPR
461 **1** **Stars Over The Sea (USA)**[35] 4576 2-9-7 **82** JoeFanning 3 90+
(Mark Johnston) *mde all at ordinary pce: shkn up and qcknd wl over 1f out: edgd lft and kpt on wl fnl f: unchal* **9/4**[1]
31 **2** 2 ½ **Braidley (IRE)**[20] 5083 2-9-3 **78** GrahamLee 2 80
(James Bethell) *prom: hdwy to chse wnr over 2f out: rdn and flashed tail ins fnl f: kpt on: no imp* **5/2**[2]
016 **3** 2 ½ **Hatti (IRE)**[3] 5717 2-8-1 **65** (p) RaulDaSilva(3) 4 61
(Micky Hammond) *prom: rdn over 2f out: rallied fr over 1f out: plugged on fnl f: nt pce of first two* **16/1**
21 **4** 2 **New Street (IRE)**[36] 4556 2-8-13 **74** LeeTopliss 7 65
(Richard Fahey) *prom: rdn and outpcd over 2f out: kpt on fnl f: nvr able to chal* **7/2**[3]
0210 **5** ½ **Clever Miss**[16] 5284 2-9-4 **79** JamieSpencer 5 69
(Alan McCabe) *dwlt: hld up: rdn and effrt over 2f out: no imp over 1f out* **8/1**
3544 **6** ½ **Irondale Express**[19] 5136 2-8-8 **69** BarryMcHugh 6 58
(Tony Coyle) *chsd wnr to over 2f out: sn rdn: btn fnl f* **11/1**
0066 **7** 1 ¼ **Petergate**[11] 5424 2-8-2 **63** JamesSullivan 8 49
(Brian Rothwell) *hld up: rdn over 2f out: btn over 1f out* **14/1**

1m 40.57s (-2.83) **Going Correction** -0.225s/f (Firm) **7** Ran SP% **113.6**
Speed ratings (Par 100): **105,102,100,98,97 97,95**
toteswingers 1&2 £2.20, 1&3 £7.30, 2&3 £6.50 CSF £8.03 CT £67.30 TOTE £3.10: £1.80, £2.50; EX 8.60 Trifecta £88.20 Pool: £1589.12 - 13.50 winning units..
Owner R S Brookhouse **Bred** W S Farish & Watership Down Stud **Trained** Middleham Moor, N Yorks

FOCUS
A good nursery in which the winner was allowed an easy time of things on the lead towards the centre of the track. The third gives perspective.

5830 BETFRED "THE BONUS KING" FILLIES H'CAP 7f
4:35 (4:36) (Class 5) (0-75,75) 3-Y-O+ **£2,587** (£770; £384; £192) **Stalls** High

Form RPR
5312 **1** **Imaginary World (IRE)**[9] 5515 5-9-0 **66** (p) JasonHart(3) 10 75
(John Balding) *hld up: stdy hdwy 2f out: shkn up to ld wl ins fnl f: r.o* **4/1**[2]
04-6 **2** 1 ¼ **Fever Few**[19] 5152 4-9-4 **67** MichaelO'Connell 4 73
(Jane Chapple-Hyam) *chsd ldr: led over 2f out to wl ins fnl f: kpt on same pce nr fin* **14/1**
2220 **3** 1 **Push Me (IRE)**[17] 5239 6-9-7 **70** [1] GrahamLee 8 73
(Iain Jardine) *hld up: pushed along over 2f out: hdwy over 1f out: r.o ins fnl f* **7/1**
4324 **4** 1 **Alluring Star**[6] 5614 5-9-1 **64** PaulMulrennan 2 65
(Michael Easterby) *cl up: effrt and ev ch over 2f out to ins fnl f: kpt on same pce* **5/1**[3]
4001 **5** ¾ **Fab Lolly (IRE)**[16] 5290 3-8-9 **63** JamesSullivan 6 60
(James Bethell) *in tch: rdn over 2f out: effrt over 1f out: one pce ins fnl f* **14/1**
-252 **6** 1 ½ **Meeting In Paris (IRE)**[10] 5486 3-8-3 **57** (p) PatrickMathers 7 50
(Richard Fahey) *dwlt: sn pushed along in midfield: effrt and drvn wl over 1f out: wknd ins fnl f* **7/2**[1]
050 **7** 14 **Pivotal Prospect**[19] 5138 5-8-11 **60** RobertWinston 9 17
(Tracy Waggott) *in tch: rdn over 2f out: effrt over 1f out: wknd qckly last 150yds* **8/1**
0006 **8** nk **Miss Matiz**[9] 5515 6-8-4 **56** oh11 DeclanCannon(3) 3 12
(Alan Kirtley) *towards rr: drvn over 2f out: sn wknd* **66/1**
6305 **9** 6 **Light Rose (IRE)**[12] 5398 3-9-7 **75** (b[1]) JoeFanning 5 13
(Mark Johnston) *led at decent gallop: rdn and hdd over 2f out: sn btn: eased whn no ch fnl f* **13/2**
-000 **R** **Tamara Bay**[14] 5331 5-8-8 **57** oh2 ow1 TomEaves 1
(John Davies) *taken early to post: ref to r* **25/1**

1m 25.54s (-2.26) **Going Correction** -0.225s/f (Firm)
WFA 3 from 4yo+ 5lb **10** Ran SP% **114.5**
Speed ratings (Par 103): **103,101,100,99,98 96,80,80,73,**
toteswingers 1&2 £12.80, 1&3 £6.00, 2&3 £21.10 CSF £57.42 CT £387.72 TOTE £3.80: £1.30, £5.80, £2.50; EX 69.60 Trifecta £455.40 Pool: £1555.34 - 2.56 winning units..
Owner Hairy Gorrilaz **Bred** Denis McDonnell **Trained** Scrooby, Notts

FOCUS
A fair fillies' handicap in which the winner recorded the best comparative time on the card so far. The winner's best run since he was a 3yo.

5831 BETFRED TV "BONUS LUNCH" H'CAP 1m 6f 97y
5:10 (5:10) (Class 5) (0-75,75) 4-Y-O+ **£2,587** (£770; £384; £192) **Stalls** Low

Form RPR
01 **1** **Medieval Bishop (IRE)**[63] 3625 4-8-4 **61** ow2 (p) JasonHart(3) 7 69
(Tim Walford) *led 1f: cl up: led over 2f out: sn drvn along: hld on gamely fnl f* **10/1**
4140 **2** nk **Mister Pagan**[30] 4782 5-9-7 **75** GrahamLee 2 83+
(Jim Goldie) *midfield on ins: effrt and hdwy over 2f out: styd on wl to chse wnr last 100yds: kpt on: jst hld* **15/2**[3]
1250 **3** ½ **Zarosa (IRE)**[25] 4913 4-8-0 **61** JoeyHaynes(7) 9 68
(John Berry) *prom: effrt whn n.m.r briefly over 2f out: kpt on ins fnl f* **6/1**[2]
6060 **4** 1 **Authentication**[18] 5185 4-8-4 **58** AndrewElliott 5 64
(Mel Brittain) *hld up in midfield: rdn over 3f out: styd on fnl 2f: nrst fin* **33/1**
1522 **5** nk **Sally Friday (IRE)**[16] 5295 5-8-2 **63** (p) KevinStott(7) 13 68
(Edwin Tuer) *midfield: stdy hdwy 3f out: chsd wnr over 1f out to last 100yds: one pce* **8/1**
2135 **6** 1 ¾ **Madrasa (IRE)**[24] 4969 5-8-9 **70** (bt) JacobButterfield(7) 8 73
(Keith Reveley) *hld up: rdn 3f out: styd on fr over 1f out: no imp* **10/1**
6354 **7** hd **Brunello**[10] 5466 5-8-2 **59** (p) DeclanCannon(3) 1 61
(Philip Kirby) *hld up: rdn 3f out: rallied over 1f out: no imp fnl f* **14/1**
6424 **8** 1 ½ **Beat The Shower**[24] 4969 7-8-6 **60** JamesSullivan 6 60
(Peter Niven) *t.k.h: hld up on outside: rdn and outpcd 3f out: styd on fnl f: no imp* **10/1**
2 **9** ½ **Mont Blanc**[15] 5312 4-9-4 **72** (p) PaulMulrennan 11 72
(Jane Chapple-Hyam) *t.k.h: cl up: effrt and chsd wnr over 2f out to over 1f out: wknd ins fnl f* **11/2**[1]
1402 **10** 3 ½ **Tartan Jura**[11] 5423 5-9-7 **75** (p) JoeFanning 14 70
(Mark Johnston) *led after 1f: rdn over 6f out: hdd over 3f out: wknd fr 2f out* **8/1**
-004 **11** shd **Persian Peril**[21] 5055 9-9-6 **74** RobertWinston 3 69
(Alan Swinbank) *hld up: rdn over 4f out: no imp fr 2f out* **16/1**
145 **12** 2 ½ **Miss Macnamara (IRE)**[21] 5048 4-8-8 **62** TomEaves 12 53
(Martin Todhunter) *cl up: led over 3f out to over 2f out: sn btn* **14/1**
-304 **13** 3 ½ **Russian George (IRE)**[112] 2087 7-9-4 **72** JamieSpencer 10 58
(Steve Gollings) *hld up: rdn and outpcd over 3f out: btn fnl 2f* **16/1**
130- **14** 1 ¾ **Wayne Manor (IRE)**[9] 7381 4-9-3 **71** (t) LeeTopliss 4 55
(Lucinda Russell) *early reminders in rr: struggling over 3f out: nvr on terms* **28/1**

3m 11.47s (0.17) **Going Correction** -0.175s/f (Firm) **14** Ran SP% **122.4**
Speed ratings (Par 103): **92,91,91,90,90 89,89,88,88,86 86,85,83,82**
CSF £84.52 CT £501.57 TOTE £13.60: £4.70, £2.80, £2.70; EX 89.80 Trifecta £778.30 Part won. Pool: £1037.75 - 0.52 winning units..
Owner Mr & Mrs K Hamilton,D Dickson,N Skinner **Bred** Keatly Overseas Ltd **Trained** Sheriff Hutton, N Yorks

FOCUS
A fair staying handicap in which they went a steady gallop early on. A rather muddling race and it's hard to rate the bare form much higher.

5832 BETFRED MOBILE H'CAP 6f
5:45 (5:45) (Class 4) (0-80,80) 3-Y-O+ **£4,690** (£1,395; £697; £348) **Stalls** High

Form RPR
364 **1** **Right Touch**[21] 5056 3-9-3 **76** BarryMcHugh 7 85
(Richard Fahey) *cl up: rdn to ld over 1f out: kpt on strly fnl f* **10/1**
1423 **2** 1 **Tajneed (IRE)**[20] 5088 10-8-8 **71** JordanNason(7) 14 77
(David Nicholls) *chsd ldrs: rdn over 2f out: rallied and chsd wnr fnl f: r.o* **9/1**
0243 **3** ½ **Beckermet (IRE)**[21] 5049 11-8-10 **66** JamesSullivan 9 70
(Ruth Carr) *led tl rdn and hdd over 1f out: r.o ins fnl f* **18/1**
4105 **4** ½ **Indego Blues**[23] 5011 4-9-0 **70** PaulQuinn 15 73
(David Nicholls) *midfield: effrt and rdn 2f out: kpt on same pce ins fnl f* **12/1**
0342 **5** ½ **Roker Park (IRE)**[14] 5333 8-9-5 **75** (v) DanielTudhope 1 76
(David O'Meara) *cl up: rdn and ev ch over 1f out: hung lft: no ex ins fnl f* **9/2**[1]
4001 **6** shd **Showboating (IRE)**[8] 5564 5-9-8 **78** 6ex (tp) JamieSpencer 4 79
(Alan McCabe) *hld up: rdn and hdwy over 1f out: kpt on ins fnl f* **8/1**[3]
6/65 **7** ½ **Beau Amadeus (IRE)**[29] 4807 4-9-0 **70** JoeFanning 13 69
(David Nicholls) *in tch: rdn over 2f out: edgd lft and one pce appr fnl f* **12/1**
2625 **8** nk **Angelito**[33] 4620 4-9-10 **80** RobertWinston 11 78
(Ed McMahon) *dwlt: hld up: pushed along and hdwy over 1f out: nvr able to chal* **7/1**[2]
1300 **9** 1 ½ **Rasaman (IRE)**[17] 5238 9-9-10 **80** GrahamLee 10 73
(Jim Goldie) *hld up towards rr: pushed along over 2f out: no imp fnl f* **7/1**[2]
0000 **10** nk **Mission Impossible**[16] 5294 8-8-12 **68** (p) DaleSwift 8 60
(Tracy Waggott) *in tch: rdn over 2f out: no ex over 1f out* **20/1**
4014 **11** nk **Ambitious Icarus**[3] 5708 4-8-9 **65** (e) RobbieFitzpatrick 6 56
(Richard Guest) *t.k.h: towards rr: rdn 2f out: btn fnl f* **16/1**
0000 **12** ½ **Escape To Glory (USA)**[16] 5294 5-9-8 **78** PaulMulrennan 2 68
(Michael Dods) *hld up in midfield: rdn over 2f out: wknd fnl f* **16/1**
0002 **13** 1 ¾ **Towbee**[20] 5088 4-9-7 **77** (b) TomEaves 3 61
(Michael Easterby) *t.k.h: hld up in midfield: rdn 2f out: sn wknd* **14/1**
0053 **14** 1 ¼ **Meandmyshadow**[10] 5498 5-9-7 **77** MichaelO'Connell 5 57
(Alan Brown) *cl up: drvn along 1/2-way: wknd wl over 1f out* **16/1**

1m 12.5s (-2.10) **Going Correction** -0.225s/f (Firm)
WFA 3 from 4yo+ 3lb **14** Ran SP% **123.1**
Speed ratings (Par 105): **105,103,103,102,101 101,100,100,98,98 97,97,94,93**
CSF £99.38 CT £1659.21 TOTE £11.90: £2.70, £3.20, £4.80; EX 158.60 Trifecta £812.00 Part won. Pool: £1082.75 - 0.95 winning units..
Owner Nicholas Wrigley & Kevin Hart **Bred** The Athenians **Trained** Musley Bank, N Yorks

FOCUS
A fair sprint handicap in which they went a decent gallop up the centre of the track. The winner rates a length personal best.

5833 BETFRED BUNDLES H'CAP 1m 4f 93y
6:15 (6:15) (Class 6) (0-65,64) 3-Y-O+ **£1,940** (£577; £288; £144) **Stalls** Low

Form RPR
3200 **1** **Blue Top**[29] 4809 4-9-0 **53** (p) JasonHart(3) 10 62
(Tim Walford) *hld up in midfield: hdwy over 2f out: drvn to ld ins fnl f: edgd rt: kpt on wl* **12/1**
6541 **2** ½ **Vittachi**[17] 5240 6-9-1 **51** (p) MichaelO'Connell 14 59
(Alistair Whillans) *hld up in midfield: hdwy on outside over 2f out: chsd wnr ins fnl f: kpt on: hld nr fin* **10/1**
3401 **3** ¾ **Ailsa Craig (IRE)**[13] 5370 7-9-5 **62** (p) KevinStott(7) 3 69
(Edwin Tuer) *hld up in midfield on ins: hdwy over 2f out: ev ch ins fnl f: kpt on same pce last 75yds* **9/1**[3]
0040 **4** 1 ½ **Shirls Son Sam**[8] 5560 5-9-0 **50** MichaelStainton 13 54
(Chris Fairhurst) *t.k.h: prom on outside: hdwy to ld 1/2-way: kicked clr over 3f out: hdd ins fnl f: no ex* **33/1**
055 **5** 1 ½ **Korngold**[13] 5370 5-8-13 **49** BarryMcHugh 4 51
(Tracy Waggott) *plld hrd early: prom on ins: nt clr run over 3f out: effrt over 2f out: one pce fnl f* **14/1**
4623 **6** 3 ¼ **Iceman George**[39] 4455 9-9-7 **62** (v) TobyAtkinson(5) 1 59
(Alison Hutchinson) *hld up: rdn over 3f out: styd on fr 2f out: nvr able to chal* **20/1**
66-4 **7** nk **Spanish Legacy**[19] 5143 4-8-7 **50** JacobButterfield(7) 6 46
(Julie Camacho) *t.k.h: sn towards rr: rdn over 2f out: hdwy over 1f out: nrst fin* **12/1**
0045 **8** 1 ¼ **Buster Brown (IRE)**[18] 5179 4-10-0 **64** DaleSwift 11 58
(James Given) *plld hrd early in midfield: hmpd after 2f: rdn over 3f out: styd on fnl f: no imp* **9/2**[2]
0500 **9** 7 **Fine Altomis**[19] 5143 4-9-2 **52** PaulMulrennan 2 35
(Michael Dods) *hld up: pushed along over 2f out: nvr able to chal* **25/1**
0-06 **10** 1 ¼ **Inniscastle Boy**[24] 4951 4-8-13 **49** GrahamLee 8 30
(Jim Goldie) *hld up: hmpd after 2f: rdn over 3f out: nvr able to chal* **14/1**
6404 **11** 8 **Magic Lando (FR)**[18] 5204 3-9-2 **62** RobertWinston 12 45
(Ismail Mohammed) *t.k.h: trckd ldrs: effrt and rdn 3f out: wknd over 1f out: sn eased whn btn* **9/4**[1]
-600 **12** 7 **Jeer (IRE)**[11] 5420 9-9-5 **55** JamesSullivan 7 12
(Michael Easterby) *led to 1/2-way: cl up tl rdn and wknd over 2f out* **50/1**

0640 **13** 1 3/4 **Alsahil (USA)**[20] 5086 7-10-0 64 (b[1]) DanielTudhope 16 18
(Alan Swinbank) *prom on outside: rdn and outpcd over 2f out: sn btn* 22/1

066 **14** 1 **Croftamie**[11] 5420 4-8-13 49 JoeFanning 9
(Tracy Waggott) *t.k.h early: chsd ldrs tl rdn and wknd over 2f out* 33/1

4043 **15** 48 **Silver Tigress**[17] 5222 5-9-7 57 (p) TomEaves 5
(George Moore) *midfield: lost pl qckly 3f out: sn struggling: t.o* 14/1

2m 42.73s (-2.87) **Going Correction** -0.175s/f (Firm)
WFA 3 from 4yo+ 10lb 15 Ran SP% **124.2**
Speed ratings (Par 101): **102,101,101,100,99 97,96,95,91,90 85,80,79,78,46**
CSF £119.75 CT £1153.70 TOTE £13.10: £2.70, £4.40, £3.70; EX 102.60 Trifecta £163.80 Pool: £891.82 - 4.08 winning units..
Owner Brown, Evans, Lister, Cowley **Bred** Mrs Joan M Langmead **Trained** Sheriff Hutton, N Yorks

FOCUS
The concluding contest was a modest middle-distance handicap in which they went a steady gallop early on, and 3lb claiming jockey Jason Hart was particularly strong in the finish in completing a superb treble. The winner is rated back to his old best.
T/Plt: £35.40 to a £1 stake. Pool: £51072.08 - 1052.99 winning tickets T/Qpdt: £27.40 to a £1 stake. Pool: £2709.02 - 72.94 winning tickets RY

5543 RIPON (R-H)
Monday, August 26

OFFICIAL GOING: Good (good to soft in places; 8.1)
Wind: Virtually nil Weather: Sunshine

5834 FREEBETS.CO.UK (S) STKS 6f
1:55 (1:56) (Class 6) 2-Y-O **£2,726** (£805; £402) **Stalls** High

Form RPR

3124 **1** **Black Treacle (IRE)**[7] 5591 2-9-7 70 (v[1]) PJMcDonald 6 73
(Keith Dalgleish) *led 2f: trckd ldr: swtchd rt and rdn to chal over 1f out: led ent fnl f: kpt on* 2/1[2]

2300 **2** 2 1/4 **Sartori**[46] 4218 2-9-2 72 MartinHarley 4 61
(Mick Channon) *chsd ldng pair: hdwy 2f out: sn rdn: styd on u.p fnl f: nt rch wnr* 6/5[1]

2655 **3** 2 1/4 **Song Of Rowland (IRE)**[20] 5106 2-9-2 67 DavidNolan 1 55
(David O'Meara) *cl up: led after 2f: rdn along 2f out: hdd and drvn ent fnl f: sn wknd* 6/1[3]

000 **4** 7 **Casper Lee (IRE)**[23] 4977 2-9-2 44 GrahamGibbons 2 34
(Nigel Tinkler) *dwlt and in rr: rdn along 1/2-way: sme hdwy fnl 2f: nvr a factor* 22/1

00 **5** 4 1/2 **Dizzy Miss Lizzy (IRE)**[20] 5101 2-8-11 0 SeanLevey 5 15
(Richard Hannon) *sn rdn along and a in rr* 8/1

0 **6** 10 **Angus Mac Og (IRE)**[73] 3298 2-8-9 0 DanielleMooney[(7)] 3
(Nigel Tinkler) *chsd ldng pair 1f: hung lft thrght: rdn bef 1/2-way and sn bhd* 66/1

1m 14.14s (1.14) **Going Correction** 0.0s/f (Good) 6 Ran SP% **110.0**
Speed ratings (Par 92): **92,89,86,76,70 57**
toteswingers 1&2 £1.10, 1&3 £1.30, 2&3 £1.02 CSF £4.54 TOTE £2.90: £1.50, £1.10; EX 5.50 Trifecta £8.90 Pool: £1000.88 - 83.83 winning units..There was no bid for the winner. Sartori bought by Mrs Marjorie Fife for £6,000.
Owner Straightline Construction Ltd **Bred** Tally-Ho Stud **Trained** Carluke, S Lanarks

FOCUS
A seller run on ground described by winning jockey PJ McDonald as being on the easy side of good. They finished well pread out and the winner's previous Polytrack form could be rated this high.

5835 SIS VIRTUAL BETTING CHANNEL H'CAP 1m 1f 170y
2:25 (2:25) (Class 5) (0-75,75) 3-Y-O **£3,234** (£962; £481; £240) **Stalls** Low

Form RPR

24-4 **1** **Lyric Piece**[12] 5392 3-9-1 69 (p) MartinHarley 7 84+
(Sir Mark Prescott Bt) *trckd ldr: hdwy 3f out: cl up 2f out: sn led: rdn clr appr fnl f: kpt on strly* 5/1

3005 **2** 5 **Tussie Mussie**[9] 5548 3-9-0 68 (b[1]) FrannyNorton 3 73
(Mark Johnston) *mde most tl rdn along and hdd wl over 1f out: sn drvn and kpt on same pce* 8/1

3520 **3** 1 3/4 **Gioia Di Vita**[10] 5483 3-9-7 75 TonyHamilton 2 76
(David Nicholls) *trckd ldng pair on inner: rdn along wl over 2f out: drvn wl over 1f out: kpt on one pce* 10/3[2]

0133 **4** 1 1/4 **Naaz (IRE)**[10] 5483 3-9-7 75 (b) NeilCallan 4 74
(Ed Dunlop) *trckd ldng pair: hdwy 3f out: rdn 2f out: drvn over 1f out: wknd fnl f* 5/2[1]

5241 **5** 1 3/4 **Correggio**[19] 5146 3-9-6 74 PJMcDonald 6 69
(Micky Hammond) *hld up: hdwy on outer 3f out: rdn to chse ldrs 2f out: drvn over 1f out: wknd ent fnl f* 6/1

5124 **6** 13 **Lexington Blue**[5] 5642 3-8-13 67 (v) DavidNolan 1 36
(David O'Meara) *reminders s: hld up in rr: effrt and sme hdwy 3f out: sn rdn and wknd* 9/2[3]

2m 2.94s (-2.46) **Going Correction** -0.175s/f (Firm) 6 Ran SP% **111.9**
Speed ratings (Par 100): **102,98,96,95,94 83**
toteswingers 1&2 £11.90, 1&3 £6.80, 2&3 £4.70 CSF £41.50 TOTE £7.40: £5.10, £4.70; EX 48.80 Trifecta £419.30 Part won. Pool: £559.07 - 0.93 winning units..
Owner Cheveley Park Stud **Bred** Cheveley Park Stud Ltd **Trained** Newmarket, Suffolk

FOCUS
This ended up being quite a one-sided 3yo handicap. It was run at a decent pace and the runner-up is the key to the form.

5836 BILLY NEVETT MEMORIAL H'CAP 6f
3:00 (3:00) (Class 4) (0-85,85) 3-Y-O **£4,851** (£1,443; £721; £360) **Stalls** High

Form RPR

411 **1** **Monakova (IRE)**[10] 5486 3-8-13 77 ow1 DavidNolan 2 90
(David O'Meara) *trckd ldrs: hdwy 2f out: chal over 1f out: sn rdn: led last 100yds: kpt on* 9/4[1]

0311 **2** 1/2 **Sedenoo**[33] 4624 3-9-3 81 AdamKirby 1 92
(Marco Botti) *trckd ldng pair: effrt to chal 2f out: rdn to ld over 1f out: drvn ins fnl f: hdd and no ex last 100yds* 9/4[1]

0641 **3** 2 **Flighty Clarets (IRE)**[14] 5333 3-7-13 66 NeilFarley[(3)] 8 71
(Richard Fahey) *trckd ldng pair on inner: effrt 2f out: sn n.m.r and swtchd rt over 1f out: rdn and kpt on fnl f* 12/1

0530 **4** 2 **Khelman (IRE)**[23] 5011 3-8-8 72 TonyHamilton 7 71
(Richard Fahey) *slt ld: rdn along 2f out: drvn and hdd over 1f out: grad wknd* 11/2[3]

6212 **5** 2 3/4 **Scentpastparadise**[19] 5141 3-8-8 72 PJMcDonald 5 62
(Ann Duffield) *cl up: rdn along 2f out: sn wknd* 10/1

1424 **6** 1/2 **Tumblewind**[31] 4734 3-9-2 85 GeorgeChaloner[(5)] 3 73
(Richard Whitaker) *rrd and dwlt s: hdwy on outer after 2f out: cl up and ch 2f out: sn rdn and wknd* 9/2[2]

1m 12.55s (-0.45) **Going Correction** 0.0s/f (Good) 6 Ran SP% **111.9**
Speed ratings (Par 102): **103,102,99,97,93 92**
toteswingers 1&2 £1.10, 1&3 £4.40, 2&3 £3.50 CSF £7.27 CT £44.66 TOTE £2.70: £1.40, £1.90; EX 7.30 Trifecta £20.60 Pool: £1021.80 - 37.16 winning units..
Owner Dundalk Racing Club **Bred** Thomas Jones **Trained** Nawton, N Yorks

FOCUS
A couple of progressive types pulled clear in this 3yo sprint. The first two could both have been rated higher.

5837 IRISH STALLION FARMS EBF RIPON CHAMPION TWO YRS OLD TROPHY 2013 (LISTED RACE) 6f
3:35 (3:35) (Class 1) 2-Y-O **£17,013** (£6,450; £3,228; £1,608; £807) **Stalls** High

Form RPR

3251 **1** **Supplicant**[9] 5547 2-9-2 103 TonyHamilton 1 105+
(Richard Fahey) *prom: cl up 1/2-way: led wl over 1f out: rdn clr ent fnl f: kpt on: readily* 1/1[1]

120 **2** 2 3/4 **Riverboat Springs (IRE)**[69] 3422 2-9-2 93 MartinHarley 5 95
(Mick Channon) *sn rdn along and outpcd in rr: detached 1/2-way: hdwy wl over 1f out: rdn and styd on fnl f: no ch w wnr* 7/2[2]

1020 **3** 1/2 **Ventura Mist**[4] 5679 2-8-11 96 (p) DuranFentiman 2 89
(Tim Easterby) *qckly away: restrained to trck ldng pair: effrt wl over 1f out: rdn and one pce ent fnl f* 7/1

0021 **4** hd **Hoku (IRE)**[21] 5061 2-8-11 85 HarryBentley 6 88
(Olly Stevens) *trckd ldrs whn hit rail and unbalanced after 1f: hdwy 2f out: swtchd rt and rdn over 1f out: one pce ent fnl f* 11/2[3]

1103 **5** 10 **Legend Rising (IRE)**[12] 5396 2-9-2 91 (b[1]) SeanLevey 3 63
(Richard Hannon) *sn led: rdn along over 2f out: hdd wl over 1f out and sn wknd* 11/1

1m 12.49s (-0.51) **Going Correction** 0.0s/f (Good) 5 Ran SP% **108.4**
Speed ratings (Par 102): **103,99,98,98,85**
CSF £4.54 TOTE £1.50: £1.10, £1.80; EX 5.30 Trifecta £10.90 Pool: £1308.23 - 89.35 winning units..
Owner Cheveley Park Stud **Bred** Cheveley Park Stud Ltd **Trained** Musley Bank, N Yorks

FOCUS
Supplicant was the clear form choice and has the scope to rate a bit higher. The second and fourth were close to form.

5838 RIPON ROWELS H'CAP 1m
4:10 (4:10) (Class 2) (0-100,97) 3-Y-O£12,602 (£3,772; £1,886; £944; £470) **Stalls** Low

Form RPR

5420 **1** **Osteopathic Remedy (IRE)**[23] 5014 9-9-0 90 ConnorBeasley[(5)] 2 100
(Michael Dods) *in tch: hdwy 3f out and sn chsng ldrs: rdn to ld appr fnl f: sn clr: drvn out* 10/1

5111 **2** 2 **Robert The Painter (IRE)**[9] 5546 5-9-7 97 (v) DavidBergin[(5)] 11 102
(David O'Meara) *trckd ldr: cl up 1/2-way: led 3f out: rdn 2f out: hdd and drvn appr fnl f: kpt on same pce* 15/2[3]

0100 **3** shd **Captain Bertie (IRE)**[24] 4946 5-9-2 94 IanBurns[(7)] 14 99+
(Jane Chapple-Hyam) *hld up towards rr: swtchd wd and hdwy 3f out: rdn over 1f out: styng on whn edgd rt ent fnl f: nrst fin* 20/1

4650 **4** 2 **Dubai Dynamo**[9] 5546 8-9-1 86 PJMcDonald 10 87
(Ruth Carr) *hld up towards rr: hdwy over 2f out: sn rdn and styd on wl fnl f: nrst fin* 20/1

3-10 **5** 2 1/2 **Haafaguinea**[24] 4946 3-9-6 97 AdamKirby 6 92
(Clive Cox) *towards rr: hdwy wl over 2f out: sn rdn: drvn and kpt on appr fnl f: nrst fin* 3/1[1]

1632 **6** 1/2 **Suits Me**[28] 4825 10-9-8 93 GrahamGibbons 7 87
(David Barron) *led: pushed along 4f out: hdd 3f out: sn rdn: drvn and kpt on one pce fnl 2f* 12/1

3623 **7** 2 1/4 **Trail Blaze (IRE)**[23] 5014 4-9-10 95 (b) NeilCallan 3 83
(Kevin Ryan) *trckd ldrs: effrt 3f out: rdn and hung rt over 2f out: sn drvn and wknd* 4/1[2]

5402 **8** shd **No Poppy (IRE)**[9] 5546 5-8-9 85 AdamCarter[(5)] 8 73
(Tim Easterby) *in rr tl sme late hdwy* 12/1

2164 **9** 3/4 **Desert Revolution**[14] 5335 3-8-5 82 FrannyNorton 9 69
(Mark Johnston) *dwlt: a towards rr* 10/1

-000 **10** 3/4 **Anton Chigurh**[9] 5546 4-9-4 89 StephenCraine 5 74
(Tom Dascombe) *midfield: effrt on inner 1/2-way: sn rdn along and n.d* 25/1

0000 **11** 1 1/2 **Justonefortheroad**[30] 4744 7-9-5 90 TonyHamilton 12 71
(Richard Fahey) *chsd ldrs: rdn along 3f out: sn wknd* 33/1

010 **12** 1 3/4 **Ardmay (IRE)**[83] 2958 4-9-5 90 DavidNolan 1 67
(Kevin Ryan) *chsd ldng pair: rdn along over 3f out: sn wknd* 28/1

-411 **13** 4 1/2 **The Rectifier (USA)**[44] 4308 6-9-11 96 (t) MickyFenton 13 63
(Seamus Durack) *chsd ldrs: rdn along 3f out: drvn over 2f out: sn wknd* 14/1

0050 **14** 7 **Compton**[30] 4744 4-8-13 84 SeanLevey 4 35
(Robert Cowell) *a towards rr* 25/1

1m 38.1s (-3.30) **Going Correction** -0.175s/f (Firm)
WFA 3 from 4yo+ 6lb 14 Ran SP% **120.6**
Speed ratings (Par 109): **109,107,106,104,102 101,99,99,98,98 96,94,90,83**
toteswingers 1&2 £20.10, 1&3 Not won, 2&3 £76.90 CSF £74.92 CT £1533.71 TOTE £9.10: £2.90, £3.00, £9.60; EX 95.10 Trifecta £1427.20 Part won. Pool: £1903.04 - 0.24 winning units..
Owner Kevin Kirkup **Bred** Airlie Stud **Trained** Denton, Co Durham
■ Stewards' Enquiry : David Bergin four-day ban: careless riding (9-12 Sep)

FOCUS
A useful and competitive handicap. It was run at a good gallop but, as is often the case over this C&D, it wasn't easy to get into contention from off the pace, the performance of the third worth marking up. The winner looks as good as ever.

5839 SIS LIVE MAIDEN STKS 1m
4:45 (4:46) (Class 5) 3-4-Y-O **£3,234** (£962; £481; £240) **Stalls** Low

Form RPR

64- **1** **Zain Eagle**[292] 7636 3-9-5 0 NeilCallan 8 91
(Gerard Butler) *mde all: qcknd 2f out: clr over 1f out: unchal* 7/2[2]

2 **2** 9 **Endless Light**[49] 4125 3-9-0 0 SeanLevey 7 65
(Jeremy Noseda) *trckd wnr: effrt 3f out: rdn along over 2f out: drvn and no imp fr over 1f out* 6/4[1]

3 1 **Dawn Calling (IRE)** 3-9-5 0 FrannyNorton 5 68
(Mark Johnston) *trckd ldng pair: effrt over 2f out: sn rdn and kpt on same pce* 7/2[2]

226U **4** 1/2 **Jullundar (IRE)**[23] 5016 3-9-5 66 (v) MartinHarley 2 67
(Mick Channon) *in tch: hdwy over 3f out: rdn to chse ldrs over 2f out: drvn and one pce fr wl over 1f out* 12/1

The Form Book Flat, Raceform Ltd, Compton, RG20 6NL.

5 7 **Let's Go Live** 3-9-5 0 .... MickyFenton 6 51
(Paul Midgley) *s.i.s and in rr: swtchd wd and rdn 3f out: sn no imp* **33/1**

0 6 *nk* **Glasgon**[10] 5484 3-9-2 0 .... NeilFarley(3) 4 50
(Declan Carroll) *chsd ldrs: rdn along 3f out: sn wknd* **33/1**

7 *1/2* **Semai (IRE)** 3-9-5 0 .... AdamKirby 3 49
(Marco Botti) *dwlt and towards rr: hdwy over 3f out: rdn along to chse ldrs wl over 2f out: sn wknd* **13/2[3]**

8 *1 1/2* **Nowcando** 3-9-0 0 .... PJMcDonald 1 40
(K R Burke) *a bhd* **16/1**

1m 39.43s (-1.97) **Going Correction** -0.175s/f (Firm) 8 Ran SP% **117.2**
Speed ratings (Par 103): **102,93,92,91,84 84,83,82**
toteswingers 1&2 £2.50, 1&3 £4.60, 2&3 £1.30 CSF £9.42 TOTE £5.10: £1.50, £1.10, £1.80; EX 12.60 Trifecta £50.50 Pool: £1585.03 - 23.50 winning units..
Owner Asaad Al Banwan **Bred** Biddestone Stud Ltd **Trained** Newmarket, Suffolk

FOCUS
An ordinary maiden overall. The winner's form could be rated up to 5lb higher on time.

5840 BETFAIR NOVICE FLAT AMATEUR RIDERS' H'CAP (FOR NOVICE AMATEUR RIDERS) 1m 1f 170y
5:20 (5:21) (Class 6) (0-60,60) 4-Y-0+ **£2,495** (£774; £386; £193) **Stalls** Low

Form RPR

4222 1 **Euston Square**[13] 5368 7-11-4 **57** .... (v[1]) MrHAABannister 2 73
(Alistair Whillans) *hld up in midfield: hdwy over 3f out: pushed along to chse ldrs over 2f out: rdn to chse ldr ent fnl f: sn led and styd on strly* **5/2[1]**

0453 2 *5* **Outlaw Torn (IRE)**[12] 5383 4-11-7 **60** .... (e) MissBeckySmith 12 66
(Richard Guest) *led and set str pce: sn clr: 10 l ahd at 1/2-way: rdn along over 1f out: hdd ins fnl f: one pce* **14/1**

0060 3 *3/4* **Monthly Medal**[3] 5713 10-11-2 **55** .... (t) MissLWilson 5 59
(Wilf Storey) *in rr: hdwy 3f out: rdn along on inner 2f out: styd on u.p fnl f: nrst fin* **20/1**

0333 4 *nk* **Rockweiller**[11] 5427 6-11-1 **54** .... (v) MrPJohn 1 58
(Steve Gollings) *prom: rdn along over 2f out: drvn to chse ldr wl over 1f out: sn no imp* **5/1[2]**

3454 5 *1 3/4* **Rub Of The Relic (IRE)**[11] 5426 8-11-5 **58** .... (v) MissHDukes 14 58
(Paul Midgley) *chsd ldrs: rdn along 3f out: kpt on same pce fnl 2f* **10/1**

4005 6 *nk* **Glan Lady (IRE)**[11] 5426 7-10-4 **46** oh1 .... MrJLBaker(3) 7 46
(Michael Appleby) *towards rr: hdwy 3f out: rdn 2f out: kpt on fnl f: nrst fin* **28/1**

4104 7 *nk* **Amazing Blue Sky**[19] 5142 7-11-5 **58** .... MrRColley 8 57
(Ruth Carr) *sn chsng clr ldr: hdwy 3f out: tk clsr order over 2f out: sn rdn: wknd over 1f out* **15/2[3]**

642 8 *nk* **Frosty Berry**[14] 5337 4-11-2 **58** .... MrAFrench(3) 3 56
(Neville Bycroft) *in rr tl styd on fnl 2f: nvr a factor* **5/1[2]**

0650 9 *1/2* **Eium Mac**[24] 4966 4-11-3 **56** .... MrSebSpencer 6 53
(Neville Bycroft) *chsd ldrs: rdn along wl over 2f out: sn one pce* **20/1**

006- 10 *3 1/2* **Divine Success (IRE)**[343] 6316 4-10-7 **46** oh1 .... MrTHamilton 10 36
(Richard Fahey) *chsd ldrs: rdn along over 3f out: wknd over 2f out* **18/1**

600 11 *shd* **Sir George (IRE)**[26] 4893 8-10-7 **46** .... MrAaronJames 17 36
(Suzzanne France) *nvr bttr than midfield* **33/1**

0-00 12 *7* **Celtic Step**[60] 3727 9-10-8 **50** .... MrKWood(3) 16 26
(Peter Niven) *nvr bttr than midfield* **16/1**

300- 13 *3* **Come Hither**[248] 8213 4-11-4 **60** .... MrPHardy(3) 11 30
(John Norton) *a in rr* **33/1**

14 *10* **An Spailpin Fanach (USA)**[36] 4568 6-11-5 **58** .... MissLEgerton 9 7
(Paul Midgley) *a in rr* **33/1**

2m 6.32s (0.92) **Going Correction** -0.175s/f (Firm) 14 Ran SP% **122.4**
Speed ratings (Par 101): **89,85,84,84,82 82,82,82,81,78 78,73,70,62**
toteswingers 1&2 £7.50, 1&3 £25.80, 2&3 £67.70 CSF £37.68 CT £579.08 TOTE £3.10: £1.90, £3.00, £9.80; EX 48.70 Trifecta £557.90 Part won. Pool: £743.94 - 0.76 winning units..
Owner Granite City Racing & John Waugh **Bred** Juddmonte Farms Ltd **Trained** Newmill-On-Slitrig, Borders

FOCUS
A modest amateurs' handicap to round things off. The runner-up soon established a clear lead, rather ignored by the rest of the field until the straight, the winner the only one to get past him. The winner built on his recent form.
T/Plt: £48.60 to a £1 stake. Pool: £53429.57 - 802.42 winning tickets T/Qpdt: £5.10 to a £1 stake. Pool: £3139.00 - 448.40 winning tickets JR

5644 WARWICK (L-H)
Monday, August 26

OFFICIAL GOING: Good (6.5)
Wind: Light against Weather: Fine

5841 RACINGUK.COM H'CAP 6f
2:10 (2:10) (Class 5) (0-70,70) 3-Y-0+ **£2,587** (£770; £384; £192) **Stalls** Low

Form RPR

0622 1 **Rigolleto (IRE)**[7] 5583 5-9-6 **66** .... GeorgeBaker 5 74
(Anabel K Murphy) *a.p: chsd ldr 2f out: shkn up over 1f out: r.o u.p to ld nr fin* **7/2[2]**

3402 2 *hd* **Ace Master**[13] 5373 5-8-10 **59** .... (b) MarkCoumbe(3) 9 66
(Roy Bowring) *led 5f out: rdn over 1f out: hdd nr fin* **7/1**

050P 3 *1* **Bussa**[14] 5349 5-9-4 **67** .... (t) DeclanBates(3) 7 71
(David Evans) *s.i.s and hmpd s: hld up: rdn over 1f out: r.o ins fnl f: nt rch ldrs* **25/1**

1-60 4 *nse* **Ozz**[140] 1430 4-8-11 **62** .... (bt) LauraPike(5) 8 66
(Frank Sheridan) *hld up: pushed along over 1f out: r.o ins fnl f: nrst fin* **33/1**

1264 5 *1 1/4* **Planetex (IRE)**[19] 5148 4-9-3 **66** .... DarrenEgan(3) 1 66
(John Quinn) *trckd ldrs: rdn over 1f out: styd on same pce fnl f* **13/2[3]**

424 6 *3/4* **Dark Lane**[4] 5669 7-9-8 **68** .... TomQueally 3 66
(David Evans) *hld up: hdwy u.p over 1f out: styd on same pce ins fnl f* **8/1**

6044 7 *hd* **Jarrow (IRE)**[5] 5645 6-9-3 **63** .... (b) WilliamCarson 6 60
(Milton Bradley) *hld up: hdwy 2f out: sn rdn: no ex ins fnl f* **22/1**

4000 8 *1/2* **Nasri**[33] 4628 7-9-10 **70** .... (p) LiamKeniry 10 65
(Milton Bradley) *chsd ldr tl rdn 2f out: no ex ins fnl f* **20/1**

-320 9 *7* **Sakhee's Rose**[24] 4962 3-9-2 **65** .... RoystonFfrench 2 38
(Ed McMahon) *s.i.s: sn prom: rdn over 2f out: wknd fnl f* **10/1**

4130 10 *6* **See The Storm**[30] 4746 5-9-10 **70** .... JimCrowley 4 24
(Ian Williams) *led 1f: remained handy tl rdn and wknd over 1f out* **2/1[1]**

1m 12.05s (0.25) **Going Correction** +0.125s/f (Good)
WFA 3 from 4yo+ 3lb 10 Ran SP% **117.5**
Speed ratings (Par 103): **103,102,101,101,99 98,98,97,88,80**
toteswingers 1&2 £5.50, 1&3 Not won, 2&3 £20.60 CSF £26.79 CT £533.53 TOTE £4.60: £2.50, £3.50, £10.90; EX 25.60 Trifecta £342.80 Part won. Pool: £457.09 - 0.16 winning units..
Owner All The Kings Horses **Bred** Michael O'Mahony **Trained** Wilmcote, Warwicks

FOCUS
The pace was not very strong in this sprint handicap. The hold-up performers couldn't land a blow but two in-form runners filled the first two positions and the form looks solid enough. The winner is rated to his Thirsk latest.

5842 FREE RADIO NURSERY H'CAP 5f 110y
2:45 (2:45) (Class 5) (0-75,72) 2-Y-0 **£2,587** (£770; £384; £192) **Stalls** Low

Form RPR

6010 1 **Primitorio (IRE)**[24] 4948 2-9-4 **69** .... (b) JimCrowley 5 85+
(Ralph Beckett) *hmpd s: in tch: shkn up to ld and hung rt over 1f out: rdn clr: eased nr fin* **11/4[1]**

5113 2 *7* **Lilo Lil**[9] 5509 2-8-13 **67** .... (p) ThomasBrown(3) 1 60
(David C Griffiths) *sn chsng ldr: rdn over 1f out: styd on same pce ins fnl f* **4/1[2]**

312 3 *1 1/2* **Douneedahand**[7] 5595 2-8-11 **62** .... KieranO'Neill 6 50
(Seamus Mullins) *hmpd s: prom: led over 4f out: rdn and hdd over 1f out: no ex ins fnl f* **10/1**

314 4 *3/4* **Captain Whoosh (IRE)**[39] 4434 2-9-7 **72** .... LiamKeniry 7 58
(Tom Dascombe) *prom: rdn over 2f out: no ex fnl f* **11/4[1]**

4255 5 *1/2* **Dodger Marley (IRE)**[9] 5509 2-9-0 **65** .... (t) PatCosgrave 4 49
(Stuart Williams) *hmpd s: sn prom: rdn over 2f out: styd on same pce fr over 1f out* **6/1[3]**

406 6 *nse* **Thrtypointstothree (IRE)**[56] 3883 2-9-0 **68** .... WilliamTwiston-Davies(3) 2 52
(Nikki Evans) *led 1f: chsd ldrs: rdn over 2f out: styd on same pce fr over 1f out* **20/1**

5416 7 *1/2* **Honey Meadow**[39] 4431 2-9-2 **67** .... TomQueally 3 49
(Robert Eddery) *wnt rt s: hld up: rdn over 1f out: n.d* **8/1**

1m 6.06s (0.16) **Going Correction** +0.125s/f (Good) 7 Ran SP% **112.6**
Speed ratings (Par 94): **103,93,91,90,90 89,89**
toteswingers 1&2 £1.10, 1&3 £6.90, 2&3 £7.10 CSF £13.49 TOTE £3.20: £1.50, £3.10; EX 10.10 Trifecta £73.10 Pool: £205.55 - 2.10 winning units..
Owner Thurloe Thoroughbreds XXXI **Bred** Manister House Stud **Trained** Kimpton, Hants

FOCUS
This nursery looked competitive but the winner powered clear. He is going the right way but could prove flattered by this.

5843 EBFSTALLIONS.COM MAIDEN STKS 7f 26y
3:20 (3:21) (Class 5) 2-Y-0 **£2,911** (£866; £432; £216) **Stalls** Low

Form RPR

4 1 **Meteoroid (USA)**[30] 4764 2-9-5 0 .... TomQueally 3 76+
(Lady Cecil) *hld up: hdwy over 2f out: shkn up and r.o to ld wl ins fnl f: readily* **13/8[2]**

532 2 *1/2* **Captain Bob (IRE)**[12] 5399 2-9-5 79 .... FrankieDettori 12 75
(Charles Hills) *led: rdn and hung rt over 1f out: hdd wl ins fnl f* **6/4[1]**

3 *nk* **Chatez (IRE)** 2-9-5 0 .... FergusSweeney 8 74+
(Alan King) *hld up: hdwy over 1f out: rdn and r.o wl* **50/1**

4 *3/4* **Hoon (IRE)** 2-9-5 0 .... WilliamCarson 1 72+
(Rae Guest) *a.p: racd keenly: shkn up over 1f out: r.o* **40/1**

20 5 *1/2* **After The Goldrush**[23] 4987 2-9-2 0 .... WilliamTwiston-Davies(3) 11 71
(Richard Hannon) *trckd ldrs: wnt 2nd 2f out: sn rdn: styd on same pce ins fnl f* **10/1**

0 6 *1 1/2* **Flying Cape (IRE)**[15] 5299 2-9-5 0 .... LiamKeniry 10 67+
(Andrew Hollinshead) *s.i.s: hld up: rdn and r.o wl ins fnl f: nt rch ldrs* **40/1**

63 7 *3* **Tancred (IRE)**[19] 5145 2-9-5 0 .... GeorgeBaker 7 59
(Peter Chapple-Hyam) *chsd ldrs: swtchd rt 2f out: sn rdn: styd on same pce fr over 1f out* **15/2[3]**

00 8 *3/4* **Gloss (IRE)**[26] 4896 2-9-5 0 .... PatDobbs 6 57
(Richard Hannon) *chsd ldr tl pushed along 2f out: wknd ins fnl f* **25/1**

00 9 *3/4* **Barbary (IRE)**[53] 3991 2-9-5 0 .... FrederikTylicki 4 55
(James Fanshawe) *stdd s: hld up: nvr on terms* **25/1**

4 10 *9* **Captain Devious**[11] 5428 2-9-2 0 .... DeclanBates(3) 9 32
(David Evans) *hld up: pushed along and hung rt 1/2-way: wknd over 2f out* **66/1**

1m 24.75s (0.15) **Going Correction** -0.175s/f (Firm) 10 Ran SP% **115.0**
Speed ratings (Par 94): **92,91,91,90,89 87,84,83,82,72**
toteswingers 1&2 £1.40, 1&3 £64.10, 2&3 £64.10 CSF £4.02 TOTE £2.90: £1.20, £1.10, £7.10; EX 5.20 Trifecta £105.60 Pool: £784.28 - 5.56 winning units..
Owner Niarchos Family **Bred** Flaxman Holdings Limited **Trained** Newmarket, Suffolk

FOCUS
There was not much separating the first six in this maiden but the two market leaders filled the first two positions and the race should throw up winners. The runner-up helps guide the form.

5844 REWARDS4RACING.COM CONDITIONS STKS 7f 26y
3:55 (3:56) (Class 3) 3-Y-0+ **£7,439** (£2,213; £1,106; £553) **Stalls** Low

Form RPR

1063 1 **Highland Colori (IRE)**[16] 5285 5-8-11 99 .... LiamKeniry 5 106
(Andrew Balding) *trckd ldr tl pushed along and swtchd to r alone stands' side 2f out: led over 1f out: rdn out* **9/4[2]**

3065 2 *1 1/2* **Es Que Love (IRE)**[4] 5681 4-8-11 104 .... FrankieDettori 3 102
(Mark Johnston) *led: pushed along over 2f out: rdn and hdd over 1f out: styd on* **5/6[1]**

-003 3 *1* **The Cheka (IRE)**[23] 5013 7-8-11 102 .... (p) TomQueally 2 99
(Eve Johnson Houghton) *dwlt: hld up: hdwy over 1f out: rdn and r.o: nt rch ldrs* **10/1**

0641 4 *8* **Annunciation**[16] 5260 3-8-6 99 .... KieranO'Neill 4 78
(Richard Hannon) *chsd ldrs: rdn over 2f out: wknd fnl f* **13/2[3]**

1m 22.28s (-2.32) **Going Correction** -0.175s/f (Firm)
WFA 3 from 4yo+ 5lb 4 Ran SP% **107.7**
Speed ratings (Par 107): **106,104,103,94**
CSF £4.53 TOTE £4.60; EX 5.20 Trifecta £17.20 Pool: £928.70 - 40.39 winning units..
Owner Evan M Sutherland **Bred** Rathbarry Stud **Trained** Kingsclere, Hants

FOCUS
A decent conditions event. It was run at a good pace and winner scored after racing alone against the stands' rail in the straight. He is rated to form.

5845 BRITISH STALLION STUDS EBF MAIDEN STKS 7f 26y
4:30 (4:32) (Class 5) 3-Y-0+ **£3,881** (£1,155; £577; £288) **Stalls** Low

Form RPR

04 1 **Canon Law (IRE)**[84] 2931 3-9-5 0 .... KirstyMilczarek 8 76+
(Luca Cumani) *trckd ldrs: pushed along over 2f out: rdn to ld over 1f out: edgd lft ins fnl f: styd on* **5/1[2]**

30 2 *nk* **Desert Wings (IRE)**[10] 5484 3-9-5 0 .... MickaelBarzalona 6 75+
(Charlie Appleby) *plld hrd and prom: rdn and ev ch fr over 1f out: styd on* **10/11[1]**

-224 3 1 1/4 **Martial Art (IRE)**[9] 5512 3-9-5 70......(p) LiamKeniry 2 72
(Andrew Balding) *chsd ldrs: shkn up and ev ch over 1f out: rdn ins fnl f: nt qckn* **7/1**[3]

0 4 3/4 **Defiant Spirit**[12] 5386 3-9-5 0...... GeorgeBaker 5 70
(Roger Charlton) *trckd ldrs: rdn over 1f out: styd on* **8/1**

3 5 1 3/4 **Caerwyn**[11] 5444 3-9-0 0...... MichaelJMMurphy(5) 10 65
(Marcus Tregoning) *mid-div: racd keenly: hdwy over 2f out: rdn over 1f out: styd on same pce fnl f* **8/1**

6 3/4 **Aomen Rock** 3-9-5 0...... FrederikTylicki 11 63+
(James Fanshawe) *hld up: pushed along over 1f out: styd on ins fnl f: nvr nrr* **8/1**

06 7 2 1/4 **Raafa's Jigsaw**[8] 5563 4-9-5 0...... AndrewMullen 9 54
(Michael Appleby) *led: rdn over 2f out: hdd over 1f out: wknd fnl f* **80/1**

8 15 **Churt** 4-9-10 0...... SaleemGolam 3 19
(Christopher Kellett) *dwlt and hmpd s: a in rr* **80/1**

06 9 11 **Alberto**[14] 5345 3-9-5 0...... PatDobbs 4
(Paul Fitzsimons) *dwlt and wnt lft s: hld up: plld hrd: wknd over 2f out* **40/1**

1m 23.81s (-0.79) **Going Correction** -0.175s/f (Firm)
WFA 3 from 4yo 5lb **9** Ran SP% **119.8**
Speed ratings (Par 103): **97,96,95,94,92 91,88,71,59**
toteswingers 1&2 £1.90, 1&3 £10.00, 2&3 £1.60 CSF £10.31 TOTE £6.50: £2.50, £1.02, £1.30; EX 14.00 Trifecta £32.50 Pool: £1051.92 - 24.25 winning units..
Owner S Stuckey **Bred** Liam Butler **Trained** Newmarket, Suffolk

FOCUS
They went a steady pace in this maiden and the strong favourite was just held. There are one or two doubts but the third sets the standard.

5846 JENNINGSBET.COM H'CAP 1m 6f 213y
5:05 (5:05) (Class 6) (0-60,57) 3-Y-0+ **£1,940** (£577; £288; £144) **Stalls** Low

Form RPR

0306 1 **Vertueux (FR)**[17] 5216 8-9-7 **50**......(p) LiamKeniry 4 59
(Tony Carroll) *mde all: set stdy pce tl qcknd over 3f out: rdn over 1f out: styd on wl* **25/1**

0006 2 3/4 **Waving**[20] 5093 4-9-9 **55**......(t) WilliamTwiston-Davies(3) 7 63
(Tony Carroll) *s.i.s and hmpd s: hld up: hdwy over 2f out: rdn to chse wnr over 1f out: sn ev ch: unable qck nr fin* **13/2**

0042 3 3 **Mr Vendman (IRE)**[10] 5500 3-8-5 **47**......(b[1]) JimmyQuinn 3 51
(Ian Williams) *trckd wnr after 2f: rdn over 2f out: styd on same pce fnl f* **5/1**[3]

0404 4 1 **Moaning Butcher**[8] 5560 3-9-1 **57**......(v) JimCrowley 2 60
(Mark Johnston) *chsd ldrs: rdn over 1f out: no ex ins fnl f* **3/1**[2]

2132 5 3 1/4 **Noor Al Haya (IRE)**[5] 5630 3-8-13 **55**...... KieranO'Neill 1 54+
(Mark Usher) *hld up: rdn over 1f out: nvr any ch* **11/4**[1]

V432 6 1 3/4 **Honey Haven (IRE)**[11] 5432 3-8-7 **54**...... NoelGarbutt(5) 8 50
(Mark Brisbourne) *wnt lft s: hld up: rdn over 2f out: nvr on terms* **13/2**

0-40 7 1 **Venir Rouge**[56] 3884 9-9-7 **53**...... ThomasBrown(3) 5 48
(Harry Whittington) *hld up: rdn over 2f out: nvr on terms* **25/1**

5040 8 nk **Between The Lines (IRE)**[28] 4838 4-9-8 **56**..(t) MichaelJMMurphy(5) 10 51
(Anthony Middleton) *plld hrd and prom: rdn over 2f out: wknd over 1f out* **16/1**

000- 9 4 **Ponte Di Rosa**[292] 7077 5-9-13 **56**...... WilliamCarson 11 45
(Simon Hodgson) *chsd ldrs: rdn over 2f out: hung lft and wknd over 1f out* **16/1**

3m 27.63s (8.63) **Going Correction** -0.175s/f (Firm)
WFA 3 from 4yo+ 13lb **9** Ran SP% **114.5**
Speed ratings (Par 101): **69,68,67,66,64 63,63,63,60**
toteswingers 1&2 £24.80, 1&3 £29.40, 2&3 £10.30 CSF £177.10 CT £952.96 TOTE £22.60: £5.80, £2.40, £2.10; EX 376.60 Trifecta £601.60 Part won. Pool: £802.15 - 0.05 winning units..
Owner John Rutter **Bred** Roger Baudouin **Trained** Cropthorne, Worcs

FOCUS
They went a steady pace in this low-grade staying handicap. There was 25-1 front-running winner and the favourite was never involved under a patient ride. A 1-2 for Tony Carroll. The winner is rated to form.

5847 LEAMINGTON FOOD AND DRINK FESTIVAL H'CAP (JOCKEY CLUB GRASSROOTS MIDDLE DISTANCE SERIES QUALIFIER) 1m 2f 188y
5:40 (5:40) (Class 4) (0-80,79) 3-Y-0+ **£4,690** (£1,395; £697; £348) **Stalls** Low

Form RPR

0500 1 **Super Say (IRE)**[64] 3607 7-10-0 **79**......(t) AndrewMullen 2 86
(Michael Appleby) *a.p: rdn to ld over 1f out: edgd rt ins fnl f: jst hld on* **16/1**

1-50 2 nk **The Cayterers**[19] 5124 11-9-9 **77**...... ThomasBrown(3) 9 83
(Ronald Harris) *hld up: rdn over 2f out: r.o ins fnl f: jst failed* **20/1**

065 3 1 1/4 **Markttag**[16] 5286 3-8-12 **72**...... KirstyMilczarek 1 76
(Luca Cumani) *trckd ldr tl over 8f out: wnt 2nd again 7f out: rdn and ev ch over 1f out: styd on same pce ins fnl f* **8/1**

-262 4 hd **Herod The Great**[22] 5032 3-9-1 **75**...... FergusSweeney 8 79
(Alan King) *plld hrd and prom: rdn over 2f out: hung lft over 1f out: styd on same pce ins fnl f* **5/1**[2]

0250 5 3/4 **Kelpie Blitz (IRE)**[44] 4280 4-9-11 **76**......(t) GeorgeBaker 3 79
(Seamus Durack) *hld up: hdwy u.p over 1f out: nt rch ldrs* **7/1**

0/ 6 4 1/2 **Ceannline (IRE)**[602] 3492 7-9-4 **72**...... WilliamTwiston-Davies(3) 6 67
(Venetia Williams) *hld up: rdn over 2f out: n.d* **22/1**

21- 7 6 **Intiba (USA)**[336] 6535 3-9-3 **77**...... MickaelBarzalona 4 62
(Saeed bin Suroor) *led: rdn and hdd over 1f out: wknd fnl f* **7/4**[1]

3613 8 nk **Arlecchino (IRE)**[18] 5189 3-9-0 **74**......(b) RoystonFfrench 5 58
(Ed McMahon) *trckd ldrs: plld hrd: wnt 2nd over 8f out tl over 7f out: remained handy tl rdn over 2f out: wknd over 1f out* **6/1**[3]

0514 9 3 **Significant Move**[28] 4831 6-9-9 **74**......(v[1]) PatCosgrave 7 53
(Stuart Kittow) *hld up: rdn over 2f out: wknd over 1f out: eased* **8/1**

2m 17.56s (-3.54) **Going Correction** -0.175s/f (Firm)
WFA 3 from 4yo+ 9lb **9** Ran SP% **117.0**
Speed ratings (Par 105): **105,104,103,103,103 99,95,95,93**
toteswingers 1&2 £40.30, 1&3 £24.20, 2&3 £52.40 CSF £290.88 CT £2737.78 TOTE £23.10: £6.40, £6.80, £2.60; EX 191.80 Trifecta £908.00 Part won. Pool: £1210.72 - 0.03 winning units..
Owner Castle Racing **Bred** Peter Jones And G G Jones **Trained** Danethorpe, Notts

FOCUS
They went a decent pace in this handicap. The favourite was disappointing under a forcing ride and two of the oldest runners in the line-up filled the first two places. The winner is rated to the balance of this year's form.
T/Plt: £93.80 to a £1 stake. Pool: £41117.51 - 319.69 winning tickets T/Qpdt: £19.60 to a £1 stake. Pool: £1780.09 - 66.95 winning tickets CR

5805 DEAUVILLE (R-H)
Monday, August 26

OFFICIAL GOING: Turf: soft; fibresand: standard

5848a PRIX DE VALMONT (CLAIMER) (2YO COLTS & GELDINGS) (FIBRESAND) 6f 110y
3:40 (12:00) 2-Y-O **£10,975** (£4,390; £3,292; £2,195; £1,097)

RPR

1 **Cockney Bob**[9] 2-8-9 0......(p) OlivierPeslier 3 76
(D Windrif, France) **7/2**[2]

2 snk **Shepherd Gate (USA)**[9] 5508 2-8-13 0......(b) ThierryJarnet 4 80
(J S Moore) *restrained early: prom in midfield: 4th 3f out: rdn to chal over 1f out: led jst ins fnl f: r.o but worn down and hdd fnl strides* **10/1**[3]

3 1 3/4 **Simply Ozzy (IRE)**[17] 5362 2-9-0 0...... ThomasMessina 6 76
(V Luka Jr, Czech Republic) **61/1**

4 1 1/4 **Color Code (FR)**[17] 5362 2-8-9 0...... TheoBachelot 11 67
(S Wattel, France) **27/1**

5 1 1/2 **Zanthalia (FR)**[9] 2-8-9 0...... MaximeGuyon 5 63
(S Wattel, France) **16/1**

6 snk **Minley**[17] 5215 2-9-6 0...... ChristopheSoumillon 8 74
(Rae Guest) *dwlt sltly and pushed along to rcvr: sn trcking ldr in 2nd on outer: rdn to chal 2f out: led over 1f out: hdd jst ins fnl f and no ex: fdd and dropped to sixth cl home* **7/2**[2]

7 snk **Oeil De Tigre (FR)**[32] 4701 2-9-2 0...... FabriceVeron 1 69
(H-A Pantall, France) **23/10**[1]

8 1/2 **Tableforten**[44] 4300 2-9-3 0...... IoritzMendizabal 2 69
(J S Moore) *settled in midfield on inner: angled off rail and rdn whn nt clr run briefly over 1f out: kpt on same pce ins fnl f: nvr able to chal* **12/1**

9 nk **Island Kingdom (IRE)**[32] 4662 2-8-6 0...... SoufyaneMoulin(3) 10 60
(J S Moore) *hld up in last pair on outer: last 3f out: rdn 2f out: sn outpcd: kpt on u.p and sme late hdwy but n.d* **12/1**

10 2 **Petit Arc En Ciel**[34] 2-8-9 0...... Francois-XavierBertras 7 55
(E J O'Neill, France) **64/1**

11 3 **Le Magellan (FR)**[78] 2-8-10 0......(b) SebastienMartino(6) 9 53
(H De Nicolay, France) **20/1**

1m 19.47s (79.47) **11** Ran SP% **116.6**
WIN (incl. 1 euro stake): 4.50. PLACES: 1.90, 2.90, 10.60. DF: 16.60. SF: 25.80.
Owner Frederic Sarfati **Bred** Miss Deborah Wisbey **Trained** France

5819 EPSOM (L-H)
Tuesday, August 27

OFFICIAL GOING: Good (7.5)
Wind: light, against Weather: sunny and warm

5850 JRA NURSERY H'CAP 7f
2:15 (2:16) (Class 5) (0-75,70) 2-Y-O **£3,881** (£1,155; £577; £288) **Stalls** Low

Form RPR

0335 1 **Imshivalla (IRE)**[18] 5235 2-9-0 **63**...... PaulHanagan 5 69
(Richard Fahey) *chsd ldr: rdn and effrt 2f out: led ins fnl f: styd on strly and gng away at fin: readily* **5/1**[3]

41 2 3 1/4 **Smart Payer**[34] 4617 2-9-7 **70**...... J-PGuillambert 1 68
(Jo Hughes) *taken down early: led and clr after 1f: rdn 2f out: hdd and no ex ins fnl f: kpt on for clr 2nd* **8/1**

045 3 2 1/4 **M'Lady Ermyn**[10] 5524 2-8-6 **55**...... FrankieMcDonald 7 47+
(Pat Phelan) *s.i.s: bhd: rdn over 2f out: styd on strly fnl f to snatch 3rd last strides: nvr trbld ldrs* **20/1**

515 4 nk **A Childs Dream (IRE)**[46] 4232 2-9-5 **68**...... RichardHughes 4 59
(Richard Hannon) *chsd ldng pair: rdn and effrt over 2f out: outpcd 2f out: kpt on same pce and no imp after: lost 3rd last strides* **7/2**[2]

502 5 1/2 **Got To Dance**[48] 4164 2-9-6 **69**...... JimCrowley 6 59
(Ralph Beckett) *hld up off the pce in midfield: rdn and effrt over 2f out: pressing for 3rd but no threat to ldng pair 1f out: one pce fnl f* **7/2**[2]

464 6 1 1/2 **Autopilot**[29] 4827 2-9-5 **68**......(p) RyanMoore 3 54
(Brian Meehan) *hld up off the pce in midfield: effrt to dispute 3rd 2f out: no imp on ldng pair over 1f out: wknd ins fnl f* **9/4**[1]

0045 7 45 **Little Big Man**[8] 5595 2-7-11 **49** oh1...... SimonPearce(3) 2
(Sylvester Kirk) *hld up in last pair: struggling 4f out: lost tch qckly over 2f: t.o fnl f* **33/1**

1m 24.79s (1.49) **Going Correction** +0.20s/f (Good) **7** Ran SP% **110.7**
Speed ratings (Par 94): **99,95,92,92,91 90,38**
toteswingers 1&2 £3.80, 1&3 £12.10, 2&3 £10.20 CSF £40.46 TOTE £7.20: £3.10, £3.00; EX 44.90 Trifecta £356.60 Pool: £2140.04 - 4.49 winning units..
Owner Pow Partnership **Bred** M Fahy & Rathbarry Stud **Trained** Musley Bank, N Yorks

FOCUS
A moderate nursery. It was run at a sound early pace and the first pair were always up there. The winner built on her Musselburgh run.

5851 JOHN AKEHURST H'CAP 6f
2:50 (2:52) (Class 3) (0-90,89) 3-Y-0+ **£7,439** (£2,213; £1,106; £553) **Stalls** High

Form RPR

1010 1 **Hopes N Dreams (IRE)**[10] 5544 5-9-8 **87**...... JamieSpencer 1 99
(Kevin Ryan) *taken down early: mde all: shkn up and readily qcknd clr over 1f out: in command 1f out: eased towards fin: comf* **8/1**[3]

3401 2 2 3/4 **Clear Praise (USA)**[17] 5278 6-8-11 **76**...... RichardHughes 2 80
(Simon Dow) *t.k.h: chsd ldrs: rdn and effrt to chse clr wnr over 1f out: r.o but no imp* **8/1**[3]

1610 3 1 1/4 **Head Space (IRE)**[10] 5544 5-9-10 **89**......(p) JamesSullivan 5 89
(Ruth Carr) *stdd s: hld up in rr: effrt and swtchd rt 2f out: hdwy u.p over 1f out: wnt 3rd ins fnl f: styd on but no threat to wnr* **8/1**[3]

2110 4 1/2 **Picture Dealer**[24] 4983 4-9-10 **89**...... RyanMoore 6 88
(Gary Moore) *racd in last pair: outpcd over 3f out: rdn 3f out: hdwy u.p over 1f out: styd on fnl f: nvr trbld ldrs* **1/1**[1]

3010 5 1 1/4 **Noverre To Go (IRE)**[10] 5544 7-9-4 **83**......(p) SteveDrowne 3 78
(Ronald Harris) *t.k.h: hld up in midfield: swtchd lft and effrt on inner wl over 1f out: no ch w wnr and one pce fnl f* **14/1**

0250 6 1/2 **Baldemar**[32] 4730 8-8-8 **73**...... PaulHanagan 4 66
(Richard Fahey) *chsd wnr: rdn and unable qck ent fnl 2f: lost 2nd over 1f out: wknd fnl f* **8/1**[3]

2416 **7** *1 3/4* **Fortinbrass (IRE)**[16] 5303 3-9-2 **84**.................................. JimCrowley 7 72
(Ralph Beckett) *in tch in midfield: rdn and unable qck over 2f out: drvn and btn over 1f out: wknd fnl f* **7/1**[2]

1m 9.44s (0.04) **Going Correction** +0.20s/f (Good)
WFA 3 from 4yo+ 3lb **7** Ran SP% **113.6**
Speed ratings (Par 107): **107,103,101,101,99 98,96**
toteswingers 1&2 £4.90, 1&3 £6.50, 2&3 £5.80 CSF £67.00 CT £527.94 TOTE £7.30: £2.90, £2.60; EX 70.70 Trifecta £292.90 Pool: £2840.28 - 7.27 winning units..
Owner JCG Chua & CK Ong **Bred** J & Mrs Brennan & Edward & Mrs O'Regan **Trained** Hambleton, N Yorks

FOCUS
A fair sprint handicap. The winner had the run of things but is thriving. The form could be rated higher.

5852 BRITISH STALLION STUDS EBF MAIDEN STKS 1m 114y
3:25 (3:26) (Class 5) 2-Y-O **£3,881** (£1,155; £577; £288) **Stalls** Low

Form RPR
0 **1** **Solidarity**[74] 3291 2-9-5 0.. MickaelBarzalona 4 73+
(Charlie Appleby) *stdd after s: chsd ldng: hdwy to chse ldr 2f out: rdn to ld 1f out: r.o strly and drew clr fnl f: comf* **7/2**[2]

004 **2** *2 1/2* **Dalaki (IRE)**[16] 5309 2-9-5 72..(b) RyanMoore 2 68
(Clive Brittain) *shkn up leaving stalls: sn led: hdd 6f out: chsd ldr tl 2f out: kpt on same pce fr over 1f out: wnt 2nd fnl 75yds: no imp* **8/1**

0 **3** *1 3/4* **Al Khawaneej Star (USA)**[18] 5244 2-9-5 0.................... HarryBentley 5 64+
(Michael Bell) *dwlt: hld up in tch in last pair: rdn and effrt ent fnl 2f: hdwy 1f out: kpt on to go 3rd wl ins fnl f: no threat to wnr* **4/1**[3]

02 **4** *1* **Opera Fan (FR)**[20] 5122 2-9-0 0... JoeFanning 7 57
(Mark Johnston) *t.k.h: w ldr tl led 6f out: rdn ent fnl 2f: hdd over 1f out: no ex and btn ins fnl f: wknd and lost 2 pls fnl 75yds* **4/1**[3]

06 **5** *1* **Under My Wing (IRE)**[24] 4987 2-9-5 0........................ RichardHughes 3 60+
(Richard Hannon) *taken down early: in tch in midfield 5th and outpcd u.p 2f out: kpt on same pce and no threat to ldrs after* **3/1**[1]

3 **6** *21* **Astrowolf**[26] 4926 2-9-5 0.. TedDurcan 6 16
(Mark H Tompkins) *hld up in tch in last pair: pushed along 4f out: rdn and btn over 2f out: sn wknd: wl bhd and eased ins fnl f* **7/1**

1m 47.19s (1.09) **Going Correction** +0.20s/f (Good) **6** Ran SP% **110.8**
Speed ratings (Par 94): **103,100,99,98,97 78**
toteswingers 1&2 £4.60, 1&3 £3.00, 2&3 £4.50 CSF £29.07 TOTE £3.60: £1.70, £3.00; EX 29.60 Trifecta £128.80 Pool: £2670.91 - 15.54 winning units..
Owner Godolphin **Bred** Darley **Trained** Newmarket, Suffolk

FOCUS
This appeared a modest 2-y-o maiden. They went a fair early pace. Not much depth, the second and third helping with the level.

5853 TERRY MILLS H'CAP 7f
3:55 (3:56) (Class 4) (0-80,80) 3-Y-O **£6,469** (£1,925; £962; £481) **Stalls** Low

Form RPR
4360 **1** **Flashlight (IRE)**[12] 5439 3-9-7 **80**...................................... JoeFanning 2 88
(Mark Johnston) *mde all: gng best 2f out: sn rdn and qcknd clr: in command and r.o wl fnl f* **7/2**[3]

4156 **2** *2 1/2* **Fiducia**[20] 5134 3-8-8 **67**.. HarryBentley 3 69
(Simon Dow) *stdd s: t.k.h: hld up in last pair: hdwy u.p over 1f out: chsd wnr 1f out: r.o but no threat to wnr* **10/1**

0022 **3** *4* **Panther Patrol (IRE)**[11] 5477 3-9-2 **75**............................... RyanMoore 6 66
(Eve Johnson Houghton) *in tch in midfield: effrt to chse ldng pair and rdn over 3f out: chsd clr wnr over 1f out tl 1f out: wl hld and one pce fnl f* **11/4**[1]

0230 **4** *1* **Whipper Snapper (IRE)**[10] 5541 3-9-4 **77**................(p) JamieSpencer 1 66+
(William Knight) *hld up in tch in last pair: rdn and outpcd over 2f out: styd on u.p ins fnl f: no ch w wnr* **5/1**

0030 **5** *2* **Hipster**[1] 5825 3-9-4 **77**..(v) JimCrowley 5 60
(Ralph Beckett) *chsd wnr: rdn and effrt over 2f out: unable qck and lost 2nd over 1f out: wknd fnl f* **3/1**[2]

2510 **6** *3 1/4* **Hornboy**[43] 4354 3-9-0 **73**...(p) RichardHughes 4 48
(Jeremy Noseda) *chsd ldng pair tl over 3f out: outpcd and edgd lft over 2f out: bhd over 1f out: wknd fnl f* **8/1**

1m 24.63s (1.33) **Going Correction** +0.20s/f (Good) **6** Ran SP% **110.8**
Speed ratings (Par 102): **100,97,92,91,89 85**
toteswingers 1&2 £3.90, 1&3 £2.80, 2&3 £5.90 CSF £34.45 TOTE £4.40: £1.60, £5.90; EX 33.90 Trifecta £182.00 Pool: £2293.35 - 9.44 winning units..
Owner Sheikh Hamdan Bin Mohammed Al Maktoum **Bred** Gerry Smith **Trained** Middleham Moor, N Yorks

FOCUS
A fairly tight-looking 3-y-o handicap, but the winner set an ordinary pace and few got in a blow. He is rated to the best of this year's turf form.

5854 CHANTILLY H'CAP (JOCKEY CLUB GRASSROOTS MIDDLE DISTANCE SERIES QUALIFIER) 1m 4f 10y
4:30 (4:31) (Class 5) (0-75,75) 3-Y-O+ **£3,881** (£1,155; £577; £288) **Stalls** Centre

Form RPR
-003 **1** **Toptempo**[10] 5542 4-9-7 **68**... TedDurcan 5 75
(Mark H Tompkins) *hld up in last pair: hdwy to chal 2f out: ev ch and drew clr w rival over 1f out: led fnl 100yds: r.o wl and pushed out towards fin* **11/2**

465 **2** *3/4* **Rock God (IRE)**[3] 5743 3-8-13 **70**.....................................(b[1]) JohnFahy 2 76
(Eve Johnson Houghton) *chsd ldr tl 9f out: chsd ldng pair after: swtchd rt and chsd ldr over 2f out: drvn to ld and edgd rt over 1f out: hdd and no ex fnl 100yds* **7/1**

234 **3** *1 1/2* **Fantasy In Blue**[83] 2995 3-8-13 **70**..................................... RyanMoore 3 74+
(Sir Michael Stoute) *hld up in last pair: hdwy after and sltly hmpd wl over 2f out: hdwy u.p over 1f out: chsd ldng pair ins fnl f: styd on but nt rch ldrs* **7/2**[2]

0254 **4** *9* **Grandiloquent**[13] 5384 4-9-4 **65**...............................(p) JamieSpencer 7 57
(Kevin Ryan) *sn bustled along to ld: reminder 4f out: drvn over 2f out: hdd over 1f out: 3rd and btn 1f out: sn wknd: eased towards fin* **6/1**

-604 **5** *6* **Epsom Salts**[40] 4437 8-8-13 **63**...............................(p) JemmaMarshall(3) 1 44
(Pat Phelan) *bustled along leaving stalls: chsd ldrs tl shuffled bk 8f out: in tch in midfield: swtchd rt and effrt over 2f out: sn struggling: wknd wl over 1f out: eased wl ins fnl f* **14/1**

230- **6** *7* **The Bells O Peover**[110] 6584 5-10-0 **75**........................(v) JoeFanning 8 46
(Mark Johnston) *chsd ldng pair: wnt 2nd 9f out tl over 2f out: sn struggling u.p: wknd wl over 1f out: bhd and eased wl ins fnl f* **10/3**[1]

3-32 **7** *4 1/2* **Candyman Can (IRE)**[13] 5391 3-8-12 **69**............................ LiamKeniry 6 33
(Dominic Ffrench Davis) *hld up in tch in midfield: hdwy 4f out: slighly hmpd lost pl and unbalanced wl over 2f out: nt rcvr and wl bhd after: eased ins fnl f* **9/2**[3]

4251 **8** *4* **Anginola (IRE)**[20] 5123 4-9-1 **62**...................................... PatCosgrave 4 20
(Laura Mongan) *in tch in midfield: rdn and effrt over 3f out: hmpd and lost pl wl over 2f out: nt rcvr and bhd after: eased ins fnl f: t.o* **20/1**

2m 39.5s (0.60) **Going Correction** +0.20s/f (Good)
WFA 3 from 4yo+ 10lb **8** Ran SP% **117.1**
Speed ratings (Par 103): **106,105,104,98,94 89,86,84**
toteswingers 1&2 £6.50, 1&3 £4.10, 2&3 £4.80 CSF £44.40 CT £154.76 TOTE £7.20: £2.50, £2.30, £1.60; EX 40.70 Trifecta £217.10 Pool: £3053.28 - 10.54 winning units..
Owner Roalco Limited **Bred** Dullingham Park Stud & M P Bowring **Trained** Newmarket, Suffolk

FOCUS
An open-looking handicap in which the principals were clear at the finish. Ordinary form in all probability.

5855 TOTEPOOL.COM THE HOME OF POOL BETTING H'CAP 1m 2f 18y
5:05 (5:06) (Class 5) (0-75,75) 3-Y-O+ **£3,881** (£1,155; £577; £288) **Stalls** Low

Form RPR
0040 **1** **Lowther**[15] 5348 8-10-0 **75**..(v) KierenFox 2 83
(Lee Carter) *hld up in tch in last trio: clsd 3f out: rdn and qcknd to ld over 2f out: clr and drvn over 1f out: a gng to hold on: rdn out* **20/1**

5003 **2** *1/2* **Starwatch**[8] 5587 6-10-0 **75**... LiamKeniry 3 82
(John Bridger) *t.k.h: chsd ldrs: rdn and n.m.r over 2f out: rdn and chsd clr wnr wl over 1f out: styd on wl ins fnl f: nvr quite getting to wnr* **7/1**[3]

2434 **3** *1 1/4* **Mu'Ajiza**[10] 5546 3-9-5 **74**.. JoeFanning 5 79
(Mark Johnston) *hld up in tch in midfield: shuffled bk towards rr over 3f out: swtchd rt and effrt over 2f out: wnt 3rd ent fnl f: styd on: nvr gng to rch wnr: eased nr fin* **7/4**[1]

0066 **4** *3* **Woolston Ferry (IRE)**[16] 5304 7-9-7 **68**.................... FergusSweeney 6 67
(Henry Candy) *s.i.s: hld up in tch in rr: rdn and effrt over 2f out: hdwy over 1f out: chsd ldng trio and swtchd lft ins fnl f: nvr trbld ldrs* **8/1**

2126 **5** *2 1/4* **Manomine**[20] 5129 4-9-7 **68**.. RyanMoore 4 63
(Clive Brittain) *chsd ldr tl over 2f out: sn drvn and unable qck: no imp and btn whn hung lft down camber and eased ins fnl f* **3/1**[2]

6240 **6** *shd* **Norfolk Sky**[16] 5312 4-8-13 **67**...................................... AaronChave(7) 7 61
(Laura Mongan) *hld up in tch in last trio: hdwy on outer 4f out: rdn and outpcd over 2f out: no threat to ldrs after* **16/1**

2506 **7** *1/2* **April Ciel**[11] 5479 4-8-12 **66**... OisinMurphy(7) 1 60
(Ronald Harris) *led: rdn and hdd over 2f out: 3rd and btn over 1f out: wknd ins fnl f* **8/1**

5-60 **8** *49* **Hazzaat (IRE)**[87] 2874 3-8-11 **66**................................. J-PGuillambert 8
(Gary Harrison) *in tch in midfield: rdn and lost pl 3f out: sn bhd: t.o* **12/1**

2m 10.37s (0.67) **Going Correction** +0.20s/f (Good)
WFA 3 from 4yo+ 8lb **8** Ran SP% **114.4**
Speed ratings (Par 103): **105,104,103,101,99 99,98,59**
toteswingers 1&2 £10.70, 1&3 £7.00, 2&3 £4.00 CSF £151.32 CT £375.55 TOTE £23.00: £3.50, £2.00, £1.20; EX 153.10 Trifecta £697.40 Pool: £2189.25 - 2.35 winning units..
Owner P A Allard **Bred** L J Barratt **Trained** Epsom, Surrey
■ Stewards' Enquiry : Kieren Fox four-day ban: used whip above permitted level (Sep 10-13)

FOCUS
A moderate handicap. There just was an average pace on. The winner was well handicapped on his best form and the second ran to his mark.
T/Plt: £1,388.50 to a £1 stake. Pool: £58869.79 - 30.95 winning tickets T/Qpdt: £61.50 to a £1 stake. Pool: £4938.43 - 59.40 winning tickets SP

5834 RIPON (R-H)
Tuesday, August 27

OFFICIAL GOING: Good (8.2)
Wind: Breezy, half behind Weather: Hot, sunny

5856 AT THE RACES ON FACEBOOK (S) STKS 1m 1f 170y
2:00 (2:01) (Class 6) 3-4-Y-O **£2,726** (£805; £402) **Stalls** Low

Form RPR
2620 **1** **Chloe's Image**[25] 4953 3-8-4 55................................ DeclanCannon(3) 5 59
(Philip Kirby) *chsd ldrs: rdn over 4f out: rallied to ld over 2f out: hung rt: kpt on strly fnl f* **6/5**[2]

0030 **2** *3 3/4* **Rosselli (IRE)**[22] 5052 4-9-12 64.................................. DanielTudhope 3 63
(K R Burke) *cl up: led over 4f out to over 2f out: rallied: nt pce of wnr fnl f* **1/1**[1]

-400 **3** *2 1/4* **Multifact**[30] 4806 3-8-12 51.. TomEaves 1 52
(Michael Dods) *t.k.h: trckd ldrs: effrt and rdn 3f out: hung rt and outpcd fr 2f out* **12/1**[3]

0005 **4** *5* **Firefly**[19] 5200 4-9-6 43..(be) DuranFentiman 4 43
(John Weymes) *led at ordinary gallop to over 4f out: drvn and wknd fnl 2f* **40/1**

040 **5** *20* **Eaton Oak**[22] 5069 3-8-9 48... MarkCoumbe(3) 2 5
(Lisa Williamson) *s.i.s: hld up in tch: struggling over 4f out: sn lost tch: t.o* **40/1**

2m 6.05s (0.65) **Going Correction** -0.125s/f (Firm)
WFA 3 from 4yo 8lb **5** Ran SP% **108.0**
Speed ratings (Par 101): **92,89,87,83,67**
CSF £2.57 TOTE £1.80: £1.30, £1.10; EX 2.70 Trifecta £356.60 Pool: £1623.48 - 217.78 winning units..There was no bid for the winner.
Owner G Fawcett & The Gathering **Bred** J Ellis **Trained** Middleham, N Yorks

FOCUS
Drying conditions. A poor race but the form makes sense.

5857 AT THE RACES SKY 415 MAIDEN AUCTION FILLIES' STKS 5f
2:30 (2:30) (Class 5) 2-Y-O **£3,234** (£962; £481; £240) **Stalls** High

Form RPR
224 **1** **Rural Celebration**[81] 3064 2-8-4 70................................ JulieBurke(3) 4 71+
(David O'Meara) *prom: rdn over 2f out: hung rt and hdwy over 1f out: led ins fnl f: kpt on strly* **3/1**[2]

3352 **2** *1 3/4* **Fredricka**[11] 5480 2-7-13 62... PhilipPrince(5) 3 62
(Garry Moss) *cl up: effrt and rdn 2f out: ev ch ins fnl f: kpt on same pce towards fin* **5/1**[3]

4225 **3** *1/2* **Simply Black (IRE)**[31] 4783 2-8-8 76 ow1..................... PaulMulrennan 5 64
(Bryan Smart) *t.k.h: led: rdn 2f out: hdd ins fnl f: kpt on same pce* **7/4**[1]

52 **4** *1* **Baltic Spirit (IRE)**[8] 5578 2-8-4 0.................................... JasonHart(3) 7 59
(Keith Dalgleish) *in tch: rdn over 2f out: kpt on fnl f: nt pce to chal* **3/1**[2]

5 **5** *1/2* **White Flag**[132] 1606 2-8-0 0..................................... RachelRichardson(7) 6 58+
(Tim Easterby) *s.i.s: bhd and outpcd: plenty to do 1/2-way: styd on wl fnl f: nrst fin* **33/1**

4320 **6** *1* **Emily Davison (IRE)**[12] 5421 2-8-4 63 AndrewMullen 1 51
(David C Griffiths) *cl up: rdn over 2f out: wknd ins fnl f* **16/1**
1m 0.14s (0.14) **Going Correction** 0.0s/f (Good) **6** Ran SP% **111.9**
Speed ratings (Par 91): **98,95,94,92,92 90**
toteswingers 1&2 £2.40, 1&3 £2.20, 2&3 £2.20 CSF £17.88 TOTE £3.70: £1.70, £2.40; EX 19.40 Trifecta £40.60 Pool: £2366.53 - 43.67 winning units..
Owner Hambleton Racing Ltd - Two Chances **Bred** J A And M A Knox **Trained** Nawton, N Yorks
FOCUS
Just a modest fillies' maiden and the pace looked a bit too quick. Straightforward form, the winner back to her debut level.

5858 AT THE RACES VIRGIN 534 NURSERY H'CAP 6f
3:05 (3:06) (Class 4) (0-85,79) 2-Y-0 **£3,881** (£1,155; £577; £288) **Stalls** High

Form RPR
2501 **1** **Khalice**[22] 5053 2-9-3 **75** TonyHamilton 7 81
(Richard Fahey) *mde all against stands' side rail: rdn 2f out: styd on strly fnl f* **11/4**[1]
4214 **2** *2* **Bounty Hunter (IRE)**[23] 5028 2-9-5 **77** (p) RichardKingscote 3 77
(Tom Dascombe) *chsd wnr thrght: rdn 2f out: kpt on same pce ins fnl f* **5/1**[3]
651 **3** *shd* **New Bidder**[20] 5145 2-9-7 **79** MichaelO'Connell 9 79
(Jedd O'Keeffe) *trckd ldrs: rdn and outpcd wl over 1f out: styd on ins fnl f* **7/2**[2]
045 **4** *1 ¾* **Lazy Sioux**[15] 5339 2-7-13 **62** PhilipPrince(5) 5 56
(Richard Guest) *dwlt: bhd and sn pushed along: hdwy on wd outside and hung rt over 2f out: one pce fnl f* **12/1**
3305 **5** *½* **Street Boss (IRE)**[20] 5136 2-8-4 **62** (t) DuranFentiman 1 55
(Tim Easterby) *dwlt: sn in tch on outside: rdn over 2f out: one pce over 1f out* **28/1**
331 **6** *1* **Yajamila**[19] 5194 2-9-7 **79** PaulMulrennan 8 69
(James Tate) *hld up bhd ldng gp: nt clr run 1/2-way: sn rdn: no imp fnl f* **10/1**
1 **7** *nk* **We'Ll Shake Hands (FR)**[18] 5225 2-8-11 **76** JoeyHaynes(7) 6 67+
(K R Burke) *t.k.h: prom: outpcd and edgd rt 2f out: n.d after* **11/2**
3252 **8** *2 ¼* **Milly's Secret (IRE)**[10] 5547 2-9-7 **79** PJMcDonald 4 61
(Ann Duffield) *prom: rdn over 2f out: wknd wl over 1f out* **10/1**
5216 **9** *3 ½* **Soul Instinct**[14] 5366 2-8-6 **71** KevinStott(7) 2 43
(Kevin Ryan) *hld up: rdn over 2f out: btn over 1f out* **16/1**
1m 13.48s (0.48) **Going Correction** 0.0s/f (Good) **9** Ran SP% **116.1**
Speed ratings (Par 96): **96,93,93,90,90 88,88,85,80**
toteswingers 1&2 £5.40, 1&3 £3.90, 2&3 £5.10 CSF £16.82 CT £49.13 TOTE £4.00: £1.40, £1.50, £1.90; EX 17.80 Trifecta £109.50 Pool: £2762.74 - 18.90 winning units..
Owner The G-Guck Group **Bred** Limestone And Tara Studs **Trained** Musley Bank, N Yorks
FOCUS
A fair nursery in which the pace held up well. The form makes sense rated around the second and third.

5859 SAPPER CONDITIONS STKS 5f
3:40 (3:40) (Class 3) 2-Y-0 **£6,301** (£1,886; £943; £472) **Stalls** High

Form RPR
212 **1** **Northern Water**[2] 5787 2-8-9 82 JoeyHaynes(7) 2 85+
(K R Burke) *mde all: rdn 2f out: kpt on strly fnl f* **5/6**[1]
2516 **2** *3 ¼* **Muspelheim**[32] 4726 2-9-2 82 PJMcDonald 4 73
(Ann Duffield) *chsd ldrs: rdn over 2f out: wnt 2nd last 100yds: nt pce of wnr* **4/1**[2]
6515 **3** *½* **Money Team (IRE)**[11] 5468 2-8-11 80 EvaMoscrop(7) 3 73
(Philip Kirby) *chsd wnr: rdn over 2f out: edgd rt and lost 2nd last 100yds: no ex* **5/1**
2136 **4** *7* **Innocently (IRE)**[2] 5787 2-9-0 76 DanielTudhope 1 54
(David O'Meara) *t.k.h: in tch: rdn over 2f out: sn no imp: btn and eased fnl f* **9/2**[3]
59.64s (-0.36) **Going Correction** 0.0s/f (Good) **4** Ran SP% **109.4**
Speed ratings (Par 98): **102,96,96,84**
CSF £4.51 TOTE £1.50; EX 3.80 Trifecta £8.70 Pool: £1707.57 - 146.80 winning units..
Owner Market Avenue Racing Club Ltd **Bred** M Humby & Dr J Leigh **Trained** Middleham Moor, N Yorks
■ Karl Burke's first winner since taking over the licence again from his wife Elaine.
FOCUS
Uncompetitive stuff and the form is far from solid. Not a race to go overboard about.

5860 ATTHERACES.COM CITY OF RIPON STKS (H'CAP) 1m 1f 170y
4:15 (4:15) (Class 3) (0-90,87) 3-Y-0 **£7,561** (£2,263; £1,131; £566; £282) **Stalls** Low

Form RPR
1050 **1** **Maven**[17] 5269 5-9-11 **84** DavidAllan 4 92
(Tim Easterby) *t.k.h: hld up in midfield: hdwy over 2f out: wandered and led over 1f out: drvn out fnl f* **10/1**
4161 **2** *¾* **Eeny Mac (IRE)**[13] 5383 6-8-13 **72** AndrewElliott 7 79
(Neville Bycroft) *s.i.s: hld up last: hdwy on outside over 2f out: chsd wnr ins fnl f: kpt on fin* **25/1**
163 **3** *1* **Hydrant**[13] 5382 7-9-3 **81** ConnorBeasley(5) 9 86
(Richard Guest) *cl up: led over 2f out to over 1f out: rallied: one pce ins fnl f* **14/1**
0643 **4** *nse* **San Cassiano (IRE)**[22] 5055 6-9-7 **80** PJMcDonald 5 85
(Ruth Carr) *led to over 2f out: rallied: kpt on same pce fnl f* **10/1**
3163 **5** *1 ¼* **Dolphin Rock**[20] 5149 6-9-6 **79** DaleSwift 6 81
(Brian Ellison) *t.k.h: trckd ldrs: effrt and rdn over 1f out: one pce fnl f* **12/1**
3312 **6** *hd* **Triple Eight (IRE)**[13] 5382 5-9-5 **78** (b) MichaelO'Connell 2 80
(Philip Kirby) *hld up: effrt and swtchd lft over 2f out: rdn whn rdr dropped reins wl over 1f out: sn hung rt: kpt on fnl f* **3/1**[1]
0240 **7** *hd* **Barren Brook**[10] 5546 6-9-5 **78** PaulMulrennan 3 79
(Michael Easterby) *t.k.h in midfield: effrt whn no room fr 3f out to wl over 1f out: sn rdn and no imp* **5/1**[3]
-015 **8** *4* **Full Toss**[15] 5335 7-9-1 **74** GrahamLee 1 68
(Jim Goldie) *trckd ldrs: rdn 3f out: wknd wl over 1f out* **16/1**
4-51 **9** *nk* **Spirit Of Rio (IRE)**[21] 5110 3-9-1 **82** GrahamGibbons 10 75
(David Barron) *hld up: rdn over 3f out: nvr on terms* **9/2**[2]
6000 **10** *11* **St Moritz (IRE)**[25] 4946 7-10-0 **87** (t) DanielTudhope 8 59
(David O'Meara) *chsd ldrs: rdn over 3f out: wknd fr 2f out* **5/1**[3]
2m 2.51s (-2.89) **Going Correction** -0.125s/f (Firm)
WFA 3 from 5yo+ 8lb **10** Ran SP% **118.8**
Speed ratings (Par 107): **106,105,104,104,103 103,103,100,99,91**
toteswingers 1&2 £47.90, 1&3 £25.10, 2&3 £39.80 CSF £231.45 CT £3469.46 TOTE £14.20: £4.50, £6.40, £4.90; EX 393.60 Trifecta £2574.50 Pool: £3726.88 - 1.08 winning units..
Owner Mrs Jennifer E Pallister **Bred** Habton Farms **Trained** Great Habton, N Yorks
FOCUS
A competitive handicap that saw something of a surprise winner. Straightforward form, however.

5861 ATTHERACES.COM EXCLUSIVE WILLIAM BUICK BLOG H'CAP 1m
4:45 (4:47) (Class 5) (0-75,75) 3-Y-0+ **£3,234** (£962; £481; £240) **Stalls** Low

Form RPR
0644 **1** **Skyfire**[20] 5144 6-8-13 **62** (p) MichaelStainton 4 71
(Nick Kent) *cl up: led over 2f out: edgd rt and hrd pressed over 1f out: hld on gamely fnl f* **8/1**
0134 **2** *nk* **No Quarter (IRE)**[25] 4966 6-8-13 **62** MichaelO'Connell 8 70
(Tracy Waggott) *trckd ldrs: effrt over 2f out: ev ch and drvn over 1f out: kpt on fnl f: rdr dropped whip fnl 110yds: hld nr fin* **12/1**
0013 **3** *nk* **Aerodynamic (IRE)**[4] 5713 6-9-7 **70** (b) GrahamGibbons 9 78
(Michael Easterby) *dwlt: t.k.h and sn in tch: rdn 3f out: rallied wl over 1f out: styd on fnl f: hld nr fin* **11/2**[1]
-000 **4** *1 ½* **Desert Creek (IRE)**[10] 5546 7-9-5 **75** JordanNason(7) 3 79+
(David Nicholls) *hld up: rdn and hdwy over 2f out: styd on fnl f: nvr able to chal* **6/1**[2]
0003 **5** *5* **Sardanapalus**[11] 5491 4-9-8 **71** (b) GrahamLee 7 64
(Kevin Ryan) *midfield: pushed along fr over 5f out: effrt whn hung rt over 2f out: sn no imp* **13/2**[3]
6002 **6** *1 ¼* **The Osteopath (IRE)**[8] 5580 10-9-12 **75** DuranFentiman 5 65
(John Davies) *hld up: rdn and effrt 3f out: no imp fr 2f out* **8/1**
000 **7** *5* **Daddy Warbucks (IRE)**[46] 4264 4-9-5 **73** TobyAtkinson(5) 1 51
(David Nicholls) *t.k.h: led to over 2f out: rdn and wknd over 1f out* **13/2**[3]
0256 **8** *2 ½* **Jonny Lesters Hair (IRE)**[20] 5144 8-8-13 **62** DavidAllan 10 35
(Tim Easterby) *prom: rdn over 3f out: drifted rt and wknd 2f out: eased whn no ch* **7/1**
5110 **9** *5* **Running Reef (IRE)**[64] 3628 4-9-5 **68** BarryMcHugh 2 29
(Tracy Waggott) *hld up: struggling over 3f out: nvr on terms* **7/1**
-150 **10** *1 ½* **Special Mix**[56] 3573 5-9-5 **68** PaulMulrennan 6 26
(Michael Easterby) *s.i.s: hld up: struggling over 3f out: sn btn* **22/1**
1m 39.46s (-1.94) **Going Correction** -0.125s/f (Firm) **10** Ran SP% **115.6**
Speed ratings (Par 103): **104,103,103,101,96 95,90,88,83,81**
toteswingers 1&2 £11.40, 1&3 £9.50, 2&3 £5.30 CSF £98.48 CT £585.85 TOTE £12.20: £3.30, £2.70, £1.50; EX 111.10 Trifecta £1352.10 Pool: £2243.40 - 1.24 winning units..
Owner Cynthia Commons, Nick Kent **Bred** Darley **Trained** Brigg, Lincs
FOCUS
Just a modest handicap in which the first three all raced prominently.

5862 VISIT ATTHERACES.COM/MOBILE STAYERS H'CAP (DIV I) 2m
5:15 (5:16) (Class 6) (0-65,65) 3-Y-0+ **£3,234** (£962; £481; £240) **Stalls** High

Form RPR
-063 **1** **Cowslip**[20] 5137 4-9-0 **51** PJMcDonald 8 59
(George Moore) *prom: lost pl bnd over 4f out: rallied 3f out: led ins fnl f: styd on wl* **12/1**
6450 **2** *1 ½* **Jan Smuts (IRE)**[22] 5048 5-9-2 **60** (tp) KevinStott(7) 5 66
(Wilf Storey) *missed break: hld up: hdwy on outside over 4f out: led and rdr dropped reins wl over 1f out: hdd ins fnl f: one pce* **12/1**
0-06 **3** *2* **Generous Dream**[20] 5137 5-9-7 **58** DavidAllan 2 62
(Mel Brittain) *led: rdn and edgd lft over 2f out: hdd wl over 1f out: one pce fnl f* **7/2**[1]
6505 **4** *1 ¾* **Valentine's Gift**[2] 5786 5-8-12 **49** oh2 (p) DuranFentiman 6 51
(Neville Bycroft) *hld up: rdn and hdwy 3f out: kpt on fnl f: nrst fin* **8/1**
313/ **5** *1 ½* **Bouggler**[166] 6386 8-9-9 **60** MickyFenton 4 60
(Emma Lavelle) *hld up in tch on outside: effrt and hung rt over 3f out: no imp fnl 2f* **4/1**[2]
66-5 **6** *3 ½* **Not Til Monday (IRE)**[16] 5312 7-10-0 **65** DougieCostello 1 61
(J R Jenkins) *trckd ldrs: rdn over 4f out: wknd 2f* **8/1**
533 **7** *2 ½* **Naburn**[60] 3790 5-10-0 **65** TonyHamilton 3 58
(Alan Swinbank) *trckd ldrs: lost pl over 4f out: sn n.d* **4/1**[2]
0205 **8** *42* **Altnaharra**[17] 5267 4-8-12 **49** oh3 (v) GrahamLee 9
(Jim Goldie) *bhd: struggling over 5f out: t.o* **16/1**
3405 **9** *nk* **Kayef (GER)**[38] 4530 6-9-11 **65** (p) WilliamTwiston-Davies(3) 7 7
(Michael Scudamore) *trckd ldrs: drvn over 4f out: wknd over 3f out: t.o* **7/1**[3]
3m 31.01s (-0.79) **Going Correction** -0.125s/f (Firm) **9** Ran SP% **118.2**
Speed ratings (Par 101): **96,95,94,93,92 90,89,68,68**
toteswingers 1&2 £13.00, 1&3 £16.20, 2&3 £9.10 CSF £148.19 CT £616.94 TOTE £15.40: £4.20, £5.80, £1.70; EX 213.10 Trifecta £1145.00 Part won. Pool: £1526.78 - 0.38 winning units..
Owner Mrs Susan Moore **Bred** G Reed **Trained** Middleham Moor, N Yorks
FOCUS
The first division of a modest staying handicap. The form fits in.

5863 VISIT ATTHERACES.COM/MOBILE STAYERS H'CAP (DIV II) 2m
5:50 (5:50) (Class 6) (0-65,65) 3-Y-0+ **£3,234** (£962; £481; £240) **Stalls** High

Form RPR
2235 **1** **Kodicil (IRE)**[47] 4204 5-10-0 **65** GrahamGibbons 7 72
(Tim Walford) *mde all: rdn over 2f out: styd on strly: unchal* **11/4**[1]
6230 **2** *3 ½* **Petella**[9] 5560 7-9-4 **60** (p) ConnorBeasley(5) 2 63
(George Moore) *hld up: hdwy on outside over 3f out: chsd wnr over 1f out: hung rt: no imp* **7/1**
563 **3** *2 ¼* **Mister Carter (IRE)**[15] 5337 6-10-0 **65** (v) MichaelO'Connell 3 65
(Ian Williams) *trckd ldrs: drvn over 2f out: one pce over 1f out* **3/1**[2]
1003 **4** *3 ½* **Grammar**[12] 5420 4-8-11 **51** (e) RaulDaSilva(3) 6 47
(David Thompson) *prom: chsd wnr over 2f out to over 1f out: wknd ins fnl f* **11/1**
4045 **5** *4* **Uncut Stone (IRE)**[9] 5560 5-8-13 **50** (v[1]) TomEaves 1 41
(Peter Niven) *s.i.s: hld up: hdwy on outside over 3f out: edgd rt 2f out: no imp* **8/1**
5406 **6** *1* **Raleigh Quay (IRE)**[15] 5337 6-9-4 **55** (v) PJMcDonald 4 45
(Micky Hammond) *midfield: rdn over 3f out: btn fnl 2f* **16/1**
-630 **7** *1 ¾* **Joe The Coat**[48] 4166 4-9-12 **63** PaulMulrennan 9 51
(Mark H Tompkins) *mid-div: rdn and outpcd 3f out: btn 2f out* **11/2**[3]
0465 **8** *3 ½* **Ferney Boy**[15] 5337 7-8-12 **49** oh4 MichaelStainton 8 33
(Chris Fairhurst) *chsd wnr to over 3f: rdn and wknd over 2f out* **40/1**
63- **9** *7* **Dan's Heir**[322] 6956 11-8-12 **49** oh3 (p) GrahamLee 10 24
(Wilf Storey) *bhd: rdn over 5f out: nvr on terms* **16/1**
3m 31.14s (-0.66) **Going Correction** -0.125s/f (Firm) **9** Ran SP% **113.2**
Speed ratings (Par 101): **96,94,93,91,89 88,88,86,82**
toteswingers 1&2 £4.30, 1&3 £2.70, 2&3 £5.30 CSF £21.98 CT £59.98 TOTE £3.60: £1.10, £1.70, £1.70; EX 22.80 Trifecta £55.20 Pool: £1225.13 - 16.61 winning units..
Owner D & S Woodall **Bred** Tally-Ho Stud **Trained** Sheriff Hutton, N Yorks
FOCUS
The second leg of the staying handicap. Limited but straightforward form.

The Form Book Flat, Raceform Ltd, Compton, RG20 6NL.

T/Plt: £431.80 to a £1 stake. Pool: £52679.65 - 89.05 winning tickets T/Qpdt: £174.50 to a £1 stake. Pool: £3914.90 - 16.60 winning tickets RY

[5192] SOUTHWELL (L-H)

Tuesday, August 27

OFFICIAL GOING: Standard

Wind: Virtually nil Weather: Sunny with cloudy periods

5864 LADBROKES H'CAP 5f (F)

4:40 (4:40) (Class 6) (0-55,55) 3-Y-0+ **£1,940** (£577; £288; £144) **Stalls** High

Form RPR

4064 **1** **Beach Rhythm (USA)**[18] 5230 6-8-9 **46**..................(v[1]) DeclanBates(3) 4 57
(Jim Allen) *prom: led after 2f: rdn over 1f out: jnd and drvn ins fnl f: kpt on strly towards fin* **9/2**[1]

-424 **2** ¾ **Exkaliber**[201] 551 4-8-9 **48**..............................(t) RobertTart(5) 1 56
(Jeremy Gask) *in tch on wd outside: hdwy over 2f out: effrt to chal over 1f out: rdn ins fnl f and ev ch tl drvn: edgd rt and no ex towards fin* **9/2**[1]

0003 **3** 1 ¾ **Sarah Berry**[18] 5230 4-9-7 **55**..............................(v) AdamKirby 5 57
(Chris Dwyer) *towards rr: pushed along and hdwy 1/2-way: chsd ldng pair wl over 1f out: sn rdn and no imp fnl f* **13/2**[2]

6000 **4** 1 ¼ **Kwanto**[19] 5192 3-8-12 **48**.............................. AndrewMullen 10 46
(Michael Appleby) *chsd ldrs: rdn along over 1f out: drvn and one pce fnl f* **8/1**

001 **5** ½ **Lord Buffhead**[11] 5470 4-9-6 **54**..........................(v) RobbieFitzpatrick 13 50
(Richard Guest) *racd nr stands' rail: prom: rdn along wl over 1f out: grad wknd* **12/1**

64-0 **6** 3 **Angel Grigio**[19] 5184 3-8-12 **48**..............................(e) PatrickMathers 2 33
(Geoffrey Oldroyd) *in tch on outer: rdn along to chse ldrs 1/2-way: wknd wl over 1f out* **14/1**

6000 **7** 1 **Code Six (IRE)**[11] 5486 4-9-1 **49**..............................(p) RoystonFfrench 9 30
(Bryan Smart) *led 2f: cl up: rdn along wl over 1f out: sn wknd* **16/1**

4050 **8** 1 ½ **Southern Sapphire**[22] 5067 3-8-7 **48**..................... JacobButterfield(5) 7 24
(Kristin Stubbs) *chsd ldrs: rdn along 1/2-way: sn wknd* **25/1**

5005 **9** 1 ½ **Red Star Lady (IRE)**[43] 4353 3-8-10 **46** oh1.................. JimmyQuinn 8 17
(Shaun Harris) *in tch: rdn along wl over 2f out: sn outpcd* **66/1**

0040 **10** ¾ **Depden (IRE)**[21] 5097 5-8-7 **46** oh1.................. MichaelJMMurphy(5) 12 14
(Richard Price) *in tch 1f: sn rdn along and towards rr fr 1/2-way* **8/1**

0-54 **11** 1 **Heart Beat Song**[83] 2977 5-8-5 **46** oh1........................ VictorSantos(7) 6 10
(James Moffatt) *dwlt: a in rr* **7/1**[3]

4364 **12** 3 ¾ **Island Express (IRE)**[111] 2169 6-9-0 **53**....................(tp) AnnStokell(5) 11
(Ann Stokell) *s.i.s: a in rr* **33/1**

0060 **13** ½ **Bird Dog**[21] 5085 7-8-7 **46** oh1..................................(v) DannyBrock(5) 3
(Phil McEntee) *chsd ldrs: rdn along bef 1/2-way: sn wknd* **25/1**

59.42s (-0.28) **Going Correction** -0.025s/f (Stan)
WFA 3 from 4yo+ 2lb **13** Ran SP% **116.8**
Speed ratings (Par 101): **101,99,97,95,94 89,87,85,83,81 80,74,73**
toteswingers 1&2 £4.30, 1&3 £6.80, 2&3 £4.80 CSF £21.77 CT £118.81 TOTE £6.40: £2.50, £2.10, £2.80; EX 25.30 Trifecta £109.30 Pool: £2588.47 - 17.76 winning units..
Owner J P Allen **Bred** Christoph Amerian **Trained** Stoodleigh, Devon
■ Jim Allen's first winner.

FOCUS
A very moderate sprint handicap that was dominated by the market leaders, who were all drawn low. The form is rated around the principals.

5865 LADBROKES NURSERY H'CAP 7f (F)

5:10 (5:10) (Class 6) (0-65,65) 2-Y-0 **£2,045** (£603; £302) **Stalls** Low

Form RPR

005 **1** **Madame Mirasol (IRE)**[65] 3605 2-8-11 **55**.......................... NeilCallan 8 69+
(Kevin Ryan) *cl up: led wl over 2f out: rdn clr wl over 1f out: unchal* **7/2**[2]

0000 **2** 8 **Cabaan (IRE)**[6] 5634 2-9-7 **65**..(p) DaneO'Neill 2 55
(Brian Meehan) *slt ld on inner: rdn along 3f out: sn hdd: drvn and one pce fnl 2f* **7/1**

5525 **3** ¾ **Evacusafe Lady**[19] 5167 2-9-2 **60**..............................(p) KirstyMilczarek 4 48
(John Ryan) *trckd ldrs: hdwy to chse ldng pair 3f out: rdn over 2f out: sn drvn and one pce* **20/1**

5003 **4** 1 ½ **Claudia Octavia**[24] 4990 2-8-1 **45**...................................... LukeMorris 3 29
(Brian Ellison) *chsd ldrs on inner: rdn along 3f out: drvn and one pce fnl 2f* **14/1**

040 **5** ½ **Aspenbreeze**[21] 5101 2-8-12 **56**.................................... RobertWinston 6 39
(Alan Bailey) *sn rdn along and bhd tl styd on fnl 2f: nrst fin* **8/1**

5044 **6** ½ **By The Light (IRE)**[12] 5424 2-9-5 **63**........................... FrannyNorton 10 45
(Mark Johnston) *sn pushed along to chse ldrs: rdn along and outpcd over 3f out: drvn and plugged on one pce fnl 2f* **7/4**[1]

050 **7** 12 **Bertha Burnett (IRE)**[24] 4977 2-8-12 **61**............ MichaelJMMurphy(5) 5 11
(Brian Rothwell) *in tch: pushed along 1/2-way: rdn along over 3f out: sn outpcd* **16/1**

0002 **8** 7 **Volodina (IRE)**[19] 5193 2-8-9 **53**................................(v[1]) AndrewMullen 7
(Alan McCabe) *dwlt: sn in tch: hdwy to chse ldrs on outer over 3f out: wd st: sn rdn and wknd* **6/1**[3]

000 **9** 25 **Bridge Of Avon**[13] 5380 2-8-1 **45**...................................... JimmyQuinn 1
(Mel Brittain) *dwlt: a in rr: bhd fnl 3f* **50/1**

1m 29.47s (-0.83) **Going Correction** -0.10s/f (Stan) **9** Ran SP% **115.8**
Speed ratings (Par 92): **100,90,90,88,87 87,73,65,36**
toteswingers 1&2 £5.90, 1&3 £6.80, 2&3 £10.10 CSF £28.34 CT £429.18 TOTE £4.60: £1.40, £2.30, £3.50; EX 36.50 Trifecta £509.40 Pool: £1275.75 - 1.87 winning units..
Owner Mrs Margaret Forsyth **Bred** John Cullinan **Trained** Hambleton, N Yorks

FOCUS
This modest nursery that was turning into a procession by the winner. There was no depth to the race and it's hard to be confident about the standard in behind.

5866 LADBROKES MEDIAN AUCTION MAIDEN STKS 6f (F)

5:45 (5:45) (Class 6) 2-Y-0 **£1,940** (£577; £288; £144) **Stalls** Low

Form RPR

32 **1** **Zal Zilhom (IRE)**[10] 5543 2-9-5 0.......................... PhillipMakin 2 64+
(Kevin Ryan) *led 1f: cl up: n.m.r bnd at 1/2-way: rdn along to chse ldr over 2f out: drvn to chal over 1f out: led ent fnl f: kpt on* **10/11**[1]

03 **2** 1 ¼ **Black Vale (IRE)**[19] 5193 2-9-5 0..............................(p) NeilCallan 6 60
(James Tate) *wnt rt s: sn rdn and edgd lft: led after 1f: edgd lft bnd agt 1/2-way: sn rdn clr: jnd and drvn over 1f out: hdd ent fnl f one pce* **5/2**[2]

06 **3** 2 ½ **Red Biba (IRE)**[141] 1432 2-8-11 0.......................... NataliaGemelova(3) 5 48
(Alan McCabe) *prom whn hmpd and bmpd after s: chsd ldng pair whn n.m.r bnd at 1/2-way: rdn wl over 2f out: kpt on same pce fr wl over 1f out* **50/1**

0 **4** 3 ¾ **Misu's Maite**[11] 5494 2-8-11 0.......................... MarkCoumbe(3) 1 37
(Roy Bowring) *chsd ldrs on inner whn n.m.r bnd at 1/2-way: sn rdn along and one pce fnl 2f* **20/1**

4063 **5** 1 **Donny Rover (IRE)**[35] 4610 2-9-5 69..........................(p) RobertWinston 4 39
(David C Griffiths) *a in rr* **4/1**[3]

6 4 ½ **Birikyno** 2-9-5 0.. RenatoSouza 3 25
(Mark Usher) *dwlt: a in rr* **33/1**

1m 18.14s (1.64) **Going Correction** -0.10s/f (Stan) **6** Ran SP% **110.6**
Speed ratings (Par 92): **85,83,80,75,73 67**
toteswingers 1&2 £1.10, 1&3 £6.10, 2&3 £12.50 CSF £3.26 TOTE £1.40: £1.10, £1.70; EX 3.90 Trifecta £38.90 Pool: £1993.06 - 38.36 winning units..
Owner Abdulla Ahmad Al Shaikh **Bred** Liam Queally **Trained** Hambleton, N Yorks

FOCUS
A weak auction maiden, but the winner is going the right way.

5867 LADBROKES MAIDEN STKS 1m (F)

6:15 (6:15) (Class 5) 3-Y-0 **£2,587** (£770; £384; £192) **Stalls** Low

Form RPR

532 **1** **Akeed Dubawi**[39] 4495 3-9-5 73..(p) NeilCallan 5 80+
(William Haggas) *cl up: led wl over 2f out: clr whn hung lft to inner over 1f out: drvn and kpt on strly* **4/5**[1]

205 **2** 8 **China Creek (IRE)**[11] 5484 3-9-0 78.............................. FrannyNorton 4 57
(Mark Johnston) *cl up: led over 3f out: sn rdn and hdd wl over 2f out: drvn and edgd lft over 1f out: plugged on same pce* **13/8**[2]

206 **3** 12 **Reminisce (IRE)**[75] 3253 3-9-5 77..................................(b[1]) AdamKirby 1 34
(Marco Botti) *slt ld on inner: rdn along and hdd over 3f out: sn drvn and outpcd* **7/1**[3]

50 **4** 25 **Heroes Welcome (IRE)**[26] 4927 3-8-11 0.......................... BillyCray(3) 3
(Deborah Sanderson) *dwlt: sn rdn along and outpcd in rr: bhd fr 1/2-way* **100/1**

1m 42.66s (-1.04) **Going Correction** -0.10s/f (Stan) **4** Ran SP% **107.1**
Speed ratings (Par 100): **101,93,81,56**
CSF £2.32 TOTE £1.40; EX 2.00 Trifecta £2.70 Pool: £841.73 - 227.93 winning units..
Owner Jaber Abdullah **Bred** Theobalds Stud **Trained** Newmarket, Suffolk

FOCUS
A fair maiden on paper with three of the runners officially rated in the 70s, but they finished well strung out behind the dominant winner. Not form to get too carried away with.

5868 DOWNLOAD THE LADBROKES MOBILE APP H'CAP 1m 6f (F)

6:45 (6:46) (Class 4) (0-80,80) 3-Y-0+ **£4,690** (£1,395; £697; £348) **Stalls** Low

Form RPR

0036 **1** **Cosimo de Medici**[17] 5288 6-9-11 **77**.............................. GeorgeBaker 8 90
(Hughie Morrison) *trckd ldrs on outer: clsd up 1/2-way: led wl over 2f out: rdn wl over 1f out: styd on strly* **11/4**[1]

3341 **2** 6 **Wadaa (USA)**[30] 4804 3-9-2 **80**.. NeilCallan 4 85
(James Tate) *hld up in tch: hdwy 5f out: trckd ldng pair over 3f out: effrt on outer and rdn wl over 2f out: drvn to chse wnr over 1f out: sn no imp* **3/1**[2]

4111 **3** 4 **Slip Of The Tongue**[10] 5526 3-9-2 **80**............................... LukeMorris 2 80
(Sir Mark Prescott Bt) *led: pushed along 4f out: rdn and hdd wl over 2f out: sn drvn and one pce fr wl over 1f out* **3/1**[2]

0215 **4** 11 **Proud Times (USA)**[42] 4380 7-9-1 **67**..............................(p) JimmyQuinn 7 53
(Ali Brewer) *hld up towards rr: pushed along over 4f out: rdn and sme hdwy 2f out: sn drvn and plugged on: nvr a factor* **14/1**

0-01 **5** ½ **Yasir (USA)**[21] 5087 5-9-8 **74**...(p) DaneO'Neill 5 59
(Conor Dore) *hld up in rr: hdwy 6f out: chsd ldrs 4f out: rdn along over 3f out: sn outpcd* **16/1**

0000 **6** 5 **Jacobs Son**[9] 5560 5-9-6 **72**.. AndrewMullen 1 51
(Michael Appleby) *trckd ldrs on inner: rdn along 6f out: wknd over 4f out* **25/1**

2400 **7** 1 ¼ **Northside Prince (IRE)**[20] 5147 7-9-12 **78**................. RobertWinston 6 55
(Alan Swinbank) *hld up towards rr: hdwy 1/2-way: rdn along over 4f out: sn outpcd* **12/1**

4-00 **8** 9 **Suzi's A Class Act**[17] 5288 5-9-11 **77**..........................(p) FrederikTylicki 3 42
(Paul D'Arcy) *cl up: rdn along over 5f out: sn wknd* **33/1**

-651 **P** **Picalily**[19] 5196 4-8-7 **64**.. RobertTart(5) 9
(Brendan Powell) *hld up in rr tl rn wd and p.u 1m out: bit slipped through* **9/1**[3]

3m 4.68s (-3.62) **Going Correction** -0.10s/f (Stan)
WFA 3 from 4yo+ 12lb **9** Ran SP% **113.7**
Speed ratings (Par 105): **106,102,100,94,93 90,90,85,**
toteswingers 1&2 £3.00, 1&3 £2.30, 2&3 £3.00 CSF £10.96 CT £25.06 TOTE £3.70: £1.90, £1.20, £1.50; EX 12.70 Trifecta £30.90 Pool: £1511.58 - 36.58 winning units..
Owner Bevan, Doyle & Lawrence **Bred** Shortgrove Manor Stud **Trained** East Ilsley, Berks

FOCUS
The feature race and quite a competitive staying handicap on paper, but only three mattered in the straight. Strong form for the grade.

5869 BET ON YOUR MOBILE WITH LADBROKES H'CAP 7f (F)

7:15 (7:20) (Class 6) (0-55,55) 3-Y-0+ **£1,940** (£577; £288; £144) **Stalls** Low

Form RPR

5006 **1** **Elusive Warrior (USA)**[19] 5198 10-8-5 **46** oh1..........(p) AaronJones(7) 2 57
(Alan McCabe) *trckd ldrs: hdwy over 2f out: rdn along wl over 1f out: swtchd rt ent fnl f: led last 110yds: styd on* **20/1**

0500 **2** 1 **Poppy Bond**[22] 5054 3-8-8 **47**.. FrannyNorton 10 53
(Alan Bailey) *trckd ldrs: n.m.r and lost pl after 1f: sn towards rr: wd st and gd hdwy on outer wl over 1f out: sn rdn and styd on strly fnl f* **25/1**

4560 **3** 1 **Viennese Verse**[20] 5135 3-9-2 **55**....................................... DaneO'Neill 4 59
(Henry Candy) *cl up: rdn to ld 2f out: drvn over 1f out: hdd ins fnl f: kpt on same pce* **8/1**[3]

06-3 **4** 1 **Lilly White (USA)**[13] 5407 3-8-13 **52**........................... WilliamCarson 11 53
(John Butler) *chsd ldrs: rdn over 2f out: drvn over 1f out: kpt on fnl f: nrst fin* **7/2**[2]

-003 **5** 1 **Coach Montana (IRE)**[61] 3738 4-8-12 **46**...................... FrederikTylicki 1 47
(Jane Chapple-Hyam) *slt ld: rdn along 3f out: hdd 2f out and sn drvn: wknd ent fnl f* **11/1**

6051 **6** ¾ **Nonaynever**[19] 5198 5-9-3 **51**..(b) JamesSullivan 7 50
(Ruth Carr) *in tch on inner: rdn along over 3f out: styd on to chse ldrs over 1f out: sn drvn and no imp fnl f* **3/1**[1]

3404 **7** 1 ¼ **Poetic Belle**[7] 5617 3-9-1 **54**..(t) JimmyQuinn 12 47
(Shaun Harris) *chsd ldrs: wd st: rdn over 2f out: sn no imp* **50/1**

5-35 **8** 3 ½ **Hidden Asset**[49] 4144 3-8-12 **51**................................ AndrewMullen 13 35
(Michael Appleby) *sn cl up on outer: rdn along over 2f out: drvn and wkng whn hung lft over 1f out* **3/1**[1]

0200 **9** 2 **Kings 'n Dreams**[14] 5373 6-9-1 **49**...............................(e[1]) LukeMorris 9 30
(Dean Ivory) *sn rdn along and a towards rr* **12/1**

-064 **10** 3/4 **Joeluke**[31] 4763 3-8-5 **47** DeclanCannon(3) 3 24
(Philip Kirby) *dwlt: a in rr* **33/1**
0044 **11** 14 **One In A Thousand (IRE)**[7] 5616 3-8-7 **51** (p) RobertTart(5) 8
(Chris Dwyer) *a in rr* **20/1**
0250 **12** 24 **Queen Flush (IRE)**[22] 5054 3-8-9 **55** JordanNason(7) 5
(David Nicholls) *dwlt: a in rr* **25/1**
1m 29.4s (-0.90) **Going Correction** -0.10s/f (Stan)
WFA 3 from 4yo+ 5lb **12** Ran SP% **121.5**
Speed ratings (Par 101): **101,99,98,97,96 95,94,90,87,87 71,43**
toteswingers 1&2 £22.50, 1&3 £33.30, 2&3 £40.80 CSF £422.43 CT £4348.53 TOTE £15.70: £5.00, £9.00, £2.70; EX 186.80 Trifecta £1375.70 Part won. Pool: £1834.26 - 0.04 winning units..
Owner Mrs M J McCabe **Bred** Steve Peskoff **Trained** Averham Park, Notts
FOCUS
A big field for this moderate handicap. The winner is obviously still capable at this lowly level.

5870 LADBROKES APPRENTICE H'CAP 1m (F)
7:45 (7:45) (Class 5) (0-75,75) 3-Y-O **£2,520** (£754; £377; £188; £94) **Stalls** Low

Form RPR
5525 **1** **Megamunch (IRE)**[15] 5342 3-9-2 **70** (p) JacobButterfield(3) 3 78
(Kristin Stubbs) *trckd ldrs: chsd ldng pair wl over 2f out: sn swtchd rt and rdn to chal: led wl over 1f out: drvn and edging lft whn rdr dropped reins ent fnl f: sn rcvrd and drvn out: hld on wl* **4/1**[3]
6022 **2** 1/2 **Emperatriz**[19] 5192 3-8-9 **63** JoeyHaynes(3) 1 70
(John Holt) *cl up: effrt 3f out and sn rdn: ev ch tl drvn and no ex wl ins fnl f* **10/3**[2]
1150 **3** 1 **Apache Rising**[116] 1991 3-9-7 **75** ThomasGarner(3) 6 80
(Bryan Smart) *hld up: hdwy on inner over 3f out and sn led: rdn over 2f out: hdd wl over 1f out: ev ch tl drvn and one pce wl ins fnl f* **13/8**[1]
2040 **4** 7 **Birdy Boy (USA)**[14] 5369 3-9-0 **65** MichaelJMMurphy 5 54
(Mark Johnston) *awkwards s: in rr: hdwy on outer over 3f out: sn rdn along and no imp fnl 2f* **5/1**
6405 **5** 6 **East Texas Red (IRE)**[27] 4881 3-8-5 **56** oh3 RobertTart 2 31
(Mick Quinn) *prom: effrt over 3f out: sn drvn and wd st: wknd over 2f out* **16/1**
2113 **6** 10 **Mick Dundee (IRE)**[197] 615 3-8-9 **67** JordonMcMurray(7) 4 19
(John Ryan) *led: rdn along and hdd 3f out: sn wknd* **14/1**
1m 43.4s (-0.30) **Going Correction** -0.10s/f (Stan) **6** Ran SP% **110.4**
Speed ratings (Par 100): **97,96,95,88,82 72**
toteswingers 1&2 £2.80, 1&3 £2.70, 2&3 £2.30 CSF £16.97 CT £27.19 TOTE £4.70: £1.60, £1.80; EX 18.60 Trifecta £29.40 Pool: £884.39 - 22.50 winning units..
Owner P & L Partners **Bred** Ardrums House Stud **Trained** Norton, N Yorks
■ Stewards' Enquiry : Thomas Garner four-day ban: used whip above permitted level (Sep 10-13)
FOCUS
A couple of AW winners returning from breaks in this apprentice handicap. The time was 0.74secs slower than the earlier maiden.
T/Jkpt: £17,750.00 to a £1 stake. Pool: £25000.00 - 1 winning ticket T/Plt: £130.00 to a £1 stake. Pool: £53426.11 - 299.83 winning tickets T/Qpdt: £25.50 to a £1 stake. Pool: £4282.74 - 123.95 winning tickets JR

5848 DEAUVILLE (R-H)
Tuesday, August 27
OFFICIAL GOING: Turf: good, fibresand: standard

5875a PRIX DU LOGIS SAINT-GERMAIN (CONDITIONS) (2YO) (TURF) 1m (R)
1:20 (12:00) 2-Y-O **£13,821** (£5,528; £4,146; £2,764; £1,382)

RPR
1 **Honeymoon Cocktail (FR)**[23] 5039 2-9-0 0 ChristopheSoumillon 4 90
(J-C Rouget, France) **1/1**[1]
2 2 **Rising Breeze (FR)**[26] 4926 2-9-0 0 MartinHarley 5 85
(K R Burke) *trckd ldr: shkn up to ld 2f out: rdn over 1 1/2f out and r.o: hdd 1f out: sn dropped to 3rd: rallied u.p to regain 2nd cl home: wl hld by wnr* **9/2**
3 3/4 **Rangali**[20] 2-9-0 0 FabriceVeron 1 84
(H-A Pantall, France) **4/1**[3]
4 2 1/2 **Blyde River (IRE)** 2-8-7 0 MaximeGuyon 3 71
(F Doumen, France) **15/1**
5 snk **Ashkannd (FR)**[18] 2-8-10 0 Christophe-PatriceLemaire 2 74
(A De Royer-Dupre, France) **33/10**[2]
6 3/4 **Artemus Gordon (IRE)**[33] 2-8-10 0 PanagiotisDimitsanis 6 72
(Robert Collet, France) **54/1**
1m 45.4s (4.60) **6** Ran SP% **119.5**
WIN (incl. 1 euro stake): 2.00. PLACES: 1.50, 2.40. SF: 8.20.
Owner Daniel-Yves Treves **Bred** Mme G Forien & G Forien **Trained** Pau, France

5364 CARLISLE (R-H)
Wednesday, August 28
OFFICIAL GOING: Good to firm (8.0)
Stable bend and old stable bend moved out, adding 10yds to 1m and 1m1f races and 20yds to 1m6f race.
Wind: Breezy, half against Weather: Overcast

5876 BETFAIR NOVICE FLAT AMATEUR RIDERS' H'CAP (FOR NOVICE AMATEUR RIDERS) 5f 193y
2:00 (2:01) (Class 6) (0-65,64) 4-Y-O+ **£2,495** (£774; £386; £193) **Stalls** Low

Form RPR
4025 **1** **Lothair (IRE)**[16] 5341 4-10-4 **50** MrORJSangster(3) 8 65
(Alan Swinbank) *w ldr: led over 2f out: rdn and r.o wl fnl f* **4/1**[2]
0000 **2** 3/4 **Kuanyao (IRE)**[25] 5011 7-11-4 **64** MrDPCostello(3) 7 77
(David Nicholls) *in tch: effrt and chsd wnr over 1f out: kpt on to pull clr of rest fnl f: hld nr fin* **10/1**
0301 **3** 4 1/2 **Silly Billy (IRE)**[13] 5427 5-10-5 **51** MissJLambert(3) 1 49
(Brian Ellison) *prom: pushed along over 2f out: edgd lft and styd on fnl f: no ch w first two* **7/2**[1]
020 **4** 1 1/4 **Triskaidekaphobia**[9] 5583 10-10-2 **45** (t) MissHDoyle 10 39
(Wilf Storey) *led to over 2f out: rallied: outpcd fnl f* **50/1**
4204 **5** 3/4 **Adiator**[35] 4623 5-11-2 **59** MrSebSpencer 4 51
(Neville Bycroft) *hld up: shkn up and hdwy over 1f out: styd on: nvr able to chal* **7/2**[1]
05 **6** 1 **Medecis Mountain**[18] 5290 4-9-13 **45** (p) MrAFrench(3) 2 34
(Neville Bycroft) *bhd: rdn over 3f out: styd on fnl f: n.d* **33/1**
0002 **7** 2 **Cheyenne Red (IRE)**[15] 5365 7-10-5 **48** MrRSmith 12 30
(Michael Herrington) *trckd ldrs: rdn and edgd lft 2f out: wknd fnl f* **20/1**
62-0 **8** 3/4 **Beachwood Bay**[28] 4884 5-10-9 **52** (p) MrJamesHughes 5 32
(Jo Hughes) *hld up bhd ldng gp: rdn over 2f out: btn fnl f* **16/1**
-633 **9** 1 **Carrie's Magic**[5] 5708 6-10-3 **46** CallumBewley 6 23
(Alistair Whillans) *s.i.s: sn pushed along in rr: effrt on outside over 2f out: wknd over 1f out* **6/1**[3]
4600 **10** 1 **Hab Reeh**[9] 5583 5-10-11 **54** (t) MrRColley 9 27
(Ruth Carr) *dwlt: hld up on outside: shortlived effrt over 2f out: sn btn* **8/1**
1m 13.21s (-0.49) **Going Correction** -0.15s/f (Firm) **10** Ran SP% **114.5**
Speed ratings (Par 101): **97,96,90,88,87 86,83,82,81,79**
toteswingers 1&2 £8.00, 1&3 £4.40, 2&3 £8.80 CSF £41.69 CT £155.82 TOTE £5.10: £2.00, £2.70, £1.70; EX 37.00 Trifecta £148.50 Pool: £3335.68 - 16.84 winning units..
Owner Mrs J Porter **Bred** Lynch Bages Ltd & Samac Ltd **Trained** Melsonby, N Yorks
■ The first winner for 16-y-o rider Ollie Sangster, son of Ben and grandson of Robert.
■ Stewards' Enquiry : Miss J Lambert caution: careless riding
FOCUS
Following a dry start to the week the ground was officially described as good to firm. After the second race Robert Winston described it as lovely ground. A moderate race for novice amateur riders' and there was a scarcity of recent winning form on offer. It paid to be prominent and the first two were clear. A personal-best from the winner with the runner-up to the best of his form in the past year.

5877 BRITISH STALLION STUDS E B F MAIDEN STKS 5f 193y
2:30 (2:39) (Class 5) 2-Y-O **£2,911** (£866; £432; £216) **Stalls** Low

Form RPR
2 **1** **No Leaf Clover (IRE)**[21] 5140 2-9-5 0 RobertWinston 1 74
(Ollie Pears) *hld up bhd ldng gp: stdy hdwy over 2f out: led and edgd rt over 1f out: idled ins fnl f: drvn out* **2/1**[1]
3 **2** nk **Captain Myles (IRE)**[16] 5350 2-9-5 0 StevieDonohoe 6 73
(Nicky Vaughan) *bhd: pushed along over 3f out: gd hdwy on outside 2f out: styd on wl fnl f: hld nr fin* **20/1**
3 1 3/4 **Our Channel (USA)** 2-9-5 0 GrahamLee 9 67
(William Haggas) *dwlt: hld up: pushed along and edgd rt 2f out: styd on wl fnl f: nrst fin* **3/1**[2]
4263 **4** 3/4 **Heroique (IRE)**[11] 5543 2-9-0 70 DavidAllan 7 60
(Tim Easterby) *led: rdn and edgd lft over 2f out: hdd over 1f out: kpt on same pce* **11/2**[3]
46 **5** 1 3/4 **Damaah (USA)**[20] 5180 2-9-0 0 FrannyNorton 11 54
(Mark Johnston) *pressed ldr: rdn and ev ch 2f out: outpcd fnl f* **10/1**
06 **6** 2 1/2 **Lomond Lassie**[62] 3724 2-8-11 0 JasonHart(3) 10 46
(Keith Dalgleish) *prom on outside: rdn over 2f out: wknd over 1f out* **28/1**
3 **7** 2 1/4 **Too Elusive**[86] 2913 2-9-5 0 GrahamGibbons 4 44
(Kristin Stubbs) *trckd ldrs: drvn and outpcd 1/2-way: btn over 1f out* **8/1**
0 **8** 1 **Genax (IRE)**[27] 4924 2-8-7 0 EvaMoscrop(7) 2 36
(Philip Kirby) *dwlt: bhd: pushed along over 2f out: n.d* **80/1**
9 3 1/2 **Royal Connoisseur (IRE)** 2-9-5 0 (p) TonyHamilton 3 30
(Richard Fahey) *plld hrd: trckd ldrs tl rdn and wknd wl over 1f out* **9/1**
1m 13.12s (-0.58) **Going Correction** -0.15s/f (Firm) **9** Ran SP% **113.4**
Speed ratings (Par 94): **97,96,94,93,90 87,84,83,78**
toteswingers 1&2 £4.90, 1&3 £2.00, 2&3 £7.90 CSF £45.44 TOTE £2.90: £1.20, £3.90, £1.70; EX 23.30 Trifecta £127.60 Pool: £3081.24 - 18.10 winning units..
Owner Charles Wentworth **Bred** Tally-Ho Stud **Trained** Norton, N Yorks
FOCUS
A fair maiden. The form could be rated slightly better.

5878 CHRISTMAS PARTIES AT CARLISLE RACECOURSE H'CAP (JOCKEY CLUB GRASSROOTS SPRINT SERIES QUALIFIER) 5f 193y
3:00 (3:12) (Class 5) (0-70,70) 3-Y-O **£2,587** (£770; £384; £192) **Stalls** Low

Form RPR
5531 **1** **Gold Beau (FR)**[5] 5704 3-9-2 **70** 6ex (p) JacobButterfield(5) 5 78
(Kristin Stubbs) *trckd ldrs: led and edgd rt over 1f out: rdn out fnl f* **9/2**[2]
1233 **2** 1 1/4 **Salvatore Fury (IRE)**[5] 5705 3-9-3 **69** (p) JasonHart(3) 7 73+
(Keith Dalgleish) *hld up: stdy hdwy gng wl over 1f out: shkn up and chsd wnr ins fnl f: r.o* **7/2**[1]
3350 **3** hd **Teetotal (IRE)**[21] 5150 3-9-7 **70** GrahamGibbons 3 73
(Nigel Tinkler) *trckd ldrs: rdn over 2f out: r.o ins fnl f* **33/1**
5223 **4** nk **Hazza The Jazza**[12] 5487 3-8-9 **63** (b) ConnorBeasley(5) 4 65
(Richard Guest) *hld up in tch: effrt over 1f out: edgd rt: kpt on fnl f: no imp* **6/1**[3]
5340 **5** 1 1/2 **Mitchell**[34] 4670 3-9-0 **66** LMcNiff(3) 12 64
(David Thompson) *w ldr: led over 2f out to over 1f out: kpt on same pce ins fnl f* **16/1**
0500 **6** 1 1/4 **Opt Out**[16] 5333 3-9-2 **65** PJMcDonald 8 59
(Alistair Whillans) *s.i.s: bhd and outpcd: hdwy over 1f out: r.o fnl f* **10/1**
25 **7** nse **Findog**[30] 4821 3-9-1 **69** DavidBergin(5) 2 62
(Linda Perratt) *hld up: stdy hdwy over 2f out: rdn over 1f out: no imp fnl f* **12/1**
-210 **8** 1 **Rapscallion Deep (IRE)**[83] 3025 3-9-6 **69** FrannyNorton 11 59
(Kevin Ryan) *taken early to post: led to over 2f out: rallied: wknd ins fnl f* **6/1**[3]
2124 **9** 3/4 **Abraham Monro**[12] 5487 3-8-7 **56** JamesSullivan 9 44
(Ruth Carr) *hld up on outside: effrt on outside over 2f out: no imp fr over 1f out* **11/1**
452 **10** 1 1/4 **Thornton Lady (USA)**[11] 5517 3-9-5 **68** GrahamLee 1 52
(Jim Goldie) *bhd and sn pushed along: no imp fr 1/2-way* **10/1**
056 **11** 1 1/4 **Dream Ally (IRE)**[53] 4069 3-9-2 **65** (t) PhillipMakin 6 45
(Jedd O'Keeffe) *towards rr: outpcd over 2f out: n.d after* **20/1**
0-45 **12** 18 **Millie N Aire**[100] 2512 3-8-8 **57** AndrewElliott 13
(Danielle McCormick) *prom on outside: lost pl over 2f out: sn btn* **66/1**
6-00 **13** 3 **Colours Of Nature**[5] 5704 3-8-11 60 ow1 (b[1]) RobertWinston 10
(Eric Alston) *t.k.h early: trckd ldrs tl rdn and wknd fr 2f out* **66/1**
1m 12.71s (-0.99) **Going Correction** -0.15s/f (Firm) **13** Ran SP% **119.8**
Speed ratings (Par 100): **100,98,98,97,95 94,93,92,91,89 88,64,60**
toteswingers 1&2 £3.70, 1&3 £22.30, 2&3 £11.20 CSF £20.05 CT £468.00 TOTE £4.60: £1.70, £1.70, £7.70; EX 23.50 Trifecta £128.60 Pool: £3437.30 - 6.30 winning units..
Owner D Arundale **Bred** Haras Du Quesnay **Trained** Norton, N Yorks

FOCUS
Just a modest sprint. The time was quicker than the first two races over the same distance. The form is taken at face value rated around the placed horses.

5879 EMMA HUMPLEBY H'CAP — 1m 6f 32y
3:30 (3:33) (Class 4) (0-85,84) 3-Y-O+ **£6,469** (£1,925; £962; £481) **Stalls** Low

Form RPR

6202 **1** **Linguine (FR)**[22] 5086 3-9-2 **84** MickyFenton 6 96
(Seamus Durack) *t.k.h early: mde all: rdn clr over 1f out: kpt on strly fnl f* **11/4**[2]

0-01 **2** *5* **Ampleforth**[14] 5409 5-9-0 **70** (b) GrahamLee 2 75
(Ian Williams) *pressed wnr: rdn over 2f out: edgd rt: kpt on same pce fnl f* **14/1**

0411 **3** *½* **Silver Samba**[20] 5185 4-9-4 **81** OisinMurphy(7) 1 85
(Andrew Balding) *trckd ldrs: effrt on outside over 2f out: edgd rt over 1f out: kpt on same pce fnl f* **5/2**[1]

2000 **4** *1 ¼* **Ethics Girl (IRE)**[11] 5514 7-9-5 **75** (t) FrannyNorton 5 78
(John Berry) *trckd ldrs: rdn over 2f out: one pce appr fnl f* **15/2**[3]

-631 **5** *2 ¾* **Embsay Crag**[10] 5560 7-8-10 **69** 6ex DeclanCannon(3) 3 68
(Philip Kirby) *hld up: rdn over 2f out: no imp over 1f out* **11/4**[2]

5554 **6** *4* **Mojolika**[13] 5423 5-9-1 **71** GrahamGibbons 4 64
(Tim Easterby) *hld up in tch: rdn over 2f out: btn over 1f out* **12/1**

3m 4.95s (-2.55) **Going Correction** -0.15s/f (Firm)
WFA 3 from 4yo+ 12lb **6** Ran SP% **108.0**
Speed ratings (Par 105): **101,98,97,97,95 93**
toteswingers 1&2 £5.10, 1&3 £2.10, 2&3 £4.70 CSF £33.85 TOTE £2.90: £1.60, £5.60; EX 35.30 Trifecta £111.70 Pool: £2416.74 - 16.22 winning units..
Owner Mrs Anne Cowley **Bred** Rupert Piersch **Trained** Baydon, Wilts

FOCUS
Only a small field for this fair staying handicap but with three last-time-out winners taking their chance it was quietly competitive. It was run over 20 yards further than advertised due to rail movements. The winner is rated in line with his latest Musselburgh form, while the placed horses are also close to recent marks.

5880 JD PIPES H'CAP — 7f 200y
4:00 (4:00) (Class 4) (0-85,85) 3-Y-O+ **£5,498** (£1,636; £817; £408) **Stalls** Low

Form RPR

0100 **1** **King Torus (IRE)**[11] 5546 5-9-9 **82** JamesSullivan 7 90
(Ruth Carr) *trckd ldr: led and qcknd over 2f out: hung rt over 1f out: drvn and hld on wl towards fin* **25/1**

1231 **2** *nk* **Silver Rime (FR)**[16] 5332 8-9-6 **79** PhillipMakin 5 86
(Linda Perratt) *hld up: hdwy on outside over 2f out: chsd wnr fnl f: kpt on fin* **17/2**

1164 **3** *¾* **Talent Scout (IRE)**[29] 4850 7-9-3 **83** (p) GemmaTutty(7) 4 88
(Karen Tutty) *t.k.h: led to over 2f out: rallied: kpt on same pce ins fnl f* **9/2**[3]

6001 **4** *3* **Tellovoi (IRE)**[24] 5026 5-9-12 **85** (v) GrahamLee 1 83
(Ian Williams) *trckd ldrs: rdn over 2f out: kpt on same pce ins fnl f* **6/4**[1]

4612 **5** *hd* **Hot Rod Mamma (IRE)**[11] 5548 6-9-7 **80** PJMcDonald 3 78
(Dianne Sayer) *stdd s: hld up: rdn and effrt 2f out: outpcd fnl f* **7/2**[2]

3144 **6** *3* **Act Your Shoe Size**[32] 4760 4-9-5 **81** JasonHart(3) 8 72
(Keith Dalgleish) *prom: rdn and outpcd over 2f out: n.d after* **9/1**

4050 **7** *2 ½* **Shadowtime**[29] 4850 8-9-1 **74** RobertWinston 2 59
(Tracy Waggott) *hld up in tch: drvn over 2f out: btn over 1f out* **14/1**

1m 38.57s (-1.43) **Going Correction** -0.15s/f (Firm) **7** Ran SP% **111.4**
Speed ratings (Par 105): **101,100,99,96,96 93,91**
toteswingers 1&2 £13.50, 1&3 £14.60, 2&3 £5.60 CSF £202.90 CT £1120.51 TOTE £27.30: £6.70, £2.40; EX 140.20 Trifecta £1995.70 Pool: £2735.20 - 1.02 winning units..
Owner Sprint Thoroughbred Racing **Bred** Whisperview Trading Ltd **Trained** Huby, N Yorks
■ Stewards' Enquiry : James Sullivan caution: careless riding.

FOCUS
The remainder of the races were over 10 yards further than advertised due to rail movement. This looked to be a decent race with lots of recent winning form on offer, but it was an out-of-form horse at a big price who managed to lead them home. The front-running third helps set the level.

5881 JOAN KEDDY'S 60TH BIRTHDAY CELEBRATION FILLIES' H'CAP — 7f 200y
4:30 (4:30) (Class 5) (0-75,69) 3-Y-O+ **£2,587** (£770; £384; £192) **Stalls** Low

Form RPR

0000 **1** **First Class Favour (IRE)**[31] 4807 5-8-13 **56** DavidAllan 4 64
(Tim Easterby) *led 1f: chsd clr ldr: rdn and hdwy to ld over 1f out: hld on wl fnl f* **9/1**

4113 **2** *¾* **Absent Amy (IRE)**[21] 5153 4-9-12 **69** (t) GrahamLee 7 75
(Amy Weaver) *in tch: rdn and hdwy whn checked briefly over 1f out: kpt on ins fnl f* **3/1**[2]

0-0 **3** *shd* **Slim Chance (IRE)**[21] 5124 4-9-10 **67** AndrewElliott 5 73
(Simon West) *dwlt: t.k.h and led after 1f: sn clr: hdd over 1f out: rallied: hld towards fin* **13/2**[3]

1131 **4** *nk* **True Pleasure (IRE)**[15] 5369 6-9-4 **61** PJMcDonald 6 66
(James Bethell) *hld up: rdn: hdwy and ev ch over 1f out: kpt on same pce wl ins fnl f* **11/10**[1]

2324 **5** *9* **My New Angel (IRE)**[20] 5192 4-9-7 **64** PhillipMakin 2 49
(Jason Ward) *prom: rdn and outpcd wl over 2f out: sn btn* **13/2**[3]

1m 39.92s (-0.08) **Going Correction** -0.15s/f (Firm) **5** Ran SP% **109.3**
Speed ratings (Par 100): **94,93,93,92,83**
CSF £34.67 TOTE £10.80: £4.10, £2.50; EX 30.80 Trifecta £196.90 Pool: £2129.34 - 8.10 winning units..
Owner S A Heley **Bred** Oghill House Stud **Trained** Great Habton, N Yorks

FOCUS
An uncompetitive fillies' handicap. The runner-up was close to his AW form with the third not far off his best.

5882 HAPPY BIRTHDAY ALEX DARROCH H'CAP — 1m 1f 61y
5:05 (5:05) (Class 5) (0-70,70) 3-Y-O+ **£2,587** (£770; £384; £192) **Stalls** Low

Form RPR

-004 **1** **Judicious**[20] 5179 6-9-9 **65** PJMcDonald 9 73
(Geoffrey Harker) *chsd ldr and sn clr of rest: led over 2f out: drvn and hld on wl fnl f* **9/1**

3405 **2** *hd* **Tectonic (IRE)**[16] 5332 4-9-3 **62** (p) JasonHart(3) 12 70
(Keith Dalgleish) *in tch: shkn up and hdwy whn edgd rt over 1f out: chsd wnr ins fnl f: kpt on: hld nr fin* **5/1**[2]

0643 **3** *1* **May's Boy**[140] 1466 5-8-10 **52** JamesSullivan 8 58
(James Moffatt) *hld up in midfield: effrt and hdwy over 2f out: kpt on ins fnl f* **20/1**

0311 **4** *hd* **Remix (IRE)**[7] 5631 4-9-6 **67** 6ex DannyBrock(5) 13 72
(Ian Williams) *hld up on outside: effrt and hdwy 2f out: kpt on fnl f: nt pce to chal* **9/4**[1]

0655 **5** *nk* **Sinatramania**[38] 4562 6-8-9 **51** oh5 FrannyNorton 1 56
(Tracy Waggott) *t.k.h early: chsd clr ldrs: effrt and pressed wnr over 1f out to ins fnl f: sn outpcd* **11/1**

266 **6** *1 ½* **Spes Nostra**[28] 4889 5-9-13 **69** (b) GrahamGibbons 10 70
(David Barron) *t.k.h: led and sn clr w wnr: hdd over 2f out: outpcd ins fnl f* **13/2**[3]

5340 **7** *¾* **Call Of Duty (IRE)**[12] 5466 8-9-2 **58** (p) GrahamLee 7 58
(Dianne Sayer) *dwlt: bhd: rdn and hdwy 2f out: no imp fnl f* **15/2**

3425 **8** *1 ½* **Royal Straight**[19] 5239 8-9-10 **66** (t) PhillipMakin 5 62
(Linda Perratt) *stdd s: hld up: effrt on outside over 2f out: no imp over 1f out* **14/1**

2004 **9** *nk* **District Attorney (IRE)**[13] 5427 4-8-9 **51** oh2 MichaelStainton 4 47
(Chris Fairhurst) *hld up: rdn along 3f out: nvr on terms* **14/1**

530- **10** *29* **Early Applause**[24] 6239 5-9-9 **70** ConnorBeasley(5) 2
(Nicky Richards) *midfield on ins: struggling over 3f out: sn btn: t.o* **12/1**

1m 55.53s (-2.07) **Going Correction** -0.15s/f (Firm) **10** Ran SP% **116.7**
Speed ratings (Par 103): **103,102,101,101,101 100,99,98,97,72**
toteswingers 1&2 £7.10, 1&3 £16.60, 2&3 £18.80 CSF £53.62 CT £885.30 TOTE £11.30: £2.90, £1.50, £3.40; EX 48.30 Trifecta £1430.10 Part won. Pool: £1906.90 - 0.70 winning units..
Owner Michael Reay **Bred** Cheveley Park Stud Ltd **Trained** Thirkleby, N Yorks

FOCUS
A modest handicap to close out the card. The runner-up sets the standard with the third not far off his winter AW form.
T/Plt: £328.10 to a £1 stake. Pool: £59,465.49 - 132.27 winning tickets T/Qpdt: £107.00 to a £1 stake. Pool: £3819.85 - 26.4 winning tickets RY

5466 CATTERICK (L-H)
Wednesday, August 28

OFFICIAL GOING: Good (8.0)
Wind: moderate 1/2 against Weather: fine

5883 BETFRED MOBILE CASINO MEDIAN AUCTION MAIDEN STKS — 5f
2:10 (2:10) (Class 6) 2-Y-O **£2,385** (£704; £352) **Stalls** Low

Form RPR

25 **1** **Skye's The Limit**[137] 1541 2-9-5 0 DavidNolan 3 70
(Richard Fahey) *chsd ldr: drvn to ld over 2f out: edgd lft 1f out: edgd rt ins fnl f: jst hld on* **1/1**[1]

0 **2** *shd* **Noble Asset**[47] 4259 2-9-5 0 MichaelO'Connell 2 70
(John Quinn) *t.k.h: led: hdd over 2f out: swtchd rt 1f out: upsides whn carried rt clsng stages: jst hld* **2/1**[2]

36 **3** *2 ½* **Thornaby Princess**[21] 5140 2-8-11 0 RaulDaSilva(3) 4 56
(Marjorie Fife) *t.k.h: hdwy over 2f out: sn drvn: kpt on to take 3rd towards fin* **10/1**[3]

0544 **4** *½* **Princess Myla (IRE)**[15] 5366 2-9-0 59 (p) LeeTopliss 6 54
(Paul Midgley) *dwlt: sn chsng ldrs: drvn over 2f out: one pce* **20/1**

5 *5* **Traditionelle** 2-9-0 0 DuranFentiman 5 36
(Tim Easterby) *dwlt: sn chsng ldrs: drvn over 2f out: wknd fnl f* **28/1**

60 **6** *4 ½* **Lady Dancer (IRE)**[16] 5339 2-8-11 0 JulieBurke(3) 7 20
(George Moore) *in rr: drvn and lost pl over 2f out* **100/1**

7 *hd* **Marlismamma (FR)** 2-9-0 0 DanielTudhope 1 19+
(David O'Meara) *in rr: lost pl over 2f out* **10/1**[3]

1m 0.6s (0.80) **Going Correction** +0.075s/f (Good) **7** Ran SP% **110.7**
Speed ratings (Par 92): **96,95,91,91,83 75,75**
toteswingers 1&2 £1.10, 1&3 £1.90, 2&3 £3.40 CSF £2.87 TOTE £1.80: £1.20, £1.70; EX 1.80 Trifecta £14.90 Pool: £2913.52 - 146.11 winning units..
Owner The Fairweather Foursome **Bred** Whatton Manor Stud **Trained** Musley Bank, N Yorks
■ Stewards' Enquiry : David Nolan caution: careless riding.

FOCUS
A weak contest, unlikely to produce too many winners during the remainder of the season.

5884 BETFRED MOBILE SPORTS MAIDEN STKS — 5f 212y
2:40 (2:40) (Class 5) 3-Y-O+ **£2,911** (£866; £432; £216) **Stalls** Low

Form RPR

-355 **1** **Sky Garden**[16] 5345 3-9-0 64 (p) JoeFanning 6 67
(William Haggas) *w ldr: led after 1f: drvn over 2f out: hdd narrowly appr fnl f: regained ld last 75yds: drvn out* **11/8**[1]

3 **2** *nk* **Discussiontofollow (IRE)**[18] 5290 3-9-5 0 PaulMulrennan 3 71
(Geoffrey Harker) *trckd ldrs: shkn up and narrow ld appr fnl f: hdd ins fnl f: no ex* **10/3**[2]

3440 **3** *3 ½* **Shillito**[25] 4976 3-9-5 64 BarryMcHugh 2 60
(Tony Coyle) *led 1f: t.k.h: trckd ldrs: swtchd rt over 1f out: kpt on same pce* **9/2**[3]

5005 **4** *4* **Stoneacre Hull (IRE)**[162] 1078 4-8-12 44 SladeO'Hara(5) 4 42
(Peter Grayson) *in rr: outpcd over 2f out: kpt on fnl f: tk 4th nr fin* **66/1**

000 **5** *nk* **Partner's Gold (IRE)**[11] 5517 3-9-5 48 TomEaves 7 46
(Alan Berry) *mid-div: outpcd over 2f out: one pce* **50/1**

\- **6** *6* **Jiminy** 3-9-5 0 LukeMorris 1 27
(Scott Dixon) *mid-div: drvn 3f out: sn wknd* **7/1**

5450 **7** *11* **Red Red Wine**[24] 5030 3-9-0 61 (v[1]) ShirleyTeasdale(5) 5
(Alan McCabe) *s.i.s: detached in last: reminders over 4f out: sn bhd* **10/1**

1m 12.97s (-0.63) **Going Correction** -0.125s/f (Firm)
WFA 3 from 4yo 3lb **7** Ran SP% **108.4**
Speed ratings (Par 103): **99,98,93,88,88 80,65**
toteswingers 1&2 £1.90, 1&3 £1.80, 2&3 £3.30 CSF £5.35 TOTE £2.20: £1.30, £2.20; EX 5.50 Trifecta £17.60 Pool: £1043.32 - 44.25 winning units..
Owner Lael Stable **Bred** Lael Stables **Trained** Newmarket, Suffolk

FOCUS
Plenty of reasons to think this was weak event. The form is rated a bit cautiously given the favourite's profile.

5885 BETFRED BETTER ODDS ON GOALS GALORE H'CAP — 1m 7f 177y
3:10 (3:15) (Class 5) (0-70,69) 3-Y-O+ **£3,067** (£905; £453) **Stalls** Centre

Form RPR

2333 **1** **Nashville (IRE)**[13] 5423 4-9-13 **68** (p) JoeFanning 7 79
(Richard Fahey) *chsd ldr: chal over 7f out: led over 4f out: drvn clr over 2f out: eased towards fin* **7/2**[2]

-002 **2** *6* **Danceintothelight**[23] 5048 6-8-12 **56** NeilFarley(3) 3 59
(Micky Hammond) *chsd ldrs: drvn 5f out: kpt on fnl 2f: tk 2nd nr fin* **9/1**

2122 **3** *½* **Jebulani**[16] 5343 3-7-11 **55** oh2 JulieBurke(3) 2 57
(Barry Murtagh) *trckd ldr: t.k.h: drvn over 5f out: 2nd over 3f out: kpt on one pce fnl 2f* **7/2**[2]

331 **4** *1 ¼* **Strikemaster (IRE)**[16] 5337 7-8-8 **54** (t) NoelGarbutt(5) 6 55
(Lee James) *dwlt: sn pushed along in last: sme hdwy over 3f out: kpt on to take 4th nr fin* **7/1**

2165 **5** 1/2 **Looks Like Rain**[40] 4506 4-10-0 **69** AidanColeman 4 69
(Brian Ellison) *s.i.s: hld up in rr: drvn over 4f out: 3rd over 3f out: one pce* **11/2**[3]

6060 **6** 14 **Bijou Dan**[26] 4969 12-8-12 **53** oh7 TomEaves 1 37
(George Moore) *hld up in mid-div: drvn 9f out: lost pl over 3f out: bhd fnl 2f* **50/1**

633 **7** 30 **Mister Carter (IRE)**[1] 5863 6-9-10 **65** (v) MichaelO'Connell 5 13
(Ian Williams) *led: hdd over 4f out: lost pl over 2f out: sn bhd: t.o whn eased ins fnl f* **9/4**[1]

3m 28.51s (-3.49) **Going Correction** -0.125s/f (Firm)
WFA 3 from 4yo+ 14lb **7** Ran SP% **115.1**
Speed ratings (Par 103): **103,100,99,99,98 91,76**
toteswingers 1&2 £4.60, 1&3 £2.00, 2&3 £5.20 CSF £34.36 TOTE £3.90: £2.00, £4.60; EX 26.90 Trifecta £58.20 Pool: £1559.42 - 20.07 winning units..
Owner Dr Marwan Koukash **Bred** B L Harvey & Balmerino Bloodstock **Trained** Musley Bank, N Yorks

FOCUS
There was plenty here that appeared to want to lead, meaning this staying event was run at a solid tempo. A clear personal best from the winner but the form is rated a bit cautiously.

5886 BETFRED "TREBLE ODDS ON LUCKY 15'S" H'CAP 7f
3:40 (3:41) (Class 4) (0-85,85) 3-Y-O **£5,175** (£1,540; £769; £384) **Stalls** Centre

Form RPR

1001 **1** **Skytrain**[13] 5437 3-9-3 **81** JoeFanning 2 88
(Mark Johnston) *led 1f: trckd ldr: led narrowly over 1f out: hld on wl towards fin* **4/1**[3]

1250 **2** 1/2 **Al Mukhdam**[47] 4236 3-9-6 **84** PaulMulrennan 1 90
(Peter Chapple-Hyam) *led after 1f: qckd pce 3f out: hdd over 1f out: kpt on: no ex clsng stages* **10/3**[2]

4041 **3** hd **Bluegrass Blues (IRE)**[25] 5004 3-9-7 **85** LukeMorris 5 90
(Paul Cole) *chsd ldrs: effrt over 2f out: kpt on same pce last 50yds* **6/4**[1]

4235 **4** 1 1/2 **Penny Garcia**[11] 5510 3-9-1 **79** DuranFentiman 4 80
(Tim Easterby) *dwlt: sn trcking ldrs: effrt 2f out: n.m.r over 1f out: kpt on same pce* **7/1**

1300 **5** 1 1/2 **Baltic Prince (IRE)**[6] 5676 3-7-9 **66** JoeyHaynes(7) 3 63
(Paul Green) *s.i.s: hld up in rr: effrt over 2f out: kpt on one pce appr fnl f* **10/1**

1505 **6** 9 **Deepest Blue**[6] 5673 3-8-4 **68** BarryMcHugh 6 41
(Declan Carroll) *t.k.h in rr: effrt over 2f out: sn lost pl and bhd* **14/1**

1m 26.11s (-0.89) **Going Correction** -0.125s/f (Firm) **6** Ran SP% **111.3**
Speed ratings (Par 102): **100,99,99,97,95 85**
toteswingers 1&2 £3.00, 1&3 £1.40, 2&3 £1.40 CSF £17.28 TOTE £4.10: £2.30, £1.70; EX 15.80 Trifecta £30.30 Pool: £2409.55 - 59.47 winning units..
Owner A D Spence **Bred** Brook Stud Bloodstock Ltd **Trained** Middleham Moor, N Yorks

FOCUS
A competitive handicap that appeared to develop into a bit of a sprint in the home straight. A length best from the winner with the next two close to their marks.

5887 BETFRED "DOUBLE DELIGHT" H'CAP 5f 212y
4:10 (4:10) (Class 5) (0-75,74) 3-Y-O+ **£2,911** (£866; £432; £216) **Stalls** Low

Form RPR

0233 **1** **Wild Sauce**[14] 5381 4-9-5 **74** (bt) GeorgeChaloner(5) 4 83
(Bryan Smart) *trckd ldrs: 2nd 3f out: upsides over 1f out: led jst ins fnl f: hld on nr fin* **2/1**[1]

1620 **2** nk **Majestic Manannan (IRE)**[22] 5088 4-9-8 **72** AdrianNicholls 3 80
(David Nicholls) *led 5f: hdd and edgd rt jst ins fnl f: kpt on towards fin* **4/1**[2]

4260 **3** 1 1/2 **Perfect Words (IRE)**[12] 5470 3-8-4 **62** ShirleyTeasdale(5) 6 65
(Marjorie Fife) *s.i.s: hdwy to chse ldrs over 3f out: 3rd over 2f out: kpt on same pce fnl f* **6/1**

1300 **4** 2 1/4 **Red Cape (FR)**[9] 5583 10-9-2 **66** (b) DaleSwift 1 62
(Ruth Carr) *trckd ldrs: one pce and hung rt over 1f out: eased nr fin* **8/1**

6656 **5** 3 1/4 **Rutterkin (USA)**[12] 5470 5-8-2 **55** oh8 JulieBurke(3) 8 41
(James Moffatt) *dwlt: swtchd lft after s: in rr: sme hdwy on ins over 2f out: wknd over 1f out* **25/1**

0006 **6** 2 1/4 **M J Woodward**[6] 5673 4-8-11 **61** JoeFanning 5 39
(Paul Green) *trckd ldrs on outer: hung rt and lost pl bnd over 3f out: sme hdwy over 1f out: sn wknd* **6/1**

4505 **7** 3/4 **Blue Shoes (IRE)**[15] 5365 4-8-9 **59** (b) DuranFentiman 7 35
(Tim Easterby) *in rr: drvn 3f out: wknd over 1f out* **11/2**[3]

1m 12.89s (-0.71) **Going Correction** -0.125s/f (Firm)
WFA 3 from 4yo+ 3lb **7** Ran SP% **112.2**
Speed ratings (Par 103): **99,98,96,93,89 86,85**
toteswingers 1&2 £1.60, 1&3 £2.80, 2&3 £5.30 CSF £9.69 CT £38.74 TOTE £2.90: £1.60, £1.80; EX 10.70 Trifecta £44.00 Pool: £2802.79 - 47.72 winning units..
Owner Richard Page **Bred** Ashbrittle Stud **Trained** Hambleton, N Yorks

FOCUS
A fair event dominated by the two that headed the weights. Pretty straightforward form.

5888 BETFRED "HAT TRICK HEAVEN" H'CAP (QUALIFIER FOR 2013 CATTERICK TWELVE FURLONG SERIES FINAL) 1m 3f 214y
4:40 (4:40) (Class 4) (0-85,81) 3-Y-O **£6,817** (£2,013; £1,007) **Stalls** Centre

Form RPR

2140 **1** **Dolphin Village (IRE)**[54] 4023 3-8-8 **73** GeorgeChaloner(5) 5 80
(Richard Fahey) *hld up in rr: effrt and swtchd outside over 2f out: upsides whn rdr dropped whip 1f out: sn led: edgd lft towards fin: hld on* **5/1**[3]

4110 **2** hd **Ambleside**[4] 5764 3-9-4 **78** JoeFanning 1 85
(Mark Johnston) *s.i.s: sn chsng ldrs: nt clr run over 2f out: upsides and n.m.r 1f out: kpt on: jst hld* **7/4**[2]

2251 **3** 1 1/4 **Corton Lad**[25] 4995 3-9-3 **77** (tp) TomEaves 4 82
(Keith Dalgleish) *trckd ldrs: upsides over 6f out: led over 1f out: hdd jst ins fnl f: kpt on same pce: n.m.r nr fin* **11/1**

2134 **4** hd **Sunblazer (IRE)**[14] 5390 3-8-10 **70** PatrickMathers 3 75
(William Muir) *trckd ldrs: pushed along over 4f out: chal over 2f out: keeping on same pce whn hmpd nr fin* **9/1**

1113 **5** 11 **Portrait**[13] 5448 3-9-7 **81** LukeMorris 2 73
(Sir Mark Prescott Bt) *set stdy pce: drvn and qcknd gallop over 4f out: hdd over 2f out: wkng whn hmpd on ins over 1f out: sn eased* **6/4**[1]

2m 37.47s (-1.43) **Going Correction** -0.125s/f (Firm) **5** Ran SP% **111.4**
Speed ratings (Par 102): **99,98,98,97,90**
CSF £14.40 TOTE £4.50: £1.70, £1.40; EX 15.70 Trifecta £64.90 Pool: £2377.79 - 27.47 winning units..
Owner Y Nasib **Bred** Gerrardstown House Stud **Trained** Musley Bank, N Yorks
■ Stewards' Enquiry : George Chaloner one-day ban: careless riding (Sep 11)

FOCUS
This wasn't a strongly run contest and the first four were seperated by little at the line. The form reads sound.

5889 COLLECT TOTEPOOL RETURNS AT ANY BETFRED SHOP H'CAP 5f
5:15 (5:17) (Class 6) (0-65,72) 3-Y-O+ **£2,385** (£704; £352) **Stalls** Low

Form RPR

4104 **1** **Captain Royale (IRE)**[15] 5365 8-9-7 **60** (p) BarryMcHugh 11 73
(Tracy Waggott) *hld up in rr: smooth hdwy 2f out: led jst ins fnl f: wnt clr: v readily* **25/1**

1050 **2** 2 1/2 **Choc'A'Moca (IRE)**[12] 5470 6-9-9 **62** (v) MickyFenton 12 66
(Paul Midgley) *swtchd lft after s: sn w ldrs: led 2f out: hdd jst ins fnl f: kpt on same pce* **22/1**

4500 **3** 1/2 **Windforpower (IRE)**[12] 5470 3-8-10 **51** (p) JoeFanning 5 53
(Tracy Waggott) *t.k.h towards rr: hdwy 2f out: n.m.r 1f out: kpt on towards fin* **11/1**

3651 **4** 1 3/4 **Tuibama (IRE)**[32] 4762 4-9-9 **62** (p) DaleSwift 2 58
(Tracy Waggott) *led: hdd 2f out: one pce fnl f* **9/2**[2]

3312 **5** 1 1/4 **Megaleka**[3] 5800 3-8-13 **59** NatashaEaton(5) 9 50+
(Alan Bailey) *s.i.s: swtchd lft after s: hdwy on ins over 2f out: chsng ldrs over 1f out: one pce* **5/1**[3]

6564 **6** 1 1/4 **Lady Poppy**[12] 5470 3-9-7 **62** PaulMulrennan 7 49
(George Moore) *chsd ldrs: drvn over 2f out: one pce* **9/1**

6250 **7** 1/2 **Tongalooma**[15] 5365 7-9-3 **56** LukeMorris 1 41
(James Moffatt) *in rr: hdwy over 2f out: one pce over 1f out* **7/1**

00-0 **8** 1 1/4 **Kyzer Chief**[9] 5579 8-9-7 **60** MichaelO'Connell 8 41
(Tina Jackson) *chsd ldrs on outer: drvn over 2f out: lost pl over 1f out* **40/1**

0-00 **9** 1 **Baybshambles (IRE)**[28] 4892 9-8-7 **51** GeorgeChaloner(5) 4 28
(Tina Jackson) *rrd s: a in rr* **33/1**

3311 **10** 1 3/4 **Gottcher**[5] 5708 5-10-5 **72** 12ex TomEaves 3 43
(Keith Dalgleish) *w ldrs: drvn and lost pl 2f out: eased nr fin* **2/1**[1]

1m 0.02s (0.22) **Going Correction** +0.075s/f (Good)
WFA 3 from 4yo+ 2lb **10** Ran SP% **112.6**
Speed ratings (Par 101): **101,97,96,93,91 89,88,86,85,82**
toteswingers 1&2 £22.80, 1&3 £23.50, 2&3 £16.10 CSF £417.87 CT £5519.77 TOTE £20.60: £6.80, £6.10, £3.20; EX 171.60 Trifecta £1674.30 Part won. Pool: £2232.41 - 0.72 winning units..
Owner H Conlon **Bred** Skymarc Farm Inc **Trained** Spennymoor, Co Durham

FOCUS
A modest event. Not for to take too literally but still the winner's best for the best part of two years.
T/Plt: £36.20 to a £1 stake. Pool: £41,975.63 - 844.49 winning tickets T/Qpdt: £25.90 to a £1 stake. Pool: £2085.30 - 59.40 winning tickets WG

5392 KEMPTON (A.W) (R-H)
Wednesday, August 28

OFFICIAL GOING: Standard
Wind: Nil Weather: Fine, warm

5890 LADIES DAY WITH TOBY ANSTIS 07.09.13 H'CAP 6f (P)
6:10 (6:12) (Class 6) (0-60,60) 3-Y-O **£1,940** (£577; £288; £144) **Stalls** Low

Form RPR

0452 **1** **Marmalady (IRE)**[14] 5393 3-9-7 **60** RyanMoore 3 82
(Gary Moore) *trckd ldng pair: led over 2f out: rdn wl clr over 1f out: unchal* **15/8**[1]

0322 **2** 7 **Brynford**[14] 5397 3-9-6 **59** AdamKirby 10 59+
(Chris Dwyer) *restrained into last after s: stl last and rdn 2f out: gd prog over 1f out: styd on to take modest 2nd last 50yds* **7/1**

2453 **3** 1/2 **Imperial Spirit**[13] 5431 3-8-10 **49** (v) MartinHarley 4 47
(Mick Channon) *mde most to over 2f out: no ch w wnr after: clung on to modest 2nd tl last 50yds* **12/1**

-435 **4** 3/4 **Speronella**[75] 3268 3-9-7 **60** AndreaAtzeni 2 56
(Hughie Morrison) *chsd ldrs: rdn to go 3rd 2f out: no ch w wnr and no hdwy after* **12/1**

0324 **5** hd **Sally Bruce**[8] 5602 3-8-8 **54** JenniferFerguson(7) 5 49
(Edward Creighton) *trckd ldrs: effrt to chal for a pl over 1f out but no ch w wnr: fdd* **33/1**

5032 **6** 3/4 **Compton Albion (IRE)**[23] 5067 3-8-9 **53** (p) RobertTart(5) 9 46
(Jeremy Gask) *dwlt: hld up in last trio: shkn up over 2f out: modest prog fnl f* **3/1**[2]

4600 **7** 1 **Man In The Arena**[14] 5407 3-8-11 **50** (b) WilliamCarson 8 39
(Dr Jon Scargill) *chsd ldrs: rdn over 2f out on outer: no ch after: wknd fnl f* **50/1**

5432 **8** 1 **Admirals Walk (IRE)**[11] 5525 3-9-7 **60** (bt[1]) PatDobbs 6 46
(Sylvester Kirk) *t.k.h: chsd ldrs: rdn over 2f out: sn btn: wknd fnl f* **9/2**[3]

4000 **9** hd **Whitford (IRE)**[14] 5407 3-8-10 **52** SimonPearce(3) 7 38
(Chris Dwyer) *dwlt: a wl in rr: shkn up and no prog 2f out* **50/1**

464 **10** nk **Borough Boy (IRE)**[17] 5305 3-9-1 **54** (v) MartinDwyer 1 39
(Derek Shaw) *taken down early: plld hrd: hld up in last trio: rdn and no prog 2f out* **14/1**

5046 **11** 1 1/4 **Marvelino**[57] 3921 3-9-7 **60** (b) DaneO'Neill 11 41
(Pat Eddery) *w ldr to over 2f out: wknd qckly* **16/1**

1m 12.02s (-1.08) **Going Correction** -0.05s/f (Stan) **11** Ran SP% **125.3**
Speed ratings (Par 98): **105,95,95,94,93 92,91,90,89,89 87**
toteswingers 1&2 £3.20, 1&3 £4.50, 2&3 £11.00 CSF £17.08 CT £134.05 TOTE £3.00: £1.50, £2.20, £3.80; EX 14.30 Trifecta £96.90 Pool: £2049.51 - 15.85 winning units..
Owner Heart Of The South Racing **Bred** Tribes Man Syndicate **Trained** Lower Beeding, W Sussex

FOCUS
This 3-y-o sprint handicap looked fairly open on paper, but the winner hacked up. The form is fluid, with the runner-up rated 6lb below her latest C&D form.

5891 CONOR MAYNARD 14.09.13 MAIDEN AUCTION STKS 7f (P)
6:40 (6:41) (Class 6) 2-Y-O **£1,940** (£577; £288; £144) **Stalls** Low

Form RPR

30 **1** **Ajig**[37] 4589 2-8-10 0 JohnFahy 4 75
(Eve Johnson Houghton) *pressed ldr: rdn fr 1/2-way: persistent chal fr 2f out: looked hld fnl f tl styd on to ld post* **16/1**

35 **2** shd **Baars Causeway (IRE)**[40] 4484 2-8-3 0 MichaelJMMurphy(5) 1 73
(Alan Jarvis) *led: drvn and hrd pressed 2f out: kpt on fnl f: hdd post* **4/5**[1]

3 1 1/2 **Top Dollar** 2-8-12 0 RyanMoore 10 73
(James Tate) *chsd ldng pair: shkn up 2f out: urged along and styd on but nvr able to bridge the gap* **9/2**[2]

0 **4** 1 **Encore Encore (FR)**[21] 5131 2-8-6 0 .... PaulHanagan 9 65
(Harry Dunlop) *dwlt: settled in rr: shkn up and prog 2f out: chsd ldng trio over 1f out: kpt on but no real imp* **14/1**

0 **5** hd **Cadmium**[13] 5443 2-8-8 0 .... DavidProbert 3 66
(Harry Dunlop) *dwlt: towards rr: prog over 2f out: rdn to dispute 4th fr over 1f out: kpt on but no real imp on ldrs* **66/1**

6 1 1/2 **Donncha (IRE)** 2-9-3 0 .... AndreaAtzeni 14 71
(Robert Eddery) *in rr of main gp: shkn up over 2f out: prog over 1f out: kpt on fnl f: nrst fin* **20/1**

2 **7** 2 1/2 **Water For Life**[21] 5151 2-8-6 0 .... WilliamCarson 12 54
(Dave Morris) *t.k.h: trckd ldrs on outer: rdn 2f out: sn outpcd and btn: fdd* **12/1**[3]

0 **8** 3/4 **Diffident Beats**[7] 5646 2-8-11 0 .... MartinHarley 11 57
(Mick Channon) *stdd s: hld up in rr: nudged along fr 2f out: nvr remotely involved* **20/1**

04 **9** 2 1/4 **Black Sceptre (IRE)**[20] 5167 2-8-8 0 .... JenniferFerguson(7) 2 55
(Edward Creighton) *prom tl wknd 2f out* **66/1**

04 **10** 1/2 **Morgans Bluff**[48] 4206 2-8-1 0 .... JemmaMarshall(3) 8 42
(Pat Phelan) *chsd ldrs tl wknd over 2f out* **50/1**

11 10 **Sir Percy Blakeney** 2-9-1 0 .... MartinDwyer 6 27
(Marcus Tregoning) *dwlt: sn detached in 12th: no prog: t.o* **16/1**

12 1/2 **Permsiri (IRE)** 2-8-6 0 .... MartinLane 7 17+
(Malcolm Saunders) *s.v.s: a t.o: lost no further grnd fr 1/2-way* **100/1**

33 **13** 16 **Hannah Louise (IRE)**[19] 5229 2-8-4 0 .... (t) ChrisCatlin 5
(Olivia Maylam) *taken down early: plld v hrd: taken out wd after 1f: steered wd after and wknd 3f out: eased and wl t.o* **16/1**

1m 27.47s (1.47) **Going Correction** -0.05s/f (Stan) **13 Ran SP% 121.2**
Speed ratings (Par 92): **89,88,87,86,85 84,81,80,77,77 65,65,46**
toteswingers 1&2 £5.80, 1&3 £9.00, 2&3 £1.70 CSF £28.50 TOTE £17.00: £3.50, £1.20, £1.50; EX 47.90 Trifecta £253.20 Pool: £1712.70 - 5.07 winning units..
Owner Eden Racing Club **Bred** Southcourt Stud **Trained** Blewbury, Oxon

FOCUS
No great strength in depth to this juvenile maiden. The main action developed down the middle of the home straight. The form is rated at face value through the runner-up for now.

5892 BETDAQ 1ST UK COMMISSION FREE MEDIAN AUCTION MAIDEN STKS 1m 4f (P)

7:10 (7:11) (Class 5) 3-5-Y-0 **£2,587** (£770; £384; £192) **Stalls Centre**

Form RPR

3-32 **1** **Omnipresent**[12] 5469 3-9-3 72 .... RyanMoore 1 84
(Sir Michael Stoute) *mde all: rdn over 2f out: styd on wl fr over 1f out* **8/1**

42 **2** 1 1/2 **Certification (IRE)**[23] 5058 3-9-3 0 .... SilvestreDeSousa 13 81+
(Mark Johnston) *chsd ldrs: rdn 3f out: prog over 2f out: wnt 2nd over 1f out and looked a real threat: hanging and disorganised after: no imp last 100yds* **13/2**[2]

2 **3** 3 1/4 **Mahdiyah**[22] 5100 3-8-12 0 .... PaulHanagan 4 71
(Saeed bin Suroor) *t.k.h early: trckd ldrs: rdn to chse wnr over 2f out: nt qckn and no imp over 1f out: sn lost 2nd* **4/5**[1]

33 **4** 1 1/4 **Al Arish (IRE)**[19] 5233 3-9-3 0 .... TomQueally 7 74
(Lady Cecil) *chsd wnr to over 2f out: steadily outpcd u.p* **7/1**[3]

03 **5** 2 1/2 **Mount Macedon**[33] 4719 3-9-3 0 .... AdamKirby 2 70+
(Luca Cumani) *towards rr: sme prog fr over 3f out: pushed along and kpt on steadily fnl 2f: nvr involved* **25/1**

6 3 3/4 **Arty Campbell (IRE)** 3-9-3 0 .... MartinLane 3 64
(David Simcock) *settled in midfield on inner: shkn up and outpcd fr over 2f out: no imp after: kpt on* **66/1**

6 **7** 4 **Martagon Lily**[35] 4632 3-8-12 0 .... WilliamBuick 11 53
(John Gosden) *hld up in midfeld: rdn over 2f out: wknd over 1f out: fin tired* **16/1**

46 **8** 5 **Rancho Montoya (IRE)**[22] 5100 3-8-12 0 .... DavidProbert 6 45
(Andrew Balding) *a in rr: rdn 3f out: no prog* **16/1**

0 **9** 1/2 **Gentlemax (FR)**[23] 5064 3-9-3 0 .... JimCrowley 9 49
(Alan Jarvis) *settled wl in rr: wl outpcd and one reminder over 2f out: nursed home after but kpt on* **50/1**

0-4 **10** 14 **Wild Anthem**[90] 2803 3-8-12 0 .... PatDobbs 8 21
(Hughie Morrison) *a wl in rr: wknd over 4f out: t.o* **33/1**

2-60 **11** 8 **Catch The Cider**[21] 5133 3-9-3 0 .... GeorgeBaker 5 14
(Hans Adielsson) *prog to go prom after 2f: wknd qckly over 3f out: t.o* **25/1**

0 **12** 49 **Zorro's Blade**[12] 5469 5-9-8 0 .... (v1) RobertTart(5) 10
(Michael Mullineaux) *drvn fr s: a in last pair: wknd 5f out: wl t.o* **100/1**

2m 33.4s (-1.10) **Going Correction** -0.05s/f (Stan)
WFA 3 from 4yo+ 10lb **12 Ran SP% 119.3**
Speed ratings (Par 103): **101,100,97,97,95 92,90,86,86,77 71,39**
toteswingers 1&2 £4.00, 1&3 £2.20, 2&3 £2.50 CSF £56.42 TOTE £9.60: £3.00, £2.40, £1.10; EX 42.50 Trifecta £78.90 Pool: £1653.51 - 15.71 winning units..
Owner K Abdullah **Bred** Juddmonte Farms Ltd **Trained** Newmarket, Suffolk

FOCUS
This well-contested maiden was run at a stop-start pace and as a result it paid to race handy. The winner, who is related to a couple that were better on this surface, looked better suited by it. The second is rated a few pounds off, backed up by the fourth and fifth.

5893 BOOK NOW FOR LADIES DAY 07.09.13 NURSERY H'CAP 1m (P)

7:40 (7:43) (Class 6) (0-60,59) 2-Y-0 **£1,940** (£577; £288; £144) **Stalls Low**

Form RPR

0044 **1** **Jazri**[23] 5068 2-8-8 51 .... MatthewLawson(5) 7 57+
(Milton Bradley) *wl in rr: rdn 3f out: sustained prog on outer over 2f out: maintained effrt to ld last 75yds: hld on* **11/1**

0546 **2** nk **Aristocracy**[24] 5034 2-9-5 57 .... MartinHarley 3 63
(Mick Channon) *rousted to ld after 1f: hrd rdn over 2f out: fended off pursuers tl hdd last 75yds: tried to rally but jst hld* **6/1**[3]

4450 **3** 2 1/4 **Tyrsal (IRE)**[7] 5634 2-9-2 54 .... AndreaAtzeni 8 54
(Robert Eddery) *broke best but sn restrained bhd ldrs: prog to go 2nd over 2f out: drvn and nt qckn over 1f out: one pce fnl f* **10/1**

5054 **4** 2 **May Whi (IRE)**[25] 4990 2-9-7 59 .... (v1) RichardKingscote 1 55
(Tom Dascombe) *pressed ldrs: rdn on inner over 2f out: one pce fr over 1f out* **10/1**

660 **5** 2 1/2 **Moving Waves (IRE)**[23] 5053 2-9-5 57 .... ShaneKelly 6 47
(Ollie Pears) *hld up in midfield: rdn over 2f out: no imp on ldrs over 1f out: wl hld after* **3/1**[2]

0602 **6** 3/4 **Jazzy Lady (IRE)**[43] 4387 2-9-0 52 .... TomQueally 14 40
(David Evans) *wl in rr: rdn in last 1/2-way: kpt on past btn horses fnl 2f* **25/1**

6660 **7** nk **Jana**[24] 5034 2-9-3 55 .... SilvestreDeSousa 10 43
(Sylvester Kirk) *led briefly in 1st f: mostly chsd ldr after: drvn over 2f out: wknd over 1f out* **20/1**

600 **8** 3/4 **Big Kenny**[56] 3948 2-8-11 52 .... DeclanBates(3) 4 38
(David Evans) *a towards rr: rdn and struggling 3f out: no ch after* **40/1**

056 **9** nk **Freddie Kilroy**[22] 5105 2-9-3 55 .... RyanMoore 5 40
(Ed Dunlop) *hld up in midfield: rdn wl over 2f out: no prog over 1f out: wknd fnl f* **2/1**[1]

044 **10** nk **Escarlata Rossa**[19] 5243 2-8-13 51 .... JohnFahy 2 35
(J S Moore) *led briefly early: chsd ldrs: rdn over 3f out: steadily wknd over 2f out* **20/1**

0045 **11** 2 1/2 **Mildenhall**[16] 5347 2-9-4 56 .... SeanLevey 9 35
(Richard Hannon) *settled towards rr: rdn 3f out: no prog* **12/1**

2005 **12** 2 **Kitty Brown (IRE)**[43] 4387 2-9-5 57 .... (v) AdamKirby 12 31
(David Evans) *reluctant to enter stalls: s.s: a in last trio: wl btn fnl 2f* **25/1**

040 **13** 3 1/4 **Village Cricket**[55] 3991 2-9-1 53 .... (p) DaneO'Neill 11 20
(Pam Sly) *chsd ldrs on outer early: rdn and wknd over 3f out* **33/1**

1m 41.56s (1.76) **Going Correction** -0.05s/f (Stan) **13 Ran SP% 129.4**
Speed ratings (Par 92): **89,88,86,84,81 81,80,80,79,79 77,75,71**
toteswingers 1&2 £13.80, 1&3 £17.80, 2&3 £7.20 CSF £75.24 CT £710.94 TOTE £6.30: £2.40, £2.40, £4.00; EX 92.70 Trifecta £1103.80 Part won. Pool: £1471.81 - 0.16 winning units..
Owner Dab Hand Racing **Bred** Broughton Bloodstock **Trained** Sedbury, Gloucs

FOCUS
An ordinary nursery. They went a fair pace and few counted seriously. The lack of depth limits enthusiasm for the form.

5894 £200 FREE BETS AT BETDAQ H'CAP (LONDON MILE SERIES QUALIFIER) 1m (P)

8:10 (8:11) (Class 3) (0-95,95) 3-Y-0+
£7,158 (£2,143; £1,071; £535; £267; £134) **Stalls Low**

Form RPR

1516 **1** **Ehtedaam (USA)**[33] 4733 4-9-10 95 .... [1] PaulHanagan 6 107+
(Saeed bin Suroor) *s.i.s: t.k.h early: towards rr: prog over 2f out: rdn to ld jst ins fnl f: styd on wl: readily* **4/1**[2]

12-1 **2** 1 1/2 **Seek Again (USA)**[13] 5439 3-9-4 95 .... WilliamBuick 12 104+
(John Gosden) *hld up in midfield: drvn jst over 2f out: prog over 1f out but wnr already gone past: styd on to take 2nd last 75yds* **5/4**[1]

3000 **3** 3/4 **Maverik**[27] 4923 5-9-3 88 .... JimCrowley 11 95
(William Knight) *led 1f: trckd ldr: led again over 2f out gng strly: drvn over 1f out: hdd and one pce jst ins fnl f* **25/1**

0-06 **4** 1/2 **Well Painted (IRE)**[99] 2541 4-9-2 87 .... (t) RyanMoore 3 93+
(William Haggas) *towards rr: rdn and no prog over 2f out: styd on fr over 1f out: gng on at fin* **9/1**[3]

0520 **5** 3/4 **Shahdaroba (IRE)**[18] 5260 3-8-9 93 .... PatMillman(7) 8 97
(Rod Millman) *trckd ldrs: shoved along fr over 2f out: disp 2nd over 1f out: nt qckn: kpt on* **25/1**

4000 **6** 1/2 **Emilio Largo**[23] 5056 5-9-8 93 .... FrederikTylicki 1 96
(James Fanshawe) *trckd ldrs: rdn to dispute 2nd over 1f out: steadily fdd fnl f* **9/1**[3]

2512 **7** 2 1/4 **Clockmaker (IRE)**[61] 3754 7-9-9 94 .... FergusSweeney 5 92
(Conor Dore) *led after 1f to over 2f out: wknd over 1f out* **25/1**

4210 **8** nk **Silverheels (IRE)**[29] 4859 4-9-3 88 .... TomQueally 14 85
(Paul Cole) *racd on outer in midfield: lost pl and rdn over 2f out: nvr on terms after* **16/1**

3-30 **9** 1/2 **Shamir**[135] 1585 6-9-2 87 .... DaneO'Neill 7 83
(Jo Crowley) *sn in rr: rdn over 2f out: no imp on ldrs after* **25/1**

/004 **10** 1/2 **Prompter**[40] 4488 6-9-3 88 .... DougieCostello 9 83
(Jonjo O'Neill) *hld up in last pair: jst pushed along fnl 2f: nvr remotely involved* **33/1**

-000 **11** 3/4 **Jacob Cats**[18] 5255 4-9-5 90 .... JamieSpencer 10 83
(Olly Stevens) *sn stdd into last: rdn and no prog wl over 2f out* **14/1**

1200 **12** 3 **Loyalty**[165] 1036 6-9-6 91 .... (v) MartinDwyer 2 77
(Derek Shaw) *prom on inner: rdn over 2f out: nt qckn: wknd over 1f out* **33/1**

2500 **13** 11 **Nazreef**[81] 3108 6-9-10 95 .... GeorgeBaker 13 56
(Hughie Morrison) *prom on outer tl wknd rapidly wl over 2f out: t.o* **25/1**

1m 37.41s (-2.39) **Going Correction** -0.05s/f (Stan)
WFA 3 from 4yo+ 6lb **13 Ran SP% 122.1**
Speed ratings (Par 107): **109,107,106,106,105 105,102,102,101,101 100,97,86**
toteswingers 1&2 £1.80, 1&3 £30.70, 2&3 £15.70 CSF £8.66 CT £114.65 TOTE £3.10: £1.10, £1.40, £4.50; EX 11.50 Trifecta £210.70 Pool: £1108.27 - 3.94 winning units..
Owner Godolphin **Bred** Grapestock Llc **Trained** Newmarket, Suffolk

FOCUS
A decent handicap run at an average pace and the form looks solid enough, with the third and fifth backing up the winner's form.

5895 COMMISSION FREE 1ST MONTH AT BETDAQ H'CAP 2m (P)

8:40 (8:40) (Class 4) (0-85,85) 4-Y-0+ **£4,690** (£1,395; £697; £348) **Stalls Low**

Form RPR

2-34 **1** **Spiritoftomintoul**[25] 5008 4-8-13 77 .... TomQueally 8 93+
(Lady Cecil) *hld up in last pair: gd prog on wd outside over 2f out: led over 1f out: rdn clr: impressive* **9/4**[1]

1630 **2** 3 1/4 **Cousin Khee**[46] 4301 6-9-6 84 .... RyanMoore 5 91+
(Hughie Morrison) *hld up in 9th: nt clr run over 2f out tl over 1f out: gd prog after but wnr already flown: styd on to take 2nd nr fin* **7/1**[3]

0-30 **3** 1 **Saborido (USA)**[54] 4029 7-9-4 82 .... JimCrowley 14 88
(Amanda Perrett) *hld up in 10th: gd prog on outer over 2f out alongside wnr: chal over 1f out but sn outpcd: lost 2nd nr fin* **25/1**

22 **4** 1 1/4 **Presto Volante (IRE)**[27] 4913 5-9-2 80 .... (v1) PatDobbs 3 84
(Amanda Perrett) *hld up in 7th: rdn and sme prog on inner over 2f out: swtchd lft over 1f out: kpt on but nvr able to threaten* **8/1**

2544 **5** shd **Spice Fair**[20] 5185 6-9-2 80 .... SeanLevey 9 84+
(Mark Usher) *stdd s: hld up in last: nt clr run over 2f out tl forced way through over 1f out: styd on but nt pce to threaten* **16/1**

34-0 **6** nk **Halling's Quest**[56] 3960 4-9-7 85 .... DougieCostello 7 89+
(Hughie Morrison) *hld up in last trio: prog on inner fr 2f out: styd on but nt pce to threaten* **25/1**

0010 **7** 3 3/4 **Mexicali (IRE)**[28] 4873 5-9-1 79 .... SebSanders 12 78
(Dean Ivory) *trckd ldrs: prog to ld after 5f: hdd & wknd over 1f out* **6/1**[2]

-500 **8** 1/2 **Sohar**[28] 4873 5-9-4 82 .... KirstyMilczarek 2 81
(James Toller) *chsd ldrs in 5th: drvn over 2f out: wknd over 1f out* **10/1**

0311 **9** 2 **Meetings Man (IRE)**[19] 5231 6-9-2 80 .... (p) AdamKirby 10 76
(Ali Brewer) *t.k.h: hld up in 8th: rdn over 2f out: wknd over 1f out* **8/1**

1205 **10** 4 **Italian Riviera**[13] 5423 4-9-2 80 .... (p) ChrisCatlin 11 72
(Sir Mark Prescott Bt) *pressed ldrs: rdn and wknd over 2f out: no ch whn bmpd over 1f out* **16/1**

2311 **11** 5 **Hi Note**[11] 5535 5-8-13 82 .... HarryPoulton(5) 4 68
(Sheena West) *pestered ldr: led after 3f tl after 5f: wknd over 2f out* **20/1**

1005 **12** *1* **Desert Recluse (IRE)**[33] 4704 6-9-4 **82**.......................... WilliamBuick 1 66
(Pat Eddery) *rousted to ld: hdd after 3f: tried to ld again after 5f but unable to do so: wknd qckly over 2f out* **14/1**

4030 **13** *½* **Danvilla**[18] 5288 6-9-1 **79**................................(p) WilliamCarson 6 63
(Paul Webber) *chsd ldrs in 6th: rdn over 3f out: sn wknd* **40/1**

3m 26.07s (-4.03) **Going Correction** -0.05s/f (Stan) 13 Ran SP% **122.2**
Speed ratings (Par 105): **108,106,105,105,105 105,103,102,101,99 97,96,96**
toteswingers 1&2 £2.70, 1&3 £21.70, 2&3 £21.30 CSF £17.00 CT £326.28 TOTE £3.50: £1.40, £1.70, £6.80; EX 24.90 Trifecta £374.40 Pool: £1823.24 - 3.65 winning units..
Owner Angus Dundee Distillers plc **Bred** Barry Walters Farms **Trained** Newmarket, Suffolk

FOCUS
Not a bad staying handicap and there was a fair pace on. The third and fourth help set the standard.

5896 WINNERS ARE WELCOME AT BETDAQ FILLIES' H'CAP 7f (P)
9:10 (9:11) (Class 4) (0-85,83) 3-Y-O+ **£4,690** (£1,395; £697; £348) **Stalls** Low

Form RPR

-321 **1** **Trucanini**[21] 5152 3-9-3 **79**.. GeorgeBaker 10 88+
(Chris Wall) *pressed ldr: led 2f out gng strly: shkn up to assert jst over 1f out: readily* **3/1**[1]

0163 **2** *1¾* **Hidden Belief (IRE)**[14] 5398 3-8-13 **75**.......................... JimCrowley 4 78
(Ralph Beckett) *trckd ldng pair: rdn to chal wl over 1f out: readily hld fnl f: jst hld on for 2nd* **5/1**[3]

3133 **3** *nk* **Truly Madly (IRE)**[2] 5820 3-8-7 **69**........................... JohnFahy 7 71
(Hans Adielsson) *hld up in midfield: prog fr 2f out: wnt 3rd over 1f out: styd on and nrly snatched 2nd* **14/1**

0603 **4** *1¼* **Califante**[20] 5202 3-9-7 **83**.. MartinDwyer 5 82
(William Muir) *hld up: rdn in last trio 2f out: prog over 1f out: styd on to take 4th ins fnl f* **12/1**

01-4 **5** *1¼* **Sugar House (USA)**[26] 4941 3-9-0 **76**.................... MickaelBarzalona 11 72
(Charlie Appleby) *chsd ldrs in 4th: one of first u.p wl over 2f out: plugged on but nt pce to threaten* **4/1**[2]

4600 **6** *hd* **Fanrouge (IRE)**[17] 5308 4-9-11 **82**............................ AndreaAtzeni 9 79
(Rod Millman) *hld up towards rr: rdn 2f out: kpt on same pce: n.d* **33/1**

4200 **7** *4* **Fulney**[21] 5125 4-9-5 **76**.. DaneO'Neill 2 62
(James Eustace) *led at gd pce: rdn and hdd 2f out: wknd over 1f out: eased ins fnl f* **33/1**

123- **8** *½* **Spokeswoman (IRE)**[299] 7523 3-9-7 **83**................. SilvestreDeSousa 8 66
(Saeed bin Suroor) *awkward s: t.k.h: hld up in last: shkn up and no prog on outer over 2f out: wl btn after* **3/1**[1]

256 **9** *¾* **Entwined (IRE)**[20] 5187 3-8-2 **71**.......................... JenniferFerguson(7) 3 52
(Clive Cox) *hld up in rr: rdn on inner jst over 2f out: no prog: wknd fnl f* **20/1**

2252 **10** *hd* **It's Taboo**[13] 5444 3-8-9 **71**...................................... DavidProbert 1 51
(Mark Usher) *pushed along to chse ldrs: wknd over 1f out* **20/1**

1m 25.33s (-0.67) **Going Correction** -0.05s/f (Stan)
WFA 3 from 4yo 5lb 10 Ran SP% **116.4**
Speed ratings (Par 102): **101,99,98,97,95 95,91,90,89,89**
toteswingers 1&2 £5.50, 1&3 £11.40, 2&3 £11.50 CSF £17.24 CT £181.21 TOTE £6.60: £2.20, £1.10, £3.80; EX 23.00 Trifecta £271.10 Pool: £1355.62 - 3.74 winning units..
Owner Dolly's Dream Syndicate **Bred** The National Stud Never Say Die Club Ltd **Trained** Newmarket, Suffolk

FOCUS
This modest fillies' handicap was largely made up of 3-y-os. It was run at a fair enough pace, but those held up struggled to make an impact. The winner is progressing while the placed horses help set the level.
T/Jkpt: Not won. T/Plt: £20.00 to a £1 stake. Pool: £80,351.65 - 2923.25 winning tickets T/Qpdt: £17.70 to a £1 stake. Pool: £4966.06 - 206.55 winning tickets JN

5864 SOUTHWELL (L-H)
Wednesday, August 28

OFFICIAL GOING: Standard
Wind: Light behind Weather: Cloudy

5897 LADBROKES H'CAP 1m 4f (F)
4:50 (4:50) (Class 6) (0-55,55) 4-Y-O+ **£1,940** (£577; £288; £144) **Stalls** Low

Form RPR

-052 **1** **Royal Alcor (IRE)**[7] 5633 6-9-0 **55**..........................(t) DanielMuscutt(7) 9 77
(Gay Kelleway) *trckd ldrs: smooth hdwy 4f out: cl up over 3f out: led wl over 2f out: sn pushed clr: unchal* **9/2**[1]

3012 **2** *12* **Torero**[7] 5643 4-9-6 **54**..(p) BrianHughes 2 57
(Kevin Ryan) *hld up in midfield: hdwy on inner to trck ldrs bef 1/2-way: effrt and cl up 3f out: sn rdn and ev ch tl drvn and one pce fr wl over 1f out* **6/1**[3]

6006 **3** *2¾* **Lacey**[13] 5432 4-8-11 **50**..(e[1]) JackDuern(5) 10 48
(Andrew Hollinshead) *towards rr: stdy hdwy 1/2-way: chsd ldrs over 3f out: rdn along wl over 2f out: styd on to chse ldng pair over 1f out: sn drvn: hung rt and no imp* **12/1**

0345 **4** *hd* **Eanans Bay (IRE)**[22] 5084 4-8-12 **46** oh1...............................(b) LiamJones 5 44
(Mark H Tompkins) *bhd: swtchd wd and rdn along 1/2-way: hdwy over 3f out: drvn over 2f out: kpt on: nrst fin* **10/1**

0006 **5** *2* **Dubara Reef (IRE)**[9] 5592 6-8-9 **46**............ WilliamTwiston-Davies(3) 6 41
(Paul Green) *chsd ldrs on outer: rdn along and outpcd 1/2-way: plugged on fnl 3f: n.d* **25/1**

5025 **6** *6* **Light The City (IRE)**[13] 5420 6-8-9 **46**.................... RaulDaSilva(3) 1 31
(Ruth Carr) *disp ld: chsd ldr fr 1/2-way: rdn along 4f out: drvn over 3f out and sn wknd* **5/1**[2]

/001 **7** *5* **Mr Dream Maker (IRE)**[35] 4622 5-8-8 **49** ow1....... LukeLeadbitter(7) 11 26
(Noel Wilson) *disp ld tl led 1/2-way: rdn along 4f out: hdd wl over 2f out and sn wknd* **10/1**

0-66 **8** *14* **Sygnature**[196] 646 4-9-4 **52**.. NeilCallan 4
(Alan Swinbank) *rdn along s: sn chsng ldrs: pushed along 1/2-way: rdn over 5f out: sn wknd* **7/1**

5062 **9** *½* **Soweto Star (IRE)**[50] 4147 5-9-5 **53**............................... SteveDrowne 7
(John Best) *chsd ldrs: rdn along and lost pl over 5f out: sn bhd* **7/1**

0-40 **10** *3¾* **Fleeting Fashion**[31] 4809 4-9-2 **50**........................... AndrewMullen 8
(Michael Appleby) *a in rr* **10/1**

/00- **11** *12* **Northgate Lodge (USA)**[403] 4350 8-8-12 **46** oh1............ JimmyQuinn 3
(Mel Brittain) *midfield whn n.m.r on inner and lost pl over 1m out: bhd fr 1/2-way* **50/1**

2m 38.7s (-2.30) **Going Correction** -0.10s/f (Stan) 11 Ran SP% **114.9**
Speed ratings (Par 101): **103,95,93,93,91 87,84,75,74,72 64**
toteswingers 1&2 £5.70, 1&3 £14.90, 2&3 £15.70 CSF £30.39 CT £301.92 TOTE £6.30: £2.00, £1.90, £4.10; EX 25.20 Trifecta £352.20 Pool: £2403.88 - 5.11 winning units..
Owner Gay Kelleway & Paul Kerridge **Bred** John Hayes **Trained** Exning, Suffolk

FOCUS
A strong pace soon had them sorted out, with only a handful ever looking comfortable. A marginal personal-best from the winner with the second slightly below his recent turf form.

5898 LADBROKES NURSERY H'CAP 6f (F)
5:20 (5:20) (Class 6) (0-60,60) 2-Y-O **£2,045** (£603; £302) **Stalls** Low

Form RPR

000 **1** **Mornin Mr Norris**[33] 4724 2-8-3 **45**............................ RaulDaSilva(3) 4 47
(John Quinn) *mde most: rdn wl over 2f out: drvn over 1f out: kpt on fnl f: hld on gamely towards fin* **7/1**

5254 **2** *nk* **The Dukkerer (IRE)**[30] 4820 2-9-7 **60**......................... DanielTudhope 7 62
(David O'Meara) *trckd ldrs: swtchd lft to inner and hdwy 2f out: rdn to chal over 1f out: drvn ins fnl f and ev ch tl no ex nr fin* **4/1**[3]

130 **3** *½* **It's All A Game**[13] 5424 2-8-13 **57**...............................(v) PhilipPrince(5) 6 57
(Richard Guest) *sn rdn along and outpcd in rr: wd st: hdwy 2f out: kpt on wl u.p appr fnl f: nrst fin* **3/1**[1]

5441 **4** *2* **She Can Jig**[12] 5480 2-9-0 **60**..................................... KevinStott(7) 5 54+
(Kevin Ryan) *rdn along s and sn outpcd in rr: drvn along 1/2-way: wd st: hdwy 2f out: kpt on appr fnl f: nrst fin* **10/3**[2]

443 **5** *hd* **Hot Stock (FR)**[42] 4412 2-9-7 **60**................................... CathyGannon 3 53
(Jo Hughes) *in tch: hdwy wl over 2f out: sn rdn: kpt on fnl f: nrst fin* **5/1**

0000 **6** *4½* **Baileys Celebrate**[7] 5634 2-8-6 **45**............................... LiamJones 8 25
(Mark Johnston) *cl up: rdn along over 2f out: drvn and wknd over 1f out* **12/1**

0603 **7** *3½* **Reale Silenzio**[12] 5480 2-8-3 **45**................................ RyanPowell(3) 9 14
(John Weymes) *chsd ldrs: rdn along wl over 2f out: drvn and wknd over 1f out* **16/1**

000 **8** *½* **Suni Dancer**[15] 5364 2-8-11 **50**.................................... SteveDrowne 1 18
(Paul Green) *chsd ldrs on inner: rdn along wl over 2f out: drvn wl over 1f out and sn wknd* **25/1**

1m 17.78s (1.28) **Going Correction** -0.10s/f (Stan) 8 Ran SP% **114.7**
Speed ratings (Par 92): **87,86,85,83,83 77,72,71**
toteswingers 1&2 £6.00, 1&3 £7.20, 2&3 £2.30 CSF £35.19 CT £102.12 TOTE £5.60: £1.50, £1.50, £1.20; EX 47.00 Trifecta £214.30 Pool: £1233.21 - 4.31 winning units..
Owner Mrs E Wright **Bred** Mrs E Wright **Trained** Settrington, N Yorks

FOCUS
They went a good pace, but the surface favours those who raced handily. The form looks weak.

5899 BET ON YOUR MOBILE WITH LADBROKES H'CAP 7f (F)
5:50 (5:52) (Class 5) (0-75,75) 4-Y-O+ **£2,587** (£770; £384; £192) **Stalls** Low

Form RPR

6500 **1** **Caldercruix (USA)**[47] 4237 6-9-2 **75**....................(v) GeorgeDowning(5) 8 84
(James Evans) *chsd ldrs: hdwy and cl up over 3f out: rdn to chal over 2f out: drvn over 1f out: led ins fnl f: edgd lft and kpt on wl towards fin* **4/1**[1]

4005 **2** *1½* **Piceno (IRE)**[9] 5580 5-8-9 **66**...(p) BillyCray(3) 7 71
(Scott Dixon) *cl up whn sltly hmpd after 1f: sn led: jnd and rdn wl over 2f out: drvn over 1f out: hdd ins fnl f: no ex towards fin* **6/1**[3]

0300 **3** *2¾* **Flying Pickets (IRE)**[20] 5195 4-8-8 **65**....(be) WilliamTwiston-Davies(3) 1 63
(Alan McCabe) *towards rr and pushed along after 2f: wd st: hdwy 2f out: sn rdn and edgd lft over 1f out: kpt on fnl f: nrst fin* **16/1**

-004 **4** *2* **Last Supper**[50] 4145 4-8-3 **57**..(p) JimmyQuinn 5 50+
(James Bethell) *chsd ldrs on inner: rdn along 3f out: drvn 2f out: sn one pce* **25/1**

1250 **5** *1¾* **Fluctuation (IRE)**[12] 5479 5-8-12 **69**.......................(v) MarkCoumbe(3) 6 57
(Ian Williams) *dwlt: hdwy to chse ldrs after 2f: rdn along over 2f out: drvn wl over 1f out: sn no imp* **9/2**[2]

3451 **6** *2* **Fairy Wing (IRE)**[22] 5097 6-9-0 **68**...................................(b) NeilCallan 9 51+
(Violet M Jordan) *slt ld whn edgd lft and then rt after 1f: sn hdd: swtchd wd and stdd: in tch: hdwy on outer to chse ldrs 3f out: rdn over 2f out: sn btn* **7/1**

5-35 **7** *¾* **Kimbali (IRE)**[14] 5378 4-9-3 **71**..............................(p) DanielTudhope 4 52
(Richard Fahey) *dwlt: hdwy to chse ldrs after 2f: rdn along to chse ldng pair 3f out: drvn over 2f out and sn wknd* **10/1**

1060 **8** *¾* **Kingscombe (USA)**[8] 5614 4-8-9 **63** ow2....................(p) SteveDrowne 3 42
(Linda Jewell) *sn outpcd and rdn along in rr: a bhd* **6/1**[3]

1m 28.96s (-1.34) **Going Correction** -0.10s/f (Stan) 8 Ran SP% **98.1**
Speed ratings (Par 103): **103,101,98,95,93 91,90,89**
toteswingers 1&2 £5.20, 1&3 £8.30, 2&3 £5.40 CSF £20.21 CT £205.25 TOTE £4.90: £2.10, £1.60, £4.10; EX 21.20 Trifecta £243.80 Pool: £1106.19 - 3.40 winning units..
Owner David Mantle **Bred** Bjorn Nielsen **Trained** Broadwas, Worcs

FOCUS
There were plenty of track favourites in this decent race, the first two among them. The winner is rated close to his best in the past year, with the second in line with his best since the winter, despite being hampered.

5900 LADBROKES MAIDEN AUCTION STKS 5f (F)
6:20 (6:22) (Class 6) 2-Y-O **£1,940** (£577; £288; £144) **Stalls** High

Form RPR

04 **1** **Britain (IRE)**[49] 4177 2-8-4 0.. CathyGannon 6 65
(David C Griffiths) *led: rdn 2f out: drvn and edgd lft wl over 1f out: clr ent fnl f: kpt on* **17/2**

4 **2** *2¾* **Annie's Rose**[7] 5638 2-8-4 0..................................... RoystonFfrench 1 55
(Bryan Smart) *prom: chsd wnr 1/2-way: rdn to chal 2f out: drvn and one pce appr fnl f* **6/5**[1]

43 **3** *3* **Highland Princess (IRE)**[18] 5289 2-8-4 43................... JimmyQuinn 4 44
(Paul Midgley) *cl up: rdn along 2f out: sn drvn and one pce* **14/1**

5 **4** *2¼* **Royal Bushida**[9] 5590 2-8-9 0................................ AdamMcLean(7) 5 48
(Derek Shaw) *sn pushed along and outpcd in rr: rdn 2f out: sme late hdwy* **12/1**

0 **5** *nk* **Maidana (IRE)**[11] 5543 2-8-4 0....................................... LiamJones 2 35
(Tim Easterby) *dwlt: in tch: rdn along 1/2-way: wknd 2f out* **5/1**[3]

6 *14* **Wilberfoss (IRE)** 2-8-9 0... KierenFallon 3
(Mel Brittain) *dwlt in tch: rdn along and outpcd over 3f out: sn bhd and eased fr wl over 1f out* **3/1**[2]

1m 0.13s (0.43) **Going Correction** -0.075s/f (Stan) 6 Ran SP% **112.0**
Speed ratings (Par 92): **93,88,83,80,79 57**
toteswingers 1&2 £2.00, 1&3 £9.90, 2&3 £3.90 CSF £19.27 TOTE £9.50: £4.60, £1.10; EX 31.80 Trifecta £200.20 Pool: £1519.95 - 5.69 winning units..
Owner Morton Racing **Bred** Jill Finegan & Noel Cogan **Trained** Bawtry, S Yorks

FOCUS
This was a weak maiden in which the favourite probably didn't run her race, so it took little winning. The placed horses are the best guides to the level.

5901 DOWNLOAD THE LADBROKES APP H'CAP 5f (F)
6:50 (6:50) (Class 4) (0-80,79) 3-Y-O+ £4,690 (£1,395; £697; £348) Stalls High

Form RPR
4000 1 **First In Command (IRE)**[24] 5036 8-9-4 **76**(t) WilliamTwiston-Davies(3) 4 86
(John Stimpson) *swtchd lft after s and hld up in tch: hdwy on outer over 2f out: rdn to chal and hung lft over 1f out: led jst ins fnl f: sn drvn and jst hld on* **14/1**
3012 2 *shd* **Clubland (IRE)**[28] 4884 4-9-6 **75** JimmyQuinn 6 85
(Roy Bowring) *trckd ldrs: smooth hdwy to chal wl over 1f out: rdn and led jst over 1f out: hdd and drvn jst ins fnl f: rallied wl towards fin* **5/2**[1]
1424 3 2 ¾ **Pull The Pin (IRE)**[6] 5674 4-8-7 **65** RaulDaSilva(3) 2 65
(Paul Green) *slt ld: rdn along 2f out: drvn and hdd jst over 1f out: kpt on same pce fnl f* **6/1**[2]
4450 4 ½ **Captain Scooby**[28] 4884 7-8-6 **66** PhilipPrince(5) 10 64
(Richard Guest) *towards rr and rdn along 1/2-way: hdwy over 1f out: styd on wl u.p fnl f: nrst fin* **14/1**
5464 5 *shd* **Lenny Bee**[14] 5381 7-8-11 **73** (t) KevinStott(7) 7 71
(Garry Moss) *prom: rdn along 2f out: drvn and wknd over 1f out* **7/1**[3]
2030 6 ½ **Shawkantango**[6] 5673 6-8-8 **70** (v) AdamMcLean(7) 12 66
(Derek Shaw) *racd nr stands' rail: sn rdn along and outpcd in rr: hdwy wl over 1f out: styng on wl whn sltly hmpd appr fnl f: kpt on: nrst fin* **25/1**
4200 7 *shd* **Monnoyer**[27] 4930 4-8-7 **67** (be) TimClark(5) 9 62
(Scott Dixon) *cl up: disp ld 1/2-way: rdn and ev ch wl over 1f out: drvn appr fnl f: wknd* **10/1**
0000 8 1 **Hazelrigg (IRE)**[22] 5108 8-9-7 **76** (e[1]) DanielTudhope 11 68
(Tim Easterby) *chsd ldrs: rdn along 2f out: sn btn* **25/1**
00-6 9 ¾ **R Woody**[23] 5062 6-9-9 **78** (p) KierenFallon 5 67
(Robert Cowell) *dwlt and in rr: rdn along 1/2-way: sme late hdwy* **10/1**
6012 10 *nk* **We Have A Dream**[7] 5645 8-9-3 **72** (p) NeilCallan 13 60
(Violet M Jordan) *in tch on outer: rdn along 2f out: drvn and hung rt jst over 1f out: wknd* **20/1**
0600 11 ½ **Cardinal**[103] 2425 8-9-5 **74** SteveDrowne 3 60
(Robert Cowell) *dwlt: a in rr* **25/1**
5000 12 1 ¾ **Speightowns Kid (USA)**[130] 1681 5-8-10 **65** AndrewMullen 8 45
(Richard Ford) *a towards rr* **16/1**
3114 13 ½ **Desert Strike**[49] 4165 7-9-10 **79** (p) LiamKeniry 1 57
(Conor Dore) *in tch on outer: rdn along 1/2-way: sn wknd* **10/1**

58.94s (-0.76) **Going Correction** -0.075s/f (Stan) 13 Ran SP% **118.1**
Speed ratings (Par 105): **103,102,98,97,97 96,96,94,93,93 92,89,88**
toteswingers 1&2 £17.90, 1&3 £19.00, 2&3 £3.40 CSF £45.99 CT £236.71 TOTE £23.60: £4.80, £1.20, £1.90; EX 73.30 Trifecta £666.60 Pool: £1361.81 - 1.53 winning units..
Owner Mrs C Loughnane **Bred** Peter And Mrs McCutcheon **Trained** Butterton, Staffs

FOCUS
This was a competitive sprint contested by horses of a good standard for the track. The winner is rated to last year's best with the second stepping up on recent turf form.

5902 LADBROKES MAIDEN STKS 1m 4f (F)
7:20 (7:20) (Class 5) 3-4-Y-O £2,587 (£770; £384; £192) Stalls Low

Form RPR
65 1 **Hunting Ground (USA)**[73] 3364 3-9-3 0 LiamJones 3 92
(Mark Johnston) *mde all: rdn along 3f out: drvn clr wl over 1f out: kpt on wl* **8/1**[3]
3222 2 7 **Saddaqa (USA)**[12] 5478 3-8-12 84 (p) KierenFallon 5 76
(Saeed bin Suroor) *prom: cl up after 4f: effrt 3f out: rdn over 2f out: drvn and wandered wl over 1f out: sn one pce* **8/13**[1]
0-6 3 7 **Shemaal (IRE)**[111] 2198 3-9-3 0 DominicFox 6 70
(Roger Varian) *chsd ldrs: rdn along 4f out: drvn 3f out and plugged on one pce* **10/1**
4 1 **Waha (IRE)** 3-8-5 0 AhmadAlSubousi(7) 2 63
(Saeed bin Suroor) *dwlt and bhd: hdwy and in tch on outer 1/2-way: rdn along over 3f out: drvn and plugged on one pce fnl 2f* **20/1**
225- 5 4 ½ **Ruwaiyan (USA)**[389] 4797 4-9-13 85 NeilCallan 4 61
(James Tate) *t.k.h: trckd ldng pair: effrt 4f out: rdn along 3f out: drvn over 2f out and sn wknd* **3/1**[2]
450 6 5 **Una Bella Cosa**[20] 5192 3-8-9 48 (v) WilliamTwiston-Davies(3) 7 48
(Alan McCabe) *hld up in tch: hdwy over 4f out: rdn along over 3f out: drvn and outpcd over 2f out* **100/1**
7 67 **Generous George (IRE)** 4-9-13 0 JimmyQuinn 1
(Mel Brittain) *in tch: rdn along after 3f: lost pl and bhd bef 1/2-way: t.o fnl 4f* **100/1**

2m 36.4s (-4.60) **Going Correction** -0.10s/f (Stan)
WFA 3 from 4yo 10lb 7 Ran SP% **113.9**
Speed ratings (Par 103): **111,106,101,101,98 94,50**
toteswingers 1&2 £1.10, 2&3 £2.90, 1&3 £11.50 CSF £13.44 TOTE £7.10: £3.60, £1.10; EX 20.30 Trifecta £91.90 Pool: £1338.17 - 10.92 winning units..
Owner Sheikh Hamdan Bin Mohammed Al Maktoum **Bred** Darley **Trained** Middleham Moor, N Yorks

FOCUS
There were some famous owners and top stables represented in this maiden, but the runners were strung out like chasers at the finish and the race has a thin look to it. The third is rated in line with his turf form.

5903 LADBROKES FOLLOW US ON TWITTER H'CAP 1m (F)
7:50 (7:50) (Class 6) (0-60,63) 3-Y-O+ £1,940 (£577; £288; £144) Stalls Low

Form RPR
4225 1 **Master Of Song**[8] 5614 6-9-4 **57** (p) MarkCoumbe(3) 14 71+
(Roy Bowring) *v.s.a and lost many l s: gd hdwy after 3f: chsd ldrs over 3f out: chal over 2f out: rdn to ld wl over 1f out: drvn and styd on gamely fnl f* **9/4**[1]
5620 2 2 **Arabian Flight**[9] 5596 4-9-4 **54** AndrewMullen 3 63
(Michael Appleby) *led: rdn along 3f out: jnd and drvn over 2f out: hdd wl over 1f out: one pce u.p fnl f* **10/1**
2-0 3 2 **Uncle Brit**[115] 2042 7-9-10 **60** BrianHughes 1 64
(Malcolm Jefferson) *in tch on inner: hdwy over 3f out: rdn to chse ldrs over 2f out: kpt on u.p fnl f: nrst fin* **14/1**
661 4 ½ **Throwing Roses**[16] 5341 3-8-5 **50** RaulDaSilva(3) 8 53
(Lawrence Mullaney) *chsd ldrs: rdn along 3f out: drvn 2f out: kpt on u.p appr fnl f* **8/1**[3]
5304 5 8 **Maggie Mey (IRE)**[20] 5198 5-8-13 **49** DanielTudhope 2 34
(Lawrence Mullaney) *chsd ldrs on inner: hdwy wl over 2f out: sn rdn and no imp* **8/1**[3]
0006 6 ½ **Secretori**[26] 4939 3-8-8 **50** (b[1]) CathyGannon 7 34
(Jo Hughes) *dwlt and towards rr: hdwy 2f out: sn rdn and plugged on: n.d* **8/1**[3]
005 7 4 ½ **Imperial Bond**[21] 5139 4-8-10 **46** oh1 (t) TomEaves 9 19
(Jason Ward) *dwlt and towards rr: hdwy and in tch 1/2-way: chsd ldrs 3f out and sn rdn: drvn over 2f out and sn wknd* **16/1**
3006 8 6 **Multisure**[16] 5334 3-8-1 **46** oh1 (b[1]) JulieBurke(3) 12 6
(Ruth Carr) *cl up: rdn along 3f out: sn drvn and wknd over 2f out* **16/1**
0030 9 *shd* **Aureolin Gulf**[13] 5429 4-8-5 **46** oh1 JackDuern(5) 10 5
(Andrew Hollinshead) *chsd ldng pair: rdn along 3f out: sn drvn and wknd* **16/1**
0040 10 20 **Smokey Oakey (IRE)**[127] 1752 9-9-7 **57** NeilCallan 6
(Mark H Tompkins) *a towards rr* **9/1**
5366 11 4 **Multilicious**[42] 4401 3-8-11 **53** (e[1]) KierenFallon 4
(Tim Easterby) *dwlt: a in rr: bhd whn eased wl over 2f out* **13/2**[2]

1m 43.31s (-0.39) **Going Correction** -0.10s/f (Stan)
WFA 3 from 4yo+ 6lb 11 Ran SP% **120.8**
Speed ratings (Par 101): **97,95,93,92,84 84,79,73,73,53 49**
toteswingers 1&2 £7.50, 1&3 £6.40, 2&3 £29.90 CSF £26.69 CT £272.02 TOTE £3.90: £1.50, £3.30, £3.30; EX 26.50 Trifecta £261.30 Pool: £771.83 - 2.21 winning units..
Owner S R Bowring **Bred** S R Bowring **Trained** Edwinstowe, Notts
■ Stewards' Enquiry : Cathy Gannon two-day ban: careless riding (Sep 12-13)

FOCUS
This modest event looked competitive on paper, but the winner landed a gamble in extraordinary circumstances. The second is rated in line with the balance of his winter form, while the third is rated close to last year's turf level.
T/Plt: £22.80 to a £1 stake. Pool: £53,223.09 - 1702.28 winning tickets T/Qpdt: £5.10 to a £1 stake. Pool: £5123.90 - 739.45 winning tickets JR

5904 - 5910a (Foreign Racing) - See Raceform Interactive

5804 BADEN-BADEN (L-H)
Wednesday, August 28
OFFICIAL GOING: Turf: good to soft

5911a ZUKUNFTS-RENNEN (GROUP 3) (2YO) (TURF) 7f
5:25 (12:00) 2-Y-O

£26,016 (£8,943; £4,471; £2,439; £1,626; £1,219)

RPR
1 **Abendwind (GER)** 2-9-0 0 APietsch 1 103
(W Hickst, Germany) *midfield: smooth hdwy to ld 2f out: sn rdn and r.o appr fnl f: kpt on wl u.p ins fnl f: a holding runner-up fnl 75yds: readily* **10/1**
2 *hd* **Magic Artist (IRE)** 2-9-0 0 LennartHammer-Hansen 4 102
(W Figge, Germany) *towards rr: hdwy on ins 2f out: 3rd and ev ch 1 1/2f out: rdn to chse wnr 1f out: r.o u.p but a hld by the wnr fnl 75yds* **109/10**
3 2 **Kerosin (GER)** 2-9-0 0 ADeVries 7 97
(W Giedt, Germany) *chsd ldr: hrd rdn and nt qckn 2f out: styd on ins fnl f: nt pce to trble first two* **74/10**
4 *nse* **Imperiator**[23] 2-9-0 0 OlivierPeslier 3 97
(P Decouz, France) *led: hdd 2f out: rdn and sltly outpcd 1 1/2f out: kpt on again u.p fnl f* **12/5**[2]
5 ¾ **High Duty** 2-9-0 0 AStarke 6 95
(P Schiergen, Germany) *towards rr: hdwy over 2f out: rdn to chal 1 1/2f out: nt qckn appr 1f out: one pce fnl f* **19/10**[1]
6 4 **Indikova (IRE)**[24] 2-8-10 0 EPedroza 8 81
(A Wohler, Germany) *midfield on outer: rdn to chse ldrs 2f out: wknd u.p fnl f* **124/10**
7 2 ½ **Victory Tiger (GER)**[59] 2-9-0 0 CristianDemuro 2 78
(W Hefter, Germany) *chsd ldr on inner: rdn and outpcd over 1 1/2f out: wknd ins fnl f* **112/10**
8 12 **Smoke On The Water (GER)**[46] 2-9-2 0 StefanieHofer 5 49
(Mario Hofer, Germany) *hld up towards rr: t.k.h: rapid hdwy on outside to press ldr 2 1/2f out: c wd fnl bnd: sn rdn and lost pl: bhd whn eased ins fnl f* **37/10**[3]

1m 27.02s (3.12) 8 Ran SP% **130.2**
WIN (incl. 10 euro stake): 110. PLACES: 31, 27, 23. SF: 1338.
Owner Frau Gisela Remmert **Bred** Gestut Trona **Trained** Germany

5779 CLAIREFONTAINE (R-H)
Wednesday, August 28
OFFICIAL GOING: Turf: soft

5912a PRIX DU LIEU DES FIEFFES (CONDITIONS) (4YO) (TURF) 1m
1:20 (12:00) 4-Y-O £11,382 (£4,552; £3,414; £2,276; £1,138)

RPR
1 **Riverkaye (FR)**[26] 4-8-9 0 IoritzMendizabal 5 76
(J-C Rouget, France) **33/10**[2]
2 1 ½ **Relizane**[58] 4-8-9 0 AntoineHamelin 1 73
(A De Royer-Dupre, France) **9/5**[1]
3 1 **Hippolyte (FR)**[26] 4-8-13 0 FlavienPrat 4 75
(T Clout, France) **9/5**[1]
4 ½ **Evervescent (IRE)**[5] 5735 4-8-9 0 (b) SoufyaneMoulin(4) 2 74
(J S Moore) *settled in next to last: effrt to go 3rd under 1 1/2f out: rdn and styd on appr fnl f: no ex u.p 150yds: dropped to 4th fnl 75yds* **23/1**
5 2 ½ **Ice Cool (FR)**[100] 4-9-5 0 MaximeGuyon 6 74
(W Hefter, Germany) **15/2**[3]
6 1 ½ **Latino (SWI)** 4-8-5 0 SebastienMartino(8) 3 64
(H-A Pantall, France) **25/1**

1m 37.3s (97.30) 6 Ran SP% **114.5**
WIN (incl. 1 euro stake): 4.30. PLACES: 2.20, 1.80. SF: 11.80.
Owner Gerard Laboureau **Bred** S C E A Haras Du Ma **Trained** Pau, France

5913a PRIX DES NYMPHEAS (CLAIMER) (3YO FILLIES) (TURF) 1m 3f
1:50 (12:00) 3-Y-O £9,349 (£3,739; £2,804; £1,869; £934)

RPR
1 **Pixie Cut (IRE)**[6] 5692 3-8-13 0 SoufyaneMoulin(3) 2 70
(J S Moore) *led: set stdy gallop: shkn up and qcknd 2f out: jnd over 1 1/2f out and briefly hdd: rallied and asserted over 1f out: r.o gamely to hold on u.p* **43/10**[3]

2 snk **Inchelle (IRE)**[46] 3-8-6 0 .... SoufianeSaadi(5) 4 65
(E Lellouche, France) **19/1**

3 1 1/4 **Prairie Sunset (FR)**[18] 3-8-13 0 .... CesarPasserat(3) 7 68
(S Wattel, France) **9/5**[1]

4 1 1/4 **Bizzy Nizzy (FR)**[62] 3-8-11 0 .... EnzoCorallo(4) 8 65
(S Wattel, France) **11/2**

5 2 1/2 **Lavilla (FR)**[256] 3-8-9 0 .... ThibaultSpeicher(6) 1 60
(D Allard, France) **34/1**

6 1 1/2 **Kaabamix (FR)**[60] 3-8-6 0 .... ValentinGambart(5) 5 53
(D Windrif, France) **7/2**[2]

7 1 3/4 **Signorellina (FR)** 3-8-6 0 .... (p) FabienMasse(5) 3 50
(J Rossi, France) **37/1**

8 4 **Morny's Place (IRE)**[68] 3-8-11 0 .... NicolasLarenaudie(8) 6 51
(G Collet, France) **17/2**

9 2 1/2 **Will O'The Wisp (FR)** 3-8-13 0 .... MatthiasLauron(5) 9 45
(Mme A-C Trouve, France) **38/1**

2m 22.4s (142.40) **9** Ran SP% **115.8**
WIN (incl. 1 euro stake): 5.30. PLACES: 1.80, 3.00, 1.40. DF: 45.70. SF: 73.80.
Owner G V March & J S Moore **Bred** Rocal Bloodstock **Trained** Upper Lambourn, Berks

5914a PRIX DES COLCHIQUES (CLAIMER) (3YO COLTS & GELDINGS) (TURF) 1m 3f

3:55 (12:00) 3-Y-O **£9,349** (£3,739; £2,804; £1,869; £934)

RPR

1 **Teolagi (IRE)**[26] 4950 3-9-2 0 .... SoufyaneMoulin(3) 6 74
(J S Moore) *w.w towards rr: smooth prog to take clsr order 2 1/2f out: rdn to chal 1 1/2f out: led ins fnl f: r.o: asserted fnl 50yds* **76/10**

2 1/2 **Star Of Namibia (IRE)**[6] 5692 3-8-6 0 .... (b) MatthiasLauron(5) 5 65
(J S Moore) *chsd clr ldr: 3rd and sltly outpcd 3f out: rdn to chal ldrs over 1 1/2f out: 2nd and ev ch 1f out: r.o u.p: hld by wnr fnl 50yds* **11/2**

3 hd **Bibactic (IRE)**[33] 3-8-11 0 .... MathieuTavaresDaSilva(4) 1 69
(J E Pease, France) **4/1**[2]

4 1 1/4 **Livento (FR)**[63] 3-8-6 0 .... (p) NicolasLarenaudie(5) 7 62
(A Bonin, France) **27/1**

5 1 3/4 **Clef D'Or (FR)**[38] 4575 3-8-11 0 .... EnzoCorallo(4) 2 63
(Y Durepaire, France) **2/1**[1]

6 snk **Jee Pee And Jeremy (FR)**[36] 3-9-1 0 .... CesarPasserat(3) 3 66
(Mme Pia Brandt, France) **48/10**[3]

7 2 **Chef Chaudard (FR)**[17] 3-8-4 0 .... (p) SoufianeSaadi(7) 8 55
(J-C Rouget, France) **63/10**

8 3 **Next Time (FR)**[78] 3-8-9 0 .... JeremyBonin(6) 4 54
(Mlle S Sine, France) **53/1**

2m 19.6s (139.60) **8** Ran SP% **116.7**
WIN (incl. 1 euro stake): 8.60. PLACES: 2.30, 2.10, 2.00. DF: 17.00. SF: 37.10.
Owner Mrs Fitri Hay **Bred** Mrs Fitriani Hay **Trained** Upper Lambourn, Berks

5703 HAMILTON (R-H)

Thursday, August 29

OFFICIAL GOING: Good to firm (good in places; 8.0)
Wind: Breezy, half behind Weather: Overcast

5915 EBF STALLIONS WALTER GLYNN'S "LUDICROUS" DEBUTANTS' MAIDEN STKS 6f 5y

2:10 (2:10) (Class 5) 2-Y-O **£3,234** (£962; £481; £240) **Stalls** High

Form RPR

1 **Invincible Strike (IRE)** 2-9-5 0 .... PaulMulrennan 3 80+
(James Tate) *t.k.h: trckd ldr: rdn to ld over 1f out: edgd lft ins fnl f: kpt on strly* **11/4**[2]

2 2 1/2 **Quickaswecan** 2-9-5 0 .... JoeFanning 6 75+
(Mark Johnston) *led: rdn and hdd over 1f out: one pce whn n.m.r ins fnl f* **5/6**[1]

3 3 3/4 **In Vino Veritas (IRE)** 2-9-5 0 .... PJMcDonald 2 61
(Ann Duffield) *noisy in paddock: chsd ldrs: outpcd over 2f out: kpt on fnl f: no ch w first two: bttr for r* **14/1**

4 hd **Shore Patrol (IRE)** 2-9-5 0 .... TonyHamilton 4 61
(Richard Fahey) *prom: rdn and outpcd over 2f out: no imp fr over 1f out* **6/1**[3]

5 3/4 **Reflection** 2-9-0 0 .... LeeTopliss 5 53
(Richard Fahey) *dwlt: sn prom: rdn and outpcd over 2f out: sn n.d* **33/1**

6 1 1/4 **Ronya (IRE)** 2-9-0 0 .... RobertWinston 1 50
(K R Burke) *hld up in tch: rdn and outpcd 1/2-way: n.d* **18/1**

1m 12.17s (-0.03) **Going Correction** -0.075s/f (Good) **6** Ran SP% **110.4**
Speed ratings (Par 94): **97,93,88,88,87 85**
toteswingers 1&2 £1.50, 2&3 £3.00, 1&3 £2.30 CSF £5.20 TOTE £3.70: £1.30, £1.10; EX 5.60 Trifecta £21.00 Pool: £2547.21 - 90.81 winning units..
Owner Sheikh Juma Dalmook Al Maktoum **Bred** J Hanly, Castlemartin Sky & Skymarc Farm **Trained** Newmarket, Suffolk

FOCUS
A 6f race for unraced 2-y-os. The winner looks a nice recruit.

5916 DM HALL H'CAP 6f 5y

2:40 (2:41) (Class 6) (0-60,55) 3-Y-O **£2,045** (£603; £302) **Stalls** Centre

Form RPR

6044 1 **Bix (IRE)**[40] 4514 3-8-13 **47** .... GrahamLee 5 52
(Alan Berry) *mde all in centre: overall ldr appr fnl f: kpt on wl last 100yds* **9/1**

0056 2 1/2 **Annie Gogh**[40] 4544 3-9-7 **55** .... (b[1]) DavidAllan 6 58
(Tim Easterby) *missed break: sn rcvrd and chsd stands' side ldr: overall ldr and wandered wl over 1f out: hdd appr fnl f: kpt on* **3/1**[1]

4001 3 2 3/4 **Blue Clumber**[14] 5431 3-8-13 **52** .... ShirleyTeasdale(5) 4 46
(Shaun Harris) *chsd centre ldrs: rdn over 2f out: rallied over 1f out: kpt on: nt pce of first two* **10/1**

054 4 3 **Senora Lobo (IRE)**[23] 5089 3-9-1 **49** .... (p) RoystonFfrench 8 34
(Lisa Williamson) *overall ldr stands' rail: hdd wl over 1f out: sn one pce* **14/1**

023 5 3/4 **Baker's Pursuit**[8] 5641 3-9-6 **54** .... TomEaves 2 36
(Jim Goldie) *in tch centre: effrt and rdn over 2f out: edgd lft and outpcd over 1f out* **5/1**[3]

00-6 6 shd **Windsor Secret**[19] 5261 3-8-11 **45** .... JoeFanning 3 27
(Keith Dalgleish) *prom centre: rdn and outpcd over 2f out: styd on fnl f: nvr able to chal* **10/1**

3405 7 2 3/4 **Faither**[6] 5704 3-8-8 **45** .... JasonHart(3) 7 18
(Keith Dalgleish) *upset in stalls: in tch centre: rdn over 2f out: wknd wl over 1f out* **7/2**[2]

300 8 1 3/4 **Helterskelter Girl**[43] 4400 3-8-12 **46** .... PJMcDonald 1 13
(Ann Duffield) *prom centre: drvn over 2f out: wknd wl over 1f out* **6/1**

1m 12.17s (-0.03) **Going Correction** -0.075s/f (Good) **8** Ran SP% **113.0**
Speed ratings (Par 98): **97,96,92,88,87 87,83,81**
toteswingers 1&2 £5.70, 2&3 £4.80, 1&3 £8.30 CSF £35.37 CT £276.61 TOTE £10.60: £4.10, £1.10, £4.80; EX 51.80 Trifecta £311.70 Pool: £3096.59 - 7.45 winning units..
Owner Alan Berry **Bred** Longfort Stud **Trained** Cockerham, Lancs

FOCUS
A low-grade 6f 3-y-o handicap. The time was identical to the opener, suggesting that the winner ran to a mark in the mid-70s. Just three previous winners in the line-up and two raced virtually alone against the stands' side rail.

5917 TAGGARTS PEUGEOT CLAIMING STKS 5f 4y

3:10 (3:10) (Class 6) 3-Y-O+ **£2,045** (£603; £302) **Stalls** Centre

Form RPR

5113 1 **Last Sovereign**[40] 4536 9-9-2 94 .... (b) JacobButterfield(5) 5 82
(Ollie Pears) *cl up: led after 1f: rdn 2f out: edgd rt and kpt on fnl f: jst hld on* **2/7**[1]

0110 2 hd **Hamoody (USA)**[30] 4860 9-9-2 80 .... AdrianNicholls 2 76
(David Nicholls) *chsd ldrs: rdn and drifted lft over 1f out: kpt on wl fnl f: jst hld* **11/4**[2]

000- 3 3 **Running Water**[380] 5190 5-8-0 40 .... JordanHibberd(7) 1 56?
(Alan Berry) *led 1f: cl up: effrt and ev ch over 1f out: outpcd ins fnl f* **100/1**

0005 4 2 1/4 **Distant Sun (USA)**[6] 5708 9-8-10 49 .... (p) PaulMulrennan 4 51
(Linda Perratt) *t.k.h early: stdd in tch: outpcd over 2f out: n.d after* **33/1**[3]

59.38s (-0.62) **Going Correction** -0.075s/f (Good) **4** Ran SP% **108.4**
Speed ratings (Par 101): **101,100,95,92**
CSF £1.36 TOTE £1.40; EX 1.60 Trifecta £9.80 Pool: £1979.91 - 151.19 winning units..
Owner Richard Walker **Bred** Gestut Hof Ittlingen & Cheveley Park Stud Ltd **Trained** Norton, N Yorks

FOCUS
This claimer was, on official ratings, a match with two no-hopers completing the line-up.

5918 TAGGARTS MOTOR GROUP SCOTTISH TROPHY H'CAP 1m 1f 36y

3:40 (3:40) (Class 4) (0-80,80) 3-Y-O+ **£5,175** (£1,540; £769; £384) **Stalls** Low

Form RPR

4104 1 **Wellingrove (IRE)**[15] 5383 3-9-1 **69** .... JoeFanning 5 79
(Mark Johnston) *mde all: rdn clr wl over 1f out: kpt on fnl f: unchal* **9/2**[3]

666 2 2 **Spes Nostra**[1] 5882 5-9-8 **69** .... (b) GrahamGibbons 4 75
(David Barron) *prom: rdn and hung rt over 3f out: rallied to chse (clr) wnr ins fnl f: no imp* **15/2**

1510 3 2 **Size (IRE)**[48] 4264 4-9-9 **70** .... LeeTopliss 3 73+
(Richard Fahey) *hld up: rdn over 3f out: hdwy over 1f out: kpt on: nrst fin* **10/3**[1]

2201 4 hd **Argaki (IRE)**[8] 5642 3-9-9 **80** 6ex .... JasonHart(3) 1 81
(Keith Dalgleish) *chsd ldrs: rdn over 3f out: chsd wnr over 1f out to ins fnl f: no ex* **7/2**[2]

4250 5 2 1/4 **Royal Straight**[1] 5882 8-9-5 **66** .... (t) PhillipMakin 7 62
(Linda Perratt) *hld up: rdn and hdwy over 2f out: no imp fnl f* **20/1**

4304 6 hd **Another For Joe**[17] 5332 5-9-11 **72** .... GrahamLee 10 68
(Jim Goldie) *hld up: hdwy over 3f out: rdn and hung rt over 2f out: no imp over 1f out* **6/1**

6636 7 7 **High Resolution**[24] 5051 6-9-1 **67** .... ConnorBeasley(5) 9 47
(Linda Perratt) *s.i.s: hld up: rdn over 3f out: n.d* **12/1**

21-0 8 1 3/4 **Dark Ruler (IRE)**[16] 5368 4-9-8 **69** .... TonyHamilton 8 46
(Alan Swinbank) *midfield: hung rt and wknd over 3f out* **25/1**

6360 9 1 **Assizes**[17] 5355 4-10-0 **75** .... (b[1]) JamesSullivan 6 49
(Ruth Carr) *chsd wnr: rdn 3f out: wknd wl over 1f out* **14/1**

1m 55.42s (-4.28) **Going Correction** -0.35s/f (Firm)
WFA 3 from 4yo+ 7lb **9** Ran SP% **112.5**
Speed ratings (Par 105): **105,103,101,101,99 99,92,91,90**
toteswingers 1&2 £6.20, 2&3 £6.10, 1&3 £3.70 CSF £36.82 CT £124.58 TOTE £3.30: £1.30, £3.20, £1.10; EX 35.30 Trifecta £194.30 Pool: £2491.96 - 9.50 winning units..
Owner Sheikh Hamdan Bin Mohammed Al Maktoum **Bred** Hascombe And Valiant Studs **Trained** Middleham Moor, N Yorks

FOCUS
On paper a competitive handicap, but very few entered the argument.

5919 GRIFFITHS & ARMOUR MAIDEN STKS 6f 5y

4:10 (4:15) (Class 5) 3-Y-O+ **£3,408** (£1,006; £503) **Stalls** Centre

Form RPR

505 1 **Baron Run**[21] 5184 3-8-12 66 .... JoeyHaynes(7) 8 68
(K R Burke) *reluctant to enter stalls: chsd ldrs: rdn to ld over 3f out: r.o wl fnl f* **9/4**[2]

-045 2 1 1/2 **Hanalei Bay (IRE)**[10] 5581 3-9-5 69 .... (p) TomEaves 4 63
(Keith Dalgleish) *led to over 3f out: rdn and edgd rt over 2f out: kpt on same pce ins fnl f* **9/4**[2]

3 2 1/4 **Penny Stock (IRE)** 3-9-0 0 .... JoeFanning 3 51
(Mark Johnston) *cl up: rdn over 2f out: rallied: kpt on same pce fnl f* **2/1**[1]

6503 4 1 **Lady Calantha**[23] 5089 3-9-0 44 .... PaddyAspell 5 48
(Alan Berry) *chsd ldrs: outpcd and hung rt over 2f out: kpt on fnl f: no imp* **33/1**

5-0 5 12 **Classy Anne**[12] 5517 3-9-0 0 .... PhillipMakin 6 10
(Jim Goldie) *sn outpcd: rdn and struggling fr 1/2-way* **40/1**

6 nk **Blue Sonic** 3-9-0 0 .... GrahamLee 2 9
(Jim Goldie) *s.i.s and wnt rt s: outpcd: no ch fr 1/2-way* **9/1**[3]

1m 11.59s (-0.61) **Going Correction** -0.075s/f (Good) **6** Ran SP% **110.3**
Speed ratings (Par 103): **101,99,96,94,78 78**
toteswingers 1&2 £1.80, 2&3 £1.50, 1&3 £1.70 CSF £7.43 TOTE £3.30: £1.80, £1.90; EX 7.80 Trifecta £14.30 Pool: £3631.52 - 190.15 winning units..
Owner Mrs Elaine M Burke **Bred** Mrs D Hughes **Trained** Middleham Moor, N Yorks

FOCUS
A very modest 3yo sprint maiden. The three market leaders were in a line soon after halfway.

5920 PRESTIGE SCOTLAND H'CAP (QUALIFIER FOR THE £15000 BETFAIR SCOTTISH STAYERS' SERIES FINAL) 1m 4f 17y

4:45 (4:45) (Class 5) (0-70,71) 3-Y-O+ **£3,234** (£962; £481; £240) **Stalls** Low

Form RPR

323 1 **St Ignatius**[7] 5666 6-9-7 **63** .... (v) RobertWinston 6 68
(Alan Bailey) *t.k.h: led at stdy pce: hmpd by loose horse over 5f out: qcknd over 3f out: jnd over 1f out: kpt on gamely fnl f* **10/3**[1]

5263 **2** 1 1/4 **Geanie Mac (IRE)**[8] 5643 4-8-9 **51** oh3........................(v) PJMcDonald 3 54
(Linda Perratt) *chsd ldrs: wnt 2nd over 4f out: rdn over 2f out: hdwy and ev ch over 1f out: one pce ins fnl f* **9/1**

1612 **3** 1/2 **A Southside Boy (GER)**[31] 4822 5-9-9 **65**........................ TomEaves 4 68+
(Jim Goldie) *hld up in last in steadily run r: rdn over 4f out: hdwy over 1f out: kpt on fnl f: nvr able to chal* **4/1**[2]

233 **4** 1 **Saffron Town (IRE)**[13] 5469 4-10-0 **70**........................ AndrewMullen 5 71
(Alan Swinbank) *prom: rdn over 4f out: rallied over 3f out: kpt on same pce fr over 1f out* **6/1**

0-00 **5** 1 3/4 **Hail Bold Chief (USA)**[93] 2753 6-9-5 **61**........................ JoeFanning 1 59
(Alan Swinbank) *hld up in tch: rdn along over 4f out: rallied over 2f out: no imp over 1f out* **10/1**

3044 **6** 3 1/4 **Hello Gorgeous**[17] 5334 3-7-11 **52** oh5........................ RaulDaSilva(3) 2 45
(Keith Dalgleish) *chsd wnr to over 4f out: cl up tl rdn and wknd wl over 1f out* **11/2**[3]

4321 **U** **Bayan Kasirga (IRE)**[17] 5343 3-9-1 **67**........................ TonyHamilton 7
(Richard Fahey) *prom: sddle sn slipped: uns rdr after 1f* **4/1**[2]

2m 38.44s (-0.16) **Going Correction** -0.35s/f (Firm)
WFA 3 from 4yo+ 10lb **7** Ran SP% **111.8**
Speed ratings (Par 103): **86,85,84,84,83 80,**
toteswingers 1&2 £5.10, 2&3 £5.30, 1&3 £3.50 CSF £31.65 CT £120.53 TOTE £4.70: £2.70, £4.70; EX 37.70 Trifecta £275.90 Pool: £2245.22 - 6.10 winning units..
Owner A J H **Bred** Simon And Helen Plumbly **Trained** Newmarket, Suffolk

FOCUS
The pace was very steady here with the leader encountering traffic problems round the loop with the loose horse getting in his way.

5921 TAGGARTS NISSAN "HANDS & HEELS" APPRENTICE SERIES H'CAP (ROUND 4 RACING EXCELLENCE INITIATIVE) 1m 65y
5:15 (5:15) (Class 6) (0-55,54) 3-Y-O+ **£2,045** (£603; £302) **Stalls** Low

Form RPR

43-4 **1** **Cheers Buddy (IRE)**[16] 5369 5-9-0 **51**........................ RobJFitzpatrick(5) 4 63
(Keith Dalgleish) *trckd ldrs: led 3f out: pushed along wl over 1f out: hld on wl fnl f* **7/2**[1]

0065 **2** 3/4 **Taxiformissbyron**[17] 5334 3-8-12 **50**........................ KevinStott 7 60
(Michael Herrington) *led at ordinary gallop: hdd 3f out: rallied: edgd rt over 1f out: kpt on fnl f* **9/2**[2]

0054 **3** 2 1/2 **Tukitinyasok (IRE)**[6] 5713 6-9-3 **49**........................ SamanthaBell 11 54
(Clive Mulhall) *s.i.s: hld up on outside: hdwy and prom over 3f out: drifted rt and one pce over 1f out* **7/1**[3]

1204 **4** 2 **Crucis Abbey (IRE)**[15] 5387 5-8-12 **49**........................(p) GaryMahon(5) 1 49
(Mark Brisbourne) *t.k.h: hld up in tch: rdn over 3f out: rallied over 1f out: no imp fnl f* **8/1**

6040 **5** hd **Yourholidayisover (IRE)**[19] 5295 6-8-12 **49**........................ JackGarritty(5) 10 48+
(Patrick Holmes) *s.i.s: bhd: rdn over 4f out: styd on fr 2f out: nvr able to chal* **20/1**

2460 **6** 1 3/4 **Kyle Of Bute**[83] 3043 7-9-3 **49**........................ ConnorBeasley 9 44
(Richard Ford) *trckd ldr: rdn over 2f out: edgd rt and wknd over 1f out* **16/1**

4301 **7** 2 **Captain Baldwin**[19] 5261 4-9-5 **51**........................(v) JordanNason 5 42
(Jim Goldie) *t.k.h: in tch: rdn and outpcd over 3f out: n.d after* **7/2**[1]

0333 **8** 1/2 **Remember Rocky**[31] 4826 4-8-11 **48**........................(p) DanielleMooney(5) 2 38
(Lucy Normile) *t.k.h: hld up towards rr: pushed along over 3f out: sme late hdwy: nvr on terms* **10/1**

3500 **9** 10 **Hellbender (IRE)**[65] 3657 7-9-8 **54**........................(t) ShelleyBirkett 8 21
(Shaun Harris) *hld up: struggling over 3f out: sn btn* **14/1**

35-0 **10** 3 **Wind Shuffle (GER)**[16] 5370 10-8-8 **47**........................ NicolaCurrie(7) 6 7
(Lucinda Russell) *s.i.s: bhd: rdn over 3f out: sn btn* **40/1**

00-0 **11** 6 **Spoken Words**[235] 87 4-8-8 **45**........................(p) JordanHibberd(5) 3
(Alan Berry) *midfield: struggling over 3f out: sn btn* **66/1**

1m 47.25s (-1.15) **Going Correction** -0.35s/f (Firm)
WFA 3 from 4yo+ 6lb **11** Ran SP% **116.6**
Speed ratings (Par 101): **91,90,87,85,85 83,81,81,71,68 62**
toteswingers 1&2 £4.90, 2&3 £5.30, 1&3 £3.80 CSF £18.47 CT £106.77 TOTE £4.30: £1.60, £1.30, £2.10; EX 21.10 Trifecta £154.60 Pool: £2421.63 - 11.74 winning units..
Owner Robert Reid **Bred** Jaykayenn Syndicate **Trained** Carluke, S Lanarks
■ Stewards' Enquiry : Jordan Nason four-day ban: careless riding (Sep 12,13,15,16)

FOCUS
A low-grade 'hands and heels' apprentice handicap run at a sound gallop and it paid to race up with the pace.
T/Plt: £27.00 to a £1 stake. Pool of £49199.95 - 1326.0 winning tickets. T/Qpdt: £10.10 to a £1 stake. Pool of £2655.02 - 193.78 winning tickets. RY

5890 KEMPTON (A.W) (R-H)
Thursday, August 29

OFFICIAL GOING: Standard
Wind: Moderate half across Weather: Sunny early

5922 LADIES DAY WITH TOBY ANSTIS 07.09.13 MEDIAN AUCTION MAIDEN STKS 1m (P)
6:20 (6:25) (Class 6) 2-Y-O **£1,940** (£577; £288; £144) **Stalls** Low

Form RPR

3 **1** **Top Tug (IRE)**[29] 4896 2-9-5 0........................ RyanMoore 9 80+
(Sir Michael Stoute) *in tch: drvn over 2f out: hdwy over 1f out chsd ldr ins fnl f: hung lft and led fnl 110yds: pushed out* **10/11**[1]

5 **2** nk **Toast Of New York (USA)**[18] 5299 2-9-5 0........................ JamieSpencer 1 77
(Jamie Osborne) *slt ld: pushed along and qcknd over 2f out: hung lft fr over 1f out: hdd fnl 110yds: no ex: bit c through horses mouth* **4/1**[2]

0 **3** 2 1/4 **Template (IRE)**[13] 5472 2-9-5 0........................ RichardHughes 12 72
(Richard Hannon) *t.k.h: in tch: hdwy to cl on ldrs 4f out: drvn to chse ldr over 1f out: edgd lft and outpcd ins fnl f* **10/1**[3]

23 **4** hd **Rudi Five One (FR)**[18] 5309 2-9-5 0........................ AndreaAtzeni 7 71
(Robert Eddery) *in rr: hdwy fr 2f out: styd on fnl f and edgd lft: nvr gng pce to rch ldrs* **12/1**

5 3 3/4 **Lady Tyne** 2-9-0 0........................ JamesDoyle 3 57
(Roger Charlton) *in tch but sn pushed along and green: hdwy over 2f out: no ex over 1f out* **16/1**

2 **6** 3 1/2 **Goleador (USA)**[40] 4518 2-9-5 0........................ AdamKirby 11 54
(Marco Botti) *sn chsng ldrs: rdn over 2f out: wknd wl over 1f out* **14/1**

0 **7** nse **Maid Of Tuscany (IRE)**[36] 4640 2-9-0 0........................ PatCosgrave 2 49
(Mark Usher) *chsd ldrs: wnt 2nd and rdn appr fnl 2f: no imp wknd appr fnl f* **40/1**

63 **8** 1 1/4 **Strassman**[19] 5262 2-9-5 0........................ SilvestreDeSousa 14 51
(Mark Johnston) *chsd ldrs: rdn 2f out: wknd over 1f out* **20/1**

9 1/2 **Ventura Ice (IRE)** 2-9-0 0........................ PatDobbs 6 45
(Richard Hannon) *s.i.s: in rr: sme late hdwy* **25/1**

64 **10** 10 **Shaheen Shah (GER)**[21] 5193 2-9-5 0........................ MartinDwyer 4 26
(Conrad Allen) *pressed ldr: rdn over 2f out: sn wknd* **50/1**

11 1/2 **Luna Sunrise** 2-8-9 0........................ MichaelJMMurphy(5) 13 19
(Alan Jarvis) *slowly away: green and a in rr* **66/1**

1m 40.75s (0.95) **Going Correction** -0.025s/f (Stan) **11** Ran SP% **116.2**
Speed ratings (Par 92): **94,93,91,91,87 84,83,82,82,72 71**
toteswingers 1&2 £1.10, 2&3 £4.00, 1&3 £3.20 CSF £4.00 TOTE £2.00: £1.10, £1.60, £1.70; EX 4.90 Trifecta £24.70 Pool: £2138.21 - 64.70 winning units..
Owner Mrs Denis Haynes **Bred** Wretham Stud **Trained** Newmarket, Suffolk

FOCUS
They went a steady pace in this maiden but the hot favourite stayed on strongly to score with something in hand and his main market rival finished second. The third and fourth help set the level.

5923 CONOR MAYNARD 14.09.13 H'CAP 1m (P)
6:50 (6:53) (Class 6) (0-60,60) 3-Y-O **£1,940** (£577; £288; £144) **Stalls** Low

Form RPR

3534 **1** **Red Tulip**[29] 4885 3-9-4 **57**........................ FrederikTylicki 8 67
(James Fanshawe) *in tch: hdwy 2f out: drvn to ld over 1f out: hdd briefly fnl 120yds: sn rallied to ld again: pushed out* **9/2**[2]

66-2 **2** nk **Sword Of The Lord**[19] 5275 3-9-6 **59**........................ JamieSpencer 3 68
(Michael Bell) *t.k.h: hld up in rr: drvn and qcknd ins fnl 2f to chse wnr appr fnl f: slt ld fnl 120yds: sn fnd no ex u.p and hdd: kpt on one pce* **9/4**[1]

6054 **3** 3 1/4 **Carrera**[74] 3376 3-9-3 **56**........................ SebSanders 6 58
(J W Hills) *in rr: hrd drvn over 2f out: styd on to chse ldrs ins fnl f: no imp* **15/2**[3]

1603 **4** 2 1/4 **Napinda**[12] 5527 3-9-1 **54**........................ WilliamCarson 14 51
(Philip McBride) *chsd ldrs: rdn over 2f out: wknd fnl f* **20/1**

0-50 **5** 3/4 **Substantivo (IRE)**[77] 3241 3-9-2 **60**........................ MichaelJMMurphy(5) 9 55
(Alan Jarvis) *chsd ldrs: rdn over 2f out: wknd over 1f out* **9/2**[2]

0056 **6** 2 3/4 **Elle Rebelle**[15] 5391 3-9-0 **53**........................ TomMcLaughlin 7 42
(Mark Brisbourne) *chsd ldr over 3f out: wknd over 1f out* **20/1**

-600 **7** 1/2 **Lars Krister (IRE)**[15] 5393 3-9-7 **60**........................(b) DavidProbert 10 47
(Hans Adielsson) *in rr: hdwy over 1f out: styd on in clsng stages* **12/1**

3020 **8** 1/2 **Fair Comment**[9] 5604 3-9-6 **59**........................ SteveDrowne 5 45
(Michael Blanshard) *in tch: rdn over 2f out: wknd wl over 1f out* **14/1**

6-66 **9** 3/4 **Lucilla**[31] 4830 3-9-5 **58**........................ AndreaAtzeni 2 43
(Stuart Williams) *in rr: drvn over 2f out: styd on same pce* **16/1**

5450 **10** 3 1/2 **Sweet Vintage (IRE)**[81] 3137 3-9-1 **54**........................(t) MartinDwyer 12 31
(Mark Brisbourne) *led tl hdd & wknd qckly wl over 1f out* **33/1**

3000 **11** 7 **Maisie's Moon (USA)**[15] 5395 3-8-13 **52**........................(b) SilvestreDeSousa 13 12
(Hughie Morrison) *in tch over 4f* **33/1**

0-00 **12** 6 **Zarla**[13] 5495 3-9-2 **55**........................ RichardKingscote 4
(Tom Dascombe) *chsd ldrs: rdn and btn 3f out* **12/1**

1m 40.07s (0.27) **Going Correction** -0.025s/f (Stan) **12** Ran SP% **122.2**
Speed ratings (Par 98): **97,96,93,91,90 87,87,86,85,82 75,69**
toteswingers 1&2 £2.10, 2&3 £4.10, 1&3 £7.00 CSF £14.74 CT £77.08 TOTE £5.60: £2.10, £1.80, £2.70; EX 16.80 Trifecta £77.40 Pool: £1975.27 - 19.13 winning units..
Owner Mrs Doreen M Swinburn **Bred** Genesis Green Stud Ltd **Trained** Newmarket, Suffolk
■ Stewards' Enquiry : Jamie Spencer one-day ban: careless riding (Sep 12)

FOCUS
The pace was not very strong in this minor handicap but two of the market leaders pulled clear and the form looks solid.

5924 BETVICTOR.COM/BRITISH STALLION STUDS EBF MAIDEN STKS 7f (P)
7:20 (7:21) (Class 5) 2-Y-O **£2,911** (£866; £432; £216) **Stalls** Low

Form RPR

1 **Lightning Spear** 2-9-5 0........................ JamieSpencer 4 86+
(Ralph Beckett) *t.k.h trckd ldrs: drvn and hdwy over 1f out: qcknd to ld fnl 110yds: readily* **11/4**[2]

2 3/4 **Alpine Retreat (USA)** 2-9-5 0........................ MickaelBarzalona 13 85+
(Charlie Appleby) *chsd ldrs: pushed along and green over 3f out: drvn 2f out: qcknd fnl f and r.o strly to chse wnr in clsng stages but a jst hld* **10/1**

26 **3** hd **Intermedium**[6] 5718 2-9-5 0........................ SilvestreDeSousa 3 81
(Charlie Appleby) *chsd ldr: led over 1f out and sn drvn: hdd fnl 110ydsyds: no ex and dropped to 3rd clsng stages* **3/1**[3]

4 1/2 **Fracking (IRE)** 2-9-5 0........................ JamesDoyle 9 80
(Olly Stevens) *unruly stalls: sn led: rdn 2f out: hdd over 1f out: styd on same pce fnl f* **33/1**

2 **5** 1 1/4 **Shafrah (IRE)**[18] 5299 2-9-5 0........................ PaulHanagan 6 77
(Richard Hannon) *chsd ldrs: pushed along 2f out: outpcd fnl f* **7/4**[1]

6 3/4 **Extremity (IRE)** 2-9-5 0........................ MartinDwyer 1 74
(Hugo Palmer) *in tch: pushed along and hdwy to chse ldrs 2f out: outpcd ins fnl f* **8/1**

0 **7** 4 1/2 **Sellingallthetime (IRE)**[26] 4987 2-9-5 0........................ RyanMoore 10 62
(Charles Hills) *s.i.s: in rr: hdwy on outer over 3f out: nvr rchd ldrs and outpcd fnl 2f* **8/1**

06 **8** 1 1/4 **Nashmi**[13] 5488 2-9-5 0........................ MartinHarley 11 59
(Fawzi Abdulla Nass, Bahrain) *towards rr: hdwy 3f out: rdn and no imp over 2f out: sn wknd* **33/1**

0 **9** 1 1/4 **Rehanaat (USA)**[22] 5131 2-9-0 0........................ AndreaAtzeni 12 50
(Ed Dunlop) *towards rr most of way* **33/1**

10 2 1/2 **Si Senor (IRE)** 2-9-5 0........................ FrederikTylicki 7 49
(Ed Vaughan) *slowly away: sme hdwy into mid-div 4f out: wknd over 2f out* **66/1**

11 8 **Hostile Fire (IRE)** 2-9-5 0........................ LiamKeniry 2 27
(Ed de Giles) *slowly away: gren: a in rr* **66/1**

12 27 **Bourbondi** 2-9-5 0........................(b[1]) TomMcLaughlin 5
(Michael Murphy) *v.s.a green: a wl bhd* **100/1**

13 3 1/2 **Wildling** 2-9-0 0........................ PatCosgrave 8
(Jim Boyle) *slowly away: green and a bhd* **100/1**

1m 26.56s (0.56) **Going Correction** -0.025s/f (Stan) **13** Ran SP% **133.1**
Speed ratings (Par 94): **95,94,93,93,91 91,85,84,83,80 71,40,36**
toteswingers 1&2 £9.00, 2&3 £5.90, 1&3 £4.20 CSF £33.85 TOTE £4.20: £1.90, £2.60, £1.40; EX 51.50 Trifecta £138.50 Pool: £2288.90 - 12.39 winning units..
Owner Qatar Racing Limited **Bred** Newsells Park Stud **Trained** Kimpton, Hants

FOCUS
An interesting maiden best rated through the third. The pace was fair and two potentially useful newcomers filled the first two places.

5925 £25 FREE BET AT BETVICTOR.COM MEDIAN AUCTION MAIDEN FILLIES' STKS 1m 4f (P)
7:50 (7:52) (Class 6) 3-5-Y-0 **£1,940** (£577; £288; £144) **Stalls** Centre

Form RPR
45 1 **Silk Train**[66] 3618 3-9-0 0 JamieSpencer 7 68
(David Simcock) *trckd ldr: drvn over 2f out: led wl over 1f out: pushed out* **11/8**[1]
2 2 **Chattanooga Line** 3-9-0 0 PatCosgrave 1 65
(George Baker) *chsd ldrs: rdn and led on ins wl over 2f out: hdd wl over 1f out: kpt on same pce fnl f* **8/1**
3 4 **Quality Alliance** 3-9-0 0 FrederikTylicki 3 58
(James Fanshawe) *in tch: chsd ldrs and rdn over 2f out: no ch w ldng duo fnl f* **9/2**[3]
0 4 2 3/4 **Lady Theodora**[13] 5478 3-8-9 0 MichaelJMMurphy[(5)] 8 54
(Alan Jarvis) *towards rr but in tch: rdn: hung rt and green over 2f out: mod prog fnl f* **10/1**
5 nse **Ginjo** 3-9-0 0 RyanMoore 6 54
(Charles Hills) *chsd ldrs: rdn over 2f out: no imp: wknd fnl f* **7/2**[2]
00 6 3/4 **Karitza (FR)**[19] 5281 3-9-0 0 JamesDoyle 2 53
(Jeremy Gask) *led: rdn and edgd lft fr 4f out: hdd & wknd wl over 2f out* **33/1**
7 12 **Ballyshonagh** 3-9-0 0 TedDurcan 5 34
(Chris Wall) *green: a towards rr* **14/1**
8 40 **Donard Lass** 3-9-0 0 PatDobbs 4
(Jimmy Fox) *s.i.s: in rr: lost tch fnl 4f* **40/1**

2m 37.8s (3.30) **Going Correction** -0.025s/f (Stan) **8 Ran SP% 114.8**
Speed ratings (Par 98): **88,86,84,82,82 81,73,46**
toteswingers 1&2 £3.80, 2&3 £4.70, 1&3 £1.40 CSF £13.63 TOTE £2.30: £1.10, £1.60, £1.70; EX 15.20 Trifecta £72.30 Pool: £1584.32 - 16.43 winning units..
Owner Windborne Partnership **Bred** Meon Valley Stud **Trained** Newmarket, Suffolk
FOCUS
The went a steady pace in this maiden but the favourite scored with authority.

5926 DOWNLOAD THE BETVICTOR APP NURSERY H'CAP 7f (P)
8:20 (8:20) (Class 5) (0-75,74) 2-Y-O **£2,587** (£770; £384; £192) **Stalls** Low

Form RPR
034 1 **Punk**[12] 5539 2-8-12 65 LukeMorris 5 72+
(Fawzi Abdulla Nass, Bahrain) *t.k.h: trckd ldrs: drvn to ld 1f out: pushed out* **5/1**[3]
243 2 2 **Salford Secret (IRE)**[45] 4351 2-9-2 74 TobyAtkinson[(5)] 8 75+
(Marco Botti) *s.i.s: hld up in rr: shkn up and hdwy over 1f out: sn rdn: styd on fnl f to chse wnr in clsng stages but no imp* **9/4**[1]
4104 3 3/4 **Atheera (IRE)**[20] 5235 2-9-1 68 PaulHanagan 7 67
(Mark Johnston) *chsd ldr: led 2f out and sn rdn: hdd 1f out: sn one pce* **10/1**
3100 4 1 1/4 **One Penny Piece**[12] 5536 2-9-6 73 WilliamCarson 4 69
(Philip McBride) *sn led: hdd 2f out: wknd fnl f* **9/1**
424 5 1 1/4 **Sebs Sensei (IRE)**[28] 4906 2-9-2 69 RichardHughes 3 61
(Richard Hannon) *s.i.s: in rr: hdwy on ins and rdn over 2f out: no imp on ldrs and wknd fnl f* **5/2**[2]
503 6 hd **Craftsmanship (FR)**[18] 5307 2-9-5 72 AndreaAtzeni 6 64
(Robert Eddery) *in rr: rdn over 2f out: sme hdwy fnl f* **13/2**
436 7 2 **Jersey Brown (IRE)**[14] 5443 2-9-1 68 MartinHarley 9 54
(Mick Channon) *t.k.h: chsd ldrs: rdn over 2f out: wknd over 1f out* **25/1**
4530 8 1 3/4 **Dancing Sal (IRE)**[24] 5068 2-8-11 64 PatCosgrave 1 46
(David Evans) *chsd ldrs: rdn over 2f out: wknd wl over 1f out* **20/1**

1m 27.13s (1.13) **Going Correction** -0.025s/f (Stan) **8 Ran SP% 121.5**
Speed ratings (Par 94): **92,89,88,87,86 85,83,81**
toteswingers 1&2 £3.30, 2&3 £8.10, 1&3 £5.30 CSF £17.87 CT £112.80 TOTE £7.70: £2.20, £1.40, £3.00; EX 21.50 Trifecta £155.00 Pool: £1187.94 - 5.74 winning units..
Owner Fawzi Abdulla Nass **Bred** Aislabie Bloodstock Ltd **Trained** Bahrain
FOCUS
They went a steady pace in this nursery. The winner scored in good style but the favourite didn't get much luck and the form behind is messy.

5927 BETVICTOR CASINO ON YOUR MOBILE NURSERY H'CAP 6f (P)
8:50 (8:51) (Class 4) (0-85,82) 2-Y-O **£3,752** (£1,116; £557; £278) **Stalls** Low

Form RPR
16 1 **Claim The Roses (USA)**[34] 4717 2-9-5 80 [1] RyanMoore 4 86+
(Ed Vaughan) *hld up in rr: pushed along and gd hdwy wl over 1f out to ld jst ins fnl f: r.o strly* **5/1**[3]
2461 2 1 3/4 **Lady Frances**[15] 5396 2-9-7 82 SilvestreDeSousa 1 82
(Mark Johnston) *chsd ldr: rdn and styd on fr 2f out: chal 1f out: styd chsng wnr but no imp* **9/4**[2]
541 3 1 1/2 **Constantine**[73] 3413 2-9-2 77 RichardHughes 2 73
(Richard Hannon) *led: rdn 2f out: jnd 1f out and sn hdd: no ex* **8/1**
5162 4 3/4 **Chord Chart (IRE)**[40] 4519 2-9-7 82 MickaelBarzalona 6 75
(Charlie Appleby) *in tch: rdn and hdwy ins fnl 2f: no imp fnl f* **7/4**[1]
6113 5 4 **Threetimesalady**[16] 5366 2-9-2 77 LukeMorris 5 60
(Sir Mark Prescott Bt) *in tch: hdwy 4f out to chse ldrs 3f out: rdn to dispute 2nd 2f out: wknd qckly fnl f* **8/1**
401 6 5 **Value (IRE)**[29] 4880 2-8-13 74 SeanLevey 3 38
(Richard Hannon) *chsd ldrs: rdn over 2f out and sn btn* **20/1**

1m 12.72s (-0.38) **Going Correction** -0.025s/f (Stan) **6 Ran SP% 110.8**
Speed ratings (Par 96): **101,98,96,95,90 83**
toteswingers 1&2 £2.50, 2&3 £3.80, 1&3 £3.70 CSF £16.22 TOTE £4.20: £1.50, £2.10; EX 17.70 Trifecta £121.30 Pool: £1514.64 - 9.35 winning units..
Owner Salem Rashid **Bred** Woodford Thoroughbreds LLC **Trained** Newmarket, Suffolk
FOCUS
This nursery featured three last-time-out winners. It was run at a good pace and the winner scored under a hold-up ride. The runner-up is rated to her recent course win with the third close to his pre-race mark.

5928 FOLLOW US ON TWITTER @BETVICTOR H'CAP 7f (P)
9:20 (9:21) (Class 4) (0-80,80) 3-Y-O+ **£4,690** (£1,395; £697; £348) **Stalls** Low

Form RPR
5504 1 **Ocean Legend (IRE)**[24] 5062 8-9-7 75 LukeMorris 1 84
(Tony Carroll) *chsd ldrs: rdn over 1f out: led fnl 150yds: hld on wl* **14/1**
003 2 nk **Noble Citizen (USA)**[4] 5799 8-9-12 80 (be) JamieSpencer 4 88
(David Simcock) *in rr: hdwy on ins over 1f out: str run fnl f: fin wl: nt quite get up* **7/1**
1113 3 hd **Levi Draper**[27] 4960 4-9-9 77 FrederikTylicki 8 85
(James Fanshawe) *in rr: hdwy 2f out: sn rdn: styd on u.p fnl f: kpt on cl home: nt quite pce of ldng duo* **11/4**[1]
3321 4 1 1/4 **Kinglami**[24] 5062 4-9-9 80 (p) ThomasBrown[(3)] 6 84+
(Brian Gubby) *chsd ldrs: led 2f out: sn rdn: hdd fnl 150yds: wknd in clsng stages* **13/2**[3]
1000 5 2 1/4 **Restaurateur (IRE)**[42] 4440 4-9-12 80 DavidProbert 14 78+
(Andrew Balding) *in rr: rdn 2f out: styd on wl fnl f: fin wl* **7/1**
1122 6 nse **Intomist (IRE)**[73] 3404 4-9-7 75 (p) PatCosgrave 3 73
(Jim Boyle) *chsd ldrs: rdn over 2f out: wknd ins fnl f* **14/1**
3201 7 1/2 **You're The Boss**[29] 4887 3-9-7 80 (p) GeorgeBaker 2 77
(Ed Walker) *in tch: drvn over 2f out: no imp over 1f out* **15/2**
6605 8 1/2 **Sewn Up**[12] 5511 3-9-1 74 (p) ShaneKelly 11 69
(Andrew Hollinshead) *in rr: drvn and hdwy over 2f out: no imp over 1f out: wknd ins fnl f* **50/1**
0545 9 1 1/4 **Another Try (IRE)**[20] 5219 8-8-12 71 MichaelJMMurphy[(5)] 9 63
(Alan Jarvis) *chsd ldr: led 4f out: hdd 2f out: wknd fnl f* **16/1**
0624 10 2 **Prince Of Burma (IRE)**[15] 5389 5-9-7 75 AdamKirby 13 62
(David Evans) *s.i.s: in rr: pushed along 3f out: sme hdwy fnl f* **20/1**
3020 11 1 1/2 **Exceedexpectations (IRE)**[22] 5124 4-9-9 77 LiamKeniry 7 60
(Conor Dore) *mid-div and rdn over 2f out: sn btn* **33/1**
00 12 6 **Top Diktat**[50] 4167 5-9-1 69 SamHitchcott 12 35
(Gary Moore) *s.i.s: a in rr* **33/1**
0-60 13 1 **Torres Del Paine**[15] 5398 6-9-3 71 WilliamCarson 10 35
(Brett Johnson) *sn bhd* **50/1**
-401 14 3 3/4 **Pivotal Movement**[19] 5280 3-9-6 79 RichardHughes 5 33
(Richard Hannon) *sn led: hdd 4f out: wknd fr 2f out* **5/1**[2]

1m 25.24s (-0.76) **Going Correction** -0.025s/f (Stan)
WFA 3 from 4yo+ 5lb **14 Ran SP% 127.2**
Speed ratings (Par 105): **103,102,102,101,98 98,97,97,95,93 91,84,83,79**
toteswingers 1&2 £2.50, 2&3 £3.80, 1&3 £3.70 CSF £110.42 CT £370.10 TOTE £16.20: £4.70, £2.90, £1.30; EX 73.80 Trifecta £368.40 Pool: £1469.75 - 2.99 winning units..
Owner W McLuskey **Bred** Mark Commins **Trained** Cropthorne, Worcs
FOCUS
They went a decent pace in this competitive handicap and there was a tight three-way finish.
T/Plt: £14.60 to a £1 stake. Pool of £66109.28 - 3284.22 winning tickets. T/Qpdt: £9.20 to a £1 stake. Pool of £5456.22 - 436.87 winning tickets. ST

5630 LINGFIELD (L-H)
Thursday, August 29

OFFICIAL GOING: Turf course -good (good to firm in places) changing to good to firm (good in places) after race 1 (4.40); all-weather - standard
Stands rail moved in 3 metres on turf course.
Wind: Light, across Weather: Fine, warm

5929 STONEGATE HOMES AFFORDABLE HOUSING SOLUTIONS MEDIAN AUCTION MAIDEN FILLIES' STKS 5f
4:40 (4:40) (Class 6) 2-Y-O **£2,045** (£603; £302) **Stalls** High

Form RPR
2205 1 **Go Glamorous (IRE)**[31] 4828 2-9-0 75 LukeMorris 10 77
(Ronald Harris) *racd against rail: pressed ldr: led after 2f: rdn over 1f out: sn drew clr* **10/11**[1]
2 2 1/2 **Hipz (IRE)** 2-9-0 0 PatCosgrave 7 68
(George Baker) *trckd ldrs: clsd to go 2nd wl over 1f out: one pce and no imp on wnr fnl f* **16/1**
3 3 3 1/4 **Kuala Queen (IRE)**[9] 5609 2-9-0 0 JohnFahy 5 56
(Denis Coakley) *trckd ldrs on outer: shkn up over 1f out: outpcd after* **2/1**[2]
4 3/4 **Dazza** 2-9-0 0 ShaneKelly 11 54+
(Gary Moore) *s.s: outpcd in last pair and pushed along: stl only 7th and wl off the pce over 1f out: styd on wl fnl f* **10/1**[3]
00 5 2 **Little Briar Rose**[18] 5307 2-9-0 0 ChrisCatlin 8 46
(John Spearing) *led 2f: pressed wnr to wl over 1f out: wknd qckly* **50/1**
6 3/4 **Shirley Vanessa (IRE)** 2-9-0 0 SeanLevey 3 44
(Luke Dace) *chsd ldrs: rdn wl over 1f out: sn wknd* **33/1**
0 7 1/2 **Spider Lily**[64] 3694 2-9-0 0 SteveDrowne 2 42
(Peter Makin) *in tch: effrt on wd outside 2f out: sn wknd* **12/1**
8 4 1/2 **Forest Glen (IRE)** 2-9-0 0 LiamKeniry 1 26
(Sylvester Kirk) *s.s: bdly outpcd in last pair: a bhd* **33/1**

57.97s (-0.23) **Going Correction** -0.275s/f (Firm) **8 Ran SP% 116.2**
Speed ratings (Par 89): **90,86,80,79,76 75,74,67**
toteswingers 1&2 £3.90, 2&3 £4.50, 1&3 £1.40 CSF £18.58 TOTE £2.70: £1.10, £3.40, £1.40; EX 17.80 Trifecta £50.90 Pool: £3342.52 - 49.23 winning units..
Owner Robert & Nina Bailey **Bred** Carlo Soria & Razza Del Pian Del Lago **Trained** Earlswood, Monmouths
FOCUS
Just an ordinary maiden in which the winner had the best pre-race form. The race looks weak and could be rated too high.

5930 STONEGATE HOMES 3 YEAR CELEBRATIONS H'CAP 5f
5:10 (5:11) (Class 6) (0-65,65) 3-Y-O+ **£2,045** (£603; £302) **Stalls** High

Form RPR
002 1 **Tom Sawyer**[26] 4992 5-9-5 63 (b) WilliamTwiston-Davies[(3)] 2 74
(Julie Camacho) *mounted on crse: mde virtually all and sn racd one off the rail: grabbed rail slot 2f out: drvn clr ins fnl f* **8/1**
6005 2 2 **Aaranyow (IRE)**[4] 5798 5-8-6 52 (p) NathanAlison[(5)] 1 56
(Clifford Lines) *trckd ldng pair: wnt 2nd 2f out: pressed wnr tl one pce ins fnl f* **8/1**
4236 3 1 1/4 **Proper Charlie**[26] 4996 5-8-5 46 oh1 (v) KierenFox 10 46
(Lee Carter) *n.m.r sn after s and wl in rr: swtchd to nr side rail over 1f out: r.o wl fnl f to take 3rd* **4/1**[3]
00-0 4 3 **College Doll**[13] 5499 4-8-2 46 oh1 RyanPowell[(3)] 6 35
(Christine Dunnett) *chsd ldrs: rdn to go 3rd over 1f out but nt on terms: fdd ins fnl f* **50/1**
5255 5 3/4 **Charming (IRE)**[4] 5796 4-9-4 62 (p) MarkCoumbe[(3)] 8 48
(Olivia Maylam) *hld up towards rr: nt clr run over 2f out to over 1f out: one pce whn in the clr* **14/1**
123 6 nk **Friendship Is Love**[14] 5422 3-9-5 62 LiamKeniry 3 47
(David Elsworth) *racd on outer and wl in rr: rdn over 2f out: modest late prog: no ch* **11/4**[1]
0 7 5 **Ziefhd**[126] 1783 4-8-10 54 (p) RyanClark[(3)] 5 21
(Tim McCarthy) *racd against rail and pressed wnr to 2f out: sn wknd qckly* **25/1**

5435 **8** 3 ¾ **Mossgo (IRE)**[16] 5376 3-9-3 **60**...(t) LukeMorris 4 13
(John Best) *chsd ldrs on outer: drvn 1/2-way: wknd over 1f out* **20/1**

414 **9** *shd* **Josefa Goya**[14] 5422 3-9-8 **65**.. KierenFallon 11 18+
(Hughie Morrison) *taken down early and steadily to post: tried to grab prom pl against nr side rail but unable to do so: chsd ldrs: struggling 2f out: no ch whn hmpd over 1f out: eased* **3/1**[2]

5060 **10** *17* **Give Us A Belle (IRE)**[13] 5499 4-8-8 **49** oh1 ow3..(bt) AdamBeschizza 9
(Christine Dunnett) *stmbld sn after s: a bhd: t.o* **50/1**

0-06 **11** *48* **Laura's Bairn**[30] 4866 4-9-10 **65**.....................................(v) ShaneKelly 12
(J R Jenkins) *restless stalls: rring as they opened and c out sideways: lost all ch and allowed to amble home* **16/1**

56.69s (-1.51) **Going Correction** -0.275s/f (Firm)
WFA 3 from 4yo+ 2lb **11** Ran SP% **119.0**
Speed ratings (Par 101): **101,97,95,91,89 89,81,75,75,47**
toteswingers 1&2 £7.10, 2&3 £8.40, 1&3 £5.50 CSF £68.55 CT £300.28 TOTE £8.50: £2.50, £2.20, £1.30; EX 85.10 Trifecta £612.60 Pool: £2827.37 - 3.46 winning units..
Owner Bolingbroke J Howard FAO Mersey R & Ptns **Bred** Newsells Park Stud **Trained** Norton, N Yorks

■ Stewards' Enquiry : William Twiston-Davies one-day ban: failed to ride to draw (Sep 12)
Kieren Fox one-day ban: careless riding (Sep 15)

FOCUS
A modest sprint that was effectively decided at the start, the first and second both coming across sharply from low draws to dominate, and very few ever threatening a serious blow.

5931 DARRELL HINDS MEMORIAL H'CAP 6f
5:40 (5:40) (Class 5) (0-70,69) 3-Y-O+ **£2,726** (£805; £402) **Stalls** High

Form RPR

2433 **1** **Rambo Will**[26] 4999 5-9-1 **59**.. CathyGannon 12 72
(J R Jenkins) *mde all and racd against nr side rail: shkn up over 1f out: wl in command fnl f* **5/2**[1]

4413 **2** 2 ½ **Jay Bee Blue**[17] 5346 4-9-9 **67**.....................................(bt) TomQueally 11 72
(Sean Curran) *trckd ldng trio and racd against rail: waiting for a gap jst over 2f out: got through to chse wnr over 1f out: one pce fnl f* **5/2**[1]

4246 **3** 2 ¾ **Dark Lane**[3] 5841 7-9-7 **68**... DeclanBates(3) 8 64
(David Evans) *pressed ldng pair: nt qckn and lost pl 2f out: kpt on u.p to take 3rd again ins fnl f* **8/1**[3]

5634 **4** 1 ¼ **Ghostwing**[87] 2918 6-9-7 **65**..(vt) SeanLevey 6 57
(Luke Dace) *pressed wnr to wl over 1f out: wknd fnl f* **5/1**[2]

2160 **5** *1* **Song Of Parkes**[13] 5498 6-9-5 **68**..............................(p) SladeO'Hara(5) 5 57
(Peter Grayson) *sn off the pce in 7th: urged along and no prog on outer 1/2-way: plugged on fnl f* **12/1**

4600 **6** ¾ **Night Trade (IRE)**[29] 4884 6-9-1 **66**........................(p) OisinMurphy(7) 10 53
(Ronald Harris) *restless in stalls and awkward s: in tch: effrt in 5th on outer 2f out: wknd fnl f* **8/1**[3]

0004 **7** *2* **Zaheeb**[33] 4752 5-8-9 **53**...(p) JimmyQuinn 7 33
(Dave Morris) *chsd ldrs in 5th: no imp 2f out: sn wknd* **12/1**

U00 **8** *7* **Midnight Feast**[12] 5522 5-9-9 **67**.......................................(v) KierenFox 1 25
(Lee Carter) *s.s and then impeded sltly: a wl off the pce in last pair* **20/1**

3500 **9** 1 ½ **Overrider**[13] 5477 3-9-6 **67**..(t) JamieMackay 2 20
(Alastair Lidderdale) *blindfold sltly late off and slowly away: a off the pce in last pair* **33/1**

1m 8.99s (-2.21) **Going Correction** -0.275s/f (Firm)
WFA 3 from 4yo+ 3lb **9** Ran SP% **119.1**
Speed ratings (Par 103): **103,99,96,94,93 92,89,80,78**
toteswingers 1&2 £1.90, 2&3 £4.80, 1&3 £4.60 CSF £8.60 CT £43.60 TOTE £3.80: £1.60, £1.80, £2.40; EX 10.20 Trifecta £64.00 Pool: £1622.41 - 18.99 winning units..
Owner Mrs S Bambridge **Bred** T H Bambridge **Trained** Royston, Herts

FOCUS
Yet another sprint on the turf course in which a position against the stands' rail proved vital, the winner making all.

5932 CHANTRY LAND WORKING WITH STONEGATE HOMES MAIDEN STKS 7f
6:10 (6:11) (Class 5) 3-Y-O **£2,726** (£805; £402) **Stalls** High

Form RPR

3532 **1** **Rufoof**[12] 5512 3-9-0 68.. DaneO'Neill 3 74
(Charles Hills) *trckd ldng pair: wnt 2nd after 3f: shkn up over 2f out: clsd fr over 1f out: led ins fnl f: styd on wl* **2/1**[1]

2426 **2** 1 ½ **Disco Inferno (IRE)**[12] 5512 3-9-5 77...........................(bt[1]) SeanLevey 7 75
(Brian Meehan) *led against rail: 2 l up and gng strly 3f out: hrd rdn wl over 1f out: hdd and nt qckn ins fnl f* **3/1**[3]

3 **3** *6* **St Georges Hill (IRE)**[215] 396 3-9-5 0............................ JimCrowley 6 59
(Michael Wigham) *chsd ldng trio: pushed along fr 1/2-way and nt on terms: wnt 3rd 2f out: no imp after* **9/4**[2]

0350 **4** *1* **Persian Patriot**[69] 3537 3-9-0 68...................................... CathyGannon 1 51
(William Jarvis) *sltly awkward s: racd on outer early: mostly in 5th and nvr on terms w ldrs: no real prog fnl 2f* **7/1**

0 **5** 2 ½ **Kindlelight Storm (USA)**[31] 4839 3-9-5 0........................ RobertHavlin 9 49
(Nick Littmoden) *s.s: rousted along in last trio: nvr a factor: plugged on fnl 2f* **25/1**

05 **6** 3 ¼ **Presumido (IRE)**[19] 5277 3-9-5 0...................................... AmirQuinn 8 41
(Simon Dow) *chsd ldr 3f: wknd 2f out* **50/1**

00 **7** *18* **First Peninsular**[89] 2872 3-9-5 0.................................... GeorgeBaker 5
(Chris Wall) *a in last trio: bhd fr 1/2-way: t.o* **20/1**

0 **8** *26* **Be Gifted**[19] 5277 3-9-0 0.. KirstyMilczarek 4
(John E Long) *dwlt: sn wl t.o* **100/1**

1m 21.55s (-1.75) **Going Correction** -0.275s/f (Firm) **8** Ran SP% **113.2**
Speed ratings (Par 100): **99,97,90,89,86 82,62,32**
toteswingers 1&2 £1.50, 2&3 £2.20, 1&3 £1.90 CSF £7.97 TOTE £3.20: £1.20, £1.40, £1.10; EX 8.40 Trifecta £15.60 Pool: £1754.88 - 83.97 winning units..
Owner Hamdan Al Maktoum **Bred** Shadwell Estate Company Limited **Trained** Lambourn, Berks

FOCUS
The leading pair pulled clear in what turned out to be a weak maiden.

5933 HUGH & PAT 40TH ANNIVERSARY H'CAP 2m (P)
6:40 (6:40) (Class 5) (0-75,73) 4-Y-O+ **£2,726** (£805; £402) **Stalls** Low

Form RPR

3222 **1** **Story Writer**[20] 5233 4-9-7 **73**.. JimCrowley 4 83
(William Knight) *trckd ldrs: mostly in 2nd fr 1/2-way: gng easily 3f out: led over 2f out and kicked for home: rdn and pressed briefly fnl f: styd on wl* **2/1**[1]

0-02 **2** 1 ¼ **While You Wait (IRE)**[10] 5586 4-9-6 **72**.......................... GeorgeBaker 7 81
(Gary Moore) *hld up in last: stdy prog fr 3f out: rdn to chse wnr over 1f out and tried to cl: no imp last 100yds* **14/1**

5316 **3** *8* **Star Alliance (IRE)**[23] 5084 5-8-10 **62**.............................(b) KierenFallon 3 61
(Ian Williams) *cl up: rdn in 3rd over 2f out: wl outpcd by ldng pair over 1f out* **8/1**

36-3 **4** 1 ¼ **Alfraamsey**[20] 5231 5-9-1 **72**.. HarryPoulton(5) 1 69
(Sheena West) *led 6f: brief effrt to ld again over 6f out: cl up and rdn over 2f out: sn wl outpcd* **8/1**

2-64 **5** ½ **Squad**[225] 224 7-9-6 **72**..(v) LukeMorris 5 69
(Simon Dow) *dwlt: hld up in last trio: shkn up over 3f out: no real prog 2f out: wknd over 1f out* **16/1**

214/ **6** 3 ¾ **Hunting Tower**[16] 6224 9-8-10 **69**..............................(t) DanielMuscutt(7) 6 61
(Tim Vaughan) *hld up in last trio: effrt on wd outside over 3f out: no prog over 2f out: sn wknd* **5/1**[3]

111 **7** 1 ¾ **Almost Gemini (IRE)**[85] 2980 4-9-3 **69**............................(p) ShaneKelly 2 59
(Don Cantillon) *pressed ldr: led after 6f: rdn fr 4f out: hdd over 2f out: wknd qckly* **11/4**[2]

2344 **8** *13* **Double Cee**[40] 4530 4-8-12 **71**...................................(p) OisinMurphy(7) 8 46
(Warren Greatrex) *chsd ldrs: rdn 5f out: wknd 3f out: t.o* **20/1**

3m 26.06s (0.36) **Going Correction** +0.10s/f (Slow) **8** Ran SP% **116.2**
Speed ratings (Par 103): **103,102,98,97,97 95,94,88**
toteswingers 1&2 £6.20, 2&3 £13.80, 1&3 £4.20 CSF £32.34 CT £189.28 TOTE £3.80: £2.20, £4.60, £4.50; EX 33.10 Trifecta £369.50 Pool: £1435.73 - 2.91 winning units..
Owner The Pheasant Rew Partnership **Bred** Oakhill Stud **Trained** Patching, W Sussex

FOCUS
A run-of-the-mill staying event, although the leading pair deserve some credit for pulling so far clear. The pace was steady until halfway.

5934 STONEGATE HOMES CLIENT APPRECIATION H'CAP 1m 4f (P)
7:10 (7:12) (Class 6) (0-60,58) 3-Y-O+ **£2,045** (£603; £302) **Stalls** Low

Form RPR

-420 **1** **Ebony Roc (IRE)**[64] 3675 3-9-0 **54**.. SeanLevey 8 65+
(Amanda Perrett) *led 1f: trckd ldr: led again 3f out: drvn for home over 2f out: 3 l up fnl f: clung on nr fin* **9/2**[1]

4460 **2** ¾ **Rodrigo De Freitas (IRE)**[23] 5099 6-9-8 **52**..................(v) JimCrowley 9 60
(Jim Boyle) *dwlt: pushed along at various stages in last trio: prog on outer fr 3f out: gd hdwy to go 2nd ins fnl f: clsd on wnr qckly fin* **6/1**[2]

0/30 **3** *nk* **Cabuchon (GER)**[23] 5093 6-9-0 **47**.............................(t) DeclanBates(3) 4 55
(David Evans) *chsd ldrs: rdn 3f out: prog to dispute 2nd 1f out: clsd on wnr nr fin* **10/1**[3]

0624 **4** 1 ¼ **Chasin' Rainbows**[22] 5127 5-9-7 **51**.................................. DaneO'Neill 2 57
(Sylvester Kirk) *hld up in 9th: prog on inner over 2f out: drvn to dispute 2nd 1f out: one pce after* **6/1**[2]

2464 **5** 2 ½ **Aphrodite Spirit (IRE)**[21] 5178 3-8-5 **45**........................... ChrisCatlin 12 47
(Pat Eddery) *led after 1f to 3f out: chsd wnr after tl wknd 1f out* **16/1**

4433 **6** 4 ½ **Another Squeeze**[14] 5434 5-9-6 **50**...............................(p[1]) CathyGannon 5 45
(Peter Hiatt) *nvr bttr than midfield: pushed along over 3f out: outpcd fr 2f out: no imp after* **10/1**[3]

0-44 **7** *hd* **Like Clockwork**[16] 5370 4-10-0 **58**..................................... KierenFallon 11 52
(Mark H Tompkins) *mostly chsd ldng pair to wl over 1f out: wknd qckly* **6/1**[2]

0-05 **8** *nse* **Awesome Rock (IRE)**[225] 226 4-9-4 **48**............................ RobertHavlin 1 42
(Roger Ingram) *stdd s: hld up in last trio: stl there 3f out: plld out wd over 2f out: kpt on fr over 1f out: no ch to threaten* **16/1**

0300 **9** *6* **Highly Likely (IRE)**[20] 5216 4-9-11 **58**.....................(t) ThomasBrown(3) 6 43
(Steve Woodman) *chsd ldrs: rdn over 3f out: wknd 2f out* **10/1**[3]

5500 **10** *12* **Queenie's Star (IRE)**[12] 5528 6-8-8 **45**.....................(t) OisinMurphy(7) 3 11
(Michael Attwater) *nvr bttr than midfield: wknd over 2f out: t.o* **40/1**

0-00 **11** 2 ¼ **Ay Tay Tate (IRE)**[24] 5059 7-10-0 **58**............................(p) GeorgeBaker 10 20
(Noel Wilson) *chsd ldrs on outer: rdn 5f out: wknd over 3f out: t.o* **10/1**[3]

6403 **12** *2* **Mariet**[22] 5123 4-9-5 **49**.. TomQueally 7 8
(Suzy Smith) *dwlt: a in last trio: pushed along and wknd 3f out: t.o* **16/1**

2m 32.4s (-0.60) **Going Correction** +0.10s/f (Slow)
WFA 3 from 4yo+ 10lb **12** Ran SP% **117.5**
Speed ratings (Par 101): **106,105,105,104,102 99,99,99,95,87 86,84**
toteswingers 1&2 £6.70, 2&3 £15.90, 1&3 £18.70 CSF £30.13 CT £258.79 TOTE £7.70: £2.30, £2.20, £5.10; EX 32.80 Trifecta £408.40 Pool: £1332.34 - 2.44 winning units..
Owner The To-Agori-Mou Partnership **Bred** Joe Rogers **Trained** Pulborough, W Sussex

FOCUS
A low-grade handicap that went the way of one of the few unexposed sorts in the line-up. The pace soon appeared sound, the field finishing quite well strung out.

5935 JUST ONE MOORE THEN WE'LL ALL GO H'CAP 1m 2f (P)
7:40 (7:42) (Class 6) (0-60,59) 3-Y-O **£2,726** (£805; £402) **Stalls** Low

Form RPR

1514 **1** **Winslow Arizona (IRE)**[24] 5073 3-9-7 **59**......................... TomQueally 5 69+
(Michael Bell) *settled in midfield: prog on outer over 2f out: swept into ld 1f out: sn rdn clr* **2/1**[1]

2000 **2** *3* **Nepalese Pearl**[44] 4385 3-8-12 **50**.................................. RobertHavlin 6 53
(Pat Eddery) *trckd ldrs: rdn in 3rd 2f out: tried to chal over 1f out: sn outpcd by wnr but styd on* **25/1**

0436 **3** ½ **Tornado Battle**[12] 5527 3-8-13 **51**................................. CathyGannon 1 53
(Phil McEntee) *in tch in midfield: hrd rdn over 1f out: styd on wl after to take 3rd ins fnl f* **14/1**

504 **4** 1 ¼ **Marguerite St Just**[12] 5527 3-8-5 **48**........................... NathanAlison(5) 2 48
(Olivia Maylam) *trckd ldrs: rdn over 2f out: cl enough over 1f out: sn outpcd* **25/1**

0010 **5** *shd* **Szabo's Art**[17] 5334 3-9-5 **57**...(b[1]) ChrisCatlin 11 56
(Sir Mark Prescott Bt) *slowest away: rapid prog on outer to ld after 2f: drvn 2f out: hdd & wknd 1f out* **6/1**[3]

0-00 **6** *nse* **Wedding Speech (IRE)**[38] 4590 3-9-7 **59**......................... ShaneKelly 8 58
(James Fanshawe) *settled in midfield: pushed along on outer over 2f out: rdn and nt qckn over 1f out: kpt on fnl f* **5/1**[2]

0504 **7** 1 ½ **Bullseye Babe**[70] 3495 3-8-13 **51**..................................(e[1]) DaneO'Neill 7 47
(Mark Usher) *hld up in last pair: stl there 2f out: rdn over 1f out: kpt on ins fnl f: no ch* **10/1**

0504 **8** ½ **Entrapping**[12] 5528 3-9-1 **53**.. KirstyMilczarek 9 48
(John E Long) *plld hrd: hld up in rr: rdn and no prog wl over 2f out* **6/1**[3]

6300 **9** *shd* **World Freight Girl**[22] 5126 3-8-11 **49**............................ JimmyQuinn 12 44
(Dean Ivory) *prom: chsd ldr 6f out: drvn to chal over 1f out: wknd qckly fnl f* **33/1**

0000 **10** 3 ¾ **Terpsichore**[9] 5604 3-8-7 **45**.. RenatoSouza 4 33
(Sylvester Kirk) *nvr bttr than midfield: lost pl fr 3f out: no ch over 1f out* **66/1**

1556 **11** 2 ¾ **Compton Silver**[66] 3621 3-9-7 **59**.................................... GeorgeBaker 3 41
(Hans Adielsson) *reluctant ldr 2f: styd prom tl wknd over 2f out* **8/1**

6-00 **12** *12* **Iffley Fields**[44] 4391 3-8-10 **48**................................(b[1]) AdamBeschizza 10
(Michael Squance) *a in last pair: wknd over 3f out: t.o* **50/1**

2m 8.12s (1.52) **Going Correction** +0.10s/f (Slow) **12** Ran SP% **119.5**
Speed ratings (Par 98): **97,94,94,93,93 93,91,91,91,88 86,76**
toteswingers 1&2 £13.10, 2&3 £49.90, 1&3 £8.80 CSF £66.15 CT £580.00 TOTE £2.50: £1.10, £29.00, £12.20; EX 54.70 Trifecta £1218.20 Part won. Pool: £1624.29 - 0.53 winning units..
Owner Rathordan Partnership **Bred** Sir E J Loder **Trained** Newmarket, Suffolk

FOCUS
An ordinary handicap overall, but the ready winner is going the right way. The pace was steady for much of the way.
T/Jkpt: £5,071.40 to a £1 stake. Pool of £25000.00 - 3.50 winning tickets. T/Plt: £25.00 to a £1 stake. Pool of £71245.43 - 2072.74 winning ticket. T/Qpdt: £6.00 to a £1 stake. Pool of £6594.50 - 807.20 winning tickets. JN

5936 - 5938a (Foreign Racing) - See Raceform Interactive

5911

BADEN-BADEN (L-H)

Thursday, August 29

OFFICIAL GOING: Turf: good

5939a KRONIMUS-RENNEN (LISTED RACE) (2YO) (TURF) 6f
1:40 (12:00) 2-Y-O **£9,756** (£4,065; £1,626; £813)

RPR

1 **Suzi's Connoisseur**[8] 5656 2-9-2 0........................... IoritzMendizabal 8 96
(Mark Johnston) *wnt rt s: pushed along to chse ldrs: rdn to chal over 1f out: led ins fnl f: edgd lft u.p but asserted: readily* **42/10**[3]

2 *½* **Sugar Love (GER)** 2-8-6 0.. AStarke 5 85
(P Schiergen, Germany) **4/1**[2]

3 *1 ¾* **Oxanueva (FR)**[36] 4651 2-8-13 0.................................... FabriceVeron 4 86
(H-A Pantall, France) **5/2**[1]

4 *1 ¾* **Key To Fun (GER)**[29] 2-9-2 0........................ LennartHammer-Hansen 6 84
(Frau E Mader, Germany) **61/10**

5 *shd* **Mr Pommeroy (FR)**[67] 2-9-2 0.................................... CristianDemuro 3 84
(Mario Hofer, Germany) **122/10**

6 *nse* **Oriental Magic (GER)** 2-8-6 0.................................... FilipMinarik 2 74
(J Hirschberger, Germany) **26/5**

7 *hd* **Andrina (IRE)**[47] 2-8-13 0.. VSchulepov 7 80
(H J Groschel, Germany) **122/10**

8 *5* **Sharin (GER)**[47] 2-8-10 0.. DPorcu 1 62
(Markus Klug, Germany) **92/10**

9 *6* **German Rules** 2-9-0 0... EPedroza 9 48
(H-W Hiller, Germany) **148/10**

1m 9.41s (-0.88) **9** Ran SP% **129.3**
WIN (incl. 10 euro stake): WIN: 52. PLACES: 20, 18, 15. SF: 283..
Owner Greenstead Hall Racing Ltd **Bred** Greenstead Hall Racing Ltd **Trained** Middleham Moor, N Yorks

5940a DARLEY OETTINGEN-RENNEN (GROUP 2) (3YO+) (TURF) 1m
4:00 (12:00) 3-Y-O+
£32,520 (£12,601; £5,284; £3,252; £2,032; £1,219)

RPR

1 **Gereon (GER)**[46] 4333 5-9-1 0.................................... LiamJones 2 108
(C Zschache, Germany) *mde all: rdn 2f out: r.o strly and asserted: drvn clr* **16/1**

2 *1 ¾* **Felician (GER)**[46] 4333 5-9-4 0..................... LennartHammer-Hansen 10 107
(Ferdinand J Leve, Germany) *hld up: rdn over 2f out: r.o and wnt 2nd ins fnl f: no imp on wnr* **17/5**[1]

3 *¾* **Empire Storm (GER)**[25] 6-9-1 0.................................... JBojko 12 102
(A Wohler, Germany) *midfield: rdn over 2f out: outpcd by wnr over 1f out: kpt on u.p and wnt 3rd towards fin* **208/10**

4 *hd* **Samba Brazil (GER)**[67] 3612 4-8-11 0...................... CristianDemuro 6 98
(J Hirschberger, Germany) *midfield in tch: clsd 3f out: rdn over 2f out: 2nd but outpcd by wnr ent fnl f: kpt on but dropped to 4th towards fin* **218/10**

5 *¾* **Dux Scholar**[39] 5-9-1 0.. MircoDemuro 9 100
(A Savujev, Czech Republic) *hld up: rdn 2f out: r.o but nt gng pce to chal* **26/5**

6 *nk* **Indriya (FR)**[88] 4-8-11 0.. OlivierPeslier 7 95
(F Rohaut, France) *t.k.h: hld up in last pair: rdn over 2f out: r.o but nvr threatened* **10/1**

7 *nk* **Combat Zone (IRE)**[39] 7-9-4 0..................................... NRichter 3 102
(Mario Hofer, Germany) *trckd ldr: rdn 3f out: kpt on same pce and lost multiple pls ins fnl f* **244/10**

8 *shd* **Peace At Last (IRE)**[18] 5314 3-8-13 0........................ FabriceVeron 11 101
(H-A Pantall, France) *hld up in last pair: last 1/2-way: rdn over 2f out: r.o but nvr threatened* **51/10**[3]

9 *nk* **Global Thrill**[46] 4333 4-9-1 0.................................... ADeVries 4 98
(J Hirschberger, Germany) *squeezed s: midfield: rdn over 2f out: kpt on but outpcd ent fnl f and n.d after* **19/5**[2]

10 *½* **Royal Fox**[46] 4333 3-8-10 0 ow1.......................... MrDennisSchiergen 5 97
(P Schiergen, Germany) *squeezed s: hld up in midfield: rdn over 2f out: nt clr run over 1f out: swtchd lft and keeping on whn short of room again ins fnl f: nt rcvr* **23/1**

11 *nk* **Akua'da (GER)**[61] 3852 3-8-9 0.................................... EPedroza 8 95
(A Wohler, Germany) *midfield in tch: rdn over 2f out: outpcd ent fnl f: no ex and dropped to rr* **68/10**

12 *shd* **Quixote (GER)**[46] 4333 3-8-9 0.................................... AStarke 1 95
(P Schiergen, Germany) *prom: rdn 3f out: kpt on tl no ex ent fnl f: fdd and dropped to last fnl strides* **11/1**

1m 38.96s (-0.15)
WFA 3 from 4yo+ 6lb **12** Ran SP% **129.3**
WIN (incl. 10 euro stake): 170. PLACES: 27, 20, 42, 38. SF: 1,057.
Owner C Zschache **Bred** Gestut Ebbesloh **Trained** Germany

5508

CHESTER (L-H)

Friday, August 30

OFFICIAL GOING: Good (6.9)

Rail between 6f and 1.5f moved out 3yds, with drop in at that point adding 13yds to races 1, 3, 5 and 7, 14yds to races 2 and 4 and 26yd to race 6.
Wind: Moderate; across Weather: Fine

5941 FREE SCRATCH CARD WITH CHESTERBET EASY 6 / EBF MAIDEN STKS 7f 122y
2:00 (2:01) (Class 4) 2-Y-O **£6,469** (£1,925; £962; £481) **Stalls** Low

Form RPR

043 **1** **Bow Creek (IRE)**[7] 5727 2-9-0 0.................................... FrannyNorton 2 87
(Mark Johnston) *mde all: drvn clr fnl f: unchal* **5/6**[1]

3 **2** *3 ¼* **Mukaynis (IRE)**[16] 5405 2-9-0 0.................................... TomQueally 7 79+
(Lady Cecil) *chsd wnr: drvn over 3f out: styd on same pce fnl f* **8/1**

50 **3** *3 ½* **Haayil**[69] 3581 2-9-0 0.. RobertHavlin 8 71
(John Gosden) *s.i.s: sn chsng ldrs: nt clr run 1f out: styd on to take 3rd nr fin* **16/1**

4 *½* **Yenhaab (IRE)** 2-9-0 0.. JamieSpencer 3 70+
(William Haggas) *trckd ldrs: drvn 2f out: kpt on same pce* **7/1**[3]

5 *¾* **Mountain Lion (IRE)** 2-9-0 0.................................... SilvestreDeSousa 4 68+
(Saeed bin Suroor) *s.i.s: in rr: hdwy over 1f out: styng on at fin* **13/2**[2]

4 **6** *nk* **Samtu (IRE)**[15] 5438 2-9-0 0...................................... MartinLane 6 67
(Clive Brittain) *trckd ldrs: drvn over 2f out: one pce* **50/1**

5 **7** *¾* **Rasameel (USA)**[21] 5244 2-9-0 0.................................. DaneO'Neill 9 66+
(J W Hills) *swtchd lft after s: in rr: drvn 3f out: kpt on fnl f* **16/1**

0062 **8** *10* **Arrowzone**[14] 5482 2-9-0 70.................................(p) GrahamGibbons 1 42
(Garry Moss) *stmbld s: sn chsng ldrs: drvn 3f out: lost pl 2f out: sn bhd* **20/1**

9 *36* **Right Behind You** 2-9-0 0.................................... RichardKingscote 5
(Tom Dascombe) *s.i.s: sn drvn along detached in last: bhd after 2f: t.o 3f out* **25/1**

1m 35.29s (1.49) **Going Correction** +0.175s/f (Good) **9** Ran SP% **113.8**
Speed ratings (Par 96): **99,95,92,91,91 90,89,79,43**
toteswingers 1&2 £2.30, 1&3 £4.60, 2&3 £11.00 CSF £7.68 TOTE £1.60: £1.10, £1.60, £4.30; EX 7.40 Trifecta £39.30 Pool: £3,251.73 - 61.91 winning units..
Owner Sheikh Hamdan Bin Mohammed Al Maktoum **Bred** Round Hill Stud **Trained** Middleham Moor, N Yorks

FOCUS
Not a bad juvenile maiden with the winner confirming the improvement shown at York.

5942 CHESTERBET EASY 6 STARTS HERE MAIDEN FILLIES' STKS 1m 2f 75y
2:30 (2:33) (Class 4) 3-Y-O+ **£6,469** (£1,925; £962; £481) **Stalls** High

Form RPR

3-03 **1** **Vicksburg**[106] 2389 3-9-0 72.................................... MartinDwyer 4 86+
(Andrew Balding) *mde all: drvn over 2f out: styd on wl* **13/2**

5 **2** *2 ¼* **Empress Adelaide**[14] 5495 3-9-0 0.............................. JamieSpencer 9 84+
(William Haggas) *in rr: outpcd over 4f out: hdwy on outside over 2f out: chsng ldrs and edgd lft 1f out: styd on to take 2nd last 50yds* **14/1**

34 **3** *1 ¾* **Annawi**[26] 5038 3-9-0 0.. DaneO'Neill 8 78
(Henry Candy) *trckd ldrs: 2nd over 4f out: drvn over 2f out: keeping on same pce whn hung lft over 1f out* **8/1**

633 **4** *¾* **Snow Powder (IRE)**[14] 5478 3-9-0 83.............................. RobertHavlin 5 77
(John Gosden) *chsd ldrs: drvn and outpcd over 2f out: hdwy and n.m.r over 1f out: styd on towards fin* **4/1**[2]

0-22 **5** *½* **Conserve (IRE)**[8] 5678 3-9-0 0.................................... TomQueally 7 76
(Lady Cecil) *in rr: outpcd over 4f out: hdwy 3f out: kpt on fnl f* **11/4**[1]

-362 **6** *½* **Madame Elizabeth**[22] 5181 3-9-0 72.......................... GrahamGibbons 6 75
(Andrew Hollinshead) *trckd ldrs: t.k.h: one pce fnl 2f* **12/1**

64 **7** *9* **Perfect Summer (IRE)**[24] 5100 3-9-0 0.............................. ChrisCatlin 11 58
(Lady Cecil) *s.i.s: swtchd lft after s: sn detached in last: sme hdwy over 2f out: nvr on terms* **20/1**

04 **8** *1 ¼* **Evermore (IRE)**[14] 5495 3-9-0 0.................................... FrannyNorton 2 55
(Mark Johnston) *s.i.s: sn chsng ldrs: wknd over 1f out: eased ins fnl f* **15/2**

0420 **9** *1 ¼* **Ella Motiva (IRE)**[16] 5391 3-9-0 47.......................... RobbieFitzpatrick 3 53?
(Mark Brisbourne) *in rr-div: drvn over 4f out: sn lost pl* **80/1**

02 **10** *3* **Sharareh**[25] 5064 3-9-0 0.. FrankieDettori 10 47
(Luca Cumani) *chsd ldrs: reminders over 3f out: wkng whn n.m.r over 1f out: sn eased: lame* **6/1**[3]

6 **11** *81* **Come On Flo**[19] 5301 3-8-9 0..............................(p) SladeO'Hara(5) 1
(Michael Mullineaux) *w ldrs 2f: lost pl over 5f out: sn bhd: t.o 3f out: eventually completed* **100/1**

2m 14.13s (2.93) **Going Correction** +0.225s/f (Good) **11** Ran SP% **118.5**
Speed ratings (Par 102): **97,95,93,93,92 92,85,84,83,80 16**
toteswingers 1&2 £15.40, 1&3 £9.20, 2&3 £14.90 CSF £92.81 TOTE £6.90: £1.80, £5.80, £2.50; EX 105.40 Trifecta £1035.30 Pool: £3,269.72 - 2.36 winning units..
Owner Richard Wilmot-Smith **Bred** Highclere Stud **Trained** Kingsclere, Hants

FOCUS
A modest fillies' maiden and a persoanl-best from the winner, although not an easy race to rate.

5943 CHESTERBET POWERED BY DATATOTE H'CAP 7f 2y
3:00 (3:01) (Class 3) (0-95,94) 3-Y-O+ **£7,762** (£2,310; £1,154; £577) **Stalls** Low

Form RPR

0035 **1** **Laffan (IRE)**[21] 5238 4-9-5 **86**.............................. SilvestreDeSousa 6 96
(Tim Easterby) *mid-div: hdwy to chse ldrs whn hmpd over 1f out: led last 75yds: drvn out* **7/1**

0-00 **2** *1 ¼* **Sir Reginald**[97] 2665 5-9-5 **86**.................................... LeeTopliss 2 93
(Richard Fahey) *s.i.s: in rr: hdwy on inner over 2f out: c wd over 1f out: styd on wl to take 2nd nr fin* **11/2**[2]

0520 **3** *½* **Chosen Character (IRE)**[20] 5268 5-9-8 **94**...........(vt) NatashaEaton(5) 7 99
(Tom Dascombe) *mid-div: hdwy on outside over 1f out: chsd wnr last 75yds: styd on same pce* **18/1**

3100 **4** *1 ½* **The Confessor**[13] 5533 6-9-10 **91**.............................. CathyGannon 1 93
(Henry Candy) *chsd ldrs: upsides over 1f out: kpt on same pce last 150yds* **4/1**[1]

1053 **5** *nk* **Verse Of Love**[18] 5348 4-9-2 **83**.................................... TomQueally 5 84+
(David Evans) *stmbld and hmpd s: sn drvn along: hdwy and swtchd to outer over 1f out: styd on ins fnl f* **12/1**

4031 **6** *nk* **Secret Look**[27] 5009 3-9-5 **91**.................................... GrahamGibbons 11 89
(Ed McMahon) *prom: hdwy to ld over 1f out: hdd ins fnl f: fdd* **8/1**

3230 **7** 1 1/4 **Zacynthus (IRE)**[13] 5545 5-9-9 **90** FrankieDettori 4 87
(Kevin Ryan) *in rr: hdwy over 1f out: kpt on: nvr a threat* **13/2**[3]
1310 **8** 1 **Rusty Rocket (IRE)**[48] 4285 4-9-4 **85** FrannyNorton 10 79
(Paul Green) *chsd ldrs: upsides over 1f out: wknd last 150yds* **16/1**
0003 **9** 3 **King Of Eden (IRE)**[14] 5481 7-9-1 **85** (b) NeilFarley(3) 3 71
(Eric Alston) *in rr: hdwy on ins over 1f out: wknd jst ins fnl f* **9/1**
5300 **10** hd **Dr Red Eye**[13] 5545 5-9-9 **93** (p) BillyCray(3) 12 79
(Scott Dixon) *swtchd lft after s: sn w ldr: wknd 1f out: eased ins fnl f* **12/1**
5000 **11** 3 **Yair Hill (IRE)**[13] 5518 5-9-6 **87** (b) JamieSpencer 8 65
(Noel Wilson) *stdd s: hld up in rr: sme hdwy on outer whn hung lft over 1f out: sn wknd* **33/1**
0000 **12** 3 1/4 **Xilerator (IRE)**[13] 5546 6-9-2 **83** (p) RobertHavlin 14 53
(David Nicholls) *chsd ldrs: lost pl over 1f out* **33/1**
0104 **13** 1 1/2 **Snow Bay**[13] 5518 7-8-13 **85** ShirleyTeasdale(5) 9 51
(Paul Midgley) *swtchd lft after s: led: hdd over 1f out: sn lost pl* **20/1**

1m 29.01s (2.51) **Going Correction** +0.275s/f (Good)
WFA 3 from 4yo+ 5lb **13** Ran SP% **119.5**
Speed ratings (Par 107): **96,94,94,92,91 91,90,89,85,85 81,78,76**
toteswingers 1&2 £8.20, 1&3 £25.60, 2&3 £19.00 CSF £44.32 TOTE £6.60: £2.10, £2.50, £5.90; EX 62.00 Trifecta £1131.40 Pool: £3,379.95 - 2.24 winning units..
Owner Middleham Park Racing XI & Partners **Bred** Vincent Dunne **Trained** Great Habton, N Yorks

FOCUS
A fair handicap, run at a strong pace and straightforward for rated around the first two.

5944 CHESTERBET PUTTING PROFITS BACK INTO RACING H'CAP 1m 2f 75y
3:35 (3:36) (Class 3) (0-90,90) 3-Y-O **£7,762** (£2,310; £1,154; £577) **Stalls** High

Form RPR
-302 **1** **Yarroom (IRE)**[22] 5182 3-9-7 **90** DaneO'Neill 1 102+
(Roger Varian) *trckd ldrs: led over 1f out: styd on wl* **7/2**[1]
1512 **2** 1 1/4 **Ningara**[20] 5283 3-9-3 **86** CathyGannon 3 96+
(Andrew Balding) *trckd ldrs: t.k.h: stdd to rr after 2f: pushed along over 4f out: outpcd over 2f out: hdwy and swtchd rt over 1f out: hung lft and styd on to take 2nd last 50yds* **4/1**[2]
5051 **3** 1 3/4 **Phaenomena (IRE)**[26] 5038 3-9-1 **84** TomQueally 4 90
(Lady Cecil) *lost pl after 2f: in rr: pushed along 6f out: hdwy on outer over 2f out: styd on fnl f: tk 4th nr fin* **9/1**
5122 **4** 1/2 **Velox**[27] 5006 3-9-5 **88** FrankieDettori 5 93
(Luca Cumani) *dwlt: in rr: effrt over 2f out: hdwy over 1f out: kpt on to take 4th nr fin* **7/2**[1]
3112 **5** 1 **Sadiq**[36] 4683 3-9-4 **87** (v[1]) SilvestreDeSousa 9 90
(Saeed bin Suroor) *led after 1f: qcknd pce 5f out: hdd over 1f out: wknd clsng stages* **6/1**[3]
12 **6** hd **Mulakim**[43] 4452 3-9-7 **90** RobertHavlin 7 93
(Saeed bin Suroor) *dwlt: swtchd lft after s: hld up in rr: drvn 4f out: kpt on fnl f* **16/1**
2311 **7** nk **Rocket Ronnie (IRE)**[15] 5425 3-8-8 **84** JordanNason(7) 8 87
(David Nicholls) *fast away: led 1f: trckd ldrs: t.k.h: edgd lft and wknd jst ins fnl f* **16/1**
5211 **8** 1 3/4 **Topamichi**[26] 5030 3-8-7 **76** MartinLane 2 75
(Mark H Tompkins) *trckd ldrs: t.k.h: wknd jst ins fnl f* **9/1**
1240 **9** 2 3/4 **Pitchoun (IRE)**[27] 4984 3-9-5 **88** FrannyNorton 6 82
(Mark Johnston) *chsd ldrs: nt clr run over 1f out: wknd and eased fnl f* **22/1**

2m 13.38s (2.18) **Going Correction** +0.325s/f (Good) **9** Ran SP% **114.8**
Speed ratings (Par 104): **104,103,101,101,100 100,100,98,96**
toteswingers 1&2 £4.30, 1&3 £8.20, 2&3 £9.00 CSF £17.42 CT £114.71 TOTE £4.80: £1.40, £1.90, £4.40; EX 23.40 Trifecta £132.80 Pool: £3,817.59 - 21.55 winning units..
Owner Sheikh Ahmed Al Maktoum **Bred** Darley **Trained** Newmarket, Suffolk

FOCUS
A good-quality 3-y-o handicap, dominated by some progressive sorts, and a case for rating the race a little higher.

5945 CHESTERSPORT IN ASSOCIATION WITH STAN JAMES NURSERY H'CAP 7f 2y
4:05 (4:05) (Class 3) (0-95,87) 2-Y-O **£7,115** (£2,117; £1,058; £529) **Stalls** Low

Form RPR
123 **1** **Nezar (IRE)**[8] 5679 2-9-1 **81** FrankieDettori 8 88+
(William Haggas) *swtchd lft after s: hld up in rr: hdwy on outside over 2f out: hung bdly lft over 1f out: led jst ins fnl f: drvn out* **8/13**[1]
4210 **2** 1 1/4 **Party Ruler (IRE)**[8] 5679 2-9-1 **81** RichardKingscote 3 83
(Tom Dascombe) *led: hdd jst ins fnl f: styd on same pce* **10/1**
5522 **3** 2 **Our Gabrial (IRE)**[33] 4802 2-8-8 **74** SilvestreDeSousa 7 72
(Richard Fahey) *mid-div: drvn over 3f out: chsng ldrs whn hmpd over 1f out: swtchd lft: styd on ins fnl f* **7/1**[2]
023 **4** 1 **Intermath (IRE)**[13] 5524 2-9-5 **85** TomQueally 4 79
(David Evans) *chsd ldrs: outpcd over 2f out: kpt on ins fnl f* **9/1**[3]
634 **5** 1/2 **Hulcolt (IRE)**[18] 5338 2-8-7 **73** RobertHavlin 1 66
(Garry Moss) *w ldr: hmpd over 1f out: one pce* **20/1**
2332 **6** 2 **Split Rock**[21] 5235 2-8-12 **78** FrannyNorton 6 66
(Mark Johnston) *chsd ldrs: drvn over 4f out: hmpd over 1f out: swtchd rt jst ins fnl f: kpt on* **12/1**
1056 **7** nk **Know Your Name**[26] 5029 2-8-8 **74** CathyGannon 2 61
(David Evans) *mid-div: drvn over 2f out: sn outpcd: kpt on ins fnl f: nvr a factor* **20/1**

1m 29.75s (3.25) **Going Correction** +0.375s/f (Good) **7** Ran SP% **110.7**
Speed ratings (Par 98): **96,94,92,91,90 88,87**
toteswingers 1&2 £2.00, 1&3 £2.40, 2&3 £4.10 CSF £7.12 CT £21.71 TOTE £1.30: £1.10, £5.00; EX 5.90 Trifecta £27.40 Pool: £1,708.19 - 46.67 winning units..
Owner Saleh Al Homaizi & Imad Al Sagar **Bred** Edgeridge Ltd And Glenvale Stud **Trained** Newmarket, Suffolk

FOCUS
A modest nursery in which the winner did not need to replicate his sales race form to score.

5946 CHESTERBET SUPPORTS THE SPORT H'CAP 1m 7f 195y
4:40 (4:41) (Class 3) (0-95,90) 3-Y-O+ **£7,762** (£2,310; £1,154; £577) **Stalls** Low

Form RPR
1534 **1** **Statutory (IRE)**[14] 5475 3-9-0 **90** FrannyNorton 5 104+
(Mark Johnston) *trckd ldrs on outer: led 3f out: drvn clr over 1f out: won gng rt away* **9/4**[1]
0266 **2** 9 **Moidore**[34] 4782 4-9-13 **89** MichaelO'Connell 7 92
(John Quinn) *led: hdd 3f out: outpcd and 4th over 1f out: swtchd rt: rallied to take 2nd nr fin* **9/2**[2]
223 **3** 3/4 **Twelve Strings (IRE)**[63] 3765 4-9-6 **82** (p) JamieSpencer 4 84
(Brian Ellison) *chsd ldrs: drvn 6f out: kpt on and 3rd over 1f out: chsd wnr 1f out: one pce* **5/1**[3]
1110 **4** 1/2 **Kashgar**[29] 4913 4-8-7 **76** DanielMuscutt(7) 8 77
(Bernard Llewellyn) *trckd ldrs: effrt over 3f out: 2nd 2f out: one pce* **16/1**
0050 **5** 3/4 **Softsong (FR)**[20] 5256 5-9-11 **87** ChrisCatlin 3 87
(Philip Hobbs) *hld up in rr: effrt 4f out: kpt on fnl f: nvr a factor* **10/1**
2211 **6** hd **Zenafire**[26] 5031 4-9-1 **77** (p) PaulQuinn 6 77
(Andrew Hollinshead) *t.k.h in rr: effrt on outer 3f out: kpt on fnl f: no threat* **11/2**
1033 **7** 101 **Sir Bedivere (IRE)**[14] 5475 4-9-10 **86** (t) FrankieDettori 1
(Brian Meehan) *trckd ldr: drvn 4f out: lost pl over 2f out: sn bhd and heavily eased: virtually p.u* **5/1**[3]

3m 31.61s (3.61) **Going Correction** +0.425s/f (Yiel)
WFA 3 from 4yo+ 14lb **7** Ran SP% **112.6**
Speed ratings (Par 107): **107,102,102,101,101 101,**
toteswingers 1&2 £2.70, 1&3 £3.20, 2&3 £4.30 CSF £12.11 CT £44.07 TOTE £3.60: £2.90, £2.20; EX 16.20 Trifecta £59.00 Pool: £3,125.26 - 39.71 winning units..
Owner Sheikh Hamdan Bin Mohammed Al Maktoum **Bred** Darley **Trained** Middleham Moor, N Yorks
■ Stewards' Enquiry : Michael O'Connell two-day ban: excessive use (13 Sep & 15 Sep)

FOCUS
A fair staying handicap and an impressive winner. The third was below form and the fourth helps with perspective.

5947 CHESTERBET H'CAP (FOR GENTLEMAN AMATEUR RIDERS) 7f 122y
5:15 (5:16) (Class 4) (0-80,79) 3-Y-O+ **£6,239** (£1,935; £967; £484) **Stalls** Low

Form RPR
0052 **1** **Piceno (IRE)**[2] 5899 5-10-1 **66** (p) MrKLocking(7) 6 75
(Scott Dixon) *in tch: effrt over 2f out: 3rd over 1f out: styd on to ld last 75yds* **11/1**
3013 **2** 1 **Ralphy Boy (IRE)**[9] 5637 4-10-7 **65** MrWHogg 7 72
(Alistair Whillans) *led: hdd ins fnl f: no ex* **9/1**
6630 **3** nk **Barwick**[28] 4957 5-10-11 **74** MrCSmith(5) 3 80
(Mark H Tompkins) *in rr: hdwy on outside over 1f out: styd on to take 2nd nr fin* **14/1**
6111 **4** 1 1/4 **Dream Walker (FR)**[23] 5138 4-11-0 **77** MrHAABannister(5) 8 80
(Brian Ellison) *chsd ldrs on outer: 2nd over 1f out: kpt on same pce* **5/2**[1]
4225 **5** nse **My Single Malt (IRE)**[23] 5138 5-10-7 **72** (p) MrKWood(7) 4 75
(Julie Camacho) *mid-div: hdwy and edgd lft over 1f out: one pce* **7/1**[2]
2362 **6** 1 1/4 **Silvas Romana (IRE)**[15] 5430 4-10-11 **69** MrSWalker 12 69
(Mark Brisbourne) *carried lft s: in rr: hdwy on outer over 1f out: hung lft and kpt on fnl f* **8/1**[3]
0204 **7** 1 1/4 **Capitol Gain (IRE)**[25] 5065 4-10-1 **66** MrORJSangster(7) 14 63
(Brian Meehan) *swtchd lft s: detached in last: hdwy 2f out: styd on ins fnl f* **33/1**
0605 **8** 3 3/4 **Viva Ronaldo (IRE)**[72] 3464 7-10-2 **65** MrTHamilton(5) 9 53
(Richard Fahey) *chsd ldrs on outer: lost pl 2f out* **20/1**
4250 **9** 2 **See Clearly**[11] 5583 4-10-4 **67** (p) MrWEasterby(5) 5 50
(Tim Easterby) *chsd ldrs: wkng whn crowded over 1f out* **25/1**
0020 **10** 3 **One Scoop Or Two**[26] 5026 7-11-1 **73** (v) MrRossBirkett 1 49
(Andrew Hollinshead) *swvd rt s: mid-div: hdwy over 3f out: drvn and wknd over 1f out* **8/1**[3]
0-00 **11** nk **Kyllachy Star**[31] 4859 7-11-1 **73** MrJHamilton 10 48
(Richard Fahey) *mid-div: lost pl over 3f out* **7/1**[2]
1000 **12** 9 **Ferdy (IRE)**[10] 5613 4-10-7 **70** MrRColley(5) 2 24
(Paul Green) *trckd ldrs: t.k.h: lost pl 2f out: sn bhd* **10/1**

1m 37.33s (3.53) **Going Correction** +0.475s/f (Yiel) **12** Ran SP% **121.4**
Speed ratings (Par 105): **101,100,99,98,98 97,95,92,90,87 86,77**
toteswingers 1&2 £14.30, 1&3 £23.00, 2&3 £29.10 CSF £106.43 CT £1413.67 TOTE £13.50: £3.30, £3.60, £4.30; EX 86.70 Trifecta £1550.60 Part won. Pool: £2,067.52 - 0.65 winning units..

Owner Ontoawinner 4 **Bred** Miss Wendy Fox **Trained** Babworth, Notts
■ Stewards' Enquiry : Mr O R J Sangster two-day ban: careless riding (tbc)
Mr W Hogg two-day ban: excessive use (tbc)

FOCUS
A moderate handicap, confined to gentleman amateur riders. The form looks pretty straightforward.
T/Jkpt: £5,916.60 to a £1 stake. Pool: £25,000.00 - 3.00 winning units T/Plt: £146.40 to a £1 stake. Pool: £80,368.60 - 400.58 winning units T/Qpdt: £9.70 to a £1 stake. Pool: £5,811.32 - 440.34 winning units WG

5442 SALISBURY (R-H)
Friday, August 30

OFFICIAL GOING: Good to firm (good in places; 9.0)
Rail 16ft off permanent rail on far side of straight.
Wind: Virtually nil Weather: Mainly sunny with rain from 7.30

5948 4COM PLC LADY RIDERS' H'CAP (FOR LADY AMATEUR RIDERS) 1m
4:30 (4:31) (Class 5) (0-70,76) 3-Y-O+ **£2,807** (£870; £435; £217) **Stalls** Centre

Form RPR
403 **1** **Mahadee (IRE)**[16] 5387 8-10-0 **66** (b) MissCBoxall(3) 6 80
(Ed de Giles) *little slowly away: towards rr: hdwy whn nt clr run 3f out tl swtchd to rails wl over 1f out: r.o strly to ld ent fnl f: drew clr: comf* **9/2**[2]
3351 **2** 7 **Jewelled**[10] 5605 7-10-13 **76** 6ex (v) MrsCBartley 10 74
(Lady Herries) *mid-div: smooth hdwy in centre fr over 2f out: led wl over 1f out: rdn and hdd ent fnl f: nt pce of wnr* **4/1**[1]
3453 **3** 3/4 **Takitwo**[13] 5525 10-9-7 **56** MissCWalton 12 52
(Geoffrey Deacon) *prom tl rdn over 2f out: kpt chsng ldrs: styd on ins fnl f to regain 3rd fnl 100yds* **12/1**
0550 **4** 1/2 **Space War**[25] 5051 6-10-1 **69** (t) AnnaHesketh(5) 13 64
(Michael Easterby) *wnt to s early: slowly away: sn mid-div: rdn 3f out: no imp tl r.o ins fnl f: wnt 4th fnl 75yds* **8/1**
3426 **5** 2 3/4 **Lutine Charlie (IRE)**[10] 5622 6-10-0 **63** MissRachelKing 7 52
(Pat Eddery) *led tl rdn wl over 1f out: no ex ins fnl f* **16/1**
/400 **6** 1/2 **Kilburn**[18] 5346 9-9-13 **62** (p) MissZoeLilly 1 50
(Alastair Lidderdale) *wnt to s early: mid-div: pushed along whn dropped to last 3f out: swtchd to stands' side sn after: plenty to do but r.o wl ent fnl f: clsng wl at fin* **25/1**
0640 **7** 1 1/4 **Saint Irene**[22] 5191 4-9-7 **59** MissAliceMills(3) 8 44
(Michael Blanshard) *nvr bttr than mid-div* **12/1**
004 **8** 1 **Uncle Dermot (IRE)**[25] 5063 5-9-11 **65** MissJenniferPowell(5) 11 47
(Brendan Powell) *v awkwardly away: bhd: stdy hdwy whn swtchd to centre fr over 2f out: no further imp fnl f* **8/1**
3264 **9** 1 1/2 **Delightful Sleep**[4] 5816 5-9-6 **60** MissHDoyle(5) 4 39
(David Evans) *s.i.s: mid-div: pushed along over 3f out: nvr any imp: wknd fnl f* **11/2**[3]

0005 **10** 2 1/2 **Rapid Water**[22] 5172 7-8-13 **51** oh6..................(p) MissJoannaMason(3) 2 24
(Pat Eddery) *s.i.s: sn trcking ldrs: wnt 2nd over 3f out: rdn and ev ch over 2f out tl over 1f out: wknd ent fnl f* **25/1**

2605 **11** 1/2 **Shifting Star (IRE)**[18] 5346 8-10-3 **66**..........................(vt) MissADeniel 14 38
(John Bridger) *trckd ldrs: rdn over 2f out: sn wknd* **12/1**

0304 **12** 4 1/2 **Silver Marizah (IRE)**[11] 5586 4-8-9 **51** oh6..........(v1) MissRBIngram(7) 5 13
(Roger Ingram) *prom: rdn over 3f out: wknd 2f out* **40/1**

1m 43.23s (-0.27) **Going Correction** +0.05s/f (Good) **12** Ran SP% **114.9**
Speed ratings (Par 103): **103,96,95,94,92 91,90,89,87,85 84,80**
toteswingers 1&2 £4.20, 1&3 £12.80, 2&3 £7.70 CSF £21.53 CT £204.03 TOTE £5.00: £1.60, £1.30, £4.60; EX 19.20 Trifecta £293.30 Pool: £2,028.40 - 5.18 winning units..
Owner 2 1/2 - 3 1/2 Club **Bred** Darley **Trained** Ledbury, H'fords

FOCUS
There was a temporary rail up 16feet from the permanent far rail on the straight course. The leaders looked to go a bit too quickly. The winner is rated in line with his turf best in the past year.

5949 BATHWICK TYRES MAIDEN AUCTION STKS (DIV I) 6f
5:10 (5:11) (Class 5) 2-Y-O **£2,911** (£866; £432; £216) **Stalls** Low

Form RPR

0 **1** **Arranger (IRE)**[30] 4877 2-8-11 0.................................. JimCrowley 2 77+
(Richard Hannon) *trckd ldr: swtchd off rails jst over 2f out: led over 1f out: r.o wl: rdn out* **3/1**[2]

0 **2** 2 **Our Duchess (IRE)**[15] 5443 2-8-6 0.......................... MickaelBarzalona 1 65+
(Richard Hannon) *in tch: rdn whn outpcd over 3f out: hdwy over 1f out: kpt on to go 2nd ins fnl f but a being hld* **15/2**[3]

2 **3** 3/4 **Tides Reach (IRE)**[16] 5385 2-8-6 0.................................... LukeMorris 6 63+
(Roger Charlton) *in tch: rdn whn outpcd over 3f out: prog jst over 1f out: r.o to go 3rd ins fnl f* **5/6**[1]

4 3/4 **Tanojin (IRE)** 2-8-8 0... MartinHarley 7 62
(Mick Channon) *s.i.s: sn in tch: rdn to chse ldrs over 2f out: kpt on but nt gng pce to chal fnl f* **14/1**

5 2 3/4 **Desert Ace (IRE)** 2-9-2 0.. SteveDrowne 3 62
(Clive Cox) *trckd ldr: rdn and ev ch 2f out: sn hung lft: no ex fnl f* **14/1**

0 **6** hd **Dream Impossible (IRE)**[15] 5442 2-8-8 0 ow2..................... JohnFahy 4 53
(Peter Makin) *sn outpcd in last: stl there tl r.o ins fnl f: fin wl* **50/1**

6 **7** 1 1/4 **Katja**[32] 4827 2-8-6 0.. PaulHanagan 8 47
(J W Hills) *sn led: rdn and hdd over 1f out: wknd fnl f* **20/1**

8 8 **Smidgen (IRE)** 2-8-11 0... LiamKeniry 9 26
(Ed de Giles) *s.i.s: hld up in last pair: effrt to cl over 2f out: sn hung lft: wknd whn rchd stands' side rail ent fnl f* **18/1**

1m 15.56s (0.76) **Going Correction** +0.05s/f (Good) **8** Ran SP% **116.6**
Speed ratings (Par 94): **96,93,92,91,87 87,85,75**
toteswingers 1&2 £3.70, 1&3 £1.40, 2&3 £2.50 CSF £26.30 TOTE £4.00: £1.10, £2.30, £1.10; EX 20.60 Trifecta £45.40 Pool: £2,347.77 - 38.75 winning units..
Owner Mrs J Wood **Bred** Tally-Ho Stud **Trained** East Everleigh, Wilts

FOCUS
The first division of a maiden auction event and an interesting little race. Hand-timed sectionals, taken at the path over 3f out, showed the pace was around half a second faster than the other leg to that point, and the final time was an impressive 1.42 seconds quicker. At the start of the day Richard Hannon had a 29% strike-rate with second-time-out juveniles in 2013, compared with 16% with newcomers, and here he had the one-two with a couple of fillies who had the benefit of a previous run. Not the easiest race to set a level for, but the race average is pretty strong and the winner looks value for a bit more.

5950 BATHWICK TYRES MAIDEN AUCTION STKS (DIV II) 6f
5:45 (5:46) (Class 5) 2-Y-O **£2,911** (£866; £432; £216) **Stalls** Low

Form RPR

4 **1** **Go For Broke**[19] 5307 2-8-11 0... JimCrowley 5 71+
(Richard Hannon) *trckd ldr: led 2f out: sn rdn: a holding on fnl f: r.o wl* **8/11**[1]

2 3/4 **High Accolade** 2-8-11 0.. AndreaAtzeni 2 69+
(Roger Varian) *trckd ldrs: rdn whn sltly hmpd ent fnl f: swtchd rt: kpt on but a being hld by wnr* **4/1**[2]

3 nk **Marmarus** 2-8-11 0.. SteveDrowne 9 68+
(Clive Cox) *in rr running green early: hdwy whn short of room 2f out: running on whn short of room again ent fnl f: fin strly to snatch 3rd towards fin* **12/1**

5 **4** 3/4 **Monte Viso**[28] 4937 2-8-6 0.................................. MichaelJMMurphy(5) 4 65
(Stuart Kittow) *t.k.h early in tch: rdn jst over 2f out: sn chsng ldrs: kpt on same pce fnl f* **8/1**[3]

00 **5** nk **Ambria's Fury (IRE)**[14] 5472 2-8-9 0............................. SamHitchcott 8 62
(Mick Channon) *s.i.s: mid-div: rdn and prog over 2f out: chsd ldrs over 1f out: kpt on same pce fnl f* **14/1**

0 **6** 1 **Fisher Lane**[9] 5635 2-8-8 0.. CharlesBishop(3) 7 61
(Olly Stevens) *trckd ldr: hanging lft 1st f: rdn and ch fr 2f out: fdd fnl 120yds* **14/1**

7 2 3/4 **Mishnah** 2-8-7 0 ow3.. JohnFahy 6 48
(John Holt) *in last pair: pushed along over 3f out: short-lived effrt 2f out: wknd ent fnl f* **40/1**

00 **8** 8 **Khloe**[15] 5442 2-8-6 0.. LukeMorris 3 22
(Michael Blanshard) *racd keenly w awkward hd-carriage: led tl 2f out: sn wknd* **33/1**

1m 16.98s (2.18) **Going Correction** +0.05s/f (Good) **8** Ran SP% **115.4**
Speed ratings (Par 94): **87,86,85,84,84 82,79,68**
toteswingers 1&2 £1.90, 1&3 £3.80, 2&3 £5.10 CSF £3.88 TOTE £1.70: £1.10, £1.50, £3.50; EX 5.60 Trifecta £21.00 Pool: £2,169.00 - 77.13 winning units..
Owner Lady Whent **Bred** Raffin Bloodstock **Trained** East Everleigh, Wilts

FOCUS
Another second-time-out 2-y-o winner for Richard Hannon, who had a one-two with such types in the first leg. The time was 1.42 seconds slower than the other division. The field was compressed and rated cautiously with that in mind.

5951 BATHWICK TYRES NURSERY H'CAP 1m
6:15 (6:15) (Class 5) (0-75,75) 2-Y-O **£2,911** (£866; £432; £216) **Stalls** Centre

Form RPR

021 **1** **Anglophile**[23] 5122 2-9-6 **74**.................................... MickaelBarzalona 3 81+
(Charlie Appleby) *trckd ldrs: pushed along whn sltly outpcd and lost position over 3f out: hdwy over 2f out: rdn to ld over 1f out: kpt on fnl f: a holding on: pushed out* **7/4**[1]

320 **2** 3/4 **Aqlaam Vision**[30] 4877 2-9-3 **71**................................. FrederikTylicki 10 75
(Clive Brittain) *travelled wl: trckd ldrs: led over 3f out: rdn 2f out: sn hdd: kpt on ins fnl f but a being hld* **11/2**

3312 **3** 2 **Ocean Storm (IRE)**[15] 5424 2-9-7 **75**............................... JimCrowley 1 75
(James Tate) *trckd ldrs: rdn over 2f out: kpt on fnl f but nt pce to chal* **5/1**[3]

6401 **4** 1 **Lady Marl**[25] 5068 2-8-10 **64**.. ShaneKelly 4 62
(Gary Moore) *little slowly away: in last trio: hdwy over 2f out: sn rdn: abt to chal for hld 3rd whn whipped arnd hd by rivals whip ent fnl f: kpt on same pce after* **9/1**

0062 **5** 1/2 **Rising Dawn (IRE)**[18] 5347 2-8-10 **64**............................. RichardHughes 2 61
(Richard Hannon) *hld up in last pair: pushed along for prog but nvr clrest of runs fr over 2f out: swtchd lft and rt but nvr able to get on terms: kpt on towards fin* **9/2**[2]

615 **6** 1 **Hedge End (IRE)**[105] 2414 2-8-13 **67**.................................. PatDobbs 6 60+
(Richard Hannon) *hld up in last pair: sltly outpcd and detached over 3f out: styd on again fr over 1f out but nvr any threat* **20/1**

006 **7** 2 1/2 **My My My Diliza**[36] 4668 2-8-6 **60**................................. AndreaAtzeni 5 47
(J S Moore) *mid-div: rdn 3f out: wknd jst over 1f out* **40/1**

3056 **8** 2 1/4 **Khee Society**[18] 5347 2-8-9 **63**... LukeMorris 7 45
(David Evans) *led tl over 3f out: sn rdn: wknd over 1f out* **14/1**

5526 **9** hd **Mawzoona**[16] 5400 2-9-0 **68**... MartinHarley 9 50
(Mick Channon) *trckd ldr: rdn over 2f out: wknd ent fnl f* **25/1**

1m 44.21s (0.71) **Going Correction** +0.05s/f (Good) **9** Ran SP% **114.3**
Speed ratings (Par 94): **98,97,95,94,93 92,90,88,87**
toteswingers 1&2 £9.30, 1&3 £3.00, 2&3 £5.20 CSF £11.10 CT £40.21 TOTE £2.80: £1.40, £2.40, £1.50; EX 12.60 Trifecta £51.80 Pool: £2,297.06 - 33.22 winning units..
Owner Godolphin **Bred** Darley **Trained** Newmarket, Suffolk
■ Stewards' Enquiry : Jim Crowley one-day ban: careless riding (13 Sep)

FOCUS
Probably a pretty fair nursery for the grade. The winner scored fluently and the form should be reasonably good.

5952 WEATHERBYS BANK STONEHENGE STKS (LISTED RACE) 1m
6:45 (6:45) (Class 1) 2-Y-O **£15,595** (£5,912; £2,959; £1,474) **Stalls** Centre

Form RPR

131 **1** **Washaar (IRE)**[34] 4747 2-9-2 104.................................... PaulHanagan 1 96+
(Richard Hannon) *t.k.h trcking ldr: settled after 2f: swtchd off rails jst over 4f out: led 3f out: sn hrd rdn and narrowly hdd: rallied gamely u.str.p to ld over 1f out: drifted lft fnl 120yds: kpt on: drvn rt out* **2/5**[1]

5143 **2** 1/2 **Cool Bahamian (IRE)**[26] 5028 2-8-13 87..............................[1] JohnFahy 5 92
(Eve Johnson Houghton) *hmpd leaving stalls: racd in 4th: hdwy 2f out: sn rdn: mounted str chal jst ins fnl f: kpt on: hld nring fin* **10/1**

2431 **3** 1 1/2 **Dancealot**[13] 5536 2-8-8 81... FrederikTylicki 4 83
(Clive Brittain) *wnt lft s: trckd ldng pair: jnd ldrs 3f out: led over 2f out: sn hrd rdn: hdd over 1f out: ev ch ins fnl f: hld in cl 3rd whn squeezed out fnl 50yds* **5/1**[2]

6211 **4** 25 **Chinese Jade**[21] 5242 2-8-13 78....................................(p) LukeMorris 3 28
(Sir Mark Prescott Bt) *racd keenly: led tl rdn 3f out: sn hld: wknd over 1f out: eased ins fnl f* **15/2**[3]

1m 43.62s (0.12) **Going Correction** +0.05s/f (Good) **4** Ran SP% **109.0**
Speed ratings (Par 102): **101,100,99,74**
CSF £5.12 TOTE £1.20; EX 5.10 Trifecta £12.70 Pool: £1,034.37 - 61.01 winning units..
Owner Hamdan Al Maktoum **Bred** Gerard Corry & Cristian Healy **Trained** East Everleigh, Wilts
■ Stewards' Enquiry : Paul Hanagan one-day ban: careless riding (13 Sep)
John Fahy two-day ban: excessive use (Sep 13,15)

FOCUS
A disappointing turnout for this Listed contest and the winner, who had upwards of 12lb in hand on RPRs, even with his 3lb penalty for winning at the same level last time, made harder work of it than expected. However, hand-timed sectionals, taken at the path after halfway, show the pace was around two seconds faster to that point than the earlier nursery, and they came home slower, with the final time only 0.59 seconds quicker than the race won by Anglophile. A modest contest for the grade with the odds-on winner below par in success.

5953 PARTY CONTINUES AT CHAPEL NIGHTCLUB H'CAP 1m 4f
7:15 (7:15) (Class 4) (0-85,84) 3-Y-O **£4,851** (£1,443; £721; £360) **Stalls** High

Form RPR

0-11 **1** **Plutocracy (IRE)**[102] 2500 3-9-5 **82**................................ TedDurcan 6 96+
(David Lanigan) *in tch: pushed along and hdwy over 2f out: shkn up to ld sn after: styd on wl and in command fnl f: comf* **7/2**[2]

5225 **2** 1 3/4 **Lady Pimpernel**[15] 5448 3-9-3 **80**.................................... PaulHanagan 4 90
(Henry Candy) *led: upped tempo over 3f out: sn rdn: hdd 2f out: sn hld by wnr: styd on* **7/2**[2]

2122 **3** 2 3/4 **Duke Of Perth**[27] 4980 3-9-7 **84**.. KierenFallon 7 90
(Luca Cumani) *t.k.h early: trckd ldrs: rdn and ev ch 2f out: sn hld: styd on same pce fnl f* **12/5**[1]

3120 **4** 1 1/4 **Royal Signaller**[27] 4984 3-9-3 **80**....................................(p) PatDobbs 2 84
(Amanda Perrett) *trckd ldrs: nudged along over 4f out: rdn 3f out: styd on same pce fnl 2f* **9/2**[3]

2222 **5** 1 **Astrum**[30] 4899 3-8-12 **75**.. AndreaAtzeni 3 77
(Rod Millman) *trckd ldr: rdn 3f out: styd on same pce fr 2f out tl no ex fnl 120yds* **15/2**

5506 **6** 12 **Ronaldinho (IRE)**[13] 5534 3-9-4 **81**.............................. RichardHughes 5 64
(Richard Hannon) *hld up last: swtchd wd over 5f out: effrt but little imp 3f out: wknd over 1f out* **14/1**

1344 **7** 27 **Khelac**[26] 5032 3-8-0 **66**..(v1) RyanPowell(3) 1
(Philip Hide) *t.k.h early: in tch: dropped to joint last 5f out: struggling 4f out: bhd fr over 2f out: t.o* **25/1**

2m 36.53s (-1.47) **Going Correction** +0.05s/f (Good) **7** Ran SP% **114.3**
Speed ratings (Par 102): **106,104,103,102,101 93,75**
toteswingers 1&2 £5.20, 1&3 £1.40, 2&3 £2.50 CSF £16.15 CT £33.90 TOTE £4.10: £2.20, £2.40; EX 21.80 Trifecta £48.60 Pool: £1,317.11 - 20.28 winning units..
Owner B E Nielsen **Bred** Bjorn Nielsen **Trained** Upper Lambourn, Berks

FOCUS
A fair handicap run at what looked a reasonable enough pace. The runner-up sets the level to his sound recent form.

5954 WESTOVER GROUP H'CAP 1m 6f 21y
7:45 (7:45) (Class 5) (0-75,74) 3-Y-O+ **£2,911** (£866; £432; £216)

Form RPR

2040 **1** **Laser Blazer**[22] 5168 5-10-0 **70**.....................................(p) JimCrowley 11 78
(Jeremy Gask) *detached last: racing keenly whn latched onto main gp after 3f: swtchd out over 4f out: pushed along and stdy prog fr over 3f out: drvn 2f out: edgd rt but styd on strly to ld jst ins fnl f* **33/1**

0320 **2** 1 1/4 **Honourable Knight (IRE)**[21] 5231 5-9-7 **63**..................... LiamKeniry 4 69
(Mark Usher) *in tch: rdn and stdy prog fr 3f out: clsd on ldr over 2f out: disp ld over 1f out tl jst ins fnl f: styd on* **20/1**

0631 **3** nse **Don Padeja**[10] 5612 3-9-6 **74** 6ex.................................... AndreaAtzeni 8 80
(Luca Cumani) *t.k.h in mid-div: hdwy over 3f out: sn rdn: clsd on ldr in disp 2nd over 2f out: styd on fnl f* **5/6**[1]

The Form Book Flat, Raceform Ltd, Compton, RG20 6NL.

5603 **4** *2* **Mick Duggan**[24] 5099 3-8-13 **67**.. LukeMorris 2 70
(Simon Hodgson) *mid-div: hdwy over 3f out: sn rdn: clsd on clr ldr in disp 2nd fr over 2f out: disp ld over 1f out tl jst ins fnl f: no ex fnl 75yds* **12/1**

2234 **5** *½* **Guards Chapel**[15] 4754 5-9-12 **68**..............................(v) GeorgeBaker 10 70
(Gary Moore) *hld up towards rr: pushed along 4f out: sme prog 3f out: styd on fr over 1f out but nvr threatened* **10/1**[3]

0405 **6** *hd* **Perfect Spell**[28] 4961 3-8-13 **67**...................................(p) DavidProbert 1 69
(Andrew Balding) *trckd ldr: pushed along whn ldr kicked 4f out: clsd on ldr in disp 2nd over 2f out: no ex ins fnl f* **9/2**[2]

6212 **7** *1 ½* **Green To Gold (IRE)**[16] 5409 8-10-0 **70**..................(b) RichardHughes 5 70
(Don Cantillon) *led: kicked clr 4f out: rdn 3f out: hdd over 1f out: fdd fnl f* **10/1**[3]

500- **8** *5* **Shot In The Dark (IRE)**[51] 7811 4-9-3 **59**.........................(t) PatDobbs 7 52
(Jonathan Geake) *trckd ldrs: rdn wl over 3f out: sn btn* **50/1**

040 **9** *27* **Sammyman**[79] 3209 6-9-4 **60**.. KierenFallon 3 15
(Michael Blanshard) *trckd ldrs tl dropped to rr qckly 5f out: bhd after: t.o* **14/1**

000- **10** *dist* **Dance With Me (IRE)**[264] 5796 4-9-13 **69**....................[1] SteveDrowne 9
(Jonathan Geake) *racd keenly: hld up in rr of main gp: hdwy to trck ldr over 7f out tl dropped away qckly over 4f out: t.o* **66/1**

3m 6.38s (-1.02) **Going Correction** +0.05s/f (Good)
WFA 3 from 4yo+ 12lb **10** Ran SP% **116.4**
Speed ratings (Par 103): **104,103,103,102,101 101,100,98,82,**
toteswingers 1&2 £47.40, 1&3 £15.20, 2&3 £11.50 CSF £532.99 CT £1187.68 TOTE £40.50: £6.50, £4.10, £1.10; EX 792.40 Trifecta £1331.10 Part won. Pool: £1,774.85 - 0.56 winning units..
Owner Calne Engineering Ltd **Bred** Edward J G Young **Trained** Sutton Veny, Wilts

FOCUS
Perhaps this form shouldn't be taken too literally as it was run in a downpour (rain and watered ground never a good combination) and Laser Blazer, hard to find beforehand, as a starting price of 33-1 suggests, was followed home by a 20-1 shot. The fourth sets the standard judged on his Polytrack form.
T/Plt: £6.40 to a £1 stake. Pool: £44,008.19 - 4,989.86 winning units T/Qpdt: £4.80 to a £1 stake. Pool: £4,633.10 - 705.20 winning units TM

5186 SANDOWN (R-H)
Friday, August 30

OFFICIAL GOING: Good (good to firm in places; sprint course 8.2, round course 8.3)
Far rail of sprint track in 3yds. Round course rail out 4yds from 7f to 2.5f, with drop-in at that point increasing distances on round course by 5yds.
Wind: Light; against Weather: Fine; warm

5955 ORLEANS NURSERY H'CAP 5f 6y
2:20 (2:21) (Class 4) (0-85,91) 2-Y-O **£3,881** (£1,155; £577; £288) **Stalls** Low

Form RPR

211 **1** **Strategical (USA)**[11] 5590 2-9-13 **91** 6ex.................. MickaelBarzalona 4 97+
(Charlie Appleby) *wnt lft s: rcvrd to trck ldng pair after 1f: clsd to ld over 1f out: pushed clr: comf* **11/8**[2]

0233 **2** *2* **Urban Dreamer (IRE)**[12] 5558 2-8-8 **72**......................... AndreaAtzeni 2 70
(Rod Millman) *led against rail: rdn and hdd over 1f out: kpt on but no ch w wnr* **10/1**[3]

3010 **3** *5* **Foxy Clarets (IRE)**[8] 5679 2-8-13 **77**................................ RyanMoore 3 57
(Richard Fahey) *nvr gng wl: hanging lft and last after 1f: rdn into modest 3rd ins fnl f* **1/1**[1]

6104 **4** *4 ½* **Mahlah (IRE)**[20] 5272 2-9-4 **82**.................................... RichardHughes 1 46
(Richard Hannon) *stdd s but jnd ldr after 1f: lost 2nd and wknd over 1f out: eased fnl f* **12/1**

1m 2.07s (0.47) **Going Correction** +0.125s/f (Good) **4** Ran SP% **108.9**
Speed ratings (Par 96): **101,97,89,82**
CSF £12.51 TOTE £2.20; EX 11.80 Trifecta £15.20 Pool: £598.63 - 29.42 winning units..
Owner Godolphin **Bred** Daniel J Burke **Trained** Newmarket, Suffolk

FOCUS
A dry night and the ground was given as good, good to firm in places (GoingStick: Sprint 8.2; Round 8.3). With the favourite running no sort of race this didn't take much winning. The winner looks up to Listed class with the winner rated to his recent level.

5956 EDGELEY PARK HOLIDAY HOMES SURREY H'CAP 5f 6y
2:50 (2:52) (Class 5) (0-75,75) 3-Y-0+ **£3,234** (£962; £481; £240) **Stalls** Low

Form RPR

2062 **1** **Rocket Rob (IRE)**[8] 5673 7-9-10 **75**................................ WilliamBuick 8 87
(Willie Musson) *hld up in last: stl there over 1f out: swtchd out wd and gd prog after: led ins fnl f: sn clr* **5/1**[2]

5423 **2** *2* **The Strig**[7] 5701 6-8-13 **64**..(v) J-PGuillambert 13 69
(Stuart Williams) *settled in last quartet: prog on outer over 1f out: clsng to chal whn wnr swept past jst ins fnl f: styd on to take 2nd* **20/1**

0423 **3** *2* **Macdillon**[15] 5441 7-9-2 **67**...(t) KierenFallon 9 69
(Stuart Kittow) *trckd ldng quartet on outer: nt clr run and lost pl 1f out: styd on to take 3rd nr fin* **8/1**

2412 **4** *1* **Wooden King (IRE)**[5] 5796 8-9-4 **69**.......................... TomMcLaughlin 1 63
(Malcolm Saunders) *racd against rail: led or disp ld: rdn 2f out: hdd and fdd ins fnl f* **7/1**[3]

2621 **5** *hd* **Angel Way (IRE)**[15] 5441 4-9-9 **74**................................... RyanMoore 3 67
(Mike Murphy) *led or disp ld: rdn 2f out: hdd and fdd ins fnl f* **9/4**[1]

332 **6** *1 ¼* **Best Be Careful (IRE)**[17] 5376 5-9-4 **69**.................. RichardHughes 12 58
(Mark Usher) *racd on outer of ldng quartet: fdd jst over 1f out* **16/1**

6140 **7** *hd* **Crimson Queen**[42] 4487 6-9-7 **72**....................................(b) LiamJones 7 60
(Roy Brotherton) *pushed along in last quartet after 2f: gng bttr but in last whn nt clr run fr 1f out: no ch after* **25/1**

01-3 **8** *nk* **Greenery (IRE)**[11] 5585 3-9-4 **71**......................................[1] JamesDoyle 5 67+
(Roger Charlton) *trckd ldng quartet: pushed along 2f out: gng wl enough whn trapped bhd rivals fr jst over 1f out: no ch to rcvr* **10/1**

5102 **9** *nk* **Irish Boy (IRE)**[10] 5620 5-9-3 **68**...............................(tp) SebSanders 6 66+
(Christine Dunnett) *trckd ldng quartet: gng wl whn trapped bhd rivals fr jst over 1f out: no ch to rcvr* **20/1**

1442 **10** *1* **Picansort**[7] 5701 6-8-11 **62**...(b) ShaneKelly 10 44
(Peter Crate) *disp ld to jst ins fnl f: wknd* **14/1**

0466 **11** *nk* **The Wee Chief (IRE)**[18] 5349 7-8-13 **64**.............................. PatDobbs 4 54+
(Jimmy Fox) *hld up in last quartet against rail: nt clr run fr over 1f out: no ch to rcvr* **8/1**

1m 1.61s (0.01) **Going Correction** +0.125s/f (Good)
WFA 3 from 4yo+ 2lb **11** Ran SP% **117.2**
Speed ratings (Par 103): **104,100,97,96,95 93,93,92,92,90 90**
toteswingers 1&2 £34.10, 1&3 £12.60, 2&3 £15.40 CSF £102.83 CT £792.14 TOTE £4.80: £2.00, £7.40, £2.00; EX 132.20 TRIFECTA Not won..
Owner John Searchfield **Bred** Mrs Marita Rogers **Trained** Newmarket, Suffolk

FOCUS
There was a strong, contested lead here, with a line of four out in front. As they predictably weakened, falling back into the faces of those ridden more patiently, there was plenty of trouble in running, and that set things up nicely for the first two, who switched wide for a clear run, having initially been held up in rear. The form cannot be taken totally literally but could rate higher through the runner-up.

5957 BRITISH STALLION STUDS EBF MAIDEN STKS 7f 16y
3:20 (3:23) (Class 5) 2-Y-O **£3,881** (£1,155; £577; £288) **Stalls** Low

Form RPR

1 **Ensuring** 2-9-5 0.. ShaneKelly 1 79+
(James Fanshawe) *trckd ldrs: clsd over 1f out: brought between ldng pair fnl f: pushed into narrow ld last 100yds: shade cosily* **7/1**

5 **2** *nk* **Early Morning (IRE)**[22] 5188 2-9-5 0.............................. JamesDoyle 10 78
(Harry Dunlop) *trckd ldr: led after 2f: pressed and shkn up wl over 1f out: styd on wl but hdd and hld last 100yds* **11/1**

0 **3** *2 ¾* **Irish Tears**[14] 5488 2-9-5 0.. WilliamBuick 7 71
(John Gosden) *trckd ldng pair to 2f out: shkn up and kpt on again fnl f to take 3rd nr fin* **16/1**

4 *nk* **Exchequer (IRE)** 2-9-5 0.. RichardHughes 2 70+
(Richard Hannon) *led 2f: trckd ldr: shkn up to chal again 2f out: rdn and nt qckn 1f out: fdd* **2/1**[1]

5 *1 ½* **Berkeley Vale** 2-9-5 0.. SebSanders 14 66+
(Roger Teal) *rn green in last pair: pushed along more vigorously than most and prog over 2f out: styd on to take 5th wl ins fnl f* **66/1**

6 *1 ¼* **Flag War (GER)** 2-9-5 0.. KierenFallon 6 63
(Saeed bin Suroor) *trckd ldrs: shkn up and nt qckn 2f out: kpt on one pce after* **4/1**[2]

7 *shd* **Maraayill (IRE)** 2-9-5 0... AdamKirby 4 63+
(Marco Botti) *trckd ldrs: wl in tch and pushed along over 1f out: fdd* **5/1**[3]

0 **8** *1 ¼* **Douman (USA)**[7] 5718 2-9-5 0......................................(t) HarryBentley 15 59
(Ed Dunlop) *settled in 8th and sltly off the pce: pushed along over 2f out: lost pl and rdn over 1f out: kpt on again fnl f* **66/1**

9 *3 ¼* **Black Caesar (IRE)** 2-9-5 0... PatDobbs 12 51+
(Richard Hannon) *wl in tch on outer: pushed along over 2f out: wknd over 1f out* **25/1**

10 *¾* **Mind** 2-9-5 0.. PatCosgrave 5 49
(Henry Candy) *rrd jst bef stalls opened and slowly away: a in rr: pushed along and no prog 2f out* **25/1**

11 *hd* **Arable** 2-9-5 0.. WilliamCarson 13 48
(Charles Hills) *dwlt: mostly in last pair: pushed along and no progs over 2f out* **40/1**

12 *nk* **Cape Summit** 2-9-5 0... TedDurcan 3 48
(Ed Dunlop) *dwlt: a wl in rr: pushed along and no prog 2f out* **50/1**

13 *1 ½* **Stampede (IRE)** 2-9-5 0... RyanMoore 9 44
(Sir Michael Stoute) *n.m.r sn after s: a wl in rr: pushed along and no prog 2f out* **9/1**

1m 31.35s (1.85) **Going Correction** +0.05s/f (Good) **13** Ran SP% **121.8**
Speed ratings (Par 94): **91,90,87,87,85 84,83,82,78,77 77,77,75**
toteswingers 1&2 £6.90, 1&3 £18.30, 2&3 £14.20 CSF £78.39 TOTE £10.90: £3.00, £2.70, £4.60; EX 82.40 Trifecta £1060.00 Part won. Pool: £1,413.39 - 0.62 winning units..
Owner Ben CM Wong **Bred** Rabbah Bloodstock Limited **Trained** Newmarket, Suffolk

FOCUS
The pace held up in this maiden and it proved hard to come from behind. Quite a bunched finish suggests this may be one of the weaker recent renewals.

5958 EDGELEY PARK CLASSIC H'CAP 1m 14y
3:55 (3:56) (Class 3) (0-90,90) 3-Y-0
£9,337 (£2,796; £1,398; £699; £349; £175) **Stalls** Low

Form RPR

13-1 **1** **Brownsea Brink**[28] 4957 3-8-13 **82**...................................... PatDobbs 2 92+
(Richard Hannon) *mde all: set mod pce: wound it up fr 2f out: styd on and a holding rivals* **12/1**

2221 **2** *¾* **Thouwra (IRE)**[14] 5495 3-8-13 **82**...................................(p) KierenFallon 3 90
(Saeed bin Suroor) *hld up in tch: shkn up 2f out: prog over 1f out: chsd wnr ins fnl f: styd on but nvr quite able to chal* **15/2**

2-06 **3** *1* **Tobacco Road (IRE)**[7] 5721 3-8-12 **81**........................... PatCosgrave 1 86
(Richard Hannon) *t.k.h: trckd ldng pair: rdn over 2f out: nt qckn over 1f out: styd on ins fnl f* **33/1**

3-11 **4** *nse* **Breden (IRE)**[20] 5287 3-9-4 **87**.. WilliamBuick 8 92
(John Gosden) *hld up in midfield: prog on outer 2f out: rdn to chse wnr jst over 1f out to ins fnl f: one pce* **13/8**[1]

4421 **5** *1* **Gracious George (IRE)**[22] 5187 3-8-8 **77**....................(b[1]) TedDurcan 4 80
(Jimmy Fox) *hld up in last trio in modly run event: tried to make prog on outer fr 2f out: kpt on but nvr able to threaten* **20/1**

2251 **6** *hd* **George Cinq**[30] 4897 3-9-5 **88**.. AdamKirby 7 90
(Michael Bell) *stdd s: hld up in last in modly run event: tried to make prog on outer fr 2f out: kpt on but no ch of threatening* **13/2**[3]

2012 **7** *1 ½* **Regal Silk**[18] 5348 3-8-13 **82**.. JamesDoyle 9 82
(Jeremy Noseda) *chsd wnr: rdn 2f out: lost 2nd and btn jst over 1f out: wknd and eased* **9/1**

12-0 **8** *nk* **Janoub Nibras (IRE)**[13] 5533 3-9-7 **90**......................... JimmyFortune 5 89
(Richard Hannon) *hld up in last trio in modly run event: shkn up and no prog 2f out: wl btn over 1f out* **25/1**

3-15 **9** *nse* **Enobled**[97] 2666 3-9-5 **88**... RyanMoore 6 86
(Sir Michael Stoute) *trckd ldrs: rdn and nt qckn 2f out: lost pl and fdd over 1f out* **4/1**[2]

1m 44.62s (1.32) **Going Correction** +0.05s/f (Good) **9** Ran SP% **112.4**
Speed ratings (Par 104): **95,94,93,93,92 92,90,90,90**
toteswingers 1&2 £12.20, 1&3 £24.20, 2&3 £20.70 CSF £92.83 CT £1911.67 TOTE £12.90: £3.50, £1.70, £6.60; EX 96.20 Trifecta £1297.30 Part won. Pool: £1,729.77 - 0.74 winning units..
Owner The Heffer Syndicate **Bred** Carmel Stud **Trained** East Everleigh, Wilts

FOCUS
The early pace was pretty steady. The runner-up is rated to his pre-race best, while the winner can do better.

5959 SURBITON MAIDEN FILLIES' STKS — 1m 14y
4:25 (4:26) (Class 5) 3-Y-O — **£3,234** (£962; £481; £240) **Stalls** Low

Form — RPR

4 **1** **Electra Spectra**[42] 4495 3-9-0 0 .... KierenFallon 1 79+
(Luca Cumani) *s.s: chsd ldr sn after s tl after 3f: rdn to go 2nd again wl over 2f out: clsd to ld over 1f out: styd on to draw clr fnl f* **8/13**[1]

2 *3 ¾* **Dark Amber** 3-9-0 0 .... SebSanders 3 68
(Brendan Powell) *broke in 2nd but sn hld up in last: prog over 2f out: chsd wnr over 1f out and cl enough: fdd ins fnl f* **10/1**[3]

2434 **3** *3* **Society Pearl (IRE)**[16] 5403 3-9-0 68 .... (b[1]) HarryBentley 4 61
(Charles Hills) *led and untrbld in front: shkn up and hdd over 1f out: immediately caved in* **9/4**[2]

4 *32* **Sultry Lady** 3-8-9 0 .... HarryPoulton(5) 2
(Jamie Poulton) *s.s: plld hrd and chsd ldr after 3f to wl over 2f out: wknd qckly: t.o* **16/1**

1m 46.17s (2.87) **Going Correction** +0.05s/f (Good) **4** Ran SP% **107.7**
Speed ratings (Par 97): **87,83,80,48**
CSF £7.12 TOTE £1.70; EX 4.60 Trifecta £9.90 Pool: £1,751.32 - 132.03 winning units..
Owner Helena Springfield Ltd **Bred** Meon Valley Stud **Trained** Newmarket, Suffolk

FOCUS
A poor maiden for the track and the form looks shaky.

5960 HWFA WILLIAMS H'CAP — 1m 2f 7y
5:00 (5:00) (Class 4) (0-80,80) 3-Y-O — **£4,690** (£1,395; £697; £348) **Stalls** Low

Form — RPR

2310 **1** **Close At Hand**[30] 4878 3-9-2 **75** .... WilliamBuick 8 87+
(John Gosden) *trckd ldr and racd wd early: led wl over 2f out: drvn over 1f out: hrd pressed nr fin: hld on wl* **4/1**[2]

41 **2** *nk* **Alegra**[28] 4968 3-9-6 **79** .... PatCosgrave 4 89+
(Lady Cecil) *trckd ldng trio: rdn to chse wnr 2f out: grad clsd fnl f: nvr quite got there* **5/4**[1]

1-65 **3** *4* **Aussie Lyrics (FR)**[45] 4384 3-9-2 **75** .... JamesDoyle 7 77
(George Baker) *hld up in last pair: rdn and prog to go 3rd over 1f out: edgd rt and no imp on ldng pair* **7/1**

063 **4** *3 ¼* **The Wizard Of Aus (IRE)**[20] 5281 3-8-7 **66** .... DavidProbert 2 62
(Andrew Balding) *chsd ldng pair to 2f out: wkng whn short of room briefly over 1f out* **8/1**

2-00 **5** *1 ¼* **Gilded Frame**[122] 1900 3-8-9 **68** .... HarryBentley 3 62
(Marcus Tregoning) *trckd ldrs in 5th: rdn over 2f out: no prog: wkng whn short of room briefly over 1f out* **20/1**

403 **6** *10* **Legends (IRE)**[23] 5133 3-9-2 **75** .... RyanMoore 6 59
(Sir Michael Stoute) *led to wl over 2f out: sn btn: eased over 1f out* **9/2**[3]

-105 **7** *80* **Barnaby Brook (CAN)**[98] 2641 3-8-10 **69** .... (b[1]) J-PGuillambert 5
(Nick Littmoden) *rdn fr s and tk no interest: t.o fr 1/2-way* **33/1**

2m 8.87s (-1.63) **Going Correction** +0.05s/f (Good) **7** Ran SP% **113.9**
Speed ratings (Par 102): **108,107,104,101,100 92,28**
toteswingers 1&2 £2.70, 1&3 £6.30, 2&3 £1.90 CSF £9.35 CT £32.23 TOTE £3.90: £2.30, £1.20; EX 9.80 Trifecta £47.20 Pool: £1,966.47 - 31.24 winning units..
Owner Normandie Stud Ltd **Bred** Hesmonds Stud Ltd **Trained** Newmarket, Suffolk
■ Stewards' Enquiry : Pat Cosgrave two-day ban: excessive use (13 Sep & 15 Sep)

FOCUS
The two fillies in the line-up came clear here and the form has a sound feel.
T/Plt: £588.60 to a £1 stake. Pool: £64,866.33 - 80.44 winning units T/Qpdt: £71.50 to a £1 stake. Pool: £3,996.05 - 41.35 winning units JN

5897 SOUTHWELL (L-H)
Friday, August 30

OFFICIAL GOING: Standard
Wind: Light; behind Weather: Cloudy with sunny spells

5961 32REDBINGO.COM APPRENTICE H'CAP — 1m (F)
4:20 (4:20) (Class 6) (0-60,60) 3-Y-O+ — **£1,940** (£577; £288; £144) **Stalls** Low

Form — RPR

2000 **1** **Mcconnell (USA)**[23] 5123 8-9-0 **52** .... (b) OisinMurphy(5) 5 61
(Violet M Jordan) *awkward leaving stalls: sn pushed along in rr: hdwy over 4f out: led over 1f out: edgd rt ins fnl f: rdn out* **6/1**[3]

6505 **2** *3* **Marina Ballerina**[22] 5192 5-8-13 **46** oh1 .... (p) RyanClark 7 48
(Roy Bowring) *sn pushed along in rr: outpcd 5f out: hdwy over 1f out: r.o to go 2nd post: nt rch wnr* **16/1**

6532 **3** *shd* **Moe's Place (IRE)**[11] 5594 3-9-2 **60** .... (p) JacobButterfield(5) 4 62
(Kristin Stubbs) *led: rdn: edgd lft and hdd over 1f out: styd on same pce fnl f: lost 2nd post* **6/5**[1]

3336 **4** *3 ¼* **Handsome Stranger (IRE)**[25] 5072 3-9-0 **58** .... TimClark(5) 6 52
(Alan Bailey) *sn pushed along to chse ldrs: rdn over 3f out: styd on same pce fr over 1f out* **7/2**[2]

5050 **5** *3 ½* **Bladewood Girl**[23] 5135 5-9-7 **57** .... (p) DannyBrock(3) 3 43
(J R Jenkins) *chsd ldr: rdn over 2f out: wknd fnl f* **7/1**

6504 **6** *1* **Lexi's Dancer**[10] 5605 3-8-13 **52** .... WilliamTwiston-Davies 8 36
(Ian Williams) *sn pushed along to chse ldrs: rdn 1/2-way: hung lft fr over 2f out tl wknd over 1f out* **6/1**[3]

0060 **7** *32* **Multisure**[2] 5903 3-8-7 **46** oh1 .... (b) JulieBurke 1
(Ruth Carr) *prom tl rdn and wknd over 3f out* **14/1**

1m 43.66s (-0.04) **Going Correction** -0.025s/f (Stan)
WFA 3 from 4yo+ 6lb **7** Ran SP% **121.3**
Speed ratings (Par 101): **99,96,95,92,89 88,56**
toteswingers 1&2 £8.30, 1&3 £1.90, 2&3 £5.60 CSF £95.04 CT £192.46 TOTE £5.80: £3.70, £7.30; EX 69.50 Trifecta £354.30 Pool: £778.67 - 1.64 winning units..
Owner Rakebackmypoker.com **Bred** Hall Et Al Farm **Trained** Moreton Morrell, Warwicks

FOCUS
Exposed performers in a moderate apprentice handicap. The gallop was reasonable and the winner came down the centre. This was his best performance of the year with the third rated in line with his Polytrack form.

5962 32RED.COM MEDIAN AUCTION MAIDEN STKS — 1m (F)
4:55 (4:56) (Class 5) 3-4-Y-O — **£2,587** (£770; £384; £192) **Stalls** Low

Form — RPR

22 **1** **Blighty (IRE)**[29] 4927 3-9-5 0 .... StevieDonohoe 6 78+
(Lady Cecil) *trckd ldrs: wnt 2nd over 3f out: led on bit over 2f out: clr over 1f out: easily* **1/7**[1]

0- **2** *6* **Roger Thorpe**[393] 4746 4-9-8 0 .... RyanClark(3) 4 57
(Deborah Sanderson) *s.i.s: hdwy over 6f out: led over 4f out: rdn and hdd over 2f out: sn outpcd* **40/1**

6 **3** *½* **Pretty Bubbles**[29] 4927 4-9-6 0 .... TonyHamilton 5 51
(J R Jenkins) *prom: rdn over 2f out: styd on same pce* **6/1**[2]

00 **4** *15* **Get Going**[45] 4382 3-9-5 0 .... DougieCostello 7 22
(Hughie Morrison) *sn pushed along and prom: rdn over 4f out: wknd over 3f out* **7/1**[3]

00 **5** *35* **Tarmo (IRE)**[20] 5281 3-9-0 0 .... (b[1]) RobertTart(5) 3
(Marco Botti) *led: pushed along and hdd over 4f out: rdn and wknd over 2f out* **16/1**

- **6** *7* **Truth Hurts** 3-9-5 0 .... JimmyQuinn 2
(Violet M Jordan) *prom: lost pl over 5f out: sn bhd* **7/1**[3]

7 *3 ½* **Bridge To My Heart** 3-8-11 0 .... (t) WilliamTwiston-Davies(3) 8
(Olivia Maylam) *s.i.s: outpcd* **12/1**

0 **8** *¾* **Alfred The Great**[59] 3932 3-8-12 0 .... VictorSantos(7) 1
(Richard Ford) *plld hrd and prom: hung rt and lost pl over 5f out: sn bhd* **25/1**

1m 42.89s (-0.81) **Going Correction** -0.025s/f (Stan)
WFA 3 from 4yo 6lb **8** Ran SP% **146.6**
Speed ratings (Par 103): **103,97,96,81,46 39,36,35**
toteswingers 1&2 £6.20, 1&3 £1.50, 2&3 £19.70 CSF £27.45 TOTE £1.10: £1.02, £15.00, £1.60; EX 23.70 Trifecta £82.00 Pool: £2,859.13 - 26.12 winning units..
Owner Ennismore Racing I **Bred** Ennismore Racing I **Trained** Newmarket, Suffolk

FOCUS
A most uncompetitive maiden and one run at a fair gallop. The very easy winner came down the centre and the race is given a token rating through the second.

5963 32RED CASINO CLAIMING STKS — 7f (F)
5:30 (5:30) (Class 5) 2-Y-O — **£2,587** (£770; £384; £192) **Stalls** Low

Form — RPR

156U **1** **Cascadia (IRE)**[14] 5467 2-8-0 59 .... JoeyHaynes(7) 2 58
(K R Burke) *w ldr tl led over 3f out: rdn over 1f out: r.o: eased nr fin* **14/1**

0562 **2** *2 ¼* **Chilly In Rio (IRE)**[14] 5467 2-8-2 55 ow2 .... (p) OisinMurphy(7) 3 54
(William Muir) *chsd ldrs: sn pushed along: rdn over 2f out: styd on to go 2nd ins fnl f: nt trble wnr* **8/1**[3]

2461 **3** *1 ½* **Limegrove**[11] 5591 2-8-1 65 .... NoelGarbutt(5) 5 47
(David Evans) *trckd ldrs: racd keenly: wnt 2nd over 3f out: rdn over 2f out: styd on same pce ins fnl f* **15/8**[2]

10 **4** *12* **Mr Carbonfootprint**[27] 4988 2-9-4 78 .... TonyHamilton 1 26
(Richard Fahey) *sn led: pushed along and hdd over 3f out: rdn and wknd 2f out* **4/5**[1]

5 *25* **Quick Decision** 2-8-5 0 .... JakePayne(5) 4
(Bill Turner) *sn outpcd* **16/1**

1m 31.67s (1.37) **Going Correction** -0.025s/f (Stan) **5** Ran SP% **114.0**
Speed ratings (Par 94): **91,88,86,73,44**
CSF £106.30 TOTE £14.50: £6.10, £3.20; EX 61.10 Trifecta £97.40 Pool: £2,129.28 - 16.37 winning units..
Owner Mrs Elaine M Burke **Bred** John Wholey **Trained** Middleham Moor, N Yorks

FOCUS
An uncompetitive claimer in which the two market leaders disappointed to varying degrees. The gallop was reasonable and the winner came down the centre. The improved runner-up helps set the level.

5964 £32 BONUS AT 32RED.COM FILLIES' (S) STKS — 5f (F)
6:00 (6:01) (Class 6) 2-Y-O — **£1,940** (£577; £288; £144) **Stalls** High

Form — RPR

0004 **1** **Scarborough (IRE)**[14] 5480 2-8-12 50 .... (p) JimmyQuinn 6 54
(Paul Midgley) *mde all: rdn over 1f out: styd on* **11/8**[1]

405 **2** *1 ¼* **Red Tiger Lily**[11] 5578 2-8-5 40 .... DanielleMooney(7) 5 50
(Nigel Tinkler) *sn pushed along in rr: hdwy 1/2-way: rdn and ev ch over 1f out: styd on same pce ins fnl f* **16/1**

0446 **3** *4 ½* **Dotesy (IRE)**[27] 4990 2-8-12 55 .... DougieCostello 1 33
(John Quinn) *sn pushed along to chse ldrs: rdn and outpcd 1/2-way: rallied over 1f out: styd on same pce fnl f* **5/2**[2]

0042 **4** *3 ¼* **Countess Lupus (IRE)**[21] 5229 2-8-7 45 .... JacobButterfield(5) 7 22
(Kristin Stubbs) *chsd ldrs: rdn 1/2-way: wknd fnl f* **5/2**[2]

310 **5** *4 ½* **Music Stop**[21] 5229 2-8-13 58 .... (bt) DannyBrock(5) 2 16
(Phil McEntee) *sn outpcd: hdwy over 3f out: rdn 1/2-way: hung lft and wknd over 1f out* **7/1**[3]

1m 0.74s (1.04) **Going Correction** +0.025s/f (Slow) **5** Ran SP% **117.6**
Speed ratings (Par 89): **92,90,82,77,70**
toteswingers 1&2 £3.10, 1&3 £3.70, 2&3 £4.80 CSF £23.41 TOTE £2.70: £2.30, £5.50; EX 24.50 Trifecta £52.80 Pool: £1,435.01 - 20.38 winning units..The winner was bought in for 4,250guineas
Owner Taylor's Bloodstock Ltd **Bred** Tom Foley **Trained** Westow, N Yorks

FOCUS
A moderate fillies' seller. The gallop was sound and the winner came down the centre. The first two pulled clear.

5965 32REDBET.COM H'CAP — 6f (F)
6:30 (6:31) (Class 6) (0-65,65) 3-Y-O+ — **£1,940** (£577; £288; £144) **Stalls** Low

Form — RPR

3042 **1** **Solarmaite**[8] 5674 4-9-0 **58** .... (b) MarkCoumbe(3) 5 67
(Roy Bowring) *a.p: rdn over 1f out: r.o to ld wl ins fnl f* **7/4**[1]

015 **2** *½* **Lord Buffhead**[3] 5864 4-8-8 **54** .... (v) ConnorBeasley(5) 8 61
(Richard Guest) *s.i.s: sn pushed along in rr: hdwy 1/2-way: rdn and ev ch ins fnl f: r.o* **14/1**

5026 **3** *1* **Putin (IRE)**[5] 5798 5-9-4 **64** .... (bt) DannyBrock(5) 3 68
(Phil McEntee) *led: hdd over 4f out: led again over 3f out: rdn over 1f out: hdd and unable qck wl ins fnl f* **3/1**[2]

3006 **4** *3* **Time To Begin (IRE)**[18] 5354 3-8-9 **56** ....(b) WilliamTwiston-Davies(3) 9 51
(Alan McCabe) *w ldrs: rdn over 2f out: ev ch over 1f out: no ex ins fnl f* **8/1**

-466 **5** *1 ¾* **Spitfire**[79] 3210 8-9-10 **65** .... (t) DougieCostello 6 54
(J R Jenkins) *s.i.s: sn pushed along in rr: hdwy u.p over 1f out: nt trble ldrs* **7/1**[3]

2301 **6** *nk* **John Coffey (IRE)**[7] 5709 4-8-9 **57** .... AliRawlinson(7) 7 45
(Michael Appleby) *broke wl sn lost pl: rdn over 2f out: nt trble ldrs* **3/1**[2]

6605 **7** *12* **Moss The Boss (IRE)**[25] 5054 3-8-2 **46** oh1 .... JimmyQuinn 1
(Paul Midgley) *prom: led over 4f out: pushed along and hdd over 3f out: rdn and wknd over 1f out* **33/1**

1m 15.56s (-0.94) **Going Correction** -0.025s/f (Stan)
WFA 3 from 4yo+ 3lb **7** Ran SP% **119.6**
Speed ratings (Par 101): **105,104,103,99,96 96,80**
toteswingers 1&2 £5.10, 1&3 £1.80, 2&3 £5.70 CSF £30.17 CT £73.49 TOTE £2.30: £1.20, £5.20; EX 24.90 Trifecta £122.70 Pool: £2,002.18 - 12.23 winning units..
Owner S R Bowring **Bred** S R Bowring **Trained** Edwinstowe, Notts

FOCUS
A very ordinary handicap in which the gallop was sound throughout. The winner came down the centre and the form looks straightforward rated around the placed horses.

5966 32RED H'CAP 1m 4f (F)
7:00 (7:00) (Class 5) (0-70,69) 3-Y-0+ **£3,234** (£962; £481; £240) **Stalls** Low

Form RPR
651P **1** **Picalily**[3] 5868 4-9-4 **64** RobertTart(5) 7 89+
(Brendan Powell) *hld up: hdwy over 5f out: chsd ldr 4f out: rdn over 1f out: edgd rt ins fnl f: styd on wl: eased towards fin* **11/4**[1]
1316 **2** *4 ½* **Golden Jubilee (USA)**[24] 5099 4-9-5 **63**...(v) WilliamTwiston-Davies(3) 2 79
(Nigel Twiston-Davies) *chsd ldr tl led over 4f out: rdn and hdd over 2f out: swtchd rt over 1f out: styd on same pce fnl f* **5/1**
0612 **3** *11* **Exclusion (USA)**[21] 5234 3-8-11 **62**(b) DougieCostello 5 60
(Noel Quinlan) *chsd ldrs: rdn over 3f out: wknd 2f out* **9/2**[3]
-134 **4** *4* **Decana**[23] 5130 5-9-4 **66** CharlieBennett(7) 8 58
(Hughie Morrison) *s.i.s: hld up: hdwy u.p over 3f out: wknd over 2f out* **7/2**[2]
-000 **5** *4 ½* **Adili (IRE)**[25] 5052 4-9-13 **68** DaleSwift 6 53
(Brian Ellison) *hld up: rdn over 4f out: a in rr* **8/1**
4006 **6** *9* **Mohawk Ridge**[14] 5466 7-9-5 **65** ConnorBeasley(5) 1 35
(Michael Dods) *led: rdn and hdd over 4f out: wknd over 2f out* **7/1**
2315 **7** *34* **Town Mouse**[24] 5087 3-9-4 **69** JimmyQuinn 4
(Neil King) *s.i.s: sn prom: rdn and lost pl over 5f out: sn bhd* **7/1**

2m 37.62s (-3.38) **Going Correction** -0.025s/f (Stan)
WFA 3 from 4yo+ 10lb **7** Ran SP% **119.8**
Speed ratings (Par 103): **110,107,99,97,94 88,65**
toteswingers 1&2 £5.60, 1&3 £4.40, 2&3 £4.60 CSF £18.06 CT £61.42 TOTE £4.00: £2.30, £2.80; EX 16.80 Trifecta £129.00 Pool: £1,207.21 - 7.01 winning units..
Owner W A Harrison-Allan **Bred** W A Harrison-Allan **Trained** Upper Lambourn, Berks

FOCUS
A modest handicap in which six of the seven were winners this season. The gallop was no more than fair to the home turn and the first two, who finished clear, came down the centre. The form is fluid but the first two are both improvers.

5967 32REDPOKER.COM H'CAP 1m 3f (F)
7:30 (7:31) (Class 6) (0-65,65) 3-Y-0+ **£1,940** (£577; £288; £144) **Stalls** Low

Form RPR
5630 **1** **Madeira Girl (IRE)**[25] 5070 4-9-12 **63** DougieCostello 4 72+
(Jonjo O'Neill) *a.p: pushed along over 4f out: rdn to ld over 1f out: edgd rt ins fnl f: styd on* **8/1**
2040 **2** *1 ¾* **Miss Ella Jade**[23] 5144 4-8-13 **50** TonyHamilton 7 55
(Richard Whitaker) *led 1f: remained handy: chsd ldr over 2f out: rdn and hung lft fr over 1f out: styd on* **12/1**
005 **3** *½* **Goldie Horn**[16] 5386 5-8-10 **50**(t) WilliamTwiston-Davies(3) 6 54
(Nigel Twiston-Davies) *s.i.s: hld up: pushed along 1/2-way: rdn over 3f out: hdwy over 1f out: r.o: nt rch ldrs* **14/1**
430 **4** *nk* **Star Date (IRE)**[36] 4679 4-9-4 **62** OisinMurphy(7) 1 66
(Michael Attwater) *led after 1f: rdn over 2f out: hdd over 1f out: no ex ins fnl f* **7/1**[3]
3600 **5** *6* **Tornado Force (IRE)**[52] 4150 5-9-9 **65** ConnorBeasley(5) 5 58
(Alan McCabe) *hld up: hdwy over 3f out: rdn and wknd over 1f out* **3/1**[2]
3423 **6** *6* **Sixties Queen**[10] 5615 3-8-6 **57** TimClark(5) 2 40
(Alan Bailey) *trckd ldrs: plld hrd: rdn over 2f out: wknd over 1f out* **3/1**[2]
0000 **7** *10* **Whistle We Go (GER)**[51] 4161 5-8-4 **46** oh1[1] PhilipPrince(5) 8 12
(Nick Kent) *hld up: rdn over 4f out: wknd 3f out* **33/1**
006 **8** *½* **Le Tigre De Bronze**[20] 5281 3-8-9 **55** JimmyQuinn 3 37
(Hughie Morrison) *trckd ldrs: rdn over 4f out: wknd 2f out: eased fnl f* **2/1**[1]

2m 28.1s (0.10) **Going Correction** -0.025s/f (Stan)
WFA 3 from 4yo+ 9lb **8** Ran SP% **124.2**
Speed ratings (Par 101): **98,96,96,96,91 87,80,79**
toteswingers 1&2 £15.50, 1&3 £7.50, 2&3 £10.90 CSF £104.61 CT £1347.18 TOTE £9.90: £3.30, £5.10, £5.70; EX 112.60 Trifecta £1071.30 Part won. Pool: £1,428.51 - 0.77 winning units..
Owner Jonjo O'Neill Racing Club **Bred** Keatly Overseas Ltd **Trained** Cheltenham, Gloucs

FOCUS
A modest handicap run at an ordinary gallop. The winner came down the centre. The third is rated close to her latest maiden form.
T/Plt: £521.70 to a £1 stake. Pool: £40,133.36 - 56.15 winning units T/Qpdt: £72.10 to a £1 stake. Pool: £5,485.67 - 56.30 winning units CR

5577 THIRSK (L-H)
Friday, August 30

OFFICIAL GOING: Good (good to firm in places; 8.8)
Wind: Moderate; behind Weather: Cloudy with sunny periods

5968 BRITISH STALLION STUDS EBF MAIDEN STKS (DIV I) 1m
2:10 (2:18) (Class 4) 2-Y-0 **£4,204** (£1,251; £625; £312) **Stalls** Low

Form RPR
422 **1** **Greed Is Good**[13] 5539 2-9-5 **75** DanielTudhope 8 78
(K R Burke) *trckd ldrs: hdwy to chse ldng pair over 3f out: chal over 1f out: rdn to ld ent fnl f: kpt on* **3/1**[2]
0 **2** *1 ¼* **Hartnell**[35] 4731 2-9-5 0 JoeFanning 7 75
(Mark Johnston) *led 3f: cl up: led again over 3f out: rdn along 2f out: jnd over 1f out: hdd and drvn ent fnl f: kpt on same pce* **10/1**
44 **3** *3 ¾* **Rock 'N' Roll Star**[14] 5490 2-9-5 0 RobertWinston 11 67
(Charles Hills) *uns rdr and bolted 6f bef s: chsd ldrs: rdn along and hdwy over 2f out: sn rdn to chse ldng pair: kpt on same pce appr fnl f* **3/1**[2]
4 **4** *1 ¼* **Innocent Touch (IRE)**[16] 5379 2-9-5 0 TonyHamilton 2 64
(Richard Fahey) *trckd ldng pair: hdwy over 3f out: rdn along 2f out: sn one pce* **10/1**
0 **5** *4* **Good Value**[49] 4256 2-9-5 0 GrahamLee 1 54
(Sir Michael Stoute) *cl up: led after 3f: pushed along over 3f out: sn hdd and rdn: grad wknd* **11/4**[1]
5 **6** *3* **Chivers (IRE)**[40] 4556 2-9-5 0 DavidAllan 3 48
(Tim Easterby) *s.i.s: bhd tl sme late hdwy* **50/1**
0 **7** *1 ¼* **Nam Ma Prow**[17] 5364 2-9-2 0 JasonHart(3) 6 45
(Simon West) *a in rr* **100/1**
8 *5* **Aramadyh** 2-9-0 0 PaulMulrennan 4 28+
(James Tate) *midfield: rdn along 1/2-way: sn outpcd and bhd fnl 2f* **28/1**
0 **9** *nk* **Desert Skywalker (IRE)**[19] 5299 2-9-5 0 AhmedAjtebi 9 32
(Charlie Appleby) *green: a in rr: bhd fnl 3f* **6/1**[3]
10 *16* **Tortoise** 2-8-9 0 PhilipPrince(5) 10
(Richard Guest) *v s.i.s: green: a outpcd and wl bhd* **100/1**

1m 39.71s (-0.39) **Going Correction** -0.075s/f (Good) **10** Ran SP% **116.5**
Speed ratings (Par 96): **98,96,93,91,87 84,83,78,78,62**
toteswingers 1&2 £7.10, 1&3 £2.00, 2&3 £10.10 CSF £32.29 TOTE £3.20: £1.40, £3.50, £1.50; EX 30.90 Trifecta £148.80 Pool: £2,508.98 - 12.64 winning units..
Owner M Charge & Mrs E Burke **Bred** Northcombe Stud **Trained** Middleham Moor, N Yorks

FOCUS
Fair form from the principals in a maiden run at a sound pace, the field well strung out from an early stage.

5969 BRITISH STALLION STUDS EBF MAIDEN STKS (DIV II) 1m
2:40 (2:42) (Class 4) 2-Y-0 **£4,204** (£1,251; £625; £312) **Stalls** Low

Form RPR
3 **1** **Emef Diamond**[14] 5473 2-9-5 0 TomEaves 8 77
(Mick Channon) *mde all: rdn 2f out: drvn over 1f out: kpt on gamely u.p fnl f* **15/8**[1]
2 *1* **Mustamir (IRE)** 2-9-5 0 PaulMulrennan 4 75+
(James Tate) *trckd ldrs: hdwy on inner over 2f out: rdn to chse ldng pair over 1f out: styd on u.p and ev ch ins fnl f tl no ex towards fin* **8/1**
62 **3** *1* **Eddiemaurice (IRE)**[18] 5338 2-9-5 0 PhillipMakin 5 72
(Richard Guest) *towards rr: hdwy over 2f out: swtchd rt and rdn wl over 1f out: styd on strly fnl f: nrst fin* **11/2**[3]
3 **4** *1* **Major Surprise (USA)**[22] 5180 2-9-5 0 DanielTudhope 10 70
(K R Burke) *trckd ldng pair: hdwy to trck wnr 1/2-way: effrt over 2f out: sn chal: rdn over 1f out and ev ch tl drvn: edgd lft and wknd ins fnl f* **5/2**[2]
5 *1 ½* **Notarised** 2-9-5 0 JoeFanning 7 67
(Mark Johnston) *in tch: hdwy 3f out: rdn to chse ldng trio wl over 1f out: no imp fnl f* **11/1**
6 *8* **Little Bruv** 2-9-5 0 DuranFentiman 6 48
(Tim Easterby) *in tch: pushed along and hdwy 3f out: rdn 2f out and sn outpcd* **50/1**
7 *4 ½* **Highway Pursuit** 2-9-5 0 PJMcDonald 2 38
(George Moore) *green: a towards rr* **66/1**
0 **8** *1 ¾* **State Law (IRE)**[21] 5244 2-9-5 0 AhmedAjtebi 1 34
(Charlie Appleby) *dwlt: green and a in rr* **9/1**
0 **9** *14* **Northern Reach**[66] 3648 2-9-0 0 DavidAllan 9
(Geoffrey Harker) *cl up: pushed along 1/2-way: rdn wl over 3f out and sn wknd* **100/1**

1m 40.76s (0.66) **Going Correction** -0.075s/f (Good) **9** Ran SP% **112.6**
Speed ratings (Par 96): **93,92,91,90,88 80,76,74,60**
toteswingers 1&2 £12.30, 1&3 £1.30, 2&3 £13.30 CSF £17.23 TOTE £2.70: £1.10, £3.20, £1.40; EX 19.60 Trifecta £77.40 Pool: £1,687.08 - 16.34 winning units..
Owner Mrs Margaret Forsyth & MF Logistic **Bred** Bearstone Stud **Trained** West Ilsley, Berks

FOCUS
A similar standard to the first division, though it wasn't as truly run, that reflected in a slower time.

5970 WATCH RACING UK ON SKY 432 MAIDEN CLAIMING STKS 6f
3:10 (3:11) (Class 4) 2-Y-0 **£3,881** (£1,155; £577; £288) **Stalls** High

Form RPR
6553 **1** **Song Of Rowland (IRE)**[4] 5834 2-9-0 67 DanielTudhope 5 69+
(David O'Meara) *sn trcking ldrs: smooth hdwy and cl up over 2f out: led wl over 1f out: sn clr: readily* **11/4**[2]
2364 **2** *4 ½* **Classy Lassy (IRE)**[52] 4154 2-9-3 75 GrahamLee 4 53
(Brian Ellison) *sn led: rdn along 2f out: hdd wl over 1f out and sn drvn: kpt on one pce* **2/1**[1]
00 **3** *hd* **Valued Opinion (IRE)**[55] 4065 2-8-7 0(tp) JoeFanning 2 42
(Tim Pitt) *prom: cl up after 2f: effrt 2f out and ev ch: sn rdn and one pce* **12/1**
0004 **4** *½* **Casper Lee (IRE)**[4] 5834 2-8-10 44(v[1]) PaulMulrennan 10 43
(Nigel Tinkler) *dwlt and in rr: rdn along over 2f out: hdwy and n.m.r over 1f out: styng on whn nt clr run and swtchd lft ins fnl f: kpt on: nrst fin* **25/1**
420 **5** *nk* **Elualla (IRE)**[31] 4847 2-8-4 58 AndrewMullen 9 37
(Nigel Tinkler) *towards rr: hdwy over 2f out: swtchd to inner and rdn wl over 1f out: sn drvn and no imp* **9/1**
0525 **6** *2* **Autumn Tide (IRE)**[14] 5480 2-8-1 50 JamesSullivan 8 28
(John Quinn) *prom: pushed along 1/2-way: sn rdn and wknd 2f out* **9/1**
7 *1 ½* **Rievaulx Ranger (IRE)** 2-9-0 0 PhillipMakin 6 36
(Kevin Ryan) *dwlt: a towards rr* **7/2**[3]
6045 **8** *4 ½* **Astral Pursuits**[37] 4617 2-7-12 43 ow1 DeclanCannon(3) 7 10
(Nigel Tinkler) *chsd ldrs: rdn along 1/2-way: sn wknd* **80/1**
0 **9** *41* **Lunesdale Buddy**[17] 5364 2-8-9 0 ow1 TomEaves 3
(Alan Berry) *towards rr: rdn along 1/2-way: sn outpcd and bhd* **100/1**

1m 12.17s (-0.53) **Going Correction** -0.25s/f (Firm) **9** Ran SP% **116.0**
Speed ratings (Par 96): **93,87,86,86,85 83,81,75,20**
toteswingers 1&2 £1.70, 1&3 £8.20, 2&3 £8.20 CSF £8.65 TOTE £5.30: £1.10, £1.10, £4.70; EX 9.30 Trifecta £55.30 Pool: £2,448.58 - 33.20 winning units..
Owner Dr Marwan Koukash **Bred** Southern Bloodstock **Trained** Nawton, N Yorks
■ Stewards' Enquiry : Paul Mulrennan two-day ban: careless riding (13 Sep & 15 Sep)

FOCUS
This turned into a one-sided claimer, the winner doing it easily.

5971 THEAKSTON LIGHTFOOT H'CAP 6f
3:45 (3:45) (Class 4) (0-80,80) 3-Y-0+ **£4,851** (£1,443; £721; £360) **Stalls** High

Form RPR
2662 **1** **Ashpan Sam**[25] 5062 4-9-10 **78** PhillipMakin 8 92+
(John Spearing) *trckd ldrs: hdwy wl over 1f out: rdn to ld jst ins fnl f: sn qcknd clr: kpt on strly* **14/1**
4041 **2** *3 ¾* **George Fenton**[11] 5583 4-8-5 **64** 6ex(p) PhilipPrince(5) 13 67
(Richard Guest) *towards rr: hdwy 2f out: n.m.r and swtchd lft to wd outside over 1f out: styd on strly fnl f* **9/1**
4210 **3** *hd* **Sunrise Dance**[20] 5294 4-9-4 **77** ConnorBeasley(5) 7 79
(Robert Johnson) *sn cl up: rdn to ld 1 1/2f out: drvn and hdd jst ins fnl f: kpt on same pce* **8/1**[3]
5354 **4** *nk* **Silvanus (IRE)**[9] 5639 8-9-11 **79** PaulMulrennan 9 80
(Paul Midgley) *trckd ldrs: effrt and n.m.r over 1f out: swtchd lft and rdn ent fnl f: kpt on* **28/1**
2300 **5** *hd* **Sir Pedro**[35] 4730 4-9-4 **75** PatrickHills(3) 2 76
(Charles Hills) *trckd ldrs: hdwy 2f out: rdn and ev ch over 1f out: drvn and one pce fnl f* **33/1**
4444 **6** *1* **Waseem Faris (IRE)**[11] 5579 4-9-6 **74** TomEaves 16 73
(Mick Channon) *trckd ldrs: effrt and n.m.r over 1f out: swtchd lft and rdn ent fnl f: no imp* **13/2**[2]
4504 **7** *hd* **Captain Scooby**[2] 5901 7-8-9 **68** DavidBergin(5) 10 65
(Richard Guest) *towards rr: hdwy and pushed along 2f out: rdn over 1f out: swtchd lft and styd on fnl f: nrst fin* **22/1**

0000 **8** *hd* **Escape To Glory (USA)**[4] 5832 5-9-10 **78** GrahamLee 5 74
(Michael Dods) *in rr: rdn along over 2f out: sme late hdwy* **16/1**

1243 **9** *½* **Imperial Legend (IRE)**[9] 5639 4-9-12 **80** (p) AndrewMullen 15 75
(David Nicholls) *led: rdn 2f out: hdd 1 1/2f out: grad wknd* **12/1**

4605 **10** *nk* **Cocktail Charlie**[16] 5381 5-9-3 **71** (p) DavidAllan 3 65
(Tim Easterby) *racd wd: cl up: rdn along 2f out: sn edgd rt: wkng whn n.m.r jst ins fnl f* **20/1**

0060 **11** *1* **Johannes (IRE)**[30] 4879 10-9-6 **79** GeorgeChaloner(5) 6 70
(Richard Fahey) *towards rr: swtchd lft and sme hdwy wl over 2f out: sn rdn and n.d* **9/1**

0100 **12** *hd* **Pea Shooter**[22] 5183 4-9-3 **78** (p) KevinStott(7) 11 68
(Kevin Ryan) *towards rr: rdn along and sme hdwy 2f out: n.m.r over 1f out: sn wknd* **8/1**[3]

4205 **13** *¾* **Sunraider (IRE)**[7] 5705 6-9-11 **79** MickyFenton 4 67
(Paul Midgley) *dwlt: a in rr* **28/1**

3425 **14** *½* **Roker Park (IRE)**[4] 5832 8-9-7 **75** DanielTudhope 12 62
(David O'Meara) *a towards rr* **11/2**[1]

2663 **15** *5* **Holy Angel (IRE)**[20] 5273 4-9-2 **70** (e) RobertWinston 1 42
(Tim Easterby) *racd wd: chsd ldrs: rdn along over 1f out: sn wknd* **9/1**

1m 10.31s (-2.39) **Going Correction** -0.25s/f (Firm) **15** Ran SP% **120.1**
Speed ratings (Par 105): **105,100,99,99,99 97,97,97,96,96 94,94,93,92,86**
toteswingers 1&2 £15.60, 1&3 £21.50, 2&3 £19.00 CSF £124.33 CT £1114.57 TOTE £12.00: £3.90, £3.40, £3.70; EX 83.10 Trifecta £941.80 Pool: £2,645.71 - 2.10 winning units..
Owner Advantage Chemicals Holdings Ltd **Bred** Advantage Chemicals Holdings Ltd **Trained** Kinnersley, Worcs

FOCUS
This looked quite competitive beforehand but the winner did it easily. A step forward from the progressive winner.

5972 RACING UK YOUR RACING HOME FROM HOME H'CAP 2m
4:15 (4:15) (Class 4) (0-80,78) 3-Y-0+ £4,851 (£1,443; £721; £360) Stalls Low

Form RPR

4115 **1** **Dr Irv**[34] 4782 4-9-6 **73** DeclanCannon(3) 7 81+
(Philip Kirby) *hld up in rr: smooth hdwy on outer wl over 2f out: cl up over 1f out: rdn to ld ins fnl f: sn edgd lft and drvn out* **9/4**[1]

-602 **2** *nk* **Rosairlie (IRE)**[24] 5109 5-9-7 **71** PJMcDonald 6 79
(Micky Hammond) *trckd ldrs: hdwy 3f out: rdn to chal over 1f out: drvn and edging lft ent fnl f: ev ch whn n.m.r last 50yds: no ex nr fin* **11/2**

650 **3** *3 ½* **Gabrial's Star**[29] 4913 4-10-0 **78** (v[1]) TomEaves 3 82
(Ian Williams) *prom: cl up after 6f: rdn to ld 3f out: drvn wl over 1f out: hdd ins fnl f: hld whn n.m.r and wknd last 100yds* **5/1**

2114 **4** *7* **Miss Tiger Lily**[24] 5102 3-8-10 **74** JoeFanning 2 69
(Harry Dunlop) *led: rdn along and hdd 3f out: drvn 2f out and grad wknd* **3/1**[2]

6426 **5** *5* **My Destination (IRE)**[13] 5514 4-8-13 **66** JasonHart(3) 4 55
(Declan Carroll) *hld up in tch: pushed along 5f out: rdn along over 3f out: outpcd fnl 2f* **4/1**[3]

0410 **6** *10* **Major Domo (FR)**[9] 5640 5-9-5 **69** AndrewMullen 1 46
(Alan Swinbank) *t.k.h: trckd ldr 6f: chsd ldng pair: rdn along over 3f out: wknd over 2f out: sn bhd and eased* **16/1**

3m 27.0s (-1.30) **Going Correction** -0.075s/f (Good)
WFA 3 from 4yo+ 14lb **6** Ran SP% **113.7**
Speed ratings (Par 105): **100,99,98,94,92 87**
toteswingers 1&2 £3.50, 1&3 £3.30, 2&3 £3.10 CSF £15.30 CT £54.92 TOTE £3.00: £1.70, £3.00; EX 12.60 Trifecta £40.20 Pool: £2,255.77 - 42.07 winning units..
Owner Irvine Lynch **Bred** Whitsbury Manor Stud & Pigeon House Stud **Trained** Middleham, N Yorks

FOCUS
A fair staying event, though it wasn't much of a test at the trip, the race not really beginning in earnest until the final 4f. The placed horses set the level.

5973 WATCH RACING UK ON FREEVIEW 231 CLASSIFIED (S) STKS 6f
4:50 (4:50) (Class 6) 3-Y-0+ £1,940 (£577; £288; £144) Stalls High

Form RPR

1505 **1** **Colbyor**[27] 4992 4-9-0 65 GeorgeChaloner(5) 4 74
(Richard Fahey) *trckd ldrs: hdwy 2f out: swtchd lft and effrt over 1f out: rdn to ld ent fnl f: kpt on wl* **7/1**

3060 **2** *1 ¼* **Above The Stars**[8] 5674 5-9-5 73 GrahamLee 1 70
(Conor Dore) *hld up: hdwy wl over 1f out: rdn and ch ent fnl f: kpt on* **16/1**

U432 **3** *1 ¼* **Llewellyn**[5] 5783 5-8-13 72 AdrianNicholls 3 61
(David Nicholls) *trckd ldr: cl up over 2f out: rdn to ld over 1f out: drvn and hdd ent fnl f: sn one pce* **1/1**[1]

6004 **4** *2 ¼* **Partner (IRE)**[16] 5378 7-8-10 63 (p) JasonHart(3) 5 54
(Noel Wilson) *trckd ldrs: swtchd lft and effrt wl over 1f out: sn rdn and one pce* **8/1**

3004 **5** *hd* **Red Cape (FR)**[2] 5887 10-9-5 66 (b) JamesSullivan 6 59
(Ruth Carr) *hld up: effrt and n.m.r over 1f out: sn rdn and n.d* **6/1**[3]

0140 **6** *4* **Roland**[30] 4881 3-9-2 71 (b) TomEaves 7 47
(Kevin Ryan) *reminders s: led: rdn along 2f out: hdd wl over 1f out: sn wknd* **14/1**

4562 **7** *nk* **Commanche Raider (IRE)**[14] 5470 6-8-13 68 PaulMulrennan 2 40
(Michael Dods) *trckd ldrs on outer: effrt 2f out: sn rdn and btn* **11/2**[2]

1m 11.31s (-1.39) **Going Correction** -0.25s/f (Firm)
WFA 3 from 4yo+ 3lb **7** Ran SP% **115.8**
Speed ratings (Par 101): **99,97,95,92,92 87,86**
toteswingers 1&2 £9.80, 1&3 £2.10, 2&3 £3.30 CSF £105.22 TOTE £9.50: £3.60, £6.60; EX 111.20 Trifecta £222.80 Pool: £2,500.84 - 8.41 winning units..The winner was bought in for £3,800
Owner E Bruce **Bred** Mr And Mrs E Bruce **Trained** Musley Bank, N Yorks

FOCUS
Fair form from the principals in this seller. The first two set a straightforward level.

5974 JW 4X4 NORTHALLERTON - MYLES 7 TODAY H'CAP 7f
5:25 (5:25) (Class 4) (0-80,80) 3-Y-0+ £4,851 (£1,443; £721; £360) Stalls Low

Form RPR

6244 **1** **Celtic Sixpence (IRE)**[12] 5564 5-9-0 **68** (p) MichaelStainton 16 79
(Nick Kent) *led: hdd over 4f out: chsd ldr tl led again jst over 2f out: rdn clr and edgd lft ent fnl f: kpt on* **25/1**

3250 **2** *1 ½* **Our Boy Jack (IRE)**[14] 5481 4-9-4 **77** GeorgeChaloner(5) 7 84
(Richard Fahey) *trckd ldrs: hdwy 3f out: rdn to chse ldng pair 2f out: drvn to chse wnr ins fnl f: no imp towards fin* **5/1**[2]

1026 **3** *¾* **Blue Maisey**[28] 4967 5-8-4 **65** KevinStott(7) 14 70
(Edwin Tuer) *bhd: swtchd rt to outer and hdwy 2f out: rdn over 1f out: styd on strly fnl f: nrst fin* **12/1**

5452 **4** *hd* **Mutafaakir (IRE)**[7] 5711 4-9-2 **70** (p) PJMcDonald 12 74
(Ruth Carr) *chsd ldr: led over 4f out: rdn along and hdd over 2f out: cl up tl drvn over 1f out and one pce ins fnl f* **6/1**[3]

-003 **5** *1 ¼* **Evanescent (IRE)**[28] 4967 4-8-9 **70** JoeDoyle(7) 2 71
(John Quinn) *trckd ldng pair on inner: rdn along over 2f out: drvn over 1f out: one pce fnl f* **10/1**

5052 **6** *hd* **Tarooq (USA)**[7] 5696 7-9-11 **79** (t) DanielTudhope 15 79
(Stuart Williams) *chsd ldrs: hdwy on outer 3f out: rdn 2f out: drvn and one pce appr fnl f* **3/1**[1]

5-66 **7** *½* **Eurystheus (IRE)**[111] 2256 4-9-8 **76** AndrewMullen 11 75
(Michael Appleby) *dwlt and towards rr: hdwy on wd outside 3f out: rdn to chse ldrs 2f out: sn stly outpcd: swtchd lft and drvn ent fnl f: kpt on fin* **17/2**

4550 **8** *3* **Steel Stockholder**[14] 5481 7-9-6 **74** DavidAllan 1 65
(Mel Brittain) *chsd ldrs on inner: rdn along over 2f out: drvn wl over 1f out and grad wknd* **20/1**

0-20 **9** *2 ¼* **President Lincoln (USA)**[142] 1485 5-9-8 **79** JasonHart(3) 9 64
(Declan Carroll) *a towards rr* **12/1**

1126 **10** *nk* **West Leake Hare (IRE)**[20] 5292 4-9-10 **78** AdrianNicholls 5 64
(David Nicholls) *in tch: hdwy 3f out: rdn to chse ldrs 2f out: sn drvn and no imp appr fnl f* **8/1**

0-00 **11** *18* **Tarrsille (IRE)**[13] 5544 7-9-12 **80** MickyFenton 3 16
(Paul Midgley) *a towards rr: bhd and eased fnl 2f* **50/1**

4-00 **12** *8* **Half A Crown (IRE)**[93] 2781 8-8-4 **65** ShelleyBirkett(7) 6
(Nick Kent) *rrd s and s.i.s: a in rr: bhd and eased fnl 2f* **66/1**

5314 **13** *13* **Barney McGrew (IRE)**[14] 5481 10-9-10 **78** PaulMulrennan 8
(Michael Dods) *midfield: hdwy on inner wl over 2f out: rdn over 1f out: wkng whn lost action and virtually p.u ins fnl f* **16/1**

1m 25.68s (-1.52) **Going Correction** -0.075s/f (Good) **13** Ran SP% **120.0**
Speed ratings (Par 105): **105,103,102,102,100 100,99,96,93,93 73,63,49**
toteswingers 1&2 £19.40, 1&3 £28.10, 2&3 £25.20 CSF £143.27 CT £1667.74 TOTE £26.80: £4.50, £3.00, £6.30; EX 396.70 Trifecta £1649.10 Part won. Pool: £2,198.81 - 0.38 winning units..
Owner Cynthia Commons, Nick Kent **Bred** Burns Farm Stud **Trained** Brigg, Lincs

FOCUS
Typical of many handicaps over this C&D in that it wasn't easy to get into contention from off the pace, three of the first four home in front rank throughout. Straightforward form that perhaps could be rated a couple of pounds higher.

5975 BET & WATCH WITH RACINGUK'S APP H'CAP 1m
5:55 (5:55) (Class 5) (0-70,69) 3-Y-O £2,726 (£805; £402) Stalls Low

Form RPR

1322 **1** **Bousatet (FR)**[11] 5581 3-8-10 **65** KevinStott(7) 3 73
(Kevin Ryan) *trckd ldrs: hdwy 3f out: rdn to chse ldng pair 2f out: drvn to chal ent fnl f: kpt on gamely u.p to ld nr line* **5/2**[1]

513 **2** *shd* **Mandy's Boy (IRE)**[9] 5632 3-9-6 **68** (p) GrahamLee 7 75
(Ian Williams) *chsd ldr: hdwy 3f out: led 2f out: drvn ent fnl f: hdd and no ex nr line* **7/2**[2]

4463 **3** *½* **Medici Dancer**[18] 5342 3-9-6 **68** (p) DavidAllan 8 74
(Tim Easterby) *towards rr: hdwy on wd outside over 2f out: rdn wl over 1f out: styd on to chal jst ins fnl f and ev ch tl edgd lft and no ex towards fin* **11/2**[3]

1403 **4** *2* **Callmeakhab (IRE)**[24] 5096 3-9-7 **69** RobertWinston 9 71
(Charles Hills) *hld up towards rr: hdwy over 2f out: rdn wl over 1f out: drvn to chse ldrs whn n.m.r and swtchd lft ins fnl f: kpt on: nrst fin* **10/1**

5425 **5** *2* **Gabrial The Thug (FR)**[33] 4806 3-9-1 **68** (t) GeorgeChaloner(5) 2 65
(Richard Fahey) *towards rr: hdwy on inner over 2f out: sn rdn along: styd on u.p fnl f: nrst fin* **8/1**

4506 **6** *nk* **Midnight Warrior**[18] 5342 3-8-0 **55** JoeDoyle(7) 4 51
(Ron Barr) *chsd ldrs: rdn along 3f out: drvn and outpcd wl over 1f out: kpt on fnl f* **20/1**

0213 **7** *nk* **Marcus Caesar (IRE)**[11] 5581 3-9-2 **64** JamesSullivan 11 60
(Ruth Carr) *led: rdn along 3f out: hdd 2f out and grad wknd* **8/1**

6633 **8** *nk* **The Scuttler (IRE)**[8] 5668 3-9-3 **65** TomEaves 6 60
(Mick Channon) *chsd ldng pair: rdn along wl over 2f out: drvn wl over 1f out: wknd fnl f* **14/1**

2424 **9** *20* **Tanawar (IRE)**[55] 4048 3-9-4 **66** PaulMulrennan 1 15
(Tim Etherington) *sn outpcd: a bhd* **16/1**

1m 39.41s (-0.69) **Going Correction** -0.075s/f (Good) **9** Ran SP% **114.8**
Speed ratings (Par 100): **100,99,99,97,95 95,94,94,74**
toteswingers 1&2 £3.10, 1&3 £3.70, 2&3 £4.80 CSF £11.02 CT £43.10 TOTE £2.50: £1.70, £1.70, £2.60; EX 14.40 Trifecta £60.60 Pool: £1,660.92 - 20.54 winning units..
Owner Highbank Stud **Bred** F Bayrou & F A Mc Nulty **Trained** Hambleton, N Yorks

FOCUS
A modest handicap which was soundly run. The form is straightforward, rated around the first three.
T/Plt: £128.50 to a £1 stake. Pool: £59,639.99 - 338.59 winning units T/Qpdt: £69.80 to a £1 stake. Pool: £3,052.20 - 32.35 winning units JR

5665 BATH (L-H)
Saturday, August 31

OFFICIAL GOING: Firm (9.4)
Far side rail dolled out about 4yds from 5f to just beyond 3f to provide fresh line where sprint races meet main track and no change to advertised distances.
Wind: Moderate; across Weather: Sunny spells early

5976 BRITISH STALLION STUDS /TED BAKER E B F NOVICE STKS 5f 161y
4:45 (4:46) (Class 5) 2-Y-O £2,911 (£866; £432; £216) Stalls Centre

Form RPR

0 **1** **Fear Or Favour (IRE)**[63] 3836 2-9-0 0 JohnFahy 5 79+
(Clive Cox) *chsd ldrs: drvn 3f out: chal fr 2f out: led ins fnl f: pushed clr: readily* **4/1**[2]

00 **2** *2 ¾* **China In My Hands**[7] 5740 2-8-9 0 CathyGannon 3 65
(Mick Channon) *chsd ldrs: rdn 3f out: styd on fr over 1f out to take 2nd last strides but no ch w wnr* **10/1**

622 **3** *nk* **Sunset Shore**[17] 5396 2-9-0 77 ChrisCatlin 1 69
(Sir Mark Prescott Bt) *led: jnd and pushed along 2f out: hdd ins fnl f: sn fnd no ex: dropped to 3rd last strides* **1/2**[1]

3100 **4** *8* **Sakuramachi**[23] 5175 2-8-9 62 ow3 WilliamTwiston-Davies(3) 2 40
(Nikki Evans) *in rr and outpcd: drvn and hung lft fr 2f out: nvr any ch* **50/1**

The Form Book Flat, Raceform Ltd, Compton, RG20 6NL.

3123 **5** 3 ½ **Douneedahand**[5] 5842 2-8-11 66 .... LiamKeniry 4 27
(Seamus Mullins) *pressed ldr tl over 2f out: hung lft and wknd wl over 1f out* **7/1**[3]

1m 12.08s (0.88) **Going Correction** +0.025s/f (Good) **5** Ran SP% **110.2**
Speed ratings (Par 94): **95,91,90,80,75**
CSF £36.83 TOTE £5.70: £2.30, £3.30; EX 22.90 Trifecta £72.60 Pool: £1935.19 - 19.96 winning units..
Owner Lakes Bathrooms Ltd **Bred** Shadwell Estate Company Limited **Trained** Lambourn, Berks

FOCUS
Far side rail dolled out about 4yds from 5f to just beyond 3f to provide fresh line where sprint races meet main track and no change to advertised distances. Not a bad little conditions event rated through the third to previous course form. There was no hanging about and that suited the closers.

5977 HOBBS H'CAP 2m 1f 34y
5:15 (5:15) (Class 6) (0-60,62) 4-Y-0+ **£1,940** (£577; £288; £144) **Stalls** Centre

Form RPR

5121 **1** **Chapter Five**[9] 5666 6-9-6 **62** .... (p) RyanPowell(3) 1 68
(Ian Williams) *trckd ldrs: rdn 3f out: hdwy over 2f out: chal over 1f out: slt ld ins fnl f: hld on all out* **10/11**[1]

6-44 **2** *shd* **Manshoor (IRE)**[17] 5409 8-8-11 **50** .... DougieCostello 6 56
(Lucy Wadham) *led: jnd 6f out: hdd 9f out: dropped to 3rd 6f out: rdn and hdwy over 3f out: chal over 2f out: sn led: narrowly hdd ins fnl f: rallied and kpt on: jst hld* **12/1**

5064 **3** 3 ¼ **Lucky Diva**[37] 4655 6-8-10 **54** .... (v) JakePayne(5) 3 56
(Bill Turner) *in rr: drvn along over 3f out: hdwy u.p fr 2f out: kpt on to take 3rd fnl 100yds: no imp on ldng duo* **7/1**[3]

00-1 **4** 3 **Princesse Fleur**[16] 5432 5-8-11 **53** .... WilliamTwiston-Davies(3) 5 52
(Michael Scudamore) *chsd ldr: chal 6f out: led 9f out: drvn and qcknd over 3f out: jnd over 2f out: sn hdd: wknd fnl f* **9/4**[2]

6000 **5** 10 **Inffiraaj (IRE)**[9] 5671 4-8-7 **46** oh1 .... CathyGannon 4 34
(Mick Channon) *in rr but in tch: drvn and hdwy to chse ldr 6f out: rdn 4f out: wknd 2f out* **16/1**

3m 57.98s (6.08) **Going Correction** +0.025s/f (Good) **5** Ran SP% **109.2**
Speed ratings (Par 101): **86,85,84,83,78**
CSF £12.26 TOTE £1.70: £1.10, £2.20; EX 14.00 Trifecta £41.50 Pool: £854.05 - 15.40 winning units..
Owner Mr & Mrs Hutton & Mrs Laing **Bred** Mrs Lesley A Hutton **Trained** Portway, Worcs
■ Stewards' Enquiry : Ryan Powell two-day ban: used whip above permitted level (Sep 15-16)

FOCUS
A moderate little staying handicap, run at a routine pace until nearing the home turn. The first pair came away from the furlong marker. The runner-up is rated a slight improver on AW form with the third to her latest mark.

5978 L K BENNETT H'CAP 1m 5y
5:45 (5:45) (Class 5) (0-75,82) 3-Y-0+ **£2,587** (£770; £384; £192) **Stalls** Low

Form RPR

0301 **1** **Siouxperhero (IRE)**[20] 5304 4-9-5 **68** .... (p) WilliamCarson 5 74
(William Muir) *trckd ldrs: rdn to ld over 1f out: hrd pressed ins fnl f: all out* **5/1**[3]

2533 **2** *nk* **New Falcon (IRE)**[24] 5125 3-9-0 **72** .... (p) ThomasBrown(3) 3 78
(James Tate) *chsd ldrs: rdn over 2f out: str run on outside over 1f out to chal thrght fnl f: no ex last strides* **9/4**[1]

0106 **3** *nk* **Poor Duke (IRE)**[15] 5491 3-9-2 **71** .... (p) FergusSweeney 4 76
(Jamie Osborne) *hld up in rr but in tch: rdn along 3f out: hdwy on ins over 1f out and squeezed through ins fnl f: kpt on wl: nt quite rch ldng duo* **8/1**

0001 **4** 1 ¼ **Silverware (USA)**[17] 5378 5-9-12 **75** .... CathyGannon 6 77
(Kristin Stubbs) *led: rdn ins fnl 3f: keept slt advantage tl hdd over 1f out: outpcd fnl 75yds* **8/1**

0321 **5** *nk* **Yojimbo (IRE)**[5] 5815 5-10-2 **82** 6ex .... (v) CharlesBishop(3) 1 83
(Mick Channon) *in rr but in tch: hdwy fr 2f out: chsd ldrs fr 1f out: outpcd fnl 75yds* **11/4**[2]

-124 **6** ¾ **Emmuska**[58] 3983 4-9-4 **67** .... SteveDrowne 7 67
(Clive Cox) *chsd ldr: drvn to chal fr 2f out tl 1f out: wknd fnl 110yds* **6/1**

1m 39.91s (-0.89) **Going Correction** +0.025s/f (Good)
WFA 3 from 4yo+ 6lb **6** Ran SP% **110.6**
Speed ratings (Par 103): **105,104,104,103,102 102**
toteswingers 1&2 £2.40, 1&3 £7.60, 2&3 £5.00 CSF £16.16 TOTE £5.10: £2.30, £1.80; EX 15.40 Trifecta £113.70 Pool: £1441.74 - 9.5 winning units..
Owner Muir Racing Partnership - Bath **Bred** J & J Waldron **Trained** Lambourn, Berks

FOCUS
This was competitive and there was a tight finish. The form looks ordinary but sound enough, with the first five pretty much to recent marks.

5979 CREW CLOTHING H'CAP 1m 5f 22y
6:15 (6:15) (Class 6) (0-55,54) 3-Y-0+ **£1,940** (£577; £288; £144) **Stalls** High

Form RPR

4124 **1** **See And Be Seen**[8] 5702 3-8-11 **52** .... (p) RenatoSouza 6 58
(Sylvester Kirk) *chsd ldrs: rdn along fr 3f out: styd on fr over 1f out to ld fnl 100yds: hld on all out* **9/2**[3]

000- **2** *shd* **Amantius**[18] 7654 4-9-1 **45** .... (b[1]) CathyGannon 2 50
(Johnny Farrelly) *hld up in rr: rdn over 2f out and hdwy on ins over 1f out: styd on wl u.p to chal fnl 100yds: nt qckn last strides* **20/1**

2532 **3** ¾ **Eyeline**[10] 5650 3-8-13 **54** .... (p) PaulQuinn 4 58
(Andrew Hollinshead) *t.k.h: led: rdn along fr 3f out: hrd pressed fnl f: hdd and outpcd fnl 100yds* **3/1**[2]

6343 **4** 1 ½ **Finch Flyer (IRE)**[5] 5671 6-9-2 **46** .... (p) ChrisCatlin 5 48
(Aytach Sadik) *chsd ldr: rdn to chal 2f out: wknd fnl 110yds* **10/1**

0054 **5** 2 ¼ **Sugar Coated (IRE)**[45] 4405 3-8-9 **53** .... WilliamTwiston-Davies(3) 1 52
(Michael Bell) *chsd ldrs: rdn over 2f out: one pce 2f out: wknd fnl f* **6/4**[1]

0063 **6** 7 **Walter De La Mare (IRE)**[10] 5650 6-9-3 **47** .... (b) LiamKeniry 9 35
(Anabel K Murphy) *in rr: rdn and sme hdwy over 2f out: nvr rchd ldrs and sn wknd* **10/1**

000 **7** 28 **Holli Deya**[25] 5100 3-8-0 **46** .... (p) PhilipPrince(5) 7
(Andi Brown) *t.k.h: stmbld after 3f and sn in rr: lost tch fr over 2f out* **12/1**

2m 53.44s (1.44) **Going Correction** +0.025s/f (Good)
WFA 3 from 4yo+ 11lb **7** Ran SP% **113.8**
Speed ratings (Par 101): **96,95,95,94,93 88,71**
toteswingers 1&2 £6.50, 1&3 £2.40, 2&3 £10.30 CSF £79.94 CT £309.63 TOTE £5.50: £2.90, £6.50; EX 35.10 Trifecta £261.70 Pool: £2223.70 - 6.37 winning units..
Owner Timothy Pearson **Bred** Exors Of The Late T E Pocock **Trained** Upper Lambourn, Berks
■ Stewards' Enquiry : Renato Souza five-day ban: used whip above permitted level without giving gelding time to respond (Sep 14-18)

FOCUS
An ordinary staying handicap. The winner's previous run here was sound enough and the third helps set the standard.

5980 OSPREY LONDON H'CAP 1m 2f 46y
6:45 (6:45) (Class 6) (0-65,66) 3-Y-0+ **£1,940** (£577; £288; £144) **Stalls** Low

Form RPR

1462 **1** **Bold Cross (IRE)**[9] 5671 10-9-11 **65** .... ThomasBrown(3) 7 73
(Edward Bevan) *in tch: hdwy over 2f out: rdn to ld wl over 1f out: strly pressed thrght fnl f: kpt on gamely clsng stages* **13/2**[3]

1205 **2** *nk* **Taro Tywod (IRE)**[15] 5479 4-9-10 **61** .... TomMcLaughlin 4 68
(Mark Brisbourne) *chsd ldrs: chal ins fnl 2f: pressed wnr u.p thrght fnl f no ex last strides* **8/1**

4121 **3** 3 ½ **Precision Five**[9] 5667 4-9-10 **66** .... (p) TobyAtkinson(5) 5 67
(Jeremy Gask) *s.i.s: in rr: rdn and nt clr run 2f out: u.p and swtchd rt over 1f out but continually carrying hd high: kpt on to take 3rd fnl 110yds: no ch w ldng duo* **5/2**[1]

0631 **4** 1 ¼ **Dawn Rock**[24] 5126 3-8-6 **51** .... CathyGannon 3 49
(Simon Dow) *chsd ldr 3f: rdn on rail whn nt clr run 2f out: styd on same pce fr over 1f out* **9/2**[2]

-060 **5** ½ **Geeaitch**[22] 5234 4-9-11 **62** .... WilliamCarson 8 59
(Anthony Carson) *led: rdn over 2f out: sn edgd lft: hdd wl over 1f out: wknd fnl f* **5/2**[1]

6650 **6** 4 ½ **Daneside (IRE)**[16] 5426 6-9-7 **58** .... (t[1]) J-PGuillambert 2 47
(Gary Harrison) *s.i.s: in rr: sme hdwy on outside fr 2f out: nvr rchd ldrs and sn wknd* **14/1**

5226 **7** 2 ½ **Petersboden**[11] 5615 4-8-9 **46** .... FergusSweeney 6 30
(Michael Blanshard) *chsd ldr after 3f: rdn over 3f out: wknd ins fnl 2f* **12/1**

2m 10.3s (-0.70) **Going Correction** +0.025s/f (Good)
WFA 3 from 4yo+ 8lb **7** Ran SP% **114.1**
Speed ratings (Par 101): **103,102,99,98,98 94,92**
toteswingers 1&2 £7.70, 1&3 £4.10, 2&3 £5.70 CSF £55.37 CT £163.88 TOTE £8.00: £3.00, £2.60; EX 33.00 Trifecta £77.70 Pool: £2274.10 - 21.95 winning units..
Owner E G Bevan **Bred** M Hosokawa **Trained** Ullingswick, H'fords
■ Stewards' Enquiry : Thomas Brown two-day ban: careless riding (Sep 15-16)

FOCUS
The first pair drew clear in this weak handicap. The winner is rated to his best in the last two years, backed up by the runnerup to her former best.

5981 SUPERDRY H'CAP 5f 161y
7:15 (7:17) (Class 6) (0-60,60) 3-Y-0 **£1,940** (£577; £288; £144) **Stalls** Centre

Form RPR

0000 **1** **Scarlet Strand**[22] 5227 3-8-7 **46** oh1 .... PaulQuinn 9 52
(Andrew Hollinshead) *in tch: hdwy to chse ldrs 2f out: led u.p appr fnl f: kpt on wl* **10/1**

6346 **2** ¾ **New Rich**[17] 5404 3-8-13 **52** .... JohnFahy 1 55
(Eve Johnson Houghton) *in rr: hdwy and hung lft over 1f out: swtchd lft and chsd wnr fnl 110yds: no imp* **7/2**[2]

0045 **3** 3 ½ **Gregori (IRE)**[9] 5674 3-9-1 **57** .... (t) WilliamTwiston-Davies(3) 3 48
(Brian Meehan) *chsd ldr: led 2f out: sn rdn: hung lft over 1f out: sn hdd: wknd fnl 110yds* **3/1**[1]

4533 **4** 1 **Imperial Spirit**[3] 5890 3-8-7 **49** .... (v) CharlesBishop(3) 4 37
(Mick Channon) *led: hdd 2f out and edgd lft: hmpd on rail over 1f out: no ch after* **3/1**[1]

00-0 **5** ½ **Little Miss Zuri (IRE)**[240] 31 3-8-7 **46** oh1 .... CathyGannon 5 32
(Sylvester Kirk) *in rr: rdn along 3f out: clsd on ldrs 2f out but nvr on terms: wknd ins fnl f* **16/1**

0326 **6** 2 ¼ **Sunny Hollow**[37] 4654 3-9-2 **55** .... LiamKeniry 2 34
(James Toller) *chsd ldrs: rdn and wknd over 2f out* **8/1**[3]

1m 11.89s (0.69) **Going Correction** +0.025s/f (Good) **6** Ran SP% **98.3**
Speed ratings (Par 98): **96,95,90,89,88 85**
toteswingers 1&2 £8.50, 1&3 £2.40, 2&3 £2.00 CSF £33.38 CT £81.93 TOTE £10.40: £4.70, £2.10; EX 35.30 Trifecta £103.90 Pool: £1080.19 - 7.79 winning units..
Owner M Johnson **Bred** R Hollinshead And M Johnson **Trained** Upper Longdon, Staffs

FOCUS
A very weak sprint handicap with the winner getting back to something like her best 2-y-o mark.

5982 LINDT H'CAP 5f 11y
7:45 (7:45) (Class 6) (0-55,53) 3-Y-0+ **£1,940** (£577; £288; £144) **Stalls** Centre

Form RPR

4362 **1** **Burnt Cream**[17] 5408 6-9-5 **51** .... (t) RobertHavlin 5 60
(Martin Bosley) *bmpd s: hld up in rr: stdy hdwy 2f out to ld 1f out: hung rt fnl 110yds: hld on all out* **8/1**

6222 **2** *hd* **Chester'Slittlegem (IRE)**[9] 5670 4-9-3 **49** .... CathyGannon 8 57
(Jo Hughes) *chsd ldrs: drvn and styd on wl fnl f: chal clsng stages: jst hld* **5/4**[1]

0510 **3** 2 ¼ **Little China**[28] 4999 4-9-4 **50** .... (b) SteveDrowne 2 50
(William Muir) *chsd ldr: drvn to chal fr 2f out: outpcd and hld whn hmpd fnl 75yds* **5/1**[3]

5053 **4** 2 **Volcanic Dust (IRE)**[9] 5670 5-8-12 **51** .... (t) WillPettis(7) 6 44
(Milton Bradley) *wnt lft s: in tch: chsd ldrs and rdn 2f out: wknd ins fnl f* **4/1**[2]

0006 **5** ¾ **Ishetoo**[17] 5408 9-8-8 **45** .... (b) SladeO'Hara(5) 4 35
(Peter Grayson) *wnt rt s: sn rdn: mod prog fnl f* **25/1**

1050 **6** *nk* **Spic 'n Span**[9] 5670 8-9-7 **53** .... (b) WilliamCarson 1 42
(Ronald Harris) *led: rdn over 2f out: hdd 1f out: wknd ins fnl f* **9/1**

5664 **7** 1 ¼ **Brandywell Boy (IRE)**[9] 5670 10-8-10 **45** .... BillyCray(3) 9 29
(Dominic Ffrench Davis) *sn rdn: nvr gng pce to trble ldrs* **12/1**

00 **8** 4 ½ **Perlachy**[134] 1665 9-8-13 **50** .... (p) PhilipPrince(5) 7 18
(Ronald Harris) *chsd ldrs: rdn over 2f out: wknd fr 2f out* **16/1**

1m 2.67s (0.17) **Going Correction** +0.025s/f (Good) **8** Ran SP% **119.6**
Speed ratings (Par 101): **99,98,95,91,90 90,88,81**
toteswingers 1&2 £2.20, 1&3 £7.20, 2&3 £4.60 CSF £19.40 CT £59.43 TOTE £7.80: £2.20, £1.20, £1.60; EX 24.70 Trifecta £351.40 Pool: £2422.08 - 5.16 winning units..
Owner Mrs Patricia Brown **Bred** C Eddington And Partners **Trained** Chalfont St Giles, Bucks
■ Stewards' Enquiry : Robert Havlin one-day ban: careless riding (Sep 15)

FOCUS
A moderate sprint handicap and a small personal-best from the winner.

T/Plt: £1,158.90 to a £1 stake. Pool: £42,311.24 - 26.65 winning units T/Qpdt: £141.20 to a £1 stake. Pool: £5,401.50 - 28.30 winning units ST

5783 BEVERLEY (R-H)

Saturday, August 31

OFFICIAL GOING: Good to firm (8.9)

Inside rail around bottom bend moved out to provide fresh ground, increasing race distances of 7f and beyond by 19yds.

Wind: moderate, 1/2 against Weather: cloudy with sunny periods

5983 EBF RACEHORSETRADER.COM MAIDEN FILLIES' STKS (DIV I) 7f 100y

1:55 (1:56) (Class 4) 2-Y-O £4,075 (£1,212; £606; £303) Stalls Low

Form RPR

3 1 **Illuminating Dream (IRE)**[37] 4668 2-9-0 0 .... JamieSpencer 1 76+
(David Brown) *wnt lft s: sn led: pushed along and rn green over 2f out: rdn and edgd lft over 1f out: kpt on u.p fnl f* **11/10**[1]

6 2 2 ½ **Thurayaat**[44] 4432 2-9-0 0 .... DaneO'Neill 10 70+
(Roger Varian) *towards rr: hdwy 3f out: chsd ldrs over 1f out: swtchd rt and rdn ins fnl f: styd on wl to take 2nd nr fin* **5/1**[2]

06 3 hd **Bajan Beauty (IRE)**[30] 4921 2-9-0 0 .... RobertWinston 3 70
(Charles Hills) *trckd ldrs on inner whn stmbld 1/2-way: hdwy over 2f out: swtchd lft and rdn to chse wnr appr fnl f: sn drvn and no imp towards fin: lost 2nd nr line* **5/1**[2]

45 4 3 ¾ **Eleventh Hour (IRE)**[36] 4723 2-9-0 0 .... AhmedAjtebi 7 61
(Charlie Appleby) *chsd ldrs on outer: effrt over 2f out: rdn wl over 1f out: sn one pce* **12/1**

5 shd **La Havrese (FR)** 2-9-0 0 .... PJMcDonald 2 61
(Ann Duffield) *in tch: hdwy over 2f out: rdn wl over 1f out: kpt on one pce* **50/1**

35 6 3 **Nowinaminute (IRE)**[18] 5364 2-9-0 0 .... JamesSullivan 6 54
(James Given) *cl up: rdn along wl over 2f out: drvn wl over 1f out: grad wknd* **20/1**

0 7 ½ **Thatchereen (IRE)**[21] 5282 2-9-0 0 .... MickyFenton 5 52
(Michael Bell) *t.k.h: rn green and towards rr: pushed along wl over 2f out: sme late hdwy* **28/1**

0 8 2 ¼ **Soul Artist (IRE)**[12] 5577 2-9-0 0 .... DuranFentiman 8 47
(Tim Easterby) *a towards rr* **33/1**

9 2 ¾ **Capelena** 2-9-0 0 .... FrederikTylicki 4 40
(Clive Brittain) *in tch: rdn along over 2f out: sn wknd* **16/1**

10 nse **Connexion Francais** 2-8-11 0 .... PaulPickard(3) 9 40
(Tim Etherington) *dwlt: a bhd* **100/1**

11 1 ½ **Crafty Spell** 2-9-0 0 .... JoeFanning 11 37
(Mark Johnston) *wnt lft s: a bhd* **11/1**[3]

1m 34.4s (0.60) **Going Correction** -0.325s/f (Firm) 11 Ran SP% **117.0**

Speed ratings (Par 93): **83,80,79,75,75 72,71,68,65,65 64**

Tote Swingers 1&2 £3.00, 2&3 £4.10, 1&3 £2.40 CSF £6.14 TOTE £1.90: £1.10, £2.10, £1.80; EX 8.70 Trifecta £47.20 Pool: £5,066.06 - 80.41 winning tickets..

Owner Qatar Racing Limited **Bred** Barbara Keller **Trained** Averham Park, Notts

FOCUS

Ordinary maiden form.

5984 BETFRED BEVERLEY BULLET SPRINT STKS (LISTED RACE) 5f

2:30 (2:31) (Class 1) 3-Y-O+ £23,680 (£8,956; £4,476; £2,236) Stalls Low

Form RPR

0331 1 **Stepper Point**[18] 5375 4-9-0 104 ....(p) MartinDwyer 2 109
(William Muir) *mde all: rdn over 1f out: drvn ins fnl f: hld on gamely towards fin* **10/1**

2100 2 nk **York Glory (USA)**[8] 5726 5-9-0 109 ....(b) JamieSpencer 4 108+
(Kevin Ryan) *hld up and bhd: gng wl whn stdd 1/2-way: hdwy 2f out: swtchd rt wl over 1f out: gd hdwy whn n.m.r and swtchd lft ent fnl f: sn rdn and fin strly: edgd rt towards fin: jst failed* **11/4**[1]

-600 3 ¾ **Borderlescott**[14] 5545 11-9-0 102 .... PaulMulrennan 1 105
(Robin Bastiman) *chsd ldrs: hdwy on inner over 1f out: rdn to chal ins fnl f and ev ch tl drvn and no ex towards fin* **12/1**

0210 4 1 **Masamah (IRE)**[29] 4947 7-9-0 106 ....(p) DaneO'Neill 11 102
(Marco Botti) *chsd ldrs: hdwy wl over 1f out: rdn appr fnl f: kpt on* **8/1**[3]

2122 5 1 **Minalisa**[13] 5561 4-8-9 101 .... TedDurcan 9 93
(Rae Guest) *wnt lft s: towards rr: pushed along 1/2-way: hdwy over 1f out: sn rdn and hanging rt: swtchd lft and drvn ins fnl f: styd on wl: nrst fin* **15/2**[2]

1300 6 ¾ **Tangerine Trees**[49] 4311 8-9-0 105 ....(v) TomEaves 6 95
(Bryan Smart) *prom: rdn along wl over 1f out: drvn and wknd appr fnl f* **9/1**

0000 7 nk **Doc Hay (USA)**[74] 3420 6-9-0 101 .... DanielTudhope 7 94
(David O'Meara) *t.k.h: hld up in rr: hdwy on inner wl over 1f out: rdn and kpt on fnl f: nrst fin* **16/1**

0010 8 1 ½ **Cheviot (USA)**[10] 5651 7-9-0 96 ....(p) DuranFentiman 3 89
(Ian Semple) *chsd ldrs: rdn along 1/2-way: wkng whn sltly hmpd wl over 1f out* **33/1**

-000 9 ¾ **Stonefield Flyer**[191] 746 4-9-0 95 .... PJMcDonald 10 86
(Keith Dalgleish) *sltly hmpd s and in rr tl sme late hdwy* **80/1**

3044 10 2 **Pearl Sea (IRE)**[13] 5561 3-8-7 92 .... HarryBentley 8 74
(David Brown) *nvr bttr than midfield* **28/1**

4043 11 shd **Excelette (IRE)**[49] 4311 4-8-9 102 .... RoystonFfrench 12 74
(Bryan Smart) *prom: rdn along 2f out: sn drvn and wknd* **12/1**

-300 12 1 **Caledonia Lady**[8] 5726 4-8-9 102 .... FrederikTylicki 15 70
(Jo Hughes) *swtchd rt s: towards rr: hdwy on outer and in tch 2f out: sn rdn and wknd* **10/1**

6002 13 3 ¼ **Inxile (IRE)**[18] 5375 8-9-0 101 ....(p) AdrianNicholls 5 63
(David Nicholls) *in tch: rdn along bef 1/2-way: sn wknd* **33/1**

23-0 14 12 **Baileys Jubilee**[136] 1622 3-8-7 104 .... JoeFanning 14 15
(Mark Johnston) *chsd ldrs on outer: rdn along 2f out: sn wknd* **16/1**

0103 15 6 **Ballista (IRE)**[27] 5027 5-9-4 110 .... RobertWinston 13
(Tom Dascombe) *prom: rdn along over 2f out: wkng whn hmpd appr fnl f* **16/1**

1m 1.72s (-1.78) **Going Correction** -0.10s/f (Good)

WFA 3 from 4yo+ 2lb 15 Ran SP% **121.3**

Speed ratings (Par 111): **110,109,108,106,105 103,103,101,99,96 96,94,89,70,60**

Tote Swingers 1&2 £7.20, 2&3 £12.40, 1&3 £25.30 CSF £36.51 TOTE £13.50: £3.50, £1.50, £4.70; EX 45.20 Trifecta £759.00 Pool: £81,929.25 - 80.95 winning tickets..

Owner C L A Edginton **Bred** Whitsbury Manor Stud **Trained** Lambourn, Berks

■ Stewards' Enquiry : Jamie Spencer one-day ban: careless riding (Sep 15)

Ted Durcan one-day ban: careless riding (Sep 15)

FOCUS

A good-quality Listed sprint, loaded with front-runners, and predictably they went fast up front. Still, not much got into it from off the pace. The winner sets the level rated to his former best.

5985 BETFRED WISHES INDIAN TRAIL A HAPPY RETIREMENT H'CAP 5f

3:05 (3:06) (Class 5) (0-75,75) 3-Y-O+ £3,234 (£962; £481; £240) Stalls Low

Form RPR

6050 1 **Bronze Beau**[17] 5381 6-9-3 73 ....(tp) JacobButterfield(5) 2 86
(Kristin Stubbs) *mde all: rdn over 1f out: drvn clr ins fnl f: styd on* **6/1**[2]

3502 2 2 ¾ **Rich Again (IRE)**[21] 5273 4-9-0 65 .... JamieSpencer 1 68+
(James Bethell) *dwlt and in rr: gd hdwy on inner over 1f out: squeezed through and rdn ent fnl f: styd on wl towards fin* **15/8**[1]

0400 3 shd **Rangooned**[16] 5422 3-8-13 66 .... PJMcDonald 7 69
(Ann Duffield) *in tch: hdwy to chse ldrs over 1f out: swtchd lft and rdn ins fnl f: styd on strly towards fin* **28/1**

4256 4 2 **Hit The Lights (IRE)**[25] 5088 3-9-3 70 .... RobertWinston 4 66
(Ollie Pears) *cl up on inner: rdn and ev ch whn n.m.r over 1f out: swtchd lft and drvn ent fnl f: kpt on same pce* **6/1**[2]

1215 5 ½ **Ingenti**[15] 5470 5-8-12 70 .... KevinStott(7) 6 64
(Christopher Wilson) *trckd ldrs: hdwy and cl up 1/2-way: rdn over 1f out: wknd fnl f* **13/2**[3]

3520 6 nk **Indian Trail**[17] 5381 13-8-12 70 ....(b) JordanNason(7) 12 63
(David Nicholls) *dwlt and swtchd rt s: in rr: hdwy wl over 1f out: rdn and styd on wl fnl f: nrst fin* **12/1**

3400 7 1 **Boxing Shadows**[9] 5673 3-9-1 68 ....(p) PaulMulrennan 9 57
(Bryan Smart) *midfield: effrt 2f out: sn rdn and no imp fnl f* **16/1**

0605 8 hd **Chunky Diamond (IRE)**[12] 5579 4-9-4 72 ....(t) LMcNiff(3) 13 60
(Ruth Carr) *towards rr: effrt and sme hdwy wl over 1f out: sn rdn and no imp fnl f* **16/1**

0200 9 nk **Medici Time**[14] 5537 8-9-9 74 .... TomEaves 14 61
(Tim Easterby) *in rr: hdwy wl over 1f out: sn rdn and kpt on fnl f: nt rch ldrs* **20/1**

0202 10 2 ¾ **Mey Blossom**[16] 5422 8-9-0 65 ....(p) RussKennemore 15 42
(Richard Whitaker) *chsd ldrs: rdn along 2f out: sn wknd* **20/1**

-606 11 2 ½ **Marine Commando**[18] 5376 5-9-3 68 ....(be) JamesSullivan 5 36
(Ruth Carr) *in tch: effrt whn n.m.r and hmpd over 1f out: sn wknd* **28/1**

2030 12 nk **Mercers Row**[17] 5381 6-9-3 68 .... DanielTudhope 10 35
(Karen Tutty) *cl up: rdn wl over 1f out: sn drvn and wknd* **11/1**

020 13 2 ¼ **Dreaming Of Rubies**[57] 4017 4-9-8 73 ....(t) DaneO'Neill 17 32
(Ben Haslam) *cl up on outer: rdn along 2f out: sn wknd* **20/1**

1m 2.5s (-1.00) **Going Correction** -0.10s/f (Good)

WFA 3 from 4yo+ 2lb 13 Ran SP% **125.7**

Speed ratings (Par 103): **104,99,99,96,95 94,93,93,92,88 84,83,80**

Tote Swingers 1&2 £5.20, 2&3 £14.70, 1&3 £66.50 CSF £17.07 CT £308.14 TOTE £10.30: £3.50, £1.10, £10.10; EX 28.50 Trifecta £661.50 Pool: £2,660.70 - 3.01 winning tickets..

Owner D Arundale **Bred** Meon Valley Stud **Trained** Norton, N Yorks

■ Stewards' Enquiry : Jordan Nason one-day ban: careless riding (Sep 15)

FOCUS

Another race in which it paid to race on the speed. The time suggests the winner ran to somewhere near his best.

5986 BETFRED "DOUBLE DELIGHT" H'CAP 1m 1f 207y

3:40 (3:40) (Class 2) (0-105,104) 3-Y-O £12,938 (£3,850; £1,924; £962) Stalls Low

Form RPR

5422 1 **London Citizen (USA)**[20] 5326 3-8-0 88 .... JoeyHaynes(5) 1 98
(K R Burke) *qckly into stride and sn clr: pushed along over 2f out: rdn over 1f out: kpt on strly fnl f* **4/1**[3]

6002 2 1 ½ **Windhoek**[9] 5681 3-9-7 104 .... JoeFanning 5 111
(Mark Johnston) *chsd clr ldr: hdwy over 2f out: rdn over 1f out: drvn and no imp fnl f* **1/1**[1]

2151 3 6 **Circus Turn (USA)**[6] 5792 3-8-7 90 6ex .... FrederikTylicki 2 85
(Sir Michael Stoute) *trckd ldng pair: hdwy 3f out: rdn along 2f out: sn drvn and one pce* **7/2**[2]

1246 4 7 **Danat Al Atheer**[27] 5035 3-8-6 89 ....(b) MartinDwyer 4 70
(William Haggas) *hld up: a in rr* **8/1**

1040 5 10 **Cruck Realta**[30] 4917 3-8-10 93 .... TomEaves 3 54
(Mick Channon) *chsd ldrs: rdn along wl over 2f out: sn btn* **14/1**

2m 1.84s (-5.16) **Going Correction** -0.325s/f (Firm) 5 Ran SP% **110.0**

Speed ratings (Par 106): **107,105,101,95,87**

CSF £8.51 TOTE £6.00: £3.50, £1.10; EX 8.80 Trifecta £30.40 Pool: £2,571.89 - 63.38 winning tickets..

Owner H Strecker & Mrs E Burke **Bred** Stonestreet Thoroughbred Holdings LLC **Trained** Middleham Moor, N Yorks

FOCUS

Early pace prevailed once again, London Citizen being the fourth winner on the card to make all. A clear personal-best from the winner, while the second ran to somewhere near his form from earlier in the season.

5987 BETFRED "GOALS GALORE" H'CAP 7f 100y

4:15 (4:15) (Class 4) (0-85,84) 3-Y-O+ £4,690 (£1,395; £697; £348) Stalls Low

Form RPR

1153 1 **Consign**[16] 5437 3-9-6 83 ....(v) JamieSpencer 6 92
(Jeremy Noseda) *in tch: hdwy over 2f out: chsd ldrs over 1f out: rdn to ld ins fnl f: edgd rt and kpt on wl towards fin* **7/4**[1]

0500 2 ¾ **Shadowtime**[3] 5880 8-9-2 74 .... BarryMcHugh 3 81
(Tracy Waggott) *in rr: pushed along 2f out: rdn over 1f out: swtchd lft and drvn ent fnl f: styd on strly towards fin* **14/1**

1021 3 1 **Fathsta (IRE)**[10] 5645 8-9-0 75 .... NeilFarley(3) 7 80
(Declan Carroll) *trckd ldng pair: hdwy 2f out: chsd ldr over 1f out: rdn to chal ent fnl f: ev ch tl drvn and no ex last 75yds* **10/1**

3006 4 2 ¼ **Al Muheer (IRE)**[11] 5613 8-9-12 84 ....(b) JamesSullivan 8 83
(Ruth Carr) *towards rr: hdwy on outer over 2f out: rdn wl over 1f out: kpt on fnl f: nrst fin* **20/1**

-003 5 2 **Polish World (USA)**[13] 5564 9-8-12 70 .... MickyFenton 5 64
(Paul Midgley) *sn led: rdn along 3f out: hdd 2f out: sn drvn and wknd* **5/1**[2]

-400 6 1 **Maria's Choice (IRE)**[59] 3960 4-9-7 79 ....(v[1]) MartinDwyer 1 70
(Alan McCabe) *bhd tl styd on fnl 2f: nvr rchd ldrs* **14/1**

1105 7 1 ¾ **Relight My Fire**[6] 5784 3-8-12 75 ....(b) DavidAllan 9 62
(Tim Easterby) *chsd ldr: hdwy to ld 2f out: sn rdn and edgd rt: jnd and drvn ent fnl f: sn hdd & wknd* **10/1**

0005 8 2 ¾ **Copperwood**[11] 5613 8-9-4 76 .... JoeFanning 2 56
(Mark Johnston) *chsd ldrs: rdn along wl over 2f out: sn wknd* **8/1**

1240 **9** *17* **Red Explorer (USA)**[22] 5247 3-9-7 **84**................................ TedDurcan 4 37
(Charles Hills) *chsd ldrs: rdn along wl over 2f out: drvn wl over 1f out: sn wknd and eased* **6/1**[3]

1m 31.8s (-2.00) **Going Correction** -0.325s/f (Firm)
WFA 3 from 4yo+ 5lb **9** Ran SP% **114.7**
Speed ratings (Par 105): **98,97,96,93,91 90,88,84,65**
Tote Swingers 1&2 £6.50, 2&3 £21.10, 1&3 £5.00 CSF £28.93 CT £195.43 TOTE £2.20: £1.30, £4.40, £2.50; EX 28.70 Trifecta £339.90 Pool: £3,393.33 - 7.48 winning tickets..
Owner Miss Yvonne Jacques **Bred** Natton House Thoroughbreds & Mark Woodall **Trained** Newmarket, Suffolk

FOCUS
In contrast to the earlier races, the winner came from off the pace this time, with the leaders going too hard up front early and then kicking for home 3f out. The runner-up is rated slightly below his early season form.

5988 EBF RACEHORSETRADER.COM MAIDEN FILLIES' STKS (DIV II) 7f 100y
4:50 (4:51) (Class 4) 2-Y-O **£4,075** (£1,212; £606; £303) **Stalls** Low

Form RPR
50 **1** **Dance Bid**[17] 5394 2-9-0 0................................ FrederikTylicki 5 77
(Clive Brittain) *trckd ldrs: hdwy 2f out: cl up over 1f out: rdn to ld ins fnl f: kpt on* **22/1**
03 **2** *1 ¼* **Anipa**[21] 5279 2-9-0 0................................ PaulMulrennan 12 74+
(Ed Dunlop) *s.i.s and bhd: hdwy wl over 2f out: rdn over 1f out: kpt on wl fnl f: nrst fin* **10/3**[2]
4 **3** *½* **Sound Of Summer (IRE)**[14] 5529 2-9-0 0.................... TedDurcan 6 73+
(Charles Hills) *dwlt and towards rr: hdwy over 2f out: rdn to chse ldrs over 1f out: drvn and kpt on fnl f: nrst fin* **6/4**[1]
03 **4** *2* **Spring Carnival (USA)**[14] 5516 2-9-0 0.................... AhmedAjtebi 8 68
(Charlie Appleby) *trckd ldrs: hdwy on outer and cl up 3f out: led wl over 1f out: sn rdn: drvn and hdd ins fnl f: wknd* **8/1**
05 **5** *nk* **Ultraviolet (IRE)**[43] 4491 2-9-0 0........................ JamieSpencer 4 67
(David Simcock) *chsd ldr: hdwy 3f out: sn cl up: rdn and ev ch over 1f out: drvn and wknd ent fnl f* **5/1**[3]
6 *1* **Percy's Gal** 2-9-0 0................................ RoystonFfrench 10 65
(Karen Tutty) *dwlt: green and outpcd in rr: hdwy on outer over 2f out: rdn over 1f out: kpt on fnl f: nrst fin* **22/1**
6 **7** *2 ¾* **Christmas Wish**[21] 5282 2-9-0 0........................ TomEaves 9 59
(Mick Channon) *midfield: rdn along over 2f out: n.d* **10/1**
00 **8** *nk* **Roving Bunny**[19] 5338 2-9-0 0............................ JamesSullivan 3 58
(James Given) *a towards rr* **66/1**
04 **9** *4* **Tell Me When**[14] 5543 2-9-0 0............................ MickyFenton 1 49
(Brian Rothwell) *chsd ldrs on inner: rdn along 3f out: wkng whn n.m.r wl over 1f out* **40/1**
63 **10** *4 ½* **Ibecke**[44] 4443 2-9-0 0................................ JoeFanning 2 38
(Mark Johnston) *led: rdn along over 2f out: drvn and hdd wl over 1f out: sn wknd* **12/1**

1m 34.63s (0.83) **Going Correction** -0.325s/f (Firm) **10** Ran SP% **120.3**
Speed ratings (Par 93): **82,80,80,77,77 76,73,72,68,63**
Tote Swingers 1&2 £13.90, 2&3 £2.30, 1&3 £10.60 CSF £94.85 TOTE £40.90: £7.50, £1.40, £1.10; EX 137.10 Trifecta £604.90 Pool: £2,535.35 - 3.14 winning tickets..
Owner Saeed Manana **Bred** Dr J M Leigh **Trained** Newmarket, Suffolk

FOCUS
This looked more open than division one.

5989 BETFRED "HAT TRICK HEAVEN" MAIDEN STKS 5f
5:20 (5:23) (Class 5) 3-Y-O+ **£3,234** (£962; £481; £240) **Stalls** Low

Form RPR
32 **1** **Be Lucky**[115] 2169 3-9-0 0................................ PaulMulrennan 6 71+
(Michael Easterby) *trckd ldrs: hdwy 2f out: rdn to ld ent fnl f: drvn and hld on wl towards fin* **2/1**[2]
3222 **2** *¾* **Hi Filwah (USA)**[11] 5618 3-9-5 68........................(v) JamieSpencer 3 73
(Jeremy Noseda) *dwlt and towards rr: hdwy 2f out: rdn to chse ldrs over 1f out: styd on to chal ins fnl f and ev ch tl drvn and no ex towards fin* **7/4**[1]
5 **3** *2 ½* **Shotgun Start**[26] 5069 3-9-5 0............................ JoeFanning 9 64
(Michael Wigham) *in tch: hdwy wl over 1f out: rdn and hung sharply lft ent fnl f: kpt on* **7/1**[3]
4460 **4** *4 ½* **Headstight (IRE)**[24] 5139 4-9-2 49........................(p) MickyFenton 14 43
(Paul Midgley) *swtchd rt s and hld up in rr: hdwy 2f out: swtchd lft to outer and rdn over 1f out: no imp fnl f* **18/1**
4-6 **5** *1 ½* **Mon Chic**[21] 5290 3-9-0 0................................ RoystonFfrench 13 38
(Geoffrey Oldroyd) *towards rr: hdwy 2f out: sn rdn and no imp fnl f* **80/1**
50-0 **6** *3 ¼* **Chorister Choir (IRE)**[14] 5517 3-9-0 62.................... DuranFentiman 5 26
(Tim Easterby) *sn led: hdd 1/2-way: cl up tl rdn to ld again briefly over 1f out: sn drvn: hdd & wknd qckly* **50/1**
24 **7** *nk* **Idle Warrior**[70] 3593 3-9-5 0............................ BarryMcHugh 11 30
(Richard Fahey) *chsd ldrs: rdn along wl over 1f out: sn outpcd* **12/1**
0 **8** *¾* **Perci French**[8] 5715 3-9-5 0............................ DanielTudhope 4 27
(David O'Meara) *nvr bttr then midfield* **20/1**
0 **9** *3 ½* **Playful Promises (IRE)**[9] 5685 3-9-0 0.................(b[1]) FrederikTylicki 12 10
(W P Browne, Ire) *cl up: led 1/2-way: rdn and hdd over 1f out: wknd qckly* **25/1**
0 **10** *3 ¾* **Baby Mac**[6] 5783 5-9-2 0............................[1] AdamCarter(5) 1
(Neville Bycroft) *a in rr* **40/1**
005- **11** *1* **Mariella**[255] 8166 3-9-0 49................................ TomEaves 7
(Neville Bycroft) *a in rr* **50/1**
-02 **12** *nk* **Spirit Of Parkes**[102] 2535 3-9-5 0........................ TedDurcan 2
(Eric Alston) *chsd ldrs: rdn along 2f out: sn wknd* **10/1**

1m 3.23s (-0.27) **Going Correction** -0.10s/f (Good)
WFA 3 from 4yo+ 2lb **12** Ran SP% **120.4**
Speed ratings (Par 103): **98,96,92,85,83 78,77,76,70,64 63,62**
Tote Swingers 1&2 £1.80, 2&3 £3.80, 1&3 £5.70 CSF £5.59 TOTE £3.00: £1.30, £1.30, £2.60; EX 7.00 Trifecta £38.80 Pool: £1,942.97 - 37.46 winning tickets..
Owner The Sangster Family & M W Easterby **Bred** Jeremy Green And Sons **Trained** Sheriff Hutton, N Yorks

FOCUS
A typically modest 3-y-o plus sprint maiden for the time of year. The form makes sense with the first two to form.

5990 STARS OF THE FUTURE APPRENTICE H'CAP 1m 1f 207y
5:55 (5:56) (Class 6) (0-65,65) 3-Y-O **£2,587** (£770; £384; £192) **Stalls** Low

Form RPR
0043 **1** **Ningbo Express (IRE)**[17] 5386 3-9-10 **65**.................. JordanVaughan 7 78
(Rae Guest) *hld up and bhd: gd hdwy over 3f out: led wl over 1f out: rdn and hung lft ins fnl f: sn clr* **5/2**[2]
0111 **2** *5* **Artful Prince**[15] 5497 3-9-6 **64**........................(b) JackGarritty(3) 2 68
(James Given) *sn led and set str pce: jnd 3f out: sn hdd and rdn: drvn and rallied to chse wnr ent fnl f: sn no imp* **11/10**[1]
2023 **3** *8* **Special Report (IRE)**[9] 5667 3-8-4 **48**.................... DanielleMooney(3) 6 36
(Peter Hiatt) *hld up in tch: hdwy over 3f out: chal over 2f out and ev ch tl rdn and one pce appr fnl f* **14/1**
2445 **4** *½* **Betty Boo (IRE)**[23] 5197 3-8-2 **46** oh1........................ GaryMahon(3) 5 33
(Shaun Harris) *chsd ldrs: hdwy over 3f out: cl up and ev ch over 2f out: sn rdn and one pce fr wl over 1f out* **25/1**
0154 **5** *5* **Bahamamay**[15] 5483 3-9-2 **62**............................ EireannCagney(5) 4 40
(Richard Fahey) *chsd ldrs: hdwy over 3f out: led wl over 2f out: sn rdn: hdd wl over 1f out and sn wknd* **9/2**[3]
3044 **6** *¾* **Precision Strike**[5] 5433 3-8-13 **57**........................(v) LukeLeadbitter(3) 1 33
(Richard Guest) *chsd clr ldr: tk clsr order over 3f out: cl up wl over 2f out: sn rdn and wknd wl over 1f out* **11/1**

2m 5.36s (-1.64) **Going Correction** -0.325s/f (Firm) **6** Ran SP% **113.2**
Speed ratings (Par 98): **93,89,82,82,78 77**
Tote Swingers 1&2 £1.40, 2&3 £2.80, 1&3 £5.20 CSF £5.73 TOTE £3.60: £2.00, £1.20; EX 7.50 Trifecta £31.10 Pool: £1,813.42 - 43.61 winning tickets..
Owner Maze Rattan Limited **Bred** Brian Williamson **Trained** Newmarket, Suffolk

FOCUS
This was run at a furious gallop early and the pace collapsed. The winner is unexposed at the trip and could be on a good mark on Ayr form.
T/Jkpt: Not won. T/Plt: £10.40 to a £1 stake. Pool: £80,969.61 - 5,639.55 winning units T/Qpdt: £4.80 to a £1 stake. Pool: £2,902.20 - 445.90 winning units JR

5941 CHESTER (L-H)
Saturday, August 31

OFFICIAL GOING: Good (7.6)
Rail from 6f to 1.5f out a further 3yds from Friday, adding 22yds to races 1 & 6, 24yds to races 2, 4 & 5, 44yds to race 3 and 46yds to race 7.
Wind: Fresh; half against Weather: Fine but overcast

5991 MINSTRELL RECRUITMENT H'CAP 5f 110y
2:20 (2:21) (Class 2) (0-100,98) 3-Y-O+ **£12,938** (£3,850; £1,924; £962) **Stalls** Low

Form RPR
200 **1** **El Viento (FR)**[14] 5545 5-9-0 **91**........................(v) GeorgeChaloner(5) 5 103
(Richard Fahey) *s.i.s: in rr and drvn along: swtchd outside over 1f out: styd on strly to ld last 75yds: won gng away* **9/2**[2]
3001 **2** *2 ¾* **New Fforest**[51] 4221 3-8-6 **88**............................ OisinMurphy(7) 1 91
(Andrew Balding) *mid-div: hdwy on ins 2f out: styd on ins fnl f: tk 2nd towards fin* **4/1**[1]
2133 **3** *½* **Smart Daisy K**[14] 5511 3-8-11 **86**........................ ShaneKelly 7 87+
(Andrew Hollinshead) *trckd ldrs: t.k.h: kpt on to take 3rd nr fin* **5/1**[3]
0654 **4** *nk* **L'Ami Louis (IRE)**[15] 5489 5-8-11 **83**.................... LukeMorris 9 83
(Henry Candy) *wnt r s: sn chsng ldrs: nt clr run and lost pl over 1f out: styd on wl ins fnl f: tk 4th post* **7/1**
0644 **5** *1* **Addictive Dream (IRE)**[18] 5375 6-9-12 **98**.................. KierenFallon 8 95
(David Nicholls) *sn w ldr: led over 1f out: hdd last 75yds: no ex* **12/1**
0000 **6** *1* **Captain Dunne (IRE)**[14] 5519 8-8-11 **83**.................. GrahamGibbons 4 76
(Tim Easterby) *led: hdd over 1f out: wknd fnl 50yds* **11/1**
010 **7** *hd* **Doctor Parkes**[10] 5651 7-9-11 **97**........................ J-PGuillambert 2 89
(Stuart Williams) *chsd ldrs: nt clr run jst ins fnl f: kpt on same pce* **6/1**
0-24 **8** *½* **Even Stevens**[203] 584 5-8-10 **85**........................(p) BillyCray(3) 6 76
(Scott Dixon) *mid-div: hdwy over 1f out: kpt on ins fnl f* **20/1**
4000 **9** *2 ¼* **Al's Memory (IRE)**[8] 5696 4-8-12 **87**.................... DeclanBates(3) 3 70
(David Evans) *s.s: nvr on terms* **12/1**
3100 **10** *7* **Rusty Rocket (IRE)**[1] 5943 4-8-13 **85**.................... FrannyNorton 11 54
(Paul Green) *sn chsng ldrs on outer: hung rt and lost pl over 1f out: heavily eased ins fnl f* **14/1**

1m 7.31s (1.11) **Going Correction** +0.30s/f (Good)
WFA 3 from 4yo+ 2lb **10** Ran SP% **116.8**
Speed ratings (Par 109): **104,100,99,99,97 96,96,95,92,83**
toteswingers 1&2 £7.20, 1&3 £4.20, 2&3 £6.20 CSF £22.92 CT £95.83 TOTE £5.70: £2.10, £1.70, £1.40; EX 32.50 Trifecta £78.00 Pool: £1,981.69 - 19.03 winning units..
Owner John Nicholls Ltd/David Kilburn **Bred** Ballykilbride Stud **Trained** Musley Bank, N Yorks

FOCUS
The going was given as good (GoingStick 7.6) and the rail was out 3yds after racing on Friday; Actual race distances 5f132yds; 6f42yds; 1m5f133yds; 7f146yds; 7f26yds; 1m7f241yds. The pace collapsed here but the runner-up is rated pretty much to form.

5992 CRABBIE'S ALCOHOLIC GINGER BEER H'CAP 7f 122y
2:55 (2:57) (Class 2) 3-Y-O+
£28,012 (£8,388; £4,194; £2,097; £1,048; £526) **Stalls** Low

Form RPR
5120 **1** **Clockmaker (IRE)**[3] 5894 7-8-11 **91**........................ PhillipMakin 1 102
(Conor Dore) *chsd ldrs: led over 1f out: forged clr ins fnl f* **8/1**
0001 **2** *3 ½* **Brae Hill (IRE)**[31] 4895 7-8-7 **92**........................ GeorgeChaloner(5) 3 94
(Richard Fahey) *dwlt: in rr: hdwy on inner over 2f out: styd on wl to take 2nd last 50yds* **7/1**
0652 **3** *2* **Es Que Love (IRE)**[5] 5844 4-9-10 **104**.................... GrahamLee 2 101
(Mark Johnston) *led: hdd over 1f out: kpt on same pce* **7/2**[1]
0235 **4** *1* **Mabait**[7] 5738 7-8-1 **88**................................ ShelleyBirkett(7) 10 88
(David Simcock) *in rr: nt clr run on inner 2f out: chsng ldrs whn nt clr run on ins and swtchd rt ins fnl f: r.o* **12/1**
0001 **5** *½* **Marcret (ITY)**[64] 3754 6-9-6 **100**........................ DavidProbert 12 94
(James Unett) *swtchd lft after s: sn chsng ldrs: one pce fnl f* **25/1**
0004 **6** *nse* **Regal Parade**[14] 5545 9-8-12 **97**........................(t) MatthewLawson(5) 7 90
(Milton Bradley) *in rr: effrt on outer over 2f out: styd on wl ins fnl f* **20/1**
4121 **7** *shd* **Alejandro (IRE)**[22] 5238 4-8-10 **90**........................ LeeTopliss 4 83
(Richard Fahey) *w ldr: wknd over 1f out* **11/2**[3]
053 **8** *3* **Ayaar (IRE)**[14] 5510 3-8-10 **96**............................(v) SamHitchcott 5 82
(Mick Channon) *mid-div: effrt over 2f out: chsng ldrs over 1f out: n.m.r 100yds out: wknd* **9/1**
006 **9** *¾* **Thunderball**[14] 5545 7-8-10 **90**............................(p) LukeMorris 9 74
(Scott Dixon) *mid-div: drvn over 3f out: wknd over 1f out* **25/1**
2003 **10** *nk* **Enrol**[13] 5561 4-9-0 **94**................................(v) ShaneKelly 6 77
(Sir Michael Stoute) *dwlt: t.k.h early: effrt over 2f out: rdn over 1f out: nvr a factor* **5/1**[2]

1401 **11** 2 1/2 **Correspondent**14 5510 3-9-4 **104** MartinLane 11 81
(Brian Meehan) *swtchd lft after s: sn chsng ldrs on outer: lost pl 4f out: eased clsng stages* **8/1**

1m 34.02s (0.22) **Going Correction** +0.30s/f (Good)
WFA 3 from 4yo+ 6lb **11** Ran SP% **119.1**
Speed ratings (Par 109): **110,106,104,103,103 102,102,99,99,98 96**
toteswingers 1&2 £21.20, 1&3 £8.70, 2&3 £5.00 CSF £62.15 CT £202.31 TOTE £13.50: £3.90, £3.40, £1.70; EX 72.40 Trifecta £169.00 Pool: £2,422.15 - 10.74 winning units..
Owner CHP Consulting **Bred** Lemongrove Stud & Brendan Arthur **Trained** Hubbert's Bridge, Lincs

FOCUS
A good quality handicap in which the winner looked better than ever, while the runner-up is rated to his best Polytrack mark.

5993 GOLDEN SQUARE SHOPPING CENTRE CHESTER (H'CAP) (LISTED RACE) 1m 5f 89y
3:30 (3:32) (Class 1) (0-110,108) 3-Y-0+
£20,982 (£7,955; £3,981; £1,983; £995; £499) **Stalls** Low

Form RPR
121 **1** **Sun Central (IRE)**49 4309 4-9-11 **108** (p) SebSanders 10 117
(William Haggas) *in rr: hdwy to chse ldrs 3f out: 2nd over 2f out: hung lft: edgd rt then lft: led jst ins fnl f: drvn out* **4/1**2

2600 **2** 1 1/4 **Bite Of The Cherry**9 5683 4-8-11 **94** oh1 (v1) DavidProbert 1 101
(Michael Bell) *chsd ldrs: led 4f out: hdd jst ins fnl f: styd on same pce last 50yds* **20/1**

220 **3** 2 1/4 **Handsome Man (IRE)**63 3824 4-9-0 **97** KierenFallon 6 101
(Saeed bin Suroor) *hld up in rr: hdwy over 3f out: 3rd 2f out: kpt on same pce* **6/1**3

151- **4** 9 **Tempest Fugit (IRE)**303 7510 4-9-2 **99** NickyMackay 7 89
(John Gosden) *dwlt: detached in last: drvn over 3f out: swtchd lft and tk modest 4th ins fnl f* **9/1**

1014 **5** 2 1/4 **Star Lahib (IRE)**9 5683 4-9-2 **99** FrannyNorton 2 86
(Mark Johnston) *mid-div: drvn over 4f out: modest 4th over 1f out: wknd ins fnl f* **7/2**1

-554 **6** 5 **Savanna La Mar (USA)**27 5035 3-8-2 **96** (p) LukeMorris 5 75
(Sir Mark Prescott Bt) *chsd ldrs: drvn over 5f out: lost pl over 2f out* **8/1**

54 **7** 16 **Montaser (IRE)**29 4944 4-9-4 **101** SamHitchcott 3 56
(David Simcock) *mid-div: chsng ldrs 3f out: lost pl over 2f out: sn bhd* **12/1**

2233 **8** 1 1/2 **Alta Lilea (IRE)**7 5779 3-8-8 **102** GrahamLee 8 55
(Mark Johnston) *w ldr: drvn over 4f out: lost pl over 2f out: sn bhd* **9/1**

0400 **P** **Guarantee**7 5766 4-9-2 **99** (p) PhillipMakin 4
(William Haggas) *led: eased and hdd 4f out: t.o whn p.u 2f out: lame* **13/2**

2m 54.75s (2.05) **Going Correction** +0.30s/f (Good)
WFA 3 from 4yo+ 11lb **9** Ran SP% **113.4**
Speed ratings (Par 111): **105,104,102,97,95 92,83,82,**
toteswingers 1&2 £12.60, 1&3 £5.20, 2&3 £12.70 CSF £76.97 CT £472.36 TOTE £3.30: £1.10, £7.50, £2.20; EX 89.50 Trifecta £734.70 Pool: £2,188.60 - 2.23 winning units..
Owner Lael Stable **Bred** Lael Stables **Trained** Newmarket, Suffolk

FOCUS
They went a good gallop in this Listed handicap, Alta Lilea and Guarantee rather taking each other on in front. The runner-up looks the best guide to the level.

5994 IRISH STALLION FARMS EBF COMBERMERE FILLIES' CONDITIONS STKS 6f 18y
4:05 (4:06) (Class 2) 2-Y-0 **£12,602** (£3,772; £1,886; £944; £470) **Stalls** Low

Form RPR
2201 **1** **Blockade (IRE)**15 5468 2-8-12 90 GrahamLee 6 92+
(James Tate) *chsd ldrs: drvn over 2f out: led 1f out: styd on* **5/2**2

1213 **2** 2 **Lilbourne Lass**15 5476 2-9-1 96 SeanLevey 2 89
(Richard Hannon) *chsd ldrs: drvn 3f out: swtchd rt over 1f out: styd on to take 2nd last 50yds* **6/5**1

6662 **3** hd **Rough Courte (IRE)**26 5053 2-8-12 78 SamHitchcott 7 85
(Mick Channon) *carried wd and lost pl over 4f out: carried wd bnd over 1f out: styd on wl ins fnl f: tk 3rd last 30yds: gng on at fin* **33/1**

5020 **4** 2 3/4 **Quatuor (IRE)**16 5460 2-9-5 88 RichardKingscote 1 84
(Tom Dascombe) *led: hdd 1f out: wknd last 50yds* **8/1**

100 **5** 12 **Fire Blaze (IRE)**50 4253 2-9-1 93 KierenFallon 3 50
(Charlie Appleby) *gave problems s: dwlt: t.k.h: swtchd outside and trckd ldr over 4f out: hung bdly rt bnd over 2f out: sn wknd: eased ins fnl f* **7/2**3

1m 16.86s (3.06) **Going Correction** +0.30s/f (Good) **5** Ran SP% **110.3**
Speed ratings (Par 97): **91,88,88,84,68**
CSF £5.94 TOTE £3.40: £1.40, £1.60; EX 7.30 Trifecta £29.90 Pool: £2,074.21 - 51.87 winning units..
Owner Saeed Manana **Bred** Patrick A Cassidy **Trained** Newmarket, Suffolk

FOCUS
A fairly tight little conditions event, and dubious form. Straightforward form rated through the fourth.

5995 BRITISH STALLION STUDS E B F MAIDEN STKS 7f 2y
4:40 (4:41) (Class 4) 2-Y-0 **£6,469** (£1,925; £962; £481) **Stalls** Low

Form RPR
336 **1** **Edge (IRE)**50 4256 2-9-5 78 SeanLevey 5 80
(Richard Hannon) *chsd ldng pair: 2nd 2f out: styd on to ld towards fin* **4/1**3

5422 **2** 3/4 **Lincoln (IRE)**5 5819 2-9-5 80 SamHitchcott 4 78
(Mick Channon) *bmpd s: led after 1f: hdd and no ex clsng stages* **7/2**2

4 **3** 2 1/2 **My Painter (IRE)**21 5282 2-9-0 0 RichardKingscote 3 72+
(Charles Hills) *dwlt and wnt rt s: stmbld and lost pl bend after 1f: hdwy over 2f out: hung lft over 1f out: styd on to take 3rd last 50yds* **5/4**1

0 **4** 2 1/4 **Telegraph (IRE)**27 5033 2-9-5 0 DavidProbert 7 65
(Andrew Balding) *chsd ldr: drvn over 2f out: wknd fnl 50yds* **10/1**

5 3 3/4 **Sherston** 2-9-5 0 FrannyNorton 2 55
(Mark Johnston) *led 1f: chsd ldrs: outpcd over 2f out: one pce* **7/1**

0565 **6** 1 **Mfiftythreedotcom (IRE)**27 5025 2-9-5 68 LeeTopliss 9 52
(Richard Fahey) *wnt rt s: sn chsng ldrs: rdn and outpcd over 2f out: hung rt and lost pl bnd over 1f out* **25/1**

7 nse **Enfys Hud** 2-8-11 0 DeclanBates(3) 8 47
(David Evans) *s.i.s: sn outpcd and bhd: sme hdwy over 1f out: nvr on terms* **50/1**

0 **8** 3 **Streethowlingmama (USA)**85 3049 2-9-0 0 GrahamGibbons 6 39
(William Jarvis) *mid-div: outpcd over 2f out: 4th over 1f out: sltly hmpd 1f out: sn wknd* **40/1**

9 9 **Enquiring** 2-9-5 0 GrahamLee 1 20
(Mark Johnston) *lost pl after 1f: sn wl outpcd and wl bhd* **16/1**

1m 29.48s (2.98) **Going Correction** +0.30s/f (Good) **9** Ran SP% **122.4**
Speed ratings (Par 96): **94,93,90,87,83 82,82,78,68**
toteswingers 1&2 £2.70, 1&3 £2.30, 2&3 £2.50 CSF £19.45 TOTE £4.10: £1.30, £1.40, £1.50; EX 18.70 Trifecta £49.60 Pool: £4,038.06 - 61.03 winning units..
Owner Hughes, Morecombe, Anderson **Bred** Swordlestown Stud **Trained** East Everleigh, Wilts

FOCUS
This looked a fair maiden and the form is straightforward, with the first two running to their marks.

5996 CONTROLLED SOLUTIONS GROUP H'CAP 5f 110y
5:10 (5:11) (Class 4) (0-85,85) 3-Y-O **£6,469** (£1,925; £962; £481) **Stalls** Low

Form RPR
2100 **1** **Space Artist (IRE)**84 3097 3-9-1 **79** GrahamLee 2 86
(Bryan Smart) *mde all: hld on gamely* **11/2**

136 **2** 1/2 **Trinityelitedotcom (IRE)**19 5340 3-8-13 **77** RichardKingscote 11 82
(Tom Dascombe) *w wnr: no ex towards fin* **10/1**

1021 **3** hd **Sharaarah (IRE)**10 5639 3-9-6 **84** DavidNolan 5 89
(David O'Meara) *trckd ldrs: drvn 2f out: kpt on to take cl 3rd nr fin* **5/2**1

0530 **4** 1/2 **Layla's Oasis**23 5184 3-8-2 **66** oh2 PatrickMathers 3 69
(Richard Fahey) *dwlt: sn chsng ldrs: effrt on ins over 1f out: kpt on same pce last 50yds* **16/1**

0600 **5** 3/4 **Storm Moon (USA)**7 5769 3-9-5 **83** FrannyNorton 10 83
(Mark Johnston) *chsd ldrs: effrt over 2f out: n.m.r over 1f out: kpt on same pce last 100yds* **10/1**

5500 **6** 2 1/4 **Top Boy**50 4255 3-9-0 **85** AdamMcLean(7) 4 78+
(Derek Shaw) *dwlt: hdwy on outside to chse ldrs over 3f out: one pce over 1f out* **7/2**2

2241 **7** nse **Jontleman (IRE)**15 5477 3-9-2 **80** SamHitchcott 6 73
(Mick Channon) *mid-div: hdwy to chse ldrs over 1f out: one pce fnl f* **9/2**3

4660 **8** 2 1/4 **Hardy Blue (IRE)**26 5067 3-8-2 **66** oh1 LukeMorris 1 51
(Danielle McCormick) *in rr: drvn over 2f out: nvr on terms* **14/1**

1m 8.69s (2.49) **Going Correction** +0.30s/f (Good) **8** Ran SP% **115.1**
Speed ratings (Par 102): **95,94,94,93,92 89,89,86**
toteswingers 1&2 £10.10, 1&3 £3.90, 2&3 £5.50 CSF £58.47 CT £172.65 TOTE £7.30: £2.00, £1.90, £1.20; EX 71.30 Trifecta £644.20 Pool: £2,053.70 - 2.39 winning units..
Owner The Smart Dame Laura Partnership **Bred** Rathasker Stud **Trained** Hambleton, N Yorks

FOCUS
Nothing came from off the pace. The form makes sense at face value, rated around the in-form placed horses.

5997 GOLDEN SQUARE WARRINGTON H'CAP 1m 7f 195y
5:40 (5:42) (Class 4) (0-85,83) 3-Y-0+ **£6,469** (£1,925; £962; £481) **Stalls** Low

Form RPR
3331 **1** **Nashville (IRE)**3 5885 4-9-5 **74** 6ex GrahamLee 1 81
(Richard Fahey) *led: qcknd pce over 6f out: hdd over 1f out: rallied to ld last stride* **15/8**1

3236 **2** shd **Gabrial's King (IRE)**30 4913 4-9-8 **77** KierenFallon 8 84
(David Simcock) *mid-div: swtchd outside over 5f out: chsng ldrs 3f out: led over 12f out: faltered and hung lft: hdd post* **5/1**3

2314 **3** 1/2 **Nateeja (IRE)**31 4899 3-8-5 **74** FrannyNorton 9 80
(J W Hills) *swtchd lft after s: sn chsng ldrs: drvn and outpcd over 2f out: styd on to join ldrs last 100yds: no ex nr fin* **7/2**2

214 **4** 1 **Eshtyaaq**14 5520 6-8-11 **69** DeclanBates(3) 4 74
(David Evans) *n.m.r sn after s: sn chsng ldrs: 2nd over 4f out: kpt on same pce last 75yds* **9/1**

311 **5** 23 **Tijori (IRE)**59 3952 5-8-13 **68** (p) MartinLane 10 45
(Bernard Llewellyn) *in rr and sn pushed along: bhd and reminders 7f out: tk distant 5th ins fnl f* **16/1**

1623 **6** 1 1/2 **Filatore (IRE)**30 4913 4-8-11 **73** (p) DanielMuscutt(7) 12 49
(Bernard Llewellyn) *chsd ldrs: drvn 7f out: lost pl over 4f out: sn bhd* **12/1**

5 **7** 3 **Villa Royale**27 5031 4-10-0 **83** DavidNolan 5 55
(David O'Meara) *wnt lft s: in rr: drvn over 5f out: outpcd over 3f out: poot 5th 2f out: wknd ins fnl f* **10/1**

3542 **8** 28 **Uncle Bernie (IRE)**12 5592 3-8-2 **71** oh9 ow2 (p) DavidProbert 11 9
(Andrew Hollinshead) *mid-div: lost pl 4f out: sn bhd: t.o whn eased over 1f out* **20/1**

-550 **9** 29 **L Frank Baum (IRE)**30 4913 6-8-13 **75** OisinMurphy(7) 2
(Bernard Llewellyn) *hmpd sn after s: in rr: rdn along after 7f: sn wl bhd: t.o 7f out: eventually completed* **12/1**

3m 31.59s (3.59) **Going Correction** +0.30s/f (Good)
WFA 3 from 4yo+ 14lb **9** Ran SP% **118.8**
Speed ratings (Par 105): **103,102,102,102,90 89,88,74,59**
toteswingers 1&2 £3.50, 1&3 £4.00, 2&3 £5.80 CSF £11.84 CT £31.12 TOTE £2.70: £1.10, £1.90, £1.90; EX 10.40 Trifecta £62.60 Pool: £2,083.47 - 24.92 winning units..
Owner Dr Marwan Koukash **Bred** B L Harvey & Balmerino Bloodstock **Trained** Musley Bank, N Yorks

FOCUS
They went a steady early gallop here and it proved hard to come from off the pace. The first four were clear and the fourth helps set the level.
T/Plt: £14.80 to a £1 stake. Pool: £112,869.12 - 5,539.85 winning units T/Qpdt: £4.00 to a £1 stake. Pool: £4,538.10 - 829.20 winning units WG

5955 SANDOWN (R-H)
Saturday, August 31

OFFICIAL GOING: Good to firm (sprint course 8.3, round course 8.5)
Far side of sprint track moved in 3yds. Round course on inner line and all distances as advertised.
Wind: Light; against Weather: Sunny

5998 BETFRED GOALS GALORE H'CAP 5f 6y
2:05 (2:06) (Class 3) (0-95,93) 3-Y-0+
£12,450 (£3,728; £1,864; £932; £466; £234) **Stalls** Low

Form RPR
02 **1** **Burning Thread (IRE)**14 5519 6-9-3 **86** (b) AdamBeschizza 3 97
(Tim Etherington) *chsd ldr tl led 1/2-way: rdn clr over 1f out: styd on wl and in command after: rdn out* **7/1**3

121 **2** 2 **Tidal's Baby**32 4860 4-8-7 **77** PaulHanagan 2 81
(Tony Carroll) *hld up trcking ldrs: effrt and rdn to chse clr wnr over 1f out: styd on u.p but no imp* **6/1**1

4250 **3** 3/4 **Sir Maximilian (IRE)**14 5519 4-9-5 **88** StevieDonohoe 11 89
(Nicky Vaughan) *hld up in tch in midfield: effrt and n.m.r over 1f out: hdwy u.p 1f out: chsd ldng pair ins fnl f: styd on wl but no threat to wnr* **12/1**

 The Form Book Flat, Raceform Ltd, Compton, RG20 6NL.

0060 **4** 1 1/4 **Dungannon**[14] 5519 6-9-3 **86**....(v[1]) JimmyFortune 10 86+
(Andrew Balding) *hld up in midfield: switching lft looking for run wl over 1f out: nvr much room but sme hdwy ins fnl f: swtchd lft again and r.o cl home: nvr able to chal* **8/1**

-143 **5** nk **Mission Approved**[38] 4641 3-8-9 **80**.... RyanMoore 16 76+
(Sir Michael Stoute) *swtchd rt after s: hld up in rr: clsd but nt clr run 2f out: hdwy jst ins fnl f: squeezed between horses and styd on wl ins fnl f: nvr trbld ldrs* **9/1**

2110 **6** 1/2 **Swendab (IRE)**[8] 5696 5-9-4 **87**....(v) FergusSweeney 13 81
(John O'Shea) *chsd ldrs: drvn and outpcd in 3rd 2f out: no imp and lost 3 pls ins fnl f* **16/1**

2004 **7** hd **Joe Packet**[22] 5247 6-9-8 **91**.... JimCrowley 9 84
(Jonathan Portman) *chsd ldrs: rdn and unable qck 1/2-way: rallied u.p and chsd ldrs again over 1f out: no ex fnl f* **13/2**[2]

0000 **8** 1/2 **Fratellino**[22] 5247 6-8-13 **82**....(tp) MartinHarley 12 73
(Alan McCabe) *in tch in midfield: rdn 1/2-way: no imp tl styd on ins fnl f: nvr trbld ldrs* **25/1**

0056 **9** 4 **Pandar**[21] 5257 4-9-10 **93**....(p) JamesDoyle 5 70
(Robert Cowell) *hld up trcking ldrs: rdn and no rspnse 2f out: sn btn: wknd fnl f* **14/1**

50 **10** nk **B Fifty Two (IRE)**[78] 3299 4-9-3 **86**....(t) WilliamBuick 15 62
(J W Hills) *bhd: rdn 1/2-way: hdwy but no threat to ldrs ent fnl f: no prog ins fnl f: wl hld and eased towards fin* **18/1**

0405 **11** 1 3/4 **Ask The Guru**[117] 2083 3-8-11 **82**....(v[1]) RobertHavlin 1 51
(Michael Attwater) *led tl 1/2-way: sn rdn and struggling: wknd ent fnl f* **28/1**

000 **12** hd **Edge Closer**[32] 4860 9-8-13 **87**.... GeorgeDowning(5) 7 56
(Tony Carroll) *chsd ldrs tl rdn and unable qck 1/2-way: wknd over 1f out* **16/1**

41 **13** 3/4 **O'Gorman**[75] 3415 4-9-2 **85**.... RichardHughes 4 51
(Gary Brown) *taken down early: stdd s: hld up in rr: n.d* **7/1**[3]

1030 **14** 1 1/4 **Lupo D'Oro (IRE)**[14] 5533 4-9-2 **85**.... SteveDrowne 6 47
(John Best) *v.s.a: a bhd: n.d* **11/1**

59.87s (-1.73) **Going Correction** -0.125s/f (Firm)
WFA 3 from 4yo+ 2lb **14** Ran SP% **120.7**
Speed ratings (Par 107): **108,104,103,101,101 100,100,99,92,92 89,89,88,86**
toteswingers 1&2 £5.50, 1&3 £13.90, 2&3 £16.20 CSF £48.76 CT £520.05 TOTE £6.40: £2.30, £2.10, £4.50; EX 26.50 Trifecta £924.30 Pool: £3,987.37 - 3.23 winning units..
Owner Tim Etherington **Bred** James Lombard **Trained** Norton, N Yorks

FOCUS
A drying day, and there was fresh ground from the 7f start to the 2f pole. This was a typically competitive Sandown sprint handicap, with low-drawn runners just having the edge, and a few finding trouble, although they didn't go overly quick. The winner stepped up on this year's form, while the runner-up ran close to his Goodwood mark backed up by the third.

5999 BETFRED MOBILE SOLARIO STKS (GROUP 3) 7f 16y
2:40 (2:42) (Class 1) 2-Y-O **£22,684** (£8,600; £4,304; £2,144) **Stalls** Low

Form RPR
1 **1** **Kingman**[63] 3833 2-9-0 0.... JamesDoyle 4 112+
(John Gosden) *stdd after s: hld up in tch: smooth hdwy to join ldr 2f out: rdn hands and heels and qcknd to ld over 1f out: in command but signs of greeness fnl f: pushed out: comf* **2/7**[1]

1512 **2** 2 **Emirates Flyer**[35] 4747 2-9-0 100.... SilvestreDeSousa 2 104
(Saeed bin Suroor) *chsd ldr: rdn whn gallop qcknd jst over 2f out: unable qck w wnr over 1f out: no imp on fnl f but styd on to go 2nd last strides* **10/1**[3]

211 **3** hd **Music Theory (IRE)**[16] 5438 2-9-0 105.... MickaelBarzalona 1 103
(Charlie Appleby) *led and set stdy gallop: rdn and qcknd jst over 2f out: hdd and unable qck w wnr over 1f out: styd on same pce fnl f: lost 2nd last strides* **9/2**[2]

0524 **4** 7 **Rosso Corsa**[31] 4876 2-9-0 95.... MartinHarley 3 84
(Mick Channon) *stdd s: t.k.h: hld up in tch: rdn over 2f out: sn struggling and outpcd over 1f out: wknd fnl f* **33/1**

1m 28.38s (-1.12) **Going Correction** -0.20s/f (Firm) **4** Ran SP% **108.0**
Speed ratings (Par 104): **98,95,95,87**
CSF £3.90 TOTE £1.20; EX 3.40 Trifecta £5.00 Pool: £3,141.75 - 466.99 winning units..
Owner K Abdullah **Bred** Juddmonte Farms Ltd **Trained** Newmarket, Suffolk

FOCUS
John Gosden had already won the Solario three times, notably with subsequent Breeders' Cup Classic hero Raven's Pass, and while the trainer's latest winner still has a way to go before reaching such a level, Kingman, who was following up a seriously impressive debut win, is another potential top notcher. Hand-timed sectionals, taken at the marker just over 3f out, showed the pace was around two seconds slower than the later nursery to that point, yet the final time was 0.16 seconds quicker, and the speed Kingman produced to brush aside some decent enough rivals (runner-up earned 98 RPR last time, third 100, fourth 96) was really quite impressive. The time and the race averages suggest this form is no better than rated.

6000 THOROUGHBRED BREEDERS' ASSOCIATION ATALANTA STKS (GROUP 3) (F&M) 1m 14y
3:15 (3:16) (Class 1) 3-Y-O+
£23,463 (£23,463; £6,456; £3,216; £1,614; £810) **Stalls** Low

Form RPR
6223 **1** **Ladys First**[36] 4732 4-9-1 105.... TonyHamilton 8 109
(Richard Fahey) *sn led: rdn and hdd over 2f out: sustained duel w ldr and battled on gamely: hrd drvn to ld again fnl 100yds: jnd on post* **7/1**[3]

110 **1** dht **Integral**[28] 4985 3-8-9 106.... RyanMoore 6 109+
(Sir Michael Stoute) *wnt rt s: hld up in tch in last pair: swtchd lft 3f out: rdn and gd hdwy to ld over 2f out: clr w rival over 1f out: hrd drvn and hdd fnl 100yds: battled on gamely to join ldr on post* **13/8**[1]

2100 **3** 1 3/4 **Shuruq (USA)**[29] 4949 3-8-13 110....(p) SilvestreDeSousa 2 109
(Saeed bin Suroor) *t.k.h: chsd ldr tl 6f out: styd chsng ldrs: rdn over 2f out: sltly outpcd over 1f out: kpt on ins fnl f: wnt 3rd on post* **12/1**

111 **4** nse **Zibelina (IRE)**[16] 5461 3-8-13 109.... MickaelBarzalona 10 109
(Charlie Appleby) *stdd after s: t.k.h: hld up towards rr tl hdwy to chse ldr 6f out: rdn over 2f out: sltly outpcd over 1f out: kpt on same pce ins fnl f: lost 3rd on post* **2/1**[2]

4664 **5** 4 **Falls Of Lora (IRE)**[21] 5271 4-9-1 96.... WilliamBuick 11 96
(Charlie Appleby) *chsd ldrs: rdn over 2f out: drvn and outpcd over 1f out: wknd ins fnl f* **14/1**

-602 **6** 1 **Reyaadah**[21] 5271 3-8-9 101.... PaulHanagan 7 93
(Charles Hills) *t.k.h: hld up in tch in midfield: shuffled bk into last trio 5f out: swtchd lft and effrt over 2f out: sn edging rt and outpcd: wl hld but plugged on fnl f* **16/1**

6-03 **7** nk **Winter's Night (IRE)**[36] 4705 5-9-1 97.... AdamKirby 5 93
(Clive Cox) *hld up in tch in last trio: rdn and effrt over 2f out: sn drvn and struggling: wl btn over 1f out: plugged on* **16/1**

-065 **8** 2 1/4 **Aquatinta (GER)**[35] 4792 3-8-9 102.... SteveDrowne 3 87
(Clive Cox) *in tch in midfield: rdn over 2f out: sn drvn and outpcd wl over 1f out: wknd ent fnl f* **25/1**

6364 **9** 26 **Private Alexander (IRE)**[36] 4732 3-8-9 95.... JamesDoyle 9 28
(David O'Meara) *hld up in touuch in midfield: rdn and no hdwy over 2f out: btn whn eased jst over 1f out: t.o* **40/1**

1m 39.2s (-4.10) **Going Correction** -0.20s/f (Firm)
WFA 3 from 4yo+ 6lb **9** Ran SP% **116.3**
TRIFECTA Tote Trif27 Owner.
Owner Mrs H Steel **Bred** Sparsholt Stud **Trained** Musley Bank, N Yorks

FOCUS
This decent fillies' Group 3 saw a dead-heat between Integral and Ladys First, but the former looked much the best on the day. Rounding the bend into the straight, four of the first five finishers filled the first four positions, with Ladys First in front, and the exception was Integral, who was last. Sir Michael Stoute's filly was then asked to make a big effort once in line for home, and she got there easily, before understandably getting tired, and that gave the Fahey runner another chance. The form makes sense, with the first four close to recent marks and the fifth to form.

6001 BETFRED TV & LEVY BOARD H'CAP 1m 2f 7y
3:50 (3:51) (Class 2) 3-Y-O+
£37,350 (£11,184; £5,592; £2,796; £1,398; £702) **Stalls** Low

Form RPR
125 **1** **Vasily**[21] 5269 5-8-12 **97**.... RobertTart(5) 2 105
(Robert Eddery) *chsd ldrs: n.m.r on inner wl over 1f out: swtchd lft and chalng between horses whn rdr dropped whip 1f out: rn wl to ld fnl wl ins fnl f* **12/1**

5401 **2** nk **Fennell Bay (IRE)**[13] 5559 4-8-10 **90**.... MickaelBarzalona 13 97
(Mark Johnston) *chsd ldrs: rdn and sltly outpcd over 2f out: rallied u.p to chal over 1f out: led jst ins fnl f: hdd wl ins fnl f: kpt on* **16/1**

4644 **3** 1/2 **Proud Chieftain**[21] 5283 5-9-0 **94**....(p) JamesDoyle 3 100
(Clifford Lines) *hld up in tch in midfield: effrt u.p 2f out: hdwy 1f out: styd on wl u.p ins fnl f* **20/1**

2122 **4** 1 3/4 **Sennockian Star**[7] 5768 3-8-13 **101**....(v) LiamJones 9 104
(Mark Johnston) *sn led: rdn over 2f out: hrd drvn and hdd jst ins fnl f: no ex and wknd fnl 75yds* **5/1**[1]

-052 **5** 1/2 **Trade Commissioner (IRE)**[14] 5540 5-9-10 **104**.... WilliamBuick 7 106+
(John Gosden) *t.k.h: hld up in tch in rr: stl plenty to do but hdwy wl over 1f out: swtchd lft over 1f out: styd on wl ins fnl f: nt rch ldrs* **7/1**[3]

0051 **6** nse **Mister Music**[7] 5742 4-9-3 **97**....(b) RichardHughes 14 98
(Richard Hannon) *hld up in tch towards rr: rdn and effrt 2f out: hdwy u.p 1f out: styd on wl fnl f: nt rch ldrs* **20/1**

2610 **7** 3/4 **Danchai**[21] 5269 4-9-5 **99**....(p) AndreaAtzeni 12 99
(William Haggas) *t.k.h: hld up wl in tch in midfield: rdn and effrt over 2f out: hdwy to press ldrs over 1f out: no ex and wknd ins fnl f* **8/1**

110 **8** 3/4 **Whispering Warrior (IRE)**[32] 4854 4-8-13 **93**.... JimCrowley 1 91
(David Simcock) *hld up in tch in midfield: rdn and effrt over 2f out: edging rt and swtchd lft over 1f out: kpt on but no threat to ldrs fnl f* **8/1**

4214 **9** 3/4 **Gabrial The Great (IRE)**[21] 5269 4-9-2 **96**.... AdamKirby 4 93
(Luca Cumani) *t.k.h: hld up in tch towards rr: effrt and swtchd lft over 1f out: nt clr run 1f out: plugged on same pce fnl f* **13/2**[2]

4131 **10** nk **Nemushka**[14] 5548 4-8-0 **80**.... JimmyQuinn 6 76
(Richard Fahey) *hld up in tch in midfield: rdn and effrt ent fnl 2f: swtchd lft and drvn over 1f out: no ex and wknd ins fnl f* **20/1**

2-10 **11** 1/2 **Resurge (IRE)**[63] 3832 8-9-4 **98**....(t) TomQueally 8 93
(Stuart Kittow) *hld up in tch in last trio: rdn and no imp 2f out: kpt on but no threat to ldrs ins fnl f* **50/1**

6340 **12** 1 1/2 **Chapter Seven**[71] 3525 4-9-6 **100**.... GeorgeBaker 10 92
(Stuart Williams) *hld up in tch in midfield: rdn and effrt 3f out: sme hdwy u.p wl over 1f out: wknd fnl f* **12/1**

0430 **13** 1 3/4 **Beaufort Twelve**[21] 5259 4-8-2 **87** ow1....(v[1]) MichaelJMMurphy(5) 15 76
(William Jarvis) *t.k.h: hld up in tch in midfield hdwy to chse ldr 6f out tl over 1f out: btn and short of room sn after: wknd fnl f* **16/1**

-030 **14** 6 **Labarinto**[21] 5269 5-9-5 **99**.... RyanMoore 5 76
(Sir Michael Stoute) *in tch in midfield: rdn 3f out: no imp and wknd over 1f out: bhd and eased wl ins fnl f* **9/1**

0150 **15** 13 **Asatir (USA)**[29] 4946 4-9-1 **95**....(p) SilvestreDeSousa 11 46
(Saeed bin Suroor) *hld up in tch towards rr: rdn and no hdwy over 3f out: wknd 2f out: bhd and eased ins fnl f* **20/1**

2m 5.83s (-4.67) **Going Correction** -0.20s/f (Firm)
WFA 3 from 4yo+ 8lb **15** Ran SP% **122.9**
Speed ratings (Par 109): **110,109,109,107,107 107,106,106,105,105 105,103,102,97,87**
toteswingers 1&2 £42.50, 1&3 £54.90, 2&3 £58.90 CSF £177.95 CT £3793.14 TOTE £14.40: £4.80, £6.30, £6.50; EX 242.60 Trifecta £5043.90 Part won. Pool: £6,725.28 - 0.66 winning units..
Owner Owen O'Brien & David Bannon **Bred** Cheveley Park Stud Ltd **Trained** Newmarket, Suffolk

FOCUS
A good handicap, but it proved hard to make up ground. Rounding the bend into the straight, three of the first four finishers held a top-four position. The winner recorded a marginal personal-best.

6002 BETFRED.COM NURSERY H'CAP 7f 16y
4:25 (4:27) (Class 4) (0-85,80) 2-Y-O **£5,175** (£1,540; £769; £384) **Stalls** Low

Form RPR
226 **1** **Gown (IRE)**[14] 5508 2-8-13 **72**.... RyanMoore 1 77
(Charles Hills) *t.k.h: chsd ldrs: swtchd lft and rdn to ld over 1f out: styd on wl fnl f: rdn out* **14/1**

1 **2** 1 **Lilyfire (USA)**[36] 4702 2-9-7 **80**.... JamesDoyle 2 85+
(Roger Charlton) *t.k.h: hld up in tch in last trio: swtchd lft and nt clr run 2f out: sme hdwy whn hmpd and swtchd lft jst over 1f out: gap opened and r.o wl ins fnl f to go 2nd cl home: nt rch wnr* **5/2**[1]

5343 **3** nk **Needless Shouting (IRE)**[6] 5790 2-8-8 **67**.... MartinHarley 7 68
(Mick Channon) *led and crossed to inner rail: rdn ent fnl 2f: drvn and hdd over 1f out: kpt on same pce ins fnl f: lost 2nd cl home* **13/2**[3]

21 **4** 1/2 **Hunters Creek (IRE)**[21] 5279 2-9-6 **79**.... WilliamBuick 4 79
(John Gosden) *dwlt: in tch in last trio: rdn and hdwy over 2f out: chsd ldrs and drvn ent fnl f: kpt on but no imp on wnr fnl 100yds* **5/2**[1]

21 **5** 1/2 **Smart Salute**[31] 4886 2-9-6 **79**.... GeorgeBaker 5 78
(Ed Walker) *t.k.h: hld up wl in tch in midfield: nt clr run 2f out: swtchd lft and effrt to chse ldrs 1f out: kpt on same pce ins fnl f* **4/1**[2]

452 **6** hd **Officer Drivel (IRE)**[10] 5635 2-9-0 **73**.... JimmyFortune 3 71
(Luke Dace) *stdd after s: hld up in tch in rr: effrt on outer and edgd rt 2f out: kpt on ins fnl f: nt pce to chal* **25/1**

633 **7** 2 1/2 **Miaplacidus (IRE)**[36] 4723 2-8-9 **68**.... PaulHanagan 8 59
(Richard Fahey) *chsd ldr tl over 1f out: no ex u.p ent fnl f: wknd fnl 100yds* **20/1**

531 **8** *11* **The Alamo (IRE)**[20] 5309 2-9-5 **78** .... RichardHughes 6 39
(Richard Hannon) *t.k.h: chsd ldrs: rdn and effrt jst over 2f out: no ex and btn ent fnl f: bhd and eased ins fnl f* **10/1**

1m 28.54s (-0.96) **Going Correction** -0.20s/f (Firm) **8** Ran SP% **114.8**
Speed ratings (Par 96): **97,95,95,94,94 94,91,78**
toteswingers 1&2 £6.70, 1&3 £7.90, 2&3 £5.30 CSF £49.48 CT £259.84 TOTE £15.80: £2.90, £1.30, £2.00; EX 69.00 Trifecta £470.30 Pool: £3,855.38 - 6.14 winning units..
Owner Mrs J K Powell **Bred** J Collins **Trained** Lambourn, Berks

FOCUS
A fair nursery run at a much better pace than the Solario Stakes. The form looks straightforward.

6003 BETFRED DOUBLE DELIGHT/HAT TRICK HEAVEN H'CAP 1m 14y
5:00 (5:01) (Class 4) (0-80,80) 3-Y-O **£5,175** (£1,540; £769; £384) **Stalls** Low

Form RPR

41- **1** **Rainbow Beauty**[299] 7592 3-8-9 **68** .... (p) JamesDoyle 4 79
(Gerard Butler) *hld up in midfield: effrt over 2f out: hdwy u.p to ld over 1f out: r.o wl fnl f: rdn out* **16/1**

125 **2** *1 1/4* **Starlight Symphony (IRE)**[23] 5202 3-9-1 **74** .... (b) TomQueally 1 82
(Eve Johnson Houghton) *hld up in midfield: rdn and effrt over 2f out: hdwy u.p over 1f out: styd on wl ins fnl f: wnt 2nd cl home* **20/1**

5132 **3** *hd* **Silver Dixie (USA)**[16] 5440 3-9-7 **80** .... RyanMoore 10 88
(Jeremy Noseda) *hld up in tch in midfield: rdn and effrt over 2f out: hdwy u.p over 1f out: chsd wnr ins fnl f: kpt on same pce fnl 100yds: lost 2nd towards fin* **2/1**[1]

1652 **4** *1* **Aint Got A Scooby (IRE)**[40] 4593 3-9-1 **74** .... AdamKirby 6 79
(Clive Cox) *chsd ldrs: rdn and effrt over 2f out: swtchd lft over 1f out: kpt on same pce ins fnl f* **8/1**

4236 **5** *1 1/2* **Strong Conviction**[16] 5440 3-9-0 **73** .... MartinHarley 8 75
(Mick Channon) *chsd ldr for 2f: chsd ldrs after: rdn to chal 2f out: drvn to ld over 1f out: sn hdd: wknd ins fnl f* **14/1**

2412 **6** *1* **Mazaaher**[28] 5004 3-9-3 **76** .... PaulHanagan 7 75
(J W Hills) *wl in tch in midfield: rdn and unable qck over 2f out: styd on same pce u.p ins fnl f* **9/2**[2]

34 **7** *1 1/2* **Big Whiskey (IRE)**[14] 5541 3-9-4 **77** .... GeorgeBaker 11 73
(Edward Creighton) *chsd ldrs tl wnt 2nd 6f out: upsides ldr and travelling wl 2f out: sn rdn and fnd little: btn 1f out: wknd ins fnl f* **18/1**

-465 **8** *nse* **Living The Life (IRE)**[113] 2223 3-9-0 **73** .... WilliamBuick 9 69
(Jamie Osborne) *stdd s: hld up in rr: effrt and swtchd lft 2f out: sme hdwy over 1f out: kpt on same pce ins fnl f* **20/1**

3042 **9** *2* **Emulating (IRE)**[10] 5632 3-8-13 **72** .... RichardHughes 12 63
(Richard Hannon) *stdd and dropped in bhd after s: hld up in rr: effrt u.p over 2f out: no real imp: nvr trbld ldrs* **11/2**[3]

2350 **10** *1* **Strictly Ballroom (IRE)**[24] 5125 3-8-12 **71** .... SilvestreDeSousa 3 62
(Mark Johnston) *hld up in tch in midfield: rdn and unable qck jst over 2f out: plugging on same pce and wl hld whn nt clr run ins fnl f* **25/1**

2500 **11** *2 1/4* **Atlantis City (FR)**[62] 3858 3-8-2 **61** oh1 .... JimmyQuinn 2 45
(Richard Hannon) *s.i.s and bustled along early: rdn 3f out: no imp and stl plenty to do whn swtchd lft over 1f out: nvr trbld ldrs* **40/1**

0610 **12** *4 1/2* **Orbison (IRE)**[40] 4593 3-9-2 **75** .... AndreaAtzeni 5 49
(Roger Varian) *taken down early: racd keenly: led tl rdn and hdd over 1f out: btn 1f out: fdd ins fnl f* **16/1**

1m 40.29s (-3.01) **Going Correction** -0.20s/f (Firm) **12** Ran SP% **117.5**
Speed ratings (Par 102): **107,105,105,104,103 102,100,100,98,97 95,90**
toteswingers 1&2 £41.70, 1&3 £7.60, 2&3 £10.70 CSF £302.47 CT £935.15 TOTE £18.20: £4.70, £6.10, £1.40; EX 235.40 Trifecta £1076.10 Pool: £3,673.70 - 2.56 winning units..
Owner D O'Donohoe & J Cavanagh **Bred** Mascalls Stud **Trained** Newmarket, Suffolk

FOCUS
A fair handicap run at what looked a good pace. The fourth and fifth help set the standard in a sound-looking race.

6004 WATCH FRED'S PUSHES ON BETFRED TV H'CAP 1m 2f 7y
5:30 (5:32) (Class 4) (0-85,85) 3-Y-O+ **£5,175** (£1,540; £769; £384) **Stalls** Low

Form RPR

2020 **1** **Opera Box**[31] 4878 5-9-13 **84** .... GeorgeBaker 3 92
(Marcus Tregoning) *chsd ldr: rdn to ld 2f out: hdd but stl ev ch fr over 1f out: led wl ins fnl f: hld on wl* **7/1**[3]

0436 **2** *shd* **Tinshu (IRE)**[61] 3899 7-9-7 **78** .... (p) PaulHanagan 4 86
(Derek Haydn Jones) *hld up in tch in midfield: smooth hdwy to ld over 1f out: sn rdn: hdd wl ins fnl f: r.o but jst hld* **14/1**

2044 **3** *nk* **Purple 'n Gold (IRE)**[5] 5348 4-9-5 **76** .... (p) RyanMoore 12 83
(David Pipe) *hld up in midfield: shuffled bk towards rr and rdn over 2f out: hdwy 1f out: str run ins fnl f: nt quite rch ldrs* **12/1**

331 **4** *shd* **I'm Fraam Govan**[25] 5100 5-9-10 **81** .... (t) PatCosgrave 8 88+
(George Baker) *hld up in midfield: clsd and nt clr run 2f out: hdwy to chse ldrs jst ins fnl f: kpt on wl u.p fnl 100yds: nt quite rch ldrs* **5/1**[2]

3650 **5** *1 3/4* **Hefner (IRE)**[35] 4744 4-9-9 **85** .... MichaelJMMurphy[(5)] 13 89
(William Jarvis) *stdd after s: hld up in rr: rdn and no hdwy over 2f out: hdwy on outer 1f out: r.o wl fnl f: edgd rt nr fin: nt rch ldrs* **14/1**

300/ **6** *2* **World Heritage**[707] 5483 7-10-0 **85** .... AndreaAtzeni 7 85
(Robert Eddery) *hld up towards rr: hdwy on inner over 2f out: chsng ldrs whn nt clr run 1f out: kpt on same pce ins fnl f* **25/1**

00-5 **7** *1* **My Lord**[30] 2808 5-8-13 **70** .... JimmyFortune 1 68
(Luke Dace) *s.i.s: bhd: hdwy 3f out: drvn and no imp over 1f out: wknd ins fnl f* **20/1**

0-04 **8** *1 1/4* **Freddy Q (IRE)**[30] 4907 4-9-1 **77** .... RobertTart[(5)] 5 72
(Roger Teal) *t.k.h: hld up in midfield: effrt over 2f out: keeping on same pce whn hmpd 1f out: styd on same pce fnl f* **20/1**

2556 **9** *1* **Dandy (GER)**[28] 5006 4-9-3 **74** .... (v) WilliamBuick 14 67
(Andrew Balding) *chsd ldrs: rdn and ev ch over 2f out: no ex ent fnl f: wknd fnl 100yds* **16/1**

0/00 **10** *2 1/2* **Togiak (IRE)**[43] 4488 6-9-1 **72** .... MartinHarley 11 60
(David Pipe) *led tl rdn and hdd 2f out: sn struggling: wknd ent fnl f* **40/1**

2416 **11** *1/2* **Lucky Henry**[19] 5348 4-9-13 **84** .... AdamKirby 10 71
(Clive Cox) *chsd ldrs: rdn and effrt over 2f out: no ex over 1f out: wknd ins fnl f* **10/1**

133 **12** *2 1/2* **Broadway Duchess (IRE)**[16] 5440 3-9-3 **82** .... RichardHughes 6 64
(Richard Hannon) *stdd after s: hld up towards rr: swtchd lft and effrt u.p over 2f out: no prog over 1f out: wknd fnl f* **15/8**[1]

6640 **13** *14* **Kaafel (IRE)**[122] 1922 4-9-4 **80** ....[1] JimCrowley 2 34
(Peter Hedger) *taken down early: chsd ldrs: rdn and unable qck over 2f out: wknd over 1f out: eased ins fnl f* **20/1**

14 **15** **Johnnys Legacy (IRE)**[295] 7681 6-9-0 **71** .... LiamJones 9
(Conor Dore) *nvr gng wl and a towards rr: rdn and lost tch over 2f out: t.o over 1f out* **50/1**

2m 6.71s (-3.79) **Going Correction** -0.20s/f (Firm)
WFA 3 from 4yo+ 8lb **14** Ran SP% **122.5**
Speed ratings (Par 105): **107,106,106,106,105 103,102,101,101,99 98,96,85,73**
toteswingers 1&2 £23.10, 1&3 £8.80, 2&3 £25.90 CSF £92.44 TOTE £7.70: £2.90, £5.00, £3.80; EX 118.90 Trifecta £1380.20 Pool: £2,528.49 - 1.37 winning units..
Owner Efemera Stud **Bred** Efemera Stud **Trained** Whitsbury, Hants

FOCUS
The favourite flopped, Broadway Duchess caught a bit wide and not improving as anticipated for the step up in trip, and there was a bunch finish. The form looks sound but ordinary.
T/Plt: £346.70 to a £1 stake. Pool: £159,614.95 - 336.07 winning units T/Qpdt: £148.60 to a £1 stake. Pool: £8,272.76 - 41.17 winning units SP

6005 - 6009a (Foreign Racing) - See Raceform Interactive

5939 BADEN-BADEN (L-H)
Saturday, August 31

OFFICIAL GOING: Turf: good

6010a T VON ZASTROW STUTENPREIS (GROUP 3) (3YO+ FILLIES & MARES) (TURF) 1m 3f
4:15 (12:00) 3-Y-O+
£26,016 (£8,943; £4,471; £2,439; £1,626; £1,219)

RPR

1 **Adoya (GER)**[27] 5044 3-8-10 0 .... FabienLefebvre 2 105
(Andreas Lowe, Germany) *dwlt and hld up in last: rdn and hdwy 2f out: c across to nr side rail in st and styd on to chal ins fnl f: led 100yds out and drew clr: readily* **4/1**[2]

2 *1 1/4* **Fitful Skies (IRE)**[38] 4652 4-9-5 0 .... FabriceVeron 4 103
(H-A Pantall, France) *hld up towards rr: rdn and hdwy 2f out: styd on and wnt 2nd wl ins fnl f: nt pce of wnr* **7/2**[1]

3 *1 3/4* **Adriana (GER)**[29] 5-9-5 0 .... MircoDemuro 1 100
(M Rulec, Germany) *t.k.h: restrained in rr early but sn stdy hdwy on outer and led after 4f: 2 l advantage whn rdn 2f out: styd on but clsd down and strly pressed ins fnl f: hdd 100yds out: no ex and dropped to 3rd* **179/10**

4 *1 3/4* **Pearls Or Passion (FR)**[48] 4336 4-9-5 0 .... Francois-XavierBertras 6 97
(F Rohaut, France) *prom early: settled in midfield after 4f: rdn 2f out: sn outpcd by ldrs: styd on u.p and jst prevailed for 4th* **57/10**

5 *hd* **Oriental Lady (GER)**[27] 5044 3-8-10 0 .... ADeVries 8 96
(J Hirschberger, Germany) *t.k.h: hld up: hdwy into midfield on outer 1/2-way: rdn over 2f out: outpcd by ldrs over 1f out: styd on u.p and jst denied 4th* **91/10**

6 *4* **Path Wind (FR)**[56] 4-9-5 0 .... EPedroza 9 89
(A Wohler, Germany) *midfield: rdn over 2f out: sltly hmpd as wnr cut across in st: sn outpcd: plugged on for mod 6th* **32/5**

7 *2 1/2* **Ars Nova (GER)**[27] 5044 3-8-10 0 .... CristianDemuro 7 85
(W Figge, Germany) *led: hdd after 4f and trckd ldr: rdn over 2f out: outpcd and btn ent fnl f: fdd* **59/10**

8 *5* **Quilita (GER)**[27] 5044 3-8-10 0 .... AStarke 10 76
(P Schiergen, Germany) *trckd ldr: rdn over 3f out: outpcd and lost pl 2f out: sn no ex and btn* **43/10**[3]

9 *3/4* **Molly Amour (GER)**[48] 4-9-5 0 .... JBojko 3 74
(M Rulec, Germany) *t.k.h: midfield in tch on inner: rdn over 2f out: no ex and btn over 1f out: fdd* **243/10**

10 *13* **Artemisia (IRE)**[83] 3146 3-8-10 0 .... MrDennisSchiergen 5 51
(P Schiergen, Germany) *hld up in midfield: rdn over 3f out: sn dropped to rr: last and btn 2f out: t.o and eased ins fnl f* **149/10**

2m 21.64s (2.37)
WFA 3 from 4yo+ 9lb **10** Ran SP% **129.5**
WIN (incl. 10 euro stake): 50. PLACES: 19, 18, 37. SF: 215.
Owner Stall Waldecker Stern **Bred** Frau Doris & Dr Harald Mitze **Trained** Germany

6011 - 6012a (Foreign Racing) - See Raceform Interactive

5602 BRIGHTON (L-H)
Sunday, September 1

OFFICIAL GOING: Good to firm (watered; 7.6)
Rail moved out between 4.5f and 2f to provide fresh ground, increasing distances by 9yds
Wind: light across Weather: dry and sunny

6013 GATWICK AIRPORT SUPPORTS ROCKINGHORSE CHILDREN'S CHARITY MAIDEN AUCTION STKS 5f 59y
2:00 (2:00) (Class 6) 2-Y-O **£2,045** (£603; £302) **Stalls** Centre

Form RPR

46 **1** **Penny's Boy**[18] 5399 2-8-11 0 .... RichardHughes 2 72
(Sylvester Kirk) *mde virtually all: rdn 2f out: drvn and forged clr 1f out: styd on wl* **2/1**[1]

26 **2** *1/2* **Flashy Queen (IRE)**[13] 5593 2-8-8 0 .... JoeFanning 1 67
(Joseph Tuite) *t.k.h: chsd ldrs: rdn and effrt 2f out: str chal ins fnl f: r.o but hld towards fin* **7/2**[2]

24 **3** *3/4* **Amadaffair**[13] 5593 2-8-4 0 .... HayleyTurner 5 60
(Tom Dascombe) *w ldr: rdn and ev ch 2f out: no ex jst ins fnl f: one pce fnl 100yds* **7/2**[2]

3 **4** *1/2* **Kiss From A Rose**[38] 4686 2-8-6 0 .... ChrisCatlin 4 61
(Rae Guest) *stdd s: t.k.h: hld up in tch: swtchd lft over 2f out: rdn and effrt over 1f out: styd on same pce ins fnl f* **12/1**[3]

34 **5** *1 1/4* **Orlando Star (CAN)**[11] 5635 2-8-11 0 .... RobertTart[(5)] 6 66
(Roger Teal) *hld up in tch in last pair: rdn and swtchd lft over 1f out: no imp fnl f* **7/2**[2]

0 **6** *9* **Mini Light**[15] 5529 2-8-6 0 .... SamHitchcott 3 24
(Mick Channon) *chsd ldrs tl 1/2-way: sn lost pl and bhd fnl f* **40/1**

1m 3.81s (1.51) **Going Correction** +0.075s/f (Good) **6** Ran SP% **110.1**
Speed ratings (Par 93): **90,89,88,87,85 70**
toteswingers 1&2 £2.30, 1&3 £1.60, 2&3 £2.60 CSF £8.89 TOTE £2.80: £1.30, £2.00; EX 9.70 Trifecta £39.20 Pool: £2810.73 - 53.74 winning units..
Owner Malcolm Brown & Mrs Penny Brown **Bred** Peter Webb **Trained** Upper Lambourn, Berks
■ Stewards' Enquiry : Richard Hughes two-day ban: used whip above permitted level (Sep 15-16)

FOCUS
Rail moved out between 4.5 f and 2f to provide fresh ground increasing distances by 9yds. Modest maiden form, with there being little between the first five at the line. They came stands' side. The form is rated around those in behinmd the winner.

6014 LONDON GATWICK TO BEIJING MAIDEN STKS 6f 209y
2:30 (2:31) (Class 5) 2-Y-O £2,587 (£770; £384; £192) Stalls Centre

Form RPR
422 1 **Peak Royale**[45] 4439 2-9-5 77 RichardHughes 1 75+
(Richard Hannon) *stdd s: hld up in last: clsd and chal 2f out: rdn to ld over 1f out: edging lft but drew clr ins fnl f: comf* **10/11**[1]
56 2 4 ½ **Sahra Al Khadra**[16] 5494 2-9-5 0 PaulHanagan 2 63
(Charles Hills) *t.k.h: chsd ldr for 2f: chsd ldrs after: rdn and effrt 2f out: 3rd and btn 1f out: plugged on to go 2nd fnl 50yds* **10/1**
4 3 ½ **Sullivan Street (IRE)**[22] 5279 2-9-5 0 MickaelBarzalona 5 62
(Charlie Appleby) *led: swtchd lft and rdn over 2f out: hdd over 1f out: wknd ins fnl f: lost 2nd fnl 50yds* **11/4**[2]
552 4 10 **Nakeeta**[7] 5785 2-9-5 0 SamHitchcott 4 35
(Mick Channon) *t.k.h: chsd ldrs: wnt 2nd 5f out tl 2f out: sn wknd bhd fnl f* **7/2**[3]

1m 24.37s (1.27) **Going Correction** +0.075s/f (Good) 4 Ran SP% **110.4**
Speed ratings (Par 95): **95,89,89,77**
CSF £9.89 TOTE £1.70; EX 10.60 Trifecta £18.20 Pool: £2138.75 - 87.94 winning units..
Owner Malih Lahej Al Basti **Bred** Brookside Breeders Club **Trained** East Everleigh, Wilts

FOCUS
Little depth to this ordinary small-field maiden. The winner is rated pretty much to his mark.

6015 LONDON GATWICK TO MOSCOW H'CAP 1m 3f 196y
3:00 (3:03) (Class 6) (0-65,65) 3-Y-O £2,045 (£603; £302) Stalls High

Form RPR
6652 1 **Jan De Heem**[23] 5216 3-9-7 65 (v) JimCrowley 4 72+
(Ralph Beckett) *stdd s: hld up in tch in rr: rdn and effrt in centre 2f out: drvn to ld ent fnl f: hung lft u.p but in command fnl 100yds: idling and pushed out towards fin* **11/8**[1]
43-0 2 ½ **Syrenka**[35] 4799 3-9-5 63 HayleyTurner 3 67
(Marcus Tregoning) *led and set stdy gallop: rdn and qcknd over 2f out: edgd lft u.p over 1f out: hdd ent fnl f: kpt on again towards fin* **3/1**[3]
00-2 3 2 ¾ **Simple Joys**[69] 3632 3-9-0 61 (p) ThomasBrown(3) 2 61
(Andrew Balding) *chsd ldr: rdn whn gallop qcknd over 2f out: 3rd and outpcd 1f out: one pce fnl f* **11/4**[2]
0043 4 nk **Point Of Control**[18] 5411 3-8-8 59 LouisSteward(7) 1 58
(Michael Bell) *chsd ldng pair: rdn and effrt whn gallop qcknd over 2f out: 4th and btn 1f out: one pce after* **11/2**

2m 36.37s (3.67) **Going Correction** +0.075s/f (Good) 4 Ran SP% **109.2**
Speed ratings (Par 99): **90,89,87,87**
CSF £5.76 TOTE £1.90; EX 5.90 Trifecta £9.30 Pool: £1886.14 - 150.67 winning units..
Owner Larksborough Stud Limited **Bred** Larksborough Stud Limited **Trained** Kimpton, Hants

FOCUS
This was always likely to be tactical and the runner-up set just a steady gallop.

6016 EBF / LONDON GATWICK TO HO CHI MINH CITY FILLIES' H'CAP 1m 1f 209y
3:30 (3:30) (Class 4) (0-85,85) 3-Y-O+ £6,469 (£1,925; £962; £481) Stalls High

Form RPR
4213 1 **Soryah (IRE)**[26] 5095 3-9-5 84 RichardHughes 6 95+
(Luca Cumani) *chsd ldr tl 6f out: styd chsng ldrs: rdn and effrt 3f out: ev ch over 1f out: led ins fnl f: r.o wl* **11/4**[2]
4212 2 1 **Qawaafy (USA)**[11] 5649 3-9-2 81 PaulHanagan 7 90
(Roger Varian) *t.k.h: hld up in tch: jnd ldrs 3f out: rdn to ld 2f out: hdd and one pce ins fnl f* **9/4**[1]
4343 3 2 ¼ **Mu'Ajiza**[5] 5855 3-8-9 74 JoeFanning 4 79
(Mark Johnston) *led and set stdy gallop: rdn and hdd over 2f out: styd pressing ldrs tl no ex u.p over 1f out: plugged on same pce ins fnl f* **9/2**
1111 4 ¾ **Beacon Lady**[6] 5823 4-9-6 85 6ex OisinMurphy(7) 2 88
(William Knight) *stdd s: t.k.h: hld up in tch in rr: hdwy 1/2-way: jnd ldr 4f out: rdn to ld over 2f out: hdd 2f out and sn outpcd: dropped to last over 1f out: no threat to wnr but kpt on again fnl 100yds* **3/1**[3]
2131 5 2 ¼ **Curly Come Home**[24] 5169 4-9-10 82 (t) GeorgeBaker 5 81
(Chris Wall) *t.k.h: chsd ldrs: shuffled bk to rr but stl wl in tch 3f out: effrt to chal wl over 1f out: 3rd and no ex 1f out: wknd ins fnl f* **9/1**

2m 8.32s (4.72) **Going Correction** +0.075s/f (Good)
WFA 3 from 4yo 7lb 5 Ran SP% **110.6**
Speed ratings (Par 102): **84,83,81,80,79**
CSF £9.38 TOTE £4.20: £1.80, £1.40; EX 8.80 Trifecta £31.00 Pool: £2652.42 - 64.07 winning units..
Owner Sheikh Mohammed Obaid Al Maktoum **Bred** Liam Queally **Trained** Newmarket, Suffolk

FOCUS
A good fillies' handicap for the level, with a pair of progressive 3-y-os drawing clear. It was run at just a steady gallop and they came centre-field late on.

6017 LONDON GATWICK TO OSLO H'CAP 5f 59y
4:05 (4:05) (Class 6) (0-60,60) 3-Y-O+ £2,045 (£603; £302) Stalls Centre

Form RPR
4435 1 **Pharoh Jake**[15] 5522 5-8-5 49 MichaelJMMurphy(5) 7 58
(John Bridger) *chsd ldrs: rdn to chse ldr over 1f out: led 1f out and clr ins fnl f: r.o wl* **13/2**
5203 2 1 ½ **Volito**[12] 5608 7-9-3 56 GeorgeBaker 5 59
(Anabel K Murphy) *stdd s: t.k.h: hld up in tch in last pair: swtchd rt and effrt over 1f out: chsd wnr ins fnl f: r.o but nvr gng to rch wnr* **9/2**[3]
2222 3 1 ½ **Chester'Slittlegem (IRE)**[1] 5982 4-8-10 49 CathyGannon 4 47
(Jo Hughes) *in tch in midfield: effrt u.p 2f out: chsd clr wnr briefly ins fnl f: no imp* **13/8**[1]
50/5 4 1 **Coalburn**[18] 5408 5-8-7 46 oh1 ChrisCatlin 3 41
(Gary Harrison) *chsd ldr: rdn 2f out: lost 2nd and outpcd over 1f out: no threat to wnr and plugged on same pce fnl f* **25/1**
0102 5 nk **Idle Curiosity (IRE)**[12] 5602 3-9-6 60 WilliamCarson 1 53
(Jim Boyle) *led: rdn and hdd to far rail over 2f out: hdd and no ex 1f out: wknd ins fnl f* **15/2**
1452 6 1 ¾ **Renoir's Lady**[17] 5447 5-9-2 55 JimCrowley 6 42
(Joseph Tuite) *hld up in tch in last pair: rdn and no hdwy 2f out: drvn and btn over 1f out: bhd fnl f* **3/1**[2]

1m 2.89s (0.59) **Going Correction** +0.075s/f (Good)
WFA 3 from 4yo+ 1lb 6 Ran SP% **110.2**
Speed ratings (Par 101): **98,95,93,91,91 88**
toteswingers 1&2 £3.50, 1&3 £2.40, 2&3 £2.00 CSF £33.64 TOTE £7.60: £3.10, £2.70; EX 24.40 Trifecta £19.65 Pool: £2618.10 - 99.80 winning units..
Owner The Hair & Haberdasher Partnership **Bred** J J Bridger **Trained** Liphook, Hants

FOCUS
A weak sprint handicap.

6018 LONDON GATWICK TO COLOMBO SRI LANKA H'CAP (THE SUNDAY £5K BONUS RACE) 5f 213y
4:35 (4:35) (Class 5) (0-75,75) 3-Y-O+ £2,587 (£770; £384; £192) Stalls Centre

Form RPR
5005 1 **Gabrial's Gift (IRE)**[15] 5537 4-9-0 68 JimCrowley 8 77
(David Simcock) *hld up in tch in last pair: trcking ldrs and nt clr run on stands' rail 2f out: swtchd lft and effrt u.p over 1f out: r.o to ld wl ins fnl f: gng away at fin* **9/4**[1]
60-1 2 1 **Jinker Noble**[20] 5349 4-9-6 74 LiamKeniry 7 80
(Ed de Giles) *t.k.h: hld up in tch in midfield: c towards stands' rail and chsd ldr 2f out: rdn to ld 1f out: drvn ins fnl f: hdd wl ins fnl f: no ex* **3/1**[2]
3000 3 3 ½ **Where's Reiley (USA)**[9] 5697 7-8-10 64 (b) RobertHavlin 4 59
(Michael Attwater) *sn bustled along: chsd ldrs after 1f: led 3f out: c to stands' rail over 2f out: drvn and hdd 1f out: sn outpcd and btn: hld on for 3rd fnl 100yds* **22/1**
4031 4 ¾ **Griffin Point (IRE)**[10] 5670 6-8-8 62 (b) WilliamCarson 5 54
(William Muir) *t.k.h: led for 1f: stdd bk into midfield: styd towards centre over 2f out: effrt u.p to chse ldrs over 1f out: no ex and outpcd fnl f* **14/1**
2110 5 2 ½ **Bosham**[25] 5150 3-8-8 69 MichaelJMMurphy(5) 3 53
(William Jarvis) *stdd s: hld up in rr: effrt u.p in centre 2f out: no ex over 1f out: wknd fnl f* **7/2**[3]
0120 6 12 **We Have A Dream**[4] 5901 8-8-9 70 (tp) OisinMurphy(7) 2 16
(Violet M Jordan) *sn bustled along: led after 1f tl hdd 3f out: wknd u.p 2f out: wl bhd 1f out* **8/1**
0356 7 7 **Red Larkspur (IRE)**[21] 5308 4-9-7 75 (p) RichardHughes 1
(Roger Teal) *mostly chsd ldr: c towards stands' side and rdn whn stmbld 2f out: nt rcvr and sn btn: eased ent fnl f: t.o* **6/1**

1m 10.0s (-0.20) **Going Correction** +0.075s/f (Good)
WFA 3 from 4yo+ 2lb 7 Ran SP% **114.4**
Speed ratings (Par 103): **104,102,98,97,93 77,68**
toteswingers 1&2 £2.50, 1&3 £6.50, 2&3 £10.00 CSF £9.22 CT £111.99 TOTE £2.60: £1.60, £2.30; EX 10.40 Trifecta £103.10 Pool: £3679.16 - 26.76 winning units..
Owner Dr Marwan Koukash **Bred** Skymarc Farm **Trained** Newmarket, Suffolk

FOCUS
No hanging around here and the runners came towards the stands' side.

6019 LONDON GATWICK TO DUBAI APPRENTICE H'CAP 6f 209y
5:05 (5:05) (Class 6) (0-60,59) 3-Y-O+ £2,045 (£603; £302) Stalls Centre

Form RPR
4500 1 **Olney Lass**[33] 4864 6-9-6 59 JoeyHaynes(5) 6 69
(Lydia Pearce) *hld up in tch in rr of main gp: pushed along and gd hdwy to ld over 1f out: clr fnl f: r.o wl: comf* **8/1**
2445 2 3 ½ **Fairy Mist (IRE)**[24] 5170 6-8-8 45 MichaelJMMurphy(3) 8 46
(John Bridger) *stdd s: t.k.h: hld up towards rr early: hdwy to ld 5f out: hdd 3f out: outpcd and swtchd lft over 1f out: chsd wnr ent fnl f: kpt on but no imp* **12/1**
2203 3 nk **Chevise (IRE)**[9] 5697 5-9-8 59 (p) RyanTate(3) 1 59
(Steve Woodman) *t.k.h: chsd ldrs: rdn and effrt in centre over 2f out: no ch w wnr and kpt on same pce fnl f* **4/1**[2]
6254 4 nk **Loraine**[13] 5596 3-9-4 59 MatthewLawson(3) 2 58
(Jamie Osborne) *s.i.s: hld up in tch in rr: effrt towards inner over 2f out: no threat to wnr but pressing for placings fnl f: kpt on* **7/1**
5 5 nk **Amy Farah Fowler (IRE)**[29] 4999 4-8-11 45 WilliamTwiston-Davies 4 43
(Ian Williams) *hld in tch towards rr: rdn and effrt 2f out: edging lft and no imp over 1f out: styd on same pce fnl f* **11/4**[1]
6054 6 hd **Baby Dottie**[31] 4909 6-9-0 55 (t) SophieRalston(7) 9 53
(Pat Phelan) *t.k.h: chsd ldrs: rdn and effrt over 2f out: outpcd over 1f out: battling for placings and kpt on same pce fnl f* **9/1**
4116 7 2 ¼ **Just Isla**[18] 5407 3-9-3 55 (be[1]) DeclanBates 5 47
(Peter Makin) *chsd ldrs tl hdwy to ld 3f out: rdn and hdd over 1f out: sn outpcd by wnr and btn: wknd ins fnl f* **5/1**[3]
0455 8 2 **Jackie Love (IRE)**[6] 5817 5-8-9 48 (v) IanBurns(5) 7 34
(Olivia Maylam) *t.k.h: led for 2f: chsd ldrs: rdn over 2f out: outpcd and btn over 1f out: wl hld fnl f* **16/1**
0660 9 6 **Toffee Shot**[24] 5198 3-8-6 49 ShelleyBirkett(5) 3 19
(J W Hills) *walked out of stalls and veered bdly lft: lost many l and wl bhd: clsd and in tch 4f out: rdn and effrt on inner over 2f out: wknd over 1f out* **20/1**

1m 24.67s (1.57) **Going Correction** +0.075s/f (Good)
WFA 3 from 4yo+ 4lb 9 Ran SP% **115.3**
Speed ratings (Par 101): **94,90,89,89,88 88,86,83,77**
toteswingers 1&2 £10.00, 1&3 £4.10, 2&3 £5.80 CSF £98.11 CT £445.18 TOTE £11.10: £3.40, £2.80, £1.70; EX 94.30 Trifecta £384.40 Pool: £2223.15 - 4.33 winning units..
Owner Mrs Louise Marsh **Bred** T H Rossiter **Trained** Newmarket, Suffolk

FOCUS
Runners were spread across the track in what was a moderate handicap.
T/Jkpt: £1,350.00 to a £1 stake. Pool: £24,718.38 - 13.00 winning units T/Plt: £98.00 to a £1 stake. Pool: £78,339.53 - 583.37 winning units T/Qpdt: £36.40 to a £1 stake. Pool: £4167.86 - 84.50 winning units SP

6020 - (Foreign Racing) - See Raceform Interactive

5770 CURRAGH (R-H)
Sunday, September 1

OFFICIAL GOING: Good to firm

6021a GO AND GO ROUND TOWER STKS (GROUP 3) 6f
2:40 (2:43) 2-Y-O £31,707 (£9,268; £4,390; £1,463)

RPR
1 **Great White Eagle (USA)**[27] 5074 2-9-3 JosephO'Brien 2 107+
(A P O'Brien, Ire) *w.w towards rr: smooth hdwy on outer fr 2f out: sn pushed along and qcknd to ld 1f out: kpt on wl towards fin: comf* **1/3**[1]
2 2 **Remember You (IRE)**[27] 5074 2-9-0 92 WayneLordan 1 95
(David Wachman, Ire) *sn trckd ldrs on outer: cl 5th 1/2-way: hdwy on outer to dispute ld 2f out: sn rdn and hdd 1f out: no ch w wnr: kpt on same pce* **16/1**
3 ½ **Expedition (IRE)**[8] 5771 2-9-3 (v[1]) RyanMoore 3 97
(A P O'Brien, Ire) *prom: disp 1/2-way: sn led narrowly tl hdd 1f out: no ex u.p in 3rd ins fnl f: kpt on same pce* **8/1**[2]

4 ½ **Boom The Groom (IRE)**[8] 5771 2-9-3 100........................ FergalLynch 8 95
(David Marnane, Ire) *on toes befhand: hld up in tch: t.k.h: pushed along over 2f out and clsd on nrside into 4th ent fnl f: no ex u.p: kpt on same pce* **10/1**[3]

5 1 ¼ **Bluebell (IRE)**[18] 5413 2-9-0 82.................................. SeamieHeffernan 5 88
(A P O'Brien, Ire) *chsd ldrs: 6th 1/2-way: rdn 1 1/2f out and sn no imp on ldrs in 5th: kpt on same pce* **33/1**

6 3 **Free Code (IRE)**[23] 5226 2-9-3 .... JohnnyMurtagh 6 81
(James Tate) *chsd ldrs: 7th 1/2-way: pushed along and short of room bhd horses 2f out: sn swtchd lft: rdn in rr ent fnl f and sme late hdwy* **8/1**[2]

7 1 ½ **Intensical (IRE)**[8] 5771 2-9-3 .... KevinManning 7 77
(J S Bolger, Ire) *cl up: disp 1/2-way: sn pushed along and lost action briefly: rdn and no imp whn sltly hmpd 1 1/2f out: one pce fnl f* **25/1**

8 nk **Sign From Heaven (IRE)**[11] 5661 2-9-0 93...................... ConnorKing 4 73
(David Wachman, Ire) *on toes befhand: broke wl to r promly: disp 1/2-way: pushed along and outpcd 2f out: sn no ex u.p: one pce fnl f* **16/1**

9 4 ¾ **Danehill Brook (IRE)** 2-9-3 .... WJLee 9 60
(David Wachman, Ire) *dwlt sltly: sn cl up on nrside: disp 1/2-way: pushed along 2f out and sn no ex whn edgd rt: dropped to rr ins fnl f* **16/1**

1m 10.59s (-4.91) **Going Correction** -0.675s/f (Hard) **9** Ran SP% **130.8**
Speed ratings: **105,102,101,101,99 95,93,92,86**
CSF £11.11 TOTE £1.20: £1.10, £2.20, £1.80; DF 7.50.

Owner Michael Tabor & Derrick Smith & Mrs John Magnier **Bred** Rosemont Farm Llc & Darley **Trained** Ballydoyle, Co Tipperary

FOCUS
The most noticeable thing when reviewing past renewals of this contest was that Aidan O'Brien hadn't been successful since Cherokee back in 2004. He brought a particularly strong hand to the table this year with a third of the field residing at Ballydoyle. There was no shortage of pace through the opening stages and the winning time was good.

6023a DANCE DESIGN STKS (GROUP 3) (F&M) 1m 1f
3:40 (3:42) 3-Y-0+ **£31,707** (£9,268; £4,390; £1,463)

RPR

1 **Say (IRE)**[10] 5683 3-9-1 110 ow1...................................... JosephO'Brien 6 108+
(A P O'Brien, Ire) *hld up in tch: 5th 1/2-way: swtchd lft over 2f out: sn pushed along and qcknd on outer to ld over 150yds out: kpt on wl* **4/1**[2]

2 1 ¼ **Aloof (IRE)**[18] 5415 4-9-6 105.. WayneLordan 1 105
(David Wachman, Ire) *sn led: 1 l clr 1/2-way: rdn 1 1/2f out and sn strly pressed: hdd over 150yds out: no ex* **10/1**[3]

3 ½ **Pearl Of Africa (IRE)**[43] 4546 3-9-0 98.......................... JamieSpencer 2 104+
(Edward Lynam, Ire) *dwlt: w.w in rr: clsr in 6th 1/2-way: pushed along into st: and clsd u.p in mod 6th ins fnl f: kpt on wl and wnt 3rd on outer cl home wout troubling principals* **10/1**[3]

4 ¾ **Bunairgead (IRE)**[26] 5115 3-9-0 101.........................(b) KevinManning 3 102
(J S Bolger, Ire) *chsd ldrs: 3rd 1/2-way: rdn in 4th ins fnl f and no ex u.p: kpt on same pce* **12/1**

5 1 ¼ **One Spirit (IRE)**[10] 5688 5-9-6 100................................ NGMcCullagh 7 100
(F Dunne, Ire) *prom: sn settled bhd ldr: t.k.h early: cl 2nd 1/2-way: rdn fr 2f out and no imp on ldr: dropped to 3rd ins fnl f and wknd cl home* **33/1**

6 1 **Hanky Panky (IRE)**[4] 5907 3-9-0 98................................. RyanMoore 4 98
(A P O'Brien, Ire) *racd towards rr: niggled along in rr after 1/2-way: rdn over 1f out and kpt on towards fin* **20/1**

7 nk **Along Came Casey (IRE)**[18] 5415 5-9-6 113..................... PatSmullen 5 97
(D K Weld, Ire) *hld up bhd ldrs in 4th: niggled along over 2f out: sn rdn in 5th and no imp on ldrs 1f out: eased nr fin* **4/7**[1]

1m 51.3s (-3.60) **Going Correction** -0.10s/f (Good)
WFA 3 from 4yo+ 6lb **7** Ran SP% **117.2**
Speed ratings: **112,110,110,109,108 107,107**
CSF £43.55 TOTE £4.00: £1.90, £4.60; DF 33.50.

Owner Derrick Smith & Mrs John Magnier & Michael Tabor **Bred** Smythson **Trained** Ballydoyle, Co Tipperary

FOCUS
Rivalries were renewed here with the winner reversing form with the odds-on favourite from their recent Gowran Park clash. The early gallop was generous. The winner and fourth set the standard.

6024a MOYGLARE STUD STKS (GROUP 1) (FILLIES) 7f
4:15 (4:16) 2-Y-0

£106,097 (£34,756; £16,463; £5,487; £3,658; £1,829)

RPR

1 **Rizeena (IRE)**[14] 5573 2-9-0 .... JamesDoyle 1 113
(Clive Brittain) *settled bhd ldrs: 6th 1/2-way: hdwy in 5th 1 1/2f out: rdn 1f out and edgd sltly rt u.p to ld ins fnl 100yds: kpt on wl* **9/2**[3]

2 hd **Tapestry (IRE)**[21] 5318 2-9-1 109 ow1............................. JosephO'Brien 5 111
(A P O'Brien, Ire) *chsd ldrs in 3rd: tk clsr order fr 2f out: n.m.r in 4th ent fnl f: rdn and nt clr run between horses fnl 100yds: kpt on same pce: fin 3rd: plcd 2nd* **2/1**[2]

3 ¾ **Kiyoshi**[72] 3522 2-9-0 .... JamieSpencer 3 111
(Charles Hills) *chsd ldrs in 4th: rdn in 3rd fr 2f out and qcknd wl to ld 1f out: sn wnt rt and strly pressed: hdd ins fnl 100yds: no ex: fin 2nd: disqualified and plcd 3rd* **13/8**[1]

4 3 ¼ **Carla Bianca (IRE)**[43] 4545 2-9-0 .... PatSmullen 7 102
(D K Weld, Ire) *chsd ldrs: 5th 1/2-way: outpcd 2f out: pushed along in mod 6th ent fnl f and styd on into nvr threatening 4th cl home* **14/1**

5 ¾ **Perhaps (IRE)**[21] 5318 2-9-0 104...........................(p) SeamieHeffernan 4 100
(A P O'Brien, Ire) *sn led at gd pce: reduced advantage fr 2f out: sn rdn and hdd 1f out: no ex* **18/1**

6 1 ¾ **Wonderfully (IRE)**[45] 4462 2-9-0 105.............................. RyanMoore 2 97
(A P O'Brien, Ire) *sn trckd ldr in 2nd: hdwy to chal 1f out: sn hdd and bdly hmpd: dropped to 6th and eased* **8/1**

7 32 **Touch Of Snow (IRE)**[29] 5018 2-9-0 72............................. ShaneFoley 6 12
(John Joseph Murphy, Ire) *w.w in rr: struggling at 1/2-way: rdn over 2f out and no imp: wknd* **100/1**

1m 22.91s (-7.89) **Going Correction** -1.025s/f (Hard) **7** Ran SP% **113.6**
Speed ratings: **104,102,103,99,98 96,59**
CSF £12.10 TOTE £4.80: £1.60, £1.50; DF 14.40.

Owner Sheikh Rashid Dalmook Al Maktoum **Bred** Round Hill Stud **Trained** Newmarket, Suffolk

■ Stewards' Enquiry : Jamie Spencer four-day ban: careless riding (Sep 16-19)

FOCUS
It should not be underestimated what Rizeena achieved in winning this contest, taking the step up in trip in her stride and looking as though running over further won't be an issue. They went a good clip from the start, but the principals quickened well over a furlong out. A strong renewal and possibly better than rated.

6025a IRISH STALLION FARMS EUROPEAN BREEDERS FUND IRISH CAMBRIDGESHIRE (PREMIER H'CAP) 1m
4:45 (4:51) 3-Y-0+

£48,780 (£15,447; £7,317; £2,439; £1,626; £813)

RPR

1 **Moran Gra (USA)**[39] 4648 6-8-13 95......................(p) RonanWhelan(3) 9 103+
(Ms Joanna Morgan, Ire) *hld up in tch: 8th 1/2-way: hdwy on outer fr 2f out to ld over 150yds out: kpt on wl* **12/1**

2 1 ¾ **Regulation (IRE)**[21] 5322 4-8-12 91.................................. ShaneFoley 6 95+
(M Halford, Ire) *racd in mid-div: 10th 1/2-way: prog on outer fr 2f out: rdn in 6th ent fnl f and kpt on wl u.p into 2nd fnl strides: nt trble wnr* **11/1**

3 nk **Campanology**[18] 5416 4-8-13 92..............................(t) NGMcCullagh 5 95
(J P Murtagh, Ire) *chsd ldrs: 7th 1/2-way: hdwy fr 2f out on outer: rdn in 2nd ins fnl f and sn no imp on wnr: dropped to 3rd fnl strides* **20/1**

4 1 **Ansgar (IRE)**[17] 5453 5-9-13 106.............................(t) RoryCleary 10 107
(Sabrina J Harty, Ire) *chsd ldr: 2nd 1/2-way: rdn over 2f out and clsd u.p to ld over 1 1/2f out: sn strly pressed and hdd over 150yds out: sn no ex in 4th: kpt on same pce* **12/1**

5 ½ **Tobann (IRE)**[10] 5688 3-9-6 104..............................(t) KevinManning 1 103
(J S Bolger, Ire) *racd in mid-div: 9th 1/2-way: hdwy fr 3f out to chse ldrs: rdn in 3rd 1 1/2f out: n.m.r between horses and sn no ex: kpt on same pce in 5th nr fin* **10/1**

6 2 ¾ **Mordanmijobsworth (IRE)**[18] 5416 3-7-8 88 oh3.....(b) IanQueally(10) 8 81
(G M Lyons, Ire) *chsd ldrs: 5th 1/2-way: rdn and no imp on ldrs ent fnl f: kpt on* **20/1**

7 ¾ **Sweet Lightning**[38] 4696 8-9-13 106.........................(t) JohnnyMurtagh 17 98
(J P Murtagh, Ire) *w.w in rr of mid-div: rdn 2f out and sme hdwy into mod 10th ent fnl f: kpt on* **12/1**

8 hd **Cash Or Casualty (IRE)**[8] 5775 5-8-8 87..................(t) MichaelHussey 3 78
(Damian Joseph English, Ire) *cl up: settled bhd ldr: 3rd 1/2-way: rdn and wknd over 2f out* **33/1**

9 hd **Target Acquired (IRE)**[4] 5906 3-8-1 88 oh4.........(b[1]) ConorHoban(3) 18 78
(A Oliver, Ire) *sn led: 3 l clr 1/2-way: sn rdn and hdd over 1 1/2f out: wknd ins fnl f* **33/1**

10 ½ **Vastonea (IRE)**[33] 4869 5-8-13 95.................................... SHJames(3) 12 85
(Kevin Prendergast, Ire) *hld up in mid-div: pushed along in 12th after 1/2-way and no ex: kpt on one pce* **25/1**

11 1 ¾ **Dance And Dance (IRE)**[15] 5533 7-9-2 95...................(b) RyanMoore 14 81
(Ed Vaughan) *towards rr for most: pushed along over 2f out and no imp: kpt on one pce ins fnl f* **6/1**[1]

12 1 **Anderiego (IRE)**[10] 5681 5-9-1 94.. FMBerry 4 77
(David O'Meara) *in rr of mid-div: rdn and no imp over 2f out* **20/1**

13 1 **Abbey Vale (IRE)**[14] 5572 3-8-8 92.................................... GaryCarroll 7 72
(G M Lyons, Ire) *in rr of mid-div: rdn and no imp fr under 2f out: kpt on one pce fnl f* **8/1**[3]

14 shd **Golden Shoe (IRE)**[21] 5322 5-7-13 83 oh2................. ConnorKing(5) 19 64
(J T Gorman, Ire) *chsd ldrs: 4th 1/2-way: rdn and no ex u.p over 2f out: wknd* **20/1**

15 1 ¼ **Northern Rocked (IRE)**[17] 5454 7-8-8 90.............(v) LeighRoche(3) 20 68
(D K Weld, Ire) *in rr of mid-div: rdn and no imp fr 2f out: one pce fnl f* **25/1**

16 1 ¼ **Stuccodor (IRE)**[29] 5019 4-9-11 104..............................(v) PatSmullen 11 79
(D K Weld, Ire) *hld up in tch: rdn and no imp fr 2f out: eased fnl f* **10/1**

17 nk **Line Drummer (FR)**[123] 1938 3-9-1 99.................... SeamieHeffernan 16 72
(A P O'Brien, Ire) *a bhd: rdn and no imp fr 3f out* **14/1**

18 2 ¾ **Francis Of Assisi (IRE)**[161] 1167 3-9-6 104...........(p) JosephO'Brien 15 71
(A P O'Brien, Ire) *w.w towards rr: pushed along and no imp 2f out: eased fnl f* **7/1**[2]

19 shd **Global Village (IRE)**[33] 4869 8-9-4 97............................... ChrisHayes 13 65
(Brian Ellison) *towards rr: rdn and no imp fr 3f out* **14/1**

20 9 ½ **Karamaya (IRE)**[21] 5322 3-8-11 95......................(b[1]) DeclanMcDonogh 2 40
(John M Oxx, Ire) *chsd ldrs: 6th 1/2-way: sn pushed along and no ex: wknd and eased* **10/1**

1m 35.64s (-10.36) **Going Correction** -1.025s/f (Hard)
WFA 3 from 4yo+ 5lb **20** Ran SP% **142.5**
Speed ratings: **110,108,107,106,106 103,102,102,102,102 100,99,98,98,96 95,95,92,92,83**
CSF £140.25 CT £2696.22 TOTE £15.80: £3.70, £3.10, £5.40, £2.80; DF 183.80.
Owner D T Breen & Micheal D Ryan **Bred** Airlie Stud & Robert N Clay **Trained** Ballivor, Co Meath

FOCUS
Without a win this year, apparently due to a foot problem on his last couple of starts, Moran Gra ran out a good winner of a competitive handicap that not many horses got into. The fourth and fifth help set the standard.

6026 - 6027a (Foreign Racing) - See Raceform Interactive

6010 BADEN-BADEN (L-H)
Sunday, September 1

OFFICIAL GOING: Turf: good

6028a LONGINES - GROSSER PREIS VON BADEN (GROUP 1) (3YO+) (TURF) 1m 4f
4:05 (12:00) 3-Y-0+ **£121,951** (£48,780; £20,325; £12,195)

RPR

1 **Novellist (IRE)**[36] 4745 4-9-6 0... EPedroza 4 113+
(A Wohler, Germany) *tk v t.k.h: reluctant ldr: set stdy gallop: hdd 1/2-way: trckd ldr: rdn to ld over 1f: grad asserted u.p ins fnl f: in control fnl 100yds: workmanlike* **1/6**[1]

2 ¾ **Seismos (IRE)**[21] 5324 5-9-6 0.. AndreaAtzeni 5 112
(A Wohler, Germany) *trckd ldr: led 1/2-way: rdn and 2 l clr 2 1/2f out: hdd over 1f out: kpt on u.p fnl f: wl hld by wnr fnl 100yds* **12/1**[3]

3 ¾ **Meandre (FR)**[42] 4571 5-9-6 0...................................... MircoDemuro 3 111+
(A Savujev, Czech Republic) *trckd ldng pair: tk clsr order on outer 2 1/2f out: cl 3rd and rdn over 1f out: kpt on at same pce u.p fnl f* **7/1**[2]

4 ½ **Empoli (GER)**[21] 5324 3-8-11 0... AStarke 1 110
(P Schiergen, Germany) *trckd ldng pair: outpcd and dropped to last 2 1/2f out: rdn and no imp 1 1/2f out: styd on ins fnl f: nt pce to chal* **25/1**

The Form Book Flat, Raceform Ltd, Compton, RG20 6NL.

5 *4* **Quinzieme Monarque (USA)**[56] 4103 3-8-11 0.................. ADeVries 2 104+
(J Hirschberger, Germany) *hld up in rr: tk clsr order 2 1/2f out: chsd ldr into st over 2f out: sn hrd rdn and nt qckn: outpcd appr fnl f and dropped away: eased fnl 100yds* **25/1**

2m 33.9s (0.44)
WFA 3 from 4yo+ 9lb **5** Ran SP% **113.6**
WIN (incl. 10 euro stake): 13. PLACES: 12, 17. SF: 33.
Owner Dr Christoph Berglar **Bred** Christoph Berglar **Trained** Germany

FOCUS
They dawdled through the early part of the race and the winner was always doing just enough.

6029 - 6030a (Foreign Racing) - See Raceform Interactive

4322 LONGCHAMP (R-H)

Sunday, September 1

OFFICIAL GOING: Turf: good to soft

6031a PRIX DE LIANCOURT (LISTED RACE) (3YO FILLIES) (TURF) 1m 2f 110y
2:40 (12:00) 3-Y-O **£22,357** (£8,943; £6,707; £4,471; £2,235)

RPR
1 **Odeliz (IRE)**[16] 5496 3-8-11 0.......................... DanielTudhope 2 99
(K R Burke) *trckd ldr on inner: cl 3rd travelling wl but hemmed in bhd two ldrs over 2f out: once gap appeared chal between horses to ld 1f out: r.o u.p: appeared to idle fnl 50yds: jst hld on* **94/10**
2 *nse* **Piana (FR)**[36] 4792 3-9-2 0.......................... RonanThomas 7 104+
(A Bonin, France) **11/1**
3 *snk* **Shared Account**[15] 3-8-11 0.......................... ChristopheSoumillon 4 99
(P Bary, France) **58/10**
4 *2* **Dakatari (FR)**[102] 3-8-11 0.......................... OlivierPeslier 6 95
(F Head, France) **4/1[2]**
5 *hd* **Commute**[21] 5315 3-8-11 0.......................... GregoryBenoist 1 95
(D Smaga, France) **3/1[1]**
6 *3* **Regal Hawk**[24] 5190 3-8-11 0.......................... GeraldMosse 3 89
(James Tate) *tk v t.k.h: prom tl shuffled bk after 1 1/2f: hld up towards rr on inner: rdn but short of room 2f out: no imp once in clr: one pce fnl f* **9/2[3]**
7 *nk* **Magic Art (IRE)**[17] 3-8-11 0.......................... ThierryThulliez 8 88
(W Figge, Germany) **21/1**
8 *3 ½* **Amarysia (FR)**[20] 5361 3-8-11 0.......................... AnthonyCrastus 9 81
(C Laffon-Parias, France) **18/1**
9 *1* **Herminia (IRE)**[35] 3-8-11 0.......................... MaximeGuyon 10 80
(A Fabre, France) **6/1**

2m 10.57s (0.37) **9** Ran SP% **119.9**
WIN (incl. 1 euro stake): 10.40. PLACES: 2.90, 3.30, 2.00. DF: 68.40. SF: 200.20..
Owner McMahon Thoroughbreds Ltd & Mrs E Burke **Bred** Aleyrion Bloodstock Ltd **Trained** Middleham Moor, N Yorks

6032 - (Foreign Racing) - See Raceform Interactive

6013 BRIGHTON (L-H)

Monday, September 2

OFFICIAL GOING: Good to firm (firm in places; 7.8)
Wind: light, across Weather: dry and sunny

6033 IAN CARNABY (S) H'CAP 5f 213y
2:30 (2:30) (Class 6) (0-60,60) 3-Y-O+ **£2,045** (£603; £302) **Stalls** Centre

Form RPR
5560 1 **Father Fred**[23] 5275 3-8-6 **47**.......................... JimmyQuinn 8 59
(Chris Dwyer) *in tch towards rr: c nrest stands' rail over 2f out: rdn and hdwy to ld 1f out: r.o strly and drew clr fnl 100yds: readily* **25/1**
0440 2 *3 ¼* **Jarrow (IRE)**[7] 5841 6-9-7 **60**..........................(p) RichardKingscote 4 62
(Milton Bradley) *chsd ldrs: jnd ldrs and travelling wl 2f out: rdn to ld over 1f out: hdd 1f out: outpcd ins fnl f but kpt on to hold 2nd* **3/1[2]**
6146 3 *1* **Surrey Dream (IRE)**[16] 5525 4-8-9 **48** ow1.......................... RichardHughes 6 47
(John Bridger) *chsd ldr: rdn and ev ch 2f out tl no ex u.p ent fnl f: 3rd and plugged on same pce after* **11/4[1]**
0624 4 *4 ½* **Scommettitrice (IRE)**[15] 3623 5-8-9 **55**..........................(bt) OisinMurphy(7) 7 39
(Mark Gillard) *s.i.s: rdn along in rr: styd on past btn horses fnl f to snatch 4th cl home: nvr trbld ldrs* **6/1**
0-05 5 *nk* **Little Miss Zuri (IRE)**[2] 5981 3-8-5 **46** oh1.......................... ChrisCatlin 3 29
(Sylvester Kirk) *led tl rdn and hdd over 1f out: sn struggling and btn 1f out: wknd* **20/1**
3546 6 *hd* **Ingleby Star (IRE)**[10] 5701 8-9-5 **58**..........................(p) ShaneKelly 5 41
(John Stimpson) *broke wl: sn stdd and hld up in tch in midfield: effrt and hung lft over 1f out: fnd little and sn btn: wknd fnl f* **7/1**
4366 7 *nk* **Flaxen Lake**[7] 5818 6-8-7 **46** oh1..........................(p) CathyGannon 2 28
(Milton Bradley) *dwlt: in tch in last trio: effrt towards inner 2f out: drvn and no imp over 1f out: wknd fnl f* **14/1**
0000 8 *22* **Confirmed**[27] 5098 4-8-7 **46** oh1..........................(bt[1]) WilliamCarson 9
(Sean Curran) *wl in tch in midfield: rdn and lost pl over 2f out: bhd over 1f out* **4/1[3]**

1m 10.15s (-0.05) **Going Correction** -0.025s/f (Good)
WFA 3 from 4yo+ 2lb **8** Ran SP% **113.7**
Speed ratings (Par 101): **99,94,93,87,86 86,86,56**
toteswingers 1&2 £16.10, 1&3 £11.40, 2&3 £2.60 CSF £98.05 CT £283.75 TOTE £30.20: £8.30, £1.30, £1.80; EX 166.20 Trifecta £648.60 Pool: £3951.08 - 4.56 winning units..There were no bids.
Owner Mrs C M Goode **Bred** Pedro Rosas **Trained** Newmarket, Suffolk

FOCUS
Rail dolled out from 4.5f to 2f adding about 9yds to all race distances. A desperately poor race, even by selling handicap standards and it saw something of an upset. The winner showed his first form and the race is rated at face value.

6034 GOOD LAW SOLICITORS MAIDEN FILLIES' STKS 5f 213y
3:00 (3:00) (Class 5) 2-Y-O **£2,587** (£770; £384; £192) **Stalls** Centre

Form RPR
03 1 **Amnesia (IRE)**[32] 4912 2-9-0 0.......................... RichardHughes 3 77+
(William Haggas) *trckd ldrs: swtchd rt and effrt 2f out: edgd lft u.p and led over 1f out: styd on wl and forged clr fnl 100yds* **5/2[2]**
222 2 *1 ¼* **Genuine Quality (USA)**[44] 4539 2-9-0 76.......................... JamieSpencer 1 73
(Ed Vaughan) *led: rdn and hdd over 1f out: hrd drvn and styd on same pce ins fnl f: btn and eased cl home* **4/9[1]**
0 3 *6* **Laughing Dove (IRE)**[8] 5797 2-9-0 0.......................... PaulHanagan 4 54
(William Haggas) *chsd ldr tl 2f out: sn rdn and outpcd: 3rd and wl hld fnl f* **12/1[3]**
00 4 *18* **Zaftual**[35] 4828 2-9-0 0.......................... JimmyQuinn 2
(K F Clutterbuck) *stdd s: t.k.h: hld up in rr: rdn and lost tch over 1f out* **100/1**

1m 10.24s (0.04) **Going Correction** -0.025s/f (Good) **4** Ran SP% **106.5**
Speed ratings (Par 92): **98,96,88,64**
CSF £3.95 TOTE £2.60; EX 4.60 Trifecta £5.50 Pool: £3148.43 - 426.32 winning units..
Owner St Albans Bloodstock LLP **Bred** Norelands Stud & Lofts Hall Stud **Trained** Newmarket, Suffolk

FOCUS
A modest maiden. The winner was well on top but the second was below par.

6035 FREEDOM LEISURE, WHERE YOU MATTER, NURSERY H'CAP 5f 213y
3:30 (3:30) (Class 5) (0-75,75) 2-Y-O **£2,587** (£770; £384; £192) **Stalls** Centre

Form RPR
15 1 **La Tinta Bay**[38] 4717 2-9-7 **74**.......................... RichardHughes 2 82+
(Richard Hannon) *chsd ldr tl rdn to ld wl over 1f out: drvn and r.o strly to draw clr ins fnl f: readily* **7/2[2]**
0101 2 *3 ½* **Primitorio (IRE)**[7] 5842 2-9-8 **75** 6ex..........................(b) JimCrowley 4 72
(Ralph Beckett) *racd in midfield: rdn and effrt to chse wnr over 1f out: drvn and pressing wnr 1f out: no ex and readily brushed aside fnl 100yds* **1/2[1]**
4160 3 *2 ½* **Honey Meadow**[7] 5842 2-9-0 **67**.......................... AndreaAtzeni 3 56
(Robert Eddery) *chsd ldng pair: effrt u.p to chse ldng pair over 1f out: no imp and wl hld fnl f* **16/1**
060 4 *nk* **Maysville (IRE)**[21] 5352 2-8-6 **59**.......................... WilliamCarson 5 47
(Charles Hills) *hld up in rr: rdn and effrt 2f out: no ch w ldrs but battling for 3rd fnl f: kpt on same pce* **20/1**
5000 5 *½* **Flying Kyte**[12] 5634 2-8-1 **54** oh7 ow1..........................(v[1]) FrankieMcDonald 6 40
(Pat Phelan) *hld up in last pair: rdn and struggling 3f out: n.d after: plugging on same pce whn swtchd rt ins fnl f* **100/1**
405 6 *25* **Shamardyh (IRE)**[36] 4801 2-8-9 **62**..........................(b[1]) NeilCallan 1
(James Tate) *racd freely: led and sn clr: rdn and hdd wl over 1f out: sn struggling and wknd qckly jst over 1f out: wl bhd and heavily eased ins fnl f* **10/1[3]**

1m 10.18s (-0.02) **Going Correction** -0.025s/f (Good) **6** Ran SP% **109.6**
Speed ratings (Par 95): **99,94,91,90,89 56**
CSF £5.33 TOTE £3.70: £1.90, £1.10; EX 7.50 Trifecta £21.40 Pool: £3652.97 - 127.56 winning units..
Owner J R Shannon **Bred** J R Shannon **Trained** East Everleigh, Wilts

FOCUS
An ordinary nursery. The favourite was nowhere near the level of his Warwick win.

6036 ERIN MCDONNELL MAIDEN STKS 1m 1f 209y
4:00 (4:00) (Class 5) 3-Y-O+ **£2,587** (£770; £384; £192) **Stalls** High

Form RPR
-532 1 **Dance King**[73] 3542 3-9-5 **80**.......................... TedDurcan 1 80+
(David Lanigan) *led: rdn and hrd pressed ent fnl 2f: hdd narrowly over 1f out: bmpd and carried lft ent fnl f: edgd rt u.p ins fnl f: battled on wl and led again nr fin* **4/5[1]**
2 *hd* **My History (IRE)** 3-9-5 0.......................... NeilCallan 4 79+
(Mark Johnston) *chsd ldr: jnd ldr and racing against stands' rail over 2f out: rdn to ld over 1f out: edgd lft u.p ent fnl f: kpt on wl tl hdd and no ex nr fin* **5/1[3]**
55 3 *2 ¼* **Entrenched (USA)**[46] 4454 3-9-5 0..........................(p) SilvestreDeSousa 3 74
(Charlie Appleby) *chsd ldng pair: drvn and effrt to press ldrs over 1f out: unable qck 1f out: wknd fnl 100yds* **3/1[2]**
00 4 *1 ½* **Wolfs Breath (TUR)**[75] 3469 3-9-0 0.......................... RichardHughes 6 66
(Charles Hills) *t.k.h early: in tch in midfield: rdn over 2f out: 4th and outpcd 2f out: pushed along and looked wl hld over 1f out: kpt on again ins fnl f* **12/1**
5 *7* **Seabougg**[29] 5-9-7 0.......................... RyanTate(5) 8 57?
(James Eustace) *hld up in tch towards rr: rdn and effrt over 2f out: sn struggling and btn: wknd wl over 1f out* **40/1**
00 6 *36* **Majnon Fajer (IRE)**[14] 5588 3-9-5 0..........................[1] RobertHavlin 5
(Roger Ingram) *dwlt: hld up in tch in rr: rdn and struggling over 3f out: sn lost tch: t.o fnl 2f* **100/1**
00 7 *41* **Tumbleweed Finale**[59] 4013 3-9-0 0.......................... ChrisCatlin 2
(Rae Guest) *t.k.h: hld up in rr: rdn and struggling over 4f out: lost tch 3f out: t.o and eased fnl 2f* **66/1**

2m 5.49s (1.89) **Going Correction** -0.025s/f (Good)
WFA 3 from 5yo 7lb **7** Ran SP% **109.8**
Speed ratings (Par 103): **91,90,89,87,82 53,20**
toteswingers 1&2 £1.40, 1&3 £1.20, 2&3 £1.80 CSF £4.81 TOTE £1.70: £1.20, £2.20; EX 5.80 Trifecta £9.90 Pool: £4618.69 - 346.65 winning units..
Owner B E Nielsen **Bred** Meon Valley Stud **Trained** Upper Lambourn, Berks

FOCUS
There was suspicion that this was stronger than the majority of maiden races run at the seaside track and it might just be a race to follow. However it was steadily run. The winner didn't need to match his best.

6037 SQUAREONEFINANCIAL.CO.UK PROPERTY FINANCE SPECIALISTS H'CAP 1m 1f 209y
4:30 (4:30) (Class 5) (0-70,70) 3-Y-O+ **£2,587** (£770; £384; £192) **Stalls** High

Form RPR
6222 1 **Mizyen (IRE)**[13] 5606 3-9-1 **68**.......................... NeilCallan 4 77
(James Tate) *t.k.h: led: rdn and c to stands' rail over 2f out: drvn and hdd over 1f out: battled bk gamely to ld again ins fnl f: forged ahd fnl 50yds* **5/6[1]**
5400 2 *1* **Emman Bee (IRE)**[30] 5001 4-9-6 **66**.......................... RichardHughes 2 74
(Luke Dace) *chsd wnr: effrt and upsides over 2f out: rdn to ld over 1f out: drvn ins fnl f: hdd and no ex fnl 50yds: btn and eased cl home* **15/2**
1140 3 *3 ¼* **Green Earth (IRE)**[25] 5168 6-8-12 **61**..........................(p) JemmaMarshall(3) 3 62
(Pat Phelan) *chsd ldng pair: swtchd lft and effrt 2f out: drvn and styd on same pce fr over 1f out* **7/1[3]**
3053 4 *1 ¼* **Brown Pete (IRE)**[13] 5605 5-8-10 **63**.......................... OisinMurphy(7) 5 61
(Violet M Jordan) *hld up in tch in last pair: rdn and effrt over 1f out: edgd lft and no imp 1f out: plugged on same pce fnl f* **9/1**

0464 5 10 **Fabled City (USA)**[22] 5310 4-9-5 **70**...............(t) RyanTate(5) 6 48
(Clive Cox) *taken down early: stdd s: t.k.h: hld up in tch in last pair: rdn and effrt 2f out: btn over 1f out: sn wknd* **4/1**[2]

2m 3.92s (0.32) **Going Correction** -0.025s/f (Good)
WFA 3 from 4yo+ 7lb **5** Ran SP% **108.8**
Speed ratings (Par 103): **97,96,93,92,84**
CSF £7.41 TOTE £1.80: £1.50, £3.80; EX 6.90 Trifecta £36.90 Pool: £2869.54 - 58.26 winning units..
Owner Sheikh Juma Dalmook Al Maktoum **Bred** Mrs A Brudenell **Trained** Newmarket, Suffolk

FOCUS
A fair race for the grade. The winner stepped up a bit on his recent efforts, but there was no depth to this.

6038 HARRINGTONS LETTINGS H'CAP 7f 214y
5:00 (5:02) (Class 6) (0-55,55) 3-Y-0+ **£1,940** (£577; £288; £144) **Stalls** Centre

Form RPR
6034 1 **Napinda**[4] 5923 3-9-1 **54**............... SilvestreDeSousa 16 63
(Philip McBride) *chsd ldrs: rdn to chse clr ldr over 2f out: swtchd lft wl over 1f out: styd on u.p to ld fnl 100yds: rdn out* **5/1**[1]

5050 2 1 3/4 **Hail Promenader (IRE)**[25] 5204 7-9-7 **55**...............(bt) WilliamCarson 8 60
(Anthony Carson) *taken down early: sn bustled along to ld: clr and c to stands' rail over 2f out: hung bdly lft over 1f out: drvn and hdd fnl 100yds: wknd towards fin* **6/1**[2]

5360 3 hd **Who's That Chick (IRE)**[58] 4071 4-8-12 **51**............... RyanTate(5) 12 55
(Ralph Smith) *racd off the pce in midfield: hdwy u.p to chse clr ldng pair over 1f out: styd on wl ins fnl f* **9/1**

R632 4 2 1/2 **Sakhee's Alround**[19] 5407 3-8-11 **50**...............(p) AdamBeschizza 4 48+
(K F Clutterbuck) *taken down early: s.i.s: wl bhd in rr: rdn 3f out: hdwy in centre over 1f out: styd on wl ins fnl f: nvr trbld ldrs* **6/1**[2]

0340 5 1 **Polish Rider**[13] 5615 3-8-7 **46** oh1............... KieranO'Neill 6 42
(Richard Hannon) *chsd ldrs: unable qck u.p over 2f out: kpt on same pce fr over 1f out* **18/1**

-030 6 2 1/4 **Soubrette**[26] 5127 3-8-4 **46** oh1............... RyanPowell(3) 13 37
(George Margarson) *midfield: rdn and effrt 3f out: chsd clr ldng pair wl over 1f out: no imp: wknd ins fnl f* **66/1**

0000 7 1 1/4 **Cristaliyev**[7] 5818 5-8-5 **46**............... EoinWalsh(7) 9 34
(David Evans) *taken down early: hld up wl off the pce in last quartet: rdn and hdwy towards centre 2f out: kpt on: nvr trbld ldrs* **20/1**

3000 8 3/4 **Byrd In Hand (IRE)**[30] 4996 6-8-12 **51**............... MichaelJMMurphy(5) 7 37
(John Bridger) *racd off the pce in midfield: rdn and struggling over 3f out: plugged on but wl hld fnl 2f* **10/1**

0015 9 nk **King Of Wing (IRE)**[13] 5622 4-9-4 **52**...............(be) CathyGannon 3 38
(Phil McEntee) *hld up off the pce in last quartet: hmpd bnd over 4f out: stl bhd and hmpd again 3f out: sme late hdwy: nvr trbld ldrs* **12/1**

2404 10 3 1/2 **Benandonner (USA)**[25] 5171 10-8-9 **50**...............(v[1]) OisinMurphy(7) 14 27
(Paddy Butler) *broke wl but sn rdn along: chsd ldrs: struggling u.p 4f out: wknd over 2f out* **10/1**

163 11 10 **Litmus (USA)**[201] 630 4-9-3 **51**...............(b) NeilCallan 15
(Simon Dow) *chsd ldr tl over 2f out: sn lost pl u.p: bhd fnl f* **10/1**

6530 12 3 3/4 **Ishisoba**[23] 5275 3-8-13 **52**...............(p) AndreaAtzeni 1
(Alastair Lidderdale) *hld up off the pce in last quartet: hmpd bnd over 4f out: n.d* **11/1**

0250 13 30 **Our Three Graces (IRE)**[26] 5128 3-9-0 **53**............... RichardHughes 5
(Gary Moore) *off the pce in midfield: hmpd and lost pl bnd 4f out: bhd after: lost tch 2f out: sn eased: t.o* **17/2**[3]

1m 35.49s (-0.51) **Going Correction** -0.025s/f (Good)
WFA 3 from 4yo+ 5lb **13** Ran SP% **120.6**
Speed ratings (Par 101): **101,99,99,96,95 93,92,91,91,87 77,73,43**
toteswingers 1&2 £5.60, 1&3 £9.10, 2&3 £11.00 CSF £34.12 CT £277.24 TOTE £5.40: £2.20, £1.80, £3.70; EX 31.40 Trifecta £218.90 Pool: £3702.46 - 12.68 winning units..
Owner Peter Wagstaffe **Bred** Stuart McPhee Bloodstock Ltd **Trained** Newmarket, Suffolk

FOCUS
A devilishly competitive, if only moderate handicap. The form is rated on the negative side.

6039 GENTING CASINO BRIGHTON H'CAP 6f 209y
5:30 (5:30) (Class 5) (0-70,70) 3-Y-0+ **£2,587** (£770; £384; £192) **Stalls** Centre

Form RPR
4231 1 **Pilates (IRE)**[11] 5668 3-9-0 **64**............... SilvestreDeSousa 10 79
(Mark Johnston) *chsd ldrs tl led wl over 2f out: edgd lft u.p over 1f out: styd on strly and drew clr ins fnl f: readily* **5/2**[1]

0644 2 4 **Saskia's Dream**[45] 4496 5-9-1 **61**...............(v) RichardHughes 8 65
(Jane Chapple-Hyam) *hld up in tch in midfield: rdn and effrt whn hung lft over 1f out: sn chsng wnr: outpcd by wnr but kpt on ins fnl f* **9/2**[3]

5003 3 3/4 **Golden Desert (IRE)**[30] 4998 9-9-10 **70**............... NeilCallan 3 72
(Simon Dow) *s.i.s: hld up in tch in last pair: rdn and hdwy whn swtchd rt over 1f out: styd on wl ins fnl f: no threat to wnr* **20/1**

5443 4 2 1/2 **Patavium Prince (IRE)**[13] 5607 10-9-7 **67**............... DaneO'Neill 4 62
(Jo Crowley) *in tch: rdn and hdwy in centre 2f out: chsd ldrs over 1f out: no ex 1f out and wknd ins fnl f* **16/1**

1104 5 2 **The Mongoose**[7] 5815 5-9-1 **68**...............(t) EoinWalsh(7) 7 58
(David Evans) *w ldr: rdn and chsd wnr over 2f out: struggling and losing pl whn pushed lft over 1f out: wknd fnl f* **7/1**

604 6 1/2 **Frognal (IRE)**[23] 5278 7-8-13 **66**...............(b) OisinMurphy(7) 2 54
(Paddy Butler) *s.i.s: hld up in last pair: swtchd rt and effrt jst over 2f out: no imp u.p over 1f out: wknd ins fnl f* **20/1**

5045 7 nse **Admiralofthesea (USA)**[23] 5273 3-9-0 **64**............... AndreaAtzeni 11 52
(Robert Eddery) *in tch towards rr: hdwy into midfield and c towards stands' rail 3f out: sn struggling u.p: wknd over 1f out* **4/1**[2]

6344 8 11 **Ghostwing**[4] 5931 6-9-5 **65**...............(vt) HayleyTurner 9 24
(Luke Dace) *in tch in midfield: rdn and lost pl over 2f out: bhd over 1f out: wknd and bhd whn eased wl ins fnl f* **11/2**

0456 9 16 **Fletcher Christian**[84] 3159 3-9-3 **67**............... ChrisCatlin 1
(John Gallagher) *led tl wl over 2f out: sn rdn and lost pl 2f out: wl bhd and eased ins fnl f* **33/1**

1m 22.36s (-0.74) **Going Correction** -0.025s/f (Good)
WFA 3 from 4yo+ 4lb **9** Ran SP% **113.0**
Speed ratings (Par 103): **103,98,97,94,92 91,91,79,60**
toteswingers 1&2 £3.70, 1&3 £5.10, 2&3 £14.20 CSF £12.97 CT £178.09 TOTE £2.50: £1.10, £1.70, £5.80; EX 14.00 Trifecta £204.20 Pool: £2883.51 - 10.58 winning units..
Owner Sheikh Hamdan Bin Mohammed Al Maktoum **Bred** Michael O'Mahony **Trained** Middleham Moor, N Yorks

FOCUS
A modest handicap. The winner progressed again.
T/Plt: £20.60 to a £1 stake. Pool: £69,334.93 - 2455.52 winning units T/Qpdt: £3.20 to a £1 stake. Pool: £3327.45 - 396.70 winning units SP

5693 FFOS LAS (L-H)
Monday, September 2

OFFICIAL GOING: Good to firm (8.7)
Wind: fresh against Weather: overcast

6040 32RED H'CAP 5f
2:20 (2:21) (Class 6) (0-65,64) 3-Y-0+ **£1,940** (£577; £288; £144) **Stalls** Centre

Form RPR
3163 1 **Dangerous Age**[11] 5673 3-9-4 **62**............... RyanMoore 5 68
(J W Hills) *trckd ldrs: drvn over 1f out: led early ins fnl f: hld on wl* **11/4**[2]

0314 2 nk **Griffin Point (IRE)**[1] 6018 6-9-0 **62**...............(b) ThomasGarner(5) 6 67
(William Muir) *led: pushed along fr 1/2-way: hdd over 1f out: drvn and kpt on wl* **2/1**[1]

5510 3 shd **Catflap (IRE)**[41] 4608 4-8-13 **59**...............(p) RosieJessop(3) 7 64
(Derek Haydn Jones) *walked to post v early: cl up: tk narrow ld over 1f out: hdd early ins fnl f: kpt on: jst hld* **6/1**[3]

20-0 4 nk **Dawn Catcher**[18] 5447 3-9-5 **63**............... SebSanders 4 67
(Geoffrey Deacon) *t.k.h: hld up bhd ldrs: drvn and hdwy over 1f out: sn ev ch: kpt on same pce fnl f* **16/1**

4100 5 1 3/4 **Reginald Claude**[11] 5674 5-9-3 **60**............... DavidProbert 1 57
(Mark Usher) *s.i.s: in rr: r.o ins fnl f: nvr trbld ldrs* **8/1**

6544 6 1 1/4 **Ryan Style (IRE)**[26] 5154 7-9-4 **64**...............(p) MarkCoumbe(3) 3 57
(Lisa Williamson) *chsd ldrs: drvn 2f out: one pce appr fnl f* **7/1**

150- 7 6 **My Meteor**[273] 7969 6-9-7 **64**............... JamesDoyle 2 35
(Tony Newcombe) *hld up: drvn over 1f out: sn wknd* **8/1**

57.6s (-0.70) **Going Correction** -0.175s/f (Firm)
WFA 3 from 4yo+ 1lb **7** Ran SP% **114.9**
Speed ratings (Par 101): **98,97,97,96,94 92,82**
toteswingers 1&2 £1.40, 1&3 £2.70, 2&3 £3.40 CSF £8.79 CT £28.89 TOTE £3.60: £1.70, £1.70; EX 8.30 Trifecta £23.90 Pool: £1723.90 - 54.09 winning units..
Owner R Hunter, D Klein, M Hoodless **Bred** Mrs T Brudenell **Trained** Upper Lambourn, Berks

FOCUS
There was a tight finish to this moderate sprint handicap, with the first four closely covered. The second and third set the standard.

6041 32RED CASINO NURSERY H'CAP 1m (R)
2:50 (2:50) (Class 4) (0-85,82) 2-Y-0 **£3,752** (£1,116; £557; £278) **Stalls** Low

Form RPR
01 1 **Hala Hala (IRE)**[21] 5330 2-9-2 **77**............... RyanMoore 4 78+
(Michael Bell) *hld up wl in tch in last: wnt 3rd over 5f out: clsd to chal 2f out: sn led: drvn out fnl f* **6/4**[2]

0560 2 1/2 **Know Your Name**[3] 5945 2-8-10 **74**............... DeclanBates(3) 1 74
(David Evans) *racd in 3rd tl relegated to last over 5f out: pushed along 3f out: edgd lft u.p over 1f out: swtchd rt and r.o fnl f: tk 2nd last strides* **5/1**[3]

021 3 nk **If (GER)**[25] 5167 2-9-2 **80**............... ThomasBrown(3) 5 79
(Andrew Balding) *rdn along fr stalls to ld after 1f: hdd over 1f out: drvn and kpt on wl: lost 2nd last strides* **11/10**[1]

5300 4 2 **Dancing Sal (IRE)**[4] 5926 2-8-3 **64**............... LukeMorris 3 58
(David Evans) *led 1f: trckd ldr: chal 2f out: sn drvn: one pce fnl f* **12/1**

1m 39.36s (-1.64) **Going Correction** -0.175s/f (Firm) 2y crse rec **4** Ran SP% **112.0**
Speed ratings (Par 97): **101,100,100,98**
CSF £8.96 TOTE £2.20; EX 5.90 Trifecta £19.60 Pool: £1055.29 - 40.31 winning units..
Owner Sultan Ali **Bred** Forenaghts Stud Farm Ltd **Trained** Newmarket, Suffolk

FOCUS
Not a bad little nursery and another tight finish. Not easy to pin down what the winner achieved.

6042 32RED.COM H'CAP 1m (R)
3:20 (3:21) (Class 6) (0-65,65) 3-Y-0+ **£1,940** (£577; £288; £144) **Stalls** Low

Form RPR
430 1 **Mcdelta**[23] 5277 3-9-1 **61**............... SebSanders 5 71
(Geoffrey Deacon) *hld up: drvn and hdwy over 2f out: r.o to ld ins fnl f: drawing away towards fin* **20/1**

5621 2 1 1/2 **Wordismybond**[21] 5346 4-9-7 **62**............... RyanMoore 3 69
(Peter Makin) *trckd ldr: led 2f out: drvn and hdd ins fnl f: kpt on: no ex towards fin* **7/4**[1]

1 3 2 **Song Of Snowdon**[19] 5386 3-9-5 **65**............... SteveDrowne 7 67
(William Muir) *hld up: rdn over 2f out: sn sltly outpcd by ldrs: r.o ins fnl f* **5/2**[2]

3333 4 1 1/4 **McCool Bannanas**[45] 4482 5-9-6 **61**............... DavidProbert 1 61
(James Unett) *chsd ldrs: nt clr run 2f out tl over 1f out: sn rdn and unable qck* **7/2**[3]

4330 5 1 3/4 **Admirable Art (IRE)**[35] 4829 3-9-4 **64**............... LukeMorris 4 60
(Tony Carroll) *chsd ldrs: rdn over 2f out: one pce fnl f* **6/1**

000 6 7 **Bertie Blu Boy**[24] 5232 5-8-7 **51** oh4...............(b) MarkCoumbe(3) 8 30
(Lisa Williamson) *led: hdd 2f out: sn wknd* **20/1**

1m 39.03s (-1.97) **Going Correction** -0.175s/f (Firm)
WFA 3 from 4yo+ 5lb **6** Ran SP% **111.0**
Speed ratings (Par 101): **102,100,98,97,95 88**
toteswingers 1&2 £13.00, 2&3 £1.90, 1&3 £3.20 CSF £54.37 CT £118.39 TOTE £17.80: £10.30, £1.30; EX 63.40 Trifecta £266.40 Pool: £2010.51 - 5.65 winning units..
Owner P D Cundell **Bred** Roden House Stud **Trained** Compton, Berks

FOCUS
An ordinary handicap, run at a fair pace. Improvement from the winner.

6043 £32 FREE AT 32RED.COM MEDIAN AUCTION MAIDEN STKS 6f
3:50 (3:51) (Class 6) 3-5-Y-0 **£1,940** (£577; £288; £144) **Stalls** Centre

Form RPR
2520 1 **It's Taboo**[5] 5896 3-9-0 71............... DavidProbert 4 56+
(Mark Usher) *trckd ldr: disp ld after 2f tl led 2f out: pushed out* **8/13**[1]

6 2 3/4 **Pearl Style (FR)**[16] 5517 3-9-5 0............... HarryBentley 5 59+
(Olly Stevens) *hld up: rdn and clsd over 1f out: chsd ldr ins fnl f: r.o but a being hld* **5/2**[2]

0203 3 1 1/4 **Winnie Perry**[12] 5644 3-9-5 57...............(b[1]) JamesDoyle 1 55
(Rod Millman) *hld up in tch: clsd to chse wnr 2f out: sn drvn: lost 2nd ins fnl f* **5/1**[3]

0000 4 5 **Cool And Clear (IRE)**[48] 4378 3-9-5 43...............(b[1]) LiamKeniry 3 39?
(Pat Eddery) *led: jnd after 2f: rdn and hdd 2f out: sn wknd* **50/1**

4006 5 14 **Kaahen (USA)**[53] 4193 3-9-2 37...............(p) ThomasBrown(3) 2
(Pat Eddery) *chsd ldrs to 1/2-way: sn edgd lft u.p and wknd: t.o* **66/1**

1m 10.68s (0.68) **Going Correction** -0.175s/f (Firm) **5** Ran SP% **110.6**
Speed ratings (Par 101): **88,87,85,78,60**
CSF £2.45 TOTE £1.50: £1.10, £1.50; EX 2.70 Trifecta £3.40 Pool: £3782.29 - 826.51 winning units..
Owner Mrs T Channing-Williams **Bred** Mrs T J Channing-Williams **Trained** Upper Lambourn, Berks

The Form Book Flat, Raceform Ltd, Compton, RG20 6NL.

FOCUS
A weak maiden which consisted of 3yos. It was run at an average pace for a sprint. A very modest level set around the third.

6044 32RED ON THE APP STORE H'CAP — 1m 4f (R)
4:20 (4:20) (Class 6) (0-55,55) 3-Y-O+ — **£1,940** (£577; £288; £144) **Stalls** Low

Form — RPR
303 **1** **Cabuchon (GER)**[4] 5934 6-8-10 **47**.....(t) DeclanBates(3) 8 59
(David Evans) *hld up in last pair: stdy hdwy over 2f out: led 1f out: pushed out: comf* **5/2**[2]
660 **2** 3 **Dumbfounded (FR)**[27] 5100 5-9-5 **53**..... RyanMoore 4 60
(Lady Herries) *trckd ldr: relegated to 3rd at 1/2-way: wnt 2nd again 3f out: drvn and unable qck 2f out: disputing 3rd 1f out: styd on to take 2nd nr fin* **9/4**[1]
2613 **3** ¾ **Men Don't Cry (IRE)**[12] 5633 4-9-3 **54**.....(b) MarkCoumbe(3) 1 60
(Ed de Giles) *led: shkn up 2f out: drvn over 1f out: sn hdd and one pce: lost 2nd nr fin* **3/1**[3]
6405 **4** ½ **Hawaiian Freeze**[12] 5633 4-8-9 **46** oh1.....[1] WilliamTwiston-Davies(3) 2 51
(John Stimpson) *midfield: hdwy over 2f out: sn drvn and hung lft: kpt on same pce fnl f* **25/1**
0062 **5** 7 **Waving**[7] 5846 4-9-7 **55**.....(t) LukeMorris 7 49
(Tony Carroll) *racd in 3rd tl chsd ldr 1/2-way: lost 2nd 3f out: sn drvn: wknd fnl f* **5/1**
0000 **6** 3½ **A Good Year (IRE)**[14] 5592 3-8-3 **49**..... SimonPearce(3) 6 37
(J W Hills) *s.s and flashed tail repeatedly 1f: hld up in last pair: effrt over 2f out: no imp: wknd over 1f out: flashed tail again fnl f* **20/1**
6006 **7** 16 **Ernie**[103] 2563 6-9-4 **52**..... SebSanders 5 15
(Geoffrey Deacon) *midfield: drvn over 3f out: wknd over 2f out: t.o* **10/1**

2m 34.81s (-2.59) **Going Correction** -0.175s/f (Firm)
WFA 3 from 4yo+ 9lb — 7 Ran SP% **118.7**
Speed ratings (Par 101): **101,99,98,98,93 91,80**
toteswingers 1&2 £2.50, 1&3 £2.00, 2&3 £2.40 CSF £9.12 CT £17.28 TOTE £3.30: £2.00, £2.90; EX 11.20 Trifecta £36.50 Pool: £3133.52 - 64.34 winning units..
Owner Mrs E Evans **Bred** Gestut Schlenderhan **Trained** Pandy, Monmouths

FOCUS
A moderate handicap, run at an ordinary early pace. Fair form for the grade.

6045 BARRY WALTERS CATERING FILLIES' H'CAP — 6f
4:50 (4:50) (Class 4) (0-80,78) 3-Y-O+ — **£4,690** (£1,395; £697; £348) **Stalls** Centre

Form — RPR
1046 **1** **Finesse**[26] 5125 4-9-2 **73**..... SebSanders 6 84+
(Ralph Beckett) *trckd ldrs gng wl: qcknd to ld over 1f out: sn clr: comf* **9/2**[3]
-412 **2** 1¾ **Abated**[41] 4603 3-9-2 **75**..... JamesDoyle 1 78
(Roger Charlton) *led tl hdd over 1f out: sn outpcd by wnr but kpt on wl u.p for clr 2nd* **9/4**[1]
2046 **3** 3¼ **Queen Aggie (IRE)**[11] 5676 3-9-2 **78**..... DeclanBates(3) 3 71
(David Evans) *in rr: sltly hmpd and swtchd lft after 2f: drvn 2f out: r.o to go 3rd nr fin* **7/1**
4012 **4** ½ **Edged Out**[31] 4942 3-9-0 **73**..... DavidProbert 5 64
(Christopher Mason) *chsd ldr tl over 1f out: sn hung lft and one pce: lost 3rd nr fin* **14/1**
1443 **5** 3 **Ginzan**[22] 5308 5-9-6 **77**..... LukeMorris 4 58
(Malcolm Saunders) *s.i.s: in tch after 1f: rdn over 2f out: outpcd by ldrs over 1f out: wknd ins fnl f* **4/1**[2]
13 **P** **My Own Way Home**[18] 5447 5-8-10 **67**..... RyanMoore 2
(David Evans) *chsd ldrs tl p.u after 2f: fatally injured* **4/1**[2]

1m 8.48s (-1.52) **Going Correction** -0.175s/f (Firm)
WFA 3 from 4yo+ 2lb — 6 Ran SP% **108.1**
Speed ratings (Par 102): **103,100,96,95,91**
toteswingers 1&2 £2.90, 1&3 £5.10, 2&3 £2.90 CSF £13.90 TOTE £7.00: £2.90, £1.10; EX 24.30 Trifecta £83.90 Pool: £2006.15 - 17.91 winning units..
Owner P K Gardner **Bred** Springcombe Park Stud **Trained** Kimpton, Hants

FOCUS
A modest sprint handicap for fillies, run at a routine pace. The winner was value for extra but the form isn't rated too positively.

6046 DAVIES CHEMISTS "LLANELLI" MAIDEN STKS — 1m 4f (R)
5:20 (5:20) (Class 5) 3-Y-O+ — **£2,587** (£770; £384; £192) **Stalls** Low

Form — RPR
0033 **1** **Bohemian Dance (IRE)**[28] 5064 3-8-12 78..... RyanMoore 1 53+
(Sir Michael Stoute) *mde all: set stdy pce tl wound it up 4f out: drew clr over 1f out: unchal* **1/25**[1]
2 5 **Willow Island (IRE)**[219] 4-9-9 0..... RichardEvans(3) 4 44
(David Evans) *racd in 3rd tl wnt 2nd 4f out: sn rdn and no ch w wnr: kpt on u.p to hold 2nd* **16/1**[2]
0-5 **3** nk **Hendry Trigger**[7] 5813 4-9-7 0..... RobertWilliams(5) 2 44
(Bernard Llewellyn) *t.k.h early: chsd wnr 8f: rdn 3f out: hung rt but plugged on to press for 2nd fnl f* **50/1**
4 nk **Mr Burbidge**[108] 5-9-12 0.....(b) LiamKeniry 3 43
(Neil Mulholland) *dwlt: hld up in last: drvn 3f out: plugged on one pce* **33/1**[3]

2m 42.21s (4.81) **Going Correction** -0.175s/f (Firm)
WFA 3 from 4yo+ 9lb — 4 Ran SP% **106.9**
Speed ratings (Par 103): **76,72,72,72**
CSF £1.65 TOTE £1.10; EX 1.90 Trifecta £4.30 Pool: £840.65 - 144.94 winning units..
Owner Ballymacoll Stud **Bred** Ballymacoll Stud Farm Ltd **Trained** Newmarket, Suffolk

FOCUS
A straightforward task for the choicely bred winner. The form is rated around the poor third.
T/Plt: £32.20 to a £1 stake. Pool: £50,973.12 - 1152.25 winning units T/Qpdt: £6.20 to a £1 stake. Pool: £3327.45 - 396.70 winning units RL

5915 HAMILTON (R-H)
Monday, September 2

OFFICIAL GOING: Good to firm (good in places; 7.8)
Wind: Fresh, across Weather: Overcast

6047 OVERTON FARM NURSERY H'CAP — 6f 5y
2:10 (2:10) (Class 5) (0-75,74) 2-Y-O — **£3,881** (£1,155; £577; £288) **Stalls** High

Form — RPR
4042 **1** **Bandolier**[30] 4990 2-8-8 **66**..... GeorgeChaloner(5) 3 66
(Richard Fahey) *chsd ldrs: rdn over 2f out: led ins fnl f: jst hld on* **15/2**
2350 **2** nse **Supa U**[37] 4756 2-8-9 **62**.....(e[1]) DavidAllan 9 62
(Tim Easterby) *bhd and sn outpcd: hdwy over 1f out: rdn and styd on strly fnl f: jst hld* **7/1**[3]
14 **3** 1 **Les Gar Gan (IRE)**[12] 5656 2-9-7 **74**..... PaulMulrennan 7 75+
(Keith Dalgleish) *trckd ldrs: effrt whn no room fr over 1f out tl swtchd rt ins fnl f: kpt on fin* **5/4**[1]
104 **4** nk **Pigeon Pie**[63] 3890 2-9-4 **71**..... JoeFanning 1 67
(Mark Johnston) *cl up: rdn and ev ch over 1f out to ins fnl f: kpt on same pce towards fin* **14/1**
6241 **5** 3 **Omanome (IRE)**[10] 5703 2-9-3 **70**..... DanielTudhope 2 57
(David O'Meara) *led: rdn over 2f out: hdd ins fnl f: sn outpcd* **7/2**[2]
450 **6** 4½ **Uncle Bobby**[79] 3350 2-8-7 **60**..... JamesSullivan 8 33
(Michael Easterby) *bhd and outpcd after 2f: shortlived effrt over 2f out: hung rt and sn btn* **16/1**
025 **7** 6 **Sukari Gold (IRE)**[28] 5053 2-8-9 **62**..... GrahamLee 4 16
(Kevin Ryan) *prom: drvn over 3f out: wknd over 2f out* **14/1**

1m 10.91s (-1.29) **Going Correction** -0.30s/f (Firm) — 7 Ran SP% **110.1**
Speed ratings (Par 95): **96,95,94,94,90 84,76**
toteswingers 1&2 £5.50, 1&3 £2.20, 2&3 £3.10 CSF £53.26 CT £101.33 TOTE £4.60: £2.40, £2.70; EX 66.70 Trifecta £146.50 Pool: £4365.70 - 22.33 winning units..
Owner N H T Wrigley **Bred** Wrigley & Mrs Kennard **Trained** Musley Bank, N Yorks

FOCUS
Rail at normal position and all distances as advertised. Modest nursery form, and quite a messy race, with the favourite looking unfortunate back in third. A minor personal best from the winner.

6048 ST ANDREWS AMBULANCE H'CAP — 1m 65y
2:40 (2:41) (Class 5) (0-75,74) 3-Y-O+ — **£3,234** (£962; £481; £240) **Stalls** Low

Form — RPR
0122 **1** **Red Charmer (IRE)**[18] 5425 3-9-1 **70**..... PJMcDonald 7 82
(Ann Duffield) *mde all: rdn over 2f out: styd on strly fnl f* **7/1**
1 **2** 1¾ **Nightster (IRE)**[10] 5707 3-9-5 **74**..... JoeFanning 6 82
(Mark Johnston) *pressed wnr: rdn and ev ch over 1f out: kpt on same pce wl ins fnl f* **4/1**[2]
3160 **3** 2 **Ted's Brother (IRE)**[10] 5711 5-9-2 **71**.....(e) PhilipPrince(5) 3 74
(Richard Guest) *t.k.h: trckd ldrs: rdn and effrt over 2f out: edgd lft: kpt on same pce fnl f* **9/2**[3]
2203 **4** ½ **Push Me (IRE)**[7] 5830 6-9-6 **70**..... GrahamLee 2 72
(Iain Jardine) *hld up in tch: outpcd over 2f out: sn rdn: rallied over 1f out: kpt on: nvr able to chal* **9/2**[3]
6440 **5** 2 **Jebel Tara**[19] 5382 8-9-10 **74**.....(bt) MichaelO'Connell 4 72
(Alan Brown) *hld up in tch: rdn over 2f out: edgd lft: no imp fr over 1f out* **28/1**
4052 **6** 1½ **Tectonic (IRE)**[5] 5882 4-8-12 **62**.....(p) TomEaves 8 56
(Keith Dalgleish) *t.k.h: trckd ldrs: rdn and outpcd 2f out: sn no imp* **11/4**[1]
405 **7** 2¼ **I'm Super Too (IRE)**[67] 3715 6-9-7 **71**..... BenCurtis 5 60
(Alan Swinbank) *hld up in tch: rdn and outpcd over 2f out: n.d after* **20/1**
6360 **8** 1¾ **High Resolution**[4] 5918 6-9-3 **67**..... PaulMulrennan 1 52
(Linda Perratt) *s.i.s: hld up: rdn over 3f out: nvr on terms* **11/1**

1m 45.81s (-2.59) **Going Correction** -0.30s/f (Firm)
WFA 3 from 4yo+ 5lb — 8 Ran SP% **112.1**
Speed ratings (Par 103): **100,98,96,95,93 92,90,88**
toteswingers 1&2 £3.90, 1&3 £5.50, 2&3 £3.30 CSF £33.64 CT £139.20 TOTE £9.30: £2.30, £1.80, £1.50; EX 35.10 Trifecta £134.10 Pool: £3640.91 - 20.35 winning units..
Owner I Farrington & R Chapman **Bred** Tally-Ho Stud **Trained** Constable Burton, N Yorks

FOCUS
Little got into this with the two 3yos, who sat first and second throughout, maintaining their positions. The form could be rated higher.

6049 DOWNLOAD THE FREE RACING UK APP H'CAP — 1m 1f 36y
3:10 (3:11) (Class 6) (0-60,59) 3-Y-O — **£1,940** (£577; £288; £144) **Stalls** Low

Form — RPR
0652 **1** **Taxiformissbyron**[4] 5921 3-8-12 **50**..... GrahamLee 1 59
(Michael Herrington) *led 1f: chsd clr ldr: led over 3f out: rdn wl over 1f out: hld on wl fnl f* **13/8**[1]
2 **2** nk **Minot Street (CAN)**[46] 4449 3-8-7 **45**.....(bt) PJMcDonald 10 53
(John C McConnell, Ire) *in tch: hdwy on outside over 2f out: chal fnl f: kpt on: hld nr fin* **8/1**
6230 **3** 1½ **Polar Forest**[17] 5500 3-9-0 **57**..... PhilipPrince(5) 2 62
(Richard Guest) *taken early to post: s.i.s: hld up: stdy hdwy 3f out: sn rdn: kpt on fnl f: nt rch first two* **15/2**
3004 **4** 2¾ **Dutch Gal**[8] 5784 3-9-6 **58**..... GrahamGibbons 8 57
(John Holt) *prom: hdwy and cl up over 3f out: rdn and outpcd appr fnl fq* **16/1**
5 2 **Dalandra**[48] 4395 3-9-6 **58**..... PaulMulrennan 4 53
(Michael Dods) *taken early to post: t.k.h: prom: rdn over 2f out: outpcd over 1f out* **13/2**[2]
3230 **6** 1 **Mudaawem (USA)**[123] 1966 3-9-7 **59**..... JoeFanning 3 51
(Mark Johnston) *w ldr 1f: cl up: rdn over 2f out: edgd lft over 1f out: sn btn* **7/1**[3]
3660 **7** ¾ **Multilicious**[5] 5903 3-9-1 **53**..... DavidAllan 9 44
(Tim Easterby) *hld up: rdn over 3f out: sme late hdwy: nvr on terms* **14/1**
003 **8** ½ **Bitusa (USA)**[12] 5642 3-9-6 **58**..... BenCurtis 6 48
(Alan Swinbank) *hld up: rdn over 2f out: nvr on terms* **12/1**
0-66 **9** 2¾ **Windsor Secret**[4] 5916 3-8-7 **45**..... TomEaves 7 29
(Keith Dalgleish) *hld up: rdn over 3f out: btn fnl 2f* **28/1**
0600 **10** 42 **Hayley**[21] 5334 3-8-0 **45**.....(p) SophieRobertson(7) 11
(Jim Goldie) *s.i.s: plld hrd and rapid hdwy on outside to ld after 1f: sn clr: hdd over 3f out: wknd over 2f out: t.o* **100/1**

1m 57.07s (-2.63) **Going Correction** -0.30s/f (Firm) — 10 Ran SP% **111.5**
Speed ratings (Par 99): **99,98,97,94,93 92,91,91,88,51**
toteswingers 1&2 £2.80, 1&3 £3.10, 2&3 £6.80 CSF £14.14 CT £72.82 TOTE £2.10: £1.20, £2.30, £2.10; EX 12.70 Trifecta £49.30 Pool: £4149.39 - 63.02 winning units..
Owner H Hurst **Bred** Hugh M Hurst **Trained** Cold Kirby, N Yorks

FOCUS
A weak handicap but the form makes sense. The winner was well in on her AW form.

6050 HAMILTON-PARK.CO.UK MAIDEN STKS — 1m 1f 36y
3:40 (3:40) (Class 5) 3-Y-O+ — **£3,408** (£1,006; £503) **Stalls** Low

Form — RPR
2 **1** **Mahican (IRE)**[15] 5563 3-9-5 0..... JoeFanning 3 74+
(Mark Johnston) *mde all: shkn up and qcknd clr over 1f out: styd on strly: unchal* **1/7**[1]
2 4 **Swehan (IRE)** 3-9-5 0..... GrahamLee 2 65+
(Kevin Ryan) *dwlt: sn chsng wnr and sn niggled along: effrt and rdn over 2f out: one pce over 1f out: bttr for r* **6/1**[2]

0340 3 17 **Captain Rhyric**[20] 5370 4-9-11 47 PhillipMakin 4 47
(James Moffatt) *chsd ldrs tl rdn and wknd fr 2f out* **33/1**[3]
1m 58.42s (-1.28) **Going Correction** -0.30s/f (Firm)
WFA 3 from 4yo 6lb **3** Ran SP% **104.7**
Speed ratings (Par 103): **93,89,74**
CSF £1.28 TOTE £1.20; EX 1.40 Trifecta £1.60 Pool: £2130.71 - 967.72 winning units..
Owner Sheikh Hamdan Bin Mohammed Al Maktoum **Bred** Ken Lynch **Trained** Middleham Moor, N Yorks
FOCUS
No Llanarmon Lad, so this looked an easy opportunity for the winner. The time was slow and it's difficult to know what the 1-2 achieved.

6051 RACING UK ON SKY CHANNEL 432 H'CAP 1m 3f 16y
4:10 (4:10) (Class 5) (0-75,73) 3-Y-0+ **£3,234** (£962; £481; £240) **Stalls** High

Form RPR
1 **Lindenhurst (IRE)**[18] 5459 3-8-11 66 (t) JoeFanning 4 75+
(John C McConnell, Ire) *chsd clr ldr: clsd 1/2-way: rdn over 1f out: led over 1f out: styd on wl fnl f* **13/8**[1]
5531 2 2 **Aneedh**[31] 4940 3-9-4 73 MichaelO'Connell 2 78
(Jedd O'Keeffe) *chsd ldrs: rdn and effrt over 2f out: styd on fnl f to take 2nd nr fin: nt rch wnr* **7/1**
3552 3 hd **King Of Paradise (IRE)**[24] 5222 4-9-6 70 JasonHart(3) 7 75
(Eric Alston) *t.k.h: led and clr to 1/2-way: rdn over 2f out: hdd over 1f out: one pce ins fnl f: lost 2nd nr fin* **7/2**[2]
5221 4 5 **Hernando Torres**[34] 4853 5-9-1 62 GrahamGibbons 8 58
(Michael Easterby) *towards rr: rdn over 3f out: effrt 2f out: sn no imp* **5/1**[3]
032 5 ½ **Aryizad (IRE)**[10] 5707 4-9-7 68 BenCurtis 6 63
(Alan Swinbank) *t.k.h: hld up: hdwy on outside over 3f out: wknd 2f out* **10/1**
00-3 6 1 **Hot Spice**[13] 5612 5-9-10 71 JamesSullivan 5 64
(Michael Easterby) *t.k.h: chsd ldrs: rdn over 3f out: wknd 2f out* **13/2**
2m 20.48s (-5.12) **Going Correction** -0.30s/f (Firm)
WFA 3 from 4yo+ 8lb **6** Ran SP% **111.9**
Speed ratings (Par 103): **106,104,104,100,100 99**
toteswingers 1&2 £3.00, 1&3 £1.70, 2&3 £4.70 CSF £13.48 CT £34.06 TOTE £3.20: £2.50, £3.60; EX 13.00 Trifecta £51.70 Pool: £2988.32 - 43.27 winning units..
Owner Derek Kierans **Bred** K Maginn **Trained** Stamullen, Co Meath
FOCUS
Ok form for the level with them going a decent gallop and a pair of progressive 3yos claiming first and second. The form makes sense.

6052 BETFAIR SCOTTISH SPRINT SERIES FINAL H'CAP 6f 5y
4:40 (4:42) (Class 3) 3-Y-0+ **£9,703** (£2,887; £1,443; £721) **Stalls** Centre

Form RPR
1324 1 **Feel The Heat**[39] 4669 6-8-4 66 (v) RoystonFfrench 2 76
(Bryan Smart) *hld up on outside: effrt and hdwy over 2f out: led appr fnl f: kpt on strly* **11/1**
2433 2 1½ **Beckermet (IRE)**[7] 5832 11-8-4 66 JamesSullivan 12 71
(Ruth Carr) *led tl edgd rt and hdd appr fnl f: kpt on* **11/1**
1643 3 1 **Alexandrakollontai (IRE)**[10] 5704 3-7-11 64 oh2 JulieBurke(3) 14 66+
(Alistair Whillans) *wnt down as stall opened and missed break: bhd: hdwy 1/2-way: styd on fr over 1f out: nrst fin* **7/1**[2]
3141 4 nk **Circuitous**[23] 5263 5-8-12 74 (v) TomEaves 7 75
(Keith Dalgleish) *cl up: rdn over 2f out: kpt on ins fnl f* **12/1**
6563 5 nk **The Nifty Fox**[23] 5266 9-9-0 76 (p) PhillipMakin 13 76
(Tim Easterby) *hld up in tch: smooth hdwy over 1f out: rdn and one pce ins fnl f* **20/1**
0140 6 1 **Ambitious Icarus**[7] 5832 4-7-12 65 (e) PhilipPrince(5) 3 62
(Richard Guest) *hld up: rdn over 2f out: styd on fnl f: nvr able to chal* **22/1**
4160 7 nk **Jinky**[10] 5705 5-8-13 75 GrahamLee 11 71
(Linda Perratt) *in tch: rdn over 2f out: one pce fr over 1f out* **16/1**
1534 8 1¼ **Mandalay King (IRE)**[23] 5294 8-8-0 67 (b) ShirleyTeasdale(5) 6 59
(Marjorie Fife) *bhd: rdn over 2f out: kpt on ins fnl f: n.d* **14/1**
6413 9 nk **Flighty Clarets (IRE)**[7] 5836 3-8-2 66 PatrickMathers 10 57
(Richard Fahey) *t.k.h early: hld up: rdn over 2f out: no imp fr over 1f out* **9/1**
6215 10 1 **Secret Advice**[30] 4976 3-8-5 69 JoeFanning 9 57
(Keith Dalgleish) *t.k.h: in tch: rdn over 2f out: no ex appr fnl f* **14/1**
5111 11 ½ **Gran Canaria Queen**[10] 5714 4-8-8 70 DavidAllan 4 56
(Tim Easterby) *cl up tl rdn and no ex over 1f out* **9/2**[1]
50 12 2¼ **Findog**[5] 5878 3-8-2 69 NeilFarley(3) 5 48
(Linda Perratt) *midfield: pushed along 2f out: sn no imp* **18/1**
2660 13 1¾ **Chester Aristocrat**[45] 4472 4-9-7 86 JasonHart(3) 8 59
(Eric Alston) *t.k.h: cl up tl rdn and wknd over 1f out* **8/1**[3]
5006 14 7 **Opt Out**[5] 5878 3-7-12 65 RaulDaSilva(3) 1 16
(Alistair Whillans) *cl up: rdn over 2f out: wknd wl over 1f out* **12/1**
1m 10.77s (-1.43) **Going Correction** -0.30s/f (Firm)
WFA 3 from 4yo+ 2lb **14** Ran SP% **117.4**
Speed ratings (Par 107): **97,95,93,93,92 91,91,89,89,87 87,84,81,72**
toteswingers 1&2 £19.80, 1&3 £13.70, 2&3 £15.90 CSF £123.65 CT £938.02 TOTE £10.50: £2.20, £4.10, £3.00; EX 133.00 Trifecta £1086.00 Pool: £4245.12 - 2.93 winning units..
Owner B Smart **Bred** Bearstone Stud **Trained** Hambleton, N Yorks
FOCUS
An open sprint, in which the runners were spread centre-to-stands' side, and it was one of the lower-drawn runners who came out on top. The runner-up helps set the standard.

6053 RACING UK AMATEUR RIDERS' H'CAP 6f 5y
5:10 (5:15) (Class 6) (0-65,63) 4-Y-0+ **£1,975** (£607; £303) **Stalls** Centre

Form RPR
0251 1 **Lothair (IRE)**[5] 5876 4-10-7 56 6ex MrSWalker 3 65
(Alan Swinbank) *cl up: rdn to ld over 1f out: r.o wl fnl f* **6/4**[1]
0500 2 1½ **Compton Heights**[21] 5336 4-10-6 55 MrsCBartley 4 59
(Jim Goldie) *hld up bhd ldrs: effrt and hdwy over 1f out: chsd wnr fnl f: kpt on* **16/1**
00-0 3 1½ **Camerooney**[10] 5713 10-10-4 58 MissNHayes(5) 2 57
(Marjorie Fife) *chsd ldrs: pushed along 2f out: kpt on ins fnl f* **33/1**
0412 4 1¼ **George Fenton**[3] 5971 4-10-6 62 (p) MrRAsquith(7) 10 57
(Richard Guest) *hld up: shkn up and hdwy over 1f out: edgd lft: kpt on: no imp* **11/4**[2]
3226 5 nk **Saxonette**[10] 5708 5-10-5 54 MissCWalton 1 48
(Linda Perratt) *in tch: shkn up 2f out: no imp fnl f* **9/1**
440 6 shd **Spread Boy (IRE)**[23] 5261 6-9-7 45 MissJRRichards(3) 7 39
(Alan Berry) *prom: edgd rt and outpcd over 2f out: kpt on last 100yds* **28/1**
6000 7 nk **Hab Reeh**[5] 5876 5-10-3 52 (t) MissSBrotherton 8 45
(Ruth Carr) *dwlt: t.k.h and sn in tch: effrt 2f out: outpcd fnl f* **7/1**[3]
6352 8 1¾ **Rock Canyon (IRE)**[10] 5708 4-10-0 49 (p) MrJHamilton 6 36
(Linda Perratt) *led to over 1f out: wknd ins fnl f* **14/1**
0603 9 1 **Monthly Medal**[7] 5840 10-10-0 52 (t) MissSMDoolan(3) 9 36
(Wilf Storey) *hld up bhd ldng gp: shkn up and outpcd whn n.m.r wl over 1f out: sn btn* **14/1**
1m 12.09s (-0.11) **Going Correction** -0.30s/f (Firm) **9** Ran SP% **114.8**
Speed ratings (Par 101): **88,86,84,82,81 81,81,79,77**
toteswingers 1&2 £5.70, 1&3 £13.90, 2&3 £26.60 CSF £28.59 CT £564.00 TOTE £2.90: £1.10, £4.20, £9.90; EX 27.30 Trifecta £503.00 Pool: £3924.67 - 5.85 winning units..
Owner Mrs J Porter **Bred** Lynch Bages Ltd & Samac Ltd **Trained** Melsonby, N Yorks
FOCUS
The main action unfolded centre-field in what was a weak handicap for amateurs. The winner is the best guide.
T/Jkpt: £7100.00 to a £1 stake. Pool: £10,000.00 - 1.0 winning units T/Plt: £182.40 to a £1 stake. Pool: £63,320.82 - 253.41 winning units T/Qpdt: £12.30 to a £1 stake. Pool: £4581.39 - 273.99 winning units RY

BEAUMONT-DE-LOMAGNE (R-H)
Monday, September 2
OFFICIAL GOING: Turf: good

6058a PRIX GASTON COMBES (CONDITIONS) (4YO+) (LADY AMATEUR RIDERS) (TURF) 1m 3f 110y
4:30 (4:30) 4-Y-0+ **£2,845** (£1,138; £853; £569; £284)

RPR
1 **Volochope (FR)**[1767] 10-9-11 0 MlleIngridGrard 3 43
(M Delaplace, France) **56/10**[3]
2 shd **Qurqui**[296] 7-10-3 0 MlleLaraLeGeay 5 49
(Pierrick Le Geay, France) **6/4**[2]
3 1½ **Lichtlein (FR)**[155] 6-9-3 0 MlleGabrielleBarone(4) 7 36
(D Barone, France) **15/2**
4 ½ **Sunny Cat (FR)**[263] 5-9-11 0 MlleSolangeGourdain(4) 1 43
(C Gourdain, France) **13/10**[1]
5 7 **Bienvenido (FR)**[679] 8-9-6 0 (b) MlleIngridPrunet-Foch(5) 2 28
(P Prunet-Foch, France) **36/1**
6 5 **Aldershot (FR)**[1554] 7-8-10 0 MlleLinePayet-Burin(5) 6 9
(Mlle L Payet-Burin, France) **187/1**
7 3½ **Irons On Fire (USA)**[18] 5464 5-9-0 0 (p) MlleCharleyLauffer(4) 4 6
(Gay Kelleway) *barrier s: chsd clr ldr: lost pl over 2 1/2f out: bhd fnl 1 1/2f* **24/1**
2m 26.1s (146.10) **7** Ran SP% **117.6**
WIN (incl. 1 euro stake): 6.60. PLACES: 1.90, 1.10. SF: 19.90.
Owner Martial Delaplace **Bred** Alain Chopard & Mme Maryse Delteil **Trained** France

3614 SAINT-CLOUD (L-H)
Monday, September 2
OFFICIAL GOING: Turf: good

6059a PRIX DE FONTENAY (CLAIMER) (2YO) (TURF) 7f
1:50 (1:51) 2-Y-0 **£7,723** (£3,089; £2,317; £1,544; £772)

RPR
1 **Ascot Memory (IRE)**[24] 5363 2-8-13 0 TheoBachelot 12 76
(S Wattel, France) **104/10**
2 hd **Victorianvalentine (FR)**[7] 2-9-2 0 AntoineHamelin 9 78
(Matthieu Palussiere, France) **14/5**[1]
3 4½ **Jack Beauregard (IRE)** 2-9-4 0 Pierre-CharlesBoudot 5 68
(Gianluca Bietolini, Italy) **47/1**
4 nk **Donibane (FR)**[42] 4599 2-8-8 0 DavidBreux 6 58
(Mlle V Dissaux, France) **104/1**
5 ½ **Infolinia (USA)**[8] 2-8-3 0 JimmyTastayre(5) 8 56
(C Lerner, France) **15/1**
6 ¾ **Almond Grace**[40] 4651 2-8-11 0 AlexisBadel 1 57
(Mme M Bollack-Badel, France) **8/1**
7 ¾ **Syrina (FR)** 2-8-11 0 CesarPasserat(4) 11 59
(F-X De Chevigny, France) **93/1**
8 nse **Stake Winning (FR)**[24] 5363 2-8-11 0 RonanThomas 16 55
(S Wattel, France) **26/1**
9 hd **Blues Orchestra (FR)** 2-9-1 0 ThomasMessina 7 58
(J-V Toux, France) **55/1**
10 ¾ **Stella Indiana (FR)**[24] 5363 2-8-11 0 MarcLerner 3 52
(J Heloury, France) **68/10**[3]
11 shd **Boogy Man (ITY)**[16] 2-9-1 0 UmbertoRispoli 10 56
(G Botti, France) **6/1**[2]
12 10 **Nidoran (ITY)** 2-9-1 0 ChristopheSoumillon 4 29
(L Riccardi, Italy) **44/5**
13 nk **Pleats (FR)**[25] 5213 2-8-11 0 EddyHardouin 2 24
(Matthieu Palussiere, France) **50/1**
14 2½ **L'Oublieuse (FR)** 2-8-3 0 NicolasLarenaudie(5) 13 15
(J Bertran De Balanda, France) **116/1**
15 dist **Qasima (FR)** 2-8-8 0 (b1) FlavienPrat 15
(Mme L Audon, France) **96/1**
16 2½ **Chanceuse**[24] 5229 2-8-11 0 MaximeGuyon 14
(Gay Kelleway) *chsd ldrs early: sn dropped towards rr: rdn and no imp 2 1/2f out: sn wknd: t.o* **7/1**
1m 26.42s (-5.78) **16** Ran SP% **115.7**
WIN (incl. 1 euro stake): 11.40. PLACES: 3.30, 2.00, 12.00. DF: 18.10. SF: 41.20.
Owner Ecurie Ascot **Bred** M O'Mahony **Trained** France

6060a PRIX DE BRUNOY (CLAIMER) (4YO+) (TURF) 1m 2f 110y
2:50 (2:49) 4-Y-0+ **£9,349** (£3,739; £2,804; £1,869; £934)

RPR
1 **Stelway (FR)**[305] 4-9-4 0 ChristopheSoumillon 3 75+
(P Bary, France) **13/10**[1]
2 3½ **Diodoros (FR)**[16] 7-9-5 0 AnthonyCrastus 2 69+
(F Chappet, France) **5/2**[2]
3 shd **Mrs Miller (GER)**[29] 5-8-8 0 EddyHardouin 1 58+
(S Smrczek, Germany) **19/1**

4 snk **Uphold**[14] 5601 6-9-2 0 (b) MaximeGuyon 4 66+
(Gay Kelleway) *trckd ldr on outer: jnd ldr over 3f out: rdn and sltly outpcd 2f out: hmpd and lost pl 1 1/2f out: styd on again ins fnl f to be involved in blanket fin for 2nd* **19/5**[3]
5 nk **Kentucky Winner (FR)**[110] 4-9-5 0 UmbertoRispoli 6 68
(A Lyon, France) **9/1**
6 hd **Eldarion (IRE)**[84] 5-9-2 0 (b) TheoBachelot 7 65
(A Lyon, France) **38/1**
7 4 **Minor Swing (FR)**[78] 5-8-6 0 (p) NicolasLarenaudie(5) 5 52+
(R Houthoofd, Belgium) **24/1**
8 6 **Sandoka (FR)**[117] 4-8-8 0 (b) CesarPasserat(3) 8 40+
(J-P Delaporte, France) **26/1**
2m 10.12s (-9.48) 8 Ran SP% **118.2**
WIN (incl. 1 euro stake): 2.30. PLACES: 1.20, 1.30, 2.50. DF: 3.00. SF: 4.50.
Owner Mme Chris Jacob **Bred** Stella Maris **Trained** Chantilly, France

6061 - (Foreign Racing) - See Raceform Interactive

5790 **GOODWOOD** (R-H)
Tuesday, September 3

OFFICIAL GOING: Good to firm (good in places)
Wind: Moderate across (away from stands) Weather: Fine, very warm

6062 GOODWOOD RACEHORSE OWNERS GROUP MAIDEN STKS 1m 1f 192y
2:20 (2:23) (Class 5) 3-Y-O **£3,234** (£962; £481; £240) **Stalls** Low

Form RPR
5 1 **Martian (IRE)**[31] 4978 3-9-5 0 RyanMoore 3 87+
(William Haggas) *str: lw: trckd ldng pair: pushed along wl over 2f out: clsd to ld 1f out: styd on wl: readily* **9/4**[2]
-255 2 1 1/2 **Nickels And Dimes (IRE)**[11] 5720 3-9-0 76 WilliamBuick 9 73
(John Gosden) *pressed ldr: pushed upsides 3f out: drvn and stl upsides whn wnr wnt past 1f out: styd on* **8/1**
3533 3 1/2 **Are You Mine (IRE)**[17] 5548 3-9-0 71 (v1) JimCrowley 1 72
(Ralph Beckett) *led: jnd 3f out: drvn and hdd 1f out: one pce* **5/1**[3]
53 4 hd **Angus Glens**[18] 5495 3-9-5 0 SteveDrowne 10 80+
(David Dennis) *leggy: athletic: t.k.h early: hld up towards rr: shkn up over 2f out: prog on wd outside wl over 1f out: styd on and nrly snatched 3rd* **12/1**
4 5 1 1/2 **Wizara (IRE)**[18] 5478 3-9-0 0 SilvestreDeSousa 8 69
(Saeed bin Suroor) *leggy: cls cpld: trckd ldng pair: shkn up and nt qckn jst over 2f out: one pce* **2/1**[1]
5 6 3 1/4 **Advisory**[37] 4805 3-9-5 0 JoeFanning 2 67
(Mark Johnston) *leggy: athletic: awkward on way to s: slowest away: hld up in last pair: shkn up and no prog 3f out: kpt on fr over 1f out* **16/1**
7 2 3/4 **Diamond Mine** 3-9-5 0 AndreaAtzeni 6 62
(Luca Cumani) *leggy: dwlt: sn in midfield: pushed along 3f out: steadily outpcd fr over 2f out* **14/1**
60 8 2 **Bold Citizen (IRE)**[12] 5678 3-9-5 0 AdamKirby 7 58
(Ed Dunlop) *lengthy: a in last pair: struggling over 3f out: n.d after* **100/1**
0 9 8 **Maygo's Joy**[24] 5281 3-9-5 0 RobertHavlin 4 42
(Jamie Poulton) *leggy: nvr bttr than midfield: wknd 3f out: t.o* **100/1**
2m 8.34s (0.24) **Going Correction** -0.125s/f (Firm) 9 Ran SP% **114.1**
Speed ratings (Par 101): **94,92,92,92,91 88,86,84,78**
Tote Swingers: 1&2 £4.70, 1&3 £3.00, 2&3 £4.00 CSF £20.54 TOTE £3.00: £1.20, £2.20, £1.40; EX 21.50 Trifecta £104.40 Pool: £4,258.44 - 30.56 winning units..
Owner The Starship Partnership **Bred** T Hirschfeld **Trained** Newmarket, Suffolk

FOCUS
The lower bend was dolled out 7yds from the 6f marker to the 2f marker in the straight, increasing distances on that course by 12yds. The top bend was dolled out by 3yds, increasing distances on that course by 6yds. The official ground description was amended to good to firm, good in places after the opener, a fair maiden which was run at an average pace. The time was fairly slow and the bare form is limited, but the winner is sure to rate higher.

6063 EBF RACING UK MAIDEN FILLIES' STKS 1m
2:55 (2:55) (Class 5) 2-Y-O **£3,234** (£962; £481; £240) **Stalls** Low

Form RPR
0 1 **Uchenna (IRE)**[20] 5394 2-9-0 0 JamieSpencer 8 80+
(David Simcock) *str: trckd ldr: chal fr 2f out: drvn into narrow ld ins fnl f: hld on wl* **9/2**[3]
42 2 hd **Tea In Transvaal (IRE)**[17] 5529 2-9-0 0 RichardHughes 5 80
(Richard Hannon) *lw: led: rdn and hrd pressed fr 2f out: narrowly hdd ins fnl f: kpt on wl but a jst hld* **5/2**[2]
3625 3 1 1/4 **Tinga (IRE)**[24] 5284 2-9-0 87 MartinHarley 1 77
(Mick Channon) *cl up: shkn up and nt qckn 2f out as ldng pair wnt for home: styd on same pce fnl f* **9/4**[1]
4 1 1/4 **Criteria (IRE)** 2-9-0 0 WilliamBuick 6 74+
(John Gosden) *tall: athletic: s.s: hld up in last trio: pushed along 2f out: sme prog into 4th over 1f out but nt on terms: reminder jst ins fnl f: styd on encouragingly after* **5/1**
5 5 3 **Arabian Comet (IRE)**[27] 5131 2-9-0 0 MickaelBarzalona 2 67
(Charlie Appleby) *unf: dwlt: sn wl in tch: rn green whn asked for effrt 2f out: wknd over 1f out* **10/1**
00 6 1 3/4 **Division Belle**[22] 5352 2-9-0 0 SteveDrowne 9 63
(William Muir) *w'like: mostly in last pair: effrt on inner whn short of room briefly over 1f out: sn wknd* **100/1**
7 1 3/4 **Honor Bound** 2-9-0 0 JimCrowley 7 59
(Ralph Beckett) *athletic: a towards rr: shkn up and no prog over 2f out: wknd over 1f out* **16/1**
00 8 hd **Nyanza (GER)**[46] 4491 2-9-0 0 FergusSweeney 4 59
(Alan King) *chsd ldrs: pushed along on outer over 2f out: wknd qckly over 1f out* **50/1**
1m 40.66s (0.76) **Going Correction** -0.125s/f (Firm) 8 Ran SP% **112.1**
Speed ratings (Par 92): **91,90,89,88,85 83,81,81**
Tote Swingers: 1&2 £2.60, 1&3 £2.60, 2&3 £2.00 CSF £15.51 TOTE £3.70: £1.30, £1.50, £1.10; EX 17.20 Trifecta £52.30 Pool: £4,168.46 - 59.70 winning units..
Owner The Black Gold Partnership **Bred** Knockaney Stud **Trained** Newmarket, Suffolk

FOCUS
Musidora winner Liber Nauticus took a division of this maiden last year. This looked a decent race on paper, but the pace was not strong. The first three were always to the fore. The winner improved and the second is rated to her mark.

6064 PETER WILLETT CONDITIONS STKS 7f
3:30 (3:30) (Class 2) 2-Y-O **£15,562** (£4,660; £2,330; £1,165; £582) **Stalls** Low

Form RPR
4221 1 **Lyn Valley**[17] 5539 2-9-2 89 JoeFanning 2 98+
(Mark Johnston) *trckd clr ldr: clsd over 2f out: shkn up to ld over 1f out: hdd briefly ins fnl f: styd on wl nr fin* **2/1**[2]
5244 2 nk **Rosso Corsa**[3] 5999 2-9-2 95 MartinHarley 6 97
(Mick Channon) *hld up in 4th: clsd over 2f out: rdn to chal over 1f out: led briefly ins fnl f: edgd lft and nt qckn nr fin* **9/2**[3]
10 3 5 **Wahaab (IRE)**[77] 3422 2-9-2 0 PaulHanagan 1 84
(Richard Hannon) *free to post: racd freely: led and sn 3 l clr: hdd & wknd over 1f out* **13/8**[1]
3 4 4 1/2 **Classified Weapon (USA)**[75] 3493 2-8-12 0 JamieSpencer 3 67
(David Simcock) *w'like: hld up in last: clsd on ldrs over 2f out: wknd qckly over 1f out* **8/1**
2151 5 18 **Al Baz**[36] 4833 2-9-4 83 RyanMoore 4 25
(James Tate) *chsd ldng pair to over 2f out: wknd qckly: t.o* **10/1**
1m 25.65s (-1.35) **Going Correction** -0.125s/f (Firm) 5 Ran SP% **109.8**
Speed ratings (Par 101): **102,101,95,90,70**
CSF £11.03 TOTE £3.30: £1.30, £2.30; EX 10.40 Trifecta £20.20 Pool: £3,129.36 - 115.78 winning units..
Owner J Barson **Bred** Highclere Stud And Floors Farming **Trained** Middleham Moor, N Yorks

FOCUS
Quite a valuable conditions event, and useful form rated around the second who ran right to his best. A nice step up from the winner.

6065 BADGER ALES NURSERY STKS (H'CAP) 6f
4:05 (4:05) (Class 2) 2-Y-O **£9,703** (£2,887; £1,443; £721) **Stalls** High

Form RPR
2344 1 **Deeds Not Words (IRE)**[20] 5399 2-8-2 **72** SilvestreDeSousa 5 80+
(Mick Channon) *led: rdn 2f out: hdd jst ins fnl f: rallied to ld last 75yds: styd on wl* **4/1**[3]
2154 2 1/2 **Expert (IRE)**[17] 5530 2-9-7 **91** RichardHughes 1 98+
(Richard Hannon) *lw: hld up in last pair: prog on outer to chse wnr over 1f out: rdn to ld jst ins fnl f: styd on but hdd and hld last 75yds* **5/2**[1]
0224 3 6 **Memory Styx**[11] 5699 2-8-8 **78** MartinHarley 6 67
(Mick Channon) *hld up in last: rdn and prog to take 3rd over 1f out: lost grnd on ldng pair after* **12/1**
0340 4 2 **Tableforten**[8] 5848 2-8-5 **75** LiamJones 2 58
(J S Moore) *swtg: pressed wnr: rdn over 2f out: lost 2nd over 1f out: wknd qckly* **14/1**
241 5 nk **Captain Midnight (IRE)**[9] 5787 2-8-11 **81** 6ex RyanMoore 4 63
(David Brown) *chsd ldrs: rdn over 2f out: wknd quite qckly over 1f out* **11/4**[2]
6465 6 1 1/2 **Crowdmania**[28] 5083 2-8-7 **77** JoeFanning 7 54
(Mark Johnston) *racd against nr side rail: pressed wnr to wl over 1f out: shkn up and fnd nil: wknd qckly fnl f* **4/1**[3]
1m 10.39s (-1.81) **Going Correction** -0.325s/f (Firm) 6 Ran SP% **109.6**
Speed ratings (Par 101): **99,98,90,87,87 85**
Tote Swingers: 1&2 £4.70, 1&3 £3.00, 2&3 £4.00 CSF £13.68 TOTE £4.80: £2.10, £1.50; EX 14.70 Trifecta £52.30 Pool: £3,321.76 - 47.58 winning units..
Owner George Materna **Bred** B Holland, S Hillen & J Cullinan **Trained** West Ilsley, Berks

FOCUS
Decent nursery form. The first two pulled a long way clear, coming close together late on. An improved effort from the winner with a fione effort in defeat from the second.

6066 ROYAL SUSSEX REGIMENT STKS (H'CAP) 2m
4:40 (4:41) (Class 2) (0-105,97) 3-Y-O+ **£12,938** (£3,850; £1,924; £962) **Stalls** Low

Form RPR
6212 1 **Aquilonius (IRE)**[23] 5302 4-8-9 **78** oh1 (t) MickaelBarzalona 7 87
(Stuart Williams) *mde all at decent pce: urged along wl over 2f out: pressed briefly jst over 1f out: styd on wl fnl f* **16/1**
3412 2 2 1/4 **Mutual Regard (IRE)**[24] 5256 4-9-11 **94** (p) LukeMorris 6 100
(Sir Mark Prescott Bt) *hld up disputing 7th: prog wl over 3f out: rdn 2f out: wandered u.p but tk 2nd over 1f out and looked a threat: wl hld fnl f* **8/1**
1104 3 nk **Arch Villain (IRE)**[24] 5288 4-9-7 **90** RyanMoore 5 96
(Amanda Perrett) *chsd ldng pair to over 3f out: lost pl u.p: kpt on again fr over 1f out to take 3rd ins fnl f* **5/1**[3]
-032 4 1/2 **Waterclock (IRE)**[24] 5288 4-9-5 **88** JamesDoyle 8 93
(Roger Charlton) *mostly chsd ldng trio: rdn 3f out: nt qckn on outer 2f out: kpt on again fnl f* **6/1**
-460 5 hd **Martin Chuzzlewit (IRE)**[13] 5655 4-9-2 **85** WilliamBuick 9 90
(David Simcock) *lw: chsd wnr: shkn up 3f out: nt qckn 2f out: lost 2nd over 1f out: one pce* **14/1**
1161 6 2 3/4 **Broxbourne (IRE)**[13] 5655 4-9-11 **94** JoeFanning 4 96
(Mark Johnston) *trckd ldrs disputing 5th: prog to chse ldng pair over 3f out: drvn and no imp over 2f out: steadily fdd over 1f out* **5/1**[3]
0262 7 2 1/4 **Mawaqeet (USA)**[13] 5655 4-9-11 **94** PaulHanagan 3 94+
(Sir Michael Stoute) *lw: hld up in last: pushed along over 3f out: limited rspnse and no great hdwy* **10/1**
5250 8 4 **Ray Ward (IRE)**[54] 4211 3-9-1 **97** JamieSpencer 2 91+
(David Simcock) *hld up disputing 7th: tried to make prog 3f out but fnd little whn asked: wknd over 1f out* **9/2**[2]
2411 9 2 3/4 **Argent Knight**[24] 5288 3-8-7 **89** (v) SteveDrowne 1 80
(William Jarvis) *trckd ldrs disputing 5th: lost pl over 3f out: sn wknd* **4/1**[1]
3m 26.95s (-2.05) **Going Correction** -0.125s/f (Firm) 9 Ran SP% **118.6**
WFA 3 from 4yo 13lb
Speed ratings (Par 109): **100,98,98,98,98 97,95,93,92**
Tote Swingers: 1&2 £15.50, 1&3 £20.10, 2&3 £7.40 CSF £140.47 CT £745.03 TOTE £24.50: £5.30, £2.00, £1.90; EX 270.80 Trifecta £1263.50 Pool: £4,722.48 - 2.80 winning units..
Owner T W Morley & Mrs J Morley **Bred** Redmondstown Stud **Trained** Newmarket, Suffolk

FOCUS
This good staying handicap looked well contested on paper, but it was dominated by the winner under a nicely judged ride. He might well match his AW form. Straightforward form in many respects.

6067 GOLF AT GOODWOOD STKS (H'CAP) 6f
5:10 (5:14) (Class 4) (0-80,80) 3-Y-0+ **£6,469** (£1,925; £962; £481) **Stalls** High

Form RPR

2-00 **1** **Slip Sliding Away (IRE)**[13] 5636 6-9-2 **75**........................ AdamKirby 5 85
(Peter Hedger) *swtg: hld up in rr: prog on wd outside over 2f out and pushed along: led jst over 1f out: edgd lft u.p but styd on wl* **20/1**

1320 **2** 1 ¼ **Tidentime (USA)**[34] 4879 4-9-7 **80**.................................... MartinHarley 2 86
(Mick Channon) *pressed ldr: led 2f out: hdd jst over 1f out: wl hld by wnr but fended off rivals to hold on for 2nd* **9/2[1]**

3214 **3** nk **Kinglami**[5] 5928 4-9-7 **80**...(p) SteveDrowne 10 85
(Brian Gubby) *trckd ldrs: pushed along over 2f out: trying to cl whn squeezed for room briefly 1f out: styd on same pce* **6/1[3]**

00-0 **4** nk **Jubilee Brig**[27] 5124 3-9-2 **77**...(v[1]) RyanMoore 6 81
(Gary Moore) *trckd ldrs on outer: others mde move bef him 2f out: n.m.r whn rdn 1f out: plld out and styd on to press for a pl nr fin* **10/1**

0233 **5** ½ **Commanche**[18] 5489 4-8-12 **76**.. RobertTart(5) 1 79
(Chris Dwyer) *racd towards centre: pressed ldrs: nrly upsides jst over 1f out: stl chalng for 2nd tl wknd last 50yds* **6/1[3]**

2105 **6** ¾ **Bravo Echo**[26] 5187 7-9-7 **80**... RobertHavlin 9 80
(Michael Attwater) *lw: mde most against nr side rail to 2f out: nt qckn over 1f out: one pce fnl f* **6/1[3]**

0-03 **7** 2 ½ **Valmina**[65] 3855 6-8-10 **74**.......................................(t) GeorgeDowning(5) 4 67
(Tony Carroll) *hld up towards rr: smooth prog on wd outside fr 1/2-way to press ldrs 2f out: nt qckn over 1f out: wknd fnl f* **20/1**

3211 **8** shd **Royal Guinevere**[36] 4830 3-9-4 **79**.................................. JimmyQuinn 11 72
(Dean Ivory) *walked to post: trckd ldrs: rdn 2f out: wknd over 1f out* **8/1**

0304 **9** ½ **Johnny Castle**[11] 5722 5-9-7 **80**... PatDobbs 8 71+
(Amanda Perrett) *dwlt: chsd ldrs towards nr side rail tl wknd over 1f out* **12/1**

4012 **10** 8 **Clear Praise (USA)**[7] 5851 6-9-3 **76**........................ RichardHughes 3 43
(Simon Dow) *stdd s: hld up in last: no prog 2f out: sn wknd: t.o* **5/1[2]**

0000 **11** nk **Time Medicean**[15] 5594 7-9-2 **75**.. LukeMorris 7 41
(Tony Carroll) *racd towards nr side rail: a in rr: wknd 2f out: t.o* **25/1**

1m 10.61s (-1.59) **Going Correction** -0.325s/f (Firm)
WFA 3 from 4yo+ 2lb **11 Ran SP% 119.0**
Speed ratings (Par 105): **97,95,94,94,93 92,89,89,88,78 77**
Tote Swingers: 1&2 £15.90, 1&3 £23.50, 2&3 £6.20 CSF £106.61 CT £633.37 TOTE £16.30: £5.00, £1.40, £2.50; EX 162.80 Trifecta £803.90 Pool: £4,285.27 - 3.99 winning units..
Owner Bernard Keay & Partners **Bred** S Holt & A C Beggan & R J Beggan **Trained** Dogmersfield, Hampshire

■ Stewards' Enquiry : Adam Kirby caution: careless riding

FOCUS
A fair handicap. The second and third set the level.

6068 GOODWOOD AVIATION & FLYING SCHOOL H'CAP 1m 3f
5:40 (5:41) (Class 5) (0-70,69) 4-Y-0+ **£3,234** (£962; £481; £240) **Stalls** High

Form RPR

-424 **1** **Mister Fizz**[23] 5312 5-8-10 **65**...................................... DanielCremin(7) 7 72
(Miss Imogen Pickard) *trckd ldr: shkn up to ld 2f out: jnd jst ins fnl f: urged along and hld on gamely* **6/1[3]**

0-51 **2** shd **Spiritual Art**[13] 5633 7-8-12 **60**.....................................(v) RichardHughes 1 67
(Luke Dace) *trckd ldng pair: stalked wnr gng strly over 1f out: brought to chal and upsides jst ins fnl f: cajoled along and couldn't go past* **5/1[2]**

0355 **3** 2 **James Pollard (IRE)**[12] 5434 8-8-6 **59**...................(t) DanielMuscutt(5) 6 63
(Bernard Llewellyn) *trckd ldng trio: rdn over 1f out: styd on same pce after: tk 3rd last stride* **20/1**

1311 **4** shd **Minority Interest**[13] 5650 4-8-9 **64**..........................(b) OisinMurphy(7) 10 67
(Brett Johnson) *sn led: drvn 3f out: hdd 2f out: one pce after and lost 3rd last stride* **7/2[1]**

000- **5** ½ **Minty Fox**[266] 8060 4-8-11 **59**... FergusSweeney 3 62
(Eve Johnson Houghton) *a abt same pl: rdn and nt qckn over 1f out: one pce after* **25/1**

06-3 **6** ½ **Swift Blade (IRE)**[36] 4832 5-9-7 **69**...................................(p) AdamKirby 8 71+
(Lady Herries) *hld up and last after 3f: swtchd to far rail and drvn over 1f out: kpt on same pce: n.d* **7/2[1]**

4326 **7** hd **Royal Etiquette (IRE)**[29] 5065 6-8-13 **61**................(vt) DougieCostello 5 63
(Lawney Hill) *hld up and last early: clsd on ldrs 2f out and stl hld together: pushed along and one pce fr over 1f out: nvr chal* **16/1**

4233 **8** ¾ **Batgirl**[9] 5802 6-9-5 **67**..(p) BrettDoyle 9 67
(Martin Smith) *hld up in last trio: rdn and tried to make prog on outer 2f out: one pce and no hdwy jst over 1f out* **5/1[2]**

2150 **9** 9 **Shirataki (IRE)**[26] 5168 5-9-6 **68**.................................. WilliamCarson 4 54
(Peter Hiatt) *dwlt: sn in midfield: shkn up 2f out: wknd qckly jst over 1f out* **14/1**

660/ **10** 5 **Penchesco (IRE)**[681] 6402 8-8-7 **55** oh1............................ JoeFanning 2 33
(Amanda Perrett) *hld up in rr: shkn up and no prog 2f out: wl btn whn lost action bdly last 100yds* **14/1**

2m 27.12s (0.62) **Going Correction** -0.125s/f (Firm) **10 Ran SP% 119.9**
Speed ratings (Par 103): **92,91,90,90,90 89,89,88,82,78**
Tote Swingers: 1&2 £5.50, 1&3 £18.00, 2&3 £20.60 CSF £37.21 CT £574.93 TOTE £6.80: £2.10, £2.20, £5.00; EX 51.60 Trifecta £1465.40 Pool: £2,543.17 - 1.30 winning units..
Owner Mrs Margaret J Wilson **Bred** Mrs Margaret J Wilson **Trained** Ullingswick, Herefordshire
■ Imogen Pickard's first winner.

FOCUS
A modest handicap, but not without interest. The first four home comprised the leading quartet all the way. Pretty straightforward form.

T/Plt: £98.60 to a £1 stake. Pool: £88,897.00 - 657.55 winning units T/Qpdt: £50.70 to a £1 stake. Pool: £4,494.00 - 65.50 winning units JN

5609 LEICESTER (R-H)
Tuesday, September 3

OFFICIAL GOING: Good to firm (good in places)
Wind: Light; behind Weather: Cloudy with sunny spells

6069 NELSON RESTAURANT MAIDEN AUCTION STKS 7f 9y
2:00 (2:01) (Class 5) 2-Y-O **£2,587** (£770; £384; £192) **Stalls** Centre

Form RPR

60 **1** **Peacemaker (IRE)**[20] 5394 2-8-6 0.. JohnFahy 8 69+
(Eve Johnson Houghton) *a.p: racd alone on stands' side rail to 1/2-way: shkn up to ld over 1f out: rdn out* **9/2[2]**

2 **2** 1 ¾ **Mocacha (IRE)**[15] 5584 2-9-1 0... DaneO'Neill 7 73
(William Haggas) *hld up: hdwy 1/2-way: rdn over 2f out: styd on same pce ins fnl f* **1/2[1]**

0 **3** hd **Miss Lucy Jane**[18] 5482 2-8-7 0.................................... TonyHamilton 1 64
(Richard Fahey) *sn outpcd: r.o ins fnl f: nrst fin* **12/1**

53 **4** 1 ½ **The Doyle Machine (IRE)**[27] 5140 2-8-11 0.............. AdamBeschizza 3 65
(Noel Quinlan) *led: rdn and hdd over 1f out: no ex ins fnl f* **7/1[3]**

00 **5** nk **Ultimate Warrior (IRE)**[17] 5539 2-9-0 0............................ SeanLevey 2 67+
(Richard Hannon) *prom: pushed along 1/2-way: sn outpcd: styd on fnl f* **33/1**

00 **6** hd **Rosina Jay (IRE)**[29] 5061 2-8-4 0.................................... RyanTate(5) 6 61
(Clive Cox) *chsd ldrs: pushed along 1/2-way: styd on same pce fnl f* **33/1**

7 2 **Red Cossack (CAN)** 2-8-13 0.. JimmyFortune 4 62+
(Paul Webber) *s.i.s: plld hrd and sn trcking ldrs: rdn and edgd rt over 1f out: wknd and eased wl ins fnl f* **14/1**

45 **8** 13 **Shrewd Bob (IRE)**[17] 5539 2-8-13 0............................... CathyGannon 5 26
(Robert Eddery) *hld up: hdwy 1/2-way: rdn over 2f out: wknd over 1f out* **20/1**

1m 26.34s (0.14) **Going Correction** -0.275s/f (Firm) **8 Ran SP% 122.4**
Speed ratings (Par 95): **88,86,85,84,83 83,81,66**
Tote Swingers: 1&2 £1.50, 1&3 £6.40, 2&3 £2.80 CSF £7.54 TOTE £3.90: £1.10, £1.02, £3.00; EX 7.80 Trifecta £49.30 Pool: £4,020.27 - 61.10 winning units..
Owner R L Maynard & B McNamee **Bred** Watership Down Stud **Trained** Blewbury, Oxon

FOCUS
A maiden lacking strength in depth. A straightforward approach to the form has been taken.

6070 CLUBROOM FILLIES' NURSERY H'CAP 5f 218y
2:30 (2:31) (Class 4) (0-85,82) 2-Y-O **£3,881** (£1,155; £577; £288) **Stalls** Centre

Form RPR

5210 **1** **Musicora**[31] 5005 2-9-7 **82**.. SeanLevey 4 87
(Richard Hannon) *racd keenly: mde virtually all: shkn up over 1f out: rdn out* **3/1[1]**

3340 **2** 1 ½ **State Anthem**[17] 5536 2-8-8 **72**.................................... CharlesBishop(3) 5 73
(Mick Channon) *racd keenly: sn trcking wnr: rdn over 1f out: styd on* **16/1**

3406 **3** nk **Ixelles Diamond (IRE)**[18] 5468 2-8-7 **68**.......................... TonyHamilton 2 68
(Richard Fahey) *hld up: hdwy over 1f out: sn rdn: styd on* **10/1**

410 **4** 2 ½ **Mops Angel**[97] 2767 2-8-12 **73**.. AndrewMullen 6 65
(Michael Appleby) *prom: rdn over 1f out: styd on same pce ins fnl f* **11/1**

3240 **5** ½ **Princess Rose**[17] 5508 2-8-11 **72**...................................... DaneO'Neill 8 63
(William Haggas) *hld up: pushed along over 2f out: hdwy over 1f out: styd on same pce ins fnl f* **10/3[2]**

435 **6** 3 **Lady Tiana**[19] 5435 2-8-8 **69**.. CathyGannon 1 51
(Lucy Wadham) *hld up: racd keenly: effrt and nt clr run 2f out: sn rdn: n.d* **9/2[3]**

3310 **7** 3 ½ **Sandsman's Girl (IRE)**[17] 5536 2-9-3 **78**..................... JamesSullivan 3 49
(James Given) *chsd ldrs: rdn over 2f out: wknd fnl f* **12/1**

61 **8** 1 ¼ **Lady Stella**[14] 5603 2-9-1 **76**... TomQueally 7 43
(Rae Guest) *chsd ldrs: rdn over 2f out: wknd over 1f out* **11/2**

1m 11.96s (-1.04) **Going Correction** -0.275s/f (Firm) **8 Ran SP% 112.6**
Speed ratings (Par 94): **95,93,92,89,88 84,79,78**
Tote Swingers: 1&2 £13.00, 1&3 £5.50, 2&3 £11.70 CSF £48.82 CT £421.78 TOTE £3.70: £1.30, £5.70, £2.00; EX 75.70 Trifecta £375.60 Pool: £2,903.46 - 5.79 winning units..
Owner The Three Points Partnership **Bred** Sir Eric Parker **Trained** East Everleigh, Wilts

FOCUS
A fair fillies' nursery in which it paid to race prominently. Straightforward form in behind the winner.

6071 ARTHUR GADSBY MEMORIAL H'CAP 1m 3f 183y
3:05 (3:05) (Class 5) (0-75,73) 3-Y-0+ **£2,587** (£770; £384; £192) **Stalls** Low

Form RPR

-410 **1** **Quest For More (IRE)**[27] 5134 3-9-2 **72**......................... GeorgeBaker 1 86+
(Roger Charlton) *hld up in tch: lost pl 7f out: hdwy u.p and hung rt fr over 1f out: styd on to ld nr fin* **9/4[1]**

4613 **2** nk **Lisa's Legacy**[9] 5789 3-9-2 **72**................................. RichardKingscote 2 85
(Daniel Kubler) *a.p: trckd ldr over 6f out tl led wl over 2f out: rdn over 1f out: hdd nr fin* **15/2[3]**

0-04 **3** 6 **Grey Blue (IRE)**[15] 5582 3-8-11 **67**................................ KierenFallon 6 70
(Mark Johnston) *hld up: hdwy over 3f out: chsd ldr 2f out: sn rdn and hung rt: no ex ins fnl f* **11/1**

3260 **4** 1 **Strike Force**[9] 5802 9-8-10 **62**.......................................(t) TobyAtkinson(5) 4 63
(Alison Hutchinson) *prom: lost pl over 6f out: rdn over 3f out: styd on same pce fr over 1f out* **33/1**

-363 **5** ½ **Gamble**[32] 4961 3-9-3 **73**.. TomQueally 9 74
(Michael Bell) *trckd ldrs: led 8f out: hdd wl over 2f out: rdn over 1f out: wknd ins fnl f* **5/2[2]**

5565 **6** nk **Royal Peculiar**[11] 5712 5-9-11 **72**..............................(b[1]) AndrewMullen 7 72
(Michael Appleby) *s.i.s: hld up: hdwy 1/2-way: rdn over 2f out: hung rt and wknd fnl f* **8/1**

0025 **7** ½ **Grayswood**[22] 5343 3-8-6 **62**.. HarryBentley 5 61
(William Muir) *hld up: hdwy over 5f out: rdn over 2f out: wknd over 1f out* **10/1**

544 **8** 8 **Duke Of Grazeon (IRE)**[28] 5110 3-8-10 **66**.............(b) RoystonFfrench 8 53
(Mrs Ilka Gansera-Leveque) *trckd ldr: led over 8f out: sn hdd: remained handy: pushed along over 3f out: wknd wl over 1f out* **28/1**

3-25 **9** 8 **Alborz (IRE)**[202] 642 4-9-10 **71**.................................... CathyGannon 3 45
(Tim Vaughan) *led: hdd over 8f out: remained handy tl rdn and wknd wl over 2f out* **22/1**

2m 31.53s (-2.37) **Going Correction** -0.275s/f (Firm)
WFA 3 from 4yo+ 9lb **9 Ran SP% 110.4**
Speed ratings (Par 103): **96,95,91,91,90 90,90,84,79**
Tote Swingers: 1&2 £4.00, 1&3 £5.90, 2&3 £7.70 CSF £17.99 CT £140.60 TOTE £3.90: £2.00, £1.80, £2.90; EX 20.20 Trifecta £111.70 Pool: £3,475.96 - 23.33 winning units..
Owner H R H Sultan Ahmad Shah **Bred** Epona Bloodstock Ltd **Trained** Beckhampton, Wilts

The Form Book Flat, Raceform Ltd, Compton, RG20 6NL.

FOCUS
A fair handicap. They went steady early and the pace only quickened once in the home straight. The first two were clear and showed useful form.

6072 WEATHERBYS BANK FOREIGN EXCHANGE H'CAP 7f 9y
3:40 (3:40) (Class 4) (0-80,80) 3-Y-0+ £4,690 (£1,395; £697; £348) Stalls Centre

Form RPR
P543 1 **Breccbennach**[8] 5815 3-8-10 70 (tp) DaneO'Neill 2 77
(Seamus Durack) *trckd ldrs: rdn to ld 1f out: edgd rt: styd on* 6/1[2]
4-36 2 ½ **Diamond Belle**[18] 5493 4-9-8 78 TomQueally 5 86
(Noel Quinlan) *w ldrs tl led over 4f out: rdn and hdd 1f out: edgd rt styd on* 12/1
4213 3 1 ¼ **Liberty Jack (IRE)**[12] 5676 3-9-3 77 (p) GeorgeBaker 7 79
(Roger Charlton) *hld up: racd keenly: hdwy over 1f out: rdn and hung rt ins fnl f: nt run on* 2/1[1]
0146 4 1 **Ortac Rock (IRE)**[30] 5026 4-9-6 76 (t) TonyHamilton 8 78
(Richard Fahey) *sn pushed along towards rr: r.o u.p ins fnl f: nt rch ldrs* 13/2[3]
0100 5 ½ **Available (IRE)**[40] 4671 4-9-8 78 (tp) GrahamGibbons 4 78
(John Mackie) *a.p: rdn over 1f out: styd on same pce ins fnl f* 33/1
0240 6 1 ¼ **Ceelo**[37] 4797 3-8-12 72 JimmyFortune 1 67
(Sylvester Kirk) *hld up: hdwy u.p over 1f out: no ex ins fnl f* 9/1
1025 7 nk **Illustrious Prince (IRE)**[11] 5711 6-9-2 75 NeilFarley(3) 3 71
(Declan Carroll) *chsd ldrs: rdn over 2f out: ev ch over 1f out: no ex ins fnl f* 10/1
6243 8 1 ¾ **Dance With Dragons (IRE)**[17] 5541 3-9-6 80 (p) KirstyMilczarek 6 69
(William Stone) *trckd ldrs: rdn over 2f out: wknd fnl f* 15/2
0062 9 3 **Bogsnog (IRE)**[14] 5611 3-8-8 73 JacobButterfield(5) 10 54
(Kristin Stubbs) *led: hdd over 4f out: sn pushed along: rdn and edgd lft over 1f out: wknd fnl f* 12/1
1251 10 10 **Jonnie Skull (IRE)**[9] 5799 7-9-2 77 6ex (vt) TobyAtkinson(5) 9 33
(Phil McEntee) *w ldr tl pushed along over 4f out: wknd over 2f out* 20/1

1m 24.6s (-1.60) **Going Correction** -0.275s/f (Firm)
WFA 3 from 4yo+ 4lb 10 Ran SP% 114.9
Speed ratings (Par 105): **98,97,96,94,94 92,92,90,87,75**
Tote Swingers: 1&2 £14.70, 1&3 £3.40, 2&3 £7.50 CSF £74.24 CT £197.43 TOTE £7.40: £2.10, £3.90, £1.60; EX 112.10 Trifecta £574.10 Pool: £3,490.14 - 4.55 winning units..
Owner Mrs Anne Cowley **Bred** Bloomsbury Stud **Trained** Baydon, Wilts

FOCUS
A fair handicap run at a solid pace. The winner is rated back to his 2yo best.

6073 CROPSTON NURSERY H'CAP 5f 2y
4:15 (4:17) (Class 6) (0-65,63) 2-Y-0 £2,587 (£770; £384; £192) Stalls Centre

Form RPR
3220 1 **Anytimeatall (IRE)**[15] 5595 2-9-4 60 KierenFallon 5 64
(Alan Bailey) *mde all: rdn over 1f out: edgd rt ins fnl f: styd on* 9/2[1]
0300 2 ½ **Tinsill**[29] 5066 2-8-6 51 (v) DeclanCannon(3) 13 53
(Nigel Tinkler) *chsd ldrs: rdn and ev ch ins fnl f: kpt on* 40/1
065 3 ½ **Romantic Bliss (IRE)**[25] 5225 2-7-13 46 (b[1]) JoeyHaynes(5) 12 46
(K R Burke) *mid-div: pushed along and hdwy 1/2-way: rdn and edgd rt fr over 1f out: r.o* 5/1[2]
F245 4 nk **Cheeky Peta'S**[17] 5543 2-9-6 62 JamesSullivan 3 61
(James Given) *chsd ldrs: rdn over 1f out: styd on* 10/1
0004 5 ½ **Tricksome (IRE)**[11] 5710 2-8-6 55 RowanScott(7) 2 52
(Ann Duffield) *mid-div: hdwy 1/2-way: rdn over 1f out: styd on* 16/1
4223 6 1 **Anfield**[13] 5648 2-8-11 53 PaoloSirigu 4 47
(Mick Quinn) *w wnr: rdn and ev ch over 1f out: styd on same pce ins fnl f* 11/1
5046 7 3 ¾ **Shelley's Choice (IRE)**[15] 5595 2-9-5 61 RichardKingscote 8 41
(Tom Dascombe) *sn pushed along in rr: rdn over 1f out: r.o ins fnl f: nvr nrr* 7/1[3]
3533 8 1 ¼ **Goadby**[25] 5215 2-9-6 62 GrahamGibbons 1 38
(John Holt) *chsd ldrs: rdn 1/2-way: wknd over 1f out* 8/1
0006 9 2 ½ **Monsieur Blanc (IRE)**[8] 5814 2-9-1 57 CathyGannon 6 24
(Denis Coakley) *s.i.s: outpcd* 20/1
3350 10 ½ **Yellow Lady (IRE)**[29] 5066 2-8-13 55 HarryBentley 11 20
(Olly Stevens) *hld up: rdn and wknd over 1f out* 5/1[2]
5065 11 1 **Zac's Princess**[8] 5814 2-8-0 45 (t) SimonPearce(3) 9 6
(Milton Bradley) *prom: lost pl 1/2-way: sn bhd* 28/1
3000 12 2 ¾ **Abisko (IRE)**[20] 5380 2-9-4 60 SeanLevey 7 11+
(Brian Ellison) *swvd lft s: rdn 1/2-way: a in rr* 12/1

1m 0.77s (0.77) **Going Correction** -0.275s/f (Firm) 12 Ran SP% 116.8
Speed ratings (Par 93): **82,81,80,79,79 77,71,69,65,64 63,58**
Tote Swingers: 1&2 £38.30, 1&3 £5.60, 2&3 £34.10 CSF £191.10 CT £950.70 TOTE £4.50: £1.60, £13.20, £2.40; EX 220.60 Trifecta £1566.10 Pool: £3,211.08 - 1.53 winning units..
Owner Yo Delice Partnership **Bred** Patrick A Cassidy **Trained** Newmarket, Suffolk

FOCUS
A low-grade nursery run at a good pace. Not a race t odewll on.

6074 INTERACTIVE H'CAP 7f 9y
4:50 (4:52) (Class 6) (0-60,60) 3-Y-0 £1,940 (£577; £288; £144) Stalls Centre

Form RPR
505 1 **Pearl Queen (USA)**[15] 5588 3-9-7 60 HarryBentley 3 75+
(Chris Wall) *racd centre: in rr: hdwy 1/2-way: led overall over 2f out: rdn and hung lft ins fnl f: styd on: 1st of 8 in gp* 7/1
6045 2 2 ½ **Two No Bids (IRE)**[21] 5373 3-9-0 53 (be) CathyGannon 10 59
(Phil McEntee) *overall ldr stands' side tl rdn and hdd over 2f out: styd on same pce fnl f: 1st of 3 in gp* 12/1
330 3 3 ½ **Copper Trade**[24] 5277 3-9-7 60 TomQueally 11 57
(Eve Johnson Houghton) *racd stands' side: chsd ldr: rdn and ev ch that side over 1f out: sn hung rt: no ex ins fnl f: 2nd of 3 in gp* 11/2[3]
4-34 4 nk **Tammuz (IRE)**[28] 5096 3-9-5 58 KierenFallon 5 54
(Tony Carroll) *racd centre: hld up: hdwy over 1f out: styd on: nt trble ldrs: 2nd of 8 in gp* 7/1
6-50 5 2 ¼ **Fantasy Invader (IRE)**[20] 5393 3-9-0 53 SeanLevey 1 43
(John Quinn) *racd centre: chsd ldrs: rdn 1/2-way: wknd fnl f: 3rd of 8 in gp* 14/1
0440 6 1 ¼ **One In A Thousand (IRE)**[7] 5869 3-8-12 51 (p) SaleemGolam 4 38
(Chris Dwyer) *racd centre: chsd ldr: led that gp 1/2-way tl hdd over 2f out: sn rdn: wknd over 1f out: 4th of 8 in gp* 66/1
0120 7 ½ **Absolute Diamond**[18] 5471 3-9-3 59 RaulDaSilva(3) 2 44
(John Quinn) *racd centre: prom: rdn 1/2-way: wknd wl over 1f out: 5th of 8 in gp* 9/2[2]
00-3 8 nse **Ri Na Si**[17] 5517 3-9-7 60 AndrewMullen 6 45
(Michael Appleby) *racd centre: prom: rdn over 2f out: wknd wl over 1f out: 6th of 8 in gp* 8/1
4040 9 4 ½ **Poetic Belle**[7] 5869 3-8-13 52 (t) KirstyMilczarek 7 25
(Shaun Harris) *racd centre: prom: rdn over 2f out: sn wknd: 7th of 8 in gp* 20/1
0365 10 10 **Grey Gazelle**[54] 4193 3-8-13 55 CharlesBishop(3) 9 1
(Mick Channon) *racd stands' side: hld up: rdn and wknd wl over 1f out: eased: last of 3 in gp* 16/1
000 11 3 ¼ **Rocky Couloir**[90] 2989 3-8-13 52 GrahamGibbons 8
(Michael Easterby) *racd centre: led to 1/2-way: wknd over 2f out: eased fnl f: last of 8 in gp* 4/1[1]

1m 25.07s (-1.13) **Going Correction** -0.275s/f (Firm) 11 Ran SP% 116.2
Speed ratings (Par 99): **95,92,88,87,85 83,83,83,78,66 62**
Tote Swingers: 1&2 £12.10, 1&3 £9.30, 2&3 £7.30 CSF £86.81 CT £505.74 TOTE £8.30: £4.10, £3.90, £1.90; EX 97.90 Trifecta £591.60 Pool: £2,430.43 - 3.08 winning units..
Owner Pearl Bloodstock Ltd **Bred** Adrian Regan, Kildare Stud & Darley **Trained** Newmarket, Suffolk

FOCUS
A modest but competitive 3yo handicap. The field split into two groups. The winner deserves plenty of credit and can rate higher.

6075 SIX HILLS H'CAP 5f 218y
5:20 (5:20) (Class 5) (0-70,70) 3-Y-0+ £2,587 (£770; £384; £192) Stalls Centre

Form RPR
2515 1 **The Dark Wizard (IRE)**[20] 5389 3-9-5 70 (b[1]) GeorgeBaker 3 80
(Roger Charlton) *a.p: chsd ldr over 2f out: led over 1f out: rdn out* 4/1[2]
1333 2 1 ¾ **Shaolin (IRE)**[17] 5515 3-9-4 69 (t) DaneO'Neill 4 73
(Seamus Durack) *hld up: hdwy 2f out: rdn over 1f out: r.o: nt rch wnr* 13/8[1]
561 3 hd **Clock Opera (IRE)**[23] 5300 3-8-10 61 KirstyMilczarek 5 64
(William Stone) *led: rdn and hdd over 1f out: styd on same pce ins fnl f* 8/1
0005 4 5 **Grace Hull**[49] 4378 3-8-8 59 AndrewMullen 2 46
(Garry Moss) *chsd ldr tl rdn over 2f out: no ex fnl f* 40/1
400 5 4 ½ **Black Annis Bower**[17] 5537 5-9-2 65 GrahamGibbons 7 38
(Michael Easterby) *prom: rdn over 2f out: wknd over 1f out* 8/1
3000 6 ¾ **Meshardal (GER)**[15] 5580 3-8-9 60 JamesSullivan 6 31
(Ruth Carr) *hld up: pushed along 1/2-way: nvr on terms* 25/1
-030 7 3 ½ **Portrush Storm**[59] 4064 8-8-2 56 oh1 JoeyHaynes(5) 9 15
(Ray Peacock) *chsd ldrs: rdn over 2f out: wknd wl over 1f out* 33/1
4610 8 2 ¼ **Dancing Maite**[17] 5515 8-8-9 61 (b) MarkCoumbe(3) 11 13
(Roy Bowring) *prom: rdn over 2f out: wknd wl over 1f out* 15/2[3]
21 9 4 **Pastureyes**[25] 5220 3-8-9 65 TimClark(5) 8 4
(Scott Dixon) *prom: rdn over 2f out: edgd rt and wknd wl over 1f out* 14/1
3101 10 6 **Artful Lady (IRE)**[14] 5602 4-9-0 63 TomQueally 1
(George Margarson) *sn outpcd* 12/1

1m 10.86s (-2.14) **Going Correction** -0.275s/f (Firm)
WFA 3 from 4yo+ 2lb 10 Ran SP% 115.7
Speed ratings (Par 103): **103,100,100,93,87 86,82,79,73,65**
Tote Swingers: 1&2 £4.40, 1&3 £8.20, 2&3 £2.70 CSF £10.57 CT £48.62 TOTE £4.40: £2.20, £1.10, £2.40; EX 16.30 Trifecta £71.90 Pool: £1,757.93 - 18.32 winning units..
Owner P Inglett & D Carter **Bred** Rossenarra Bloodstock Limited **Trained** Beckhampton, Wilts

FOCUS
A modest handicap dominated by runners on the far side. The form is taken at face value.
T/Jkpt: Part won. £17,750.00 to a £1 stake. Pool: £25,000 - 0.50 winning tickets. T/Plt: £50.80 to a £1 stake. Pool: £71,546.00 - 1,027.83 winning units T/Qpdt: £19.80 to a £1 stake. Pool: £5,315.00 - 198.50 winning units CR

5929 LINGFIELD (L-H)
Tuesday, September 3

OFFICIAL GOING: Turf course - good to firm (firm in places; 8.4); all weather - standard
Wind: nil Weather: dry, light cloud

6076 LINGFIELD PARK SUPPORTS YOUNG EPILEPSY NURSERY H'CAP 7f
4:45 (4:45) (Class 5) (0-75,74) 2-Y-0 £2,587 (£770; £384; £192) Stalls High

Form RPR
1123 1 **Finn Class (IRE)**[11] 5717 2-9-3 73 ThomasBrown(3) 3 79
(Michael Bell) *in tch in midfield: rdn and hdwy to ld jst over 1f out: asserting and edgd rt 1f out: r.o wl: pushed out* 6/4[1]
031 2 2 ¼ **Pyjama Day**[15] 5593 2-9-6 73 (b) MartinDwyer 8 73
(Hugo Palmer) *w ldr: rdn 2f out: led over 1f out: sn hdd: outpcd by wnr and kpt on same pce ins fnl f* 8/1
2303 3 1 **Royal Connection**[25] 5242 2-8-13 69 WilliamTwiston-Davies(3) 5 66
(Richard Hannon) *led: rdn 2f out: hdd over 1f out: struggling to qckn whn swtchd lft 1f out: plugged on same pce after* 5/1[3]
11 4 1 ¾ **Cape Factor (IRE)**[13] 5634 2-9-1 68 ChrisCatlin 2 61
(Rae Guest) *in tch in midfield: rdn and effrt 2f out: no imp and btn ent fnl f: plugged on* 5/2[2]
005 5 5 **Queenie's Home**[20] 5394 2-9-7 74 FrederikTylicki 6 53
(James Given) *chsd ldrs: rdn and unable qck 2f out: drvn and btn over 1f out: wknd fnl f* 7/1
2444 6 1 ¼ **Senorita Guest (IRE)**[13] 5634 2-8-12 65 SamHitchcott 7 41
(Mick Channon) *taken down early: squeezed for room and sltly hmpd leaving stalls: sn rcvrd and in tch in midfield: lost pl and rdn over 2f out: wknd over 1f out* 7/1
0000 7 ½ **Brockholes Flyer (IRE)**[14] 5610 2-7-9 53 oh4 NoelGarbutt(5) 1 27
(Brendan Powell) *stdd and swtchd rt after s: hld up in tch in rr: swtchd lft and rdn over 2f out: no hdwy: wknd over 1f out* 50/1

1m 22.63s (-0.67) **Going Correction** -0.125s/f (Firm) 7 Ran SP% 121.9
Speed ratings (Par 95): **98,95,94,92,86 85,84**
Tote Swingers: 1&2 £4.80, 1&3 £3.00, 2&3 £5.20 CSF £16.22 CT £52.67 TOTE £2.00: £1.50, £3.10; EX 22.50 Trifecta £98.20 Pool: £1,490.32 - 11.38 winning units..
Owner Saif Ali **Bred** Rabbah Bloodstock Limited **Trained** Newmarket, Suffolk

FOCUS
Stands' side rail of straight course moved in 3m. They went a fair pace in this modest nursery and predictably the stands' rail was the place to be late on.

6077 TANDRIDGE H'CAP 5f
5:15 (5:15) (Class 5) (0-75,74) 3-Y-0+ £2,587 (£770; £384; £192) Stalls High

Form RPR
0011 1 **Royal Bajan (USA)**[14] 5608 5-9-7 74 (p) FrederikTylicki 8 81
(James Given) *taken down early: chsd clr ldr: rdn over 1f out: grad clsd u.p ins fnl f: r.o to ld last stride* 6/4[1]
6131 2 shd **Pucon**[17] 5522 4-9-2 69 LiamKeniry 7 76
(Roger Teal) *broke fast: led and sn clr: rdn jst over 1f out: drvn and kpt on ins fnl f: hdd last stride* 5/1[3]

1206 **3** ¾ **We Have A Dream**[2] 6018 8-8-12 **70**........................(tp) DannyBrock(5) 3 74
(Violet M Jordan) *racd off the pce in midfield: rdn and hdwy jst over 1f out: styd on wl ins fnl f: nt rch ldrs* **14/1**

0-44 **4** 1½ **Somoud (IRE)**[15] 5585 3-9-2 **70**........................ AndreaAtzeni 2 69
(J R Jenkins) *dwlt: sn rcvrd to chse clr ldng pair: rdn and unable qck over 1f out: one pce fnl f* **6/1**

31-5 **5** 1¼ **Million Faces**[14] 5620 4-9-5 **72**........................ ChrisCatlin 5 66
(Rae Guest) *hld up off the pce in last pair: pushed along 1/2-way: rdn and sme hdwy over 1f out: no ex jst ins fnl f: wknd fnl 100yds* **8/1**

2113 **6** 2½ **Excellent Aim**[14] 5620 6-8-11 **67**........................ RyanPowell(3) 1 52
(George Margarson) *racd furthest fr stands' rail: a in rr: rdn and no hdwy wl over 1f out: bhd ins fnl f* **11/4**[2]

57.25s (-0.95) **Going Correction** -0.125s/f (Firm)
WFA 3 from 4yo+ 1lb **6** Ran SP% **115.4**
Speed ratings (Par 103): **102,101,100,98,96 92**
Tote Swingers: 1&2 £2.30, 1&3 £6.20, 2&3 £8.30 CSF £9.93 CT £74.80 TOTE £3.10: £1.30, £2.70; EX 12.60 Trifecta £81.20 Pool: £824.31 - 7.61 winning units..
Owner The Cool Silk Partnership **Bred** West Wind Farm **Trained** Willoughton, Lincs

FOCUS
This was competitive and there was no hanging about.

6078 LINGFIELD PARK OWNERS GROUP H'CAP 6f
5:50 (5:50) (Class 3) (0-95,94) 3-Y-0+ **£7,762** (£2,310; £1,154; £577) **Stalls** High

Form RPR

3040 **1** **Zero Money (IRE)**[13] 5651 7-9-5 **92**........................(b) MartinDwyer 6 103
(Hugo Palmer) *rdn along leaving stalls: chsd ldr: swtchd lft over 3f out: rdn to ld jst over 1f out: clr and hung lft ins fnl f: r.o wl: rdn out* **5/1**

2413 **2** 2¾ **Clear Spring (IRE)**[11] 5696 5-9-4 **94**........... WilliamTwiston-Davies(3) 3 96
(John Spearing) *s.i.s: bhd and urged along: swtchd lft and effrt u.p over 2f out: chsd ldrs over 1f out: styd on wl to go 2nd cl home: no threat to wnr* **3/1**[2]

2612 **3** nk **La Fortunata**[8] 5821 6-9-2 **92**........................ RyanPowell(3) 4 93
(Mike Murphy) *led and crossed to r against stands' rail: rdn and hdd jst over 1f out: no ex and one pce fnl f: lost 2nd cl home* **4/1**[3]

4004 **4** 1¾ **Fair Value (IRE)**[8] 5821 5-9-2 **89**........................ SebSanders 2 85
(Simon Dow) *awkward leaving stalls: in tch in midfield: chsd ldng pair 2f out: effrt u.p over 1f out: no ex jst ins fnl f: wknd towards fin* **8/1**

11 **5** 2 **Spin Artist (USA)**[11] 5705 3-8-12 **87**........................ NeilCallan 1 76
(Mark Johnston) *chsd ldrs and moving rt after s: rdn and no rspnse 2f out: 5th and wl btn 1f out* **11/4**[1]

0000 **6** shd **Tioman Legend**[35] 4860 4-8-12 **85**........................(p) MartinLane 7 74
(Roger Charlton) *hld up in last pair: swtchd lft and effrt over 2f out: no imp over 1f out: nvr trbld ldrs* **10/1**

0600 **7** ½ **Piscean (USA)**[17] 5533 8-8-12 **85**........................ FrederikTylicki 5 72
(Tom Keddy) *in tch in midfield: rdn 1/2-way: outpcd u.p over 1f out: n.d after* **16/1**

1m 9.24s (-1.96) **Going Correction** -0.125s/f (Firm)
WFA 3 from 4yo+ 2lb **7** Ran SP% **114.4**
Speed ratings (Par 107): **108,104,103,101,98 98,98**
Tote Swingers: 1&2 £3.80, 1&3 £4.10, 2&3 £2.70 CSF £20.39 CT £65.17 TOTE £4.80: £4.10, £1.40; EX 22.20 Trifecta £97.90 Pool: £1,749.27 - 6.29 winning units..
Owner Kremlin Cottage III **Bred** Carrigbeg Stud **Trained** Newmarket, Suffolk

FOCUS
A fair sprint handicap.

6079 BREATHE SPA AT LINGFIELD MARRIOTT MAIDEN AUCTION STKS 1m (P)
6:20 (6:26) (Class 5) 2-Y-0 **£2,587** (£770; £384; £192) **Stalls** High

Form RPR

0 **1** **Elysian Prince**[9] 5790 2-9-1 0........................ DavidProbert 8 75+
(Paul Cole) *chsd ldr tl rdn to ld 2f out: clr over 1f out: r.o strly: easily* **7/4**[1]

0 **2** 4½ **Black Label**[19] 5442 2-9-1 0........................ JohnFahy 4 65
(Harry Dunlop) *hld up in last quartet: hdwy into 6th but stl plenty to do 2f out: swtchd rt over 1f out and styd on wl fnl f: wnt 2nd fnl 75yds: no ch w wnr* **8/1**

3 1¾ **Duly Acclaimed (IRE)** 2-8-4 0........................ LiamJones 3 50
(J S Moore) *rn green: in tch in midfield: 5th and outpcd jst over 2f out: rallied and styd on wl ins fnl f: snatched 3rd last stride: no ch w wnr* **8/1**

00 **4** shd **Diffident Beats**[6] 5891 2-8-11 0........................ SamHitchcott 2 57
(Mick Channon) *chsd ldrs: effrt in 3rd 2f out: drvn and chsd clr wnr over 1f out: no imp and lost 2 pls fnl 75yds* **8/1**

5 **5** 2 **Solent Lad (USA)**[27] 5151 2-8-11 0........................ AndreaAtzeni 1 52
(Robert Eddery) *unruly on way to s: chsd ldrs: rdn and unable qck 2f out: 3rd and btn 1f out: wknd ins fnl f* **9/2**[2]

4 **6** 3¼ **Winter Picnic (IRE)**[14] 5603 2-8-8 0........................ MartinLane 6 42
(Tobias B P Coles) *led: rdn and hdd 2f out: sn drvn and outpcd by wnr: wknd over 1f out: fdd fnl f* **7/1**[3]

0 **7** 1¾ **Charleys Angel**[41] 4631 2-8-1 0........................ JemmaMarshall(3) 5 34
(Pat Phelan) *hld up in last quartet: outpcd and edging lft over 2f out: wl btn over 1f out* **20/1**

0 **8** 8 **Lucky Dottie**[13] 5635 2-8-4 0........................ FrankieMcDonald 12 15
(Pat Phelan) *rrd as stalls opened and slowly away: rn green in rr: reminder sn after s: lost tch over 2f out: wl bhd and hung rt ins fnl f* **33/1**

0 **9** hd **Craftybird**[20] 5394 2-8-8 0........................ ChrisCatlin 7 19
(Brett Johnson) *chsd ldrs: rdn 3f out: sn struggling and losing pl whn wd bnd 2f out: sn fdd* **33/1**

00 **10** 3¼ **No Second Thoughts (IRE)**[19] 5443 2-8-10 0................ LiamKeniry 9
(Michael Blanshard) *rn green: in tch in midfield: rdn and lost pl wl over 2f out: wl bhd over 1f out* **33/1**

11 1¾ **Brave Mariner** 2-8-2 0........................ RyanWhile(7) 10
(Bill Turner) *s.i.s: a in last pair and sn rdn along: lost tch over 2f out: t.o* **20/1**

P **Ican'Tknow** 2-8-8 0........................ HectorCrouch(7) 11
(Gary Moore) *rn green: in tch in midfield on outer: rdn and wknd over 2f out: wl btn whn stmbld and lost action over 1f out: p.u and dismntd 1f out: fatally injured* **10/1**

1m 39.99s (1.79) **Going Correction** -0.075s/f (Stan) **12** Ran SP% **127.8**
Speed ratings (Par 95): **88,83,81,81,79 76,74,66,66,63 61,**
Tote Swingers: 1&2 £3.60, 1&3 £4.70, 2&3 £7.40 CSF £16.98 TOTE £2.40: £1.10, £3.00, £3.40; EX 15.40 Trifecta £244.20 Pool: £2,050.02 - 6.29 winning units..
Owner D S Lee **Bred** D S Lee **Trained** Whatcombe, Oxon

FOCUS
A modest 2yo maiden. There was an average pace on.

6080 FREDDIE PARKER WINNING FASHION H'CAP 1m 2f (P)
6:50 (6:56) (Class 5) (0-75,75) 3-Y-0+ **£2,587** (£770; £384; £192) **Stalls** Low

Form RPR

1522 **1** **Qanan**[9] 5802 4-9-6 **72**........................ AshleyMorgan(3) 3 80
(Chris Wall) *chsd ldrs: effrt and swtchd rt over 1f out: qcknd u.p to ld wl ins fnl f: rdn out* **8/1**[2]

2055 **2** ½ **Spring Tonic**[90] 2981 4-9-7 **70**........................ SebSanders 13 77
(Simon Dow) *styd wd fr outside draw: chsd ldr after 2f: rdn and ev ch ent fnl 2f: drvn and led ins fnl f: hdd and no ex wl ins fnl f* **12/1**

-000 **3** nk **Modernism**[81] 3301 4-9-10 **73**........................ NeilCallan 5 79
(David Simcock) *led: rdn and sustained duel w rival fr jst over 2f out: hdd and styd on same pce ins fnl f* **14/1**

63-2 **4** 2½ **Heezararity**[43] 4591 5-9-1 **69**........................ RyanTate(5) 1 71
(Jonathan Geake) *hld up in last quartet: rdn and hdwy over 2f out: styd on steadily u.p fnl f: nt rch ldrs* **20/1**

4442 **5** 1¼ **Opera Buff**[28] 5099 4-9-6 **69**........................(p) AidanColeman 10 68
(Sean Curran) *in tch in midfield: rdn and outpcd over 2f out: wd and plenty to do bnd 2f out: styd on u.p fnl f: no threat to ldrs* **10/1**[3]

2436 **6** 1¾ **Wilfred Pickles (IRE)**[25] 5245 7-9-11 **74**........................ LiamKeniry 6 70
(Jo Crowley) *hld up in tch in midfield: rdn and effrt over 1f out: drvn and no hdwy 1f out: wknd ins fnl f* **20/1**

3623 **6** dht **Take A Note**[26] 5191 4-9-12 **75**........................ JimCrowley 4 71
(Patrick Chamings) *hld up in tch in midfield: swtchd rt and effrt u.p wl over 1f out: styd on fnl f: nvr trbld ldrs* **8/1**[2]

-622 **8** 2 **Plenum (GER)**[94] 2874 3-9-2 **72**........................ TedDurcan 7 64
(David Lanigan) *chsd ldrs: rdn and unable qck over 2f out: outpcd and btn over 1f out: wknd ins fnl f* **5/2**[1]

1143 **9** nk **Drahem**[26] 5181 3-9-2 **72**........................ FrederikTylicki 11 64
(James Fanshawe) *hld up in tch in midfield: sddle slipped 5f out and rdr unable to offer any assistance after: kpt on same pce fr wl over 1f out* **5/2**[1]

0300 **10** nk **Dimitar (USA)**[18] 5479 4-9-5 **68**........................ JackMitchell 8 59
(Brendan Powell) *stdd s: hld up in rr: rdn and effrt on outer but stl plenty to do bnd 2f out: styd on but n.d* **50/1**

-340 **11** 2¾ **Olympic Jule**[41] 4637 3-8-11 **67**........................ LiamJones 2 53
(Harry Dunlop) *hld up in tch in midfield: rdn and struggling over 2f out: wknd wl over 1f out* **50/1**

3305 **12** ½ **Watcheroftheskies**[20] 5387 3-9-0 **70**........................ MartinLane 12 55
(J W Hills) *stdd s: hld up in rr: rdn and no hdwy 2f out: n.d* **33/1**

5440 **13** 5 **Punditry**[19] 5440 3-9-0 **70**........................ HayleyTurner 9 45
(James Toller) *a towards rr: rdn 7f out: bhd 2f out* **33/1**

2m 4.93s (-1.67) **Going Correction** -0.075s/f (Stan)
WFA 3 from 4yo+ 7lb **13** Ran SP% **122.1**
Speed ratings (Par 103): **103,102,102,100,99 97,97,96,96,95 93,93,89**
Tote Swingers: 1&2 £22.80, 1&3 £19.10, 2&3 £39.50 CSF £93.76 CT £1335.05 TOTE £7.80: £2.30, £4.40, £4.60; EX 125.10 Trifecta £1429.40 Part won. Pool: £1,905.96 - 0.46 winning units..
Owner Alan & Jill Smith **Bred** Genesis Green Stud Ltd **Trained** Newmarket, Suffolk

FOCUS
This well-contested handicap looked pretty tight on paper, but few got seriously involved as the principals fought it out.

6081 VINES BMW H'CAP 1m 4f (P)
7:20 (7:20) (Class 5) (0-75,75) 3-Y-0 **£2,587** (£770; £384; £192) **Stalls** Low

Form RPR

3114 **1** **Prospera (IRE)**[19] 5445 3-9-7 **75**........................(b) JimCrowley 5 87
(Ralph Beckett) *hld up in tch in midfield: effrt u.p to chal over 2f out: led wl over 1f out: pressed but hld on wl ins fnl f: rdn out* **3/1**[2]

-444 **2** ½ **Mistral Wind (IRE)**[82] 3251 3-8-7 **61**........................ AndreaAtzeni 6 72
(Ed Dunlop) *hld up in last pair: rdn and hdwy over 2f out: pressed ldrs 2f out: hung rt but chsd wnr jst over 1f out: pressing wnr wl ins fnl f: no ex and hld towards fin* **12/1**

3525 **3** 8 **Sweet Martoni**[9] 5795 3-9-2 **70**........................ SebSanders 4 69
(William Knight) *chsd ldr tl led 10f out: rdn and hdd wl over 1f out: 3rd and btn 1f out: wknd but hung to 3rd fnl f* **9/2**

-433 **4** hd **Candoluminescence**[27] 5132 3-9-2 **70**........................ JamesDoyle 1 69
(Roger Charlton) *led for 2f: chsd ldr tl rdn and unable qck ent fnl 2f: 4th and wl btn 1f out: plugged on and pressing for modest 3rd wl ins fnl f* **5/4**[1]

04-0 **5** 1½ **Sweeping Rock (IRE)**[10] 5743 3-8-7 **61** oh1................ HayleyTurner 7 57
(Marcus Tregoning) *stdd and dropped in bhd after s: hld up in rr: rdn and effrt over 2f out: no real imp: modest 5th 1f out* **25/1**

2-03 **6** 8 **Codebreaker**[65] 3861 3-9-0 **68**........................ LiamKeniry 3 52
(Hughie Morrison) *chsd ldng pair tl rdn and outpcd over 2f out: wknd u.p over 1f out: fdd fnl f* **14/1**

4652 **7** 1½ **Rock God (IRE)**[7] 5854 3-8-12 **66**........................(b) JohnFahy 2 48
(Eve Johnson Houghton) *in tch in midfield: rdn 4f out: dropped to rr and struggling u.p 3f out: bhd over 1f out* **4/1**[3]

2m 31.19s (-1.81) **Going Correction** -0.075s/f (Stan) **7** Ran SP% **125.8**
Speed ratings (Par 101): **103,102,97,97,96 90,89**
Tote Swingers: 1&2 £5.70, 1&3 £2.40, 2&3 £9.60 CSF £41.72 CT £169.53 TOTE £5.10: £2.60, £3.80; EX 56.00 Trifecta £171.90 Pool: £1,936.32 - 8.44 winning units..
Owner The Millennium Madness Partnership **Bred** Mount Coote Stud **Trained** Kimpton, Hants

FOCUS
There was a sound pace on in this moderate 3yo handicap and the first pair dominated the final furlong.
T/Plt: £541.60 to a £1 stake. Pool: £47,408.64 - 63.90 winning units T/Qpdt: £168.50 to a £1 stake. Pool: £6,694.87 - 29.40 winning units SP

5637 MUSSELBURGH (R-H)
Tuesday, September 3

OFFICIAL GOING: Good to firm (8.1)
Wind: Breezy, half against Weather: Cloudy, warm

6082 32RED (S) STKS 5f
2:10 (2:11) (Class 6) 2-Y-0 **£1,940** (£577; £288; £144) **Stalls** High

Form RPR

425 **1** **Kano's Ghirl (IRE)**[13] 5638 2-8-7 66........................ TomEaves 4 58
(Keith Dalgleish) *trckd ldrs: led over 1f out: sn rdn: kpt on wl fnl f: jst hld on* **10/3**[2]

0430 **2** *nse* **Secret Applause**11 5710 2-8-12 61 PaulMulrennan 7 63
(Michael Dods) *in tch: effrt and swtchd rt over 1f out: styd on wl fnl f: jst hld* **13/2**

3 *nk* **Bifocal** 2-8-12 0 GrahamLee 2 62
(David Brown) *taken early and walked to s: s.i.s: bhd and outpcd: hdwy 1/2-way: rdn and kpt on wl fnl f* **11/2**3

2641 **4** *3/4* **Bountiful Forest**15 5578 2-8-9 62 JasonHart(3) 1 59
(Noel Wilson) *cl up: rdn and disp ld over 1f out: one pce wl ins fnl f* **9/1**

06 **5** *4* **Robynelle**11 5703 2-8-12 70 PJMcDonald 5 45
(Keith Dalgleish) *led tl rdn and hdd over 1f out: wknd ins fnl f* **11/8**1

544 **6** *1/2* **Straight Gin**15 5578 2-8-12 60 BarryMcHugh 6 43
(Alan Berry) *trckd ldrs: drvn along 1/2-way: wknd ins fnl f* **20/1**

1m 0.57s (0.17) **Going Correction** -0.10s/f (Good) **6** Ran SP% **108.7**
Speed ratings (Par 93): **94,93,93,92,85 85**
Tote Swingers: 1&2 £3.90, 1&3 £3.30, 2&3 £6.00 CSF £22.69 TOTE £4.80: £2.10, £3.40; EX 27.30 Trifecta £55.70 Pool: £1,178.70 - 15.85 winning units..The winner was bought in for £7,500. Bifocal bought by Mr Ian Semple for £12,000.
Owner Lamont Racing **Bred** Tally-Ho Stud **Trained** Carluke, S Lanarks
■ Stewards' Enquiry : P J McDonald caution: careless riding.

FOCUS
Stands' bend moved out 3m. A modest juvenile seller rated par for the grade.

6083 CMYK DIGITAL SOLUTIONS H'CAP 1m
2:40 (2:40) (Class 6) (0-60,59) 3-Y-O+ **£1,940** (£577; £288; £144) **Stalls** Low

Form RPR

225- **1** **Goal (IRE)**9 7593 5-9-4 53 (t) RobertWinston 1 61
(Gordon Elliott, Ire) *in tch: effrt whn nt clr run over 2f out to over 1f out: rallied and chalng whn rdr dropped reins briefly ins fnl f: sn led: drvn out* **7/4**1

0503 **2** *nk* **Summer Dancer (IRE)**22 5341 9-9-8 57 MickyFenton 11 64
(Paul Midgley) *taken early to post: t.k.h in rr: hdwy to chse ldrs whn nt clr run over 1f out: swtchd lft and styd on wl to take 2nd cl home* **8/1**3

6066 **3** *nk* **Joshua The First**13 5637 4-9-9 58 (p) TomEaves 12 65
(Keith Dalgleish) *chsd ldrs: effrt and ev ch over 2f out to ins fnl f: kpt on: hld cl home* **16/1**

4566 **4** *3/4* **Conjuror's Bluff**9 5783 5-8-8 46 (p) JasonHart(3) 6 51
(Frederick Watson) *in tch: hdwy to ld over 1f out: hdd ins fnl f: hld towards fin* **25/1**

0044 **5** *1/2* **Dutch Gal**1 6049 3-9-4 58 FrannyNorton 3 61
(John Holt) *s.i.s: hld up on ins: rdn over 2f out: styd on wl fnl f: nrst fin* **16/1**

3330 **6** *1/2* **Remember Rocky**5 5921 4-8-8 48 (p) DavidBergin(5) 2 50
(Lucy Normile) *towards rr: drvn over 2f out: kpt on fnl f: nvr able to chal* **16/1**

4522 **7** *nk* **Eilean Mor**24 5261 5-8-5 47 DanielleMooney(7) 9 49
(R Mike Smith) *hld up: rdn and hdwy 2f out: kpt on same pce fnl f* **16/1**

4615 **8** *1 1/2* **Look On By**13 5642 3-9-4 58 PJMcDonald 13 55
(Ruth Carr) *led to over 1f out: rdn and wknd ins fnl f* **8/1**3

004 **9** *1/2* **Maillot Jaune (IRE)**24 5290 3-8-11 51 ow1 RussKennemore 14 47+
(Patrick Holmes) *s.i.s: hld up on outside: rdn over 2f out: rallied over 1f out: no imp* **66/1**

4410 **10** *1 3/4* **Goninodaethat**22 5331 5-9-8 57 1 GrahamLee 5 50
(Jim Goldie) *cl up: effrt over 2f out: wknd ins fnl f* **14/1**

560 **11** *nk* **Military Call**46 4469 6-8-7 45 (p) JulieBurke(3) 4 37
(R Mike Smith) *in tch: rdn and effrt over 2f out: wknd ins fnl f* **28/1**

0400 **12** *2* **Fife Jo**22 5331 3-8-2 49 JordanNason(7) 7 35
(Jim Goldie) *t.k.h: hld up: struggling wl over 2f out: sn btn* **28/1**

22 **13** *18* **Minot Street (CAN)**1 6049 3-8-5 45 (bt) BarryMcHugh 10
(John C McConnell, Ire) *hld up on outside: struggling 3f out: sn btn: t.o* **11/2**2

1m 40.15s (-1.05) **Going Correction** -0.10s/f (Good)
WFA 3 from 4yo+ 5lb **13** Ran SP% **116.4**
Speed ratings (Par 101): **101,100,100,99,99 98,98,96,96,94 94,92,74**
Tote Swingers: 1&2 £2.80, 1&3 £5.90, 2&3 £6.30 CSF £14.35 CT £176.09 TOTE £3.80: £1.40, £3.70, £5.90; EX 14.10 Trifecta £191.70 Pool: £1,332.26 - 5.21 winning units..
Owner Willie McKay **Bred** A M F Persse **Trained** Trim, Co Meath

FOCUS
A moderate handicap, but dramatic for those who waded in on the favourite. The compressed finish limits the form.

6084 VISITEASTLOTHIAN.ORG MAIDEN STKS 7f 30y
3:15 (3:16) (Class 5) 3-Y-O+ **£2,587** (£770; £384; £192) **Stalls** Low

Form RPR

4325 **1** **Mishaal (IRE)**12 5676 3-9-5 67 BarryMcHugh 9 76
(Michael Herrington) *chsd clr ldr: smooth hdwy to ld over 1f out: sn shkn up: clr whn hung rt ins fnl f: r.o* **7/2**2

0452 **2** *5* **Hanalei Bay (IRE)**5 5919 3-9-5 67 (b1) TomEaves 5 63
(Keith Dalgleish) *t.k.h: led and clr: rdn and hdd over 1f out: kpt on: no ch w wnr* **7/1**

5036 **3** *1 3/4* **Mowhoob**13 5642 3-9-5 67 GrahamLee 4 58
(Jim Goldie) *chsd ldrs: effrt over 2f out: one pce fr over 1f out* **5/1**3

4 *shd* **Favourite Treat (USA)** 3-9-5 0 FrannyNorton 6 58+
(Mark Johnston) *in tch: rn green and outpcd over 3f out: rallied over 1f out: drifted rt: no imp fnl f* **11/2**

0-02 **5** *2 1/4* **Gambino (IRE)**11 5704 3-9-5 47 PaddyAspell 7 51
(Alan Berry) *hld up in tch: effrt and cl up 2f out: sn rdn: outpcd fnl f* **40/1**

43 **6** *1/2* **Gaspard**16 5563 3-9-5 0 DanielTudhope 8 50
(David O'Meara) *in tch: rdn over 2f out: sn edgd rt and outpcd: no imp whn edgd lft appr fnl f* **6/4**1

0400 **7** *7* **Pastoral Prey**22 5336 3-9-5 52 (p) PaulMulrennan 3 31
(Ian Semple) *t.k.h: hld up in tch: struggling over 2f out: sn btn* **66/1**

-000 **8** *10* **Artillery Train (IRE)**62 3946 4-9-9 38 (b) BrianHughes 2
(Tim Etherington) *s.i.s: bhd: struggling 1/2-way: nvr on terms* **100/1**

9 *12* **Sapphire Sky** 4-9-4 0 AndrewElliott 1
(Jim Goldie) *s.i.s: bhd and detached: lost tch fr 1/2-way* **33/1**

1m 27.67s (-1.33) **Going Correction** -0.10s/f (Good)
WFA 3 from 4yo 4lb **9** Ran SP% **114.6**
Speed ratings (Par 103): **103,97,95,95,92 92,84,72,58**
Tote Swingers: 1&2 £4.70, 1&3 £3.90, 2&3 £5.60 CSF £27.14 TOTE £3.80: £1.50, £2.40, £1.60; EX 25.60 Trifecta £103.30 Pool: £2,191.66 - 15.90 winning units..
Owner Kelvyn Gracie & Lawrence McCaughey **Bred** Darley **Trained** Cold Kirby, N Yorks

FOCUS
A moderate older-horse maiden dominated by those with plenty of previous experience. The pace was fair and the winner rates a minor personal best.

6085 32RED.COM NURSERY H'CAP 7f 30y
3:50 (3:50) (Class 5) (0-75,75) 2-Y-O **£3,234** (£962; £481; £240) **Stalls** Low

Form RPR

2010 **1** **Bureau (IRE)**31 4988 2-9-7 75 FrannyNorton 2 80+
(Mark Johnston) *cl up: led 2f out: rdn and styd on strly fnl f* **8/13**1

3104 **2** *3/4* **Boogangoo (IRE)**11 5703 2-9-5 73 PaulMulrennan 5 75
(Keith Dalgleish) *trckd ldrs: effrt and swtchd lft wl over 1f out: sn chsng wnr: kpt on ins fnl f* **16/1**

0500 **3** *1 3/4* **Fair Flutter (IRE)**19 5424 2-8-3 57 PatrickMathers 4 54
(Richard Fahey) *s.i.s: sn in tch: effrt over 2f out: rdn and hung lft over 1f out: one pce ins fnl f* **11/1**

054 **4** *4 1/2* **Camatini (IRE)**37 4801 2-9-0 68 PJMcDonald 3 53
(Michael Dods) *in tch: rdn over 2f out: no imp fr over 1f out* **10/1**3

4035 **5** *1 1/4* **Angel Rosa**11 5703 2-8-9 63 TomEaves 7 45
(Keith Dalgleish) *chsd ldrs on outside: rdn over 2f out: wknd over 1f out* **25/1**

1303 **6** *nk* **It's All A Game**6 5898 2-7-12 57 (v) PhilipPrince(5) 6 38
(Richard Guest) *t.k.h: hld up in tch: rdn over 2f out: sn no imp* **7/1**2

6355 **7** *10* **Nelson's Pride**26 5194 2-8-7 66 ShaneGray(5) 1 20
(Kevin Ryan) *led to 2f out: sn rdn and wknd* **10/1**3

1m 29.8s (0.80) **Going Correction** -0.10s/f (Good) **7** Ran SP% **110.7**
Speed ratings (Par 95): **91,90,88,83,81 81,69**
Tote Swingers: 1&2 £12.60, 1&3 £3.20, 2&3 £3.40 CSF £11.45 TOTE £2.00: £1.20, £5.00; EX 11.30 Trifecta £108.60 Pool: £2,883.21 - 19.90 winning units..
Owner Sheikh Hamdan Bin Mohammed Al Maktoum **Bred** Darley **Trained** Middleham Moor, N Yorks

FOCUS
A one-sided nursery according to the market. It was run at a decent enough pace and the form is straightforward.

6086 CALA HOMES UK'S BEST HOUSEBUILDER H'CAP (A QUALIFIER FOR THE BETFAIR STAYERS' SERIES FINAL) 1m 4f 100y
4:25 (4:25) (Class 5) (0-70,72) 3-Y-O+ **£3,234** (£962; £481; £240) **Stalls** Low

Form RPR

5313 **1** **Discay**11 5712 4-10-0 70 FrannyNorton 9 81+
(Mark Johnston) *t.k.h: pressed ldr: led over 2f out: rdn whn veered lft appr fnl f: kpt on strly* **5/2**2

1 **2** *3 1/2* **Lindenhurst (IRE)**1 6051 3-9-7 72 6ex (t) GrahamLee 6 77
(John C McConnell, Ire) *prom: effrt over 2f out: sn rdn: chsd wnr ins fnl f: kpt on* **6/4**1

5351 **3** *2 3/4* **Valantino Oyster (IRE)**7 5420 6-9-4 60 (p) DaleSwift 5 61
(Tracy Waggott) *t.k.h: led: rdn and hdd over 2f out: rallied: kpt on same pce ins fnl f* **18/1**

0252 **4** *1 1/2* **Dean Iarracht (IRE)**19 5420 7-8-6 51 oh3 (p) JasonHart(3) 2 49
(Tracy Waggott) *t.k.h: chsd ldrs: rdn over 2f out: swtchd lft over 1f out: sn one pce* **16/1**

6133 **5** *1 3/4* **La Bacouetteuse (FR)**13 5640 8-9-11 67 (b) DavidAllan 3 62+
(Iain Jardine) *dwlt: hld up: rdn over 2f out: sme late hdwy: nvr rchd ldrs* **9/1**3

1134 **6** *nk* **Grand Diamond (IRE)**13 5643 9-8-9 58 (p) JordanNason(7) 7 53
(Jim Goldie) *hld up in tch: effrt and pushed along over 2f out: sn no imp* **12/1**

0000 **7** *shd* **Jawaab (IRE)**11 5712 9-9-6 62 (p) MichaelO'Connell 10 57
(Philip Kirby) *hld up in tch: rdn and outpcd over 2f out: n.d after* **16/1**

023- **8** *5* **Coax**245 5622 5-9-6 62 DuranFentiman 1 49
(Patrick Holmes) *in tch: rdn over 3f out: wknd fnl 2f* **16/1**

/006 **9** *3/4* **Non Dom (IRE)**13 5643 7-8-9 51 oh1 (v) PJMcDonald 4 37
(Wilf Storey) *sn pushed along in rr: hdwy on outside and prom 1/2-way: rdn and wknd over 3f out* **25/1**

0010 **P** **Mr Dream Maker (IRE)**6 5897 5-8-9 51 oh3 PaulMulrennan 8
(Noel Wilson) *midfield on outside: rdn and lost pl whn p.u over 5f out* **28/1**

2m 41.46s (-0.54) **Going Correction** -0.10s/f (Good)
WFA 3 from 4yo+ 9lb **10** Ran SP% **116.5**
Speed ratings (Par 103): **97,94,92,91,90 90,90,87,86,**
Tote Swingers: 1&2 £1.90, 1&3 £7.40, 2&3 £5.30 CSF £6.57 CT £51.59 TOTE £2.90: £1.30, £1.10, £5.00; EX 8.40 Trifecta £91.20 Pool: £3,067.01 - 25.20 winning units..
Owner C H Greensit & W A Greensit **Bred** C H And W A Greensit **Trained** Middleham Moor, N Yorks

FOCUS
They didn't go much of a pace in this modest handicap and the front four raced handily throughout. The second more than matched his previous day's form at Hamilton.

6087 32RED H'CAP 2m
5:00 (5:00) (Class 6) (0-65,65) 3-Y-O+ **£2,587** (£770; £384; £192) **Stalls** High

Form RPR

1 **Diyala (IRE)**7 5872 4-10-0 65 (t) RobertWinston 6 80+
(Gordon Elliott, Ire) *t.k.h: hld up: stdy hdwy over 3f out: led gng wl over 1f out: sn shkn up and drew clr fnl f* **2/1**1

4502 **2** *6* **Jan Smuts (IRE)**7 5862 5-9-4 60 (tp) GeorgeChaloner(5) 4 68
(Wilf Storey) *t.k.h early: in tch: hdwy and ev ch over 2f out: kpt on fnl f: no ch w wnr* **9/2**3

2632 **3** *2 1/2* **Geanie Mac (IRE)**5 5920 4-8-11 48 (p) PJMcDonald 2 53
(Linda Perratt) *prom: rdn over 2f out: kpt on same pce fr over 1f out* **13/2**

56-5 **4** *1* **Passion Planet (IRE)**18 5506 5-9-12 63 TomEaves 1 67
(John C McConnell, Ire) *hld up: rdn and effrt over 3f out: styd on fnl f: no imp* **25/1**

5511 **5** *nk* **Lochiel**15 5592 9-10-0 65 PaulMulrennan 5 68
(Ian Semple) *chsd ldrs: smooth hdwy to ld over 2f out: rdn and hdd over 1f out: wknd ins fnl f* **7/1**

3540 **6** *1 1/2* **Brunello**8 5831 5-9-8 59 (p) RussKennemore 3 61
(Philip Kirby) *chsd ldr: led over 5f out to over 2f out: edgd rt and wknd over 1f out* **4/1**2

1334 **7** *5* **Forrest Flyer (IRE)**24 5267 9-9-13 64 (p) GrahamLee 8 60
(Jim Goldie) *led: reminders 1/2-way: rdn and hdd over 5f out: rallied: wknd over 1f out* **16/1**

3025 **8** *29* **Sohcahtoa (IRE)**13 5643 7-9-8 62 LMcNiff(3) 7 23
(Andrew Crook) *hld up: struggling over 6f out: btn fnl 3f: t.o* **16/1**

3m 31.98s (-1.52) **Going Correction** -0.10s/f (Good) **8** Ran SP% **113.0**
Speed ratings (Par 101): **99,96,94,94,94 93,90,76**
Tote Swingers: 1&2 £3.80, 1&3 £4.40, 2&3 £6.70 CSF £10.78 CT £47.44 TOTE £3.10: £1.30, £2.70, £2.20; EX 15.40 Trifecta £66.80 Pool: £2,255.27 - 25.31 winning units..

Owner Barstool Prophets Syndicate **Bred** His Highness The Aga Khan's Studs S C **Trained** Trim, Co Meath
FOCUS
A moderate staying handicap, but the winner looks much better than this grade. The form is rated on the positive side.

6088 32RED.COM H'CAP 5f
5:30 (5:31) (Class 6) (0-65,66) 3-Y-0+ **£1,940** (£577; £288; £144) **Stalls** High

Form RPR
1041 **1** **Captain Royale (IRE)**[6] 5889 8-9-12 **66** 6ex..............(p) BarryMcHugh 6 75+
(Tracy Waggott) *hld up: hdwy whn nt clr run over 1f out: qcknd to ld ins fnl f: hld on wl* **4/1**[1]
6662 **2** *nk* **Here Now And Why (IRE)**[13] 5641 6-9-2 **56**..............(p) DavidAllan 7 64
(Iain Jardine) *prom: effrt over 1f out: led briefly ins fnl f: kpt on: hld nr fin* **13/2**[2]
0600 **3** *3/4* **Mr Snooks**[14] 5614 3-8-5 **46**.. PaulQuinn 11 51
(David Nicholls) *in tch: effrt whn n.m.r and swtchd lft over 1f out: r.o ins fnl f* **33/1**
0000 **4** *1/2* **Irish Girls Spirit (IRE)**[102] 2611 4-8-13 **53**..................... MickyFenton 2 56
(Paul Midgley) *prom: hdwy over 1f out: edgd lft and ev ch ins fnl f: one pce nr fin* **20/1**
534 **5** *1 1/4* **Beauty Pageant (IRE)**[9] 5796 6-9-5 **59**.......................... GrahamLee 5 58
(David Brown) *chsd ldrs: rdn over 2f out: one pce whn checked appr fnl f* **9/1**
6000 **6** *shd* **Fol Hollow (IRE)**[22] 5336 8-9-3 **57**.......................... MichaelO'Connell 13 56
(Stuart Coltherd) *hld up: nt clr run over 2f out: hdwy fnl f: nvr able to chal* **22/1**
6514 **7** *nk* **Tuibama (IRE)**[6] 5889 4-9-8 **62**..(p) DaleSwift 12 59
(Tracy Waggott) *w ldrs: effrt and rdn over 1f out: kpt on same pce fnl f* **7/1**[3]
0200 **8** *1/2* **Pavers Star**[28] 5085 4-9-5 **59**.. RobertWinston 1 55+
(Noel Wilson) *bhd: rdn and hdwy 1/2-way: edgd lft and one pce appr fnl f* **16/1**
-046 **9** *nk* **Mandy Layla (IRE)**[18] 5485 3-9-4 **64**..................... GeorgeChaloner(5) 8 59
(Bryan Smart) *cl up: led over 1f out to ins fnl f: sn btn* **4/1**[1]
0134 **10** *hd* **Quality Art (USA)**[13] 5641 5-9-2 **61**.......................... PhilipPrince(5) 10 55+
(Richard Guest) *dwlt: hld up: n.m.r 1/2-way: sn rdn: sme late hdwy: nvr on terms* **10/1**
4332 **11** *1* **See Vermont**[38] 4762 5-8-6 **49**......................................(p) JasonHart(3) 9 39
(Robin Bastiman) *led to over 1f out: wknd ins fnl f* **13/2**[2]
2060 **12** *nse* **Royal Duchess**[11] 5708 3-8-7 **48** ow1.......................... TomEaves 3 38+
(Lucy Normile) *dwlt: bhd: rdn 2f out: n.m.r ins fnl f: sn btn* **66/1**

59.97s (-0.43) **Going Correction** -0.10s/f (Good)
WFA 3 from 4yo+ 1lb 12 Ran SP% **117.7**
Speed ratings (Par 101): **99,98,97,96,94 94,93,93,92,92 90,90**
Tote Swingers: 1&2 £5.60, 1&3 £15.90, 2&3 £18.80 CSF £28.14 CT £770.05 TOTE £3.70: £1.20, £2.40, £12.40; EX 19.20 Trifecta £785.30 Pool: £1,610.91 - 1.53 winning units..
Owner H Conlon **Bred** Skymarc Farm Inc **Trained** Spennymoor, Co Durham
■ Stewards' Enquiry : David Allan four-day ban: used whip above permitted level (Sep 17-20)
FOCUS
A moderate, if competitive sprint handicap. Straightforward, limited form in behind the winner.
T/Plt: £51.50 to a £1 stake. Pool: £47,324.00 - 670.50 winning units T/Qpdt: £11.90 to a £1 stake. Pool: £3,339.00 - 206.29 winning units RY

LAYTOWN
Tuesday, September 3
OFFICIAL GOING: Standard

6089a TOTE MOBILE BETTING H'CAP 6f
4:20 (4:20) (50-70,70) 4-Y-0+ **£4,768** (£1,105; £483; £276)

RPR
1 **Enigma Code (UAE)**[2] 6026 8-10-8 **67**........................(t) IanMcCarthy(3) 73
(Damian Joseph English, Ire) *sn led narrowly: rdn and strly pressed fr over 2f out: kpt on best u.p ins fnl f* **11/1**
2 *1/2* **Ucanchoose (IRE)**[10] 5775 7-11-0 **70**........................ DeclanMcDonogh 74
(Andrew Slattery, Ire) *trckd ldrs in 4th: tk clsr order after 1/2-way: rdn in 2nd 1 1/2f out: ev ch ent fnl f: kpt on wl towards fin wout matching wnr* **11/2**[3]
3 *2 1/2* **Little Arrows (IRE)**[19] 5451 7-10-7 **63**................................. ShaneFoley 59+
(K J Condon, Ire) *in rr: pushed along and stl plenty to do 1 1/2f out: rdn ins fnl f and styd on wl into nvr nrr 3rd fnl strides* **8/1**
4 *nk* **Jembatt (IRE)**[1] 6055 6-10-12 **68** 5ex.............................. ChrisHayes 63
(Michael Mulvany, Ire) *chsd ldrs: pushed along in 6th 1/2-way: wnt mod 3rd ent fnl f: sn no ex u.p: denied 3rd fnl strides* **5/1**[2]
5 *nk* **Lily's Star (IRE)**[23] 5321 6-10-13 **69**.. RWalsh 63
(H Rogers, Ire) *hld up in tch: sme hdwy on outer fr 1/2-way: rdn in 5th and no ex ent fnl f: kpt on same pce* **13/2**
6 *shd* **Dana's Present**[45] 4517 4-11-0 **70**................................ SeamieHeffernan 64
(George Baker) *trckd ldrs in 3rd: pushed along after 1/2-way and sn no imp on ldrs: one pce fnl 2f* **7/2**[1]
7 *1/2* **Sweet Annathea (IRE)**[1] 6055 4-10-5 **61**................................ RoryCleary 53
(Thomas Cleary, Ire) *towards rr: rdn and no imp fr 2f out: kpt on ins fnl f* **20/1**
8 *1* **Emkanaat**[17] 5522 5-11-0 **70**.. GaryCarroll 59
(Amy Weaver) *chsd ldrs in 5th: rdn fr 1/2-way and clsd briefly on inner: no ex u.p ins fnl f: wknd nr fin* **11/2**[3]
9 *6* **Wandering Heart (IRE)**[10] 5775 5-10-10 **66**..................... DavyCondon 36
(Liam P Cusack, Ire) *w.w towards rr: rdn and no imp fr 2f out* **25/1**
10 *1 1/2* **Ellell Duke (IRE)**[394] 4852 4-10-8 **64**.......................... EmmetMcNamara 29
(Seamus Fahey, Ire) *sn settled bhd ldr in 2nd: rdn fr 1/2-way and sn no ex u.p: wknd fnl 2f* **16/1**

1m 14.6s (74.60) 10 Ran SP% **116.9**
CSF £70.62 CT £528.28 TOTE £11.60: £3.70, £2.20, £2.80; DF 162.20.
Owner Joseph M English **Bred** Darley **Trained** Naul, Co Dublin
FOCUS
The course was positioned as close to the enclosures as ever before and, as a consequence, the surface was very slow and deep. The jockeys reported plenty of kickback and the winning time was 4.7 seconds slower than the corresponding contest 12 months ago. It paid to race prominently.

5976 BATH (L-H)
Wednesday, September 4
OFFICIAL GOING: Firm (9.4)
Wind: Virtually nil Weather: Sunny

6095 WEATHERBYS HAMILTON INSURANCE MAIDEN AUCTION STKS 5f 161y
2:00 (2:03) (Class 5) 2-Y-0 **£2,587** (£770; £384; £192) **Stalls** Centre

Form RPR
22 **1** **Shilla (IRE)**[15] 5609 2-8-4 0.. CathyGannon 3 69+
(Henry Candy) *mde all: jnd 2f out: sn shkn up and c comf clr appr fnl f: easily* **1/6**[1]
64 **2** *2 3/4* **Castagna Girl**[40] 4708 2-8-8 0.. ShaneKelly 1 64
(Denis Coakley) *chsd ldrs: rdn and outpcd over 2f out: styd on to take wl hld 2nd appr fnl f* **5/1**[2]
05 **3** *1 1/4* **Gower Princess**[21] 5385 2-8-1 0.................................. PhilipPrince(5) 4 58
(Ronald Harris) *t.k.h: chsd wnr: rdn to chal 2f out: easily outpcd appr fnl and styd on same pce into 3rd sn after* **33/1**[3]
00 **4** *9* **Benoordenhout (IRE)**[20] 5442 2-8-9 0.................................. JohnFahy 2 30
(Jonathan Portman) *s.i.s: sn rcvrd to chse ldrs: rdn over 2f out: sn btn* **66/1**

1m 10.58s (-0.62) **Going Correction** -0.30s/f (Firm) 4 Ran SP% **106.8**
Speed ratings (Par 95): **92,88,86,74**
CSF £1.32 TOTE £1.10; EX 1.30 Trifecta £2.10 Pool: £1895.39 - 659.85 winning units..
Owner Henry Candy & Partners III **Bred** Thomas Smullen **Trained** Kingston Warren, Oxon
FOCUS
As uncompetitive a maiden as you are likely to see.

6096 WEATHERBYS BANK FOREIGN EXCHANGE H'CAP 5f 161y
2:30 (2:30) (Class 5) (0-75,75) 4-Y-0+ **£2,587** (£770; £384; £192) **Stalls** Centre

Form RPR
1400 **1** **Crimson Queen**[5] 5956 6-8-13 **72**........................(b) GeorgeChaloner(5) 4 85
(Roy Brotherton) *mde all: 6 l clr 1/2-way: rdn over 1f out: styd on wl fnl f: unchal* **3/1**[1]
2463 **2** *6* **Dark Lane**[6] 5931 7-8-7 **68**.. EoinWalsh(7) 8 61
(David Evans) *in rr and drvn along 3f out: hdwy on outer over 1f out and styd on wl to go 2nd fnl 75yds but nvr any ch w unchal wnr* **10/1**
4002 **3** *1* **Annes Rocket (IRE)**[21] 5404 8-8-12 **73**.................. CameronHardie(7) 3 63
(Jimmy Fox) *stdd s: in rr: pushed along 3f out: hdwy appr fnl f: styd on to take 3rd fnl 50yds but nvr any ch w unchal wnr* **7/1**[3]
3102 **4** *nk* **Dreams Of Glory**[13] 5669 5-8-13 **67**.................................. GrahamLee 1 56
(Ron Hodges) *chsd unchal wnr: rdn 3f out: no ch sn after but hld 2nd tl wknd into 4th fnl 75yds* **7/2**[2]
2145 **5** *1* **Comptonspirit**[28] 5148 9-8-12 **69**.......................... MatthewLawson(3) 6 55
(Brian Baugh) *in tch and rdn 3f out: nvr nr unchal wnr but disp 2nd u.p over 1f out: wknd fnl 50yds* **18/1**
3525 **6** *1 1/2* **Belle Bayardo (IRE)**[13] 5669 5-8-12 **66**.......................... CathyGannon 7 47
(Ronald Harris) *in rr: sn drvn along: sme hdwy over 1f out but nvr nr unchal wnr and btn sn after* **7/1**[3]
4103 **7** *9* **Kakapuka**[15] 5621 6-9-5 **73**.. MartinHarley 2 24
(Anabel K Murphy) *disp 2nd bhd unchal wnr 2f: sn u.p: wknd ins fnl 2f* **3/1**[1]

1m 8.74s (-2.46) **Going Correction** -0.30s/f (Firm) 7 Ran SP% **111.6**
Speed ratings (Par 103): **104,96,94,94,92 90,78**
toteswingers 1&2 £5.70, 1&3 £5.70, 2&3 £9.20 CSF £31.23 CT £187.42 TOTE £3.30: £2.10, £6.00; EX 34.90 Trifecta £340.50 Pool: £1167.50 - 2.57 winning units..
Owner Arthur Clayton **Bred** Cheveley Park Stud Ltd **Trained** Elmley Castle, Worcs
FOCUS
An ordinary sprint handicap with six of the seven runners previous C&D winners. The pace was searing. All about the winner but probably not form to get carried away with.

6097 BBC RADIO BRISTOL H'CAP 1m 2f 46y
3:00 (3:00) (Class 6) (0-55,58) 4-Y-0+ **£1,940** (£577; £288; £144) **Stalls** Low

Form RPR
2260 **1** **Petersboden**[4] 5980 4-9-1 **46**.................................. FergusSweeney 2 52
(Michael Blanshard) *towards rr but in tch: hdwy 3f out: drvn to chse ldrs 2f out: rdn to ld wl over 1f out: styd on wl u.p clsng stages* **10/1**
-552 **2** *1* **Saint Boniface**[13] 5667 4-9-7 **52**...................................... SebSanders 5 56
(Peter Makin) *plld hrd in rr: drvn and hdwy to chse ldrs 2f out: chal u.p between horses 1f out: sn chsng wnr: kpt on but a hld* **2/1**[1]
2140 **3** *1 1/2* **Devon Diva**[20] 5429 7-8-12 **48**.......................... MichaelJMMurphy(5) 1 49
(John Gallagher) *chsd ldrs: wnt 2nd over 4f out: rdn 3f out: chal u.p 2f out: stl ev ch 1f out: one pce into 3rd fnl 110yds* **11/4**[2]
526 **4** *1/2* **Omega Omega**[28] 5123 4-9-0 **45**..............................(b) AdamBeschizza 3 45
(Julia Feilden) *stdd in rr but in tch: drvn and hdwy 2f out: styd on u.p fnl f but no imp on ldng trio clsng stages* **20/1**
4336 **5** *2* **Another Squeeze**[6] 5934 5-9-5 **50**..........................(p) CathyGannon 4 47
(Peter Hiatt) *led: rdn and hrd pressed fr over 2f out: hdd wl over 1f out: wknd fnl 120yds* **3/1**[3]
6/00 **6** *13* **Appyjack**[27] 5171 5-9-5 **50**.. GrahamLee 7 22
(Tony Carroll) *chsd ldr tl over 4f out: styd pressing for 2nd: rdn over 3f out: wknd ins fnl 2f* **8/1**

2m 11.1s (0.10) **Going Correction** -0.30s/f (Firm) 6 Ran SP% **110.0**
Speed ratings (Par 101): **87,86,85,84,83 72**
toteswingers 1&2 £3.20, 1&3 £6.30, 2&3 £1.80 CSF £29.21 TOTE £13.80: £5.40, £2.00; EX 28.80 Trifecta £131.80 Pool: £1784.52 - 10.15 winning units..
Owner N C D Hall **Bred** J And Mrs Bowtell **Trained** Upper Lambourn, Berks
FOCUS
A weak handicap run in a slow time. The winner is rated to form.

6098 BBC RADIO SOMERSET FILLIES' H'CAP 1m 2f 46y
3:30 (3:30) (Class 5) (0-75,75) 3-Y-0+ **£2,587** (£770; £384; £192) **Stalls** Low

Form RPR
4316 **1** **Familliarity**[35] 4898 3-9-5 **74**.. DaneO'Neill 1 85
(Roger Varian) *mde all: drvn over 2f out: styd on wl thrght fnl f* **5/2**[2]
51 **2** *1 3/4* **Quantify (USA)**[30] 5071 3-9-5 **74**.............................. KirstyMilczarek 4 82
(Luca Cumani) *chsd wnr thrght: rdn to chal 2f out: no ex u.p fnl f* **9/2**[3]
4-41 **3** *1 3/4* **Lyric Piece**[9] 5835 3-9-6 **75** 6ex..................................(p) MartinHarley 2 79
(Sir Mark Prescott Bt) *racd in 3rd thrght: rdn over 3f out: effrt to cl on ldrs u.p over 1f out: nvr on terms and styd on same pce* **5/6**[1]
6203 **4** *4 1/2* **Dama De La Noche (IRE)**[40] 4715 3-8-7 **62**.................. KieranO'Neill 3 58
(Richard Hannon) *a in last pl: rdn and no imp 3f out: wknd 2f out* **12/1**

2m 7.23s (-3.77) **Going Correction** -0.30s/f (Firm) 4 Ran SP% **109.0**
Speed ratings (Par 100): **103,101,100,96**
CSF £12.71 TOTE £3.10; EX 14.40 Trifecta £13.10 Pool: £1429.47 - 81.61 winning units..

The Form Book Flat, Raceform Ltd, Compton, RG20 6NL.

Owner Helena Springfield Ltd **Bred** Meon Valley Stud **Trained** Newmarket, Suffolk
FOCUS
An ordinary fillies' handicap in which the order barely changed. The time was almost four seconds quicker than the previous race. A chance has been taken that the form is ok.

6099 BATH CHRONICLE H'CAP 1m 5f 22y
4:00 (4:00) (Class 6) (0-60,56) 4-Y-O+ **£1,940** (£577; £288; £144) **Stalls** High

Form RPR
3061 **1** **Vertueux (FR)**[9] 5846 8-9-13 **56** 6ex....(p) LiamKeniry 1 62
(Tony Carroll) *sn led: jnd 7f out: hrd pressed and u.p fr 2f out tl hdd 1f out: rallied to ld again fnl 100yds: kpt on wl* **5/2**[2]
0636 **2** *hd* **Walter De La Mare (IRE)**[4] 5979 6-9-4 **47**.... MartinHarley 3 53
(Anabel K Murphy) *racd in 4th but wl in tch: hdwy on outside fr 2f out: led u.p 1f out: hdd and no ex fnl 100yds* **9/2**
4253 **3** *3 ¾* **Glens Wobbly**[20] 5433 5-9-2 **45**.... FergusSweeney 2 45
(Jonathan Geake) *trckd ldr: pressed wnr fr 7f out: chal u.p 2f out: wknd appr fnl f* **6/4**[1]
/556 **4** *8* **Fair Breeze**[22] 3473 6-9-2 **45**....(t) GrahamLee 4 33
(Richard Phillips) *chsd ldrs in 3rd: rdn over 3f out: wknd wl over 2f out* **7/2**[3]
2m 51.95s (-0.05) **Going Correction** -0.30s/f (Firm) 4 Ran SP% **109.0**
Speed ratings (Par 101): **88,87,85,80**
CSF £12.71 TOTE £1.90; EX 9.90 Trifecta £18.80 Pool: £1187.18 - 47.25 winning units..
Owner John Rutter **Bred** Roger Baudouin **Trained** Cropthorne, Worcs
FOCUS
A poor contest and shaky form. The winner's best figure on turf for two years.

6100 BATH MAGAZINE H'CAP 5f 11y
4:30 (4:31) (Class 5) (0-70,69) 3-Y-O **£2,587** (£770; £384; £192) **Stalls** Centre

Form RPR
41 **1** **Emjayem**[23] 5345 3-9-2 **69**.... GrahamLee 4 76+
(Ed McMahon) *mde all: drvn and qcknd fnl f: readily* **13/8**[2]
6253 **2** *1* **Hot Secret**[10] 5796 3-8-13 **69**.... ThomasBrown(3) 1 72
(Andrew Balding) *trckd ldrs on rails in cl 3rd: a little tight for room whn rdn jst ins fnl f but sn chsng wnr and no imp: hld on wl for 2nd* **5/4**[1]
1333 **3** *hd* **Truly Madly (IRE)**[7] 5896 3-9-2 **69**.... JohnFahy 2 71
(Hans Adielsson) *in cl 4th: drvn and hdwy to cl 2f out: disp 2nd ins fnl f but no imp on wnr and kpt on same pce clsng stages* **9/2**[3]
1450 **4** *5* **Ada Lovelace**[30] 5060 3-8-11 **69**.... PhilipPrince(5) 3 53
(Dean Ivory) *chsd wnr: drvn to chal 2f out: sn outpcd: wknd into 4th jst ins fnl f* **12/1**
1m 1.03s (-1.47) **Going Correction** -0.30s/f (Firm) 4 Ran SP% **108.4**
Speed ratings (Par 101): **99,97,97,89**
CSF £4.04 TOTE £2.00; EX 3.80 Trifecta £4.40 Pool: £1797.36 - 305.09 winning units..
Owner Mrs J McMahon **Bred** Mrs J McMahon **Trained** Lichfield, Staffs
FOCUS
A handicap in name only as all four runners had the same mark of 69. The second and third are rated to form.

6101 BATH PUB COMPANY APPRENTICE TRAINING SERIES H'CAP (PART OF THE RACING EXCELLENCE INITIATIVE) 5f 161y
5:00 (5:00) (Class 6) (0-55,51) 4-Y-O+ **£1,940** (£577; £288; £144) **Stalls** Centre

Form RPR
2223 **1** **Chester'Slittlegem (IRE)**[3] 6017 4-8-8 **49**.... JosephineGordon(7) 4 56
(Jo Hughes) *chsd ldr over 3f out: pushed along to ld over 1f out: sn hrd pressed and jnd fnl 120yds: fnd ex last strides* **2/1**[1]
4405 **2** *shd* **Ridgeway Sapphire**[15] 5602 6-8-11 **45**....(v) DanielMuscutt 6 52
(Mark Usher) *in tch: hdwy 2f out: chal ins fnl f and upsides fnl 120yds: no ex last strides* **10/1**
6640 **3** *1 ½* **Brandywell Boy (IRE)**[4] 5982 10-8-11 **45**....(b) JoshBaudains 7 47
(Dominic Ffrench Davis) *led: drvn 3 l clr over 3f out: hdd over 1f out: one pce fnl 110yds* **14/1**
5003 **4** *nk* **The Name Is Frank**[9] 5817 8-9-2 **50**....(t) ShelleyBirkett 2 51
(Mark Gillard) *chsd ldrs: drvn 3f out: styd on fnl f: nvr quite gng pce to rch ldrs* **8/1**
0353 **5** *¾* **Chester Deelyte (IRE)**[9] 5818 5-8-12 **46**....(v) EoinWalsh 3 44
(Lisa Williamson) *early spd: sn outpcd and rdn: styd on appr fnl f: r.o clsng stages* **5/1**[3]
051 **6** *2 ¾* **All Right Now**[9] 5817 6-9-3 **51** 6ex....(p) OisinMurphy 5 40
(Tony Newcombe) *chsd ldrs: rdn over 2f out: sn btn* **9/4**[2]
000- **7** *20* **My Best Man**[532] 986 7-8-9 **48**.... AidenBlakemore(5) 1
(Tony Carroll) *v.s.a and lost all ch* **20/1**
1m 10.63s (-0.57) **Going Correction** -0.30s/f (Firm) 7 Ran SP% **112.4**
Speed ratings (Par 101): **91,90,88,88,87 83,57**
toteswingers 1&2 £4.00, 1&3 £5.40, 2&3 £13.60 CSF £21.67 TOTE £2.50: £1.50, £4.60; EX 15.70 Trifecta £256.80 Pool: £2016.05 - 5.88 winning units..
Owner Chester Racing Club Ltd **Bred** Pat Todd **Trained** Lambourn, Berks
FOCUS
A poor apprentice handicap with the top weight rated 51 including a penalty. The winner only needed to run to last week's form.
T/Plt: £431.00 to a £1 stake. Pool: £48,535.07 - 82.19 winning units T/Qpdt: £51.00 to a £1 stake. Pool: £2915.89 - 42.29 winning units ST

5922 KEMPTON (A.W) (R-H)
Wednesday, September 4

OFFICIAL GOING: Standard
Wind: Moderate, across (away from stands), races 1-5. Almost nil, remainder
Weather: Sunny, very warm

6102 BOOK NOW FOR JUMP SUNDAY 20.10.13 CLASSIFIED STKS (DIV I) 1m 2f (P)
5:30 (5:30) (Class 6) 3-Y-O+ **£1,940** (£577; £288; £144) **Stalls** Low

Form RPR
-310 **1** **Jamaica Grande**[40] 4718 5-9-4 53.... WilliamCarson 9 59
(Dave Morris) *slowly away: hld up in last: prog over 3f out: rdn over 2f out: clsd on ldrs over 1f out: styd on to ld last 75yds* **16/1**
0002 **2** *¾* **Nepalese Pearl**[6] 5935 3-8-11 50.... RobertHavlin 2 58
(Pat Eddery) *led: kicked on 3f out: hrd pressed jst over 1f out: kpt on wl but hdd last 75yds* **5/1**[2]
0503 **3** *¾* **Princess Spirit**[28] 5135 4-8-11 50....(p) JenniferFerguson(7) 5 56
(Edward Creighton) *awkward s: sn wl in tch: prog 3f out: chsd ldr 2f out: clsd to chal 1f out: nt qckn and sn lost 2nd* **5/1**[2]
0-05 **4** *nk* **Ryedale Lass**[18] 5528 5-9-4 53.... HayleyTurner 4 55
(Geoffrey Deacon) *trckd ldrs: sltly outpcd over 2f out and pushed along: clsd over 1f out but hanging and nt qckn: kpt on* **4/1**[1]
0053 **5** *6* **Goldie Horn**[5] 5967 5-9-1 53....(t) WilliamTwiston-Davies(3) 1 43
(Nigel Twiston-Davies) *trckd ldng pair: rdn to chse ldr over 3f out to 2f out: wknd rapidly* **5/1**[2]
05 **6** *1 ¼* **Culture Trip**[28] 5126 3-8-11 45....(v) AndreaAtzeni 7 41
(Gary Moore) *hld up towards rr: outpcd and rdn fr 3f out: nvr on terms after* **7/1**[3]
3133 **7** *hd* **Supa Seeker (USA)**[27] 5172 7-8-13 52.... GeorgeDowning(5) 8 41
(Tony Carroll) *a towards rr: struggling 3f out: nvr on terms after* **4/1**[1]
100/ **8** *17* **Mister Fantastic**[644] 7370 7-9-4 50.... SamHitchcott 3 7
(Dai Burchell) *chsd ldr to over 3f out: wknd rapidly: t.o* **25/1**
0500 **9** *nk* **Mr Mallo**[15] 5615 4-9-4 35.... ShaneKelly 6 6
(John Stimpson) *t.k.h early: trckd ldrs 4f: sn lost pl and u.p: t.o* **33/1**
2m 8.06s (0.06) **Going Correction** +0.025s/f (Slow)
WFA 3 from 4yo+ 7lb 9 Ran SP% **115.2**
Speed ratings (Par 101): **100,99,98,98,93 92,92,79,78**
toteswingers 1&2 £8.30, 1&3 £17.60, 2&3 £5.00 CSF £93.69 TOTE £25.10: £5.00, £2.60, £1.60; EX 116.50 Trifecta £744.00 Pool: £1664.45 - 1.67 winning units..
Owner Stuart Wood **Bred** Mrs J A Gawthorpe **Trained** Baxter's Green, Suffolk
FOCUS
An open race, with 3lb covering all but two of the runners.

6103 BOOK NOW FOR JUMP SUNDAY 20.10.13 CLASSIFIED STKS (DIV II) 1m 2f (P)
6:00 (6:00) (Class 6) 3-Y-O+ **£1,940** (£577; £288; £144) **Stalls** Low

Form RPR
0532 **1** **Sudden Wish (IRE)**[29] 5092 4-9-4 55.... RyanMoore 8 55
(Gary Moore) *trapped out wd early: chsd ldrs in 5th after 3f: rdn to go 3rd over 2f out: chsd ldr 1f out: styd on to ld last 120yds* **5/4**[1]
0600 **2** *1* **Pink Mischief**[21] 5404 3-8-11 47.... RichardHughes 7 53
(Harry Dunlop) *stdd s: hld up and last early: rapid prog on wd outside fr 3f out: chsd ldng trio wl over 1f out but hanging rt: styd on ins fnl f to take 2nd last stride* **16/1**
6522 **3** *shd* **Tatting**[16] 5596 4-9-4 55.... LukeMorris 3 53
(Chris Dwyer) *prom: trckd ldr over 3f out and gng best: rdn to ld over 1f out: hung rt and idled sn after: hdd last 120yds: hung lft after: lost 2nd post* **2/1**[2]
4645 **4** *1 ¼* **Aphrodite Spirit (IRE)**[6] 5934 3-8-11 45.... LiamJones 6 50
(Pat Eddery) *led after 1f: rdn over 2f out: hdd over 1f out: hld whn sltly checked sn after: one pce* **10/1**[3]
0306 **5** *8* **Planchette**[41] 4688 3-8-4 42.... IanBurns(7) 1 34
(Jane Chapple-Hyam) *trckd ldrs tl wknd qckly over 2f out* **33/1**
1600 **6** *8* **Poetry Writer**[64] 3919 4-9-4 53....(p) NeilCallan 9 18
(Michael Blanshard) *in tch in rr: rdn over 2f out: sn wknd and wl bhd* **10/1**[3]
040- **7** *1* **Polydamos**[326] 4214 4-9-4 54.... JimmyQuinn 4 16
(Tony Carroll) *sn towards rr: rdn and wknd over 2f out: sn wl bhd* **16/1**
00-6 **8** *5* **Kapunda**[28] 5127 5-9-4 41.... SamHitchcott 2 6
(Sean Curran) *led 1f: chsd ldr to over 3f out: wknd rapidly: t.o* **25/1**
0400 **9** *7* **One Dark Night**[28] 5127 3-8-11 40.... AndreaAtzeni 5
(Gary Moore) *a in rr: wknd rapidly over 2f out: t.o* **50/1**
2m 7.11s (-0.89) **Going Correction** +0.025s/f (Slow)
WFA 3 from 4yo+ 7lb 9 Ran SP% **116.5**
Speed ratings (Par 101): **104,103,103,102,95 89,88,84,78**
toteswingers 1&2 £4.90, 1&3 £1.50, 2&3 £4.70 CSF £23.95 TOTE £2.40: £1.10, £2.80, £1.30; EX 19.00 Trifecta £42.30 Pool: £2025.46 - 35.88 winning units..
Owner M&R Refurbishments Ltd **Bred** Catridge Farm Stud & S Von Schilcher **Trained** Lower Beeding, W Sussex
■ Stewards' Enquiry : Luke Morris two-day ban: careless riding (Sep 18-19)
FOCUS
This was nowhere near as competitive as the first division, but it was the quicker of the two races by 0.95sec.

6104 WINNERS ARE WELCOME AT BETDAQ NURSERY H'CAP 5f (P)
6:30 (6:31) (Class 5) (0-75,75) 2-Y-O **£2,587** (£770; £384; £192) **Stalls** Low

Form RPR
654 **1** **Aspirant**[47] 4477 2-8-11 **65**.... RichardHughes 5 68+
(Roger Charlton) *racd three off the rail bnd after 1f: reminder wl over 2f out in 3rd and racd awkwardly: rdn over 1f out and hd in the air: r.o properly fnl f to ld last strides* **5/4**[1]
1024 **2** *nk* **Weisse Socken (IRE)**[18] 5509 2-9-4 **72**....(p) JimCrowley 3 74
(Ralph Beckett) *pressed ldr: rdn to chal over 1f out: led jst ins fnl f: hdd and no ex last strides* **11/4**[2]
0311 **3** *½* **Fine Art Fair (IRE)**[16] 5595 2-9-4 **72**.... RyanMoore 6 72
(Gary Moore) *trapped out v wd bnd after 1f and sn struggling in 4th: drvn over 1f out: r.o wl fnl f: gaining at fin* **11/4**[2]
3033 **4** *2* **Debt Settler (IRE)**[16] 5595 2-8-3 **57**.... JimmyQuinn 2 50
(Luke Dace) *pushed up to ld: drvn over 1f out: hdd jst ins fnl f: fdd* **10/1**[3]
430 **5** *23* **Boston Alex (IRE)**[32] 5000 2-8-8 **62**.... HayleyTurner 1
(Conor Dore) *stdd s: sn outpcd and t.o* **25/1**
1m 1.01s (0.51) **Going Correction** +0.025s/f (Slow) 5 Ran SP% **110.7**
Speed ratings (Par 95): **96,95,94,91,54**
CSF £5.02 TOTE £1.90: £1.10, £2.90; EX 5.00 Trifecta £13.80 Pool: £1870.65 - 101.63 winning units..
Owner K Abdullah **Bred** Juddmonte Farms Ltd **Trained** Beckhampton, Wilts
FOCUS
The early pace was hot and there were four in line as they headed to the turn.

6105 LADIES DAY WITH TOBY ANSTIS 07.09.13 CLASSIFIED CLAIMING STKS 1m (P)
7:00 (7:00) (Class 6) 3-Y-O+ **£1,940** (£577; £288; £144) **Stalls** Low

Form RPR
4244 **1** **Four Winds**[28] 5153 7-8-6 66....(v[1]) LiamJones 7 83
(Robert Cowell) *pressed ldr at str pce: led over 3f out: clr whn hung lft bnd sn after: continued to hang lft and ended against nr side rail: kpt on wl: unchal* **2/1**[1]
0-55 **2** *3* **Checkpoint**[77] 3468 4-8-6 67....(p) SamHitchcott 4 76
(Gary Moore) *taken down early: s.i.s: wl off the pce in last pair: rdn and prog over 2f out: chsd wnr wl over 1f out: kpt on but nvr able to threaten* **4/1**[3]
0066 **3** *4 ½* **Warbond**[27] 5170 5-8-6 57....(p) LukeMorris 5 65
(Michael Madgwick) *sn off the pce in 5th: rdn over 2f out: prog to dispute 2nd wl over 1f out: one pce after* **8/1**

0453 **4** *6* **Shaunas Spirit (IRE)**[146] 1503 5-9-3 67 PaulBooth(7) 8 69
(Dean Ivory) *hld up bhd ldng pair: chsd clr wnr jst over 2f out to wl over 1f out: wknd* **10/1**

0-34 **5** *3 1/4* **Three Crowns**[27] 5173 3-8-9 68 WilliamCarson 3 50
(Jonathan Portman) *s.i.s: wl off the pce in last pair: rdn over 2f out: no real prog* **16/1**

0020 **6** *1* **Blue Deer (IRE)**[26] 5234 5-8-6 52 (p) KierenFox 2 40
(Lee Carter) *chsd ldng trio but nt on terms: shoved along bef 1/2-way: struggling after* **20/1**

410 **7** *8* **Beauchamp Xerxes**[65] 3889 7-8-1 68 (t) RyanTate(5) 1 21
(Hans Adielsson) *led at decent pce but pressed: hdd over 3f out and no rspnse: lost 2nd jst over 2f out and wknd* **5/2**[2]

1m 38.65s (-1.15) **Going Correction** +0.025s/f (Slow)
WFA 3 from 4yo+ 5lb 7 Ran SP% **112.8**
Speed ratings (Par 101): **106,103,98,92,89 88,80**
toteswingers 1&2 £2.60, 1&3 £3.70, 2&3 £5.90 CSF £10.06 TOTE £2.90: £1.90, £2.30; EX 10.00 Trifecta £54.70 Pool: £1485.23 - 20.33 winning units..

Owner T W Morley **Bred** The Queen **Trained** Six Mile Bottom, Cambs

FOCUS
A modest race featuring several with question marks next to their names.

6106 COMMISSION FREE 1ST MONTH AT BETDAQ H'CAP 1m (P)
7:30 (7:30) (Class 5) (0-75,74) 3-Y-O **£2,587** (£770; £384; £192) **Stalls** Low

Form RPR

304 **1** **For Posterity**[12] 5720 3-9-4 71 MickaelBarzalona 8 80+
(Charlie Appleby) *trckd ldr: rdn whn pce lifted over 2f out: clsng whn impeded wl over 1f out: drvn to ld last 150yds: styd on wl* **10/3**[2]

1 **2** *1 1/4* **Araqella (IRE)**[15] 5618 3-9-2 69 RyanMoore 9 75+
(William Haggas) *chsd ldrs and sn in 4th: rdn over 2f out whn pce lifted: swtchd rt wl over 1f out and sn chsd ldng pair: styd on to take 2nd nr fin: no threat to wnr* **5/1**[3]

150- **3** *1/2* **Zain Spirit (USA)**[308] 7478 3-9-3 70 (p) NeilCallan 7 75
(Gerard Butler) *led at mod pce: kicked on wl over 2f out: edgd lft wl over 1f out: hdd and one pce last 150yds: lost 2nd nr fin* **16/1**

4103 **4** *nk* **Moma Lee**[21] 5395 3-9-4 71 WilliamBuick 5 75
(John Gosden) *trckd ldng pair: rdn over 2f out whn pce lifted: lost 3rd over 1f out: kpt on but unable to chal* **10/1**

0301 **5** *1* **Gone Dutch**[21] 5395 3-9-6 73 FrederikTylicki 6 75+
(James Fanshawe) *hld up in 6th in steadily run event: rdn over 2f out: tried to cl fr over 1f out: kpt on but ldrs nt stopping* **7/4**[1]

0560 **6** *3* **The Gatling Boy (IRE)**[21] 5401 3-9-7 74 RichardHughes 3 69
(Richard Hannon) *awkward s: t.k.h and hld up in last: rdn over 2f out and racd v awkwardly: drvn and passed 2 toiling rivals over 1f out* **8/1**

4004 **7** *2 1/4* **Perfect Haven**[19] 5493 3-9-5 72 JimCrowley 1 61
(Ralph Beckett) *hld up in 7th in steadily run event: outpcd and shkn up over 2f out: nvr on terms after* **9/1**

05-5 **8** *3 1/4* **Tigerish**[135] 1729 3-8-13 66 PatDobbs 4 47
(Amanda Perrett) *t.k.h: hld up and sn in 5th: outpcd over 2f out: wknd over 1f out* **50/1**

1m 40.38s (0.58) **Going Correction** +0.025s/f (Slow) 8 Ran SP% **114.2**
Speed ratings (Par 101): **98,96,96,95,94 91,89,86**
toteswingers 1&2 £3.80, 1&3 £7.50, 2&3 £12.20 CSF £20.31 CT £201.29 TOTE £4.40: £1.50, £1.60, £7.10; EX 20.00 Trifecta £181.20 Pool: £1225.91 - 5.07 winning units..

Owner Godolphin **Bred** New England, Myriad & Mount Coote **Trained** Newmarket, Suffolk

■ Stewards' Enquiry : Neil Callan two-day ban: careless riding (Sep 18-19)

FOCUS
An interesting handicap, but the early pace was steady and it paid to race prominently.

6107 £200 FREE BETS AT BETDAQ/BRITISH STALLION STUDS EBF MAIDEN FILLIES' STKS 6f (P)
8:00 (8:02) (Class 5) 2-Y-O **£2,911** (£866; £432; £216) **Stalls** Low

Form RPR

32 **1** **Perfect Alchemy (IRE)**[20] 5435 2-9-0 0 JimCrowley 6 71+
(Ralph Beckett) *trckd ldrs: shkn up over 2f out: clsd over 1f out: drvn to ld last 150yds: styd on* **6/4**[1]

2 *1/2* **Acclio (IRE)** 2-9-0 0 LukeMorris 5 69
(Clive Brittain) *hld up in midfield on inner: prog 2f out: tried to chal 1f out: styd on wl but hld last 75yds* **40/1**

6 **3** *1/2* **Pretty Flemingo (IRE)**[18] 5529 2-9-0 0 RichardHughes 2 68
(Richard Hannon) *trckd ldng pair: clsd to ld over 1f out: rdn and hdd last 150yds: kpt on same pce* **5/2**[2]

6 **4** *1* **Miss Buckshot (IRE)**[34] 4924 2-9-0 0 ChrisCatlin 3 65+
(Rae Guest) *v awkward s: settled in last trio: pushed along jst over 2f out: styd on wl fnl 2f to take 4th ins fnl f* **50/1**

5 *nk* **Pageant Belle** 2-9-0 0 RyanMoore 10 64+
(Roger Charlton) *racd on outer in last trio: pushed along over 2f out: styd on steadily fr over 1f out: nt disgracd* **8/1**

5 **6** *3/4* **Clapperboard**[27] 5174 2-9-0 0 RichardKingscote 7 61
(Paul Fitzsimons) *t.k.h early: trckd ldrs on outer: pushed along 2f out: kpt on one pce after* **100/1**

0 **7** *1* **Prim And Proper**[18] 5529 2-9-0 0 KierenFallon 11 58
(Brendan Powell) *trckd ldr to 2f out: steadily lost pl: nt knocked abt* **33/1**

6 **8** *1* **Artemis (IRE)**[15] 5609 2-9-0 0 (t) AndreaAtzeni 8 55
(Conrad Allen) *a in midfield: pushed along 2f out: no imp on ldrs 1f out: eased last 75yds* **33/1**

0 **9** *1* **Sweet Amaalie (IRE)**[47] 4484 2-9-0 0 LiamJones 4 52
(William Haggas) *towards rr: shkn up over 2f out: one pce and no imp on ldrs over 1f out* **20/1**

10 *2 1/4* **Rose Buck** 2-9-0 0 TomQueally 1 44
(Paul Cole) *dwlt: rn green in last trio: reminder and detached in last over 1f out: styd on fnl 150yds* **16/1**

3 **11** *1/2* **Qatar Princess (IRE)**[23] 5344 2-9-0 0 HarryBentley 9 43
(Olly Stevens) *racd freely: led but at mod pce: hdd over 1f out: wknd qckly fnl f* **5/1**[3]

1m 14.89s (1.79) **Going Correction** +0.025s/f (Slow) 11 Ran SP% **118.3**
Speed ratings (Par 92): **89,88,87,86,85 84,83,82,80,77 77**
toteswingers 1&2 £9.10, 1&3 £1.40, 2&3 £21.20 CSF £84.27 TOTE £2.40: £1.10, £8.90, £1.50; EX 44.10 Trifecta £169.60 Pool: £1848.44 - 8.17 winning units..

Owner The Perfect Partnership & D H Caslon **Bred** W Maxwell Ervine **Trained** Kimpton, Hants

FOCUS
Once again the pace was fairly steady early and it developed into a dash in the straight.

6108 BETDAQ 1ST UK RACE COMMISSION FREE H'CAP 1m 4f (P)
8:30 (8:31) (Class 4) (0-85,82) 3-Y-O+ **£4,690** (£1,395; £697; £348) **Stalls** Centre

Form RPR

0460 **1** **Aegaeus**[12] 5712 4-9-12 82 RyanMoore 1 95
(Ed Dunlop) *mde all: allowed to dictate mod pce: stretched on over 2f out: sn clr: drvn out: unchal* **10/1**

2136 **2** *4* **Burnham**[18] 5513 4-9-9 79 (p) RichardHughes 9 86
(Hughie Morrison) *racd on outer: wl in tch: outpcd and rdn over 2f out: styd on to take 2nd jst over 1f out: no ch w wnr* **14/1**

213 **3** *1 1/4* **Portmonarch (IRE)**[41] 4681 3-9-3 82 (p) TedDurcan 3 87
(David Lanigan) *trckd wnr: drvn wl over 2f out: sn outpcd: kpt on to hold on to 2nd tl jst over 1f out: one pce* **7/2**[1]

35-5 **4** *3/4* **Infinite Hope (USA)**[20] 5445 4-9-8 78 KirstyMilczarek 2 81
(Luca Cumani) *trckd wnr: rdn and outpcd over 2f out: no imp after: fdd fnl f* **7/1**[3]

-016 **5** *nk* **Ikhtisas (USA)**[27] 5189 3-8-12 77 SilvestreDeSousa 6 80
(Saeed bin Suroor) *wl in tch: trckd ldng trio 1/2-way: outpcd over 2f out: one pce after* **7/2**[1]

6042 **6** *1 3/4* **Takeitfromalady (IRE)**[28] 5129 4-9-10 80 (v) KierenFox 8 80
(Lee Carter) *hld up and mostly in last trio: no ch once wnr had gone for home over 2f out: drvn and kpt on fnl f* **12/1**

0251 **7** *nk* **Royal Dutch**[18] 5542 4-9-6 76 PatCosgrave 4 76
(Denis Coakley) *cl up 2f: sn hld up: dropped to last trio 4f out: tried to make prog 3f out: no imp on ldrs over 1f out* **10/1**

543 **8** *1/2* **Layline (IRE)**[28] 5129 6-9-7 77 LukeMorris 7 76
(Gay Kelleway) *awkward s: sn in midfield: rdn and outpcd over 2f out: no prog after* **25/1**

454 **9** *2* **Mutanaweb (IRE)**[19] 5484 3-8-13 78 PaulHanagan 10 74
(John Gosden) *dwlt: racd wd thrght: in rr: rdn over 3f out: sn struggling* **9/2**[2]

6425 **10** *1 1/4* **Tingo In The Tale (IRE)**[26] 5231 4-9-1 71 LiamKeniry 11 65
(David Arbuthnot) *hld up in last trio: no ch once wnr had kicked on over 2f out: no prog* **16/1**

1150 **11** *6* **Standpoint**[28] 5129 7-9-7 77 HayleyTurner 5 61
(Conor Dore) *stdd s: hld up in last: pushed along and detached fnl 2f* **33/1**

2m 33.94s (-0.56) **Going Correction** +0.025s/f (Slow)
WFA 3 from 4yo+ 9lb 11 Ran SP% **120.3**
Speed ratings (Par 105): **102,99,98,98,97 96,96,96,94,93 89**
toteswingers 1&2 £22.20, 1&3 £15.40, 2&3 £9.80 CSF £144.61 CT £595.06 TOTE £10.90: £3.80, £3.60, £1.50; EX 163.80 Trifecta £931.40 Pool: £1241.91 - 0.50 winning units..

Owner Lord Derby **Bred** Stanley Estate And Stud Co **Trained** Newmarket, Suffolk

6109 BOOK NOW FOR LADIES DAY 07.09.13 H'CAP 1m 3f (P)
9:00 (9:01) (Class 6) (0-65,65) 3-Y-O **£1,940** (£577; £288; £144) **Stalls** Low

Form RPR

3324 **1** **Runninglikethewind (IRE)**[15] 5606 3-9-6 64 GeorgeBaker 10 73
(Chris Wall) *led after 1f: mde rest: gng strly over 2f out: drew 2 l clr over 1f out: hung lft ins fnl f: styd on* **7/2**[2]

6055 **2** *1 1/4* **Lybica (IRE)**[35] 4898 3-9-6 64 RyanMoore 6 71+
(Gary Moore) *trckd ldrs: rdn over 2f out: prog to go 2nd 1f out: kpt on but nvr able to chal* **5/4**[1]

500 **3** *1 1/4* **Calon Lad (IRE)**[30] 5064 3-9-6 64 PatCosgrave 12 69+
(George Baker) *hld up in last trio: drvn over 2f out and no prog: hdwy over 1f out: r.o to take 3rd nr fin* **20/1**

0503 **4** *3/4* **Hero's Story**[11] 5762 3-9-2 60 (p) PatDobbs 1 63
(Amanda Perrett) *wl in tch: shkn up over 2f out: chsd ldrs over 1f out but no imp: styd on ins fnl f* **16/1**

5515 **5** *1/2* **Diletta Tommasa (IRE)**[27] 5204 3-9-5 63 AndreaAtzeni 8 65
(John Stimpson) *hld up bhd ldrs: prog to go 2nd over 4f out and tried to chal: hld fr 2f out: lost 2nd 1f out and fdd* **20/1**

2126 **6** *3/4* **Bertie Moon**[21] 5387 3-9-6 64 HayleyTurner 5 65
(Geoffrey Deacon) *led 1f: chsd wnr to 5f out: styd prom: rdn and pressed for a pl over 1f out: fdd fnl f* **16/1**

0006 **7** *hd* **El Massivo (IRE)**[10] 5802 3-9-4 62 JimmyQuinn 11 63
(William Jarvis) *hld up in rr: tried for a run up inner 2f out and n.m.r briefly: one pce after* **14/1**

126 **8** *1/2* **Alpine Mysteries (IRE)**[44] 4584 3-9-3 64 ThomasBrown(3) 7 64
(Harry Dunlop) *trckd ldrs: wnt 2nd briefly 5f out: nt qckn over 2f out: steadily fdd* **6/1**[3]

6401 **9** *1 1/4* **Jacobella**[27] 5178 3-9-4 65 MatthewLawson(3) 9 62
(Jonathan Portman) *dwlt: last early: sme prog 7f out but stl in rr: rdn on outer over 2f out: no great prog* **20/1**

4360 **10** *shd* **Perpetual Ambition**[27] 5204 3-9-5 63 (p) FrederikTylicki 4 60
(Paul D'Arcy) *hld up towards rr: no prog over 2f out: sme hdwy over 1f out but no ch: fdd nr fin* **33/1**

000 **11** *2* **Capetown Kid**[44] 4590 3-9-3 61 LiamKeniry 3 55
(Sylvester Kirk) *trckd ldrs: edgd rt and struggling 2f out: wknd* **33/1**

003 **12** *11* **Minimee**[57] 4143 3-9-7 65 LukeMorris 2 39
(Phil McEntee) *n.m.r sn after s and dropped to last trio: wknd over 2f out: t.o* **33/1**

2m 21.38s (-0.52) **Going Correction** +0.025s/f (Slow) 12 Ran SP% **122.5**
Speed ratings (Par 99): **102,101,100,99,99 98,98,98,97,97 95,87**
toteswingers 1&2 £2.60, 1&3 £15.90, 2&3 £8.80 CSF £7.65 CT £73.70 TOTE £5.60: £1.60, £1.20, £5.30; EX 13.80 Trifecta £166.20 Pool: £2110.03 - 9.50 winning units..

Owner Des Thurlby **Bred** Gerrardstown House Stud **Trained** Newmarket, Suffolk

FOCUS
The market only really wanted to know about two of these, and they filled the first two spots.

T/Plt: £43.10 to a £1 stake. Pool: £76,439.88 - 1291.91 winning units T/Qpdt: £17.70 to a £1 stake. Pool: £7935.66 - 330.29 winning units JN

6076 LINGFIELD (L-H)

Wednesday, September 4

OFFICIAL GOING: Turf course - good to firm (firm in places; 8.6); all-weather - standard

Wind: virtually nil Weather: warm and sunny

6110 AT THE RACES MAIDEN STKS 6f

2:20 (2:21) (Class 5) 2-Y-O **£2,726** (£805; £402) **Stalls** High

Form RPR

4 **1** **Outback Traveller (IRE)**[11] 5744 2-9-5 0 WilliamBuick 6 77
(Jeremy Noseda) *wnt rt s: crossed to r against stands' rail: mde all: rdn and styd on strly ins fnl f: readily* **7/4**[1]

2 **2** 1 1/2 **Travis Bickle (IRE)**[32] 5000 2-9-5 0 RichardHughes 12 72+
(Sylvester Kirk) *bustled along early: in tch in midfield: swtchd lft and trcking ldng pair over 1f out: kpt on u.p fnl f: wnt 2nd fnl 50yds: no threat to wnr* **2/1**[2]

3 1 **Almargo (IRE)** 2-9-5 0 MickaelBarzalona 8 69+
(Charlie Appleby) *hmpd s: bhd: wnt lft over 4f out: swtchd lft and hdwy furthest fr stands' rail over 2f out: chsd ldrs whn edgd rt and bmpd rival 1f out: sn chsng wnr: no ex and lost 2nd fnl 50yds: wknd towards fin* **7/1**[3]

4 1 **Bereka** 2-9-0 0 RyanMoore 3 61
(James Tate) *swtchd rt after s: pressing wnr: rdn wl over 1f out: rn green: edgd lft and bmpd rival 1f out: no ex and outpcd ins fnl f* **8/1**

45 **5** 4 **Drive On (IRE)**[34] 4912 2-9-5 0 JimmyFortune 7 53
(Eve Johnson Houghton) *in tch in midfield: effrt and squeezed between horses wl over 1f out: sn rdn and no ex ent fnl f: wknd ins fnl f* **50/1**

0 **6** 1/2 **Midnight Rambler (IRE)**[16] 5584 2-9-5 0 PatDobbs 11 51
(Richard Hannon) *sn outpcd in last trio: rdn 1/2-way: wl bhd over 2f out: styd on past btn horses fnl f: nvr trbld ldrs* **14/1**

7 1 3/4 **Torchlighter (IRE)** 2-9-5 0 JoeFanning 9 46
(Mark Johnston) *in tch in midfield: hdwy to chse ldrs 3f out: rdn and unable qck ent fnl 2f: wknd over 1f out* **14/1**

0 **8** 8 **Illegal Action (USA)**[21] 5399 2-9-5 0 (t) NeilCallan 2 20
(Olly Stevens) *chsd ldrs: rdn and lost pl over 2f out: bhd and eased ins fnl f* **25/1**

9 8 **Maymyo (IRE)** 2-9-5 0 LiamJones 5
(Sylvester Kirk) *s.i.s: rn green in rr: pushed lft over 4f out: wl bhd fr 1/2-way* **33/1**

1m 10.55s (-0.65) **Going Correction** -0.25s/f (Firm) 9 Ran SP% **115.4**
Speed ratings (Par 95): **94,92,90,89,84 83,81,70,59**
toteswingers 1&2 £1.60, 1&3 £3.10, 2&3 £3.10 CSF £5.30 TOTE £2.70: £1.80, £1.02, £2.50; EX 6.60 Trifecta £25.60 Pool: £3628.44 - 106.27 winning units..
Owner Saeed Suhail **Bred** Tally-Ho Stud **Trained** Newmarket, Suffolk

FOCUS
Stands' side rail of straight course moved in 3m. A warm day with ground conditions described as good to firm, firm in places. 3mm of water was applied to the last 5f on the eve of raceday. A 6f maiden for 2yos opened the four races run on the turf course.

6111 ANN PAGE NURSERY H'CAP 6f

2:50 (2:51) (Class 6) (0-65,65) 2-Y-O **£2,045** (£603; £302) **Stalls** High

Form RPR

3521 **1** **Dovil's Duel (IRE)**[15] 5610 2-9-7 **65** AndreaAtzeni 11 74
(Rod Millman) *travelled strly: chsd ldr tl rdn to ld over 1f out: clr and r.o strly ins fnl f: readily* **3/1**[1]

542 **2** 2 1/2 **Vallila**[11] 5757 2-8-9 **58** JoeyHaynes(5) 1 59+
(Roger Charlton) *hld up in midfield: pushed along and hdwy towards centre over 2f out: chsd ldrs and rdn over 1f out: chsd clr wnr ins fnl f: r.o wl but no imp* **16/1**

5360 **3** 3 **Touch Paper (IRE)**[12] 5699 2-9-5 **63** RichardHughes 12 54
(Richard Hannon) *led: rdn and hdd over 1f out: outpcd by wnr and btn 1f out: wknd ins fnl f* **8/1**

5414 **4** 2 3/4 **Oxlip**[15] 5610 2-8-13 **57** PatDobbs 6 40
(Richard Hannon) *hld up towards rr: rdn and hdwy over 1f out: wnt 4th ins fnl f: styd on but no ch w ldrs* **20/1**

3134 **5** 3 3/4 **Captain Ryan**[16] 5595 2-9-7 **65** SteveDrowne 10 36
(Peter Makin) *t.k.h: chsd ldrs: rdn and unable qck 2f out: outpcd and btn over 1f out: wknd fnl f* **16/1**

3306 **6** hd **Jersey Cream (IRE)**[14] 5634 2-9-5 **63** RyanMoore 4 33
(Gary Moore) *v.s.a: detached in last: styd on past btn horses ins fnl f: nvr trbld ldrs* **8/1**

6050 **7** 1 **Desert Colours**[15] 5610 2-9-2 **60** (b[1]) NeilCallan 13 27
(Kevin Ryan) *chsd ldrs: rdn over 2f out: drvn and outpcd over 1f out: sn wknd and wl btn fnl f* **8/1**

0525 **8** 1 1/4 **Vodka Chaser (IRE)**[26] 5363 2-9-7 **65** LiamJones 8 28
(J S Moore) *in tch in midfield: rdn and unable qck over 2f out: wknd u.p over 1f out* **25/1**

055 **9** 2 3/4 **Connaught Water (IRE)**[72] 3631 2-9-1 **59** RichardKingscote 14 13
(Jonathan Portman) *in tch in midfield: shuffled bk and in rr whn n.m.r over 2f out: rdn and no hdwy over 1f out: wl btn fnl f* **5/1**[2]

000 **10** 1/2 **Fiftyshadesfreed (IRE)**[19] 5473 2-9-6 **64** PatCosgrave 7 16
(George Baker) *s.i.s: hld up in rr of main gp: swtchd lft and nt clr run 2f out: wl hld whn swtchd lft ins fnl f: nvr trbld ldrs* **14/1**

2532 **11** 1 3/4 **Zafraaj**[9] 5814 2-9-7 **65** (p) LukeMorris 5 12
(Ronald Harris) *in tch towards rr: effrt u.p over 2f out: hrd drvn and wknd over 1f out: fdd ins fnl f* **20/1**

2534 **12** 3/4 **Queen Of The Tarts**[27] 5175 2-9-5 **63** MickaelBarzalona 9 7
(Olly Stevens) *in tch in midfield: rdn and lost pl over 2f out: bhd over 1f out* **6/1**[3]

5000 **13** 4 **Dawnfromthepast (IRE)**[30] 5066 2-8-1 **45** JimmyQuinn 2
(Luke Dace) *in tch: rdn and struggling over 2f out: wknd qckly over 1f out: wl bhd and eased ins fnl f* **50/1**

1m 10.52s (-0.68) **Going Correction** -0.25s/f (Firm) 13 Ran SP% **123.0**
Speed ratings (Par 93): **94,90,86,83,78 77,76,74,71,70 68,67,61**
toteswingers 1&2 £8.40, 1&3 £6.60, 2&3 £31.70 CSF £54.49 CT £375.63 TOTE £3.40: £1.20, £5.10, £3.40; EX 59.40 Trifecta £635.90 Pool: £2877.74 - 3.39 winning units..
Owner Always Hopeful Partnership **Bred** David Allan **Trained** Kentisbeare, Devon

FOCUS
A low-grade nursery, in which there was money for several of those drawn high.

6112 CELEBRATING 15 YEARS OF SKY SPORTS NEWS/EBF STALLIONS MAIDEN FILLIES STKS 7f

3:20 (3:20) (Class 5) 2-Y-O **£3,067** (£905; £453) **Stalls** High

Form RPR

5 **1** **Radiator**[34] 4921 2-9-0 0 RyanMoore 2 99+
(Sir Michael Stoute) *mde all and crossed to r against stands' rail: pushed wl clr over 1f out: r.o wl: unchal* **11/10**[1]

62 **2** 15 **Zawiyah**[23] 5344 2-9-0 0 KierenFallon 9 61
(Luca Cumani) *chsd ldrs: swtchd lft and wnt 3rd 3f out: rdn and unable qck: no ch w wnr fr over 1f out: wnt 2nd ins fnl f* **2/1**[2]

3 1/2 **Minnaloushe (IRE)** 2-9-0 0[1] WilliamBuick 5 57
(John Gosden) *s.i.s: bhd: pushed along and sme hdwy over 1f out: wnt between horses and styd on fnl f to press for 2nd cl home: no ch w wnr* **12/1**

0 **4** 1 **Kinloss**[18] 5529 2-9-0 0 RichardHughes 4 54
(Richard Hannon) *chsd ldng pair: rdn 1/2-way: 4th and wl btn over 1f out: plugged on same pce fnl f* **25/1**

0 **5** 1 1/2 **Pacquita**[30] 5053 2-9-0 0 JoeFanning 6 50
(Mark Johnston) *restless in stalls: chsd wnr: rdn: hung lft and btn over 1f out: wknd and lost 3 pls ins fnl f* **25/1**

00 **6** 1 3/4 **Trinity Lorraine (IRE)**[30] 5061 2-9-0 0 SamHitchcott 3 45
(Alan Bailey) *s.i.s: hld up wl off the pce in rr: no ch but rdn and sme hdwy over 1f out: no prog fnl f* **50/1**

0 **7** 1 1/2 **Step Away**[25] 5282 2-9-0 0 SteveDrowne 1 41
(Charles Hills) *wnt lft s: a bhd: n.d* **50/1**

8 hd **Arctic Moon (USA)** 2-9-0 0 MickaelBarzalona 8 41
(Charlie Appleby) *rn green: off the pce towards rr: swtchd lft and effrt towards centre 3f out: wknd wl over 1f out: wl bhd over 1f out* **5/1**[3]

5 **9** 2 1/4 **Dangerous Flower (USA)**[18] 5516 2-9-0 0 HarryBentley 7 35
(Mick Channon) *chsd ldrs: rdn and struggling 1/2-way: sn lost pl and wl bhd over 1f out* **33/1**

1m 21.56s (-1.74) **Going Correction** -0.25s/f (Firm) 9 Ran SP% **119.9**
Speed ratings (Par 95): **99,81,81,80,78 76,74,74,71**
toteswingers 1&2 £1.70, 1&3 £3.90, 2&3 £4.20 CSF £3.44 TOTE £1.70: £1.02, £1.10, £3.50; EX 2.80 Trifecta £27.70 Pool: £4338.64 - 117.43 winning units..
Owner K Abdullah **Bred** Juddmonte Farms Ltd **Trained** Newmarket, Suffolk

FOCUS
A pair of impeccably bred fillies with Group 1 entries headed the market for this fillies' maiden. The winner demolished these, admittedly with the heldp of the rail, and looks smart.

6113 GREYHOUND PUB LINGFIELD MEDIAN AUCTION MAIDEN STKS 7f

3:50 (3:50) (Class 6) 3-5-Y-O **£2,045** (£603; £302) **Stalls** High

Form RPR

6334 **1** **Poitin**[21] 5393 3-9-0 62[1] TomQueally 5 65
(Harry Dunlop) *trckd ldr: led over 1f out: shkn up and readily asserted ins fnl f: r.o: comf* **7/4**[1]

5306 **2** 4 1/2 **Moss Hill**[26] 5232 4-9-9 51 FrankieDettori 6 58
(Charles Hills) *awkward leaving stalls: led: rdn and hdd over 1f out: unable qck and brushed aside ins fnl f: plugged on to hold 2nd* **7/4**[1]

0 **3** nk **Tingle Tangle (USA)**[28] 5133 3-9-5 65 LukeMorris 7 57
(Tony Carroll) *chsd ldng pair: swtchd lft and drvn over 1f out: outpcd and btn 1f out: no ch w wnr but plugged on to press for 2nd cl home* **3/1**[2]

4 **4** 7 **Another Name (IRE)**[65] 3898 3-9-5 0 SilvestreDeSousa 2 38
(Paul Cole) *a same pl: rdn 1/2-way: drvn and struggling over 2f out: wknd over 1f out* **10/1**[3]

0 **5** 7 **Churt**[9] 5845 4-9-9 0 SaleemGolam 1 19
(Christopher Kellett) *hld up in last pair: rdn and short-lived effrt over 2f out: sn btn: wknd and bhd over 1f out* **66/1**

6 3/4 **Pastoral Dancer** 4-9-9 0 PatDobbs 3 17
(Richard Rowe) *s.i.s: a bhd: rdn and edgd lft over 2f out: sn btn: bhd over 1f out* **20/1**

1m 23.8s (0.50) **Going Correction** -0.25s/f (Firm)
WFA 3 from 4yo 4lb 6 Ran SP% **113.1**
Speed ratings (Par 101): **87,81,81,73,65 64**
toteswingers 1&2 £1.60, 1&3 £1.60, 2&3 £2.20 CSF £5.09 TOTE £2.80: £1.10, £1.80; EX 5.40 Trifecta £9.20 Pool: £1701.89 - 137.86 winning units..
Owner David & Paul Hearson **Bred** David & Paul Hearson **Trained** Lambourn, Berks

FOCUS
A weak maiden for older horses to close the turf proceedings.

6114 COMPLETE PLUMBING SERVICES (S) STKS 1m 2f (P)

4:20 (4:20) (Class 6) 3-Y-O+ **£2,045** (£603; £302) **Stalls** Low

Form RPR

1240 **1** **Conducting**[31] 5042 5-9-9 68 LukeMorris 5 71
(Gay Kelleway) *led tl 7f out: comf chsd ldr tl rdn to ld again ent fnl 2f: clr over 1f out: r.o wl: pushed out* **10/11**[1]

003 **2** 4 1/2 **Elusive Band (USA)**[9] 5813 3-8-11 64 (p) MartinLane 3 57
(Bernard Llewellyn) *chsd ldng pair: rdn and effrt over 2f out: chsd clr wnr over 1f out: no imp* **7/1**[3]

0300 **3** 17 **Bert The Alert**[39] 4771 5-9-4 70 (b[1]) GeorgeBaker 6 23
(Gary Moore) *t.k.h: pressed ldr tl led 7f out: clr 6f out tl rdn and hdd ent fnl 2f: lost 2nd and btn over 1f out: heavily eased ins fnl f* **5/4**[2]

0/ **4** 30 **Stanwell**[626] 7807 5-8-13 0 ThomasGarner(5) 4
(H Edward Haynes) *a in rr: rdn 7f out: lost tch 4f out: wl t.o over 2f out* **50/1**

2m 6.82s (0.22) **Going Correction** +0.05s/f (Slow)
WFA 3 from 4yo+ 7lb 4 Ran SP% **111.3**
Speed ratings (Par 101): **101,97,83,59**
CSF £7.63 TOTE £1.50; EX 5.10 Trifecta £6.10 Pool: £753.97 - 91.25 winning units..There were no bids.
Owner J Farley, M Brunner & M Whatley **Bred** David J Brown **Trained** Exning, Suffolk

FOCUS
Just the four of the declared six runners went to post for this seller.

6115 ARC SUPPORTS RETRAINING OF RACEHORSES H'CAP 1m 2f (P)

4:50 (4:51) (Class 4) (0-85,85) 3-Y-O **£4,690** (£1,395; £697; £348) **Stalls** Low

Form RPR

514 **1** **Tinghir (IRE)**[93] 2927 3-9-4 **82** TedDurcan 6 94+
(David Lanigan) *in tch in midfield: effrt to chse ldrs 2f: rdn and qcknd to ld over 1f out: r.o wl ins fnl f: rdn out* **3/1**[2]

3224 **2** 1 3/4 **Autun (USA)**[32] 4980 3-9-7 **85** TomQueally 4 93
(Lady Cecil) *s.i.s: hld up: wl in tch in rr: hdwy on outer wl over 1f out: chsd wnr 1f out: kpt on but no imp on wnr* **7/2**[3]

1-61 **3** *1 3/4* **Al Jamal**[16] 5589 3-9-4 **82**.. SilvestreDeSousa 1 87
(Saeed bin Suroor) *t.k.h: chsd ldr for 2f: stdd bk into last trio but stl t.k.h: rdn and effrt jst over 2f out: nt clr run over 1f out: 3rd and one pce fnl f* **2/1**[1]

5012 **4** *2 3/4* **High Time Too (IRE)**[21] 5395 3-9-0 **78**.. MartinDwyer 3 77
(Hugo Palmer) *in tch in last pair: rdn and swtchd lft over 1f out: no ex jst ins fnl f: wknd fnl 100yds* **20/1**

100 **5** *4* **Tribal Path (IRE)**[130] 1829 3-8-11 **75**.. JoeFanning 7 66
(Mark Johnston) *t.k.h: chsd ldr 8f out: rdn to ld 2f out: hdd and unable qck over 1f out: sn btn: lost 2nd 1f out: fdd fnl f* **7/1**

2104 **6** *3 1/2* **Stresa**[28] 5134 3-9-3 **81**.. WilliamBuick 2 65
(John Gosden) *led for 2f: chsd ldng pair after tl rdn and lost pl qckly wl over 1f out: bhd fnl f* **5/1**

1-00 **7** *1* **Empiricist (IRE)**[33] 4950 3-8-12 **76**..(p) PatDobbs 5 58
(Amanda Perrett) *chsd ldrs tl led 8f out: rdn and hdd 2f out: sn btn and wknd over 1f out* **33/1**

2m 4.87s (-1.73) **Going Correction** +0.05s/f (Slow) 7 Ran SP% **117.4**
Speed ratings (Par 103): **108,106,105,103,99 97,96**
totewingers 1&2 £2.90, 1&3 £2.50, 2&3 £2.00 CSF £14.60 TOTE £4.40: £2.00, £2.00; EX 17.20 Trifecta £43.30 Pool: £3469.19 - 59.98 winning units..
Owner B E Nielsen **Bred** Bjorn Nielsen **Trained** Upper Lambourn, Berks

FOCUS
An interesting 3yo handicap containing several well-bred, in-form participants. All seven runners were in with a chance at the top of the straight.

6116 WORLD HORSE WELFARE MEDIAN AUCTION MAIDEN STKS 1m 4f (P)
5:20 (5:20) (Class 6) 3-4-Y-0 **£2,045** (£603; £302) **Stalls** Low

Form RPR

3403 **1** **Dragon City**[21] 5392 3-9-5 73.. WilliamBuick 6 75
(Harry Dunlop) *chsd ldr tl led 10f out: mde rest: rdn and qcknd over 3f out: clr w runner-up fnl 3f: edgd rt wl over 1f out: hld on u.p ins fnl f* **9/4**[2]

2 *1/2* **My Direction** 3-9-5 0.. JoeFanning 4 74
(Mark Johnston) *led for 2f: chsd wnr after: drew clr of field and rdn over 3f out: swtchd lft wl over 1f out: kpt on gamely and pressing wnr ins fnl f: hld towards fin* **5/1**[3]

0200 **3** *7* **Kenny's Girl (IRE)**[71] 3666 3-9-0 66.. MartinDwyer 3 58
(William Muir) *in tch in midfield: rdn and outpcd whn gallop qcknd over 3f out: 3rd and no imp fr over 2f out* **6/1**

6 **4** *1 1/2* **Wall Street Boss (USA)**[13] 5678 3-9-5 0.. GeorgeBaker 2 61
(James Fanshawe) *stdd s: hld up in last pair: rdn along over 4f out: racing awkwardly and outpcd over 3f out: no ch after: sme hdwy and pressing for 3rd 1f out: nudged along and no ex* **8/1**

42 **5** *6* **Al Guwair (IRE)**[25] 5281 3-9-5 0..(p) FrankieDettori 7 51
(Lady Cecil) *chsd ldrs: rdn and outpcd whn gallop qcknd over 3f out: wl btn after: 5th and wknd over 1f out* **7/4**[1]

6 *2 3/4* **Bethan** 4-9-9 0.. TedDurcan 5 42
(Julia Feilden) *stdd s: hld up in tch in midfield: rdn and outpcd whn gallop qcknd over 3f out: n.d after* **33/1**

00 **7** *41* **Scala Santa**[16] 5586 4-9-9 0.. SteveDrowne 1
(Martin Bosley) *a in last pair: last and struggling whn rdn over 5f out: t.o fnl 3f* **100/1**

2m 33.15s (0.15) **Going Correction** +0.05s/f (Slow)
WFA 3 from 4yo 9lb 7 Ran SP% **113.1**
Speed ratings (Par 101): **101,100,96,95,91 89,61**
toteswingers 1&2 £2.70, 1&3 £2.90, 2&3 £5.30 CSF £13.64 TOTE £2.40: £1.50, £4.00; EX 10.90 Trifecta £54.20 Pool: £1503.24 - 20.78 winning units..
Owner The Blue Bar Partnership **Bred** Sir Eric Parker **Trained** Lambourn, Berks

FOCUS
A modest auction maiden to close the card.
T/Jkpt: £1461.90 to a £1 stake. Pool: £11,324.70 - 5.50 winning units T/Plt: £23.60 to a £1 stake. Pool: £81,062.59 - 2500.72 winning units T/Qpdt: £11.60 to a £1 stake. Pool: £4085.43 - 259.84 winning units SP

6117 - 6123a (Foreign Racing) - See Raceform Interactive

4700 CHANTILLY (R-H)
Wednesday, September 4

OFFICIAL GOING: Turf: good; polytrack: standard

6124a PRIX DE LA COCHERE (LISTED RACE) (3YO FILLIES) (TURF) 1m
4:50 (12:00) 3-Y-0 **£22,357** (£8,943; £6,707; £4,471; £2,235)

RPR

1 **Akemi (IRE)**[48] 4468 3-8-11 0.. ChristopheSoumillon 1 102
(X Thomas-Demeaulte, France) **89/10**

2 *1* **Butterfly McQueen (USA)**[39] 4743 3-8-11 0.. DavidProbert 7 100
(Andrew Balding) *sn led: rdn and strly pressed 2f out: hdd over 1f out and readily outpcd by wnr: kpt on wl for 2nd* **11/1**

3 *1 1/4* **Punta Stella (IRE)**[76] 3521 3-8-11 0..(p) CristianDemuro 9 97
(S Kobayashi, France) **47/1**

4 *snk* **Kenbella (FR)**[23] 5361 3-8-11 0.. FabriceVeron 3 97
(H-A Pantall, France) **20/1**

5 *snk* **Nuit D'Amour (FR)**[41] 4700 3-8-11 0.. ThierryJarnet 10 96
(Mme Pia Brandt, France) **33/10**[3]

6 *nk* **Belonging**[20] 5461 3-8-11 0.. MaximeGuyon 6 96
(A Fabre, France) *t.k.h: prom on outer: rdn to chal 2f out: nt qckn over 1f out: 3rd and hld ent fnl f: kpt on but lost 3 pls ins fnl 100yds* **3/1**[2]

7 *2* **Askania Nova (IRE)**[20] 5461 3-8-11 0.. GeraldMosse 4 91
(A De Royer-Dupre, France) **49/1**

8 *6* **Her Star (USA)**[41] 4700 3-8-11 0..(b) Christophe-PatriceLemaire 2 77
(P Bary, France) **20/1**

9 *3 1/2* **Snow Bell (FR)**[66] 3877 3-9-2 0.. GregoryBenoist 5 74
(N Clement, France) **5/2**[1]

10 *1 1/4* **Reponds Moi (USA)**[76] 3521 3-8-11 0.. OlivierPeslier 11 66
(F Head, France) **13/1**

1m 35.2s (-2.80) 10 Ran SP% **116.0**
WIN (incl. 1 euro stake): 9.90. PLACES: 3.10, 3.50, 12.30. DF: 56.30. SF: 127.70.
Owner Prime Equestrian S.A.R.L. **Bred** J Hernon **Trained** France

5268 HAYDOCK (L-H)
Thursday, September 5

OFFICIAL GOING: Good to firm (8.2)
Wind: Light to moderate; against Weather: Cloudy

6125 BETFRED SALFORD RED DEVILS' FOUNDATION EBF MAIDEN STKS 1m
2:00 (2:00) (Class 5) 2-Y-0 **£2,911** (£866; £432; £216) **Stalls** Low

Form RPR

0 **1** **Gold Trail (IRE)**[28] 5188 2-9-5 0.. SilvestreDeSousa 2 79
(Charlie Appleby) *trckd ldrs: rdn over 1f out: r.o to ld ins fnl f: green but kpt on wl towards fin* **7/1**[3]

34 **2** *3/4* **Tahadee (IRE)**[13] 5727 2-9-5 0.. MartinHarley 10 77
(Mick Channon) *chsd ldrs: rdn 2f out: chal 1f out: nt qckn ins fnl f: kpt on towards fin* **10/3**[2]

3 *3/4* **Rangi Chase (IRE)** 2-9-5 0.. GrahamLee 4 75
(Richard Fahey) *midfield: nt clr run on inner over 2f out: effrt whn nt clr run over 1f out: styd on towards fin: tk 3rd fnl stride* **25/1**

3 **4** *shd* **Snow Sky**[27] 5244 2-9-5 0.. RyanMoore 3 75
(Sir Michael Stoute) *rdn along s and sn led: rdn 2f out: hdd ins fnl f: no ex towards fin* **4/7**[1]

5 *1 3/4* **Blazers Rock (IRE)** 2-9-0 0.. ShaneGray(5) 7 71
(Kevin Ryan) *midfield: rdn over 3f out: kpt on u.p ins fnl f: nvr able to chal* **50/1**

3 **6** *1 1/4* **Ralphy Lad (IRE)**[20] 5482 2-9-5 0.. AndrewMullen 5 68
(Alan Swinbank) *chsd ldrs: rdn over 2f out: hung rt over 1f out: kpt on same pce fnl f* **25/1**

7 *hd* **Whitby High Light** 2-9-5 0.. PaulMulrennan 14 68+
(Andrew Hollinshead) *hld up: pushed along and hung lft whn green over 1f out: kpt on one pce fnl f: nvr able to trble ldrs* **66/1**

8 *1 1/2* **Caridadi (IRE)** 2-9-5 0.. AhmedAjtebi 8 67
(Charlie Appleby) *broke wl: racd keenly: w ldr: rdn and ev ch 2f out: wknd and eased fnl 100yds* **25/1**

6 **9** *2 1/2* **Inevitable**[10] 5827 2-9-5 0.. JoeFanning 11 58
(Mark Johnston) *w ldrs: rdn and wknd 2f out: btn whn hmpd 1f out* **14/1**

10 *nse* **Asteroidea** 2-9-0 0.. LiamKeniry 12 53
(Pam Sly) *stdd s: hld up: green and hung rt on bnd wl over 5f out: nvr on terms w ldrs* **50/1**

11 *14* **Empress Ali (IRE)** 2-9-0 0.. MickyFenton 6 21
(Tom Tate) *carried wd and rt over 5f out: in rr: green and outpcd after: wl adrift fnl 2f* **66/1**

12 *12* **Sea Monkey** 2-9-5 0.. StevieDonohoe 9
(Nicky Vaughan) *bhd: sn struggling: wl adrift fnl 2f* **66/1**

1m 43.69s (-0.01) **Going Correction** -0.25s/f (Firm) 12 Ran SP% **125.8**
Speed ratings (Par 95): **90,89,88,88,86 85,85,83,81,81 67,55**
toteswingers 1&2 £2.50, 1&3 £10.60, 2&3 £10.90 CSF £30.93 TOTE £8.10: £1.80, £1.20, £6.20; EX 31.10 Trifecta £337.30 Pool: £3,884.03 - 8.63 winning units..
Owner Godolphin **Bred** Mrs S M Rogers & Sir Thomas Pilkington **Trained** Newmarket, Suffolk

FOCUS
All races on Inner Home straight and one yard added to races on Round Course. A fair 2-y-o maiden.

6126 BETFRED MOBILE SPORTS H'CAP 1m
2:30 (2:30) (Class 4) (0-80,83) 3-Y-0+ **£5,175** (£1,540; £769; £384) **Stalls** Low

Form RPR

2-35 **1** **Multi Bene**[37] 4850 4-9-10 **80**.. GrahamGibbons 9 93
(Ed McMahon) *midfield: hdwy 3f out whn travelling wl: led over 1f out: r.o to draw clr ins fnl f: eased down towards fin* **9/1**[3]

544- **2** *3 1/2* **Dixie's Dream (IRE)**[337] 6789 4-9-3 **80**.. KevinStott(7) 2 85
(William Jarvis) *midfield: pushed along over 2f out: hdwy u.p over 1f out: kpt on to take 2nd fnl 75yds: no ch w wnr* **11/1**

0200 **3** *1/2* **One Scoop Or Two**[6] 5947 7-9-3 **73**..(v) RussKennemore 3 77
(Andrew Hollinshead) *trckd ldrs: nt clr run 2f out: rdn over 1f out: kpt on ins fnl f but no ch w wnr* **33/1**

0251 **4** *1 1/2* **Storming (IRE)**[25] 5310 3-8-12 **73**..(p) CathyGannon 11 73
(Andrew Balding) *prom: led 2f out: rdn and hdd over 1f out: no ex fnl 100yds* **9/2**[2]

0010 **5** *shd* **Fazza**[17] 5580 6-9-2 **72**.. PaulMulrennan 12 72
(Edwin Tuer) *hld up: hdwy whn nt clr run over 1f out: pushed along and kpt on ins fnl f: no imp* **10/1**

321 **6** *3* **Paradise Watch**[21] 5444 3-9-5 **80**.. KierenFallon 6 73
(Luca Cumani) *midfield: pushed along over 3f out: hdwy over 2f out: nt qckn whn chsng ldrs 1f out: no ex fnl 100yds* **4/1**[1]

0012 **7** *1/2* **Investment Expert (IRE)**[34] 4957 3-9-1 **76**.. RyanMoore 7 68
(Jeremy Noseda) *hld up: pushed along 2f out and carried hd high: nvr able to get on terms w ldrs* **4/1**[1]

1041 **8** *2 3/4* **Wellingrove (IRE)**[7] 5918 3-9-0 **75** 6ex.. JoeFanning 10 61
(Mark Johnston) *trckd ldrs: rdn over 1f out: wknd 1f out* **9/1**[3]

2464 **9** *nk* **Bling King**[23] 5367 4-9-3 **73**..(p) SilvestreDeSousa 1 58
(Geoffrey Harker) *midfield: pushed along over 3f out: rdn over 1f out: wknd fnl f* **16/1**

5200 **10** *1 3/4* **Snooky**[37] 4859 4-9-3 **78**.. GeorgeChaloner(5) 13 59
(Richard Fahey) *bhd: pushed along 3f out: rdn over 1f out: no imp* **9/1**[3]

2110 **11** *1 3/4* **Cono Zur (FR)**[24] 5332 6-9-0 **70**.. JamesSullivan 4 47
(Ruth Carr) *led: rdn and hdd 2f out: wknd over 1f out* **20/1**

0-00 **12** *22* **Chellalla**[12] 5742 4-9-10 **80**.. StevieDonohoe 5 6
(Ian Williams) *a bhd: u.p 3f out: sn wl adrift* **100/1**

1m 40.58s (-3.12) **Going Correction** -0.25s/f (Firm)
WFA 3 from 4yo+ 5lb 12 Ran SP% **120.2**
Speed ratings (Par 105): **105,101,101,99,99 96,95,93,92,91 89,67**
toteswingers 1&2 £20.10, 1&3 £68.10, 2&3 £24.30 CSF £103.81 CT £3168.56 TOTE £11.70: £3.10, £3.30, £6.90; EX 102.00 Trifecta £2375.80 Part won. Pool: £3,167.85 - 0.40 winning units..
Owner Mrs Richards & Mrs Brazier **Bred** Mickley Stud **Trained** Lichfield, Staffs

The Form Book Flat, Raceform Ltd, Compton, RG20 6NL.

FOCUS
A fair 1m handicap that pitted a handful of progressive 3yos against some seemingly exposed older horses. There was plenty of competition for the lead, resulting in a furious gallop.

6127 BETFRED SALFORD RED DEVILS' "TACKLE HEALTH" EBF MAIDEN STKS 6f
3:00 (3:04) (Class 5) 2-Y-O **£2,911** (£866; £432; £216) **Stalls** Centre

Form RPR
1 **Brian Noble** 2-9-0 0 GrahamLee 5 81+
(Richard Fahey) *s.i.s: racd bhd ldrs: rdn and no imp wl over 1f out tl styd on ins fnl f: led fnl 75yds: wl in command fin* **9/4**[2]
020 2 2 ¼ **Rogue Wave (IRE)**[13] 5727 2-9-0 85 DanielTudhope 1 74
(Alan Jarvis) *edgy in preliminaries: a.p: rdn over 1f out: stl ev ch ins fnl f: kpt on same pce and no ch w wnr towards fin* **5/4**[1]
52 3 *hd* **Gold Club**[27] 5225 2-9-0 0 GrahamGibbons 4 73
(Ed McMahon) *led: rdn over 1f out: hdd fnl 75yds: kpt on same pce towards fin* **4/1**[3]
4 57 **Our Red Devil (IRE)** 2-9-0 0 AdrianNicholls 2
(David Nicholls) *rn green: racd bhd ldrs: outpcd over 2f out: eased whn wl btn fnl f* **11/2**

1m 15.86s (2.06) **Going Correction** +0.225s/f (Good) **4 Ran SP% 110.6**
Speed ratings (Par 95): **95,92,91,15**
CSF £5.63 TOTE £3.50; EX 5.60 Trifecta £13.40 Pool: £1,492.68 - 83.30 winning units..
Owner Dr Marwan Koukash **Bred** Mrs D Du Feu And Trickledown Stud **Trained** Musley Bank, N Yorks

FOCUS
Not a bad little 2-yo maiden.

6128 BETFRED DUKE OF LANCASTER'S REGIMENT CUP H'CAP 1m 3f 200y
3:35 (3:35) (Class 2) (0-100,92) 3-Y-0+ **£14,231** (£4,235; £2,116; £1,058) **Stalls** Centre

Form RPR
0-11 1 **Venue**[48] 4476 3-9-3 92 RyanMoore 1 101
(Lady Cecil) *trckd ldrs: pushed along 3f out: swtchd rt 2f out: styd on to ld 1f out: mainly pushed out cl home: gd ride* **10/11**[1]
3110 2 *hd* **Guising**[113] 2369 4-9-3 83 SilvestreDeSousa 2 92
(David Brown) *led: rdn whn pressed over 1f out: sn hdd: rallied for press cl home* **12/1**
4012 3 1 ½ **Fennell Bay (IRE)**[5] 6001 4-9-10 90 JoeFanning 5 97
(Mark Johnston) *chsd ldr: rdn whn chalng 1f out: stl ev ch ins fnl f: no ex towards fin* **11/4**[2]
530 4 ¾ **Incendo**[27] 5237 7-8-13 82 (v) MichaelJMMurphy(3) 4 87
(Ian Williams) *in rr: plld out 2f out: rdn over 1f out whn chsng ldng trio: nvr able to chal* **33/1**
1211 5 4 ½ **Mankini (IRE)**[43] 4626 4-9-6 86 KirstyMilczarek 3 84
(Luca Cumani) *trckd ldrs: rdn over 1f out: sn btn* **4/1**[3]

2m 32.83s (-0.97) **Going Correction** -0.25s/f (Firm)
WFA 3 from 4yo+ 9lb **5 Ran SP% 109.7**
Speed ratings (Par 109): **93,92,91,91,88**
CSF £12.58 TOTE £1.80: £1.20, £3.00; EX 10.30 Trifecta £33.60 Pool: £1,483.85 - 33.06 winning units..
Owner K Abdullah **Bred** Juddmonte Farms Ltd **Trained** Newmarket, Suffolk

FOCUS
Only five runners but an interesting puzzle with a few in-form, progressive participants.

6129 BETFRED SALFORD RED DEVILS' IN THE COMMUNITY EBF CONDITIONS STKS 7f
4:05 (4:07) (Class 3) 3-Y-0+ **£11,320** (£3,368; £1,683; £841) **Stalls** Low

Form RPR
6322 1 **Intransigent**[12] 5738 4-8-12 100 LiamKeniry 6 109
(Andrew Balding) *hld up: hdwy 2f out: chsd ldr over 1f out: r.o to ld fnl 150yds: sn readily drew clr: eased down towards fin* **15/8**[1]
2-00 2 4 **Firebeam**[187] 869 5-8-12 106 SilvestreDeSousa 3 98
(Charlie Appleby) *led: tried to slip field 2f out: rdn 1f out: hdd fnl 150yds: sn no ch w wnr* **2/1**[2]
6550 3 3 ½ **Bear Behind (IRE)**[26] 5257 4-8-12 100 RichardKingscote 1 89
(Tom Dascombe) *chsd ldrs: rdn over 2f out: wl btn fnl f* **14/1**
-503 4 *nk* **Spiritual Star (IRE)**[19] 5518 4-8-12 99 WilliamCarson 5 88
(Anthony Carson) *hld up: effrt whn carried hd high over 1f out: no imp* **17/2**
2250 5 1 ½ **Smarty Socks (IRE)**[14] 5681 9-8-12 97 DanielTudhope 2 84
(David O'Meara) *in rr: pushed along over 2f out: nvr able to get on terms* **5/1**[3]
5104 6 14 **Set The Trend**[12] 5763 7-9-11 103 KierenFallon 4 59
(David O'Meara) *chsd ldr tl rdn over 2f out: wknd over 1f out* **10/1**

1m 27.34s (-3.36) **Going Correction** -0.25s/f (Firm) **6 Ran SP% 111.1**
Speed ratings (Par 107): **109,104,100,100,98 82**
toteswingers 1&2 £1.80, 1&3 £4.10, 2&3 £4.90 CSF £5.79 TOTE £2.40: £2.00, £1.20; EX 7.00 Trifecta £47.70 Pool: £2,781.30 - 43.70 winning units..
Owner Kingsclere Racing CLub **Bred** Kingsclere Stud **Trained** Kingsclere, Hants

FOCUS
A good-quality conditions event.

6130 BETFRED MOBILE CASINO H'CAP (FOR GENTLEMAN AMATEUR RIDERS) 1m 3f 200y
4:40 (4:41) (Class 5) (0-70,70) 4-Y-0+ **£2,495** (£774; £386; £193) **Stalls** Centre

Form RPR
4013 1 **Ailsa Craig (IRE)**[10] 5833 7-10-6 62 (p) MrPDennis(7) 11 76
(Edwin Tuer) *chsd ldrs: led over 1f out: styd on to draw clr ins fnl f* **8/1**
330/ 2 6 **Clarion Call**[12] 5630 5-11-2 65 MrSWalker 8 69
(Graeme McPherson) *hld up: hdwy 4f out: u.p over 1f out: kpt on to take 2nd fnl 75yds: no imp on wnr* **7/1**
1461 3 1 ½ **Automotive**[11] 5793 5-10-13 62 6ex MrRossBirkett 7 64
(Julia Feilden) *hld up: hdwy over 3f out: rdn whn chsng ldrs over 1f out: kpt on same pce ins fnl f* **11/2**[3]
0122 4 *nk* **Shahrazad (IRE)**[14] 5672 4-10-2 56 (t) JackGilligan(5) 4 58
(Patrick Gilligan) *led: rdn over 2f out: hdd over 1f out: no ex wl ins fnl f* **9/2**[2]
5331 5 2 ¼ **Spanish Plume**[14] 5671 5-11-1 64 (p) MrWHogg 1 62
(Andrew Hollinshead) *chsd ldr: chal over 1f out: nt qckn: wknd fnl 75yds* **7/1**
5-55 6 13 **Hyperlink (IRE)**[20] 5466 4-11-2 70 MrAlexFerguson(5) 6 47
(Michael Bell) *hld up: sme hdwy over 2f out: nvr able to get nr ldrs* **9/2**[2]
2221 7 4 **Euston Square**[10] 5840 7-11-0 63 6ex (v) MrJHamilton 3 34
(Alistair Whillans) *s.v.s: hdwy to go in rr of main gp after 2f: in tch 6f out: rdn and wknd over 3f out* **4/1**[1]
1200 8 2 ¾ **Maybeme**[11] 5786 7-10-13 67 (p) MrSebSpencer(5) 10 33
(Neville Bycroft) *hld up bhd: pushed along over 3f out: nvr on terms* **20/1**
60-0 9 10 **Overrule (USA)**[219] 430 9-10-8 62 (p) MrMatthewStanley(5) 2 12
(Chris Bealby) *chsd ldrs tl rdn and wknd 3f out* **33/1**
500- 10 5 **Swords**[364] 5967 11-10-2 56 oh11 MrDLevey(5) 5
(Ray Peacock) *chsd ldrs tl wknd over 4f out* **66/1**
00-5 11 3 ½ **De Lesseps (USA)**[17] 5596 5-10-0 56 oh6 MrTGreenwood(7) 9
(James Moffatt) *in tch: rdn and wknd over 3f out* **50/1**

2m 32.3s (-1.50) **Going Correction** -0.25s/f (Firm) **11 Ran SP% 119.0**
Speed ratings (Par 103): **95,91,90,89,88 79,76,75,68,65 62**
toteswingers 1&2 £11.00, 1&3 £8.10, 2&3 £8.70 CSF £61.79 CT £339.67 TOTE £9.60: £2.80, £2.60, £2.10; EX 70.70 Trifecta £536.20 Pool: £4,209.18 - 5.88 winning units..
Owner Ontoawinner **Bred** P J B O'Callaghan **Trained** Birkby, N Yorks

FOCUS
An ordinary handicap, confined to gentleman amateur riders.
T/Jkpt: Not won. T/Plt: £1,799.40 to a £1 stake. Pool: £72,101.13 - 29.25 winning units T/Qpdt: £58.00 to a £1 stake. Pool: £4,948.67 - 63.10 winning units DO

6102 KEMPTON (A.W) (R-H)
Thursday, September 5

OFFICIAL GOING: Standard
Wind: Almost nil Weather: Sunny, hot

6131 BOOK NOW FOR JUMP SUNDAY 20.10.13 CLAIMING STKS 7f (P)
5:10 (5:10) (Class 6) 2-Y-O **£1,940** (£577; £288; £144) **Stalls** Low

Form RPR
064 1 **Morally Bankrupt**[10] 5819 2-9-3 0 RichardHughes 7 73
(Richard Hannon) *cl up: chsd ldr 3f out: rdn over 2f out: clsd over 1f out: led last 150yds: pushed clr* **10/11**[1]
006 2 2 ¼ **Hickster (IRE)**[28] 5175 2-8-7 50 (v1) FergusSweeney 6 56
(Tom Dascombe) *led: rdn over 2f out: sn clr w wnr: hdd and no ex last 150yds* **12/1**
0002 3 2 ¾ **Cabaan (IRE)**[9] 5865 2-8-12 62 (b1) DaneO'Neill 4 54
(Brian Meehan) *chsd ldng trio: rdn 1/2-way: chsd ldng pair over 2f out: no imp but kpt on* **4/1**[2]
00 4 1 **Plough Boy (IRE)**[27] 5243 2-8-9 0 TedDurcan 3 48
(Willie Musson) *t.k.h early: hld up in last quartet: nt on terms 3f out: prog and reminder 2f out: 4th over 1f out: pushed along and no hdwy after* **66/1**
5622 5 1 ¾ **Chilly In Rio (IRE)**[6] 5963 2-8-5 55 (p) MartinDwyer 1 39
(William Muir) *chsd ldrs: rdn and no prog 2f out: steadily fdd* **9/1**
6600 6 ½ **Jana**[8] 5893 2-8-4 55 LukeMorris 5 37
(Sylvester Kirk) *chsd ldrs: drvn and no prog over 2f out: fdd over 1f out* **20/1**
5 7 4 ½ **Brean Splash Susie**[27] 5229 2-8-1 0 ow1 RyanWhile(7) 8 29
(Bill Turner) *chsd ldr to 3f out: urged along and wknd 2f out* **50/1**
0000 8 7 **Crazy Brenda (IRE)**[24] 5350 2-8-2 25 FrannyNorton 10 4
(Sylvester Kirk) *a in rr: struggling over 3f out: sn wl bhd* **66/1**
0025 9 6 **Mr Childrey (IRE)**[27] 5243 2-8-6 49 (b) LiamJones 9
(J S Moore) *a wl in rr: drvn after 3f and no prog: t.o* **25/1**
03 10 3 ½ **Secret Ocean (IRE)**[27] 5243 2-8-4 0 (b) JoeyHaynes(5) 2
(J S Moore) *dwlt: nvr gng wl and sn detached in last: t.o* **6/1**[3]

1m 26.85s (0.85) **Going Correction** -0.025s/f (Stan) **10 Ran SP% 117.9**
Speed ratings (Par 93): **94,91,88,87,85 84,79,71,64,60**
toteswingers 1&2 £5.40, 1&3 £2.20, 2&3 £6.80 CSF £13.29 TOTE £2.30: £1.10, £2.80, £2.10; EX 21.10 Trifecta £70.40 Pool: £2,835.87 - 30.19 winning units..
Owner J Sullivan & C Giles **Bred** Horizon Bloodstock Limited **Trained** East Everleigh, Wilts

FOCUS
Some very limited juveniles on show in this claimer and it's hard to get excited about many of them.

6132 BETVICTOR.COM NOVICE AUCTION STKS 7f (P)
5:40 (5:40) (Class 5) 2-Y-O **£2,587** (£770; £384; £192) **Stalls** Low

Form RPR
31 1 **Captain Secret**[42] 4668 2-8-6 79 LukeMorris 4 77+
(Marco Botti) *mde all: set mod pce: kicked on over 2f out: hrd pressed fr over 1f out: drvn and hld on* **1/1**[1]
1003 2 *nk* **Beau Nash (IRE)**[12] 5745 2-9-3 85 RichardHughes 3 87+
(Richard Hannon) *trckd ldng pair: wnt 2nd over 2f out: drvn to chal wl over 1f out: kpt trying but jst hld fnl f* **6/5**[2]
3 8 **Manipulation (IRE)** 2-8-9 0 MartinLane 2 58
(David Simcock) *stdd s: t.k.h early: hld up in last pair: rn green briefly over 2f out: sn outpcd: shkn up to take modest 3rd ins fnl f* **16/1**[3]
00 4 2 **Starlight Princess (IRE)**[48] 4484 2-8-7 0 LiamJones 5 50
(J S Moore) *dwlt: chsd wnr at mod pce to over 2f out: sn btn* **66/1**
0 5 1 ½ **Sydney James (IRE)**[25] 5307 2-8-11 0 DaneO'Neill 1 50
(Richard Hannon) *hld up in last pair: outpcd over 2f out: rdn and no prog after* **20/1**

1m 27.21s (1.21) **Going Correction** -0.025s/f (Stan) **5 Ran SP% 107.6**
Speed ratings (Par 95): **92,91,82,80,78**
CSF £2.30 TOTE £2.40: £1.20, £1.10; EX 3.20 Trifecta £6.00 Pool: £1,712.53 - 213.91 winning units..
Owner Scuderia Blueberry **Bred** R G Percival **Trained** Newmarket, Suffolk

FOCUS
A decent little race and it served up a thrilling finish.

6133 £25 FREE BET AT BETVICTOR.COM MAIDEN STKS (DIV I) 1m (P)
6:10 (6:19) (Class 5) 3-Y-0+ **£2,587** (£770; £384; £192) **Stalls** Low

Form RPR
6 1 **Cornrow**[20] 5495 3-9-5 0 WilliamBuick 13 89
(John Gosden) *trckd ldrs: led after 3f: mde rest: kicked on 2f out: rdn and kpt on wl fnl f* **8/1**
5-3 2 1 **Magic Hurricane (IRE)**[13] 5720 3-9-5 0 FrederikTylicki 10 87
(James Fanshawe) *trckd ldrs: rdn and prog to chse wnr wl over 1f out: tried to chal fnl f: no imp last 100yds* **2/1**[1]
3 3 3 **Dawn Calling (IRE)**[10] 5839 3-9-5 0 FrannyNorton 7 80
(Mark Johnston) *trckd ldr over 2f: styd prom: rdn to chse wnr over 3f out to wl over 1f out: steadily outpcd* **9/2**[3]
24 4 6 **Bejeweled (IRE)**[29] 5133 3-9-0 0 TomQueally 11 61
(Lady Cecil) *in tch in midfield: rdn over 3f out and outpcd: nvr on terms after: plugged on* **8/1**
3- 5 ½ **La Belle Epoque (USA)**[308] 7506 3-9-0 0 (p) LukeMorris 14 60
(Gerard Butler) *in tch in midfield: outpcd over 3f out: rdn over 2f out: plugged on after* **20/1**

0 **6** 1 ¾ **Intrinsic**[14] 5678 3-9-5 0..............................(p) RichardHughes 6 61
(Sir Michael Stoute) *led 3f out: chsd wnr to over 3f out: urged along and steadily wknd* **20/1**

0 **7** 7 **Semai (IRE)**[10] 5839 3-9-0 0.............................. TobyAtkinson(5) 4 45
(Marco Botti) *trckd ldrs: rdn over 3f out: wknd over 2f out* **33/1**

6-6 **8** 2 ¼ **The Best Doctor (IRE)**[13] 5720 3-9-5 0.............................. SebSanders 12 40
(Jeremy Noseda) *a wl in rr: t.o 1/2-way: v modest late prog* **14/1**

9 2 ¼ **Boboli Gardens** 3-9-5 0..............................(t) RoystonFfrench 1 35
(Mrs Ilka Gansera-Leveque) *in tch to 1/2-way: sn wknd: wl bhd fnl 2f* **33/1**

60 **10** 5 **Dreaming Again**[21] 5444 3-9-5 0.............................. KieranO'Neill 3 23
(Jimmy Fox) *nvr on terms: wl adrift in 10th sn after 1/2-way: t.o* **100/1**

06 **11** 1 ½ **Crystal Tiger**[22] 5386 3-9-0 0.............................. DaneO'Neill 9 15
(Alan Jarvis) *s.i.s: wl in rr: sme prog to latch on to bk of main gp over 3f out: sn wknd: t.o* **100/1**

0-0 **12** 7 **Spirit Man**[234] 211 3-9-5 0.............................. MartinDwyer 2
(Derek Shaw) *a wl in rr: t.o fr 1/2-way* **100/1**

P **West Riding (IRE)** 3-9-5 0.............................. MickaelBarzalona 5
(Charlie Appleby) *dwlt: a in rr: t.o 1/2-way: p.u over 2f out: fatally injured* **4/1**[2]

1m 38.41s (-1.39) **Going Correction** -0.025s/f (Stan) **13 Ran SP% 118.8**
Speed ratings (Par 103): **105,104,101,95,94 92,85,83,81,76 74,67,**
toteswingers 1&2 £4.50, 1&3 £6.40, 2&3 £3.70 CSF £22.96 TOTE £7.00: £3.00, £1.40, £1.90; EX 35.20 Trifecta £132.30 Pool: £2,370.29 - 13.42 winning units..
Owner HRH Princess Haya Of Jordan **Bred** Darley **Trained** Newmarket, Suffolk

FOCUS
Some big yards represented but, with the twice-raced and seemingly limited Magic Hurricane heading the market, there was a likelihood that this was nothing more than an ordinary contest.

6134 £25 FREE BET AT BETVICTOR.COM MAIDEN STKS (DIV II) 1m (P)
6:40 (6:47) (Class 5) 3-Y-O+ **£2,587** (£770; £384; £192) **Stalls** Low

Form RPR

1 **Deglet Noor** 3-9-0 0.............................. DaneO'Neill 4 82+
(Roger Varian) *in tch in midfield: last of those w a ch fr 1/2-way: rdn over 2f out: prog over 1f out: styd on wl after to ld nr fin* **33/1**

-360 **2** nk **Hanzada (USA)**[97] 2850 3-9-0 80.............................. AndreaAtzeni 9 81
(Ed Dunlop) *trckd ldrs: rdn to cl 2f out: led jst ins fnl f: styd on but hdd nr fin* **12/1**[3]

3 **3** 1 ¾ **Proximate**[17] 5588 3-9-5 0.............................. RichardHughes 12 82
(Sir Michael Stoute) *prom: rdn to chal 2f out: pressed ldr tl jst ins fnl f: one pce* **7/2**[2]

2 **4** ¾ **Ennobled Friend (USA)**[29] 5133 3-9-5 0.............. MickaelBarzalona 10 80
(Charlie Appleby) *led 1f: chsd ldr: clsng to chal whn nudged jst over 2f out: led wl over 1f out but hrd pressed: hdd jst ins fnl f: fdd* **8/11**[1]

5 3 ¼ **Busatto (USA)** 3-9-5 0.............................. FrannyNorton 11 73+
(Mark Johnston) *s.i.s: sn rcvrd to chse ldrs: shkn up over 2f out: no imp and rn green over 1f out: one pce after* **16/1**

0-44 **6** 1 ¼ **Smart Eighteen**[13] 5715 3-9-5 63.............................. FrederikTylicki 13 70
(Paul D'Arcy) *led after 1f and sn clr: wandered over 2f out: hdd wl over 1f out: steadily wknd* **33/1**

7 2 **Pomodoro** 3-9-5 0.............................. WilliamBuick 3 65+
(John Gosden) *s.s: mostly in last trio and sn wl off the pce: sme prog over 2f out: styd on steadily fnl 2f: by no means disgracd* **12/1**[3]

54 **8** 1 ½ **Speedy Writer**[17] 5588 3-9-5 0.............................. FergusSweeney 5 62
(Henry Candy) *chsd ldrs but sn pushed along: in tch over 2f out: steadily wknd* **14/1**

60 **9** 8 **Millies Quest**[13] 5720 4-8-12 0.............................. JordanVaughan(7) 6 38
(Martin Smith) *hld up and sn wl in rr: hmpd on inner over 4f out: no ch in 8th over 2f out: fdd* **66/1**

00 **10** 6 **Mignonne**[64] 3957 3-8-9 0.............................. RyanTate(5) 7 25
(Hans Adielsson) *s.i.s: wl in rr: reminder 5f out: no prog and wl bhd fr 1/2-way* **66/1**

00 **11** 4 **Vol Freak**[29] 5133 3-9-5 0.............................. SaleemGolam 1 20
(Willie Musson) *a towards rr: rdn 1/2-way: wl bhd after* **100/1**

12 15 **Byron Again** 3-9-5 0.............................. FrankieMcDonald 8
(Sean Curran) *a wl in rr: t.o 3f out* **100/1**

00 **13** 2 ½ **Up Tipp**[20] 5495 3-9-5 0.............................. TedDurcan 2
(Mike Murphy) *a towards rr: rdn 1/2-way: t.o* **100/1**

1m 38.6s (-1.20) **Going Correction** -0.025s/f (Stan)
WFA 3 from 4yo 5lb **13 Ran SP% 119.9**
Speed ratings (Par 103): **105,104,102,102,98 97,95,94,86,80 76,61,58**
toteswingers 1&2 £22.00, 1&3 £16.10, 2&3 £5.70 CSF £382.75 TOTE £35.10: £8.20, £3.80, £1.70; EX 130.70 Trifecta £1718.30 Part won. Pool: £2,291.13 - 0.65 winning units..
Owner Hamdan Al Maktoum **Bred** Shadwell Estate Company Limited **Trained** Newmarket, Suffolk
■ Stewards' Enquiry : Andrea Atzeni one-day ban: careless riding (Sep 19)

FOCUS
The second division of this maiden looked stronger than the first.

6135 DOWNLOAD THE BETVICTOR APP H'CAP 6f (P)
7:10 (7:15) (Class 5) (0-70,70) 3-Y-O+ **£2,587** (£770; £384; £192) **Stalls** Low

Form RPR

202 **1** **Dominium (USA)**[13] 5697 6-8-13 68..............................(b) RobertTart(5) 6 77
(Jeremy Gask) *hld up towards rr: prog 1/2-way: rdn and clsd fr over 1f out: styd on wl to ld last 50yds* **5/2**[1]

0030 **2** ¾ **Dream Catcher (FR)**[19] 5537 5-9-4 68..............................(b[1]) CathyGannon 11 75
(Henry Candy) *led: crossed fr wd draw and sn clr: 4 l up over 2f out: grad c bk to rivals: hdd last 50yds* **10/1**

6345 **3** nk **Glastonberry**[30] 5104 5-9-4 68.............................. HayleyTurner 4 74
(Geoffrey Deacon) *trckd ldrs: prog over 2f out: drvn to chse clr ldr wl over 1f out: grad clsd fnl f but wnr wnt past last 75yds* **8/1**

4165 **4** 1 **Oasis Spirit**[26] 5280 3-9-4 70.............................. DavidProbert 3 72
(Andrew Balding) *chsd ldrs: drvn to go 3rd over 1f out on inner: kpt on but nvr able to chal* **9/2**[2]

5402 **5** 1 ¼ **Emerald Sea**[16] 5617 3-9-2 68.............................. TedDurcan 7 66
(Chris Wall) *settled in rr: sme prog fr 2f out: rdn fnl f: styd on but no ch to chal* **6/1**[3]

5046 **6** hd **Rondeau (GR)**[20] 5474 8-9-5 69.............................. GeorgeBaker 8 67
(Patrick Chamings) *taken down early: hld up in last trio and racd wd: prog 2f out: rdn over 1f out: kpt on but no ch to threaten* **8/1**

0000 **7** hd **Nasri**[10] 5841 7-9-6 70..............................(p) LukeMorris 1 67
(Milton Bradley) *chsd clr ldr to wl over 1f out: fdd u.p* **14/1**

0040 **8** 2 **Roy's Legacy**[13] 5708 4-9-2 66..............................(t) JimmyQuinn 9 57
(Shaun Harris) *chsd ldrs: steadily wknd fnl 2f* **33/1**

0606 **9** hd **Blazing Knight (IRE)**[26] 5278 3-9-4 70.............................. JimCrowley 10 60
(Ralph Beckett) *hld up and last early: prog on inner over 2f out: rdn over 1f out: effrt petered out ins fnl f* **11/1**

0-00 **10** 7 **Dark Ages (IRE)**[111] 2425 4-9-1 70..............................(t) DanielMuscutt(5) 12 38
(Paul Burgoyne) *racd wd in midfield: lost grnd 3f out: sn wl in rr* **20/1**

0000 **11** 10 **Pick A Little**[14] 5673 5-9-3 67.............................. JackMitchell 2 3
(Michael Blake) *struggling in last trio after 2f: t.o* **33/1**

/040 **12** 1 ¾ **Appointee (IRE)**[25] 5308 4-9-6 70..............................(v[1]) WilliamBuick 5
(Robert Cowell) *t.k.h: chsd ldng pair to 1/2-way: wknd rapidly: t.o* **20/1**

1m 12.74s (-0.36) **Going Correction** -0.025s/f (Stan)
WFA 3 from 4yo+ 2lb **12 Ran SP% 122.8**
Speed ratings (Par 103): **101,100,99,98,96 96,96,93,93,83 70,68**
toteswingers 1&2 £5.90, 1&3 £5.50, 2&3 £8.80 CSF £28.54 CT £183.73 TOTE £3.60: £1.10, £3.30, £2.60; EX 31.80 Trifecta £177.60 Pool: £1,437.99 - 6.06 winning units..
Owner Horses First Racing Limited **Bred** Corbett Farm **Trained** Sutton Veny, Wilts

FOCUS
There was no hanging around in this sprint handicap.

6136 BETVICTOR CASINO ON YOUR MOBILE H'CAP (LONDON MIDDLE DISTANCE SERIES QUALIFIER) 1m 3f (P)
7:40 (7:40) (Class 4) (0-85,83) 3-Y-O **£4,690** (£1,395; £697; £348) **Stalls** Low

Form RPR

1422 **1** **Tajheez (IRE)**[28] 5189 3-9-7 83.............................. PaulHanagan 8 94
(Roger Varian) *t.k.h: trckd ldr: led over 2f out: rdn and edgd rt over 1f out: styd on wl to assert fnl f* **11/10**[1]

1214 **2** 2 ½ **Grendisar (IRE)**[85] 3206 3-9-1 77..............................(p) AdamKirby 7 83
(Marco Botti) *trckd ldng pair: rdn to chse wnr jst over 2f out: tried to chal jst over 1f out: one pce fnl f* **7/2**[2]

6-3 **3** 2 ¾ **Flemish School**[13] 5695 3-8-9 71 ow1..............................(p) NeilCallan 3 72
(Gerard Butler) *hld up in 4th: rdn whn jockey dropped whip over 2f out: encouraged along to take 3rd over 1f out: no imp* **12/1**

4366 **4** hd **Poetic Verse**[35] 4914 3-8-13 75.............................. AndreaAtzeni 1 76
(Rod Millman) *hld up in last: clsd 3f out: rdn and nt qckn jst over 2f out: no ch after: plugged on* **16/1**

0514 **5** ¾ **Strawberry Jam**[13] 5719 3-8-11 73.............................. TomQueally 5 72
(Paul Cole) *hld up in 5th: easily outpcd over 2f out: no ch after: plugged on ins fnl f* **8/1**

2110 **6** ¾ **Couloir Extreme (IRE)**[34] 4950 3-9-2 78.............................. GeorgeBaker 4 76
(Gary Moore) *led: set sedate pce to 1/2-way: hdd and btn over 2f out: wknd fnl f* **6/1**[3]

2m 26.27s (4.37) **Going Correction** -0.025s/f (Stan) **6 Ran SP% 108.8**
Speed ratings (Par 103): **83,81,79,79,78 77**
toteswingers 1&2 £1.60, 1&3 £2.20, 2&3 £3.60 CSF £4.70 CT £22.69 TOTE £2.00: £1.20, £1.90; EX 3.50 Trifecta £15.60 Pool: £1,011.27 - 48.61 winning units..
Owner Hamdan Al Maktoum **Bred** Shadwell Estate Company Limited **Trained** Newmarket, Suffolk

FOCUS
It paid to be handy in this tactically run affair.

6137 FOLLOW US ON TWITTER @BETVICTOR H'CAP 1m 3f (P)
8:10 (8:10) (Class 6) (0-55,55) 3-Y-O+ **£1,940** (£577; £288; £144) **Stalls** Low

Form RPR

0033 **1** **Compton Bird**[21] 5429 4-8-12 51.............................. RyanTate(5) 14 63
(Hans Adielsson) *awkward s: hld up in last trio: gd prog over 2f out: rdn and clsd qckly to ld jst over 1f out: sn clr* **7/1**[3]

-044 **2** 4 ½ **Lucky Black Star (IRE)**[20] 5497 3-8-13 55.............................. PatCosgrave 3 59
(George Baker) *wl in tch: rdn over 2f out: prog but wnr flew past over 1f out: styd on fnl f to take 2nd last strides* **6/1**[2]

2624 **3** nk **Princess Willow**[50] 4411 5-9-7 55.............................. KirstyMilczarek 8 58
(John E Long) *trckd ldr: led 100yds: trckd ldr: led 3f out: tried to go for home over 2f out: hdd and outpcd jst over 1f out: lost 2nd last strides* **4/1**[1]

6244 **4** 1 ¾ **Chasin' Rainbows**[7] 5934 5-9-3 51.............................. DaneO'Neill 2 51
(Sylvester Kirk) *hld up towards rr: prog over 2f out: sn drvn: outpcd wl over 1f out: kpt on fnl f* **6/1**[2]

6400 **5** nk **Our Golden Girl**[24] 5346 3-8-6 53..............................(b[1]) RobertTart(5) 9 53
(Shaun Lycett) *prom on outer: rdn to chse ldr over 2f out to over 1f out: steadily fdd* **16/1**

0332 **6** ¾ **Laconicos (IRE)**[20] 5492 11-9-7 55..............................(t) LukeMorris 6 53
(William Stone) *chsd ldrs: rdn over 3f out: outpcd fr 2f out: kpt on fnl f* **7/1**[3]

0050 **7** 4 ½ **Arte Del Calcio**[52] 4350 4-8-11 50.............................. GeorgeDowning(5) 11 40
(Tony Carroll) *stdd s: hld up in last: prog over 2f out: reminders over 1f out: kpt on but nvr involved* **16/1**

60 **8** 2 ¼ **The Yank**[30] 5093 4-9-4 52.............................. JimmyQuinn 5 38
(Tony Carroll) *trckd ldng pair: rdn to dispute 2nd over 2f out to wl over 1f out: wknd* **8/1**

000 **9** 3 ¾ **Hundred Acre Wood**[128] 1904 3-8-13 55.............................. JackMitchell 13 35
(Olivia Maylam) *chsd ldrs: rdn 5f out: no prog 3f out: steadily wknd* **50/1**

2U34 **10** 1 ½ **Lady Barastar (IRE)**[21] 5126 5-9-4 52..............................(b) GeorgeBaker 4 29
(Amanda Perrett) *stdd s: hld up in last trio: effrt on inner over 2f out: no prog over 1f out: eased* **10/1**

0310 **11** 12 **Frosty Secret**[27] 5216 4-9-4 52..............................(b) LiamJones 1 7
(Jane Chapple-Hyam) *racd freely: led after 100yds: hdd 3f out: wknd qckly: t.o* **14/1**

0-00 **12** 45 **Electrickery**[19] 5515 4-8-12 46.............................. AdamBeschizza 10
(Mark Buckley) *in tch to 1/2-way: sn wknd: wl t.o* **40/1**

2m 21.77s (-0.13) **Going Correction** -0.025s/f (Stan)
WFA 3 from 4yo+ 8lb **12 Ran SP% 116.6**
Speed ratings (Par 101): **99,95,95,94,94 93,90,88,85,84 76,43**
toteswingers 1&2 £8.20, 1&3 £5.20, 2&3 £5.80 CSF £47.82 CT £192.43 TOTE £8.10: £2.80, £2.80, £1.90; EX 62.00 Trifecta £771.60 Pool: £1,178.94 - 1.14 winning units..
Owner Erik Penser **Bred** Whitsbury Manor Stud **Trained** Kingston Lisle, Oxon

FOCUS
Moderate form.

6138 LADIES DAY WITH TOBY ANSTIS 07.09.13 H'CAP 6f (P)
8:40 (8:41) (Class 6) (0-65,66) 3-Y-O **£1,940** (£577; £288; £144) **Stalls** Low

Form RPR

4521 **1** **Marmalady (IRE)**[8] 5890 3-9-8 66 6ex.............................. GeorgeBaker 6 78+
(Gary Moore) *led after 1f: 3 l clr over 3f out: rdn over 1f out: nvr seriously threatened* **2/5**[1]

0310 **2** 2 **Sweet Talking Guy (IRE)**[29] 5128 3-8-8 55..............(t) SimonPearce(3) 4 61
(Lydia Pearce) *in tch: prog over 2f out: drvn and styd on to take 2nd ins fnl f: nvr able to chal* **10/1**[3]

-043 **3** nk **Secret Success**[71] 3679 3-9-0 58..............................(t) TomQueally 3 63
(Paul Cole) *s.i.s: drvn in last early: no prog tl styd on fr over 1f out: tk 3rd nr fin and clsd on runner-up* **11/2**[2]

2043 **4** 1 ¼ **Harrogate Fair**[99] 2779 3-9-4 62.............................. JimmyQuinn 2 63
(Michael Squance) *in tch: rdn to chse wnr 2f out: no imp: lost 2nd and fdd ins fnl f* **16/1**

-000 **5** *4* **Iffley Fields**[7] 5935 3-8-2 **51** oh3..............................(p) NatashaEaton(5) 8 39
(Michael Squance) *taken down early: chsd ldrs: rdn over 2f out: steadily wknd* **66/1**
-003 **6** *¾* **Pearl Noir**[11] 5788 3-8-13 **57**..............................(t) LukeMorris 5 43
(Scott Dixon) *led 1f: chsd wnr to 2f out: wknd over 1f out* **12/1**
6430 **7** *10* **Mighty Mata**[22] 5397 3-8-13 **57**..............................(p) DavidProbert 7 11
(Mark Usher) *chsd ldrs: drvn and wknd 1/2-way: t.o* **25/1**

1m 12.79s (-0.31) **Going Correction** -0.025s/f (Stan) **7** Ran SP% **114.8**
Speed ratings (Par 99): **101,98,97,96,90 89,76**
toteswingers 1&2 £2.60, 1&3 £1.80, 2&3 £3.30 CSF £5.73 CT £11.30 TOTE £1.10: £1.02, £5.70; EX 6.30 Trifecta £17.60 Pool: £1,950.29 - 82.67 winning units..
Owner Heart Of The South Racing **Bred** Tribes Man Syndicate **Trained** Lower Beeding, W Sussex
FOCUS
The market was dominated by recent C&D scorer Marmalady and those who got involved at very skinny odds were duly rewarded
T/Plt: £14.90 to a £1 stake. Pool: £65,287.41 - 3,178.56 winning units T/Qpdt: £9.50 to a £1 stake. Pool: £7,541.32 - 584.67 winning units JN

5948 SALISBURY (R-H)
Thursday, September 5

OFFICIAL GOING: Good to firm (good in places last 2f; watered; 8.8)
Wind: Virtually nil Weather: Sunny

6139 BREEDERS BACK RACING/WHITSBURY MANOR STUD E B F NOVICE STKS 1m
2:10 (2:10) (Class 4) 2-Y-O **£4,528** (£1,347; £673; £336) **Stalls** Centre

Form RPR
1 **Shankly** 2-8-12 0.............................. PaulHanagan 3 80+
(Clive Cox) *lengthy: str: bit bkwd: slowly away: trckd ldng trio: pushed along over 3f out: swtchd to centre over 1f out: rdn and str run jst ins fnl f: led fnl 75yds: comf* **6/1**[3]
0314 **2** *¾* **Faintly (USA)**[19] 5524 2-9-3 82.............................. PatDobbs 2 83
(Amanda Perrett) *travelled wl trcking ldrs: shkn up to ld ent fnl f: sn rdn: no ex whn hdd fnl 75yds* **5/1**[2]
4 **3** *2½* **Sebastian Beach (IRE)**[27] 5244 2-8-12 0.............................. RichardHughes 4 72
(Richard Hannon) *lengthy: str: disp ld after 1f: rdn over 2f out: hdd jst ins fnl f: kpt on same pce* **4/11**[1]
5 **4** *2* **Avocadeau (IRE)**[10] 5819 2-8-12 0.............................. MartinDwyer 1 67
(William Muir) *w'like: led: jnd after 1f: rdn over 2f out: hdd jst ins fnl f: kpt on same pce tl no ex fnl 75yds* **33/1**

1m 44.49s (0.99) **Going Correction** +0.075s/f (Good) **4** Ran SP% **107.2**
Speed ratings (Par 97): **98,97,94,92**
CSF £29.81 TOTE £4.10; EX 25.60 Trifecta £28.90 Pool: £1,447.51 - 37.50 winning units..
Owner D J Burke **Bred** Whitley Stud **Trained** Lambourn, Berks
FOCUS
The going was officially good to firm, good in places in the last 4f (watered). This novice event has been won by some high-class horses over the past ten years, such as subsequent Group 1 winners Punctilious and Cityscape, while recent Gordon Stakes winner Cap O'Rushes took it last year. The four runners didn't go much of a pace and the time was nearly five seconds outside standard, but this was still a taking winning debut.

6140 E B F & SAM SHEPPARD QUIDHAMPTON MAIDEN FILLIES' STKS (DIV I) 6f 212y
2:40 (2:42) (Class 3) 2-Y-O **£7,115** (£2,117; £1,058; £529) **Stalls** Centre

Form RPR
62 **1** **Rosehill Artist (IRE)**[20] 5488 2-9-0 0.............................. AndreaAtzeni 10 76
(Charles Hills) *w'like: mid-div: pushed along 3f out: sn rdn and hdwy: chal jst over 1f out: kpt on wl to ld fnl 75yds: rdn out* **11/4**[2]
4 **2** *½* **Alys Love**[12] 5740 2-9-0 0.............................. MartinDwyer 9 75
(William Muir) *athletic: trckd ldrs: rdn to chal 2f out: led ent fnl f: hdd fnl 75yds: kpt on but no ex* **12/1**
3 *shd* **Dianora** 2-9-0 0.............................. PatDobbs 7 74+
(Sir Michael Stoute) *athletic: s.i.s: towards rr: hdwy on rails 2f out: nt clr run bhd ldrs sn after: swtchd lft ent fnl f: r.o wl to go 3rd nring fin: nrly snatched 2nd* **25/1**
0 **4** *¾* **Wedding Wish (IRE)**[26] 5282 2-9-0 0.............................. TomQueally 6 72
(Michael Bell) *str: hld up towards rr: rdn and stdy prog fr wl over 1f out: fin strly to snatch 4th towards fin* **14/1**
5 *½* **Persian Bolt (USA)** 2-9-0 0.............................. JohnFahy 4 71+
(Eve Johnson Houghton) *unf: hld up in midfield: nt clear run and switchd rt 2f out: prog whn nowhere to go over 1f out: switched lft just ins fnl f: shaken up and styd on wl last 100yds* **50/1**
6 *shd* **On Demand** 2-9-0 0.............................. DavidProbert 3 71
(Andrew Balding) *w'like: lengthy: led: rdn 2f out: hdd ent fnl f: no ex fnl 120yds* **10/1**
3 **7** *1* **Dime Dancer (IRE)**[26] 5282 2-9-0 0.............................. RichardHughes 2 68
(Richard Hannon) *unf: trckd ldrs: struggling to mount chal whn short of room over 1f out: one pce and hld after* **9/4**[1]
00 **8** *nk* **All Yours (IRE)**[22] 5394 2-9-0 0.............................. NeilCallan 1 67
(William Knight) *w ldr: rdn 3f out: kpt on gamely jst bhd ldrs tl short of room on rails fnl 120yds whn hld* **100/1**
0 **9** *9* **Highland Stardust**[19] 5529 2-9-0 0.............................. AdamKirby 11 43
(Clive Cox) *a towards rr* **100/1**
342 **10** *nk* **Gratzie**[10] 5812 2-9-0 0.............................. SamHitchcott 12 42
(Mick Channon) *sn trcking ldrs: rdn over 2f out: wknd over 1f out* **10/1**
0 **11** *9* **Cordial**[48] 4491 2-9-0 0.............................. WilliamBuick 8 18
(John Gosden) *str: mid-div: rdn over 2f out: sn wknd* **9/2**[3]

1m 29.46s (0.86) **Going Correction** +0.075s/f (Good) **11** Ran SP% **115.9**
Speed ratings (Par 96): **98,97,97,96,95 95,94,94,84,83 73**
toteswingers 1&2 £7.80, 1&3 £12.30, 2&3 £20.40 CSF £34.51 TOTE £4.10: £1.30, £3.20, £4.60; EX 40.50 Trifecta £627.30 Pool: £2,903.28 - 3.47 winning units..
Owner John C Grant **Bred** Tullamaine Castle Stud **Trained** Lambourn, Berks
FOCUS
With not much covering the front eight at the line, it's doubtful this is outstanding form, but a few caught the eye.

6141 E B F & SAM SHEPPARD QUIDHAMPTON MAIDEN FILLIES' STKS (DIV II) 6f 212y
3:15 (3:16) (Class 3) 2-Y-O **£7,115** (£2,117; £1,058; £529) **Stalls** Centre

Form RPR
1 **Lustrous** 2-9-0 0.............................. RichardHughes 6 80+
(Richard Hannon) *athletic: mid-div: hdwy over 2f out: rdn to ld ent fnl f: kpt on wl to assert towards fin: readily* **7/1**
00 **2** *2* **Placidia (IRE)**[22] 5394 2-9-0 0.............................. TedDurcan 2 75
(David Lanigan) *str: trckd ldrs: rdn to chse ldr 2f out: chsd wnr ins fnl f: hung rt: kpt on same pce* **10/1**
443 **3** *1* **An Chulainn (IRE)**[12] 5773 2-9-0 0.............................. NeilCallan 3 72
(Mark Johnston) *lw: led: rdn 2f out: hdd ent fnl f: kpt on same pce* **9/4**[1]
4 *1* **Asyad (IRE)** 2-9-0 0.............................. FrankieDettori 8 69+
(Sir Michael Stoute) *lengthy: s.i.s: in last pair: hdwy fr over 2f out: rdn to chse ldng trio over 1f out: no further imp: kpt on same pce* **4/1**[3]
0 **5** *3¾* **Mahatta (IRE)**[22] 5394 2-9-0 0.............................. PaulHanagan 4 59
(Charles Hills) *w'like: racd keenly trcking ldrs: rdn 3f out: nvr gng pce to chal: fdd ins fnl f* **11/1**
6 *nk* **Sweet P** 2-9-0 0.............................. HayleyTurner 7 58
(Marcus Tregoning) *w'like: hung lft and reminder after 1f: nvr bttr than mid-div* **16/1**
7 *16* **Stybba** 2-9-0 0.............................. JamieSpencer 5 15
(Andrew Balding) *w'like: str: s.i.s: towards rr: rdn over 2f out: wknd over 1f out* **3/1**[2]
8 *5* **Petale Noir** 2-9-0 0.............................. AndreaAtzeni 11
(Jonathan Portman) *w'like: bit bkwd: dwlt: a in rr* **40/1**
0 **9** *17* **Spirited Silver**[13] 5698 2-9-0 0.............................. SamHitchcott 10
(John Bridger) *sn prom: rdn over 3f out: wknd over 2f out: t.o* **250/1**

1m 29.87s (1.27) **Going Correction** +0.075s/f (Good) **9** Ran SP% **114.4**
Speed ratings (Par 96): **95,92,91,90,86 85,67,61,42**
toteswingers 1&2 £7.40, 1&3 £4.60, 2&3 £4.50 CSF £73.46 TOTE £7.90: £2.70, £2.80, £1.10; EX 100.90 Trifecta £366.40 Pool: £3,684.21 - 7.53 winning units..
Owner Mrs P Good **Bred** Mrs P Good **Trained** East Everleigh, Wilts
FOCUS
This looked the weaker division and the winning time was 0.41sec slower than the first leg.

6142 EBF STALLIONS & COUNTRY GENTLEMEN'S ASSOCIATION DICK POOLE FILLIES' STKS (LISTED RACE) 6f
3:45 (3:46) (Class 1) 2-Y-O
£19,848 (£7,525; £3,766; £1,876; £941; £472) **Stalls** Low

Form RPR
13 **1** **Joyeuse**[76] 3522 2-8-12 0.............................. TomQueally 5 103+
(Lady Cecil) *lw: travelled wl in tch: tk clsr order over 2f out: rdn to ld ent fnl f: edgd rt: enough in hand and a holding on nring fin: rdn out* **8/11**[1]
41 **2** *nk* **Dorothy B (IRE)**[35] 4924 2-8-12 85.............................. WilliamBuick 6 102+
(John Gosden) *str: hld up last of 6: pushed along 3f out: swtchd lft to centre 2f out: sn rdn: str run ins fnl f: clsng qckly on wnr at fin* **10/1**
153 **3** *2¾* **Wedding Ring (IRE)**[26] 5284 2-8-12 97.............................. MickaelBarzalona 1 93
(Charlie Appleby) *trckd ldrs: rdn over 2f out: ev ch briefly ent fnl f: kpt on same pce* **4/1**[2]
1055 **4** *shd* **Alutiq (IRE)**[14] 5680 2-8-12 95.............................. JamieSpencer 2 93
(Eve Johnson Houghton) *in tch: pushed along and hdwy whn swtchd rt and nt clr run whn abt to mount chal over 1f out: snatched up: swtchd bk lft: no ch after but r.o fnl 120yds* **8/1**[3]
5136 **5** *1* **Lamar (IRE)**[26] 5284 2-8-12 88.............................. NeilCallan 3 90
(James Tate) *led: rdn over 2f out: hdd ent fnl f: fdd* **40/1**
2132 **6** *1* **Lilbourne Lass**[5] 5994 2-8-12 96..............................(p) RichardHughes 4 87
(Richard Hannon) *trckd ldr: rdn and ev ch 2f out tl jst over 1f out: fdd fnl f* **8/1**[3]

1m 14.75s (-0.05) **Going Correction** +0.075s/f (Good) **6** Ran SP% **111.7**
Speed ratings (Par 100): **103,102,98,98,97 96**
toteswingers 1&2 £3.20, 1&3 £1.50, 2&3 £2.90 CSF £9.07 TOTE £1.60: £1.30, £3.60; EX 8.70 Trifecta £25.00 Pool: £3,211.01 - 96.18 winning units..
Owner K Abdullah **Bred** Juddmonte Farms Ltd **Trained** Newmarket, Suffolk
FOCUS
This Listed event can go to a smart filly, with the 2008 winner Serious Attitude going on to win the Cheveley Park and a Grade 1 in Canada, while last year's winner Winning Express went on to finish runner-up in the Cheveley Park and fourth in this year's 1000 Guineas. It was encouraging that this year's finish was fought out between the two most lightly raced fillies in the field.

6143 "CHOOSE EBF NOMINATED" LOCHSONG FILLIES' STKS (H'CAP) 6f 212y
4:20 (4:20) (Class 2) (0-100,98) 3-Y-0+ **£14,006** (£4,194; £2,097; £1,048; £524) **Stalls** Centre

Form RPR
0126 **1** **Tantshi (IRE)**[40] 4766 3-8-12 **90**.............................. AndreaAtzeni 3 103
(Roger Varian) *travelled wl: hld up last of 5 wl in tch: tk clsr order over 2f out: shkn up to chal ent fnl f: led fnl 100yds: edgd rt: rdn out* **7/2**[2]
-132 **2** *nk* **Ghanaian (FR)**[20] 5493 3-8-12 **90**.............................. MickaelBarzalona 1 102
(Charlie Appleby) *swtg: travelled wl: trckd ldrs: swtchd out to chal over 1f out: rdn to ld jst ins fnl f: hdd fnl 100yds: carried rt: kpt on* **6/4**[1]
1211 **3** *3* **Floating Along (IRE)**[29] 5125 3-8-6 **84** oh2.............................. PaulHanagan 2 88
(William Haggas) *lw: led: rdn and hrd pressed fr over 1f out: hdd jst ins fnl f: no ex* **7/2**[2]
2066 **4** *7* **Poetic Dancer**[19] 5533 4-8-6 **85**.............................. RyanTate(5) 4 70
(Clive Cox) *trckd ldrs: rdn over 2f out: wknd fnl f* **6/1**[3]
306 **5** *1* **I'm So Glad**[26] 5285 4-9-0 **91**.............................. CharlesBishop(3) 6 73
(Mick Channon) *trckd ldr: rdn over 2f out: wknd fnl f* **10/1**

1m 27.98s (-0.62) **Going Correction** +0.075s/f (Good)
WFA 3 from 4yo 4lb **5** Ran SP% **107.8**
Speed ratings (Par 96): **106,105,102,94,93**
CSF £8.82 TOTE £4.00: £1.50, £1.50; EX 9.90 Trifecta £22.40 Pool: £2,499.09 - 83.50 winning units..
Owner Sheikh Ahmed Al Maktoum **Bred** Darley **Trained** Newmarket, Suffolk
FOCUS
The 3-y-o fillies dominated this handicap and that generation were winning this for the eighth time in ten years.

6144 CGA "PERSIAN PUNCH" CONDITIONS STKS 1m 6f 21y
4:50 (4:50) (Class 2) 3-Y-0+
£12,450 (£3,728; £1,864; £932; £466; £234)

Form RPR
0000 **1** **Viking Storm**[15] 5655 5-9-2 94.............................. JamieSpencer 6 100
(Harry Dunlop) *hld up in last pair: pushed along over 4f out: outpcd over 3f out: gd hdwy in centre over 2f out: led over 1f out: styd on wl to assert ins fnl f* **14/1**
041 **2** *¾* **Asbaab (USA)**[41] 4719 3-8-7 98.............................. PaulHanagan 2 101
(Brian Meehan) *lw: led: qcknd pce wl over 3f out: rdn over 2f out: hdd over 1f out: ev ch tl edgd lft and no ex fnl 120yds: jst hld on for 2nd* **7/1**[3]
3541 **3** *shd* **Mysterious Man (IRE)**[12] 5746 4-9-2 94.............................. JimmyFortune 1 99
(Andrew Balding) *trckd ldng trio: outpcd 4f out: styd on fr over 1f out: fin strly: jst failed to snatch 2nd* **3/1**[2]

3-40 **4** 1 **Cavaleiro (IRE)**[37] 4857 4-9-2 97 .... HayleyTurner 4 97
(Marcus Tregoning) *trckd ldng pair: swtchd lft 3f out: sn rdn: nvr gng pce to mount chal: styd on fnl f* **7/1**[3]

2042 **5** ½ **Suegioo (FR)**[12] 5746 4-9-2 92 .... (p) PaoloSirigu 5 97
(Marco Botti) *hld up last of 6: pushed along over 6f out: outpcd and plenty to do wl over 3f out: stdy prog fr 2f out: styd on fnl f wout threatening to rch ldrs* **8/1**

1365 **6** 3 **No Heretic**[35] 4919 5-9-2 100 .... JimCrowley 3 93
(David Simcock) *trckd ldr: sltly outpcd wl over 3f out: kpt chsng ldr tl over 1f out: no ex ins fnl f* **6/4**[1]

3m 4.51s (-2.89) **Going Correction** +0.075s/f (Good)
WFA 3 from 4yo+ 11lb **6** Ran SP% **107.8**
Speed ratings (Par 109): **111,110,110,109,109 107**
toteswingers 1&2 £9.10, 1&3 £6.00, 2&3 £3.20 CSF £94.09 TOTE £16.00: £5.60, £3.60; EX 59.20 Trifecta £499.00 Pool: £2,532.07 - 3.80 winning units..
Owner Be Hopeful Partnership **Bred** Charlie Wyatt **Trained** Lambourn, Berks

FOCUS
A strange staying conditions event in some ways, as despite the gallop looking solid there wasn't much covering the front five at the line.

6145 SYDENHAMS MAIDEN STKS 5f
5:20 (5:20) (Class 4) 3-Y-0+ **£5,175** (£1,540; £769; £384) **Stalls** Low

Form RPR

0 **1** **Threave**[106] 2576 5-8-8 0 .... OisinMurphy(7) 6 70
(Violet M Jordan) *taken steadily to s: mde all: shkn up over 1f out: r.o strly: readily* **20/1**

25 **2** 4 **Perfect Muse**[21] 5444 3-9-0 0 .... AdamKirby 1 55
(Clive Cox) *trckd wnr: rdn for brief effrt over 1f out: sn outpcd* **11/8**[1]

30 **3** 1¼ **Spiraea**[68] 3837 3-9-0 0 .... PatDobbs 2 51
(Mark Rimell) *trckd wnr: rdn over 1f out: nt pce to mount chal* **2/1**[2]

3462 **4** ½ **New Rich**[5] 5981 3-9-5 52 .... (p) JohnFahy 5 54
(Eve Johnson Houghton) *hld up but wl in tch: rdn wl over 1f out: nvr gng pce to get involved* **3/1**[3]

3640 **5** 6 **Island Express (IRE)**[9] 5864 6-9-1 53 .... (tp) AnnStokell(5) 4 32
(Ann Stokell) *slowly away: sn trcking ldrs: rdn wl over 2f out: wknd ent fnl f* **25/1**

50 **6** ¾ **Lady Rain**[38] 4839 4-8-8 0 .... ShelleyBirkett(7) 3 25
(Milton Bradley) *chsd ldrs: rdn over 2f out: wknd ent fnl f* **50/1**

1m 1.8s (0.80) **Going Correction** +0.075s/f (Good)
WFA 3 from 4yo+ 1lb **6** Ran SP% **111.0**
Speed ratings (Par 105): **96,89,87,86,77 76**
toteswingers 1&2 £5.50, 1&3 £5.10, 2&3 £1.60 CSF £47.42 TOTE £20.80: £6.60, £1.30; EX 46.40 Trifecta £253.30 Pool: £2,784.22 - 8.24 winning units..
Owner Mrs Jackie Cornwell **Bred** Mrs J A Cornwell **Trained** Moreton Morrell, Warwicks

FOCUS
This wasn't great for an £8,000 contest and the front pair in the market had both disappointed on their seconds starts following promising debuts, so perhaps the race was set up for a shock.

6146 CGA RACING EXCELLENCE APPRENTICE H'CAP (WHIPS SHALL BE CARRIED BUT NOT USED) 1m
5:50 (5:50) (Class 5) (0-70,69) 3-Y-0+ **£2,911** (£866; £432; £216) **Stalls** Centre

Form RPR

4620 **1** **Lady Sylvia**[11] 5793 4-9-8 65 .... PatMillman 3 74
(Joseph Tuite) *hld up bhd ldrs: swtchd lft and hdwy 2f out: led ent fnl f: r.o wl: readily* **9/2**[3]

6005 **2** 1 **Lambert Pen (USA)**[21] 5429 3-8-2 55 oh3 .... DanielCremin(5) 4 62
(Mick Channon) *hld up but in tch: swtchd lft and hdwy over 1f out: chsd wnr jst ins fnl f: r.o for clr 2nd but a being hld* **8/1**

304 **3** 6 **Moortahan**[21] 5444 3-9-0 69 .... CameronHardie(7) 7 62
(Richard Hannon) *trckd ldrs: ev ch briefly ent fnl f: no ex* **6/1**

3522 **4** nk **South Cape**[33] 4996 10-9-0 64 .... JayneFarwell(7) 2 57
(Gary Moore) *led for 1f: trckd ldr: led 2f out: hdd ent fnl f: no ex* **3/1**[2]

4355 **5** 4½ **Catchanova (IRE)**[11] 5793 6-8-9 57 .... CharlieBennett(5) 8 39
(Eve Johnson Houghton) *led after 1f tl 2f out: wknd ent fnl f* **11/4**[1]

000 **6** 2½ **Olivers Mount**[84] 3250 3-8-7 55 oh8 .... OisinMurphy 6 31
(Ed Vaughan) *s.i.s: sn cl up: chal 2f out tl wknd ent fnl f* **10/1**

046 **7** hd **Beep**[17] 5588 3-9-5 67 .... ShelleyBirkett 1 43
(Lydia Richards) *trckd ldrs: rdn 3f out: wknd ent fnl f* **10/1**

1m 45.42s (1.92) **Going Correction** +0.075s/f (Good)
WFA 3 from 4yo+ 5lb **7** Ran SP% **113.4**
Speed ratings (Par 103): **93,92,86,85,81 78,78**
toteswingers 1&2 £5.70, 1&3 £4.60, 2&3 £9.30 CSF £38.47 CT £215.65 TOTE £3.60: £2.50, £4.20; EX 47.40 Trifecta £287.70 Pool: £2,062.33 - 5.37 winning units..
Owner David J Keast **Bred** Highclere Stud **Trained** Great Shefford, Berks

FOCUS
A modest apprentice handicap in which the first two home occupied the last two positions at halfway.
T/Plt: £410.80 to a £1 stake. Pool: £53,375.51 - 94.83 winning units T/Qpdt: £18.20 to a £1 stake. Pool: £4,663.25 - 188.70 winning units TM

6147 - 6151a (Foreign Racing) - See Raceform Interactive

5811

CHEPSTOW (L-H)
Friday, September 6

OFFICIAL GOING: Good to soft (good in places;7.6)
Wind: Moderate across Weather: Overcast

6152 32REDPOKER.COM MAIDEN AUCTION STKS 1m 14y
2:20 (2:21) (Class 6) 2-Y-0 **£1,940** (£577; £288; £144) **Stalls** Centre

Form RPR

3 **1** **Top Dollar**[9] 5891 2-8-9 0 ow1 .... NeilCallan 7 66+
(James Tate) *fly j. stalls: sn trcking ldrs: led gng wl appr fnl 2f: readily* **11/10**[1]

000 **2** 1¼ **My Anchor**[44] 4631 2-8-9 45 .... LiamKeniry 5 63
(Sylvester Kirk) *chsd ldrs: wnt 2nd over 3f out: chal wl over 2f out: chsd wnr fnl 2f but no imp fnl f* **20/1**

005 **3** 1 **Ambria's Fury (IRE)**[7] 5950 2-8-9 0 .... SamHitchcott 1 61
(Mick Channon) *chsd ldrs: rdn over 2f out: kpt on to take 3rd jst ins fnl f but nvr gng pce to trble wnr* **7/1**[3]

00 **4** hd **Kaizen Factor**[26] 5309 2-8-13 0 .... DavidProbert 10 64
(Rod Millman) *chsd ldr tl over 3f out: styd on same pce fr over 1f out* **33/1**

0 **5** ½ **Trigger Park (IRE)**[11] 5811 2-8-11 0 .... CathyGannon 12 61
(Ronald Harris) *wnt rt s: sn in tch: rdn over 2f out: styd on fnl f* **33/1**

06 **6** 4½ **Stagewise (IRE)**[22] 5442 2-8-6 0 .... WilliamCarson 11 46
(Jonathan Portman) *chsd ldrs: rdn 3f out: wknd over 1f out* **10/1**

06 **7** 1½ **Dandys Perier (IRE)**[11] 5811 2-8-11 0 .... LukeMorris 4 47
(Ronald Harris) *led tl hdd wl over 2f out: sn btn* **16/1**

6 **8** 6 **Gold Class**[25] 5338 2-8-11 0 .... ShaneKelly 3 34
(Ed McMahon) *outpcd* **11/4**[2]

0 **9** shd **Permsiri (IRE)**[9] 5891 2-7-13 0 .... PhilipPrince(5) 2 26
(Malcolm Saunders) *s.i.s: sn rdn: a in rr* **66/1**

0 **10** 1¾ **Holy Water (IRE)**[22] 5443 2-8-8 0 .... MatthewLawson(3) 6 29
(Jonathan Portman) *s.i.s: rdn: green and a in rr* **33/1**

1m 35.78s (-0.42) **Going Correction** -0.175s/f (Firm) **10** Ran SP% **116.8**
Speed ratings (Par 93): **95,93,92,92,92 87,86,80,79,78**
toteswingers 1&2 £9.90, 2&3 £8.70, 1&3 £2.60 CSF £31.69 TOTE £2.10: £1.10, £5.40, £2.10; EX 20.20 Trifecta £103.30 Pool: £862.45 - 6.25 winning units..
Owner Saeed Manana **Bred** Shawahed Thoroughbred Corporation **Trained** Newmarket, Suffolk

FOCUS
The ground had eased from its overnight description of good all over. Neil Callan described conditions as "just on the easy side." A very moderate maiden with no depth, in which the first five finished clear.

6153 32RED.COM H'CAP 1m 14y
2:50 (2:52) (Class 6) (0-65,65) 3-Y-0+ **£1,940** (£577; £288; £144) **Stalls** Centre

Form RPR

54-0 **1** **Amulet**[30] 5152 3-9-2 62 .... ShaneKelly 8 70
(Eve Johnson Houghton) *mde all: drvn 2f out: styd on wl: u.p fnl f* **25/1**

4005 **2** ½ **Bursledon (IRE)**[14] 5694 3-9-4 64 .... (v[1]) SeanLevey 1 71
(Richard Hannon) *in rr: hdwy fr 2f out: drvn over 1f out: styd on to chse wnr fnl 110yds but a hld* **7/1**[3]

0502 **3** 1 **Hail Promenader (IRE)**[4] 6038 7-9-0 55 .... (bt) WilliamCarson 7 60
(Anthony Carson) *sn chsng wnr: rdn over 2f out: no imp fnl f and lost 2nd fnl 110yds* **7/2**[1]

5435 **4** nk **Bobs Her Uncle**[46] 4584 4-9-7 62 .... TedDurcan 10 66
(James Bethell) *chsd ldrs: rdn over 2f out: kpt on fnl f but nvr gng pce to chal* **6/1**[2]

6-22 **5** 2 **Sword Of The Lord**[8] 5923 3-8-10 59 .... WilliamTwiston-Davies(3) 3 58
(Michael Bell) *in tch: rdn and hdwy over 2f out: no imp appr fnl f* **7/2**[1]

-040 **6** 2¾ **Signature Dish (IRE)**[29] 5181 3-9-5 65 .... DavidProbert 11 58
(Andrew Balding) *in tch: rdn 3f out: hung lft over 2f out and sn btn* **12/1**

2640 **7** hd **Delightful Sleep**[7] 5948 5-8-11 59 .... EoinWalsh(7) 4 52
(David Evans) *in rr: hdwy and in tch over 2f out: sn rdn and no further prog* **16/1**

5012 **8** 4½ **Tanforan**[22] 5429 11-8-11 59 .... ShelleyBirkett(7) 12 41
(Brian Baugh) *chsd ldrs over 5f* **7/1**[3]

-004 **9** ½ **Captain Oats (IRE)**[22] 5432 10-8-10 51 oh1 .... CathyGannon 6 32
(Pam Ford) *s.i.s: a towards rr* **50/1**

0605 **10** 10 **Nezami (IRE)**[20] 5521 8-9-7 62 .... NeilCallan 9 20
(Patrick Clinton) *chsd ldrs 5f* **10/1**

3300 **11** 22 **Offbeat Safaris (IRE)**[11] 5816 5-9-1 56 .... (p) LukeMorris 2
(Ronald Harris) *chsd ldrs to 1/2-way* **25/1**

1m 33.7s (-2.50) **Going Correction** -0.175s/f (Firm)
WFA 3 from 4yo+ 5lb **11** Ran SP% **116.0**
Speed ratings (Par 101): **105,104,103,103,101 98,98,93,93,83 61**
toteswingers 1&2 £39.40, 2&3 £5.50, 1&3 £21.90 CSF £186.14 CT £788.11 TOTE £25.80: £6.60, £2.60, £1.50; EX 264.40 Trifecta £1092.30 Part won. Pool: £1456.44 - 0.84 winning units..
Owner Mrs Virginia Neale **Bred** Cherry Park Stud **Trained** Blewbury, Oxon

FOCUS
Modest handicap form. Few got involved.

6154 32RED CASINO H'CAP 7f 16y
3:20 (3:22) (Class 6) (0-65,65) 3-Y-0+ **£1,940** (£577; £288; £144) **Stalls** Centre

Form RPR

5610 **1** **The Great Gabrial**[21] 5471 4-9-5 60 .... (v[1]) AidanColeman 6 72
(Ian Williams) *trckd ldr: led appr fnl f: readily* **7/1**

-213 **2** 2¼ **Thankyou Very Much**[64] 3983 3-9-3 62 .... TedDurcan 12 67
(James Bethell) *in tch: rdn over 2f out: styd on fnl f to chse wnr fnl 75yds but nvr any ch: hld on wl for 2nd* **5/2**[1]

6302 **3** nk **Emiratesdotcom**[11] 5816 7-9-10 65 .... (p) LiamKeniry 5 70
(Milton Bradley) *in rr: rdn: swtchd rt and hdwy over 1f out: styd on u.p fnl f to press 2nd in clsng stages but nvr any ch w wnr* **7/2**[2]

0650 **4** ¾ **My Learned Friend (IRE)**[56] 4237 9-8-12 60 .... (p) RobHornby(7) 9 63
(Andrew Balding) *chsd ldrs: rdn along over 2f out: styd on same pce fnl f* **20/1**

406 **5** ½ **Thewestwalian (USA)**[109] 2496 5-8-10 51 oh1 .... WilliamCarson 4 53
(Peter Hiatt) *led: rdn 2f out: hdd appr fnl f: wknd fnl 110yds* **20/1**

-604 **6** 2¼ **Ozz**[11] 5841 4-9-7 62 .... (bt) LukeMorris 1 58
(Frank Sheridan) *in rr and sn hrd drvn: stl plenty to do over 1f out: r.o u.p fnl f: kpt on in clsng stages* **6/1**[3]

5-00 **7** hd **Carlarajah**[20] 5541 3-9-2 64 .... (v[1]) WilliamTwiston-Davies(3) 3 58
(Michael Bell) *disp 2nd tl over 2f out: wknd ins fnl f* **10/1**

6424 **8** nk **Little Choosey**[25] 5349 3-9-1 65 .... (p) RyanTate(5) 8 59
(Clive Cox) *chsd ldrs: rdn 3f out: wknd over 1f out* **8/1**

-560 **9** 2½ **Frosted Off**[21] 5499 3-8-7 52 .... SamHitchcott 7 39
(John Spearing) *in rr: drvn over 2f out: sme hdwy fnl f* **50/1**

0560 **10** 1½ **Schoolboy Champ**[11] 5816 6-8-3 51 oh6 .... (tp) EoinWalsh(7) 2 35
(Lisa Williamson) *in tch: rdn 1/2-way and sn outpcd: no ch after* **25/1**

6005 **11** 2¾ **Annie Besant**[20] 5512 3-8-6 51 oh2 .... JimmyQuinn 11 27
(Michael Mullineaux) *rdn 3f out: a outpcd* **20/1**

1m 22.59s (-0.61) **Going Correction** -0.175s/f (Firm)
WFA 3 from 4yo+ 4lb **11** Ran SP% **117.9**
Speed ratings (Par 101): **96,93,93,92,91 89,88,88,85,83 80**
toteswingers 1&2 £6.40, 2&3 £2.40, 1&3 £6.30 CSF £23.02 CT £74.72 TOTE £8.90: £3.00, £1.20, £1.40; EX 35.60 Trifecta £124.50 Pool: £1567.87 -9.43 winning units..
Owner Dr Marwan Koukash **Bred** Juddmonte Farms Ltd **Trained** Portway, Worcs

FOCUS
Another very ordinary handicap. This time the field raced towards the far side.

6155 32RED ON THE APP STORE APPRENTICE (S) STKS 7f 16y
3:50 (3:50) (Class 6) 3-4-Y-0 **£1,940** (£577; £288; £144) **Stalls** Centre

Form RPR

524 **1** **Peak Storm**[29] 5172 4-9-3 66 .... (p) CiaranMckee(5) 1 71
(John O'Shea) *s.i.s: in tch: pressed ldrs fr 3f out tl rdn to take slt ld 1f out: styd on wl* **6/4**[2]

4-66 **2** 1 **Billyrayvalentine (CAN)**[14] 5722 4-9-3 77 ....[1] CharlesBishop 4 63
(George Baker) *t.k.h: trckd ldrs: chal 3f out: led over 2f out: rdn and hdd 1f out: styd on same pce* **5/4**[1]

0060 **3** *5* **Ficelle (IRE)**[11] 5817 4-8-7 52........................ OisinMurphy(5) 2 45
(Ronald Harris) *in tch: drvn to chse ldrs 3f out: outpcd over 1f out: wknd fnl 110yds* **16/1**

4320 **4** *2* **Admirals Walk (IRE)**[9] 5890 3-8-8 60..........(tp) JoshBaudains(5) 6 45
(Sylvester Kirk) *led: jnd 3f out: hdd over 2f out: wknd 1f out* **5/1**[3]

0 **5** *7* **Mobley Chaos**[11] 5813 3-8-10 0........................ PhilipPrince(3) 3 27
(Ronald Harris) *early spd: wknd 3f out* **100/1**

-00U **6** *2 1/4* **Buds Bruvver**[32] 5073 4-8-12 25........................ EoinWalsh(5) 7 21
(Brian Baugh) *sn rdn: wnt lft u.p and wl bhd fnl 4f* **100/1**

1m 24.09s (0.89) **Going Correction** -0.175s/f (Firm)
WFA 3 from 4yo 4lb **6** Ran SP% **109.0**
Speed ratings (Par 101): **87,85,80,77,69 67**
toteswingers 1&2 £1.10, 2&3 £1.90, 1&3 £2.90 CSF £3.44 TOTE £2.70: £2.00, £1.10; EX 4.30 Trifecta £14.00 Pool: £2467.32 - 131.78 winning units..The winner was bought in for £5500.
Owner The Cross Racing Club **Bred** Redhill Bloodstock Limited **Trained** Elton, Gloucs

FOCUS
They went a fair gallop in this seller, which was run in a time 1.5sec slower than the previous handicap.

6156 FOWNHOPE MITSUBISHI H'CAP 6f 16y
4:20 (4:22) (Class 6) (0-60,60) 3-Y-0+ **£1,940** (£577; £288; £144) **Stalls** Centre

Form RPR

0062 **1** **Euroquip Boy (IRE)**[11] 5818 6-8-0 46 oh1........................ IanBurns(7) 8 56
(Michael Scudamore) *chsd ldrs: led 2f out: rdn over 1f out: kpt on fnl f: jst lasted* **9/2**[2]

060 **2** *shd* **Diamond Vine (IRE)**[11] 5817 5-9-0 53........................(v) LukeMorris 1 63
(Ronald Harris) *chsd ldrs: chal fr 2f out: upsides u.p fnl f: jst failed* **20/1**

1223 **3** *nse* **Verus Delicia (IRE)**[31] 5097 4-9-7 60........................ ShaneKelly 7 70+
(John Stimpson) *in rr: nt clr run and swtchd rt 2f out: rapid hdwy fnl f: fin fast: jst failed* **7/1**

4261 **4** *2 1/4* **Dancing Welcome**[11] 5818 7-8-12 58 6ex..........(bt) WillPettis(7) 14 60
(Milton Bradley) *chsd ldrs: rdn over 2f out: styd on same pce ins fnl f* **10/1**

3560 **5** *2 1/2* **Hamis Al Bin (IRE)**[24] 5373 4-9-5 58........................ SteveDrowne 3 52
(Milton Bradley) *hdwy 3f out: chsd ldrs and rdn 2f out: wknd ins fnl f* **20/1**

0-02 **6** *1 1/4* **Monty Fay (IRE)**[11] 5817 4-8-8 47 oh1 ow1........................ TedDurcan 12 37
(Derek Haydn Jones) *pressed ldr 3f: sn rdn: wknd fnl f* **6/1**[3]

0006 **7** *1/2* **Superior Edge**[31] 5094 6-8-13 59........................(p) OisinMurphy(7) 15 48
(Christopher Mason) *chsd ldrs: wknd fnl f* **16/1**

0013 **8** *1 3/4* **Blue Clumber**[8] 5916 3-8-11 52........................ JimmyQuinn 6 35
(Shaun Harris) *chsd ldrs: outpcd 3f out: spome prog again fnl f* **16/1**

0400 **9** *3/4* **Depden (IRE)**[10] 5864 5-8-0 46 oh1........................(p) LouisSteward(7) 10 27
(Richard Price) *in tch: rdn and outpcd over 2f out* **25/1**

4402 **10** *nk* **Jarrow (IRE)**[4] 6033 6-9-7 60........................(p) JohnFahy 2 40
(Milton Bradley) *slt ld tl hdd 2f out: sn btn* **8/1**

5263 **11** *1 1/4* **One Last Dream**[77] 3529 4-9-3 56........................ WilliamCarson 13 32
(Ron Hodges) *early spd: sn bhd* **7/2**[1]

6244 **12** *nk* **Scommettitrice (IRE)**[4] 6033 5-8-11 55..........(b) PhilipPrince(5) 4 30
(Mark Gillard) *s.i.s: outpcd* **16/1**

2/5- **13** *1 3/4* **Interchoice Star**[357] 6195 8-9-1 54........................(p) FergusSweeney 5 23
(Ray Peacock) *chsd ldrs over 3f* **33/1**

1m 10.74s (-1.26) **Going Correction** -0.175s/f (Firm)
WFA 3 from 4yo+ 2lb **13** Ran SP% **121.3**
Speed ratings (Par 101): **101,100,100,97,94 92,92,89,88,88 86,86,84**
toteswingers 1&2 £25.70, 2&3 £36.80, 1&3 £5.10 CSF £98.22 CT £656.80 TOTE £7.60: £2.60, £8.30, £2.30; EX 135.10 Trifecta £1262.80 Part won. Pool: £1683.74 - 0.26 winning units..
Owner Ted Bennett **Bred** Gerard And Yvonne Kennedy **Trained** Bromsash, H'fords

FOCUS
A very modest sprint with a tight finish.

6157 32RED H'CAP 5f 16y
4:50 (4:51) (Class 6) (0-55,54) 3-Y-0+ **£1,940** (£577; £288; £144) **Stalls** Centre

Form RPR

4006 **1** **Trending (IRE)**[17] 5602 4-9-7 54........................(bt) SeanLevey 8 64+
(Jeremy Gask) *chsd ldrs: rdn to ld 1f out: drvn out* **3/1**[2]

5103 **2** *2 1/2* **Little China**[6] 5982 4-9-3 50........................(b) SteveDrowne 3 51
(William Muir) *chsd ldrs: rdn over 1f out: kpt on to take 2nd in clsng stages but no ch w wnr* **5/2**[1]

5005 **3** *hd* **Chelsea Grey (IRE)**[30] 5128 3-8-11 45........................(b) CathyGannon 6 45
(Ronald Harris) *racd stands' side: chsd ldrs: rdn 2f out: kpt on u.p fnl f to press for 2nd in clsng stages but no ch w wnr* **12/1**

5334 **4** *1/2* **Imperial Spirit**[6] 5981 3-8-8 49........................(v) DanielCremin(7) 2 47
(Mick Channon) *pressed ldr: slt ld fr 3f out: hdd 1f out: wknd fnl 110yds* **5/1**

0505 **5** *1/2* **Courageous (IRE)**[28] 5221 7-9-2 49........................ JohnFahy 4 46
(Milton Bradley) *in rr: sn pushed along and outpcd: hdwy appr fnl f: kpt on in clsng stages* **12/1**

0604 **6** *4* **Dropping Zone**[23] 5407 3-9-1 49........................ MickyFenton 9 31+
(Des Donovan) *s.i.s: sn chsng ldrs: wknd over 1f out: eased whn no ch* **7/2**[3]

0000 **7** *1* **Bheleyf (IRE)**[30] 5128 3-9-4 52........................ PatCosgrave 1 31
(Joseph Tuite) *slt ld tl hdd 3f out: wknd over 1f out: eased whn no ch* **16/1**

59.31s (0.01) **Going Correction** -0.175s/f (Firm)
WFA 3 from 4yo+ 1lb **7** Ran SP% **113.7**
Speed ratings (Par 101): **92,88,87,86,86 79,78**
toteswingers 1&2 £2.60, 2&3 £3.80, 1&3 £2.80 CSF £10.83 CT £75.09 TOTE £3.60: £1.30, £2.60; EX 13.10 Trifecta £67.90 Pool: £3223.60 - 35.56 winning units..
Owner The Twitterati **Bred** Thomas Hassett **Trained** Sutton Veny, Wilts

FOCUS
A weak handicap.

6158 £32 FREE AT 32RED.COM H'CAP 1m 4f 23y
5:20 (5:20) (Class 5) (0-70,70) 3-Y-0+ **£2,587** (£770; £384; £192) **Stalls** Low

Form RPR

4001 **1** **Eton Rambler (USA)**[28] 5217 3-9-1 68........................(p) PatCosgrave 7 77
(George Baker) *in rr: hdwy over 2f out: styd on u.p to ld fnl 150yds: drvn out* **8/1**

6265 **2** *1 1/4* **Musikhani**[64] 3990 3-8-10 70........................ OisinMurphy(7) 12 77
(Andrew Balding) *chsd ldrs: rdn to ld over 1f out: hdd and outpcd fnl 150yds* **9/4**[1]

3-15 **3** *3/4* **Afro**[31] 5102 3-8-9 65........................ CharlesBishop(3) 1 71
(Peter Hedger) *in tch drvn and hdwy to chse ldrs fr 2f out: styd on fnl f to take 3rd fnl 50yds: nt rch ldng duo* **10/1**

6425 **4** *1 1/4* **Knight's Parade (IRE)**[17] 5606 3-9-3 70........................ SeanLevey 10 74
(Amanda Perrett) *in tch: hdwy 4f out: chsd ldrs and drvn 2f out: one pce fnl f* **7/1**[3]

4331 **5** *hd* **Whitefall (USA)**[22] 5434 3-8-6 59........................ JimmyQuinn 9 63
(David Evans) *chsd ldrs: led over 2f out: hdd over 1f out: wknd fnl f* **7/1**[3]

6031 **6** *1/2* **Flash Crash**[12] 5803 4-9-0 58........................(t) WilliamCarson 13 61
(Anthony Carson) *in rr: rdn and hdwy 3f out: one pce u.p over 1f out* **6/1**[2]

2040 **7** *8* **The Quarterjack**[26] 5312 4-9-10 68........................ CathyGannon 6 58
(Ron Hodges) *in rr: rdn along over 5f out: nvr nr ldrs* **12/1**

6543 **8** *3/4* **Silk Route**[23] 5403 3-8-13 66........................ FergusSweeney 5 55
(Henry Candy) *chsd ldrs: wknd over 2f out* **8/1**

4600 **9** *3/4* **Highlife Dancer**[15] 5312 5-8-12 63........................(v) DanielCremin(7) 11 51
(Mick Channon) *led after 2f: hdd over 2f out: sn wknd* **25/1**

500- **10** *53* **Almail (USA)**[315] 7380 7-9-7 65........................ SteveDrowne 3
(Jamie Osborne) *led 2f: wknd 3f out: virtually p.u fnl f* **33/1**

0463 **U** **Batchelors Star (IRE)**[14] 5694 5-9-8 66........................(t) MickyFenton 8
(Seamus Durack) *in rr: rdn and no ch whn stmbld and uns rdr appr fnl f* **12/1**

2m 36.32s (-2.68) **Going Correction** -0.175s/f (Firm)
WFA 3 from 4yo+ 9lb **11** Ran SP% **123.5**
Speed ratings (Par 103): **101,100,99,98,98 98,93,92,92,56**
toteswingers 1&2 £6.30, 2&3 £7.80, 1&3 £14.50 CSF £27.66 CT £193.41 TOTE £11.40: £2.70, £1.70, £4.00; EX 46.10 Trifecta £505.00 Pool: £2274.87 - 3.37 winning units..
Owner The Eton Ramblers **Bred** Darley, Bengal B'Stock Llc, J D Vice,Dvm **Trained** Manton, Wilts

FOCUS
Just a Class 5 handicap but the best race on the card, as well as the only one on the round course. The first six finished in a heap, well clear of the others.
T/Plt: £18.90 to a £1 stake. Pool of £73916.25 - 2844.56 winning tickets. T/Qpdt: £4.60 to a £1 stake. Pool of £5192.18 - 826.78 winning tickets ST

6125 HAYDOCK (L-H)
Friday, September 6

OFFICIAL GOING: Good to soft changing to soft after race 3 (3.00)
Wind: Light, across Weather: Overcast and showers

6159 BETFRED SHARPLES GROUP H'CAP 5f
2:00 (2:02) (Class 4) (0-85,85) 3-Y-0+ **£5,175** (£1,540; £769; £384) **Stalls** Centre

Form RPR

2430 **1** **Imperial Legend (IRE)**[7] 5971 4-9-2 80........................(p) TomQueally 11 90
(David Nicholls) *hld up in midfield: hdwy ent fnl f: r.o to ld towards fin* **9/1**

1000 **2** *1/2* **Rusty Rocket (IRE)**[6] 5991 4-9-7 85........................ JoeFanning 14 93
(Paul Green) *sn led: rdn over 1f out: hdd towards fin* **7/1**[2]

2351 **3** *3/4* **Diman Waters (IRE)**[29] 5183 6-9-1 82........................ JasonHart(3) 13 87
(Eric Alston) *s.i.s: chsd ldrs: effrt over 1f out: chal ins fnl f: styd on: hld towards fin* **8/1**[3]

1000 **4** *2 1/4* **Pea Shooter**[7] 5971 4-9-0 78........................(p) GrahamLee 5 75+
(Kevin Ryan) *in tch in centre: effrt to chse ldrs over 1f out: one pce fnl 75yds* **8/1**[3]

3025 **5** *3/4* **Moorhouse Lad**[20] 5519 10-9-6 84........................ AdamKirby 10 79
(Garry Moss) *chsd ldrs: n.m.r and lost pl over 1f out: rallied and kpt on towards fin* **9/1**

6040 **6** *1/2* **Whitecrest**[21] 5498 5-8-13 77........................ ChrisCatlin 12 70
(John Spearing) *prom: pushed along and ev ch 2f out: one pce ins fnl f* **20/1**

300 **7** *nse* **Perfect Blossom**[19] 5561 6-9-1 79........................ PaulMulrennan 2 72
(Alan Berry) *towards rr: hdwy over 2f out: chsd ldrs over 1f out: no ex wl ins fnl f* **33/1**

102- **8** *hd* **Senator Bong**[303] 7635 3-8-11 76........................ RyanMoore 7 68
(David Elsworth) *stdd s: hld up in midfield: effrt over 1f out: edgd lft and no imp ins fnl f* **9/2**[1]

0300 **9** *1/2* **Oldjoesaid**[31] 5108 9-8-12 76 ow1........................ PhillipMakin 4 66
(Paul Midgley) *hld up: pushed along over 1f out: no imp* **14/1**

6050 **10** *nse* **Chunky Diamond (IRE)**[6] 5985 4-8-8 72..........(t) JamesSullivan 3 62
(Ruth Carr) *s.i.s: hld up in rr: rdn over 1f out: kpt on ins fnl f: no imp* **25/1**

0600 **11** *1/2* **Profile Star (IRE)**[84] 3299 4-8-12 76........................ GrahamGibbons 9 64
(David Barron) *prom: rdn over 1f out: fdd wl ins fnl f* **14/1**

-050 **12** *1/2* **Mayoman (IRE)**[35] 4954 8-9-6 84........................(v) DanielTudhope 6 70
(David O'Meara) *hld up bhd: pushed along 2f out: nvr a threat* **9/1**

5631 **13** *6* **Triple Dream**[49] 4487 8-8-12 76..........(tp) RichardKingscote 8 41
(Milton Bradley) *chsd ldrs: pushed along over 2f out: wknd over 1f out* **11/1**

10/0 **14** *2 3/4* **Your Gifted (IRE)**[20] 5519 6-8-8 77........................ ShaneGray(5) 1 32
(Lisa Williamson) *hld up: rdn 2f out: bhd and struggling fnl f* **50/1**

1m 1.49s (0.69) **Going Correction** +0.30s/f (Good)
WFA 3 from 4yo+ 1lb **14** Ran SP% **118.1**
Speed ratings (Par 105): **106,105,104,100,99 98,98,98,97,97 96,95,85,81**
toteswingers 1&2 £14.00, 2&3 £6.10, 1&3 £7.00 CSF £66.55 CT £394.60 TOTE £8.30: £3.20, £2.80, £1.90; EX 80.00 Trifecta £668.50 Pool: £3531.82 - 3.96 winning units..
Owner Pinnacle Mujadil Partnership **Bred** Newlands House Stud **Trained** Sessay, N Yorks

FOCUS
All races on Inner Home straight and one yard added to races on Round Course. Rain on watered ground saw conditions ease considerably. A fair sprint handicap.

6160 BETFRED APPLIANCES ON LINE EBF MAIDEN FILLIES' STKS 6f
2:30 (2:32) (Class 5) 2-Y-0 **£2,911** (£866; £432; £216) **Stalls** Centre

Form RPR

3 **1** **Coral Mist**[37] 4877 2-9-0 0........................ TomQueally 2 88+
(Charles Hills) *racd keenly: a.p: rdn and hung lft fr 2f out: led over 1f out: r.o and drew clr wl ins fnl f* **11/10**[1]

644 **2** *3* **Merletta**[15] 5680 2-9-0 97........................ RyanMoore 3 76
(Jeremy Noseda) *led: rdn and hdd over 1f out: no imp on wnr fnl 100yds* **6/4**[2]

55 **3** *2* **Scots Law (IRE)**[11] 5827 2-9-0 0........................ JoeFanning 1 70
(Keith Dalgleish) *a.p: pushed along 2f out: nt qckn over 1f out: one pce fnl f* **20/1**

0 **4** *4 1/2* **Penny Pursuits**[19] 5558 2-9-0 0........................ GrahamLee 7 57
(Alan Berry) *chsd ldrs: lost pl over 2f out: sn outpcd: plugged on fnl f whn no ch* **100/1**

5 *3 1/4* **Sitting Pretty (IRE)** 2-9-0 0........................ RichardKingscote 6 47
(Tom Dascombe) *in tch: pushed along 1/2-way: rdn and hung lft whn outpcd over 1f out* **13/2**[3]

0 **6** *1/2* **Jaeger Connoisseur (IRE)**[37] 4886 2-9-0 0........................ DanielTudhope 4 45
(K R Burke) *hld up: rdn over 1f out: outpcd after* **33/1**

7 **7** 4 **Aussie Sky (IRE)** 2-9-0 0 .... StevieDonohoe 5 33
(John Stimpson) *s.i.s: sn pushed along: alway bhd: nvr on terms* **66/1**
1m 15.98s (2.18) **Going Correction** +0.30s/f (Good) **7** Ran SP% **111.1**
Speed ratings (Par 92): **97,93,90,84,80 79,74**
toteswingers 1&2 £1.30, 2&3 £2.20, 1&3 £1.80 CSF £2.75 TOTE £2.60: £1.50, £1.10; EX 3.30 Trifecta £8.90 Pool: £3162.73 - 266.20 winning units..
Owner Triermore Stud & R A Scarborough **Bred** Serpentine B'Stock & Genesis Green Stud **Trained** Lambourn, Berks
FOCUS
Hard to know exactly what the winner achieved given the runner-up, officially rated 97, was below form.

6161 BETFRED BOLTON LADS & GIRLS CLUB H'CAP (DIV I) 6f
3:00 (3:01) (Class 4) (0-85,84) 3-Y-0+ **£5,175** (£1,540; £769; £384) **Stalls** Centre

Form RPR
0433 **1** **Bop It**[27] 5294 4-9-4 **81** .... DanielTudhope 8 94+
(David O'Meara) *a.p: hung lft and led over 1f out: rdn clr ins fnl f: a doing enough towards fin* **4/1**[1]
6301 **2** 1 ¾ **Corporal Maddox**[13] 5775 6-9-6 **83** .... (p) RichardKingscote 2 90
(Ronald Harris) *dwlt: hld up: hdwy over 1f out: sn wnt 2nd: styd on ins fnl f: clsd on wnr towards fin* **9/1**
0216 **3** 4 **Beau Mistral (IRE)**[13] 5775 4-8-7 **70** .... JoeFanning 12 64
(Paul Green) *chsd ldr tl pushed along over 2f out: edgd lft ent fnl f: kpt on same pce* **7/1**
0100 **4** 1 **Mount Hollow**[29] 5183 8-9-1 **78** .... (p) TomQueally 5 69
(Andrew Hollinshead) *in rr: rdn 2f out: hdwy over 1f out: edgd lft and styd on ins fnl f: nt trble ldrs* **25/1**
1324 **5** hd **Mon Brav**[25] 5355 6-9-5 **82** .... MartinLane 10 72
(Brian Ellison) *pushed along towards rr: rdn over 2f out: styd on ins fnl f: nt rch ldrs* **5/1**[3]
50 **6** hd **Al Khan (IRE)**[13] 5738 4-9-7 **84** .... SaleemGolam 11 74
(Violet M Jordan) *dwlt: hld up: stdy hdwy 1/2-way: chsd ldrs ent fnl 2f: rdn and no imp 1f out: one pce after* **8/1**
1410 **7** 1 ½ **Lionheart**[28] 5219 3-9-5 **84** .... RyanMoore 9 69
(Luca Cumani) *in tch: pushed along over 2f out: rdn over 1f out: no extxra wl ins fnl f* **9/2**[2]
6224 **8** 2 ½ **Kingscroft (IRE)**[60] 4111 5-9-7 **84** .... PaulMulrennan 3 61
(Richard Ford) *midfield: pushed along 1/2-way: wknd over 1f out* **12/1**
4430 **9** 2 ½ **Midnight Dynamo**[16] 5639 6-8-13 **76** .... GrahamLee 4 45
(Jim Goldie) *hld up: pushed along 1/2-way: rdn and no imp wl over 1f out* **20/1**
0000 **10** 3 ¾ **Klynch**[32] 5056 7-9-6 **83** .... (b) JamesSullivan 6 40
(Ruth Carr) *racd in centre of trck: led: rdn and hdd over 1f out: sn wknd* **11/1**
020- **11** 2 **Invincible Lad (IRE)**[389] 5165 9-8-13 **76** .... GrahamGibbons 1 27
(Ed McMahon) *chsd ldrs tl rdn and wknd 2f out* **25/1**
1m 15.47s (1.67) **Going Correction** +0.45s/f (Yiel)
WFA 3 from 4yo+ 2lb **11** Ran SP% **116.9**
Speed ratings (Par 105): **106,103,98,97,96 96,94,91,87,82 80**
toteswingers 1&2 £5.40, 2&3 £10.90, 1&3 £6.70 CSF £38.86 CT £245.93 TOTE £5.20: £2.10, £3.00, £2.20; EX 29.00 Trifecta £371.10 Pool: £2546.09 - 5.14 winning units..
Owner A Turton, J Blackburn & R Bond **Bred** Bond Thoroughbred Corporation **Trained** Nawton, N Yorks
FOCUS
There was much to like about the performance of the winner.

6162 BETFRED BOLTON LADS & GIRLS CLUB H'CAP (DIV II) 6f
3:30 (3:30) (Class 4) (0-85,84) 3-Y-0+ **£5,175** (£1,540; £769; £384) **Stalls** Centre

Form RPR
6621 **1** **Ashpan Sam**[7] 5971 4-9-7 **84** 6ex .... PhillipMakin 11 96
(John Spearing) *mde all: rdn ins fnl f: r.o: in command towards fin* **3/1**[1]
0016 **2** 2 ¼ **Showboating (IRE)**[11] 5832 5-8-13 **76** .... (tp) RyanMoore 12 81
(Alan McCabe) *hld up: hdwy over 1f out: styd on to take 2nd towards fin: nt trble wnr* **11/2**[3]
5641 **3** ½ **Hadaj**[21] 5489 4-9-5 **82** .... FrederikTylicki 5 85
(Ruth Carr) *a.p: rdn and tried to chal over 1f out: no ex towards fin* **9/2**[2]
4005 **4** ¾ **Best Trip (IRE)**[20] 5544 6-9-5 **82** .... GrahamLee 10 83
(Brian Ellison) *midfield: hdwy 2f out: rdn and chsd ldrs ins fnl f: kpt on but unable to chal* **3/1**[1]
5-02 **5** ½ **Rio's Pearl**[31] 5103 3-9-0 **79** .... (b) SebSanders 6 78
(Ralph Beckett) *hld up: hdwy 2f out: chsd ldrs over 1f out: rdn and tried to chal ent fnl f: one pce fnl 75yds* **7/1**
0312 **6** 4 ½ **Light From Mars**[20] 5537 8-9-6 **83** .... (p) RichardKingscote 7 68
(Tom Dascombe) *hld up: rdn over 1f out: no imp* **9/1**
0000 **7** 2 ¼ **Xilerator (IRE)**[7] 5943 6-9-6 **83** .... (b[1]) PaulMulrennan 8 61
(David Nicholls) *plld hrd: prom: rdn 2f out: wknd over 1f out* **16/1**
0000 **8** 2 ¾ **Evens And Odds (IRE)**[16] 5636 9-8-12 **80** .... SladeO'Hara(5) 4 49
(Peter Grayson) *in rr: pushed along 1/2-way: nvr a threat* **50/1**
1m 15.59s (1.79) **Going Correction** +0.45s/f (Yiel)
WFA 3 from 4yo+ 2lb **8** Ran SP% **113.9**
Speed ratings (Par 105): **106,103,102,101,100 94,91,88**
toteswingers 1&2 £4.30, 2&3 £4.00, 1&3 £3.00 CSF £19.73 CT £72.45 TOTE £3.90: £1.20, £2.00, £2.30; EX 19.60 Trifecta £103.80 Pool: £2747.18 - 19.83 winning units..
Owner Advantage Chemicals Holdings Ltd **Bred** Advantage Chemicals Holdings Ltd **Trained** Kinnersley, Worcs
FOCUS
This was straightforward for the winner.

6163 BETFRED BOLTON ATLANTIC ROWING CHALLENGE H'CAP 1m 2f 95y
4:00 (4:00) (Class 3) (0-95,95) 3-Y-0+ **£8,086** (£2,406; £1,202; £601) **Stalls** Centre

Form RPR
2-15 **1** **Ennistown**[72] 3698 3-8-12 **88** .... FrederikTylicki 11 100+
(Charlie Appleby) *hld up in rr: hdwy 2f out: r.o to ld fnl 150yds: drew clr towards fin* **11/2**
2014 **2** 2 ¾ **Gworn**[29] 5182 3-8-11 **87** .... RyanMoore 1 94
(Ed Dunlop) *hld up: hdwy 3f out: rdn to ld 1f out: hdd fnl 150yds: unable to go wr towards fin* **11/4**[1]
036 **3** hd **Centurius**[34] 4979 3-9-4 **94** .... AdamKirby 4 101
(Marco Botti) *chsd ldrs: rdn over 2f out: kpt on ins fnl f but nt gng pce to mount serious chal* **10/1**
1-25 **4** nk **Mujazif (IRE)**[20] 5540 3-9-1 **91** .... (t) MartinLane 3 97
(Brian Meehan) *hld up: rdn 2f out: kpt on ins fnl f: clsd towards fin: nvr able to chal* **15/2**
14-0 **5** 1 **Anomaly**[27] 5283 4-9-9 **92** .... PhillipMakin 10 96
(Charlie Appleby) *led: rdn over 1f out: sn hdd: no ex fnl 75yds* **4/1**[2]
1120 **6** 2 ¼ **Double Discount (IRE)**[36] 4917 3-8-13 **89** .... RichardKingscote 9 89
(Tom Dascombe) *hld up: rdn over 2f out: nvr a threat* **9/2**[3]
2350 **7** 2 ¼ **Love Marmalade (IRE)**[13] 5768 3-8-6 **82** .... JoeFanning 8 78
(Mark Johnston) *chsd ldr tl rdn over 1f out: sn wknd* **9/1**
06/ **8** 50 **Egotist (IRE)**[410] 5-9-12 **95** .... SebSanders 6
(Milton Bradley) *chsd ldrs tl wknd over 3f out: bhd fnl 2f: t.o* **33/1**
2m 15.99s (0.49) **Going Correction** +0.175s/f (Good)
WFA 3 from 4yo+ 7lb **8** Ran SP% **114.0**
Speed ratings (Par 107): **105,102,102,102,101 99,98,58**
toteswingers 1&2 £3.70, 2&3 £5.90, 1&3 £10.50 CSF £20.90 CT £146.35 TOTE £4.90: £1.10, £1.60, £4.10; EX 20.90 Trifecta £170.00 Pool: £3637.40 - 16.04 winning units..
Owner Godolphin **Bred** Darley **Trained** Newmarket, Suffolk
FOCUS
Perhaps not much strength in depth, but a tidy performance from the winner.

6164 BETFRED UOB FIBRELEC H'CAP 7f
4:30 (4:30) (Class 3) (0-90,90) 3-Y-0+ **£8,086** (£2,406; £1,202; £601) **Stalls** Low

Form RPR
-311 **1** **Big Johnny D (IRE)**[27] 5292 4-9-8 **88** .... GrahamGibbons 6 103+
(David Barron) *mde all: a travelling wl: rdn briefly ins fnl f: comf* **2/1**[1]
0000 **2** 2 **Sam Nombulist**[34] 5014 5-9-0 **80** .... (p) PhillipMakin 2 86
(Ian Semple) *t.k.h: a.p: rdn to take 2nd and carried hd awkwardly over 1f out: no imp on wnr fnl f* **8/1**
6100 **3** 1 ¾ **Lord Of The Dance (IRE)**[15] 5681 7-9-5 **90** .... SladeO'Hara(5) 4 91
(Michael Mullineaux) *midfield: pushed along and hdwy 2f out: chsd ldrs over 1f out: no ex towards fin* **20/1**
0040 **4** 2 ¼ **Head Of Steam (USA)**[13] 5738 6-9-8 **88** .... RichardKingscote 1 83
(Amanda Perrett) *chsd ldrs: rdn over 1f out: kpt on but unable to chal* **7/1**[3]
3000 **5** 1 ½ **Alfred Hutchinson**[114] 2365 5-9-7 **87** .... GrahamLee 9 79
(Geoffrey Oldroyd) *towards rr: rdn over 1f out: kpt on ins fnl f: nt trble ldrs* **14/1**
0040 **6** nk **Powerful Presence (IRE)**[20] 5544 7-9-7 **87** .... DanielTudhope 3 78
(David O'Meara) *chsd wnr: rdn over 2f out: lost 2nd over 1f out: wknd ins fnl f* **12/1**
0001 **7** hd **Green Howard**[21] 5481 5-9-1 **81** .... FrederikTylicki 8 71
(Robin Bastiman) *hld up: u.p 2f out: no imp* **6/1**[2]
4156 **8** 1 **Ginger Jack**[25] 5335 6-9-9 **89** .... PaulMulrennan 12 77
(Geoffrey Harker) *hld up: rdn over 2f out: no imp* **12/1**
1522 **9** 1 **Ready (IRE)**[15] 5676 3-8-13 **83** .... (p) TomQueally 11 68
(Garry Moss) *midfield: rdn 2f out: wknd ins fnl f* **6/1**[2]
0030 **10** 9 **King Of Eden (IRE)**[7] 5943 7-9-2 **85** .... (b) JasonHart(3) 7 47
(Eric Alston) *edgy in stalls: chsd ldrs: rdn 3f out: sn wknd* **25/1**
1m 30.56s (-0.14) **Going Correction** +0.175s/f (Good)
WFA 3 from 4yo+ 4lb **10** Ran SP% **116.2**
Speed ratings (Par 107): **107,104,102,100,98 98,97,96,95,85**
toteswingers 1&2 £4.30, 2&3 £4.00, 1&3 £3.00 CSF £18.39 CT £249.43 TOTE £2.60: £1.40, £2.40, £5.10; EX 29.40 Trifecta £439.00 Pool: £3529.66 - 6.03 winning units..
Owner Clive Washbourn **Bred** David McGuinness **Trained** Maunby, N Yorks
FOCUS
Not form to get carried away with.

6165 BETFRED BOLTON CENTRAL BNI H'CAP 1m 6f
5:00 (5:00) (Class 4) (0-85,81) 3-Y-0+ **£5,175** (£1,540; £769; £384) **Stalls** Low

Form RPR
503 **1** **Gabrial's Star**[7] 5972 4-9-11 **78** .... (b[1]) RichardKingscote 6 88
(Ian Williams) *mde all and set stdy pce tl steadily increased tempo over 3f out: rdn over 1f out: styd on wl: unchal* **7/4**[2]
-000 **2** 3 ¾ **Bowdler's Magic**[114] 2369 6-9-8 **78** .... (t) LMcNiff(3) 1 83
(David Thompson) *hld up in rr: pushed along over 2f out: impr for press to take 2nd wl over 1f out: no imp on wnr fnl f* **12/1**
0003 **3** 8 **The Betchworth Kid**[24] 5374 8-9-13 **80** .... TomQueally 3 75
(Michael Bell) *chsd wnr: pushed along over 3f out: rdn over 2f out: lost 2nd wl over 1f out: one pce and wl btn after* **7/2**[3]
0601 **4** 12 **Handsome Ransom**[14] 5712 4-10-0 **81** .... DanielTudhope 4 65
(David O'Meara) *chsd ldrs: pushed along and failed to pick-up over 2f out: sn in last pl: eased whn wl btn over 1f out* **6/4**[1]
3m 11.29s (9.29) **Going Correction** +0.325s/f (Good)
WFA 3 from 4yo+ 11lb **4** Ran SP% **106.3**
Speed ratings (Par 105): **86,83,79,72**
CSF £16.32 TOTE £2.20; EX 11.70 Trifecta £28.70 Pool: £1781.56 - 46.51 winning units..
Owner Dr Marwan Koukash **Bred** Miss K Rausing **Trained** Portway, Worcs
FOCUS
Uncompetitive stuff.

6166 BETFRED CLYDE & CO MAIDEN STKS 1m 3f 200y
5:30 (5:32) (Class 5) 3-Y-0+ **£3,234** (£962; £481; £240) **Stalls** Centre

Form RPR
23 **1** **Refectory (IRE)**[27] 5286 3-9-5 0 .... RyanMoore 5 82+
(Andrew Balding) *a.p: nosed ahd 3f out: rdn clr over 1f out: wl in command and styd on wl fnl f* **4/9**[1]
3 **2** 9 **Copybook**[58] 4157 3-9-0 0 .... JoeFanning 8 62
(Mark Johnston) *hld up: hdwy over 3f out: chsd ldrs over 2f out: sn lugged lft: wnt 2nd jst over 1f out: no ch w wnr fnl f* **4/1**[2]
430 **3** ¾ **Caledonia**[21] 5484 6-10-0 0 .... GrahamLee 4 66+
(Jim Goldie) *sweating: prom: rdn and outpcd over 3f out: kpt on u.p to take 3rd wl ins fnl f: clsd on runner-up cl home* **8/1**[3]
4 1 ¾ **Lineman**[86] 3230 3-9-5 0 .... TomQueally 6 63
(Andrew Hollinshead) *s.i.s: in rr: sme hdwy 3f out: plugged on fnl f but n.d* **25/1**
5- **5** 2 **Colour My World**[263] 8147 3-9-5 0 .... GrahamGibbons 3 60
(Ed McMahon) *led: hdd narrowly 3f out: sn rdn: lost 2nd jst over 1f out: wknd fnl f* **11/1**
00 **6** 6 **Cape Rosa**[14] 5715 3-9-0 0 .... PaulMulrennan 7 45
(James Moffatt) *hld up: pushed along over 5f out: bhd over 4f out: nvr a threat* **100/1**
7 14 **Muraafiq (USA)** 4-9-11 0 .... JasonHart(3) 2 28
(Simon West) *s.i.s: sn prom: rdn over 3f out: wknd over 2f out* **66/1**
2m 39.22s (5.42) **Going Correction** +0.325s/f (Good)
WFA 3 from 4yo+ 9lb **7** Ran SP% **115.0**
Speed ratings (Par 103): **94,88,87,86,85 81,71**
toteswingers 1&2 £1.10, 2&3 £2.60, 1&3 £2.00 CSF £2.63 TOTE £1.50: £1.40, £1.70; EX 3.10 Trifecta £7.30 Pool: £3480.36 - 355.32 winning units..
Owner Brook Farm Bloodstock **Bred** Barronstown Stud And Pacelco S A **Trained** Kingsclere, Hants
FOCUS
The clear form pick won as expected

The Form Book Flat, Raceform Ltd, Compton, RG20 6NL.

T/Jkpt: Not won. T/Plt: £18.90 to a £1 stake. Pool of £88074.03 - 3386.87 winning ticket. T/Qpdt: £6.60 to a £1 stake. Pool of £5751.62 - 640.64 winning tickets. DO

6131 KEMPTON (A.W) (R-H)
Friday, September 6

OFFICIAL GOING: Standard
Wind: Light, across Weather: Fine

6167 MIDLAND FACILITIES APPRENTICE H'CAP 1m (P)
6:20 (6:21) (Class 4) (0-85,85) 3-Y-0+ **£4,690** (£1,395; £697; £348) **Stalls** Low

Form RPR
0205 **1** **Uppercut**[13] 5742 5-9-3 **81** RobertTart(3) 8 93
(Stuart Kittow) *hld up in last trio: shkn up over 2f out: gd prog on wd outside over 1f out: sustained effrt to ld last 100yds: won gng away* **6/1**[3]
322 **2** *1 1/4* **Ocean Tempest**[25] 5355 4-9-9 **84** (p) RyanClark 1 93
(John Ryan) *trckd ldr: led over 2f out: sn drvn: hdd and outpcd last 100yds* **9/2**[2]
2-00 **3** *1 3/4* **Border Legend**[112] 2424 4-9-9 **84** WilliamTwiston-Davies 9 89
(Roger Charlton) *wl in tch: shkn up on outer over 2f out: prog over 1f out: disp 2nd jst ins fnl f: wnr sn wnt past and one pce after* **5/2**[1]
0520 **4** *2 3/4* **Mingun Bell (USA)**[12] 5802 6-9-2 **77** (p) DeclanBates 12 75
(Ed de Giles) *cl up: rdn over 2f out: kpt on same pce fnl 2f and nvr able to threaten* **25/1**
142 **5** *nk* **Cruiser**[26] 5310 5-9-5 **85** (p) ThomasGarner(5) 14 82
(William Muir) *racd wd early: chsd ldng pair: rdn over 2f out: disp 2nd briefly 1f out but no imp: outpcd after* **8/1**
U000 **6** *1* **Midnight Feast**[8] 5931 5-8-8 **72** (v) DannyBrock(3) 11 67
(Lee Carter) *led to over 2f out: steadily wknd over 1f out* **40/1**
2500 **7** *hd* **Weapon Of Choice (IRE)**[64] 3984 5-9-7 **85** MichaelJMMurphy(3) 6 80
(Stuart Kittow) *w.w towards rr: shkn up over 2f out: one pce and no imp on ldrs over 1f out* **8/1**
0114 **8** *1/2* **Tevez**[12] 5799 8-8-10 **76** (p) DanielMuscutt(5) 10 69
(Des Donovan) *hld up in last trio: shkn up over 2f out: prog to chse ldrs jst over 1f out: effrt rather petered out fnl f* **16/1**
2250 **9** *1 1/2* **Savanna Days (IRE)**[34] 5014 4-9-1 **76** (v) AshleyMorgan 5 67
(Mick Channon) *trckd ldrs: prog 2f out: edgd towards far rail whn pressing for a pl over 1f out: wknd fnl f* **16/1**
5000 **10** *1/2* **Swiftly Done (IRE)**[20] 5546 6-9-3 **85** LukeLeadbitter(7) 7 74
(Declan Carroll) *urged along early in rr: rchd midfield 1/2-way: trying to mount an effrt on inner whn squeezed out over 1f out: nt rcvr and swiftly done w* **12/1**
6-00 **11** *5* **Embankment**[123] 2085 4-8-11 **77** (p) NoelGarbutt(5) 3 54
(William Jarvis) *dwlt and urged along early: a in rr: rdn and no prog over 2f out* **25/1**
0125 **12** *9* **Idol Deputy (FR)**[123] 2085 7-9-4 **82** (p) NathanAlison(3) 2 37
(James Bennett) *chsd ldrs: rdn sn after 1/2-way: wknd wl over 2f out* **33/1**
1100 **13** *45* **Travelling**[21] 5491 4-8-11 **75** GeorgeDowning(3) 4
(Tony Carroll) *dwlt and awkward s: a in rr: wknd 3f out: wl t.o* **25/1**

1m 37.89s (-1.91) **Going Correction** -0.025s/f (Stan) 13 Ran SP% **119.6**
Speed ratings (Par 105): **108,106,105,102,101 100,100,100,98,98 93,84,39**
toteswingers 1&2 £3.90, 2&3 £4.10, 1&3 £4.00 CSF £31.14 CT £89.32 TOTE £7.80: £2.70, £1.30, £1.30; EX 41.60 Trifecta £184.00 Pool: £1718.19 - 7.00 winning units..
Owner H A Cushing **Bred** The Hon Mrs R Pease **Trained** Blackborough, Devon
■ Stewards' Enquiry : Danny Brock three-day ban: careless riding (Sep 20-22)

FOCUS
This modest handicap looked wide open. It was run at a fair pace.

6168 LETCHWORTH COURIERS/IRISH STALLION FARMS EBF MAIDEN STKS 1m (P)
6:50 (6:50) (Class 5) 2-Y-0 **£2,911** (£866; £432; £216) **Stalls** Low

Form RPR
64 **1** **Adventure Seeker (IRE)**[29] 5188 2-9-5 0 WilliamBuick 11 75
(Ed Vaughan) *slowest away: rapid prog on outer to ld after 3f: mde rest: at least 2 l clr fr 2f out: rdn out* **9/2**[2]
2 *1 1/4* **Laugharne** 2-9-5 0 JamesDoyle 6 72
(Roger Charlton) *wl in tch: shkn up and prog jst over 2f out: chsd wnr ins fnl f: no real imp* **20/1**
0 **3** *3/4* **Storm Force Ten**[37] 4896 2-9-5 0 DavidProbert 5 71
(Andrew Balding) *pressed ldrs: rdn 2f out: nvr gng pce to chal but styd on fr over 1f out* **6/1**[3]
4 *1/2* **Kingdom's Call (USA)** 2-9-5 0 MickaelBarzalona 10 69+
(Charlie Appleby) *s.i.s: wl in rr and rn green: in last pair and hd high whn rdn over 2f out: styd on wl fr over 1f out: nrst fin* **3/1**[1]
0 **5** *1/2* **Lunar Spirit**[64] 3986 2-9-0 0 JimCrowley 4 63
(Ralph Beckett) *led 3f: styd prom: chsd wnr over 2f out: no imp over 1f out: lost 2nd and fdd ins fnl f* **7/1**
35 **6** *1 3/4* **Glebe Spirit (IRE)**[21] 5473 2-9-5 0 PatDobbs 1 64
(Richard Hannon) *mostly in midfield: tried to cl on ldrs 2f out: kpt on but nvr gng pce to threaten* **10/1**
7 *1 1/4* **Rochambeau (IRE)** 2-9-5 0 JimmyFortune 12 61
(Sir Michael Stoute) *wl in rr: last 3f out: nudged along and light reminder 2f out: kpt on steadily fr over 1f out* **20/1**
3 **8** *shd* **Lightning Shower (USA)**[15] 5675 2-9-5 0 AndreaAtzeni 9 61
(Marco Botti) *t.k.h: hld up in rr: rdn and no prog over 2f out: kpt on one pce fr over 1f out* **8/1**
0 **9** *shd* **Always Resolute**[49] 4483 2-9-2 0 MichaelJMMurphy(3) 8 61
(Alan Jarvis) *wl in rr: rdn and struggling over 2f out: looked like fining last 1f out: r.o fnl 100yds* **50/1**
5 **10** *nse* **Marengo**[37] 4883 2-9-5 0 LiamKeniry 3 60
(Ed de Giles) *nvr bttr than midfield: rdn and no prog over 2f out: one pce after* **66/1**
0 **11** *3/4* **Dover The Moon (IRE)**[63] 4026 2-9-5 0 DaneO'Neill 7 59
(Richard Hannon) *nvr bttr than midfield: shkn up over 2f out: steadily fdd over 1f out* **16/1**
12 *3/4* **Bombardment (USA)** 2-9-5 0 KierenFallon 13 57
(Charlie Appleby) *s.i.s: sn prom: chsd wnr over 4f out: rdn over 2f out and sn lost 2nd: wknd over 1f out* **10/1**

1m 40.53s (0.73) **Going Correction** -0.025s/f (Stan) 12 Ran SP% **118.1**
Speed ratings (Par 95): **95,93,93,92,92 90,89,88,88,88 88,87**
toteswingers 1&2 £46.50, 2&3 £63.40, 1&3 £9.00 CSF £96.03 TOTE £5.30: £1.80, £7.90, £2.00; EX 92.90 Trifecta £1118.90 Part won. Pool: £1491.90 - 0.12 winning units..
Owner Hamed Rashed Bin Ghadayer **Bred** Runnymede Farm Inc And Catesby W Clay **Trained** Newmarket, Suffolk

FOCUS
A fair 2-y-o maiden in which it paid to race handily.

6169 ADVANCED TREE SERVICES LIMITED/IRISH STALLIONS EBF MAIDEN STKS 6f (P)
7:20 (7:21) (Class 5) 2-Y-0 **£2,911** (£866; £432; £216) **Stalls** Low

Form RPR
33 **1** **Mystique Rider**[38] 4858 2-9-5 0 HarryBentley 9 84
(Olly Stevens) *forced to r wd first half of r: chsd ldrs: clsd 2f out: rdn to ld over 1f out: drvn out and hld on wl* **6/4**[1]
6 **2** *1/2* **Charles Molson**[33] 5033 2-9-5 0 DaneO'Neill 7 82+
(Henry Candy) *hld up in tch: waiting for a gap over 2f out: prog wl over 1f out: wnt 2nd and pressed wnr hrd fnl f: jst hld* **7/1**[3]
32 **3** *1 1/4* **Gilmer (IRE)**[43] 4676 2-9-5 0 MickaelBarzalona 6 78
(Charlie Appleby) *w ldr: led jst over 2f out: rdn and hdd over 1f out: one pce* **3/1**[2]
4 *1* **Hesbaan (IRE)** 2-9-5 0 PaulHanagan 4 75+
(Marcus Tregoning) *towards rr: pushed along over 2f out: styd on wl fr jst over 1f out to take 4th nr fin* **20/1**
0 **5** *1/2* **Highland Acclaim (IRE)**[118] 2250 2-9-5 0 DavidProbert 2 74
(Andrew Balding) *t.k.h: prom: rdn 2f out: cl up jst over 1f out: nt qckn* **8/1**
6 *nk* **Crystal Lake (IRE)** 2-9-5 0 JimCrowley 5 73
(Ralph Beckett) *wl in tch: clsd on ldrs 2f out: shkn up over 1f out: one pce fnl f* **8/1**
7 *2 3/4* **Zugzwang (IRE)** 2-9-5 0 MartinHarley 10 64
(Ed de Giles) *towards rr: shkn up over 2f out: nt on terms after: kpt on fnl f* **66/1**
5 **8** *2 1/2* **Vanvidd (FR)**[87] 3167 2-9-5 0 GeorgeBaker 8 56+
(Hans Adielsson) *hld up and mostly in last pair: nudged along 2f out: limited prog over 1f out: fdd ins fnl f* **66/1**
5 **9** *1/2* **Danzki (IRE)**[42] 4724 2-9-5 0 LukeMorris 3 54
(Gay Kelleway) *chsd ldrs: rdn over 2f out: cl up over 1f out: sn wknd* **16/1**
54 **10** *3 1/4* **Royal Bushida**[9] 5900 2-8-12 0 AdamMcLean(7) 12 44
(Derek Shaw) *fractious bef ent stalls: slowly away: a in rr: urged along and wknd 2f out* **100/1**
0 **11** *2* **Kopenhagen (IRE)**[35] 4937 2-9-5 0 LiamKeniry 1 37
(Ed de Giles) *led to jst over 2f out: wknd qckly over 1f out* **66/1**

1m 13.32s (0.22) **Going Correction** -0.025s/f (Stan) 11 Ran SP% **115.8**
Speed ratings (Par 95): **97,96,94,93,92 92,88,85,84,80 77**
toteswingers 1&2 £3.50, 2&3 £4.70, 1&3 £1.30 CSF £12.20 TOTE £2.60: £1.10, £2.40, £1.50; EX 12.60 Trifecta £37.80 Pool: £1245.34 - 24.68 winning units..
Owner K Altaji,R Sayegh & Pearl Bloodstock Ltd **Bred** Mrs J A Rawding **Trained** Chiddingfold, Surrey

FOCUS
This wasn't a bad 2-y-o maiden.

6170 CA CONTRACTS LTD. NURSERY H'CAP 6f (P)
7:50 (7:50) (Class 5) (0-75,73) 2-Y-0 **£2,587** (£770; £384; £192) **Stalls** Low

Form RPR
0035 **1** **Basil Berry**[16] 5634 2-8-7 **64** RobertTart(5) 4 69
(Chris Dwyer) *hld up in last pair: plld out wd and prog over 1f out: drvn and r.o wl to ld last 100yds* **4/1**[3]
330 **2** *1* **Misty Sparkler**[70] 3760 2-9-5 **71** HayleyTurner 3 73
(Brian Meehan) *trckd ldr after 2f: led over 2f out but sn hrd pressed: hdd over 1f out: edgd lft but rallied to ld jst ins fnl f: hdd last 100yds: styd on* **10/1**
5415 **3** *1 1/2* **Inspiriter**[34] 5005 2-9-7 **73** MickaelBarzalona 7 70
(Charlie Appleby) *trckd ldrs: clsd over 2f out: rdn to ld over 1f out: hdd and nt qckn jst ins fnl f* **3/1**[2]
036 **4** *2 1/2* **Sandy Cove**[18] 5584 2-8-10 **62** JamesDoyle 5 54
(Roger Charlton) *hld up in last pair: rdn and racing awkwardly whn hmpd over 1f out: kpt on to take 4th ins fnl f: no ch* **9/2**
0341 **5** *3 1/2* **Punk**[8] 5926 2-9-5 **71** 6ex LukeMorris 6 49
(Fawzi Abdulla Nass, Bahrain) *in tch: clsd on ldrs to chal 2f out: upsides over 1f out: wknd tamely sn after* **9/4**[1]
453 **6** *1 1/2* **Skinny Love**[22] 5421 2-9-1 **67** AndreaAtzeni 1 40
(Robert Cowell) *chsd ldr 2f: wknd wl over 1f out* **9/1**
1605 **7** *13* **Classical Diva**[16] 5648 2-9-0 **73** (b[1]) LukeLeadbitter(7) 2 4
(Declan Carroll) *awkward s and rousted along: sn led and t.k.h: hdd over 2f out: wknd rapidly: t.o* **25/1**

1m 12.69s (-0.41) **Going Correction** -0.025s/f (Stan) 7 Ran SP% **116.9**
Speed ratings (Par 95): **101,99,97,94,89 87,70**
toteswingers 1&2 £10.70, 2&3 £4.80, 1&3 £4.00 CSF £43.42 TOTE £4.10: £2.10, £5.70; EX 41.10 Trifecta £284.30 Pool: £1267.10 - 3.34 winning units..
Owner Strawberry Fields Stud **Bred** Strawberry Fields Stud **Trained** Newmarket, Suffolk

FOCUS
A modest nursery, run at a strong early pace.

6171 4-RAIL SERVICES LIMITED/IRISH STALLION FARMS EBF FILLIES' CONDITIONS STKS 7f (P)
8:20 (8:20) (Class 3) 2-Y-0 **£9,337** (£2,796; £1,398; £699) **Stalls** Low

Form RPR
1 **1** **Sound Reflection (USA)**[34] 5003 2-9-2 0 MickaelBarzalona 3 92+
(Charlie Appleby) *mde all: set mod pce tl kicked on jst over 2f out: shkn up over 1f out: styd on wl* **8/15**[1]
1 **2** *1 3/4* **Night Song**[27] 5282 2-9-2 0 WilliamBuick 1 87
(John Gosden) *trckd wnr: shkn up 2f out: styd on but nvr able to chal fr over 1f out* **7/4**[2]
3 *5* **Mia San Triple** 2-8-12 0 AndreaAtzeni 4 70
(Peter Chapple-Hyam) *stdd s: hld up in last: wnt 3rd 2f out: shkn up and rn green over 1f out: sn lft bhd* **33/1**[3]
4 *2 1/2* **Classic Princess** 2-8-12 0 [1] LukeMorris 2 63
(Gay Kelleway) *stdd s: chsd ldng pair to 2f out: steadily wknd* **100/1**

1m 29.28s (3.28) **Going Correction** -0.025s/f (Stan) 4 Ran SP% **105.5**
Speed ratings (Par 96): **80,78,72,69**
CSF £1.59 TOTE £1.50; EX 1.40 Trifecta £2.60 Pool: £614.67 - 172.99 winning units..
Owner Godolphin **Bred** Darley **Trained** Newmarket, Suffolk

FOCUS
An interesting fillies' conditions event, taken last year by subsequent Oaks winner Talent.

6172 MAINDEC CHAIRMANS BIRTHDAY H'CAP (LONDON MIDDLE DISTANCE SERIES QUALIFIER) 1m 3f (P)
8:50 (8:51) (Class 3) (0-95,94) 3-Y-0+

£7,158 (£2,143; £1,071; £535; £267; £134) **Stalls** Low

Form RPR

-435 **1** **Cat O'Mountain (USA)**[13] 5749 3-8-12 **88**.............. MickaelBarzalona 4 99+
(Charlie Appleby) *trckd ldng pair: rdn to go 2nd over 1f out: clsd to ld last 100yds: r.o wl* **3/1**[1]

5626 **2** 1 1/4 **Castilo Del Diablo (IRE)**[14] 5723 4-9-8 **90**...............(b[1]) JimCrowley 10 99
(David Simcock) *hld up in last: pushed along 3f out: stl last over 2f out: gd prog on wd outside after: r.o wl to take 2nd nr fin: no ch to chal* **9/2**[2]

0433 **3** 3/4 **Ruscello (IRE)**[34] 4979 4-9-10 **92**.............................. GeorgeBaker 3 100
(Ed Walker) *led 3f: w ldr tl led again over 2f out gng strly: rdn over 1f out: hdd and fdd last 100yds* **6/1**[3]

05 **4** 1 1/2 **Voodoo Prince**[69] 3838 5-9-10 **92**.............................. NeilCallan 9 97
(Ed Dunlop) *hld up in last trio: prog jst over 2f out: chsd ldrs and 3rd briefly ins fnl f: one pce after* **12/1**

4441 **5** 1 **She's Late**[27] 5286 3-8-12 **88**.............................. WilliamBuick 6 92
(John Gosden) *trckd ldrs on inner: angled out and rdn over 2f out: tried to cl over 1f out: one pce* **16/1**

2003 **6** 1/2 **Icebuster**[27] 5259 5-9-4 **86**.............................. AndreaAtzeni 8 89
(Rod Millman) *s.i.s: hld up in last trio: rdn and prog on inner fr 2f out: one pce fnl f* **16/1**

-100 **7** 2 1/4 **Expert Fighter (USA)**[38] 4854 4-9-11 **93**.................... HarryBentley 11 92
(Saeed bin Suroor) *towards rr: sltly impeded over 2f out: sn rdn and no prog: plugged on* **14/1**

3235 **8** 3/4 **Villoresi (IRE)**[13] 5746 4-9-5 **87**.............................. JamesDoyle 12 85
(James Fanshawe) *trckd ldrs: rdn over 2f out: wknd over 1f out* **9/1**

31-5 **9** 1 3/4 **Saytara (IRE)**[40] 4796 4-9-12 **94**.............................. KierenFallon 2 89
(Saeed bin Suroor) *w ldr: led after 3f to over 2f out: wknd wl over 1f out* **8/1**

61 **10** 1 1/2 **Jeeraan (USA)**[21] 5484 3-8-12 **88**.............................. PaulHanagan 5 81
(Ed Dunlop) *trckd ldng pair tl rdn and wknd jst over 2f out* **10/1**

3123 **11** 5 **Duroble Man**[68] 3862 3-8-10 **86**.............................. FergusSweeney 7 71
(Alan King) *in tch in midfield tl wknd over 2f out: sn bhd* **20/1**

2m 18.32s (-3.58) **Going Correction** -0.025s/f (Stan)
WFA 3 from 4yo+ 8lb **11** Ran SP% **118.6**
Speed ratings (Par 107): **112,111,110,109,108 108,106,106,104,103 100**
toteswingers 1&2 £4.90, 2&3 £6.20, 1&3 £3.10 CSF £15.97 CT £77.24 TOTE £3.80: £1.40, £1.30, £2.60; EX 20.70 Trifecta £81.10 Pool: £1222.24 - 11.30 winning units..
Owner Godolphin **Bred** Darley **Trained** Newmarket, Suffolk

FOCUS
A fair handicap and another race where it paid to race handily.

6173 EVENTMASTERS.CO.UK H'CAP 2m (P)
9:20 (9:20) (Class 5) (0-75,73) 4-Y-0+ **£2,587** (£770; £384; £192) **Stalls** Low

Form RPR

3202 **1** **Honourable Knight (IRE)**[7] 5954 5-9-2 **68**.................... LiamKeniry 8 75
(Mark Usher) *trckd ldrs: wnt 2nd over 2f out: sn rdn: clsd to ld over 1f out: clr ins fnl f: eased nr fin* **7/1**

252 **2** 1 3/4 **Jezza**[20] 5535 7-8-11 **63**..............................(bt) LukeMorris 6 68
(Karen George) *awkward s: in tch: rdn and prog on outer over 2f out: styd on fnl f to take 2nd last strides* **6/1**[3]

2204 **3** nk **King Olav (UAE)**[30] 5129 8-9-3 **72**.............. WilliamTwiston-Davies(3) 10 77
(Tony Carroll) *trckd ldr: led over 3f out: kicked on over 2f out: hdd over 1f out: fdd and lost 2nd last strides* **10/1**

6400 **4** 1 3/4 **Bow To No One (IRE)**[71] 3726 7-9-1 **70**........... MichaelJMMurphy(3) 4 72
(Alan Jarvis) *hld up in last pair: rdn 3f out: styd on fr wl over 1f out: nvr able to threaten* **10/1**

0400 **5** 1/2 **Topolski (IRE)**[77] 3531 7-9-6 **72**.............................. WilliamBuick 1 74
(David Arbuthnot) *lost pl after 4f and sn in last pair: rdn and prog over 2f out: disp 3rd briefly 1f out: one pce after* **7/1**

5206 **6** 1 3/4 **Where's Susie**[101] 2749 8-9-2 **68**.............................. RobertHavlin 5 68
(Michael Madgwick) *hld up in tch: prog to chse ldng pair over 2f out: no imp: lost 3rd and wknd fnl f* **20/1**

0-60 **7** 2 1/4 **Natural High (IRE)**[149] 1464 8-9-4 **70**..............................(t) JamesDoyle 7 67
(Sean Curran) *hld up towards rr: drvn on inner over 2f out: prog wl over 1f out: fdd fnl f* **33/1**

-333 **8** 1 1/4 **Diamond Penny (IRE)**[29] 5185 5-9-7 **73**....................(b[1]) SteveDrowne 9 69
(Seamus Durack) *trckd ldrs on outer: rdn and nt qckn wl over 2f out: struggling after* **11/4**[1]

-600 **9** 18 **Valid Reason**[20] 5520 6-9-3 **69**..............................(p) JimCrowley 2 43
(Dean Ivory) *led at modest pce: rdn and hdd over 3f out: sn wknd: t.o* **5/1**[2]

1-65 **10** 3 1/4 **Petaluma**[123] 2069 4-9-5 **71**.............................. MartinHarley 3 41
(Mick Channon) *prog and prom after 4f: rdn and wknd 3f out: t.o* **12/1**

3m 32.34s (2.24) **Going Correction** -0.025s/f (Stan) **10** Ran SP% **116.2**
Speed ratings (Par 103): **93,92,91,91,90 89,88,88,79,77**
toteswingers 1&2 £6.80, 2&3 £9.40, 1&3 £15.00 CSF £48.47 CT £422.29 TOTE £7.50: £2.30, £2.10, £2.60; EX 26.50 Trifecta £198.00 Pool: £1172.81 - 4.44 winning units..
Owner Mrs T Channing-Williams **Bred** Mohammed Al Sulaim **Trained** Upper Lambourn, Berks

FOCUS
A modest staying handicap.
T/Plt: £110.70 to a £1 stake. Pool of £93122.38 - 613.81 winning tickets. T/Qpdt: £27.50 to a £1 stake. Pool of £6594.65 - 177.10 winning tickets. JN

5826 NEWCASTLE (L-H)
Friday, September 6

OFFICIAL GOING: Good (7.2) changing to good to soft after race 1 (2.10) changing to soft after race 5 (4.10)
Wind: Fresh, half behind Weather: Overcast, showers

6174 WATERAID/BRITISH STALLION STUDS EBF MAIDEN STKS (DIV I) 6f
2:10 (2:12) (Class 5) 2-Y-0 **£2,911** (£866; £432; £216) **Stalls** Low

Form RPR

4 **1** **Royal Banker**[55] 4312 2-9-5 0.............................. MichaelO'Connell 6 81+
(Jedd O'Keeffe) *prom: pushed along over 2f out: edgd rt and hdwy to ld appr fnl f: kpt on strly last 150yds* **5/1**[3]

2 **2** 2 **Sandra's Diamond (IRE)**[16] 5638 2-9-0 0.............................. TomEaves 4 70
(Keith Dalgleish) *taken early to post: led: rdn and hdd appr fnl f: rallied ins fnl f: kpt on* **10/1**

35 **3** shd **Missouri Spirit**[18] 5577 2-9-5 0.............................. BrianHughes 3 75
(Kevin Ryan) *cl up: effrt and ev ch over 1f out to ins fnl f: kpt on same pce wl ins fnl f* **25/1**

3 **4** 3 **Elsie Partridge (IRE)**[22] 5435 2-9-0 0.............................. PJMcDonald 2 61
(Noel Quinlan) *prom: effrt over 2f out: edgd lft and one pce appr fnl f* **7/1**

04 **5** nse **Dream And Search (GER)**[91] 3044 2-9-5 0.............. JamieSpencer 10 66
(Charles Hills) *hld up in tch: effrt and pushed along 2f out: no imp fnl f* **9/4**[1]

2 **6** 2 **Red Pike (IRE)**[139] 1680 2-9-5 0.............................. RoystonFfrench 7 60
(Bryan Smart) *dwlt: sn rdn along in rr: hdwy over 1f out: kpt on: nvr able to chal* **11/4**[2]

00 **7** 1 3/4 **Genax (IRE)**[9] 5877 2-8-7 0.............................. EvaMoscrop(7) 8 49
(Philip Kirby) *t.k.h: hld up bhd ldrs: shkn up 2f out: sn outpcd* **100/1**

8 3/4 **Ty Cobb (IRE)** 2-9-2 0.............................. RaulDaSilva(3) 5 52
(John Quinn) *chsd ldng gp: rdn and outpcd over 2f out: n.d after* **25/1**

9 18 **Truancy (IRE)** 2-9-5 0.............................. RobertWinston 9
(Alan Berry) *t.k.h early: cl up tl rdn and wknd over 2f out: t.o* **7/1**

0 **10** 3 1/4 **Gravy Dipper (IRE)**[53] 4351 2-9-5 0.............................. DougieCostello 1
(John Quinn) *hung lft thrght: hld up: struggling wl over 2f out: sn btn: t.o* **100/1**

1m 14.87s (0.27) **Going Correction** -0.075s/f (Good) **10** Ran SP% **117.9**
Speed ratings (Par 95): **95,92,92,88,88 85,83,82,58,53**
toteswingers 1&2 £8.10, 2&3 £11.80, 1&3 £10.90 CSF £52.58 TOTE £6.10: £2.50, £1.90, £2.70; EX 45.30 Trifecta £1195.80 Part won. Pool: £1594.44 - 0.76 winning units..
Owner Paul & Dale Chapman Racing **Bred** Cheveley Park Stud Ltd **Trained** Middleham Moor, N Yorks

FOCUS
After 9mm of rain, the ground was eased to good. A fair maiden, run at an honest pace. It paid to race prominently.

6175 WATERAID/BRITISH STALLION STUDS EBF MAIDEN STKS (DIV II) 6f
2:40 (2:40) (Class 5) 2-Y-0 **£2,911** (£866; £432; £216) **Stalls** Low

Form RPR

0320 **1** **Kenny The Captain (IRE)**[20] 5508 2-9-5 74................ DuranFentiman 1 73
(Tim Easterby) *chsd ldrs: led over 2f out: clr over 1f out: pushed out* **9/4**[1]

54 **2** 2 **Crakehall Lad (IRE)**[62] 4044 2-9-5 0.............................. BenCurtis 7 67
(Alan Swinbank) *hld up bhd ldng gp: pushed along over 2f out: hdwy to chse (clr) wnr over 1f out: kpt on fnl f* **7/1**[3]

5 **3** 2 **Sketch Map (IRE)**[21] 5482 2-9-5 0.............................. RussKennemore 8 61
(Jedd O'Keeffe) *missed break: bhd: pushed along and hdwy 2f out: kpt on fnl f: no imp* **10/1**

0 **4** 1 1/4 **Pure Impressions**[18] 5577 2-9-0 0.............................. JoeyHaynes(5) 6 57+
(K R Burke) *trckd ldrs: rdn over 2f out: one pce fr over 1f out* **3/1**[2]

00 **5** 3 **Trinity Star (IRE)**[25] 5338 2-9-5 0.............................. TomEaves 4 48
(Michael Dods) *hld up: shkn up and stdy hdwy whn checked over 1f out: no imp fnl f* **50/1**

02 **6** nk **Noble Asset**[9] 5883 2-9-5 0.............................. MichaelO'Connell 3 47
(John Quinn) *plld hrd: cl up tl edgd rt and hdd over 2f out: sn no ex* **3/1**[2]

0 **7** 1/2 **Victory Danz (IRE)**[37] 4886 2-9-5 0.............................. DavidNolan 9 46
(David O'Meara) *hld up in tch: drvn and outpcd over 2f out: sme late hdwy: nvr on terms* **25/1**

00 **8** 3 **Poco Piccolo**[31] 5083 2-9-2 0.............................. BillyCray(3) 5 37
(Deborah Sanderson) *t.k.h: cl up tl rdn and wknd over 2f out* **80/1**

63 **9** nk **Idamante**[127] 1960 2-9-5 0.............................. TonyHamilton 2 36
(Kristin Stubbs) *chsd ldrs to 2f out: sn rdn and wknd* **16/1**

1m 16.2s (1.60) **Going Correction** +0.15s/f (Good) **9** Ran SP% **115.3**
Speed ratings (Par 95): **95,92,89,88,84 83,82,78,78**
toteswingers 1&2 £4.00, 2&3 £7.40, 1&3 £7.20 CSF £18.66 TOTE £3.40: £1.40, £1.70, £3.10; EX 19.50 Trifecta £170.80 Pool: £2212.29 - 9.71 winning units..
Owner Reality Partnerships V **Bred** Joe Foley & John Grimes **Trained** Great Habton, N Yorks

FOCUS
After the first race the going was changed from good, to good to soft. This was not as strong as the first division. The pace was fair.

6176 ESH CONSTRUCTION MAIDEN STKS 5f
3:10 (3:12) (Class 5) 3-Y-0+ **£2,587** (£770; £384; £192) **Stalls** Low

Form RPR

2222 **1** **Hi Filwah (USA)**[6] 5989 3-9-5 68..............................(p) JamieSpencer 8 71
(Jeremy Noseda) *dwlt: sn pushed along and prom: smooth hdwy to ld over 1f out: qcknd clr fnl f: comf* **4/6**[1]

4403 **2** 3 **Shillito**[9] 5884 3-9-5 64..............................(b[1]) BarryMcHugh 2 54
(Tony Coyle) *cl up: led over 2f out to over 1f out: kpt on fnl f: no ch w wnr* **5/1**[3]

6050 **3** 1 1/2 **Moss The Boss (IRE)**[7] 5965 3-9-0 43.................... ShirleyTeasdale(5) 1 49
(Paul Midgley) *trckd ldrs: smooth hdwy over 2f out: effrt and ev ch over 1f out: one pce fnl f* **50/1**

4 3 3/4 **Chessfield Park** 3-9-5 0.............................. RoystonFfrench 6 36
(Bryan Smart) *dwlt: rn green in rr: effrt 2f out: no imp fnl f* **11/1**

043 **5** 6 **Cracking Choice (IRE)**[21] 5485 3-9-5 57......................(b) TomEaves 5 14
(Michael Dods) *racd on outside of gp: led to over 2f out: wknd over 1f out* **9/2**[2]

6/0- **6** 8 **Mrs Medley**[588] 334 7-8-10 27.............................. AnnStokell(5) 7
(Ann Stokell) *bhd and sn outpcd: no ch fr 1/2-way* **100/1**

-020 **7** 3 3/4 **Spirit Of Parkes**[6] 5989 3-9-5 0.............................. RobertWinston 3
(Eric Alston) *cl up to 1/2-way: sn rdn and wknd* **12/1**

1m 1.38s (0.28) **Going Correction** +0.15s/f (Good)
WFA 3 from 7yo 1lb **7** Ran SP% **113.8**
Speed ratings (Par 103): **103,98,95,89,80 67,61**
toteswingers 1&2 £1.60, 2&3 £10.20, 1&3 £8.10 CSF £4.45 TOTE £1.60: £1.10, £2.50; EX 4.90 Trifecta £85.70 Pool: £2150.48 - 18.81 winning units..
Owner Faisal Alsheikh **Bred** Peter Redekop Bc Limited **Trained** Newmarket, Suffolk

FOCUS
Plenty of exposed types in this maiden. It was run at a sound pace.

6177 J N BENTLEY H'CAP 2m 19y
3:40 (3:40) (Class 6) (0-60,65) 3-Y-0+ **£1,940** (£577; £288; £144) **Stalls** Low

Form RPR

023- **1** **Madam Lilibet (IRE)**[182] 7603 4-9-11 **57**.............................. PaulQuinn 15 65
(Sharon Watt) *hld up: rdn and plenty to do over 2f out: gd hdwy over 1f out: led ins fnl f: flashed tail: r.o strly* **20/1**

6/50 **2** *1 ¾* **Wee Giant (USA)**[74] 3627 7-9-6 **52** BarryMcHugh 8 58
(Tony Coyle) *hld up in midfield: effrt and edgd lft over 2f out: hdwy to chse wnr wl ins fnl f: r.o* **33/1**

0455 **3** *hd* **Uncut Stone (IRE)**[10] 5863 5-9-4 **50** (b) DaleSwift 4 56
(Peter Niven) *hld up: rdn and plenty to do over 2f out: gd hdwy fnl f: fin strly* **20/1**

0604 **4** *½* **Authentication**[11] 5831 4-9-12 **58** AndrewElliott 1 63
(Mel Brittain) *led: hdd over 3f out: sn rdn: rallied: led briefly ins fnl f: one pce* **14/1**

/000 **5** *1 ¾* **High On A Hill (IRE)**[14] 5712 6-9-12 **58** (v[1]) DavidAllan 12 61
(Iain Jardine) *prom: hdwy to ld over 3f out: sn kicked few l clr: hdd ins fnl f: sn btn* **14/1**

0122 **6** *½* **Torero**[9] 5897 4-9-8 **54** (p) BrianHughes 7 56
(Kevin Ryan) *prom: rdn over 3f out: edgd lft 2f out: sn one pce* **10/1**[3]

0001 **7** *hd* **Filia Regina**[12] 5801 3-9-6 **65** 6ex JamieSpencer 11 67
(Ed Dunlop) *missed break: t.k.h in rr: stdy hdwy over 5f out: rdn over 2f out: hdwy u.p over 1f out: btn and eased ins fnl f* **4/7**[1]

5054 **8** *¾* **Valentine's Gift**[10] 5862 5-9-1 **47** DuranFentiman 13 48
(Neville Bycroft) *hld up: rdn over 3f out: hdwy over 1f out: nvr able to chal* **25/1**

0423 **9** *1* **Mr Vendman (IRE)**[11] 5846 3-8-2 **47** (b) FrannyNorton 10 47
(Ian Williams) *t.k.h: chsd ldrs: rdn over 3f out: rallied: wknd fnl f* **8/1**[2]

3300 **10** *5* **Moheebb (IRE)**[11] 5828 9-10-0 **60** (p) DougieCostello 6 54
(Robert Johnson) *midfield: rdn and edgd lft over 2f out: wknd over 1f out* **33/1**

3-0 **11** *6* **Dan's Heir**[10] 5863 11-8-7 **46** (p) SamanthaBell(7) 5 33
(Wilf Storey) *hld up: struggling wl over 3f out: sn n.d* **50/1**

-031 **12** *2 ¾* **Lady Gargoyle**[16] 5643 5-8-8 **47** SophieRobertson(7) 14 31
(Jim Goldie) *t.k.h: trckd ldrs tl rdn and wknd over 2f out* **20/1**

0-00 **13** *59* **Idarose (IRE)**[24] 5370 4-9-1 **47** oh1 ow1 PaddyAspell 2
(Alan Berry) *in tch on ins: struggling over 4f out: sn btn: t.o* **100/1**

3m 41.67s (2.27) **Going Correction** +0.15s/f (Good)
WFA 3 from 4yo+ 13lb **13** Ran SP% **124.2**
Speed ratings (Par 101): **100,99,99,98,97 97,97,97,96,94 91,89,60**
toteswingers 1&2 £11.60, 2&3 £52.80, 1&3 £39.00 CSF £534.60 CT £12574.55 TOTE £29.10: £5.50, £11.30, £4.30; EX 822.40 Trifecta £1253.00 Part won. Pool: £1670.67 - 0.01 winning units..
Owner D H Montgomerie **Bred** Mrs Clodagh McStay **Trained** Brompton-on-Swale, N Yorks

FOCUS
This long-distance contest was run at a sound pace which suited the finishers.

6178 FASTFLOW MAIDEN STKS 1m (R)
4:10 (4:11) (Class 5) 3-Y-O+ **£2,587** (£770; £384; £192) **Stalls** Low

Form RPR

23/2 **1** **Llanarmon Lad (IRE)**[21] 5484 4-9-10 83 DaleSwift 2 77
(Brian Ellison) *chsd ldrs: effrt and drvn 2f out: led last 110yds: kpt on wl* **4/7**[1]

2 *1* **Abbotsfield (IRE)** 3-9-0 0 AndrewElliott 3 69
(Ben Haslam) *hld up towards rr: rdn and hung lft over 2f out: gd hdwy over 1f out: chsd wnr wl ins fnl f: r.o* **50/1**

5/ **3** *hd* **Life And Times (USA)**[110] 4096 5-9-10 0 FrannyNorton 7 74+
(Mark Johnston) *t.k.h towards rr: pushed along over 2f out: hdwy over 1f out: hung lft and styd on towards fin* **5/1**[3]

052 **4** *½* **Red Warrior (IRE)**[21] 5495 3-9-5 75 RobertWinston 4 72
(Ismail Mohammed) *t.k.h: led: rdn and qcknd 2f out: hdd last 110yds: sn one pce* **3/1**[2]

0- **5** *2* **Witch Way Went**[361] 6099 3-8-11 0 [1] PaulPickard(3) 1 62
(Brian Ellison) *sn chsng ldr: effrt and edgd lft over 2f out: one pce fnl f* **20/1**

5 **6** *4 ½* **Let's Go Live**[11] 5839 3-9-5 0 BarryMcHugh 10 57
(Paul Midgley) *t.k.h: in tch tl rdn and wknd appr fnl f* **50/1**

7 *5* **Miss Rebero** 3-9-0 0 PJMcDonald 9 41
(Tim Fitzgerald) *s.i.s: hld up: rdn 3f out: no imp fr 2f out* **66/1**

8 *5* **Redalani (IRE)** 3-9-0 0 MichaelO'Connell 12 29
(Alan Brown) *hld up: rdn and outpcd over 3f out: hung lft 2f out: n.d* **20/1**

U0 **9** *8* **Top Line Banker**[20] 5517 3-9-5 0 TomEaves 6 16
(Brian Ellison) *bhd: struggling wl over 3f out: nvr on terms* **50/1**

0 **10** *5* **Moissanite**[19] 5563 4-9-2 0 DeclanCannon(3) 8
(Sean Regan) *plld hrd in tch: rdn: hung lft and wknd over 2f out* **100/1**

60 **11** *6* **Slip Of A Girl (IRE)**[21] 5484 3-9-0 0 RussKennemore 5
(Patrick Holmes) *towards rr: struggling wl over 2f out: sn btn* **66/1**

1m 46.93s (1.63) **Going Correction** +0.35s/f (Good)
WFA 3 from 4yo+ 5lb **11** Ran SP% **124.7**
Speed ratings (Par 103): **105,104,103,103,101 96,91,86,78,73 67**
toteswingers 1&2 £14.40, 2&3 £23.20, 1&3 £1.40 CSF £61.38 TOTE £1.90: £1.10, £9.60, £1.60; EX 44.70 Trifecta £197.10 Pool: £3119.12 - 11.86 winning units..
Owner Middleham Park Racing XLIII & Partner **Bred** Miss Sarah Thompson **Trained** Norton, N Yorks

FOCUS
Plenty of pace on for this uncompetitive maiden, which saw Middleham Park Racing account for the first two home.

6179 GOWLAND & DAWSON H'CAP 1m 4f 93y
4:40 (4:41) (Class 6) (0-65,65) 3-Y-O+ **£1,940** (£577; £288; £144) **Stalls** Low

Form RPR

2524 **1** **Dean Iarracht (IRE)**[3] 6086 7-8-12 **51** oh3 (p) RobertWinston 7 56
(Tracy Waggott) *trckd ldrs: led and qcknd over 2f out: sn rdn: hld on wl fnl f* **7/1**

0656 **2** *½* **Young Jay**[17] 5612 3-8-13 **61** FrannyNorton 9 65
(Mark Johnston) *trckd ldr: rdn over 2f out: outpcd over 1f out: styd on wl fnl f: regained 2nd last stride* **5/1**[2]

4545 **3** *nse* **Rub Of The Relic (IRE)**[11] 5840 8-9-5 **58** (v) BarryMcHugh 1 62
(Paul Midgley) *t.k.h: led at stdy pce: rdn and hdd over 2f out: rallied: kpt on ins fnl f: lost 2nd last stride* **12/1**

5412 **4** *½* **Vittachi**[11] 5833 6-8-12 **51** (p) MichaelO'Connell 3 54
(Alistair Whillans) *trckd ldrs: n.m.r over 2f out: sn rdn and outpcd: rallied over 1f out: r.o* **5/4**[1]

5604 **5** *1 ¼* **Latin Rebel (IRE)**[27] 5264 6-8-12 **51** oh1 TomEaves 4 52
(Jim Goldie) *t.k.h: in tch: rdn and outpcd over 2f out: styd on fnl f: no imp* **8/1**

1003 **6** *hd* **Spiekeroog**[27] 5295 7-9-12 **65** DavidNolan 5 66
(David O'Meara) *hld up: n.m.r briefly over 2f out: effrt over 1f out: kpt on: nvr able to chal* **6/1**[3]

060 **7** *13* **Liliargh (IRE)**[37] 4893 4-9-10 **63** PJMcDonald 8 45
(Ben Haslam) *hld up: struggling 2f out: sn btn* **12/1**

2m 53.31s (7.71) **Going Correction** +0.35s/f (Good)
WFA 3 from 4yo+ 9lb **7** Ran SP% **114.4**
Speed ratings (Par 101): **88,87,87,87,86 86,77**
toteswingers 1&2 £4.80, 2&3 £6.00, 1&3 £6.80 CSF £41.33 CT £413.43 TOTE £7.50: £3.40, £3.30; EX 53.50 Trifecta £348.40 Pool: £2858.78 - 6.15 winning units..
Owner Michael Howarth **Bred** Ken Carroll **Trained** Spennymoor, Co Durham

FOCUS
The going was changed to soft after the fifth race. A weak handicap run at a steady pace.

6180 NORTHUMBRIAN WATER H'CAP 6f
5:10 (5:12) (Class 6) (0-55,62) 3-Y-O+ **£1,940** (£577; £288; £144) **Stalls** Low

Form RPR

2511 **1** **Lothair (IRE)**[4] 6053 4-10-0 **62** 12ex BenCurtis 7 72
(Alan Swinbank) *pressed ldr: led and rdn 2f out: styd on strly fnl f* **3/1**[1]

3406 **2** *1 ¼* **Graceful Act**[22] 5427 5-9-2 **50** (p) DaleSwift 13 56
(Ron Barr) *bhd: rdn over 2f out: hdwy over 1f out: styd on wl fnl f to take 2nd last stride* **7/1**[3]

0300 **3** *nse* **Lees Anthem**[37] 4891 6-9-2 **50** PJMcDonald 15 56
(Mel Brittain) *hld up: smooth hdwy over 2f out: chal and rdn appr fnl f: one pce wl ins fnl f: lost 2nd last stride* **16/1**

3-05 **4** *1* **Fleurtille**[14] 5715 4-9-7 **55** RobertWinston 1 58
(Robert Johnson) *prom: effrt and pushed along over 2f out: rallied: one pce wl ins fnl f* **33/1**

3410 **5** *½* **Monel**[27] 5263 5-9-6 **54** AndrewElliott 11 55
(Jim Goldie) *hld up: gd hdwy over 1f out: styd on ins fnl f: nvr able to chal* **12/1**

645 **6** *1 ½* **Mysterious Wonder**[14] 5709 3-8-10 **53** EvaMoscrop(7) 12 50
(Philip Kirby) *hld up in midfield: shkn up 2f out: no imp fnl f* **6/1**[2]

-000 **7** *2 ¾* **Baybshambles (IRE)**[9] 5889 9-8-12 **51** GeorgeChaloner(5) 16 40
(Tina Jackson) *chsd ldrs: rdn and outpcd over 2f out: styd on ins fnl f* **25/1**

0000 **8** *¾* **Novalist**[23] 5408 5-9-2 **50** (b) DuranFentiman 9 36
(Robin Bastiman) *led to 2f out: sn rdn and outpcd* **14/1**

0562 **9** *nse* **Annie Gogh**[8] 5916 3-9-5 **55** (b) DavidAllan 4 43
(Tim Easterby) *hld up: rdn and drifted to far rail fr over 2f out: sn n.d* **7/1**[3]

0441 **10** *nk* **Black Douglas**[21] 5487 4-9-5 **53** TomEaves 6 38
(Jim Goldie) *dwlt: hld up: effrt whn hung bdly lft fr 2f out: sn btn* **6/1**[2]

0441 **11** *1* **Bix (IRE)**[8] 5916 3-9-3 **53** 6ex DavidNolan 14 35
(Alan Berry) *in tch: outpcd over 2f out: n.d after* **20/1**

6603 **12** *shd* **Mr Man In The Moon (IRE)**[23] 5408 5-9-0 **53** (p) DavidBergin(5) 3 35
(Mandy Rowland) *chsd ldrs tl wknd fr 2f out* **16/1**

0-00 **13** *1* **Ursus**[35] 4966 8-9-2 **50** PaddyAspell 8 29
(Christopher Wilson) *hld up: rdn over 2f out: edgd lft and sn btn* **50/1**

3405 **14** *4* **Tony Hollis**[21] 5471 5-8-9 **50** GemmaTutty(7) 2 17
(Karen Tutty) *in tch tl hung lft and wknd fr over 2f out* **16/1**

406- **U** **The Kicking Lord**[304] 7616 4-8-12 **53** RobJFitzpatrick(7) 10
(Noel Wilson) *rrd and uns rdr s* **33/1**

1m 16.17s (1.57) **Going Correction** +0.35s/f (Good)
WFA 3 from 4yo+ 2lb **15** Ran SP% **127.0**
Speed ratings (Par 101): **103,101,101,99,99 97,93,92,92,92 90,90,89,84,**
toteswingers 1&2 £5.40, 2&3 £25.10, 1&3 £17.40 CSF £23.04 CT £313.82 TOTE £3.00: £1.10, £2.40, £3.10; EX 27.50 Trifecta £629.90 Pool: £3411.98 - 4.06 winning units..
Owner Mrs J Porter **Bred** Lynch Bages Ltd & Samac Ltd **Trained** Melsonby, N Yorks

FOCUS
The pace was fair for this modest contest.

6181 WATERAID H'CAP 7f
5:45 (6:07) (Class 5) (0-70,70) 3-Y-O+ **£2,587** (£770; £384; £192) **Stalls** Low

Form RPR

0520 **1** **Jupiter Fidius**[21] 5471 6-8-10 **63** GemmaTutty(7) 6 72
(Karen Tutty) *trckd ldrs: hdwy to ld appr fnl f: pushed out* **14/1**

0225 **2** *1 ¼* **Rio Cobolo (IRE)**[22] 5427 7-9-0 **60** AdrianNicholls 14 66
(David Nicholls) *led: rdn: edgd lft and hdd appr fnl f: rallied: kpt on same pce last 100yds* **5/1**[2]

3451 **3** *2* **Red Paladin (IRE)**[20] 5515 3-9-6 **70** (p) BrianHughes 4 69
(Kevin Ryan) *dwlt: hld up: stdy hdwy gng wl 3f out: pushed along appr fnl f: kpt on same pce* **5/1**[2]

3265 **4** *3 ½* **Keep It Dark**[19] 5564 4-9-1 **61** (e[1]) DavidNolan 1 53
(Tony Coyle) *hld up in tch: effrt and rdn over 2f out: kpt on same pce fnl f* **8/1**

1100 **5** *2 ¾* **Running Reef (IRE)**[10] 5861 4-9-8 **68** FrannyNorton 7 53
(Tracy Waggott) *chsd ldrs: rdn and outpcd over 2f out: rallied over 1f out: kpt on fnl f* **25/1**

0003 **6** *6* **Whispered Times (USA)**[11] 5828 6-9-1 **61** (p) BarryMcHugh 3 31
(Tracy Waggott) *w ldr: pushed along over 2f out: wknd qckly 1f out* **12/1**

2234 **7** *nk* **Hazza The Jazza**[9] 5878 3-8-13 **63** RobertWinston 8 31
(Richard Guest) *in tch: drvn and outpcd over 2f out: n.d after* **6/1**[3]

0630 **8** *nk* **Bunce (IRE)**[14] 5713 5-8-12 **65** JoshDoyle(7) 13 34
(David O'Meara) *in tch: pushed along over 2f out: sn btn* **12/1**

0-06 **9** *4* **Orwellian**[139] 1686 4-9-2 **62** RoystonFfrench 15 21
(Bryan Smart) *t.k.h: hld up: struggling over 2f out: sn btn* **16/1**

100 **10** *5* **Mitchum**[18] 5583 4-9-6 **66** (p) DaleSwift 12 12
(Ron Barr) *t.k.h bhd ldng gp: struggling over 3f out: sn btn* **20/1**

00 **11** *3 ¼* **Live Dangerously**[14] 5705 3-9-6 **70** (t) TomEaves 16 6
(Keith Dalgleish) *t.k.h: hld up: struggling wl over 2f out: sn btn* **16/1**

4-62 **12** *19* **Fever Few**[11] 5830 4-9-7 **67** MichaelO'Connell 10
(Jane Chapple-Hyam) *stall opened fractionally early but dwlt: t.k.h and sn in tch: rdn and wknd over 3f out: t.o* **3/1**[1]

1m 29.65s (1.85) **Going Correction** +0.35s/f (Good)
WFA 3 from 4yo+ 4lb **12** Ran SP% **126.2**
Speed ratings (Par 103): **103,101,99,95,92 85,84,84,80,74 70,48**
toteswingers 1&2 £20.30, 2&3 £9.60, 1&3 £9.40 CSF £87.94 CT £421.83 TOTE £17.00: £4.70, £2.40, £2.00; EX 121.80 Trifecta £982.80 Pool: £2415.74 - 1.84 winning units..
Owner Grange Park Racing **Bred** A C Birkle **Trained** Osmotherley, N Yorks

FOCUS
A competitive finale, despite the four absentees.

T/Plt: £5,195.70 to a £1 stake. Pool of £73452.83 - 10.32 winning tickets. T/Qpdt: £283.90 to a £1 stake. Pool of £6025.28 - 15.70 winning tickets. RY

6182 - (Foreign Racing) - See Raceform Interactive

5255 ASCOT (R-H)

Saturday, September 7

OFFICIAL GOING: Good
Wind: almost nil Weather: fine, but cloudy

6183 FLY LONDON SOUTHEND AIRPORT H'CAP 7f
1:55 (1:55) (Class 2) 3-Y-O+ **£51,752** (£15,400; £7,696; £3,848) **Stalls** High

Form RPR
1050 **1** **Redvers (IRE)**[42] 4744 5-9-0 **95**..........(b) RichardKingscote 5 105
(Ed Vaughan) *trckd ldrs in centre: smooth prog to ld gp 2f out: overall ldr 1f out but hrd pressed: drvn and hld on* **8/1**[3]
2001 **2** *nk* **Gabriel's Lad (IRE)**[28] 5285 4-9-4 **99**.......... RobertWinston 8 108
(Denis Coakley) *dwlt: hld up in rr in centre: gd prog and nrest to far side rail fr 2f out: chal 1f out: chsd wnr after: styd on but a hld* **7/1**[2]
1360 **3** *1* **Hasopop (IRE)**[21] 5538 3-9-5 **104**.......... MartinHarley 1 109
(Marco Botti) *hld up in rr in centre: prog on far side of gp over 2f out: cl up over 1f out but nt qckn: styd on ins fnl f* **20/1**
6230 **4** *shd* **Trail Blaze (IRE)**[12] 5838 4-8-9 **95**..........(b) ShaneGray(5) 17 101
(Kevin Ryan) *racd nr side early: overall ldr and clr: hung rt fr 2f out: hdd 1f out: styd on* **14/1**
6150 **5** *1* **Field Of Dream**[36] 4946 6-9-8 **103**..........(b) JimmyFortune 11 107
(Jamie Osborne) *dwlt: hld up in centre: stl last 2f out: nt clr run over 1f out: styd on fnl f: nt gng pce to threaten* **10/1**
1450 **6** *1* **Galician**[14] 5738 4-9-6 **101**.......... FrannyNorton 9 102
(Mark Johnston) *pressed ldr in centre: drvn over 2f out: stl chalng over 1f out: outpcd after* **12/1**
4326 **7** *1* **Pythagorean**[14] 5738 3-8-11 **96**.......... SteveDrowne 2 93
(Roger Charlton) *hld up in rr in centre: shkn up over 2f out: nt clr run briefly over 1f out: styd on same pce fnl f: n.d* **6/1**[1]
0000 **8** *3/4* **Excellent Guest**[14] 5738 6-8-12 **96**.......... RyanPowell(3) 12 92
(George Margarson) *hld up on nr side: prog whn n.m.r over 1f out: drvn and kpt on fnl f: n.d* **20/1**
2246 **9** *4 1/2* **Don't Call Me (IRE)**[42] 4744 6-9-3 **105**..........(t) KevinStott(7) 10 89
(David Nicholls) *chsd ldrs in centre: rdn and cl up jst over 2f out: sn lost pl qckly* **10/1**
0550 **10** *nk* **Monsieur Chevalier (IRE)**[14] 5738 6-9-0 **98**.......... ThomasBrown(3) 15 81
(P J O'Gorman) *trckd ldrs nr side: effrt 2f out: no prog jst over 1f out: sn wknd* **16/1**
0425 **11** *2 1/2* **Summerinthecity (IRE)**[21] 5545 6-8-12 **93**.......... CathyGannon 7 69
(David Nicholls) *chsd ldrs in centre: lost pl qckly jst over 2f out: swtchd rt over 1f out: no prog after* **20/1**
6200 **12** *shd* **Light Up My Life (IRE)**[24] 5402 3-9-0 **99**.......... PatDobbs 18 74
(Richard Hannon) *chsd nr side ldrs: rdn and no prog 2f out: sn wknd* **33/1**
2660 **13** *shd* **Les Troyens**[28] 5268 5-8-11 **92**..........(v) HarryBentley 14 68
(Saeed bin Suroor) *chsd clr ldr nr side to 2f out: sn wknd* **33/1**
0604 **14** *1/2* **Born To Surprise**[21] 5533 4-8-8 **92**.......... WilliamTwiston-Davies(3) 13 66
(Michael Bell) *chsd ldrs in centre: wknd over 1f out* **14/1**
0420 **15** *1/2* **Democretes**[21] 5533 4-8-12 **93**.......... BrettDoyle 16 66
(Richard Hannon) *chsd nr side ldrs to 2f out: sn wknd* **20/1**
1410 **16** *1/2* **Glen Moss (IRE)**[14] 5738 4-9-3 **98**.......... JimmyQuinn 6 70
(Charles Hills) *led gp in centre to 2f out: wknd rapidly* **10/1**
4410 **17** *1 1/4* **Shebebi (USA)**[14] 5738 3-9-1 **100**..........(b) DaneO'Neill 3 67
(Mark Johnston) *pressed ldr in centre to 2f out: wknd rapidly* **16/1**

1m 27.73s (0.13) **Going Correction** +0.275s/f (Good)
WFA 3 from 4yo+ 4lb **17 Ran SP% 122.9**
Speed ratings (Par 109): **110,109,108,108,107 106,104,104,98,98 95,95,95,94,94 93,92**
toteswingers 1&2 £7.90, 2&3 £131.30, 1&3 £52.50 CSF £56.10 CT £1096.35 TOTE £8.20: £2.20, £2.10, £6.20, £3.20; EX 60.40 Trifecta £1090.10 Pool: £2821.58 - 1.94 winning units..
Owner M J C Hawkes and E J C Hawkes **Bred** Peter Jones And G G Jones **Trained** Newmarket, Suffolk

FOCUS
Straight course stands' side rail positioned 7yds inside normal position. Round course rails 4yds inside from 1m2f increasing to 9yds at home bend straight and down the far side of the straight. Old Mile increased by 10yds and 1m4f by 16yds. A really competitive handicap, and Trail Blaze lived up to his name and took them along at a good clip. That suited the winner down to the ground. The first three all challenged towards the far side of the main bunch. Straightforward form.

6184 MCGEE GROUP E B F MAIDEN STKS 7f
2:25 (2:29) (Class 4) 2-Y-O **£5,175** (£1,540; £769; £384) **Stalls** High

Form RPR
0 **1** **Stealth Missile (IRE)**[43] 4702 2-9-0 0.......... FrannyNorton 11 86
(Clive Brittain) *mde all: rdn and hrd pressed fr 2f out: wandered but fnd more to assert ins fnl f* **25/1**
2 *3/4* **Art Of War (IRE)** 2-9-5 0.......... RichardKingscote 8 89+
(Tom Dascombe) *dwlt: wl in rr: rn green but gd prog fr jst over 2f out: shkn up and styd on wl fnl f to take 2nd last strides* **16/1**
2 **3** *nk* **Bon Voyage**[15] 5718 2-9-5 0.......... JimmyFortune 4 88
(Richard Hannon) *prom: edgd lft 3f out: pressed wnr over 2f out: upsides tl no ex ins fnl f: lost 2nd last strides* **7/4**[1]
4 *3/4* **Monsea (IRE)** 2-9-5 0.......... MartinHarley 1 86
(Richard Hannon) *towards rr: prog fr over 2f out: jnd ldng pair 1f out: fdd last 100yds* **25/1**
4 **5** *3* **Fracking (IRE)**[9] 5924 2-9-5 0.......... HarryBentley 7 78
(Olly Stevens) *pressed wnr to over 2f out: steadily fdd over 1f out* **6/1**[3]
3 **6** *6* **Amood (IRE)**[21] 5539 2-9-5 0.......... DaneO'Neill 5 63
(Charles Hills) *chsd ldrs: shkn up over 2f out: wknd over 1f out* **9/4**[2]
0 **7** *1 1/4* **Golden Journey (IRE)**[24] 5399 2-9-5 0.......... JohnFahy 2 59
(Clive Cox) *pressed ldrs to 2f out: wknd over 1f out* **20/1**
8 *2* **Majestic Sun (IRE)** 2-9-5 0.......... FergusSweeney 3 54
(Peter Chapple-Hyam) *dwlt: in tch: rdn whn bmpd over 2f out: sn wknd* **20/1**
9 *hd* **Pershing** 2-9-5 0.......... MartinLane 6 54
(Brian Meehan) *pressed ldrs: rdn and sing to lose pl whn bmpd 3f out: bmpd again sn after: wknd* **40/1**
10 *1 3/4* **Bilimbi (IRE)** 2-9-5 0.......... LiamJones 10 49
(William Haggas) *in tch: pushed along 1/2-way: wknd over 2f out* **16/1**
11 *8* **Frosty The Snowman (IRE)** 2-9-5 0.......... SteveDrowne 12 28
(Charles Hills) *dwlt: mostly in last and nvr gng wl: t.o* **20/1**
12 *1/2* **Danglydontask** 2-9-5 0.......... CathyGannon 9 27
(David Arbuthnot) *chsd ldrs 3f: sn struggling: t.o* **33/1**

1m 29.79s (2.19) **Going Correction** +0.275s/f (Good) **12 Ran SP% 119.6**
Speed ratings (Par 97): **98,97,96,95,92 85,84,81,81,79 70,70**
toteswingers 1&2 £38.60, 2&3 £8.20, 1&3 £7.00 CSF £346.98 TOTE £31.20: £5.80, £4.80, £1.30; EX 477.00 Trifecta £1323.70 Part won. Pool: £1764.99 - 0.44 winning units..
Owner Saeed Manana **Bred** Sommerville Bloodstock **Trained** Newmarket, Suffolk

FOCUS
Telescope finished second in this on his debut last season, but it'll be a surprise if anything as good took part this year.

6185 NYETIMBER HYPERION FILLIES' CONDITIONS STKS 1m (R)
3:00 (3:02) (Class 2) 2-Y-O **£9,703** (£2,887; £1,443; £721) **Stalls** Low

Form RPR
140 **1** **Feedyah (USA)**[21] 5555 2-8-12 0.......... MartinLane 3 92
(Charlie Appleby) *hld up in last: clsd 2f out: swtchd ins over 1f out: drvn to ld last 100yds: styd on wl* **11/2**
0214 **2** *nk* **Adhwaa**[28] 5284 2-8-12 93.......... DaneO'Neill 4 91
(J W Hills) *led: rdn over 2f out: sn hrd pressed: kpt on u.p but hdd and hld last 100yds* **9/4**[2]
2 **3** *1* **Casual Smile**[28] 5282 2-8-12 0.......... JimmyFortune 1 89
(Andrew Balding) *hld up in 3rd: clsd to chal fr 2f out: drvn and upsides 1f out: nt qckn last 150yds* **2/1**[1]
10 **4** *shd* **Hot Coffee (IRE)**[21] 5555 2-8-12 0.......... RichardKingscote 2 88
(Tom Dascombe) *trckd ldr: clsd to chal 2f out: sn rdn: nt qckn and leaned on rival 1f out: one pce after* **11/4**[3]

1m 44.84s (4.14) **Going Correction** +0.275s/f (Good) **4 Ran SP% 106.2**
Speed ratings (Par 98): **90,89,88,88**
CSF £17.00 TOTE £5.20; EX 14.20 Trifecta £21.40 Pool: £123.69 - 43.10 winning units..
Owner Godolphin **Bred** Darley **Trained** Newmarket, Suffolk

FOCUS
This looked a pretty tight affair on paper, they went no more than a fair gallop, and finished in a heap.

6186 LADBROKES MOBILE H'CAP (HERITAGE HANDICAP) 1m 4f
3:30 (3:30) (Class 2) 3-Y-O **£97,035** (£28,875; £14,430; £7,215) **Stalls** Low

Form RPR
-010 **1** **Excellent Result (IRE)**[79] 3486 3-9-0 **94**.......... RobertWinston 2 103
(Saeed bin Suroor) *t.k.h early: trckd ldng pair: rdn over 2f out: clsd to ld jst over 1f out: sn in command: styd on* **14/1**
2311 **2** *1* **Elhaame (IRE)**[27] 5302 3-9-0 **94**.......... RichardKingscote 8 101+
(Luca Cumani) *trckd ldrs on inner in 7th: rdn and angled out fr over 1f out: styd on to take 2nd ins fnl f: unable to chal* **8/1**[3]
1106 **3** *hd* **Eshtiaal (USA)**[14] 5746 3-8-13 **93**..........(bt[1]) DaneO'Neill 15 100
(Brian Meehan) *trckd ldrs in 6th: rdn and nt qckn over 2f out: styd on wl fnl f to take 3rd last stride* **16/1**
3221 **4** *shd* **Glenard**[28] 5274 3-8-11 **91**.......... JimmyQuinn 6 98
(Charles Hills) *trckd ldng trio: rdn and leaned upon by rival wl over 2f out: kpt on u.p fr over 1f out: nvr able to chal* **14/1**
2312 **5** *1* **Cafe Society (FR)**[56] 4279 3-8-9 **89**.......... MartinLane 7 94+
(David Simcock) *heavily restrained s: hld up in last: rdn 2f out: styd on fr over 1f out to take 5th last strides: far too much to do* **3/1**[1]
1111 **6** *nk* **Special Meaning**[15] 5706 3-8-12 **92**.......... FrannyNorton 4 97
(Mark Johnston) *led: rdn and jnd 2f out: hdd and no ex jst over 1f out* **6/1**[2]
-230 **7** *nse* **Wadi Al Hattawi (IRE)**[28] 5258 3-8-8 **88**..........(p) NickyMackay 1 93
(Saeed bin Suroor) *dwlt and pushed along in rr early: stl wl in rr and rdn 2f out: styd on wl fnl f: nrst fin* **16/1**
2150 **8** *nk* **Elidor**[14] 5764 3-8-12 **92**.......... MartinHarley 11 96
(Mick Channon) *a in midfield: rdn and no prog 2f out: kpt on u.p fr over 1f out: nt gng pce to threaten* **14/1**
1061 **9** *1 1/4* **Royal Skies (IRE)**[28] 5258 3-9-6 **100**.......... LiamJones 12 102
(Mark Johnston) *t.k.h early: chsd ldr: rdn to chal and upsides 2f out tl jst over 1f out: fdd* **14/1**
0136 **10** *hd* **Shrewd**[28] 5274 3-8-9 **92**.......... ThomasBrown(3) 16 94
(Michael Bell) *stdd s fr wd draw: hld up in last pair: shkn up 2f out: prog over 1f out: styng on but no ch whn nt clr run ins fnl f: eased* **20/1**
2154 **11** *nk* **Dare To Achieve**[28] 5274 3-9-1 **95**.......... SteveDrowne 5 96
(William Haggas) *dwlt: hld up in rr: rdn and no real prog fr 2f out* **12/1**
-125 **12** *nk* **Romantic Settings**[86] 3240 3-8-10 **95**.......... GeorgeChaloner(5) 3 96
(Richard Fahey) *dwlt: rcvrd to chse ldrs in 5th: rdn 2f out: wknd over 1f out* **20/1**
455 **13** *6* **Another Cocktail**[56] 4279 3-8-13 **93**..........(b[1]) JohnFahy 13 84
(Hughie Morrison) *nvr bttr than midfield: rdn 3f out: sn btn* **33/1**
4142 **14** *29* **Goodwood Mirage (IRE)**[36] 4950 3-9-0 **94**.......... TedDurcan 14 39
(William Knight) *stdd s: racd wd and t.k.h in rr: no prog over 3f out: sn eased: t.o* **6/1**[2]

2m 33.94s (1.44) **Going Correction** +0.275s/f (Good) **14 Ran SP% 123.3**
Speed ratings (Par 107): **106,105,105,105,104 104,104,104,103,103 102,102,98,79**
toteswingers 1&2 £26.00, 2&3 £59.80, 1&3 £34.20 CSF £121.71 CT £1840.77 TOTE £18.20: £5.70, £2.90, £6.90; EX 173.30 Trifecta £2102.90 Part won. Pool: £2803.91 - 0.43 winning units..
Owner Godolphin **Bred** Tom & Geraldine Molan **Trained** Newmarket, Suffolk

FOCUS
A valuable handicap but despite the decent-sized field they went no pace and it turned into a dash for the line. Improvement from the first two and the form should work out.

6187 WONDERING WINE COMPANY NURSERY H'CAP 5f
4:05 (4:05) (Class 2) 2-Y-O **£11,644** (£3,465; £1,731; £865) **Stalls** High

Form RPR
2410 **1** **Flying Bear (IRE)**[17] 5656 2-8-8 **75**.......... HayleyTurner 3 78
(Jeremy Gask) *s.s: hld up in last: prog over 1f out: drvn and r.o fnl f: led post* **7/2**[2]
3404 **2** *nse* **Tableforten**[4] 6065 2-8-6 **73**.......... LiamJones 2 76
(J S Moore) *sn pushed along to stay in tch: drvn 2f out: swtchd rt jst over 1f out: sn chsd ldr: clsd to ld nr fin: hdd post* **8/1**
0115 **3** *nk* **Zalzilah**[35] 5012 2-9-7 **88**..........(b[1]) MartinHarley 5 90
(James Tate) *led: gng bttr than rest over 1f out: drvn fnl f: hdd on both sides nr fin* **10/1**
400 **4** *1 1/2* **Gym Shoes**[25] 5364 2-8-3 **70**.......... JimmyQuinn 1 67
(Richard Fahey) *hld up: outpcd and rdn 1/2-way: sn bhd: styd on fr over 1f out to take 4th nr fin* **16/1**
0350 **5** *nk* **Ifwecan**[17] 5656 2-9-6 **87**.......... FrannyNorton 7 82
(Mark Johnston) *trckd ldrs: rdn and nt qckn over 1f out: sn btn* **5/2**[1]
1405 **6** *3/4* **Steventon Star**[57] 4248 2-9-7 **88**.......... DaneO'Neill 4 81
(Richard Hannon) *cl up: chsd ldr 2f out: sn rdn: lost 2nd and wknd 1f out* **7/2**[2]
513 **7** *3* **Straits Of Malacca**[35] 5012 2-8-4 **76**.......... ShaneGray(5) 6 58
(Kevin Ryan) *chsd ldr to 2f out: wknd* **5/1**[3]

1m 1.67s (1.17) **Going Correction** +0.275s/f (Good) **7 Ran SP% 115.8**
Speed ratings (Par 101): **101,100,100,98,97 96,91**
toteswingers 1&2 £5.30, 2&3 £20.50, 1&3 £5.00 CSF £31.65 TOTE £4.00: £2.10, £4.70; EX 28.30 Trifecta £249.60 Pool: £2231.21 - 6.70 winning units..

Owner Flying Bear Partnership **Bred** Joseph Flanagan & Jarlath Fahey **Trained** Sutton Veny, Wilts

FOCUS

This nursery was run at a good gallop, and that suited the winner.

6188 RITZ CLUB FILLIES' H'CAP 1m (S)

4:40 (4:41) (Class 3) (0-95,95) 3-Y-O+ **£8,409** (£2,502; £1,250; £625) **Stalls** High

Form RPR

15- **1** **Lanansaak (IRE)**[351] 6448 3-8-8 **82**....[1] DaneO'Neill 6 101
(Roger Varian) *stdd s: hld up in last pair: cruised through to go 2nd 2f out: cajoled into ld jst over 1f out: hd at awkward angle but bolted up* **6/1**

0331 **2** 4 ½ **Forgive**[29] 5246 4-9-6 **94**.... RobertTart(5) 1 103
(Richard Hannon) *pressed ldr: led 3f out: rdn 2f out: hdd jst over 1f out: wl clr of rest but no ch w wnr* **7/2**[1]

-633 **3** 10 **Penny Rose**[22] 5496 3-8-8 **82**.... FrannyNorton 5 68
(Mark Johnston) *sn in rr: rdn over 3f out: no ch 2f out: tk modest 3rd jst over 1f out: lost further grnd on ldng pair after* **5/1**[3]

2103 **4** ¾ **Great Timing (USA)**[29] 5246 3-9-7 **95**.... MartinLane 9 79
(Charlie Appleby) *led: rdn and hdd 3f out: sn btn: lost modest 3rd over 1f out: wknd* **4/1**[2]

0405 **5** 3 ½ **Sorella Bella (IRE)**[49] 4525 3-9-4 **92**.... MartinHarley 11 68
(Mick Channon) *chsd ldng pair to over 3f out: sn struggling and btn* **14/1**

2145 **6** 9 **Plover**[42] 4766 3-8-12 **86**.... SteveDrowne 8 41
(Sir Michael Stoute) *hld up in last pair: rdn 1/2-way: prog u.p wl over 2f out: sn wknd: wl bhd fnl f* **8/1**

1254 **7** shd **Saucy Minx (IRE)**[19] 5589 3-8-7 **81**.... NickyMackay 3 36
(Amanda Perrett) *cl up: rdn to chse ldng pair over 3f out to over 2f out: wknd rapidly* **7/1**

252 **8** nse **Starlight Symphony (IRE)**[7] 6003 3-8-2 **76**....(b) JimmyQuinn 2 31
(Eve Johnson Houghton) *chsd ldrs to 1/2-way: sn wknd* **7/1**

1m 40.6s (-0.20) **Going Correction** +0.275s/f (Good)
WFA 3 from 4yo 5lb **8** Ran SP% **116.0**
Speed ratings (Par 104): **112,107,97,96,93 84,84,84**
toteswingers 1&2 £4.30, 2&3 £5.00, 1&3 £8.40 CSF £27.72 CT £114.35 TOTE £4.80: £1.90, £1.70, £1.90; EX 21.70 Trifecta £146.40 Pool: £2596.69 - 13.15 winning units..

Owner Hamdan Al Maktoum **Bred** Shadwell Estate Company Limited **Trained** Newmarket, Suffolk

FOCUS

Two came well clear in this fillies' handicap, and the winner looks pattern class. The second ran a personal best to beat the rest easily.

6189 LAST CALL FROM "THE CROC" H'CAP 5f

5:10 (5:11) (Class 3) (0-90,90) 3-Y-O+ **£8,409** (£2,502; £1,250; £625) **Stalls** High

Form RPR

0604 **1** **Dungannon**[7] 5998 6-9-3 **86**....(v) JimmyFortune 18 96
(Andrew Balding) *hld up in midfield: stdy prog 2f out: clsd fnl f: drvn ahd last 100yds: hld on* **3/1**[1]

3630 **2** hd **Lady Gibraltar**[17] 5651 4-9-2 **88**....(v) MichaelJMMurphy(3) 16 97
(Alan Jarvis) *trckd ldrs: rdn and prog to ld over 1f out: hdd last 100yds: battled on wl: jst hld* **14/1**

0106 **3** ½ **Fitz Flyer (IRE)**[33] 5056 7-9-4 **87**....(v) FrannyNorton 7 94
(David Nicholls) *chsd ldrs: rdn and swtchd rt over 1f out: chsd ldng pair fnl f: styd on but nvr quite able to chal* **12/1**

6210 **4** ¾ **Gabbiano**[21] 5544 4-9-1 **89**.... RobertTart(5) 12 94
(Jeremy Gask) *wl in rr: pushed along 1/2-way: brought to nr side rail over 1f out: styd on strly fnl f: nrst fin* **4/1**[2]

4662 **5** ¾ **Titus Gent**[23] 5441 8-8-12 **84**.... CharlesBishop(3) 8 86+
(Jeremy Gask) *wl in rr: sltly hmpd 3f out: prog on far side over 1f out: styd on fnl f: nrst fin* **16/1**

0404 **6** nk **Diamond Charlie (IRE)**[43] 4707 5-9-0 **83**.... JimmyQuinn 17 84
(Simon Dow) *s.i.s: towards rr: rdn 2f out: styd on fr over 1f out: nt gng pce to chal* **9/1**[3]

5324 **7** nk **Rylee Mooch**[21] 5537 5-8-7 **81**....(e) PhilipPrince(5) 15 81
(Richard Guest) *mde most to over 1f out: grad fdd* **14/1**

3631 **8** 1 ¼ **Monumental Man**[44] 4675 4-8-13 **82**....(p) HayleyTurner 11 77
(James Unett) *w ldrs: drvn and upsides jst over 1f out: wknd fnl f* **16/1**

2142 **9** ¾ **Port Alfred**[19] 5585 3-9-0 **84**.... MartinLane 13 76
(Charlie Appleby) *pressed ldr: upsides wl over 1f out: wknd fnl f* **9/1**[3]

1006 **10** ¾ **Church Music (IRE)**[71] 3786 4-8-11 **80**....(v) NickyMackay 9 70
(Michael Scudamore) *chsd ldrs: rdn and no imp over 1f out: fdd fnl f* **33/1**

4446 **11** nk **Waseem Faris (IRE)**[8] 5971 4-8-7 **76** oh2....(v[1]) RobertHavlin 2 65
(Mick Channon) *s.s: swtchd fr wd draw and hld up wl in rr: shkn up and modest prog over 1f out: no hdwy after* **14/1**

0240 **12** 2 **Gladiatrix**[20] 5561 4-8-12 **88**....(b) PatMillman(7) 10 69
(Rod Millman) *squeezed out s: rcvrd to chse ldrs: wknd wl over 1f out* **14/1**

000 **13** 1 ½ **Stone Of Folca**[21] 5519 5-9-7 **90**.... SteveDrowne 14 66
(John Best) *chsd ldrs: rdn 2f out: wknd over 1f out* **20/1**

2026 **14** 37 **Jillnextdoor (IRE)**[14] 5769 3-9-6 **90**.... MartinHarley 5
(Mick Channon) *stmbld bdly s: a wl in rr: no ch whn sltly hmpd 3f out: allowed to coast home* **20/1**

1402 **15** 7 **Rebecca Romero**[14] 5750 6-8-13 **82**.... RobertWinston 3
(Denis Coakley) *wl in rr whn almost b.d 3f out: allowed to coast home* **20/1**

120 **F** **Arctic Lynx (IRE)**[33] 5062 6-8-12 **81**.... LiamJones 4
(Robert Cowell) *pushed along in midfield whn stmbld bdly and fell 3f out* **33/1**

1m 1.05s (0.55) **Going Correction** +0.275s/f (Good)
WFA 3 from 4yo+ 1lb **16** Ran SP% **131.3**
Speed ratings (Par 107): **106,105,104,103,102 102,101,99,98,97 96,93,91,31,20**
toteswingers 1&2 £15.50, 2&3 £140.10, 1&3 £14.90 CSF £47.01 CT £489.93 TOTE £4.10: £1.40, £3.60, £3.20, £1.90; EX 56.20 Trifecta £654.40 Pool: £2824.67 - 3.23 winning units..

Owner DR E Harris **Bred** J A E Hobby **Trained** Kingsclere, Hants

FOCUS

The whole field came up the centre of the track, but the first two raced on the stands' side of the bunch before drifting across in the closing stages. Straightforward form to a good handicap.

T/Plt: £1,310.60 to a £1 stake. Pool of £129860.98 - 72.33 winning tickets. T/Qpdt: £162.20 to a £1 stake. Pool of £5337.80 - 24.35 winning tickets. JN

6159 HAYDOCK (L-H)

Saturday, September 7

OFFICIAL GOING: Good to soft (soft in places in back straight; 7.6)

Wind: Half against Weather: Cloudy with showers

6190 BETFRED MOBILE BE FRIENDLY H'CAP 5f

2:05 (2:05) (Class 2) (0-100,99) 3-Y-O+ **£17,789** (£5,293; £2,645; £1,322) **Stalls** Centre

Form RPR

0000 **1** **Confessional**[21] 5545 6-9-2 **94**....(e) DavidAllan 8 105
(Tim Easterby) *a handy in centre of trck: led over 1f out: kpt on wl: pushed out towards fin* **15/2**

011 **2** ¾ **Harrison George (IRE)**[72] 3720 8-8-12 **95**....(bt) NatashaEaton(5) 10 103
(P J O'Gorman) *a.p in centre of trck: rdn to take 2nd over 1f out: kpt on u.p ins fnl f but nt quite able to chal wnr* **13/2**[2]

6500 **3** 2 ¾ **Judge 'n Jury**[14] 5772 9-9-4 **96**....(t) LukeMorris 11 94
(Ronald Harris) *w ldr on nr side tl rdn over 1f out: kpt on same pce ins fnl f* **12/1**

5400 **4** 1 **Kyleakin Lass**[29] 5247 4-8-13 **91**.... RichardHughes 6 86
(Jonathan Portman) *hld up in centre of trck: effrt to chse ldrs over 1f out: one pce fnl 100yds* **12/1**

0245 **5** 1 ¼ **Racy**[28] 5257 6-9-6 **98**.... GrahamLee 5 88
(Brian Ellison) *hld up in centre of trck: rdn over 1f out: kpt on wout threatening ldrs ins fnl f* **7/1**[3]

1146 **6** 1 **Above Standard (IRE)**[17] 5651 5-8-12 **90**....[1] GrahamGibbons 14 76
(Michael Easterby) *racd bhd ldrs on nr side: niggled along 1/2-way: kpt on one pce ins fnl f: no imp* **4/1**[1]

4353 **7** nk **Normal Equilibrium**[14] 5769 3-8-12 **91**.... NeilCallan 13 76
(Robert Cowell) *racd bhd ldrs on nr side: u.p wl over 1f out: plugged on ins fnl f wout threatening* **13/2**[2]

130 **8** 3 ¼ **Jack Luey**[32] 5108 6-8-5 **86**.... RaulDaSilva(3) 2 60
(Lawrence Mullaney) *racd in centre of trck: a bhd: u.p 1/2-way: nvr on terms* **8/1**

2003 **9** 4 **Jedward (IRE)**[12] 5821 6-8-7 **85** oh1....(b) PaulHanagan 12 44
(Kevin Ryan) *racd on nr side: led: rdn and hdd over 1f out: wknd ins fnl f* **15/2**

5003 **10** 3 **Prohibit**[25] 5375 8-9-7 **99**....(p) JimCrowley 3 47
(Robert Cowell) *chsd ldrs in cntre of trck tl rdn and lost pl 2f out: bhd after* **12/1**

1m 0.14s (-0.66) **Going Correction** +0.10s/f (Good)
WFA 3 from 4yo+ 1lb **10** Ran SP% **116.9**
Speed ratings (Par 109): **109,107,103,101,99 98,97,92,86,81**
Tote Swingers: 1&2 £8.00, 1&3 £14.20, 2&3 £10.10 CSF £55.73 CT £583.85 TOTE £8.40: £2.30, £2.30, £4.00; EX 44.70 Trifecta £291.80 Pool: £2,329.42 - 5.98 winning units..

Owner T G & Mrs M E Holdcroft **Bred** Bearstone Stud **Trained** Great Habton, N Yorks

FOCUS

All races on stands' side home straight, and rail movement added 50yds to 1m races and 100yds to 1m6f races. The going had dried a little since Friday and they were racing on some fresh ground. Luke Morris said the ground was "good to soft, not as soft as I thought." The time for the opener was only 1.64sec outside the standard, suggesting conditions weren't too taxing. A decent sprint handicap, They split into two groups, a larger bunch of six down the centre and the others on the stands' side. It proved hard to make ground from the rear and the first two were always to the fore in their group. The winner has been rated back to his old handicap best, 5lb off his peak handicap form.

6191 BETFRED.COM SUPERIOR MILE (GROUP 3) 1m

2:40 (2:40) (Class 1) 3-Y-O+

£34,026 (£12,900; £6,456; £3,216; £1,614; £810) **Stalls** Low

Form RPR

312 **1** **Top Notch Tonto (IRE)**[28] 5287 3-8-11 95.... DaleSwift 4 113
(Brian Ellison) *midfield: pushed along and hdwy 3f out: led over 2f out: rdn and edgd lft over 1f out: r.o wl fnl f* **22/1**

4315 **2** 2 ¼ **Hay Dude**[15] 5728 3-8-11 99.... DanielTudhope 10 108
(K R Burke) *hld up: smooth hdwy on outer 2f out: rdn ins fnl f: tk 2nd fnl 150yds: no imp on wnr* **14/1**

0523 **3** nk **Gabrial (IRE)**[15] 5725 4-9-2 110.... PaulHanagan 7 107
(Richard Fahey) *trckd ldrs: rdn to chse wnr wl over 1f out: sn no imp: lost 2nd fnl 150yds: kpt on same pce* **11/1**

3323 **4** ¾ **Tawhid**[21] 5532 3-8-11 111.... GeraldMosse 3 106
(Saeed bin Suroor) *hld up in rr: swtchd rt arnd the whole field wl over 1f out: sn rdn to prog: carried hd high: styd on ins fnl f: nvr able to mount serious chal* **7/2**[2]

1211 **5** 2 **Montiridge (IRE)**[36] 4945 3-9-1 115.... RichardHughes 2 105
(Richard Hannon) *racd keenly: hld up: pushed along 3f out: effrt to chse ldrs over 1f out: sn no imp: btn ins fnl f: fdd fnl 100yds* **10/11**[1]

5224 **6** 5 **Highland Knight (IRE)**[23] 5446 6-9-2 110....(t) DavidProbert 9 89
(Andrew Balding) *prom tl rdn and wknd wl over 1f out* **14/1**

1-01 **7** 2 **Nine Realms**[28] 5255 4-9-2 97.... RyanMoore 1 85
(William Haggas) *trckd ldrs: lost pl 3f out: struggling fnl 2f* **7/1**[3]

010 **8** 3 ½ **Anna's Pearl**[69] 3876 3-8-11 105....(b) JimCrowley 5 77
(Ralph Beckett) *led: hdd over 2f out: sn rdn: wknd over 1f out* **28/1**

1m 43.35s (-0.35) **Going Correction** +0.30s/f (Good)
WFA 3 from 4yo+ 5lb **8** Ran SP% **116.6**
Speed ratings (Par 113): **113,110,110,109,107 102,100,97**
Tote Swingers: 1&2 £17.30, 1&3 £15.70, 2&3 £10.00 CSF £289.91 TOTE £27.10: £4.70, £2.40, £2.60; EX 255.00 Trifecta £1821.20 Pool: £3,329.64 - 1.37 winning units..

Owner Keith Brown **Bred** Seamus Finucane **Trained** Norton, N Yorks

■ Dale Swift's first Group winner.

FOCUS

This event had Group 3 status for the first time. It looked up to scratch for the grade on paper, and was run at a reasonable gallop, but there was a surprise outcome with the spoils going to the lowest-rated horse in the line-up, with form pair Montiridge and Tawhid not seen at their best. This was out of line with the rest of the winner's form, with the race rated around the runner-up.

6192 BETFRED "GOALS GALORE" OLD BOROUGH CUP (H'CAP) 1m 6f

3:15 (3:15) (Class 2) (0-105,100) 3-Y-O **£38,814** (£11,550; £5,772; £2,886) **Stalls** Low

Form RPR

211 **1** **Platinum (IRE)**[17] 5640 6-9-0 **90**....(p) RussKennemore 12 100+
(Philip Kirby) *in tch: rdn over 2f out: led over 1f out: styd on thrght fnl f: wl in control clsng stages* **10/1**

1363 **2** 1 ¼ **Clowance Estate (IRE)**[14] 5746 4-9-3 **93**.... GrahamLee 9 101
(Roger Charlton) *w ldr: rdn to ld 2f out: hdd over 1f out: kpt on: wl hld fnl 100yds* **6/1**[2]

111- **3** 1/2 **Pallasator**[344] 6625 4-9-10 **100**.. LukeMorris 13 107+
(Sir Mark Prescott Bt) *hld up: pushed along 4f out: hdwy 3f out: rdn and hung lft whn chsng ldrs over 1f out: styd on ins fnl f but nvr gng to get there* **7/2**[1]

0350 **4** 1 3/4 **Wyborne**[17] 5655 4-7-13 **78**.. RaulDaSilva(3) 4 83
(Brian Ellison) *chsd ldrs: rdn over 2f out: tried to chal over 1f out: one pce towards fin* **22/1**

3113 **5** shd **Kiama Bay (IRE)**[15] 5723 7-9-1 **91**.................................. PaulHanagan 5 96
(Richard Fahey) *chsd ldrs: rdn over 1f out: drifted lft ins fnl f: kpt on same pce* **10/1**

0025 **6** 1 1/4 **Scatter Dice (IRE)**[15] 5723 4-8-12 **88**............................ NeilCallan 2 91
(Mark Johnston) *led: rdn and hdd 2f out: stl wl there: no ex fnl 100yds* **14/1**

6302 **7** 5 **Cousin Khee**[10] 5895 6-8-11 **87**.. RyanMoore 8 83
(Hughie Morrison) *hld up: struggling 3f out: styd on fr over 1f out: nvr a threat* **10/1**

0030 **8** 1 1/4 **Suraj**[17] 5655 4-9-1 **91**.. AdamKirby 1 85
(Michael Bell) *s.s: rdn along early on: in rr: u.p 3f out: plugged on over 1f out but nvr a threat* **9/1**

6006 **9** 1 **Blue Bajan (IRE)**[17] 5655 11-9-1 **91**..........................(p) DanielTudhope 7 84
(David O'Meara) *midfield: rdn over 2f out: one pce and no imp on ldrs over 1f out* **16/1**

1511 **10** 1/2 **Poyle Thomas**[22] 5475 4-8-8 **84**...................................... JimCrowley 11 76
(Ralph Beckett) *midfield: pushed along 3f out: no imp fnl 2f* **7/1**[3]

622- **11** 7 **Gassin Golf**[136] 5905 4-9-4 **94**.. GeorgeBaker 16 76
(Richard Lee) *hld up in rr: toiling 3f out: nvr a threat* **14/1**

2045 **12** 3/4 **Oriental Fox (GER)**[14] 5766 5-9-10 **100**............................ JoeFanning 6 81
(Mark Johnston) *in tch: rdn 3f out: wknd 2f out* **10/1**

3060 **13** 1 3/4 **Itlaaq**[15] 5723 7-8-12 **88**..(t) GrahamGibbons 15 67
(Michael Easterby) *midfield: rdn over 2f out: wknd over 1f out* **40/1**

0316 **14** 32 **Nanton (USA)**[57] 4262 11-8-9 **85**.................................... ShaneKelly 3 19
(Jim Goldie) *midfield tl rdn and wknd 3f out: t.o* **50/1**

3m 6.51s (4.51) **Going Correction** +0.475s/f (Yiel) **14** Ran SP% **123.3**
Speed ratings (Par 109): **106,105,105,104,103 103,100,99,99,98 94,94,93,75**
Tote Swingers: 1&2 £14.60, 1&3 £6.60, 2&3 £7.40 CSF £69.62 CT £259.86 TOTE £12.30: £3.30, £3.30, £1.60; EX 107.80 Trifecta £670.30 Pool: £45,864.72 - 51.31 winning units..
Owner Mrs Philippa Kirby **Bred** Lodge Park Stud **Trained** Middleham, N Yorks

FOCUS
A competitive and valuable handicap, but it wasn't strong run. They arrowed down the centre of the track in the home straight and the first six finished clear, among them the four who had been up there throughout. The winenr surpassed even his early French form.

6193 BETFRED SPRINT CUP (BRITISH CHAMPIONS SERIES) (GROUP 1) 6f
3:50 (3:53) (Class 1) 3-Y-O+
£141,775 (£53,750; £26,900; £13,400; £6,725; £3,375) **Stalls** Centre

Form RPR

4231 **1** **Gordon Lord Byron (IRE)**[23] 5453 5-9-3 114.............. JohnnyMurtagh 2 121
(T Hogan, Ire) *in tch: led over 2f out: rdn clr over 1f out: r.o wl: eased down cl home* **7/2**[2]

1310 **2** 3 **Slade Power (IRE)**[15] 5726 4-9-3 115........................ WayneLordan 14 111
(Edward Lynam, Ire) *trckd ldrs travelling wl: rdn over 1f out: sn tk 2nd: kpt on ins fnl f but no ch w wnr* **9/1**

-000 **3** 3/4 **Hoof It**[21] 5545 6-9-3 107.. GrahamGibbons 13 108
(Michael Easterby) *pushed along s: prom: led over 4f out: hdd over 2f out: rdn over 1f out: kpt on ins fnl f but hld* **33/1**

6500 **4** 3/4 **Hawkeyethenoo (IRE)**[35] 4986 7-9-3 106........................ GrahamLee 16 106
(Jim Goldie) *towards rr: rdn and hdwy over 1f out: styd on ins fnl f: nvr able to chal ldrs* **22/1**

2-05 **5** hd **Soul (AUS)**[34] 5027 6-9-3 112.. JoeFanning 15 105
(Saeed bin Suroor) *prom: rdn over 1f out: nt qckn: styd on same pce ins fnl f* **16/1**

1041 **6** 3/4 **Garswood**[39] 4856 3-9-1 111.. RyanMoore 10 103
(Richard Fahey) *sluggish s: bhd and outpcd: styd on ins fnl f: nt trble ldrs* **5/1**[3]

0222 **7** 1 1/2 **Hamza (IRE)**[14] 5772 4-9-3 108...(b) JimCrowley 7 98
(Kevin Ryan) *prom: pushed along over 2f out: rdn and nt qckn over 1f out: no ex fnl 100yds* **25/1**

2166 **8** 2 **Kavanagh (SAF)**[14] 5747 6-9-3 115..............................(t) PatCosgrave 8 92
(M F De Kock, South Africa) *midfield: rdn 2f out: no imp over 1f out* **50/1**

2112 **9** 8 **Lethal Force (IRE)**[34] 5040 4-9-3 121................................ AdamKirby 1 67
(Clive Cox) *chsd ldrs: rdn 2f out: wknd over 1f out* **5/2**[1]

1-30 **10** 1 **Intense Pink**[77] 3557 4-9-0 104.. SebSanders 5 61
(Chris Wall) *towards rr: niggled along 1/2-way: effrt u.p 2f out: no imp on ldrs: wknd over 1f out* **40/1**

6212 **11** 2 1/4 **Rex Imperator**[14] 5763 4-9-3 110.................................(p) NeilCallan 9 57
(William Haggas) *hld up: rdn over 2f out: btn over 1f out* **12/1**

2621 **12** 1 1/4 **Heeraat (IRE)**[49] 4527 4-9-3 112.................................... PaulHanagan 3 54
(William Haggas) *led: hdd over 4f out: remained prom tl wknd wl over 1f out: eased whn wl btn ins fnl f* **14/1**

2020 **13** 15 **Swiss Spirit**[15] 5726 4-9-3 111...................................... RichardHughes 11 7
(John Gosden) *hld up: outpcd 2f out: toiling after* **14/1**

1m 12.25s (-1.55) **Going Correction** +0.10s/f (Good)
WFA 3 from 4yo+ 2lb **13** Ran SP% **119.9**
Speed ratings (Par 117): **114,110,109,108,107 106,104,102,91,90 87,85,65**
Tote Swingers: 1&2 £6.90, 1&3 £38.80, 2&3 £38.60 CSF £33.22 CT £936.37 TOTE £4.70: £1.60, £3.10, £8.50; EX 48.40 Trifecta £1735.10 Pool: £10,321.76 - 4.46 winning units..
Owner Dr Cyrus Poonawalla & Morgan J Cahalan **Bred** Roland H Alder **Trained** Nenagh, Co Tipperary

FOCUS
Probably an ordinary renewal of this Group 1 sprint, partcicularly with the favourite below his best. Notable absentees were last year's winner Society Rock, ruled out after sustaining concussion in the week, and Reckless Abandon who was slightly lame. There are grounds for thinking Gordon Lord Byron ran a personal best, but the time was ordinary and caution has been taken with the form.

6194 BETFRED "TREBLE ODDS ON LUCKY 15'S" NURSERY H'CAP 6f
4:25 (4:27) (Class 2) 2-Y-O **£11,320** (£3,368; £1,683; £841) **Stalls** Centre

Form RPR

3124 **1** **Kickboxer (IRE)**[15] 5693 2-8-11 **74**.................................... PaulHanagan 9 81
(Mick Channon) *chsd ldr: rdn to ld over 1f out: sn pressed: edgd sltly lft fnl 100yds: hld on wl* **6/1**[3]

01 **2** nk **Musical Comedy**[14] 5757 2-9-4 **81**.................................. RichardHughes 8 87
(Richard Hannon) *racd keenly: trckd ldr: rdn appr fnl f: sn ev ch: carried sltly lft fnl 100yds: kpt on but a jst hld* **5/6**[1]

10 **3** 2 3/4 **Belayer (IRE)**[36] 4948 2-9-2 **79**.. NeilCallan 7 77
(Kevin Ryan) *in tch: rdn 2f out: one pce: wnt 3rd ins fnl f: no threat to ldng pair* **8/1**

3320 **4** 3 3/4 **Bounty Girl (IRE)**[41] 4808 2-8-8 **71**................................ DavidAllan 6 58
(Tim Easterby) *led: rdn and edgd rt over 2f out: hdd over 1f out: wknd fnl f* **20/1**

5531 **5** 2 1/2 **Song Of Rowland (IRE)**[8] 5970 2-8-10 **73**.................. DanielTudhope 5 52
(David O'Meara) *hld up in tch: rdn 2f out: sn wknd* **11/1**

2050 **6** hd **Morning Post**[16] 5679 2-9-5 **82**.. RyanMoore 1 60
(Kevin Ryan) *hld up in tch: pushed along 1/2-way: wknd over 1f out* **5/1**[2]

1m 13.79s (-0.01) **Going Correction** +0.10s/f (Good) **6** Ran SP% **109.7**
Speed ratings (Par 101): **104,103,99,94,91 91**
Tote Swingers: 1&2 £1.50, 1&3 £2.40, 2&3 £3.50 CSF £11.00 CT £35.17 TOTE £5.90: £2.30, £1.20; EX 17.10 Trifecta £56.40 Pool: £1,821.55 - 24.19 winning units..
Owner Mrs T Burns **Bred** Rathasker Stud **Trained** West Ilsley, Berks

FOCUS
The first two drew clear in this fairly valuable nursery.

6195 BETFRED TV STKS (REGISTERED AS THE ASCENDANT STAKES) (LISTED RACE) 1m
5:00 (5:01) (Class 1) 2-Y-O **£14,461** (£5,482; £2,743; £1,366; £685) **Stalls** Low

Form RPR

11 **1** **Chief Barker (IRE)**[15] 5717 2-9-0 0.............................. RichardHughes 6 100+
(Richard Hannon) *trckd ldr: pushed along to chal over 2f out: briefly outpcd and l down over 1f out: drvn appr fnl f: styd on to ld towards fin* **5/4**[1]

010 **2** nk **Chriselliam (IRE)**[21] 5555 2-8-9 0.................................. GeraldMosse 4 94+
(Charles Hills) *hld up in tch: sltly awkward rnd bnd: hdwy over 2f out: qcknd to ld wl over 1f out: sn l up: rdn fnl f: no ex fnl 75yds: hdd towards fin* **11/2**

1212 **3** 1 1/2 **Lily Rules (IRE)**[21] 5536 2-8-9 90.................................. BarryMcHugh 2 91
(Tony Coyle) *in tch: rdn 2f out: kpt on: edgd lft fnl 100yds* **8/1**

1202 **4** 4 **Riverboat Springs (IRE)**[12] 5837 2-9-0 95...................... RyanMoore 3 87
(Mick Channon) *hld up: pushed along over 3f out: nvr threatened* **9/2**[3]

4611 **5** hd **Stars Over The Sea (USA)**[12] 5829 2-9-0 88.................. JoeFanning 1 87
(Mark Johnston) *led: rdn whn hdd wl over 1f out: sn wknd* **7/2**[2]

1m 45.69s (1.99) **Going Correction** +0.30s/f (Good) **5** Ran SP% **111.3**
Speed ratings (Par 103): **102,101,100,96,96**
CSF £8.66 TOTE £2.00: £1.20, £2.60; EX 8.80 Trifecta £43.80 Pool: £1,592.17 - 27.24 winning units..
Owner Middleham Park Racing Xxiii **Bred** Eimear Mulhern **Trained** East Everleigh, Wilts

FOCUS
The fifth running of this Listed race. Richard Hannon had won two of the previous four, taking it with the smart Havana Gold last year, and Chief Barker made it three for the stable.

6196 BETFRED DOUBLE DELIGHT HAT TRICK HEAVEN H'CAP 1m 6f
5:30 (5:30) (Class 2) (0-100,100) 3-Y-O **£16,172** (£4,812; £2,405; £1,202) **Stalls** Low

Form RPR

131 **1** **Nearly Caught (IRE)**[31] 5132 3-8-6 **85**........................ RichardHughes 7 96+
(Hughie Morrison) *prom: pushed along over 4f out: rdn to ld wl over 2f out: edgd persisently rt fnl 2f: ended up against stands' rail: styd on* **3/1**[1]

213 **2** 1 1/2 **Alwilda**[32] 5109 3-8-2 **81**.. LukeMorris 6 90
(Sir Mark Prescott Bt) *hld up: pushed along and hdwy 3f out: rdn to chse wnr over 1f out: kpt on* **6/1**[3]

212 **3** 1 **Renew (IRE)**[28] 5274 3-9-5 **98**.. RyanMoore 4 105
(Marco Botti) *hld up in midfield: rdn over 3f out: kpt on one pce: wnt 3rd ins fnl f* **3/1**[1]

5341 **4** 2 1/4 **Statutory (IRE)**[8] 5946 3-9-7 **100**.................................... JoeFanning 1 104
(Mark Johnston) *trckd ldng pair: rdn 3f out: edgd rt and wknd ins fnl f* **4/1**[2]

2311 **5** nk **Lemon Pearl**[21] 5514 3-8-6 **85**.. JimCrowley 8 89
(Ralph Beckett) *led: rdn whn hdd wl over 2f out: wknd ins fnl f* **6/1**[3]

1404 **6** 3 3/4 **Red Runaway**[54] 4349 3-8-2 **81** oh1................................ KieranO'Neill 3 79
(Ed Dunlop) *hld up: rdn over 3f out: brief hdwy over 2f out: edgd lft and wknd over 1f out* **14/1**

-550 **7** 7 **Hollowina**[79] 3482 3-8-6 **85**.. PaulHanagan 5 74
(David Brown) *midfield: rdn over 3f out: wknd fnl 2f: eased* **12/1**

3m 5.88s (3.88) **Going Correction** +0.475s/f (Yiel) **7** Ran SP% **112.9**
Speed ratings (Par 107): **107,106,105,104,104 101,97**
Tote Swingers 1&2 £5.30, 2&3 £4.40, 1&3 £1.70. CSF £20.79 CT £56.86 TOTE £4.40: £2.70, £3.60; EX 33.40 Trifecta £67.40 Pool: £1,262.66 - 14.02 winning units..
Owner A N Solomons **Bred** Irish National Stud **Trained** East Ilsley, Berks

FOCUS
A good staying handicap run at a steady gallop but in a slightly quicker time than the earlier Old Borough Cup for older handicappers. Winners should come out of it and there's more to come from Nearly Caught.
T/Jkpt: Not won. T/Plt: £1,016.00 to a £1 stake. Pool: £144,472.78 - 103.8 winning tickets. T/Qpdt: £14.90 to a £1 stake. Pool: £9,639.59 - 476.63 winning tickets. DO

6167 KEMPTON (A.W) (R-H)
Saturday, September 7

OFFICIAL GOING: Standard
Wind: Moderate across Weather: Sunny spells

6197 TOTEPLACEPOT CONDITIONS STKS 7f (P)
1:45 (1:45) (Class 4) 2-Y-O **£3,752** (£1,116; £557; £278) **Stalls** Low

Form RPR

1 **1** **Evening Attire**[35] 4977 2-8-12 0.. SeanLevey 2 88
(David Brown) *led: drvn along ins fnl 2f: jnd fnl f whn hung lft but a jst doing enough in clsng stages* **7/2**[2]

1 **2** nk **Hors De Combat**[22] 5488 2-8-12 0................................ FrederikTylicki 4 87
(James Fanshawe) *trckd ldrs: wnt 2nd 2f out: drvn to chal fnl f: kpt on but no ex in clsng stages* **1/4**[1]

3 11 **Passover** 2-8-12 0.. LiamKeniry 6 57
(Andrew Balding) *s.i.s: sn chsng ldr: dropped to 3rd 2f out: sn btn* **25/1**[3]

4 11 **Kingsway Lad (IRE)** 2-8-12 0.. MichaelO'Connell 1 28
(Derek Shaw) *a in last pl: lost tch over 2f out* **66/1**

1m 26.89s (0.89) **Going Correction** -0.05s/f (Stan) **4** Ran SP% **107.6**
Speed ratings (Par 97): **92,91,79,66**
CSF £4.88 TOTE £4.20; EX 6.60 Trifecta £8.40 Pool: £1038.81 - 92.39 winning units..
Owner J C Fretwell **Bred** Howard Barton Stud **Trained** Averham Park, Notts

 The Form Book Flat, Raceform Ltd, Compton, RG20 6NL.

FOCUS

The race was all about the pair who had been successful in their only previous starts, but there was a big discrepancy in their respective odds and those who waded in on the 1-4 favourite were blowing furiously on their burnt fingers immediately afterwards. The early stages were run at a dawdle.

6198 TOTEPOOL SEPTEMBER STKS (GROUP 3) 1m 4f (P)

2:20 (2:20) (Class 1) 3-Y-0+

£34,026 (£12,900; £6,456; £3,216; £1,614; £810) **Stalls** Centre

Form RPR

-330 **1** **Prince Bishop (IRE)**[161] 1268 6-9-4 112 (v) KierenFallon 2 114
(Saeed bin Suroor) *chsd ldrs: wnt 2nd ins fnl 2f: str chal u.p thrght fnl f: led last strides* **7/1**[3]

2011 **2** *hd* **Royal Empire (IRE)**[21] 5531 4-9-7 112 SilvestreDeSousa 6 117
(Saeed bin Suroor) *chsd ldrs: led 2f out and sn rdn: jnd fnl f but kpt narrow ld tl hdd last strides* **9/4**[1]

-324 **3** *3½* **Main Sequence (USA)**[76] 3608 4-9-4 112 TedDurcan 9 108
(David Lanigan) *chsd ldrs rdn over 2f out: styd on same pce appr fnl f* **4/1**[2]

30-3 **4** *nk* **Prince Alzain (USA)**[12] 5822 4-9-4 103 FrederikTylicki 4 108
(Gerard Butler) *in rr: hdwy over 2f out: styd on to press for 3rd fnl f but no imp on ldng duo* **25/1**

6105 **5** *3¼* **Rewarded**[17] 5654 4-9-4 109 KirstyMilczarek 7 102
(James Toller) *in tch: drvn and hdwy over 2f out: kpt on same pce fnl f* **16/1**

2410 **6** *½* **Robin Hoods Bay**[15] 5725 5-9-4 107 LiamKeniry 1 102
(Ed Vaughan) *in rr: drvn over 2f out: sme hdwy over 1f out but nvr any ch* **14/1**

7 *¾* **Sabor A Triunfo (CHI)**[175] 4-9-6 111 RobertHavlin 3 102
(Ed Dunlop) *chsd ldrs: rdn 3f out: wknd over 2f out* **25/1**

13-5 **8** *5* **Masterstroke (USA)**[36] 4944 4-9-4 114 MickaelBarzalona 10 92
(Charlie Appleby) *led: hdd 2f out: wknd over 1f out: eased fnl f* **4/1**[2]

0031 **9** *nk* **Sinaadi (IRE)**[27] 5311 3-8-6 75 HayleyTurner 11 89?
(Clive Brittain) *chsd ldr to 3f out: sn btn* **100/1**

3535 **10** *1¾* **Wigmore Hall (IRE)**[21] 5550 6-9-4 112 (p) JamieSpencer 5 89
(Michael Bell) *s.i.s: hld up in rr: plld lft to outside and rdn wl over 2f out: no imp and sn wknd* **9/1**

2m 30.02s (-4.48) **Going Correction** -0.05s/f (Stan)
WFA 3 from 4yo+ 9lb **10** Ran SP% **114.5**
Speed ratings (Par 113): **112,111,109,109,107 106,106,103,102,101**
toteswingers 1&2 £3.70, 2&3 £2.00, 1&3 £6.40 CSF £22.33 TOTE £8.50: £2.50, £1.20, £1.80; EX 27.70 Trifecta £86.70 Pool: £2142.74 - 18.52 winning units..
Owner Godolphin **Bred** Thurso Limited **Trained** Newmarket, Suffolk

FOCUS

A fascinating Group 3, with a few of these on retrieval missions, and the pace looked generous. Two of the three previous course winners dominated the finish and it resulted in a 1-2 for Godolphin. A good Group 3 but the winner did not need to match his very best old form.

6199 TOTESCOOP6 LONDON MILE H'CAP (SERIES FINAL) 1m (P)

2:55 (2:55) (Class 2) 3-Y-0+

£31,125 (£9,320; £4,660; £2,330; £1,165; £585) **Stalls** Low

Form RPR

4341 **1** **Graphic (IRE)**[28] 5268 4-8-13 **90** (p) JamieSpencer 3 101
(William Haggas) *led 1f: styd trcking ldrs: drvn to ld again ins fnl 2f: kpt on strly in clsng stages* **9/1**[3]

0516 **2** *1¼* **Mister Music**[7] 6001 4-9-3 **97** (b) WilliamTwiston-Davies(3) 5 105
(Richard Hannon) *wl in tch: hdwy 2f out: styd on wl u.p to chse wnr fnl f but no imp in clsng stages* **18/1**

0630 **3** *1¼* **Loving Spirit**[14] 5738 5-9-2 **98** RobertTart(5) 15 103
(James Toller) *hld up in rr: c wd into st and racd towards stands' side: gd hdwy wl over 1f out: kpt on to take 3rd in clsng stages but no imp on ldng duo* **10/1**

2-12 **4** *½* **Seek Again (USA)**[10] 5894 3-9-2 **98** RobertHavlin 2 102
(John Gosden) *chsd ldrs: rdn over 2f out: disp 2nd appr fnl f: no ex fnl 100yds* **9/2**[2]

1130 **5** *nse* **Solar Deity (IRE)**[119] 2254 4-9-4 **95** PaoloSirigu 12 99
(Marco Botti) *chsd ldr: rdn and outpcd over 2f out: rallied u.p and styd on wl fnl f: gng on cl home* **16/1**

5161 **6** *nk* **Ehtedaam (USA)**[10] 5894 4-9-10 **101** SilvestreDeSousa 10 104+
(Saeed bin Suroor) *s.i.s: hld up in rr: hdwy and drvn over 1f out: styd on wl in clsng stages: nt rch ldrs* **5/2**[1]

5105 **7** *hd* **Storm King**[28] 5268 4-9-3 **94** (p) MichaelO'Connell 7 97
(Jane Chapple-Hyam) *sn in tch: hdwy on ins 3f out: chsd ldrs fr 2f out: one pce ins fnl f* **9/1**[3]

0006 **8** *½* **Emilio Largo**[10] 5894 5-9-0 **91** (t) FrederikTylicki 8 93
(James Fanshawe) *towards rr: rdn over 2f out: styd on appr fnl f and kpt on in clsng stages: nt rch ldrs* **14/1**

2000 **9** *½* **Loyalty**[10] 5894 6-8-6 **90** (v) AdamMcLean(7) 9 91
(Derek Shaw) *in rr: drvn along over 2f out: kpt on fnl f: nt rch ldrs* **33/1**

0061 **10** *½* **Shavansky**[31] 5129 9-8-3 **87** ShelleyBirkett(7) 1 86
(Rod Millman) *s.i.s: in rr: hdwy over 2f out: sn rdn: nvr gng pce to rch ldrs* **16/1**

1201 **11** *1¼* **Clockmaker (IRE)**[7] 5992 7-9-7 **98** HayleyTurner 6 95
(Conor Dore) *led after 1f: hdd u.p ins fnl 2f: wknd appr fnl f* **14/1**

4046 **12** *hd* **Chapter And Verse (IRE)**[36] 4957 7-8-12 **89** PatDobbs 13 85
(Mike Murphy) *s.i.s: drvn along 2f out: a outpcd* **33/1**

0003 **13** *1¼* **Maverik**[10] 5894 5-8-11 **88** MickaelBarzalona 16 81
(William Knight) *chsd ldr after 2f: chal appr fnl 2f: btn sn after* **14/1**

1014 **14** *1¼* **Postscript (IRE)**[28] 5268 5-9-0 **91** KirstyMilczarek 11 81
(David Simcock) *racd on outside: rdn 3f out: a towards rr* **33/1**

5000 **15** *14* **Nazreef**[10] 5894 6-9-3 **94** (vt) DougieCostello 14 52
(Hughie Morrison) *chsd ldrs: wknd ins fnl 3f* **66/1**

1m 36.7s (-3.10) **Going Correction** -0.05s/f (Stan)
WFA 3 from 4yo+ 5lb **15** Ran SP% **123.2**
Speed ratings (Par 109): **113,111,110,110,109 109,109,108,108,107 106,106,105,104,90**
toteswingers 1&2 £21.10, 2&3 £52.80, 1&3 £20.10 CSF £159.42 CT £1705.66 TOTE £6.30: £2.30, £4.90, £3.40; EX 177.20 Trifecta £1556.80 Part won. Pool: £2075.85 - 0.20 winning units..
Owner The Royal Ascot Racing Club **Bred** Kevin & Meta Cullen **Trained** Newmarket, Suffolk

FOCUS

A fiercely competitive handicap, run at a strong pace. Seven of these ran in the qualifier here ten days ago, while the 2010 and 2012 winners of this race were back for another try. The winner is rated better than ever.

6200 TOTEEXACTA H'CAP (LONDON MIDDLE DISTANCE SERIES QUALIFIER) 1m 3f (P)

3:35 (3:36) (Class 4) (0-80,79) 3-Y-0+ **£4,690** (£1,395; £697; £348) **Stalls** Low

Form RPR

5242 **1** **Jazz Master**[14] 5743 3-8-9 **70** (b) SilvestreDeSousa 5 82
(Luca Cumani) *chsd ldr after 2f: led appr fnl 2f: pushed clr fnl f: readily* **7/4**[1]

0442 **2** *3½* **Scottish Star**[30] 5190 5-9-6 **78** RyanTate(5) 6 83
(James Eustace) *chsd ldrs: rdn to chse wnr over 1f out but nvr any ch* **7/1**

10-6 **3** *1½* **Uriah Heep (FR)**[22] 5475 4-9-12 **79** FergusSweeney 3 81
(Alan King) *chsd ldrs: rdn and one pce over 2f out: styd on fnl f: kpt on to take 3rd in clsng stages* **25/1**

4425 **4** *1¾* **Opera Buff**[4] 6080 4-9-2 **69** (p) LiamKeniry 4 68
(Sean Curran) *chsd ldrs: rdn to chse wnr over 1f out but no imp: wknd in clsng stages* **8/1**

3312 **5** *½* **Nimiety**[15] 5706 4-9-12 **79** KierenFallon 7 77
(Mark Johnston) *t.k.h: led: hdd appr fnl 2f: wknd fnl f* **9/2**[2]

11-2 **6** *2¾* **Ty Gwr**[26] 5356 4-9-4 **71** JamieSpencer 2 64
(Brian Ellison) *stdd s: hld up in rr: shake up 2f out: sme hdwy: sn btn* **11/2**[3]

-042 **7** *½* **Bobbyscot (IRE)**[40] 4831 6-9-1 **75** HectorCrouch(7) 9 67
(Gary Moore) *in rr: hdwy 4f out: wknd 2f out* **16/1**

0010 **8** *3* **Oetzi**[57] 4264 5-9-6 **73** MickaelBarzalona 8 60
(Alan Jarvis) *towards rr most of way* **20/1**

5210 **9** *6* **Stiff Upper Lip (IRE)**[31] 5132 3-9-0 **75** PatDobbs 1 51
(Richard Hannon) *chsd ldrs: rdn 4f out: wknd 3f out* **12/1**

2m 18.9s (-3.00) **Going Correction** -0.05s/f (Stan)
WFA 3 from 4yo+ 8lb **9** Ran SP% **115.7**
Speed ratings (Par 105): **108,105,104,103,102 100,100,98,93**
toteswingers 1&2 £3.00, 2&3 £10.60, 1&3 £8.90 CSF £14.57 CT £226.47 TOTE £2.50: £1.10, £2.30, £8.40; EX 13.40 Trifecta £340.80 Pool: £1237.66 - 2.72 winning units..
Owner Castle Down Racing **Bred** Meon Valley Stud **Trained** Newmarket, Suffolk

FOCUS

A fair middle-distance handicap. They didn't seem to go that quick early, but still finished well spread out. This didn't have great depth but the winner earned a 4lb personal best.

6201 TOTEPOOL.COM SIRENIA STKS (GROUP 3) 6f (P)

4:10 (4:10) (Class 1) 2-Y-O

£22,684 (£8,600; £4,304; £2,144; £1,076; £540) **Stalls** Low

Form RPR

1015 **1** **Brown Sugar (IRE)**[20] 5573 2-9-3 109 PatDobbs 8 110
(Richard Hannon) *chsd ldrs: rdn: hdwy and edgd lft over 1f out: led ins fnl f: edgd rt sn after: jst hld on* **11/2**

1240 **2** *shd* **Figure Of Speech (IRE)**[20] 5573 2-9-0 103 (p) MickaelBarzalona 1 107
(Charlie Appleby) *in rr: rdn and gd hdwy over 1f out: chsd wnr ins fnl f: styd on strly in clsng stages: jst failed* **9/2**[3]

031 **3** *4* **Simple Magic (IRE)**[26] 5352 2-8-11 91 RobertHavlin 4 91
(John Gosden) *led: rdn 2f out: hdd ins fnl f: sn outpcd by ldng duo but hld on wl for 3rd* **7/1**

1001 **4** *nk* **Bahamian Heights**[17] 5656 2-9-0 96 (b) KierenFallon 6 93
(Clive Brittain) *chsd ldr: rdn over 2f out: outpcd ins fnl f* **12/1**

11 **5** *¾* **Hot Streak (IRE)**[14] 5767 2-9-0 0 JamieSpencer 10 91
(Kevin Ryan) *stdd s: t.k.h and hld up in rr: pushed along over 2f out: sme hdwy over 1f out: nvr nr ldrs and styd on same pce* **3/1**[2]

311 **6** *nk* **Brave Boy (IRE)**[25] 5372 2-9-0 103 SilvestreDeSousa 7 90
(Saeed bin Suroor) *chsd ldrs: rdn over 2f out: wknd fnl f* **9/4**[1]

121 **7** *2¼* **Northern Water**[11] 5859 2-9-0 82 FrederikTylicki 3 82
(K R Burke) *chsd ldrs: rdn ins fnl 3f: wknd ins fnl 2f* **28/1**

1m 11.78s (-1.32) **Going Correction** -0.05s/f (Stan) **7** Ran SP% **113.0**
Speed ratings (Par 105): **106,105,100,100,99 98,95**
toteswingers 1&2 £3.40, 2&3 £6.90, 1&3 £6.70 CSF £29.42 TOTE £5.40: £2.40, £2.00; EX 25.50 Trifecta £204.40 Pool: £1392.99 - 5.11 winning units..
Owner De La Warr Racing **Bred** Ballylinch Stud **Trained** East Everleigh, Wilts

FOCUS

A race hit by three non-runners, but still an interesting Group 3 and the finish was fought out between the two horses with proven Group-race form.

6202 TOTEQUICKPICK H'CAP 2m (P)

4:45 (4:48) (Class 4) (0-80,77) 3-Y-O **£4,690** (£1,395; £697; £348) **Stalls** Low

Form RPR

-332 **1** **Ballinderry Boy**[32] 5102 3-8-12 **71** ThomasBrown(3) 6 86
(Andrew Balding) *led after 3f: pushed 4 l clr over 2f out: drvn fnl f: styd on strly* **13/2**

2315 **2** *1¼* **Deficit (IRE)**[44] 4681 3-9-1 **71** JamieSpencer 3 84
(Michael Bell) *trckd ldrs: rdn to chse wnr over 2f out: styd on u.p fnl f but a readily hld* **5/1**[2]

3234 **3** *13* **The Welsh Wizard (IRE)**[33] 5058 3-9-6 **76** (b[1]) MickaelBarzalona 9 73
(Charles Hills) *in rr: pushed along and hdwy on outside 3f out: styd on u.p to take mod 3rd ins fnl f* **8/1**

2253 **4** *2½* **Thorpe (IRE)**[24] 5390 3-9-6 **76** (p) RichardKingscote 5 70
(Ralph Beckett) *led 3f: styd chsng ldrs and wnt 2nd again over 3f out: dropped to 3rd over 2f out: sn wknd: lost mod 3rd ins fnl f* **5/1**[2]

5401 **5** *3¾* **Mallory Heights (IRE)**[26] 5356 3-9-6 **76** SilvestreDeSousa 10 66
(Luca Cumani) *chsd ldrs: wnt 2nd 7f out: rdn over 3f out: sn wknd* **11/4**[1]

1413 **6** *4½* **Choral Prince (IRE)**[31] 5157 3-8-13 **69** PatDobbs 1 54
(Mike Murphy) *rdn 3f out: a towards rr* **25/1**

2225 **7** *1* **Astrum**[8] 5953 3-9-3 **73** SeanLevey 2 56
(Rod Millman) *in rr but in tch: sme hdwy 4f out: wknd wl over 2f out* **14/1**

4430 **8** *¾* **Conquestadim**[14] 5762 3-9-0 **70** DougieCostello 4 52
(Hughie Morrison) *a in rr* **33/1**

0605 **9** *14* **Federal Blue (USA)**[15] 5706 3-9-7 **77** KierenFallon 7 43
(Mark Johnston) *rdn 5f out: a in rr* **6/1**[3]

6401 **10** *25* **Cherry Princess**[15] 5702 3-8-2 **58** oh2 KirstyMilczarek 8
(Stuart Williams) *chsd ldrs: wknd 4f out: t.o* **25/1**

3m 26.63s (-3.47) **Going Correction** -0.05s/f (Stan) **10** Ran SP% **116.0**
Speed ratings (Par 103): **106,105,98,97,95 93,93,92,85,73**
toteswingers 1&2 £4.70, 2&3 £9.20, 1&3 £13.70 CSF £37.94 CT £265.52 TOTE £6.00: £2.10, £2.40, £2.70; EX 42.60 Trifecta £49.30 Pool: £744.41 - 11.31 winning units..
Owner Rainbow Racing **Bred** Spring Bloodstock Ltd **Trained** Kingsclere, Hants

FOCUS
They didn't go a great pace in this staying handicap and those that raced in the front half of the field were favoured, but they still finished well spread out. A clear personal best from the winner.

6203 TOTETRIFECTA H'CAP (DIV I) 7f (P)
5:20 (5:22) (Class 4) (0-85,85) 3-Y-0+ **£4,690** (£1,395; £697; £348) **Stalls Low**

Form RPR
-222 1 **Footstepsintherain (IRE)**[59] 4183 3-9-0 **79** TedDurcan 2 89+
(David Lanigan) *chsd ldrs: led jst ins fnl f: drvn out* **10/1**
-153 2 1 **Twenty One Choice (IRE)**[54] 4340 4-9-6 **81** LiamKeniry 6 89
(Ed de Giles) *chsd ldrs: drvn to chal 1f out: styd on wl fnl f but nt gng pce of wnr* **7/2**[1]
2210 3 ¾ **Sir Mike**[14] 5742 4-9-7 **82** PatDobbs 12 88
(Amanda Perrett) *in rr: drvn and hdwy over 1f out: str run between horses fnl f to take 3rd in clsng stages: nt rch ldng duo* **12/1**
035 4 shd **Signor Sassi**[39] 4863 4-9-8 **83** JamieSpencer 9 89
(William Knight) *hld up in rr: pushed along and gd hdwy over 1f out: styd on fnl f but nvr gng pce to rch ldrs* **14/1**
-601 5 nk **Red Art (IRE)**[27] 5301 4-8-12 **78** DanielMuscutt(5) 5 83
(Charles Hills) *towards rr: drvn 3f out: hdwy over 1f out: kpt on fnl f* **16/1**
5026 6 nk **Royal Prize**[24] 5401 3-9-6 **85** RichardKingscote 8 88+
(Ralph Beckett) *in rr: drvn 2f out: hdwy over 1f out: kpt on wl fnl f: nt rch ldrs* **13/2**[3]
-005 7 2¾ **Novellen Lad (IRE)**[17] 5636 8-9-0 **75** JohnFahy 10 72
(Willie Musson) *in tch: rdn over 2f out: outpcd fnl f* **50/1**
114 8 3 **Admiralty**[59] 4181 4-9-7 **85** ThomasBrown(3) 11 74
(Ismail Mohammed) *chsd ldrs: rdn over 2f out: wknd over 1f out* **8/1**
5216 9 ½ **Satwa Story**[13] 5799 3-9-4 **83** MickaelBarzalona 7 69
(Charlie Appleby) *sn led: rdn over 2f out: hdd jst ins fnl f: wknd qckly* **9/2**[2]
1053 10 1¾ **The Tichborne (IRE)**[59] 4165 5-9-3 **78** (v) FrederikTylicki 3 61
(Roger Teal) *chsd ldrs: rdn over 2f out: wknd u.p appr fnl f* **14/1**
5001 11 3½ **Caldercruix (USA)**[10] 5899 6-9-0 **80** (v) GeorgeDowning(5) 1 53
(James Evans) *towards rr most of way* **25/1**
0000 12 8 **Lastkingofscotland (IRE)**[17] 5636 7-8-12 **73** (b) FergusSweeney 13 24
(Conor Dore) *in tch: rdn and wknd 3f out* **50/1**
041 13 ¾ **Canon Law (IRE)**[12] 5845 3-8-9 **74** KierenFallon 4 23
(Luca Cumani) *plld hrd: chsd ldrs: wknd 3f out* **13/2**[3]

1m 25.07s (-0.93) **Going Correction** -0.05s/f (Stan)
WFA 3 from 4yo+ 4lb **13 Ran SP% 121.9**
Speed ratings (Par 105): **103,101,101,100,100 100,97,93,91,91 87,77,77**
toteswingers: 1&2 £2.40, 1&3 £18.70, 2&3 £19.90 CSF £45.30 CT £455.75 TOTE £7.40: £2.00, £2.10, £5.90; EX 33.10 Trifecta £337.60 Pool: £1282.49 - 2.84 winning units..
Owner Favourites Racing **Bred** Ken Carroll **Trained** Upper Lambourn, Berks

FOCUS
A competitive handicap which was faster than division II. A personal best from the winner.

6204 TOTETRIFECTA H'CAP (DIV II) 7f (P)
5:50 (5:52) (Class 4) (0-85,85) 3-Y-0+ **£4,690** (£1,395; £697; £348) **Stalls Low**

Form RPR
2122 1 shd **Future Reference (IRE)**[30] 5187 3-9-3 **82** (t) SilvestreDeSousa 6 92+
(Saeed bin Suroor) *chsd ldrs: rdn and str run to press wnr fnl f: upsides fnl 50yds whn pushed lft: jst failed: fin 2nd, shd: awrdd r* **5/2**[1]
0413 2 **Bluegrass Blues (IRE)**[10] 5886 3-9-6 **85** JohnFahy 8 94
(Paul Cole) *chsd ldrs: led over 1f out: hrd rdn fnl f: edgd lft u.p whn hrd pressed fnl 50yds: hld on all out: fin first: disq: plcd 2nd* **9/2**[2]
6303 3 1 **Extrasolar**[15] 5721 3-9-6 **85** (t) PatDobbs 2 91+
(Amanda Perrett) *in rr: hdwy fr 2f out: styd on wl fnl f but nt gng pce of ldng duo* **14/1**
5533 4 1 **Light Burst (USA)**[30] 5195 4-9-4 **82** ThomasBrown(3) 4 86
(Ismail Mohammed) *in tch: drvn and r.o fnl f: no imp fnl 110yds* **8/1**
-630 5 hd **Axiom**[14] 5738 9-9-10 **85** (b) JamieSpencer 9 89
(Ed Walker) *in rr: pushed along and hdwy appr fnl f: r.o cl home* **15/2**
0424 6 nk **Afkar (IRE)**[65] 3993 5-8-10 **71** KierenFallon 11 74
(Clive Brittain) *chsd ldr: led over 2f out: hdd over 1f out: no ex fnl 110yds* **16/1**
0330 7 4 **Top Cop**[15] 5696 4-9-4 **79** (p) LiamKeniry 12 71
(Andrew Balding) *in rr: drvn over 2f out: nvr gng pce to get into contention* **22/1**
6024 8 1 **Alnoomaas (IRE)**[17] 5636 4-9-1 **76** MickaelBarzalona 10 65
(Luke Dace) *sn led: hdd over 2f out: wknd qckly fnl f* **12/1**
U014 9 1¾ **Order Of Service**[63] 4056 3-8-13 **78** SeanLevey 5 62
(David Brown) *towards rr most of way* **11/2**[3]
0200 10 ¾ **Exceedexpectations (IRE)**[9] 5928 4-9-0 **75** FergusSweeney 7 58
(Conor Dore) *chsd ldrs: rdn over 2f out and sn btn* **40/1**
610 11 3¼ **Messila Star**[75] 3633 3-9-3 **82** (t) TedDurcan 1 56
(Jeremy Noseda) *rdn 3 out: a in rr* **14/1**

1m 25.88s (-0.12) **Going Correction** -0.05s/f (Stan)
WFA 3 from 4yo+ 4lb **11 Ran SP% 118.7**
Speed ratings (Par 105): **97,98,96,95,95 95,90,89,87,86 82**
CSF £13.28 CT £135.63 TOTE £3.40: £1.60, £1.10, £5.70; EX 16.50 Trifecta £132.80 Pool: £815.24 - 4.60 winning units..
Owner Godolphin **Bred** Darley **Trained** Newmarket, Suffolk
■ Stewards' Enquiry : John Fahy two-day ban: careless riding (Sep 21-22)

FOCUS
The pace looked ordinary and the winning time was 0.81sec slower than the first division. The form makes sense.
T/Plt: £908.20 to a £1 stake. Pool of £67258.70 - 54.06 winning tickets. T/Qpdt: £85.70 to a £1 stake. Pool of £4521.60 - 39.0 winning tickets. ST

5968 THIRSK (L-H)
Saturday, September 7

OFFICIAL GOING: Good to soft (soft in places; 7.0)
Wind: Fresh half against Weather: Cloudy with sunny periods

6205 BARKERS OF NORTHALLERTON H'CAP (DIV I) 6f
2:00 (2:00) (Class 4) (0-80,80) 4-Y-0+ **£6,469** (£1,925; £962; £481) **Stalls High**

Form RPR
4524 1 **Mutafaakir (IRE)**[8] 5974 4-8-11 **70** (p) PJMcDonald 4 80
(Ruth Carr) *qckly away and sn swtchd rt to stands' rail: mde all: rdn over 1f out: kpt on strly fnl f* **3/1**[2]
2321 2 ½ **Lulu The Zulu (IRE)**[22] 5498 5-8-13 **72** AndrewMullen 6 80+
(Michael Appleby) *dwlt and towards rr: pushed along and hdwy 1/2-way: rdn wl over 1f out: styd on to chse wnr ins fnl f: sn ev ch tl drvn and no ex towards fin* **11/4**[1]
4064 3 2½ **Bonnie Charlie**[15] 5705 7-9-1 **74** PaulQuinn 9 74
(David Nicholls) *hld up in rr: hdwy 2f out: rdn over 1f out: styd on fnl f: nrst fin* **13/2**[3]
2331 4 ¾ **Wild Sauce**[10] 5887 4-8-13 **77** (bt) ThomasGarner(5) 3 75
(Bryan Smart) *sn chsng ldng pair on outer: hdwy and cl up 1/2-way: rdn wl over 1f out: drvn ent fnl f: kpt on same pce* **8/1**
1102 5 1 **Hamoody (USA)**[9] 5917 9-9-7 **80** AdrianNicholls 5 75
(David Nicholls) *trckd ldrs: hdwy over 2f out: rdn to chse wnr and hung lft appr fnl f: sn drvn and wknd last 100yds* **14/1**
5030 6 2½ **Waking Warrior**[19] 5579 5-9-2 **75** (tp) PaulMulrennan 2 62
(Kevin Ryan) *chsd ldrs on outer: rdn along 2f out: wknd over 1f out* **8/1**
4000 7 ½ **Burnhope**[53] 4389 4-8-8 **70** (p) BillyCray(3) 1 55
(Scott Dixon) *sn cl up: rdn along over 2f out: grad wknd* **25/1**
0010 8 2½ **Solar Spirit (IRE)**[20] 5564 8-9-7 **80** TonyHamilton 11 57
(Tracy Waggott) *stdd s: t.k.h: hld up towards rr: effrt and sme hdwy 1/2-way: n.m.r over 2f out: sn rdn and n.d* **11/1**
00 9 5 **Fama Mac**[32] 5088 6-8-8 **67** AndrewElliott 8 28
(Neville Bycroft) *prom: rdn along 1/2-way: wknd over 2f out* **12/1**

1m 13.41s (0.71) **Going Correction** +0.20s/f (Good) **9 Ran SP% 113.8**
Speed ratings (Par 105): **103,102,99,98,96 93,92,89,82**
Tote Swingers: 1&2 £2.70, 1&3 £9.40, 2&3 £4.70 CSF £11.48 CT £48.32 TOTE £3.90: £1.50, £1.30, £2.00; EX 9.50 Trifecta £90.80 Pool: £726.46 - 5.99 winning units..
Owner Michael Hill **Bred** Shadwell Estate Company Limited **Trained** Huby, N Yorks

FOCUS
The going was Good to Soft, soft in places after the previous day's rain and as a result there were quite a few withdrawals. The jockeys reported the ground as riding somewhere between "on the soft side of good" and "soft". The first division of a fair sprint handicap. The winner is rated back to his Newcastle June form.

6206 BRITISH STALLION STUDS E B F MAIDEN STKS 7f
2:30 (2:37) (Class 4) 2-Y-O **£4,528** (£1,347; £673; £336) **Stalls Low**

Form RPR
1 **Comino (IRE)** 2-9-5 0 PaulMulrennan 12 81+
(Kevin Ryan) *trckd ldr: led over 2f out: drvn over 1f out: styd on ins fnl f* **7/1**[3]
4222 2 1½ **Lincoln (IRE)**[7] 5995 2-9-5 77 SamHitchcott 9 77
(Mick Channon) *led: hdd over 2f out: styd on same pce ins fnl f* **8/11**[1]
3040 3 4 **Chamberlain**[63] 4053 2-9-5 70 (p[1]) TomEaves 8 67
(Alan McCabe) *s.i.s: reminders and hdwy to chse ldrs on outside over 5f out: hung lft and 3rd 1f out: kpt on same pce* **20/1**
4 ½ **Lady Heidi** 2-9-0 0 PhillipMakin 13 60+
(Philip Kirby) *mid-div: hdwy over 3f out: styd on to take 4th last 50yds* **20/1**
0 5 2½ **False Witness (IRE)**[26] 5338 2-8-12 0 JordanNason(7) 6 59
(David Nicholls) *dwlt: sn chsng ldrs: drvn over 3f out: one pce fnl 2f* **80/1**
0440 6 2¾ **Dry Your Eyes (IRE)**[35] 5005 2-9-0 71 AdrianNicholls 7 47
(Mark Johnston) *chsd ldrs: drvn over 3f out: one pce* **7/2**[2]
00 7 ½ **Emerahldz (IRE)**[21] 5508 2-9-0 0 TonyHamilton 1 45
(Richard Fahey) *s.s: bhd: kpt on fnl 2f: nvr nr ldrs* **20/1**
8 2½ **Mestizo** 2-8-11 0 NeilFarley(3) 10 39
(Declan Carroll) *s.i.s: in rr: kpt on fnl 2f: nvr a factor* **28/1**
9 hd **Bearskin (IRE)** 2-9-5 0 PJMcDonald 4 43
(Ann Duffield) *sn chsng ldrs: outpcd over 3f out: kpt on fnl 2f* **14/1**
00 10 2¾ **Sandfield (IRE)**[21] 5543 2-9-0 0 ShirleyTeasdale(5) 3 36
(Paul Midgley) *unruly s: mid-div: lost pl over 4f out: no threat after* **40/1**
00 11 13 **Halloween Moon**[19] 5577 2-9-5 0 JamesSullivan 5
(James Bethell) *mid- div: drvn over 3f out: sn lost pl: bhd fnl 2f* **66/1**
06 12 6 **Angus Mac Og (IRE)**[12] 5834 2-8-12 0 DanielleMooney(7) 11
(Nigel Tinkler) *in rr: bhd fnl 3f: t.o* **150/1**

1m 30.15s (2.95) **Going Correction** +0.30s/f (Good) **12 Ran SP% 122.9**
Speed ratings (Par 97): **95,93,88,88,85 82,81,78,78,75 60,53**
Tote Swingers: 1&2 £2.70, 1&3 £16.10, 2&3 £4.30 CSF £12.11 TOTE £7.70: £2.10, £1.10, £4.40; EX 18.20 Trifecta £101.30 Pool: £1,155.97 - 8.55 winning units..
Owner D W Barker **Bred** Tom Twomey **Trained** Hambleton, N Yorks

FOCUS
A fair maiden judged on the ratings of those with experience, but the market only featured three and the race concerned just two in the straight.

6207 MARC FINDLAY 21ST BIRTHDAY NURSERY H'CAP 1m
3:05 (3:05) (Class 3) (0-95,85) 2-Y-O **£8,086** (£2,406; £1,202; £601) **Stalls Low**

Form RPR
4114 1 **Fire Fighting (IRE)**[36] 4959 2-9-7 **85** AdrianNicholls 3 91
(Mark Johnston) *set stdy pce: hung rt home bnd: pushed along and qcknd 3f out: rdn and edgd rt 2f out: sn jnd: drvn ent fnl f and styd on strly* **3/1**[3]
126 2 2½ **Shot In The Sun (IRE)**[21] 5536 2-8-11 **75** TonyHamilton 6 75
(Richard Fahey) *trckd wnr: hdwy 1/2-way: rdn along whn n.m.r 2f out: sn swtchd lft and drvn: kpt on fnl f* **7/2**
132 3 2¾ **Snow Squall**[21] 5524 2-9-7 **85** TomMcLaughlin 4 79
(Charlie Appleby) *hld up in tch: hdwy on outer over 3f out: chal 2f out: sn rdn and ev ch tl drvn and wknd jst ins fnl f* **13/8**[1]
41 4 4½ **Master Of Finance (IRE)**[21] 5508 2-9-7 **85** PaulMulrennan 5 69
(Mark Johnston) *trckd wnr on inner: rdn along over 3f out: sn outpcd and bhd fnl 2f* **11/4**[2]

1m 43.8s (3.70) **Going Correction** +0.30s/f (Good) **4 Ran SP% 112.0**
Speed ratings (Par 99): **93,90,87,83**
CSF £13.22 TOTE £4.10; EX 18.80 Trifecta £47.30 Pool: £209.88 - 3.32 winning units..
Owner A D Spence **Bred** P Bellaiche **Trained** Middleham Moor, N Yorks

FOCUS
A decent nursery despite the small field.

6208 PERSONAL TOUCHES H'CAP 1m
3:40 (3:41) (Class 3) (0-95,92) 3-Y-O **£9,703** (£2,887; £1,443; £721) **Stalls Low**

Form RPR
4120 1 **Altharoos (IRE)**[28] 5287 3-9-2 **87** PaulMulrennan 8 97
(Sir Michael Stoute) *hld up in rr: gd hdwy over 2f out: chsd ldrs whn n.m.r and swtchd lft over 1f out: rdn to chal ins fnl f: styd on wl on inner to ld last 40yds* **3/1**[2]
0431 2 nk **Gabrial's Kaka (IRE)**[20] 5562 3-9-7 **92** TomEaves 9 101
(Richard Fahey) *trckd ldr: hdwy to chal over 2f out: sn rdn and led jst ins fnl f: sn drvn: hdd and no ex last 40yds* **9/2**[3]
0310 3 ¾ **Party Royal**[15] 5728 3-8-13 **84** AdrianNicholls 5 91
(Mark Johnston) *led: rdn along over 2f out: sn jnd and drvn over 1f out: hdd jst ins fnl f: kpt on same pce last 100yds* **16/1**

1002 **4** 3 ¾ **Equity Risk (USA)**[15] 5728 3-9-6 **91** ..... PhillipMakin 2 90
(Kevin Ryan) *trckd ldrs on inner: hdwy over 2f out: rdn and ch over 1f out: drvn and one pce fnl f* **11/8**[1]

2353 **5** 2 ¼ **Asgardella (IRE)**[91] 3080 3-9-3 **88** ..... TonyHamilton 6 81
(Richard Fahey) *trckd ldrs on outer: hdwy 3f out: rdn over 2f out: drvn and wknd wl over 1f out* **20/1**

1315 **6** *shd* **Woody Bay**[30] 5182 3-8-10 **81** ..... JamesSullivan 4 74
(James Given) *chsd ldrs: rdn along wl over 2f out: drvn wl over 1f out: sn wknd* **9/1**

5-0 **7** 12 **Patrona Ciana (FR)**[16] 5684 3-8-13 **84** ..... DavidNolan 1 50
(David O'Meara) *in tch on inner: rdn along 3f out: sn outpcd* **14/1**

-000 **8** 3 ¾ **Jamesbo's Girl**[21] 5518 3-8-10 **84** ..... DeclanCannon(3) 10 41
(Philip Kirby) *hld up: a towards rr* **25/1**

1m 41.21s (1.11) **Going Correction** +0.30s/f (Good) **8** Ran SP% **116.4**
Speed ratings (Par 105): **106,105,104,101,98 98,86,83**
Tote Swingers: 1&2 £4.00, 1&3 £13.00, 2&3 £7.40 CSF £17.35 CT £184.67 TOTE £4.10: £1.70, £1.60, £3.00; EX 17.10 Trifecta £188.50 Pool: £985.46 - 3.91 winning units..
Owner Hamdan Al Maktoum **Bred** Shadwell Estate Company Limited **Trained** Newmarket, Suffolk

FOCUS
A good mile handicap for 3yos run 2.59secs faster than the preceding nursery and it produced a cracking finish. A clear best from the winner.

6209 BARKERS OF NORTHALLERTON H'CAP (DIV II) 6f
4:20 (4:28) (Class 4) (0-80,80) 4-Y-0+ **£6,469** (£1,925; £962; £481) **Stalls** High

Form RPR

1054 **1** **Indego Blues**[12] 5832 4-8-11 **70** ..... PaulQuinn 4 83
(David Nicholls) *hld up in tch: hdwy 1/2-way: rdn to ld ent fnl f: clr whn edgd rt: rdn out* **4/1**[3]

/650 **2** 3 **Beau Amadeus (IRE)**[12] 5832 4-8-9 **68** .....(b) AdrianNicholls 1 71
(David Nicholls) *sn cl up: led over 3f out: rdn and hdd over 2f out: drvn and rallied ent fnl f: kpt on same pce towards fin* **11/2**

0122 **3** 1 **Clubland (IRE)**[10] 5901 4-9-4 **80** ..... MarkCoumbe(3) 3 80
(Roy Bowring) *trckd ldrs: hdwy to ld over 2f out: rdn wl over 1f out: hdd ent fnl f: sn one pce* **3/1**[1]

-000 **4** 4 **Tarrsille (IRE)**[8] 5974 7-8-11 **75** ..... ShirleyTeasdale(5) 9 62
(Paul Midgley) *chsd ldrs: rdn along and hung lft 2f out: sn one pce* **33/1**

4120 **5** 5 **Big Wave (IRE)**[13] 5798 5-8-13 **77** .....(t) TobyAtkinson(5) 10 48
(Alison Hutchinson) *chsd ldrs: rdn along wl over 2f out: sn wknd* **14/1**

2103 **6** *nk* **Sunrise Dance**[8] 5971 4-8-13 **77** ..... ConnorBeasley(5) 5 47
(Robert Johnson) *led: pushed along and hdd over 3f out: sn rdn and wknd over 2f out* **7/2**[2]

000 **7** 8 **Tango Sky (IRE)**[35] 5011 4-9-1 **74** ..... PaulMulrennan 7 19
(David Nicholls) *s.i.s: a outpcd and bhd* **9/1**

1m 13.1s (0.40) **Going Correction** +0.20s/f (Good) **7** Ran SP% **102.2**
Speed ratings (Par 105): **105,101,99,94,87 87,76**
Tote Swingers: 1&2 £3.10, 1&3 £2.00, 2&3 £2.40 CSF £20.26 CT £46.61 TOTE £4.00: £2.40, £2.80; EX 12.10 Trifecta £38.40 Pool: £459.34 - 8.95 winning units..
Owner Pinnacle Indesatchel Partnership **Bred** Bearstone Stud **Trained** Sessay, N Yorks

FOCUS
The second leg of the sprint handicap was run 1.11secs faster than the first division. There was a false start after Meandmyshadow burst the stalls and the mare was withdrawn, and that probably resulted in a couple of these not running their races. The winner is rated back to his best.

6210 ADORN HATS FILLIES' H'CAP 1m
4:55 (4:57) (Class 4) (0-85,85) 3-Y-0+ **£6,469** (£1,925; £962; £481) **Stalls** Low

Form RPR

1225 **1** **Aeronwyn Bryn (IRE)**[22] 5496 3-8-8 **82** ..... ConnorBeasley(5) 14 95
(Michael Dods) *swtchd lft after 1f: sn chsng ldrs: led 2f out: sn clr: drvn out* **7/1**

6125 **2** 3 ¼ **Hot Rod Mamma (IRE)**[10] 5880 6-9-2 **80** ..... PJMcDonald 12 86
(Dianne Sayer) *stdd and swtchd lft s: hld up in rr: hdwy over 2f out: chsd wnr 1f out: no real imp* **11/2**[2]

1436 **3** 3 ½ **Sharqawiyah**[30] 5202 3-9-0 **83** ..... TomMcLaughlin 13 81
(Luca Cumani) *in rr: effrt and swtchd wd 3f out: styd on to take 3rd 1f out* **8/1**

3416 **4** 1 ¾ **Shesastar**[16] 5684 5-9-1 **79** ..... PhillipMakin 4 73
(David Barron) *hood removed late: s.s: in rr: effrt on outside 3f out: styd on to take 4th jst ins fnl f* **10/1**

6000 **5** 3 ½ **Steer By The Stars (IRE)**[40] 4825 3-8-8 **77** ..... AdrianNicholls 1 63
(Mark Johnston) *drvn to sn chse ldrs: led 5f out: hdd 2f out: sn wknd* **18/1**

1125 **6** 2 **Lilac Lace (IRE)**[81] 3443 3-9-0 **83** ..... DuranFentiman 7 64
(Tim Easterby) *dwlt: in rr: hdwy over 3f out: chsng ldrs over 1f out: wknd fnl f* **12/1**

2332 **7** ½ **Simply Shining (IRE)**[13] 5784 3-7-13 **75** .....(p) SamanthaBell(7) 2 55
(Richard Fahey) *s.i.s: sn mid-div: hdwy on inner whn nt clr run over 1f out: no threat* **13/2**[3]

4020 **8** ¾ **No Poppy (IRE)**[12] 5838 5-9-2 **85** ..... AdamCarter(5) 5 63
(Tim Easterby) *chsd ldrs: drvn over 2f out: lost pl over 1f out* **4/1**[1]

0115 **9** 1 ½ **Angel Cake (IRE)**[26] 5354 4-8-7 **71** oh5 ..... AndrewMullen 11 46
(Michael Appleby) *led tl 5f out: lost pl over 1f out* **25/1**

0231 **10** 4 **Jadesnumberone (IRE)**[15] 5695 3-7-11 **73** ow1 ..... LouisSteward(7) 8 39
(Michael Bell) *t.k.h: trckd ldrs: lost pl over 1f out* **15/2**

0052 **11** *nk* **Tussie Mussie**[12] 5835 3-8-2 **71** oh3 .....(b) JamesSullivan 6 36
(Mark Johnston) *t.k.h: trckd ldrs: lost pl 2f out* **20/1**

220 **12** 13 **Jeannie Galloway (IRE)**[17] 5637 6-8-8 **72** ..... TomEaves 10 7
(Keith Dalgleish) *chsd ldrs: lost pl and heavily eased over 1f out: t.o* **22/1**

1m 41.14s (1.04) **Going Correction** +0.30s/f (Good)
WFA 3 from 4yo+ 5lb **12** Ran SP% **119.1**
Speed ratings (Par 102): **106,102,99,97,94 92,91,90,89,85 84,71**
Tote Swingers: 1&2 £7.50, 1&3 £12.00, 2&3 £9.70 CSF £44.23 CT £257.14 TOTE £7.20: £2.00, £2.10, £3.20; EX 47.00 Trifecta £434.40 Pool: £2,120.85 - 3.66 winning units..
Owner Andrew Tinkler **Bred** Owenstown Stud **Trained** Denton, Co Durham

FOCUS
A competitive fillies' handicap and the time was similar to the earlier 3-y-o handicap over the trip. The winner tracked the pace but the next three home came from the rear. Fillies' form, but fair depth to the race.

6211 HAMBLETON CUP (H'CAP) 1m 4f
5:25 (5:25) (Class 4) (0-85,83) 3-Y-0+ **£8,086** (£2,406; £1,202; £601) **Stalls** High

Form RPR

3124 **1** **Rhombus (IRE)**[13] 5792 3-9-2 **82** ..... ChrisCatlin 14 95+
(Ismail Mohammed) *midfield: hdwy over 4f out: trckd ldrs 3f out: effrt and n.m.r over 1f out: swtchd rt and rdn to chal ent fnl f: sn led and styd on strly* **7/2**[1]

0305 **2** 3 ½ **War Poet**[37] 4929 6-9-11 **82** .....(t) TomEaves 13 89
(Brian Ellison) *hld up towards rr: hdwy over 4f out: chsd ldrs over 2f out: rdn wl over 1f out: ev ch ent fnl f: sn drvn and kpt on same pce* **9/2**[2]

3406 **3** ¾ **Be Perfect (USA)**[24] 5382 4-9-4 **82** ..... JordanNason(7) 8 88
(David Nicholls) *trckd ldrs: hdwy 5f out: cl up over 3f out: rdn to ld 2f out: drvn and hdd jst ins fnl f: kpt on same pce* **14/1**

3235 **4** 3 **Eric The Grey (IRE)**[34] 5030 3-8-6 **72** ..... PatrickMathers 11 73
(Richard Fahey) *chsd ldrs: pushed along over 4f out: rdn 3f out: drvn and kpt on one pce fnl 2f* **11/2**[3]

5143 **5** ¾ **Now My Sun**[27] 5302 4-9-6 **77** ..... PhillipMakin 6 77
(K R Burke) *t.k.h: hld up in rr: hdwy 5f out: effrt on wd outside wl over 2f out: sn rdn and kpt on: nrst fin* **8/1**

0002 **6** 2 ½ **Calaf**[20] 5559 5-9-5 **81** ..... ConnorBeasley(5) 12 77
(Brian Ellison) *t.k.h: hld up in rr: hdwy 3f out: rdn along 2f out: nt rch ldrs* **7/1**

0034 **7** 2 **Harry Buckle**[21] 5542 4-9-5 **83** ..... LouisSteward(7) 3 76
(Philip McBride) *trckd ldr: led 1/2-way: rdn along 3f out: hdd 2f out: grad wknd* **9/1**

3644 **8** 3 ¼ **Bright Applause**[33] 5059 5-9-0 **71** ..... TonyHamilton 5 58
(Tracy Waggott) *trckd ldng pair: effrt 4f out: rdn along 3f out: drvn over 2f out and sn wknd* **25/1**

1612 **9** 5 **Eeny Mac (IRE)**[11] 5860 6-9-3 **74** ..... AndrewElliott 7 53
(Neville Bycroft) *a in midfield* **16/1**

6434 **10** 3 **San Cassiano (IRE)**[11] 5860 6-9-9 **80** ..... JamesSullivan 10 55
(Ruth Carr) *led: hdd 1/2-way: rdn along over 3f out: sn wknd* **16/1**

1-64 **11** 1 ¾ **Braveheart Move (IRE)**[20] 5559 7-9-9 **80** ..... PaulMulrennan 9 52
(Geoffrey Harker) *a towards rr* **25/1**

0210 **12** ¾ **Choisan (IRE)**[15] 5706 4-9-9 **80** ..... DuranFentiman 1 51
(Tim Easterby) *chsd ldrs on inner: pushed along 5f out: rdn over 3f out and sn wknd* **20/1**

30-6 **13** 99 **The Bells O Peover**[11] 5854 5-9-1 **72** .....(v) AdrianNicholls 4
(Mark Johnston) *t.k.h early: in tch: pushed along 1/2-way: lost pl over 5f out: sn bhd and eased fnl 3f* **20/1**

2m 39.29s (3.09) **Going Correction** +0.30s/f (Good)
WFA 3 from 4yo+ 9lb **13** Ran SP% **125.0**
Speed ratings (Par 105): **101,98,98,96,95 94,92,90,87,85 84,83,17**
CSF £18.40 CT £201.96 TOTE £3.80: £1.10, £2.80, £4.40; EX 19.10 Trifecta £415.60 Pool: £1,154.45 - 2.08 winning units..
Owner Sheikh Rashid Dalmook Al Maktoum **Bred** Ruskerne Ltd **Trained** Newmarket, Suffolk

FOCUS
A decent handicap which was sound run. A clear step forward from the winner to see off a couple of well-treated older horses.

6212 THIRSK CURRY & COMEDY NIGHT 11TH OCTOBER H'CAP 5f
5:55 (5:56) (Class 4) (0-85,85) 3-Y-0 **£6,469** (£1,925; £962; £481) **Stalls** High

Form RPR

6005 **1** **Storm Moon (USA)**[7] 5996 3-9-4 **82** ..... AdrianNicholls 6 91
(Mark Johnston) *cl up on outer: led 2f out and sn rdn: drvn and edgd lft ins fnl f: kpt on* **10/1**

4052 **2** 1 **Millkwood**[22] 5485 3-8-8 **72** ow1 .....(tp) TomEaves 5 77
(John Davies) *hmpd s: sn trcking ldrs: hdwy on outer 2f out: rdn to chse wnr ent fnl f: drvn and no imp towards fin* **8/1**

4246 **3** *nk* **Tumblewind**[12] 5836 3-9-1 **84** ..... ConnorBeasley(5) 10 88
(Richard Whitaker) *trckd ldrs: hdwy wl over 1f out: rdn and edgd lft ent fnl f: sn drvn and kpt on: nrst fin* **9/2**[3]

0213 **4** 2 **Sharaarah (IRE)**[7] 5996 3-9-6 **84** ..... DavidNolan 9 81
(David O'Meara) *chsd ldrs: rdn to chse wnr over 1f out: drvn and wknd ent fnl f* **9/4**[1]

3340 **5** 1 ¼ **Dream Maker (IRE)**[14] 5769 3-9-2 **80** ..... DuranFentiman 8 73
(Tim Easterby) *dwlt and in rr: rdn and sme hdwy over 1f out: n.d* **12/1**

1132 **6** ½ **Jofranka**[33] 5057 3-8-13 **77** ..... PhillipMakin 1 68
(David Barron) *qckly away: sn led and swtchd rt to stands' rail: pushed along 1/2-way: rdn and hdd 2f out: drvn and wknd over 1f out* **3/1**[2]

0600 **7** ½ **Strange Magic (IRE)**[35] 4993 3-9-7 **85** ..... TonyHamilton 2 74
(Richard Fahey) *a in rr* **16/1**

0050 **8** 3 ¼ **Mayfield Girl (IRE)**[14] 5769 3-8-13 **77** ..... PaulMulrennan 7 54
(Mel Brittain) *cl up: rdn along 1/2-way: drvn and wknd over 1f out: btn whn n.m.r ent fnl f* **10/1**

59.9s (0.30) **Going Correction** +0.20s/f (Good) **8** Ran SP% **116.8**
Speed ratings (Par 103): **105,103,102,99,97 96,96,90**
Tote Swingers 1&2 £10.20, 2&3 £5.30, 1&3 £9.00 CSF £87.83 CT £416.52 TOTE £13.50: £2.60, £2.00, £1.60; EX 106.50 Trifecta £425.10 Pool: £613.79 - 1.08 winning units..
Owner Sheikh Hamdan Bin Mohammed Al Maktoum **Bred** Darley **Trained** Middleham Moor, N Yorks

FOCUS
Another competitive sprint handicap. The winner is rated to his 3yo turf form.
T/Plt: £277.20 to a £1 stake. Pool: £47,322.77 - 124.62 winning tickets. T/Qpdt: £293.10 to a £1 stake. Pool: £1,901.2 - 4.80 winning tickets. JR

5672 WOLVERHAMPTON (A.W) (L-H)
Saturday, September 7

OFFICIAL GOING: Standard to slow
Wind: Light behind Weather: Cloudy with sunny spells

6213 QUICKSILVERSLOTS ON THE HIGH STREET E B F MAIDEN STKS 5f 20y(P)
6:00 (6:01) (Class 5) 2-Y-0 **£3,234** (£962; £481; £240) **Stalls** Low

Form RPR

02 **1** **Muir Lodge**[20] 5558 2-9-5 0 .....(t) DavidProbert 2 84+
(Andrew Balding) *trckd ldrs: shkn up to ld and hung rt ins fnl f: rdn out* **8/13**[1]

44 **2** 1 ¾ **Chorlton Manor (IRE)**[20] 5558 2-9-5 0 ..... StevieDonohoe 9 78
(Nicky Vaughan) *chsd ldr tl shkn up to ld over 1f out: rdn and hdd ins fnl f: styd on* **10/1**

54 **3** 6 **Exceed Areeda (IRE)**[26] 5352 2-9-0 0 ..... ShaneKelly 6 51+
(James Tate) *s.i.s: sn pushed along in rr: hmpd wl over 3f out: rdn over 1f out: r.o ins fnl f: nrst fin* **8/1**[3]

00 **4** 2 **The Boss Of Me**[20] 5558 2-9-5 0 ..... J-PGuillambert 8 49
(Kevin Ryan) *led: rdn and hdd over 1f out: wknd ins fnl f* **33/1**

42 **5** ¾ **Dynamo Walt (IRE)**[19] 5590 2-9-5 0 ..... MichaelO'Connell 3 46
(Derek Shaw) *prom: rdn over 1f out: sn wknd* **33/1**

0 **6** *hd* **Marlismamma (FR)**[10] 5883 2-8-11 0 ..... JulieBurke(3) 5 40
(David O'Meara) *mid-div: drvn along 1/2-way: nvr trbld ldrs* **66/1**

0 **7** 1 ¼ **Back On Baileys**[142] 1634 2-9-0 0 ..... CathyGannon 4 36
(Chris Dwyer) *prom tl rdn and wknd over 1f out* **40/1**

0 **8** ½ **Vadara**[22] 5494 2-9-5 0 DaleSwift 7 39
(Michael Easterby) *sn pushed along towards rr: nvr on terms* **66/1**

2 **9** 1¼ **Clumber Street**[16] 5665 2-9-5 0 GrahamGibbons 1 35
(Ed McMahon) *trckd ldrs: plld hrd: hmpd 4f out: rdn and hung lft fr over 1f out: wknd fnl f* **4/1**[2]

00 **10** ¾ **Clear Focus (IRE)**[21] 5529 2-9-0 0 JackMitchell 10 27
(Brendan Powell) *in rr whn swtchd lft 4f out: shkn up over 1f out: nvr nr to chal* **50/1**

0 **11** 2¾ **Miss Lawlass (IRE)**[18] 5609 2-8-11 0 WilliamTwiston-Davies(3) 12 17
(James Given) *sn pushed along and a in rr* **80/1**

1m 4.87s (2.57) **Going Correction** +0.45s/f (Slow) 11 Ran SP% **116.6**
Speed ratings (Par 95): **97,94,84,81,80 79,77,77,75,73 69**
Tote Swingers: 1&2 £2.70, 1&3 £2.50, 2&3 £4.60 CSF £7.58 TOTE £1.50: £1.10, £1.40, £1.70; EX 6.50 Trifecta £14.60 Pool: £871.49 - 44.63 winning units..
Owner Mrs Fitri Hay **Bred** Langton Stud **Trained** Kingsclere, Hants
■ Stewards' Enquiry : J-P Guillambert three-day ban: careless riding (Sep 21-23)

FOCUS
This was the first meeting at Wolverhampton in two weeks, following maintenance work to the surface to ensure the track can cope when the temperature dips in the winter. As a result the going remained standard to slow. After the opener Shane Kelly said: "It's slower, no doubt, but this is the first meeting back so it will take time. It's just harder work for the horses and deeper down on the inside", while David Probert remarked: "It's just standard to slow, no real isues." An ordinary maiden with little depth.

6214 PLAY £500 ROULETTE AT QUICKSILVERSLOTS H'CAP 7f 32y(P)
6:30 (6:32) (Class 5) (0-75,73) 3-Y-O **£2,587** (£770; £384; £192) **Stalls** High

Form RPR

646 **1** **Glanely (IRE)**[44] 4667 3-9-7 73 ShaneKelly 4 85+
(James Fanshawe) *s.i.s: sn pushed along in rr: hdwy over 1f out: r.o u.p to ld towards fin* **5/1**[3]

1436 **2** nk **Benoni**[23] 5437 3-9-6 72 CathyGannon 1 83
(Henry Candy) *trckd ldrs: rdn to ld over 1f out: hdd towards fin* **4/1**[2]

2133 **3** 2 **Fossa**[26] 5349 3-9-1 67 DavidProbert 2 73
(Dean Ivory) *mid-div: hdwy and nt clr run over 1f out: sn rdn: styd on* **6/1**

2406 **4** ¾ **Ceelo**[4] 6072 3-9-6 72 (p) StevieDonohoe 5 76
(Sylvester Kirk) *s.i.s: sn pushed along in rr: rdn over 2f out: r.o u.p ins fnl f: nt rch ldrs* **14/1**

2344 **5** 1¼ **On With The Dance (IRE)**[24] 5395 3-9-2 71(p) WilliamTwiston-Davies(3) 6 71
(Ed Vaughan) *s.i.s: hld up: hdwy 1/2-way: rdn over 2f out: hung lft over 1f out: ev ch ins fnl f: wknd towards fin* **10/1**

3545 **6** 2½ **Work Ethic (IRE)**[24] 5395 3-8-10 69 (p) OisinMurphy(7) 9 62
(Gerard Butler) *s.s: in rr: hdwy u.p over 1f out: edgd lft ins fnl f: nt trble ldrs* **22/1**

6531 **7** 2¼ **Nordikhab (IRE)**[19] 5594 3-9-1 67 (p) NeilCallan 8 54
(Kevin Ryan) *chsd ldr tl led over 2f out: sn rdn and hung rt: hdd over 1f out: wknd ins fnl f* **3/1**[1]

6654 **8** 2¼ **Keene's Pointe**[28] 5280 3-9-6 72 SebSanders 3 53
(J W Hills) *chsd ldrs: rdn over 1f out: wknd ins fnl f* **16/1**

2140 **9** 21 **Lager Time (IRE)**[22] 5477 3-9-0 69 DeclanBates(3) 11
(David Evans) *sn led: rdn and hdd over 2f out: wknd over 1f out* **40/1**

0500 **10** 2¾ **Iberis**[54] 4354 3-9-5 71 PatCosgrave 10
(Lady Cecil) *s.i.s: sn pushed along in rr: rdn and wknd over 2f out* **10/1**

1505 **11** 4½ **Clock On Tom**[43] 4725 3-8-11 63 GrahamGibbons 7
(Michael Easterby) *wnt lft s: prom tl wknd 1/2-way* **16/1**

1m 32.15s (2.55) **Going Correction** +0.45s/f (Slow) 11 Ran SP% **119.4**
Speed ratings (Par 101): **103,102,100,99,98 95,92,90,66,62 57**
Tote Swingers: 1&2 £4.00, 1&3 £11.60, 2&3 £3.10 CSF £25.74 CT £114.70 TOTE £6.00: £2.20, £2.20, £1.60; EX 26.80 Trifecta £126.80 Pool: £963.42 - 5.69 winning units..
Owner Simon Gibson **Bred** R Hannon & J Cullinan **Trained** Newmarket, Suffolk

FOCUS
A competitive 3yo handicap.

6215 MORE WAYS TO WIN £500 @ QUICKSILVERSLOTS CLAIMING STKS 7f 32y(P)
7:05 (7:05) (Class 5) 3-Y-O+ **£2,587** (£770; £384; £192) **Stalls** High

Form RPR

2420 **1** **Mr David (USA)**[13] 5799 6-9-7 81 (b) DavidProbert 3 85
(Jamie Osborne) *mid-div: hdwy and nt clr run over 1f out: rdn ins fnl f: r.o to ld nr fin* **10/1**

321 **2** nk **Secret Beau**[28] 5277 3-9-1 75 (v) SebSanders 2 81
(Ralph Beckett) *hld up: hdwy over 2f out: rdn to chse ldr and hung lft over 1f out: styd on u.p to ld wl ins fnl f: hdd nr fin* **5/1**[3]

015 **3** ½ **Elusive Hawk (IRE)**[15] 5696 9-9-5 82 (v) DeclanBates(3) 12 84
(David Evans) *s.i.s: hld up: hdwy u.p over 1f out: edgd lft ins fnl f: r.o* **8/1**

406 **4** ½ **Azrael**[18] 5621 5-9-1 78 (p) DavidBergin(5) 9 80
(Alan McCabe) *trckd ldr tl led 1/2-way: rdn over 1f out: hdd and unable qck wl ins fnl f* **14/1**

0336 **5** 6 **Prime Exhibit**[12] 5815 8-9-3 75 (t) ShaneKelly 4 61
(John Stimpson) *hld up: hdwy over 1f out: sn rdn: styd on same pce fnl f* **14/1**

5556 **6** shd **Juvenal (IRE)**[14] 5759 4-9-5 77 WilliamTwiston-Davies(3) 5 66
(Richard Hannon) *hld up: rdn 1/2-way: r.o ins fnl f: nvr nrr* **4/1**[2]

0004 **7** nk **Seek The Fair Land**[51] 4438 7-9-3 82 (b) CathyGannon 10 60
(Jim Boyle) *s.i.s and stmbld sn after s: hdwy over 5f out: rdn over 2f out: hung rt over 1f out: wknd ins fnl f* **10/1**

0050 **8** 3½ **Green Park (IRE)**[22] 5481 10-8-11 83 (b) JasonHart(3) 11 48
(Declan Carroll) *trckd ldrs: racd keenly: rdn and wknd over 1f out* **22/1**

0213 **9** 2 **Fathsta (IRE)**[7] 5987 8-8-12 79 NeilFarley(3) 8 43+
(Declan Carroll) *sn led: hdd 1/2-way: rdn and edgd rt over 1f out: sn wknd* **3/1**[1]

2152 **10** 5 **Officer In Command (USA)**[131] 1890 7-9-4 74 FrankieMcDonald 6 33
(John Butler) *s.i.s: sn pushed along and a in rr* **25/1**

-000 **11** 32 **Esprit De Midas**[38] 4879 7-9-5 87 (p) PaulBooth(7) 1
(Dean Ivory) *chsd ldrs tl rdn and wknd 1/2-way* **14/1**

1m 32.55s (2.95) **Going Correction** +0.45s/f (Slow)
WFA 3 from 4yo+ 4lb 11 Ran SP% **119.2**
Speed ratings (Par 103): **101,100,100,99,92 92,92,88,85,80 43**
Tote Swingers: 1&2 £11.10, 1&3 £10.70, 2&3 £10.60 CSF £60.23 TOTE £11.50: £3.70, £2.20, £2.40; EX 59.80 Trifecta £320.10 Pool: £936.51 - 2.19 winning units..Secret Beau claimed by Mr P. D. Evans £11,000.
Owner Steve Jakes & S J Piper Partnership **Bred** Mr & Mrs R David Randal **Trained** Upper Lambourn, Berks

FOCUS
A fair claimer in which the early pace was strong, which favoured the closers. The winenr and third are rated to their Polytrack bests.

6216 GET UP TO £200 FREEPLAYS @ QUICKSILVERSLOTS H'CAP 1m 4f 50y(P)
7:35 (7:35) (Class 6) (0-60,65) 3-Y-O+ **£1,940** (£577; £288; £144) **Stalls** Low

Form RPR

0521 **1** **Royal Alcor (IRE)**[10] 5897 6-9-10 65 ShelleyBirkett(7) 9 80
(Gay Kelleway) *a.p: led over 2f out: shkn up and sn clr: easily* **5/2**[1]

3543 **2** 9 **Giantstepsahead (IRE)**[22] 5492 4-9-11 59 SebSanders 4 60
(Michael Wigham) *trckd ldr tl led 4f out: rdn and hdd over 2f out: sn outpcd* **5/2**[1]

0020 **3** 1¾ **Ground Ginger**[22] 5500 3-8-3 46 oh1 JimmyQuinn 6 44
(James Bethell) *hld up: hdwy 8f out: rdn over 4f out: styd on same pce fnl 2f* **10/1**

3244 **4** 6 **Waahej**[16] 5672 7-9-6 59 LauraPike(5) 3 48
(Peter Hiatt) *awkward leaving stalls: hld up in tch: plld hrd: lost pl 8f out: hdwy over 2f out: rdn and wknd over 1f out* **11/2**[3]

6305 **5** 6 **Souter Point (USA)**[19] 5592 7-9-1 49 AdamBeschizza 1 28
(William Kinsey) *s.s: hld up: rdn and wknd over 2f out* **18/1**

1044 **6** 17 **Corn Maiden**[13] 5803 4-9-1 56 LewisWalsh(7) 10 8
(Lydia Pearce) *led 8f: rdn and wknd over 2f out* **25/1**

-153 **7** nk **Weybridge Light**[11] 5370 8-9-2 53 (b) RaulDaSilva(3) 8 4
(David Thompson) *s.i.s: hdwy over 8f out: rdn over 3f out: wknd over 2f out* **5/1**[2]

0-66 **8** 36 **So Cheeky**[12] 5196 4-8-9 46 oh1 JasonHart(3) 5
(Richard Guest) *chsd ldrs: pushed along over 6f out: sn lost pl: rdn and wknd 5f out* **33/1**

6300 **9** 79 **Smirfy's Silver**[18] 5615 9-8-9 48 TimClark(5) 7
(Michael Mullineaux) *s.v.s: a wl bhd* **28/1**

2m 46.64s (5.54) **Going Correction** +0.45s/f (Slow)
WFA 3 from 4yo+ 9lb 9 Ran SP% **113.8**
Speed ratings (Par 101): **99,93,91,87,83 72,72,48,**
Tote Swingers: 1&2 £2.40, 1&3 £2.40, 2&3 £7.30 CSF £8.02 CT £50.23 TOTE £3.60: £1.30, £1.80, £3.60; EX 11.40 Trifecta £81.10 Pool: £578.84 - 5.35 winning units..
Owner Gay Kelleway & Paul Kerridge **Bred** John Hayes **Trained** Exning, Suffolk

FOCUS
A low-grade handicap, which was turned into a procession by the winner.

6217 £1 TO WIN £500 @ QUICKSILVERSLOTS CLAIMING STKS 1m 4f 50y(P)
8:05 (8:05) (Class 6) 3-Y-O+ **£1,940** (£577; £288; £144) **Stalls** Low

Form RPR

30/1 **1** **Mungo Park**[19] 5586 5-9-6 70 (t) SaleemGolam 5 82
(Sophie Leech) *hld up: hdwy over 3f out: rdn to ld 1f out: styd on u.p* **16/1**

6060 **2** 1¼ **Perennial**[15] 5706 4-10-0 84 DanielTudhope 10 88
(David O'Meara) *a.p: chsd ldr over 2f out: led over 1f out: sn rdn and hdd: edgd lft ins fnl f: styd on same pce towards fin* **5/4**[1]

1010 **3** 8 **City Ground (USA)**[36] 4951 6-9-6 66 GrahamGibbons 7 67
(Michael Easterby) *led: rdn and hdd over 1f out: wknd ins fnl f* **9/1**

2154 **4** nk **Just Lille (IRE)**[32] 5087 10-9-3 72 (p) PJMcDonald 8 64
(Ann Duffield) *chsd ldr tl rdn over 2f out: wknd over 1f out* **10/1**

400- **5** 13 **Anton Dolin (IRE)**[7] 7147 5-9-1 77 (p) WilliamTwiston-Davies(3) 1 44
(Dr Richard Newland) *prom tl rdn and wknd over 2f out* **13/2**[3]

0400 **6** 1½ **English Summer**[31] 5129 6-9-10 79 (t) NeilCallan 4 48
(David Simcock) *chsd ldrs: rdn over 2f out: wknd over 1f out* **5/2**[2]

1500 **7** 2¼ **Special Mix**[11] 5861 5-9-5 66 NeilFarley(3) 6 42
(Michael Easterby) *hld up: pushed along over 4f out: rdn and wknd 3f out* **50/1**

2 **8** 2¼ **Willow Island (IRE)**[5] 6046 4-9-8 0 ow1 RichardEvans(3) 9 41
(David Evans) *sn pushed along in rr: rdn and wknd over 3f out* **25/1**

00- **9** dist **Bull Market (IRE)**[291] 6323 10-9-3 45 DeclanBates(3) 2
(Alan Jones) *hld up: wknd over 5f out* **100/1**

2m 46.16s (5.06) **Going Correction** +0.45s/f (Slow) 9 Ran SP% **118.1**
Speed ratings (Par 101): **101,100,94,94,85 84,83,81,**
Tote Swingers 1&2 £4.40, 2&3 £4.30, 1&3 £13.10 CSF £37.30 TOTE £14.30: £3.00, £1.20, £2.00; EX 64.20 Trifecta £694.10 Part won. Pool: £925.57 - 0.20 winning units..Mungo Park claimed by Miss Gay Kelleway for £6,000.
Owner C J Leech **Bred** Newsells Park Stud **Trained** Elton, Gloucs

FOCUS
The front two pulled clear in this fair claimer.

6218 GREAT JOBS @ QUICKSILVERSLOTS.CO.UK H'CAP 1m 141y(P)
8:35 (8:36) (Class 6) (0-65,65) 3-Y-O+ **£1,940** (£577; £288; £144) **Stalls** Low

Form RPR

5155 **1** **Diletta Tommasa (IRE)**[3] 6109 3-9-2 63 ShaneKelly 13 69
(John Stimpson) *hld up: swtchd lft sn after s: hdwy over 1f out: rdn: edgd lft and r.o to ld wl ins fnl f* **14/1**

5-00 **2** ¾ **Baile Atha Cliath (IRE)**[110] 2507 4-8-7 51 oh6 NeilFarley(3) 9 55
(Declan Carroll) *hld up in tch: rdn over 2f out: led ins fnl f: sn hdd: styd on* **33/1**

3043 **3** 1 **Peter's Friend**[16] 5677 4-9-6 61 PJMcDonald 5 63
(Michael Herrington) *a.p: led wl over 1f out: sn rdn: hdd ins fnl f: kpt on* **9/2**[2]

000 **4** 1¼ **Testa Rossa (IRE)**[37] 4928 3-9-4 65 SebSanders 12 64
(J W Hills) *hld up: rdn over 2f out: hdwy over 1f out: hmpd ins fnl f: styd on same pce* **11/1**

4050 **5** 2¼ **Tenessee**[59] 4169 6-9-7 62 PatCosgrave 4 56
(Jamie Osborne) *chsd ldr tl rdn over 2f out: no ex ins fnl f* **12/1**

0031 **6** nse **Warden Bond**[33] 5073 5-9-10 65 (p) NeilCallan 8 59
(William Stone) *prom: chsd ldr over 2f out: rdn and ev ch over 1f out: edgd rt and no ex ins fnl f* **7/1**[3]

2640 **7** 4 **Moment In The Sun**[42] 4754 4-8-8 56 (b) OisinMurphy(7) 7 41
(David Flood) *sn led: racd keenly: rdn and hdd wl over 1f out: wknd ins fnl f* **14/1**

050- **8** 2¾ **Rock Band**[38] 4901 4-9-9 64 [1] GrahamGibbons 6 42
(Emmet Michael Butterly, Ire) *s.i.s: hld up: rdn over 1f out: n.d* **9/2**[2]

0605 **9** 2¾ **Geeaitch**[7] 5980 4-9-5 60 WilliamCarson 1 32
(Anthony Carson) *hld up: rdn over 2f out: wknd over 1f out* **2/1**[1]

2013 **10** 12 **Glenridding**[26] 5354 9-9-8 63 (p) DaleSwift 10 7
(James Given) *prom: pushed along over 3f out: rdn over 2f out: sn wknd* **16/1**

1m 54.66s (4.16) **Going Correction** +0.45s/f (Slow)
WFA 3 from 4yo+ 6lb 10 Ran SP% **120.4**
Speed ratings (Par 101): **99,98,97,96,94 94,90,88,85,75**
Tote Swingers 1&2 £51.30, 2&3 £27.70, 1&3 £12.20 CSF £395.88 CT £2461.43 TOTE £14.80: £4.40, £6.00, £1.80; EX 271.80 Trifecta £753.50 Part won. Pool: £1,004.76 - 0.02 winning units..

The Form Book Flat, Raceform Ltd, Compton, RG20 6NL.

Owner J T Stimpson **Bred** Ms Sheila Lavery **Trained** Butterton, Staffs
FOCUS
A modest handicap.

6219 TRY ROULETTE @ QUICKSILVERSLOTS H'CAP 5f 216y(P)
9:05 (9:07) (Class 6) (0-65,64) 3-Y-0+ **£1,940** (£577; £288; £144) **Stalls** Low

Form RPR
560 **1** **Dream Ally (IRE)**[10] 5878 3-9-3 **62**.........................(tp) MichaelO'Connell 9 75
(Jedd O'Keeffe) *chsd ldrs: led over 1f out: rdn and edgd rt ins fnl f: styd on* **9/4**[1]
0152 **2** *1 3/4* **Lord Buffhead**[8] 5965 4-8-12 **55**.............................(v) RobbieFitzpatrick 11 62
(Richard Guest) *hld up: hdwy over 1f out: sn rdn and edgd rt: r.o* **7/2**[2]
6050 **3** *nk* **Methaaly (IRE)**[28] 5273 10-8-10 **58**..........................(be) TimClark(5) 3 64
(Michael Mullineaux) *broke wl: sn lost pl: hdwy over 1f out: n.m.r ins fnl f: r.o: nt rch ldrs* **10/1**
6565 **4** *3* **Rutterkin (USA)**[10] 5887 5-8-7 **50** oh3.............................. JimmyQuinn 10 46
(James Moffatt) *mid-div: hdwy over 2f out: sn rdn: edgd lft and styd on same pce fnl f* **18/1**
0300 **5** *2* **Art Dzeko**[16] 5674 4-9-7 **64**.. WilliamCarson 7 54
(Brian Baugh) *prom: rdn over 2f out: no ex ins fnl f* **16/1**
1466 **6** *3/4* **Rise To Glory (IRE)**[12] 1995 5-8-9 **55**............................(b) JasonHart(3) 4 43
(Shaun Harris) *sn led: rdn and hdd over 1f out: wknd ins fnl f* **5/1**[3]
0400 **7** *4* **Unassailable**[24] 5407 3-8-9 **54** ow1.................................(b) NeilCallan 5 29
(Kevin Ryan) *chsd ldrs: rdn 1/2-way: wknd fnl f* **11/2**
3000 **8** *6* **Magic Ice**[15] 5708 3-8-4 **52**..(p) RaulDaSilva(3) 8 8
(Brian Ellison) *chsd ldr: rdn over 2f out: wknd over 1f out* **12/1**
0004 **9** *3/4* **Lady Cricketer**[13] 5800 4-8-2 **50** oh5...........................(p) NatashaEaton(5) 2 3
(Michael Squance) *hld up: rdn and wknd over 2f out* **50/1**
0542 **10** *3* **Gracie's Games**[22] 5499 7-8-7 **50** oh5..........................(b) CathyGannon 6
(John Spearing) *sn outpcd* **12/1**

1m 18.28s (3.28) **Going Correction** +0.45s/f (Slow)
WFA 3 from 4yo+ 2lb **10** Ran SP% **122.6**
Speed ratings (Par 101): **96,93,93,89,86 85,80,72,71,67**
Tote Swingers 1&2 £4.00, 2&3 £14.10, 1&3 £11.50 CSF £10.60 CT £69.60 TOTE £3.70: £1.70, £1.60, £3.00; EX 16.20 Trifecta £83.90 Pool: £1,181.29 - 10.55 winning units..
Owner Caron & Paul Chapman **Bred** Noel & Roger O'Callaghan **Trained** Middleham Moor, N Yorks
FOCUS
A modest but competitive handicap.
T/Plt: £146.20 to a £1 stake. Pool: £68,539.00 - 342.00 winning tickets. T/Qpdt: £59.70 to a £1 stake. Pool: £6,745.00 - 83.50 winning tickets. CR

5449 LEOPARDSTOWN (L-H)
Saturday, September 7
OFFICIAL GOING: Good (good to yielding in places)

6223a ICON BREEDERS' CUP JUVENILE TURF TRIAL STKS (GROUP 3) 1m
5:15 (5:15) 2-Y-0 **£31,707** (£9,268; £4,390; £1,463)

RPR
1 **Australia**[49] 4545 2-9-3 .... JosephO'Brien 3 113+
(A P O'Brien, Ire) *sn settled in 3rd: niggled along to press ldr under 2f out: led over 1f out and sn qcknd clr: impressive* **2/1**[1]
2 *6* **Free Eagle (IRE)**[23] 5452 2-9-3 .... PatSmullen 5 99
(D K Weld, Ire) *trckd ldr in 2nd tl on terms 2f out and sn led: hdd over 1f out and sn no match for wnr* **5/2**[2]
3 *3 1/2* **Kingfisher (IRE)**[10] 5904 2-9-3 .... SeamieHeffernan 1 91
(A P O'Brien, Ire) *led tl hdd under 2f out: sn one pce* **8/1**[3]
4 *11* **Wexford Town (IRE)**[23] 5452 2-9-3 .... KevinManning 2 66
(J S Bolger, Ire) *sn in rr: pushed along over 3f out and sn adrift* **25/1**

1m 40.3s (-0.90) **Going Correction** +0.10s/f (Good) **4** Ran SP% **115.0**
Speed ratings: **108,102,98,87**
CSF £4.25 TOTE £3.20; DF 4.90.
Owner D Smith & Mrs J Magnier & M Tabor & T Ah Khing **Bred** Stanley Estate And Stud Co **Trained** Ballydoyle, Co Tipperary
FOCUS
Last term this proved an informative heat with regard to the following year's Classics with Derby fourth Battle Of Marengo easily accounting for Irish Derby winner Trading Leather. This year's renewal could prove even better. A small field but the entire quartet had shown plenty of ability and the ante-post Derby favourite was present.

6224a COOLMORE FUSAICHI PEGASUS MATRON STKS (GROUP 1) (F&M) 1m
5:45 (5:49) 3-Y-0+ **£105,691** (£30,894; £14,634; £4,878)

RPR
1 **La Collina (IRE)**[44] 4696 4-9-5 106...................................... ChrisHayes 4 111
(Kevin Prendergast, Ire) *w.w: prog in 7th 2f out: swtchd rt appr fnl f in 4th: styd on wl to ld cl home* **25/1**
2 *1/2* **Lily's Angel (IRE)**[66] 3964 4-9-5 105.................................. GaryCarroll 6 110
(G M Lyons, Ire) *racd in mid-div: tk clsr order in 3rd 2f out: qcknd to ld ent fnl f: hdd cl home* **14/1**
3 *shd* **Say (IRE)**[6] 6023 3-9-0 110.. SeamieHeffernan 7 109
(A P O'Brien, Ire) *hld up towards rr: 10th 2f out: styd on wl towards inner to press ldr in 2nd ins fnl f: kpt on wl but dropped to 3rd cl home* **8/1**
4 *3 1/2* **Kenhope (FR)**[41] 4817 3-9-0 .... ThierryJarnet 11 101+
(H-A Pantall, France) *hld up towards rr: 11th 2f out: prog in 7th 1f out: styd on wl into 4th cl home: nvr nrr* **5/2**[1]
5 *1 1/4* **Fiesolana (IRE)**[16] 5688 4-9-5 110... WJLee 2 99
(W McCreery, Ire) *trckd ldrs: prog into cl 2nd after 1/2-way: led briefly over 1f out: sn hdd and no ex: dropped to 5th clsng stages* **4/1**[2]
6 *1* **Scintillula (IRE)**[16] 5682 3-9-0 113................................(t) KevinManning 8 96
(J S Bolger, Ire) *trckd ldrs in 3rd: pushed along under 3f out: nt qckn appr fnl f: kpt on one pce* **14/1**
7 *2* **Chigun**[41] 4817 4-9-5 .... TomQueally 9 92
(Lady Cecil) *hld up in rr: strly rdn in last 3f out: kpt on wl ins fnl f* **6/1**[3]
8 *1 1/2* **Just Pretending (USA)**[35] 4985 3-9-0 113.................. JosephO'Brien 1 87
(A P O'Brien, Ire) *led to 1/2-way: led again off home turn tl hdd over 1f out: sn wknd* **8/1**
9 *2* **One Spirit (IRE)**[6] 6023 5-9-5 100...................................... NGMcCullagh 10 84
(F Dunne, Ire) *racd in mid-div tl nt qckn under 2f out: sn one pce* **50/1**
10 *hd* **Caponata (USA)**[27] 5317 4-9-5 109..................................(v[1]) PatSmullen 12 83
(D K Weld, Ire) *chsd ldrs towards outer: clsd to trck ldrs appr home turn: no imp under 2f out: eased fnl f* **13/2**
11 *2* **Magical Dream (IRE)**[35] 4985 3-9-0 105.......................... MichaelHussey 3 78
(A P O'Brien, Ire) *chsd ldrs on inner tl nt qckn under 2f out: sn no ex* **20/1**

12 *nk* **Wannabe Better (IRE)**[10] 5907 3-9-0 102.......................... WayneLordan 5 77
(T Stack, Ire) *trckd ldr in 2nd tl led 1/2-way: hdd home turn: wknd qckly appr fnl f* **14/1**

1m 39.0s (-2.20) **Going Correction** +0.10s/f (Good)
WFA 3 from 4yo+ 5lb **12** Ran SP% **129.0**
Speed ratings: **115,114,114,110,109 108,106,105,103,102 100,100**
CSF £359.86 TOTE £32.10: £5.60, £3.50, £2.90; DF 410.60.
Owner J Vasicek **Bred** Manister House Stud **Trained** Friarstown, Co Kildare
FOCUS
The absence of ante-post favourite Elusive Kate due to an unsatisfactory blood test was disappointing and a substandard renewal was littered with Group 3 performers, but that shouldn't detract from the performance of the winner who was very brave. The first two set the standard which is a bit low on race averages.

6225a KPMG ENTERPRISE STKS (GROUP 3) 1m 2f
6:15 (6:15) 3-Y-0+ **£31,707** (£9,268; £4,390; £1,463)

RPR
1 **The United States (IRE)**[16] 5691 3-9-3 102..............(p) JosephO'Brien 3 107
(A P O'Brien, Ire) *sn led: strly pressed and jnd 1f out: rallied wl to reassert clsng stages* **2/1**[1]
2 *1/2* **Elleval (IRE)**[10] 5907 3-9-3 106.. FergalLynch 6 106
(David Marnane, Ire) *hld up in rr: gd hdwy to press ldr in 2nd appr fnl f and sn on terms: kpt on wl: jst hld* **14/1**
3 *1 1/4* **Tandem**[39] 4869 4-9-10 103..(v) PatSmullen 7 104
(D K Weld, Ire) *w.w in 5th: c wd early in st: travelled wl to chse ldrs in 3rd appr fnl f: sn rdn and one pce* **7/2**[3]
4 *1 3/4* **Belle De Crecy (IRE)**[24] 5415 4-9-7 103........................ NGMcCullagh 4 97
(J P Murtagh, Ire) *trckd ldr in cl 2nd tl nt qckn appr fnl f: kpt on same pce* **6/1**
5 *shd* **Uleavemebreathless**[24] 5415 3-9-0 94.................................. ChrisHayes 5 97
(A Oliver, Ire) *w.w tl gd prog on inner off home turn: wnt 3rd appr fnl f: no imp and dropped to 5th on line* **33/1**
6 *7 1/2* **Zand (IRE)**[90] 3142 3-9-3 99...................................... DeclanMcDonogh 2 85
(John M Oxx, Ire) *chsd ldrs in 4th: nt qckn 2f out: sn no ex* **5/2**[2]
7 *2 1/4* **Manalapan (IRE)**[16] 5691 3-9-3 97................................... KevinManning 1 80
(P J Prendergast, Ire) *trckd ldr in cl 3rd tl nt qckn 2f out: sn wknd* **9/1**

2m 5.59s (-2.61) **Going Correction** +0.10s/f (Good)
WFA 3 from 4yo 7lb **7** Ran SP% **118.0**
Speed ratings: **114,113,112,111,111 105,103**
CSF £32.29 TOTE £2.70: £1.40, £3.80; DF 27.60.
Owner Derrick Smith & Mrs John Magnier & Michael Tabor **Bred** Beauty Is Truth Syndicate **Trained** Ballydoyle, Co Tipperary
FOCUS
The progressive winner ran a personal best.

6226a RED MILLS IRISH CHAMPION STKS (GROUP 1) 1m 2f
6:50 (6:50) 3-Y-0+
£353,252 (£115,447; £54,471; £17,886; £11,788; £5,691)

RPR
1 **The Fugue**[16] 5682 4-9-4 .... WilliamBuick 8 123+
(John Gosden) *w.w: tk clsr order in 4th 1/2-way: travelled wl to ld over 1f out: sn pushed clr: styd on wl: comf* **4/1**[2]
2 *1 1/4* **Al Kazeem**[17] 5654 5-9-7 .... JamesDoyle 3 123+
(Roger Charlton) *chsd ldr in 3rd: pushed along into 2nd over 2f out: nt qckn w wnr ins fnl f: kpt on same pce* **9/10**[1]
3 *2* **Trading Leather (IRE)**[17] 5654 3-9-0 120....................... KevinManning 4 119
(J S Bolger, Ire) *led: pressed under 2f out: hdd over 1f out and dropped to 3rd: kpt on same pce* **5/1**[3]
4 *3 3/4* **Parish Hall (IRE)**[124] 2105 4-9-7 110............................... RonanWhelan 2 112
(J S Bolger, Ire) *trckd ldr in 2nd: niggled along 3f out: nt qckn and dropped to 4th over 2f out: sn no ex* **33/1**
5 *21* **Euphrasia (IRE)**[32] 5114 4-9-4 104...................................... GaryCarroll 6 67
(Joseph G Murphy, Ire) *hld up in rr: lft modest 5th 1/2-way: no imp fr early in st* **100/1**
6 *dist* **Kingsbarns (IRE)**[315] 7398 3-9-0 116............................... JosephO'Brien 1
(A P O'Brien, Ire) *sn settled in 4th: qckly dropped to rr 1/2-way: sn eased* **4/1**[2]

2m 5.22s (-2.98) **Going Correction** +0.10s/f (Good)
WFA 3 from 4yo+ 7lb **6** Ran SP% **113.2**
Speed ratings: **115,114,112,109,92**
CSF £8.18 TOTE £3.70: £1.90, £1.40; DF 9.70.
Owner Lord Lloyd-Webber **Bred** Watership Down Stud **Trained** Newmarket, Suffolk
FOCUS
The withdrawal of Declaration Of War certainly took a bit away from this race and it would have been more than interesting to see how he would have coped with the winner. The time was fairly slow and The Fugue is given a generic top filly mark, with the next two to par.

6227 - 6230a (Foreign Racing) - See Raceform Interactive

VELIEFENDI
Saturday, September 7
OFFICIAL GOING: Polytrack: fast; turf: good

6231a INTERNATIONAL ISTANBUL TROPHY (GROUP 3) (3YO+ FILLIES & MARES) (TURF) 1m
5:30 (12:00) 3-Y-0+ **£93,495** (£37,398; £18,699; £9,349)

RPR
1 **Beatrice**[63] 4092 3-9-0 0 ow1.. FabriceVeron 8 104
(H-A Pantall, France) *midfield: rdn over 2f out: r.o to chal ins fnl f: led cl home: shade cosily* **69/10**
2 *1/2* **Arsaadi (IRE)**[41] 4811 4-9-6 0..(p) AhmedAjtebi 1 105
(William Haggas) *prom in main body of field: rdn over 2f out: r.o to chal ins fnl f: wnt 2nd cl home: hld by wnr* **1/20**[1]
3 *1* **Willpower (TUR)**[17] 3-9-3 0.. SelimKaya 9 104
(Z Bektas, Turkey) *dwlt sltly: hld up in last pair: rdn 3f out: swtchd lft over 2f out: kpt on steadily u.p and wnt 3rd post: nvr nrr* **22/5**
4 *nse* **Lady Jacamira (GER)**[48] 4-9-6 0.. APietsch 5 103
(R Dzubasz, Germany) *dwlt sltly and pushed along early: hld up towards rr on outer: rdn 3f out: kpt on steadily u.p and wnt 4th post: nvr nrr* **12/5**[2]
5 *shd* **Elevato (TUR)**[17] 3-8-13 0.. GokhanKocakaya 2 99
(Z Guneli, Turkey) *chsd clr ldr: rdn 3f out: clsd 2f out: led ent fnl f: kpt on but strly pressed and hdd cl home: no ex and dropped to 5th post* **209/10**

6 1 ½ **Iphigeneia (TUR)**[69] 4-9-6 0 ... HalisKaratas 6 99
(E Sengel, Turkey) *hld up towards rr: rdn 3f out: hung both ways u.p: kpt on but nt pce to chal* **42/10**[3]

7 1 ½ **Balcibin (TUR)**[17] 5-9-6 0 ... FuatCakar 7 95
(Z Bektas, Turkey) *pushed along to go forward and led: sn clr: rdn 3f out: reeled in 2f out: hdd ent fnl f: sn no ex and btn: fdd and eased towards fin* **22/5**

8 2 ½ **Xanim Qiz (IRE)** 4-9-6 0 ... YBilik 4 90
(Y Musayev, Turkey) *dwlt and pushed along early: midfield on inner: rdn 3f out: outpcd over 1f out: sn in rr and btn* **115/10**

9 6 ½ **Mihrimahal (TUR)**[17] 4-9-6 0 ... SadettinBoyraz 3 75
(S Altundag, Turkey) *stdd and hld up in last pair on inner: rdn 3f out: last and btn over 1f out: eased ins fnl f: nvr a factor* **187/10**

1m 36.28s (0.95)
WFA 3 from 4yo+ 5lb **9** Ran SP% **211.2**
DIVIDENDS (INCLUDING 1 UNIT STAKE): WIN 7.85; DF 4.50; SF 13.30.
Owner Alexandre Pereira **Bred** Alexandre Pereira **Trained** France

6232a INTERNATIONAL FRANCE GALOP FRBC ANATOLIA TROPHY (LOCAL GROUP 2) (3YO+) (POLYTRACK) 1m 2f (P)

7:00 (12:00) 3-Y-O+ **£93,495** (£37,398; £18,699; £9,349)

RPR

1 **Danadana (IRE)**[15] 5725 5-9-6 0 ... AndreaAtzeni 2 110
(Luca Cumani) *midfield in tch: clsd 4f out: rdn to chal 2f out: led over 1f out: drvn clr: pushed out towards fin: comf* **1/5**[1]

2 3 ½ **King Drok (TUR)** 4-9-6 0 ...(bt) FuatCakar 6 103
(T Turkmen, Turkey) *stdd and hld up in last pair on inner: clsd 3f out: swtchd out and rdn over 2f out: 3rd but outpcd by wnr ent fnl f: styd on and wnt 2nd towards fin* **11/1**

3 1 **Cakal Carlos (TUR)** 3-8-11 0 ... AhmetCelik 4 99
(I Kapusiz, Turkey) *trckd ldr: led over 3f out: rdn and strly pressed 2f out: hdd over 1f out and sn outpcd by wnr: styd on but dropped to 3rd towards fin* **13/10**[2]

4 5 **Step By Step (TUR)**[20] 5-9-6 0 ... GokhanKocakaya 3 91
(M Kaya, Turkey) *stdd and hld up in last: rdn over 3f out: wnt 4th 2f out: plugged on but nt pce to chal: eased whn hld towards fin* **78/10**

5 11 ½ **Rampoldi (TUR)**[371] 5848 4-9-6 0 ... HalisKaratas 1 68
(S Keresteci, Turkey) *midfield in tch on inner: rdn over 2f out: no ex and btn over 1f out: sn eased* **7/4**[3]

6 26 **Red Fighter (AZE)** 3-9-0 0 ow3 ...(t) SelimKaya 5 17
(Anar Balahuseynov, Azerbaijan) *t.k.h: trckd ldr on inner: led over 5f out: rdn and hdd over 3f out: sn no ex and btn: wknd and eased: t.o* **91/20**

7 25 **Walks In Dark (TUR)** 3-8-11 0 ...(bt) MehmetKaya 7
(Sab Arslan, Turkey) *wnt lft and lost grnd s: pushed along to rcvr and sn led: taken wd and hdd over 5f out: eased and sn last: tailed rt off* **40/1**

2m 3.79s (-1.21)
WFA 3 from 4yo+ 7lb **7** Ran SP% **203.3**
DIVIDENDS (INCLUDING 1 UNIT STAKE): WIN 1.20; DF 11.55; SF 12.05.
Owner Sheikh Mohammed Obaid Al Maktoum **Bred** Darley **Trained** Newmarket, Suffolk

5763 YORK (L-H)

Sunday, September 8

OFFICIAL GOING: Good (good to soft in places; 6.6)
Wind: Moderate; half behind Weather: Fine

6233 JUDITH MARSHALL MEMORIAL STKS (NURSERY H'CAP) 7f

2:00 (2:02) (Class 4) (0-85,84) 2-Y-O **£6,469** (£1,925; £962; £481) **Stalls** Low

Form RPR

01 1 **Remember**[24] 5435 2-9-5 **82** ... RyanMoore 6 87+
(Richard Hannon) *trckd ldr: led over 2f out: edgd rt ins fnl f: drvn out* **7/2**[3]

41 2 1 ¼ **Makin The Rules (IRE)**[26] 5364 2-8-11 **74** ... MichaelO'Connell 8 76
(John Quinn) *mid-div: hdwy over 2f out: styd on to take 2nd last 50yds* **20/1**

3351 3 ¾ **Imshivalla (IRE)**[12] 5850 2-8-9 **72** ... PaulHanagan 2 72
(Richard Fahey) *led: hdd over 2f out: kpt on same pce fnl f* **16/1**

3330 4 hd **Major Crispies**[37] 4948 2-8-11 **79** ... RyanTate(5) 11 78
(James Eustace) *mid-div: hdwy over 2f out: carried hd high: hung lft and kpt on ins fnl f* **7/1**

2610 5 2 ½ **Porteous**[37] 4948 2-8-2 **65** ... MartinLane 1 58
(Mick Channon) *mid-div: hdwy to chse ldrs over 3f out: wknd fnl 150yds* **33/1**

0163 6 shd **Hatti (IRE)**[13] 5829 2-7-11 **63** oh1 ...(p) RaulDaSilva(3) 10 56
(Micky Hammond) *dwlt: swtchd lft after s: bhd: kpt on fnl 2f: nt rch ldrs* **33/1**

6513 7 1 ¼ **New Bidder**[12] 5858 2-9-4 **81** ... RussKennemore 4 70
(Jedd O'Keeffe) *chsd ldrs: drvn over 3f out: wknd last 150yds* **9/1**

1050 8 1 **Neighbother**[43] 4783 2-8-8 **71** ... TonyHamilton 7 58
(Richard Fahey) *dwlt: t.k.h in rr: hdwy over 2f out: wknd fnl f* **33/1**

3002 9 2 ¾ **Sartori**[13] 5834 2-8-1 **69** ... ShirleyTeasdale(5) 3 49
(Marjorie Fife) *mid-div: drvn over 2f out: wknd over 1f out* **50/1**

31 10 ½ **Zeshov (IRE)**[86] 3290 2-9-4 **81** ... WilliamBuick 5 59
(Jeremy Noseda) *trckd ldrs: lost pl over 1f out* **10/3**[2]

0431 11 8 **Bow Creek (IRE)**[9] 5941 2-9-7 **84** ... JoeFanning 13 41
(Mark Johnston) *sn chsng ldrs: drvn over 2f out: lost pl over 1f out* **3/1**[1]

1m 25.31s (0.01) **Going Correction** +0.125s/f (Good) **11** Ran SP% **114.2**
Speed ratings (Par 97): **104,102,101,101,98 98,97,95,92,92 83**
toteswingers 1&2 £12.70, 1&3 £6.60, 2&3 £29.90 CSF £75.29 CT £1005.80 TOTE £4.20: £2.00, £4.60, £2.70; EX 60.50 Trifecta £677.10 Pool: £2,657.32 - 2.94 winning units..
Owner Saeed Manana **Bred** Fittocks Stud **Trained** East Everleigh, Wilts

FOCUS
Rail moved on home bend from 1m1f to entrance to home straight reducing races of 1mile and beyond by 20yds. The going was Good, good to soft in places after a dry night, although the jockeys' opinions varied from "horrible and tacky" to "beautiful, just on the easy side." A decent nursery that was won in 2012 by the subsequent Group 3 winner Waterway Run.

6234 MINSTER ALARMS E B F STALLIONS MAIDEN STKS 5f 89y

2:30 (2:35) (Class 3) 2-Y-O **£7,439** (£2,213; £1,106; £553) **Stalls** Centre

Form RPR

3 1 **Alphabet Rap (IRE)**[25] 5380 2-9-5 0 ... GrahamGibbons 11 88+
(David Barron) *trckd ldrs: hdwy wl over 1f out: rdn to ld jst ins fnl f: kpt on strly* **13/2**

6623 2 ½ **Rough Courte (IRE)**[8] 5994 2-9-0 85 ... SamHitchcott 10 81
(Mick Channon) *in tch on outer: hdwy wl over 1f out: sn rdn and styd on to chse wnr ins fnl f: kpt on* **10/1**

4 3 1 ¼ **Rock N Rouge (IRE)**[27] 5339 2-9-0 0 ... JimCrowley 9 77
(David Brown) *prom: cl up 1/2-way: rdn to ld over 1f out: hdd jst ins fnl f: kpt on u.p* **22/1**

2625 4 1 ¼ **Sacha Park (IRE)**[40] 4858 2-9-5 97 ... SeanLevey 7 77
(Richard Hannon) *prom: led 1/2-way: rdn and hdd over 1f out: one pce fnl f* **11/4**[1]

5 shd **My Inspiration (IRE)** 2-9-0 0 ... RyanMoore 1 72+
(William Haggas) *cl up: green: pushed along and outpcd 1/2-way: hdwy over 1f out: styd on fnl f* **4/1**[3]

552 6 1 ¾ **The Hooded Claw (IRE)**[20] 5577 2-9-5 75 ... DavidAllan 8 71
(Tim Easterby) *chsd ldrs: rdn along 2f out: sn no imp* **16/1**

7 2 ¼ **Royal Birth** 2-9-5 0 ... JamieSpencer 3 63
(Stuart Williams) *dwlt: a towards rr* **9/1**

8 nk **Cordite (IRE)** 2-9-0 0 ... TobyAtkinson(5) 6 62
(Michael Appleby) *dwlt: a towards rr* **50/1**

255 9 ½ **Bahamian C**[21] 5558 2-9-5 75 ... PaulHanagan 4 60
(Richard Fahey) *sn led: rdn along and hdd 1/2-way: wknd over 1f out* **12/1**

5 10 1 ¼ **Oak Bluffs (IRE)**[23] 5494 2-8-12 0 ... JoshQuinn(7) 2 56
(Richard Fahey) *cl up: rdn along 1/2-way: wknd wl over 1f out* **50/1**

11 28 **Galvanize** 2-9-5 0 ... GrahamLee 5
(Kevin Ryan) *unruly in stalls: slowly away and green: a outpcd in rr: detached and eased fr 1/2-way* **7/2**[2]

1m 5.1s (1.00) **Going Correction** +0.125s/f (Good) **11** Ran SP% **123.2**
Speed ratings (Par 99): **97,96,94,92,92 89,85,85,84,82 37**
toteswingers 1&2 £8.50, 1&3 £24.90, 2&3 £20.20 CSF £72.16 TOTE £8.20: £2.20, £2.80, £5.30; EX 72.10 Trifecta £1723.80 Pool: £4,021.58 - 1.74 winning units..
Owner Miss N J Barron **Bred** Stephanie Hanly **Trained** Maunby, N Yorks

FOCUS
A good maiden but something of a turn-up.

6235 BETFRED GARROWBY STKS (LISTED RACE) 6f

3:00 (3:02) (Class 1) 3-Y-O+
£20,982 (£7,955; £3,981; £1,983; £995; £499) **Stalls** Centre

Form RPR

-143 1 **Hallelujah**[72] 3784 5-8-9 100 ...(t) HayleyTurner 1 104
(James Fanshawe) *mid-div: hdwy on outer over 2f out: chsng ldrs over 1f out: styd on ins fnl f: led post* **7/1**

5150 2 nse **Ladies Are Forever**[16] 5726 5-9-2 105 ...(b) GrahamLee 7 111
(Geoffrey Oldroyd) *chsd ldrs: led narrowly ins fnl f: hdd post* **6/1**[3]

0303 3 hd **Mince**[64] 4079 4-8-9 105 ...(v[1]) RyanMoore 8 103
(Roger Charlton) *mde most stands' side: hrd rdn and hdd ins fnl f: no ex nr fin* **7/2**[1]

0105 4 1 **Lightning Cloud (IRE)**[15] 5763 5-9-0 99 ... JamieSpencer 12 105
(Kevin Ryan) *swtchd lft after s: hld up in rr: hdwy 2f out: styd on stands' side ins fnl f* **12/1**

101 5 ¾ **Hitchens (IRE)**[35] 5027 8-9-7 109 ... GrahamGibbons 11 110
(David Barron) *wnt lft s: chsd ldrs stands' side: kpt on same pce fnl f* **9/1**

3120 6 1 ¾ **Smoothtalkinrascal (IRE)**[37] 4947 3-8-12 106 ... DanielTudhope 5 97
(David O'Meara) *hld up in rr: effrt 2f out: styd on last 150yds* **8/1**

0035 7 ½ **Mirza**[38] 4935 6-9-0 103 ...(p) SebSanders 9 95
(Rae Guest) *mid-div: effrt over 2f out: kpt on fnl f: nvr a threat* **20/1**

2102 8 ¾ **Nocturn**[15] 5747 4-9-0 102 ...(p) WilliamBuick 3 93
(Jeremy Noseda) *w ldr racing towards far side: t.k.h: wknd last 150yds* **5/1**[2]

-203 9 ½ **Royal Rock**[36] 4981 9-9-0 100 ... TedDurcan 2 91
(Chris Wall) *dwlt: in rr: drvn over 2f out: kpt on fnl f: nvr a factor* **33/1**

1025 10 2 ½ **Mass Rally (IRE)**[28] 5320 6-9-0 105 ...(b) PaulMulrennan 6 83
(Michael Dods) *dwlt: hld up in mid-div: effrt 2f out: wknd last 100yds* **7/1**

3-00 11 3 ¾ **Baileys Jubilee**[8] 5984 3-8-7 100 ... JoeFanning 4 66
(Mark Johnston) *chsd ldrs: lost pl over 1f out* **33/1**

3553 12 23 **Superboot (IRE)**[19] 5616 3-8-12 92 ... JimCrowley 10
(Michael Wigham) *s.i.s: in rr and drvn along: bhd fnl 2f: virtually p.u: t.o* **80/1**

1m 10.87s (-1.03) **Going Correction** +0.125s/f (Good)
WFA 3 from 4yo+ 2lb **12** Ran SP% **118.9**
Speed ratings (Par 111): **111,110,110,109,108 106,105,104,103,100 95,64**
toteswingers 1&2 £9.10, 1&3 £4.20, 2&3 £5.00 CSF £47.21 TOTE £7.70: £2.70, £2.30, £2.00; EX 55.50 Trifecta £288.80 Pool: £5,055.06 - 13.12 winning units..
Owner CLS (Chippenham) Limited **Bred** Chippenham Lodge Stud Ltd **Trained** Newmarket, Suffolk
■ Stewards' Enquiry : Ryan Moore two-day ban: used whip above permitted level (Sep 22-23)

FOCUS
A good Listed sprint.

6236 COOPERS MARQUEES STKS (H'CAP) 1m 2f 88y

3:35 (3:35) (Class 4) (0-80,83) 3-Y-O+ **£6,469** (£1,925; £962; £481) **Stalls** Low

Form RPR

2200 1 **Cosmic Halo**[16] 5706 4-9-4 **74** ... PaulHanagan 12 85
(Richard Fahey) *hld up towards rr: stdy hdwy on wd outside 3f out: rdn 2f out: drvn and styd on to ld last 100yds: hld on wl towards fin* **33/1**

2/50 2 ¾ **Fragonard**[46] 4633 4-9-5 **75** ... TomQueally 8 85
(Lady Cecil) *hld up towards rr: hdwy and reminders over 3f out: swtchd rt and rdn 2f out: styd on wl appr fnl f and ev ch tl drvn and no ex last 50yds* **14/1**

3-12 3 ¾ **Bishop's Castle (USA)**[22] 5521 4-9-6 **76** ... RyanMoore 10 85
(Brian Ellison) *hld up in midfield: gd hdwy 3f out: pushed along 2f out: led ent fnl f: sn rdn and edgd rt: drvn and hdd last 100yds: kpt on same pce* **5/1**[1]

2111 4 ¾ **Save The Bees**[26] 5368 5-8-13 **72** ... JasonHart(3) 15 79
(Declan Carroll) *led: pushed along 3f out: rdn 2f out: drvn and hdd ent fnl f: kpt on same pce* **12/1**

2400 5 1 **Barren Brook**[12] 5860 6-9-7 **77** ... PaulMulrennan 3 82
(Michael Easterby) *trckd ldrs: smooth hdwy 4f out: cl up 3f out ev ch tl rdn and wknd over 1f out* **15/2**

2511 6 1 ½ **Morocco**[31] 5179 4-9-11 **81** ... DanielTudhope 1 83
(David O'Meara) *hld up in rr: stdy hdwy towards inner over 3f out: chsd ldrs whn sltly hmpd 1 1/2f out: sn rdn and ev ch tl drvn ent fnl f and kpt on same pce* **6/1**[2]

4515 7 ½ **Arc Light (IRE)**[25] 5382 5-9-6 **76** ... DavidAllan 13 77
(Tim Easterby) *hld up: gd hdwy 3f out: rdn to chse ldrs whn edgd lft 1 1/2f out: sn drvn and one pce* **7/1**[3]

0436 8 nk **Invincible Hero (IRE)**[20] 5580 6-9-2 **79** ... LukeLeadbitter(7) 9 80
(Declan Carroll) *prom: effrt over 3f out: rdn along 2f out: grad wknd* **25/1**

0133 **9** 2 1/4 **Aerodynamic (IRE)**[12] 5861 6-9-2 **72**....................(b) GrahamGibbons 20 69
(Michael Easterby) *stdd s and swtchd lft towards inner: hld up in rr: hdwy 3f out: rdn along 2f out: styd on appr fnl f: nrst fin* **25/1**

3342 **10** 1 **Bank On Me**[32] 5124 4-9-9 **79**.. WilliamCarson 2 74
(Philip McBride) *trckd ldrs: effrt 4f out: rdn along wl over 2f out: sn no imp* **8/1**

-200 **11** 1 1/2 **President Lincoln (USA)**[9] 5974 5-9-7 **77**............ MichaelO'Connell 16 69
(Declan Carroll) *chsd ldrs: rdn along over 3f out: wknd over 2f out* **50/1**

5001 **12** 2 1/2 **Super Say (IRE)**[13] 5847 7-9-13 **83**...........................(t) AndrewMullen 14 70
(Michael Appleby) *hld up in midfield: sme hdwy over 4f out: rdn along over 3f out: sn wknd* **16/1**

0420 **13** nk **Patriotic (IRE)**[72] 3785 5-9-2 **77**....................................(p) RobertTart(5) 17 64
(Chris Dwyer) *hld up towards rr: sme hdwy 3f out: sn rdn and n.d* **25/1**

302 **14** hd **Day Of Destiny (IRE)**[29] 5264 8-9-2 **72**.......................... GrahamLee 4 58
(James Given) *prom: rdn along over 4f out: drvn 3f out and sn wknd* **25/1**

1140 **15** nk **Laughing Jack**[38] 4923 5-9-1 **76**.......................... GeorgeDowning(5) 19 62
(Tony Carroll) *a towards rr* **25/1**

1310 **16** 2 1/2 **Nemushka**[8] 6001 4-9-4 **79**.. GeorgeChaloner(5) 5 60
(Richard Fahey) *in tch: hdwy on inner over 3f out: rdn to chse ldrs over 2f out: sn ev ch: drvn wl over 1f out and sn wknd* **14/1**

1456 **17** 2 1/4 **Christmas Light**[43] 4777 6-9-8 **78**.................................. JamieSpencer 6 55
(Brian Ellison) *a in rr* **16/1**

0640 **18** 23 **Tiger Reigns**[20] 5580 7-9-4 **74**.......................................(t) PhillipMakin 11 7
(Michael Dods) *a towards rr* **33/1**

321- **19** 1 1/2 **King Of The Celts (IRE)**[412] 4396 5-9-6 **76**...................... TomEaves 7 6
(Tim Easterby) *prom: effrt and cl up 4f out: sn rdn along and wknd wl over 2f out* **50/1**

2m 8.51s (-3.99) **Going Correction** -0.225s/f (Firm) **19** Ran SP% **128.2**
Speed ratings (Par 105): **106,105,104,104,103 102,101,101,99,98 97,95,95,95,95 93,91,72,71**
toteswingers 1&2 £27.60, 1&3 £36.90, 2&3 £12.30 CSF £421.05 CT £2723.56 TOTE £46.90: £9.00, £2.40, £1.40, £3.30; EX 691.40 Trifecta £2434.40 Part won. Pool: £3,245.94 - 0.36 winning units..
Owner The Cosmic Cases **Bred** The Cosmic Cases **Trained** Musley Bank, N Yorks

FOCUS
The rail had been moved on the home bend from 9f to the 4f point, reducing race distances of 1m and over by 20 yards. A big field for this competitive handicap and another good finish.

6237 CASTLES UK EDUCATIONAL AND RESIDENTIAL FURNITURE STKS (H'CAP) (THE SUNDAY £5K BONUS RACE) 2m 88y

4:05 (4:05) (Class 4) (0-85,84) 3-Y-0+ **£6,469** (£1,925; £962; £481) **Stalls** Low

Form RPR

4135 **1** **Eagle Rock (IRE)**[18] 5655 5-9-10 **80**..........................(p) FrannyNorton 17 89
(Tom Tate) *swtchd lft to chse ldr after s: led after 3f: increased gallop 5f out: hdd over 3f out: rallied over 1f out: styd on to ld last 30yds* **8/1**[3]

4210 **2** nk **Flashman**[18] 5655 4-9-9 **79**.. PaulHanagan 10 88
(Richard Fahey) *mid-div: hdwy over 3f out: 2nd over 1f out: led jst ins fnl f: hdd and no ex clsng stages* **7/1**[2]

6620 **3** 3 3/4 **Rocktherunway (IRE)**[33] 5109 4-9-6 **81**..............(p) ConnorBeasley(5) 13 86
(Michael Dods) *hld up in rr: rapid hdwy on ins over 4f out: led over 3f out: hdd jst ins fnl f: kpt on same pce* **12/1**

0660 **4** 1/2 **Hit The Jackpot (IRE)**[20] 5580 4-9-5 **75**...................... DanielTudhope 5 79
(David O'Meara) *hld up in rr: hdwy 3f out: chsng ldrs over 1f out: kpt on same pce* **25/1**

0612 **5** 3 1/4 **Hawk Mountain (UAE)**[18] 5640 8-9-6 **76**...................... WilliamBuick 11 76
(John Quinn) *trckd ldrs: outpcd over 3f out: hdwy stands' side 2f out: one pce* **10/1**

601 **6** 2 **Body Language (IRE)**[54] 4372 5-9-12 **82**.......................(p) GrahamLee 8 80
(Ian Williams) *mid-div: sn drvn along: hdwy stands' side over 2f out: nvr trbld ldrs* **8/1**[3]

0633 **7** hd **Getabuzz**[13] 5823 5-9-7 **77**... DavidAllan 7 74
(Tim Easterby) *dwlt: hld up in rr: hdwy over 3f out: chsng ldrs 2f out: fdd fnl f* **14/1**

0210 **8** 1 1/4 **Sula Two**[39] 4873 6-9-8 **83**.. PhilipPrince(5) 14 79
(Ron Hodges) *hld up in rr: hdwy over 4f out: chsng ldrs 3f out: wknd fnl f* **16/1**

500/ **9** 9 **Recession Proof (FR)**[908] 5743 7-9-12 **82**..........(p) MichaelO'Connell 16 67
(John Quinn) *mid-div: hdwy 5f out: lost pl over 2f out* **16/1**

4114 **10** 7 **Pearl Spice (IRE)**[30] 5240 3-8-11 **80**............................(b) RyanMoore 15 57
(Tim Pitt) *hld up in rr: hdwy 7f out: chsng ldrs over 3f out: sn wknd* **3/1**[1]

4265 **11** 1/2 **My Destination (IRE)**[9] 5972 4-8-6 **65**..........................(b) JasonHart(3) 1 41
(Declan Carroll) *dwlt: t.k.h: sn trcking ldrs: hmpd and stdd to rr after 1f: hdwy on ins to chse ldrs over 4f out: edgd rt and lost pl 3f out* **40/1**

011 **12** 1/2 **Medieval Bishop (IRE)**[13] 5831 4-8-10 **66**.............(p) DuranFentiman 6 41
(Tim Walford) *chsd ldrs: drvn over 4f out: lost pl over 2f out* **25/1**

4020 **13** 1 1/2 **Tartan Jura**[13] 5831 5-9-4 **74**..(p) JoeFanning 3 48
(Mark Johnston) *chsd ldrs: drvn over 5f out: lost pl over 2f out* **25/1**

6022 **14** 2 1/2 **Rosairlie (IRE)**[9] 5972 5-9-5 **75**.................................... PJMcDonald 2 46
(Micky Hammond) *chsd ldrs: lost pl over 2f out* **20/1**

3311 **15** nse **Nashville (IRE)**[8] 5997 4-9-8 **78**...............................(p) JamieSpencer 4 49
(Richard Fahey) *led: reminders after s: hdd after 3f: drvn over 6f out: lost pl over 2f out* **8/1**[3]

3m 33.73s (-0.77) **Going Correction** -0.225s/f (Firm)
WFA 3 from 4yo+ 13lb **15** Ran SP% **124.8**
Speed ratings (Par 105): **92,91,89,89,88 87,87,86,81,78 78,77,77,75,75**
toteswingers 1&2 £13.50, 1&3 £19.90, 2&3 £19.20 CSF £60.63 CT £689.10 TOTE £7.60: £2.90, £2.70, £4.10; EX 64.30 Trifecta £950.40 Pool: £1,954.93 - 1.54 winning units..
Owner The Ivy Syndicate **Bred** Silk Fan Syndicate **Trained** Tadcaster, N Yorks

FOCUS
Another good turnout for this stayers' handicap but three came clear in the closing stages.

6238 HANSON SPRINGS 50TH ANNIVERSARY STKS (H'CAP) 6f

4:40 (4:41) (Class 3) (0-95,92) 3-Y-0 **£9,703** (£2,887; £1,443; £721) **Stalls** Centre

Form RPR

0041 **1** **Lancelot Du Lac (ITY)**[15] 5748 3-9-7 **92**......................... JimCrowley 10 102
(Dean Ivory) *dwlt and hld up in rr: swtchd lft to outer and smooth hdwy 2f out: rdn to ld 1f out: drvn and hld on wl towards fin* **3/1**[1]

1410 **2** 1/2 **Secondo (FR)**[43] 4767 3-9-5 **90**... RyanMoore 9 98
(Roger Charlton) *hld up in rr: hdwy wl over 1f out: rdn ent fnl f: styd on to chal ins fnl f: sn drvn and ev ch tl no ex nr fin* **5/1**[2]

641 **3** shd **Right Touch**[13] 5832 3-8-9 **80**... PaulHanagan 7 88
(Richard Fahey) *cl up: rdn to ld briefly over 1f out: hdd 1f out: sn drvn and ev ch tl no ex last 50yds* **8/1**

5000 **4** 2 1/4 **Mary's Daughter**[15] 5769 3-8-11 **82**.............................. TonyHamilton 6 82
(Richard Fahey) *trckd ldrs: effrt over 1f out: sn rdn and kpt on same pce fnl f* **20/1**

1341 **5** nse **Bondesire**[34] 5057 3-9-1 **86**.. DanielTudhope 4 86
(David O'Meara) *led: rdn along 2f out: hdd over 1f out: drvn and one pce fnl f* **16/1**

-062 **6** 3/4 **Lastchancelucas**[22] 5511 3-8-11 **85**.................................. JasonHart(3) 8 83
(Declan Carroll) *cl up: rdn along over 2f out: grad wknd* **17/2**

2100 **7** 2 **Robot Boy (IRE)**[43] 4767 3-9-4 **89**..................................... JamieSpencer 2 81
(David Barron) *trckd ldrs: rdn along wl over 1f out: sn wknd* **13/2**[3]

3153 **8** 1 1/4 **Red Refraction (IRE)**[15] 5748 3-8-12 **83**............................ SeanLevey 5 71
(Richard Hannon) *trckd ldrs: effrt 2f out: sn rdn and wknd over 1f out* **20/1**

5560 **9** hd **Dominate**[36] 4983 3-9-3 **88**... JimmyFortune 11 75
(Richard Hannon) *a towards rr* **22/1**

0400 **10** 1/2 **Bachotheque (IRE)**[34] 5056 3-8-7 **78** oh1......................... DavidAllan 14 63
(Tim Easterby) *hld up: a towards rr* **25/1**

6200 **11** nk **Jadanna (IRE)**[29] 5260 3-9-2 **87**... GrahamLee 12 71
(James Given) *in tch: effrt 2f out: sn rdn and wknd over 1f out* **33/1**

1152 **U** **Hoofalong**[15] 5769 3-9-2 **87**..(p) GrahamGibbons 15
(Michael Easterby) *rrd stalls and uns rdr s: tk no part* **5/1**[2]

1m 11.37s (-0.53) **Going Correction** +0.125s/f (Good) **12** Ran SP% **119.8**
Speed ratings (Par 105): **108,107,107,104,104 103,100,98,98,97 97,**
toteswingers 1&2 £5.50, 1&3 £6.70, 2&3 £8.70 CSF £16.09 CT £111.47 TOTE £4.50: £2.10, £2.30, £2.30; EX 22.60 Trifecta £140.50 Pool: £3,397.60 - 18.13 winning units..
Owner M J Yarrow **Bred** Elektra Di Fausto Martellozzo & C Sas **Trained** Radlett, Herts

FOCUS
Another competitive handicap, this time a sprint for 3-y-os, and it was dominated by the top weights and market leaders. The time was half a second slower than the earlier Listed race.

6239 FUTURE CLEANING SERVICES APPRENTICE STKS (H'CAP) (GO RACING IN YORKSHIRE FUTURE STARS SERIES) 1m 4f

5:10 (5:10) (Class 4) (0-80,83) 4-Y-0+ **£6,469** (£1,925; £962; £481) **Stalls** Centre

Form RPR

32/5 **1** **Montefeltro**[21] 5563 5-9-3 **79**.. RobertTart(3) 18 90
(Brian Ellison) *hld up in rr: gd hdwy over 2f out: n.m.r over 1f out: styd on wl to ld nr fin* **7/1**[3]

3036 **2** 1 1/2 **Next Edition (IRE)**[16] 5712 5-9-1 **79**............................ EvaMoscrop(5) 1 88
(Philip Kirby) *hld up in rr: hdwy on ins 4f out: led over 1f out: hdd and no ex clsng stages* **10/1**

0403 **3** 3 3/4 **Cosmic Sun**[16] 5706 7-9-0 **73**..(t) LeeTopliss 17 76
(Richard Fahey) *s.s: swtchd lft after s: hdwy over 3f out: chsng ldr over 1f out: kpt on same pce* **6/1**[1]

0460 **4** 1 3/4 **High Office**[18] 5655 7-9-1 **77**...................................... GeorgeChaloner(3) 6 77
(Richard Fahey) *dwlt: in rr: hdwy 7f out: effrt stands' side over 2f out: kpt on fnl f* **13/2**[2]

4241 **5** 3/4 **Mister Fizz**[5] 6068 5-8-7 **71** 6ex.................................... DanielCremin(5) 2 70
(Miss Imogen Pickard) *trckd ldrs on inner: t.k.h: n.m.r bnd over 5f out: kpt on one pce fnl 2f* **10/1**

5352 **6** 1 **Prophesy (IRE)**[19] 5612 4-9-2 **75**... JasonHart 9 72
(Declan Carroll) *led tl over 6f out: led over 3f out tl over 1f out: one pce* **7/1**[3]

0402 **7** 2 1/2 **Al Furat (USA)**[23] 5466 5-8-2 **66** oh8.............................. NoelGarbutt(5) 5 59
(Ron Barr) *s.i.s: in rr: drvn and hdwy over 3f out: one pce fnl 2f* **40/1**

2234 **8** 1/2 **Gran Maestro (USA)**[13] 5823 4-9-1 **74**................................(b) LMcNiff 3 67
(Ruth Carr) *in tch: effrt 3f out: one pce* **20/1**

6546 **9** 1/2 **Gala Casino Star (IRE)**[22] 5521 8-8-9 **73**..............(p) JordanNason(5) 14 65
(Geoffrey Harker) *hld up in rr: hdwy stanbds' side 3f out: hung lft over 1f out: sn wknd* **16/1**

0666 **10** 4 1/2 **Dancing Primo**[30] 5222 7-8-11 **70**...................................... RyanClark 12 55
(Mark Brisbourne) *in tch: effrt on outside 3f out: wknd over 1f out* **16/1**

446 **11** shd **Watts Up Son**[35] 5031 5-8-9 **75**................................(v) LukeLeadbitter(7) 7 59
(Declan Carroll) *w ldrs: chal over 3f out: wknd over 1f out* **20/1**

5501 **12** 4 **Tetbury (USA)**[14] 5786 4-9-7 **83**..................................(v) DavidBergin(3) 8 61
(David O'Meara) *sn chsng ldrs: wknd over 2f out* **8/1**

0123 **13** 2 1/2 **Demolition**[26] 5367 9-8-11 **75**.. JoeyHaynes(5) 4 49
(Noel Wilson) *in tch: drvn over 3f out: lost pl 2f out* **16/1**

0134 **14** 2 3/4 **Flying Power**[14] 5786 5-8-10 **74**................................... JacobButterfield(5) 11 44
(John Norton) *sn chsng ldrs: lost pl over 3f out* **16/1**

0041 **15** hd **Tinseltown**[15] 5466 7-8-6 **68**.. ShirleyTeasdale(3) 15 37
(Brian Rothwell) *sn chsng ldrs: led over 6f out: hdd over 3f out: sn lost pl and bhd* **25/1**

2m 30.49s (-2.71) **Going Correction** -0.225s/f (Firm) **15** Ran SP% **121.3**
Speed ratings (Par 105): **100,99,96,95,94 94,92,92,91,88 88,86,84,82,82**
toteswingers 1&2 £17.30, 1&3 £11.30, 2&3 £15.00 CSF £71.51 CT £453.23 TOTE £9.60: £3.70, £6.30, £2.40; EX 87.40 Trifecta £1029.10 Pool: £2,120.10 - 1.54 winning units..
Owner D Gilbert, M Lawrence, A Bruce **Bred** Darley **Trained** Norton, N Yorks

FOCUS
Yet another big field for this apprentice handicap and the pace was sound.
T/Jkpt: Not won. T/Plt: £954.80 to a £1 stake. Pool: £171,220.52 - 130.90 winning units T/Qpdt: £49.90 to a £1 stake. Pool: £11,704.80 - 173.48 winning units WG

6244 - 6247a (Foreign Racing) - See Raceform Interactive

3612 DORTMUND (R-H)

Sunday, September 8

OFFICIAL GOING: Turf: good to soft

6248a GROSSER PREIS VON DSW21 - 129TH DEUTSCHES ST.LEGER (GROUP 3) (3YO+) (TURF) 1m 6f

4:15 (12:00) 3-Y-0+

£26,016 (£8,943; £4,471; £2,439; £1,626; £1,219)

RPR

1 **Hey Little Gorl (GER)**[21] 3-8-6 0.. AHelfenbein 2 101
(Markus Klug, Germany) *wnt rt and bmpd s: restrained and hld up in tch: in rr 3f out: fanned wd and rdn on turn into st: drifted rt u.p but styd on to chal ins fnl f: wore down runner-up and led fnl strides* **6/1**

2 shd **Saratino (GER)**[14] 3-8-9 0.. CristianDemuro 3 104
(Mario Hofer, Germany) *stdd and hld up towards rr: rdn over 2f out: edgd rt u.p but styd on to chal ent fnl f: sn led but immediately pressed by eventual wnr: worn down and hdd fnl strides* **56/10**[3]

3 1 1/2 **Arango (GER)**[39] 3-8-9 0.. LennartHammer-Hansen 6 102
(S Smrczek, Germany) *midfield in tch: rdn to chal 2f out: led over 1f out: strly pressed ent fnl f: sn hdd and dropped to 3rd: styd on but wl hld* **39/10**[2]

4 nk **Tres Rock Danon (FR)**[14] 7-9-6 0.. SHellyn 5 101
(Gerald Geisler, Germany) *trckd ldr: rdn to chal over 2f out: outpcd by ldrs over 1f out: styd on wl u.p ins fnl f and jst prevailed for 4th* **14/1**

5 *nk* **Altano (GER)**38 4919 7-9-6 0 EPedroza 4 101
(A Wohler, Germany) *hld up in rr: rdn 3f out: plugged on u.p in st and jst denied 4th: nt pce to chal* **3/5**1
6 *2 1/2* **Slowfoot (GER)**14 5-9-6 0 HarryBentley 1 98
(Markus Klug, Germany) *wnt lft and bmpd s: pushed along in early stages: prom on inner: rdn to chal on turn into st: led 2f out: hdd over 1f out and sn outpcd: plugged on* **108/10**
7 *12* **Andreas (GER)**63 4-9-6 0 KClijmans 7 81
(Markus Klug, Germany) *pushed along to go forward fr wdst draw: sn crossed over and led: rdn 3f out: strly pressed and hdd 2f out: sn no ex and btn: fdd and dropped to last: eased ins fnl f* **147/10**
3m 2.88s (-2.62)
WFA 3 from 4yo+ 11lb 7 Ran SP% **133.9**
WIN (incl. 10 euro stake): 70. PLACES: 29, 31. SF: 908.
Owner Gestut Gorlsdorf **Bred** Gestut Gorlsdoff **Trained** Germany

6030 LONGCHAMP (R-H)

Sunday, September 8

OFFICIAL GOING: Turf: good

6249a PRIX LA ROCHETTE (GROUP 3) (2YO) (TURF) 7f
1:25 (12:00) 2-Y-O £32,520 (£13,008; £9,756; £6,504; £3,252)

RPR
1 **Karakontie (JPN)**28 5313 2-8-11 0 OlivierPeslier 7 106
(J E Pease, France) *hld up in rr on outer: rdn and gd hdwy 1 1/2f out: r.o wl ins fnl f: led cl home: drvn out* **4/1**3
2 *3/4* **Decathlete (USA)**38 2-8-11 0 Pierre-CharlesBoudot 5 104
(A Fabre, France) *midfield on outer: tk clsr order under 1 1/2f out: rdn and qcknd to ld 150yds out: r.o u.p: hdd cl home: no ex* **7/4**1
3 *1 1/4* **Stillman (FR)**29 2-8-11 0 ChristopheSoumillon 3 101
(Mario Hofer, Germany) *trckd ldng pair: pressed ldr under 2f out: rdn to ld over 1f out: hdd 150yds out: no ex* **8/1**
4 *1 3/4* **Daraybi (FR)**45 2-8-11 0 Christophe-PatriceLemaire 1 96
(A De Royer-Dupre, France) *towards rr on inner: last bhd wall of horses 1 1/2f out: rdn and r.o whn gap appeared on rail 1f out: swtchd outside wkng rival 100yds out: styd on but nvr on terms* **5/2**2
5 *1 1/2* **Stormyra (FR)**22 5555 2-8-8 0 ThierryJarnet 4 89
(J-P Gallorini, France) *towards rr taking a t.k.h: rdn and no imp 1 1/2f out: kpt on at same pce u.p fnl f* **16/1**
6 *nk* **Little Big Shot (IRE)**40 2-8-11 0 UmbertoRispoli 2 91
(F-H Graffard, France) *trckd ldr taking a t.k.h: shkn up to hold pl 2 1/2f out: rdn and outpcd over 1 1/2f out: kpt on at one pce u.p fnl f* **16/1**
7 *nse* **Muharaaj (IRE)**21 5573 2-8-11 0 AntoineHamelin 6 91
(Matthieu Palussiere, France) *sn led: hdd over 1f out: wknd ins fnl f* **16/1**
1m 22.45s (1.75) 7 Ran SP% **113.7**
WIN (incl. 1 euro stake): 4.40. PLACES: 2.30, 1.50. SF: 16.20.
Owner Niarchos Family **Bred** Flaxman Holdings Limited **Trained** Chantilly, France

6250a PRIX DE LUTECE (GROUP 3) (3YO) (TURF) 1m 7f
2:40 (12:00) 3-Y-O £32,520 (£13,008; £9,756; £6,504; £3,252)

RPR
1 **Valirann (FR)**37 3-8-9 0 Christophe-PatriceLemaire 6 111+
(A De Royer-Dupre, France) *w ldr: led after 4f: hdd 1/2-way and dropped to midfield: pushed along over 3f out: swtchd to outer and rdn over 1f out: styd on to ld fnl strides* **7/2**2
2 *snk* **Lucky Look (FR)**29 5297 3-8-6 0 GregoryBenoist 2 107
(D Smaga, France) *led: hdd after 4f and trckd ldr on inner: rdn 3f out: angled out to chal 2f out: led over 1f out: strly pressed thrght fnl f: styd on but hdd fnl strides* **7/1**
3 *snk* **Montclair (IRE)**35 5041 3-8-11 0 (b) Pierre-CharlesBoudot 3 112
(A Fabre, France) *hld up in tch: racd in last pair on inner 5f out: rdn 3f out: styd on to chal ins fnl f: 2nd and ev ch 100yds out: nt quite pce of front pair and dropped to 3rd cl home* **5/4**1
4 *snk* **Au Revoir (IRE)**15 5779 3-8-9 0 FlavienPrat 4 110
(A Fabre, France) *prom early: midfield in tch 1/2-way: rdn to chal 2f out: cl 2nd and ev ch ent fnl f: styd on but nt quite pce of front trio and dropped to 4th cl home* **5/1**3
5 *1 1/4* **Mohicane (FR)**24 5463 3-8-6 0 MickaelForest 1 105
(W Walton, France) *hld up in last: rdn 3f out: hdwy on outer 2f out: styd on wl but nt quite pce to chal: 5th and hld whn squeezed for room and snatched up cl home* **10/1**
6 *nk* **Diyamindar (FR)**69 3912 3-8-9 0 (p) AlexandreRoussel 7 108
(J Boisnard, France) *midfield in tch early: prom on outer after 4f: led 1/2-way: rdn over 2f out: hdd over 1f out: no ex and fdd ins fnl f* **16/1**
7 *8* **Green Byron (FR)**24 5463 3-8-9 0 IoritzMendizabal 5 98
(J-M Lefebvre, France) *hld up in tch: hdwy on outer to trck ldr 1/2-way: rdn and brief effrt to chal over 2f out: no ex and btn over 1f out: fdd and dropped to last: eased ins fnl f* **20/1**
3m 14.37s (-1.63) 7 Ran SP% **115.6**
WIN (incl. 1 euro stake): 4.10. PLACES: 2.80, 3.30. SF: 25.20.
Owner H H Aga Khan **Bred** Haras De S.A. Aga Khan Scea **Trained** Chantilly, France
FOCUS
They went steady and finished in a bunch. The winner should improve.

6251a PRIX DU PIN (GROUP 3) (3YO+) (TURF) 7f
3:10 (12:00) 3-Y-O+ £32,520 (£13,008; £9,756; £6,504; £3,252)

RPR
1 **Desert Blanc**15 5-9-1 0 GregoryBenoist 12 112+
(C Baillet, France) *w.w towards rr: rdn and hdwy on outside 2f out: r.o wl u.p fnl f: led fnl strides* **12/1**
2 *nk* **Mayyadah (IRE)**24 5461 3-8-8 0 ThierryJarnet 8 106
(F Head, France) *chsd ldr: pushed along to ld 1 1/2f out: r.o u.p fnl f: hdd fnl strides* **14/1**
3 *hd* **Sommerabend**28 6-9-1 0 GeraldMosse 7 111
(M Rulec, Germany) *disp 3rd on outer: rdn to chse ldr over 1f out: hrd rdn and r.o fnl f: nvr quite on terms* **20/1**
4 *1 1/4* **What A Name (IRE)**24 5461 3-8-13 0 Christophe-PatriceLemaire 10 107+
(M Delzangles, France) *towards rr: prog 2f out: r.o u.p fnl f: nt pce to chal* **6/1**3
5 *1 1/4* **Monsieur Playboy (GER)**28 4-9-1 0 UmbertoRispoli 11 104+
(Mme Pia Brandt, France) *burst through stalls bef s: dwlt: in rr: rdn and hdwy 2f out: styd on u.p fnl f: nvr plcd to chal* **18/1**
6 *snk* **Tulips (IRE)**14 5806 4-8-11 0 Pierre-CharlesBoudot 5 99
(A Fabre, France) *midfield: rdn over 2 1/2f out: hdwy towards inner over 1 1/2f out: one pce fnl f: nvr on terms* **15/8**1
7 *1 3/4* **So Long Malpic (FR)**40 6-8-11 0 OlivierPeslier 2 95
(T Lemer, France) *towards rr: last 1/2-way: styd on ins fnl f: nvr in contention* **8/1**
8 *1 1/2* **Princedargent (FR)**14 5806 3-8-11 0 ThierryThulliez 6 93
(H-A Pantall, France) *sn led: 4 l clr 1/2-way: rdn 2f out: hdd 1 1/2f out: sn wknd and bhd fnl f* **20/1**
9 *snk* **Gengis (FR)**71 3851 3-9-2 0 IoritzMendizabal 4 97
(G Doleuze, France) *towards rr: rdn and shortlived effrt over 1 1/2f out: no further imp: one pce fnl f* **10/1**
10 *3/4* **Us Law (IRE)**35 5040 3-8-11 0 ChristopheSoumillon 9 90
(P Bary, France) *midfield on outer: hrd rdn 2 1/2f out: no imp: wknd ins fnl f* **16/1**
11 *2 1/2* **Kendam (FR)**64 4093 4-8-11 0 FabriceVeron 1 82
(H-A Pantall, France) *midfield on inner: nowhere to go and snatched up sn after 1/2-way: rdn and one pce 1f out: short of room and eased fnl 150yds* **16/1**
12 *6* **Market Share**33 5120 3-8-11 0 JamesDoyle 3 67
(P Bary, France) *disp 3rd on inner: rdn over 3f out: no imp: wknd fr 2f out: bhd fnl f* **5/1**2
1m 20.31s (-0.39)
WFA 3 from 4yo+ 4lb 12 Ran SP% **126.8**
WIN (incl. 1 euro stake): 13.20. PLACES: 4.50, 4.40, 5.40. DF: 83.10. SF: 159.90.
Owner Ecurie Jarlan **Bred** Haras Du Mezeray **Trained** France

5465 SAN SEBASTIAN (R-H)

Sunday, September 8

OFFICIAL GOING: Turf: soft

6252a GRAN PREMIO DE SAN SEBASTIAN (CONDITIONS) (3YO+) (TURF) 1m 6f
6:35 (12:00) 3-Y-O+ £12,195 (£4,878; £2,439; £1,219)

RPR
1 **Entre Copas**70 9-9-6 0 J-LMartinez 7 94
(J-M Osorio, Spain) **5/2**2
2 *3/4* **Azafata (SPA)** 4-9-3 0 JHorcajada 9 90
(J Lopez Sanchez, Spain) **139/10**
3 *nk* **Seaside Sizzler**39 4873 6-9-2 0 (v) Roberto-CarlosMontenegro 1 89
(Ralph Beckett) *towards rr on inner: rdn and hdwy over 2f out: styd on u.p fnl f: tk 3rd post: nrest at fin* **13/10**1
4 *hd* **Australia Day (IRE)**24 5465 10-9-6 0 OscarUrbina 4 92
(Paul Webber) *led: rdn 2 1/2f out: hdd over 1 1/2f out: rallied u.p ins fnl f: no ex last 100yds: lost 3rd post* **16/5**3
5 *nk* **Achtung (SPA)**70 5-9-8 0 MGomes 8 94
(J Lopez Sanchez, Spain) **96/10**
6 *1/2* **Coside (USA)** 5-9-2 0 Francois-XavierBertras 6 87
(E Leon Penate, Spain) **77/10**
7 *7 1/4* **Le Feu Du Ciel (FR)**542 7-9-4 0 (p) VJanacek 2 79
(G Arizkorreta Elosegui, Spain) **161/10**
8 *2 1/2* **Roatan**24 5465 8-9-4 0 IBorrego 5 75
(Mlle A Imaz-Ceca, France) **27/1**
9 *dist* **Baranain (SPA)** 4-8-13 0 JeremyCrocquevieille 3
(T Martins, Spain) **29/1**
3m 1.65s (181.65) 9 Ran SP% **136.3**
TOTE DIVIDENDS (all including 1 euro stakes): WIN 3.50; PLACE 2.10, 14.40; DF 21.70.
Owner Cuadra Africa **Bred** Almagro De Activadades Comerciales **Trained** Spain

6231 VELIEFENDI

Sunday, September 8

OFFICIAL GOING: Turf: good

6253a INTERNATIONAL BOSPHORUS CUP (GROUP 2) (3YO+) (TURF) 1m 4f
2:00 (12:00) 3-Y-O+ £146,341 (£58,536; £29,268; £14,631)

RPR
1 **Lost In The Moment (IRE)**22 5531 6-9-6 0 (p) MickaelBarzalona 4 108+
(Saeed bin Suroor) *towards rr: last and pushed along 3f out: rdn and hdwy 2 1/2f out: short of room: stdd and swtchd outside 1 1/2f out: r.o wl u.p fnl f to ld cl home* **7/4**2
2 *1* **Ambivalent (IRE)**36 4985 4-9-2 0 AndreaAtzeni 11 102+
(Roger Varian) *dwlt fr wd draw: led on inner after 1f: set stdy gallop: qcknd 3f out: sn pressed: rdn 2f out: hdd briefly over 1f out: rallied to ld 1f out: r.o gamely u.p: hdd cl home: no ex* **56/10**
3 *nse* **Nymphea (IRE)**49 4571 4-9-2 0 AStarke 9 102+
(P Schiergen, Germany) *t.k.h and trckd ldr: pressed ldr 2 1/2f out: hrd rdn and edgd rt 1 1/2f out: led briefly over 1f out: hdd 1f out: r.o u.p: jst failed to get bk up for 2nd* **5/4**1
4 *nk* **Talip Han (IRE)**23 3-9-0 0 ow4 SelimKaya 5 109+
(B Dag, Turkey) *trckd ldng gp: lost pl sn after 1/2-way: 7th and rdn over 3f out: styd on u.p fnl f: nvr quite getting there* **47/20**3
5 *1/2* **David Livingston (IRE)**29 5270 4-9-6 0 JohnnyMurtagh 1 105+
(M F De Kock, South Africa) *midfield on inner: 6th and pushed along over 3f out: styd on into 3rd over 1f out: kpt on ins fnl f: nt pce to chal* **51/20**
6 *1/2* **Matador Yasar (TUR)**23 4-9-6 0 AhmetCelik 3 104
(H Derinsu, Turkey) *towards rr: hdwy on inner 2 1/2f out: 4th and hrd rdn over 1f out: kpt on at one pce fnl f* **159/10**
7 *3* **Sanzatu (TUR)**11 4-9-6 0 (t) HalisKaratas 2 99
(S Aydogdi, Turkey) *led: hdd after 1f: trckd ldrs: hrd rdn and nt qckn 2f out: grad outpcd by ldrs: plugged on at same pce fnl f* **107/20**
8 *1* **Nordvulkan (GER)**49 4571 3-8-10 0 APietsch 6 97+
(R Dzubasz, Germany) *towards rr: pushed v wd fnl bnd: rdn and no imp 2f out: kpt on late ins fnl f: nvr in contention* **184/10**

9 *hd* **Cihanim (TUR)**[23] 4-9-6 0 GokhanKocakaya 8 98
(S Bektas, Turkey) *in rr: effrt and c wd fnl bnd: no imp fr 2f out: styd on wl ins fnl f: nvr in contention* **17/1**

10 2 **Feuerblitz (GER)**[28] 5324 4-9-6 0 RichardHughes 7 94+
(M Figge, Germany) *t.k.h: trckd ldng pair on outer: 4th and scrubbed along 3f out: rdn and wknd fr 1 1/2f out* **89/10**

11 4 ½ **Mitico (TUR)**[23] 5-9-6 0 GokhanGokce 10 87+
(Z Guneli, Turkey) *midfield: hdwy on outside 3 1/2f out: 5th and rdn over 2 1/2f out: wknd u.p over 2f out: sn btn* **208/10**

2m 28.87s (0.07)
WFA 3 from 4yo+ 9lb **11** Ran SP% **201.0**
DIVIDENDS (INCLUDING 1 UNIT STAKE): WIN 2.75; PLACE (1-2): 3.55, 5.75; DF 14.35; SF 19.50.

Owner Godolphin **Bred** Rockhart Trading Ltd **Trained** Newmarket, Suffolk
FOCUS
The pace was very steady

6254a INTERNATIONAL TOPKAPI TROPHY (GROUP 2) (3YO+) (TURF) 1m
3:30 (12:00) 3-Y-O+ £219,512 (£95,575; £47,787; £23,893)

RPR

1 **Producer**[40] 4856 4-9-6 0 RichardHughes 1 111+
(Richard Hannon) *hld up in last pair: last 3f out: rdn over 2f out: 6th and stl plenty to do ent fnl f: str run towards fin: led post* **9/10**[1]

2 *hd* **Chil The Kite**[15] 5760 4-9-6 0 GeorgeBaker 3 111
(Hughie Morrison) *t.k.h early: hld up in last pair: hdwy fr 3f out: swtchd ins and rdn to chal over 1f out: led ent fnl f and qcknd clr: r.o but clsd down rapidly towards fin and hdd post* **2/1**[3]

3 *nk* **White Ram (TUR)**[21] 5-9-6 0 (t) HalisKaratas 2 110
(Hakan El, Turkey) *trckd ldr on inner: angled out and rdn over 2f out: wnt 2nd 100yds out: r.o and fin strly but nvr quite able to chal and dropped to 3rd fnl strides* **19/10**[2]

4 2 **Astorya (TUR)**[21] 4-9-6 0 SelimKaya 4 105
(U Bilik, Turkey) *trckd ldr on outer: rdn to chal 3f out: disputing 2nd and ev ch ent fnl f: kpt on but outpcd by front trio towards fin and dropped to 4th* **51/10**

5 ½ **Libranno**[14] 5794 5-9-6 0 PatCosgrave 8 104
(Richard Hannon) *midfield on inner: rdn over 3f out: r.o but nt pce to chal* **59/10**

6 2 ½ **Fast Stars Line (TUR)**[21] 4-9-6 0 MehmetKaya 9 98
(N Kocken, Turkey) *sent forward fr wdst draw and led: rdn and strly pressed fr 3f out: hdd ent fnl f: sn no ex: steadily fdd and eased towards fin* **177/10**

7 1 **Quick Wit**[29] 5270 6-9-6 0 (p) MickaelBarzalona 6 96
(Saeed bin Suroor) *dwlt and wnt rt s: pushed along to rcvr: hld up towards rr on outer: rdn over 2f out: outpcd in rr over 1f out: hung rt u.p: kpt on but nvr threatened* **5/2**

8 4 **Dutyfree (TUR)**[42] 5-9-6 0 (b) SadettinBoyraz 7 87
(G Igdir, Turkey) *stmbld s and pushed along early: midfield in tch on outer: rdn 3f out: no ex over 1f out: sn in rr and btn: eased ins fnl f* **147/10**

9 ½ **Agresivo (USA)**[71] 4-9-6 0 AkinSozen 5 86
(S Ozolke, Turkey) *dwlt sltly: midfield: rdn 3f out: no ex over 1f out: sn in rr and btn: eased ins fnl f* **9/1**

1m 35.33s **9** Ran SP% **201.6**
DIVIDENDS (INCLUDING 1 UNIT STAKE): WIN 1.90; DF 2.85; SF 4.60.
Owner J Palmer-Brown **Bred** Cheveley Park Stud Ltd **Trained** East Everleigh, Wilts
FOCUS
This was run at a decent pace.

6033 BRIGHTON (L-H)
Monday, September 9

OFFICIAL GOING: Good to soft (soft in places) changing to soft after race 1 (2:30)
Wind: Almost nil Weather: Cloudy, heavy rain race 4

6255 BRASSERIE ITALIAN BRIGHTON MARINA FILLIES' H'CAP 5f 213y
2:30 (2:30) (Class 5) (0-75,69) 3-Y-O+ £2,587 (£770; £384; £192) Stalls Low

Form RPR

6442 1 **Saskia's Dream**[7] 6039 5-8-13 61 (v) RichardHughes 3 66
(Jane Chapple-Hyam) *hld up: hdwy and swtchd lft over 1f out: drvn to ld ins fnl f* **8/11**[1]

1-00 2 1 **Take The Lead**[17] 5697 3-9-1 65 PatDobbs 2 67
(Richard Hannon) *broke wl: disp 2nd: hrd rdn and edgd lft over 1f out: unable qck ins fnl f* **8/1**

1060 3 *hd* **Commandingpresence (USA)**[17] 5701 7-9-6 68 KieranO'Neill 7 69
(John Bridger) *sn led: rdn 2f out: hdd ins fnl f: one pce* **12/1**

0602 4 *nse* **Above The Stars**[10] 5973 5-9-7 69 HayleyTurner 5 70
(Conor Dore) *sn disputing 2nd: pressed ldr over 1f out: hrd rdn and one pce ins fnl f* **4/1**[2]

0000 5 2 **Interakt**[95] 3010 6-8-12 63 MichaelJMMurphy(3) 6 58
(Joseph Tuite) *hld up: n.m.r on outside rail over 2f out: sn rdn and no hdwy* **7/1**[3]

1m 12.0s (1.80) **Going Correction** +0.30s/f (Good)
WFA 3 from 5yo+ 2lb **5** Ran SP% **109.2**
Speed ratings (Par 100): **100,98,98,98,95**
CSF £7.04 TOTE £1.60: £1.10, £3.80; EX 7.10 Trifecta £29.90 Pool: £1568.10 - 39.25 winning units..
Owner Peter Bottomley & Jane Chapple-Hyam **Bred** Psb Holdings Ltd **Trained** Dalham, Suffolk
FOCUS
After 6mm of overnight rain the going was good to soft, soft in places. The rail was doled out from the 4.5f to 3.5f markers, adding six yards to race distances. This modest handicap was run at a sound pace with the field racing up the stands' rail before hanging to the centre late on. Afterwards, Richard Hughes felt the ground was riding soft. The form is weak and is rated cautiously.

6256 32RED/BRITISH STALLION STUDS EBF MAIDEN STKS 6f 209y
3:00 (3:00) (Class 5) 2-Y-O £2,911 (£866; £432; £216) Stalls Low

Form RPR

632 1 **Juan Alonso (IRE)**[15] 5790 2-9-5 75 RichardHughes 4 77
(Richard Hannon) *mde all: led field to stands' rail st: rdn and hld on wl fnl 2f* **2/1**[1]

3 2 ½ **Our Channel (USA)**[12] 5877 2-9-5 GeorgeBaker 5 76
(William Haggas) *hld up: hdwy over 2f out: chsd wnr fnl f: kpt on: a hld* **5/2**[2]

43 3 2 ¾ **Sullivan Street (IRE)**[8] 6014 2-9-5 HarryBentley 9 69
(Charlie Appleby) *prom: chsd wnr 2f out tl 1f out: no ex ins fnl f* **13/2**

4 1 ¼ **Approach The West (IRE)** 2-9-0 MartinHarley 6 60
(James Tate) *hld up towards rr: effrt over 2f out: styng on steadily at fin* **9/1**

00 5 1 ¼ **Sellingallthetime (IRE)**[11] 5924 2-9-5 SteveDrowne 1 62
(Charles Hills) *prom: chsd wnr after 3f tl 2f out: wknd over 1f out* **5/1**[3]

0 6 1 ¾ **Rathealy (IRE)**[17] 5718 2-9-5 SebSanders 8 58+
(Alan Bailey) *stdd s: hld up in rr: rdn over 2f out: n.d* **100/1**

7 *shd* **Filament Of Gold (USA)** 2-9-5 KierenFallon 3 60+
(Mark Johnston) *chsd ldrs: rn green and sn pushed along: wknd over 1f out: eased whn btn* **12/1**

0 8 10 **Sir Percy Blakeney**[12] 5891 2-9-5 HayleyTurner 7 31
(Marcus Tregoning) *in tch tl wknd over 2f out* **33/1**

1m 25.38s (2.28) **Going Correction** +0.30s/f (Good) **8** Ran SP% **113.5**
Speed ratings (Par 95): **98,97,94,92,91 89,89,77**
toteswingers 1&2 £2.20, 1&3 £4.40, 2&3 £2.40 CSF £7.03 TOTE £2.10: £1.20, £1.40, £2.00; EX 7.60 Trifecta £27.50 Pool: £3007.78 - 81.47 winning units..
Owner J N Reus & Mrs Anna Doyle **Bred** Churchtown House Stud & Liam Butler **Trained** East Everleigh, Wilts
FOCUS
Some powerful stables in opposition for this maiden which was run at a fair pace. Once again they headed stands side. The winner had the run of things and this is routine form.

6257 32RED CASINO H'CAP 1m 3f 196y
3:30 (3:30) (Class 6) (0-60,57) 3-Y-O £1,940 (£577; £288; £144) Stalls High

Form RPR

2624 1 **Uganda Glory (USA)**[24] 5500 3-9-7 57 (v[1]) PatCosgrave 2 68
(George Baker) *mde all: led field to stands' rail st: qcknd 4f out: pushed along and in control fnl 2f: comf* **9/4**[1]

0233 2 5 **Special Report (IRE)**[9] 5990 3-8-12 48 WilliamCarson 4 51
(Peter Hiatt) *hld up towards rr: rdn 4f out: styd on to chse wnr over 1f out: no imp* **9/2**[2]

4363 3 6 **Tornado Battle**[11] 5935 3-9-1 51 (p) CathyGannon 1 45
(Phil McEntee) *t.k.h: prom: chsd wnr 1/2-way: rdn 4f out: wknd over 1f out* **5/1**[3]

3660 4 ¾ **Bell'Arte (IRE)**[23] 5528 3-9-2 52 FergusSweeney 7 45
(Laura Mongan) *t.k.h in rr: rdn over 3f out: sme hdwy over 1f out: unable to chal* **8/1**

0000 5 3 ½ **Terpsichore**[11] 5935 3-8-9 45 RenatoSouza 3 33
(Sylvester Kirk) *in tch: outpcd and dropped to last 4f out: n.d after* **33/1**

0-25 6 *hd* **Orla's Rainbow (IRE)**[19] 5630 3-8-11 47 (b) SamHitchcott 5 34
(Gary Moore) *chsd ldrs: rdn 1/2-way: wknd 2f out* **6/1**

-530 7 45 **Frederick Alfred**[39] 4931 3-8-13 49 (b[1]) KierenFallon 6
(Mark H Tompkins) *chsd ldrs: rdn and lost pl 5f out: wl bhd and eased fnl 2f* **5/1**[3]

2m 36.41s (3.71) **Going Correction** +0.30s/f (Good) **7** Ran SP% **110.6**
Speed ratings (Par 99): **99,95,91,91,88 88,58**
toteswingers 1&2 £2.30, 1&3 £2.30, 2&3 £3.50 CSF £11.62 CT £41.58 TOTE £2.50: £1.60, £2.70; EX 9.40 Trifecta £32.60 Pool: £2101.93 - 48.32 winning units..
Owner George Baker & Partners **Bred** Walmac Farm Llc **Trained** Manton, Wilts
FOCUS
This was a weak affair, run at a steady pace. The winner recorded a personal-best but the form is weak.

6258 £32 FREE AT 32RED.COM H'CAP 1m 1f 209y
4:00 (4:00) (Class 5) (0-75,75) 3-Y-O+ £2,587 (£770; £384; £192) Stalls High

Form RPR

1060 1 **Hunting Rights (USA)**[25] 5440 3-9-5 75 KierenFallon 3 86
(Mark Johnston) *disp ld: led 6f out: led field to stands' rail st: rdn and styd on wl fnl 2f: clr fnl f* **7/1**

0534 2 4 ½ **Brown Pete (IRE)**[7] 6037 5-8-7 63 OisinMurphy(7) 7 65
(Violet M Jordan) *prom: chsd wnr over 3f out: hrd rdn and one pce appr fnl f* **9/1**

2221 3 2 ½ **Mizyen (IRE)**[7] 6037 3-9-4 74 6ex MartinHarley 5 72
(James Tate) *disp ld 4f: chsd wnr after tl over 3f out: btn 2f out* **9/4**[1]

-432 4 *nse* **Red Shuttle**[26] 5403 6-9-11 74 AdamKirby 4 72
(Andi Brown) *bhd: rdn and sme hdwy 2f out: nt rch ldrs* **5/1**[3]

6130 5 24 **Arlecchino (IRE)**[14] 5847 3-9-2 72 (b) RichardHughes 1 58
(Ed McMahon) *nvr nr ldrs: eased whn no ch over 1f out* **3/1**[2]

512 6 31 **Jewelled**[10] 5948 7-9-12 75 (v) SebSanders 6
(Lady Herries) *bhd: wnt mod 4th 6f out: wknd 4f out: bhd and eased over 2f out* **11/2**

2m 8.28s (4.68) **Going Correction** +0.425s/f (Yiel)
WFA 3 from 4yo+ 7lb **6** Ran SP% **110.3**
Speed ratings (Par 103): **98,94,92,92,73 48**
toteswingers 1&2 £8.40, 1&3 £3.40, 2&3 £4.10 CSF £60.77 TOTE £7.80: £3.40, £4.60; EX 76.40 Trifecta £393.20 Pool: £2289.05 - 4.36 winning units..
Owner Sheikh Hamdan Bin Mohammed Al Maktoum **Bred** Darley **Trained** Middleham Moor, N Yorks
FOCUS
It began to rain heavily before the fourth race. The pace was honest for this tight handicap. It paid to race handily and the runner-up is rated to his recent best for now.

6259 32REDPOKER.COM H'CAP 6f 209y
4:30 (4:31) (Class 5) (0-75,74) 3-Y-O+ £2,587 (£770; £384; £192) Stalls Low

Form RPR

6U01 1 **Kamchatka**[20] 5607 3-9-4 72 (bt) LiamKeniry 3 83
(Philip Hide) *led after 1f and set gd pce: led field to stands' rail st: hrd rdn over 1f out: clr fnl f* **3/1**[2]

0026 2 3 ¾ **Charitable Act (FR)**[26] 5398 4-9-10 74 GeorgeBaker 8 76
(Gary Moore) *chsd clr ldrs: hrd rdn 3f out: styd on to take 2nd ins fnl f: no ch w wnr* **15/8**[1]

4516 3 3 ¾ **Fairy Wing (IRE)**[12] 5899 6-8-11 68 (b) OisinMurphy(7) 4 60
(Violet M Jordan) *led 1f: chsd wnr after tl wknd ins fnl f* **11/2**

4040 4 4 **Perfect Pastime**[26] 5398 5-9-1 65 (p) PatCosgrave 6 47
(Jim Boyle) *outpcd in rr: mod hdwy 2f out: no imp* **9/2**[3]

6204 5 2 ½ **Rough Rock (IRE)**[15] 5798 8-8-11 61 HayleyTurner 2 36
(Chris Dwyer) *modest 4th most of way: wknd over 1f out* **7/1**

00-0 6 17 **Red Bay**[33] 5154 4-8-12 62 LukeMorris 1
(Jane Chapple-Hyam) *chsd ldrs 2f: bhd and rdn 4f out* **20/1**

1m 26.29s (3.19) **Going Correction** +0.425s/f (Yiel)
WFA 3 from 4yo+ 4lb **6** Ran SP% **110.6**
Speed ratings (Par 103): **98,93,89,84,82 62**
toteswingers 1&2 £2.00, 1&3 £3.40, 2&3 £2.90 CSF £8.77 CT £25.61 TOTE £3.40: £1.60, £1.50; EX 8.00 Trifecta £26.30 Pool: £2598.31 - 73.83 winning units..
Owner S P C Woods **Bred** Whitsbury Manor Stud **Trained** Findon, W Sussex

FOCUS
Four withdrawals took some off the interest from this contest. The pace was strong in the testing ground, with once again the winner making all. The winner is rated as recording a personal-best.

6260 32RED.COM H'CAP — 7f 214y
5:00 (5:01) (Class 6) (0-60,59) 3-Y-O — £1,940 (£577; £288; £144) Stalls Low

Form — RPR
3364 1 **Handsome Stranger (IRE)**[10] 5961 3-8-13 56..........(b[1]) RobertTart(5) 6 66
(Alan Bailey) *prom: rdn 4f out: led 1f out: sn clr: comf* 6/1[2]
5123 2 5 **Pour La Victoire (IRE)**[14] 5816 3-9-2 54.................... RichardHughes 4 53
(Tony Carroll) *mainly 2nd: chsd wnr fnl f: no imp* 9/4[1]
6035 3 3/4 **Thomasina**[20] 5604 3-8-8 46.. CathyGannon 1 43
(Denis Coakley) *chsd ldrs: led 3f out tl 1f out: one pce* 10/1
5566 4 3 **Haatefina**[40] 4885 3-9-7 59.. DavidProbert 5 49
(Mark Usher) *sn pushed along towards rr: sme hdwy over 2f out: no imp over 1f out* 7/1[3]
0052 5 1 **Lambert Pen (USA)**[4] 6146 3-9-0 52.............................. MartinHarley 9 40
(Mick Channon) *bhd: rdn 4f out: mod effrt 2f out: nt trble ldrs* 9/4[1]
0566 6 2 **Elle Rebelle**[11] 5923 3-8-11 49.. LiamKeniry 8 32
(Mark Brisbourne) *hld up towards rr: rdn over 2f out: n.d* 9/1
-660 7 3 1/2 **Lucilla**[11] 5923 3-9-2 54.. AdamBeschizza 3 29
(Stuart Williams) *sn pushed along in 5th: wknd 3f out: sn bhd* 12/1
56 8 42 **Culture Trip**[5] 6102 3-8-7 45..................................(b[1]) SamHitchcott 2
(Gary Moore) *sn led: hdd & wknd 3f out: bhd whn eased over 1f out* 25/1
1m 39.61s (3.61) **Going Correction** +0.425s/f (Yiel) **8** Ran SP% **119.0**
Speed ratings (Par 99): **98,93,92,89,88 86,82,40**
toteswingers 1&2 £3.40, 1&3 £7.40, 2&3 £3.20 CSF £20.82 CT £138.04 TOTE £6.00: £1.80, £1.10, £2.80; EX 21.10 Trifecta £144.90 Pool: £3069.46 - 15.88 winning units..
Owner John Stocker **Bred** Gerrardstown House Stud **Trained** Newmarket, Suffolk

FOCUS
A weak contest run at a sound pace. The winner was on a good mark and the race could be rated higher.

6261 THERMOLAST ROOFING LTD APPRENTICE H'CAP — 7f 214y
5:30 (5:30) (Class 6) (0-60,60) 4-Y-O+ — £1,940 (£577; £288; £144) Stalls Low

Form — RPR
3603 1 **Who's That Chick (IRE)**[7] 6038 4-8-9 51.................. DanielCremin(3) 6 61
(Ralph Smith) *chsd ldr: led 2f out: drvn to hold on fnl f* 5/1[2]
0043 2 hd **Ela Goog La Mou**[15] 5803 4-8-6 48 oh1 ow2............ GeorgeBuckell(3) 11 58
(Peter Charalambous) *led at gd pce tl 2f out: rallied wl fnl f* 12/1
0001 3 3 1/2 **Mcconnell (USA)**[10] 5961 8-8-11 50.............................(b) NoraLooby 2 51
(Violet M Jordan) *chsd ldrs: wnt 3rd 2f out: styd on same pce* 20/1
0450 4 3 1/2 **Katmai River (IRE)**[32] 5177 6-8-7 46........................(v) DanielMuscutt 9 39
(Mark Usher) *in tch: effrt over 2f out: no imp* 11/2[3]
0341 5 nk **Cape Crossing**[26] 5387 4-8-13 52.................................(t) OisinMurphy 7 45
(Andrew Balding) *prom tl outpcd fnl 2f* 9/4[1]
6400 6 1 3/4 **Saint Irene**[10] 5948 4-9-4 57.. PatMillman 4 46
(Michael Blanshard) *hld up towards rr: nvr rchd ldrs* 5/1[2]
4452 7 1/2 **Fairy Mist (IRE)**[8] 6019 6-8-7 46 oh1............................ RyanWhile 1 34
(John Bridger) *chsd ldrs: hmpd on rail and lost pl over 4f out: no hdwy fnl 3f* 14/1
6163 8 8 **Lightning Spirit**[32] 5170 5-8-10 56..............................(p) JayneFarwell(7) 3 25
(Gary Moore) *hld up in rr: nvr trbld ldrs* 10/1
0-00 9 3/4 **Percythepinto (IRE)**[20] 5622 4-9-5 58............................(t) IanBurns 12 25
(George Baker) *a towards rr* 16/1
0-00 10 10 **Princess Gail**[26] 5387 5-8-7 46 oh1...............................(t) EoinWalsh 5
(Mark Brisbourne) *s.i.s: a bhd* 25/1
050 11 26 **Cadeaux Royale**[19] 5645 5-8-7 46 oh1.........................(t) JoshBaudains 8
(Dominic Ffrench Davis) *mid-div on outer: wknd over 4f out: bhd and eased fnl 2f* 33/1
1m 39.2s (3.20) **Going Correction** +0.425s/f (Yiel) **11** Ran SP% **120.4**
Speed ratings (Par 101): **101,100,97,93,93 91,91,83,82,72 46**
toteswingers 1&2 £9.80, 1&3 £14.50, 2&3 £35.20 CSF £63.41 CT £1143.48 TOTE £5.50: £1.70, £3.90, £4.40; EX 66.90 Trifecta £2031.70 Part won. Pool: £2709.06 - 0.58 winning units..
Owner Piper, Harris, Churchill, Hirschfeld **Bred** T Hirschfeld **Trained** Epsom, Surrey

FOCUS
Plenty of pace on for this handicap, confined to apprentice riders. The field raced up the centre with once again the prominent runners dominating. The winner built on her latest mark.
T/Jkpt: £7,271.10 to a £1 stake. Pool: £128012.66 - 12.50 winning tickets T/Plt: £49.80 to a £1 stake. Pool: £98865.30 - 1447.93 winning tickets T/Qpdt: £43.50 to a £1 stake. Pool: £5859.63 - 99.60 winning tickets LM

5983 BEVERLEY (R-H)
Tuesday, September 10

OFFICIAL GOING: Good to firm (8.6)
Wind: Fresh half against Weather: Heavy cloud and showers

6271 RACE HORSE TRADER XTRA MAIDEN AUCTION STKS — 7f 100y
4:35 (4:36) (Class 5) 2-Y-O — £2,911 (£866; £432; £216) Stalls Low

Form — RPR
623 1 **Eddiemaurice (IRE)**[11] 5969 2-8-11 72..................... PatrickMathers 10 72
(Richard Guest) *towards rr: hdwy on wd outside 2f out: rdn and edgd rt jst over 1f out: sn chal: styd on to ld ins fnl f* 13/8[1]
0320 2 nk **El Beau (IRE)**[24] 5508 2-8-13 71.............................. MichaelO'Connell 6 73
(John Quinn) *trckd ldrs: effrt 2f out: swtchd lft and rdn over 1f out: sn chal and ev ch ins fnl f: drvn and kpt on towards fin* 5/1[3]
00 3 3/4 **Miss Sophisticated**[29] 5338 2-8-8 0.......................... GrahamGibbons 9 67
(David Barron) *trckd ldrs: cl up after 3f: rdn to ld over 1f out: drvn ent fnl f: sn hdd: kpt on u.p* 25/1
4230 4 2 **Island Kingdom (IRE)**[15] 5848 2-8-9 69.................... AndreaAtzeni 2 63
(J S Moore) *trckd ldrs: n.m.r and sltly hmpd after 2 1/2f: hdwy over 2f out: effrt to chse ldrs whn hmpd over 1f out: kpt on fnl f: nrst fin* 8/1
23 5 1/2 **George The First**[66] 4044 2-8-13 0.............................. PaulMulrennan 4 66
(Kevin Ryan) *led: rdn along over 2f out: drvn and hdd over 1f out: grad wknd* 3/1[2]
06 6 1 1/4 **Scottish Academy**[15] 5812 2-8-8 0.............................. JoeFanning 11 58
(Mark Johnston) *trckd ldrs: effrt over 2f out: rdn along wl over 1f out: sn one pce* 16/1
45 7 1 **Ainmire**[15] 5826 2-8-11 0.. DaleSwift 7 59
(John Quinn) *prom on inner: awkward and edgd rt after 2 1/2f: rdn along wl over 2f out: drvn over 1f out: sn wknd* 20/1
8 3 **Quest Of Colour (IRE)** 2-8-10 0.................................. TonyHamilton 8 50
(Richard Fahey) *dwlt: a towards rr* 10/1
9 11 **Scrafton** 2-8-8 0... MichaelJMMurphy(3) 1 26
(James Bethell) *s.i.s: a in rr* 25/1
00 10 12 **That Be Grand**[40] 4926 2-8-2 0 ow1.................................. BillyCray(3) 3
(Shaun Harris) *towards rr whn hmpd on inner after 1 1/2f: bhd after* 100/1
1m 35.43s (1.63) **Going Correction** 0.0s/f (Good) **10** Ran SP% **119.3**
Speed ratings (Par 95): **90,89,88,86,85 84,83,79,67,53**
Tote Swingers: 1&2 £3.20, 1&3 £16.50, 2&3 £22.00 CSF £9.92 TOTE £2.10: £1.30, £1.70, £7.30; EX 10.50 Trifecta £322.30 Pool: £1,184.82 - 2.75 winning units..
Owner Maze Rattan Limited **Bred** Declan Murphy **Trained** Wetherby, W Yorks

FOCUS
Despite there being rain around, the track had been watered and the ground was cutting up. The inside rail around the bottom bend was moved out to provide fresh ground, increasing all races over 7f plus by 19yds. The form is straightforward with the winner to his mark.

6272 RACEHORSETRADER.COM BEST PLACE TO SELL RACEHORSES MAIDEN STKS — 1m 1f 207y
5:05 (5:07) (Class 5) 3-Y-O+ — £2,911 (£866; £432; £216) Stalls Low

Form — RPR
2 1 **My History (IRE)**[8] 6036 3-9-5 0.................................. JoeFanning 2 76+
(Mark Johnston) *sn led and set str pce: pushed along over 2f out: jnd and rdn wl over 1f out: drvn ins fnl f: kpt on wl towards fin* 8/13[1]
3322 2 1 **Response**[35] 5110 3-9-5 75... GrahamGibbons 4 72
(William Haggas) *t.k.h early: trckd wnr: hdwy and cl up wl over 2f out: rdn to chal wl over 1f out: drvn and ev ch ent fnl f tl no ex last 75yds* 5/2[2]
05- 3 1 1/4 **Hurry Home Poppa (IRE)**[262] 8223 3-9-5 0.......................... DaleSwift 7 70
(John Mackie) *chsd ldrs: rdn along over 2f out: kpt on wl u.p fnl f* 33/1
4240 4 1 1/2 **Tanawar (IRE)**[11] 5975 3-9-5 66.................................. PaulMulrennan 6 67
(Tim Etherington) *chsd ldng pair: rdn wl over 1f out: drvn and one pce appr fnl f* 20/1
4 5 4 1/2 **Razera (IRE)**[25] 5469 3-9-5 0.................................. MichaelO'Connell 10 58
(John Quinn) *dwlt and towards rr: t.k.h early: hdwy 1/2-way: chsd ldrs wl over 2f out: sn rdn: drvn and one pce fr wl over 1f out* 16/1
6 1 1/4 **El Cordobes (IRE)** 3-9-5 0.. TonyHamilton 5 56
(Richard Fahey) *green and sn pushed along in rr: sme hdwy over 3f out: n.d* 6/1[3]
7 23 **Lucky North** 3-9-5 0.. DavidAllan 3 12
(Mel Brittain) *in tch: rdn along over 4f out: sn outpcd and bhd fnl 3f* 50/1
8 73 **Bad Medicine** 3-8-9 0.. DanielMuscutt(5) 1
(Colin Teague) *dwlt: a in rr: t.o fnl 3f* 66/1
2m 7.74s (0.74) **Going Correction** 0.0s/f (Good)
WFA 3 from 4yo 7lb **8** Ran SP% **121.8**
Speed ratings (Par 103): **97,96,95,94,90 89,71,12**
Tote Swingers: 1&2 £1.60, 1&3 £7.60, 2&3 £9.80 CSF £2.56 TOTE £1.50: £1.10, £1.10, £7.80; EX 3.70 Trifecta £28.50 Pool: £1,761.47 - 46.30 winning units..
Owner Sheikh Hamdan Bin Mohammed Al Maktoum **Bred** Haras De La Perelle **Trained** Middleham Moor, N Yorks

FOCUS
A weak maiden dominated by the first two. The third and those behind help to set the level.

6273 BET & WATCH WITH RACINGUK'S APP H'CAP — 5f
5:40 (5:40) (Class 3) (0-95,89) 3-Y-O+ — £7,762 (£2,310; £1,154; £577) Stalls Low

Form — RPR
6413 1 **Hadaj**[4] 6162 4-8-7 82.. KevinStott(7) 5 90
(Ruth Carr) *led 1f: cl up tl led again over 1f out: sn rdn and hung lft ent fnl f: kpt on* 3/1[2]
0266 2 3/4 **Singeur (IRE)**[24] 5544 6-9-7 89.................................. PaulMulrennan 2 94
(Robin Bastiman) *hld up in rr: effrt and nt clr run on inner wl over 1f out: rdn and qcknd through ent fnl f: kpt on wl towards fin* 7/1
3111 3 3/4 **Bondi Beach Boy**[22] 5579 4-9-0 82.............................. PJMcDonald 4 84
(James Turner) *t.k.h: hld up: effrt and swtchd lft wl over 1f out: rdn to chse ldrs ent fnl f: keeping on whn sltly hmpd and swtchd rt last 100yds: one pce after* 4/1[3]
0000 4 nk **Mister Manannan (IRE)**[36] 5056 6-9-0 82........................ KierenFallon 3 83
(David Nicholls) *hld up in rr: swtchd lft to wd outside and rdn over 1f out: styd on fnl f: nrst fin* 8/1
1343 5 1 **Avon Breeze**[24] 5544 4-8-10 83.............................. GeorgeChaloner(5) 1 81
(Richard Whitaker) *trckd ldrs on inner: effrt and n.m.r over 1f out: sn rdn and edgd lft ent fnl f: sn one pce* 2/1[1]
6103 6 3/4 **Head Space (IRE)**[14] 5851 5-9-7 89............................(p) DaleSwift 8 84
(Ruth Carr) *t.k.h: cl up: rdn along over 1f out: sn wknd* 14/1
1000 7 nk **Lucky Numbers (IRE)**[35] 5108 7-9-6 88......................... DavidNolan 6 82
(David O'Meara) *t.k.h: chsd ldrs: rdn along over 1f out: sn wknd* 25/1
0105 8 1 1/4 **Lost In Paris (IRE)**[22] 5639 7-8-11 79............................(p) DavidAllan 7 68
(Tim Easterby) *prom: led after 1f: rdn along and hdd over 1f out: sn wknd* 25/1
1m 2.61s (-0.89) **Going Correction** 0.0s/f (Good) **8** Ran SP% **116.3**
Speed ratings (Par 107): **107,105,104,104,102 101,100,98**
Tote Swingers: 1&2 £4.50, 1&3 £3.70, 2&3 £7.20 CSF £24.76 CT £82.92 TOTE £5.80: £1.90, £2.40, £1.40; EX 28.20 Trifecta £172.80 Pool: £2,166.28 - 9.40 winning units..
Owner Sprint Thoroughbred Racing **Bred** Rabbah Bloodstock Limited **Trained** Huby, N Yorks

FOCUS
A decent enough sprint handicap and straightforward form, with the second to his best mark in the last year.

6274 RACING UK PROFITS ALL RETURNED TO RACING H'CAP — 7f 100y
6:10 (6:10) (Class 4) (0-85,85) 3-Y-O+ — £4,851 (£1,443; £721; £360) Stalls Low

Form — RPR
1113 1 **Kohlaan (IRE)**[59] 4306 3-9-1 80.................................. AndreaAtzeni 1 92
(Roger Varian) *sn led and clr at sound pce: pushed along wl over 1f out: rdn ent fnl f: styd on strly* 7/4[1]
5141 2 2 3/4 **Lunar Deity**[15] 5825 4-9-7 82.. KierenFallon 5 89
(Eve Johnson Houghton) *hld up in tch: hdwy 2f out: rdn over 1f out: chsd wnr jst ins fnl f: sn drvn and no imp* 9/2[2]
6504 3 2 1/4 **Dubai Dynamo**[15] 5838 8-9-10 85.................................. PJMcDonald 3 87
(Ruth Carr) *hld up in rr: hdwy wl over 1f out: rdn and kpt on fnl f: nrst fin* 9/2[2]
0011 4 1 1/2 **Skytrain**[13] 5886 3-9-3 82.. JoeFanning 8 78
(Mark Johnston) *trckd ldrs: hdwy over 2f out: rdn to chse wnr over 1f out: drvn and wknd appr fnl f* 9/2[2]
5002 5 3 **Shadowtime**[10] 5987 8-9-1 76.................................. MichaelO'Connell 6 67
(Tracy Waggott) *t.k.h: prom: chsd wnr 1/2-way: rdn over 2f out: drvn and wknd over 1f out* 14/1[3]
0426 6 nk **Rich Forever (IRE)**[46] 4725 3-8-3 71 oh1.......(v[1]) MichaelJMMurphy(3) 4 59
(James Bethell) *hld up in rr: effrt over 2f out: sn rdn and nvr a factor* 14/1[3]
1005 7 1 1/2 **Available (IRE)**[7] 6072 4-9-3 78.............................(tp) GrahamGibbons 7 64
(John Mackie) *chsd ldrs: rdn along 2f out: sn wknd* 20/1

0003 **8** 2 3/4 **Gouray Girl (IRE)**[16] 5783 6-9-2 77 .... DaleSwift 2 57
(Brian Ellison) *dwlt and towards rr: sme hdwy 3f out: swtchd lft and rdn over 2f out: n.d* **16/1**

1m 32.73s (-1.07) **Going Correction** 0.0s/f (Good)
WFA 3 from 4yo+ 4lb **8** Ran SP% **114.9**
Speed ratings (Par 105): **106,102,100,98,95 94,93,89**
Tote Swingers: 1&2 £2.50, 1&3 £2.70, 2&3 £4.30 CSF £9.77 CT £30.06 TOTE £2.60: £1.30, £1.30, £1.90; EX 8.40 Trifecta £41.90 Pool: £1,739.79 - 31.12 winning units..
Owner Sheikh Ahmed Al Maktoum **Bred** Old Carhue Stud **Trained** Newmarket, Suffolk

FOCUS
A fair handicap but nothing could live with the winner. He can do better again with the second rated a slight improver.

6275 RACEHORSETRADER.COM TO BUY FUTURE WINNERS NURSERY H'CAP 1m 100y
6:40 (6:40) (Class 4) (0-75,75) 2-Y-O **£2,911** (£866; £432; £216) **Stalls** Low

Form RPR
5003 **1** *shd* **Fair Flutter (IRE)**[7] 6085 2-8-3 **57** .... PatrickMathers 5 61
(Richard Fahey) *towards rr: hdwy on outer 3f out: rdn to chse ldrs wl over 1f out: drvn and styd on wl fnl f: cl up and ev ch whn hmpd nr fin: fin 2nd, shd: awrdd r* **14/1**
3123 **2** **Ocean Storm (IRE)**[11] 5951 2-9-7 **75** .... PaulMulrennan 6 79
(James Tate) *sn led: and clr: rdn along wl over 1f out: drvn and edgd lft and rt ins fnl f: hung sharply lft nr fin: jst hld on: fin 1st: disq: plcd 2nd* **5/1**[3]
623 **3** *7* **Blue Atlantic (USA)**[40] 4906 2-9-5 **73** .... JoeFanning 4 61
(Mark Johnston) *chsd ldrs: rdn along wl over 2f out: styd on fnl f: tk 3rd nr line* **11/2**
3321 **4** *1/2* **Lucky Visione**[42] 4861 2-9-1 **74** .... DanielMuscutt[(5)] 7 61
(Gay Kelleway) *chsd ldrs: rdn along and outpcd 1/2-way: drvn over 2f out: styd on appr fnl f: n.d* **14/1**
0363 **5** *hd* **Baltic Fire (IRE)**[26] 5424 2-8-0 **59** ....(b) JoeyHaynes[(5)] 2 46
(K R Burke) *chsd ldr: rdn along over 2f out: drvn over 1f out: wknd fnl f* **6/1**
2046 **6** *1 1/4* **Ahoy There (IRE)**[24] 5543 2-8-11 **65** .... AndrewElliott 3 49
(Tom Tate) *chsd ldng pair: rdn along 1/2-way: drvn 2f out and grad wknd* **7/1**
003 **7** *3/4* **Blue Talisman (IRE)**[16] 5785 2-8-5 **59** .... AndreaAtzeni 1 41
(Tim Easterby) *in tch: rdn along 3f out: n.d* **9/2**[2]
065 **8** *15* **Sirpertan**[40] 4926 2-7-11 **54** oh4 .... JulieBurke[(3)] 9
(Tim Walford) *a bhd* **16/1**
440 **9** *20* **Starlit Cantata**[18] 5716 2-8-13 **67** .... KierenFallon 8
(Eve Johnson Houghton) *dwlt: towards rr whn hung lft after 3f: sn bhd* **7/2**[1]

1m 48.37s (0.77) **Going Correction** 0.0s/f (Good) **9** Ran SP% **118.5**
Speed ratings (Par 97): **95,96,88,88,88 86,86,71,51**
Tote Swingers: 1&2 £20.90, 1&3 £26.50, 2&3 £7.20 CSF £73.45 CT £403.02 TOTE £18.80: £4.60, £1.40, £2.00; EX 103.20 Trifecta £256.50 Pool: £1,746.18 - 5.10 winning units..
Owner Mr And Mrs J D Cotton **Bred** Thomas G Cooke **Trained** Musley Bank, N Yorks
■ Stewards' Enquiry : Paul Mulrennan one-day ban: careless riding (Sep 24)

FOCUS
The stewards had a straightforward decision to reverse the placings. The form has a sound feel with the first two clear.

6276 DOWNLOAD THE FREE RACING UK APP H'CAP 1m 100y
7:10 (7:10) (Class 6) (0-65,64) 3-Y-O+ **£1,940** (£577; £288; £144) **Stalls** Low

Form RPR
0622 **1** **Moral Issue**[18] 5713 5-9-4 **58** .... RobertWinston 6 73
(Alan Swinbank) *hld up towards rr: smooth hdwy 3f out: cl up on bit 2f out: shkn up to ld over 1f out: clr fnl f: readily* **5/2**[1]
0021 **2** *6* **Violent Velocity (IRE)**[20] 5637 10-9-3 **64** .... JoeDoyle[(7)] 5 66
(John Quinn) *in tch: hdwy on inner 2f out and sn cl up: rdn and ev ch over 1f out: drvn and one kpt fnl f: no ch w wnr* **9/1**
3013 **3** *nk* **Silly Billy (IRE)**[13] 5876 5-8-11 **51** .... DaleSwift 15 52
(Brian Ellison) *hld up towards rr: swtchd wd and hdwy wl over 2f out: rdn to chse ldrs over 1f out: kpt on fnl f: nrst fin* **5/1**[2]
0445 **4** *3 1/4* **Icy Blue**[16] 5783 5-8-7 **52** ....(p) GeorgeChaloner[(5)] 2 46+
(Richard Whitaker) *chsd ldrs: hdwy 3f out: led over 2f out: sn jnd and rdn: drvn and hdd over 1f out: wknd ent fnl f* **7/1**[3]
1540 **5** *2 1/4* **Snap Music (USA)**[20] 5642 3-9-2 **61** .... JoeFanning 12 49
(Mark Johnston) *dwlt and towards rr: wd st and sn rdn along: plugged on fnl 2f: n.d* **14/1**
0546 **6** *2 3/4* **The Blue Banana (IRE)**[41] 4893 4-8-10 **50** ....(b) PaulMulrennan 10 33
(Edwin Tuer) *chsd ldrs: effrt on wd outside 3f out: rdn over 2f out: grad wknd* **9/1**
0516 **7** *1* **Nonaynever**[14] 5869 5-8-11 **51** ....(b) JamesSullivan 13 32
(Ruth Carr) *in rr tl styd on fnl 2f: nvr a factor* **20/1**
3440 **8** *1/2* **Khelac**[11] 5953 3-9-3 **62** ....(b) TomEaves 11 41
(Philip Hide) *chsd ldrs: hdwy 3f out: rdn over 2f out: wknd over 1f out* **16/1**
3303 **9** *1/2* **Cabal**[24] 5521 6-8-9 **56** ....(b) GaryMahon[(7)] 9 35
(Andrew Crook) *dwlt: a towards rr* **16/1**
-656 **10** *2* **Rosy Ryan (IRE)**[18] 5715 3-8-2 **50** oh5 .... JulieBurke[(3)] 14 23
(Tina Jackson) *a in rr* **66/1**
-030 **11** *1 1/2* **Auto Mac**[29] 5341 5-9-4 **58** ....(b) AndrewElliott 3 29
(Neville Bycroft) *chsd ldrs on inner: rdn along 3f out: sn wknd* **16/1**
0000 **12** *3 1/4* **Thrust Control (IRE)**[29] 5341 6-8-10 **50** oh1 ....(p) GrahamGibbons 4 14
(Tracy Waggott) *led: rdn along 3f out: sn hdd & wknd* **20/1**
6202 **13** *2 1/4* **Arabian Flight**[13] 5903 4-8-12 **52** .... AndrewMullen 8 11
(Michael Appleby) *prom: rdn along wl over 2f out: sn wknd* **12/1**
6500 **14** *1 1/2* **Eium Mac**[15] 5840 4-8-13 **53** .... DuranFentiman 1 8
(Neville Bycroft) *a towards rr* **33/1**
4340 **15** *2 1/2* **Duchess Of Dreams**[26] 5432 3-8-0 **50** oh5 .... JoeyHaynes[(5)] 7
(Richard Guest) *cl up on outer: rdn along over 3f out: sn wknd* **33/1**

1m 47.0s (-0.60) **Going Correction** 0.0s/f (Good)
WFA 3 from 4yo+ 5lb **15** Ran SP% **126.6**
Speed ratings (Par 101): **103,97,96,93,91 88,87,86,86,84 82,79,77,75,73**
Tote Swingers: 1&2 £5.40, 1&3 £3.90, 2&3 £7.00 CSF £24.85 CT £115.57 TOTE £3.90: £1.50, £2.70, £2.20; EX 30.80 Trifecta £50.40 Pool: £1,082.86 - 16.10 winning units..
Owner Brian Valentine **Bred** Redmyre Bloodstock Ltd **Trained** Melsonby, N Yorks

FOCUS
A moderate contest in which the winner looks back in top form.
T/Plt: £11.20 to a £1 stake. Pool: £56,275.64 - 3,663.20 winning tickets. T/Qpdt: £5.80 to a £1 stake. Pool: £5,770.94 - 731.50 winning tickets. JR

6069 LEICESTER (R-H)
Tuesday, September 10

OFFICIAL GOING: Good to firm (good in places; 8.3)
Wind: Light half-against Weather: Overcast

6277 BRITISH STALLION STUDS APOLLO EBF MAIDEN STKS 7f 9y
2:20 (2:22) (Class 4) 2-Y-O **£4,851** (£1,443; £721; £360) **Stalls** Centre

Form RPR
1 **Maverick Wave (USA)** 2-9-5 0 .... WilliamBuick 9 81+
(John Gosden) *chsd ldrs: shkn up to ld over 1f out: r.o wl: edgd rt towards fin* **5/1**[3]
6 **2** *2 1/4* **Alisios (GR)**[33] 5199 2-9-5 0 .... KirstyMilczarek 7 75+
(Luca Cumani) *chsd ldrs: rdn over 1f out: r.o* **66/1**
5 **3** *nk* **Sherston**[10] 5995 2-9-5 0 .... FrannyNorton 12 74
(Mark Johnston) *led: rdn and hdd over 1f out: styd on same pce ins fnl f* **10/1**
4 *3* **Freemason** 2-9-5 0 .... RyanMoore 4 66+
(Sir Michael Stoute) *chsd ldrs: pushed along over 2f out: no ex ins fnl f* **7/2**[2]
0 **5** *nk* **Beach Bar (IRE)**[38] 4987 2-9-5 0 ....[1] JimCrowley 2 65
(William Knight) *prom: pushed along over 2f out: rdn over 1f out: styd on same pce fnl f* **8/1**
4 **6** *3/4* **Hoon (IRE)**[15] 5843 2-9-5 0 .... WilliamCarson 13 63
(Rae Guest) *chsd ldrs: rdn over 2f out: no ex fnl f* **14/1**
7 *2* **Weekendatbernies (IRE)** 2-9-5 0 .... LiamKeniry 6 58+
(Ed de Giles) *hld up: outpcd over 2f out: rdn over 1f out: styd on ins fnl f* **33/1**
8 *hd* **Syros (IRE)** 2-9-5 0 .... JamesDoyle 10 57
(Brian Meehan) *chsd ldrs: shkn up over 1f out: wknd fnl f* **33/1**
9 *2 3/4* **Despot (IRE)** 2-9-5 0 .... SteveDrowne 5 50
(Charles Hills) *s.i.s: sn pushed along in rr: sme hdwy over 1f out: wknd ins fnl f* **33/1**
42 **10** *1 1/2* **Raise Your Gaze**[25] 5472 2-9-5 0 .... AdamKirby 11 46
(Clive Cox) *chsd ldrs: shkn up over 2f out: wknd over 1f out* **9/4**[1]
06 **11** *shd* **Frederic Chopin**[25] 5490 2-9-5 0 .... HarryBentley 3 45
(Stuart Williams) *mid-div: pushed along over 2f out: wknd over 1f out* **100/1**
12 *1 3/4* **Intense Effort (IRE)** 2-9-5 0 .... MickaelBarzalona 8 41
(Charlie Appleby) *sn pushed along and a in rr* **16/1**
13 *hd* **Moxey** 2-9-5 0 .... DaneO'Neill 1 40
(Henry Candy) *s.i.s and wnt rt s: in rr: rdn over 2f out: sn wknd* **20/1**

1m 26.59s (0.39) **Going Correction** +0.125s/f (Good) **13** Ran SP% **118.5**
Speed ratings (Par 97): **102,99,99,95,95 94,92,91,88,87 86,84,84**
Tote Swingers: 1&2 £44.80, 1&3 £11.40, 2&3 £63.00 CSF £322.01 TOTE £6.80: £2.20, £12.60, £2.50; EX 555.20 Trifecta £1486.20 Part won. Pool: £1,981.68 - 0.56 winning units..
Owner HRH Princess Haya Of Jordan **Bred** Jim Plemmons & Darley **Trained** Newmarket, Suffolk

FOCUS
William Buick described the ground as "beautiful". Just a fair maiden and the form is fluid.

6278 NANPANTON H'CAP 7f 9y
2:50 (2:50) (Class 3) (0-95,91) 3-Y-O+ **£7,762** (£2,310; £1,154; £577) **Stalls** Centre

Form RPR
3000 **1** **Mezzotint (IRE)**[32] 5247 4-9-5 **91** .... TobyAtkinson[(5)] 1 104
(Marco Botti) *s.i.s: hld up: hdwy over 2f out: rdn to ld ins fnl f: r.o* **10/1**
1 **2** *1 1/2* **Talented Kid**[22] 5588 4-9-6 **87** .... FrannyNorton 8 96
(Mark Johnston) *w ldrs: racd keenly: led over 5f out: rdn over 1f out: hdd ins fnl f: styd on same pce* **6/4**[1]
1241 **3** *1/2* **Tatlisu (IRE)**[25] 5474 3-8-11 **82** .... RyanMoore 7 88
(Richard Fahey) *hld up: pushed along and hdwy 2f out: rdn and ev ch fr over 1f out tl no ex wl ins fnl f* **3/1**[2]
0000 **4** *8* **Webbow (IRE)**[17] 5738 11-9-4 **85** .... LiamKeniry 4 71
(Julie Camacho) *led: hdd over 5f out: chsd ldrs: rdn over 2f out: wknd over 1f out* **20/1**
3451 **5** *1/2* **Albaqaa**[21] 5613 8-8-13 **85** .... RobertTart[(5)] 3 70
(P J O'Gorman) *w ldrs: rdn and ev ch wl over 1f out: sn hung rt: wknd fnl f* **6/1**
0305 **6** *2 3/4* **Nassau Storm**[24] 5533 4-9-7 **88** .... JimCrowley 5 65
(William Knight) *chsd ldrs: rdn over 2f out: wknd over 1f out* **9/2**[3]
2000 **7** *1 1/4* **King Of Jazz (IRE)**[18] 5696 5-9-3 **84** ....(v) DougieCostello 2 58
(Peter Bowen) *hld up: rdn over 2f out: wknd wl over 1f out* **33/1**

1m 25.7s (-0.50) **Going Correction** +0.125s/f (Good)
WFA 3 from 4yo+ 4lb **7** Ran SP% **114.3**
Speed ratings (Par 107): **107,105,104,95,95 91,90**
Tote Swingers: 1&2 £5.10, 1&3 £4.50, 2&3 £1.70 CSF £25.53 CT £57.74 TOTE £6.80: £1.40, £3.30; EX 36.70 Trifecta £124.30 Pool: £2,338.33 - 14.10 winning units..
Owner GIB Bloodstock Ltd & J Allison **Bred** David Barry **Trained** Newmarket, Suffolk

FOCUS
Fair form with the winner basically to his best in a straightforward race.

6279 RANCLIFFE (S) STKS 7f 9y
3:20 (3:51) (Class 6) 2-Y-O **£1,940** (£577; £288; £144) **Stalls** Centre

Form RPR
4646 **1** **Autopilot**[14] 5850 2-8-12 68 ....(b) JimmyFortune 1 70+
(Brian Meehan) *hld up: hdwy over 2f out: shkn up to ld over 1f out; edgd rt ins fnl f: styd on wl: comf* **3/1**[1]
100 **2** *3 3/4* **Der Blaue Reiter (IRE)**[52] 4528 2-9-3 79 .... PatCosgrave 10 65
(George Baker) *chsd ldrs: led over 2f out: rdn and hdd over 1f out: styd on same pce ins fnl f* **7/2**[2]
0250 **3** *1 3/4* **Sukari Gold (IRE)**[8] 6047 2-8-7 62 ....(b[1]) JimmyQuinn 14 50
(Kevin Ryan) *a.p: rdn over 2f out: edgd rt over 1f out: styd on same pce fnl f* **14/1**
030 **4** *3 1/4* **Secret Ocean (IRE)**[5] 6131 2-8-5 0 ....(b) OisinMurphy[(7)] 7 46
(J S Moore) *led over 4f: rdn over 1f out: wknd ins fnl f* **14/1**
3326 **5** *3* **Sleepy Joe (IRE)**[22] 5591 2-8-10 62 .... DanielCremin[(7)] 6 43
(Mick Channon) *hld up: hdwy 1/2-way: rdn and wknd over 1f out* **6/1**
0 **6** *2 1/4* **Flower Arranger (IRE)**[74] 3753 2-8-4 0 .... DeclanBates[(3)] 2 27
(David Evans) *chsd ldrs: rdn 1/2-way: wknd wl over 1f out* **50/1**
6 *dht* **Kantara Castle (IRE)** 2-8-12 0 .... DaneO'Neill 9 32
(Richard Hannon) *s.s: outpcd: rdn over 2f out: nvr nrr* **5/1**[3]
0044 **8** *1 1/2* **Casper Lee (IRE)**[11] 5970 2-8-12 55 ....(v) J-PGuillambert 5 28
(Nigel Tinkler) *prom: rdn 1/2-way: wknd over 1f out* **20/1**

0440 **9** 4 ½ **Escarlata Rossa**[13] 5893 2-8-7 49....................(b[1]) JohnFahy 12 11
(J S Moore) *prom: racd alone stands' side fnl 4f: rdn over 2f out: sn wknd* **25/1**

0250 **10** 3 **Mr Childrey (IRE)**[5] 6131 2-8-12 49....................(b) LiamKeniry 11 8
(J S Moore) *reminder after s: sn prom: rdn and wknd over 2f out* **50/1**

00 **11** 4 **Lovely Lily**[29] 5351 2-8-1 0 ow1.................... RyanWhile(7) 15
(Bill Turner) *prom tl rdn and wknd over 2f out* **33/1**

60 **12** 7 **Lambeth Palace**[46] 4708 2-8-12 0.................... WilliamCarson 8
(Ronald Harris) *sn outpcd* **66/1**

13 3 ½ **Viking Hall (IRE)** 2-8-12 0.................... MartinLane 4
(Rae Guest) *sn outpcd* **6/1**

1m 27.29s (1.09) **Going Correction** +0.125s/f (Good) **13** Ran SP% **122.8**
Speed ratings (Par 93): **98,93,91,88,84 82,82,80,75,71 67,59,55**
Tote Swingers: 1&2 £3.50, 1&3 £6.00, 2&3 £8.50 CSF £12.91 TOTE £4.60: £1.40, £2.00, £4.40; EX 15.90 Trifecta £140.50 Pool: £2,689.49 - 14.35 winning units..Winner sold to Whitson Bloodstock for 7,200gns. Der Blaue Reite was bought by Claus Bjorling for 7,000.
Owner Bayardo **Bred** The Pocock Family **Trained** Manton, Wilts

FOCUS
The runners were spread across the track in this seller, which saw the two at the head of the market emerge. The winner could do better but not totally convincing form.

6280 MARKFIELD H'CAP — 1m 3f 183y
3:50 (4:20) (Class 4) (0-85,84) 3-Y-O+ — **£4,851** (£1,443; £721; £360) **Stalls** Low

Form RPR

4212 **1** **Nautilus**[18] 5719 3-9-2 **84**.................... WilliamBuick 4 99+
(John Gosden) *a.p: trckd ldr 1/2-way: shkn up to ld over 1f out: styd on wl* **6/5**[1]

-424 **2** 4 ½ **Hassle (IRE)**[33] 5190 4-9-5 **78**.................... AdamKirby 3 84
(Clive Cox) *hld up: hdwy over 4f out: rdn and edgd rt over 1f out: styd on same pce ins fnl f* **9/2**[2]

3131 **3** ½ **Discay**[7] 6086 4-9-3 **76** 6ex.................... RyanMoore 5 81
(Mark Johnston) *chsd ldrs: rdn over 3f out: styd on same pce fnl f* **9/2**[2]

2524 **4** 1 ¼ **Jack Who's He (IRE)**[15] 5825 4-9-2 **75**.................... MartinDwyer 1 78
(William Muir) *racd keenly: led 2f: trckd ldr to 1/2-way: remained handy: rdn over 2f out: no ex ins fnl f* **10/1**

2312 **5** 8 **Livia's Dream (IRE)**[26] 5436 4-9-9 **82**.................... TomMcLaughlin 6 72
(Ed Walker) *racd keenly: trckd ldr tl led 10f out: rdn over 2f out: hdd over 1f out: wknd ins fnl f* **6/1**[3]

/60- **6** 17 **Taaresh (IRE)**[22] 5944 8-9-2 **75**.................... JimmyQuinn 2 38
(Kevin Morgan) *hld up: wknd over 3f out* **20/1**

2m 31.51s (-2.39) **Going Correction** -0.025s/f (Good)
WFA 3 from 4yo+ 9lb **6** Ran SP% **110.0**
Speed ratings (Par 105): **106,103,102,101,96 85**
Tote Swingers 1&2 £2.30, 2&3 £3.00, 1&3 £1.10 CSF £6.55 TOTE £1.90: £1.10, £3.40; EX 6.40 Trifecta £22.60 Pool: £1,893.09 - 62.81 winning units..
Owner Abdulla Al Khalifa **Bred** Sheikh Abdulla Bin Isa Al Khalifa **Trained** Newmarket, Suffolk

FOCUS
A fair handicap for the level and it was won in good style by a progressive 3-y-o.

6281 BRITISH STALLION STUDS FILBERT EBF MAIDEN FILLIES' STKS — 1m 60y
4:20 (4:52) (Class 4) 2-Y-O — **£4,851** (£1,443; £721; £360) **Stalls** Low

Form RPR

1 **Surcingle (USA)** 2-9-0 0.................... RyanMoore 2 82+
(Sir Michael Stoute) *s.i.s: sn pushed along into mid-div: hdwy over 3f out: shkn up to ld over 1f out: r.o wl* **5/1**[3]

2 4 **Sweeping Up** 2-9-0 0.................... JimmyFortune 11 72+
(Hughie Morrison) *a.p: rdn to chse wnr over 1f out: styd on same pce ins fnl f* **20/1**

0 **3** hd **Ghinia (IRE)**[31] 5282 2-9-1 0 ow1.................... AdamKirby 7 73
(Pam Sly) *s.i.s: hdwy u.p over 1f out: styd on same pce ins fnl f* **33/1**

0 **4** 2 ¼ **Cosette (IRE)**[53] 4483 2-9-0 0.................... DaneO'Neill 6 67
(Henry Candy) *mid-div: hdwy over 2f out: sn rdn: styd on same pce fnl f* **25/1**

5 4 ½ **Dorset Cream** 2-9-0 0.................... JamesDoyle 9 56+
(Lady Cecil) *s.i.s and n.m.r s: hdwy over 2f out: rdn over 1f out: wknd ins fnl f* **7/2**[2]

6 nk **Chortle** 2-9-0 0.................... MickaelBarzalona 10 55
(Charlie Appleby) *sn pushed along in rr: hdwy u.p over 1f out: wknd ins fnl f* **6/1**

7 1 ¾ **Mrs Pat** 2-9-0 0.................... SeanLevey 3 51
(Richard Fahey) *mid-div: pushed along over 2f out: swtchd rt over 1f out: nvr on terms* **33/1**

43 **8** nse **My Painter (IRE)**[10] 5995 2-9-0 0.................... WilliamBuick 12 51
(Charles Hills) *trckd ldr tl hung lft 6f out: remained handy: wnt 2nd again over 2f out tl rdn and edgd rt over 1f out: wknd ins fnl f* **7/4**[1]

0 **9** ½ **La Faisan Blanche (USA)**[38] 5003 2-9-0 0..........(b[1]) KirstyMilczarek 4 50
(Luca Cumani) *racd keenly: prom: trckd ldr 6f out tl rdn over 2f out: wknd over 1f out* **50/1**

0 **10** 3 ¼ **Snow Conditions**[34] 5131 2-9-0 0.................... LiamKeniry 8 42
(Philip Hide) *hld up: effrt over 2f out: wknd over 1f out* **100/1**

6 **11** 18 **Heartily (IRE)**[24] 5516 2-9-0 0.................... AhmedAjtebi 5
(Charlie Appleby) *led: rdn: hdd & wknd over 1f out: eased* **16/1**

00 **12** hd **Satin Waters**[15] 5812 2-9-0 0.................... JohnFahy 1
(Eve Johnson Houghton) *prom: pushed along over 3f out: wknd over 2f out* **100/1**

1m 46.65s (1.55) **Going Correction** -0.025s/f (Good) **12** Ran SP% **113.9**
Speed ratings (Par 94): **91,87,86,84,80 79,78,77,77,74 56,56**
Tote Swingers: 1&2 £17.80, 1&3 £16.60, 2&3 £54.50 CSF £99.12 TOTE £6.10: £2.10, £4.80, £4.90; EX 115.40 Trifecta £893.20 Pool: £2,107.57 - 1.76 winning units..
Owner K Abdullah **Bred** Juddmonte Farms Inc **Trained** Newmarket, Suffolk

FOCUS
This looked a fair fillies' maiden and it should produce winners. They went off fast and it turned into a proper test at the distance. The winner looks sure to do better.

6282 PRESTWOLD CONDITIONS STKS — 5f 2y
4:50 (5:20) (Class 3) 3-Y-O+ — **£7,561** (£2,263; £1,131; £566; £282) **Stalls** Centre

Form RPR

-430 **1** **Noble Storm (USA)**[108] 2669 7-8-9 95.................... SeanLevey 2 104
(Ed McMahon) *mde all: rdn 1f out: r.o: unchal* **7/1**[3]

20-0 **2** 1 ¾ **Rocky Ground (IRE)**[24] 5538 3-8-8 97....................[1] JamieSpencer 1 98
(Roger Varian) *a.p: chsd wnr 2f out: shkn up over 1f out: no imp ins fnl f* **6/4**[1]

2040 **3** nk **Humidor (IRE)**[38] 4986 6-8-9 102....................(t) JamesDoyle 5 97
(George Baker) *sn outpcd: r.o u.p ins fnl f: nrst fin* **7/4**[2]

20 **4** shd **Bern Me Baby (USA)**[45] 4767 3-8-3 95.................... PaoloSirigu 3 91
(Marco Botti) *chsd wnr tl rdn 2f out: styd on* **12/1**

0000 **5** 9 **Monsieur Joe (IRE)**[91] 3187 6-9-0 103.................... JimCrowley 4 69
(Robert Cowell) *prom: rdn 1/2-way: wknd over 1f out* **7/1**[3]

59.26s (-0.74) **Going Correction** +0.125s/f (Good)
WFA 3 from 6yo+ 1lb **5** Ran SP% **109.1**
Speed ratings (Par 107): **110,107,106,106,92**
CSF £17.74 TOTE £10.40: £5.90, £1.10; EX 25.10 Trifecta £50.40 Pool: £2,076.99 - 30.87 winning units..
Owner Mrs R L Bedding **Bred** Brereton C Jones **Trained** Lichfield, Staffs

FOCUS
Not form to put much faith in, although it makes sense with the winner rated back to last year's peak level. There was no hanging around and little changed during the race.

6283 SWAN APPRENTICE H'CAP — 1m 1f 218y
5:20 (5:51) (Class 6) (0-65,65) 4-Y-O+ — **£1,940** (£577; £288; £144) **Stalls** Low

Form RPR

-024 **1** **Be My Rock**[17] 5758 4-9-7 **65**.................... OisinMurphy 7 75+
(Rae Guest) *hld up: pushed along over 3f out: hdwy over 2f out: rdn to ld ins fnl f: r.o wl* **6/4**[1]

2052 **2** 2 ¾ **Taro Tywod (IRE)**[10] 5980 4-9-7 **65**.................... EoinWalsh 3 69
(Mark Brisbourne) *trckd ldr: racd keenly: led over 2f out: rdn over 1f out: hdd and unable qck ins fnl f* **6/1**[2]

0555 **3** ½ **Having A Ball**[77] 3656 9-8-2 **51** oh3.................... CharlieBennett(5) 9 54
(Geoffrey Deacon) *hld up: hdwy 2f out: rdn and edgd lft ins fnl f: styd on same pce* **16/1**

2452 **4** 1 **Stag Hill (IRE)**[15] 5813 4-8-11 **60**....................(p) JackGarritty(5) 2 61
(Bernard Llewellyn) *s.i.s: hdwy over 8f out: rdn and ev ch over 1f out: styd on same pce ins fnl f* **8/1**[3]

0056 **5** 2 ¾ **Glan Lady (IRE)**[15] 5840 7-8-4 **51** oh6.................... LouisSteward(3) 5 47
(Michael Appleby) *hld up: pushed along over 2f out: swtchd rt and hdwy over 1f out: nt trble ldrs* **25/1**

4023 **6** 2 ½ **Vastly (USA)**[90] 3222 4-9-5 **63**.................... PatMillman 10 54
(Julia Feilden) *prom: pushed along over 3f out: wknd over 1f out* **8/1**[3]

0305 **7** ¾ **Transfer**[71] 3882 8-8-7 **51** oh2.................... IanBurns 1 40
(Richard Price) *trckd ldrs: rdn over 2f out: wknd over 1f out* **16/1**

0302 **8** 2 ½ **Rosselli (IRE)**[14] 5856 4-9-0 **63**....................(p) BTTreanor(5) 6 47
(K R Burke) *led over 7f: wknd over 1f out* **6/1**[2]

6010 **9** 1 **Thewinningmachine**[22] 5596 4-8-3 **54**.................... HarryBurns(7) 4 36
(Jo Hughes) *mid-div: hdwy over 2f out: rdn and wknd over 1f out* **10/1**

50-0 **10** 3 **Rock Band**[3] 6218 4-9-6 **64**.................... RyanWhile 8 40
(Emmet Michael Butterly, Ire) *hld up: rdn over 2f out: hung rt and wknd over 1f out* **20/1**

2m 10.3s (2.40) **Going Correction** -0.025s/f (Good) **10** Ran SP% **120.3**
Speed ratings (Par 101): **89,86,86,85,83 81,80,78,78,75**
Tote Swingers 1&2 £4.20, 2&3 £12.10, 1&3 £7.60 CSF £11.01 CT £108.88 TOTE £3.30: £1.20, £2.10, £3.50; EX 13.90 Trifecta £208.00 Pool: £2,032.35 - 7.32 winning units..
Owner Willis, Jennings & Carter **Bred** Arbib Bloodstock Partnership **Trained** Newmarket, Suffolk

FOCUS
A moderate handicap run at a decent pace. The second and third set a straightforward standard.
T/Plt: £174.60 to a £1 stake. Pool: £72,263.70 - 302.11 winning units. T/Qpdt: £17.80 to a £1 stake. Pool: £5,640.15 - 234.20 winning units. CR

5289 REDCAR (L-H)
Tuesday, September 10

OFFICIAL GOING: Soft (good to soft in places; 6.9)
Wind: strong 1/2 against Weather: overcast, showers, very windy

6284 WEATHERBYS HAMILTON INSURANCE NURSERY H'CAP (DIV I) — 7f
2:00 (2:05) (Class 5) (0-75,75) 2-Y-O — **£2,587** (£770; £384; £192) **Stalls** Centre

Form RPR

020 **1** **Shirocco Passion**[33] 5180 2-8-5 **59**.................... BarryMcHugh 6 76+
(Tony Coyle) *mid-div: hdwy over 3f out: led 2f out: edgd lft and drew clr fnl f* **11/2**[3]

6501 **2** 7 **Mount Cheiron (USA)**[25] 5467 2-8-9 **63**.................... PJMcDonald 2 59
(Dianne Sayer) *in rr: hdwy over 2f out: sn chsng ldrs: 2nd jst ins fnl f* **13/2**

0500 **3** ½ **Bertha Burnett (IRE)**[14] 5865 2-8-1 **55**.................... LukeMorris 9 50
(Brian Rothwell) *fly-jmpd s: sn chsng ldrs: 3rd jst ins fnl f: kpt on same pce* **28/1**

3642 **4** nk **Classy Lassy (IRE)**[11] 5970 2-9-2 **70**.................... DanielTudhope 1 64
(Brian Ellison) *swvd lft s: in rr: hdwy over 2f out: kpt on to take 4th ins fnl f* **5/1**[2]

3036 **5** 2 ¼ **It's All A Game**[7] 6085 2-7-13 **58**....................(e[1]) PhilipPrince(5) 3 46
(Richard Guest) *sn chsng ldrs far side: drvn and lost pl over 3f out: edgd rt and kpt on over 1f out* **12/1**

3316 **6** 1 ¼ **Yajamila**[14] 5858 2-9-7 **75**.................... GrahamLee 5 60
(James Tate) *chsd ldrs: wknd fnl f* **5/1**[2]

2665 **7** 2 ¼ **Bajan Rebel**[28] 5366 2-8-3 **57**.................... JamesSullivan 10 37
(Michael Easterby) *t.k.h: led: hdd 2f out: lost pl over 1f out* **10/1**

004 **8** shd **Bar Shy**[51] 4556 2-8-4 **58**.................... DuranFentiman 11 37
(Tim Easterby) *mid-div: drvn and outpcd over 3f out: kpt on fnl f* **16/1**

606 **9** 16 **Lady Dancer (IRE)**[13] 5883 2-7-11 **54** oh9.................... JulieBurke(3) 4
(George Moore) *w ldrs: drvn and lost pl over 3f out: bhd whn heavily eased ins fnl f: t.o* **50/1**

433 **10** 1 ¼ **Red Tide (IRE)**[27] 5379 2-9-0 **71**..........(p) WilliamTwiston-Davies(3) 7 7
(Alan McCabe) *chsd ldrs: wknd 2f out: heavily eased ins fnl f: t.o* **10/3**[1]

1m 29.41s (4.91) **Going Correction** +0.70s/f (Yiel) **10** Ran SP% **113.2**
Speed ratings (Par 95): **99,91,90,90,87 86,83,83,65,63**
Tote Swingers: 1&2 £8.30, 1&3 £23.80, 2&3 £30.80 CSF £39.83 CT £932.53 TOTE £5.50: £2.90, £1.90, £8.30; EX 38.90 Trifecta £1743.40 Pool: £2,341.74 - 1.00 winning units..
Owner P D Smith Holdings Ltd **Bred** P D Smith Holdings Ltd **Trained** Norton, N Yorks

FOCUS
The first leg of this open nursery was run 0.2sec faster than the second division. The winner impressed, with moderate, straightforward form in behind.

6285 WEATHERBYS HAMILTON INSURANCE NURSERY H'CAP (DIV II) — 7f
2:30 (2:31) (Class 5) (0-75,74) 2-Y-O — **£2,587** (£770; £384; £192) **Stalls** Centre

Form RPR

2540 **1** **Thornaby Nash**[20] 5656 2-9-3 **70**.................... DanielTudhope 5 77+
(David O'Meara) *t.k.h in mid-div: hdwy and swtchd rt over 1f out: led last 150yds: styd on strly* **9/2**[2]

6045 **2** 2 ¼ **Please Let Me Go**[38] 4990 2-8-4 **57**.................... LukeMorris 9 58+
(Julie Camacho) *in rr: drvn over 3f out: hdwy 2f out: styd on to take 2nd last 50yds* **20/1**

3663 **3** 1 ¾ **Another Royal**[18] 5703 2-8-4 **57**.................... DuranFentiman 3 54
(Tim Easterby) *chsd ldrs: styd on same pce fnl f* **6/1**

6345 **4** 3/4 **Hulcolt (IRE)**[11] 5945 2-9-1 **71** .... JasonHart(3) 4 66
(Garry Moss) *led: edgd lft over 1f out: hdd ins fnl f: no ex* **8/1**

035 **5** 3 **Lendal Bridge**[112] 2553 2-8-5 **58** .... JamesSullivan 10 46
(Tony Coyle) *s.i.s: swtchd lft after s: hdwy 3f out: fdd fnl f* **18/1**

065 **6** 1/2 **Mister Uno (IRE)**[27] 5379 2-7-10 **57** oh1 ow3 .... RowanScott(7) 8 42
(Ann Duffield) *in rr: edgd lft over 2f out: kpt on: nvr a factor* **25/1**

10 **7** nk **We'Ll Shake Hands (FR)**[14] 5858 2-9-2 **74** .... JoeyHaynes(5) 7 60+
(K R Burke) *hld up towards rr: hdwy to chse ldrs over 2f out: wknd over 1f out* **3/1**[1]

0030 **8** nk **Bowsers Bold**[38] 4988 2-9-0 **67** .... HayleyTurner 2 52
(Marcus Tregoning) *chsd ldrs: drvn over 2f out: lost pl over 1f out* **5/1**[3]

051 **9** 2 1/4 **Strictly Glitz (IRE)**[81] 3541 2-7-12 **58** .... JoeDoyle(7) 1 37
(John Quinn) *chsd ldrs: lost pl over 1f out* **12/1**

360 **10** 26 **Nevada Blue**[45] 4756 2-8-9 **62** .... BarryMcHugh 6 +
(Tony Coyle) *chsd ldrs: lost pl over 2f out: sn bhd: heavily eased ins fnl f: t.o: struck into* **12/1**

1m 29.61s (5.11) **Going Correction** +0.70s/f (Yiel) **10** Ran SP% **114.5**
Speed ratings (Par 95): **98,95,93,92,89 88,88,87,85,55**
Tote Swingers: 1&2 £16.00, 1&3 £6.90, 2&3 £20.80 CSF £87.56 CT £555.77 TOTE £4.30: £1.60, £6.60, £1.90; EX 112.80 Trifecta £458.80 Pool: £1,881.30 - 3.07 winning units..
Owner Dave Scott **Bred** Dave Scott **Trained** Nawton, N Yorks

FOCUS
The second division of an open nursery. Modest form, but there's every chance of more to come for the winner.

6286 MARKET CROSS JEWELLERS MAIDEN AUCTION STKS 5f
3:00 (3:02) (Class 6) 2-Y-O **£2,045** (£603; £302) **Stalls** Centre

Form RPR

55 **1** **White Flag**[14] 5857 2-8-1 0 .... RachelRichardson(7) 8 61+
(Tim Easterby) *w ldr: led over 2f out: rdn over 1f out: kpt on* **8/1**

0 **2** 1 **Scoreline**[127] 2075 2-9-1 0 .... DanielTudhope 9 62
(David O'Meara) *in tch: rdn to chse wnr jst ins fnl f: kpt on but a hld* **11/4**[1]

3 1/2 **Focusofourthoughts (IRE)** 2-8-13 0 .... PJMcDonald 3 58+
(Ann Duffield) *dwlt: hld up in midfield: rdn and rn green over 1f out: r.o strly ins fnl f: swtchd lft fnl 50yds: gaining at fin* **4/1**[2]

505 **4** 3/4 **Red Forever**[32] 5226 2-8-11 52 .... RobertWinston 5 53
(Alan Berry) *prom: rdn and ev ch over 1f out: no ex fnl f* **12/1**

063 **5** hd **Red Biba (IRE)**[14] 5866 2-8-4 50 .... DavidProbert 2 45
(Alan McCabe) *in tch: rdn over 2f out: kpt on one pce* **15/2**

000 **6** 1 1/2 **Nu Form Fire (IRE)**[27] 5380 2-9-1 52 .... LeeTopliss 11 51
(Nigel Tinkler) *chsd ldr: rdn over 2f out: grad wknd fnl f* **18/1**

7 1/2 **Sooqaan** 2-8-9 0 .... TomEaves 7 43
(Mel Brittain) *s.i.s: hld up: in rr tl kpt on fnl f* **16/1**

8 nse **Garfunkel (IRE)** 2-9-1 0 .... GrahamLee 4 49
(Ann Duffield) *midfield: pushed along 1/2-way: rn green: nvr threatened ldrs* **9/2**[3]

0 **9** 1/2 **Mavree (IRE)**[39] 4963 2-8-6 0 .... DuranFentiman 6 38
(Tim Easterby) *led narrowly: rdn whn hdd over 2f out: wknd over 1f out* **33/1**

05 **10** 2 1/4 **Maidana (IRE)**[13] 5900 2-7-11 0 .... GaryMahon(7) 1 28
(Tim Easterby) *wnt lft s: a towards rr* **33/1**

0 **11** 3 1/2 **Miss Tallulah (IRE)**[96] 3023 2-7-13 0 .... RobertDodsworth(7) 12 17
(Mel Brittain) *racd keenly: hld up: rdn over 2f out: sn wknd* **33/1**

1m 2.79s (4.19) **Going Correction** +0.70s/f (Yiel) **11** Ran SP% **115.4**
Speed ratings (Par 93): **94,92,91,90,90 87,86,86,86,82 76**
Tote Swingers: 1&2 £5.90, 1&3 £5.20, 2&3 £4.20 CSF £29.17 TOTE £10.60: £2.40, £1.30, £2.10; EX 40.60 Trifecta £136.50 Pool: £2,010.02 - 11.03 winning units..
Owner Habton Farms **Bred** Exors Of The Late T E Pocock **Trained** Great Habton, N Yorks

FOCUS
A moderate maiden run at solid pace. Plating-class form, and the winner didn't need to improve.

6287 WEATHERBYS BANK FOREIGN EXCHANGE H'CAP 6f
3:30 (3:32) (Class 5) (0-75,72) 3-Y-O+ **£2,587** (£770; £384; £192) **Stalls** Centre

Form RPR

5406 **1** **Barkston Ash**[18] 5705 5-9-4 **72** ....(p) JasonHart(3) 12 83+
(Eric Alston) *s.i.s: n.m.r after 1f: hdwy over 2f out: led 1f out: drvn out* **6/1**[1]

5040 **2** 2 **Captain Scooby**[11] 5971 7-8-11 **67** .... ConnorBeasley(5) 17 72
(Richard Guest) *s.i.s: hdwy over 2f out: styd on to take 2nd jst ins fnl f: no imp* **8/1**[2]

0512 **3** nk **Lucky Lodge**[16] 5788 3-8-11 **64** .... AndrewElliott 16 68
(Mel Brittain) *s.i.s: hdwy over 2f out: n.m.r and swtchd stands' side over 1f out: fin wl to take 3rd nr fin* **16/1**

0554 **4** 1 1/4 **Dark Opal (IRE)**[25] 5485 3-9-2 **69** .... LukeMorris 4 69
(John Weymes) *chsd ldrs: kpt on same pce appr fnl f* **16/1**

1406 **5** 1/2 **Ambitious Icarus**[8] 6052 4-8-8 **64** ....(e) PhilipPrince(5) 15 63
(Richard Guest) *hld up in mid-div: hdwy over 2f out: hung lft over 1f out: kpt on same pce* **10/1**

0214 **6** 1 3/4 **Little Jimmy Odsox (IRE)**[29] 5333 5-9-1 **66** ....(b) DuranFentiman 9 60
(Tim Easterby) *chsd ldrs: led over 2f out: hdd over 1f out: kpt on one pce* **8/1**[2]

3503 **7** nse **Teetotal (IRE)**[13] 5878 3-9-3 **70** .... GrahamLee 11 63
(Nigel Tinkler) *s.i.s: hdwy over 2f out: one pce appr fnl f* **12/1**

2645 **8** nk **Planetex (IRE)**[15] 5841 4-8-11 **65** .... RaulDaSilva(3) 14 57
(John Quinn) *chsd ldrs: led over 1f out: sn hdd and fdd* **8/1**[2]

1645 **9** 2 **Foreign Rhythm (IRE)**[26] 5422 8-8-7 **63** .... ShirleyTeasdale(5) 6 49
(Ron Barr) *chsd ldrs: drvn over 2f out: wknd over 1f out* **18/1**

3405 **10** 2 1/2 **Mitchell**[13] 5878 3-8-10 **66** ow1 .... LMcNiff(3) 8 45
(David Thompson) *chsd ldrs: lost pl over 1f out* **11/1**

0300 **11** 3 **Mercers Row**[10] 5985 6-8-8 **66** .... GemmaTutty(7) 2 36
(Karen Tutty) *chsd ldrs: wknd over 1f out: wnt lft ins fnl f* **33/1**

6060 **12** nk **Marine Commando**[10] 5985 5-9-0 **65** ....(be) JamesSullivan 7 34
(Ruth Carr) *in rr: hdwy and swtchd lft over 2f out: wknd over 1f out: hmpd ins fnl f* **33/1**

2500 **13** 8 **See Clearly**[11] 5947 4-8-13 **64** ....(p) RobertWinston 5 9
(Tim Easterby) *w ldrs: wknd and eased over 1f out* **17/2**[3]

0004 **14** 10 **El McGlynn (IRE)**[22] 5583 4-8-9 **63** .... NeilFarley(3) 10
(Eric Alston) *led tl over 2f out: sn wknd: bhd whn eased over 1f out* **9/1**

1m 15.05s (3.25) **Going Correction** +0.70s/f (Yiel)
WFA 3 from 4yo+ 2lb **14** Ran SP% **116.2**
Speed ratings (Par 103): **106,103,102,101,100 98,98,97,95,91 87,87,76,63**
Tote Swingers: 1&2 £21.70, 1&3 £10.70, 2&3 £17.20 CSF £49.69 CT £520.09 TOTE £2.80: £2.20, £2.40, £4.30; EX 46.90 Trifecta £853.70 Part won. Pool: £1,138.33 - 0.66 winning units..
Owner The Selebians **Bred** Jonathan Shack **Trained** Longton, Lancs

FOCUS
A modest sprint handicap which favoured those ridden with restraint. Straightforward form.

6288 WATCH RACING UK ON SKY 432 STKS (H'CAP) (STRAIGHT-MILE CHAMPIONSHIP QUALIFIER) 1m
4:00 (4:01) (Class 4) (0-85,85) 3-Y-O+ **£6,469** (£1,925; £962; £481) **Stalls** Centre

Form RPR

0000 **1** **Swiftly Done (IRE)**[4] 6167 6-9-7 **85** .... JasonHart(3) 6 95
(Declan Carroll) *hld up in midfield: smooth hdwy over 1f out: sn trckd ldrs: rdn jst ins fnl f: kpt on to ld fnl 50yds* **7/1**[3]

0520 **2** 1/2 **No Dominion (IRE)**[30] 5304 4-8-13 **74** .... GrahamLee 2 82
(James Given) *hld up: gng wl whn briefly n.m.r over 1f out: sn gd hdwy: rdn and ev ch ins fnl f: kpt on* **16/1**

2514 **3** 3/4 **Toto Skyllachy**[16] 5783 8-9-10 **85** .... DanielTudhope 12 92
(David O'Meara) *rrd at s: sn midfield: rdn and hdwy 1f out: led appr fnl f: hdd fnl 50yds: no ex* **18/1**

0025 **4** 2 1/4 **Satanic Beat (IRE)**[33] 5195 4-9-2 **77** .... PhillipMakin 11 79
(Jedd O'Keeffe) *midfield: rdn over 2f out: hdwy over 1f out: kpt on fnl f* **15/2**

0026 **5** 1 1/2 **The Osteopath (IRE)**[14] 5861 10-9-1 **76** .... DuranFentiman 1 74
(John Davies) *hld up in midfield: rdn over 2f out: kpt on fnl f: nvr threatened ldrs* **20/1**

4006 **6** nse **Maria's Choice (IRE)**[10] 5987 4-8-11 **79** .... AaronJones(7) 3 77
(Alan McCabe) *hld up: rdn over 2f out: kpt on fnl f: nvr threatened* **40/1**

0635 **7** 1/2 **Hakuna Matata**[24] 5546 6-8-11 **77** ....(b) ConnorBeasley(5) 10 74
(Michael Dods) *hld up in midfield: hdwy and briefly ev ch appr fnl f: wknd fnl f* **10/1**

1042 **8** 2 3/4 **Victoire De Lyphar (IRE)**[25] 5481 6-9-5 **80** ....(e) JamesSullivan 5 71
(Ruth Carr) *racd keenly: led: rdn whn hdd over 1f out: sn wknd* **16/1**

4041 **9** 1 3/4 **Sound Advice**[22] 5580 4-9-6 **81** .... WilsonRenwick 8 68
(Keith Dalgleish) *racd keenly: prom: rdn to ld narrowly over 1f out: sn hdd: wknd fnl f* **10/1**

0202 **10** 2 3/4 **Kiwi Bay**[31] 5291 8-9-2 **77** .... TomEaves 7 57
(Michael Dods) *in tch: t.k.h early: rdn over 2f out: wknd over 1f out* **8/1**

633 **11** 4 1/2 **Hydrant**[14] 5860 7-9-1 **81** .... PhilipPrince(5) 14 51
(Richard Guest) *prom: wknd fnl 2f* **16/1**

-003 **12** 1/2 **Arabian Star (IRE)**[21] 5613 5-9-3 **81** .... WilliamTwiston-Davies(3) 9 50
(Alan McCabe) *strubled s: sn prom: wknd over 1f out* **33/1**

5441 **13** 2 **On My Own (TUR)**[46] 4718 4-9-3 **78** .... SebSanders 15 42
(J W Hills) *in tch: rdn over 2f out: wknd over 1f out* **6/1**[1]

1640 **14** 12 **Desert Revolution**[15] 5838 3-9-0 **80** .... AdrianNicholls 4 16
(Mark Johnston) *hld up in midfield: chsd ldrs 3f out: wknd fnl 2f* **13/2**[2]

6-05 **15** 2 1/4 **Certral**[61] 4201 5-8-10 **74** .... PaulPickard(3) 13 5
(Mel Brittain) *midfield: wknd over 2f out* **22/1**

1m 40.9s (4.30) **Going Correction** +0.70s/f (Yiel)
WFA 3 from 4yo+ 5lb **15** Ran SP% **118.6**
Speed ratings (Par 105): **106,105,104,102,101 100,100,97,95,93 88,88,86,74,71**
Tote Swingers: 1&2 £21.60, 1&3 £21.50, 2&3 £29.90 CSF £106.31 CT £1977.77 TOTE £5.70: £2.90, £5.40, £6.60; EX 159.90 Trifecta £1707.10 Part won. Pool: £2,276.25 - 0.22 winning units..
Owner D Watts, Miss C King, J Syme & M Syme **Bred** Joe Fogarty **Trained** Sledmere, E Yorks

FOCUS
A decent handicap run at a reasonable pace. The winner is rated back towards last year's soft-ground form.

6289 HARRY FROOM BIRTHDAY CELEBRATION MAIDEN STKS 6f
4:30 (4:32) (Class 5) 3-Y-O+ **£2,587** (£770; £384; £192) **Stalls** Centre

Form RPR

0/ **1** **Brother Tiger**[726] 6099 4-9-7 0 .... DavidProbert 17 72+
(David C Griffiths) *trckd ldrs: 2nd over 3f out: r.o to ld ins fnl f: styd on wl* **11/1**

5- **2** 2 **Dutiful Son (IRE)**[396] 5040 3-9-5 0 .... SebSanders 1 66
(Jeremy Noseda) *s.i.s: hdwy to chse ldrs over 3f out: led over 1f out: hdd and no ex ins fnl f* **7/2**[1]

33 **3** hd **Yarn**[18] 5715 3-9-0 0 .... PhillipMakin 7 60
(William Haggas) *hld up in mid-div: effrt over 1f out: styd on ins fnl f* **7/2**[1]

4062 **4** 1 **Graceful Act**[4] 6180 5-8-11 50 ....(p) ConnorBeasley(5) 6 57
(Ron Barr) *chsd ldrs: drvn 3f out: kpt on same pce fnl f* **4/1**[2]

0356 **5** 2 3/4 **Busy Bimbo (IRE)**[18] 5709 4-9-2 48 .... RobertWinston 4 49
(Alan Berry) *in tch: hdwy to chse ldrs over 2f out: wknd fnl f* **22/1**

0060 **6** 1 1/4 **Dolly Diva**[54] 4430 4-8-9 47 ....(p) JordanNason(7) 10 45
(Paul Midgley) *s.i.s: hdwy over 3f out: one pce fnl 2f* **50/1**

3 **7** 3/4 **Penny Stock (IRE)**[12] 5919 3-9-0 0 .... AdrianNicholls 16 43
(Mark Johnston) *led after 1f: hdd over 1f out: sn wknd* **12/1**

4-65 **8** 1 **Mon Chic**[10] 5989 3-9-0 45 .... TomEaves 14 40
(Geoffrey Oldroyd) *mid-div: drvn and outpcd over 2f out: no threat after* **66/1**

00- **9** 3/4 **Dinkie**[412] 4448 3-9-0 0 .... BarryMcHugh 5 38
(Geoffrey Oldroyd) *mid-div: drvn 4f out: kpt on appr fnl f: nvr a factor* **100/1**

4 **10** 2 1/4 **Chessfield Park**[4] 6176 3-9-2 0 .... MarkCoumbe(3) 9 36
(Bryan Smart) *chsd ldrs: rdn over 2f out: wknd over 1f out* **25/1**

6 **11** 1/2 **Cataria Girl (USA)**[26] 5444 4-9-2 0 .... HayleyTurner 2 30
(Marcus Tregoning) *chsd ldrs: drvn 3f out: lost pl wl over 1f out* **12/1**

-665 **12** 1 **Lichen Angel**[31] 5265 3-9-0 47 ....(p) RussKennemore 3 27
(Richard Whitaker) *mid-div: sme hdwy over 2f out: wknd over 1f out* **80/1**

13 nse **Kalani's Diamond** 3-9-0 0 .... GrahamLee 15 26
(Bryan Smart) *s.i.s: wnt rt after s: nvr on terms* **25/1**

-060 **14** 7 **Swift Code (IRE)**[36] 5054 3-9-5 17 .... LeeTopliss 8 10
(Nigel Tinkler) *led 1f: lost pl over 2f out: sn bhd* **150/1**

15 11 **Tasrih (USA)** 4-9-4 0 .... WilliamTwiston-Davies(3) 11
(Alan McCabe) *s.i.s: in rr: bhd whn eased over 1f out* **8/1**[3]

0400 **16** 2 **Storma Norma**[19] 5677 3-9-0 62 .... DuranFentiman 12
(Tim Easterby) *in rr: bhd fnl 3f* **16/1**

1m 16.11s (4.31) **Going Correction** +0.70s/f (Yiel)
WFA 3 from 4yo+ 2lb **16** Ran SP% **123.5**
Speed ratings (Par 103): **99,96,96,94,91 89,88,87,86,83 82,81,81,71,57 54**
Tote Swingers: 1&2 £14.00, 1&3 £13.60, 2&3 £4.60 CSF £47.59 TOTE £16.10: £5.60, £2.10, £2.00; EX 85.10 Trifecta £965.30 Pool: £2,016.58 - 1.58 winning units..
Owner Norcroft Park Stud **Bred** Norcroft Park Stud **Trained** Bawtry, S Yorks

FOCUS
A modest 3yo-plus maiden with lack of depth behind the winner.

6290 CONGRATULATIONS MR & MRS RIGG H'CAP 1m 6f 19y
5:00 (5:02) (Class 6) (0-65,65) 3-Y-O+ £2,045 (£603; £302) Stalls Low

Form RPR

2001 **1** **Blue Top**[15] [5833] 4-9-4 **58**....(p) JasonHart(3) 10 65
(Tim Walford) *hld up in rr: pushed along and hdwy over 2f out: swtchd to outer over 1f out: styd on wl to ld fnl 100yds* **9/1**[3]

5022 **2** ½ **Jan Smuts (IRE)**[7] [6087] 5-9-12 **63**....(tp) GrahamLee 5 69
(Wilf Storey) *midfield: smooth hdwy 3f out: stl gng wl over 1f out: rdn and upsides ins fnl f: kpt on* **16/1**

555 **3** ¾ **Korngold**[15] [5833] 5-8-12 **49**.... DanielTudhope 12 54
(Tracy Waggott) *midfield: hdwy over 2f out: rdn and upsides over 1f out: edgd lft: one pce fnl 100yds* **9/1**[3]

4240 **4** shd **Beat The Shower**[15] [5831] 7-9-8 **59**....[1] WilsonRenwick 13 64
(Peter Niven) *midfield: rdn to chse ldrs over 2f out: swtchd rt and n.m.r appr fnl f: kpt on* **14/1**

330 **5** 1 **Naburn**[14] [5862] 5-9-13 **64**.... TomEaves 1 68
(Alan Swinbank) *trckd ldrs: rdn to chal 3f out: led over 1f out: hdd 100yds out: wknd* **22/1**

1444 **6** shd **Duke Of Yorkshire**[24] [5549] 3-9-0 **65**.... NeilFarley(3) 8 68
(Declan Carroll) *midfield: rdn and hdwy to chse ldrs over 1f out: one pce fnl f* **11/1**

/502 **7** 2½ **Wee Giant (USA)**[4] [6177] 7-9-1 **52**.... BarryMcHugh 9 52
(Tony Coyle) *hld up on inner: hdwy over 3f out: sn rdn to chse ldrs: wknd fnl f* **10/1**

6-40 **8** 1¼ **Spanish Legacy**[15] [5833] 4-8-12 **49**.... PhillipMakin 6 48
(Julie Camacho) *midfield: rdn over 2f out: wknd fnl f* **25/1**

0034 **9** 3 **Grammar**[14] [5863] 4-8-11 **51**....(e) RaulDaSilva(3) 2 46
(David Thompson) *led: rdn over 3f out: hdd over 1f out: wknd* **25/1**

-610 **10** shd **Man From Seville**[40] [4931] 3-8-13 **61**.... LukeMorris 4 56
(Sir Mark Prescott Bt) *prom: rdn and upsides over 3f out: wknd fnl 2f* **11/4**[1]

00 **11** 7 **Sendiym (FR)**[15] [5052] 6-9-7 **58**.... BrianHughes 14 43
(Dianne Sayer) *trckd ldrs: rdn and wknd over 2f out* **40/1**

0-03 **12** 1 **Crystal Monarch (IRE)**[24] [5526] 4-9-3 **54**.... ChrisCatlin 11 38
(Lady Cecil) *hld up: a towards rr* **16/1**

436 **13** 1½ **Summerlea (IRE)**[78] [3625] 7-9-2 **53**.... DuranFentiman 15 35
(Patrick Holmes) *in tch: rdn over 3f out: wknd over 2f out* **20/1**

323 **14** ½ **Bavarian Nordic (USA)**[36] [5059] 8-9-7 **58**.... RussKennemore 3 40
(Richard Whitaker) *trckd ldrs: rdn over 3f out: already wkng whn n.m.r over 2f out* **14/1**

6236 **15** 9 **Iceman George**[15] [5833] 9-9-5 **61**....(v) PhilipPrince(5) 16 31
(Alison Hutchinson) *hld up: a towards rr* **20/1**

1451 **P** **Spats Colombo**[31] [5295] 3-8-10 **58**.... JamesSullivan 7
(Micky Hammond) *hld up: eased fr over 2f out: p.u ins fnl f* **7/1**[2]

3m 7.91s (3.21) **Going Correction** +0.30s/f (Good)
WFA 3 from 4yo+ 11lb **16** Ran SP% **125.7**
Speed ratings (Par 101): **102,101,101,101,100 100,99,98,96,96 92,92,91,90,85**
Tote Swingers 1&2 £9.40, 2&3 £21.80, 1&3 £14.80 CSF £134.50 CT £1357.77 TOTE £12.30: £3.20, £2.30, £2.90, £3.60; EX 171.30 Trifecta £1078.50 Part won. Pool: £1,438.07 - 0.56 winning units..
Owner Brown, Evans, Lister, Cowley **Bred** Mrs Joan M Langmead **Trained** Sheriff Hutton, N Yorks
■ Stewards' Enquiry : Neil Farley one-day ban: careless riding (Sep 24)

FOCUS
A low-grade staying handicap, and straightforward form.

6291 RACING REPLAY, ALL TODAY'S RACING SKY 432 APPRENTICE H'CAP 7f
5:30 (5:31) (Class 5) (0-75,75) 3-Y-O+ £2,587 (£770; £384; £192) Stalls Centre

Form RPR

0250 **1** **Illustrious Prince (IRE)**[7] [6072] 6-9-4 **75**.... LukeLeadbitter(7) 12 85
(Declan Carroll) *towards rr: hdwy to trck ldrs over 4f out: led 3f out: drew clr fnl f* **16/1**

0020 **2** 3½ **Kung Hei Fat Choy (USA)**[32] [5238] 4-9-10 **74**....(b) LeeTopliss 3 75
(James Given) *in rr: hdwy over 2f out: styd on to take 2nd last 50yds* **9/1**

1603 **3** 1¼ **Ted's Brother (IRE)**[8] [6048] 5-9-4 **71**....(e) PhilipPrince(3) 2 69
(Richard Guest) *hld up in rr: hdwy far side over 2f out: chsd wnr over 1f out: hrd rdn and kpt on same pce* **5/1**[1]

0-25 **4** 1¾ **Messageinabottle (USA)**[24] [5517] 3-8-5 **64**.... JacobButterfield(5) 7 55
(James Bethell) *chsd ldrs: edgd rt over 1f out: kpt on same pce* **16/1**

4332 **5** hd **Beckermet (IRE)**[8] [6052] 11-9-2 **66**.... LMcNiff 6 59
(Ruth Carr) *w ldrs: n.m.r over 2f out: hmpd over 1f out: kpt on ins fnl f* **5/1**[1]

2255 **6** ¾ **My Single Malt (IRE)**[11] [5947] 5-9-8 **72**....(v[1]) WilliamTwiston-Davies 13 63
(Julie Camacho) *wnt lft s: mid-div: effrt over 2f out: hung lft and one pce over 1f out* **6/1**[2]

0-00 **7** nse **Nelson's Bay**[86] [3368] 4-9-3 **72**.... SamanthaBell(5) 10 63
(Wilf Storey) *mid-div: n.m.r over 1f out: kpt on one pce* **33/1**

1342 **8** 1¾ **No Quarter (IRE)**[14] [5861] 6-9-0 **64**.... CharlesBishop 4 50
(Tracy Waggott) *chsd ldrs: drvn over 2f out: one pce* **7/1**[3]

0230 **9** hd **Repetition**[57] [4354] 3-8-10 **67**.... ShaneGray(3) 1 50
(Kevin Ryan) *led: hdd 3f out: hung rt and wknd over 1f out* **6/1**[2]

5210 **10** nk **Dennis**[22] [5581] 3-8-10 **67**.... DarylByrne(3) 8 50
(Tim Easterby) *w ldrs: drvn over 2f out: edgd rt and wknd over 1f out* **18/1**

4500 **11** 6 **Red Red Wine**[13] [5884] 3-8-0 **61** oh1....(v) AaronJones(7) 11 28
(Alan McCabe) *dwlt: in rr: sn drvn along: bhd fnl 3f* **40/1**

5061 **12** 26 **Destination Aim**[39] [4967] 6-9-4 **68**.... JasonHart 14
(Frederick Watson) *in rr: reminders over 3f out: bhd and hung rt over 2f out: eased over 1f out: t.o: virtually p.u* **9/1**

1m 29.1s (4.60) **Going Correction** +0.70s/f (Yiel)
WFA 3 from 4yo+ 4lb **12** Ran SP% **116.8**
Speed ratings (Par 103): **101,97,95,93,93 92,92,90,90,89 83,53**
Tote Swingers 1&2 £20.90, 2&3 £9.20, 1&3 £22.00 CSF £150.82 CT £844.35 TOTE £20.90: £5.30, £3.20, £1.80; EX 186.90 Trifecta £1125.20 Part won. Pool: £1,500.39 - 0.40 winning units..
Owner Ray Flegg **Bred** Rathbarry Stud **Trained** Sledmere, E Yorks
■ Stewards' Enquiry : Philip Prince four-day ban: used whip above permitted level (Sep 24-26,tbn)

FOCUS
A fair apprentice handicap. This rates one of the winner's better career efforts.
T/Jkpt: Not won. T/Plt: £549.80 to a £1 stake. Pool: £58,550.65 - 77.74 winning tickets. T/Qpdt: £36.40 to a £1 stake. Pool: £5,285.03 - 107.30 winning tickets. WG

6124 CHANTILLY (R-H)
Tuesday, September 10

OFFICIAL GOING: Turf: soft

6292a PRIX D'AUMALE (GROUP 3) (2YO FILLIES) (TURF) 1m
1:50 (1:51) 2-Y-O £32,520 (£13,008; £9,756; £6,504; £3,252)

RPR

1 **Lesstalk In Paris (IRE)**[37] 2-8-9 0.... IoritzMendizabal 1 105
(J-C Rouget, France) *dwlt: sn trcking ldr on inner taking a t.k.h: hemmed in fr 3f out: sat and suffered tl able to switch outside and take narrow gap ent fnl f: qcknd to ld 110yds out: pushed out hands and heels: readily* **69/10**[3]

2 ¾ **Straight Thinking (USA)**[24] [5555] 2-8-9 0.... MaximeGuyon 4 103
(A Fabre, France) *trckd ldr between horses: pressed ldr fr 2 1/2f out: led 1 1/2f out: sn rdn and 1 l clr ent fnl f: r.o: hdd 110yds out: no ex* **1/1**[1]

3 2 **Marbre Rose (IRE)**[36] 2-8-9 0.... ThierryJarnet 7 99
(F Head, France) *trckd ldr on outer: rdn and no imp 1 1/2f out: 4th and briefly outpcd over 1f out: kpt on u.p ins fnl f: tk 3rd cl home: nt pce to chal* **8/1**

4 shd **Lacarolina (FR)**[24] [5555] 2-8-9 0.... GregoryBenoist 2 98
(J-C Rouget, France) *led: scubbed along and hdd 1 1/2f out: kpt on at one pce u.p fnl f: lost 3rd cl home* **14/5**[2]

5 ¾ **Kenzadargent (FR)**[47] [4701] 2-8-9 0.... AnthonyCrastus 6 97
(J-M Capitte, France) *settled in rr on outer: rdn and no imp fr 2f out: kpt on wl u.p ins fnl f: nvr on terms* **12/1**

6 nk **Malka (FR)**[24] [5555] 2-8-9 0.... AntoineHamelin 5 96
(Matthieu Palussiere, France) *dwlt: towards rr on inner: styd on u.p fnl f: nvr in contention* **17/1**

7 4 **Marie D'o (FR)**[21] [5628] 2-8-9 0.... UmbertoRispoli 3 87
(K Borgel, France) *settled in 5th: rdn and short of room 2f out: lost pl over 1f out: eased ins fnl f* **26/1**

1m 38.91s (0.91) **7** Ran SP% **117.0**
WIN (incl. 1 euro stake): 7.90. PLACES: 2.80, 1.50. SF: 19.60.
Owner SARL Ecurie J-L Tepper **Bred** Skymarc Farm Inc **Trained** Pau, France

FOCUS
The form fits with the consistent race averages.

6293a PRIX D'ARENBERG (GROUP 3) (2YO) (TURF) 5f 110y
2:20 (2:22) 2-Y-O £32,520 (£13,008; £9,756; £6,504; £3,252)

RPR

1 **This Time (FR)**[28] 2-8-8 0.... FabriceVeron 4 104
(H-A Pantall, France) *t.k.h in rr: rdn and hdwy 2f out: short of room 1 1/2f out: hrd rdn to chal ins fnl f: r.o u.p: led cl home* **17/2**

2 snk **Another Party (FR)**[36] [5082] 2-8-11 0.... AntoineHamelin 3 106
(Matthieu Palussiere, France) *chsd ldrs: swtchd outside and hdwy 2f out: rdn to ld appr fnl f: r.o u.p: hdd cl home* **12/1**

3 1¼ **Haikbidiac (IRE)**[19] [5679] 2-8-11 0....(p) Christophe-PatriceLemaire 7 102
(William Haggas) *led on rail: jnd after 2f but wnt on again 1/2-way: rdn and hdd over 1f out: kpt on u.p fnl f: no ex fnl 50yds* **2/1**[1]

4 2 **Make It Reel (FR)**[44] [4816] 2-8-11 0.... ChristopheSoumillon 5 95
(P Bary, France) *trckd ldrs: lost pl bef 1/2-way: prog to chse ldrs over 1 1/2f out: 4th and hrd rdn ins fnl f: one pce* **7/1**

5 1 **Al Muthana (FR)**[23] [5573] 2-8-11 0.... FrankieDettori 1 92
(F-H Graffard, France) *towards rr on inner: prog and short of room under 2f out: shuffled bk and swtchd outside appr 1f out: styd on u.p ins fnl f: nvr on terms* **4/1**[2]

6 ¾ **Konkan (IRE)**[21] 2-8-8 0.... CristianDemuro 6 87
(L Riccardi, Italy) *midfield on inner: dropped towards rr bef 1/2-way: hdwy on outside 1 1/2f out: styng on in 5th 1f out: run flattened out fnl 110yds* **6/1**[3]

7 5 **Kanz**[21] [5609] 2-8-8 0.... MartinHarley 2 70
(Mick Channon) *chsd ldrs on inner: rdn 2f out: n.m.r but unable qck 1 1/2f out: grad lost tch w ldrs* **20/1**

8 3 **Winshine (FR)**[26] [5460] 2-8-8 0.... Pierre-CharlesBoudot 8 60
(J-M Capitte, France) *trckd ldr: jnd ldr after 2f: rdn and wknd fr over 1 1/2f out: eased ins fnl f* **34/1**

9 1½ **Aztec Brave (FR)**[33] 2-8-11 0.... OlivierPeslier 10 58
(E J O'Neill, France) *t.k.h towards rr on outer: nvr in contention* **13/1**

10 ½ **Blu Axara (ITY)**[32] [5363] 2-8-8 0.... UmbertoRispoli 9 54
(F Chappet, France) *t.k.h and prom on outer: outpcd over 2f out: sn rdn and wknd* **30/1**

1m 4.99s (0.49) **10** Ran SP% **116.3**
WIN (incl. 1 euro stake): 9.50. PLACES: 2,40, 2.80, 1.50. DF: 64.10. SF: 148.20.
Owner Mme Antoinette Tamagni **Bred** Mme A Tamagni & Mme M-E Binswanger **Trained** France

FOCUS
The form fits with the race averages.

6294a PRIX DES TOURELLES (LISTED RACE) (3YO+ FILLIES & MARES) (TURF) 1m 4f
2:55 (2:55) 3-Y-O+ £21,138 (£8,455; £6,341; £4,227; £2,113)

RPR

1 **Quiz Mistress**[31] [5297] 5-9-3 0.... IoritzMendizabal 9 105+
(Hughie Morrison) *w.w in rr: swtchd outside and hdwy 1 1/2f out: r.o wl u.p: led 110yds out: drvn out* **93/10**

2 1 **Pagera (FR)**[31] [5298] 5-9-3 0....(p) ThierryJarnet 2 103+
(H-A Pantall, France) **10/1**

3 snk **Gosh (IRE)**[30] [5315] 3-8-8 0.... AntoineHamelin 4 103+
(Mme Pia Brandt, France) **11/2**

4 hd **Court Pastoral**[38] [5015] 3-8-8 0.... TomQueally 5 103
(Lady Cecil) *led: hdd after 2f and trckd ldr: led again 2f out: rdn 1f out: hdd 110yds out: no ex: lost 3rd on line* **5/1**[3]

5 1 **Linda Radlett (IRE)**[19] 4-9-3 0.... MaximeGuyon 6 101
(A Fabre, France) *towards rr: nowhere to go 2f out tl gap opened ent fnl f: styd on but nt pce to chal* **3/1**[1]

6 4 **Myrtlewood (IRE)**[304] [7694] 4-9-3 0.... FrankieDettori 8 95
(F-H Graffard, France) **17/1**

7 hd **Mahnaz**[27] 4-9-3 0.... Pierre-CharlesBoudot 1 94
(A Fabre, France) **68/10**

8 snk **Queen Bubble (IRE)**[29] [5360] 4-9-3 0....(p) FlavienPrat 10 94
(Y De Nicolay, France) **41/1**

9 ½ **Last Born (FR)**[48] 4652 4-9-3 0.. OlivierPeslier 7 93
(A Fabre, France) **19/5**[2]

2m 30.87s (-0.13)
WFA 3 from 4yo+ 9lb **9** Ran SP% **117.4**
WIN (incl. 1 euro stake): 10.30. PLACES: 2.90, 2.90, 2.10. DF: 45.30. SF: 79.60.
Owner The Fairy Story Partnership **Bred** Deepwood Farm Stud **Trained** East Ilsley, Berks

5876 CARLISLE (R-H)

Wednesday, September 11

OFFICIAL GOING: Good (good to soft in places) changing to soft after race 1 (2:20)

Wind: Light, half against Weather: Overcast, showers

6295 CHEVIOT NURSERY H'CAP 5f 193y

2:20 (2:20) (Class 5) (0-75,75) 2-Y-0 **£2,587** (£770; £384; £192) **Stalls** Low

Form RPR

465 **1** **Damaah (USA)**[14] 5877 2-8-4 **58**.. JoeFanning 5 66+
(Mark Johnston) *cl up: led over 2f out: rdn and drifted rt appr fnl f: kpt on strly* **7/1**

2310 **2** 2½ **Instant Attraction (IRE)**[21] 5656 2-9-7 **75**................ MichaelO'Connell 1 75
(Jedd O'Keeffe) *led 2f: cl up: effrt whn checked and swtchd lft 1f out: kpt on ins fnl f: nt gng pce of wnr* **10/3**[1]

2634 **3** 1¼ **Heroique (IRE)**[14] 5877 2-8-12 **66**.. DavidAllan 9 62
(Tim Easterby) *prom: effrt and rdn 2f out: edgd rt: kpt on same pce ins fnl f* **17/2**

265 **4** 3 **Henke (IRE)**[47] 4731 2-8-11 **65**.. GrahamLee 3 52
(Nigel Tinkler) *dwlt: hld up: stdy hdwy 1/2-way: rdn and kpt on fr over 1f out: no imp* **7/2**[2]

5453 **5** 5 **Noble Reach**[22] 5610 2-8-0 **54** oh1.. PaulQuinn 10 26
(Geoffrey Harker) *hld up on outside: rdn over 2f out: hld whn edgd rt over 1f out* **20/1**

6030 **6** 2½ **Reale Silenzio**[14] 5898 2-8-0 **54** oh9..........................(p) JamesSullivan 4 19
(John Weymes) *t.k.h: hld up: n.m.r over 3f out: rdn 2f out: nvr able to chal* **100/1**

0125 **7** 2½ **Tweety Pie (IRE)**[32] 5272 2-9-1 **72**.. NeilFarley(3) 2 29
(Declan Carroll) *led 2f: rdn and hdd over 2f out: wknd over 1f out* **16/1**

4414 **8** 1 **She Can Jig**[14] 5898 2-8-1 **60**.. ShaneGray(5) 6 14
(Kevin Ryan) *hld up: rdn along 1/2-way: sn no imp: btn over 1f out* **12/1**

434 **9** 2¼ **Hello Beautiful (IRE)**[26] 5468 2-9-0 **68**..........................(p) PJMcDonald 8 16
(Ann Duffield) *t.k.h early: cl up tl rdn and wknd fr 2f out* **7/1**

0454 **10** 3 **Lazy Sioux**[15] 5858 2-8-7 **61**.. LukeMorris 7
(Richard Guest) *towards rr: drvn along 1/2-way: struggling fr 2f out* **6/1**[3]

1m 14.43s (0.73) **Going Correction** +0.025s/f (Good) **10** Ran SP% **114.4**
Speed ratings (Par 95): **96,92,91,87,80 77,73,72,69,65**
toteswingers 1&2 £4.00, 1&3 £9.90, 2&3 £7.50 CSF £29.96 CT £206.50 TOTE £7.70: £2.40, £2.50, £2.00; EX 28.10 Trifecta £127.00 Pool: £757.02 - 4.46 winning units..
Owner Hamdan Al Maktoum **Bred** Shadwell Farm LLC **Trained** Middleham Moor, N Yorks

FOCUS
Rail on inside and all distances as advertised. A decent pace for this nursery with the field racing far side. It paid to race handily, the runner-up is rated to his turf mark with the third to the balance of her form.

6296 READ RACINGUK.COM/COLUMNISTS H'CAP (DIV I) 1m 1f 61y

2:50 (2:50) (Class 5) (0-70,76) 3-Y-O+ **£2,587** (£770; £384; £192) **Stalls** Low

Form RPR

0526 **1** **Tectonic (IRE)**[9] 6048 4-9-1 **64**..........................(p) JasonHart(3) 1 76
(Keith Dalgleish) *t.k.h: trckd ldrs: led centre over 1f out: hrd pressed ins fnl f: hld on wl* **6/1**[3]

504 **2** shd **Jordaura**[37] 5050 7-9-1 **64**.. MarkCoumbe(3) 9 75
(Alan Berry) *s.i.s: hld up: gd hdwy on wd outside over 1f out: chal wl ins fnl f: jst hld* **20/1**

0-05 **3** 6 **Vicky Valentine**[36] 5107 3-8-1 **56**.. JulieBurke(3) 6 54
(Alistair Whillans) *midfield: drvn and outpcd over 4f out: rallied centre 2f out: kpt on: no ch w first two* **28/1**

0523 **4** ½ **Magic Skyline (IRE)**[19] 5707 3-8-13 **65**.. DaleSwift 10 62
(Brian Ellison) *prom: effrt and carried towards stands' side 2f out: sn rdn: one pce appr fnl f* **7/1**

0044 **5** 1 **Plunder**[16] 5828 3-9-1 **67**..[1] RobertHavlin 7 62
(Richard Ford) *hld up towards rr: effrt and drvn centre 2f out: no imp appr fnl f* **10/1**

4532 **6** 1¼ **Outlaw Torn (IRE)**[16] 5840 4-9-0 **60**..........................(e) RobbieFitzpatrick 5 52
(Richard Guest) *led to 1/2-way: rdn centre over 2f out: fdd appr fnl f* **9/1**

1221 **7** hd **Red Charmer (IRE)**[9] 6048 3-9-10 **76** 6ex........................ PJMcDonald 2 68
(Ann Duffield) *cl up: led 1/2-way: swtchd to stands' side over 2f out: hdd over 1f out: sn btn* **9/2**[2]

3400 **8** ½ **Call Of Duty (IRE)**[14] 5882 8-8-10 **56** oh1........................ GrahamLee 3 47
(Dianne Sayer) *towards rr: rdn along centre over 2f out: no imp over 1f out* **7/1**

4343 **9** ½ **Obboorr**[23] 5580 4-9-4 **64**.. JamesSullivan 4 53
(Brian Rothwell) *hld up: rdn along and hdwy in centre over 2f out: wknd over 1f out* **3/1**[1]

005 **10** ½ **Hail Bold Chief (USA)**[13] 5920 6-8-11 **57**................ RobertWinston 11 45
(Alan Swinbank) *hld up in midfield on outside: struggling over 3f out: sn btn* **25/1**

0206 **11** ¾ **Orions Hero (IRE)**[28] 5383 3-9-4 **70**..........................(p) TonyHamilton 8 57
(Richard Fahey) *trckd ldrs: drvn and c centre over 2f out: sn btn* **22/1**

1m 58.03s (0.43) **Going Correction** +0.15s/f (Good)
WFA 3 from 4yo+ 6lb **11** Ran SP% **118.0**
Speed ratings (Par 103): **104,103,98,98,97 96,95,95,95,94 93**
toteswingers 1&2 £39.50, 1&3 Not won, 2&3 Not won CSF £123.21 CT £3095.32 TOTE £9.10: £2.60, £3.20, £7.20; EX 198.20 Trifecta £824.90 Pool: £1099.97 - 0.01 winning units..
Owner Mrs L A Ogilvie **Bred** W Maxwell Ervine **Trained** Carluke, S Lanarks
■ Stewards' Enquiry : P J McDonald two-day ban: careless riding (Sep 25-26)

FOCUS
After the first race, the going was changed to soft. An open handicap run at a fair pace. The field headed middle to stands' side, with the first two home racing up the centre. They finished clear in a similar time to division II.

6297 READ RACINGUK.COM/COLUMNISTS H'CAP (DIV II) 1m 1f 61y

3:25 (3:25) (Class 5) (0-70,70) 3-Y-O+ **£2,587** (£770; £384; £192) **Stalls** Low

Form RPR

1112 **1** **Artful Prince**[11] 5990 3-8-13 **65**..........................(b) GrahamLee 3 75+
(James Given) *dwlt: hld up towards rr: gd hdwy far side to ld ins fnl f: kpt on strly* **5/2**[1]

2303 **2** 1¾ **Polar Forest**[9] 6049 3-8-0 **57**.. PhilipPrince(5) 9 63
(Richard Guest) *hld up: stdy hdwy in centre 2f out: chsd wnr ins fnl f: kpt on* **12/1**

1534 **3** ¾ **Ebony Express**[19] 5712 4-9-5 **65**.. BenCurtis 1 69
(Alan Swinbank) *trckd ldrs: effrt and rdn centre over 2f out: kpt on ins fnl f* **13/2**[3]

5023 **4** hd **Mixed Message (IRE)**[29] 5368 3-9-4 **70**........................ DaleSwift 7 74
(Brian Ellison) *hld up on outside: effrt and rdn 2f out: kpt on fnl f: nrst fin* **4/1**[2]

4150 **5** ½ **Fraserburgh (IRE)**[16] 5815 3-9-4 **70**........................ JoeFanning 8 73
(Mark Johnston) *chsd ldr: led centre over 2f out: hdd ins fnl f: kpt on same pce* **15/2**

6531 **6** 1½ **Woodacre**[32] 5264 6-9-4 **64**.. RussKennemore 10 64
(Richard Whitaker) *chsd ldrs on outside: rdn over 2f out: hung rt and no ex over 1f out* **8/1**

2560 **7** ¾ **Jonny Lesters Hair (IRE)**[15] 5861 8-9-0 **60**..................(t) DavidAllan 2 58
(Tim Easterby) *led to over 2f out: styd towards far side: fdd appr fnl f* **16/1**

U002 **8** 4 **Voice From Above (IRE)**[22] 5615 4-8-11 **64**................ JackGarritty(7) 4 53
(Patrick Holmes) *towards rr: rdn towards over 3f out: btn far side over 1f out* **25/1**

0663 **9** 1 **Joshua The First**[8] 6083 4-8-12 **58**..........................(p) TomEaves 5 45
(Keith Dalgleish) *in tch: rdn along over 3f out: wknd centre over 1f out* **17/2**

060 **10** 19 **Edas**[37] 5051 11-8-7 **56**.. JasonHart(3) 6
(Thomas Cuthbert) *hld up: drvn along towards far side 3f out: sn wknd: t.o* **25/1**

600- **11** 37 **Illawalla**[348] 6643 5-8-10 **56** oh11.. AndrewElliott 11
(Alan Berry) *midfield: drvn and outpcd 4f out: btn and eased fnl 2f* **125/1**

1m 58.04s (0.44) **Going Correction** +0.15s/f (Good)
WFA 3 from 4yo+ 6lb **11** Ran SP% **117.4**
Speed ratings (Par 103): **104,102,101,101,101 99,99,95,94,77 44**
toteswingers 1&2 £7.80, 1&3 £5.00, 2&3 £1.60 CSF £34.01 CT £178.30 TOTE £3.20: £1.20, £4.20, £2.70; EX 43.50 Trifecta £199.90 Pool: £722.18 - 2.70 winning units..
Owner Ingram Racing **Bred** Graham Wilson **Trained** Willoughton, Lincs

FOCUS
This was competitive enough and was run in a similar time to division I. It was run at a sound pace with the field heading middle to far side. The winner is rated back to form.

6298 WATCH RACING UK ON SKY 432 MAIDEN FILLIES' STKS 6f 192y

4:00 (4:01) (Class 5) 2-Y-O **£2,587** (£770; £384; £192) **Stalls** Low

Form RPR

5 **1** **Zumurudah (FR)**[43] 4848 2-9-0 0.. JoeFanning 6 82+
(Mark Johnston) *mde all: rdn and clr over 1f out: kpt on strly fnl f* **12/1**

2 3¾ **Dynaglow (USA)** 2-9-0 0.. RobertHavlin 10 73+
(John Gosden) *hmpd s: hld up on outside: gd hdwy to chse (clr) wnr over 1f out: kpt on fnl f: no imp* **7/2**[2]

3 **3** hd **Tears Of The Sun**[35] 5131 2-9-0 0.. DanielTudhope 11 72+
(Roger Varian) *carried lft s: plld hrd and sn cl up on outside: chsd wnr over 2f out to over 1f out: styd disputing 2nd pl: one pce ins fnl f* **4/5**[1]

4 6 **Maiden Approach** 2-9-0 0.. TonyHamilton 3 56+
(Richard Fahey) *trckd ldrs: rdn over 2f out: outpcd by first three fr over 1f out* **11/2**[3]

5 ½ **Moon Over Rio (IRE)** 2-9-0 0.. AndrewElliott 7 55+
(Ben Haslam) *cl up: drvn and lost pl over 2f out: n.d after* **66/1**

6 2 **Lady Bubbles** 2-9-0 0.. JamesSullivan 8 50
(Michael Easterby) *t.k.h in rr: pushed along and effrt over 2f out: sn no imp* **66/1**

7 nse **Wannabe Magic** 2-9-0 0.. MichaelO'Connell 4 50
(Jedd O'Keeffe) *midfield: drvn and outpcd 3f out: n.d after* **40/1**

00 **8** 1 **Kashstaree**[28] 5379 2-9-0 0.. PhillipMakin 1 47
(David Barron) *hld up: rdn over 3f out: no imp fr 2f out* **80/1**

9 ½ **Updated (FR)** 2-9-0 0.. RobertWinston 2 46
(Ismail Mohammed) *dwlt: t.k.h and sn midfield: outpcd over 3f out: sn btn* **16/1**

0 **10** 16 **Bonnie Fairy**[35] 5140 2-9-0 0.. TomEaves 5 4
(Keith Dalgleish) *dwlt: sn in tch: rdn over 3f out: sn btn* **50/1**

11 9 **Petite Cadeaux (IRE)** 2-9-0 0.. GrahamLee 9
(Tom Tate) *wnt bdly lft s: bhd: struggling over 3f out: sn btn* **25/1**

1m 29.34s (2.24) **Going Correction** +0.15s/f (Good) **11** Ran SP% **119.2**
Speed ratings (Par 92): **93,88,88,81,81 78,78,77,77,58 48**
toteswingers 1&2 £7.80, 1&3 £5.00, 2&3 £1.60 CSF £53.13 TOTE £11.10: £2.50, £1.40, £1.10; EX 68.60 Trifecta £119.60 Pool: £1590.10 - 9.97 winning units..
Owner Jaber Abdullah **Bred** S R L Az Agr Razza Della Sila **Trained** Middleham Moor, N Yorks

FOCUS
Little form to go on for this fillies' maiden. It was run at a fair pace with the front three finishing clear. The form will take time to settle.

6299 BRITISH STALLION STUDS E B F MAIDEN STKS 7f 200y

4:35 (4:37) (Class 5) 2-Y-O **£3,067** (£905; £453) **Stalls** Low

Form RPR

42 **1** **Stormardal (IRE)**[16] 5826 2-9-5 0.. RobertWinston 6 88+
(Ismail Mohammed) *t.k.h: cl up: led over 2f out: shkn up and drew clr fr over 1f out* **11/8**[1]

024 **2** 4½ **All Talk N No Do (IRE)**[19] 5698 2-9-5 75........................ GrahamLee 12 76
(Seamus Durack) *cl up on outside: effrt and ev ch over 2f out: edgd rt and one pce fr over 1f out* **11/4**[2]

62 **3** 6 **Porthos Du Vallon**[32] 5262 2-9-5 0.. TomEaves 2 62
(Keith Dalgleish) *t.k.h: led to over 2f out: outpcd by first two fr over 1f out* **33/1**

3 **4** 1½ **In Vino Veritas (IRE)**[13] 5915 2-9-5 0.. PJMcDonald 1 59
(Ann Duffield) *hld up in tch: drvn and outpcd over 3f out: rallied 2f out: plugged on fnl f: no imp* **11/1**

44 **5** 1 **Innocent Touch (IRE)**[12] 5968 2-9-5 0.. TonyHamilton 8 56+
(Richard Fahey) *towards rr: drvn over 3f out: rallied over 1f out: kpt on: nvr able to chal* **12/1**

5 **6** 3/4 **Ice Mayden**[30] 5338 2-8-11 0 .... MarkCoumbe(3) 3 50
(Bryan Smart) *in tch: outpcd 3f out: rallied over 1f out: nt pce to chal* **22/1**

50 **7** 1 1/4 **Paddy's Bay**[76] 3724 2-8-12 0 .... KevinStott(7) 4 52
(Kevin Ryan) *chsd ldrs tl rdn and wknd fr 2f out* **66/1**

8 *hd* **Where's Tiger** 2-9-5 0 .... PhillipMakin 10 51+
(Jedd O'Keeffe) *towards rr: drvn along whn n.m.r briefly over 2f out: sn n.d* **50/1**

56 **9** *shd* **Chivers (IRE)**[12] 5968 2-9-5 0 .... DavidAllan 11 51
(Tim Easterby) *bhd: rdn 4f out: nvr on terms* **66/1**

36 **10** 5 **Ralphy Lad (IRE)**[6] 6125 2-9-5 0 .... BenCurtis 9 39
(Alan Swinbank) *hld up in tch: outpcd over 2f out: edgd rt and sn btn* **10/1**[3]

11 4 **It's Just George** 2-9-2 0 .... JasonHart(3) 14 30
(Keith Dalgleish) *s.i.s: bhd and sn pushed along: nvr on terms* **40/1**

12 9 **Tizlove Regardless (USA)** 2-9-5 0 .... JoeFanning 7 10
(Mark Johnston) *sn pushed along towards rr: shortlived effrt on outside wl over 2f out: sn btn* **10/1**[3]

1m 41.67s (1.67) **Going Correction** +0.15s/f (Good) **12** Ran SP% **117.7**
Speed ratings (Par 95): **97,92,86,85,84 83,82,81,81,76 72,63**
toteswingers 1&2 £1.60, 1&3 £8.60, 2&3 £9.90 CSF £4.57 TOTE £2.50: £1.50, £1.10, £7.20; EX 6.50 Trifecta £98.30 Pool: £1095.22 - 8.35 winning units..
Owner Sheikh Juma Dalmook Al Maktoum **Bred** Kevin & Meta Cullen **Trained** Newmarket, Suffolk

FOCUS
A modest maiden run at a fair pace. The field finished very well strung out. The winner was impressive and the form could rate a few pounds higher.

6300 COMLONGON CASTLE H'CAP — 7f 200y
5:05 (5:05) (Class 3) (0-95,94) 3-Y-O+ **£8,086** (£2,406; £1,202; £601) **Stalls** Low

Form RPR

2131 **1** **Pacific Heights (IRE)**[46] 4758 4-9-5 **89** .... DaleSwift 3 99
(Brian Ellison) *trckd ldrs: rdn 2f out: slt ld and hrd pressed appr fnl f: hld on gamely u.p* **9/4**[1]

3521 **2** *nse* **Dutch Rose (IRE)**[20] 5684 4-9-10 **94** .... DanielTudhope 5 104
(David O'Meara) *hld up in tch: rdn over 2f out: hdwy to dispute ld appr fnl f: kpt on wl: jst hld* **5/1**[3]

1252 **3** 4 1/2 **Hot Rod Mamma (IRE)**[4] 6210 6-8-10 **80** .... DuranFentiman 10 80
(Dianne Sayer) *s.i.s and swtchd rt s: hld up: stdy hdwy over 2f out: chsng ldrs and rdn over 1f out: outpcd by first two ins fnl f* **9/2**[2]

305 **4** 1 1/2 **Jo'Burg (USA)**[16] 5828 9-8-13 **83** .... GrahamLee 2 79
(David O'Meara) *hld up: rdn over 2f out: styd on fnl f: nvr able to chal* **40/1**

2330 **5** 1 1/4 **Dubai Hills**[47] 4733 7-9-3 **87** .... TomEaves 7 80
(Bryan Smart) *dwlt: hld up on outside: rdn and edgd rt 2f out: sn no imp* **16/1**

1001 **6** *nk* **King Torus (IRE)**[14] 5880 5-9-2 **86** .... JamesSullivan 9 79
(Ruth Carr) *pressed ldr: led and rdn over 2f out: hung rt and hdd appr fnl f: sn btn* **20/1**

4516 **7** 3 1/4 **Wannabe King**[33] 5238 7-9-1 **92** .... (v) JordanNason(7) 4 77
(Geoffrey Harker) *led to over 2f out: rdn and wknd over 1f out* **12/1**

6326 **8** 5 **Suits Me**[16] 5838 10-9-8 **92** .... PhillipMakin 1 66
(David Barron) *t.k.h: hld up in tch: struggling over 2f out: n.d after* **8/1**

2164 **9** 2 3/4 **Mushaakis (IRE)**[24] 5562 3-8-10 **85** .... JoeFanning 8 52
(Mark Johnston) *chsd ldrs tl hung rt and wknd over 2f out* **9/2**[2]

1m 40.67s (0.67) **Going Correction** +0.15s/f (Good)
WFA 3 from 4yo+ 5lb **9** Ran SP% **115.7**
Speed ratings (Par 107): **102,101,97,95,94 94,91,86,83**
toteswingers 1&2 £9.50, 1&3 £5.10, 2&3 £4.90 CSF £13.58 CT £46.66 TOTE £3.60: £1.50, £2.70, £2.30; EX 12.10 Trifecta £43.00 Pool: £1086.77 - 18.95 winning units..
Owner A Barnes **Bred** Smythson **Trained** Norton, N Yorks

■ Stewards' Enquiry : Daniel Tudhope two-day ban: used whip above permitted level (Sep 25-26)
Dale Swift four-day ban: used whip above permitted level (Sep 25,26,29,30)

FOCUS
A sound gallop for this decent handicap with the front two pulling clear and fighting out a thrilling finish.

6301 BET & WATCH WITH RACING UK'S APP H'CAP — 7f 200y
5:35 (5:36) (Class 5) (0-70,70) 3-Y-O+ **£2,726** (£805; £402) **Stalls** Low

Form RPR

3323 **1** **Confusing**[27] 5425 3-9-3 **68** .... DanielTudhope 6 77
(David O'Meara) *hld up in midfield: hdwy on outside over 2f out: led and hrd pressed ins fnl f: hld on wl* **9/1**

1022 **2** *nk* **Border Bandit (USA)**[21] 5637 5-9-1 **61** .... JoeFanning 3 69
(Tracy Waggott) *prom: effrt and rdn over 2f out: chal ins fnl f: kpt on: jst hld* **9/2**[2]

0001 **3** *hd* **First Class Favour (IRE)**[14] 5881 5-8-12 **58** .... DavidAllan 4 66
(Tim Easterby) *led: rdn over 2f out: hdd ins fnl f: kpt on: hld cl home* **16/1**

444 **4** 3/4 **Aramist (IRE)**[106] 2754 3-9-3 **68** .... BenCurtis 12 74
(Alan Swinbank) *s.i.s: bhd: rdn 1/2-way: gd hdwy on outside over 1f out: kpt on strly towards fin* **16/1**

334 **5** 1 1/2 **Dance For Georgie**[21] 5637 4-8-13 **64** .... GeorgeChaloner(5) 15 66
(Ben Haslam) *t.k.h: hld up in tch: effrt over 2f out: edgd rt over 1f out: kpt on same pce ins fnl f* **11/2**[3]

0-01 **6** 4 **Cape Samba**[19] 5713 4-9-8 **68** .... RobertWinston 10 61
(Ismail Mohammed) *prom: effrt and rdn over 2f out: wknd appr fnl f* **8/1**

0263 **7** 1 1/4 **Blue Maisey**[12] 5974 5-8-12 **65** .... KevinStott(7) 5 55
(Edwin Tuer) *hld up: drvn and outpcd over 2f out: n.d after* **4/1**[1]

0-0 **8** 1/2 **Indian Giver**[29] 5369 5-8-13 **62** .... PaulPickard(3) 7 51
(Alan Berry) *bhd: rdn along 3f out: no imp fr 2f out* **33/1**

3326 **9** 3 1/4 **Rex Romanorum (IRE)**[68] 4007 5-9-0 **67** .... JackGarritty(7) 13 49
(Patrick Holmes) *chsd ldr: rdn over 3f out: wknd fr 2f out* **9/1**

1503 **10** *shd* **Apache Rising**[15] 5870 3-9-5 **70** .... GrahamLee 8 51
(Bryan Smart) *hld up in midfield on outside: hdwy wl over 2f out: rdn and wknd wl over 1f out* **12/1**

3-41 **11** 2 **Cheers Buddy (IRE)**[13] 5921 5-8-10 **56** .... TomEaves 2 33
(Keith Dalgleish) *s.i.s: hld up: stdy hdwy over 3f out: rdn and wknd over 2f out* **15/2**

1m 41.28s (1.28) **Going Correction** +0.15s/f (Good)
WFA 3 from 4yo+ 5lb **11** Ran SP% **118.8**
Speed ratings (Par 103): **99,98,98,97,96 92,91,90,87,87 85**
toteswingers 1&2 £5.20, 1&3 £29.60, 2&3 £16.40 CSF £49.81 CT £651.45 TOTE £12.50: £4.40, £3.20, £4.10; EX 65.80 Trifecta £515.80 Pool: £734.82 - 1.06 winning units..
Owner P D Player **Bred** Whatton Manor Stud **Trained** Nawton, N Yorks

FOCUS
Four non-runners on account of the ground, but still an open contest. A 4lb personal best from the winner.

6302 LLOYD LTD H'CAP — 1m 6f 32y
6:05 (6:05) (Class 3) (0-90,90) 3-Y-O+ **£8,086** (£2,406; £1,202; £601) **Stalls** Low

Form RPR

0050 **1** **Sirvino**[19] 5706 8-9-7 **86** .... LMcNiff(3) 8 97
(David Barron) *hld up: smooth hdwy to ld over 1f out: pushed clr ins fnl f: readily* **20/1**

4206 **2** 3 **Hepworth**[47] 4720 4-9-4 **80** .... (p) RobertHavlin 11 87
(John Gosden) *hld up: pushed along 3f out: edgd rt over 1f out: chsd wnr fnl f: kpt on: no imp* **16/1**

1102 **3** 3 3/4 **Lion Beacon**[27] 5448 3-8-11 **84** .... GrahamLee 2 86
(Amanda Perrett) *pressed ldr: rdn 3f out: ev ch over 1f out: sn one pce* **12/5**[1]

5422 **4** 1 1/2 **Rio's Rosanna (IRE)**[19] 5723 6-9-11 **87** .... RussKennemore 5 87+
(Richard Whitaker) *t.k.h early: chsd ldrs: drvn and ev ch briefly over 1f out: sn outpcd* **7/2**[2]

532 **5** 1 **Good Speech (IRE)**[25] 5549 3-7-11 **73** oh1 .... RaulDaSilva(3) 6 72
(Tom Tate) *hld up in tch: hdwy on outside and ev ch over 1f out: sn rdn and outpcd* **5/1**

-116 **6** 1/2 **O Ma Lad (IRE)**[33] 5237 5-10-0 **90** .... (p) MichaelO'Connell 9 88
(John Quinn) *hld up towards rr: rdn over 2f out: edgd rt and no imp over 1f out* **17/2**

0000 **7** 3 1/2 **Crackentorp**[21] 5655 8-9-9 **85** .... DavidAllan 7 79
(Tim Easterby) *hld up: drvn along over 4f out: no imp fr 2f out* **14/1**

651 **8** 9 **Hunting Ground (USA)**[14] 5902 3-8-13 **86** .... JoeFanning 4 68
(Mark Johnston) *t.k.h: led: rdn and hdd over 1f out: sn wknd* **9/2**[3]

0040 **9** 5 **Persian Peril**[16] 5831 9-8-11 **73** .... BenCurtis 10 48
(Alan Swinbank) *hld up in tch: rdn 3f out: wknd wl over 1f out* **40/1**

3m 14.4s (6.90) **Going Correction** +0.15s/f (Good)
WFA 3 from 4yo+ 11lb **9** Ran SP% **116.8**
Speed ratings (Par 107): **86,84,82,81,80 80,78,73,70**
toteswingers 1&2 £17.00, 1&3 £10.40, 2&3 £5.60 CSF £299.63 CT £1053.88 TOTE £17.90: £5.90, £5.50, £2.00; EX 293.10 Trifecta £518.10 Pool: £690.91 - 0.05 winning units..
Owner Theo Williams and Charles Mocatta **Bred** Allan Perry **Trained** Maunby, N Yorks

FOCUS
A number of progressive types in the field but it was an old-timer who landed this in fine style. The winner is rated in line with his best form in the past year.
T/Plt: £37.60 to a £1 stake. Pool: £63409.55 - 1230.12 winning tickets T/Qpdt: £2.50 to a £1 stake. Pool: £4918.89 - 1424.19 winning tickets RY

5515 DONCASTER (L-H)
Wednesday, September 11

OFFICIAL GOING: Good changing to good to soft after race 1 (2:00)
Wind: Light half against Weather: Overcast and rain

6303 ARENA GROUP NURSERY H'CAP — 7f
2:00 (2:01) (Class 2) 2-Y-O **£9,703** (£2,887; £1,443; £721) **Stalls** High

Form RPR

312 **1** **Braidley (IRE)**[16] 5829 2-8-11 **79** .... TedDurcan 14 90+
(James Bethell) *hld up in rr: swtchd rt to outer and gd hdwy 3f out: rdn to ld 1 1/2f out: clr whn flashed tail ins fnl f: kpt on strly* **9/1**

3100 **2** 3 1/4 **Master Carpenter (IRE)**[62] 4212 2-9-7 **89** .... AndreaAtzeni 6 91
(Rod Millman) *dwlt: hld up towards rr: pushed along and sltly outpcd over 3f out: swtchd rt 2f out: rdn to chse ldrs whn edgd lft over 1f out: styd on to chse wnr fnl f: no imp* **7/1**

2036 **3** 1 1/2 **Jazz (IRE)**[21] 5656 2-9-1 **83** .... WilliamBuick 3 81
(Charles Hills) *lw: t.k.h: trckd ldrs: hdwy over 2f out: sn cl up: rdn and ev ch over 1f out: kpt on same pce* **9/2**[1]

436 **4** *nk* **Supersta**[19] 5727 2-8-5 **73** .... HarryBentley 13 70
(Ronald Harris) *trckd ldrs on outer: hdwy over 2f out: sn disputing ld: rdn and hung lft wl over 1f out: sn drvn and one pce* **6/1**[2]

1231 **5** 1 1/4 **Finn Class (IRE)**[8] 6076 2-8-4 **79** 6ex .... LouisSteward(7) 1 73
(Michael Bell) *lw: prom: cl up 1/2-way: rdn to ld briefly 2f out: sn hdd and drvn: grad wknd* **13/2**[3]

4310 **6** 3/4 **Latenightrequest**[39] 4988 2-8-3 **71** .... PatrickMathers 7 63
(Richard Fahey) *trckd ldrs: pushed along and sltly outpcd over 2f out: rdn and hmpd wl over 1f out: swtchd rt and kpt on fnl f* **28/1**

0635 **7** 3/4 **Donny Rover (IRE)**[15] 5866 2-8-4 **72** ow3 .... (p) DavidProbert 9 62
(David C Griffiths) *chsd ldrs: rdn and hung lft wl over 1f out: sn btn* **16/1**

104 **8** 8 **Mr Carbonfootprint**[12] 5963 2-8-4 **72** .... BarryMcHugh 5 40
(Richard Fahey) *plld hrd: cl up: pushed along 1/2-way: sn wknd* **33/1**

4036 **9** 1 **Street Force (USA)**[18] 5745 2-9-4 **86** .... (b) TomQueally 2 52
(Clive Brittain) *dwlt: hld up in tch: effrt and sme hdwy on outer 3f out: rdn along over 2f out: sn wknd* **18/1**

1210 **10** 2 1/4 **Fair Ranger**[20] 5679 2-9-5 **87** .... RichardHughes 12 47
(Richard Hannon) *hld up in tch: pushed along 3f out: rdn and wknd 2f out* **9/2**[1]

6324 **11** 3 1/4 **Emaad (USA)**[18] 5745 2-8-5 **73** .... PaulHanagan 8 24
(Mark Johnston) *lw: led: rdn along 3f out: hdd 2f out and sn wknd* **8/1**

1m 27.76s (1.46) **Going Correction** +0.35s/f (Good) **11** Ran SP% **115.1**
Speed ratings (Par 101): **105,101,99,99,97 96,96,86,85,83 79**
toteswingers 1&2 £15.50, 1&3 £6.00, 2&3 £6.50 CSF £69.16 CT £328.26 TOTE £10.30: £2.60, £2.30, £2.20; EX 74.60 Trifecta £688.10 Pool: £1227.10 - 1.33 winning units..
Owner Clarendon Thoroughbred Racing **Bred** A Pettinari **Trained** Middleham Moor, N Yorks

FOCUS
The stalls were placed against the stands' rail for this decent nursery, but the jockeys decided to race up the centre and those held up seemed to be at an advantage. The winner impressed and the form looks solid.

6304 IRISH STALLION FARMS E B F CONDITIONS STKS — 6f
2:30 (2:30) (Class 2) 2-Y-O **£12,450** (£3,728; £1,864; £932; £466) **Stalls** High

Form RPR

1 **1** **Lightning Thunder**[25] 5529 2-8-8 0 .... HarryBentley 4 96+
(Olly Stevens) *lw: stdd and plld hrd early stages: trckd ldrs: hdwy to chse ldr over 1f out: rdn to chal ent fnl f: narrow advantage fnl 100yds: jst hld on* **5/2**[3]

1205 **2** *shd* **Justice Day (IRE)**[18] 5765 2-9-1 103 .... RyanMoore 1 103
(David Elsworth) *led: rdn and qcknd over 1f out: drvn ent fnl f: hdd narrowly last 100yds: rallied nr line: jst failed* **9/4**[2]

1542 **3** hd **Expert (IRE)**[8] 6065 2-8-13 91 RichardHughes 2 100
(Richard Hannon) *trckd ldrs: hdwy over 1f out: swtchd lft to chal on outer ent fnl f and sn ev ch tl rdn and nt qckn nr line* **2/1**[1]

1122 **4** 3 ¾ **Scruffy Tramp (IRE)**[33] 5228 2-8-11 92 SeanLevey 3 87
(Michael Wigham) *hld up in rr: hdwy over 1f out: rdn and no imp fnl f* **20/1**

2116 **5** hd **Free Code (IRE)**[10] 6021 2-8-13 86 (b[1]) PaulMulrennan 5 89
(James Tate) *trckd ldr: cl up 2f out: sn rdn and wknd over 1f out* **8/1**

1m 15.34s (1.74) **Going Correction** +0.35s/f (Good) **5** Ran SP% **108.5**
Speed ratings (Par 101): **102,101,101,96,96**
CSF £8.25 TOTE £3.90: £2.10, £1.50; EX 9.30 Trifecta £19.00 Pool: £1552.22 - 61.01 winning units..
Owner Mohd Al Kubasi & Pearl Bloodstock Ltd **Bred** S A Douch **Trained** Chiddingfold, Surrey

FOCUS
A decent conditions race and there little between the front three at the line. The form looks straightforward and the winner might have more to come.

6305 CROWN HOTEL BAWTRY SCARBROUGH STKS (LISTED RACE) 5f
3:00 (3:00) (Class 1) 2-Y-0+ **£23,680** (£8,956; £4,476; £2,236) **Stalls** High

Form RPR

2513 **1** **Justineo**[40] 4947 4-9-11 108 (b) WilliamBuick 6 109+
(Roger Varian) *qckly away and mde all: qcknd clr 2f out: rdn and edgd rt ins fnl f: kpt on* **4/1**[1]

2104 **2** 1 ½ **Masamah (IRE)**[11] 5984 7-9-11 106 (p) RyanMoore 7 104
(Marco Botti) *lw: in tch: hdwy 2f out: rdn to chse wnr ent fnl f: sn drvn and no imp towards fin* **4/1**[1]

5003 **3** hd **Judge 'n Jury**[4] 6190 9-9-11 96 (t) FrankieDettori 11 103
(Ronald Harris) *racd nr stands' rail: prom: rdn and cl up 2f out: drvn ins fnl f: kpt on same pce towards fin* **14/1**

0430 **4** 1 ¼ **Excelette (IRE)**[11] 5984 4-9-6 102 PaulHanagan 4 93
(Bryan Smart) *chsd ldrs: rdn 2f out: drvn and one pce appr fnl f* **10/1**

6003 **5** 1 ¼ **Borderlescott**[11] 5984 11-9-11 106 PaulMulrennan 5 94
(Robin Bastiman) *chsd ldrs: rdn along and outpcd 1/2-way: styd on fnl f* **16/1**

3050 **6** 1 ½ **Hoyam**[18] 5772 3-9-5 99 TomQueally 10 83
(Michael Bell) *dwlt and towards rr: rdn along and hdwy wl over 1f out: kpt on u.p fnl f: n.d* **12/1**

3006 **7** ¾ **Tangerine Trees**[11] 5984 8-9-11 104 (v) JoeFanning 1 86
(Bryan Smart) *prom on wd outside: effrt 2f out: sn rdn and wknd over 1f out* **8/1**[3]

-501 **8** ½ **Magical Macey (USA)**[75] 3776 6-9-11 102 (b) GrahamGibbons 2 84
(David Barron) *prom: rdn along 2f out: sn wknd* **8/1**[3]

1050 **9** nk **Medicean Man**[40] 4947 7-10-0 107 (p) SteveDrowne 3 86
(Jeremy Gask) *dwlt: a towards rr* **15/2**[2]

0031 **10** ½ **Swan Song**[16] 5821 4-9-6 93 DavidProbert 8 76
(Andrew Balding) *racd towards stands' rail: in tch: rdn along over 2f out: sn outpcd* **16/1**

0400 **11** 6 **Bungle Inthejungle**[19] 5726 3-9-10 102 MartinHarley 9 60
(Mick Channon) *lw: a towards rr: outpcd and bhd fnl 2f* **12/1**

59.92s (-0.58) **Going Correction** +0.10s/f (Good)
WFA 3 from 4yo+ 1lb **11** Ran SP% **116.9**
Speed ratings: **108,105,105,103,101 98,97,96,96,95 86**
toteswingers 1&2 £1.90, 1&3 £11.30, 2&3 £9.80 CSF £18.11 TOTE £4.00: £2.00, £1.60, £3.70; EX 17.10 Trifecta £149.20 Pool: £2814.33 - 14.13 winning units..
Owner Saleh Al Homaizi & Imad Al Sagar **Bred** Saleh Al Homaizi & Imad Al Sagar **Trained** Newmarket, Suffolk

FOCUS
Little got into this Listed race. The time compared quite well with the later handicap and the third sets the standard.

6306 CLIPPER LOGISTICS LEGER LEGENDS CLASSIFIED STKS 1m (S)
3:35 (3:37) (Class 5) 3-Y-0+ **£6,469** (£1,443; £1,443; £481) **Stalls** High

Form RPR

0126 **1** **Dana's Present**[8] 6089 4-11-0 70 WillieSupple 8 76
(George Baker) *trckd ldrs: hdwy and cl up over 2f out: rdn over 1f out: drvn ins fnl f: styd on wl towards fin to ld on line* **12/1**

0112 **2** nse **Pelmanism**[37] 5070 6-11-0 67 GayKelleway 12 76+
(Brian Ellison) *hld up towards rr: hdwy 3f out: swtchd rt to stands' rail 2f out: rdn and str run to ld over 1f out: drvn and wknd towards fin: hdd on line* **11/1**

1040 **2** dht **Excellent Puck (IRE)**[17] 5802 3-10-9 70 JimmyMcCarthy 10 76
(Jamie Osborne) *lw: in tch: hdwy 3f out: chsd ldrs 2f out: sn rdn and styd on wl fnl f: jst failed* **12/1**

1-60 **4** 2 ½ **Self Employed**[116] 2463 6-11-0 69 CarlLlewellyn 15 70
(Garry Woodward) *prom: hdwy to ld 2f out: rdn and hdd over 1f out: wknd ins fnl f* **10/1**

4132 **5** 3 **Jay Bee Blue**[13] 5931 4-11-0 67 (bt) LukeHarvey 7 63
(Sean Curran) *in tch: hdwy 3f out: rdn to chse ldrs over 1f out: drvn and one pce fnl f* **20/1**

-000 **6** 1 ¼ **Mr Spiggott (IRE)**[98] 2981 4-11-0 70 (v) NickConnorton 6 60
(Gary Moore) *trckd ldrs: hdwy 3f out: cl up 2f out: sn rdn and wknd ent fnl f* **14/1**

0521 **7** 6 **Piceno (IRE)**[12] 5947 5-11-0 70 (p) TonyCulhane 19 47
(Scott Dixon) *lw: trckd ldr: hdwy and cl up 1/2-way: disp ld 3f out: rdn 2f out and grad wknd* **13/2**[2]

0440 **8** 2 **Berlusca (IRE)**[29] 5369 4-11-0 69 DavidO'Meara 16 42
(David O'Meara) *dwlt: a towards rr* **20/1**

0004 **9** shd **Sword In Hand**[26] 5474 4-11-0 70 (t) DaleGibson 18 42
(Alan Jarvis) *led: rdn along 3f out: hdd 2f out and sn wknd* **9/1**

4600 **10** ½ **Orders From Rome (IRE)**[78] 3661 4-11-0 67 (t) GaryBardwell 4 41
(Eve Johnson Houghton) *nvr bttr than midfield* **40/1**

0613 **11** 1 **My Guardian Angel**[91] 3218 4-11-0 69 JohnLowe 13 38
(Mark H Tompkins) *swtg: prom: rdn along 1/2-way: sn wknd* **16/1**

4034 **12** 3 ¾ **Callmeakhab (IRE)**[12] 5975 3-10-9 69 MichaelHills 2 30
(Charles Hills) *chsd ldrs: rdn along 3f out: sn drvn and wknd over 2f out* **11/2**[1]

5141 **13** 1 **Winslow Arizona (IRE)**[13] 5935 3-10-9 69 WillieRyan 9 27
(Michael Bell) *a towards rr* **8/1**[3]

0035 **14** 2 ¼ **Sardanapalus**[15] 5861 4-11-0 70 (p) KevinDarley 11 22
(Kevin Ryan) *dwlt: a towards rr* **10/1**

-260 **15** ¾ **Waltz Darling (IRE)**[25] 3545 5-11-0 67 WillieNewton 17 21
(Keith Reveley) *a towards rr* **50/1**

1m 43.18s (3.88) **Going Correction** +0.35s/f (Good)
WFA 3 from 4yo+ 5lb **15** Ran SP% **118.2**
Speed ratings (Par 103): **94,93,93,91,88 87,81,79,79,78 77,73,72,70,69**
PLACE: Pelmanism £3.40, Excellent Puck £5.10 EX: DP/P £77.90, DP/EP £104.00 CSF: DP/P £64.44, DP/EP £69.49 TOTE £12.50: £3.70 Trifecta £873.70 3-8-15 & 3-15-8. Part won. Pool: £0.62 - 2330.09 winning units..
Owner Whitsbury Racing Club **Bred** Newsells Park Stud **Trained** Manton, Wilts

FOCUS
The fourth running of this "legends" contest and it was as dramatic a renewal as any. The form may not be reliable, however. The winner took his turf form to his 3yo AW level.

6307 PARK HILL HOSPITAL CONDITIONS STKS 1m 2f 60y
4:10 (4:10) (Class 2) 3-5-Y-0 **£12,450** (£3,728; £1,864; £932) **Stalls** Low

Form RPR

203 **1** **Out Of Bounds (USA)**[193] 871 4-9-2 110 SilvestreDeSousa 2 110
(Saeed bin Suroor) *well made: lengthy: lw: mde all: pushed along 3f out: rdn 2f out: drvn ins fnl f: edgd lft and styd on wl* **11/4**[2]

016- **2** ½ **Gatewood**[158] 1407 5-9-2 109 WilliamBuick 1 109
(John Gosden) *trckd wnr: hdwy over 3f out: effrt over 2f out: sn rdn: drvn ent fnl f: kpt on* **1/1**[1]

0/05 **3** 13 **Ocean War**[53] 4526 5-9-2 106 MickaelBarzalona 3 84
(Charlie Appleby) *stdd s and hld up: t.k.h: hdwy to trck ldng pair after 3f: effrt over 3f out: rdn wl over 2f out: sn drvn and one pce* **4/1**[3]

0-55 **4** 9 **Whipper's Boy (IRE)**[16] 5822 3-8-9 100 PaulMulrennan 5 67
(Brian Meehan) *trckd ldng pair on outer: effrt 3f out: rdn along over 2f out: sn btn and eased wl over 1f out* **9/1**

2m 11.38s (1.98) **Going Correction** +0.425s/f (Yiel)
WFA 3 from 4yo+ 7lb **4** Ran SP% **106.7**
Speed ratings (Par 109): **109,108,98,91**
CSF £5.84 TOTE £2.80; EX 4.80 Trifecta £9.90 Pool: £1425.47 - 107.89 winning units..
Owner Godolphin **Bred** Darley **Trained** Newmarket, Suffolk

FOCUS
Not form to take much notice of going forward with doubts over the field. The winner is rated to his AW form with the second a length off his old British form.

6308 BEAUTY AT DONCASTER H'CAP 7f
4:45 (4:47) (Class 2) (0-100,95) 3-Y-0
£12,450 (£3,728; £1,864; £932; £466; £234) **Stalls** High

Form RPR

1-20 **1** **Breton Rock (IRE)**[109] 2655 3-9-4 **92** MartinLane 1 103
(David Simcock) *hld up and bhd: stdy run on wd outside fr over 2f out: led over 1f out: sn rdn and edgd rt: drvn ins fnl f and kpt on wl* **12/1**

1000 **2** ½ **One Word More (IRE)**[19] 5728 3-9-6 **94** GrahamGibbons 10 104
(Charles Hills) *trckd ldrs: hdwy over 2f out: n.m.r over 1f out: sn rdn and styd on to chse wnr ins fnl f: no imp nr fin* **25/1**

-145 **3** ¾ **Gold Hunter (IRE)**[27] 5439 3-9-4 **92** SilvestreDeSousa 8 100+
(Saeed bin Suroor) *hld up in rr: effrt and n.m.r over 2f out: swtchd rt to outer and rdn over 1f out: sn edgd rt: styd on strly fnl f: nrst fin* **7/1**[3]

2503 **4** ½ **Regal Dan (IRE)**[41] 4922 3-8-13 **87** RyanMoore 16 94
(Charles Hills) *prom: effrt 2f out and ev ch tl rdn over 1f out and kpt on same pce fnl f* **5/1**[1]

-260 **5** ½ **Flyman**[81] 3563 3-9-2 **90** LeeTopliss 15 95
(Richard Fahey) *lw: prom: cl up 1/2-way: rdn to ld wl over 1f out: sn hung lft and hdd appr fnl f: sn drvn and kpt on same pce* **33/1**

0226 **6** ½ **Fils Anges (IRE)**[27] 5439 3-9-2 **90** FrankieDettori 3 94
(Michael Bell) *trckd ldrs: hdwy over 2f out: pushed along whn n.m.r and hmpd over 1f out: kpt on same pce after* **14/1**

4026 **7** ½ **Makafeh**[46] 4743 3-9-4 **92** AndreaAtzeni 11 95
(Luca Cumani) *swtg: hld up towards rr: hdwy 2f out: rdn and kpt on fnl f: nrst fin* **9/1**

0532 **8** hd **Secretinthepark**[25] 5538 3-9-7 **95** SteveDrowne 9 97
(Ed McMahon) *swtg: hld up in midfield: hdwy over 2f out: sn rdn and kpt on u.p fnl f: nrst fin* **11/1**

4434 **9** ¾ **Secret Art (IRE)**[19] 5728 3-8-13 **87** JimCrowley 14 87
(Ralph Beckett) *lw: in tch: pushed along and sltly outpcd over 2f out: sn rdn and kpt on fnl f: nrst fin* **11/2**[2]

20 **10** 3 ½ **Homage (IRE)**[41] 4922 3-9-2 **90** WilliamBuick 17 81
(Jeremy Noseda) *hld up towards rr: hdwy over 2f out: sn rdn and no imp fnl f* **12/1**

0600 **11** ½ **Ahern**[25] 5538 3-9-1 **89** HarryBentley 2 78
(David Barron) *dwlt and swtchd rt s: a towards rr* **25/1**

0046 **12** 2 ½ **Chilworth Icon**[25] 5538 3-9-7 **95** MartinHarley 5 77
(Mick Channon) *in tch: hdwy to chse ldrs over 2f out: sn rdn and wknd over 1f out* **25/1**

5205 **13** 2 ½ **Shahdaroba (IRE)**[14] 5894 3-8-11 **92** (v[1]) PatMillman(7) 7 68
(Rod Millman) *prom: rdn along wl over 2f out: sn wknd* **22/1**

0000 **14** 1 ¼ **Masarah (IRE)**[19] 5728 3-9-5 **93** TomQueally 12 65
(Clive Brittain) *led: rdn along over 2f out: hdd wl over 1f out and sn wknd* **33/1**

311 **15** 2 ½ **Life Partner (IRE)**[19] 5721 3-9-6 **94** MickaelBarzalona 6 60
(Charlie Appleby) *hld up towards rr: effrt 3f out: sn rdn and btn: bhd and eased over 1f out* **7/1**[3]

5056 **16** ¾ **Steelriver (IRE)**[42] 4890 3-8-7 **81** oh1 PaulHanagan 13 45
(James Bethell) *chsd ldrs: rdn along wl over 2f out: sn wknd and bhd: eased over 1f out* **20/1**

1m 27.46s (1.16) **Going Correction** +0.35s/f (Good) **16** Ran SP% **124.0**
Speed ratings (Par 107): **107,106,105,105,104 103,103,103,102,98 97,94,91,90,87 86**
toteswingers 1&2 £64.20, 1&3 £10.90, 2&3 £31.50 CSF £290.45 CT £2354.86 TOTE £15.80: £3.40, £6.30, £2.30, £1.70; EX 398.10 Trifecta £2196.40 Pool: £2928.55 - 0.20 winning units..
Owner John Cook **Bred** George Kent **Trained** Newmarket, Suffolk

FOCUS
A decent handicap and again they raced as one group up the centre. The form is rated on the positive side around the fifth to seventh.

6309 BERENDSEN WORKWEAR H'CAP 5f
5:15 (5:19) (Class 4) (0-85,85) 3-Y-0+ **£6,469** (£1,925; £962; £481) **Stalls** High

Form RPR

3005 **1** **Sir Pedro**[12] 5971 4-8-10 **74** WilliamBuick 21 85
(Charles Hills) *lw: racd nr stands' rail: trckd ldr: hdwy to ld 2f out: rdn over 1f out: jnd and drvn ins fnl f: hld on gamely towards fin* **7/1**[2]

2335 **2** nk **Commanche**[8] 6067 4-8-7 **76** RobertTart(5) 18 86
(Chris Dwyer) *in tch: hdwy wl over 1f out: rdn and str run to chal ins fnl f: ev ch tl drvn and no ex nr fin* **8/1**[3]

3544 **3** 3 **Silvanus (IRE)**[12] 5971 8-9-0 **78** PaulHanagan 9 77+
(Paul Midgley) *trckd ldrs: swtchd lft and hdwy wl over 1f out: effrt whn nt clr run ent fnl f: sn swtchd rt and rdn: styd on wl towards fin* **14/1**

00 **4** hd **Perfect Blossom**[5] 6159 6-9-1 **79** PaulMulrennan 7 77
(Alan Berry) *lw: hld up and bhd: hdwy 2f out: nt clr run over 1f out: sn swtchd rt and styd on fnl f: nrst fin* **33/1**

1332 **5** shd **Haajes**[41] 4930 9-9-1 **79** (v) LeeTopliss 10 77
(Paul Midgley) *midfield: rdn along: lost pl and bhd 1/2-way: swtchd rt and hdwy over 1f out: styd on wl u.p fnl f: nrst fin* **12/1**

3240 **6** 1 **Rylee Mooch**[4] 6189 5-9-3 **81**.....(e) MartinHarley 14 75
(Richard Guest) *prom: cl up 2f out: sn rdn and one pce ent fnl f* **14/1**
0000 **7** nse **Hazelrigg (IRE)**[14] 5901 8-8-9 **73**.....(e) BarryMcHugh 13 67
(Tim Easterby) *in tch: hdwy wl over 1f out: rdn and kpt on fnl f: nrst fin* **20/1**
6120 **8** 1 **Adam's Ale**[28] 5381 4-8-7 **76**..... ShirleyTeasdale(5) 4 67
(Paul Midgley) *chsd ldrs: rdn along over 1f out: sn one pce* **16/1**
6000 **9** 2 **Profile Star (IRE)**[5] 6159 4-8-12 **76**..... GrahamGibbons 2 59
(David Barron) *lw: prom in centre: rdn along wl over 1f out: drvn and wknd appr fnl f* **25/1**
0501 **10** 3/4 **Bronze Beau**[11] 5985 6-8-12 **81**.....(tp) JacobButterfield(5) 22 62
(Kristin Stubbs) *racd nr stands' rail: led: rdn along and hdd 2f out: grad wknd* **16/1**
0016 **11** 3 1/2 **Noodles Blue Boy**[25] 5519 7-9-2 **80**.....(p) RyanMoore 11 48
(Ollie Pears) *chsd ldrs: rdn along wl over 1f out: drvn and wknd appr fnl f* **14/1**
0626 **12** 1 **Satsuma**[47] 4734 3-8-13 **83**..... ConnorBeasley(5) 8 48
(David Brown) *prom: rdn along 2f out: sn drvn and wknd over 1f out* **16/1**
0041 **13** hd **Threes Grand**[18] 5769 3-9-1 **85**..... TimClark(5) 17 49
(Scott Dixon) *b.hind: dwlt and in rr: sme hdwy 2f out: sn rdn and btn whn n.m.r over 1f out* **9/2**[1]
-240 **14** 3/4 **Even Stevens**[11] 5991 5-9-5 **83**.....(p) TomQueally 5 44
(Scott Dixon) *chsd ldrs: rdn along 2f out: sn wknd* **10/1**
-005 **15** 1 1/4 **Cheveton**[48] 4690 9-9-4 **82**..... SteveDrowne 1 39
(Richard Price) *lw: dwlt: a bhd* **16/1**
1123 **16** 1 **Sleepy Blue Ocean**[25] 5519 7-9-1 **79**.....(p) AndrewMullen 12 32
(John Balding) *prom: rdn along wl over 1f out: sn drvn and wknd over 1f out* **12/1**

1m 0.2s (-0.30) **Going Correction** +0.10s/f (Good)
WFA 3 from 4yo+ 1lb **16** Ran SP% **121.3**
Speed ratings (Par 105): **106,105,100,100,100 98,98,96,93,92 86,85,85,83,81 80**
toteswingers 1&2 £19.50, 1&3 £14.90, 2&3 Not won CSF £60.11 CT £807.46 TOTE £9.20: £2.30, £3.10, £3.20, £7.20; EX 93.70 Trifecta £1250.40 Pool: £1667.29 - 0.70 winning units..
Owner R Morecombe, J Netherthorpe, C Wright **Bred** C J Mills **Trained** Lambourn, Berks

FOCUS
Little got into what was a fair sprint handicap. Small steps up from the first two, who were always prominent towards the stands' side.
T/Jkpt: Not won. T/Plt: £374.00 to a £1 stake. Pool: £134865.27 - 263.23 winning tickets T/Qpdt: £73.90 to a £1 stake. Pool: £8330.89 - 83.40 winning tickets JR

6197
KEMPTON (A.W) (R-H)
Wednesday, September 11

OFFICIAL GOING: Standard
Wind: Moderate, half against Weather: Raining

6310 COMMISSION FREE 1ST MONTH AT BETDAQ CLASSIFIED CLAIMING STKS 6f (P)
5:45 (5:46) (Class 5) 3-Y-0+ **£2,587** (£770; £384; £192) **Stalls** Low

Form RPR
0051 **1** **Gabrial's Gift (IRE)**[10] 6018 4-9-1 75..... KierenFallon 8 84
(David Simcock) *sn trckd ldr: led jst over 2f out: pushed clr over 1f out: comf* **4/5**[1]
3510 **2** 3 1/4 **Assembly**[26] 5477 3-8-9 70.....(b) JamesDoyle 5 70
(William Haggas) *rousted early to chse ldrs: prog 1/2-way: chsd wnr over 1f out: sn rdn and nt qckn: kpt on but wl hld after* **5/1**[2]
-600 **3** 3 **Torres Del Paine**[13] 5928 6-8-7 68.....(v[1]) WilliamCarson 3 56
(Brett Johnson) *settled in last trio: prog on wd outside jst over 2f out: hanging but chsd ldng pair jst over 1f out: no imp: fin tired* **16/1**
1605 **4** 1 1/4 **Song Of Parkes**[13] 5931 6-8-9 73.....(p) SladeO'Hara(5) 4 59
(Peter Grayson) *trckd ldrs on inner: urged along over 2f out: no imp over 1f out: outpcd* **20/1**
2063 **5** 1 3/4 **We Have A Dream**[8] 6077 8-8-8 70.....(tp) CharlesBishop(3) 7 50
(Violet M Jordan) *led to jst over 2f out: steadily wknd over 1f out* **12/1**
046 **6** nk **Frognal (IRE)**[9] 6039 7-8-2 72.....(bt) OisinMurphy(7) 2 47
(Paddy Butler) *stdd s: hld up in last: pushed along bef 1/2-way: no prog tl kpt on fr over 1f out* **14/1**
0466 **7** 3 1/2 **Rondeau (GR)**[6] 6135 8-8-8 69..... ThomasBrown(3) 10 38
(Patrick Chamings) *racd wd: chsd ldrs: wknd jst over 2f out* **8/1**[3]
004 **8** 1/2 **Danziger (IRE)**[36] 5094 4-8-6 70.....(p) DeclanBates(3) 9 35
(David Evans) *chsd ldrs tl wknd jst over 2f out* **25/1**
400- **9** 3 1/4 **Jemimaville (IRE)**[364] 6150 6-8-2 49.....(v) RyanPowell(3) 1 20
(Giles Bravery) *a in last trio: wknd over 2f out* **100/1**
210/ **10** 16 **Alkhataaf (USA)**[1144] 4398 6-8-12 70..... SimonPearce(3) 11
(Lydia Pearce) *racd v wd in midfield: wknd bef 1/2-way: t.o* **25/1**

1m 11.6s (-1.50) **Going Correction** -0.125s/f (Stan)
WFA 3 from 4yo+ 2lb **10** Ran SP% **117.0**
Speed ratings (Par 103): **105,100,96,95,92 92,87,86,82,61**
toteswingers 1&2 £2.10, 1&3 £4.60, 2&3 £13.00 CSF £4.61 TOTE £1.70: £1.10, £2.50, £7.60; EX 6.30 Trifecta £44.20 Pool: £2044.84 - 34.69 winning units..Gabrial's Gift was claimed by Mr Paul J. Dixon for £10,000. Assembly was claimed by Mr P. M. Phelan for £8,000.
Owner Dr Marwan Koukash **Bred** Skymarc Farm **Trained** Newmarket, Suffolk

FOCUS
Drizzly, cool conditions at the start of this eight-race card. An easy winner in this claimer.

6311 RUCKUSWIRELESS.COM NURSERY H'CAP 7f (P)
6:15 (6:15) (Class 6) (0-65,65) 2-Y-0 **£1,940** (£577; £288; £144) **Stalls** Low

Form RPR
406 **1** **Relation Alexander (IRE)**[27] 5435 2-9-4 **62**..... FrederikTylicki 8 73+
(Paul D'Arcy) *in tch: pushed along 1/2-way: rdn and prog on outer wl over 2f out: led wl over 1f out: hung to nr side rail but clr fnl f: styd on wl* **9/2**[3]
003 **2** 2 1/2 **Acquaint (IRE)**[22] 5603 2-9-6 **64**..... RichardHughes 9 68+
(Richard Hannon) *hld up in rr: rdn wl over 2f out: prog over 1f out: tk 2nd ins fnl f: styd on wl but no ch to rch wnr* **8/1**
5260 **3** 2 3/4 **Mawzoona**[12] 5951 2-9-1 **62**..... CharlesBishop(3) 4 59
(Mick Channon) *wl in tch: shkn up over 2f out: kpt on at one pce after and tk 3rd ins fnl f* **12/1**
465 **4** 3/4 **Herbah**[56] 4409 2-9-5 **63**..... DaneO'Neill 13 58
(Roger Varian) *nt that wl away: prog on outer fr wd draw and prom after 2f: circled rivals to go 2nd over 3f out to jst over 2f out: chsd wnr over 1f out to ins fnl f: wknd* **3/1**[2]
4014 **5** 3 1/4 **Lady Marl**[12] 5951 2-9-6 **64**..... GeorgeBaker 5 50
(Gary Moore) *blanket c off after horse lft stalls: hld up in rr: rdn and prog on inner over 2f out: no imp over 1f out: wknd fnl f* **11/4**[1]
665 **6** 2 1/4 **Speed Society**[22] 5603 2-8-12 **56**..... PatCosgrave 1 36
(Jim Boyle) *chsd ldng pair: pushed along over 4f out: wknd 2f out* **14/1**
000 **7** 1/2 **Assoluta (IRE)**[17] 5790 2-9-4 **62**..... LiamKeniry 11 41
(Sylvester Kirk) *dwlt: hld up in last pair: shkn up over 2f out: no great prog* **25/1**
0023 **8** 1 1/2 **Cabaan (IRE)**[6] 6131 2-9-7 **65**.....(b) JimmyFortune 7 40
(Brian Meehan) *led to wl over 1f out: wknd qckly* **12/1**
6001 **9** 1/2 **Notnow Penny**[16] 5814 2-8-0 **47**..... SimonPearce(3) 3 20
(Milton Bradley) *chsd ldr: pushed along over 4f out: lost 2nd over 3f out: sn wknd* **40/1**
0000 **10** 1 1/4 **Brockholes Flyer (IRE)**[8] 6076 2-8-10 **54**.....(v[1]) JackMitchell 12 24
(Brendan Powell) *plld hrd and sn hld up in last: shoved along and struggling 3f out* **66/1**
6400 **11** nk **Black Geronimo**[21] 5634 2-9-1 **62**..... DeclanBates(3) 6 31
(David Evans) *chsd ldrs to 1/2-way: sn wknd u.p* **25/1**

1m 25.86s (-0.14) **Going Correction** -0.125s/f (Stan) **11** Ran SP% **114.6**
Speed ratings (Par 93): **95,92,89,88,84 81,81,79,79,77 77**
toteswingers 1&2 £7.20, 1&3 £10.90, 2&3 £15.90 CSF £37.75 CT £409.46 TOTE £8.40: £2.80, £3.70, £3.30; EX 69.20 Trifecta £480.60 Pool: £1499.63 - 2.33 winning units..
Owner K Snell **Bred** Gerry Flannery Developments **Trained** Newmarket, Suffolk

FOCUS
A modest nursery in which the winner looks capable of scoring off higher marks and the second looks capable of winning before long.

6312 BETDAQ 1ST UK RACE COMMISSION FREE MAIDEN FILLIES' STKS 1m 4f (P)
6:45 (6:45) (Class 5) 3-4-Y-0 **£2,587** (£770; £384; £192) **Stalls** Centre

Form RPR
3 **1** **Speckled (USA)**[144] 1698 3-9-0 0..... AhmedAjtebi 9 83
(Charlie Appleby) *w.w: shkn up and prog on wd outside over 2f out: clsd qckly to ld over 1f out: styd on wl* **5/1**[3]
3350 **2** 3 1/4 **Whippy Cream (IRE)**[38] 5035 3-9-1 96 ow1..... AdamKirby 8 78
(Marco Botti) *forced to r wd: trckd ldrs: clsd over 3f out: led over 2f out: sn drvn: hdd and one pce over 1f out* **10/11**[1]
6555 **3** 1 3/4 **Near Time**[33] 5245 3-9-0 73.....[1] JimmyFortune 11 75
(Andrew Balding) *slowly away and pushed along early: mostly in 8th: rdn 3f out and sn outpcd: styd on fr 2f out to take 3rd last 100yds: nvr nrr* **8/1**
06 **4** 1 1/2 **Oscilate Wildly (IRE)**[107] 2713 3-9-0 0..... JamesDoyle 7 72
(Peter Chapple-Hyam) *wl in tch: drvn over 2f out: sn outpcd and btn* **25/1**
6334 **5** 3/4 **Snow Powder (IRE)**[12] 5942 3-9-0 83..... NickyMackay 6 71
(John Gosden) *mostly chsd ldr: rdn to chal and upsides over 2f out: chsd new ldr to over 1f out: wknd* **7/2**[2]
6 8 **Caterina De Medici (FR)**[271] 4-9-9 80..... KirstyMilczarek 10 58
(Ed Walker) *led to over 2f out: wknd qckly* **20/1**
0 **7** 20 **Ballyshonagh**[13] 5925 3-9-0 0..... TedDurcan 1 26
(Chris Wall) *chsd ldrs to over 3f out: wknd rapidly: t.o* **66/1**
06 **8** 27 **Feather Dancer**[72] 3902 3-8-11 0 ow2..... HarryPoulton(5) 4
(Jamie Poulton) *sn detached in last: wl t.o* **100/1**
5 **9** 3 1/4 **Ginjo**[13] 5925 3-9-0 0..... RichardKingscote 3
(Charles Hills) *chsd ldng pair to over 4f out: wknd rapidly: wl t.o* **20/1**

2m 32.4s (-2.10) **Going Correction** -0.125s/f (Stan)
WFA 3 from 4yo 9lb **9** Ran SP% **118.2**
Speed ratings (Par 100): **102,99,98,97,97 91,78,60,58**
toteswingers 1&2 £2.00, 1&3 £8.60, 2&3 £2.60 CSF £9.80 TOTE £4.80: £1.50, £1.10, £2.60; EX 11.00 Trifecta £75.40 Pool: £2269.91 - 22.55 winning units..
Owner Godolphin **Bred** Darley **Trained** Newmarket, Suffolk

FOCUS
Not an entirely satisfying contest, given the absence of Saddaqa and the uneven pace.

6313 £200 FREE BETS AT BETDAQ H'CAP 1m 4f (P)
7:15 (7:15) (Class 5) (0-75,75) 3-Y-0 **£2,587** (£770; £384; £192) **Stalls** Centre

Form RPR
6132 **1** **Lisa's Legacy**[8] 6071 3-9-4 **72**..... RichardKingscote 6 85
(Daniel Kubler) *trckd ldng pair: clsd to ld 2f out: rdn clr over 1f out: styd on wl* **7/2**[2]
256 **2** 5 **Apparently**[26] 5484 3-9-7 **75**..... AhmedAjtebi 4 80
(Charlie Appleby) *slowly away: hld up in last pair and detached early: shkn up over 2f out: prog on wd outside wl over 1f out: styd on to take 2nd last 75yds: no ch w wnr* **9/4**[1]
2314 **3** 3/4 **Kastini**[39] 5001 3-8-11 **65**..... RichardHughes 3 69
(Denis Coakley) *trckd ldrs in 5th: rdn and prog to chal jst over 2f out: chsd wnr after but lft bhd: fdd and lost 2nd last 75yds* **8/1**[3]
324 **4** 3/4 **Astorgs Galaxy**[33] 5233 3-9-1 **69**.....(p) PatDobbs 7 72
(Sir Michael Stoute) *chsd ldr: lost 2nd and squeezed out over 2f out: no ch after: kpt on again fnl f* **12/1**
0413 **5** hd **Tenor (IRE)**[67] 4075 3-9-3 **71**.....(t) DaneO'Neill 1 73
(Roger Varian) *trckd ldng pair: rdn and nt qckn over 2f out: kpt on same pce fr over 1f out* **9/4**[1]
036 **6** 5 **Bossa Nova Baby (IRE)**[87] 3364 3-9-2 **70**..... GeorgeBaker 2 64
(Charles Hills) *hld up in 6th: rdn and no prog over 2f out: wl btn over 1f out* **20/1**
2236 **7** 2 **Spieta (IRE)**[35] 5130 3-8-13 **67**..... KirstyMilczarek 5 58
(Luca Cumani) *led: kicked on over 3f out: hdd & wknd 2f out* **20/1**
-366 **8** 6 **Squeeze My Brain (IRE)**[30] 5356 3-9-4 **72**.....(t) JamesDoyle 8 53
(Ralph Beckett) *stdd s: hld up in last pair and detached early: no prog 3f out: wknd over 1f out* **20/1**

2m 32.5s (-2.00) **Going Correction** -0.125s/f (Stan) **8** Ran SP% **116.8**
Speed ratings (Par 101): **101,97,97,96,96 93,91,87**
toteswingers 1&2 £3.10, 1&3 £3.50, 2&3 £2.30 CSF £11.72 CT £55.58 TOTE £4.50: £1.50, £1.50, £2.20; EX 13.80 Trifecta £89.60 Pool: £1138.71 - 9.52 winning units..
Owner Mrs P Wilson & C Wilson **Bred** Mrs Patricia Wilson **Trained** Whitsbury, Hants

FOCUS
Another 1m4f race in which the pace slackened as they turned out with a circuit to go, and the winning time was 0.1secs slower than the preceding maiden.

6314 WINNERS ARE WELCOME AT BETDAQ CONDITIONS STKS 1m (P)
7:45 (7:45) (Class 4) 2-Y-0 **£3,752** (£1,116; £557; £278) **Stalls** Low

Form RPR
31 **1** **Day Of Conquest**[31] 5299 2-9-0 0..... RichardHughes 6 95
(Richard Hannon) *hld up in last: rousted and quick prog on wd outside over 2f out: ended against nr side rail and led over 1f out: drvn out* **5/2**[2]
1521 **2** 1 3/4 **Safety Check (IRE)**[18] 5745 2-9-0 95..... MickaelBarzalona 4 91
(Charlie Appleby) *t.k.h: hld up in last: prog 3f out: chsd on ldrs over 2f out: chal down centre over 1f out: styd on but hld ins fnl f* **5/4**[1]

415 **3** *2* **Zampa Manos (USA)**[18] 5745 2-8-11 81 ThomasBrown(3) 5 86
(Andrew Balding) *led 100yds: sn in 3rd: rdn to ld over 2f out to over 1f out: one pce* **17/2**

4221 **4** *1 3/4* **Greed Is Good**[12] 5968 2-8-9 78 JoeyHaynes(5) 3 82+
(K R Burke) *hld up in 4th: waiting for room on inner over 2f out: rdn and effrt wl over 1f out: one pce after* **8/1**

1536 **5** *1/2* **Lone Warrior (IRE)**[25] 5530 2-9-0 99 CathyGannon 1 81
(David Evans) *chsd ldr after 100yds tl wl over 2f out: brief rally wl over 1f out: sn no ex* **6/1**[3]

46 **6** *10* **Samtu (IRE)**[12] 5941 2-9-0 0 JamesDoyle 2 58
(Clive Brittain) *led after 100yds: rdn and hdd over 2f out: wknd over 1f out: eased* **25/1**

1m 39.66s (-0.14) **Going Correction** -0.125s/f (Stan) 6 Ran SP% **112.8**
Speed ratings (Par 97): **95,93,91,89,89 79**
toteswingers 1&2 £1.10, 1&3 £3.80, 2&3 £2.90 CSF £6.08 TOTE £3.10: £2.40, £1.10; EX 7.10 Trifecta £28.10 Pool: £1279.32 - 34.09 winning units..
Owner Mohammed Sultan **Bred** Bearstone Stud **Trained** East Everleigh, Wilts

FOCUS
A decent conditions' event, contested by six Polytrack debutants. The third and fourth are rated to their marks.

6315 RUCKUS WIRELESS H'CAP 1m (P)
8:15 (8:15) (Class 6) (0-65,65) 3-Y-0+ **£1,940** (£577; £288; £144) **Stalls** Low

Form RPR

-050 **1** **Silver Lace (IRE)**[26] 5491 4-9-7 62 TedDurcan 5 71
(Chris Wall) *sn in rr: rdn and stl wl in rr over 2f out: prog on wd outside over 1f out: sustained effrt to ld last stride* **9/1**

0010 **2** *hd* **Exclusive Waters (IRE)**[22] 5615 3-9-3 63 AdamKirby 7 71
(William Knight) *reminder after 100yds and urged along to chse ldrs: hrd rdn on outer over 2f out: styd on fr over 1f out to ld last 75yds: hdd post* **7/2**[1]

120 **3** *1/2* **Bowstar**[191] 878 4-9-7 62 (p) GeorgeBaker 9 69
(Michael Attwater) *prom: trckd ldr after 3f: led gng strly wl over 1f out: sn rdn: hdd and nt qckn last 75yds* **16/1**

6201 **4** *1/2* **Lady Sylvia**[6] 6146 4-9-10 65 PatDobbs 11 71
(Joseph Tuite) *wl in rr: sltly checked over 4f out and dropped to last: prog over 2f out: rdn over 1f out: styd on after but jst outpcd by finers out wd* **8/1**[3]

1121 **5** *3/4* **Victorian Number (FR)**[33] 5230 5-9-10 65 HayleyTurner 3 69
(Geoffrey Deacon) *mostly in midfield: rdn and nt qckn over 2f out: short of room briefly sn after: kpt on fr over 1f out: nt pce to chal* **10/1**

6006 **6** *3/4* **Tagalaka (IRE)**[35] 5135 3-9-1 61 JohnFahy 2 63
(Eve Johnson Houghton) *towards rr: prog fr 3f out: chsd ldr briefly over 1f out: fdd ins fnl f* **25/1**

5341 **7** *2 1/2* **Red Tulip**[13] 5923 3-9-3 63 FrederikTylicki 4 60
(James Fanshawe) *wl in rr: rdn over 2f out: prog to chse ldrs over 1f out: fdd ins fnl f* **8/1**[3]

0232 **8** *3/4* **Mishrif (USA)**[22] 5622 7-9-10 65 (v) RichardHughes 14 60
(J R Jenkins) *racd wd early: led after 2f: drvn and hdd over 1f out: wknd* **10/1**

2400 **9** *2* **Pat's Legacy (USA)**[18] 5762 7-9-5 60 FergusSweeney 1 50
(Pat Phelan) *prom on inner: rdn over 2f out: nt qckn over 1f out: fdd ins fnl f* **10/1**

000 **10** *3 1/4* **Diplomatic (IRE)**[35] 5135 8-9-8 63 (p) JimmyQuinn 10 46
(Michael Squance) *s.i.s: towards rr: rdn on inner over 2f out: no prog over 1f out* **20/1**

0304 **11** *hd* **Solvanna**[35] 5135 3-8-9 62 (p) OisinMurphy(7) 8 44
(Heather Main) *racd wd: mostly in rr: lost grnd bnd 3f out: nvr on terms after* **20/1**

0350 **12** *21* **Samoan (IRE)**[16] 5823 4-9-10 65 (b) DaneO'Neill 13
(Brian Meehan) *slowest away: prog on wd outside to chse ldrs 1/2-way: wknd rapidly wl over 2f out: t.o* **20/1**

31 **13** *9* **Arcadian Legend (USA)**[63] 4176 3-9-4 64 SebSanders 12
(Jeremy Noseda) *led 2f: rdn and wknd rapidly over 3f out: t.o* **5/1**[2]

1m 38.45s (-1.35) **Going Correction** -0.125s/f (Stan)
WFA 3 from 4yo+ 5lb 13 Ran SP% **122.4**
Speed ratings (Par 101): **101,100,100,99,99 98,95,95,93,89 89,68,59**
toteswingers 1&2 £10.30, 1&3 £45.60, 2&3 £13.50 CSF £39.11 CT £516.43 TOTE £9.20: £3.30, £1.80, £4.50; EX 71.60 Trifecta £726.30 Part won. Pool: £968.47 - 0.36 winning units..
Owner The Equema Partnership **Bred** Liam Queally **Trained** Newmarket, Suffolk

FOCUS
A generous-looking pace, and a winning time 1.2 seconds quicker than that of the preceding conditions event.

6316 RUCKUSWIRELESS.COM H'CAP (DIV I) 7f (P)
8:45 (8:45) (Class 5) (0-70,70) 3-Y-0+ **£2,587** (£770; £384; £192) **Stalls** Low

Form RPR

5500 **1** **Hierarch (IRE)**[35] 5135 6-8-9 62 LewisWalsh(7) 6 72
(David Simcock) *trckd ldrs: prog to go 2nd 2f out: urged into ld jst ins fnl f: hanging lft but kpt on: jst hld on* **14/1**

0252 **2** *hd* **Fantasy Gladiator**[17] 5799 7-9-10 70 (p) PatCosgrave 3 79+
(John Quinn) *towards rr: looking for room over 2f out: brought wd and prog over 1f out: styd on wl fnl f: jst failed* **11/1**

0056 **3** *1 1/2* **Scottish Lake**[174] 1096 5-9-10 70 (b) GeorgeBaker 10 75
(Olivia Maylam) *led: rdn over 1f out: hdd jst ins fnl f: nt qckn sn after: kpt on* **8/1**[2]

0064 **4** *hd* **Greensward**[28] 5406 7-9-8 68 (b) PatDobbs 11 72
(Mike Murphy) *dwlt: mostly in last trio: brought to nr side and prog over 1f out: styd on fnl f: nrst fin* **10/1**[3]

0430 **5** *nk* **Eager To Bow (IRE)**[28] 5398 7-9-3 70 OisinMurphy(7) 7 74
(Patrick Chamings) *towards rr: brought to nr side and drvn 2f out: styd on fr jst over 1f out: unable to chal* **8/1**[2]

0-54 **6** *1/2* **Jillywinks**[161] 1329 3-8-13 63 FrederikTylicki 12 64
(Scott Dixon) *wl in rr: last whn urged along over 2f out: kpt on fr over 1f out: nt pce to chal* **20/1**

5023 **7** *nk* **Black Truffle (FR)**[23] 5594 3-8-10 60 (e[1]) DavidProbert 1 60
(Mark Usher) *stdd s: sn in midfield: pushed along to chse ldrs over 1f out: nt qckn and one pce after* **8/1**[2]

3023 **8** *1/2* **Emiratesdotcom**[5] 6154 7-9-10 70 (p) RichardKingscote 2 70
(Milton Bradley) *hld up in midfield: rdn 2f out: one pce and no imp fnl f* **8/1**[2]

0551 **9** *nk* **Quintet (IRE)**[20] 5677 3-9-6 70 JimCrowley 13 68
(Ralph Beckett) *pressed ldrs: rdn and nt qckn over 2f out: lost 2nd sn after: fdd fnl f* **2/1**[1]

4534 **10** *2 1/2* **Shaunas Spirit (IRE)**[7] 6105 5-9-0 67 (p) PaulBooth(7) 5 60
(Dean Ivory) *t.k.h in midfield: brought towards nr side in st: nt qckn over 1f out: wknd* **20/1**

000- **11** *3 1/2* **Know No Fear**[348] 6638 8-9-6 66 TedDurcan 8 49
(Alastair Lidderdale) *stdd s: hld up in last: shuffled along on inner over 2f out: nvr involved: eased last 100yds* **25/1**

51-0 **12** *1* **Beam Of Light**[18] 5758 3-9-5 69 FergusSweeney 9 48
(Jamie Osborne) *racd on outer in midfield: wknd 2f out* **20/1**

0300 **13** *3 1/4* **Dvinsky (USA)**[55] 4424 12-8-10 56 oh10 (b) JimmyQuinn 4 28
(Roger Ingram) *drvn to chse ldng pair: wknd over 2f out* **50/1**

1m 25.43s (-0.57) **Going Correction** -0.125s/f (Stan)
WFA 3 from 5yo+ 4lb 13 Ran SP% **122.0**
Speed ratings (Par 103): **98,97,96,95,95 94,94,94,93,90 86,85,81**
toteswingers 1&2 £22.30, 1&3 £15.80, 2&3 £13.90 CSF £150.29 CT £1373.59 TOTE £17.30: £4.50, £2.50, £2.60; EX 177.60 Trifecta £398.10 Pool: £1166.30 - 2.19 winning units..
Owner Tick Tock Partnership **Bred** Castlemartin Stud And Skymarc Farm **Trained** Newmarket, Suffolk
■ Stewards' Enquiry : George Baker three-day ban: careless riding (Sep 25,26,29)

6317 RUCKUSWIRELESS.COM H'CAP (DIV II) 7f (P)
9:15 (9:15) (Class 5) (0-70,70) 3-Y-0+ **£2,587** (£770; £384; £192) **Stalls** Low

Form RPR

2453 **1** **First Class**[46] 4752 5-9-1 61 (p) DavidProbert 7 70
(Rae Guest) *trckd ldrs: shkn up over 2f out: prog after: led jst over 1f out: kpt on wl* **7/2**[1]

3100 **2** *1/2* **Sheikh The Reins (IRE)**[28] 5398 4-9-10 70 (v) GeorgeBaker 2 77
(John Best) *trckd clr ldng pair: clsd over 2f out gng strly: chal over 1f out: chsd wnr after: nt qckn* **9/1**

0033 **3** *3/4* **Golden Desert (IRE)**[9] 6039 9-9-6 66 HayleyTurner 9 71
(Simon Dow) *slowly away: hld up in last: drvn over 2f out: prog over 1f out: styd on to take 3rd nr fin: unable to chal* **9/1**

4020 **4** *1* **Only Ten Per Cent (IRE)**[188] 912 5-9-10 70 RichardHughes 12 73
(J R Jenkins) *hld up in midfield: rdn 2f out: styd on fr over 1f out: nt pce to chal* **8/1**

0P3 **5** *2* **Bussa**[16] 5841 5-9-7 70 (t) DeclanBates(3) 13 67
(David Evans) *towards rr: drvn over 2f out: no prog tl kpt on fr over 1f out: nrst fin* **10/1**

0640 **6** *nk* **South Kenter (USA)**[33] 5230 4-8-3 56 oh11 (p) OisinMurphy(7) 4 52
(Heather Main) *led at str pce but hdd after 2f: lost 2nd over 1f out: steadily fdd* **50/1**

0304 **7** *1/2* **The Happy Hammer (IRE)**[112] 2573 7-9-4 67 ThomasBrown(3) 6 62
(Eugene Stanford) *towards rr: rdn over 2f out: nt clr run over 1f out and dropped to rr: kpt on again ins fnl f* **12/1**

4431 **8** *shd* **Excellent Jem**[30] 5354 4-9-10 70 (b) MartinDwyer 5 65
(Jane Chapple-Hyam) *pressed ldr at str pce and clr of rest: led after 2f: hdd jst over 1f out: wknd* **11/2**[2]

-000 **9** *3/4* **Sea Soldier (IRE)**[100] 2920 5-9-0 67 JonathanWilletts(7) 11 60
(Andrew Balding) *hld up in rr: last and pushed along jst over 2f out: no prog tl styd on ins fnl f* **12/1**

0335 **10** *1/2* **Magical Rose (IRE)**[17] 5799 3-9-5 69 FrederikTylicki 10 60
(Paul D'Arcy) *wl in rr: drvn and limited prog wl over 1f out: fdd fnl f* **7/1**[3]

0040 **11** *3 1/2* **Zaheeb**[13] 5931 5-8-10 56 (b) WilliamCarson 1 38
(Dave Morris) *chsd clr ldrs: wknd qckly wl over 1f out* **16/1**

1136 **12** *7* **Mick Dundee (IRE)**[15] 5870 3-9-2 66 (bt[1]) AdamKirby 3 29
(John Ryan) *awkward s: sn in midfield: rdn on inner 2f out: wknd qckly over 1f out* **20/1**

1m 25.18s (-0.82) **Going Correction** -0.125s/f (Stan)
WFA 3 from 4yo+ 4lb 12 Ran SP% **118.3**
Speed ratings (Par 103): **99,98,97,96,94 93,93,93,92,91 87,79**
toteswingers 1&2 £10.10, 1&3 £10.50, 2&3 £15.90 CSF £35.08 CT £269.98 TOTE £5.90: £1.70, £2.80, £3.20; EX 37.90 Trifecta £570.90 Pool: £874.46 - 1.14 winning units..
Owner Brian Cooper And Miss Elaine Reffo **Bred** Amethyst Stud **Trained** Newmarket, Suffolk

FOCUS
The quicker division of the 7f handicap, although the trailblazing antics of South Kenter and Excellent Jem were basically ignored.
T/Plt: £64.20 to a £1 stake. Pool: £68969.51 - 783.55 winning tickets T/Qpdt: £12.20 to a £1 stake. Pool: £7241.25 - 437.70 winning tickets JN

6152 CHEPSTOW (L-H)
Thursday, September 12

OFFICIAL GOING: Good (good to soft in places)
Wind: Virtually nil Weather: Overcast early, sunny spells later

6318 32RED CASINO E B F MAIDEN FILLIES' STKS 7f 16y
1:55 (1:56) (Class 5) 2-Y-0 **£2,911** (£866; £432; £216) **Stalls** Centre

Form RPR

2 **1** **Laurelita (IRE)**[38] 5061 2-9-0 0 PatCosgrave 2 78+
(George Baker) *mde all: shkn up over 1f out: styd on strly fnl f: unchal* **5/1**[3]

0 **2** *2 1/2* **Regardez**[42] 4921 2-9-0 0 JimCrowley 9 72+
(Ralph Beckett) *towards rr: hdwy over 2f out: styd on wl fnl f to take 2nd fnl 110yds but no ch w unchal wnr* **6/4**[1]

63 **3** *hd* **Cay Dancer**[70] 3986 2-9-0 0 DavidProbert 7 71+
(Richard Hannon) *chsd ldrs: drvn to dispute 2nd fnl 110yds but no ch w unchal wnr* **6/1**

43 **4** *1* **Sound Of Summer (IRE)**[12] 5988 2-9-0 0 SteveDrowne 8 68
(Charles Hills) *chsd wnr: rdn and no imp fr 2f out: no ex and dropped to 4th fnl 110yds* **3/1**[2]

5 *3/4* **Miss Brazil (IRE)** 2-8-11 0 WilliamTwiston-Davies(3) 11 66+
(Richard Hannon) *hld up towards rr: hdwy over 2f out: kpt on same pce ins fnl f* **14/1**

0 **6** *4 1/2* **Goodwood Storm**[38] 5061 2-9-0 0 LukeMorris 5 55
(William Knight) *chsd ldrs: rdn 3f out: wknd ins fnl 2f* **33/1**

4 **7** *3* **Tanojin (IRE)**[13] 5949 2-9-0 0 SamHitchcott 10 47
(Mick Channon) *chsd ldrs: rdn over 2f out: wknd sn after* **25/1**

8 *5* **Spring Lady** 2-9-0 0 WilliamCarson 6 34
(Alan Jarvis) *sn bhd* **50/1**

40 **9** *1 1/4* **Ormer**[29] 5385 2-9-0 0 CathyGannon 1 31
(David Evans) *chsd ldrs 3f: sn rdn and btn* **100/1**

10 *7* **Mystical Maze** 2-8-11 0 RyanClark(3) 4 12
(Mark Brisbourne) *chsd ldrs: rdn over 3f out: sn btn* **100/1**

11 6 **Cider Time (IRE)** 2-8-11 0 .... DeclanBates(3) 3
(David Evans) *a wl bhd* **100/1**

1m 23.48s (0.28) **Going Correction** +0.075s/f (Good) **11** Ran SP% **114.3**
Speed ratings (Par 92): **101,98,97,96,95 90,87,81,80,72 65**
toteswingers 1&2 £1.90, 2&3 £2.70, 1&3 £4.30 CSF £12.22 TOTE £6.30: £2.10, £1.10, £1.70; EX 15.70 Trifecta £70.90 Pool: £1119.42 - 11.84 winning units..
Owner Mr & Mrs J Pittam & Peter Gleeson **Bred** Mrs E J O'Grady **Trained** Manton, Wilts
FOCUS
A suspicion that this may have been an above average juvenile event and it saw a visually impressive front-running performance. The third helps with the level.

6319 32REDPOKER.COM E B F MAIDEN FILLIES' STKS 7f 16y
2:30 (2:30) (Class 5) 3-Y-O **£3,881** (£1,155; £577; £288) **Stalls** Centre

Form RPR
-204 1 **Bountybeamadam**[96] 3091 3-9-0 72 .... (p) PatCosgrave 3 62
(George Baker) *mde all: pushed along over 2f out: drvn out fnl f* **7/2**[3]
-026 2 1 ¼ **Candy Kitten**[46] 4799 3-9-0 69 .... LukeMorris 5 58
(Alastair Lidderdale) *chsd ldrs: rdn and outpcd 3f out: rallied over 1f out and chsd wnr ins fnl f: kpt on cl home but a hld* **11/4**[2]
4500 3 3 ¾ **Sweet Vintage (IRE)**[14] 5923 3-8-11 51 .... (t) RyanClark(3) 2 49
(Mark Brisbourne) *chsd wnr: rdn and dropped to 3rd ins fnl 2f: kpt on same pce fnl f* **16/1**
6600 4 hd **Toffee Shot**[11] 6019 3-9-0 49 .... (b[1]) SteveDrowne 7 48
(J W Hills) *disputed 2nd over 3f: drvn and outpcd over 2f out: kpt on again in clsng stages* **66/1**
0-23 5 1 **Nur Jahan (IRE)**[49] 4687 3-9-0 73 .... TedDurcan 4 45
(David Lanigan) *s.i.s: in rr but in tch: hdwy3f out: drvn to chse wnr ins fnl 2f: sn no imp: wknd ins fnl f* **6/4**[1]
6 7 **Felice (IRE)** 3-8-11 0 .... RobertTart(3) 6 27
(Scott Dixon) *chsd ldrs: rdn 3f out: sn btn* **7/1**
0- 7 5 **Incognita**[457] 3010 3-9-0 0 .... RobertHavlin 8 14
(Chris Down) *s.i.s: a outpcd: lost tch fr 3f out* **33/1**
05 8 18 **Finalee**[20] 5695 3-9-0 0 .... ChrisCatlin 1
(John Gallagher) *sn wl bhd* **20/1**

1m 25.22s (2.02) **Going Correction** +0.075s/f (Good) **8** Ran SP% **116.5**
Speed ratings (Par 98): **91,89,85,85,83 75,70,49**
toteswingers 1&2 £3.80, 2&3 £3.10, 1&3 £36.80 CSF £13.65 TOTE £6.20: £1.10, £1.50, £3.80; EX 14.30 Trifecta £89.50 Pool: £928.93 - 7.78 winning units..
Owner Whitsbury Hopefuls **Bred** Brightwalton Stud **Trained** Manton, Wilts
FOCUS
With the 73-rated Nur Jahan dominating the market, this was a weak race. The time was slow and the third and fourth limit the form.

6320 32RED NURSERY H'CAP 5f 16y
3:00 (3:01) (Class 5) (0-70,71) 2-Y-O **£2,587** (£770; £384; £192) **Stalls** Centre

Form RPR
435 1 **Alfie Lunete (IRE)**[24] 5593 2-9-2 65 .... TedDurcan 2 68
(J S Moore) *s.i.s: in rr: drvn and hdwy over 1f out: str run ins fnl f: led last strides* **14/1**
3232 2 hd **Stellarta**[22] 5648 2-9-6 69 .... LiamKeniry 3 71
(Michael Blanshard) *pressed ldrs: slt ld fr 1/2-way: kpt on wl fnl f: hdd last strides* **10/1**
233 3 hd **Flicksta (USA)**[41] 4937 2-9-5 68 .... LukeMorris 4 70
(Ronald Harris) *chsd ldrs: rdn over 2f out: pressed wnr ins fnl f: no ex in clsng stages* **7/1**[3]
1603 4 nk **Honey Meadow**[10] 6035 2-9-1 64 .... AdamBeschizza 6 64
(Robert Eddery) *chsd ldr: rdn 1/2-way: kpt on u.p fnl 100yds: no ex in clsng stages* **14/1**
2201 5 2 **Anytimeatall (IRE)**[9] 6073 2-9-0 66 6ex .... RobertTart(3) 8 59
(Alan Bailey) *pressed ldrs: chal 3f out tl ins fnl 2f: outpcd fnl f* **8/1**
5211 6 3 ¾ **Dovil's Duel (IRE)**[8] 6111 2-9-8 71 6ex .... DavidProbert 5 51
(Rod Millman) *chsd ldrs: rdn over 2f out and sn btn* **6/4**[1]
6423 7 1 ¾ **Narborough**[17] 5814 2-8-12 61 .... SamHitchcott 9 34
(Mick Channon) *chsd ldrs: rdn 1/2-way: wknd ins fnl 2f* **16/1**
4325 8 1 **Prisca**[36] 5121 2-9-4 70 .... WilliamTwiston-Davies(3) 10 40
(Richard Hannon) *bdly outpcd in rr tl styd on ins fnl f* **14/1**
032 9 3 ¾ **Black Vale (IRE)**[16] 5866 2-8-11 60 .... (p) JimCrowley 1 16
(James Tate) *pressed ldrs: wknd qckly wl over 1f out* **6/1**[2]
105 10 2 ½ **Music Stop**[13] 5964 2-8-9 58 .... (b) CathyGannon 2 5
(Phil McEntee) *slt ld tl narrowly hdd 1/2-way: wknd qckly 2f out* **66/1**

1m 0.02s (0.72) **Going Correction** +0.075s/f (Good) **10** Ran SP% **114.4**
Speed ratings (Par 95): **97,96,96,95,92 86,83,82,76,72**
toteswingers 1&2 £21.80, 2&3 £12.10, 1&3 £14.90 CSF £143.17 CT £1066.85 TOTE £21.30: £4.30, £3.00, £3.40; EX 184.30 Trifecta £1078.10 Part won. Pool: £1437.51 - 0.91 winning units..
Owner Ross Peters & J S Moore **Bred** K Molloy **Trained** Upper Lambourn, Berks
FOCUS
A competitive nursery and it served up a thrilling finish. The front four were all pretty exposed and the form looks sound enough.

6321 32RED.COM H'CAP 1m 14y
3:35 (3:35) (Class 6) (0-60,60) 3-Y-O **£1,940** (£577; £288; £144) **Stalls** Centre

Form RPR
0055 1 **Let Me In (IRE)**[85] 3475 3-8-8 47 .... (v[1]) DavidProbert 12 57
(Patrick Chamings) *chsd ldrs tl slt advantage 3f out: drvn ins fnl f: styd on strly in clsng stages* **6/1**
4236 2 1 ½ **Sixties Queen**[13] 5967 3-9-0 56 .... RobertTart(3) 7 63
(Alan Bailey) *in rr but in tch: hdwy over 3f out: styd on fnl f: tk 2nd in clsng stages but no ch w wnr* **3/1**[1]
0525 3 1 **Lambert Pen (USA)**[3] 6260 3-8-6 52 .... DanielCremin(7) 9 57
(Mick Channon) *in rr: hdwy over 2f out: chsd wnr appr fnl f: no imp and styd on same pce into 3rd in clsng stages* **4/1**[2]
-303 4 2 ½ **Black Eyed Girl (IRE)**[35] 5173 3-8-11 50 .... TedDurcan 3 49
(J S Moore) *sn led: narrowly hdd 3f out: lost 2nd over 1f out: sn edgd lft: wknd ins fnl f* **20/1**
0200 5 nse **Fair Comment**[14] 5923 3-9-5 58 .... LiamKeniry 6 57
(Michael Blanshard) *chsd ldrs: rdn and outpcd over 2f out: styd on again ins fnl f* **14/1**
0 6 1 ¾ **Xclusive**[95] 3137 3-9-0 58 .... PhilipPrince(5) 2 53
(Ronald Harris) *chsd ldrs: rdn and outpcd 3f out: kpt on again in clsng stages* **14/1**
405 7 ¾ **Polish Rider**[10] 6038 3-8-7 46 oh1 .... KieranO'Neill 10 39
(Richard Hannon) *chsd ldrs: wknd over 1f out* **10/1**
-050 8 2 **Miss Mocca**[106] 2770 3-9-4 60 .... MatthewLawson(3) 8 48
(Jonathan Portman) *in rr: hdwy fr 4f out: outpcd ins fnl 3f: mod prog again fnl f* **20/1**
5-06 9 1 ¼ **Norphin**[31] 5346 3-9-6 59 .... PatCosgrave 5 45
(Denis Coakley) *chsd ldrs: rdn 3f out: wknd qckly 2f out* **9/2**[3]
1500 10 4 ½ **Double Star**[23] 5615 3-8-11 50 .... JohnFahy 11 25
(Jonathan Portman) *in rr: hdwy over 3f out: wknd ins fnl 2f* **20/1**
0204 11 3 ¾ **Isle Of Beauty**[49] 4656 3-8-8 47 .... (v[1]) FergusSweeney 1 14
(Tom Dascombe) *chsd ldrs: wknd qckly 3f out* **20/1**

1m 36.91s (0.71) **Going Correction** +0.075s/f (Good) **11** Ran SP% **118.9**
Speed ratings (Par 99): **99,97,96,94,93 92,91,89,88,83 79**
toteswingers 1&2 £4.60, 2&3 £4.30, 1&3 £8.20 CSF £23.01 CT £80.71 TOTE £12.30: £3.30, £1.50, £1.70; EX 32.50 Trifecta £158.20 Pool: £914.53 - 4.33 winning units..
Owner Select Racing Bloodstock Ltd **Bred** Epona Bloodstock Ltd **Trained** Baughurst, Hants
FOCUS
A low-grade handicap but a personal best from the winner.

6322 £32 FREE AT 32RED.COM NURSERY H'CAP 1m 14y
4:10 (4:18) (Class 6) (0-65,65) 2-Y-O **£1,940** (£577; £288; £144) **Stalls** Centre

Form RPR
0625 1 **Rising Dawn (IRE)**[13] 5951 2-9-3 64 .... WilliamTwiston-Davies(3) 2 69+
(Richard Hannon) *in tch: rdn 3f out: led 1f out: hung rt u.p fnl 75yds: rdn out* **7/2**[1]
6026 2 ¾ **Jazzy Lady (IRE)**[15] 5893 2-8-3 50 .... DeclanBates(3) 13 53
(David Evans) *in rr: hdwy 3f out: styd on wl fnl f to chse wnr whn carried lft in clsng stages* **25/1**
4503 3 1 **Tyrsal (IRE)**[15] 5893 2-8-7 54 ow1 .... RobertTart(3) 8 55
(Robert Eddery) *chsd ldr: led over 3f out: hdd 1f out: styng on same pce whn pushed rt fnl 50yds and lost 2nd sn after* **9/2**[2]
5040 4 1 ½ **Double Czech (IRE)**[41] 4948 2-9-7 65 .... RobertHavlin 10 63
(Amanda Perrett) *chsd ldrs: rdn 2f out: wknd ins fnl f* **8/1**
6156 5 1 ¾ **Hedge End (IRE)**[13] 5951 2-9-7 65 .... JimCrowley 15 59
(Richard Hannon) *in rr: hdwy 3f out: styd on fnl f but nvr gng pce to rch ldrs* **5/1**[3]
0000 6 nk **Brockholes Flyer (IRE)**[1] 6311 2-8-5 49 .... (v) ChrisCatlin 11 42
(Brendan Powell) *chsd ldrs: rdn over 2f out: wknd fnl f* **50/1**
503 7 3 **Mimbleberry**[34] 5225 2-9-3 61 .... FergusSweeney 16 47
(Tom Dascombe) *in rr: hdwy 3f out: sn rdn: no prog 2f out: wknd fnl f* **8/1**
0060 8 2 ½ **My My My Diliza**[13] 5951 2-8-11 55 .... (b[1]) LiamKeniry 7 35
(J S Moore) *chsd ldrs: rdn 3f out: wknd 2f out* **25/1**
4343 9 2 **Ding Ding**[27] 5467 2-8-10 54 .... SamHitchcott 12 30
(Mick Channon) *in rr: rdn over 3f out: sme hdwy over 2f out: nvr rchd ldrs and sn btn* **14/1**
550 10 3 ½ **Unfashionable (IRE)**[28] 5442 2-8-1 45 .... (b[1]) LukeMorris 5 13
(Stuart Kittow) *led tl hdd over 3f out: wknd over 2f out* **50/1**
600 11 4 ½ **Indie Star**[17] 5812 2-8-11 55 .... DavidProbert 14 12
(Harry Dunlop) *a in rr* **14/1**
0560 12 4 ½ **Freddie Kilroy**[15] 5893 2-8-9 53 .... (b[1]) SteveDrowne 6
(Ed Dunlop) *in tch 4f* **8/1**
0650 13 3 ½ **Loving Your Work**[27] 5472 2-9-7 65 .... (p) PatCosgrave 9 4
(George Baker) *plld hrd: sutmbled after 1f: sn in tch: wknd 3f out* **14/1**
030 14 2 ½ **Oakley Dancer**[31] 5350 2-7-13 46 .... RaulDaSilva(3) 17
(Tony Carroll) *a in rr* **40/1**
6 15 1 ¼ **Flying Author (IRE)**[26] 5524 2-8-11 55 .... CathyGannon 4
(Phil McEntee) *hmpd after 1f: a in rr* **33/1**

1m 36.69s (0.49) **Going Correction** +0.075s/f (Good) **15** Ran SP% **127.4**
Speed ratings (Par 93): **100,99,98,96,95 94,91,89,87,83 79,74,71,68,67**
toteswingers 1&2 £6.00, 2&3 £31.40, 1&3 £5.70 CSF £105.58 CT £427.28 TOTE £4.40: £2.00, £7.00, £2.10; EX 155.60 Trifecta £532.50 Part won. Pool: £710.02 - 0.44 winning units..
Owner Mohamed Saeed Al Shahi **Bred** Ms Ashley O'Leary **Trained** East Everleigh, Wilts
FOCUS
A devilishly difficult race on paper. Modest form with the winner stepping up a little.

6323 32RED ON THE APP STORE H'CAP (DIV I) 7f 16y
4:45 (4:46) (Class 6) (0-60,60) 3-Y-O+ **£1,940** (£577; £288; £144) **Stalls** Centre

Form RPR
1160 1 **Just Isla**[11] 6019 3-9-1 55 .... (p) SteveDrowne 10 64
(Peter Makin) *in rr: hdwy 2f out: led and hung lft appr fnl f: styd on u.p and hung rt in clsng stages* **14/1**
3303 2 1 ¾ **Copper Trade**[9] 6074 3-9-6 60 .... JohnFahy 3 67+
(Eve Johnson Houghton) *chsd ldrs: n.m.r and lost pl over 2f out drvn and hdwy over 1f out: styd on wl to take 2nd last strides but nt trble wnr* **8/1**[3]
3466 3 shd **Ishiamiracle**[35] 5192 4-8-10 46 .... (p) CathyGannon 4 51
(Phil McEntee) *led: rdn 2f out: hdd appr fnl f: styd on same pce: lost 2nd last strides* **16/1**
P430 4 ¾ **Copper To Gold**[31] 5331 4-8-11 47 .... AdamBeschizza 2 50
(Robin Bastiman) *chsd ldrs: rdn over 2f out: styd on same pce fnl f* **14/1**
4020 5 ½ **Jarrow (IRE)**[6] 6156 6-9-7 60 .... (p) WilliamTwiston-Davies(3) 6 61
(Milton Bradley) *in tch: hdwy fr 2f out: kpt on same pce ins fnl f* **16/1**
0300 6 ¾ **Spinning Ridge (IRE)**[28] 5429 8-9-3 53 .... (b) LukeMorris 11 52
(Ronald Harris) *towards rr and rdn 1/2-way: n.m.r u.p ins fnl 2f: kpt on same pce* **16/1**
0034 7 2 ½ **The Name Is Frank**[8] 6101 8-8-13 49 .... (t) FergusSweeney 9 42
(Mark Gillard) *chsd ldrs: rdn over 2f out: wknd over 1f out* **20/1**
4065 8 3 ½ **Thewestwalian (USA)**[6] 6154 5-9-0 50 .... WilliamCarson 8 33
(Peter Hiatt) *pressed ldrs: rdn over 2f out: wknd wl over 1f out* **6/1**[2]
023 9 1 ¼ **Blackamoor Harry**[37] 5092 4-8-5 46 oh1 .... (t) NoelGarbutt(5) 1 26
(Richard Ford) *s.i.s: hdwy to cl on ldrs over 3f out: sn wknd* **8/1**[3]
34-4 10 ½ **Game All (IRE)**[26] 5522 4-9-7 57 .... (p) LiamKeniry 5 35
(Hugo Palmer) *chsd ldrs: rdn 3f out: wknd qckly wl over 1f out* **7/4**[1]
5000 11 14 **Bankroll**[21] 5677 6-9-7 57 .... (tp) GeorgeBaker 7
(Jonjo O'Neill) *early spd: bhd fr 1/2-way* **14/1**

1m 23.78s (0.58) **Going Correction** +0.075s/f (Good)
WFA 3 from 4yo+ 4lb **11** Ran SP% **115.3**
Speed ratings (Par 101): **99,97,96,96,95 94,91,87,86,85 69**
toteswingers 1&2 £10.80, 2&3 £19.20, 1&3 £33.60 CSF £119.16 CT £1853.02 TOTE £11.30: £3.40, £2.00, £5.50; EX 56.60 Trifecta £606.60 Pool: £2484.48 - 3.07 winning units..
Owner D A Poole **Bred** David Poole **Trained** Ogbourne Maisey, Wilts
■ Stewards' Enquiry : Adam Beschizza one-day ban: careless riding (Sep 26)
FOCUS
Some exposed handicappers were on show in this handicap and it came as no real surprise to see the finish fought out by the two 3yos in the line-up. Sound if limited form.

6324 32RED ON THE APP STORE H'CAP (DIV II) 7f 16y
5:20 (5:24) (Class 6) (0-60,59) 3-Y-O+ **£1,940** (£577; £288; £144) **Stalls** Centre

Form RPR
5603 1 **Viennese Verse**[16] 5869 3-9-2 55 .... FergusSweeney 7 63
(Henry Candy) *chsd ldrs: slt ld fr 3f out: rdn 2f out: hung rt u.p fnl 50yds: hld on all out* **7/1**[3]

5556 **2** *hd* **Monsieur Pontaven**[31] 5341 6-8-12 **47**....................(b) AdamBeschizza 6 55
(Robin Bastiman) *in rr: hdwy over 2f out: chsd wnr fnl f: str run fnl 110yds: jst failed* **7/1**[3]

0452 **3** *3* **Two No Bids (IRE)**[9] 6074 3-9-0 **53**..........................(be) CathyGannon 2 52
(Phil McEntee) *s.i.s: sn chsng ldrs: chsd wnr 2f out and sn u.p: no ex and one pce into 3rd fnl f* **5/1**[2]

5001 **4** *1/2* **Olney Lass**[11] 6019 6-9-7 **59**.. SimonPearce(3) 5 58
(Lydia Pearce) *in rr: rdn 3f out: hdwy appr fnl 2f: styd on fnl f: nvr gng pce to rch ldrs* **7/2**[1]

2614 **5** *2 3/4* **Dancing Welcome**[6] 6156 7-9-1 **57**...............................(bt) WillPettis(7) 8 48
(Milton Bradley) *chsd ldrs: rdn 3f out: wknd 2f out* **5/1**[2]

500 **6** *2 1/2* **Cheers Big Ears (IRE)**[17] 5816 7-8-7 **45**....................(t) RaulDaSilva(3) 4 29
(Richard Price) *in tch: rdn 1/2-way: wknd wl over 2f out* **7/1**[3]

6-00 **7** *nk* **Seraphiel**[71] 3949 4-9-1 **50**.. SteveDrowne 10 34
(Chris Down) *in rr: hdwy to cl on ldrs 4f out: wknd ins fnl 3f* **33/1**

3000 **8** *1/2* **George Benjamin**[59] 4357 6-9-4 **53**................................(t) JimCrowley 3 35
(Christopher Kellett) *chsd ldr: rdn over 2f out: wknd qckly over 1f out* **5/1**[2]

405 **9** *15* **Compton Prince**[34] 5220 4-9-9 **58**..................................(b) LukeMorris 1
(Milton Bradley) *led tl hdd 3f out wknd qckly fnl 2f: eased whn no ch* **20/1**

1m 23.86s (0.66) **Going Correction** +0.075s/f (Good)
WFA 3 from 4yo+ 4lb **9** Ran SP% **117.4**
Speed ratings (Par 101): **99,98,95,94,91 88,88,87,70**
toteswingers 1&2 £8.20, 2&3 £7.70, 1&3 £4.20 CSF £56.03 CT £271.61 TOTE £8.80: £2.50, £2.50, £2.50; EX 50.80 Trifecta £244.50 Pool: £2656.61 - 8.14 winning units..
Owner The Chevaliers **Bred** Tony Hirschfeld & L K Piggott **Trained** Kingston Warren, Oxon
■ Stewards' Enquiry : Jim Crowley caution: entered wrong stall.

FOCUS
A similar time and similar form to the first division. The runner-up is probably the key.

6325 32REDBINGO.COM H'CAP — 1m 4f 23y
5:50 (5:52) (Class 6) (0-65,65) 3-Y-O+ **£1,940** (£577; £288; £144) **Stalls** Low

Form RPR

000/ **1** **Highway Code (USA)**[15] 4347 7-9-5 **58**......................... SteveDrowne 15 69
(Richard Lee) *trckd ldrs: led 2f out: pushed clr fnl f: comf* **12/1**

1203 **2** *4* **Flamingo Beat**[20] 5702 3-9-3 **65**.. ChrisCatlin 3 70
(Rae Guest) *chsd ldrs: rdn over 2f out: chsd wnr fnl f but no imp* **10/1**

4305 **3** *1 1/2* **Muskat Link**[37] 5099 3-9-0 **62**...................................... FergusSweeney 11 65
(Henry Candy) *chsd ldr: slt ld 3f out: hdd 2f out: outpcd by wnr sn after and dropped to 3rd fnl f* **12/1**

4201 **4** *3/4* **Ebony Roc (IRE)**[14] 5934 3-8-13 **61**................................ RobertHavlin 14 62
(Amanda Perrett) *chsd ldrs: rdn over 3f out: styd on fr over 1f out to take one pce 4th last strides* **5/1**[2]

5060 **5** *nse* **April Ciel**[16] 5855 4-9-9 **62**... LukeMorris 1 63
(Ronald Harris) *led: rdn 4f out: narrowly hdd 3f out: one pce appr fnl f: lost 4th last strides* **16/1**

-600 **6** *1* **Paddy's Saltantes (IRE)**[50] 4634 3-9-3 **65**...................(b[1]) JohnFahy 12 65
(J S Moore) *broke wl: dropped in rr 1/2-way: rdn over 3f out: styd on fr over 1f out: nt rch ldrs* **33/1**

2546 **7** *1/2* **Rowlestone Lad**[45] 4838 6-8-11 **55**......................... GeorgeDowning(5) 10 54
(John Flint) *in rr: rdn over 3f out: styd on fnl f: nt rch ldrs* **25/1**

2-20 **8** *1/2* **Wily Fox**[114] 2545 6-9-6 **62**... RosieJessop(3) 7 60
(James Eustace) *chsd ldrs: rdn over 3f out: one pce fnl 2f* **20/1**

0-05 **9** *1 1/4* **Motion Lass**[119] 2390 3-9-2 **64**..[1] JimCrowley 13 60
(Ralph Beckett) *chsd ldrs: rdn 3f out: wknd fr 2f out* **7/2**[1]

5-64 **10** *3/4* **Eightfold**[24] 5592 4-9-7 **60**...(t) GeorgeBaker 5 55
(Seamus Durack) *in rr: styd on fr over 2f out: nvr rchd ldrs* **8/1**[3]

3031 **11** *1* **Cabuchon (GER)**[10] 6044 6-9-0 **56** 6ex.....................(t) DeclanBates(3) 6 49
(David Evans) *nvr beyond mid-div* **14/1**

2504 **12** *3/4* **Balady (IRE)**[19] 5762 4-9-12 **65**.. LiamKeniry 16 57
(Dominic Ffrench Davis) *in rr: nvr gng pce to get beyond mid-div* **25/1**

0-23 **13** *1/2* **Simple Joys**[11] 6015 3-8-13 **61**...................................(p) CathyGannon 8 52
(Andrew Balding) *in rr: sme hdwy over 3f out: nvr beyond mid-div* **16/1**

-215 **14** *3/4* **On Stage**[42] 4915 4-9-0 **60**.. PatMillman(7) 17 50
(Stuart Kittow) *s.i.s: a towards rr* **10/1**

-530 **15** *nse* **Cuckoo Rock (IRE)**[39] 5032 6-9-0 **56**................(p) MatthewLawson(3) 4 46
(Jonathan Portman) *a in rr* **25/1**

0400 **16** *1 1/4* **Missionaire (USA)**[38] 5065 6-8-11 **53**.......(p) WilliamTwiston-Davies(3) 2 41
(Tony Carroll) *chsd ldr to 3f out* **50/1**

6305 **17** *29* **Star Of Mayfair (USA)**[29] 5391 3-9-1 **63**..................(v[1]) WilliamCarson 9
(Alan Jarvis) *a in rr: t.o* **33/1**

2m 39.04s (0.04) **Going Correction** +0.075s/f (Good)
WFA 3 from 4yo+ 9lb **17** Ran SP% **126.1**
Speed ratings (Par 101): **102,99,98,97,97 97,96,96,95,95 94,93,93,93,93 92,72**
toteswingers 1&2 £10.20, 2&3 £27.50, 1&3 £40.60 CSF £120.41 CT £1501.82 TOTE £16.60: £3.70, £2.60, £3.20, £1.80; EX 143.50 Trifecta £901.00 Pool: £2116.07 - 1.76 winning units..
Owner D E Edwards **Bred** T Leung **Trained** Byton, H'fords

FOCUS
A modest finale but an impressive performance from the winner who can do better on the Flat. The second and third set the standard.
T/Plt: £201.50 to a £1 stake. Pool of £61718.66 - 223.50 winning tickets T/Qpdt: £46.50 to a £1 stake. Pool of £4871.50 - 77.50 winning tickets. ST

6303 DONCASTER (L-H)
Thursday, September 12

OFFICIAL GOING: Good to soft (6.8)
Wind: light 1/2 against Weather: fine

6326 EUROPEAN BREEDERS' FUND CARRIE RED FILLIES' NURSERY STKS (H'CAP) — 6f 110y
1:40 (1:43) (Class 2) 2-Y-O **£19,407** (£5,775; £2,886; £1,443) **Stalls** High

Form RPR

3202 **1** **Aqlaam Vision**[13] 5951 2-8-8 **75**...................................... WilliamBuick 10 85
(Clive Brittain) *lw: sn bhd: gd hdwy stands' side 2f out: styd on strly to ld last 50yds* **9/1**

2122 **2** *1 1/4* **Ticking Katie (IRE)**[19] 5745 2-8-7 **79**......................... JoeyHaynes(5) 2 86
(K R Burke) *led: clr over 1f out: hdd and no ex wl ins fnl f* **8/1**[3]

6125 **3** *2 1/4* **Cornish Path**[26] 5536 2-8-10 **77**.. DaneO'Neill 14 77
(Henry Candy) *mid-div: hdwy towards stands' side over 2f out: kpt on ins fnl f* **15/2**[2]

2261 **4** *nk* **Gown (IRE)**[12] 6002 2-8-9 **76**... RyanMoore 7 76
(Charles Hills) *hld up in rr: hdwy whn nt clr run over 1f out: styd on ins fnl f* **9/1**

01 **5** *3/4* **Arranger (IRE)**[13] 5949 2-8-10 **77**... SeanLevey 4 74
(Richard Hannon) *lw: wnt rt s: chsd ldrs: effrt over 2f out: kpt on same pce over 1f out* **20/1**

1206 **6** *shd* **Suite (IRE)**[41] 4948 2-9-7 **88**.. PatDobbs 6 85
(Richard Hannon) *chsd ldrs: effrt over 2f out: kpt on same pce over 1f out* **16/1**

002 **7** *1/2* **Nakuti (IRE)**[28] 5443 2-8-7 **74**.. JamieSpencer 5 70
(Sylvester Kirk) *hmpd s: hld up in rr: hdwy towards stands' side 2f out: styd on ins fnl f* **14/1**

143 **8** *1/2* **Les Gar Gan (IRE)**[10] 6047 2-8-7 **74**.................... SilvestreDeSousa 9 68
(Keith Dalgleish) *lw: chsd ldrs: drvn and lost pl over 3f out: kpt on fnl f* **7/2**[1]

5321 **9** *nk* **Inyordreams**[24] 5577 2-8-9 **76**.. DaleSwift 8 70
(James Given) *stmbld s: mid-div: hdwy over 2f out: nt clr run over 1f out: one pce* **8/1**[3]

3402 **10** *1* **State Anthem**[9] 6070 2-8-5 **72**.. PaulHanagan 11 63
(Mick Channon) *awkward s: t.k.h: sn trcking ldrs stands' side: cl 2nd over 4f out: wknd over 1f out* **33/1**

6510 **11** *1/2* **Lady In Blue (IRE)**[26] 5536 2-8-4 **71**................................ JimmyQuinn 1 61
(William Haggas) *dwlt: hld up far side: sme hdwy over 2f out: sn wknd* **12/1**

1332 **12** *4* **Atlantic Affair (IRE)**[19] 5773 2-9-1 **82**............................. JoeFanning 12 61
(Mark Johnston) *chsd ldrs: drvn over 2f out: wknd fnl f* **12/1**

010 **13** *4 1/2* **Chutney (IRE)**[40] 5005 2-8-11 **78**................................ RichardHughes 13 44
(Richard Hannon) *in rr: drvn over 4f out: bhd whn eased ins fnl f* **12/1**

0055 **14** *19* **Queenie's Home**[9] 6076 2-8-6 **73**................................... JamesSullivan 3
(James Given) *stmbld s: in rr: lost pl over 3f out: sn bhd: eased fnl f: t.o* **66/1**

1m 20.5s (0.60) **Going Correction** +0.125s/f (Good) **14** Ran SP% **121.0**
Speed ratings (Par 98): **101,99,97,96,95 95,95,94,94,93 92,87,82,61**
toteswingers 1&2 £15.00, 2&3 £9.40, 1&3 £15.40 CSF £78.38 CT £594.40 TOTE £11.40: £3.40, £2.00, £3.30; EX 75.20 Trifecta £947.20 Pool: £2928.48 - 2.31 winning units..
Owner Saeed Manana **Bred** Mrs T Brudenell & Trickledown Stud **Trained** Newmarket, Suffolk

FOCUS
William Buick, successful in the opener, described the ground as "dead, and hard work". This is usuually a warm fillies' nursery and it should produce winners. Most of the action played out down the centre of the track and there appeared no real bias here.

6327 JAPAN RACING ASSOCIATION SCEPTRE STKS (GROUP 3) (F&M) — 7f
2:10 (2:10) (Class 1) 3-Y-O+ **£35,520** (£13,434; £6,714; £3,354) **Stalls** High

Form RPR

4000 **1** **Nargys (IRE)**[25] 5561 3-8-10 103.. AndreaAtzeni 3 109
(Luca Cumani) *lw: t.k.h in rr: effrt over 2f out: edgd rt over 1f out: styd on wl to ld last 150yds: drvn out* **8/1**

63 **2** *1 3/4* **Switcher (IRE)**[19] 5763 4-9-0 95...................................... TonyHamilton 6 105
(Richard Fahey) *led at stdy pce: increased pce over 2f out: hdd over 1f out: kpt on wl in clsng stages* **25/1**

3412 **3** *nse* **Winning Express (IRE)**[41] 4949 3-8-10 107...................... GrahamLee 1 104
(Ed McMahon) *trckd ldrs on outer: upsides over 1f out: kpt on same pce ins fnl f* **11/4**[2]

1141 **4** *nk* **Annecdote**[41] 4949 3-8-13 107.............................. RichardKingscote 5 106
(Jonathan Portman) *hld up: effrt over 3f out: edgd rt over 1f out: sn upsides: kpt on same pce wl ins fnl f* **9/2**[3]

6640 **5** *shd* **Maureen (IRE)**[46] 4817 3-8-13 107.................................. RichardHughes 2 106
(Richard Hannon) *lw: trckd ldr: led narrowly over 1f out: hdd jst ins fnl f: kpt on same pce* **15/8**[1]

140 **6** *3 1/2* **Zurigha (IRE)**[85] 3460 3-8-10 105... RyanMoore 8 93
(Richard Hannon) *racd stands' side: w ldr: wknd fnl f* **10/1**

01 **7** *9* **Bethany Bay (IRE)**[74] 3874 3-8-10 84................................ TadhgO'Shea 9 69
(John Patrick Shanahan, Ire) *swtchd lft after 1f: chsd ldrs: lost pl over 1f out: sn bhd* **50/1**

360- **8** *11* **Boastful (IRE)**[355] 6468 5-9-0 99................................... DanielTudhope 7 40
(K R Burke) *t.k.h: w ldrs: drvn over 2f out: sn lost pl and bhd* **16/1**

1m 26.3s **Going Correction** +0.125s/f (Good)
WFA 3 from 4yo+ 4lb **8** Ran SP% **111.5**
Speed ratings (Par 113): **105,103,102,102,102 98,88,75**
toteswingers 1&2 £18.30, 2&3 £9.50, 1&3 £3.80 CSF £165.27 TOTE £9.30: £2.30, £3.70, £1.30; EX 226.00 Trifecta £901.80 Pool: £4034.58 - 3.35 winning units..
Owner Sheikh Mohammed Obaid Al Maktoum **Bred** Ballylinch Stud **Trained** Newmarket, Suffolk

FOCUS
An ordinary fillies' Group 3 and they raced stands' side, although only Zurigha stuck to the rail. The pace was ordinary, set by the second who's the key. Nargys was back to her Royal Ascot form.

6328 WEATHERBYS HAMILTON INSURANCE £300,000 2-Y-O STKS — 6f 110y
2:40 (2:42) (Class 2) 2-Y-O
£175,129 (£70,080; £35,040; £17,484; £8,760; £8,760) **Stalls** High

Form RPR

0506 **1** **Morning Post**[5] 6194 2-9-2 82..................................(b[1]) PaulMulrennan 15 100
(Kevin Ryan) *swtchd lft over 5f out: sn chsng ldrs: led appr fnl f: hung bdly lft: hld on nr fin* **100/1**

1106 **2** *1/2* **Azagal (IRE)**[21] 5680 2-8-4 95................................... DuranFentiman 17 87
(Tim Easterby) *hld up stands' side: chsng ldrs 3f out: led over 1f out: hdd jst ins fnl f: kpt on gamely towards fin* **12/1**

210 **3** *hd* **Mawfoor (IRE)**[86] 3422 2-8-9 95.................................... JimmyFortune 21 91
(Brian Meehan) *swtg: in rr stands' side: gd hdwy 2f out: chsng ldrs appr fnl f: kpt on same pce in clsng stages* **12/1**

4056 **4** *shd* **Steventon Star**[5] 6187 2-8-9 88...(b[1]) PatDobbs 6 91
(Richard Hannon) *lw: hld up in rr: gd hdwy over 2f out: chsng ldrs 1f out: edgd lft: styd on towards fin* **33/1**

2442 **5** *1 1/2* **Rosso Corsa**[9] 6064 2-8-9 93.. MartinHarley 16 87
(Mick Channon) *mid-div: hdwy over 2f out: chsng ldrs over 1f out: kpt on same pce* **12/1**

1314 **6** *nk* **Stormy Paradise (IRE)**[32] 5313 2-8-9 95..................... FrankieDettori 18 86
(Brian Meehan) *in rr stands' side: hdwy over 2f out: styd on same pce fnl f* **14/1**

0232 **7** *nk* **Coulsty (IRE)**[22] 5656 2-8-9 97..................................... RichardHughes 7 85
(Richard Hannon) *lw: trckd ldrs: upsides 2f out: edgd lft and kpt on same pce appr fnl f: lame* **9/2**[1]

1212 **8** *2 1/2* **Malachim Mist (IRE)**[61] 4300 2-8-12 90............................. SeanLevey 1 82
(Richard Hannon) *chsd ldrs far side: wknd fnl f* **28/1**

0103 **9** *4 1/2* **Foxy Clarets (IRE)**[13] 5955 2-8-6 82............................ PatrickMathers 9 63
(Richard Fahey) *chsd ldrs: wknd over 1f out* **50/1**

4106 **10** *1 1/4* **Ben Hall (IRE)**[42] 4918 2-8-12 100.................................. WilliamBuick 8 66
(John Gosden) *swtg: led: hdd over 1f out: sn wknd: eased nr fin* **7/1**[2]

2136 **11** *1/2* **Tobougg Happy**[21] 5679 2-8-1 87.......................... SilvestreDeSousa 10 53
(James Tate) *chsd ldrs: wkng whn wnt rt over 1f out* **16/1**

5011 **12** ½ **Khalice**[16] 5858 2-8-7 82 TonyHamilton 3 58
(Richard Fahey) *mid-div towards far side: hdwy over 2f out: nvr a factor* 25/1

2061 **13** ¾ **Finflash (IRE)**[28] 5428 2-8-6 79 AndreaAtzeni 12 55
(Mick Channon) *trckd ldrs: edgd rt and wknd over 1f out* 50/1

4211 **14** ½ **Art Official (IRE)**[40] 4988 2-8-9 89 RyanMoore 11 57
(Richard Hannon) *lw: chsd ldrs: lost pl 2f out* 15/2[3]

5322 **15** 4 **Captain Bob (IRE)**[17] 5843 2-8-12 79 (p) JamieSpencer 13 49
(Charles Hills) *hld up in rr: hmpd and carried lft over 5f out: drvn and sme hdwy 3f out: lost pl over 1f out* 33/1

1201 **16** 1¼ **Suzi's Connoisseur**[14] 5939 2-8-12 97 JoeFanning 14 45
(Mark Johnston) *on toes: chsd ldrs: wkng whn hmpd over 1f out* 12/1

121 **17** hd **Zaraee (IRE)**[39] 5028 2-9-2 89 DaneO'Neill 20 49
(William Haggas) *lw: in rr stands' side: nvr on terms* 16/1

2312 **18** hd **Tanseeb**[41] 4948 2-9-0 88 GrahamLee 19 46
(Mark Johnston) *lw: stmbld s: a in rr stands' side* 25/1

21 **19** 2¾ **Tanzeel (IRE)**[48] 4716 2-8-12 85 PaulHanagan 4 36
(Charles Hills) *chsd ldrs far side: rdn over 2f out: sn lost pl: eased ins fnl f* 7/1[2]

4624 **20** 6 **Stella Clavisque (IRE)**[21] 5675 2-8-6 77 (b) NGMcCullagh 5 14
(Brian Meehan) *swtg: mid-div: drvn and lost pl over 2f out: eased whn bhd in clsng stages* 100/1

5120 **U** **Regiment**[41] 4948 2-8-6 84 BarryMcHugh 2
(Richard Fahey) *lw:awkward leaving stalls: rdr lost iron and sn uns rdr after s* 100/1

1m 20.84s (0.94) **Going Correction** +0.125s/f (Good) **21** Ran SP% **128.1**
Speed ratings (Par 101): **99,98,98,98,96 96,95,92,87,86 85,85,84,83,79 77,77,77,74,67**
toteswingers 1&2 £0.00, 2&3 £40.90, 1&3 £0.00 CSF £1048.93 TOTE £109.60: £25.90, £4.40, £5.30; EX 3507.50 TRIFECTA Not won..
Owner Matt & Lauren Morgan **Bred** T J Cooper **Trained** Hambleton, N Yorks
■ Stewards' Enquiry : Jimmy Fortune two-day ban: used whip above permitted level (Sep 26,29)
Duran Fentiman two-day ban: used whip above permitted level (Sep 26,29)

FOCUS
The time was 0.34sec slower than the opening fillies' nursery. Subsequent Group 1 winner Wootton Bassett and the Classic-placed Reply are the best winners so far of this hugely valuable sales race. The field raced down the centre, but five of the first six home were drawn in the highest seven stalls. There was a shock result, the winner showing big improement for the blinkers. The form is rated around the third and fourth.

6329 DFS PARK HILL STKS (GROUP 2) (F&M) 1m 6f 132y
3:15 (3:15) (Class 1) 3-Y-O+
£51,039 (£19,350; £9,684; £4,824; £2,421; £1,215) **Stalls** Low

Form RPR

335 **1** **The Lark**[81] 3614 3-8-6 107 JamieSpencer 8 107+
(Michael Bell) *lw: hld up towards rr: smooth hdwy over 2f out: upsides over 1f out: led jst ins fnl f: pushed out* 15/8[1]

561 **2** 1¼ **Phiz (GER)**[34] 5233 3-8-6 70 WilliamBuick 10 104
(John Gosden) *wnt rt s: mid-div: hdwy to chal over 2f out: edgd lft and led over 1f out: hdd jst ins fnl f: styd on same pce* 14/1

2330 **3** 4 **Alta Lilea (IRE)**[12] 5993 3-8-6 101 JoeFanning 3 99
(Mark Johnston) *trckd ldr: led over 3f out: hdd over 1f out: kpt on same pce* 9/1[3]

4253 **4** 3¾ **Jathabah (IRE)**[21] 5683 3-8-8 97 ow2 RichardHughes 4 96
(Clive Brittain) *trckd ldrs: lft 4th and one pce over 1f out* 9/1[3]

3066 **5** hd **Jehannedarc (IRE)**[19] 5741 5-9-4 97 (p) RyanMoore 5 94
(Ed Dunlop) *t.k.h in rr: effrt over 2f out: kpt on fnl f* 18/1

3412 **6** 5 **Wadaa (USA)**[16] 5868 3-8-6 82 PaulHanagan 6 88
(James Tate) *detached in last: drvn 4f out: nvr a factor* 16/1

434 **7** 2¼ **Saint Hilary**[19] 5761 4-9-4 87 MartinDwyer 7 85
(William Muir) *chsd ldrs: drvn over 3f out: lost pl over 2f out* 33/1

-606 **8** 44 **Coquet**[21] 5683 4-9-4 98 SilvestreDeSousa 1 27
(Hughie Morrison) *led: qcknd pce over 4f out: hdd over 3f out: lost pl over 2f out: sn bhd: eased: t.o* 20/1

1-11 **F** **Seal Of Approval**[39] 5035 4-9-4 99 HayleyTurner 2
(James Fanshawe) *hld up in mid-div: effrt over 3f out: n.m.r and swtchd ins over 2f out: 4th and styng on whn clipped heels and fell over 1f out* 2/1[2]

3m 8.95s (1.55) **Going Correction** +0.425s/f (Yiel)
WFA 3 from 4yo+ 12lb **9** Ran SP% **113.6**
Speed ratings (Par 115): **112,111,109,107,107 104,103,79,**
toteswingers 1&2 £8.30, 2&3 £10.00, 1&3 £4.00 CSF £28.77 TOTE £2.90: £1.30, £3.10, £2.30; EX 30.00 Trifecta £211.60 Pool: £3804.81 - 13.48 winning units..
Owner Lady Bamford **Bred** Lady Bamford **Trained** Newmarket, Suffolk

FOCUS
The result of this Group 2 was overshadowed by Seal Of Approval taking a sickening fall in the straight. The pace seemed fair but the form looks weak for a Group 2. The race is taken at face value with The Lark back to her Oaks form.

6330 CROWNHOTEL-BAWTRY.COM EBF MAIDEN STKS 1m (S)
3:50 (4:26) (Class 3) 2-Y-O **£7,762** (£2,310; £1,154; £577) **Stalls** High

Form RPR

0 **1** **Pupil (IRE)**[27] 5472 2-9-5 0 RichardHughes 8 86+
(Richard Hannon) *w'like: str: scope: hld up in rr: hdwy stands' side over 2f out: str run appr fnl f: led last 100yds: drvn out* 4/1[2]

2 1½ **Double Bluff (IRE)** 2-9-5 0 JoeFanning 7 82+
(Mark Johnston) *w'like: leggy: led: set stdy pce: qcknd gallop over 3f out: hdd over 1f out: rallied and 2nd 100yds out: kpt on wl* 12/1

3 3¾ **Raven Ridge (IRE)** 2-9-5 0 WilliamBuick 3 74+
(Michael Bell) *w'like: trckd ldrs: effrt 3f out: styd on ins fnl f: tk 3rd nr fin* 11/2[3]

4 ½ **Fast Delivery** 2-9-5 0 SilvestreDeSousa 5 73+
(Saeed bin Suroor) *leggy: dwlt: hld up: t.k.h: trckd ldrs: stdd over 5f out: hdwy to trck ldrs over 2f out: led over 1f out: hdd 100yds out wknd* 5/2[1]

5 ¾ **Courageous Rock (USA)** 2-9-5 0 JimmyFortune 6 71+
(Ed Vaughan) *w'like: str: dwlt: t.k.h in rr: hdwy 3f out: kpt on same pce over 1f out* 20/1

020 **6** 7 **Miss Acclaimed (IRE)**[29] 5419 2-9-0 0 DaleSwift 9 51
(Brian Ellison) *hld up in mid-div: t.k.h: outpcd over 2f out: grad wknd* 10/1

7 shd **Hard Divorce (USA)** 2-9-5 0 JamieSpencer 10 56
(David Brown) *unf: scope: chsd ldrs: drvn 3f out: lost pl over 1f out* 11/2[3]

35 **8** 3¾ **Newgate Queen**[35] 5180 2-9-0 0 BarryMcHugh 11 43
(Tony Coyle) *leggy: hld up in mid-div: outpcd over 2f out: edgd lft and sn wknd* 28/1

9 3¼ **Come On Sunshine** 2-9-5 0 TonyHamilton 2 40
(Richard Fahey) *unf: scope: wnt lft s: t.k.h: sn w ldr: lost pl 2f out* 9/1

10 13 **Leisure Cruise (USA)** 2-9-5 0 PatDobbs 4 12
(Richard Hannon) *leggy: unf: in rr: bhd fnl 2f* 16/1

1m 42.48s (3.18) **Going Correction** +0.125s/f (Good) **10** Ran SP% **120.2**
Speed ratings (Par 99): **89,87,83,83,82 75,75,71,68,55**
toteswingers 1&2 £12.10, 2&3 £15.30, 1&3 £6.20 CSF £53.02 TOTE £5.40: £1.90, £4.00, £2.40; EX 60.80 Trifecta £201.80 Pool: £4747.39 - 17.63 winning units..
Owner Andrew Tinkler **Bred** Camas Park Stud **Trained** East Everleigh, Wilts

FOCUS
This maiden has produced plenty of smart types over the years, with Nathaniel (2010) and Encke (2011) notable runners-up, and the latest edition could prove to be a decent contest, despite the time being slow. It fits with the pretty strong race average. The race was delayed by more than half an hour due to lack of ambulance cover after the incident in the 3.15.

6331 DOWNLOAD THE LADBROKES BINGO APP H'CAP 6f
4:25 (5:01) (Class 3) (0-90,90) 3-Y-O+ **£9,703** (£2,887; £1,443; £721) **Stalls** High

Form RPR

6620 **1** **Pearl Ice**[26] 5545 5-9-7 90 GrahamGibbons 6 100
(David Barron) *swtg: mde all: fnd ex and hld on gamely nr fin* 11/1

61-5 **2** nk **Fairway To Heaven (IRE)**[35] 5183 4-9-1 84 FrankieDettori 14 93+
(Michael Wigham) *dwlt: hld up in rr: stdy hdwy over 2f out: swtchd lft ins fnl f: upsides last 50yds: no ex nr fin* 9/2[1]

0060 **3** nk **Thunderball**[12] 5992 7-9-5 88 (p) TomQueally 16 96
(Scott Dixon) *b: lw: chsd ldrs: upsides 1f out: no ex in clsng stages* 6/1[3]

300 **4** 1 **Jack Luey**[5] 6190 6-9-3 86 TomEaves 9 91
(Lawrence Mullaney) *chsd ldrs: kpt on same pce last 100yds* 25/1

0621 **5** ¾ **Rocket Rob (IRE)**[13] 5956 7-8-12 81 WilliamBuick 12 83
(Willie Musson) *lw: hld up in rr: hdwy 2f out: styd on fnl f* 20/1

103 **6** ½ **Baby Strange**[26] 5537 9-8-11 87 AdamMcLean(7) 13 88
(Derek Shaw) *hld up in rr: hdwy over 2f out: edgd rt and chsng ldrs stands' side 1f out: kpt on same pce* 11/2[2]

1301 **7** 2 **If So**[22] 5636 4-9-4 87 RyanMoore 21 81+
(James Fanshawe) *trckd two others stands' side: effrt and nt clr run swtchd lft over 1f out: kpt on: nvr trbld ldrs* 8/1

1143 **8** 1 **Dark Castle**[34] 5247 4-9-2 85 PJMcDonald 8 76
(Micky Hammond) *mid-div: effrt over 2f out: kpt on: nvr a threat* 11/1

0 **9** shd **Line Of Reason (IRE)**[47] 4780 3-9-2 87 GrahamLee 19 78
(Paul Midgley) *lw: mid-div: effrt over 2f out: nvr trbld ldrs* 16/1

0526 **10** nse **Tarooq (USA)**[13] 5974 7-9-0 83 (t) AndreaAtzeni 20 74
(Stuart Williams) *chsd ldr on stands' side: drvn over 2f out: nvr a threat* 9/1

-000 **11** 1 **West Leake Diman (IRE)**[40] 5009 4-9-3 86 RichardKingscote 7 74
(Charles Hills) *sn chsng ldrs: effrt over 2f out: wknd over 1f out* 25/1

0300 **12** 2¼ **Lupo D'Oro (IRE)**[12] 5998 4-9-2 85 RobertWinston 5 65
(John Best) *s.v.s: hdwy over 2f out: nt clr run 1f out: nvr a factor* 22/1

6500 **13** ¾ **Arctic Feeling (IRE)**[26] 5544 5-9-1 84 TonyHamilton 1 62
(Richard Fahey) *chsd ldrs: drvn over 2f out: wknd appr fnl f* 20/1

506 **14** 2¾ **Al Khan (IRE)**[6] 6161 4-9-1 84 (p) AdamKirby 2 53
(Violet M Jordan) *mid-div: hdwy on outer over 2f out: lost pl over 1f out* 20/1

2032 **15** hd **Mayaasem**[20] 5722 3-8-13 84 PaulHanagan 22 53
(Charles Hills) *led two others stands' side: drvn over 2f out: sn lost pl* 11/1

1m 13.23s (-0.37) **Going Correction** +0.125s/f (Good)
WFA 3 from 4yo+ 2lb **15** Ran SP% **126.2**
Speed ratings (Par 107): **107,106,106,104,103 103,100,99,99,99 97,94,93,90,89**
toteswingers 1&2 £11.90, 2&3 £8.90, 1&3 £16.50 CSF £55.68 CT £344.02 TOTE £12.70: £4.30, £2.20, £2.20; EX 97.40 Trifecta £463.30 Pool: £2224.21 - 3.60 winning units..
Owner Laurence O'Kane & Paul Murphy **Bred** Canary Thoroughbreds **Trained** Maunby, N Yorks

FOCUS
This fair sprint handicap was diluted by seven non-runners. They split into two groups, with three on the stands' rail and the rest down the middle, before the main body of the field came over to the stands' side with 2f left. The winner is rated pretty much back to his best.

6332 DFS H'CAP 1m 2f 60y
5:00 (5:35) (Class 2) (0-110,103) 3-Y-O+ **£16,172** (£4,812; £2,405; £1,202) **Stalls** Low

Form RPR

1150 **1** **Clon Brulee (IRE)**[44] 4854 4-9-2 93 GrahamGibbons 11 102
(David Barron) *trckd ldrs: upsides over 1f out: shkn up to ld last 50yds: drvn out* 7/1

0102 **2** ¾ **Tha'ir (IRE)**[17] 5822 3-9-4 102 SilvestreDeSousa 7 109
(Saeed bin Suroor) *trckd ldr: led 2f out: hdd last 50yds: no ex* 13/2

/2-5 **3** nk **Conduct (IRE)**[33] 5283 6-9-5 96 RyanMoore 8 103
(William Haggas) *lw: hld up in mid-div: hdwy over 2f out: sn drvn: hung lft and styd on ins fnl f* 7/2[1]

-040 **4** nk **Black Spirit (USA)**[33] 5270 6-9-10 101 (t) AdamKirby 9 107
(Clive Cox) *chsd ldrs: nt clr run over 2f out tl over 1f out: kpt on last 75yds* 10/1

6443 **5** 2½ **Proud Chieftain**[12] 6001 5-9-6 97 (p) WilliamBuick 2 98
(Clifford Lines) *trckd ldrs: nt clr run over 2f out tl swtchd rt over 1f out: kpt on same pce* 12/1

4313 **6** 1¼ **Viewpoint (IRE)**[26] 5540 4-9-5 96 RichardHughes 5 95
(Richard Hannon) *stdd s: hld up in rr: hdwy on ins over 3f out: kpt on same pce over 1f out* 8/1

-100 **7** hd **Resurge (IRE)**[12] 6001 8-9-6 97 (t) TomQueally 6 95
(Stuart Kittow) *hld up in rr: effrt on outer over 3f out: kpt on: nvr a threat* 20/1

2622 **8** 1 **Aussie Reigns (IRE)**[18] 5792 3-8-8 92 (v) PaulHanagan 12 89
(William Knight) *dwlt: t.k.h in rr: effrt over 3f out: nvr a threat* 11/1

1224 **9** 7 **Sennockian Star**[12] 6001 3-9-3 101 (v) JoeFanning 3 84
(Mark Johnston) *led: qcknd pce over 3f out: hdd 2f out: sn lost pl* 11/2[2]

0-21 **10** 7 **Greek War (IRE)**[19] 5749 4-9-8 99 AhmedAjtebi 1 69
(Charlie Appleby) *t.k.h in rr: drvn over 2f out: hung rt and lost pl over 1f out: sn eased and bhd* 6/1[3]

2m 12.71s (3.31) **Going Correction** +0.425s/f (Yiel)
WFA 3 from 4yo+ 7lb **10** Ran SP% **118.7**
Speed ratings (Par 109): **103,102,102,101,99 98,98,97,92,86**
toteswingers 1&2 £10.60, 2&3 £6.80, 1&3 £6.00 CSF £52.98 CT £188.88 TOTE £8.40: £2.90, £2.00, £1.80; EX 60.50 Trifecta £286.60 Pool: £1914.21 - 5.00 winning units..
Owner Ms Colette Twomey **Bred** Collette Twomey **Trained** Maunby, N Yorks

FOCUS
A good handicap, although they didn't look to go that quick and there was nothing really progressive in the race. The form is fairly ordinary for the grade.
T/Jkpt: Not won. T/Plt: £746.00 to a £1 stake. Pool of £183095.84 -179.16 winning tickets. T/Qpdt: £99.20 to a £1 stake. Pool of £13336.31 - 99.40 winning tickets. WG

5850 EPSOM (L-H)

Thursday, September 12

OFFICIAL GOING: Soft (good to soft in places; overall 6.7; home straight: stands' side 6.9, far side 6.1)

Wind: virtually nil Weather: overcast

6333 CHEAM MAIDEN STKS 6f

2:20 (2:24) (Class 4) 2-Y-O **£3,881** (£1,155; £577; £288) **Stalls** High

Form RPR

3 **1** **Star Code (IRE)**[19] 5757 2-9-5 0 .... SebSanders 3 73+
(Richard Hannon) *mde all: rdn wl over 1f out: drvn and asserted ent fnl f: in command and r.o wl ins fnl f* **4/1**[2]

33 **2** ½ **Pool House**[19] 5744 2-9-2 0 .... ThomasBrown(3) 2 71
(Andrew Balding) *trckd ldr: effrt to chal over 1f out: nt qckn u.p ent fnl f: a hld and r.o one pce fnl f* **2/5**[1]

002 **3** 3¼ **China In My Hands**[12] 5976 2-8-11 67 .... CharlesBishop(3) 1 56
(Mick Channon) *s.i.s and flashed tail leaving stalls: sn rcvrd and hld up in tch: rdn and effrt 2f out: outpcd over 1f out: no threat to ldng pair and one pce fnl f: wnt 3rd nr fin* **8/1**[3]

4 shd **Roring Samson (IRE)** 2-9-5 0 .... JamesDoyle 5 61
(George Baker) *chsd ldrs: rdn and effrt 2f out: unable qck and btn ent fnl f: wl hld and kpt on same pce after: lost 3rd nr fin* **16/1**

0 **5** 2 **Classic Mission**[31] 5344 2-9-0 0 .... RyanTate(5) 4 55
(Jonathan Portman) *s.i.s: in tch in rr: clsd 1/2-way: rdn and unable qck 2f out: wknd over 1f out* **66/1**

1m 13.24s (3.84) **Going Correction** +0.50s/f (Yiel) **5 Ran SP% 109.9**
Speed ratings (Par 97): **94,93,89,88,86**
CSF £6.06 TOTE £4.20: £1.70, £1.10; EX 6.80 Trifecta £13.60 Pool: £2598.82 - 143.25 winning units..
Owner Sheikh Rashid Dalmook Al Maktoum **Bred** Holborn Trust Co **Trained** East Everleigh, Wilts

FOCUS
Races largely on Inner line and distances as advertised. A modest juvenile maiden in which the order hardly changed and the runners came centre-to-stands' side in the home straight, but not all the way across. This rating could underestimate the winner.

6334 BRITISH STALLION STUDS EBF MEDIAN AUCTION MAIDEN STKS 7f

2:50 (2:51) (Class 5) 2-Y-O **£3,881** (£1,155; £577; £288) **Stalls** Low

Form RPR

335 **1** **Mime Dance**[40] 4987 2-9-2 71 .... ThomasBrown(3) 6 71
(Andrew Balding) *chsd ldrs: clsd and upsides ldrs over 2f out: rdn to ld narrowly wl over 1f out: doing little in front tl fnd ex fnl 75yds: r.o and holding rival towards fin* **10/11**[1]

00 **2** nk **Thatchereen (IRE)**[12] 5983 2-9-0 0 .... JamesDoyle 4 65
(Michael Bell) *dwlt: hld up in tch in rr: rdn and effrt wl over 1f out: swtchd lft and str run to chal fnl 75yds: r.o but hld towards fin* **20/1**

3433 **3** 2½ **Needless Shouting (IRE)**[12] 6002 2-9-2 68 .... CharlesBishop(3) 3 64
(Mick Channon) *led: jnd 3f out: rdn and hdd wl over 1f out: kpt on and ev ch after tl no ex and btn ins fnl f: wknd fnl 100yds* **3/1**[2]

05 **4** 1½ **Cameley Dawn**[17] 5812 2-9-0 0 .... SebSanders 8 55
(Malcolm Saunders) *in tch in midfield: rdn and effrt 2f out: styng on same pce whn pushed lft and sltly hmpd jst ins fnl f: no threat to ldrs but kpt on again towards fin* **20/1**

6 **5** 1 **Nova Princesse (GER)**[40] 4997 2-9-0 0 .... (t) MartinLane 2 52
(Marco Botti) *t.k.h: chsd ldr: rdn and ev ch ent fnl 2f: hanging lft over 1f out: no ex and btn jst ins fnl f: sn wknd* **8/1**

0 **6** hd **Dark Crystal**[22] 5646 2-8-11 0 .... MichaelJMMurphy(3) 1 52
(John Gallagher) *in tch in midfield tl lost pl after 2f: stl in tch in last pair after: effrt and hdwy 2f out: no ex 1f out: wknd ins fnl f* **50/1**

0 **7** 3¼ **Presidente**[31] 5344 2-9-5 0 .... TomMcLaughlin 7 48
(Ed Walker) *stdd s: t.k.h: hld up in tch in last pair: hdwy into midfield 4f out: rdn and unable qck 2f out: wknd jst over 1f out: bhd and eased wl ins fnl f* **7/1**[3]

1m 27.81s (4.51) **Going Correction** +0.50s/f (Yiel) **7 Ran SP% 112.5**
Speed ratings (Par 95): **94,93,90,89,87 87,84**
toteswingers 1&2 £5.00, 2&3 £5.70, 1&3 £1.30 CSF £23.53 TOTE £1.80: £1.50, £7.60; EX 19.50 Trifecta £124.70 Pool: £2700.49 - 16.23 winning units..
Owner David Brownlow **Bred** The Stanley Estate And Stud Company **Trained** Kingsclere, Hants

FOCUS
A modest 2yo maiden in which the runners came slightly further towards the stands' side than in the opener and it may be no coincidence that the first two home came closest to the rail. The winner is rated to his pre-race mark.

6335 SCREWFIX LIVE 2013 H'CAP 1m 114y

3:25 (3:26) (Class 5) (0-75,75) 3-Y-O **£4,528** (£1,347; £673; £336) **Stalls** Low

Form RPR

4301 **1** **Mcdelta**[10] 6042 3-8-13 67 6ex .... SebSanders 1 79
(Geoffrey Deacon) *hld up in last trio: shkn up and hdwy 3f out: chsd ldr 2f out: rdn to ld over 1f out: sn in command and r.o wl fnl f: readily* **16/1**

2365 **2** 2¾ **Strong Conviction**[12] 6003 3-9-1 72 .... CharlesBishop(3) 3 78
(Mick Channon) *led: rdn ent fnl 2f: hdd and unable qck over 1f out: no ch w wnr but kpt on for clr 2nd fnl f* **7/1**

1443 **3** 2½ **Capella's Song (IRE)**[19] 5758 3-9-1 72 .... ThomasBrown(3) 2 72
(Michael Bell) *chsd ldrs: 3rd and effrt ent fnl 2f: no ex and outpcd over 3f out: wl hld and plugged on same pce fnl f* **4/1**[2]

0305 **4** shd **Hipster**[16] 5853 3-9-7 75 .... (b) MartinLane 4 75
(Ralph Beckett) *bustled along leaving stalls: chsd ldr: rdn over 3f out: drvn and outpcd 2f out: wl hld but plugged on ins fnl f* **14/1**

4304 **5** 1¼ **Astrosapphire**[35] 5203 3-8-8 62 .... KirstyMilczarek 5 59
(Mark H Tompkins) *racd in last trio: rdn and effrt over 2f out: no imp and btn over 1f out: wl hld and plugged on same pce fnl f* **33/1**

6524 **6** 2¾ **Aint Got A Scooby (IRE)**[12] 6003 3-9-1 74 .... RyanTate(5) 8 65
(Clive Cox) *in tch in midfield: rdn and effrt ent fnl 2f: sn outpcd and wl btn over 1f out: wknd fnl f* **11/4**[1]

12 **7** 14 **Nightster (IRE)**[10] 6048 3-9-3 74 .... MichaelJMMurphy(3) 6 33
(Mark Johnston) *chsd ldrs tl lost pl qckly 3f out: lost tch 2f out* **5/1**[3]

3015 **8** 2¾ **Gone Dutch**[8] 6106 3-9-5 73 .... FrederikTylicki 7 25
(James Fanshawe) *s.i.s: sn pushed along and nvr gng wl in rr: lost tch 2f out* **4/1**[2]

50-3 **9** 10 **Zain Spirit (USA)**[8] 6106 3-9-2 70 .... (p) JamesDoyle 9
(Gerard Butler) *in tch in midfield: lost pl and bhd 3f out: lost tch 2f out: eased ins fnl f: t.o* **16/1**

1m 48.03s (1.93) **Going Correction** +0.50s/f (Yiel) **9 Ran SP% 117.2**
Speed ratings (Par 101): **111,108,106,106,105 102,90,87,78**
toteswingers 1&2 £16.70, 2&3 £6.50, 1&3 £10.40 CSF £124.68 TOTE £20.00: £5.80, £2.50, £1.50; EX 106.60 Trifecta £860.10 Pool: £2861.63 - 2.49 winning units..
Owner P D Cundell **Bred** Roden House Stud **Trained** Compton, Berks

FOCUS
An ordinary handicap and this time the jockeys came right across on reaching the straight. The second sets the standard with the winner improving again.

6336 ERS MEDICAL JUMP JOCKEYS DERBY H'CAP (TO BE RIDDEN BY PROFESSIONAL NATIONAL HUNT JOCKEYS) 1m 4f 10y

4:00 (4:03) (Class 4) (0-80,80) 4-Y-O+ **£7,762** (£2,310; £1,154; £577) **Stalls** Centre

Form RPR

4255 **1** **Rossetti**[19] 5762 5-10-13 69 .... (p) JamieMoore 14 81
(Gary Moore) *t.k.h: led early: sn hdd and chsd ldng trio: clsd to ld and gng wl 3f out: clr and rdn over 1f out: hanging lft and rdn out fnl f* **12/1**

0031 **2** 1¼ **Toptempo**[16] 5854 4-11-3 73 .... ColinBolger 11 82
(Mark H Tompkins) *hld up in midfield: swtchd rt wl over 2f out: rdn and hdwy 2f out: chsd clr wnr and swtchd lft ent fnl f: r.o wl ins fnl f: nvr gng to rch wnr* **8/1**[3]

1214 **3** 4 **Certavi (IRE)**[20] 5706 4-11-1 71 .... AlainCawley 4 74
(Brendan Powell) *hld up in midfield: rdn and effrt over 2f out: chsd clr wnr ent fnl 2f: no imp: lost 2nd ent fnl f and one pce after* **8/1**[3]

-040 **4** 2 **Freddy Q (IRE)**[12] 6004 4-11-3 73 .... AidanColeman 5 72
(Roger Teal) *t.k.h: chsd ldrs: rdn and chsd wnr briefly over 2f out: sn outpcd and btn: 4th and plugged on same pce fr over 1f out* **25/1**

0033 **5** 1 **The Betchworth Kid**[6] 6165 8-11-10 80 .... (v) DavidBass 2 78
(Michael Bell) *dwlt: racd in last quintet: hdwy and swtchd lft over 2f out: drvn and no prog over 1f out: wl hld and styd on same pce after* **25/1**

4003 **6** nk **Saint Helena (IRE)**[26] 5535 5-11-6 76 .... SamTwiston-Davies 7 73
(Harry Dunlop) *hld up in rr: hdwy over 3f out: drvn and no imp wl over 1f out: wl hld and plugged on same pce after* **25/1**

30/2 **7** 1¼ **Clarion Call**[7] 6130 5-10-10 66 oh1 .... (p) PaulMoloney 6 61
(Graeme McPherson) *chsd ldrs: rdn and effrt over 2f out: unable qck and sn outpcd: wknd over 1f out* **20/1**

5-13 **8** 3½ **Hilali (IRE)**[17] 5824 4-11-10 80 .... APMcCoy 1 70+
(Gary Brown) *stdd s: hld up in last quintet: hdwy over 3f out: drvn and no prog whn squeezed for room and sltly hmpd 2f out: sn wknd* **11/4**[2]

5/05 **9** 1 **Zafisio (IRE)**[42] 4923 7-11-10 80 .... MarkGrant 9 68
(Jo Hughes) *hld up in last quintet: effrt on stands' rail whn nt clr run and hmpd wl over 2f out: n.d after* **16/1**

5140 **10** nk **Significant Move**[17] 5847 6-11-2 72 .... (b) PaddyBrennan 10 60
(Stuart Kittow) *hld up in last pair: short-lived effrt u.p 3f out: sn btn* **16/1**

4050 **11** 7 **Kayef (GER)**[16] 5862 6-10-10 66 oh4 .... (v[1]) TomScudamore 3 42
(Michael Scudamore) *led tl rdn and hdd 3f out: sn struggling and wknd: bhd over 1f out* **66/1**

204 **12** nk **Priors Gold**[24] 5231 6-11-1 71 .... DominicElsworth 8 47
(Laura Mongan) *w ldr tl over 3f out: wkng whn hmpd over 2f out: bhd over 1f out* **33/1**

0401 **13** 20 **Lowther**[16] 5855 8-11-9 79 .... (v) LeightonAspell 13 23
(Lee Carter) *hld up in tch in midfield: lost pl 3f out: sn bhd: t.o and eased fnl f* **25/1**

3-12 **14** 119 **Azrag (USA)**[17] 5823 5-11-10 80 .... (p) DenisO'Regan 12
(Gerard Butler) *in tch in midfield: rdn and dropped to rr 6f out: lost tch and eased fr over 4f out: wl t.o after* **9/4**[1]

2m 46.89s (7.99) **Going Correction** +0.50s/f (Yiel) **14 Ran SP% 123.7**
Speed ratings (Par 105): **93,92,89,88,87 87,86,84,83,83 78,78,65,**
toteswingers 1&2 £22.90, 2&3 £11.20, 1&3 £12.20 CSF £99.04 CT £834.12 TOTE £11.80: £2.80, £3.20, £2.40; EX 121.90 Trifecta £1520.50 Pool: £2178.21 - 1.07 winning units..
Owner Sheikh A'Leg Racing **Bred** Bricklow Ltd **Trained** Lower Beeding, W Sussex
■ Stewards' Enquiry : Colin Bolger two-day ban: careless riding (Sep 26,29)

FOCUS
A unique chance for the jump jockeys to test their skills over the Derby course, but Kayef and Priors Gold went off far too quick and it was little surprise that the pace collapsed. The winner is rated back to his best.

6337 HYPERION H'CAP 7f

4:35 (4:35) (Class 4) (0-80,80) 3-Y-O+ **£6,469** (£1,925; £962; £481) **Stalls** Low

Form RPR

0102 **1** **Brocklebank (IRE)**[23] 5621 4-9-5 80 .... JackDuern(5) 10 88
(Simon Dow) *stdd s: sn wl off the pce in last: rdn 3f out: clsng but stl last over 1f out: swtchd rt and str run against stands' rail ins fnl f: led towards fin* **14/1**

2003 **2** ¾ **My Kingdom (IRE)**[20] 5722 7-9-6 76 .... (t) J-PGuillambert 7 82+
(Stuart Williams) *wl in tch in midfield: swtchd lft and hdwy u.p jst over 1f out: drvn to ld ins fnl f: hdd and no ex towards fin* **10/1**

1226 **3** ¾ **Intomist (IRE)**[14] 5928 4-9-5 75 .... (p) FrederikTylicki 1 79
(Jim Boyle) *broke wl: sn lost pl: wl off the pce in last pair and rdn 1/2-way: drvn 3f out: clsd and carried lft 1f out: squeezed between horses and styd on fnl 100yds* **14/1**

1140 **4** ½ **Swift Cedar (IRE)**[33] 5268 3-9-3 80 .... MichaelJMMurphy(3) 4 83
(Alan Jarvis) *racd off the pce in last quartet: swtchd lft and clsd 2f out: pressing ldrs u.p 1f out: no ex and one pce ins fnl f* **8/1**[3]

3300 **5** ¾ **Top Cop**[5] 6204 4-9-2 79 .... (b) OisinMurphy(7) 5 80
(Andrew Balding) *chsd ldrs: rdn and ev ch 2f out: no extxra u.p jst ins fnl f: outpcd fnl 100yds* **8/1**[3]

3-25 **6** hd **Abigails Angel**[204] 720 6-8-13 69 .... KirstyMilczarek 9 69
(Brett Johnson) *pressed ldrs: rdn and ev ch 2f out but wanting to hang lft 2f out: led over 1f out but stl hanging lft: hdd ins fnl f: no ex and outpcd fnl 100yds* **33/1**

6446 **7** 1¼ **Sharp And Smart (IRE)**[61] 4278 4-9-5 75 .... DougieCostello 11 72
(Hughie Morrison) *chsd ldrs: travelling wl enough but bhd horses 2f out: swtchd lft and then rt over 1f out: switching bk lft 1f out: nvr enough room tl too late: unable to chal* **8/1**[3]

2311 **8** 1¾ **Pilates (IRE)**[10] 6039 3-8-10 70 6ex .... MartinLane 8 63
(Mark Johnston) *bustled along leaving stalls: chsd ldrs tl led over 5f out: rdn over 2f out: carried lft and hdd over 1f out: wknd ins fnl f* **3/1**[1]

3202 **9** 6 **Tidentime (USA)**[9] 6067 4-9-7 80 .... CharlesBishop(3) 3 57
(Mick Channon) *racd off the pce in last quintet: rdn and hdwy 3f out: no ex and btn over 1f out: sn wknd* **4/1**[2]

2213 **10** *shd* **Sarangoo**[24] 5589 5-9-8 **78**........ JamesDoyle 6 55
(Malcolm Saunders) *led tl over 5f out: styd w ldrs: rdn and struggling whn bmpd and sltly hmpd over 1f out: sn btn and wknd fnl f* **8/1**[3]

1m 26.61s (3.31) **Going Correction** +0.50s/f (Yiel)
WFA 3 from 4yo+ 4lb **10** Ran SP% **114.8**
Speed ratings (Par 105): **101,100,99,98,97 97,96,94,87,87**
toteswingers 1&2 £21.50, 2&3 £18.60, 1&3 £20.70 CSF £143.72 CT £2036.78 TOTE £19.90: £4.00, £3.60, £3.90; EX 187.10 Trifecta £1583.80 Part won. Pool: £2111.77 - 0.63 winning units..
Owner J C G Chua **Bred** Vincent Reen **Trained** Epsom, Surrey

FOCUS
This looked a fair handicap beforehand, but it became a messy contest and the form should be treated with the utmost caution. There was a three-way battle for the early lead and those responsible went off far too quick. The second and third help set the standard.

6338 HAPPY 21ST BIRTHDAY ADAM AND CHRIS H'CAP (JOCKEY CLUB GRASSROOTS SPRINT FLAT SERIES QUALIFIER) 6f

5:10 (5:10) (Class 5) (0-75,75) 3-Y-O **£5,175** (£1,540; £769; £384) **Stalls** High

Form RPR
-405 **1** **Prince Regal**[90] 3289 3-9-2 **73**........ MichaelJMMurphy(3) 5 80
(Alan Jarvis) *mde all: rdn and asserted over 1f out: in command wandering ins fnl f: styd on* **8/1**

5321 **2** *3/4* **Marjong**[22] 5647 3-9-7 **75**........ SebSanders 6 79
(Simon Dow) *stdd s: hld up wl off the pce in rr: clsd and gng wl 2f out: hit rail and wnt lft over 1f out: rdn to chse ldrs and carried lft ins fnl f: r.o to go 2nd nr fin* **5/1**

4363 **3** *nk* **Silkelly**[20] 5714 3-9-5 **73**........ DavidNolan 7 76
(David O'Meara) *w wnr: rdn and ev ch over 2f out: no ex over 1f out: styd on same pce and edgd lft ins fnl f: lost 2nd nr fin* **10/1**

2532 **4** *3 1/2* **Hot Secret**[8] 6100 3-8-12 **69**........ ThomasBrown(3) 4 61
(Andrew Balding) *racd off the pce in last pair: clsd 2f out: rdn and hung lft ent fnl f: sn wknd* **4/1**[3]

4331 **5** *1* **Lucky Di**[20] 5697 3-9-2 **73**........ CharlesBishop(3) 3 62
(Peter Hedger) *chsd clr ldrs: rdn and effrt ent fnl 2f: no imp over 1f out: wknd fnl f* **9/4**[1]

0-31 **6** *6* **Mukhabarat (IRE)**[26] 5517 3-9-7 **75**........ FrederikTylicki 1 44
(Saeed bin Suroor) *chsd clr ldng pair tl rdn and no prog over 2f out: wknd over 1f out: bhd ins fnl f* **7/2**[2]

1m 12.04s (2.64) **Going Correction** +0.50s/f (Yiel) **6** Ran SP% **109.9**
Speed ratings (Par 101): **102,101,100,95,94 86**
toteswingers 1&2 £3.50, 2&3 £2.80, 1&3 £7.50 CSF £44.18 TOTE £9.10: £3.50, £2.40; EX 52.30 Trifecta £265.10 Pool: £2639.02 - 7.46 winning units..
Owner T&J Partnership **Bred** Mrs Ann Jarvis **Trained** Twyford, Bucks

FOCUS
A modest 3yo sprint handicap and, although the leaders appeared to go off quickly enough, the pace held up this time. The winner is rated pretty much back to his 2yo form.
T/Plt: £1,222.00 to a £1 stake. Pool of £51977.69- 31.05 winning tickets. T/Qpdt: £369.30 to a £1 stake. Pool of £3693.93 - 7.40 winning tickets SP

6213 WOLVERHAMPTON (A.W) (L-H)

Thursday, September 12

OFFICIAL GOING: Standard to slow
Wind: Light behind Weather: Cloudy with sunny spells

6339 32REDPOKER.COM APPRENTICE H'CAP 1m 1f 103y(P)

5:30 (5:30) (Class 6) (0-60,62) 3-Y-O+ **£1,940** (£577; £288; £144) **Stalls** Low

Form RPR
4606 **1** **Kyle Of Bute**[14] 5921 7-9-1 **48**........ JoshBaudains 13 58
(Richard Ford) *hld up in tch: rdn to chse ldr fnl f: styd on to ld nr fin* **16/1**

044 **2** *nk* **Keene**[79] 3665 3-9-2 **58**........ LouisSteward(3) 1 67
(Philip McBride) *led: rdn clr 2f out: hdd nr fin* **5/2**[1]

6335 **3** *1* **Elizabeth Coffee (IRE)**[18] 5803 5-9-5 **52**........(t) JoeyHaynes 10 59
(John Weymes) *prom: nt clr run and lost pl over 2f out: rallied over 1f out: r.o* **12/1**

3641 **4** *4* **Handsome Stranger (IRE)**[3] 6260 3-9-9 **62** 6ex........(b) TimClark 5 61
(Alan Bailey) *chsd ldr: rdn over 3f out: lost 2nd 1f out: no ex* **3/1**[2]

4200 **5** *1 1/2* **Ella Motiva (IRE)**[13] 5942 3-8-3 **47**........ GaryMahon(5) 9 42
(Mark Brisbourne) *hld up: rdn wd over 2f out: r.o ins fnl f: nvr nrr* **16/1**

6000 **6** *3/4* **Justcallmehandsome**[39] 5032 11-8-8 **46** oh1(be) JosephineGordon(5) 12 40
(Dominic Ffrench Davis) *s.i.s: hld up: hdwy over 2f out: no ex fr over 1f out* **28/1**

140 **7** *nk* **Tyrur Ted**[59] 4355 8-9-6 **58**........(t) DanaZamecnikova(5) 7 51
(Frank Sheridan) *chsd ldrs: rdn over 2f out: styd on same pce fr over 1f out* **12/1**

1514 **8** *1 3/4* **Barton Bounty**[54] 4516 6-9-12 **59**........ KevinStott 6 48
(Peter Niven) *hld up: pushed along 5f out: nvr on terms* **7/2**[3]

2203 **9** *10* **Azelle**[33] 5275 3-9-7 **60**........ DanielMuscutt 4 28
(Brendan Powell) *sn pushed along to chse ldrs: rdn over 3f out: wknd wl over 1f out* **12/1**

540 **10** *4 1/2* **Heart Beat Song**[16] 5864 5-8-13 **46** oh1........ JacobButterfield 2
(James Moffatt) *prom: rdn over 2f out: sn wknd* **33/1**

2m 5.17s (3.47) **Going Correction** +0.35s/f (Slow)
WFA 3 from 4yo+ 6lb **10** Ran SP% **117.0**
Speed ratings (Par 101): **98,97,96,93,91 91,91,89,80,76**
toteswingers 1&2 £15.30, 2&3 £10.20, 1&3 £35.30 CSF £56.28 CT £517.33 TOTE £14.10: £5.30, £1.60, £3.90; EX 64.70 Trifecta £845.70 Part won. Pool: £1127.63 - 0.70 winning units..
Owner J H Chrimes And Mr & Mrs G W Hannam **Bred** Chippenham Lodge Stud Ltd **Trained** Garstang, Lancs
■ Stewards' Enquiry : Josh Baudains two-day ban: careless riding (Sep 26,29); one-day ban: failed to ride to draw (Sep 30)

FOCUS
They went a solid pace in this moderate apprentice rider's handicap and few managed to land a blow. The winner was close to his best this year off higher marks.

6340 32RED.COM EBF MAIDEN STKS 7f 32y(P)

6:00 (6:01) (Class 5) 2-Y-O **£2,911** (£866; £432; £216) **Stalls** High

Form RPR
362 **1** **Art Wave (IRE)**[33] 5279 2-9-5 **76**........ MartinHarley 9 76
(Marco Botti) *chsd ldrs: led 2f out: sn rdn: r.o u.p* **11/8**[1]

34 **2** *1/2* **Archibald Thorburn (IRE)**[17] 5826 2-9-5 **0**........ PaulMulrennan 1 75
(Ed McMahon) *hld up: hdwy over 1f out: rdn to chse wnr and edgd lft ins fnl f: r.o* **15/2**

34 **3** *2 1/2* **Major Surprise (USA)**[13] 5969 2-9-5 **0**........ DanielTudhope 5 69
(K R Burke) *a.p: swtchd lft over 1f out: sn rdn: hung lft and ev ch: styd on same pce ins fnl f* **9/4**[2]

06 **4** *nk* **Flying Cape (IRE)**[17] 5843 2-9-5 **0**........ RussKennemore 6 68
(Andrew Hollinshead) *hld up: hdwy and nt clr run over 2f out: rdn over 1f out: styd on* **11/2**[3]

0 **5** *7* **Mumtaza**[70] 3978 2-9-0 **0**........ SeanLevey 8 46
(Richard Hannon) *prom: shkn up over 1f out: wknd ins fnl f* **20/1**

0 **6** *6* **Hostile Fire (IRE)**[14] 5924 2-9-2 **0**........ MarkCoumbe(3) 7 36
(Ed de Giles) *sn pushed along in rr: nvr nrr* **100/1**

0506 **7** *15* **Creative Spirit**[65] 4141 2-8-7 **56**........ ClaireMurray(7) 4
(David Brown) *led 1f: led again 5f out: rdn and hdd 2f out: sn wknd* **50/1**

0 **8** *3 1/4* **Razin' Hell**[17] 5827 2-9-5 **0**........ AndrewElliott 3
(Alan McCabe) *sn pushed along to chse ldr: led 6f out tl 5f out: styd 2nd tl rdn over 2f out: wknd over 1f out* **100/1**

9 *8* **Don Ottavio** 2-9-5 **0**........ TedDurcan 2
(David Lanigan) *s.i.s: outpcd: lost tch over 2f out* **14/1**

1m 31.99s (2.39) **Going Correction** +0.35s/f (Slow) **9** Ran SP% **115.4**
Speed ratings (Par 95): **100,99,96,96,88 81,64,60,51**
toteswingers 1&2 £2.10, 2&3 £4.40, 1&3 £1.90 CSF £12.51 TOTE £2.60: £1.10, £1.80, £1.60; EX 12.70 Trifecta £26.30 Pool: £1960.19 - 55.82 winning units..
Owner Mohamed Albousi Alghufli **Bred** Sherbourne Lodge **Trained** Newmarket, Suffolk

FOCUS
An ordinary 2yo maiden and, thanks to a brisk early pace, the form is straightforward. The first four were clear.

6341 32RED FILLIES' H'CAP 7f 32y(P)

6:30 (6:31) (Class 4) (0-80,78) 3-Y-O+ **£4,690** (£1,395; £697; £348) **Stalls** High

Form RPR
-213 **1** **Star Pearl (USA)**[47] 4769 3-9-6 **78**........ HarryBentley 10 90
(Roger Varian) *trckd ldrs: wnt 2nd 5f out tl led over 2f out: sn pushed clr: rdn out* **15/8**[1]

0625 **2** *2 1/4* **Small Fury (IRE)**[41] 4942 3-8-7 **72**........ HarryBurns(7) 2 77
(Jo Hughes) *led: hdd over 2f out: rdr dropped whip over 1f out: kpt on* **40/1**

3121 **3** *3* **Imaginary World (IRE)**[17] 5830 5-8-13 **70**........(p) JasonHart(3) 3 68
(John Balding) *hld up: nt clr run 2f out: hdwy over 1f out: sn rdn: r.o: nt rch ldrs* **10/1**[3]

0233 **4** *nk* **Summer Dream (IRE)**[31] 5353 3-9-3 **75**........(b) MartinHarley 1 71
(Marco Botti) *prom: rdn over 1f out: styd on* **10/1**[3]

1- **5** *1 1/2* **Mrs Bannock (IRE)**[315] 7505 3-9-1 **73**........ MickaelBarzalona 9 65
(Charlie Appleby) *s.i.s: hld up: hdwy over 2f out: rdn over 1f out: styd on same pce ins fnl f* **5/2**[2]

5100 **6** *nse* **Balti's Sister (IRE)**[19] 5758 4-9-9 **77**........ BrettDoyle 8 70
(Martin Smith) *s.i.s: hld up: r.o ins fnl f: nvr on terms* **12/1**

3430 **7** *1* **Lisiere (IRE)**[21] 5684 4-9-3 **76**........(b) JoeyHaynes(5) 4 66
(K R Burke) *mid-div: pushed along 5f out: rdn and lost pl 1/2-way: n.d after* **10/1**[3]

6123 **8** *nk* **Perfect Venture**[32] 5300 3-8-10 **68**........ DavidProbert 5 56
(Clive Cox) *racd keenly: trckd ldr 2f: remained handy: rdn over 2f out: wknd ins fnl f* **25/1**

1420 **9** *3/4* **Lovesome**[29] 5406 3-8-10 **75**........ LouisSteward(7) 11 61
(Michael Bell) *s.i.s: hdwy over 5f out: rdn over 2f out: wknd fnl f* **25/1**

3333 **10** *1 1/2* **Truly Madly (IRE)**[8] 6100 3-8-4 **69**........ KevinStott(7) 7 51
(Hans Adielsson) *prom: pushed along 1/2-way: wknd 2f out* **16/1**

1m 30.88s (1.28) **Going Correction** +0.35s/f (Slow)
WFA 3 from 4yo+ 4lb **10** Ran SP% **114.3**
Speed ratings (Par 102): **106,103,100,99,97 97,96,96,95,93**
toteswingers 1&2 £18.40, 2&3 £29.00, 1&3 £1.80 CSF £90.01 CT £619.80 TOTE £2.50: £1.10, £7.90, £2.10; EX 131.70 Trifecta £1299.00 Pool: £1935.85 - 1.11 winning units..
Owner Pearl Bloodstock Ltd **Bred** Stephen E Quick **Trained** Newmarket, Suffolk

FOCUS
Not a bad handicap. It was run at an uneven pace, though, and racing handily was a must. The runner-up is probably the key to the form.

6342 32RED CASINO MAIDEN STKS 5f 216y(P)

7:00 (7:01) (Class 5) 2-Y-O **£2,587** (£770; £384; £192) **Stalls** Low

Form RPR
306 **1** **Fiftyshadesofgrey (IRE)**[44] 4858 2-9-5 **87**........ PatCosgrave 2 76
(George Baker) *sn w ldr: led 1/2-way: rdn and hung rt over 1f out: styd on u.p* **6/5**[1]

63 **2** *1* **Gamgoom**[29] 5399 2-9-5 **0**........ MickaelBarzalona 8 73
(Harry Dunlop) *s.i.s: sn pushed along in rr: hdwy over 1f out: r.o wl: nt rch wnr* **13/8**[2]

4 **3** *nk* **Look Here's Al**[27] 5494 2-9-5 **0**........ PaulMulrennan 11 72
(Ed McMahon) *chsd ldrs: rdn and ev ch over 1f out: styd on same pce ins fnl f* **7/1**[3]

56 **4** *2 3/4* **Clapperboard**[8] 6107 2-9-0 **0**........ FrankieMcDonald 5 59
(Paul Fitzsimons) *led to 1/2-way: rdn and ev ch whn hmpd over 1f out: no ex ins fnl f* **33/1**

06 **5** *2 1/2* **Midnight Rambler (IRE)**[8] 6110 2-9-5 **0**........ SeanLevey 10 56+
(Richard Hannon) *s.i.s: hld up: pushed along over 2f out: rdn over 1f out: nvr nrr* **20/1**

4 **6** *hd* **Wadi Alamardi**[21] 5665 2-9-5 **0**........ HarryBentley 9 56
(Michael Bell) *chsd ldrs: rdn over 2f out: wknd ins fnl f* **16/1**

06 **7** *1 3/4* **Golly Miss Molly**[29] 5385 2-9-0 **0**........ MartinHarley 6 46
(Jeremy Gask) *s.i.s: hdwy over 4f out: rdn over 2f out: wknd over 1f out* **50/1**

8 *3 1/4* **Twelve Bore** 2-9-5 **0**........ StevieDonohoe 4 41
(Willie Musson) *s.i.s: outpcd* **22/1**

0 **9** *3 1/2* **Dutch Lady**[42] 4924 2-9-0 **0**........ JimmyQuinn 12 25
(John Holt) *prom: rdn over 2f out: wknd over 1f out* **66/1**

1m 18.05s (3.05) **Going Correction** +0.35s/f (Slow) **9** Ran SP% **117.4**
Speed ratings (Par 95): **93,91,91,87,84 84,81,77,72**
toteswingers 1&2 £1.10, 2&3 £3.20, 1&3 £2.80 CSF £3.18 TOTE £2.10: £1.10, £1.10, £2.00; EX 4.00 Trifecta £10.80 Pool: £1843.44 - 126.97 winning units..
Owner Team Fifty **Bred** Doc Bloodstock **Trained** Manton, Wilts

FOCUS
A modest juvenile maiden. The winner was below his Windsor Castle form in success.

6343 32REDBET.COM H'CAP (DIV I) 5f 216y(P)

7:30 (7:32) (Class 6) (0-60,60) 3-Y-O+ **£1,940** (£577; £288; £144) **Stalls** Low

Form RPR
0-55 **1** **Big Storm Coming**[219] 525 3-8-11 **52**........ HarryBentley 7 65
(Brian Ellison) *a.p: pushed along over 2f out: rdn to ld over 1f out: r.o* **9/2**[2]

1654 **2** 1 1/4 **Loyal N Trusted**[24] 5594 5-9-5 **58**................................(p) MartinHarley 9 67+
(Richard Price) *s.i.s: hld up: hdwy over 1f out: edgd lft and r.o: nt rch wnr* **7/2**[1]
0004 **3** 1 1/2 **Kwanto**[16] 5864 3-8-6 **47**................................(p) AndrewMullen 6 51
(Michael Appleby) *sn led: rdn and hdd over 1f out: styd on same pce ins fnl f* **12/1**
0500 **4** *nk* **Ivestar (IRE)**[27] 5470 8-9-3 **56**................................(p) PaulMulrennan 11 59
(Michael Easterby) *a.p: chsd ldr over 4f out: rdn over 1f out: styd on same pce ins fnl f* **6/1**[3]
1005 **5** 1 **Reginald Claude**[10] 6040 5-9-7 **60**................................ DavidProbert 10 60
(Mark Usher) *hld up: hdwy over 2f out: styd on same pce ins fnl f* **9/2**[2]
505 **6** 1 **Fantasy Invader (IRE)**[9] 6074 3-8-12 **53**................(v[1]) PatCosgrave 5 50
(John Quinn) *s.i.s: in rr: rdn and edgd lft over 1f out: r.o ins fnl f: nrst fin* **8/1**
0000 **7** 2 3/4 **Lady Kildare (IRE)**[28] 5422 5-8-9 **48**................(t) MichaelO'Connell 12 36
(Jedd O'Keeffe) *s.i.s: sn prom: rdn over 2f out: wknd fnl f* **20/1**
0406 **8** 1/2 **Copper Leyf**[34] 5230 3-8-5 **46** oh1................................(tp) RenatoSouza 2 32
(Jeremy Gask) *hld up: nt clr run over 2f out: rdn over 1f out: hung lft ins fnl f: n.d* **33/1**
05 **9** 1 1/2 **Imjin River (IRE)**[129] 2096 6-8-12 **54**................................(t) RobertTart(3) 4 36
(William Stone) *mid-div: hdwy over 2f out: rdn over 1f out: wknd ins fnl f* **14/1**
2000 **10** 6 **Stonecrabstomorrow (IRE)**[17] 5816 10-9-3 **59**......... MarkCoumbe(3) 1 21
(Roy Brotherton) *sn pushed along in rr: n.d* **12/1**
/303 **11** 10 **Spirit Of Dixie**[20] 5709 6-8-0 **46** oh1................................ AaronJones(7) 8
(Alan McCabe) *chsd ldrs tl rdn and wknd over 2f out* **28/1**
0000 **12** 2 1/2 **Forever Janey**[31] 5354 4-8-4 **46** oh1................................ RaulDaSilva(3) 3
(Paul Green) *chsd ldrs: pushed along 1/2-way: wknd over 1f out* **50/1**

1m 17.18s (2.18) **Going Correction** +0.35s/f (Slow)
WFA 3 from 4yo+ 2lb **12** Ran SP% **119.1**
Speed ratings (Par 101): **99,97,95,94,93 92,88,87,85,77 64,61**
toteswingers 1&2 £5.90, 2&3 £10.90, 1&3 £7.70 CSF £19.90 CT £180.08 TOTE £6.50: £1.80, £1.70, £3.30; EX 25.20 Trifecta £217.00 Pool: £1450.23 - 5.01 winning units..
Owner Fishlake Commercial Motors Ltd **Bred** Bearstone Stud **Trained** Norton, N Yorks

FOCUS
The first division of a weak sprint handicap, run in a similar time to division II. The form should work out and the winner can do better.

6344 32REDBET.COM H'CAP (DIV II) 5f 216y(P)
8:00 (8:02) (Class 6) (0-60,60) 3-Y-O+ **£1,940** (£577; £288; £144) **Stalls** Low

Form RPR
5060 **1** **Gaelic Wizard (IRE)**[65] 4155 5-8-10 **56**................(p) JoshBaudains(7) 11 68
(Dominic Ffrench Davis) *chsd ldr tl led 1/2-way: rdn over 2f out: styd on u.p* **12/1**
2360 **2** 2 1/2 **Whipphound**[21] 5674 5-9-7 **60**................................ RobertWinston 9 64
(Mark Brisbourne) *chsd ldr: rdn to chse wnr over 1f out: styd on same pce ins fnl f* **7/2**[1]
-025 **3** *nk* **Gambino (IRE)**[9] 6084 3-8-6 **47**................................ PatrickMathers 10 50
(Alan Berry) *s.i.s: sn pushed along in rr: hdwy over 2f out: rdn over 1f out: styd on* **11/2**[3]
0064 **4** 3/4 **Time To Begin (IRE)**[13] 5965 3-8-13 **54**................................(bt) SeanLevey 5 55
(Alan McCabe) *sn pushed along and prom: lost pl 5f out: hdwy u.p over 1f out: hung lft ins fnl f: styd on* **10/1**
4555 **5** *shd* **Cymeriad**[22] 5644 3-8-5 **46**................................(p) LukeMorris 6 46
(Michael Easterby) *prom: rdn over 1f out: no ex ins fnl f* **17/2**
0503 **6** 1 **Methaaly (IRE)**[5] 6219 10-9-2 **58**................................(be) RobertTart(3) 12 55
(Michael Mullineaux) *hld up: hdwy u.p over 1f out: styd on same pce ins fnl f* **11/2**[3]
0040 **7** 3 1/2 **Direct Trade**[31] 5354 3-8-5 **46** oh1................................(e[1]) DavidProbert 7 32
(Mark Usher) *prom: rdn and edgd lft over 1f out: wknd ins fnl f* **20/1**
4324 **8** 2 3/4 **Molly Jones**[97] 3042 4-8-11 **50**................................(p) PatCosgrave 2 27
(Derek Haydn Jones) *sn pushed along in rr: n.d* **12/1**
1522 **9** 1 1/4 **Lord Buffhead**[5] 6219 4-9-2 **55**................................(v) RobbieFitzpatrick 3 28
(Richard Guest) *s.i.s: sn drvn along in rr: nvr on terms* **9/2**[2]
200- **10** 2 1/2 **Avonlini**[317] 7465 7-8-4 **50**................................(v[1]) KevinStott(7) 8 15
(Richard Ford) *led to 1/2-way: rdn and wknd over 1f out* **22/1**
0/00 **11** *nk* **Musical Strike**[23] 5622 4-8-2 **46** oh1................................ ShirleyTeasdale(5) 4 10
(Shaun Harris) *prom: rdn over 2f out: sn wknd* **66/1**

1m 17.28s (2.28) **Going Correction** +0.35s/f (Slow)
WFA 3 from 4yo+ 2lb **11** Ran SP% **116.8**
Speed ratings (Par 101): **98,94,94,93,93 91,87,83,81,78 78**
toteswingers 1&2 £10.80, 2&3 £4.90, 1&3 £12.80 CSF £52.38 CT £228.26 TOTE £14.20: £4.10, £2.00, £2.90; EX 76.80 Trifecta £606.50 Pool: £1468.67 - 1.81 winning units..
Owner D J Ffrench Davis **Bred** Mrs Mary Gallagher **Trained** Lambourn, Berks

FOCUS
This second division of the weak sprint handicap, run at a sound pace. The winner is rated close to his earlier efforts.

6345 32REDBINGO.COM H'CAP 5f 20y(P)
8:30 (8:30) (Class 6) (0-60,60) 3-Y-O+ **£1,940** (£577; £288; £144) **Stalls** Low

Form RPR
053 **1** **Never A Quarrel (IRE)**[31] 5345 3-9-6 **60**................................ FergusSweeney 3 72
(Jeremy Gask) *trckd ldr: rdn to ld ins fnl f: r.o* **5/1**[2]
0010 **2** 2 1/2 **Little Eli**[27] 5485 3-9-2 **59**................................ JasonHart(3) 8 62
(Eric Alston) *led: rdn over 1f out: hdd and unable qck ins fnl f* **10/3**[1]
3125 **3** 1 1/2 **Megaleka**[15] 5889 3-9-1 **60**................................ TimClark(5) 6 58+
(Alan Bailey) *hld up: rdn over 1f out: r.o ins fnl f: nvr nrr* **6/1**[3]
0033 **4** *nk* **Sarah Berry**[16] 5864 4-9-2 **55**................................(v) LukeMorris 1 52
(Chris Dwyer) *prom: sn pushed along: rdn 1/2-way: styd on same pce fr over 1f out* **8/1**
00-3 **5** *hd* **Running Water**[14] 5917 5-8-4 **50**................................ JordanHibberd(7) 9 46
(Alan Berry) *hld up: r.o ins fnl f: nvr on nrr* **28/1**
6003 **6** 1 1/2 **Mr Snooks**[9] 6088 3-8-6 **46**................................ PaulQuinn 4 36
(David Nicholls) *chsd ldrs: rdn over 1f out: wknd ins fnl f* **5/1**[2]
0630 **7** 3 1/2 **Sabrina's Secret**[27] 5485 3-9-6 **60**................................ AndrewElliott 5 38
(Tom Tate) *hld up: racd keenly: nt clr run 1/2-way: n.d* **8/1**
0000 **8** 1 3/4 **Magic Ice**[5] 6219 3-8-12 **52**................................(p) HarryBentley 7 24
(Brian Ellison) *in rr: hdwy 1/2-way: rdn and wknd over 1f out* **12/1**
0460 **9** 5 **Marvelino**[15] 5890 3-9-3 **57**................................(p) RobertWinston 2 11
(Pat Eddery) *prom: nt clr run and lost pl after 1f: drvn along 1/2-way: eased whn btn over 1f out* **8/1**

1m 3.91s (1.61) **Going Correction** +0.35s/f (Slow)
WFA 3 from 4yo+ 1lb **9** Ran SP% **115.2**
Speed ratings (Par 101): **101,97,94,94,93 91,85,83,75**
toteswingers 1&2 £6.10, 2&3 £5.20, 1&3 £10.00 CSF £21.98 CT £102.56 TOTE £5.50: £1.70, £1.50, £2.60; EX 36.00 Trifecta £132.50 Pool: £1589.28 - 8.99 winning units..
Owner Coral Champions Club **Bred** Mount Coote Stud **Trained** Sutton Veny, Wilts

FOCUS
Another weak handicap. The first pair dominated with the winner rating a cler personal best.

6346 £32 BONUS AT 32RED.COM H'CAP 1m 4f 50y(P)
9:00 (9:00) (Class 5) (0-75,75) 3-Y-O+ **£2,587** (£770; £384; £192) **Stalls** Low

Form RPR
5656 **1** **Royal Peculiar**[9] 6071 5-9-9 **72**................................ AndrewMullen 5 84
(Michael Appleby) *trckd ldrs: led over 2f out: rdn over 1f out: all out* **4/1**[2]
231 **2** *shd* **St Ignatius**[14] 5920 6-9-4 **67**................................(v) RobertWinston 12 79
(Alan Bailey) *a.p: trckd ldr 10f out: led wl over 3f out: rdn and hdd over 2f out: rallied ins fnl f: r.o* **15/2**
3230 **3** 7 **Lean On Pete (IRE)**[32] 5304 4-9-12 **75**................................ ShaneKelly 11 76
(Ollie Pears) *hld up: hdwy over 2f out: rdn over 1f out: styd on same pce* **5/1**[3]
0203 **4** 2 1/2 **Snow Hill**[31] 5356 5-9-11 **74**................................(b) SebSanders 2 71
(Chris Wall) *s.i.s: hld up: hdwy and nt clr run over 2f out: rdn over 1f out: no ex ins fnl f* **7/2**[1]
-015 **5** 5 **Yasir (USA)**[16] 5868 5-9-9 **72**................................(p) FergusSweeney 8 61
(Conor Dore) *hld up: hdwy over 4f out: rdn over 2f out: wknd over 1f out* **10/1**
460 **6** 10 **Watts Up Son**[4] 6239 5-9-5 **75**................................(v) LukeLeadbitter(7) 10 48
(Declan Carroll) *sn led: rdn and hdd wl over 3f out: wknd over 2f out* **12/1**
2604 **7** 2 1/2 **Strike Force**[9] 6071 9-9-3 **71**................................(tp) TobyAtkinson(5) 7 40
(Alison Hutchinson) *prom: rdn over 3f out: wknd over 2f out* **25/1**
20 **8** 1 **Mont Blanc**[17] 5831 4-9-9 **72**................................ LukeMorris 6 39
(Jane Chapple-Hyam) *hld up in tch: rdn and wknd over 2f out* **11/2**
5-60 **9** 21 **Isdaal**[96] 3095 6-9-3 **66**................................ JimmyQuinn 9
(Kevin Morgan) *hld up: rdn and wknd over 3f out* **28/1**
050- **10** 3 **Spirit Of Adjisa (IRE)**[158] 5830 9-9-5 **68**................................ DavidProbert 3
(David C Griffiths) *chsd ldrs: rdn over 4f out: wknd over 3f out* **20/1**
3130 **11** *nk* **Blades Lad**[134] 1936 4-9-10 **73**................................ PaulMulrennan 1
(Peter Niven) *prom: pushed along over 5f out: wknd 4f out* **14/1**
0 **12** 1/2 **Johnnys Legacy (IRE)**[12] 6004 6-8-13 **65**................(p) SimonPearce(3) 4
(Conor Dore) *hld up: pushed along over 6f out: wknd over 4f out* **33/1**

2m 43.48s (2.38) **Going Correction** +0.35s/f (Slow) **12** Ran SP% **124.5**
Speed ratings (Par 103): **106,105,101,99,96 89,87,87,73,71 71,70**
toteswingers 1&2 £9.60, 2&3 £5.60, 1&3 £9.00 CSF £34.42 CT £159.32 TOTE £6.80: £2.70, £1.40, £1.50; EX 58.70 Trifecta £332.20 Pool: £1394.28 - 3.14 winning units..
Owner Terry Pryke **Bred** Newsells Park Stud **Trained** Danethorpe, Notts

FOCUS
A modest handicap which saw the first pair fight it out off the home turn in a cracking finish, clear of the rest. The winner is rated in line with his early summer turf form.
T/Plt: £17.70 to a £1 stake. Pool of £87793.14 - 3613.39 winning tickets. T/Qpdt: £8.90 to a £1 stake. Pool of £10580.56, 875.60 winning tickets. CR

6326 DONCASTER (L-H)
Friday, September 13

OFFICIAL GOING: Good to soft (6.7)
Wind: Light half against Weather: Cloudy with sunny periods

6347 POLYPIPE FLYING CHILDERS STKS (GROUP 2) 5f
1:40 (1:43) (Class 1) 2-Y-O
£39,697 (£15,050; £7,532; £3,752; £1,883; £945) **Stalls** High

Form RPR
0310 **1** **Green Door (IRE)**[22] 5679 2-9-0 94................................(b) JimCrowley 3 108
(Olly Stevens) *t.k.h early: trckd ldrs: hdwy on outer 1/2-way: rdn over 1f out: qckn to chal ins fnl f: led last 100yds* **18/1**
3513 **2** 1 1/4 **Wind Fire (USA)**[22] 5680 2-8-11 103................................ JamieSpencer 2 101
(David Brown) *lw: trckd ldng pair: hdwy 2f out: rdn to ld over 1f out: jnd and drvn ins fnl f: hdd and no ex last 100yds* **4/1**[2]
1410 **3** 1/2 **Extortionist (IRE)**[54] 4572 2-9-0 104................................ MickaelBarzalona 4 102
(Olly Stevens) *swtg: on toes: t.k.h: hld up in rr: swtchd lft to outer and hdwy 2f out: rdn to chse ldng pair ent fnl f: kpt on* **7/1**
1061 **4** 3/4 **Fast (IRE)**[50] 4653 2-8-11 91................................ RyanMoore 8 96
(Richard Hannon) *cl up on inner: led after 2f: rdn and hdd over 1f out: kpt on same pce* **10/1**
4532 **5** 3 1/4 **Thunder Strike**[22] 5679 2-9-0 101................................ RichardHughes 7 87
(Richard Hannon) *led 2f: cl up: rdn along 2f out: wknd over 1f out* **10/3**[1]
1044 **6** *nk* **Sleeper King (IRE)**[22] 5679 2-9-0 103................................ JamesDoyle 5 86
(Kevin Ryan) *lw: chsd ldrs: rdn along 2f out: sn wknd* **10/3**[1]
1634 **7** 11 **Ambiance (IRE)**[33] 5319 2-9-0 104................................(v) SilvestreDeSousa 6 47
(Mick Channon) *in tch: pushed along bef 1/2-way: rdn over 2f out: sn btn and eased* **5/1**[3]

59.94s (-0.56) **Going Correction** -0.075s/f (Good) **7** Ran SP% **109.7**
Speed ratings (Par 107): **101,99,98,97,91 91,73**
toteswingers 1&2 £6.50, 1&3 £15.30, 2&3 £5.40 CSF £80.85 TOTE £16.30: £7.90, £3.10; EX 101.10 Trifecta £914.00 Pool: £3729.63 - 3.06 winning units..
Owner D Redvers & Michael H Watt **Bred** Mrs Sue Lenehan **Trained** Chiddingfold, Surrey
■ A first Group winner in his debut season for Olly Stevens.

FOCUS
The course endured 2mm of overnight rain and the ground was expected to ride similarly to the opening day as a result. There were conflicting reports amongst riders after the opener, though the winning time suggested it was slightly quicker than the official assessment. This was an open running of the Flying Childers and not the strongest affair by Group 2 standards. They went a solid pace with the leaders keen to race near the stands' rail and the runner-up and third set the standard.

6348 LADBROKES MALLARD STKS (H'CAP) 1m 6f 132y
2:10 (2:10) (Class 2) (0-110,108) 3-Y-O+**£25,876** (£7,700; £3,848; £1,924) **Stalls** Low

Form RPR
5-24 **1** **Camborne**[20] 5741 5-10-0 **108**................................(p) RobertHavlin 1 116
(John Gosden) *hld up in rr: swtchd rt to outer wl over 1f out: rdn and qcknd wl to ld ent fnl f: sn clr* **7/1**[3]
3231 **2** 2 **Shwaiman (IRE)**[27] 5520 3-8-2 **94**................................ AndreaAtzeni 3 99
(James Fanshawe) *dwlt: t.k.h: hld up in rr: gd hdwy on outer wl over 2f out: chal wl over 1f out and ev ch tl rdn and kpt on same pce fnl f* **9/4**[1]
2021 **3** 2 3/4 **Pether's Moon (IRE)**[41] 4984 3-8-9 **101**................................ RichardHughes 7 103
(Richard Hannon) *trckd ldrs: hdwy to trck ldr after 3f: cl up over 5f out: tk narrow advantage 3f out: rdn 2f out: drvn and hdd ent fnl f: sn one pce* **9/4**[1]
2-2 **4** 1/2 **Tropical Beat**[35] 5237 5-9-5 **99**................................ DanielTudhope 6 100
(David O'Meara) *lw: trckd ldrs: hdwy on inner 2f out: rdn whn n.m.r over 1f out: sn drvn and one pce* **6/1**[2]

1620 **5** *2* **Songcraft (IRE)**[20] 5741 5-9-13 **107**.......................(p) SilvestreDeSousa 4 106
(Saeed bin Suroor) *t.k.h: led 2f: trckd ldng pair: hdwy 3f out: cl up 2f out: sn rdn and wknd appr fnl f* **10/1**

-406 **6** *55* **Tenenbaum**[62] 4309 4-9-13 **107**.......................MickaelBarzalona 5 34
(Charlie Appleby) *trckd ldr: led after 2f and set stdy pce: rdn along and hdd 3f out: wknd 2f out: sn bhd and eased* **15/2**

3m 13.36s (5.96) **Going Correction** +0.375s/f (Good)
WFA 3 from 4yo+ 12lb **6** Ran SP% **109.2**
Speed ratings (Par 109): **99,97,96,96,95 65**
toteswingers 1&2 £3.30, 1&3 £2.70, 2&3 £1.70 CSF £21.86 CT £41.84 TOTE £8.40: £3.50, £1.60; EX 25.30 Trifecta £73.10 Pool: £2924.16 - 29.99 winning units..
Owner HRH Princess Haya Of Jordan **Bred** Southill Stud **Trained** Newmarket, Suffolk

FOCUS
A strong staying handicap, despite a smaller field than usual, in which 3-y-os had the best recent record in the race. The pair representing that age group made the places, but were no match for the winner. The early pace was steady and everything had a chance halfway up the straight. This rates a personal best from the winner with two progressive 3yos in behind.

6349 SPEEDY SERVICES DONCASTER CUP (BRITISH CHAMPIONS SERIES) (GROUP 2) 2m 2f
2:40 (2:40) (Class 1) 3-Y-O+
£56,710 (£21,500; £10,760; £5,360; £2,690; £1,350) **Stalls** Low

Form RPR
-603 **1** **Times Up**[21] 5724 7-9-3 112.......................RyanMoore 4 115
(Ed Dunlop) *hld up towards rr: smooth hdwy 3f out: led 1 1/2f out: rdn ent fnl f: drvn and edgd rt last 100yds: kpt on wl* **3/1**[3]

22-4 **2** *1 1/4* **High Jinx (IRE)**[106] 2810 5-9-3 112.......................(t) JamesDoyle 3 113
(James Fanshawe) *lw: trckd ldrs: hdwy to trck ldr 1/2-way: cl up over 6f out: effrt to ld wl over 3f out: rdn 2f out: drvn and hdd 1 1/2f out: sn edgd sltly rt: kpt on u.p fnl f* **2/1**[1]

-040 **3** *1/2* **Repeater**[43] 4919 4-9-3 102.......................[1] DanielTudhope 7 112
(David O'Meara) *hld up in rr gng wl: smooth hdwy on bit 3f out: trckd ldrs 2f out: effrt whn n.m.r and sltly hmpd over 1f out: sn rdn and chsd wnr ins fnl f: drvn: one pce and lost 2nd last 75yds* **20/1**

-420 **4** *1 1/4* **Biographer**[27] 5531 4-9-3 109.......................TedDurcan 1 111
(David Lanigan) *lw: hld up in tch: hdwy over 3f out: cl up and rdn over 2f out: ev ch tl drvn over 1f out and kpt on same pce* **5/2**[2]

0406 **5** *3 1/4* **Colour Vision (FR)**[21] 5724 5-9-3 110.......................SilvestreDeSousa 2 107
(Saeed bin Suroor) *trckd ldrs: pushed along and sltly outpcd over 3f out: hdwy u.p 2f out: drvn to chse ldrs on outer and edgd lft over 1f out: sn wknd* **13/2**

-513 **6** *17* **Chiberta King**[69] 4083 7-9-3 102.......................(p) JimmyFortune 6 87
(Andrew Balding) *lw: trckd ldr to 1/2-way: prom: effrt and cl up 4f out: rdn along 3f out: sn drvn and wknd* **16/1**

0050 **7** *26* **Desert Recluse (IRE)**[16] 5895 6-9-3 80.......................RobertWinston 5 55
(Pat Eddery) *led: qcknd pce after 4f: rdn along over 4f out: hdd wl over 3f out and sn wknd* **66/1**

3m 59.09s (4.09) **Going Correction** +0.375s/f (Good) **7** Ran SP% **112.4**
Speed ratings (Par 115): **105,104,104,103,102 94,83**
toteswingers 1&2 £2.00, 1&3 £11.20, 2&3 £7.80 CSF £9.08 TOTE £2.40: £1.60, £1.90; EX 7.90 Trifecta £80.60 Pool: £6704.14 - 62.34 winning units..
Owner Mrs I H Stewart-Brown & M J Meacock **Bred** I Stewart-Brown And M Meacock **Trained** Newmarket, Suffolk

FOCUS
There was a cracking finish and it saw a virtual repeat of last year's placings. The pace was an uneven one and the race thus a little messy, but the form is clearly straightforward rated around the front pair.

6350 BARRETT STEEL MAY HILL STKS (GROUP 2) (FILLIES) 1m (S)
3:15 (3:15) (Class 1) 2-Y-O
£39,697 (£15,050; £7,532; £3,752; £1,883; £945) **Stalls** High

Form RPR
2231 **1** **Ihtimal (IRE)**[34] 5284 2-8-12 104.......................SilvestreDeSousa 7 107+
(Saeed bin Suroor) *trckd ldrs: hdwy 2f out: rdn over 1f out: qcknd wl ent fnl f to ld last 100yds: readily* **11/10**[1]

151 **2** *2* **Majeyda (USA)**[50] 4682 2-8-12 97.......................MickaelBarzalona 1 101
(Charlie Appleby) *lw: trckd ldr: cl up 1/2-way: rdn to ld over 1f out: drvn and edgd lft ins fnl f: hdd and kpt on same pce last 100yds* **9/2**[2]

0264 **3** *2* **Lady Lara (IRE)**[23] 5652 2-8-12 90.......................JimCrowley 2 96
(Alan Jarvis) *hld up in rr: hdwy on outer wl over 2f out: chsd ldrs wl over 1f out: sn rdn and ev ch tl drvn and one pce ins fnl f* **12/1**

1 **4** *1* **Lustrous**[8] 6141 2-8-12 0.......................RichardHughes 3 94
(Richard Hannon) *lw: hld up in rr: pushed along and hdwy 2f out: swtchd lft and rdn over 1f out: kpt on u.p fnl f: n.d* **10/1**

333 **5** *nk* **Halljoy (IRE)**[20] 5737 2-8-12 93.......................RyanMoore 4 93
(Clive Brittain) *lw: trckd ldng pair: hdwy on outer over 2f out: rdn to chal wl over 1f out: drvn and wknd appr fnl f* **9/1**

3 **6** *2 3/4* **Vivere (IRE)**[32] 5330 2-8-12 0.......................DanielTudhope 5 87
(David O'Meara) *w'like: trckd ldrs: pushed along wl over 2f out: sn rdn and wknd wl over 1f out* **25/1**

3122 **7** *2 1/2* **Qawaasem (IRE)**[20] 5737 2-8-12 100.......................PaulHanagan 6 82
(Charles Hills) *set stdy pce: qcknd wl over 2f out: rdn and hdd over 1f out: sn wknd* **11/2**[3]

1m 43.3s (4.00) **Going Correction** +0.375s/f (Good) **7** Ran SP% **111.8**
Speed ratings (Par 104): **95,93,91,90,89 86,84**
toteswingers 1&2 £2.00, 1&3 £3.80, 2&3 £6.70 CSF £5.92 TOTE £2.10: £1.80, £2.40; EX 8.00 Trifecta £44.50 Pool: £21043.52 - 354.04 winning units..
Owner Godolphin **Bred** Darley **Trained** Newmarket, Suffolk

FOCUS
One of the top races for staying juvenile fillies and a very good guide to the Fillies' Mile, with the last five winners of this to have contested that race having been successful. Godolphin had been responsible for the last three winners, and completed the four-timer with a one-two here. Probably an ordinary renewal but the winner can do better.

6351 ONE CALL INSURANCE FLYING SCOTSMAN STKS (LISTED RACE) 7f
3:50 (3:51) (Class 1) 2-Y-O **£15,311** (£5,805; £2,905; £1,447; £726) **Stalls** Low

Form RPR
2 **1** **Be Ready (IRE)**[27] 5530 2-9-0 0.......................SilvestreDeSousa 2 105+
(Saeed bin Suroor) *str: swtg: t.k.h early: trckd ldng pair on outer: hdwy 2f out: rdn to ld stj over 1f out: edgd rt and shkn up ins fnl f: sn qcknd and kpt on stly: impressive* **13/8**[1]

1 **2** *3* **Barley Mow (IRE)**[28] 5473 2-9-0 0.......................RichardHughes 4 97+
(Richard Hannon) *lw: t.k.h early: trckd ldng pair on inner: effrt 2f out: sn swtchd lft and rdn over 1f out: chsd wnr ent fnl f: sn no imp* **2/1**[2]

31 **3** *2 3/4* **Voice Of A Leader (IRE)**[44] 4896 2-9-0 0.......................JamieSpencer 3 90
(Peter Chapple-Hyam) *lw: led: rdn along 2f out: drvn and hdd jst over 1f out: sn one pce* **10/3**[3]

2215 **4** *2 3/4* **Brazos (IRE)**[23] 5652 2-9-0 90.......................JamesDoyle 6 83
(Clive Brittain) *hld up in rr: effrt over 2f out: sn rdn and n.d* **8/1**

1432 **5** *5* **Cool Bahamian (IRE)**[14] 5952 2-9-0 93.......................JimmyFortune 1 70
(Eve Johnson Houghton) *cl up: rdn along over 2f out: sn wknd* **16/1**

1m 28.76s (2.46) **Going Correction** +0.375s/f (Good) **5** Ran SP% **111.5**
Speed ratings (Par 103): **100,96,93,90,84**
CSF £5.27 TOTE £2.50: £1.30, £1.20; EX 6.20 Trifecta £12.80 Pool: £3792.26 - 232.28 winning units..
Owner Godolphin **Bred** Thomas Hassett **Trained** Newmarket, Suffolk

FOCUS
A compelling Listed prize for juveniles and the form, which should work out, looks well worth following. The winner is an exciting prospect and the third is the best guide.

6352 TOWNDOOR LIMITED COMMERCIAL PROPERTY RENTAL H'CAP 6f 110y
4:25 (4:27) (Class 2) (0-105,103) 3-Y-O+ **£12,938** (£3,850; £1,924; £962) **Stalls** Low

Form RPR
-002 **1** **Sir Reginald**[14] 5943 5-8-10 **89** oh2.......................PaulHanagan 10 99
(Richard Fahey) *in rr stands' side: pushed along and hdwy over 2f out: rdn wl over 1f out: styd on u.p to chal ins fnl f: kpt on gamely to ld nr fin* **10/1**

0200 **2** *nk* **Bertiewhittle**[48] 4744 5-9-3 **96**.......................GrahamGibbons 2 105
(David Barron) *trckd ldrs far side: hdwy 2f out: rdn to ld that gp and overall ldr jst over 1f out: drvn ins fnl f: hdd and no ex nr fin* **5/1**[1]

0006 **3** *1 1/4* **Yeeoow (IRE)**[41] 4983 4-8-13 **92**.......................DanielTudhope 13 98
(K R Burke) *trckd ldng pair stands' side: hdwy to ld that gp over 1f out: sn rdn and edgd rt: ev ch tl drvn and nt qckn wl ins fnl f: 2nd of 5 in gp* **8/1**[3]

2420 **4** *3/4* **Shropshire (IRE)**[41] 4986 5-9-10 **103**.......................RobertWinston 12 107
(Charles Hills) *hld up in tch on stands' rail: n.m.r wl over 1f out: sn rdn and styd on wl fnl f: 3rd of 5 in gp* **13/2**[2]

0040 **5** *1* **Joe Packet**[13] 5998 6-8-11 **90**.......................JimCrowley 9 91
(Jonathan Portman) *lw: hld up far side: hdwy 2f out: sn rdn: kpt on fnl f: nrst fin: 2nd of 9 in gp* **14/1**

0031 **6** *1/2* **Gramercy (IRE)**[21] 5696 6-9-1 **94**.......................(b) SilvestreDeSousa 11 93
(David Simcock) *clsd up stands' side: rdn along and edgd lft over 1f out: sn drvn and one pce: 4th of 5 in gp* **8/1**[3]

0304 **7** *shd* **Dubawi Sound**[41] 4981 5-9-5 **98**.......................(t) JamieSpencer 4 97
(David Brown) *overall ldr far side: rdn along 2f out: hdd appr fnl f: grad wknd: 3rd of 9 in gp* **8/1**[3]

3012 **8** *1* **Corporal Maddox**[7] 6161 6-8-3 **89** oh6.......................(p) OisinMurphy(7) 3 85
(Ronald Harris) *chsd ldrs far side: rdn along 2f out: sn drvn and wknd over 1f out: 4th of 9 in gp* **14/1**

0020 **9** *3 1/4* **Secret Witness**[27] 5545 7-9-5 **98**.......................(b) GrahamLee 1 85
(Ronald Harris) *chsd ldrs far side: rdn along 2f out: sn btn: 5th of 9 in gp* **16/1**

6010 **10** *1* **Norse Blues**[22] 5681 5-9-0 **96**.......................LMcNiff(3) 6 81
(David Barron) *lw: chsd ldrs far side: rdn along 2f out: sn wknd: 6th of 9 in gp* **12/1**

5034 **11** *nse* **Spiritual Star (IRE)**[8] 6129 4-9-6 **99**.......................WilliamCarson 7 84
(Anthony Carson) *racd far side: hld up towards rr: swtchd lft and sme hdwy 2f out: sn rdn and btn: 7th of 9 in gp* **40/1**

3000 **12** *7* **Dr Red Eye**[14] 5943 5-8-10 **92**.......................(p) BillyCray(3) 5 57
(Scott Dixon) *t.k.h: chsd ldr far side: rdn along wl over 2f out: sn wknd: 8th of 9 in gp* **25/1**

2310 **13** *1/2* **Elusive Flame**[26] 5561 4-9-0 **93**.......................RyanMoore 14 57
(David Elsworth) *led stands' side gp: rdn along 2f out: hdd and wkng whn hmpd over 1f out: 5th of 5 in gp* **8/1**[3]

5-00 **14** *1 3/4* **Mac's Power (IRE)**[41] 4986 7-8-13 **92**.......................(t) JamesDoyle 8 51
(Willie Musson) *a bhd far side: 9th of 9 in gp* **22/1**

1m 20.73s (0.83) **Going Correction** +0.375s/f (Good) **14** Ran SP% **121.1**
Speed ratings (Par 109): **110,109,108,107,106 105,105,104,100,99 99,91,90,88**
CSF £58.44 CT £441.36 TOTE £7.60: £2.80, £2.10, £3.30; EX 50.00 Trifecta £632.90 Pool: £5529.64 - 6.55 winning units..
Owner Jim McGrath **Bred** Jeremy Green And Sons **Trained** Musley Bank, N Yorks

FOCUS
A good-class sprint handicap over an unusual, intermediate distance. Three of the last four winners came from a very low draw but that was not the case this time, as the winner raced in a group of five stands' side, three of whom made the frame. The winner is rated back in top form.

6353 FRANK WHITTLE PARTNERSHIP CLASSIFIED STKS 1m 2f 60y
5:00 (5:00) (Class 3) 3-Y-O+
£8,092 (£2,423; £1,211; £605; £302; £152) **Stalls** High

Form RPR
64-1 **1** **Zain Eagle**[18] 5839 3-8-11 85.......................JamesDoyle 8 100+
(Gerard Butler) *lw: hld up in rr: swtchd to outer and smooth hdwy 3f out: cl up 2f out: shkn up and qcknd to ld appr fnl f: sn clr: readily* **5/2**[2]

51-3 **2** *3 3/4* **Amralah (IRE)**[30] 5401 3-8-11 84.......................SilvestreDeSousa 5 92
(Mick Channon) *sn trcking ldr: hdwy and cl up 3f out: led wl over 1f out: sn rdn: hdd appr fnl f: drvn and kpt on but no ch w wnr* **9/4**[1]

0623 **3** *2 3/4* **Las Verglas Star (IRE)**[85] 3503 5-9-4 84.......................PaulHanagan 9 87
(Richard Fahey) *trckd ldrs on inner: hdwy 3f out: rdn 2f out and ev ch tl drvn and one pce ent fnl f* **8/1**

5116 **4** *2* **Morocco**[5] 6236 4-9-4 81.......................DanielTudhope 7 83
(David O'Meara) *hld up in rr: hdwy over 3f out: effrt to chse ldrs 2f out: sn rdn and no imp* **8/1**

4123 **5** *4* **Stellar Express (IRE)**[43] 4929 4-9-1 85.......................AndrewMullen 1 73
(Michael Appleby) *led: rdn along 3f out: drvn 2f out: sn hdd and grad wknd* **7/1**[3]

-502 **6** *1 1/4* **The Cayterers**[18] 5847 11-8-11 79.......................OisinMurphy(7) 4 74
(Ronald Harris) *chsd ldrs: rdn along 4f out: drvn and wknd 3f out* **25/1**

5224 **7** *nk* **Muharrer**[37] 5147 4-9-4 85.......................[1] GrahamLee 10 73
(Michael Dods) *trckd ldrs on outer: hdwy 1/2-way: rdn along 3f out: wknd over 2f out* **8/1**

020 **8** *2 1/2* **Lady Chaparral**[39] 5051 6-9-1 82.......................TomEaves 3 66
(Michael Dods) *trckd ldrs on inner: hdwy over 3f out: rdn along wl over 2f out: sn wknd* **16/1**

2m 11.42s (2.02) **Going Correction** +0.375s/f (Good)
WFA 3 from 4yo+ 7lb **8** Ran SP% **114.9**
Speed ratings (Par 107): **106,103,100,99,96 95,94,92**
toteswingers 1&2 £2.70, 1&3 £5.10, 2&3 £3.30 CSF £8.61 TOTE £3.70: £1.40, £1.40, £2.20; EX 10.30 Trifecta £50.70 Pool: £3980.03 - 58.87 winning units..
Owner Asaad Al Banwan **Bred** Biddestone Stud Ltd **Trained** Newmarket, Suffolk

FOCUS
There was a fair pace on in this classified event and, a race that often goes the way of the classic generation, the form looks solid enough. The winner was perhaps value for more.

T/Jkpt: Part won. £39148.30 to a £1 stake. 0.50 winning tickets. T/Plt: £41.30 to a £1 stake. Pool: £176378.12 - 3116.10 winning tickets T/Qpdt: £5.10 to a £1 stake. Pool: £12251.33 - 1749.42 winning tickets JR

5998 SANDOWN (R-H)

Friday, September 13

OFFICIAL GOING: Sprint course - good to soft (good in places); round course - good to soft (soft in places) changing to soft all over after race 1 (2:30) changing to soft (heavy in places) after race 4 (3:40)

Wind: virtually nil Weather: rain

6354 BRITISH STALLION STUDS E B F MAIDEN STKS 5f 6y

2:00 (2:01) (Class 5) 2-Y-O **£3,881** (£1,155; £577; £288) **Stalls** Low

Form RPR

5 **1** **Desert Ace (IRE)**[14] 5949 2-9-5 0 AdamKirby 3 77+
(Clive Cox) *mde all: restrained and set stdy gallop tl rdn and readily qcknd clr over 1f out: r.o wl: comf* **6/1**[3]

2 4 1/2 **Invoke (IRE)** 2-9-0 0 TomQueally 2 56+
(Michael Bell) *chsd ldng pair tl 1/2-way: outpcd and rn green over 1f out: kpt on to chse clr wnr fnl 100yds: no imp* **7/1**

6 **3** 1 1/2 **Birikyno**[17] 5866 2-9-5 0 RenatoSouza 4 55
(Mark Usher) *chsd ldr tl 1/2-way: rdn to chse wnr again but immediately outpcd over 1f out: lost 2nd fnl 100yds* **66/1**

4 7 **Dutch Interior** 2-9-5 0 GeorgeBaker 5 30
(Gary Moore) *wnt lft s: t.k.h: hld up in tch in midfield: hdwy to chse wnr 1/2-way tl over 1f out: sn btn and fdd fnl f* **9/4**[2]

5 2 1/4 **Touzr** 2-9-5 0 FrankieDettori 1 22
(Richard Hannon) *rn green: stdd s: in tch in last pair: switching lft but stl bhd horses 1/2-way: rdn 2f out: v green and sn totally outpcd: wl btn whn j. path 1f out: wknd* **5/4**[1]

06 **6** nse **Crystalized (IRE)**[20] 5740 2-9-0 0 PatDobbs 7 17
(Richard Hannon) *in tch in last pair: rdn ent fnl 2f: sn btn: bhd fnl f* **16/1**

1m 5.9s (4.30) **Going Correction** +0.75s/f (Yiel) **6** Ran SP% **109.4**

Speed ratings (Par 95): **95,87,85,74,70 70**

toteswingers 1&2 £5.80, 1&3 £11.30, 2&3 £3.80 CSF £42.67 TOTE £5.60: £3.50, £2.70; EX 30.20 Trifecta £142.00 Pool: £1430.74 -7.55 winning units..

Owner Arabian Knights **Bred** Kildaragh Stud **Trained** Lambourn, Berks

FOCUS

Sprint course at full width and Round course dolled out up to 5yds from 7f to winning post. With a couple of the well-touted newcomers failing to live up to expectations this maiden didn't take a great deal of winning, but it was still an impressive performance from the winner. Not easy to quantify the form.

6355 EPG INSURANCE SERVICES/BRITISH STALLION STUDS E B F MAIDEN STKS 1m 14y

2:30 (2:31) (Class 5) 2-Y-O **£3,881** (£1,155; £577; £288) **Stalls** Low

Form RPR

1 **Windshear** 2-9-5 0 SeanLevey 11 78+
(Richard Hannon) *dwlt: sn rcvrd and in tch in midfield: effrt and rdn 2f out: hdwy to chse ldr and edgd rt over 1f out: styd on wl to ld wl ins fnl f: gng away at fin* **8/1**

0 **2** 3/4 **Arantes**[21] 5698 2-9-5 0 MartinHarley 10 76
(Mick Channon) *t.k.h early: chsd ldng pair tl led and travelling strly ent fnl 2f: rdn over 1f out: kpt on tl hdd and no ex wl ins fnl f* **16/1**

3 2 1/4 **Scotland (GER)** 2-9-5 0 DavidProbert 2 71+
(Andrew Balding) *dwlt: hld up in tch towards rr: clsd to trck ldrs and gng wl ent fnl 2f: rdn and effrt to chse ldrs over 1f out: styd on same pce ins fnl f* **4/1**[3]

4 nk **Venezia (IRE)** 2-9-5 0 TomQueally 6 71+
(Lady Cecil) *in tch in midfield: dropped towards rr and rdn 4f out: hdwy past btn horses over 1f out: styd on ins fnl fand pressing for 3rd cl home: no threat to ldng pair* **7/4**[1]

4 **5** hd **Yaakooum (IRE)**[40] 5033 2-9-5 0 PatDobbs 3 70
(Richard Hannon) *in tch in midfield: outpcd and rdn over 2f out: rallied ent fnl f: styd on steadily ins fnl f: no threat to ldng pair* **11/4**[2]

6 **6** 7 **Gavlar**[44] 4896 2-9-5 0 ShaneKelly 8 55
(William Knight) *in tch in midfield: lost pl and pushed along 5f out: drvn and struggling over 2f out: bhd over 1f out: no ch but styd on past btn horses fnl f* **33/1**

00 **7** 3/4 **Douman (USA)**[14] 5957 2-9-5 0 (t) GeorgeBaker 9 53
(Ed Dunlop) *led tl hdd ent fnl 2f: 4th and btn over 1f out: fdd fnl f* **25/1**

8 1 3/4 **Lochalsh (IRE)** 2-9-5 0 AdamKirby 1 49
(William Knight) *s.i.s: rn green and rdn along in rr: toiling u.p and losing tch 2f out: n.d* **33/1**

0 **9** 5 **Luna Sunrise**[15] 5922 2-9-0 0 KierenFallon 7 33
(Alan Jarvis) *t.k.h: sn pressing ldr: rdn ent fnl 2f: sn btn: fdd over 1f out: bhd fnl f* **50/1**

10 nk **Arab Dawn** 2-9-5 0 SebSanders 4 38
(Hughie Morrison) *lost pl sn after s: in tch towards rr: hdwy 3f out: rdn ent fnl 2f: sn btn and fdd over 1f out: bhd fnl f* **14/1**

1m 50.94s (7.64) **Going Correction** +0.70s/f (Yiel) **10** Ran SP% **118.4**

Speed ratings (Par 95): **89,88,86,85,85 78,77,76,71,70**

toteswingers 1&2 £33.40, 1&3 £6.20, 2&3 £13.40 CSF £120.64 TOTE £6.20: £1.50, £6.00, £1.70; EX 122.50 Trifecta £1151.80 Part won. Pool: £1535.83 - 0.08 winning units..

Owner Michael Daniels **Bred** Cheveley Park Stud Ltd **Trained** East Everleigh, Wilts

FOCUS

Fair form in a maiden in which the front five pulled clear. The form fits with the race averages. As is often the case on rain-softened ground on the round course here, they came over towards the stands' side in the straight.

6356 SUNGARD H'CAP 1m 14y

3:05 (3:05) (Class 3) (0-90,90) 3-Y-O **£7,439** (£2,213; £1,106; £553) **Stalls** Low

Form RPR

-063 **1** **Tobacco Road (IRE)**[14] 5958 3-8-12 **81** PatDobbs 5 89
(Richard Hannon) *mde all: hrd pressed and rdn 2f out: battled on wl u.p ins fnl f: gamely: all out* **14/1**

-031 **2** nk **Russian Realm**[30] 5401 3-9-0 **83** GeorgeBaker 12 90
(Sir Michael Stoute) *hld up in tch in last trio: rdn and hdwy ent fnl 2f: chal u.p ins fnl f: styd on but no ex and hld towards fin* **9/2**[3]

-220 **3** 1 1/2 **Jodies Jem**[77] 3763 3-9-4 **87** JoeFanning 6 91
(William Jarvis) *hld up in tch in midfield: travelling wl but nt clr run ent fnl 2f: swtchd rt and sltly hmpd over 1f out: sn rdn and effrt: styd on wl ins fnl f: nt rch ldrs* **25/1**

2516 **4** 3/4 **George Cinq**[14] 5958 3-9-5 **88** [1] AdamKirby 7 90
(Michael Bell) *chsd ldrs: rdn to chal and edgd lft over 1f out: no ex and btn ins fnl f: lost 3rd towards fin* **10/1**

-114 **5** 2 3/4 **Breden (IRE)**[14] 5958 3-9-4 **87** WilliamBuick 8 83
(John Gosden) *chsd ldrs: rdn and effrt ent fnl 2f: swtchd rt and hdwy to press ldrs over 1f out tl no ex 1f out: wknd ins fnl f* **3/1**[1]

1021 **6** 4 1/2 **Bartack (IRE)**[37] 5134 3-8-13 **82** (b) KierenFallon 3 67
(Luca Cumani) *chsd ldr tl ent fnl 2f: struggling u.p whn short of room over 1f out: sn wknd* **14/1**

4344 **7** 2 **Ocean Applause**[27] 5540 3-8-10 **79** (tp) BrettDoyle 10 60
(John Ryan) *dwlt: a in rr but in tch: drvn 4f out: struggling over 2f out: no ch but sme hdwy past btn horses ent fnl f: n.d* **25/1**

1- **8** 1 3/4 **Annina (IRE)**[357] 6437 3-9-7 **90** FergusSweeney 2 67
(Henry Candy) *styd nr on inner rail in bk st: chsd ldrs: rdn ent fnl 2f: btn whn short of room over 1f out: sn wknd* **14/1**

22-1 **9** 4 1/2 **Ostaad (IRE)**[22] 5678 3-9-3 **86** (v) DaneO'Neill 11 52
(Saeed bin Suroor) *in tch in midfield: rdn and effrt 2f out: no hdwy and sn btn: wknd over 1f out: fdd and eased ins fnl f* **4/1**[2]

4114 **10** 2 **Monsieur Rieussec**[30] 5401 3-8-13 **82** ShaneKelly 15 44
(Jonathan Portman) *hld up in tch in rr: shkn up and no rspnse ent fnl 2f: rdn edgd lft and wknd over 1f out: bhd and eased ins fnl f* **12/1**

4154 **11** 9 **Yourartisonfire**[27] 5510 3-9-3 **86** ChrisCatlin 9 27
(K R Burke) *t.k.h: hld up in tch towards rr: rdn and short-lived 2f out: sn wknd: wl bhd and heavily eased ins fnl f* **14/1**

2-00 **12** 3 **Janoub Nibras (IRE)**[14] 5958 3-9-5 **88** SeanLevey 13 22
(Richard Hannon) *chsd ldrs tl rdn and lost pl 3f out: wl bhd and heavily eased ins fnl f: t.o* **20/1**

1m 47.86s (4.56) **Going Correction** +0.70s/f (Yiel) **12** Ran SP% **119.1**

Speed ratings (Par 105): **105,104,103,102,99 95,93,91,86,84 75,72**

toteswingers 1&2 £23.20, 1&3 £25.20, 2&3 £28.90 CSF £74.44 CT £1596.95 TOTE £23.20: £5.20, £1.50, £8.70; EX 135.20 Trifecta £1102.50 Part won. Pool: £1470.07 - 0.23 winning units..

Owner Noodles Racing **Bred** Minch Bloodstock **Trained** East Everleigh, Wilts

FOCUS

A pretty useful 3yo handicap. The early gallop didn't look particularly strong and the runners came stands' side in the straight. The principals have the scope to do a bit better at least.

6357 PIPER HEIDSIECK CHAMPAGNE CLAIMING STKS 1m 2f 7y

3:40 (3:41) (Class 4) 3-Y-O **£6,469** (£1,925; £962; £481) **Stalls** Low

Form RPR

6311 **1** **Calm Attitude (IRE)**[38] 5092 3-8-6 66 ChrisCatlin 6 67
(Rae Guest) *stdd s: hld up in tch in rr: swtchd rt and rdn over 2f out: swtchd lft and chsd ldrs 2f out: racing against stands' rail and drvn over 1f out: str chal ins fnl f: led fnl 75yds: drvn out* **11/4**[3]

2016 **2** 1/2 **Harbinger Lass**[21] 5694 3-8-4 62 JoeFanning 5 64
(Mick Channon) *led: gng best over 2f out: rdn wl over 1f out: hrd pressed ins fnl f: hdd and one pce fnl 75yds* **7/1**

0230 **3** 3 **Bold And Free**[38] 5099 3-8-9 64 (p) DaneO'Neill 4 64
(David Elsworth) *chsd ldr: drvn over 2f out: 3rd and no ex u.p over 1f out: plugged on same pce fnl f* **7/1**

132 **4** 14 **Mandy's Boy (IRE)**[14] 5975 3-8-11 71 (p) TomQueally 3 41
(Ian Williams) *stdd s: hld up in last pair: rdn and effrt over 2f out: sn btn: wl bhd over 1f out* **9/4**[1]

5 3/4 **Tabaayun (IRE)**[78] 3-9-1 82 KierenFallon 7 43
(David O'Meara) *chsd ldng piar: clsd and wnt 2nd over 5f out tl over 3f out: sn struggling: bhd 2f out: sn lost tch* **5/2**[2]

2m 18.02s (7.52) **Going Correction** +0.825s/f (Soft) **5** Ran SP% **111.0**

Speed ratings (Par 103): **102,101,99,88,87**

CSF £20.58 TOTE £3.50: £1.30, £3.00; EX 20.50 Trifecta £73.40 Pool: £1697.16 - 17.32 winning units..

Owner The Calm Again Partnership **Bred** R N Auld **Trained** Newmarket, Suffolk

FOCUS

A few failed to live up to expectations in this very ordinary claimer. The winner is only rated to form.

6358 INKERMAN LONDON H'CAP 1m 2f 7y

4:15 (4:16) (Class 4) (0-80,79) 3-Y-O+ **£5,175** (£1,540; £769; £384) **Stalls** Low

Form RPR

215- **1** **Headline News (IRE)**[356] 6492 4-9-8 **75** ChrisCatlin 9 93+
(Rae Guest) *s.i.s: hld up in rr: swtchd rt and gd hdwy 2f out: chal ent fnl f: sn led and drew clr fnl f: readily* **20/1**

2110 **2** 4 1/2 **Topamichi**[14] 5944 3-9-2 **76** TomQueally 1 85
(Mark H Tompkins) *broke wl: stdd sn after s and hld up in tch in midfield: smooth hdwy to ld over 2f out: rdn and shifting lft towards stands' rail over 1f out: hdd jst ins fnl f: sn brushed aside but kpt on for clr 2nd* **6/1**[1]

3660 **3** 3 1/4 **Sheila's Buddy**[32] 5348 4-9-6 **73** LiamKeniry 11 76
(J S Moore) *hld up in midfield: clsd and gng wl jst over 2f out: chsd ldr briefly over 1f out: sn rdn and unable qck: wknd u.p fnl f* **8/1**[3]

5001 **4** 3 1/4 **Guilded Spirit**[21] 5694 3-8-9 **72** MichaelJMMurphy(3) 3 69
(Stuart Kittow) *dwlt: sn rcvrd and in tch in midfield: effrt u.p to chse ldr briefly 2f out: sn outpcd wl btn 1f out: plugged on* **7/1**[2]

1336 **5** 1/2 **Choral Festival**[29] 5445 7-9-8 **75** AdamKirby 5 71
(John Bridger) *hld up towards rr: swtchd rt and effrt 2f out: no threat to ldrs but battling for modest 4th fnl f: plugged on* **16/1**

4126 **6** 1/2 **Mazaaher**[13] 6003 3-9-2 **76** DaneO'Neill 12 71
(J W Hills) *in tch in midfield: rdn and effrt over 2f out: outpcd and btn wl over 1f out: 6th and wl hld whn swtchd rt 1f out* **9/1**

346 **7** 1 3/4 **Munhamer (IRE)**[37] 5133 3-8-10 **70** WilliamBuick 4 61
(John Gosden) *chsd ldr for 2f: styd chsng ldrs tl struggling u.p over 2f out: wknd over 1f out* **6/1**[1]

3330 **8** 1 **Diamond Penny (IRE)**[7] 6173 5-9-6 **73** (b) SteveDrowne 2 63
(Seamus Durack) *sn led: rdn and hdd over 2f out: btn 2f out: sn wknd* **14/1**

5066 **9** 5 **Ronaldinho (IRE)**[14] 5953 3-9-0 **74** (p) PatDobbs 7 54
(Richard Hannon) *chsd ldrs tl lost pl qckly u.p over 2f out: bhd over 1f out* **10/1**

3-24 **10** nk **Heezararity**[10] 6080 5-8-11 **69** RyanTate(5) 10 48
(Jonathan Geake) *in tch in midfield: rdn and unable qck over 2f out: sn btn: wknd over 1f out* **16/1**

31 **11** 6 **He's A Striker (IRE)**[123] 2322 3-8-12 **75** RyanClark(3) 8 43
(Michael Blake) *hld up towards rr: hdwy into midfield 1/2-way: lost pl 3f out: bhd over 1f out* **8/1**[3]

2505 **12** 6 **Kelpie Blitz (IRE)**[18] 5847 4-9-8 **75** (t) GeorgeBaker 13 32
(Seamus Durack) *broke wl: stdd and chsd ldrs tl wnt 2nd 8f out: lost 2nd and losing pl whn short of room over 2f out: sn wknd: wl bhd fnl f: t.o* **8/1**[3]

4000 **13** *31* **Right Step**[43] 4923 6-9-12 **79**......(v) KierenFallon 6
(Alan Jarvis) *a towards rr: rdn and struggling 3f out: lost tch 2f out: t.o and eased ins fnl f* 14/1

2m 17.32s (6.82) **Going Correction** +0.825s/f (Soft)
WFA 3 from 4yo+ 7lb **13** Ran SP% **123.4**
Speed ratings (Par 105): **105,101,98,96,95 95,94,93,89,88 84,79,54**
toteswingers 1&2 £19.00, 1&3 £30.30, 2&3 £7.60 CSF £140.16 CT £1070.16 TOTE £25.20: £7.20, £2.20, £3.40; EX 210.80 Trifecta £792.80 Part won. Pool: £1057.12 - 0.71 winning units..

Owner Chestnuts **Bred** Airlie Stud **Trained** Newmarket, Suffolk

FOCUS
It started to rain again before the start of this race and they finished well strung out, quite a few clearly failing to cope with the ground. The winner impressed and the form looks at least this good.

6359 BDO PROJECT FINANCE H'CAP (DIV I) 1m 14y
4:50 (4:50) (Class 4) (0-80,80) 3-Y-O+ **£5,175** (£1,540; £769; £384) **Stalls** Low

Form RPR

1334 **1** **Naaz (IRE)**[18] 5835 3-9-1 **76** ow1......(b) AdamKirby 3 83
(Ed Dunlop) *hld up in tch in last pair: hdwy u.p over 1f out: led ins fnl f: styd on wl: drvn out* 7/1

4313 **2** *3/4* **Hector's Chance**[19] 5793 4-8-5 **66**...... RyanTate(5) 10 72
(Heather Main) *w ldr: rdn over 2f out: led and wandered lft over 1f out: hdd ins fnl f: styd on same pce fnl 100yds* 6/1[3]

0032 **3** *1/2* **Starwatch**[17] 5855 6-9-5 **78**...... MichaelJMMurphy(3) 6 83
(John Bridger) *t.k.h: hld up wl in tch in midfield: rdn and lost pl over 3f out: last and looked wl hld over 1f out: rallied and edging rt ins fnl f: styd on strly fnl 100yds* 8/1

1-35 **4** *2 1/4* **Anya**[75] 3864 4-9-7 **77**...... DaneO'Neill 2 77
(Ed Walker) *hld up in tch in last pair: rdn and hdwy to chse ldrs wl over 1f out: outpcd and btn jst ins fnl f: kpt on again towards fin* 5/1[2]

0602 **5** *nse* **Canadian Run (IRE)**[57] 4442 3-9-2 **77**...... SeanLevey 5 76
(Robert Mills) *led: rdn over 2f out: hdd and drvn over 1f out: no ex 1f out: wknd fnl 75yds* 16/1

21 **6** *1/2* **Noble Protector**[59] 4381 3-9-4 **79**...... TomQueally 1 77
(Stuart Kittow) *wl in tch in midfield: lost pl and rdn over 3f out: rallied to chse ldrs ent fnl 2f: no ex u.p 1f out: wknd ins fnl f* 5/2[1]

1210 **7** *1 1/2* **Breakheart (IRE)**[27] 5521 6-8-12 **75**......(v) JackGarritty(7) 8 70
(Andrew Balding) *dwlt: rcvrd to chse ldrs after 2f: rdn and unable qck over 2f out: wknd over 1f out* 10/1

44-2 **8** *3/4* **Dixie's Dream (IRE)**[8] 6126 4-9-3 **80**...... KevinStott(7) 4 74
(William Jarvis) *wl in tch in midfield: rdn and effrt ent fnl 2f: no ex and btn over 1f out: wknd fnl f* 5/1[2]

1m 51.04s (7.74) **Going Correction** +0.825s/f (Soft)
WFA 3 from 4yo+ 5lb **8** Ran SP% **114.8**
Speed ratings (Par 105): **94,93,92,90,90 89,88,87**
toteswingers 1&2 £7.10, 1&3 £6.70, 2&3 £7.20 CSF £48.43 CT £345.90 TOTE £7.40: £1.60, £1.60, £3.00; EX 50.40 Trifecta £279.70 Pool: £2427.76 - 6.50 winning units..

Owner Robert Ng **Bred** T J Pabst And Newtown Stud **Trained** Newmarket, Suffolk

FOCUS
A fair handicap. Straightforward form, with the placed horses helping the level.

6360 BDO PROJECT FINANCE H'CAP (DIV II) 1m 14y
5:20 (5:21) (Class 4) (0-80,80) 3-Y-O+ **£5,175** (£1,540; £769; £384) **Stalls** Low

Form RPR

4453 **1** **First Post (IRE)**[20] 5759 6-9-1 **71**...... DaneO'Neill 1 81+
(Derek Haydn Jones) *broke wl: hld up in tch in midfield: hdwy to chse ldrs 2f: rdn to ld and veered lft ent fnl f: clr and idling ins fnl f: rdn out* 5/1[2]

4645 **2** *2 1/4* **Rocky Reef**[18] 5815 4-9-3 **73**......(b[1]) PatDobbs 10 78
(Philip Hide) *t.k.h: chsd ldrs: wnt 2nd 6f out tl over 2f out: styd chsng ldrs and drvn over 1f out: chsd clr wnr fnl 100yds: kpt on* 7/1

6303 **3** *shd* **Barwick**[14] 5947 5-9-6 **76**...... TomQueally 7 81
(Mark H Tompkins) *hld up off the pce in last quartet: rdn and effrt over 2f out: hdwy u.p over 1f out: swtchd rt ent fnl f: battling for 2nd and kpt on fnl 100yds* 5/1[2]

6212 **4** *3* **Ishikawa (IRE)**[36] 5191 5-8-12 **75**...... RobJFitzpatrick(7) 3 73
(K R Burke) *chsd ldrs tl hdwy to ld over 2f out: drvn and hdd over 1f out: unable qck and sltly hmpd ent fnl f: lost 2nd and wknd fnl 100yds* 9/2[1]

3011 **5** *4* **Siouxperhero (IRE)**[13] 5978 4-9-0 **70**......(p) SteveDrowne 8 59
(William Muir) *chsd ldr for 2f: styd chsng ldrs: rdn over 2f out: no ex and btn over 1f out: wknd fnl f* 16/1

3215 **6** *1 1/4* **Yojimbo (IRE)**[13] 5978 5-9-7 **80**......(v) CharlesBishop(3) 4 67
(Mick Channon) *led: rdn and hdd over 2f out: drvn and btn over 1f out: sn wknd* 8/1

4160 **7** *1* **Great Expectations**[79] 3693 5-9-4 **74**...... DavidProbert 9 58
(J R Jenkins) *in tch in midfield: rdn and effrt over 2f out: no imp u.p over 1f out: sn wknd* 6/1[3]

1444 **8** *2* **Echo Brava**[78] 3735 3-8-7 **68**...... JimmyQuinn 5 47
(Luke Dace) *hld up off the pce in last pair: rdn and effrt over 2f out: no imp: n.d* 16/1

2433 **9** *1 1/2* **Kickingthelilly**[18] 5825 4-9-8 **78**...... ChrisCatlin 6 55
(Rae Guest) *nvr travelling and sn niggled along in last quartet: rdn 3f out: wknd 2f out* 8/1

000 **10** *4 1/2* **Dellbuoy**[45] 4859 4-9-2 **72**...... FergusSweeney 2 39
(Pat Phelan) *s.i.s: a in rr: lost tch 2f out* 14/1

1m 49.25s (5.95) **Going Correction** +0.825s/f (Soft)
WFA 3 from 4yo+ 5lb **10** Ran SP% **119.0**
Speed ratings (Par 105): **103,100,100,97,93 92,91,89,87,83**
toteswingers 1&2 £7.10, 1&3 £5.10, 2&3 £7.80 CSF £40.84 CT £190.46 TOTE £5.10: £1.60, £3.40, £2.10; EX 26.20 Trifecta £182.00 Pool: £2251.44 - 9.27 winning units..

Owner Llewelyn, Runeckles **Bred** D Llewelyn & J Runeckles **Trained** Efail Isaf, Rhondda C Taff

FOCUS
The second division of the 0-80 handicap was taken in clear-cut fashion by First Post, who can win again if finding similar conditions.

T/Plt: £2,360.80 to a £1 stake. Pool: £66420.00 - 20.53 winning tickets T/Qpdt: £138.70 to a £1 stake. Pool: £5933.29 - 31.65 winning tickets SP

6339 WOLVERHAMPTON (A.W) (L-H)
Friday, September 13

OFFICIAL GOING: Standard to slow
Wind: Light half-against Weather: Raining

6361 £32 BONUS AT 32RED.COM APPRENTICE H'CAP 1m 4f 50y(P)
5:30 (5:30) (Class 6) (0-55,55) 3-Y-O **£1,940** (£577; £288; £144) **Stalls** Low

Form RPR

0446 **1** **Precision Strike**[13] 5990 3-9-2 **55**......(v) ConnorBeasley(3) 8 64
(Richard Guest) *trckd ldrs: racd keenly: led 3f out: rdn clr fr over 1f out: styd on* 10/1

4005 **2** *2 1/4* **Our Golden Girl**[8] 6137 3-9-3 **53**......(b) RobertTart 5 58
(Shaun Lycett) *hld up: pushed along over 4f out: hdwy over 2f out: rdn to go 2nd wl ins fnl f: nt rch wnr* 16/1

V120 **3** *4* **Helamis**[23] 5633 3-9-1 **54**......(p) TobyAtkinson(3) 11 53
(Alison Hutchinson) *trckd ldrs: led 10f out: rdn and hdd 3f out: styd on same pce fr over 1f out* 20/1

000 **4** *1 1/4* **Switch On**[101] 2952 3-8-12 **48**......(bt[1]) AshleyMorgan 6 45
(Chris Wall) *hld up: hdwy over 4f out: rdn over 1f out: no ex fnl f* 10/1

0045 **5** *1* **Penang Power**[23] 5650 3-8-7 **48**...... LouisSteward(5) 10 43
(Michael Bell) *sn prom: rdn over 2f out: edgd lft and no ex fnl f* 14/1

5040 **6** *1/2* **Bullseye Babe**[15] 5935 3-8-8 **51**......(e) CharlotteJenner(7) 2 45+
(Mark Usher) *hld up: pushed along over 1f out: edgd lft and r.o ins fnl f: nvr nrr* 25/1

0442 **7** *5* **Lucky Black Star (IRE)**[8] 6137 3-9-5 **55**...... ThomasBrown 9 41
(George Baker) *sn led: hdd 10f out: chsd ldrs: rdn over 2f out: wknd over 1f out* 2/1[1]

3404 **8** *1 3/4* **Halfwaytocootehill (IRE)**[45] 4849 3-8-9 **50**......(t) JacobButterfield(5) 1 33
(Ollie Pears) *hld up: rdn over 3f out: wknd over 2f out* 5/1[2]

3633 **9** *2* **Tornado Battle**[4] 6257 3-9-1 **51**......(p) JasonHart 3 31
(Phil McEntee) *prom: racd keenly: rdn over 3f out: wknd over 1f out* 6/1[3]

06-0 **10** *3/4* **Poste Restante**[139] 1828 3-8-12 **55**...... LewisWalsh(7) 4 34
(David Simcock) *s.i.s: a in rr: bhd fnl 6f* 12/1

0050 **11** *7* **Annie Besant**[7] 6154 3-8-8 **49**...... TimClark(5) 7 17
(Michael Mullineaux) *hld up: rdn over 3f out: a in rr* 33/1

4454 **12** *66* **Betty Boo (IRE)**[13] 5990 3-8-5 **48** oh1 ow2...... AlexHopkinson(7) 12
(Shaun Harris) *trckd ldr: racd wd early: pushed along over 4f out: sn wknd* 50/1

2m 46.14s (5.04) **Going Correction** +0.325s/f (Slow) **12** Ran SP% **116.2**
Speed ratings (Par 99): **96,94,91,91,90 90,86,85,84,83 79,35**
CSF £148.36 CT £3106.20 TOTE £8.90: £3.00, £4.80, £4.80; EX 217.20 Trifecta £1522.60 Pool: £2355.88 - 1.16 winning units..

Owner Resdev **Bred** Mickley Stud **Trained** Wetherby, W Yorks

FOCUS
A moderate handicap run at an ordinary gallop and, as at the course the previous evening, the time was slow. The winner came down the centre in the straight. Straightforward form.

6362 32RED H'CAP 5f 216y(P)
6:00 (6:01) (Class 5) (0-70,70) 3-Y-O **£2,911** (£866; £432; £216) **Stalls** Low

Form RPR

3222 **1** **Brynford**[16] 5890 3-8-7 **59**...... RobertTart(3) 4 67
(Chris Dwyer) *broke wl: sn stdd and lost pl: hdwy over 1f out: rdn and r.o to ld wl ins fnl f* 7/2[1]

5020 **2** *nk* **King Bertie (IRE)**[30] 5398 3-9-3 **69**...... RaulDaSilva(3) 10 76+
(Michael Wigham) *hdwy over 4f out: led over 2f out: rdn: edgd rt and hdd wl ins fnl f* 8/1

0400 **3** *3 1/4* **Poetic Belle**[10] 6074 3-8-2 **56** oh4......(t) ShirleyTeasdale(5) 7 53
(Shaun Harris) *chsd ldrs: rdn over 2f out: styd on* 66/1

5044 **4** *1 3/4* **Indian Affair**[18] 5820 3-9-7 **70**...... RichardKingscote 13 61
(Milton Bradley) *prom: outpcd over 2f out: rallied over 1f out: styd on* 10/1

50-3 **5** *1 3/4* **My Boy Bill**[50] 4670 3-9-3 **66**...... JamesSullivan 5 52
(Michael Easterby) *chsd ldrs: sn pushed along: rdn 1/2-way: styd on same pce fr over 1f out* 8/1

12-0 **6** *1 3/4* **Meet Me Halfway**[115] 2544 3-9-4 **70**...... AshleyMorgan(3) 1 50
(Chris Wall) *prom: lost pl over 4f out: styd on ins fnl f* 16/1

31-4 **7** *1/2* **Cross My Heart**[129] 2135 3-9-5 **68**...... AndreaAtzeni 12 47
(William Haggas) *hdwy to join ldr 5f out: ev ch over 2f out: sn rdn: wknd ins fnl f* 4/1[2]

5000 **8** *2* **Overrider**[15] 5931 3-9-0 **63**......(t) JamieMackay 3 35
(Alastair Lidderdale) *s.s: outpcd: nvr nrr* 33/1

2564 **9** *nk* **Hit The Lights (IRE)**[13] 5985 3-9-1 **69**...... JacobButterfield(5) 2 40
(Ollie Pears) *mid-div: rdn over 2f out: wknd ins fnl f* 10/1

0155 **10** *1* **Alhaarth Beauty (IRE)**[33] 5300 3-9-2 **68**...... ThomasBrown(3) 6 36
(Ismail Mohammed) *sn led: rdn and hdd over 2f out: wknd fnl f* 6/1[3]

4400 **11** *5* **Star Of Rohm**[42] 4962 3-9-4 **67**...... LukeMorris 8 19
(Michael Bell) *mid-div: rdn over 2f out: sn wknd* 8/1

0001 **12** *2* **Scarlet Strand**[13] 5981 3-8-7 **56** oh4...... PaulQuinn 9 2
(Andrew Hollinshead) *sn pushed along in rr: wknd over 2f out* 33/1

1m 16.63s (1.63) **Going Correction** +0.325s/f (Slow) **12** Ran SP% **121.3**
Speed ratings (Par 101): **102,101,97,94,92 90,89,86,86,85 78,75**
toteswingers 1&2 £5.70, 1&3 £47.00, 2&3 £94.10 CSF £32.36 CT £1616.63 TOTE £4.00: £1.60, £3.20, £18.20; EX 40.90 Trifecta £1043.10 Pool: £2033.82 - 1.46 winning units..

Owner R S G Jones **Bred** Old Suffolk Stud **Trained** Newmarket, Suffolk

FOCUS
A modest handicap but one run at a strong gallop before the pace collapsed. The winner came down the centre in the straight and the first two pulled clear.

6363 32RED.COM H'CAP 1m 5f 194y(P)
6:30 (6:30) (Class 5) (0-70,70) 3-Y-O **£2,911** (£866; £432; £216) **Stalls** Low

Form RPR

1241 **1** **See And Be Seen**[13] 5979 3-8-7 **56**......(p) RenatoSouza 4 60
(Sylvester Kirk) *chsd ldrs: rdn to ld 1f out: styd on* 14/1

50-4 **2** *1 1/2* **Luckster**[23] 5630 3-8-2 **51** oh6...... CathyGannon 7 53
(David Evans) *trckd ldr: rdn over 3f out: styd on u.p* 33/1

1344 **3** *1/2* **Sunblazer (IRE)**[16] 5888 3-9-7 **70**...... MartinDwyer 3 71
(William Muir) *sn led at stdy pce: qcknd over 3f out: rdn and hdd 1f out: styd on same pce ins fnl f* 4/1[2]

4442 **4** *1 1/2* **Mistral Wind (IRE)**[10] 6081 3-8-12 **61**...... AndreaAtzeni 5 60
(Ed Dunlop) *hld up: racd keenly: hdwy over 2f out: rdn over 1f out: styd on same pce fnl f* 1/1[1]

6300 **5** *6* **Aiyana**[20] 5762 3-9-3 **66**...... RichardKingscote 1 57
(Hughie Morrison) *chsd ldrs: rdn over 2f out: wknd over 1f out* 7/1[3]

The Form Book Flat, Raceform Ltd, Compton, RG20 6NL.

0-00 **6** *14* **Sings Poet**[35] 5233 3-7-11 **51** oh6 NoelGarbutt(5) 2 22
(Peter Hiatt) *s.i.s: sn prom: rdn over 4f out: wknd over 3f out* **20/1**
5420 **7** *4 1/2* **Uncle Bernie (IRE)**[13] 5997 3-8-11 **60** (p) ShaneKelly 6 25
(Andrew Hollinshead) *hld up: plld hrd: hdwy over 4f out: rdn and wknd over 2f out* **7/1**[3]
0551 **8** *4 1/2* **Hattie Jacques**[28] 5500 3-9-0 **63** SamHitchcott 8 22
(Mick Channon) *dwlt: hld up: racd keenly: pushed along over 4f out: wknd over 3f out* **12/1**

3m 14.71s (8.71) **Going Correction** +0.325s/f (Slow) **8** Ran SP% **117.1**
Speed ratings (Par 101): **88,87,86,86,82 74,72,69**
toteswingers 1&2 £49.30, 1&3 £4.70, 2&3 £14.70 CSF £359.89 CT £2186.30 TOTE £19.40: £5.00, £4.90, £1.10; EX 348.80 Trifecta £848.50 Pool: £1891.68 - 1.67 winning units..
Owner Timothy Pearson **Bred** Exors Of The Late T E Pocock **Trained** Upper Lambourn, Berks

FOCUS
A weak handicap. A steady gallop only increased leaving the back straight and this bare form doesn't look reliable, with the second the best guide. The winner raced centre-to-far side in the straight.

6364 32REDPOKER.COM CLAIMING STKS 5f 20y(P)
7:00 (7:00) (Class 6) 2-Y-O **£1,940** (£577; £288; £144) **Stalls** Low

Form RPR
4613 **1** **Limegrove**[14] 5963 2-7-12 65 NoelGarbutt(5) 3 57+
(David Evans) *sn pushed along in rr: hdwy: nt clr run and swtchd rt over 1f out: rdn to ld wl ins fnl f: r.o wl* **3/1**[3]
0450 **2** *1 1/4* **Little Big Man**[17] 5850 2-8-5 40 (b[1]) RenatoSouza 6 55
(Sylvester Kirk) *awkward leaving stalls: hdwy 1/2-way: rdn to ld ins fnl f: sn edgd lft: hdd and unable qck* **33/1**
4251 **3** *2 1/4* **Kano's Ghirl (IRE)**[10] 6082 2-8-5 66 LukeMorris 5 46
(Keith Dalgleish) *prom: rdn over 1f out: styd on* **11/4**[2]
4305 **4** *1* **Boston Alex (IRE)**[9] 6104 2-8-3 62 (p) HarryBentley 7 41
(Conor Dore) *chsd ldrs: rdn and ev ch over 1f out: no ex ins fnl f* **16/1**
4050 **5** *3/4* **Faye Belle**[24] 5610 2-7-13 45 (v) RaulDaSilva(3) 8 37
(Derek Shaw) *prom: lost pl over 3f out: styd on ins fnl f* **50/1**
604 **6** *1* **Sing Out Sister**[25] 5590 2-7-12 45 SimonPearce(3) 9 33
(Mick Channon) *trckd ldrs: racd keenly: rdn and ev ch 2f out: n.m.r over 1f out: wknd ins fnl f* **16/1**
5423 **7** *hd* **Outback Lover (IRE)**[25] 5591 2-8-3 67 (b) AndreaAtzeni 1 34
(J S Moore) *led: hdd over 3f out: pushed along 1/2-way: eased wl over 1f out: n.d after* **2/1**[1]
0035 **8** *1* **Marilyn Marquessa**[25] 5591 2-8-0 57 (b) CathyGannon 2 27
(Jo Hughes) *trckd ldr: plld hrd: led over 3f out: rdn over 1f out: hdd & wknd ins fnl f* **8/1**

1m 4.95s (2.65) **Going Correction** +0.325s/f (Slow) **8** Ran SP% **112.8**
Speed ratings (Par 93): **91,89,85,83,82 81,80,79**
toteswingers 1&2 £16.70, 1&3 £2.20, 2&3 £9.80 CSF £85.06 TOTE £4.50: £1.90, £5.40, £1.10; EX 57.10 Trifecta £432.10 Pool: £1617.32 - 2.80 winning units..
Owner J E Abbey **Bred** Mark Windsor **Trained** Pandy, Monmouths

FOCUS
Little to enthuse about in a modest claimer. The pace was sound and the winner came down the centre. She didn't even need to match her recent level.

6365 32REDBET.COM MEDIAN AUCTION MAIDEN STKS 1m 141y(P)
7:30 (7:30) (Class 6) 2-Y-O **£1,940** (£577; £288; £144) **Stalls** Low

Form RPR
52 **1** **Toast Of New York (USA)**[15] 5922 2-9-5 0 JamieSpencer 6 83+
(Jamie Osborne) *mde all: qcknd clr fnl 2f: easily* **1/3**[1]
6 **2** *12* **Byron Gala**[30] 5405 2-9-5 0 AndreaAtzeni 4 54
(Marco Botti) *hld up: hdwy over 3f out: outpcd fnl 2f: wnt 2nd wl ins fnl f* **25/1**
0 **3** *1* **Magnus Romeo**[28] 5488 2-9-5 0 (t) MartinHarley 9 52
(Marco Botti) *chsd wnr: rdn over 2f out: sn outpcd: lost 2nd wl ins fnl f* **6/1**[2]
0 **4** *1 3/4* **Aramadyh**[14] 5968 2-9-0 0 (p) LukeMorris 7 43
(James Tate) *chsd ldrs: drvn along over 5f out: styd on same pce fnl 2f* **50/1**
5 *3 3/4* **Ice Falcon (IRE)** 2-9-0 0 RyanMoore 2 35
(James Tate) *chsd ldrs: shkn up over 2f out: wknd over 1f out* **8/1**[3]
00 **6** *1 1/4* **Sexy Secret**[28] 5488 2-9-5 0 (b[1]) StevieDonohoe 1 38
(Noel Quinlan) *s.i.s: hdwy on outer over 2f out: sn wknd* **100/1**
0 **7** *6* **Enfys Hud**[13] 5995 2-8-11 0 DeclanBates(3) 3 20
(David Evans) *hld up: rdn over 3f out: sn wknd* **33/1**
00 **8** *19* **Laughing Musketeer (IRE)**[74] 3905 2-9-5 0 (t) PJMcDonald 5
(Paul Cole) *hld up: hdwy over 5f out: hung lft fr over 3f out: wknd over 2f out* **50/1**

1m 52.75s (2.25) **Going Correction** +0.325s/f (Slow) **8** Ran SP% **112.1**
Speed ratings (Par 93): **103,92,91,89,86 85,80,63**
toteswingers 1&2 £4.40, 1&3 £1.70, 2&3 £2.90 CSF £15.93 TOTE £1.30: £1.02, £3.50, £1.10; EX 8.70 Trifecta £42.10 Pool: £2146.88 - 38.21 winning units..
Owner Michael Buckley **Bred** Ashleigh Stud, F Ramos And J Ramos **Trained** Upper Lambourn, Berks

FOCUS
A most uncompetitive maiden but fair form from the winner, who won with a good deal in hand from some moderate opposition. The gallop was only fair and the winner came down the centre.

6366 32RED CASINO MAIDEN STKS 1m 141y(P)
8:00 (8:00) (Class 5) 3-Y-O+ **£2,587** (£770; £384; £192) **Stalls** Low

Form RPR
33 **1** **Duchess Of Seville**[22] 5678 3-9-0 0 MartinHarley 1 84+
(Marco Botti) *trckd ldr tl led over 2f out: sn pushed clr: r.o strly* **4/1**
0-3 **2** *8* **Muthafar (IRE)**[55] 4535 3-9-5 0 AndreaAtzeni 3 72
(William Haggas) *a.p: chsd wnr over 2f out: rdn over 1f out: styd on same pce* **7/2**[3]
3 *1 1/2* **Hawker** 3-9-5 0 JamieSpencer 8 69+
(Charlie Appleby) *s.i.s: hld up: shkn up over 1f out: r.o ins fnl f: wnt 3rd post: nrst fin* **10/1**
6- **4** *hd* **Takaathur (USA)**[324] 7324 3-9-5 0 [1] FrederikTylicki 2 68
(Saeed bin Suroor) *prom: racd keenly: rdn over 2f out: styd on same pce* **11/4**[1]
03 **5** *3 3/4* **Stomachion (IRE)**[91] 3278 3-9-5 0 RyanMoore 4 61
(Sir Michael Stoute) *hld up: hdwy 1/2-way: pushed along over 2f out: nt trble ldrs* **3/1**[2]
6 *1 3/4* **Wandsworth (IRE)** 3-9-2 0 RossAtkinson(3) 7 57
(Roger Varian) *mid-div: rdn over 2f out: nt trble ldrs* **16/1**
7 *3 1/2* **Zeteah** 3-9-0 0 TedDurcan 6 45
(David Lanigan) *s.i.s: nvr on terms* **25/1**
44 **8** *nk* **Another Name (IRE)**[9] 6113 3-9-5 0 LukeMorris 10 49
(Paul Cole) *hld up: plld hrd: hdwy over 5f out: rdn over 2f out: wknd over 1f out* **66/1**
20 **9** *9* **Willow Island (IRE)**[6] 6217 4-9-9 0 ow1 RichardEvans(3) 11 34
(David Evans) *hld up: pushed along over 3f out: wknd over 2f out* **66/1**
0 **10** *13* **Polvere D'Oro**[39] 5069 3-9-0 0 SladeO'Hara(5) 9 3
(Michael Mullineaux) *sn led: rdn and hdd over 2f out: sn wknd* **100/1**

1m 52.74s (2.24) **Going Correction** +0.325s/f (Slow)
WFA 3 from 4yo 6lb **10** Ran SP% **116.7**
Speed ratings (Par 103): **103,95,94,94,91 89,86,86,78,66**
toteswingers 1&2 £3.60, 1&3 £18.90, 2&3 £9.20 CSF £18.20 TOTE £4.60: £1.60, £1.30, £2.90; EX 18.90 Trifecta £241.80 Pool: £1333.26 - 4.13 winning units..
Owner Newsells Park Stud **Bred** Newsells Park Stud **Trained** Newmarket, Suffolk

FOCUS
Several big yards represented in a useful maiden. The gallop was no more than fair and the easy winner came down the centre, showing improved form.

6367 32REDBINGO.COM H'CAP (DIV I) 7f 32y(P)
8:30 (8:30) (Class 6) (0-65,71) 3-Y-O+ **£1,940** (£577; £288; £144) **Stalls** High

Form RPR
4124 **1** **George Fenton**[11] 6053 4-9-4 **64** (p) ConnorBeasley(5) 9 75
(Richard Guest) *s.i.s: pushed along early in rr: hdwy over 2f out: rdn to ld wl ins fnl f: r.o* **5/1**[2]
3251 **2** *1 1/2* **Mishaal (IRE)**[10] 6084 3-9-12 **71** 6ex BarryMcHugh 11 76
(Michael Herrington) *plld hrd and prom: rdn and ev ch fr over 1f out tl edgd rt and unable qck wl ins fnl f* **7/4**[1]
3244 **3** *1 1/2* **Alluring Star**[18] 5830 5-9-9 **64** GrahamGibbons 10 67
(Michael Easterby) *trckd ldr tl led over 2f out: rdn over 1f out: hdd and no ex wl ins fnl f* **5/1**[2]
4602 **4** *3* **Piccolo Express**[32] 5354 7-9-5 **60** ShaneKelly 12 56
(Brian Baugh) *hld up: hdwy on outer over 2f out: rdn over 1f out: edgd lft and wknd ins fnl f* **12/1**
4-00 **5** *3 1/2* **King Of Kudos (IRE)**[91] 3289 3-9-5 **64** (p) PJMcDonald 8 49
(Scott Dixon) *prom: rdn over 2f out: wknd fnl f* **14/1**
4500 **6** *2* **Star Up In The Sky (USA)**[28] 5487 3-8-11 **61** ShaneGray(5) 1 42
(Kevin Ryan) *chsd ldrs: rdn over 2f out: wknd over 1f out* **20/1**
2606 **7** *8* **True Prince (USA)**[81] 3644 4-8-9 **53** (b) JasonHart(3) 7 16
(Brian Ellison) *sn pushed along and a in rr* **8/1**[3]
2001 **8** *nse* **Dhhamaan (IRE)**[28] 5471 8-8-11 **52** (b) JamesSullivan 2 15
(Ruth Carr) *led over 4f: wknd over 1f out* **8/1**[3]
5221 **9** *14* **Gebayl**[100] 2992 3-9-3 **62** CathyGannon 3
(Olivia Maylam) *prom: pushed along over 4f out: rdn and wknd over 2f out* **14/1**

1m 31.66s (2.06) **Going Correction** +0.325s/f (Slow)
WFA 3 from 4yo+ 4lb **9** Ran SP% **117.7**
Speed ratings (Par 101): **101,99,97,94,90 87,78,78,62**
toteswingers 1&2 £4.40, 1&3 £4.60, 2&3 £2.80 CSF £14.44 CT £46.69 TOTE £5.70: £1.90, £1.30, £2.60; EX 16.20 Trifecta £70.90 Pool: £1352.86 - 14.29 winning units..
Owner Mrs Alison Guest **Bred** R P Williams **Trained** Wetherby, W Yorks

FOCUS
Division one of a modest handicap. The gallop was only fair and the winner came down the centre. he posted a personal best, helped by the winner.

6368 32REDBINGO.COM H'CAP (DIV II) 7f 32y(P)
9:00 (9:00) (Class 6) (0-65,65) 3-Y-O+ **£1,940** (£577; £288; £144) **Stalls** High

Form RPR
0536 **1** **Malaysian Boleh**[21] 5697 3-9-6 **65** HarryBentley 11 74+
(Simon Dow) *hld up: hdwy over 1f out: hung lft and led wl ins fnl f: sn clr: comf* **8/1**
5504 **2** *3* **Orpsie Boy (IRE)**[22] 5677 10-9-5 **63** JulieBurke(3) 10 66
(Ruth Carr) *mid-div: hdwy over 2f out: led ins fnl f: sn edgd lft and hdd: styd on same pce* **5/1**[2]
0263 **3** *1 3/4* **Putin (IRE)**[14] 5965 5-9-9 **64** (bt) LukeMorris 12 62
(Phil McEntee) *led: hdd over 2f out: rdn to ld over 1f out: hdd and unable qck ins fnl f* **8/1**
3503 **4** *hd* **Hoppy's Flyer (FR)**[28] 5471 5-9-4 **59** TomMcLaughlin 2 57
(Mark Brisbourne) *trckd ldrs 2f: remained handy: rdn and ev ch ins fnl f: styd on same pce* **10/1**
552- **5** *2* **Nelina**[302] 7728 3-9-3 **62** GrahamGibbons 4 53
(Robert Cowell) *trckd ldrs: rdn and ev ch 1f out: no ex ins fnl f* **7/1**[3]
2340 **6** *2 1/4* **Hazza The Jazza**[7] 6181 3-9-0 **64** (p) ConnorBeasley(5) 3 49
(Richard Guest) *hld up: hdwy over 1f out: sn rdn: no ex ins fnl f* **7/2**[1]
6046 **7** *1* **Ozz**[7] 6154 4-9-2 **62** (bt) LauraPike(5) 7 47
(Frank Sheridan) *hld up: plld hrd: hdwy to trck ldr 5f out: led over 2f out: rdn and hdd over 1f out: wknd in side fnl f* **25/1**
0105 **8** *1 3/4* **Stoneacre Oskar**[27] 5515 4-8-8 **54** ow1 SladeO'Hara(5) 9 35
(Peter Grayson) *s.i.s: nvr on terms* **14/1**
053 **9** *3 1/2* **Logans Lad (IRE)**[72] 3950 3-9-2 **61** ShaneKelly 1 31
(John Stimpson) *plld hrd and prom: stl gng wl enough whn nt clr run over 1f out: wknd fnl f* **14/1**
0000 **10** *1* **Whitford (IRE)**[16] 5890 3-8-3 **51** oh2 RaulDaSilva(3) 5 19
(Chris Dwyer) *chsd ldrs: rdn over 2f out: wknd fnl f* **25/1**
405 **11** *1 3/4* **New Decade**[92] 3246 4-9-10 **65** RichardKingscote 6 30
(Milton Bradley) *hld up: pushed along over 2f out: wknd over 1f out* **5/1**[2]

1m 31.51s (1.91) **Going Correction** +0.325s/f (Slow)
WFA 3 from 4yo+ 4lb **11** Ran SP% **120.4**
Speed ratings (Par 101): **102,98,96,96,94 91,90,88,84,83 81**
toteswingers 1&2 £13.00, 1&3 £7.60, 2&3 £12.20 CSF £48.97 CT £269.49 TOTE £8.80: £1.90, £3.00, £1.60; EX 65.90 Trifecta £496.00 Pool: £1079.94 - 1.63 winning units..
Owner JCG Chua & CK Ong **Bred** John & Sue Davis **Trained** Epsom, Surrey

FOCUS
A couple of unexposed sorts in a modest handicap. The pace wasn't strong and the winner came down the centre. He was arguably value for a few more lengths.

T/Plt: £418.80 to £1 stake. Pool: £94624.85 - 164.90 winning tickets T/Qpdt: £14.80 to a £1 stake. Pool: £13422.70 - 670.83 winning tickets CR

6369 - 6375a (Foreign Racing) - See Raceform Interactive

6095 BATH (L-H)

Saturday, September 14

OFFICIAL GOING: Good (7.9)

Wind: Moderate across Weather: Overcast

6376 BATHWICK TYRES CHIPPENHAM NURSERY H'CAP 5f 161y

2:15 (2:15) (Class 4) (0-85,83) 2-Y-O **£3,752** (£1,116; £557; £278) **Stalls** Centre

Form RPR

3441 **1** **Deeds Not Words (IRE)**[11] 6065 2-8-11 **76**............ CharlesBishop(3) 1 87+
(Mick Channon) *mde all: drvn clr appr fnl f: unchal* **5/2**[1]

01 **2** 3¾ **Fear Or Favour (IRE)**[14] 5976 2-9-4 **80**............................ AdamKirby 3 79
(Clive Cox) *chsd ldrs: wnt 2nd wl over 1f out but nvr any ch w wnr: hld on wl for 2nd* **11/2**

6541 **3** 1¼ **Aspirant**[10] 6104 2-8-7 **69**................................ TedDurcan 5 64
(Roger Charlton) *hld up in rr: drvn and hdwy on outside fr 2f out: kpt on fnl f to press for 2nd cl home but nvr any ch w wnr* **3/1**[2]

251 **4** ½ **Pensax Lad (IRE)**[28] 5543 2-8-12 **74**................................ LukeMorris 7 67
(Ronald Harris) *chsd ldrs: rdn and one pce over 2f out: styd on fnl f* **11/1**

4210 **5** 1¼ **Trinity River**[29] 5476 2-8-13 **78**............................ ThomasBrown(3) 6 67
(Daniel Kubler) *chsd wnr: rdn over 2f out: lost 2nd wl over 1f out: outpcd fnl f* **10/1**

1600 **6** 2½ **Corncockle**[71] 4019 2-9-7 **83**................................ PatDobbs 4 63
(Richard Hannon) *in tch: rdn over 2f out and sn btn* **20/1**

3216 **7** 2 **Minley**[19] 5848 2-9-2 **78**................................ SteveDrowne 8 52
(Rae Guest) *in rr but in tch: rdn over 2f out and sme prog: sn btn* **10/1**

2415 **8** 3¼ **Baytown Kestrel**[21] 5767 2-9-0 **76**................................ CathyGannon 2 39
(Brian Ellison) *s.i.s: a outpcd* **7/1**

1m 10.95s (-0.25) **Going Correction** -0.05s/f (Good) 8 Ran SP% **112.7**

Speed ratings (Par 97): **99,94,92,91,90 86,84,79**

toteswingers 1&2 £3.10, 1&3 £3.10, 2&3 £3.90 CSF £16.10 CT £41.77 TOTE £4.00: £1.50, £2.20, £1.10; EX 15.10 Trifecta £44.40 Pool: £992.55 - 16.76 winning units..

Owner George Materna **Bred** B Holland, S Hillen & J Cullinan **Trained** West Ilsley, Berks

FOCUS

Far side rail dolled out 4yds from 5f to just after 3f to provide fresh running line where sprint races meet the main track. No change to race distances. The ground had been eased to good due to 21mm of rain the previous day. The jockeys reported it was riding in line with the official description. A fair but competitive-looking sprint nursery but a race dominated by the favourite, who built on his solid Goodwood win.

6377 BATHWICK TYRES SWINDON H'CAP 1m 5f 22y

2:50 (2:50) (Class 4) (0-80,80) 3-Y-O+ **£4,690** (£1,395; £697; £348) **Stalls** High

Form RPR

1204 **1** **Royal Signaller**[15] 5953 3-9-3 **79**................................(p) PatDobbs 9 87
(Amanda Perrett) *mde all: jnd fr 5f out: stl hrd pressed and u.p fr over 2f out: hld on gamely fnl f* **11/4**[1]

1211 **2** ½ **Chapter Five**[14] 5977 6-8-11 **66** oh1........................(b[1]) RyanPowell(3) 13 73
(Ian Williams) *chsd ldr: chal fr 5f out and stl upside fr over 2f out and pressed wnr fnl f: no ex cl home* **10/1**

3315 **3** nk **Spanish Plume**[9] 6130 5-8-9 **66** oh1............................(p) JackDuern(5) 7 72
(Andrew Hollinshead) *chsd ldrs: drvn over 2f out: chal ins fnl f: no ex clsng stages* **16/1**

5335 **4** shd **No Such Number**[19] 5823 5-8-11 **70**........................(p) ShelleyBirkett(7) 4 76
(Julia Feilden) *in tch hdwy on outside fr 3f out: pressed ldrs u.p fnl f: nt qckn clsng stages* **16/1**

1104 **5** ½ **Kashgar**[15] 5946 4-9-4 **75**................................ OisinMurphy(5) 14 80
(Bernard Llewellyn) *hdwy on outside 3f out: pressed ldrs fnl f: outpcd fnl 50yds* **10/1**

2400 **6** shd **Abundantly**[21] 5746 4-9-7 **73**................................ JimmyFortune 2 78
(Hughie Morrison) *chsd ldrs: outpcd and drvn 3f out: rallied fr 2f out and chsd ldrs over 1f out: no ex ins fnl f* **8/1**[3]

0004 **7** 1¼ **Ethics Girl (IRE)**[17] 5879 7-9-7 **73**................................(t) AdamKirby 6 76
(John Berry) *in rr: hdwy on outside fr 3f out: chsd ldrs u.p 2f out: wknd fnl 110yds* **8/1**[3]

6432 **8** hd **Hurakan (IRE)**[23] 5666 7-9-1 **70**............................ ThomasBrown(3) 5 73
(Richard Price) *chsd ldrs: rdn 2f out: wknd ins fnl f* **14/1**

-513 **9** 1½ **Bridgehampton**[28] 5520 4-9-8 **77**................ WilliamTwiston-Davies(3) 3 78
(Michael Bell) *in rr: hdwy to cl on ldrs 4f out: rdn 3f out: wknd ins fnl f* **5/1**[2]

-600 **10** nk **Shades Of Grey**[28] 5535 6-9-1 **72**................................ RyanTate(5) 1 72
(Clive Cox) *in tch: rdn to chse ldrs over 3f out: wknd fr 2f out* **20/1**

10 **11** 12 **Evergreen Forest (IRE)**[20] 5793 5-8-7 **66**.................... NoraLooby(7) 8 48
(Natalie Lloyd-Beavis) *bhd most of way* **40/1**

1422 **R** **Kittens**[47] 4832 4-9-3 **69**................................ SteveDrowne 12
(William Muir) *restless in stalls: ref to r* **10/1**

2m 52.37s (0.37) **Going Correction** +0.075s/f (Good)

WFA 3 from 4yo+ 10lb 12 Ran SP% **118.5**

Speed ratings (Par 105): **101,100,100,100,100 100,99,99,98,98 90,**

toteswingers 1&2 £25.20, 1&3 £25.20, 2&3 £19.10 CSF £30.99 CT £378.82 TOTE £4.00: £1.50, £3.10, £7.20; EX 40.50 Trifecta £608.10 Part won. Pool: £810.90 - 0.01 winning units..

Owner Woodcote Stud Ltd **Bred** Woodcote Stud Ltd **Trained** Pulborough, W Sussex

FOCUS

A big field for this fair staying handicap and it produced a bunched finish, but the first two held those positions throughout. The winner was back to form down in grade.

6378 BATHWICK TYRES BATH MAIDEN STKS 1m 5y

3:25 (3:25) (Class 4) 2-Y-O **£3,752** (£1,116; £557; £278) **Stalls** Low

Form RPR

1 **Spark Plug (IRE)** 2-9-5 0................................ JimmyFortune 4 76+
(Brian Meehan) *trckd ldrs: led over 2f out and sn drvn along: r.o strly fnl f: readily* **12/1**

6 **2** 1½ **Act Of Charity (IRE)**[22] 5698 2-9-5 0................................ PaoloSirigu 9 73
(Marco Botti) *t.k.h: trckd ldr: rdn 2f out: hung rt u.p ins fnl f and no imp on wnr* **4/1**[3]

442 **3** 1¼ **Charlotte's Day**[33] 5330 2-9-0 74................................ LukeMorris 5 65
(Sir Mark Prescott Bt) *led: drvn along fr 4f out and stl rousted whn hdd over 2f out and one pce: kpt on fnl f but no imp on ldng duo* **5/2**[1]

0 **4** 1¼ **Dullingham**[92] 3290 2-9-5 0................................ AhmedAjtebi 10 67
(Charlie Appleby) *sn chsng ldrs: rdn ins fnl 3f and green: effrt on outside to press ldrs over 1f out: sn edgd lft u.p: wknd ins fnl f* **11/4**[2]

0 **5** 5 **Buy Out Boy**[39] 5101 2-9-5 0................................ SteveDrowne 11 56
(Jo Hughes) *in rr: rdn 3f out: styd on fnl 2f but nvr gng pce to rch ldrs* **40/1**

6 hd **Gannicus** 2-9-0 0................................ RyanTate(5) 3 55
(Brendan Powell) *chsd ldrs: rdn 3f out: outpcd 2f out* **50/1**

7 1¾ **Sweetheart Abbey** 2-9-0 0................................ TedDurcan 8 46
(William Knight) *towards rr but in tch: pushed along 4f out: sme hdwy 3f out: wknd 2f out* **40/1**

8 4½ **Nos Galan (IRE)** 2-9-5 0................................ PatDobbs 2 41
(Richard Hannon) *s.i.s: a bhd* **7/1**

9 22 **Wedgwood (IRE)** 2-9-2 0........................ WilliamTwiston-Davies(3) 6
(Richard Hannon) *s.i.s: rdn: green and no ch 4f out* **15/2**

1m 44.16s (3.36) **Going Correction** +0.075s/f (Good) 9 Ran SP% **114.0**

Speed ratings (Par 97): **86,84,83,82,77 76,75,70,48**

toteswingers 1&2 £16.20, 1&3 £4.60, 2&3 £1.90 CSF £58.26 TOTE £12.00: £2.10, £1.50, £1.80; EX 48.20 Trifecta £168.20 Pool: £1266.29 - 5.64 winning units..

Owner The Pony Club **Bred** Airlie Stud **Trained** Manton, Wilts

FOCUS

Limited experience amongst the runners in this juvenile maiden and it was a newcomer who beat the three market leaders. The winner is a likely improver and the second showed improved form.

6379 BATHWICK TYRES TETBURY H'CAP 1m 5y

4:00 (4:00) (Class 4) (0-80,80) 3-Y-O **£4,690** (£1,395; £697; £348) **Stalls** Low

Form RPR

3626 **1** **Madame Elizabeth**[15] 5942 3-8-8 **72**........................ JackDuern(5) 3 81
(Andrew Hollinshead) *chsd ldr: rdn over 2f out: led jst ins fnl f: drvn out* **8/1**

0145 **2** 1¼ **Saint Jerome (IRE)**[36] 5218 3-9-4 **80**.......... WilliamTwiston-Davies(3) 1 86
(Jamie Osborne) *led: drvn over 2f out: hdd jst ins fnl f: kpt on but no imp on wnr* **8/1**

5332 **3** 2¾ **New Falcon (IRE)**[14] 5978 3-9-0 **73**............................(p) SteveDrowne 7 73
(James Tate) *chsd ldrs: pushed along and outpcd 5f out: rdn and hdwy on outside over 2f out: kpt on fnl f but no imp on ldng duo* **7/2**[2]

1245 **4** 2½ **Freeport**[57] 4508 3-9-4 **77**................................ JimmyFortune 6 71
(Brian Meehan) *in rr but in tch: pushed along 4f out: hdwy 3f out: nvr gng pce to rch ldrs and one pce fnl 2f* **3/1**[1]

010 **5** 1¼ **Not Rigg (USA)**[44] 4928 3-8-12 **74**............................(t) RyanPowell(3) 2 65
(Gary Harrison) *sn pushed along to chse ldrs: rdn 3f out: styd on same pce fnl 2f* **14/1**

-000 **6** ½ **Empiricist (IRE)**[10] 6115 3-8-10 **69**............................(bt[1]) PatDobbs 8 59
(Amanda Perrett) *rdn along 3f out: a towards rr* **4/1**[3]

-021 **7** 2¾ **Unison (IRE)**[31] 5391 3-8-8 **70**................................ DeclanBates(3) 4 54
(Peter Makin) *rdn 3f out: a towards rr: uns rdr sn after line* **5/1**

1m 40.61s (-0.19) **Going Correction** +0.075s/f (Good) 7 Ran SP% **112.8**

Speed ratings (Par 103): **103,101,99,96,95 94,92**

toteswingers 1&2 £16.70, 1&3 £16.70, 2&3 £6.50 CSF £66.03 CT £263.60 TOTE £10.20: £4.00, £5.80; EX 94.70 Trifecta £262.90 Pool: £1357.63 - 3.87 winning units..

Owner David Lockwood & Fred Lockwood **Bred** Finbar And Aoifa Kent **Trained** Upper Longdon, Staffs

FOCUS

Another tight little handicap run at a brisk gallop and the time was 3.55secs faster than the preceding juvenile maiden. The first two held those positions throughout and were clear of the rest. The form is not entirely convincing.

6380 BATHWICK TYRES TROWBRIDGE H'CAP 1m 3f 144y

4:35 (4:35) (Class 3) (0-95,95) 3-Y-O **£7,439** (£2,213; £1,106; £553) **Stalls** Low

Form RPR

2141 **1** **Evangelist**[24] 5649 3-8-7 **81**................................(p) LukeMorris 5 91
(Sir Michael Stoute) *mde all: hrd rdn and edgd rt over 1f out: hld on wl fnl f* **4/1**

-111 **2** ¾ **Plutocracy (IRE)**[15] 5953 3-9-2 **90**................................ TedDurcan 4 99
(David Lanigan) *chsd wnr: rdn and edgd rt wl over 1f out: styng on whn hung lft jst ins fnl f: fnd no ex u.p* **6/4**[1]

4101 **3** 1¾ **Quest For More (IRE)**[11] 6071 3-8-6 **80**........................ CathyGannon 3 86+
(Roger Charlton) *t.k.h: chsd ldrs: rdn along 3f out: wnt 3rd over 1f out: kpt on same pce* **11/4**[2]

-310 **4** 12 **Chesterfield (IRE)**[35] 5258 3-9-1 **89**................................ AhmedAjtebi 1 83
(Charlie Appleby) *chsd ldrs in 3rd: rdn over 2f out: wknd fnl f: eased* **3/1**[3]

2m 32.76s (2.16) **Going Correction** +0.075s/f (Good) 4 Ran SP% **111.7**

Speed ratings (Par 105): **95,94,93,85**

CSF £10.71 TOTE £3.80; EX 9.00 Trifecta £11.40 Pool: £1160.11 - 75.96 winning units..

Owner Philip Newton **Bred** Philip Newton **Trained** Newmarket, Suffolk

FOCUS

The feature race of the day but a disappointing turnout. The winner was the third to make all on the afternoon. Hard to be too positive given the muddling nature of the race, but the 1-2-3 all been on the up.

6381 BATHWICK TYRES MIDSOMER NORTON FILLIES' H'CAP 5f 11y

5:05 (5:05) (Class 4) (0-85,84) 3-Y-O+ **£4,690** (£1,395; £697; £348) **Stalls** Centre

Form RPR

6430 **1** **Maglietta Fina (IRE)**[28] 5537 4-9-5 **82**................................ PatDobbs 10 92
(Robert Cowell) *hld up towards rr: drvn and gd hdwy over 1f out: led jst ins fnl f: readily* **7/1**

2156 **2** ¾ **Celestial Bay**[50] 4709 4-8-2 **70** oh3................................ RyanTate(5) 9 77
(Sylvester Kirk) *broke wl: drvn and outpcd 3f out: hdwy fr 2f out: styd on fnl f to take 2nd clsng stages: no imp on wnr* **8/1**

326 **3** 1¼ **Best Be Careful (IRE)**[15] 5956 5-8-2 **70** oh1.............. OisinMurphy(5) 4 73
(Mark Usher) *led: rdn 2f out: hdd jst ins fnl f: kpt on same pce and dropped to 3rd clsng stages* **10/3**[1]

4435 **4** 1¾ **Ginzan**[12] 6045 5-8-8 **76**................................ PhilipPrince(5) 11 73
(Malcolm Saunders) *chsd ldrs: chal 2f out: sn rdn: rdr dropped whip over 1f out: wknd fnl 75yds* **7/2**[2]

0406 **5** 2¼ **Whitecrest**[8] 6159 5-8-13 **76**................................ CathyGannon 6 65
(John Spearing) *rdn over 3f out: a outpcd* **11/2**

6000 **6** 2¾ **Heartsong (IRE)**[66] 4165 4-8-7 **73**............................(v) ThomasBrown(3) 1 52
(John Gallagher) *chsd ldr: chal u.p 2f out: wknd sn after* **10/1**

6006 **7** ¾ **Fanrouge (IRE)**[17] 5896 4-9-0 **80**................ WilliamTwiston-Davies(3) 3 56
(Rod Millman) *sn chsng ldrs: rdn over 2f out: sn btn* **9/2**[3]

1m 1.62s (-0.88) **Going Correction** -0.05s/f (Good)

WFA 3 from 4yo+ 1lb 7 Ran SP% **111.6**

Speed ratings (Par 102): **105,103,101,99,95 91,89**

toteswingers 1&2 £7.30, 1&3 £3.80, 2&3 £3.20 CSF £56.82 CT £215.74 TOTE £7.90: £3.70, £3.00; EX 45.20 Trifecta £513.20 Pool: £836.61 - 1.22 winning units..

Owner Scuderia Archi Romani **Bred** Sc Archi Romani **Trained** Six Mile Bottom, Cambs

FOCUS
Several course specialists on view in this fair fillies' handicap but the field was reduced by a number of withdrawals. The leaders went off hard early, leaving themselves vulnerable to the closers. The form has been given a chance.

6382 BATHWICK TYRES APPRENTICE H'CAP 5f 161y
5:40 (5:40) (Class 4) (0-85,85) 3-Y-O+ **£4,690** (£1,395; £697; £348) **Stalls** Centre

Form RPR
0100 1 **Milly's Gift**[42] 4983 3-9-1 **82**.. RyanTate(3) 7 95
(Clive Cox) *in tch: hdwy over 2f out: rdn and nt clr run over 1f out: led ins fnl f: r.o wl* **7/1**[3]
4124 2 1 ¾ **Wooden King (IRE)**[15] 5956 8-8-7 **72**.......................... PhilipPrince(3) 12 79
(Malcolm Saunders) *chsd ldrs: rdn 2f out: ev ch 1f out: one pce ins fnl f* **16/1**
410 3 1 ¼ **Shore Step (IRE)**[42] 4989 3-9-7 **85**.................................. CharlesBishop 5 88
(Mick Channon) *sn led: rdn 2f out: hdd ins fnl f: styd on same pce fnl 110yds* **7/1**[3]
5311 4 1 ½ **Gold Beau (FR)**[17] 5878 3-8-5 **74**.......................(p) JacobButterfield(5) 13 72
(Kristin Stubbs) *in rr: hdwy fr 2f out: kpt on fnl f: nt rch ldrs* **7/1**[3]
140 5 1 **Bilash**[28] 5537 6-8-4 **71** oh4.. JackDuern(5) 9 66
(Andrew Hollinshead) *pressed ldr early: styd in cl 2nd tl over 1f out: wknd ins fnl f* **20/1**
-030 6 nk **Valmina**[11] 6067 6-8-8 **73**.......................................(t) GeorgeDowning(5) 10 67
(Tony Carroll) *s.i.s: in rr: hdwy fr 2f out: styd on fnl f: nvr a threat* **12/1**
060 7 ½ **Italian Tom (IRE)**[21] 5775 6-8-11 **73**............................ ThomasBrown 4 65
(Ronald Harris) *chsd ldrs: rdn on rail whn nt clr run wl over 1f out: wknd fnl f* **9/1**
2-02 8 1 ¼ **Miliika**[34] 5308 4-9-2 **83**.. OisinMurphy(5) 3 71
(Rae Guest) *chsd ldrs: rdn over 2f out: wknd fnl f* **5/2**[1]
1143 9 ¾ **Grand Denial (IRE)**[29] 5477 3-8-13 **77**..........(b) WilliamTwiston-Davies 8 62
(Clive Cox) *rdn 1/2-way: a struggling to go pce* **6/1**[2]
4160 10 4 **Fortinbrass (IRE)**[18] 5851 3-8-12 **83**................................ JaneElliott(7) 6 55
(Ralph Beckett) *outpcd* **16/1**
060 11 5 **Taurus Twins**[76] 3855 7-9-1 **77**..(b) RyanClark 1 32
(Richard Price) *sn bhd* **20/1**

1m 10.36s (-0.84) **Going Correction** -0.05s/f (Good)
WFA 3 from 4yo+ 2lb 11 Ran SP% **119.3**
Speed ratings (Par 105): **103,100,99,97,95 95,94,92,91,86 79**
toteswingers 1&2 £23.20, 1&3 £6.80, 2&3 £16.80 CSF £114.60 CT £824.82 TOTE £7.90: £2.60, £5.00, £1.50; EX 189.50 Trifecta £982.50 Part won. Pool: £1310.00 - 0.53 winning units..
Owner Ken Lock Racing **Bred** Ken Lock Racing **Trained** Lambourn, Berks

FOCUS
A good race of its type, run in a time 0.59 secs faster than the opening nursery. Sound form with a turf best from the winner.
T/Plt: £1035.70 to a £1 stake. Pool: £52,778.66 - 37.20 winning tickets T/Qpdt: £240.90 to a £1 stake. Pool: £2637.38 - 8.10 winning tickets ST

5991 CHESTER (L-H)
Saturday, September 14

OFFICIAL GOING: Good to soft (soft in places) changing to soft after race 1 (1:50)
Wind: moderate 1/2 against Weather: fine

6383 STELLA CIDRE PEAR/BRITISH STALLION STUDS EBF MAIDEN STKS 6f 18y
1:50 (1:50) (Class 4) 2-Y-O **£6,469** (£1,925; £962; £481) **Stalls** Low

Form RPR
5 1 **Aeolus**[57] 4505 2-9-5 0.. RoystonFfrench 5 85+
(Ed McMahon) *mid-div and sn drvn along: nt clr run over 2f out and over 1f out: swtchd ins 1f out: nt clr run and swtchd rt: led last 75yds: won gng rt away* **11/4**[2]
04 2 7 **Telegraph (IRE)**[14] 5995 2-9-5 0...................................... DavidProbert 3 62
(Andrew Balding) *led: narrowly hdd appr fnl f: kpt on to take 2nd clsng stages* **5/4**[1]
40 3 ¾ **Signore Piccolo**[56] 4539 2-9-2 0...................................... JasonHart(3) 6 60
(Eric Alston) *w ldr: narrow ld appr fnl f: hdd last 75yds: fdd towards fin* **6/1**[3]
50 4 2 ¼ **Miguela McGuire**[113] 2625 2-8-11 0................................ NeilFarley(3) 4 48
(Eric Alston) *chsd ldrs: drvn over 3f out: one pce over 1f out* **33/1**
5 10 **Orient Class** 2-9-5 0.. LeeTopliss 1 23
(Paul Midgley) *sn outpcd and drvn along: lost pl over 1f out: sn bhd* **8/1**
06 6 nk **Slanderous**[80] 3680 2-9-0 0.. PJMcDonald 7 17
(Scott Dixon) *chsd ldrs: wknd over 1f out* **20/1**
0 7 hd **No Easy Day**[92] 3275 2-9-5 0.. TomEaves 2 22
(Kevin Ryan) *s.i.s: sn drvn along: nvr on terms: bhd fnl 2f* **12/1**

1m 22.97s (9.17) **Going Correction** +1.00s/f (Soft) 7 Ran SP% **111.9**
Speed ratings (Par 97): **78,68,67,64,51 50,50**
toteswingers 1&2 £1.40, 1&3 £1.70, 2&3 £1.80 CSF £6.25 TOTE £3.60: £1.10, £1.80; EX 6.10 Trifecta £21.00 Pool: £974.04 - 34.65 winning units..
Owner A Buxton **Bred** Andrew Buxton **Trained** Lichfield, Staffs

FOCUS
Entire rail moved out between 3 and 9yds, increasing distance of races 1 & 2 by 37yds, race 3 by 60yds, races 4 & 6 by 30yds, race 5 by 41yds and race 7 by 72yds. A modest juvenile maiden opened the card in which they went a contested gallop on ground which was officially changed to soft after the race. An impressive winner but the depth of the form is open to question.

6384 AEJIS H'CAP 7f 122y
2:20 (2:21) (Class 3) (0-90,90) 3-Y-O+ **£9,056** (£2,695; £1,346; £673) **Stalls** Low

Form RPR
222 1 **Ocean Tempest**[8] 6167 4-9-5 **85**.. BrettDoyle 7 99
(John Ryan) *chsd ldr: edgd lft ins fnl f: led towards fin* **8/1**
6321 2 hd **Balty Boys (IRE)**[20] 5783 4-9-7 **87**.................................. BarryMcHugh 3 100
(Brian Ellison) *led: crowded and bmpd wl ins fnl f: hdd cl home* **11/2**[3]
1305 3 7 **You Da One (IRE)**[64] 4236 3-9-2 **87**................................ DavidProbert 8 83
(Andrew Balding) *mid-div: effrt over 2f out: styd on fnl f: tk 3rd nr fin* **5/1**[2]
1210 4 ½ **Alejandro (IRE)**[14] 5992 4-9-3 **90**............................ SamanthaBell(7) 10 84
(Richard Fahey) *chsd ldrs on outer: clr 3rd 1f out: wknd towards fin* **12/1**
0064 5 1 ½ **Al Muheer (IRE)**[14] 5987 8-8-13 **82**................................(b) JasonHart(3) 5 73
(Ruth Carr) *chsd ldrs: drvn 3f out: one pce over 1f out* **9/1**
3045 6 ¾ **Gatepost (IRE)**[49] 4758 4-9-2 **82**...................................... TomEaves 11 71
(Richard Fahey) *in rr: hdwy on outer 2f out: kpt on ins fnl f* **16/1**
0050 7 nk **Mr Red Clubs (IRE)**[44] 4929 4-8-11 **77**............................ AndrewMullen 9 65
(Michael Appleby) *s.i.s: swtchd lft after s: in rr: swtchd rt over 1f out: kpt on ins fnl f* **12/1**
2003 8 3 **One Scoop Or Two**[9] 6126 7-8-10 **76** oh3..............(v) RussKennemore 6 56
(Andrew Hollinshead) *in rr: sme hdwy over 2f out: nvr a factor* **28/1**
011- 9 2 **Conry (IRE)**[319] 7452 7-9-5 **85**.. StevieDonohoe 4 60
(Ian Williams) *hld up in rr: drvn over 2f out: nvr a factor* **16/1**
005- 10 2 **Apostle (IRE)**[344] 6831 4-9-8 **88**...................................... AndreaAtzeni 12 58
(David Simcock) *swtchd lft after s: in rr: drvn over 3f out: nvr on terms* **14/1**
115 11 12 **Spin Artist (USA)**[11] 6078 3-9-2 **87**...................................... JoeFanning 2 27
(Mark Johnston) *mid-div: lost pl over 1f out: bhd whn eased ins fnl f* **7/1**
0022 12 39 **Mehdi (IRE)**[28] 5544 4-9-8 **88**...(t) AdrianNicholls 1
(David Nicholls) *chsd ldng pair on inner: heavily eased 1f out: virtually p.u: t.o* **9/2**[1]

1m 40.3s (6.50) **Going Correction** +1.00s/f (Soft)
WFA 3 from 4yo+ 5lb 12 Ran SP% **121.1**
Speed ratings (Par 107): **107,106,99,99,97 96,96,93,91,89 77,38**
toteswingers 1&2 £16.70, 1&3 £7.00, 2&3 £4.80 CSF £52.77 CT £252.16 TOTE £9.00: £3.00, £2.50, £2.90; EX 65.70 Trifecta £295.70 Pool: £1073.54 - 2.72 winning units..
Owner W McLuskey & C Little **Bred** Old Mill Stud Ltd And Oomswell Ltd **Trained** Newmarket, Suffolk

FOCUS
A decent handicap which developed into a thrilling two-horse race in the home straight and it paid to be prominent as making up ground on this turning track on soft ground is a difficult task. Dramatic improvement on the face of it from the winner and the form has been rated cautiously.

6385 STELLA ARTOIS STAND CUP (LISTED RACE) 1m 4f 66y
2:55 (2:55) (Class 1) 3-Y-O+ **£21,904** (£8,284; £4,140; £2,068) **Stalls** Low

Form RPR
60-3 1 **Tac De Boistron (FR)**[21] 5741 6-9-1 109.......................... MartinHarley 7 115
(Marco Botti) *led 1f: trckd ldrs: str run to ld over 1f out: sn qcknd clr: v readily* **11/2**[3]
1-53 2 8 **Cubanita**[90] 3381 4-8-10 102.. MartinLane 3 98
(Ralph Beckett) *hld up towards rr: effrt over 2f out: wnt 2nd 1f out: no ch w wnr* **7/2**[2]
-555 3 10 **Allied Powers (IRE)**[120] 2407 8-9-1 105........................ StevieDonohoe 5 88
(Michael Bell) *in rr: effrt on outside over 3f out: kpt on to take modest 3rd fnl 100yds* **11/1**
0145 4 ½ **Star Lahib (IRE)**[14] 5993 4-8-10 98.................................... JoeFanning 4 82
(Mark Johnston) *hld up towards rr: hdwy 5f out: drvn over 3f out: swtchd rt over 1f out: kpt on to take modest 4th last 100yds* **11/2**[3]
1044 5 5 **Area Fifty One**[21] 5760 5-9-1 105.. DavidNolan 1 80
(Richard Fahey) *trckd ldrs: led after 2f: hdd over 2f out: wknd ins fnl f* **15/2**
4411 6 ½ **Cameron Highland (IRE)**[21] 5761 4-9-6 105..............(p) AndreaAtzeni 6 84
(Roger Varian) *t.k.h early: led after 1f: led over 2f out: hdd over 1f out: wknd ins fnl f: b.b.v* **2/1**[1]
540 7 37 **Montaser (IRE)**[14] 5993 4-9-1 100.. TomEaves 2 24
(David Simcock) *s.i.s: sn trcking ldrs: drvn over 3f out: sn lost pl and bhd: t.o* **25/1**
-040 8 dist **Ile De Re (FR)**[77] 3824 7-9-1 98.. JasonHart 8
(Donald McCain) *chsd ldrs: drvn after 4f: sn reminders and lost pl: t.o 5f out: eventually completed* **20/1**

2m 49.83s (11.33) **Going Correction** +1.15s/f (Soft) 8 Ran SP% **115.0**
Speed ratings (Par 111): **108,102,96,95,92 92,67,**
toteswingers 1&2 £4.10, 1&3 £16.10, 2&3 £6.10 CSF £25.25 TOTE £5.50: £1.90, £1.10, £3.10; EX 23.60 Trifecta £158.40 Pool: £1097.36 - 5.19 winning units..
Owner Australian Thoroughbred Bloodstock **Bred** Mme Isabelle Reverseau **Trained** Newmarket, Suffolk

FOCUS
An interesting middle-distance Listed contest in which an ability to act on the testing surface was paramount, and the race rather fell apart. The winner is worth more at face value but there are doubts over what else ran their race.

6386 BOODLES DIAMOND NURSERY H'CAP 5f 110y
3:30 (3:31) (Class 3) (0-95,88) 2-Y-O **£6,931** (£2,074; £1,037; £519; £258) **Stalls** Low

Form RPR
1320 1 **De Repente (IRE)**[21] 5773 2-7-13 **69**............................ RaulDaSilva(3) 3 76
(Paul Green) *led 1f: trckd ldr: led appr fnl f: rdn out* **11/4**[1]
2243 2 2 ¼ **Memory Styx**[11] 6065 2-8-8 **75**.. JoeFanning 8 74
(Mick Channon) *hld up: hdwy over 1f out: hung lft and kpt on to take 2nd last 75yds* **11/2**[3]
5315 3 1 **Song Of Rowland (IRE)**[7] 6194 2-8-1 **71**........................ JulieBurke(3) 1 67
(David O'Meara) *dwlt: hdwy to ld after 1f: hdd appr fnl f: kpt on same pce* **7/1**
0541 4 1 ¼ **Intense Feeling (IRE)**[22] 5693 2-8-0 **72**...................... NoelGarbutt(5) 6 64
(David Evans) *mid-div: drvn over 1f out: kpt on to take 3rd last 50yds* **8/1**
32 5 1 ½ **Lilo Lil**[19] 5842 2-7-7 **67**..(p) JackGarritty(7) 4 54
(David C Griffiths) *chsd ldng pair: drvn over 1f out: one pce* **6/1**
251 6 10 **Skye's The Limit**[17] 5883 2-8-7 **74**.................................. BarryMcHugh 7 28
(Richard Fahey) *gave problems in stalls: wnt rt s: t.k.h: sn swtchd lft: drvn over 1f out: sn hung rt and wknd: eased towards fin* **4/1**[2]
1143 7 20 **Mick's Yer Man**[32] 5372 2-8-12 **86**................................(b) RyanWhile(7) 2
(Bill Turner) *dwlt: sn detached in last and drvn along: sn bhd: t.o 3f out* **6/1**

1m 13.37s (7.17) **Going Correction** +1.15s/f (Soft) 7 Ran SP% **114.2**
Speed ratings (Par 99): **98,95,93,92,90 76,50**
toteswingers 1&2 £5.60, 1&3 £13.20, 2&3 £13.20 CSF £18.10 CT £94.43 TOTE £3.50: £1.70, £1.10; EX 16.40 Trifecta £192.90 Pool: £1286.74 - 5.00 winning units..
Owner Mike Nolan **Bred** O Bourke **Trained** Lydiate, Merseyside

FOCUS
The withdrawal of the topweight and the continuing recalcitrance of Mick's Yer Man took some of the gloss off the level of form required to land this nursery, but it still looked a fair contest. The form is sound enough with the second a good yardstick.

6387 JUSTFORKICX CHARITY H'CAP 1m 2f 75y
4:10 (4:10) (Class 4) (0-80,80) 3-Y-O **£6,469** (£1,925; £962; £481) **Stalls** High

Form RPR
21 1 **Mahican (IRE)**[12] 6050 3-9-7 **80**.. JoeFanning 1 96+
(Mark Johnston) *sn led: qcknd gallop over 4f out: drvn clr over 1f out: heavily eased clsng stages* **1/1**[1]
4255 2 9 **Gabrial The Thug (FR)**[15] 5975 3-8-7 **66** oh1............(t) BarryMcHugh 2 59
(Richard Fahey) *sn trcking ldr: drvn over 2f out: hung rt over 1f out: no ch w wnr* **6/1**

2140 **3** 3 ¾ **Invincible Cara (IRE)**[45] 4878 3-9-3 **76**........................ PaulMulrennan 3 62
(Ed Dunlop) *stdd s: t.k.h: trckd ldrs: effrt over 3f out: one pce* **4/1**[3]

0310 **4** 8 **Sinaadi (IRE)**[7] 6198 3-9-6 **79**.. BrettDoyle 6 55
(Clive Brittain) *led early: sn in last: drvn 5f out: wknd over 1f out: eased ins fnl f* **3/1**[2]

2m 26.64s (15.44) **Going Correction** +1.30s/f (Soft) **4** Ran SP% **109.3**
Speed ratings (Par 103): **90,82,79,73**
CSF £7.21 TOTE £1.30; EX 5.60 Trifecta £11.60 Pool: £588.36 - 37.88 winning units..
Owner Sheikh Hamdan Bin Mohammed Al Maktoum **Bred** Ken Lynch **Trained** Middleham Moor, N Yorks

FOCUS
A fair 3yo handicap but the initial gallop was sedate with the winner enjoying an easy lead. He looks very useful, although there are doubts over the form.

6388 STELLA ARTOIS H'CAP 5f 16y
4:45 (4:46) (Class 4) (0-80,79) 3-Y-O+ **£6,469** (£1,925; £962; £481) **Stalls** Low

Form RPR

0232 **1** **Da'Quonde (IRE)**[26] 5579 5-9-3 **75**................................ PaulMulrennan 4 83
(Bryan Smart) *led early: chsd ldr: led appr fnl f: drvn out* **7/2**[1]

4460 **2** 1 **Waseem Faris (IRE)**[7] 6189 4-9-1 **73**............................(v) JoeFanning 11 78
(Mick Channon) *carried rt s: mid-div: chsd wnr last 150yds: kpt on same pce* **13/2**

3325 **3** ½ **Haajes**[3] 6309 9-9-7 **79**..(v) LeeTopliss 6 82
(Paul Midgley) *wnt rt s: chsd ldrs: drvn over 2f out: kpt on to take 3rd last 50yds* **9/2**[2]

2601 **4** 1 ¼ **Storm Lightning**[23] 5673 4-9-2 **74**............................(b) TomMcLaughlin 8 72+
(Mark Brisbourne) *carried rt s: in rr: hdwy 2f out: kpt on fnl f: tk 4th clsng stages* **13/2**

0-50 **5** 2 ¼ **Electric Qatar**[176] 1121 4-9-5 **77**................................ RichardKingscote 2 68
(Tom Dascombe) *chsd ldrs: effrt on ins over 1f out: wknd fnl 50yds* **15/2**

0/00 **6** 3 ¾ **Your Gifted (IRE)**[8] 6159 6-9-1 **73**................................(e) TomEaves 7 50
(Lisa Williamson) *carried rt s: swtchd lft after s: hld up in rr: sme hdwy fnl f: nvr a factor* **33/1**

0130 **7** nk **Jack My Boy (IRE)**[29] 5489 6-9-4 **76**................................ MartinHarley 1 52
(David Evans) *mid-div: drvn over 2f out: wknd over 1f out* **7/1**

6240 **8** 2 ¾ **Prince Of Burma (IRE)**[16] 5928 5-8-10 **73**.................... NoelGarbutt(5) 3 40
(David Evans) *s.s: nvr on terms* **16/1**

0433 **9** 3 ½ **Come On Dave (IRE)**[26] 5579 4-9-3 **75**........................ AdrianNicholls 10 52
(David Nicholls) *wnt rt s: swtchd lft and sn led: hdd appr fnl f: wknd and heavily eased ins fnl f* **11/2**[3]

1m 6.79s (5.79) **Going Correction** +1.30s/f (Soft) **9** Ran SP% **115.5**
Speed ratings (Par 105): **105,103,102,100,97 91,90,86,80**
toteswingers 1&2 £5.00, 1&3 £7.10, 2&3 £5.10 CSF £26.51 CT £104.43 TOTE £4.10: £1.50, £2.30, £1.20; EX 29.90 Trifecta £169.80 Pool: £1012.76 - 4.47 winning units..
Owner The Barber Girls **Bred** Gestut Sohrenhof **Trained** Hambleton, N Yorks

FOCUS
A fair sprint handicap in which they went a solid gallop. The form is sound enough.

6389 STELLA CIDRE H'CAP 1m 7f 195y
5:15 (5:16) (Class 4) (0-80,78) 3-Y-O **£6,469** (£1,925; £962; £481) **Stalls** Low

Form RPR

-513 **1** **Chocala (IRE)**[39] 5102 3-9-4 **75**.. MartinHarley 8 89+
(Alan King) *trckd ldrs: led 4f out: drvn and styd on wl fnl 2f* **11/8**[1]

6442 **2** 5 **Gabrial The Master (IRE)**[28] 5514 3-9-4 **75**.......................... TomEaves 6 82
(Richard Fahey) *trckd ldrs: kpt on to chse wnr over 1f out: no imp* **9/1**

2312 **3** 3 ¾ **Fitzwilly**[22] 5702 3-8-3 **60**.. DuranFentiman 5 63
(Mick Channon) *hld up in rr: hdwy 5f out: chsng ldrs over 3f out: one pce over 1f out* **5/1**[2]

0424 **4** 2 ¼ **Montjess (IRE)**[32] 5374 3-9-2 **73**............................(v) RichardKingscote 7 73
(Tom Dascombe) *led: qcknd pce over 6f out: hdd 4f out: one pce* **16/1**

4326 **5** 8 **Honey Haven (IRE)**[19] 5846 3-7-11 **59** oh5.................. NoelGarbutt(5) 3 49
(Mark Brisbourne) *s.i.s: in rr and sn drvn along: lost pl 6f out: poor 7th 3f out: modest 4th over 1f out* **33/1**

-206 **6** 14 **Mombasa**[92] 3277 3-9-5 **76**..(b[1]) AndreaAtzeni 2 50
(Ralph Beckett) *hld up in rr: drvn 5f out: sn btn: bhd whn eased ins fnl f* **15/2**

322 **7** 34 **White Month**[31] 5390 3-9-2 **73**..(p) DavidProbert 4
(Andrew Balding) *chsd ldrs: drvn 5f out: sn lost pl: t.o whn eased ins fnl f: virtually p.u: t.o* **6/1**[3]

6562 **8** 1 **Young Jay**[8] 6179 3-8-4 **61**.. JoeFanning 1
(Mark Johnston) *chsd ldrs: drvn 7f out: lost pl 5f out: t.o whn eased 1f out: virtually p.u* **7/1**

3m 53.2s (25.20) **Going Correction** +1.45s/f (Soft) **8** Ran SP% **116.1**
Speed ratings (Par 103): **95,92,90,89,85 78,61,61**
toteswingers 1&2 £2.20, 1&3 £1.90, 2&3 £3.10 CSF £15.33 CT £50.08 TOTE £2.30: £1.60, £3.00, £1.10; EX 15.70 Trifecta £53.50 Pool: £1097.18 - 15.37 winning units..
Owner High 5 **Bred** Peter Harris **Trained** Barbury Castle, Wilts

FOCUS
A reasonable staying handicap in which the tempo increased about 6f from home. The bare form is ordinary with doubts over the slow ground.
T/Plt: £25.30 to a £1 stake. Pool: £75387.86 - 2172.68 winning tickets T/Qpdt: £15.20 to a £1 stake. Pool: £2839.80 - 137.70 winning tickets WG

6347 DONCASTER (L-H)
Saturday, September 14

OFFICIAL GOING: Good to soft (soft in places; 6.8)
Race 7 was a valuable Group 1 race for Arabians.
Wind: Light across Weather: Cloudy with sunny periods

6390 AT THE RACES CHAMPAGNE STKS (GROUP 2) (C&G) 7f
2:05 (2:05) (Class 1) 2-Y-O **£50,585** (£19,178; £9,597; £4,781) **Stalls** High

Form RPR

12 **1** **Outstrip**[45] 4876 2-8-12 0.. MickaelBarzalona 5 114+
(Charlie Appleby) *dwlt: green and t.k.h in rr: pushed along wl over 2f out: gd prog on outer wl over 1f out: qcknd to ld 1f out: edgd rt and sn clr: readily* **13/8**[1]

12 **2** 3 **The Grey Gatsby (IRE)**[24] 5652 2-8-12 0.......................... GrahamLee 6 106
(Kevin Ryan) *lw: led: pushed along and qcknd wl over 2f out: jnd and rdn wl over 1f out: hdd and drvn 1f out: kpt on same pce* **13/8**[1]

4124 **3** hd **Cable Bay (IRE)**[21] 5765 2-8-12 108.............................. JamieSpencer 7 105
(Charles Hills) *trckd ldng pair: hdwy 3f out: effrt 2f out: rdn to chal wl over 1f out: kpt on same pce fnl f* **5/1**[2]

2121 **4** 13 **Treaty Of Paris (IRE)**[24] 5652 2-8-12 99.......................... JamesDoyle 1 79
(Henry Candy) *trckd ldr: cl up 4f out: rdn along wl over 2f out: wknd qckly wl over 1f out* **6/1**[3]

1m 26.9s (0.60) **Going Correction** +0.225s/f (Good) **4** Ran SP% **107.1**
Speed ratings (Par 107): **105,101,101,86**
CSF £4.39 TOTE £2.20; EX 4.20 Trifecta £9.90 Pool: £2177.72 - 164.13 winning units..
Owner Godolphin **Bred** Darley **Trained** Newmarket, Suffolk

FOCUS
Roderick Duncan, clerk of the course, said before racing that the track had taken 3.8mm of rainfall overnight, which was a bit less than some of the forecasts predicted. He therefore slightly altered the overnight going good to soft, soft in places. Mickael Barzalona described it as "soft" after the opener, while Graham Lee reported it to be "a bit dead". James Doyle went further, saying "it is tacky, very tacky". This had looked a decent renewal of a contest won by Toronado last season, but it was significantly weakened by three non-runners, most notably the likely market leader Anjaal. Whether this form will prove strong considering the field size is open to debate, but it fits with the race averages and could even prove slightly better.

6391 LADBROKES PORTLAND H'CAP 5f 140y
2:40 (2:42) (Class 2) 3-Y-O+
£37,350 (£11,184; £5,592; £2,796; £1,398; £702) **Stalls** High

Form RPR

0400 **1** **Angels Will Fall (IRE)**[24] 5651 4-9-2 **96**.................... RobertWinston 12 106
(Charles Hills) *lw: in tch stands' side: hdwy 2f out: swtchd rt and rdn over 1f out: led ins fnl f: sn drvn and jst hld on* **16/1**

3022 **2** nse **Steps (IRE)**[35] 5257 5-9-7 **101**..(b) WilliamBuick 11 111
(Roger Varian) *racd towards stands' side: trckd ldrs: gd hdwy 2f out: cl up over 1f out: rdn and ev ch ins fnl f: sn drvn and jst hld: 2nd of 16 in gp* **11/2**[1]

0200 **3** nk **Secret Witness**[1] 6352 7-9-4 **98**......................................(b) ShaneKelly 14 107
(Ronald Harris) *dwlt and towards rr stands' side gp: hdwy 2f out: sn rdn and styd on wl fnl f: nrst fin: 3rd of 16 in gp* **25/1**

2455 **4** nk **Racy**[7] 6190 6-9-3 **97**.. RyanMoore 17 105
(Brian Ellison) *towards rr stands' side: hdwy wl over 1f out: sn rdn and styd on strly fnl f: nrst fin: 4th of 16 in gp* **12/1**

5010 **5** 1 ½ **Magical Macey (USA)**[3] 6305 6-9-8 **102**..............(b) GrahamGibbons 18 104
(David Barron) *overall ldr stands' side: rdn along over 1f out: drvn ent fnl f: sn hdd and one pce: 5th of 16 in gp* **16/1**

6445 **6** 1 ¼ **Addictive Dream (IRE)**[14] 5991 6-8-10 **97**.................. JordanNason(7) 9 95
(David Nicholls) *chsd ldrs stands' side: hdwy 1/2-way: cl up 2f out: sn rdn: edgd lft and wknd appr fnl f: 6th of 16 in gp* **33/1**

0200 **7** ¾ **Ancient Cross**[24] 5651 9-9-3 **97**......................................(t) GrahamLee 10 92
(Michael Easterby) *towards rr stands' side: hdwy 2f out: sn rdn and kpt on fnl f: nrst fin: 7th of 16 in gp* **25/1**

0000 **8** 1 ¼ **Doc Hay (USA)**[14] 5984 6-9-6 **100**................................ DanielTudhope 16 94+
(David O'Meara) *dwlt and in rr stands' side: effrt and nt clr run wl over 1f out: kpt on ins fnl f: nrst fin: 8th of 16 in gp* **8/1**[2]

1002 **9** ½ **Ajjaadd (USA)**[42] 4986 7-8-11 **98**................................ KevinStott(7) 13 87
(Ted Powell) *chsd ldrs stands' side: effrt whn n.m.r and swtchd rt over 1f out: sn rdn and one pce: 9th of 16 in gp* **10/1**

2001 **10** nk **El Viento (FR)**[14] 5991 5-8-13 **98**..........................(v) GeorgeChaloner(5) 5 86
(Richard Fahey) *swtchd rt s: in tch on outer of stands' side gp: pushed along and hdwy 2f out: sn rdn and no imp fnl f: 10th of 16 in gp* **20/1**

4006 **11** hd **Elusivity (IRE)**[32] 5375 5-9-6 **100**..................................... KierenFallon 20 87
(David O'Meara) *in tch stands' side: effrt 2f out: sn rdn along and n.d: 11th of 16 in gp* **12/1**

0406 **12** ½ **Our Jonathan**[22] 5696 6-9-3 **97**................................ SilvestreDeSousa 8 82
(David Simcock) *racd on outer of stands' side gp: effrt over 2f out: sn rdn along and n.d: 12th of 16 in gp* **9/1**[3]

0400 **13** ½ **Prodigality**[28] 5545 5-9-4 **98**... JimCrowley 4 81
(Ronald Harris) *trckd ldrs far side: hdwy to ld that gp and ch wl over 1f out: sn rdn and wknd: 1st of 5 in gp* **14/1**

00U1 **14** hd **Bogart**[24] 5651 4-9-8 **102**.. NeilCallan 7 85
(Kevin Ryan) *lw: cl up stands' side: rdn along and ev ch 2f out: drvn and wknd over 1f out: 13th of 16 in gp* **11/1**

5500 **15** 1 **Monsieur Chevalier (IRE)**[7] 6183 6-8-11 **96**........(v[1]) NatashaEaton(5) 6 75
(P J O'Gorman) *dwlt: a towards rr far side: 2nd of 5 in gp* **25/1**

30-0 **16** ¾ **Definightly**[148] 1672 7-9-10 **104**....................................(b) JamesDoyle 15 80
(Roger Charlton) *prom stands' side: rdn along 2f out: sn wknd: 14th of 16 in gp* **20/1**

0105 **17** nk **Barnet Fair**[24] 5651 5-8-11 **96**.................................. ConnorBeasley(5) 21 71
(Richard Guest) *a towards rr stands' side: 15th of 16 in gp* **11/1**

0001 **18** ¾ **Confessional**[7] 6190 6-9-6 **100**..(e) DavidAllan 3 73
(Tim Easterby) *chsd ldng pair far side: hdwy 2f out: sn rdn and btn: 3rd of 5 in gp* **16/1**

0030 **19** 9 **Burwaaz**[34] 5314 4-9-2 **96**..(b) PaulHanagan 2 36
(Ed Dunlop) *chsd ldr far side: led that gp after 2f: rdn along 2f out: sn wknd: 4th of 5 in gp* **14/1**

0100 **20** 2 ¾ **Doctor Parkes**[14] 5991 7-9-3 **97**.................................. J-PGuillambert 22 27
(Stuart Williams) *a in rr stands' side: last of 16 in gp* **33/1**

0401 **21** 17 **Zero Money (IRE)**[11] 6078 7-9-5 **99**............................(b) MartinDwyer 1
(Hugo Palmer) *led far side gp: hdd after 2f: sn rdn along and wknd: bhd fnl 2f: last of 5 in gp* **33/1**

1m 8.14s (-0.66) **Going Correction** +0.225s/f (Good) **21** Ran SP% **138.5**
Speed ratings (Par 109): **113,112,112,112,110 108,107,105,105,104 104,103,103,102,101 100,100,99,87,83 60**
toteswingers 1&2 £32.60, 1&3 £176.50, 2&3 £25.90 CSF £100.66 CT £2277.08 TOTE £26.00: £5.50, £1.70, £6.90, £3.40; EX 202.00 TRIFECTA Not won..
Owner Mrs E O'Leary **Bred** Islanmore Stud **Trained** Lambourn, Berks

FOCUS
A seriously competitive handicap as one would expect for the prize-money on offer. The leaders went off predictably quickly, and the five who remained towards the inside of the track never had a chance. The winner was on a fair mark based on her Group-race best, with a personal best from the second.

6392 OLBG PARK STKS (GROUP 2) 7f
3:15 (3:16) (Class 1) 3-Y-O+
£56,710 (£21,500; £10,760; £5,360; £2,690; £1,350) **Stalls** High

Form RPR

2-16 **1** **Viztoria (IRE)**[85] 3524 3-8-11 109.................................. WayneLordan 10 114+
(Edward Lynam, Ire) *trckd ldrs: hdwy 2f out: rdn over 1f out: chal ent fnl f: kpt on wl to ld last 100yds* **7/2**[2]

4311 **2** ¾ **Lockwood**[20] 5794 4-9-4 109...................................... SilvestreDeSousa 9 116
(Saeed bin Suroor) *lw: prom: led after 2f: rdn along wl over 1f out: sn jnd: drvn ent fnl f: hdd and one pce last 100yds* **5/1**[3]

1351 **3** *1 1/4* **Gregorian (IRE)**[28] 5532 4-9-4 116 WilliamBuick 6 113
(John Gosden) *lw: prom: sn trcking ldr: effrt 2f out: sn rdn and ev ch tl drvn ins fnl f and one pce last 100yds* **9/4**[1]

4-24 **4** *1 1/4* **Caspar Netscher**[28] 5532 4-9-4 112 ShaneKelly 1 110
(David Simcock) *hld up towards rr: hdwy 3f out: trckd ldrs 2f out: rdn over 1f out: kpt on same pce* **10/1**

0101 **5** *1* **Sirius Prospect (USA)**[21] 5763 5-9-4 105 RobertWinston 8 107
(Dean Ivory) *trckd ldrs: rdn along over 2f out: kpt on same pce fr over 1f out* **8/1**

3004 **6** *1* **Pastoral Player**[20] 5794 6-9-4 107 GrahamLee 11 105
(Hughie Morrison) *hld up in rr: effrt and sme hdwy over 2f out: sn rdn and no imp* **20/1**

11 **7** *1 3/4* **Arnold Lane (IRE)**[136] 1944 4-9-4 108 SamHitchcott 3 100
(Mick Channon) *trckd ldrs: rdn along wl over 2f out: grad wknd* **28/1**

2002 **8** *hd* **Sovereign Debt (IRE)**[42] 5007 4-9-4 110 (p) JamieSpencer 4 99
(Michael Bell) *hld up: a towards rr* **8/1**

3320 **9** *3/4* **Red Jazz (USA)**[63] 4276 6-9-4 109 RyanMoore 5 98
(Charles Hills) *lw: led 2f: cl up: rdn along 3f out: wknd over 2f out* **14/1**

1m 25.54s (-0.76) **Going Correction** +0.225s/f (Good)
WFA 3 from 4yo+ 4lb **9** Ran SP% **115.8**
Speed ratings (Par 115): **113,112,110,109,108 107,105,104,103**
toteswingers 1&2 £5.00, 1&3 £2.70, 2&3 £3.50 CSF £21.51 TOTE £4.00: £1.50, £1.90, £1.40; EX 21.70 Trifecta £56.30 Pool: £7016.22 - 93.38 winning units..
Owner Mrs K Lavery **Bred** Airlie Stud **Trained** Dunshaughlin, Co Meath

FOCUS
A reasonable edition of this Group 2 contest, although the visual impression was they didn't go that quick early on. They raced middle to stands' side. Viztoria is rated in line with her 2yo best.

6393 LADBROKES ST LEGER STKS (BRITISH CHAMPIONS SERIES) (GROUP 1) (ENTIRE COLTS & FILLIES) 1m 6f 132y
3:50 (3:50) (Class 1) 3-Y-O
£340,260 (£129,000; £64,560; £32,160; £16,140; £8,100) **Stalls** Low

Form RPR
11 **1** **Leading Light (IRE)**[85] 3526 3-9-0 110 (p) JosephO'Brien 7 118+
(A P O'Brien, Ire) *lw: trckd ldr: cl up 3f out: led wl over 2f out: rdn over 1f out: drvn and styd on wl fnl f* **7/2**[1]

-110 **2** *1 1/4* **Talent**[56] 4550 3-8-11 114 JimCrowley 4 113
(Ralph Beckett) *hld up in rr: stdy hdwy over 3f out: trckd ldrs 2f out: effrt whn n.m.r and hmpd 1 1/2f out: sn rdn and styd on to chse wnr ins fnl f: kpt on* **9/1**

-332 **3** *3/4* **Galileo Rock (IRE)**[77] 3849 3-9-0 117 WayneLordan 1 115
(David Wachman, Ire) *lw: trckd ldng pair: hdwy 3f out: cl up 2f out: sn rdn and edgd rt over 1f out: ev ch tl drvn and one pce ins fnl f* **6/1**

4120 **4** *1/2* **Libertarian**[77] 3849 3-9-0 117 (p) WilliamBuick 2 114
(Charlie Appleby) *lw: in tch: rdn along and outpcd 4f out: hdwy 2f out: sn drvn and kpt on u.p fnl f: nrst fin* **5/1**[2]

2 **5** *3/4* **Foundry (IRE)**[24] 5653 3-9-0 0 RyanMoore 9 113
(A P O'Brien, Ire) *hld up towards rr: pushed along 4f out: hdwy 3f out: rdn to chse ldrs over 1f out: drvn and one pce ins fnl f* **5/1**[2]

6453 **6** *1/2* **Secret Number**[24] 5653 3-9-0 108 SilvestreDeSousa 5 112
(Saeed bin Suroor) *trckd ldrs: effrt 3f out: rdn along 2f out: sltly hmpd 1 1/2f out: sn drvn and one pce* **11/1**

1000 **7** *2 1/2* **Ralston Road (IRE)**[28] 5531 3-9-0 98 TadhgO'Shea 8 109?
(John Patrick Shanahan, Ire) *hld up in rr: stdy hdwy on outer 3f out: rdn to chse ldrs on outer over 2f out: sn drvn and one pce* **100/1**

3530 **8** *5* **Havana Beat (IRE)**[45] 4874 3-9-0 100 LiamKeniry 6 103
(Andrew Balding) *hld up: effrt and rdn along on inner 3f out: n.d* **40/1**

-611 **9** *3 3/4* **Great Hall**[72] 3982 3-9-0 98 KierenFallon 3 98
(Brian Meehan) *lw: in tch on inner: hdwy 3f out: rdn to chse ldrs 2f out: sn drvn and wknd* **20/1**

0-32 **10** *7* **Excess Knowledge**[45] 4874 3-9-0 107 JamesDoyle 11 89
(John Gosden) *hld up towards rr: effrt and sme hdwy on outer 4f out: rdn along over 3f out: sn btn* **11/2**[3]

4416 **11** *23* **Cap O'Rushes**[24] 5653 3-9-0 110 MickaelBarzalona 10 59
(Charlie Appleby) *sn led: rdn along 4f out: hdd wl over 2f out: sn wknd: bhd and eased fr wl over 1f out* **20/1**

3m 9.2s (1.80) **Going Correction** +0.225s/f (Good) **11** Ran SP% **116.5**
Speed ratings (Par 115): **104,103,102,102,102 102,100,98,96,92 80**
toteswingers 1&2 £8.30, 1&3 £5.70, 2&3 £14.50 CSF £34.13 CT £184.30 TOTE £3.50: £1.40, £2.90, £2.60; EX 37.20 Trifecta £300.20 Pool: £113,893.16 - 284.54 winning units..
Owner Derrick Smith & Mrs John Magnier & Michael Tabor **Bred** Lynch-Bages Ltd **Trained** Ballydoyle, Co Tipperary

FOCUS
A decent running of the season's final Classic and the pace seemed genuine thanks to Cap O'Rushes. A year on from Camelot's surprise defeat when chasing the Triple Crown, Aidan O'Brien produced a fine training performance. This rates a competitive St Leger but not a quality one, the level in line with lesser renewals. The form among the principals makes sense, with a personal best from Leading Light.

6394 NAPOLEONS CASINOS AND RESTAURANTS H'CAP 1m 4f
4:25 (4:25) (Class 2) (0-105,103) 3-Y-O+**£16,172** (£4,812; £2,405; £1,202) **Stalls** Low

Form RPR
0046 **1** **Forgotten Hero (IRE)**[21] 5768 4-8-12 **89** oh3 JamieSpencer 6 97
(Charles Hills) *hld up in rr: pushed along 1/2-way: niggled over 3f out: swtchd rt to outer wl over 2f out: str run to chal over 1f out: rdn to ld ins fnl f: drvn out* **12/1**

-200 **2** *nk* **Greatwood**[85] 3523 3-9-3 **103** KierenFallon 10 110
(Luca Cumani) *hld up towards rr: hdwy 1/2-way: trckd ldrs 3f out: effrt to chal 2f out: sn rdn and slt advantage ent fnl f: sn drvn and ev ch tl no ex nr fin* **5/1**[3]

054 **3** *nk* **Voodoo Prince**[8] 6172 5-9-0 **91** (p) GrahamLee 4 98
(Ed Dunlop) *lw: trckd ldng pair: hdwy 3f out: slt ld 2f out and sn rdn: drvn and hdd ent fnl f: ev ch tl no ex towards fin* **9/2**[2]

0000 **4** *1 1/4* **Saptapadi (IRE)**[21] 5766 7-9-0 **91** RyanMoore 3 96
(Brian Ellison) *in tch: hdwy to chse ldrs over 2f out: rdn along wl over 1f out: kpt on fnl f* **6/1**

4310 **5** *5* **Bishop Roko**[21] 5766 4-9-5 **96** JamesDoyle 9 93
(Roger Charlton) *hld up towards rr: rdn along and outpcd 3f out: plugged on u.p fnl 2f: nvr nr ldrs* **11/2**

0600 **6** *3/4* **Itlaaq**[7] 6192 7-8-12 **89** oh3 (t) GrahamGibbons 5 85
(Michael Easterby) *hld up in tch: hdwy 3f out: rdn along to chse ldrs 2f out: sn drvn and wknd* **33/1**

2000 **7** *1/2* **Hanoverian Baron**[21] 5766 8-8-8 **90** ConnorBeasley(5) 1 85
(Tony Newcombe) *trckd ldng trio: effrt on inner over 2f out: sn rdn and wknd wl over 1f out* **14/1**

4300 **8** *2 1/2* **Mister Impatience**[21] 5764 3-8-11 **97** NeilCallan 2 88
(Mark Johnston) *chsd ldr: rdn along wl over 3f out: wknd wl over 2f out* **7/2**[1]

1102 **9** *13* **Guising**[9] 6128 4-8-12 **89** oh4 SilvestreDeSousa 8 59
(David Brown) *lw: sn led: rdn along wl over 3f out: hdd 2f out: sn wknd and eased* **8/1**

2m 34.43s (-0.47) **Going Correction** +0.225s/f (Good)
WFA 3 from 4yo+ 9lb **9** Ran SP% **115.2**
Speed ratings (Par 109): **110,109,109,108,105 104,104,102,94**
toteswingers 1&2 £9.20, 1&3 £9.00, 2&3 £4.70 CSF £70.68 CT £315.29 TOTE £15.40: £3.50, £2.10, £1.70; EX 85.40 Trifecta £532.80 Pool: £3493.42 - 4.91 winning units..
Owner Mrs Julie Martin And David R Martin **Bred** James Burns And A Moynan **Trained** Lambourn, Berks

FOCUS
Considering the going, Guising set decent fractions, meaning this was always going to be a test. Sound form.

6395 AGRIARGO UK TRACTOR CHALLENGE NURSERY H'CAP 1m (S)
5:00 (5:01) (Class 2) 2-Y-O **£9,703** (£2,887; £1,443; £721) **Stalls** High

Form RPR
045 **1** **Photography (IRE)**[34] 5307 2-8-0 **71** oh5 PatrickMathers 5 75+
(Hugo Palmer) *trckd ldrs: cl up 3f out: led 2f out and sn rdn: drvn ent fnl f: hdd last 100yds: rallied to ld again on line* **20/1**

21 **2** *shd* **Extra Noble**[80] 3689 2-8-11 **82** JimCrowley 6 86+
(Ralph Beckett) *swtg: t.k.h early: trckd ldrs: effrt and nt clr run over 1f out: swtchd lft and rdn to chal ent fnl f: drvn to ld last 100yds: hdd on line* **5/2**[1]

501 **3** *1 1/2* **Dance Bid**[14] 5988 2-8-6 **77** MartinDwyer 2 77
(Clive Brittain) *dwlt: t.k.h in rr: hdwy on outer over 2f out: rdn to chal over 1f out: ev ch tl drvn and one pce ins fnl f* **12/1**

0201 **4** *3/4* **Sir Jack Layden**[69] 4096 2-8-13 **84** GrahamLee 4 83
(David Brown) *lw: cl up: rdn along 2f out: ev ch tl drvn and one pce ins fnl f* **9/2**[3]

3301 **5** *3 3/4* **Showpiece**[31] 5399 2-9-0 **85** RyanMoore 7 76
(Richard Hannon) *lw: hld up: a in rr* **9/2**[3]

1423 **6** *5* **Heskin (IRE)**[28] 5536 2-8-6 **77** (p) PaulHanagan 9 57
(Richard Fahey) *trckd ldrs: rdn along wl over 2f out: sn wknd* **8/1**

1141 **7** *29* **Fire Fighting (IRE)**[7] 6207 2-9-7 **92** NeilCallan 8 8
(Mark Johnston) *lw: led: rdn along 3f out: hdd 2f out: sn wknd* **11/4**[2]

1m 40.52s (1.22) **Going Correction** +0.225s/f (Good) **7** Ran SP% **115.2**
Speed ratings (Par 101): **102,101,100,99,95 90,61**
toteswingers 1&2 £8.50, 1&3 £10.50, 2&3 £5.30 CSF £70.83 CT £649.31 TOTE £19.10: £5.30, £2.00; EX 120.90 Trifecta £584.90 Pool: £3644.28 - 4.67 winning units..
Owner Weybridge Mafia **Bred** Noel Finegan And Noel Cogan **Trained** Newmarket, Suffolk

FOCUS
Not an easy race to assess with so many of these making their handicap debuts. The winner stepped forward and the third fits in.

6396 HARRIET DE-VERE POWELL H'CAP 1m (S)
6:05 (6:05) (Class 2) (0-110,107) 3-Y-O+**£16,172** (£4,812; £2,405; £1,202) **Stalls** High

Form RPR
12 **1** **Ascription (IRE)**[35] 5268 4-9-1 **98** (t) WilliamBuick 1 113
(Hugo Palmer) *lw: trckd ldr centre: smooth hdwy to ld 1 1/2f out: pushed clr fnl f: readily* **2/1**[1]

2140 **2** *5* **Gabrial The Great (IRE)**[14] 6001 4-8-13 **96** JamesDoyle 4 99
(Luca Cumani) *trckd ldng pair in centre: hdwy 2f out: rdn to chse wnr ent fnl f: sn drvn and no imp* **11/2**[2]

-104 **3** *5* **Levitate**[106] 2841 5-8-10 **93** (v) RobertWinston 5 85
(John Quinn) *hld up in tch: swtchd lft to centre and chsd ldrs wl over 2f out: rdn wl over 1f out: styd on fnl f to take 3rd nr fin* **13/2**

0002 **4** *nk* **Pied A Terre (AUS)**[28] 5518 5-9-2 **99** MickaelBarzalona 2 90
(Saeed bin Suroor) *racd centre: led: rdn along and qcknd over 2f out: hdd and drvn 1 1/2f out: sn wknd* **9/1**

0030 **5** *1 3/4* **Sandagiyr (FR)**[23] 5681 5-9-10 **107** SilvestreDeSousa 7 94
(Saeed bin Suroor) *t.k.h: racd towards stands' rail: trckd ldrs: effrt 3f out: rdn along over 2f out: sn btn* **9/1**

2400 **6** *3 1/4* **Global Village (IRE)**[13] 6025 8-8-11 **94** TadhgO'Shea 10 73
(Brian Ellison) *racd nr stands' rail: in tch: rdn along wl over 2f out: n.d* **6/1**[3]

0000 **7** *2* **Anderiego (IRE)**[13] 6025 5-8-10 **93** oh3 GrahamGibbons 3 68
(David O'Meara) *racd nr stands' rail: prom: rdn along 3f out: sn drvn and wknd* **16/1**

144 **8** *1 3/4* **Stepping Ahead (FR)**[63] 4295 3-8-5 **93** oh3 MartinDwyer 11 64
(K R Burke) *in tch nr stands' rail: rdn along and sme hdwy 3f out: sn wknd* **10/1**

-360 **9** *6* **Stand My Ground (IRE)**[116] 2559 6-9-5 **102** DanielTudhope 9 59
(David O'Meara) *hld up nr stands' rail: a in rr* **12/1**

1m 38.93s (-0.37) **Going Correction** +0.225s/f (Good)
WFA 3 from 4yo+ 5lb **9** Ran SP% **119.0**
Speed ratings (Par 109): **110,105,100,99,97 94,92,90,84**
toteswingers 1&2 £3.00, 1&3 £3.20, 2&3 £8.80 CSF £13.44 CT £62.51 TOTE £3.40: £1.50, £2.20, £2.20; EX 18.20 Trifecta £58.80 Pool: £2415.14 - 30.76 winning units..
Owner V I Araci **Bred** Haras De Manneville **Trained** Newmarket, Suffolk

FOCUS
Three of these raced up the middle of the track, while the main bunch were positioned stands' side for much of the way, and the smaller group provided three of the first four finishers, including the first two. A few of these were keen early. Only the first two really ran their races.
T/Jkpt: Not won. T/Plt: £39.00 to a £1 stake. Pool: £199,635.31 - 3729.08 winning tickets T/Qpdt: £10.80 to a £1 stake. Pool: £10,900.43 - 742.80 winning tickets JR

6310 KEMPTON (A.W) (R-H)
Saturday, September 14

OFFICIAL GOING: Standard
Wind: Moderate, against Weather: Overcast

6397 WILLIAM HILL JUMP SUNDAY 20.10.13 H'CAP 5f (P)
5:30 (5:31) (Class 6) (0-65,65) 3-Y-O **£1,940** (£577; £288; £144) **Stalls** Low

Form RPR
-423 **1** **Oh So Sassy**[94] 3221 3-9-3 **61** GeorgeBaker 7 79+
(Chris Wall) *mde all: clr fr 2f out: easily* **11/4**[2]

6600 **2** *4 1/2* **Outbid**[19] 5818 3-8-13 **57** KirstyMilczarek 1 57
(Tony Carroll) *prom: chsd wnr 2f out: sn rdn and no imp: one pce* **20/1**

4350 **3** *1/2* **Mossgo (IRE)**[16] 5930 3-8-11 **58** (t) RobertTart(3) 2 56
(John Best) *t.k.h: hld up bhd ldrs: pushed along over 1f out: kpt on to take 3rd ins fnl f: n.d* **10/1**

0215 4 ½ **Welsh Moonlight**[25] 5611 3-9-5 **63**.................. FergusSweeney 5 59
(Stuart Williams) *towards rr: shkn up and struggling 1/2-way: kpt on fr over 1f out to take 4th nr fin* **9/2**[3]

02 5 ½ **Golden Secret**[52] 4627 3-9-7 **65**.................. AdamKirby 6 60
(Clive Cox) *chsd ldrs: rdn wl over 1f out: no prog* **9/4**[1]

6530 6 1¼ **Somethingboutmary**[42] 4982 3-9-4 **62**..................(b) WilliamCarson 9 52
(Tim Pitt) *chsd wnr to 2f out: steadily wknd u.p* **16/1**

1026 7 1½ **Hand In Glove**[60] 4390 3-9-4 **62**.................. RobertHavlin 10 47
(Robert Cowell) *ponied to post: stdd s fr wd draw: hld up: rchd midfield 1/2-way: wknd over 1f out* **12/1**

6-55 8 ½ **Max The Machine**[82] 3638 3-8-13 **64**.................. AdamMcLean(7) 4 47
(Derek Shaw) *wnt rt s: a in rr: last and struggling 1/2-way* **14/1**

4650 9 4½ **Al Gharrafa**[102] 2962 3-9-2 **63**..................(b) MichaelJMMurphy(3) 3 30
(Rae Guest) *hmpd s: a in rr: wknd over 1f out* **14/1**

59.18s (-1.32) **Going Correction** -0.10s/f (Stan) 9 Ran SP% **116.4**
Speed ratings (Par 99): **106,98,98,97,96 94,92,91,84**
toteswingers 1&2 £10.50, 1&3 £4.00, 2&3 £25.50 CSF £55.97 CT £490.43 TOTE £3.90: £1.50, £3.60, £2.90; EX 49.60 Trifecta £370.20 Pool: £1845.43 - 3.73 winning units..
Owner The Eight Of Diamonds **Bred** Mrs C J Walker **Trained** Newmarket, Suffolk

FOCUS
It was one-way traffic in this moderate sprint handicap for 3-y-os. There was little depth, but the winner recorded a good time and looks potentially decent.

6398 BOOK WILLIAM HILL WINTER FESTIVAL H'CAP (JOCKEY CLUB GRASSROOTS MIDDLE DISTANCE SERIES QUALIFIER) 1m 2f (P)
6:00 (6:00) (Class 5) (0-70,70) 3-Y-0+ **£2,587** (£770; £384; £192) **Stalls** Low

Form RPR

0102 1 **Exclusive Waters (IRE)**[3] 6315 3-8-12 **63**.................. JimmyQuinn 3 72
(William Knight) *awkward s: sn chsd ldng pair: wnt 2nd over 3f out: drvn to ld over 1f out: jst hld on* **2/1**[1]

0664 2 nse **Woolston Ferry (IRE)**[18] 5855 7-9-9 **67**.................. FergusSweeney 10 76
(Henry Candy) *hld up in 8th: prog 2f out: rdn to chse wnr fnl f: clsd nr fin: jst failed* **10/1**

3101 3 2 **Jamaica Grande**[10] 6102 5-8-12 **56** oh3.................. WilliamCarson 6 61+
(Dave Morris) *awkward s: hld up in last trio: stl only 8th whn plld out jst over 1f out: rdn and styd on wl to take 3rd last stride* **16/1**

1213 4 nse **Precision Five**[14] 5980 4-9-8 **66**..................(p) AdamKirby 7 71
(Jeremy Gask) *rn in snatches: chsd ldrs: drvn to dispute 2nd briefly 1f out: kpt on but lost 3rd last stride* **8/1**[2]

6-40 5 ¾ **Everlasting Light**[29] 5478 3-9-3 **68**.................. RobertHavlin 5 71
(Luca Cumani) *trckd ldrs: shkn up over 2f out: trying to cl whn nt clr run over 1f out: styd on same pce fnl f* **10/1**

0434 6 1 **My Manekineko**[25] 5615 4-8-12 **56**.................. PatCosgrave 8 57
(J R Jenkins) *t.k.h: trckd ldrs: rdn to dispute 2nd briefly 1f out: wknd ins fnl f* **9/1**[3]

4205 7 1½ **Whitby Jet (IRE)**[19] 5825 5-9-5 **70**.................. CameronHardie(7) 4 68
(Ed Vaughan) *settled in midfield: shkn up over 2f out on inner: tried to cl over 1f out: no hdwy fnl f* **9/1**[3]

0643 8 shd **Claude Monet (BRZ)**[24] 5631 4-9-5 **63**.................. SebSanders 1 61
(Simon Dow) *led: drvn and hdd over 1f out: wknd fnl f* **20/1**

0331 9 nk **Compton Bird**[9] 6137 4-8-12 **59**.................. RobertTart(3) 11 57
(Hans Adielsson) *hld up in last trio: nt on terms w main gp 2f out: kpt on fnl f: nvr involved* **8/1**[2]

00-2 10 ¾ **Cool Hand Jake**[38] 5135 7-9-8 **66**.................. SteveDrowne 9 62
(Ben De Haan) *awkward s: mostly in last: pushed along over 2f out: nt on terms w main gp over 1f out: one pce after* **14/1**

0500 11 60 **Bravestar (IRE)**[33] 5356 3-9-5 **70**.................. GeorgeBaker 2
(David Lanigan) *t.k.h: trckd ldr on outer to over 3f out: wknd rapidly and eased: t.o* **12/1**

2m 5.49s (-2.51) **Going Correction** -0.10s/f (Stan)
WFA 3 from 4yo+ 7lb 11 Ran SP% **118.7**
Speed ratings (Par 103): **106,105,104,104,103 102,101,101,101,100 52**
toteswingers 1&2 £8.20, 1&3 £18.80, 2&3 £66.00 CSF £23.09 CT £259.11 TOTE £3.00: £1.40, £5.30, £4.40; EX 32.60 Trifecta £284.70 Pool: £976.30 - 2.57 winning units..
Owner The Old Brokers **Bred** M M Sammon **Trained** Patching, W Sussex

FOCUS
This ordinary handicap was run at a routine sort of pace and the winner was never far away. Straightforward form.

6399 STUB HUB TICKET H'CAP (DIV I) 1m (P)
6:30 (6:30) (Class 6) (0-60,60) 3-Y-0+ **£1,940** (£577; £288; £144) **Stalls** Low

Form RPR

0433 1 **Secret Success**[9] 6138 3-9-3 **58**..................(t) AdamKirby 11 68+
(Paul Cole) *mostly chsd ldr: rdn to chal jst over 2f out: led over 1f out: drvn to assert fnl f* **4/1**[1]

4413 2 1¾ **Sonnetation (IRE)**[37] 5204 3-8-12 **53**.................. PatCosgrave 10 59
(Jim Boyle) *led: drvn and pressed 2f out: hdd over 1f out: clung on for 2nd nr fin* **13/2**

-650 3 hd **Estibdaad (IRE)**[47] 4829 3-9-5 **60**..................(t) SteveDrowne 3 66+
(Anthony Honeyball) *t.k.h: hld up in midfield: lost pl after 1f: rdn over 2f out: nt qckn and racd awkwardly over 1f out: styd on after and nrly snatched 2nd* **9/2**[2]

/006 4 shd **Appyjack**[10] 6097 5-8-7 **46** oh1..................(t) RobertTart(3) 8 51
(Tony Carroll) *prom: rdn and nt qckn over 2f out: styd on fnl f to press for 2nd nr fin* **10/1**

0543 5 nse **Carrera**[16] 5923 3-9-1 **56**.................. SebSanders 9 61
(J W Hills) *chsd ldrs: rdn over 2f out: nt qckn wl over 1f out: styd on fnl f to press for 2nd nr fin* **6/1**[3]

6400 6 2 **Moment In The Sun**[7] 6218 4-9-1 **54**..........(b) MichaelJMMurphy(3) 13 55
(David Flood) *plld hrd: hld up on outer tl prog on wd outside over 3f out: pressed ldrs 2f out: sn fdd* **10/1**

0006 7 nk **Olivers Mount**[9] 6146 3-8-6 **47**..................(t) JimmyQuinn 7 47
(Ed Vaughan) *s.i.s: mostly in last trio: rdn and nt qckn over 2f out: plugged on one pce fr over 1f out* **25/1**

0430 8 nk **Chez Vrony**[25] 5614 7-8-10 **46** oh1.................. WilliamCarson 5 45
(Dave Morris) *broke wl but heavily restrained into rr: rdn on wd outside over 2f out: modest late prog: nvr in it* **25/1**

4136 9 1¼ **Archelao (IRE)**[24] 5631 5-8-13 **56**..................(t) PatMillman(7) 6 52
(Richard Rowe) *sn in midfield: lost pl over 2f out and bmpd along: no prog after* **8/1**

5500 10 1¾ **Kindia (IRE)**[66] 4169 5-9-6 **56**..................(p) RobertHavlin 4 48
(Michael Attwater) *s.i.s: t.k.h early: hld up in last trio: shkn up and no real prog over 2f out* **20/1**

/00- 11 1½ **Fitz**[451] 2586 7-9-2 **52**.................. FergusSweeney 1 41
(Martin Bosley) *hld up wl in rr: shkn up and no prog over 2f out* **20/1**

-264 12 1 **Squirrel Wood (IRE)**[28] 5525 5-9-5 **55**..................(b) GeorgeBaker 2 42
(Mary Hambro) *prom tl wknd qckly 2f out* **14/1**

000 13 2½ **Shelling Peas**[23] 5678 4-8-10 **53**.................. AdamMcLean(7) 12 34
(Derek Shaw) *prom tl wknd rapidly over 2f out* **33/1**

1m 39.94s (0.14) **Going Correction** -0.10s/f (Stan)
WFA 3 from 4yo+ 5lb 13 Ran SP% **121.9**
Speed ratings (Par 101): **95,93,93,92,92 90,90,90,89,87 85,84,82**
toteswingers 1&2 £5.60, 1&3 £4.00, 2&3 £6.60 CSF £28.01 CT £128.98 TOTE £4.50: £2.20, £2.90, £2.30; EX 30.70 Trifecta £149.90 Pool: £1006.35 - 5.03 winning units..
Owner A D Spence **Bred** Ray Bailey **Trained** Whatcombe, Oxon

FOCUS
A weak handicap that looked wide open. It paid to race prominently as they went a steady pace and there was a blanket finish for the places. The winner looks capable of better, at least on this surface.

6400 STUB HUB TICKET H'CAP (DIV II) 1m (P)
7:00 (7:00) (Class 6) (0-60,60) 3-Y-0+ **£1,940** (£577; £288; £144) **Stalls** Low

Form RPR

544 1 **Loraine**[13] 6019 3-9-3 **58**.................. GeorgeBaker 10 68
(Jamie Osborne) *hld up in last pair: brought wd in st and hdd towards nr side: gd prog fr 2f out: led ins fnl f: sn clr* **9/1**

350 2 2½ **Knight Charm**[31] 5395 3-9-5 **60**..................(p) AdamKirby 1 64
(Eve Johnson Houghton) *chsd ldrs in 6th: rdn over 2f out: chsd clr ldr briefly over 1f out: kpt on to take 2nd again ins fnl f* **14/1**

5033 3 ¾ **Princess Spirit**[10] 6102 4-8-7 **50**..................(p) JenniferFerguson(7) 2 53
(Edward Creighton) *dwlt: hld up in last quartet: prog on inner whn nt clr run over 2f out: kpt on fr over 1f out to take 3rd last strides* **7/1**[3]

6324 4 nk **Sakhee's Alround**[12] 6038 3-8-9 **50**..................(p) AdamBeschizza 9 52
(K F Clutterbuck) *prog fr midfield to go 2nd after 3f: led over 3f out: sn clr: 5 l up 2f out: wilted and hdd ins fnl f* **16/1**

0400 5 ¾ **Zaheeb**[3] 6317 5-9-6 **56**.................. WilliamCarson 4 56
(Dave Morris) *pushed along early: mostly in 7th: rdn and nt qckn over 2f out: kpt on fr over 1f out: nrst fin* **12/1**

4550 6 hd **Rock Anthem (IRE)**[33] 5346 9-9-5 **55**.................. KieranO'Neill 8 54
(Mike Murphy) *dwlt: hld up in last pair: prog over 2f out: disp 2nd briefly over 1f out: one pce after* **10/1**

2633 7 ½ **Do More Business (IRE)**[51] 4658 6-9-1 **51**..................(bt) JimmyQuinn 7 49
(Liam Corcoran) *hld up in last quartet: pushed along in last pair over 2f out: sme prog over 1f out: rdn and nt qckn after* **12/1**

0003 8 3 **Bajan Story**[26] 5596 4-9-6 **56**.................. FergusSweeney 3 47
(Michael Blanshard) *settled in 8th: rdn over 2f out: tried to cl w others over 1f out: sn no hdwy: wknd fnl f* **14/1**

5436 9 2¾ **Petrify**[29] 5492 3-9-3 **58**.................. KirstyMilczarek 11 43
(Luca Cumani) *led 1f: rdn in 3rd over 3f out: chsd ldr wl over 2f out to over 1f out: wknd qckly* **5/2**[1]

50-4 10 3½ **Ottavino (IRE)**[75] 3906 4-8-4 **47**.................. IanBurns(7) 5 24
(Jane Chapple-Hyam) *chsd ldrs in 5th: drvn and wknd over 2f out* **25/1**

606 11 1 **Marmot Bay (IRE)**[31] 5397 3-8-9 **50**.................. LukeMorris 6 25
(David Flood) *plld hrd: chsd ldng trio: wknd over 2f out* **16/1**

-505 12 18 **Substantivo (IRE)**[16] 5923 3-8-13 **57**.................. MichaelJMMurphy(3) 12
(Alan Jarvis) *drvn to ld after 1f and set gd pce: hdd over 3f out: wknd rapidly over 2f out: t.o* **4/1**[2]

1m 38.08s (-1.72) **Going Correction** -0.10s/f (Stan)
WFA 3 from 4yo+ 5lb 12 Ran SP% **124.5**
Speed ratings (Par 101): **104,101,100,100,99 99,99,96,93,89 88,70**
toteswingers 1&2 £20.80, 1&3 £7.90, 2&3 £26.70 CSF £134.90 CT £961.43 TOTE £7.10: £3.20, £5.70, £2.40; EX 203.90 Trifecta £494.60 Part won. Pool: £659.51 - 0.16 winning units..
Owner Mrs F Walwyn Mr & Mrs A Pakenham A Taylor **Bred** Mr & Mrs A E Pakenham **Trained** Upper Lambourn, Berks

FOCUS
The second division of the weak 1m handicap. It was run at a decent pace and suited the closers. Although it was quicker than division I, it looked the weaker race. The winner was on a good mark on her Salisbury June form.

6401 COME EXPERIENCE NEW PANORAMIC RESTAURANT NURSERY H'CAP 1m (P)
7:30 (7:30) (Class 5) (0-75,75) 2-Y-0 **£2,587** (£770; £384; £192) **Stalls** Low

Form RPR

0641 1 **Morally Bankrupt**[9] 6131 2-9-6 **74**.................. RichardHughes 8 76
(Richard Hannon) *hld up in rr: rdn and prog over 2f out: clsd on ldrs 1f out: styd on wl to ld last 50yds* **4/1**[2]

443 2 nk **Killing Time (IRE)**[77] 3836 2-9-0 **68** ow1..................(b[1]) SebSanders 4 69
(Ralph Beckett) *trckd ldrs: prog fr 2f out to chal over 1f out: led ins fnl f: hdd last 50yds* **9/2**[3]

453 3 ½ **M'Lady Ermyn**[18] 5850 2-8-1 **55** ow1.................. FrankieMcDonald 7 55
(Pat Phelan) *dwlt: mostly in last pair: brought wdst of all in st and prog u.p over 2f out: clsd on ldrs and looked a danger 1f out: nt qckn but kpt on to take 3rd nr fin* **40/1**

503 4 1 **Haayil**[15] 5941 2-9-2 **70**.................. RobertHavlin 9 67
(John Gosden) *wl in tch: prog to trck ldng pair over 3f out: gng strly over 2f out: rdn to ld over 1f out: hdd and nt qckn ins fnl f* **11/4**[1]

4526 5 1¼ **Officer Drivel (IRE)**[14] 6002 2-9-4 **72**.................. JimmyFortune 5 66
(Luke Dace) *t.k.h: hld up: dropped to last pair over 2f out: sme prog wl over 1f out: sn nt qckn: kpt on again ins fnl f* **10/1**

5302 6 ½ **Jive**[24] 5634 2-9-1 **69**.................. PatDobbs 3 62
(Richard Hannon) *restrained into last pair sn after s: stl there and nt asked for effrt 2f out: shkn up and sme prog over 1f out: one pce fnl f* **7/1**

5602 7 ¾ **Know Your Name**[12] 6041 2-9-4 **75**..................(v[1]) DeclanBates(3) 2 66
(David Evans) *wl in tch on inner: rdn over 2f out: no imp over 1f out: one pce after* **20/1**

534 8 5 **Diplomatic Force (USA)**[39] 5101 2-9-7 **75**.................. AhmedAjtebi 11 54
(Charlie Appleby) *racd v wd early: led after 3f: drvn and hdd 3f out: wknd over 1f out: eased* **12/1**

630 9 ¾ **Strassman**[16] 5922 2-8-6 **60**.................. LukeMorris 10 41+
(Mark Johnston) *chsd ldrs: u.p over 3f out: lost pl rapidly and wl in rr over 2f out* **25/1**

462 10 5 **Aristocracy**[17] 5893 2-8-6 **60**.................. SamHitchcott 6 26
(Mick Channon) *racd in ldng trio to over 3f out: sn drvn: stl in tch 2f out: wkng whn hmpd jst over 1f out* **16/1**

301 11 2½ **Ajig**[17] 5891 2-9-5 **73**.................. AdamKirby 1 33
(Eve Johnson Houghton) *led 3f: rdn to ld again 3f out: hdd & wknd rapidly over 1f out* **16/1**

1m 39.34s (-0.46) **Going Correction** -0.10s/f (Stan) 11 Ran SP% **116.9**
Speed ratings (Par 95): **98,97,97,96,94 94,93,88,87,82 80**
toteswingers 1&2 £3.30, 1&3 £20.80, 2&3 £79.50 CSF £21.70 CT £627.99 TOTE £3.50: £2.20, £2.20, £12.90; EX 23.70 Trifecta £530.40 Part won. Pool: £707.32 - 0.37 winning units..
Owner J Sullivan & C Giles **Bred** Horizon Bloodstock Limited **Trained** East Everleigh, Wilts

FOCUS
Not a bad nursery for the class and it saw a host of chances from 2f out. Ordinary form rated at face value.

6402 CONFERENCE & EVENTS DDR £39/HEAD MAIDEN STKS 1m 4f (P)
8:00 (8:01) (Class 5) 3-Y-0+ £2,587 (£770; £384; £192) Stalls Centre

Form RPR
05 1 **Hamelin (IRE)**[128] 2198 3-9-5 0 RichardHughes 6 83+
(Lady Cecil) *led 2f: trckd ldr: led again 2f out: shkn up and readily asserted over 1f out* 11/8[1]
2 2 2½ **My Direction**[10] 6116 3-9-5 0 LukeMorris 3 77
(Mark Johnston) *led after 2f: rdn and hdd 2f out: kpt on but no match for wnr fnl f* 11/4[2]
0 3 1¼ **Diamond Mine**[11] 6062 3-9-5 0 KirstyMilczarek 13 75
(Luca Cumani) *t.k.h: mostly chsd ldng pair: outpcd fr 2f out: styd on fnl f* 20/1
4 3¼ **Shanti** 3-9-5 0 AdamKirby 14 70+
(Michael Bell) *s.s: settled in last trio tl gd prog fr 3f out to dispute 3rd jst over 2f out: no ex over 1f out* 12/1
5 4½ **Balder Succes (FR)**[167] 5-10-0 0 FergusSweeney 11 63
(Alan King) *sn chsd ldrs: shkn up to dispute 3rd 3f out: hung lft and wknd 2f out* 8/1[3]
6 1 **Robertson (IRE)** 3-9-5 0 FrederikTylicki 7 61
(James Fanshawe) *rn green in midfield and pushed along at various stages: outpcd fr over 2f out* 16/1
7 2½ **Rhinestone Rebel (IRE)**[492] 7-10-0 0 WilliamCarson 12 57?
(Peter Hiatt) *s.s: t.k.h towards rr: rdn 3f out: wl outpcd fr over 2f out* 100/1
8 ¾ **Sir Tyto (IRE)**[87] 5-10-0 0 SteveDrowne 4 56?
(Peter Makin) *s.s: mostly in last: stl there 3f out and virtually t.o: pushed along and kpt on fr over 2f out* 100/1
4 9 nk **Waha (IRE)**[17] 5902 3-9-0 0 AhmedAjtebi 2 50
(Saeed bin Suroor) *dwlt: a towards rr: pushed along fr over 2f out: sn outpcd* 8/1[3]
5500 10 1 **Three Choirs (IRE)**[29] 5491 3-8-11 60 RobertTart(3) 1 49
(William Stone) *chsd ldng pair tl wknd wl over 2f out* 33/1
4 11 ½ **Mr Burbidge**[12] 6046 5-10-0 0 (b) DougieCostello 10 53
(Neil Mulholland) *chsd ldrs: drvn over 3f out: wknd over 2f out* 100/1
00 12 7 **Gentlemax (FR)**[17] 5892 3-9-2 0 MichaelJMMurphy(3) 5 42
(Alan Jarvis) *dwlt: plld hrd in rr: rdn and wknd over 3f out: sn bhd* 40/1
0 13 8 **Cardinal Pioneer (TUR)**[23] 5678 3-9-5 0 SebSanders 9 29
(J W Hills) *awkward s: nvr bttr than midfield: wknd 3f out: t.o* 66/1
4 14 7 **Alpetetim**[19] 5813 4-10-0 0 MartinLane 8 18
(Stuart Kittow) *wl in tch tl wknd rapidly 3f out: t.o* 66/1

2m 33.39s (-1.11) **Going Correction** -0.10s/f (Stan)
WFA 3 from 4yo+ 9lb 14 Ran SP% 120.7
Speed ratings (Par 103): **99,97,96,94,91 90,89,88,88,87 87,82,77,72**
toteswingers 1&2 £1.20, 1&3 £11.80, 2&3 £15.50 CSF £4.65 TOTE £2.20: £1.10, £1.50, £5.40; EX 6.20 Trifecta £62.20 Pool: £954.99 - 11.50 winning units..
Owner Lordship Stud **Bred** Lordship Stud **Trained** Newmarket, Suffolk

FOCUS
The form of this maiden should work out as there were plenty of positives about the first five or six. The form is rated around the first two.

6403 NEW O&T BAR COMING IN OCTOBER H'CAP 7f (P)
8:30 (8:30) (Class 4) (0-85,88) 3-Y-0+ £4,690 (£1,395; £697; £348) Stalls Low

Form RPR
2103 1 **Sir Mike**[7] 6203 4-9-7 82 AdamKirby 5 89
(Amanda Perrett) *mde virtually all: set mod pce tl wound it up over 2f out: drvn a l in front 1f out: hld on* 9/2[3]
0043 2 nk **Invisible Hunter (USA)**[33] 5355 4-9-7 82 (vt) AhmedAjtebi 7 88
(Saeed bin Suroor) *t.k.h: trckd ldng pair: drvn 2f out: nt qckn over 1f out: styd on to take 2nd nr fin* 4/1[2]
4131 3 nk **Bluegrass Blues (IRE)**[7] 6204 3-9-6 88 AshleyMorgan(3) 6 93
(Paul Cole) *w wnr: rdn and upsides 2f out: nt qckn 1f out: tried to rally fnl f: kpt on but lost 2nd nr fin* 11/4[1]
1133 4 1¾ **Levi Draper**[16] 5928 4-9-5 80 FrederikTylicki 1 81+
(James Fanshawe) *hld up in 7th in modly run event: outpcd fr 2f out: styd on fr over 1f out to take 4th last strides: no ch* 6/1
3033 5 hd **Extrasolar**[7] 6204 3-9-6 85 (t) PatDobbs 9 85
(Amanda Perrett) *hld up in midfield on outer: nt qckn whn pce lifted over 2f out: one pce after* 8/1
5410 6 ½ **Excuse To Linger**[29] 5489 3-9-6 85 (v) RichardHughes 3 84
(Jeremy Noseda) *stdd s: t.k.h and trckd ldng quartet: tried to cl 2f out: one pce over 1f out* 9/1
153 7 ½ **Elusive Hawk (IRE)**[7] 6215 9-9-3 81 (v) DeclanBates(3) 2 78
(David Evans) *hld up in 8th in modly run event: outpcd and no ch fr 2f out: styd on wl last 150yds* 20/1
5041 8 ¾ **Ocean Legend (IRE)**[16] 5928 8-9-4 79 LukeMorris 4 74
(Tony Carroll) *chsd ldng trio: rdn over 2f out: wknd fnl f* 16/1
0240 9 4 **Alnoomaas (IRE)**[7] 6204 4-9-0 75 JimmyFortune 8 60
(Luke Dace) *stdd s: hld up in last: lft bhd over 2f out: no prog after* 20/1

1m 25.95s (-0.05) **Going Correction** -0.10s/f (Stan)
WFA 3 from 4yo+ 4lb 9 Ran SP% 115.7
Speed ratings (Par 105): **96,95,95,93,93 92,91,91,86**
toteswingers 1&2 £6.90, 1&3 £4.40, 2&3 £3.20 CSF £22.91 CT £56.93 TOTE £4.90: £1.10, £2.00, £1.40; EX 28.60 Trifecta £63.10 Pool: £639.37 - 7.58 winning units..
Owner M H and Mrs G Tourle **Bred** M H And Mrs G Tourle **Trained** Pulborough, W Sussex

FOCUS
This fair handicap was another race on the night in which it paid to race near the pace. The winner rates a small personal best.

6404 BOOK NOW FOR JUMP SUNDAY 20.10.13 H'CAP 2m (P)
9:00 (9:00) (Class 6) (0-65,65) 3-Y-0+ £1,940 (£577; £288; £144) Stalls Low

Form RPR
3-55 1 **Superciliary**[31] 5403 4-9-5 56 PatDobbs 5 66
(Chris Gordon) *trckd ldrs: rdn to go 3rd 4f out: chsd ldr over 2f out: clsd to ld over 1f out: drvn fnl f: jst hld on* 20/1
-062 2 hd **Katie Gale**[37] 5197 3-8-1 51 oh1 (b) JimmyQuinn 1 60
(Tim Pitt) *trckd ldr: rdn and lost 2nd over 2f out: rallied to chse wnr jst over 1f out: chal last 100yds: jst hld* 11/2[3]
222 3 6 **Steely**[30] 5433 5-9-11 62 (v) RichardHughes 2 64
(Gary Moore) *led: stretched field out fr 4f out: rdn and hdd over 1f out: sn lost 2nd and fdd* 11/4[1]
313 4 1¼ **Neighbourhood (USA)**[103] 2922 5-9-11 62 (b) FergusSweeney 10 63
(James Evans) *racd wd early: hld up: dropped to last pair whn pce lifted over 4f out and sn plenty to do: prog over 3f out: wnt 4th over 2f out: kpt on but no ch* 7/1
0/0- 5 11 **Brabazon (IRE)**[71] 7791 10-9-12 63 (bt) AdamKirby 7 50
(Emmet Michael Butterly, Ire) *settled in last pair: urged along bnd 9f out: reminder 6f out: drvn to try to chse ldrs over 3f out: sn no imp: wknd 2f out* 12/1
3-16 6 5 **Entitlement**[220] 542 4-9-10 61 MartinLane 12 42
(James Fanshawe) *trckd ldrs: drvn 4f out: sn lost pl and btn* 3/1[2]
6045 7 ½ **Epsom Salts**[18] 5854 8-9-7 61 (p) JemmaMarshall(3) 11 42
(Pat Phelan) *s.i.s and pushed along early: effrt fr rr u.p 4f out: no imp over 2f out: sn fdd* 16/1
4252 8 34 **Keep Kicking (IRE)**[25] 5619 6-10-0 65 SebSanders 9 5
(Simon Dow) *sn in rr: last 1/2-way: stl there whn hmpd over 4f out: lost tch after: t.o* 8/1
305- 9 2½ **Jacob McCandles**[337] 7024 6-9-12 63 AidanColeman 8
(Shaun Lycett) *wl in tch tl wknd 4f out: t.o* 12/1
0606 10 25 **Parsons Green**[36] 5233 4-9-0 51 oh6 RobertHavlin 6
(Michael Attwater) *trckd ldr to 5f out: wknd rapidly: wl t.o* 50/1

3m 28.87s (-1.23) **Going Correction** -0.10s/f (Stan)
WFA 3 from 4yo+ 13lb 10 Ran SP% 118.7
Speed ratings (Par 101): **99,98,95,95,89 87,87,70,68,56**
toteswingers 1&2 £10.60, 1&3 £16.70, 2&3 £1.10 CSF £128.55 CT £407.31 TOTE £25.80: £5.80, £1.80, £1.60; EX 169.80 Trifecta £677.40 Part won. Pool: £903.24 - 0.21 winning units..
Owner David Henery **Bred** Prince Of Wales And Duchess Of Cornwall **Trained** Morestead, Hants

FOCUS
A moderate staying handicap, run at a fair enough pace. The winner stepped up on his previous efforts this year.
T/Plt: £75.40 to a £1 stake. Pool: £50,198.19 - 485.39 winning tickets T/Qpdt: £9.40 to a £1 stake. Pool: £6909.92 - 538.90 winning tickets JN

6110 LINGFIELD (L-H)
Saturday, September 14

OFFICIAL GOING: Straight course - soft; round course - soft (good to soft in places) changing to soft all over after race 1 (2.00)
Wind: light, half against Weather: overcast, dry

6405 YOUNG EPILEPSY H'CAP 1m 3f 106y
2:00 (2:00) (Class 5) (0-75,75) 3-Y-0+ £2,726 (£805; £402) Stalls High

Form RPR
-223 1 **Aloha**[61] 4352 3-8-10 67 DaneO'Neill 8 80
(Roger Varian) *t.k.h: chsd ldrs: effrt to chse ldr over 2f out: rdn to ld over 1f out: sn clr and styd on strly: comf* 4/1[2]
2130 2 3 **Rosie Rebel**[41] 5037 3-9-2 73 ChrisCatlin 7 80
(Rae Guest) *s.i.s: rdn along thrght: sme hdwy 7f out: swtchd rt and styd on over 2f out: wnt 3rd over 1f out: kpt on to go 2nd wl ins fnl f: no threat to wnr* 5/1
5211 3 1½ **Royal Alcor (IRE)**[7] 6216 6-9-2 70 DanielMuscutt(5) 3 75
(Gay Kelleway) *led: stl travelling wl 3f out: rdn and hdd over 1f out: no ex and plugged on same pce after: lost 2nd wl ins fnl f* 8/1
6444 4 5 **Perfect Delight**[26] 5587 4-9-3 66 JohnFahy 2 63
(Clive Cox) *racd off the pce in last trio: clsd 4f out: rdn and struggling 3f out: no ch w ldrs fnl 2f: kpt on past btn horses to go modest 4th ins fnl f* 14/1
1226 5 5 **Java Rose**[20] 5795 4-9-10 73 (p) FergusSweeney 4 62
(Henry Candy) *chsd ldrs: rdn over 3f out: struggling u.p over 2f out: 4th and wl btn over 1f out: wknd fnl f* 9/2[3]
4612 6 1¾ **First Secretary**[21] 5762 3-8-9 71 JoeyHaynes(5) 9 57
(Roger Charlton) *broke wl: t.k.h: hld up in tch in midfield: rdn and unable qck 3f out: btn whn swtchd rt 2f out: wknd* 7/2[1]
0420 7 8 **Bobbyscot (IRE)**[7] 6200 6-9-12 75 DougieCostello 6 48
(Gary Moore) *chsd ldr: rdn and no ex 3f out: sn lost 2nd and wknd: wl bhd and eased wl ins fnl f* 16/1
4254 8 8 **Knight's Parade (IRE)**[8] 6158 3-8-8 68 RobertTart(3) 1 33
(Amanda Perrett) *in tch in midfield: rdn 5f out: wknd u.p 3f out: wl bhd and eased wl ins fnl f: t.o* 8/1
4002 9 27 **Emman Bee (IRE)**[12] 6037 4-9-7 70 RichardHughes 5
(Luke Dace) *stdd s: hld up off the pce in last trio: clsd 5f out: rdn 3f out: sn btn and eased wl over 1f out: t.o* 20/1

2m 33.58s (2.08) **Going Correction** +0.30s/f (Good)
WFA 3 from 4yo+ 8lb 9 Ran SP% 116.6
Speed ratings (Par 103): **104,101,100,97,93 92,86,80,60**
toteswingers 1&2 £7.60, 1&3 £24.40, 2&3 £12.90 CSF £24.63 CT £153.27 TOTE £6.70: £2.60, £1.60, £2.80; EX 36.60 Trifecta £309.00 Pool: £426.69 - 1.03 winning units..
Owner Miss K Rausing **Bred** Miss K Rausing **Trained** Newmarket, Suffolk

FOCUS
A modest handicap to start the card and the pace looked ordinary.

6406 LEMO CONNECTIONS 40TH ANNIVERSARY H'CAP 1m 2f
2:30 (2:30) (Class 6) (0-60,59) 3-Y-0 £2,045 (£603; £302) Stalls Low

Form RPR
0345 1 **Sutton Sid**[30] 5002 3-9-1 53 (p) PatCosgrave 9 62
(Chris Gordon) *wnt lft s: rdn along leaving stalls: in tch in last trio: pushed along 7f out: rdn 5f out: responded to press and hdwy to ld 2f out: idling in front but a finding enough fnl f: rdn out* 6/1[3]
0-41 2 ½ **Ana Shababiya (IRE)**[25] 5615 3-9-5 57 HarryBentley 8 65
(Ismail Mohammed) *stdd and jostled leaving stalls: hld up in tch in rr: swtchd rt and effrt 3f out: hdwy to chse wnr over 1f out: kpt on u.p ins fnl f but a hld* 2/1[2]
3315 3 5 **Whitefall (USA)**[8] 6158 3-9-7 59 JimmyQuinn 1 58
(David Evans) *t.k.h: trckd ldrs: swtchd rt and jnd ldrs travelling wl over 2f out: rdn and fnd little 2f out: 3rd and outpcd whn drvn wl over 1f out: plugged on same pce after* 7/4[1]
6600 4 2½ **Lucilla**[5] 6260 3-9-2 54 AdamBeschizza 5 48
(Stuart Williams) *rdn along leaving stalls: in tch in last trio: drvn and struggling 3f out: wl hld 2f out: plugged on to go modest 4th ins fnl f* 20/1
2460 5 nse **Hawaiian Dream (IRE)**[38] 5135 3-9-5 57 RichardHughes 4 51
(Roger Teal) *chsd ldr: rdn over 3f out: no ex and btn 2f out: sn wknd* 16/1
4055 6 2½ **East Texas Red (IRE)**[18] 5870 3-8-13 51 DougieCostello 3 40
(Mick Quinn) *led: rdn and hdd 2f out: sn btn and wknd* 12/1

00-5 7 16 **Prairie Prince (IRE)**36 5233 3-8-5 48 DanielMuscutt(5) 2 7
(Gay Kelleway) *chsd ldrs tl rdn and lost pl qckly 3f out: bhd fnl 2f* **10/1**
2m 15.37s (4.87) **Going Correction** +0.475s/f (Yiel) 7 Ran SP% **111.4**
Speed ratings (Par 99): **99,98,94,92,92 90,77**
toteswingers 1&2 £4.90, 1&3 £2.50, 2&3 £1.10 CSF £17.48 CT £28.37 TOTE £9.50: £4.20, £1.50; EX 28.10 Trifecta £73.30 Pool: £611.65 - 6.25 winning units..
Owner Mrs Kate Digweed **Bred** Peter Hunt & Mrs Sally Hunt **Trained** Morestead, Hants
FOCUS
A poor handicap.

6407 SAVAGE & SONS ELECTRICAL MAIDEN STKS 1m 2f
3:05 (3:07) (Class 5) 3-Y-O £3,234 (£962; £481; £240) **Stalls** Low

Form RPR
45 1 **Gold Chain (IRE)**117 2519 3-9-0 0 JohnFahy 3 63+
(Clive Cox) *chsd ldr for 3f: styd chsd ldrs: effrt on inner to ld 2f out: rdn and qcknd wl clr 1f out: r.o strly: readily* **8/13**1
3-0 2 5 **Berkeley Street (USA)**103 2930 3-8-12 0 IanBurns(7) 5 58
(Jane Chapple-Hyam) *hld up in tch: effrt wl over 2f out: no ch w wnr and carried rt over 1f out: wnt 2nd ins fnl f: no imp* **7/1**3
0 3 3 **Violet Plum**102 2953 3-9-0 0 FergusSweeney 2 47?
(Laura Mongan) *led and set stdy gallop: rdn and hdd 2f out: outpcd and btn over 1f out: wknd and lost 2nd ins fnl f* **33/1**
400 4 ½ **Primo D'Oro (USA)**26 5588 3-9-5 0 RichardHughes 6 51
(Richard Hannon) *swtchd rt and racd wd tl 7f out: hld up in rr: hdwy to chse ldr 7f out tl 2f out: sn btn and hung rt: wknd* **2/1**2
2m 18.99s (8.49) **Going Correction** +0.475s/f (Yiel) 4 Ran SP% **110.7**
Speed ratings (Par 101): **85,81,78,78**
CSF £5.69 TOTE £1.50; EX 3.80 Trifecta £10.00 Pool: £611.65 - 6.25 winning units..
Owner Al Asayl Bloodstock Ltd **Bred** Sheikh Sultan Bin Khalifa Al Nahyan **Trained** Lambourn, Berks
FOCUS
Maidens for 3yos at this time of year don't come much less competitive than this. The pace was steady and the time was 3.62sec slower than the preceding handicap.

6408 EBF BREEDERS BACKING RACING MAIDEN FILLIES' STKS 5f
3:40 (3:40) (Class 5) 2-Y-O £3,067 (£905; £453) **Stalls** High

Form RPR
2 1 **Hipz (IRE)**16 5929 2-9-0 0 PatCosgrave 5 72+
(George Baker) *w ldr tl led 2f out: rdn and asserted over 1f out: pressed and drvn ins fnl f: a jst lasting home: rdn out* **3/1**2
63 2 hd **Pretty Flemingo (IRE)**10 6107 2-9-0 0 RichardHughes 10 71
(Richard Hannon) *led: rdn and hdd 2f out: sltly outpcd and looked hld over 1f out: rallied and pressing wnr ins fnl f: grad clsng towards fin* **10/11**1
0 3 6 **Arabian Sunset (IRE)**28 5529 2-9-0 0 FrederikTylicki 12 49
(Brendan Powell) *dwlt: in tch in rr: rdn and outpcd over 2f out: edging lft and rallied over 1f out: no ch w ldrs but kpt on to snatch 3rd last stride* **6/1**3
6 4 nse **Shirley Vanessa (IRE)**16 5929 2-8-9 0 JoeyHaynes(5) 2 49
(Luke Dace) *dwlt: sn in tch in midfield: chsd ldrs and rdn ent fnl 2f: outpcd and btn over 1f out: wknd ins fnl f: lost 3rd last stride* **33/1**
630 5 3 **Our Sherona**26 5584 2-9-0 59 JimmyQuinn 11 38
(Gary Harrison) *chsd ldrs: rdn and struggling ent fnl 2f: wknd over 1f out* **8/1**
6 nk **Divine Bay** 2-9-0 0 DougieCostello 4 37
(Gary Moore) *dwlt: in tch in rr: rdn and edgd lft over 2f out: sn struggling: wknd over 1f out* **14/1**
00 7 11 **Spirited Silver**9 6141 2-8-11 0 SimonPearce(3) 7
(John Bridger) *t.k.h: hld up in midfield: rdn and struggling 1/2-way: sn lost pl: wl bhd fnl f* **50/1**
1m 1.84s (3.64) **Going Correction** +0.70s/f (Yiel) 7 Ran SP% **114.3**
Speed ratings (Par 92): **98,97,88,88,83 82,65**
toteswingers 1&2 £1.20, 1&3 £15.70, 2&3 £1.50 CSF £6.08 TOTE £4.20: £2.40, £1.10; EX 8.20 Trifecta £29.80 Pool: £570.92 - 14.35 winning units..
Owner George Baker & Partners **Bred** Mrs Noelle Walsh **Trained** Manton, Wilts
FOCUS
A modest fillies' maiden hit by five non-runners and a race that only ever concerned the two form horses. Questionable depth to the race.

6409 CLIFFORD AND HELEN DEAR ANNIVERSARY MAIDEN AUCTION FILLIES' STKS 7f 140y
4:15 (4:18) (Class 6) 2-Y-O £2,045 (£603; £302) **Stalls** Centre

Form RPR
02 1 **Our Duchess (IRE)**15 5949 2-8-10 0 RichardHughes 9 76+
(Richard Hannon) *trckd ldrs: swtchd lft jst over 2f out: rdn to ld and edgd bk to stands' rail over 1f out: hld on gamely u.p fnl f: all out* **5/2**1
0 2 shd **Tullia (IRE)**22 5716 2-8-10 0 DaneO'Neill 3 76+
(William Knight) *chsd ldrs: rdn and effrt to chal over 1f out: ev ch after: r.o wl u.p: jst hld* **11/4**2
3 2 ¾ **Stosur (IRE)** 2-8-1 0 DanielMuscutt(5) 12 65
(Gay Kelleway) *dwlt: in tch in rr of main gp: swtchd lft and hdwy 5f out: rdn to chse ldng pair over 1f out: styd on same pce ins fnl f* **20/1**
60 4 8 **Christmas Wish**14 5988 2-8-7 0 SimonPearce(3) 7 50
(Mick Channon) *chsd ldr tl led over 2f out: rdn and hdd over 1f out: sn btn: wknd but hld on for modest 4th fnl f* **10/1**
3 5 nk **Duly Acclaimed (IRE)**11 6079 2-8-4 0 JimmyQuinn 13 43
(J S Moore) *in tch in rr of main gp: swtchd lft and hdwy u.p 2f out: no imp and btn over 1f out: wknd and battling for modest 4th fnl f* **8/1**
64 6 2 ¼ **Moonspring (IRE)**29 5488 2-8-8 0 FrederikTylicki 2 42
(Tobias B P Coles) *in tch in midfield: rdn and effrt ent fnl 2f: 6th and btn over 1f out: sn wknd* **8/1**
7 1 **Dalmarella Dancer (IRE)** 2-8-5 0 JoeyHaynes(5) 10 42
(K R Burke) *rn green: s.i.s: sn rcvrd and in tch in rr of main gp: swtchd lft and hmpd 2f out: sn rdn and btn* **9/2**3
00 8 6 **Craftybird**11 6079 2-8-8 0 HarryBentley 8 25
(Brett Johnson) *wl in tch in midfield: rdn and lost pl ent fnl 2f: sn btn: fdd over 1f out* **50/1**
9 1 ¾ **Fenella Foghorn** 2-8-9 0 MatthewLawson(3) 11 25
(Jonathan Portman) *hld up in tch in rr of main gp: swtchd lft and hdwy over 4f out: chsd ldrs and rdn ent fnl 2f: sn btn and fdd over 1f out* **25/1**
000 10 13 **Astral Rose**95 3174 2-8-8 52 WilliamCarson 14
(Jonathan Portman) *sn bustled along to ld: rdn and hdd over 2f out: sn dropped out: wl bhd and eased fnl f: t.o* **50/1**
11 1 **Jessy Mae** 2-8-6 0 ChrisCatlin 6
(Derek Haydn Jones) *restless in stalls: v.s.a: a wl bhd: t.o 1/2-way* **25/1**
12 14 **Macnamara** 2-8-12 0 DougieCostello 4
(Harry Dunlop) *rn green: bustled along and chsd ldrs for 3f sn dropped out: t.o fnl 2f* **20/1**
1m 37.85s (5.55) **Going Correction** +0.70s/f (Yiel) 12 Ran SP% **125.9**
Speed ratings (Par 90): **100,99,97,89,88 86,85,79,77,64 63,49**
toteswingers 1&2 £1.60, 1&3 £30.60, 2&3 £30.60 CSF £9.28 TOTE £3.00: £1.70, £2.10, £9.40; EX 11.40 Trifecta £237.50 Pool: £660.56 - 2.08 winning units..
Owner Chris Giles, Simon Brown, Potensis Ltd **Bred** International Equities Holding Inc **Trained** East Everleigh, Wilts
FOCUS
Another modest fillies' maiden dominated by the two market leaders. The first three were clear but there was little depth.

6410 FREDDIE PARKER WINNING FASHION CLAIMING STKS 7f 140y
4:50 (4:50) (Class 6) 3-Y-O £2,045 (£603; £302) **Stalls** Centre

Form RPR
3304 1 **Raging Bear (USA)**24 5632 3-8-11 73 (b) RichardHughes 2 76
(Richard Hannon) *stdd and bmpd s: t.k.h: hld up in tch: swtchd lft and rdn 2f out: chsd clr wnr jst ins fnl f: clsd relentlessly u.p to ld cl home: eased last strides* **6/4**1
1355 2 ¾ **Hartwright**29 5477 3-8-9 76 (v1) LouisSteward(7) 3 79
(Michael Bell) *wnt lft s: t.k.h: w ldr tl led 5f out: wnt clr 2f out: rdn over 1f out: kpt on but grad worn down and hdd cl home* **7/2**3
5-00 3 3 ¾ **Patrona Ciana (FR)**7 6208 3-8-13 81 DavidBergin(5) 1 72
(David O'Meara) *hld up in tch in last pair: rdn and effrt ent fnl 2f: chsd wnr wl over 1f out: no imp: lost 2nd and wknd ins fnl f* **9/2**
455 4 4 ½ **Krupskaya (FR)**35 5293 3-8-1 70 JoeyHaynes(5) 4 49
(K R Burke) *led tl 5f out: chsd ldr: rdn and unable qck ent fnl 2f: lost 2nd wl over 1f out: wknd ent fnl f* **11/4**2
1m 38.14s (5.84) **Going Correction** +0.70s/f (Yiel) 4 Ran SP% **107.1**
Speed ratings (Par 99): **98,97,93,89**
CSF £6.74 TOTE £1.60; EX 8.60 Trifecta £11.80 Pool: £737.07 - 46.67 winning units..Therre were no claims
Owner Hughes,Morecombe,Anderson,Netherthorpe **Bred** Liberation Farm **Trained** East Everleigh, Wilts
FOCUS
A tight claimer with just 4lb covering the four runners on these terms, but the time was slower than the preceding 2yo fillies' maiden, underlining the tactical nature of the contest.

6411 BRITISH STALLION STUDS EBF CONDITIONS STKS 7f
5:20 (5:20) (Class 4) 3-Y-O+ £6,469 (£1,925; £962; £481) **Stalls** High

Form RPR
1046 1 **Set The Trend**9 6129 7-9-5 100 (v1) RichardHughes 5 106
(David O'Meara) *chsd ldrs: rdn and effrt to chal over 1f out: sustained duel w three rivals fnl f: styd on wl to ld last stride* **7/1**
20 2 shd **Intibaah**41 5027 3-8-12 101 DaneO'Neill 4 103
(Brian Meehan) *t.k.h: hld up in tch in midfield: stmbld after 1f out: effrt u.p to chal over 1f out: led fnl 100yds: kpt on wl tl hdd last stride* **3/1**2
310 3 ½ **Grey Mirage**112 2649 4-8-11 94 (p) TobyAtkinson(5) 3 101
(Marco Botti) *led: rdn 2f out: battled on wl whn hrd pressed over 1f out: hdd fnl 100yds: no ex and one pce after* **6/1**3
6343 4 hd **Mar Mar (IRE)**49 4766 3-8-7 96 (b) FrederikTylicki 1 96
(Saeed bin Suroor) *stdd and dropped in bhd after s: hld up in last pair: rdn and effrt over 2f out: hdwy u.p to chal over 1f out: styd on same pce fnl 100yds* **11/4**1
065 5 ¾ **I'm So Glad**9 6143 4-8-11 89 ChrisCatlin 2 94
(Mick Channon) *hld up in tch in last pair: rdn and effrt ent fnl f: hdwy to chse ldrs 1f out: stuck bhd a wall of horses and no where to go fnl f: one pce* **16/1**
0033 6 5 **The Cheka (IRE)**19 5844 7-9-2 100 (v) DougieCostello 6 86
(Eve Johnson Houghton) *chsd ldrs: rdn over 2f out: little rspnse and sn struggling: wknd over 1f out* **3/1**2
1m 27.48s (4.18) **Going Correction** +0.70s/f (Yiel)
WFA 3 from 4yo+ 4lb 6 Ran SP% **109.3**
Speed ratings (Par 105): **104,103,103,103,102 96**
toteswingers 1&2 £1.90, 1&3 £4.30, 2&3 £4.30 CSF £26.60 TOTE £8.80: £3.40, £1.70; EX 26.40 Trifecta £223.40 Pool: £901.74 - 3.02 winning units..
Owner Corbett Stud **Bred** Old Suffolk Stud **Trained** Nawton, N Yorks
FOCUS
An interesting conditions event and a thrilling finish with four horses in a line half a furlong from home.

6412 ARC SUPPORTS RETRAINING OF RACEHORSES H'CAP 5f
5:50 (5:50) (Class 5) (0-70,70) 3-Y-O+ £2,726 (£805; £402) **Stalls** High

Form RPR
5146 1 **Monsieur Jamie**44 4930 5-9-7 70 (v) AidanColeman 3 81
(J R Jenkins) *hld up in tch in midfield: clsd to ld and travelling wl over 1f out: rdn and readily asserted 1f out: r.o wl: comf* **9/2**2
2304 2 2 ¾ **Indian Tinker**25 5620 4-9-1 67 RossAtkinson(3) 2 68+
(Robert Cowell) *rrd as stalls opened and slowly away: bhd: hdwy 1/2-way: rdn and effrt over 1f out: chsd clr wnr ins fnl f: r.o but no threat* **16/1**
0252 3 1 ¼ **Welease Bwian (IRE)**36 5221 4-8-10 59 FrederikTylicki 5 56
(Stuart Williams) *chsd ldrs: wnt 2nd over 3f out: rdn and unable qck w wnr ent fnl f: lost 2nd and one pce ins fnl f* **6/1**3
5103 4 ¾ **Catflap (IRE)**12 6040 4-8-11 60 DaneO'Neill 6 54
(Derek Haydn Jones) *taken down early and led to post: dwlt and pushed along early: in tch towards rr: hdwy and swtchd lft 2f out: rdn and effrt over 1f out: styd on same pce fnl f* **10/1**
-414 5 1 **Ladweb**29 5499 3-9-3 67 ChrisCatlin 10 57
(John Gallagher) *towards rr: swtchd lft 3f out: hdwy ent fnl 2f: drvn and no imp over 1f out: wl hld and one pce fnl f* **9/2**2
0603 6 4 ½ **Commandingpresence (USA)**5 6255 7-9-5 68 KieranO'Neill 7 42
(John Bridger) *chsd ldr tl over 3f out: lost pl and rdn 2f out: n.d and one pce fr over 1f out* **8/1**
1312 7 2 ¼ **Pucon**11 6077 4-9-7 70 RichardHughes 8 36
(Roger Teal) *led and crossed to r against stands' rail: rdn and hdd over 1f out: sn btn: fdd fnl f* **2/1**1
00-0 8 1 ¼ **Risky Rizkova**131 2098 3-8-9 62 MatthewLawson(3) 9 24
(Jonathan Portman) *in tch towards rr: rdn and racd awkwardly 3f out: n.d after* **20/1**
5-60 9 ½ **Bobby Two Shoes**35 5280 3-9-4 68 (v1) HarryBentley 1 28
(Brett Johnson) *s.i.s and sn rdn along in rr: n.d* **25/1**

The Form Book Flat, Raceform Ltd, Compton, RG20 6NL.

3041 **10** 1 1/4 **Novabridge**[19] 7143 5-9-0 **63**...(b) DougieCostello 4 18
(Neil Mulholland) *chsd ldrs: rdn and struggling ent fnl 2f: wknd over 1f out: wl btn whn hung lft and eased ins fnl f* **16/1**
1m 1.26s (3.06) **Going Correction** +0.70s/f (Yiel)
WFA 3 from 4yo+ 1lb **10** Ran SP% **124.6**
Speed ratings (Par 103): **103,98,96,95,93 86,83,81,80,78**
toteswingers 1&2 £10.00, 1&3 £6.40, 2&3 £15.30 CSF £78.99 CT £450.10 TOTE £5.60: £1.60, £6.10, £2.40; EX 72.40 Trifecta £839.80 Part won. Pool: £1119.83 - 0.74 winning units..
Owner Mark Goldstein **Bred** Greg Parsons **Trained** Royston, Herts
FOCUS
An ordinary sprint handicap nut the form could be worth a bit more. It rates a clear personal best from the winner.
T/Plt: £12.70 to a £1 stake. Pool: £54,402.36 - 3116.20 winning tickets T/Qpdt: £3.30 to a £1 stake. Pool: £2681.29 - 599.64 winning tickets SP

6413 - (Foreign Racing) - See Raceform Interactive

6020 CURRAGH (R-H)
Saturday, September 14

OFFICIAL GOING: Good (good to firm in places on round course; good to yielding in places on straight course)

6414a NEWBRIDGE GRASSROOTS FESTIVAL RENAISSANCE STKS (GROUP 3) 6f
2:25 (2:27) 3-Y-O+ **£31,707** (£9,268; £4,390; £1,463)

RPR
1 **Russian Soul (IRE)**[21] 5772 5-9-5 107.............................(p) ShaneFoley 12 110
(M Halford, Ire) *disp ld on rail: rdn whn chal over 1f out: r.o wl u.str.p ins fnl f to jst prevail* **7/1**
2 *nse* **Artistic Jewel (IRE)**[27] 5561 4-9-2 108................................ SeanLevey 2 107
(Ed McMahon) *prom: settled cl 3rd on outer: relegated to 4th bef 1/2-way: rdn to chal under 2f out: r.o wl to dispute ld u.p ins fnl f: jst denied* **7/2**[1]
3 *shd* **Farmleigh House (IRE)**[21] 5747 6-9-5 108.................... NGMcCullagh 8 110
(W J Martin, Ire) *chsd ldrs: wnt 3rd bef 1/2-way: rdn jst over 2f out: kpt on wl to dispute ld ent fnl f: r.o strly u.p: jst denied* **20/1**
4 *shd* **Scream Blue Murder (IRE)**[21] 5772 3-9-0 103............. FrankieDettori 6 106
(T Stack, Ire) *disp ld: rdn whn pressed for ld under 2f out: kpt on wl u.p fr 1f out: jst denied* **14/1**
5 3/4 **Balmont Mast (IRE)**[118] 2493 5-9-5 112...................... JohnnyMurtagh 4 107+
(Edward Lynam, Ire) *chsd ldrs: cl 6th 1/2-way: rdn under 2f out and outpcd: kpt on wl fr 1f out but no ex cl home* **11/2**[2]
6 *nk* **Cape Of Approval (IRE)**[90] 3380 4-9-5 107............................... WJLee 1 106+
(T Stack, Ire) *settled in rr of mid-div on outer: n.m.r bhd wall of horses over 1f out: sn taken to wd outside: r.o wl u.p cl home* **8/1**
7 *nk* **Hitchens (IRE)**[6] 6235 8-9-8 109.. FMBerry 5 108+
(David Barron) *chsd ldrs: cl 5th 1/2-way: pushed along over 2f out: r.o fr over 1f out but no ex cl home* **7/1**
8 *shd* **Cristoforo Colombo (USA)**[133] 2021 3-9-3 111...... SeamieHeffernan 3 105+
(A P O'Brien, Ire) *in rr of mid-div: pushed along 1/2-way: r.o wl u.p fr 1f out: nrst fin* **6/1**[3]
9 *nk* **Nocturnal Affair (SAF)**[21] 5772 7-9-5 100....................... GaryCarroll 13 104+
(David Marnane, Ire) *mid-div on rail: 8th 1/2-way: rdn wl over 1f out: r.o wl but n.m.r bhd wall of horses ins fnl f* **25/1**
10 *nk* **Dandy Boy (ITY)**[34] 5320 7-9-5 104.................................(t) FergalLynch 11 103+
(David Marnane, Ire) *bit slowly away: in rr: rdn 2f out: kpt on wl u.p ins fnl f: nvr nr to chal* **14/1**
11 5 1/2 **Maarek**[84] 3557 6-9-5 112.. RoryCleary 10 85+
(B Lalor, Ire) *in rr: rdn sn after 1/2-way: no imp and wknd appr fnl f* **6/1**[3]
12 4 3/4 **Rawaaq**[125] 2289 3-9-3 102... PatSmullen 7 70+
(D K Weld, Ire) *chsd ldrs: cl 7th 1/2-way: rdn over 2f out: no imp appr fnl f* **20/1**
13 1/2 **Scotland Forever (IRE)**[57] 4472 3-9-3 89.................. RonanWhelan 9 68+
(John Patrick Shanahan, Ire) *towards rr: rdn wl over 2f out: sn no imp on ldrs* **40/1**
1m 11.28s (-4.22) **Going Correction** -0.625s/f (Hard)
WFA 3 from 4yo+ 2lb **13** Ran SP% **131.4**
Speed ratings: **103,102,102,102,101 101,100,100,100,99 92,86,85**
CSF £33.53 TOTE £9.20: £2.10, £1.80, £7.50; DF 50.20.
Owner Mrs A G Kavanagh **Bred** Societe Civile De L'Ecurie De Meautry **Trained** Doneany, Co Kildare
FOCUS
A deep renewal but a bunchy finish and time wasn't great.

6416a LANWADES STUD BLANDFORD STKS (GROUP 2) (F&M) 1m 2f
3:35 (3:36) 3-Y-O+ **£52,845** (£15,447; £7,317; £2,439)

RPR
1 **Belle De Crecy (IRE)**[7] 6225 4-9-7 102...................... JohnnyMurtagh 2 112+
(J P Murtagh, Ire) *trckd ldr: clr of rest: 2 l 2nd 1/2-way: pushed into ld 3f out: qcknd clr: r.o wl u.p fr 2f out: kpt on strly ins fnl f* **16/1**
2 1 3/4 **Hot Snap**[42] 4985 3-9-0 113.. TomQueally 1 108+
(Lady Cecil) *chsd clr ldrs: modest 4th 1/2-way: rdn over 3f out: sn outpcd and dropped to 4th 2f out: 5th ent fnl f: rallied u.p ins fnl f to go 2nd cl home but no imp on wnr* **5/4**[1]
3 1 **Magical Dream (IRE)**[7] 6224 3-9-0 105.................... SeamieHeffernan 3 106+
(A P O'Brien, Ire) *hld up in mid-div: modest 6th 1/2-way: no room on rail 2f out and taken to outer: sme prog u.p ent fnl f: kpt on wl to go nvr threatening 3rd cl home* **25/1**
4 1 1/4 **Pearl Of Africa (IRE)**[13] 6023 3-9-0 104........................ FergalLynch 4 104
(Edward Lynam, Ire) *hld up in mid-div: modest 5th 1/2-way: rdn under 3f out and sn 3rd: kpt on same pce u.p but no imp ins fnl f: 4th cl home* **16/1**
5 1 **Purr Along**[25] 5629 3-9-0 109... FrankieDettori 5 102
(William Muir) *hld up in rr: rdn and gd prog fr 2f out to go 4th briefly ent fnl f: sn no ex u.p* **14/1**
6 *nk* **Princess Highway (USA)**[76] 3870 4-9-7 110.................... PatSmullen 8 101
(D K Weld, Ire) *chsd clr ldrs: 8 l 3rd 1/2-way: rdn 3f out to chse wnr: sn no imp and dropped to 6th cl home* **14/1**
7 20 **Alive Alive Oh**[130] 2141 3-9-0 107... FMBerry 7 61
(T Stack, Ire) *in rr: rdn fr 3f out: sn no rspnse: eased appr fnl f* **7/4**[2]
8 6 **Shirocco Star**[21] 5761 4-9-7 106...................................(b) ChrisHayes 6 49
(Hughie Morrison) *sn led: racd freely: hdd 3f out: rdn and sn wknd* **7/1**[3]
2m 4.75s (-4.55) **Going Correction** -0.025s/f (Good)
WFA 3 from 4yo 7lb **8** Ran SP% **122.3**
Speed ratings: **117,115,114,113,113 112,96,91**
CSF £39.27 TOTE £18.20: £2.20, £1.02, £6.30; DF 63.30.
Owner Andrew Tinkler **Bred** Liam Sheridan **Trained** Coolaghknock Glebe,Co Kildare
FOCUS
The winner has shown rapid progress in the two months since losing her maiden tag, and has been rated as running a big personal best. The standard is set by the third and fourth, with the time backing it up.

6417 - 6420a (Foreign Racing) - See Raceform Interactive

1231 FONTAINEBLEAU
Saturday, September 14

OFFICIAL GOING: Turf: very soft

6421a PRIX DES CHARMES (CLAIMER) (4YO+) (TURF) 1m 5f
6:00 (12:00) 4-Y-O+ **£7,723** (£3,089; £2,317; £1,544; £772)

RPR
1 **Kissavos**[44] 7-8-11 0... IoritzMendizabal 5 77
(Y Barberot, France) **92/10**
2 *hd* **Lord Emery (GER)**[83] 5-9-2 0.. UmbertoRispoli 6 82
(M Figge, Germany) **17/2**
3 *snk* **Incendo**[9] 6128 7-9-1 0.............................(b) Christophe-PatriceLemaire 13 81
(Ian Williams) *w.w in midfield on outer: 6th and travelling wl 3f out: rdn 2 1/2f out and styd on to chse ldrs over 1f out: r.o but briefly hung rt 75yds out: nvr quite on terms* **14/1**
4 1/2 **Roxy De Vindecy (FR)**[26] 5601 8-8-11 0...................... RonanThomas 2 76
(J Phelippon, France) **7/2**[2]
5 1 1/4 **Golden Beau (FR)**[30] 5-8-13 0 ow2..............(b) Pierre-CharlesBoudot 11 76
(J-P Delaporte, France) **27/1**
6 *hd* **Next Dream (FR)**[101] 6-8-11 0.. CristianDemuro 1 74
(P Monfort, France) **78/10**[3]
7 2 1/2 **Zillion Dollar Cup (FR)**[124] 5-9-4 0............................... AntoineHamelin 9 77
(F Cheyer, France) **26/1**
8 3/4 **Nostro Amico (GER)**[23] 4-9-1 0.. MaximeGuyon 7 73
(Mario Hofer, Germany) **5/2**[1]
9 *snk* **Hecate (IRE)**[105] 6-9-2 0.. ThomasMessina 8 74
(J E Pease, France) **12/1**
10 4 1/2 **Tartarin (IRE)**[44] 6-9-2 0.. BriceRaballand 3 67
(Mme C Head-Maarek, France) **19/1**
11 4 **Happy Monster (FR)**[19] 5-8-8 0..........................(p) ValentinGambart[(8)] 4 61
(M Boutin, France) **15/1**
12 2 **Uxia Du Lin (FR)** 5-8-3 0.................................(p) StephaneLaurent[(5)] 10 50
(J-P Trinquier, France) **112/1**
13 2 1/2 **Greatest (FR)**[79] 3750 4-9-1 0.. FabienLefebvre 12 53
(Mme G Rarick, France) **72/1**
(180.00) **13** Ran SP% **117.6**
WIN (incl. 1 euro stake): 10.20. PLACES: 3.50, 3.50, 5.00. DF: 37.50. SF: 109.40.
Owner Yann Barberot **Bred** Stilvi Compagnia Financiera **Trained** France

6422 - (Foreign Racing) - See Raceform Interactive

6376 BATH (L-H)
Sunday, September 15

OFFICIAL GOING: Good (good to firm in places; 8.7) changing to good after race 6 (4.50)
Wind: strong breeze against in relation to straight Weather: rain

6423 BATHWICK TYRES NEWPORT MEDIAN AUCTION MAIDEN FILLIES' STKS 5f 161y
2:10 (2:11) (Class 4) 2-Y-O **£3,752** (£1,116; £557; £278) **Stalls** Centre

Form RPR
0023 1 **Sleepy Sioux**[21] 5797 2-9-0 79.................................(b[1]) LiamKeniry 5 74
(David Elsworth) *led: rdn whn hdd and bmpd ent fnl f: rallied wl to regain ld fnl 75yds: rdn out* **9/2**[2]
2 *nk* **Miss Atomic Bomb** 2-9-0 0.. JamesDoyle 8 73
(Marco Botti) *trckd ldrs: rdn to chal wl over 1f out: edgd lft whn ldng ent fnl f: no ex whn hdd fnl 75yds* **5/1**[3]
3 1 **Perfect Pursuit** 2-8-9 0.. RyanTate[(5)] 2 70+
(Clive Cox) *towards rr: rdn and stdy prog fr 2f out: wnt 4th ins fnl f: r.o* **8/1**
6232 4 2 1/2 **Rough Courte (IRE)**[7] 6234 2-9-0 85............................. SamHitchcott 1 66
(Mick Channon) *s.i.s: sn mid-div: rdn over 2f out: kpt on to go 4th ins fnl f: nvr threatened* **11/8**[1]
60 5 1 3/4 **Katja**[16] 5949 2-9-0 0... PaulHanagan 10 56
(J W Hills) *mid-div: hdwy 2f out: sn rdn to chse ldrs: fdd ins fnl f* **25/1**
0 6 *hd* **Forest Glen (IRE)**[17] 5929 2-9-0 0.................................. DaneO'Neill 12 55
(Sylvester Kirk) *kpt on fnl f but nvr bttr than mid-div* **100/1**
7 3/4 **Thundering Cloud (IRE)** 2-9-0 0...................................... JackMitchell 7 53
(Brendan Powell) *trckd ldrs: rdn over 2f out: sn one pce* **33/1**
8 3 **Caroline's Beach (IRE)** 2-8-11 0.................... MichaelJMMurphy[(3)] 4 43
(J S Moore) *s.i.s: towards rr: nvr a threat* **40/1**
9 2 1/4 **Sutton Sioux** 2-9-0 0.. FergusSweeney 16 35
(Jeremy Gask) *prom: rdn over 2f out: wknd over 1f out* **20/1**
60 10 1 **Artemis (IRE)**[11] 6107 2-9-0 0.. CathyGannon 9 32
(Conrad Allen) *s.i.s: pushed along over 3f out: a towards rr* **33/1**
4 11 1 1/2 **Saxony**[90] 3408 2-9-0 0... DavidProbert 15 27
(Mark Usher) *prom tl rdn over 2f out: sn btn* **33/1**
02 P **Dandeena (IRE)**[25] 5646 2-9-0 0..................................... LukeMorris 6
(Ronald Harris) *p.u and dismntd after 1f* **8/1**
1m 11.48s (0.28) **Going Correction** -0.075s/f (Good) **12** Ran SP% **120.0**
Speed ratings (Par 94): **95,94,93,89,87 87,86,82,79,78 76,**
toteswingers 1&2 £7.10, 1&3 £10.20, 2&3 £8.20 CSF £25.72 TOTE £5.00: £1.80, £2.40, £2.60; EX 27.40 Trifecta £117.70 Pool: £1436.92 - 9.14 winning units..
Owner D R C Elsworth **Bred** New Hall Stud **Trained** Newmarket, Suffolk

FOCUS
Far side rail dolled out 4yds from 5f to just after 3f to provide fresh running line where sprint races meet the main track. No change to race distances. The ground remained good, good to firm in places with just a little light rain before racing. An ordinary fillies' maiden in which previous experience counted for plenty. The winner is rated roughly to form.

6424 BATHWICK TYRES GLOUCESTER H'CAP (THE SUNDAY £5K BONUS RACE) 2m 1f 34y
2:40 (2:40) (Class 4) (0-80,89) 4-Y-0+ **£4,690** (£1,395; £697; £348) **Stalls** Centre

Form RPR

2144 **1** **Eshtyaaq**[15] 5997 6-8-11 **70**.................................... CathyGannon 2 76
(David Evans) *t.k.h early: trckd ldr: rdn to chal 3f out: led over 2f out: sn strly chal: hdd ent fnl f: rallied gamely to ld towards fin: all out* **8/1**

2112 **2** *nk* **Chapter Five**[1] 6377 6-8-6 **65**.................................(p) PaulHanagan 10 71
(Ian Williams) *trckd ldrs: rdn 4f out: chal 2f out: led narrowly ent fnl f: kpt on but no ex whn hdd towards fin* **4/1**[1]

224 **3** *¾* **Presto Volante (IRE)**[18] 5895 5-9-7 **80**............................(p) PatDobbs 16 85
(Amanda Perrett) *trckd ldrs: rdn wl over 2f out: nt gng pce to chal: styd on ins fnl f* **8/1**

1220 **4** *½* **Our Folly**[37] 5231 5-8-12 **74**...........................(t) MichaelJMMurphy(3) 11 78+
(Stuart Kittow) *hld up towards rr: rn in snatches: rdn and prog fr over 2f out: styd on fnl f: wnt 4th fnl strides* **11/1**

012 **5** *hd* **Ampleforth**[18] 5879 5-8-11 **70**...............................(v) JamesDoyle 15 74
(Ian Williams) *mid-div: rdn over 3f out: hdwy over 1f out: styd on fnl f* **7/1**[3]

3115 **6** *hd* **Sunny Future (IRE)**[30] 5475 7-9-3 **76**.................... TomMcLaughlin 5 80+
(Malcolm Saunders) *hld up towards rr: rdn 3f out: no imp tl styd on fr over 1f out: keeping on wl towards fin* **14/1**

2362 **7** *nk* **Gabrial's King (IRE)**[15] 5997 4-9-7 **80**......................... SamHitchcott 13 84
(David Simcock) *s.i.s: towards rr: rdn 3f out: hdwy 2f out: ev ch ent fnl f: no ex fnl 100yds* **9/2**[2]

0401 **8** *½* **Laser Blazer**[16] 5954 5-9-2 **75**..................................(p) FergusSweeney 3 78
(Jeremy Gask) *hld up bhd: rdn and stdy prog whn swtchd to centre fr over 2f out: styd on tl no ex fnl 120yds* **16/1**

12-1 **9** *6* **Callisto Moon**[15] 2069 9-9-6 **79**.....................................(p) DaneO'Neill 17 75
(Jo Hughes) *led: rdn 3f out: hdd over 2f out: wknd ent fnl f* **10/1**

6236 **10** *½* **Filatore (IRE)**[15] 5997 4-8-8 **72**...............................(p) JoeyHaynes(5) 14 68
(Bernard Llewellyn) *mid-div: rdn over 3f out: sn btn* **10/1**

0-10 **11** *11* **Beyond (IRE)**[17] 4873 6-9-13 **89**.................(p) WilliamTwiston-Davies(3) 8 73
(David Pipe) *chsd ldrs: rdn 5f out: wknd over 2f out* **18/1**

115 **12** *1* **Tijori (IRE)**[15] 5997 5-8-3 **67**..(p) PhilipPrince(5) 1 50
(Bernard Llewellyn) *mid-div: rdn 4f out: sn btn* **33/1**

2021 **13** *42* **Honourable Knight (IRE)**[9] 6173 5-8-9 **68**..................... LiamKeniry 4 4
(Mark Usher) *mid-div: rdn over 4f out: sn wknd: virtually p.u* **14/1**

3m 50.16s (-1.74) **Going Correction** -0.075s/f (Good) **13** Ran SP% **126.8**
Speed ratings (Par 105): **101,100,100,100,100 100,99,99,96,96 91,91,71**
toteswingers 1&2 £23.70, 1&3 £4.60, 2&3 £13.20 CSF £42.51 CT £278.56 TOTE £10.40: £4.10, £3.00, £1.90; EX 66.90 Trifecta £859.20 Pool: £1374.01 - 1.19 winning units..
Owner Trevor Gallienne **Bred** P T Tellwright **Trained** Pandy, Monmouths

FOCUS
They didn't go much of a pace in this staying handicap and those who tried to come from well back faced an uphill task. The front eight finished in a heap, meaning the form is dubious.

6425 BATHWICK TYRES CARDIFF MAIDEN STKS 5f 11y
3:10 (3:10) (Class 4) 3-Y-0 **£4,690** (£1,395; £697; £348) **Stalls** Centre

Form RPR

3232 **1** **Rock Up (IRE)**[26] 5616 3-9-5 66.......................................(b) LiamKeniry 1 72
(David Elsworth) *led after 1f: rdn clr ent fnl f: readily* **4/1**[3]

2 *5* **Pucker Up** 3-9-0 0.. SeanLevey 4 49
(Ed McMahon) *s.i.s: trckd ldrs: tk clsr order over 2f out: rdn to chse wnr wl over 1f out: kpt on but readily hld ent fnl f* **6/4**[2]

4665 **3** *2* **Talqaa**[31] 5447 3-9-0 59... PaulHanagan 3 42
(Mick Channon) *led for 1f: trckd wnr: rdn over 2f out: lost 2nd wl over 1f out: kpt on same pce* **14/1**

22 **4** *1 ¾* **Teeline (IRE)**[25] 5647 3-9-0 0.. AhmedAjtebi 2 36
(Charlie Appleby) *trckd ldrs: rdn over 2f out: sn one pce* **11/8**[1]

1m 2.1s (-0.40) **Going Correction** -0.075s/f (Good) **4** Ran SP% **108.8**
Speed ratings (Par 103): **100,92,88,86**
CSF £10.42 TOTE £4.80; EX 11.20 Trifecta £26.30 Pool: £1127.42 - 32.00 winning units..
Owner Lordship Stud 1 **Bred** Martin Cullinane **Trained** Newmarket, Suffolk

FOCUS
A modest 3yo sprint maiden.

6426 BATHWICK TYRES BRISTOL FILLIES' NURSERY H'CAP 1m 5y
3:45 (3:48) (Class 4) (0-80,76) 2-Y-0 **£3,752** (£1,116; £557; £278) **Stalls** Low

Form RPR

003 **1** **Raajis (IRE)**[38] 5174 2-9-5 **74**... PaulHanagan 8 78+
(Richard Hannon) *wnt rt s: last but wl in tch: hdwy 2f out: sn rdn: chal jst ins fnl f: kpt on to ld on nod fnl strides* **5/2**[1]

412 **2** *hd* **Thewandaofu (IRE)**[102] 2993 2-9-2 **71**........................ FergusSweeney 7 74
(Jamie Osborne) *t.k.h: trckd ldr: rdn 2f out: chal over 1f out: led narrowly fnl 75yds: kpt on: hdd fnl strides* **6/1**

3430 **3** *½* **Ding Ding**[3] 6322 2-8-0 **55** oh1.. CathyGannon 6 57
(Mick Channon) *led: rdn 2f out: hrd pressed ent fnl f: hdd fnl 75yds: kpt on gamely* **10/1**

053 **4** *1 ¾* **Habdab**[20] 5812 2-9-2 **71**.. PatDobbs 3 69
(Richard Hannon) *in tch: rdn over 2f out: kpt on but nt pce to threaten* **7/1**

034 **5** *hd* **Tubeanie (IRE)**[31] 5442 2-8-3 **63**.................................. RyanTate(5) 4 61
(Clive Cox) *trckd ldrs: rdn over 2f out: kpt on but nt pce to chal* **11/4**[2]

0604 **6** *nse* **Maysville (IRE)**[13] 6035 2-8-1 **56**...................................... LukeMorris 5 53
(Charles Hills) *trckd ldrs: rdn over 2f out: kpt on same pce* **8/1**

055 **P** **Ultraviolet (IRE)**[15] 5988 2-9-0 **69**..................................... JamesDoyle 2
(David Simcock) *in tch tl p.u over 3f out: dismntd* **4/1**[3]

1m 42.97s (2.17) **Going Correction** +0.075s/f (Good) **7** Ran SP% **122.2**
Speed ratings (Par 94): **92,91,91,89,89 89,**
toteswingers 1&2 £3.40, 1&3 £4.40, 2&3 £6.70 CSF £19.73 CT £134.03 TOTE £3.70: £1.80, £2.30; EX 21.10 Trifecta £89.50 Pool: £2033.58 - 17.02 winning units..
Owner Hamdan Al Maktoum **Bred** Yeomanstown Stud **Trained** East Everleigh, Wilts

FOCUS
The rain returned before this contest. Five of the seven runners were making their nursery debuts on their fourth starts. Despite the pace looking solid, there wasn't much covering the six finishers at the line. Straightforward form with a minor personal best from the winner.

6427 BATHWICK TYRES SOMERSETSHIRE CONDITIONS STKS 1m 5y
4:20 (4:20) (Class 3) 3-Y-0+ **£7,762** (£2,310; £1,154; £577) **Stalls** Low

Form RPR

5162 **1** **Mister Music**[8] 6199 4-8-13 99..................(b) WilliamTwiston-Davies(3) 5 94
(Richard Hannon) *in tch: hdwy wl over 2f out: sn rdn: str chal fr jst over 1f out: kpt on to ld on nod fnl stride* **7/1**[3]

322 **2** *nse* **Boom And Bust (IRE)**[21] 5794 6-9-2 108........................ GeorgeBaker 6 94
(Marcus Tregoning) *trckd ldr: rdn to chal 2f out: led narrowly jst over 1f out: kpt on: hdd on nod fnl stride* **8/11**[1]

63 **3** *¾* **Bancnuanaheireann (IRE)**[43] 5007 6-9-2 90.............. AndrewMullen 7 92
(Michael Appleby) *s.i.s: last but in tch: hdwy on outer over 3f out: sn rdn: chal jst over 1f out: ev ch fnl f: no ex nring fin* **12/1**

0535 **4** *1 ¾* **Verse Of Love**[16] 5943 4-9-2 83...................................... CathyGannon 4 88
(David Evans) *trckd ldrs: rdn over 2f out: kpt on but nt pce to chal* **50/1**

2246 **5** *nk* **Highland Knight (IRE)**[8] 6191 6-9-9 108........................(t) DavidProbert 3 94
(Andrew Balding) *led: rdn whn pressed jst over 2f out: hdd jst over 1f out: kpt on same pce* **4/1**[2]

1-10 **6** *36* **Now Spun (USA)**[169] 1264 3-9-4 108............................ AhmedAjtebi 2
(Charlie Appleby) *t.k.h in tch: rdn over 3f out: wknd qckly: virtually p.u* **7/1**[3]

1m 40.13s (-0.67) **Going Correction** +0.075s/f (Good)
WFA 3 from 4yo+ 5lb **6** Ran SP% **112.6**
Speed ratings (Par 107): **106,105,105,103,103 67**
toteswingers 1&2 £2.90, 1&3 £7.30, 2&3 £2.30 CSF £12.75 TOTE £6.20: £2.60, £1.30; EX 17.80 Trifecta £84.90 Pool: £2431.42 - 21.46 winning units..
Owner Longview Stud & Bloodstock Ltd **Bred** Longview Stud & Bloodstock Ltd **Trained** East Everleigh, Wilts

■ Stewards' Enquiry : Andrew Mullen two-day ban: used whip above permitted level (Sep 29-30)

FOCUS
An interesting conditions event.

6428 BATHWICK TYRES SUPPORTING BATH RACECOURSE H'CAP 1m 2f 46y
4:50 (4:50) (Class 4) (0-85,82) 3-Y-0+ **£4,690** (£1,395; £697; £348) **Stalls** Low

Form RPR

321 **1** **Croquembouche (IRE)**[34] 5348 4-9-6 **81**..................... MarkCoumbe(3) 4 89
(Ed de Giles) *sn led: rdn 2f out: styd on strly to assert fnl 120yds* **9/2**[3]

5560 **2** *1 ¾* **Dandy (GER)**[15] 6004 4-8-13 **71**.................................(v) CathyGannon 8 76
(Andrew Balding) *trckd ldrs: rdn jst over 2f out: ev ch ent fnl f: no ex fnl 120yds* **9/1**

5026 **3** *½* **The Cayterers**[2] 6353 11-9-7 **79**.. LukeMorris 7 83
(Ronald Harris) *hld up in tch: effrt over 2f out: styd on same pce fnl f* **8/1**

0060 **4** *hd* **Ed De Gas**[43] 5006 4-9-10 **82**.. DavidProbert 3 85
(Rae Guest) *hld up: hdwy whn nt clrest of runs briefly over 1f out: sn swtchd lft and rdn: kpt on but nt pce to get involved* **3/1**[1]

3160 **5** *1 ¾* **Tuscan Fun**[49] 4810 3-8-10 **75**....................................(b[1]) DaneO'Neill 6 75
(Roger Varian) *trckd ldr: rdn over 2f out: nt quite pce to mount chal: no ex fnl f* **3/1**[1]

0000 **6** *1 ½* **Nazreef**[8] 6199 6-8-12 **70**...(v) SeanLevey 5 67
(Hughie Morrison) *trckd ldrs: rdn 3f out: wknd fnl f* **16/1**

-150 **7** *3* **Derwent (USA)**[83] 3633 3-9-3 **82**.....................................(b) JamesDoyle 2 73
(Roger Charlton) *hld up in last pair: effrt to chse ldrs over 2f out: wknd fnl f* **7/2**[2]

2m 11.87s (0.87) **Going Correction** +0.225s/f (Good)
WFA 3 from 4yo+ 7lb **7** Ran SP% **117.4**
Speed ratings (Par 105): **105,103,103,103,101 100,98**
toteswingers 1&2 £4.40, 1&3 £4.70, 2&3 £7.10 CSF £44.79 CT £317.52 TOTE £4.00: £1.80, £4.10; EX 47.00 Trifecta £126.70 Pool: £2452.66 - 14.51 winning units..
Owner John Manser **Bred** Ballymacoll Stud Farm Ltd **Trained** Ledbury, H'fords

FOCUS
A fair handicap run in unpleasant conditions, but a game front-running performance from the winner.

6429 BATHWICK TYRES BRIDGEND H'CAP 5f 11y
5:20 (5:20) (Class 4) (0-85,84) 3-Y-0 **£4,690** (£1,395; £697; £348) **Stalls** Centre

Form RPR

0510 **1** **Secret Missile**[30] 5477 3-9-1 **78**..................................... DaneO'Neill 10 84
(William Muir) *last but in tch: pushed along over 3f out: sltly outpcd over 2f out: hdwy over 1f out: r.o wl ins fnl f: led fnl strides* **11/4**[2]

2530 **2** *nse* **The Art Of Racing (IRE)**[43] 4989 3-9-6 **83**..................(t) HarryBentley 3 89
(Olly Stevens) *trckd ldrs: rdn to ld narrowly over 1f out: kpt on: hdd fnl strides* **9/4**[1]

2135 **3** *½* **Daylight**[60] 4413 3-9-0 **77**..(t) JimmyFortune 1 81
(Andrew Balding) *trckd ldrs: rdn to chal jst over 2f out: led narrowly v briefly over 1f out: kpt on w ev ch tl no ex nring fin* **7/2**[3]

1001 **4** *2 ¼* **Space Artist (IRE)**[15] 5996 3-9-4 **81**........................ RoystonFfrench 4 77
(Bryan Smart) *trckd ldrs: rdn wl over 2f out: kpt on fnl f but nvr gng pce to threaten* **11/4**[2]

4050 **5** *hd* **Ask The Guru**[15] 5998 3-9-2 **79**..................................(v) LukeMorris 8 74
(Michael Attwater) *led: rdn 2f out: hdd over 1f out: kpt on same pce* **8/1**

1m 3.3s (0.80) **Going Correction** +0.225s/f (Good) **5** Ran SP% **117.4**
Speed ratings (Par 103): **102,101,101,97,97**
CSF £10.07 TOTE £3.90: £2.50, £1.80; EX 10.00 Trifecta £32.50 Pool: £1596.69 - 36.83 winning units..
Owner Muir Racing Partnership - Manchester **Bred** Whitsbury Manor Stud **Trained** Lambourn, Berks

■ Stewards' Enquiry : Dane O'Neill two-day ban: used whip above permitted level (Sep 29-30)

FOCUS
The ground was changed to Good before this race, in which only half of the ten declared runners finally made it to post. For the first time in the afternoon the jockeys decided to make for the nearside of the track.

T/Jkpt: £46,474.70 to a £1 stake. Pool: £130,914.91 - 2.0 winning tickets T/Plt: £470.40 to a £1 stake. Pool: £96,852.02 - 150.28 winning tickets T/Qpdt: £30.10 to a £1 stake. Pool: £5713.03 - 140.37 winning tickets TM

[6040]FFOS LAS (L-H)

Sunday, September 15

OFFICIAL GOING: Soft changing to heavy after race 3 (3.30)

Wind: Blustery Weather: Raining

6430 BLUEBELL RECRUITMENT/BRITISH STALLION STUDS E B F MAIDEN STKS — 1m (R)

2:25 (2:25) (Class 5) 2-Y-O — £2,911 (£866; £432; £216) Stalls Low

Form — RPR

02 **1** **Hartnell**[16] 5968 2-9-2 0 DeclanBates(3) 6 — 80
(Mark Johnston) *trckd ldr tl led over 1f out: shkn up and sn clr: edgd lft ins fnl f: comf* 15/8[2]

4 **2** 4 **Monsea (IRE)**[8] 6184 2-9-5 0 SteveDrowne 8 — 71
(Richard Hannon) *chsd ldrs: rdn and ev ch over 1f out: styd on same pce* 1/1[1]

3 3 1/4 **Ultimate Act** 2-9-5 0 ShaneKelly 7 — 64
(Seamus Mullins) *led: clr 1/2-way: rdn and hdd over 1f out: wknd fnl f* 40/1

4 11 **Trendsetter (IRE)** 2-9-5 0 JimCrowley 4 — 40
(David Simcock) *prom: rdn over 2f out: wknd over 1f out* 10/1

0 **5** 1 1/4 **Glasgow Central**[43] 4987 2-9-5 0 RobertWinston 2 — 37
(Charles Hills) *prom: pushed along 5f out: wknd 3f out* 7/1[3]

6 7 **Eugenic** 2-9-5 0 DougieCostello 1 — 22
(Rod Millman) *s.i.s: hld up: pushed along 1/2-way: wknd over 2f out* 33/1

7 2 1/4 **Orange Grove** 2-9-5 0 MartinLane 3 — 17
(Tobias B P Coles) *hld up: effrt over 3f out: sn wknd* 25/1

8 6 **Severn Crossing** 2-9-5 0 MartinDwyer 5
(William Muir) *s.i.s: hld up: t.k.h: pushed along 5f out: bhd fr 1/2-way* 20/1

1m 49.07s (8.07) **Going Correction** +0.95s/f (Soft) — **8** Ran SP% **120.4**

Speed ratings (Par 95): **97,93,89,78,77 70,68,62**

toteswingers 1&2 £1.10, 1&3 £13.70, 2&3 £12.30 CSF £4.18 TOTE £2.90: £1.10, £1.10, £5.90; EX 5.00 Trifecta £122.30 Pool: £2296.51 - 14.08 winning units..

Owner Sheikh Hamdan Bin Mohammed Al Maktoum **Bred** Darley **Trained** Middleham Moor, N Yorks

FOCUS

Testing ground after persistent rain and miserable conditions all round, so hardly ideal circumstances for inexperienced two-year-olds, five of whom were seeing a racecourse for the first time. The winning time of this opener was over 11secs slower than RP Standard, confirming the ground to be bordering on heavy. No surprise then that they finished strung out like 3m chasers. Tricky form to pin down and a cautious approach has been taken.

6431 SAXTON DRILLING LTD MAIDEN STKS — 1m (R)

2:55 (2:57) (Class 4) 3-Y-O+ — £4,690 (£1,395; £697; £348) Stalls Low

Form — RPR

04 **1** **Defiant Spirit**[20] 5845 3-9-5 0 SteveDrowne 2 — 73
(Roger Charlton) *led 1f: chsd ldr: led again over 1f out: styd on wl* 3/1[2]

2 2 **Crow Down (IRE)**[67] 4-9-10 0 RobertWinston 5 — 68
(Charles Hills) *sn pushed along and prom: rdn to chse wnr fnl f: styd on* 12/1

3 3 1/4 **Modem** 3-9-5 0 MartinDwyer 1 — 61
(Rod Millman) *in rr: hdwy to ld over 2f out: hdd over 1f out: wknd ins fnl f* 11/1[3]

5/3 **4** 4 1/2 **Life And Times (USA)**[9] 6178 5-9-10 0 MartinLane 4 — 51
(Mark Johnston) *led 7f out: rdn and hdd over 2f out: wknd over 1f out* 8/15[1]

5 4 1/2 **Zara's Boy (IRE)**[559] 5-9-10 0 DougieCostello 3 — 40
(Evan Williams) *chsd ldr 7f out tl rdn 3f out: wknd 2f out* 25/1

1m 51.7s (10.70) **Going Correction** +1.225s/f (Soft)

WFA 3 from 4yo+ 5lb — **5** Ran SP% **110.1**

Speed ratings (Par 105): **95,93,89,85,80**

CSF £32.03 TOTE £3.70: £1.60, £4.10; EX 24.40 Trifecta £79.30 Pool: £1987.29 - 18.77 winning units..

Owner D Carter and P Inglett **Bred** Whatton Manor Stud **Trained** Beckhampton, Wilts

FOCUS

A modest maiden and the form is devalued by the disappointing performance of Life And Times, who set the standard.

6432 FELINFOEL IPA NURSERY H'CAP — 5f

3:30 (3:32) (Class 4) (0-85,79) 2-Y-O — £3,752 (£1,116; £557; £278) Stalls Centre

Form — RPR

2142 **1** **Bounty Hunter (IRE)**[19] 5858 2-9-7 79 (p) JimCrowley 3 — 83
(Tom Dascombe) *mde all in centre: shkn up over 1f out: styd on wl* 6/4[1]

2332 **2** 2 1/2 **Urban Dreamer (IRE)**[16] 5955 2-8-10 73 OisinMurphy(5) 1 — 68
(Rod Millman) *trckd wnr centre: rdn and edgd rt over 1f out: styd on same pce: last of 2 in gp* 3/1[3]

5414 **3** 8 **Intense Feeling (IRE)**[1] 6386 2-8-11 72 DeclanBates(3) 5 — 38
(David Evans) *swtchd to chse ldr stands' side 4f out: rdn 1/2-way: led that pair but wknd over 1f out: 1st of 2 that side* 2/1[2]

2051 **4** 9 **Go Glamorous (IRE)**[17] 5929 2-9-4 76 SteveDrowne 6 — 10
(Ronald Harris) *led stands' side: pushed along 1/2-way: hdd & wknd over 1f out: eased: last of 2 that side* 6/1

1m 4.68s (6.38) **Going Correction** +1.225s/f (Soft) — **4** Ran SP% **112.6**

Speed ratings (Par 97): **97,93,80,65**

CSF £6.53 TOTE £1.90; EX 6.60 Trifecta £11.30 Pool: £2006.64 - 132.17 winning units..

Owner D Ward **Bred** B Holland, S Hillen & J Cullinan **Trained** Malpas, Cheshire

FOCUS

They split into two pairs here and a slightly negative view has been taken of the form.

6433 DOUBLE DRAGON "NATIONAL ALE OF WALES" FILLIES' H'CAP — 1m 2f (R)

4:00 (4:00) (Class 4) (0-80,80) 3-Y-O+ — £4,690 (£1,395; £697; £348) Stalls Low

Form — RPR

1-44 **1** **Singersongwriter**[130] 2160 3-8-13 74 MartinLane 5 — 83+
(Ed Dunlop) *s.i.s: rcvrd to ld 8f out: shkn up over 1f out: kpt on* 15/8[1]

3130 **2** 1/2 **Rosaceous**[32] 5402 3-9-5 80 SteveDrowne 7 — 88
(Daniel Kubler) *a.p: pushed along over 3f out: chsd wnr ins fnl f: styd on* 8/1

0005 **3** 5 **Steer By The Stars (IRE)**[8] 6210 3-8-10 74 DeclanBates(3) 8 — 73
(Mark Johnston) *hld up: hdwy over 2f out: rdn over 1f out: no ex ins fnl f* 13/2

2412 **4** 6 **Play Street**[52] 4678 4-9-5 76 MatthewLawson(3) 3 — 64
(Jonathan Portman) *chsd ldr: rdn over 2f out: wknd fnl f* 8/1

4422 **5** 2 1/2 **Fatima's Gift**[32] 5411 3-8-11 72 JimCrowley 4 — 56
(David Simcock) *prom: rdn over 3f out: wknd 2f out* 5/1[3]

1-66 **6** 11 **Croeso Mawr**[93] 3269 7-9-1 69 MartinDwyer 2 — 33
(John Spearing) *hld up: rdn over 3f out: wknd over 2f out: eased* 18/1

-000 **7** 40 **Creme Anglaise**[21] 5795 5-9-4 79 LouisSteward(7) 6
(Michael Bell) *hld up: rdn over 3f out: sn wknd and eased* 9/2[2]

5652 **8** 24 **Mystical Moment**[38] 5173 3-8-10 71 (p) KieranO'Neill 1
(Richard Hannon) *hld up: pushed along 1/2-way: wknd over 3f out* 12/1

2m 21.12s (11.72) **Going Correction** +1.225s/f (Soft)

WFA 3 from 4yo+ 7lb — **8** Ran SP% **118.1**

Speed ratings (Par 102): **102,101,97,92,90 82,50,30**

toteswingers 1&2 £6.40, 1&3 £5.20, 2&3 £10.50 CSF £18.68 CT £83.72 TOTE £2.80: £1.20, £3.20, £2.10; EX 24.80 Trifecta £140.70 Pool: £2579.14 - 13.74 winning units..

Owner Cliveden Stud **Bred** Cliveden Stud Ltd **Trained** Newmarket, Suffolk

FOCUS

The ground was officially changed to heavy before this contest. Despite the fact they looked to go very steady early on it turned into a real war of attrition in the straight and over half the field were well beaten off by the two pole.

6434 CASTELL HOWELL FOOD SERVICES H'CAP (THE SUNDAY £5K BONUS RACE) — 1m 4f (R)

4:35 (4:35) (Class 3) (0-95,94) 3-Y-O+ — £7,439 (£2,213; £1,106; £553) Stalls Low

Form — RPR

4200 **1** **Miss Cap Estel**[21] 5795 4-8-9 82 OisinMurphy(5) 1 — 94
(Andrew Balding) *trckd ldrs: led over 3f out: sn clr: easily* 10/3[2]

3214 **2** 12 **Divergence (IRE)**[22] 5764 3-8-1 85 LouisSteward(7) 6 — 74
(Michael Bell) *trckd ldr: rdn and edgd rt over 2f out: sn btn* 8/11[1]

6200 **3** 23 **Solaras Exhibition (IRE)**[63] 3115 5-8-7 80 DanielMuscutt(5) 7 — 35
(Tim Vaughan) *s.i.s: sn prom: pushed along over 5f out: sn wknd* 7/1

2400 **4** 57 **Pitchoun (IRE)**[16] 5944 3-8-8 85 MartinDwyer 5
(Mark Johnston) *led over 8f: sn wknd* 11/2[3]

2m 53.3s (15.90) **Going Correction** +1.225s/f (Soft)

WFA 3 from 4yo+ 9lb — **4** Ran SP% **108.9**

Speed ratings (Par 107): **96,88,72,34**

CSF £6.34 TOTE £4.90; EX 6.80 Trifecta £13.00 Pool: £1284.49 - 74.08 winning units..

Owner J L C Pearce **Bred** J L C Pearce **Trained** Kingsclere, Hants

FOCUS

This turned into a procession.

6435 FELINFOEL CELTIC PRIDE H'CAP — 1m 4f (R)

5:05 (5:06) (Class 5) (0-70,70) 3-Y-O+ — £2,587 (£770; £384; £192) Stalls Low

Form — RPR

5430 **1** **Layline (IRE)**[11] 6108 6-9-4 67 DanielMuscutt(5) 2 — 78+
(Gay Kelleway) *trckd ldrs: led on bit over 2f out: shkn up over 1f out: styd on: eased nr fin* 10/1

-320 **2** 1 1/2 **Candyman Can (IRE)**[19] 5854 3-8-9 69 JoshBaudains(7) 12 — 76
(Dominic Ffrench Davis) *a.p: rdn over 3f out: styd on same pce ins fnl f* 9/2[3]

4335 **3** nk **Ivanhoe**[26] 5612 3-8-11 64 (p) SteveDrowne 9 — 71
(Michael Blanshard) *chsd ldrs: rdn over 2f out: styd on same pce ins fnl f* 7/2[1]

5034 **4** 7 **Hero's Story**[11] 6109 3-8-7 60 (p) JimCrowley 3 — 57
(Amanda Perrett) *chsd ldr tl led over 3f out: rdn and hdd over 2f out: wknd fnl f* 9/2[3]

436 **5** shd **Jebril (FR)**[107] 2846 3-9-3 70 ShaneKelly 8 — 67
(Jonathan Portman) *s.i.s: hld up: hdwy over 3f out: rdn and wknd over 1f out* 4/1[2]

250 **6** 1 1/2 **Pandorica**[32] 5390 5-9-9 67 (p) MartinLane 1 — 64
(Bernard Llewellyn) *led: rdn and hdd over 3f out: wknd fnl f: eased* 20/1

460 **7** 18 **Rancho Montoya (IRE)**[18] 5892 3-8-12 65 (p) MartinDwyer 5 — 34
(Andrew Balding) *hld up: rdn and wknd over 3f out* 10/1

1-60 **8** 2 **Kayalar (IRE)**[14] 4914 5-9-10 68 DougieCostello 7 — 35
(Evan Williams) *s.i.s: hld up: pushed along over 4f out: sn wknd* 28/1

06- **9** 8 **Sublime Talent (IRE)**[118] 771 7-9-3 66 (t) ThomasGarner(5) 4 — 21
(Evan Williams) *hld up: rdn and wknd over 3f out* 28/1

6605 **10** 6 **Carazam (IRE)**[35] 5302 6-9-7 70 (t) RobertWilliams(5) 6 — 17
(Bernard Llewellyn) *hld up: sme hdwy over 4f out: wknd over 3f out* 20/1

650- **11** 20 **In The Crowd (IRE)**[147] 4250 4-9-2 65 OisinMurphy(5) 11
(Richard Price) *prom tl rdn and wknd over 4f out* 16/1

2m 51.89s (14.49) **Going Correction** +1.225s/f (Soft)

WFA 3 from 4yo+ 9lb — **11** Ran SP% **119.1**

Speed ratings (Par 103): **100,99,98,94,94 93,81,79,74,70 57**

toteswingers 1&2 £9.90, 1&3 £8.90, 2&3 £3.90 CSF £52.54 CT £191.55 TOTE £10.10: £3.40, £2.00, £1.70; EX 69.60 Trifecta £221.10 Pool: £2064.57 - 7.00 winning units..

Owner M Bartram, R Smith & N Scandrett **Bred** Mrs M E Slade **Trained** Exning, Suffolk

FOCUS

This looked wide open on paper.

6436 FELINFOEL DRAGON STOUT H'CAP — 5f

5:35 (5:39) (Class 6) (0-60,61) 3-Y-O+ — £1,940 (£577; £288; £144) Stalls Centre

Form — RPR

0/54 **1** **Coalburn**[14] 6017 5-8-4 46 oh1 (v[1]) SimonPearce(3) 3 — 56
(Gary Harrison) *chsd ldrs: rdn 1/2-way: led ins fnl f: edgd lft: r.o* 18/1

4530 **2** 1 3/4 **Madame Kintyre**[24] 5670 5-8-11 50 MartinDwyer 4 — 54
(Rod Millman) *led: hdd over 3f out: chsd ldrs: led again over 1f out: rdn: hdd and unable qck ins fnl f* 12/1

5320 **3** 1/2 **Coconut Kisses**[25] 5644 3-9-6 60 KieranO'Neill 11 — 62
(Bill Turner) *chsd ldrs: rdn over 1f out: edgd lft: styd on* 10/1

5600 **4** 2 1/4 **Camache Queen (IRE)**[24] 5674 5-9-7 60 (tp) RobertWinston 9 — 54
(Joseph Tuite) *sn pushed along and prom: rdn over 1f out: no ex fnl f* 15/2

5420 **5** 3/4 **Gracie's Games**[8] 6219 7-8-11 50 (b) MartinLane 15 — 41
(John Spearing) *sn pushed along in rr: hdwy u.p over 1f out: nt trble ldrs* 5/1[2]

0603 **6** 1 1/2 **Ficelle (IRE)**[9] 6155 4-8-4 48 (b[1]) OisinMurphy(5) 10 — 34
(Ronald Harris) *sn pushed along in rr: styd on ins fnl f: nvr nrr* 5/1[2]

6-00 **7** nk **Cashel's Missile (IRE)**[20] 5818 3-8-3 50 LouisSteward(7) 6 — 35
(John Spearing) *chsd ldrs: led over 3f out tl rdn and hdd over 1f out: wknd ins fnl f* 28/1

0060 **8** 3/4 **Superior Edge**[9] 6156 6-8-13 57 (p) DanielMuscutt(5) 8 — 39
(Christopher Mason) *sn pushed along in rr: hdwy and swtchd rt 1/2-way: sn rdn: wknd fnl f* 14/1

0641 **9** 2 **Beach Rhythm (USA)**[19] 5864 6-8-10 52 (v) DeclanBates(3) 5 — 27
(Jim Allen) *chsd ldrs: rdn over 1f out: wknd fnl f* 9/2[1]

00-0 **10** 4 1/2 **Courtland Avenue (IRE)**[123] 2364 4-9-6 59 ShaneKelly 14 — 18
(Jonathan Portman) *sn outpcd* 16/1

0506 11 *hd* **Spic 'n Span**[15] 5982 8-8-13 52..................(b) SteveDrowne 12 10
(Ronald Harris) *chsd ldrs tl wknd over 1f out* 6/1[3]
3-00 12 3 3/4 **Tristessa**[54] 4607 3-8-8 51..................(v[1]) RosieJessop(3) 7
(Derek Haydn Jones) *chsd ldrs: rdn 1/2-way: wkng whn hung lft over 1f out* 33/1
6020 13 15 **Dee Aitch Dove**[30] 5499 3-9-2 56.................. JimCrowley 1
(George Baker) *chsd ldrs: lost pl over 3f out: wknd 1/2-way: eased* 12/1

1m 4.25s (5.95) **Going Correction** +1.225s/f (Soft)
WFA 3 from 4yo+ 1lb **13** Ran SP% **126.2**
Speed ratings (Par 101): **101,98,97,93,92 90,89,88,85,78 77,71,47**
toteswingers 1&2 £26.10, 1&3 £19.10, 2&3 £7.10 CSF £230.77 CT £2372.96 TOTE £18.90: £4.50, £4.40, £2.70; EX 364.70 Trifecta £1238.30 Pool: £1796.86 - 1.08 winning units..
Owner Gary Harrison **Bred** Trickledown Stud Limited **Trained** Newmarket, Suffolk

FOCUS
A weak sprint.
T/Plt: £162.40 to a £1 stake. Pool: £87,962.57 - 395.24 winning tickets T/Qpdt: £40.10 to a £1 stake. Pool: £5596.47 - 103.04 winning tickets CR

6413 CURRAGH (R-H)
Sunday, September 15

OFFICIAL GOING: Good (good to yielding in places on straight course; good to firm in places on round course)

6440a MANGUARD PLUS SOLONAWAY STKS (GROUP 3) 1m
3:15 (3:21) 3-Y-0+ **£31,707** (£9,268; £4,390; £1,463)

RPR
1 **Brendan Brackan (IRE)**[44] 4946 4-9-7 117.................. ColinKeane 10 113+
(G M Lyons, Ire) *trckd ldr: 2nd 1/2-way: hdwy fr 2f out: to chal ent fnl f: led u.p fnl 150yds and styd on wl towards fin* 9/2[2]
2 2 **Ansgar (IRE)**[14] 6025 5-9-7 107..................(t) RoryCleary 5 109
(Sabrina J Harty, Ire) *led: over 2 l clr 1/2-way: rdn 2f out and reduced advantage ent fnl f: hdd fnl 150yds and sn no ex: kpt on same pce* 10/1[3]
3 1 1/4 **Darwin (USA)**[57] 4549 3-9-5 114.................. JosephO'Brien 3 108+
(A P O'Brien, Ire) *chsd ldrs: 4th 1/2-way: clsr in 3rd under 3f out: sn rdn and no ex ins fnl f: kpt on same pce: jst hld on for 3rd* 4/7[1]
4 *nse* **Sruthan (IRE)**[94] 3262 3-9-2 106.................. ChrisHayes 8 105+
(P D Deegan, Ire) *hld up towards rr: pushed along in 7th 3f out: rdn and no imp in 5th ent fnl f: kpt on wl u.p towards fin: jst failed for 3rd* 25/1
5 2 1/2 **Stuccodor (IRE)**[14] 6025 4-9-7 104..................(v) PatSmullen 2 100+
(D K Weld, Ire) *sn settled bhd ldrs: mod 5th 1/2-way: pushed along into st and tk clsr order: rdn 2f out and sn no imp on ldrs in 4th: no ex and dropped to 5th ins fnl f* 20/1
6 2 3/4 **Fort Knox**[40] 5114 3-9-2 105.................. JohnnyMurtagh 7 93+
(J P Murtagh, Ire) *hld up: mod 6th 1/2-way: tk clsr order over 3f out: pushed along into st and sn no ex u.p: kpt on one pce* 10/1[3]
7 1 **Elleval (IRE)**[8] 6225 3-9-2 107.................. FergalLynch 6 91+
(David Marnane, Ire) *hld up towards rr: niggled along bef 1/2-way: rdn in mod 8th 1 1/2f out and no ex: kpt on one pce* 12/1
8 *nk* **Bold Thady Quill (IRE)**[40] 5114 6-9-7 103..................(p) ShaneFoley 1 91+
(K J Condon, Ire) *slowly away and racd towards rr: rdn and no imp fr 3f out: one pce fnl 2f* 33/1
9 5 **Negotiate**[40] 5114 5-9-4 88..................(tp) KevinManning 4 76
(Ms Joanna Morgan, Ire) *chsd ldrs: 3rd 1/2-way: pushed along bef st and lost pl: rdn and wknd fr 2f out* 66/1
10 15 **Indian Chief (IRE)**[15] 6009 3-9-2 106.................. SeamieHeffernan 9 44
(A P O'Brien, Ire) *a bhd: t.k.h: rdn under 3f out and no ex: eased fnl 2f* 16/1

1m 37.77s (-8.23) **Going Correction** -0.925s/f (Hard)
WFA 3 from 4yo+ 5lb **10** Ran SP% **126.6**
Speed ratings: **104,102,100,100,98 95,94,94,89,74**
CSF £50.72 TOTE £8.40: £2.10, £2.50, £1.02; DF 82.00.
Owner Anamoine Limited **Bred** Anamoine Ltd **Trained** Dunsany, Co. Meath

FOCUS
The runner-up had the run of the race and has been rated to his best.

6441a GAIN IRISH ST. LEGER (GROUP 1) 1m 6f
3:50 (3:51) 3-Y-0+
£94,308 (£30,894; £14,634; £4,878; £3,252; £1,626)

RPR
1 **Voleuse De Coeurs (IRE)**[22] 5776 4-9-8 109.................. ChrisHayes 6 118+
(D K Weld, Ire) *hld up in mid-div: 6th 1/2-way: tk clsr order fr 4f out gng wl: rdn to ld under 3f out and drvn clr 1 1/2f out: styd on strly ins fnl f: eased cl home* 9/1
2 6 **Ahzeemah (IRE)**[23] 5724 4-9-11 113..................(p) SilvestreDeSousa 4 112
(Saeed bin Suroor) *sn settled bhd ldrs: tk clsr order fr after 1/2-way: n.m.r between horses into st: sn rdn and wnt mod 2nd over 1f out: no imp on wnr: kpt on same pce towards fin to hold 2nd* 7/2[1]
3 *hd* **Saddler's Rock (IRE)**[45] 4919 5-9-11 108.................. DeclanMcDonogh 7 112
(John M Oxx, Ire) *chsd ldrs in 5th: pushed along after 1/2-way and lost pl: pushed along in cl 7th appr st: rdn on outer fr 2f out and wnt mod 3rd ins fnl f: kpt on same pce: jst hld for 2nd* 16/1
4 4 3/4 **Red Cadeaux**[29] 5531 7-9-11 115.................. GeraldMosse 8 105
(Ed Dunlop) *hld up in rr of mid-div: 8th 1/2-way: hdwy over 4f out to chal into st: rdn in 5th under 2f out and swtchd lft: no imp on wnr ent fnl f: kpt on same pce into 4th ins fnl 100yds* 4/1[2]
5 *nse* **Royal Diamond (IRE)**[22] 5776 7-9-11 112.................. JohnnyMurtagh 1 105
(J P Murtagh, Ire) *trckd ldrs tl led after 1f: strly pressed bef st and hdd under 3f out: sn no ex u.p and dropped to 6th 1 1/2f out: kpt on again ins fnl f into 5th fnl 100yds* 9/2[3]
6 1/2 **Ernest Hemingway (IRE)**[22] 5776 4-9-11 116.................. JosephO'Brien 11 105
(A P O'Brien, Ire) *w.w in rr: gd hdwy on outer over 3f out to chal into st: rdn in 2nd and sn no imp on wnr: dropped to 3rd over 1f out: wknd ins fnl f* 9/2[3]
7 4 3/4 **Pale Mimosa (IRE)**[100] 3073 4-9-8 109.................. PatSmullen 2 95
(D K Weld, Ire) *chsd ldrs: clsr in 3rd after 1/2-way: rdn in cl 6th into st and sn no ex u.p: kpt on one pce fnl 2f* 6/1
8 4 3/4 **Certerach (IRE)**[197] 870 5-9-11 108.................. ShaneFoley 5 91
(M Halford, Ire) *w.w in rr: tk clsr order in 8th bef st: sn pushed along and no imp on ldrs: kpt on one pce fnl 2f* 20/1
9 13 **Chamonix (IRE)**[106] 2864 4-9-11 110..................(p) SeamieHeffernan 3 73
(A P O'Brien, Ire) *disp early: settled bhd ldr after 1f: sn niggled along: rdn fr 1/2-way and no ex: wknd into st: eased fnl 2f* 20/1

U **Euphrasia (IRE)**[8] 6226 4-9-8 104.................. GaryCarroll 10
(Joseph G Murphy, Ire) *towards rr: 9th 1/2-way: rdn and no imp fr over 4f out: wknd and wl bhd whn uns rdr cl home: lame* 50/1

3m 0.08s (-9.32) **Going Correction** -0.225s/f (Firm)
WFA 3 from 4yo+ 11lb **10** Ran SP% **120.2**
Speed ratings: **117,113,113,110,110 110,107,105,97,**
CSF £41.02 TOTE £12.00: £2.70, £1.50, £5.40; DF 49.80.
Owner Lady O'Reilly **Bred** Irish National Stud **Trained** The Curragh, Co Kildare

FOCUS
The winner is progressive and was clear best on the day. The third helps set the standard.

6442a GOFFS VINCENT O'BRIEN NATIONAL STKS (GROUP 1) (ENTIRE COLTS & FILLIES) 7f
4:25 (4:26) 2-Y-0 **£94,308** (£30,894; £14,634; £4,878; £3,252)

RPR
1 **Toormore (IRE)**[46] 4876 2-9-3.................. RichardHughes 1 121+
(Richard Hannon) *mde all: 1 l clr 1/2-way: pressed 2f out: sn pushed along and gng best ent fnl f: rdn and kpt on wl towards fin: comf* 1/1[1]
2 2 3/4 **Sudirman (USA)**[35] 5319 2-9-3 117.................. WayneLordan 5 114
(David Wachman, Ire) *trckd ldr in 2nd: t.k.h early: rdn and clsd briefly 2f out: sn no imp on wnr: kpt on same pce* 15/8[2]
3 1 1/4 **Giovanni Boldini (USA)**[7] 6246 2-9-3.................. JosephO'Brien 2 111
(A P O'Brien, Ire) *w.w in 4th: lost pl 1/2-way: rdn on far side fr 2f out and wnt rt: clsd in 3rd u.p ent fnl f: sn no ex and kpt on same pce: nt trble wnr* 4/1[3]
4 4 1/2 **Friendship (IRE)**[22] 5774 2-9-3 108.................. SeamieHeffernan 7 98
(A P O'Brien, Ire) *w.w in rr: tk clsr order in 4th 1/2-way: rdn on outer over 2f out and sn no imp on ldrs: kpt on one pce* 14/1
5 1 3/4 **Sniper**[28] 5566 2-9-3 96.................. EmmetMcNamara 6 94
(G M Lyons, Ire) *trckd ldrs in 3rd: tk clsr order bef 1/2-way: sn pushed along and no imp on ldrs in 4th 1 1/2f out: one pce fnl f* 50/1

1m 22.67s (-8.13) **Going Correction** -0.925s/f (Hard) **5** Ran SP% **113.4**
Speed ratings: **109,105,104,99,97**
CSF £3.30 TOTE £2.20: £1.30, £1.02; DF 3.80.
Owner Middleham Park Racing IX & James Pak **Bred** BEC Bloodstock **Trained** East Everleigh, Wilts

FOCUS
A result that makes sense, but a note of caution due to a lot of winners making all on the card. The second and fifth ran to their Phoenix Stakes form and help set the standard.

6443 - 6444a (Foreign Racing) - See Raceform Interactive

6249 LONGCHAMP (R-H)
Sunday, September 15

OFFICIAL GOING: Turf: soft

6445a QATAR PRIX DU PETIT COUVERT (GROUP 3) (3YO+) (TURF) 5f (S)
12:30 (12:00) 3-Y-0+ **£22,764** (£22,764; £9,756; £6,504; £3,252)

RPR
1 **Mirza**[7] 6235 6-8-13 0..................(p) WilliamBuick 2 110
(Rae Guest) *midfield: rdn over 2f out: r.o to chal ins fnl f: led cl home: jnd post* 11/1
1 *dht* **Dibajj (FR)**[21] 5806 3-8-8 0.................. AntoineHamelin 8 106+
(A De Royer-Dupre, France) *hld up: rdn and hdwy on outer fr 2f out: r.o to chal wl ins fnl f: got up to force dead-heat post* 4/1[2]
3 *snk* **Catcall (FR)**[42] 5040 4-9-2 0.................. Francois-XavierBertras 1 112+
(P Sogorb, France) *dwlt sltly but qckly rcvrd: trckd ldng pair on inner: rdn to chal and qcknd to ld over 1f out: r.o but worn down and hdd cl home* 2/1[1]
4 *shd* **Riskit Fora Biskit (IRE)**[45] 4935 3-8-8 0.................. IoritzMendizabal 6 105
(Michael Bell) *trckd ldng pair on outer: rdn over 1f out: r.o to chal ins fnl f: w ldrs and ev ch cl home: jst hld* 4/1[2]
5 3 **A Huge Dream (IRE)**[21] 5806 4-8-9 0.................. StephanePasquier 4 94
(F Rohaut, France) *disp ld on outer: rdn over 2f out: hdd over 1f out: sn no ex and btn: fdd* 20/1
6 1 3/4 **Blarney Stone (JPN)**[175] 6-8-13 0.................. YusukeFujioka 5 92
(Yasutoshi Ikee, Japan) *last early and a towards rr: rdn 2f out: sn outpcd: kpt on and tk mod sixth cl home but nvr threatened* 33/1
7 3/4 **Caspian Prince (IRE)**[28] 4-8-13 0.................. MaximeGuyon 3 89
(E J O'Neill, France) *disp ld on inner: rdn over 2f out: hdd over 1f out: sn no ex and btn: fdd* 20/1
8 1/2 **Victory Laurel (IRE)**[119] 2491 3-9-1 0.................. JamieSpencer 7 90
(Robert Cowell) *sn towards rr and pushed along: rdn and outpcd fr 1/2-way: n.d* 8/1
9 4 **Sara Lucille**[28] 3-8-8 0..................(b) ThierryJarnet 9 69
(F Head, France) *a in rr: rdn in last 1/2-way: sn no imp and btn: nvr a factor* 7/1[3]

58.4s (2.10) **Going Correction** +0.725s/f (Yiel)
WFA 3 from 4yo+ 1lb **9** Ran SP% **117.7**
Speed ratings: **112,112,111,111,106 104,102,102,95**
WIN (incl. 1 euro stake): 7.70 (Mirza), 3.50 (Dibajj) PLACES: 3.20 (Mirza), 1.70 (Dibajj), 1.40. DF: 35.90. SF: 32.50.
Owner A Al Maddah **Bred** C Humphris **Trained** Chantilly, France
■ The photo-finish took nearly half an hour for the judge to unravel.
Owner C J Mills **Bred** C J Mills **Trained** Newmarket, Suffolk
■ The photo-finish took nearly half an hour for the judge to unravel.

6446a QATAR PRIX NIEL (GROUP 2) (3YO COLTS & FILLIES) (TURF) 1m 4f
1:30 (12:00) 3-Y-0 **£60,243** (£23,252; £11,097; £7,398; £3,699)

RPR
1 **Kizuna (JPN)**[112] 2700 3-9-2 0.................. YutakaTake 3 116+
(Shozo Sasaki, Japan) *stdd and hld up towards rr: smooth hdwy on outer fr 3f out: gng best 2f out: rdn over 1f out: styd on to chal wl ins fnl f: led cl home: strly pressed fnl strides: jst prevailed on hd bob post* 6/1
2 *shd* **Ruler Of The World (IRE)**[78] 3849 3-9-2 0..................(p) RyanMoore 1 115+
(A P O'Brien, Ire) *settled in midfield on inner: angled off rail and rdn 2f out: short of room and swtchd lft over 1f out: swtchd rt again ins fnl f: styd on and str run towards fin: chal fnl strides: jst denied on hd bob post* 11/2
3 3/4 **Ocovango**[64] 4325 3-9-2 0.................. OlivierPeslier 2 114
(A Fabre, France) *prom in main body of field on inner: pushed along over 2f out: swtchd lft for clr run and rdn over 1f out: chal ent fnl f and sn led: styd on but hdd cl home and dropped to 3rd* 10/1

 The Form Book Flat, Raceform Ltd, Compton, RG20 6NL.

4 1 **Flintshire**64 4325 3-9-2 0 MaximeGuyon 9 112
(A Fabre, France) *settled in midfield on outer: rdn 2f out: styd on steadily under firm hands and heels ins fnl f but nvr quite able to chal* **13/8**1

5 1 1/4 **Shikarpour (IRE)**56 4573 3-9-2 0 Christophe-PatriceLemaire 7 110
(A De Royer-Dupre, France) *trckd clr ldr: clsd fr 4f out: led over 2f out: sn rdn: styd on but strly pressed and hdd ins fnl f: no ex towards fin* **20/1**

6 snk **Spiritjim (FR)**97 3-9-2 0 ChristopheSoumillon 10 110
(P Bary, France) *reluctant to load: hld up towards rr: swtchd ins to rail after 2f: rdn 2f out: styd on and wnt 6th ins fnl 75yds: fin wl but nvr threatened* **33/1**

7 nk **Max Dynamite (FR)**64 4325 3-9-2 0 FrankieDettori 8 109
(J Van Handenhove, France) *dwlt sltly and hld up in last: rdn over 2f out: styd on but nt pce to chal* **100/1**

8 nk **Triple Threat (FR)**56 4573 3-9-2 0 Pierre-CharlesBoudot 5 109
(A Fabre, France) *prom in main body of field on outer: clsd fr 4f out: rdn in cl 2nd 2f out: kpt on tl no ex ins fnl f: fdd* **9/2**3

9 1/2 **Vancouverite**31 5462 3-9-2 0 MickaelBarzalona 6 108
(A Fabre, France) *hld up towards rr on outer: rdn 2f out: outpcd ent fnl f: styd on but nvr a factor* **7/2**2

10 dist **Preempt**15 3-9-2 0 ThierryThulliez 4
(P Bary, France) *led: clr 1/2-way: clsd down fr 4f out: hdd over 2f out: immediately dropped out wout coming under any press and sn last: t.o* **150/1**

2m 37.64s (7.24) **Going Correction** +0.725s/f (Yiel) **10** Ran SP% **126.6**
Speed ratings: **104,103,103,102,101 101,101,101,101,**
WIN (incl. 1 euro stake): 7.80. PLACES: 3.10, 3.10, 2.40. DF: 28.20. SF: 18.90.
Owner Shinji Maeda **Bred** North Hills Co Ltd **Trained** Japan

FOCUS
Traditionally the leading Arc trial, although most recent winners haven't been able to make an impact in the big one. Pacemaker Preempt set just an ordinary gallop early and it resulted in a dash for the line off the home bend. The time was slower than that set by Treve in the Vermeille. The narrow yet impressive winner is a genuine Group 1 horse whereas this year's Europena middle-distance 3yos look Group 2 level.

6447a QATAR PRIX GLADIATEUR-GRAND PRIX DES BENEVOLES 2013 (GROUP 3) (4YO+) (TURF) 1m 7f 110y

2:08 (12:00) 4-Y-0+ **£32,520** (£13,008; £9,756; £6,504; £3,252)

RPR

1 **Domeside**112 2695 7-9-4 0 ChristopheSoumillon 7 110
(M Delcher Sanchez, France) *hld up in tch: rdn and gd hdwy ent fnl 2f: qcknd to ld ins fnl f: r.o wl: comf* **7/1**3

2 1/2 **Les Beaufs (FR)**64 4324 4-9-6 0 AdrienFouassier 14 111
(Mme V Seignoux, France) *dwlt: sn rcvrd and trckd ldr after 1f: effrt to ld 3f out: drvn ent fnl 2f: hdd ins fnl f: kpt on gamely but a hld* **8/1**

3 2 **Goldtara (FR)**28 5575 5-8-10 0 ThierryJarnet 5 99
(A Lyon, France) *chsd ldrs: effrt u.p ent fnl 2f: kpt on but no real imp on ldng pair fnl f* **9/1**

4 1/2 **Smoky Hill (IRE)**53 4-8-11 0 UmbertoRispoli 8 99
(M Delzangles, France) *chsd ldr for 1f: styd handy: effrt u.p jst over 2f out: styd on ins fnl f: nvr gng pce to threaten ldng pair* **25/1**

5 2 **Gaterie (USA)**53 4652 4-8-8 0 MickaelBarzalona 2 94+
(A Fabre, France) *hld up in midfield: rdn over 3f out: no imp tl hdwy but stl plenty to do over 1f out: styd on ins fnl f: no threat to ldrs* **7/1**3

6 3/4 **Kasbah Bliss (FR)**16 11-8-11 0 CristianDemuro 12 96+
(F Doumen, France) *stdd and dropped in bhd after s: hld up in last trio: rdn and effrt 2f out: hdwy over 1f out: styd on fnl f: nvr trbld ldrs* **20/1**

7 1 1/2 **Almalyk (FR)**18 4-8-11 0 Christophe-PatriceLemaire 11 94+
(A De Royer-Dupre, France) *in tch in midfield on outer: rdn and effrt overt 2f out: outpcd u.p 2f out: rallied and kpt on again ins fnl f: no threat to ldrs* **20/1**

8 1/2 **Mud Hilah (FR)**31 4-8-8 0 (b) OlivierPeslier 13 90
(A De Mieulle, France) *led tl rdn and hdd 3f out: no ex u.p and btn jst over 1f out: wknd ins fnl f* **25/1**

9 1 1/4 **Dance Moves**28 5575 5-9-0 0 MaximeGuyon 4 95
(A Fabre, France) *hld up in tch towards rr: hmpd jst over 3f out: struggling after and plenty to do whn rdn ent fnl 2f: sme hdwy over 1f out: nvr trbld ldrs* **4/1**2

10 1 1/4 **Genzy (FR)**22 5766 5-8-11 0 RichardKingscote 9 90
(Ian Williams) *hld up in tch towards rr: rdn and effrt ent fnl 2f: no prog: nvr trbld ldrs* **10/1**

11 1 1/4 **Aiken**29 5531 5-9-0 0 WilliamBuick 10 92
(John Gosden) *dwlt and pushed along leaving stalls: rdn and hdwy on outer to chse ldrs after 3f: rdn and fnd little ent fnl 2f: btn 1f out: no ch and eased ins fnl f* **3/1**1

12 6 **Rain Of Melody (IRE)**26 7-8-11 0 StephanePasquier 3 82?
(Y Gourraud, France) *hld up in tch: effrt but no hdwy 3f out: wknd wl over 1f out: wl btn and eased ins fnl f* **50/1**

13 2 1/2 **Holly Polly (GER)**70 4-8-8 0 FabriceVeron 6 76
(H-A Pantall, France) *hld up in last trio: rdn and effrt over 2f out: no hdwy and sn wknd* **33/1**

14 dist **Only A Pleasure (IRE)**28 5575 4-9-0 0 Pierre-CharlesBoudot 1
(A Fabre, France) *rn in snatches: a in rr: rdn and lost tch over 2f out: wl bhd and eased fnl f* **28/1**

3m 27.24s (5.74) **Going Correction** +0.725s/f (Yiel) **14** Ran SP% **125.8**
Speed ratings: **114,113,112,112,111 111,110,110,109,108 108,105,104,**
WIN (incl. 1 euro stake): 8.20. PLACES: 3.00, 2.90, 2.90. DF: 28.10. SF: 47.90.
Owner Safsaf Canarias Srl **Bred** Appleby Lodge Stud **Trained** France

FOCUS
A trial for the Prix du Cadran, little got into it from off the pace, and it was a repeat result of the Prix Vicomtesse Vigier over C&D in May, with Domeside beating Les Beaufs.

6448a QATAR PRIX VERMEILLE (GROUP 1) (3YO+ FILLIES & MARES) (TURF) 1m 4f

2:40 (12:00) 3-Y-0+ **£162,593** (£65,048; £32,524; £16,247; £8,138)

RPR

1 **Treve (FR)**91 3385 3-8-8 0 FrankieDettori 3 118+
(Mme C Head-Maarek, France) *t.k.h: hld up in tch on inner: shuffled bk and had to wait for run on turn into st: in the clr and shkn up 2f out: styd on under hands and heels and led ins fnl f: pushed clr: v readily* **11/10**1

2 1 3/4 **Wild Coco (GER)**45 4920 5-9-2 0 TomQueally 11 114
(Lady Cecil) *got across fr wdst draw and sn led: hdd after 5f and trckd ldr: led again gng wl 3f out: rdn clr over 1f out: styd on but reeled in and hdd ins fnl f: readily outpcd by wnr but clr 2nd best* **8/1**3

3 3 1/2 **Tasaday (USA)**26 5629 3-8-8 0 MickaelBarzalona 9 109
(A Fabre, France) *stdd and hld up towards rr on outer: hdwy 3f out: rdn over 2f out: readily outpcd by front pair ent fnl f but styd on for wl hld 3rd* **6/1**2

4 snk **Orion Love**42 5044 3-8-8 0 (p) FabriceVeron 2 109
(H-A Pantall, France) *t.k.h: w ldrs early: sn restrained in midfield: rdn over 2f out: readily outpcd by front pair ent fnl f but styd on for wl hld 4th* **50/1**

5 3/4 **Galvaun (IRE)**36 5297 4-9-2 0 Pierre-CharlesBoudot 10 107
(A Fabre, France) *dropped in and hld up in last: rdn over 2f out: styd on and wnt 5th ins fnl f but n.d* **33/1**

6 1/2 **Silasol (IRE)**31 5462 3-8-8 0 OlivierPeslier 8 107
(C Laffon-Parias, France) *hld up in last pair: last 3f out: rdn whn nt clr run between rivals 2f out: styd on steadily but nvr threatened* **12/1**

7 4 **Romantica**28 5574 4-9-2 0 MaximeGuyon 6 100
(A Fabre, France) *hld up in tch: rdn 3f out: outpcd over 1f out: nt given hrd time once hld but kpt on and wnt 7th towards fin* **12/1**

8 1 1/4 **Venus De Milo (IRE)**24 5682 3-8-8 0 RyanMoore 1 99
(A P O'Brien, Ire) *trckd ldr: led after 5f: rdn and hdd 3f out: kpt on tl no ex and btn over 1f out: fdd and eased cl home* **6/1**2

9 3 **La Pomme D'Amour**36 5297 5-9-2 0 FlavienPrat 4 93
(A Fabre, France) *prom on inner: rdn over 2f out and sn lost pl: in rr and btn ent fnl f: eased* **20/1**

10 15 **Penelopa**42 5044 3-8-8 0 WilliamBuick 5 70
(M G Mintchev, Germany) *midfield in tch on outer: clsd 4f out: rdn and brief effrt to chal 3f out: sn no ex and btn: fdd and dropped to last over 2f out: eased and t.o* **14/1**

2m 36.82s (6.42) **Going Correction** +0.725s/f (Yiel)
WFA 3 from 4yo+ 9lb **10** Ran SP% **119.0**
Speed ratings: **107,105,103,103,102 102,99,99,97,87**
WIN (incl. 1 euro stake): 1.80. PLACES: 1.30, 3.00, 2.30.. DF: 12.70. SF: 14.90.
Owner HE Sh Joaan Bin Hamad Al Thani **Bred** Haras Du Quesnay **Trained** Chantilly, France

FOCUS
The great Zarkava in 2008 was the last filly to go on and win the Arc following victory in this race, and there's a very real chance that Treve can do the same following what was a hugely impressive performance. The second, fourth and fifth help with the level.

6449a QATAR PRIX FOY (GROUP 2) (4YO+ COLTS, FILLIES & MARES) (TURF) 1m 4f

3:10 (12:00) 4-Y-0+ **£60,243** (£23,252; £11,097; £7,398; £3,699)

RPR

1 **Orfevre (JPN)**168 5-9-2 0 ChristopheSoumillon 1 121+
(Yasutoshi Ikee, Japan) *travelled strly: trckd ldrs: swtchd lft and qcknd smartly to ld ent fnl f: sn drew clr: nt extended* **4/6**1

2 3 **Very Nice Name (FR)**21 5807 4-9-2 0 OlivierPeslier 2 114
(A De Mieulle, France) *hld up wl in tch in midfield: n.m.r 2f out: drvn and hdd jst over 1f out: r.o to go 2nd ins fnl f: no ch w wnr* **22/1**

3 3/4 **Pirika (IRE)**36 5297 5-8-13 0 Pierre-CharlesBoudot 5 110
(A Fabre, France) *t.k.h: hld up wl in tch in midfield: effrt u.p and hdwy over 1f out: r.o u.p to go 3rd ins fnl f: no ch w wnr* **28/1**

4 3/4 **Going Somewhere (BRZ)**113 4-9-1 0 GregoryBenoist 8 111
(D Smaga, France) *hld up wl in tch in last trio: rdn and hdwy over 2f out: kpt on u.p ins fnl f: no ch w wnr* **33/1**

5 nse **Stellar Wind (JPN)**106 4-9-2 0 YutakaTake 3 112
(Tomohito Ozeki, Japan) *led and set stdy gallop: rdn and qcknd 2f out: hdd ent fnl f and immediately brushed aside by wnr: styd on one pce and lost 3 pls fnl f* **12/1**

6 hd **Haya Landa (FR)**21 5807 5-8-13 0 FrankieDettori 10 108
(Mme L Audon, France) *stdd and dropped in bhd after s: hld up wl in tch in last trio: hdwy on inner 2f out: nt clr run and swtchd lft jst ins fnl f: r.o: no ch w wnr* **25/1**

7 nk **Now We Can**21 5807 4-9-2 0 ThierryThulliez 9 111
(N Clement, France) *chsd ldr tl rdn and unable qck 2f out: outpcd and btn over 1f out: one pce after* **25/1**

8 1 **Dunaden (FR)**84 3615 7-9-2 0 JamieSpencer 4 109
(M Delzangles, France) *chsd ldng trio: rdn and effrt ent fnl 2f: outpcd and btn over 1f out: wl hld and plugged on same pce fnl f* **9/2**2

9 3/4 **Mandour (USA)**36 5298 4-9-2 0 Christophe-PatriceLemaire 7 108
(A De Royer-Dupre, France) *hld up wl in tch in last trio: rdn and effrt whn swtchd lft 2f out: no prog* **7/1**3

2m 41.47s (11.07) **Going Correction** +0.725s/f (Yiel) **9** Ran SP% **116.8**
Speed ratings: **92,90,89,89,88 88,88,87,87**
WIN (incl. 1 euro stake): 1.80. PLACES: 1.40, 2.70, 3.30. DF: 12.70. SF: 14.80.
Owner Sunday Racing Co Ltd **Bred** Shadai Corporation Inc **Trained** Japan
■ Camelot was taken out because of the ground and worked at the Curragh instead.

FOCUS
A race that hasn't produced the Arc winner since 1992, namely Subotica, who was actually defeated in this race. Run at a very steady gallop (time the slowest of the three trials), for a second consecutive year it went to Orfevre. The third and seventh help with the standard.

6450a QATAR PRIX DU MOULIN DE LONGCHAMP (GROUP 1) (3YO+ COLTS, FILLIES & MARES) (TURF) 1m

3:45 (12:00) 3-Y-0+ **£209,048** (£83,634; £41,817; £20,890; £10,463)

RPR

1 **Maxios**88 3457 5-9-2 0 StephanePasquier 4 122+
(J E Pease, France) *chsd runaway ldr in clr 2nd: clsd fr 3f out: rdn to ld 2f out and nvr in any danger after: r.o strly: comf* **7/1**3

2 5 **Olympic Glory (IRE)**35 5314 3-8-11 0 FrankieDettori 8 110+
(Richard Hannon) *hld up: last 1/2-way: rdn and toiling in rr 2f out: fnlly responded to heavy press ins fnl f and kpt on to take mod 2nd fnl strides: nvr nrr* **8/11**1

3 shd **Anodin (IRE)**77 3876 3-8-11 0 (b) OlivierPeslier 6 109+
(F Head, France) *hld up in last pair: rdn 2f out: r.o and wnt 2nd ins fnl f: no imp on wnr and dropped to 3rd fnl strides* **14/1**

4 1 1/2 **Gale Force Ten**42 5040 3-8-11 0 (p) RyanMoore 2 106+
(A P O'Brien, Ire) *led main body of field: rdn over 2f out: kpt on u.p but nvr any threat to wnr* **12/1**

5 snk **Style Vendome (FR)**77 3876 3-8-11 0 ThierryThulliez 5 105+
(N Clement, France) *midfield on outer: rdn over 2f out: kpt on u.p but no imp on wnr* **7/1**3

6 shd **Flotilla (FR)**91 3385 3-8-8 0 Christophe-PatriceLemaire 3 102+
(M Delzangles, France) *midfield on inner: rdn over 2f out: 2nd but no imp on wnr ent fnl f: kpt on tl no ex and lost multiple pls towards fin* **5/1**2

7 *10* **Sage Melody (FR)**70 4105 3-8-8 0 .... UmbertoRispoli 7 79
(M Delzangles, France) *led and sn clr of 2nd and wl clr of remainder: reeled in fr 3f out: rdn and hdd 2f out: no ex and btn: wknd and dropped to last ent fnl f: eased* **150/1**

1m 40.73s (2.33) **Going Correction** +0.725s/f (Yiel)
WFA 3 from 5yo 5lb **7** Ran SP% **114.6**
Speed ratings: **117,112,111,110,110 110,100**
WIN (incl. 1 euro stake): 4.00. PLACES: 1.40, 1.20. DF: 3.50. SF: 10.10.
Owner Niarchos Family **Bred** Niarchos Family **Trained** Chantilly, France

FOCUS
An unsatisfactory result as Maxios was given too much rope. A personal best from him.

5324 MUNICH (L-H)
Sunday, September 15

OFFICIAL GOING: Turf: soft

6451a BAYERISCHE HAUSBAU-WERTE - GROSSE EUROPA MEILE (GROUP 3) (3YO+) (TURF) 1m
4:10 (12:00) 3-Y-0+
£26,016 (£8,943; £4,471; £2,439; £1,626; £1,219)

RPR

1 **Samba Brazil (GER)**17 5940 4-8-11 0 .... AndreaAtzeni 8 104
(J Hirschberger, Germany) *dwlt: hld up in tch in rr: gd hdwy over 1f out: chsng ldrs whn nt clr run and swtchd lft ent fnl f: sn rdn and qcknd to ld fnl 150yds: r.o wl* **10/1**

2 *3/4* **Akua'da (GER)**17 5940 3-8-11 0 .... EPedroza 5 106
(A Wohler, Germany) *chsd ldr tl led ent fnl 2f: drvn and hrd pressed over 1f out: hdd fnl 150yds: r.o wl but a jst hld* **111/10**

3 *1/2* **Point Blank (GER)**56 5-9-1 0 .... StefanieHofer 4 105
(Mario Hofer, Germany) *wl in tch in midfield: clsd to chse ldrs 2f out: rdn to chal ent fnl f: r.o but unable qck wl ins fnl f* **28/1**

4 *1/2* **Amaron**120 2446 4-9-1 0 .... AHelfenbein 11 104
(Andreas Lowe, Germany) *hld up in tch in midfield: effrt u.p to chse ldrs over 1f out: unable qck 1f out: styd on same pce fnl f* **18/5**2

5 *nk* **Empire Storm (GER)**17 5940 6-9-1 0 .... JBojko 12 103
(A Wohler, Germany) *hld up in tch towards rr: effrt on outer 2f out: styd on wl ins fnl f: nt rch ldrs* **123/10**

6 *1 1/2* **Belgian Bill**21 5808 5-9-1 0 .... TedDurcan 9 100
(George Baker) *t.k.h: hld up wl in tch in midfield: effrt to chse ldrs over 1f out: hrd drvn and no ex 1f out: wknd ins fnl f* **3/1**1

7 *2* **Royal Fox**17 5940 3-8-10 0 .... MrDennisSchiergen 7 94
(P Schiergen, Germany) *s.i.s: hld up in tch in rr: hdwy whn nt clr run on inner and swtchd rt over 1f out: kpt on ins fnl f: nvr trbld ldrs* **212/10**

8 *hd* **Felician (GER)**17 5940 5-9-5 0 .... LennartHammer-Hansen 1 99
(Ferdinand J Leve, Germany) *hld up wl in tch in midfield on inner: effrt u.p over 1f out: no imp 1f out: wknd ins fnl f* **42/10**3

9 *3/4* **Combat Zone (IRE)**17 5940 7-9-1 0 .... NRichter 10 93
(Mario Hofer, Germany) *chsd ldrs: rdn and unable qck ent fnl 2f: drvn and btn over 1f out: wknd ins fnl f* **135/10**

10 *nk* **Scoville (GER)**28 4-8-11 0 .... SHellyn 6 88
(H Hesse, Germany) *hld up in rr: effrt but stl plenty to do whn hmpd over 1f out: n.d after but kpt on ins fnl f* **43/1**

11 *8* **Superplex (FR)**31 5462 3-8-13 0 .... KKerekes 2 76
(M Figge, Germany) *led tl rdn and hdd ent fnl 2f: sn rdn and btn: bhd and eased ins fnl f* **66/10**

12 *47* **Bronze Prince**21 5794 6-9-1 0 .... SebSanders 3
(Michael Attwater) *dwlt: sn rcvrd and chsd ldrs: lost pl qckly over 2f out: bhd and virtually p.u over 1f out: t.o* **25/1**

1m 39.54s (99.54)
WFA 3 from 4yo+ 5lb **12** Ran SP% **125.0**
WIN (incl. 10 euro stake): 110. PLACES: 34, 30, 71. SF: 939.
Owner Gestut Karlshof **Bred** Gestut Karlshof **Trained** Germany

3188 TABY (R-H)
Sunday, September 15

OFFICIAL GOING: Turf: good to soft; all-weather: standard

6452a AMACITALOPNING (CONDITIONS) (2YO FILLIES) (TURF) 5f 165y
12:28 (12:00) 2-Y-0 **£18,921** (£9,460; £4,541; £3,027; £1,892)

RPR

1 **Harbour Light (DEN)** 2-9-4 0 .... ElioneChaves 1
(Soren Jensen, Denmark) **63/20**3

2 *3* **Prinsessen** 2-9-4 0 .... MRobaldo 8
(Bent Olsen, Denmark) **27/10**1

3 *1 1/2* **Ametyst (DEN)** 2-9-4 0 .... ManuelSantos 2
(Bent Olsen, Denmark) **17/2**

4 *2 1/2* **Tai She (SWE)** 2-9-4 0 .... JacobJohansen 12
(Soren Jensen, Denmark) **246/10**

5 *1/2* **Mon Fleur (DEN)** 2-9-4 0 .... (p) ValmirDeAzeredo 4
(Bodil Hallencreutz, Sweden) **38/1**

6 *1* **Mendacious Harpy (IRE)**25 5636 2-9-4 0 .... (p) FJohansson 10
(George Baker) *chsd ldrs: rdn and one pce ins fnl f* **31/10**2

7 *1* **Liebling** 2-9-4 0 .... Per-AndersGraberg 15
(Niels Petersen, Norway) **61/10**

8 *1/2* **Tamara Quest (SWE)** 2-9-4 0 .... LeonardRios 6
(Maria Johansson, Sweden) **195/10**

9 *1/2* **Red Dakota (IRE)**47 4862 2-9-4 0 .... RebeccaColldin 3
(Claes Bjorling, Sweden) **218/10**

10 *1/2* **Dream'run (ITY)** 2-9-4 0 .... OliverWilson 14
(Bettina Wilson, Denmark) **32/1**

11 *1* **Desert Chicory (SWE)** 2-9-4 0 .... NathalieMortensen 7
(Henrik Engblom, Sweden) **36/1**

12 *1/2* **Poppapp (SWE)** 2-9-4 0 .... DayversonDeBarros 9
(Jaana Alvesparr, Sweden) **50/1**

13 *3 1/2* **Lucky You (SWE)** 2-9-4 0 .... (p) RafaeldeOliveira 11
(Sandra Brolin, Sweden) **76/1**

14 *2* **Wishful (SWE)** 2-9-4 0 .... RafaelSchistl 13
(Erik Svensson, Sweden) **77/1**

1m 8.8s (2.10) **14** Ran SP% **126.1**
DIVIDENDS (all including 1sek stake): WIN 4.15; PLACE 1.71, 1.84, 2.24; SF 14.83.
Owner Stald Seaside **Bred** Stutteri Hjortebo **Trained** Denmark

6453a STOCKHOLM CUP INTERNATIONAL (GROUP 3) (3YO+) (TURF) 1m 4f
3:45 (12:00) 3-Y-0+ **£47,303** (£23,651; £11,352; £7,568; £4,730)

RPR

1 **Without Fear (FR)**21 5809 5-9-4 0 .... FJohansson 13 101
(Niels Petersen, Norway) *dwlt: sn rcvrd to chse ldrs: wnt 2nd after 2f tl led over 4f out: sn clr: rdn and kpt on wl fnl 2f* **19/2**

2 *1 1/2* **Bank Of Burden (USA)**21 5809 6-9-4 0 .... Per-AndersGraberg 2 99
(Niels Petersen, Norway) *in tch in midfield: clsd on ldrs over 4f out: nt clr run and swtchd rt 3f out: effrt u.p to chse clr wnr 2f: sme hdwy 1f out: no imp and hld fnl 75yds* **31/10**1

3 *1* **Hurricane Red (IRE)**35 5326 3-8-9 0 .... ElioneChaves 4 97
(Lennart Reuterskiold Jr, Sweden) *hld up in midfield: clsd on ldrs over 4f out: swtchd rt and effrt u.p 2f out: wnt 3rd ins fnl f and r.o wl fnl 100yds: nt rch ldrs* **31/10**1

4 *1 1/2* **Sir Lando**77 3879 6-9-4 0 .... (p) RobertHavlin 3 95
(Wido Neuroth, Norway) *hld up in midfield: shuffled bk to rr 1/2-way: swtchd rt and effrt u.p jst over 2f out: styd on wl ins fnl f: nvr trbld ldr* **63/10**3

5 *1* **Jubilance (IRE)**21 5809 4-9-4 0 .... JacobJohansen 12 93
(Bent Olsen, Denmark) *hld up in midfield: clsd but n.m.r on inner over 4f out: hdwy u.p over 1f out: styd on u.p fnl f: nvr trbld ldrs* **29/1**

6 *1* **Berling (IRE)**21 5809 6-9-4 0 .... ManuelMartinez 1 92
(Jessica Long, Sweden) *broke wl and led early: sn hdd and chsd ldrs after: effrt to chse wnr over 3f out tl 2f out: sn outpcd and btn 3rd 1f out: wknd* **32/5**

7 *1* **Bomar (IRE)**42 5045 4-9-4 0 .... RafaeldeOliveira 9 90
(Wido Neuroth, Norway) *hld up in last trio: effrt but v wd 3f out: styd on fnl f: nvr trbld ldrs* **67/1**

8 *nk* **Lataradud (IRE)**519 6-9-4 0 .... EspenSki 7 90
(Roy Arne Kvisla, Sweden) *racd in midfield: rdn and effrt 5f out: drvn and outpcd u.p over 2f out: n.d after* **22/1**

9 *4* **Lindenthaler (GER)**56 5-9-4 0 .... OliverWilson 6 83
(Fredrik Reuterskiold, Sweden) *hld up towards rr: rdn and hdwy 5f out: struggling u.p 3f out: plugged on same pce and btn fnl 2f* **26/1**

10 *1/2* **Painters Easel (IRE)**952 5-9-4 0 .... (b) ManuelSantos 11 83
(Maria Sandh, Sweden) *racd freely: sn dashed into ld and clr: hdd over 4f out: rdn and btn over 2f out: fdd fnl f* **70/1**

11 *1 1/2* **Glen's Diamond**23 5724 5-9-4 0 .... BarryMcHugh 8 80
(Richard Fahey) *s.i.s: bhd: forced wd and hdwy after 2f: midfield 1/2-way: rdn and no rspnse over 3f out: sn btn* **39/10**2

12 *3* **Touch Of Hawk (FR)**21 5809 7-9-4 0 .... Jan-ErikNeuroth 10 75
(Wido Neuroth, Norway) *chsd ldrs tl wknd u.p over 2f out: bhd fnl f* **39/1**

13 *4* **Manchester (FR)**21 5809 5-9-4 0 .... RafaelSchistl 5 69
(Niels Petersen, Norway) *hld up in rr: last 1/2-way: effrt on outer and plenty to do over 2f out: sn wknd* **29/1**

2m 28.7s (-0.50)
WFA 3 from 4yo+ 9lb **13** Ran SP% **126.0**
DIVIDENDS (all including 1sek stake): WIN 10.51; PLACE 2.96, 1.74, 1.80; SF 56.55.
Owner Stall Bonne Nuit **Bred** Zamim Ralphy Meahjohn **Trained** Norway

WOODBINE (R-H)
Sunday, September 15

OFFICIAL GOING: Turf: firm; polytrack: fast

6454a CANADIAN STKS (GRADE 2) (3YO+ FILLIES & MARES) (TURF) 1m 1f
7:59 (12:00) 3-Y-0+
£111,801 (£37,267; £22,360; £9,316; £3,726; £1,863)

RPR

1 **Minakshi (FR)**49 5-8-2 0 ow1 .... LContreras 1 103
(Michael Matz, U.S.A) *midfield: rdn over 2f out: chal over 1f out: led ent fnl f: r.o strly u.p and a holding runner-up* **71/10**

2 *1/2* **Colonial Flag (USA)**29 4-8-5 0 .... JRoccoJr 7 105
(Michael Matz, U.S.A) *hld up in last pair: last 1/2-way: hdwy on outer 2f out: rdn over 1f out: r.o and wnt 2nd ins fnl f: pressed wnr all the way to fin but a being hld* **106/10**

3 *1 3/4* **Moment Of Majesty (CAN)**21 6-8-1 0 .... EmmaJayneWilson 6 97
(Roger L Attfield, Canada) *dwlt and hld up in last pair on inner: nt clr run fr 2f out tl swtchd rt and rdn over 1f out: r.o down wd outside and wnt 3rd cl home: nvr nrr* **17/1**

4 *3/4* **La Tia (USA)**29 5552 4-8-6 0 ow3 .... KDesormeaux 9 101
(Armando de la Cerda, U.S.A) *broke wl fr wdst draw and disp ld on outer: led over 2f out: rdn and strly pressed over 1f out: hdd ent fnl f: sn no ex: fdd and dropped to 4th cl home* **42/10**3

5 *1* **Ladys First**15 6000 4-8-7 0 .... TonyHamilton 4 100
(Richard Fahey) *pushed along to go forward and disp ld on inner: hdd over 2f out: rdn over 1f out: sn outpcd by ldrs: styd on u.p ins fnl f* **18/5**2

6 *1* **No Explaining (IRE)**43 6-8-1 0 .... JRVelazquez 2 92
(Roger L Attfield, Canada) *trckd ldng pair: rdn to chal 2f out: outpcd by ldrs over 1f out: fdd ins fnl f* **23/4**

7 *hd* **Pure Blue Sky (USA)**31 4-8-2 0 ow1 .... JStein 5 92
(Sam Di Pasquale, Canada) *midfield: rdn and towards rr 3f out: last whn nt clr run 2f out: swtchd rt and r.o: wnt 7th cl home but nvr threatened* **47/1**

8 *3/4* **Solid Appeal (USA)**29 5552 4-8-9 0 .... (b) JesseMCampbell 3 98
(Reade Baker, Canada) *trckd ldng pair on inner: shuffled bk 4f out: rdn 2f out: outpcd by ldrs over 1f out: fdd ins fnl f and dropped to 8th cl home* **49/20**1

9 *13 1/2* **Meri Shika (FR)**38 3-7-13 0 ow3 .... DJMoran 8 65
(Roger L Attfield, Canada) *midfield on outer: hdwy to trck ldng pair 4f out: rdn over 2f out: no ex and btn over 1f out: fdd and dropped to last ent fnl f: eased and t.o* **216/10**

1m 44.05s (104.05)
WFA 3 from 4yo+ 6lb **9** Ran SP% **117.8**
PARI-MUTUEL (all including $2 stakes): WIN 16.20; PLACE (1-2) 9.00, 10.10; SHOW (1-2-3) 6.50, 6.40, 8.50; SF 113.60.
Owner Northern Bloodstock **Bred** Elevage Haras De Bourgeauville **Trained** USA

6456a RICOH WOODBINE MILE (GRADE 1) (3YO+) (TURF) 1m (T)

10:38 (12:00) 3-Y-0+

£372,670 (£124,223; £68,322; £37,267; £12,422; £6,211)

RPR

1 Wise Dan (USA)[36] 6-8-12 0 JRVelazquez 4 130+
(Charles LoPresti, U.S.A) 1/4[1]

2 3 1/2 Za Approval (USA)[78] 5-8-7 0 GKGomez 6 117
(Christophe Clement, U.S.A) 69/10[2]

3 1 1/4 Trade Storm[22] 5739 5-8-9 0 GaryStevens 3 116
(David Simcock) 43/5[3]

4 2 1/2 Riding The River (USA)[21] 6-8-9 0 (b) TKKabel 1 110
(David Cotey, U.S.A) 238/10

5 2 1/4 Dimension[21] 5-8-9 0 DJMoran 5 105
(Conor Murphy, U.S.A) 182/10

6 2 Excaper (USA)[21] 4-8-5 0 (b) LContreras 2 97
(Ian Black, Canada) 161/10

1m 31.75s (91.75) 6 Ran SP% 118.2

PARI-MUTUEL (all including $2 stakes): WIN 2.50; PLACE (1-2) 2.10, 3.50; SHOW (1-2-3) 2.10, 2.20, 2.60; SF 7.00.

Owner Morton Fink **Bred** Mort Fink **Trained** USA

6455 - 6456a (Foreign Racing) - See Raceform Interactive

[6255] BRIGHTON (L-H)

Monday, September 16

OFFICIAL GOING: Good to soft (soft in places; 6.4)

Wind: Fresh, against Weather: Sunny spells

6457 SIS APPRENTICE (S) H'CAP 1m 1f 209y

2:20 (2:21) (Class 6) (0-65,62) 3-Y-0+ £1,940 (£577; £288; £144) Stalls High

Form RPR

0013 1 Mcconnell (USA)[7] 6261 8-9-0 50 (b) OisinMurphy 8 58
(Violet M Jordan) *in tch: effrt over 2f out: led 1f out: styd on* 9/2[2]

0-53 2 3/4 Hendry Trigger[14] 6046 4-9-0 53 LouisSteward(3) 2 59
(Bernard Llewellyn) *hld up: rdn 6f out: hdwy 2f out: rdn to chal 1f out: kpt on* 10/1

0406 3 1 3/4 Drummond[21] 5813 4-9-0 50 (t) DanielMuscutt 3 53
(Bernard Llewellyn) *chsd ldrs: outpcd 4f out: rallied and pressed ldrs 2f out: kpt on same pce fnl f* 5/1[3]

2332 4 5 Special Report (IRE)[7] 6257 3-8-6 48 ShelleyBirkett 6 41
(Peter Hiatt) *prom: led 2f out tl 1f out: wknd fnl f* 6/4[1]

3100 5 4 Frosty Secret[11] 6137 4-9-1 51 (b) IanBurns 4 36
(Jane Chapple-Hyam) *led 2f: chsd ldr after tl led again 4f out: hdd 2f out: wknd over 1f out* 10/1

3040 6 6 Silver Marizah (IRE)[17] 5948 4-8-12 48 oh3 (p) NoelGarbutt 1 21
(Roger Ingram) *towards rr: hdwy on inner 5f out: led 3f out tl 2f out: wknd over 1f out* 20/1

4040 7 1 3/4 Benandonner (USA)[14] 6038 10-8-13 49 (p) RyanWhile 5 18
(Paddy Butler) *led after 2f tl wknd 4f out: sn bhd* 16/1

6-36 8 1/2 It's A Girl Thing (IRE)[27] 5605 4-9-5 62 HectorCrouch(7) 7 30
(Gary Moore) *towards rr: sme hdwy 4f out: wknd over 2f out* 8/1

2m 8.95s (5.35) **Going Correction** +0.25s/f (Good)

WFA 3 from 4yo+ 6lb 8 Ran SP% 114.8

Speed ratings (Par 101): **88,87,86,82,78 74,72,72**

toteswingers 1&2 £7.70, 1&3 £7.00, 2&3 £6.50 CSF £48.15 CT £232.72 TOTE £4.20: £1.20, £2.80, £2.40; EX 47.80 Trifecta £284.00 Pool: £790.54 - 2.08 winning units..Benandonner was claimed Mr M. Murphy for £3,000. Special Report was claimed by Mr Nick Croom £3,000.

Owner Rakebackmypoker.com **Bred** Hall Et Al Farm **Trained** Moreton Morrell, Warwicks

FOCUS

All races on inner all race distances as advertised. A poor race in which very few could be fancied. The winner is rated close to this year's AW form but the form behind looks far from solid.

6458 OVERLINE TELECOMS H'CAP 1m 3f 196y

2:50 (2:52) (Class 6) (0-65,61) 3-Y-0+ £1,940 (£577; £288; £144) Stalls High

Form RPR

-536 1 Panettone (IRE)[68] 4179 4-9-9 59 (b) AndreaAtzeni 1 72
(Roger Varian) *pressed ldr: led 4f out: c to stands' side st: chal by rival on far side: in control and rdn out ins fnl f* 9/4[1]

0621 2 1 1/2 Mr Fickle (IRE)[32] 5429 4-9-10 60 (b) GeorgeBaker 4 71
(Gary Moore) *chsd ldrs: hrd rdn and styd on far side st: jnd ldr 2f out: kpt on u.p* 7/2[2]

1403 3 9 Green Earth (IRE)[14] 6037 6-9-7 60 JemmaMarshall(3) 9 56
(Pat Phelan) *hld up towards rr on outer: c to stands' side st: hdwy 2f out: edgd rt and no ex fnl f* 12/1

3024 4 3 1/2 Royal Defence (IRE)[7] 3151 7-8-12 48 MartinLane 7 39
(Mick Quinn) *led tl rdn and hdd 4f out: c to stands' side st: sn outpcd* 10/1

6216 5 hd Comedy House[38] 5231 5-9-5 60 PhilipPrince(5) 10 50
(Michael Madgwick) *in tch: rdn 5f out: c to stands' side st: sn btn* 8/1

210- 6 1 1/2 Cantor[423] 4296 5-9-6 56 PatrickDonaghy 3 44
(Giles Bravery) *prom: rdn and c to stands' side st: sn outpcd* 7/1[3]

3454 7 3 3/4 Eanans Bay (IRE)[19] 5897 4-8-8 47 oh2 (b) AshleyMorgan(3) 8 29
(Mark H Tompkins) *chsd ldng pair: rdn and c to stands' side st: sn lost pl* 16/1

-050 8 1 1/2 Himalayan Peak[88] 3497 3-8-12 61 RyanTate(5) 5 40
(James Eustace) *s.s: rdn 1/2-way: styd on far side st: a bhd* 8/1

2510 9 58 Anginola (IRE)[20] 5854 4-9-10 60 FergusSweeney 6
(Laura Mongan) *mid-div on inner: styd in centre st: wknd 3f out: bhd and eased over 1f out* 14/1

2m 36.1s (3.40) **Going Correction** +0.25s/f (Good)

WFA 3 from 4yo+ 8lb 9 Ran SP% 117.0

Speed ratings (Par 101): **98,97,91,88,88 87,85,84,45**

toteswingers 1&2 £2.70, 1&3 £7.10, 2&3 £3.80 CSF £10.11 CT £76.68 TOTE £3.40: £1.30, £1.80, £1.50; EX 13.30 Trifecta £57.90 Pool: £1431.02 - 18.52 winning units..

Owner Duncan Jones & Dr Sosie Kassab **Bred** Bjorn Nielsen **Trained** Newmarket, Suffolk

FOCUS

A oderate handicap in which the winner is rated close to last year's C&D mark.

6459 MAYO WYNNE BAXTER H'CAP 7f 214y

3:20 (3:20) (Class 6) (0-65,65) 3-Y-0+ £1,940 (£577; £288; £144) Stalls Low

Form RPR

004 1 Bloodsweatandtears[109] 2787 5-9-2 57 GeorgeBaker 4 66
(William Knight) *mde all: led field to stands' rail st: rdn and hld on wl fnl 2f* 7/2[1]

5050 2 1 Poetic Lord[31] 5479 4-9-9 64 AndreaAtzeni 8 71
(Sylvester Kirk) *hld up towards rr: hdwy on stands' rail 2f out: swtchd lft into centre and chsd wnr over 1f out: hung bdly lft and stened: kpt on* 7/1

0040 3 3 1/2 Santo Prince (USA)[49] 4829 3-9-4 63 MartinLane 1 62
(Michael Bell) *chsd ldng pair: drvn along fr 4f out: one pce fnl 2f* 6/1[3]

5342 4 3/4 Brown Pete (IRE)[7] 6258 5-9-2 62 OisinMurphy(5) 10 59
(Violet M Jordan) *in tch: chsd ldrs 4f out: hrd rdn and one pce fnl 2f* 4/1[2]

6212 5 1/2 Wordismybond[14] 6042 4-9-10 65 SteveDrowne 7 61
(Peter Makin) *w wnr: rdn and edgd lft over 1f out: wknd fnl f* 6/1[3]

5224 6 1 1/4 South Cape[11] 6146 10-9-2 64 JayneFarwell(7) 3 57
(Gary Moore) *s.s: hld up in rr: effrt and swtchd lft over 1f out: nvr rchd ldrs* 10/1

0404 7 7 Perfect Pastime[7] 6259 5-9-10 65 (e[1]) MartinDwyer 2 42
(Jim Boyle) *mid-div: initially styd alone on far side in st: hdwy and jnd main bunch on stands' side 2f out: wknd jst over 1f out* 12/1

4006 8 3/4 Saint Irene[7] 6261 4-9-2 57 FergusSweeney 9 32
(Michael Blanshard) *nvr trbld ldrs* 8/1

5-50 9 7 Tigerish[12] 6106 3-9-1 60 [1] PatDobbs 5 19
(Amanda Perrett) *chsd ldrs 5f* 25/1

1m 38.23s (2.23) **Going Correction** +0.25s/f (Good)

WFA 3 from 4yo+ 4lb 9 Ran SP% 115.0

Speed ratings (Par 101): **98,97,93,92,92 91,84,83,76**

toteswingers 1&2 £7.00, 1&3 £8.00, 2&3 £11.80 CSF £28.16 CT £142.75 TOTE £4.90: £1.40, £2.20, £2.10; EX 32.40 Trifecta £157.00 Pool: £1125.79 - 5.37 winning units..

Owner Canisbay Bloodstock **Bred** Oakhill Stud **Trained** Patching, W Sussex

■ Stewards' Enquiry : Andrea Atzeni one-day ban: careless riding (Sep 30)

FOCUS

A moderate handicap, but it was run at a fair pace throughout. The winner is rated to his best in the last year.

6460 CHANDLERS BMW MAIDEN AUCTION STKS 6f 209y

3:50 (3:51) (Class 6) 2-Y-0 £1,940 (£577; £288; £144) Stalls Low

Form RPR

1 Improvized 2-8-9 0 ow1 SteveDrowne 5 65+
(William Muir) *s.i.s: bhd: hdwy in centre over 2f out: styd on wl to ld fnl 75yds* 14/1

030 2 hd Nice Arty (IRE)[25] 5675 2-8-13 68 PatDobbs 1 68
(Jamie Osborne) *chsd ldrs: hrd rdn over 1f out: styd on wl fnl f* 12/1

0002 3 1/2 My Anchor[10] 6152 2-8-9 66 AndreaAtzeni 6 63
(Sylvester Kirk) *chsd ldrs: rdn 3f out: kpt on u.p* 9/4[1]

6 4 hd Sweet P[11] 6141 2-8-8 0 MartinDwyer 11 61
(Marcus Tregoning) *prom on outer: edgd lft and led ins fnl f: hdd and unable qck fnl 75yds* 3/1[2]

06 5 3/4 Fisher Lane[17] 5950 2-8-10 0 CharlesBishop(3) 2 64
(Olly Stevens) *led: edgd lft and hdd ins fnl f: no ex* 8/1

0 6 4 Seven Lucky Seven[92] 3366 2-8-11 0 J-PGuillambert 8 52
(Gary Harrison) *chsd ldrs on outer: rdn 3f out: one pce* 5/1[3]

00 7 2 1/4 Haines[60] 4439 2-8-6 0 OisinMurphy(5) 4 46
(Brett Johnson) *chsd ldrs: rdn 4f out: sn outpcd* 50/1

00 8 shd Sir Percy Blakeney[7] 6256 2-8-9 0 MichaelJMMurphy(3) 7 46
(Marcus Tregoning) *w ldrs 3f: rdn and btn 3f out* 33/1

0045 9 5 Rural Affair[26] 5635 2-8-5 53 [1] MartinLane 10 26
(Harry Dunlop) *sn outpcd: nvr nr ldrs* 8/1

00 10 1 Commanding Force[32] 5443 2-8-9 0 KieranO'Neill 3 27
(John Bridger) *outpcd: a bhd* 100/1

11 1 1/4 Topofthedrops (IRE) 2-8-13 0 FergusSweeney 9 28
(Philip Hide) *outpcd: sn wl bhd* 25/1

1m 25.93s (2.83) **Going Correction** +0.25s/f (Good) 11 Ran SP% 118.8

Speed ratings (Par 93): **93,92,92,91,91 86,83,83,78,77 75**

toteswingers 1&2 £18.20, 1&3 £8.60, 2&3 £5.10 CSF £166.72 TOTE £15.00: £4.80, £3.40, £1.10; EX 199.30 Trifecta £851.00 Pool: £2487.55 - 2.19 winning units..

Owner Foursome Thoroughbreds **Bred** Foursome Thoroughbreds **Trained** Lambourn, Berks

FOCUS

It's unlikely this was anything other than an ordinary maiden and, with a little over a length covering the first five home, the form should be treated with a degree of caution.

6461 IT FIRST H'CAP 5f 213y

4:20 (4:20) (Class 4) (0-80,80) 3-Y-0+ £4,690 (£1,395; £697; £348) Stalls Low

Form RPR

0014 1 Olney Lass[4] 6324 6-8-4 66 SimonPearce(3) 5 76
(Lydia Pearce) *sn outpcd and bhd: hdwy 2f out: led over 1f out: pushed clr* 9/2[3]

6000 2 2 1/4 Cardinal[19] 5901 8-8-10 69 SteveDrowne 4 72
(Robert Cowell) *in tch: effrt over 2f out: chsd wnr fnl f: unable qck* 7/1

1350 3 3 1/2 Amenable (IRE)[24] 5701 6-8-9 73 (p) OisinMurphy(5) 8 65
(Violet M Jordan) *disp ld at gd pce: led over 2f out tl over 1f out: wknd fnl f* 14/1

-100 4 2 Royal Reyah[91] 3411 4-9-2 75 [1] ShaneKelly 7 60
(Stuart Kittow) *v.s.a: wl bhd tl modest late hdwy* 5/2[1]

6061 5 nk Jungle Bay[22] 5798 6-9-4 77 (b) AndreaAtzeni 6 61
(Jane Chapple-Hyam) *prom on outer: c wdr than others ent st: wknd over 1f out* 11/4[2]

0014 6 2 1/4 Aye Aye Skipper (IRE)[31] 5477 3-9-5 80 MartinLane 2 57
(Dean Ivory) *disp ld at gd pce tl over 2f out: wknd wl over 1f out* 5/1

1m 10.86s (0.66) **Going Correction** +0.25s/f (Good)

WFA 3 from 4yo+ 2lb 6 Ran SP% 109.3

Speed ratings (Par 105): **105,102,97,94,94 91**

toteswingers 1&2 £5.70, 1&3 £7.70, 2&3 £9.50 CSF £32.33 CT £366.76 TOTE £6.30: £2.70, £3.00; EX 43.80 Trifecta £177.40 Pool: £1210.36 - 5.11 winning units..

Owner Mrs Louise Marsh **Bred** T H Rossiter **Trained** Newmarket, Suffolk

FOCUS
A competitive sprint handicap, despite the relatively small field, run at a searching early pace. The form is bit fluid with the runner-up rated to this year's form.

6462 HARVEYS BREWERY H'CAP 6f 209y
4:50 (4:50) (Class 6) (0-65,61) 3-Y-O+ £1,940 (£577; £288; £144) Stalls Low

Form RPR
6000 1 **Bestfootforward**[118] 2533 4-8-2 47 oh2 ShelleyBirkett(7) 1 64+
(Julia Feilden) *mde all at gd pce: kpt to ins rail st: clr fnl 2f: easily* 12/1
064 2 5 **Silvee**[33] 5404 6-8-8 49 MichaelJMMurphy(3) 6 53
(John Bridger) *towards rr: rdn 3f out: hdwy and hung lft over 1f out: styd on to take 2nd fnl 100yds: no ch w wnr* 5/1[3]
4550 3 ½ **Jackie Love (IRE)**[15] 6019 5-8-4 47 oh2 (v) OisinMurphy(5) 5 50
(Olivia Maylam) *cl up: chsd wnr 3f out: rdn and hld fnl 2f: lost 2nd fnl 100yds* 9/2[2]
3266 4 1¾ **Wishformore (IRE)**[44] 4999 6-9-1 53 (p) RichardThomas 4 51
(Zoe Davison) *in tch: rdn 3f out: kpt on same pce: a wl hld* 7/1
1463 5 3¾ **Surrey Dream (IRE)**[14] 6033 4-8-9 47 KieranO'Neill 3 35
(John Bridger) *chsd ldrs: rdn 3f out: sn btn* 7/1
0005 6 1½ **Iffley Fields**[11] 6138 3-8-1 47 oh2 (p) NatashaEaton(5) 2 31
(Michael Squance) *chsd wnr 4f: wknd 2f out* 33/1
2000 7 4½ **Kings 'n Dreams**[20] 5869 6-9-2 54 (b) MartinLane 7 52
(Dean Ivory) *dwlt: bhd: swtchd to ins rail and sme hdwy 2f out: no imp whn n.m.r and eased ins fnl f* 10/1
0233 8 1½ **Speedfit Boy (IRE)**[27] 5604 3-9-6 61 GeorgeBaker 8 29
(George Margarson) *hld up in rr: rdn 3f out: no rspnse* 2/1[1]

1m 24.84s (1.74) **Going Correction** +0.25s/f (Good)
WFA 3 from 4yo+ 3lb 8 Ran SP% 112.9
Speed ratings (Par 101): **100,94,93,91,87 85,80,78**
toteswingers 1&2 £10.50, 1&3 £11.60, 2&3 £4.20 CSF £68.79 CT £315.72 TOTE £15.20: £5.20, £2.60, £2.80; EX 109.60 Trifecta £802.40 Pool: £1712.11 - 1.60 winning units..
Owner Northmore Stud **Bred** Elsdon Farms **Trained** Exning, Suffolk
■ Stewards' Enquiry : Natasha Eaton one-day ban: careless riding (Sep 30)

FOCUS
Some disappointing types on show in this handicap, but few could predict the ease in which the enterprisingly ridden Bestfootforward would get off the mark for her new connections. The runner-up is rated in line with her latest mark.

6463 JUICE 107.2 RADIO MADE IN BRIGHTON H'CAP 5f 59y
5:20 (5:20) (Class 5) (0-70,69) 3-Y-O+ £2,587 (£770; £384; £192) Stalls Low

Form RPR
4232 1 **The Strig**[17] 5956 6-9-4 66 (v) J-PGuillambert 4 77
(Stuart Williams) *hld up: hdwy 2f out: led over 1f out: drvn out* 5/2[2]
01 2 nk **Threave**[11] 6145 5-9-1 68 OisinMurphy(5) 3 78
(Violet M Jordan) *led tl over 1f out: rallied wl fnl 75yds: uns rdr after post* 3/1[3]
6221 3 2 **Rigolleto (IRE)**[21] 5841 5-9-7 69 GeorgeBaker 1 72
(Anabel K Murphy) *chsd ldr tl 2f out: one pce appr fnl f* 7/4[1]
6024 4 10 **Above The Stars**[7] 6255 5-9-7 69 FergusSweeney 5 37
(Conor Dore) *chsd ldrs: rdn over 2f out: sn wknd* 12/1
3142 U **Griffin Point (IRE)**[14] 6040 6-9-1 63 (b) MartinDwyer 7
(William Muir) *anticipated s: crashed through gate and uns rdr* 6/1

1m 3.52s (1.22) **Going Correction** +0.25s/f (Good) 5 Ran SP% 111.9
Speed ratings (Par 103): **100,99,96,80,**
CSF £10.50 TOTE £3.50: £2.50, £1.50; EX 13.20 Trifecta £30.40 Pool: £1568.72 - 38.62 winning units..
Owner Brian Piper & David Cobill **Bred** Old Mill Stud **Trained** Newmarket, Suffolk

FOCUS
A disappointing turnout for a race of this nature and, with last month's Bath scorer Griffin Point unseating a luckless Martin Dwyer at the start, it's dubious as to what was actually required to win this. The third sets the standard rated close to recent marks.
T/Plt: £255.40 to a £1 stake. Pool: £72689.38 - 207.75 winning tickets T/Qpdt: £49.20 to a £1 stake. Pool: £5710.69 - 85.80 winning tickets LM

6082 MUSSELBURGH (R-H)
Monday, September 16

OFFICIAL GOING: Good (good to soft in places; 7.5)
Wind: Strong half against Weather: Overcast

6464 BATLEYS FOODSERVICE H'CAP 7f 30y
2:10 (2:15) (Class 6) (0-65,64) 3-Y-O+ £1,259 (£1,259; £288; £144) Stalls Low

Form RPR
5032 1 **Summer Dancer (IRE)**[13] 6083 9-9-3 60 PaulMulrennan 6 70
(Paul Midgley) *hld up in tch: sltly hmpd home turn: gd hdwy over 2f out: swtchd lft and rdn to chse ldr appr fnl f: drvn and kpt on gamely towards fin to join ldr on line* 5/1[2]
-144 1 dht **Cara's Request (AUS)**[45] 4956 8-8-11 59 ConnorBeasley(5) 9 69
(Michael Dods) *trckd ldrs: sltly hmpd home turn: gd hdwy 3f out: led wl over 1f out: rdn ent fnl f: kpt on: jnd on line* 9/2[1]
6050 3 3 **Viva Ronaldo (IRE)**[17] 5947 7-8-12 60 GeorgeChaloner(5) 7 62
(Richard Fahey) *bhd: pushed along after 3f: hdwy on wd outside 2f out: sn rdn and styd on wl fnl f: nrst fin* 7/1
2603 4 1½ **Perfect Words (IRE)**[19] 5887 3-8-10 61 ShirleyTeasdale(5) 4 58
(Marjorie Fife) *chsd ldrs: hdwy 3f out: rdn 2f out: drvn appr fnl f: kpt on same pce* 14/1
0363 5 3½ **Mowhoob**[13] 6084 3-9-4 64 GrahamLee 2 51
(Jim Goldie) *in rr: hdwy wl over 2f out and sn pushed along: rdn over 1f out: kpt on fnl f: nvr nr ldrs* 13/2[3]
4522 6 ¾ **Hanalei Bay (IRE)**[13] 6084 3-9-4 64 (b) TomEaves 5 49
(Keith Dalgleish) *chsd ldrs: pushed along 3f out: sn rdn and wknd 2f out* 12/1
2252 7 ¾ **Rio Cobolo (IRE)**[10] 6181 7-9-5 62 AdrianNicholls 8 46
(David Nicholls) *cl up: led wl over 2f out: rdn along and hdd wl over 1f out: sn drvn: edgd rt and grad wknd* 8/1
00-6 8 ¾ **Andiamo Via**[24] 5711 6-9-0 60 (p) PaulPickard(3) 1 42
(Brian Ellison) *trckd ldrs: effrt wl over 2f out: rdn along wl over 1f out: sn drvn and btn* 5/1[2]
40 9 8 **Drive Home (USA)**[31] 5471 6-8-12 58 (p) NeilFarley(3) 3 19
(Noel Wilson) *chsd ldrs on inner: edgd lft home turn: rdn along 3f out: sn wknd* 25/1
0060 10 3½ **Ptolemy**[31] 5471 4-9-1 58 GrahamGibbons 11 9
(David Barron) *towards rr racing wd: hung lft and rn wd home turn: bhd after* 18/1
0044 11 shd **Partner (IRE)**[17] 5973 7-9-0 60 JasonHart(3) 12 11
(Noel Wilson) *led: rdn along over 3f out: hdd wl over 2f out: sn drvn and grad wknd* 33/1

1m 31.27s (2.27) **Going Correction** +0.30s/f (Good)
WFA 3 from 4yo+ 3lb 11 Ran SP% 114.9
Speed ratings (Par 101): **99,99,95,93,89 89,88,87,78,74 74**WIN: Summer Dancer £2.90, Cara's Request £2.30; PLACE: SD £2.30, CR £2.00; EXACTA: SD&CR £15.20, CR&SD £15.10; CSF SD&CR £13.53, CR&SD £12.96. T/C: SD&CR&VR £78.57, CR&SD&VR £7.36. TRICAST: SD&CR&VR£112.40, CR&SD&VR £108.30., £2.60, £27Owner Stewart Aitken Trifecta £Bred S Aitken Trained.
Owner The Howarting's Partnership **Bred** Eddie O'Leary **Trained** Westow, N Yorks

FOCUS
Paul Mulrennan described the ground as being on the soft side of good. The front pair drew clear in what was a moderate handicap and proved inseparable at the line. Cara's Request sets the level rated to this year's form.

6465 DRINKS EXPRESS (S) STKS 7f 30y
2:40 (2:41) (Class 6) 2-Y-O £1,940 (£577; £288; £144) Stalls Low

Form RPR
500 1 **Maid In Rio (IRE)**[23] 5773 2-8-6 0 JoeFanning 3 75
(Mark Johnston) *trckd ldr: hdwy and cl up 1/2-way: led 3f out and sn edgd rt: rdn clr 2f out: kpt on* 16/1
1241 2 4½ **Black Treacle (IRE)**[21] 5834 2-9-2 78 (v) TomEaves 2 69
(Keith Dalgleish) *led: rdn along and jnd 1/2-way: hdd 3f out: sn swtchd lft: drvn 2f out and one pce* 6/5[1]
4430 3 ½ **Princess Tamay (IRE)**[23] 5773 2-8-6 66 DuranFentiman 1 57
(Mark Johnston) *chsd ldng pair: hdwy 3f out: rdn over 2f out: drvn over 1f out: one pce* 11/8[2]
0355 4 3¼ **Angel Rosa**[13] 6085 2-8-5 59 ow1 GeorginaBaxter(7) 5 52
(Keith Dalgleish) *in tch: hdwy and cl up 1/2-way: pushed along 3f out: rdn over 2f out and sn btn* 15/2[3]
060 5 6 **Boy Ranger (IRE)**[31] 5482 2-8-11 45 (v[1]) PJMcDonald 4 29
(Ann Duffield) *sn outpcd in rr: bhd fr 1/2-way* 50/1

1m 32.08s (3.08) **Going Correction** +0.30s/f (Good) 5 Ran SP% 107.2
Speed ratings (Par 93): **94,88,88,84,77**
CSF £34.42 TOTE £12.50: £5.70, £1.10; EX 41.10 Trifecta £103.90 Pool: £2851.25 - 20.56 winning units..The winner was bought in for £8,500.
Owner The New Fairyhouse Partnership **Bred** Miss Susan Bates And Suzannah Dwyer **Trained** Middleham Moor, N Yorks

FOCUS
Bit of a turn up in a seller that appeared to lack depth but nevertheless straightforward form rated around the placed horses.

6466 BATLEYS CASH AND CARRY H'CAP 2m
3:10 (3:10) (Class 4) (0-85,79) 3-Y-O+ £6,469 (£1,925; £962; £481) Stalls High

Form RPR
0016 1 **Man Of Plenty**[41] 5109 4-9-12 77 (p) PaulMulrennan 2 87
(Ed Dunlop) *trckd ldrs: hdwy to trck ldr 5f out: led 3f out: rdn and edgd lft ent fnl f: drvn out* 8/1
0002 2 1 **Bowdler's Magic**[10] 6165 6-9-9 77 (t) LMcNiff(3) 8 86
(David Thompson) *hld up in rr: hdwy on outer 3f out: effrt to chse ldrs wl over 1f out: rdn to chse wnr appr fnl f: sn drvn and kpt on* 16/1
1151 3 6 **Dr Irv**[17] 5972 4-9-11 79 DeclanCannon(3) 6 81
(Philip Kirby) *hld up towards rr: hdwy 3f out: rdn to chse ldrs wl over 1f out: drvn and edgd rt appr fnl f: sn one pce* 4/1[2]
6604 4 nk **Hit The Jackpot (IRE)**[8] 6237 4-9-10 75 DavidNolan 5 76
(David O'Meara) *trckd ldrs: smooth hdwy over 3f out: effrt to chse wnr over 2f out: rdn wl over 1f out: sn one pce* 4/1[2]
0222 5 4 **Jan Smuts (IRE)**[6] 6290 5-8-10 64 (tp) JasonHart(3) 1 60
(Wilf Storey) *rrd and lost several l s: hld up in rr: hdwy on outer 6f out: chsd ldrs 3f out: rdn over 2f out: sn drvn and no imp* 6/1[3]
1226 6 3¾ **Merchant Of Dubai**[26] 5640 8-9-9 77 LucyAlexander(3) 3 69
(Jim Goldie) *trckd ldrs on inner: pushed along and lost pl 7f out: bhd fr over 3f out* 10/1
3205 7 hd **Aleksandar**[26] 5640 4-9-6 71 GrahamLee 4 63
(Jim Goldie) *slt ld 3f: cl up: rdn along 3f out: sn wknd* 8/1
6050 8 15 **Federal Blue (USA)**[9] 6202 3-8-12 75 JoeFanning 7 49
(Mark Johnston) *cl up: slt ld after 3f: rdn along 4f out: hdd 3f out: sn wknd and bhd* 7/2[1]

3m 36.25s (2.75) **Going Correction** +0.30s/f (Good)
WFA 3 from 4yo+ 12lb 8 Ran SP% 113.7
Speed ratings (Par 105): **105,104,101,101,99 97,97,89**
toteswingers 1&2 £22.60, 1&3 £5.50, 2&3 £14.70 CSF £120.57 CT £585.77 TOTE £10.90: £2.40, £4.30, £1.10; EX 173.10 Trifecta £1064.50 Pool: £2154.62 - 1.51 winning units..
Owner Bluehills Racing Limited **Bred** Hesmonds Stud Ltd **Trained** Newmarket, Suffolk

FOCUS
They appeared to go a fair gallop in this decent staying event. The winner is rated back to his 3yo best, with the runner-up building on his latest form.

6467 BEST ONE NURSERY H'CAP 5f
3:40 (3:40) (Class 5) (0-75,72) 2-Y-O £3,881 (£1,155; £432; £432) Stalls High

Form RPR
1555 1 **One Boy (IRE)**[24] 5710 2-9-5 70 PaulMulrennan 1 73+
(Michael Dods) *in tch: hdwy to trck ldrs 2f out: effrt and nt clr run over 1f out: sn swtchd lft and rdn to ld ent fnl f: kpt on* 11/4[1]
3204 2 ¾ **Bounty Girl (IRE)**[9] 6194 2-9-3 68 (e[1]) DavidAllan 2 68
(Tim Easterby) *hld up in rr: swtchd rt to outer and stdy hdwy 2f out: rdn over 1f out: chal jst ins fnl f: sn drvn and kpt on* 9/2
6050 3 4½ **Classical Diva**[10] 6170 2-9-1 69 (b) NeilFarley(3) 6 53
(Declan Carroll) *wnt rt s: trckd ldrs: effrt 2f out: sn rdn and kpt on same pce fnl f* 20/1
6414 3 dht **Bountiful Forest**[13] 6082 2-8-8 62 JasonHart(3) 4 46
(Noel Wilson) *cl up: led 2f out: rdn over 1f out: hdd and drvn ent fnl f: kpt on same pce* 16/1
026 5 2½ **Noble Asset**[10] 6175 2-9-7 72 MichaelO'Connell 8 47
(John Quinn) *led: rdn along 1/2-way: hdd 2f out: sn drvn: edgd rt over 1f out and sn wknd* 4/1[3]
5446 6 1 **Straight Gin**[13] 6082 2-8-4 55 JamesSullivan 5 31
(Alan Berry) *sltly hmpd s: in rr: swtchd rt and rdn whn hmpd over 1f out: nvr a factor* 33/1
2513 7 hd **Kano's Ghirl (IRE)**[3] 6364 2-8-13 64 TomEaves 7 43
(Keith Dalgleish) *chsd ldrs: rdn along and hld whn hmpd over 1f out* 8/1

0014 **8** 2 1/4 **Fuel Injection**[22] 5787 2-8-9 **60** .... LeeTopliss 3 23
(Paul Midgley) *cl up: rdn along over 2f out: sn wknd* **7/2**[2]

1m 2.45s (2.05) **Going Correction** +0.475s/f (Yiel) **8** Ran SP% **111.8**
Speed ratings (Par 95): **102,100,93,93,89 88,87,84**
PLACE: Bountiful Forest £1.70, Classical Diva £2.80. T/C: OB&BGBF £79.39, OB&BG&CD £98.56. TRIFECTA: OB&BGBF £75.20, OB&BG&CD £90.90 CSF £14.62 TOTE £4.30: £2.30, £1.50; EX 17.30.
Owner Sekura Group **Bred** Tom Radley **Trained** Denton, Co Durham
FOCUS
Moderate nursery form and a messy race in behind. The runner-up sets the level for now.

6468 BEST IN CLAIMING STKS 1m 1f
4:10 (4:10) (Class 6) 3-Y-0+ **£1,940** (£577; £288; £144) **Stalls** Low

Form RPR
1230 **1** **Demolition**[8] 6239 9-8-11 75 .... JasonHart(3) 3 76
(Noel Wilson) *trckd ldr: led 3f out: rdn over 1f out: kpt on strly* **11/4**[2]
1261 **2** 1 1/2 **Extraterrestrial**[21] 5828 9-9-1 73 .... GeorgeChaloner(5) 2 79
(Richard Fahey) *in tch: hdwy to trck ldrs 1/2-way: effrt on inner 2f out: sn rdn: chsd wnr ins fnl f: sn no imp* **7/2**[3]
3365 **3** 1 3/4 **Prime Exhibit**[9] 6215 8-9-6 74 .... (t) JoeFanning 7 75
(John Stimpson) *dwlt and in rr: hdwy over 2f out: sn rdn: styd on fnl f: nrst fin* **9/1**
2505 **4** 1/2 **Royal Straight**[18] 5918 8-9-2 65 .... (t) PhillipMakin 5 70
(Linda Perratt) *hld up: hdwy over 2f out: rdn to chse ldrs over 1f out: drvn and one pce fnl f* **20/1**
4405 **5** 1 **Jebel Tara**[14] 6048 8-9-3 70 .... (tp) PaulPickard(3) 8 72
(Alan Brown) *trckd ldng pair on outer: hdwy to chse wnr 2f out: sn rdn and one pce appr fnl f* **12/1**
2101 **6** 1 3/4 **Seattle Drive (IRE)**[42] 5050 5-9-10 78 .... GrahamLee 1 72
(Brian Ellison) *trckd ldrs on inner: effrt and n.m.r over 2f out: sn rdn and n.d* **5/2**[1]
4640 **7** 1 **Bling King**[11] 6126 4-9-8 71 .... (b) PJMcDonald 6 68
(Geoffrey Harker) *dwlt: a towards rr* **14/1**
6131 **8** 3 1/4 **Yorksters Prince (IRE)**[57] 4562 6-9-1 59 .... (b) ShirleyTeasdale(5) 4 58
(Marjorie Fife) *led: hdd and rdn along 3f out: drvn 2f out and sn wknd* **20/1**

1m 55.22s (1.32) **Going Correction** +0.30s/f (Good) **8** Ran SP% **111.3**
Speed ratings (Par 101): **106,104,103,102,101 100,99,96**
toteswingers 1&2 £3.20, 1&3 £4.30, 2&3 £5.60 CSF £12.11 TOTE £3.60: £1.50, £2.10, £2.80; EX 13.40 Trifecta £65.20 Pool: £2824.06 - 32.45 winning units..Seattle Drive was claimed by Mr D Pipe for 10,000.
Owner M Wormald **Bred** P D And Mrs Player **Trained** Middleham, N Yorks
FOCUS
Quite a tight claimer best rated around the second and fourth.

6469 PETRUSHKA VODKA H'CAP (DIV I) 5f
4:40 (4:41) (Class 5) (0-70,69) 3-Y-0+ **£3,234** (£962; £481; £240) **Stalls** High

Form RPR
5003 **1** **Windforpower (IRE)**[19] 5889 3-8-5 51 .... (p) JoeFanning 9 59
(Tracy Waggott) *trckd ldrs: n.m.r and swtchd rt over 1f out: sn ev ch: kpt on to ld ins fnl f* **8/1**
2440 **2** nk **Economic Crisis (IRE)**[35] 5333 4-9-8 67 .... GrahamLee 1 74
(Alan Berry) *hld up in rr: hdwy wl over 2f out: rdn ent fnl f: sn chal and ev ch tl drvn and no ex towards fin* **12/1**
66 **3** 1/2 **Mr Mo Jo**[40] 5148 5-9-6 68 .... (p) JasonHart(3) 4 73
(Lawrence Mullaney) *cl up: rdn along 2f out: ev ch ent fnl f: sn drvn and nt qckn last 100yds* **7/1**
66 **4** 1 **Go Go Green (IRE)**[28] 5579 7-9-10 69 .... PhillipMakin 5 71+
(Jim Goldie) *hld up towards rr: hdwy 2f out: n.m.r over 1f out: effrt and nt clr run ins fnl f: kpt on towards fin* **13/2**[3]
4502 **5** 1/2 **Our Diane (IRE)**[80] 3779 3-8-9 60 .... GeorgeChaloner(5) 2 60
(Richard Fahey) *awkward and hmpd s: sn in tch: hdwy 2f out: rdn to ld jst over 1f out: drvn and hdd ins fnl f: one pce* **5/1**[1]
2265 **6** hd **Saxonette**[14] 6053 5-8-8 53 .... PJMcDonald 7 52
(Linda Perratt) *towards rr: hdwy and in tch 1/2-way: rdn along 2f out: kpt on fnl f: nrst fin* **17/2**
4050 **7** 1/2 **Mitchell**[6] 6287 3-9-2 65 .... (p) LMcNiff(3) 8 62
(David Thompson) *trckd ldrs: hdwy 2f out: effrt and n.m.r over 1f out: nt clr run ins fnl f: hld whn hmpd towards fin* **11/2**[2]
4604 **8** 1 **Headstight (IRE)**[16] 5989 4-8-0 50 oh2 .... (p) ShirleyTeasdale(5) 3 44
(Paul Midgley) *in tch: hdwy on outer 2f out: rdn and ch over 1f out: sn drvn and wknd ent fnl f* **7/1**
0060 **9** 1 **Boucher Garcon (IRE)**[108] 2832 5-8-10 58 .... NeilFarley(3) 6 48
(Declan Carroll) *prom: cl up 1/2-way: led 2f out: sn rdn and hdd jst over 1f out: sn wknd* **15/2**
1000 **10** 8 **Just Like Heaven (IRE)**[56] 4588 4-9-8 67 .... DuranFentiman 10 28
(Tim Easterby) *led: rdn along and hdd 2f out: sn wknd* **25/1**

1m 3.1s (2.70) **Going Correction** +0.475s/f (Yiel)
WFA 3 from 4yo+ 1lb **10** Ran SP% **115.3**
Speed ratings (Par 103): **97,96,95,94,93 93,92,90,89,76**
toteswingers 1&2 £10.20, 1&3 £6.60, 2&3 £17.90 CSF £98.24 CT £722.43 TOTE £7.50: £2.20, £4.20, £2.40; EX 80.70 Trifecta £449.00 Pool: £3073.67 - 5.13 winning units..
Owner David Tate **Bred** Tally-Ho Stud **Trained** Spennymoor, Co Durham
FOCUS
An open, low-grade sprint handicap that went to one of the 3-y-os. The placed horses help to set the level.

6470 XTRA LOCAL H'CAP (QUALIFIER FOR THE £15,000 SCOTTISH STAYERS' SERIES FINAL) 1m 4f 100y
5:10 (5:10) (Class 5) (0-70,67) 3-Y-0+ **£3,234** (£962; £481; £240) **Stalls** Low

Form RPR
321U **1** **Bayan Kasirga (IRE)**[18] 5920 3-9-1 67 .... GeorgeChaloner(5) 11 77
(Richard Fahey) *in tch: hdwy 3f out: rdn to ld 1 1/2f out: clr whn edgd lft and rdr dropped reign ins fnl f: kpt on strly* **11/2**[2]
6323 **2** 3 1/4 **Geanie Mac (IRE)**[13] 6087 4-8-12 51 .... (p) PJMcDonald 6 56
(Linda Perratt) *trckd ldrs: hdwy and cl up 3f out: rdn to dispute ld 2f out and ev ch tl drvn and one pce ent fnl f* **14/1**
305- **3** 1 3/4 **Burns Night**[18] 7768 7-9-9 62 .... (p) PhillipMakin 4 64
(Philip Kirby) *hld up and bhd: hdwy over 3f out: chsd ldrs 2f out: sn rdn and no imp fnl f* **13/2**[3]
3513 **4** 3 1/4 **Valantino Oyster (IRE)**[13] 6086 6-9-2 60 .... (p) ConnorBeasley(5) 8 57
(Tracy Waggott) *led: hdd over 7f out: cl up: rdn to ld again wl over 2f out: drvn and hdd 1 1/2f out: grad wknd* **17/2**
0005 **5** 1 1/4 **High On A Hill (IRE)**[10] 6177 6-9-5 58 .... (p) DavidAllan 7 53
(Iain Jardine) *bhd: hdwy on outer 3f out: rdn along wl over 1f out: kpt on fnl f: n.d* **13/2**[3]
4360 **6** 1 **Summerlea (IRE)**[6] 6290 7-9-0 53 .... RussKennemore 5 47
(Patrick Holmes) *nvr bttr than midfield* **12/1**
4346 **7** 1/2 **Maybeagrey**[30] 5548 4-9-8 61 .... DuranFentiman 12 54
(Tim Easterby) *hld up towards rr: hdwy 3f out: rdn along 2f out: nvr nr ldrs* **12/1**
0000 **8** 1 1/2 **Jawaab (IRE)**[13] 6086 9-9-5 58 .... (p) MichaelO'Connell 10 49
(Philip Kirby) *a towards rr* **22/1**
1040 **9** 2 1/4 **Amazing Blue Sky**[21] 5840 7-9-3 56 .... JamesSullivan 2 43
(Ruth Carr) *cl up: led over 7f out: rdn along over 3f out: hdd wl over 2f out and sn wknd* **18/1**
-043 **10** 18 **Grey Blue (IRE)**[13] 6071 3-9-5 66 .... JoeFanning 1 25
(Mark Johnston) *prom: effrt and cl up 3f out: sn rdn and wknd over 2f out* **3/1**[1]
5241 **11** 19 **Dean Iarracht (IRE)**[10] 6179 7-8-10 52 .... (p) JasonHart(3) 3
(Tracy Waggott) *in tch: rdn along over 3f out: sn wknd* **12/1**

2m 47.04s (5.04) **Going Correction** +0.30s/f (Good)
WFA 3 from 4yo+ 8lb **11** Ran SP% **116.9**
Speed ratings (Par 103): **95,92,91,89,88 88,87,86,85,73 60**
toteswingers 1&2 £14.50, 1&3 £10.40, 2&3 £17.00 CSF £79.37 CT £514.20 TOTE £6.40: £1.40, £5.00, £2.90; EX 93.80 Trifecta £437.90 Pool: £2022.45 - 3.46 winning units..
Owner Stephen Humphreys **Bred** Lynn Lodge Stud **Trained** Musley Bank, N Yorks
FOCUS
This appeared to be run at a fair gallop and it was one of the less-exposed 3-y-os who came to the fore. The runner-up is rated to the better view of this year's form.

6471 PETRUSHKA VODKA H'CAP (DIV II) 5f
5:40 (5:40) (Class 5) (0-70,69) 3-Y-0+ **£3,234** (£962; £481; £240) **Stalls** High

Form RPR
0060 **1** **Opt Out**[14] 6052 3-9-2 62 .... PJMcDonald 8 72
(Alistair Whillans) *hld up in tch: smooth hdwy wl over 1f out: rdn and qcknd ent fnl f: led last 100yds* **15/2**
0021 **2** 1/2 **Tom Sawyer**[18] 5930 5-9-5 69 .... (b) ConnorBeasley(5) 1 77
(Julie Camacho) *cl up: led 1/2-way: rdn ent fnl f: hdd and no ex last 100yds* **3/1**[1]
6622 **3** 1 1/4 **Here Now And Why (IRE)**[13] 6088 6-8-13 58 .... (p) DavidAllan 6 62
(Iain Jardine) *hld up in tch: hdwy 2f out: effrt and n.m.r over 1f out: sn rdn and kpt on fnl f* **4/1**[2]
0004 **4** 1 3/4 **Irish Girls Spirit (IRE)**[13] 6088 4-8-3 53 .... ShirleyTeasdale(5) 7 50
(Paul Midgley) *prom: effrt 2f out: sn rdn and n.m.r over 1f out: sn one pce* **10/1**
5620 **5** 3/4 **Commanche Raider (IRE)**[17] 5973 6-9-9 68 .... GrahamLee 9 63
(Michael Dods) *hld up in rr: hdwy 2f out: nt clr run and swtchd rt over 1f out: kpt on fnl f: nrst fin* **10/1**
5466 **6** hd **Ingleby Star (IRE)**[14] 6033 8-8-10 58 ow2 .... (be) PaulPickard(3) 2 52
(John Stimpson) *led: hdd 1/2-way: sn pushed along: rdn and ev ch over 1f out: wknd ent fnl f* **10/1**
00 **7** 1 **Findog**[14] 6052 3-9-7 67 .... PaulMulrennan 5 57
(Linda Perratt) *in tch: hdwy 2f out: chsd ldr over 1f out: sn rdn and btn whn n.m.r ins fnl f* **11/2**[3]
0010 **8** 3 **Chosen One (IRE)**[28] 5579 8-9-8 67 .... JamesSullivan 10 47
(Ruth Carr) *chsd ldrs on inner: pushed along and n.m.r 1/2-way: sn wknd* **22/1**
520 **9** 3/4 **Rock Canyon (IRE)**[14] 6053 4-8-5 50 oh1 .... (p) JoeFanning 4 27
(Linda Perratt) *in tch on outer: hdwy over 2f out: rdn along wl over 1f out: sn wknd* **11/1**
5654 **10** 3/4 **Rutterkin (USA)**[9] 6219 5-7-12 50 oh3 .... VictorSantos(7) 3 24
(James Moffatt) *a in rr* **28/1**

1m 2.29s (1.89) **Going Correction** +0.475s/f (Yiel)
WFA 3 from 4yo+ 1lb **10** Ran SP% **115.6**
Speed ratings (Par 103): **103,102,100,97,96 95,94,89,88,87**
toteswingers 1&2 £7.30, 1&3 £8.70, 2&3 £2.20 CSF £29.96 CT £106.88 TOTE £8.70: £2.90, £1.60, £1.80; EX 38.60 Trifecta £241.70 Pool: £2049.19 - 6.35 winning units..
Owner Akela Construction Ltd **Bred** Darley **Trained** Newmill-On-Slitrig, Borders
FOCUS
As in the first division it was won by one of the 3-y-os. The runner-up is rated back to last year's form with the third a shade off his latest C&D mark.
T/Plt: £106.30 to a £1 stake. Pool: £64588.96 - 443.44 winning tickets T/Qpdt: £33.10 to a £1 stake. Pool: £4167.10 - 93.10 winning tickets JR

6361 WOLVERHAMPTON (A.W) (L-H)
Monday, September 16

OFFICIAL GOING: Standard to slow
Wind: Fresh half-behind Weather: Cloudy with sunny spells

6472 32RED CASINO APPRENTICE H'CAP 1m 141y(P)
2:30 (2:30) (Class 6) (0-55,55) 3-Y-0+ **£1,940** (£577; £288; £144) **Stalls** Low

Form RPR
5223 **1** **Tatting**[12] 6103 4-9-7 55 .... JoshCrane 4 66+
(Chris Dwyer) *hld up: hdwy over 1f out: led ins fnl f: shkn up and r.o wl* **3/1**[1]
4504 **2** 2 **Katmai River (IRE)**[7] 6261 6-8-7 46 .... (v) CharlotteJenner(5) 12 52
(Mark Usher) *a.p: led wl over 1f out: rdn and hdd ins fnl f: styd on same pce* **12/1**
1330 **3** 2 **Supa Seeker (USA)**[12] 6102 7-8-11 50 .... AidenBlakemore(5) 5 52
(Tony Carroll) *chsd ldrs: rdn and nt clr run over 1f out: styd on same pce fnl f* **12/1**
0006 **4** hd **Justcallmehandsome**[4] 6339 11-8-7 46 oh1 .... (be) JosephineGordon(5) 7 47
(Dominic Ffrench Davis) *hld up: hdwy over 5f out: rdn over 1f out: styd on same pce fnl f* **16/1**
-002 **5** nk **Baile Atha Cliath (IRE)**[9] 6218 4-9-5 53 .... LukeLeadbitter 10 54
(Declan Carroll) *trckd ldr: racd keenly: led over 3f out: rdn and hdd wl over 1f out: styd on same pce ins fnl f* **4/1**[2]
2044 **6** 1 3/4 **Crucis Abbey (IRE)**[18] 5921 5-8-11 48 .... (p) GaryMahon(3) 13 45
(Mark Brisbourne) *prom: rdn over 2f out: no ex fnl f* **10/1**
000 **7** 1 1/2 **Just Five (IRE)**[32] 5426 7-8-10 49 .... (vt) JackGarritty(5) 8 42
(John Weymes) *rn wout declared tongue strap: dwlt: sn pushed along in rr: styd on ins fnl f: nvr nrr* **25/1**
1403 **8** nk **Devon Diva**[12] 6097 7-8-9 48 .... JeanVanOvermeire(5) 2 40
(John Gallagher) *led: hdd over 3f out: rdn and ev ch over 1f out: wknd ins fnl f* **16/1**
2403 **9** 2 1/4 **Meglio Ancora**[32] 5426 6-8-13 52 .... CharlieBennett(5) 3 39
(Richard Ford) *s.i.s: hld up: hmpd 7f out: hdwy and edgd lft over 1f out: wknd ins fnl f* **9/1**

5265 **10** 1 ½ **Lucky Mountain**[38] 5217 3-8-7 **46** oh1 AdamMcLean 6 31
(Scott Dixon) *trckd ldrs: rdn over 2f out: wkng whn n.m.r over 1f out* **9/2**[3]

6506 **11** nk **Daneside (IRE)**[16] 5980 6-9-0 **55** JackOsborn(7) 1 38
(Gary Harrison) *mid-div: effrt 2f out: wkng whn nt clr run over 1f out* **14/1**

1m 52.58s (2.08) **Going Correction** +0.225s/f (Slow)
WFA 3 from 4yo+ 5lb **11** Ran SP% **119.9**
Speed ratings (Par 101): **99,97,95,95,95 93,92,91,89,88 88**
toteswingers 1&2 £7.50, 1&3 £8.00, 2&3 £27.70 CSF £41.68 CT £395.11 TOTE £4.30: £2.20, £2.90, £4.20; EX 40.80 Trifecta £700.40 Pool: £1131.78 - 1.21 winning units..
Owner Mrs K W Sneath **Bred** Darley **Trained** Newmarket, Suffolk
■ Stewards' Enquiry : Gary Mahon three-day ban: careless riding (Sep 30,Oct 1-2)

FOCUS
A low-grade apprentice handicap run at a sound pace and the winner came from last to first. The winner is rated back to his best.

6473 £32 BONUS AT 32RED.COM (S) STKS — 1m 141y(P)
3:00 (3:00) (Class 6) 3-5-Y-O **£1,940** (£577; £288; £144) **Stalls** Low

Form RPR

2505 **1** **Fluctuation (IRE)**[19] 5899 5-9-6 68 (v) RobertTart(3) 3 72
(Ian Williams) *hld up: nt clr run over 2f out: hdwy over 1f out: sn rdn: r.o to ld wl ins fnl f* **8/1**[3]

6406 **2** nk **Honey Of A Kitten (USA)**[46] 4904 5-9-2 73 (v) EoinWalsh(7) 6 71
(David Evans) *sn led: hdd over 6f out: led again 5f out: rdn over 1f out: hdd wl ins fnl f: kpt on* **16/1**

0502 **3** 1 ¼ **The Guru Of Gloom (IRE)**[26] 5631 5-9-4 62 (b) ThomasGarner(5) 5 68
(William Muir) *s.i.s: hld up: racd keenly: hdwy on outer over 2f out: chsd ldr over 1f out: sn rdn: styd on same pce ins fnl f* **8/1**[3]

23 **4** 3 **Well Owd Mon**[36] 5301 3-8-7 0 JackDuern(5) 4 57
(Andrew Hollinshead) *sn w ldr: led over 6f out: hdd 5f out: chsd ldr: rdn over 2f out: no ex ins fnl f* **9/1**

2401 **5** 2 ¼ **Conducting**[12] 6114 5-9-9 70 LukeMorris 8 56
(Gay Kelleway) *chsd ldrs: pushed along 1/2-way: styd on same pce fnl 2f* **11/4**[1]

0100 **6** hd **Creek Falcon (IRE)**[54] 4628 4-9-9 77 DanielTudhope 2 56
(David O'Meara) *hld up in tch: nt clr run over 2f out: rdn over 1f out: no ex fnl f* **11/4**[1]

0005 **7** ¾ **Ajeeb (USA)**[26] 5631 5-9-0 65 (t) WilliamTwiston-Davies(3) 7 48
(Michael Scudamore) *trckd ldrs: rdn over 1f out: wknd ins fnl f* **14/1**

4000 **8** 2 ½ **Cocozza (USA)**[35] 5355 5-9-3 75 (p) JimmyQuinn 10 42
(K F Clutterbuck) *prom: rdn over 1f out: wknd fnl f* **7/1**[2]

000 **9** 99 **Idolise (IRE)**[41] 5092 4-9-3 26 (t) ChrisCatlin 1
(John Spearing) *sn outpcd* **100/1**

1m 51.5s (1.00) **Going Correction** +0.225s/f (Slow)
WFA 3 from 4yo+ 5lb **9** Ran SP% **111.6**
Speed ratings (Par 101): **104,103,102,99,97 97,97,94,6**
toteswingers 1&2 £20.50, 1&3 £10.50, 2&3 £13.20 CSF £119.48 TOTE £9.90: £2.40, £2.50, £2.40; EX 57.80 Trifecta £395.90 Pool: £1894.03 - 3.58 winning units..The winner was bought in for 3,250gns.
Owner J Tredwell **Bred** Corduff Stud & T J Rooney **Trained** Portway, Worcs

FOCUS
Official ratings had little bearing on the outcome of this seller which was run at a true pace. The third looks the key to the form with his best effort since the spring.

6474 32REDPOKER.COM NURSERY H'CAP — 7f 32y(P)
3:30 (3:30) (Class 6) (0-65,68) 2-Y-O **£1,940** (£577; £288; £144) **Stalls** High

Form RPR

5422 **1** **Vallila**[12] 6111 2-8-11 **61** JoeyHaynes(5) 1 67
(Roger Charlton) *chsd ldrs: pushed along over 2f out: rdn to ld and edgd rt over 1f out: r.o* **9/1**[3]

243 **2** 1 ¾ **Amadaffair**[15] 6013 2-9-2 **61** RichardKingscote 8 63
(Tom Dascombe) *chsd ldr: rdn over 2f out: styd on* **14/1**

2542 **3** 1 ¼ **The Dukkerer (IRE)**[19] 5898 2-9-4 **63** DanielTudhope 7 62
(David O'Meara) *led: rdn and hdd over 1f out: hung lft and no ex ins fnl f* **16/1**

21 **4** 2 **Starlight Serenade**[32] 5442 2-9-6 **65** JimCrowley 4 59+
(Ralph Beckett) *prom: rdn over 2f out: styd on same pce fnl f* **2/1**[2]

4061 **5** 1 ¼ **Relation Alexander (IRE)**[5] 6311 2-9-6 **68** 6ex RobertTart(3) 9 59
(Paul D'Arcy) *hld up: pushed along 1/2-way: hdwy over 2f out: rdn and edgd lft over 1f out: nt trble ldrs* **6/4**[1]

415 **6** 1 ¼ **Born To Fly (IRE)**[24] 5699 2-9-5 **64** JimmyQuinn 5 52
(Gary Harrison) *mid-div: pushed along 1/2-way: hdwy over 2f out: sn rdn: wknd ins fnl f* **11/1**

5250 **7** 2 ½ **Vodka Chaser (IRE)**[12] 6111 2-8-13 **65** CharlotteJenner(7) 3 47
(J S Moore) *prom: pushed along 3f out: wknd over 1f out* **50/1**

053 **8** 1 ¼ **Ambria's Fury (IRE)**[10] 6152 2-9-5 **64** MartinHarley 6 43
(Mick Channon) *s.i.s: hld up: rdn over 1f out: n.d* **18/1**

4563 **9** 1 ¼ **Severnwind (IRE)**[49] 4833 2-9-2 **61** LukeMorris 10 37
(Ronald Harris) *hld up: rdn over 2f out: n.d* **33/1**

2454 **10** 14 **Cheeky Peta'S**[13] 6073 2-9-6 **65** SilvestreDeSousa 11 6
(James Given) *hld up: a in rr: rdn and wknd over 2f out* **33/1**

1m 32.84s (3.24) **Going Correction** +0.225s/f (Slow) **10** Ran SP% **117.3**
Speed ratings (Par 93): **90,88,86,84,82 81,78,77,75,59**
toteswingers 1&2 £8.90, 1&3 £5.90, 2&3 £20.30 CSF £124.61 CT £2018.49 TOTE £8.00: £2.30, £2.80, £2.40; EX 103.70 Trifecta £594.30 Pool: £2942.84 - 3.71 winning units..
Owner L Norris **Bred** L Norris **Trained** Beckhampton, Wilts

FOCUS
It paid to race handily and the first three home were in the thick of the action throughout. Fillies dominated with just two males in the line-up. This rates a step up from the winner.

6475 32RED H'CAP (DIV I) — 7f 32y(P)
4:00 (4:01) (Class 5) (0-75,75) 3-Y-O+ **£3,234** (£962; £481; £240) **Stalls** High

Form RPR

6236 **1** **Take A Note**[13] 6080 4-9-7 **75** (v[1]) JimCrowley 3 85
(Patrick Chamings) *prom: hmpd and lost pl 6f out: hdwy u.p over 1f out: led ins fnl f: r.o wl* **3/1**[2]

3050 **2** 2 **Light Rose (IRE)**[21] 5830 3-9-2 **73** SilvestreDeSousa 6 77
(Mark Johnston) *a.p: hmpd 6f out: led over 1f out: rdn and hdd ins fnl f: styd on same pce* **6/1**

0445 **3** 3 ¼ **Khajaaly (IRE)**[24] 5713 6-9-0 **68** (tp) AndrewMullen 1 64
(Michael Appleby) *a.p: rdn over 1f out: styd on same pce fnl f* **16/1**

2501 **4** ½ **Illustrious Prince (IRE)**[6] 6291 6-8-13 **74** LukeLeadbitter(7) 10 68
(Declan Carroll) *s.i.s: sn prom: led 5f out: shkn up over 2f out: rdn and hdd over 1f out: no ex ins fnl f* **9/2**[3]

2112 **5** 5 **Bapak Muda (USA)**[36] 5300 3-8-11 **75** KevinStott(7) 7 55
(Kevin Ryan) *led 2f: chsd ldr: rdn over 2f out: edgd lft and wknd ins fnl f* **11/4**[1]

1045 **6** 2 ¼ **The Mongoose**[14] 6039 5-8-7 **68** (t) EoinWalsh(7) 4 43
(David Evans) *chsd ldrs: rdn over 2f out: wknd fnl f* **14/1**

2-3 **7** 8 **Ferryview Place**[234] 376 4-8-11 **65** (vt) StevieDonohoe 9 18
(Ian Williams) *s.i.s: a in rr* **7/1**

0000 **8** 5 **Lastkingofscotland (IRE)**[9] 6203 7-9-3 **71** (b) LiamKeniry 2 11
(Conor Dore) *sn pushed along in rr: nvr on terms* **25/1**

0400 **9** 99 **Roy's Legacy**[11] 6135 4-8-10 **64** (t) JimmyQuinn 8
(Shaun Harris) *chsd ldrs tl rdn and wknd over 2f out: eased sn after* **40/1**

1m 30.56s (0.96) **Going Correction** +0.225s/f (Slow)
WFA 3 from 4yo+ 3lb **9** Ran SP% **115.5**
Speed ratings (Par 103): **103,100,97,96,90 88,79,73,**
toteswingers 1&2 £4.10, 1&3 £8.60, 2&3 £8.90 CSF £21.47 CT £247.58 TOTE £4.90: £1.70, £2.10, £2.90; EX 26.80 Trifecta £228.20 Pool: £2630.66 - 8.64 winning units..
Owner The Foxford House Partnership **Bred** P J L Wright **Trained** Baughurst, Hants

FOCUS
The first two home had work to do after both met traffic problems in the first half of the race. The runner-up is rated in line with his best form and sets the standard.

6476 32RED H'CAP (DIV II) — 7f 32y(P)
4:30 (4:30) (Class 5) (0-75,75) 3-Y-O+ **£3,234** (£962; £481; £240) **Stalls** High

Form RPR

1333 **1** **Fossa**[9] 6214 3-8-10 **67** RobertWinston 7 79
(Dean Ivory) *trckd ldrs: wnt 2nd 4f out: led 2f out: r.o wl* **5/1**[2]

3611 **2** 2 ¾ **Avatar Star (IRE)**[33] 5393 3-9-3 **74** (tp) MartinHarley 4 79
(Marco Botti) *led 1f: chsd ldrs: rdn over 1f out: styd on same pce fnl f* **13/2**

5000 **3** ½ **Grilletto (USA)**[25] 5676 3-9-4 **75** (p) NeilCallan 8 78
(James Tate) *hld up: rdn over 2f out: hdwy u.p over 1f out: hung lft ins fnl f: r.o: nt rch ldrs* **11/2**[3]

1024 **4** ½ **Burning Dawn (USA)**[25] 5676 3-9-2 **73** HarryBentley 2 75
(David Brown) *prom: pushed along over 2f out: rdn over 1f out: styd on same pce fnl f* **6/1**

6101 **5** hd **The Great Gabrial**[10] 6154 4-8-13 **67** (b) SilvestreDeSousa 6 69+
(Ian Williams) *hld up: hdwy: nt clr run and swtchd rt 1f out: hung lft and r.o ins fnl f: nt rch ldrs* **7/2**[1]

301 **6** 1 ¼ **Ambitious Boy**[37] 5273 4-9-7 **75** DanielTudhope 3 74
(Andrew Hollinshead) *hld up: hdwy and nt clr run over 1f out: nvr trbld ldrs* **7/1**

2354 **7** nk **One Way Or Another (AUS)**[157] 1521 10-8-5 **66** EoinWalsh(7) 5 64
(David Evans) *sn pushed along into mid-div: hdwy over 2f out: rdn over 1f out: no ex fnl f* **25/1**

2520 **8** 5 **Meridius (IRE)**[54] 4636 3-9-1 **72** JimmyQuinn 9 56
(Gary Harrison) *s.i.s: hdwy over 4f out: rdn over 2f out: wknd fnl f* **10/1**

2000 **9** 3 ¾ **Exceedexpectations (IRE)**[9] 6204 4-9-5 **73** LiamKeniry 10 48
(Conor Dore) *led 6f out: rdn and hdd 2f out: wknd fnl f* **33/1**

0 **10** 5 **Casa Tua (FR)**[78] 3-8-6 **66** JulieBurke(3) 1 26
(David O'Meara) *s.i.s: a in rr: lost tch fr over 2f out* **20/1**

1m 30.61s (1.01) **Going Correction** +0.225s/f (Slow)
WFA 3 from 4yo+ 3lb **10** Ran SP% **115.0**
Speed ratings (Par 103): **103,99,99,98,98 97,96,91,86,81**
toteswingers 1&2 £2.80, 1&3 £5.90, 2&3 £8.90 CSF £35.93 CT £184.77 TOTE £7.00: £2.30, £1.60, £2.10; EX 30.20 Trifecta £228.20 Pool: £2942.49 - 9.67 winning units..
Owner Geoff Copp **Bred** G B Turnbull Ltd **Trained** Radlett, Herts

FOCUS
The second division of this modest handicap. The winner stepped up on his latest C&D form.

6477 32RED.COM E B F MAIDEN STKS — 5f 20y(P)
5:00 (5:02) (Class 5) 2-Y-O **£3,234** (£962; £481; £240) **Stalls** Low

Form RPR

442 **1** **Chorlton Manor (IRE)**[9] 6213 2-9-5 72 StevieDonohoe 11 78
(Nicky Vaughan) *chsd ldrs: shkn up over 1f out: edgd lft and r.o to ld wl ins fnl f: comf* **5/1**[3]

2222 **2** 1 ¼ **Genuine Quality (USA)**[14] 6034 2-9-0 76 HarryBentley 4 69
(Ed Vaughan) *w ldr tl led 2f out: rdn and hdd wl ins fnl f* **11/4**[1]

46 **3** nk **High On Life**[26] 5646 2-9-5 0 JimCrowley 1 72
(Jamie Osborne) *chsd ldrs: rdn over 1f out: styd on* **12/1**

4 **4** 1 **Bereka**[12] 6110 2-9-0 0 NeilCallan 9 64
(James Tate) *chsd ldrs: rdn and ev ch ins fnl f: styd on same pce* **7/2**[2]

4 **5** nk **Quantum Dot (IRE)**[100] 3092 2-9-5 0 RichardKingscote 8 70
(Tom Dascombe) *chsd ldrs: shkn up over 1f out: styng on whn hmpd wl ins fnl f: nt rcvr* **11/4**[1]

60 **6** 4 **Gulland Rock**[50] 4808 2-9-5 0 WilliamCarson 6 53
(William Muir) *led 3f: sn rdn: no wknd ins fnl f* **20/1**

7 2 ¾ **Caminel (IRE)** 2-9-0 0 RobertWinston 10 38
(Jeremy Gask) *s.i.s: sn pushed along in rr: nvr nrr* **25/1**

8 ½ **Dont Tell Nan** 2-8-7 0 AdamMcLean(7) 12 37
(Derek Shaw) *mid-div: pushed along 1/2-way: wknd over 1f out* **66/1**

9 2 ½ **Bazooka (IRE)** 2-9-2 0 DeclanBates(3) 7 33
(Ed de Giles) *hld up: pushed along 1/2-way: a in rr* **80/1**

0 **10** 1 ½ **Grande Mago (IRE)**[94] 3295 2-9-5 0 LiamKeniry 5 27
(Robert Cowell) *mid-div: pushed along 1/2-way: sn wknd* **14/1**

40 **11** 1 **Bob Masnicken**[45] 4963 2-9-5 0 LukeMorris 2 24
(Scott Dixon) *sn pushed along and a in rr* **66/1**

06 **12** 3 ¼ **Marlismamma (FR)**[9] 6213 2-8-11 0 JulieBurke(3) 3
(David O'Meara) *in rr: pushed along 3f out: wknd 1/2-way* **80/1**

1m 2.99s (0.69) **Going Correction** +0.225s/f (Slow) **12** Ran SP% **120.6**
Speed ratings (Par 95): **103,101,100,98,98 92,87,86,82,80 78,73**
toteswingers 1&2 £3.60, 1&3 £6.50, 2&3 £6.80 CSF £18.75 TOTE £6.10: £1.70, £1.30, £2.80; EX 22.80 Trifecta £208.80 Pool: £3441.77 - 12.35 winning units..
Owner Paul Wildes **Bred** Sinead & Joe Bishop **Trained** Stoke Heath, Shropshire
■ Stewards' Enquiry : Harry Bentley one-day ban: careless riding (Sep 30)

FOCUS
Probably an above-average 2-y-o maiden for the track. The form is rated around the first two and the fourth.

6478 32REDBET.COM H'CAP — 5f 216y(P)
5:30 (5:31) (Class 6) (0-55,58) 3-Y-O+ **£1,940** (£577; £288; £144) **Stalls** Low

Form RPR

5601 **1** **Father Fred**[14] 6033 3-9-5 **55** JimmyQuinn 12 74
(Chris Dwyer) *sn pushed along and prom: led 1f out: rdn out* **7/1**[2]

551 **2** 1 **Big Storm Coming**[4] 6343 3-9-8 **58** 6ex HarryBentley 5 73
(Brian Ellison) *hld up: hdwy over 1f out: rdn to chse wnr ins fnl f: r.o* **11/10**[1]

1066 **3** 4 **Charlemagne Diva**[24] 5704 3-8-11 **54** (t) KevinStott(7) 7 56
(Richard Guest) *chsd ldrs: rdn and ev ch over 1f out: styd on same pce ins fnl f* **8/1**[3]

The Form Book Flat, Raceform Ltd, Compton, RG20 6NL.

2000 **4** 1 ½ **Very First Blade**[21] 5818 4-8-11 **50**............................(p) JackDuern(5) 13 47
(Mark Brisbourne) *hdwy to ld over 4f out: rdn and hdd 1f out: no ex ins fnl f* **16/1**

-026 **5** ½ **Monty Fay (IRE)**[10] 6156 4-9-1 **49**..(t) NeilCallan 4 45
(Derek Haydn Jones) *hld up: hdwy over 2f out: rdn over 1f out: styd on same pce fnl f* **16/1**

4040 **6** 2 ½ **Marshall Art**[28] 5594 4-9-1 **52**..(tp) RobertTart(3) 1 40
(Ken Wingrove) *chsd ldrs: rdn over 1f out: wknd ins fnl f* **25/1**

0130 **7** hd **Almaty Express**[25] 5674 11-9-2 **55**............................(b) JoeyHaynes(5) 6 42
(John Weymes) *sn pushed along in rr: styd on ins fnl f: nvr nrr* **16/1**

0600 **8** 2 ¼ **Flow Chart (IRE)**[25] 5670 6-8-10 **49**.......................... SladeO'Hara(5) 3 29
(Peter Grayson) *hld up: pushed along and hung rt over 2f out: n.d* **22/1**

4666 **9** ¾ **Rise To Glory (IRE)**[9] 6219 5-9-5 **53**.......................(p) RobertWinston 11 30
(Shaun Harris) *chsd ldrs: rdn and ev ch over 1f out: wknd ins fnl f* **16/1**

4000 **10** hd **Lady Mango (IRE)**[21] 5818 5-9-4 **52**.......................... LukeMorris 8 29
(Ronald Harris) *mid-div: rdn over 2f out: sn wknd* **20/1**

3356 **11** ½ **Steel City Boy (IRE)**[160] 1452 10-8-13 **52**...................... AnnStokell(5) 9 27
(Ann Stokell) *led: hdd over 4f out: rdn and wknd over 1f out* **33/1**

5220 **12** 1 ½ **Lord Buffhead**[4] 6344 4-9-7 **55**..............................(v) RobbieFitzpatrick 2 25
(Richard Guest) *s.s: outpcd* **8/1**[3]

00-0 **13** 17 **My Best Man**[12] 6101 7-9-3 **51**.. LiamKeniry 10
(Tony Carroll) *s.s: outpcd* **66/1**

1m 16.24s (1.24) **Going Correction** +0.225s/f (Slow)
WFA 3 from 4yo+ 2lb **13** Ran SP% **123.3**
Speed ratings (Par 101): **100,98,93,91,90 87,87,84,83,82 82,80,57**
toteswingers 1&2 £2.80, 1&3 £9.00, 2&3 £3.70 CSF £14.56 CT £71.64 TOTE £8.70: £2.80, £1.10, £3.50; EX 19.60 Trifecta £155.80 Pool: £2394.21 - 11.52 winning units..
Owner Mrs C M Goode **Bred** Pedro Rosas **Trained** Newmarket, Suffolk

FOCUS
A moderate sprint handicap in which the first pair came clear, but the form is fluid and lacks depth.

6479 32REDBINGO.COM H'CAP 1m 4f 50y(P)
6:00 (6:03) (Class 6) (0-60,60) 3-Y-O+ **£1,940** (£577; £288; £144) **Stalls** Low

Form RPR

00-2 **1** **Amantius**[16] 5979 4-9-0 **48**..(b) CathyGannon 4 59
(Johnny Farrelly) *a.p: rdn over 1f out: styd on to ld wl ins fnl f* **8/1**

6133 **2** ¾ **Men Don't Cry (IRE)**[14] 6044 4-9-8 **56**............................(b) LiamKeniry 5 66
(Ed de Giles) *trckd ldrs: led over 1f out: sn rdn: hdd wl ins fnl f* **9/2**[1]

0-00 **3** 4 ½ **Divea**[70] 4126 4-9-12 **60**.. WilliamCarson 1 63
(Anthony Carson) *hld up: hdwy u.p over 1f out: styd on to go 3rd nr fin: nt trble ldrs* **17/2**

0256 **4** ½ **Light The City (IRE)**[19] 5897 6-8-12 **46**.............................. LukeMorris 6 48
(Ruth Carr) *trckd ldr tl led wl over 1f out: sn rdn and hdd: edgd lft and no ex ins fnl f* **6/1**[2]

5323 **5** 7 **Eyeline**[16] 5979 3-8-9 **56**...(v) JackDuern(5) 7 47
(Andrew Hollinshead) *led: rdn and hdd wl over 1f out: wknd fnl f* **13/2**[3]

3353 **6** 1 ¼ **Elizabeth Coffee (IRE)**[4] 6339 5-9-4 **52**......................(t) JimmyQuinn 12 41
(John Weymes) *s.s: hld up: hdwy over 3f out: rdn and wknd over 1f out* **9/2**[1]

4000 **7** 21 **Satwa Laird**[93] 3329 7-9-4 **57**.. AnnStokell(5) 2 12
(Ann Stokell) *hld up: pushed along over 3f out: sn lost tch* **33/1**

04-5 **8** hd **Likelikelikelikeit**[31] 5497 3-8-13 **55**.......................... SilvestreDeSousa 9 10
(Mark H Tompkins) *prom: pushed along over 5f out: rdn and wknd over 1f out* **8/1**

9 5 **Song Of Pride (GER)**[534] 4513 9-9-12 **60**.......................... ChrisCatlin 3 7
(Mandy Rowland) *hld up: rdn over 4f out: wknd over 3f out* **25/1**

006 **10** 13 **Cape Rosa**[10] 6166 3-8-1 **46**.. RaulDaSilva(3) 10
(James Moffatt) *hld up: pushed along over 3f out: sn wknd* **22/1**

2150 **11** 11 **Midnight Bahia (IRE)**[180] 1090 4-9-4 **52**.................... RobertWinston 11
(Dean Ivory) *chsd ldrs tl rdn and wknd over 2f out* **8/1**

2m 44.28s (3.18) **Going Correction** +0.225s/f (Slow)
WFA 3 from 4yo+ 8lb **11** Ran SP% **119.0**
Speed ratings (Par 101): **98,97,94,94,89 88,74,74,71,62 55**
toteswingers 1&2 £8.40, 1&3 £20.00, 2&3 £8.70 CSF £43.48 CT £320.96 TOTE £7.50: £2.10, £1.90, £4.80; EX 51.90 Trifecta £499.40 Pool: £2384.29 - 3.58 winning units..
Owner Wayne Clifford **Bred** Mickley Stud **Trained** Bridgwater, Somerset
■ The first training success for former jump jockey Johnny Farrelly.

FOCUS
A modest middle-distance handicap but a personal-best from the winner.
T/Jkpt: Not won. T/Plt: £668.60 to a £1 stake. Pool: £79637.90 - 86.94 winning tickets T/Qpdt: £107.30 to a £1 stake. Pool: £6739.72 - 46.45 winning tickets CR

6059 SAINT-CLOUD (L-H)
Monday, September 16
OFFICIAL GOING: Turf: very soft

6484a PRIX JOUBERT (LISTED RACE) (3YO FILLIES) (TURF) 1m 4f
3:40 (12:00) 3-Y-O **£22,357** (£8,943; £6,707; £4,471; £2,235)

RPR

1 **Siljan's Saga (FR)**[27] 5629 3-9-1 0...................... Pierre-CharlesBoudot 1 107
(J-P Gauvin, France) **42/10**[2]

2 shd **Childa (IRE)**[124] 2381 3-9-1 0.................................. ChristopheSoumillon 3 107
(S Wattel, France) **10/1**

3 nk **Ebiyza (IRE)**[19] 3-8-11 0.............................. Christophe-PatriceLemaire 2 103
(A De Royer-Dupre, France) **8/1**[3]

4 1 ¾ **Perfect Queen (FR)**[50] 3-8-11 0.................................. AurelienLemaitre 4 100
(F Head, France) **12/1**

5 1 **Oriental Wind**[36] 5315 3-8-11 0.................................. StephanePasquier 8 98
(Rod Collet, France) **14/1**

6 hd **Cushion**[43] 5035 3-8-11 0.. WilliamBuick 13 98
(John Gosden) *midfield in tch on outer: rdn over 2f out: ev ch whn briefly short of room over 1f out: styd on steadily after but nt quite pce to chal* **3/1**[1]

7 3 **Soccer Mom (GER)**[39] 3-8-11 0.................................... GregoryBenoist 5 93
(X Nakkachdji, France) **9/1**

8 2 **Alta Stima (IRE)**[65] 4323 3-8-11 0.................................. OlivierPeslier 6 90
(E Lellouche, France) **13/1**

9 2 ½ **Tunkwa (FR)**[36] 5315 3-8-11 0...............................(p) AntoineHamelin 7 86
(D Sepulchre, France) **21/1**

10 1 ¼ **Snow Pine**[39] 3-8-11 0.. MlleAmelieFoulon 11 84
(A Fabre, France) *trckd ldr: rdn and lost pl over 2f out: sn no ex and btn: fdd: eased towards fin* **8/1**[3]

11 nk **Scarlet Sonnet (IRE)**[65] 4323 3-8-11 0...................... TheoBachelot 10 83
(S Wattel, France) **25/1**

12 5 **Sea Claria (FR)**[16] 3-8-11 0.. ThierryThulliez 9 83
(T Doumen, France) **69/1**

2m 43.73s (3.33) **12** Ran SP% **116.9**
WIN (incl. 1 euro stake): 5.20. PLACES: 2.20, 3.50, 2.70. DF: 30.50. SF: 31.80.
Owner E Palluat De Besset & E Tassin **Bred** Mme P Ouvry **Trained** France

6318 CHEPSTOW (L-H)
Tuesday, September 17
OFFICIAL GOING: Soft changing to heavy after race 2 (2.50)
Wind: Virtually nil Weather: Light rain

6485 32 RED CASINO EBF MAIDEN STKS 7f 16y
2:20 (2:22) (Class 5) 2-Y-O **£2,911** (£866; £432; £216) **Stalls** Centre

Form RPR

1 **Davids Park** 2-9-5 0.. JamesDoyle 2 77+
(John Joseph Murphy, Ire) *s.i.s: in rr: hdwy 3f out: pushed along to ld ins fnl 2f: styd on strly fnl f* **6/1**

0 **2** 4 ½ **Dimity (IRE)**[9] 6242 2-8-11 0.. IJBrennan(3) 8 61+
(John Joseph Murphy, Ire) *sn trcking ldrs: travelling wl 2f out: pushed along to chse wnr sn after: no imp but hld on wl for 2nd clsng stages* **3/1**[1]

00 **3** nk **Nick The Odds (IRE)**[64] 4351 2-8-12 0............... JosephineGordon(7) 4 65
(Jo Hughes) *chsd ldrs: pushed along over 2f out: kpt on to press for 2nd ins fnl f but nvr any ch w wnr* **33/1**

4 2 ¼ **Manor Way (IRE)** 2-9-2 0.............................. WilliamTwiston-Davies(3) 9 60+
(Richard Hannon) *slowly away: in rr: hdwy and in tch 1/2-way: shkn up and kpt on to take wl hld 4th clsng stages* **7/2**[2]

05 **5** ¾ **Trigger Park (IRE)**[11] 6152 2-9-5 0................................ CathyGannon 7 58
(Ronald Harris) *chsd ldrs: led ins fnl 3f: hdd u.p ins fnl 2f wknd ins fnl f* **10/1**

00 **6** hd **Ferngrove (USA)**[60] 4483 2-9-5 0........................... RichardKingscote 6 57
(Jonathan Portman) *sn led: hdd ins fnl 3f: wknd over 1f out* **10/1**

00 **7** ¾ **Allergic Reaction (IRE)**[25] 5698 2-9-5 0........................ AdamKirby 5 55
(William Knight) *in tch and rdn along 3f out: wknd over 1f out* **5/1**[3]

1m 30.71s (7.51) **Going Correction** +0.825s/f (Soft) **7** Ran SP% **99.3**
Speed ratings (Par 95): **90,84,84,81,81 80,80**
Tote Swingers: 1&2 £3.50, 1&3 £9.70, 2&3 £14.10 CSF £18.15 TOTE £5.20: £2.80, £1.60; EX 22.00 Trifecta £137.70 Pool: £750.94 - 4.09 winning units..
Owner Mrs Judith Cash & D Cash **Bred** D E And Mrs J Cash **Trained** Upton, Co. Cork

FOCUS
After heavy morning rain, the going eased to soft. This weak maiden was run at a steady pace, with the field racing middle-to-stands' side. Mind, backed at prices in the morning, got upset in the stalls and had to be withdrawn while Jessy May refused to enter the stalls. The winner impressed but it's hard to rate this form higher.

6486 32RED MAIDEN STKS 7f 16y
2:50 (2:51) (Class 5) 3-Y-O+ **£2,587** (£770; £384; £192) **Stalls** Centre

Form RPR

4 **1** **Favourite Treat (USA)**[14] 6084 3-9-5 0.............................. AdamKirby 7 93+
(Mark Johnston) *racd stands' side: disp ld tl def advantage over 2f out: drvn clr fnl f* **4/1**

22 **2** 9 **Endless Light**[22] 5839 3-9-0 0... JamesDoyle 3 66
(Jeremy Noseda) *racd towards far side: drvn to chse wnr 2f out but nvr any ch: fin 1st in gp* **11/4**[1]

4 **3** 1 ½ **Artistical (IRE)**[171] 1243 3-9-5 0...................................... GeorgeBaker 5 67
(William Haggas) *chsd ldrs on stands' side: no ch w wnr fr 2f out: fin 2nd in gp* **3/1**[2]

200 **4** nk **Pashan Garh**[76] 3961 4-9-8 **75**.. LiamKeniry 2 67
(Pat Eddery) *cashed ldrs far side: rdn 3f out: no ch w wnr fr 2f out and styd on same pce: fin 2nd in gp* **7/2**[3]

4262 **5** 4 ½ **Disco Inferno (IRE)**[19] 5932 3-9-5 **75**.......................(bt) JimmyFortune 1 55
(Brian Meehan) *racd far side and disp ld tl rdn over 2f out: sn btn: fin 3rd in gp* **5/1**

4 **6** 5 **Ninepointsixthree**[40] 5176 3-9-5 0...................................... FergusSweeney 4 42
(John O'Shea) *racd centre to far side: chsd ldrs 3f: sn wknd: fin 4th in gp* **50/1**

040 **7** hd **Bustling Darcey**[56] 4607 3-8-9 42................................ OisinMurphy(5) 6 37
(Mark Gillard) *racd stands' side: chsd ldrs 3f: sn wknd: fin 3rd in gp* **100/1**

1m 27.73s (4.53) **Going Correction** +0.825s/f (Soft)
WFA 3 from 4yo 3lb **7** Ran SP% **113.5**
Speed ratings (Par 103): **107,96,95,94,89 83,83**
Tote Swingers: 1&2 £3.40, 1&3 £3.20, 2&3 £3.10 CSF £15.19 TOTE £5.60: £2.50, £2.10; EX 21.80 Trifecta £73.70 Pool: £2,046.05 - 20.80 winning units..
Owner Sheikh Hamdan Bin Mohammed Al Maktoum **Bred** Fares Farm Inc **Trained** Middleham Moor, N Yorks

FOCUS
The pace was fair for this maiden, with the time 2.91 seconds quicker then the first division. They finished at long intervals, with the winner racing alone up the stands' rail. The winner could be rated higher but the going limits enthusiasm.

6487 32RED.COM NURSERY H'CAP 6f 16y
3:20 (3:22) (Class 5) (0-70,69) 2-Y-O **£2,587** (£770; £384; £192) **Stalls** Centre

Form RPR

424 **1** **Golden Spear**[27] 5646 2-9-5 **67**..(p) PatCosgrave 5 79+
(Noel Quinlan) *chsd ldrs: rdn over 2f out: led appr fnl f: edgd rt u.p: sn clr* **7/2**[2]

3206 **2** 4 ½ **Llyrical**[64] 4347 2-9-6 **68**.. DaneO'Neill 3 65
(Derek Haydn Jones) *pressed ldr: slt ld fr 3f out: rdn 2f out: hdd appr fnl f: sn no ch w wnr: hld on wl for 2nd* **9/2**[3]

060 **3** hd **Dandys Perier (IRE)**[11] 6152 2-8-5 **53**.......................... CathyGannon 4 49
(Ronald Harris) *in tch: rdn and outpcd over 2f out: styd on fnl f to take 3rd nr fin and clsng on 2nd but no ch w wnr* **12/1**

356 **4** ½ **Glebe Spirit (IRE)**[11] 6168 2-9-7 **69**.................................... PatDobbs 8 64
(Richard Hannon) *chsd ldrs: rdn and outpcd over 2f out: styd on again fnl f and tk 4th clsng stages* **2/1**[1]

4066 **5** 1 ¼ **Thrtypointstothree (IRE)**[22] 5842 2-8-11 **64**.............. OisinMurphy(5) 2 55
(Nikki Evans) *led: narrowly hdd 3f out: wknd ins finak f and lost 2 pls clsng stages* **16/1**

3305 **6** 9 **Tamayuz Magic (IRE)**[62] 4399 2-9-4 **66**............................ AdamKirby 6 30
(Mark Johnston) *chsd ldrs: rdn 3f out and sn btn* **5/1**

4446 **7** *1 ¾* **Senorita Guest (IRE)**[14] 6076 2-8-11 **62**.................. CharlesBishop(3) 1 21
(Mick Channon) *bhd most of way* **8/1**

1m 16.41s (4.41) **Going Correction** +0.825s/f (Soft) 7 Ran SP% **115.1**
Speed ratings (Par 95): **103,97,96,96,94 82,80**
Tote Swingers: 1&2 £4.90, 1&3 £11.90, 2&3 £10.50 CSF £19.82 CT £168.38 TOTE £4.80: £2.00, £2.80; EX 24.40 Trifecta £127.60 Pool: £1,943.89 - 11.42 winning units..
Owner Newtown Anner Stud Farm Ltd **Bred** D P And Mrs J A Martin **Trained** Newmarket, Suffolk

FOCUS
Four of the seven runners were making their nursery debut. It was run at a fair pace and the winner scoped emphatically, but again the bad ground suggests a negative stance is best form now.

6488 PICKWICK BOOKMAKERS H'CAP 7f 16y
3:50 (3:50) (Class 4) (0-85,85) 3-Y-O **£4,690** (£1,395; £697; £348) **Stalls** Centre

Form RPR

0542 **1** **Kyllachy Rise**[24] 5759 3-9-5 **83**.. PatDobbs 5 96+
(Richard Hannon) *trckd ldr: led ins fnl 3f: drvn clr over 1f out: edgd rt and styd on strly ins fnl f* **5/2**[1]

0225 **2** *5* **Related**[34] 5401 3-9-5 **83**.. AdamKirby 1 84
(Clive Cox) *s.i.s: sn in tch: chsd wnr over 2f out: no ch fr over 1f out but kpt on wl for 2nd fnl f* **4/1**[3]

3212 **3** *1 ¼* **Secret Beau**[10] 6215 3-8-11 **78**...................................... DeclanBates(3) 3 75
(David Evans) *chsd ldrs: rdn and outpcd over 2f out: styd on again fnl f to take 3rd fnl 110yds* **12/1**

1311 **4** *1 ½* **Tight Fit**[31] 5541 3-9-7 **85**.. DaneO'Neill 7 79
(Henry Candy) *chsd ldrs: drvn to dispute 2nd over 1f out: no imp on wnr: wknd fnl 150yds* **11/4**[2]

0100 **5** *1 ½* **Unknown Villain (IRE)**[48] 4879 3-9-2 **80**................. RichardKingscote 4 70
(Tom Dascombe) *t.k.h: rdn over 2f out: no prog and no ch sn after* **8/1**

1531 **6** *15* **Clement (IRE)**[52] 4772 3-8-10 **74**.. JohnFahy 2 26
(John O'Shea) *a in rr* **16/1**

1-35 **7** *3 ½* **Intrepid (IRE)**[47] 4908 3-9-0 **78**....................................(v[1]) JamesDoyle 6 31
(Jeremy Noseda) *t.k.h: led tl hdd ins fnl 3f: sn wknd* **7/1**

1m 28.36s (5.16) **Going Correction** +0.825s/f (Soft) 7 Ran SP% **112.4**
Speed ratings (Par 103): **103,97,95,94,92 75,71**
Tote Swingers: 1&2 £2.60, 1&3 £3.30, 2&3 £4.70 CSF £12.38 TOTE £3.20: £1.80, £3.30; EX 15.00 Trifecta £82.10 Pool: £1,856.97 - 16.95 winning units..
Owner Arjun Waney **Bred** Whatton Manor Stud **Trained** East Everleigh, Wilts

FOCUS
This fair handicap was run at a sound pace in the conditions and the form could be rated higher.

6489 £32 FREE AT 32RED.COM CLAIMING STKS 7f 16y
4:20 (4:20) (Class 6) 3-Y-O+ **£1,940** (£577; £288; £144) **Stalls** Centre

Form RPR

241 **1** **Peak Storm**[11] 6155 4-9-1 67.......................................(p) OisinMurphy(5) 5 79+
(John O'Shea) *chsd ldrs: led appr fnl 2f: pushed clr over 1f out: easily* **11/4**[2]

3041 **2** *5* **Raging Bear (USA)**[3] 6410 3-8-13 73...........................(v[1]) DaneO'Neill 6 61
(Richard Hannon) *in tch: rdn 3f out: outpcd u.p over 2f out and last over 1f out: styd on u.p fnl f to take wl hld 2nd fnl 30yds* **9/4**[1]

-662 **3** *1 ¼* **Billyrayvalentine (CAN)**[11] 6155 4-9-2 72...................... PatCosgrave 2 58
(George Baker) *rrd stalls: hood off late and slowly away: in tch 1/2-way: outpcd u.p over 2f out: rallied fnl f to take 3rd fnl 30yds: no ch w wnr* **6/1**

0050 **4** *½* **Rapid Water**[18] 5948 7-8-10 45.......................................(p) LiamKeniry 1 51
(Pat Eddery) *in rr but in tch: hdwy u.p over 1f out: tk one pce 4th fnl 150yds* **66/1**

06/0 **5** *1 ½* **Egotist (IRE)**[11] 6163 5-9-10 86............................ RichardKingscote 7 61
(Milton Bradley) *led: hdd appr fnl 2f: wknd fnl 120yds* **7/1**

3040 **6** *shd* **Johnny Castle**[14] 6067 5-9-10 78.......................................(p) PatDobbs 4 61
(Amanda Perrett) *chsd ldr: chsd wnr over 1f out but nvr any ch: wknd fnl 120yds* **7/2**[3]

1m 28.59s (5.39) **Going Correction** +0.825s/f (Soft)
WFA 3 from 4yo+ 3lb 6 Ran SP% **107.9**
Speed ratings (Par 101): **102,96,94,94,92 92**
Tote Swingers: 1&2 £1.70, 1&3 £3.00, 2&3 £2.00 CSF £8.58 TOTE £3.70: £2.30, £2.00; EX 10.40 Trifecta £23.50 Pool: £1,854.27 - 59.17 winning units..Raging Bear claimed by Mr James Evans £10,000.
Owner The Cross Racing Club **Bred** Redhill Bloodstock Limited **Trained** Elton, Gloucs

FOCUS
Not a bad contest for the grade, run at a steady pace. The field raced up the centre with the winner pulling clear. A personal-best from the winner with the lowly rated fourth not limiting things, having run well on similar ground here before.

6490 32REDPOKER.COM H'CAP 1m 4f 23y
4:50 (4:51) (Class 4) (0-85,83) 3-Y-O+ **£4,690** (£1,395; £697; £348) **Stalls** Low

Form RPR

3424 **1** **Princess Caetani (IRE)**[23] 5795 4-9-7 **83**.................... OisinMurphy(5) 2 93
(David Dennis) *hld up in rr: hdwy 3f out: drvn to chse ldr 2f out: chal 1f out: sn led: styd on strly* **7/2**[2]

1410 **2** *2 ¼* **Astra Hall**[23] 5795 4-9-7 **78**.. JimCrowley 6 85
(Ralph Beckett) *led: rdn 2f out: jnd 1f out: hdd jst ins fnl f: sn outpcd by wnr but wl clr of 3rd* **9/4**[1]

0426 **3** *6* **Takeitfromalady (IRE)**[13] 6108 4-9-8 **79**..................(b) CathyGannon 8 77
(Lee Carter) *chsd ldrs: wnt 2nd 7f out: rdn 3f out: dropped to 3rd 2f out: no ch w ldng duo after* **8/1**[3]

0141 **4** *nk* **Rutherglen**[24] 5762 3-8-12 **77**.. PatCosgrave 4 74
(George Baker) *chsd ldrs: rdn over 3f out: btn 2f out* **9/4**[1]

0- **5** *4 ½* **Burnt Sienna (IRE)**[20] 5910 3-8-2 **70**............................ IJBrennan(3) 5 60
(John Joseph Murphy, Ire) *in tch: rdn and outpcd 4f out: mod prog u.p fnl f* **10/1**

0/6 **6** *17* **Ceannline (IRE)**[22] 5847 7-8-9 **69**.................. WilliamTwiston-Davies(3) 7 34
(Venetia Williams) *chsd ldrs: wknd over 3f out* **20/1**

360- **7** *4 ½* **Hamilton Hill**[395] 5359 6-8-8 **70**.................................(t) DanielMuscutt(5) 1 28
(Bernard Llewellyn) *in tch: rdn 4f out: sn btn* **25/1**

6445 **8** *1 ¼* **Phoenix Flight (IRE)**[161] 1454 8-9-6 **77**....................(b) FergusSweeney 3 33
(James Evans) *a in rr: t.o fnl 4f* **33/1**

2m 47.08s (8.08) **Going Correction** +0.825s/f (Soft)
WFA 3 from 4yo+ 8lb 8 Ran SP% **115.5**
Speed ratings (Par 105): **106,104,100,100,97 85,82,82**
Tote Swingers: 1&2 £3.80, 1&3 £3.40, 2&3 £3.90 CSF £11.67 CT £57.53 TOTE £4.40: £1.80, £1.50, £2.50; EX 10.50 Trifecta £49.10 Pool: £1,757.14 - 26.79 winning units..
Owner Favourites Racing **Bred** Barronstown Stud **Trained** Hanley Swan, Worcestershire
■ The first winner as a trainer for former jump jockey David Dennis.

FOCUS
This looked competitive enough. It was run at an honest pace with the field racing up the far rail. The first two are both rated improvers.

6491 32RED ON THE APP STORE H'CAP (DIV I) 1m 2f 36y
5:20 (5:22) (Class 6) (0-65,65) 3-Y-O+ **£1,940** (£577; £288; £144) **Stalls** Low

Form RPR

0605 **1** **April Ciel**[5] 6325 4-9-7 **62**...(p) CathyGannon 9 71
(Ronald Harris) *mde all: drvn over 1f out: kpt on wl fnl f: rdr dropped whip clsng stages: unchal* **6/1**[2]

10 **2** *5* **Monopoli**[82] 3721 4-9-5 **60**... JimCrowley 10 60
(John O'Shea) *in tch: hdwy 3f out: chsd unchal wnr over 1f out but nvr any ch* **7/1**[3]

2601 **3** *nk* **Petersboden**[13] 6097 4-8-11 **52** oh2 ow1.................... FergusSweeney 3 51
(Michael Blanshard) *in tch: drvn and no prog over 2f out: styd on ins fnl f to take 3rd clsng stages and gaining on 2nd but no ch w wnr* **33/1**

0500 **4** *1* **Arte Del Calcio**[12] 6137 4-8-10 **51** oh3............................ JimmyQuinn 11 49
(Tony Carroll) *s.i.s: t.k.h after 2f and chsd wnr 5f out: rdn and no imp over 2f out: one pce into 4th fnl f* **25/1**

0660 **5** *nk* **Hallingham**[46] 4961 3-9-4 **65**....................................... RichardKingscote 7 62
(Jonathan Portman) *in rr: hdwy fr 3f out: kpt on u.p fnl f to cl on plcd horses but nvr any ch w wnr* **33/1**

650 **6** *½* **Stockhill Diva**[51] 4799 3-9-2 **63**.. PatDobbs 5 59
(Brendan Powell) *in rr: hdwy on rails and drvn over 1f out: kpt on fnl f* **12/1**

0241 **7** *1* **Be My Rock**[7] 6283 4-9-5 **65**.. OisinMurphy(5) 1 59
(Rae Guest) *chsd ldrs: rdn over 2f out: wknd fnl f* **1/1**[1]

040 **8** *6* **Evermore (IRE)**[18] 5942 3-9-3 **64**...................................... AdamKirby 2 48
(Mark Johnston) *chsd ldrs: rdn over 2f out: sn btn* **8/1**

6454 **9** *21* **Aphrodite Spirit (IRE)**[13] 6103 3-8-5 **52** oh5 ow1...........[1] ChrisCatlin 8
(Pat Eddery) *chsd ldr 5f: wknd qckly over 3f out* **16/1**

10 *4* **Hypatia (IRE)**[25] 5729 3-8-10 **60**...............................(bt[1]) IJBrennan(3) 6
(John Joseph Murphy, Ire) *in rr: rdn and sme hdwy over 3f out: wknd over 2f out: virtually p.u fnl f* **25/1**

2m 17.96s (7.36) **Going Correction** +0.825s/f (Soft)
WFA 3 from 4yo 6lb 10 Ran SP% **115.0**
Speed ratings (Par 101): **103,99,98,97,97 96,96,91,74,71**
Tote Swingers: 1&2 £10.30, 1&3 £14.90, 2&3 £17.50 CSF £44.59 CT £1257.86 TOTE £8.50: £2.10, £2.40, £5.60; EX 51.50 Trifecta £902.00 Part won. Pool: £1,202.72 - 0.70 winning units..
Owner Paul & Ann de Weck **Bred** Paul And Ann De Weck **Trained** Earlswood, Monmouths

FOCUS
A decent pace for this moderate handicap. The winner is rated back towards his best, with the next three home confirming the level.

6492 32RED ON THE APP STORE H'CAP (DIV II) 1m 2f 36y
5:50 (5:50) (Class 6) (0-65,65) 3-Y-O+ **£1,940** (£577; £288; £144) **Stalls** Low

Form RPR

4543 **1** **Bold Duke**[111] 2785 5-9-5 **65** ow1.............................. RobertWilliams(5) 10 74
(Edward Bevan) *in rr: hdwy 3f out: drvn to ld 2f out: styd on wl fnl f* **5/1**[1]

-044 **2** *3 ½* **Descaro (USA)**[53] 4713 7-9-0 **55**.................................. FergusSweeney 3 58
(John O'Shea) *in tch: hdwy and drvn 4f out: styd on fnl f to take 2nd clsng stages but no ch w wnr* **14/1**

-504 **3** *¾* **Present Day**[33] 5434 4-8-5 **51** oh4...................................(b) RyanTate(5) 5 52
(Clive Cox) *sn led: rdn 3f out: hdd 2f out: no ch w wnr fnl f and lost 2nd clsng stages* **8/1**

40-0 **4** *2* **Polydamos**[13] 6103 4-8-10 **51** oh2...................................... JimmyQuinn 6 49
(Tony Carroll) *in tch: hdwy 4f out: rdn over 2f out: styd on fnl f but nvr a threat* **25/1**

4422 **5** *1* **Banreenahreenkah (IRE)**[28] 5605 3-9-4 **65**.................... PatCosgrave 8 61
(Denis Coakley) *chsd ldrs: styd on same pce fnl 2f* **5/1**[1]

032 **6** *½* **Belle Park**[33] 5434 6-8-6 **54**.. RyanWhile(7) 4 49
(Karen George) *in rr: rdn 3f out: styd on same pce fnl 2f* **7/1**[3]

4322 **7** *½* **Greyemkay**[25] 5694 5-8-6 **52**...................................... DanielMuscutt(5) 2 46
(Richard Price) *chsd ldrs: rdn 3f out: no ch fnl 2f* **6/1**[2]

00-6 **8** *¾* **One For Joules (IRE)**[258] 20 6-9-4 **59**......................... GeorgeBaker 9 52
(John Flint) *in rr: rdn 3f out: mod prog u.p 3f out: no ch fnl 2f* **5/1**[1]

6000 **9** *2 ¼* **Highlife Dancer**[11] 6158 5-9-3 **61**.................................. CharlesBishop(3) 7 50
(Mick Channon) *in rr most of way* **16/1**

3050 **10** *32* **Watcheroftheskies**[14] 6080 3-9-2 **63**.......................................[1] PatDobbs 1
(J W Hills) *chsd ldrs early: reminder 5f out: wknd qckly 3f out: t.o* **12/1**

2m 17.77s (7.17) **Going Correction** +0.825s/f (Soft)
WFA 3 from 4yo+ 6lb 10 Ran SP% **112.0**
Speed ratings (Par 101): **104,101,100,99,98 97,97,96,95,69**
Tote Swingers: 1&2 £12.40, 1&3 £7.40, 2&3 £14.50 CSF £72.35 CT £544.41 TOTE £5.50: £2.40, £2.80, £2.10; EX 49.60 Trifecta £274.90 Pool: £976.15 - 2.66 winning units..
Owner E G Bevan **Bred** Pullen Farm Stud **Trained** Ullingswick, H'fords

FOCUS
This modest contest was run at an honest pace. The winner is rated to his best but there is not a lot of depth to the race.
T/Plt: £30.30 to a £1 stake. Pool: £57,539.33 - 1,385.50 winning tickets. T/Qpdt: £10.60 to a £1 stake. Pool: £3,817.28 - 264.27 winning tickets. ST

6205 THIRSK (L-H)
Tuesday, September 17
OFFICIAL GOING: Good to soft changing to soft after race 1 (2.10)
Wind: fresh 1/2 behind Weather: overcast, cool, very breezy, raining

6493 THIRSKRACECOURSE.NET NURSERY H'CAP 6f
2:10 (2:10) (Class 4) (0-85,82) 2-Y-O **£4,090** (£1,207; £604) **Stalls** High

Form RPR

531 **1** **See The Sun**[30] 5558 2-9-7 **82**.. DuranFentiman 2 86+
(Tim Easterby) *trckd ldrs: led jst ins fnl f: drvn out* **15/2**

2234 **2** *1 ½* **Searchlight**[66] 4314 2-9-0 **75**.. NeilCallan 4 75
(Kevin Ryan) *w ldr: t.k.h: led over 3f out: hdd and nt qckn last 150yds* **9/2**[3]

3020 **3** *nk* **Oriental Relation (IRE)**[45] 4987 2-8-13 **74**.................... GrahamLee 1 73
(James Given) *outpcd and lost pl over 4f out: hdwy over 2f out: styd on fnl f* **7/1**

2232 **4** *2 ½* **Broadcaster (IRE)**[25] 5710 2-9-2 **77**............................... SeanLevey 8 71
(Ed McMahon) *trckd ldrs: nt clr run and lost pl over 4f out: swtchd lft: kpt on same pce fnl f* **7/2**[1]

1624 **5** *4 ½* **Chord Chart (IRE)**[19] 5927 2-9-7 **82**............................. AhmedAjtebi 9 60
(Charlie Appleby) *in rr: hdwy over 2f out: chsng ldrs over 1f out: wknd fnl f* **4/1**[2]

5153 **6** *1* **Money Team (IRE)**[21] 5859 2-9-5 **80**................................ PhillipMakin 6 55
(Philip Kirby) *chsd ldrs: drvn 3f out: wknd over 1f out* **9/1**

0421 **7** *3 ¼* **Bandolier**[15] 6047 2-8-8 **69**... BarryMcHugh 5 34
(Richard Fahey) *in rr: effrt over 2f out: sn wknd* **12/1**

3540 **8** *24* **Loma Mor**[29] 5595 2-7-12 **62** ow1...........................(p) RaulDaSilva(3) 3
(Alan McCabe) *rrd s: sn chsng ldrs on outside: edgd lft and lost pl 2f out: heavily eased whn bhd: t.o* **66/1**

6221 **9** *1* **Disclosure**[60] 4470 2-9-1 **76**...(p) TomEaves 7
(Bryan Smart) *led: hdd over 2f out: sn lost pl and bhd: virtually p.u: t.o* **9/1**

1m 14.34s (1.64) **Going Correction** +0.225s/f (Good) **9** Ran SP% **113.9**
Speed ratings (Par 97): **98,96,95,92,86 84,80,48,47**
Tote Swingers: 1&2 £7.30, 1&3 £13.70, 2&3 £9.20 CSF £40.58 CT £246.93 TOTE £8.10: £2.90, £2.50, £3.00; EX 48.80 Trifecta £205.30 Pool: £1,510.63 - 5.51 winning units..

Owner C H Stevens **Bred** R C Dollar **Trained** Great Habton, N Yorks

FOCUS
With the ground officially good to soft, the home bend had been dolled out, adding approximately 8yds to 7f, 1m and 1m4f events. Racing began with a competitive nursery, in which few could be confidently discounted. Rain began to fall as the runners went to post. The winner built on his maiden win and there may be more to come.

6494 THIRSK RACECOURSE COMEDY-CURRY NIGHT 11TH OCTOBER (S) NURSERY H'CAP 7f

2:40 (2:41) (Class 5) (0-75,60) 2-Y-O **£2,726** (£805; £402) **Stalls** Low

Form RPR

0440 **1** **Casper Lee (IRE)**[7] 6279 2-9-2 **55**..............................(v) PaulMulrennan 4 66+
(Nigel Tinkler) *stdd s: in rr: reminders over 3f out: gd hdwy to chse wnr over 1f out: hung lft and led last 100yds: drvn clr* **16/1**

2503 **2** *4* **Sukari Gold (IRE)**[7] 6279 2-9-3 **56**....................................(b) NeilCallan 5 57
(Kevin Ryan) *led 1f: led 3f out: hung lft over 1f out: hdd and no ex ins fnl f* **7/2**[1]

0510 **3** *1 ¾* **Strictly Glitz (IRE)**[7] 6285 2-8-12 **58**................................ JoeDoyle(7) 11 55
(John Quinn) *s.i.s: in rr: hdwy over 2f out: swtchd rt over 1f out: kpt on to take 3rd nr fin* **11/1**

0024 **4** *¾* **Midnight Muscida (IRE)**[32] 5467 2-9-1 **54**..........(be) RobertWinston 12 49
(Tim Easterby) *trckd ldrs on outer: t.k.h: drvn over 2f out: one pce over 1f out* **15/2**

004 **5** *5* **Diffident Beats**[14] 6079 2-9-7 **60**....................................... MartinHarley 9 42
(Mick Channon) *mid-div: drvn over 2f out: nvr a threat* **7/2**[1]

6000 **6** *1 ¼* **Meconopsis**[34] 5379 2-8-6 **45**.. DuranFentiman 8 24
(Tim Easterby) *sn trcking ldrs: t.k.h: drvn over 2f out: wknd over 1f out* **14/1**

0450 **7** *2* **Astral Pursuits**[18] 5970 2-8-3 **45**.................................... RaulDaSilva(3) 1 19
(Nigel Tinkler) *drvn to sn chse ldrs: led after 2f: hdd 3f out: wknd over 1f out* **40/1**

0365 **8** *¾* **It's All A Game**[7] 6284 2-9-0 **58**..............................(v) PhilipPrince(5) 6 30
(Richard Guest) *mid-div: lost pl after 2f: sme hdwy over 2f out: nvr a factor* **6/1**[2]

3420 **9** *shd* **Sherry For Nanny (IRE)**[88] 3541 2-8-10 **54**........... ShirleyTeasdale(5) 7 26
(Marjorie Fife) *in rr: effrt over 2f out: nvr on terms* **20/1**

060 **10** *8* **Angus Mac Og (IRE)**[10] 6206 2-8-3 **45**.................(v[1]) DeclanCannon(3) 2
(Nigel Tinkler) *chsd ldrs: outpcd 3f out: wknd 2f out: eased clsng stages* **66/1**

6060 **11** *3 ¼* **Lady Dancer (IRE)**[7] 6284 2-8-3 **45**............................(b[1]) JulieBurke(3) 3
(George Moore) *mid-div: wknd over 1f out: bhd whn eased* **50/1**

060 **12** *13* **Absconder (IRE)**[46] 4963 2-8-6 **45**.................................... JoeFanning 10
(Mark Johnston) *mid-div on outer: drvn over 3f out: lost pl over 2f out: eased whn bhd* **13/2**[3]

1m 32.11s (4.91) **Going Correction** +0.575s/f (Yiel) **12** Ran SP% **115.4**
Speed ratings (Par 95): **94,89,87,86,80 79,77,76,76,67 63,48**
Tote Swingers: 1&2 £13.20, 1&3 £46.90, 2&3 £14.40 CSF £67.85 CT £667.46 TOTE £11.20: £4.60, £1.60, £3.40; EX 110.90 Trifecta £663.00 Part won. Pool: £884.10 - 0.15 winning units..There was no bid for the winner. Sukari Gold claimed by Mr T. Dascombe for £6,000.

Owner Fools Gold Racing Syndicate **Bred** E McKenna **Trained** Langton, N Yorks

FOCUS
Plenty of these seemed overburdened, even allowing for the weakness of the race. The ground was officially changed to soft before this event. The winner scored well but the form looks ordinary.

6495 FOLLOW US @THIRSKRACES H'CAP 1m

3:10 (3:11) (Class 4) (0-85,85) 3-Y-O **£5,175** (£1,540; £769; £384) **Stalls** Low

Form RPR

2052 **1** **China Creek (IRE)**[21] 5867 3-8-9 **73**.................................. JoeFanning 3 82
(Mark Johnston) *sn chsng ldrs: led over 2f out: hdd briefly jst ins fnl f: kpt on wl* **13/2**[3]

0-1 **2** *¾* **Sherzam**[25] 5715 3-8-12 **76**.. PJMcDonald 9 83
(Michael Dods) *led early: trckd ldrs: upsides over 2f out: led briefly jst ins fnl f: kpt on same pce* **8/1**

2115 **3** *2* **Nurpur (IRE)**[26] 5684 3-9-7 **85**...................................... DanielTudhope 8 88
(David O'Meara) *hld up in rr: swtchd rt over 2f out: chsng ldng pair over 1f out: edgd lft and kpt on same pce* **5/2**[1]

1256 **4** *2 ¾* **Lilac Lace (IRE)**[10] 6210 3-9-5 **83**................................. DuranFentiman 1 80
(Tim Easterby) *stdd s: sn trcking ldrs: n.m.r on inner over 2f out: fdd fnl f* **16/1**

-161 **5** *nk* **Mount Tiger**[36] 5355 3-9-3 **81**... PaulMulrennan 5 77
(James Tate) *hld up in mid-div: drvn over 2f out: one pce* **11/4**[2]

5146 **6** *6* **Off The Pulse**[93] 3369 3-8-12 **76**................................ GrahamGibbons 4 59
(John Mackie) *in rr: drvn over 4f out: lost pl 2f out* **9/1**

5230 **7** *1* **Lazarus Bell**[108] 2876 3-9-5 **83**.. DaleSwift 6 64
(Alan Brown) *chsd ldrs: lost pl after 1f: drvn over 2f out: nvr a factor* **11/1**

3010 **8** *11* **Mister Marcasite**[36] 5342 3-8-11 **75**.................................... TomEaves 2 32
(Mel Brittain) *sn led: hdd over 2f out: sn lost pl and bhd* **12/1**

1m 44.04s (3.94) **Going Correction** +0.575s/f (Yiel) **8** Ran SP% **111.6**
Speed ratings (Par 103): **103,102,100,97,97 91,90,79**
Tote Swingers: 1&2 £6.20, 1&3 £3.50, 2&3 £4.80 CSF £53.94 CT £162.16 TOTE £7.20: £2.70, £2.60, £1.10; EX 26.80 Trifecta £105.20 Pool: £1,090.37 - 7.77 winning units..

Owner Sheikh Hamdan Bin Mohammed Al Maktoum **Bred** Darley **Trained** Middleham Moor, N Yorks

FOCUS
A competitive handicap, with the top weight rated 85. The winner fulfilled his debut promise while the form behind was straightforward.

6496 ANDERSON BARROWCLIFF CENTENARY STKS (H'CAP) 7f

3:40 (3:40) (Class 4) (0-85,85) 3-Y-O+ **£5,175** (£1,540; £769; £384) **Stalls** Low

Form RPR

2502 **1** **Our Boy Jack (IRE)**[18] 5974 4-8-8 **77**.................. GeorgeChaloner(5) 11 87
(Richard Fahey) *in rr: drvn 4f out: hdwy over 2f out: chsng ldrs and swtchd rt over 1f out: styd on to ld nr fin* **4/1**[1]

0500 **2** *nk* **Green Park (IRE)**[10] 6215 10-8-6 **73**............................(b) NeilFarley(3) 12 82
(Declan Carroll) *t.k.h in mid-div on outer: effrt 3f out: led over 1f out: hdd nr fin* **22/1**

1260 **3** *2* **West Leake Hare (IRE)**[18] 5974 4-8-13 **77**................ AdrianNicholls 13 81
(David Nicholls) *s.i.s: hdwy over 2f out: swtchd rt over 1f out: styd on to take 3rd nr fin* **20/1**

0645 **4** *hd* **Al Muheer (IRE)**[3] 6384 8-9-4 **82**... DaleSwift 2 86
(Ruth Carr) *chsd ldrs: drvn over 2f out: kpt on towards fin* **7/1**

0162 **5** *nk* **Showboating (IRE)**[11] 6162 5-8-13 **77**............................(tp) SeanLevey 4 80
(Alan McCabe) *trckd ldrs: upsides over 1f out: kpt on same pce* **10/1**

0626 **6** *½* **Lastchancelucas**[9] 6238 3-9-1 **85**..................................... JasonHart(3) 9 86
(Declan Carroll) *trckd ldrs: upsides over 1f out: one pce* **13/2**[3]

3006 **7** *3 ¾* **Fieldgunner Kirkup (GER)**[32] 5481 5-9-4 **82**........... GrahamGibbons 8 74
(David Barron) *chsd ldrs: effrt over 2f out: wknd fnl f* **9/2**[2]

0000 **8** *1 ¾* **Klynch**[11] 6161 7-9-2 **80**..(b) JamesSullivan 6 68
(Ruth Carr) *s.i.s: sme hdwy 2f out: nvr a factor* **16/1**

1040 **9** *hd* **Snow Bay**[18] 5943 7-9-1 **84**.................................. ShirleyTeasdale(5) 3 72
(Paul Midgley) *led: drvn 3f out: hdd over 1f out: fdd* **20/1**

0030 **10** *1 ½* **Gouray Girl (IRE)**[7] 6274 6-8-13 **77**..................................(p) TomEaves 1 61
(Brian Ellison) *s.i.s: drvn and sme hdwy over 2f out: lost pl over 1f out* **20/1**

2441 **11** *3 ½* **Celtic Sixpence (IRE)**[18] 5974 5-8-11 **75**................(p) MichaelStainton 5 50
(Nick Kent) *chsd ldrs: hmpd 2f out: sn lost pl* **13/2**[3]

0100 **12** *3* **Solar Spirit (IRE)**[10] 6205 8-9-1 **79**................................ RobertWinston 7 47
(Tracy Waggott) *mid-div: chsng ldrs over 2f out: wknd and heavily eased ins fnl f* **28/1**

100 **13** *6* **Oil Strike**[27] 5639 6-9-0 **78**... PaulMulrennan 10 31
(Michael Easterby) *in rr: bhd fnl 2f* **33/1**

1m 30.06s (2.86) **Going Correction** +0.575s/f (Yiel)
WFA 3 from 4yo+ 3lb **13** Ran SP% **117.3**
Speed ratings (Par 105): **106,105,103,103,102 102,97,95,95,94 90,86,79**
Tote Swingers: 1&2 £12.80, 1&3 £12.20, 2&3 £33.70 CSF £98.74 CT £1109.11 TOTE £4.30: £2.10, £7.40, £4.80; EX 89.40 Trifecta £1017.80 Part won. Pool: £1,357.12 - 0.49 winning units..

Owner Middleham Park Racing XXXVI **Bred** Mrs Ian Fox **Trained** Musley Bank, N Yorks

FOCUS
An ultra-competitive handicap on paper and, remarkably, the first three home were widest drawn.

6497 THIRSK RACECOURSE FOR CONFERENCES & BANQUETING MAIDEN STKS 1m

4:10 (4:11) (Class 5) 3-Y-O+ **£2,587** (£770; £384; £192) **Stalls** Low

Form RPR

45 **1** **Princess Loulou (IRE)**[51] 4799 3-8-12 0.......................[1] AndreaAtzeni 1 92+
(Roger Varian) *chsd ldrs: modest 3rd and drvn over 3f out: styd on to ld 1f out: drvn wl clr* **11/4**[1]

5 **2** *9* **Busatto (USA)**[12] 6134 3-9-3 0... JoeFanning 3 77+
(Mark Johnston) *led after 1f: t.k.h: edgd rt over 2f out: hdd 1f out* **10/3**[2]

25-5 **3** *8* **Ruwaiyan (USA)**[20] 5902 4-9-7 79............................... PaulMulrennan 11 59
(James Tate) *w ldr: t.k.h: drvn 3f out: hung lft and wknd over 1f out* **7/2**[3]

54- **4** *1 ¾* **How Fortunate**[566] 737 5-9-2 0.. GrahamLee 12 51
(Tim Etherington) *chsd ldrs: outpcd and lost pl over 3f out: kpt on fnl 2f: tk modest 4th nr fin* **28/1**

0-5 **5** *¾* **Witch Way Went**[11] 6178 3-8-9 0.................................. PaulPickard(3) 4 49
(Brian Ellison) *chsd ldrs: outpcd and lost pl over 4f out: kpt on fnl 2f: tk modest 5th nr fin* **14/1**

2 **6** *½* **Abbotsfield (IRE)**[11] 6178 3-8-12 0.................................. AndrewElliott 7 48
(Ben Haslam) *led 1f: outpcd over 3f out: hung lft over 2f out: one pce* **11/2**

0-4 **7** *4 ½* **Kalithea**[48] 4887 3-8-12 0...(e) BarryMcHugh 6 38
(Julie Camacho) *s.i.s: sn prom: outpcd over 3f out: wknd over 1f out* **10/1**

56 **8** *8* **Let's Go Live**[11] 6178 3-9-3 0.. LeeTopliss 2 25
(Paul Midgley) *dwlt: sn mid-div: lost pl over 2f out* **50/1**

06 **9** *2* **Glasgon**[22] 5839 3-9-0 0.. NeilFarley(3) 10 21
(Declan Carroll) *in rr: sme hdwy over 2f out: sn wknd* **40/1**

00-0 **10** *1 ½* **Nakuru Breeze (IRE)**[31] 5515 4-8-11 50..........(be[1]) JacobButterfield(5) 8 13
(Suzzanne France) *rrd s: mid-div: outpcd over 4f out: sn lost pl* **100/1**

0-00 **11** *1 ¼* **Running On Faith**[175] 1187 5-9-7 30........................... KirstyMilczarek 9 15
(Garry Woodward) *lost pl after 2f: sn bhd* **200/1**

0 **12** *2 ½* **Redalani (IRE)**[11] 6178 3-8-12 0... DaleSwift 5
(Alan Brown) *trckd ldrs: t.k.h: outpcd over 3f out: sn wknd* **66/1**

13 *4 ½* **Hilda Ogden (IRE)** 3-8-12 0.. PaulQuinn 13
(David Nicholls) *s.i.s: swtchd lft after s: a bhd* **25/1**

1m 43.75s (3.65) **Going Correction** +0.575s/f (Yiel)
WFA 3 from 4yo+ 4lb **13** Ran SP% **117.8**
Speed ratings (Par 103): **104,95,87,85,84 84,79,71,69,68 66,64,59**
Tote Swingers: 1&2 £3.70, 1&3 £4.00, 2&3 £5.00 CSF £11.20 TOTE £4.00: £1.80, £1.70, £1.80; EX 16.20 Trifecta £34.30 Pool: £2,002.68 - 4.73 winning units..

Owner Saleh Al Homaizi & Imad Al Sagar **Bred** David John Brown **Trained** Newmarket, Suffolk

FOCUS
Not much worthwhile form to assess in a maiden lacking depth.

6498 THIRSK RACECOURSE FOR YOUR CHRISTMAS PARTY MAIDEN STKS (THE £5K BONUS RACE) 1m 4f

4:45 (4:45) (Class 5) 3-Y-O+ **£2,726** (£805; £402) **Stalls** High

Form RPR

4/-3 **1** **Aquilla (IRE)**[44] 5038 4-9-8 0... MartinHarley 12 84+
(David Simcock) *trckd ldrs: led on bit 3f out: wnt clr over 1f out: eased nr fin: easily* **6/4**[1]

346- **2** *2* **Perfect Heart**[347] 6839 4-9-13 77...................................... AndreaAtzeni 8 83+
(Roger Varian) *trckd ldrs: t.k.h: clr 2nd over 2f out: kpt on: no ch w wnr* **7/2**[2]

6 **3** *4 ½* **El Cordobes (IRE)**[7] 6272 3-9-5 0...................................... TonyHamilton 7 76
(Richard Fahey) *hld up: carried wd bnd after 2: hdwy 5f out: 3rd over 2f out: kpt on one pce* **14/1**

-264 **4** *13* **Heroine Required (FR)**25 5707 3-9-0 75.................. GrahamGibbons 5 52
(William Haggas) *mid-div: chsng ldrs over 4f out: sn drvn: modest 4th and one pce 2f out* **7/1**

5 *2 3/4* **Pastoral**17 4-9-8 0.. BarryMcHugh 2 48
(Tony Coyle) *hld up in rr: hdwy 5f out: drvn over 3f out: one pce* **33/1**

56 **6** *nk* **Advisory**14 6062 3-9-5 0.. JoeFanning 4 52
(Mark Johnston) *chsd ldrs: drvn and outpcd over 4f out: one pce fnl 3f* **6/1**3

04 **7** *9* **Princeofthedesert**51 4809 7-9-13 54........................... GrahamLee 11 39
(Garry Woodward) *chsd ldrs: ledafter 3f: hdd 3f out: sn wknd* **50/1**

2350 **8** *18* **Regal Swain (IRE)**43 5051 5-9-13 69....................... RobertWinston 10 12
(Alan Swinbank) *rrd s: carried wd and stmbld bnd after 2f: racd wd and hdwy to join ldrs 6f out: wknd over 2f out: heavily eased clsng stages* **14/1**

2 **9** *11* **Swehan (IRE)**15 6050 3-9-5 0.. NeilCallan 3
(Kevin Ryan) *led 3f: w ldrs: wknd over 2f out: eased ins fnl f* **14/1**

5 **10** *6* **Inka Express**58 4559 3-9-0 0.................................(t) PatrickMathers 1
(Mike Sowersby) *mid-div: rn wd bnd after 2f: lost pl over 8f out: sn bhd: t.o 5f out* **100/1**

0 **11** *13* **Generous George (IRE)**20 5902 4-9-6 0..................... JamieGormley(7) 6
(Mel Brittain) *prom: rn wd bnd after 2f: sn bhd: t.o 5f out* **100/1**

0 **12** *dist* **Bad Medicine**7 6272 3-8-11 0.. PaulPickard(3) 9
(Colin Teague) *s.s: sn bhd: t.o 7f out: virtually p.u 3f out: eventually completed* **200/1**

2m 42.2s (6.00) **Going Correction** +0.575s/f (Yiel)
WFA 3 from 4yo+ 8lb **12** Ran SP% **116.4**
Speed ratings (Par 103): **103,101,98,90,88 87,81,69,62,58 49,**
Tote Swingers: 1&2 £2.60, 1&3 £6.00, 2&3 £9.90 CSF £6.22 TOTE £2.70: £1.70, £1.80, £4.50; EX 8.20 Trifecta £73.40 Pool: £2,596.19 - 26.51 winning units..
Owner Al Asayl Bloodstock Ltd **Bred** Ennistown Stud **Trained** Newmarket, Suffolk

FOCUS
Another maiden in which solid form was at a premium.

6499 THIRSK RACECOURSE WEDDING FAYRE 6TH OCTOBER H'CAP 1m 4f
5:15 (5:17) (Class 4) (0-85,82) 3-Y-0+ **£5,175** (£1,540; £769; £384) **Stalls** High

Form RPR

2354 **1** **Eric The Grey (IRE)**10 6211 3-8-5 69..........................(p) BarryMcHugh 6 81
(Richard Fahey) *chsd ldrs: n.m.r and lost pl over 8f out: hdwy over 3f out: sn chsng ldrs: styd on fnl f: led nr fin* **5/1**3

51P1 **2** *1/2* **Picalily**18 5966 4-9-0 73.. RobertTart(3) 2 84
(Brendan Powell) *t.k.h: trckd ldr: led over 4f out: edgd rt over 2f out: hdd and no ex clsng stages* **16/1**

3052 **3** *6* **War Poet**10 6211 6-9-12 82.......................................(tp) TomEaves 8 84
(Brian Ellison) *sn trcking ldrs: 2nd over 3f out: rdn and upsides over 2f out: wknd fnl f* **9/2**2

12-4 **4** *shd* **White Nile (IRE)**25 5723 4-9-12 82.......................... GrahamLee 5 84
(David Simcock) *t.k.h: trckd ldrs: drvn over 3f out: outpcd over 2f out: kpt on to take modest 3rd nr fin* **1/1**1

0362 **5** *2 1/2* **Next Edition (IRE)**9 6239 5-9-2 79.......................... EvaMoscrop(7) 1 77
(Philip Kirby) *trckd ldrs: stdd and dropped bk last after 3f: effrt over 3f out: chsng ldrs over 2f out: wknd over 1f out* **9/1**

-640 **6** *19* **Braveheart Move (IRE)**10 6211 7-9-7 77....................(p) PJMcDonald 4 47
(Geoffrey Harker) *led: hdd over 4f out: lost pl 3f out: eased whn bhd: t.o* **40/1**

-410 **7** *2 1/4* **Waverunner**91 3443 3-9-0 78.. JoeFanning 7 44
(Mark Johnston) *t.k.h in rr: hdwy to trck ldrs 8f out: lost pl 3f out: bhd whn eased* **16/1**

2m 43.25s (7.05) **Going Correction** +0.575s/f (Yiel)
WFA 3 from 4yo+ 8lb **7** Ran SP% **109.1**
Speed ratings (Par 105): **99,98,94,94,92 80,78**
Tote Swingers: 1&2 £6.50, 1&3 £3.10, 2&3 £4.10 CSF £68.29 CT £347.58 TOTE £5.50: £2.20, £3.40; EX 45.30 Trifecta £149.90 Pool: £1,949.26 - 9.75 winning units..
Owner The Clynes & Knaggs Partnership **Bred** David Carey **Trained** Musley Bank, N Yorks

FOCUS
An interesting finale, with a top weight rated 82. The early pace looked steady.
T/Jkpt: £17,750.00 to a £1 stake. Pool: £25,000.00 - 1.00 winning tickets. T/Plt: £45.30 to a £1 stake. Pool: £68,125.96 - 1,097.65 winning tickets. T/Qpdt: £7.00 to a £1 stake. Pool: £4,791.00 - 500.30 winning tickets. WG

5797 YARMOUTH (L-H)
Tuesday, September 17

OFFICIAL GOING: Soft (good to soft in places) changing to good to soft after race 1 (2.30)
Wind: medium to fresh, half against Weather: overcast

6500 BRITISH STALLION STUDS/GREENE KING EBF MAIDEN FILLIES' STKS 6f 3y
2:30 (2:31) (Class 5) 2-Y-O **£2,911** (£866; £432; £216) **Stalls** Centre

Form RPR

1 **Al Thakhira** 2-9-0 0.. SilvestreDeSousa 5 89+
(Marco Botti) *t.k.h: early: hld up in tch towards rr of main gp: rdn and hdwy to chse ldr over 1f out: led ins fnl f: r.o strly: pushed out: readily* **5/2**1

2 *2 3/4* **Expect** 2-9-0 0.. RyanMoore 8 79+
(Jeremy Noseda) *chsd ldrs: rdn and effrt ent fnl 2f: led over 1f out: rn green and hung lft in front: hdd ins fnl f: sn outpcd by wnr but kpt on for clr 2nd* **9/2**3

3 *2 1/2* **Weekend Getaway (IRE)** 2-9-0 0.. LukeMorris 1 71
(Clive Brittain) *dwlt: sn rcvrd and in tch in midfield: rdn and effrt over 2f out: kpt on same pce fr over 1f out: wnt 3rd ins fnl f: no threat to ldng pair* **7/2**2

30 **4** *1* **Souville**41 5145 2-9-0 0..1 WilliamBuick 3 68
(Chris Wall) *led: rdn ent fnl 2f: hdd and no ex over 1f out: wandered rt and wknd ins fnl f* **7/2**2

5 *3* **Little Tinka** 2-9-0 0.. PaulHanagan 2 59
(Mark H Tompkins) *dwlt: in tch towards rr of main gp: rdn and unable qck ent fnl 2f: wknd over 1f out* **20/1**

6 *nk* **L Ge R** 2-8-11 0.. RosieJessop(3) 4 58
(Peter Charalambous) *t.k.h: chsd ldr tl over 1f out: sn btn: fdd ins fnl f* **16/1**

7 *1 1/2* **New Row** 2-9-0 0..1 RobertHavlin 9 54
(William Jarvis) *s.i.s: in tch in rr of main gp: rdn and outpcd ent fnl f: sn btn and wknd over 1f out* **16/1**

8 *9* **Perspicacity** 2-9-0 0.. FrederikTylicki 6 27
(J R Jenkins) *rn green: sn detached in last: wl bhd fnl 2f* **40/1**

1m 14.71s (0.31) **Going Correction** +0.125s/f (Good) **8** Ran SP% **110.2**
Speed ratings (Par 92): **102,98,95,93,89 89,87,75**
Tote Swingers: 1&2 £2.90, 1&3 £3.30, 2&3 £3.40 CSF £12.90 TOTE £3.10: £1.20, £1.50, £2.20; EX 9.40 Trifecta £40.60 Pool: £2,534.59 - 46.75 winning units..
Owner Mubarak Al Naemi **Bred** Qatar Bloodstock Ltd **Trained** Newmarket, Suffolk

FOCUS
Full width of back straight utilised. This was quite an interesting fillies' maiden, with seven of the eight runners newcomers, and the winner was impressive.

6501 RACHAEL KEATLEY MEMORIAL NURSERY H'CAP (FOR THE JACK LEADER CHALLENGE TROPHY) 1m 3y
3:00 (3:00) (Class 4) (0-85,85) 2-Y-O **£3,752** (£1,116; £557; £278) **Stalls** Centre

Form RPR

031 **1** **Ghaawy**22 5811 2-9-5 83.. PaulHanagan 5 90+
(Sir Michael Stoute) *mde all: grad increased gallop fr 1/2-way: rdn ent fnl 2f: clr w runner-up 1f out: hrd pressed and edgd lft ins fnl f: styd on wl and gng away at fin* **11/8**1

636 **2** *3/4* **Newmarket Warrior (IRE)**37 5309 2-8-12 76................... RyanMoore 6 81+
(Michael Bell) *in tch in rr: pushed along and outpcd 1/2-way: rdn over 2f out: gd hdwy to chse wnr over 1f out: ev ch whn carried sltly lft ins fnl f: no ex and btn towards fin* **7/2**2

01 **3** *4* **Solidarity**21 5852 2-8-13 77.. MickaelBarzalona 3 73
(Charlie Appleby) *t.k.h early: hld up wl in tch: rdn and chsd wnr over 2f out tl over 1f out: sn outpcd and wl hld fnl f* **7/2**2

0213 **4** *4 1/2* **If (GER)**15 6041 2-8-13 80.. ThomasBrown(3) 1 66
(Andrew Balding) *dwlt: sn rcvrd and chsd ldrs: wnt 2nd 1/2-way tl over 2f out: sn struggling u.p: wknd over 1f out* **10/1**

4313 **5** *1 1/4* **Dancealot**18 5952 2-9-7 85.. LukeMorris 2 68
(Clive Brittain) *t.k.h: chsd wnr tl 1/2-way: rdn over 2f out: drvn and outpcd 2f out: wknd over 1f out* **6/1**3

1m 41.3s (0.70) **Going Correction** +0.125s/f (Good) **5** Ran SP% **109.9**
Speed ratings (Par 97): **101,100,96,91,90**
toteswingers 1&2 £10.20, 2&3 £10.30, 1&3 £6.50 CSF £6.41 TOTE £2.40: £1.30, £2.30; EX 5.70 Trifecta £17.60 Pool: £2,153.06 - 91.26 winning units..
Owner Hamdan Al Maktoum **Bred** Shadwell Estate Company Limited **Trained** Newmarket, Suffolk

FOCUS
A fair nursery, but the early pace was modest.

6502 THOMAS PRIOR MEMORIAL MAIDEN STKS 6f 3y
3:30 (3:31) (Class 5) 3-Y-0+ **£2,911** (£866; £432; £216) **Stalls** Centre

Form RPR

2226 **1** **Gravitational (IRE)**28 5611 3-9-5 80.......................... WilliamBuick 7 83
(Chris Wall) *stdd s: t.k.h: hld up in tch in rr: clsd and travelling wl whn nt clr run wl over 1f out: swtchd rt and hdwy over 1f out: qcknd to ld ins fnl f: r.o wl and gng away at fin* **11/8**1

02 **2** *1 3/4* **It Must Be Faith**25 5715 3-9-5 0.......................... AndrewMullen 4 78
(Michael Appleby) *t.k.h: chsd ldrs: effrt to chal 2f out: led over 1f out: hdd and styd on same pce ins fnl f* **6/1**3

06 **3** *1/2* **Intrinsic**12 6133 3-9-5 0.. RyanMoore 5 76
(Sir Michael Stoute) *chsd ldrs: rdn and effrt 2f out: drvn and ev ch ent fnl f: no ex and one pce ins fnl f* **8/1**

4552 **4** *1* **Living Desert**43 5069 3-9-5 72..........................(p) LukeMorris 8 73
(James Toller) *t.k.h and racd awkwardly: chsd ldr tl led 2f out: wanting to hang lft u.p and hdd over 1f out: styd on same pce fnl f* **3/1**2

5002 **5** *3* **Marsh Dragon**40 5200 3-9-0 58.. TedDurcan 3 59
(Mark H Tompkins) *hld up in tch towards rr: rdn and hdwy jst over 2f out: 5th and outpcd over 1f out: wknd ins fnl f* **20/1**

53 **6** *3* **Shotgun Start**17 5989 3-9-5 0.. PaulHanagan 1 55
(Michael Wigham) *in tch in midfield tl dropped to rr over 3f out: effrt and immediately wanting to hang lft over 1f out: edging lft and no imp fnl f* **8/1**

6043 **7** *6* **Tiger's Home**48 4881 3-9-0 54..........................(p) AdamBeschizza 2 32
(Julia Feilden) *led briefly early: sn in tch in midfield: rdn and struggling ent fnl 2f: wknd and bhd 1f out* **33/1**

0040 **8** *1/2* **Lady Cricketer**10 6219 4-8-13 43..........................(b) RosieJessop(3) 6 31
(Michael Squance) *squeezed for room leaving stalls: sn rcvrd and led: rdn and hdd 2f out: sn btn: wknd and bhd 1f out* **100/1**

1m 13.97s (-0.43) **Going Correction** +0.125s/f (Good)
WFA 3 from 4yo 2lb **8** Ran SP% **112.3**
Speed ratings (Par 103): **107,104,104,102,98 94,86,86**
Tote Swingers: 1&2 £3.10, 1&3 £3.20, 2&3 £8.20 CSF £9.73 TOTE £2.30: £1.10, £2.20, £2.50; EX 10.30 Trifecta £50.20 Pool: £3,531.95 - 52.69 winning units..
Owner David Gilbert **Bred** Joseph Broderick **Trained** Newmarket, Suffolk

FOCUS
A modest older-horse sprint maiden.

6503 BOODLES DIAMOND H'CAP 1m 3f 101y
4:00 (4:00) (Class 2) (0-100,100) 3-Y-O **£12,602** (£3,772; £1,886; £944; £470) **Stalls** Low

Form RPR

5241 **1** **Battalion (IRE)**43 5058 3-8-2 81 oh1.......................... SilvestreDeSousa 3 102+
(William Haggas) *mde all: travelling best ent fnl 3f: readily drew clr on bit over 2f out: in n.d after: v easily: nt extended* **9/4**1

3011 **2** *5* **Thomas Hobson**31 5534 3-8-9 88.. WilliamBuick 5 96
(John Gosden) *t.k.h early: hld up in tch in last pair: rdn and effrt in 3rd over 2f out: chsd clr wnr over 1f out: kpt on but no imp* **9/4**1

0610 **3** *2 1/4* **Royal Skies (IRE)**10 6106 3-9-7 100.......................... KieronFallon 4 104
(Mark Johnston) *chsd wnr: rdn over 3f out: outpcd by wnr over 2f out: lost 2nd over 1f out: wl hld but battled on to hold 3rd fnl f* **6/1**3

1360 **4** *hd* **Shrewd**10 6186 3-8-5 91.. LouisSteward(7) 1 95
(Michael Bell) *hld up in tch in rr: rdn and effrt over 3f out: outpcd btn 2f out: battling for 3rd and plugged on same pce fnl f* **4/1**2

4046 **5** *15* **Red Runaway**10 6196 3-8-3 82 oh2 ow1.......................... PaulHanagan 2 62
(Ed Dunlop) *chsd ldrs: rdn and effrt over 3f out: sn struggling and dropped to last over 2f out: wl bhd and heavily eased ins fnl f* **6/1**3

2m 28.06s (-0.64) **Going Correction** +0.125s/f (Good) **5** Ran SP% **110.1**
Speed ratings (Par 107): **107,103,101,101,90**
CSF £7.47 TOTE £3.60: £2.00, £1.40; EX 6.00 Trifecta £19.10 Pool: £2,341.96 - 91.57 winning units..
Owner Sheikh Juma Dalmook Al Maktoum **Bred** Kildaragh Stud **Trained** Newmarket, Suffolk

FOCUS
Despite the small field, this looked a nice 3yo handicap beforehand but it proved extremely one-sided.

6504 NICHOLSONS OF STALHAM JCB DEALERS H'CAP 1m 6f 17y
4:30 (4:31) (Class 4) (0-85,85) 3-Y-0+ £4,690 (£1,395; £697; £348) Stalls Centre

Form RPR
0-0 1 **Shelford (IRE)**[115] 1615 4-9-13 84 AndrewMullen 3 91
(Michael Appleby) *chsd ldrs: effrt on inner over 3f out: chsd ldng pair and swtchd rt 1f out: styd on wl u.p to ld wl ins fnl f: gng away at fin* 20/1
3065 2 1 **Mawaakef (IRE)**[36] 5348 5-10-0 85 KierenFallon 7 91
(J R Jenkins) *stdd after s: hld up in rr: hdwy 3f out: rdn to chse ldrs over 2f out: wnt 2nd 2f out: drvn and ev ch 1f out: one pce fnl 100yds* 12/1
232- 3 nk **Watered Silk**[143] 6380 5-9-10 81 FrederikTylicki 1 86
(Lucy Wadham) *led tl 9f out: chsd ldr tl led again 4f out: rdn over 2f out: clr 2f out: hrd pressed and drvn 1f out: hdd and styd on same pce wl ins fnl f* 9/1
4540 4 7 **Mutanaweb (IRE)**[13] 6108 3-8-11 78 (p) PaulHanagan 5 74
(John Gosden) *in tch in midfield: rdn and effrt to chse ldr 3f out tl 2f out: sn struggling: wknd fnl f* 11/4[1]
1045 5 3 1/4 **Sign Manual**[47] 4913 4-9-7 78 WilliamBuick 8 70
(Michael Bell) *in tch in last trio: hdwy 6f out: effrt and racing wd of rivals 4f out: no ex 2f out: wknd and wl hld whn hung lft ins fnl f* 5/1[3]
1110 6 7 **Attwaal (IRE)**[124] 2385 4-9-9 80 RyanMoore 4 63
(Neil King) *hld up in last trio: effrt u.p 3f out: drvn and no hdwy 2f out: sn wknd* 11/2
031 7 6 **Gabrial's Star**[11] 6165 4-9-11 82 (b) SilvestreDeSousa 6 57
(Ian Williams) *chsd ldrs: rdn to chse ldr 4f out tl 3f out: sn lost pl u.p: bhd over 1f out* 9/2[2]
12 8 21 **Kent Ragstone (USA)**[174] 1200 4-9-3 74 ShaneKelly 2 22
(William Haggas) *chsd ldr tl led 9f out: rdn and hdd 4f out: sn dropped out: wl bhd over 1f out: eased ins fnl f: t.o* 6/1

3m 7.23s (-0.37) **Going Correction** +0.125s/f (Good)
WFA 3 from 4yo+ 10lb 8 Ran SP% 113.6
Speed ratings (Par 105): **106,105,105,101,99 95,91,79**
Tote Swingers: 1&2 £12.50, 1&3 £13.50, 2&3 £9.70 CSF £228.62 CT £2304.48 TOTE £23.20: £7.50, £5.20, £1.40; EX 91.10 Trifecta £441.00 Pool: £2,727.34 - 4.63 winning units..
Owner Carl Hodgson **Bred** Brittas & Minch Bloodstock **Trained** Danethorpe, Notts

FOCUS
The pace looked solid in this staying handicap with a couple soon scampering clear.

6505 AT THE RACES CONDITIONS STKS 6f 3y
5:00 (5:01) (Class 3) 3-Y-0+ £7,246 (£2,168; £1,084; £542) Stalls Centre

Form RPR
2030 1 **Royal Rock**[9] 6235 9-8-9 100 TedDurcan 1 107
(Chris Wall) *stdd and dropped in bhd after s: hld up in rr: clsd 1/2-way: rdn to ld 1f out: r.o wl and asserted fnl 75yds* 11/2[3]
2630 2 1 1/2 **Morache Music**[23] 5806 5-8-9 105 SteveDrowne 4 103
(Peter Makin) *hld up in tch in last pair: rdn and effrt over 1f out: drvn and kpt on same pce ins fnl f: wnt 2nd cl home* 11/4[2]
20-3 3 hd **Master Of War**[24] 5747 3-8-7 105 KierenFallon 3 102
(Richard Hannon) *chsd ldr: rdn over 2f out: styd on u.p to ld over 1f out: sn hdd: no ex and btn fnl 75yds: wknd and lost 2nd cl home* 10/11[1]
-000 4 7 **Baileys Jubilee**[9] 6235 3-8-2 100 SilvestreDeSousa 2 76
(Mark Johnston) *broke fast: led tl rdn and hdd over 1f out: sn btn: wknd ins fnl f* 13/2

1m 13.7s (-0.70) **Going Correction** +0.125s/f (Good)
WFA 3 from 5yo+ 2lb 4 Ran SP% 107.8
Speed ratings (Par 107): **109,107,106,97**
CSF £19.50 TOTE £6.20; EX 17.30 Trifecta £20.30 Pool: £2,048.73 - 75.34 winning units..
Owner Ms Aida Fustoq **Bred** Deerfield Farm **Trained** Newmarket, Suffolk
■ Stewards' Enquiry : Silvestre De Sousa caution; entered wrong stall.

FOCUS
Three of the four runners held an equal chance on adjusted official ratings in this interesting conditions event.

6506 MOULTON NURSERIES H'CAP 5f 43y
5:30 (5:31) (Class 4) (0-85,82) 3-Y-0+ £4,690 (£1,395; £697; £348) Stalls Centre

Form RPR
2401 1 **Peace Seeker**[24] 5750 5-9-5 80 WilliamCarson 4 87
(Anthony Carson) *racd in centre: chsd ldrs overall: rdn to ld overall over 1f out: edgd rt ins fnl f: styd on wl: rdn out* 7/2[1]
0000 2 1/2 **Baddilini**[45] 5009 3-9-6 82 (p) KierenFallon 2 87
(Alan Bailey) *racd in centre: sn pushed along towards rr: hdwy u.p 2f out: chsd wnr ins fnl f: pressing wnr fnl 100yds: no ex and hld towards fin* 6/1
0001 3 1 1/4 **First In Command (IRE)**[20] 5901 8-9-7 82 (t) ShaneKelly 9 83
(John Stimpson) *stdd after s: hld up in rr: swtchd lft to join centre gp after 1f: hdwy ent fnl f: drvn to chse ldng pair fnl 100yds: no imp after* 8/1
1410 4 2 **Pixilated**[45] 4989 3-8-12 81 ShelleyBirkett[(7)] 1 75
(Gay Kelleway) *racd in centre: chsd overall ldr: ev ch u.p over 1f out tl ins fnl f: wknd fnl 100yds* 14/1
0-60 5 3/4 **R Woody**[20] 5901 6-9-0 75 (p) WilliamBuick 3 66
(Robert Cowell) *racd in centre: hld up in last trio: effrt u.p ent fnl f: edgd lft and kpt on fnl 150yds: nt trble ldrs* 4/1[2]
2015 6 shd **Smokethatthunders (IRE)**[33] 5441 3-8-11 73 LukeMorris 8 63
(James Toller) *racd nr stands' rail edgd lft wl over 2f out: sn rdn: one pce and btn whn edgd lft again 1f out: wknd ins fnl f* 5/1[3]
5015 7 2 **Exotic Guest**[22] 5820 3-8-10 72 PaulHanagan 5 55
(George Margarson) *racd in centre: in tch in midfield overall: lost pl and rdn 2f out: no imp and hung lft 1f out: wknd ins fnl f* 10/1
2000 8 2 **Billy Red**[84] 3658 9-8-10 71 (b) SilvestreDeSousa 6 54
(J R Jenkins) *swtchd rt s and racd nr stands' rail: in tch in midfield overall: pushed lft and hmpd wl over 2f out: sn rdn and struggling: bhd whn hmpd again 1f out: wknd* 20/1
0111 9 3/4 **Royal Bajan (USA)**[14] 6077 5-9-1 76 (p) FrederikTylicki 7 49
(James Given) *swtchd rt after s and racd against stands' rail: overall ldr tl rdn and hdd over 1f out: fdd ins fnl f* 15/2

1m 3.39s (0.69) **Going Correction** +0.125s/f (Good)
WFA 3 from 5yo+ 1lb 9 Ran SP% 116.6
Speed ratings (Par 105): **99,98,96,93,91 91,88,85,84**
Tote Swingers: 1&2 £7.40, 1&3 £10.10, 2&3 £8.10 CSF £24.99 CT £158.35 TOTE £4.60: £1.60, £2.40, £3.60; EX 31.60 Trifecta £145.50 Pool: £1,637.36 - 8.44 winning units..
Owner Hugh & Mindi Byrne **Bred** C J Mills **Trained** Newmarket, Suffolk
■ Stewards' Enquiry : Luke Morris one-day ban; careless riding (1st oct)

FOCUS
A fair sprint handicap in which the field soon split into two. The main group raced up the centre, while Smokethatthunders, Billy Red and Royal Bajan came up the stands' rail, but events suggest that it didn't do them any favours.
T/Plt: £230.80 to a £1 stake. Pool: £71,849.89 - 227.19 winning tickets. T/Qpdt: £57.30 to a £1 stake. Pool: £3,610.78 - 46.60 winning tickets. SP

6507 - 6510a (Foreign Racing) - See Raceform Interactive

6271 BEVERLEY (R-H)
Wednesday, September 18

OFFICIAL GOING: Good

6511 BET TOTEJACKPOT TEXT TOTE TO 89660 (S) NURSERY H'CAP 5f
2:00 (2:03) (Class 6) (0-65,61) 2-Y-0 £2,385 (£704; £352) Stalls Low

Form RPR
3002 1 **Tinsill**[15] 6073 2-8-10 53 (v) DeclanCannon[(3)] 1 74
(Nigel Tinkler) *chsd ldrs: hdwy 2f out: swtchd lft and rdn to ld ent fnl f: sn clr* 13/2[2]
4230 2 7 **Narborough**[6] 6320 2-9-7 61 MartinHarley 11 57
(Mick Channon) *prom: effrt and cl up 2f out: rdn to ld briefly jst over 1f out: sn hdd and drvn: kpt on same pce* 5/1[1]
0424 3 hd **Countess Lupus (IRE)**[19] 5964 2-8-5 45 (b[1]) RoystonFfrench 2 40
(Kristin Stubbs) *chsd ldrs: effrt and hanging rt whn n.m.r over 1f out: swtchd lft and drvn ent fnl f: styd on wl towards fin* 12/1
0350 4 3/4 **Marilyn Marquessa**[5] 6364 2-9-0 57 JasonHart[(3)] 6 50
(Jo Hughes) *cl up: led over 2f out: sn rdn and hdd jst over 1f out: drvn and one pce fnl f* 7/1[3]
0045 5 hd **Tricksome (IRE)**[15] 6073 2-9-1 55 (p) PJMcDonald 9 47
(Ann Duffield) *towards rr: hdwy 1/2-way: rdn along wl over 1f out: styd on fnl f: nrst fin* 9/1
0306 6 1/2 **Reale Silenzio**[7] 6295 2-8-5 45 (b[1]) JamesSullivan 14 35
(John Weymes) *towards rr: hdwy 2f out: swtchd lft and rdn over 1f out: styd on fnl f: nrst fin* 33/1
0056 7 4 1/2 **Patisserie**[33] 5467 2-8-9 49 (v[1]) TomEaves 10 23
(Ann Duffield) *dwlt and towards rr: pushed along 1/2-way: hdwy wl over 1f out: sn rdn and kpt on fnl f: nvr nr ldrs* 16/1
4052 8 1 3/4 **Red Tiger Lily**[19] 5964 2-8-3 50 DanielleMooney[(7)] 5 18
(Nigel Tinkler) *towards rr: sme hdwy whn n.m.r wl over 1f out: sn rdn and n.d* 12/1
0650 9 3/4 **Zac's Princess**[15] 6073 2-8-2 45 (tp) RosieJessop[(3)] 13 10
(Milton Bradley) *chsd ldrs on wd outside: rdn along 2f out: sn wknd* 50/1
0565 10 3/4 **Barleycorn**[60] 4538 2-8-6 53 RachelRichardson[(7)] 12 15
(Tim Easterby) *a in rr* 16/1
0504 11 nk **Kopkap**[23] 5814 2-9-1 55 GrahamGibbons 7 16
(Ed McMahon) *sn led: rdn along and hdd over 2f out: sn wknd* 5/1[1]
33 12 1 **Highland Princess (IRE)**[21] 5900 2-8-2 47 ShirleyTeasdale[(5)] 8 4
(Paul Midgley) *a in rr* 20/1
0010 13 3 3/4 **Notnow Penny**[7] 6311 2-8-4 47 SimonPearce[(3)] 4
(Milton Bradley) *prom on inner: rdn along bef 1/2-way: sn wknd* 16/1
6640 14 nk **Danetimeranger (IRE)**[30] 5591 2-8-4 49 (b[1]) PhilipPrince[(5)] 3
(Ronald Harris) *towards rr: rdn along 1/2-way: nvr a factor* 16/1

1m 5.39s (1.89) **Going Correction** +0.35s/f (Good) 14 Ran SP% 117.7
Speed ratings (Par 93): **98,86,86,85,84 84,76,74,72,71 71,69,63,63**
toteswingers 1&2 £5.10, 2&3 £10.90, 1&3 £10.20 CSF £37.26 TOTE £6.70: £2.30, £1.40, £5.00; EX 37.60 Trifecta £613.70 Pool: £920.88 - 1.12 winning units..The winner was bought in 7,500gns.
Owner The Crawford Society **Bred** L T Roberts **Trained** Langton, N Yorks

FOCUS
All distances as advertised. The course had escaped any overnight rain and the meeting took place on ground that was officially good. After the first Royston Ffrench asserted that it was good ground, although a bit loose on top. A fresh wind against the runners was noted. This was a weak race but the winner was quite impressive. Straightforward form in behind.

6512 PLAY ROULETTE AND BLACKJACK AT TOTEPOOL.COM EBF MAIDEN FILLIES' STKS 7f 100y
2:30 (2:32) (Class 5) 2-Y-0 £3,234 (£962; £481; £240) Stalls Low

Form RPR
5 1 **Crowley's Law**[54] 4702 2-9-0 0 RichardKingscote 10 79+
(Tom Dascombe) *stdd s: swtchd rt after s: hld up in mid-div: drvn over 2f out: rdn and edgd lft over 1f out: styd on wl to ld ins fnl f: forged clr* 10/11[1]
0 2 5 **Adore**[35] 5394 2-9-0 0 PaulMulrennan 3 67
(Sir Michael Stoute) *trckd ldrs: drvn over 2f out: styd on wl ins fnl f: tk 2nd in clsng stages* 7/1[3]
03 3 1 **Rayoumti (IRE)**[77] 3958 2-9-0 0 MartinHarley 7 65
(Marco Botti) *led tl over 5f out: led 2f out: hdd and no ex ins fnl f* 9/2[2]
5 4 1 3/4 **La Havrese (FR)**[18] 5983 2-9-0 0 PJMcDonald 5 61
(Ann Duffield) *trckd ldrs: chal over 1f out: one pce* 18/1
5 5 **Testing (FR)** 2-9-0 0 LiamJones 9 49
(Mark Johnston) *w ldr: t.k.h: led over 5f out: hdd 2f out: sn wknd* 8/1
50 6 14 **Pacarama**[111] 2793 2-8-7 0 DanielleMooney[(7)] 11 16
(Jason Ward) *sn in rr and drvn along: bhd fnl 4f* 66/1
7 nse **Red Wifey (IRE)** 2-8-9 0 ShirleyTeasdale[(5)] 8 16
(Alan McCabe) *s.i.s: sn bhd* 50/1
8 1 **Marquesa Naranja (IRE)** 2-9-0 0 DavidNolan 1 14
(David O'Meara) *s.i.s: sn mid-div: effrt over 2f out: wknd qckly over 1f out* 12/1
9 29 **Bay Street Belle** 2-9-0 0 PhillipMakin 6
(Philip Kirby) *mid-div: drvn 4f out: hung lft and lost pl over 2f out: bhd whn eased 1f out: virtually p.u: hopelessly t.o* 12/1

1m 34.66s (0.86) **Going Correction** +0.225s/f (Good) 9 Ran SP% 118.3
Speed ratings (Par 92): **104,98,97,95,89 73,73,72,39**
toteswingers 1&2 £4.30, 2&3 £6.50, 1&3 £1.90 CSF £8.30 TOTE £2.40: £1.50, £1.90, £1.10; EX 7.40 Trifecta £19.10 Pool: £803.30 - 31.44 winning units..
Owner Paul Crowley & Co **Bred** Middle Park Stud Ltd **Trained** Malpas, Cheshire

FOCUS
They went a good pace in this fillies' maiden. The winner can do better, but the form is modest overall.

6513 BET TOTEQUADPOT TEXT TOTE TO 89660 MAIDEN AUCTION STKS 7f 100y
3:00 (3:01) (Class 5) 2-Y-O £3,234 (£962; £481; £240) Stalls Low

Form RPR
3454 1 **Hulcolt (IRE)**[8] 6285 2-8-8 71 JasonHart(3) 4 72
(Garry Moss) *mde all: rdn clr 2f out: styd on strly: readily* 11/4[2]
2 6 **Bold Captain (IRE)** 2-8-13 0 MichaelO'Connell 8 60+
(John Quinn) *towards rr: hdwy wl over 2f out: swtchd rt to inner and chsd ldrs over 1f out: swtchd lft and rdn ent fnl f: styd on: no ch w wnr* 12/1
60 3 nk **Gold Class**[12] 6152 2-8-11 0 GrahamGibbons 2 57
(Ed McMahon) *trckd ldrs on inner: hdwy 3f out: rdn to chse ldng pair over 2f out: drvn wl over 1f out: kpt on same pce* 14/1
4 1 3/4 **Mayfield Boy** 2-8-9 0 AndrewElliott 13 51+
(Mel Brittain) *in rr: pushed along 1/2-way: hdwy on inner 2f out: rdn over 1f out: swtchd lft and styd on wl fnl f: nrst fin* 33/1
000 5 nk **Jacbequick**[37] 5338 2-8-6 0 RaulDaSilva(3) 7 50
(Karen Tutty) *cl up: rdn along wl over 2f out: drvn wl over 1f out: grad wknd* 100/1
6 6 6 **Little Bruv**[19] 5969 2-8-13 0 RobertWinston 6 40
(Tim Easterby) *dwlt: midfield: hdwy to chse ldrs 1/2-way: rdn along over 2f out: sn no imp* 16/1
7 nk **Irene Hull (IRE)** 2-8-1 0 ConnorBeasley(5) 14 33
(Garry Moss) *dwlt and bhd: sme hdwy on wd outside over 2f out: rdn and edgd rt over 1f out: n.d* 33/1
2432 8 1/2 **Salford Secret (IRE)**[20] 5926 2-9-1 76 MartinHarley 11 40
(Marco Botti) *midfield: hdwy wl over 2f out: rdn to chse ldrs and edgd rt wl over 1f out: no imp whn rdr dropped rein ent fnl f: eased after* 5/4[1]
0 9 6 **Company Secretary (USA)**[34] 5442 2-8-11 0 PaulMulrennan 5 22
(Jo Hughes) *nvr bttr than midfield* 16/1
5 10 3/4 **Galaxy (IRE)**[24] 5785 2-8-6 0 ShirleyTeasdale(5) 10 21
(Alan McCabe) *a in rr* 25/1
00 11 2 1/4 **Notts So Blue**[87] 3605 2-8-1 0 NeilFarley(3) 9 8
(Shaun Harris) *chsd ldng pair: rdn along 1/2-way: sn wknd* 100/1
12 1 **Tinchy Ryder** 2-8-9 0 RoystonFfrench 3 11
(Bryan Smart) *dwlt: sn chsng ldrs: rdn along wl over 2f out: sn wknd* 33/1
13 3/4 **Al Wuseil (FR)** 2-9-1 0 TomEaves 12 15
(Kevin Ryan) *chsd ldrs on wd outside: green and sn rdn along: lost pl after 3f: sn bhd* 10/1[3]

1m 34.99s (1.19) **Going Correction** +0.225s/f (Good) 13 Ran SP% 121.0
Speed ratings (Par 95): **102,95,94,92,92 85,85,84,77,76 74,73,72**
toteswingers 1&2 £35.70, 2&3 £21.20, 1&3 £7.90 CSF £34.32 TOTE £4.70: £1.60, £5.00, £3.70; EX 52.80 Trifecta £641.20 Part won. Pool: £854.95 - 0.56 winning units..
Owner Ron Hull **Bred** Kilshannig Stud **Trained** Tickhill, S Yorks

FOCUS
A slightly slower time than the preceding fillies' maiden. Punters only wanted to know about the two experienced horses in this race. There was a lack of depth and the winner governs the form.

6514 PROGRESSIVE CASINO JACKPOTS AT TOTEPOOL.COM H'CAP 1m 4f 16y
3:35 (3:35) (Class 4) (0-85,81) 3-Y-O £6,469 (£1,925; £962; £481) Stalls Low

Form RPR
3160 1 **A Star In My Eye (IRE)**[33] 5496 3-9-3 77 TomEaves 2 87
(Kevin Ryan) *mde all: pushed along 3f out: rdn and edgd lft 2f out: drvn and hung bdly lft to stands' rail jst over 1f out: styd on strly* 11/2
1103 2 5 **Chant (IRE)**[30] 5582 3-8-11 71 PJMcDonald 5 73
(Ann Duffield) *trckd ldrs: hdwy 3f out: swtchd rt and rdn to chse wnr wl over 1f out: drvn ent fnl f and kpt on same pce* 5/1[3]
-321 3 3 1/2 **Omnipresent**[21] 5892 3-9-7 81 PaulMulrennan 1 77
(Sir Michael Stoute) *hld up in rr: pushed along and hdwy 3f out: swtchd lft and rdn wl over 2f out: drvn wl over 1f out and plugged on one pce* 11/8[1]
3510 4 8 **Enzaal (USA)**[53] 4765 3-9-5 79 MichaelO'Connell 3 63
(Philip Kirby) *chsd ldng pair: rdn along wl over 2f out: drvn wl over 1f out: sn outpcd* 9/1
3500 5 15 **Love Marmalade (IRE)**[12] 6163 3-9-5 79 LiamJones 4 39
(Mark Johnston) *chsd ldr: rdn along 3f out: sn drvn and wknd 2f out* 11/4[2]

2m 40.26s (0.46) **Going Correction** +0.225s/f (Good) 5 Ran SP% 110.8
Speed ratings (Par 103): **107,103,101,96,86**
CSF £31.04 TOTE £7.20: £2.90, £2.40; EX 36.20 Trifecta £69.20 Pool: £1517.45 - 16.43 winning units..
Owner Sultan Ali **Bred** Mrs Joan Murphy **Trained** Hambleton, N Yorks

FOCUS
The best race on the card, but also the smallest line-up with only five taking their chance. It took place in deteriorating weather conditions and the winner was another who made every yard. The winner improved but it's tricky to pin down the form.

6515 EXCLUSIVE OFFERS ON TOTEPOOL MOBILE H'CAP (DIV I) 5f
4:10 (4:11) (Class 5) (0-75,75) 3-Y-O+ £3,234 (£962; £481; £240) Stalls Low

Form RPR
-0U4 1 **Master Bond**[48] 4930 4-9-5 73 DavidNolan 7 87
(David O'Meara) *mid-div: hdwy 2f out: led jst ins fnl f: edgd lft: kpt on strly: readily* 13/2[3]
32 2 2 1/4 **Modern Lady**[28] 5639 3-8-7 67 PhilipPrince(5) 1 73
(Richard Guest) *w ldr: led over 3f out: hdd jst ins fnl f: crowded and kpt on same pce* 7/1
5544 3 1 3/4 **Dark Opal (IRE)**[8] 6287 3-9-0 69 MartinHarley 5 69
(John Weymes) *mid-div: effrt over 2f out: chsng ldrs over 1f out: kpt on same pce* 9/1
0066 4 shd **M J Woodward**[21] 5887 4-8-4 61 oh3 JasonHart(3) 8 60
(Paul Green) *chsd ldrs: kpt on same pce fnl f* 20/1
2163 5 1/2 **Beau Mistral (IRE)**[12] 6161 4-8-12 69 RaulDaSilva(3) 6 66
(Paul Green) *in rr: nt clr run over 2f out: nt clr run and swtchd ins over 1f out: styd on ins fnl f* 11/2[1]
2130 6 1 1/4 **Fathsta (IRE)**[11] 6215 8-9-4 75 NeilFarley(3) 13 68
(Declan Carroll) *charged gate and stall opened early: chsd ldrs on outer: kpt on same pce over 1f out* 16/1
000 7 shd **Medici Time**[18] 5985 8-9-5 73 PhillipMakin 2 66
(Tim Easterby) *sn outpcd and in rr: hdwy over 1f out: nvr nr ldrs* 7/1
6-06 8 1 **Willbeme**[92] 3441 5-8-12 71 AdamCarter(5) 10 60
(Neville Bycroft) *w ldrs: wknd over 1f out* 10/1
2125 9 2 **Scentpastparadise**[23] 5836 3-9-2 71 PJMcDonald 9 53
(Ann Duffield) *mid-div: drvn over 2f out: nvr a factor* 12/1
0502 10 1 1/4 **Choc'A'Moca (IRE)**[21] 5889 6-8-3 62 (v) ShirleyTeasdale(5) 11 39
(Paul Midgley) *chsd ldrs: edgd rt and lost pl over 1f out* 12/1
000 11 10 **Mitchum**[12] 6181 4-8-11 65 (v[1]) TomEaves 4
(Ron Barr) *s.i.s: in rr: bhd whn eased ins fnl f* 25/1
0500 12 4 1/2 **Chunky Diamond (IRE)**[12] 6159 4-9-3 71 (bt[1]) JamesSullivan 12
(Ruth Carr) *s.i.s: in rr on outside: bhd whn eased ins fnl f* 22/1
6202 13 7 **Majestic Manannan (IRE)**[21] 5887 4-9-6 74 AdrianNicholls 3
(David Nicholls) *upset in stalls: led: hdd over 3f out: hung lft and lost pl over 2f out: heavily eased over 1f out* 6/1[2]

1m 4.69s (1.19) **Going Correction** +0.225s/f (Good)
WFA 3 from 4yo+ 1lb 13 Ran SP% 121.3
Speed ratings (Par 103): **104,100,97,97,96 94,94,92,89,87 71,64,53**
toteswingers 1&2 £5.40, 2&3 £22.30, 1&3 £17.80 CSF £50.92 CT £433.41 TOTE £8.20: £2.20, £3.00, £4.90; EX 41.80 Trifecta £651.20 Part won. Pool: £868.36 - 0.75 winning units..
Owner Bonded Twentyten Partnership **Bred** Bond Thoroughbred Corporation **Trained** Nawton, N Yorks
■ Stewards' Enquiry : David Nolan one-day ban: careless riding (2 Octo)

FOCUS
The first division of a modest sprint handicap. The winner showed significant improvement, with the next two close to their marks.

6516 EXCLUSIVE OFFERS ON TOTEPOOL MOBILE H'CAP (DIV II) 5f
4:45 (4:46) (Class 5) (0-75,75) 3-Y-O+ £3,234 (£962; £481; £240) Stalls Low

Form RPR
6630 1 **Holy Angel (IRE)**[19] 5971 4-9-2 70 (e) RobertWinston 3 79
(Tim Easterby) *hld up in rr: hdwy on inner 2f out: effrt and nt clr run over 1f out: swtchd lft and rdn to chal ent fnl f: qcknd to ld last 100yds: edgd lft: kpt on* 3/1[1]
0522 2 1 **Millkwood**[11] 6212 3-9-4 73 (tp) PhillipMakin 12 78+
(John Davies) *hld up in rr: hdwy on wd outside wl over 1f out: sn rdn: styd on strly fnl f* 8/1[3]
2155 3 3/4 **Ingenti**[18] 5985 5-8-8 69 KevinStott(7) 1 72
(Christopher Wilson) *trckd ldrs on inner: effrt and nt clr run 2f out: squeezed through and rdn to ld jst over 1f out: edgd lft and drvn ins fnl f: hdd and one pce last 100yds* 5/1[2]
0400 4 1/2 **Lucky Dan (IRE)**[44] 5049 7-8-11 68 RaulDaSilva(3) 2 69
(Paul Green) *cl up: led wl over 1f out: sn rdn and hdd jst over 1f out: drvn: edgd lft and wknd fnl f* 12/1
23 5 1 1/4 **Ypres**[30] 5583 4-9-5 73 [1] TomEaves 5 69
(Jason Ward) *trckd ldrs: effrt and n.m.r over 1f out: sn swtchd rt: rdn ent fnl f: kpt on* 3/1[1]
4003 6 1/2 **Rangooned**[18] 5985 3-8-11 66 PJMcDonald 11 61
(Ann Duffield) *chsd ldrs on outer: effrt and cl up 2f out: sn rdn and ev ch tl drvn and wknd ent fnl f* 14/1
-600 7 3/4 **Fathom Five (IRE)**[85] 3667 9-8-4 61 BillyCray(3) 4 53
(Shaun Harris) *trckd ldrs: effrt 2f out: swtchd rt and rdn wl over 1f out: sn wknd* 50/1
0530 8 1 1/2 **Meandmyshadow**[23] 5832 5-9-7 75 DaleSwift 8 62
(Alan Brown) *cl up: rdn along 2f out: grad wknd* 10/1
0000 9 1 1/2 **Master Rooney (IRE)**[50] 4852 7-8-10 71 JordanNason(7) 6 52
(Geoffrey Harker) *led: rdn along over 2f out: hdd wl over 1f out: sn wknd* 20/1
0306 10 1/2 **Shawkantango**[21] 5901 6-9-0 68 (v) MichaelO'Connell 9 47
(Derek Shaw) *a in rr* 25/1
502/ 11 nk **Alis Aquilae (IRE)**[687] 7201 7-8-8 65 ow2 PaulPickard(3) 7 43
(Tim Etherington) *prom: rdn along over 2f out: sn wknd* 12/1

1m 5.71s (2.21) **Going Correction** +0.35s/f (Good)
WFA 3 from 4yo+ 1lb 11 Ran SP% 119.5
Speed ratings (Par 103): **96,94,93,92,90 89,88,86,83,82 82**
toteswingers 1&2 £5.60, 2&3 £7.50, 1&3 £5.20 CSF £27.81 CT £121.29 TOTE £3.90: £1.30, £2.80, £2.50; EX 30.50 Trifecta £146.20 Pool: £1650.93 - 8.46 winning units..
Owner Three Jolly Farmers **Bred** Yeomanstown Stud **Trained** Great Habton, N Yorks

FOCUS
The second division of the sprint handicap was a scrappy sort of affair and the time was a second slower than the first. The first two home came from the back. A small personal best from the winner.

6517 PLAY RAINBOW RICHES AT TOTEPOOL.COM MAIDEN STKS 5f
5:15 (5:16) (Class 5) 2-Y-O £3,234 (£962; £481; £240) Stalls Low

Form RPR
1 **Rozene (IRE)** 2-9-0 0 GrahamGibbons 7 70+
(David Barron) *trckd ldrs gng wl: smooth hdwy to ld appr fnl f: pushed out* 15/2
0 2 3/4 **Cordite (IRE)**[10] 6234 2-9-0 0 TobyAtkinson(5) 1 72
(Michael Appleby) *mid-div: hdwy 2f out: styd on to chse wnr wl ins fnl f* 7/2[2]
0 3 1 1/4 **Brave Imp**[132] 2189 2-9-0 0 ShaneGray(5) 2 67
(Kevin Ryan) *w ldrs: led 2f out: hdd appr fnl f: kpt on same pce* 20/1
4 4 3 1/2 **Stroll On (IRE)**[24] 5797 2-9-0 0 RobertWinston 5 50+
(Rae Guest) *in rr: sn pushed along: swtchd lft over 2f out: hdwy over 1f out: edgd rt and hmpd ins fnl f: nvr rchd ldrs* 15/8[1]
0635 5 1/2 **Red Biba (IRE)**[8] 6286 2-8-11 50 NataliaGemelova(3) 4 48
(Alan McCabe) *led: hdd 2f out: kpt on one pce appr fnl f* 25/1
2 6 shd **Meadway**[128] 2314 2-9-5 0 RoystonFfrench 14 53
(Bryan Smart) *wnt lft s: chsd ldrs on outer: wnt lft over 1f out: one pce and wnt rt ins fnl f* 6/1[3]
7 1 1/4 **Edward Elgar** 2-9-5 0 PaulQuinn 6 48
(Richard Whitaker) *s.v.s: detached in rr: edgd lft over 3f out: swtchd rt over 1f out: styd on wl: fin strly* 20/1
0006 8 nk **Nu Form Fire (IRE)**[8] 6286 2-9-2 52 DeclanCannon(3) 13 47
(Nigel Tinkler) *wnt lft s: swtchd rt after s: in rr: hdwy over 2f out: fdd fnl f* 50/1
00 9 1 **Sweet Amaalle (IRE)**[14] 6107 2-9-0 0 LiamJones 10 38
(William Haggas) *in rr and drvn along: kpt on fnl 2f: nvr on terms* 16/1
546 10 1 1/2 **Fantasy Justifier (IRE)**[103] 3035 2-9-5 71 MartinHarley 8 38
(Ronald Harris) *w ldrs: wknd fnl f* 10/1
11 3/4 **Camanche Grey (IRE)** 2-9-5 0 AndrewElliott 3 35
(Ben Haslam) *chsd ldrs: t.k.h: lost pl 3f out* 33/1
5 12 5 **Traditionelle**[21] 5883 2-9-0 0 DuranFentiman 9 12
(Tim Easterby) *mid-div: hdwy over 2f out: sn chsng ldrs: lost pl over 1f out* 25/1
13 hd **Ruby Hull (IRE)** 2-8-11 0 JasonHart(3) 11 12
(Garry Moss) *wnt lft s: swtchd rt after s: a in rr* 20/1

1m 7.09s (3.59) **Going Correction** +0.225s/f (Good) 13 Ran SP% 124.9
Speed ratings (Par 95): **85,83,81,76,75 75,73,72,71,68 67,59,59**
toteswingers 1&2 £6.30, 2&3 £18.00, 1&3 £31.60 CSF £32.33 TOTE £7.60: £2.10, £1.50, £5.40; EX 59.30 Trifecta £598.80 Part won. Pool: £798.50 - 0.38 winning units..

Owner Twinacre Nurseries Ltd **Bred** M Downey & John Osborne **Trained** Maunby, N Yorks
FOCUS
Comfortably the slowest race ran over the minimum distance on the card. In all likelihood a modest maiden, and straightforward form.

6518 FOLLOW TOTEPOOL ON FACEBOOK & TWITTER APPRENTICE TRAINING SERIES CLASSIFIED STKS — 1m 100y
5:50 (5:51) (Class 6) 3-Y-0+ — £2,385 (£704; £352) Stalls Low

Form			Horse	Jockey	RPR
5466	1		**The Blue Banana (IRE)**[8] 6276 4-9-0 50 (b)	KevinStott 4	63
			(Edwin Tuer) *hld up towards rr: smooth hdwy over 2f out: trckd ldrs over 1f out: shkn up to ld ins fnl f: sn clr* **7/2**[1]		
5460	2	4	**Attain**[71] 4144 4-9-0 51 (p)	ShelleyBirkett 5	54
			(Julia Feilden) *in tch: wd st: hdwy over 2f out: rdn to chse ldrs over 1f out: edgd lft and kpt on fnl f* **8/1**		
5066	3	¾	**Midnight Warrior**[19] 5975 3-8-7 50	EvaMoscrop(3) 6	52
			(Ron Barr) *trckd ldng pair: effrt wl over 2f out: cl up and ev ch over 1f out: sn rdn and kpt on same pce fnl f* **15/2**[3]		
5	4	nk	**Dalandra**[16] 6049 3-8-10 55	ConnorBeasley 10	51
			(Michael Dods) *trckd ldr: hdwy and cl up 3f out: led on inner over 1f out and sn rdn: drvn and hdd ins fnl f: wknd* **9/2**[2]		
0405	5	2¼	**Yourholidayisover (IRE)**[20] 5921 6-8-9 49	JackGarritty(5) 13	46
			(Patrick Holmes) *towards rr: hdwy on inner 3f out: rdn to chse ldrs 2f out: drvn over 1f out: kpt on one pce* **12/1**		
2005	6	3	**Ella Motiva (IRE)**[6] 6339 3-8-5 47	GaryMahon(5) 1	39
			(Mark Brisbourne) *bhd: hdwy wl over 2f out: rdn and hung lft wl over 1f out: kpt on fnl f: nvr nr ldrs* **10/1**		
00-0	7	1½	**Misty Eyes**[145] 1802 4-9-0 37	JordanNason 14	36
			(Geoffrey Harker) *led: rdn along over 2f out: drvn and hdd over 1f out: sn wknd* **66/1**		
4026	8	¾	**Secret Empress**[36] 5369 3-8-10 47	TimClark 3	34
			(Bryan Smart) *dwlt and in rr: hdwy on outer and wd st: rdn wl over 2f out: plugged on: n.d* **15/2**[3]		
0000	9	½	**Kept**[41] 5177 4-9-0 51	OisinMurphy 12	33
			(Ronald Harris) *trckd ldrs: hdwy 3f out: rdn along 2f out: sn drvn and btn* **17/2**		
0054	10	1¾	**Firefly**[22] 5856 4-9-0 41 (tp)	JoeyHaynes 11	29
			(John Weymes) *chsd ldrs: rdn along wl over 2f out: sn wknd* **25/1**		
0050	11	1	**Kheskianto (IRE)**[130] 2273 7-8-9 45 (t)	PaulBooth(5) 9	27
			(Michael Chapman) *dwlt: a in rr* **33/1**		
3065	12	¾	**Planchette**[14] 6103 3-8-10 42	IanBurns 2	25
			(Jane Chapple-Hyam) *chsd ldrs on inner: rdn along wl over 2f out: sn wknd* **33/1**		
0565	13	¾	**Glan Lady (IRE)**[8] 6283 7-8-9 43 (p)	AliRawlinson(5) 8	23
			(Michael Appleby) *midfield: hdwy to chse ldrs over 3f out: rdn along over 2f out: sn wknd* **14/1**		
0440	14	3¼	**Richo**[34] 5433 7-8-7 42	AlexHopkinson(7) 16	16
			(Shaun Harris) *a in rr* **40/1**		
00-0	15	¾	**Misu Mac**[74] 4050 3-8-7 24	RobJFitzpatrick(3) 17	14
			(Neville Bycroft) *a in rr* **100/1**		
00-0	16	7	**Come Hither**[23] 5840 4-9-0 55 (v[1])	JacobButterfield 15	
			(John Norton) *a bhd* **25/1**		
4000	17	2¾	**Lady Tycoon**[36] 5377 4-8-11 41	LukeLeadbitter(3) 7	
			(Mark Brisbourne) *chsd ldrs: rdn along over 3f out: sn wknd* **40/1**		

1m 49.3s (1.70) **Going Correction** +0.225s/f (Good)
WFA 3 from 4yo+ 4lb — **17** Ran SP% **130.0**
Speed ratings (Par 101): **100,96,95,94,92 89,88,87,86,85 84,83,82,79,78 71,68**
toteswingers 1&2 £8.90, 2&3 £19.30, 1&3 £8.00 CSF £31.38 TOTE £5.60: £2.00, £3.40, £5.10; EX 46.60 Trifecta £582.90 Pool: £818.76 - 1.05 winning units..
Owner E Tuer & Mr & Mrs C Tompkins **Bred** Tally-Ho Stud **Trained** Birkby, N Yorks
FOCUS
With the race conditions stipulating that horses must not have won more than one Flat race to take part, this was a desperately weak contest. The betting suggested it was wide open and 2f from home a number could have been given a chance. The winner's best form since early last year.
T/Jkpt: Not won. T/Plt: £173.30 to a £1 stake. Pool of £59,885.57 - 252.12 winning tickets.
T/Qpdt: £62.70 to a £1 stake. Pool of £3,219.90 - 38.00 winning tickets. JR

6397 KEMPTON (A.W) (R-H)
Wednesday, September 18

OFFICIAL GOING: Standard
Wind: Moderate, across Weather: Partial cloud

6519 WILLIAM HILL JUMP SUNDAY 20.10.13 MEDIAN AUCTION MAIDEN STKS — 5f (P)
5:45 (5:45) (Class 6) 3-4-Y-0 — £1,940 (£577; £288; £144) Stalls Low

Form			Horse	Jockey	RPR
54-	1		**Upper Grosvenor**[483] 2387 4-9-6	DominicFox 5	64+
			(Roger Varian) *hld up in 4th: effrt over 1f out: rdn to ld ins fnl f: readily* **4/7**[1]		
056	2	1¼	**Presumido (IRE)**[20] 5932 3-9-5 51	HarryBentley 8	59
			(Simon Dow) *in rr of main gp tl rdn and r.o fr over 1f out: tk 2nd on line* **12/1**		
-550	3	hd	**Max The Machine**[4] 6397 3-9-5 64	MartinDwyer 2	59
			(Derek Shaw) *led: rdn 2f out: hdd and unable qck ins fnl f* **7/2**[2]		
006	4	1	**Purford Green**[24] 5796 4-9-1 40 (v)	JohnFahy 3	50
			(Michael Attwater) *chsd ldrs: rdn and one pce fnl 2f* **50/1**		
5040	5	1¼	**Time For Crabbies (IRE)**[24] 5788 3-9-5 55	GrahamLee 4	51
			(Lisa Williamson) *prom tl rdn and btn over 1f out* **7/1**[3]		
	6	7	**Bossy Jane** 3-9-0	RichardThomas 6	20
			(Zoe Davison) *s.s: a bhd* **25/1**		

1m 0.71s (0.21) **Going Correction** -0.025s/f (Stan)
WFA 3 from 4yo 1lb — **6** Ran SP% **111.9**
Speed ratings (Par 101): **97,95,94,93,91 79**
toteswingers 1&2 £2.50, 2&3 £2.30, 1&3 £1.10 CSF £8.97 TOTE £1.40: £1.10, £4.40; EX 9.10 Trifecta £21.10 Pool: £630.58 - 22.38 winning units..
Owner H R H Sultan Ahmad Shah **Bred** Hrh Sultan Ahmad Shah **Trained** Newmarket, Suffolk
FOCUS
A weak maiden.

6520 £200 FREE BETS AT BETDAQ NURSERY H'CAP — 1m 2f (P)
6:15 (6:16) (Class 5) (0-75,75) 2-Y-0 — £2,587 (£770; £384; £192) Stalls Low

Form			Horse	Jockey	RPR
31	1		**Jelly Fish**[24] 5785 2-9-6 74	JamesDoyle 4	79+
			(Amanda Perrett) *t.k.h in 5th: hdwy over 2f out: led over 1f out: rdn to hold on narrowly fnl f* **13/8**[1]		
005	2	nk	**Ultimate Warrior (IRE)**[15] 6069 2-9-1 69	RichardHughes 6	73
			(Richard Hannon) *chsd ldr: str chal fnl f: r.o wl: jst hld* **14/1**		
563	3	4	**The Wallace Line (IRE)**[60] 4518 2-8-9 63	SamHitchcott 5	60
			(Mick Channon) *mid-div to rr: effrt 3f out: r.o fr over 1f out: nrst fin* **33/1**		
366	4	½	**Power Up**[24] 5785 2-8-13 67	GrahamLee 1	63
			(Mark Johnston) *prom tl no ex ent fnl f* **16/1**		
14	5	1	**Stagemanship (USA)**[26] 5717 2-9-7 75	MickaelBarzalona 7	69
			(Charlie Appleby) *restless in stalls: led tl wknd over 1f out* **7/4**[2]		
533	6	½	**M'Lady Ermyn**[4] 6401 2-8-0 54	FrankieMcDonald 8	47+
			(Pat Phelan) *s.s: bhd tl rdn and styd on fnl 2f* **8/1**[3]		
0262	7	1	**Jazzy Lady (IRE)**[6] 6322 2-7-9 54 oh4	NoelGarbutt(5) 11	45
			(David Evans) *bhd: rdn 5f out: wd into st: sme late hdwy* **33/1**		
2603	8	½	**Mawzoona**[7] 6311 2-8-5 62	CharlesBishop(3) 3	52+
			(Mick Channon) *t.k.h towards rr: last 4f out: pushed along and styd on fnl 2f* **16/1**		
004	9	1½	**Kaizen Factor**[12] 6152 2-9-0 68	MartinDwyer 10	55
			(Rod Millman) *mid-div tl outpcd and btn 2f out* **25/1**		
405	10	1¾	**Aspenbreeze**[22] 5865 2-8-0 54 oh1	KieranO'Neill 9	38
			(Alan Bailey) *chsd ldrs: rdn 4f out: wknd 2f out* **33/1**		
0050	11	8	**Kitty Brown (IRE)**[21] 5893 2-8-1 55	CathyGannon 2	24
			(David Evans) *in tch tl wknd over 2f out* **66/1**		

2m 8.02s (0.02) **Going Correction** -0.025s/f (Stan) — **11** Ran SP% **118.2**
Speed ratings (Par 95): **98,97,94,94,93 92,92,91,90,89 82**
toteswingers 1&2 £5.40, 2&3 £18.80, 1&3 £12.70 CSF £24.39 CT £562.39 TOTE £2.50: £1.30, £2.80, £15.20; EX 27.50 Trifecta £553.60 Part won. Pool: £738.22 - 0.27 winning units..
Owner K Abdullah **Bred** Millsec Limited **Trained** Pulborough, W Sussex
FOCUS
Quite a test of stamina for these 2yos. The first pair were clear and the winner can rate higher in time.

6521 COMMISSION FREE 1ST MONTH AT BETDAQ H'CAP — 1m 2f (P)
6:45 (6:46) (Class 5) (0-70,70) 3-Y-0 — £2,587 (£770; £384; £192) Stalls Low

Form			Horse	Jockey	RPR
0552	1		**Lybica (IRE)**[14] 6109 3-9-4 67	RyanMoore 9	76
			(Gary Moore) *prom: led over 1f out: drvn out* **4/1**[1]		
5446	2	nk	**Landau (IRE)**[23] 5816 3-9-0 63	LiamKeniry 14	71
			(Sylvester Kirk) *chsd ldrs: chal over 1f out: r.o* **12/1**		
-33	3	1½	**Flemish School**[13] 6136 3-9-7 70 (p)	JamesDoyle 3	75
			(Gerard Butler) *in tch: effrt over 2f out: kpt on fnl f* **12/1**		
0004	4	½	**Strategic Strike (IRE)**[58] 4591 3-9-0 63	GrahamLee 13	67
			(Paul Cole) *mid-div: effrt over 2f out: kpt on u.p* **10/1**		
2036	5	1¼	**Mesmerized (IRE)**[35] 5395 3-9-4 67	AdamKirby 2	69+
			(Marco Botti) *hld up towards rr: rdn and hdwy over 1f out: r.o* **12/1**		
2-00	6	½	**Harwoods Star (IRE)**[103] 3062 3-9-7 70 (e[1])	JimCrowley 4	71
			(Amanda Perrett) *towards rr: rdn and styd on fnl 2f: nvr nrr* **8/1**		
1350	7	½	**Typhon (USA)**[38] 5304 3-9-6 69	MickaelBarzalona 7	69
			(David Lanigan) *hld up in rr: sme hdwy on inner over 1f out: styd on same pce* **10/1**		
4400	8	1¼	**Punditry**[15] 6080 3-9-2 65 (v)	KirstyMilczarek 10	62
			(James Toller) *led after 1f: rdn 3f out: hdd & wknd over 1f out* **40/1**		
3040	9	shd	**Solvanna**[7] 6315 3-8-13 62	CathyGannon 6	59
			(Heather Main) *chsd ldrs tl outpcd 3f out* **40/1**		
6506	10	½	**Chief Executive (IRE)**[35] 5390 3-9-3 66	RichardHughes 5	62
			(Jo Hughes) *mid-div: effrt and n.m.r over 1f out: sn btn* **12/1**		
6005	11	¾	**Pearl Street (USA)**[32] 5534 3-9-3 66	HarryBentley 11	63+
			(Henry Candy) *bhd: rdn over 2f out: nvr rchd ldrs* **5/1**[2]		
4001	12	nk	**Posh Boy (IRE)**[40] 5234 3-9-2 65	GeorgeBaker 1	67+
			(Chris Wall) *led 1f: prom: rdn 2f out: cl 4th and hld whn hmpd on rail jst ins fnl f: eased* **6/1**[3]		
0000	13	nk	**Habeshia**[40] 5245 3-9-7 70 (v)	SteveDrowne 12	63
			(John Best) *a in rr: styng on at fin* **28/1**		
034	14	nse	**Florida Beat**[148] 1741 3-9-0 63 (p)	JimmyFortune 8	56
			(Andrew Balding) *mid-div: rdn 3f out: sn btn* **20/1**		

2m 7.64s (-0.36) **Going Correction** -0.025s/f (Stan) — **14** Ran SP% **124.1**
Speed ratings (Par 101): **100,99,98,98,97 96,96,95,95,94 94,94,93,93**
toteswingers 1&2 £13.00, 2&3 £35.00, 1&3 £7.00 CSF £52.77 CT £544.10 TOTE £3.90: £2.20, £3.50, £2.50; EX 40.60 Trifecta £474.10 Pool: £897.69 - 1.42 winning units..
Owner Sylvia Vrska **Bred** Tingling Syndicate **Trained** Lower Beeding, W Sussex
■ Stewards' Enquiry : Kirsty Milczarek one-day ban: careless riding (2 Oct)
FOCUS
This looked pretty competitive.

6522 NEW O&T BAR COMING IN OCTOBER H'CAP — 1m 4f (P)
7:15 (7:17) (Class 6) (0-65,65) 3-Y-0 — £1,940 (£577; £288; £144) Stalls Centre

Form			Horse	Jockey	RPR
2014	1		**Ebony Roc (IRE)**[6] 6325 3-9-3 61	RyanMoore 2	71
			(Amanda Perrett) *trckd ldrs: led 1f out: hrd rdn fnl f: jst hld on* **4/1**[2]		
0634	2	nse	**The Wizard Of Aus (IRE)**[19] 5960 3-9-6 64	JimmyFortune 11	74+
			(Andrew Balding) *hld up towards rr: rdn and gd hdwy over 1f out: fin wl: jst failed* **9/2**[3]		
0-00	3	¾	**Captain Caroline**[33] 5495 3-8-7 51 oh1	MartinDwyer 10	59
			(Mike Murphy) *sn led: rdn over 2f out: hdd 1f out: kpt on wl u.p: unable qck nr fin* **50/1**		
0202	4	3½	**Aminah**[32] 5528 3-9-2 60	JamesDoyle 12	62
			(Robert Cowell) *chsd ldr tl over 1f out: no ex fnl f* **12/1**		
5003	5	2¼	**Calon Lad (IRE)**[14] 6109 3-9-7 65	PatCosgrave 7	64
			(George Baker) *hld up in rr of midfield: effrt on outer 3f out: no imp whn hung rt 1f out* **9/4**[1]		
-005	6	1¼	**Gilded Frame**[19] 5960 3-9-7 65	GeorgeBaker 4	62
			(Marcus Tregoning) *t.k.h: prom tl wknd over 1f out* **6/1**		
-006	7	¾	**Wedding Speech (IRE)**[20] 5935 3-9-0 58	ShaneKelly 1	53
			(James Fanshawe) *chsd ldrs tl outpcd fnl 2f* **16/1**		
6002	8	1¼	**Pink Mischief**[14] 6103 3-8-8 52	DavidProbert 5	45
			(Harry Dunlop) *bhd: rdn and sme hdwy over 1f out: nvr nr to chal* **11/1**		
3236	9	½	**Zhuba (IRE)**[33] 5497 3-9-7 65	SteveDrowne 9	58
			(John Best) *mid-div: rdn 4f out: sn outpcd* **16/1**		

0-00 **10** *nk* **Sweet Louise (IRE)**[58] 4590 3-8-8 **52**........................(t[1]) KirstyMilczarek 8 44
(Barry Brennan) *in tch tl outpcd over 2f out* **40/1**
030 **11** *2 1/4* **Minimee**[14] 6109 3-9-3 **61**........................ CathyGannon 6 49
(Phil McEntee) *dwlt: hld up in rr: rdn over 2f out: no rspnse* **33/1**
-600 **12** *shd* **Hazzaat (IRE)**[22] 5855 3-9-4 **62**........................ J-PGuillambert 3 50
(Gary Harrison) *mid-div tl wknd over 2f out* **33/1**
2m 36.24s (1.74) **Going Correction** -0.025s/f (Stan) **12** Ran SP% **121.3**
Speed ratings (Par 99): **93,92,92,90,88 87,87,86,86,85 84,84**
toteswingers 1&2 £5.00, 2&3 £51.00, 1&3 £40.70 CSF £22.41 CT £800.01 TOTE £3.50: £2.10, £1.60, £18.00; EX 20.40 Trifecta £717.50 Part won. £956.69 - 0.65 winning units..
Owner The To-Agori-Mou Partnership **Bred** Joe Rogers **Trained** Pulborough, W Sussex
FOCUS
There was a steady early gallop here and those that raced up with the pace held a big advantage.

6523 TURFTV/BRITISH STALLION STUDS EBF MAIDEN FILLIES' STKS 1m (P)
7:45 (7:47) (Class 5) 2-Y-O **£2,911** (£866; £432; £216) **Stalls** Low

Form RPR
22 **1** **Psychometry (FR)**[26] 5716 2-9-0........................ RyanMoore 7 80
(Sir Michael Stoute) *trckd ldrs on outer: led over 1f out: drvn out* **5/4**[1]
6 **2** *1 1/4* **Dancing Sands (IRE)**[26] 5716 2-9-0........................ MickaelBarzalona 3 77
(Charlie Appleby) *chsd ldr: led 2f out tl over 1f out: kpt on u.p* **11/4**[2]
3 *2 3/4* **Sequined (USA)** 2-9-0........................ SilvestreDeSousa 2 70+
(Charlie Appleby) *s.s: bhd: swtchd wd and rapid hdwy 1f out: r.o strly to take 3rd ins fnl f: should improve* **14/1**
4 *1 1/2* **Nibbling (IRE)** 2-9-0........................ JimCrowley 13 66+
(Paul Cole) *in tch on outer:effrt 2f out: kept on fnl f* **25/1**
5 *hd* **Tioga Pass** 2-9-0........................ GrahamLee 9 66+
(Paul Cole) *prom: rdn over 2f out: styd on same pce* **25/1**
6 *3/4* **Emaratiya Ana (IRE)** 2-9-0........................ HarryBentley 12 64+
(Roger Varian) *towards rr tl rdn and styd on fnl 2f* **25/1**
7 *hd* **Pearlofthequarter** 2-9-0........................ DaneO'Neill 10 64
(Marco Botti) *mid-div: rdn and styd on same pce fnl 2f* **20/1**
8 *nse* **Jordan Princess** 2-9-0........................ AndreaAtzeni 8 63+
(Luca Cumani) *s.s: bhd: sme hdwy on inner over 1f out: nvr rchd ldrs* **6/1**[3]
00 **9** *1 3/4* **Star Anise (FR)**[49] 4880 2-9-0........................[1] DavidProbert 11 59
(Harry Dunlop) *mid-div: rdn over 2f out: sn btn* **100/1**
10 *hd* **Be My Icon** 2-9-0........................ JamesDoyle 4 59
(Roger Charlton) *chsd ldrs tl wknd 2f out* **40/1**
11 *3/4* **Stereo Love (FR)** 2-9-0........................ AdamKirby 6 57+
(Clive Cox) *s.s: sn in midfield: n.m.r and lost pl over 2f out* **16/1**
00 **12** *1 3/4* **Penara**[34] 5435 2-9-0........................ SamHitchcott 5 53
(Philip Hide) *led tl wknd qckly 2f out* **100/1**
0 **13** *12* **Connexion Francais**[18] 5983 2-9-0........................ AdamBeschizza 1 24
(Tim Etherington) *chsd ldrs over 5f: wknd qckly* **100/1**
1m 41.56s (1.76) **Going Correction** -0.025s/f (Stan) **13** Ran SP% **119.7**
Speed ratings (Par 92): **90,88,86,84,84 83,83,83,81,81 80,78,66**
toteswingers 1&2 £5.00, 2&3 £51.00, 1&3 £40.70 CSF £4.04 TOTE £2.30: £1.10, £1.30, £4.00; EX 5.90 Trifecta £27.60 Pool: £1134.81 - 30.74 winning units..
Owner Niarchos Family **Bred** Famille Niarchos **Trained** Newmarket, Suffolk
FOCUS
This went with the market, with the two fillies who had shown up well in their previous starts coming clear.

6524 BETDAQ 1ST RACE UK COMMISSION FREE FILLIES' H'CAP 7f (P)
8:15 (8:16) (Class 4) (0-85,84) 3-Y-O+ **£4,690** (£1,395; £697; £348) **Stalls** Low

Form RPR
3211 **1** **Trucanini**[21] 5896 3-9-4 **84**........................ GeorgeBaker 1 92
(Chris Wall) *led on bit tl jnd ins fnl f: shkn up and rallied to ld again fnl 75yds: cleverly* **6/4**[1]
1632 **2** *nk* **Hidden Belief (IRE)**[21] 5896 3-8-9 **75**........................ JimCrowley 8 82
(Ralph Beckett) *hld up towards rr: hdwy 2f out: pressed ldrs ins fnl f: kpt on* **6/1**[2]
3265 **3** *hd* **Nardin**[26] 5700 3-9-3 **83**........................ DaneO'Neill 5 90
(Ed Dunlop) *s.i.s: hld up in 6th: hdwy 2f out: jnd wnr ins fnl f: unable qckn fnl 75yds* **6/1**[2]
2540 **4** *3/4* **Saucy Minx (IRE)**[11] 6188 3-9-0 **80**........................ RyanMoore 6 85
(Amanda Perrett) *dwlt: bhd: rdn and hdwy over 1f out: styd on* **15/2**[3]
4122 **5** *2* **Abated**[16] 6045 3-8-9 **75**........................ JamesDoyle 3 74
(Roger Charlton) *chsd wnr tl rdn and one pce appr fnl f* **8/1**
5213 **6** *2 1/2* **Wakeup Little Suzy (IRE)**[132] 2195 3-8-8 **74**..............(t) AndreaAtzeni 7 66
(Marco Botti) *chsd ldrs on outer: rdn 3f out: outpcd fnl 2f* **16/1**
6034 **7** *1/2* **Califante**[21] 5896 3-9-2 **82**........................ MartinDwyer 4 73
(William Muir) *in tch tl outpcd fnl 2f* **14/1**
2000 **8** *1 1/2* **Supernova Heights (IRE)**[55] 4671 3-9-4 **84**.............. RichardHughes 2 71
(Brian Meehan) *prom tl wknd 2f out* **14/1**
1m 24.4s (-1.60) **Going Correction** -0.025s/f (Stan) **8** Ran SP% **110.7**
Speed ratings (Par 102): **108,107,107,106,104 101,100,99**
toteswingers 1&2 £2.70, 2&3 £7.10, 1&3 £3.40 CSF £9.85 CT £38.69 TOTE £2.00: £1.10, £2.40, £2.30; EX 12.00 Trifecta £30.50 Pool: £1331.24 - 32.70 winning units..
Owner Dolly's Dream Syndicate **Bred** The National Stud Never Say Die Club Ltd **Trained** Newmarket, Suffolk
FOCUS
Although the winner made just about all, there was a fair pace on and the placed horses came from behind.

6525 WINNERS ARE WELCOME AT BETDAQ H'CAP (JOCKEY CLUB GRASSROOTS SPRINT SERIES QUALIFIER) (DIV I) 6f (P)
8:45 (8:49) (Class 4) (0-85,85) 3-Y-O+ **£4,690** (£1,395; £697; £348) **Stalls** Low

Form RPR
362 **1** **Trinityelitedotcom (IRE)**[18] 5996 3-8-11 **77**........... RichardKingscote 2 87
(Tom Dascombe) *mde all: rdn 3 l clr 2f out: drvn along fnl f: jst hld on* **9/1**
1435 **2** *hd* **Mission Approved**[18] 5998 3-9-0 **80**........................ JamesDoyle 3 89
(Sir Michael Stoute) *in tch: effrt 2f out: r.o wl fnl f: clsng at fin: jst failed* **2/1**[1]
10 **3** *2 3/4* **O'Gorman**[18] 5998 4-9-7 **85**........................ LiamKeniry 7 85
(Gary Brown) *towards rr: hdwy fnl 2f: nrst fin* **16/1**
021 **4** *hd* **Dominium (USA)**[13] 6135 6-8-3 **72**........................(b) RyanTate[(5)] 4 72
(Jeremy Gask) *mid-div: hrd rdn over 1f out: styd on* **13/2**[3]
0-04 **5** *1/2* **Jubilee Brig**[15] 6067 3-8-11 **77**........................(v) RyanMoore 8 75
(Gary Moore) *t.k.h: towards rr tl r.o fr over 1f out: nvr nrr* **4/1**[2]
3233 **6** *nk* **Tagula Night (IRE)**[25] 5750 7-9-1 **79**........................(bt) RichardHughes 9 76
(Dean Ivory) *rn without declared eyeshields: prom tl outpcd fnl 2f* **9/1**
5601 **7** *1 1/2* **Aye Aye Digby (IRE)**[26] 5701 8-9-4 **82**........................ GeorgeBaker 1 74
(Patrick Chamings) *prom tl wknd over 1f out* **16/1**
0354 **8** *nk* **Signor Sassi**[11] 6203 4-9-5 **83**........................ AdamKirby 5 74
(William Knight) *prom tl n.m.r and wknd over 1f out* **4/1**[2]
-000 **9** *6* **Dark Ages (IRE)**[13] 6135 4-8-2 **71** oh3........................(t) DanielMuscutt[(5)] 10 43
(Paul Burgoyne) *nvr trbld ldrs: bhd fnl 2f* **66/1**
0003 **10** *2 3/4* **Bayleyf (IRE)**[62] 4425 4-9-2 **80**........................(t[1]) SteveDrowne 6 43
(John Best) *s.s: a bhd* **40/1**
1m 11.68s (-1.42) **Going Correction** -0.025s/f (Stan)
WFA 3 from 4yo+ 2lb **10** Ran SP% **122.4**
Speed ratings (Par 105): **108,107,104,103,103 102,100,100,92,88**
toteswingers 1&2 £6.10, 2&3 £19.80, 1&3 £24.90 CSF £28.75 CT £308.26 TOTE £7.40: £2.20, £2.10, £4.60; EX 44.30 Trifecta £782.70 Part won. Pool: £1043.62 - 0.86 winning units..
Owner Manor House Stables LLP **Bred** Natasha Newsome **Trained** Malpas, Cheshire
■ Stewards' Enquiry : James Doyle one-day ban@ careless riding (2 Oct)
FOCUS
There wasn't much competition for the lead early.

6526 WINNERS ARE WELCOME AT BETDAQ H'CAP (JOCKEY CLUB GRASSROOTS SPRINT SERIES QUALIFIER) (DIV II) 6f (P)
9:15 (9:16) (Class 4) (0-85,85) 3-Y-O+ **£4,690** (£1,395; £697; £348) **Stalls** Low

Form RPR
0112 **1** **Ziggy's Stardust**[28] 5636 4-9-3 **81**........................ DaneO'Neill 1 92
(Henry Candy) *trckd ldr: led ent fnl f: rdn out* **7/2**[2]
1532 **2** *1* **Twenty One Choice (IRE)**[11] 6203 4-9-5 **83**........................ AdamKirby 7 90
(Ed de Giles) *chsd ldrs: rdn 2f out: r.o fnl f* **11/4**[1]
6231 **3** *1 1/4* **Saloomy**[26] 5722 4-9-7 **85**........................ RichardHughes 6 88
(John Butler) *led tl ent fnl f: one pce* **9/2**[3]
5151 **4** *shd* **The Dark Wizard (IRE)**[15] 6075 3-8-11 **77**........................(b) JamesDoyle 4 80
(Roger Charlton) *mid-div: rdn and hdwy over 1f out: styd on* **7/1**
0001 **5** *2 1/4* **Shamahan**[27] 5669 4-8-13 **77**........................ RyanMoore 5 72
(Gary Moore) *prom tl outpcd fnl 2f* **6/1**
0500 **6** *3/4* **Compton**[23] 5838 4-9-2 **80**........................(v[1]) GrahamLee 2 73
(Robert Cowell) *dwlt: mid-div: rdn and no hdwy fnl 2f* **12/1**
0502 **7** *1 3/4* **Decision By One**[41] 5183 4-9-1 **79**........................(t) RichardKingscote 8 66
(Tom Dascombe) *hld up in rr: rdn 2f out: nvr trbld ldrs* **14/1**
6646 **8** *1/2* **Street Power (USA)**[28] 5636 8-8-8 **72**........................ SteveDrowne 9 58
(Jeremy Gask) *t.k.h in rr: rdn 2f out: n.d* **20/1**
-044 **9** *9* **Avonmore Star**[202] 822 5-8-8 **72**........................ MartinDwyer 3 29
(Mike Murphy) *t.k.h: a towards rr: rdn 2f out: sn bhd* **20/1**
1m 11.99s (-1.11) **Going Correction** -0.025s/f (Stan)
WFA 3 from 4yo+ 2lb **9** Ran SP% **117.7**
Speed ratings (Par 105): **106,104,103,102,99 98,96,95,83**
toteswingers 1&2 £4.10, 2&3 £4.00, 1&3 £5.20 CSF £13.88 CT £42.56 TOTE £4.50: £2.00, £1.30, £1.80; EX 17.30 Trifecta £23.50 Pool: £640.28 - 20.39 winning units..
Owner Henry Candy **Bred** Mr And Mrs L Baker **Trained** Kingston Warren, Oxon
■ Stewards' Enquiry : Steve Drowne two-day ban: weighed in heavy (2-3 Oct)
FOCUS
The slower of the two divisions by 0.31sec, and it paid to race close to the pace.
T/Plt: £14.80 to a £1 stake. Pool of £63592.81 - 3129.73 winning tickets. T/Qpdt: £6.90 to a £1 stake. Pool of £7903.35 - 839.02 winning tickets. LM

6354 SANDOWN (R-H)
Wednesday, September 18

OFFICIAL GOING: Sprint course - soft (heavy in places); round course - heavy (soft in places)
Wind: Moderate, against Weather: Fine but cloudy

6527 OLD ELLENS H'CAP (SUPPORTING THE RACEHORSE SANCTUARY) 5f 6y
2:20 (2:21) (Class 5) (0-75,75) 3-Y-O+ **£3,234** (£962; £481; £240) **Stalls** Low

Form RPR
2321 **1** **The Strig**[2] 6463 6-9-4 **72** 6ex........................(v) JamesDoyle 2 81
(Stuart Williams) *trckd ldrs and racd against rail: smooth prog 2f out: rdn to ld 1f out: drvn out* **5/1**[2]
0000 **2** *1 1/4* **Time Medicean**[15] 6067 7-9-2 **70**........................ LiamKeniry 3 75
(Tony Carroll) *hld up wl in rr and racd against far rail: smooth prog 2f out: followed wnr through but nt clr run briefly 1f out: tk 2nd last 100yds: unable to chal* **20/1**
600 **3** *3/4* **Italian Tom (IRE)**[4] 6382 6-9-5 **73**........................ CathyGannon 4 75+
(Ronald Harris) *s.i.s: hld up wl in rr: impeded over 3f out: rdn and prog towards ins rail 2f out: plld out wd over 1f out: styd on wl to take 3rd ins fnl f* **5/1**[2]
004 **4** *2 1/4* **Solemn**[27] 5673 8-9-5 **73**........................(b) AdamKirby 9 67
(Milton Bradley) *led and sn crossed to far rail: edgd away fr rail 2f out: hdd and fdd 1f out* **10/1**
434 **5** *2 3/4* **Harrogate Fair**[13] 6138 3-8-6 **61** oh3........................ JimmyQuinn 14 45+
(Michael Squance) *wl in rr and racd wdst of all: rdn and prog 2f out: chsd ldrs 1f out: sn wknd* **20/1**
0504 **6** *2 1/2* **Royal Award**[44] 5060 4-8-13 **67**........................(p) JimCrowley 1 42
(Jonathan Portman) *lw: racd against rail: cl up: trckd ldr 1/2-way: plld away fr rail and rdn to chal over 1f out: wknd fnl f* **12/1**
02-0 **7** *3/4* **Senator Bong**[12] 6159 3-9-6 **75**........................ RyanMoore 11 47
(David Elsworth) *lw: towards rr: shkn up 2f out: no prog and wl btn after* **5/1**[2]
0-00 **8** *2 1/2* **Risky Rizkova**[4] 6412 3-8-7 **62**........................(b[1]) JohnFahy 8 25
(Jonathan Portman) *in tch: chsd ldrs 2f out: rdn and wknd jst over 1f out* **50/1**
1562 **9** *7* **Celestial Bay**[4] 6381 4-8-13 **67**........................ RichardHughes 6 5
(Sylvester Kirk) *nvr bttr than midfield: wknd 2f out: heavily eased jst over 1f out: t.o* **4/1**[1]
6014 **10** *2 1/4* **Storm Lightning**[4] 6388 4-9-6 **74**........................(b) TomMcLaughlin 7 4
(Mark Brisbourne) *racd towards outer: chsd ldrs 3f: wknd v rapidly: t.o* **6/1**[3]
6003 **11** *hd* **Torres Del Paine**[7] 6310 6-8-7 **61** oh1........................(v) KieranO'Neill 5
(Brett Johnson) *chsd ldr to 1/2-way: wknd rapidly: t.o* **25/1**
1020 **12** *4* **Irish Boy (IRE)**[19] 5956 5-8-8 **69**........................(tp) EoinWalsh[(7)] 10
(Christine Dunnett) *taken down early: sn t.o* **25/1**
1m 5.22s (3.62) **Going Correction** +0.825s/f (Soft)
WFA 3 from 4yo+ 1lb **12** Ran SP% **120.2**
Speed ratings (Par 103): **104,102,100,97,92 88,87,83,72,68 68,62**
toteswingers 1&2 £23.10, 2&3 £25.20, 1&3 £7.00 CSF £107.36 TOTE £6.00: £2.00, £6.80, £2.40; EX 160.40 Trifecta £464.20 Pool: £1580.45 - 2.55 winning units..
Owner Brian Piper & David Cobill **Bred** Old Mill Stud **Trained** Newmarket, Suffolk

The Form Book Flat, Raceform Ltd, Compton, RG20 6NL.

FOCUS
Sprint track at full width, Round course at innermost configuration and distances as advertised. As is often the case in 5f sprints at the track, a low draw proved an advantage. The winner appeared better than ever.

6528 BRITISH STALLION STUDS EBF MAIDEN STKS 1m 14y
2:50 (2:50) (Class 5) 2-Y-O **£3,881** (£1,155; £577; £288) **Stalls** Low

Form RPR
4 **1** **Miner's Lamp (IRE)**[35] 5405 2-9-5 0 MickaelBarzalona 9 90
(Charlie Appleby) *w'like: scope: lw: s.i.s: wl in rr: pushed along in last pair 1/2-way: gd prog and grabbed nr side rail 3f out: chsd ldr wl over 1f out: drvn to ld ins fnl f: asserted last 75yds* **5/1**
6 **2** *1 ¼* **Flag War (GER)**[19] 5957 2-9-5 0 SilvestreDeSousa 1 87
(Saeed bin Suroor) *cmpt: s.i.s: styd on inner in bk st and wnt prom after 3f: styd out wdr than other pair w a ch in st but rdn to ld 2f out: hdd ins fnl f: no ex last 75yds* **7/2**[2]
52 **3** *9* **Early Morning (IRE)**[19] 5957 2-9-5 0 JamesDoyle 3 67
(Harry Dunlop) *mde most: failed to grab nr side rail in st and hdd 2f out: sn wknd but stl clr of rest* **9/2**[3]
2 **4** *6* **Mustamir (IRE)**[19] 5969 2-9-5 0 RyanMoore 6 54
(James Tate) *w'like: tall: racd v wd in bk st: mostly chsd ldr: lost 2nd wl over 2f out: sn wknd: wl bhd fnl f* **11/4**[1]
0 **5** *1 ¼* **Libeccio (FR)**[26] 5698 2-9-5 0 DavidProbert 2 52
(Andrew Balding) *lw: chsd ldrs: rdn and wknd 2f out: wl bhd fnl f* **12/1**
6 *1 ¾* **Zephyr** 2-9-5 0 (p) RobertHavlin 7 48
(John Gosden) *cmpt: s.s: in tch in rr tl wknd jst over 2f out: wl bhd fnl f* **8/1**
0 **7** *¾* **Frosty The Snowman (IRE)**[11] 6184 2-9-5 0 SteveDrowne 4 46
(Charles Hills) *w'like: tall: in tch in rr: wknd over 2f out: wl bhd fnl f* **50/1**
5 **8** *½* **Notarised**[19] 5969 2-9-5 0 JoeFanning 8 45
(Mark Johnston) *leggy: athletic: in tch tl wknd jst over 2f out: wl bhd fnl f* **8/1**
0 **9** *39* **Wildling**[20] 5924 2-9-0 0 PatCosgrave 10
(Jim Boyle) *leggy: in tch to 3f out: wknd rapidly: wl t.o* **100/1**

1m 49.43s (6.13) **Going Correction** +0.825s/f (Soft) **9** Ran SP% **116.6**
Speed ratings (Par 95): **102,100,91,85,84 82,82,81,42**
toteswingers 1&2 £4.70, 2&3 £2.00, 1&3 £3.60 CSF £23.12 TOTE £6.80: £2.00, £1.40, £1.60; EX 31.10 Trifecta £124.50 Pool: £2155.68 - 12.98 winning units..
Owner Godolphin **Bred** Mrs C L Weld **Trained** Newmarket, Suffolk

FOCUS
The runners came stands' side in what was a fair juvenile maiden, dominated by the two Godolphin runners. They stepped up on their debuts although the third ran below previous form.

6529 ST JAMES'S PLACE WEALTH MANAGEMENT NOVICE STKS 7f 16y
3:20 (3:21) (Class 4) 2-Y-O **£3,881** (£1,155; £577) **Stalls** Low

Form RPR
51 **1** **Signposted (IRE)**[23] 5819 2-9-0 82 DavidProbert 4 88+
(Andrew Balding) *lw: t.k.h: trckd ldr: crusied up to chal over 1f out: led jst ins fnl f: easily* **4/9**[1]
410 **2** *2 ¼* **Xanthos**[27] 5679 2-9-3 85 TomMcLaughlin 1 82
(Ed Walker) *lw: t.k.h: led: styd on far side in st w other pair: tried to kick on 2f out: hdd jst ins fnl f: no ch w wnr* **3/1**[2]
601 **3** *2 ¼* **Peacemaker (IRE)**[15] 6069 2-8-9 69 JohnFahy 3 68
(Eve Johnson Houghton) *stdd s: hld up in last: rdn 2f out: no imp and wl btn after* **6/1**[3]

1m 37.45s (7.95) **Going Correction** +0.825s/f (Soft) **3** Ran SP% **108.5**
Speed ratings (Par 97): **87,84,81**
CSF £2.12 TOTE £1.50; EX 2.40 Trifecta £3.00 Pool: £1697.23 - 423.46 winning units..
Owner N Botica, Rex & Mrs Wendy Gorell **Bred** Tullamaine Castle Stud And Partners **Trained** Kingsclere, Hants

FOCUS
Only two of the three could seriously be considered in this. The runner-up looks the best guide to the form.

6530 FORTUNE STKS (LISTED RACE) 1m 14y
3:55 (3:55) (Class 1) 3-Y-O+
£20,982 (£7,955; £3,981; £1,983; £995; £499) **Stalls** Low

Form RPR
0206 **1** **Penitent**[24] 5794 7-9-4 115 DanielTudhope 4 111
(David O'Meara) *mde all: led field up far side in st: wound up the pce fr 3f out: slt jink over 2f out: drvn over 1f out: styd on wl* **9/4**[2]
-566 **2** *1 ¼* **Boomshackerlacker (IRE)**[75] 4043 3-9-0 98 (p) PatCosgrave 2 108
(George Baker) *t.k.h early: trckd ldng pair: rdn to chse wnr over 1f out: tried to cl fnl f: styd on but no imp last 100yds* **33/1**
4435 **3** *4* **Bana Wu**[35] 5402 4-8-13 102 DavidProbert 1 94
(Andrew Balding) *lw: dwlt: hld up in rr: shkn up over 2f out: no prog and sn btn: plugged on to take 3rd nr fin* **14/1**
6200 **4** *nse* **Validus**[27] 5681 4-9-4 102 JamesDoyle 6 99
(Luca Cumani) *hld up and sn in last: shkn up over 2f out: no prog and sn btn: plugged on to press for 3rd nr fin* **16/1**
3431 **5** *¾* **Wentworth (IRE)**[47] 4946 3-9-0 106 RichardHughes 3 97
(Richard Hannon) *lw: trckd wnr: rdn 2f out: nt qckn and sn lost 2nd: wknd fnl f* **1/1**[1]
1205 **6** *¾* **Westwiththenight (IRE)**[54] 4705 4-8-13 92 RyanMoore 5 90
(William Haggas) *lw: in tch in rr: rdn and detached in last 2f out: plugged on nr fin* **16/1**
0030 **7** *nse* **Aesop's Fables (USA)**[25] 5739 4-9-4 106 [1] SilvestreDeSousa 7 95
(Saeed bin Suroor) *lw: dwlt: t.k.h and sn chsd ldng trio: drvn and no imp 2f out: wknd fnl f* **8/1**[3]

1m 48.08s (4.78) **Going Correction** +0.825s/f (Soft)
WFA 3 from 4yo+ 4lb **7** Ran SP% **113.3**
Speed ratings (Par 111): **109,107,103,103,102 102,102**
toteswingers 1&2 £4.00, 2&3 £14.40, 1&3 £4.60 CSF £62.00 TOTE £4.30: £1.90, £5.80; EX 44.40 Trifecta £257.20 Pool: £ 2906.64 - 8.47 winning units..
Owner Middleham Park Racing XVII **Bred** Cheveley Park Stud Ltd **Trained** Nawton, N Yorks

FOCUS
Not form to put much faith in, with the favourite failing to handle the ground and the third in the betting pulling his chance away. The winner did not need to run to his best.

6531 MAX PATEL WEALTH MANAGER OF CHOICE FILLIES' H'CAP 1m 14y
4:30 (4:32) (Class 4) (0-85,85) 3-Y-O **£5,175** (£1,540; £769; £384) **Stalls** Low

Form RPR
343 **1** **Annawi**[19] 5942 3-8-13 **77** FergusSweeney 9 86
(Henry Candy) *lw: trckd ldr: styd far side st: led over 2f out: pressed 1f out: styd on wl last 150yds* **16/1**
0231 **2** *1 ½* **Cosseted**[31] 5563 3-8-10 **74** ShaneKelly 6 80+
(James Fanshawe) *s.i.s: mostly in last pair: c nr side st: drvn on outer 2f out: kpt on to ld gp ins fnl f: nt on terms w wnr* **7/2**[1]
1 **3** *½* **Deglet Noor**[13] 6134 3-9-6 **84** MickaelBarzalona 8 89
(Roger Varian) *w'like: str: chsd ldrs: c nr side in st and grabbed rail: led gp u.p 2f out: edgd rt and hdd ins fnl f: kpt on: 2nd of 4 in gp* **7/1**
4311 **4** *nse* **Narmin (IRE)**[41] 5173 3-9-2 **80** DaneO'Neill 2 85+
(John Gosden) *lw: chsd ldrs: styd far side st: rdn to chse wnr over 1f out and tried to chal: no ex ins fnl f: 2nd of 4 in gp* **6/1**[3]
-613 **5** *hd* **Al Jamal**[14] 6115 3-9-4 **82** SilvestreDeSousa 10 86
(Saeed bin Suroor) *led: styd far side in st: hdd over 2f out: lost 2nd over 1f out: kpt on nr fin: 3rd of 4 in gp* **4/1**[2]
3312 **6** *2* **Playbill**[30] 5589 3-8-10 **74** RyanMoore 5 74
(Sir Michael Stoute) *lw: chsd ldrs: led quartet to nr side in st but nt against rail: lost ld 2f out: fdd: 3rd of 4 in gp* **7/1**
0224 **7** *2 ½* **Magique (IRE)**[40] 5245 3-8-9 **73** JimCrowley 4 67
(Jeremy Noseda) *stdd s: hld up in last: styd far side in st: lost tch w others 2f out: last of 4 in gp* **12/1**
4363 **8** *2 ¾* **Sharqawiyah**[11] 6210 3-9-5 **83** JamesDoyle 1 71
(Luca Cumani) *lw: in tch: c nr side in st: wknd u.p 2f out: last of 4 in gp* **7/1**

1m 48.44s (5.14) **Going Correction** +0.825s/f (Soft) **8** Ran SP% **107.6**
Speed ratings (Par 100): **107,105,105,104,104 102,100,97**
toteswingers 1&2 £2.40, 2&3 £12.10, 1&3 £8.10 CSF £63.07 CT £373.96 TOTE £22.40: £4.90, £1.40, £2.60; EX 101.10 Trifecta £601.40 Pool: £1987.40 - 2.47 winning units..
Owner Major M G Wyatt **Bred** Dunchurch Lodge Stud Co **Trained** Kingston Warren, Oxon

FOCUS
A decent fillies' handicap that saw the field split into two soon on entering the straight, with half the field coming over to race stands' side. As it turned out there was hardly anything in it, with Annawi (far side) just edging out Cosseted (stands' side). Improvement from both the first two.

6532 KEN MANLEY MEMORIAL MAIDEN FILLIES' STKS 1m 2f 7y
5:05 (5:09) (Class 5) 3-Y-O+ **£2,587** (£770; £384; £192) **Stalls** Low

Form RPR
52 **1** **Empress Adelaide**[19] 5942 3-9-0 0 RyanMoore 2 86+
(William Haggas) *lengthy: lw: disp ld tl def advantage jst over 2f out: drvn and asserted over 1f out: styd on wl* **6/4**[1]
2 *3* **Norway Cross** 3-9-0 0 JamesDoyle 3 81+
(Luca Cumani) *leggy: unf: hld up in last trio: shkn up and prog 2f out: styd on fr over 1f out to take 2nd last 75yds: no threat to wnr* **20/1**
60 **3** *1* **Martagon Lily**[21] 5892 3-9-0 0 RobertHavlin 4 79
(John Gosden) *athletic: lw: trckd ldng pair: rdn to chse wnr wl over 1f out: no imp: lost 2nd last 75yds* **12/1**
3502 **4** *2* **Whippy Cream (IRE)**[7] 6312 3-9-0 96 AdamKirby 8 75
(Marco Botti) *disp ld tl drvn and nt qckn jst over 2f out: lost 2nd wl over 1f out: fdd* **9/4**[2]
52- **5** *5* **Kalispell (IRE)**[327] 7364 3-9-0 0 MickaelBarzalona 7 66
(Charlie Appleby) *trckd ldrs in 5th: rdn and no prog over 2f out: wknd over 1f out* **3/1**[3]
6 **6** *2 ¾* **Bethan**[14] 6116 4-9-6 0 AdamBeschizza 6 61?
(Julia Feilden) *lengthy: mostly in last trio: pushed along 4f out: wknd over 2f out* **66/1**
0 **7** *13* **Camisole (IRE)**[30] 5588 3-9-0 0 SteveDrowne 5 38
(Charles Hills) *str: dwlt: mostly in last: lost tch over 3f out: sn t.o* **25/1**
8 *nse* **Mrs Micawber** 3-9-0 0 RichardHughes 1 38
(Michael Bell) *leggy: trckd ldng pair tl wknd over 2f out: sn eased: t.o* **20/1**

2m 16.49s (5.99) **Going Correction** +0.825s/f (Soft)
WFA 3 from 4yo 6lb **8** Ran SP% **118.3**
Speed ratings (Par 100): **109,106,105,104,100 98,87,87**
toteswingers 1&2 £9.10, 2&3 £11.80, 1&3 £4.10 CSF £37.28 TOTE £2.50: £1.30, £4.40, £2.50; EX 28.30 Trifecta £480.10 Pool: £3284.23 - 5.13 winning units..
Owner Cheveley Park Stud **Bred** Cheveley Park Stud Ltd **Trained** Newmarket, Suffolk

FOCUS
This was quite well run. The field stayed far side and this proved quite straightforward for the favourite. Doubts over the form but the winner should do better.

6533 WILDWOOD GOLF AND COUNTRY CLUB H'CAP (JOCKEY CLUB GRASSROOTS MIDDLE DISTANCE SERIES QUALIFIER) 1m 2f 7y
5:35 (5:35) (Class 4) (0-85,85) 3-Y-O **£5,175** (£1,540; £769; £384) **Stalls** Low

Form RPR
2252 **1** **Lady Pimpernel**[19] 5953 3-9-4 **82** DaneO'Neill 6 93
(Henry Candy) *led: hrd rdn and pressed 2f out: narrowly hdd jst over 1f out: fought bk wl to ld again ins fnl f: gamely* **7/2**[2]
1102 **2** *½* **Topamichi**[5] 6358 3-8-12 **76** RyanMoore 1 86
(Mark H Tompkins) *mostly trckd wnr: shkn up and clsd to ld narrowly on inner jst over 1f out: hdd and drvn ins fnl f: hld nr fin* **2/1**[1]
-113 **3** *5* **Lyric Ballad**[74] 4066 3-8-13 **77** SilvestreDeSousa 8 78
(Hughie Morrison) *lost pl after 3f: prog 4f out: rdn to press wnr 2f out: hanging and nt qckn over 1f out: wknd fnl f* **8/1**
6333 **4** *3* **Penny Rose**[11] 6188 3-9-3 **81** JoeFanning 5 76
(Mark Johnston) *hld up and sn in last: pushed along 4f out: prog on outer and in tch jst over 2f out: wknd over 1f out* **10/1**
0-12 **5** *½* **Powder Hound**[135] 2086 3-9-5 **83** DavidProbert 4 77
(Andrew Balding) *lw: in tch: shkn up over 2f out: sn wknd* **5/1**
1312 **6** *1 ¾* **Fast Pace**[42] 5132 3-9-5 **83** PatDobbs 2 74
(Amanda Perrett) *prom: drvn over 2f out: wknd wl over 1f out* **9/2**[3]
4-15 **7** *11* **Unmoothaj**[107] 2927 3-8-13 **77** LiamKeniry 3 47
(Pam Sly) *hld up in rr: wknd over 2f out: t.o* **25/1**

2m 18.07s (7.57) **Going Correction** +0.825s/f (Soft) **7** Ran SP% **114.5**
Speed ratings (Par 103): **102,101,97,95,94 93,84**
toteswingers 1&2 £2.40, 2&3 £4.50, 1&3 £3.60 CSF £10.97 CT £50.38 TOTE £4.90: £2.10, £1.60; EX 12.50 Trifecta £51.00 Pool: £1733.65 - 25.49 winning units..
Owner Henry Candy & Partners II **Bred** Harts Farm Stud **Trained** Kingston Warren, Oxon

FOCUS
This was a stone slower than the previous C&D maiden. Again they all stayed far side in the straight. The second is the best guide.

T/Plt: £72.70 to a £1 stake. Pool of £70611.56 - 708.75 winning tickets. T/Qpdt: £18.40 to a £1 stake. Pool of £3532.78 - 141.57 winning tickets. JN

6500 YARMOUTH (L-H)

Wednesday, September 18

OFFICIAL GOING: Good to soft (good in places in back straight; 6.4)

Wind: medium to fresh, across Weather: mainly cloudy, bright spells

6534 BRITISH STALLION STUDS/GREENE KING EBF MAIDEN STKS 7f 3y

2:10 (2:10) (Class 5) 2-Y-O **£2,911** (£866; £432; £216) **Stalls** Centre

Form RPR

0 1 **Oxsana**[24] 5797 2-9-0 0 TomQueally 1 80
(William Haggas) *t.k.h: hld up in tch in midfield: rdn and effrt to chse ldr wl over 1f out: drvn to chal 1f out: sustained effrt u.p to ld fnl 50yds: rdn out* **11/2**[3]

0 2 nk **Torchlighter (IRE)**[14] 6110 2-9-5 0 KierenFallon 4 84
(Mark Johnston) *led and set stdy gallop: rdn and fnd ex 2f out: clr w wnr 1f out: battled on wl u.p and sustained duel w wnr after tl hdd and no ex fnl 50yds* **16/1**

3 1 **Munaaser** 2-9-5 0 PaulHanagan 7 82
(Sir Michael Stoute) *wnt sltly rt s: sn rcvrd and chsd ldrs after 1f: rdn over 2f out: rn green and outpcd wl over 1f out: rallied u.p ins fnl f: styd on wl fnl 100yds* **6/4**[1]

4 4 ½ **Throne Room** 2-9-5 0 WilliamBuick 5 70
(John Gosden) *hld up wl in tch in midfield: rdn over 2f out: outpcd and btn over 1f out: no threat to ldng trio and styd on same pce fnl f* **3/1**[2]

5 ¾ **Go Sakhee** 2-9-5 0 AndreaAtzeni 9 68
(Roger Varian) *wnt rt s: hld up in tch in last trio: rdn 1/2-way: swtchd rt 3f out: outpcd and btn over 1f out: no threat to ldrs and plugged on same pce fnl f* **8/1**

0 6 1 ¾ **Yellow Emperor (IRE)**[56] 4631 2-9-5 0 (v[1]) TedDurcan 2 63
(Jeremy Noseda) *chsd ldr: rdn ent fnl 2f: lost 2nd and outpcd wl over 1f out: edgd lft and sn btn: wknd fnl f* **20/1**

5 7 2 ¼ **Daisy Boy (IRE)**[48] 4906 2-9-5 0 SeanLevey 6 58
(Stuart Williams) *dwlt: hld up in tch in last trio: rdn and struggling over 2f out: wknd over 1f out* **40/1**

8 2 ¾ **Like A Prayer** 2-9-5 0 MartinLane 3 50
(Marco Botti) *dwlt: t.k.h: hld up in tch in last pair: shkn up 1/2-way: rdn and struggling over 2f out: wknd over 1f out* **12/1**

1m 27.04s (0.44) **Going Correction** -0.15s/f (Firm) 8 Ran SP% **112.3**

Speed ratings (Par 95): **91,90,89,84,83 81,78,75**

toteswingers 1&2 £9.20, 2&3 £5.40, 1&3 £2.30 CSF £82.48 TOTE £4.40: £1.20, £3.20, £1.70; EX 54.70 Trifecta £204.00 Pool: £1153.67 - 4.24 winning units..

Owner Sultan Ali **Bred** The Kingwood Partnership **Trained** Newmarket, Suffolk

FOCUS

Full width of back straight utilised. A hugely informative maiden, dominated in recent years by the market principals with nine of the last ten winners justifying favouritism. Experience is often key in this type of race however, and it proved the case in this event with the finish fought out by two horses who had shaped with a degree of promise on their respective debuts. Not form to be totally confident about but they race was dominated by well-bred sorts from top yards and this is traditionally a good juvenile race.

6535 DANNY WRIGHT MEMORIAL FILLIES' H'CAP (FOR THE CHALLENGE TROPHY) 6f 3y

2:40 (2:41) (Class 5) (0-75,71) 3-Y-O+ **£2,587** (£770; £384; £192) **Stalls** Centre

Form RPR

0403 1 **Oh So Spicy**[42] 5154 6-9-5 **69** TedDurcan 11 80
(Chris Wall) *in tch in midfield: effrt to ld 2f out: clr w rival 1f out: styd on wl u.p and gng away at fin: rdn out* **13/2**[2]

0334 2 1 ½ **Azenzar**[41] 5181 3-9-5 **71** (p) WilliamBuick 6 77
(Roger Varian) *wl in tch in midfield: rdn and effrt to chse wnr wl over 1f out: ev ch ins fnl f tl btn wl ins fnl f: wknd towards fin* **9/4**[1]

3404 3 ¾ **Ray Of Joy**[33] 5498 7-9-4 **68** TomQueally 2 72
(J R Jenkins) *hld up in midfield: clsd on ldrs 2f out: rdn and effrt over 1f out: chsd ldng pair ins fnl f: kpt on u.p* **12/1**

2233 4 1 ½ **Verus Delicia (IRE)**[12] 6156 4-8-13 **63** AndreaAtzeni 5 62
(John Stimpson) *in tch in midfield: rdn and effrt ent fnl 2f: chsd ldng pair and drvn over 1f out: styd on same pce and lost 3rd ins fnl f* **7/1**[3]

2301 5 nk **Gift Of Silence**[29] 5617 4-9-5 **69** FrankieDettori 8 67
(John Berry) *wl bhd: hdwy 1/2-way: rdn and battling for placing over 1f out: no imp and one pce ins fnl f* **17/2**

6006 6 ½ **Caramelita**[27] 5677 6-9-4 **68** (v) FrederikTylicki 4 64
(J R Jenkins) *in tch in midfield: clsd to chse ldrs over 1f out: rdn and no ex 1f out: wknd ins fnl f* **20/1**

6343 7 2 **Meddling**[29] 5617 3-8-13 **65** PaulHanagan 9 55
(Sir Michael Stoute) *off the pce in last trio: rdn ent fnl 2f: sme hdwy over 1f out: kpt on ins fnl f: nvr trbld ldrs* **9/1**

5613 8 6 **Clock Opera (IRE)**[15] 6075 3-8-9 **61** KirstyMilczarek 3 32
(William Stone) *led tl rdn and hdd 2f out: sn lost pl and btn: wknd ent fnl f* **17/2**

0005 9 hd **Interakt**[9] 6255 6-8-10 **63** (p) ThomasBrown(3) 10 33
(Joseph Tuite) *sn wl off the pce in rr: rdn over 2f out: n.d* **20/1**

0030 10 1 ½ **El Mirage (IRE)**[77] 3956 3-9-4 **70** MartinLane 1 35
(Dean Ivory) *chsd ldr tl over 2f out: sn btn and dropped out: bhd fnl f* **28/1**

-620 11 shd **Fever Few**[12] 6181 4-9-3 **67** WilliamCarson 7 32
(Jane Chapple-Hyam) *bmpd s: sn rcvrd and chsng ldrs: rdn and unable qck 2f out: sn btn and wknd: fdd fnl f* **16/1**

1m 12.78s (-1.62) **Going Correction** -0.15s/f (Firm)

WFA 3 from 4yo+ 2lb 11 Ran SP% **114.2**

Speed ratings (Par 100): **104,102,101,99,98 97,95,87,87,85 84**

toteswingers 1&2 £3.30, 2&3 £5.70, 1&3 £14.00 CSF £20.13 TOTE £8.60: £2.10, £1.90, £3.70; EX 20.80 Trifecta £214.80 Pool: £2610.90 - 9.11 winning units..

Owner The Eight Of Diamonds **Bred** Mrs C J Walker **Trained** Newmarket, Suffolk

FOCUS

A hot race for the grade with plenty of pace on throughout. The winner is rated back to his best.

6536 EBF AT THE RACES JOHN MUSKER FILLIES' STKS (FOR THE JOHN MUSKER TROPHY) (LISTED RACE) 1m 2f 21y

3:10 (3:13) (Class 1) 3-Y-O+

£22,488 (£8,560; £4,284; £2,136; £1,072; £540) **Stalls** Low

Form RPR

2630 1 **Miss You Too**[45] 5044 3-8-10 96 ChrisCatlin 8 103
(David Simcock) *mde all: 3 l clr 4f out: stl clr and rdn over 1f out: styd on wl: unchal* **20/1**

1342 2 3 ¼ **Jabhaat (USA)**[32] 5534 3-8-10 86 PaulHanagan 3 97
(Ed Dunlop) *hld up in midfield: rdn and effrt 3f out: hdwy over 2f out: chsd clr wnr 1f out: kpt on but no imp* **16/1**

-111 3 2 ¼ **Ribbons**[49] 4878 3-8-10 95 FrederikTylicki 9 92+
(James Fanshawe) *stdd s: hld up off the pce in rr: last and rdn over 4f out: no real imp stl only modest 7th over 1f out: styd on ins fnl f: snatched 3rd last stride: no ch w wnr* **5/2**[1]

3113 4 shd **Rock Choir**[35] 5402 3-8-10 94 AndreaAtzeni 10 92+
(William Haggas) *dwlt: t.k.h: hld up in rr: hdwy into midfield 1/2-way: no imp u.p and stl modest 6th over 1f out: styd on to chse ldng pair ins fnl f: lost 3rd last stride: no ch w wnr* **5/1**[3]

2000 5 2 **Agent Allison**[47] 4949 3-8-10 100 MartinLane 1 88
(Peter Chapple-Hyam) *stdd s: hld up wl off the pce towards rr: hdwy on inner over 2f out: swtchd rt over 1f out: kpt on fnl f: n.d* **16/1**

3101 6 1 **Close At Hand**[19] 5960 3-8-10 83 WilliamBuick 6 86
(John Gosden) *chsd ldng pair: rdn and effrt over 2f out: unable qck and no imp: lost 3rd over 1f out: wknd ins fnl f* **20/1**

2-16 7 ½ **Audacia (IRE)**[62] 4468 3-8-10 84 SeanLevey 4 85
(Hugo Palmer) *t.k.h: chsd clr wnr: rdn and no imp over 2f out: lost 2nd and 1f out: wknd* **25/1**

0006 8 7 **Semayyel (IRE)**[35] 5402 4-9-2 95 (b) TedDurcan 2 71
(Clive Brittain) *chsd ldng trio: rdn and no hdwy 3f out: wl btn 2f out: wknd* **25/1**

3120 9 ¾ **Spicy Dal**[45] 5035 3-8-10 89 TomQueally 5 69
(Hughie Morrison) *racd in midfield: rdn and no hdwy 4f out: bhd fnl 2f* **22/1**

1003 10 6 **Shuruq (USA)**[18] 6000 3-8-10 109 (p) AhmedAjtebi 7 57
(Saeed bin Suroor) *hld up in midfield: rdn and no hdwy 3f out: wl btn ent fnl 2f: eased ins fnl f* **5/1**[3]

6412 11 5 **Hippy Hippy Shake**[35] 5402 4-9-6 100 KierenFallon 11 51
(Luca Cumani) *a wl off the pce towards rr and nvr gng wl: rdn and no hdwy over 4f out: wl bhd and eased fnl f* **4/1**[2]

2m 5.98s (-4.52) **Going Correction** -0.15s/f (Firm)

WFA 3 from 4yo 6lb 11 Ran SP% **115.2**

Speed ratings (Par 108): **112,109,107,107,105 105,104,99,98,93 89**

toteswingers 1&2 £32.10, 2&3 £8.10, 1&3 £10.00 CSF £275.39 TOTE £21.40: £3.40, £4.40, £1.80; EX 324.50 Trifecta £2208.10 Pool: £3386.95 - 1.15 winning units..

Owner Andrew Whitlock **Bred** Plantation Stud & Amarvilas Bloodstock **Trained** Newmarket, Suffolk

FOCUS

Semayyel had created an almighty upset when winning this corresponding race at odds of 125-1 last season and it provided another shock result. Not great form by Listed standard but this has to rate a personal best from Miss You Too.

6537 VAUXHALL HOLIDAY PARK H'CAP (FOR THE GOLDEN JUBILEE TROPHY) 1m 2f 21y

3:45 (3:45) (Class 3) (0-90,90) 3-Y-O **£7,246** (£2,168; £1,084; £542; £270) **Stalls** Low

Form RPR

224 1 **Tuscania**[25] 5742 5-9-3 **83** FrederikTylicki 5 92
(Lucy Wadham) *hld up in tch in last trio: smooth hdwy to trck ldrs 2f out: rdn to ld over 1f out: kpt on wl fnl f: rdn out* **16/1**

211 2 1 ½ **Mahican (IRE)**[4] 6387 3-9-0 **86** 6ex KierenFallon 1 92
(Mark Johnston) *dwlt: sn rcvrd and chsd ldr: rdn to ld: rdn wl over 2f out: hdd and drvn over 1f out: kpt on same pce ins fnl f* **5/2**[1]

1201 3 1 ¼ **Altharoos (IRE)**[11] 6208 3-9-4 **90** PaulHanagan 3 94
(Sir Michael Stoute) *hld up wl in tch in midfield: rdn and effrt on inner over 2f out: swtchd rt over 1f out: styd on u.p fnl f* **3/1**[2]

0340 4 ½ **Harry Buckle**[11] 6211 4-9-0 **80** (t) WilliamCarson 7 83
(Philip McBride) *t.k.h: chsd ldr tl 7f out: styd chsng ldrs: rdn wl over 2f out: drvn and kpt on same pce fr wl over 1f out* **25/1**

141 5 2 ½ **Tinghir (IRE)**[14] 6115 3-9-2 **88** TedDurcan 6 86
(David Lanigan) *wl in tch in midfield: effrt u.p on inner over 2f out: no ex and btn 1f out: wknd ins fnl f* **10/3**[3]

6143 6 ¾ **Noble Gift**[25] 5742 3-9-0 **86** WilliamBuick 2 83
(William Knight) *t.k.h: chsd ldrs: wnt 2nd 7f tl wl over 1f out: sn struggling and wknd ent fnl f* **5/1**

5003 7 3 ½ **Daghash**[100] 3157 4-8-10 **76** TomQueally 8 66
(Clive Brittain) *hld up in tch in last trio: effrt u.p 3f out: no prog: nvr trbld ldrs* **16/1**

210 8 7 **Snow Trooper**[144] 1840 5-9-5 **85** MartinLane 4 62
(Dean Ivory) *t.k.h: chsd ldrs tl lost pl over 2f out: sn wl btn: bhd 1f out* **14/1**

2m 9.52s (-0.98) **Going Correction** -0.15s/f (Firm)

WFA 3 from 4yo+ 6lb 8 Ran SP% **115.6**

Speed ratings (Par 107): **97,95,94,94,92 91,89,83**

toteswingers 1&2 £6.60, 2&3 £1.60, 1&3 £8.30 CSF £56.82 TOTE £13.90: £3.30, £1.30, £1.20; EX 54.70 Trifecta £303.50 Pool: £2376.15 - 5.87 winning units..

Owner Mr And Mrs A E Pakenham **Bred** Juddmonte Farms Ltd **Trained** Newmarket, Suffolk

FOCUS

This looked a fiercely competitive renewal of this contest. The winner's best form since her early 3yo days.

6538 SEA-DEER H'CAP 1m 3y

4:20 (4:20) (Class 4) (0-85,85) 3-Y-O+ **£4,690** (£1,395; £697; £348) **Stalls** Centre

Form RPR

2212 1 **Thouwra (IRE)**[19] 5958 3-9-5 **84** (p) WilliamBuick 8 94
(Saeed bin Suroor) *t.k.h: hld up in tch in midfield: clsd to chse ldr over 2f out: rdn to ld 1f out: hrd pressed ins fnl f: hld on towards fin: rdn out* **9/4**[1]

6203 2 hd **Buckstay (IRE)**[32] 5534 3-9-4 **83** FrankieDettori 3 92
(Peter Chapple-Hyam) *t.k.h: hld up in midfield: hdwy over 2f out: rdn and effrt over 1f out: str chal ins fnl f: r.o u.p but hld towards fin* **11/2**[3]

1 3 1 **Joe Sugden**[26] 5720 4-9-7 **82** (t) MartinLane 6 88
(Mrs Ilka Gansera-Leveque) *chsd ldr tl led 4f out: rdn and edgd rt 2f out: hdd 1f out: kpt on same pce ins fnl f* **20/1**

3033 4 1 **Barwick**[5] 6360 5-9-1 **76** TomQueally 10 80
(Mark H Tompkins) *s.i.s and bustled along leaving stalls: bhd: clsd 1/2-way: hdwy to chse ldrs and drvn over 1f out: kpt on same pce ins fnl f* **4/1**[2]

0005 5 ½ **Alfred Hutchinson**[12] 6164 5-9-7 **85** WilliamTwiston-Davies(3) 2 88
(Geoffrey Oldroyd) *hld up in midfield: clsd 3f out: rdn and chsd ldrs over 1f out: styd on same pce ins fnl f* **16/1**

440 6 nse **Ocean Applause**[5] 6356 3-9-0 **79** (tp) BrettDoyle 4 82
(John Ryan) *s.i.s: bhd and pushed along early: swtchd lft and clsd 6f out: effrt to chse ldrs and drvn 2f out: no ex 1f out: wknd ins fnl f* **16/1**

3100 7 8 **Macchiara**[38] 5310 4-9-2 **77** ChrisCatlin 7 61
(Rae Guest) *chsd ldr: rdn over 2f out: lost pl ent fnl 2f: wknd and bhd 1f out* **25/1**

The Form Book Flat, Raceform Ltd, Compton, RG20 6NL.

0050 **8** *19* **Copperwood**[18] 5987 8-9-0 **75** KierenFallon 11 16
(Mark Johnston) *broke fast: chsd ldrs: rdn and struggling over 3f out: sn dropped out: t.o fnl f* **28/1**
6000 **9** *13* **Jake's Destiny (IRE)**[48] 4923 4-9-8 **83** (t) TedDurcan 9
(George Baker) *a towards rr: rdn over 3f out and sn struggling: wl bhd and eased fnl f: t.o* **8/1**
1031 **10** *12* **Azma (USA)**[33] 5491 3-8-13 **78** PaulHanagan 1
(Conrad Allen) *led tl 1/2-way: chsd ldr tl over 2f out: sn dropped out and bhd: t.o and eased fnl f* **7/1**

1m 38.07s (-2.53) **Going Correction** -0.15s/f (Firm)
WFA 3 from 4yo+ 4lb **10** Ran SP% **113.6**
Speed ratings (Par 105): **106,105,104,103,103 103,95,76,63,51**
toteswingers 1&2 £2.40, 2&3 £12.10, 1&3 £8.10 CSF £13.69 CT £191.91 TOTE £2.30: £1.30, £1.70, £4.20; EX 14.80 Trifecta £115.90 Pool: £2111.13 - 13.65 winning units..
Owner Godolphin **Bred** Darley **Trained** Newmarket, Suffolk

FOCUS
A hotly contested handicap, run at a fair pace throughout and it served up a thrilling finish. The form is rated around the fourth and fifth, with the first three unexposed.

6539 DAN HAGUE YARMOUTH NO 1 BOOKMAKER H'CAP 5f 43y
4:55 (4:55) (Class 2) (0-100,97) 3-Y-0+ **£12,602** (£3,772; £1,886; £944; £470) **Stalls** Centre

Form RPR
6000 **1** **Free Zone**[36] 5375 4-9-5 **95** PaulHanagan 3 105
(Bryan Smart) *chsd ldrs: rdn 1/2-way: drvn and hdwy over 1f out: chal ins fnl f: led fnl 75yds: styd on wl* **10/1**[3]
5006 **2** *3/4* **Jiroft (ITY)**[23] 5821 6-9-2 **95** (p) RobertTart(3) 7 102
(Robert Cowell) *chsd ldr tl rdn to ld over 1f out: clr w wnr ins fnl f: hdd and no ex fnl 75yds* **16/1**
3 *1 1/4* **Jamaican Bolt (IRE)**[172] 1232 5-9-2 **95** WilliamTwiston-Davies(3) 10 98
(Geoffrey Oldroyd) *racd in midfield: rdn and hdwy over 1f out: styd on u.p ins fnl f: wnt 3rd nr fin: no threat to ldng pair* **11/4**[1]
3-42 **4** *nk* **Exceptionelle**[63] 4413 3-8-11 **88** WilliamBuick 5 90
(Roger Varian) *dwlt: sn rcvrd and chsd ldrs: rdn and effrt wl over 1f out: styd on same pce u.p ins fnl f* **7/2**[2]
3530 **5** *1/2* **Normal Equilibrium**[11] 6190 3-8-13 **90** (p) TomQueally 1 90
(Robert Cowell) *racd in midfield: effrt and edgd lft over 1f out: kpt on ins fnl f: no threat to ldrs* **14/1**
6402 **6** *1/2* **Goldream**[28] 5651 4-9-3 **93** (p) FrederikTylicki 8 91
(Robert Cowell) *s.i.s: bhd: hdwy u.p over 1f out: kpt on ins fnl f: nvr trbld ldrs* **7/2**[2]
0051 **7** *1/2* **Storm Moon (USA)**[11] 6212 3-8-9 **86** KierenFallon 6 82
(Mark Johnston) *led tl rdn and hdd over 1f out: no ex 1f out: wknd ins fnl f* **12/1**
5006 **8** *1/2* **Top Boy**[18] 5996 3-8-6 **83** PatrickMathers 11 78
(Derek Shaw) *stdd s: hld up in last trio: effrt over 1f out: no imp and hung lft ins fnl f: n.d* **14/1**
0013 **9** *nk* **First In Command (IRE)**[1] 6506 8-8-7 **83** oh1 (t) MartinLane 9 76
(John Stimpson) *racd off the pce in last trio: rdn and effrt over 1f out: kpt on but n.d* **16/1**
0030 **10** *1* **Prohibit**[11] 6190 8-9-4 **97** (p) ThomasBrown(3) 2 87
(Robert Cowell) *chsd ldrs: rdn 1/2-way: little rspnse and lost pl over 1f out: wknd fnl f* **25/1**

1m 1.72s (-0.98) **Going Correction** -0.15s/f (Firm)
WFA 3 from 4yo+ 1lb **10** Ran SP% **116.8**
Speed ratings (Par 109): **101,99,97,97,96 95,94,94,93,92**
toteswingers 1&2 £15.90, 2&3 £14.00, 1&3 £6.30 CSF £157.31 CT £573.39 TOTE £12.80: £3.60, £4.50, £1.50; EX 172.90 Trifecta £1118.80 Pool: £2554.52 - 1.71 winning units..
Owner Fromthestables.com Racing **Bred** R G Levin **Trained** Hambleton, N Yorks

FOCUS
Some likeable and hardened sprinters were on show in this Class 2 contest. The winner was rated back close to his best.

6540 LA CONTINENTAL CAFE IN GREAT YARMOUTH H'CAP 2m
5:25 (5:25) (Class 4) (0-85,85) 3-Y-0 **£4,690** (£1,395; £697; £348) **Stalls** Low

Form RPR
-651 **1** **Kelvingrove (IRE)**[29] 5619 3-9-2 **80** FrederikTylicki 4 91
(Ed Vaughan) *stdd s: hld up in rr: clsd and wnt 2nd 4f out: rdn and ev ch 2f out: led ent fnl f: gng clr and rn green ins fnl f: styd on wl* **11/4**[3]
3143 **2** *3* **Nateeja (IRE)**[18] 5997 3-8-12 **76** PaulHanagan 1 83
(J W Hills) *chsd ldr tl clsd to ld 4f out: drvn and hrd pressed 2f out: hdd ent fnl f: no ex and btn fnl 150yds* **5/2**[2]
132 **3** *18* **Alwilda**[11] 6196 3-9-7 **85** ChrisCatlin 2 74
(Sir Mark Prescott Bt) *hung lft thrght: racd in 3rd: clsd and pressing ldrs 4f out: rdn and hung lft 2f: sn btn: eased ins fnl f* **15/8**[1]
1140 **4** *15* **Pearl Spice (IRE)**[10] 6237 3-9-2 **80** (b) WilliamCarson 3 47
(Tim Pitt) *rn in snatches: sn rdn along to ld and wnt clr: c bk to field 10f out: sn urged along and wnt clr again: rdn and hdd 4f out: sn dropped out: t.o and eased fnl f* **5/1**

3m 30.0s (-2.40) **Going Correction** -0.15s/f (Firm) **4** Ran SP% **106.7**
Speed ratings (Par 103): **100,98,89,82**
CSF £9.45 TOTE £3.80; EX 9.10 Trifecta £18.00 Pool: £1140.20 - 47.36 winning units..
Owner The Kelvingrove Partnership **Bred** Mark Johnston Racing Ltd **Trained** Newmarket, Suffolk

FOCUS
A fair staying handicap, despite the lack of runners. The winner more than confirmed his previous romp.
T/Plt: 12.80 to a £1 stake. Pool of £80253.11 - 4576.02 winning tickets. T/Qpdt: £6.80 to a £1 stake. Pool of £6749.50 - 728.30 winning tickets. SP

6541 - 6544a (Foreign Racing) - See Raceform Interactive

5330 AYR (L-H)
Thursday, September 19

OFFICIAL GOING: Soft (8.4)
Wind: Breezy, half against Weather: Overcast, dull

6545 EBF / FRAZER COOGANS COMMERCIAL SOLICITORS NOVICE STKS 1m
1:40 (1:41) (Class 4) 2-Y-0 **£5,498** (£1,636; £817; £408) **Stalls** Low

Form RPR
31 **1** **Bremner**[40] 5262 2-9-5 0 GrahamLee 2 89+
(Kevin Ryan) *trckd ldr: rdn to ld over 2f out: clr appr fnl f: pushed out* **7/2**[3]
31 **2** *2 3/4* **Illuminating Dream (IRE)**[19] 5983 2-9-0 78 PhillipMakin 4 78
(David Brown) *edgy in preliminaries: prom: rdn and outpcd over 3f out: rallied and edgd lft 2f out: chsd wnr last 100yds: kpt on: no imp* **10/3**[2]
31 **3** *2 1/2* **Roachdale House (IRE)**[24] 5826 2-9-5 79 TonyHamilton 3 77
(Richard Fahey) *sn pushed along to trck ldr: t.k.h: effrt and chsd wnr over 1f out to last 100yds: sn btn* **10/11**[1]
1042 **4** *5* **Boogangoo (IRE)**[16] 6085 2-9-0 75 TomEaves 1 61
(Keith Dalgleish) *led to over 2f out: rdn and wknd over 1f out* **12/1**
5 *5* **Thorntoun Care** 2-9-0 0 JoeFanning 5 50+
(Jim Goldie) *s.i.s and wnt rt s: rn green in rr: shortlived effrt over 2f out: sn btn* **40/1**

1m 46.39s (2.59) **Going Correction** +0.325s/f (Good) **5** Ran SP% **107.8**
Speed ratings (Par 97): **100,97,94,89,84**
CSF £14.53 TOTE £4.10: £1.50, £1.50; EX 12.30 Trifecta £15.60 Pool: £1376.77 - 65.92 winning units..
Owner Highbank Stud **Bred** Highbank Stud **Trained** Hambleton, N Yorks

FOCUS
Track at full width and distances as advertised. Tony Hamilton said after the opener: "It's soft but nothing worse than that," and Philip Makin said: "It's soft and it will open up." The time was 7.89sec above Racing Post standard, and suggests that the ground was very much on the soft side. They were racing into a headwind too, which would have had an effect on times. High-class stayer Simenon won this in 2009. Decent juvenile form, although only the first two gave their running. There's every chance of more from the winner.

6546 S.T. ANDREW PLANT HIRE MAIDEN AUCTION STKS 6f
2:10 (2:12) (Class 5) 2-Y-0 **£3,881** (£1,155; £577; £288) **Stalls** High

Form RPR
1 **Red Stargazer (IRE)** 2-8-11 0 RobertWinston 1 87
(David Barron) *s.i.s: hld up: smooth hdwy whn nt clr run over 2f out to over 1f out: squeezed through to ld ins fnl f: pushed clr: readily* **12/1**
2 **2** *3 1/2* **Kommander Kirkup**[117] 2670 2-8-11 0 PJMcDonald 3 77
(Michael Dods) *prom on outside: effrt and ev ch over 1f out to ins fnl f: kpt on: nt pce of wnr* **5/4**[1]
23 **3** *1 1/2* **Ribbleton**[38] 5338 2-8-9 0 TonyHamilton 5 70
(Richard Fahey) *w ldrs: rdn and led over 1f out: hdd ins fnl f: sn one pce* **7/2**[2]
00 **4** *1 3/4* **Firecruise**[75] 4053 2-8-9 0 GrahamGibbons 10 65
(David Barron) *in tch: drvn and outpcd over 2f out: rallied ins fnl f: kpt on: nvr able to chal* **16/1**
4 **5** *1/2* **Lexington Abbey**[37] 5364 2-8-13 0 GrahamLee 9 67
(Kevin Ryan) *cl up: effrt and ev ch over 1f out: wknd ins fnl f* **9/2**[3]
0 **6** *1 3/4* **Mishnah**[20] 5950 2-7-13 0 JoeyHaynes(5) 8 53
(John Holt) *in tch: rdn and outpcd over 2f out: n.d after* **40/1**
22 **7** *3 1/4* **Mocacha (IRE)**[16] 6069 2-9-2 0 (b[1]) PhillipMakin 4 55
(William Haggas) *led to over 1f out: sn rdn and wknd* **17/2**
00 **8** *3 1/4* **Mavree (IRE)**[9] 6286 2-7-11 0 RachelRichardson(7) 2 34
(Tim Easterby) *hld up on outside: struggling wl over 2f out: nvr on terms* **100/1**
0 **9** *11* **Black Tie Dancer (IRE)**[34] 5490 2-8-6 0 (b[1]) DanielMuscutt(5) 7 8
(Gay Kelleway) *s.i.s: bhd: struggling 1/2-way: sn btn: t.o* **50/1**
5 **10** *7* **Reflection**[21] 5915 2-8-8 0 TomEaves 6
(Richard Fahey) *bhd and sn outpcd: hung lft 1/2-way: sn lost tch* **40/1**

1m 16.7s (4.30) **Going Correction** +0.70s/f (Yiel) **10** Ran SP% **116.8**
Speed ratings (Par 95): **99,94,92,90,89 87,82,78,63,54**
toteswingers 1&2 £4.80, 1&3 £7.90, 2&3 £1.80 CSF £27.36 TOTE £17.60: £3.50, £1.20, £1.10; EX 41.90 Trifecta £258.60 Pool: £2749.66 - 7.97 winning units..
Owner Twinacre Nurseries Ltd **Bred** Maurice Burns **Trained** Maunby, N Yorks

FOCUS
Just a fair maiden. The winner impressed but may have been flattered. The third is perhaps the best guide.

6547 BREWIN DOLPHIN H'CAP 5f
2:40 (2:43) (Class 5) (0-70,70) 3-Y-0+ **£3,881** (£1,155; £577; £288) **Stalls** High

Form RPR
00-5 **1** **Boris Grigoriev (IRE)**[38] 5333 4-9-4 **67** (b) GrahamGibbons 17 77
(Michael Easterby) *towards rr stands' side: reminders after 2f: hdwy stands' rail to ld appr fnl f: hld on wl towards fin: 1st of 10 in gp* **10/1**[3]
664 **2** *nk* **Go Go Green (IRE)**[3] 6469 7-9-6 **69** PhillipMakin 16 78
(Jim Goldie) *hld up stands' side: hdwy whn nt clr run over 1f out: chsd wnr ins fnl f: kpt on: 2nd of 10 in gp* **10/1**[3]
5025 **3** *1 1/4* **Our Diane (IRE)**[3] 6469 3-8-10 **60** TonyHamilton 18 65
(Richard Fahey) *prom stands' side: effrt and rdn 2f out: kpt on fnl f: 3rd of 10 in gp* **14/1**
1110 **4** *1 1/4* **Gran Canaria Queen**[17] 6052 4-9-7 **70** DanielTudhope 5 70+
(Tim Easterby) *cl up far side: led that gp over 1f out: plld clr fnl f: no ch w stands' side gp: 1st of 6 in gp* **9/1**[2]
402 **5** *hd* **Captain Scooby**[9] 6287 7-8-13 **67** PhilipPrince(5) 21 66
(Richard Guest) *hld up stands' side: rdn after 2f out: hdwy over 1f out: kpt on fnl f: 4th of 10 in gp* **8/1**[1]
060 **6** *1* **Foxy Music**[47] 4992 9-9-3 **69** JasonHart(3) 9 65
(Eric Alston) *led centre quartet: rdn and hung rt to outside of stands' side gp 2f out: one pce fnl f: 1st of 4 in gp* **22/1**
0411 **7** *shd* **Captain Royale (IRE)**[16] 6088 8-9-2 **70** (p) GeorgeChaloner(5) 22 65
(Tracy Waggott) *led stands' side: rdn and hdd appr fnl f: kpt on same pce: 5th of 10 in gp* **16/1**
6450 **8** *1* **Planetex (IRE)**[9] 6287 4-9-2 **65** (p) RobertWinston 10 57
(John Quinn) *prom centre: effrt 2f out: edgd rt: kpt on same pce fnl f: 2nd of 4 in gp* **14/1**
0050 **9** *1/2* **Elusive Bonus (IRE)**[35] 5422 4-8-10 **64** DavidBergin(5) 19 54
(David O'Meara) *cl up stands' side: drvn 2f out: outpcd ins fnl f: 6th of 10 in gp* **8/1**[1]
134- **10** *1/2* **Dreamy Ciara**[501] 1891 3-9-5 **69** PJMcDonald 20 57
(David Brown) *hld up stands' side: drvn over 2f out: kpt on fnl f: nvr able to chal: 7th of 10 in gp* **25/1**
0000 **11** *3/4* **Mission Impossible**[24] 5832 8-8-12 **66** (p) JacobButterfield(5) 13 51
(Tracy Waggott) *chsd centre ldrs: rdn and hung rt to outside of stands' side gp 2f out: sn no imp: 3rd of 4 in gp* **10/1**[3]
2656 **12** *nse* **Saxonette**[3] 6469 5-8-7 **56** oh3 AndrewElliott 3 41
(Linda Perratt) *in tch far side: drvn over 2f out: hdwy to chse far side ldr ins fnl f: no imp: 2nd of 6 in gp* **22/1**
0000 **13** *1* **Burnhope**[12] 6205 4-9-4 **67** (p) GrahamLee 2 49
(Scott Dixon) *led far side to over 1f out: sn no ex and lost 2nd ins fnl f: 3rd of 6 in gp* **20/1**
235 **14** *nk* **Baker's Pursuit**[21] 5916 3-8-8 **58** oh4 ow2 TomEaves 7 39
(Jim Goldie) *chsd ldng gp far side: drvn 1/2-way: no imp fr over 1f out: 4th of 6 in gp* **50/1**
5304 **15** *1/2* **Layla's Oasis**[19] 5996 3-8-8 **65** SamanthaBell(7) 12 44
(Richard Fahey) *in tch stands' side gp: rdn over 2f out: wknd over 1f out: 8th of 10 in gp* **20/1**

2332 **16** ½ **Salvatore Fury (IRE)**[22] 5878 3-9-6 **70**.....(p) JoeFanning 4 47
(Keith Dalgleish) *prom far side: effrt and edgd lft over 1f out: btn ins fnl f: 5th of 6 in gp* **11/1**

/400 **17** 2½ **Pitt Rivers**[27] 5705 4-8-13 **62**..... DaleSwift 15 30
(Linda Perratt) *chsd stands' side ldrs tl wknd fr 2f out: 9th of 10 in gp* **66/1**

2000 **18** *hd* **Monnoyer**[22] 5901 4-8-11 **65**.....(bt) TimClark(5) 8 32
(Scott Dixon) *racd centre: cl up tl wknd fr 2f out: last of 4 in gp* **25/1**

0440 **19** 2½ **Partner (IRE)**[3] 6464 7-8-6 **60**.....(b) JoeyHaynes(5) 14 18
(Noel Wilson) *in tch stands' side tl rdn and wknd fr 2f out: last of 10 in gp* **18/1**

1406 **20** 4 **Roland**[20] 5973 3-8-13 **68**.....(b) ShaneGray(5) 1 12
(Kevin Ryan) *chsd far side ldrs tl wknd 2f out: last of 4 in gp* **50/1**

1m 2.48s (3.08) **Going Correction** +0.70s/f (Yiel)
WFA 3 from 4yo+ 1lb **20** Ran SP% **123.6**
Speed ratings (Par 103): **103,102,100,98,98 96,96,94,94,93 92,91,90,89,89 88,84,83,79,73**
toteswingers 1&2 £33.20, 1&3 £41.20, 2&3 £41.20 CSF £91.63 CT £1424.16 TOTE £11.20: £2.80, £2.10, £4.50, £2.60; EX 93.60 Trifecta £647.30 Pool: £1812.59 - 2.10 winning units..
Owner Mrs L Ward **Bred** Lynch Bages Ltd **Trained** Sheriff Hutton, N Yorks

FOCUS
A big field for this modest sprint handicap and they split into three groups from the off, with the largest bunch of ten, who raced on the stands' side, containing the first three home. The winner cashed in on a good mark and the second ran his best race since his 2009 peak.

6548 QUALITY AND VALUE AT IRISH YEARLING SALES H'CAP (DIV I) 7f 50y
3:10 (3:12) (Class 5) (0-75,78) 3-Y-0+ **£3,881** (£1,155; £577; £288) **Stalls** High

Form RPR

0035 **1** **Evanescent (IRE)**[20] 5974 4-9-2 **69**..... RobertWinston 5 88
(John Quinn) *hld up in tch: smooth hdwy over 2f out: led wl over 1f out: pushed clr: readily* **8/1**[3]

1414 **2** 6 **Circuitous**[17] 6052 5-9-7 **74**.....(v) TomEaves 9 77
(Keith Dalgleish) *prom: effrt and ev ch over 2f out: kpt on fnl f: nt pce of wnr* **11/1**

4145 **3** *nk* **Makinson Lane (IRE)**[176] 1206 3-8-9 **65**..... TonyHamilton 7 66
(Richard Fahey) *hld up in tch: stdy hdwy over 2f out: effrt and edgd lft over 1f out: sn one pce* **22/1**

3046 **4** 2¼ **Another For Joe**[21] 5918 5-9-4 **71**..... GrahamLee 3 67
(Jim Goldie) *midfield: effrt and drvn over 2f out: plugged on fnl f: no imp* **8/1**[3]

2120 **5** 1½ **Strong Man**[27] 5711 5-9-6 **73**.....(b) DanielTudhope 12 65
(Michael Easterby) *cl up: led over 2f out: sn rdn and edgd lft: hdd wl over 1f out: sn outpcd* **17/2**

6033 **6** 1½ **Ted's Brother (IRE)**[9] 6291 5-8-13 **71**.....(e) PhilipPrince(5) 6 60
(Richard Guest) *dwlt: hld up: stdy hdwy on outside wl over 2f out: sn rdn: no imp over 1f out* **7/1**[2]

0504 **7** ½ **Delores Rocket**[43] 5150 3-8-7 **68**.....(b) ShaneGray(5) 8 54
(Kevin Ryan) *towards rr: drvn along over 3f out: sme hdwy on outside over 1f out: n.d* **9/1**

662 **8** *nk* **Spes Nostra**[21] 5918 5-9-4 **71**.....(b) GrahamGibbons 4 57
(David Barron) *hld up in tch: drvn and outpcd over 2f out: n.d after* **11/2**[1]

4061 **9** 1 **Barkston Ash**[9] 6287 5-9-8 **78** 6ex.....(p) JasonHart(3) 11 62
(Eric Alston) *bhd and sn struggling: nvr on terms* **7/1**[2]

6630 **10** 7 **Joshua The First**[8] 6297 4-8-7 **60**.....(p) JoeFanning 13 26
(Keith Dalgleish) *hld up: rdn over 3f out: btn 2f out* **12/1**

3115 **11** ½ **Harbour Captain (IRE)**[44] 5096 3-8-8 **71**..... JosephineGordon(7) 1 34
(Jo Hughes) *dwlt: sn chsng ldrs: hung lft and wknd over 2f out* **16/1**

0000 **12** 8 **Daddy Warbucks (IRE)**[23] 5861 4-9-3 **70**..... AdrianNicholls 10 14
(David Nicholls) *led to over 2f out: sn struggling: eased whn no ch fnl f* **14/1**

1m 34.46s (1.06) **Going Correction** +0.325s/f (Good)
WFA 3 from 4yo+ 3lb **12** Ran SP% **116.1**
Speed ratings (Par 103): **106,99,98,96,94 92,92,91,90,82 82,73**
toteswingers 1&2 £14.60, 1&3 £30.80, 2&3 £29.80 CSF £90.96 CT £1853.86 TOTE £11.00: £2.90, £3.60, £7.60; EX 127.50 Trifecta £1839.80 Part won. Pool: £2453.16 - 0.71 winning units..
Owner Charles Wentworth **Bred** Oliver Donlon **Trained** Settrington, N Yorks

FOCUS
Division one of this ordinary handicap. They went quick, and only the clear winner truly got home. This rated a 10lb personal best from him and the form could be worth more at face value.

6549 QUALITY AND VALUE AT IRISH YEARLING SALES H'CAP (DIV II) 7f 50y
3:40 (3:42) (Class 5) (0-75,75) 3-Y-0+ **£3,881** (£1,155; £577; £288) **Stalls** High

Form RPR

4323 **1** **Llewellyn**[20] 5973 5-8-10 **71**..... JordanNason(7) 6 80
(David Nicholls) *trckd ldrs: smooth hdwy to ld over 2f out: sn rdn: hld on gamely fnl f* **5/1**[1]

000 **2** *nk* **Live Dangerously**[13] 6181 3-8-5 **65**.....(t) JasonHart(3) 7 73
(Keith Dalgleish) *trckd ldrs: effrt and ev ch over 2f out: rdn and edgd lft over 1f out: kpt on fnl f* **22/1**

0000 **3** ½ **Escape To Glory (USA)**[20] 5971 5-9-7 **75**..... GrahamLee 11 82
(Michael Dods) *hld up: hdwy on outside over 2f out: sn rdn: kpt on ins fnl f: hld towards fin* **7/1**[3]

0300 **4** ½ **Eutropius (IRE)**[33] 5546 4-9-5 **73**..... DanielTudhope 12 79
(Alan Swinbank) *hld up: rdn and hdwy 2f out: kpt on ins fnl f: nt pce to chal* **6/1**[2]

2502 **5** 3¼ **Chiswick Bey (IRE)**[36] 5378 5-9-2 **70**..... TonyHamilton 5 68
(Richard Fahey) *midfield: rdn and outpcd over 2f out: edgd lft and rallied over 1f out: kpt on: nrst fin* **5/1**[1]

0506 **6** 7 **Old Man Clegg**[25] 5784 3-8-8 **65**.....(t) GrahamGibbons 13 43
(Michael Easterby) *prom: effrt over 2f out: wknd over 1f out* **15/2**

4100 **7** 1¼ **Goninodaethat**[16] 6083 5-8-7 **61** oh5..... AndrewElliott 9 37
(Jim Goldie) *chsd ldr: led over 3f out to over 2f out: wknd over 1f out* **18/1**

0003 **8** 11 **New Leyf (IRE)**[27] 5711 7-9-3 **71**..... AdrianNicholls 1 19
(David Nicholls) *hld up: struggling wl over 2f out: sn btn* **9/1**

6252 **9** 7 **Small Fury (IRE)**[7] 6341 3-8-8 **72**..... HarryBurns(7) 8
(Jo Hughes) *led to over 2f out: sn rdn and wknd* **15/2**

200 **10** 3¼ **Jeannie Galloway (IRE)**[12] 6210 6-9-2 **70**..... TomEaves 3
(Keith Dalgleish) *t.k.h: trckd ldrs tl rdn and wknd fr 2f out* **10/1**

1m 35.21s (1.81) **Going Correction** +0.325s/f (Good)
WFA 3 from 4yo+ 3lb **10** Ran SP% **112.4**
Speed ratings (Par 103): **102,101,101,100,96 88,87,74,66,63**
toteswingers 1&2 £21.20, 1&3 £8.60, 2&3 £25.20 CSF £110.44 CT £762.07 TOTE £5.30: £1.90, £4.60, £2.60; EX 96.30 Trifecta £1770.40 Pool: £2463.94 - 1.04 winning units..
Owner David Nicholls Racing Club **Bred** Elite Racing Club **Trained** Sessay, N Yorks

FOCUS
This open handicap was run in a time 0.75sec slower than the first division. The first four finished in a heap, clear of the remainder. The form is taken at face value with the winner rated back to his best.

6550 HILLHOUSE QUARRY GROUP SUPPORTING AYRSHIRE HOSPICE H'CAP 1m
4:10 (4:11) (Class 4) (0-85,89) 3-Y-0+ **£6,469** (£1,925; £962; £481) **Stalls** Low

Form RPR

1114 **1** **Dream Walker (FR)**[20] 5947 4-8-11 **77**..... PhilipPrince(5) 7 90
(Brian Ellison) *trckd ldrs: led over 2f out: sn drvn and clr over 1f out: kpt on strly* **5/1**[2]

0200 **2** 2¼ **No Poppy (IRE)**[12] 6210 5-9-3 **83**..... AdamCarter(5) 10 90
(Tim Easterby) *dwlt: hld up: rdn and hdwy over 2f out: chsd wnr appr fnl f: kpt on* **8/1**[3]

0410 **3** 1¼ **Sound Advice**[9] 6288 4-9-6 **81**..... GrahamGibbons 14 85
(Keith Dalgleish) *t.k.h in midfield on outside: effrt and chsd wnr briefly over 1f out: kpt on same pce ins fnl f* **20/1**

0001 **4** ¾ **Swiftly Done (IRE)**[9] 6288 6-9-11 **89** 6ex..... JasonHart(3) 9 91+
(Declan Carroll) *midfield: effrt whn nt clr run over 2f out: sn rdn: hdwy over 1f out: kpt on: nvr able to chal* **4/1**[1]

0224 **5** 1½ **Karaka Jack**[40] 5291 6-9-7 **82**..... AdrianNicholls 3 81
(David Nicholls) *bhd: rdn and hdwy on outside 2f out: kpt on fnl f: nvr able to chal* **12/1**

4410 **6** *shd* **Le Chat D'Or**[33] 5546 5-9-7 **82**.....(bt) GrahamLee 1 86+
(Michael Dods) *t.k.h: hld up on ins: effrt whn nt clr run over 2f out: rallied over 1f out: r.o: no imp* **17/2**

30-0 **7** 2¼ **Good Boy Jackson**[57] 4643 5-9-2 **77**..... JoeFanning 11 71
(R Mike Smith) *cl up: effrt and chsd wnr over 2f out to over 1f out: sn wknd* **33/1**

1446 **8** 2¼ **Act Your Shoe Size**[22] 5880 4-9-5 **80**..... PJMcDonald 4 68
(Keith Dalgleish) *in tch: drvn along over 2f out: wknd fr over 1f out* **28/1**

5143 **9** 3¾ **Toto Skyllachy**[9] 6288 8-9-10 **85**..... DanielTudhope 6 65
(David O'Meara) *towards rr: drvn over 2f out: btn over 1f out* **12/1**

2312 **10** ¾ **Silver Rime (FR)**[22] 5880 8-9-7 **82**..... PhillipMakin 2 60
(Linda Perratt) *hld up: rdn along 2f out: sn btn* **28/1**

-006 **11** ¾ **Venutius**[43] 5149 6-8-9 **77**..... EvaMoscrop(7) 5 53
(Philip Kirby) *towards rr: struggling over 2f out: sn btn* **25/1**

2002 **12** 1 **Chookie Royale**[45] 5051 5-9-7 **82**.....(p) TomEaves 12 56
(Keith Dalgleish) *in tch tl rdn and wknd 2f out* **22/1**

0002 **13** 6 **Sam Nombulist**[13] 6164 5-9-7 **82**.....(v) RobertWinston 8 42
(Ian Semple) *cl up: led over 3f out to over 2f out: rdn and wknd wl over 1f out* **8/1**[3]

201 **14** 1 **Polar Chief**[25] 5784 3-9-1 **85**..... JacobButterfield(5) 13 43
(Kristin Stubbs) *led: rdn and hdd over 3f out: wknd over 2f out* **10/1**

1m 45.12s (1.32) **Going Correction** +0.325s/f (Good)
WFA 3 from 4yo+ 4lb **14** Ran SP% **116.7**
Speed ratings (Par 105): **106,103,102,101,100 100,97,95,91,91 90,89,83,82**
toteswingers 1&2 £11.70, 1&3 £24.70, 2&3 £32.20 CSF £38.54 CT £761.15 TOTE £5.60: £1.90, £3.50, £7.10; EX 53.20 Trifecta £1038.90 Pool: £1925.53 - 1.39 winning units..
Owner Keith Brown **Bred** John Berry **Trained** Norton, N Yorks

FOCUS
A competitive handicap. The winner continued his progress and the form is rated around the third and fourth.

6551 WILLIAM HILL - DOWNLOAD THE APP H'CAP (FOR THE KILKERRAN CUP) 1m 2f
4:40 (4:40) (Class 2) (0-100,97) 3-Y-0+
£15,562 (£4,660; £2,330; £1,165; £582; £292) **Stalls** Low

Form RPR

4603 **1** **Hi There (IRE)**[26] 5768 4-8-13 **86**..... TonyHamilton 8 96
(Richard Fahey) *t.k.h: hld up on outside: smooth hdwy over 2f out: effrt and wnt 2nd over 1f out: styd on wl fnl f: led post* **7/1**

0000 **2** *nse* **Beaumont's Party (IRE)**[40] 5283 6-9-1 **91**..... JasonHart(3) 9 101
(Brian Ellison) *trckd ldrs: led and rdn over 2f out: kpt on fnl f: hdd post* **7/1**

013 **3** 2¼ **Grandorio (IRE)**[75] 4063 3-8-11 **90**..... DanielTudhope 6 96
(David O'Meara) *hld up: stdy hdwy 3f out: sn rdn: edgd lft and kpt on fnl f: nrst fin* **11/2**[3]

6013 **4** 2½ **Clayton**[40] 5283 4-9-10 **97**..... GrahamLee 2 98
(Kevin Ryan) *led: rdn and hdd over 2f out: rallied: outpcd appr fnl f* **7/1**

2415 **5** 1½ **Spirit Of The Law (IRE)**[26] 5768 4-8-10 **88**..... GeorgeChaloner(5) 3 86
(Richard Fahey) *trckd ldrs: effrt and rdn over 2f out: no ex fr over 1f out* **10/3**[1]

0501 **6** 6 **Maven**[23] 5860 5-9-1 **88**..... GrahamGibbons 4 75
(Tim Easterby) *hld up towards rr: stdy hdwy over 3f out: rdn and outpcd over 2f out: n.d after* **14/1**

2014 **7** 8 **Argaki (IRE)**[21] 5918 3-8-1 **83** oh2..... RaulDaSilva(3) 7 54
(Keith Dalgleish) *pressed ldr: rdn and led briefly over 2f out: wknd over 1f out* **20/1**

6000 **8** 1¼ **Spanish Duke (IRE)**[85] 3685 6-8-12 **85**..... DaleSwift 10 54
(Brian Ellison) *s.i.s: bhd: struggling over 3f out: nvr on terms* **25/1**

0320 **9** 10 **Fort Belvedere**[27] 5706 5-9-0 **87**..... TomEaves 5 37
(Keith Dalgleish) *midfield: struggling wl over 3f out: sn btn* **16/1**

-064 **10** 53 **Well Painted (IRE)**[22] 5894 4-8-13 **86**.....(t) PhillipMakin 1
(William Haggas) *towards rr: struggling over 4f out: lost tch and eased fr 3f out* **5/1**[2]

2m 15.29s (3.29) **Going Correction** +0.325s/f (Good)
WFA 3 from 4yo+ 6lb **10** Ran SP% **113.8**
Speed ratings (Par 109): **99,98,97,95,93 89,82,81,73,31**
toteswingers 1&2 £11.60, 1&3 £6.10, 2&3 £8.10 CSF £53.87 CT £288.63 TOTE £9.90: £2.70, £2.70, £1.90; EX 55.30 Trifecta £636.00 Pool: £2114.28 - 2.49 winning units..
Owner Market Avenue Racing Club Ltd **Bred** J & J Waldron **Trained** Musley Bank, N Yorks

FOCUS
A valuable handicap and the feature on the card, although it was weakened by the withdrawal of King Of The Danes. Sound form with the winner rated to his best.

6552 CAMPBELL BROTHERS H'CAP 1m 5f 13y
5:10 (5:10) (Class 5) (0-70,75) 3-Y-0+ **£3,881** (£1,155; £577; £288) **Stalls** Low

Form RPR

33-6 **1** **Calculated Risk**[47] 4995 4-9-9 **66**..... RobertWinston 2 78+
(John Quinn) *hld up towards rr: smooth hdwy over 3f out: led over 1f out: sn clr: idled ins fnl f: drvn out* **11/4**[1]

6045 **2** 1 1/2 **Latin Rebel (IRE)**[13] 6179 6-8-12 **55** oh5 JoeFanning 15 64
(Jim Goldie) *hld up: smooth hdwy over 3f out: effrt and chsd (clr) wnr over 1f out: kpt on fnl f* **25/1**
006- **3** 3 **Hunters Belt (IRE)**[26] 3307 9-9-0 **60** (vt) JasonHart(3) 10 64
(George Bewley) *bhd: rdn and hdwy on outside 3f out: kpt on fnl f: nt pce of first two* **12/1**
4301 **4** 4 **Layline (IRE)**[4] 6435 6-9-11 **73** 6ex DanielMuscutt(5) 7 71
(Gay Kelleway) *hld up in tch: smooth hdwy and prom 3f out: rdn 2f out: sn outpcd* **11/2**[2]
5354 **5** 1 **Attansky (IRE)**[40] 5295 3-8-1 **56** (p) JulieBurke(3) 6 53
(Tim Easterby) *led to over 2f out: sn drvn: wknd over 1f out* **20/1**
1346 **6** nk **Grand Diamond (IRE)**[16] 6086 9-8-7 **57** JordanNason(7) 1 53
(Jim Goldie) *hld up: stdy hdwy on ins over 2f out: sn rdn and no imp* **33/1**
-005 **7** shd **Key Gold**[43] 5137 4-9-3 **65** GeorgeChaloner(5) 11 61
(Richard Fahey) *hld up: rdn over 3f out: styd on fnl f: nvr able to chal* **11/2**[2]
6123 **8** nk **A Southside Boy (GER)**[21] 5920 5-9-8 **65** AndrewElliott 8 60
(Jim Goldie) *hld up: rdn and hdwy on outside to chse ldrs 4f out: led over 2f out to over 1f out: sn btn* **10/1**
3340 **9** 1 **Forrest Flyer (IRE)**[16] 6087 9-9-4 **61** GrahamLee 3 55
(Jim Goldie) *chsd ldrs tl rdn and wknd over 2f out* **25/1**
4124 **10** 6 **Vittachi**[13] 6179 6-8-12 **55** (p) TomEaves 14 40
(Alistair Whillans) *midfield: effrt over 4f out: wknd over 2f out* **25/1**
2000 **11** nk **Kingarrick**[44] 5084 5-8-7 **55** oh2 JoeyHaynes(5) 9 40
(Noel Wilson) *missed break: bhd: shortlived effrt over 3f out: sn btn* **33/1**
5115 **12** 1 1/2 **Lochiel**[16] 6087 9-9-8 **65** PJMcDonald 13 47
(Ian Semple) *in tch tl rdn and wknd over 2f out* **16/1**
2312 **13** 1 1/4 **St Ignatius**[7] 6346 6-9-10 **67** (v) GrahamGibbons 5 47
(Alan Bailey) *cl up: rdn and ev ch over 3f out: wknd 2f out* **11/1**
5531 **14** 23 **Woodstock (IRE)**[25] 5789 3-9-2 **68** DaleSwift 4 14
(Brian Ellison) *prom: struggling over 4f out: lost tch over 2f out: t.o* **17/2**[3]

3m 3.28s (9.28) **Going Correction** +0.325s/f (Good)
WFA 3 from 4yo+ 9lb **14** Ran SP% **121.1**
Speed ratings (Par 103): **84,83,81,78,78 77,77,77,77,73 73,72,71,57**
toteswingers 1&2 £20.00, 1&3 £10.80, 2&3 £31.30 CSF £87.68 CT £726.06 TOTE £3.70: £1.60, £7.80, £5.30; EX 116.70 Trifecta £1290.60 Part won. Pool: £1720.90 - 0.40 winning units..
Owner Terry Warner **Bred** Newsells Park Stud **Trained** Settrington, N Yorks

FOCUS
Modest handicap form, but a clear-cut winner who posted a personal best. The form could be rated at least 3lb higher.
T/Jkpt: Not won. T/Plt: £1,129.90 to a £1 stake. Pool of £83,505.58 - 53.95 winning tickets. T/Qpdt: £351.30 to a £1 stake. Pool of £8166.50 - 17.20 winning tickets. R

6519 KEMPTON (A.W) (R-H)

Thursday, September 19

OFFICIAL GOING: Standard
Wind: Moderate, across (away from stands) Weather: Rain before racing. Becoming bright

6553 BETVICTOR BACK OF THE NET OFFER H'CAP (DIV I) 1m (P)
5:40 (5:40) (Class 6) (0-55,55) 3-Y-0+ **£1,940** (£577; £288; £144) **Stalls** Low

Form RPR
4500 **1** **Kielty's Folly**[31] 5596 9-9-2 **50** JimCrowley 10 58
(Brian Baugh) *trckd ldng pair: clsd to ld 2f out and drvn for home: 2 l up fnl f but treading water: clung on* **20/1**
4132 **2** 1 **Sonnetation (IRE)**[5] 6399 3-9-1 **53** RichardHughes 5 59
(Jim Boyle) *chsd ldrs: rdn over 2f out: kpt on u.p fnl 2f: wnt 2nd 75yds out and threatened to cl wnr down: nt qckn last strides* **2/1**[1]
2021 **3** hd **I'm Harry**[24] 7145 4-9-4 **52** (vt) FergusSweeney 1 58
(George Baker) *pushed along early to rch midfield: 7th 1/2-way: drvn over 2f out: kpt on fr over 1f out: tk 3rd nr fin and clsd on ldng pair* **11/2**[2]
500 **4** 1/2 **La Rosiere (USA)**[35] 5434 4-9-7 **55** (p) JackMitchell 7 59
(Pat Murphy) *hld up in last quartet: rdn and prog over 2f out: kpt on fr over 1f out: nrst fin* **25/1**
2020 **5** 1/2 **Arabian Flight**[9] 6276 4-9-2 **55** TobyAtkinson(5) 12 58
(Michael Appleby) *led at gd pce: hdd 2f out: chsd wnr tl wknd last 75yds* **12/1**
2305 **6** 1/2 **Welsh Inlet (IRE)**[26] 5758 5-9-4 **55** MichaelJMMurphy(3) 11 57
(John Bridger) *sn in last quartet: rdn over 2f out: racd awkwardly but kpt on fr over 1f out: nrst fin* **14/1**
1630 **7** 1 1/2 **Lightning Spirit**[10] 6261 5-9-2 **50** (p) GeorgeBaker 13 49
(Gary Moore) *slowly away: hld up in last: plenty to do whn sed to make prog over 2f out: tried to cl over 1f out: one pce fnl f* **9/1**
5465 **8** 3 3/4 **Royal Caper**[36] 5407 3-9-1 **53** (v) KirstyMilczarek 2 43
(John Ryan) *chsd ldr to over 2f out: wknd jst over 1f out* **7/1**[3]
6000 **9** 9 **Lars Krister (IRE)**[21] 5923 3-8-12 **55** (bt) RyanTate(5) 6 24
(Hans Adielsson) *slowly away: nvr bttr than midfield: struggling over 2f out: sn wknd* **12/1**
5522 **10** 1/2 **Saint Boniface**[15] 6097 4-9-5 **53** SteveDrowne 3 21
(Peter Makin) *chsd ldrs: drvn and no prog over 2f out: wknd wl over 1f out: heavily eased* **10/1**
1630 **11** 1 1/4 **Litmus (USA)**[17] 6038 4-8-11 **50** (b) JackDuern(5) 8 15
(Simon Dow) *racd wd: chsd ldrs to 1/2-way: sn wknd and bhd* **16/1**
4300 **12** 9 **Mighty Mata**[14] 6138 3-8-11 **54** (e[1]) OisinMurphy(5) 4
(Mark Usher) *nvr gng wl and sn rdn in last quartet: t.o 3f out* **33/1**

1m 38.95s (-0.85) **Going Correction** -0.075s/f (Stan)
WFA 3 from 4yo+ 4lb **12** Ran SP% **119.8**
Speed ratings (Par 101): **101,100,99,99,98 98,96,93,84,83 82,73**
toteswingers 1&2 £13.90, 1&3 £19.80, 2&3 £2.20 CSF £59.47 CT £272.03 TOTE £17.40: £2.80, £1.50, £2.20; EX 109.40 Trifecta £284.60 Pool: £1064.07 - 2.80 winning units..
Owner Saddle Up Racing **Bred** Stanneylands Livery **Trained** Audley, Staffs

FOCUS
The field were soon quite well strung out, with Arabian Flight getting across from her wide draw to set what looked a reasonable pace, but nothing got involved from too far back.

6554 BETVICTOR BACK OF THE NET OFFER H'CAP (DIV II) 1m (P)
6:10 (6:11) (Class 6) (0-55,55) 3-Y-0+ **£1,940** (£577; £288; £144) **Stalls** Low

Form RPR
0333 **1** **Princess Spirit**[5] 6400 4-8-9 **50** (p) JenniferFerguson(7) 11 61
(Edward Creighton) *n.m.r after 1f and dropped to last trio: rdn and prog on outer fr over 2f out: clsd to ld 1f out: sn clr* **10/1**
4006 **2** 1 1/2 **Moment In The Sun**[5] 6399 4-9-6 **54** (be) MickaelBarzalona 10 62
(David Flood) *stl on way to paddock after all the rest had lft: hld up in rr: rdn over 2f out: prog over 1f out: styd on ins fnl f to take 2nd last strides* **8/1**
5023 **3** 1/2 **Hail Promenader (IRE)**[13] 6153 7-9-7 **55** (bt) WilliamCarson 4 62
(Anthony Carson) *led: stepped on it after 3f and sn 3 l clr: edgd lft fr 2f out: hdd 1f out: hld on nr fin* **8/1**
3415 **4** hd **Cape Crossing**[10] 6261 4-9-1 **52** (t) ThomasBrown(3) 9 58
(Andrew Balding) *chsd ldr after 2f: clsd fr 2f out: chal and upsides 1f out: wknd last 100yds* **5/1**[2]
321 **5** 1 1/4 **Sudden Wish (IRE)**[15] 6103 4-9-7 **55** GeorgeBaker 7 59
(Gary Moore) *chsd ldr 2f: styd prom: clsd w others fr 2f out: in tch 1f out: no ex* **11/2**[3]
0304 **6** 3 **Exopuntia**[30] 5622 7-9-1 **49** AdamBeschizza 6 46
(Julia Feilden) *in tch in midfield: rdn and sme prog 2f out: no imp over 1f out: fdd* **20/1**
2231 **7** 1/2 **Tatting**[3] 6472 4-9-7 **55** JimmyQuinn 5 50
(Chris Dwyer) *nt that wl away and pushed into midfield: tried to cl on inner fr 2f out: no hdwy over 1f out: fdd* **15/8**[1]
200/ **8** 1 1/4 **Looks Like Slim**[130] 7286 6-9-0 **53** RyanTate(5) 13 46
(Ben De Haan) *sn in last: shkn up 2f out: passed stragglers fr over 1f out: nvr a factor* **16/1**
4/0- **9** 2 **Dance To Destiny**[469] 2858 5-9-2 **50** KirstyMilczarek 12 38
(K F Clutterbuck) *racd wd: nvr beyond midfield: drvn over 2f out: wknd over 1f out* **66/1**
0 **10** 1/2 **Jameela's Dream**[106] 2979 3-9-3 **55** PatDobbs 8 42
(Robert Cowell) *nvr bttr than midfield: no prog 2f out: wknd over 1f out* **25/1**
0P0- **11** 4 1/2 **Dichoh**[273] 8179 10-9-0 **48** (p) FergusSweeney 3 24
(Michael Madgwick) *prom tl wknd 2f out* **50/1**
0000 **12** 3 **Shelling Peas**[5] 6399 4-9-5 **53** JackMitchell 2 23
(Derek Shaw) *a in rr: struggling over 2f out* **100/1**

1m 38.54s (-1.26) **Going Correction** -0.075s/f (Stan)
WFA 3 from 4yo+ 4lb **12** Ran SP% **117.1**
Speed ratings (Par 101): **103,101,101,100,99 96,96,94,92,92 87,84**
toteswingers 1&2 £7.70, 1&3 £14.60, 2&3 £7.40 CSF £82.78 CT £687.55 TOTE £12.40: £3.10, £2.50, £2.00; EX 131.90 Trifecta £429.40 Pool: £999.48 - 1.74 winning units..
Owner N Dyshaev **Bred** Harton Limited **Trained** Wormshill, Kent

FOCUS
Division two of a moderate handicap and the winner and second stayed on from well back, whereas the third tried to make all.

6555 £25 FREE BET AT BETVICTOR.COM MAIDEN STKS 1m (P)
6:40 (6:41) (Class 5) 3-Y-0+ **£2,587** (£770; £384; £192) **Stalls** Low

Form RPR
2- **1** **Appease**[300] 7838 4-9-9 0 RichardHughes 1 77+
(Richard Hannon) *prom: trckd ldr over 3f out: shkn up to ld jst over 1f out: styd on wl* **6/1**[2]
6 **2** 2 **Aomen Rock**[24] 5845 3-9-5 0 FrederikTylicki 11 72+
(James Fanshawe) *in tch: prog on outer over 3f out to chse ldrs: on terms 2f out: rdn and nt qckn over 1f out: styd on to take 2nd nr fin* **8/1**[3]
00 **3** 1 1/4 **Semai (IRE)**[14] 6133 3-9-0 0 TobyAtkinson(5) 2 69
(Marco Botti) *led after 2f: rdn and hdd jst over 1f out: fdd nr fin* **50/1**
4 1 **Zuhd (IRE)** 3-9-5 0 PaulHanagan 3 67+
(William Haggas) *dwlt: rn green towards rr: hrd rdn 2f out: kpt on u.p to take 4th last strides* **8/1**[3]
62 **5** nk **Pearl Style (FR)**[17] 6043 3-9-5 0 HarryBentley 5 66
(Olly Stevens) *chsd ldrs: pushed along and no imp on ldng trio wl over 1f out: one pce after* **20/1**
6 1 1/4 **Bison Grass** 3-9-5 0 (b[1]) SebSanders 14 64
(Giles Bravery) *awkward s: wl in rr: pushed along over 2f out: n.d but kpt on steadily fr over 1f out: eased nr fin* **66/1**
3-2 **7** 1/2 **Zurbriggen**[27] 5720 3-9-5 0 MickaelBarzalona 9 62
(Charlie Appleby) *t.k.h: hld up in midfield: tried to cl fr over 2f out: nt qckn and no prog over 1f out* **4/5**[1]
33 **8** 1/2 **St Georges Hill (IRE)**[21] 5932 3-9-5 0 JimCrowley 13 61+
(Michael Wigham) *hld up in last: stl there over 2f out: jst pushed along on inner after: modest prog and nvr involved: likely improver* **10/1**
05 **9** 2 1/2 **Kindlelight Storm (USA)**[21] 5932 3-8-12 0 JordanVaughan(7) 4 55
(Nick Littmoden) *trckd ldrs: jst pushed along fr over 2f out: steadily wknd* **66/1**
10 2 1/2 **White Peak (USA)** 3-9-2 0 MichaelJMMurphy(3) 6 49
(Mark Johnston) *t.k.h early: rn green in rr: no prog and btn over 2f out* **16/1**
0-0 **11** nk **Secret Woman (IRE)**[98] 3239 3-9-0 0 MartinLane 8 43
(Alan Jarvis) *chsd ldrs tl steadily wknd fr over 2f out* **66/1**
05 **12** 6 **Churt**[15] 6113 4-9-4 0 ThomasGarner(5) 7 34
(Christopher Kellett) *a towards rr: rdn and no real prog over 2f out: sn wknd* **100/1**
0 **13** 28 **Donard Lass**[21] 5925 3-9-0 0 KieranO'Neill 12
(Jimmy Fox) *led 2f: rdn over 4f out: wknd rapidly over 3f out: t.o* **100/1**

1m 39.03s (-0.77) **Going Correction** -0.075s/f (Stan)
WFA 3 from 4yo 4lb **13** Ran SP% **120.2**
Speed ratings (Par 103): **100,98,96,95,95 94,93,93,90,88 87,81,53**
toteswingers 1&2 £6.60, 1&3 £37.40, 2&3 £33.60 CSF £52.12 TOTE £5.70: £5.30, £6.70, £21.90; EX 59.70 Trifecta £1160.10 Part won. Pool: £1546.82 - 0.13 winning units..
Owner John Reddington **Bred** Juddmonte Farms Ltd **Trained** East Everleigh, Wilts

FOCUS
Just an ordinary maiden.

6556 DOWNLOAD THE BETVICTOR APP H'CAP 1m (P)
7:10 (7:10) (Class 5) (0-75,75) 3-Y-0 **£2,587** (£770; £384; £192) **Stalls** Low

Form RPR
0402 **1** **Excellent Puck (IRE)**[8] 6306 3-9-7 **75** RichardHughes 4 79+
(Jamie Osborne) *trckd ldr: rdn over 2f out: clsd u.p to chal over 1f out: narrow ld jst ins fnl f: kpt on* **7/4**[1]
3011 **2** 1/2 **Mcdelta**[7] 6335 3-9-6 **74** 6ex SebSanders 2 77+
(Geoffrey Deacon) *hld up in midfield: prog on inner 2f out: hanging lft and hrd rdn after: styd on to take 2nd last 50yds: a hld* **7/2**[2]
340 **3** shd **Big Whiskey (IRE)**[19] 6003 3-9-0 **75** JenniferFerguson(7) 9 78
(Edward Creighton) *hld up in last trio: clsd on ldrs 2f out: shkn up to chal and upsides 1f out: nt qckn last 100yds* **7/1**
0-30 **4** 1/2 **Zain Spirit (USA)**[7] 6335 3-9-2 **70** (p) FrederikTylicki 3 72
(Gerard Butler) *led: kicked on 3f out: hdd and no ex jst ins fnl f* **10/1**

6666 5 ½ **Byroness**[104] 3039 3-8-13 **72**.. RyanTate(5) 7 73
(Heather Main) *broke on terms but then awkwardly and dropped to last trio: stl there whn rdn jst over 1f out: r.o fnl f: no hope of chalng* **16/1**

005 6 1 **Tribal Path (IRE)**[15] 6115 3-9-2 **70**.................................... DaneO'Neill 6 68
(Mark Johnston) *chsd ldrs and racd on outer: rdn over 2f out: no prog over 1f out: one pce* **6/1**[3]

-546 7 ¾ **Jillywinks**[8] 6316 3-8-9 **63**.................................... AdamBeschizza 5 60
(Scott Dixon) *t.k.h: hld up in midfield: rdn and no prog 2f out: wl hld after* **33/1**

2310 8 2 ¾ **Jadesnumberone (IRE)**[12] 6210 3-9-1 **72**... WilliamTwiston-Davies(3) 1 62
(Michael Bell) *trckd ldng pair tl wknd over 1f out* **14/1**

0040 9 ½ **Perfect Haven**[15] 6106 3-8-11 **70**.................................... OisinMurphy(5) 8 59
(Ralph Beckett) *hld up: rdn in last 3f out: tried to mount an effrt over 1f out: wknd fnl f* **20/1**

1m 38.79s (-1.01) **Going Correction** -0.075s/f (Stan) 9 Ran SP% **114.7**
Speed ratings (Par 101): **102,101,101,100,100 99,98,95,95**
toteswingers 1&2 £2.50, 1&3 £2.50, 2&3 £2.90 CSF £7.62 CT £33.35 TOTE £2.70: £1.90, £1.20, £2.40; EX 9.80 Trifecta £29.10 Pool: £1731.08 - 44.47 winning units..
Owner K J P Gundlach **Bred** Swersky & Associates **Trained** Upper Lambourn, Berks

FOCUS
A modest handicap run at what looked an ordinary pace.

6557 NEW O&T BAR COMING IN OCTOBER MEDIAN AUCTION MAIDEN STKS 1m 4f (P)
7:40 (7:40) (Class 6) 3-4-Y-O **£1,940** (£577; £288; £144) **Stalls** Centre

Form RPR

2420 1 **Halling's Treasure**[33] 5514 3-9-2 77........................ ThomasBrown(3) 11 81
(Andrew Balding) *trckd ldrs disputing 5th: prog on outer over 2f out: led over 1f out: drvn and styd on wl* **3/1**[1]

0 2 ¾ **First Warning**[44] 5100 3-9-5 0.. JamesDoyle 10 80
(Amanda Perrett) *trckd ldng pair: shkn up over 2f out: clsd to chal jst over 1f out: pressed wnr after: styd on but hld* **16/1**

2343 3 1 ¼ **The Welsh Wizard (IRE)**[12] 6202 3-9-5 75.........(b) MickaelBarzalona 14 78
(Charles Hills) *t.k.h: trckd ldr: rdn to ld briefly wl over 1f out: one pce fnl f* **3/1**[1]

5430 4 4 ½ **Silk Route**[13] 6158 3-9-0 66.. DaneO'Neill 8 66
(Henry Candy) *in tch disputing 7th: prog on outer over 3f out: rdn and nt qckn 2f out: hanging but kpt on fnl f to take 4th last strides* **8/1**[3]

0526 5 nk **Happy Families**[30] 5606 3-8-9 68.. RyanTate(5) 1 66
(Heather Main) *led at gd pce: hdd & wknd wl over 1f out* **25/1**

2 6 shd **Chattanooga Line**[21] 5925 3-9-0 0.. PatCosgrave 9 65
(George Baker) *trckd ldrs disputing 5th: rdn 3f out: struggling 2f out: one pce after* **8/1**[3]

6 7 2 **Arty Campbell (IRE)**[22] 5892 3-9-5 0.. MartinLane 13 67
(David Simcock) *hld up in last trio: hrd rdn on inner over 2f out: no great prog after: no ch* **8/1**[3]

8 hd **Angelot Du Berlais (FR)**[190] 4-9-13 70........................ RichardHughes 2 67
(Dr Richard Newland) *trckd ldng pair: rdn over 2f out: no imp wl over 1f out: sn fdd: eased* **6/1**[2]

9 7 **Coconell** 3-9-0 0.. SebSanders 12 51
(Jeremy Noseda) *s.s and rousted early: mostly in last trio: wknd over 2f out* **16/1**

04 10 ½ **Lady Theodora**[21] 5925 3-9-0 0.. JimCrowley 5 50
(Alan Jarvis) *in tch disputing 7th: rdn and wknd over 2f out* **25/1**

0 11 97 **Echoe Beach**[134] 2157 3-9-0 0........................(p) CathyGannon 4
(Olivia Maylam) *last and struggling after 3f: t.o whn hung bdly lft bnd over 3f out: virtually p.u* **100/1**

2m 32.7s (-1.80) **Going Correction** -0.075s/f (Stan)
WFA 3 from 4yo 8lb 11 Ran SP% **118.1**
Speed ratings (Par 101): **103,102,101,98,98 98,97,96,92,91 27**
toteswingers 1&2 £17.40, 1&3 £2.60, 2&3 £14.90 CSF £56.73 TOTE £3.60: £1.02, £9.10, £2.00; EX 58.00 Trifecta £322.70 Pool: £1430.34 - 3.32 winning units..
Owner Mildmay Racing & D H Caslon **Bred** Mildmay Bloodstock Ltd **Trained** Kingsclere, Hants

FOCUS
An ordinary maiden.

6558 FOLLOW US ON TWITTER @BETVICTOR H'CAP 2m (P)
8:10 (8:10) (Class 6) (0-60,59) 3-Y-0+ **£1,940** (£577; £288; £144) **Stalls** Low

Form RPR

0622 1 **Katie Gale**[5] 6404 3-8-7 **50**........................(b) JimmyQuinn 10 59
(Tim Pitt) *trckd ldng trio: moved up to join ldr 7f out: led wl over 2f out: drvn over 1f out: edgd rt and hrd pressed fnl f: hld on* **3/1**[1]

4346 2 hd **My Manekineko**[5] 6398 4-9-11 **56**........................ RichardHughes 11 65
(J R Jenkins) *stdd s: t.k.h: hld up in last pair: prog on outer 4f out: clsd on ldrs 2f out: wnt 2nd 1f out: edgd rt w wnr and str chal: jst hld* **7/2**[2]

0-21 3 2 ¾ **Amantius**[3] 6479 4-9-9 **54** 6ex........................(b) CathyGannon 14 60
(Johnny Farrelly) *t.k.h: trckd ldrs in 6th: prog on wd outside to chse wnr 2f out: clsd 1f out but lost 2nd: fdd* **5/1**[3]

4-05 4 1 ¾ **Sweeping Rock (IRE)**[16] 6081 3-8-10 **56**.............. MichaelJMMurphy(3) 3 60
(Marcus Tregoning) *trckd ldrs in 5th: lost pl on inner 4f out: hmpd over 2f out: kpt on u.p after to take 4th last strides* **7/1**

0620 5 nk **Soweto Star (IRE)**[22] 5897 5-9-5 **50**........................ GeorgeBaker 12 53
(John Best) *t.k.h: trckd ldr: led over 7f out: hdd wl over 2f out: grad outpcd* **16/1**

3310 6 hd **Compton Bird**[5] 6398 4-9-9 **59**........................ RyanTate(5) 13 62
(Hans Adielsson) *hld up in last pair: prog and swtchd to inner 2f out: rdn over 1f out: kpt on but no ch of rching ldrs* **10/1**

562P 7 l **Ice Apple**[108] 2921 5-9-3 **48**........................ KirstyMilczarek 8 50
(John E Long) *hld up in 10th: rdn and prog over 2f out: no imp on ldrs wl over 1f out* **33/1**

-440 8 3 ½ **Like Clockwork**[21] 5934 4-9-11 **56**........................ SteveDrowne 6 54
(Mark H Tompkins) *hld up in 7th: lost pl on inner 4f out: wl in rr and pushed along over 2f out: shkn up over 1f out: nvr involved* **16/1**

003 9 nk **Camelopardalis**[44] 5093 4-9-11 **56**........................ MartinLane 1 53
(Tobias B P Coles) *trckd ldng pair: impeded over 7f out: chsd ldrs after tl wknd over 2f out* **16/1**

-400 10 7 **Venir Rouge**[24] 5846 9-9-2 **50**........................(p) ThomasBrown(3) 7 39
(Harry Whittington) *hld up in 8th: rdn and prog to chse ldrs over 2f out: sn wknd* **25/1**

441/ 11 5 **Bravo Bravo**[144] 1016 6-9-5 **55**........................(b) OisinMurphy(5) 4 38
(Mark Gillard) *urged along and reminders early: a towards rr: rdn 5f out: sn btn* **7/1**

0000 12 18 **Hundred Acre Wood**[14] 6137 3-8-7 **50**........................(p) SamHitchcott 5 11
(Olivia Maylam) *led: jinked over 7f out and sn hdd: wknd rapidly 3f out: t.o* **66/1**

3m 31.32s (1.22) **Going Correction** -0.075s/f (Stan)
WFA 3 from 4yo+ 12lb 12 Ran SP% **123.9**
Speed ratings (Par 101): **93,92,91,90,90 90,89,88,88,84 82,73**
toteswingers 1&2 £4.60, 1&3 £5.40, 2&3 £7.70 CSF £13.80 CT £53.35 TOTE £3.30: £1.10, £1.60, £9.00; EX 16.60 Trifecta £84.80 Pool: £1042.64 - 9.21 winning units..
Owner Ferrybank Properties Limited **Bred** Netherfield House Stud **Trained** Newmarket, Suffolk

FOCUS
A moderate staying handicap.

6559 £25 FREE BET #BACKOFTHENET H'CAP (LONDON MIDDLE DISTANCE SERIES QUALIFIER) 1m 3f (P)
8:40 (8:44) (Class 4) (0-85,85) 3-Y-0+ **£4,690** (£1,395; £697; £348) **Stalls** Low

Form RPR

2242 1 **Autun (USA)**[15] 6115 3-9-5 **85**........................ JamesDoyle 4 95+
(Lady Cecil) *sn restrained towards rr: prog on outer 2f out: rdn over 1f out: clsd to ld last 120yds: styd on wl* **5/2**[2]

2421 2 1 **Jazz Master**[12] 6200 3-8-13 **79**........................(b) RichardHughes 2 87+
(Luca Cumani) *trckd ldr 3f: styd prom: pushed along to cl 2f out: shkn up to ld 1f out: hdd and one pce last 120yds* **15/8**[1]

3252 3 1 ¾ **Pompeia**[82] 3834 3-8-12 **78**........................(p) JimCrowley 3 83
(Ralph Beckett) *trckd ldng trio: prog to ld 2f out: edgd lft after: hdd and nt qckn 1f out* **9/1**

116 4 ¾ **Nave (USA)**[47] 5008 6-9-8 **81**........................ MartinLane 10 85
(David Simcock) *trckd ldng trio: rdn wl over 2f out and struggling: styd on u.p fr over 1f out to take 4th ins fnl f* **25/1**

0526 5 1 ¾ **Greylami (IRE)**[35] 5436 8-9-7 **85**........................ RyanTate(5) 5 86
(Clive Cox) *hld up in last pair: shkn up and prog wl over 1f out: effrt flattened out fnl f* **12/1**

1600 6 1 **Jupiter Storm**[24] 5823 4-9-9 **82**........................ GeorgeBaker 1 81
(Gary Moore) *led at gd pce and sn 4 l clr: hdd and fdd 2f out* **14/1**

5145 7 1 ¼ **Strawberry Jam**[14] 6136 3-8-1 **72**........................ NathanAlison(5) 9 68
(Paul Cole) *t.k.h: hld up in last pair: sltly impeded over 7f out: effrt on inner over 2f out: sn no prog* **16/1**

0165 8 6 **Ikhtisas (USA)**[15] 6108 3-8-10 **76**........................ MickaelBarzalona 6 62
(Saeed bin Suroor) *hld up towards rr: prog over 2f out: wknd qckly over 1f out* **6/1**[3]

21-0 9 13 **Ace Of Valhalla**[117] 2671 4-9-10 **83**........................ HarryBentley 8 45
(Olly Stevens) *chsd ldr after 3f tl wknd qckly over 2f out: t.o* **8/1**

2m 17.95s (-3.95) **Going Correction** -0.075s/f (Stan)
WFA 3 from 4yo+ 7lb 9 Ran SP% **122.8**
Speed ratings (Par 105): **111,110,109,108,107 106,105,101,91**
toteswingers 1&2 £2.10, 1&3 £5.20, 2&3 £3.40 CSF £8.20 CT £37.39 TOTE £3.80: £1.40, £1.70, £2.30; EX 9.60 Trifecta £47.40 Pool: £1329.30 - 21.00 winning units..
Owner K Abdullah **Bred** Juddmonte Farms Inc **Trained** Newmarket, Suffolk

FOCUS
A fair handicap.

6560 REINDEER RACING CHRISTMAS PARTY NIGHTS H'CAP 6f (P)
9:10 (9:10) (Class 6) (0-65,71) 3-Y-0 **£1,940** (£577; £288; £144) **Stalls** Low

Form RPR

1215 1 **Batchworth Lady**[111] 2829 3-9-5 **63**........................ JimmyQuinn 2 70
(Dean Ivory) *trckd ldng pair: wnt 2nd over 1f out: rdn to ld jst ins fnl f: jst hld on* **14/1**

3200 2 nse **Sakhee's Rose**[24] 5841 3-9-5 **63**........................(b[1]) GeorgeBaker 5 70
(Ed McMahon) *stdd s: hld up in last pair: prog 2f out: drvn to go 2nd ins fnl f: styd on nr fin: jst failed* **6/1**

0630 3 1 **Ishi Honest**[42] 5184 3-9-2 **60**........................(p) DavidProbert 4 64
(Mark Usher) *mde most: rdn over 1f out: hdd jst ins fnl f: one pce* **16/1**

5361 4 1 ½ **Malaysian Boleh**[6] 6368 3-9-8 **71** 6ex........................ JackDuern(5) 9 70+
(Simon Dow) *hld up in last pair: rdn on outer wl over 1f out: prog fnl f to take 4th last 75yds: nvr on terms* **9/4**[1]

3315 5 ½ **Koharu**[30] 5607 3-9-0 **61**........................(t) DeclanBates(3) 1 58
(Peter Makin) *hld up in tch: pushed along and lft bhd over 1f out: rdn and kpt on same pce fnl f* **14/1**

1025 6 nk **Idle Curiosity (IRE)**[18] 6017 3-9-2 **60**........................ RichardHughes 7 56
(Jim Boyle) *t.k.h: w ldr to wl over 1f out: steadily fdd* **10/1**

0450 7 1 ¼ **Admiralofthesea (USA)**[17] 6039 3-9-4 **62**........................ AdamBeschizza 12 54
(Robert Eddery) *hld up in tch: rdn and no prog 2f out: sn btn* **10/3**[2]

565 8 1 ¼ **Coire Gabhail**[70] 4200 3-9-2 **60**........................ PatDobbs 3 48
(Hughie Morrison) *t.k.h: hld up in tch: rdn and fnd nil 2f out: sn btn* **11/2**[3]

4560 9 nk **Fletcher Christian**[17] 6039 3-9-3 **64**........................ MichaelJMMurphy(3) 6 51
(John Gallagher) *chsd ldng pair to 2f out: sn btn* **25/1**

1m 13.21s (0.11) **Going Correction** -0.075s/f (Stan) 9 Ran SP% **115.7**
Speed ratings (Par 99): **96,95,94,92,91 91,89,88,87**
toteswingers 1&2 £6.60, 1&3 £18.00, 2&3 £8.40 CSF £95.46 CT £1369.04 TOTE £10.90: £1.40, £1.20, £5.30; EX 102.40 Trifecta £877.80 Part won. Pool: £1170.45 - 0.83 winning units..
Owner Mrs Diana Price **Bred** Batchworth Heath Farm Stud **Trained** Radlett, Herts

FOCUS
A moderate sprint handicap.
T/Plt: £212.20 to a £1 stake. Pool of £72,939.41 - 250.83 winning tickets. T/Qpdt: £18.90 to a £1 stake. Pool of £9216.92 - 359.73 winning tickets. JN

5558 PONTEFRACT (L-H)
Thursday, September 19

OFFICIAL GOING: Good (good to firm in places; 7.4)
Wind: moderate 1/2 behind Weather: overcast becoming fine, changeable

6561 YOUR GUIDE TO PONTEFRACT AT PONTEFRACTRACECOURSETIPS.CO.UK MEDIAN AUCTION MAIDEN STKS 5f
2:30 (2:30) (Class 5) 2-Y-0 **£3,234** (£962; £481; £240) **Stalls** Low

Form RPR

223 1 **Omaha Gold (IRE)**[29] 5638 2-9-0 66........................[1] RoystonFfrench 4 75
(Bryan Smart) *mde all: qcknd clr over 1f out: eased towards fin* **3/1**[2]

5 2 5 **Shared Equity**[53] 4808 2-9-5 0........................ MichaelO'Connell 9 62
(Jedd O'Keeffe) *s.i.s: sn chsng ldrs on outside: edgd lft and kpt on to take 2nd last 50yds* **11/8**[1]

00 3 ½ **Captain Gee**[55] 4724 2-8-12 0........................ JoeDoyle(7) 7 60
(John Quinn) *chsd ldrs: effrt over 2f out: nt clr run over 1f out: styd on same pce fnl f* **50/1**

The Form Book Flat, Raceform Ltd, Compton, RG20 6NL.

5444 **4** 3/4 **Princess Myla (IRE)**[22] 5883 2-9-0 59..............................(p) LeeTopliss 6 53
(Paul Midgley) *chsd wnr: kpt on same pce over 1f out* **20/1**

46 **5** 1 1/4 **Wadi Alamardi**[7] 6342 2-9-5 0.................................... AndreaAtzeni 3 53
(Michael Bell) *in rr: swtchd lft after 1f: sme hdwy 2f out: keeping on whn nt clr run ins fnl f* **16/1**

02 **6** nse **Scoreline**[9] 6286 2-9-5 0.................................... DavidNolan 1 53
(David O'Meara) *trckd ldrs: drvn over 2f out: kpt on one pce over 1f out* **9/2**[3]

7 1/2 **Kheleyf Diamond (IRE)**[43] 5159 2-9-0 0.................... BarryMcHugh 8 47
(Tony Coyle) *chsd ldrs: drvn over 2f out: one pce whn hmpd wl ins fnl f* **40/1**

8 1 **Amahoro** 2-9-0 0.. MartinHarley 5 42+
(Mick Channon) *dwlt: in rr: t.k.h: sme hdwy 2f out: nt clr run over 1f out: nvr a factor* **7/1**

1m 3.39s (0.09) **Going Correction** +0.05s/f (Good) **8** Ran SP% **112.8**
Speed ratings (Par 95): **101,93,92,91,89 88,88,86**
toteswingers 1&2 £1.80, 1&3 £53.70, 2&3 £15.40 CSF £7.25 TOTE £2.90: £1.50, £1.10, £7.30; EX 9.70 Trifecta £132.80 Pool: £2081.95 - 11.75 winning units..
Owner Phil Shaw **Bred** Tally-Ho Stud **Trained** Hambleton, N Yorks

FOCUS
The bulk of the field, outside of the winner, finished in a heap in this ordinary maiden, suggesting the form is pretty weak.

6562 RIFLES CHALLENGE H'CAP (DIV I) 1m 4y

3:00 (3:00) (Class 4) (0-80,79) 3-Y-0+ **£5,175** (£1,540; £769; £384) **Stalls** Low

Form RPR

0105 **1** **Fazza**[14] 6126 6-8-10 **72**.................................... KevinStott(7) 5 84
(Edwin Tuer) *hld up in mid-div: effrt and swtchd rt over 1f out: styd on to ld last 75yds: drvn out* **11/4**[1]

132 **2** 1 3/4 **Ralphy Boy (IRE)**[20] 5947 4-8-12 **67**.................... MichaelO'Connell 8 75
(Alistair Whillans) *led: drvn clr wl over 1f out: hdd and no ex wl ins fnl f* **9/1**

-660 **3** 3 **Eurystheus (IRE)**[20] 5974 4-9-5 **74**.......................... AndrewMullen 9 75
(Michael Appleby) *dwlt: sn chsng ldrs: effrt over 2f out: styd on same pce over 1f out: rdr dropped whip ins fnl f* **11/2**[3]

6242 **4** 1 1/2 **Frozen Over**[25] 5793 5-9-5 **74**.................................... AndreaAtzeni 7 72
(Stuart Kittow) *hld up in rr: drvn over 3f out: hdwy over 1f out: kpt on ins fnl f* **4/1**[2]

6350 **5** 1 1/2 **Hakuna Matata**[9] 6288 6-9-3 **77**..........................(v[1]) ConnorBeasley(5) 10 71
(Michael Dods) *mid-div: effrt over 2f out: bmpd over 1f out: one pce* **6/1**

4606 **6** nk **Watts Up Son**[7] 6346 5-9-3 **75**.................................... NeilFarley(3) 3 69
(Declan Carroll) *drvn early to chse ldr: rdn to chal over 2f out: one pce over 1f out* **14/1**

0066 **7** 1 1/2 **Maria's Choice (IRE)**[9] 6288 4-9-3 **79**.......................... AaronJones(7) 4 69
(Alan McCabe) *s.i.s: in rr: drvn over 3f out: sme hdwy whn nt clr run jst ins fnl f: nvr a factor* **16/1**

1100 **8** hd **Cono Zur (FR)**[14] 6126 6-9-0 **69**.................................... JamesSullivan 2 59
(Ruth Carr) *chsd ldrs: drvn over 2f out: wknd last 150yds* **12/1**

9 5 **Collodi (GER)**[81] 4-9-8 **77**.................................... MartinHarley 6 55
(Roger Curtis) *in rr: drvn over 3f out: bhd fnl 2f* **14/1**

0/00 **10** 29 **Fred Archer (IRE)**[99] 3192 5-8-10 **65** oh5.................. RussKennemore 1
(Sue Smith) *in rr: drvn over 3f out: lost pl over 2f out: sn bhd and eased: t.o* **100/1**

1m 44.11s (-1.79) **Going Correction** -0.075s/f (Good) **10** Ran SP% **114.2**
Speed ratings (Par 105): **105,103,100,98,97 96,95,95,90,61**
toteswingers 1&2 £7.10, 1&3 £2.90, 2&3 £10.10 CSF £27.79 CT £126.83 TOTE £4.00: £1.50, £2.20, £1.90; EX 31.20 Trifecta £283.50 Pool: £928.94 - 2.45 winning units..
Owner E Tuer **Bred** D R Tucker **Trained** Birkby, N Yorks

FOCUS
They went a decent pace in this fair handicap.

6563 BOOK YOUR CHRISTMAS PARTY HERE ON 0113 2876387 H'CAP 1m 2f 6y

3:30 (3:31) (Class 4) (0-85,83) 3-Y-0+ **£5,175** (£1,540; £769; £384) **Stalls** Low

Form RPR

1- **1** **Ajman Bridge**[281] 8070 3-9-3 **82**.................................... AndreaAtzeni 1 95+
(Luca Cumani) *mid-div: effrt over 3f out: chsng ldrs whn n.m.r over 2f out: brought wd and drvn to ld 1f out: styd on wl* **9/4**[1]

5550 **2** 2 1/4 **Moccasin (FR)**[36] 5382 4-9-4 **77**.................................... RoystonFfrench 5 85
(Geoffrey Harker) *trckd ldrs: led briefly over 1f out: styd on same pce* **33/1**

2415 **3** 1 **Correggio**[24] 5835 3-8-6 **74**.................................... NeilFarley(3) 7 80
(Micky Hammond) *hld up in rr: hdwy on ins over 3f out: chsng ldrs over 2f out: kpt on same pce* **20/1**

2160 **4** 3/4 **Never Forever**[49] 4929 4-8-7 **71**.................................... ConnorBeasley(5) 4 76
(George Moore) *s.i.s: in rr: effrt over 3f out: styd on fnl f* **14/1**

221 **5** nk **Blighty (IRE)**[20] 5962 3-9-2 **81**.................................... TomQueally 3 89+
(Lady Cecil) *hld up in mid-div: nt clr run and stmbld over 2f out: hdwy on outer over 1f out: styd on ins fnl f* **3/1**[2]

4054 **6** 2 3/4 **Forget Me Not Lane (IRE)**[30] 5612 4-9-0 **73**........(b[1]) PaulMulrennan 15 71
(Kevin Ryan) *t.k.h: swtchd lft s: hdd over 1f out: wknd last 100yds* **9/1**[3]

0410 **7** 3/4 **Wellingrove (IRE)**[14] 6126 3-8-10 **75**.................................... LiamJones 10 72
(Mark Johnston) *swtchd lft s: chsd ldrs: chal 2f out: wknd ins fnl f* **25/1**

5460 **8** 3/4 **Gala Casino Star (IRE)**[11] 6239 8-8-7 **73**..................(b) KevinStott(7) 17 68
(Geoffrey Harker) *swtchd lft after s: chsd ldrs: one pce over 1f out* **25/1**

3126 **9** 1 1/2 **Triple Eight (IRE)**[23] 5860 5-9-4 **77**..........................(b) RussKennemore 6 69
(Philip Kirby) *dwlt: hld up: hdwy on ins over 2f out: sn chsng ldrs: wknd over 1f out: struck into* **11/1**

4340 **10** 3 1/4 **San Cassiano (IRE)**[12] 6211 6-9-7 **80**.......................... JamesSullivan 13 66
(Ruth Carr) *swtchd lft after s: chsd ldrs: lost pl over 1f out* **40/1**

5150 **11** 8 **Arc Light (IRE)**[11] 6236 5-9-3 **76**.................................... DuranFentiman 14 46
(Tim Easterby) *swtchd lft after s: hdwy on outer 5f out: sn chsng ldrs: wkng whn bmpd over 2f out* **12/1**

-111 **12** 4 1/2 **Tapis Libre**[63] 4437 5-9-0 **78**.................................... ShirleyTeasdale(5) 16 39
(Michael Easterby) *in rr: drvn over 4f out: bhd fnl 3f* **20/1**

520/ **13** 1 1/2 **Swindy**[143] 5235 5-8-11 **75**.................................... GeorgeDowning(5) 9 33
(Sue Smith) *in tch: lost pl 3f out: sn bhd* **66/1**

3156 **14** 7 **Woody Bay**[12] 6208 3-9-1 **80**.................................... WilliamBuick 8 24
(James Given) *chsd ldrs on outer: lost pl wl over 1f out: eased whn bhd ins fnl f* **12/1**

2m 12.74s (-0.96) **Going Correction** -0.075s/f (Good)
WFA 3 from 4yo+ 6lb **14** Ran SP% **120.2**
Speed ratings (Par 105): **100,98,97,96,96 94,93,93,91,89 82,79,78,72**
toteswingers 1&2 £23.00, 1&3 £10.50, 2&3 £35.50 CSF £93.49 CT £1236.33 TOTE £3.40: £1.60, £5.70, £9.90; EX 79.90 Trifecta £1079.50 Part won. Pool: £1439.39 - 0.42 winning units..
Owner Sheikh Mohammed Obaid Al Maktoum **Bred** Rabbah Bloodstock Limited **Trained** Newmarket, Suffolk

FOCUS
A big field for this fair handicap and the market was dominated by a couple of unexposed 3yos, one of whom proved successful.

6564 PONTEFRACT PARK FILLIES' H'CAP 6f

4:00 (4:01) (Class 3) (0-90,90) 3-Y-0+

£9,337 (£2,796; £1,398; £699; £349; £175) **Stalls** Low

Form RPR

1235 **1** **Jubilante**[69] 4252 3-9-1 **83**.................................... JimmyFortune 1 93
(Hughie Morrison) *hld up in rr: hdwy and brought to outside over 2f out: edgd lft 1f out: styd on to ld towards fin* **3/1**[1]

0120 **2** 1/2 **Love Island**[33] 5544 4-9-5 **90**.................................... ConnorBeasley(5) 10 98
(Richard Whitaker) *w ldr: led 3f out: hdd and no ex clsng stages* **4/1**[3]

3405 **3** 3/4 **Dream Maker (IRE)**[12] 6212 3-8-10 **78**.......................... JamesSullivan 3 84
(Tim Easterby) *trckd ldrs on inner: nt clr run over 2f out and over 1f out: styd on same pce last 100yds* **16/1**

0205 **4** nk **Misplaced Fortune**[45] 5056 8-9-1 **88**..............................(v) KevinStott(7) 8 93
(Nigel Tinkler) *s.i.s: in rr on outer: hdwy over 1f out: edgd lft and kpt on ins fnl f* **4/1**[3]

0100 **5** 1 1/2 **Shafaani**[33] 5538 3-9-4 **86**..............................(t) TomQueally 6 86
(Clive Brittain) *led: hdd 3f out: wkng whn n.m.r nr fin* **11/1**

221 **6** 2 **Jubilant Queen**[39] 5308 3-8-8 **76**.................................... WilliamBuick 5 70
(Clive Cox) *s.i.s: drvn over 2f out: swtchd rt 1f out: sn fdd* **7/2**[2]

2354 **7** 1/2 **Penny Garcia**[22] 5886 3-8-10 **78**.................................... DuranFentiman 11 70
(Tim Easterby) *chsd ldrs on outer: sltly hmpd 1f out: sn fdd* **12/1**

5201 **8** 4 1/2 **It's Taboo**[17] 6043 3-8-3 **71**.................................... DavidProbert 7 49
(Mark Usher) *chsd ldrs: drvn over 2f out: wknd jst ins fnl f: eased clsng stages* **20/1**

1m 16.14s (-0.76) **Going Correction** +0.05s/f (Good)
WFA 3 from 4yo+ 2lb **8** Ran SP% **113.9**
Speed ratings (Par 104): **107,106,105,104,102 100,99,93**
toteswingers 1&2 £4.40, 1&3 £7.20, 2&3 £17.20 CSF £15.08 CT £161.10 TOTE £3.40: £2.50, £2.10, £3.80; EX 14.00 Trifecta £90.80 Pool: £1352.23 - 11.16 winning units..
Owner S de Zoete & Partners **Bred** Wellsummers Stud **Trained** East Ilsley, Berks

FOCUS
A decent fillies' sprint handicap.

6565 BOOK YOUR 21ST OCTOBER TOTESPORT PACKAGE H'CAP (ROUND 6 OF PONTEFRACT STAYERS CHAMPIONSHIP) 2m 1f 22y

4:30 (4:30) (Class 5) (0-75,75) 3-Y-0+ **£3,234** (£962; £481; £240) **Stalls** Low

Form RPR

0100 **1** **Riptide**[49] 4913 7-10-0 **75**..............................(v) BrianHughes 2 87
(Michael Scudamore) *drvn early to chse ldrs: led over 3f out: forged clr over 1f out* **11/1**

2351 **2** 10 **Kodicil (IRE)**[23] 5863 5-9-9 **70**.................................... DuranFentiman 10 71
(Tim Walford) *w ldrs: chsd wnr over 2f out: no imp* **8/1**

0006 **3** 3/4 **Mr Crystal (FR)**[32] 5560 9-8-11 **58**..............................(p) PaulMulrennan 13 58
(Micky Hammond) *in rr: drvn 4f out: hdwy over 2f out: styd on to take 3rd nr fin* **20/1**

6315 **4** 1 **Embsay Crag**[22] 5879 7-9-9 **73**.................................... DeclanCannon(3) 6 72
(Philip Kirby) *s.s: hdwy over 4f out: 4th over 2f out: kpt on same pce* **4/1**[2]

2050 **5** 2 3/4 **Italian Riviera**[22] 5895 4-9-9 **70**.................................... WilliamBuick 4 66
(Sir Mark Prescott Bt) *hld up in mid-div: hdwy 6f out: chal over 3f out: 3rd and rdn over 2f out: hung lft and wknd 1f out* **3/1**[1]

2240 **6** nk **Zaplamation (IRE)**[78] 3944 8-9-7 **68**.......................... MichaelO'Connell 15 64
(John Quinn) *in rr: drvn 7f out: hdwy over 2f out: swtchd ins over 1f out: one pce* **20/1**

2302 **7** 1 **Petella**[23] 5863 7-8-9 **61**..............................(p) ConnorBeasley(5) 7 56
(George Moore) *in rr: hdwy over 3f out: kpt on fnl 2f: nvr a factor* **10/1**

-306 **8** 2 1/2 **Inside Knowledge (USA)**[19] 1601 7-8-2 **56** oh8...(p) GemmaTutty(7) 16 48
(Garry Woodward) *sn chsng ldrs: upsides over 3f out: wknd over 2f out* **50/1**

3350 **9** 5 **Dr Finley (IRE)**[32] 5560 6-8-12 **62**..............................(v) SimonPearce(3) 3 48
(Lydia Pearce) *mid-div: hdwy to chse ldrs over 4f out: wknd over 2f out* **25/1**

6044 **10** 42 **Authentication**[13] 6177 4-8-12 **59**.................................... TomQueally 9
(Mel Brittain) *t.k.h: mde most 4f: reminders over 4f out: lost pl over 3f out: sn bhd: t.o* **12/1**

4162 **11** 1 1/2 **Cape Alex**[100] 3168 4-9-2 **63**..............................(b) JimmyFortune 11 2
(Clive Brittain) *trckd ldrs: t.k.h: led after 4f: hdd over 3f out: sn lost pl: eased over 1f out: t.o* **14/1**

3040 **12** 3 3/4 **Russian George (IRE)**[24] 5831 7-9-8 **69**..................(p) MartinHarley 14 3
(Steve Gollings) *in rr: drvn 7f out: lost pl over 4f out: bhd whn hung rt over 1f out: t.o* **33/1**

0510 **13** 4 1/2 **Tobacco**[49] 4931 3-8-0 **59** oh5.................................... PaulQuinn 1
(Tim Easterby) *in rr: bhd fnl 4f: t.o whn virtually p.u over 1f out* **7/1**[3]

3m 47.48s (2.88) **Going Correction** -0.075s/f (Good)
WFA 3 from 4yo+ 12lb **13** Ran SP% **118.7**
Speed ratings (Par 103): **90,85,84,84,83 83,82,81,79,59 58,56,54**
toteswingers 1&2 £10.10, 1&3 £32.50, 2&3 £23.50 CSF £89.10 CT £1748.64 TOTE £14.10: £3.50, £2.20, £7.60; EX 127.00 Trifecta £1073.30 Pool: £2299.65 - 1.60 winning units..
Owner Middletons **Bred** D Robb **Trained** Bromsash, H'fords

FOCUS
This looked a decent stamina test with a three-way battle for the lead through the early stages.

6566 SUBSCRIBE ONLINE AT RACINGUK.COM MAIDEN STKS 1m 2f 6y

5:00 (5:02) (Class 5) 3-Y-0+ **£3,234** (£962; £481; £240) **Stalls** Low

Form RPR

1 **Innsbruck** 3-9-5 0.................................... MichaelO'Connell 7 87
(John Quinn) *hld up in rr: hdwy on ins over 2f out: chal on ins 1f out: r.o to ld clsng stages* **50/1**

02- **2** nk **Personable**[337] 7172 3-9-5 0.................................... AhmedAjtebi 5 86
(Charlie Appleby) *trckd ldrs t.k.h: narrow advantage 1f out: hdd and no ex clsng stages* **4/1**[2]

24 **3** 3 1/4 **Vermont (IRE)**[69] 4257 3-9-5 0.................................... AndreaAtzeni 2 80
(Luca Cumani) *rrd s: t.k.h: trcking ldrs after 3f: led over 2f out: hdd 1f out: fdd* **5/6**[1]

0-0 **4** 8 **Travel (USA)**[102] 3136 3-9-0 0.................................... LiamJones 3 60
(Mark Johnston) *led: hdd over 2f out: hung rt and wknd over 1f out* **25/1**

4 **5** 7 **Two Moons**[32] 5563 3-9-5 0.................................... BarryMcHugh 10 52
(Tony Coyle) *swtchd lft after s: mid-div: hdwy over 4f out: sn chsng ldrs: drvn over 2f out: wknd over 1f out* **14/1**

00 **6** 11 **Anne's Valentino**[34] 5484 3-9-0 0.................................... PaulMulrennan 1 26
(Malcolm Jefferson) *t.k.h in rr: reminders over 5f out: sn bhd* **150/1**

-054 **7** *15* **Just One Kiss**[59] 4594 3-9-0 77 TomQueally 9
(Lady Cecil) *swtchd lft after s: sn chsng ldrs: drvn over 2f out: lost pl wl over 1f out: eased whn bhd ins fnl f* **9/1**

0 **8** *7* **Pomodoro**[14] 6134 3-9-5 0 WilliamBuick 8
(John Gosden) *mid-div: t.k.h: effrt and chsng ldrs over 3f out: wknd wl over 1f out: heavily eased ins fnl f* **5/1**[3]

00 **9** *1 1/2* **Nautical Twilight**[34] 5484 3-9-0 0 JamesSullivan 6
(Malcolm Jefferson) *trckd ldrs: drvn and lost pl over 4f out: sn bhd: t.o* **150/1**

0 **10** *83* **Muraafiq (USA)**[13] 6166 4-9-11 0 DuranFentiman 4
(Simon West) *unruly: dwlt: in rr: bhd fnl 4f: t.o over 2f out: virtually p.u: eventually completed* **150/1**

2m 14.28s (0.58) **Going Correction** -0.075s/f (Good)
WFA 3 from 4yo 6lb **10** Ran SP% **115.7**
Speed ratings (Par 103): **94,93,91,84,79 70,58,52,51,**
toteswingers 1&2 £25.70, 1&3 £10.40, 2&3 £2.20 CSF £239.63 TOTE £43.30: £7.50, £1.20, £1.10; EX 176.70 Trifecta £1131.30 Pool: £3275.94 - 2.17 winning units..

Owner Mrs L Lillingston **Bred** New England, Stanley House & Mount Coote Studs **Trained** Settrington, N Yorks

FOCUS
Older-horse maidens at this time of year aren't usually very competitive and this one provided a surprise winner.

6567 RIFLES CHALLENGE H'CAP (DIV II) 1m 4y
5:30 (5:31) (Class 4) (0-80,77) 3-Y-0+ **£5,175** (£1,540; £769; £384) **Stalls** Low

Form RPR

0254 **1** **Satanic Beat (IRE)**[9] 6288 4-9-10 **77** TomQueally 1 85
(Jedd O'Keeffe) *led: controlled pce: qckngd wl over 1f out: drvn out: unchal* **2/1**[1]

-000 **2** *1 1/4* **Kyllachy Star**[20] 5947 7-9-3 **70** PatrickMathers 6 75
(Richard Fahey) *trckd ldrs: effrt 2f out: chsd wnr jst ins fnl f: styd on same pce* **14/1**

5202 **3** *hd* **No Dominion (IRE)**[9] 6288 4-9-7 **74** WilliamBuick 3 79
(James Given) *dwlt: hld up in last: t.k.h: swtchd outside and hd over 1f out: styd on ins fnl f* **11/4**[2]

3430 **4** *3/4* **Obboorr**[8] 6296 4-8-11 **64** BarryMcHugh 8 67
(Brian Rothwell) *hld up towards rr: effrt over 2f out: chsng ldrs over 1f out: kpt on same pce* **10/1**[3]

6416 **5** *3/4* **West End Lad**[49] 4928 10-9-2 **72** (b) RyanClark(3) 2 73
(Roy Bowring) *chsd ldrs: kpt on same pce appr fnl f* **20/1**

6431 **6** *nk* **Who's Shirl**[27] 5711 7-9-8 **75** MichaelStainton 5 76
(Chris Fairhurst) *dwlt: hld up towards rr: hdwy on ins over 2f out: nt clr run over 1f out: swtchd outside: styd on ins fnl f* **14/1**

2020 **7** *3/4* **Kiwi Bay**[9] 6288 8-9-10 **77** (p) PaulMulrennan 9 76
(Michael Dods) *swtchd lft after s: trckd ldr: tk keen old: drvn over 2f out: fdd last 150yds* **16/1**

0025 **8** *2* **Shadowtime**[9] 6274 8-9-9 **76** MichaelO'Connell 7 70
(Tracy Waggott) *trckd ldrs: t.k.h: effrt over 2f out: wknd last 150yds* **16/1**

1m 45.07s (-0.83) **Going Correction** -0.075s/f (Good) **8** Ran SP% **99.0**
Speed ratings (Par 105): **101,99,99,98,98 97,97,95**
toteswingers 1&2 £4.80, 1&3 £1.50, 2&3 £5.40 CSF £22.41 CT £47.18 TOTE £2.50: £1.10, £3.10, £1.40; EX 22.50 Trifecta £82.50 Pool: £1384.30 - 12.58 winning units..

Owner Caron & Paul Chapman **Bred** Patrick Gleeson **Trained** Middleham Moor, N Yorks
■ Oratory was withdrawn (11-2, ref to ent stalls). Deduct 15p in the £ under R4.

FOCUS
The winning time was nearly a second slower than the first division.

6568 RACING UK PROFITS RETURNED TO RACING APPRENTICE H'CAP 6f
6:00 (6:02) (Class 5) (0-70,70) 3-Y-0+ **£3,234** (£962; £481; £240) **Stalls** Low

Form RPR

5030 **1** **Teetotal (IRE)**[9] 6287 3-9-0 **70** DanielleMooney(5) 10 80
(Nigel Tinkler) *swtchd lft after s: mid-div: effrt over 2f out: swtchd lft over 1f out: led 1f out: styd on wl* **8/1**

3016 **2** *2* **John Coffey (IRE)**[20] 5965 4-8-10 **64** AliRawlinson(5) 7 68
(Michael Appleby) *hld up towards rr: hdwy over 2f out: styd on to take 2nd last 50yds: no imp* **11/2**[3]

2300 **3** *2 1/4* **Legal Bond**[43] 5139 4-8-5 **61** (p) JoshDoyle(7) 4 57
(David O'Meara) *led: hdd 1f out: kpt on same pce* **6/1**

2246 **4** *hd* **Amethyst Dawn (IRE)**[30] 5614 7-8-12 **64** (v) AaronJones(3) 1 60
(Alan McCabe) *rn wout declared tongue strap: chsd ldrs on inner: n.m.r after 1f: drvn over 2f out: kpt on same pce fnl f* **4/1**[1]

0250 **5** *1 1/2* **Amis Reunis**[41] 5232 4-8-4 **58** JordanHibberd(5) 11 49
(Alan Berry) *mid-div: effrt over 2f out: chsng ldrs 1f out: one pce* **22/1**

3056 **6** *4* **Errigal Lad**[37] 5373 8-8-2 **56** oh10 AnnaHesketh(5) 9 34
(Garry Woodward) *mid-div on outer: effrt over 2f out: edgd lft 1f out: nvr a threat* **33/1**

4130 **7** *2 1/4* **Flighty Clarets (IRE)**[17] 6052 3-8-8 **66** EireannCagney(7) 8 37
(Richard Fahey) *in rr: sme hdwy over 2f out: wknd over 1f out* **5/1**[2]

0040 **8** *1 1/2* **China Excels**[37] 5365 6-8-6 **58** BTTreanor(3) 5 24
(Sue Smith) *charged gate: s.s: in rr: nvr on terms* **14/1**

63 **9** *2 3/4* **Whisky Bravo**[33] 5523 4-8-12 **66** ClaireMurray(5) 6 23
(David Brown) *dwlt: in rr: drvn 3f out: nvr on terms* **12/1**

6100 **10** *1 3/4* **Dancing Maite**[16] 6075 8-8-5 **59** (b) JackGarritty(5) 3 11
(Roy Bowring) *w ldr: edgd lft after 1f: drvn over 2f out: wknd over 1f out* **5/1**[2]

1m 16.32s (-0.58) **Going Correction** +0.05s/f (Good)
WFA 3 from 4yo+ 2lb **10** Ran SP% **115.8**
Speed ratings (Par 103): **105,102,99,99,97 91,88,86,83,80**
toteswingers 1&2 £4.70, 1&3 £9.00, 2&3 £5.40 CSF £51.21 CT £291.64 TOTE £10.10: £3.10, £1.80, £1.80; EX 29.90 Trifecta £328.50 Pool: £1824.89 - 4.16 winning units..

Owner Raybould & Scott **Bred** T Jones **Trained** Langton, N Yorks

FOCUS
They went a decent pace in this apprentice handicap.

T/Plt: £37.90 to a £1 stake. Pool of £73,619.16 - 1414.55 winning tickets. T/Qpdt: £23.00 to a £1 stake. Pool of £3833.00 - 123.20 winning tickets. WG

6534 YARMOUTH (L-H)
Thursday, September 19

OFFICIAL GOING: Good (good to soft in places; 6.8)
Wind: fresh, half against Weather: light rain

6569 BRITISH STALLION STUDS EBF SPRINT MAIDEN STKS 6f 3y
2:20 (2:21) (Class 5) 2-Y-O **£2,835** (£848; £424; £212; £105) **Stalls** Centre

Form RPR

1 **Wednaan** 2-9-5 0 PatCosgrave 1 76+
(M F De Kock, South Africa) *hld up in tch in rr of main gp: smooth hdwy to chse ldrs 2f out: rdn to ld over 1f out: rn green in front and pressed ins fnl f: r.o wl and asserted fnl 75yds* **11/8**[1]

0 **2** *3/4* **Silver Treasure (FR)**[26] 5744 2-9-5 0 RobertHavlin 4 71
(Amy Weaver) *taken down early and ponied to s: s.i.s: hdwy into midfield and swtchd to r nr stands' rail after 2f: rdn and effrt to chse wnr 1f out: pressing wnr ins fnl f: kpt on but hld fnl 75yds* **16/1**

3 *1 3/4* **Al Senad** 2-9-5 0 RyanMoore 9 66+
(Peter Chapple-Hyam) *in tch in midfield: swtchd rt to r nr stands' rail after 2f: rdn and effrt 2f out: hdwy and swtchd lft 1f out: chsd ldng pair ins fnl f: kpt on* **11/4**[2]

06 **4** *2 3/4* **Rathealy (IRE)**[10] 6256 2-9-5 0 KierenFallon 8 58
(Alan Bailey) *racd in centre: t.k.h: led and set stdy gallop: hdd and rdn 2f out: outpcd and btn 1f out: no threat to ldrs and styd on same pce after* **66/1**

03 **5** *1/2* **Chainsaw**[35] 5438 2-9-5 0 HarryBentley 10 56
(Stuart Williams) *t.k.h and racd awkwardly: chsd ldrs and swtchd to r nr stands' rail after 1f: chsd ldr tl led 2f out: rdn and hdd over 1f out: wknd fnl 150yds* **11/2**[3]

6 *shd* **Mr Win (IRE)** 2-9-5 0 TedDurcan 3 56
(Chris Wall) *restless in stalls: s.i.s: in rr: rdn and effrt over 2f out: no imp tl hdwy 1f out: kpt on steadily ins fnl f: nvr trbld ldrs* **20/1**

7 *hd* **He's My Boy (IRE)** 2-9-5 0 FrederikTylicki 7 55
(James Fanshawe) *in tch in midfield: rdn and effrt 2f out: outpcd and btn over 1f out: no threat to ldrs and kpt on same pce ins fnl f* **9/1**

8 *1/2* **Exceeding Power** 2-9-5 0 AdamKirby 6 54
(Michael Bell) *in tch in midfield: swtchd lft and rn green over 2f out: sn rdn and hdwy to press ldrs 2f out: no ex and btn ent fnl f: wknd fnl 150yds* **16/1**

9 *11* **Templar Boy** 2-9-5 0 ChrisCatlin 5 21
(J R Jenkins) *stdd s: t.k.h and rn green towards rr: last and struggling whn rdn along 1/2-way: lost tch over 1f out* **100/1**

1m 16.02s (1.62) **Going Correction** -0.05s/f (Good) **9** Ran SP% **113.2**
Speed ratings (Par 95): **87,86,83,80,79 79,78,78,63**
toteswingers 1&2 £4.70, 1&3 £1.50, 2&3 £9.00 CSF £25.63 TOTE £2.20: £1.10, £3.40, £1.10; EX 20.70 Trifecta £56.60 Pool: £2258.16 - 29.88 winning units..

Owner Sheikh Mohammed Bin Khalifa Al Maktoum **Bred** Qatar Bloodstock Ltd **Trained** South Africa

FOCUS
Full width of back straight utilised. Van Der Neer won this contest on his debut last September before going on to finish third in the 2000 Guineas the following spring, but this year's race, in which they went an honest gallop, looked modest in terms of prior form. The winner could take high rank, however.

6570 BRITISH STALLION STUDS/GREENE KING EBF MAIDEN STKS 1m 3y
2:50 (2:51) (Class 5) 2-Y-O **£2,911** (£866; £432; £216) **Stalls** Centre

Form RPR

4 **1** **Mount Logan (IRE)**[62] 4483 2-9-5 0 RyanMoore 4 84+
(Luca Cumani) *chsd ldrs: effrt and rdn to chal over 1f out: led fnl 100yds: sn in command and styd on strly: rdn out* **5/4**[1]

5 **2** *2 1/4* **Istikshaf (IRE)**[27] 5718 2-9-5 0 SilvestreDeSousa 3 79
(Saeed bin Suroor) *led: jnd and rdn over 1f out: wnt lft ent fnl f: wnt lft again and hdd fnl 100yds: no ex and sn btn but kpt on for clr 2nd* **2/1**[2]

3 *3 3/4* **Latin Charm (IRE)** 2-9-5 0 PaoloSirigu 6 70+
(Marco Botti) *s.i.s: rn green and detached in last: clsd 1/2-way: rdn and no hdwy 3f out: modest 5th over 1f out: kpt on u.p ins fnl f to go 3rd cl home: nvr trbld ldrs* **16/1**

4 *nk* **Grand Meister** 2-9-5 0 AdamKirby 5 69+
(Michael Bell) *in tch in midfield: rdn and effrt over 2f out: 4th and no imp over 1f out: kpt on same pce ins fnl f* **20/1**

5 *1/2* **Deadly Approach** 2-9-5 0[1] KierenFallon 1 68
(Charlie Appleby) *s.i.s: t.k.h: stdy hdwy to press ldr 1/2-way: rdn and no ex 2f out: 3rd and btn over 1f out: wknd ins fnl f and lost 2 pls towards fin* **9/2**[3]

0 **6** *23* **Rockwood**[95] 3366 2-8-12 0 (t) IanBurns(7) 8 12
(Jane Chapple-Hyam) *s.i.s: bhd: clsd and j. path over 5f out: sn rdn: wknd over 2f out: t.o fnl f* **33/1**

36 **7** *3* **Astrowolf**[23] 5852 2-9-2 0 AshleyMorgan(3) 7 5
(Mark H Tompkins) *chsd ldrs: rdn and struggling 1/2-way: bhd fnl 2f: t.o fnl f* **25/1**

4 **8** *9* **Kingsway Lad (IRE)**[12] 6197 2-9-5 0 MartinDwyer 2
(Derek Shaw) *t.k.h: chsd ldr tl 1/2-way: lost pl over 2f out: t.o and eased ins fnl f* **100/1**

1m 42.1s (1.50) **Going Correction** -0.05s/f (Good) **8** Ran SP% **114.4**
Speed ratings (Par 95): **90,87,84,83,83 60,57,48**
toteswingers 1&2 £1.10, 1&3 £4.00, 2&3 £4.80 CSF £3.75 TOTE £2.10: £1.10, £1.10, £3.80; EX 4.50 Trifecta £22.40 Pool: £3189.61 - 106.41 winning units..

Owner Sheikh Mohammed Obaid Al Maktoum **Bred** Ladyswood Stud & Canning Downs Stud Aus **Trained** Newmarket, Suffolk

FOCUS
A fair juvenile maiden, and a race won by Main Sequence on his debut in September 2011 before he went on to finish runner-up in the 2012 Derby. They went pretty steady early on, and a horse with previous experience made it count. The second helps with the level of the form.

6571 SEAJACKS H'CAP 7f 3y
3:20 (3:21) (Class 3) (0-90,91) 3-Y-0+ **£7,439** (£2,213; £1,106; £553) **Stalls** Centre

Form RPR

2221 **1** **Ocean Tempest**[5] 6384 4-9-10 **91** 6ex BrettDoyle 9 102
(John Ryan) *hld up in tch in midfield: rdn and effrt to ld over 1f out: asserting but hung lft ent fnl f: hrd pressed cl home: jst hld on* **7/4**[1]

4164 **2** *shd* **Shesastar**[12] 6210 5-8-12 **79** RyanMoore 10 90
(David Barron) *in tch in last quartet: rdn over 3f out: swtchd rt over 1f out: str run to press wnr ins fnl f: r.o wl and clsng fnl 50yds: jst failed* **11/2**[2]

0035 **3** 3 **Comrade Bond**[51] 4864 5-8-7 **74**.. TedDurcan 5 77
(Mark H Tompkins) *chsd ldrs: rdn and effrt to chse wnr over 1f out tl ins fnl f: outpcd by ldng pair but hld on for 3rd fnl 100yds* **12/1**

6600 **4** nk **Les Troyens**[12] 6183 5-9-7 **88**..(v) SilvestreDeSousa 8 90
(Saeed bin Suroor) *t.k.h: hld up in tch in midfield: rdn and hdwy to chse ldrs 2f out: outpcd by ldng pair ins fnl f: kpt on same pce* **10/1**

00 **5** 1 1/4 **Rebellious Guest**[54] 4744 4-9-7 **88**.. JamieMackay 7 87
(George Margarson) *stdd s: t.k.h: hld up in last pair: effrt but stl plenty to do whn nt clr run: hmpd and swtchd rt over 1f out: hdwy and styd on ins fnl f: no threat to ldrs* **17/2**

4515 **6** 1/2 **Albaqaa**[9] 6278 8-9-1 **85**.. RobertTart(3) 4 82
(P J O'Gorman) *stdd s: hld up in tch in last quartet: effrt and no imp over 1f out: rdn and sme hdwy 1f out: kpt on but no threat to ldrs* **14/1**

0616 **7** 1 1/4 **Azrur (IRE)**[40] 5287 3-9-4 **88**.. AdamKirby 6 81
(Michael Bell) *led: drvn 2f out: sn drvn and hdd over 1f out: wknd fnl f* **7/1**[3]

0100 **8** 2 1/4 **Intimidate**[96] 3342 3-8-12 **82**..(p) FrankieDettori 3 69
(Jeremy Noseda) *racd along in centre to far side: chsd ldr tl 2f out: sn drvn and unable qck: btn 1f out: fdd ins fnl f* **11/1**

1600 **9** 3 1/2 **Great Expectations**[6] 6360 5-8-7 **74**.. ChrisCatlin 2 52
(J R Jenkins) *stdd s: t.k.h: hld up in tch in rr: rdn and short-lived effrt over 1f out: sn btn: wknd fnl f* **16/1**

1m 26.86s (0.26) **Going Correction** -0.05s/f (Good)
WFA 3 from 4yo+ 3lb **9** Ran SP% **112.4**
Speed ratings (Par 107): **96,95,92,92,90 90,88,86,82**
toteswingers 1&2 £2.40, 1&3 £6.10, 2&3 £6.60 CSF £10.70 CT £85.30 TOTE £2.30: £1.30, £1.40, £3.30; EX 10.80 Trifecta £58.40 Pool: £2929.56 - 37.60 winning units..
Owner W McLuskey & C Little **Bred** Old Mill Stud Ltd And Oomswell Ltd **Trained** Newmarket, Suffolk

FOCUS
A decent handicap.

6572 AT THE RACES NURSERY H'CAP 7f 3y
3:50 (3:50) (Class 4) (0-85,85) 2-Y-O **£3,752** (£1,116; £557; £278) **Stalls** Centre

Form RPR

253 **1** **Meeting Waters**[52] 4827 2-8-4 **68**.. JohnFahy 2 85+
(William Haggas) *mde all: swtchd rt to r alone against stands' rail sn after s: rdn over 1f out: styd on strly and drew wl clr fnl f: comf* **7/1**

3341 **2** 6 **Gender Agenda**[27] 5699 2-8-10 **81**.. LouisSteward(7) 7 82
(Michael Bell) *t.k.h: hld up in midfield: clsd to chse wnr and gng wl over 2f out: rdn and no ex over 1f out: btn 1f out: wknd ins fnl f* **7/2**[3]

1323 **3** 3 **Snow Squall**[12] 6207 2-9-7 **85**.. KierenFallon 5 78
(Charlie Appleby) *hld up in last pair: hdwy after 2f: chsd ldrs 1/2-way: rdn and effrt over 2f out: 3rd and btn over 1f out: wknd fnl f* **3/1**[2]

0312 **4** 4 **Pyjama Day**[16] 6076 2-8-11 **75**..(b) MartinDwyer 3 58
(Hugo Palmer) *awkward leaving stalls: led main gp and chsd wnr tl over 2f out: sn struggling u.p: wknd over 1f out* **14/1**

1 **5** 2 **Boadicee**[50] 4883 2-9-2 **80**.. ChrisCatlin 4 58
(Rae Guest) *awkward leaving stalls and slowly away: a in rr: rdn 1/2-way: drvn and no hdwy 3f out: no ch fnl 2f* **6/1**

324 **6** 2 **Istimraar (IRE)**[39] 5299 2-9-1 **79**..(p) SilvestreDeSousa 6 51
(Saeed bin Suroor) *t.k.h: chsd ldrs: rdn and no rspnse wl over 2f out: wknd wl btn over 1f out: bhd and eased wl ins fnl f* **5/2**[1]

1m 27.67s (1.07) **Going Correction** -0.05s/f (Good) **6** Ran SP% **109.2**
Speed ratings (Par 97): **91,84,80,76,73 71**
toteswingers 1&2 £4.80, 1&3 £3.30, 2&3 £3.10 CSF £29.59 TOTE £10.00: £3.20, £2.70; EX 33.60 Trifecta £130.70 Pool: £2274.81 - 13.04 winning units..
Owner Liam Sheridan **Bred** T R G Vestey **Trained** Newmarket, Suffolk

FOCUS
A good nursery handicap. The winner may be flattered by racing solo on the rail but only time will tell.

6573 STANLEY THREADWELL MEMORIAL H'CAP 1m 6f 17y
4:20 (4:20) (Class 2) (0-100,95) 3-Y-**O**£12,602 (£3,772; £1,886; £944; £470) **Stalls** Centre

Form RPR

2/51 **1** **Montefeltro**[11] 6239 5-8-9 **79**.. RobertTart(3) 2 95+
(Brian Ellison) *t.k.h early: stdd bk into last pair after 2f and hld up wl off the pce: stl plenty to do and effrt 3f out: hdwy to chse clr ldr over 1f out: led fnl 150yds: sn clr and in command: r.o wl: comf* **10/11**[1]

0316 **2** 4 1/2 **Colinca's Lad (IRE)**[70] 4208 11-8-6 **80**.. ShelleyBirkett(7) 5 84
(Peter Charalambous) *led: wnt clr 12f out: rdn and fnd ex 2f out: hdd fnl 150yds and sn brushed aside by wnr: plugged on for clr 2nd* **8/1**[3]

0-04 **3** 6 **Lyric Street (IRE)**[90] 3531 5-9-6 **87**..(p) RyanMoore 8 83
(Jeremy Noseda) *stdd after s: t.k.h and hld up wl off the pce in last: plenty to do and effrt wl over 2f out: no real imp tl plugged on fr over 1f out: wnt modest 3rd ins fnl f: nvr trbld ldrs* **9/4**[2]

3110 **4** 3 1/2 **Hi Note**[22] 5895 5-9-0 **81**.. ChrisCatlin 1 72
(Sheena West) *bustled along leaving stalls: sn chsd clr ldr: clsd 4f out: rdn and no ex over 2f out: 3rd and wl hld over 1f out: wknd fnl f* **10/1**

2200 **5** 16 **Quixote**[27] 5723 4-9-8 **89**..(bt) MartinDwyer 4 57
(Clive Brittain) *chsd ldng pair: rdn and effrt 4f out: no prog: dropped to last over 1f out and sn wl bhd* **12/1**

3m 3.7s (-3.90) **Going Correction** -0.05s/f (Good) **5** Ran SP% **111.0**
Speed ratings (Par 109): **109,106,103,101,91**
CSF £9.00 TOTE £1.80: £1.10, £3.00; EX 10.10 Trifecta £25.70 Pool: £2529.01 - 73.73 winning units..
Owner D Gilbert, M Lawrence, A Bruce **Bred** Darley **Trained** Norton, N Yorks

FOCUS
A decent staying handicap in which they went an even gallop.

6574 "GET ON" WITH DAN HAGUE FILLIES' H'CAP 1m 3f 101y
4:50 (4:53) (Class 4) (0-80,79) 3-Y-0+ **£4,690** (£1,395; £697; £348) **Stalls** Low

Form RPR

5155 **1** **The Ducking Stool**[25] 5802 6-8-7 **67**.. ShelleyBirkett(7) 4 74
(Julia Feilden) *hld up wl in tch in last pair: effrt 2f out: kpt on wanting to hang lft whn rdn but wnt 3rd 1f out: cajoled along and styd on to ld wl ins fnl f: gng away at fin* **10/1**

223 **2** 1 **Shalwa**[35] 5445 3-9-5 **79**..(p) AdamKirby 3 84
(Marco Botti) *led: rdn over 3f out: hdd and drvn over 2f out: kpt on u.p and ev ch ins fnl f: no ex and outpcd by wnr fnl 50yds* **6/4**[1]

6211 **3** 1 **Nullarbor Sky (IRE)**[36] 5411 3-8-10 **70**..(p) SilvestreDeSousa 6 73
(Lucy Wadham) *chsd ldrs: effrt and upsides ldr 3f out: rdn to ld over 2f out: drvn over 1f out: hdd and no ex wl ins fnl f: wknd towards fin* **10/3**[3]

2-14 **4** 3 3/4 **I Say (IRE)**[33] 5548 3-9-2 **76**..(p) KierenFallon 2 73
(William Haggas) *chsd ldng pair: rdn and effrt ent fnl 2f: hanging lft u.p and unable qck over 1f out: wknd ins fnl f* **5/2**[2]

422R **5** 17 **Kittens**[5] 6377 4-9-2 **69**.. MartinDwyer 7 37
(William Muir) *pushed along early: a last but wl in tch: rdn and effrt on inner over 2f out: wknd over 1f out: heavily eased wl ins fnl f* **14/1**

2m 28.84s (0.14) **Going Correction** -0.05s/f (Good)
WFA 3 from 4yo+ 7lb **5** Ran SP% **107.4**
Speed ratings (Par 102): **97,96,95,92,80**
CSF £24.43 TOTE £10.20: £2.50, £1.40; EX 29.50 Trifecta £86.00 Pool: £2415.01 - 21.04 winning units..
Owner Hoofbeats Ltd Racing Club **Bred** Cheveley Park Stud Ltd **Trained** Exning, Suffolk

FOCUS
A fair middle-distance fillies' handicap.

6575 BARTHOLOMEWS JEWELLERS H'CAP 6f 3y
5:20 (5:21) (Class 4) (0-85,85) 3-Y-O **£4,690** (£1,395; £697; £348) **Stalls** Centre

Form RPR

-141 **1** **Rocksilla**[43] 5150 3-9-1 **79**.. TedDurcan 5 90+
(Chris Wall) *niggled along in last pair: reminder 1/2-way: rdn and stl plenty to do over 2f out: swtchd lft and str run jst over 1f out: led and wnt rt fnl 75yds: sn in command and eased last strides* **9/2**[2]

0002 **2** 1 3/4 **Baddilini**[2] 6506 3-9-4 **82**..(p) KierenFallon 1 87
(Alan Bailey) *led and brought field to stands' rail: rdn and hdd over 1f out: rallied u.p to ld again fnl 100yds: sn hdd and one pce* **9/2**[2]

4230 **3** 1 3/4 **Huntsmans Close**[26] 5769 3-8-13 **84**.. LouisSteward(7) 2 83
(Michael Bell) *chsd ldr tl pushed along to ld over 1f out: rdn and hdd fnl 100yds: sn btn and wknd towards fin* **11/2**

3112 **4** 2 1/4 **Sedenoo**[24] 5836 3-9-4 **85**.. RobertTart(3) 7 77
(Marco Botti) *hld up in rr: effrt u.p and hung lft over 1f out: no imp 1f out: wknd ins fnl f* **5/2**[1]

-034 **5** 1/2 **Agerzam**[44] 5103 3-9-6 **84**..(b[1]) RyanMoore 6 75
(Roger Varian) *hld up in tch in midfield: rdn and effrt over 1f out: drvn and no hdwy 1f out: wknd ins fnl f* **5/1**[3]

2020 **6** 3/4 **Red Gift (IRE)**[84] 3730 3-8-7 **71** oh1..(p) SilvestreDeSousa 4 59
(Brian Ellison) *chsd ldrs: rdn 1/2-way: struggling u.p and lost pl over 1f out: wknd fnl f* **12/1**

2010 **7** 6 **You're The Boss**[21] 5928 3-9-0 **78**..(b[1]) TomMcLaughlin 3 47
(Ed Walker) *wnt lft leaving stalls and s.i.s: sn rcvrd and t.k.h in midfield: rdn and effrt to chse ldrs 2f out: rdn and btn over 1f out: wknd fnl f* **14/1**

1m 13.71s (-0.69) **Going Correction** -0.05s/f (Good) **7** Ran SP% **111.3**
Speed ratings (Par 103): **102,99,97,94,93 92,84**
toteswingers 1&2 £5.20, 1&3 £4.20, 2&3 £5.20 CSF £23.50 TOTE £4.50: £2.40, £3.50; EX 18.00 Trifecta £145.10 Pool: £2397.07 - 12.38 winning units..
Owner Moyns Park Stud **Bred** Moyns Park Estate And Stud Ltd **Trained** Newmarket, Suffolk

FOCUS
A good 3-y-o handicap in which they went a solid gallop.
T/Plt: £11.70 to a £1 stake. Pool of £76,394.60 - 4750.86 winning tickets. T/Qpdt: £9.40 to a £1 stake. Pool of £5053 - 394.90 winning tickets. SP

6576 - 6580a (Foreign Racing) - See Raceform Interactive

6545 AYR (L-H)
Friday, September 20

OFFICIAL GOING: Soft (good to soft in places; goingstick 8.5; sprint course: far side 8.5, centre 8.5, stands' side 8.7)
Wind: Breezy, half against Weather: Cloudy

6581 BRITISH STALLION STUDS E B F MAIDEN STKS 7f 50y
1:20 (1:21) (Class 4) 2-Y-O **£5,498** (£1,636; £817; £408) **Stalls** High

Form RPR

2222 **1** **Lincoln (IRE)**[13] 6206 2-9-5 78.. MartinHarley 2 80
(Mick Channon) *cl up: led over 3f out: drew clr fr over 1f out: readily* **4/1**[2]

2 2 3/4 **Art Obsession (IRE)** 2-9-5 0.. GrahamGibbons 3 73+
(David Barron) *prom: effrt and rdn 3f out: chsd (clr) wnr appr fnl f: kpt on: no imp* **12/1**

6 **3** 3/4 **Ronya (IRE)**[22] 5915 2-9-0 0.. JimCrowley 4 66
(K R Burke) *prom: rdn and outpcd over 2f out: rallied fnl f: kpt on fin* **66/1**

4433 **4** 1 1/4 **An Chulainn (IRE)**[15] 6141 2-9-0 82.. JoeFanning 6 63
(Mark Johnston) *cl up: hdwy to chse wnr 3f out: sn rdn and edgd lft: lost 2nd appr fnl f: sn outpcd* **7/1**[3]

3 **5** 1/2 **Beautiful Stranger (IRE)**[60] 4576 2-9-5 0.. TomEaves 1 67
(Keith Dalgleish) *led to over 3f out: rallied: no ex over 1f out* **40/1**

6 1 1/4 **Automated** 2-9-5 0.. JamieSpencer 10 64+
(Clive Brittain) *bhd and sn pushed along: drvn over 3f out: allowed to coast home last 75yds but styd on wl* **14/1**

0 **7** 1 1/4 **Derbyshire (IRE)**[28] 5727 2-9-5 0.. NeilCallan 7 61
(Kevin Ryan) *prom: effrt on outside over 2f out: wknd over 1f out* **2/1**[1]

0 **8** 2 **McCarthy Mor (IRE)**[118] 2670 2-9-5 0.. TonyHamilton 13 56
(Richard Fahey) *midfield: drvn along over 2f out: btn over 1f out* **16/1**

0 **9** nk **Excellent Royale (IRE)**[39] 5344 2-9-5 0.. RobertWinston 11 55
(Charles Hills) *prom: rdn over 2f out: hung lft and wknd over 1f out* **10/1**

00 **10** 2 1/2 **Aldreth**[35] 5482 2-9-5 0.. PhillipMakin 9 49
(Michael Easterby) *s.i.s: bhd: shkn up over 2f out: styd on steadily: nvr nr ldrs* **66/1**

11 13 **Insaany** 2-9-5 0.. PaulHanagan 14 16
(Mark Johnston) *noisy and green in paddock: towards rr: drvn along 3f out: sn wknd* **12/1**

12 2 **Magic Music Man** 2-9-5 0.. DanielTudhope 8 11
(K R Burke) *bhd and outpcd: no ch fr 1/2-way* **14/1**

13 19 **Uplifted (IRE)** 2-9-5 0.. PaulMulrennan 12
(Kevin Ryan) *bhd and sn outpcd: hung lft and lost tch fr 3f out* **33/1**

1m 36.68s (3.28) **Going Correction** +0.125s/f (Good) **13** Ran SP% **117.9**
Speed ratings (Par 97): **87,83,83,81,81 79,78,75,75,72 57,55,33**
Tote Swingers 1&2 £15.70, 2&3 £69.60, 1&3 £68.40 CSF £49.79 TOTE £4.90: £1.70, £4.10, £14.70; EX 58.70 Trifecta £841.40 Part won. Pool: £1,121.99 - 0.24 winning tickets..
Owner Billy Parish **Bred** Tipper House Stud **Trained** West Ilsley, Berks

FOCUS
Home bend moved out 2m, adding about 6yds to races on Round course. Despite 0.5mm of rain overnight, the ground had dried out slightly from the previous day and was described as soft, good to soft in places. Descriptions of the ground from the jockeys after the opener included "tacky" and "very gluey". An interesting maiden, but these juveniles seemed to find it hard work in the conditions and the time was 8.18 seconds outside standard. It proved hard to make up ground from off the pace.

6582 AL MAKTOUM COLLEGE NURSERY H'CAP 6f
1:50 (1:50) (Class 2) 2-Y-O

£12,450 (£3,728; £1,864; £932; £466; £234) **Stalls High**

Form RPR
2412 **1** **Black Treacle (IRE)**^{4} 6465 2-9-1 **78**....................(b^{1}) TomEaves 8 83
(Keith Dalgleish) *led: rdn 2f out: hdd ins fnl f: edgd lft and rallied gamely to regain ld nr fin* **33/1**

412 **2** *nse* **Makin The Rules (IRE)**^{12} 6233 2-8-11 **74**............ MichaelO'Connell 10 79
(John Quinn) *trckd ldrs: effrt and rdn 2f out: led ins fnl f: kpt on: hdd cl home* **6/1**^{2}

21 **3** *shd* **No Leaf Clover (IRE)**^{23} 5877 2-9-0 **77**.................. RobertWinston 6 82+
(Ollie Pears) *s.i.s: hld up in midfield: nt clr run over 2f out: weaved through over 1f out: kpt on wl u.p fnl f: jst hld* **5/1**^{1}

3201 **4** *1 1/2* **Kenny The Captain (IRE)**^{14} 6175 2-8-12 **75**............. DuranFentiman 9 75
(Tim Easterby) *trckd ldrs: effrt and drvn over 2f out: kpt on same pce fnl f* **10/1**

553 **5** *2 3/4* **Scots Law (IRE)**^{14} 6160 2-8-12 **75**.................. PaulMulrennan 13 70+
(Keith Dalgleish) *hld up: hdwy whn nt clr run over 2f out and over 1f out: sn rdn: one pce fnl f* **33/1**

1030 **6** *3/4* **Foxy Clarets (IRE)**^{8} 6328 2-9-5 **82**...................... TonyHamilton 5 72
(Richard Fahey) *hld up: rdn over 2f out: hdwy over 1f out: no imp fnl f* **11/1**

1241 **7** *2 1/2* **Kickboxer (IRE)**^{13} 6194 2-9-2 **79**............................ MartinHarley 14 64
(Mick Channon) *hld up: rdn over 2f out: edgd rt and n.m.r over 1f out: nvr able to chal* **6/1**^{2}

4651 **8** *1/2* **Damaah (USA)**^{9} 6295 2-8-1 **64** 6ex........................... JoeFanning 4 45
(Mark Johnston) *cl up tl rdn and wknd appr fnl f* **7/1**^{3}

1000 **9** *1 3/4* **Yorkshire Relish (IRE)**^{29} 5679 2-9-0 **77**.................. PhillipMakin 11 52
(Kevin Ryan) *bhd: drvn over 2f out: nvr able to chal* **11/1**

1110 **10** *2* **Touch The Clouds**^{29} 5679 2-8-13 **76**......................... NeilCallan 3 45
(Kevin Ryan) *chsd ldrs on outside tl rdn and wknd 2f out* **20/1**

4004 **11** *3 1/4* **Gym Shoes**^{13} 6187 2-8-6 **69**............................... PatrickMathers 16 29
(Richard Fahey) *in tch: hmpd and lost pl over 4f out: n.d after* **16/1**

4333 **12** *1* **Left Defender (IRE)**^{39} 5347 2-8-8 **71**....................(b^{1}) RobertHavlin 12 28
(Jo Hughes) *cl up tl rdn and wknd fr 2f out* **22/1**

2343 **13** *3 3/4* **Stoney Quine (IRE)**^{49} 4952 2-8-0 **63** oh2..................... CathyGannon 1 8
(Keith Dalgleish) *prom on outside: rdn and wknd over 2f out* **50/1**

1043 **14** *1 1/2* **Atheera (IRE)**^{22} 5926 2-8-5 **68**.............................. PaulHanagan 15 18
(Mark Johnston) *towards rr: sn pushed along: no imp whn hmpd over 1f out* **25/1**

1235 **U** **Mr Matthews (IRE)**^{56} 4703 2-9-7 **84**......................... DanielTudhope 2
(K R Burke) *hld up bhd ldng gp on outside: stirrup iron broke and uns rdr over 2f out* **10/1**

1m 15.81s (3.41) **Going Correction** +0.375s/f (Good) **15** Ran SP% **119.3**
Speed ratings (Par 101): **92,91,91,89,86 85,81,81,78,76 71,70,65,63,**
Tote Swingers 1&2 £23.90, 2&3 £12.40, 1&3 £46.40 CSF £205.69 CT £1185.58 TOTE £18.50: £5.50, £3.00, £2.70; EX 205.90 Trifecta £644.10 Pool: £1,205.42 - 1.40 winning tickets..
Owner Straightline Construction Ltd **Bred** Tally-Ho Stud **Trained** Carluke, S Lanarks
■ Stewards' Enquiry : Michael O'Connell one-day ban; careless riding (4th Oct)

FOCUS
A decent and competitive nursery with little covering the front three at the line.

6583 BAM PROPERTIES LTD H'CAP (FOR THE SOUTH AYRSHIRE CUP) 5f
2:20 (2:21) (Class 4) (0-85,85) 3-Y-0+ **£6,469** (£1,925; £962; £481) **Stalls Centre**

Form RPR
0000 **1** **Hazelrigg (IRE)**^{9} 6309 8-8-9 **73**....................(e) RobertHavlin 27 83
(Tim Easterby) *trckd stands' side ldrs: effrt and pushed along over 1f out: styd on strly fnl f: led cl home: 1st of 12 in gp* **20/1**

4301 **2** *nk* **Imperial Legend (IRE)**^{14} 6159 4-8-13 **84**............(p) JordanNason$^{(7)}$ 23 93
(David Nicholls) *t.k.h: trckd ldrs stands' side: rdn over 1f out: led ins fnl f: ct cl home: 2nd of 12 in gp* **9/1**^{2}

0012 **3** *shd* **Aetna**^{90} 3584 3-9-4 **83**.. PaulMulrennan 2 92+
(Michael Easterby) *trckd far side ldrs: shkn up to ld that gp over 1f out: hung rt and kpt on wl fnl f: jst hld by first two stands' side: 1st of 12 in gp* **5/1**^{1}

1525 **4** *nk* **Gowanharry (IRE)**^{41} 5266 4-8-6 **75**.................... ConnorBeasley$^{(5)}$ 15 82
(Michael Dods) *cl up stands' side: effrt and disp ld fnl f: kpt on: jst hld: 3rd of 12 in gp* **14/1**

0643 **5** *1/2* **Bonnie Charlie**^{13} 6205 7-8-10 **74**................................ PaulQuinn 19 80
(David Nicholls) *bhd stands' side: weaved through fr over 1f out: kpt on strly fnl f: nrst fin: 4th of 12 in gp* **20/1**

2400 **6** *nse* **Even Stevens**^{9} 6309 5-9-5 **83**...........................(p) RobertWinston 26 89
(Scott Dixon) *led stands' side gp to ins fnl f: kpt on same pce towards fin: 5th of 12 in gp* **25/1**

0000 **7** *1/2* **Rothesay Chancer**^{30} 5639 5-8-8 **72**........................ JoeFanning 14 76
(Jim Goldie) *hld up bhd ldng gp stands' side: rdn over 2f out: kpt on fnl f: nvr rchd ldrs: 6th of 12 in gp* **40/1**

30/0 **8** *1/2* **Son Du Silence (IRE)**^{83} 3823 4-9-4 **82**.....................(t) GrahamLee 16 84
(James Ewart) *prom stands' side: rdn over 2f out: kpt on same pce ins fnl f: 7th of 12 in gp* **16/1**

1025 **9** *1* **Hamoody (USA)**^{13} 6205 9-8-11 **78**.......................... JasonHart$^{(3)}$ 8 76
(David Nicholls) *prom far side: rdn 2f out: styd on fnl f to take 2nd that gp towards fin: no imp: 2nd of 12 in gp* **40/1**

-025 **10** *hd* **Rio's Pearl**^{14} 6162 3-8-13 **78**...........................(b) JamieSpencer 25 76
(Ralph Beckett) *hld up stands' side: effrt whn n.m.r over 2f out: rdn over 1f out: no imp fnl f: 8th of 12 in gp* **10/1**^{3}

2406 **11** *shd* **Rylee Mooch**^{9} 6309 5-9-2 **80**...........................(e) DanielTudhope 9 77
(Richard Guest) *cl up far side: drvn over 2f out: chsd far side ldr ins fnl f to nr fin: 3rd of 12 in gp* **16/1**

0306 **12** *1 3/4* **Waking Warrior**^{13} 6205 5-8-4 **73**......................(tp) ShaneGray$^{(5)}$ 17 64
(Kevin Ryan) *hld up stands' side: drvn over 2f out: sme late hdwy: nvr able to chal: 9th of 12 in gp* **22/1**

1234 **13** *nk* **Lexington Place**^{27} 5769 3-8-12 **82**...................... DavidBergin$^{(5)}$ 10 72
(David O'Meara) *cl up far side: rdn over 2f out: no ex fr over 1f out: 4th of 12 in gp* **16/1**

0410 **14** *hd* **Threes Grand**^{9} 6309 3-9-1 **85**............................... TimClark$^{(5)}$ 7 74
(Scott Dixon) *in tch on outside of far side gp: rdn over 2f out: one pce over 1f out: 5th of 12 in gp* **20/1**

0-00 **15** *3/4* **Scatty Cat (IRE)**^{27} 5775 3-8-6 **74**....................(t) IJBrennan$^{(3)}$ 3 60
(Peter McCreery, Ire) *in tch far side: outpcd over 2f out: n.d after: 6th of 12 in gp* **20/1**

4300 **16** *shd* **Midnight Dynamo**^{14} 6161 6-8-11 **75**........................ JimCrowley 6 61
(Jim Goldie) *midfield far side: drvn over 2f out: no imp fr over 1f out: 7th of 12 in gp* **40/1**

5635 **17** *hd* **The Nifty Fox**^{18} 6052 9-8-12 **76**.......................(p) PhillipMakin 13 61
(Tim Easterby) *swtchd rt and hld up stands' side: rdn over 2f out: nt pce to chal: 10th of 12 in gp* **25/1**

6000 **18** *1/2* **Strange Magic (IRE)**^{13} 6212 3-9-3 **82**.................... PaulHanagan 20 66
(Richard Fahey) *hld up stands' side: drvn over 2f out: nvr rchd ldrs: 11th of 12 in gp* **28/1**

231 **19** *3/4* **Angus Og**^{39} 5340 3-9-0 **84**................................ JoeyHaynes$^{(5)}$ 1 65
(K R Burke) *missed break: sme late hdwy but a bhd far side: 8th of 12 in gp* **11/1**

0000 **20** *3/4* **Profile Star (IRE)**^{9} 6309 4-8-11 **75**.................... GrahamGibbons 21 53
(David Barron) *cl up stands' side: rdn over 2f out: wknd wl over 1f out: last of 12 in gp* **25/1**

0004 **21** *1/2* **Mister Manannan (IRE)**^{10} 6273 6-9-4 **82**.................. AdrianNicholls 12 58
(David Nicholls) *swtchd lft and bhd far side: drvn along 1/2-way: nvr on terms: 9th of 12 in gp* **28/1**

1010 **22** *1* **Red Baron (IRE)**^{49} 4954 4-9-0 **81**............................ NeilFarley$^{(3)}$ 4 54
(Eric Alston) *led far side: drvn over 2f out: hdd over 1f out: sn btn: 10th of 12 in gp* **40/1**

0030 **23** *6* **Jedward (IRE)**^{13} 6190 6-9-6 **84**..........................(p) NeilCallan 11 35
(Kevin Ryan) *stall opened early: swtchd lft and hld up bhd ldng gp far side: rdn over 2f out: sn btn: 11th of 12 in gp* **20/1**

3110 **24** *2 3/4* **Gottcher**^{23} 5889 5-8-9 **73**.. TomEaves 5 14
(Keith Dalgleish) *chsd far side ldrs tl rdn and wknd 2f out: last of 12 in gp* **28/1**

1m 1.62s (2.22) **Going Correction** +0.375s/f (Good)
WFA 3 from 4yo+ 1lb **24** Ran SP% **128.2**
Speed ratings (Par 105): **97,96,96,95,95 95,94,93,91,91 91,88,88,87,86 86,86,85,84,82 82,80,70,66**
Tote Swingers 1&2 £21.80, 2&3 £15.50, 1&3 £54.50 CSF £153.65 CT £1068.33 TOTE £19.10: £3.60, £3.00, £2.40, £4.40; EX 161.20 Trifecta £318.30 Pool: £1,145.90 - 2.70 winning tickets..
Owner The Senators **Bred** Rathbarry Stud **Trained** Great Habton, N Yorks
■ Stewards' Enquiry : Jordan NasonJ two-day ban; used whip above permitted level (4th,5th Oct).

FOCUS
The field split into two groups early and, although there didn't seem to be that much between them during the contest and a low-drawn horse went close to winning, seven of the first eight places went to those who raced up the nearside.

6584 SHADWELL STUD/E B F STALLIONS HARRY ROSEBERY STKS (LISTED RACE) 5f
2:50 (2:51) (Class 1) 2-Y-O

£19,848 (£7,525; £3,766; £1,876; £941; £472) **Stalls High**

Form RPR
2 **1** **Hurryupharriet (IRE)**^{27} 5771 2-8-12 0.......................... TomEaves 3 98
(W McCreery, Ire) *broke smartly: mde all: edgd rt 1f out: drvn out* **5/1**^{3}

4112 **2** *3/4* **Mecca's Angel (IRE)**^{27} 5767 2-8-12 **95**.................. PaulMulrennan 9 95
(Michael Dods) *sn w wnr: drvn 2f out: n.m.r jst ins fnl f: no ex clsng stages* **3/1**^{1}

1211 **3** *hd* **Umneyati**^{30} 5648 2-8-12 **84**.................................... NeilCallan 10 95
(James Tate) *sn chsng ldrs: swtchd lft 1f out: kpt on wl* **12/1**

6130 **4** *2 1/4* **Oasis Town**^{29} 5679 2-8-12 **89**..................................... GrahamLee 5 87
(Kevin Ryan) *dwlt: in rr: styd on wl fnl f* **9/1**

1004 **5** *1* **Lady Chantilly (IRE)**^{35} 5476 2-8-12 **90**....................... JoeFanning 2 83
(Jo Hughes) *in rr: hdwy over 1f out: styd on towards fin* **25/1**

0441 **6** *3/4* **Blithe Spirit**^{34} 5509 2-8-12 **81**............................... JasonHart 4 80
(Eric Alston) *chsd ldrs: wknd fnl 150yds* **22/1**

0014 **7** *1 1/4* **Bahamian Heights**^{13} 6201 2-9-3 **96**..................(b) JamieSpencer 8 81
(Clive Brittain) *in rr: sme hdwy over 2f out: nvr a factor* **5/1**^{3}

0212 **8** *1 3/4* **Back Lane**^{42} 5236 2-9-3 **85**..................................... PaulHanagan 6 74
(Richard Fahey) *prom: early: outpcd after 2f: hdwy 2f out: sn rdn and wknd* **9/1**

411 **9** *2 1/2* **Fast Track**^{48} 5012 2-9-3 **86**................................... GrahamGibbons 1 65
(David Barron) *w ldrs: drvn over 2f out: lost pl over 1f out* **9/2**^{2}

1m 1.72s (2.32) **Going Correction** +0.375s/f (Good) **9** Ran SP% **112.4**
Speed ratings (Par 103): **96,94,94,90,89 88,86,83,79**
Tote Swingers 1&2 £6.00, 2&3 £3.90, 1&3 £11.10 CSF £19.67 TOTE £4.30: £1.80, £1.60, £2.20; EX 8.10 Trifecta £81.50 Pool: £2,044.51 - 18.79 winning tickets..
Owner John C Davies **Bred** P Burns **Trained** The Curragh, Co.Kildare

FOCUS
This Listed event has gone to some decent types in the past ten years including the subsequent Group-race winners Captain Gerrard and Garswood. The front pair dominated throughout in this year's renewal.

6585 UAE H'CAP 2m 1f 105y
3:25 (3:26) (Class 3) (0-95,90) 4-Y-0+ **£10,350** (£3,080; £1,539; £769) **Stalls Low**

Form RPR
1402 **1** **Mister Pagan**^{25} 5831 5-8-10 **79**.............................. GrahamLee 10 87+
(Jim Goldie) *hld up in midfield: effrt and rdn over 2f out: styd on wl fnl f to ld towards fin* **10/1**

2-00 **2** *1/2* **Albert Bridge**^{118} 2654 5-9-4 **87**................................ JimCrowley 5 95
(Ralph Beckett) *racd wd: hld up in midfield: effrt and hdwy over 2f out: drvn to ld over 1f out: kpt on: hdd nr fin* **9/2**^{1}

6203 **3** *1 1/2* **Rocktherunway (IRE)**^{12} 6237 4-8-7 **81**...........(p) ConnorBeasley$^{(5)}$ 1 87
(Michael Dods) *hld up in midfield: smooth hdwy over 2f out: rdn and ev ch over 1f out: kpt on same pce ins fnl f* **12/1**

2662 **4** *2 1/4* **Moidore**^{21} 5946 4-9-7 **90**..................................... MichaelO'Connell 7 93
(John Quinn) *led 2f: chsd ldr: led over 3f out: sn rdn: hdd over 1f out: outpcd ins fnl f* **6/1**^{3}

16-0 **5** *9* **Los Nadis (GER)**^{11} 1273 9-8-7 **79**........................ NeilFarley$^{(3)}$ 4 72
(Jim Goldie) *rn in snatches: towards rr: drvn after 6f: plugged on fr 2f out: nvr on terms* **25/1**

6125 **6** *3 1/2* **Hawk Mountain (UAE)**^{12} 6237 8-8-7 **76**........................ TomEaves 8 64
(John Quinn) *towards rr: pushed along after 4f: drvn over 3f out: no imp fr 2f out* **33/1**

013- **7** *1 1/4* **New Youmzain (FR)**^{336} 7211 4-8-12 **81**...................... MartinHarley 6 68
(Mick Channon) *prom: rdn over 3f out: wknd over 2f out* **16/1**

41-0 **8** *3 1/2* **Face Value**^{30} 5663 5-8-3 **75**.............................(p) IJBrennan$^{(3)}$ 11 58
(Adrian McGuinness, Ire) *sn drvn in rr: hdwy to ld after 2f: clr after 6f to over 5f out: hdd over 3f out: wknd fr 2f out* **16/1**

3611 **9** *4 1/2* **Almagest**^{36} 5423 5-9-5 **88**...................................... DanielTudhope 9 65
(David O'Meara) *hld up: rdn over 3f out: sn struggling* **9/1**

233 **10** *1 3/4* **Twelve Strings (IRE)**[21] 5946 4-8-13 **82**.................... JamieSpencer 12 57
(Brian Ellison) *chsd ldrs: drvn over 3f out: wknd 2f out* **6/1**[3]
2102 **11** *16* **Flashman**[12] 6237 4-8-10 **79**.................................... PaulHanagan 13 35
(Richard Fahey) *towards rr and sn pushed along: struggling 4f out: sn btn* **11/2**[2]
/10- **12** *62* **Bright Abbey**[20] 6933 5-8-9 **77** ow1.......................... PaulMulrennan 2
(Dianne Sayer) *bhd: lost tch 1/2-way: virtually p.u fnl 4f* **33/1**
0256 **13** *1 1/4* **Scatter Dice (IRE)**[13] 6192 4-9-4 **87**.......................... JoeFanning 3
(Mark Johnston) *in tch: lost pl over 6f out: virtually p.u fnl 3f* **10/1**
3m 59.51s (-0.19) **Going Correction** +0.125s/f (Good) **13** Ran SP% **119.5**
Speed ratings (Par 107): **105,104,104,103,98 97,96,94,92,91 84,55,54**
Tote Swingers 1&2 £6.50, 2&3 £13.50, 1&3 £17.90 CSF £53.59 CT £554.24 TOTE £13.10: £3.70, £2.10, £3.00; EX 77.70 Trifecta £826.60 Pool: £1,293.60 - 1.17 winning tickets..
Owner Richard Murray **Bred** Richard Murray & Archie Turner **Trained** Uplawmoor, E Renfrews
FOCUS
A decent staying handicap, run at a true pace, and they finished well spread out.

6586 WILLIAM HILL AYR BRONZE CUP (H'CAP) 6f
4:00 (4:01) (Class 2) 3-Y-0+
£15,562 (£4,660; £2,330; £1,165; £582; £292) **Stalls** Centre

Form RPR
4142 **1** **Circuitous**[1] 6548 5-8-11 **74**...............................(v) TomEaves 27 82
(Keith Dalgleish) *mde all stands' side: hrd pressed fnl f: hld on gamely: 1st of 14 in gp* **14/1**
0010 **2** *hd* **Green Howard**[14] 6164 5-9-1 **81**.............................. JasonHart(3) 15 89
(Robin Bastiman) *midfield stands' side: nt clr run over 2f out: hdwy over 1f out: disp ld ins fnl f: jst hld: 2nd of 14 in gp* **33/1**
2413 **3** *1/2* **Tatlisu (IRE)**[10] 6278 3-8-12 **82**...................... GeorgeChaloner(5) 18 88
(Richard Fahey) *hld up bhd ldng gp stands' side: hdwy to chse ldrs over 1f out: kpt on ins fnl f: 3rd of 14 in gp* **25/1**
0054 **4** *1* **Best Trip (IRE)**[14] 6162 6-9-5 **82**......................... GrahamGibbons 20 85
(Brian Ellison) *in tch stands' side: n.m.r over 2f out and over 1f out: effrt whn checked 1f out: kpt on towards fin: 4th of 14 in gp* **8/1**[2]
0502 **5** *hd* **Farlow (IRE)**[36] 5437 5-9-8 **85**.............................. PaulHanagan 13 87+
(Richard Fahey) *hld up far side: gd hdwy over 1f out: led that gp wl ins fnl f: nt rch stands' side gp: 1st of 13 in gp* **14/1**
6211 **6** *1 1/2* **Ashpan Sam**[14] 6162 4-9-9 **86** 8ex............................ PhillipMakin 3 84+
(John Spearing) *led far side: rdn 2f out: hdd wl ins fnl f: one pce: 2nd of 13 in gp* **10/1**[3]
4112 **7** *1 1/4* **Shady McCoy (USA)**[34] 5541 3-9-1 **80**...................... RobertWinston 4 74
(David Barron) *dwlt: hld up far side: hdwy and prom over 2f out: sn rdn: kpt on same pce fnl f: 3rd of 13 in gp* **8/1**[2]
0050 **8** *3/4* **Cheveton**[9] 6309 9-9-5 **82**.. JoeFanning 7 74
(Richard Price) *chsd far side ldrs: drvn over 2f out: kpt on same pce fnl f: 4th of 13 in gp* **20/1**
0306 **9** *nse* **Valmina**[6] 6382 6-8-8 **74**...(t) RobertTart(3) 17 66
(Tony Carroll) *hld up stands' side: nt clr run over 2f out: hdwy over 1f out: kpt on fnl f: nvr able to chal: 5th of 14 in gp* **50/1**
0402 **10** *nk* **Kimberella**[27] 5748 3-9-5 **84**.................................... RobertHavlin 24 75
(Michael Attwater) *prom stands' side: rdn 2f out: kpt on same pce fnl f: 6th of 14 in gp* **25/1**
2603 **11** *2 1/2* **West Leake Hare (IRE)**[3] 6496 4-9-1 **78**.................. AdrianNicholls 12 61
(David Nicholls) *dwlt: bhd far side: rdn and hdwy over 1f out: nvr rchd ldrs: 5th of 13 in gp* **33/1**
600 **12** *1/2* **Jinky**[18] 6052 5-8-7 **75**... ShaneGray(5) 9 57
(Linda Perratt) *prom far side: rdn over 2f out: one pce over 1f out: 6th of 13 in gp* **50/1**
1500 **13** *hd* **Personal Touch**[48] 4983 4-8-11 **81**....................... SamanthaBell(7) 5 62
(Richard Fahey) *t.k.h: midfield far side: pushed along over 2f out: no imp over 1f out: 7th of 13 in gp* **28/1**
0541 **14** *nk* **Indego Blues**[13] 6209 4-8-12 **75** 5ex................................ PaulQuinn 11 55
(David Nicholls) *in tch on outside of far side gp: drvn over 2f out: wknd over 1f out: 8th of 13 in gp* **20/1**
5241 **15** *nse* **Mutafaakir (IRE)**[13] 6205 4-8-13 **76** 5ex.......................(p) MartinHarley 2 56
(Ruth Carr) *t.k.h: trckd far side ldrs: rdn over 2f out: wknd over 1f out: 9th of 13 in gp* **25/1**
1113 **16** *1 1/2* **Bondi Beach Boy**[10] 6273 4-8-12 **82**...................... JordanNason(7) 23 58
(James Turner) *chsd stands' side ldrs: rdn over 2f out: no ex over 1f out: 7th of 14 in gp* **25/1**
6413 **17** *3/4* **Right Touch**[12] 6238 3-9-2 **81** 5ex............................... JamieSpencer 10 54
(Richard Fahey) *bhd far side: rdn along over 2f out: nvr rchd ldrs: 10th of 13 in gp* **12/1**
4131 **18** *3/4* **Hadaj**[10] 6273 4-9-5 **87** 5ex.. DavidBergin(5) 26 58
(Ruth Carr) *chsd stands' side ldrs: rdn over 2f out: wkng whn hmpd over 1f out: 8th of 14 in gp* **16/1**
441 **19** *nk* **Algar Lad**[41] 5266 3-8-11 **76**... GrahamLee 21 46
(Jim Goldie) *hld up stands' side: rdn along over 2f out: n.d: 9th of 14 in gp* **20/1**
0002 **20** *1/2* **Rusty Rocket (IRE)**[14] 6159 4-9-8 **85**....................... PaulMulrennan 19 54
(Paul Green) *in tch on outer of stands' side gp: drvn along 1/2-way: wknd over 1f out: 10th of 14 in gp* **25/1**
4300 **21** *3/4* **Lisiere (IRE)**[8] 6341 4-8-13 **76**...................................(v[1]) JimCrowley 14 43
(K R Burke) *bhd on outside of stands' side gp: drvn along 1/2-way: nvr on terms: 11th of 14 in gp* **40/1**
4331 **22** *1/2* **Bop It**[14] 6161 4-9-9 **86** 5ex.. DanielTudhope 22 51
(David O'Meara) *chsd stands' side ldrs: rdn over 2f out: wknd over 1f out: 12th of 14 in gp* **11/2**[1]
0004 **23** *nk* **Mary's Daughter**[12] 6238 3-9-3 **82**.............................. TonyHamilton 6 46
(Richard Fahey) *chsd far side ldrs: rdn over 2f out: wknd over 1f out: 11th of 13 in gp* **22/1**
0000 **24** *nk* **Yair Hill (IRE)**[21] 5943 5-9-5 **87**.............................. JoeyHaynes(5) 25 50
(Noel Wilson) *chsd stands' side ldrs: rdn over 2f out: lost pl wl over 1f out: 13th of 14 in gp* **50/1**
1100 **25** *3/4* **Nasharra (IRE)**[34] 5544 5-9-6 **83**.................................(tp) NeilCallan 16 44
(Kevin Ryan) *dwlt: bhd stands' side: rdn 1/2-way: hdwy whn hmpd over 1f out: sn btn: last of 14 in gp* **66/1**
212 **26** *2 1/2* **Tidal's Baby**[20] 5998 4-8-9 **77**.............................. GeorgeDowning(5) 1 31
(Tony Carroll) *midfield far side: drvn along over 2f out: sn btn: 12th of 13 in gp* **18/1**
0103 **27** *1 1/2* **Half A Billion (IRE)**[54] 4812 4-8-13 **81**................... ConnorBeasley(5) 8 30
(Michael Dods) *chsd far side ldrs tl wknd over 2f out: last of 13 in gp* **33/1**
1m 13.86s (1.46) **Going Correction** +0.375s/f (Good)
WFA 3 from 4yo+ 2lb **27** Ran SP% **138.8**
Speed ratings (Par 109): **105,104,104,102,102 100,98,97,97,97 94,93,93,92,92 90,89,88,88,87 86,85,85,85,84 80,78**
Tote Swingers 1&2 £88.10, 2&3 £0.00, 1&3 £88.10 CSF £427.55 CT £11017.59 TOTE £15.70: £5.30, £9.80, £7.20, £2.60; EX 999.10 TRIFECTA Not won..

Owner Alison Walker Sarah Cousins **Bred** Deepwood Farm Stud **Trained** Carluke, S Lanarks
■ Stewards' Enquiry : Tom Eaves one-day ban; careless riding (4th Oct).
FOCUS
It was inevitable the field would soon split into two and, as in the earlier sprint handicap, those who raced up the nearside just held sway with the first four coming from that group. Also, as in that contest, the winner was drawn closest to the stands' rail.

6587 LOWMAC RECYCLING H'CAP (DIV I) 1m
4:35 (4:35) (Class 5) (0-70,70) 3-Y-O **£3,881** (£1,155; £577; £288) **Stalls** Low

Form RPR
6330 **1** **The Scuttler (IRE)**[21] 5975 3-8-13 **62**............................ MartinHarley 5 72
(Mick Channon) *in tch: quicekned to ld 2f out: sn drvn clr* **12/1**
3054 **2** *4* **Dark Ocean (IRE)**[32] 5580 3-9-3 **66**........................ MichaelO'Connell 9 67
(Jedd O'Keeffe) *squeezed out s: t.k.h in rr: hdwy over 2f out: chsd wnr 1f out: no imp* **4/1**[1]
5226 **3** *2 3/4* **Hanalei Bay (IRE)**[4] 6464 3-9-1 **64**.............................. TomEaves 8 59
(Keith Dalgleish) *rr-div: hdwy over 2f out: styd on to take modest 3rd nr fin* **12/1**
6506 **4** *nk* **Kolonel Kirkup**[32] 5581 3-8-6 **60**.......................[1] ConnorBeasley(5) 10 54
(Michael Dods) *mid-div: hdwy over 2f out: kpt on ins fnl f* **10/1**
3360 **5** *1/2* **Ingleby Symphony (IRE)**[48] 4994 3-9-6 **69**...............(b[1]) PaulHanagan 1 62
(Richard Fahey) *chsd ldr: lft in ld bnd 4f out: hdd 2f out: one pce* **4/1**[1]
3305 **6** *2 3/4* **Admirable Art (IRE)**[18] 6042 3-8-11 **60**............................ GrahamLee 3 47
(Tony Carroll) *s.i.s: mid-div: hdwy over 2f out: sn chsng ldrs: wknd fnl 100yds* **6/1**[3]
0222 **7** *1 1/2* **Emperatriz**[24] 5870 3-9-2 **65**... RobertHavlin 4 49
(John Holt) *trckd ldrs: drvn over 2f out: wknd fnl 150yds* **9/2**[2]
400 **8** *2 1/2* **Echo Of Lightning**[48] 5016 3-8-2 **56** oh6........................ JoeyHaynes(5) 2 35
(Noel Wilson) *t.k.h: led: hung bdly rt bnd over 4f out: sn hdd: c stands' side: wknd fnl 2f* **40/1**
-650 **9** *9* **Winged Icarus (USA)**[43] 5195 3-8-5 **57**.....................(b[1]) JasonHart(3) 7 16
(Brian Ellison) *in rr: drvn over 3f out: nvr on terms: bhd whn eased ins fnl f* **9/1**
554 **10** *4 1/2* **Krupskaya (FR)**[6] 6410 3-9-0 **70**..................................... BTTreanor(7) 6 19
(K R Burke) *mid-div: drvn over 3f out: bhd fnl 2f: eased clsng stages* **25/1**
-005 **11** *hd* **King Of Kudos (IRE)**[7] 6367 3-9-1 **64**........................ RobertWinston 11 12
(Scott Dixon) *chsd ldrs: lft 2nd bnd over 3f out: lost pl over 1f out: eased whn bhd clsng stages* **22/1**
1m 44.49s (0.69) **Going Correction** +0.125s/f (Good) **11** Ran SP% **117.6**
Speed ratings (Par 101): **101,97,94,93,93 90,89,86,77,73 73**
Tote Swingers 1&2 £12.80, 2&3 £8.00, 1&3 £16.20 CSF £58.41 CT £602.22 TOTE £14.10: £3.40, £2.00, £4.80; EX 88.30 Trifecta £608.40 Pool: £2,350.50 - 2.89 winning tickets..
Owner Lord Ilsley Racing (Hern Syndicate) **Bred** J Hanly **Trained** West Ilsley, Berks
FOCUS
An ordinary handicap.

6588 LOWMAC RECYCLING H'CAP (DIV II) 1m
5:10 (5:11) (Class 5) (0-70,70) 3-Y-O **£3,881** (£1,155; £577; £288) **Stalls** Low

Form RPR
062 **1** **Trixie Malone**[119] 2613 3-8-2 **56** oh4............................ JoeyHaynes(5) 1 66+
(K R Burke) *trckd ldrs: led and rdn 2f out: hld on wl fnl f* **14/1**
3321 **2** *hd* **Mash Potato (IRE)**[35] 5483 3-9-3 **66**......................(p) PaulMulrennan 6 76+
(Michael Dods) *hld up towards rr: hdwy over 3f out: effrt and chsd wnr over 1f out: ev ch fnl f: hld nr fin* **2/1**[1]
100 **3** *5* **Natures Law (IRE)**[30] 5642 3-8-11 **60**.............................. JoeFanning 3 59
(Keith Dalgleish) *trckd ldrs: effrt and ev ch 2f out: sn rdn: outpcd by first two fnl f* **16/1**
2132 **4** *3 1/4* **Thankyou Very Much**[14] 6154 3-9-0 **63**...................... JamieSpencer 7 55
(James Bethell) *sn pushed along in rr: hdwy over 3f out: sn rdn: no imp fr 2f out* **7/2**[2]
4633 **5** *3/4* **Medici Dancer**[21] 5975 3-9-7 **70**.................................(p) DuranFentiman 4 60
(Tim Easterby) *prom: rdn over 2f out: hung lft over 1f out: sn btn* **6/1**[3]
5066 **6** *8* **Old Man Clegg**[1] 6549 3-9-2 **65**..............................(bt[1]) GrahamGibbons 5 38
(Michael Easterby) *t.k.h: hld up: rdn over 2f out: sn wknd* **14/1**
5610 **7** *4 1/2* **Lucy Bee**[32] 5594 3-8-9 **61**... JasonHart(3) 10 24
(R Mike Smith) *led tl rdn and hdd 2f out: sn btn* **16/1**
0440 **8** *shd* **Mujarrad (USA)**[76] 4068 3-9-4 **67**..................................... TomEaves 9 29
(Ian Semple) *hld up: pushed along wl over 2f out: sn btn* **12/1**
1320 **9** *1/2* **Just A Pound (IRE)**[84] 3772 3-8-11 **60**.......................... RobertHavlin 8 21
(Jo Hughes) *midfield: rdn and outpcd over 3f out: sn btn* **16/1**
3635 **10** *nk* **Mowhoob**[4] 6464 3-9-1 **64**... GrahamLee 2 25
(Jim Goldie) *midfield: struggling 4f out: n.d after* **8/1**
1m 44.39s (0.59) **Going Correction** +0.125s/f (Good) **10** Ran SP% **119.6**
Speed ratings (Par 101): **102,101,96,93,92 84,80,80,79,79**
Tote Swingers 1&2 £7.70, 2&3 £8.30, 1&3 £24.50 CSF £43.40 CT £492.99 TOTE £14.60: £2.50, £1.30, £5.40; EX 60.90 Trifecta £1569.70 Pool: £3,052.82 - 1.45 winning tickets..
Owner Mrs Elaine M Burke **Bred** Llety Stud **Trained** Middleham Moor, N Yorks
■ Stewards' Enquiry : Paul Mulrennan two-day ban; used whip above permitted level (4th,5th Oct).
FOCUS
They went a strong pace and the field finished well spread out, though the final time was only 0.1sec quicker than the first division. The runners raced away from the inside rail in the straight.
T/Jkpt: Not won. T/Plt: £332.80 to a £1 stake. Pool: £96,133.40 - 210.86 winning tickets. T/Qpdt: £48.00 to a £1 stake. Pool: £9,668.15 - 148.8 winning tickets. RY

5529 NEWBURY (L-H)
Friday, September 20

OFFICIAL GOING: Soft (6.2)
Wind: mild breeze against Weather: sunny

6589 FREE BETS FREEBETS.CO.UK E B F MAIDEN STKS (DIV I) 6f 8y
1:30 (1:30) (Class 4) 2-Y-O **£4,528** (£1,347; £673; £336) **Stalls** High

Form RPR
0 **1** **Black Caesar (IRE)**[21] 5957 2-9-5 0........................... RichardHughes 1 82+
(Richard Hannon) *str: led whn swtchd to stands' side rails after 1f: r.o strly fnl f: pushed out* **6/1**[2]
4 **2** *1 3/4* **Hesbaan (IRE)**[14] 6169 2-9-5 0.................................... DaneO'Neill 2 77+
(Marcus Tregoning) *w'like: str: lw: sn trcking wnr: rdn over 1f out: kpt on but nt pce to chal* **4/1**[1]
05 **3** *1 1/4* **Stomp**[30] 5646 2-9-5 0.. GeorgeBaker 5 73+
(Roger Charlton) *str: lw: broke wl: led for 1f: trckd ldrs: rdn ent fnl f: kpt on but nt pce to get on terms* **13/2**[3]
06 **4** *5* **Dream Impossible (IRE)**[21] 5949 2-9-0 0.................. JimmyFortune 10 53
(Peter Makin) *in tch: pushed along wl over 2f out: sn rdn: disputing 4th whn outpcd by ldrs wl over 1f out: kpt on same pce fnl f* **33/1**

0 5 nse **Prize**133 2204 2-9-0 0 RyanMoore 11 53
(Richard Hannon) *leggy: cl cpld: mid-div: rdn over 2f out: disputing 4th whn outpcd by ldrs wl over 1f out: kpt on same pce fnl f* **4/1**1
6 1 ½ **Lacock** 2-9-5 0 FergusSweeney 12 60+
(Henry Candy) *unf: scope: hld up towards rr on rails: nt clr run fr 3f out tl pushed along 2f out: styng on but no threat to ldrs whn nt clr run again jst over 1f out: no further imp* **4/1**1
40 7 1 ½ **Biotic**32 5584 2-9-5 0 AndreaAtzeni 7 49
(Rod Millman) *tall: mid-div tl lost pl 3f out: sn struggling: sme late prog but nvr a threat after* **25/1**
8 nk **Pendo** 2-9-5 0 LiamKeniry 9 48+
(Alastair Lidderdale) *w'like: tall: s.i.s: towards rr: swtchd lft over 1f out: sme late prog into midfield: nvr a danger* **100/1**
9 1 ¼ **See No Ships** 2-9-0 0 DavidProbert 6 39
(Mark Usher) *leggy: lean: mid-div: rdn over 2f out: wknd over 1f out* **100/1**
0 10 6 **Come On Lila**78 3986 2-9-0 0 JohnFahy 8 21
(Alex Hales) *w'like: bit bkwd: towards rr: sme prog in centre whn bmpd over 1f out: sn wknd* **100/1**
11 1 ¾ **Excedo Praecedo** 2-9-5 0 PatDobbs 3 21
(Amanda Perrett) *w'like: tall: s.i.s: towards rr: hdwy in centre after 2f: rdn whn swtchd lft over 1f out: sn wknd* **20/1**
12 1 ¼ **Strategic Force (IRE)** 2-9-5 0 AdamKirby 4 17
(Clive Cox) *w'like: tall: chsd ldrs: rdn 2f out: wknd over 1f out* **9/1**

1m 15.21s (2.21) **Going Correction** +0.325s/f (Good) **12** Ran SP% **112.1**
Speed ratings (Par 97): **98,95,94,87,87 85,83,82,81,73 70,69**
Tote Swingers 1&2 £5.20, 2&3 £3.70, 1&3 £9.00 CSF £27.01 TOTE £6.60: £2.00, £1.30, £2.50; EX 33.60 Trifecta £157.40 Pool: £2,216.74 - 10.56 winning tickets..
Owner Carmichael Humber **Bred** Miss Hilary Mullen **Trained** East Everleigh, Wilts

FOCUS
The going was officially soft on a relatively warm day. The first division of a decent maiden that has thrown up subsequent Group winners Stimulation, Pastoral Player and Mince. The runners came up the stands' rail and the first three (all drawn towards the outside) held those positions throughout. Thet finished clear and these ratings don't flatter.

6590 FREE BETS FREEBETS.CO.UK E B F MAIDEN STKS (DIV II) 6f 8y
2:00 (2:00) (Class 4) 2-Y-O **£4,528** (£1,347; £673; £336) **Stalls** High

Form RPR
1 **Cape Wrath** 2-9-5 0 RichardHughes 3 83+
(Richard Hannon) *w'like: lengthy: lw: s.i.s: towards rr: gd hdwy to ld over 1f out: rdn ent fnl f: r.o wl to assert fnl 120yds* **2/1**1
2 ¾ **Dark Leopard** 2-9-5 0 JamesDoyle 9 81+
(Roger Charlton) *cmpt: mid-div: smooth hdwy fr 2f out to chal jst over 1f out: sn rdn: ev ch ins fnl f: kpt on but hld fnl 120yds* **3/1**2
3 3 ¼ **Nissaki Kasta** 2-9-0 0 SilvestreDeSousa 8 67+
(Hughie Morrison) *lengthy: lw: mid-div: pushed along and hdwy over 2f out: rdn to chse ldng pair over 1f out: kpt on but nt pce to get on terms* **7/1**
4 1 ½ **Pipe Dream** 2-9-5 0 JimmyFortune 1 66
(Brian Meehan) *unf: scope: mid-div: rdn over 2f out: squeezed up ent fnl f: styd on to snatch 4th fnl strides* **9/1**
00 5 hd **Cueca (FR)**44 5131 2-8-11 0 MatthewLawson(3) 4 60
(Jonathan Portman) *w'like: trckd ldrs: rdn to dispute ld 2f out tl over 1f out: kpt on same pce: lost 4th fnl strides* **33/1**
0 6 1 **Zugzwang (IRE)**14 6169 2-9-2 0 MarkCoumbe(3) 2 62
(Ed de Giles) *w'like: s.i.s: t.k.h in rr: swtchd lft: rdn and hdwy over 1f out: nt clr run ent fnl f: no further imp* **16/1**
0 7 ¾ **Coiste Bodhar (IRE)**37 5399 2-8-12 0 NoraLooby(7) 10 63
(Joseph Tuite) *trckd ldrs: pushed along whn nt clr run 2f out: squeezed up ent fnl f: nt a threat after* **66/1**
8 hd **Stan Nineteen (IRE)** 2-9-5 0 PatCosgrave 11 68+
(George Baker) *w'like: tall: lw: s.i.s: towards rr on rail: stdy hdwy whn nt clr run and snatched up over 1f out: swtchd lft but no ch after* **20/1**
0 9 3 **Ignight**53 4827 2-9-5 0 DavidProbert 5 50
(Mark Usher) *trckd ldrs: rdn to dispute ld 2f out tl over 1f out: wknd ins fnl f* **66/1**
05 10 2 **Beatabout The Bush (IRE)**32 5584 2-9-5 0 WilliamBuick 7 44
(Charles Hills) *leggy: led tl rdn 2f out: sn wknd* **6/1**3
11 1 **With A Twist** 2-9-0 0 (t) LiamKeniry 6 36
(Andrew Balding) *w'like: slowly away: a in rr* **12/1**

1m 16.47s (3.47) **Going Correction** +0.325s/f (Good) **11** Ran SP% **119.4**
Speed ratings (Par 97): **89,88,83,81,81 80,79,78,74,72 70**
Tote Swingers 1&2 £2.20, 2&3 £6.40, 1&3 £4.80 CSF £7.73 TOTE £3.50: £1.20, £1.90, £2.40; EX 10.10 Trifecta £68.70 Pool: £2,338.78 - 25.52 winning tickets..
Owner Lady Rothschild **Bred** Kincorth Investments Inc **Trained** East Everleigh, Wilts
■ Stewards' Enquiry : Mark Coumbe caution; falling to ride out.
Pat Cosgrave caution; failed to ride out.

FOCUS
The second leg of the maiden and the time was 1.26secs slower than the first. Unlike that race this was dominated by newcomers. The winner looks sure to rate higher.

6591 DUBAI DUTY FREE FINEST SURPRISE H'CAP 1m 4f 5y
2:30 (2:31) (Class 3) (0-95,94) 3-Y-O+ **£7,439** (£2,213; £1,106; £553) **Stalls** Centre

Form RPR
2100 1 **Sula Two**12 6237 6-8-10 **83** PhilipPrince(5) 5 90
(Ron Hodges) *trckd ldrs: rdn wl over 3f out: chsd ldr over 2f out: chal ent fnl f: hrd rdn to ld fnl 120yds: hld on: all out* **16/1**
1420 2 hd **Goodwood Mirage (IRE)**13 6186 3-9-4 **94** FrankieDettori 7 101
(William Knight) *hld up towards rr: last 6f out: swtchd rt and stdy prog fr over 3f out: rdn 2f out: wnt 3rd ent fnl f: styd on wl to go 2nd nring fin: nt quite rching wnr* **7/2**1
0330 3 ½ **Sir Bedivere (IRE)**21 5946 4-9-4 **86** (t) JimmyFortune 9 92
(Brian Meehan) *trckd ldr: led over 3f out: rdn wl over 1f out: jnd ent fnl f: hdd fnl 120yds: styd on: lost 3rd nring finsh* **20/1**
4415 4 1 ¼ **She's Late**14 6172 3-8-10 **86** WilliamBuick 11 90
(John Gosden) *hld up in last trio: rdn and hdwy wl over 2f out: chsd ldng pair over 2f out tl ent fnl f: styd on but no ex* **7/2**1
0-50 5 ½ **Signed Up**27 5746 4-9-7 **89** PatDobbs 8 93
(Amanda Perrett) *mid-div: rdn over 3f out: styd on same pce fnl 2f* **8/1**
1122 6 ½ **Continuum**35 5475 4-9-12 **94** JamesDoyle 3 97
(Lady Cecil) *s.i.s: in rr: nudged along whn swtchd to centre over 3f out: rdn over 2f out: little imp tl styd on fnl f: nvr rching ldrs* **4/1**2
5634 7 2 **All The Aces (IRE)**30 5655 8-9-9 **91** TomQueally 2 91
(Nicky Henderson) *lw: trckd ldrs: rdn over 3f out: nvr gng pce to get on terms: fdd ins fnl f* **11/1**
004- 8 ½ **Samba King**314 7689 4-9-8 **90** MickaelBarzalona 4 89
(Charlie Appleby) *mid-div: rdn over 3f out: nvr any imp: wknd jst over 1f out* **15/2**3
2020 9 13 **Sadler's Risk (IRE)**27 5746 5-9-10 **92** (v1) SilvestreDeSousa 6 72
(Mark Johnston) *led tl rdn over 3f out: sn btn* **10/1**

2m 36.27s (0.77) **Going Correction** +0.25s/f (Good)
WFA 3 from 4yo+ 8lb **9** Ran SP% **115.4**
Speed ratings (Par 107): **107,106,106,105,105 105,103,103,94**
Tote Swingers 1&2 £9.20, 2&3 £11.40, 1&3 £34.60 CSF £71.43 CT £1147.80 TOTE £17.40: £3.70, £1.90, £5.80; EX 131.10 Trifecta £481.90 Pool: £2,501.93 - 3.89 winning tickets..
Owner Richard Prince **Bred** D R Tucker **Trained** Charlton Mackrell, Somerset
■ Stewards' Enquiry : Philip Prince nine-day ban; used whip above permitted level (4th,5th,7th-13th Oct).
Frankie Dettori two-day ban; used whip above permitted level (4th-5th Oct).

FOCUS
A good middle-distance handicap but a surprise result. A personal best for the winner, who goes well here.

6592 DUBAI DUTY FREE CONDITIONS STKS 1m 1f
3:05 (3:05) (Class 3) 3-Y-O+
£7,158 (£2,143; £1,071; £535; £267; £134) **Stalls** Centre

Form RPR
04-5 1 **Tales Of Grimm (USA)**112 2840 4-8-11 105 RyanMoore 3 106
(Richard Fahey) *hld up last but wl in tch: tk clsr order 3f out: rdn to chse ldr wl over 1f out: styd on to ld fnl 120yds: kpt on wl and a holding on after* **6/1**3
01-1 2 nk **French Navy**83 3839 5-9-6 110 MickaelBarzalona 2 114
(Charlie Appleby) *t.k.h: trckd ldrs: snatched up whn short of room on bnd 6f out: smooth prog to ld wl over 2f out: rdn over 1f out: hdd fnl 120yds: styd on but no ex* **5/4**1
6-30 3 3 ½ **Bonfire**134 2186 4-9-3 106 RichardHughes 4 104
(Andrew Balding) *racd keenly: trckd ldr: travelling wl enough whn joining ldrs 3f out: drifted rt whn rdn over 2f out: fnd little: lost 2nd over 1f out* **3/1**2
-254 4 1 **Mujazif (IRE)**14 6163 3-8-6 91 (t) MartinDwyer 5 97
(Brian Meehan) *trckd ldrs: rdn 3f out: styd on same pce fnl 2f* **8/1**
3044 5 7 **Questioning (IRE)**25 5822 5-8-11 102 (b) WilliamBuick 1 81
(John Gosden) *lw: led tl rdn wl over 2f out: sn hld: wknd ent fnl f* **8/1**
0500 6 5 **Navajo Chief**29 5681 6-9-3 102 JamesDoyle 6 77
(Alan Jarvis) *hld up in last pair but wl in tch: effrt 3f out: wknd 2f out* **20/1**

1m 56.07s (0.57) **Going Correction** +0.25s/f (Good)
WFA 3 from 4yo+ 5lb **6** Ran SP% **110.7**
Speed ratings (Par 107): **107,106,103,102,96 92**
Tote Swingers 1&2 £2.20, 2&3 £2.10, 1&3 £1.80 CSF £13.65 TOTE £5.50: £2.50, £1.40; EX 9.80 Trifecta £29.50 Pool: £3,096.43 - 78.69 winning tickets..
Owner Sir Robert Ogden **Bred** Winsong Farms **Trained** Musley Bank, N Yorks

FOCUS
A better than average conditions stakes with all but one of the runners rated in the 100s, but most of these have questions to answer. The initial pace was slow and the form makes sense as rated.

6593 HAYNES, HANSON & CLARK CONDITIONS STKS 1m (S)
3:40 (3:41) (Class 2) 2-Y-O **£9,960** (£2,982; £1,491; £745; £372) **Stalls** High

Form RPR
1 1 **Pinzolo**35 5490 2-9-2 0 MickaelBarzalona 5 97+
(Charlie Appleby) *w'like: scope: str: attractive: trckd ldng trio: nudged along over 3f out: travelling wl on heels of ldrs whn nt clr run jst over 1f out: swtchd rt and r.o strly fnl 100yds: short of room but led narrowly fnl 40yds* **5/2**2
22 2 hd **Red Galileo**28 5727 2-8-12 0 AndreaAtzeni 4 91+
(Ed Dunlop) *lw: racd freely: led: rdn ent fnl f: drifted off stands' rail: jnd whn edgd rt ins fnl 75yds: hdd ins fnl 40yds: kpt on* **6/5**1
01 3 1 ¼ **Pupil (IRE)**8 6330 2-9-2 0 RichardHughes 2 92
(Richard Hannon) *little slowly away: last of 5 but wl in tch: swtchd lft over 2f out: sn rdn: kpt on in clly disp 2nd tl no ex fnl 75yds* **11/2**3
031 4 1 ½ **What About Carlo (FR)**26 5790 2-8-12 79 WilliamBuick 6 85
(Eve Johnson Houghton) *lw: trckd ldrs: swtchd lft over 2f out: rdn and ev ch ent fnl f: fdd fnl 140yds* **7/1**
5 5 14 **Castle Combe (IRE)**26 5790 2-8-12 0 MartinDwyer 1 54
(Marcus Tregoning) *trckd ldr: rdn over 2f out: wknd ent fnl f* **16/1**

1m 40.89s (1.19) **Going Correction** +0.325s/f (Good) **5** Ran SP% **107.8**
Speed ratings (Par 101): **107,106,105,104,90**
Tote Swinger 1&2 £3.90 CSF £5.65 TOTE £3.50: £1.50, £1.60; EX 4.80 Trifecta £14.50 Pool: £2,832.48 - 145.92 winning tickets..
Owner Godolphin **Bred** Fittocks Stud **Trained** Newmarket, Suffolk
■ Stewards' Enquiry : Andrea Atzeni one-day ban; careless riding (4th Oct).

FOCUS
Often an interesting 2yo conditions stakes in which Marcus Tregoning has the best recent record, with five winners since 1999. The winner was alue for extra and looks sure to rate higher.

6594 DUBAI DUTY FREE FULL OF SURPRISES E B F FILLIES' CONDITIONS STKS 7f (S)
4:15 (4:15) (Class 2) 2-Y-O **£9,960** (£2,982; £1,491; £745; £372) **Stalls** High

Form RPR
2643 1 **Lady Lara (IRE)**7 6350 2-8-12 90 JamesDoyle 4 88+
(Alan Jarvis) *lw: trckd ldrs: shkn up to ld ent fnl f: r.o wl: readily* **5/4**1
621 2 1 ¼ **Rosehill Artist (IRE)**15 6140 2-9-2 81 AndreaAtzeni 1 89
(Charles Hills) *led: sn swtchd to stands' side rails: rdn over 1f out: hdd ent fnl f: kpt on but nt pce of wnr* **9/2**3
3 1 ¾ **Water Queen** 2-8-12 0 RyanMoore 6 82+
(William Haggas) *trckd ldrs: rdn over 1f out: nt pce to get on terms: kpt on ins fnl f* **5/2**2
30 4 1 ½ **Dime Dancer (IRE)**15 6140 2-8-12 0 RichardHughes 2 77
(Richard Hannon) *sn swtchd to stands' side rails: trckd ldr: rdn over 1f out: nvr quite ev ch: hld in 3rd fnl f: fdd fnl 75yds* **9/1**
5 5 nse **Persian Bolt (USA)**15 6140 2-8-12 0 JohnFahy 7 77
(Eve Johnson Houghton) *athletic: hld up bhd ldng 4: swtchd lft over 2f out and tk clsr order: rdn over 1f out: outpcd fnl f* **10/1**

1m 30.28s (4.58) **Going Correction** +0.325s/f (Good) **5** Ran SP% **110.3**
Speed ratings (Par 98): **86,84,82,80,80**
Tote Swinger 1&2 £4.00 CSF £7.27 TOTE £2.30: £1.40, £2.00; EX 5.70 Trifecta £15.00 Pool: £2,935.42 - 146.46 winning tickets..
Owner Cedars Two **Bred** Shanty Syndicate **Trained** Twyford, Bucks

FOCUS
A good fillies' conditions stakes that has thrown up the odd group and Listed winner in recent seasons. The time was slow and the winner didn't need to match her May Hill form.

6595 DUBAI DUTY FREE CUP (LISTED RACE) 7f (S)
4:50 (4:50) (Class 1) 3-Y-0+
£20,982 (£7,955; £3,981; £1,983; £995; £499) **Stalls** High

Form RPR
3234 **1** **Tawhid**[13] 6191 3-8-13 111..(p) SilvestreDeSousa 5 111+
(Saeed bin Suroor) *s.i.s: hld up in centre gp: gd hdwy 2f out: led 1f out: rdn clr: readily* **15/8**[1]
0030 **2** 2 1/2 **Enrol**[20] 5992 4-8-11 93.. RyanMoore 2 100
(Sir Michael Stoute) *lw: hld up in centre gp: pushed along and stdy prog fr over 2f out: rdn over 1f out: kpt on to go 2nd fnl 120yds: no ch w wnr* **9/1**
-002 **3** 1 1/4 **Firebeam**[15] 6129 5-9-2 104.. MickaelBarzalona 6 102
(Charlie Appleby) *swtg: led centre gp: rdn over 1f out: hdd ent fnl f: sn outpcd by wnr: no ex whn lost 2nd fnl 120yds* **12/1**
32 **4** 1 **Free Wheeling (AUS)**[202] 869 5-9-2 110....................(tp) JamesDoyle 3 99
(Saeed bin Suroor) *lw: trckd ldrs in centre gp: swtchd to stands' side 2f out: sn rdn: kpt on but nt pce to get involved* **5/1**[3]
3111 **5** 3/4 **Magic City (IRE)**[27] 5738 4-9-2 102.......................... RichardHughes 8 98
(Richard Hannon) *stdd s: sn swtchd to centre gp: swtchd to stands' side gp 2f out: sn rdn: kpt on same pce fnl f* **10/3**[2]
4010 **6** 1/2 **Correspondent**[20] 5992 3-8-13 103.......................... TomQueally 1 95
(Brian Meehan) *swtg: mid-div in chsng gp: rdn over 2f out: no imp* **16/1**
1-0U **7** nk **Fort Bastion (IRE)**[27] 5763 4-9-2 105.......................... JimmyFortune 4 96
(Richard Fahey) *lw: trckd ldr in centre gp: rdn over 2f out: wknd fnl f* **25/1**
10 **8** 2 **Arnold Lane (IRE)**[6] 6392 4-9-5 108.......................... SamHitchcott 7 94
(Mick Channon) *hld up bhd one other on stands' side rails: rdn to chse ldrs but nvr threatened main gp over 2f out: wknd fnl f* **18/1**
1065 **9** 1 3/4 **Well Acquainted (IRE)**[26] 5794 3-8-13 105.......................... JohnFahy 9 85
(Clive Cox) *led stands' side pair: overall chsd ldrs: rdn over 2f out: wknd over 1f out* **14/1**

1m 26.47s (0.77) **Going Correction** +0.325s/f (Good)
WFA 3 from 4yo+ 3lb **9** Ran SP% **113.9**
Speed ratings (Par 111): **108,105,103,102,101 101,100,98,96**
Tote Swingers 1&2 £4.10, 2&3 £10.10, 1&3 £4.20 CSF £19.58 TOTE £3.10: £1.10, £2.50, £2.70; EX 10.00 Trifecta £130.20 Pool: £3,972.44 - 22.87 winning tickets..
Owner Godolphin **Bred** West Lodge Stud **Trained** Newmarket, Suffolk

FOCUS
A Listed race in which Saeed bin Suroor had trained three of the last four winners. He was doubly represented this time and improved his record through Tawhid. The time was 3.81secs faster than the preceding fillies' race and not surprisingly the quickest race of the day furlong-per-furlong on the straight track. The winner was value for a bit extra.

6596 OAKLEY COACHBUILDERS H'CAP 1m 2f 6y
5:20 (5:20) (Class 4) (0-85,85) 3-Y-0+ **£5,822** (£1,299; £1,299; £432) **Stalls** Centre

Form RPR
0040 **1** **Pasaka Boy**[26] 5792 3-9-3 **84**.. PatDobbs 14 90
(Jonathan Portman) *lw: in tch: rdn 3f out: hdwy over 1f out: str run ins fnl f: led fnl stride* **17/2**
3640 **2** hd **Presburg (IRE)**[28] 5723 4-9-3 **78**.. LiamKeniry 8 85
(Joseph Tuite) *towards rr of midfield: prog whn nt clr run 3f out: rdn and hdwy wl over 1f out: c w str run upsides wnr ins fnl f: jst failed* **20/1**
330 **2** dht **Broadway Duchess (IRE)**[20] 6004 3-9-1 **82**.............. RichardHughes 1 89+
(Richard Hannon) *trckd ldrs: nt clr run 2f out tl swtchd rt jst over 1f out: r.o wl to ld fnl 50yds: hdd fnl stride* **6/1**[2]
050 **4** 3/4 **Zafisio (IRE)**[8] 6336 7-9-5 **80**.. JohnFahy 5 84
(Jo Hughes) *disp ld early: trckd ldrs: rdn over 2f out: led jst ins fnl f: hdd fnl 70yds: kpt on* **25/1**
21-3 **5** 3/4 **Flow (USA)**[36] 5436 3-9-2 **83**.. TomQueally 6 88+
(Lady Cecil) *lw: in tch: pushed along whn nt clr run over 2f out: snatched up ent fnl f: fin wl but no ch after* **4/1**[1]
0-66 **6** shd **Circumvent**[82] 3864 6-9-7 **85**.. AshleyMorgan(3) 3 88
(Paul Cole) *s.i.s: sn mid-div: hdwy fr 3f out: rdn 2f out: styd on same pce fnl f* **12/1**
6110 **7** hd **Breaking The Bank**[25] 5824 4-9-6 **81**.. MartinDwyer 2 83
(William Muir) *disp ld: rdn over 2f out: hdd ent fnl f: no ex fnl 120yds* **16/1**
0601 **8** 1/2 **Hunting Rights (USA)**[11] 6258 3-9-0 **81** 6ex........... SilvestreDeSousa 7 83
(Mark Johnston) *disp ld: rdn over 2f out: hdd ent fnl f: fdd fnl 120yds* **15/2**
5000 **9** 1 1/4 **Weapon Of Choice (IRE)**[14] 6167 5-9-8 **83**.......................... RyanMoore 4 88+
(Stuart Kittow) *mid-div: nudged along 3f out: nt clr run fr 2f out: stl nowhere to go whn squeezed up ins fnl f: eased whn no ch* **7/1**[3]
0323 **10** nk **Starwatch**[7] 6359 6-9-0 **78**.. MichaelJMMurphy(3) 10 77
(John Bridger) *b.hind: nvr bttr than mid-div* **16/1**
103/ **11** hd **Christopher Wren (USA)**[142] 5273 6-9-10 **85**.............. GeorgeBaker 16 83+
(Nick Gifford) *lw: hld up bhd: struggling 3f out: sme late prog: nvr a danger* **25/1**
140 **12** 1/2 **Granell (IRE)**[51] 4897 3-9-2 **83**..(b) JimmyFortune 12 80
(Brian Meehan) *lw: rdn over 2f out: a towards rr* **12/1**
4362 **13** 1/2 **Tinshu (IRE)**[20] 6004 7-9-6 **81**..(p) DaneO'Neill 9 78
(Derek Haydn Jones) *b: mid-div: rdn over 2f out: hld whn short of room ent fnl f* **12/1**
0100 **14** 6 **Oetzi**[13] 6200 5-8-12 **73**.. FergusSweeney 11 59
(Alan Jarvis) *lw: mid-div: rdn 3f out: sn btn* **16/1**
6000 **15** 3 3/4 **Johnno**[54] 4798 4-9-2 **77**.. SebSanders 17 56
(J W Hills) *a towards rr* **25/1**

2m 11.02s (2.22) **Going Correction** +0.25s/f (Good)
WFA 3 from 4yo+ 6lb **15** Ran SP% **126.1**
Speed ratings (Par 105): **101,100,100,100,99 99,99,99,98,97 97,97,96,92,89**PL: BD £2.80, PRES £2.80; CSF: PB & BD £29.11, PB & PRES £89.13; EX: PB & BD £50.20, PB & PRES £137.70; TRIF: PB & BD & PRES £638.70, PB & PRES & BD £638.70; TRIC: PB & PRES & BD £552.00; SW: PB & BD £12.50, PB & PRES £38.20, BD & PRES £26.60 TOTE £9.27: £Owner, £RWH Partnership, £Bred, £G Wickens And J HomanTrained Upper Lambourn, Berks.

FOCUS
A big field for this competitive handicap which has been dominated by 4yos in recent seasons. This time it fell to one of the 3yos in a very close finish, but there were several hard-luck stories in behind. The winner is rated back to form.
T/Plt: £10.60 to a £1 stake. Pool: £54,978.78 - 3769.33 winning tickets. T/Qpdt: £5.50 to a £1 stake. Pool: £3,859.89 - 517.59 winning tickets. TM

6174 NEWCASTLE (L-H)
Friday, September 20

OFFICIAL GOING: Good to soft (soft in places; 6.4)
Wind: fresh across Weather: cloudy

6597 BRITISH STALLION STUDS EBF MAIDEN FILLIES' STKS 1m 3y(S)
2:10 (2:10) (Class 5) 2-Y-0 **£2,911** (£866; £432; £216) **Stalls** Centre

Form RPR
3 **1** **Volume**[28] 5716 2-9-0 0.. KirstyMilczarek 1 78+
(Luca Cumani) *t.k.h early: trckd ldrs: led 2f out: pushed clr: comf* **8/11**[1]
0 **2** 4 1/2 **Empress Ali (IRE)**[15] 6125 2-9-0 0.. AndrewMullen 6 66
(Tom Tate) *prom: rdn over 2f out: outpcd over 1f out: kpt on fnl f: wnt 2nd post* **100/1**
4 **3** hd **Lady Heidi**[13] 6206 2-9-0 0.. RussKennemore 8 66
(Philip Kirby) *s.i.s: hld up in tch: hdwy 3f out: rdn to chse wnr over 1f out: no ex fnl 100yds: lost 2nd post* **9/1**[3]
00 **4** 1/2 **Western Sands (IRE)**[39] 5330 2-9-0 0.. BarryMcHugh 7 65
(Richard Fahey) *led narrowly: rdn whn hdd 2f out: plugged on* **20/1**
3 **5** 1/2 **Lady Yeats**[42] 5224 2-9-0 0.. PJMcDonald 5 63+
(George Moore) *midfield: rdn 3f out: kpt on ins fnl f: nvr threatened* **40/1**
0 **6** 4 **Three Heart's**[41] 5282 2-9-0 0.. MartinLane 3 55
(Hugo Palmer) *hld up in tch: pushed along 1/2-way: sn no imp* **16/1**
55 **7** nk **Arabian Comet (IRE)**[17] 6063 2-9-0 0.. AhmedAjtebi 10 57
(Charlie Appleby) *trckd ldrs: rdn over 2f out: wknd over 1f out* **9/1**[3]
3 **8** 1 1/2 **Coin Broker (IRE)**[25] 5826 2-9-0 0.. DavidNolan 4 51
(David O'Meara) *prom: rdn over 2f out: wknd over 1f out* **3/1**[2]
5 **9** 1 1/4 **Moon Over Rio (IRE)**[9] 6298 2-9-0 0.. AndrewElliott 9 48
(Ben Haslam) *hld up in tch: rdn 3f out: sn btn* **40/1**
10 20 **Hello Sweetness** 2-9-0 0.. DaleSwift 2 4
(Jason Ward) *slowly away: a in rr* **66/1**

1m 44.03s (0.63) **Going Correction** +0.125s/f (Good) **10** Ran SP% **120.9**
Speed ratings (Par 92): **101,96,96,95,95 91,91,89,88,68**
Tote Swingers 1&2 £41.60, 2&3 £93.20, 1&3 £2.50 CSF £155.36 TOTE £2.10: £1.10, £11.40, £1.50; EX 94.00 Trifecta £773.50 Pool: £2,223.22 - 2.15 winning tickets..
Owner S Stuckey **Bred** Stuart Stuckey **Trained** Newmarket, Suffolk

FOCUS
Rail after winning post moved in 2yds to allow for fresh ground. The official going remained good to soft, soft in places. After the opener Barry McHugh described the ground as "on the dead side". An interesting maiden run at an even pace, and it was dominated by the well-backed favourite. The standard looks modest in behind.

6598 VERTEM ASSET MANAGEMENT H'CAP 1m 2f 32y
2:40 (2:41) (Class 6) (0-65,71) 3-Y-0+ **£1,940** (£577; £288; £144) **Stalls** Centre

Form RPR
1121 **1** **Artful Prince**[9] 6297 3-9-10 **71** 6ex..(b) DaleSwift 4 85+
(James Given) *midfield: swtchd to outer 2f out: r.o strly to ld fnl 100yds* **2/1**[1]
1-00 **2** 1/2 **Dark Ruler (IRE)**[22] 5918 4-9-10 **65**.. AndrewMullen 8 78
(Alan Swinbank) *trckd ldrs: led 3f out: rdn 2f out: kpt on wl but hdd fnl 100yds* **22/1**
5042 **3** 6 **Jordaura**[9] 6296 7-9-4 **64**.. SladeO'Hara(5) 11 66
(Alan Berry) *hld up: pushed along and hdwy over 2f out: kpt on to go 3rd ins fnl 100yds: no threat to ldng pair* **7/1**[2]
0002 **4** 2 3/4 **Noosa Sound**[26] 5789 3-8-5 **52**..(t) RoystonFfrench 17 48
(John Davies) *midfield: hdwy to chse ldrs 2f out: no ex ins fnl f: lost 3rd fnl 100yds* **33/1**
0402 **5** hd **Miss Ella Jade**[21] 5967 4-8-10 **51**.. MartinLane 13 47
(Richard Whitaker) *trckd ldrs: rdn over 2f out: one pce* **20/1**
2302 **6** 1/2 **Dubai Celebration**[61] 4557 5-9-2 **57**.. BarryMcHugh 5 52
(Julie Camacho) *in tch: rdn over 2f out: one pce* **7/1**[2]
5553 **7** shd **Korngold**[10] 6290 5-8-10 **51** oh2.. ChrisCatlin 2 46
(Tracy Waggott) *hld up in midfield on inner: persistently short of room 3f out tl over 1f out: kpt on fnl f: nrst fin* **8/1**[3]
6030 **8** nk **Monthly Medal**[18] 6053 10-8-6 **54**..(t) KevinStott(7) 7 48
(Wilf Storey) *hld up in midfield: rdn whn hmpd 2f out: one pce after* **11/1**
0400 **9** nk **Amazing Blue Sky**[4] 6470 7-9-1 **56**..(p) LeeTopliss 6 50
(Ruth Carr) *trcaked ldrs: rdn over 2f out: grad wknd over 1f out* **16/1**
60-6 **10** 2 1/2 **Cometography (IRE)**[99] 3252 4-9-3 **58**..................(p) RussKennemore 3 47
(Lawrence Mullaney) *hld up: rdn over 2f out: minor hdwy whn n.m.r ins fnl f* **50/1**
6433 **11** 3/4 **May's Boy**[23] 5882 5-8-8 **52**.. RaulDaSilva(3) 15 40
(James Moffatt) *midfield: rdn over 2f out: sn btn* **20/1**
3000 **12** hd **Moheebb (IRE)**[14] 6177 9-9-1 **56**..(p) KirstyMilczarek 16 43
(Robert Johnson) *slowly away: sn midfield: rdn over 2f out: nvr threatened* **18/1**
3515 **13** hd **The Codger**[35] 5483 3-9-0 **64**.. JulieBurke(3) 12 51
(David O'Meara) *s.i.s: hld up: nvr threatened* **12/1**
4/00 **14** 1 3/4 **Tourtiere**[108] 2961 5-8-13 **54**.. PJMcDonald 10 37
(George Moore) *in tch: rdn over 2f out: wknd over 1f out* **33/1**
2544 **15** 18 **Grandiloquent**[24] 5854 4-9-8 **63**..(p) BrianHughes 9 12
(Kevin Ryan) *sn led: hdd 3f out: sn wknd* **20/1**
5000 **16** 9 **Hussar Ballad (USA)**[87] 3649 4-9-0 **55**.. AndrewElliott 14
(Mel Brittain) *sn w ldr towards outer: rdn over 4f out: wknd 3f out* **50/1**

2m 14.07s (2.17) **Going Correction** +0.20s/f (Good)
WFA 3 from 4yo+ 6lb **16** Ran SP% **125.1**
Speed ratings (Par 101): **99,98,93,91,91 91,90,90,90,88 87,87,87,86,71 64**
Tote Swingers 1&2 £13.00, 2&3 £58.90, 1&3 £3.50 CSF £58.29 CT £279.02 TOTE £2.70: £1.30, £5.70, £2.60, £4.50; EX 59.40 Trifecta £190.30 Pool: £1,491.83 - 5.87 winning tickets..
Owner Ingram Racing **Bred** Graham Wilson **Trained** Willoughton, Lincs
■ Stewards' Enquiry : Dale Swift one-day ban; careless riding (4th Oct).

FOCUS
A modest handicap run at a decent gallop. The winner continues on the upgrade.

6599 VERTEMASSETMANAGEMENT.COM FILLIES' H'CAP 1m 2f 32y
3:15 (3:17) (Class 5) (0-75,75) 4-Y-0+ **£2,587** (£770; £384; £192) **Stalls** Centre

Form RPR
0325 **1** **Aryizad (IRE)**[18] 6051 4-8-13 **67**.. AndrewMullen 4 74
(Alan Swinbank) *trckd ldr: rdn over 2f out: drvn appr fnl f: kpt on to ld towards fin* **16/1**
4354 **2** 1/2 **Bobs Her Uncle**[14] 6153 4-8-9 **63** ow1.. DaleSwift 1 69
(James Bethell) *led: rdn over 2f out: drvn over 1f out: kpt on: hdd towards fin* **7/2**[2]

3460 **3** *3* **Maybeagrey**[4] 6470 4-8-7 **61**.................................(p) PJMcDonald 2 61
(Tim Easterby) *trckd ldr: rdn over 2f out: one pce and hld in 3rd over 1f out* **5/1**[3]
233 **4** *1 1/4* **Waveguide (IRE)**[72] 4180 4-9-1 **69**................................ MartinLane 6 67
(David Simcock) *midfield: rdn over 2f out: one pce* **7/1**
110 **5** *nse* **Yojojo (IRE)**[39] 5360 4-9-2 **75**................................ DanielMuscutt(5) 9 73
(Gay Kelleway) *hld up in tch: rdn over 2f out: one pce: nvr threatened ldrs* **6/1**
0340 **6** *4* **Gold Show**[51] 4889 4-8-6 **67**................................ KevinStott(7) 3 57
(Edwin Tuer) *midfield: rdn over 2f out: wknd over 1f out* **2/1**[1]
0600 **7** *3 1/2* **Liliargh (IRE)**[14] 6179 4-8-7 **61** oh1................................ AndrewElliott 7 45
(Ben Haslam) *hld up: rdn over 2f out: sn btn* **40/1**

2m 15.61s (3.71) **Going Correction** +0.20s/f (Good) **7** Ran SP% **107.3**
Speed ratings (Par 100): **93,92,90,89,85 83,83**
Tote Swingers 1&2 £8.30, 2&3 £3.70, 1&3 £4.60 CSF £62.07 CT £278.54 TOTE £10.70: £5.40, £1.70; EX 74.70 Trifecta £402.90 Pool: £1,567.76 - 2.91 winning tickets..
Owner Mrs J Porter **Bred** Ger Hayes **Trained** Melsonby, N Yorks

FOCUS
A modest fillies' handicap, the early pace was steady and the tempo didn't increase until 3f out. It's hard to think the bare form is much better.

6600 BOOKMAKERS.CO.UK H'CAP — 1m 3y(S)
3:50 (3:51) (Class 6) (0-65,65) 3-Y-0+ **£1,940** (£577; £288; £144) **Stalls** Centre

Form RPR
2-03 **1** **Uncle Brit**[23] 5903 7-9-4 **59**................................ PJMcDonald 13 67
(Malcolm Jefferson) *midfield: rdn and hdwy to chse ldrs over 1f out: kpt on to ld fnl 75yds* **7/1**[3]
1130 **2** *3/4* **Royal Holiday (IRE)**[43] 5195 6-9-7 **62**...................(p) RussKennemore 2 68
(Marjorie Fife) *led narrowly: rdn whn hdd over 1f out: kpt on* **20/1**
02 **3** *shd* **King Pin**[25] 5828 8-9-10 **65**................................(p) DaleSwift 3 71
(Tracy Waggott) *hld up: rdn and hdwy over 2f out: ev ch over 1f out: kpt on* **17/2**
6221 **4** *hd* **Moral Issue**[10] 6276 5-9-9 **64** 6ex................................ AndrewMullen 7 70
(Alan Swinbank) *midfield: pushed along 1/2-way: rdn and hdwy over 2f out: led narrowly over 1f out: hdd fnl 75yds: no ex and lost 2 pls post* **5/2**[1]
6614 **5** *2 3/4* **Throwing Roses**[23] 5903 3-8-3 **51** oh1................................ RaulDaSilva(3) 12 50
(Lawrence Mullaney) *midfield: rdn over 3f out: kpt on fnl f: nvr threatened* **16/1**
4105 **6** *1 1/4* **Monel**[14] 6180 5-8-13 **54**................................ AndrewElliott 1 50
(Jim Goldie) *hld up in rr: swtchd lft over 2f out: rdn and hdwy over 1f out: one pce fnl f* **25/1**
430- **7** *2 1/4* **Charles De Mille**[458] 3254 5-9-3 **61**................................ DeclanCannon(3) 10 52
(George Moore) *hld up: rdn over 2f out: plugged on: nvr threatened* **66/1**
6430 **8** *2 1/2* **Baraboy (IRE)**[39] 5334 3-8-4 **52**................................ JulieBurke(3) 14 37
(Barry Murtagh) *prom: rdn over 2f out: wknd over 1f out* **22/1**
-00 **9** *1/2* **Indian Giver**[9] 6301 5-9-2 **62**................................(b[1]) SladeO'Hara(5) 8 46
(Alan Berry) *hld up: rdn over 2f out: nvr threatened* **33/1**
6441 **10** *4 1/2* **Skyfire**[24] 5861 6-9-3 **65**................................(p) KevinStott(7) 11 39
(Nick Kent) *chsd ldrs: rdn 3f out: wknd over 1f out* **6/1**[2]
0060 **11** *1/2* **Hayek**[36] 5427 6-8-7 **55**................................(b) GaryMahon(7) 15 28
(Tim Easterby) *chsd ldrs: rdn over 3f out: wknd over 2f out* **16/1**
0212 **12** *2 1/4* **Violent Velocity (IRE)**[10] 6276 10-9-2 **64**................................ JoeDoyle(7) 4 32
(John Quinn) *midfield: rdn 3f out: wknd over 1f out* **12/1**
346 **13** *3 1/4* **Dandarrell**[49] 4953 6-9-7 **62**................................ BarryMcHugh 6 22
(Julie Camacho) *chsd ldrs: rdn 3f out: wknd over 1f out* **17/2**
00-5 **14** *11* **Thackeray**[191] 987 6-9-10 **65**................................ MichaelStainton 16
(Chris Fairhurst) *midfield: rdn 1/2-way: wknd over 2f out* **33/1**
5160 **15** *7* **Nonaynever**[10] 6276 5-8-10 **51**................................(b) KirstyMilczarek 9
(Ruth Carr) *in tch: wknd over 2f out* **33/1**

1m 43.85s (0.45) **Going Correction** +0.125s/f (Good)
WFA 3 from 5yo+ 4lb **15** Ran SP% **119.1**
Speed ratings (Par 101): **102,101,101,100,98 96,94,92,91,87 86,84,81,70,63**
Tote Swingers 1&2 £24.20, 2&3 £18.80, 1&3 £13.10 CSF £143.11 CT £1242.48 TOTE £8.40: £2.00, £6.00, £3.00; EX 157.90 Trifecta £690.50 Pool: £2,566.28 - 2.78 winning tickets..
Owner J M Jefferson **Bred** Heather Raw **Trained** Norton, N Yorks

FOCUS
A modest handicap run at a good pace. Straightforward form.

6601 APEX RADIO H'CAP — 1m 4f 93y
4:25 (4:28) (Class 5) (0-75,75) 3-Y-0 **£2,587** (£770; £384; £192) **Stalls** Low

Form RPR
-053 **1** **Vicky Valentine**[9] 6296 3-8-4 **61** oh5................................ JulieBurke(3) 6 66
(Alistair Whillans) *trckd ldr: pushed along to ld over 2f out: idled ins fnl f: hld on towards fin* **9/1**
5312 **2** *1/2* **Aneedh**[18] 6051 3-9-7 **75**................................ RussKennemore 2 79
(Jedd O'Keeffe) *trckd ldrs: rdn over 2f out: kpt on: hld towards fin* **9/2**[2]
5620 **3** *1* **Young Jay**[6] 6389 3-8-7 **61**................................ LiamJones 3 64
(Mark Johnston) *led: rdn whn hdd over 2f out: kpt on one pce* **9/1**
2333 **4** *nk* **Arr' Kid (USA)**[41] 5264 3-9-3 **71**................................ PJMcDonald 4 73+
(Keith Dalgleish) *s.i.s: hld up in tch: pushed along 4f out: kpt on fnl f: nrst fin* **9/4**[1]
-365 **5** *1* **Perfect Calm (USA)**[70] 4240 3-8-13 **67**................................ BarryMcHugh 5 68
(Julie Camacho) *hld up: rdn 3f out: one pce and nvr threatened* **18/1**
5234 **6** *1 3/4* **Magic Skyline (IRE)**[9] 6296 3-8-11 **65**................................ DaleSwift 8 63
(Brian Ellison) *in tch: rdn 3f out: wknd ins fnl f* **5/1**[3]

2m 51.1s (5.50) **Going Correction** +0.20s/f (Good) **6** Ran SP% **90.9**
Speed ratings (Par 101): **89,88,88,87,87 85**
Tote Swingers 1&2 £3.40, 2&3 £3.10, 1&3 £6.10 CSF £30.05 CT £159.70 TOTE £8.40: £4.00, £1.30; EX 33.90 Trifecta £148.70 Pool: £1,664.53 - 8.39 winning tickets..
Owner Frank Lowe **Bred** Frank Lowe **Trained** Newmill-On-Slitrig, Borders
■ Flamingo Beat was withdrawn (3-1, upset in stalls). Deduct 25p in the £ under R4.

FOCUS
An ordinary 3yo handicap, and fairly shaky form. The winner is rated back to her 2yo form.

6602 BOOKER CASH AND CARRY H'CAP — 7f
5:00 (5:00) (Class 5) (0-75,75) 3-Y-0 **£2,587** (£770; £384; £192) **Stalls** Centre

Form RPR
3221 **1** **Bousatet (FR)**[21] 5975 3-8-8 **69**................................ KevinStott(7) 5 79+
(Kevin Ryan) *trckd ldr: led on bit over 1f out: rdn and kpt on fnl f* **11/8**[1]
1050 **2** *1 1/2* **Relight My Fire**[20] 5987 3-9-1 **74**................................(b) DarylByrne(5) 4 80
(Tim Easterby) *in tch: rdn over 2f out: chsd wnr over 1f out: kpt on but a hld* **15/2**
5030 **3** *4 1/2* **Apache Rising**[9] 6301 3-9-2 **70**................................(v[1]) RoystonFfrench 6 64
(Bryan Smart) *led: rdn whn hdd over 1f out: wknd* **8/1**
0100 **4** *1* **Mister Marcasite**[3] 6495 3-9-7 **75**................................ AndrewElliott 3 66
(Mel Brittain) *dwlt: hld up: rdn over 2f out: nvr threatened* **11/2**[3]
2134 **5** *1/2* **Black Rider (IRE)**[51] 4890 3-9-4 **72**................................ BarryMcHugh 1 62
(Julie Camacho) *hld up in rr: rdn over 2f out: nvr threatened* **5/2**[2]

1m 29.07s (1.27) **Going Correction** +0.125s/f (Good) **5** Ran SP% **108.9**
Speed ratings (Par 101): **97,95,90,89,88**
Tote Swinger 1&2 £7.70 CSF £11.62 TOTE £2.30: £1.30, £4.50; EX 11.20 Trifecta £34.60 Pool: £2,411.84 - 52.13 winning tickets..
Owner Highbank Stud **Bred** F Bayrou & F A Mc Nulty **Trained** Hambleton, N Yorks

FOCUS
A fair 3yo handicap run at a decent pace. The winner was perhaps slightly better than the bare result.

6603 FREEBETTING WITH BOOKMAKERS.CO.UK H'CAP (DIV I) — 5f
5:30 (5:33) (Class 6) (0-65,65) 3-Y-0+ **£1,940** (£577; £288; £144) **Stalls** Centre

Form RPR
4065 **1** **Ambitious Icarus**[10] 6287 4-9-6 **64**................................(e) RobbieFitzpatrick 8 73
(Richard Guest) *hld up: rdn and hdwy over 1f out: led jst ins fnl f: kpt on* **7/1**
3003 **2** *1* **Lees Anthem**[14] 6180 6-8-8 **52**................................ PJMcDonald 12 57
(Mel Brittain) *hld up: rdn 2f out: swtchd rt appr fnl f: r.o: wnt 2nd fnl 100yds* **5/1**[2]
6450 **3** *1* **Foreign Rhythm (IRE)**[10] 6287 8-9-0 **63**................................ ShirleyTeasdale(5) 4 65
(Ron Barr) *chsd ldrs: rdn to ld over 1f out: hdd jst ins fnl f: no ex* **14/1**
0622 **4** *1/2* **One Kool Dude**[28] 5709 4-8-13 **57**................................(b) AndrewElliott 1 57
(Neville Bycroft) *hld up: rdn 1/2-way: kpt on fnl f* **11/2**[3]
5022 **5** *1/2* **Rich Again (IRE)**[20] 5985 4-9-7 **65**................................ BrianHughes 11 63
(James Bethell) *s.i.s: hld up: rdn and hdwy to chse ldrs over 1f out: no ex fnl f* **3/1**[1]
0500 **6** *1/2* **Pivotal Prospect**[25] 5830 5-9-0 **58**................................ RoystonFfrench 13 54
(Tracy Waggott) *chsd ldrs: no ex fnl f* **7/1**
0455 **7** *3 1/2* **Sir Geoffrey (IRE)**[28] 5701 7-8-11 **55**................................(p) RussKennemore 7 39
(Scott Dixon) *prom tl wknd ins fnl f* **9/1**
000 **8** *3 1/2* **Sharp Shoes**[45] 5085 6-8-3 **54** oh4 ow3................................(p) KevinStott(7) 5 25
(Christopher Wilson) *led: rdn whn hdd over 1f out: wknd* **20/1**
060- **9** *1/2* **Fair Bunny**[420] 4547 6-8-7 **51** oh3................................(e[1]) AndrewMullen 9 20
(Alan Brown) *chsd ldrs: wknd over 1f out* **33/1**
0 **10** *hd* **Red Roar (IRE)**[46] 5049 6-8-7 **54**................................ JulieBurke(3) 3 23
(Alan Berry) *midfield: wknd fnl 2f* **16/1**

1m 1.6s (0.50) **Going Correction** +0.125s/f (Good) **10** Ran SP% **112.3**
Speed ratings (Par 101): **101,99,97,97,96 95,89,84,83,83**
Tote Swingers 1&2 £6.70, 2&3 £10.10, 1&3 £14.10 CSF £38.54 CT £422.32 TOTE £8.70: £2.40, £2.00, £2.10; EX 44.10 Trifecta £906.50 Pool: £1,378.33 - 1.14 winning tickets..
Owner ABS Metals & Waste **Bred** L T Roberts **Trained** Wetherby, W Yorks
■ Sir Nod was withdrawn (14-1, ref to ent stalls). Deduct 5p in the £ under R4.

FOCUS
The first division of modest sprint handicap was run 0.17secs quicker than the second heat. Pretty straightforward form.

6604 COOPERS MARQUEES H'CAP (DIV II) — 5f
6:00 (6:02) (Class 6) (0-65,65) 3-Y-0+ **£1,940** (£577; £288; £144) **Stalls** Centre

Form RPR
4500 **1** **Planetex (IRE)**[1] 6547 4-9-4 **65**................................(p) RaulDaSilva(3) 7 74+
(John Quinn) *midfield: smooth hdwy fr 1/2-way: led fnl 100yds: pushed out* **5/2**[1]
4410 **2** *1/2* **Black Douglas**[14] 6180 4-8-9 **53**................................ AndrewElliott 9 60
(Jim Goldie) *hld up: rdn and hdwy over 1f out: kpt on fnl f: wnt 2nd towards fin* **17/2**
0430 **3** *3/4* **Balinka**[36] 5422 3-9-0 **59**................................(v) PJMcDonald 4 63
(Mel Brittain) *led: rdn 2f out: hdd fnl 100yds: no ex and lost 2nd towards fin* **9/1**
5140 **4** *1 1/4* **Tuibama (IRE)**[17] 6088 4-9-3 **61**................................(p) DaleSwift 1 61
(Tracy Waggott) *midfield: hdwy to chse ldrs over 1f out: kpt on* **8/1**[3]
2200 **5** *shd* **Lord Buffhead**[4] 6478 4-8-13 **57**................................(v) RobbieFitzpatrick 6 56
(Richard Guest) *s.i.s: early reminders in rr: rdn 1/2-way: kpt on fnl f: nrst fin* **9/1**
5100 **5** *dht* **A J Cook (IRE)**[51] 4892 3-9-0 **64**................................(p) ShirleyTeasdale(5) 10 63
(Ron Barr) *midfield: rdn 1/2-way: kpt on* **33/1**
6030 **7** *1 1/2* **Mr Man In The Moon (IRE)**[14] 6180 5-8-7 **51**................................ AndrewMullen 8 45
(Alan Swinbank) *midfield: rdn 1/2-way: sn no imp* **8/1**[3]
0041 **8** *1 1/4* **Edith Anne**[46] 5054 3-9-2 **61**................................(p) LeeTopliss 12 50
(Paul Midgley) *prom: rdn 1/2-way: wknd fnl f* **11/2**[2]
3565 **9** *3/4* **Busy Bimbo (IRE)**[10] 6289 4-8-4 **51** oh3................................ JulieBurke(3) 3 38
(Alan Berry) *hld up: nvr threatened* **16/1**
1054 **10** *nse* **Ichimoku**[44] 5141 3-8-11 **56**................................(t) RoystonFfrench 11 42
(Bryan Smart) *chsd ldrs: wknd fnl f* **9/1**
30- **11** *3 1/4* **On The High Tops (IRE)**[325] 7457 5-8-12 **56**................................ BarryMcHugh 2 31
(Colin Teague) *hld up: a towards rr* **33/1**
4-06 **12** *9* **Angel Grigio**[24] 5864 3-8-1 **51** oh4................................(b[1]) NoelGarbutt(5) 5
(Geoffrey Oldroyd) *chsd ldrs: wknd over 1f out: eased* **33/1**

1m 1.77s (0.67) **Going Correction** +0.125s/f (Good)
WFA 3 from 4yo+ 1lb **12** Ran SP% **121.4**
Speed ratings (Par 101): **99,98,97,95,94 94,92,90,89,89 83,69**
Tote Swingers 1&2 £6.40, 2&3 £15.50, 1&3 £7.50 CSF £24.49 CT £168.01 TOTE £3.20: £1.20, £3.70, £3.10; EX 29.00 Trifecta £282.60 Pool: £1,732.27 - 4.59 winning tickets..
Owner Mrs S Quinn **Bred** Mrs Diane Williams **Trained** Settrington, N Yorks

FOCUS
The second division of a modest sprint handicap was a length slower than the first division. Similar form.
T/Plt: £278.50 to a £1 stake. Pool: £73,752.45 - 193.26 winning tickets. T/Qpdt: £81.70 to a £1 stake. Pool: £5,070.4 - 45.9 winning tickets. AS

6472 WOLVERHAMPTON (A.W) (L-H)
Friday, September 20

OFFICIAL GOING: Standard to slow
Wind: Light behind Weather: Cloudy with sunny spells

6605 SPONSOR A RACE BY CALLING 01902 390000 NURSERY H'CAP — 7f 32y(P)
5:40 (5:41) (Class 5) (0-70,68) 2-Y-0 **£2,587** (£770; £384; £192) **Stalls** High

Form RPR
555 **1** **More Aspen (USA)**[26] 5797 2-9-5 **66**................................ SaleemGolam 10 74
(Marco Botti) *chsd ldrs: shkn up to ld over 1f out: rdn out* **11/2**[3]
2432 **2** *3* **Amadaffair**[4] 6474 2-9-0 **61**................................ RichardKingscote 6 62
(Tom Dascombe) *trckd ldr tl led over 2f out: rdn and hdd over 1f out: styd on same pce ins fnl f* **11/2**[3]

The Form Book Flat, Raceform Ltd, Compton, RG20 6NL.

056 **3** *hd* **The Grumpy Gnome (IRE)**[39] 5339 2-9-4 **65**..............(p) JimmyQuinn 1 66
(Richard Fahey) *chsd ldrs: rdn over 2f out: styd on* **14/1**

024 **4** *3/4* **Opera Fan (FR)**[24] 5852 2-9-2 **63**.................................. KierenFallon 3 62
(Mark Johnston) *chsd ldrs: pushed along 1/2-way: styd on* **9/2**[2]

060 **5** *nk* **Drinkuptrig (IRE)**[63] 4505 2-9-2 **63**............................ AdamBeschizza 9 61+
(Stuart Williams) *hld up: rdn over 2f out: hdwy over 1f out: r.o* **9/1**

003 **6** *2 1/4* **Sheacheval (IRE)**[32] 5593 2-9-4 **65**................................... LukeMorris 7 57
(J S Moore) *mid-div: rdn over 2f out: styd on ins fnl f: nvr trbld ldrs* **18/1**

0364 **7** *1 1/4* **Sandy Cove**[14] 6170 2-8-13 **60**.. FrederikTylicki 5 49
(Roger Charlton) *led: rdn and hdd over 2f out: wknd ins fnl f* **7/2**[1]

543 **8** *nk* **Exceed Areeda (IRE)**[13] 6213 2-9-6 **67**.............................. ShaneKelly 4 56
(James Tate) *hld up: hdwy over 2f out: rdn over 1f out: n.m.r and wknd ins fnl f* **17/2**

356 **9** *9* **Nowinaminute (IRE)**[20] 5983 2-8-13 **60**...................... JamesSullivan 12 27
(James Given) *hld up: rdn 1/2-way: wknd over 2f out: eased fnl f* **33/1**

034 **10** *7* **Earl's Bridge**[124] 2474 2-8-5 **59**....................................... RyanWhile(7) 11 8
(Bill Turner) *s.i.s: outpcd* **100/1**

004 **11** *33* **St Vincent (IRE)**[81] 3905 2-9-7 **68**..................................(b[1]) TedDurcan 8 +
(David Lanigan) *s.i.s: hit rails over 5f out: hdwy over 4f out: rdn and wknd over 2f out: eased over 1f out* **10/1**

1m 30.3s (0.70) **Going Correction** +0.025s/f (Slow) **11** Ran SP% **116.7**
Speed ratings (Par 95): **97,93,93,92,92 89,88,87,77,69 31**
Tote Swingers 1&2 £7.70, 2&3 £8.30, 1&3 £14.30 CSF £35.54 CT £411.26 TOTE £7.00: £2.40, £1.40, £4.00; EX 40.10 Trifecta £793.80 Pool: £1,425.18 - 1.34 winning tickets..
Owner Mohamed Albousi Alghufli **Bred** Barry Weisbord **Trained** Newmarket, Suffolk

FOCUS
The Polytrack was standard to slow again, but the relaid surface continues to bed in and it probably won't be long before it's back to standard. Richard Kingscote said after riding in the first: "It's getting there." Not many managed to get into this modest nursery. The winner showed big improvement, with straightforward form in behind.

6606 FREYA FELTON PROMISE DREAMS CLASSIFIED CLAIMING STKS 7f 32y(P)
6:10 (6:13) (Class 6) 3-Y-0+ **£1,940** (£577; £288; £144) **Stalls** High

Form RPR

0644 **1** **Greensward**[9] 6316 7-9-8 68..(b) ShaneKelly 6 81
(Mike Murphy) *hld up: hdwy on outer over 2f out: rdn to ld towards fin* **7/2**[1]

4453 **2** *1/2* **Khajaaly (IRE)**[4] 6475 6-9-1 68..............................(tp) TobyAtkinson(5) 7 78
(Michael Appleby) *a.p: racd keenly: pushed along to chse ldr 3f out: rdn to ld ins fnl f: hdd towards fin* **7/2**[1]

-350 **3** *2 3/4* **Kimbali (IRE)**[23] 5899 4-9-2 70... JimmyQuinn 5 67
(Richard Fahey) *s.i.s: hld up: hdwy u.p over 1f out: r.o: nt rch ldrs* **6/1**[3]

6300 **4** *1 1/4* **Bunce (IRE)**[14] 6181 5-9-2 63......................................(b[1]) KierenFallon 9 63
(David O'Meara) *trckd ldr tl led 1/2-way: rdn over 1f out: hdd and no ex ins fnl f* **7/1**

0023 **5** *1* **Annes Rocket (IRE)**[16] 6096 8-8-9 66................(b[1]) CameronHardie(7) 8 61
(Jimmy Fox) *hld up: plld hrd: r.o ins fnl f: nvr trbld ldrs* **7/1**

0300 **6** *4* **Portrush Storm**[17] 6075 8-8-10 50..............................(p) DavidProbert 4 44
(Ray Peacock) *trckd ldrs: racd keenly: rdn over 2f out: wknd fnl f* **40/1**

P35 **7** *2 1/4* **Bussa**[9] 6317 5-8-13 70...(t) DeclanBates(3) 2 44
(David Evans) *hld up: shkn up over 1f out: wknd ins fnl f* **4/1**[2]

0635 **8** *11* **We Have A Dream**[9] 6310 8-8-13 70.....................(p) CharlesBishop(3) 3 14
(Violet M Jordan) *sn led: hdd 1/2-way: rdn and wknd over 2f out* **14/1**

0006 **9** *1 1/4* **Vogarth**[37] 5378 9-7-13 36..(b) IanBurns(7) 11
(Michael Chapman) *s.i.s: hdwy over 5f out: rdn 1/2-way: wknd over 2f out* **100/1**

00-4 **10** *21* **Berrymead**[157] 1598 8-8-13 43... AnnStokell(5) 1
(Ann Stokell) *led early: chsd ldrs tl wknd 1/2-way* **125/1**

1m 29.91s (0.31) **Going Correction** +0.025s/f (Slow) **10** Ran SP% **114.6**
Speed ratings (Par 101): **99,98,95,93,92 88,85,73,71,47**
Tote Swingers 1&2 £4.20, 2&3 £5.50, 1&3 £4.90 CSF £15.44 TOTE £4.50: £2.00, £1.10, £2.90; EX 19.60 Trifecta £102.20 Pool: £1,338.85 - 9.81 winning tickets..
Owner The Furlong Friends **Bred** Kincorth Investments Inc **Trained** Westoning, Beds
■ Stewards' Enquiry : Charles Bishop two-day ban; used whip down the shoulder in the forehand (5th,7th Oct).

FOCUS
A very ordinary claimer and dubious form. The first two were among the better treated.

6607 UNCLE BOB'S MEDIAN AUCTION MAIDEN FILLIES' STKS 5f 216y(P)
6:40 (6:41) (Class 6) 2-Y-0 **£1,940** (£577; £288; £144) **Stalls** Low

Form RPR

65 **1** **Nova Princesse (GER)**[8] 6334 2-9-0 0......................(t) SaleemGolam 11 70
(Marco Botti) *hld up: hdwy over 2f out: rdn to ld wl ins fnl f: styd on* **16/1**

330 **2** *1/2* **Mimi Luke (USA)**[69] 4277 2-9-0 68..................................... AdamKirby 9 68
(Alan Bailey) *chsd ldr: rdn over 1f out: led and edgd lft ins fnl f: sn hdd: styd on* **7/1**

3 **3** *nk* **Rocksee (IRE)**[39] 5352 2-9-0 0.................................. RichardKingscote 7 67
(Tom Dascombe) *prom: lost pl over 3f out: hdwy over 1f out: r.o* **3/1**[2]

5 **4** *3/4* **Pageant Belle**[16] 6107 2-9-0 0.. TedDurcan 6 65
(Roger Charlton) *trckd ldrs: racd keenly: rdn over 1f out: styd on* **9/4**[1]

34 **5** *1 1/4* **Elsie Partridge (IRE)**[14] 6174 2-9-0 0.............................. PatCosgrave 1 61
(Noel Quinlan) *sn led: rdn and hung rt over 1f out: hdd and no ex ins fnl f* **4/1**[3]

0 **6** *5* **Poetic Choice**[41] 5282 2-9-0 0.................................. TomMcLaughlin 10 46
(Nick Littmoden) *s.i.s: sn pushed along in rr: kpt on ins fnl f: nvr nrr* **40/1**

7 *1 3/4* **Naivasha** 2-9-0 0... SteveDrowne 5 41+
(Robert Cowell) *s.i.s: sn pushed along in rr: nvr on terms* **25/1**

00 **8** *hd* **Prim And Proper**[16] 6107 2-9-0 0...................................... KierenFallon 4 40
(Brendan Powell) *chsd ldrs: sn pushed along: eased whn btn ins fnl f* **10/1**

9 *3 1/4* **Sky Ranger (IRE)** 2-9-0 0.. ShaneKelly 12 31
(James Tate) *sn pushed along and prom: rdn over 2f out: wknd over 1f out* **18/1**

00 **10** *3 1/2* **Miss Lawlass (IRE)**[13] 6213 2-9-0 0............................ JamesSullivan 2 20
(James Given) *prom: lost pl after 1f: wknd 1/2-way* **100/1**

11 *1 1/4* **Sweet Angelica** 2-9-0 0.. FrederikTylicki 8 16
(James Given) *s.i.s: outpcd* **25/1**

1m 16.05s (1.05) **Going Correction** +0.025s/f (Slow) **11** Ran SP% **119.6**
Speed ratings (Par 90): **94,93,92,91,90 83,81,81,76,72 70**
Tote Swingers 1&2 £15.10, 2&3 £4.20, 1&3 £5.60 CSF £122.15 TOTE £12.60: £3.90, £1.70, £1.40; EX 119.40 Trifecta £490.60 Pool: £1,302.77 - 1.99 winning tickets..
Owner Scuderia Blueberry **Bred** Gestut Isarland **Trained** Newmarket, Suffolk

FOCUS
Ordinary form as befits the grade. The second and fourth help set the standard.

6608 EVENTMASTERS.CO.UK "IT'S BEEN EMOTIONAL TRENCHY" H'CAP (DIV I) 7f 32y(P)
7:10 (7:11) (Class 4) (0-85,85) 3-Y-0+ **£4,690** (£1,395; £697; £348) **Stalls** High

Form RPR

21- **1** **Horsted Keynes (FR)**[310] 7706 3-8-9 **76**.......................... WilliamBuick 9 89+
(Roger Varian) *trckd ldr: shkn up to ld 1f out: r.o: readily* **7/4**[1]

0432 **2** *1 1/4* **Invisible Hunter (USA)**[6] 6403 4-9-4 **82**.......................(vt) KierenFallon 5 93
(Saeed bin Suroor) *led: rdn and hdd 1f out: styd on same pce ins fnl f* **9/4**[2]

0500 **3** *2 1/4* **Capo Rosso (IRE)**[34] 5510 3-9-4 **85**....................... RichardKingscote 3 89
(Tom Dascombe) *mid-div: n.m.r over 6f out: hdwy over 1f out: r.o: nt rch ldrs* **12/1**

5220 **4** *1 3/4* **Ready (IRE)**[14] 6164 3-9-2 **83**...(p) AdamKirby 7 82
(Garry Moss) *a.p: rdn over 1f out: styd on same pce fnl f* **10/1**[3]

0202 **5** *3 1/4* **Greyfriarschorista**[44] 5153 6-8-13 **77**................................ LukeMorris 4 68
(Tom Keddy) *chsd ldrs: rdn over 2f out: wknd ins fnl f* **28/1**

1006 **6** *1 3/4* **Balti's Sister (IRE)**[8] 6341 4-8-13 **77**.................................... BrettDoyle 6 64
(Martin Smith) *s.i.s: hdwy over 2f out: rdn over 1f out: wknd fnl f* **33/1**

336 **7** *1 1/4* **Lutine Bell**[34] 5518 6-9-3 **81**..(p) ShaneKelly 10 64
(Mike Murphy) *s.i.s: hld up: nvr on terms* **12/1**

0005 **8** *1/2* **Restaurateur (IRE)**[22] 5928 4-8-11 **80**....................(v) OisinMurphy(5) 2 62
(Andrew Balding) *in rr: rdn over 1f out: n.d* **12/1**

0406 **9** *1 3/4* **Powerful Presence (IRE)**[14] 6164 7-9-7 **85**................... PatCosgrave 8 62
(David O'Meara) *mid-div: pushed along over 2f out: wknd over 1f out* **20/1**

4250 **10** *3/4* **Summerinthecity (IRE)**[13] 6183 6-8-13 **77**........................ TedDurcan 1 52
(David Nicholls) *hld up: rdn over 1f out: n.d* **10/1**[3]

1m 27.94s (-1.66) **Going Correction** +0.025s/f (Slow)
WFA 3 from 4yo+ 3lb **10** Ran SP% **119.5**
Speed ratings (Par 105): **110,108,106,104,100 98,96,96,94,93**
Tote Swingers 1&2 £2.00, 2&3 £7.20, 1&3 £6.80 CSF £5.72 CT £36.33 TOTE £3.40: £1.10, £1.10, £3.10; EX 9.50 Trifecta £66.50 Pool: £1,482.18 - 16.70 winning tickets..
Owner Mrs Fitri Hay **Bred** Oceanic Bloodstock & Mme A Gravereaux **Trained** Newmarket, Suffolk

FOCUS
They pace was solid in this fair handicap, in which the first two were always to the fore. The form looks good for the grad and the winner is capable of better.

6609 EVENTMASTERS.CO.UK "IT'S BEEN EMOTIONAL TRENCHY" H'CAP (DIV II) 7f 32y(P)
7:40 (7:40) (Class 4) (0-85,85) 3-Y-0+ **£4,690** (£1,395; £697; £348) **Stalls** High

Form RPR

2002 **1** **Free Spin (IRE)**[28] 5705 4-9-4 **85**... LMcNiff(3) 5 95
(David Barron) *mid-div: hdwy over 2f out: rdn over 1f out: edgd lft and styd on to ld wl ins fnl f* **4/1**[3]

5334 **2** *1* **Light Burst (USA)**[13] 6204 4-9-1 **82**......................... ThomasBrown(3) 7 89
(Ismail Mohammed) *chsd ldrs: led over 1f out: rdn: edgd lft and hdd wl ins fnl f* **7/2**[2]

-362 **3** *5* **Diamond Belle**[17] 6072 4-9-3 **81**...................................... PatCosgrave 6 75
(Noel Quinlan) *led: rdn and hdd over 1f out: edgd rt and no ex fnl f* **9/1**

0500 **4** *1 3/4* **Mr Red Clubs (IRE)**[6] 6384 4-8-8 **77**......................... TobyAtkinson(5) 9 66
(Michael Appleby) *hld up: drvn along over 2f out: styd on ins fnl f: nvr nrr* **11/4**[1]

0010 **5** *1/2* **Caldercruix (USA)**[13] 6203 6-8-11 **80**............................(b) RyanTate(5) 8 68
(James Evans) *s.i.s: hld up: rdn over 1f out: styd on ins fnl f: nrst fin* **28/1**

0202 **6** *nk* **Kung Hei Fat Choy (USA)**[10] 6291 4-9-0 **78**..........(b) JamesSullivan 10 65
(James Given) *chsd ldrs: rdn over 2f out: wknd over 1f out* **8/1**

2610 **7** *1 1/4* **Yahilwa (USA)**[29] 5676 3-8-13 **80**.................................(p) LukeMorris 3 63
(James Tate) *w ldr: rdn over 2f out: wknd fnl f* **25/1**

201 **8** *1 3/4* **Mr David (USA)**[13] 6215 6-9-3 **81**..................................(b) DavidProbert 1 60
(Jamie Osborne) *hld up: rdn over 1f out: nvr on terms* **9/1**

4422 **9** *nk* **Ssafa**[108] 2963 5-8-9 **73**... SteveDrowne 4 51
(Alastair Lidderdale) *hld up: a in rr* **25/1**

0046 **10** *1/2* **Living Leader**[35] 5489 4-8-13 **77**..............................(v) TomMcLaughlin 2 54
(Nick Littmoden) *sn pushed along and prom: rdn over 2f out: wknd over 1f out* **14/1**

1m 28.79s (-0.81) **Going Correction** +0.025s/f (Slow)
WFA 3 from 4yo+ 3lb **10** Ran SP% **117.8**
Speed ratings (Par 105): **105,103,98,96,95 95,93,91,91,90**
Tote Swingers 1&2 £4.60, 2&3 £14.10, 1&3 £7.00 CSF £18.20 CT £119.80 TOTE £6.70: £2.00, £1.50, £2.20; EX 28.20 Trifecta £144.60 Pool: £1,428.36 - 7.40 winning tickets..
Owner Laurence O'Kane **Bred** Glending Bloodstock **Trained** Maunby, N Yorks

FOCUS
This was run in a time 0.85sec slower than the previous division. The first two finished clear and the winner produced a personal best.

6610 NAME A RACE TO ENHANCE YOUR BRAND H'CAP 7f 32y(P)
8:10 (8:11) (Class 6) (0-60,60) 3-Y-0+ **£1,940** (£577; £288; £144) **Stalls** High

Form RPR

0036 **1** **Sleek**[29] 5674 3-9-4 **60**...(b) AndreaAtzeni 4 68+
(Marco Botti) *chsd ldr tl led 3f out: rdn over 1f out: hung rt ins fnl f: hung lft nr fin: styd on* **3/1**[2]

5034 **2** *3/4* **Hoppy's Flyer (FR)**[7] 6368 5-9-6 **59**......................... TomMcLaughlin 11 66
(Mark Brisbourne) *hld up: hdwy 1/2-way: rdn to chse wnr over 1f out: sn hung rt: styd on: hung lft nr fin* **14/1**

0133 **3** *nk* **Silly Billy (IRE)**[10] 6276 5-9-5 **58**............................ RichardKingscote 9 64+
(Brian Ellison) *hld up: hdwy over 1f out: r.o: nt rch ldrs* **10/3**[3]

6024 **4** *1 1/4* **Piccolo Express**[7] 6367 7-9-7 **60**.. ShaneKelly 10 63
(Brian Baugh) *a.p: rdn over 1f out: styng on same pce whn nt clr run towards fin* **11/1**

2660 **5** *8* **Bitaphon (IRE)**[144] 1887 4-8-13 **57**.............................. TobyAtkinson(5) 1 38
(Michael Appleby) *led 4f: sn rdn: wknd over 1f out* **25/1**

5060 **6** *4* **Seamster**[38] 5365 6-9-2 **55**..(vt) FrederikTylicki 7 25
(Richard Ford) *chsd ldrs: rdn and ev ch over 2f out: wknd over 1f out* **25/1**

3000 **7** *1/2* **High On The Hog (IRE)**[32] 5594 5-9-1 **54**........................(p) JimmyQuinn 3 23
(Mark Brisbourne) *mid-div: rdn over 2f out: sn wknd* **50/1**

1-5 **8** *1* **Ioannou**[250] 194 4-9-6 **59**.. PatCosgrave 2 25
(Noel Quinlan) *prom: rdn over 2f out: wknd over 1f out* **9/4**[1]

5560 **9** *1 1/2* **Compton Silver**[22] 5935 3-8-10 **57**................................(b) RyanTate(5) 5 18
(Hans Adielsson) *hld up: rdn and wknd over 2f out* **14/1**

0105 **10** *nk* **Brown Volcano (IRE)**[44] 5154 4-9-3 **56**.......................(p) LukeMorris 12 18
(John O'Shea) *s.i.s: sn pushed along in rr: rdn over 2f out: sn wknd* **25/1**

2230 **11** *16* **Mucky Molly**[73] 4145 5-9-1 **54**..(vt) SteveDrowne 6
(Alison Hutchinson) *s.i.s: outpcd* **25/1**

1m 30.38s (0.78) **Going Correction** +0.025s/f (Slow)
WFA 3 from 4yo+ 3lb **11** Ran SP% **117.9**
Speed ratings (Par 101): **96,95,94,93,84 79,79,77,76,75 57**
Tote Swingers 1&2 £5.40, 2&3 £5.80, 1&3 £2.60 CSF £40.57 CT £151.70 TOTE £3.40: £2.00, £3.20, £1.70; EX 56.50 Trifecta £339.00 Pool: £1,153.77 - 2.55 winning tickets..
Owner Miss Yvonne Jacques **Bred** London Thoroughbred Services Ltd **Trained** Newmarket, Suffolk

FOCUS
A weak handicap with a spread of just 6lb. They went a strong gallop and the first four finished clear. The placed horses set the standard.

6611 FOLLOW US ON TWITTER @WOLVESRACES MAIDEN FILLIES' STKS 1m 141y(P)
8:40 (8:40) (Class 5) 3-Y-0+ **£2,587** (£770; £384; £192) **Stalls** Low

Form RPR

-642 **1** **Vanity Rules**[32] 5588 3-9-0 79.. WilliamBuick 9 85
(John Gosden) *chsd ldrs: rdn over 2f out: styd on u.p to ld nr fin* **15/8**[2]

60 **2** *1* **Fossola (USA)**[35] 5478 3-9-0 0.. AdamKirby 2 83
(Charlie Appleby) *led: rdn over 2f out: hdd nr fin* **33/1**

3602 **3** *¾* **Hanzada (USA)**[15] 6134 3-9-0 83.. AndreaAtzeni 1 81
(Ed Dunlop) *chsd ldrs: rdn over 1f out: styd on same pce ins fnl f* **13/8**[1]

2024 **4** *½* **Running Deer (IRE)**[26] 5802 4-8-12 75.................... LouisSteward[(7)] 10 79
(Lady Cecil) *a.p: chsd ldr 5f out: pushed along over 1f out: styd on same pce ins fnl f* **5/1**[3]

3-5 **5** *7* **La Belle Epoque (USA)**[15] 6133 3-9-0 0....................(b[1]) LukeMorris 6 64
(Gerard Butler) *hld up: hdwy over 3f out: rdn over 2f out: wknd over 1f out* **16/1**

52 **6** *27* **Invincible Magic (IRE)**[28] 5695 3-9-0 0........................ AhmedAjtebi 5
(Charlie Appleby) *hld up: wknd over 2f out* **14/1**

30 **7** *3 ½* **Penny Stock (IRE)**[10] 6289 3-9-0 0.................................. KierenFallon 4
(Mark Johnston) *prom: pushed along over 3f out: wknd over 2f out* **16/1**

0 **8** *8* **Ismaali**[103] 3136 3-9-0 0.. JamesSullivan 7
(James Given) *s.i.s: outpcd* **100/1**

00P/ **9** *11* **Tea And Sympathy**[812] 3596 5-9-0 0........................ TobyAtkinson[(5)] 3
(Michael Appleby) *sn pushed along in rr: nt clr run over 7f out: bhd fnl 5f* **100/1**

/0-6 **10** *2 ½* **Mrs Medley**[14] 6176 7-9-0 27.. AnnStokell[(5)] 8
(Ann Stokell) *plld hrd: trckd ldr over 3f: wknd 4f out* **200/1**

1m 49.77s (-0.73) **Going Correction** +0.025s/f (Slow)
WFA 3 from 4yo+ 5lb **10** Ran SP% **113.4**
Speed ratings (Par 100): **104,103,102,102,95 71,68,61,51,49**
Tote Swingers 1&2 £7.20, 2&3 £9.80, 1&3 £1.60 CSF £63.84 TOTE £3.00: £1.10, £6.00, £1.10; EX 54.20 Trifecta £186.80 Pool: £1,563.30 - 6.27 winning tickets..
Owner A E Oppenheimer **Bred** Hascombe And Valiant Studs **Trained** Newmarket, Suffolk

FOCUS
Fair fillies' form, rated at face value.

6612 BOOK NOW FOR CHRISTMAS H'CAP 1m 1f 103y(P)
9:10 (9:14) (Class 6) (0-65,69) 3-Y-0+ **£1,940** (£577; £288; £144) **Stalls** Low

Form RPR

0000 **1** **Monzino (USA)**[56] 4718 5-8-12 **60**.................................. PaulBooth[(7)] 8 69
(Michael Chapman) *s.s: hld up: hdwy over 1f out: r.o to ld nr fin* **25/1**

1021 **2** *nk* **Exclusive Waters (IRE)**[6] 6398 3-9-9 **69** 6ex.................... AdamKirby 5 78
(William Knight) *prom: lost pl over 3f out: rallied over 1f out: rdn to ld ins fnl f: edgd lft: hdd nr fin* **5/4**[1]

0406 **3** *2* **Signature Dish (IRE)**[14] 6153 3-9-3 **63**........................ DavidProbert 9 68
(Andrew Balding) *a.p: rdn over 2f out: styd on* **9/1**

6414 **4** *nk* **Handsome Stranger (IRE)**[8] 6339 3-9-2 **62** 6ex..........(b) KierenFallon 10 66
(Alan Bailey) *hld up: hdwy 1/2-way: rdn and ev ch ins fnl f: styd on same pce* **10/1**

004 **5** *1* **Testa Rossa (IRE)**[13] 6218 3-9-4 **64**........................ SebSanders 12 66
(J W Hills) *chsd ldrs: rdn to ld over 1f out: hdd and no ex ins fnl f* **10/1**

-234 **6** *¾* **Malih**[35] 5479 4-9-6 **64**.. MichaelJMMurphy[(3)] 6 64
(Jamie Osborne) *hld up: rdn over 2f out: hdwy over 1f out: nt clr run and swtchd lft ins fnl f: nt rch ldrs* **6/1**[3]

3600 **7** *3 ¼* **Perpetual Ambition**[16] 6109 3-9-1 **61**........................(p) FrederikTylicki 1 55
(Paul D'Arcy) *led: rdn and hdd 2f out: wknd ins fnl f* **28/1**

4040 **8** *4 ½* **Magic Lando (FR)**[25] 5833 3-8-12 **61**.................... ThomasBrown[(3)] 13 45
(Ismail Mohammed) *sn chsng ldr: led 2f out: rdn and hdd over 1f out: wknd ins fnl f* **7/2**[2]

4006 **9** *5* **Kilburn**[21] 5948 9-9-10 **65**..(b) SteveDrowne 2 38
(Alastair Lidderdale) *hld up: a in rr: wknd over 2f out* **28/1**

600 **10** *4* **Millies Quest**[15] 6134 4-9-10 **65**.. BrettDoyle 4 39
(Martin Smith) *got loose prior to the s: trckd ldrs: racd keenly: rdn over 2f out: sn wknd* **33/1**

064- **11** *3 ¾* **Straight Shot (IRE)**[330] 7352 4-9-8 **63**........................ JimmyQuinn 11 20
(John Butler) *hld up: rdn and wknd over 2f out* **33/1**

2m 2.65s (0.95) **Going Correction** +0.025s/f (Slow)
WFA 3 from 4yo+ 5lb **11** Ran SP% **125.8**
Speed ratings (Par 101): **96,95,93,93,92 92,89,85,80,77 73**
Tote Swingers 1&2 £13.50, 2&3 £3.50, 1&3 £12.60 CSF £58.43 CT £343.49 TOTE £19.50: £6.10, £1.20, £2.50; EX 102.50 Trifecta £963.80 Part won. Pool: £1,285.19 - 0.93 winning tickets..
Owner Mrs M Chapman **Bred** Pillar Property Services Inc **Trained** Market Rasen, Lincs
■ Stewards' Enquiry : David Probert two-day ban; used whip above permitted level (4th-5th Oct).

FOCUS
A moderate handicap and a rapidly changing picture in the straight. The form is not entirely convincing.
T/Plt: £61.70 to a £1 stake. Pool: £96,296.9 - 1138.2 winning tickets. T/Qpdt: £10.90 to a £1 stake. Pool: £11,670.72 - 790.27 winning tickets. CR

6613 - 6617a (Foreign Racing) - See Raceform Interactive

4651 MAISONS-LAFFITTE (R-H)
Friday, September 20

OFFICIAL GOING: Turf: good to soft

6618a LA COUPE DE MAISONS-LAFFITTE (GROUP 3) (3YO+) (TURF) 1m 2f (S)
2:20 (2:22) 3-Y-0+ **£32,520** (£13,008; £9,756; £6,504; £3,252)

RPR

1 **Cirrus Des Aigles (FR)**[26] 5807 7-9-0 0............ ChristopheSoumillon 5 116
(Mme C Barande-Barbe, France) *led: set stdy pce: rdn whn jnd 2f out: styd on u.p and asserted again ins fnl 120yds: in control and pushed out towards fin* **2/1**[2]

2 *2 ½* **Vally Jem (FR)**[33] 5574 4-8-10 0..................................(p) AntoineHamelin 6 107
(D Sepulchre, France) *hld up in last but wl in tch: rdn over 2f out: styd on and wnt 2nd post: no threat to wnr* **18/1**

3 *hd* **Smoking Sun (USA)**[41] 5298 4-9-0 0........................ StephanePasquier 2 111
(P Bary, France) *trckd ldr on outer: rdn to chal and jnd ldr 2f out: styd on and upsides wnr tl no ex ins fnl 120yds: fdd and dropped to 3rd post* **19/5**[3]

4 *¾* **Pilote (IRE)**[36] 5462 3-8-8 0.. OlivierPeslier 3 109
(A Fabre, France) *trckd ldr on inner: rdn over 2f out: nt qckn u.p: kpt on same pce fnl f and nvr able to chal* **13/10**[1]

5 *4 ½* **Grace Lady (FR)**[33] 5574 4-9-2 0.. GeraldMosse 4 102
(Mlle T Puitg, France) *t.k.h: hld up in tch on outer: rdn over 2f out: outpcd in last ent fnl f: coasted home once btn* **15/2**

2m 11.19s (8.79)
WFA 3 from 4yo+ 6lb **5** Ran SP% **114.7**
WIN (incl. 1 euro stake): 3.00. PLACES: 2.30, 5.30. SF: 29.90.
Owner Jean-Claude-Alain Dupouy **Bred** M Yvon Lelimouzin & M Benoit Deschamps **Trained** France

6581 AYR (L-H)
Saturday, September 21

OFFICIAL GOING: Good to soft (soft in places; 8.7, sprint course: far side 8.6, centre 8.7, stands' side 8.8)
Wind: Light, half behind Weather: Overcast

6619 SKED CONSTRUCTION - CONCRETE'S WHAT WE DO NURSERY H'CAP 1m
1:30 (1:31) (Class 2) 2-Y-0
£12,450 (£3,728; £1,864; £932; £466; £234) **Stalls** Low

Form RPR

3106 **1** **Latenightrequest**[10] 6303 2-8-2 **70**........................ PatrickMathers 9 75
(Richard Fahey) *s.i.s: bhd and pushed along: gd hdwy 2f out: led appr fnl f: kpt on wl* **25/1**

3202 **2** *¾* **El Beau (IRE)**[11] 6271 2-8-2 **73**.. RaulDaSilva[(3)] 10 76
(John Quinn) *prom: rdn over 2f out: kpt on wl fnl f to take 2nd nr fin* **6/1**

0310 **3** *nk* **Tiger Twenty Two**[31] 5656 2-8-11 **84**........................ GeorgeChaloner[(5)] 7 86
(Richard Fahey) *prom: rdn over 2f out: ev ch appr fnl f: one pce last 100yds: lost 2nd nr fin* **9/1**

0424 **4** *3* **Boogangoo (IRE)**[2] 6545 2-8-7 **75**.. TomEaves 4 71
(Keith Dalgleish) *led: rdn 2f out: hdd appr fnl f: wknd last 75yds* **18/1**

1430 **5** *1* **Les Gar Gan (IRE)**[9] 6326 2-8-9 **77** ow1........................ PaulMulrennan 5 71
(Keith Dalgleish) *t.k.h: hld up: rdn over 2f out: no imp tl styd on fnl f: nvr able to chal* **11/2**[3]

3121 **6** *½* **Braidley (IRE)**[10] 6303 2-9-7 **89**.. GrahamLee 11 81
(James Bethell) *hld up: pushed along over 3f out: rallied 2f out: no imp fnl f* **10/3**[1]

6231 **7** *9* **Eddiemaurice (IRE)**[11] 6271 2-8-0 **73** ow1............ ConnorBeasley[(5)] 2 46
(Richard Guest) *hld up towards rr: rdn and outpcd over 2f out: sn btn* **13/2**

2144 **8** *1* **Culdaff (IRE)**[38] 5400 2-9-1 **83**.. TomQueally 6 53
(Charles Hills) *t.k.h: pressed ldr: rdn over 2f out: wknd over 1f out* **12/1**

01 **9** *16* **Light Weight (IRE)**[26] 5827 2-8-8 **76**........................ JamieSpencer 3 11
(Kevin Ryan) *t.k.h: trckd ldrs tl rdn and wknd over 2f out: t.o* **9/2**[2]

044 **10** *1* **Citizen Kaine (IRE)**[67] 4386 2-8-2 **70**........................ DuranFentiman 12
(Jo Hughes) *prom: rdn over 2f out: sn wknd: t.o* **16/1**

1m 44.3s (0.50) **Going Correction** +0.20s/f (Good) **10** Ran SP% **116.9**
Speed ratings (Par 101): **105,104,103,100,99 99,90,89,73,72**
toteswingers 1&2 £26.20, 2&3 £10.30, 1&3 £33.90 CSF £168.88 CT £1477.49 TOTE £33.70: £8.00, £2.70, £3.00; EX 183.00 Trifecta £1728.00 Part won. Pool: £2304.00 - 0.45 winning units..
Owner Middleham Park Racing XVI & Partner **Bred** Mrs S J Walker **Trained** Musley Bank, N Yorks

FOCUS
Home bend moved out 6m adding about 18yds to races on Round course. The ground was drying out and not as soft as it had been on the first two days and was described as tacky by riders in the first, although Raul da Silva thought it was good. The opener was run in a time 5.80sec outside the standard. Recent Group 3 winner Top Notch Tonto won this nursery last year. The pace was sound and this is fair form.

6620 WILLIAM HILL - BET ON THE MOVE DOONSIDE CUP STKS (LISTED RACE) 1m 2f
2:05 (2:05) (Class 1) 3-Y-0+
£34,026 (£12,900; £6,456; £3,216; £1,614; £810) **Stalls** Low

Form RPR

1300 **1** **Sharestan (IRE)**[175] 1268 5-9-0 111........................ KierenFallon 7 108
(Saeed bin Suroor) *prom on outside: stdy hdwy to ld 2f out: sn rdn: hld on wl fnl f* **11/4**[2]

-465 **2** *nk* **Willie The Whipper**[31] 5653 3-8-8 107........................ JamieSpencer 2 107
(Ann Duffield) *hld up in tch: rdn over 2f out: hdwy over 1f out: chsd wnr ins fnl f: r.o* **6/1**

1501 **3** *1 ¼* **Clon Brulee (IRE)**[9] 6332 4-9-0 96........................ GrahamGibbons 6 105
(David Barron) *trckd ldrs: ev ch gng wl over 2f out: rdn over 1f out: kpt on same pce fnl f* **9/1**

1250 **4** *½* **Romantic Settings**[14] 6186 3-8-3 93........................ PatrickMathers 4 99
(Richard Fahey) *led at slow pce: rdn and hdd 2f out: rallied: kpt on same pce fnl f* **25/1**

The Form Book Flat, Raceform Ltd, Compton, RG20 6NL.

-130 **5** *1* **First Mohican**[27] 5807 5-9-0 108 TomQueally 3 102
(Lady Cecil) *s.i.s: sn pushed along and prom: hdwy and ev ch over 2f out to over 1f out: outpcd fnl f* **7/4**[1]

012- **6** *2 ¾* **Hajras (IRE)**[322] 7557 4-9-0 105 PaulHanagan 5 97
(Mark Johnston) *w ldr: rdn over 2f out: wknd fnl f* **11/2**[3]

341- **7** *3 ½* **Media Hype**[297] 7895 6-9-0 105 JimCrowley 1 90
(K R Burke) *t.k.h: in tch: struggling over 2f out: sn btn* **16/1**

2m 14.31s (2.31) **Going Correction** +0.20s/f (Good)
WFA 3 from 4yo+ 6lb **7** Ran SP% **112.4**
Speed ratings (Par 111): **98,97,96,96,95 93,90**
toteswingers 1&2 £5.20, 2&3 £5.00, 1&3 £4.90 CSF £18.78 TOTE £3.50: £2.10, £2.30; EX 14.80 Trifecta £116.90 Pool: £3141.94 - 20.15 winning units..
Owner Godolphin **Bred** His Highness The Aga Khan's Studs S C **Trained** Newmarket, Suffolk

FOCUS
The early pace was slow and the race turned into a sprint from the turn in. Saeed Bin Suroor sent out his fourth winner of the race in the last ten years.

6621 WILLIAM HILL AYR SILVER CUP (H'CAP) 6f
2:40 (2:40) (Class 2) 3-Y-0+

£31,125 (£9,320; £4,660; £2,330; £1,165; £585) **Stalls** Centre

Form RPR

2000 **1** **Ancient Cross**[7] 6391 9-9-10 **97** (tp) PatCosgrave 26 106
(Michael Easterby) *s.i.s: hld up stands' side: hdwy over 2f out: led ins fnl f: drvn out: 1st of 18 in gp* **33/1**

0200 **2** *nk* **Fast Shot**[35] 5544 5-9-0 **87** DavidAllan 20 95+
(Tim Easterby) *midfield stands' side: effrt whn nt clr run over 1f out: styd on wl fnl f: jst hld: 2nd of 18 in gp* **25/1**

-604 **3** *shd* **An Saighdiur (IRE)**[34] 5567 6-9-9 **96** WJLee 27 104+
(Andrew Slattery, Ire) *trckd ldrs: effrt whn no room over 1f out: swtchd lft ins fnl f: kpt on strly: 3rd of 18 in gp* **17/2**[2]

1104 **4** *1 ¼* **Picture Dealer**[25] 5851 4-9-2 **89** FergusSweeney 15 93+
(Gary Moore) *hld up stands' side: short of room fr 1/2-way: hdwy and prom whn checked ins fnl f: kpt on wl: 4th of 18 in gp* **28/1**

003 **5** *nse* **Boots And Spurs**[28] 5738 4-9-4 **91** (v) JimCrowley 17 95
(K R Burke) *hld up: hdwy whn nt clr run and swtchd lft over 1f out: r.o wl fnl f: 5th of 18 in gp* **16/1**

0021 **6** *¾* **Sir Reginald**[8] 6352 5-9-4 **91** 5ex PaulHanagan 2 92+
(Richard Fahey) *hld up in tch centre: hdwy to ld that gp over 1f out: kpt on fnl f: nt rch stands' side ldrs: 1st of 9 in gp* **14/1**

02-2 **7** *1* **Take Cover**[49] 4983 6-9-6 **93** GrahamLee 22 91
(David C Griffiths) *trckd stands' side ldrs: effrt and rdn over 2f out: one pce fnl f: 6th of 18 in gp* **8/1**[1]

0063 **8** *½* **Yeeoow (IRE)**[8] 6352 4-9-0 **92** JoeyHaynes(5) 21 88
(K R Burke) *trckd stands' side ldrs: rdn 2f out: drifted lft and one pce ins fnl f: 7th of 18 in gp* **12/1**

1004 **9** *2* **The Confessor**[22] 5943 6-9-4 **91** CathyGannon 24 81
(Henry Candy) *cl up stands' side: rdn 2f out: outpcd ins fnl f: 8th of 18 in gp* **22/1**

0100 **10** *1* **Cheviot (USA)**[21] 5984 7-9-6 **96** (p) JasonHart(3) 25 83
(Ian Semple) *led stands' side: rdn 2f out: hdd ins fnl f: sn btn: 9th of 18 in gp* **33/1**

4132 **11** *shd* **Clear Spring (IRE)**[18] 6078 5-9-7 **94** PhillipMakin 13 80
(John Spearing) *chsd ldng gp stands' side: rdn over 2f out: no imp over 1f out: 10th of 18 in gp* **25/1**

0034 **12** *nk* **Chooseday (IRE)**[35] 5544 4-9-0 **87** (p) PatSmullen 8 72+
(Kevin Ryan) *cl up centre: led over 2f out to over 1f out: sn one pce: 2nd of 9 in gp* **20/1**

3051 **13** *¾* **Crew Cut (IRE)**[35] 5537 5-8-11 **87** (b) RobertTart(3) 23 70
(Jeremy Gask) *s.i.s: hld up stands' side: hdwy over 1f out: kpt on fnl f: nrst fin: 11th of 18 in gp* **16/1**

2202 **14** *¾* **Links Drive Lady**[29] 5700 5-9-1 **88** RobertWinston 6 69
(Dean Ivory) *hld up centre: swtchd to r on outside of stands' side gp: 1/2-way: effrt and prom 2f out: wknd ins fnl f: 12th of 18 in gp* **25/1**

4000 **15** *1 ¾* **Polski Max**[35] 5545 3-9-2 **96** GeorgeChaloner(5) 10 71
(Richard Fahey) *prom centre: rdn over 2f out: one pce fr over 1f out: 3rd of 9 in gp* **28/1**

2662 **16** *1 ¾* **Singeur (IRE)**[11] 6273 6-9-2 **89** PaulMulrennan 5 58
(Robin Bastiman) *hld up centre: rdn over 2f out: no imp over 1f out: 4th of 9 in gp* **33/1**

112 **17** *¾* **Harrison George (IRE)**[14] 6190 8-9-3 **95** (bt) NatashaEaton(5) 11 62
(P J O'Gorman) *prom on outside of stands' side gp: rdn over 2f out: edgd rt and wknd over 1f out: 13th of 18 in gp* **25/1**

2304 **18** *nk* **Trail Blaze (IRE)**[14] 6183 4-9-8 **95** (b) NeilCallan 9 61
(Kevin Ryan) *chsd centre ldrs: rdn along 1/2-way: outpcd fr 2f out: 5th of 9 in gp* **12/1**

6201 **19** *½* **Pearl Ice**[9] 6331 5-9-8 **95** 5ex JamieSpencer 19 59
(David Barron) *hld up stands' side: rdn 2f out: nvr able to chal: 14th of 18 in gp* **12/1**

0603 **20** *1 ¼* **Thunderball**[9] 6331 7-9-3 **90** (p) TomQueally 1 50
(Scott Dixon) *w centre ldr: rdn 1/2-way: wknd wl over 1f out: 6th of 9 in gp* **25/1**

2400 **21** *2 ¼* **Dick Bos**[35] 5545 4-9-3 **90** DanielTudhope 12 43
(David O'Meara) *in tch on outside of stands' side gp: rdn over 2f out: wknd over 1f out: 15th of 18 in gp* **20/1**

1400 **22** *½* **Gandalak (FR)**[98] 3335 4-8-13 **91** (b[1]) DavidBergin(5) 18 43
(David O'Meara) *in tch stands' side: rdn and wknd 2f out: 16th of 18 in gp* **25/1**

3103 **23** *shd* **Rodrigo De Torres**[35] 5545 6-9-7 **94** BarryMcHugh 4 45
(David Nicholls) *t.k.h early: trckd centre ldrs: rdn over 2f out: wkng whn hmpd over 1f out: 7th of 9 in gp* **40/1**

0316 **24** *1 ¾* **Gramercy (IRE)**[8] 6352 6-9-8 **95** (b) KierenFallon 3 41
(David Simcock) *bhd and sn drvn along centre: nvr on terms: 8th of 9 in gp* **20/1**

0612 **25** *1 ½* **Colonel Mak**[49] 5009 6-9-8 **95** GrahamGibbons 7 36
(David Barron) *led centre to over 2f out: sn wknd: last of 9 in gp* **10/1**[3]

0530 **26** *nk* **Nameitwhatyoulike**[35] 5544 4-9-2 **89** DuranFentiman 14 29
(Michael Easterby) *in tch stands' side tl rdn and wknd 2f out: 17th of 18 in gp* **28/1**

0000 **27** *1* **Stonefield Flyer**[21] 5984 4-9-8 **95** TomEaves 16 32
(Keith Dalgleish) *chsd stands' side ldrs to 1/2-way: sn rdn and wknd: last of 18 in gp* **33/1**

1m 13.45s (1.05) **Going Correction** +0.325s/f (Good)
WFA 3 from 4yo+ 2lb **27** Ran SP% **140.5**
Speed ratings (Par 109): **106,105,105,103,103 102,101,100,98,96 96,96,95,94,91 89,88,88,87,85 82,82,82,79,77 77,75**
toteswingers 1&2 £87.70, 2&3 £109.70, 1&3 £23.10 CSF £706.39 CT £7519.54 TOTE £37.30: £8.40, £5.70, £2.60, £8.00; EX 416.70 Trifecta £2248.10 Part won. Pool: £2997.46 - 0.40 winning units..
Owner Pete Bown,BackUp Technology & Steve Hull **Bred** Darley **Trained** Sheriff Hutton, N Yorks

FOCUS
A high-class handicap and very open, with only a 10lb spread between the runners. They split into two groups with ten coming down the centre and the rest on the stands' side, with the fair rail avoided altogether. The groups merged in the latter stages. High numbers dominated, with seven of the first ten home drawn in the 20s and only one of the first 11 coming from a single-figure draw. The winner is rated back to his best.

6622 WILLIAM HILL - IN THE APP STORE FIRTH OF CLYDE STKS (GROUP 3) (FILLIES) 6f
3:15 (3:15) (Class 1) 2-Y-O

£34,026 (£12,900; £6,456; £3,216; £1,614; £810) **Stalls** Centre

Form RPR

31 **1** **Coral Mist**[15] 6160 2-8-12 0 TomQueally 7 98+
(Charles Hills) *hld up in rr: gd hdwy and swtchd outside over 2f out: rn to ld in clsng stages* **11/2**[3]

0214 **2** *nse* **Hoku (IRE)**[26] 5837 2-8-12 88 HarryBentley 5 98
(Olly Stevens) *s.i.s: sn w ldrs: led jst ins fnl f: hdd and no ex in clsng stages* **16/1**

0203 **3** *nk* **Ventura Mist**[26] 5837 2-8-12 93 (p) DuranFentiman 4 97
(Tim Easterby) *w ldrs: kpt on wl ins fnl f: no ex towards fin* **20/1**

21 **4** *½* **Valonia**[52] 4877 2-8-12 0 JamieSpencer 15 96
(Henry Candy) *led: hdd jst ins fnl f: kpt on same pce last 50yds* **9/4**[1]

2 **5** *shd* **Remember You (IRE)**[20] 6021 2-8-12 0 WayneLordan 11 95
(David Wachman, Ire) *chsd ldrs on ins: n.m.r and swtchd lft appr fnl f: kpt on ins fnl f* **3/1**[2]

41 **6** *½* **Veiled Intrigue**[28] 5740 2-8-12 76 FergusSweeney 8 94
(Henry Candy) *s.i.s: hdwy on outer to chse ldrs 3f out: kpt on same pce fnl f* **28/1**

0045 **7** *hd* **Lady Chantilly (IRE)**[1] 6584 2-8-12 90 KierenFallon 14 93
(Jo Hughes) *in rr: hmpd over 2f out: hdwy over 1f out: styd on ins fnl f* **20/1**

2011 **8** *nk* **Blockade (IRE)**[21] 5994 2-8-12 94 GrahamLee 9 92
(James Tate) *chsd ldrs: one pce over 1f out* **14/1**

223 **9** *1 ¾* **City Zen (IRE)**[28] 5767 2-8-12 92 BarryMcHugh 1 87
(Tony Coyle) *in rr: hdwy over 2f out: chsng ldrs over 1f out: sn wknd* **25/1**

1062 **10** *2* **Azagal (IRE)**[9] 6328 2-8-12 92 DavidAllan 12 81
(Tim Easterby) *in rr: swtchd rt to stands' side rail after 1f: swtchd lft and sme hdwy over 2f out: wknd appr fnl f* **7/1**

22 **11** *1 ½* **Sandra's Diamond (IRE)**[15] 6174 2-8-12 0 TomEaves 2 77
(Keith Dalgleish) *chsd ldrs: lost pl over 2f out: sn bhd* **25/1**

0313 **12** *3 ¼* **Simple Magic (IRE)**[14] 6201 2-8-12 94 JimCrowley 6 67
(John Gosden) *hld up in mid-div: effrt over 2f out: lost pl over 1f out* **12/1**

1m 14.24s (1.84) **Going Correction** +0.325s/f (Good) **12** Ran SP% **124.6**
Speed ratings (Par 102): **100,99,99,98,98 98,97,97,95,92 90,86**
toteswingers 1&2 £28.80, 2&3 £37.80, 1&3 £32.30 CSF £85.48 TOTE £6.90: £2.30, £4.20, £6.90; EX 102.40 Trifecta £2256.70 Pool: £70399.62 - 23.39 winning units..
Owner Triermore Stud & R A Scarborough **Bred** Serpentine B'Stock & Genesis Green Stud **Trained** Lambourn, Berks

■ Stewards' Enquiry : Duran Fentiman two-day ban; used whip above permitted level (5th-7th Oct).

FOCUS
The field came over to the stands' side after a furlong or so. The first eight were separated by around two lengths at the line so the form is questionable and has to rate poor for the grade, but the winner produced a likeable performance.

6623 WILLIAM HILL AYR GOLD CUP (HERITAGE H'CAP) 6f
3:50 (3:51) (Class 2) 3-Y-0+

£96,487 (£28,892; £14,446; £7,223; £3,611; £1,813) **Stalls** Centre

Form RPR

0631 **1** **Highland Colori (IRE)**[26] 5844 5-8-13 **104** 5ex OisinMurphy(5) 19 116
(Andrew Balding) *prom stands' side gp: led over 1f out: kpt on strly fnl f* **20/1**

0100 **2** *2 ¼* **Louis The Pious**[35] 5545 5-8-12 **98** DanielTudhope 18 103
(David O'Meara) *prom stands' side: effrt and ev ch over 1f out to ins fnl f: kpt on same pce* **25/1**

0641 **3** *½* **Jack Dexter**[84] 3822 4-9-10 **110** GrahamLee 22 113
(Jim Goldie) *trckd stands' side ldrs: n.m.r briefly over 2f out: effrt over 1f out: kpt on fnl f* **8/1**[3]

4100 **4** *1* **Heaven's Guest (IRE)**[28] 5738 3-8-7 **100** GeorgeChaloner(5) 16 100
(Richard Fahey) *towards rr on outside of stands' side gp: hdwy over 1f out: r.o ins fnl f* **25/1**

1061 **5** *hd* **Baccarat (IRE)**[35] 5545 4-9-1 **101** PaulHanagan 14 100
(Richard Fahey) *in tch on outside of stands' side gp: drvn over 2f out: hdwy over 1f out: kpt on: no imp* **15/2**[2]

0046 **6** *hd* **Regal Parade**[21] 5992 9-8-8 **97** (t) RobertTart(3) 5 96
(Milton Bradley) *hld up centre gp: gd hdwy on outside over 1f out: kpt on ins fnl f: no imp* **25/1**

4060 **7** *nk* **Our Jonathan**[7] 6391 6-8-11 **97** HarryBentley 12 95
(David Simcock) *s.i.s: sn midfield centre: rdn over 2f out: effrt and hdwy over 1f out: kpt on same pce fnl f* **20/1**

0003 **8** *nk* **Hoof It**[14] 6193 6-9-7 **107** GrahamGibbons 24 104
(Michael Easterby) *chsd stands' side ldrs: effrt and ev ch over 2f out: outpcd fnl f* **9/1**

0012 **9** *1* **Gabriel's Lad (IRE)**[14] 6183 4-8-13 **99** RobertWinston 13 93
(Denis Coakley) *hld up on outside of stands' side gp: effrt and swtchd lft over 1f out: nvr rchd ldrs* **12/1**

1012 **10** *nk* **Spinatrix**[35] 5545 5-9-0 **105** (p) ConnorBeasley(5) 25 98
(Michael Dods) *led and overall ldr whn gps merged over 2f out: hdd over 1f out: btn ins fnl f* **16/1**

0250 **11** *hd* **Mass Rally (IRE)**[13] 6235 6-9-5 **105** (b) PaulMulrennan 21 97
(Michael Dods) *s.i.s: hld up: hdwy over 1f out: nvr able to chal* **16/1**

0403 **11** *dht* **Humidor (IRE)**[11] 6282 6-9-2 **102** (t) PatCosgrave 27 94
(George Baker) *hld up stands' side: effrt and rdn over 1f out: no imp fnl f* **33/1**

0330 **13** *1 ¾* **Red Dubawi (IRE)**[7] 6415 5-8-8 **99** ConnorKing(5) 17 85
(David Marnane, Ire) *bhd stands' side tl hdwy over 1f out: nvr rchd ldrs* **25/1**

3040 **14** *2* **Dubawi Sound**[8] 6352 5-8-12 **98** (v[1]) JamieSpencer 3 78
(David Brown) *hld up centre: rdn over 2f out: nvr able to chal* **40/1**

2220 **15** *shd* **Hamza (IRE)**[14] 6193 4-9-8 **108** (b) NeilCallan 4 88
(Kevin Ryan) *cl up centre: ev ch whn gps merged over 2f out: wknd fnl f* **25/1**

22-3 **16** *hd* **Joe Eile (IRE)**[62] 4569 5-8-13 **99** EmmetMcNamara 6 78
(G M Lyons, Ire) *prom in centre: effrt and ev ch whn gps merged over 2f out: wknd ins fnl f* **33/1**

5004 **17** *shd* **Hawkeyethenoo (IRE)**[14] 6193 7-9-6 **106**........................ KierenFallon 9 85
(Jim Goldie) *sn pushed along bhd centre ldrs: shortlived effrt 2f out: btn fnl f* **14/1**

3603 **18** *1 ¾* **Hasopop (IRE)**[14] 6183 3-9-2 **104**........................ PaoloSirigu 11 77
(Marco Botti) *cl up centre: rdn over 2f out: lost pl whn hmpd over 1f out* **40/1**

0U10 **19** *1 ¾* **Bogart**[7] 6391 4-9-2 **102**........................ PatSmullen 7 70
(Kevin Ryan) *cl up centre: ev ch whn gps merged over 2f out: edgd rt over 1f out: wknd fnl f* **40/1**

4460 **20** *1 ¾* **Majestic Myles (IRE)**[31] 5651 5-8-11 **97**........................ BarryMcHugh 15 59
(Richard Fahey) *prom on outside of stands' side gp tl wknd 2f out* **40/1**

1060 **21** *3 ¾* **Duke Of Firenze**[50] 4947 4-9-1 **101**........................ CathyGannon 20 51
(Sir Michael Stoute) *hld up stands' side: rdn 2f out: nvr on terms* **25/1**

1054 **22** *2* **Lightning Cloud (IRE)**[13] 6235 5-8-13 **99**........................ TomQueally 1 43
(Kevin Ryan) *hld up centre: struggling over 2f out: sn btn* **33/1**

1161 **23** *½* **Tropics (USA)**[28] 5747 5-9-7 **107**........................ JimCrowley 26 49
(Dean Ivory) *hld up stands' side: rdn over 2f out: nvr on terms* **6/1**[1]

4346 **24** *1 ½* **Khubala (IRE)**[27] 5804 4-8-13 **99**........................(b) PhillipMakin 23 36
(Hugo Palmer) *chsd stands' side ldrs: rdn and lost pl whn hmpd over 2f out* **12/1**

1020 **25** *nse* **Nocturn**[13] 6235 4-8-13 **102**........................(p) WilliamTwiston-Davies(3) 2 39
(Jeremy Noseda) *hld up centre: rdn over 2f out: sn btn* **50/1**

1 **26** *9* **Lover Man (IRE)**[102] 3187 4-9-1 **101**........................ TomEaves 10 9
(Keith Dalgleish) *led centre gp: hdd whn gps merged over 2f out: sn wknd* **25/1**

1m 12.65s (0.25) **Going Correction** +0.325s/f (Good)
WFA 3 from 4yo+ 2lb **26** Ran SP% **138.0**
Speed ratings (Par 109): **111,108,107,106,105 105,105,104,103,102 102,102,100,97,97 97,97,94,92,90 85,82,81,79,79 67**
toteswingers 1&2 £259.80, 2&3 £71.30, 1&3 £22.00 CSF £448.12 CT £4334.38 TOTE £27.50: £5.50, £6.20, £2.80, £6.80; EX 779.10 Trifecta £7507.00 Pool: £1009.34 - 0.42 winning units..
Owner Evan M Sutherland **Bred** Rathbarry Stud **Trained** Kingsclere, Hants
■ Stewards' Enquiry : Connor Beasley two-day ban; used whip above permitted level (5th,7th Oct)

FOCUS
Another fine renewal of this valuable and prestigious sprint, in which the bottomweights were rated 97. As in the Silver Cup, they raced in two groups at first, before the smaller group of 11 tacked over to join the stands' side bunch at halfway. That was clearly the place to be and 12 of the first 13 home were drawn in double figures. The time was 0.8sec quicker than the Silver Cup. The winner rates a clear personal best, with the next two to form.

6624 WILLIAM HILL - IPHONE, IPAD, IPAD MINI AYRSHIRE H'CAP 1m
4:25 (4:25) (Class 2) (0-105,105) 3-Y-0+
£15,562 (£4,660; £2,330; £1,165; £582; £292) **Stalls** Low

Form RPR

1043 **1** **Levitate**[7] 6396 5-8-7 **93**........................(v) OisinMurphy(5) 8 101
(John Quinn) *swtchd lft after s: trckd ldr: chal over 1f out: led jst ins fnl f: styd on wl* **5/1**[1]

0012 **2** *2 ¼* **Brae Hill (IRE)**[21] 5992 7-8-11 **92**........................ PaulHanagan 9 95
(Richard Fahey) *swtchd lft after s: led: hdd jst ins fnl f: no ex* **6/1**[3]

1112 **3** *½* **Robert The Painter (IRE)**[26] 5838 5-9-4 **99**........................(v) GrahamLee 10 101
(David O'Meara) *swtchd lft after s: chsd ldr: upsides over 1f out: kpt on same pce last 75yds* **6/1**[3]

0600 **4** *hd* **Two For Two (IRE)**[28] 5768 5-9-4 **99**........................ DanielTudhope 3 100
(David O'Meara) *hmpd s: mid-div: hdwy over 2f out: chal over 1f out: kpt on same pce last 75yds* **11/2**[2]

2245 **5** *½* **Karaka Jack**[2] 6550 6-8-10 **91** oh9........................ BarryMcHugh 1 91?
(David Nicholls) *in rr and sn pushed along: hdwy on wd outside 2f out: styd on ins fnl f* **20/1**

0520 **6** *1* **Pintura**[30] 5681 6-9-10 **105**........................(p) NeilCallan 6 103
(Kevin Ryan) *chsd ldrs: pushed along over 2f out: kpt on same pce appr fnl f* **12/1**

4201 **7** *1 ¼* **Osteopathic Remedy (IRE)**[26] 5838 9-8-10 **96**...... ConnorBeasley(5) 5 91
(Michael Dods) *chsd ldrs: one pce fnl 2f* **8/1**

0100 **8** *hd* **Norse Blues**[8] 6352 5-9-1 **96**........................ GrahamGibbons 7 90
(David Barron) *stdd s: hld up in rr: hdwy over 3f out: drvn and one pce fnl 2f* **12/1**

2251 **9** *1 ½* **Aeronwyn Bryn (IRE)**[14] 6210 3-8-1 **91** oh1........................ JoeyHaynes(5) 4 82
(Michael Dods) *wnt lft s: hld up in rr: smooth hdwy over 2f out: chsng ldrs over 1f out: sn fdd* **5/1**[1]

100 **10** *13* **Anna's Pearl**[14] 6191 3-9-1 **100**........................(v¹) JamieSpencer 2 61
(Ralph Beckett) *hmpd s: hld up in rr: rdn over 2f out: sn lost pl: eased whn bhd* **11/1**

1m 43.28s (-0.52) **Going Correction** +0.20s/f (Good)
WFA 3 from 5yo+ 4lb **10** Ran SP% **116.9**
Speed ratings (Par 109): **110,107,107,107,106 105,104,104,102,89**
toteswingers 1&2 £8.00, 2&3 £9.40, 1&3 £8.40 CSF £34.86 CT £160.59 TOTE £6.50: £2.00, £2.80, £2.20; EX 38.70 Trifecta £255.30 Pool: £3824.14 - 11.23 winning units..
Owner Charles Wentworth **Bred** Cheveley Park Stud Ltd **Trained** Settrington, N Yorks
■ Stewards' Enquiry : Joey Haynes two-day ban; careless riding (5th,7th Oct).

FOCUS
It didn't pay to sit too far off the pace here. A personal best from the winner, but ordinary form for the grade.

6625 MICROTECH SUPPORT H'CAP 7f 50y
5:00 (5:00) (Class 3) (0-95,93) 3-Y-0+ **£9,703** (£2,887; £1,443; £721) **Stalls** Low

Form RPR

3120 **1** **Silver Rime (FR)**[2] 6550 8-8-6 **83** ow1........................ OisinMurphy(5) 9 92
(Linda Perratt) *hld up: hdwy on outside 2f out: led ins fnl f: drvn and kpt on wl* **20/1**

1240 **2** *nk* **Magic Destiny**[30] 5684 4-8-13 **85**........................ DanielTudhope 3 93
(K R Burke) *t.k.h in midfield: smooth hdwy to ld over 2f out: rdn over 1f out: hdd ins fnl f: rallied: hld nr fin* **15/2**[3]

0351 **3** *1 ½* **Laffan (IRE)**[22] 5943 4-9-6 **92**........................ DavidAllan 6 96
(Tim Easterby) *hld up: rdn over 2f out: hdwy over 1f out: kpt on strly fnl f* **7/1**[2]

1130 **4** *1 ¼* **Elle Woods (IRE)**[30] 5684 3-8-12 **87**........................(p) PaulMulrennan 12 87
(Michael Dods) *hld up: rdn along 2f out: kpt on wl fnl f: nrst fin* **12/1**

0016 **5** *1* **King Torus (IRE)**[10] 6300 5-9-0 **86**........................ GrahamLee 10 84
(Ruth Carr) *slt ld to over 2f out: sn rdn and rallied: no ex ins fnl f* **25/1**

0000 **6** *½* **Justonefortheroad**[26] 5838 7-9-2 **88**........................ PaulHanagan 5 85
(Richard Fahey) *towards rr: rdn and outpcd over 2f out: styd on fnl f: nvr able to chal* **7/1**[2]

50 **7** *¾* **Tariq Too**[35] 5533 6-9-7 **93**........................ HarryBentley 7 88
(Amy Weaver) *s.i.s: hld up on ins: hdwy and prom 2f out: sn rdn: btn ins fnl f* **12/1**

0000 **8** *½* **Capaill Liath (IRE)**[42] 5285 5-9-1 **87**........................(p) NeilCallan 11 81
(Kevin Ryan) *in tch on outside: rdn and outpcd 2f out: n.d after* **16/1**

0020 **9** *½* **Chookie Royale**[2] 6550 5-8-10 **82**........................(p) TomEaves 2 74
(Keith Dalgleish) *trckd ldrs: effrt over 2f out: wknd 1f out* **16/1**

0020 **10** *2* **Sam Nombulist**[2] 6550 5-8-10 **82**........................(v) BarryMcHugh 1 69
(Ian Semple) *w ldr: rdn over 2f out: wknd over 1f out* **14/1**

100 **11** *2 ½* **Ardmay (IRE)**[26] 5838 4-9-3 **89**........................ PatSmullen 4 70
(Kevin Ryan) *in tch: outpcd whn n.m.r wl over 1f out* **16/1**

4310 **12** *1 ¾* **Haaf A Sixpence**[133] 2254 4-9-4 **90**........................ JimCrowley 8 66
(Ralph Beckett) *hld up in tch: rdn over 2f out: no imp over 1f out* **12/5**[1]

5-00 **13** *1 ½* **Radio Gaga**[121] 2585 4-9-6 **92**........................ GrahamGibbons 14 64
(Ed McMahon) *prom tl rdn and wknd over 2f out* **12/1**

1m 33.2s (-0.20) **Going Correction** +0.20s/f (Good)
WFA 3 from 4yo+ 3lb **13** Ran SP% **122.2**
Speed ratings (Par 107): **109,108,106,105,104 103,102,102,101,99 96,94,92**
toteswingers 1&2 £17.30, 2&3 £11.70, 1&3 £12.30 CSF £166.84 CT £1224.38 TOTE £20.10: £4.70, £2.70, £3.10; EX 122.60 Trifecta £619.20 Pool: £3153.95 - 3.81 winning units..
Owner Ken McGarrity **Bred** Jean-Philippe Dubois **Trained** East Kilbride, S Lanarks

FOCUS
A pretty open handicap. The pace was decent and the first four were all patiently ridden. The winner was close to his old best.

6626 JORDAN ELECTRICS LTD H'CAP 1m 5f 13y
5:35 (5:35) (Class 3) (0-90,92) 3-Y-0+ **£9,703** (£2,887; £1,443; £721) **Stalls** Low

Form RPR

3-62 **1** **Cockney Sparrow**[29] 5712 4-9-1 **82**........................ OisinMurphy(5) 17 91
(John Quinn) *chsd ldr: led 3f out: hld on gamely u.p fnl f* **5/2**[1]

3040 **2** *1* **Jonny Delta**[31] 5655 6-9-1 **77**........................ GrahamLee 12 84
(Jim Goldie) *hld up: hdwy over 2f out: effrt and rdn over 1f out: styd on fnl f: tk 2nd towards fin* **9/1**

3504 **3** *nk* **Wyborne**[14] 6192 4-9-2 **78**........................ GrahamGibbons 2 85
(Brian Ellison) *hld up: hdwy over 2f out: chsd wnr over 1f out: kpt on: lost 2nd towards fin* **12/1**

1150 **4** *nk* **Hawdyerwheesht**[29] 5706 5-9-1 **77**........................ DanielTudhope 10 83
(Jim Goldie) *hld up: rdn and hdwy 2f out: kpt on ins fnl f* **20/1**

-002 **5** *1 ¼* **Albert Bridge**[1] 6585 5-9-11 **87**........................ JimCrowley 8 91
(Ralph Beckett) *trckd ldrs: effrt and rdn over 2f out: kpt on same pce fnl f* **5/1**[3]

3541 **6** *4* **Eric The Grey (IRE)**[4] 6499 3-8-4 **75** 6ex........................(p) PaulHanagan 15 73
(Richard Fahey) *prom: effrt and pushed along over 2f out: wknd ins fnl f* **4/1**[2]

4604 **7** *¾* **High Office**[13] 6239 7-8-8 **75**........................ GeorgeChaloner(5) 14 72
(Richard Fahey) *s.i.s: sn in midfield: outpcd over 2f out: rallied fnl f: no imp* **10/1**

2513 **8** *hd* **Corton Lad**[24] 5888 3-8-7 **78** ow1........................(tp) TomEaves 9 75
(Keith Dalgleish) *trckd ldrs on outside: rdn over 2f out: wknd appr fnl f* **22/1**

0005 **9** *1* **Memory Cloth**[39] 5367 6-9-1 **77**........................ JamieSpencer 4 72
(Brian Ellison) *bhd: rdn over 3f out: hdwy over 1f out: nvr rchd ldrs* **22/1**

0501 **10** *3 ½* **Sirvino**[10] 6302 8-9-13 **92**........................ LMcNiff(3) 11 82
(David Barron) *hld up: rdn over 3f out: nvr on terms* **16/1**

4063 **11** *1* **Be Perfect (USA)**[14] 6211 4-9-0 **81**........................ ConnorBeasley(5) 5 70
(David Nicholls) *midfield: effrt over 2f out: wknd wl over 1f out* **16/1**

2036 **12** *½* **Noble Alan (GER)**[29] 5706 10-9-11 **87**........................ PaulMulrennan 6 75
(Nicky Richards) *t.k.h: in tch tl wknd fr 2f out* **16/1**

2050 **13** *1* **Aleksandar**[5] 6466 4-8-9 **71**........................ BarryMcHugh 1 57
(Jim Goldie) *trckd ldrs: effrt and rdn over 2f out: sn btn* **16/1**

2100 **14** *3* **Choisan (IRE)**[14] 6211 4-9-3 **79**........................ DuranFentiman 7 61
(Tim Easterby) *led at stdy pce: styd alone far side and hdd 3f out: sn btn* **33/1**

3m 0.64s (6.64) **Going Correction** +0.20s/f (Good)
WFA 3 from 4yo+ 9lb **14** Ran SP% **131.9**
Speed ratings (Par 107): **87,86,86,86,85 82,82,82,81,79 78,78,77,76**
toteswingers 1&2 £10.80, 2&3 £32.70, 1&3 £9.90 CSF £27.35 CT £252.00 TOTE £3.90: £2.00, £3.40, £3.80; EX 42.00 Trifecta £817.30 Pool: £2362.30 - 2.16 winning units..
Owner Mr & Mrs Paul Gaffney **Bred** P Cunningham **Trained** Settrington, N Yorks
■ A 9,260-1 four-timer for Oisin Murphy on his only rides on the card.

FOCUS
They went a fairly steady pace in this decent handicap. They headed down the centre in the home straight, with the exception of Choisan who stuck to the inside and finished last. The winner didn't need to improve with the second setting the standard.
T/Jkpt: Not won. T/Plt: £8,428.20 to a £1 stake. Pool of £149168.05 - 12.92 winning tickets.
T/Qpdt: £543.70 to a £1 stake. Pool of £17966.70 - 24.45 winning tickets. RY

5883 CATTERICK (L-H)
Saturday, September 21

OFFICIAL GOING: Good (7.8)
Wind: Light across Weather: Cloudy

6627 BRITISH STALLION STUDS EBF MAIDEN STKS 5f 212y
2:10 (2:11) (Class 5) 2-Y-0 **£3,234** (£962; £481; £240) **Stalls** Low

Form RPR

4020 **1** **State Anthem**[9] 6326 2-9-0 72........................ AdrianNicholls 1 73
(Mick Channon) *dwlt: sn trcking ldrs on inner: cl up 1/2-way: led wl over 1f out: sn rdn and edgd rt: drvn ins fnl f: hdd narrowly last 75yds: rallied to ld on line* **13/8**[1]

0 **2** *shd* **Royal Connoisseur (IRE)**[24] 5877 2-9-5 0........................[1] DavidNolan 10 78
(Richard Fahey) *towards rr: hdwy 2f out: chsd ldrs over 1f out: swtchd lft and rdn to chal ins fnl f: tk slt advantage last 75yds: hdd on line* **25/1**

64 **3** *1 ¼* **Breakable**[59] 4616 2-8-9 0........................ DarylByrne(5) 7 69
(Tim Easterby) *in tch: hdwy over 2f out: rdn to chse ldrs over 1f out: kpt on u.p fnl f* **16/1**

353 **4** *¾* **Missouri Spirit**[15] 6174 2-9-0 79........................ ShaneGray(5) 4 72
(Kevin Ryan) *led 2f: cl up rdn to chal 2f out and ev ch: drvn over 1f out: kpt on same pce fnl f* **2/1**[2]

05 **5** *nk* **False Witness (IRE)**[14] 6206 2-8-12 0........................ JordanNason(7) 5 71
(David Nicholls) *prom: effrt on outer 2f out: sn rdn and one pce ins fnl f* **25/1**

53 **6** *8* **Sketch Map (IRE)**[15] 6175 2-9-5 0........................ MichaelO'Connell 2 47
(Jedd O'Keeffe) *dwlt: a towards rr* **5/1**[3]

5 **7** *1 ¼* **Orient Class**[7] 6383 2-9-5 0........................ LeeTopliss 8 43+
(Paul Midgley) *a towards rr* **50/1**

The Form Book Flat, Raceform Ltd, Compton, RG20 6NL.

42 **8** 3/4 **Annie's Rose**[24] 5900 2-9-0 0 .... RoystonFfrench 3 36
(Bryan Smart) *cl up: led after 2f: pushed along over 2f out: sn rdn: hdd wl over 1f out and sn wknd* **14/1**

0 **9** 2 1/2 **Garfunkel (IRE)**[11] 6286 2-9-5 0 .... PJMcDonald 6 33
(Ann Duffield) *sn outpcd and a bhd* **20/1**

0 **10** 17 **Take A Break**[26] 5826 2-9-0 0 .... JamesSullivan 9
(Robert Johnson) *chsd ldrs on outer: rdn along 1/2-way: sn wknd* **200/1**

1m 13.85s (0.25) **Going Correction** +0.025s/f (Good) **10** Ran SP% **115.6**
Speed ratings (Par 95): **99,98,97,96,95 85,83,82,79,56**
toteswingers 1&2 £9.60, 2&3 £27.60, 1&3 £6.40 CSF £51.30 TOTE £2.30: £1.10, £6.50, £3.00; EX 74.10 Trifecta £1157.60 Pool: £2429.20 - 1.57 winning units..
Owner Saeed Manana **Bred** Mrs R D Peacock **Trained** West Ilsley, Berks

FOCUS
The going was good. Plenty of pace on for this maiden with the front five home clear. The winner is just rated to form.

6628 33 RACECOURSES LIVE ON SKY 432 NURSERY H'CAP 7f
2:45 (2:46) (Class 4) (0-85,84) 2-Y-O **£3,881** (£1,155; £577; £288) **Stalls** Centre

Form RPR

1515 **1** **Al Baz**[18] 6064 2-9-0 **80** .... ThomasBrown(3) 1 87
(James Tate) *led: rdn along wl over 1f out: hdd narrowly ent fnl f: sn drvn and rallied wl to ld again nr fin* **15/2**

1135 **2** *nse* **Threetimesalady**[23] 5927 2-8-11 **77** .... RosieJessop(3) 2 84
(Sir Mark Prescott Bt) *trckd ldng pair: hdwy and cl up 2f out: rdn to ld ent fnl f: sn drvn and edgd rt: hdd nr fin* **6/1**[1]

2102 **3** *8* **Party Ruler (IRE)**[22] 5945 2-9-2 **84** .... JackDuern(5) 10 69
(Tom Dascombe) *cl up: rdn along 2f out: drvn and one pce appr fnl f* **13/2**[2]

4333 **4** *1* **Needless Shouting (IRE)**[9] 6334 2-8-5 **68** .... JamesSullivan 5 51
(Mick Channon) *chsd ldrs: hdwy on inner over 2f out: sn rdn: kpt on one pce* **9/1**

542 **5** *shd* **Crakehall Lad (IRE)**[15] 6175 2-8-7 **70** .... BenCurtis 6 52+
(Alan Swinbank) *dwlt: in rr and sn rdn along: bhd 1/2-way: styd on u.p fnl 2f: n.d* **9/1**

4333 **6** *hd* **Beltor**[26] 5827 2-8-9 **72** .... PJMcDonald 8 54+
(Michael Dods) *hld up: pushed along after 2f: rdn along and rr 1/2-way: styd on u.p fnl 2f: n.d* **6/1**[1]

6343 **7** *1/2* **Heroique (IRE)**[10] 6295 2-8-1 **64** ....(e[1]) PaulQuinn 4 44
(Tim Easterby) *plld hrd: chsd ldrs: rdn along over 2f out: wknd wl over 1f out* **12/1**

01 **8** *2 1/2* **Picks Pinta**[88] 3659 2-8-6 **69** .... AdrianNicholls 9 43
(Jo Hughes) *dwlt: in tch: rdn along to chse ldrs over 2f out: wknd wl over 1f out* **16/1**

4622 **9** *1 1/4* **Handwoven (IRE)**[29] 5703 2-8-9 **72** .... LiamJones 7 42
(Mark Johnston) *midfield: rdn along 1/2-way: sn outpcd* **7/1**[3]

321 **10** *22* **Zal Zilhom (IRE)**[25] 5866 2-8-2 **70** .... ShaneGray(5) 3
(Kevin Ryan) *sn outpcd and rdn along: a bhd* **6/1**[1]

1m 26.43s (-0.57) **Going Correction** +0.025s/f (Good) **10** Ran SP% **114.0**
Speed ratings (Par 97): **104,103,94,93,93 93,92,89,88,63**
toteswingers 1&2 £10.50, 2&3 £5.00, 1&3 £7.00 CSF £50.81 CT £315.29 TOTE £10.20: £3.10, £2.00, £1.80; EX 69.80 Trifecta £342.00 Pool: £2038.44 - 4.46 winning units..
Owner Saif Ali **Bred** Norman Court Stud **Trained** Newmarket, Suffolk

FOCUS
A wide-open handicap run at a fair pace. The first three home were in control throughout. Improvement from the first two.

6629 PIN POINT RECRUITMENT H'CAP 1m 5f 175y
3:20 (3:20) (Class 4) (0-80,71) 3-Y-O **£5,453** (£1,610; £805) **Stalls** Low

Form RPR

4446 **1** **Duke Of Yorkshire**[11] 6290 3-8-12 **65** .... NeilFarley(3) 4 73
(Declan Carroll) *trckd ldng pair: hdwy to chse ldr 3f out: led 1 1/2f out: jnd and rdn ent fnl f: sn drvn and jst hld on* **6/1**

3443 **2** *shd* **Sunblazer (IRE)**[8] 6363 3-9-6 **70** .... DougieCostello 2 78
(William Muir) *trckd ldrs: hdwy 3f out: rdn to chse wnr over 1f out: chal ent fnl f: sn drvn and ev ch: jst failed* **4/1**[1]

4-02 **3** *3 1/4* **Estinaad (USA)**[27] 5791 3-8-11 **61** .... DaleSwift 1 64
(Brian Ellison) *hld up towards rr: hdwy on inner 3f out: rdn to chse ldng pair over 1f out: drvn and no imp fnl f* **9/2**[2]

1223 **4** *8* **Jebulani**[24] 5885 3-8-1 **54** .... JulieBurke(3) 3 46
(Barry Murtagh) *led: rdn along 3f out: hdd 1 1/2f out: sn drvn and grad wknd* **11/2**[3]

2411 **5** *4* **See And Be Seen**[8] 6363 3-8-10 **60** ....(p) RenatoSouza 5 47
(Sylvester Kirk) *hld up in tch: hdwy over 4f out: rdn along 3f out: sn btn* **13/2**

4244 **6** *nk* **Montjess (IRE)**[7] 6389 3-9-2 **71** ....(v) JackDuern(5) 6 57
(Tom Dascombe) *trckd ldr: effrt 4f out: rdn along 3f out: sn wknd* **9/2**[2]

354 **7** *68* **Samoset**[101] 3201 3-8-10 **60** .... BenCurtis 7
(Alan Swinbank) *in rr: hdwy on outer to chse ldrs 6f out: rdn along 4f out: sn wknd and wl bhd fnl 3f: fin lame* **15/2**

3m 2.65s (-0.95) **Going Correction** +0.025s/f (Good) **7** Ran SP% **111.1**
Speed ratings (Par 103): **103,102,101,96,94 94,55**
toteswingers 1&2 £3.30, 2&3 £7.10, 1&3 £10.10 CSF £28.29 TOTE £8.90: £4.90, £2.90; EX 45.10 Trifecta £227.30 Pool: £1776.10 - 5.86 winning units..
Owner M Stewart **Bred** Redhill Bloodstock & Tweenhills Stud **Trained** Sledmere, E Yorks

FOCUS
An open handicap run at a steady pace. Modest form with small bests from the first two.

6630 RACING REPLAY ALL TODAY'S RACING SKY432 MAIDEN STKS 7f
3:55 (3:57) (Class 5) 3-4-Y-O **£3,234** (£962; £481; £240) **Stalls** Centre

Form RPR

33 **1** **Dawn Calling (IRE)**[16] 6133 3-9-5 0 .... AdrianNicholls 7 76
(Mark Johnston) *mde all: rdn and qcknd clr over 2f out: styd on strly: unchal* **15/8**[2]

050 **2** *8* **Imperial Bond**[24] 5903 4-9-1 42 ....(t) KevinStott(7) 6 55
(Jason Ward) *chsd ldrs: hdwy over 2f out: rdn to chse wnr over 1f out: sn drvn and no imp* **33/1**

303- **3** *4 1/2* **Global Icon**[33] 5598 3-9-5 72 ....(p) LeeTopliss 9 42
(Michael Dods) *in rr and pushed along after 3f: hdwy wl over 2f out: rdn wl over 1f out: styd on wl appr fnl f* **6/1**[3]

00 **4** *nk* **Spring Bird**[34] 5563 4-8-10 0 .... JordanNason(7) 5 37
(David Nicholls) *chsd wnr: rdn along over 2f out: drvn wl over 1f out: one pce* **40/1**

5003 **5** *hd* **Sweet Vintage (IRE)**[9] 6319 3-8-11 51 ....(t) RyanClark(3) 11 36
(Mark Brisbourne) *chsd ldng pair: hdwy to chse wnr 3f out: rdn 2f out: drvn and hung lft appr fnl f: one pce* **33/1**

-0 **6** *3/4* **Flying Giant (IRE)**[45] 5133 3-9-5 0 .... BenCurtis 8 39
(Jo Hughes) *in tch: rdn along and sme hdwy over 2f out: sn drvn and n.d* **25/1**

0524 **7** *3 1/4* **Red Warrior (IRE)**[15] 6178 3-9-2 82 .... ThomasBrown(3) 1 30
(Ismail Mohammed) *trckd ldrs on inner: pushed along 3f out: swtchd rt and rdn 2f out: sn wknd* **4/5**[1]

0 **8** *3 3/4* **Miss Rebero**[15] 6178 3-9-0 0 .... PJMcDonald 4 15
(Tim Fitzgerald) *dwlt: a in rr* **40/1**

00 **9** *11* **Moissanite**[15] 6178 4-9-0 0 .... DeclanCannon(3) 3
(Sean Regan) *a towards rr* **100/1**

5034 **10** *5* **Lady Calantha**[23] 5919 3-9-0 45 .... PaulQuinn 10
(Alan Berry) *a in rr* **33/1**

1m 26.23s (-0.77) **Going Correction** +0.025s/f (Good)
WFA 3 from 4yo 3lb **10** Ran SP% **123.2**
Speed ratings (Par 103): **105,95,90,90,90 89,85,81,68,63**
toteswingers 1&2 £6.80, 2&3 £11.00, 1&3 £3.00 CSF £66.77 TOTE £3.20: £1.10, £7.10, £2.20; EX 60.90 Trifecta £328.40 Pool: £3405.58 - 7.77 winning units..
Owner Sheikh Hamdan Bin Mohammed Al Maktoum **Bred** Airlie Stud And Sir Thomas Pilkington **Trained** Middleham Moor, N Yorks

■ Stewards' Enquiry : Paul Quinn jockey said that the filly lost her action
Thomas Brown trainer's representative said that the colt was unsuited by the track

FOCUS
This modest maiden was run at a sound pace. The winner made all in the bset of the four C&D times but there are doubts over the bare form.

6631 2013 CATTERICK TWELVE FURLONG SERIES FINAL H'CAP 1m 3f 214y
4:30 (4:30) (Class 2) 3-Y-O+ **£12,938** (£3,850; £1,924; £962) **Stalls** Centre

Form RPR

1401 **1** **Dolphin Village (IRE)**[24] 5888 3-7-11 **77** .... SamanthaBell(7) 1 85
(Richard Fahey) *trckd ldrs on inner: hdwy 2f out: rdn to ld jst ins fnl f: kpt on wl towards fin* **4/1**[2]

0410 **2** *2* **Tinseltown**[13] 6239 7-7-11 **67** .... ShirleyTeasdale(5) 9 72
(Brian Rothwell) *led: pushed along 3f out: rdn 2f out: drvn and hdd jst ins fnl f: kpt on* **16/1**

2340 **3** *1/2* **Gran Maestro (USA)**[13] 6239 4-8-7 **72** ....(b) PJMcDonald 6 76
(Ruth Carr) *prom: trckd ldr over 5f outg: cl up 3f out: rdn 2f out: drvn over 1f out: kpt on same pce fnl f* **9/1**

0131 **4** *nk* **Ailsa Craig (IRE)**[16] 6130 7-8-2 **74** ow3 ....(p) KevinStott(7) 5 78+
(Edwin Tuer) *hld up in rr: hdwy 4f out: rdn to chse ldrs wl over 1f out: swtchd rt to outer and drvn ent fnl f: kpt on: nrst fin* **13/2**[3]

50 **5** *1/2* **Villa Royale**[21] 5997 4-9-3 **82** .... DavidNolan 4 85
(David O'Meara) *trckd ldrs: hdwy over 2f out: rdn wl over 1f out: sn drvn and kpt on same pce fnl f* **9/1**

6440 **6** *1* **Bright Applause**[14] 6211 5-8-5 **70** .... RoystonFfrench 8 71
(Tracy Waggott) *trckd ldrs: hdwy 4f out: cl up over 2f out: sn rdn and ev ch tl drvn over 1f out and grad wknd* **16/1**

21U1 **7** *3/4* **Bayan Kasirga (IRE)**[5] 6470 3-8-0 **76** 6ex ow3 .... NeilFarley(3) 3 76
(Richard Fahey) *hld up in rr: pushed along over 3f out: rdn over 2f out: kpt on u.p fnl f: n.d* **3/1**[1]

0155 **8** *1 1/2* **Yasir (USA)**[9] 6346 5-8-5 **70** ....(p) JamesSullivan 2 68
(Conor Dore) *trckd ldrs on inner: pushed along 4f out: rdn over 3f out: drvn and one pce fnl 2f* **12/1**

1166 **9** *14* **O Ma Lad (IRE)**[10] 6302 5-9-10 **89** ....(b[1]) MichaelO'Connell 7 64
(John Quinn) *hld up in rr: effrt and sme hdwy over 3f out: rdn along over 2f out: sn btn and eased* **4/1**[2]

2m 39.5s (0.60) **Going Correction** +0.025s/f (Good)
WFA 3 from 4yo+ 8lb **9** Ran SP% **117.8**
Speed ratings (Par 109): **99,97,97,97,96 96,95,94,85**
toteswingers 1&2 £12.70, 2&3 £20.10, 1&3 £7.90 CSF £66.32 CT £549.38 TOTE £4.30: £1.40, £5.00, £2.50; EX 68.40 Trifecta £342.70 Pool: £1551.17 - 3.39 winning units..
Owner Y Nasib **Bred** Gerrardstown House Stud **Trained** Musley Bank, N Yorks

■ Stewards' Enquiry : Michael O'Connell jockeys said that the gelding lost its action

FOCUS
Not a strong handicap for the grade. It was run at a steady pace, which suited those handy. Shaky form, rated around the second and third.

6632 CATTERICKBRIDGE.CO.UK H'CAP 1m 5f 175y
5:05 (5:10) (Class 6) (0-65,65) 4-Y-O+ **£2,726** (£805; £402) **Stalls** Low

Form RPR

305 **1** **Naburn**[11] 6290 5-9-6 **64** .... BenCurtis 11 75
(Alan Swinbank) *prom: led after 4f: pushed clr over 2f out: rdn over 1f out: styd on strly* **15/2**

0022 **2** *3 1/2* **Danceintothelight**[24] 5885 6-8-9 **56** .... NeilFarley(3) 7 62
(Micky Hammond) *led 4f: prom: chsd wnr 4f out: rdn along 2f out: drvn over 1f out: kpt on: no imp* **8/1**

0036 **3** *2* **Spiekeroog**[15] 6179 7-9-6 **64** .... MichaelO'Connell 13 67
(David O'Meara) *hld up towards rr: hdwy 4f out: rdn along over 2f out: chsd ldrs over 1f out: drvn to chse ldng pair ent fnl f: no imp* **10/1**

5225 **4** *1* **Sally Friday (IRE)**[26] 5831 5-8-12 **63** ....(p) KevinStott(7) 3 65
(Edwin Tuer) *hld up towards rr: hdwy 3f out: rdn 2f out: drvn over 1f out: kpt on: nrst fin* **9/2**[2]

2404 **5** *hd* **Beat The Shower**[11] 6290 7-9-2 **60** .... DavidNolan 6 62
(Peter Niven) *hld up in rr: hdwy wl over 2f out: rdn along wl over 1f out: kpt on appr fnl f: nrst fin* **7/1**[3]

2503 **6** *1 3/4* **Zarosa (IRE)**[26] 5831 4-9-1 **64** .... NoelGarbutt(5) 5 63
(John Berry) *trckd ldrs on inner: hdwy over 3f out: rdn along over 2f out: sn chsng ldrs: drvn appr fnl f: sn wknd* **4/1**[1]

4020 **7** *1 3/4* **Al Furat (USA)**[13] 6239 5-8-8 **57** .... ShirleyTeasdale(5) 9 54
(Ron Barr) *trckd ldrs: effrt 3f out: rdn along over 2f out: grad wknd* **10/1**

0005 **8** *hd* **Adili (IRE)**[22] 5966 4-8-11 **58** .... PaulPickard(3) 4 54
(Brian Ellison) *hld up and bhd: pushed along 4f out: hdwy on inner 2f out: sn rdn and n.d* **12/1**

0430 **9** *nk* **Silver Tigress**[26] 5833 5-8-11 **55** .... LeeTopliss 2 51
(George Moore) *midfield: hdwy on inner to trck ldrs over 3f out: rdn along 2f out: sn drvn and wknd* **16/1**

2606 **10** *2* **Badea**[47] 5059 4-9-7 **65** .... PJMcDonald 8 58
(Martin Todhunter) *a towards rr* **16/1**

2360 **11** *3/4* **Iceman George**[11] 6290 9-9-1 **59** ....(p) DougieCostello 12 51
(Alison Hutchinson) *in tch: hdwy on outer over 3f out: rdn along wl over 2f out: sn wknd* **25/1**

35-0 **12** *5* **Tropical Bachelor (IRE)**[54] 4835 7-8-12 **56** .... StevieDonohoe 10 41
(Nicky Vaughan) *prom: rdn along 4f out: wknd wl over 2f out* **40/1**

0-62 **13** 2¾ **Ravi River (IRE)**[8] 5370 9-8-12 **61** ow1.................... GarryWhillans(5) 14 42
(Alistair Whillans) *hld up in rr: sme hdwy on outer 5f out: rdn along wl over 3f out: sn wknd* **20/1**

3m 5.07s (1.47) **Going Correction** +0.025s/f (Good) **13** Ran SP% **122.2**
Speed ratings (Par 101): **96,94,92,92,92 91,90,90,89,88 88,85,83**
toteswingers 1&2 £11.50, 2&3 £12.90, 1&3 £13.90 CSF £66.51 CT £616.48 TOTE £8.60: £2.90, £2.90, £4.10; EX 77.30 Trifecta £657.80 Pool: £1759.55 - 2.00 winning units..
Owner Elsa Crankshaw & G Allan **Bred** Old Mill Stud **Trained** Melsonby, N Yorks

FOCUS
An open if modest handicap, run at a steady pace. Again it paid to race handy. The race is rated around the runner-up to this year's form.

6633 BOOK NOW FOR SATURDAY 19TH OCTOBER H'CAP (DIV I) 7f
5:40 (5:41) (Class 6) (0-65,70) 3-Y-0+ **£2,726** (£805; £402) **Stalls** Centre

Form RPR
4322 **1** **Lil Sophella (IRE)**[32] 5614 4-8-1 **52**................................ JackGarritty(7) 2 60+
(Patrick Holmes) *dwlt: in rr: hdwy 3f out: swtchd rt and chsd clr ldr 1f out: styd on wl to ld towards fin* **7/2**[1]

6000 **2** ½ **Red Cobra (IRE)**[29] 5704 3-8-9 **56**.............................. JamesSullivan 12 62
(Tim Easterby) *led: clr over 2f out: hdd and no ex towards fin* **20/1**

6034 **3** 1 **Perfect Words (IRE)**[5] 6464 3-8-9 **61**.................. ShirleyTeasdale(5) 11 64
(Marjorie Fife) *chsd ldrs: effrt over 2f out: styd on same pce ins fnl f* **8/1**[3]

5042 **4** 2 **Orpsie Boy (IRE)**[8] 6368 10-9-2 **63**.................................. JulieBurke(3) 6 62
(Ruth Carr) *in rr: hdwy over 2f out: kpt on fnl f* **11/2**[2]

0430 **5** 3 **Clumber Place**[40] 5331 7-8-12 **56**.. DaleSwift 4 47
(James Given) *chsd ldr: fdd appr fnl f* **9/1**

4400 **6** ½ **Logans Legend (IRE)**[36] 5471 5-8-1 **52**........................[1] JoeDoyle(7) 13 41
(Lawrence Mullaney) *in rr: hdwy over 2f out: kpt on: nvr nr ldrs* **14/1**

3245 **7** nse **My New Angel (IRE)**[24] 5881 4-9-5 **63**.......................... PJMcDonald 9 52
(Jason Ward) *mid-div: effrt 3f out: one pce fnl 2f* **10/1**

3003 **8** nk **Legal Bond**[2] 6568 4-8-10 **61**..................................(p) JoshDoyle(7) 10 49
(David O'Meara) *stmbld s: chsd ldrs: wknd over 1f out* **11/2**[2]

3420 **9** 1 **No Quarter (IRE)**[11] 6291 6-9-6 **64**........................ MichaelO'Connell 5 50
(Tracy Waggott) *hld up in mid-div: t.k.h: effrt over 2f out: wknd over 1f out* **11/2**[2]

3044 **10** 7 **Wotalad**[92] 3547 3-8-11 **58**......................................[1] RussKennemore 8 24
(Richard Whitaker) *mid-div: hung rt and lost pl bnd 4f out: bhd fnl 3f* **20/1**

1m 26.99s (-0.01) **Going Correction** +0.025s/f (Good)
WFA 3 from 4yo+ 3lb **10** Ran SP% **114.8**
Speed ratings (Par 101): **101,100,99,97,93 93,92,92,91,83**
toteswingers 1&2 £21.40, 2&3 £32.70, 1&3 £7.50 CSF £77.02 CT £526.81 TOTE £4.70: £1.90, £3.30, £2.60; EX 68.90 Trifecta £598.20 Part won. Pool: £797.71 - 0.14 winning units..
Owner Foulrice Park Racing Limited **Bred** Waterford Hall Stud **Trained** Middleham, N Yorks

■ Stewards' Enquiry : Michael O'Connell jockey said that the gelding ran too free
Russ Kennemore jockey said that the gelding failed to handle the bend

FOCUS
Five withdrawals but this was still open enough. It was run at a sound pace and in a similar time to division II. The winner looks capable of a bit better.

6634 BOOK NOW FOR SATURDAY 19TH OCTOBER H'CAP (DIV II) 7f
6:10 (6:12) (Class 6) (0-65,69) 3-Y-0+ **£2,726** (£805; £402) **Stalls** Centre

Form RPR
1241 **1** **George Fenton**[8] 6367 4-9-4 **69**..................................(p) KevinStott(7) 14 78
(Richard Guest) *trckd ldrs: hdwy 3f out: rdn and ev ch over 1f out: drvn ins fnl f: styd on wl to ld on line* **6/1**[3]

345 **2** shd **Dance For Georgie**[10] 6301 4-9-3 **64**........................ DeclanCannon(3) 4 73
(Ben Haslam) *led: rdn wl over 1f out: drvn and edgd rt wl ins fnl f: hdd on line* **9/2**[1]

0624 **3** 1¾ **Graceful Act**[11] 6289 5-8-3 **52**.............................(p) ShirleyTeasdale(5) 1 56
(Ron Barr) *hld up: hdwy on inner over 2f out: rdn to chse ldrs over 1f out: kpt on fnl f* **9/1**

0006 **4** 1¾ **Meshardal (GER)**[18] 6075 3-8-10 **57**.................................. PJMcDonald 5 56
(Ruth Carr) *trckd ldrs on inner: hdwy 2f out: rdn to chse ldr over 1f out: drvn and wknd fnl f* **16/1**

1000 **5** 1½ **Rasselas (IRE)**[40] 5341 6-8-10 **61**.............................. AnnaHesketh(7) 10 57
(David Nicholls) *towards rr: hdwy on inner 2f out: rdn and kpt on fnl f: nrst fin* **28/1**

0130 **6** nse **Glenridding**[14] 6218 9-9-5 **63**....................................(p) DaleSwift 8 58
(James Given) *in tch: swtchd rt and effrt over 2f out: rdn along wl over 1f out: styd on fnl f: nrst fin* **25/1**

0034 **7** nse **Deliberation (IRE)**[26] 5818 5-8-9 **53** ow1............... MichaelO'Connell 13 48
(John Quinn) *cl up: rdn along over 2f out: drvn wl over 1f out: grad wknd* **16/1**

402 **8** ½ **Dialogue**[73] 4160 7-9-0 **65**... JordanNason(7) 2 59
(Geoffrey Harker) *s.i.s and in rr: hdwy over 2f out: sn rdn: styd on fnl f: nrst fin* **9/1**

0503 **9** ¾ **Viva Ronaldo (IRE)**[5] 6464 7-8-9 **60**.......................... SamanthaBell(7) 3 52
(Richard Fahey) *in rr tl styd on fnl 2f: n.d* **6/1**[3]

0013 **10** ¾ **First Class Favour (IRE)**[10] 6301 5-9-2 **60**...................... PaulQuinn 6 50
(Tim Easterby) *midfield: hdwy 3f out: chsd ldrs 2f out: sn rdn and wknd over 1f out* **5/1**[2]

-054 **11** 2 **Fleurtille**[15] 6180 4-8-6 **55**................................ JacobButterfield(5) 12 39
(Robert Johnson) *dwlt: a towards rr* **25/1**

5500 **12** 1 **Viking Warrior (IRE)**[36] 5471 6-8-13 **57**........................(p) LeeTopliss 11 39
(Michael Dods) *prom: rdn along wl over 2f out: sn drvn and wknd* **16/1**

6000 **13** 47 **Kai**[156] 1656 4-8-7 **51** oh1..(b) BenCurtis 9
(Alan McCabe) *v.s.a and lost many l s: a wl bhd* **40/1**

0010 **F** **Dhhamaan (IRE)**[8] 6367 8-9-0 **58**...........................(b) JamesSullivan 7
(Ruth Carr) *s.i.s and bhd: rdn along and sme hdwy over 2f out: stmbld and fell wl over 1f out* **18/1**

1m 27.1s (0.10) **Going Correction** +0.025s/f (Good)
WFA 3 from 4yo+ 3lb **14** Ran SP% **119.9**
Speed ratings (Par 101): **100,99,97,95,94 94,94,93,92,91 89,88,34,**
toteswingers 1&2 £4.00, 2&3 £11.60, 1&3 £14.30 CSF £31.57 CT £253.03 TOTE £4.50: £2.40, £1.90, £2.00; EX 30.80 Trifecta £326.50 Pool: £1127.36 - 2.58 winning units..
Owner Mrs Alison Guest **Bred** R P Williams **Trained** Wetherby, W Yorks

■ Stewards' Enquiry : Jordan Nason jockey that the gelding was slowly away

FOCUS
A eventful low-grade handicap, run at a strong pace. Another personal best from the winner.
T/Plt: £743.00 to a £1 stake. Pool of £50947.26 - 50.05 winning tickets. T/Qpdt: £53.90 to a £1 stake. Pool of £2757.0 - 37.80 winning tickets. JR

6589 NEWBURY (L-H)
Saturday, September 21

OFFICIAL GOING: Soft (good to soft in places; 6.2)
Wind: Virtually nil Weather: Overcast

6635 WEDGEWOOD ESTATES EBF MAIDEN STKS (DIV I) 7f (S)
1:20 (1:23) (Class 4) 2-Y-0 **£4,528** (£1,347; £673; £336) **Stalls** High

Form RPR
6 **1** **Extremity (IRE)**[23] 5924 2-9-5 0...................................... MartinDwyer 2 81+
(Hugo Palmer) *trckd ldrs: led over 1f out: pushed clr fnl f: easily* **5/2**[1]

05 **2** 3¼ **Maxie T**[56] 4756 2-9-5 0.................................... SilvestreDeSousa 1 73
(Mark Johnston) *chsd ldrs: drvn along fr 3f out: styd on wl fnl f to take and hold 2nd fnl 50yds but no ch w wnr* **7/1**

3 nse **Magnus Maximus** 2-9-5 0.. JimmyFortune 4 72+
(Richard Hannon) *sn in tch: hdwy 3f out: styd on fr over 1f out: kpt on to press for 2nd clsng stages but no ch w wnr* **11/2**[3]

4 nk **Dutch Romance** 2-9-0 0.. SteveDrowne 11 67+
(Charles Hills) *in rr: shkn up 3f out: hdwy fr 2f out: kpt on fnl f to cl on 3rd nr fin but no ch w wnr* **14/1**

5 **5** ½ **Baker Man (IRE)**[102] 3175 2-9-5 0................................... JamesDoyle 10 70
(Sylvester Kirk) *t.k.h: led: drvn and hdd over 1f out: sn outpcd by wnr but hld 2nd tl no ex fnl 50yds* **7/1**

06 **6** 2 **Hostile Fire (IRE)**[9] 6340 2-9-2 0.......................... MarkCoumbe(3) 5 65
(Ed de Giles) *in tch: hdwy over 2f out: edgd lft over 1f out: kpt on same pce fnl f* **100/1**

7 2¾ **White Russian** 2-9-0 0.. AdamKirby 3 53
(Henry Candy) *in rr: pushed along over 2f out: sme prog fnl f but nvr a threat* **12/1**

8 1 **Danzeno** 2-9-0 0.. TobyAtkinson(5) 6 55
(Michael Appleby) *in rr: sme hdwy fr 3f out: edgd lft 2f out: sn wknd* **40/1**

9 1½ **Characterise** 2-9-5 0.. SamHitchcott 9 51
(Mick Channon) *rdn over 2f out: nvr beyond mid-div* **25/1**

10 3½ **Urban Sanctuary** 2-9-5 0.. TomMcLaughlin 8 42
(Ed Walker) *in tch: rdn 3f out: wknd sn after* **33/1**

11 ¾ **Storm Rider (IRE)** 2-9-5 0.. RichardHughes 7 40
(Richard Hannon) *s.i.s: towards rr most of way* **4/1**[2]

00 **12** ½ **Always Resolute**[15] 6168 2-9-2 0...................... MichaelJMMurphy(3) 12 39
(Alan Jarvis) *chsd ldrs: rdn 3f out: sn wknd* **25/1**

1m 27.55s (1.85) **Going Correction** +0.275s/f (Good) **12** Ran SP% **117.4**
Speed ratings (Par 97): **100,96,96,95,95 93,89,88,87,83 82,81**
toteswingers 1&2 £3.60, 1&3 £2.80, 2&3 £7.50 CSF £19.12 TOTE £3.50: £1.60, £2.40, £2.40; EX 23.10 Trifecta £80.40 Pool: £1010.65 - 9.42 winning units..
Owner Kremlin Cottage II **Bred** B Holland, S Hillen & J Cullinan **Trained** Newmarket, Suffolk

FOCUS
Rail moved out from Friday between 5f and 7f adding about 12m to races on Round course. In truth this looked nothing more than an ordinary maiden by course standards, but it should still produce winners. They raced down the centre of the track. The form rates at the lower end of the race averages.

6636 DUBAI DUTY FREE LEGACY CUP (REGISTERED AS THE ARC TRIAL) (GROUP 3) 1m 3f 5y
1:50 (1:50) (Class 1) 3-Y-0+
£34,026 (£12,900; £6,456; £3,216; £1,614; £810) **Stalls** Centre

Form RPR
-241 **1** **Camborne**[8] 6348 5-9-3 114..(p) RobertHavlin 4 116
(John Gosden) *stdd s: hld up in rr: hdwy on outside over 2f out: rdn and edgd lft over 1f out: led jst ins fnl f: r.o strly* **4/1**[2]

1212 **2** 1¾ **Gifted Girl (IRE)**[35] 5552 4-9-0 108.......................... FrankieDettori 2 110
(Paul Cole) *trckd ldrs in 3rd: qcknd to chal 2f out: rdn to ld over 1f out: hdd jst ins fnl f and sn outpcd by wnr: kpt on wl to hold 2nd cl home* **6/1**[3]

3243 **3** nse **Main Sequence (USA)**[14] 6198 4-9-3 112.....................(p) TedDurcan 1 113
(David Lanigan) *chsd ldr: led over 2f out: sn rdn: hdd over 1f out: outpcd by wnr fnl f but kpt on to press for 2nd tl dropped to 3rd last stride* **10/1**

3034 **4** 1½ **Spillway**[31] 5653 3-8-10 106.. JamesDoyle 6 110
(Eve Johnson Houghton) *in rr: hdwy fr 3f out: chsd ldrs and drvn 2f out: one pce fnl f* **12/1**

0501 **5** 2 **Fattsota**[26] 5822 5-9-3 103.. TonyHamilton 3 107
(David O'Meara) *led: rdn and hdd over 2f out: wknd over 1f out* **16/1**

1201 **6** hd **Kassiano (GER)**[35] 5540 4-9-3 113.......................... SilvestreDeSousa 7 107
(Saeed bin Suroor) *t.k.h towards rr: hdwy 3f out: drvn to chse ldrs and edgd lft 2f out: wknd fnl f* **10/11**[1]

2m 20.19s (-1.01) **Going Correction** +0.175s/f (Good)
WFA 3 from 4yo+ 7lb **6** Ran SP% **109.3**
Speed ratings (Par 113): **110,108,108,107,106 106**
toteswingers 1&2 £3.80, 1&3 £3.10, 2&3 £4.20 CSF £25.72 TOTE £4.40: £2.00, £1.80; EX 24.50 Trifecta £112.30 Pool: £3192.68 - 21.31 winning units..
Owner HRH Princess Haya Of Jordan **Bred** Southill Stud **Trained** Newmarket, Suffolk

FOCUS
The field were soon strung out in this Group 3 contest, courtesy of Fattsota setting a good gallop, and the race set up nicely for the closers. Camborne matched his Doncaster form.

6637 DUBAI DUTY FREE MILL REEF STKS (GROUP 2) 6f 8y
2:20 (2:23) (Class 1) 2-Y-0
£36,861 (£13,975; £6,994; £3,484; £1,748; £877) **Stalls** High

Form RPR
2511 **1** **Supplicant**[26] 5837 2-9-1 103.. TonyHamilton 8 111
(Richard Fahey) *chsd ldrs: rdn over 2f out: styd on wl u.p to chal to chal whn rdr dropped whip fnl 120yds: led sn after and bmpd: styd on gamely* **7/2**[1]

135 **2** ¾ **Rufford (IRE)**[30] 5679 2-9-1 92.. AdamKirby 4 109
(Richard Fahey) *led: rdn over 2f out: hrd pressed over 1f out and hdd jst ins fnl f: rallied clsng stages to take 2nd but no imp on wnr* **20/1**

115 **3** ½ **Hot Streak (IRE)**[14] 6201 2-9-1 104........................ DeclanMcDonogh 9 107
(Kevin Ryan) *t.k.h: trckd ldrs: chal over 1f out: led jst ins fnl f: hdd fnl 110yds: no ex and one pce into 3rd clsng stages* **8/1**[3]

2402 **4** shd **Figure Of Speech (IRE)**[14] 6201 2-9-1 107..........(p) SilvestreDeSousa 7 107
(Charlie Appleby) *in rr but in tch: hdwy 2f out: pressed ldrs fr 1f out: bmpd fnl 110yds and styd on same pce* **4/1**[2]

11 **5** ½ **Shamshon (IRE)**[37] 5460 2-9-1 0...................................... FrankieDettori 6 105
(Richard Hannon) *trckd ldrs: drvn 2f out: chal 1f out: no ex fnl 110yds* **7/2**[1]

The Form Book Flat, Raceform Ltd, Compton, RG20 6NL.

3520 **6** *nse* **Anticipated (IRE)**[34] 5573 2-9-1 108 RichardHughes 3 105
(Richard Hannon) *in rr but in tch: rdn 2f out: styd on ins fnl f but nvr quite gng pce to rch ldrs* **4/1**[2]

01 **7** *3/4* **Trading Profit**[68] 4347 2-9-1 0 JimmyFortune 5 103
(Andrew Balding) *in rr but in tch: hdwy over 2f out: sn rdn: styd on same pce fr over 1f out* **16/1**

1m 13.59s (0.59) **Going Correction** +0.275s/f (Good) **7** Ran SP% **106.2**
Speed ratings (Par 107): **107,106,105,105,104 104,103**
toteswingers 1&2 £8.70, 1&3 £4.70, 2&3 £12.90 CSF £57.96 TOTE £4.50: £2.30, £7.70; EX 50.20 Trifecta £699.70 Pool: £2481.64 - 2.65 winning units..
Owner Cheveley Park Stud **Bred** Cheveley Park Stud Ltd **Trained** Musley Bank, N Yorks
■ Complicit was withdrawn (10-1, ref to ent stalls). Deduct 5p in the £ under R4.

FOCUS
A weak Group 2, with the form looking more worthy of Listed level, and the runners were quite well bunched at the line, with them having gone relatively steady up front early on. The form has been rated as high as it's plausible.

6638 DUBAI DUTY FREE H'CAP 1m 2f 6y
2:55 (2:57) (Class 2) (0-105,104) 3-Y-O+

£46,687 (£13,980; £6,990; £3,495; £1,747; £877) **Stalls** Centre

Form RPR

-105 **1** **Haafaguinea**[26] 5838 3-8-6 **97** RyanTate(5) 1 106
(Clive Cox) *chsd ldrs: drvn to ld 2f out: narrowly hdd 1f out: styd chalng and led again fnl 110yds: drvn out* **9/1**

3400 **2** *3/4* **Chapter Seven**[21] 6001 4-9-6 **100** DeclanMcDonough 8 108
(Stuart Williams) *towards rr: hdwy on outside over 2f out: slt ld u.p ins fnl f: hdd and nt qckn fnl 110yds* **16/1**

543 **3** *nk* **Voodoo Prince**[7] 6394 5-8-12 **92** (p) AndreaAtzeni 11 99
(Ed Dunlop) *chsd ldrs: rdn over 2f out: slt ld 1f out and sn hdd: styd chalng tl nt qckn fnl 110yds* **7/1**[3]

4 *3/4* **Saxo Jack (FR)**[34] 5572 3-8-11 **97** GaryCarroll 4 106+
(G M Lyons, Ire) *in tch: nt clr run and lost position appr fnl 2f: shkn up and plenty to do appr fnl f: qckd wl fnl 150yds: fin strly: gng on cl home* **9/2**[1]

1110 **5** *3/4* **Disclaimer**[92] 3526 3-9-2 **102** JamesDoyle 6 107
(Lady Cecil) *towards rr: hdwy and pushed along over 2f out: sn rdn: kpt on same pce u.p ins fnl f* **6/1**[2]

0525 **6** *nse* **Trade Commissioner (IRE)**[21] 6001 5-9-10 **104** RobertHavlin 7 108
(John Gosden) *hld up in rr: hdwy on outside to chse ldrs 2f out: sn rdn: kpt on fnl f but nvr quite gng pce to press ldrs* **12/1**

2240 **7** *1* **Sennockian Star**[9] 6332 3-9-1 **101** (v) SilvestreDeSousa 9 104
(Mark Johnston) *in rr: drvn along over 3f out: hdwy u.p towards outside fnl f: nt rch ldrs* **16/1**

5422 **8** *3 1/4* **Trader Jack**[28] 5742 4-8-13 **93** JimmyFortune 14 89
(Roger Charlton) *in rr: hdwy to cl on ldrs over 2f out and sn rdn: wknd over 1f out* **10/1**

5542 **9** *3 1/4* **Benzanno (IRE)**[26] 5824 4-8-2 **87** DanielMuscutt(5) 2 77
(Andrew Balding) *t.k.h and sn led: hrd pressed fr over 4f out: rdn 3f out: hdd 2f out: wknd over 1f out* **8/1**

0404 **10** *1/2* **Black Spirit (USA)**[9] 6332 6-9-7 **101** (tp) AdamKirby 3 90
(Clive Cox) *chsd ldrs: drvn to chal over 2f out: wknd wl over 1f out* **12/1**

2356 **11** *5* **Salutation (IRE)**[28] 5749 3-8-3 **92** MichaelJMMurphy(3) 12 72
(Mark Johnston) *chsd ldr: upsides 7f out and stl chalng 3f out: wknd over 2f out* **25/1**

3136 **12** *2* **Viewpoint (IRE)**[9] 6332 4-9-2 **96** RichardHughes 13 72
(Richard Hannon) *in rr: sme hdwy over 2f out: nvr quite rchd ldrs and sn wknd* **12/1**

0123 **13** *2 1/4* **Fennell Bay (IRE)**[16] 6128 4-8-10 **90** FrederikTylicki 10 62
(Mark Johnston) *chsd ldrs: chal 4f out tl wl over 2f out: sn wknd* **20/1**

2m 8.05s (-0.75) **Going Correction** +0.175s/f (Good)
WFA 3 from 4yo+ 6lb **13** Ran SP% **118.6**
Speed ratings (Par 109): **110,109,109,108,107 107,107,104,101,101 97,95,94**
toteswingers 1&2 £29.90, 1&3 £12.60, 2&3 £25.70 CSF £143.79 CT £1073.38 TOTE £10.10: £3.60, £6.50, £2.40; EX 221.70 Trifecta £1477.10 Part won. Pool: £1969.59 - 0.91 winning units..
Owner Mrs Olive Shaw **Bred** Bishop Wilton Stud **Trained** Lambourn, Berks
■ Stewards' Enquiry : Ryan Tate four-day ban; used whip above permitted level (5,7-9th Oct).

FOCUS
Usually a pretty hot handicap. The early pace wasn't hectic. The winner built on his reappearance effort and the fourth was perhaps unlucky.

6639 DUBAI INTERNATIONAL AIRPORT WORLD TROPHY (GROUP 3) 5f 34y
3:30 (3:32) (Class 1) 3-Y-O+

£34,026 (£12,900; £6,456; £3,216; £1,614; £810) **Stalls** High

Form RPR

500 **1** **Maarek**[7] 6414 6-9-0 111 DeclanMcDonough 8 116
(B Lalor, Ire) *in rr and sn pushed along: hdwy and nt clr run and swtchd lft appr fnl f: rapid hdwy to ld fnl 75yds: r.o strly* **9/2**[2]

1002 **2** *1* **York Glory (USA)**[21] 5984 5-9-0 109 (b) JamesDoyle 10 112
(Kevin Ryan) *towards rr: hdwy and rdn over 1f out: c rt and styd on wl u.p fnl 150yds: tk 2nd last strides but no imp on wnr* **7/1**[3]

0205 **3** *hd* **Kingsgate Native (IRE)**[29] 5726 8-9-5 112 ShaneKelly 7 116
(Robert Cowell) *trckd ldrs: hrd drvn to chal fnl 150yds: chsd wnr fnl 75yds but a outpcd: lost 2nd last strides* **12/1**

3311 **4** *3/4* **Stepper Point**[21] 5984 4-9-0 109 (p) MartinDwyer 3 109
(William Muir) *trckd ldr: led ins fnl 2f: drvn and hdd fnl 75yds: no ex clsng stages* **14/1**

0-00 **5** *hd* **Ballesteros**[95] 3420 4-9-0 104 JimmyFortune 2 108
(Brian Meehan) *in rr: hdwy over 1f out: pressed ldrs u.p fnl 150yds: styd on same pce* **25/1**

5106 **6** *2* **Tickled Pink (IRE)**[29] 5726 4-9-0 109 RichardHughes 6 101
(Lady Cecil) *chsd ldrs: rdn ins fnl 2f: wknd fnl 150yds* **4/1**[1]

3201 **7** *1/2* **Miss Lahar**[59] 4647 4-8-11 102 SilvestreDeSousa 12 96
(Mick Channon) *racd towards stands' side: rdn 2f out: nvr gng pce to rch ldrs* **20/1**

2154 **8** *1/2* **Demora**[31] 5651 4-8-11 90 AndrewMullen 1 94
(Michael Appleby) *dipped s but sn led: hdd ins fnl 2f: wknd ins fnl f* **20/1**

4001 **9** *1/2* **Angels Will Fall (IRE)**[7] 6391 4-8-11 100 TedDurcan 14 92
(Charles Hills) *racd towards stands' side: rdn over 2f out: nvr gng pce to rch ldrs* **14/1**

0222 **10** *1/2* **Steps (IRE)**[7] 6391 5-9-0 104 (b) AndreaAtzeni 11 93
(Roger Varian) *racd towards stands' side: rdn 2f out and nvr gng pce to rch ldrs* **4/1**[1]

3000 **11** *shd* **Caledonia Lady**[21] 5984 4-8-11 100 FrederikTylicki 4 90
(Jo Hughes) *chsd ldrs: rdn over 2f out: werakening whn hmpd 1f out* **14/1**

033 **12** *3/4* **Judge 'n Jury**[10] 6305 9-9-0 100 (t) FrankieDettori 9 90
(Ronald Harris) *racd towards stands' side: chsd ldrs over 3f* **25/1**

3450 **13** *1* **Place In My Heart**[27] 5806 4-8-11 100 SteveDrowne 13 84
(Clive Cox) *racd towards stands' side: rdn along 1/2-way and sn outpcd* **33/1**

1m 1.04s (-0.36) **Going Correction** +0.275s/f (Good) **13** Ran SP% **118.5**
Speed ratings (Par 113): **113,111,111,109,109 106,105,104,103,103 103,101,100**
toteswingers 1&2 £12.40, 1&3 £6.80, 2&3 £7.20 CSF £32.69 TOTE £4.80: £2.00, £2.70, £3.50; EX 41.50 Trifecta £697.60 Pool: £3197.71 - 3.43 winning units..
Owner Lisbunny Syndicate **Bred** New England Stud & P J & P M Vela **Trained** Fethard, Co Tipperary

FOCUS
A good, competitive sprint, run at a strong gallop, and the race set up for the closers. The winner was the pick of these on his best form and the next four were within a couple of pounds of their marks.

6640 DUBAI DUTY FREE NURSERY H'CAP 7f (S)
4:05 (4:05) (Class 3) (0-95,92) 2-Y-O

£6,225 (£1,864; £932; £466; £233; £117) **Stalls** High

Form RPR

4310 **1** **Bow Creek (IRE)**[13] 6233 2-8-13 **84** SilvestreDeSousa 1 100+
(Mark Johnston) *mde all: drvn 2f out: c clr appr fnl f: unchal* **9/2**[3]

41 **2** *6* **Meteoroid (USA)**[26] 5843 2-8-8 **79** SteveDrowne 3 79+
(Lady Cecil) *chsd ldrs: drvn over 2f out: styd on to take 2nd fnl 110yds but no ch w unchal wnr* **13/8**[1]

1002 **3** *1 1/4* **Master Carpenter (IRE)**[10] 6303 2-9-7 **92** AndreaAtzeni 2 89
(Rod Millman) *chsd ldrs: wnt 2nd and drvn over 2f out: no imp on unchal wnr sn after: no ex and lost 2nd fnl 110yds* **9/2**[3]

461 **4** *1/2* **Penny's Boy**[20] 6013 2-7-12 **72** SimonPearce(3) 5 68
(Sylvester Kirk) *towards rr: drvn 2f out: styd on fnl f to cl on 3rd nr fin but nvr any ch w unchal wnr* **25/1**

2120 **5** *3 1/4* **Malachim Mist (IRE)**[9] 6328 2-9-5 **90** RichardHughes 4 77
(Richard Hannon) *in tch: pushed along and dropped towards rr over 2f out: no ch after* **4/1**[2]

564 **6** *2 1/4* **Charlie Wells (IRE)**[26] 5811 2-7-12 **72** RyanPowell(3) 6 54
(Eve Johnson Houghton) *wnt rt s: towards rr: hdwy to cl on ldrs and rdn 3f out: wknd 2f out* **16/1**

214 **7** *3* **Harwoods Volante (IRE)**[39] 5372 2-8-8 **79** RobertHavlin 8 53
(Amanda Perrett) *bmpd s: t.k.h: sn disputing 2nd: rdn 2f out: wknd qckly* **11/1**

1m 26.27s (0.57) **Going Correction** +0.275s/f (Good) **7** Ran SP% **112.5**
Speed ratings (Par 99): **107,100,98,98,94 91,88**
toteswingers 1&2 £2.10, 1&3 £1.80, 2&3 £1.90 CSF £11.85 CT £33.28 TOTE £5.50: £2.70, £1.80; EX 16.10 Trifecta £69.30 Pool: £1961.22 - 21.21 winning units..
Owner Sheikh Hamdan Bin Mohammed Al Maktoum **Bred** Round Hill Stud **Trained** Middleham Moor, N Yorks

FOCUS
A decent nursery blown apart from the front by the winner. The third is a solid guide.

6641 WEDGEWOOD ESTATES EBF MAIDEN STKS (DIV II) 7f (S)
4:40 (4:41) (Class 4) 2-Y-O **£4,528** (£1,347; £673; £336) **Stalls** High

Form RPR

1 **Kingston Hill** 2-9-5 0 AndreaAtzeni 2 82+
(Roger Varian) *trckd ldrs: wnt 2nd over 1f out: green and hung lft whn drvn to ld fnl 100yds: readily* **4/1**[2]

4 **2** *1 1/2* **Exchequer (IRE)**[22] 5957 2-9-5 0 RichardHughes 9 78
(Richard Hannon) *trckd ldr: led and hung lft fr over 1f out: stl edging lft whn hdd and outpcd fnl 100yds* **4/6**[1]

0 **3** *2 3/4* **Berrahri (IRE)**[38] 5399 2-9-5 0 SilvestreDeSousa 10 71
(John Best) *sn led: drvn hung lft and hdd over 1f out: styd on same pce fnl f* **33/1**

4 *3 1/2* **Be Seeing You** 2-9-5 0 JamesDoyle 11 62+
(Roger Charlton) *s.i.s: in rr: hdwy and drvn over 2f out: nvr rchd ldrs and one pce fnl 2f* **10/1**[3]

04 **5** *1/2* **Jersey Royal**[56] 4773 2-9-5 0 JimmyFortune 7 60+
(Richard Hannon) *chsd ldrs: drvn 2f out: sn one pce: wknd over 1f out* **12/1**

50 **6** *1 1/2* **Marengo**[15] 6168 2-9-2 0 MarkCoumbe(3) 4 57
(Ed de Giles) *chsd ldrs: rdn over 2f out and one pce: wknd wl over 1f out* **25/1**

7 *2* **Squaw King** 2-9-5 0 ShaneKelly 3 51
(Eve Johnson Houghton) *sn in tch: wknd over 2f out* **25/1**

8 *8* **Keep Close** 2-9-0 0 TedDurcan 5 26
(Mick Channon) *in rr: rdn and sme prog 3f out: wknd over 2f out* **14/1**

9 *1 1/2* **Vaguely Spanish** 2-9-5 0 AdamKirby 1 27
(Tony Carroll) *a in rr* **50/1**

10 *4* **Summerling (IRE)** 2-8-11 0 MatthewLawson(3) 6 11
(Jonathan Portman) *s.i.s: sn in tch: chsd ldrs 3f out: wknd appr fnl 2f* **50/1**

11 *63* **Exceed Policy** 2-9-5 0 SteveDrowne 8
(David Dennis) *sn t.o* **33/1**

1m 28.03s (2.33) **Going Correction** +0.275s/f (Good) **11** Ran SP% **120.9**
Speed ratings (Par 97): **97,95,92,88,87 85,83,74,72,68**
toteswingers 1&2 £1.60, 1&3 £13.60, 2&3 £8.80 CSF £6.79 TOTE £4.80: £1.60, £1.10, £6.30; EX 8.60 Trifecta £107.50 Pool: £2203.63 - 15.63 winning units..
Owner Paul Smith **Bred** Ridgecourt Stud **Trained** Newmarket, Suffolk

FOCUS
Little depth to what was the second division of this ordinary maiden and the front pair in the market duly drew clear. There's more to come from the winner.

6642 HEATHERWOLD STUD H'CAP 7f (S)
5:10 (5:13) (Class 4) (0-80,81) 3-Y-O **£4,851** (£1,443; £721; £360) **Stalls** High

Form RPR

2304 **1** **Whipper Snapper (IRE)**[25] 5853 3-9-2 **75** AdamKirby 1 84
(William Knight) *in rr: hdwy 3f out: rdn 2f out: chsd ldr 1f out: led fnl 110yds: kpt on wl* **20/1**

3341 **2** *1* **Naaz (IRE)**[8] 6359 3-9-8 **81** (b) FrankieDettori 2 87
(Ed Dunlop) *chsd ldrs: rdn to ld over 1f out: hdd and no ex fnl 110yds* **9/2**[1]

1542 **3** *1 1/4* **Front Page News**[29] 5721 3-9-1 **74** AndreaAtzeni 5 77
(Robert Eddery) *sn chsng ldrs: rdn over 1f out: tk 3rd fnl 110yds but no imp on ldng duo* **7/1**

6461 **4** *1* **Glanely (IRE)**[14] 6214 3-9-5 **78** ShaneKelly 10 78+
(James Fanshawe) *in rr: swtchd rt to stands' side over 1f out: continued to hang rt fnl f but styd on strly fnl 110yds: fin wl* **6/1**[3]

001 **5** ½ **Evident (IRE)**[112] 2872 3-9-3 **76**.................................... JamesDoyle 4 75+
(Jeremy Noseda) *hld up in rr: drvn: swtchd lft and hdwy over 1f out: kpt on clsng stages: nt rch ldrs* **12/1**
4460 **6** ¾ **Movementneverlies**[48] 5037 3-8-11 **70**........................ SteveDrowne 13 67
(Charles Hills) *chsd ldrs: rdn and one pce 2f out: styd on again fnl f* **25/1**
4010 **7** nk **Pivotal Movement**[23] 5928 3-9-6 **79**......................... RichardHughes 3 75
(Richard Hannon) *chsd ldrs: led over 2f out: hdd over 1f out: wknd ins fnl f* **7/1**
4362 **8** shd **Benoni**[14] 6214 3-9-2 **75**.. TedDurcan 12 71
(Henry Candy) *in rr: drvn 2f out: styd on clsng stages but nvr a threat* **5/1**[2]
5606 **8** dht **The Gatling Boy (IRE)**[17] 6106 3-8-13 **72**.................. JimmyFortune 8 68
(Richard Hannon) *led 2f: chsd ldrs: wknd ins fnl 2f* **25/1**
354 **10** ¾ **Strictly Silca**[29] 5700 3-9-6 **79**............................(v) SilvestreDeSousa 14 73
(Mick Channon) *sn chsng ldrs: wknd over 1f out* **14/1**
4215 **11** ¾ **Gracious George (IRE)**[22] 5958 3-9-4 **77**..................(b) BrettDoyle 6 69
(Jimmy Fox) *in tch: chsd ldrs over 2f out: btn whn wnt lft over 1f out* **14/1**
1335 **12** ¾ **Al Raqeeb (IRE)**[29] 5721 3-9-4 **77**.............................. TonyHamilton 7 67
(Gary Harrison) *chsd ldrs: wknd 2f out* **25/1**
2121 **13** 1 **Combustible (IRE)**[46] 5096 3-9-5 **78**........................ GaryCarroll 9 66
(John Stimpson) *t.k.h: led after 2f: hdd over 2f out: sn btn* **10/1**

1m 26.99s (1.29) **Going Correction** +0.275s/f (Good) **13** Ran SP% **120.6**
Speed ratings (Par 103): **103,101,100,99,98 97,97,97,97,96 95,94,93**
toteswingers 1&2 £19.50, 1&3 £20.30, 2&3 £13.20 CSF £104.57 CT £537.41 TOTE £17.60: £4.40, £2.20, £2.80; EX 168.20 Trifecta £508.90 Part won. Pool: £678.58 - 0.01 winning units..
Owner The Oil Merchants **Bred** Michael Mullins **Trained** Patching, W Sussex

FOCUS
The early pace was steady, but picked up when the hard pulling filly Combustible went to the front, and there were plenty in with a chance inside the final 2f. The first three raced on the far side. The winner is rated in line with the better view of his form.
T/Plt: £407.80 to a £1 stake. Pool: £95500.29 - 170.91 winning tickets T/Qpdt: £87.10 to a £1 stake. Pool: £5347.80 - 45.40 winning tickets ST

5744 NEWMARKET (R-H)
Saturday, September 21

OFFICIAL GOING: Good (7.1)
Wind: light, half behind Weather: light rain, drizzle, mild

6643 FEDERATION OF BLOODSTOCK AGENTS EBF MAIDEN FILLIES' STKS 1m
1:55 (1:56) (Class 4) 2-Y-O **£4,528** (£1,347; £673; £336) **Stalls** Centre

Form RPR
1 **Taghrooda** 2-9-0 0.. DaneO'Neill 3 85+
(John Gosden) *hld up in tch in rr: rdn: gd hdwy and edging lft over 1f out: led 1f out: r.o wl and a jst holding runner-up fnl f: pushed out* **20/1**
23 **2** nk **Casual Smile**[14] 6185 2-9-0 0................................ DavidProbert 13 84
(Andrew Balding) *hld up wl in tch and travelled wl: effrt over 1f out: rdn and ev ch 1f out: r.o wl u.p fnl f: a jst hld* **15/8**[1]
422 **3** 2¼ **Tea In Transvaal (IRE)**[18] 6063 2-9-0 78....................... RyanMoore 14 79
(Richard Hannon) *hld up in tch in last trio: effrt and edgd rt over 2f out: hdwy wl over 1f out: pressed ldrs and drvn 1f out: no ex and one pce fnl 100yds* **5/1**[3]
4 ½ **Brown Diamond (IRE)** 2-9-0 0.......................... MickaelBarzalona 11 78+
(Charles Hills) *s.i.s: in tch in last trio: rdn and effrt jst over 2f out: hdwy to press ldrs u.p 1f out: no ex and one pce fnl 100yds* **33/1**
4 **5** 1¼ **Criteria (IRE)**[18] 6063 2-9-0 0.............................. WilliamBuick 1 75
(John Gosden) *wl in tch in midfield: effrt ent fnl 2f: drvn and pressing ldrs over 1f out: no ex and btn 1f out: wknd ins fnl f* **2/1**[2]
6 ½ **Gold Approach** 2-9-0 0.. JohnnyMurtagh 4 73
(William Haggas) *in tch in midfield: effrt u.p 2f out: no imp tl styd on ins fnl f: no threat to ldrs* **7/1**
7 ½ **Fray** 2-9-0 0.. RichardKingscote 5 72+
(Roger Charlton) *rn green: t.k.h: hld up in tch in midfield: effrt and edgd rt ent fnl 2f: stl green and no imp whn edgd rt over 1f out: styd on same pce fnl f* **33/1**
6 **8** ½ **Yeah Baby (IRE)**[47] 5061 2-9-0 0.............................. SebSanders 6 71
(Charles Hills) *pressed ldr tl led 1/2-way: rdn 2f out: drvn and hdd 1f out: wknd ins fnl f* **33/1**
9 1¼ **Groovejet** 2-9-0 0.. LukeMorris 9 68
(Peter Chapple-Hyam) *dwlt and bmpd sn after s: sn in tch in midfield: pushed along 1/2-way: rdn and lost pl over 2f out: rallied 1f out and styd on ins fnl f and gng on at fin: no threat to ldrs* **50/1**
00 **10** 1¾ **Mollasses**[29] 5716 2-9-0 0.. JoeFanning 2 64
(Jonathan Portman) *chsd ldrs: rdn ent fnl 2f: struggling and outpcd whn short of room and sltly hmpd over 1f out: sn wknd* **80/1**
11 shd **By Jupiter** 2-9-0 0.. MartinHarley 8 64
(Michael Bell) *wnt lft and stdd s: hld up in tch in last trio: rdn and effrt jst over 2f out: no imp after: n.d* **50/1**
12 2¼ **Malory Towers** 2-9-0 0.. PatDobbs 7 58
(Richard Hannon) *led tl 1/2-way: rdn and lost pl over 2f out: bhd over 1f out* **33/1**
0 **13** 1 **Asteroidea**[16] 6125 2-9-0 0.. LiamKeniry 12 56
(Pam Sly) *t.k.h: chsd ldrs: rdn and struggling ent fnl 2f: sn lost pl and wknd over 1f out* **50/1**
20 **14** 2¼ **Water For Life**[24] 5891 2-9-0 0.............................. WilliamCarson 10 50
(Dave Morris) *in tch in midfield: rdn andlost pl over 2f out: bhd over 1f out* **100/1**

1m 40.67s (2.07) **Going Correction** +0.125s/f (Good) **14** Ran SP% **121.9**
Speed ratings (Par 94): **94,93,91,90,89 89,88,88,86,85 85,82,81,79**
toteswingers 1&2 £10.00, 2&3 £3.00, 1&3 £10.70 CSF £56.15 TOTE £36.20: £6.10, £1.20, £1.70; EX 126.60 Trifecta £270.50 Pool: £1045.01 - 2.89 winning units..
Owner Hamdan Al Maktoum **Bred** Shadwell Estate Company Limited **Trained** Newmarket, Suffolk

FOCUS
Far side of Rowley Mile track used and stalls: centre. First meeting on the Rowley Mile since May. The going was good and the far side course was used with the stalls in the centre. This fillies' maiden has produced some subsequent high-class winners in the past, including Light Shift in 2006 and Midday in 2008. The pace was not very strong in this decent renewal but a newcomer beat the leading form contender and the pair finished clear of the rest. The form makes sense.

6644 £100,000 TATTERSALLS MILLIONS FILLIES' MEDIAN AUCTION STKS 6f
2:30 (2:35) (Class 2) 2-Y-O
£54,100 (£24,590; £9,840; £4,910; £2,960; £1,970) **Stalls** Centre

Form RPR
1533 **1** **Wedding Ring (IRE)**[16] 6142 2-9-1 97.................... MickaelBarzalona 6 90+
(Charlie Appleby) *hld up in tch and travelled wl: clsd to ld 2f out: rdn over 1f out: hrd pressed and drvn ins fnl f: fnd ex and r.o gamely fnl 75yds* **6/4**[1]
01 **2** nk **Oxsana**[3] 6534 2-9-1 0... MartinHarley 8 89
(William Haggas) *hld up in tch in rr: gd hdwy u.p over 1f out: drvn and str chal ins fnl f: r.o but hld fnl 75yds* **20/1**
03 **3** 1¼ **Fashion Fund**[35] 5529 2-8-13 0.................................. WilliamBuick 4 83
(Brian Meehan) *in tch in midfield: effrt u.p ent fnl 2f: chsd wnr wl over 1f out tl ent fnl f: kpt on same pce fnl 150yds* **16/1**
622 **4** 1 **Zawiyah**[17] 6112 2-8-13 71... JoeFanning 3 80
(Luca Cumani) *dwlt: in tch towards rr: hdwy midfield: rdn 2f out: pressed wnr ent fnl f tl fnl 150yds: no ex and wknd fnl 75yds* **25/1**
04 **5** 1 **Johara (IRE)**[33] 5577 2-8-5 0...................................... LukeMorris 7 69
(Chris Wall) *in tch towards rr: rdn and effrt ent fnl 2f: drvn and hdwy over 1f out: chsd ldrs 1f out: styd on same pce ins fnl f* **50/1**
2021 **6** nk **Aqlaam Vision**[9] 6326 2-9-1 85..................................... RyanMoore 1 78
(Clive Brittain) *in tch towards rr: rdn and over 2f out: outpcd wl over 1f out: rallied and styd on u.p ins fnl f: no threat to ldrs* **4/1**[2]
6 **7** ½ **Two Smart (IRE)**[27] 5797 2-8-11 0........................ RichardKingscote 5 73
(K R Burke) *sn led: rdn and hdd 2f out: styd on same pce u.p fr over 1f out* **9/1**
0310 **8** 2 **Oriel**[35] 5536 2-9-1 81... PatDobbs 9 71
(Richard Hannon) *chsd ldrs: rdn to chse wnr 2f out tl wl over 1f out: no ex u.p over 1f out: wknd ins fnl f* **16/1**
031 **9** nk **Amnesia (IRE)**[19] 6034 2-9-1 78......................... JohnnyMurtagh 12 70
(William Haggas) *in tch in midfield: rdn and effrt ent fnl 2f: no imp and one pce fr over 1f out* **8/1**[3]
13 **10** nk **Chess Valley**[39] 5371 2-8-11 74.................................. ChrisCatlin 13 65
(Rae Guest) *hld up in tch in midfield: rdn and effrt 2f out: no imp u.p over 1f out: wknd ins fnl f* **33/1**
403 **11** shd **Manderley (IRE)**[38] 5394 2-8-5 76.......................... KieranO'Neill 11 59
(Richard Hannon) *chsd ldrs: rdn 1/2-way: outpcd and lost pl whn swtchd rt ent fnl f: plugged on same pce after* **25/1**
12 nk **Broughtons Secret** 2-8-9 0...................................... JamieMackay 14 62
(Willie Musson) *s.i.s: detached in last: rdn along 4f out: swtchd rt 1f out: kpt on ins fnl f: n.d* **100/1**
00 **13** ½ **Black Rodded**[35] 5529 2-8-7 0.................................. DavidProbert 10 58
(Hughie Morrison) *led briefly early: chsd ldr tl 2f out: sn drvn and no ex: btn over 1f out: wknd fnl f* **100/1**
33 **14** 1¼ **Tears Of The Sun**[10] 6298 2-8-7 0.............................. MartinLane 2 55
(Roger Varian) *in tch in midfield: rdn and unable qck 2f out: wknd over 1f out: bhd fnl f* **16/1**

1m 13.22s (1.02) **Going Correction** +0.125s/f (Good) **14** Ran SP% **118.1**
Speed ratings (Par 98): **98,97,95,94,93 92,92,89,89,88 88,88,87,85**
toteswingers 1&2 £12.20, 2&3 £99.70, 1&3 £6.10 CSF £40.11 TOTE £2.10: £1.10, £6.80, £4.00; EX 48.10 Trifecta £557.70 Pool: £1846.18 - 2.48 winning units..
Owner Godolphin **Bred** Swettenham Stud **Trained** Newmarket, Suffolk

FOCUS
A decent renewal of this valuable fillies' sales race. The pace was just fair but the leading form contender battled well to justify favouritism. There are concerns about how literally to take this.

6645 £100,000 TATTERSALLS MILLIONS MEDIAN AUCTION TROPHY 6f
3:05 (3:05) (Class 2) 2-Y-O
£54,100 (£24,590; £9,840; £4,910; £2,960; £1,970) **Stalls** Centre

Form RPR
32 **1** **Toofi (FR)**[50] 4958 2-8-7 0...................................... WilliamBuick 9 97+
(Roger Varian) *wl in tch in midfield: rdn and effrt to chse ldrs wl over 1f out: led 1f out: styd on strly: rdn out* **4/1**[2]
3454 **2** 1 **Jallota**[34] 5573 2-8-9 112... MartinHarley 11 96
(Mick Channon) *chsd ldr and travelled wl: rdn to ld over 1f out: hdd and drvn 1f out: kpt on but no ex and one pce fnl 100yds* **5/4**[1]
021 **3** 2½ **Muir Lodge**[14] 6213 2-8-13 77...............................(t[1]) LiamKeniry 7 92
(Andrew Balding) *t.k.h: hld up in midfield: hdwy u.p over 1f out: styd on steadily ins fnl f to snatch 3rd cl home: no threat to ldng pair* **22/1**
23 **4** shd **Bon Voyage**[14] 6184 2-8-9 0...................................... RyanMoore 1 88
(Richard Hannon) *dwlt: sn rcvrd and in midfield: effrt over 2f out: hdwy u.p over 1f out: kpt on ins fnl f and pressing for 3rd towards fin: no threat to ldng pair* **12/1**
05 **5** nse **Highland Acclaim (IRE)**[15] 6169 2-8-9 0................ DavidProbert 10 88
(Andrew Balding) *hld up in midfield: effrt and edgd rt ent fnl 2f: hdwy u.p over 1f out: kpt on fnl f and pressing for 3rd towards fin: no threat to ldng pair* **66/1**
2 **6** ¾ **Quickaswecan**[23] 5915 2-8-11 0.................................. FMBerry 3 87
(Mark Johnston) *led: rdn and hdd over 1f out: 3rd and btn ins fnl f: wknd and lost 3 pls towards fin* **20/1**
3335 **7** 3¼ **Halljoy (IRE)**[8] 6350 2-8-0 93...................................... LukeMorris 2 66
(Clive Brittain) *chsd ldrs: rdn 1/2 way: drvn and outpcd wl over 1f out: wl hld and plugged on same pce fnl f* **14/1**
120U **8** nse **Regiment**[9] 6328 2-8-5 84... JimmyQuinn 8 71
(Richard Fahey) *chsd ldrs: rdn 1/2-way: lost pl u.p wl over 1f out: wl hld and plugged on same pce fnl f* **80/1**
5413 **9** shd **Constantine**[23] 5927 2-8-9 77...................................... SeanLevey 6 74
(Richard Hannon) *wl in tch in midfield: rdn and unable qck over 2f out: btn over 1f out wknd fnl f* **66/1**
10 nk **Newton's Law (IRE)** 2-8-7 0............................ MickaelBarzalona 5 71
(Brian Meehan) *s.i.s: bhd: rdn and sme hdwy against stands' rail over 1f out: no imp ins fnl f: nvr trbld ldrs* **22/1**
11 ¾ **Sir Guy Porteous (IRE)** 2-8-11 0................................ DaneO'Neill 15 73
(Mark Johnston) *towards rr: rdn and effrt then swtchd lft ent fnl 2f: sme hdwy over 1f out: no imp fnl f: nvr trbld ldrs* **66/1**

2100 **12** *1 ½* **Speed The Plough**[31] 5656 2-8-11 75................................ PatDobbs 16 68
(Richard Hannon) *dwlt: a towards rr: effrt and hdwy u.p ent 2f out: sn drvn and no hdwy over 1f out: wknd fnl f* **100/1**

1450 **13** *2* **Vine De Nada**[78] 4019 2-8-7 78................................ MartinLane 12 58
(Mark Johnston) *veered lft sn after s and sn bhd: n.d* **100/1**

0216 **14** *hd* **Lanark (IRE)**[52] 4876 2-8-13 95................................ JoeFanning 14 63
(Mark Johnston) *in tch in midfield: rdn 1/2-way: lost pl and bhd over 1f out* **14/1**

2211 **15** *½* **Lyn Valley**[18] 6064 2-9-3 94................................ JohnnyMurtagh 4 65
(Mark Johnston) *s.i.s: rcvrd and in tch in midfield after 2f: rdn and struggling 1/2-way: bhd over 1f out* **7/1**[3]

1m 12.4s (0.20) **Going Correction** +0.125s/f (Good) **15** Ran SP% **119.1**
Speed ratings (Par 101): **103,101,98,98,98 97,92,92,92,92 91,89,86,86,85**
toteswingers 1&2 £2.70, 2&3 £8.90, 1&3 £9.40 CSF £8.44 TOTE £5.00: £1.80, £1.30, £5.60; EX 13.00 Trifecta £263.10 Pool: £1352.27 - 3.85 winning units..
Owner Saleh Al Homaizi & Imad Al Sagar **Bred** Sudstrom Team Hogdala A B **Trained** Newmarket, Suffolk

FOCUS
The strong favourite was overhauled by his main market rival in this valuable sales race and the pair pulled clear. The third and ninth suggest the bare form is no better than rated.

6646 BETFRED CESAREWITCH TRIAL (H'CAP) 2m 2f
3:40 (3:43) (Class 2) (0-105,99) 3-Y-O+ **£32,345** (£9,625; £4,810; £2,405) **Stalls** Centre

Form RPR

0450 **1** **Oriental Fox (GER)**[14] 6192 5-9-10 99................................ JohnnyMurtagh 8 111
(Mark Johnston) *hld up: gd hdwy to trck ldrs 3f out: rdn to ld over 1f out: clr 1f out: styd on strly: readily* **9/1**

16 **2** *3 ¼* **Body Language (IRE)**[13] 6237 5-8-6 81..............(p) MickaelBarzalona 11 89
(Ian Williams) *hld up in last trio: rdn over 8f out: str run over 3f out and pressing ldrs 3f out: chsd wnr over 1f out: kpt on one pce fnl f* **16/1**

4350 **3** *1 ¾* **Brockwell**[42] 5256 4-9-2 91................................ RichardKingscote 5 97
(Tom Dascombe) *chsd ldrs: wnt 2nd 5f out: led 3f out and sn rdn: hdd and unable qck over 1f out: plugged on same pce fnl f* **9/2**[1]

0361 **4** *11* **Cosimo de Medici**[25] 5868 6-8-12 87................................ RyanMoore 4 81
(Hughie Morrison) *taken down early: hld up towards rr: hdwy 5f out: rdn and effrt to chse ldrs 3f out: 4th and outpcd over 2f out: wl btn after: plugged on* **10/1**

1362 **5** *1 ¼* **Burnham**[17] 6108 4-8-4 79................................(p) LukeMorris 19 72
(Hughie Morrison) *hld up in tch: effrt u.p over 3f out: 5th and outpcd whn edgd rt over 2f out: plugged on but wl btn after* **20/1**

1043 **6** *3* **Arch Villain (IRE)**[18] 6066 4-9-1 90................................ PatDobbs 16 79
(Amanda Perrett) *hld up in tch: effrt u.p over 3f out: sn drvn and outpcd over 2f out: 6th and wl btn fnl 2f: edgd rt ins fnl f* **7/1**[3]

4113 **7** *2 ¾* **Silver Samba**[24] 5879 4-8-6 81................................ DavidProbert 2 67
(Andrew Balding) *hld up in midfield: clsd on ldrs and travelling wl 5f out: rdn and fnd nil 3f out: sn wknd and wl btn fnl 2f* **11/1**

6000 **8** *½* **Valid Reason**[15] 6173 6-8-1 76 oh10 ow1..............(p) FrankieMcDonald 9 62
(Dean Ivory) *t.k.h: hld up in tch in midfield: clsd on ldrs 5f out: drvn and no ex over 3f out: wknd and wl btn fnl 2f* **33/1**

24 **9** *½* **Teak (IRE)**[10] 4782 6-8-1 76................................ MartinLane 15 61
(Ian Williams) *hld up in midfield: drvn and struggling whn swtchd lft over 5f out: lost pl and bhd over 3f out: no ch after* **16/1**

1114 **10** *nk* **Beacon Lady**[20] 6016 4-8-11 86................................ DaneO'Neill 13 71
(William Knight) *taken down early: stdd and dropped in after s: hld up in rr: effrt and sme hdwy 4f out: edgd rt and no hdwy over 2f out: sn wknd* **14/1**

1144 **11** *5* **Miss Tiger Lily**[22] 5972 3-8-0 88 oh15................................ KieranO'Neill 14 68
(Harry Dunlop) *led tl rdn and hdd 3f out: sn btn: fdd fnl 2f* **50/1**

1616 **12** *7* **Broxbourne (IRE)**[18] 6066 4-9-5 94................................ JoeFanning 7 66
(Mark Johnston) *hld up in midfield: effrt and switching lft over 3f out: no hdwy and sn btn: wknd wl over 2f out: t.o and eased ins fnl f* **6/1**[2]

1351 **13** *12* **Eagle Rock (IRE)**[13] 6237 5-8-10 85..........................(p) WilliamBuick 18 43
(Tom Tate) *racd away fr rivals in centre: chsd ldr: rdn 6f out: lost 2nd 5f out: wknd 3f out: t.o and eased ins fnl f* **8/1**

3160 **14** *7* **Nanton (USA)**[14] 6192 11-8-9 84................................ AndrewElliott 12 35
(Jim Goldie) *hld up in last quartet: rdn and effrt 4f out: no hdwy: t.o fnl 2f: eased over 1f out* **33/1**

3110 **15** *¾* **Nashville (IRE)**[13] 6237 4-8-3 78................................ JimmyQuinn 17 28
(Richard Fahey) *t.k.h: chsd ldrs tl wknd qckly 3f out: eased fr wl over 1f out: t.o* **25/1**

-303 **16** *23* **Saborido (USA)**[24] 5895 7-8-8 83................................ SeanLevey 3 8
(Amanda Perrett) *hld up in midfield: rdn and wknd over 3f out: t.o and eased fr wl over 1f out* **25/1**

-040 **17** *29* **Sergeant Ablett (IRE)**[42] 5288 5-8-0 75................................ NickyMackay 10
(Luke Dace) *chsd ldrs tl rdn and lost plce 4f out: eased fr 2f out: wl t.o* **33/1**

5115 **18** *42* **Porcini**[35] 5520 4-8-9 84................................(p) WilliamCarson 6
(Philip McBride) *midfield: rdn 5f out: lost pl qckly and dropped to last 4f out: wl t.o and eased fnl 2f* **16/1**

3m 49.81s (-2.19) **Going Correction** +0.125s/f (Good)
WFA 3 from 4yo+ 13lb **18** Ran SP% **131.1**
Speed ratings (Par 109): **109,107,106,101,101 100,98,98,98,98 95,92,87,84,84 73,60,42**
toteswingers 1&2 £27.80, 2&3 £27.80, 1&3 £12.80 CSF £143.25 CT £756.21 TOTE £13.20: £3.60, £4.00, £2.00, £3.10; EX 206.10 Trifecta £1144.50 Part won. Pool: £1526.01 - 0.32 winning units..
Owner Markus Graff **Bred** Gestut Auenquelle **Trained** Middleham Moor, N Yorks

FOCUS
The went a decent pace in this Cesarewitch trial. The top weight scored in decent style and the first three finished a long way clear. Sound form.

6647 ASIA VIP CLUB H'CAP (DIV I) 6f
4:15 (4:16) (Class 4) (0-85,85) 3-Y-O+ **£4,851** (£1,443; £721; £360) **Stalls** Centre

Form RPR

5030 **1** **Equitania**[28] 5769 3-8-13 79 ow1................................ SebSanders 9 87
(Alan Bailey) *mde all: rdn ent fnl f: kpt on gamely: a holding on fnl 120yds* **25/1**

0063 **2** *nk* **Vallarta (IRE)**[64] 4478 3-8-7 73................................ MartinLane 10 80
(Mick Channon) *trckd wnr: rdn 2f out: r.o to cl on wnr jst ins fnl f: keeping on wl nring fin* **14/1**

-002 **3** *¾* **Midnight Rider (IRE)**[36] 5489 5-9-7 85................................ GeorgeBaker 6 89
(Chris Wall) *s.i.s: in last trio: shkn up and hdwy over 1f out: sn rdn: r.o wl fnl f: wnt cl 3rd nring fin but nvr getting there* **3/1**[1]

5431 **4** *½* **Breccbennach**[18] 6072 3-8-8 74................................(tp) DaneO'Neill 11 76
(Seamus Durack) *mid-div: hdwy 3f out: rdn 2f out: no imp tl r.o ent fnl f: sn chsng ldng pair: no ex whn lost 3rd nr fin* **8/1**[3]

2400 **5** *2* **Alnoomaas (IRE)**[7] 6403 4-8-9 73................................ JimmyQuinn 1 68
(Luke Dace) *s.i.s: sn trcking wnr: rdn over 2f out: no ex fnl f* **22/1**

0105 **6** *1 ¼* **Noverre To Go (IRE)**[25] 5851 7-9-4 82................................ LukeMorris 2 73
(Ronald Harris) *mid-div: rdn over 2f out: kpt on same pce* **14/1**

0000 **7** *1 ¼* **Fratellino**[21] 5998 6-9-2 80................................(tp) MartinHarley 8 66
(Alan McCabe) *mid-div: rdn 3f out: one pce fnl 2f* **20/1**

2360 **8** *1 ¼* **Jack Of Diamonds (IRE)**[70] 4281 4-9-0 78................................ JoeFanning 7 60
(Roger Teal) *s.i.s: in last pair: rdn 2f out: little imp* **8/1**[3]

2320 **9** *½* **Cruise Tothelimit (IRE)**[29] 5696 5-9-1 79................................ RyanMoore 3 59
(Ian Williams) *in tch: rdn 2f out: wknd fnl f* **8/1**[3]

1115 **10** *1 ¼* **Nenge Mboko**[52] 4879 3-9-5 85................................(v) WilliamBuick 5 60
(George Baker) *s.i.s: nvr travelling towards rr: nvr threatened* **4/1**[2]

1-00 **11** *3 ¾* **Magic Secret**[55] 4812 5-9-6 84................................ JohnnyMurtagh 4 46
(William Muir) *trckd ldrs: rdn over 2f out: wknd over 1f out* **8/1**[3]

1m 12.4s (0.20) **Going Correction** +0.125s/f (Good)
WFA 3 from 4yo+ 2lb **11** Ran SP% **115.7**
Speed ratings (Par 105): **103,102,101,100,98 96,94,93,92,90 85**
toteswingers 1&2 £64.00, 2&3 £9.40, 1&3 £8.60 CSF £324.99 CT £1363.66 TOTE £28.70: £5.80, £4.70, £1.60; EX 199.90 Trifecta £1299.40 Pool: £1732.61 - 0.02 winning units..
Owner John Stocker **Bred** Longdon Stud **Trained** Newmarket, Suffolk

FOCUS
The outsider made all in this competitive sprint handicap. Possibly not form to take too literally.

6648 ASIA VIP CLUB H'CAP (DIV II) 6f
4:50 (4:50) (Class 4) (0-85,85) 3-Y-O+ **£4,851** (£1,443; £721; £360) **Stalls** Centre

Form RPR

00 **1** **B Fifty Two (IRE)**[21] 5998 4-9-5 83..........................(bt[1]) SebSanders 10 92
(J W Hills) *mde all: rdn and fnd ex over 1f out: in command and r.o wl fnl f* **7/1**

0050 **2** *1 ¼* **Novellen Lad (IRE)**[14] 6203 8-8-9 73................................ WilliamBuick 4 78
(Willie Musson) *chsd ldrs: rdn and chsd wnr over 1f out: swtchd rt ent fnl f: kpt on but no real imp* **13/2**[3]

3000 **3** *½* **Rasaman (IRE)**[26] 5832 9-9-1 79................................ AndrewElliott 11 82
(Jim Goldie) *dwlt: sn rcvrd and in tch in midfield: lost pl over 2f out: rdn wl over 1f out: rallied u.p and styd on wl ins fnl f* **12/1**

406- **4** *1 ¾* **Kylladdie**[429] 4255 6-8-7 71................................(b) JoeFanning 7 69
(Steve Gollings) *stdd s: hld up in tch in midfield: hdwy ent fnl 2f: rdn and chsd ldrs over 1f out: no ex and wknd fnl 100yds* **25/1**

2130 **5** *shd* **Bajan Bear**[36] 5489 5-8-10 74................................ DaneO'Neill 2 71
(Michael Blanshard) *dwlt: hld up in tch in last trio: rdn and effrt wl over 1f out: styd on ins fnl f: no threat to wnr* **4/1**[1]

11-0 **6** *1 ½* **Conry (IRE)**[7] 6384 7-9-2 85................................ GeorgeDowning[(5)] 1 78
(Ian Williams) *stdd s: hld up in tch in midfield: rdn and effrt 2f out: no imp and one pce fr over 1f out* **11/1**

4246 **7** *¾* **Afkar (IRE)**[14] 6204 5-8-7 71 oh1................................ LukeMorris 3 61
(Clive Brittain) *chsd wnr: rdn and unable qck ent fnl 2f: lost pl over 1f out: wl hld and one pce fnl f* **11/2**[2]

3126 **8** *nk* **Light From Mars**[15] 6162 8-9-4 82..........................(p) RichardKingscote 5 71
(Tom Dascombe) *s.i.s: hld up in tch in last trio: effrt wl over 1f out: no imp: nvr trbld ldrs* **7/1**

2410 **9** *4* **Jontleman (IRE)**[21] 5996 3-9-0 80................................ MartinHarley 8 57
(Mick Channon) *hld up in tch in midfield: rdn and effrt wl over 1f out: sn outpcd: wknd fnl f* **11/2**[2]

6000 **10** *1 ¾* **Piscean (USA)**[18] 6078 8-9-5 83................................(b) GeorgeBaker 9 54
(Tom Keddy) *stdd s: t.k.h: hld up in tch in rr: swtchd lft and effrt 2f out: no hdwy: wknd ent fnl f* **16/1**

1m 12.75s (0.55) **Going Correction** +0.125s/f (Good)
WFA 3 from 4yo+ 2lb **10** Ran SP% **114.9**
Speed ratings (Par 105): **101,99,98,96,96 94,93,92,87,85**
toteswingers 1&2 £11.00, 2&3 £13.00, 1&3 £19.10 CSF £51.15 CT £548.75 TOTE £8.10: £2.20, £3.10, £4.00; EX 57.10 Trifecta £1562.90 Pool: £2637.29 - 1.26 winning units..
Owner Gary And Linnet Woodward **Bred** Mull Enterprises Ltd **Trained** Upper Lambourn, Berks

FOCUS
They went a steady pace in the second division of this sprint handicap. The winner made all and the hold-up performers couldn't get involved. The first two were on good marks on their old form.

6649 PRESTIGE VEHICLES EBF FILLIES' H'CAP 1m 4f
5:25 (5:26) (Class 3) (0-95,95) 3-Y-O+ **£8,409** (£2,502; £1,250; £625) **Stalls** Centre

Form RPR

0513 **1** **Phaenomena (IRE)**[22] 5944 3-8-9 84................................ MartinHarley 5 97
(Lady Cecil) *hld up in last trio: rdn whn swtchd lft fr over 2f out: gd hdwy ent fnl f: fin v strly to ld fnl 75yds: won gng away* **5/1**[3]

-312 **2** *1* **Astonishing (IRE)**[27] 5795 3-9-3 92................................ RyanMoore 4 103
(Sir Michael Stoute) *trckd ldrs: rdn to chal over 1f out: kpt on ins fnl f: tk def 2nd nring fin: no answer for late thrust of wnr* **6/4**[1]

1112 **3** *½* **Willow Beck**[28] 5749 4-9-5 86................................ WilliamBuick 2 96
(John Gosden) *in tch: nudged along to take clsr over 2f out: rdn to ld over 1f out: hrd pressed ins fnl f: no ex whn hdd fnl 75yds* **4/1**[2]

01 **4** *¾* **Silk Sari**[74] 4139 3-8-9 84................................ PatDobbs 7 93
(Luca Cumani) *sn in tch: trckd ldrs 3f out: rdn 2f out: kpt on ins fnl f* **12/1**

-021 **5** *1 ¼* **Zipp (IRE)**[47] 5064 3-8-5 80................................ MartinLane 10 87
(Charles Hills) *hld up in last trio: rdn wl over 2f out: no imp tl styd on ins fnl f: fin wl but nvr any ch* **20/1**

2114 **6** *1 ½* **Paris Rose**[77] 4066 3-8-9 84................................ JoeFanning 3 89
(William Haggas) *hld up in last trio: hdwy to trck ldrs over 4f out: rdn and ev ch over 1f out tl ent fnl f: fdd fnl 120yds* **20/1**

3-00 **7** *15* **Lily In Pink**[140] 2012 5-10-0 95................................ RichardKingscote 8 76
(Jonathan Portman) *in tch tl over 3f out: sn struggling in rr* **33/1**

2216 **8** *7* **Arbaah (USA)**[58] 4681 3-8-8 83................................ DaneO'Neill 6 52
(Brian Meehan) *led tl over 2f out: wknd over 1f out: eased fnl f* **33/1**

0201 **9** *1 ¾* **Opera Box**[21] 6004 5-9-7 88................................ GeorgeBaker 9 55
(Marcus Tregoning) *trckd ldrs: rdn over 3f out: sn btn: eased fnl f* **25/1**

1-50 **10** *10* **Saytara (IRE)**[15] 6172 4-9-13 94................................ JohnnyMurtagh 1 86
(Saeed bin Suroor) *trckd ldr: led over 2f out: rdn and hdd over 1f out: wknd qckly: heavily eased ins fnl f* **7/1**

2m 31.4s (-0.60) **Going Correction** +0.125s/f (Good)
WFA 3 from 4yo+ 8lb **10** Ran SP% **116.1**
Speed ratings (Par 104): **107,106,106,105,104 103,93,89,87,81**
toteswingers 1&2 £2.40, 2&3 £1.40, 1&3 £4.30 CSF £11.92 CT £31.93 TOTE £6.40: £1.90, £1.30, £2.00; EX 14.00 Trifecta £56.10 Pool: £3318.43 - 44.34 winning units..
Owner Niarchos Family **Bred** Mrs C L Weld **Trained** Newmarket, Suffolk

FOCUS
They went a fair pace in this fillies' handicap and the winner finished well from some way back. Solid form.

6650 MARTYN HEYES 40 YEARS OF SERVICE H'CAP 1m
5:55 (5:59) (Class 2) (0-100,100) 3-Y-0+ **£12,291** (£3,657; £1,827; £913) **Stalls** Centre

Form RPR
3-11 **1** **Brownsea Brink**[22] 5958 3-8-6 **86** KieranO'Neill 14 97
(Richard Hannon) *t.k.h trcking ldrs: led over 2f out: sn rdn: hld on wl whn pressed fnl 120yds: all out* **12/1**
2030 **2** ½ **Rockalong (IRE)**[28] 5768 4-9-0 **90** JohnnyMurtagh 5 100
(Luca Cumani) *mid-div: rdn 3f out: hdwy over 1f out: str chal fnl 120yds: hld nring fin* **4/1**[1]
1531 **3** 1 **Consign**[21] 5987 3-8-7 **87** (v) ChrisCatlin 9 95
(Jeremy Noseda) *s.i.s: towards rr: rdn and hdwy into midfield over 2f out: stdy prog to chse ldrs ent fnl f: styd on wl to go 3rd nring fin* **18/1**
4110 **4** nk **The Rectifier (USA)**[26] 5838 6-9-6 **96** (t) GeorgeBaker 8 103
(Seamus Durack) *chsd ldrs: rdn whn sltly outpcd 3f out: styd on again ins fnl f* **20/1**
-001 **5** hd **Modern Tutor**[28] 5759 4-8-12 **88** RyanMoore 10 95
(Sir Michael Stoute) *hld up towards rr: pushed along over 3f out: rdn and stdy prog fr 2f out: swtchd lft: styd on fnl f* **7/1**[3]
1131 **6** nk **Kohlaan (IRE)**[11] 6274 3-8-7 **87** DominicFox 19 93
(Roger Varian) *led: rdn and hdd over 2f out: kpt on same pce fnl f* **6/1**[2]
530 **7** 1 ¾ **Ayaar (IRE)**[21] 5992 3-9-1 **95** MartinHarley 3 97
(Mick Channon) *mid-div: rdn to chse ldrs and racd alone on far side 2f out: no ex fnl 120yds* **25/1**
5-00 **8** ¾ **Myboyalfie (USA)**[123] 2541 6-8-10 **86** oh1 (v) DavidProbert 11 86
(J R Jenkins) *chsd ldrs: rdn 3f out: nt pce to chal: kpt on but no ex fnl 120yds* **33/1**
0140 **9** nk **Postscript (IRE)**[14] 6199 5-9-0 **90** PatDobbs 16 89
(David Simcock) *mid-div: travelling wl bhd ldrs 2f out: sn rdn: nt pce to chal: no ex fnl 75yds* **25/1**
1050 **10** ½ **Storm King**[14] 6199 4-9-4 **94** (b[1]) WilliamCarson 17 92
(Jane Chapple-Hyam) *mid-div: rdn to chse ldrs over 2f out: drifted to nrside rails: styd on same pce fnl f* **33/1**
161 **11** 15 **Askaud (IRE)**[36] 5493 5-9-4 **94** (p) LukeMorris 12 58
(Scott Dixon) *prom: rdn wl over 2f out: wknd over 1f out: eased fnl 75yds* **25/1**
2010 **12** 3 **Clockmaker (IRE)**[14] 6199 7-9-8 **98** LiamKeniry 6 55
(Conor Dore) *chsd ldrs: rdn over 3f out: sn wknd: eased fnl f* **33/1**
1100 **13** 7 **Ajraam (USA)**[35] 5510 3-9-0 **94** DaneO'Neill 1 35
(Charles Hills) *prom tl rdn over 2f out: sn wknd: eased fnl f* **25/1**
-554 **14** 19 **Whipper's Boy (IRE)**[10] 6307 3-9-5 **99** (b[1]) AndrewElliott 15
(Brian Meehan) *prom early: pushed along to chse ldrs over 4f out: wknd over 3f out: eased fnl f* **50/1**
2110 **15** 2 ¾ **Yeager (USA)**[35] 5551 3-9-0 **94** (t) WilliamBuick 18
(Jeremy Noseda) *hld up towards rr: rdn over 4f out: nvr any imp: eased fnl f* **4/1**[1]
0056 **16** 1 **Heavy Metal**[35] 5510 3-8-7 **87** JoeFanning 2
(Mark Johnston) *mid-div tl over 3f out: sn bhd: eased fnl f* **25/1**
211- **17** 68 **Tamarkuz (USA)**[346] 6980 3-9-2 **96** MartinLane 7
(Saeed bin Suroor) *unruly loading: mid-div: lost pl tamely over 5f out: sn bhd: virtually p.u fr 3f out* **7/1**[3]

1m 38.09s (-0.51) **Going Correction** +0.125s/f (Good)
WFA 3 from 4yo+ 4lb **17** Ran SP% **127.0**
Speed ratings (Par 109): **107,106,105,105,105 104,102,102,101,101 86,83,76,57,54 53,**
toteswingers 1&2 £15.00, 2&3 £17.30, 1&3 £26.30 CSF £54.36 CT £930.41 TOTE £15.20: £3.10, £1.70, £4.40, £4.40; EX 81.60 Trifecta £80.40 Pool: £1010.65 - 9.42 winning units..
Owner The Heffer Syndicate **Bred** Carmel Stud **Trained** East Everleigh, Wilts
FOCUS
Six last-time-out winners lined up in this hot handicap. The pace was not very strong and a couple of the market leaders were disappointing but the progressive winner deserves credit for scoring after taking a strong hold. The form is essentially sound.
T/Plt: £49.40 to a £1 stake. Pool of £82287.94 - 1215.47 winning tickets. T/Qpdt: £42.40 to a £1 stake. Pool of £3574.40 - 62.27 winning tickets. TM

6605 WOLVERHAMPTON (A.W) (L-H)
Saturday, September 21
OFFICIAL GOING: Standard to slow
Wind: Light behind Weather: Fine

6651 32RED CASINO H'CAP 5f 20y(P)
5:50 (5:51) (Class 6) (0-55,55) 3-Y-0+ **£1,940** (£577; £288; £144) **Stalls** Low

Form RPR
3344 **1** **Imperial Spirit**[15] 6157 3-8-13 **48** (v) SamHitchcott 12 56
(Mick Channon) *mde all: rdn over 1f out: r.o* **12/1**
0-04 **2** 1 ½ **College Doll**[23] 5930 4-8-5 **46** oh1 (t) EoinWalsh(7) 13 49
(Christine Dunnett) *a.p: chsd wnr 2f out: rdn and ev ch 1f out: styd on same pce ins fnl f* **28/1**
1300 **3** ½ **Almaty Express**[5] 6478 11-9-1 **54** (b) AdamCarter(5) 11 55
(John Weymes) *chsd ldrs: rdn over 1f out: styd on same pce ins fnl f* **12/1**
0326 **4** nse **Compton Albion (IRE)**[24] 5890 3-9-4 **53** (b[1]) AndrewMullen 5 54+
(Jeremy Gask) *mid-div: pushed along 1/2-way: rdn and edgd lft ins fnl f: r.o: nt rch ldrs* **4/1**[2]
6000 **5** shd **Flow Chart (IRE)**[5] 6478 6-8-10 **49** SladeO'Hara(5) 6 50
(Peter Grayson) *hld up: rdn over 1f out: r.o ins fnl f: nt rch ldrs* **8/1**
665 **6** 1 ¼ **Princess Bounty**[32] 5616 3-8-10 **50** NathanAlison(5) 8 46
(Phil McEntee) *s.i.s: hdwy over 3f out: rdn 1/2-way: styd on same pce ins fnl f* **33/1**
0043 **7** ¾ **Kwanto**[9] 6343 3-8-7 **47** (tp) TobyAtkinson(5) 3 40
(Michael Appleby) *prom: rdn 1/2-way: styd on same pce fnl f* **7/2**[1]
640 **8** 4 **Borough Boy (IRE)**[24] 5890 3-9-3 **52** (v) TomMcLaughlin 2 31
(Derek Shaw) *hmpd sn after s: a in rr* **9/1**
4242 **9** 2 **Exkaliber**[25] 5864 4-8-10 **51** (tp) DavidParkes(7) 1 23
(Jeremy Gask) *hld up: pushed along 1/2-way: a in rr* **6/1**[3]
6060 **10** 1 ½ **Marmot Bay (IRE)**[7] 6400 3-8-8 **48** PhilipPrince(5) 10 14
(David Flood) *w wnr tl pushed along 1/2-way: wknd over 1f out* **16/1**
3456 **11** 51 **Christopher Chua (IRE)**[138] 2096 4-8-13 **50** (v[1]) CharlesBishop(3) 7
(Michael Scudamore) *prom: hmpd over 4f out: bdly hmpd and lost pl wl over 3f out: eased* **12/1**

1m 3.16s (0.86) **Going Correction** +0.15s/f (Slow)
WFA 3 from 4yo+ 1lb **11** Ran SP% **113.0**
Speed ratings (Par 101): **99,96,95,95,95 93,92,85,82,80**
toteswingers 1&2 £36.80, 2&3 £109.10, 1&3 £14.60 CSF £290.05 CT £2509.04 TOTE £15.50: £4.40, £8.60, £3.80; EX 273.50 Trifecta £697.90 Part won. Pool: £930.55 - 0.11 winning units..
Owner Tytherley Partnership **Bred** J P Coggan **Trained** West Ilsley, Berks
■ Stewards' Enquiry : Adam Carter four-day ban; careless riding (5th,7th-9th Oct).
Eoin Walsh three-day ban; careless riding (5th,7th,8th Oct).
FOCUS
A low-grade handicap to kick things off. The first three home were all prominent from the off. Weak form.

6652 TONY SHRIVE MEMORIAL H'CAP (DIV I) 5f 216y(P)
6:20 (6:21) (Class 5) (0-75,74) 3-Y-0+ **£2,911** (£866; £432; £216) **Stalls** Low

Form RPR
4310 **1** **Excellent Jem**[10] 6317 4-8-10 **70** (b) IanBurns(7) 1 77
(Jane Chapple-Hyam) *s.i.s: hdwy over 2f out: rdn and hung rt over 1f out: r.o to ld nr fin* **8/1**[3]
0003 **2** nk **Where's Reiley (USA)**[20] 6018 7-9-2 **69** (b) RobertHavlin 10 75
(Michael Attwater) *chsd ldrs: rdn over 1f out: ev ch ins fnl f: r.o* **12/1**
1032 **3** hd **Little China**[15] 6157 4-8-9 **62** (b) FrederikTylicki 6 67
(William Muir) *chsd ldrs: rdn to ld over 1f out: hdd nr fin* **16/1**
6215 **4** 2 **Angel Way (IRE)**[22] 5956 4-9-7 **74** SeanLevey 5 73
(Mike Murphy) *led 5f out: rdn and hdd over 1f out: styd on same pce ins fnl f* **11/4**[2]
-303 **5** 1 ½ **Going French (IRE)**[54] 4837 6-9-1 **68** SamHitchcott 7 62
(Dai Burchell) *led 1f: chsd ldr: rdn 2f out: no ex ins fnl f* **12/1**
0466 **6** 2 ¾ **Frognal (IRE)**[10] 6310 7-9-0 **70** (bt) CharlesBishop(3) 2 55
(Violet M Jordan) *s.i.s: in rr tl styd on ins fnl f: nvr nrr* **12/1**
000 **7** nse **Speightowns Kid (USA)**[24] 5901 5-8-10 **63** AndrewMullen 8 48
(Richard Ford) *sn pushed along in rr: styd on ins fnl f: nvr nrr* **11/1**
5044 **8** 1 ¾ **Danzoe (IRE)**[45] 5155 6-9-0 **67** TomMcLaughlin 3 47
(Christine Dunnett) *hld up: hdwy u.p over 1f out: wknd and eased ins fnl f* **33/1**
0302 **9** 6 **Dream Catcher (FR)**[16] 6135 5-9-2 **69** (b) MartinDwyer 4 29
(Henry Candy) *prom: pushed along over 3f out: wknd over 1f out* **15/8**[1]

1m 15.67s (0.67) **Going Correction** +0.15s/f (Slow)
WFA 3 from 4yo+ 2lb **9** Ran SP% **112.8**
Speed ratings (Par 103): **101,100,100,97,95 92,91,89,81**
toteswingers 1&2 £16.20, 2&3 £29.40, 1&3 £12.50 CSF £95.84 CT £1499.36 TOTE £7.10: £1.40, £3.10, £3.60; EX 87.60 Trifecta £642.00 Pool: £973.38 - 1.13 winning units..
Owner Mrs Jane Chapple-Hyam **Bred** Norcroft Park Stud **Trained** Dalham, Suffolk
FOCUS
A modest contest which was run at a good pace, the field well strung out from an early stage. There's a chance the form is up to a length better.

6653 TONY SHRIVE MEMORIAL H'CAP (DIV II) 5f 216y(P)
6:50 (6:51) (Class 5) (0-75,74) 3-Y-0+ **£2,911** (£866; £432; £216) **Stalls** Low

Form RPR
3453 **1** **Glastonberry**[16] 6135 5-8-12 **68** DeclanBates(3) 7 81
(Geoffrey Deacon) *a.p: led over 1f out: sn rdn and hung lft: r.o* **12/1**
6050 **2** 1 ¾ **Cocktail Charlie**[22] 5971 5-8-9 **69** (p) GaryMahon(7) 9 76
(Tim Easterby) *a.p: chsd ldr 1/2-way: led over 2f out: rdn and hdd over 1f out: styd on same pce ins fnl f* **7/1**
601 **3** hd **Dream Ally (IRE)**[14] 6219 3-8-12 **67** (tp) FrederikTylicki 8 73
(Jedd O'Keeffe) *chsd ldr tl led over 3f out: hdd over 2f out: rdn and ev ch over 1f out: styd on same pce ins fnl f* **15/8**[1]
2633 **4** 1 ¾ **Putin (IRE)**[8] 6368 5-8-5 **63** (bt) NathanAlison(5) 1 52
(Phil McEntee) *chsd ldrs: rdn over 2f out: no ex wknd ins fnl f: fin 5th: plcd 4th* **14/1**
5102 **5** 1 ¼ **Point North (IRE)**[54] 4837 6-9-7 **74** (b) RobertHavlin 3 69
(John Balding) *trckd ldrs: rdn over 1f out: wknd fnl f: fin 6th: plcd 5th* **9/2**[3]
6050 **6** 2 **Sewn Up**[23] 5928 3-9-3 **72** (tp) LiamJones 5 50
(Andrew Hollinshead) *s.i.s: hdwy over 2f out: rdn and wknd over 1f out: fin 7th: plcd 6th* **16/1**
0000 **7** 9 **Evens And Odds (IRE)**[15] 6162 9-8-11 **69** SladeO'Hara(5) 4 19
(Peter Grayson) *s.i.s: sn pushed along and a in rr: fin 8th: plcd 7th* **33/1**
2150 **8** 22 **La Sylphe**[104] 3134 3-8-2 **60** oh2 RosieJessop(3) 6
(Derek Shaw) *led: hdd over 3f out: wknd over 2f out: fin 9th: plcd 8th* **40/1**
-316 **D** 3 ½ **Mukhabarat (IRE)**[9] 6338 3-9-4 **73** MickaelBarzalona 2 68+
(Saeed bin Suroor) *s.i.s: hld up: pushed along over 2f out: r.o ins fnl f: nvr nrr: fin 4th: disqualified and plcd last: rdr failed to weigh in* **7/2**[2]

1m 15.06s (0.06) **Going Correction** +0.15s/f (Slow)
WFA 3 from 5yo+ 2lb **9** Ran SP% **113.3**
Speed ratings (Par 103): **105,102,102,95,93 91,79,49,97**
toteswingers 1&2 £16.20, 2&3 £29.40, 1&3 £12.50 CSF £91.19 CT £218.76 TOTE £10.90: £2.30, £2.50, £1.10; EX 57.60 Trifecta £294.70 Pool: £1450.18 - 3.68 winning units..
Owner Geoffrey Deacon **Bred** Geoffrey Deacon **Trained** Compton, Berks
■ Stewards' Enquiry : Mickael Barzalona three-day ban; failed to weigh-in (5th,7th,8th Oct).
FOCUS
A sound pace here and no reason why the form won't prove solid for the level. The time was a bit quicker than division II.

6654 £32 BONUS AT 32RED.COM (S) STKS 5f 216y(P)
7:20 (7:20) (Class 6) 2-Y-0 **£1,940** (£577; £288; £144) **Stalls** Low

Form RPR
0045 **1** **Diffident Beats**[4] 6494 2-8-11 60 (v[1]) SamHitchcott 2 59
(Mick Channon) *sn outpcd: hdwy over 1f out: r.o u.p to ld nr fin* **10/1**
0 **2** nk **Buy And Sell (IRE)**[67] 4379 2-8-11 0 SeanLevey 9 58
(David Brown) *a.p: pushed along over 2f out: led over 1f out: sn rdn and hung lft: hdd nr fin* **7/2**[2]
062 **3** 1 ½ **Hickster (IRE)**[16] 6131 2-8-11 59 (v) StephenCraine 5 53
(Tom Dascombe) *led: rdn and hdd over 1f out: styd on same pce ins fnl f* **9/2**[3]
3153 **4** 3 ¼ **Song Of Rowland (IRE)**[7] 6386 2-9-3 70 RichardHughes 1 49
(David O'Meara) *chsd ldrs: pushed along over 2f out: rdn over 1f out: no ex ins fnl f* **6/4**[1]
3U **5** 5 **Kodafine (IRE)**[73] 4174 2-8-9 73 DeclanBates(3) 4 28
(David Evans) *s.i.s: hdwy over 4f out: rdn over 2f out: wknd over 1f out* **13/2**
6 ¾ **Ivory** 2-8-3 0 BillyCray(3) 8 19
(Garry Moss) *s.i.s: outpcd* **40/1**

3054 7 4 ½ **Boston Alex (IRE)**[8] 6364 2-8-3 53.........................(p) SimonPearce(3) 10 5
(Conor Dore) *chsd ldrs: ev ch over 2f out: sn rdn: wknd fnl f* **28/1**
00 8 ½ **Streethowlingmama (USA)**[21] 5995 2-8-6 0.............. AndrewMullen 7 3
(William Jarvis) *chsd ldr: rdn and ev ch over 2f out: wknd over 1f out* **16/1**
1m 16.72s (1.72) **Going Correction** +0.15s/f (Slow) 8 Ran SP% **114.6**
Speed ratings (Par 93): **94,93,91,87,80 79,73,72**
toteswingers 1&2 £3.60, 2&3 £3.40, 1&3 £6.80 CSF £45.09 TOTE £11.30: £2.60, £1.40, £1.80; EX 80.70 Trifecta £423.70 Pool: £1410.21 - 2.49 winning units..There was no bid for the winner. Song Of Rowland was claimed by A P Jones for £6000.
Owner M Channon **Bred** P Balding **Trained** West Ilsley, Berks
FOCUS
Modest form in a seller run at a good pace. The winner is rated back to form, the third giving perspective.

6655 PAUL (FRANKO) FRANKLIN MEMORIAL H'CAP 7f 32y(P)
7:50 (7:50) (Class 6) (0-65,65) 3-Y-O **£1,940** (£577; £288; £144) **Stalls** High

Form RPR
6031 1 **Viennese Verse**[9] 6324 3-9-1 59.. SeanLevey 3 69
(Henry Candy) *chsd ldr 5f out tl led over 2f out: rdn and edgd lft over 1f out: styd on* **4/1**[2]
0141 2 nk **Burren View Lady (IRE)**[30] 5674 3-9-6 64....................(v) TedDurcan 10 73+
(Tim Easterby) *hld up: hdwy 1/2-way: rdn over 1f out: r.o* **7/2**[1]
4140 3 1 **Josefa Goya**[23] 5930 3-9-7 65...................................... RichardHughes 12 71
(Hughie Morrison) *led over 4f: rdn over 1f out: styd on* **7/1**
-344 4 nk **Tammuz (IRE)**[18] 6074 3-8-7 56.. RyanTate(5) 11 61+
(Tony Carroll) *s.i.s: hld up: hdwy over 1f out: r.o: nt rch ldrs* **16/1**
5620 5 1 ½ **Annie Gogh**[15] 6180 3-8-7 58................................ RachelRichardson(7) 4 59
(Tim Easterby) *s.i.s: hdwy over 5f out: lost pl over 3f out: nt clr run over 2f* **20/1**
2221 6 ½ **Brynford**[8] 6362 3-9-7 65.. JimmyQuinn 8 65
(Chris Dwyer) *hld up: hdwy over 1f out: rdn and edgd lft ins fnl f: styd on same pce* **9/2**[3]
6040 7 1 ¾ **Excellent Addition (IRE)**[31] 5644 3-8-10 61........... LukeLeadbitter(7) 9 56
(Declan Carroll) *prom: rdn over 1f out: no ex ins fnl f* **15/2**
2304 8 8 **Clary (IRE)**[68] 4356 3-9-4 62...(p) LiamJones 7 35
(James Unett) *sn pushed along and a in rr* **16/1**
-440 9 3 ¾ **Princess Patsky (USA)**[116] 2763 3-8-11 62............(v) LouisSteward(7) 5 25
(Michael Bell) *prom: rdn 1/2-way: wknd over 1f out* **16/1**
0000 10 ½ **Shatin Secret**[27] 5788 3-8-10 54.................................. FrederikTylicki 6 16
(Noel Wilson) *mid-div: lost pl 4f out: wknd over 2f out* **28/1**
060 11 2 **Lincolnrose (IRE)**[45] 5128 3-8-7 51 oh1.....................(p) AndrewMullen 2 8
(Michael Appleby) *chsd ldr 2f: remained handy tl rdn and wknd over 2f out* **25/1**
1m 30.89s (1.29) **Going Correction** +0.15s/f (Slow) 11 Ran SP% **114.4**
Speed ratings (Par 99): **98,97,96,96,94 93,91,82,78,77 75**
toteswingers 1&2 £3.40, 2&3 £4.80, 1&3 £4.20 CSF £17.29 CT £95.26 TOTE £4.20: £2.10, £1.80, £2.90; EX 19.80 Trifecta £109.90 Pool: £1654.79 - 11.28 winning units..
Owner The Chevaliers **Bred** Tony Hirschfeld & L K Piggott **Trained** Kingston Warren, Oxon
■ Stewards' Enquiry : Ted Durcan two-day ban; used whip above permitted level (5th,7th Oct).
FOCUS
Another ordinary handicap, although the winner is progressive. The second improved too.

6656 32RED EBF MAIDEN STKS 1m 141y(P)
8:20 (8:21) (Class 5) 2-Y-O **£2,911** (£866; £432; £216) **Stalls** Low

Form RPR
0 1 **Hard Divorce (USA)**[9] 6330 2-9-5 0............................ RichardHughes 5 71+
(David Brown) *prom: jnd ldr over 6f out: pushed along to ld 2f out: sn rdn: hdd ins fnl f: rallied to ld post* **11/4**[2]
4 2 shd **Kingdom's Call (USA)**[15] 6168 2-9-5 0.................. MickaelBarzalona 1 71
(Charlie Appleby) *w ldr tl led over 7f out: rdn and hdd 2f out: rallied to ld ins fnl f: hdd post* **8/15**[1]
54 3 1 ¾ **Avocadeau (IRE)**[16] 6139 2-9-5 0..................................... MartinDwyer 4 67
(William Muir) *led 1f: chsd ldrs: rdn over 2f out: nt clr run ins fnl f: styd on same pce towards fin* **10/1**[3]
040 4 nk **Heska (IRE)**[26] 5811 2-9-5 63.. SamHitchcott 6 66
(Mick Channon) *hdwy over 6f out: rdn over 3f out: styd on same pce ins fnl f* **16/1**
0 5 14 **Mizzeni (FR)**[41] 5323 2-9-0 0.......................................[1] DanielMuscutt(5) 7 34
(Gay Kelleway) *s.i.s and wnt lft s: hld up: rdn and wknd over 2f out* **25/1**
400 6 9 **Ormer**[9] 6318 2-8-11 43..(v[1]) DeclanBates(3) 2 8
(David Evans) *sn pushed along in rr: wknd over 3f out* **100/1**
1m 54.02s (3.52) **Going Correction** +0.15s/f (Slow) 6 Ran SP% **111.7**
Speed ratings (Par 95): **90,89,88,88,75 67**
toteswingers 1&2 £1.10, 2&3 £1.70, 1&3 £1.60 CSF £4.49 TOTE £4.80: £1.20, £1.10; EX 5.20 Trifecta £11.80 Pool: £1421.91 - 90.07 winning units..
Owner Qatar Racing Limited **Bred** Estate Of Edward P Evans **Trained** Averham Park, Notts
FOCUS
Fair efforts from the leading pair, who dominated throughout, but the bare form is ordinary.

6657 32RED.COM H'CAP 1m 141y(P)
8:50 (8:50) (Class 5) (0-70,70) 3-Y-O **£2,587** (£770; £384; £192) **Stalls** Low

Form RPR
0445 1 **Plunder**[10] 6296 3-9-2 65.. RobertHavlin 6 76
(Richard Ford) *sn pushed along and prom: chsd ldr over 6f out: led wl over 2f out: rdn clr fr over 1f out* **9/1**
5504 2 3 **Konzert (ITY)**[30] 5668 3-8-10 62...................................... RyanPowell(3) 5 66
(Ian Williams) *s.i.s: outpcd: hdwy 2f out: rdn to go 2nd 1f out: r.o: no ch w wnr* **14/1**
12 3 1 ¾ **Araqella (IRE)**[17] 6106 3-9-7 70.. LiamJones 4 70
(William Haggas) *trckd ldrs: rdn over 2f out: styd on same pce fr over 1f out* **15/8**[1]
4064 4 1 ½ **Ceelo**[14] 6214 3-9-7 70...(p) RichardHughes 10 67
(Sylvester Kirk) *hld up: pushed along and hdwy over 2f out: rdn over 1f out: styd on same pce* **10/3**[2]
0404 5 2 ¾ **Birdy Boy (USA)**[25] 5870 3-9-0 63.................................. JoeFanning 7 53
(Mark Johnston) *led: rdn and hdd wl over 2f out: wknd fnl f* **9/1**
0-50 6 6 **Prairie Prince (IRE)**[7] 6406 3-8-2 56 oh11.................. ShelleyBirkett(5) 3 32
(Gay Kelleway) *hld up: rdn over 2f out: nvr on terms* **66/1**
0162 7 2 ¼ **Harbinger Lass**[8] 6357 3-8-13 62.................................... SamHitchcott 1 33
(Mick Channon) *chsd ldrs: rdn over 3f out: wknd over 2f out* **10/1**
4-00 8 6 **Platinum Proof (USA)**[112] 2874 3-8-8 57............................ SeanLevey 9 14
(David O'Meara) *chsd ldrs: rdn over 3f out: wknd over 2f out* **11/2**[3]

60 9 25 **Continental Divide (IRE)**[27] 5789 3-9-6 69............... FergusSweeney 2
(Jamie Osborne) *prom: hmpd and lost pl over 6f out: rdn and wknd over 3f out* **14/1**
1m 51.35s (0.85) **Going Correction** +0.15s/f (Slow) 9 Ran SP% **117.2**
Speed ratings (Par 101): **102,99,97,96,94 88,86,81,59**
toteswingers 1&2 £9.00, 2&3 £7.00, 1&3 £5.30 CSF £126.89 CT £337.95 TOTE £11.90: £3.00, £6.30, £1.10; EX 138.90 Trifecta £1198.50 Pool: £1662.18 - 1.04 winning units..
Owner Darren & Annaley Yates **Bred** Millsec Limited **Trained** Garstang, Lancs
FOCUS
This ended up being a very one-sided handicap and the winner was perhaps bit more dominant than the bare form.

6658 32REDPOKER.COM H'CAP 1m 4f 50y(P)
9:20 (9:20) (Class 6) (0-65,65) 3-Y-O+ **£1,940** (£577; £288; £144) **Stalls** Low

Form RPR
0434 1 **Getaway Car**[12] 4961 3-9-2 65.....................................(b) FrederikTylicki 8 85
(Gerard Butler) *hld up: hdwy over 3f out: led over 2f out: sn rdn clr: easily* **11/4**[1]
2650 2 11 **My Destination (IRE)**[13] 6237 4-9-1 63.................... LukeLeadbitter(7) 2 65
(Declan Carroll) *hld up: hdwy over 3f out: rdn over 1f out: styd on to go 2nd wl ins fnl f: no ch w wnr* **16/1**
0510 3 ¾ **Royal Sea (IRE)**[36] 5466 4-9-1 61.................................(be) TimClark(5) 5 62
(Michael Mullineaux) *s.i.s: sn pushed along in rr: hdwy 3f out: rdn to chse wnr over 1f out: edgd rt and wknd ins fnl f* **16/1**
0-04 4 4 ½ **Maoi Chinn Tire (IRE)**[16] 5666 6-9-5 60.................... StephenCraine 12 54
(Jennie Candlish) *hld up: styd on appr fnl f: nvr nrr* **25/1**
3310 5 8 **Nolecce**[40] 5356 6-9-2 62.. JackDuern(5) 9 43
(Tony Forbes) *chsd ldrs: led over 4f out: rdn and hdd over 2f out: wknd over 1f out* **10/1**[3]
0-60 6 8 **The Bells O Peover**[14] 6211 5-9-8 63..........................(b) JoeFanning 11 31
(Mark Johnston) *led over 10f out: hdd over 4f out: rdn and wknd over 1f out* **11/2**[2]
304 7 4 ½ **Star Date (IRE)**[22] 5967 4-9-7 62................................(p) RobertHavlin 3 23
(Michael Attwater) *prom: racd keenly: sddle slipped sn after s: chsd ldr 7f out tl pushed along over 3f out: wknd over 2f out* **10/1**[3]
3-02 8 1 ½ **Syrenka**[20] 6015 3-9-2 65.. RichardHughes 10 23
(Marcus Tregoning) *prom: racd keenly: rdn over 2f out: sn wknd and eased* **11/4**[1]
56-0 9 5 **The Winged Assasin (USA)**[23] 2328 7-9-4 62.......(bt[1]) RyanPowell(3) 1 12
(Shaun Lycett) *led: hdd over 10f out: remained handy tl rdn and wknd over 3f out* **25/1**
6050 10 11 **Sondeduro**[83] 3854 4-9-8 63... FergusSweeney 4
(Jamie Osborne) *chsd ldrs over 8f* **10/1**[3]
-003 11 nse **Urban Space**[33] 5586 7-9-5 60... JimmyQuinn 6
(Tony Carroll) *hld up: bhd fnl 5f* **20/1**
2m 41.09s (-0.01) **Going Correction** +0.15s/f (Slow)
WFA 3 from 4yo+ 8lb 11 Ran SP% **120.2**
Speed ratings (Par 101): **106,98,98,95,89 84,81,80,77,69 69**
toteswingers 1&2 £7.50, 2&3 £53.80, 1&3 £6.50 CSF £52.56 CT £600.31 TOTE £4.70: £1.60, £4.70, £4.70; EX 46.40 Trifecta £485.10 Pool: £1237.55 - 1.91 winning units..
Owner A D Spence **Bred** Mascalls Stud **Trained** Newmarket, Suffolk
FOCUS
Thet went a decent pace and this proved all about the winner, who showed big improvement.
T/Plt: £373.20 to a £1 stake. Pool of £64338.97- 125.85 winning tickets. T/Qpdt: £8.90 to a £1 stake. Pool of £8954.62 - 740.73 winning tickets. CR

6659 - 6662a (Foreign Racing) - See Raceform Interactive

6047 HAMILTON (R-H)
Sunday, September 22

OFFICIAL GOING: Good to soft (7.6)
Wind: Breezy, half behind Weather: Cloudy, bright

6663 WIN BIG WITH THE TOTEJACKPOT NURSERY H'CAP 6f 5y
2:20 (2:22) (Class 5) (0-75,71) 2-Y-O **£3,881** (£1,155; £577; £288) **Stalls** High

Form RPR
6350 1 **Donny Rover (IRE)**[11] 6303 2-9-4 68.......................(v[1]) GrahamGibbons 2 72
(David C Griffiths) *in tch on outside: hdwy over 1f out: rdn to ld ent fnl f: hung lft: shkn up and kpt on wl towards fin* **11/2**[1]
0565 2 nk **Rockie Road (IRE)**[33] 5610 2-7-13 52 ow2.................. RaulDaSilva(3) 8 55
(Paul Green) *hld up: effrt whn n.m.r and swtchd rt over 1f out: chsd wnr ins fnl f: kpt on fin* **8/1**
1044 3 4 ½ **Pigeon Pie**[20] 6047 2-9-6 70.. JoeFanning 6 60
(Mark Johnston) *cl up: led over 1f out: hdd ent fnl f: sn outpcd by first two* **6/1**[2]
3330 4 1 ½ **Left Defender (IRE)**[2] 6582 2-9-7 71.................................. BenCurtis 1 56
(Jo Hughes) *cl up on outside: rdn over 2f out: rallied: outpcd fnl f* **7/1**
0004 5 shd **Two Shades Of Grey (IRE)**[40] 5371 2-9-0 64.............. TonyHamilton 7 55+
(Richard Fahey) *prom: pushed along over 2f out: effrt whn n.m.r fr over 1f out: hmpd ins fnl f: styd on fin* **11/2**[1]
446 6 ¾ **Elite Freedom (IRE)**[41] 5352 2-8-9 62........................ JasonHart(3) 4 45
(Jo Hughes) *dwlt: bhd: rdn and hung lft 2f out: repeatedly denied room ins fnl f: kpt on towards fin: nvr any ch of rching ldrs* **6/1**[2]
1400 7 2 **Overstep (IRE)**[28] 5787 2-9-6 70......................................(b[1]) GrahamLee 9 47
(Mark Johnston) *t.k.h: led to over 1f out: sn rdn and wknd* **13/2**[3]
2415 8 ½ **Omanome (IRE)**[20] 6047 2-9-6 70............................... DanielTudhope 5 45
(David O'Meara) *t.k.h: prom: rdn over 2f out: rallied: wknd fnl f* **8/1**
24 9 1 ½ **Baltic Spirit (IRE)**[26] 5857 2-8-13 63................................ TomEaves 3 34
(Keith Dalgleish) *trckd ldrs: lost pl 2f out: sn struggling* **10/1**
1m 12.9s (0.70) **Going Correction** -0.05s/f (Good) 9 Ran SP% **116.5**
Speed ratings (Par 95): **93,92,86,84,84 83,80,80,78**
Tote Swingers: 1&2 £10.80, 2&3 £7.80 CSF £49.54 CT £275.89 TOTE £7.20: £2.50, £3.60, £1.60; EX 71.00 Trifecta £653.40 Pool: £2,031.36 - 2.33 winning units..
Owner Willie McKay **Bred** Lynn Lodge Stud **Trained** Bawtry, S Yorks
FOCUS
Rail realignment around the loop reduced races on Round course by about 25 yards. Modest nursery form with the first pair clear.

6664 TOTEQUADPOT FOUR PLACES IN FOUR RACES H'CAP 6f 5y
2:50 (2:50) (Class 5) (0-75,75) 3-Y-O **£3,234** (£962; £481; £240) **Stalls** Centre

Form RPR
051 1 **Baron Run**[24] 5919 3-8-9 68.. JoeyHaynes(5) 4 76
(K R Burke) *mde all centre: rdn along 1/2-way: hld on gamely fnl f* **12/1**
5304 2 hd **Khelman (IRE)**[27] 5836 3-8-11 70............................. GeorgeChaloner(5) 3 77
(Richard Fahey) *prom centre: effrt and swtchd lft 2f out: ev ch ins fnl f: edgd rt: kpt on: jst hld* **5/1**[2]

402 **3** *1* **Chasing Dreams**[109] 2994 3-9-6 **74**..............................[1] GrahamLee 6 77
(Kevin Ryan) *slowly away: bhd and pushed along: hdwy in centre over 2f out: kpt on ins fnl f* **13/2**[3]
6433 **4** *2 1/2* **Alexandrakollontai (IRE)**[20] 6052 3-8-7 **64**................. JulieBurke(3) 11 59
(Alistair Whillans) *missed break: bhd on nr side of gp: hdwy over 2f out: effrt and hung rt over 1f out: no imp ins fnl f* **15/8**[1]
0-40 **5** *5* **Bond Club**[46] 5150 3-9-0 **68**...(p) TomEaves 8 47
(Geoffrey Oldroyd) *towards rr in centre: drvn along 1/2-way: styd on fnl f: nvr able to chal* **20/1**
2326 **6** *2 3/4* **Exzachary**[37] 5477 3-9-7 **75**.. DanielTudhope 2 46
(Jo Hughes) *cl up on far side of gp: rdn over 2f out: wknd over 1f out* **15/2**
0500 **7** *1 3/4* **Laudation**[28] 5784 3-8-6 **60**..(v) AndrewElliott 10 25
(Danielle McCormick) *chsd ldrs on nr side of gp: rdn over 2f out: hung lft and wknd over 1f out* **40/1**
0620 **8** *1/2* **Bogsnog (IRE)**[19] 6072 3-9-0 **73**...........................(p) JacobButterfield(5) 7 36
(Kristin Stubbs) *chsd ldrs centre: rdn 1/2-way: wknd over 1f out* **16/1**
1150 **9** *2* **Harbour Captain (IRE)**[3] 6548 3-9-0 **71**......................... JasonHart(3) 1 28
(Jo Hughes) *prom towards far side of gp: rdn over 2f out: wknd over 1f out: eased whn no ch ins fnl f* **8/1**
0600 **10** *1/2* **Loch Moy**[35] 5564 3-8-10 **64**..(v) TonyHamilton 9 19
(Richard Fahey) *towards rr on nr side of gp: struggling over 2f out: sn btn* **16/1**
1m 12.24s (0.04) **Going Correction** -0.05s/f (Good) 10 Ran SP% **114.3**
Speed ratings (Par 101): **97,96,95,92,85 81,79,78,76,75**
Tote Swingers: 1&2 £6.90, 1&3 £8.60, 2&3 £5.10 CSF £69.61 CT £428.66 TOTE £10.10: £3.40, £2.00, £3.40; EX 49.00 Trifecta £332.50 Pool: £1,991.31 - 4.49 winning units..
Owner Mrs Elaine M Burke **Bred** Mrs D Hughes **Trained** Middleham Moor, N Yorks
FOCUS
An open sprint handicap.

6665 TOTEPOOL EBF STALLIONS FLOWER OF SCOTLAND FILLIES' H'CAP (THE SUNDAY £5K BONUS RACE) 6f 5y
3:20 (3:21) (Class 3) (0-95,91) 3-Y-0+ **£9,703** (£2,887; £1,443; £721) **Stalls** Centre

Form RPR
0250 **1** **Dancheur (IRE)**[30] 5700 4-8-6 **79**.................................. JoeyHaynes(5) 7 92
(K R Burke) *taken early to post: mde virtually all in centre: rdn over 2f out: kpt on strly fnl f* **16/1**
0440 **2** *2 3/4* **Pearl Sea (IRE)**[22] 5984 3-9-7 **91**.................................. PJMcDonald 5 95
(David Brown) *disp ld centre to over 2f out: sn rdn: kpt on ins fnl f: nt pce of wnr* **17/2**
1-25 **3** *hd* **Athenian (IRE)**[114] 2848 4-9-4 **86**... LukeMorris 6 89
(Sir Mark Prescott Bt) *in tch centre: drvn along and effrt over 2f out: kpt on ins fnl f* **9/2**[1]
4220 **4** *1 3/4* **Dusky Queen (IRE)**[31] 5684 3-8-13 **83**......................... TonyHamilton 13 81
(Richard Fahey) *towards rr centre: hdwy over 2f out: rdn and edgd lft over 1f out: kpt on fnl f: nvr able to chal* **6/1**[3]
3435 **5** *nk* **Avon Breeze**[12] 6273 4-8-10 **83**............................... GeorgeChaloner(5) 14 80
(Richard Whitaker) *chsd stands' side ldr: rdn and edgd rt 2f out: kpt on ins fnl f* **6/1**[3]
5000 **6** *1* **Tartiflette**[31] 5684 4-9-6 **88**...(b) GrahamGibbons 2 82
(Ed McMahon) *in tch on far side of centre gp: rdn and hung rt over 1f out: sn outpcd* **5/1**[2]
2131 **7** *hd* **Someone's Darling**[34] 5581 3-8-3 **73**........................... BarryMcHugh 11 66
(Jim Goldie) *chsd stands' side ldrs: rdn over 2f out: sn no imp* **16/1**
4111 **8** *3/4* **Monakova (IRE)**[27] 5836 3-8-13 **83**............................. DanielTudhope 1 74
(David O'Meara) *hld up on far side of centre gp: rdn over 2f out: hdwy over 1f out: kpt on: no imp* **8/1**
4402 **9** *2* **Economic Crisis (IRE)**[6] 6469 4-8-5 **73** oh6............... PatrickMathers 3 57
(Alan Berry) *chsd centre ldrs: rdn over 2f out: wknd wl over 1f out* **28/1**
-040 **10** *1* **Lasilia (IRE)**[99] 3340 3-9-0 **84**.. GrahamLee 4 65
(Kevin Ryan) *chsd centre ldrs: rdn over 2f out: wknd over 1f out* **33/1**
1036 **11** *2 3/4* **Sunrise Dance**[15] 6209 4-8-3 **76**............................... ConnorBeasley(5) 9 48
(Robert Johnson) *in tch on nr side of centre gp: drvn over 2f out: wknd over 1f out* **20/1**
3000 **12** *hd* **Midnight Dynamo**[2] 6583 6-8-7 **75**..................................... TomEaves 10 47
(Jim Goldie) *prom centre: drvn over 2f out: wknd over 1f out* **28/1**
1300 **13** *5* **Aubrietia**[120] 2647 4-9-2 **89**...(b) DavidBergin(5) 8 45
(Alan McCabe) *taken early to post: hld up centre: rdn over 2f out: sn btn: eased whn no ch fnl f* **40/1**
2520 **14** *1* **Small Fury (IRE)**[3] 6549 3-8-4 **74**..................................(b[1]) JoeFanning 12 26
(Jo Hughes) *led stands' side trio to over 2f out: sn wknd* **25/1**
1m 11.37s (-0.83) **Going Correction** -0.05s/f (Good)
WFA 3 from 4yo+ 2lb **14** Ran SP% **117.7**
Speed ratings (Par 104): **103,99,99,96,96 95,94,93,91,89 86,85,79,77**
Tote Swingers: 1&2 £22.30, 1&3 £13.20, 2&3 £6.20 CSF £130.85 CT £724.04 TOTE £20.00: £5.50, £2.90, £2.20; EX 224.00 Trifecta £1199.20 Pool: £2,938.15 - 1.83 winning units..
Owner Mark James & Mrs Elaine Burke **Bred** A F O'Callaghan **Trained** Middleham Moor, N Yorks
FOCUS
Little got into this decent sprint.

6666 BRITISH STALLION STUDS EBF MAIDEN STKS 1m 65y
3:50 (3:51) (Class 5) 2-Y-O **£3,234** (£962; £481; £240) **Stalls** Low

Form RPR
4 **1** **Mr Gallivanter (IRE)**[28] 5785 2-9-5 0....................... MichaelO'Connell 1 76
(John Quinn) *dwlt: sn prom: rdn and outpcd over 3f out: rallied over 1f out: styd on wl to ld last stride* **11/2**[3]
36 **2** *shd* **Vivere (IRE)**[9] 6350 2-9-0 0... DanielTudhope 3 71
(David O'Meara) *t.k.h: disp ld: led and rdn over 1f out: edgd lft ins fnl f: hdd last stride* **2/1**[2]
3 **3** *1/2* **Rangi Chase (IRE)**[17] 6125 2-9-5 0.. GrahamLee 5 75
(Richard Fahey) *t.k.h: trckd ldrs: pushed along over 2f out: hdwy over 1f out: edgd lft: ev ch ins fnl f: hld nr fin* **5/4**[1]
60 **4** *3 1/4* **Inevitable**[17] 6125 2-9-5 0.. JoeFanning 4 68
(Mark Johnston) *t.k.h: led to over 1f out: outpcd ins fnl f* **15/2**
0 **5** *20* **It's Just George**[11] 6299 2-9-5 0.. TomEaves 2 24
(Keith Dalgleish) *hld up: rdn along over 3f out: hung rt and wknd over 2f out* **50/1**
05 **6** *1 3/4* **Buy Out Boy**[8] 6378 2-9-2 0.. JasonHart(3) 7 20
(Jo Hughes) *cl up: rdn over 3f out: edgd rt and wknd over 2f out* **28/1**
1m 47.97s (-0.43) **Going Correction** -0.325s/f (Firm) 6 Ran SP% **110.3**
Speed ratings (Par 95): **89,88,88,85,65 63**
Tote Swingers: 1&2 £2.10, 1&3 £2.20, 2&3 £1.40 CSF £16.36 TOTE £10.10: £3.10, £1.20; EX 19.40 Trifecta £38.20 Pool: £3,112.92 - 60.98 winning units..
Owner Ross Harmon **Bred** Keogh Family **Trained** Settrington, N Yorks

FOCUS
Ordinary maiden form, with their being just half a length between the first three at the line. Significant improvement from the winner, with the second rated more in line with her debut than her Group 2 run.

6667 TOTEPOOL HOME OF KING SIZE POOLS H'CAP 1m 1f 36y
4:20 (4:20) (Class 5) (0-70,70) 3-Y-O+ **£3,234** (£962; £481; £240) **Stalls** Low

Form RPR
0423 **1** **Jordaura**[2] 6598 7-9-4 **69**.. SladeO'Hara(5) 5 79
(Alan Berry) *s.i.s: hld up: hdwy over 2f out: led ins fnl f: kpt on wl* **8/1**
1432 **2** *2 1/4* **Lord Franklin**[42] 5304 4-9-6 **69**....................................... JasonHart(3) 3 74
(Eric Alston) *led: rdn over 3f out: rallied: hdd ins fnl f: kpt on same pce* **4/1**[2]
3600 **3** *1* **High Resolution**[20] 6048 6-8-11 **62**.......................... ConnorBeasley(5) 1 65
(Linda Perratt) *hld up in midfield on ins: rdn over 2f out: hdwy over 1f out: kpt on: nrst fin* **7/1**[3]
5103 **4** *1* **Size (IRE)**[24] 5918 4-9-5 **70**..................................... GeorgeChaloner(5) 2 71
(Richard Fahey) *chsd ldrs: stdy hdwy over 3f out: effrt and rdn over 2f out: one pce fnl f* **3/1**[1]
4454 **5** *nk* **Icy Blue**[12] 6276 5-8-10 **56** oh5.......................................(p) BarryMcHugh 6 56
(Richard Whitaker) *cl up gng wl: effrt and rdn over 1f out: edgd both ways: no ex ins fnl f* **20/1**
0530 **6** *2* **Commissar**[29] 5742 4-9-7 **70**..(t) RyanPowell(3) 7 66
(Ian Williams) *hld up in tch: hdwy and ldng gp: rdn over 2f out: edgd rt: sn no imp* **9/1**
2214 **7** *1* **Hernando Torres**[20] 6051 5-8-9 **62**..................................(p) AnnaHesketh(7) 9 55
(Michael Easterby) *hld up: pushed along over 3f out: sme hdwy over 1f out: nvr able to chal* **14/1**
2212 **8** *1* **North Pole**[31] 5668 3-9-4 **69**..(p) LukeMorris 4 61
(Sir Mark Prescott Bt) *in tch: effrt and drvn over 2f out: hung lft wl over 1f out: sn wknd* **4/1**[2]
2306 **9** *19* **Mudaawem (USA)**[20] 6049 3-8-5 **56**................................. JoeFanning 12 6
(Mark Johnston) *sn towards rr: struggling over 4f out: sn lost tch: t.o* **25/1**
1m 57.02s (-2.68) **Going Correction** -0.325s/f (Firm)
WFA 3 from 4yo+ 5lb 9 Ran SP% **113.9**
Speed ratings (Par 103): **98,96,95,94,93 92,91,90,73**
Tote Swingers: 1&2 £4.00, 1&3 £7.60, 2&3 £7.00 CSF £39.45 CT £235.93 TOTE £9.10: £2.80, £1.60, £3.00; EX 41.40 Trifecta £243.00 Pool: £1,868.14 - 5.76 winning units..
Owner A B Parr **Bred** Pendley Farm **Trained** Cockerham, Lancs
FOCUS
Moderate form, with a couple of the key contenders failing to give their running.

6668 BET TOTEEXACTA ON EVERY RACE H'CAP 1m 5f 9y
4:50 (4:52) (Class 4) (0-80,78) 3-Y-O+ **£5,175** (£1,540; £769; £384) **Stalls** High

Form RPR
5523 **1** **King Of Paradise (IRE)**[20] 6051 4-9-5 **72**.................... JasonHart(3) 5 80
(Eric Alston) *mde all: sn clr: pushed along over 2f out: hld on wl fnl f* **6/1**
1313 **2** *nk* **Discay**[12] 6280 4-10-0 **78**.. JoeFanning 2 85
(Mark Johnston) *chsd (clr) wnr: rdn over 2f out: edgd rt: styd on fnl f: jst hld* **6/1**
-104 **3** *9* **Swinging Hawk (GER)**[36] 5514 7-9-7 **74**...................... RyanPowell(3) 6 67
(Ian Williams) *hld up and bhd: hdwy to chse clr ldng pair over 1f out: kpt on fnl f: nvr any ch of rching first two* **7/2**[3]
6330 **4** *3* **Getabuzz**[14] 6237 5-9-11 **75**... DavidAllan 1 64
(Tim Easterby) *hld up bhd clr ldng pair: pushed along over 2f out: sn no imp: btn over 1f out* **11/4**[2]
4303 **5** *3 3/4* **Caledonia**[16] 6166 6-9-2 **66**... GrahamLee 3 49
(Jim Goldie) *hld up in tch: sn niggled along: drvn and outpcd wl over 4f out: n.d after* **5/2**[1]
164/ **6** *25* **Captain Brown**[27] 4050 5-9-8 **75**.............................. LucyAlexander(3) 4 21
(James Moffatt) *t.k.h: hld up: struggling over 4f out: t.o* **25/1**
2m 50.26s (-3.64) **Going Correction** -0.325s/f (Firm) 6 Ran SP% **109.9**
Speed ratings (Par 105): **98,97,92,90,88 72**
Tote Swingers: 1&2 £3.10, 1&3 £3.60, 2&3 £4.60 CSF £38.34 TOTE £6.00: £2.70, £1.90; EX 20.40 Trifecta £40.70 Pool: £2,793.82 - 51.44 winning units..
Owner P G Buist **Bred** Sandro Garavelli **Trained** Longton, Lancs
FOCUS
Not form to take much notice of going forward, with the front pair racing clear from an early stage and the first two in the betting labouring from some way out, having been taken out of their comfort zone.

6669 COLLECT TOTEPOOL WINNINGS AT BETFRED SHOPS H'CAP 5f 4y
5:20 (5:22) (Class 6) (0-65,69) 3-Y-O+ **£1,940** (£577; £288; £144) **Stalls** Centre

Form RPR
4243 **1** **Pull The Pin (IRE)**[25] 5901 4-8-8 **52**.............................(b) RaulDaSilva(3) 5 60
(Paul Green) *mde all: rdn over 2f out: kpt on wl fnl f: jst lasted* **9/4**[1]
00 **2** *hd* **Rock Canyon (IRE)**[6] 6471 4-8-8 **49**................................... JoeFanning 9 56
(Linda Perratt) *hld up in tch: hdwy and rdn over 1f out: kpt on wl fnl f: jst hld* **13/2**[3]
6560 **3** *1/2* **Saxonette**[3] 6547 5-8-12 **53**.. TomEaves 8 58
(Linda Perratt) *in tch: effrt and hdwy over 1f out: kpt on ins fnl f* **10/1**
2231 **4** *nse* **Chester'Slittlegem (IRE)**[18] 6101 4-8-4 **52** .... JosephineGordon(7) 10 57
(Jo Hughes) *chsd wnr: effrt over 1f out: kpt on ins fnl f: no ex and lost 2nd towards fin* **7/1**
0054 **5** *1* **Distant Sun (USA)**[24] 5917 9-8-3 **49**...................(p) ConnorBeasley(5) 11 50
(Linda Perratt) *hld up: rdn and hdwy over 1f out: kpt on ins fnl f* **16/1**
0400 **6** *2* **Wicked Wilma (IRE)**[30] 5708 9-8-5 **46** oh1.................. PatrickMathers 7 40
(Alan Berry) *chsd ldng gp: pushed along over 2f out: kpt on same pce ins fnl f* **12/1**
3261 **7** *hd* **Chloe's Dream (IRE)**[28] 5788 3-9-8 **64**............................ PJMcDonald 1 58
(Ann Duffield) *cl up: rdn over 2f out: no ex over 1f out* **9/2**[2]
2500 **8** *7* **Tongalooma**[25] 5809 7-8-13 **54**.. GrahamLee 6 22
(James Moffatt) *chsd ldrs: rdn over 2f out: wknd over 1f out* **13/2**[3]
0-35 **9** *hd* **Running Water**[10] 6345 5-8-5 **49**...................................... JasonHart(3) 2 17
(Alan Berry) *dwlt: bhd: shortlived effrt over 2f out: sn btn* **20/1**
1m 0.43s (0.43) **Going Correction** -0.05s/f (Good)
WFA 3 from 4yo+ 1lb 9 Ran SP% **115.5**
Speed ratings (Par 101): **94,93,92,92,91 88,87,76,76**
Tote Swingers 1&2 £4.80, 2&3 £10.30, 1&3 £6.50 CSF £17.16 CT £122.16 TOTE £3.40: £1.10, £2.50, £2.60; EX 20.20 Trifecta £150.80 Pool: £2,321.65 - 11.54 winning units..
Owner Paddy Mason **Bred** T J Ryan **Trained** Lydiate, Merseyside
FOCUS
Low-grade handicap form.
T/Plt: £475.90 to a £1 stake. Pool: £60,314.62 - 92.51 winning tickets. T/Qpdt: £61.10 to a £1 stake. Pool: £4,045.00 - 48.95 winning tickets. RY

The Form Book Flat, Raceform Ltd, Compton, RG20 6NL.

6670 - 6673a (Foreign Racing) - See Raceform Interactive

6117 GOWRAN PARK (R-H)

Sunday, September 22

OFFICIAL GOING: Good (good to firm in places)

6674a DENNY CORDELL LAVARACK & LANWADES STUD FILLIES STKS (GROUP 3) 1m 1f 100y

3:55 (3:57) 3-Y-O+ **£36,991** (£10,813; £5,121; £1,707)

RPR

1 **Mango Diva**[39] 5402 3-9-1 98 ow1 JohnnyMurtagh 6 103+
(Sir Michael Stoute) *w.w: 5th 1/2-way: swtchd lft 2f out: niggled to ld ins fnl f: extended advantage cl home: comf* **7/4**[1]

2 1 **Uleavemebreathless**[15] 6225 3-9-0 98 ChrisHayes 3 100
(A Oliver, Ire) *trckd ldrs in 3rd: pushed along 3f out: led under 2f out tl hdd ins fnl f: kpt on wl though no match for wnr cl home* **14/1**

3 2 **Scintillula (IRE)**[15] 6224 3-9-3 112 (t) KevinManning 7 99+
(J S Bolger, Ire) *chsd ldrs in 4th: pushed along 3f out: nt qckn under 2f out where dropped to rr: styd on again ins fnl f* **7/2**

4 shd **Aloof (IRE)**[21] 6023 4-9-5 105 WayneLordan 2 95
(David Wachman, Ire) *led tl hdd under 2f out: kpt on same pce fnl f* **3/1**[2]

5 3 **Sleeping Beauty (IRE)**[47] 5115 3-9-0 89 LeighRoche 4 90
(D K Weld, Ire) *hld up: in rr 1/2-way: nt qckn over 2f out: kpt on one pce* **25/1**

6 ½ **Caponata (USA)**[15] 6224 4-9-5 109 PatSmullen 1 88
(D K Weld, Ire) *trckd ldr in 2nd tl pushed along and nt qckn 2f out: sn no ex* **10/3**[3]

1m 59.69s (-7.31)
WFA 3 from 4yo+ 5lb 6 Ran SP% **117.2**
CSF £28.25 TOTE £2.50: £1.40, £5.00; DF 25.20 Trifecta £156.30.
Owner Antoniades Family **Bred** A G Antoniades **Trained** Newmarket, Suffolk

FOCUS
A decent renewal but it's hard to know how good the form is, with at least one of these not running her race. The second and fifth help set the standard, and the averages support.

6675 - 6677a (Foreign Racing) - See Raceform Interactive

3389 COLOGNE (R-H)

Sunday, September 22

OFFICIAL GOING: Turf: soft

6678a PREIS VON EUROPA (GROUP 1) (3YO+) (TURF) 1m 4f

3:50 (12:00) 3-Y-O+ **£81,300** (£24,390; £12,195; £5,691; £2,439)

RPR

1 **Meandre (FR)**[21] 6028 5-9-6 0 ADeVries 3 114
(A Savujev, Czech Republic) *towards rr: hdwy on outer 3f out: wnt rt and bmpd Earl Of Tinsdal 2f out: rdn to ld 1 1/2f out: r.o gamely whn chal thrght fnl f: a jst holding Empoli: fin 1st: disq & plcd 3rd* **21/10**[1]

2 3 **Vif Monsieur (GER)**[35] 5576 3-8-13 0 KClijmans 6 108
(J Hirschberger, Germany) *led after 1 1/2f and qcknd tempo: 2 l clr over 2f out: sn rdn: hdd 1 1/2f out: no ex: fin 3rd, nk, 3l: awrdd r* **94/10**

3 2 **Earl Of Tinsdal (GER)**[29] 5778 5-9-6 0 EPedroza 4 105
(A Wohler, Germany) *led: hdd after 1 1/2f: chsd ldr: rdn and inching clsr to ldr whn bdly bmpd fr both sides 2f out: dropped to 4th and nt rcvr: fin 4th, nk, 3l, 2l: plcd 2nd* **13/5**[2]

4 nk **Empoli (GER)**[21] 6028 3-8-13 0 AStarke 1 113
(P Schiergen, Germany) *midfield on inner: rdn and effrt 2 1/2f out: wnt lft and bmpd Earl Of Tinsdal 2f out: cl 3rd and hrd rdn over 1f out: r.o u.p fnl f: a jst hld by Meandre: fin 2nd, nk: disq and plcd 4th* **14/5**[3]

5 nk **Berlin Berlin**[35] 4-9-3 0 AHelfenbein 2 101
(Markus Klug, Germany) *w.w towards rr: rdn to chse ldng quartet 2f out: kpt on at one pce ins fnl f* **66/10**

6 4 ½ **Donn Halling (IRE)**[28] 5807 5-9-6 0 UmbertoRispoli 7 97
(V Luka Jr, Czech Republic) *towards rr: last and rdn over 3f out: shortlived effrt fr 2f out: one pce ins fnl f* **187/10**

7 1 ¾ **See The Rock (IRE)**[28] 3-8-13 0 JBojko 5 95
(A Wohler, Germany) *chsd ldrs: outpcd 2 1/2f out: sn rdn and wknd* **56/10**

2m 29.88s (-3.02)
WFA 3 from 4yo+ 8lb 7 Ran SP% **129.4**
WIN (incl. 10 euro stake): 104. PLACES: 37, 24. SF: 533.
Owner Ramzan Kadyrov **Bred** Famille Rothschild **Trained** Czech Republic

3880 SAN SIRO (R-H)

Sunday, September 22

OFFICIAL GOING: Turf: good

6679a PREMIO FEDERICO TESIO (GROUP 2) (3YO+) (TURF) 1m 3f

4:00 (12:00) 3-Y-O+ **£38,617** (£16,991; £9,268; £4,634)

RPR

1 **Biz The Nurse (IRE)**[105] 3147 3-8-9 0 CristianDemuro 2 111+
(S Botti, Italy) *t.k.h: restrained in main gp bhd two clr ldrs: rdn and hdwy towards outside 2f out: 3rd and styng on appr 1f out but 5 l off ldr: r.o wl u.p ins fnl f: led post* **51/100**[1]

2 nse **Orsino (GER)**[49] 6-8-11 0 LManiezzi 5 106
(R Rohne, Germany) *led: kicked clr over 2 1/2f out: rdn and edgd lft 2f out: edgd rt appr 1f out: r.o gamely u.p fnl f: hdd post* **8/5**[2]

3 ¾ **Wild Wolf (IRE)**[84] 3881 4-8-11 0 (b) CFiocchi 6 105
(S Botti, Italy) *chsd ldr: rdn and outpcd by ldr 2 1/2f out: styd on wl u.p fnl f* **9/2**[3]

4 3 ½ **Romantic Wave (IRE)**[105] 3147 4-8-11 0 FabioBranca 9 98
(S Botti, Italy) *hdd main gp bhd two clr ldrs: rdn and nt qckn 2f out: one pce fnl f* **9/2**[3]

5 1 ½ **Frankenstein**[105] 3147 6-8-11 0 DarioVargiu 3 96
(B Grizzetti, Italy) *hld up in rr: rdn and sme hdwy on outside over 2f out: kpt on ins fnl f: nvr in contention* **15/1**

6 2 ½ **Teixidor (ITY)**[133] 2295 4-8-11 0 SSulas 1 91
(Ottavio Di Paolo, Italy) *towards rr: rdn and no imp fr over 2 1/2f out* **20/1**

7 1 ¼ **Demeteor (ITY)**[91] 3-8-5 0 GMarcelli 7 90
(R Menichetti, Italy) *midfield: rdn and btn fr over 2f out: nvr a factor* **25/1**

2m 14.5s (-4.10)
WFA 3 from 4yo+ 7lb 7 Ran SP% **155.9**
WIN (incl. 1 euro stake): 1.51. PLACES: 1.21, 1.30. DF: 2.17.
Owner Scuderia Aleali Srl **Bred** Massimo Parri **Trained** Italy

CAZAUBON-BARBOTAN-LES-THERMES (R-H)

Sunday, September 22

OFFICIAL GOING: Turf: good

6680a PRIX DES PYRENEES (CONDITIONS) (5YO+) (TURF) 1m 4f 165y

5:30 (12:00) 5-Y-O+ **£2,439** (£975; £731; £487; £243)

RPR

1 **Grande Vision (FR)** 5-9-3 0 EdouardLacaille 4
(T Larriviere, France) **42/10**[1]

2 hd **Ashdeuzo (FR)**[1433] 7-9-6 0 (p) CarlosAndresLoaiza 5
(E Puente Simon, Spain)

3 1 ½ **Brillantissimo (FR)**[641] 8-9-2 0 (p) BaptisteFouchet 10
(J-M Reillier, France)

4 2 ½ **Bolt (FR)**[512] 5-8-8 0 (p) FlavienGarnier(6) 2
(P Vidotto, France)

5 2 **Palo Dancer (FR)**[1110] 5-8-8 0 MlleMarionLanave(6) 6
(T Roumazeilles, France)

6 snk **Hot Chili Peper (FR)**[1171] 7-8-8 0 MlleLilyLePemp(6) 3
(F Seguin, France)

7 nk **Rezia (FR)**[632] 5-8-7 0 (p) MlleMarie-AnneBernadet(6) 8
(A Mesnil, France)

8 snk **Cap Honor (FR)** 8-9-2 0 (p) MrLudovicMorcell 9
(D Turquet, France)

9 8 **Sabianga (FR)**[1131] 6-9-3 0 (p) GuillaumeHeurtault 7
(P Prunet-Foch, France)

10 10 **Irons On Fire (USA)**[20] 6058 5-9-2 0 ow2 (p) MlleIngridGrard 1
(Gay Kelleway)

2m 48.2s (168.20) 10 Ran SP% **19.2**
WIN (incl. 1 euro stake): 5.20.
Owner Mme Marie-Louise Fischini **Bred** Ecurie Biraben & Sarl Haras De Saint-Faust **Trained** France

6663 HAMILTON (R-H)

Monday, September 23

OFFICIAL GOING: Good to soft (good in places; 7.5)
Wind: Almost nil Weather: Overcast

6681 BRITISH STALLION STUDS EBF MAIDEN STKS 6f 5y

2:10 (2:10) (Class 5) 2-Y-O **£3,234** (£962; £481; £240) **Stalls High**

Form RPR

3 1 **Focusofourthoughts (IRE)**[13] 6286 2-9-5 0 PJMcDonald 1 74+
(Ann Duffield) *prom on outside: effrt and rdn 2f out: led ins fnl f: hld on wl* **6/1**[3]

26 2 hd **Red Pike (IRE)**[17] 6174 2-9-5 0 (v[1]) RoystonFfrench 2 73
(Bryan Smart) *t.k.h: w ldr: rdn 2f out: led over 1f out to ins fnl f: kpt on: hld nr fin* **5/1**[2]

0 3 1 ¾ **Upholland**[55] 4858 2-9-5 0 TonyHamilton 7 68
(Richard Fahey) *trckd ldrs: rdn 2f out: kpt on same pce ins fnl f* **5/6**[1]

0 4 shd **Pure Amber (IRE)**[61] 4616 2-9-5 0 JoeFanning 9 67
(Mark Johnston) *led: rdn and hdd over 1f out: rallied: kpt on same pce ins fnl f* **12/1**

0 5 2 **Injaz**[38] 5494 2-9-5 0 PaulMulrennan 8 61+
(Kevin Ryan) *trckd ldrs: rdn and edgd rt over 2f out: kpt on same pce fnl f* **14/1**

0 6 7 **Vosne Romanee**[58] 4756 2-9-5 0 TomEaves 4 40
(Keith Dalgleish) *chsd ldng gp: drvn and outpcd over 2f out: sn btn* **50/1**

7 1 ¾ **Unfinishedbusiness** 2-9-5 0 LeeTopliss 3 35+
(Richard Fahey) *green in preliminaries: missed break: bhd: hdwy over 3f out: rdn and wknd fr 2f out* **9/1**

46 8 ¾ **Raise A Billion**[33] 5638 2-9-0 0 SladeO'Hara(5) 5 33
(Alan Berry) *prom: rdn 1/2-way: sn lost pl* **100/1**

9 3 ¼ **The Cat** 2-9-0 0 BarryMcHugh 6 18
(Linda Perratt) *s.i.s: bhd: struggling 2f out: sn btn* **50/1**

1m 13.03s (0.83) **Going Correction** +0.075s/f (Good) 9 Ran SP% **114.8**
Speed ratings (Par 95): **97,96,94,94,91 82,79,78,74**
toteswingers 1&2 £2.70, 2&3 £1.60, 1&3 £2.30 CSF £35.59 TOTE £7.20: £2.20, £1.10, £1.10; EX 24.20 Trifecta £43.60 Pool: £1993.54 - 34.23 winning units..
Owner Eshwin Racing, Hibbert & Starkie **Bred** James Hughes **Trained** Constable Burton, N Yorks

FOCUS
Due to rail movements all races beyond 6f were run over 25 yards less than the advertised distance. The ground had continued to dry out and was generally reckoned to be just on the easy side of good, if a bit dead and tacky. With the stalls on the straight track on the stands' side they raced in one group on that wing. This is rated as ordinary form.

6682 TRY A TOTETRIFECTA AT TOTEPOOL.COM H'CAP 5f 4y

2:40 (2:40) (Class 5) (0-70,69) 3-Y-O **£3,408** (£1,006; £503) **Stalls High**

Form RPR

0565 1 **Manatee Bay**[38] 5486 3-8-3 51 JoeFanning 1 62
(David Nicholls) *t.k.h: cl up on outside: led 1f out: sn shkn up and edgd lft: kpt on wl* **11/4**[2]

0301 2 2 **Teetotal (IRE)**[4] 6568 3-9-0 69 DanielleMooney(7) 8 73
(Nigel Tinkler) *t.k.h: prom: shkn up 2f out: chsd wnr ins fnl f: kpt on same pce* **1/1**[1]

5106 3 2 ¼ **Amelia Jay**[29] 5788 3-8-4 52 ow1 AndrewElliott 9 48
(Danielle McCormick) *cl up: rdn and led briefly over 1f out: outpcd ins fnl f* **12/1**

005 4 1 ½ **Partner's Gold (IRE)**[26] 5884 3-8-4 52 oh2 ow2 RoystonFfrench 3 43
(Alan Berry) *trckd ldrs: rdn over 2f out: outpcd whn hmpd over 1f out*

4000 **F** **Boxing Shadows**[23] 5985 3-9-4 **66**............................(p) PaulMulrennan 7 62
(Bryan Smart) *led tl rdn and hdd over 1f out: one pce whn short of room, clipped heels and fell ent fnl f* **4/1**[3]

1m 0.63s (0.63) **Going Correction** +0.075s/f (Good) **5** Ran SP% **108.7**
Speed ratings (Par 101): **97,93,90,87,**
CSF £5.77 TOTE £4.90: £2.60, £1.20; EX 8.10 Trifecta £30.80 Pool: £1081.66 - 26.32 winning units..
Owner Pinnacle Royal Applause Partnership **Bred** Miss A J Rawding & P M Crane **Trained** Sessay, N Yorks
■ Stewards' Enquiry : Joe Fanning seven-day ban: careless riding (7-13 Oct)

FOCUS
A depleted field and the race was marred by the fall of Boxing Shadows, who hampered the already beaten Partner's Gold. The form might be alright for the grade with the winner relatively unexposed.

6683 TOTEPOOL MOBILE TEXT TOTE TO 89660 CLAIMING STKS 1m 1f 36y
3:10 (4:11) (Class 6) 3-5-Y-O **£2,587** (£770; £384; £192) **Stalls** Low

Form RPR
5 **1** **Tabaayun (IRE)**[10] 6357 3-9-1 75...............................(v[1]) DanielTudhope 4 70
(David O'Meara) *trckd ldr: led over 2f out: clr whn drifted rt fr over 1f out: kpt on strly: eased cl home* **4/1**[3]

4460 **2** *4 1/2* **Act Your Shoe Size**[4] 6550 4-9-0 80.................................... TomEaves 2 53
(Keith Dalgleish) *led at stdy pce: rdn over 3f out: hdd over 2f out: kpt on same pce appr fnl f* **8/13**[1]

3020 **3** *1* **Rosselli (IRE)**[13] 6283 4-9-0 60.................................... GrahamLee 1 51
(K R Burke) *trckd ldrs: drvn 3f out: outpcd fr 2f out* **3/1**[2]

6000 **4** *1/2* **Armada Bay (IRE)**[144] 1967 3-8-9 46.........................(t) RoystonFfrench 3 51?
(Bryan Smart) *in tch: rdn over 3f out: outpcd 2f out: n.d after* **50/1**

1m 59.38s (-0.32) **Going Correction** 0.0s/f (Good)
WFA 3 from 4yo 5lb **4** Ran SP% **108.9**
Speed ratings (Par 101): **101,97,96,95**
CSF £7.12 TOTE £5.40; EX 7.00 Trifecta £5.50 Pool: £2982.31 - 401.46 winning units..
Owner Middleham Park Racing LVII & Partner **Bred** Ecurie Des Monceaux **Trained** Nawton, N Yorks
■ Stewards' Enquiry : Tom Eaves one-day ban: careless riding (7 Oct)

FOCUS
This claimer was run an hour after the advertised time due to Paul Mulrennan having to be taken to hospital under medical supervision after his fall in the previous race. The pace was very steady until the final two and a half furlongs and the form must be taken with a punch of salt. The winner was way off his peak level.

6684 YOUR FAVOURITE POOL BETS AT TOTEPOOL.COM MAIDEN STKS 1m 1f 36y
3:40 (4:41) (Class 5) 3-4-Y-O **£3,234** (£962; £481; £240) **Stalls** Low

Form RPR
5333 **1** **Are You Mine (IRE)**[20] 6062 3-9-0 71.............................(v) GrahamLee 3 77
(Ralph Beckett) *mde virtually all: hrd pressed fr over 2f out: edgd lft u.p ins fnl f: hld on gamely towards fin* **5/2**[2]

33 **2** *nse* **Proximate**[18] 6134 3-9-5 0.. LukeMorris 1 82
(Sir Michael Stoute) *chsd ldr: smooth hdwy and ev ch fr over 2f out: str chal fnl f: jst failed* **8/13**[1]

3 *13* **Bound Copy (USA)** 3-9-0 0.. JoeFanning 2 59
(Mark Johnston) *in tch: hdwy and cl up over 2f out: sn rdn: wknd appr fnl f* **5/1**[3]

4 *25* **Mystical King** 3-9-5 0.. TomEaves 4
(Linda Perratt) *chsd ldrs tl rdn and wknd fr 3f out: t.o* **50/1**

1m 59.64s (-0.06) **Going Correction** 0.0s/f (Good) **4** Ran SP% **109.1**
Speed ratings (Par 103): **100,99,88,66**
CSF £4.54 TOTE £3.20; EX 5.40 Trifecta £5.00 Pool: £1447.86 - 214.33 winning units..
Owner P D Savill **Bred** Oak Hill Stud **Trained** Kimpton, Hants

FOCUS
The first two were closely matched on pre-race figures and basically to form.

6685 TOTEPOOL.COM EBF STALLIONS CONDITIONS STKS 6f 5y
4:10 (5:10) (Class 2) 3-Y-O+
£14,317 (£4,287; £2,143; £1,071; £535; £269) **Stalls** High

Form RPR
0101 **1** **Hopes N Dreams (IRE)**[27] 5851 5-8-5 95.................. BarryMcHugh 3 102
(Kevin Ryan) *mde all: rdn and qcknd over 1f out: kpt on strly: unchal* **5/2**[2]

3-50 **2** *3* **El Manati (IRE)**[93] 3562 3-8-3 99.................................(p) LukeMorris 1 92
(James Tate) *racd wd of remainder: t.k.h: cl up: rdn 2f out: edgd lft and kpt on fnl f: nt rch wnr* **17/2**

6120 **3** *nk* **Colonel Mak**[2] 6621 6-8-10 95.................................... GrahamGibbons 5 96
(David Barron) *chsd ldrs: effrt and rdn 2f out: kpt on same pce ins fnl f* **6/4**[1]

0316 **4** *1 3/4* **Secret Look**[24] 5943 3-8-8 91.. RobertWinston 2 91
(Ed McMahon) *in tch: effrt over 2f out: edgd rt: no imp fr over 1f out* **3/1**[3]

0004 **5** *hd* **Baileys Jubilee**[6] 6505 3-8-3 95.. JoeFanning 6 85
(Mark Johnston) *prom: effrt and pushed along over 1f out: no imp fnl f* **12/1**

4410 **6** *10* **Bix (IRE)**[17] 6180 3-8-8 52.. JordanHibberd 7 58?
(Alan Berry) *bhd: struggling 1/2-way: btn fr 2f out* **200/1**

1m 11.55s (-0.65) **Going Correction** +0.075s/f (Good)
WFA 3 from 5yo+ 2lb **6** Ran SP% **112.3**
Speed ratings (Par 109): **107,103,102,100,100 86**
toteswingers 1&2 £2.60, 2&3 £4.30, 1&3 £1.70 CSF £22.91 TOTE £3.30: £1.60, £3.20; EX 23.20 Trifecta £59.00 Pool: £1117.55 - 14.18 winning units..
Owner JCG Chua & CK Ong **Bred** J & Mrs Brennan & Edward & Mrs O'Regan **Trained** Hambleton, N Yorks

FOCUS
A decent prize for this Class 2 sprint and a competitive line-up. The time was relatively ordinary and there are doubts over the form.

6686 MORE FOOTBALL THAN EVER AT TOTEPOOL.COM H'CAP 1m 3f 16y
4:40 (5:40) (Class 5) (0-70,68) 3-Y-O **£3,234** (£962; £481; £240) **Stalls** High

Form RPR
4444 **1** **Aramist (IRE)**[12] 6301 3-9-7 **68**.. BenCurtis 4 78
(Alan Swinbank) *prom: effrt and rdn over 2f out: led over 1f out: styd on wl* **6/4**[1]

433 **2** *2 3/4* **Inherited**[29] 5801 3-8-10 **57**.......................................(p) LukeMorris 2 62
(Sir Mark Prescott Bt) *led: rdn over 3f out: hrd pressed fr over 2f out: edgd lft and hdd over 1f out: kpt on same pce fnl f* **7/4**[2]

663 **3** *1 3/4* **Henpecked**[48] 5110 3-8-13 **60**.. PJMcDonald 1 62
(Alistair Whillans) *chsd ldrs: outpcd over 3f out: rallied 2f out: kpt on fnl f: nvr able to chal* **7/1**

1545 **4** *1 1/4* **Bahamamay**[23] 5990 3-8-13 **60**.. LeeTopliss 3 60
(Richard Fahey) *chsd ldr: rdn and chal over 2f out: outpcd fnl f* **9/2**[3]

2m 24.42s (-1.18) **Going Correction** 0.0s/f (Good) **4** Ran SP% **107.0**
Speed ratings (Par 101): **104,102,100,99**
CSF £4.35 TOTE £2.70; EX 4.40 Trifecta £12.00 Pool: £1169.51 - 73.08 winning units..
Owner Pam & Richard Ellis **Bred** Fiona Craig & S Couldridge **Trained** Melsonby, N Yorks

FOCUS
Just one previous winner in this four horse line-up. A truly-run 3yo handicap and a decisive winner in the end after three were in a line over a furlong out. The form is rated around the second.

6687 COLLECT TOTEPOOL WINNINGS AT BETFRED SHOPS H'CAP 6f 5y
5:10 (6:10) (Class 6) (0-65,59) 3-Y-O+ **£1,940** (£577; £288; £144) **Stalls** High

Form RPR
456 **1** **Mysterious Wonder**[17] 6180 3-8-10 **52**.....................(b[1]) EvaMoscrop(7) 4 64
(Philip Kirby) *mde virtually all: rdn over 1f out: kpt on strly fnl f* **6/1**

0-00 **2** *1 3/4* **Hills Of Dakota**[44] 5261 5-9-12 **59**.....................(b[1]) TomEaves 3 65
(Keith Dalgleish) *taken early to post: w ldrs: rdn 2f out: edgd rt and kpt on fnl f* **10/1**

2005 **3** *1/2* **Lord Buffhead**[3] 6604 4-9-5 **57**.....................(v) PhilipPrince(5) 6 62
(Richard Guest) *taken early to post: cl up: rdn over 2f out: edgd lft and styd on fnl f* **15/2**

5002 **4** *2* **Compton Heights**[21] 6053 4-9-12 **59**.................................... GrahamLee 11 57
(Jim Goldie) *hld up: rdn and hdwy 2f out: edgd rt: kpt on ins fnl f: nvr able to chal* **4/1**[1]

002 **5** *1 1/4* **Rock Canyon (IRE)**[1] 6669 4-9-2 **49**.................................... LeeTopliss 12 43
(Linda Perratt) *hld up: rdn over 2f out: styd on fnl f: nvr rchd ldrs* **5/1**[3]

6330 **6** *nk* **Carrie's Magic**[26] 5876 6-8-10 **46**.................................... JasonHart(3) 1 39
(Alistair Whillans) *cl up: rdn over 2f out: one pce over 1f out* **13/2**

406 **7** *hd* **Spread Boy (IRE)**[21] 6053 6-8-5 **45**.................................... JordanHibberd(7) 7 38
(Alan Berry) *in tch: rdn and outpcd over 2f out: n.d after* **20/1**

4665 **8** *3/4* **Don't Tell**[63] 4585 3-8-10 **45**.. PJMcDonald 10 35
(George Moore) *in tch: outpcd over 2f out: n.d after* **25/1**

0253 **9** *3/4* **Gambino (IRE)**[11] 6344 3-8-12 **47**.................................... RobertWinston 13 35
(Alan Berry) *bhd: rdn over 3f out: nvr able to chal* **9/2**[2]

5600 **10** *3/4* **Schoolboy Champ**[17] 6154 6-8-12 **45**.....................(tp) RoystonFfrench 9 31
(Lisa Williamson) *chsd ldrs: drvn and outpcd over 2f out: btn fnl f* **40/1**

1050 **U** **Stoneacre Oskar**[10] 6368 4-9-7 **59**.................................... SladeO'Hara(5) 2
(Peter Grayson) *s.i.s: bhd: hdwy 2f out: 4th and styng on whn sddle slipped and uns rdr ins fnl f* **16/1**

1m 13.6s (1.40) **Going Correction** +0.075s/f (Good)
WFA 3 from 4yo+ 2lb **11** Ran SP% **120.3**
Speed ratings (Par 101): **93,90,90,87,85 85,85,84,83,82**
toteswingers 1&2 £4.50, 2&3 £5.60, 1&3 £4.20 CSF £64.57 CT £426.20 TOTE £8.20: £2.30, £4.10, £3.10; EX 76.70 Trifecta £99.30 Pool: £2112.09 - 3.71 winning units..
Owner Two Ladies And A Gentleman **Bred** Wellsummers Stud **Trained** Middleham, N Yorks

FOCUS
The first three home were in the firing line throughout. The form is rated around them, and at face value.
T/Plt: £70.40 to a £1 stake. Pool of £47005.06 - 487.02 winning tickets. T/Qpdt: £41.90 to a £1 stake. Pool of £2454.15 - 43.30 winning tickets. RY

6553 KEMPTON (A.W) (R-H)
Monday, September 23

OFFICIAL GOING: Standard
Wind: Virtually nil Weather: While cloud

6688 BETVICTOR.COM/BRITISH STALLION STUDS EBF MAIDEN STKS 1m 2f (P)
2:20 (2:20) (Class 5) 2-Y-O **£2,911** (£866; £432; £216) **Stalls** Low

Form RPR
42 **1** **Devilment**[28] 5811 2-9-5 0.. MickaelBarzalona 5 79
(Charlie Appleby) *hld up in rr: gd hdwy over 2f out: drvn to ld ins fnl f: r.o strly* **11/8**[1]

02 **2** *4* **Black Label**[20] 6079 2-9-5 0.. JimCrowley 2 71
(Harry Dunlop) *chsd ldrs: rdn 2f out and sn narrow 2nd: one pce 1f out: rallied in clsng stages to retake 2nd but no ch w wnr* **8/1**

03 **3** *nse* **Storm Force Ten**[17] 6168 2-9-5 0.. DavidProbert 4 71
(Andrew Balding) *led: rdn 2f out: hdd ins fnl f: sn outpcd by wnr: lost 2nd last strides* **11/2**[3]

032 **4** *1 3/4* **Anipa**[23] 5988 2-9-0 74.. WilliamBuick 7 63
(Ed Dunlop) *hld up in rr: hdwy 2f out: kpt on fnl f: nt rch ldrs* **3/1**[2]

30 **5** *1 1/2* **Lightning Shower (USA)**[17] 6168 2-9-5 0.. MartinHarley 1 65
(Marco Botti) *in tch: drvn and styd on 3f out: one pce fnl f* **25/1**

03 **6** *6* **Al Khawaneej Star (USA)**[27] 5852 2-9-5 0.. JamieSpencer 8 54
(Michael Bell) *chsd ldr: rdn 3f out: wknd 2f out* **9/1**

0 **7** *7* **Lingfield Lupus (IRE)**[51] 4997 2-9-5 0.. SteveDrowne 6 40
(John Best) *rdn 4f out: a towards rr* **66/1**

0 **8** *9* **Wedgwood (IRE)**[9] 6378 2-9-5 0.. PatDobbs 3 23
(Richard Hannon) *chsd ldrs: rdn and wknd 3f out* **33/1**

2m 6.56s (-1.44) **Going Correction** -0.175s/f (Stan) **8** Ran SP% **111.9**
Speed ratings (Par 95): **98,94,94,93,92 87,81,74**
toteswingers 1&2 £3.20, 2&3 £3.70, 1&3 £2.60 CSF £12.65 TOTE £2.30: £1.60, £1.80, £1.20; EX 10.80 Trifecta £25.60 Pool: £917.86 - 26.85 winning units..
Owner Godolphin **Bred** Cliveden Stud **Trained** Newmarket, Suffolk

FOCUS
All of these were tackling this trip for the first time but the market principles had pedigrees that suggested they should improve for it.

6689 DAY DELEGATE RATES FROM £39 MEDIAN AUCTION MAIDEN STKS 7f (P)
2:50 (2:52) (Class 5) 2-Y-O **£2,587** (£770; £384; £192) **Stalls** Low

Form RPR
54 **1** **Ninety Minutes (IRE)**[39] 5443 2-9-5 0.. SteveDrowne 11 73+
(John Best) *sn chsng ldr: rdn over 2f out: sn chalng: led ins fnl f: pushed out* **7/1**[2]

2 *1 1/4* **Desert Society (IRE)** 2-9-5 0.. SeanLevey 2 70+
(Richard Hannon) *in tch: hdwy fr 2f out: styd on wl fnl f to take 2nd in clsng stages: nt rch wnr* **10/1**

3 *1/2* **Space Walker (IRE)** 2-9-5 0.. JohnFahy 14 68
(Harry Dunlop) *sn led: rdn and jnd fr 2f out: hdd ins fnl f: no ex and dropped to 3rd in clsng stages* **33/1**

0 **4** *nk* **Red Cossack (CAN)**[20] 6069 2-9-5 0.. DaneO'Neill 9 67
(Paul Webber) *s.i.s: in rr: drvn and hdwy on ins fr 2f out: kpt on in clsng stages* **7/1**[2]

26 5 ¾ **Goleador (USA)**[25] 5922 2-9-5 0 ... MartinHarley 3 65
(Marco Botti) *chsd ldrs: rdn over 2f out: one pce ins fnl f* **8/1**[3]
03 6 1 **Template (IRE)**[25] 5922 2-9-5 0 ... PatDobbs 1 63
(Richard Hannon) *trckd ldrs: rdn 2f out: styd on same pce fr over 1f out* **7/4**[1]
3 7 1¼ **Passover**[16] 6197 2-9-5 0 ... (t) LiamKeniry 13 59
(Andrew Balding) *t.k.h in rr: hdwy appr fnl f: kpt on in clsng stages: nt rch ldrs* **8/1**[3]
64 8 4 **Shirley Vanessa (IRE)**[9] 6408 2-9-0 0 ... SamHitchcott 7 47
(Luke Dace) *mid-div: rdn and no prog over 2f out* **66/1**
9 nk **Nirva (IRE)** 2-9-0 0 ... TomQueally 4 43
(Lady Cecil) *s.i.s: sn pushed along a towards rr* **7/1**[2]
0 10 3 **Pacific Trip**[33] 5646 2-9-5 0 ... DavidProbert 5 40
(Andrew Balding) *chsd ldrs: rdn 3f out: wknd over 2f out* **50/1**
00 F **Silvercombe**[47] 5145 2-9-5 0 ... RenatoSouza 8 52+
(Sylvester Kirk) *in tch: pushed along and styng on whn fell fnl 75yds: fatally injured* **66/1**
B **Synonym (ITY)** 2-9-0 0 ... SebSanders 10 47+
(J W Hills) *in rr: sme hdwy fnl f: styng on but nvr a threat whn b.d fnl 75yds* **50/1**
0 B **Don Ottavio**[11] 6340 2-9-5 0 ... TedDurcan 12 52+
(David Lanigan) *chsd ldrs: wkng whn b.d fnl 75yds* **50/1**

1m 27.9s (1.90) **Going Correction** -0.175s/f (Stan) **13** Ran SP% **117.0**
Speed ratings (Par 95): **82,80,80,79,78 77,76,71,71,67 , ,**
toteswingers 1&2 £16.60, 2&3 £73.40, 1&3 £49.20 CSF £70.62 TOTE £5.90: £1.70, £3.00, £10.40; EX 112.30 Trifecta £1021.90 Part won. Pool: £1362.59 - 0.95 winning units..
Owner Andy Carroll, Kevin Nolan & Mark Curtis **Bred** Louis A Walshe **Trained** Hucking, Kent

FOCUS
This looked an ordinary enough maiden on paper with the short-priced favourite, who hardly set an exacting standard, proving disappointing. A few of these are sure to progress from the bare form. The race was marred by a horrific incident in the final furlong where three horses came down.

6690 DOWNLOAD THE BETVICTOR APP/BRITISH STALLION STUDS EBF MAIDEN FILLIES' STKS (DIV I) 7f (P)

3:20 (3:32) (Class 5) 2-Y-O **£2,911** (£866; £432; £216) **Stalls** Low

Form RPR
03 1 **Spiritual Flame**[33] 5646 2-9-0 0 ... SebSanders 9 77+
(William Haggas) *chsd ldrs: rdn to chal 2f out: slt ld sn after but a hrd pressed: kpt on wl to assert in clsng stages* **11/2**[3]
2 nk **Oh Star (USA)** 2-9-0 0 ... WilliamBuick 11 76+
(John Gosden) *chsd ldrs: chal fr 2f out and stl upsides whn green and hung lft ins fnl f: stl upsides tl no ex in clsng stages* **7/1**
3 2 **Maria Bella (IRE)** 2-9-0 0 ... MickaelBarzalona 7 71
(Charlie Appleby) *chsd ldrs: rdn 2f out: kpt on fnl f to take 3rd last strides: no imp on ldng duo* **8/1**
4 nk **Amaseena (IRE)** 2-9-0 0 ... JamieSpencer 10 70
(Roger Varian) *chsd ldrs: rdn over 2f out: styd on same pce fnl f* **10/3**[1]
5 5 nk **Serena Grae**[30] 5740 2-9-0 0 ... MartinDwyer 13 69
(Marcus Tregoning) *sn led: jnd 2f out: hdd sn after: styd on same pce fnl f* **16/1**
0 6 2¾ **Terhaab (USA)**[66] 4484 2-9-0 0 ... DaneO'Neill 1 62+
(John Gosden) *in rr: hdwy 2f out: styd on fnl f: nvr a threat* **4/1**[2]
0 7 ½ **Ventura Ice (IRE)**[25] 5922 2-9-0 0 ... PatDobbs 8 60
(Richard Hannon) *chsd ldrs: pushed along over 2f out: sn outpcd* **16/1**
8 3 **Heho** 2-9-0 0 ... TomQueally 6 54+
(Sir Michael Stoute) *in rr: pushed along 3f out: styd on fr over 1f out: nvr a threat* **8/1**
00 9 ½ **Lady Emmuska**[47] 5131 2-9-0 0 ... SeanLevey 12 51
(Richard Hannon) *s.i.s: in rr: sme hdwy fnl 2f* **33/1**
10 1 **Namely (IRE)** 2-9-0 0 ... ChrisCatlin 2 48
(Sir Mark Prescott Bt) *rdn and in tch 3f out: styd on same pce fr over 2f out* **40/1**
00 11 3¼ **La Faisan Blanche (USA)**[13] 6281 2-9-0 0 ... KirstyMilczarek 4 39
(Luca Cumani) *bhd most of way* **66/1**
12 2 **Sweet Lily Pea (USA)** 2-9-0 0 ... JimCrowley 3 34
(Olly Stevens) *chsd ldrs: hung rt: green and wknd over 2f out* **16/1**
06 13 nk **Forest Glen (IRE)**[8] 6423 2-9-0 0 ... LiamKeniry 5 33
(Sylvester Kirk) *stdd s: a in rr* **66/1**

1m 26.74s (0.74) **Going Correction** -0.175s/f (Stan) **13** Ran SP% **119.2**
Speed ratings (Par 92): **88,87,85,85,84 81,80,77,76,75 72,69,69**
toteswingers 1&2 £11.30, 2&3 £3.40, 1&3 £10.10 CSF £42.99 TOTE £8.10: £1.90, £2.00, £2.40; EX 57.30 Trifecta £339.30 Pool: £1316.99 - 2.91 winning units..
Owner Cheveley Park Stud **Bred** Cheveley Park Stud Ltd **Trained** Newmarket, Suffolk

FOCUS
Some very attractive pedigrees on show and they recorded a time over a second faster than the previous 7f maiden, but there was a compressed finish and it's hard to rate the bare form any higher. As has been the case often at this rack in recent meetings, those that raced deepest on the track fared best.

6691 DOWNLOAD THE BETVICTOR APP/BRITISH STALLION STUDS EBF MAIDEN FILLIES' STKS (DIV II) 7f (P)

3:50 (4:02) (Class 5) 2-Y-O **£2,911** (£866; £432; £216) **Stalls** Low

Form RPR
1 **Queen's Prize** 2-9-0 0 ... TomQueally 9 77+
(Sir Michael Stoute) *towards rr: pushed along over 2f out: styd on strly fnl f to ld fnl 20yds: won gng away* **9/1**
3 2 1 **Mia San Triple**[17] 6171 2-9-0 0 ... MartinHarley 8 74
(Peter Chapple-Hyam) *led: rdn 2f out: kpt advantage tl hdd and no ex fnl 20yds* **7/1**[3]
00 3 1¼ **Cordial**[18] 6140 2-9-0 0 ... WilliamBuick 1 71
(John Gosden) *chsd ldrs: rdn to dispute 2nd fr 2f out: no imp fnl f and one pce into 3rd in clsng stages* **9/1**
002 4 shd **Placidia (IRE)**[18] 6141 2-9-0 76 ... TedDurcan 10 71
(David Lanigan) *chsd ldrs: rdn 2f out: kpt on fnl f: nt rch ldrs* **4/1**[2]
5 1½ **Big Boned (USA)** 2-9-0 0 ... JamieSpencer 12 67+
(Ed Dunlop) *chsd ldr: rdn over 2f out: wknd into 5th fnl 110yds* **12/1**
6 3 **A Legacy Of Love (IRE)** 2-9-0 0 ... JimCrowley 11 59+
(Amanda Perrett) *in rr: hdwy on outside 3f out: styd on fnl f but nvr a threat* **8/1**
7 5 **Irradiance (IRE)** 2-9-0 0 ... MickaelBarzalona 6 45
(Charlie Appleby) *in rr: mod prog fnl f* **11/4**[1]
0 8 1¼ **Spring Lady**[11] 6318 2-8-11 0 ... MichaelJMMurphy(3) 2 42
(Alan Jarvis) *chsd ldrs: wknd over 2f out* **66/1**
0 9 2¼ **Updated (FR)**[12] 6298 2-9-0 0 ... SeanLevey 7 36
(Ismail Mohammed) *chsd ldrs: wknd ins fnl 3f* **14/1**
10 nk **Lady Crossmar (IRE)** 2-9-0 0 ... PatDobbs 5 35+
(Richard Hannon) *slowly away: a in rr* **16/1**
11 2½ **Trillian Astra (IRE)** 2-9-0 0 ... SteveDrowne 3 28
(Clive Cox) *s.i.s: a towards rr* **20/1**

1m 25.44s (-0.56) **Going Correction** -0.175s/f (Stan) **11** Ran SP% **116.8**
Speed ratings (Par 92): **96,94,93,93,91 88,82,81,78,78 75**
toteswingers 1&2 £10.90, 2&3 £19.20, 1&3 £18.40 CSF £70.19 TOTE £8.00: £1.30, £3.00, £2.30; EX 110.30 Trifecta £985.50 Part won. Pool: £1314.00 - 0.14 winning units..
Owner The Queen **Bred** The Queen **Trained** Newmarket, Suffolk

FOCUS
They seemed to go a sound gallop here and the time was quicker than the more steadily run previous contest. The second and fourth offer perspective and the winner looks a sure-fire improver.

6692 £25 FREE BET AT BETVICTOR.COM H'CAP 6f (P)

4:20 (4:28) (Class 3) (0-95,92) 3-Y-O

£7,158 (£2,143; £1,071; £535; £267; £134) **Stalls** Low

Form RPR
23-0 1 **Hoodna (IRE)**[127] 2476 3-9-7 **92** ... AhmedAjtebi 8 102
(Saeed bin Suroor) *in tch: hdwy 2f out: qcknd fnl f to ld fnl 110yds: styd on wl* **25/1**
3003 2 1 **Barracuda Boy (IRE)**[44] 5260 3-9-7 **92** ... RichardKingscote 9 99
(Tom Dascombe) *chsd ldr: rdn 2f out: kpt on wl fnl f to chse wnr in clsng stages but no imp* **13/2**
31 3 nk **Purcell (IRE)**[37] 5511 3-9-3 **88** ... DavidProbert 6 94
(Andrew Balding) *led: rdn 2f out: kpt on tl hdd and outpcd fnl 110yds: lost 2nd in clsng stages* **7/2**[2]
0116 4 ½ **Badr Al Badoor (IRE)**[31] 5700 3-9-5 **90** ... (v) WilliamBuick 2 94
(James Fanshawe) *in tch: drvn to dispute 2nd jst ins fnl f: kpt on same pce* **9/2**[3]
0223 5 1¼ **Panther Patrol (IRE)**[27] 5853 3-8-7 **78** oh1 ... JohnFahy 3 78
(Eve Johnson Houghton) *towards rr: hdwy 2f out: styd on fnl f but nvr a ch* **20/1**
4100 6 1¼ **Lionheart**[17] 6161 3-8-12 **83** ... KirstyMilczarek 5 79
(Luca Cumani) *in rr: pushed along 2f out: styd on fr over 1f out: kpt on in clsng stages* **16/1**
2104 7 nk **Lewisham**[30] 5748 3-9-2 **87** ... JimCrowley 7 82
(Ralph Beckett) *chsd ldrs: rdn 2f out: sn btn* **14/1**
1050 8 ½ **Rivellino**[73] 4255 3-9-5 **90** ... MartinHarley 1 84
(K R Burke) *chsd ldrs: rdn over 2f out: wknd appr fnl f* **3/1**[1]
220 9 1¾ **Freddy With A Y (IRE)**[43] 5303 3-9-1 **86** ... TomQueally 11 74
(Gary Moore) *sn chsng ldrs: rdn and btn 2f out* **10/1**
2100 10 hd **Upavon**[131] 2371 3-9-2 **87** ... LiamKeniry 10 75
(David Elsworth) *s.i.s: a towards rr* **33/1**
23-0 11 nk **Spokeswoman (IRE)**[26] 5896 3-8-11 **82** ... MickaelBarzalona 4 69
(Saeed bin Suroor) *rdn over 2f out: a towards rr* **16/1**

1m 10.98s (-2.12) **Going Correction** -0.175s/f (Stan) **11** Ran SP% **117.8**
Speed ratings (Par 105): **107,105,105,104,102 101,100,100,97,97 97**
toteswingers 1&2 £16.50, 2&3 £6.80, 1&3 £17.30 CSF £176.93 CT £723.01 TOTE £19.00: £6.60, £2.60, £1.80; EX 126.40 Trifecta £747.30 Pool: £1330.02 - 1.33 winning units..
Owner Godolphin **Bred** Petra Bloodstock Agency Ltd **Trained** Newmarket, Suffolk

FOCUS
A good-quality handicap, run at a sound pace, and there appears no reason why this form shouldn't work out. The race is rated around the runner-up's solid turf form.

6693 BETVICTOR CASINO ON YOUR MOBILE H'CAP 1m 4f (P)

4:50 (4:58) (Class 4) (0-85,82) 3-Y-O **£4,690** (£1,395; £697; £348) **Stalls** Centre

Form RPR
1141 1 **Prospera (IRE)**[20] 6081 3-9-6 **81** ... (b) JimCrowley 8 90
(Ralph Beckett) *hld up in rr: hdwy on outside over 2f out: led appr fnl f: hld on all out* **9/2**[1]
0250 2 hd **Grayswood**[20] 6071 3-8-7 **68** oh1 ... (p) MartinDwyer 4 76
(William Muir) *in rr but in tch: hdwy to chal 2f out: led wl over 1f out: sn hdd: styd chalng tl no ex u.p fnl 110yds* **20/1**
2142 3 ½ **Grendisar (IRE)**[18] 6136 3-9-2 **77** ... (p) MartinHarley 6 84+
(Marco Botti) *in rr: nt clr run 2f out: swtchd lft and gd hdwy over 1f out: str run ins fnl f to cl on ldng duo: no ex in clsng stages* **9/2**[1]
1321 4 2¼ **Lisa's Legacy**[12] 6313 3-9-5 **80** ... RichardKingscote 3 84
(Daniel Kubler) *led 1f: styd trcking ldrs: rdn to press ldrs ins fnl 2f: outpcd ins fnl f* **9/2**[1]
0133 5 1¾ **Madame Vestris (IRE)**[37] 5514 3-9-5 **80** ... PatDobbs 7 81
(Sir Michael Stoute) *sn pressing ldr: led 2f out: hdd u.p wl over 1f out: wknd fnl f* **9/2**[1]
1135 6 shd **Portrait**[26] 5888 3-9-5 **80** ... (p) ChrisCatlin 5 81
(Sir Mark Prescott Bt) *chsd ldrs: rdn 3f out: outpcd over 2f out: kpt on again in clsng stages* **16/1**
3650 7 1½ **King Muro**[52] 4950 3-8-12 **73** ... LiamKeniry 1 71
(Andrew Balding) *t.k.h: chsd ldrs: ev ch 2f out: wknd u.p over 1f out* **6/1**[3]
133 8 7 **Portmonarch (IRE)**[19] 6108 3-9-7 **82** ... (p) TedDurcan 2 69
(David Lanigan) *led after 1f: sn jnd: hdd 2f out: sn btn* **11/2**[2]

2m 31.94s (-2.56) **Going Correction** -0.175s/f (Stan) **8** Ran SP% **113.0**
Speed ratings (Par 103): **101,100,100,99,97 97,96,92**
toteswingers 1&2 £11.40, 2&3 £9.70, 1&3 £5.20 CSF £89.11 CT £424.23 TOTE £5.80: £2.30, £4.50, £1.60; EX 87.80 Trifecta £398.20 Pool: £2628.49 - 4.95 winning units..
Owner The Millennium Madness Partnership **Bred** Mount Coote Stud **Trained** Kimpton, Hants

FOCUS
This had a wide-open feel to it but yet again the horse that raced widest in the straight finished in front. The pace was sound and the first three came from the rear. Another personal best from the winner.

6694 FOLLOW US ON TWITTER @BETVICTOR H'CAP 1m (P)

5:20 (5:27) (Class 4) (0-85,85) 3-Y-O+ **£4,690** (£1,395; £697; £348) **Stalls** Low

Form RPR
61 1 **Cornrow**[18] 6133 3-9-3 82 ... WilliamBuick 8 94+
(John Gosden) *in rr: hdwy on outside over 2f out: sn hrd drvn: styd on u.p fnl f: led last strides* **15/8**[1]
0266 2 nk **Royal Prize**[16] 6203 3-9-5 84 ... JimCrowley 4 95
(Ralph Beckett) *in tch: rdn and hdwy over 2f out: styd on wl u.p to take narrow ld fnl 110yds: ct last strides* **6/1**[2]
-114 3 ¾ **Pleasure Bent**[68] 4416 3-8-12 77 ... KierenFallon 3 87
(Luca Cumani) *chsd ldrs: rdn over 2f out: led over 1f out: hdd and nt qckn fnl 110yds* **7/1**[3]
5312 4 2 **Angelic Upstart (IRE)**[28] 5825 5-9-2 77 ... LiamKeniry 12 82+
(Andrew Balding) *in rr: sme hdwy whn hmpd on bnd over 3f out: swtchd lft to outside and hdwy fr 2f out: styd on fnl f: gng on in clsng stages* **12/1**

1031 **5** ½ **Sir Mike**[9] 6403 4-9-9 84 .... PatDobbs 14 88
(Amanda Perrett) *in tch: hdwy and rdn over 2f out: kpt on same pce ins fnl f* **16/1**

0560 **6** ½ **Steelriver (IRE)**[12] 6308 3-8-13 78 .... TedDurcan 5 81
(James Bethell) *chsd ldrs: rdn over 2f out: kpt on ins fnl f* **20/1**

3420 **7** 1½ **Bank On Me**[15] 6236 4-9-6 81 .... WilliamCarson 11 80
(Philip McBride) *in rr: rdn 2f out: kpt on fnl f: nt rch ldrs* **10/1**

425 **8** 2¾ **Cruiser**[17] 6167 5-9-9 84 ....(p) MartinDwyer 7 77
(William Muir) *in tch: hdwy over 2f out and sn chsng ldrs: wknd fnl f* **14/1**

5520 **9** 1¼ **Dark Emerald (IRE)**[37] 5534 3-9-6 85 ....(v) SebSanders 6 75
(Brendan Powell) *led after 2f: hdd & wknd over 1f out* **20/1**

-000 **10** 4½ **Rustic Deacon**[35] 5580 6-9-2 77 .... TomQueally 13 57
(Willie Musson) *s.i.s: towards rr most of way* **25/1**

10 **11** 6 **Air Of Glory (IRE)**[96] 3470 3-9-5 84 .... MickaelBarzalona 2 50
(Charlie Appleby) *chsd ldrs: wknd ins fnl 2f* **10/1**

0220 **12** ½ **Reflect (IRE)**[82] 3960 5-9-3 78 ....(vt) DaneO'Neill 10 43
(Derek Shaw) *a in rr* **33/1**

1246 **13** 33 **Emmuska**[23] 5978 4-9-0 80 .... RyanTate(5) 9
(Clive Cox) *a in rr* **33/1**

6400 **14** 3½ **Kaafel (IRE)**[23] 6004 4-9-4 82 ....(p) CharlesBishop(3) 1
(Peter Hedger) *led 2f: chsd ldrs tl wknd ins fnl 3f* **33/1**

1m 36.63s (-3.17) **Going Correction** -0.175s/f (Stan)
WFA 3 from 4yo+ 4lb **14 Ran SP% 122.2**
Speed ratings (Par 105): **108,107,106,104,104 103,102,99,98,93 87,87,54,50**
toteswingers 1&2 £4.50, 2&3 £5.60, 1&3 £4.20 CSF £11.10 CT £65.23 TOTE £2.70: £1.30, £2.30, £2.80; EX 16.70 Trifecta £99.30 Pool: £2354.42 - 17.77 winning units.
Owner HRH Princess Haya Of Jordan **Bred** Darley **Trained** Newmarket, Suffolk

FOCUS
This was a soundly run contest and the overall time was faster than RP standard. Good handicap form, rated around the fourth to sixth.
T/Plt: £269.40 to a £1 stake. Pool of £58864.86 - 159.45 winning tickets. T/Qpdt: £33.10 to a £1 stake. Pool of £6006.62 - 134.08 winning tickets. ST

6277 LEICESTER (R-H)
Monday, September 23

OFFICIAL GOING: Good (7.7)
Wind: Light across Weather: Overcast

6695 ASTON FLAMVILLE FILLIES' NURSERY H'CAP 5f 218y
2:00 (2:01) (Class 5) (0-75,75) 2-Y-O **£3,234** (£962; £481; £240) **Stalls** Centre

Form RPR

5025 **1** **Got To Dance**[27] 5850 2-8-13 67 .... JamesDoyle 17 71+
(Ralph Beckett) *hld up: hdwy over 1f out: sn rdn and edgd rt: r.o to ld nr fin* **12/1**

4153 **2** nk **Inspiriter**[17] 6170 2-9-5 73 .... SilvestreDeSousa 7 76
(Charlie Appleby) *chsd ldr: rdn over 2f out: led wl over 1f out: hdd nr fin* **12/1**

2212 **3** ½ **Sefaat**[31] 5693 2-9-6 74 .... PaulHanagan 15 76
(Brian Meehan) *a.p: rdn to chse ldr fnl f: styd on* **8/1**[3]

21 **4** 2½ **Hipz (IRE)**[9] 6408 2-9-4 72 .... PatCosgrave 6 66
(George Baker) *hld up: drvn along 1/2-way: hdwy and edgd lft over 1f out: styd on* **7/1**[2]

3210 **5** nk **Inyordreams**[11] 6326 2-9-7 75 .... DaleSwift 10 68+
(James Given) *mid-div: rdn over 2f out: hdwy and edgd rt over 1f out: styd on* **5/1**[1]

4654 **6** 2 **Herbah**[12] 6311 2-8-7 61 ....(b[1]) AndreaAtzeni 3 48
(Roger Varian) *led: rdn and hdd wl over 1f out: no ex ins fnl f* **8/1**[3]

022 **7** 1¾ **Nimble Kimble**[35] 5593 2-8-11 68 .... RosieJessop(3) 5 50
(James Eustace) *prom: rdn over 2f out: styd on same pce fnl f* **20/1**

2252 **8** 1 **Secret Kode (IRE)**[34] 5603 2-9-3 71 .... GeorgeBaker 14 50
(Brendan Powell) *hld up: hdwy u.p over 1f out: hung rt and no ex fnl f* **25/1**

5154 **9** ¾ **A Childs Dream (IRE)**[27] 5850 2-8-10 67.. WilliamTwiston-Davies(3) 18 44
(Richard Hannon) *mid-div: rdn 1/2-way: hdwy over 1f out: no pce fnl f* **20/1**

4351 **10** nk **Alfie Lunete (IRE)**[11] 6320 2-9-0 68 .... LiamJones 11 44
(J S Moore) *mid-div: drvn along 1/2-way: nt trble ldrs* **16/1**

6034 **11** 4½ **Honey Meadow**[11] 6320 2-8-10 64 .... AdamBeschizza 13 26
(Robert Eddery) *sn pushed along in rr: nvr nrr* **20/1**

0205 **12** 1¼ **Where The Boys Are (IRE)**[34] 5609 2-8-11 65 .... NeilCallan 1 23
(Ed McMahon) *trckd ldrs: plld hrd: rdn over 1f out: wknd fnl f* **50/1**

3453 **13** ¾ **Rosebay Coral (IRE)**[31] 5710 2-9-0 68 .... JimmyQuinn 8 24
(Tony Coyle) *mid-div: pushed along 1/2-way: wknd 2f out* **33/1**

4540 **14** nk **Cheeky Peta'S**[7] 6474 2-8-3 62 .... ConnorBeasley(5) 16 17
(James Given) *prom: rdn over 2f out: wknd over 1f out* **66/1**

221 **15** 1¾ **Shilla (IRE)**[19] 6095 2-9-4 72 .... CathyGannon 4 22
(Henry Candy) *prom: lost pl over 4f out: rdn over 2f out: sn wknd* **8/1**[3]

3302 **16** 2½ **Misty Sparkler**[17] 6170 2-9-7 75 .... MartinLane 12 22
(Brian Meehan) *s.i.s and hmpd s: hld up: pushed along 1/2-way: wknd 2f out* **20/1**

4133 **17** 7 **Emperor's Hope (IRE)**[73] 4239 2-9-7 75 .... RichardHughes 9
(Richard Hannon) *trckd ldrs: racd keenly: pushed along over 2f out: wkng whn hmpd wl over 1f out: eased* **14/1**

1m 12.01s (-0.99) **Going Correction** -0.025s/f (Good) **17 Ran SP% 119.7**
Speed ratings (Par 92): **105,104,103,100,100 97,95,93,92,92 86,84,83,83,81 77,68**
toteswingers 1&2 £13.20, 2&3 £30.20, 1&3 £39.20 CSF £128.31 CT £1273.98 TOTE £17.70: £5.30, £4.10, £2.10, £2.60; EX 216.50 Trifecta £736.60 Part won. Pool: £982.21 - 0.01 winning units..
Owner Landmark Racing Limited **Bred** Landmark Racing Limited **Trained** Kimpton, Hants

FOCUS
A competitive nursery, littered with potential improvers. Ordinary form though, rated around the second and third.

6696 KIRBY GATE MAIDEN STKS 1m 3f 183y
2:30 (2:34) (Class 5) 3-Y-O+ **£3,881** (£1,155; £577; £288) **Stalls** Low

Form RPR

4242 **1** **Hassle (IRE)**[13] 6280 4-9-13 79 ....(p) AdamKirby 6 76+
(Clive Cox) *hld up: hdwy over 3f out: led over 2f out: rdn and hung rt over 1f out: styd on* **4/1**[2]

0004 **2** 2½ **Maraweh (IRE)**[91] 3618 3-9-5 72 .... PaulHanagan 12 69
(J W Hills) *trckd ldrs: rdn and ev ch over 2f out: styd on same pce ins fnl f* **50/1**

0-66 **3** ¾ **Red Pilgrim (IRE)**[47] 5132 3-9-2 61 ....(t[1]) RobertTart(3) 10 68
(James Toller) *chsd ldrs: rdn over 2f out: edgd rt over 1f out: styd on same pce ins fnl f* **50/1**

5 **4** 2 **Balder Succes (FR)**[9] 6402 5-9-13 0 .... FergusSweeney 2 65+
(Alan King) *hld up: hdwy over 3f out: sn pushed along: styd on: nt rch ldrs* **12/1**

2 **5** 2¾ **Obstacle**[94] 3539 3-9-5 0 .... JamesDoyle 1 60
(John Gosden) *chsd ldrs: rdn over 2f out: sn outpcd: styd on ins fnl f* **9/4**[1]

6 hd **Great Fighter** 3-9-5 0 .... FrederikTylicki 13 60
(Saeed bin Suroor) *s.i.s: hdwy 10f out: rdn and outpcd over 3f out: edgd rt and styd on ins fnl f* **12/1**

7 nse **Wannabe Your Man** 3-9-5 0 .... AndreaAtzeni 5 60+
(Roger Varian) *mid-div: pushed along over 3f out: sn outpcd: styd on ins fnl f* **10/1**

8 ½ **Summerfree (USA)** 3-9-5 0 .... AdrianNicholls 3 59
(Mark Johnston) *sn led: rdn and hdd over 2f out: wknd fnl f* **8/1**[3]

040- **9** 7 **Night's Watch**[271] 8240 3-9-5 67 .... RobertHavlin 8 48
(William Jarvis) *hld up: plld hrd: sme hdwy over 2f out: rdn and wknd over 1f out* **100/1**

2222 **10** 1¼ **Saddaqa (USA)**[26] 5902 3-9-0 84 ....(p) SilvestreDeSousa 11 41
(Saeed bin Suroor) *hld up: hdwy 8f out: rdn over 2f out: wkng whn hung rt over 1f out* **4/1**[2]

5 **11** 14 **Seabougg**[21] 6036 5-9-10 0 .... RosieJessop(3) 7 24
(James Eustace) *hld up: drvn along over 3f out: sn wknd* **100/1**

12 1¼ **Jowhara** 3-9-0 0 .... NeilCallan 14 17
(Gerard Butler) *s.i.s: hdwy 10f out: rdn over 4f out: wknd over 2f out* **50/1**

13 1 **Santayana (GER)**[85] 4-9-5 49 .... DeclanBates(3) 4 15
(David Evans) *hld up: a in rr: bhd fr 1/2-way* **100/1**

/030 **14** 9 **Sure Fire (GER)**[32] 5672 8-9-10 48 .... RichardEvans(3) 15 6
(David Evans) *hld up: a in rr: bhd fr 1/2-way* **100/1**

00 **15** 18 **Lady Cliche**[61] 4633 4-9-5 0 .... JemmaMarshall(3) 9
(Roger Curtis) *s.s: a in rr: bhd fr 1/2-way* **200/1**

2m 35.07s (1.17) **Going Correction** +0.20s/f (Good)
WFA 3 from 4yo+ 8lb **15 Ran SP% 116.7**
Speed ratings (Par 103): **104,102,101,100,98 98,98,98,93,92 83,82,81,75,63**
toteswingers 1&2 £24.30, 2&3 £59.20, 1&3 £21.90 CSF £200.25 TOTE £4.90: £1.80, £8.70, £11.60; EX 156.50 Trifecta £1179.10 Part won. Pool: £1572.24 - 0.01 winning units..
Owner A D Spence **Bred** Cheval Court Stud **Trained** Lambourn, Berks

FOCUS
Some big yards represented and a thoroughly likeable performance by the winner, but this is muddling, ordinary form. The winner did not need to improve.

6697 BRITISH STALLION STUDS EBF KEGWORTH NOVICE STKS 5f 218y
3:00 (3:00) (Class 4) 2-Y-O **£5,175** (£1,540; £769; £384) **Stalls** Centre

Form RPR

2 **1** **Stars Above Me**[54] 4877 2-8-2 0 .... JoeyHaynes(5) 3 86+
(Roger Charlton) *plld hrd: led 5f out: rdn over 1f out: styd on* **7/4**[1]

1 **2** ¾ **Invincible Strike (IRE)**[25] 5915 2-9-3 0 .... NeilCallan 6 94+
(James Tate) *trckd ldrs: wnt 2nd 2f out: sn rdn: hung lft ins fnl f: styd on* **4/1**[3]

234 **3** 4½ **Intermath (IRE)**[24] 5945 2-9-3 83 .... CathyGannon 2 81
(David Evans) *chsd ldrs: outpcd 1/2-way: styd on ins fnl f* **25/1**

33 **4** ½ **Kuala Queen (IRE)**[25] 5929 2-8-7 0 .... JimmyQuinn 5 69
(Denis Coakley) *sn outpcd: styd on ins fnl f: nvr nrr* **50/1**

31 **5** 3 **Storm Trooper (IRE)**[68] 4412 2-9-3 0 .... RichardHughes 4 70
(Richard Hannon) *led 1f: chsd ldr tl rdn 2f out: hung rt and wknd over 1f out* **6/1**

1 **6** ¾ **Almuheet**[45] 5244 2-9-3 0 .... PaulHanagan 1 68
(Sir Michael Stoute) *s.i.s: hdwy 1/2-way: rdn over 2f out: wknd fnl f* **2/1**[2]

1m 12.22s (-0.78) **Going Correction** -0.025s/f (Good) **6 Ran SP% 109.8**
Speed ratings (Par 97): **104,103,97,96,92 91**
toteswingers 1&2 £2.10, 2&3 £4.90, 1&3 £4.30 CSF £8.74 TOTE £1.70: £2.10, £1.30; EX 8.30 Trifecta £63.90 Pool: £2013.84 - 23.62 winning units..
Owner Elite Racing Club **Bred** Elite Racing Club **Trained** Beckhampton, Wilts

FOCUS
An intriguing juvenile contest. A likeable effort from the winner and a fine effort at the weights from the second.

6698 GOLDEN HAND (S) STKS 7f 9y
3:30 (3:30) (Class 6) 3-Y-O **£1,940** (£577; £288; £144) **Stalls** Centre

Form RPR

0025 **1** dht **Marsh Dragon**[6] 6502 3-8-6 58 .... PaulHanagan 9 56
(Mark H Tompkins) *hld up: hdwy over 2f out: rdn and carried rt ins fnl f: jnd wnr post: fin dead-heat 1st: awrdd the r outright* **7/2**[3]

3204 **2** **Admirals Walk (IRE)**[17] 6155 3-8-11 58 ....(tp) RichardHughes 5 61
(Sylvester Kirk) *chsd ldrs: rdn over 2f out: led and hung rt ins fnl f: jnd post: fin dead-heat 1st: disq & plcd 2nd* **9/2**

0216 **3** 1¾ **Angels Calling**[33] 5644 3-8-6 61 .... JoeyHaynes(5) 2 56
(K R Burke) *a.p: led 2f out: rdn: hdd and hung rt ins fnl f: unable qck towards fin* **3/1**[2]

1400 **4** 1¼ **Schottische**[108] 3040 3-8-3 50 ....(v[1]) RosieJessop(3) 6 48
(Derek Haydn Jones) *chsd ldrs: rdn over 2f out: hung rt and outpcd over 1f out: r.o towards fin* **25/1**

3330 **5** nk **Truly Madly (IRE)**[11] 6341 3-8-11 68 .... JamesDoyle 3 52
(Hans Adielsson) *hld up: hdwy 2f out: sn rdn: styd on same pce ins fnl f* **9/4**[1]

5000 **6** 1¾ **Double Star**[11] 6321 3-8-8 48 .... MatthewLawson(3) 8 47
(Jonathan Portman) *hld up: hdwy over 2f out: sn rdn: no ex ins fnl f* **33/1**

3000 **7** 2¾ **World Freight Girl**[25] 5935 3-8-6 47 ....(b) JimmyQuinn 7 35
(Dean Ivory) *s.i.s: rdn over 2f out: nvr trbld ldrs* **33/1**

6004 **8** 1½ **Toffee Shot**[11] 6319 3-8-6 49 ....(b) MartinLane 4 31
(J W Hills) *s.i.s: sn pushed along in rr: sme hdwy over 3f out: wknd over 2f out* **25/1**

0644 **9** 5 **Time To Begin (IRE)**[11] 6344 3-8-8 53....(bt) WilliamTwiston-Davies(3) 1 22
(Alan McCabe) *led: hdd 2f out: sn rdn and wknd* **14/1**

1m 26.81s (0.61) **Going Correction** -0.025s/f (Good) **9 Ran SP% 116.4**
Speed ratings (Par 99): **95,95,93,91,91 89,86,84,78**
toteswingers 1&2 £2.70, 2&3 £3.60, 1&3 £3.40 CSF £18.91 TOTE £5.20: £1.90, £1.60, £1.20; EX 18.10 Trifecta £74.70 Pool: £848.31 - 8.50 winning units..There was no bid for the winner.
Owner Ken Lawrence **Bred** Dullingham Park & Ian Lochhead **Trained** Newmarket, Suffolk

The Form Book Flat, Raceform Ltd, Compton, RG20 6NL.

FOCUS
Marsh Dragon and Admirals Walk could not be separated, but the latter was disqualified. A poor race, even for the grade, which has been rated on the negative side.

6699 SIS LIVE H'CAP 5f 2y
4:00 (4:05) (Class 3) (0-95,95) 3-Y-O **£7,561** (£2,263; £1,131; £566; £282) **Stalls** Centre

Form RPR
0012 1 **New Fforest**[23] 5991 3-8-8 **88** .... OisinMurphy(5) 15 100
(Andrew Balding) *s.i.s: hdwy over 3f out: rdn to ld 1f out: r.o* **5/1**[2]
4004 2 1 ¼ **Kyleakin Lass**[16] 6190 4-9-2 **90** .... RichardHughes 14 97
(Jonathan Portman) *hld up: swtchd lft and hdwy over 1f out: edgd rt ins fnl f: r.o* **8/1**
1063 3 nk **Fitz Flyer (IRE)**[16] 6189 7-8-7 **88** ....(v) JordanNason(7) 3 94
(David Nicholls) *trckd ldrs: led 3f out: rdn and hdd 1f out: styd on* **8/1**
1-00 4 nk **Pearl Blue (IRE)**[115] 2848 5-9-4 **92** .... GeorgeBaker 9 97+
(Chris Wall) *hld up: hdwy and nt clr run over 1f out: hmpd ins fnl f: r.o* **14/1**
3352 5 nk **Commanche**[12] 6309 4-8-5 **82** ow1 .... RobertTart(3) 8 86
(Chris Dwyer) *chsd ldrs: pushed along 1/2-way: rdn over 1f out: styd on* **4/1**[1]
4020 6 1 **Rebecca Romero**[16] 6189 6-8-9 **83** ow1 .... JamesDoyle 11 83
(Denis Coakley) *hld up: pushed along 1/2-way: r.o ins fnl f: nt rch ldrs* **16/1**
0255 7 ½ **Moorhouse Lad**[17] 6159 10-8-9 **83** .... AndrewMullen 4 81
(Garry Moss) *led 2f: remained handy: rdn over 1f out: edgd rt ins fnl f: styd on same pce* **16/1**
0160 8 nk **Noodles Blue Boy**[12] 6309 7-8-2 **81** oh2 ....(p) ConnorBeasley(5) 13 78
(Ollie Pears) *mid-div: drvn along 1/2-way: hdwy u.p over 1f out: nt clr run ins fnl f: styd on same pce* **16/1**
1000 9 nk **Another Wise Kid (IRE)**[37] 5519 5-9-0 **88** .... JimmyQuinn 6 84
(Paul Midgley) *s.i.s: hdwy over 3f out: rdn over 1f out: styd on same pce ins fnl f* **20/1**
0500 10 ½ **Taajub (IRE)**[57] 4800 6-9-3 **91** .... AdamKirby 12 85
(Peter Crate) *mid-div: rdn whn nt clr run ins fnl f: nt rch ldrs* **6/1**[3]
2055 11 2 ½ **Bispham Green**[30] 5769 3-8-6 **81** ....(t) PaulHanagan 10 66
(Richard Fahey) *chsd ldrs: rdn 1/2-way: wknd fnl f* **8/1**
0560 12 1 ½ **Pandar**[23] 5998 4-9-3 **91** ....(v[1]) LiamJones 1 71
(Robert Cowell) *chsd ldrs: drvn along 1/2-way: wknd fnl f* **25/1**
015 13 hd **Forest Edge (IRE)**[102] 3249 4-9-4 **95** .... DeclanBates(3) 7 74
(David Evans) *a in rr* **20/1**

59.81s (-0.19) **Going Correction** -0.025s/f (Good)
WFA 3 from 4yo+ 1lb **13 Ran SP% 122.0**
Speed ratings (Par 107): **100,98,97,97,96 94,94,93,93,92 88,86,85**
toteswingers 1&2 £11.60, 2&3 £13.00, 1&3 £3.90 CSF £44.49 CT £334.61 TOTE £3.10: £1.60, £4.10, £3.20; EX 35.60 Trifecta £710.60 Pool: £993.59 - 1.04 winning units..
Owner Elite Racing Club **Bred** Elite Racing Club **Trained** Kingsclere, Hants

FOCUS
A strong renewal of this handicap. The winner continues to progress and the third is a solid guide.

6700 HENRY ALKEN CLASSIFIED CLAIMING STKS 1m 1f 218y
4:30 (4:31) (Class 5) 3-4-Y-O **£2,587** (£770; £384; £192) **Stalls** Low

Form RPR
6400 1 **Bling King**[7] 6468 4-8-11 71 .... JordanNason(7) 4 72
(Geoffrey Harker) *a.p: rdn to ld over 1f out: styd on* **9/2**[3]
5566 2 1 ¼ **Juvenal (IRE)**[16] 6215 4-9-7 75 .... RichardHughes 5 73
(Richard Hannon) *hld up: swtchd lft and hdwy over 2f out: rdn to chse wnr fnl f: unable qck towards fin* **9/4**[1]
2323 3 1 ¾ **Thereabouts (USA)**[160] 1600 4-9-5 66 .... AndrewMullen 9 67
(Michael Appleby) *hld up: hdwy over 2f out: rdn over 1f out: hung rt and styd on same pce ins fnl f* **6/1**
3633 4 3 ½ **Suspension**[29] 5791 3-8-9 51 .... RobertHavlin 3 56
(Hughie Morrison) *led: rdn and hdd over 1f out: wknd ins fnl f* **16/1**
0020 5 1 ¼ **Voice From Above (IRE)**[12] 6297 4-9-3 63 .... RussKennemore 6 56
(Patrick Holmes) *hld up: pushed along over 4f out: hdwy over 2f out: wknd fnl f* **10/1**
4524 6 7 **Stag Hill (IRE)**[13] 6283 4-8-12 60 ....(p) JoeyHaynes(5) 2 42
(Bernard Llewellyn) *prom: rdn over 2f out: wknd over 1f out* **10/1**
10 7 7 **Mandy The Nag (USA)**[46] 5181 3-8-13 75 .... NeilCallan 7 39
(Ian Williams) *trckd ldr: rdn over 2f out: wknd over 1f out* **7/2**[2]
6000 8 38 **Thecornishwren (IRE)**[29] 5803 4-8-10 31 ....(v[1]) RyanPowell(3) 1
(John Ryan) *chsd ldrs: rdn over 3f out: wknd over 2f out* **200/1**
000 9 18 **Inigo Montoya**[117] 2770 3-8-5 51 .... DeclanCannon(3) 8
(Alan McCabe) *s.i.s: a in rr: wknd 1/2-way* **100/1**

2m 8.93s (1.03) **Going Correction** +0.20s/f (Good)
WFA 3 from 4yo 6lb **9 Ran SP% 111.0**
Speed ratings (Par 103): **103,102,100,97,96 91,85,55,40**
toteswingers 1&2 £4.90, 2&3 £5.30, 1&3 £15.40 CSF £14.10 TOTE £7.20: £1.90, £1.10, £2.60; EX 16.50 Trifecta £97.10 Pool: £499.20 - 3.85 winning units..
Owner P I Harker **Bred** Whitsbury Manor Stud And Mrs M E Slade **Trained** Thirkleby, N Yorks

FOCUS
A modes trestricted claimer, and the form is limited by the fourth.

6701 HIGHFIELDS H'CAP 1m 60y
5:00 (5:02) (Class 5) (0-75,75) 3-Y-O+ **£3,234** (£962; £481; £240) **Stalls** Low

Form RPR
3331 1 **Knight Owl**[53] 4928 3-9-3 **74** .... ShaneKelly 13 83+
(James Fanshawe) *a.p: shkn up over 1f out: styd on to ld wl ins fnl f* **8/1**
0515 2 ½ **Soaring Spirits (IRE)**[33] 5632 3-9-3 **74** ....(b) AndreaAtzeni 5 82
(Roger Varian) *led: rdn over 2f out: hdd wl ins fnl f* **6/1**[3]
1 3 ¾ **Rainbow Beauty**[23] 6003 3-9-3 **74** ....(p) NeilCallan 9 80+
(Gerard Butler) *hld up: hdwy over 3f out: nt clr run over 1f out: sn rdn: edgd rt ins fnl f: r.o* **5/1**[2]
1123 4 ¾ **Aqua Ardens (GER)**[47] 5124 5-9-4 **71** ....(t) PatCosgrave 8 76
(George Baker) *chsd ldrs: rdn over 1f out: styd on same pce ins fnl f* **10/1**
6603 5 2 ¼ **Eurystheus (IRE)**[4] 6562 4-9-7 **74** .... AndrewMullen 6 73
(Michael Appleby) *dwlt: hld up: hdwy over 3f out: rdn over 1f out: styng on same pce whn nt clr run ins fnl f* **9/2**[1]
216 6 ½ **Ethel**[70] 4348 3-9-4 **75** .... RobertHavlin 7 73
(John Gosden) *trckd ldrs: racd keenly: rdn over 1f out: styd on same pce fnl f* **12/1**
2000 7 2 **President Lincoln (USA)**[15] 6236 5-9-5 **75** .... NeilFarley(3) 14 69
(Declan Carroll) *trckd ldr: rdn over 2f out: no ex fnl f* **16/1**
5203 8 ½ **Gioia Di Vita**[28] 5835 3-9-2 **73** .... AdrianNicholls 11 65
(David Nicholls) *mid-div: rdn over 2f out: no imp fnl f* **16/1**
0115 9 1 ¼ **Siouxperhero (IRE)**[10] 6360 4-9-2 **69** ....(p) JamesDoyle 4 59
(William Muir) *hld up: rdn over 2f out: nt trble ldrs* **12/1**
0460 10 1 ½ **Chapter And Verse (IRE)**[16] 6199 7-9-6 **73** .... RichardHughes 2 59+
(Mike Murphy) *hld up: hmpd 3f out: n.d* **6/1**[3]
4165 11 ½ **West End Lad**[4] 6567 10-9-2 **72** ....(b) MarkCoumbe(3) 1 57
(Roy Bowring) *hld up: rdn over 3f out: wknd over 1f out* **14/1**
-000 12 81 **Embankment**[17] 6167 4-9-5 **72** ....(p) GeorgeBaker 10
(William Jarvis) *reluctant to s: a wl bhd* **25/1**

1m 46.03s (0.93) **Going Correction** +0.20s/f (Good)
WFA 3 from 4yo+ 4lb **12 Ran SP% 121.3**
Speed ratings (Par 103): **103,102,101,101,98 98,96,95,94,93 92,11**
toteswingers 1&2 £8.70, 2&3 £7.20, 1&3 £6.30 CSF £56.79 CT £275.29 TOTE £7.60: £3.40, £2.60, £1.70; EX 56.90 Trifecta £296.40 Part won. Pool: £395.24 - 0.49 winning units..
Owner Miss Annabelle Condon **Bred** Car Colston Hall Stud **Trained** Newmarket, Suffolk
■ Stewards' Enquiry : Mark Coumbe three-day ban: careless riding (7-9 Sep)

FOCUS
A hugely competitive handicap run at stern pace. The first three were all 3yos and the form seems fine.

6702 RACING EXCELLENCE "HANDS AND HEELS" APPRENTICE SERIES H'CAP 7f 9y
5:30 (5:30) (Class 5) (0-70,75) 3-Y-O+ **£2,587** (£770; £384; £192) **Stalls** Centre

Form RPR
4650 1 **Living The Life (IRE)**[23] 6003 3-9-0 **70** ....(b[1]) JohnLawson(5) 1 83
(Jamie Osborne) *sn led: clr 3f out: sn hung lft: shkn up over 1f out: styd on: unchal* **8/1**[3]
1000 2 6 **Dancing Maite**[4] 6568 8-8-8 **59** ....(b) JonathanWilletts(3) 17 57
(Roy Bowring) *chsd wnr: pushed along over 2f out: styd on same pce fr over 1f out* **25/1**
5051 3 3 **Pearl Queen (USA)**[20] 6074 3-8-12 **68** .... SamuelClarke(5) 11 57+
(Chris Wall) *hld up: racd keenly: hdwy over 2f out: styd on: nt trble ldrs* **5/1**[2]
6163 4 nk **Hamble**[34] 5622 4-8-8 **56** ....(t) ShelleyBirkett 15 45
(Julia Feilden) *hld up: hdwy over 1f out: r.o: nt rch ldrs* **12/1**
4513 5 ½ **Red Paladin (IRE)**[17] 6181 3-9-5 **70** ....(p) KevinStott 12 57+
(Kevin Ryan) *hld up: hdwy over 2f out: pushed along and edgd lft over 1f out: no ex fnl f* **9/2**[1]
0211 6 hd **Tenbridge**[28] 5816 4-9-2 **64** ....(v) EoinWalsh 14 51
(Derek Haydn Jones) *sn outpcd: hdwy over 1f out: r.o: nt rch ldrs* **8/1**[3]
0501 7 nk **Imperator Augustus (IRE)**[34] 5614 5-9-5 **70** .... JackGarritty(3) 5 56
(Patrick Holmes) *hld up: hdwy 1/2-way: no ex fnl f* **12/1**
2045 8 2 ¼ **Rough Rock (IRE)**[14] 6259 8-8-12 **60** ....(v) ConnorBeasley 10 40
(Chris Dwyer) *prom: pushed along 1/2-way: wknd fnl f* **33/1**
5136 9 nk **Bold Ring**[58] 4746 7-8-11 **62** .... DavidParkes(3) 8 41
(Edward Creighton) *chsd ldrs: pushed along 1/2-way: wknd fnl f* **25/1**
1150 10 1 ¾ **Angel Cake (IRE)**[16] 6210 4-9-1 **66** .... AaronJones(3) 2 41
(Michael Appleby) *trckd ldrs: stmbld over 4f out: sn lost pl: n.d after* **25/1**
0555 11 4 ½ **Danz Choice (IRE)**[32] 5668 3-8-10 **66** .... StephenKing(5) 18 27
(Richard Hannon) *hld up: pushed along 1/2-way: nvr on terms* **33/1**
4600 12 hd **Quadriga (IRE)**[97] 3434 3-8-12 **63** ....(v[1]) LouisSteward 7 24
(Robert Eddery) *trckd ldrs: pushed along over 2f out: wkng whn hung rt fr over 1f out* **25/1**
3043 13 ½ **Moortahan**[18] 6146 3-8-11 **67** .... CameronHardie(5) 4 27
(Richard Hannon) *sn pushed along towards rr: bhd fnl 2f* **25/1**
6554 14 1 ¼ **True Spirit**[52] 4962 3-8-5 **61** .... StaceyKidd(5) 6 17
(Paul D'Arcy) *mid-div: hdwy over 4f out: wknd over 2f out* **33/1**
3332 15 2 ¼ **Shaolin (IRE)**[20] 6075 3-9-4 **69** ....(t) PatMillman 16 19
(Seamus Durack) *s.s: swtchd rt sn after s: sme hdwy 1/2-way: wknd 2f out* **9/2**[1]
0000 16 40 **Esprit De Midas**[16] 6215 7-9-5 **70** .... PaulBooth(3) 3
(Dean Ivory) *chsd ldrs: pushed along 1/2-way: wknd over 2f out* **25/1**

1m 25.97s (-0.23) **Going Correction** -0.025s/f (Good)
WFA 3 from 4yo+ 3lb **16 Ran SP% 122.5**
Speed ratings (Par 103): **100,93,89,89,88 88,88,85,85,83 78,77,77,75,73 27**
toteswingers 1&2 £30.60, 2&3 £27.30, 1&3 £4.30 CSF £200.20 CT £1143.94 TOTE £9.70: £4.00, £6.80, £2.60, £1.10; EX 263.20 TRIFECTA Not won..
Owner Michael Buckley **Bred** Michael Begley **Trained** Upper Lambourn, Berks

FOCUS
A devilishly competitive handicap, but it was turned into a procession by the winner. The first two dominated and it's hard to know how literally to take the form.
T/Jkpt: Not won. T/Plt: £160.70 to a £1 stake. Pool of £92628.83 - 420.77 winning tickets.
T/Qpdt: £11.40 to a £1 stake. Pool of £7817.53 - 504.04 winning tickets.. CR

6703 - 6709a (Foreign Racing) - See Raceform Interactive

6445 LONGCHAMP (R-H)
Saturday, September 21
OFFICIAL GOING: Turf: soft

6710a PRIX DES CHENES (GROUP 3) (2YO COLTS & GELDINGS) (TURF) 1m
11:30 (12:00) 2-Y-O **£32,520** (£13,008; £9,756; £6,504; £3,252)

RPR
1 **Ectot**[32] 5628 2-9-2 0 .... GregoryBenoist 4 108
(E Lellouche, France) *hld up in tch: 4th 1/2-way: hdwy to chal 2f out: shkn up and led over 1f out: edgd rt but qcknd smartly and sn clr: coasted home ins fnl 100yds: easily* **6/5**[1]
2 3 **Elliptique (IRE)**[32] 5628 2-9-2 0 .... MaximeGuyon 1 101
(A Fabre, France) *stdd and hld up in last: rdn over 2f out: r.o and wnt 2nd towards fin: no ch w easy wnr* **9/2**[3]
3 2 ½ **Daraybi (FR)**[13] 6249 2-9-2 0 .... ChristopheSoumillon 3 96
(A De Royer-Dupre, France) *trckd ldr in 2nd: chal gng wl 2f out: sn led: rdn and hdd over 1f out: readily outpcd by wnr: no ex and dropped to 3rd towards fin* **6/4**[2]
4 5 ½ **Under The Radar (FR)**[28] 2-9-2 0 .... GeraldMosse 5 84
(F Doumen, France) *led: jnd 3f out: rdn 2f out: sn hdd: no ex and btn: fdd* **13/1**
5 1 **Rising Breeze (FR)**[25] 5875 2-9-2 0 .... IoritzMendizabal 2 82
(K R Burke) *midfield in tch: 3rd 1/2-way: hdwy to join ldr 3f out: rdn and hdd 2f out: no ex and btn: fdd and dropped to last over 1f out* **11/1**

1m 43.11s (4.71) **5 Ran SP% 119.1**
WIN (incl. 1 euro stake): 2.20. PLACES: 1.30, 1.80. SF: 5.70.
Owner G Augustin-Normand & Mme E Vidal **Bred** Ecurie Des Monceaux & Skymarc Farm **Trained** Lamorlaye, France

6711a PRIX DU PALAIS D'ART MODERNE (CLAIMER) (3YO) (TURF) 1m 4f
12:00 (12:00) 3-Y-O £7,723 (£3,089; £2,317; £1,544; £772)

RPR
1 Monastrella (FR) 3-8-8 0 GeraldMosse 12 75
(A Wohler, Germany) 119/10
2 4 Zamfara 3-8-8 0 UmbertoRispoli 6 68
(P Schiergen, Germany) 9/1
3 1 1/2 Portland River (FR)[70] 3-9-5 0 AntoineHamelin 11 77
(A De Royer-Dupre, France) 19/5[1]
4 3/4 Peaceful Mind (GER) 3-8-13 0 TheoBachelot 4 70
(P Schiergen, Germany) 21/1
5 8 Dublin (GER)[5] 3-8-8 0 (b) AlexisBadel 14 52
(M Nigge, France) 38/1
6 2 Les Affres (FR)[270] 3-8-13 0 JimmyTastayre(5) 2 59
(C Boutin, France) 96/1
7 nk Magical Empress (IRE)[60] 3-9-1 0 MaximeGuyon 13 55
(Mme Pia Brandt, France) 4/1[2]
8 1/2 Star Of Namibia (IRE)[24] [5914] 3-8-11 0 (b) SoufyaneMoulin(4) 9 55
(J S Moore) *prom: rdn 3f out: sn outpcd and btn: fdd* 58/10[3]
9 3 Silver Axe (FR)[42] 3-9-5 0 GregoryBenoist 5 54
(Mme P Butel, France) 32/1
10 6 Magic Mirage (FR)[21] 3-8-8 0 (b) CesarPasserat(3) 7 36
(Y Barberot, France) 14/1
11 2 Spanish Art[21] 3-9-2 0 (b) SylvainRuis 1 38
(Mlle M Henry, France) 13/2
12 4 Touch Of Fire (IRE) 3-9-1 0 MarcLerner 10 31
(C Lerner, France) 33/1
13 3/4 Krymka (IRE) 3-8-8 0 JeromeClaudic 3 22
(C Laffon-Parias, France) 10/1
2m 41.19s (10.79) 13 Ran SP% 116.5
WIN (incl. 1 euro stake): 12.90. PLACES: 3.60, 3.30, 2.10. DF: 53.70. SF: 132.20.
Owner Stall Bodega **Bred** Stall Bodega **Trained** Germany

6712a PRIX DU PRINCE D'ORANGE (GROUP 3) (3YO) (TURF) 1m 2f
1:00 (12:00) 3-Y-O £32,520 (£13,008; £9,756; £6,504; £3,252)

RPR
1 Intello (GER)[41] [5314] 3-9-2 0 OlivierPeslier 6 116+
(A Fabre, France) *midfield in tch on outer: 3rd 1/2-way: shkn up to chal 2f out: led over 1f out: in control and pushed out ins fnl f: comf* 2/5[1]
2 3/4 Morandi (FR)[37] [5462] 3-9-2 0 ChristopheSoumillon 1 113
(J-C Rouget, France) *trckd ldr: led gng wl over 2f out: rdn and hdd over 1f out: styd on but no match for wnr ins fnl f* 3/1[2]
3 1/2 Zhiyi (USA)[37] [5462] 3-9-2 0 StephanePasquier 2 112
(P Bary, France) *dwlt sltly: midfield in tch on inner: rdn and looking for run 2f out: swtchd rt and wnt 3rd over 1f out: styd on but nt pce to chal* 6/1[3]
4 2 1/2 Lion D'Anvers (FR)[82] [3911] 3-9-2 0 UmbertoRispoli 3 107
(J Van Handenhove, France) *hld up in tch: rdn 2f out: sn outpcd by ldrs: styd on and jst hld on for 4th* 46/1
5 nse Royal Law (IRE)[40] [5361] 3-9-2 0 AdrienFouassier 5 107
(A Couetil, France) *dwlt and wnt lft s: hld up in last: rdn 2f out: sn outpcd by ldrs: styd on and almost snatched 4th post* 22/1
6 12 Paan (IRE)[21] 3-9-2 0 Pierre-CharlesBoudot 4 83
(A Fabre, France) *led: rdn and hdd over 2f out: no ex and btn: fdd and dropped to last over 1f out: eased* 32/1
2m 12.23s (8.23) 6 Ran SP% 120.2
WIN (incl. 1 euro stake): 1.40 (Intello coupled with Paan). PLACES: 1.10, 1.10. SF: 2.20.
Owner Wertheimer & Frere **Bred** Wertheimer Et Frere **Trained** Chantilly, France

6713a PRIX PERPLEXITE (H'CAP) (3YO) (TURF) 1m 2f
1:30 (12:00) 3-Y-O £12,195 (£4,878; £3,658; £2,439; £1,219)

RPR
1 Cubalibre (FR) 3-8-11 0 (b) ChristopheSoumillon 10 82
(P Sogorb, France) 67/10[2]
2 2 1/2 Maximum Velocity (FR)[95] [3454] 3-9-2 0 StephanePasquier 1 82
(J E Hammond, France) 6/1[1]
3 1 1/4 Sole Reign (FR)[20] 3-9-1 0 (b) Christophe-PatriceLemaire 9 78
(T Clout, France) 32/1
4 hd Golden Buck (FR)[25] 3-9-5 0 RonanThomas 3 82
(P Van De Poele, France) 14/1
5 snk Murillo (FR)[27] [5805] 3-8-10 0 CristianDemuro 18 72
(J-M Beguigne, France) 83/10[3]
6 1 3/4 Chene Boppe (FR)[29] 3-9-3 0 CesarPasserat 11 76
(F-X De Chevigny, France) 17/2
7 snk Sermoneta (IRE)[60] 3-9-5 0 Pierre-CharlesBoudot 2 78
(G Botti, France) 25/1
8 shd Dynamoon (FR)[29] 3-8-13 0 (b) ThierryJarnet 16 71
(H-A Pantall, France) 28/1
9 shd La Messalina (FR)[17] 3-9-3 0 SylvainRuis 20 75
(Alex Fracas, France) 34/1
10 hd Pearl Goddess[19] 3-9-4 0 UmbertoRispoli 4 76
(M Delzangles, France) 9/1
11 nk Valley Girl (FR)[101] 3-9-5 0 FabriceVeron 15 76
(H-A Pantall, France) 31/1
12 1 1/4 Victory De Rebecq (USA)[29] 3-8-11 0 PaulineProd'homme 14 66
(D Prod'Homme, France) 73/1
13 1 1/4 Zigzag (FR)[19] 3-9-3 0 FabienLefebvre 17 69
(J E Hammond, France) 17/1
14 1 1/2 Secret Taboo (FR)[89] 3-8-10 0 TheoBachelot 8 59
(A Lyon, France) 62/1
15 3/4 Alito[25] 3-9-6 0 OlivierPeslier 5 68
(W Hickst, Germany) 11/1
16 9 Chaudhary (SWI)[13] 3-9-4 0 AntoineHamelin 7 48
(U Suter, France) 18/1
17 1/2 Jee Pee And Jeremy (FR)[24] [5914] 3-8-9 0 MaximeGuyon 12 38
(Mme Pia Brandt, France) 28/1
18 3 Just Hurricane (FR)[25] 3-9-4 0 (p) IoritzMendizabal 6 41
(F Chappet, France) 28/1
19 13 Lucax (FR) 3-9-2 0 EddyHardouin 19 13
(Mlle V Dissaux, France) 106/1
20 15 Teolagi (IRE)[24] [5914] 3-9-3 0 SoufyaneMoulin 13
(J S Moore) *midfield on outer: rdn over 2f out: lost pl rapidly and dropped to last w rdr looking down as if smething amiss: eased and tailed rt off* 19/1
2m 14.16s (10.16) 20 Ran SP% 116.4
WIN (incl. 1 euro stake): 7.70. PLACES: 3.20, 2.70, 7.80. DF: 19.20. SF: 38.50.
Owner S Kinast & J Levallois **Bred** O Piraud **Trained** France

6714a PRIX D'AUTOMNE - FONDS EUROPEEN DE L'ELEVAGE (LISTED RACE) (3YO+ FILLIES & MARES) (TURF) 1m 1f
2:08 (12:00) 3-Y-O+ £19,512 (£7,804; £5,853; £3,902; £1,951)

RPR
1 Glowing Cloud[27] 4-9-2 JulienAuge 9 103+
(C Ferland, France) 172/10
2 snk Topaze Blanche (IRE)[55] [4817] 3-8-11 0 Christophe-PatriceLemaire 8 104
(C Laffon-Parias, France) 23/10[1]
3 1 Odeliz (IRE)[20] [6031] 3-8-11 0 AntoineHamelin 2 102
(K R Burke) *restrained and settled in midfield on inner: nt clr run fr 2f out tl swtchd lft and rdn over 1f out: r.o strly ins fnl f and wnt 3rd post* 11/2[3]
4 shd Table Ronde (IRE)[37] [5461] 3-8-11 0 ChristopheSoumillon 6 101
(J-C Rouget, France) 33/10[2]
5 3/4 Kenbella (FR)[17] [6124] 3-8-11 0 FabriceVeron 3 100
(H-A Pantall, France) 16/1
6 1 Matauri Pearl (IRE)[22] 4-9-2 0 MaximeGuyon 5 97
(Mme Pia Brandt, France) 38/1
7 3/4 Keegsquaw (IRE)[22] 4-9-2 0 Pierre-CharlesBoudot 10 95
(Mme A Fabre, France) 15/1
8 snk L'Espagna (FR)[63] [4555] 4-9-2 0 AnthonyCrastus 11 95
(P Khozian, France) 24/1
9 1/2 Shahad (IRE)[58] [4700] 3-8-11 OlivierPeslier 7 95
(F Head, France) 20/1
10 3/4 Shanjia (GER)[40] [5360] 4-9-2 IoritzMendizabal 12 92
(Frau C Brandstatter, Germany) 13/1
11 1 1/4 Elenya (IRE)[24] 4-9-2 0 UmbertoRispoli 1 90
(M Cesandri, France) 26/1
12 snk Hasna (FR)[22] 4-9-2 0 StephanePasquier 4 89
(P Bary, France) 14/1
1m 57.44s (5.84)
WFA 3 from 4yo 5lb 12 Ran SP% 115.4
WIN (incl. 1 euro stake): 18.20. PLACES: 4.10, 1.70, 2.40. DF: 28.50. SF: 78.20.
Owner Simon Springer **Bred** Yeguada Milagro & Balmerino Bloodstock **Trained** France

6715 - (Foreign Racing) - See Raceform Interactive

6511 BEVERLEY (R-H)
Tuesday, September 24

OFFICIAL GOING: Good to firm (9.2)
Wind: Virtually nil Weather: Overcast

6716 BRITISH STALLION STUDS EBF MAIDEN STKS 7f 100y
2:10 (2:10) (Class 5) 2-Y-O £3,408 (£1,006; £503) Stalls Low

Form RPR
32 1 Our Channel (USA)[15] [6256] 2-9-5 0 LiamJones 2 87
(William Haggas) *cl up: led wl over 2f out: rdn clr over 1f out: styd on strly* 2/1[2]
02 2 8 Rawoof (IRE)[38] [5516] 2-9-0 0 PaulHanagan 5 63
(Ed Dunlop) *chsd ldrs: hdwy 1/2-way: chsd ldng pair over 2f out and sn rdn: drvn over 1f out: kpt on to take mod 2nd ins fnl f: no ch w wnr* 6/4[1]
5 3 1/2 Blazers Rock (IRE)[19] [6125] 2-9-5 0 NeilCallan 1 67
(Kevin Ryan) *awkward s and t.k.h: sn led: pushed along 3f out: hdd wl over 2f out: sn rdn: drvn and one pce appr fnl f* 4/1[3]
04 4 1 Native Falls (IRE)[123] [2631] 2-9-5 0 AndrewMullen 3 65
(Alan Swinbank) *t.k.h: trckd ldrs: effrt wl over 2f out: sn rdn along and no imp* 50/1
00 5 3 1/2 Victory Danz (IRE)[18] [6175] 2-9-5 0 DavidNolan 7 56
(David O'Meara) *a in rr* 100/1
06 6 1 1/4 Modify[36] [5577] 2-9-0 0 (v[1]) RoystonFfrench 6 49
(Bryan Smart) *t.k.h early: a in rr* 40/1
0 7 1/2 Filament Of Gold (USA)[15] [6256] 2-9-5 0 AdrianNicholls 4 52
(Mark Johnston) *chsd ldrs: pushed along bef 1/2-way: sn rdn: and lost pl: outpcd and btb fnl 3f* 8/1
1m 32.0s (-1.80) **Going Correction** -0.275s/f (Firm) 7 Ran SP% 109.8
Speed ratings (Par 95): **99,89,89,88,84 82,82**
Tote Swingers: 1&2 £1.60, 1&3 £1.70, 2&3 £1.40 CSF £4.90 TOTE £3.40: £2.50, £1.20; EX 4.90 Trifecta £12.70 Pool: £3,833.14 - 226.00 winning units..
Owner Abdulla Al Mansoori **Bred** Bluegrass Hall Llc **Trained** Newmarket, Suffolk
FOCUS
Track at normal configuration and distances as advertised. Not a maiden with a great deal of depth.

6717 BEVERLEY ANNUAL BADGEHOLDERS (S) STKS 1m 4f 16y
2:40 (2:40) (Class 5) 3-4-Y-O £3,234 (£962; £481; £240) Stalls Low

Form RPR
2303 1 Bold And Free[11] [6357] 3-8-8 62 (p) JamieSpencer 1 66+
(David Elsworth) *trckd ldng pair: hdwy 3f out: swtchd lft and effrt to chal 2f out: sn led: rdn clr appr fnl f: readily* 13/8[1]
4040 2 9 Halfwaytocootehill (IRE)[11] [6361] 3-8-8 49 (tp) PaulHanagan 6 52
(Ollie Pears) *trckd ldrs: hdwy 3f out: chal on outer 2f out: sn rdn and ev ch tl drvn appr fnl f and kpt on same pce* 6/1
4-50 3 3/4 Likelikelikelikeit[8] [6479] 3-8-3 55 (b[1]) LiamJones 3 45
(Mark H Tompkins) *hld up and bhd: pushed along over 3f out: swtchd lft to outer and rdn 2f out: styd on u.p appr fnl f: nrst fin* 14/1
3600 4 4 1/2 Assizes[26] [5918] 4-9-2 70 DaleSwift 5 43
(Ruth Carr) *led: pushed along 3f out: rdn over 2f out: hdd wl over 1f out: grad wknd* 9/4[2]
545 5 shd Jd Rockefeller[30] [5801] 3-8-8 40 (b) ChrisCatlin 7 43
(Paul D'Arcy) *dwlt: hld up in rr: sme hdwy 3f out: rdn along 2f out: n.d* 25/1
0053 6 2 1/4 Threepence[52] [5010] 3-8-8 45 (p) PaulQuinn 4 39
(Richard Whitaker) *awkward s: t.k.h: chsd ldrs: rdn along wl over 3f out: sn outpcd* 20/1
0340 7 3 1/2 Grammar[14] [6290] 4-9-4 50 (e) JasonHart(3) 8 39
(David Thompson) *cl up: rdn along wl over 2f out: drvn wl over 1f out: sn wknd* 5/1[3]

50 **8** *15* **Inka Express**[7] 6498 3-8-3 0....................(t) PatrickMathers 2 5
(Mike Sowersby) *in tch: pushed along and lost pl over 4f out: bhd fnl 2f* **100/1**

2m 35.86s (-3.94) **Going Correction** -0.275s/f (Firm)
WFA 3 from 4yo 8lb **8** Ran SP% **116.1**
Speed ratings (Par 103): **102,96,95,92,92 90,88,78**
Tote Swingers: 1&2 £3.30, 1&3 £5.30, 2&3 £7.70 CSF £12.11 TOTE £2.20: £1.30, £1.50, £3.00; EX 12.80 Trifecta £90.20 Pool: £2,910.40 - 24.10 winning units..Winner sold to Mrs A.Duffield for £7,000.
Owner Ten Green Bottles II **Bred** M E Broughton **Trained** Newmarket, Suffolk

FOCUS
A one-sided seller.

6718 THANKS FOR YOUR SUPPORT IN 2013 MAIDEN AUCTION STKS 5f
3:10 (3:10) (Class 4) 2-Y-O **£4,690** (£1,395; £697; £348) **Stalls** Low

Form RPR

2322 **1** **Stellarta**[12] 6320 2-8-5 70.................... PaulHanagan 3 69
(Michael Blanshard) *trckd ldrs: hdwy over 1f out: rdn to ld ent fnl f: kpt on* **7/4**[1]

3522 **2** *2 ¼* **Fredricka**[28] 5857 2-8-4 65 ow2.................... JasonHart(3) 5 63
(Garry Moss) *slt ld: rdn wl over 1f out: drvn and hdd ent fnl f: kpt on same pce* **11/2**[3]

30 **3** *¾* **Too Elusive**[27] 5877 2-8-8 0.................... JacobButterfield(5) 4 66
(Kristin Stubbs) *in tch: rdn along 1/2-way: drvn and hung lft over 1f out: edgd rt and kpt on ins fnl f: nrst fin* **17/2**

523 **4** *nk* **Gold Club**[19] 6127 2-8-9 74.................... GrahamGibbons 6 61
(Ed McMahon) *cl up: effrt 2f out: sn rdn and ev ch tl drvn appr fnl f and kpt on one pce* **12/5**[2]

545 **5** *4 ½* **Chuckamental**[43] 5350 2-8-12 64....................(t) RoystonFfrench 2 48
(Bryan Smart) *cl up: rdn along 2f out: ev ch tl drvn and wknd appr fnl f* **14/1**

6 *5* **Spinner Lane** 2-8-6 0.................... PaulQuinn 1 24+
(Richard Whitaker) *green: sn rdn along and a outpcd in rr* **10/1**

04 **7** *7* **Penny Pursuits**[18] 6160 2-8-5 0.................... BarryMcHugh 7
(Alan Berry) *green: sn rdn along in rr: a outpcd and bhd fr 1/2-way* **25/1**

1m 2.38s (-1.12) **Going Correction** -0.375s/f (Firm) **7** Ran SP% **111.3**
Speed ratings (Par 97): **93,89,88,87,80 72,61**
Tote Swingers: 1&2 £1.40, 1&3 £4.70, 2&3 £8.30 CSF £11.20 TOTE £2.20: £1.20, £1.90; EX 7.30 Trifecta £67.30 Pool: £2,243.75 - 24.99 winning units..
Owner Vincent Ward **Bred** Whitsbury Manor Stud & Pigeon House Stud **Trained** Upper Lambourn, Berks

FOCUS
A very ordinary maiden.

6719 EDDIE AND VIOLET SMITH CONDITIONS STKS 5f
3:40 (3:42) (Class 3) 3-Y-O+
£7,158 (£2,143; £1,071; £535; £267; £134) **Stalls** Low

Form RPR

0-02 **1** **Rocky Ground (IRE)**[14] 6282 3-8-8 96.................... JamieSpencer 1 104
(Roger Varian) *hld up in rr: hdwy and swtchd rt wl over 1f out: swtchd lft and rdn ent fnl f: styd on strly to squeeze through nr the fin and ld on line* **4/1**[1]

4456 **2** *hd* **Addictive Dream (IRE)**[10] 6391 6-8-2 96.................... JordanNason(7) 3 103
(David Nicholls) *trckd ldrs gng wl: smooth hdwy to chal ent fnl f: rdn and hung lft last 100yds: led nr fin: hdd on line* **10/1**

4304 **3** *nk* **Excelette (IRE)**[13] 6305 4-8-4 102.................... RoystonFfrench 8 97
(Bryan Smart) *sn led: rdn over 1f out: drvn ins fnl f: hdd and no ex nr fin* **13/2**[3]

0035 **4** *1 ¼* **Borderlescott**[13] 6305 11-8-6 105.................... JasonHart(3) 10 97
(Robin Bastiman) *trckd ldrs: rdn along wl over 1f out: kpt on same pce fnl f* **8/1**

0005 **5** *1 ¾* **Monsieur Joe (IRE)**[14] 6282 6-8-9 100.................... GrahamGibbons 2 91
(Robert Cowell) *cl up: rdn along wl over 1f out: drvn appr fnl f: grad wknd* **25/1**

0000 **6** *nse* **Doc Hay (USA)**[10] 6391 6-8-9 100.................... TonyHamilton 7 91
(David O'Meara) *dwlt and swtchd rt to inner s: bhd: effrt and n.m.r on inner wl over 1f out: swtchd lft and rdn ent fnl f: styd on towards fin* **8/1**

1106 **7** *¾* **Swendab (IRE)**[24] 5998 5-8-4 86....................(v) OisinMurphy(5) 5 88
(John O'Shea) *nvr bttr than midfield* **20/1**

0506 **8** *¾* **Hoyam**[13] 6305 3-8-3 99.................... ChrisCatlin 4 81
(Michael Bell) *dwlt and towards rr: swtchd to outer and sme hdwy 1/2-way: rdn along wl over 1f out: n.d* **12/1**

0000 **9** *3 ¾* **Tiddliwinks**[32] 5726 7-8-9 104.................... NeilCallan 6 72
(Kevin Ryan) *trckd ldrs: effrt wl over 1f out: sn rdn and wknd* **4/1**[1]

0-24 **10** *2* **Valbchek (IRE)**[31] 5747 4-8-9 102....................(p) PaulHanagan 9 65
(Jeremy Noseda) *chsd ldrs on outer: rdn along 2f out: sn wknd* **5/1**[2]

1m 0.35s (-3.15) **Going Correction** -0.375s/f (Firm)
WFA 3 from 4yo+ 1lb **10** Ran SP% **117.6**
Speed ratings (Par 107): **110,109,109,107,104 104,103,101,95,92**
Tote Swingers: 1&2 £7.30, 1&3 £6.80, 2&3 £14.10 CSF £45.28 TOTE £3.80: £1.50, £4.40, £1.80; EX 45.20 Trifecta £436.70 Pool: £2,164.66 - 3.71 winning units..
Owner Clipper Logistics & Cheveley Park Stud **Bred** Messrs Mark Hanly & James Hanly **Trained** Newmarket, Suffolk

FOCUS
A very useful sprint which was run at a good pace.

6720 GEORGE KILBURN MEMORIAL H'CAP 7f 100y
4:10 (4:11) (Class 5) (0-75,75) 3-Y-O+ **£3,234** (£962; £481; £240) **Stalls** Low

Form RPR

0350 **1** **Sardanapalus**[13] 6306 4-9-1 69....................(p) TonyHamilton 1 77
(Kevin Ryan) *trckd ldrs on inner: swtchd lft 2f out: rdn over 1f out: drvn and styd on wl fnl f to ld nr fin* **14/1**

2600 **2** *hd* **Majestic Dream (IRE)**[39] 5481 5-9-2 70.................... GrahamGibbons 3 78
(Michael Easterby) *trckd ldrs on inner: hdwy 2f out: swtchd lft over 1f out: sn rdn to chal: led last 100yds: edgd lft: drvn: hdd and no ex nr fin* **20/1**

0000 **3** *1 ¾* **Mujaadel (USA)**[43] 5341 8-8-7 61....................(p) AndrewMullen 2 64
(David Nicholls) *dwlt and hld up in rr: hdwy 2f out: rdn over 1f out: styd on ins fnl f: nrst fin* **9/1**

0035 **4** *hd* **Polish World (USA)**[24] 5987 9-9-0 68.................... BarryMcHugh 5 71
(Paul Midgley) *led: pushed along wl over 2f out: rdn over 1f out: drvn ent fnl f: hdd & wknd last 100yds* **7/1**[2]

1005 **5** *1* **Running Reef (IRE)**[18] 6181 4-8-13 67.................... RobertWinston 10 68
(Tracy Waggott) *t.k.h: hld up in rr: hdwy 2f out: swtchd lft and rdn wl over 1f out: drvn and kpt on fnl f: nrst fin* **20/1**

4266 **6** *nse* **Rich Forever (IRE)**[14] 6274 3-8-11 68....................(v) PaulHanagan 4 67
(James Bethell) *midfield: hdwy over 2f out: rdn along wl over 1f out: kpt on fnl f: nrst fin* **8/1**[3]

5504 **7** *½* **Space War**[25] 5948 6-8-10 67.................... JasonHart(3) 7 68
(Michael Easterby) *s.i.s and hld up in rr: hdwy on inner 2f out: effrt and n.m.r over 1f out: trckd ldrs whn nt clr run ins fnl f: no ch after* **14/1**

2411 **8** *½* **Peak Storm**[7] 6489 4-9-0 73 6ex....................(p) DanielMuscutt(5) 9 71
(John O'Shea) *chsd ldrs: rdn along over 2f out: drvn and wknd over 1f out* **10/1**

0004 **9** *5* **Desert Creek (IRE)**[28] 5861 7-9-0 75.................... AnnaHesketh(7) 13 61
(David Nicholls) *hld up: a towards rr* **7/1**[2]

3110 **10** *¾* **Pilates (IRE)**[12] 6337 3-9-1 72.................... NeilCallan 6 56
(Mark Johnston) *trckd ldr: cl up over 3f out: rdn along 2f out and ev ch tl drvn and wknd appr fnl f* **7/2**[1]

0502 **11** *3* **Relight My Fire**[4] 6602 3-8-12 74....................(b) DarylByrne(5) 14 51
(Tim Easterby) *trckd ldng pair: pushed along wl over 2f out: rdn wl over 1f out: grad wknd* **8/1**[3]

4404 **12** *53* **Evervescent (IRE)**[27] 5912 4-9-2 70....................(b) JamieSpencer 11
(J S Moore) *midfield on outer whn hung bdly lft bnd at 1/2-way: wd st: sn bhd and eased* **10/1**

1m 31.34s (-2.46) **Going Correction** -0.275s/f (Firm)
WFA 3 from 4yo+ 3lb **12** Ran SP% **120.5**
Speed ratings (Par 103): **103,102,100,100,99 99,98,98,92,91 88,27**
Tote Swingers: 1&2 £34.70, 1&3 £39.60, 2&3 £50.00 CSF £269.18 CT £1684.11 TOTE £19.00: £4.10, £6.50, £4.50; EX 230.40 Trifecta £639.30 Pool: £1,509.41 - 1.77 winning units..
Owner J Nixon **Bred** Rosyground Stud **Trained** Hambleton, N Yorks

FOCUS
A run-of-the-mill handicap. The gallop looked sound enough, possibly just steadying briefly at the end of the back straight.

6721 MPH LABEL H'CAP 1m 100y
4:40 (4:40) (Class 5) (0-75,75) 3-Y-O+ **£3,234** (£962; £481; £240) **Stalls** Low

Form RPR

0222 **1** **Border Bandit (USA)**[13] 6301 5-8-9 63....................(p) RobertWinston 6 70
(Tracy Waggott) *trckd ldr: cl up over 2f out: rdn along wl over 1f out: drvn to chal ent fnl f: kpt on wl to ld nr fin* **5/1**[2]

0014 **2** *hd* **Silverware (USA)**[24] 5978 5-9-7 75.................... GrahamGibbons 3 81
(Kristin Stubbs) *reminders s and sn led: rdn along 2f out: drvn ent fnl f: hdd and no ex nr fin* **9/1**

1-26 **3** *hd* **Ty Gwr**[17] 6200 4-9-3 71....................[1] DaleSwift 5 77
(Brian Ellison) *dwlt and in rr: hdwy 2f out: swtchd lft and rdn wl over 1f out: styd on ent fnl f: fin wl* **9/2**[1]

2140 **4** *½* **Hernando Torres**[2] 6667 5-8-1 62....................(p) AnnaHesketh(7) 1 67
(Michael Easterby) *hld up: hdwy on inner over 2f out: rdn to chse ldrs over 1f out: kpt on u.p fnl f* **5/1**[2]

21-0 **5** *1* **King Of The Celts (IRE)**[16] 6236 5-9-3 71.................... TonyHamilton 8 73
(Tim Easterby) *trckd ldrs on inner: hdwy over 2f out: swtchd lft and rdn to chse ldng pair over 1f out: drvn and kpt on same pce fnl f* **10/1**

0250 **6** *3* **Shadowtime**[5] 6567 8-9-7 75.................... BarryMcHugh 2 70
(Tracy Waggott) *hld up: hdwy wl over 2f out: rdn wl over 1f out: no imp fnl f* **8/1**[3]

0321 **7** *1 ¾* **Summer Dancer (IRE)**[8] 6464 9-8-12 66 6ex.................... RoystonFfrench 4 57
(Paul Midgley) *hld up in rr: effrt and sme hdwy on wd outside 2f out: sn rdn and n.d* **9/1**

120 **8** *3 ¼* **Nightster (IRE)**[12] 6335 3-9-3 75.................... NeilCallan 9 59
(Mark Johnston) *trckd ldrs: effrt over 2f out: sn rdn and wknd over 1f out* **5/1**[2]

6130 **9** *3 ¾* **My Guardian Angel**[13] 6306 4-8-13 67....................(p) PaulHanagan 7 42
(Mark H Tompkins) *trckd ldng pair on outer: effrt over 2f out: sn rdn along and wknd wl over 1f out* **12/1**

1m 44.43s (-3.17) **Going Correction** -0.275s/f (Firm)
WFA 3 from 4yo+ 4lb **9** Ran SP% **116.1**
Speed ratings (Par 103): **104,103,103,103,102 99,97,94,90**
Tote Swingers 1&2 £8.30, 2&3 £10.70, 1&3 £5.70 CSF £49.39 CT £217.52 TOTE £4.70: £1.80, £3.00, £1.60; EX 59.80 Trifecta £431.70 Pool: £768.34 - 1.33 winning units..
Owner Elsa Crankshaw Gordon Allan **Bred** Darley **Trained** Spennymoor, Co Durham

FOCUS
A fair handicap. The pace didn't look that strong, the leading pair in front rank throughout, and the performance of the third, who came from a long way back, is worth marking up slightly.

6722 BRIAN AND JASON MERRINGTON MEMORIAL AMATEUR RIDERS' H'CAP (DIV I) 1m 1f 207y
5:10 (5:10) (Class 6) (0-60,60) 3-Y-O+ **£2,183** (£677; £338; £169) **Stalls** Low

Form RPR

6-04 **1** **Haymarket**[30] 5793 4-10-9 60.................... MrAlexFerguson(5) 9 77+
(Michael Bell) *hld up in tch: smooth hdwy over 3f out: led wl over 1f out: sn rdn and styd on* **5/2**[1]

0540 **2** *1 ¼* **Valentine's Gift**[18] 6177 5-9-10 47.................... MissBeckySmith(5) 2 62
(Neville Bycroft) *dwlt and towards rr: gd hdwy over 3f out: chsd ldrs over 2f out: rdn to chse wnr over 1f out: no imp ins fnl f* **7/1**

4055 **3** *10* **Yourholidayisover (IRE)**[6] 6518 6-10-3 49.................... MissADeniel 4 45
(Patrick Holmes) *hld up: hdwy over 3f out: rdn 2f out: plugged on same pce to take modest 3rd ins fnl f* **9/2**[3]

5140 **4** *3 ¼* **Barton Bounty**[12] 6339 6-10-13 59.................... MrJHamilton 6 48
(Peter Niven) *towards rr: sme hdwy over 2f out: sn rdn and nvr nr ldrs* **7/1**

-000 **5** *5* **Ay Tay Tate (IRE)**[26] 5934 7-10-4 55....................(p) MrHAABannister(5) 5 35
(Noel Wilson) *slt ld at str pce: rdn over 3f out: hdd wl over 1f out and sn wknd* **12/1**

00/- **6** *5* **Classical Chloe**[750] 5792 5-10-0 46 oh1....................(t) MissHBethell 8 16
(Tim Fitzgerald) *dwlt: a towards rr* **25/1**

044/ **7** *3 ¾* **Xenophon**[116] 5022 5-9-11 46 oh1.................... MissAliceMills(3) 1
(Michael Chapman) *prom early: lost pl bef 1/2-way: bhd fnl 3f* **20/1**

3334 **8** *5* **Rockweiller**[29] 5840 6-10-3 54....................(v) MrPJohn(5) 7
(Steve Gollings) *cl up: disp ld 1/2-way: rdn over 3f out: drvn over 2f out and sn wknd* **11/4**[2]

2m 5.31s (-1.69) **Going Correction** -0.275s/f (Firm) **8** Ran SP% **114.7**
Speed ratings (Par 101): **95,94,86,83,79 75,72,68**
Tote Swingers 1&2 £4.30, 2&3 £6.50, 1&3 £4.20 CSF £20.67 CT £74.23 TOTE £3.80: £1.30, £1.70, £2.00; EX 21.70 Trifecta £126.10 Pool: £1,457.30 - 8.66 winning units..
Owner Mrs John Ferguson **Bred** J Breslin **Trained** Newmarket, Suffolk
■ Stewards' Enquiry : Mr P John two-day ban: use of whip (8 & 13 Oct)

FOCUS
They went a suicidal gallop, the field well strung out from an early stage, and the two pacesetters predictably had nothing left in the straight.

6723 BRIAN AND JASON MERRINGTON MEMORIAL AMATEUR RIDERS' H'CAP (DIV II) 1m 1f 207y
5:45 (5:45) (Class 6) (0-60,59) 3-Y-0+ **£2,183** (£677; £338; £169) **Stalls** Low

Form RPR

0500 **1** **Kheskianto (IRE)**[6] 6518 7-9-11 **45**.........................(t) MissAliceMills(3) 1 54
(Michael Chapman) *trckd ldng pair: hdwy on inner over 2f out: led wl over 1f out: rdn appr fnl f: kpt on* **16/1**

6050 **2** ¾ **Nezami (IRE)**[18] 6153 8-10-11 **56**............................... MissSBrotherton 4 64
(Patrick Clinton) *trckd ldrs: hdwy over 2f out: swtchd rt to inner over 1f out: rdn to chse wnr ent fnl f: sn swtchd lft and styd on towards fin* **11/1**

050 **3** 2 ¾ **Hail Bold Chief (USA)**[13] 6296 6-10-10 **55**...................... MrSWalker 5 58
(Alan Swinbank) *trckd ldrs: hdwy over 2f out: rdn wl over 1f out: drvn and kpt on same pce fnl f* **5/2**[1]

6362 **4** 5 **Walter De La Mare (IRE)**[20] 6099 6-10-0 **48**..... MissJoannaMason(3) 3 41
(Anabel K Murphy) *hld up: hdwy over 2f out: rdn wl over 1f out: kpt on one pce fnl f* **12/1**

6521 **5** 2 **Taxiformissbyron**[22] 6049 3-10-4 **55**............................ MissCWalton 10 44
(Michael Herrington) *prom: cl up 1/2-way: led over 2f out: sn rdn and hdd wl over 1f out: drvn and wknd appr fnl f* **4/1**[2]

23-0 **6** nk **Coax**[21] 6086 5-11-0 **59**.. MissADeniel 7 48
(Patrick Holmes) *midfield: sme hdwy over 3f out: sn rdn along and n.d* **9/1**

6555 **7** 9 **Sinatramania**[27] 5882 6-10-7 **52**....................................... MrsCBartley 8 24
(Tracy Waggott) *chsd ldrs: rdn along wl over 2f out: sn wknd* **11/2**[3]

0/0- **8** 1 ¼ **Marino Prince (FR)**[190] 3440 8-9-10 **46**................. MrHAABannister(5) 9 15
(Joanne Foster) *a towards rr* **20/1**

5453 **9** 5 **Rub Of The Relic (IRE)**[18] 6179 8-10-8 **58**............(v) MissHDukes(5) 11 18
(Paul Midgley) *a towards rr* **7/1**

000 **10** 1 ¼ **Sir George (IRE)**[29] 5840 8-9-8 **46** ow1.......................... MrJPearce(7) 6 4
(Suzzanne France) *s.i.s: a wl bhd* **20/1**

0000 **11** shd **Penderyn**[104] 3191 6-9-9 **45**..................................(p) MissBeckySmith(5) 2
(Charles Smith) *slt ld: rdn along 3f out: hdd over 2f out and sn wknd* **50/1**

2m 5.65s (-1.35) **Going Correction** -0.275s/f (Firm)
WFA 3 from 5yo+ 6lb 11 Ran SP% **119.8**
Speed ratings (Par 101): **94,93,91,87,85 85,78,77,73,72 72**
Tote Swingers 1&2 £38.70, 2&3 £8.80, 1&3 £15.70 CSF £179.18 CT £597.05 TOTE £21.90: £5.00, £5.70, £1.50; EX 274.80 Trifecta £898.50 Part won. Pool: £1,198.01 - 0.11 winning units..

Owner F A Dickinson **Bred** Tinnakill Partnership II **Trained** Market Rasen, Lincs

FOCUS
Another modest contest, though they at least went a more sensible gallop than the first division.
T/Plt: £170.90 to £1 stake. Pool: £54,917.96 - 234.58 winning tickets. T/Qpdt: £61.70 to £1 stake. Pool: £3,624.20 - 43.40 winning tickets. JR

6295 CARLISLE (R-H)
Tuesday, September 24

OFFICIAL GOING: Good (good to soft between 1m & 1m 4f; 6.9)
Wind: Almost nil Weather: Overcast

6724 APOLLOBET ONLINE CASINO MAIDEN AUCTION STKS 7f 200y
3:35 (3:35) (Class 6) 2-Y-0 **£1,940** (£577; £288; £144) **Stalls** Low

Form RPR

00 **1** **Running Wolf (IRE)**[43] 5338 2-8-5 0........................ ConnorBeasley(5) 7 71
(Michael Dods) *trckd ldrs: rdn to ld over 2f out: hrd pressed ins fnl f: hld on wl towards fin* **40/1**

3502 **2** hd **Supa U**[22] 6047 2-8-5 64.......................................(e) DuranFentiman 6 66
(Tim Easterby) *t.k.h in rr: effrt on outside over 2f out: drvn and ev ch ins fnl f: kpt on: jst hld* **2/1**[1]

2304 **3** 5 **Island Kingdom (IRE)**[14] 6271 2-8-9 67........................... JoeFanning 2 60
(J S Moore) *pressed ldr: led briefly over 2f out: sn rdn: outpcd by first two fnl f* **11/4**[2]

4 2 ¼ **Scurr Mist (IRE)** 2-8-10 0... TomEaves 1 54
(Keith Dalgleish) *t.k.h: led at modest gallop: rdn and hdd over 2f out: wknd fnl f* **5/1**[3]

604 **5** 1 ¾ **Christmas Wish**[10] 6409 2-8-7 63.................................. SamHitchcott 5 47
(Mick Channon) *chsd ldrs: drvn over 2f out: wknd over 1f out* **11/2**

6 ½ **D'Arcy Indiana** 2-8-10 0... GrahamLee 3 49
(Amy Weaver) *dwlt: hld up: drvn and outpcd over 2f out: n.d after* **16/1**

0 **7** hd **Mestizo**[17] 6206 2-8-3 0.. NeilFarley(3) 4 45
(Declan Carroll) *t.k.h: in tch: rdn over 2f out: wknd wl over 1f out* **17/2**

1m 42.91s (2.91) **Going Correction** +0.25s/f (Good) 7 Ran SP% **110.9**
Speed ratings (Par 93): **95,94,89,87,85 85,85**
Tote Swingers 1&2 £8.30, 2&3 £2.00, 1&3 £10.70 CSF £112.86 TOTE £7.50: £7.00, £2.10; EX 156.40 Trifecta £572.00 Pool: £1,305.19 - 1.71 winning units..
Owner M J K Dods **Bred** Ben Browne **Trained** Denton, Co Durham

FOCUS
The inside rail had been moved out 3yds from 7f start to winning line, adding 7yds to all races over 6f. Moderate maiden form.

6725 APOLLOBET MOBILE GAMES NURSERY H'CAP (DIV I) 6f 192y
4:05 (4:08) (Class 6) (0-60,60) 2-Y-0 **£1,940** (£577; £288; £144) **Stalls** Low

Form RPR

000 **1** **Roving Bunny**[24] 5988 2-9-7 **60**.................................. GrahamLee 1 68
(James Given) *prom: rdn to ld over 1f out: styd on strly fnl f* **16/1**

0001 **2** 3 **Mornin Mr Norris**[27] 5898 2-8-7 **49**........................ RaulDaSilva(3) 5 49
(John Quinn) *t.k.h early: hld up: hdwy on outside 2f out: chsd wnr fnl f: no imp towards fin* **5/1**[2]

500 **3** 3 **Paddy's Bay**[13] 6299 2-8-13 **57**.....................................(b[1]) ShaneGray(5) 2 49
(Kevin Ryan) *dwlt: sn in midfield on ins: outpcd over 2f out: rallied over 1f out: no imp fnl f* **7/1**

630 **4** ¾ **Ibecke**[24] 5988 2-8-12 **51**.. JoeFanning 6 41
(Mark Johnston) *t.k.h: led: rdn and hdd over 1f out: outpcd fnl f* **8/1**

4303 **5** 1 ¼ **Ding Ding**[9] 6426 2-9-1 **54**.. SamHitchcott 10 41
(Mick Channon) *hld up: rdn on outside and hdwy over 2f out: no imp over 1f out* **9/1**

4401 **6** 1 ½ **Casper Lee (IRE)**[7] 6494 2-8-13 **59** 6ex........................(v) KevinStott(7) 7 42+
(Nigel Tinkler) *bhd: rdn 3f out: sme late hdwy: nvr on terms* **5/2**[1]

0000 **7** shd **Suni Dancer**[27] 5898 2-8-8 **47** ow2.............................. TomEaves 4 30
(Paul Green) *t.k.h early: prom on outside: hdwy 3f out: wknd over 1f out* **33/1**

0653 **8** nk **Romantic Bliss (IRE)**[21] 6073 2-8-8 **47**............................ BenCurtis 3 29
(K R Burke) *t.k.h early: prom: drvn over 2f out: rallied: wknd over 1f out* **6/1**[3]

4200 **9** 6 **Sherry For Nanny (IRE)**[7] 6494 2-9-1 **54**...................... DanielTudhope 8 20
(Marjorie Fife) *hld up: struggling over 2f out: sn btn* **25/1**

1m 30.46s (3.36) **Going Correction** +0.25s/f (Good) 9 Ran SP% **105.8**
Speed ratings (Par 93): **90,86,83,82,80 79,79,78,71**
Tote Swingers 1&2 £24.60, 2&3 £7.90, 1&3 £24.60 CSF £80.23 CT £509.03 TOTE £13.50: £2.70, £1.50, £2.40; EX 100.60 Trifecta £518.50 Part won. Pool: £691.34 - 0.06 winning units..
Owner Miss Susanna Ballinger **Bred** Andrew Sime & Co Ltd & Susanna Ballinger **Trained** Willoughton, Lincs

FOCUS
The first division of this low-grade nursery.

6726 APOLLOBET MOBILE GAMES NURSERY H'CAP (DIV II) 6f 192y
4:35 (4:37) (Class 6) (0-60,60) 2-Y-0 **£1,940** (£577; £288; £144) **Stalls** Low

Form RPR

000 **1** **Emerahldz (IRE)**[17] 6206 2-9-2 **55**.................................. LeeTopliss 5 62+
(Richard Fahey) *trckd ldrs: rdn over 2f out: rallied and led ent fnl f: kpt on wl* **5/1**[2]

6650 **2** 1 ½ **Bajan Rebel**[14] 6284 2-9-1 **54**...................................... PhillipMakin 1 57
(Michael Easterby) *t.k.h: hld up: rdn over 2f out: hdwy over 1f out: styd on to take 2nd nr fin: nt rch wnr* **14/1**

5652 **3** ½ **Rockie Road (IRE)**[2] 6663 2-8-8 **50**........................... RaulDaSilva(3) 10 52
(Paul Green) *t.k.h: hld up in tch: hdwy to ld over 2f out: rdn and hdd ent fnl f: kpt on same pce: lost 2nd towards fin* **6/5**[1]

5030 **4** 1 ¼ **Mimbleberry**[12] 6322 2-9-7 **60**..............................(p) RichardKingscote 4 58
(Tom Dascombe) *in tch: drvn and outpcd over 2f out: rallied appr fnl f: kpt on: no imp* **11/2**[3]

0656 **5** nse **Mister Uno (IRE)**[14] 6285 2-9-0 **53**...............................(p) PJMcDonald 2 51
(Ann Duffield) *chsd ldrs: drvn and outpcd over 2f out: rallied and edgd rt appr fnl f: sn one pce* **17/2**

0006 **6** 6 **Brockholes Flyer (IRE)**[12] 6322 2-8-6 **45**........................(v) BenCurtis 8 27
(Brendan Powell) *slt ld to over 2f out: rdn and wknd over 1f out* **16/1**

3554 **7** 15 **Angel Rosa**[8] 6465 2-9-6 **59**.. TomEaves 3
(Keith Dalgleish) *w ldr to over 2f out: sn rdn and btn: t.o* **25/1**

0304 **8** 2 ¾ **Secret Ocean (IRE)**[14] 6279 2-9-0 **53**............................(b) GrahamLee 6
(J S Moore) *awkward s: plld hrd: hld up towards rr: struggling over 2f out: sn lost tch* **16/1**

050 **9** 1 **Maidana (IRE)**[14] 6286 2-8-0 **46**................................ GaryMahon(7) 9
(Tim Easterby) *dwlt: bhd: struggling over 3f out: nvr on terms* **33/1**

1m 29.59s (2.49) **Going Correction** +0.25s/f (Good) 9 Ran SP% **113.3**
Speed ratings (Par 93): **95,93,92,91,91 84,67,64,62**
Tote Swingers 1&2 £9.10, 2&3 £4.10, 1&3 £2.50 CSF £70.04 CT £134.84 TOTE £3.90: £1.90, £3.60, £1.60; EX 68.90 Trifecta £384.10 Pool: £2,069.26 - 4.03 winning units..
Owner Mrs H Steel **Bred** D G Iceton **Trained** Musley Bank, N Yorks

FOCUS
This was run in a time 0.87secs quicker than the first division and again went to a nursery debutante.

6727 APOLLOBET BEST ODDS GUARANTEED H'CAP 6f 192y
5:05 (5:05) (Class 4) (0-85,85) 3-Y-0+ **£4,851** (£1,443; £721; £360) **Stalls** Low

Form RPR

5025 **1** **Chiswick Bey (IRE)**[5] 6549 5-8-0 **71** oh1................(p) SamanthaBell(7) 7 78+
(Richard Fahey) *hld up in tch: effrt and hdwy on outside over 1f out: qcknd to ld ins fnl f: comf* **5/1**[3]

1643 **2** ¾ **Talent Scout (IRE)**[27] 5880 7-9-0 **85**........................... GemmaTutty(7) 6 90
(Karen Tutty) *led: rdn over 2f out: hdd ins fnl f: kpt on: nt pce of wnr* **11/2**

5043 **3** 1 ¼ **Dubai Dynamo**[14] 6274 8-9-6 **84**................................... PJMcDonald 5 86
(Ruth Carr) *hld up: rdn over 2f out: no imp tl hdwy over 1f out: kpt on ins fnl f* **9/2**[2]

4221 **4** nk **Al Freej (IRE)**[43] 5353 4-8-11 **75**.................................. TomEaves 4 76
(Brian Ellison) *plld hrd: in tch: effrt and rdn over 2f out: one pce fnl f* **11/2**

0114 **5** 1 ¼ **Skytrain**[14] 6274 3-9-1 **82**.. JoeFanning 1 78
(Mark Johnston) *chsd ldr: rdn over 2f out: outpcd fnl f* **11/4**[1]

5002 **6** ½ **Green Park (IRE)**[7] 6496 10-8-6 **73**...............................(b) NeilFarley(3) 2 69
(Declan Carroll) *t.k.h: chsd ldrs: stdy hdwy over 2f out: rdn over 1f out: outpcd fnl f* **14/1**

4500 **7** shd **Day Of The Eagle (IRE)**[36] 5580 7-8-10 **74**...................... GrahamLee 3 70
(Michael Easterby) *dwlt: in tch: rdn over 2f out: sn no imp* **8/1**

1m 28.02s (0.92) **Going Correction** +0.25s/f (Good)
WFA 3 from 4yo+ 3lb 7 Ran SP% **110.1**
Speed ratings (Par 105): **104,103,101,101,99 99,99**
Tote Swingers 1&2 £5.20, 2&3 £4.00, 1&3 £11.00 CSF £29.68 TOTE £7.60: £3.20, £2.30; EX 29.10 Trifecta £182.60 Pool: £1,446.19 - 5.93 winning units..
Owner Leods Contracts Limited **Bred** Mrs Kay Egan **Trained** Musley Bank, N Yorks

FOCUS
Ordinary handicap form.

6728 APOLLOBET FREE DOWNLOAD APP H'CAP 5f 193y
5:40 (5:40) (Class 5) (0-75,74) 3-Y-0+ **£2,587** (£770; £384; £192) **Stalls** Low

Form RPR

3351 **1** **Perfect Pasture**[52] 4992 3-8-12 **67**............................(v) DuranFentiman 7 79+
(Michael Easterby) *dwlt: sn cl up: led over 2f out: rdn and edgd rt ins fnl f: kpt on strly* **6/1**[3]

1010 **2** 1 ¾ **Just The Tonic**[32] 5711 6-9-0 **72**............................ ShirleyTeasdale(5) 3 78
(Marjorie Fife) *chsd ldrs: rdn over 2f out: styd on fnl f: tk 2nd nr fin: nt rch wnr* **18/1**

5111 **3** hd **Lothair (IRE)**[18] 6180 4-9-1 **68**...................................... BenCurtis 8 74
(Alan Swinbank) *trckd ldrs: ev ch over 2f out to over 1f out: kpt on same pce fnl f: lost 2nd nr fin* **9/2**[1]

3320 **4** 2 **Salvatore Fury (IRE)**[5] 6547 3-9-0 **69**.............................(p) TomEaves 4 68
(Keith Dalgleish) *hld up bhd ldng gp: effrt and swtchd lft over 1f out: one pce fnl f* **7/1**

6502 **5** ½ **Beau Amadeus (IRE)**[17] 6209 4-9-1 **68**.....................(b) AdrianNicholls 5 68
(David Nicholls) *t.k.h: hld up: rdn over 2f out: kpt on fnl f: nvr able to chal* **7/1**

5000 **6** 3 ½ **See Clearly**[14] 6287 4-8-9 **62**..................................(b) PJMcDonald 6 49
(Tim Easterby) *in tch on outside: drvn over 2f out: edgd rt and outpcd appr fnl f* **14/1**

5443 **7** 1 ½ **Dark Opal (IRE)**[6] 6515 3-8-9 **69**.............................. ConnorBeasley(5) 9 51
(John Weymes) *hld up: rdn and effrt on outside over 2f out: no imp fr over 1f out* **15/2**

3-54 **8** ¾ **Rust (IRE)**[109] 3068 3-8-12 **67**..................................... GrahamLee 2 46
(Ann Duffield) *dwlt: sn in tch: drvn and outpcd over 2f out: n.d after* **5/1**[2]

4250 **9** *1 ¾* **Roker Park (IRE)**[25] 5971 8-9-4 **74**..............................(v) JulieBurke(3) 10 48
(David O'Meara) *bhd: struggling 1/2-way: nvr on terms* **12/1**
3633 **10** *8* **Silkelly**[12] 6338 3-9-5 **74**..............................(t) DanielTudhope 1 22
(David O'Meara) *led to over 2f out: rdn and wknd over 1f out* **17/2**
1m 13.3s (-0.40) **Going Correction** +0.25s/f (Good)
WFA 3 from 4yo+ 2lb **10** Ran SP% **116.0**
Speed ratings (Par 103): **112,109,109,106,106 101,99,98,96,85**
Tote Swingers 1&2 £23.10, 2&3 £19.90, 1&3 £4.30 CSF £106.39 CT £543.62 TOTE £6.50: £2.00, £5.50, £2.00; EX 152.60 Trifecta £944.60 Pool: £2,165.14 - 1.71 winning units..
Owner Mrs Jean Turpin **Bred** Mrs Jean Turpin **Trained** Sheriff Hutton, N Yorks
■ Stewards' Enquiry : Tom Eaves two-day ban: careless riding (8-9 Oct)
FOCUS
Sound form for the level.

6729 APOLLOBET £50 MATCH BET H'CAP 1m 3f 107y
6:15 (6:15) (Class 3) (0-90,90) 3-Y-O+ **£7,439** (£2,213; £1,106; £553) **Stalls** High

Form RPR
1 **Open Eagle (IRE)**[90] 4-9-10 **88**.............................. DanielTudhope 1 100+
(David O'Meara) *t.k.h: mde all: rdn and qcknd clr wl over 1f out: eased ins fnl f: readily* **10/1**
4224 **2** *2 ¾* **Rio's Rosanna (IRE)**[13] 6302 6-9-9 **87**.............. RussKennemore 8 93
(Richard Whitaker) *in tch: effrt and hdwy on outside to chse wnr over 2f out: sn rdn: kpt on fnl f: no imp* **7/2**[1]
6511 **3** *1 ½* **Kiwayu**[74] 4262 4-9-5 **88**..............................(p) AdamNicol(5) 2 92
(Philip Kirby) *hld up bhd ldng gp: stdy hdwy over 2f out: sn rdn: one pce fnl f* **4/1**[2]
4000 **4** *shd* **Easy Terms**[101] 3345 6-9-5 **90**.............................. KevinStott(7) 4 94
(Edwin Tuer) *in tch: effrt on outside over 2f out: hung rt over 1f out: kpt on same pce* **5/1**[3]
-200 **5** *¾* **Entihaa**[32] 5706 5-9-1 **79**.............................. BenCurtis 3 81
(Alan Swinbank) *trckd ldrs: effrt and drvn over 2f out: one pce appr fnl f* **10/1**
1435 **6** *2* **Now My Sun**[17] 6211 4-8-13 **77**.............................. TomEaves 5 76
(K R Burke) *dwlt: plld hrd in rr: rdn over 2f out: kpt on fnl f: n.d* **9/1**
020- **7** *nk* **Last Shadow**[14] 6833 4-9-6 **84**..............................(t) GrahamLee 7 83
(Jonjo O'Neill) *hld up: rdn and outpcd over 2f out: rallied 1f out: nvr rchd ldrs* **8/1**
6510 **8** *5* **Hunting Ground (USA)**[13] 6302 3-9-1 **86**.............. JoeFanning 6 77
(Mark Johnston) *t.k.h: cl up: lost pl over 2f out: sn struggling* **6/1**
1110 **9** *1 ¼* **Tapis Libre**[5] 6563 5-9-0 **78**.............................. PhillipMakin 9 67
(Michael Easterby) *trckd wnr tl rdn and lost pl 3f out: sn struggling* **18/1**
2m 27.36s (4.26) **Going Correction** +0.25s/f (Good)
WFA 3 from 4yo+ 7lb **9** Ran SP% **117.7**
Speed ratings (Par 107): **94,92,90,90,90 88,88,84,84**
Tote Swingers 1&2 £9.40, 2&3 £4.50, 1&3 £7.80 CSF £45.92 CT £167.55 TOTE £14.40: £3.40, £2.30, £1.10; EX 56.00 Trifecta £575.50 Pool: £1,415.74 - 1.84 winning units..
Owner Middleham Park Racing LXXIV & Partner **Bred** F Bayrou **Trained** Nawton, N Yorks
FOCUS
What had looked a decent handicap was won in good style by the ex-French winner.

6730 APOLLOBET IN-PLAY BETTING H'CAP 1m 1f 61y
6:50 (6:50) (Class 5) (0-70,70) 3-Y-O+ **£2,587** (£770; £384; £192) **Stalls** Low

Form RPR
1132 **1** **Absent Amy (IRE)**[27] 5881 4-9-9 **69**.............. MichaelO'Connell 10 80
(Amy Weaver) *hld up in tch: pushed along over 2f out: effrt and swtchd lft over 1f out: led ins fnl f: sn clr: eased nr fin* **7/1**
1505 **2** *3 ¼* **Fraserburgh (IRE)**[13] 6297 3-9-5 **70**.............................. JoeFanning 7 75
(Mark Johnston) *cl up: led over 2f out: sn hrd pressed: hdd ins fnl f: kpt on same pce* **9/2**[2]
5261 **3** *shd* **Tectonic (IRE)**[13] 6296 4-9-10 **70**..............................(p) TomEaves 2 74
(Keith Dalgleish) *in tch: nt clr run over 2f out: swtchd lft and effrt over 1f out: r.o ins fnl f* **13/2**
50 **4** *½* **I'm Super Too (IRE)**[22] 6048 6-9-8 **68**.............................. BenCurtis 8 71
(Alan Swinbank) *t.k.h: prom: smooth hdwy on outside over 2f out: chal and rdn over 1f out: one pce ins fnl f* **16/1**
0041 **5** *¾* **Judicious**[27] 5882 6-9-8 **68**.............................. PJMcDonald 1 69
(Geoffrey Harker) *t.k.h: trckd ldrs: effrt and rdn 2f out: one pce fnl f* **10/3**[1]
000 **6** *1 ¼* **Indian Giver**[4] 6600 5-8-9 **60**.............................. SladeO'Hara(5) 5 59
(Alan Berry) *hld up: rdn over 2f out: hdwy over 1f out: nvr rchd ldrs* **25/1**
0450 **7** *2 ¼* **Buster Brown (IRE)**[29] 5833 4-9-3 **63**.............................. PhillipMakin 3 57
(James Given) *hld up: stdy hdwy 3f out: rdn 2f out: sn no imp* **13/2**
000- **8** *3 ½* **Landaho**[322] 7619 4-8-3 **56** oh11.............................. JordanHibberd(7) 4 42
(Alan Berry) *bhd: rdn and outpcd over 2f out: sn btn* **100/1**
2362 **9** *nse* **Sixties Queen**[12] 6321 3-8-7 **58**.............................. SamHitchcott 9 45
(Alan Bailey) *t.k.h: cl up: led 4f out to over 2f out: sn btn* **12/1**
020 **10** *1* **Day Of Destiny (IRE)**[16] 6236 8-9-10 **70**.............................. GrahamLee 6 54
(James Given) *t.k.h: led to 4f out: wknd fr 2f out* **11/2**[3]
1m 59.33s (1.73) **Going Correction** +0.25s/f (Good)
WFA 3 from 4yo+ 5lb **10** Ran SP% **114.2**
Speed ratings (Par 103): **102,99,99,98,97 96,94,91,91,90**
Tote Swingers: 1&2 £6.10, 1&3 £5.60, 2&3 £5.70 CSF £37.70 CT £214.78 TOTE £8.70: £2.90, £1.90, £2.30; EX 39.00 Trifecta £158.30 Pool: £1,959.05 - 9.27 winning units..
Owner Nigel Hardy **Bred** Tally-Ho Stud **Trained** Newmarket, Suffolk
FOCUS
They went steady up front early.
T/Plt: £256.60 to a £1 stake. Pool: £37,922.40 - 107.85 winning tickets. T/Qpdt: £20.40 to a £1 stake. Pool: £4,265.69 - 154.40 winning tickets. RY

6405 LINGFIELD (L-H)
Tuesday, September 24
OFFICIAL GOING: Standard
Wind: virtually nil Weather: sunny and quite warm

6731 AT THE RACES NURSERY H'CAP 5f (P)
2:00 (2:00) (Class 5) (0-75,75) 2-Y-O **£2,726** (£805; £402) **Stalls** High

Form RPR
4150 **1** **Baytown Kestrel**[10] 6376 2-9-7 **75**.............................. AdamKirby 2 81
(Brian Ellison) *mde all: edgd out rt and rdn over 1f out: in command and r.o wl fnl f: rdn out* **5/1**[3]
0223 **2** *1 ½* **Ice Slice (IRE)**[32] 5693 2-9-7 **75**.............................. RichardHughes 3 76
(Richard Hannon) *bustled along leaving stalls: chsd ldrs: effrt u.p over 1f out: chsd wnr jst ins fnl f: kpt on but no imp* **3/1**[1]
2105 **3** *shd* **Trinity River**[10] 6376 2-9-7 **75**.............................. SilvestreDeSousa 4 76
(Daniel Kubler) *chsd wnr: rdn over 1f out: slty hmpd: swtchd rt 1f out: lost 2nd and sltly outpcd jst ins fnl f: rallied and kpt on again towards fin* **8/1**
5100 **4** *¾* **Lady In Blue (IRE)**[12] 6326 2-9-2 **70**..............................(b[1]) SebSanders 1 68
(William Haggas) *dwlt and rdn along leaving stalls: sn rcvrd and in tch in midfield: effrt u.p 2f out: styd on same pce fnl f* **6/1**
4536 **5** *1 ¼* **Skinny Love**[18] 6170 2-8-13 **67**.............................. AndreaAtzeni 7 60
(Robert Cowell) *chsd ldng trio: rdn and effrt 2f out: unable qck u.p over 1f out: one pce after* **33/1**
0351 **6** *hd* **Basil Berry**[18] 6170 2-9-0 **71**.............................. RobertTart(3) 9 64
(Chris Dwyer) *hld up in last trio: rdn and wd bnd wl over 1f out: hung lft over 1f out: stl hanging but kpt on ins fnl f: no threat to ldrs* **9/2**[2]
0242 **7** *3* **Weisse Socken (IRE)**[20] 6104 2-9-6 **74**..............(b[1]) JimCrowley 5 56
(Ralph Beckett) *s.i.s: sn rdn along in rr: travelling bttr and clsd over 2f out: rdn and effrt over 1f out: wknd ins fnl f* **5/1**[3]
345 **8** *¾* **Orlando Star (CAN)**[23] 6013 2-9-2 **70**.............................. JamesDoyle 6 49
(Roger Teal) *wl in tch in midfield: rdn and effrt over 1f out: no ex u.p over 1f out: wknd ins fnl f* **16/1**
2610 **9** *7* **M'Selle (IRE)**[31] 5771 2-9-7 **75**.............................. LukeMorris 8 29
(Ronald Harris) *dwlt: a towards rr: rdn and wd bnd wl over 1f out: last and drvn w no rspnse over 1f out: sn wknd* **16/1**
59.36s (0.56) **Going Correction** -0.075s/f (Stan) **9** Ran SP% **116.6**
Speed ratings (Par 95): **92,89,89,88,86 85,81,79,68**
Tote Swingers: 1&2 £3.80, 1&3 £6.80, 2&3 £5.00 CSF £20.62 CT £118.94 TOTE £8.20: £2.40, £1.50, £2.90; EX 20.00 Trifecta £227.80 Pool: £2,306.82 - 7.59 winning units..
Owner The Acorn Partnership **Bred** R F And S D Knipe **Trained** Norton, N Yorks
FOCUS
This was a decent nursery, but the trip and sharp track suited the winner more than some of her main opponents.

6732 C W ENERGY H'CAP 5f (P)
2:30 (2:30) (Class 6) (0-60,60) 3-Y-O+ **£2,045** (£603; £302) **Stalls** High

Form RPR
2523 **1** **Welease Bwian (IRE)**[10] 6412 4-9-4 **58**.............................. RyanMoore 4 66+
(Stuart Williams) *dwlt: hld up in tch in rr of main gp: rdn and effrt on inner over 1f out: str run under mainly hands and heels to ld wl ins fnl f: kpt on* **5/2**[1]
3503 **2** *nk* **Mossgo (IRE)**[10] 6397 3-9-3 **58**..............................(t) GeorgeBaker 7 65
(John Best) *led: rdn and fnd ex over 1f out: drvn 1f out: hdd wl ins fnl f: styd on same pce towards fin* **16/1**
2434 **3** *1 ¼* **Johnny Splash (IRE)**[35] 5608 4-9-4 **58**..............(v) RichardHughes 1 60
(Roger Teal) *chsd ldng trio: effrt u.p 2f out: styd on same pce fnl f* **8/1**
0042 **4** *1 ¼* **Multitask**[52] 4999 3-9-2 **57**.............................. AdamKirby 8 55
(Michael Madgwick) *chsd ldr: pressing ldng and rdn 2f out: no ex and sltly outpcd u.p jst over 1f out: wknd wl ins fnl f* **11/4**[2]
4351 **5** *hd* **Pharoh Jake**[23] 6017 5-8-13 **56**.............................. MichaelJMMurphy(3) 3 53
(John Bridger) *wl in tch in midfield: rdn 2f out: drvn and outpcd over 1f out: styd on same pce fnl f* **8/1**
602 **6** *1 ½* **Diamond Vine (IRE)**[18] 6156 5-9-2 **56**..............................(v) LukeMorris 5 48
(Ronald Harris) *short of room and dropped to rr of main gp over 4f out: sn rdn: drvn and no imp over 1f out: plugged on but nvr trbld ldrs* **7/1**[3]
2555 **7** *shd* **Charming (IRE)**[26] 5930 4-9-6 **60**..............................(b[1]) SebSanders 2 51
(Olivia Maylam) *wl in tch in midfield: rdn and effrt wl over 1f out: no prog ent fnl f: wknd fnl 100yds* **10/1**
206 **8** *4 ½* **Green Millionaire**[41] 5388 3-9-5 **60**..............................(p) FergusSweeney 6 35
(Jeremy Gask) *hld up in tch in rr of main gp: effrt u.p 2f out: sn outpcd and btn: wknd over 1f out* **33/1**
0200 **9** *15* **Irish Boy (IRE)**[6] 6527 5-8-12 **59**..............................(tp) EoinWalsh(7) 10
(Christine Dunnett) *taken down early: s.i.s: sn rdn and nvr travelling: lost tch 1/2-way* **10/1**
59.5s (0.70) **Going Correction** -0.075s/f (Stan)
WFA 3 from 4yo+ 1lb **9** Ran SP% **117.0**
Speed ratings (Par 101): **91,90,88,86,86 83,83,76,52**
Tote Swingers: 1&2 £7.90, 1&3 £3.10, 2&3 £9.10 CSF £44.12 CT £287.01 TOTE £3.50: £1.30, £2.80, £2.70; EX 47.80 Trifecta £573.70 Pool: £2,063.03 - 2.69 winning units..
Owner W E Enticknap **Bred** Nils Koop **Trained** Newmarket, Suffolk
FOCUS
This was a modest sprint, but the first two (both running off a mark of 58) had been rated in the high 60s earlier in the year.

6733 AIREY MILLER PARTNERSHIP/EBFSTALLIONS.COM MAIDEN STKS 1m (P)
3:00 (3:03) (Class 5) 2-Y-O **£3,067** (£905; £453) **Stalls** High

Form RPR
3 **1** **Alex Vino (IRE)**[32] 5718 2-9-5 0.............................. RyanMoore 3 79
(Sir Michael Stoute) *led and set stdy gallop: rdn and qcknd 2f out: clr w rival and drvn over 1f out: hdd ins fnl f: battled on gamely u.p to ld again last stride* **9/4**[2]
2 *shd* **Dursey Island (USA)** 2-9-5 0.............................. RichardHughes 1 79+
(Richard Hannon) *chsd ldrs: rdn and effrt to chse ldr wl over 1f out: ev ch 1f out: led ins fnl f: kpt on but hdd last stride* **10/1**
3 *2* **Cape Caster (IRE)** 2-9-5 0.............................. JimCrowley 4 74+
(Ralph Beckett) *s.i.s: hld up in tch in rr: swtchd lft and hdwy over 1f out: kpt on wl fnl f to go 3rd fnl 50yds: no threat to ldng pair* **16/1**
4 *hd* **Ian's Memory (USA)** 2-9-5 0.............................. FrankieDettori 7 73+
(Jeremy Noseda) *hld up wl in tch in midfield: rdn and effrt 2f out: chsd clr ldng pair jst over 1f out: kpt on but no imp: lost 3rd fnl 50yds* **7/1**[3]
5 *shd* **Montaly** 2-9-5 0.............................. DavidProbert 6 73+
(Andrew Balding) *s.i.s: sn in tch in midfield: rdn and effrt over 2f out: hdwy and battling for 3rd 1f out: kpt on: no threat to ldng pair* **50/1**
2 **6** *2 ¼* **Alpine Retreat (USA)**[26] 5924 2-9-5 0.............................. MickaelBarzalona 5 68
(Charlie Appleby) *wl in tch in tch in midfield: rdn 4f out and nvr travelling after: drvn and dropped to last trio over 2f out: bhd and swtchd rt jst over 1f out: styd on fnl f but no threat to ldrs* **4/5**[1]
0 **7** *1* **One Man Band (IRE)**[32] 5718 2-9-5 0.............................. SilvestreDeSousa 8 65
(Charlie Appleby) *free to post: t.k.h: hld up in tch in midfield: hdwy to chse ldrs 4f out: effrt and rdn 2f out: wnt 3rd briefly over 1f out: sn lost pl: wknd ins fnl f* **33/1**
60 **8** *½* **Son Of Feyan (IRE)**[47] 5188 2-9-5 0.............................. LiamKeniry 10 64
(Roger Teal) *chsd ldr tl wl over 1f out: sn drvn and outpcd: wknd fnl f* **66/1**
9 *6* **Gimme Five** 2-9-5 0.............................. FergusSweeney 9 50
(Alan King) *s.i.s: in tch towards rr: rdn and effrt 2f out: sn struggling and wknd over 1f out* **50/1**

10 8 **Palace Dragon (IRE)** 2-9-5 0 .... LukeMorris 2 31
(Sir Mark Prescott Bt) *in tch in midfield: lost pl and rdn over 4f out: wknd over 1f out* **50/1**

1m 39.03s (0.83) **Going Correction** -0.075s/f (Stan) 10 Ran SP% **124.1**
Speed ratings (Par 95): **92,91,89,89,89 87,86,85,79,71**
Tote Swingers: 1&2 £4.20, 1&3 £5.40, 2&3 £8.90 CSF £25.92 TOTE £3.60: £1.30, £2.60, £4.00; EX 30.90 Trifecta £177.10 Pool: £5,246.00 - 22.21 winning units..
Owner Nurlan Bizakov **Bred** Hesmonds Stud Ltd **Trained** Newmarket, Suffolk

FOCUS
This was an above-average maiden with good stables involved, several expensive purchases on show and a number of future winners likely to have been in the line-up.

6734 AIREY MILLER CONSTRUCTION MANAGEMENT H'CAP (DIV I) 1m (P)
3:30 (3:31) (Class 5) (0-75,75) 3-Y-O **£2,726** (£805; £402) **Stalls** High

Form RPR

6025 **1** **Canadian Run (IRE)**[11] 6359 3-9-7 **75** .... KierenFox 12 89+
(Robert Mills) *mde all: rdn and qcknd clr over 2f out: wnt further clr and in n.d over 1f out: styd on strly* **12/1**

5246 **2** 6 **Aint Got A Scooby (IRE)**[12] 6335 3-9-1 **74** .... RyanTate(5) 5 74
(Clive Cox) *chsd ldrs: rdn and outpcd by wnr over 2f out: no ch w wnr over 1f out: styd on u.p to go 2nd wl ins fnl f* **7/1**[3]

0262 **3** ½ **Candy Kitten**[12] 6319 3-9-1 **69** .... LukeMorris 10 67
(Alastair Lidderdale) *in tch in midfield: hdwy to chse ldr over 5f out: drvn and outpcd by wnr over 2f out: no ch w wnr but hld on to 2nd tl wl ins fnl f* **25/1**

0052 **4** 1¼ **Bursledon (IRE)**[18] 6153 3-8-12 **66** ....(v) RichardHughes 3 61
(Richard Hannon) *hld up in midfield: no ch w wnr but sme hdwy u.p over 1f out: no imp fnl f* **9/2**[2]

531- **5** 1 **Absolutely Right (IRE)**[284] 8102 3-9-4 **72** .... TomQueally 6 65
(George Margarson) *t.k.h: hld up wl in tch in midfield: rdn over 2f out: lost pl bnd wl over 1f out: rallied and kpt on ins fnl f: no ch w wnr* **10/1**

324 **6** ½ **Mandy's Boy (IRE)**[11] 6357 3-9-3 **71** ....(p) JimCrowley 8 63
(Ian Williams) *chsd ldrs: 3rd and outpcd over 2f out: drvn and no hdwy 2f out: wl hld and styd on same pce after* **10/1**

3350 **7** shd **Magical Rose (IRE)**[13] 6317 3-8-13 **67** ....(p) FrederikTylicki 7 59
(Paul D'Arcy) *hld up in tch in midfield: rdn and effrt jst over 2f out: kpt on ins fnl f: no ch w wnr* **20/1**

620 **8** nk **Mr Fitzroy (IRE)**[30] 5792 3-9-6 **74** .... RyanMoore 2 65
(Andrew Balding) *t.k.h: chsd ldrs: outpcd over 2f out: drvn and no hdwy over 1f out: no ch and plugged on same pce fnl f* **11/4**[1]

2334 **9** 1¼ **Summer Dream (IRE)**[12] 6341 3-9-2 **75** ....(b) TobyAtkinson(5) 11 63
(Marco Botti) *s.i.s: sn rcvrd and in tch in midfield: outpcd over 2f out: swtchd ins and effrt over 1f out: no hdwy: n.d* **14/1**

-605 **10** ½ **Keep The Secret**[48] 5152 3-9-0 **68** .... AdamKirby 4 55
(William Knight) *stdd s: t.k.h: hld up in rr: n.d* **8/1**

2243 **11** 4½ **Tilstarr (IRE)**[55] 4898 3-9-1 **72** .... RobertTart(3) 1 48
(Roger Teal) *taken down early: hld up in tch towards rr: hmpd bnd over 5f out: n.d* **10/1**

1m 36.9s (-1.30) **Going Correction** -0.075s/f (Stan) 11 Ran SP% **118.7**
Speed ratings (Par 101): **103,97,96,95,94 93,93,93,92,91 87**
Tote Swingers: 1&2 £1.60, 1&3 £1.70, 2&3 £1.40 CSF £94.45 CT £2110.56 TOTE £17.00: £4.40, £2.90, £8.50; EX 115.90 Trifecta £2730.20 Part won. Pool: £3,640.31 - 0.57 winning units..
Owner Brendan Kerr **Bred** Stuart Weld **Trained** Headley, Surrey

FOCUS
This middling handicap looked competitive on paper, but the winner was suddenly asked to quicken up approaching the straight and nothing else could go with him.

6735 AIREY MILLER CONSTRUCTION MANAGEMENT H'CAP (DIV II) 1m (P)
4:00 (4:01) (Class 5) (0-75,75) 3-Y-O **£2,726** (£805; £402) **Stalls** High

Form RPR

3403 **1** **Big Whiskey (IRE)**[5] 6556 3-9-0 **75** .... JenniferFerguson(7) 7 83
(Edward Creighton) *chsd ldrs: wnt 2nd wl over 2f out: rdn and effrt to ld 1f out: pushed along and r.o wl fnl f* **7/2**[1]

4-01 **2** 1 **Amulet**[18] 6153 3-8-11 **65** .... ShaneKelly 8 71
(Eve Johnson Houghton) *led: rdn ent fnl 2f: hdd 1f out: kpt on wl u.p and styd pressing wnr tl no ex fnl 75yds* **8/1**[3]

0410 **3** 1¼ **Canon Law (IRE)**[17] 6203 3-9-6 **74** .... RyanMoore 10 77
(Luca Cumani) *in tch in midfield: effrt but outpcd in 4th 2f out: chsd clr ldng pair over 1f out: styd on u.p but nvr threatened ldng pair* **7/2**[1]

00-4 **4** hd **Funky Cold Medina**[154] 1754 3-9-2 **70** .... FrankieDettori 11 72+
(Charles Hills) *flashed tail leaving stalls: hld up in last pair: effrt but stl plenty whn swtchd lft over 1f out: r.o wl ins fnl f: nvr trbld ldrs* **8/1**[3]

4440 **5** 3½ **Echo Brava**[11] 6360 3-8-13 **67** .... RichardHughes 3 61
(Luke Dace) *hld up in tch in last trio: hdwy 3f out: drvn and no imp wl over 1f out: one pce after* **10/1**

1063 **6** ½ **Poor Duke (IRE)**[24] 5978 3-9-3 **71** ....(p) JamesDoyle 1 64
(Jamie Osborne) *in tch in last pair: pushed along 6f out: drvn and struggling 3f out: bhd and wd bnd wl over 1f out: kpt on fnl f: nvr trbld ldrs* **9/2**[2]

1 **7** 1½ **Welsh Sunrise**[228] 564 3-9-0 **68** .... LukeMorris 12 57
(Ed Walker) *in tch in midfield: rdn and outpcd over 2f out: drvn and no hdwy over 1f out: sn wknd* **25/1**

105 **8** 1¼ **Not Rigg (USA)**[10] 6379 3-9-1 **72** ....(t) RyanPowell(3) 4 58
(Gary Harrison) *chsd ldr tl wl over 2f out: 3rd and outpcd u.p 2f out: wknd over 1f out* **20/1**

01 **9** nse **Laura Secord (CAN)**[98] 3435 3-9-5 **73** .... AndreaAtzeni 2 59
(Heather Main) *in tch in midfield: lost pl 4f out: bhd and struggling u.p over 2f out: n.d fnl 2f* **14/1**

32-3 **10** 15 **Mosman**[256] 168 3-8-13 **67** .... JimCrowley 6 17
(Dean Ivory) *in tch in midfield: lost pl and struggling over 2f out: bhd over 1f out: eased ins fnl f* **10/1**

1m 36.9s (-1.30) **Going Correction** -0.075s/f (Stan) 10 Ran SP% **118.3**
Speed ratings (Par 101): **103,102,100,100,97 96,95,93,93,78**
Tote Swingers: 1&2 £5.70, 1&3 £3.90, 2&3 £6.70 CSF £32.65 CT £106.28 TOTE £4.90: £1.60, £2.70, £1.90; EX 41.30 Trifecta £134.60 Pool: £2,661.01 - 14.82 winning units..
Owner N Dyshaev **Bred** Michael Coogan **Trained** Wormshill, Kent

FOCUS
The second division of this race produced a much closer finish than the first, with several relatively unexposed sorts chasing home the battle-hardened winner.

6736 WORLD HORSE WELFARE H'CAP 2m (P)
4:30 (4:30) (Class 6) (0-65,65) 3-Y-O+ **£2,045** (£603; £302) **Stalls** Low

Form RPR

6100 **1** **Man From Seville**[14] 6290 3-8-11 **60** .... LukeMorris 10 75+
(Sir Mark Prescott Bt) *in tch in midfield: hdwy to chse wnr jst over 3f out: rdn to ld 2f out: sn clr and in command over 1f out: eased towards fin* **9/2**[2]

2406 **2** 5 **Norfolk Sky**[28] 5855 4-10-0 **65** .... FergusSweeney 5 71
(Laura Mongan) *hld up in last quartet: hdwy 4f out: chsd ldng pair and rdn over 2f out: chsd clr wnr wl over 1f out: kpt on but no imp* **16/1**

3/06 **3** 1 **Sinbad The Sailor**[59] 4754 8-9-13 **64** ....(v) PatCosgrave 8 69
(George Baker) *dwlt and pushed along early: hld up in rr: hdwy 4f out: 4th and drvn over 1f out: kpt on but no ch w wnr* **9/2**[2]

2223 **4** 3¼ **Steely**[10] 6404 5-9-10 **61** .... RyanMoore 14 62
(Gary Moore) *led: hung rt fr 9f out: rdn and hdd 2f out: sn btn: wknd fnl f* **11/4**[1]

2154 **5** 6 **Proud Times (USA)**[28] 5868 7-10-0 **65** ....(p) AdamKirby 3 59
(Ali Brewer) *hld up in last pair: reminder over 5f out: rdn and effrt on outer over 3f out: 7th and wl btn 2f out* **12/1**

3500 **6** 2¼ **Dr Finley (IRE)**[5] 6565 6-9-8 **62** ....(v) SimonPearce(3) 13 53
(Lydia Pearce) *hld up in midfield: rdn over 4f out: 6th and btn whn swtchd lft over 2f out: no ch fnl 2f* **16/1**

330 **7** 2¾ **Mister Carter (IRE)**[27] 5885 6-9-13 **64** ....(vt) RichardHughes 11 52
(Ian Williams) *chsd ldr: rdn 4f out: lost pl and btn over 2f out: wknd 2f out* **6/1**[3]

5450 **8** 19 **Ginger Fizz**[108] 3110 6-10-0 **65** ....[1] ShaneKelly 2 30
(Ben Case) *in tch in midfield: rdn and struggling over 4f out: wl bhd fnl 2f: t.o* **16/1**

6300 **9** ¾ **Joe The Coat**[28] 5863 4-9-9 **60** .... TomQueally 4 24
(Mark H Tompkins) *chsd ldrs tl lost pl qckly u.p over 3f out: wl bhd fnl 2f: t.o* **6/1**[3]

00-0 **10** 16 **Ponte Di Rosa**[29] 5846 5-8-8 **50** .... JoeyHaynes(5) 6
(Simon Hodgson) *chsd ldrs: rdn 5f out: lost pl qckly 4f out: t.o fnl 2f* **33/1**

3m 21.76s (-3.94) **Going Correction** -0.075s/f (Stan)
WFA 3 from 4yo+ 12lb 10 Ran SP% **119.9**
Speed ratings (Par 101): **106,103,103,101,98 97,95,86,86,78**
Tote Swingers 1&2 £17.50, 2&3 £14.90, 1&3 £4.30 CSF £75.81 CT £348.21 TOTE £5.60: £2.30, £4.30, £1.40; EX 88.90 Trifecta £481.50 Pool: £2,315.98 - 3.60 winning units..
Owner Mr & Mrs William Rucker **Bred** Lady Bamford **Trained** Newmarket, Suffolk

FOCUS
This was a moderate staying event run at an ordinary pace.

6737 GREYHOUND PUB LINGFIELD H'CAP 1m 2f (P)
5:00 (5:00) (Class 6) (0-60,60) 3-Y-O+ **£2,045** (£603; £302) **Stalls** Low

Form RPR

0400 **1** **Solvanna**[6] 6521 3-9-3 **60** .... AndreaAtzeni 11 70
(Heather Main) *dwlt and short of room sn after s: hdwy on outer to ld over 7f out: mde rest: rdn clr 2f out: drvn fnl f: kpt on wl whn pressed fnl 50yds* **16/1**

442 **2** 1 **Keene**[12] 6339 3-9-3 **60** .... WilliamCarson 6 68
(Philip McBride) *t.k.h: chsd ldrs: drvn to chse clr wnr 2f out: styd on and clsd to press wnr wl ins fnl f: no ex and hld fnl 50yds* **11/4**[2]

51P **3** 1 **Santadelacruze**[38] 5528 4-9-9 **60** ....(b) RyanMoore 7 66+
(Gary Moore) *hld up in tch in midfield: swtchd lft and effrt to chse ldng pair 1f out: styd on same pce u.p fnl f* **9/4**[1]

1360 **4** 2½ **Archelao (IRE)**[10] 6399 5-9-4 **55** ....(t) KierenFox 3 56
(Richard Rowe) *hld up in last quartet: rdn and hdwy into midfield over 2f out: swtchd lft 1f out: styd on fnl f: nvr trbld ldrs* **20/1**

3145 **5** 1 **Lady Lunchalot (USA)**[147] 1897 3-8-9 **59** ....(p) KirstyFrench(7) 10 59
(J S Moore) *hld up towards rr: swtchd rt and hdwy into midfield but stuck wd 7f out: hdwy to chse wnr over 2f out tl 2f out: no ex and wknd ins fnl f* **20/1**

6500 **6** 3¾ **Cherry Tiger**[49] 5098 3-9-3 **60** .... LukeMorris 8 52
(James Toller) *hld up in midfield: rdn and unable qck over 2f out: swtchd ins and rallied briefly over 1f out: wknd fnl f* **7/1**[3]

0030 **7** 2¼ **Bajan Story**[10] 6400 4-9-3 **54** ....(p) FergusSweeney 13 42
(Michael Blanshard) *hld up in tch in midfield: rdn and outpcd over 2f out: wknd over 1f out* **33/1**

063 **8** ¾ **El Libertador (USA)**[87] 3819 7-8-11 **53** ....[1] JoeyHaynes(5) 12 40
(Eric Wheeler) *hld up in last quartet: effrt and sme hdwy jst over 2f out: no imp and wl btn over 1f out* **16/1**

266- **9** 4 **Mohair**[287] 8060 4-9-8 **59** .... SeanLevey 14 38
(Luke Dace) *stdd and dropped in bhd after s: rdn 4f out: n.d* **25/1**

5100 **10** ½ **Anginola (IRE)**[8] 6458 4-9-8 **59** .... GeorgeBaker 1 37
(Laura Mongan) *in tch in midfield: rdn and lost pl over 2f out: bhd over 1f out* **33/1**

3555 **11** nk **Catchanova (IRE)**[19] 6146 6-9-4 **55** ....(p) JohnFahy 9 33
(Eve Johnson Houghton) *dwlt and pushed along early: a towards rr: struggling u.p 3f out: bhd over 1f out* **16/1**

1300 **12** ½ **Salient**[69] 4411 9-9-3 **54** .... SebSanders 4 31
(Michael Attwater) *t.k.h: mainly chsd ldr tl over 2f out: sn wknd: bhd fnl f* **25/1**

6031 **13** 12 **Who's That Chick (IRE)**[15] 6261 4-9-4 **55** .... RichardHughes 2 9
(Ralph Smith) *led tl over 7f out: styd chsng ldrs tl wknd jst over 2f out: wl btn and eased over 1f out* **8/1**

2m 5.61s (-0.99) **Going Correction** -0.075s/f (Stan)
WFA 3 from 4yo+ 6lb 13 Ran SP% **121.8**
Speed ratings (Par 101): **100,99,98,96,95 92,90,90,87,86 86,85,76**
Tote Swingers 1&2 £9.90, 2&3 £2.30, 1&3 £9.40 CSF £55.80 CT £142.94 TOTE £24.40: £5.80, £1.60, £1.30; EX 69.60 Trifecta £313.80 Pool: £2,935.11 - 7.01 winning units..
Owner Wetumpka Racing & Andrew Knott **Bred** Usk Valley Stud **Trained** Kingston Lisle, Oxon

FOCUS
This was a modest event, won by a longstanding maiden.

6738 COMPLETE PLUMBING SERVICES MAIDEN STKS 1m 2f (P)
5:30 (5:31) (Class 5) 3-Y-O+ **£2,726** (£805; £402) **Stalls** Low

Form RPR

3-44 **1** **Squire Osbaldeston (IRE)**[138] 2198 3-9-5 82 .... TomQueally 1 86+
(Lady Cecil) *a travelling wl: trckd ldrs: chsd ldr over 1f out: shkn up and qcknd to ld jst ins fnl f: r.o wl: comf* **5/4**[1]

3 **2** *2 ½* **Hawker**[11] 6366 3-9-5 0 MickaelBarzalona 2 79
(Charlie Appleby) *led tl hung rt bnd after 1f and hdd: chsd ldr after tl led again 2f: drvn over 1f out: hdd and unable qck w wnr jst ins fnl f: one pce after* **10/1**

0653 **3** *1 ½* **Markttag**[29] 5847 3-9-5 72 RyanMoore 4 76
(Luca Cumani) *in tch in midfield: rdn and effrt over 2f out: outpcd over 1f out: rallied and styd on again ins fnl f: no threat to ldrs* **10/1**

4 *nk* **Musaddas** 3-9-5 0 SilvestreDeSousa 10 76
(Saeed bin Suroor) *wnt rt s: t.k.h: hld up in last trio: rdn and hdwy on inner over 1f out: styd on same pce fnl f* **3/1**[2]

5 *1 ¾* **Freedom's Light** 3-9-0 0 WilliamBuick 8 67+
(John Gosden) *s.i.s: in tch in rr: rn green and outpcd over 2f out: rallied and stl running green ent fnl f: kpt on same pce ins fnl f* **14/1**

-542 **6** *3* **Dalgig**[116] 2833 3-9-5 80 RichardHughes 6 67
(Jamie Osborne) *chsd ldr tl led 9f out: rdn and hdd 2f out: no ex and btn over 1f out: wknd ins fnl f* **9/2**[3]

-20 **7** *14* **Mawj Tamy (USA)**[126] 2547 3-9-5 0 DaneO'Neill 3 40
(Charles Hills) *sn chsng ldrs: rdn 3f out: lost pl ent fnl 2f: sn wknd: wl bhd fnl f* **33/1**

8 *35* **Asian Prince (IRE)**[90] 4-9-11 0 (t) GeorgeBaker 5
(Alastair Lidderdale) *dwlt: hld up in tch in last trio: rdn and btn over 2f out: sn wknd: t.o and heavily eased ins fnl f* **100/1**

2m 4.54s (-2.06) **Going Correction** -0.075s/f (Stan)
WFA 3 from 4yo 6lb **8** Ran SP% **116.4**
Speed ratings (Par 103): **105,103,101,101,100 97,86,58**
Tote Swingers 1&2 £3.90, 2&3 £7.20, 1&3 £3.40 CSF £16.06 TOTE £2.60: £1.40, £2.50, £2.20; EX 12.90 Trifecta £61.50 Pool: £2,700.96 - 32.89 winning units..
Owner P Hickman & G Johns **Bred** Kushnarenkovo Syndicate **Trained** Newmarket, Suffolk

FOCUS
This was an interesting maiden contested by a number of late developers from big stables.
T/Jkpt: £53,556.50 to a £1 stake. Pool: £113,147.61 - 1.50 winning tickets. T/Plt: £538.10 to a £1 stake. Pool: £82,898.51 - 112.45 winning tickets. T/Qpdt: £231.40 to a £1 stake. Pool: £6,066.62 - 19.40 winning tickets. SP

6062 GOODWOOD (R-H)
Wednesday, September 25

OFFICIAL GOING: Round course - good; straight course - good to soft (good in places)
Wind: Almost nil Weather: Fine becoming hazy, warm

6739 BRITISH STALLION STUDS E B F MAIDEN STKS 7f
2:00 (2:01) (Class 5) 2-Y-O **£3,234** (£962; £481; £240) **Stalls** Low

Form RPR

45 **1** **Fracking (IRE)**[18] 6184 2-9-5 0 MickaelBarzalona 6 87
(Olly Stevens) *w'like: str: mde all and spreadeagled field: pushed along and drew clr over 2f out: unchal* **9/2**[1]

0 **2** *5* **Wilde Inspiration (IRE)**[75] 4231 2-9-5 0 JimCrowley 3 73
(Ralph Beckett) *leggy: chsd ldng pair: rdn over 2f out: no ch w wnr but kpt on to take 2nd ins fnl f* **8/1**

20 **3** *nk* **Rock Of Dreams (IRE)**[88] 3836 2-9-5 0 WilliamBuick 13 72
(Charles Hills) *w'like: swtg: chsd wnr: lft bhd and shkn up over 2f out: no imp after: lost 2nd ins fnl f* **20/1**

22 **4** *1 ¼* **Travis Bickle (IRE)**[21] 6110 2-9-5 0 RichardHughes 4 69
(Sylvester Kirk) *w'like: chsd ldng trio but sn pushed along: nt qckn over 2f out: one pce after* **6/1**[3]

05 **5** *½* **Classic Mission**[13] 6333 2-9-5 0 RichardKingscote 1 68
(Jonathan Portman) *leggy: swtg: a in same pl: pushed along and no prog 2f out: shkn up briefly over 1f out: one pce: nt disgracd* **100/1**

6 *shd* **High Master (IRE)** 2-9-5 0 FrankieDettori 7 67
(Richard Hannon) *w'like: dwlt: sme way off the pce in 8th: pushed along over 2f out: kpt on fr over 1f out: n.d* **5/1**[2]

7 *½* **Arbaab** 2-9-5 0 PaulHanagan 2 66+
(Sir Michael Stoute) *str: chsd ldrs in 6th and rn green: pushed along and no prog over 2f out: one pce after* **13/2**

8 *3* **Aertex (IRE)** 2-9-0 0 PatDobbs 9 53
(Richard Hannon) *leggy: attractive: dwlt and sltly impeded s: chsd ldrs in 7th: no prog over 2f out: wknd over 1f out* **33/1**

9 *¾* **Matravers** 2-9-5 0 RyanMoore 15 56
(Sir Michael Stoute) *athletic: bit bkwd: dwlt: sn in last pair fr wd draw and wl off the pce: pushed along over 2f out: kpt on fr over 1f out* **16/1**

10 *shd* **Best Kept** 2-9-5 0 AndreaAtzeni 8 56
(Amanda Perrett) *lengthy: bit bkwd: sn in last quartet: pushed along over 2f out: nvr a factor but kpt on fnl f* **20/1**

5 **11** *3* **Berkeley Vale**[26] 5957 2-9-5 0 SebSanders 12 48
(Roger Teal) *w'like: dwlt: sn in last quartet: pushed along 3f out: hanging and no prog* **14/1**

12 *2 ¾* **Kelamita (IRE)** 2-9-0 0 JimmyFortune 14 35
(Hughie Morrison) *leggy: dwlt: a wl in rr* **50/1**

00 **13** *hd* **Maid Of Tuscany (IRE)**[27] 5922 2-9-0 0 DavidProbert 11 35
(Mark Usher) *w'like: nvr beyond midfield and nvr on terms: bhd over 1f out* **100/1**

0 **14** *14* **Exceed Policy**[4] 6641 2-9-5 0 SteveDrowne 5 2
(David Dennis) *lengthy: lw: in tch in midfield 2f: sn dropped to rr: wknd 3f out: t.o* **100/1**

U **Idea (USA)** 2-9-5 0 JamesDoyle 10
(Sir Michael Stoute) *lengthy: str: v restless in stalls: jinked and uns rdr s* **5/1**[2]

1m 28.63s (1.63) **Going Correction** +0.20s/f (Good) **15** Ran SP% **120.2**
Speed ratings (Par 95): **98,92,91,90,89 89,89,85,84,84 81,78,78,62,**
toteswingers 1&2 £9.20, 1&3 £13.70, 2&3 £29.90 CSF £38.07 TOTE £5.00: £1.90, £3.90, £4.20; EX 51.50 Trifecta £576.20 Pool: £2809.12 - 3.65 winning units..
Owner P Winkworth **Bred** Airlie Stud **Trained** Chiddingfold, Surrey

FOCUS
Rail from 6f on lower bend to Winning Post dolled out about 7yds increasing distances by circa 10yds and top bend dolled out 3yds increasing distances on that course by circa 5yds. A dry couple of days leading up to the meeting meant the ground was given as good on the round course and good to soft, with good places, on the straight course. The jockeys seemed to think that it was on the slow side of that description after the first. Some decent types have taken this maiden in the past, most notably Derby winner Workforce in 2009. There were a few well-bred newcomers but it was those with previous experience that filled the first five places.

6740 BIBENDUM E B F MAIDEN STKS 1m 1f
2:30 (2:31) (Class 4) 2-Y-O **£5,175** (£1,540; £769; £384) **Stalls** Low

Form RPR

2 **1** **Double Bluff (IRE)**[13] 6330 2-9-5 0 JoeFanning 1 89+
(Mark Johnston) *lw: mde all: gng much bttr than rivals 3f out: pushed along and drew 3 l clr wl over 1f out: in n.d after but shkn up fnl f* **13/8**[1]

02 **2** *1 ¾* **Pack Leader (IRE)**[33] 5698 2-9-5 0 RichardKingscote 3 86+
(Amanda Perrett) *awkward bef gng to post: trckd ldng pair: rdn 3f out: chsd wnr over 2f out but sn lft bhd: hung rt and lft fnl f but styd on and clsd gap nr fin* **3/1**[2]

342 **3** *6* **Tahadee (IRE)**[20] 6125 2-9-5 79 MartinHarley 4 74
(Mick Channon) *swtg: trckd ldng trio: gng wl 4f out: rdn 3f out: wnt 3rd over 1f out but lft bhd by first pair* **4/1**[3]

43 **4** *2* **Sebastian Beach (IRE)**[20] 6139 2-9-5 0 RichardHughes 7 70
(Richard Hannon) *trckd wnr: rdn 3f out: lost 2nd over 2f out: wknd wl over 1f out* **7/1**

5 *3 ¼* **Vent De Force** 2-9-5 0 JimmyFortune 2 63
(Hughie Morrison) *w'like: bit bkwd: s.s: nvr on terms w ldrs: rdn and no prog 4f out* **33/1**

6 **6** *8* **Zephyr**[7] 6528 2-9-5 0 (p) WilliamBuick 6 47
(John Gosden) *dwlt: nvr on terms w ldrs: rdn and no prog 4f out: wknd fnl f* **8/1**

7 *43* **Taws** 2-9-0 0 AndreaAtzeni 5
(Rod Millman) *leggy: s.s: sn wl bhd and rn green: t.o* **66/1**

1m 57.44s (1.14) **Going Correction** +0.20s/f (Good) **7** Ran SP% **111.1**
Speed ratings (Par 97): **102,100,95,93,90 83,45**
toteswingers 1&2 £1.90, 1&3 £1.80, 2&3 £2.10 CSF £6.23 TOTE £2.60: £2.10, £1.80; EX 7.10 Trifecta £19.50 Pool: £2721.04 - 104.58 winning units..
Owner R W Huggins **Bred** Michael G Daly **Trained** Middleham Moor, N Yorks

FOCUS
Embryonic stayers on show in this juvenile maiden, which doesn't have a great record for producing smart performers. However, the winner looks decent and made every yard.

6741 SANTA MARIA FOODSERVICE STKS (H'CAP) 1m 4f
3:05 (3:05) (Class 2) (0-105,97) 3-Y-O+ **£12,938** (£3,850; £1,924; £962) **Stalls** High

Form RPR

10-0 **1** **Gospel Choir**[33] 5723 4-10-0 **97** RyanMoore 1 106+
(Sir Michael Stoute) *trckd ldrs: pushed along over 3f out: clsd to chal fr 2f out: drvn to ld 1f out: styd on* **2/1**[1]

3000 **2** *½* **Mister Impatience**[11] 6394 3-9-3 **94** JoeFanning 2 102
(Mark Johnston) *lw: trckd ldr: led 2f out: drvn and hdd 1f out: styd on but a hld nr fin* **8/1**

2150 **3** *1 ¼* **Duke Of Clarence (IRE)**[32] 5746 4-9-11 **94** RichardHughes 7 100
(Richard Hannon) *hld up in last: pushed along over 3f out: no prog tl styd on fr over 1f out: nvr able to chal* **6/1**[3]

4025 **4** *1 ½* **Haylaman (IRE)**[46] 5259 5-9-10 **93** JimCrowley 5 97
(David Simcock) *hld up in 5th: rdn and trying to cl whn n.m.r 2f out: kpt on one pce after* **12/1**

4006 **5** *shd* **Blue Surf**[32] 5766 4-9-13 **96** PatDobbs 3 99
(Amanda Perrett) *lw: trckd ldrs: rdn and nt qckn over 2f out: n.d over 1f out: plugged on* **7/1**

10 **6** *3* **Charles Camoin (IRE)**[32] 5768 5-9-11 **94** LiamKeniry 6 93
(Sylvester Kirk) *swtg: hld up in 6th: clsd on ldrs towards far rail 3f out: nt qckn 2f out: wknd over 1f out* **10/1**

6-51 **7** *nk* **Pearl Castle (IRE)**[48] 5189 3-8-10 **87** JamieSpencer 4 85
(Andrew Balding) *racd freely: led to 2f out: sn wknd* **10/3**[2]

2m 40.75s (2.35) **Going Correction** +0.20s/f (Good)
WFA 3 from 4yo+ 8lb **7** Ran SP% **111.1**
Speed ratings (Par 109): **100,99,98,97,97 95,95**
toteswingers 1&2 £3.70, 1&3 £2.30, 2&3 £6.70 CSF £17.52 TOTE £2.50: £1.20, £3.50; EX 17.70 Trifecta £69.40 Pool: £2722.77 - 29.41 winning units..
Owner Cheveley Park Stud **Bred** Cheveley Park Stud Ltd **Trained** Newmarket, Suffolk

FOCUS
A good handicap, in which some sort of case could be made for all seven of these. The gallop was uneven and a few could be given a chance at the 2f pole. The form seems sound enough.

6742 GREENE KING FOUNDATION STKS (LISTED RACE) 1m 1f 192y
3:40 (3:41) (Class 1) 3-Y-O+
£22,684 (£8,600; £4,304; £2,144; £1,076; £540) **Stalls** Low

Form RPR

-420 **1** **Grandeur (IRE)**[39] 5553 4-9-0 118 RyanMoore 7 112+
(Jeremy Noseda) *hld up in last pair: prog over 3f out but plenty to do: sustained hdwy after to ld jst over 1f out: drvn and styd on wl* **6/4**[1]

2100 **2** *1 ¼* **Quick Wit**[17] 6254 6-9-0 107 (p) SilvestreDeSousa 8 109
(Saeed bin Suroor) *lw: trckd ldrs: disp 3rd fr 4f out: rdn over 2f out: clsd to chal jst over 1f out: chsd wnr after: styd on but wl hld* **16/1**

015 **3** *1 ½* **Making Eyes (IRE)**[70] 4421 5-8-9 99 MartinDwyer 2 101
(Hugo Palmer) *prom: trckd ldr 1/2-way: clsd 3f out: stl gng strly 2f out: rdn to chal over 1f out: sn outpcd but kpt on* **33/1**

5233 **4** *¾* **Gabrial (IRE)**[18] 6191 4-9-0 110 PaulHanagan 4 105
(Richard Fahey) *t.k.h: hld up in 6th: prog to chse ldng pair 4f out: rdn to cl fr over 2f out: on terms but hld whn n.m.r jst over 1f out: kpt on* **11/1**

0-11 **5** *1 ¼* **Brown Panther**[55] 4919 5-9-5 113 RichardKingscote 1 107
(Tom Dascombe) *lw: led: wnt clr 5f out to over 3f out: shkn up and hdd jst over 1f out: fdd* **3/1**[2]

1055 **6** *5* **Rewarded**[18] 6198 4-9-0 109 KirstyMilczarek 6 92
(James Toller) *had to be dismntd and led last 2f to post: in tch towards rr: rdn and struggling 3f out: wl btn after* **14/1**

210 **7** *14* **Sugar Boy (IRE)**[88] 3849 3-8-11 112 MartinHarley 9 67
(Marco Botti) *chsd ldr to 1/2-way: wknd 4f out: t.o* **4/1**[3]

1621 **8** *11* **Mister Music**[10] 6427 4-9-0 99 (b) RichardHughes 3 42
(Richard Hannon) *hld up in last pair: urged along and no prog over 3f out: wknd and eased: t.o* **25/1**

5063 **9** 4 ½ **Dick Doughtywylie**[67] 4526 5-9-0 102............................ WilliamBuick 5 33
(John Gosden) *lw: trckd ldrs: rdn and wknd wl over 3f out: t.o and eased* **20/1**

2m 6.6s (-1.50) **Going Correction** +0.20s/f (Good)
WFA 3 from 4yo+ 6lb **9** Ran SP% **117.4**
Speed ratings (Par 111): **114,113,111,111,110 106,95,86,82**
toteswingers 1&2 £5.80, 1&3 £15.30, 2&3 £32.20 CSF £28.75 TOTE £2.20: £1.30, £4.70, £8.00; EX 23.90 Trifecta £464.70 Pool: £4841.76 - 7.81 winning units..
Owner Miss Yvonne Jacques **Bred** Mrs Cherry Faeste **Trained** Newmarket, Suffolk

FOCUS
This Listed contest has sometimes gone to a top-notch performer, most notably Twice Over (2009) and Hunter's Light (2011). This renewal looked right up to standard, with a few of these capable of plying their trade at a higher level. The winner was best in and didn't need to be at his best.

6743 HILDON NATURAL MINERAL WATER STKS (H'CAP) 1m 3f
4:15 (4:16) (Class 4) (0-80,86) 3-Y-O **£6,469** (£1,925; £962; £481) **Stalls** High

Form RPR

41-4 **1** **Sweet Deal (IRE)**[32] 5743 3-9-3 **76**............................ WilliamBuick 9 88+
(Jeremy Noseda) *hld up in last pair: pushed along and prog fr 3f out: wandered both lft and rt but clsd fr over 1f out to ld ins fnl f: drvn and styd on strly* **4/1**[1]

-653 **2** 1 ¼ **Aussie Lyrics (FR)**[26] 5960 3-9-1 **74**..........................(p) JamesDoyle 5 84
(George Baker) *led: tk field to centre in st: gng strly over 2f out: rdn over 1f out: hdd ins fnl f: styd on but outpcd nr fin* **9/2**[2]

1-30 **3** 2 ¾ **Ice Pie**[132] 2387 3-9-0 **73**............................ RichardKingscote 12 78
(Tom Dascombe) *lw: trckd ldng trio: chsd ldr jst over 2f out to over 1f out: one pce* **4/1**[1]

4462 **4** 1 ¼ **Landau (IRE)**[7] 6521 3-8-7 **66** oh3............................ LiamKeniry 3 69
(Sylvester Kirk) *trckd ldng pair to 2f out: readily outpcd after* **20/1**

534 **5** 3 ¼ **Angus Glens**[22] 6062 3-9-3 **76**............................ SteveDrowne 11 73
(David Dennis) *t.k.h: hld up towards rr: rdn 3f out: no prog tl kpt on fr over 1f out: n.d* **8/1**

-341 **6** *shd* **Deserted**[31] 5802 3-9-3 **76**............................ KirstyMilczarek 4 73
(Luca Cumani) *lw: trckd ldrs: shkn up and nt qckn over 2f out: steadily outpcd after* **6/1**[3]

2100 **7** 1 ½ **Stiff Upper Lip (IRE)**[18] 6200 3-8-13 **75**(b[1]) WilliamTwiston-Davies(3) 10 70
(Richard Hannon) *lw: mostly chsd ldr to jst over 2f out: wknd* **25/1**

3353 **8** ½ **Ivanhoe**[10] 6435 3-8-7 **66** oh2..........................(p) DavidProbert 7 60
(Michael Blanshard) *in tch in midfield: nt qckn over 2f out: trying to keep on but no ch whn short of room over 1f out: one pce* **10/1**

2540 **9** 4 ½ **Knight's Parade (IRE)**[11] 6405 3-8-8 **67**............................ PatDobbs 2 53
(Amanda Perrett) *hld up in rr: shkn up over 2f out: no prog and nvr involved* **20/1**

10 **10** 1 ½ **He's A Striker (IRE)**[12] 6358 3-8-11 **73**............................ RyanClark(3) 13 57
(Michael Blake) *s.s: hld up in last: rdn wl over 2f out: no great prog* **20/1**

-006 **11** 5 **Harwoods Star (IRE)**[7] 6521 3-8-11 **70**..........................(e) JimCrowley 1 45
(Amanda Perrett) *dwlt and swvd rt s: nvr beyond midfield: shkn up and wknd over 2f out* **16/1**

6520 **12** 2 ½ **Rock God (IRE)**[22] 6081 3-9-0 **73**..........................(b) JohnFahy 8 44
(Eve Johnson Houghton) *s.i.s and pushed up into midfield: prog to go prom over 3f out: wknd qckly over 2f out* **25/1**

2m 29.45s (2.95) **Going Correction** +0.20s/f (Good) **12** Ran SP% **120.5**
Speed ratings (Par 103): **97,96,94,93,90 90,89,89,86,84 81,79**
toteswingers 1&2 £4.90, 1&3 £5.80, 2&3 £6.50 CSF £20.13 CT £76.63 TOTE £5.00: £1.70, £1.80, £2.30; EX 30.30 Trifecta £114.00 Pool: £2972.49 - 19.54 winning units..
Owner Mrs Susan Roy **Bred** M Henochsberg & Pontchartrain Stud **Trained** Newmarket, Suffolk

FOCUS
This race was weakened significantly by the morning defection of Battalion, who would have dominated the market. In the event it was an open sort of race but the market got it spot on with the first three in the betting coming home in the places. The field came down the centre. Fair form, assessed at face value.

6744 3663 INSPIRED BY YOU STKS (H'CAP) 6f
4:50 (4:51) (Class 4) (0-80,80) 3-Y-O+ **£6,469** (£1,925; £962; £481) **Stalls** High

Form RPR

0661 **1** **Joey's Destiny (IRE)**[36] 5611 3-8-13 **77**.................. ThomasBrown(3) 2 86
(George Baker) *towards rr: prog on outer fr 2f out: edgd lft but styd on wl fnl f to ld last strides* **5/1**[1]

21 **2** *nse* **Dilgura**[117] 2824 3-8-10 **71**............................ ShaneKelly 9 80
(Stuart Kittow) *lengthy: trckd ldrs gng wl: prog to ld wl over 1f out: drvn fnl f: edgd rt and hdd last strides* **10/1**

120 **3** ½ **Tidal's Baby**[5] 6586 4-9-0 **78**............................ GeorgeDowning(5) 8 85
(Tony Carroll) *dwlt: wl in rr: rdn and prog over 2f out: chsd ldr jst ins fnl f: nt qckn and lost 2nd nr fin* **7/1**[3]

-001 **4** ¾ **Slip Sliding Away (IRE)**[22] 6067 6-9-6 **79**.................. JamesDoyle 10 88+
(Peter Hedger) *hld up wl in rr: trying to cl whn nt clr run over 1f out: swtchd rt ins fnl f: running on strly and would have gone cl but rn out of room nr fin: eased* **11/2**[2]

4-51 **5** ¾ **Apricot Sky**[128] 2499 3-9-0 **75**............................ DaneO'Neill 14 77
(Henry Candy) *in tch on nr side: prog 2f out: rdn and nt qckn over 1f out: kpt on* **8/1**

0214 **6** *hd* **Dominium (USA)**[7] 6525 6-8-10 **72**..........................(b) RobertTart(3) 3 74
(Jeremy Gask) *prom on outer: rdn jst over 2f out: nt qckn over 1f out: kpt on* **8/1**

6010 **7** ¾ **Aye Aye Digby (IRE)**[7] 6525 8-9-4 **77**............................ JimCrowley 15 76
(Patrick Chamings) *racd against nr side rail: w ldrs: rdn and nt qckn over 1f out: one pce after* **12/1**

5-00 **8** ½ **Fat Gary**[48] 5182 3-9-3 **78**..........................(p) RichardKingscote 1 76
(Tom Dascombe) *led to over 2f out: one pce over 1f out: fdd ins fnl f* **12/1**

0406 **9** 1 ¼ **Johnny Castle**[8] 6489 5-9-5 **78**............................ WilliamBuick 6 72
(Amanda Perrett) *lw: s.i.s: wl in rr: plld out wdst of all and sme prog over 1f out: wknd last 100yds* **12/1**

2400 **10** 1 ¼ **Prince Of Burma (IRE)**[11] 6388 5-8-4 **70**............................ EoinWalsh(7) 13 60
(David Evans) *s.v.s and lost all ch: detached in last tl kpt on fr over 1f out* **50/1**

1056 **11** *nk* **Bravo Echo**[22] 6067 7-9-6 **79**............................ RobertHavlin 7 68
(Michael Attwater) *racd on outer: chsd ldrs: no prog 2f out: wknd over 1f out* **15/2**

0615 **12** ¾ **Jungle Bay**[9] 6461 6-9-4 **77**..........................(b) LiamJones 4 63
(Jane Chapple-Hyam) *racd freely early: chsd ldr: led over 2f out to wl over 1f out: wknd qckly* **25/1**

4421 **13** 2 ¼ **Saskia's Dream**[16] 6255 5-8-2 **66** oh2..........................(b) IanBurns(5) 11 45
(Jane Chapple-Hyam) *cl up: rdn over 2f out: sn wknd* **25/1**

1m 12.14s (-0.06) **Going Correction** -0.075s/f (Good)
WFA 3 from 4yo+ 2lb **13** Ran SP% **120.4**
Speed ratings (Par 105): **97,96,96,95,94 94,93,92,90,89 88,87,84**
toteswingers 1&2 £14.90, 1&3 £6.60, 2&3 £9.20 CSF £54.20 CT £368.87 TOTE £7.20: £2.60, £3.10, £2.50; EX 81.80 Trifecta £715.50 Pool: £2835.84 - 2.97 winning units..
Owner Delancey **Bred** Brian Wallace **Trained** Manton, Wilts
■ Stewards' Enquiry : George Downing two-day ban: used whip above permitted level (Oct 9-10)

FOCUS
A tight-knit sprint handicap in which the majority of the field raced towards the stands' rail. However, the winner came down the centre. The form makes sense.

6745 MERBURY CATERING CONSULTANTS APPRENTICE STKS (H'CAP) 5f
5:20 (5:20) (Class 5) (0-75,74) 3-Y-O+ **£3,234** (£962; £481; £240) **Stalls** High

Form RPR

012 **1** **Threave**[9] 6463 5-9-1 **68**............................ CharlesBishop 10 78
(Violet M Jordan) *taken down early: mde all: rdn over 2f out: edgd rt fr over 1f out: hrd pressed fnl f: hld on wl* **4/1**[1]

3060 **2** *nk* **Valmina**[5] 6586 6-9-1 **71**..........................(t) GeorgeDowning(3) 4 80
(Tony Carroll) *hld up in last pair: stdy prog on outer fr 1/2-way: wnt 2nd jst ins fnl f and sn chal: jst hld last strides* **6/1**[3]

142U **3** 1 ¾ **Griffin Point (IRE)**[9] 6463 6-8-7 **63**..........................(b) RyanTate(3) 1 66
(William Muir) *racd wdst of all in midfield and sn urged along: prog over 1f out: styd on fnl f to take 3rd nr fin* **12/1**

4233 **4** *nk* **Macdillon**[26] 5956 7-8-9 **67**..........................(t) DanielMuscutt(5) 5 69
(Stuart Kittow) *trckd ldrs: pushed along and cl up 2f out: nt clr run and swtchd lft 1f out: kpt on same pce fnl f* **11/2**[2]

6501 **5** 1 **Alpha Delta Whisky**[31] 5796 5-9-3 **70**..................(v) MichaelJMMurphy 7 68
(John Gallagher) *pressed wnr to 1f out: wknd* **14/1**

4602 **6** 1 ¼ **Waseem Faris (IRE)**[11] 6388 4-9-2 **74**..........................(v) DanielCremin(5) 8 67
(Mick Channon) *hld up wl in rr: urged along and no real prog 2f out: kpt on fnl f: n.d* **11/2**[2]

0032 **7** *nk* **Where's Reiley (USA)**[4] 6652 7-8-10 **63**..........................(b) RyanClark 3 55
(Michael Attwater) *prom on outer: rdn 1/2-way: lost pl u.p over 1f out: plugged on* **8/1**

044 **8** *hd* **Solemn**[7] 6527 8-8-13 **73**..........................(b) WillPettis(7) 2 65
(Milton Bradley) *pressed ldrs on outer: nt qckn over 1f out: wknd ins fnl f* **16/1**

5324 **9** ¾ **Hot Secret**[13] 6338 3-9-0 **68**............................ ThomasBrown 14 57
(Andrew Balding) *taken down early: sltly awkward s: racd against nr side rail and in tch: tried to cl on ldrs 2f out: no hdwy fnl f* **12/1**

0531 **10** 1 ½ **Never A Quarrel (IRE)**[13] 6345 3-8-13 **67**............................ RobertTart 11 51
(Jeremy Gask) *taken down early: chsd ldrs: rdn over 2f out: steadily wknd over 1f out* **8/1**

263 **11** 3 ¼ **Best Be Careful (IRE)**[11] 6381 5-8-12 **68**.................. JoeyHaynes(3) 13 40
(Mark Usher) *racd towards nr side: chsd ldrs: wknd over 1f out* **20/1**

6464 **12** 1 ¼ **Princess Cammie (IRE)**[42] 5397 3-8-1 **60** oh8.................. IanBurns(5) 12 27
(John Bridger) *a wl in rr: no ch over 1f out* **50/1**

20-0 **13** 6 **Invincible Lad (IRE)**[19] 6161 9-9-6 **73**.........(p) WilliamTwiston-Davies 6 19
(Ed McMahon) *s.i.s: a wl in rr: wl bhd over 1f out* **33/1**

050- **14** 10 **Marygold**[359] 6739 4-8-7 **63**............................ DannyBrock(3) 9
(Lee Carter) *nvr gng wl: a in rr: t.o* **50/1**

58.57s (-1.63) **Going Correction** -0.075s/f (Good)
WFA 3 from 4yo+ 1lb **14** Ran SP% **126.8**
Speed ratings (Par 103): **110,109,106,106,104 102,102,101,100,98 93,91,81,65**
toteswingers 1&2 £8.80, 1&3 £10.50, 2&3 £15.90 CSF £27.99 CT £283.07 TOTE £4.40: £1.60, £3.10, £5.70; EX 38.90 Trifecta £562.40 Pool: £2248.89 - 2.99 winning units..
Owner Mrs Jackie Cornwell **Bred** Mrs J A Cornwell **Trained** Moreton Morrell, Warwicks

FOCUS
Just a modest apprentice handicap to end the card but it served up another exciting finish. Sound form.
T/Plt: £34.60 to £1 stake. Pool: £83,715.05 - 1763.68 winning tickets. T/Qpdt: £10.30 to £1 stake. Pool: £7021.18 - 503.02 winning tickets. JN

6688 KEMPTON (A.W) (R-H)
Wednesday, September 25

OFFICIAL GOING: Standard
Wind: Nil Weather: Bright early

6746 REINDEER RACING ON 06.12.13 MAIDEN STKS 5f (P)
5:25 (6:34) (Class 5) 2-Y-O **£2,587** (£770; £384; £192) **Stalls** Low

Form RPR

4 **1** **Dutch Interior**[12] 6354 2-9-5 0............................ JimmyFortune 4 76+
(Gary Moore) *trckd ldrs: drvn to ld 1f out: rdn out fnl 150yds* **3/1**[2]

20 **2** 1 ¼ **Clumber Street**[18] 6213 2-9-5 0............................ SeanLevey 7 72
(Ed McMahon) *led: rdn and hdd 1f out: styd on same pce fnl 110yds* **25/1**

43 **3** 1 ¼ **Rock N Rouge (IRE)**[17] 6234 2-9-0 0............................ JamieSpencer 6 62
(David Brown) *chsd ldrs: rdn 2f out: styd on same pce appr fnl f* **4/5**[1]

0 **4** 1 ½ **Groundworker (IRE)**[52] 5033 2-9-5 0............................ CathyGannon 5 62+
(Sylvester Kirk) *in tch: pushed along and one pce 1/2-way: styd on u.p fnl f kpt on clsng stages* **33/1**

00 **5** 1 **Spirit Of Alsace (IRE)**[55] 4924 2-9-0 0............................[1] AndreaAtzeni 2 53
(Roger Varian) *chsd ldrs: rdn over 2f out: styd on same pce* **4/1**[3]

40 **6** ¾ **Tanojin (IRE)**[13] 6318 2-9-0 0............................ SamHitchcott 8 50+
(Mick Channon) *s.i.s: in rr: rdn over 2f out: kpt on fnl f: nt rch ldrs* **16/1**

0 **7** ¾ **Bazooka (IRE)**[9] 6477 2-9-5 0............................ PatCosgrave 12 53+
(Ed de Giles) *s.i.s: in rr: pushed along and hdwy over 1f out: kpt on clsng stages but nvr a threat* **50/1**

63 **8** 1 ½ **Birikyno**[12] 6354 2-9-0 0............................ ThomasGarner(5) 10 47
(Mark Usher) *in tch early: sn rdn and outpcd* **33/1**

0 **9** 1 **Sutton Sioux**[10] 6423 2-9-0 0............................ FergusSweeney 3 39
(Jeremy Gask) *chsd ldrs to 1/2-way* **25/1**

00 **10** 2 ½ **Back On Baileys**[18] 6213 2-9-0 0............................ LukeMorris 1 30
(Chris Dwyer) *chsd ldrs tl wknd qckly over 1f out* **33/1**

40 **11** 10 **Saxony**[10] 6423 2-9-0 0............................ HarryBentley 11
(Mark Usher) *s.i.s: a bhd* **50/1**

1m 0.1s (-0.40) **Going Correction** -0.05s/f (Stan) **11** Ran SP% **126.9**
Speed ratings (Par 95): **101,99,97,94,93 91,90,88,86,82 66**
toteswingers 1&2 £7.90, 1&3 £1.60, 2&3 £5.50 CSF £81.29 TOTE £4.80: £1.60, £6.30, £1.10; EX 89.60 Trifecta £211.80 Pool: £7471.04 - 26.44 winning units..
Owner R A Green **Bred** Cheveley Park Stud Ltd **Trained** Lower Beeding, W Sussex

The Form Book Flat, Raceform Ltd, Compton, RG20 6NL.

FOCUS
The runners tended to stick more towards the far side than at recent meetings, where it's generally been a case of the horse who challenges widest wins.

6747 £500 FREE BETS AT BETDAQ MAIDEN STKS 6f (P)
5:55 (6:34) (Class 5) 2-Y-O **£2,587** (£770; £384; £192) **Stalls** Low

Form RPR

1 **Mushir** 2-9-5 0 PaulHanagan 1 86+
(Roger Varian) *in rr: drvn over 2f out: styd on wl on far rail fnl f to chse ldr fnl 100yds: led last stride* **4/5**[1]

042 **2** *nse* **Speedfiend**[40] 5494 2-9-5 81 PatCosgrave 5 86
(Noel Quinlan) *led: jnd fr 2f out: shkn up and asserted again fnl f: kpt on wl: ct last stride* **5/1**[3]

0363 **3** *1 ¾* **Jazz (IRE)**[14] 6303 2-9-5 83 JamieSpencer 3 81
(Charles Hills) *chsd ldrs: chal fr 2f out and sn rdn: outpcd fnl f: wknd into 3rd fnl 110yds* **9/4**[2]

4 *8* **Pushkin Museum (IRE)** 2-9-5 0 JimmyFortune 6 57
(Gary Moore) *in tch: rdn to chse ldrs 2f out: wknd over 1f out* **50/1**

5423 **5** *2 ¼* **Wickhambrook (IRE)**[44] 5339 2-9-5 75 SeanLevey 2 50
(Ismail Mohammed) *in rr: shkn up: hung rt and no ch 2f out* **10/1**

05 **6** *24* **Sydney James (IRE)**[20] 6132 2-9-5 0 RichardHughes 8
(Richard Hannon) *drvn to chse ldr and faltered after 1f: rdn over 3f out: wknd qckly wl over 2f out* **33/1**

1m 12.57s (-0.53) **Going Correction** -0.05s/f (Stan) **6** Ran SP% **117.0**
Speed ratings (Par 95): **101,100,98,87,84 52**
toteswingers 1&2 £1.90, 1&3 £1.50, 2&3 £1.80 CSF £5.95 TOTE £2.40: £1.80, £3.30; EX 7.30 Trifecta £16.20 Pool: £13,669.67 - 631.21 winning units..
Owner Hamdan Al Maktoum **Bred** Shadwell Estate Company Limited **Trained** Newmarket, Suffolk

FOCUS
A fair maiden, dominated by those at the head of the market.

6748 BETDAQ - THE SPORTS BETTING EXCHANGE MEDIAN AUCTION MAIDEN STKS 1m (P)
6:30 (6:31) (Class 5) 3-5-Y-O **£2,587** (£770; £384; £192) **Stalls** Low

Form RPR

1 **Havelovewilltravel (IRE)** 3-9-0 0 RyanMoore 6 70+
(Jeremy Noseda) *in rr: hdwy on outside over 2f out: str run fnl f: led last strides* **5/2**[1]

-552 **2** *hd* **Checkpoint**[21] 6105 4-9-9 65 (p) SamHitchcott 5 74
(Gary Moore) *chsd ldrs: rdn to ld over 1f out: kpt on: hdd last strides* **8/1**

0 **3** *3 ¼* **You Look So Good**[120] 2760 3-9-0 0 NeilCallan 9 62
(Roger Varian) *chsd ldrs: rdn: hung rt and green 2f out: styd on to take 3rd fnl f but nt pce of ldng duo* **7/2**[3]

63 **4** *½* **Pretty Bubbles**[26] 5962 4-9-4 0 DavidProbert 2 61
(J R Jenkins) *in tch: hdwy to chse ldrs 2f out: one pce fnl f* **14/1**

0000 **5** *3 ¾* **Habeshia**[7] 6521 3-9-5 70 (v) SteveDrowne 12 57
(John Best) *pressed ldrs after 3f: rdn over 2f out: wknd appr fnl f* **16/1**

0024 **6** *3 ¼* **Rioja Day (IRE)**[44] 5346 3-9-5 63 (b) SebSanders 11 50
(J W Hills) *led: jnd after 3f: rdn over 2f out: hdd over 1f out: sn wknd* **8/1**

0236 **7** *1 ½* **Vastly (USA)**[15] 6283 4-9-4 70 (p) ShelleyBirkett(5) 13 46
(Julia Feilden) *chsd ldrs: wknd 2f out* **3/1**[2]

6 **8** *3* **Pastoral Dancer**[21] 6113 4-9-9 0 PatDobbs 10 39
(Richard Rowe) *in rr: sme hdwy over 2f out: sn wknd* **66/1**

9 *1* **Thomas Blossom (IRE)** 3-9-5 0 J-PGuillambert 14 37
(Nigel Tinkler) *in tch 5f* **20/1**

10 *11* **Broon Troot (IRE)** 3-9-5 0 MartinDwyer 7 12
(Marcus Tregoning) *s.i.s: a in rr* **20/1**

0 **11** *23* **Bridge To My Heart**[26] 5962 3-9-0 0 (v1) CathyGannon 3
(Olivia Maylam) *sn wl bhd* **66/1**

1m 39.65s (-0.15) **Going Correction** -0.05s/f (Stan)
WFA 3 from 4yo 4lb **11** Ran SP% **123.1**
Speed ratings (Par 103): **98,97,94,94,90 87,85,82,81,70 47**
toteswingers 1&2 £6.40, 1&3 £2.60, 2&3 £7.00 CSF £23.91 TOTE £4.20: £2.00, £1.20, £1.80; EX 24.80 Trifecta £126.30 Pool: £5052.64 - 30.00 winning units..
Owner Joseph Barton **Bred** Lynch Bages Ltd **Trained** Newmarket, Suffolk

FOCUS
A weak maiden for the track. The pre-race standard was modest and the form is far from solid.

6749 REINDEER RACING AT KEMPTON 13.12.13 NURSERY H'CAP 7f (P)
7:00 (7:01) (Class 6) (0-65,65) 2-Y-O **£1,940** (£577; £288; £144) **Stalls** Low

Form RPR

0000 **1** **Fiftyshadesfreed (IRE)**[21] 6111 2-9-4 62 PatCosgrave 9 64
(George Baker) *chsd ldrs: chal over 1f out: sn slt ld: hld on gamely u.p thrght fnl f* **16/1**

004 **2** *½* **Starlight Princess (IRE)**[20] 6132 2-8-9 53 (p) LiamJones 8 54
(J S Moore) *in rr: drvn and hdwy on outside fr 2f out: str run fnl f to press wnr clsng stages but a jst hld* **50/1**

006 **3** *shd* **Division Belle**[22] 6063 2-9-4 62 MartinDwyer 4 63
(William Muir) *chsd ldrs: rdn and outpcd fr 2f out: swtchd rt and styd on fnl 110yds: gng on nr fin* **16/1**

000 **4** *½* **Gloss (IRE)**[30] 5843 2-9-7 65 PatDobbs 7 64
(Richard Hannon) *chsd ldrs: rdn and slt ld over 1f out: sn hdd no ex fnl 110yds* **10/1**

455 **5** *1* **Drive On (IRE)**[21] 6110 2-8-10 54 (t) JohnFahy 11 51
(Eve Johnson Houghton) *chsd ldrs: rdn over 2f out: chal over 1f out: outpcd fnl 110yds* **7/1**[3]

0023 **6** *hd* **China In My Hands**[13] 6333 2-9-7 65 MartinHarley 13 61
(Mick Channon) *sn led: rdn over 2f out: hdd over 1f out: outpcd fnl 110yds* **16/1**

065 **7** *½* **Midnight Rambler (IRE)**[13] 6342 2-9-2 60 RichardHughes 3 55
(Richard Hannon) *trckd ldrs: rdn 2f out: effrt on ins over 1f out: wknd fnl 110yds* **7/2**[2]

000 **8** *½* **Syrian Pearl**[37] 5593 2-9-7 65 TedDurcan 2 60
(Chris Wall) *in tch: drvn: sme hdwy and nt clr run ins fnl f: nt rch ldrs* **7/1**[3]

530 **9** *1 ¾* **Ambria's Fury (IRE)**[9] 6474 2-9-6 64 (v1) SamHitchcott 14 53
(Mick Channon) *s.i.s: in rr: rdn over 2f out: sme hdwy fnl f* **50/1**

3066 **10** *½* **Jersey Cream (IRE)**[21] 6111 2-9-2 60 RyanMoore 1 47
(Gary Moore) *sn in rr: pushed along 2f out: no imp* **3/1**[1]

6002 **11** *1* **Choral Clan (IRE)**[46] 5276 2-8-13 57 (v1) JackMitchell 10 42
(Philip Mitchell) *in rr: hdwy fr 3f out: chsd ldrs 2f out: btn whn hmpd ins fnl f* **14/1**

5033 **12** *1 ¼* **Tyrsal (IRE)**[13] 6322 2-8-11 55 AndreaAtzeni 5 41
(Robert Eddery) *in tch: chsd ldrs and rdn over 1f out: hld whn hmpd and stmbld ins fnl f* **7/1**[3]

5340 **13** *2 ¾* **Queen Of The Tarts**[21] 6111 2-9-3 61 NeilCallan 6 35
(Olly Stevens) *bhd most of way* **20/1**

1m 27.86s (1.86) **Going Correction** -0.05s/f (Stan) **13** Ran SP% **126.8**
Speed ratings (Par 93): **87,86,86,85,84 84,83,83,81,80 79,78,74**
toteswingers 1&2 £196.70, 1&3 £66.70, 2&3 £133.80 CSF £681.37 CT £12265.29 TOTE £29.00: £9.50, £11.30, £7.70; EX 529.70 Trifecta £1892.70 Pool: £2523.63 - 0.01 winning units..
Owner Team Fifty **Bred** Bernard Cloney **Trained** Manton, Wilts

FOCUS
Those who challenged widest came out on top in this wide-open nursery, so not form to put much faith in.

6750 BETDAQ 1ST UK RACE COMMISSION FREE H'CAP 1m 4f (P)
7:30 (7:31) (Class 4) (0-85,83) 4-Y-0+ **£4,690** (£1,395; £697; £348) **Stalls** Centre

Form RPR

4614 **1** **Uphold**[23] 6060 6-9-6 82 (v) RyanMoore 6 89
(Gay Kelleway) *chsd ldrs: str run on outside over 1f out to ld fnl 110yds: kpt on strly* **12/1**

4422 **2** *½* **Scottish Star**[18] 6200 5-8-11 78 RyanTate(5) 8 84
(James Eustace) *towards rr: hdwy 4f out: str run on outside over 1f out: kpt on wl to take 2nd last strides but nt pce of wnr* **5/1**[1]

2510 **3** *nse* **Royal Dutch**[21] 6108 4-8-11 73 PatCosgrave 2 79
(Denis Coakley) *chsd ldrs: drvn to chal ins fnl f: outpcd fnl 50yds: lost 2nd last strides* **10/1**

164 **4** *1* **Nave (USA)**[6] 6559 6-9-5 81 MartinLane 3 85
(David Simcock) *in rr: hdwy on outside fr 2f out: kpt on wl clsng stages: nt rch ldrs* **14/1**

0003 **5** *1 ¼* **Modernism**[22] 6080 4-9-0 76 NeilCallan 5 78+
(David Simcock) *chsd ldrs: rdn over 2f out: wknd fnl 50yds* **6/1**[2]

5221 **6** *nk* **Qanan**[22] 6080 4-8-11 76 AshleyMorgan(3) 10 78+
(Chris Wall) *led: styd on far side and drvn 2f out: jnd fr 1f out: hdd & wknd fnl 110yds* **7/1**[3]

2240 **7** *¾* **Muharrer**[12] 6353 4-9-7 83 PaulHanagan 13 84+
(Michael Dods) *chsd ldr: rdn over 2f out: chal appr fnl f: wknd fnl 150yds* **6/1**[2]

110 **8** *2 ¼* **Meetings Man (IRE)**[28] 5895 6-9-3 79 (p) JamesDoyle 11 76
(Ali Brewer) *in rr: drvn over 2f out: kpt on fr over 1f out: nvr rchd ldrs* **20/1**

/000 **9** *1 ½* **Togiak (IRE)**[25] 6004 6-8-7 69 oh1 (p) CathyGannon 9 64
(David Pipe) *in tch: rdn and no prog over 2f out* **8/1**

250- **10** *3 ½* **Bilidn**[327] 7522 5-9-6 82 RichardHughes 7 71
(Ben De Haan) *s.i.s: towards rr most of way* **25/1**

0-63 **11** *2 ¼* **Uriah Heep (FR)**[18] 6200 4-9-2 78 FergusSweeney 12 63
(Alan King) *chsd ldrs: rdn 3f out: wknd over 2f out* **5/1**[1]

2005 **12** *1 ¾* **Sir Boss (IRE)**[49] 5129 8-8-13 80 SladeO'Hara(5) 1 63
(Michael Mullineaux) *in rr: sme hdwy 3f out: nvr rchd ldrs and sn wknd* **33/1**

2043 **13** *1* **King Olav (UAE)**[19] 6173 8-8-9 74 WilliamTwiston-Davies(3) 4 55
(Tony Carroll) *in rr: rdn and sme hdwy over 3f out: sn wknd* **20/1**

2m 32.23s (-2.27) **Going Correction** -0.05s/f (Stan) **13** Ran SP% **125.3**
Speed ratings (Par 105): **105,104,104,103,103 102,102,100,99,97 96,94,94**
toteswingers 1&2 £9.40, 1&3 £38.20, 2&3 £19.70 CSF £71.06 CT £646.80 TOTE £7.30: £2.20, £1.50, £5.00; EX 40.80 Trifecta £427.70 Pool: £2466.12 - 4.32 winning units..
Owner Miss Gay Kelleway **Bred** Juddmonte Farms Ltd **Trained** Exning, Suffolk

FOCUS
A fair handicap that was run at just an ordinary gallop. The winner was close to his old British best with the next three close to their marks.

6751 WINNERS ARE WELCOME AT BETDAQ H'CAP (LONDON MIDDLE DISTANCE SERIES QUALIFIER) 1m 3f (P)
8:00 (8:00) (Class 3) (0-95,95) 3-Y-O
£7,158 (£2,143; £1,071; £535; £267; £134) **Stalls** Low

Form RPR

4351 **1** **Cat O'Mountain (USA)**[19] 6172 3-9-5 93 MickaelBarzalona 5 108
(Charlie Appleby) *in tch: hdwy 4f out: drvn to ld appr fnl f: pushed clr* **10/11**[1]

5122 **2** *3* **Ningara**[26] 5944 3-9-1 89 DavidProbert 7 98
(Andrew Balding) *in tch: hdwy 2f out: drvn and kpt on fnl f to chse wnr fnl 110yds but nvr any ch* **7/2**[2]

2330 **3** *1 ¼* **Masquerading (IRE)**[40] 5475 3-9-0 88 TedDurcan 1 95
(David Lanigan) *chsd ldrs: rdn and slt ld 2f out: hdd over 1f out: sn outpcd by wnr: one pce and lost 2nd fnl 110yds* **8/1**

-135 **4** *2 ½* **Vital Evidence (USA)**[48] 5189 3-8-8 82 ow1 JamesDoyle 3 85
(Sir Michael Stoute) *trckd ldr: rdn and ev ch 2f out: wknd u.p 1f out* **8/1**

3610 **5** *shd* **Ajmany (IRE)**[55] 4917 3-9-4 92 (b) RichardHughes 6 94
(Luca Cumani) *stdd s: in rr: rdn and no prog over 2f out: kpt on fnl f* **7/1**[3]

5546 **6** *2 ½* **Savanna La Mar (USA)**[25] 5993 3-9-7 95 (p) LukeMorris 4 93
(Sir Mark Prescott Bt) *led: rdn and hdd 2f out: wknd sn after* **16/1**

2m 18.78s (-3.12) **Going Correction** -0.05s/f (Stan) **6** Ran SP% **115.2**
Speed ratings (Par 105): **109,106,105,104,104 102**
toteswingers 1&2 £1.10, 1&3 £4.10, 2&3 £6.50 CSF £4.55 TOTE £1.60: £1.10, £2.00; EX 5.00 Trifecta £27.00 Pool: £11,257.94 - 311.94 winning units..
Owner Godolphin **Bred** Darley **Trained** Newmarket, Suffolk

FOCUS
A small field, but a good race and a positive view has been taken of this form.

6752 BOOK CHRISTMAS PARTIES ON 01932 753518 H'CAP (DIV I) 6f (P)
8:30 (8:30) (Class 6) (0-60,60) 3-Y-0+ **£1,940** (£577; £288; £144) **Stalls** Low

Form RPR

40 **1** **Game All (IRE)**[13] 6323 4-9-4 57 (b1) MartinDwyer 10 65
(Hugo Palmer) *chsd ldrs: styd on wl u.p fnl f to ld last strides* **10/1**

333 **2** *nk* **Yarn**[15] 6289 3-9-3 58 RyanMoore 7 65+
(William Haggas) *towards rr: hdwy on ins fr 2f out: led u.p fnl 75yds: hdd last strides* **6/4**[1]

4004 **3** *nk* **Primo D'Oro (USA)**[11] 6407 3-9-5 60 RichardHughes 8 66
(Richard Hannon) *in tch on outside whn rdn fr ins fnl 3f: r.o u.p ins fnl f: styng on clsng stages* **5/1**[2]

6145 **4** *nk* **Dancing Welcome**[13] 6324 7-9-5 58 (bt) RichardKingscote 2 63
(Milton Bradley) *led: rdn over 2f out: kpt narrow ld u.p tl hdd and no ex fnl 75yds* **12/1**

0334 **5** *nk* **Sarah Berry**[13] 6345 4-9-1 54 (v) LukeMorris 9 58
(Chris Dwyer) *chsd ldrs: rdn to chal appr fnl f: styd on same pce fnl 110yds* **20/1**

-000 **6** *1* **Skidby Mill (IRE)**[93] 3630 3-9-2 57 PatCosgrave 1 58
(Laura Mongan) *chsd ldrs: rdn over 2f out: styd on same pce fnl f* **25/1**

1404 **7** *nk* **My Sweet Lord**[43] 5373 3-9-4 **59**......................(v[1]) LiamKeniry 5 59+
(Mark Usher) *slowly away: in rr: drvn and sme hdwy on ins over 2f out: styd on u.p ins fnl f: nt rch ldrs* **16/1**

-000 **8** *½* **Carlarajah**[19] 6154 3-9-2 **60**......................(v) WilliamTwiston-Davies(3) 11 58
(Michael Bell) *in rr: drvn and kpt on fr over 1f out: nt rch ldrs* **12/1**

0056 **9** *¾* **Kasbhom**[42] 5406 3-9-3 **58**...................... WilliamCarson 4 54
(Anthony Carson) *chsd ldrs: wknd fnl f* **16/1**

-020 **10** *1 ¾* **Our Sweet Art**[43] 5373 3-9-0 **55**...................... SteveDrowne 12 45
(John Best) *bmpd after 1f: outpcd* **33/1**

0403 **11** *hd* **Steelcut**[34] 5674 9-9-7 **60**......................(p) LiamJones 6 50
(Mark Buckley) *chsd ldrs: rdn 2f out: no ch after* **8/1**[3]

020 **12** *2 ¾* **Trisara**[44] 5345 3-9-3 **58**...................... JamesDoyle 3 39
(Harry Dunlop) *chsd ldrs: rdn 2f out: wknd appr fnl f* **8/1**[3]

1m 13.69s (0.59) **Going Correction** -0.05s/f (Stan)
WFA 3 from 4yo+ 2lb **12** Ran SP% **126.7**
Speed ratings (Par 101): **94,93,93,92,92 91,90,90,89,86 86,82**
toteswingers 1&2 £4.80, 1&3 £15.70, 2&3 £1.80 CSF £26.50 CT £93.78 TOTE £12.40: £2.80, £1.30, £2.20; EX 38.50 Trifecta £178.60 Pool: £1044.59 - 4.38 winning units..
Owner Astor,Brudenell,Deal,Fellowes,Palmer&2JC **Bred** K Molloy **Trained** Newmarket, Suffolk
FOCUS
The slower division and the first five were covered by very little. However the form is taken at face value around the fourth, with the first three all unexposed.

6753 BOOK CHRISTMAS PARTIES ON 01932 753518 H'CAP (DIV II) 6f (P)
9:00 (9:00) (Class 6) (0-60,60) 3-Y-O+ **£1,940** (£577; £288; £144) **Stalls** Low

Form RPR

4624 **1** **New Rich**[20] 6145 3-9-0 **55**......................(p) JohnFahy 3 64
(Eve Johnson Houghton) *in rr: hdwy over 1f out: str run undet press fnl f to ld clsng stages* **8/1**

45 **2** *½* **Harrogate Fair**[7] 6527 3-9-5 **60**...................... JimmyQuinn 4 67
(Michael Squance) *trckd ldrs: led over 1f out: drvn ins fnl f: edgd rt u.p and hdd clsng stages* **4/1**[1]

345 **3** *¾* **Beauty Pageant (IRE)**[22] 6088 6-9-4 **57**...................... SeanLevey 2 62
(David Brown) *led: rdn and hdd over 1f out: styng on same pce whn bmpd clsng stages* **8/1**

5605 **4** *2* **Hamis Al Bin (IRE)**[19] 6156 4-9-3 **56**...................... RichardKingscote 9 54
(Milton Bradley) *in rr: pushed along 2f out: styd on fnl f: nt rch ldrs* **5/1**[2]

0460 **5** *1 ½* **Ozz**[12] 6368 4-9-7 **60**......................(t) JamesDoyle 5 53
(Frank Sheridan) *in rr: hdwy over 1f out: kpt on clsng stages: nvr a threat* **14/1**

6002 **6** *nk* **Outbid**[11] 6397 3-9-2 **57**...................... KirstyMilczarek 7 49
(Tony Carroll) *in rr: hdwy and pushed along over 2f out: styd on same pce ins fnl f* **20/1**

5110 **7** *1 ¼* **Red Ramesses (IRE)**[191] 1063 4-9-5 **58**...................... SteveDrowne 1 46
(John Best) *chsd ldrs: rdn and wknd over 2f out* **7/1**[3]

4354 **8** *1* **Speronella**[28] 5890 3-9-4 **59**......................(p) JimmyFortune 10 44
(Hughie Morrison) *rdn over 2f out: towards rr most of way* **8/1**

003 **9** *1 ¾* **Cape Appeal**[110] 3036 3-9-5 **60**...................... RichardHughes 12 40
(Richard Hannon) *chsd ldr: rdn ins fnl 2f: wknd appr fnl f* **4/1**[1]

0-50 **10** *3 ¾* **Thrasos (IRE)**[159] 1660 4-9-0 **53**...................... LiamKeniry 8 21
(Jo Crowley) *chsd ldrs: wknd over 1f out* **7/1**[3]

1m 12.8s (-0.30) **Going Correction** -0.05s/f (Stan)
WFA 3 from 4yo+ 2lb **10** Ran SP% **126.4**
Speed ratings (Par 101): **100,99,98,95,93 93,91,90,87,82**
toteswingers 1&2 £7.90, 1&3 £12.10, 2&3 £12.90 CSF £43.63 CT £233.67 TOTE £11.10: £3.00, £1.30, £3.50; EX 52.00 Trifecta £464.60 Pool: £826.89 - 1.33 winning units..
Owner Eden Racing Club **Bred** Whitsbury Manor Stud And Mrs M E Slade **Trained** Blewbury, Oxon
FOCUS
They went a good gallop and, unlike in the first division, the runners finished strung out. It was the quicker division but lacked improvers.
T/Plt: £357.40 to £1 stake. Pool: £71,337.09 - 145.69 winning tickets. T/Qpdt: £234.00 to £1 stake. Pool: £8128.97 - 25.70 winning tickets. ST

6284 REDCAR (L-H)
Wednesday, September 25

OFFICIAL GOING: Good (good to soft in places) changing to good to soft after race 6 (5.00)
Wind: moderate 1/2 against Weather: overcast, light rain

6754 BRITISH STALLION STUDS EBF MAIDEN STKS 7f
2:10 (2:17) (Class 5) 2-Y-O **£2,911** (£866; £432; £216) **Stalls** Centre

Form RPR

4 **1** **Approach The West (IRE)**[16] 6256 2-9-0 0...................... DavidAllan 6 73+
(James Tate) *in tch: pushed along wl over 2f out: swtchd to outer and rdn to chse ldrs over 1f out: styd on ent fnl f to ld last 100yds* **9/2**[1]

6 **2** *nk* **Percy's Gal**[25] 5988 2-9-0 0...................... BarryMcHugh 11 72
(Karen Tutty) *trckd ldrs: hdwy over 2f out: rdn to ld ent fnl f: drvn: hdd and no ex last 100yds* **11/1**[3]

0 **3** *2* **Syros (IRE)**[15] 6277 2-9-5 0...................... PhillipMakin 4 72
(Brian Meehan) *prom: cl up 1/2-way: effrt 2f out and sn ev ch tl rdn and one pce ins fnl f* **9/2**[1]

4 *¾* **Aran Sky (IRE)** 2-8-12 0...................... RobJFitzpatrick(7) 12 70
(K R Burke) *midfield: hdwy 1/2-way: sn trcking ldrs: led 2f out: rdn over 1f out: drvn and hdd ent fnl f: one pce* **33/1**

5 *3* **Mighty Missile (IRE)** 2-9-5 0...................... AndrewElliott 15 62
(Tom Tate) *wnt rt s: green and bhd: hdwy over 2f out: sn pushed along: styd on fnl f: nrst fin* **22/1**

0 **6** *1 ¼* **Kalahari Kingdom (IRE)**[61] 4731 2-9-5 0...................... TonyHamilton 10 59
(Richard Fahey) *hld up towards rr: stdy hdwy 1/2-way: rdn to chse ldrs whn hung lft over 1f out: sn no imp* **9/2**[1]

7 *½* **Beautiful Forest** 2-9-0 0...................... KierenFallon 8 53
(Saeed bin Suroor) *s.i.s: green and in rr: hdwy 3f out: rdn to chse ldrs 2f out: sn one pce* **13/2**[2]

8 *1 ¼* **Private Dancer** 2-9-5 0...................... AndrewMullen 7 54
(Alan Swinbank) *s.i.s: green and in rr tl styd on fnl 2f: n.d* **40/1**

0 **9** *½* **Where's Tiger**[14] 6299 2-9-5 0...................... MichaelO'Connell 5 53
(Jedd O'Keeffe) *towards rr: sme late hdwy: n.d* **40/1**

0 **10** *2* **Tinchy Ryder**[7] 6513 2-9-5 0...................... RoystonFfrench 13 48
(Bryan Smart) *plld hrd in midfield: rdn along over 2f out: n.d* **100/1**

11 *1* **Mindblowing** 2-9-5 0...................... TomEaves 2 45
(Kevin Ryan) *s.i.s: sn rdn along and in tch: cl up on outer 1/2-way: rdn wl over 2f out: sn wknd* **20/1**

04 **12** *¾* **Pure Impressions**[19] 6175 2-9-5 0...................... RobertWinston 14 43
(K R Burke) *prom: led 3f out: rdn along and hdd 2f out: wknd over 1f out* **16/1**

13 *6* **Master Clockmaker (IRE)** 2-9-5 0...................... GrahamLee 9 28
(Ann Duffield) *trckd ldrs: pushed along 1/2-way: sn wknd* **14/1**

14 *13* **Loot** 2-9-5 0...................... LeeTopliss 3
(Richard Fahey) *green: a towards rr* **11/1**[3]

00 **15** *hd* **Vadara**[18] 6213 2-9-5 0...................... GrahamGibbons 1
(Michael Easterby) *led: rdn along and hdd 3f out: sn wknd* **100/1**

1m 26.5s (2.00) **Going Correction** +0.275s/f (Good) **15** Ran SP% **116.0**
Speed ratings (Par 95): **99,98,96,95,92 90,90,88,88,85 84,83,76,62,61**
toteswingers 1&2 £8.50, 1&3 £6.40, 2&3 £12.00 CSF £49.49 TOTE £4.30: £1.50, £3.50, £2.30; EX 47.00 Trifecta £315.40 Pool: £1117.22 - 2.65 winning units..
Owner Saeed Manana **Bred** Deerfield Farm **Trained** Newmarket, Suffolk
FOCUS
The going was good, good to soft in places from an overnight prediction of good, good to firm in places. Little form to go on for this maiden which was run at a fair pace. The first three home all had experience.

6755 HOLD YOUR CHRISTMAS PARTY HERE NURSERY H'CAP 1m
2:40 (2:42) (Class 6) (0-65,65) 2-Y-O **£1,940** (£577; £288; £144) **Stalls** Low

Form RPR

1636 **1** **Hatti (IRE)**[17] 6233 2-9-3 **61**......................(p) MichaelStainton 9 65
(Micky Hammond) *in rr: hdwy over 2f out: nt clr run and swtchd rt over 1f out: hung bdly lft and styd on to ld towards fin* **8/1**[2]

0000 **2** *½* **Suni Dancer**[1] 6725 2-8-2 **46** ow1...................... DuranFentiman 12 49
(Paul Green) *hld up in rr: edgd lft over 3f out: hdwy over 2f out: led last 50yds: hdd towards fin* **50/1**

0550 **3** *1 ½* **Queenie's Home**[13] 6326 2-9-7 **65**...................... GrahamLee 5 64
(James Given) *trckd ldr: led over 2f out: hdd last 50yds: hmpd nr fin* **8/1**[2]

0452 **4** *1* **Please Let Me Go**[15] 6285 2-9-2 **60**...................... BarryMcHugh 11 57
(Julie Camacho) *hld up towards rr: hdwy over 2f out: kpt on same pce over 2f out* **8/1**[2]

0030 **5** *nk* **Blue Talisman (IRE)**[15] 6275 2-8-13 **57**......................(e[1]) DavidAllan 8 53
(Tim Easterby) *mid-div: rdn 3f out: sn chsng ldrs: one pce appr fnl f: sltly hmpd nr fin* **5/1**[1]

2620 **6** *¾* **Jazzy Lady (IRE)**[7] 6520 2-8-6 **53**...................... DeclanBates(3) 6 47
(David Evans) *chsd ldrs: one pce over 1f out* **14/1**

000 **7** *hd* **Barbara Elizabeth**[37] 5577 2-7-12 **45**...................... RaulDaSilva(3) 13 39
(Tony Coyle) *in rr: hdwy over 2f out: one pce* **11/1**

0544 **8** *1 ¼* **Camatini (IRE)**[22] 6085 2-8-12 **61**...................... ConnorBeasley(5) 7 52
(Michael Dods) *mid-div: rdn and outpcd over 2f out: kpt on fnl f* **5/1**[1]

0660 **9** *½* **Petergate**[30] 5829 2-8-11 **60**...................... JacobButterfield(5) 1 49
(Brian Rothwell) *chsd ldrs: outpcd over 4f out: drvn 3f out: one pce* **17/2**[3]

3650 **10** *1 ¾* **It's All A Game**[8] 6494 2-8-6 **57**......................(v) KevinStott(7) 3 42
(Richard Guest) *chsd ldrs: wknd over 1f out* **12/1**

6240 **11** *1 ¼* **Mitcd (IRE)**[81] 4061 2-9-1 **64**...................... GeorgeChaloner(5) 4 46
(Richard Fahey) *chsd ldrs: drvn 3f out: lost pl over 1f out* **8/1**[2]

0500 **12** *8* **Desert Colours**[21] 6111 2-9-0 **58**......................(p) TomEaves 2 21
(Kevin Ryan) *led: hdd over 2f out: lost pl over 1f out: sn bhd* **16/1**

1m 40.74s (4.14) **Going Correction** +0.275s/f (Good) **12** Ran SP% **118.8**
Speed ratings (Par 93): **90,89,88,87,86 85,85,84,84,82 81,73**
toteswingers 1&2 £77.70, 1&3 £14.90, 2&3 £56.30 CSF £339.08 CT £3331.92 TOTE £7.20: £2.30, £15.30, £2.20; EX 472.50 Trifecta £625.40 Pool: £833.96 - 0.01 winning units..
Owner 50/50 Racing Club **Bred** Miss Imelda O'Shaughnessy **Trained** Middleham Moor, N Yorks
■ Stewards' Enquiry : Michael Stainton two-day ban: careless riding (Oct 9-10); two-day ban: used whip above permitted level (Oct 11,13)
FOCUS
A low-grade nursery run at a steady pace. The field raced up the centre.

6756 WATCH RACING UK ON CHANNEL 432 (S) STKS 1m
3:15 (3:17) (Class 5) 3-Y-O+ **£2,587** (£770; £384; £192) **Stalls** Low

Form RPR

0-00 **1** **Alakhan (IRE)**[36] 5613 7-9-0 75...................... MichaelO'Connell 2 81
(Ian Williams) *trckd ldrs: hdwy over 2f out: chsd ldr over 1f out: rdn to ld ent fnl f: sn drvn and kpt on wl towards fin* **4/1**[3]

6454 **2** *½* **Al Muheer (IRE)**[8] 6496 8-9-2 81...................... JasonHart(3) 7 85
(Ruth Carr) *hld up: hdwy to trck ldrs over 2f out: rdn to chse wnr ins fnl f: sn drvn and no imp towards fin* **13/8**[1]

054 **3** *3* **Jo'Burg (USA)**[14] 6300 9-9-0 82...................... DavidBergin(5) 6 78
(David O'Meara) *dwlt: hld up in tch: hdwy over 2f out: rdn over 1f out: styd on fnl f: nrst fin* **7/2**[2]

-050 **4** *1 ¾* **Certral**[15] 6288 5-8-9 69...................... BarryMcHugh 8 64
(Mel Brittain) *in tch: hdwy to chse ldrs 3f out: rdn along 2f out: drvn and one pce appr fnl f* **20/1**

1500 **5** *7* **Staff Sergeant**[35] 5637 6-9-5 73...................... GrahamLee 5 58
(Iain Jardine) *prom: pushed along to chse clr ldr wl over 2f out: rdn wl over 1f out: sn wknd* **12/1**

2600 **6** *nk* **Waltz Darling (IRE)**[14] 6306 5-9-0 67...................... TomEaves 3 52
(Keith Reveley) *hld up in tch: pushed along 3f out: sn rdn and n.d* **40/1**

5455 **7** *½* **Patently (IRE)**[39] 5527 3-8-10 67......................(bt) KierenFallon 1 54
(Brian Meehan) *sn led: hung lft to far rail and clr after 2f: 10 l advantage at 1/2-way: rdn along over 2f out: hdd & wknd ent fnl f* **11/2**

50 **8** *15* **Lenderking (IRE)**[37] 5586 5-8-7 0......................(t) DavidParkes(7) 10 16
(Michael Chapman) *prom: rdn along 3f out: sn wknd* **200/1**

006- **9** *3 ¼* **Orpen Wide (IRE)**[323] 7605 11-8-7 41...................... PaulBooth(7) 9 9
(Michael Chapman) *towards rr: rdn along 3f out: sn outpcd and bhd fnl 2f* **125/1**

1m 39.23s (2.63) **Going Correction** +0.275s/f (Good)
WFA 3 from 5yo+ 4lb **9** Ran SP% **111.9**
Speed ratings (Par 103): **97,96,93,91,84 84,83,68,65**
toteswingers 1&2 £2.90, 1&3 £4.20, 2&3 £2.80 CSF £10.37 TOTE £6.30: £1.60, £1.20, £1.60; EX 12.20 Trifecta £37.90 Pool: £2425.88 - 47.94 winning units..There was no bid for the winner
Owner Patrick Kelly **Bred** Juergen Imm **Trained** Portway, Worcs
FOCUS
A fair contest for the grade, run at a fierce gallop, but the form is rated a bit cautiously.

6757 DOWNLOAD THE RACING UK APP H'CAP 5f
3:50 (3:52) (Class 5) (0-70,70) 3-Y-O+ **£2,587** (£770; £384; £192) **Stalls** Centre

Form RPR

1635 **1** **Beau Mistral (IRE)**[7] 6515 4-9-3 **69**...................... RaulDaSilva(3) 15 79
(Paul Green) *trckd ldrs: effrt 2f out: r.o to ld nr fin* **5/1**[1]

050 **2** *½* **Eland Ally**[37] 5579 5-9-7 **70**......................(p) AndrewElliott 11 78
(Tom Tate) *chsd ldrs: led jst ins fnl f: hdd and no ex towards fin* **9/1**

403- **3** 1 1/4 **Marabout (IRE)**[360] 6707 3-8-6 **56** oh1 .... DuranFentiman 8 60+
(Mel Brittain) *dwlt: hdwy over 2f out: chsng ldrs over 1f out: styd on same pce last 75yds* **33/1**

5646 **4** 1/2 **Lady Poppy**[28] 5889 3-8-10 **60** .... AndrewMullen 1 62
(George Moore) *led: hdd jst ins fnl f: no ex* **20/1**

4022 **5** shd **Ace Master**[30] 5841 5-8-8 **60** .... (b) MarkCoumbe(3) 2 61
(Roy Bowring) *w ldrs: kpt on same pce jst ins fnl f* **5/1**[1]

63 **6** nse **Mr Mo Jo**[9] 6469 5-9-2 **68** .... (p) JasonHart(3) 13 69
(Lawrence Mullaney) *w ldrs: kpt on same pce fnl f* **9/1**

0460 **7** 1 1/2 **Mandy Layla (IRE)**[22] 6088 3-8-12 **62** .... RoystonFfrench 9 58
(Bryan Smart) *in rr: hdwy 2f out: styd on ins fnl f* **16/1**

0500 **8** 1/2 **Mitchell**[9] 6469 3-8-13 **63** .... (p) RobertWinston 4 57
(David Thompson) *chsd ldrs: swvd lft over 3f out: one pce over 1f out* **7/1**[2]

1404 **9** 1/2 **Tuibama (IRE)**[5] 6604 4-8-12 **61** ....[1] MichaelO'Connell 5 53
(Tracy Waggott) *chsd ldrs: one pce over 1f out* **17/2**[3]

02/0 **10** nk **Alis Aquilae (IRE)**[7] 6516 7-9-0 **63** .... AdamBeschizza 14 54
(Tim Etherington) *in rr: sme hdwy over 1f out: nvr a factor* **25/1**

5020 **11** shd **Choc'A'Moca (IRE)**[7] 6515 6-8-13 **62** .... (v) LeeTopliss 7 53
(Paul Midgley) *mid-div: sn drvn along: wkng whn n.m.r and eased towards fin* **20/1**

6205 **12** 1/2 **Commanche Raider (IRE)**[9] 6471 6-9-5 **68** .... GrahamLee 10 57
(Michael Dods) *hld up in rr: stmbld wl over 1f out: nvr a factor* **10/1**

4332 **13** 2 1/2 **Mother Jones**[192] 1052 5-8-5 **61** .... ClaireMurray(7) 12 41
(David Brown) *hood removed v late: s.s: a in rr* **16/1**

0-0 **14** 1/2 **On The High Tops (IRE)**[5] 6604 5-8-7 **56** .... BarryMcHugh 16 34
(Colin Teague) *hld up in rr: effrt over 2f out: wknd over 1f out* **40/1**

0-00 **15** 2 1/2 **Kyzer Chief**[28] 5889 8-8-8 **57** ow1 .... TomEaves 17 26
(Tina Jackson) *chsd ldrs: lost pl over 1f out* **50/1**

59.53s (0.93) **Going Correction** +0.275s/f (Good)
WFA 3 from 4yo+ 1lb **15** Ran SP% **117.9**
Speed ratings (Par 103): **103,102,100,99,99 99,96,95,95,94 94,93,89,88,84**
toteswingers 1&2 £13.20, 1&3 £40.40, 2&3 £54.00 CSF £43.52 CT £1374.66 TOTE £5.50: £2.70, £3.70, £12.60; EX 57.00 Trifecta £853.70 Pool: £1138.36 - 0.04 winning units..
Owner The Winsor Not Group **Bred** John McEnery **Trained** Lydiate, Merseyside

FOCUS
A wide-open sprint handicap run at a sound pace. It paid to race handy.

6758 VOLTIGEUR RESTAURANT 2 COURSE SPECIAL FOR £10.95 H'CAP — 1m 2f
4:25 (4:27) (Class 5) (0-75,79) 3-Y-0+ **£2,587** (£770; £384; £192) **Stalls** Low

Form RPR

5343 **1** **Ebony Express**[14] 6297 4-9-0 **65** .... BenCurtis 4 74
(Alan Swinbank) *prom: effrt to chse ldr 3f out: rdn to chal 2f out: drvn and styd on ins fnl f to ld last 40yds* **8/1**

3526 **2** 1/2 **Prophesy (IRE)**[17] 6239 4-9-7 **75** .... NeilFarley(3) 11 83
(Declan Carroll) *led: pushed along wl over 2f out: rdn wl over 1f out: drvn ins fnl f: hdd and no ex last 40yds* **5/1**[2]

-056 **3** 2 1/2 **Brockfield**[153] 1775 7-9-2 **67** .... DavidAllan 3 70
(Mel Brittain) *t.k.h: hld up: hdwy over 3f out: chsd ldrs over 2f out: sn rdn: drvn to chse ldng pair ent fnl f: kpt on same pce* **25/1**

3403 **4** hd **Gran Maestro (USA)**[4] 6631 4-9-4 **72** .... (p) JasonHart(3) 6 75
(Ruth Carr) *towards rr: hdwy 3f out: rdn to chse ldrs 2f out: swtchd rt and drvn ent fnl f: kpt on* **11/2**[3]

50-1 **5** 1/2 **Returntobrecongill**[100] 3398 3-9-2 **73** .... RussKennemore 2 75
(Sally Hall) *dwlt and plld hrd in rr: hdwy on inner 3f out: rdn to chse ldrs wl over 1f out: drvn and no imp fnl f* **33/1**

004 **6** 2 1/2 **Coincidently**[62] 4690 3-9-1 **72** ....[1] RobertWinston 1 69
(Alan Bailey) *trckd ldrs on inner: hdwy 4f out: rdn 2f out: drvn appr fnl f: sn one pce* **20/1**

5553 **7** 1 1/2 **Nordic Quest (IRE)**[83] 3976 4-9-8 **73** .... (p) FrederikTylicki 8 67
(Gerard Butler) *hld up in rr: hdwy 3f out: swtchd rt and rdn to chse ldrs 2f out: drvn over 1f out and no imp* **9/2**[1]

10- **8** 1 **Dynastic**[97] 3519 4-9-3 **68** .... BarryMcHugh 7 60
(Tony Coyle) *hld up in rr: sme hdwy over 2f out: n.d* **33/1**

0212 **9** nk **Unex Michelangelo (IRE)**[34] 5677 4-9-5 **70** .... GrahamGibbons 9 61
(Michael Easterby) *hld up: effrt and sme hdwy wl over 2f out: sn rdn along and n.d* **11/2**[3]

0305 **10** nk **Wyldfire (IRE)**[43] 5368 3-8-9 **66** .... TonyHamilton 14 56
(Richard Fahey) *sn chsng ldr: rdn along wl over 3f out: wknd over 2f out* **11/1**

0350 **11** 1 **Rock Supreme (IRE)**[44] 5332 4-9-2 **72** .... (p) ConnorBeasley(5) 13 60
(Michael Dods) *towards rr: hdwy on wd outside 3f out: rdn over 2f out: n.d* **16/1**

000 **12** nk **Nelson's Bay**[15] 6291 4-9-5 **70** .... GrahamLee 12 58
(Wilf Storey) *a in rr* **28/1**

2301 **13** shd **Demolition**[9] 6468 9-9-7 **79** 6ex .... KevinStott(7) 10 67
(Noel Wilson) *chsd ldrs: rdn along 3f out: sn wknd* **16/1**

2404 **14** 3/4 **Tanawar (IRE)**[15] 6272 3-8-9 **66** .... TomEaves 5 52
(Tim Etherington) *trckd ldrs: pushed along 3f out: rdn over 2f out: sn wknd* **50/1**

2m 7.46s (0.36) **Going Correction** +0.15s/f (Good)
WFA 3 from 4yo+ 6lb **14** Ran SP% **116.7**
Speed ratings (Par 103): **104,103,101,101,101 99,97,97,96,96 95,95,95,94**
toteswingers 1&2 £5.70, 1&3 £33.50, 2&3 £34.30 CSF £42.43 CT £964.07 TOTE £6.30: £1.70, £2.60, £11.00; EX 57.30 Trifecta £1294.10 Pool: £1725.54 - 0.63 winning units..
Owner Mrs T Blackett **Bred** Miss E J Wright **Trained** Melsonby, N Yorks

FOCUS
An open handicap, run at a fair pace. The field raced far side and again it paid to race handy.

6759 RACING REPLAY, ALL TODAY'S RACING SKY432 (S) STKS — 1m 2f
5:00 (5:01) (Class 6) 3-5-Y-0 **£2,045** (£603; £302) **Stalls** Low

Form RPR

0300 **1** **Auto Mac**[15] 6276 5-8-10 56 .... AdamCarter(5) 4 66
(Neville Bycroft) *chsd ldrs: drvn to join ldrs over 2f out: led 1f out: edgd lft towards fin: all out* **12/1**

4000 **2** 1/2 **Sunnybridge Boy (IRE)**[31] 5802 4-9-1 65 .... RobertWinston 2 65
(K R Burke) *sn chsng ldrs: chal over 3f out: hld whn hmpd fnl strides* **5/2**[1]

4015 **3** 2 **Conducting**[9] 6473 5-9-7 65 .... GrahamLee 6 67
(Gay Kelleway) *mid-div: hdwy over 3f out: kpt on same pce to take 3rd nr fin* **4/1**[2]

6004 **4** 1 1/2 **Assizes**[1] 6717 4-8-12 70 .... JasonHart(3) 10 58
(Ruth Carr) *sn trcking ldrs: led 4f out: hdd 1f out: wknd clsng stages* **5/2**[1]

4062 **5** 4 1/2 **Honey Of A Kitten (USA)**[9] 6473 5-9-4 69 .... (v) DeclanBates(3) 11 55
(David Evans) *mid-div: effrt over 3f out: edgd rt over 1f out: nvr a factor* **11/2**[3]

0 **6** 5 **Hilda Ogden (IRE)**[8] 6497 3-8-4 0 .... PaulQuinn 8 34
(David Nicholls) *in rr: swtchd lft after 1f: drvn 4f out: kpt on fnl 2f: nvr a factor* **33/1**

4003 **7** 3 3/4 **Multifact**[29] 5856 3-8-9 50 .... TomEaves 1 32
(Michael Dods) *sn chsng ldrs: drvn over 3f out: wknd 2f out* **16/1**

-000 **8** 1 1/4 **Idarose (IRE)**[19] 6177 4-8-3 15 .... (b[1]) JordanHibberd(7) 5 24
(Alan Berry) *dwlt: sn mid-div: wknd over 2f out* **200/1**

0-00 **9** 6 **Nakuru Breeze (IRE)**[8] 6497 4-8-5 50 .... (be) JacobButterfield(5) 9 12
(Suzzanne France) *t.k.h: led: hdd 4f out: lost pl 3f out* **100/1**

0/0- **10** 6 **Spokesperson (USA)**[460] 3352 5-8-12 52 .... (v) NeilFarley(3) 7 5
(Frederick Watson) *s.i.s: reminders sn after s: sme hdwy 7f out: drvn over 4f out: lost pl over 3f out* **33/1**

05-0 **11** 23 **Mariella**[25] 5989 3-8-6 45 ow2 .... BarryMcHugh 3
(John Wainwright) *stdd s: in rr: bhd fnl 4f: t.o whn eased over 1f out* **50/1**

2m 8.56s (1.46) **Going Correction** +0.15s/f (Good)
WFA 3 from 4yo+ 6lb **11** Ran SP% **115.4**
Speed ratings (Par 101): **100,99,98,96,93 89,86,85,80,75 57**
toteswingers 1&2 £6.90, 1&3 £6.70, 2&3 £3.50 CSF £40.94 TOTE £16.80: £4.60, £1.10, £1.80; EX 62.70 Trifecta £226.00 Pool: £2016.58 - 6.69 winning units..There was no bid for the winner
Owner Mrs C M Whatley **Bred** Roger Ingram **Trained** Brandsby, N Yorks

FOCUS
A modest contest run at a steady pace. Rather shaky form with the second and fourth not having been at their best recently.

6760 TWO YEAR OLD TROPHY COMES NEXT H'CAP (DIV I) — 6f
5:30 (5:31) (Class 6) (0-65,65) 3-Y-0+ **£2,045** (£603; £302) **Stalls** Centre

Form RPR

3000 **1** **Mercers Row**[15] 6287 6-8-13 **64** .... GemmaTutty(7) 6 74
(Karen Tutty) *trckd ldrs: hdwy wl over 1f out: rdn and rdr dropped whip ent fnl f: styd on wl to ld last 100yds* **16/1**

500- **2** 1 **Ad Vitam (IRE)**[519] 1583 5-8-7 **51** oh4 .... DavidAllan 11 58
(Mel Brittain) *hld up: hdwy 2f out: rdn to ld over 1f out: drvn and edgd lft ent fnl f: hdd and no ex last 100yds* **28/1**

304 **3** hd **Music Festival (USA)**[39] 5515 6-8-8 **52** .... TomEaves 12 58
(Jim Goldie) *hld up towards rr: hdwy 2f out: rdn to chse ldrs over 1f out: drvn and ch ins fnl f: sn edgd lft and kpt on same pce* **8/1**

0426 **4** nk **Thatcherite (IRE)**[33] 5713 5-9-0 **58** .... (t) BarryMcHugh 5 68+
(Tony Coyle) *dwlt: sn in tch: hdwy to chse ldrs whn nt clr run over 1f out: swtchd rt and rdn ent fnl f: kpt on: nrst fin* **11/4**[1]

3035 **5** 1 1/4 **Done Dreaming (IRE)**[40] 5485 3-8-3 **56** .... SamanthaBell(7) 10 57
(Richard Fahey) *trckd ldrs: hdwy 2f out: rdn over 1f out: sn drvn and edgd lft ent fnl f: one pce* **12/1**

1240 **6** 2 1/4 **Abraham Monro**[28] 5878 3-8-6 **55** .... JasonHart(3) 7 49
(Ruth Carr) *rrd s and s.i.s: hdwy 1/2-way: rdn to chse ldrs over 1f out: hld whn sltly hmpd and swtchd rt ins fnl f* **8/1**

6000 **7** 4 **Fathom Five (IRE)**[7] 6516 9-8-12 **61** .... ShirleyTeasdale(5) 14 42
(Shaun Harris) *cl up: led 1/2-way: rdn along and hdd over 1f out: sn drvn and wknd fnl f* **28/1**

0-00 **8** 1/2 **Spoken Words**[27] 5921 4-8-0 **51** oh6 .... (b) JordanHibberd(7) 8 31
(Alan Berry) *in tch: hdwy to trck ldrs 2f out: sn n.m.r: swtchd lft and rdn over 1f out: sn no imp* **100/1**

0000 **9** 1/2 **Baybshambles (IRE)**[19] 6180 9-8-2 **51** oh2 .... (p) ConnorBeasley(5) 9 29
(Tina Jackson) *s.i.s and bhd: hdwy over 2f out: sn rdn and n.d* **28/1**

2146 **10** 1 1/4 **Little Jimmy Odsox (IRE)**[15] 6287 5-9-7 **65** .... (b) DuranFentiman 4 39
(Tim Easterby) *cl up: rdn 2f out: ev ch tl drvn and wknd appr fnl f* **4/1**[2]

3505 **11** 4 **Maakirr (IRE)**[34] 5677 4-8-10 **57** .... (p) MarkCoumbe(3) 2 18
(Roy Bowring) *prom: rdn along over 2f out: sn drvn and wknd* **13/2**[3]

200/ **12** 1/2 **Wyatt Earp (IRE)**[1040] 7526 12-8-11 **62** .... (p) KevinStott(7) 13 22
(Richard Guest) *led to 1/2-way: sn rdn along and wknd wl over 1f out* **11/1**

0U00 **13** 7 **Lucy Minaj**[56] 4891 3-8-5 **51** oh3 .... (v[1]) RoystonFfrench 1
(Bryan Smart) *wnt lft s: sn prom on outer: rdn along 1/2-way: sn wknd* **28/1**

1m 13.83s (2.03) **Going Correction** +0.275s/f (Good)
WFA 3 from 4yo+ 2lb **13** Ran SP% **118.9**
Speed ratings (Par 101): **97,95,95,95,93 90,85,84,83,82 76,76,66**
toteswingers 1&2 £103.30, 1&3 £26.70, 2&3 £28.40 CSF £410.07 CT £3921.91 TOTE £26.60: £7.80, £13.10, £3.30; EX 434.70 Trifecta £673.40 Pool: £897.91 - 0.02 winning units..
Owner K Fitzsimons **Bred** Heather Raw **Trained** Osmotherley, N Yorks

FOCUS
The going was changed to good to soft following the sixth race. This moderate handicap was run at an honest pace. The winner had slipped to a good mark.

6761 TWO YEAR OLD TROPHY COMES NEXT H'CAP (DIV II) — 6f
6:05 (6:06) (Class 6) (0-65,65) 3-Y-0+ **£2,045** (£603; £151; £151) **Stalls** Centre

Form RPR

0032 **1** **Lees Anthem**[5] 6603 6-8-8 **52** .... DavidAllan 7 60
(Mel Brittain) *chsd ldrs: led over 1f out: edgd lft ins fnl f: hld on* **13/2**

2334 **2** 3/4 **Verus Delicia (IRE)**[7] 6535 4-9-5 **63** .... GrahamLee 12 69+
(John Stimpson) *s.i.s: in rr: hdwy over 1f out: styd on wl to take 2nd post* **11/2**[3]

4102 **3** shd **Black Douglas**[5] 6604 4-8-9 **53** .... TomEaves 5 58
(Jim Goldie) *hld up in mid-div: effrt over 2f out: chsd wnr ins fnl f: styd on same pl clsng stages* **5/1**[2]

460 **3** dht **Niceonemyson**[40] 5470 4-8-6 **57** .... KevinStott(7) 10 62
(Christopher Wilson) *chsd ldrs: 2nd 1f out: kpt on same pce last 50yds* **14/1**

3204 **5** 1 3/4 **Haadeeth**[78] 4149 6-9-4 **65** .... DeclanBates(3) 8 65
(David Evans) *in rr: hdwy over 2f out: edgd lft 1f out: kpt on same pce* **25/1**

-060 **6** hd **Orwellian**[19] 6181 4-9-2 **60** .... RoystonFfrench 9 59
(Bryan Smart) *dwlt: in rr: drvn over 2f out: edgd rt over 1f out: kpt on wl ins fnl f* **9/1**

2505 **7** nk **Amis Reunis**[6] 6568 4-9-0 **58** .... PatrickMathers 4 56
(Alan Berry) *chsd ldrs: drvn over 2f out: one pce over 1f out* **18/1**

2443 **8** 2 1/2 **Alluring Star**[12] 6367 5-9-4 **62** .... GrahamGibbons 11 52
(Michael Easterby) *led: hdd over 1f out: sn wknd* **7/2**[1]

06-U **9** 3/4 **The Kicking Lord**[19] 6180 4-8-6 **53** .... JasonHart(3) 6 41
(Noel Wilson) *hood removed late: s.i.s: effrt over 2f out: wkng whn n.m.r 1f out* **28/1**

/003 **10** 1/2 **Durham Express (IRE)**[49] 5139 6-8-2 **51** oh3 .... (p) ConnorBeasley(5) 2 37
(Tina Jackson) *chsd ldr: wknd appr fnl f* **10/1**

0306 **11** nse **Emily Hall**[43] 5365 4-8-7 **51** oh3 .... DuranFentiman 3 37
(Bryan Smart) *dwlt: hdwy over 2f out: wknd over 1f out* **16/1**

3005 **12** *7* **Belinsky (IRE)**[40] 5487 6-8-12 **56**................................(p) BarryMcHugh 1 20
(Julie Camacho) *in rr: edgd rt and n.m.r appr fnl f: sn lost pl: eased clsng stages* **20/1**

0050 **13** *hd* **Piste**[40] 5470 7-8-7 **51** oh6..(e) AndrewMullen 13 14
(Tina Jackson) *dwlt: in rr: sme hdwy over 2f out: sn lost pl: eased whn bhd clsng stages* **50/1**

1m 13.83s (2.03) **Going Correction** +0.275s/f (Good) **13** Ran SP% **118.5**
Speed ratings (Par 101): **97,96,95,95,93 93,92,89,88,87 87,78,78**PL: N £2.10, BD £1.20; Trifecta: LA/VD/BD £91.80; LA/VD/N £281.90; Tricast: LA/VD/BD £101.23; LA/VD/N £245.37; toteswingers LA&VD £8.00, LA&N £7.20, LA&BD £3.50, VD&BD £2.80, VD&N £8.70 CSF £39.96 TOTE £7.30: £1.90, £2.00; EX 41.30 TRIFECTA Pool: £1602.27 Owner.

FOCUS
Plenty of pace on for this handicap. Little got involved and this was ordinary form. It's a long time since the winner rated any higher.
T/Jkpt: Not won. T/Plt: £93.80 to £1 stake. Pool: £69,074.73 - 537.35 winning tickets. T/Qpdt: £12.40 to £1 stake. Pool: £5773.30 - 343.20 winning tickets. WG

6643 NEWMARKET (R-H)
Thursday, September 26

OFFICIAL GOING: Good (good to firm in places; 8.1; stands' side 8.1, centre 8.0, far side 8.2)
Wind: light, across Weather: dry and bright

6762 NGK SPARK PLUGS EBF MAIDEN STKS (C&G) 1m
2:00 (2:02) (Class 4) 2-Y-O **£4,528** (£1,347; £673; £336) **Stalls** High

Form RPR

25 **1** **Master The World (IRE)**[34] 5727 2-9-0 0................................ NeilCallan 17 86+
(Gerard Butler) *mde all: rdn and qcknd clr wl over 1f out: in command fr over 1f out: styd on* **13/2**[2]

2 *2* **Divisional** 2-9-0 0................................ WilliamBuick 10 81+
(John Gosden) *hld up in midfield: switching lft and hdwy wl over 1f out: styd on to chse wnr ins fnl f: gng on wl fin but nvr gng to rch wnr* **8/1**

3 *2 1/4* **King's Land** 2-9-0 0................................ SilvestreDeSousa 3 76
(Saeed bin Suroor) *s.i.s: t.k.h and sn hld up in midfield: rdn and hdwy wl over 1f out: styd on to go 3rd ins fnl f: kpt on but no threat to wnr* **6/1**[1]

4 *1/2* **Touch The Sky** 2-9-0 0................................ TomQueally 12 75+
(Lady Cecil) *s.i.s: hld up in tch in rr: effrt and edging rt whn swtchd lft wl over 1f out: hdwy 1f out: styd on strly ins fnl f: no threat to wnr* **6/1**[1]

5 *3/4* **Mustadaam (IRE)** 2-9-0 0................................ PaulHanagan 11 73
(Brian Meehan) *chsd ldrs: drvn and unable qck wl over 1f out: no imp on wnr and battling for 2nd 1f out: plugged on same pce fnl f* **10/1**

6 *3/4* **Carthage (IRE)** 2-9-0 0................................ RichardHughes 14 72+
(Richard Hannon) *s.i.s: hld up in tch in rr: effrt wl over 1f out: hdwy and swtchd rt 1f out: styd on strly fnl 100yds: no threat to wnr* **9/1**

0 **7** *shd* **Arable**[27] 5957 2-9-0 0................................ JamesDoyle 18 71
(Charles Hills) *in tch in midfield: rdn and effrt over 2f out: hdwy wl over 1f out: chsd clr wnr 1f out tl ins fnl f: no ex and plugged on same pce fnl 100yds* **33/1**

0 **8** *1 3/4* **Roskilly (IRE)**[41] 5473 2-8-9 0................................ OisinMurphy(5) 7 67
(Andrew Balding) *chsd ldrs: rdn and struggling wl over 2f out: outpcd and btn wl over 1f out: plugged on same pce after* **16/1**

6 **9** *1* **Rainbow Rock (IRE)**[96] 3581 2-9-0 0................................ JoeFanning 2 65
(Mark Johnston) *chsd wnr: rdn ent fnl 2f: outpcd and btn wl over 1f out: lost 2nd 1f out and wknd ins fnl f* **7/1**[3]

10 *1* **Love Tangle (IRE)** 2-9-0 0................................ MartinLane 6 63
(Brian Meehan) *wl in tch in midfield: rdn 3f out: sn drvn and outpcd: plugged on same pce and no threat to ldrs fnl 2f* **25/1**

11 *1/2* **Mustadrik (USA)** 2-9-0 0................................ DaneO'Neill 13 62
(J W Hills) *chsd ldrs: rdn and struggling ent fnl 3f: lost pl and btn 2f out: plugged on* **66/1**

12 *1* **Norse Star (IRE)** 2-9-0 0................................ LiamKeniry 8 59
(Sylvester Kirk) *in tch in midfield: rdn and struggling over 3f out: lost pl and btn 2f out: wl hld and plugged on same pce after* **100/1**

00 **13** *4* **Prairie Prize**[34] 5718 2-9-0 0................................ JamieSpencer 5 50
(David Elsworth) *hld up towards rr: rdn and sme hdwy over 2f out: no imp and racd awkwardly over 1f out: nvr trbld ldrs* **25/1**

14 *1* **Masterpaver** 2-9-1 0 ow1................................ SebSanders 15 49
(Alan Bailey) *hld up in tch in rr: rdn and effrt over 2f out: no imp and wl hld whn hmpd wl over 1f out: n.d* **50/1**

15 *3 1/4* **Oracle Boy** 2-9-0 0................................ MartinDwyer 9 40
(William Muir) *in tch in midfield: rdn and lost pl 3f out: bhd over 1f out* **40/1**

0 **16** *2* **Moxey**[16] 6277 2-9-0 0................................ FergusSweeney 4 36
(Henry Candy) *pressed ldrs tl 3f out: sn rdn and lost pl ent fnl 2f: wknd and bhd fnl f* **66/1**

17 *3/4* **Dalarosso** 2-9-0 0................................ RyanMoore 1 34
(Ed Dunlop) *in tch towards rr: rdn and struggling 3f out: sn btn and bhd fnl 2f* **14/1**

18 *1/2* **Chinotto (IRE)** 2-9-0 0................................ DavidProbert 16 33
(Andrew Balding) *hld up towards rr: short-lived effrt ent fnl 2f: bhd over 1f out* **20/1**

1m 39.85s (1.25) **Going Correction** +0.10s/f (Good) **18** Ran SP% **120.9**
Speed ratings (Par 97): **97,95,92,92,91 90,90,88,87,86 86,85,81,80,77 75,74,73**
toteswingers 1&2 £10.20, 2&3 £10.30, 1&3 £6.50 CSF £51.41 TOTE £6.70: £2.10, £2.70, £2.40; EX 61.60 Trifecta £318.80 Pool: £2715.45 - 6.38 winning units..
Owner K Quinn/ C Benham/ I Saunders **Bred** A Hanahoe **Trained** Newmarket, Suffolk
■ Stewards' Enquiry : Tom Queally one-day ban: careless riding (Oct 10)

FOCUS
Far side of Rowley Mile used and stalls 1m4f &1m6f: centre, rest far side. A good-looking maiden.

6763 EBM-PAPST NURSERY H'CAP 1m
2:35 (2:42) (Class 2) 2-Y-O **£9,056** (£2,695; £1,346; £673) **Stalls** High

Form RPR

5212 **1** **Safety Check (IRE)**[15] 6314 2-9-7 **94**................................ SilvestreDeSousa 9 100+
(Charlie Appleby) *mde all: rdn wl over 1f out: drvn and styd on wl and a holding rival ins fnl f* **7/2**[3]

6362 **2** *3/4* **Newmarket Warrior (IRE)**[9] 6501 2-7-13 **77** ow1..... OisinMurphy(5) 10 81+
(Michael Bell) *trckd ldrs: rdn and swtchd rt over 1f out: pressing wnr fnl f: hld hd high and edgd rt ins fnl f: one pce and a hld* **9/4**[1]

421 **3** *2* **Stormardal (IRE)**[15] 6299 2-9-1 **88**................................ NeilCallan 1 88
(Ismail Mohammed) *chsd ldrs: rdn and effrt to chse wnr 3f out: unable qck over 1f out: 3rd and styd on same pce fnl f* **3/1**[2]

4130 **4** *1* **Gold Top (IRE)**[40] 5536 2-8-9 **82** ow1................................ RichardHughes 5 79
(Richard Hannon) *in tch in midfield: rdn and outpcd over 2f out: kpt on again u.p ins fnl f* **16/1**

234 **5** *1/2* **Rudi Five One (FR)**[28] 5922 2-8-2 **75**................................ AndreaAtzeni 4 71
(Robert Eddery) *awkward leaving stalls and s.i.s: in tch towards rr: rdn and effrt 3f out: outpcd wl over 1f out: kpt on same pce fnl f* **12/1**

0451 **6** *2 1/4* **Photography (IRE)**[12] 6395 2-8-2 **75**................................ PatrickMathers 2 66
(Hugo Palmer) *s.i.s: in tch in midfield: rdn and outpcd 3f out: no threat to ldrs and kpt on same pce fnl 2f* **13/2**

5310 **7** *nk* **The Alamo (IRE)**[26] 6002 2-8-4 **77**................................ JimmyQuinn 8 67
(Richard Hannon) *chsd wnr tl 3f out: sn drvn and unable qck: outpcd and btn over 1f out: wknd fnl f* **25/1**

0042 **8** *11* **Dalaki (IRE)**[30] 5852 2-8-0 **73** oh1................................ MartinLane 7 38
(Clive Brittain) *rdr late removing the hood and v.s.a: a bustled along in rr: rdn over 3f out: sn lost tch: wl bhd over 1f out* **12/1**

1m 39.76s (1.16) **Going Correction** +0.10s/f (Good) **8** Ran SP% **116.4**
Speed ratings (Par 101): **98,97,95,94,93 91,91,80**
toteswingers 1&2 £2.60, 2&3 £2.20, 1&3 £2.20 CSF £12.07 CT £25.89 TOTE £3.70: £1.40, £1.60, £1.40; EX 12.20 Trifecta £36.60 Pool: £3396.83 - 69.48 winning units..
Owner Godolphin **Bred** Malih Al Basti **Trained** Newmarket, Suffolk

FOCUS
The field raced stands' side in what looked a decent nursery.

6764 PRINCESS ROYAL RICHARD HAMBRO E B F STKS (LISTED RACE) (F&M) 1m 4f
3:10 (3:14) (Class 1) 3-Y-O+
£22,684 (£8,600; £4,304; £2,144; £1,076; £540) **Stalls** Centre

Form RPR

3122 **1** **Astonishing (IRE)**[5] 6649 3-8-9 92................................ RyanMoore 12 110+
(Sir Michael Stoute) *stdd s: hld up in tch in rr: swtchd lft and hdwy 3f out: rdn and qcknd to ld 2f out: sn clr and in command: styd on wl: readily* **11/4**[1]

1120 **2** *7* **Songbird (IRE)**[35] 5683 4-9-3 97................................ JamesDoyle 4 99
(Lady Cecil) *hld up in tch in midfield: rdn and effrt 3f out: hdwy to chse clr wnr and edgd lft over 1f out: no imp on wnr but kpt on for clr 2nd* **10/1**

1116 **3** *3 3/4* **Special Meaning**[19] 6186 3-8-9 92................................ SilvestreDeSousa 8 93
(Mark Johnston) *chsd ldr: rdn 3f out: drvn and outpcd 2f out: no ch w wnr but kpt on u.p ins fnl f to snatch 3rd last stride* **8/1**[3]

1116 **4** *shd* **Regal Hawk**[25] 6031 3-8-9 85................................ NeilCallan 1 93
(James Tate) *bmpd s: sn in tch in midfield: rdn and effrt 3f out: drvn and outpcd 2f out: and wl hld 1f out: lost 3rd last stride* **20/1**

1215 **5** *1 1/2* **Kikonga**[53] 5035 3-8-9 93................................ RichardHughes 11 90
(Luca Cumani) *stdd and dropped in bhd after s: hld up in tch in last quartet: rdn and effrt over 2f out: no imp wl over 1f out: wl hld and plugged on same pce fnl f* **17/2**

3125 **6** *2 1/2* **Livia's Dream (IRE)**[16] 6280 4-9-3 82................................ DaneO'Neill 6 86
(Ed Walker) *led: clr 10f out: rdn and hdd 2f out: immediately outpcd by wnr and btn: lost 2nd over 1f out: wknd fnl f* **100/1**

5612 **7** *3* **Phiz (GER)**[14] 6329 3-8-9 103................................ WilliamBuick 2 81
(John Gosden) *wnt rt s: chsd ldrs: rdn over 3f out: sn struggling and lost pl over 2f out: wl btn over 1f out: wknd* **9/2**[2]

1114 **8** *1 3/4* **Court Pastoral**[16] 6294 3-8-9 103................................ TomQueally 5 79
(Lady Cecil) *hld up in tch in midfield: rdn over 3f out: struggling u.p and lost pl over 2f out: wl btn over 1f out* **9/2**[2]

311 **9** *1/2* **Miss Dashwood**[32] 5795 4-9-3 90................................ FrederikTylicki 3 78
(James Fanshawe) *t.k.h: chsd ldrs: rdn and lost pl 3f out: btn 2f out and sn wknd* **11/1**

4243 **10** *9* **Souviens Toi**[33] 5761 4-9-3 99................................[1] FrankieDettori 7 63
(Marco Botti) *hld up in tch in last quartet: rdn over 3f out: sn struggling: bhd 2f: eased ins fnl f* **10/1**

2m 30.85s (-1.15) **Going Correction** +0.10s/f (Good)
WFA 3 from 4yo 8lb **10** Ran SP% **116.9**
Speed ratings (Par 111): **107,102,99,99,98 97,95,93,93,87**
toteswingers 1&2 £6.50, 2&3 £11.50, 1&3 £4.00 CSF £31.90 TOTE £3.40: £1.60, £3.80, £2.50; EX 25.30 Trifecta £125.80 Pool: £6066.24 - 36.16 winning units..
Owner Lady Rothschild **Bred** Azienda Agricola Rosati Colarieti **Trained** Newmarket, Suffolk

FOCUS
The runners headed centre-field for this fillies' Listed race, which was run at a good gallop, but it's hard to know what to make of the form.

6765 SOMERVILLE TATTERSALL STKS (GROUP 3) (C&G) 7f
3:40 (3:43) (Class 1) 2-Y-O
£22,684 (£8,600; £4,304; £2,144; £1,076; £540) **Stalls** High

Form RPR

100 **1** **Miracle Of Medinah**[35] 5679 2-8-12 99................................ LiamKeniry 5 105
(Mark Usher) *chsd ldr: led and travelling strly wl over 1f out: rdn and fnd ex over 1f out: r.o wl and a in command ins fnl f* **25/1**

1243 **2** *1 1/4* **Cable Bay (IRE)**[12] 6390 2-8-12 108................................ FrankieDettori 1 102
(Charles Hills) *chsd ldrs: rdn and effrt 2f out: chsd wnr jst over 1f out: r.o but a readily hld fnl 100yds* **11/4**[1]

1231 **3** *2* **Nezar (IRE)**[27] 5945 2-8-12 96................................ WilliamBuick 3 97
(William Haggas) *t.k.h early: hld up wl in tch in midfield: rdn and effrt 2f out: chsd ldng pair 1f out: styd on same pce after* **5/1**[3]

2154 **4** *hd* **Brazos (IRE)**[13] 6351 2-8-12 90................................ RyanMoore 4 96
(Clive Brittain) *bmpd leaving stalls: in tch in last pair: rdn 3f out: swtchd rt over 1f out: kpt on u.p ins fnl f: no threat to wnr* **14/1**

1 **5** *hd* **God Willing**[41] 5472 2-8-12 0................................ JamieSpencer 2 96
(Ed Dunlop) *hld up in tch in last pair: rdn and effrt 2f out: hdwy u.p to chse ldng pair over 1f out tl 1f out: styd on same pce after* **8/1**

10 **6** *2 1/2* **Championship (IRE)**[100] 3422 2-8-12 0................................ RichardHughes 6 89
(Richard Hannon) *wl in tch in midfield: rdn 2f out: unable qck and n.m.r over 1f out: wknd ins fnl f* **4/1**[2]

2103 **7** *1 3/4* **Mawfoor (IRE)**[14] 6328 2-8-12 95................................ PaulHanagan 8 85
(Brian Meehan) *wl in tch in midfield: n.m.r ent fnl 2f: rdn and unable qck wl over 1f out: wknd fnl f* **6/1**

11 **8** *3 1/4* **Silent Bullet (IRE)**[48] 5224 2-8-12 0................................ SilvestreDeSousa 7 76
(Saeed bin Suroor) *led: rdn 2f out: drvn and hdd over 1f out: wknd fnl f* **6/1**

1m 25.92s (0.52) **Going Correction** +0.10s/f (Good) **8** Ran SP% **113.5**
Speed ratings (Par 105): **101,99,97,97,96 93,91,88**
toteswingers 1&2 £11.90, 2&3 £3.50, 1&3 £13.70 CSF £91.93 TOTE £31.60: £5.80, £1.40, £1.50; EX 126.70 Trifecta £785.30 Pool: £4900.22 - 4.67 winning units..
Owner The High Jinks Partnership **Bred** A C M Spalding **Trained** Upper Lambourn, Berks

FOCUS
They raced stands' side. Not a strong race for the grade, as can sometimes be the case, and the form looks questionable, with a couple of the leading contenders failing to give their running and the race falling to a 25-1 outsider. The winner was a surprise improver.

6766 JOCKEY CLUB ROSE BOWL (FORMERLY FENWOLF STKS) (LISTED RACE) 2m
4:15 (4:20) (Class 1) 3-Y-0+

£20,982 (£7,955; £3,981; £1,983; £995; £499) **Stalls** Centre

Form RPR
2104 **1** **Caucus**[34] 5724 6-9-6 **110** WilliamBuick 8 110
(John Gosden) *hld up in tch in midfield: hdwy to chse ldrs 3f out: rdn and chsd ldr over 1f out: led ent fnl f: styd on strly: readily* **15/8**[1]
3414 **2** 2 ¼ **Statutory (IRE)**[19] 6196 3-8-5 **100** JoeFanning 6 104
(Mark Johnston) *chsd ldr tl led 12f out: rdn 3f out: drvn: edgd rt and hdd over 1f out: kpt on same pce ins fnl f* **4/1**[2]
62 **3** *nk* **Body Language (IRE)**[5] 6646 5-8-12 **81** (p) SilvestreDeSousa 10 99
(Ian Williams) *hld up in last quartet: rdn and effrt over 3f out: modest 4th 2f out: styd on wl ins fnl f to go 3rd towards fin: no threat to wnr* **16/1**
0505 **4** ½ **Model Pupil**[33] 5741 4-9-3 **105** JamesDoyle 2 103
(Charles Hills) *chsd ldrs: hdwy to chse ldr over 4f out: rdn 3f out: 3rd and unable qck over 1f out: kpt on same pce fnl f* **12/1**
-24 **5** 6 **Tropical Beat**[13] 6348 5-9-3 **98** JamieSpencer 4 96
(David O'Meara) *stdd s: hld up in rr: in tch whn bdly hmpd 4f out: no threat to ldrs after: kpt on fnl f* **10/1**
0403 **6** 12 **Repeater**[13] 6349 4-9-3 **109** RyanMoore 3 91
(David O'Meara) *rdr late removing hood and slowly away: hld up in last pair: rdn and effrt 3f out: no hdwy and btn 2f out: eased fnl f* **5/1**[3]
-404 **7** 20 **Cavaleiro (IRE)**[21] 6144 4-9-3 **94** MartinDwyer 9 58
(Marcus Tregoning) *hld up in tch in last trio: hdwy into midfield 1/2-way: rdn 3f out: sn btn: heavily eased ins fnl f: t.o* **25/1**
0 **8** 23 **Sabor A Triunfo (CHI)**[19] 6198 4-9-0 **106** RichardHughes 1 27
(Ed Dunlop) *led for 4f: chsd ldr tl over 4f out: sn u.p: wknd 3f out: t.o over 1f out* **14/1**
4340 **9** 3 ¾ **Saint Hilary**[14] 6329 4-8-12 **87** (p) NeilCallan 7 21
(William Muir) *chsd ldrs: losing pl whn bdly hmpd 4f out: sn bhd: t.o over 1f out* **66/1**
2420 **P** **Genzy (FR)**[11] 6447 5-9-3 **104** RichardKingscote 5
(Ian Williams) *hld up in tch in midfield: effrt whn lost action and p.u 4f out: fatally injured* **9/1**

3m 25.74s (-4.76) **Going Correction** +0.10s/f (Good)
WFA 3 from 4yo+ 12lb **10** Ran SP% **116.1**
Speed ratings (Par 111): **115,113,113,113,110 104,94,82,81,**
toteswingers 1&2 £2.20, 2&3 £7.50, 1&3 £6.90 CSF £8.98 TOTE £3.00: £1.40, £1.80, £4.90; EX 12.70 Trifecta £161.30 Pool: £11357.33 - 52.78 winning units..
Owner Normandie Stud Ltd **Bred** Normandie Stud Ltd **Trained** Newmarket, Suffolk

FOCUS
Not as strong as last year's edition.

6767 ARKLE FINANCE H'CAP 1m
4:50 (4:54) (Class 3) (0-95,95) 3-Y-0+

£7,470 (£2,236; £1,118; £559; £279; £140) **Stalls** High

Form RPR
2354 **1** **Mabait**[26] 5992 7-8-9 **87** GeorgeBuckell(7) 5 94
(David Simcock) *hld up in tch in last pair: nt clr run 2f out: swtchd rt and effrt over 1f out: str run ins fnl f to ld last strides* **5/1**[2]
2051 **2** *hd* **Uppercut**[20] 6167 5-9-0 **85** NeilCallan 3 92
(Stuart Kittow) *in tch in midfield: rdn 3f out: hdwy u.p and ev ch over 1f out: led 1f out: hdd wl ins fnl f: kpt on* **13/2**
1500 **3** *nse* **Asatir (USA)**[26] 6001 4-9-10 **95** (v) SilvestreDeSousa 6 101
(Saeed bin Suroor) *s.i.s: in tch in last pair: rdn 1/2-way: hdwy u.p over 1f out: chal ins fnl f: kpt on to ld wl ins fnl f: hdd and lost 2 pls last strides* **12/1**
610 **4** 1 ½ **Jeeraan (USA)**[20] 6172 3-8-13 **88** PaulHanagan 1 91
(Ed Dunlop) *chsd ldrs: rdn and effrt over 2f out: led over 1f out: drvn and hdd 1f out: wknd wl ins fnl f* **8/1**
1240 **5** ½ **George Guru**[75] 4297 6-9-8 **93** RobertHavlin 2 95
(Michael Attwater) *s.i.s: hld up in last pair: hdwy over 2f out: rdn and effrt to press ldrs ent fnl f: no ex and wknd fnl 75yds* **12/1**
2100 **6** 2 ¼ **Silverheels (IRE)**[29] 5894 4-9-2 **87** RyanMoore 4 84
(Paul Cole) *chsd ldr tl rdn to ld 2f out: hdd over 1f out: styng on same pce whn hmpd ins fnl f: nt rcvr and wl hld after* **6/1**[3]
1-0 **7** ½ **Annina (IRE)**[13] 6356 3-9-1 **90** DaneO'Neill 9 86
(Henry Candy) *chsd ldrs: rdn and lost pl whn swtchd rt ent fnl 2f: no imp u.p over 1f out: one pce fnl f* **7/2**[1]
3103 **8** 11 **Party Royal**[19] 6208 3-8-9 **84** JoeFanning 8 54
(Mark Johnston) *led: rdn and hdd 2f out: sn btn and dropped to rr over 1f out: wknd fnl f* **7/2**[1]

1m 38.32s (-0.28) **Going Correction** +0.10s/f (Good)
WFA 3 from 4yo+ 4lb **8** Ran SP% **115.2**
Speed ratings (Par 107): **105,104,104,103,102 100,100,89**
toteswingers 1&2 £3.70, 2&3 £11.30, 1&3 £10.80 CSF £37.49 CT £369.57 TOTE £6.70: £2.20, £2.60, £3.30; EX 37.40 Trifecta £228.50 Pool: £3792.92 - 12.44 winning units..
Owner Khalifa Dasmal **Bred** L A C Ashby Newhall Estate Farm **Trained** Newmarket, Suffolk

FOCUS
A race that set up for the closers.

6768 E B F VINDIS BENTLEY FILLIES' H'CAP 6f
5:25 (5:25) (Class 2) (0-100,97) 3-Y-0+

£12,450 (£3,728; £1,864; £932; £466; £234) **Stalls** High

Form RPR
0160 **1** **Ladyship**[36] 5651 4-9-7 **97** RyanMoore 6 105
(Sir Michael Stoute) *in tch in midfield: clsd on ldrs 1/2-way: drvn to ld ent fnl f: r.o wl drvn out* **11/4**[1]
2054 **2** ¾ **Misplaced Fortune**[7] 6564 8-8-12 **88** (v) SilvestreDeSousa 3 94
(Nigel Tinkler) *racd in last pair: rdn 1/2-way: swtchd rt and drvn over 1f out: r.o strly ins fnl f: wnt 2nd towards fin* **12/1**
01 **3** *nk* **Reqaaba**[38] 5585 3-8-1 **84** OisinMurphy(5) 7 91+
(Robert Cowell) *bhd: clsd 1/2-way: nt clr run 2f out tl swtchd rt ins fnl f: r.o strly fnl 100yds: nt rch ldrs* **7/1**[3]
-424 **4** ½ **Exceptionelle**[8] 6539 3-8-10 **88** AndreaAtzeni 4 91
(Roger Varian) *chsd ldrs: clsd 1/2-way: rdn and effrt wl over 1f out: chsd wnr ins fnl f: styd on same pce fnl 100yds and lost 2 pls towards fin* **8/1**

1001 **5** *hd* **Milly's Gift**[12] 6382 3-8-5 **88** RyanTate(5) 10 91
(Clive Cox) *t.k.h: hld up in tch in midfield: nt clr run and swtchd rt over 1f out: kpt on same pce u.p ins fnl f* **5/1**[2]
2113 **6** 2 **Floating Along (IRE)**[21] 6143 3-8-6 **84** JoeFanning 2 80
(William Haggas) *in tch in midfield: clsd on ldrs 1/2-way: effrt u.p over 1f out: no ex ins fnl f: wknd fnl 100yds* **9/1**
216- **7** 1 **Malilla (IRE)**[385] 5979 3-9-0 **92** PaulHanagan 5 85
(Clive Cox) *hld up in last trio: clsd on ldrs 1/2-way: rdn and no imp wl over 1f out: styd on same pce fnl f* **20/1**
6123 **8** *hd* **La Fortunata**[23] 6078 6-9-2 **95** MichaelJMMurphy(3) 9 88
(Mike Murphy) *chsd ldr tl led 1/2-way: rdn and hdd ent fnl f: wknd fnl 150yds* **12/1**
4230 **9** 1 ½ **Victrix Ludorum (IRE)**[55] 4949 3-9-2 **94** RichardHughes 1 82
(Richard Hannon) *racd in last trio: clsd 1/2-way: hdwy u.p over 1f out: no ex 1f out: wknd ins fnl f* **7/1**[3]
3100 **10** *hd* **Elusive Flame**[13] 6352 4-9-2 **92** (b[1]) WilliamBuick 8 79
(David Elsworth) *led tl 1/2-way: rdn and lost pl over 1f out: wknd ins fnl f* **14/1**

1m 11.76s (-0.44) **Going Correction** +0.10s/f (Good)
WFA 3 from 4yo+ 2lb **10** Ran SP% **116.3**
Speed ratings (Par 96): **106,105,104,103,103 101,99,99,97,97**
toteswingers 1&2 £8.30, 2&3 £9.50, 1&3 £5.10 CSF £37.63 CT £211.56 TOTE £3.20: £1.30, £4.60, £2.70; EX 39.20 Trifecta £276.90 Pool: £2427.35 - 6.57 winning units..
Owner Cheveley Park Stud **Bred** Cheveley Park Stud Ltd **Trained** Newmarket, Suffolk

FOCUS
This was always likely to be run at a strong pace, with a few front-runners lining up.
T/Jkpt: Not won. T/Plt: £57.70 to a £1 stake. Pool of £71329.08 - 901.47 winning tickets. T/Qpdt: £27.90 to a £1 stake. Pool of £5351.35 - 141.90 winning tickets. SP

6561 PONTEFRACT (L-H)
Thursday, September 26

OFFICIAL GOING: Good (good to firm in places; 7.6)
Wind: Light half against Weather: Cloudy

6769 BRITISH STALLION STUDS EBF STRAWBERRY HILL MAIDEN STKS 6f
2:20 (2:20) (Class 4) 2-Y-O **£4,528** (£1,347; £673; £336) **Stalls** Low

Form RPR
02 **1** **Torchlighter (IRE)**[8] 6534 2-9-5 0 LiamJones 6 88+
(Mark Johnston) *wnt lft s: mde most: rdn clr and hung rt wl over 1f out: readily* **6/4**[1]
0 **2** 7 **Smidgen (IRE)**[27] 5949 2-9-2 0 MarkCoumbe(3) 3 67
(Ed de Giles) *prom on inner: chsd wnr fr 1/2-way: rdn wl over 1f out: sn edgd rt and no imp* **80/1**
3 1 ½ **Smart Alec (IRE)** 2-9-5 0 AndrewMullen 1 63+
(Alan Swinbank) *in tch on inner: hdwy 1/2-way: rdn to chse ldrs 2f out: kpt on same pce* **16/1**
0 **4** *nk* **Bearskin (IRE)**[19] 6206 2-9-5 0 (p) MichaelO'Connell 8 62
(Ann Duffield) *plld hrd: trckd ldrs: rdn along over 2f out: drvn and one pce appr fnl f* **22/1**
5 3 **Soviet Courage (IRE)** 2-9-5 0 GrahamGibbons 4 53+
(William Haggas) *sltly hmpd s: towards rr: green and pushed along 1/2-way: hdwy 2f out: swtchd lft and rdn over 1f out: kpt on fnl f* **7/2**[3]
6 2 **My Target (IRE)** 2-9-5 0 MickaelBarzalona 5 47+
(Saeed bin Suroor) *sltly hmpd s: trckd ldrs on outer: green and pushed along wl over 2f out: sn rdn and wknd wl over 1f out* **9/4**[2]
7 1 ¾ **Starlite Jewel** 2-9-0 0 RobertWinston 7 36
(Ollie Pears) *green and towards rr: hdwy over 2f out: rdn along and swtchd rt over 1f out: sn no imp* **50/1**
8 ½ **Mighty Force (IRE)** 2-9-5 0 LukeMorris 2 40
(Nick Littmoden) *a towards rr* **33/1**
9 ½ **Naggers (IRE)** 2-9-5 0 LeeTopliss 11 38
(Paul Midgley) *dwlt: a towards rr* **50/1**
10 6 **Eastern Dynasty** 2-9-5 0 AndrewElliott 10 20
(Ben Haslam) *cl up: rdn along over 2f out: wknd wl over 1f out* **66/1**
0 **11** *nk* **Queen Of Arts**[43] 5380 2-9-0 0 TonyHamilton 12 14
(Richard Fahey) *in tch on outer: rdn along wl over 2f out: sn wknd* **20/1**

1m 16.68s (-0.22) **Going Correction** -0.10s/f (Good) **11** Ran SP% **117.6**
Speed ratings (Par 97): **97,87,85,85,81 78,76,75,74,66 66**
toteswingers 1&2 £23.40, 2&3 £55.50, 1&3 £6.90 CSF £164.97 TOTE £2.70: £1.20, £8.50, £3.80; EX 100.70 Trifecta £2438.20 Part won. Pool of £3250.99 - 0.78 winning units..
Owner Sheikh Hamdan Bin Mohammed Al Maktoum **Bred** Darley **Trained** Middleham Moor, N Yorks

FOCUS
The going was good, good to firm in places. Only four of the field had run before. This maiden was run at a fair pace with the first three home racing up the inside rail.

6770 BEST HORSE RACING - SKY CHANNEL 432 FILLIES' NURSERY H'CAP 1m 4y
2:55 (2:55) (Class 4) (0-85,79) 2-Y-O **£4,528** (£1,347; £505; £505) **Stalls** Low

Form RPR
01 **1** **Tender Emotion**[43] 5394 2-9-7 **79** MickaelBarzalona 2 87+
(Charlie Appleby) *trckd ldrs: swtchd to outer after 2f: qcknd to ld 3f out and sn edgd lft to inner: rdn and qcknd clr wl over 1f out: rdn ins fnl f: styd on wl* **5/4**[1]
01 **2** 3 ¼ **Mutatis Mutandis (IRE)**[40] 5516 2-9-5 **77** TomMcLaughlin 3 77
(Ed Walker) *trckd ldng pair: pushed along and sltly outpcd 3f out: rdn over 2f out: styd on to chse wnr fr over 1f out: no imp towards fin* **5/2**[2]
11 **3** 3 ½ **Flora Medici**[42] 5424 2-9-4 **76** LukeMorris 5 68
(Sir Mark Prescott Bt) *cl up: rdn and sltly outpcd 3f out: drvn 2f out: kpt on one pce* **7/2**[3]
0201 **3** *dht* **Shirocco Passion**[16] 6284 2-9-0 **72** BarryMcHugh 4 64
(Tony Coyle) *slt ld: hdd: rdn and sltly outpcd 3f out: drvn 2f out: kpt on one pce* **7/1**

1m 46.1s (0.20) **Going Correction** -0.10s/f (Good) **4** Ran SP% **107.7**
Speed ratings (Par 94): **95,91,88,88**
TRIFECTA: Tender Emotion/Mutatis Mutandis/Flora Medici £3.50 TE/MM/Shirocco Passion £5.00. CSF £4.57 TOTE £1.70; EX 4.70 Trifecta £5.00 Pool: £1870.89 - 197.47 winning units..
Owner Godolphin **Bred** Darley **Trained** Newmarket, Suffolk

FOCUS
All four of the runners had won on their previous start. This fillies' handicap was run at a steady pace.

6771 CGC EVENTS FOR CONFERENCE & BANQUETING H'CAP 5f
3:30 (3:30) (Class 5) (0-75,76) 3-Y-0+ £3,234 (£962; £481; £240) Stalls Low

Form RPR

3000 **1** **Oldjoesaid**[20] 6159 9-9-2 **74** .... GeorgeChaloner(5) 9 82
(Paul Midgley) *trckd ldrs: pushed along and lost pl 1/2-way: rdn 2f out: styd on and swtchd rt ent fnl f: sn drvn and fin strly to ld on line* **12/1**

235 **2** *shd* **Ypres**[8] 6516 4-8-13 **73** .... KevinStott(7) 2 81
(Jason Ward) *trckd ldrs: smooth hdwy and cl up 2f out: rdn to ld ent fnl f: hdd and no ex on line* **4/1**[2]

3503 **3** *nk* **Amenable (IRE)**[10] 6461 6-9-6 **73** .... (p) MartinHarley 4 80
(Violet M Jordan) *cl up: effrt wl over 1f out: sn rdn and ev ch tl drvn ins fnl f and no ex towards fin* **12/1**

6301 **4** *1* **Holy Angel (IRE)**[8] 6516 4-9-9 **76** 6ex .... (e) RobertWinston 6 79
(Tim Easterby) *dwlt and hld up in rr: hdwy on inner 2f out: trckd ldrs over 1f out: rdn and ev ch ent fnl f: sn drvn and no imp towards fin* **11/2**[3]

4110 **5** *nk* **Captain Royale (IRE)**[7] 6547 8-9-3 **70** .... (p) BarryMcHugh 5 72
(Tracy Waggott) *trckd ldrs: hdwy wl over 1f out: rdn ent fnl f: no imp last 100yds* **16/1**

1200 **6** *hd* **Adam's Ale**[15] 6309 4-9-2 **74** .... ShirleyTeasdale(5) 1 75
(Paul Midgley) *sn led: rdn along wl over 1f out: hdd and drvn ent fnl f: kpt on same pce* **5/2**[1]

5640 **7** *1 1/2* **Hit The Lights (IRE)**[13] 6362 3-8-8 **67** .... JacobButterfield(5) 11 63
(Ollie Pears) *prom: rdn along 2f out: grad wknd appr fnl f* **14/1**

0061 **8** *3/4* **Trending (IRE)**[20] 6157 4-8-8 **61** .... (bt) SeanLevey 7 54
(Jeremy Gask) *dwlt: a towards rr* **11/1**

2020 **9** *3/4* **Mey Blossom**[26] 5985 8-8-6 **64** .... (p) ConnorBeasley(5) 8 54
(Richard Whitaker) *a towards rr* **25/1**

5123 **10** *1/2* **Lucky Lodge**[16] 6287 3-8-11 **65** .... (b) DavidAllan 10 54
(Mel Brittain) *a towards rr* **11/1**

0100 **11** *3* **Chosen One (IRE)**[10] 6471 8-8-11 **67** .... JasonHart(3) 13 45
(Ruth Carr) *chsd ldrs on outer: cl up 1/2-way: sn rdn and wknd wl over 1f out* **33/1**

1m 3.31s (0.01) **Going Correction** -0.10s/f (Good)
WFA 3 from 4yo+ 1lb **11** Ran SP% **115.3**
Speed ratings (Par 103): **95,94,94,92,92 91,89,88,87,86 81**
toteswingers 1&2 £20.10, 2&3 £8.70, 1&3 £24.90 CSF £58.39 CT £607.89 TOTE £18.00: £4.90, £1.20, £2.90; EX 120.20 Trifecta £652.60 Pool: £2588.61 - 2.97 winning units..
Owner Pee Dee Tee Syndicate & T W Midgley **Bred** Mrs R D Peacock **Trained** Westow, N Yorks

FOCUS
The pace was fair for this open sprint handicap.

6772 SIMON SCROPE DALBY SCREW-DRIVER H'CAP 1m 2f 6y
4:05 (4:05) (Class 2) (0-105,103) 3-Y-0+
£12,450 (£3,728; £1,864; £932; £466; £234) Stalls Low

Form RPR

-151 **1** **Ennistown**[20] 6163 3-9-1 **96** .... MickaelBarzalona 3 103+
(Charlie Appleby) *hld up towards rr: gd hdwy on outer wl over 2f out: rdn over 1f out: styd on wl to ld last 50yds* **9/4**[1]

211 **2** *3/4* **Croquembouche (IRE)**[11] 6428 4-8-9 **87** 6ex .... MarkCoumbe(3) 4 92
(Ed de Giles) *led and sn clr: rdn along over 2f out: drvn over 1f out: hdd and no ex last 50yds* **5/1**[2]

200 **3** *nk* **Spifer (IRE)**[89] 3832 5-9-1 **90** .... (p) MartinHarley 8 94
(Marco Botti) *dwlt and hld up in rr: hdwy and nt clr run over 2f out: squeezed through and rdn to chse ldrs wl over 1f out: drvn and kpt on fnl f: nrst fin* **10/1**

6233 **4** *3/4* **Las Verglas Star (IRE)**[13] 6353 5-8-4 **84** oh1 .... GeorgeChaloner(5) 7 86
(Richard Fahey) *trckd ldrs: cl up over 2f out: rdn wl over 1f out: drvn and kpt on same pce fnl f* **11/2**[3]

0034 **5** *7* **Redact (IRE)**[47] 5255 4-9-1 **90** .... SeanLevey 1 78
(Richard Hannon) *trckd ldrs: effrt over 3f out: sn rdn along and outpcd whn n.m.r over 2f out: swtchd rt to outer and drvn wl over 1f out: sn no imp* **15/2**

3400 **6** *3 1/2* **Awake My Soul (IRE)**[47] 5269 4-9-1 **95** .... DavidBergin(5) 6 76
(David O'Meara) *chsd clr ldr: rdn along 3f out: drvn and hld whn hmpd and wknd wl over 1f out* **11/1**

5140 **7** *4* **Ottoman Empire (FR)**[70] 4465 7-10-0 **103** .... HarryBentley 2 76
(John Butler) *trckd ldrs: effrt 3f out: rdn along 2f out: sn drvn and wknd* **9/1**

3200 **8** *2 1/2* **Muharrib (IRE)**[34] 5728 3-8-12 **93** .... RobertWinston 5 61
(Saeed bin Suroor) *hld up towards rr: hdwy on inner 3f out: rdn and squeezed through 2f out: sn drvn and wknd over 1f out* **9/1**

2m 10.06s (-3.64) **Going Correction** -0.10s/f (Good)
WFA 3 from 4yo+ 6lb **8** Ran SP% **112.0**
Speed ratings (Par 109): **110,109,109,108,102 100,96,94**
toteswingers 1&2 £2.30, 2&3 £3.00, 1&3 £6.20 CSF £12.75 CT £89.67 TOTE £2.30: £1.10, £1.20, £4.00; EX 8.50 Trifecta £42.00 Pool: £1926.83 - 34.36 winning units..
Owner Godolphin **Bred** Darley **Trained** Newmarket, Suffolk

FOCUS
A decent handicap run at a sound pace.

6773 BRITISH STALLION STUDS EBF FRIER WOOD MAIDEN STKS 1m 4y
4:40 (4:40) (Class 4) 2-Y-0 £4,528 (£1,347; £673; £336) Stalls Low

Form RPR

62 **1** **Act Of Charity (IRE)**[12] 6378 2-9-5 0 .... SaleemGolam 1 82+
(Marco Botti) *trckd ldrs on inner: hdwy 2f out: effrt whn nt clr run and hmpd wl over 1f out: rdn to ld jst over 1f out: edgd rt ins fnl f: kpt on strly* **5/2**[2]

2 *3* **Man Of Harlech** 2-9-2 0 .... ThomasBrown(3) 6 75+
(Andrew Balding) *hld up in tch: hdwy to trck ldrs over 2f out: effrt and nt clr run wl over 1f out: squeezed through and rdn to chse wnr ent fnl f: sn drvn and no imp* **7/2**[3]

02 **3** *5* **Arantes**[13] 6355 2-9-5 0 .... MartinHarley 7 64
(Mick Channon) *hld up in tch: hdwy on outer 3f out: chal wl over 1f out: sn rdn and sltly hmpd: ev ch tl drvn and one pce ent fnl f* **2/1**[1]

0 **4** *4* **Tizlove Regardless (USA)**[15] 6299 2-9-5 0 .... LiamJones 3 54
(Mark Johnston) *led: rdn along 3f out: drvn and edgd lft and rt over 1f out: sn hdd & wknd* **10/1**

00 **5** *14* **State Law (IRE)**[27] 5969 2-9-5 0 .... MickaelBarzalona 5 31
(Charlie Appleby) *trckd ldrs: hdwy 3f out: sn cl up: rdn wl over 1f out and ev ch: drvn and hld whn hmpd over 1f out: sn eased* **12/1**

00 **6** *4 1/2* **Rocky Hill Ridge**[31] 5826 2-9-5 0 .... (b[1]) SeanLevey 4 12
(Alan McCabe) *cl up: rdn along over 3f out: sn wknd* **100/1**

7 *3* **Deep Resolve (IRE)** 2-9-5 0 .... AndrewMullen 2 5
(Alan Swinbank) *dwlt: a in rr: rdn along and outpcd fr wl over 2f out* **8/1**

1m 46.07s (0.17) **Going Correction** -0.10s/f (Good) **7** Ran SP% **113.0**
Speed ratings (Par 97): **95,92,87,83,69 64,61**
toteswingers 1&2 £2.40, 2&3 £2.60, 1&3 £1.70 CSF £11.43 TOTE £2.80: £1.10, £3.50; EX 14.30 Trifecta £31.00 Pool: £2659.08 - 64.16 winning units..
Owner Mrs Lucie Botti **Bred** J Kenny **Trained** Newmarket, Suffolk

FOCUS
Plenty of pace on in this maiden, and the field was well strung out at the line.

6774 BET & WATCH WITH RACINGUK'S APP STKS (H'CAP) 6f
5:15 (5:18) (Class 4) (0-80,80) 3-Y-0+ £4,690 (£1,395; £697; £348) Stalls Low

Form RPR

0351 **1** **Evanescent (IRE)**[7] 6548 4-9-2 75 6ex .... RobertWinston 11 90
(John Quinn) *qckly away: mde all: rdn clr wl over 1f out: readily* **5/2**[1]

1625 **2** *3* **Showboating (IRE)**[9] 6496 5-9-4 77 .... (tp) SeanLevey 7 82
(Alan McCabe) *wnt lft s: towards rr: n.m.r 1/2-way: hdwy 2f out: sn rdn: styd on to chse wnr ins fnl f: no imp* **7/1**

505R **3** *1 1/4* **Defence Council (IRE)**[62] 4730 5-9-2 75 .... TonyHamilton 8 76
(Mel Brittain) *towards rr: hdwy 2f out: swtchd rt to outer and rdn wl over 1f out: styd on fnl f: nrst fin* **20/1**

5506 **4** *shd* **Johnny Cavagin**[60] 4812 4-9-5 78 .... (t) BarryMcHugh 4 79
(Richard Guest) *t.k.h: trckd ldrs: hdwy to chse wnr over 2f out: rdn wl over 1f out: drvn and one pce ent fnl f* **6/1**[3]

0000 **5** *1/2* **Trade Secret**[49] 5183 6-8-13 72 .... DavidAllan 3 71
(Mel Brittain) *cl up on inner: rdn along 2f out: sn drvn and wknd appr fnl f* **7/1**

5014 **6** *5* **Illustrious Prince (IRE)**[10] 6475 6-9-0 80 .... LukeLeadbitter(7) 9 63
(Declan Carroll) *chsd ldrs on wd outside: rdn along 2f out: sn one pce* **14/1**

3114 **7** *1/2* **Gold Beau (FR)**[12] 6382 3-8-8 74 .... (p) JacobButterfield(5) 2 56
(Kristin Stubbs) *trckd ldrs on inner: effrt and n.m.r 2f out: sn rdn and wknd* **9/2**[2]

1000 **8** *hd* **Solar Spirit (IRE)**[9] 6496 8-9-6 79 .... MichaelO'Connell 5 60
(Tracy Waggott) *broke wl: plld hrd: trckd ldrs: n.m.r and lost pl after 2f: towards rr fr wl over 2f out* **25/1**

150 **9** *3* **Azzurra Du Caprio (IRE)**[103] 3351 5-9-3 79 .... DeclanCannon(3) 10 51
(Ben Haslam) *chsd ldng pair: effrt over 2f out: rdn wl over 1f: sn drvn and wknd* **40/1**

1m 16.43s (-0.47) **Going Correction** -0.10s/f (Good)
WFA 3 from 4yo+ 2lb **9** Ran SP% **103.8**
Speed ratings (Par 105): **99,95,93,93,92 85,85,84,80**
toteswingers 1&2 £3.70, 2&3 £9.80, 1&3 £8.60 CSF £15.87 CT £199.93 TOTE £3.40: £1.30, £2.30, £5.30; EX 15.10 Trifecta £161.10 Pool: £1697.37 - 7.89 winning units..
Owner Charles Wentworth **Bred** Oliver Donlon **Trained** Settrington, N Yorks

FOCUS
The pace was solid for this fair handicap.

6775 PONTEFRACT PARK APPRENTICE H'CAP 1m 4f 8y
5:50 (5:50) (Class 5) (0-75,73) 3-Y-0+ £3,234 (£962; £481; £240) Stalls Low

Form RPR

3440 **1** **Thecornishcowboy**[41] 5491 4-9-4 **69** .... (tp) JordonMcMurray(6) 4 77
(John Ryan) *trckd ldrs: pushed along 3f out: effrt wl over 1f out: swtchd rt and rdn ent fnl f: sn led and kpt on wl towards fin* **9/1**

5630 **2** *1/2* **Pertuis (IRE)**[41] 5466 7-9-1 **62** .... EvaMoscrop(5) 6 71
(Micky Hammond) *hld up and bhd: hdwy over 4f out: effrt 2f out: rdn and styd on wl to chse wnr ins fnl f: nrst fin* **17/2**

1032 **3** *2 1/2* **Chant (IRE)**[8] 6514 3-9-0 **71** .... RowanScott(4) 9 75
(Ann Duffield) *prom: cl up 1/2-way: led wl over 2f out and sn rdn: drvn over 1f out: hdd ins fnl f: kpt on same pce* **4/1**[2]

6342 **4** *hd* **The Wizard Of Aus (IRE)**[8] 6522 3-8-7 **64** .... JackGarritty(4) 3 67
(Andrew Balding) *hld up in tch: smooth hdwy over 3f out: jnd ldr 2f out: chal over 1f out: shkn up and ev ch ent fnl f: sn rdn and n.m.r: grad wknd* **10/11**[1]

4140 **5** *19* **Underwritten**[39] 5560 4-9-9 **68** .... (b) DanielMuscutt 7 43
(John Weymes) *set str pce: rdn along over 4f out: hdd wl over 2f out and sn wknd* **25/1**

0-36 **6** *3 1/4* **Hot Spice**[24] 6051 5-9-7 **70** .... AnnaHesketh(4) 5 40
(Michael Easterby) *chsd ldrs: rdn along and lost pl over 1/2-way: sn bhd* **8/1**[3]

1500 **7** *41* **Shirataki (IRE)**[23] 6068 5-9-7 **66** .... ThomasGarner 2
(Peter Hiatt) *in tch: hdwy to trck ldrs after 4f: cl up 1/2-way: rdn along wl over 2f out: sn drvn: and wknd: heavily eased over 1f out* **20/1**

2m 40.48s (-0.32) **Going Correction** -0.10s/f (Good)
WFA 3 from 4yo+ 8lb **7** Ran SP% **112.6**
Speed ratings (Par 103): **97,96,95,94,82 80,52**
toteswingers 1&2 £5.90, 2&3 £7.20, 1&3 £3.70 CSF £77.39 CT £353.49 TOTE £6.80: £2.20, £3.50; EX 82.80 Trifecta £166.00 Pool: £1210.66 - 5.46 winning units..
Owner C Letcher & J Ryan **Bred** Hadi Al Tajir **Trained** Newmarket, Suffolk

FOCUS
This handicap, confined to apprentice riders, was run at a sound pace.
T/Plt: £74.40 to a £1 stake. Pool of £39625.60 - 388.34 winning tickets. T/Qpdt: £16.70 to a £1 stake. Pool of £3223.20 - 142.80 winning tickets. JR

6651 WOLVERHAMPTON (A.W) (L-H)
Thursday, September 26

OFFICIAL GOING: Standard to slow
Wind: Moderate half against Weather: Overcast

6776 32REDPOKER.COM MAIDEN AUCTION STKS 5f 216y(P)
5:45 (5:45) (Class 6) 2-Y-0 £1,940 (£577; £288; £144) Stalls Low

Form RPR

34 **1** **Kiss From A Rose**[25] 6013 2-8-7 0 .... ChrisCatlin 2 70
(Rae Guest) *mde all: rdn 2f out: drvn and edgd lft ins fnl f: kpt on* **7/1**

54 **2** *2 1/2* **Monte Viso**[27] 5950 2-8-12 0 .... ShaneKelly 4 71
(Stuart Kittow) *chsd ldrs: rdn over 2f out: keeping on and 3/4 l down whn hmpd by wnr 110yds out: swtchd rt: nt rcvr* **5/2**[1]

534 **3** *2 3/4* **The Doyle Machine (IRE)**[23] 6069 2-8-12 66 .... AdamBeschizza 5 59
(Noel Quinlan) *pressed ldr: rdn 2f out: hung lft and one pce in 3rd fnl f* **3/1**[2]

00 **4** *2 1/2* **Spider Lily**[28] 5929 2-7-13 0 .... JoeyHaynes(5) 8 44
(Peter Makin) *chsd ldrs: rdn over 2f out: grad wknd over 1f out* **12/1**

56 **5** *1/2* **Pelagian (USA)**[36] 5635 2-8-12 0 .... LukeMorris 1 50
(Dean Ivory) *chsd ldrs: rdn over 2f out: grad wknd over 1f out* **14/1**

The Form Book Flat, Raceform Ltd, Compton, RG20 6NL.

0 6 *hd* **Caroline's Beach (IRE)**[11] 6423 2-8-4 0.......................... JimmyQuinn 3 41
(J S Moore) *hld up: rdn 1/2-way: nvr threatened ldrs* **14/1**

5 7 *14* **Lawman's Lady (IRE)**[180] 1240 2-8-7 0.......................... AdrianNicholls 7 2
(Mark Johnston) *midfield: sn pushed along: wknd 2f out* **7/2**[3]

8 *10* **Copper Cavalier** 2-8-12 0.......................... SteveDrowne 6
(Robert Cowell) *slowly away: loooked bit reluctant early and sn detached* **22/1**

1m 17.23s (2.23) **Going Correction** +0.35s/f (Slow) **8** Ran SP% **113.7**
Speed ratings (Par 93): **99,95,92,88,88 87,69,55**
toteswingers 1&2 £4.40, 2&3 £1.70, 1&3 £3.20 CSF £24.59 TOTE £5.20: £1.50, £1.40, £1.20; EX 21.40 Trifecta £32.20 Pool: £2193.82 - 50.96 winning units..
Owner Sakal, Davies & Jennings **Bred** Southcourt Stud **Trained** Newmarket, Suffolk
■ Stewards' Enquiry : Chris Catlin four-day ban: careless riding (Oct 10,11,13,14)

FOCUS
With no significant rain the Polytrack continued to ride on the slow side. After the opener Luke Morris said "The kickback is not so bad but is a bit dead."

6777 32RED H'CAP 5f 216y(P)
6:15 (6:15) (Class 5) (0-75,73) 3-Y-O+ **£2,587** (£770; £384; £192) **Stalls** Low

Form RPR

6060 **1** **Blazing Knight (IRE)**[21] 6135 3-9-0 **68**.......................... (b) JimCrowley 4 80
(Ralph Beckett) *trckd ldrs: rdn to ld appr fnl f: kpt on: hld on towards fin* **4/1**[2]

2221 **2** *nk* **Hi Filwah (USA)**[20] 6176 3-9-0 **68**.......................... (p) SebSanders 2 79
(Jeremy Noseda) *dwlt: in tch: rdn to chse wnr appr fnl f: kpt on: jst hld* **11/8**[1]

6006 **3** *6* **Night Trade (IRE)**[28] 5931 6-8-9 **64**.......................... (p) RaulDaSilva(3) 5 57
(Ronald Harris) *midfield: rdn over 2f out: one pce: wnt 3rd ins fnl f: no threat to ldng pair* **20/1**

6542 **4** *3/4* **Loyal N Trusted**[14] 6343 5-8-9 **61**.......................... (p) LukeMorris 6 52
(Richard Price) *hld up: rdn and sme hdwy on outer 2f out: one pce* **5/1**[3]

6300 **5** *1/2* **Sabrina's Secret**[14] 6345 3-8-5 **59** oh1.......................... AdrianNicholls 8 48
(Tom Tate) *slowly away: rapid hdwy on wd outside to ld over 4f out: rdn 2f out: hung lft and hdd appr fnl f: wknd* **20/1**

0031 **6** *1 3/4* **Invigilator**[161] 1650 5-8-8 **67**.......................... (t) AdamMcLean(7) 7 51
(Derek Shaw) *in tch on outer: rdn over 2f out: wknd over 1f out* **10/1**

0300 **7** *3* **El Mirage (IRE)**[8] 6535 3-9-5 **73**.......................... AdamKirby 3 48
(Dean Ivory) *led: hdd over 4f out: trckd ldr: rdn over 2f out: wknd over 1f out* **12/1**

1440 **8** *7* **Run It Twice (IRE)**[139] 2209 3-9-1 **72**.......................... DeclanBates(3) 1 26
(David Evans) *s.i.s: a in rr* **12/1**

1m 16.04s (1.04) **Going Correction** +0.35s/f (Slow)
WFA 3 from 5yo+ 2lb **8** Ran SP% **112.8**
Speed ratings (Par 103): **107,106,98,97,96 94,90,81**
toteswingers 1&2 £2.70, 2&3 £10.80, 1&3 £14.50 CSF £9.59 CT £91.24 TOTE £4.00: £1.10, £1.80, £3.70; EX 12.90 Trifecta £299.20 Pool: £1826.53 - 4.57 winning units..
Owner Circuit Racing **Bred** Tally-Ho Stud **Trained** Kimpton, Hants

6778 32RED.COM NURSERY H'CAP 5f 216y(P)
6:45 (6:45) (Class 5) (0-70,69) 2-Y-O **£2,587** (£770; £384; £192) **Stalls** Low

Form RPR

060 **1** **Lawyer (IRE)**[33] 5744 2-9-4 **66**.......................... AdamKirby 4 77+
(Luca Cumani) *trckd ldrs: pushed along to chal whn short of room between ldng pair over 1f out: swtchd lft appr fnl f: sn short of room again: swtchd rt: r.o strly fnl 100yds to ld post* **8/1**[11]

100 **2** *nk* **Madagascar Moll (IRE)**[34] 5710 2-9-2 **67**.......................... JulieBurke(3) 10 69
(David O'Meara) *trckd ldr: rdn to chal over 1f out: led ins fnl f: kpt on: hdd post* **28/1**

5423 **3** *1* **The Dukkerer (IRE)**[10] 6474 2-9-1 **63**.......................... DavidNolan 8 62
(David O'Meara) *led: rdn over 2f out: strly pressed over 1f out: hdd ins fnl f: kpt on* **10/1**[3]

2333 **4** *2 3/4* **Flicksta (USA)**[14] 6320 2-9-7 **69**.......................... LukeMorris 6 59
(Ronald Harris) *chsd ldrs: rdn over 2f out: one pce* **9/2**[2]

6131 **5** *3/4* **Limegrove**[13] 6364 2-8-12 **65**.......................... NoelGarbutt(5) 7 53
(David Evans) *in tch on outer: rdn over 2f out: one pce* **14/1**

262 **6** *nk* **Flashy Queen (IRE)**[25] 6013 2-9-5 **67**.......................... LiamKeniry 3 54
(Joseph Tuite) *midfield on inner: rdn over 2f out: one pce and nvr threatened ldrs* **18/1**

4540 **7** *nse* **Lazy Sioux**[15] 6295 2-8-10 **58**.......................... RobbieFitzpatrick 1 45
(Richard Guest) *hld up: rdn over 2f out: nvr threatened ldrs* **22/1**

0620 **8** *3/4* **Dream Sika (IRE)**[31] 5814 2-8-12 **60**.......................... JohnFahy 5 45
(Clive Cox) *hld up in midfield: rdn over 2f out: sn btn* **18/1**

500 **9** *10* **Red Oasis**[110] 3112 2-8-7 **55**.......................... JimmyQuinn 2 10
(Robert Eddery) *slowly away: a in rr* **22/1**

003 **10** *3* **Valued Opinion (IRE)**[27] 5970 2-8-8 **56**.......................... (tp) StevieDonohoe 9 2
(Tim Pitt) *hld up: a towards rr* **33/1**

1m 17.56s (2.56) **Going Correction** +0.35s/f (Slow) **10** Ran SP% **117.5**
Speed ratings (Par 95): **96,95,94,90,89 89,89,88,74,70**
toteswingers 1&2 £9.40, 2&3 £19.10, 1&3 £2.80 CSF £34.10 CT £136.71 TOTE £1.70: £1.10, £11.60, £1.40; EX 36.00 Trifecta £248.30 Pool: £2230.84 - 6.73 winning units..
Owner Sheikh Mohammed Obaid Al Maktoum **Bred** Drumlin Bloodstock **Trained** Newmarket, Suffolk

FOCUS
The market told the story in this 6f nursery.

6779 32REDBET.COM CLAIMING STKS 7f 32y(P)
7:15 (7:15) (Class 6) 2-Y-O **£1,940** (£577; £288; £144) **Stalls** High

Form RPR

0544 **1** **May Whi (IRE)**[29] 5893 2-8-6 58.......................... (v) RichardKingscote 3 61
(Tom Dascombe) *mde all: pushed along over 1f out: kpt on: comf* **2/1**[2]

610 **2** *6* **Lady Stella**[23] 6070 2-9-0 72.......................... LukeMorris 4 56
(Rae Guest) *trckd ldrs in 3rd: rdn to chse wnr wl over 1f out: one pce and sn hld in 2nd* **15/8**[1]

6225 **3** *8* **Chilly In Rio (IRE)**[21] 6131 2-8-8 59.......................... (p) CathyGannon 6 29
(William Muir) *chsd ldr: drvn over 2f out: sn btn in poor 3rd* **15/2**

600 **4** *3/4* **Lambeth Palace**[16] 6279 2-8-8 35 ow1.......................... (v[1]) ShaneKelly 2 27
(Ronald Harris) *slowly away: hld up: brief hdwy over 3f out: sn drvn and btn in poor 4th* **50/1**

4303 **5** *1 3/4* **Princess Tamay (IRE)**[10] 6465 2-8-6 66.......................... AdrianNicholls 1 21
(Mark Johnston) *hld up: rdn over 4f out: nvr threatened* **10/3**[3]

0 **6** *8* **Mrs Sands**[38] 5591 2-8-4 0.......................... JimmyQuinn 7
(J S Moore) *midfield: wknd 3f out* **20/1**

1m 31.78s (2.18) **Going Correction** +0.35s/f (Slow) **6** Ran SP% **109.7**
Speed ratings (Par 93): **101,94,85,84,82 73**
toteswingers 1&2 £1.10, 2&3 £1.70, 1&3 £1.60 CSF £5.83 TOTE £3.10: £1.80, £2.20; EX 6.10 Trifecta £21.80 Pool: £2605.81 - 89.43 winning units..May Whi was claimed by J. J. Quinn for £6000.
Owner The Whipper Partnership **Bred** Mrs M Hervet **Trained** Malpas, Cheshire

6780 32RED CASINO FILLIES' H'CAP 1m 141y(P)
7:45 (7:45) (Class 5) (0-75,75) 3-Y-O+ **£2,587** (£770; £384; £192) **Stalls** Low

Form RPR

0244 **1** **Burning Dawn (USA)**[10] 6476 3-9-3 **73**.......................... JamieSpencer 7 81
(David Brown) *trckd ldrs: rdn to ld over 2f out: wandered u.str.p fr over 1f out: kpt on* **5/1**[3]

6322 **2** *3/4* **Hidden Belief (IRE)**[8] 6524 3-9-5 **75**.......................... JimCrowley 3 81
(Ralph Beckett) *trckd ldrs: rdn to chse wnr wl over 1f out: kpt on* **9/4**[1]

0430 **3** *shd* **Elnadwa (USA)**[41] 5498 3-9-4 **74**.......................... [1] AhmedAjtebi 6 80
(Saeed bin Suroor) *hld up: rdn over 2f out: hdwy on outside over 1f out: styd on fnl f: nrst fin* **12/1**

3323 **4** *nk* **New Falcon (IRE)**[12] 6379 3-9-2 **72**.......................... (b) MartinHarley 4 77
(James Tate) *trckd ldr: rdn over 2f out: kpt on* **12/1**

5 *2 1/2* **Lookbeforeyouleap**[89] 3-9-2 **72**.......................... DavidNolan 11 72
(David O'Meara) *midfield: rdn over 2f out: one pce and nvr threatened ldrs* **33/1**

1652 **6** *1 1/4* **Russian Royale**[31] 5815 3-9-1 **71**.......................... ShaneKelly 1 68
(Stuart Kittow) *in tch: rdn over 2f out: grad wknd* **12/1**

4433 **7** *3* **Capella's Song (IRE)**[14] 6335 3-8-9 **72**.......................... LouisSteward(7) 9 62
(Michael Bell) *hld up: rdn over 2f out: nvr threatened* **9/2**[2]

1-5 **8** *14* **Mrs Bannock (IRE)**[14] 6341 3-9-2 **72**.......................... MickaelBarzalona 2 30
(Charlie Appleby) *led: rdn whn hdd over 2f out: sn wknd* **5/1**[3]

3626 **9** *17* **Silvas Romana (IRE)**[27] 5947 4-8-12 **63**.......................... TomMcLaughlin 5
(Mark Brisbourne) *hld up: rdn over 3f out: wknd and eased* **25/1**

1m 51.66s (1.16) **Going Correction** +0.35s/f (Slow)
WFA 3 from 4yo 5lb **9** Ran SP% **112.1**
Speed ratings (Par 100): **108,107,107,106,104 103,100,88,73**
toteswingers 1&2 £3.50, 2&3 £9.10, 1&3 £13.50 CSF £15.98 CT £124.95 TOTE £4.80: £1.30, £1.30, £4.70; EX 23.20 Trifecta £245.90 Pool: £2198.74 - 6.70 winning units..
Owner Qatar Racing Limited **Bred** Clearsky Farms **Trained** Averham Park, Notts
■ Stewards' Enquiry : Louis Steward one-day ban: careless riding (Oct 10)

FOCUS
Little to choose between the first four home in this truly-run fillies' handicap.

6781 £32 BONUS AT 32RED.COM MAIDEN STKS 1m 4f 50y(P)
8:15 (8:15) (Class 5) 3-Y-O+ **£2,587** (£770; £384; £192) **Stalls** Low

Form RPR

4 **1** **Lineman**[20] 6166 3-9-5 0.......................... ShaneKelly 2 73
(Andrew Hollinshead) *trckd ldr: rdn to ld over 2f out: drvn over 1f out: styd on* **5/1**[2]

4 **2** *1 1/4* **Shanti**[12] 6402 3-9-5 0.......................... JamieSpencer 1 71
(Michael Bell) *hld up in tch: trckd ldng pair gng wl 3f out: rdn to chal 2f out: drvn and hung lft over 1f out: one pce and a hld fnl f* **1/3**[1]

40 **3** *12* **Mr Burbidge**[12] 6402 5-9-13 0.......................... (b) LiamKeniry 5 52
(Neil Mulholland) *hld up in rr: rdn over 3f out: sn no imp: wnt poor 3rd ins fnl f* **40/1**

5-5 **4** *12* **Colour My World**[20] 6166 3-9-5 0.......................... GrahamGibbons 4 33
(Ed McMahon) *led: rdn whn hdd over 2f out: wknd over 1f out* **6/1**[3]

000/ **5** *68* **Joan's Legacy**[1035] 3052 6-9-5 37.......................... RaulDaSilva(3) 3
(Dave Roberts) *trckd ldr tl wknd qckly 4f out: t.o* **100/1**

2m 48.18s (7.08) **Going Correction** +0.35s/f (Slow)
WFA 3 from 5yo+ 8lb **5** Ran SP% **109.4**
Speed ratings (Par 103): **90,89,81,73,27**
CSF £7.12 TOTE £6.30: £2.30, £1.10; EX 9.60 Trifecta £77.10 Pool: £3883.93 - 37.75 winning units..
Owner The HRH Trio **Bred** Millsec Limited **Trained** Upper Longdon, Staffs

FOCUS
A surprise result to this very modest maiden.

6782 32REDBINGO.COM H'CAP (DIV I) 1m 4f 50y(P)
8:45 (8:45) (Class 6) (0-60,65) 3-Y-O+ **£1,940** (£577; £288; £144) **Stalls** Low

Form RPR

0060 **1** **El Massivo (IRE)**[22] 6109 3-9-4 **60**.......................... JimmyQuinn 4 70
(William Jarvis) *midfield: rdn and gd hdwy over 2f out: led wl over 1f out: kpt on wl* **3/1**[2]

5406 **2** *2* **Brunello**[23] 6087 5-9-5 **58** ow1.......................... (b[1]) AdamNicol(5) 2 65
(Philip Kirby) *midfield: smooth hdwy to trck ldr 3f out: rdn 2f out: kpt on but a hld by wnr* **9/2**[3]

0310 **3** *4* **Cabuchon (GER)**[14] 6325 6-9-3 **54**.......................... (t) DeclanBates(3) 3 55
(David Evans) *hld up: rdn over 2f out: kpt on to go modest 3rd jst ins fnl f* **8/1**

5361 **4** *1 1/2* **Panettone (IRE)**[10] 6458 4-10-3 **65** 6ex.......................... (b) AndreaAtzeni 8 63
(Roger Varian) *led: rdn 3f out: hdd wl over 1f out: grad wknd* **15/8**[1]

0203 **5** *nse* **Ground Ginger**[19] 6216 3-8-1 **46** oh1.......................... RaulDaSilva(3) 5 44
(James Bethell) *trckd ldr: rdn over 2f out: wknd ins fnl f* **10/1**

4054 **6** *10* **Hawaiian Freeze**[24] 6044 4-8-12 **46** oh1.......................... ShaneKelly 10 28
(John Stimpson) *racd keenly: midfield: rdn over 2f out: wknd over 1f out* **28/1**

6 **7** *25* **Xclusive**[14] 6321 3-8-13 **55**.......................... LukeMorris 6
(Ronald Harris) *trckd ldrs: rdn over 3f out: wknd over 2f out* **16/1**

00 **8** *19* **Addikt (IRE)**[54] 5002 8-9-9 **57**.......................... AdamKirby 7
(John Spearing) *racd keenly: hld up in rr: wknd over 3f out: t.o* **25/1**

2m 46.71s (5.61) **Going Correction** +0.35s/f (Slow)
WFA 3 from 4yo+ 8lb **8** Ran SP% **111.3**
Speed ratings (Par 101): **95,93,91,90,89 83,66,53**
toteswwingers 1&2 £3.40, 2&3 £5.10, 1&3 £7.30 CSF £15.98 CT £92.33 TOTE £3.40: £1.10, £2.40, £2.80; EX 17.70 Trifecta £134.70 Pool: £2731.26 - 15.20 winning units..
Owner The B A D D Partnership **Bred** Laundry Cottage Stud Farm **Trained** Newmarket, Suffolk

FOCUS
The pace was very steady for the first mile.

6783 32REDBINGO.COM H'CAP (DIV II) 1m 4f 50y(P)
9:15 (9:15) (Class 6) (0-60,60) 3-Y-O+ **£1,940** (£577; £288; £144) **Stalls** Low

Form RPR

2444 **1** **Waahej**[19] 6216 7-9-9 **57**.......................... WilliamCarson 3 65+
(Peter Hiatt) *trckd ldrs: led 2f out: sn pushed clr: eased towards fin* **2/1**[1]

000/ **2** *3* **Poncho**[714] 6820 4-8-12 **46** oh1 ....(p) LiamKeniry 1 48
(Mark Rimell) *midfield: rdn over 2f out: styd on to go 2nd jst ins fnl f: no ch w wnr* **40/1**

0535 **3** *6* **Goldie Horn**[22] 6102 5-8-13 **50**..................(t) WilliamTwiston-Davies(3) 7 42
(Nigel Twiston-Davies) *trckd ldr: rdn to ld over 2f out: sn hdd and one pce: lost 2nd jst ins fnl f: wknd* **6/1**

0-00 **4** *8* **Overrule (USA)**[21] 6130 9-9-8 **56**..............................(p) MichaelStainton 2 36
(Chris Bealby) *midfield: rdn over 4f out: sn no imp* **16/1**

4-00 **5** *1 3/4* **Pearla**[42] 5434 3-9-4 **60**.. AdamBeschizza 6 37
(Robert Stephens) *led: rdn whn hdd over 2f out: wknd* **9/1**

000 **6** *43* **Mrs Mann (USA)**[85] 3957 3-8-12 **54**................................ StevieDonohoe 4
(Willie Musson) *hld up: a bhd: t.o* **14/1**

000 **7** *72* **Tannhauser Gate (IRE)**[107] 3176 3-8-4 **46** oh1................. ChrisCatlin 9
(Jamie Osborne) *hld up in rr: rdn over 7f out: sn t.o* **9/2**[3]

25/0 **P** **Sea The Flames (IRE)**[45] 5337 5-8-12 **46** oh1........... GrahamGibbons 5
(David O'Meara) *s.i.s: sn trckd ldrs: wnt wrong and p.u 5f out* **4/1**[2]

2m 48.42s (7.32) **Going Correction** +0.35s/f (Slow)
WFA 3 from 4yo+ 8lb **8** Ran SP% **110.8**
Speed ratings (Par 101): **89,87,83,77,76 47, ,**
toteswingers 1&2 £21.20, 2&3 £6.90, 1&3 £3.50 CSF £80.25 CT £394.03 TOTE £2.30: £1.10, £5.20, £2.10; EX 78.40 Trifecta £1175.20 Pool: £4751.34 - 3.03 winning units..
Owner P W Hiatt **Bred** David John Brown **Trained** Hook Norton, Oxon

FOCUS
The pace was generous but the race rather fell apart.
T/Plt: £6.10 to a £1 stake. Pool of £71374.90 - 8488.40 winning tickets. T/Qpdt: £3.40 to a £1 stake. Pool of £8456.10 - 1800.55 winning tickets. AS

6618 MAISONS-LAFFITTE (R-H)
Thursday, September 26

OFFICIAL GOING: Turf: good

6786a PRIX DE PORT MARLY (CLAIMER) (2YO) (TURF) 6f (S)
1:50 (12:00) 2-Y-O **£10,975** (£4,390; £3,292; £2,195; £1,097)

RPR

1 **La Cumbia (IRE)**[52] 5082 2-9-1 0.................................. MaximeGuyon 1 80
(X Thomas-Demeaulte, France) **2/1**[1]

2 *3* **Golden Surprise (FR)**[15] 2-8-8 0..................................... FlavienPrat 8 64
(D Windrif, France) **13/1**

3 *nk* **Uma Mia (IRE)**[49] 2-8-0 0.. MatthiasLauron(8) 6 63
(T Lemer, France) **78/10**

4 *3/4* **Stella Clavisque (IRE)**[14] 6328 2-8-11 0........... ChristopheSoumillon 3 64
(Brian Meehan) *midfield in tch on rail: rdn 2f out: r.o and wnt 4th cl home: no ch w wnr* **9/2**[2]

5 *snk* **Ascot Memory (IRE)**[15] 2-8-8 0.................................... TheoBachelot 11 60
(S Wattel, France) **5/1**[3]

6 *nk* **Jack Beauregard (IRE)**[24] 6059 2-8-11 0.......................... AnthonyCrastus 9 63
(Gianluca Bietolini, Italy) **33/1**

7 *2 1/2* **Ceramick (FR)** 2-8-8 0... CristianDemuro 5 52
(F Doumen, France) **81/1**

8 *3* **Blu Axara (ITY)**[16] 6293 2-8-13 0................................ UmbertoRispoli 12 48
(F Chappet, France) **15/2**

9 *nk* **Fudgeit (FR)**[58] 2-8-11 0... StephanePasquier 7 45
(N Clement, France) **16/1**

10 *2* **Django James (IRE)**[9] 2-9-1 0................................... GregoryBenoist 13 43
(Robert Collet, France) **37/1**

11 *5* **Ameli (FR)**[84] 2-8-8 0.. IoritzMendizabal 4 21
(J Heloury, France) **19/1**

12 *3* **Lavistahermosa (FR)** 2-8-8 0...................... Francois-XavierBertras 10 12
(B De Montzey, France) **73/1**

1m 12.5s (-0.90) **12** Ran SP% **117.5**
WIN (incl 1 euro stake): 3.00. Places: 1.60, 3.10, 2.20. DF: 18.50. SF: 30.50..
Owner Roberto Cocheteux Tierno **Bred** Sunland Holdings & J K Thoroughbreds **Trained** France

6190 HAYDOCK (L-H)
Friday, September 27

OFFICIAL GOING: Good (7.5)
Wind: Light, half behind Weather: Sunny

6787 PETER & OLLY HUGHES GOLDEN WEDDING H'CAP (DIV I) 1m 3f 200y
1:30 (1:31) (Class 5) (0-70,70) 3-Y-O+ **£2,587** (£770; £384; £192) **Stalls** Centre

Form RPR

2415 **1** **Mister Fizz**[19] 6239 5-9-2 **69**.. DanielCremin(7) 8 80
(Miss Imogen Pickard) *mde all: rdn over 1f out: kpt on wl fnl f* **3/1**[1]

006- **2** *1 3/4* **Four Nations (USA)**[31] 7409 5-9-9 **69**.............................. LiamKeniry 9 77
(George Baker) *hld up: hdwy over 2f out: rdn to take 2nd 1f out: kpt on ins fnl f: unable to chal wnr* **22/1**

1013 **3** *4 1/2* **Jamaica Grande**[13] 6398 5-8-10 **56**........................... WilliamCarson 10 57
(Dave Morris) *stdd s: hld up: hdwy on inner over 2f out: swtchd rt and hung rt over 1f out: sn unable qck: styd on towards fin* **8/1**

2000 **4** *3/4* **Gold Medal (IRE)**[51] 5132 3-8-13 **67**................................ SeanLevey 11 67
(Richard Hannon) *chsd wnr: pushed along over 5f out: hrd at work over 3f out: lost 2nd over 2f out: kpt on same pce and wl hld ins fnl f* **5/1**[2]

4461 **5** *hd* **Precision Strike**[14] 6361 3-8-0 **59**........................(v) ConnorBeasley(5) 3 58
(Richard Guest) *racd on inner in midfield: hdwy over 3f out: wnt 2nd over 2f out: u.p and lost 2nd 1f out: kpt on same pce and wl hld ins fnl f* **9/1**

2065 **6** *9* **Wordiness**[70] 4489 5-9-7 **70**....................... WilliamTwiston-Davies(3) 12 55
(Brendan Powell) *hld up: rdn 3f out: no imp over 1f out: nvr able to trble ldrs* **7/1**[3]

5504 **7** *3/4* **Bold Assertion**[62] 4753 3-8-7 **61**...............................(v) LukeMorris 2 45
(John Best) *prom: rdn over 4f out: wknd 2f out* **14/1**

3-60 **8** *nse* **Aegean Destiny**[80] 973 6-8-7 **56** oh1..................... DeclanCannon(3) 1 40
(John Mackie) *midfield: rdn over 3f out: sn lost pl: struggling whn hmpd over 2f out: n.d after* **33/1**

5103 **9** *6* **Royal Sea (IRE)**[6] 6658 4-8-10 **61**.............................(be) TimClark(5) 7 35
(Michael Mullineaux) *s.i.s: racd in rr-div: u.p 5f out: toiling fnl 3f* **10/1**

0-50 **10** *27* **My Lord**[17] 6004 5-9-8 **68**.. LiamTreadwell 4
(Luke Dace) *midfield: hdwy over 4f out: sn chsd ldrs: rdn and wknd 2f out* **9/1**

3-02 **11** *2 3/4* **Berkeley Street (USA)**[13] 6407 3-8-2 **61**........................ IanBurns(5) 6
(Jane Chapple-Hyam) *trckd ldrs: rdn over 3f out: sn wknd* **9/1**

2m 32.28s (-1.52) **Going Correction** -0.325s/f (Firm)
WFA 3 from 4yo+ 8lb **11** Ran SP% **118.3**
Speed ratings (Par 103): **92,90,87,87,87 81,80,80,76,58 56**
toteswingers 1&2 £21.50, 1&3 £8.10, 2&3 £64.90 CSF £76.51 CT £490.14 TOTE £4.00: £1.80, £6.50, £3.30; EX 81.30 Trifecta £692.50 Part won. Pool: £923.34 - 0.99 winning units..
Owner Mrs Margaret J Wilson **Bred** Mrs Margaret J Wilson **Trained** Ullingswick, Herefordshire

FOCUS
All races on Inner Home straight and races on Round course reduced in distance by 2yds. A fair handicap in which the winner made virtually all.

6788 PETER & OLLY HUGHES GOLDEN WEDDING H'CAP (DIV II) 1m 3f 200y
2:00 (2:00) (Class 5) (0-70,76) 3-Y-O+ **£2,587** (£770; £384; £192) **Stalls** Centre

Form RPR

02-1 **1** **Sporting Gold (IRE)**[267] 33 4-9-8 **68**..............................[1] NeilCallan 8 78+
(Roger Varian) *midfield: hdwy over 3f out: rdn to press ldr over 1f out: led fnl 150yds: kpt on wl cl home* **4/1**[3]

640 **2** *3/4* **Perfect Summer (IRE)**[28] 5942 3-8-9 **63**......................... TomQueally 11 72
(Lady Cecil) *s.i.s: in rr: niggled along 6f out: hdwyh 3f out: hung lft over 2f out: str chal ins fnl f: no ex fnl strides* **11/4**[2]

00/1 **3** *2* **Highway Code (USA)**[15] 6325 7-9-10 **70**......................... SteveDrowne 5 76
(Richard Lee) *in tch: led over 2f out: rdn whn pressed over 1f out: hdd fnl 150yds: no ex towards fin* **10/1**

064 **4** *1 1/4* **Oscilate Wildly (IRE)**[16] 6312 3-9-2 **70**........................ RobertWinston 1 74
(Peter Chapple-Hyam) *midfield: hdwy 4f out: rdn to chse ldrs 2f out: swtchd rt over 1f out: kpt on same pce fnl 100yds* **12/1**

1366 **5** *4 1/2* **Tawseef (IRE)**[47] 5311 5-9-6 **69**................................... MarkCoumbe(3) 9 66
(Roy Brotherton) *missed break: in rr: sme hdwy over 3f out: one pce over 1f out* **33/1**

1211 **6** *1* **Artful Prince**[7] 6598 3-9-8 **76** 6ex..................................(b) GrahamLee 2 71
(James Given) *led for 1f: remained prom: regained ld wl over 3f out: rdn and hdd over 2f out: wknd wl ins fnl f* **7/4**[1]

004 **7** *2 1/2* **Wolfs Breath (TUR)**[25] 6036 3-9-1 **69**............................ AndreaAtzeni 10 60
(Charles Hills) *hld up: hdwy over 3f out: rdn whn chsng ldrs over 2f out: wknd over 1f out* **22/1**

0504 **8** *28* **Azabitmour (FR)**[70] 4509 3-8-8 **62** ow1........................(v) RobertHavlin 3 8
(John Best) *in tch: led after 4f: pushed along and hdd wl over 3f out: sn wknd* **28/1**

2360 **9** *nk* **Zhuba (IRE)**[9] 6522 3-8-11 **65**.................................... WilliamCarson 7 11
(John Best) *in tch: rdn over 3f out: wknd over 2f out* **33/1**

010- **10** *20* **Brasingaman Espee**[382] 6103 4-8-10 **56** oh4.................. AndrewElliott 6
(George Moore) *led after 1f: hdd after 4f: remained prom: rdn and wknd over 3f out* **66/1**

2m 30.67s (-3.13) **Going Correction** -0.325s/f (Firm)
WFA 3 from 4yo+ 8lb **10** Ran SP% **115.0**
Speed ratings (Par 103): **97,96,95,94,91 90,89,70,70,56**
toteswingers 1&2 £1.20, 1&3 £5.10, 2&3 £8.70 CSF £14.38 CT £101.20 TOTE £4.80: £2.00, £1.70, £1.70; EX 13.00 Trifecta £112.20 Pool: £1740.11 - 11.63 winning units..
Owner A D Spence **Bred** J M Beever **Trained** Newmarket, Suffolk

FOCUS
The second leg of this fair handicap was run 1.61secs faster than the first division.

6789 E B F VALE UK MAIDEN FILLIES' STKS 6f
2:30 (2:30) (Class 5) 2-Y-O **£2,911** (£866; £432; £216) **Stalls** Centre

Form RPR

1 **Dutch S** 2-8-10 0.. JohnFahy 11 76+
(Clive Cox) *cl up: rdn to chal fnl f: r.o: led post* **16/1**

5 **2** *shd* **My Inspiration (IRE)**[19] 6234 2-9-0 0................................ NeilCallan 10 80
(William Haggas) *trckd ldrs: led wl over 1f out: rdn whn pressed fnl f: hdd post* **6/4**[1]

3 *1 3/4* **Destiny's Kitten (IRE)** 2-8-10 0............................... RichardKingscote 9 71+
(Tom Dascombe) *hld up: rdn and hdwy over 1f out: styd on ins fnl f: clsd towards fin* **16/1**

5 **4** *1 1/2* **Miss Brazil (IRE)**[15] 6318 2-9-0 0...................................... SeanLevey 1 70
(Richard Hannon) *racd keenly w ldrs: rdn and ch over 1f out: edgd lft ins fnl f: no ex fnl 75yds* **11/2**[3]

54 **5** *2* **Alfaayza (IRE)**[44] 5385 2-9-0 0.. GrahamLee 3 64
(Brian Meehan) *wnt rt s: led: hdd wl over 1f out: u.p after: one pce ins fnl f* **14/1**

6 *nk* **Jolly Red Jeanz (IRE)** 2-8-10 0.................................... SteveDrowne 12 59+
(J W Hills) *in rr and rn green: rdn over 1f out: prog ins fnl f: nvr trbld ldrs* **50/1**

7 *hd* **Aurelia Cotta (IRE)** 2-8-10 0...................................... RobertWinston 8 59+
(Charles Hills) *hld up towards rr: nt clr run over 1f out: kpt on under hand ride ins fnl f and rn green: nt trble ldrs* **25/1**

8 *1 1/2* **Silver Mirage** 2-8-10 0... TomQueally 2 54
(Michael Bell) *in tch: rdn over 1f out: sn wknd* **13/2**

0 **9** *4* **Mystical Maze**[15] 6318 2-9-0 0.................................. TomMcLaughlin 6 46
(Mark Brisbourne) *w ldr: pushed along over 2f out: wknd over 1f out* **100/1**

2 **10** *2 1/4* **High Accolade**[28] 5950 2-9-0 0.......................................[1] AndreaAtzeni 4 40
(Roger Varian) *bmpd s: chsd ldrs: pushed along over 1f out: sn wknd* **7/2**[2]

11 *1/2* **Crazee Diamond** 2-8-10 0.. SamHitchcott 5 34
(Mick Channon) *n.m.r s and s.i.s: in rr: rdn over 1f out: nvr a threat* **25/1**

1m 14.32s (0.52) **Going Correction** -0.25s/f (Firm) **11** Ran SP% **120.0**
Speed ratings (Par 92): **86,85,83,81,78 78,78,76,70,67 67**
toteswingers 1&2 £7.20, 1&3 £73.30, 2&3 £9.70 CSF £40.45 TOTE £26.50: £8.60, £2.10, £5.20; EX 78.30 Trifecta £970.10 Part won. Pool: £1293.56 - 0.38 winning units..
Owner Mondial Racing & Robert Haim **Bred** R Haim & Templeton Stud **Trained** Lambourn, Berks

FOCUS
An interesting fillies' maiden, won by one of the debutantes.

6790 E B F VALE UK MAIDEN STKS (C&G) 6f
3:00 (3:02) (Class 5) 2-Y-O **£2,911** (£866; £432; £216) **Stalls** Centre

Form RPR

1 **True Comment** 2-9-0 0.. NeilCallan 4 89+
(Ed Walker) *in tch: rdn to ld over 1f out: r.o and a in command ins fnl f* **14/1**

0 **2** *3 1/2* **Galvanize**[19] 6234 2-9-0 0.. TomEaves 8 79+
(Kevin Ryan) *led: rdn and hdd over 1f out: unable to go w wnr ins fnl f* **14/1**

53 **3** *2 1/4* **Sherston**[17] 6277 2-9-0 0.. GrahamLee 5 72
(Mark Johnston) *a.p: rdn and nt qckn over 1f out: kpt on same pce ins fnl f* **3/1**[2]

6 **4** ½ **Lacock**[7] 6589 2-9-0 0 FergusSweeney 10 71
(Henry Candy) *trckd ldrs: rdn over 2f out: nt qckn over 1f out: kpt on same pce ins fnl f* **7/4**[1]
6 **5** 3 **Rolling Dice**[123] 2723 2-9-0 0 LiamKeniry 6 62
(Dominic Ffrench Davis) *midfield: rdn over 1f out: sn btn* **66/1**
6 nk **Boy In The Bar** 2-9-0 0 RobertWinston 1 64+
(David Barron) *v green and bhd: sn detached: kpt on ins fnl f: nvr trbld ldrs* **20/1**
7 ¾ **Kaheyll** 2-9-0 0 AndreaAtzeni 3 58
(William Haggas) *dwlt: bhd: outpcd 1/2-way: nvr on terms w ldrs* **7/1**
632 **8** 4 **Gamgoom**[15] 6342 2-9-0 75 LukeMorris 2 46
(Harry Dunlop) *prom: rdn whn chalng 2f out: rdr sn dropped whip: wknd 1f out: eased whn wl btn fnl 75yds* **5/1**[3]
00 **9** 1 ½ **Bashiba (IRE)**[52] 5105 2-9-0 0 GrahamGibbons 7 42
(Nigel Tinkler) *hld up: rdn over 2f out: sn btn* **80/1**
0 **10** ¾ **Exceeding Power**[8] 6569 2-9-0 0 TomQueally 12 40
(Michael Bell) *trckd ldrs: rdn over 2f out: sn wknd* **14/1**
0 **11** 10 **Oriental Dream (IRE)**[51] 5145 2-9-0 0 PhillipMakin 11 10
(Nigel Tinkler) *bhd: outpcd 1/2-way: n.d after* **66/1**

1m 13.72s (-0.08) **Going Correction** -0.25s/f (Firm) **11** Ran SP% **119.5**
Speed ratings (Par 95): **90,85,82,81,77 77,76,70,68,67 54**
toteswingers 1&2 £23.50, 1&3 £6.00, 2&3 £7.30 CSF £190.94 TOTE £13.50: £3.30, £4.10, £1.20; EX 253.50 Trifecta £1021.90 Pool: £1953.41 - 1.43 winning units..
Owner C F Ma **Bred** Mrs J A Cornwell **Trained** Newmarket, Suffolk

FOCUS
Another impressive winning newcomer in what was a fair maiden.

6791 GRIFFITHS & ARMOUR NURSERY H'CAP 5f
3:35 (3:35) (Class 2) 2-Y-O £9,703 (£2,887; £1,443; £721) Stalls Centre

Form RPR
4411 **1** **Deeds Not Words (IRE)**[13] 6376 2-8-12 84 CharlesBishop(3) 9 91
(Mick Channon) *chsd ldrs: swtchd lft over 1f out: edgd lft ins fnl f and led: rdn out* **5/2**[1]
3322 **2** ¾ **Urban Dreamer (IRE)**[12] 6432 2-8-4 73 (b[1]) WilliamCarson 12 77
(Rod Millman) *led: rdn over 1f out: hdd ins fnl f: kpt on but hld cl home* **10/1**
231 **3** 3 ½ **Jamboree Girl**[37] 5638 2-8-6 75 DuranFentiman 2 67
(Tim Easterby) *in tch: rdn to chal over 1f out: kpt on same pce fnl 100yds whn no ch w front two* **20/1**
14 **4** nse **Montaigne**[149] 1917 2-9-2 85 SebSanders 4 77
(Ralph Beckett) *in tch: rdn 2f out: chsd ldrs over 1f out: kpt on u.p ins fnl f but nt pce of ldrs* **8/1**[3]
5551 **5** ½ **One Boy (IRE)**[11] 6467 2-8-2 76 6ex ConnorBeasley(5) 8 66
(Michael Dods) *hld up: rdn over 1f out: kpt on ins fnl f: nvr able to chal* **5/1**[2]
4210 **6** nk **Lexington Rose**[69] 4528 2-8-5 79 GeorgeChaloner(5) 6 68
(Bryan Smart) *prom: rdn to chal over 1f out: hung lft ins fnl f: no ex ins fnl 100yds* **8/1**[3]
5100 **7** 1 ¾ **Hopefilly (IRE)**[53] 5082 2-8-10 79 GrahamLee 3 61
(Ed Walker) *hld up: rdn over 1f out: no imp: one pce fnl f* **12/1**
5162 **8** 1 ¾ **Muspelheim**[31] 5859 2-8-13 82 (p) PJMcDonald 7 58
(Ann Duffield) *hld up: rdn over 1f out: no imp* **18/1**
1153 **9** 1 ¼ **Zalzilah**[20] 6187 2-9-7 90 (b) NeilCallan 1 64
(James Tate) *racd alone on far side: in tch: rdn over 1f out: no ex wl ins fnl f: eased whn btn towards fin* **10/1**
1040 **10** 1 ¾ **Mr Carbonfootprint**[16] 6303 2-8-1 70 PatrickMathers 11 35
(Richard Fahey) *pushed along and a outpcd: nvr on terms* **25/1**
4220 **11** 3 **Proclamationofwar**[69] 4528 2-8-7 76 TomEaves 10 30
(Kevin Ryan) *prom tl rdn and wknd 2f out* **10/1**

59.66s (-1.14) **Going Correction** -0.25s/f (Firm) 2y crse rec **11** Ran SP% **116.3**
Speed ratings (Par 101): **99,97,92,92,91 90,88,85,83,80 75**
toteswingers 1&2 £5.90, 1&3 £8.70, 2&3 £7.20 CSF £28.07 CT £419.07 TOTE £3.20: £2.00, £3.10, £3.90; EX 27.20 Trifecta £503.70 Pool: £1613.86 - 2.40 winning units..
Owner George Materna **Bred** B Holland, S Hillen & J Cullinan **Trained** West Ilsley, Berks

FOCUS
A competitive nursery, run at a good gallop and won by a progressive juvenile.

6792 FRANK AND TOM FITZGERALD H'CAP 1m
4:10 (4:10) (Class 3) (0-90,90) 3-Y-O+ £8,086 (£2,406; £1,202; £601) Stalls Low

Form RPR
0461 **1** **Ingleby Angel (IRE)**[48] 5291 4-9-1 86 DavidBergin(5) 11 97
(David O'Meara) *hld up in midfield: hdwy over 2f out: rdn over 1f out: r.o ins fnl f: led towards fin* **12/1**
2156 **2** ½ **Yojimbo (IRE)**[14] 6360 5-8-10 79 (v) CharlesBishop(3) 4 89
(Mick Channon) *a.p: rdn to chal over 2f out: led over 1f out: hdd towards fin* **25/1**
615 **3** ½ **African Oil (FR)**[51] 5134 3-8-12 82 SteveDrowne 12 91
(Charles Hills) *racd keenly and no bttr than midfield tl rdn and hdwy over 1f out: styd on ins fnl f: gng on at fin* **16/1**
12 **4** shd **Talented Kid**[17] 6278 4-9-8 88 GrahamLee 2 97
(Mark Johnston) *racd keenly: trckd ldrs on inner: rdn over 2f out: styd on u.p ins fnl f but a hld* **3/1**[1]
3260 **5** 2 ¼ **Suits Me**[16] 6300 10-9-10 90 GrahamGibbons 8 93
(David Barron) *led: rdn over 2f out: hdd over 1f out: stl ch ins fnl f: no ex fnl 75yds* **16/1**
6305 **6** 1 ¼ **Axiom**[20] 6204 9-9-4 84 (p) LukeMorris 5 85
(Ed Walker) *hld up: rdn over 1f out: kpt on ins fnl f: nvr able to trble ldrs* **12/1**
1560 **7** ½ **Ginger Jack**[21] 6164 6-9-8 88 PJMcDonald 6 87
(Geoffrey Harker) *midfield: rdn over 3f out: kpt on ins fnl f: nvr able to chal* **20/1**
0105 **8** hd **Caldercruix (USA)**[7] 6609 6-8-7 80 (p) DanielCremin(7) 9 79
(James Evans) *prom: rdn over 2f out: nt qckn over 1f out: one pce ins fnl f: eased whn wl hld towards fin* **66/1**
1003 **9** 2 ¼ **Lord Of The Dance (IRE)**[21] 6164 7-9-6 89 SladeO'Hara(3) 3 83
(Michael Mullineaux) *hld up in midfield: hdwy on inner over 2f out: rdn over 1f out: one pce fnl f* **20/1**
000 **10** 1 ¾ **Ardmay (IRE)**[6] 6625 4-9-9 89 (b[1]) NeilCallan 10 79
(Kevin Ryan) *trckd ldrs: rdn over 2f out: lost pl over 1f out* **28/1**
5403 **11** hd **Lord Aeryn (IRE)**[41] 5546 6-9-2 87 GeorgeChaloner(5) 13 76
(Richard Fahey) *midfield: rdn 3f out: no imp over 1f out: one pce fnl f* **11/2**[3]
2112 **12** 2 ¾ **Magic Of Reality (FR)**[49] 5246 3-9-6 90 TomQueally 7 75
(Lady Cecil) *hld up: rdn on outer over 2f out: nvr a danger* **4/1**[2]
2455 **13** 2 ¼ **Karaka Jack**[6] 6624 6-9-2 82 AdrianNicholls 1 60
(David Nicholls) *in rr: pushed along over 4f out: nvr on terms* **17/2**
0000 **14** 12 **Ask Dad**[43] 5454 3-9-5 89 TomEaves 14 39
(Michael Dods) *midfield on outer: rdn and wknd 3f out* **16/1**

1m 41.08s (-2.62) **Going Correction** -0.325s/f (Firm)
WFA 3 from 4yo+ 4lb **14** Ran SP% **122.3**
Speed ratings (Par 107): **100,99,99,98,96 95,94,94,92,90 90,87,85,73**
toteswingers 1&2 £86.20, 1&3 £87.70, 2&3 £78.10 CSF £293.16 CT £4871.10 TOTE £13.30: £3.60, £5.80, £6.10; EX 261.00 Trifecta £927.50 Part won. Pool: £1236.76 - 0.11 winning units..
Owner Dave Scott **Bred** Dave Scott **Trained** Nawton, N Yorks

FOCUS
An open handicap and a decent one for the grade, but the pace was only ordinary.

6793 VALE UK H'CAP 1m 6f
4:45 (4:45) (Class 3) (0-95,97) 3-Y-O £8,086 (£2,406; £1,202; £601) Stalls Low

Form RPR
1115 **1** **Big Thunder**[48] 5274 3-9-5 93 LukeMorris 3 102
(Sir Mark Prescott Bt) *racd in cl 2nd pl after 2f: led narrowly 3f out: over 2 l clr 2f out: rdn whn edgd lft over 1f out: styd on gamely fnl f: a doing enough cl home* **9/2**[3]
3152 **2** ¾ **Deficit (IRE)**[20] 6202 3-8-5 79 AndreaAtzeni 4 87
(Michael Bell) *led at stdy pce: pushed along and hdd narrowly 3f out: over 2 l down 2f out: swtchd rt over 1f out: rallied ins fnl f: styd on but hld cl home* **17/2**
1500 **3** 1 ¼ **Elidor**[20] 6186 3-9-4 92 SamHitchcott 6 98
(Mick Channon) *hld up: pushed along 3f out: hdwy 2f out: rdn over 1f out: styd on and ch ins fnl f: no imp on front two towards fin* **12/1**
2110 **4** ¾ **Fledged**[34] 5746 3-9-9 97 RobertHavlin 1 102
(John Gosden) *prom: rdn and outpcd over 2f out: kpt on u.p ins fnl f: no imp on ldrs* **15/2**
3120 **5** 1 ¼ **Hawk High (IRE)**[34] 5764 3-8-6 80 DavidAllan 2 84
(Tim Easterby) *hld up: pushed along over 2f out: rdn over 1f out: one pce and no imp fnl f* **7/2**[1]
2214 **6** 1 ¼ **Glenard**[20] 6186 3-9-5 93 TomQueally 5 95
(Charles Hills) *hld up in rr: rdn over 2f out: edgd rt over 1f out: nvr able to trble ldrs* **4/1**[2]
1063 **7** hd **Eshtiaal (USA)**[20] 6186 3-9-7 95 (bt) GrahamLee 7 97
(Brian Meehan) *in tch: rdn over 2f out: hmpd whn n.m.r over 1f out: wl btn ins fnl f* **4/1**[2]

3m 4.18s (2.18) **Going Correction** -0.325s/f (Firm) **7** Ran SP% **110.4**
Speed ratings (Par 105): **80,79,78,78,77 77,76**
toteswingers 1&2 £3.50, 1&3 £11.40, 2&3 £10.20 CSF £38.18 TOTE £3.30: £1.60, £3.70; EX 58.50 Trifecta £391.30 Pool: £2165.12 - 4.14 winning units..
Owner John Brown & Megan Dennis **Bred** Stanley House Stud **Trained** Newmarket, Suffolk

■ Stewards' Enquiry : Andrea Atzeni two-day ban: careless riding (Oct 11,13)

FOCUS
This competitive 3yo handicap was run at a steady pace, and that suited those ridden prominently.

6794 BETDAQ HAYDOCK PARK APPRENTICE TRAINING SERIES H'CAP (PART OF THE RACING EXCELLENCE INITIATIVE) 1m 2f 95y
5:20 (5:20) (Class 5) (0-70,75) 3-Y-O+ £3,234 (£962; £481; £240) Stalls High

Form RPR
5431 **1** **Bold Duke**[10] 6492 5-9-10 70 6ex EoinWalsh(3) 5 80
(Edward Bevan) *midfield: hdwy 3f out: led over 1f out: r.o ins fnl f* **14/1**
4333 **2** 1 ¼ **Rex Whistler (IRE)**[90] 3809 3-9-4 67 ConnorBeasley 1 75
(Julie Camacho) *in tch: effrt over 2f out: rdn to chal over 1f out: sn nt qckn: kpt on towards fin* **4/1**[1]
1030 **3** 5 **Balmoral Castle**[33] 5793 4-9-5 67 KeneganDeniel(5) 2 66
(Jonathan Portman) *chsd ldrs: rdn to ld over 2f out: hdd over 1f out: outpcd by ldrs whn edgd lft wl ins fnl f: one pce after* **25/1**
4401 **4** 1 **Thecornishcowboy**[1] 6775 4-9-11 75 6ex (tp) JordonMcMurray(7) 3 72
(John Ryan) *hld up: rdn and hdwy 2f out: chsd ldrs: n.m.r on inner whn hmpd fnl 100yds: kpt on* **7/1**[2]
2330 **5** 2 ½ **Batgirl**[24] 6068 6-9-5 67 GeorgeBuckell(5) 10 59
(Martin Smith) *hld up: rdn and hdwy on outer over 2f out: one pce and no imp ins fnl f* **16/1**
244 **6** 2 **Bejeweled (IRE)**[22] 6133 3-8-9 65 AmeliaGreen(7) 9 53+
(Lady Cecil) *s.i.s: in rr: niggled along over 3f out: sme hdwy over 1f out: one pce fnl f* **4/1**[1]
0552 **7** 3 **Miss Blink**[45] 5377 6-9-3 60 JasonHart 6 42
(Robin Bastiman) *in tch: pushed along over 3f out: rdn over 2f out: outpcd wl over 1f out* **9/1**
4613 **8** 4 ½ **Automotive**[22] 6130 5-9-5 65 ShelleyBirkett(3) 13 39
(Julia Feilden) *midfield: lost pl 3f out: plugged on fnl f but n.d* **8/1**[3]
2651 **9** 2 **Duke Of Destiny (IRE)**[38] 5622 4-9-8 70 (p) BradleyBosley(5) 11 40
(Ed Walker) *hld up: u.p over 3f out: no imp over 1f out* **16/1**
326 **10** 1 ½ **Outlaw Torn (IRE)**[16] 6296 4-9-0 60 (e) KevinStott(3) 14 27
(Richard Guest) *led: clr over 5f out: hdd over 2f out: sn wknd* **14/1**
0020 **11** hd **Emman Bee (IRE)**[13] 6405 4-9-12 69 DeclanBates 8 36
(Luke Dace) *chsd ldrs tl rdn and wknd over 2f out* **25/1**
3300 **12** ¾ **Market Puzzle (IRE)**[33] 5803 6-8-8 56 oh10 (p) GaryMahon(5) 4 21
(Mark Brisbourne) *midfield early: bhd fnl 4f* **50/1**
3301 **13** 3 ¼ **The Scuttler (IRE)**[7] 6587 3-9-0 68 6ex DanielCremin(5) 7 27
(Mick Channon) *chsd ldr to 3f out: wknd over 2f out* **8/1**[3]

2m 11.16s (-4.34) **Going Correction** -0.325s/f (Firm)
WFA 3 from 4yo+ 6lb **13** Ran SP% **119.5**
Speed ratings (Par 103): **104,103,99,98,96 94,92,88,87,85 85,85,82**
toteswingers 1&2 £11.70, 1&3 £65.70, 2&3 £16.80 CSF £68.07 CT £1421.19 TOTE £16.60: £4.40, £1.70, £7.50; EX 76.40 Trifecta £920.00 Pool: £1728.50 - 1.40 winning units..
Owner E G Bevan **Bred** Pullen Farm Stud **Trained** Ullingswick, H'fords

■ Stewards' Enquiry : Jordon McMurray caution: careless riding.

FOCUS
A competitive apprentices' handicap.

T/Plt: £653.50 to a £1 stake. Pool: £64144.95 - 71.65 winning tickets T/Qpdt: £207.40 to a £1 stake. Pool: £4639.0 - 16.55 winning tickets DO

6762 NEWMARKET (R-H)

Friday, September 27

OFFICIAL GOING: Good to firm (good in places; 8.1; stands' side 8.1, centre 8.0, far side 8.2)

Wind: light to meduim, half against Weather: dry and bright

6795 AQLAAM OH SO SHARP STKS (GROUP 3) (FILLIES) 7f

1:40 (1:42) (Class 1) 2-Y-O

£22,684 (£8,600; £4,304; £2,144; £1,076; £540) **Stalls** Low

Form RPR

1 **Miss France (IRE)**[27] 2-8-12 0................................ MickaelBarzalona 3 112+
(A Fabre, France) *leggy: athletic: lw: hld up in last trio: smooth hdwy over 1f out: rdn hands and heels and effrt to chse ldr 1f out: led fnl 100yds: holding rival but doing little in front whn pricked ears and edgd rt cl home* **7/2**[2]

11 2 *hd* **Lightning Thunder**[16] 6304 2-8-12 0................................ HarryBentley 4 109
(Olly Stevens) *str: chsd ldrs: wnt 2nd ent fnl 2f: rdn to ld over 1f out: hung lft ent fnl f: hdd fnl 100yds: kpt on but a hld after: bmpd cl home* **15/2**[3]

1 3 *5* **Sweet Acclaim (IRE)**[33] 5797 2-8-12 0................................ PatCosgrave 6 96
(Noel Quinlan) *leggy: lengthy: hld up in tch in midfield: rdn and effrt ent fnl 2f: 3rd and outpcd by ldng pair 1f out: plugged on same pce after* **20/1**

51 4 *5* **Radiator**[23] 6112 2-8-12 0................................ JamesDoyle 9 83
(Sir Michael Stoute) *tall: swtg: stdd after s: hld up in tch in midfield: rdn and effrt over 2f out: no prog and outpcd over 1f out: plugged on same pce fnl f* **11/10**[1]

01 5 *½* **Stealth Missile (IRE)**[20] 6184 2-8-12 0................................ RyanMoore 7 82
(Clive Brittain) *lengthy: lw: s.i.s: racd in last pair: rdn over 2f out: outpcd and wl btn over 1f out: swtchd rt and styd on u.p ins fnl f: nvr trbld ldrs* **12/1**

3224 6 *½* **Midnite Angel (IRE)**[34] 5737 2-8-12 97................................ FrankieDettori 2 81
(Richard Hannon) *lw: hld up in tch in midfield: rdn and effrt over 2f out: unable qck and outpcd wl over 1f out: sn wknd* **8/1**

2066 7 *shd* **Suite (IRE)**[15] 6326 2-8-12 88................................ RichardHughes 8 80
(Richard Hannon) *stdd s: hld up in last pair: rdn and no hdwy ent fnl 2f: n.d* **25/1**

0231 8 *1 ¼* **Sleepy Sioux**[12] 6423 2-8-12 79................................(b) WilliamBuick 1 77
(David Elsworth) *swtg: racd freely: led and sn clr: rdn and hdd over 1f out: sn btn: fdd fnl f* **66/1**

2614 9 *14* **Gown (IRE)**[15] 6326 2-8-12 76................................ DaneO'Neill 5 41
(Charles Hills) *chsd ldr tl ent fnl 2f: sn lost pl u.p: wl bhd 1f out* **50/1**

1m 24.98s (-0.42) **Going Correction** +0.225s/f (Good) 9 Ran SP% **112.5**

Speed ratings (Par 102): **111,110,105,99,98 98,98,96,80**

toteswingers 1&2 £4.50, 1&3 £9.90, 2&3 £11.70 CSF £27.42 TOTE £4.40: £1.70, £2.60, £5.60; EX 28.20 Trifecta £202.30 Pool: £4686.49 - 17.36 winning units..

Owner Ballymore Thoroughbred Ltd **Bred** Dayton Investments Ltd **Trained** Chantilly, France

FOCUS

Far side of Rowley Mile used and stalls 1m4f : centre, rest far side. This was run at a quick pace, in a time 2.48sec outside the standard. The first two finished clear. They came close together near the line and the Stewards had a look. None of the last five winners of this event, which was promoted to Group 3 status in 2007, have managed to win a race since, but this was a cracking renewal. Strong form, and a positive view has been taken.

6796 SHADWELL INTERNATIONAL STALLIONS ROSEMARY STKS (LISTED RACE) (F&M) 1m

2:10 (2:11) (Class 1) 3-Y-O+

£20,982 (£7,955; £3,981; £1,983; £995; £499) **Stalls** Low

Form RPR

406 1 **Zurigha (IRE)**[15] 6327 3-8-10 103................................ RyanMoore 7 108
(Richard Hannon) *lw: hmpd sn after s: hld up in last pair: swtchd lft and hdwy over 1f out: str run u.p fnl f to ld wl ins fnl f: gng away at fin* **16/1**

3650 2 *¾* **Igugu (AUS)**[152] 1872 6-9-0 0................................ PatCosgrave 3 106+
(M F De Kock, South Africa) *swtg: chsd ldrs tl wnt 2nd 6f out: led and travelling wl over 2f out: rdn over 1f out: kpt on wl tl hdd and no ex wl ins fnl f* **5/1**[3]

15-1 3 *1 ½* **Lanansaak (IRE)**[20] 6188 3-8-10 100................................ DaneO'Neill 5 103
(Roger Varian) *hld up in tch in midfield: hdwy wl over 1f out: rdn to chse ldr ent fnl f: pressing wnr fnl 150yds: no ex and outpcd fnl 75yds* **11/4**[1]

6405 4 *1 ½* **Maureen (IRE)**[15] 6327 3-8-13 107................................ RichardHughes 4 102
(Richard Hannon) *lw: stdd after s: hld up in midfield: swtchd lft and effrt 2f out: clsng whn nt clr run and swtchd lft ent fnl f: chsd ldng trio and edgd rt fnl f: r.o but no threat to ldrs* **9/2**[2]

0445 5 *7* **Purr Along**[13] 6416 3-8-10 108................................ FrankieDettori 8 83
(William Muir) *lw: stdd and wnt rt s: hld up in tch in midfield: rdn and effrt ent fnl 2f: no ex over 1f out: wknd fnl f* **8/1**

6645 6 *½* **Falls Of Lora (IRE)**[27] 6000 4-9-0 97................................ SilvestreDeSousa 11 82
(Charlie Appleby) *racd in centre early: jnd field on far side over 6f out: chsd ldrs: wnt 2nd over 2f out: rdn and unable qck over 1f out: btn 1f out: wknd fnl f* **20/1**

1153 7 *1* **Nurpur (IRE)**[10] 6495 3-8-10 85................................ WilliamBuick 9 80
(David O'Meara) *hmpd s: hld up in rr: rdn and effrt over 2f out: sn outpcd and btn 2f out: n.d* **40/1**

16 8 *nse* **Expressly (IRE)**[48] 5271 3-8-10 92................................ MickaelBarzalona 6 80
(Charlie Appleby) *unf: leggy: in tch in midfield: rdn and effrt ent fnl 2f: hdwy to chse ldrs wl over 1f out: no ex jst over 1f out: wknd fnl f* **20/1**

111 9 *3 ½* **Estiqaama (USA)**[50] 5202 3-8-10 99................................ PaulHanagan 2 72
(William Haggas) *swtg: led tl rdn and hdd over 2f out: no ex u.p over 1f out: sn wknd* **11/2**

3640 10 *shd* **Private Alexander (IRE)**[27] 6000 3-8-11 90 ow1....... DanielTudhope 10 72
(David O'Meara) *in tch in midfield: swtchd lft and racd along on stands' side after 1f out: rdn and struggling over 2f: wknd over 1f out* **50/1**

632 11 *1 ½* **Switcher (IRE)**[15] 6327 4-9-0 99................................ TonyHamilton 1 68
(Richard Fahey) *rdn along leaving stalls: chsd ldr for 2f: chsd ldrs tl rdn and lost pl wl over 2f out: bhd over 1f out* **14/1**

1m 36.94s (-1.66) **Going Correction** +0.225s/f (Good)

WFA 3 from 4yo+ 4lb 11 Ran SP% **114.5**

Speed ratings (Par 111): **117,116,114,113,106 105,104,104,101,101 99**

toteswingers 1&2 £10.20, 1&3 £12.10, 2&3 £2.60 CSF £88.01 TOTE £19.70: £3.80, £1.80, £1.40; EX 128.50 Trifecta £1006.80 Pool: £4436.91 - 3.30 winning units..

Owner Saeed H Altayer **Bred** Sir Nicholas & Lady Nugent **Trained** East Everleigh, Wilts

FOCUS

This looked pretty competitive and there was a solid gallop on. The field raced up the far rail, apart from Private Alexander, who tacked over to race alone on the stands' side. The winner has been afforded some improvement and the second was below her foreign mark.

6797 NAYEF JOEL STKS (BRITISH CHAMPIONS SERIES) (GROUP 2) 1m

2:40 (2:41) (Class 1) 3-Y-O+

£51,039 (£19,350; £9,684; £4,824; £2,421; £1,215) **Stalls** Low

Form RPR

1112 1 **Soft Falling Rain (SAF)**[41] 5532 4-9-3 0................................ PaulHanagan 5 125+
(M F De Kock, South Africa) *swtg: racd in centre thrght: chsd ldr after 1f tl rdn to ld over 2f out: styd on strly fr over 1f out: rdn out* **13/8**[1]

2115 2 *3 ½* **Montiridge (IRE)**[20] 6191 3-8-13 115................................ RichardHughes 4 117
(Richard Hannon) *racd in centre thrght: stdd s: hld up in last pair: clsd on but ent fnl 2f: chsd wnr over 1f out: rdn ent fnl f: kpt on but no imp* **5/2**[2]

2014 3 *5* **Premio Loco (USA)**[34] 5739 9-9-3 111................................ GeorgeBaker 3 106
(Chris Wall) *swtg: stdd after s: swtchd to centre after 2f: bhd 1/2-way: rdn and sme hdwy whn swtchd lft over 1f out: styd on past btn horses ins fnl f: no threat to ldrs* **16/1**

2061 4 *1 ½* **Penitent**[9] 6530 7-9-3 115................................ DanielTudhope 2 102
(David O'Meara) *racd alone against far rail thrght: led for 1f: chsd ldrs after: rdn over 2f out: 3rd and outpcd over 1f out: wknd ins fnl f* **11/1**

3222 5 *¾* **Boom And Bust (IRE)**[12] 6427 6-9-3 108................................ MartinDwyer 1 100
(Marcus Tregoning) *lw: chsd ldrs: swtchd to r in centre over 5f out: rdn and unable qck 3f out: outpcd and btn over 1f out: wknd ins fnl f* **16/1**

254 6 *½* **Glory Awaits (IRE)**[56] 4945 3-8-13 112................................(b) JamieSpencer 7 99
(Kevin Ryan) *lw: racd in centre thrght: rdn along leaving stalls: hdwy to ld after 1f: rdn and hdd over 2f out: wknd u.p over 1f out* **16/1**

2130 7 *7* **Guest Of Honour (IRE)**[41] 5553 4-9-3 112................................(p) MartinHarley 6 83
(Marco Botti) *racd in centre thrght: hld up towards rr: hdwy into midfield 1/2-way: rdn over 2f out: sn struggling and lost pl: bhd over 1f out* **5/1**[3]

1m 37.2s (-1.40) **Going Correction** +0.225s/f (Good)

WFA 3 from 4yo+ 4lb 7 Ran SP% **109.3**

Speed ratings (Par 115): **116,112,107,106,105 104,97**

toteswingers 1&2 £1.50, 1&3 £4.70, 2&3 £8.90 CSF £5.20 TOTE £1.90: £1.40, £1.70; EX 4.30 Trifecta £37.50 Pool: £19729.14 - 393.64 winning units..

Owner Hamdan Al Maktoum **Bred** Highlands Farm Stud (pty) Ltd **Trained** South Africa

FOCUS

This event is in its third year as a Group 2. Despite the small field they split into three groups at first, with Penitent racing alone on the far rail and a couple more taking a separate line before joining up with the main group. The initial pace was strong. A clewar personal best from Soft Falling Rain, with Montiridge the bset guide.

6798 SHADWELL FILLIES MILE (GROUP 1) 1m

3:15 (3:15) (Class 1) 2-Y-O

£103,949 (£39,409; £19,723; £9,824; £4,930; £2,474) **Stalls** Low

Form RPR

0102 1 **Chriselliam (IRE)**[20] 6195 2-8-12 95................................ RichardHughes 1 114
(Charles Hills) *lengthy: str: lw: hld up in tch in last pair: swtchd lft and rdn over 1f out: str run u.p to ld fnl 75yds: r.o wl* **28/1**

1231 2 *1* **Rizeena (IRE)**[26] 6024 2-8-12 115................................ JamesDoyle 5 112
(Clive Brittain) *hld up in tch in midfield: rdn and effrt wl over 1f out: hdwy u.p to ld jst ins fnl f: hdd and styd on same pce fnl 75yds* **7/4**[1]

2311 3 *2* **Ihtimal (IRE)**[14] 6350 2-8-12 104................................ SilvestreDeSousa 4 107
(Saeed bin Suroor) *lw: t.k.h: hld up in tch in last pair: rdn and effrt ent fnl 2f: no imp whn pushed sltly lft over 1f out: hdwy 1f out: styd on wl ins fnl f* **5/2**[2]

016 4 *1 ¼* **Wonderfully (IRE)**[26] 6024 2-8-12 0................................ RyanMoore 3 105
(A P O'Brien, Ire) *led early: sn hdd and chsd ldrs: rdn over 2f out: drvn and unable qck over 1f out: styd on same pce fnl f* **5/1**[3]

33 5 *hd* **Avenue Gabriel**[12] 6438 2-8-12 0................................ ChrisHayes 7 104
(P D Deegan, Ire) *athletic: jostled leaving stalls: sn chsng ldr: rdn and effrt 2f out: drvn to ld over 1f out: hdd jst ins fnl f: wknd fnl 100yds* **9/1**

11 6 *1 ¾* **Sound Reflection (USA)**[21] 6171 2-8-12 0............. MickaelBarzalona 2 100
(Charlie Appleby) *tall: leggy: t.k.h early: hld up in tch in midfield: nt enough room and trying to switch lft over 1f out: swtchd lft and hdwy ent fnl f: no ex and wknd ins fnl f* **7/1**

01 7 *3 ¼* **Uchenna (IRE)**[24] 6063 2-8-12 79................................ JimCrowley 8 93
(David Simcock) *swtg: chsd ldrs: rdn and unable qck ent fnl 2f: lost pl over 1f out: wknd fnl f* **66/1**

8 *6* **Ballybacka Queen (IRE)**[12] 6438 2-8-12 0................................ PatSmullen 6 79
(P A Fahy, Ire) *lengthy: leggy: jostled leaving stalls: sn rcvrd to ld: rdn over 2f out: hdd over 1f out: losing pl whn hmpd over 1f out: sn bhd* **25/1**

1m 40.0s (1.40) **Going Correction** +0.225s/f (Good) 8 Ran SP% **112.9**

Speed ratings (Par 109): **102,101,99,97,97 95,92,86**

toteswingers 1&2 £11.30, 1&3 £4.80, 2&3 £2.10 CSF £75.68 TOTE £29.60: £6.40, £1.10, £1.50; EX 117.20 Trifecta £266.40 Pool: £16214.15 - 45.63 winning units..

Owner W Carson, Miss E Asprey, C Wright **Bred** Ballylinch Stud **Trained** Lambourn, Berks

FOCUS

This looked a strong enough Fillies' Mile on paper, but they went no pace early on and it turned into a burn-up over the final 2f. Improvent from Chriselliam but no fluke, with Rizeena just off her 7f form and the fourth and fifth fitting in.

6799 SAKHEE E B F MAIDEN STKS 7f

3:50 (3:53) (Class 4) 2-Y-O **£5,175** (£1,540; £769; £384) **Stalls** Low

Form RPR

1 **Mitraad (IRE)** 2-9-5 0................................ DaneO'Neill 1 90+
(William Haggas) *w'like: scope: lengthy: in tch in midfield: rdn and hdwy ent 2f out: chsd ldr over 1f out: led ins fnl f: styd on wl: rdn out* **16/1**

2 *1 ¼* **Baarez (USA)** 2-9-5 0................................ PaulHanagan 2 87+
(Roger Varian) *str: tall: rrd as stalls opened: in tch in midfield: pushed along and hdwy ent fnl 2f: led over 1f out but immediately hung bdly lft: hdd ins fnl f: racing against stands' rail and one pce after* **4/1**[2]

2 3 *1 ¾* **Yuften**[42] 5473 2-9-5 0................................ RichardHughes 13 82
(William Haggas) *in tch in midfield: rdn and effrt ent fnl 2f: swtchd rt over 1f out: styd on same pce fnl f* **5/4**[1]

4 4 *3* **Ifrika**[97] 3574 2-9-0 0................................ JamesDoyle 7 69
(Clive Brittain) *lengthy: wl in tch in midfield: rdn and effrt 2f out: drvn and unable qck ent fnl f: outpcd fnl 150yds* **50/1**

5 *1* **Ganges (IRE)** 2-9-5 0................................ KirstyMilczarek 12 71+
(James Toller) *w'like: cl cpld: dwlt: in tch towards rr: rdn and sltly outpcd over 2f out: rallied 1f out: no threat to ldrs but styd on again ins fnl f* **40/1**

6 *shd* **Gothic** 2-9-5 0................................ PatDobbs 4 71
(Sir Michael Stoute) *lengthy: scope: s.i.s: hld up in tch towards rr: rdn and hdwy over 1f out: rdn and kpt on same pce ins fnl f* **33/1**

The Form Book Flat, Raceform Ltd, Compton, RG20 6NL.

7 *hd* **Tall Ship (IRE)** 2-9-5 0 .... RyanMoore 11 70+
(Sir Michael Stoute) *w'like: str: bit bkwd: in tch towards rr: rdn over 2f out: outpcd 2f out: rallied ent fnl f: styd on wl fnl 100yds: nvr trbld ldrs* **7/1**[3]

62 **8** *1* **Iftaar (IRE)**[121] 2778 2-9-5 0 .... FrankieDettori 6 68
(Charles Hills) *w'like: str: led: rdn over 2f out: hdd and carried bdly lft over 1f out: nt rcvr and wknd ins fnl f* **12/1**

9 *3/4* **Salmon Sushi** 2-9-5 0 .... TedDurcan 5 66
(David Lanigan) *str: tall: bit bkwd: slowly into stride: rn green: in tch towards rr: rdn and effrt whn racd awkwardly on downhill run over 1f out: styd on same pce after* **66/1**

53 **10** *3/4* **Gilbey's Mate**[78] 4218 2-9-5 0 .... WilliamBuick 10 64
(John Gosden) *unf: scope: tall: dwlt: t.k.h: hdwy to chse ldrs over 5f out: rdn ent fnl 2f: losing pl whn carried lft and hmpd over 1f out: wknd ins fnl f* **9/1**

20 **11** *3/4* **Man Amongst Men (IRE)**[90] 3833 2-9-5 0 ....(t) JamieSpencer 3 62
(Brian Meehan) *lw: chsd ldr tl ent fnl 2f: sn rdn and no rspnse: lost pl over 1f out: wknd fnl f* **12/1**

12 *1/2* **Royal Preserve** 2-9-5 0 .... DavidProbert 16 60
(Andrew Balding) *str: tall: lw: s.i.s: rn green: in tch towards rr: rdn and unable qck whn wandered on downhill run over 1f out: plugged on: nvr trbld ldrs* **33/1**

13 *3/4* **Deauville Dancer (IRE)** 2-9-5 0 .... MartinLane 14 58
(Lady Herries) *str: bit bkwd: s.i.s: a bhd: n.d* **100/1**

14 *1/2* **Captain Swift (IRE)** 2-9-5 0 .... JimmyFortune 15 57
(Brian Meehan) *w'like: leggy: in tch in midfield: rdn jst over 2f out: losing pl and towards rr whn hmpd over 1f out: bhd ins fnl f* **100/1**

0 **15** *1/2* **Ravenous**[141] 2194 2-9-5 0 .... JimCrowley 9 55
(Ralph Beckett) *bit bkwd: chsd ldrs: rdn over 2f out: wknd over 1f out: bhd ins fnl f* **40/1**

1m 26.65s (1.25) **Going Correction** +0.225s/f (Good) **15** Ran SP% **124.4**
Speed ratings (Par 97): **101,99,97,94,93 92,92,91,90,89 88,88,87,86,86**
toteswingers 1&2 £15.10, 1&3 £9.30, 2&3 £3.10 CSF £78.79 TOTE £21.90: £6.40, £2.40, £1.30; EX 110.20 Trifecta £610.20 Pool: £5187.27 - 6.37 winning units..
Owner Hamdan Al Maktoum **Bred** Shadwell Estate Company Limited **Trained** Newmarket, Suffolk

FOCUS
Rob Roy and Evasive, who both won in Group company, are the best winners of this maiden in the past decade. There was a 1-2 for race sponsor Hamdan Al Maktoum.

6800 MAWATHEEQ GODOLPHIN STKS (LISTED RACE) 1m 4f
4:25 (4:25) (Class 1) 3-Y-0+ **£20,982** (£7,955; £3,981; £1,983; £995) **Stalls** Centre

Form RPR

123 **1** **Renew (IRE)**[20] 6196 3-8-10 100 .... MartinHarley 5 108
(Marco Botti) *chsd ldr: clsd to ld 3f out: hrd pressed and drvn 2f out: forged ahd ins fnl f: styd on wl: rdn out* **9/4**[2]

5350 **2** *1* **Wigmore Hall (IRE)**[20] 6198 6-9-4 108 .... JamieSpencer 7 106
(Michael Bell) *stdd and dropped in bhd after s: clsd to trck ldrs over 2f out: swtchd rt and effrt 1f out: drvn ins fnl f: wnt 2nd towards fin: kpt on* **7/2**[3]

1440 **3** *1/2* **Testudo (IRE)**[41] 5531 3-8-10 105 .... JimmyFortune 6 106
(Brian Meehan) *chsd ldng pair: clsd over 3f out: upsides wnr 2f out: sn rdn: no ex fnl 100yds: outpcd towards fin* **6/1**

1101 **4** *1 3/4* **Chancery (USA)**[35] 5723 5-9-4 98 .... DanielTudhope 4 103
(David O'Meara) *lw: hld up in 4th: clsd over 3f: jnd ldrs ent fnl 2f: rdn and ev ch over 1f out: edgd rt and no ex ins fnl f: wknd towards fin* **7/4**[1]

003 **5** *24* **Soho Dancer**[69] 4532 3-8-5 89 .... PaulHanagan 1 59
(James Toller) *led: clr 10f out tl rdn and hdd 3f out: sn dropped out: wl bhd over 1f out* **16/1**

2m 34.51s (2.51) **Going Correction** +0.225s/f (Good)
WFA 3 from 5yo+ 8lb **5** Ran SP% **109.5**
Speed ratings (Par 111): **100,99,99,97,81**
CSF £10.24 TOTE £2.30: £1.10, £2.70; EX 9.90 Trifecta £26.80 Pool: £3996.49 - 111.74 winning units..
Owner Giuliano Manfredini **Bred** Premier Bloodstock **Trained** Newmarket, Suffolk

FOCUS
A rather weak Listed contest.

6801 HAAFHD H'CAP (SILVER CAMBRIDGESHIRE) 1m 1f
5:00 (5:01) (Class 2) 3-Y-0+
£18,675 (£5,592; £2,796; £1,398; £699; £351) **Stalls** Low

Form RPR

33 **1** **Bancnuanaheireann (IRE)**[12] 6427 6-9-9 90 .... AndrewMullen 15 100
(Michael Appleby) *t.k.h: hld up wl in tch in midfield: rdn and effrt 2f out: hdwy to ld over 1f out: gng clr whn shifted rt u.p 1f out: styd on and a doing enough after: rdn out* **14/1**

6603 **2** *1* **Sheila's Buddy**[14] 6358 4-8-6 73 .... LiamJones 8 81
(J S Moore) *stdd s: hld up in tch in rr: rdn and hdwy over 1f out: swtchd rt 1f out: styd on strly to go 2nd last strides: nvr gng to rch wnr* **33/1**

6220 **3** *nk* **Tigers Tale (IRE)**[83] 4080 4-9-4 85 ....(v) RichardHughes 18 92
(Roger Teal) *wl in tch in midfield: rdn and effrt to chse ldrs over 1f out: styd on u.p to chse clr wnr fnl 100yds: kpt on but lost 2nd last strides* **20/1**

1141 **4** *1 1/4* **Morpheus**[43] 5440 3-9-3 89 .... JamesDoyle 22 95
(Lady Cecil) *lw: hld up in tch in midfield: rdn and effrt 2f out: hdwy over 1f out: chsd clr wnr and edgd rt jst ins fnl f: no imp: lost 2 pls fnl 100yds* **10/3**[1]

0036 **5** *hd* **Icebuster**[21] 6172 5-9-4 85 .... DavidProbert 24 90
(Rod Millman) *chsd ldrs tl hdwy to ld over 3f out: rdn and hdd 2f out: 3rd and unable qck over 1f out: kpt on same pce ins fnl f* **16/1**

4560 **6** *3/4* **Christmas Light**[19] 6236 6-8-6 78 .... OisinMurphy(5) 17 81
(Brian Ellison) *in tch in midfield: rdn and hdwy over 1f out: kpt on ins fnl f: no threat to wnr* **20/1**

6505 **7** *3/4* **Hefner (IRE)**[27] 6004 4-9-1 85 .... MichaelJMMurphy(3) 19 87
(William Jarvis) *lw: t.k.h: hld up in tch in midfield: rdn and hdwy u.p over 1f out: kpt on ins fnl f: no threat to wnr* **25/1**

0610 **8** *nk* **Shavansky**[20] 6199 9-8-13 87 .... PatMillman(7) 2 88
(Rod Millman) *t.k.h: hld up wl in tch in midfield: rdn and outpcd and lost pl over 2f out: rallied u.p 1f out: styd on wl fnl f: no threat to wnr* **50/1**

5156 **9** *1/2* **Albaqaa**[8] 6571 8-9-4 85 .... KieranO'Neill 26 85
(P J O'Gorman) *stdd s: t.k.h: hld up in rr: swtchd lft and hdwy wl over 1f out: edgd rt 1f out: styd on same pce ins fnl f: nvr trbld ldrs* **40/1**

1122 **10** *1 1/4* **Pelmanism**[16] 6306 6-8-0 67 .... SilvestreDeSousa 14 64
(Brian Ellison) *lw: wl in tch in midfield: rdn and unable qck 2f out: outpcd and btn over 1f out: plugged on same pce after* **14/1**

4410 **11** *1* **On My Own (TUR)**[17] 6288 4-8-11 78 .... PatDobbs 4 73
(J W Hills) *t.k.h: hld up in tch in midfield: rdn and effrt 2f out: hdwy u.p over 1f out: no ex 1f out: wknd ins fnl f* **25/1**

4200 **12** *shd* **Bank On Me**[4] 6694 4-8-12 79 .... DaneO'Neill 27 74
(Philip McBride) *hld up in tch towards rr: gd hdwy over 3f out: led 2f out tl rdn and hdd over 1f out: no ex 1f out: btn whn hmpd ins fnl f: fdd fnl 100yds* **20/1**

1141 **13** *2 1/2* **Dream Walker (FR)**[8] 6550 4-8-9 81 4ex .... PhilipPrince(5) 12 71
(Brian Ellison) *pressed ldrs: rdn over 2f out: lost pl and drvn 2f out: wknd u.p over 1f out* **20/1**

1323 **14** *hd* **Silver Dixie (USA)**[27] 6003 3-8-10 82 .... WilliamBuick 9 73
(Jeremy Noseda) *hld up in tch in rr: effrt whn hmpd and outpcd wl over 1f out: sn swtchd rt: plugged on fnl f: nvr trbld ldrs* **10/1**[2]

0002 **15** *nk* **Beaumont's Party (IRE)**[8] 6551 6-9-10 91 .... RyanMoore 11 80
(Brian Ellison) *t.k.h: wl in tch in midfield: rdn and outpcd 2f out: losing pl whn short of room and hmpd 2f out: n.d after* **12/1**[3]

1635 **16** *nse* **Dolphin Rock**[31] 5860 6-8-6 78 .... RyanTate(5) 16 67
(Brian Ellison) *led tl over 3f out: drvn and unable qck over 2f out: wknd over 1f out* **50/1**

5164 **17** *1 1/4* **George Cinq**[14] 6356 3-9-2 88 .... JamieSpencer 7 76
(Michael Bell) *stdd s: hld up in tch in rr: swtchd rt and effrt on far side 2f out: no hdwy: n.d* **20/1**

2662 **18** *1* **Royal Prize**[4] 6694 3-8-13 85 .... MartinLane 5 71
(Ralph Beckett) *hld up in tch in midfield: hdwy u.p over 2f out: drvn and no imp wl over 1f out: wknd fnl f* **20/1**

4222 **19** *hd* **Scottish Star**[2] 6750 5-8-11 78 .... MartinHarley 28 62
(James Eustace) *chsd ldrs: ev ch over 3f out tl rdn and lost pl ent fnl 2f: wknd over 1f out* **20/1**

400 **20** *hd* **Stevie Thunder**[41] 5546 8-8-13 83 .... RyanPowell(3) 6 67
(Ian Williams) *in tch in rr: nt clr run 3f out: rdn and no hdwy ent fnl 2f: n.d* **28/1**

1100 **21** *nse* **Niceofyoutotellme**[48] 5269 4-9-10 91 .... JimCrowley 23 75
(Ralph Beckett) *lw: hld up in tch towards rr: rdn and effrt over 2f out: struggling and no hdwy 2f out: wknd over 1f out* **10/1**[2]

0500 **22** *7* **Copperwood**[9] 6538 8-8-8 75 .... JoeFanning 10 45
(Mark Johnston) *wl in tch in midfield: rdn and no rspnse wl over 2f out: wknd over 1f out: bhd and eased wl ins fnl f* **50/1**

0026 **23** *2 3/4* **Calaf**[20] 6211 5-8-11 81 .... RobertTart(3) 21 45
(Brian Ellison) *taken down early: pressed ldrs tl rdn and lost pl over 3f out: bhd over 1f out* **33/1**

0626 **24** *1 3/4* **Classic Colori (IRE)**[46] 5355 6-9-2 83 ....(v) DanielTudhope 25 44
(David O'Meara) *wl in tch in midfield: rdn and lost pl qckly over 2f out: bhd fnl f* **20/1**

4155 **25** *3/4* **Spirit Of The Law (IRE)**[8] 6551 4-9-7 88 .... PaulHanagan 3 47
(Richard Fahey) *chsd ldrs: drvn and no rspnse over 2f out: sn dropped out: bhd and eased ins fnl f* **33/1**

1m 52.01s (0.31) **Going Correction** +0.225s/f (Good)
WFA 3 from 4yo+ 5lb **25** Ran SP% **134.5**
Speed ratings (Par 109): **107,106,105,104,104 103,103,102,102,101 100,100,98,98,97 97,96,95,95,95 95,89,86,85,84**
toteswingers 1&2 £95.70, 1&3 £105.20, 2&3 £70.10 CSF £412.33 CT £9015.75 TOTE £19.70: £3.70, £7.80, £3.50, £1.80; EX 552.90 TRIFECTA Not won..
Owner Dallas Racing **Bred** J S Bolger **Trained** Danethorpe, Notts

■ Stewards' Enquiry : Pat Dobbs two-day ban: careless riding (Oct 11,13)
James Doyle two-day ban: careless riding (Oct 11,13)

FOCUS
The fourth running of this consolation race, and not a particularly strong race for the grade despite the big field. The pace was ordinary and they raced in one pack.

6802 NEWMARKET CHALLENGE WHIP (H'CAP) 1m 2f
5:30 (5:31) (Class 6) (0-85,80) 3-Y-0+ **£0Stalls** Low

Form RPR

0150 **1** **Gone Dutch**[15] 6335 3-8-8 73 .... FrederikTylicki 4 81
(James Fanshawe) *hld up in midfield: clsd on ldrs over 3f out: 3rd and drvn wl over 1f out: led jst ins fnl f: styd on wl and drew clr towards fin* **9/2**[2]

/05- **2** *2 3/4* **Fremont (IRE)**[433] 4334 6-8-2 66 .... NoelGarbutt(5) 5 69
(Hugo Palmer) *chsd ldrs: wnt 2nd 3f out: sn rdn to ld hrd pressed and drvn over 1f out: hdd jst ins fnl f: no ex and one pce fnl 100yds* **14/1**

2100 **3** *1/2* **Breakheart (IRE)**[14] 6359 6-8-9 75 ....(v) JackGarritty(7) 2 77
(Andrew Balding) *short of room leaving stalls: hld up off the pce in last pair: clsd 3f out: chsd ldng trio and swtchd rt jst over 1f out: rdn and chsd wnr ins fnl f: no ex fnl 75yds: wknd and lost 2nd cl home* **11/2**[3]

3106 **4** *1 1/2* **Compton Bird**[8] 6558 4-7-9 59 .... JoeyHaynes(5) 3 58
(Hans Adielsson) *hld up in midfield clsd to chse ldr wl over 2f out: rdn and pressing ldr over 1f out: no ex 1f out: wknd towards fin* **11/1**

2004 **5** *39* **Dr Livingstone (IRE)**[41] 5535 8-8-11 70 .... RichardHughes 6
(Charles Egerton) *hld up wl off the pce in last pair: clsd on ldrs over 3f out: 5th and drvn 2f out: sn btn: wl bhd and eased fnl f: t.o* **8/1**

361- **6** *8* **Zenarinda**[289] 8079 6-8-9 68 .... TedDurcan 9
(Mark H Tompkins) *hld up in midfield: clsd on ldrs over 3f out: rdn over 2f out: sn wl btn and bhd: eased and t.o over 1f out* **12/1**

4601 **7** *20* **Aegaeus**[23] 6108 4-9-7 80 .... RyanMoore 7
(Ed Dunlop) *chsd ldr tl 3f out: lost pl qckly and bhd over 2f out: sn eased and wl t.o over 1f out* **11/8**[1]

100 **8** *9* **Beauchamp Xerxes**[23] 6105 7-8-2 66 .... RyanTate(5) 1
(Hans Adielsson) *led tl hdd and rdn 3f out: dropped out qckly ent fnl 2f: t.o and eased fnl f* **28/1**

2m 7.44s (1.64) **Going Correction** +0.225s/f (Good)
WFA 3 from 4yo+ 6lb **8** Ran SP% **112.9**
Speed ratings (Par 101): **102,99,99,98,67 60,44,37**
toteswingers 1&2 £12.00, 1&3 £5.20, 2&3 £13.30 CSF £61.81 CT £350.46 TOTE £5.40: £2.00, £4.30, £2.60; EX 74.50 Trifecta £467.00 Pool: £2221.53 - 3.56 winning units..
Owner The Ice Syndicate **Bred** Cheveley Park Stud Ltd **Trained** Newmarket, Suffolk

FOCUS
A handicap restricted to horses owned by members of the Jockey Club.

T/Jkpt: Not won. T/Plt: £25.90 to a £1 stake. Pool: £130191.03 - 3666.16 winning tickets T/Qpdt: £2.90 to a £1 stake. Pool: £9700.24 - 2417.27 winning tickets SP

6776 WOLVERHAMPTON (A.W) (L-H)

Friday, September 27

OFFICIAL GOING: Standard to slow

Wind: light across Weather: fine

6803 32RED CASINO H'CAP (DIV I) — 1m 141y(P)

5:40 (5:42) (Class 6) (0-60,60) 3-Y-O+ £1,940 (£577; £288; £144) Stalls Low

Form RPR

55 1 **Dancing Cosmos (IRE)**[5] 6673 3-9-3 56 .... TadhgO'Shea 10 69
(John Patrick Shanahan, Ire) *prom: swtchd rt and chsd ldrs over 2f out: led over 1f out: styd on wl* 25/1

5002 2 3 **Poppy Bond**[31] 5869 3-8-5 49 .... TimClark(5) 3 56
(Alan Bailey) *wnt rt s: chsd ldrs: led over 2f out: hdd over 1f out: styd on same pce* 11/2[2]

150 3 1 ¾ **King Of Wing (IRE)**[5] 6038 4-9-2 50 .... (be) TomMcLaughlin 9 52
(Phil McEntee) *in tch: chsng ldrs over 2f out: kpt on same pce fnl f* 33/1

25-1 4 1 ¼ **Goal (IRE)**[24] 6083 5-9-9 57 .... (t) PatCosgrave 11 57
(Gordon Elliott, Ire) *in tch: drvn over 3f out: hdwy 2f out: kpt on ins fnl f* 6/4[1]

0502 5 nk **Nezami (IRE)**[3] 6723 8-9-3 56 .... JackDuern(5) 1 55
(Patrick Clinton) *prom: drvn over 2f out: one pce* 13/2[3]

5200 6 1 ¼ **On The Cusp (IRE)**[52] 5091 6-9-5 53 .... (b) SeanLevey 13 49
(Violet M Jordan) *s.s: in rr: hdwy over 2f out: nvr nr ldrs* 50/1

5042 7 3 ¾ **Katmai River (IRE)**[11] 6472 6-8-5 46 .... (v) CharlotteJenner(7) 6 35
(Mark Usher) *in rr: sme hdwy over 2f out: nvr a factor* 14/1

6605 8 3 ½ **Bitaphon (IRE)**[7] 6610 4-9-4 57 .... ShirleyTeasdale(5) 12 38
(Michael Appleby) *sn led: hdd over 2f out: wknd over 1f out* 28/1

2003 9 1 ¼ **Pippy**[64] 4666 3-9-4 57 .... (p) RichardKingscote 8 37
(Tom Dascombe) *sn chsng ldrs: wknd over 1f out* 7/1

00-0 10 1 ½ **Valley Dreamer**[32] 5817 3-8-8 47 .... AdamBeschizza 7 23
(Robert Stephens) *mid-div: drvn over 3f out: nvr a factor* 100/1

56 11 19 **Medecis Mountain**[30] 5876 4-8-7 46 oh1 .... (p) ShaneGray(5) 4
(John Wainwright) *hmpd s: hld up in rr: lost pl 3f out: sn bhd: t.o* 100/1

5134 12 14 **Sovereign Power**[38] 5604 3-9-7 60 .... AdamKirby 2
(Paul Cole) *led early: drvn 4f out: lost pl 3f out and sn bhd: t.o* 8/1

0120 13 13 **Tanforan**[21] 6153 11-9-11 59 .... CathyGannon 5
(Brian Baugh) *in rr: drvn 5f out: sn bhd: t.o* 25/1

1m 50.74s (0.24) **Going Correction** +0.175s/f (Slow)
WFA 3 from 4yo+ 5lb 13 Ran SP% **117.0**
Speed ratings (Par 101): **105,102,100,99,99 98,94,91,90,89 72,60,48**
toteswingers 1&2 £49.00, 1&3 £95.10, 2&3 £37.80 CSF £149.31 CT £4673.57 TOTE £25.90: £9.30, £2.20, £12.60; EX 319.90 Trifecta £1876.70 Part won. Pool: £2502.30 - 0.68 winning units..
Owner Thistle Bloodstock Limited **Bred** Thistle Bloodstock Ltd **Trained** Danesfort, Co. Kilkenny

FOCUS
A moderate handicap in which the gallop was no more than fair. The winner came down the centre in the straight and, as has been the case since the track was relaid, Tadhg O'Shea confirmed the ground was "riding quite deep".

6804 32RED CASINO H'CAP (DIV II) — 1m 141y(P)

6:10 (6:13) (Class 6) (0-60,60) 3-Y-O+ £1,940 (£577; £288; £144) Stalls Low

Form RPR

2310 1 **Tatting**[8] 6554 4-9-4 55 .... RaulDaSilva(3) 11 69+
(Chris Dwyer) *dwlt: hld up in rr: hdwy 5f out: 2nd over 2f out: led on bit over 1f out: pushed out towards fin* 5/4[1]

0341 2 3 **Napinda**[25] 6038 3-9-5 58 .... WilliamCarson 1 63
(Philip McBride) *chsd ldrs: drvn 4f out: kpt on to take 2nd last 50yds: no ch w wnr* 7/1[3]

0000 3 2 ¼ **Holli Deya**[27] 5979 3-8-7 46 oh1 .... (p) ChrisCatlin 6 46
(Andi Brown) *wnt lft s: sn bhd and drvn along: hdwy over 2f out: kpt on to take 3rd nr fin* 66/1

5003 4 ¾ **Perseverent Pete (USA)**[38] 5618 3-8-6 48 .... TadhgO'Shea(3) 12 46
(Christine Dunnett) *led: hdd over 1f out: one pce* 66/1

0131 5 3 ½ **Mcconnell (USA)**[11] 6457 8-9-10 58 .... (b) SeanLevey 5 48
(Violet M Jordan) *s.i.s: hdwy over 5f out: one pce fnl 2f* 8/1

0446 6 1 ¼ **Crucis Abbey (IRE)**[11] 6472 5-9-0 48 .... (p) TomMcLaughlin 2 35
(Mark Brisbourne) *t.k.h in mid-div: drvn over 2f out: one pce* 14/1

55 7 1 ½ **Amy Farah Fowler (IRE)**[26] 6019 4-8-9 46 oh1 .... MarkCoumbe(3) 4 30
(Ian Williams) *in rr: drvn over 3f out: kpt on fnl 2f: nvr a factor* 7/2[2]

6330 8 1 ¼ **Tornado Battle**[14] 6361 3-8-11 50 .... (tp) CathyGannon 10 33
(Phil McEntee) *chsd ldrs: wknd over 1f out* 10/1

0000 9 6 **Satwa Laird**[11] 6479 7-9-4 57 .... (p) AnnStokell(5) 8 26
(Ann Stokell) *mid-div: hdwy to chse ldrs 4f out: lost pl over 2f out* 20/1

2005 10 2 **Mistress Shy**[37] 5645 6-8-13 52 .... (t) ShirleyTeasdale(5) 9 17
(Peter Hiatt) *chsd ldrs: lost pl over 1f out: sn bhd* 50/1

1m 52.85s (2.35) **Going Correction** +0.175s/f (Slow)
WFA 3 from 4yo+ 5lb 10 Ran SP% **115.7**
Speed ratings (Par 101): **96,93,91,90,87 86,85,84,78,76**
toteswingers 1&2 £2.50, 1&3 £13.60, 2&3 £26.00 CSF £10.30 CT £375.51 TOTE £2.70: £1.40, £2.30, £8.40; EX 12.90 Trifecta £548.80 Pool: £1739.46 - 2.37 winning units..
Owner Mrs K W Sneath **Bred** Darley **Trained** Newmarket, Suffolk

FOCUS
Division Two of a moderate handicap. The pace was an ordinary one and the winner came down the centre in the straight.

6805 £32 BONUS AT 32RED.COM (S) STKS — 1m 141y(P)

6:40 (6:40) (Class 6) 3-4-Y-O £1,940 (£577; £288; £144) Stalls Low

Form RPR

0062 1 **Moment In The Sun**[8] 6554 4-8-12 53 .... (v) NeilCallan 4 61
(David Flood) *in tch: effrt over 4f out: chsng ldrs over 2f out: led over 1f out: drvn out* 9/2[2]

0000 2 2 **Jake's Destiny (IRE)**[9] 6538 4-9-3 83 .... (bt[1]) PatCosgrave 6 62
(George Baker) *sn chsng ldrs: rdn over 2f out: kpt on one pce fnl f: tk 2nd post* 4/6[1]

620 3 nse **Trulee Scrumptious**[38] 5622 4-8-9 52 .... (be) RosieJessop(3) 3 57
(Peter Charalambous) *led: drvn over 3f out: hdd over 1f out: kpt on same pce* 11/1

0066 4 13 **Tagalaka (IRE)**[16] 6315 3-9-4 60 .... JohnFahy 1 41
(Eve Johnson Houghton) *hld up in rr: effrt over 4f out: rdn over 2f out: wknd over 1f out* 5/1[3]

0000 5 1 **Dansili Dutch (IRE)**[79] 4161 4-8-9 36 .... JulieBurke(3) 2 27
(David O'Meara) *chsd ldrs: drvn over 3f out: wknd 2f out* 20/1

1m 52.07s (1.57) **Going Correction** +0.175s/f (Slow)
WFA 3 from 4yo 5lb 5 Ran SP% **107.9**
Speed ratings (Par 101): **100,98,98,86,85**
CSF £7.72 TOTE £3.80: £2.40, £1.10; EX 7.50 Trifecta £21.00 Pool: £1186.20 - 42.27 winning units..There was no bid for the winner.
Owner Adam Lemon **Bred** Foursome Thoroughbreds **Trained** Exning, Suffolk

FOCUS
Not much to dwell on in an uncompetitive seller, especially with two of the three market leaders underperforming. The gallop was an ordinary one and the winner came down the centre.

6806 32REDPOKER.COM MEDIAN AUCTION MAIDEN STKS — 7f 32y(P)

7:10 (7:10) (Class 6) 3-5-Y-O £1,940 (£577; £288; £144) Stalls High

Form RPR

0- 1 **That's Plenty (IRE)**[8] 6578 4-9-8 0 .... TadhgO'Shea 10 74+
(John Patrick Shanahan, Ire) *chsd ldrs: drvn over 3f out: led over 2f out: forged clr fnl f* 1/2[1]

0- 2 8 **Red Invader (IRE)**[418] 4846 3-9-5 0 .... SteveDrowne 3 53
(Charles Hills) *w ldr: led over 3f out: hdd over 2f out: kpt on same pce over 1f out* 11/4[2]

00 3 7 **Valley Fire**[53] 5069 3-9-0 0 .... NeilCallan 9 31
(Ed McMahon) *s.i.s: hdwy over 5f out: tk modest 3rd over 1f out: one pce* 33/1

-000 4 ½ **Spoken Words**[2] 6760 4-8-10 39 .... (b) JordanHibberd(7) 8 31
(Alan Berry) *dwlt: sn mid-div: drvn over 3f out: kpt on one pce* 66/1

00 5 5 **Perci French**[27] 5989 3-9-5 0 .... DavidNolan 6 23
(David O'Meara) *chsd ldrs: drvn 3f out: sn wknd* 12/1[3]

-660 6 3 ½ **Benidorm**[72] 4400 5-9-3 45 .... [1] AdamCarter(5) 1 15
(John Wainwright) *chsd ldrs: drvn over 3f out: sn lost pl* 40/1

00-0 7 18 **Illawalla**[16] 6297 5-9-8 40 .... (b[1]) PatrickMathers 5
(Alan Berry) *led: hdd over 3f out: outpcd 3f out: wknd over 1f out: sn bhd: t.o* 200/1

60 8 8 **Come On Flo**[28] 5942 3-9-0 0 .... AdamBeschizza 7
(Michael Mullineaux) *mid-div: lost pl over 5f out: sn wl bhd: t.o 3f out* 200/1

9 2 ½ **Stoneacre Brigitte (IRE)** 4-9-5 0 .... SladeO'Hara(3) 2
(Peter Grayson) *s.s: in rr: bhd fnl 5f: t.o 3f out* 40/1

1m 30.87s (1.27) **Going Correction** +0.175s/f (Slow)
WFA 3 from 4yo+ 3lb 9 Ran SP% **111.3**
Speed ratings (Par 101): **99,89,81,81,75 71,51,41,39**
toteswingers 1&2 £1.10, 1&3 £4.40, 2&3 £2.90 CSF £1.83 TOTE £1.40: £1.02, £1.20, £4.10; EX 2.60 Trifecta £17.00 Pool: £1990.77 - 87.67 winning units..
Owner Thistle Bloodstock Limited **Bred** Denis Brosnan **Trained** Danesfort, Co. Kilkenny

FOCUS
A most uncompetitive maiden. The gallop was just fair and the winner came down the centre.

6807 BRIAN OLIVER'S 80 AND STILL GAMBLING MAIDEN STKS — 7f 32y(P)

7:40 (7:41) (Class 5) 2-Y-O £2,587 (£770; £384; £192) Stalls High

Form RPR

342 1 **Archibald Thorburn (IRE)**[15] 6340 2-9-5 75 .... GrahamLee 4 75
(Ed McMahon) *mid-div: sn pushed along: hdwy over 3f out: hmpd 2f out: sn cl 2nd: edgd rt and led jst ins fnl f: all out* 7/4[1]

2 shd **Hagree (IRE)** 2-9-5 0 .... PaoloSirigu 7 75+
(Marco Botti) *dwlt: hdwy over 4f out: led on outer and edgd lft 2f out: hdd jst ins fnl f: edgd rt: kpt on wl: jst hld* 14/1

3 4 **Wellesbourne** 2-9-5 0 .... AhmedAjtebi 6 66+
(Charlie Appleby) *chsd ldrs: drvn and outpcd over 3f out: hmpd and lost pl 2f out: kpt on to take modest 3rd jst ins fnl f* 6/1

4 4 ½ **Dolce N Karama (IRE)** 2-9-5 0 .... TadhgO'Shea 5 54
(John Patrick Shanahan, Ire) *s.i.s: sn chsng ldrs: n.m.r over 2f out: one pce* 5/1[3]

5 ¾ **Kalon Brama (IRE)** 2-8-11 0 .... RosieJessop(3) 8 47
(Peter Charalambous) *chsd ldrs: n.m.r over 2f out: one pce* 100/1

6 3 ¾ **Wunderkind (USA)** 2-9-0 0 .... LukeMorris 1 38
(Sir Mark Prescott Bt) *s.i.s: sn drvn along: hdwy 4f out: nvr a threat* 7/2[2]

000 7 2 ½ **All Yours (IRE)**[22] 6140 2-9-0 72 .... NeilCallan 2 32
(William Knight) *chsd ldrs: sn drvn along: reminders over 4f out: sn lost pl* 14/1

8 4 **Tashtu** 2-8-7 0 .... RyanWhile(7) 3 22
(Bill Turner) *dwlt: in rr: wl bhd 4f out* 100/1

60 9 ¾ **Mathematics**[56] 4958 2-9-5 0 .... AdamKirby 10 25
(Charlie Appleby) *led: hdd and hmpd 2f out: sn lost pl: bhd whn heavily eased clsng stages* 13/2

1m 31.06s (1.46) **Going Correction** +0.175s/f (Slow) 9 Ran SP% **118.2**
Speed ratings (Par 95): **98,97,93,88,87 83,80,75,74**
toteswingers 1&2 £4.80, 1&3 £3.20, 2&3 £14.60 CSF £30.73 TOTE £3.00: £1.10, £4.10, £2.70; EX 19.40 Trifecta £110.30 Pool: £1515.64 - 10.30 winning units..
Owner Robert Allcock **Bred** W J Kennedy **Trained** Lichfield, Staffs
■ Stewards' Enquiry : Paolo Sirigu three-day ban: careless riding (Oct 11,13,14)

FOCUS
A fair maiden in which the gallop was reasonable. The winner came down the centre in the straight and the first two pulled clear.

6808 32REDBET.COM H'CAP — 5f 216y(P)

8:10 (8:10) (Class 6) (0-55,61) 3-Y-O+ £1,940 (£577; £288; £144) Stalls Low

Form RPR

6011 1 **Father Fred**[11] 6478 3-9-8 61 6ex .... RaulDaSilva(3) 11 77+
(Chris Dwyer) *t.k.h: sn trcking ldr: rdn 2f out: led appr fnl f: wandered ins fnl f: styd on strly to forge clr* 4/5[1]

0623 2 4 ½ **Prigsnov Dancer (IRE)**[42] 5470 8-8-8 49 .... (p) DavidParkes(7) 9 51
(Deborah Sanderson) *chsd ldrs: kpt on fnl f: tk 2nd clsng stages* 12/1

3560 3 ½ **Steel City Boy (IRE)**[11] 6478 10-8-13 52 .... AnnStokell(5) 6 53
(Ann Stokell) *mid-div: hdwy over 2f out: kpt on to take 3rd nr fin* 40/1

6660 4 1 ¼ **Rise To Glory (IRE)**[11] 6478 5-9-5 53 .... (v[1]) DuranFentiman 10 50
(Shaun Harris) *led: hdd appr fnl f: wknd and lost 2 pls clsng stages* 25/1

0004 5 ½ **Very First Blade**[11] 6478 4-8-11 50 .... (p) JackDuern(5) 4 45
(Mark Brisbourne) *in rr: hdwy over 2f out: kpt on fnl f* 16/1

0005 6 1 ¼ **Flow Chart (IRE)**[6] 6651 6-8-12 49 .... SladeO'Hara(3) 7 41
(Peter Grayson) *s.i.s: in rr: hdwy 2f out: styd on ins fnl f* 12/1

0663 7 1 ½ **Charlemagne Diva**[11] 6478 3-8-13 54 .... (t) PhilipPrince(5) 1 41
(Richard Guest) *chsd ldrs: wknd over 1f out: eased clsng stages* 7/1[2]

0406 8 2 **Marshall Art**[11] 6478 4-9-4 52 .... (tp) AdamKirby 12 33
(Ken Wingrove) *chsd ldrs: lost pl over 1f out: eased nr fin* 16/1

000 9 6 **Perlachy**[27] 5982 9-9-0 **48**....(p[1]) LukeMorris 2 11
(Ronald Harris) *mid-div: lost pl over 3f out: bhd whn eased clsng stages* **20/1**

3003 10 3 ¼ **Almaty Express**[6] 6651 11-9-1 **54**....(b) AdamCarter(5) 3 7
(John Weymes) *in rr: bhd fnl 3f: eased clsng stages* **10/1**[3]

1m 15.82s (0.82) **Going Correction** +0.175s/f (Slow)
WFA 3 from 4yo+ 2lb **10** Ran SP% **115.3**
Speed ratings (Par 101): **101,95,94,92,92 90,88,85,77,73**
toteswingers 1&2 £2.60, 1&3 £16.90, 2&3 £47.90 CSF £11.10 CT £224.48 TOTE £2.10: £1.02, £2.70, £4.70; EX 13.20 Trifecta £348.90 Pool: £1174.88 - 2.52 winning units..
Owner Mrs C M Goode **Bred** Pedro Rosas **Trained** Newmarket, Suffolk

FOCUS
Another moderate handicap. The gallop was sound and the progressive winner was another to come down the centre.

6809 32RED H'CAP 1m 5f 194y(P)
8:40 (8:40) (Class 4) (0-80,80) 3-Y-O+ **£4,690** (£1,395; £697; £348) **Stalls** Low

Form RPR

3620 1 **Gabrial's King (IRE)**[12] 6424 4-10-0 **80**.... NeilCallan 8 87
(David Simcock) *mid-div: hdwy to chse ldrs over 3f out: 2nd over 1f out: hung rt and styd on to ld last 75yds* **7/2**[2]

2113 2 1 ¼ **Royal Alcor (IRE)**[13] 6405 6-9-4 **75**.... DanielMuscutt(5) 4 80
(Gay Kelleway) *trckd ldrs: t.k.h: led on bit over 1f out: rdn and hdd ins fnl f: no ex* **9/1**

1060 3 1 ¾ **Admirable Duque (IRE)**[32] 5823 7-8-12 **71**....(be) JoshBaudains(7) 9 74
(Dominic Ffrench Davis) *s.i.s: in rr: hdwy 4f out: styd on to take 3rd ins fnl f* **12/1**

6561 4 1 ¾ **Royal Peculiar**[15] 6346 5-10-0 **80**.... AndrewMullen 3 81
(Michael Appleby) *mid-div: chsd ldrs 5f out: led over 2f out: hdd over 1f out: one pce* **11/2**

4031 5 1 ¼ **Dragon City**[23] 6116 3-9-2 **78**.... GrahamLee 7 77
(Harry Dunlop) *trckd ldrs: led over 3f out: hdd over 2f out: one pce* **3/1**[1]

2034 6 4 ½ **Snow Hill**[15] 6346 5-9-7 **73**....(b) SebSanders 6 66
(Chris Wall) *s.i.s: hld up towards rr: hdwy over 4f out: sn drvn: wknd appr fnl f* **5/1**[3]

2003 7 10 **Kenny's Girl (IRE)**[23] 6116 3-8-4 **66** ow1.... MartinDwyer 2 45
(William Muir) *dwlt: in rr: sme hdwy over 4f out: wknd over 1f out* **25/1**

2510 8 39 **Jonnie Skull (IRE)**[20] 6072 7-9-9 **75**....(t) AdamKirby 1
(Phil McEntee) *led: hdd over 8f out: drvn to ld over 4f out: hdd over 3f out: sn lost pl and bhd: t.o over 1f out* **10/1**

0505 9 12 **Italian Riviera**[8] 6565 4-9-12 **78**....(b[1]) LukeMorris 5
(Sir Mark Prescott Bt) *t.k.h: sn trcking ldr: led over 8f out: hdd over 4f out: nt run on and sn dropped to rr: t.o 2f out: virtually p.u* **9/1**

3m 6.28s (0.28) **Going Correction** +0.175s/f (Slow)
WFA 3 from 4yo+ 10lb **9** Ran SP% **119.9**
Speed ratings (Par 105): **106,105,104,103,102 100,94,72,65**
toteswingers 1&2 £7.20, 1&3 £9.20, 2&3 £9.40 CSF £36.51 CT £348.02 TOTE £6.30: £1.60, £2.80, £2.80; EX 44.20 Trifecta £268.20 Pool: £1345.69 - 3.76 winning units..
Owner Dr Marwan Koukash **Bred** Danella Partnership **Trained** Newmarket, Suffolk

FOCUS
A fair handicap in which a reasonable gallop steadied around halfway. The winner came down the centre in the straight.

6810 32RED.COM H'CAP 1m 1f 103y(P)
9:10 (9:21) (Class 5) (0-75,74) 3-Y-O **£2,587** (£770; £384; £192) **Stalls** Low

Form RPR

4036 1 **Legends (IRE)**[28] 5960 3-9-7 **74**.... SebSanders 7 95+
(Sir Michael Stoute) *trckd ldrs: led over 2f out: sn qcknd wl clr: heavily eased ins fnl f: v easily* **9/4**[1]

2213 2 11 **Mizyen (IRE)**[18] 6258 3-9-5 **72**.... NeilCallan 10 69
(James Tate) *led after 1f: hdd 3f out: sn outpcd: kpt on to take modest 2nd appr fnl f* **10/3**[2]

2552 3 1 ¼ **Gabrial The Thug (FR)**[13] 6387 3-8-11 **64**....(t) TomEaves 9 59
(Richard Fahey) *mid-div: drvn 4f out: kpt on to take modest 3rd ins fnl f* **8/1**

13 4 5 **Song Of Snowdon**[25] 6042 3-8-12 **65**.... MartinDwyer 5 50
(William Muir) *led 1f: sn chsng ldr: led 3f out: sn hdd: wknd fnl f* **9/1**

436 5 10 **Gaspard**[24] 6084 3-9-5 **72**.... DanielTudhope 6 38
(David O'Meara) *s.i.s: hld up in mid-div: hdwy 6f out: drvn to chse ldrs over 3f out: wknd over 1f out* **6/1**[3]

0340 6 1 ¼ **Calling**[35] 5694 3-9-1 **68**.... GrahamLee 1 32
(Brian Meehan) *prom: lost pl over 5f out: bhd fnl 3f* **28/1**

3344 7 11 **Hidden Link**[78] 4193 3-9-0 **67**.... LukeMorris 2 10
(Ronald Harris) *t.k.h in rr: drvn over 3f out: sn lost pl and bhd: eased over 1f out* **33/1**

1360 8 1 ½ **Back On The Trail**[51] 5132 3-9-3 **70**.... DaleSwift 3 10
(Brian Ellison) *chsd ldrs: drvn over 4f out: lost pl over 3f out: sn bhd* **8/1**

0200 9 12 **Mad About Harry (IRE)**[106] 3243 3-9-1 **68**.... SteveDrowne 4
(John Best) *sn detached in last: t.o 3f out* **14/1**

2m 3.27s (1.57) **Going Correction** +0.175s/f (Slow) **9** Ran SP% **113.4**
Speed ratings (Par 101): **100,90,89,84,75 74,64,63,52**
toteswingers 1&2 £2.10, 1&3 £7.60, 2&3 £6.80 CSF £9.39 CT £48.50 TOTE £5.40: £1.70, £1.10, £2.30; EX 12.20 Trifecta £84.60 Pool: £1326.85 - 11.75 winning units..
Owner Prince A A Faisal **Bred** Nawara Stud Company Ltd S A **Trained** Newmarket, Suffolk

FOCUS
A fair handicap in which the gallop was just an ordinary one. The winner raced against the far rail in the straight.
T/Plt: £38.70 to a £1 stake. Pool: £81263.05 - 1529.93 winning tickets T/Qpdt: £1.90 to a £1 stake. Pool: £9854.00 - 3662.00 winning tickets WG

6811 - 6820a (Foreign Racing) - See Raceform Interactive

6383 CHESTER (L-H)
Saturday, September 28

OFFICIAL GOING: Good (7.0)
Wind: Almost nil Weather: Sunny

6821 STELLA ARTOIS MAIDEN FILLIES' STKS 7f 2y
1:55 (1:55) (Class 4) 2-Y-O **£6,469** (£1,925; £962; £481) **Stalls** Low

Form RPR

2 1 **Dynaglow (USA)**[17] 6298 2-9-0 0.... RobertHavlin 5 79+
(John Gosden) *mde all: qcknd over 1f out: r.o wl and in command fnl f* **15/8**[1]

2324 2 2 ¼ **Rough Courte (IRE)**[13] 6423 2-9-0 83.... SamHitchcott 4 73
(Mick Channon) *chsd ldrs: rdn over 2f out: wnt 2nd over 1f out: no imp on wnr* **5/2**[2]

04 3 2 ¼ **Kinloss**[24] 6112 2-9-0 0.... SeanLevey 1 67
(Richard Hannon) *racd keenly: trckd ldrs: pushed along over 2f out: rdn over 1f out: nt qckn ins fnl f: kpt on same pce* **10/1**

4 1 **Tiffany Bay (IRE)** 2-9-0 0.... TadhgO'Shea 3 64
(John Patrick Shanahan, Ire) *hld up in midfield: effrt over 2f out: kpt on u.p ins fnl f: nvr able to chal ldrs* **12/1**

00 5 nk **Enfys Hud**[15] 6365 2-8-9 0.... NoelGarbutt(5) 2 63
(David Evans) *pushed along s: in rr: hdwy over 2f out: kpt on u.p ins fnl f: nvr able to chal* **66/1**

6 shd **Layla's Red Devil (IRE)** 2-9-0 0.... TomEaves 8 63
(Richard Fahey) *s.i.s: in rr: rdn and stdy hdwy over 1f out: styd on u.p ins fnl f: nt pce to trble ldrs* **12/1**

0 7 9 **Stybba**[23] 6141 2-9-0 0.... DavidProbert 6 38
(Andrew Balding) *dwlt: hld up: pushed along over 2f out: nvr able to get on terms* **16/1**

3004 8 1 **Dancing Sal (IRE)**[26] 6041 2-8-11 60.... DeclanBates(3) 7 36
(David Evans) *w ldr tl rdn and outpcd over 2f out: wknd over 1f out* **20/1**

352 9 ½ **Baars Causeway (IRE)**[31] 5891 2-8-11 70.... MichaelJMMurphy(3) 10 34
(Alan Jarvis) *prom on outer tl rdn and wknd over 2f out* **13/2**[3]

6 10 5 **Lady Bubbles**[17] 6298 2-8-11 0.... JasonHart(3) 9 21
(Michael Easterby) *s.i.s: midfield: rdn and wknd over 2f out* **33/1**

05 11 12 **Pacquita**[24] 6112 2-9-0 0.... JoeFanning 11
(Mark Johnston) *edgy in preliminaries: midfield on outer: rdn and wknd over 2f out: bhd after* **33/1**

1m 27.39s (0.89) **Going Correction** +0.10s/f (Good) **11** Ran SP% **119.2**
Speed ratings (Par 94): **98,95,92,91,91 91,80,79,79,73 59**
toteswingers 1&2 £1.60, 1&3 £2.50, 2&3 £7.60 CSF £6.32 TOTE £2.70: £1.50, £1.40, £4.70; EX 7.50 Trifecta £85.40 Pool: £787.81 - 6.91 winning units..
Owner Chasemore Farm **Bred** Highclere **Trained** Newmarket, Suffolk

FOCUS
Rails at innermost position and all distances as advertised. An interesting card got underway with a fair juvenile fillies' maiden in which they went an honest gallop on ground officially described as good. The form makes sense.

6822 WINTER WONDERLAND AT CHESTER RACECOURSE H'CAP 6f 18y
2:30 (2:30) (Class 4) (0-85,85) 3-Y-O+ **£6,469** (£1,925; £962; £481) **Stalls** Low

Form RPR

200 1 **Cruise Tothelimit (IRE)**[7] 6647 5-9-0 **78**.... NeilCallan 1 87
(Ian Williams) *mde all: rdn and tried to stretch field over 1f out: hld on wl towards fin* **13/2**[2]

0606 2 ½ **Naabegha**[70] 4536 6-9-7 **85**.... LeeTopliss 12 92+
(Ed de Giles) *s.i.s: in rr: hld up: nt clr run over 2f out: hdwy on inner wl over 1f out: r.o ins fnl f: tk 2nd fnl 150yds: clsd on wnr towards fin but hld* **25/1**

250 3 1 ½ **Angelito**[33] 5832 4-9-1 **79**.... SeanLevey 6 82
(Ed McMahon) *racd in 2nd pl: rdn and unable to go w wnr fr over 2f out: lost 2nd fnl 150yds: styd on same pce* **13/2**[2]

4542 4 1 ¼ **Al Muheer (IRE)**[3] 6756 8-8-11 **82**.... JordanNason(7) 5 81
(Ruth Carr) *in tch: effrt wl over 1f out: styd on u.p ins fnl f: no imp on ldrs* **5/1**[1]

0000 5 ¾ **Al's Memory (IRE)**[28] 5991 4-9-4 **85**.... DeclanBates(3) 3 81
(David Evans) *in tch: rdn over 1f out: kpt on ins fnl f: nvr able to chal* **12/1**

1223 6 ½ **Clubland (IRE)**[21] 6209 4-8-13 **80**.... MarkCoumbe(3) 7 75
(Roy Bowring) *in tch: rdn over 1f out: one pce ins fnl f* **10/1**[3]

0511 7 hd **Gabrial's Gift (IRE)**[17] 6310 4-9-2 **80**.... ChrisCatlin 2 74
(Scott Dixon) *hld up: rdn and hdwy over 1f out: kpt on ins fnl f: nt trble ldrs* **5/1**[1]

0026 8 4 ½ **Green Park (IRE)**[4] 6727 10-8-13 **77**....(b) JoeFanning 10 57
(Declan Carroll) *midfield: pushed along and outpcd wl over 1f out: n.d after* **18/1**

450 9 ¾ **Mappin Time (IRE)**[64] 4730 5-8-13 **77**....(p) RobertHavlin 8 54
(Tim Easterby) *hld up: rdn over 1f out: no imp* **16/1**

0610 10 ½ **Barkston Ash**[9] 6548 5-8-11 **78**....(b) NeilFarley(3) 4 54
(Eric Alston) *hld up: pushed along over 2f out: nvr able to trble ldrs* **14/1**

0456 11 1 **Gatepost (IRE)**[14] 6384 4-9-1 **79**.... TomEaves 16 51
(Richard Fahey) *in tch on outer: rdn and wknd over 2f out* **16/1**

0004 12 nk **Pea Shooter**[22] 6159 4-8-13 **77**....(p) DeclanMcDonogh 15 48
(Kevin Ryan) *hld up: pushed along over 2f out: struggling after* **20/1**

6266 13 ¾ **Lastchancelucas**[11] 6496 3-9-1 **84**.... JasonHart(3) 9 53
(Declan Carroll) *prom: rdn over 2f out: wknd wl over 1f out* **5/1**[1]

1m 14.06s (0.26) **Going Correction** +0.10s/f (Good)
WFA 3 from 4yo+ 2lb **13** Ran SP% **125.8**
Speed ratings (Par 105): **102,101,99,97,96 95,95,89,88,88 86,86,85**
toteswingers 1&2 £0.00, 1&3 £9.60, 2&3 £19.80 CSF £165.96 CT £1156.62 TOTE £9.70: £4.70, £11.10, £1.10; EX 87.80 Trifecta £267.00 Part won. Pool: £356.02 - 0.01 winning units..
Owner Odysian Ltd T/A Cruise Nightspot **Bred** D And Mrs D Veitch **Trained** Portway, Worcs

FOCUS
A decent sprint handicap. A small personal best from the well drawn winner.

6823 SPORTINGBET.COM H'CAP 1m 2f 75y
3:05 (3:05) (Class 2) (0-105,95) 3-Y-O
£28,012 (£8,388; £4,194; £2,097; £1,048; £526) **Stalls** High

Form RPR

-125 1 **Powder Hound**[10] 6533 3-8-9 **83**.... DavidProbert 1 95
(Andrew Balding) *mde all: rdn over 1f out: in command and r.o wl to draw clr ins fnl f* **8/1**

406 2 3 ¼ **Ocean Applause**[10] 6538 3-8-0 **77**....(t) RyanPowell(3) 2 83
(John Ryan) *a.p: rdn over 1f out: outpcd by wnr ins fnl f: no ch and all out to hold on for 2nd cl home* **25/1**

2504 3 nse **Romantic Settings**[7] 6620 3-9-5 **93**.... LeeTopliss 4 99
(Richard Fahey) *hld up: hdwy on inner 2f out: styd on u.p ins fnl f: pressed runner-up: no ch w wnr* **10/1**

-211 4 4 **King Of The Danes**[128] 2584 3-9-1 **89**.... JoeFanning 3 87
(Mark Johnston) *midfield: effrt and hdwy 2f out: no imp over 1f out: one pce fnl f* **11/4**[2]

4312 5 nse **Gabrial's Kaka (IRE)**[21] 6208 3-9-6 **94**.... TomEaves 8 92
(Richard Fahey) *prom: rdn 2f out: nt qckn over 1f out: one pce fnl f* **9/1**

4-11 6 2 **Zain Eagle**[15] 6353 3-9-7 **95**.... NeilCallan 5 89
(Gerard Butler) *racd keenly: hld up in rr: rdn over 1f out: failed to pick-up: hung lft ins fnl f and no imp: eased whn wl btn fnl 100yds* **7/4**[1]

3535 7 4 ½ **Asgardella (IRE)**[21] 6208 3-8-8 **85**.... NeilFarley(3) 7 71
(Richard Fahey) *prom: pushed along over 3f out: wknd 2f out* **25/1**

4221 8 12 **Tajheez (IRE)**[23] 6136 3-9-2 **90** DaneO'Neill 6 68
(Roger Varian) *hld up: hdwy on outer 3f out: in tch over 2f out: sn wknd: eased whn wl btn over 1f out* **5/1**[3]

2m 10.68s (-0.52) **Going Correction** +0.10s/f (Good) **8** Ran SP% **117.6**
Speed ratings (Par 107): **106,103,103,100,100 98,94,85**
toteswingers 1&2 £0.00, 1&3 £7.40, 2&3 Not won CSF £177.40 CT £1999.06 TOTE £5.70: £1.80, £3.20, £3.00; EX 148.70 Trifecta £484.50 Part won. Pool: £646.00 - 0.32 winning units..
Owner George Strawbridge **Bred** George Strawbridge **Trained** Kingsclere, Hants

FOCUS
A good quality 3yo handicap, but it proved very difficult to pick up well-drawn front-runners on this card. The form has been taken at face value.

6824 STELLA ARTOIS CIDRE MAIDEN STKS — 1m 2f 75y
3:40 (3:40) (Class 4) 3-Y-O+ £6,469 (£1,925; £962; £481) Stalls High

Form RPR
52 1 **Busatto (USA)**[11] 6497 3-9-5 0 JoeFanning 1 82+
(Mark Johnston) *midfield: pushed along over 2f out: hdwy over 1f out: tk 2nd fnl 150yds: r.o to ld towards fin* **7/4**[1]

6-22 2 ¾ **Puligny (IRE)**[117] 2930 3-9-0 75 DaneO'Neill 5 72
(Charles Hills) *led: pressed 2f out: rdn to assert and over 2 l clr over 1f out: all out fnl 75yds: hdd and no ex towards fin* **7/4**[1]

5523 3 4 ½ **Gabrial The Thug (FR)**[1] 6810 3-9-5 64 (t) TomEaves 4 68
(Richard Fahey) *in tch: rdn over 1f out: kpt on u.p ins fnl f: one pce and no imp on ldrs fnl 100yds* **9/2**[2]

6 4 2 ¾ **Wandsworth (IRE)**[15] 6366 3-9-2 0 RossAtkinson(3) 8 63
(Roger Varian) *chsd ldr: ev ch 2f out: unable to go w ldr over 1f out: lost 2nd fnl 150yds: wknd sn after* **13/2**[3]

000 5 ¾ **Gentlemax (FR)**[14] 6402 3-9-5 0 SeanLevey 2 61
(Alan Jarvis) *chsd ldrs: rdn over 2f out: wknd ins fnl f* **20/1**

0- 6 14 **Cote Reveur**[378] 6237 3-9-0 0 RobertHavlin 9 30
(Michael Mullineaux) *in rr: struggling 3f out: plugged on into poor 6th pl 2f out: nvr a threat* **100/1**

7 nk **Lady Faye** 4-9-1 0 TimClark(5) 3 29
(Alan Bailey) *niggled along early: hld up after: rdn over 3f out: sn wknd* **14/1**

00 8 3 **Polvere D'Oro**[15] 6366 3-9-2 0 SladeO'Hara(3) 10 28
(Michael Mullineaux) *prom tl rdn and wknd over 2f out* **100/1**

9 41 **Dutch Barney** 3-9-5 0 ChrisCatlin 7
(Mark Brisbourne) *s.s: rdn along: bhd and detached tl 5f out: toiling again and lft bhd 3f out: t.o* **40/1**

2m 14.37s (3.17) **Going Correction** +0.10s/f (Good)
WFA 3 from 4yo 6lb **9** Ran SP% **120.1**
Speed ratings (Par 105): **91,90,86,84,84 72,72,70,37**
toteswingers 1&2 £1.20, 1&3 £1.10, 2&3 £2.30 CSF £4.85 TOTE £2.70: £1.50, £2.00, £1.10; EX 8.80 Trifecta £14.30 Pool: £1767.52 - 92.56 winning units.
Owner Sheikh Hamdan Bin Mohammed Al Maktoum **Bred** Palides Investments N V Inc **Trained** Middleham Moor, N Yorks

FOCUS
A fair maiden, but a muddling race in a relatively slow time. The winner was value for a bit extra.

6825 ADVANCED INSULATION NURSERY H'CAP — 5f 110y
4:15 (4:15) (Class 2) 2-Y-O £9,703 (£2,887; £1,443; £721) Stalls Low

Form RPR
4416 1 **Blithe Spirit**[8] 6584 2-8-11 **81** NeilFarley(3) 3 88
(Eric Alston) *mde all: qcknd clr 2f out: r.o wl and in command fnl f* **13/2**[3]

1 2 1 ½ **Secret Romance**[37] 5665 2-8-11 **78** StephenCraine 5 80
(Tom Dascombe) *a.p: unable to go w wnr 2f out: no imp after* **8/1**

042 3 ¾ **Telegraph (IRE)**[14] 6383 2-8-0 **67** oh1 DavidProbert 4 67+
(Andrew Balding) *s.s: towards rr: hdwy over 2f out: nt clr run over 1f out: r.o and clsd towards fin* **9/2**[1]

1012 4 ¾ **Primitorio (IRE)**[26] 6035 2-9-2 **83** (v[1]) NeilCallan 6 80
(Ralph Beckett) *in tch: rdn over 1f out: kpt on u.p ins fnl f: nt quite pce of ldrs* **7/1**

4614 5 2 ¼ **Penny's Boy**[7] 6640 2-8-1 **71** (t) SimonPearce(3) 12 61
(Sylvester Kirk) *s.i.s: in rr: pushed along over 2f out: prog and styd on ins fnl f: nrst fin* **25/1**

0204 6 ½ **Quatuor (IRE)**[28] 5994 2-9-2 **88** NatashaEaton(5) 2 76
(Tom Dascombe) *prom: rdn over 1f out: edgd rt whn one pce ins fnl f: wl hld towards fin* **6/1**[2]

151 7 ½ **La Tinta Bay**[26] 6035 2-9-4 **85** SeanLevey 9 71
(Richard Hannon) *s.i.s: midfield: rdn and outpcd over 2f out: kpt on steadily ins fnl f: nt trble ldrs* **8/1**

2432 8 2 **Memory Styx**[14] 6386 2-8-8 **75** SamHitchcott 8 55
(Mick Channon) *prom tl rdn and wknd over 1f out* **14/1**

2042 9 nk **Bounty Girl (IRE)**[12] 6467 2-8-5 **72** (e) TadhgO'Shea 1 51
(Tim Easterby) *hld up: rdn bef nt clr run over 1f out: btn fnl f: eased* **6/1**[2]

4042 10 nse **Tableforten**[21] 6187 2-8-9 **76** RobertHavlin 7 55
(J S Moore) *midfield tl rdn and wknd over 2f out* **12/1**

3201 11 1 ¾ **De Repente (IRE)**[14] 6386 2-8-5 **75** RaulDaSilva(3) 10 48
(Paul Green) *prom and racd 3 wd: rdn over 2f out: wknd over 1f out* **10/1**

1m 7.49s (1.29) **Going Correction** +0.10s/f (Good) **11** Ran SP% **122.1**
Speed ratings (Par 101): **95,93,92,91,88 87,86,84,83,83 81**
toteswingers 1&2 £43.90, 1&3 £11.10, 2&3 £6.20 CSF £60.09 CT £264.23 TOTE £4.70: £4.70, £1.60, £1.90; EX 114.60 Trifecta £547.00 Pool: £1020.60 - 1.39 winning units.
Owner Liam & Tony Ferguson **Bred** Liam & Tony Ferguson **Trained** Longton, Lancs

FOCUS
A decent nursery in which the winner became the fourth horse on the card to grab an early lead from a good draw and successfully make all the running. The second was well placed too.

6826 INNOSPEC H'CAP — 7f 2y
4:50 (4:50) (Class 3) (0-95,95) 3-Y-O+ £16,172 (£4,812; £2,405; £1,202) Stalls Low

Form RPR
2211 1 **Ocean Tempest**[9] 6571 4-9-7 **95** BrettDoyle 3 109
(John Ryan) *chsd ldrs: rdn to ld over 1f out: qcknd clr ins fnl f: r.o wl* **11/4**[1]

2352 2 4 ½ **Rene Mathis (GER)**[42] 5510 3-8-12 **89** TomEaves 2 90
(Richard Fahey) *midfield: hdwy on inner 2f out: rdn over 1f out: kpt on to take 2nd fnl 150yds: no ch w wnr* **3/1**[2]

5000 3 ½ **Monsieur Chevalier (IRE)**[14] 6391 6-9-6 **94** SeanLevey 1 95+
(P J O'Gorman) *missed break: hld up: hdwy over 1f out: styd on ins fnl f* **8/1**

5340 4 hd **Country Western**[60] 4859 3-8-11 **88** DaneO'Neill 8 87
(Charles Hills) *racd keenly: chsd ldrs: rdn over 1f out: kpt on ins fnl f: nt pce to mount serious chal* **8/1**

0000 5 1 ¼ **Dr Red Eye**[15] 6352 5-8-11 **90** (p) TimClark(5) 4 87
(Scott Dixon) *led: rdn and hdd over 1f out: outpcd by wnr ins fnl f: lost 2nd fnl 150yds: no ex* **7/1**[3]

3513 6 ½ **Laffan (IRE)**[7] 6625 4-9-4 **92** RobertHavlin 10 87+
(Tim Easterby) *hld up: niggled along over 4f out: rdn over 1f out: styd on ins fnl f: nt pce to trble ldrs* **10/1**

5160 7 1 ½ **Wannabe King**[17] 6300 7-8-9 **90** (v) JordanNason(7) 9 81
(Geoffrey Harker) *midfield: rdn over 1f out: kpt on ins fnl f: nvr able to chal* **25/1**

5203 8 ½ **Chosen Character (IRE)**[29] 5943 5-9-1 **94** (vt) NatashaEaton(5) 7 84
(Tom Dascombe) *hld up: hdwy over 1f out: no imp fnl f* **16/1**

2104 9 1 ¾ **Alejandro (IRE)**[14] 6384 4-9-2 **90** LeeTopliss 11 75
(Richard Fahey) *midfield: pushed along 2f out: outpcd over 1f out* **16/1**

0020 10 ½ **Rusty Rocket (IRE)**[8] 6586 4-8-10 **87** RaulDaSilva(3) 5 71
(Paul Green) *chsd ldr tl rdn over 1f out: wknd ins fnl f* **14/1**

05-0 11 1 **Apostle (IRE)**[14] 6384 4-8-13 **87** ChrisCatlin 12 68
(David Simcock) *hld up: pushed along over 1f out: nvr on terms* **33/1**

2300 12 3 ¾ **Zacynthus (IRE)**[29] 5943 5-9-1 **89** DeclanMcDonogh 6 60
(Kevin Ryan) *chsd ldrs: effrt on outer over 2f out: wknd over 1f out* **14/1**

1m 25.73s (-0.77) **Going Correction** +0.10s/f (Good)
WFA 3 from 4yo+ 3lb **12** Ran SP% **127.4**
Speed ratings (Par 107): **108,102,102,102,100 100,98,97,95,95 94,89**
toteswingers 1&2 £2.10, 1&3 £8.90, 2&3 £12.70 CSF £11.92 CT £63.42 TOTE £4.30: £1.60, £1.10, £3.90; EX 13.10 Trifecta £51.40 Pool: £1610.46 - 23.49 winning units.
Owner W McLuskey & C Little **Bred** Old Mill Stud Ltd And Oomswell Ltd **Trained** Newmarket, Suffolk

FOCUS
Another good quality handicap in which they went a solid gallop, but this time the early leader didn't stay there. Another improved effort from the winner.

6827 STELLA ARTOIS H'CAP — 1m 5f 89y
5:20 (5:20) (Class 4) (0-85,77) 3-Y-O £6,469 (£1,925; £962; £481) Stalls Low

Form RPR
4422 1 **Gabrial The Master (IRE)**[14] 6389 3-9-7 **77** TomEaves 2 83
(Richard Fahey) *mde all: rdn over 1f out: kpt on wl fnl f* **4/1**[3]

4461 2 1 **Duke Of Yorkshire**[7] 6629 3-8-11 **70** NeilFarley(3) 7 75
(Declan Carroll) *hld up: rdn and hdwy over 1f out: styd on to take 2nd towards fin: nt quite rch wnr* **5/1**

0531 3 nk **Vicky Valentine**[8] 6601 3-8-6 **65** JulieBurke(3) 6 69
(Alistair Whillans) *chsd wnr: rdn over 1f out: tried to chal ins fnl f: lost 2nd and no ex towards fin* **11/1**

1343 4 4 **Edwyn Ralph**[51] 5168 3-9-6 **76** ChrisCatlin 3 74
(David Simcock) *chsd ldrs: pushed along 2f out: rdn over 1f out: one pce ins fnl f* **5/2**[2]

0011 5 5 **Eton Rambler (USA)**[22] 6158 3-9-2 **72** (p) DaneO'Neill 1 63
(George Baker) *in tch: rdn over 2f out: hung lft and wknd ins fnl f: eased whn btn fnl 150yds* **15/8**[1]

4200 6 ¾ **Uncle Bernie (IRE)**[15] 6363 3-7-13 **58** (p) RyanPowell(3) 4 47
(Andrew Hollinshead) *racd keenly: hld up in rr: struggling over 1f out: wl btn ins fnl f* **16/1**

2m 57.47s (4.77) **Going Correction** +0.10s/f (Good) **6** Ran SP% **114.2**
Speed ratings (Par 103): **89,88,88,85,82 82**
toteswingers 1&2 £3.70, 1&3 £12.30, 2&3 £10.40 CSF £24.30 TOTE £4.50: £5.10, £1.20; EX 23.50 Trifecta £105.70 Pool: £1182.75 - 8.38 winning units.
Owner Dr Marwan Koukash **Bred** Paul Giles **Trained** Musley Bank, N Yorks

FOCUS
A fair staying handicap brought down the curtain on Chester's Flat season. Another all- the-way winner, and the form is rated cautiously.
T/Plt: £6,671.60 to a £1 stake. Pool: £1,587,948.80 - 173.75 winning units T/Qpdt: £97.50 to a £1 stake. Pool: £2,584.90 - 19.60 winning units DO

6787 HAYDOCK (L-H)
Saturday, September 28

OFFICIAL GOING: Good (good to firm in places; 8.0)
Wind: Moderate; behind Weather: Dry with warm sunshine

6828 BETFAIR SUPPORTS PRIDE OF RACING AWARDS EBF MAIDEN FILLIES' STKS — 1m
2:25 (2:26) (Class 5) 2-Y-O £2,911 (£866; £432; £216) Stalls Low

Form RPR
54 1 **Flippant (IRE)**[72] 4432 2-9-0 0 TomQueally 1 80
(William Haggas) *trckd ldr: effrt and cl up over 2f out: n.m.r: green and sltly outpcd wl over 1f out: swtchd rt and rdn ent fnl f: styd on wl to ld nr fin* **5/1**[2]

62 2 ½ **Dancing Sands (IRE)**[10] 6523 2-9-0 0 MartinLane 7 79
(Charlie Appleby) *trckd ldrs: smooth hdwy over 3f out: cl up over 2f out: rdn to ld wl over 1f out: drvn ins fnl f: hdd and no ex towards fin* **9/4**[1]

5 3 3 ¾ **Testing (FR)**[10] 6512 2-9-0 0 FrederikTylicki 6 70
(Mark Johnston) *led and sn clr: pushed along and jnd over 2f out: rdn and hdd wl over 1f out: cl up and ev ch tl drvn and kpt on same pce fnl f* **7/1**

4 1 ¼ **Cascading** 2-9-0 0 JimmyFortune 3 67
(Hughie Morrison) *dwlt and in rr: hdwy on outer over 3f out: pushed along over 2f out: rdn and edgd lft ent fnl f: kpt on: nrst fin* **25/1**

03 5 ½ **Ghinia (IRE)**[18] 6281 2-9-0 0 PatDobbs 11 66
(Pam Sly) *chsd ldrs: rdn along wl over 2f out: drvn wl over 1f out: one pce* **9/1**

3 6 1 ¼ **Minnalousha (IRE)**[24] 6112 2-9-0 0 NickyMackay 8 63
(John Gosden) *hld up: hdwy 3f out: rdn along 2f out: chsd ldrs over 1f out: sn one pce* **13/2**[3]

0 7 nk **Bella Varenna (IRE)**[49] 5282 2-9-0 0 MartinHarley 2 63
(Marco Botti) *trckd ldrs on inner: pushed along wl over 2f out: rdn wl over 1f out: one pce* **25/1**

8 ¾ **Betty The Thief (IRE)** 2-9-0 0 RichardKingscote 5 61+
(Tom Dascombe) *towards rr tl sme hdwy fnl 2f: n.d* **10/1**

0 9 3 **Quest Of Colour (IRE)**[18] 6271 2-9-0 0 SebSanders 4 54
(Richard Fahey) *a towards rr* **50/1**

0 10 ½ **Dalmarella Dancer (IRE)**[14] 6409 2-8-9 0 JoeyHaynes(5) 12 53+
(K R Burke) *t.k.h in midfield: rdn along 3f out: sn wknd* **11/1**

11 2 **Cradle Of Life (IRE)** 2-9-0 0 SteveDrowne 10 48+
(Ed Dunlop) *dwlt: a in rr* **22/1**

The Form Book Flat, Raceform Ltd, Compton, RG20 6NL.

0 **12** *3 1/4* **Mrs Pat**[18] 6281 2-9-0 0 TonyHamilton 9 41
(Richard Fahey) *chsd ldng pair: rdn along 3f out: sn wknd* **25/1**
1m 42.7s (-1.00) **Going Correction** -0.20s/f (Firm) **12** Ran SP% **118.5**
Speed ratings (Par 92): **97,96,92,91,91 89,89,88,85,85 83,79**
toteswingers 1&2 £2.00, 1&3 £15.60, 2&3 £4.30 CSF £15.48 TOTE £5.00: £2.10, £1.20, £2.70; EX 10.40 Trifecta £125.90 Pool: £959.08 - 5.71 winning units.
Owner Bernard Kantor **Bred** Wentworth Racing (pty) Ltd **Trained** Newmarket, Suffolk

FOCUS
All races on outer home straight and races on Round course increased in distance by 33yds, except race six which was increased by 83yds. The pace was good.

6829 EBF CELEBRATING THE UNSUNG HEROES OF RACING MAIDEN STKS (C&G) 1m
3:00 (3:02) (Class 5) 2-Y-O **£2,911** (£866; £432; £216) **Stalls** Low

Form RPR
42 **1** **Monsea (IRE)**[13] 6430 2-9-0 0 PatDobbs 11 82
(Richard Hannon) *trckd ldrs: hdwy 3f out: slt ld 2f out: sn rdn: jnd and drvn ent fnl f: styd on wl* **5/1**[3]
3 **2** *1* **El Najmm (IRE)**[33] 5811 2-9-0 0 DominicFox 4 80
(Roger Varian) *hld up towards rr: stdy hdwy 3f out: trckd ldrs 2f out: rdn over 1f out: styd on u.p fnl f* **2/1**[1]
0 **3** *1/2* **Caridadi (IRE)**[23] 6125 2-9-0 0 FrederikTylicki 5 79
(Charlie Appleby) *trckd ldrs: hdwy 3f out: swtchd rt and rdn to chal wl over 1f out: disp ld and ev ch whn hung bdly rt ent fnl f: kpt on towards fin* **25/1**
4 *1 3/4* **Beyond Smart (USA)** 2-9-0 0 NickyMackay 12 75+
(John Gosden) *trckd ldr: hdwy and cl up 3f out: sn disputing ld: rdn along wl over 1f out: one pce fnl f* **16/1**
5 *shd* **Personal Opinion** 2-9-0 0 MartinLane 9 74
(Charlie Appleby) *dwlt and in rr: swtchd rt to outer and hdwy 3f out: rdn along 2f out: styd on appr fnl f: nrst fin* **20/1**
0202 **6** *1 1/4* **Rogue Wave (IRE)**[23] 6127 2-9-0 83 MartinDwyer 7 71
(Alan Jarvis) *led: rdn along 3f out: hdd over 2f out: drvn wl over 1f out: grad wknd* **20/1**
4 **7** *3/4* **Year Of Glory (IRE)**[51] 5180 2-9-0 0 MartinHarley 10 70
(Marco Botti) *midfield: hdwy 3f out: rdn along 2f out: no imp fr over 1f out* **25/1**
4 **8** *nk* **Ehtifaal (IRE)**[43] 5472 2-9-0 0 TomQueally 8 69
(William Haggas) *hld up towards rr: sme hdwy 3f out and sn rdn along: swtchd rt 2f out: sn no imp* **4/1**[2]
0 **9** *1* **Pershing**[21] 6184 2-9-0 0 JimmyFortune 14 67
(Brian Meehan) *trckd ldrs: hdwy 3f out: rdn along 2f out: sn drvn and wknd* **50/1**
10 *hd* **Mountain Fighter** 2-9-0 0 SebSanders 3 66
(Saeed bin Suroor) *in tch on inner: hdwy 3f out: rdn along 2f out: sn btn* **15/2**
11 *hd* **Express Himself (IRE)** 2-9-0 0 SteveDrowne 2 66
(Ed McMahon) *dwlt: sn pushed along on inner into midfield: t.k.h: n.m.r bnd bef 1/2-way: in rr after* **16/1**
12 *2 1/4* **Ujagar (IRE)** 2-9-0 0 RichardKingscote 6 61
(Tom Dascombe) *dwlt: a in rr* **33/1**
0 **13** *6* **Application**[43] 5482 2-9-0 0 DavidAllan 15 47
(Bryan Smart) *hld up: a towards rr* **100/1**
0 **14** *nk* **Whitby High Light**[23] 6125 2-9-0 0 AndrewMullen 1 46
(Andrew Hollinshead) *chsd ldng pair on inner: rdn along over 3f out: sn wknd* **40/1**
0 **15** *6* **Come On Sunshine**[16] 6330 2-9-0 0 TonyHamilton 13 32
(Richard Fahey) *a in rr* **50/1**
1m 44.27s (0.57) **Going Correction** -0.20s/f (Firm) **15** Ran SP% **121.0**
Speed ratings (Par 95): **89,88,87,85,85 84,83,83,82,82 81,79,73,73,67**
toteswingers 1&2 £2.80, 1&3 £35.10, 2&3 £29.10 CSF £13.61 TOTE £4.90: £2.00, £1.60, £8.30; EX 20.50 Trifecta £346.00 Pool: £1,664.75 - 3.60 winning units.
Owner Saeed Manana **Bred** Timmy & Michael Hillman **Trained** East Everleigh, Wilts

FOCUS
The actual race distance was 1m33yds. There wasn't much form on show but many of these have been slow to come to hand and there is more to come as they mature.

6830 BETFAIR SUPPORTS RACING WELFARE H'CAP 5f
3:30 (3:32) (Class 2) (0-105,105) 3-Y-O+**£32,345** (£9,625; £4,810; £2,405) **Stalls** Centre

Form RPR
1540 **1** **Demora**[7] 6639 4-8-11 92 AndrewMullen 12 103
(Michael Appleby) *qckly away: mde all: rdn wl over 1f out: drvn and kpt on gamely fnl f* **8/1**
4554 **2** *1* **Racy**[14] 6391 6-9-3 98 FrederikTylicki 13 105
(Brian Ellison) *towards rr: gd hdwy 2f out: rdn over 1f out: styd on strly fnl f* **15/2**[3]
4301 **3** *1* **Noble Storm (USA)**[18] 6282 7-9-5 100 SebSanders 5 104
(Ed McMahon) *prom on wd outside: effrt 2f out: sn rdn and ev ch ent fnl f: drvn and one pce last 100yds* **12/1**
0010 **4** *hd* **Confessional**[14] 6391 6-9-5 100 (e) DavidAllan 11 103
(Tim Easterby) *prom: cl up 2f out: sn rdn and ev ch tl drvn and one pce wl ins fnl f* **12/1**
1050 **5** *1/2* **Barnet Fair**[14] 6391 5-8-9 95 JoeyHaynes[(5)] 3 96
(Richard Guest) *towards rr: hdwy on wd outside over 2f out: rdn to chse ldrs wl over 1f out: kpt on same pce fnl f* **12/1**
6302 **6** *nse* **Lady Gibraltar**[21] 6189 4-8-9 90 (v) MartinDwyer 14 91
(Alan Jarvis) *chsd wnr: rdn and ev chyance over 1f out: drvn and one pce ins fnl f* **11/1**
1042 **7** *1/2* **Masamah (IRE)**[17] 6305 7-9-10 105 (p) MartinHarley 16 104
(Marco Botti) *chsd ldrs: rdn along 2f out: drvn and one pce appr fnl f* **7/1**[2]
1000 **8** *hd* **Cheviot (USA)**[7] 6621 7-9-0 95 (b) JimmyFortune 17 94
(Ian Semple) *racd towards stands' rail: towards rr: hdwy 2f out: rdn whn n.m.r and swtchd lft over 1f out: kpt on fnl f: nrst fin* **12/1**
0032 **9** *1 1/4* **Barracuda Boy (IRE)**[5] 6692 3-8-10 92 (p) RichardKingscote 7 86
(Tom Dascombe) *hld up towards rr: hdwy 2f out and sn rdn: drvn over 1f out and no imp* **5/1**[1]
2003 **10** *3/4* **Secret Witness**[14] 6391 7-9-5 100 (p) LukeMorris 9 91
(Ronald Harris) *dwlt and towards rr: sme hdwy 1/2-way: sn rdn along and n.d* **12/1**
0060 **11** *1 1/4* **Elusivity (IRE)**[14] 6391 5-9-3 98 TomQueally 1 85
(David O'Meara) *a towards rr* **16/1**
21 **12** *hd* **Burning Thread (IRE)**[28] 5998 6-8-12 93 (b) AdamBeschizza 4 79
(Tim Etherington) *towards rr: hdwy 2f out: sn rdn and no imp appr fnl f* **16/1**
5503 **13** *3 1/4* **Bear Behind (IRE)**[23] 6129 4-9-3 98 MartinLane 6 72
(Tom Dascombe) *chsd ldrs: rdn along 2f out: grad wknd* **25/1**
0100 **14** *1 3/4* **Secret Asset (IRE)**[38] 5651 8-9-4 99 (p) MichaelO'Connell 10 67
(Jane Chapple-Hyam) *a towards rr* **25/1**
0062 **15** *1* **Jiroft (ITY)**[10] 6539 6-9-2 97 (p) SteveDrowne 8 62
(Robert Cowell) *dwlt: a bhd* **20/1**
1000 **16** *2* **Doctor Parkes**[14] 6391 7-9-1 96 J-PGuillambert 15 53
(Stuart Williams) *a towards rr* **25/1**
58.01s (-2.79) **Going Correction** -0.30s/f (Firm)
WFA 3 from 4yo+ 1lb **16** Ran SP% **126.9**
Speed ratings (Par 109): **110,108,106,106,105 105,104,104,102,101 99,98,93,90,89 86**
toteswingers 1&2 £42.70, 1&3 £18.90, 2&3 £33.60 CSF £66.15 CT £752.45 TOTE £10.10: £2.50, £2.40, £3.60, £4.30; EX 64.00 Trifecta £1278.70 Pool: £112,508.72 - 65.98 winning units.

Owner Goldform Racing **Bred** A M Wragg **Trained** Danethorpe, Notts

FOCUS
This was a hot sprint handicap, with the runners rated 90-105, and the time was predictably good. A clear best from the winner with the next two to form.

6831 RACING WELFARE PRIDE OF RACING STKS (H'CAP) (SPONSORED BY BETFAIR) 6f
4:05 (4:06) (Class 3) (0-90,89) 3-Y-O+ **£8,086** (£2,406; £1,202; £601) **Stalls** Centre

Form RPR
6041 **1** **Dungannon**[21] 6189 6-9-7 89 (b[1]) JimmyFortune 2 101
(Andrew Balding) *trckd ldrs in centre gng wl: smooth hdwy to chal over 1f out: rdn to ld ent fnl f: kpt on* **8/1**[3]
0405 **2** *1 1/4* **Joe Packet**[15] 6352 6-9-7 89 MartinHarley 7 97
(Jonathan Portman) *trckd ldrs in centre: hdwy over 1f out: rdn to chse wnr ins fnl f: no imp towards fin: 2nd of 13 in gp* **9/1**
3010 **3** *nse* **If So**[16] 6331 4-9-5 87 FrederikTylicki 11 95
(James Fanshawe) *trckd ldrs in centre: hdwy wl over 1f out: rdn ent fnl f: kpt on same pce towards fin: 3rd of 13 in gp* **6/1**[1]
5260 **4** *hd* **Tarooq (USA)**[16] 6331 7-8-13 81 (t) AdamBeschizza 17 88
(Stuart Williams) *trckd ldr stands' side: effrt 2f out: sn swtchd lft and rdn: styd on wl fnl f: nrst fin: 1st of 2 in gp* **12/1**
1036 **5** *nse* **Baby Strange**[16] 6331 9-8-11 86 AdamMcLean[(7)] 9 93
(Derek Shaw) *hld up towards rr in centre: swtchd lft to outer and hdwy over 1f out: sn rdn and styd on strly fnl f: nrst fin: 4th of 13 in gp* **16/1**
0120 **6** *1 3/4* **Corporal Maddox**[15] 6352 6-9-4 86 (p) LukeMorris 6 87
(Ronald Harris) *dwlt and towards rr in centre: hdwy over 2f out: rdn along wl over 1f out: kpt on same pce fnl f: 5th of 13 in gp* **20/1**
0500 **7** *hd* **Cheveton**[8] 6586 9-8-12 80 SaleemGolam 16 81
(Richard Price) *led stands' side gp: prom: rdn along 2f out: sn drvn and wknd over 1f out: 2nd of 2 in gp* **16/1**
3056 **8** *1 1/4* **Nassau Storm**[18] 6278 4-9-3 85 (t) PatDobbs 14 82
(William Knight) *midfield in centre: effrt over 2f out: sn rdn along and no imp: 6th of 13th in gp* **13/2**[2]
6600 **9** *nk* **Chester Aristocrat**[26] 6052 4-9-3 85 DavidAllan 1 81
(Eric Alston) *cl up: led wl over 2f out: rdn wl over 1f out: hdd ent fnl f: sn wknd: 7th of 13 in gp* **25/1**
5000 **10** *3/4* **Arctic Feeling (IRE)**[16] 6331 5-9-0 82 TonyHamilton 15 75
(Richard Fahey) *towards rr in centre: rdn along and sme hdwy 2f out: n.d 8th of 13 in gp* **25/1**
2104 **11** *1 1/4* **Gabbiano**[21] 6189 4-9-7 89 RichardKingscote 5 78
(Jeremy Gask) *chsd ldrs centre: rdn along over 2f out: sn wknd: 9th of 13 in gp* **17/2**
00 **12** *shd* **Line Of Reason (IRE)**[16] 6331 3-9-2 86 MichaelO'Connell 12 75
(Paul Midgley) *in tch in centre: hdwy wl over 1f out: sn rdn and n.m.r ent fnl f: sn wknd 10th of 13 in gp* **16/1**
2501 **13** *3/4* **Dancheur (IRE)**[6] 6665 4-8-12 85 6ex JoeyHaynes[(5)] 3 72
(K R Burke) *overall ldr in centre: pushed along and hdd wl over 2f out: rdn wl over 1f out: sn wknd 11th of 13 in gp* **9/1**
1036 **14** *5* **Head Space (IRE)**[18] 6273 5-9-2 87 (p) LMcNiff[(3)] 13 58
(Ruth Carr) *a towards rr centre: 12th of 13 in gp* **14/1**
01 **15** *6* **B Fifty Two (IRE)**[7] 6648 4-9-6 88 (bt) SebSanders 4 40
(J W Hills) *cl up centre: rdn along over 2f out: wknd wl over 1f out: last of 13 in gp* **11/1**
1m 11.58s (-2.22) **Going Correction** -0.30s/f (Firm)
WFA 3 from 4yo+ 2lb **15** Ran SP% **122.1**
Speed ratings (Par 107): **102,100,100,100,99 97,97,95,95,94 92,92,91,84,76**
toteswingers 1&2 £4.50, 1&3 £5.60, 2&3 £4.60 CSF £76.69 CT £477.60 TOTE £5.90: £2.80, £3.50, £2.10; EX 39.10 Trifecta £32.00 Pool: £1,188.89 - 27.84 winning units.
Owner DR E Harris **Bred** J A E Hobby **Trained** Kingsclere, Hants

FOCUS
This didn't have the quality of the 5f race that preceded it, but there were still some decent handicap sprinters on show. The form looks sound.

6832 JOCKEY CLUB #PRIDEOFRACING EBF "REPROCOLOR" FILLIES' H'CAP 1m 2f 95y
4:40 (4:40) (Class 3) (0-90,90) 3-Y-O+ **£12,938** (£3,850; £1,924; £962) **Stalls** Centre

Form RPR
2120 **1** **Wall Of Sound**[47] 5361 3-8-12 84 RichardKingscote 10 94+
(Tom Dascombe) *led 2f: cl up: led again wl over 2f out: rdn clr appr fnl f: styd on strly* **7/2**[2]
0405 **2** *2 1/2* **Cruck Realta**[28] 5986 3-9-4 90 MartinHarley 7 97+
(Mick Channon) *trckd ldrs: hdwy on inner 3f out: effrt whn nt clr run 1 1/2f out: swtchd rt to outer and rdn to chse wnr ins fnl f: no imp towards fin* **12/1**
-031 **3** *2* **Vicksburg**[29] 5942 3-8-13 85 JimmyFortune 4 86
(Andrew Balding) *trckd ldng pair: effrt 3f out: rdn to chse wnr wl over 1f out: sn drvn and one pce ent fnl f* **5/1**[3]
41 **4** *nk* **Electra Spectra**[29] 5959 3-8-8 80 FrederikTylicki 8 81
(Luca Cumani) *trckd ldrs: hdwy 3f out: rdn wl over 1f out: sltly hmpd and drvn appr fnl f: one pce* **11/4**[1]
1 **5** *5* **Heavenly Sound**[176] 1371 3-8-5 77 LukeMorris 1 68
(Marco Botti) *hld up in rr: sme hdwy 3f out: sn rdn along and nvr nr ldrs* **12/1**
6211 **6** *1 1/4* **Sureness (IRE)**[45] 5410 3-8-4 76 oh1 (t) PaoloSirigu 9 65
(Marco Botti) *cl up: led after 2f: pushed along over 3f out: rdn and hdd wl over 2f out: sn drvn and wknd wl over 1f out* **14/1**
4241 **7** *1/2* **Princess Caetani (IRE)**[11] 6490 4-9-4 89 JoeyHaynes[(5)] 3 77
(David Dennis) *hld up: a in rr* **13/2**

2001 8 hd **Cosmic Halo**[20] 6236 4-9-0 **80** .... TonyHamilton 5 67
(Richard Fahey) *hld up in tch: pushed along on outer over 3f out: rdn wl over 2f out and sn wknd* **8/1**

2m 11.72s (-3.78) **Going Correction** -0.20s/f (Firm)
WFA 3 from 4yo 6lb **8** Ran SP% **112.1**
Speed ratings (Par 104): **107,105,103,103,99 98,97,97**
toteswingers 1&2 £9.60, 1&3 £3.30, 2&3 £14.30 CSF £42.16 CT £206.13 TOTE £5.60: £2.00, £4.90, £2.00; EX 56.50 Trifecta £433.10 Pool: £1,564.87 - 2.70 winning units.
Owner Chasemore Farm **Bred** A Black **Trained** Malpas, Cheshire
■ Stewards' Enquiry : Martin Harley caution: careless riding
Paolo Sirigu two-day ban: careless riding (Oct 15-16)

FOCUS
The actual distance of this race was 1m2f 128yds. There were some good yardsticks in the line-up but the most interesting runners were the less-experienced ones, including the winner. A personal best for her, the form rated around the runner-up.

6833 BET365 H'CAP 1m 6f
5:15 (5:15) (Class 2) (0-100,95) 3-Y-O+ **£19,407** (£5,775; £2,886; £1,443) **Stalls** Low

Form RPR

1043 1 **Swinging Hawk (GER)**[6] 6668 7-8-9 **76** oh2 .... StevieDonohoe 2 85
(Ian Williams) *hld up towards rr: gd hdwy 3f out: chsd ldrs wl over 1f out: swtchd rt and rdn ent fnl f: styd on strly to ld last 100yds* **16/1**

0425 2 2 **Suegioo (FR)**[23] 6144 4-9-10 **91** ....(p) MartinHarley 4 97
(Marco Botti) *trckd ldng pair: hdwy 3f out: cl up 2f out: rdn and edgd lft wl over 1f out: sn led: drvn ins fnl f: hdd and one pce last 100yds* **11/4**[1]

0402 3 2 **Jonny Delta**[7] 6626 6-8-6 **80** .... JackGarritty(7) 8 83
(Jim Goldie) *in tch: hdwy over 4f out: rdn along wl over 2f out: kpt on u.p fnl f* **7/1**

5003 4 1 **Theology**[87] 3959 6-9-5 **86** .... FrederikTylicki 7 88
(Steve Gollings) *led after 1f and sn clr: pushed along and jnd 3f out: rdn over 2f out: hdd and drvn wl over 1f out: grad wknd* **11/1**

0001 5 1 3/4 **Viking Storm**[23] 6144 5-10-0 **95** .... TomQueally 3 94
(Harry Dunlop) *hld up in rr: hdwy 3f out: rdn over 2f out: sn drvn and n.d* **5/1**[2]

2116 6 nk **Zenafire**[29] 5946 4-8-10 **77** .... PaulQuinn 5 76
(Andrew Hollinshead) *hld up in rr: effrt and sme hdwy on outer wl over 3f out: rdn along wl over 2f out: n.d* **6/1**[3]

0004 7 3 1/2 **Saptapadi (IRE)**[14] 6394 7-9-9 **90** .... MichaelO'Connell 6 84
(Brian Ellison) *led 1f: trckd clr ldr: tk clsr order 4f out: rdn to chal wl over 2f out: sn ev ch tl drvn and wknd appr fnl f* **5/1**[2]

1135 8 1 1/4 **Kiama Bay (IRE)**[21] 6192 7-9-10 **91** .... TonyHamilton 1 83
(Richard Fahey) *trckd ldng pair: effrt over 3f out: rdn along wl over 2f out: sn wknd* **7/1**

3m 0.65s (-1.35) **Going Correction** -0.20s/f (Firm) **8** Ran SP% **113.5**
Speed ratings (Par 109): **95,93,92,92,91 90,88,88**
toteswingers 1&2 £10.10, 1&3 £9.20, 2&3 £5.10 CSF £59.12 CT £344.49 TOTE £24.90: £6.10, £1.10, £1.70; EX 94.00 Trifecta £765.90 Pool: £2,851.76 - 2.79 winning units.
Owner Jamie Roberts & Jack Turton **Bred** Gestut Wittekindshof **Trained** Portway, Worcs
■ Stewards' Enquiry : Jack Garritty one-day ban: careless riding (Oct 13)
Martin Harley two-day ban: used whip above permitted level (Oct 13-14)

FOCUS
There was a surprise result in this staying event, run over 1m6f 83yds, but most of the winner's rivals aren't well-handicapped at present. The winner is rated back towards last year's best.

6834 RACING WELFARE H'CAP 1m
5:50 (5:50) (Class 2) (0-105,105) 3-Y-O+**£16,172** (£4,812; £2,405; £1,202) **Stalls** Low

Form RPR

5311 1 **Short Squeeze (IRE)**[36] 5728 3-8-11 **94** .... MartinDwyer 1 111
(Hugo Palmer) *dwlt: sn trcking ldrs: smooth hdwy 3f out: cl up 2f out: rdn and qcknd to ld appr fnl f: sn clr: readily* **1/1**[1]

3212 2 4 1/2 **Balty Boys (IRE)**[14] 6384 4-8-13 **92** .... MichaelO'Connell 3 99
(Brian Ellison) *led: rdn along over 2f out: drvn and hdd jst over 1f out: kpt on u.p fnl f: no ch w wnr* **5/1**[2]

0305 3 1 1/2 **Sandagiyr (FR)**[14] 6396 5-9-12 **105** .... JimmyFortune 8 109
(Saeed bin Suroor) *hld up in rr: hdwy 3f out: rdn to chse ldrs wl over 1f out: swtchd lft to inner and drvn appr fnl f: kpt on same pce* **9/1**

1400 4 3/4 **Postscript (IRE)**[7] 6650 5-8-10 **89** .... FrederikTylicki 2 91
(David Simcock) *trckd ldng pair: hdwy 3f out: cl up over 2f out: sn rdn and ev ch tl drvn 1 1/2f out and grad wknd* **12/1**

363 5 1/2 **Centurius**[22] 6163 3-8-11 **94** .... MartinHarley 6 95
(Marco Botti) *hld up in rr: hdwy wl over 2f out: rdn along wl over 1f out: no imp fnl f* **17/2**

0161 6 1/2 **Mont Ras (IRE)**[37] 5681 6-9-5 **103** .... DavidBergin(5) 10 103
(David O'Meara) *trckd ldr: hdwy and cl up over 3f out: rdn along wl over 2f out: grad wknd* **7/1**[3]

0122 7 16 **Brae Hill (IRE)**[7] 6624 7-8-13 **92** .... TonyHamilton 5 55
(Richard Fahey) *trckd ldrs: pushed along over 3f out: rdn wl over 2f out: sn wknd* **14/1**

5006 8 14 **Navajo Chief**[8] 6592 6-9-7 **100** ....(v[1]) TomQueally 7 31
(Alan Jarvis) *in tch: pushed along wl over 3f out: sn rdn and wknd* **25/1**

1m 41.06s (-2.64) **Going Correction** -0.20s/f (Firm)
WFA 3 from 4yo+ 4lb **8** Ran SP% **117.9**
Speed ratings (Par 109): **105,100,99,98,97 97,81,67**
toteswingers 1&2 £2.40, 1&3 £3.70, 2&3 £6.20 CSF £6.55 CT £30.25 TOTE £1.90: £1.60, £2.30, £2.50; EX 7.90 Trifecta £50.90 Pool: £2,547.58 - 37.49 winning units.
Owner W Duff Gordon, R Smith, B Mathieson **Bred** Des Swan **Trained** Newmarket, Suffolk

FOCUS
There were some classy performers in this event, run over 1m 33yds, and the rapidly improving winner is one of them. The form stacks up well.
T/Plt: £83.20 to a £1 stake. Pool: £64,184.28 - 563.02 winning units T/Qpdt: £34.10 to a £1 stake. Pool: £3,583.21 - 77.70 winning units JR

6795 NEWMARKET (R-H)
Saturday, September 28

OFFICIAL GOING: Good to firm (8.5; stands' side 8.4, centre 8.5, far side 8.6)
Wind: Medium; half against Weather: Dry and bright

6835 JUDDMONTE ROYAL LODGE STKS (GROUP 2) (C&G) 1m
2:00 (2:00) (Class 1) 2-Y-O **£56,710** (£21,500; £10,760; £5,360; £2,690) **Stalls** Centre

Form RPR

31 1 **Berkshire (IRE)**[98] 3555 2-8-12 0........ JimCrowley 3 111+
(Paul Cole) *lw: racd nr side of centre: stdd s: racd keenly bhd ldng trio: swtchd to far side of centre whn nudged along over 3f out: rdn and drifted lft to nr side over 1f out: str run ins fnl f: led fnl 75yds: all out* **11/8**[1]

1421 2 nk **Somewhat (USA)**[42] 5530 2-8-12 **112** .... GeraldMosse 4 110
(Mark Johnston) *racd far side of centre: led: rdn and strly pressed fr 2f out: kpt on v gamely whn narrowly hdd fnl 75yds* **11/8**[1]

2014 3 nk **Sir Jack Layden**[14] 6395 2-8-12 **83** .... RichardHughes 1 109
(David Brown) *athletic: racd far side of centre: trckd ldng trio: swtchd rt over 1f out: edgd lft u.p fnl f: styd on strly: clsng wl at fin* **40/1**

1311 4 1/2 **Washaar (IRE)**[29] 5952 2-8-12 **104** .... PaulHanagan 2 108
(Richard Hannon) *lw: w ldr: rdn and ev ch fr 2f out: kpt on wl tl no ex fnl 75yds* **9/1**[3]

3 5 2 3/4 **Kingfisher (IRE)**[21] 6223 2-8-12 0........ RyanMoore 5 102
(A P O'Brien, Ire) *racd nr side of centre: trckd ldrs: pushed along over 3f out: rdn over 2f out: sn one pce* **7/1**[2]

1m 39.97s (1.37) **Going Correction** +0.20s/f (Good) **5** Ran SP% **109.1**
Speed ratings (Par 107): **101,100,100,99,97**
CSF £3.33 TOTE £2.30: £1.30, £1.40; EX 3.50 Trifecta £38.90 Pool: £3,163.86 - 60.92 winning units.
Owner H R H Sultan Ahmad Shah **Bred** Newsells Park Stud **Trained** Whatcombe, Oxon
■ Stewards' Enquiry : Jim Crowley two-day ban: used whip above permitted level (Oct 13-14)

FOCUS
Far side of Rowley Mile track used and stalls: centre. The Royal Lodge went through a period of being a somewhat unfashionable race, but it's produced loads of really smart types over the last few years, including among the beaten runners, and the most notable winner was the great Frankel in 2010. This has to rate an ordinary renewal though, with the time slow and the third seemingly improved. The form has to be given some sort of a chance, however.

6836 CONNOLLY'S RED MILLS CHEVELEY PARK STKS (GROUP 1) (FILLIES) 6f
2:35 (2:35) (Class 1) 2-Y-O
£103,949 (£39,409; £19,723; £9,824; £4,930; £2,474) **Stalls** Centre

Form RPR

112 1 **Vorda (FR)**[41] 5573 2-8-12 0........ OlivierPeslier 5 113+
(P Sogorb, France) *str: trckd ldrs: shkn up over 1f out: rdn to ld ins fnl f: r.o wl: shade cosily* **11/8**[1]

1051 2 3/4 **Princess Noor (IRE)**[63] 4742 2-8-12 **105** ....(b) JohnnyMurtagh 8 110
(Roger Varian) *racd alone on nr side of centre: prom: led over 3f out: rdn over 1f out: hdd ins fnl f: kpt on but nt pce of wnr* **11/1**

4112 3 1 1/4 **Kiyoshi**[27] 6024 2-8-12 **114** .... JamieSpencer 4 106
(Charles Hills) *lw: rrd leaving stalls: in last pair: pushed along and hdwy over 2f out: rdn and ev ch ent fnl f: no ex fnl 75yds* **9/4**[2]

1 4 nk **Come To Heel (IRE)**[35] 5771 2-8-12 0........ WayneLordan 7 105
(David Wachman, Ire) *lengthy: unf: t.k.h early: trckd ldrs: rdn 2f out: nt quite pce to chal but kpt on wl clsng stages: snatched 4th fnl strides* **9/1**

412 5 nk **Dorothy B (IRE)**[23] 6142 2-8-12 **102** .... WilliamBuick 3 104
(John Gosden) *led tl over 3f out: kpt pressing ldr: rdn over 1f out: kpt on tl no ex fnl 75yds: lost 4th fnl strides* **14/1**

131 6 1 **Joyeuse**[23] 6142 2-8-12 **103** .... JamesDoyle 6 101
(Lady Cecil) *lw: racd keenly: hld up bhd ldrs: rdn 2f out: styd on fnl f but nvr gng pce to get on terms* **7/1**[3]

0554 7 3 **Alutiq (IRE)**[23] 6142 2-8-12 **95** ....(p) JimCrowley 1 92
(Eve Johnson Houghton) *prom: rdn 2f out: sn hld: wknd fnl f* **50/1**

1m 13.34s (1.14) **Going Correction** +0.20s/f (Good) **7** Ran SP% **112.3**
Speed ratings (Par 106): **100,99,97,96,96 95,91**
toteswingers 1&2 £4.10, 1&3 £1.50, 2&3 £3.60 CSF £17.23 TOTE £1.80: £1.10, £5.30; EX 16.30 Trifecta £42.40 Pool: £15,283.91 - 270.17 winning units.
Owner H H Sheikh Mohammed Bin Khalifa Al Thani **Bred** Edy S.R.L. **Trained** France

FOCUS
They raced up the middle in what looked a solid enough running of the Cheveley Park and Vorda became the third French-trained filly in the last seven years to take this Group 1 prize, following on from subsequent 1000 Guineas winners Natagora (2007) and Special Duty (2009). Vorda is a likeable filly who can rate higher again, with another step up from Princess Noor.

6837 KINGDOM OF BAHRAIN SUN CHARIOT STKS (GROUP 1) (F&M) 1m
3:10 (3:10) (Class 1) 3-Y-O+
£110,130 (£41,753; £20,895; £10,409; £5,223; £2,621) **Stalls** Centre

Form RPR

1125 1 **Sky Lantern (IRE)**[56] 4985 3-8-13 **119** .... RichardHughes 2 119+
(Richard Hannon) *hld up last but wl in tch: crept clsr fr over 2f out: qcknd up wl whn shkn up jst over 1f out: led fnl 120yds: drifted rt: comf* **7/4**[1]

1101 2 1 **Integral**[28] 6000 3-8-13 **109** .... RyanMoore 1 116
(Sir Michael Stoute) *lw: hld up in last pair: hdwy 2f out: led over 1f out: sn rdn: kpt on but nt pce of wnr whn hdd fnl 120yds* **8/1**

1120 3 2 **Duntle (IRE)**[42] 5552 4-9-3 **111** .... WayneLordan 4 111
(David Wachman, Ire) *travelled wl trcking ldrs: rdn to chse ldr over 1f out: kpt on but nt pce to chal* **8/1**

4110 4 2 1/2 **Elusive Kate (USA)**[48] 5314 4-9-3 **117** .... WilliamBuick 5 105
(John Gosden) *trckd ldr: led over 2f out tl hung lft u.p wl over 1f out: no ex fnl f* **11/4**[2]

2661 5 3/4 **La Collina (IRE)**[21] 6224 4-9-3 **111** .... ChrisHayes 7 104
(Kevin Prendergast, Ire) *trckd ldrs: rdn 2f out: sn outpcd: clsng on 4th at fin* **20/1**

2130 6 9 **Just The Judge (IRE)**[56] 4985 3-8-13 **110** .... JamieSpencer 6 83
(Charles Hills) *little slowly away: sn led: rdn and hdd 2f out: sn hld: wknd over 1f out* **6/1**[3]

1600 7 6 **Chigun**[21] 6224 4-9-3 **112** ....(p) JamesDoyle 3 69
(Lady Cecil) *trckd ldr: rdn 3f out: sn hld: wknd over 1f out* **18/1**

1m 38.02s (-0.58) **Going Correction** +0.20s/f (Good)
WFA 3 from 4yo 4lb **7** Ran SP% **109.6**
Speed ratings (Par 117): **110,109,107,104,103 94,88**
toteswingers 1&2 £2.10, 1&3 £3.70, 2&3 £5.10 CSF £15.00 TOTE £2.40: £1.60, £2.20; EX 8.90 Trifecta £37.50 Pool: £27,521.36 - 549.56 winning units.
Owner B Keswick **Bred** Tally-Ho Stud **Trained** East Everleigh, Wilts

FOCUS
A good edition of the Sun Chariot and they were soon going a decent pace. They raced middle-to-far side. The form is rated in line with recent renewals, with Sky Lantern close to her best and a clear step up from Integral.

6838 BETFRED CAMBRIDGESHIRE (HERITAGE H'CAP) 1m 1f
3:50 (3:52) (Class 2) 3-Y-O+
£99,600 (£29,824; £14,912; £7,456; £3,728; £1,872) **Stalls** Centre

Form RPR

0035 1 **Educate**[35] 5739 4-9-9 **104** .... JohnnyMurtagh 4 117+
(Ismail Mohammed) *lw: racd far side: hld up in tch in midfield: rdn and effrt 2f out: hdwy to ld jst over 1f out: hung lft fnl f: jst hld on: 1st of 12 in gp* **8/1**[1]

The Form Book Flat, Raceform Ltd, Compton, RG20 6NL.

0153 **2** *shd* **Code Of Honor**[34] 5792 3-8-13 **99** FergusSweeney 28 112+
(Henry Candy) *racd stands' side: hld up in rr: effrt and forced to switch rt into centre of crse and hdwy over 1f out: edgd lft but str run ins fnl f: jst failed: 1st of 17 in gp* **12/1**[3]

2133 **3** *2* **Tres Coronas (IRE)**[77] 4310 6-8-12 **93** MickaelBarzalona 3 101
(David Barron) *racd far side: in tch in midfield: hdwy u.p 2f out: chsd ldrs 1f out: styd on same pce ins fnl f: 2nd of 12 in gp* **25/1**

3411 **4** *nse* **Graphic (IRE)**[21] 6199 4-8-13 **94** 4ex (p) FrankieDettori 20 102+
(William Haggas) *lw: racd stands' side: led gp and chsd ldrs overall tl outrt ldr 3f out: hdd jst over 1f out: no ex and one pce ins fnl f: 2nd of 17 in gp* **16/1**

-124 **5** *2 1/4* **Seek Again (USA)**[21] 6199 3-8-12 **98** JamesDoyle 17 102
(John Gosden) *lw: racd stands' side: hld up in rr: rdn and effrt 2f out: hdwy u.p over 1f out: kpt on fnl f: 3rd of 17 in gp* **14/1**

4020 **6** *3/4* **Dance And Dance (IRE)**[27] 6025 7-9-0 **95** (p) JimCrowley 33 96+
(Ed Vaughan) *lw: racd stands' side: t.k.h: hld up in rr: nt clr run over 2f out: hdwy ent fnl f: r.o wl fnl 100yds: nt rch ldrs: 4th of 17 in gp* **20/1**

0-40 **7** *hd* **Fury**[101] 3458 5-9-3 **98** (p) JosephO'Brien 27 99
(William Haggas) *racd stands' side: chsd ldrs and wl in tch overall: rdn ent fnl 2f: kpt on same pce fnl f: 5th of 17 in gp* **25/1**

1402 **8** *nk* **Gabrial The Great (IRE)**[14] 6396 4-9-1 **96** AndreaAtzeni 1 96
(Luca Cumani) *lw: racd far side: hld up in midfield overall: rdn and hdwy over 1f out: kpt on same pce ins fnl f: 3rd of 12 in gp* **20/1**

4435 **9** *3/4* **Proud Chieftain**[16] 6332 5-9-2 **97** (p) TedDurcan 30 99+
(Clifford Lines) *racd stands' side: hld up in rr: hdwy u.p over 1f out: styng on but stl plenty to do whn bdly hmpd and swtchd rt ins fnl f: r.o wl towards fin: nvr trbld ldrs: 6th of 17 in gp* **33/1**

1026 **10** *nk* **Belgian Bill**[13] 6451 5-9-9 **104** (tp) PatCosgrave 19 102
(George Baker) *lw: racd stands' side: in tch in midfield: rdn and hdwy 2f out: no imp over 1f out: kpt on ins fnl f: 7th of 17 in gp* **20/1**

1022 **11** *nse* **Tha'ir (IRE)**[16] 6332 3-9-2 **102** SilvestreDeSousa 2 101
(Saeed bin Suroor) *lw: racd far side: in tch in midfield: rdn and effrt 2f out: imp fr over 1f out: kpt on ins fnl f: 4th of 12 in gp* **16/1**

1261 **12** *nk* **Sam Sharp (USA)**[35] 5768 7-9-2 **97** PaulHanagan 9 94
(Ian Williams) *racd far side: hld up in rr: rdn and effrt ent fnl 2f: hdwy over 1f out: kpt on ins fnl f: nvr trbld ldrs: 5th of 12 in gp* **33/1**

1311 **13** *3/4* **Pacific Heights (IRE)**[17] 6300 4-8-12 **93** 4ex DaleSwift 5 88
(Brian Ellison) *racd far side: hld up in rr: effrt u.p ent fnl 2f: styd on steadily fnl f: nvr trbld ldrs: 6th of 12 in gp* **25/1**

0614 **14** *nk* **Strictly Silver (IRE)**[35] 5768 4-9-7 **102** (p) RobertWinston 32 97
(Alan Bailey) *racd stands' side: mid-div: swtchd lft and hdwy u.p to chse ldrs over 1f out: wknd ins fnl f: 8th of 17 in gp* **16/1**

1505 **15** *hd* **Field Of Dream**[21] 6183 6-9-8 **103** (b) AdamKirby 13 97
(Jamie Osborne) *racd far side: hld up in rr: rdn and hdwy over 1f out: no ex jst ins fnl f: fdd towards fin: 7th of 12 in gp* **33/1**

-010 **16** *7* **Nine Realms**[21] 6191 4-9-2 **97** LiamJones 6 76
(William Haggas) *racd far side: overall ldr tl 3f out: sn rdn: wknd over 1f out: 8th of 12 in gp* **33/1**

1003 **17** *1* **Captain Bertie (IRE)**[33] 5838 5-9-1 **96** PatSmullen 31 73
(Jane Chapple-Hyam) *racd stands' side: in tch in midfield: rdn 3f out: no hdwy and drvn 2f out: wknd over 1f out: 9th of 17 in gp* **40/1**

0445 **18** *1* **Area Fifty One**[14] 6385 5-9-7 **105** WilliamTwiston-Davies(3) 26 80
(Richard Fahey) *racd stands' side: chsd ldrs: rdn 3f out: lost pl 2f out: wknd over 1f out: 10th of 17 in gp* **66/1**

1104 **19** *1* **The Rectifier (USA)**[7] 6650 6-9-1 **96** (t) SeamieHeffernan 25 68
(Seamus Durack) *racd stands' side: chsd gp ldr tl drvn over 1f out: wknd fnl f: 11th of 17 in gp* **33/1**

3306 **20** *hd* **Queensberry Rules (IRE)**[37] 5681 3-9-0 **100** (t) RyanMoore 18 73
(William Haggas) *swtg: racd stands' side: hld up in rr: rdn and effrt over 2f out: no imp: wknd fnl f: 12th of 17 in gp* **12/1**[3]

6234 **21** *1* **Jack's Revenge (IRE)**[35] 5738 5-8-7 **93** (bt) OisinMurphy(5) 7 63
(George Baker) *racd far side: chsd ldr tl led gp and pressing overall ldr 3f out tl 2f out: sn wknd: 9th of 12 in gp* **14/1**

2603 **22** *hd* **King George River (IRE)**[36] 5728 3-8-11 **100** RobertTart(3) 35 70
(Alan Bailey) *racd stands' side: in tch in midfield: rdn and lost pl ent fnl 2f: sn wknd: 13th of 17 in gp* **10/1**[2]

315- **23** *1/2* **Bronze Angel (IRE)**[350] 7054 4-9-6 **101** (p) GeorgeBaker 22 69
(Marcus Tregoning) *racd stands' side: in tch in midfield: rdn and effrt 2f out: sn btn: wknd fnl f: 14th of 17 in gp* **16/1**

6100 **24** *3/4* **Danchai**[28] 6001 4-9-3 **98** (b[1]) WilliamBuick 8 65
(William Haggas) *racd far side: chsd ldrs tl wknd u.p 2f out: bhd fnl f: 10th of 12 in gp* **20/1**

1225 **25** *6* **Red Avenger (USA)**[36] 5725 3-9-0 **100** GeraldMosse 34 54
(Ed Dunlop) *racd stands' side: in tch in midfield: rdn and unable qck ent fnl 2f: wknd over 1f out: 15th of 17 in gp* **16/1**

100 **26** *5* **Prince Of Johanne (IRE)**[37] 5681 7-9-8 **103** (p) GrahamLee 15 45
(Tom Tate) *racd stands' side: in tch in midfield: rdn whn lost plave wl over 2f out: wl bhd and eased ins fnl f: 16th of 17 in gp* **28/1**

1123 **27** *2 1/4* **Robert The Painter (IRE)**[7] 6624 5-9-4 **99** (v) DanielTudhope 21 36
(David O'Meara) *racd stands' side: in tch in midfield: rdn and no rspnse over 2f out: sn wknd: bhd and eased fnl f: 17th of 17 in gp* **33/1**

0015 **28** *5* **Marcret (ITY)**[28] 5992 6-9-5 **100** TomMcLaughlin 12 26
(James Unett) *racd far side: in tch in midfield tl rdn 3f out: t.o and eased fnl f* **100/1**

6500 **29** *15* **Boonga Roogeta**[49] 5255 4-8-9 **93** RosieJessop(3) 14
(Peter Charalambous) *racd in centre pair: nvr bttr than midfield overall: rdn 3f out: sn wknd: t.o fnl f* **66/1**

3312 **30** *1* **Forgive**[21] 6188 4-8-13 **94** RichardHughes 10
(Richard Hannon) *racd far side: hld up in midfield: effrt over 2f out: sn wknd: t.o and eased fr over 1f out: 12th of 12 in gp* **25/1**

3242 **31** *11* **Arsaadi (IRE)**[21] 6231 4-9-4 **99** (b) AhmedAjtebi 11
(William Haggas) *racd in centre pair: nvr bttr than midfield: rdn and dropped to rr 3f out: t.o and eased fr over 1f out* **50/1**

1m 51.05s (-0.65) **Going Correction** +0.20s/f (Good)
WFA 3 from 4yo+ 5lb **31** Ran SP% **142.2**
Speed ratings (Par 109): **110,109,108,108,106 105,105,104,104,104 104,103,103,102,102 96,95,94,93,93 92,92,92,91,86 81,**
toteswingers 1&2 £17.00, 1&3 £108.30, 2&3 £101.10 CSF £80.39 CT £2409.67 TOTE £10.70: £3.10, £3.20, £6.70, £5.10; EX 119.00 Trifecta £6927.90 Part won. Pool: £9,237.29 - 0.80 winning units..
Owner Sultan Ali **Bred** Lady Legard **Trained** Newmarket, Suffolk
■ Stewards' Enquiry : Pat Cosgrave one-day ban: careless riding (Oct 13)

FOCUS
In the previous day's 'Silver Cambridgeshire', the field raced mainly in one pack, but there were three distinct bunches in this, although the middle one only contained two horses. The usual mix of hardened handicappers faced up to some less-exposed types, and William Haggas supplied almost a fifth of the field. Antepost punters were dealt a blow before the race even started when Top Notch Tonto and Ascription, 13lb and 7lb well in, were taken out at various stages of the day due to the ground. Educate posted a clear personal best and Code Of Honor is up taking on to minor Group company now too. The form is sound enough.

6839 IRISH STALLION FARMS "JERSEY LILY" EBF FILLIES' NURSERY H'CAP 7f

4:25 (4:26) (Class 2) 2-Y-O

£12,450 (£3,728; £1,864; £932; £466; £234) **Stalls** Centre

Form RPR

1010 **1** **Autumn Lily (USA)**[42] 5536 2-9-7 **93** MickaelBarzalona 3 99
(Charlie Appleby) *lw: hld up towards rr: hdwy fr 3f out: sn rdn: r.o ent fnl f: led fnl 120yds: drvn rt out* **9/1**

4122 **2** *1/2* **Thewandaofu (IRE)**[13] 6426 2-8-1 **73** KieranO'Neill 5 78
(Jamie Osborne) *led: rdn whn pressed over 2f out: kpt on gamely tl hdd fnl 120yds: drifted rt and no ex* **20/1**

1222 **3** *nk* **Ticking Katie (IRE)**[16] 6326 2-8-13 **85** DanielTudhope 4 89
(K R Burke) *trckd ldr: rdn 2f out: r.o ins fnl f: looking hld in cl 3rd whn squeezed up nr fin* **13/2**[2]

011 **4** *1* **Remember**[20] 6233 2-9-2 **88** RichardHughes 6 90
(Richard Hannon) *lw: slowly away: mid-div: hdwy 2f out: abt to mount chal whn nt clr run and swtchd lft jst over 1f out: sn rdn: nt pce to threaten* **5/2**[1]

4236 **5** *2 1/2* **Heskin (IRE)**[14] 6395 2-8-4 **76** [1] PaulHanagan 2 71
(Richard Fahey) *lw: mid-div: hdwy 3f out: sn rdn: kpt on same pce fnl 2f* **16/1**

1253 **6** *1 3/4* **Cornish Path**[16] 6326 2-8-5 **77** CathyGannon 10 67
(Henry Candy) *hmpd whn slowly away: towards rr: rdn over 2f out: styd on fr jst over 1f out: nvr trbld ldrs* **10/1**

2531 **7** *2* **Meeting Waters**[9] 6572 2-8-8 **80** JohnFahy 12 65
(William Haggas) *racd alone on stands' side: bhd: sme late prog: nvr trbld ldrs* **13/2**[2]

0101 **8** *shd* **Bureau (IRE)**[25] 6085 2-8-8 **80** SilvestreDeSousa 7 65
(Mark Johnston) *mid-div: rdn 3f out: nvr any imp* **12/1**

5013 **9** *3 1/4* **Dance Bid**[14] 6395 2-8-5 **77** LiamJones 1 53
(Clive Brittain) *prom tl rdn over 2f out: sn hld: wknd fnl f* **20/1**

011 **10** *1* **Hala Hala (IRE)**[26] 6041 2-8-2 **79** OisinMurphy(5) 8 53
(Michael Bell) *wnt lft s: sn mid-div: outpcd over 2f out: nt a threat after* **8/1**[3]

6210 **11** *10* **Kanz**[18] 6293 2-8-5 **77** WilliamCarson 11 25
(Mick Channon) *hmpd whn slowly away: a towards rr* **25/1**

311 **12** *3 3/4* **Captain Secret**[23] 6132 2-8-3 **75** AndreaAtzeni 9 13
(Marco Botti) *hmpd whn slowly away: sn chsng ldrs: rdn over 2f out: sn btn* **10/1**

1m 26.31s (0.91) **Going Correction** +0.20s/f (Good) **12** Ran SP% **121.5**
Speed ratings (Par 98): **102,101,101,99,97 95,92,92,88,87 76,72**
toteswingers 1&2 £43.90, 1&3 £9.60, 2&3 £20.60 CSF £181.57 CT £1262.22 TOTE £9.70: £3.20, £5.30, £2.10; EX 101.20 Trifecta £219.80 Pool: £3,130.71 - 10.67 winning units..
Owner Godolphin **Bred** Darley **Trained** Newmarket, Suffolk

FOCUS
All of these raced up the middle for the most part, with the exception of the well-beaten Meeting Waters, who was positioned stands' side.

6840 1ST SECURITY SOLUTIONS H'CAP 7f

5:00 (5:00) (Class 2) (0-100,100) 3-Y-O+

£11,827 (£3,541; £1,770; £885; £442; £222) **Stalls** Centre

Form RPR

5300 **1** **Ayaar (IRE)**[7] 6650 3-8-11 **93** RyanMoore 8 102
(Mick Channon) *swtg: hld up bhd: hdwy fr over 2f out: swtchd rt wl over 1f: qcknd up wl to ld sn after: enough in hand and a holding on fnl f: drvn out* **6/1**[3]

0001 **2** *nk* **Mezzotint (IRE)**[18] 6278 4-9-3 **96** AdamKirby 11 104
(Marco Botti) *s.i.s: towards rr: hdwy over 2f out: sn rdn to chse ldrs: wnt 2nd ins fnl f: clsng fast on wnr nring fin* **6/1**[3]

2605 **3** *3/4* **Flyman**[17] 6308 3-8-7 **89** PaulHanagan 4 95
(Richard Fahey) *mid-div: hdwy 2f out: sn rdn: disp 2nd ent fnl f: kpt on same pce* **8/1**

1116 **4** *1 3/4* **Majestic Moon (IRE)**[36] 5728 3-8-10 **92** ow1 RichardHughes 7 93
(Richard Fahey) *led: rdn 2f out: sn hdd: no ex fnl f* **10/3**[1]

00 **5** *hd* **Tariq Too**[7] 6625 6-8-12 **91** FergusSweeney 1 92
(Amy Weaver) *swtg: stdd s: swtchd lft and hdwy wl over 1f out: sn rdn: styd on fnl f: nvr threatened* **20/1**

5034 **6** *nk* **Regal Dan (IRE)**[17] 6308 3-8-5 **87** AndreaAtzeni 10 87+
(Charles Hills) *mid-div: on heels of ldrs travelling ok whn nt clr run over 2f out tl over 1f out: rdn but nt pce to cl: nt clr run again jst ins fnl f: kpt on but no ch after* **9/2**[2]

1235 **7** *3/4* **Frontier Fighter**[116] 2958 5-8-12 **91** DanielTudhope 6 89
(David O'Meara) *trckd ldr: rdn over 2f out: one pce fnl f* **12/1**

0014 **8** *nk* **Tellovoi (IRE)**[31] 5880 5-8-2 **86** oh1 (v) OisinMurphy(5) 5 83
(Ian Williams) *lw: trckd ldr: rdn 2f out: one pce fnl f* **14/1**

0404 **9** *nk* **Head Of Steam (USA)**[22] 6164 6-8-9 **88** ow1 (p) GrahamLee 12 84
(Amanda Perrett) *taken to s early: mid-div: rdn 2f out: nt pce to get involved* **10/1**

1150 **10** *3* **Spin Artist (USA)**[14] 6384 3-8-5 **87** LiamJones 14 75
(Mark Johnston) *lw: trckd ldr: rdn to chal 2f out tl wknd over 1f out* **20/1**

0340 **11** *9* **Spiritual Star (IRE)**[15] 6352 4-9-3 **96** WilliamCarson 13 60
(Anthony Carson) *swtg: towards rr: hdwy over 3f out: rdn over 2f out: wknd over 1f out* **25/1**

1m 24.71s (-0.69) **Going Correction** +0.20s/f (Good)
WFA 3 from 4yo+ 3lb **11** Ran SP% **117.8**
Speed ratings (Par 109): **111,110,109,107,107 107,106,106,105,102 91**
toteswingers 1&2 £6.30, 1&3 £4.90, 2&3 £10.40 CSF £40.67 CT £299.80 TOTE £7.20: £1.80, £2.30, £2.80; EX 38.90 Trifecta £256.10 Pool: £1,464.36 - 4.28 winning units..
Owner Sheikh Mohammed Bin Khalifa Al Maktoum **Bred** Blue Bloodstock Ltd **Trained** West Ilsley, Berks

FOCUS
The two heading the weights were withdrawn in the morning, as was the likely favourite Gold Hunter, so this wasn't as competitive as it might have been. The third and fourth help set the standard.

6841 PAUL & LESLEY STEVENS SILVER WEDDING ANNIVERSARY H'CAP 1m 4f
5:35 (5:35) (Class 2) (0-100,99) 3-Y-O **£12,291** (£3,657; £1,827; £913) **Stalls** Centre

Form RPR
1-32 **1** **Amralah (IRE)**[15] 6353 3-8-7 **85**................ SilvestreDeSousa 2 96
(Mick Channon) *lw: t.k.h: trckd ldrs: pulling hrd whn swtchd out to trck ldr over 7f out (bmpd 3rd): shken up 2f out: led jst over 1f out: drifted rt: kpt on strly to assert nr fin* **10/3**[3]
11 **2** 1 3/4 **Urban Dance (IRE)**[56] 5006 3-9-6 **98**................ MickaelBarzalona 6 106
(Charlie Appleby) *settled in last: smooth prog fr over 2f out: rdn to chse wnr ent fnl f: a being hld: no ex fnl 75yds: jst hld on for 2nd* **2/1**[1]
1346 **3** *shd* **Van Percy**[35] 5764 3-8-4 **87**................ OisinMurphy(5) 1 95
(Andrew Balding) *swtg: wnt rt s: in last trio tl hdwy to trck ldr over 7f out: sn hmpd: rdn over 2f out: kpt on but nt quite pce to chal and nt best of runs fnl f: nrly snatched 2nd fnl strides* **11/4**[2]
6103 **4** 5 **Royal Skies (IRE)**[11] 6503 3-9-7 **99**................ WilliamBuick 3 99
(Mark Johnston) *swtg: led: qcknd pce 4f out: rdn over 2f out: hdd jst over 1f out: fdd fnl f* **15/2**
5111 **5** 4 1/2 **Marju's Quest (IRE)**[39] 5606 3-8-2 **80**................ AndreaAtzeni 7 73
(David Simcock) *t.k.h: hld up in last trio: pushed along over 4f out: rdn over 3f out: nvr threatened: wknd ent fnl f* **9/1**
1310 **6** 41 **Emerging**[49] 5274 3-8-7 **85**................(p) LiamKeniry 8 12
(David Elsworth) *trckd ldr tl over 7f out: trckd ldrs: rdn over 3f out: wknd wl over 1f out: t.o* **10/1**

2m 34.0s (2.00) **Going Correction** +0.20s/f (Good) **6 Ran SP% 113.9**
Speed ratings (Par 107): **101,99,99,96,93 66**
toteswingers 1&2 £2.60, 1&3 £2.90, 2&3 £2.00 CSF £10.71 CT £19.63 TOTE £4.80: £2.10, £1.80; EX 10.90 Trifecta £47.60 Pool: £1,236.72 - 19.48 winning units.
Owner Prince A A Faisal **Bred** Nawara Stud Co Ltd **Trained** West Ilsley, Berks

FOCUS
A useful contest using official figures as a guide but the early gallop wasn't quick. Improved form from all the first three.
T/Jkpt: £25,511.80 to a £1 stake. Pool: £35,932.16 - 1.00 winning unit T/Plt: £184.50 to a £1 stake. Pool: £139,230.45 - 550.64 winning units T/Qpdt: £103.80 to a £1 stake. Pool: £8,532.40 - 60.80 winning units SP

5856 RIPON (R-H)
Saturday, September 28

OFFICIAL GOING: Good (8.4)
Wind: Light; half behind Weather: Cloudy; bright

6842 TREVOR INGHAM CELEBRATION EBF MAIDEN STKS 6f
2:10 (2:12) (Class 5) 2-Y-O **£4,528** (£1,347; £673; £336) **Stalls** High

Form RPR
1 **King Of Macedon (IRE)** 2-9-5 0................ AdrianNicholls 7 79+
(Mark Johnston) *mde virtually all: rdn 2f out: hld on gamely fnl f* **15/2**[3]
5526 **2** 3/4 **The Hooded Claw (IRE)**[20] 6234 2-9-5 75................ DuranFentiman 1 77
(Tim Easterby) *chsd ldrs: effrt and wnt 2nd over 2f out: kpt on wl u.p fnl f: hld nr fin* **5/1**[2]
2 **3** 1 1/4 **Jacob's Pillow**[51] 5186 2-9-5 0................ PhillipMakin 8 73
(William Haggas) *t.k.h early: chsd ldrs: rdn and edgd rt over 2f out: rallied over 1f out: kpt on ins fnl f* **4/9**[1]
0 **4** 8 **Edward Elgar**[10] 6517 2-9-0 0................ GeorgeChaloner(5) 10 49
(Richard Whitaker) *towards rr: drvn over 2f out: hung rt: kpt on fnl f: no imp* **12/1**
56 **5** 2 **Different Scenario**[145] 2075 2-9-0 0................ JimmyQuinn 11 38
(Mel Brittain) *hld up in tch: rdn over 2f out: sn outpcd* **33/1**
0 **6** 1/2 **First Commandment**[63] 4781 2-9-5 0................ PJMcDonald 9 42
(Tim Easterby) *t.k.h: pressed wnr: rdn over 2f out: wknd over 1f out* **12/1**
7 2 **Thiang (IRE)** 2-9-0 0................ PaulQuinn 5 31
(Tim Easterby) *upset in stalls: dwlt: hld up on outside: struggling over 2f out: sn btn* **28/1**
8 1 **Sleeper Class** 2-9-0 0................ BarryMcHugh 6 28
(Jim Goldie) *dwlt: hld up: shkn up over 2f out: sn btn* **28/1**
0050 **9** 6 **Rokeby**[40] 5577 2-9-5 55................ AndrewElliott 3 15
(George Moore) *s.i.s: bhd: rdn and hung rt 1/2-way: sn struggling* **50/1**
10 1/2 **Cahal (IRE)** 2-9-5 0................ GrahamGibbons 2 13
(David Nicholls) *s.i.s: bhd: pushed along over 2f out: sn btn* **25/1**

1m 13.33s (0.33) **Going Correction** -0.075s/f (Good) **10 Ran SP% 128.7**
Speed ratings (Par 95): **94,93,91,80,78 77,74,73,65,64**
toteswingers 1&2 £2.10, 1&3 £2.60, 2&3 £1.50 CSF £47.00 TOTE £8.50: £2.30, £1.60, £1.02; EX 49.50 Trifecta £130.50 Pool: £1,357.94 - 7.80 winning units.
Owner Sheikh Hamdan Bin Mohammed Al Maktoum **Bred** Gerrardstown House Stud **Trained** Middleham Moor, N Yorks

FOCUS
Rails at innermost position and all distances as advertised. Not a particularly competitive maiden.

6843 CAROLE HOGG AND ANDRENE DICKINS CONGRATULATORY APPRENTICE (S) STKS 6f
2:45 (2:45) (Class 6) 3-4-Y-O **£2,587** (£770; £384; £192) **Stalls** High

Form RPR
340 **1** **Shamrocked (IRE)**[30] 5614 4-9-2 60................ JacobButterfield(5) 3 64
(Ollie Pears) *w ldr: led after 1f: mde rest: drvn out fnl f* **9/2**[3]
4032 **2** 1 **Shillito**[22] 6176 3-9-0 59................(p) LauraBarry(5) 1 61
(Tony Coyle) *prom on outside: effrt and ev ch whn edgd lft over 1f out: kpt on fnl f: hld nr fin* **5/1**
1006 **3** 1 1/4 **Creek Falcon (IRE)**[12] 6473 4-9-5 74................(v[1]) JoshDoyle(7) 4 62
(David O'Meara) *in tch: rdn and outpcd over 1f out: edgd rt and kpt on ins fnl f* **5/2**[1]
6205 **4** 3/4 **Annie Gogh**[7] 6655 3-8-7 57................ RachelRichardson(7) 6 49
(Tim Easterby) *hld up in tch: outpcd after 2f: rallied and hung rt 2f out: kpt on fnl f: no imp* **7/2**[2]
5555 **5** 1/2 **Cymeriad**[16] 6344 3-8-11 45................(p) ShirleyTeasdale(3) 8 48
(Michael Easterby) *led 1f: cl up tl rdn and no ex over 1f out* **25/1**
5000 **6** 1 1/4 **Chunky Diamond (IRE)**[10] 6515 4-9-7 69................(tp) KevinStott(5) 2 54
(Ruth Carr) *cl up: rdn along whn n.m.r briefly over 1f out: wknd ins fnl f* **9/2**[3]
4106 **7** 12 **Bix (IRE)**[5] 6685 3-9-3 52................ NicolaGrundy(7) 5 15
(Alan Berry) *t.k.h early: prom: outpcd after 2f: struggling fr 1/2-way: t.o* **25/1**

1m 12.9s (-0.10) **Going Correction** -0.075s/f (Good)
WFA 3 from 4yo 2lb **7 Ran SP% 111.5**
Speed ratings (Par 101): **97,95,94,93,92 90,74**
toteswingers 1&2 £3.40, 1&3 £4.20, 2&3 £1.70 CSF £25.58 TOTE £3.20: £1.20, £2.90; EX 30.20 Trifecta £84.90 Pool: £1,390.93 - 12.28 winning units.There was no bid for the winner
Owner John H Sissons & Partners **Bred** Lodge Park Stud **Trained** Norton, N Yorks

FOCUS
A poor race even for this grade with most of these with plenty to prove.

6844 RIPON LAND ROVER NURSERY H'CAP 1m
3:15 (3:15) (Class 4) (0-85,89) 2-Y-O **£6,301** (£1,886; £943; £472; £235) **Stalls** Low

Form RPR
2214 **1** **Greed Is Good**[17] 6314 2-9-4 **82**................ PhillipMakin 5 91+
(K R Burke) *chsd clr ldrs: smooth hdwy over 2f out: led over 1f out: rdn and r.o strly* **5/2**[1]
0032 **2** 3 **Fair Flutter (IRE)**[18] 6275 2-8-0 **64**................ PatrickMathers 2 66
(Richard Fahey) *hld up: hdwy over 2f out: rdn and chsng ldrs whn hung rt over 1f out: wnt 2nd ins fnl f: no imp* **9/2**
4102 **3** 1 1/4 **Xanthos**[10] 6529 2-8-12 **83**................ BradleyBosley(7) 1 82
(Ed Walker) *t.k.h: slt ld to over 1f out: no ex and lost 2nd ins fnl f* **7/2**[3]
6530 **4** 12 **Shimba Hills**[78] 4246 2-8-2 **66**................ DuranFentiman 3 38
(Mick Channon) *hld up in tch: rdn over 4f out: hdwy on outside over 2f out: edgd rt and sn btn* **9/1**
5151 **5** 2 1/4 **Al Baz**[7] 6628 2-9-8 **89**................ ThomasBrown(3) 6 55
(James Tate) *disp ld: rdn over 3f out: wknd fr 2f out* **11/4**[2]
4500 **6** *nse* **Vine De Nada**[7] 6645 2-9-0 **78**................ AdrianNicholls 4 44
(Mark Johnston) *in tch: rdn over 3f out: checked over 2f out: sn btn* **12/1**

1m 38.77s (-2.63) **Going Correction** -0.35s/f (Firm) 2y crse rec **6 Ran SP% 113.3**
Speed ratings (Par 97): **99,96,94,82,80 80**
toteswingers 1&2 £1.02, 1&3 £4.30, 2&3 £13.10 CSF £14.30 TOTE £3.60: £1.40, £2.80; EX 14.80 Trifecta £50.20 Pool: £1,359.08 - 20.30 winning units.
Owner M Charge & Mrs E Burke **Bred** Northcombe Stud **Trained** Middleham Moor, N Yorks

FOCUS
This looked quite open on paper but it proved a different story in the track.

6845 RIPON CATHEDRAL CITY OF THE DALES H'CAP 6f
3:45 (3:47) (Class 2) (0-105,105) 3-Y-O+
£18,675 (£5,592; £2,796; £1,398; £699; £351) **Stalls** High

Form RPR
0006 **1** **Doc Hay (USA)**[4] 6719 6-9-5 **100**................[1] DavidNolan 12 109
(David O'Meara) *dwlt: hld up: angled rt and hdwy over 1f out: led ins fnl f: rdn out* **10/1**
0120 **2** 3/4 **Spinatrix**[7] 6623 5-9-5 **105**................(p) ConnorBeasley(5) 5 112
(Michael Dods) *cl up: rdn to ld over 1f out: hdd ins fnl f: kpt on: hld nr fin* **7/2**[1]
1331 **3** 1 1/4 **Seeking Magic**[56] 4983 5-8-12 **98**................(t) RyanTate(5) 7 101+
(Clive Cox) *hld up towards rr: nt clr run over 2f out to over 1f out: rdn and r.o fnl f: nrst fin* **5/1**[2]
1202 **4** 1/2 **Love Island**[9] 6564 4-8-12 **93** ow1................ PhillipMakin 4 94
(Richard Whitaker) *cl up: effrt and ev ch over 1f out to ins fnl f: sn no ex* **14/1**
2500 **5** 3/4 **Summerinthecity (IRE)**[8] 6608 6-8-10 **91**................ BarryMcHugh 9 90
(David Nicholls) *prom: effrt and rdn 2f out: kpt on same pce ins fnl f* **14/1**
0010 **6** 1 **El Viento (FR)**[14] 6391 5-8-11 **97**................(v) GeorgeChaloner(5) 10 92
(Richard Fahey) *prom: rdn 2f out: effrt whn no room against stands' rail 1f out: sn n.d* **9/1**
1466 **7** *nk* **Above Standard (IRE)**[21] 6190 5-8-8 **89**................ GrahamGibbons 11 83
(Michael Easterby) *led to over 1f out: wknd ins fnl f* **15/2**[3]
2002 **8** 1 3/4 **Fast Shot**[7] 6621 5-8-9 **90**................ DuranFentiman 6 79
(Tim Easterby) *hld up towards rr: rdn and hdwy on outside over 2f out: no imp over 1f out* **9/1**
6030 **9** *nk* **Thunderball**[7] 6621 7-8-9 **90**................(p) PJMcDonald 2 78
(Scott Dixon) *prom on outside: rdn over 2f out: wknd over 1f out* **20/1**
0340 **10** 1 3/4 **Chooseday (IRE)**[7] 6621 4-8-0 **86**................(p) ShaneGray(5) 8 68
(Kevin Ryan) *dwlt: bhd: rdn along over 3f out: nvr on terms* **5/1**[2]
1030 **11** 7 **Rodrigo De Torres**[7] 6621 6-8-7 **93**................ TobyAtkinson(5) 1 53
(David Nicholls) *prom on outside: rdn over 2f out: sn wknd* **16/1**

1m 10.91s (-2.09) **Going Correction** -0.075s/f (Good) **11 Ran SP% 120.4**
Speed ratings (Par 109): **110,109,107,106,105 104,103,101,101,98 89**
toteswingers 1&2 £7.90, 1&3 £6.30, 2&3 £5.70 CSF £46.06 CT £206.91 TOTE £10.30: £4.30, £1.10, £2.70; EX 46.40 Trifecta £38.60 Pool: £913.47 - 17.71 winning units.
Owner S Laffan **Bred** Colts Neck Stables Llc **Trained** Nawton, N Yorks
■ Stewards' Enquiry : David Nolan four-day ban: used whip above permitted level (Oct 13-16)
Graham Gibbons two-day ban: careless riding (Oct 13-14); one-day ban: failed to ride out for 6th (Oct 15)

FOCUS
A competitive sprint which unfolded towards the middle of the track.

6846 RIPON BET "OUR PROFITS STAY IN RACING" H'CAP 1m 4f 10y
4:20 (4:21) (Class 4) (0-85,83) 3-Y-O+ **£6,301** (£1,886; £943; £472; £235) **Stalls** Low

Form RPR
3132 **1** **Discay**[6] 6668 4-9-7 **78**................ AdrianNicholls 6 89+
(Mark Johnston) *hld up: hdwy whn nt clr run over 2f out and over 1f out: kpt on strly fnl f: led towards fin* **10/3**[1]
5010 **2** 3/4 **Tetbury (USA)**[20] 6239 4-9-12 **83**................(v) GrahamGibbons 3 90
(David O'Meara) *t.k.h in midfield: hdwy on ins to ld over 1f out: sn drvn: kpt on fnl f: hdd towards fin* **8/1**[3]
0630 **3** 1 1/4 **Be Perfect (USA)**[7] 6626 4-9-9 **80**................ BarryMcHugh 5 85
(David Nicholls) *prom: effrt and rdn over 2f out: kpt on same pce ins fnl f* **8/1**[3]
5325 **4** *nk* **Good Speech (IRE)**[17] 6302 3-8-7 **72**................ AndrewElliott 4 77
(Tom Tate) *t.k.h: led: rdn and hdd over 1f out: kpt on same pce fnl f* **9/2**[2]
2210 **5** 1 **Red Charmer (IRE)**[17] 6296 3-8-10 **75**................ PJMcDonald 1 78
(Ann Duffield) *trckd ldrs: effrt and led briefly over 1f out: no ex ins fnl f* **10/1**
3251 **6** 1 **Aryizad (IRE)**[8] 6599 4-8-11 **71**................ ThomasBrown(3) 7 72
(Alan Swinbank) *t.k.h: hld up towards rr: rdn and outpcd over 2f out: styd on fnl f: no imp* **9/1**
13-0 **7** 1 3/4 **New Youmzain (FR)**[8] 6585 4-9-5 **79**................ CharlesBishop(3) 2 78
(Mick Channon) *dwlt: hld up: rdn and outpcd over 4f out: rallied over 1f out: nvr on terms* **9/2**[2]
3400 **8** 4 **San Cassiano (IRE)**[9] 6563 6-9-7 **78**................ PhillipMakin 8 70
(Ruth Carr) *cl up tl rdn and wknd fr 2f out* **20/1**

505 **9** *18* **Villa Royale**[7] 6631 4-9-10 **81** .... DavidNolan 10 44
(David O'Meara) *trckd ldrs: rdn and wknd over 2f out: eased whn no ch fnl f* **14/1**

1000 **10** *3* **Choisan (IRE)**[7] 6626 4-9-5 **76** .... DuranFentiman 9 35
(Tim Easterby) *midfield on outside: struggling over 3f out: sn btn: eased whn no ch ins fnl f* **16/1**

2m 33.16s (-3.54) **Going Correction** -0.35s/f (Firm)
WFA 3 from 4yo+ 8lb **10** Ran SP% **118.1**
Speed ratings (Par 105): **97,96,95,95,94 94,92,90,78,76**
toteswingers 1&2 £5.40, 1&3 £3.30, 2&3 £10.20 CSF £30.96 CT £200.47 TOTE £4.10: £1.20, £3.40, £4.10; EX 28.00 Trifecta £92.10 Pool: £1,389.84 - 11.31 winning units.
Owner C H Greensit & W A Greensit **Bred** C H And W A Greensit **Trained** Middleham Moor, N Yorks

FOCUS
Probably not the most competitive of races for the grade.

6847 FREEBETS.CO.UK MAIDEN STKS 1m 4f 10y
4:55 (4:56) (Class 5) 3-Y-O+ **£4,528** (£1,347; £673; £336) **Stalls** Low

Form RPR

45 **1** **Wizara (IRE)**[25] 6062 3-8-12 0 .... HarryBentley 1 80+
(Saeed bin Suroor) *hld up: stdy hdwy over 2f out: led over 1f out: rdn and hld on wl fnl f* **11/4**[2]

333 **2** *¾* **Flemish School**[10] 6521 3-9-0 72 ow2 .... (p) PhillipMakin 7 81
(Gerard Butler) *awkward s: hld up: hdwy over 2f out: effrt and drvn over 1f out: chsd wnr ins fnl f: r.o* **15/2**

2343 **3** *¾* **Fantasy In Blue**[32] 5854 3-8-9 71 .... ThomasBrown(3) 2 78
(Sir Michael Stoute) *prom: hdwy to ld over 2f out: rdn and hdd over 1f out: rallied: kpt on same pce ins fnl f* **9/4**[1]

3635 **4** *3 ¼* **Gamble**[25] 6071 3-8-5 72 .... LouisSteward(7) 3 73
(Michael Bell) *chsd ldr: hdwy and ev ch over 2f out to over 1f out: outpcd fnl f* **5/1**[3]

20 **5** *3* **Stopped Out**[98] 3560 8-9-11 0 .... (p) RussKennemore 6 73
(Philip Kirby) *led: rdn and hdd over 2f out: wknd over 1f out* **8/1**

32 **6** *26* **Copybook**[22] 6166 3-8-12 0 .... AdrianNicholls 10 26
(Mark Johnston) *chsd ldrs: drvn and outpcd over 3f out: sn btn: t.o* **8/1**

5 **7** *12* **Pastoral**[11] 6498 4-9-6 0 .... BarryMcHugh 8 7
(Tony Coyle) *chsd ldrs: drvn over 3f out: sn struggling: t.o* **50/1**

0 **8** *12* **Nowcando**[33] 5839 3-8-5 0 .... BTTreanor(7) 5
(K R Burke) *s.i.s: bhd: struggling over 5f out: nvr on terms: t.o* **66/1**

45 **9** *24* **Razera (IRE)**[18] 6272 3-9-3 0 .... JimmyQuinn 4
(John Quinn) *dwlt: plld hrd and sn midfield: struggling over 4f out: sn btn: t.o* **25/1**

0-0 **10** *15* **High Flame (IRE)**[144] 2121 3-8-12 0 .... DuranFentiman 9
(Tim Easterby) *t.k.h in rr: struggling over 5f out: t.o* **66/1**

2m 33.06s (-3.64) **Going Correction** -0.35s/f (Firm)
WFA 3 from 4yo+ 8lb **10** Ran SP% **116.9**
Speed ratings (Par 103): **98,97,97,94,92 75,67,59,43,33**
toteswingers 1&2 £5.10, 1&3 £2.00, 2&3 £5.40 CSF £23.28 TOTE £4.00: £2.90, £1.40, £1.20; EX 25.70 Trifecta £92.70 Pool: £2,776.71 - 22.45 winning units.
Owner Godolphin **Bred** Darley **Trained** Newmarket, Suffolk
■ Stewards' Enquiry : Phillip Makin six-day ban: 2nd offence in 6mths, weighed-in 2lb heavy (Oct 12-17)

FOCUS
No stars on show in this maiden but the step up in trip brought about an improved display from the winner.

6848 SIS LIVE H'CAP 5f
5:25 (5:25) (Class 4) (0-85,85) 3-Y-O+ **£6,301** (£1,886; £943; £472; £235) **Stalls** High

Form RPR

0651 **1** **Ambitious Icarus**[8] 6603 4-8-7 **71** oh3 .... (e) KirstyMilczarek 8 83
(Richard Guest) *hld up towards rr: hdwy over 1f out: led ins fnl f: drvn out* **16/1**

2463 **2** *1 ¾* **Tumblewind**[21] 6212 3-9-0 **84** .... GeorgeChaloner(5) 17 90
(Richard Whitaker) *chsd ldrs: rdn and led over 1f out: hdd ins fnl f: kpt on same pce* **10/1**

0-12 **3** *¾* **Jinker Noble**[27] 6018 4-8-13 **77** .... PhillipMakin 15 80
(Ed de Giles) *t.k.h: trckd ldrs: effrt over 1f out: one pce ins fnl f* **3/1**[1]

00-0 **4** *½* **Ruby's Day**[58] 4935 4-8-9 **80** .... ClaireMurray(7) 14 82+
(David Brown) *dwlt: sn in tch: rdn 2f out: kpt on ins fnl f* **25/1**

5443 **5** *½* **Silvanus (IRE)**[17] 6309 8-9-0 **78** .... PJMcDonald 4 78
(Paul Midgley) *hld up bhd ldng gp: rdn 2f out: kpt on fnl f: nvr able to chal* **5/1**[2]

04 **6** *1 ¾* **Perfect Blossom**[17] 6309 6-8-9 **78** .... ConnorBeasley(5) 13 71+
(Alan Berry) *towards rr: rdn and hdwy over 1f out: kpt on: n.d* **10/1**

4004 **7** *½* **Sunny Side Up (IRE)**[68] 4580 4-8-8 **72** .... PatrickMathers 3 64
(Richard Fahey) *towards rr: rdn over 2f out: edgd rt and hdwy appr fnl f: nrst fin* **22/1**

5010 **8** *hd* **Bronze Beau**[17] 6309 6-8-11 **80** .... (tp) JacobButterfield(5) 6 71
(Kristin Stubbs) *chsd ldrs: rdn over 1f out: wknd ins fnl f* **22/1**

3253 **9** *½* **Haajes**[14] 6388 9-8-10 **79** .... (v) ShirleyTeasdale(5) 5 68
(Paul Midgley) *towards rr: drvn along 1/2-way: sme late hdwy: n.d* **12/1**

6260 **10** *1* **Satsuma**[17] 6309 3-9-2 **81** .... MichaelStainton 16 66
(David Brown) *led to over 1f out: rdn and wknd ins fnl f* **25/1**

0040 **11** *hd* **Mister Manannan (IRE)**[8] 6583 6-9-2 **80** .... AdrianNicholls 2 65
(David Nicholls) *dwlt: t.k.h and sn in tch on outside: pushed along and wknd 1f out* **12/1**

0006 **12** *½* **Captain Dunne (IRE)**[28] 5991 8-9-3 **81** .... DuranFentiman 1 64
(Tim Easterby) *cl up tl rdn and wknd appr fnl f* **8/1**

5302 **13** *1 ½* **The Art Of Racing (IRE)**[13] 6429 3-9-6 **85** .... (t) HarryBentley 11 63
(Olly Stevens) *hld up: rdn along 2f out: nvr on terms* **6/1**[3]

1050 **14** *3 ¼* **Lost In Paris (IRE)**[18] 6273 7-8-13 **77** .... (p) GrahamGibbons 10 43
(Tim Easterby) *missed break: bhd and pushed along 1/2-way: nvr on terms* **22/1**

58.47s (-1.53) **Going Correction** -0.075s/f (Good)
WFA 3 from 4yo+ 1lb **14** Ran SP% **127.2**
Speed ratings (Par 105): **109,106,105,104,103 100,99,99,98,97 96,95,93,88**
toteswingers 1&2 £19.10, 1&3 £21.40, 2&3 £10.70 CSF £164.08 CT £638.41 TOTE £27.40: £7.10, £1.50, £1.10; EX 192.50 Trifecta £831.90 Part won. Pool: £1,109.23 - 0.33 winning units..
Owner ABS Metals & Waste **Bred** L T Roberts **Trained** Wetherby, W Yorks

FOCUS
A wide-open finale.
T/Plt: £30.10 to a £1 stake. Pool: £45,415.83 - 1,099.82 winning units T/Qpdt: £4.90 to a £1 stake. Pool: £2,862.75 - 428.10 winning units RY

6803 WOLVERHAMPTON (A.W) (L-H)
Saturday, September 28

OFFICIAL GOING: Standard to slow
Wind: moderate 1/2 against Weather: fine

6849 BET365.COM MEDIAN AUCTION MAIDEN STKS 5f 216y(P)
5:30 (5:33) (Class 6) 3-Y-O **£1,940** (£577; £288; £144) **Stalls** Low

Form RPR

4240 **1** **Little Choosey**[22] 6154 3-9-0 63 .... JoeFanning 5 64
(Anabel K Murphy) *sn led: hdd after 1f: trckd ldrs: led over 1f out: rdn and styd on* **11/10**[1]

3266 **2** *3* **Sunny Hollow**[28] 5981 3-8-9 54 .... (v[1]) DanielMuscutt(5) 3 54
(James Toller) *dwlt: hdwy 3f out: kpt on fnl f: tk 2nd last 50yds* **8/1**

005 **3** *2 ¾* **Daneglow (IRE)**[80] 4176 3-8-9 34 .... GeorgeDowning(5) 7 46
(Mike Murphy) *led after 1f: hdd over 1f out: kpt on same pce* **28/1**

6-00 **4** *¾* **Princess Sheila (IRE)**[137] 2345 3-8-11 52 .... MichaelJMMurphy(3) 4 43
(J S Moore) *chsd ldrs: hung lft and one pce fnl 2f* **11/2**[3]

0440 **5** *¾* **Wotalad**[7] 6633 3-9-5 56 .... MartinLane 2 46
(Richard Whitaker) *led early: drvn and lost pl over 4f out: hdwy over 1f out: kpt on* **5/1**[2]

6 *1 ¾* **Diva Delight (IRE)** 3-9-0 0 .... ShaneKelly 1 35
(Robert Cowell) *dwlt: in rr: drvn over 3f out: sme hdwy over 1f out: sn hung rt and wknd* **7/1**

0056 **7** *4* **Iffley Fields**[12] 6462 3-9-1 37 ow1 .... (p) HarryPoulton(5) 6 28
(Michael Squance) *chsd ldrs: drvn over 3f out: edgd lft over 1f out: sn wknd* **28/1**

1m 15.13s (0.13) **Going Correction** +0.05s/f (Slow) **7** Ran SP% **110.2**
Speed ratings (Par 99): **101,97,93,92,91 89,83**
toteswingers 1&2 £2.00, 1&3 £7.10, 2&3 £20.40 CSF £9.85 TOTE £2.00: £2.20, £2.60; EX 10.00 Trifecta £111.30 Pool: £1,890.04 - 12.73 winning units.
Owner Mrs Anabel K Murphy **Bred** Mrs Sandra Fox **Trained** Wilmcote, Warwicks

FOCUS
he going, described as standard to slow, rode as advertised. The kickback, courtesy of recent work on the surface which has yet to bed in, was noticeable. A very poor 3yo sprint maiden, run at a fair pace, with six of the seven participants previously having 49 unsuccessful runs between them.

6850 BET365 CLAIMING STKS 5f 20y(P)
6:00 (6:00) (Class 6) 3-Y-O+ **£1,940** (£577; £288; £144) **Stalls** Low

Form RPR

-605 **1** **R Woody**[11] 6506 6-8-9 73 .... (e[1]) MartinLane 5 77
(Robert Cowell) *chsd ldr: led over 1f out: sn jnd: fnd ex nr line* **8/1**

4000 **2** *nk* **Dick Bos**[7] 6621 4-9-12 88 .... JoeFanning 7 93
(David O'Meara) *short of room sn after s: hdwy to chse ldrs over 3f out: chal 1f out: no ex nr fin* **6/4**[1]

4420 **3** *2 ½* **Picansort**[29] 5956 6-9-4 85 .... (b) ShaneKelly 2 76
(Peter Crate) *s.i.s: hdwy over 2f out: swtchd rt over 1f out: kpt on to take 3rd post* **9/2**[2]

6625 **4** *shd* **Titus Gent**[21] 6189 8-8-13 84 .... DavidParkes(7) 6 78
(Jeremy Gask) *mid-div: hdwy over 2f out: one pce* **15/2**[3]

4004 **5** *1 ½* **Lucky Dan (IRE)**[10] 6516 7-8-11 79 .... JasonHart(3) 9 66
(Paul Green) *mid-div: effrt over 2f out: one pce* **14/1**

5020 **6** *hd* **Decision By One**[10] 6526 4-9-0 79 .... (vt) StephenCraine 3 65
(Tom Dascombe) *led: hdd over 1f out: sn wknd* **15/2**[3]

040 **7** *2 ¾* **Danziger (IRE)**[17] 6310 4-7-10 68 .... (v) NoelGarbutt(5) 1 43
(David Evans) *mid-div: effrt over 2f out: wknd over 1f out* **33/1**

0600 **8** *1 ¼* **Dorback**[42] 5544 6-8-9 80 .... MichaelJMMurphy(3) 4 49
(Tony Newcombe) *chsd ldrs: wknd over 1f out* **9/1**

0600 **9** *5* **Taurus Twins**[14] 6382 7-8-7 70 .... (b) DeclanBates(3) 8 29
(Richard Price) *sn outpcd and in rr: bhd fnl 2f* **20/1**

1m 2.02s (-0.28) **Going Correction** +0.05s/f (Slow) **9** Ran SP% **117.2**
Speed ratings (Par 101): **104,103,99,99,96 96,92,90,82**
toteswingers 1&2 £9.90, 1&3 £8.90, 2&3 £1.40 CSF £20.72 TOTE £14.30: £3.80, £1.10, £2.70; EX 31.40 Trifecta £205.60 Pool: £1,440.47 - 5.25 winning units.
Owner Quintessential Thoroughbreds & Partner **Bred** R, D And M Close **Trained** Six Mile Bottom, Cambs

FOCUS
A decent sprint claimer and they spread across the track off the final bend to avoid the kickback.

6851 CASINO AT BET365 H'CAP 1m 1f 103y(P)
6:30 (6:30) (Class 6) (0-60,59) 3-Y-O+ **£1,940** (£577; £288; £144) **Stalls** Low

Form RPR

5-14 **1** **Goal (IRE)**[1] 6803 5-9-8 **57** .... (t) RobertWinston 1 70
(Gordon Elliott, Ire) *chsd ldrs: 2nd over 3f out: carried wd bnd over 2f out: led over 1f out: hung lft: pushed clr* **9/4**[1]

10-6 **2** *2 ¼* **Cantor**[12] 6458 5-9-6 **55** .... PatrickDonaghy 9 63
(Giles Bravery) *w ldr: led over 5f out: rn wd bnd over 2f out: hdd over 1f out: kpt on same pce* **12/1**

3220 **3** *1 ½* **Greyemkay**[11] 6492 5-8-12 **52** .... DanielMuscutt(5) 10 57
(Richard Price) *mid-div: effrt over 2f out: kpt on to take 3rd jst ins fnl f* **16/1**

4650 **4** *5* **Impeccability**[89] 3910 3-8-8 **48** .... JoeFanning 3 44
(John Mackie) *chsd ldrs: drvn 3f out: one pce fnl 2f* **25/1**

6061 **5** *3* **Kyle Of Bute**[16] 6339 7-8-9 **51** .... JoshBaudains(7) 5 39
(Richard Ford) *mid-div: hdwy over 3f out: chsng ldrs over 2f out: one pce* **6/1**[3]

5602 **6** *hd* **Cane Cat (IRE)**[34] 5803 6-9-3 **57** .... (t) GeorgeDowning(5) 7 45
(Tony Carroll) *in rr: sme hdwy 3f out: nvr a factor* **14/1**

030 **7** *1 ½* **Cabal**[18] 6276 6-9-4 **56** .... (b) JasonHart(3) 4 41
(Andrew Crook) *in rr: hdwy to chse ldrs over 4f out: wknd over 1f out* **10/1**

0064 **8** *2 ½* **Appyjack**[14] 6399 5-8-11 **46** .... (t) LukeMorris 6 26
(Tony Carroll) *mid-div: drvn to chse ldrs over 4f out: wknd over 1f out: eased towards fin* **8/1**

5435 **9** *11* **Carrera**[14] 6399 3-9-2 **56** .... SebSanders 8 13
(J W Hills) *hld up in rr: drvn over 3f out: sn bhd* **4/1**[2]

06-0 **10** *4 ½* **Divine Success (IRE)**[33] 5840 4-8-3 **45** .... SamanthaBell(7) 11
(Richard Fahey) *wnt lft s: in rr: bhd over 3f out: t.o whn hung bdly rt bnd over 2f out* **33/1**

11 *29* **Until Midnight (IRE)**[6] 2379 3-9-2 **59**.........(t) WilliamTwiston-Davies(3) 2
(Alexandra Dunn) *led: hdd over 5f out: lost pl 3f out: sn bhd: t.o 2f out: virtually p.u* **40/1**

2m 1.95s (0.25) **Going Correction** +0.05s/f (Slow)
WFA 3 from 4yo+ 5lb **11** Ran SP% **114.7**
Speed ratings (Par 101): **100,98,96,92,89 89,88,85,76,72 46**
toteswingers 1&2 £16.20, 1&3 £7.30, 2&3 £46.50 CSF £29.75 CT £348.97 TOTE £3.10: £1.50, £4.60, £3.80; EX 37.40 Trifecta £404.70 Pool: £1,585.41 - 2.93 winning units.
Owner Willie McKay **Bred** A M F Persse **Trained** Trim, Co Meath

FOCUS
Nothing more than a moderate handicap in which the pace was no more than fair, but it produced an easy winner and they finished strung out.

6852 BET365.COM NURSERY H'CAP 1m 141y(P)
7:00 (7:00) (Class 5) (0-75,75) 2-Y-0 **£2,587** (£770; £384; £192) **Stalls** Low

Form RPR
31 **1** **Top Dollar**[22] 6152 2-9-3 **71**.................................... NeilCallan 8 81+
(James Tate) *t.k.h early: trckd ldng pair: led 2f out: styd on strly to go clr: v readily* **9/4**[2]
3214 **2** *6* **Lucky Visione**[18] 6275 2-9-6 **74**................................ LukeMorris 3 70
(Gay Kelleway) *dwlt: in rr: plld wd and hdwy over 4f out: styd on to take 2nd ins fnl f: no ch w wnr* **16/1**
0446 **3** *1 1/4* **By The Light (IRE)**[32] 5865 2-8-8 **62**.............................. JoeFanning 9 56
(Mark Johnston) *sn trcking ldrs: drvn over 3f out: outpcd over 2f out: styd on to take modest 3rd clsng stages* **25/1**
6020 **4** *nk* **Know Your Name**[14] 6401 2-9-4 **75**..........................(v) DeclanBates(3) 6 68
(David Evans) *mid-div: effrt over 2f out: chsng ldrs over 1f out: kpt on one pce* **11/1**
306 **5** *1 1/2* **Full Day**[45] 5394 2-9-5 **73**.................................... JimCrowley 2 63
(Ralph Beckett) *hld up in rr: kpt on fnl 2f: nvr a factor* **2/1**[1]
5340 **6** *nk* **Diplomatic Force (USA)**[14] 6401 2-9-4 **72**.................. MartinLane 7 61
(Charlie Appleby) *led 1f: w ldr: led over 2f out: sn hdd: wknd fnl f* **16/1**
0052 **7** *15* **Ultimate Warrior (IRE)**[10] 6520 2-9-3 **74**..... WilliamTwiston-Davies(3) 5 32
(Richard Hannon) *mid-div: drvn over 4f out: lost pl 3f out: sn bhd: eased clsng stages* **4/1**[3]
235 **8** *2 1/2* **George The First**[18] 6271 2-9-3 **71**......................... RobertWinston 1 26
(Kevin Ryan) *led after 1f: hdd over 2f out: lost pl over 1f out: eased whn bhd* **16/1**

1m 50.92s (0.42) **Going Correction** +0.05s/f (Slow) **8** Ran SP% **113.9**
Speed ratings (Par 95): **100,94,93,93,91 91,78,76**
toteswingers 1&2 £6.00, 1&3 £7.80, 2&3 £24.10 CSF £36.96 CT £714.61 TOTE £4.00: £1.50, £3.20, £4.60; EX 28.80 Trifecta £218.20 Pool: £1,956.17 - 6.72 winning units.
Owner Saeed Manana **Bred** Shawahed Thoroughbred Corporation **Trained** Newmarket, Suffolk

FOCUS
The pace was fair for this reasonable nursery, which turned into something of a rout.

6853 BET365.COM H'CAP 2m 119y(P)
7:30 (7:31) (Class 6) (0-60,66) 3-Y-0+ **£1,940** (£577; £288; £144) **Stalls** Low

Form RPR
1001 **1** **Man From Seville**[4] 6736 3-9-8 **66** 6ex.......................... LukeMorris 9 83+
(Sir Mark Prescott Bt) *hld up in mid-div: hdwy over 6f out: led over 3f out: drvn clr over 1f out: eased ins fnl f* **4/9**[1]
1226 **2** *4 1/2* **Torero**[22] 6177 4-9-8 **54**..(p) NeilCallan 13 61
(Kevin Ryan) *hld up in rr: hdwy over 6f out: chsd wnr over 3f out: kpt on: no imp* **8/1**[2]
50-0 **3** *2 3/4* **Tigerino (IRE)**[67] 4614 5-9-4 **50**............................... JimCrowley 11 54
(Chris Fairhurst) *hld up in rr: gd hdwy over 5f out: 3rd 3f out: one pce: fin lame* **20/1**
0500 **4** *12* **Kayef (GER)**[16] 6336 6-10-0 **60**...............................(v) JoeFanning 7 49
(Michael Scudamore) *mid-div: lost pl over 3f out: poor 4th over 1f out* **20/1**
2533 **5** *8* **Glens Wobbly**[24] 6099 5-8-9 **46** oh1................................ RyanTate(5) 2 26
(Jonathan Geake) *chsd ldrs: drvn over 3f out: lost pl over 2f out: wknd over 1f out* **20/1**
6-6 **6** *2 1/2* **Lac Sacre (FR)**[154] 1700 4-8-11 **46** oh1........................(p) RobertTart(3) 8 23
(Tony Carroll) *mid-div: lost pl 3f out* **12/1**
4230 **7** *7* **Mr Vendman (IRE)**[22] 6177 3-7-13 **46**......................(v) RyanPowell(3) 12 14
(Ian Williams) *sn trcking ldr: led 6f out: hdd over 3f out: sn wknd* **11/1**[3]
055- **8** *21* **Cloudy Start**[33] 5683 7-9-9 **58**....................... WilliamTwiston-Davies(3) 6
(Violet M Jordan) *hld up in rr: reminders over 5f out: sn lost pl and bhd: t.o over 2f out* **40/1**
-006 **9** *1/2* **Sings Poet**[15] 6363 3-7-11 **46** oh1................................ NoelGarbutt(5) 5
(Peter Hiatt) *chsd ldrs: lost pl 6f out: t.o 3f out* **66/1**
0065 **10** *25* **Dubara Reef (IRE)**[31] 5897 6-8-11 **46** oh1........................ RaulDaSilva(3) 1
(Paul Green) *led: drvn 8f out: hdd 6f out: sn lost pl: t.o 3f out: virtually p.u* **25/1**

3m 44.82s (3.02) **Going Correction** +0.05s/f (Slow)
WFA 3 from 4yo+ 12lb **10** Ran SP% **118.5**
Speed ratings (Par 101): **94,91,90,84,81 80,76,66,66,54**
toteswingers 1&2 £1.40, 1&3 £4.90, 2&3 £15.10 CSF £3.75 CT £36.47 TOTE £1.30: £1.10, £3.10, £4.10; EX 5.60 Trifecta £69.90 Pool: £2,459.01 - 26.37 winning units.
Owner Mr & Mrs William Rucker **Bred** Lady Bamford **Trained** Newmarket, Suffolk

FOCUS
A modest pace for this desperately weak handicap.

6854 BET365 H'CAP 5f 20y(P)
8:00 (8:01) (Class 4) (0-85,84) 3-Y-0+ **£4,690** (£1,395; £697; £348) **Stalls** Low

Form RPR
1631 **1** **Dangerous Age**[26] 6040 3-8-6 **70**................................ JoeFanning 10 82
(J W Hills) *trckd ldrs on outer: led over 1f out: hld on wl* **12/1**
621 **2** *3/4* **Trinityelitedotcom (IRE)**[10] 6525 3-9-5 **83**.............. RichardKingscote 5 92
(Tom Dascombe) *chsd ldr: kpt on same pce ins fnl f* **5/2**[1]
55 **3** *nk* **Exotic Isle**[40] 5585 3-9-1 **79**....................................(v[1]) JamieSpencer 9 87
(Ralph Beckett) *wnt lft s: sn mid-div: hdwy over 2f out: kpt on same pce ins fnl f* **10/1**
0345 **4** *2* **Agerzam**[9] 6575 3-9-6 **84**.......................................(b) DaneO'Neill 7 85+
(Roger Varian) *stmbld s: in rr: hdwy over 1f out: styd on: nt rch ldrs* **10/3**[2]
3306 **5** *5* **West Coast Dream**[55] 5036 6-8-11 **77**......................... MarkCoumbe(3) 6 60
(Roy Brotherton) *chsd ldr: led over 3f out: hdd over 1f out: sn wknd* **16/1**
4305 **6** *nk* **Sandfrankskipsgo**[33] 5821 4-9-4 **81**............................... ShaneKelly 8 63
(Peter Crate) *stmbld s: sn mid-div: drvn and sme hdwy over 2f out: wknd appr fnl f* **5/1**[3]
50 **7** *1/2* **Rowe Park**[64] 4707 10-9-3 **80**.....................................(p) SaleemGolam 4 60
(Linda Jewell) *prom: drvn over 2f out: wknd over 1f out* **25/1**
1300 **8** *4 1/2* **Jack My Boy (IRE)**[14] 6388 6-9-0 **80**......................... DeclanBates(3) 11 44
(David Evans) *s.i.s: bhd: nvr on terms* **40/1**

1110 **9** *1 3/4* **Royal Bajan (USA)**[11] 6506 5-9-6 **83**..........................(p) FrederikTylicki 3 41
(James Given) *led: hdd over 3f out: wknd over 1f out* **16/1**
1140 **10** *nk* **Desert Strike**[31] 5901 7-9-2 **79**...........................(p) DougieCostello 1 36
(Conor Dore) *a in rr* **25/1**
6205 **11** *6* **Foxtrot Jubilee (IRE)**[85] 4033 3-9-5 **83**........................ JimCrowley 2 18
(Ralph Beckett) *mid-div: drvn over 2f out: sn wknd* **8/1**

1m 1.65s (-0.65) **Going Correction** +0.05s/f (Slow)
WFA 3 from 4yo+ 1lb **11** Ran SP% **118.1**
Speed ratings (Par 105): **107,105,105,102,94 93,92,85,82,82 72**
toteswingers 1&2 £3.30, 1&3 £11.70, 2&3 £5.40 CSF £41.58 CT £331.32 TOTE £12.30: £3.10, £1.30, £5.50; EX 52.00 Trifecta £234.90 Pool: £2,433.53 - 7.76 winning units.
Owner R Hunter, D Klein, M Hoodless **Bred** Mrs T Brudenell **Trained** Upper Lambourn, Berks

FOCUS
A decent sprint handicap where it paid to race prominently and a gamble came unstuck.

6855 POKER AT BET365 H'CAP (DIV I) 7f 32y(P)
8:30 (8:30) (Class 5) (0-70,73) 3-Y-0+ **£2,587** (£770; £384; £192) **Stalls** High

Form RPR
3000 **1** **Dimitar (USA)**[25] 6080 4-9-2 **65**................................ JackMitchell 8 74
(Brendan Powell) *dwlt: hdwy on wd outside over 4f out: led 2f out: hld on wl* **13/2**[3]
1306 **2** *1 1/4* **Glenridding**[7] 6634 9-8-13 **62**.....................................(p) DaleSwift 7 68
(James Given) *chsd ldrs: upsides 2f out: styd on same pce ins fnl f* **10/1**
52-5 **3** *nk* **Nelina**[15] 6368 3-8-8 **60**.. ShaneKelly 2 64
(Robert Cowell) *chsd ldrs: drvn and outpcd over 4f out: hdwy 2f out: styd on wl ins fnl f to take 3rd fnl strides* **8/1**
2411 **4** *3/4* **George Fenton**[7] 6634 4-9-3 **73**............................(p) KevinStott(7) 4 76
(Richard Guest) *trckd ldrs: upsides 2f out: wknd towards fin* **7/4**[1]
0424 **5** *6* **Orpsie Boy (IRE)**[7] 6633 10-9-0 **63**................................ LukeMorris 1 50
(Ruth Carr) *mid-div: drvn over 3f out: kpt on over 1f out: nvr on terms* **9/2**[2]
0664 **6** *6* **M J Woodward**[10] 6515 4-9-1 **67**.............................. RaulDaSilva(3) 6 38
(Paul Green) *led 1f: chsd ldrs: drvn 4f out: lost pl over 2f out* **14/1**
30 **7** *2 1/2* **Ferryview Place**[12] 6475 4-8-12 **64**................(p) MichaelJMMurphy(3) 5 28
(Ian Williams) *s.i.s: outpcd and in rr: drvn over 3f out: nvr on terms* **12/1**
0-03 **8** *3* **Slim Chance (IRE)**[31] 5881 4-9-4 **67**.......................... AndrewElliott 3 23
(Simon West) *led after 1f: hdd 2f out: sn wknd* **13/2**[3]
00-0 **9** *5* **Dance With Me (IRE)**[29] 5954 4-8-9 **63**.......................... RyanTate(5) 9 5
(Jonathan Geake) *s.v.s: a detached in last* **50/1**

1m 30.4s (0.80) **Going Correction** +0.05s/f (Slow)
WFA 3 from 4yo+ 3lb **9** Ran SP% **117.7**
Speed ratings (Par 103): **97,95,95,94,87 80,77,74,68**
toteswingers 1&2 £11.50, 1&3 £38.10, 2&3 £15.60 CSF £70.46 CT £535.63 TOTE £10.30: £2.80, £2.40, £2.90; EX 80.90 Trifecta £1803.70 Part won. Pool: £2,405.04 - 0.97 winning units..
Owner M Foley **Bred** Ashbrittle Stud **Trained** Upper Lambourn, Berks

FOCUS
They went a reasonable gallop for this well-contested handicap and plenty had chances off the final bend.

6856 POKER AT BET365 H'CAP (DIV II) 7f 32y(P)
9:00 (9:00) (Class 5) (0-70,70) 3-Y-0+ **£2,587** (£770; £384; £192) **Stalls** High

Form RPR
6441 **1** **Greensward**[8] 6606 7-9-7 **70**.......................................(b) ShaneKelly 1 81
(Mike Murphy) *mid-div: hdwy on outer over 2f out: wnt 2nd jst ins fnl f: styd on to ld post* **8/1**
6501 **2** *hd* **Living The Life (IRE)**[5] 6702 3-8-11 **70**....................(b) JohnLawson(7) 3 79
(Jamie Osborne) *s.i.s: gd hdwy to trck ldrs over 4f out: led over 2f out: clr over 1f out: wknd ins fnl f: collided w running rail: hdd last stride* **1/1**[1]
3000 **3** *2 1/4* **Elspeth's Boy (USA)**[126] 2673 6-9-0 **63**......................... JoeFanning 5 67
(Philip Kirby) *chsd ldrs: 2nd over 1f out: kpt on same pce* **16/1**
5310 **4** *8* **Nordikhab (IRE)**[21] 6214 3-9-1 **67**..............................(p) NeilCallan 7 49
(Kevin Ryan) *trckd ldrs: 2nd over 2f out: wknd over 1f out* **13/2**[3]
1015 **5** *5* **The Great Gabrial**[12] 6476 4-9-4 **67**..........................(b) AidanColeman 6 36
(Ian Williams) *led after 1f: hdd over 2f out: wknd over 1f out* **10/3**[2]
2106 **6** *3 1/4* **Mambo Spirit (IRE)**[37] 5669 9-9-1 **67**............... MichaelJMMurphy(3) 8 28
(Tony Newcombe) *in rr: bhd 4f out: nvr on terms* **28/1**
3540 **7** *1 1/4* **One Way Or Another (AUS)**[12] 6476 10-8-13 **65**....... DeclanBates(3) 9 22
(David Evans) *dwlt: a in rr* **28/1**
0234 **8** *4 1/2* **Elusive Gold (IRE)**[38] 5644 3-9-1 **67**..........................(t) SebSanders 2 11
(J W Hills) *led 1f: chsd ldrs: drvn over 3f out: lost pl over 2f out: sn bhd: eased ins fnl f* **20/1**

1m 29.51s (-0.09) **Going Correction** +0.05s/f (Slow)
WFA 3 from 4yo+ 3lb **8** Ran SP% **115.1**
Speed ratings (Par 103): **102,101,99,90,84 80,79,74**
toteswingers 1&2 £1.60, 1&3 £5.20, 2&3 £7.50 CSF £16.29 CT £125.21 TOTE £10.00: £2.40, £1.10, £4.80; EX 21.90 Trifecta £325.30 Pool: £3,628.32 - 8.36 winning units.
Owner The Furlong Friends **Bred** Kincorth Investments Inc **Trained** Westoning, Beds

FOCUS
The second division of this modest handicap was not nearly as competitive as the first and it produced a tight finish.
T/Plt: £18.40 to a £1 stake. Pool: £58,795.95 - 2,328.44 winning units T/Qpdt: £7.10 to a £1 stake. Pool: £7,520.82 - 776.95 winning units WG

6863 - 6864a (Foreign Racing) - See Raceform Interactive

6333
EPSOM (L-H)
Sunday, September 29

OFFICIAL GOING: Good (7.6)
Wind: medium, half behind Weather: dry and bright

6865 WIN BIG WITH THE TOTEJACKPOT NURSERY H'CAP 7f
2:15 (2:15) (Class 4) (0-85,84) 2-Y-0 **£6,469** (£1,925; £962; £481) **Stalls** Low

Form RPR
6321 **1** **Juan Alonso (IRE)**[20] 6256 2-9-0 **77**........................... RichardHughes 8 81
(Richard Hannon) *hld up in last trio: rdn and effrt over 2f out: str run ent fnl f: led ins fnl f: kpt on wl whn pressed towards fin* **3/1**[2]
3351 **2** *hd* **Mime Dance**[17] 6334 2-8-8 **74**................................ ThomasBrown(3) 1 77
(Andrew Balding) *in tch in midfield: rdn and effrt 2f out: swtchd rt and hdwy ent fnl f: str chal wl ins fnl f: r.o but a jst hld* **11/4**[1]
343 **3** *3* **Intermath (IRE)**[6] 6697 2-9-6 **83**................................ TomQueally 2 78
(David Evans) *led briefly: t.k.h and chsd ldr for 2f: outpcd u.p 2f out: rallied and kpt on ins fnl f to snatch 3rd on last stride* **7/1**[3]
215 **4** *shd* **Floating Ballerino (IRE)**[37] 5717 2-9-0 **77**................... HarryBentley 7 72
(Olly Stevens) *t.k.h: in tch in midfield: hdwy to chse ldr 5f out: led and stl travelling strly 2f out: rdn and over 1f out: hdd ins fnl f: sn btn and wknd towards fin* **10/1**

The Form Book Flat, Raceform Ltd, Compton, RG20 6NL.

0360 **5** 1 **Street Force (USA)**[18] 6303 2-9-7 **84** RyanMoore 5 76+
(Clive Brittain) *hld up in last pair: outpcd 3f out: rallied and swtchd rt 1f out: styd on wl ins fnl f: nvr trbld ldrs* **8/1**

4656 **6** ½ **Crowdmania**[26] 6065 2-8-10 **73** (b¹) NeilCallan 4 64
(Mark Johnston) *sn led: rdn and hdd 2f out: no ex u.p 1f out: wknd ins fnl f* **8/1**

3142 **7** 1¾ **Faintly (USA)**[24] 6139 2-9-5 **82** JamesDoyle 6 68
(Amanda Perrett) *t.k.h: hld up wl in tch in midfield: rdn and outpcd ent fnl 2f: wknd 1f out* **10/1**

3325 **8** ½ **Solo Hunter**[37] 5693 2-8-7 **70** CathyGannon 3 55
(David Evans) *bustled along leaving stalls: sn shuffled bk towards rr: in last pair and rdn over 3f out: sn outpcd: rallied 1f out: styng on but n.d whn nt enough room ins fnl f* **16/1**

1m 25.4s (2.10) **Going Correction** +0.35s/f (Good) **8** Ran SP% **110.5**
Speed ratings (Par 97): **102,101,98,98,97 96,94,93**
toteswingers 1&2 £2.10, 1&3 £4.40, 2&3 £4.70 CSF £10.83 CT £47.71 TOTE £3.20: £1.40, £1.70, £2.20; EX 11.60 Trifecta £45.60 Pool: £2601.28 - 42.71 winning units.
Owner J N Reus & Mrs Anna Doyle **Bred** Churchtown House Stud & Liam Butler **Trained** East Everleigh, Wilts

FOCUS
The rail was out seven yards from the 1m start to the winning post, adding 21 yards to races of 1m+, and 15 yards to 7f races. There was a smattering of rain overnight and, after riding in the first race, Richard Hughes felt the ground was on the soft side of good.

6866 ARC DE TRIOMPHE BETTING AT TOTEPOOL.COM CONDITIONS STKS (THE SUNDAY £5K BONUS RACE) 1m 114y
2:45 (2:48) (Class 3) 2-Y-O **£6,225** (£1,864; £932; £466; £233) **Stalls** Low

Form RPR
3 **1** **Scotland (GER)**[16] 6355 2-8-11 0 JimCrowley 2 95+
(Andrew Balding) *stdd s: hld up in rr: hdwy on outer to press ldrs travelling wl over 2f out: effrt and edgd lft down camber over 1f out: led 1f out: r.o wl and drew clr fnl 100yds: readily* **9/2**[3]

311 **2** 2½ **Day Of Conquest**[18] 6314 2-9-3 95 RichardHughes 6 96
(Richard Hannon) *chsd ldr: rdn and effrt to chal ent fnl 2f: led over 1f out: edgd lft and hdd 1f out: outpcd and btn fnl 100yds: hld on for 2nd cl home* **9/4**[2]

5365 **3** nk **Lone Warrior (IRE)**[18] 6314 2-8-11 94 (p) TomQueally 3 91
(David Evans) *led: rdn wl over 2f out: hdd over 1f out: unable qck whn short of room and hmpd jst ins fnl f: swtchd rt and rallied fnl 100yds* **10/1**

613 **4** 2¼ **Speedy Approach**[43] 5530 2-9-0 93 JamieSpencer 5 89
(Michael Bell) *hld up in 4th: clsd on ldrs 3f out: rdn and pressing ldrs whn pushed lft and hmpd over 1f out: one pce and no imp after* **2/1**[1]

2024 **5** 1 **Riverboat Springs (IRE)**[22] 6195 2-9-0 99 MartinHarley 1 86
(Mick Channon) *chsd ldng pair tl rdn and dropped last 3f out: wknd u.p ent fnl f* **9/2**[3]

1m 48.83s (2.73) **Going Correction** +0.35s/f (Good) **5** Ran SP% **109.6**
Speed ratings (Par 99): **101,98,98,96,95**
CSF £14.79 TOTE £5.10: £1.80, £1.80; EX 13.80 Trifecta £67.60 Pool: £2454.91 - 27.21 winning units.
Owner Mrs Fitri Hay **Bred** Dr Christoph Berglar **Trained** Kingsclere, Hants

FOCUS
A reasonable conditions event and it went to the least-exposed runner in the field.

6867 TOTEQUADPOT FOUR PLACES IN FOUR RACES H'CAP 1m 114y
3:20 (3:21) (Class 3) (0-90,87) 3-Y-O
£9,337 (£2,796; £1,398; £699; £349; £175) **Stalls** Low

Form RPR
2121 **1** **Thouwra (IRE)**[11] 6538 3-9-7 **87** (p) MickaelBarzalona 6 101+
(Saeed bin Suroor) *in tch in last: clsd to trck ldrs 2f out: swtchd lft: rdn and qcknd to ld over 1f out: sn clr and r.o strly: readily* **6/4**[1]

1356 **2** 3½ **Melvin The Grate (IRE)**[59] 4922 3-9-0 **80** DavidProbert 1 85
(Andrew Balding) *t.k.h: hld up wl in tch: rdn to ld over 2f out: hdd over 1f out: no ch w wnr but hld for 2nd fnl f* **7/2**[3]

5200 **3** ½ **Dark Emerald (IRE)**[6] 6694 3-9-5 **85** (v) SebSanders 2 89
(Brendan Powell) *t.k.h: hld up in tch: swtchd rt and effrt over 2f out: no ch w wnr but battling for 2nd fnl f: kpt on* **14/1**

0631 **4** 3¾ **Tobacco Road (IRE)**[16] 6356 3-9-5 **85** PatDobbs 4 80
(Richard Hannon) *taken down early: chsd ldrs: rdn and effrt over 2f out: outpcd and btn ent fnl f: wknd* **11/4**[2]

3652 **5** 9 **Strong Conviction**[17] 6335 3-8-7 **73** oh1 SamHitchcott 3 48
(Mick Channon) *led: rdn and hdd over 2f out: lost pl over 1f out: sn wknd* **8/1**

3552 **6** 1¼ **Hartwright**[15] 6410 3-8-10 **76** TomQueally 5 48
(Michael Bell) *chsd ldr: ev ch over 2f out: sn rdn and unable qck: wknd over 1f out* **20/1**

1m 45.77s (-0.33) **Going Correction** +0.35s/f (Good) **6** Ran SP% **111.4**
Speed ratings (Par 105): **115,111,111,108,100 99**
toteswingers 1&2 £1.70, 1&3 £4.70, 2&3 £5.90 CSF £6.94 TOTE £2.30: £1.30, £2.70; EX 7.60 Trifecta £35.00 Pool: £2949.25 - 63.03 winning units.
Owner Godolphin **Bred** Darley **Trained** Newmarket, Suffolk

FOCUS
Probably not a strong race for the grade, but an improving winner.

6868 TOTEPOOL HOME OF KING SIZE POOLS H'CAP 1m 2f 18y
3:55 (3:55) (Class 3) (0-95,92) 3-Y-O+
£12,450 (£3,728; £1,864; £932; £466; £234) **Stalls** Low

Form RPR
0000 **1** **Weapon Of Choice (IRE)**[9] 6596 5-9-1 **83** TomQueally 9 92
(Stuart Kittow) *chsd ldrs: effrt to ld 2f out: sn rdn: edgd rt 1f out: r.o wl and a holding rivals ins fnl f* **7/1**[3]

5420 **2** ¾ **Benzanno (IRE)**[8] 6638 4-9-8 **90** DavidProbert 1 98
(Andrew Balding) *stdd s: t.k.h: hld up in tch in midfield: switching out rt 3f out: rdn and hdwy to chse ldr over 1f out: kpt on but a hld ins fnl f* **5/1**[2]

220 **3** hd **Aussie Reigns (IRE)**[17] 6332 3-9-4 **92** (v) JimCrowley 10 99
(William Knight) *stdd s: hld up in tch in rr: hdwy u.p over 1f out: styd on wl ins fnl f: nt rch ldrs* **7/1**[3]

2135 **4** 1 **Cashpoint**[63] 4798 8-8-12 **80** JamieSpencer 2 85
(Ian Williams) *stdd after s: hld up in last pair: rdn ent fnl 2f: stl plenty to do and hdwy over 1f out: styng on whn swtchd lft ins fnl f: r.o: nt rch ldrs* **8/1**

0530 **5** 3 **Cayuga**[52] 5190 4-8-7 **80** OisinMurphy(5) 7 79
(Brett Johnson) *wl in tch in midfield: rdn and effrt over 2f out: 3rd and edgd lft ent fnl f: wknd ins fnl f* **12/1**

6166 **6** ¾ **Broughton (GER)**[35] 5792 3-9-4 **92** NeilCallan 4 90
(Mark Johnston) *chsd ldr: ev ch and rdn ent fnl 2f: unable qck and sltly hmpd ent fnl f: wknd ins fnl f* **9/2**[1]

4263 **7** nk **Takeitfromalady (IRE)**[12] 6490 4-8-10 **78** (b) KierenFox 8 75
(Lee Carter) *dwlt: sn rcvrd and in tch in midfield: rdn and unable qck over 2f out: styd on same pce fnl 2f* **25/1**

5354 **8** 4½ **Verse Of Love**[14] 6427 4-9-1 **83** CathyGannon 5 71
(David Evans) *led: rdn and pressed over 2f out: hdd 2f out: no ex 1f out: wknd 1f out* **8/1**

414- **9** 5 **Ex Oriente (IRE)**[386] 6033 4-9-5 **87** AdamBeschizza 3 65
(Stuart Williams) *hld up in last trio: rdn and no hdwy over 2f out: wl btn fnl 2f* **20/1**

-302 **10** 1 **Beedee**[46] 5401 3-8-13 **87** RichardHughes 11 63
(Richard Hannon) *in tch in midfield on outer: rdn and struggling over 3f out: lost pl and bhd 2f out* **5/1**[2]

2m 12.31s (2.61) **Going Correction** +0.35s/f (Good)
WFA 3 from 4yo+ 6lb **10** Ran SP% **115.0**
Speed ratings (Par 107): **103,102,102,101,99 98,98,94,90,89**
toteswingers 1&2 £8.80, 1&3 £12.20, 2&3 £6.50 CSF £41.33 CT £255.26 TOTE £9.60: £2.70, £2.10, £2.50; EX 43.10 Trifecta £296.20 Pool: £3123.79 - 7.90 winning units.
Owner Chris & David Stam **Bred** Stone Ridge Farm **Trained** Blackborough, Devon
■ Stewards' Enquiry : Oisin Murphy caution: careless riding.

FOCUS
A fair, competitive handicap.

6869 ARC DAY SUPERSCOOP6 AT TOTEPOOL.COM APPRENTICES' DERBY H'CAP 1m 4f 10y
4:30 (4:31) (Class 4) (0-80,79) 3-Y-O+ **£6,469** (£1,925; £962; £481) **Stalls** Centre

Form RPR
31-0 **1** **Omar Khayyam**[136] 2385 4-9-11 **79** (t) OisinMurphy(3) 12 92
(Andrew Balding) *hld up in midfield: hdwy over 2f out: rdn to ld wl over 1f out: in command and r.o wl fnl f: rdn out* **8/1**

2143 **2** 1¾ **Certavi (IRE)**[17] 6336 4-9-6 **71** WilliamTwiston-Davies 14 81
(Brendan Powell) *hld up in tch in last quartet: rdn and hdwy over 2f out: chsd wnr over 1f out: edgd lft and styd on same pce ins fnl f* **5/1**[2]

0036 **3** 4 **Saint Helena (IRE)**[17] 6336 5-9-4 **72** NathanAlison(3) 7 76
(Harry Dunlop) *s.i.s: hld up in rr: rdn and hdwy on outer 2f out: chsd clr ldng pair 1f out: kpt on but no threat to ldrs* **16/1**

0552 **4** 4 **Spring Tonic**[26] 6080 4-9-5 **73** JackDuern(3) 1 70
(Simon Dow) *mde most tl rdn and hdd wl over 1f out: sn outpcd and btn: wknd but hld on for modest 4th fnl f* **14/1**

0404 **5** ½ **Freddy Q (IRE)**[17] 6336 4-9-5 **70** RobertTart 10 66
(Roger Teal) *in tch in midfield: rdn and effrt over 2f out: outpcd and wl btn over 1f out: plugged on fnl f* **10/1**

4341 **6** ½ **Getaway Car**[8] 6658 3-9-2 **75** (p) ThomasBrown 4 71
(Gerard Butler) *rn in snatches towards rr: last and rdn 6f out: sn outpcd: styd on past btn horses and swtchd lft 1f out: kpt on: nvr trbld ldrs* **6/1**[3]

5244 **7** ¾ **Jack Who's He (IRE)**[19] 6280 4-9-4 **74** ThomasGarner(5) 11 68
(William Muir) *w ldr tl rdn and lost pl over 2f out: wknd over 1f out* **10/1**

105 **8** 2¼ **Xinbama (IRE)**[34] 5824 4-9-7 **77** (t) ShelleyBirkett(5) 9 68
(J W Hills) *hld up in midfield: rdn and lost pl over 2f out: n.d after* **14/1**

0235 **9** ¾ **May Be Some Time**[46] 5390 5-9-2 **67** MichaelJMMurphy 2 57
(Stuart Kittow) *chsd ldrs: rdn and effrt on inner over 2f out: outpcd 2f out: wknd over 1f out* **16/1**

-012 **10** ½ **Young Dottie**[41] 5587 7-8-11 **69** SophieRalston(7) 5 58
(Pat Phelan) *t.k.h: chsd ldrs: wnt 2nd briefly over 2f out: sn btn: wknd qckly over 1f out* **20/1**

1400 **11** 3 **Laughing Jack**[21] 6236 5-9-7 **75** GeorgeDowning(3) 3 59
(Tony Carroll) *chsd ldrs: rdn and lost pl 3f out: bhd over 1f out* **25/1**

1641 **P** **Bee Jay Kay**[35] 5791 3-8-9 **71** PhilipPrince(3) 6
(Brian Ellison) *hld up in last quartet: rdn and struggling over 5f out: lost action and p.u over 3f out: dismntd* **11/4**[1]

2m 41.36s (2.46) **Going Correction** +0.35s/f (Good)
WFA 3 from 4yo+ 8lb **12** Ran SP% **120.6**
Speed ratings (Par 105): **105,103,101,98,98 97,97,95,95,95 93,**
toteswingers 1&2 £5.50, 1&3 £26.10, 2&3 £18.60 CSF £48.61 CT £639.71 TOTE £8.40: £3.10, £2.00, £5.70; EX 51.00 Trifecta £887.60 Pool: £4057.68 - 3.42 winning units.
Owner J L C Pearce **Bred** Fittocks Stud **Trained** Kingsclere, Hants

FOCUS
A fair running of the Apprentices' Derby and, with the pace good, they finished strung out.

6870 TOTEPOOL SIR DAVID PROSSER MAIDEN STKS 1m 2f 18y
5:00 (5:00) (Class 5) 3-Y-O **£3,234** (£962; £481; £240) **Stalls** Low

Form RPR
0- **1** **Jakey (IRE)**[319] 7705 3-9-5 0 RichardHughes 2 78
(Pat Phelan) *t.k.h: chsd ldrs: stl travelling wl but nt clr run 2f out: swtchd lft and rdn to ld 1f out: r.o wl and sn in command: readily* **10/1**

42 **2** 2¼ **Song And Dance Man**[120] 2885 3-9-5 0 (b¹) RyanMoore 6 73
(William Haggas) *dwlt: in tch towards rr: rdn and hdwy to ld over 2f out: hdd and nt qckn u.p 1f out: edgd lft and one pce fnl f* **5/4**[1]

2 **3** 3¼ **Dark Amber**[30] 5959 3-9-1 0 ow1 SebSanders 4 63
(Brendan Powell) *stdd s: hld up in tch in rr: rdn and hdwy on outer ent fnl 2f: chal over 1f out: btn 1f out: wknd ins fnl f* **9/2**[3]

40 **4** ½ **Mansoreen**[67] 4633 3-9-5 0 MickaelBarzalona 1 66
(Saeed bin Suroor) *in tch: effrt on inner over 2f out: outpcd and btn over 1f out: plugged on fnl f* **9/4**[2]

6244 **5** 10 **Qibtee (FR)**[35] 5789 3-9-5 61 SamHitchcott 3 46
(Mick Channon) *rdn along leaving stalls: led: rdn and hdd over 3f out: wknd u.p over 1f out: bhd and eased wl ins fnl f* **16/1**

0 **6** 5 **White Peak (USA)**[10] 6555 3-9-5 0 NeilCallan 5 36
(Mark Johnston) *chsd ldr tl rdn to ld over 3f out: hdd over 2f out: lost pl and wknd over 1f out: wl bhd and eased ins fnl f* **14/1**

2m 12.06s (2.36) **Going Correction** +0.35s/f (Good) **6** Ran SP% **115.0**
Speed ratings (Par 101): **104,102,99,99,91 87**
toteswingers 1&2 £3.10, 1&3 £3.60, 2&3 £1.80 CSF £23.97 TOTE £8.00: £3.40, £1.40; EX 32.60 Trifecta £57.00 Pool: £3362.57 - 44.18 winning units.
Owner Allen B Pope **Bred** Cliveden Stud Ltd **Trained** Epsom, Surrey

FOCUS
A weak maiden, but an interesting winner.

6871 COLLECT TOTEPOOL WINNINGS AT BETFRED SHOPS H'CAP 7f
5:30 (5:33) (Class 4) (0-85,92) 3-Y-O+ **£6,469** (£1,925; £962; £481) **Stalls** Low

Form RPR
221 **1** **Iptisam**[43] 5512 4-9-0 **78** NeilCallan 14 88+
(James Tate) *travelled strly: w ldr tl led over 3f out: sn clr: rdn 2f out: stl 6 l clr over 1f out: coming bk to field but a gng to hold on fnl f* **6/1**[3]

1000 **2** ¾ **Intimidate**[10] 6571 3-8-13 **80**..........(v[1]) JamesDoyle 9 87
(Jeremy Noseda) *hld up off the pce towards rr: hdwy but stl plenty to do wl over 1f out: swtchd lft and wnt 3rd over 1f out: chsd clr wnr ins fnl f: r.o wl but nvr quite getting to wnr* **20/1**

5421 **3** 1 ¼ **Kyllachy Rise**[12] 6488 3-9-11 **92**.......... RichardHughes 1 96
(Richard Hannon) *chsd ldrs and clr in ldng quartet: chsd clr ldr over 2f out: no imp and lost 2nd jst ins fnl f: kpt on fnl 100yds: no threat to wnr* **5/2**[1]

1412 **4** 1 **Lunar Deity**[19] 6274 4-9-5 **83**.......... RyanMoore 7 85
(Eve Johnson Houghton) *racd off the pce in midfield: rdn and effrt on inner over 2f out: styd on u.p fnl f: no threat to wnr* **3/1**[2]

4051 **5** 2 ¼ **Prince Regal**[17] 6338 3-8-10 **77**.......... JimCrowley 2 72
(Alan Jarvis) *chsd ldrs and clr in ldng quartet: rdn and outpcd in 3rd 2f out: plugged on same pce after* **14/1**

0032 **6** ½ **My Kingdom (IRE)**[17] 6337 7-8-13 **77**..........(t) JamieSpencer 12 72
(Stuart Williams) *wl off the pce towards rr: rdn and no imp over 2f out: hdwy and hanging lft ent fnl f: kpt on: nvr trbld ldrs* **7/1**

6060 **7** hd **Operation Chariot (IRE)**[43] 5510 3-8-7 **79**.......... OisinMurphy(5) 10 72
(Andrew Balding) *racd off the pce in midfield: rdn over 2f out: no imp tl kpt on steadily ins fnl f: no threat to ldrs* **16/1**

0141 **8** ¾ **Olney Lass**[13] 6461 6-8-5 **72**.......... SimonPearce(3) 11 64
(Lydia Pearce) *off the pce in midfield: rdn and effrt over 2f out: sme hdwy over 1f out: kpt on: nvr trbld ldrs* **25/1**

1-06 **9** 1 ½ **Conry (IRE)**[8] 6648 7-9-0 **83**.......... GeorgeDowning(5) 15 71
(Ian Williams) *wnt rt s and slowly away: wl bhd in rr: sme hdwy and swtchd lft over 1f out: kpt on: nvr trbld ldrs* **25/1**

1021 **10** 1 ¾ **Brocklebank (IRE)**[17] 6337 4-9-0 **83**.......... JackDuern(5) 8 66
(Simon Dow) *t.k.h: hld up wl off the pce in rr: rdn and effrt 2f out: n.d* **8/1**

5300 **11** 1 ½ **Meandmyshadow**[11] 6516 5-8-9 **73**.......... CathyGannon 4 52
(Alan Brown) *led tl over 3f out: rdn and sn outpcd and wl btn 2f out: wknd over 1f out* **33/1**

5503 **12** 8 **Jackie Love (IRE)**[13] 6462 5-8-2 **71** oh26.......... NoelGarbutt(5) 5 29
(Olivia Maylam) *s.i.s: a bhd* **100/1**

1m 24.78s (1.48) **Going Correction** +0.35s/f (Good)
WFA 3 from 4yo+ 3lb **12** Ran SP% **120.4**
Speed ratings (Par 105): **105,104,102,101,99 98,98,97,95,93 91,82**
toteswingers 1&2 £21.40, 1&3 £4.20, 2&3 £12.40 CSF £126.00 CT £386.71 TOTE £6.40: £2.40, £6.10, £1.60; EX 148.90 Trifecta £850.60 Pool: £2756.35 - 2.43 winning units.
Owner Saeed Manana **Bred** Darley **Trained** Newmarket, Suffolk

FOCUS
A fair handicap and the winner took this with a good deal more authority than the margin suggests.
T/Jkpt: Not won. T/Plt: £70.50 to a £1 stake. Pool: £89,837.46 - 929.36 winning units T/Qpdt: £29.00 to a £1 stake. Pool: £6104.42 - 155.45 winning units SP

6464 MUSSELBURGH (R-H)
Sunday, September 29

OFFICIAL GOING: Good to firm (8.1)
Wind: Breezy, half behind Weather: Sunny

6872 ROYAL SCOTS CLUB NURSERY H'CAP — 5f
2:00 (2:01) (Class 6) (0-65,70) 2-Y-O £2,587 (£770; £384; £192) Stalls High

Form RPR

606 **1** **Gulland Rock**[13] 6477 2-9-0 **58**.......... DougieCostello 8 59
(William Muir) *mde all: rdn 2f out: hld on wl fnl f* **11/4**[1]

240 **2** nk **Baltic Spirit (IRE)**[7] 6663 2-9-5 **63**.......... TomEaves 7 63
(Keith Dalgleish) *chsd ldng gp: effrt and hdwy over 1f out: styd on wl to take 2nd cl home* **10/1**

0006 **3** nse **Saffire Song**[40] 5610 2-9-0 **58**.......... SilvestreDeSousa 2 58
(Alan Bailey) *cl up: effrt and rdn 2f out: ev ch ins fnl f: kpt on: hld nr fin* **13/2**

4444 **4** 1 ¾ **Princess Myla (IRE)**[10] 6561 2-9-1 **59**..........(p) LeeTopliss 1 53
(Paul Midgley) *dwlt: sn in tch on outside: rdn 2f out: kpt on same pce ins fnl f* **14/1**

0021 **5** hd **Tinsill**[11] 6511 2-9-5 **70**..........(v) DanielleMooney(7) 3 63
(Nigel Tinkler) *hld up: hdwy over 1f out: shkn up and kpt on ins fnl f* **9/1**

4143 **6** 1 ½ **Bountiful Forest**[13] 6467 2-8-13 **60**.......... JasonHart(3) 4 48
(Noel Wilson) *in tch: n.m.r over 2f out: effrt and edgd lft over 1f out: outpcd ins fnl f* **11/1**

4466 **7** 1 ¼ **Straight Gin**[13] 6467 2-8-6 **50**..........(p) BarryMcHugh 5 33
(Alan Berry) *chsd ldrs: rdn over 2f out: wknd ins fnl f* **28/1**

0136 **8** 6 **Local Flier**[37] 5710 2-9-1 **64**.......... JacobButterfield(5) 9 25
(Brian Ellison) *chsd ldrs tl rdn and lost pl over 2f out: sn struggling* **7/2**[2]

551 **9** 1 ¾ **White Flag**[19] 6286 2-8-10 **61**.......... RachelRichardson(7) 10 16
(Tim Easterby) *bhd and outpcd: no ch fr 1/2-way* **6/1**[3]

59.92s (-0.48) **Going Correction** -0.25s/f (Firm) **9** Ran SP% **114.0**
Speed ratings (Par 93): **93,92,92,89,89 86,84,75,72**
toteswingers 1&2 £10.70, 1&3 £4.90, 2&3 £9.40 CSF £30.74 CT £163.29 TOTE £4.10: £1.40, £3.30, £2.30; EX 32.60 Trifecta £209.60 Pool: £2291.66 - 8.19 winning units.
Owner C L A Edginton & K Mercer **Bred** Whitsbury Manor Stud **Trained** Lambourn, Berks

FOCUS
Home bend moved out 2m. Largely exposed types in this 5f nursery and one of two making their handicap debut prevailed.

6873 BRITISH STALLION STUDS EBF MAIDEN STKS (THE SUNDAY £5K BONUS RACE) — 7f 30y
2:30 (2:30) (Class 4) 2-Y-O £4,204 (£1,251; £625; £312) Stalls Low

Form RPR

56 **1** **Neuf Des Coeurs**[47] 5364 2-9-0 0.......... PJMcDonald 4 67
(Keith Dalgleish) *chsd clr ldng pair: rdn 3f out: rallied over 1f out: led ins fnl f: drvn out* **25/1**

623 **2** nk **Porthos Du Vallon**[18] 6299 2-9-5 67.......... TomEaves 1 71
(Keith Dalgleish) *led to over 2f out: rallied and regained ld briefly ins fnl f: kpt on: jst hld* **16/1**

4 **3** ½ **Wealth (IRE)**[43] 5508 2-9-5 0.......... TonyHamilton 5 70
(Richard Fahey) *in tch: effrt and hdwy 2f out: kpt on ins fnl f: hld nr fin* **8/11**[1]

343 **4** 1 ¼ **Major Surprise (USA)**[17] 6340 2-9-5 71.......... DanielTudhope 2 66
(K R Burke) *pressed ldr: led and rdn over 2f out: hung lft over 1f out: hdd ins fnl f: one pce* **9/4**[2]

5 **5** 17 **Maracuja** 2-9-0 0.......... JoeFanning 3 17
(Mark Johnston) *dwlt: t.k.h in rr: rdn and rn green over 2f out: sn struggling: t.o* **7/1**[3]

1m 29.95s (0.95) **Going Correction** -0.25s/f (Firm) **5** Ran SP% **110.9**
Speed ratings (Par 97): **84,83,83,81,62**
CSF £271.64 TOTE £14.40: £3.70, £5.50; EX 64.20 Trifecta £213.70 Pool: £2119.87 - 7.43 winning units.
Owner C J Colgan **Bred** Conor J Colgan **Trained** Carluke, S Lanarks

FOCUS
A modest maiden with four horses almost in a line inside the final furlong.

6874 RSP CONSULTING ENGINEERS H'CAP — 7f 30y
3:00 (3:00) (Class 4) (0-85,85) 3-Y-O £5,175 (£1,540; £769; £384) Stalls Low

Form RPR

1512 **1** **Just Paul (IRE)**[39] 5642 3-8-5 **72**.......... DeclanCannon(3) 2 80
(Philip Kirby) *in tch on ins: effrt and hdwy over 1f out: led ins fnl f: kpt on strly* **9/2**[2]

2512 **2** 1 ½ **Mishaal (IRE)**[16] 6367 3-8-8 **72**.......... BarryMcHugh 7 76
(Michael Herrington) *taken early to post: dwlt: plld hrd in rr: effrt whn n.m.r over 2f out and over 1f out: styd on wl fnl f: tk 2nd towards fin* **7/1**[3]

1222 **3** hd **Future Reference (IRE)**[22] 6204 3-9-7 **85**..........(t) SilvestreDeSousa 4 88
(Saeed bin Suroor) *led: hrd pressed and rdn 2f out: hdd ins fnl f: kpt on same pce* **2/1**[1]

2300 **4** hd **Lazarus Bell**[12] 6495 3-8-13 **80**.......... PaulPickard(3) 8 83
(Alan Brown) *t.k.h: prom on outside: hdwy to chal over 2f out to ins fnl f: kpt on same pce nr fin* **22/1**

5003 **5** ¾ **Capo Rosso (IRE)**[9] 6608 3-9-7 **85**..........(p) StephenCraine 11 86
(Tom Dascombe) *chsd ldrs: rdn over 2f out: kpt on same pce ins fnl f* **10/1**

0213 **6** ¾ **Funding Deficit (IRE)**[74] 4402 3-8-8 **72**.......... GrahamGibbons 9 71
(David Barron) *awkward s: t.k.h: hdwy whn n.m.r over 1f out: kpt on ins fnl f* **20/1**

0-12 **7** ¾ **Sherzam**[12] 6495 3-9-2 **80**.......... PJMcDonald 1 77
(Michael Dods) *chsd ldrs: rdn over 2f out: outpcd fnl f* **8/1**

-003 **8** 1 **Patrona Ciana (FR)**[15] 6410 3-9-1 **79**..........(v[1]) DanielTudhope 3 73
(David O'Meara) *t.k.h: prom: effrt on outside over 2f out: wknd fnl f* **28/1**

3110 **9** 2 ½ **Rocket Ronnie (IRE)**[30] 5944 3-8-13 **84**.......... JordanNason(7) 10 71
(David Nicholls) *hld up: rdn over 2f out: no imp fr over 1f out* **10/1**

1310 **10** 8 **Someone's Darling**[7] 6665 3-8-9 **73**.......... GrahamLee 6 39
(Jim Goldie) *stmbld sn after s: t.k.h: hld up on outside: struggling over 2f out: sn btn* **14/1**

2100 **11** 11 **Rapscallion Deep (IRE)**[32] 5878 3-8-0 **67**.......... RaulDaSilva(3) 5 3
(Kevin Ryan) *taken early to post: t.k.h in midfield: lost pl 1/2-way: sn struggling* **16/1**

1m 28.23s (-0.77) **Going Correction** -0.25s/f (Firm) **11** Ran SP% **118.4**
Speed ratings (Par 103): **94,92,92,91,90 90,89,88,85,76 63**
toteswingers 1&2 £8.10, 1&3 £4.00, 2&3 £5.10 CSF £35.32 CT £84.06 TOTE £5.30: £1.20, £2.90, £1.40; EX 35.20 Trifecta £124.30 Pool: £1808.95 - 10.91 winning units.
Owner Mr and Mrs Paul Chapman **Bred** Oghill House Stud **Trained** Middleham, N Yorks

FOCUS
A competitive 7f handicap and not a lot between the first eight at the line.

6875 CHOOSE EBF NOMINATED FILLIES' H'CAP — 1m
3:35 (3:35) (Class 3) (0-90,88) 3-Y-O+ £8,403 (£2,516; £1,258; £629; £314; £157) Stalls Low

Form RPR

046 **1** **Coincidently**[4] 6758 3-8-5 **72**.......... SilvestreDeSousa 5 80
(Alan Bailey) *chsd ldrs: led 2f out: rdn and edgd rt over 1f out: styd on strly fnl f* **13/2**

0502 **2** 1 ¼ **Light Rose (IRE)**[13] 6475 3-8-6 **73**.......... JoeFanning 2 79+
(Mark Johnston) *t.k.h: trckd ldrs: n.m.r over 2f out: effrt whn hmpd appr fnl f: hdwy to chse wnr ins fnl f: kpt on* **6/1**[3]

1304 **3** ½ **Elle Woods (IRE)**[8] 6625 3-9-5 **86**..........(p) GrahamLee 1 90
(Michael Dods) *in tch on ins: effrt 2f out: n.m.r briefly ins fnl f: r.o towards fin* **12/5**[1]

0500 **4** 2 **How's Life**[42] 5561 3-9-7 **88**.......... DavidAllan 8 87
(Tim Easterby) *led: rdn and hdd 2f out: edgd lft appr fnl f: nt qckn* **16/1**

3320 **5** 2 ¼ **Simply Shining (IRE)**[22] 6210 3-8-8 **75**..........(p) TonyHamilton 4 69
(Richard Fahey) *chsd ldrs: effrt over 2f out: edgd rt and outpcd over 1f out* **9/1**

1160 **6** nk **Oddysey (IRE)**[57] 5014 4-9-10 **87**.......... LeeTopliss 7 80
(Michael Dods) *hld up in tch: rdn over 2f out: outpcd over 1f out* **14/1**

2523 **7** shd **Hot Rod Mamma (IRE)**[18] 6300 6-9-3 **80**.......... PJMcDonald 3 73
(Dianne Sayer) *s.i.s: t.k.h in rr: stdy hdwy over 2f out: shkn up and no imp over 1f out* **9/2**[2]

4330 **8** ¾ **Kickingthelilly**[16] 6360 4-9-0 **77**.......... ChrisCatlin 6 68
(Rae Guest) *bhd: rdn and effrt over 2f out: no imp* **8/1**

4602 **9** 12 **Act Your Shoe Size**[6] 6683 4-9-1 **78**.......... TomEaves 9 42
(Keith Dalgleish) *hld up on outside: rdn along over 2f out: sn btn* **18/1**

1m 39.52s (-1.68) **Going Correction** -0.25s/f (Firm)
WFA 3 from 4yo+ 4lb **9** Ran SP% **114.1**
Speed ratings (Par 104): **98,96,96,94,92 91,91,90,78**
toteswingers 1&2 £8.70, 1&3 £6.10, 2&3 £4.50 CSF £44.58 CT £120.14 TOTE £10.00: £3.00, £2.80, £1.20; EX 58.70 Trifecta £497.70 Pool: £2064.35 - 3.11 winning units.
Owner Tom Mohan & AJH **Bred** Langton Stud **Trained** Newmarket, Suffolk
■ Stewards' Enquiry : Silvestre De Sousa one-day ban: careless riding (Oct 13)

FOCUS
A competitive and quite valuable fillies' handicap and the younger generation dominated. It paid to race up with the pace.

6876 THOMSON HOLIDAYS H'CAP — 1m 5f
4:10 (4:10) (Class 3) (0-90,90) 3-Y-O+ £10,997 (£3,272; £1,635; £817) Stalls Low

Form RPR

1110 **1** **Alcaeus**[49] 5326 3-9-5 **90**.......... LukeMorris 2 100+
(Sir Mark Prescott Bt) *t.k.h: trckd ldrs: led over 2f out: rdn and edgd rt over 1f out: styd on wl fnl f* **15/8**[1]

4033 **2** ½ **Cosmic Sun**[21] 6239 7-8-11 **73**..........(t) TonyHamilton 6 80
(Richard Fahey) *hld up in tch: rdn over 2f out: hdwy to chse wnr over 1f out: edgd rt: kpt on fnl f* **8/1**

1504 **3** 1 **Hawdyerwheesht**[8] 6626 5-9-3 **79**.......... DanielTudhope 5 84
(Jim Goldie) *s.i.s: hld up: stdy hdwy over 2f out: rdn over 1f out: kpt on ins fnl f* **10/1**

2560 **4** nse **Scatter Dice (IRE)**[9] 6585 4-9-10 **86**.......... JoeFanning 1 91
(Mark Johnston) *prom: effrt and drvn over 2f out: kpt on same pce fnl f* **4/1**[2]

The Form Book Flat, Raceform Ltd, Compton, RG20 6NL.

-002 5 7 **Muntasir (IRE)**[47] 5374 4-9-7 **83**................................ SilvestreDeSousa 3 77
(Saeed bin Suroor) *hld up in tch: rdn and edgd rt over 2f out: hdwy whn nt clr run wl over 1f out: sn btn* **5/1**[3]

2266 6 2 1/4 **Merchant Of Dubai**[13] 6466 8-8-13 **75**...........................(v) GrahamLee 4 66
(Jim Goldie) *led: rdn and hdd over 2f out: wknd over 1f out* **16/1**

1020 7 4 **Guising**[15] 6394 4-9-4 **85**.. ConnorBeasley(5) 7 70
(David Brown) *cl up: drvn over 2f out: sn wknd* **7/1**

2m 46.41s (-5.59) **Going Correction** -0.25s/f (Firm) course record
WFA 3 from 4yo+ 9lb **7** Ran SP% **110.0**
Speed ratings (Par 107): **107,106,106,106,101 100,97**
toteswingers 1&2 £2.60, 1&3 £5.90, 2&3 £1.30 CSF £16.18 TOTE £2.60: £1.50, £3.90; EX 17.30 Trifecta £79.70 Pool: £2665.00 - 25.04 winning units.
Owner Ne'er Do Wells IV **Bred** Miss K Rausing **Trained** Newmarket, Suffolk

FOCUS
A good-class staying handicap run at a sound pace.

6877 STEADFAST SCOTLAND H'CAP 1m 1f
4:45 (4:46) (Class 5) (0-70,70) 3-Y-0+ **£3,234** (£962; £481; £240) **Stalls** Low

Form RPR

4400 1 **Berlusca (IRE)**[18] 6306 4-9-7 **67**.................................... DanielTudhope 6 79
(David O'Meara) *hld up: smooth hdwy over 2f out: rdn to ld ins fnl f: sn clr* **12/1**

2613 2 5 **Tectonic (IRE)**[5] 6730 4-9-10 **70**..(p) TomEaves 7 71
(Keith Dalgleish) *hld up in tch: gd hdwy on outside to ld over 2f out: rdn and edgd rt over 1f out: hdd ins fnl f: no ch w wnr* **4/1**[3]

5054 3 2 3/4 **Royal Straight**[13] 6468 8-9-5 **65**..................................(t) PJMcDonald 3 60
(Linda Perratt) *in tch: hdwy and ev ch over 2f out: sn rdn: outpcd fnl f* **12/1**

0520 4 7 **Tussie Mussie**[22] 6210 3-9-3 **68**..(b) JoeFanning 8 49
(Mark Johnston) *t.k.h: cl up: effrt and ev ch over 2f out: sn rdn: wknd over 1f out* **7/2**[2]

4451 5 3 3/4 **Plunder**[8] 6657 3-9-2 **67**.. TonyHamilton 4 39
(Richard Ford) *t.k.h: cl up: rdn and ev ch over 2f out: wknd over 1f out* **3/1**[1]

-606 6 1/2 **Up Ten Down Two (IRE)**[75] 4372 4-9-6 **66**.............(t) GrahamGibbons 2 36
(Michael Easterby) *hld up in tch: drvn and outpcd over 2f out: n.d after* **11/1**

0430 7 3 3/4 **Titus Bolt (IRE)**[79] 4264 4-9-5 **65**.. GrahamLee 1 27
(Jim Goldie) *chsd ldrs: effrt whn nt clr run and swtchd lft over 2f out: sn rdn and wknd* **11/2**

1310 8 4 **Yorksters Prince (IRE)**[13] 6468 6-8-8 **59**............(b) ShirleyTeasdale(5) 5 12
(Marjorie Fife) *led to over 2f out: sn rdn and wknd* **9/1**

1m 51.35s (-2.55) **Going Correction** -0.25s/f (Firm)
WFA 3 from 4yo+ 5lb **8** Ran SP% **116.3**
Speed ratings (Par 103): **101,96,94,87,84 84,80,77**
toteswingers 1&2 £7.10, 1&3 £14.30, 2&3 £6.60 CSF £60.50 CT £604.79 TOTE £12.10: £3.50, £1.20, £2.90; EX 63.30 Trifecta £414.70 Pool: £3562.75 - 6.44 winning units.
Owner Peter R Ball **Bred** Value Bloodstock **Trained** Nawton, N Yorks

FOCUS
The pace was strong and the first three home were in the last three to halfway.

6878 ROYAL SCOTS APPRENTICE H'CAP (DIV I) 5f
5:15 (5:16) (Class 6) (0-60,59) 3-Y-0+ **£1,940** (£577; £288; £144) **Stalls** High

Form RPR

0044 1 **Irish Girls Spirit (IRE)**[13] 6471 4-8-12 **52**...........(p) ShirleyTeasdale(3) 1 61
(Paul Midgley) *mde all and sn crossed to stands' rail: rdn over 1f out: kpt on wl fnl f* **7/2**[2]

0024 2 2 **Compton Heights**[6] 6687 4-9-8 **59**............................ LucyAlexander 4 61
(Jim Goldie) *hld up: rdn and hdwy on outside over 1f out: chsd wnr ins fnl f: r.o* **6/1**

4006 3 1 **Wicked Wilma (IRE)**[7] 6669 9-8-1 **45**.....................(p) JordanHibberd(7) 6 43
(Alan Berry) *t.k.h: chsd ldrs: effrt and chsd wnr over 1f out to ins fnl f: one pce* **12/1**

6040 4 1 **Headstight (IRE)**[13] 6469 4-8-11 **48**..................................(p) LeeTopliss 8 43
(Paul Midgley) *hld up in tch: rdn and hdwy over 1f out: kpt on fnl f: nvr able to chal* **13/2**

-000 5 1/2 **Kyzer Chief**[4] 6757 8-9-2 **56**... ShaneGray(3) 2 49
(Tina Jackson) *chsd ldrs: drvn 2f out: one pce appr fnl f* **25/1**

000 6 1 **Pavers Star**[26] 6088 4-9-7 **58**... JasonHart 7 47
(Noel Wilson) *chsd wnr to over 1f out: sn rdn and outpcd* **4/1**[3]

/000 7 3 3/4 **Musical Strike**[17] 6344 4-8-3 **47** ow2...................(vt[1]) AlexHopkinson(7) 3 23
(Shaun Harris) *in tch on outside: rdn over 2f out: wknd over 1f out* **50/1**

0006 8 1 1/2 **Fol Hollow (IRE)**[26] 6088 8-8-11 **55**................................ BTTreanor(7) 9 25
(Stuart Coltherd) *chsd ldrs on ins: n.m.r and lost pl 1/2-way: n.d after* **14/1**

650 9 1 3/4 **True That (IRE)**[60] 4887 3-8-2 **45**................................ JordanNason(5) 5 9
(David Nicholls) *sn pushed along bhd ldng gp: drvn along 1/2-way: nvr on terms* **5/2**[1]

58.85s (-1.55) **Going Correction** -0.25s/f (Firm)
WFA 3 from 4yo+ 1lb **9** Ran SP% **118.6**
Speed ratings (Par 101): **102,98,97,95,94 93,87,84,82**
toteswingers 1&2 £3.70, 1&3 £6.00, 2&3 £8.70 CSF £25.66 CT £231.73 TOTE £3.90: £1.30, £1.70, £3.50; EX 21.30 Trifecta £207.90 Pool: £3437.26 - 12.36 winning units.
Owner Sheard, Banks, Jackson & Johnson **Bred** Seamus McMullan **Trained** Westow, N Yorks

FOCUS
Division one of a low-grade apprentice sprint handicap.

6879 ROYAL SCOTS APPRENTICE H'CAP (DIV II) 5f
5:45 (5:46) (Class 6) (0-60,58) 3-Y-0+ **£1,940** (£577; £288; £144) **Stalls** High

Form RPR

3453 1 **Beauty Pageant (IRE)**[4] 6753 6-9-0 **57**........................ ClaireMurray(7) 7 65
(David Brown) *mde all: pushed along over 1f out: kpt on wl fnl f* **7/2**[2]

0020 2 3/4 **Cheyenne Red (IRE)**[32] 5876 7-8-5 **48**........................ PaulMcGiff(7) 2 53
(Michael Herrington) *cl up: ev ch over 1f out to ins fnl f: hld towards fin* **16/1**

6223 3 nk **Here Now And Why (IRE)**[13] 6471 6-9-8 **58**..................(p) JasonHart 4 62
(Iain Jardine) *chsd ldrs: drvn 1/2-way: effrt over 1f out: edgd lft and r.o towards fin* **15/8**[1]

0-00 4 2 **Tadalavil**[135] 2409 8-8-12 **55**.. RossSmith(7) 6 52
(Linda Perratt) *hld up in tch: effrt whn n.m.r and swtchd lft over 1f out: kpt on fnl f: no imp* **22/1**

0500 5 3 3/4 **Piste**[4] 6761 7-8-6 **45**..(be) GeorgeChaloner(3) 5 28
(Tina Jackson) *dwlt: sn rdn in rr: effrt on outside over 1f out: sn no imp* **16/1**

0503 6 1 1/4 **Moss The Boss (IRE)**[23] 6176 3-8-5 **45**................ ShirleyTeasdale(3) 1 24
(Paul Midgley) *in tch: rdn along 2f out: btn fnl f* **10/1**

0036 7 1 1/2 **Mr Snooks**[17] 6345 3-8-4 **46**.. JordanNason(5) 9 19
(David Nicholls) *t.k.h early: chsd ldrs tl rdn and wknd appr fnl f* **9/2**[3]

5-05 8 1 **Classy Anne**[31] 5919 3-8-1 **45**.................................. SophieRobertson(7) 8 15
(Jim Goldie) *bhd and outpcd: no ch fr 1/2-way* **33/1**

59.09s (-1.31) **Going Correction** -0.25s/f (Firm)
WFA 3 from 4yo+ 1lb **8** Ran SP% **103.3**
Speed ratings (Par 101): **100,98,98,95,89 87,84,83**
toteswingers 1&2 £5.80, 1&3 £1.40, 2&3 £5.40 CSF £44.61 CT £98.46 TOTE £4.50: £1.60, £3.60, £1.20; EX 39.10 Trifecta £109.50 Pool: £2279.41 - 15.60 winning units.
Owner D H Brown **Bred** Mesnil, Mount Coote, New England Stud **Trained** Averham Park, Notts

FOCUS
More of the same and the first two were one-two throughout.
T/Plt: £832.30 to a £1 stake. Pool: £67,667.51 - 59.35 winning units T/Qpdt: £12.20 to a £1 stake. Pool: £7463.00 - 451.88 winning units RY

6880 - (Foreign Racing) - See Raceform Interactive

6437 CURRAGH (R-H)
Sunday, September 29

OFFICIAL GOING: Straight course - good; round course - good to firm

6881a C.L. WELD PARK STKS (GROUP 3) (FILLIES) 7f
2:40 (2:42) 2-Y-0 **£31,707** (£9,268; £4,390; £1,463)

RPR

1 **My Titania (IRE)**[22] 6220 2-9-0 .... DeclanMcDonogh 3 105+
(John M Oxx, Ire) *chsd ldrs: cl 4th 1/2-way: clsd gng wl between horses over 2f out into 2nd: led over 1f out and kpt on wl u.p towards fin to hold on* **11/10**[1]

2 1/2 **Chicago Girl (IRE)**[31] 5936 2-9-0 **86**........................... JohnnyMurtagh 7 104
(J P Murtagh, Ire) *dwlt and racd in rr: prog gng wl bhd ldrs fr over 2f out: n.m.r 1 1/2f out and sn clsd into 2nd: flashed tail: kpt on wl and edgd lft ins fnl f to press wnr cl home: a hld* **14/1**

3 5 1/2 **Tarfasha (IRE)**[61] 4868 2-9-0 .... PatSmullen 1 89
(D K Weld, Ire) *prom: sn settled bhd ldr in 2nd: clsd to ld over 2f out: sn jnd and hdd over 1f out: no ex whn disputing 3rd ins fnl f: kpt on towards fin* **2/1**[2]

4 1/2 **Colour Blue (IRE)**[13] 6483 2-9-0 **88**.................................. GaryCarroll 6 88
(W McCreery, Ire) *chsd ldrs: cl 5th 1/2-way: rdn disputing 2nd fr 2f out and sn no imp on wnr in 4th: kpt on same pce* **25/1**

5 2 1/2 **Intense Debate (IRE)** 2-9-0 .... RoryCleary 4 82+
(J S Bolger, Ire) *w.w: 7th 1/2-way: rdn fr over 2f out and wnt mod 5th ins fnl f: kpt on same pce* **40/1**

6 1 1/4 **Diamond Stilettos (IRE)**[6] 6704 2-9-0 .... AndrewPThornton 5 78
(Mrs A M O'Shea, Ire) *trckd ldrs: cl 3rd 1/2-way: niggled along 1/2-way: rdn over 2f out and sn no ex u.p: one pce ins fnl f* **14/1**

7 hd **Chroussa (IRE)**[13] 6480 2-9-0 .... KevinManning 8 78
(J S Bolger, Ire) *w.w: 6th 1/2-way: rdn on outer 2f out and wnt 5th briefly 1 1/2f out: sn no ex u.p: wknd ins fnl f* **9/1**

8 14 **Minorette (USA)**[14] 6438 2-9-0 **98**........................... JosephO'Brien 2 41
(A P O'Brien, Ire) *sn led: niggled along fr 1/2-way and hdd over 2f out: sn no ex u.p and wknd: eased over 1f out* **6/1**[3]

1m 24.2s (-6.60) **Going Correction** -0.80s/f (Hard) **8** Ran SP% **124.9**
Speed ratings: **105,104,98,97,94 93,93,77**
CSF £21.97 TOTE £1.90: £1.02, £4.50, £1.02; DF 17.90 Trifecta £54.80.
Owner Christopher Tsui **Bred** Sunderland Holdings Ltd **Trained** Currabeg, Co Kildare

FOCUS
It was a good effort by the winner who should have more to come. The race average and the fourth set the opening level.

6883a MONGEY COMMUNICATIONS JOE MCGRATH H'CAP (PREMIER HANDICAP) 6f
3:45 (3:46) 3-Y-0+
£24,390 (£7,723; £3,658; £1,219; £813; £406)

RPR

1 **Nero Emperor (IRE)**[15] 6415 4-9-10 **96**........................... WayneLordan 7 103
(T Stack, Ire) *dwlt sltly and racd towards rr: gd hdwy far side fr over 2f out: rdn ent fnl f to ld ins fnl 150yds: kpt on wl* **10/1**[3]

2 hd **English Deer (IRE)**[16] 6373 3-8-11 **85**.............................. ChrisHayes 14 92+
(P D Deegan, Ire) *w.w in mid-div: swtchd rt 2f out and hdwy on far side into 2nd wl ins fnl f: kpt on wl towards fin to press wnr: hld* **16/1**

3 1 3/4 **Tylery Wonder (IRE)**[14] 6439 3-8-11 **85**..........................(b) WJLee 20 86
(W McCreery, Ire) *prom on nrside: led 1/2-way: stl in front ent fnl f: sn strly pressed and hdd ins fnl 150yds: no ex* **20/1**

4 shd **Invincible Ridge (IRE)**[14] 6439 5-8-6 **81**..................(t) LeighRoche(3) 3 82
(D J Bunyan, Ire) *hld up in mid-div: hdwy in 10th on far side fr 2f out: wnt 4th ins fnl f and kpt on same pce towards fin wout threatening principals* **16/1**

5 hd **Sassaway (IRE)**[15] 6415 6-8-12 **84**................................ FergalLynch 24 84
(Eamonn O'Connell, Ire) *chsd ldrs on nrside: 6th 1/2-way: rdn 1 1/2f out and wnt 4th briefly ins fnl f: kpt on same pce* **12/1**

6 1 1/4 **Twenty One Choice (IRE)**[11] 6526 4-8-13 **85**....... SeamieHeffernan 15 81
(Ed de Giles) *racd in mid-div: 10th 1/2-way: rdn over 1f out and n.m.r: sn swtchd lft and kpt on u.p towards fin wout ever threatening principals* **7/1**[2]

7 1/2 **Six Of Hearts**[42] 5567 9-9-9 **95**...(b) FMBerry 4 89
(Cecil Ross, Ire) *in rr of mid-div: hdwy on far side fr 1/2-way into 7th ins fnl f: no ex u.p: kpt on same pce* **33/1**

8 1 **Greek Canyon (IRE)**[55] 5077 4-9-6 **92**........................... GaryCarroll 12 83
(G M Lyons, Ire) *chsd ldrs: 7th 1/2-way: rdn and no imp on ldrs ent fnl f: kpt on same pce* **14/1**

9 nk **Elusive Time (IRE)**[42] 5567 5-9-6 **99**......................... RossCoakley(7) 25 89
(Takashi Kodama, Ire) *racd in mid-div: 11th 1/2-way: rdn and no imp on ldrs over 1f out: kpt on one pce* **20/1**

10 1 1/4 **Almadaa**[21] 6240 6-8-1 **76** oh1.. ConorHoban(3) 18 62
(David Marnane, Ire) *nvr bttr than mid-div: rdn and no imp fr 2f out: kpt on one pce* **25/1**

11 1/2 **Srucahan (IRE)**[11] 6542 4-9-2 **88**........................... DeclanMcDonogh 21 73
(P D Deegan, Ire) *in rr of mid-div: niggled along 1/2-way and no imp ent fnl f: kpt on* **25/1**

12 shd **Machete Mark (IRE)**[37] 5728 3-9-3 **94**............................ ColinKeane(3) 19 78
(G M Lyons, Ire) *trckd ldrs: 5th 1/2-way: sn pushed along and no ex u.p over 1f out: wknd* **5/1**[1]

13 *shd* **Bubbly Bellini (IRE)**[15] 6415 6-9-5 **94**..........................(p) IJBrennan(3) 9 78
(Adrian McGuinness, Ire) *chsd ldrs early: rdn and no imp fr 2f out: one pce fnl f* **20/1**

14 *1* **Kiss The Stars (IRE)**[15] 6415 3-8-4 **78**.............................. BenCurtis 22 59
(T G McCourt, Ire) *trckd ldrs on nrside: 4th 1/2-way: rdn fr 2f out and sn no ex u.p: wknd fnl f* **11/1**

15 *3/4* **Gathering Power (IRE)**[92] 3845 3-9-1 **89**................ JohnnyMurtagh 17 67
(Edward Lynam, Ire) *dwlt sltly and racd in rr: pushed along fr 2f out and sme hdwy: n.m.r over 1f out: no ex ins fnl f* **7/1**[2]

16 *hd* **Jembatt (IRE)**[12] 6508 6-8-4 **76** oh5..........................(p) NGMcCullagh 11 54
(Michael Mulvany, Ire) *in rr of mid-div: rdn and no imp fr 2f out: one pce fnl f* **33/1**

17 *nk* **Seal Rock**[11] 6542 5-8-12 **84**...................................(b) ShaneFoley 10 61
(A Oliver, Ire) *chsd ldrs early: rdn and wknd fr 2f out* **20/1**

18 *1 3/4* **Wexford Opera (IRE)**[7] 6677 3-9-0 **88**........................ KevinManning 23 59
(J S Bolger, Ire) *trckd ldr on nrside: cl 2nd 1/2-way: rdn and no ex u.p over 2f out: sn wknd and eased* **12/1**

19 *shd* **Joe Eile (IRE)**[8] 6623 5-9-2 **98**...................................(b) IanQueally(10) 16 69
(G M Lyons, Ire) *trckd ldrs: 3rd 1/2-way: rdn and wknd fr 2f out* **14/1**

20 *1/2* **Ramone (IRE)**[36] 5775 3-8-4 **78**.. DannyGrant 13 47
(W T Farrell, Ire) *dwlt sltly: in rr of mid-div: rdn and no imp fr 2f out* **33/1**

21 *1* **Cash Or Casualty (IRE)**[11] 6542 5-9-2 **88**......................(t) RoryCleary 1 54
(Damian Joseph English, Ire) *cl up on far side early: pushed along bef 1/2-way and sn wknd* **33/1**

22 *3 1/2* **Ghaamer (USA)**[118] 2941 3-9-1 **89**... PatSmullen 5 44
(D K Weld, Ire) *racd in mid-div: dropped towards rr fr 2f out: eased ins fnl f* **16/1**

23 *1* **My Good Brother (IRE)**[15] 6415 4-9-2 **95**............... LukeDempsey(7) 8 47
(T G McCourt, Ire) *chsd ldrs: 8th 1/2-way: rdn and wknd fr 2f out* **16/1**

24 *1 3/4* **Fastidious**[41] 5598 4-8-6 **85**.. CharlieElliott(7) 6 31
(M D O'Callaghan, Ire) *cl up on far side early: rdn in 7th bef 1/2-way and sn no ex: wknd* **33/1**

1m 12.03s (-3.47) **Going Correction** -0.35s/f (Firm)
WFA 3 from 4yo+ 2lb **24** Ran SP% **152.8**
Speed ratings: **109,108,106,106,106 104,103,102,101,100 99,99,99,98,97 96,96,94,93,93 91,87,85,83**
CSF £167.57 CT £3253.74 TOTE £10.80: £2.30, £6.00, £4.60, £6.00; DF 277.60 TRIFECTA Not won..
Owner Pension Fund Syndicate **Bred** Blue Iris Syndicate **Trained** Golden, Co Tipperary

FOCUS
The first and third, making their handicap debuts, both ran personal bests. The runner-up was just denied.

6884a JUDDMONTE BERESFORD STKS (GROUP 2) 1m
4:15 (4:16) 2-Y-O **£52,845** (£15,447; £7,317; £2,439)

RPR

1 **Geoffrey Chaucer (USA)**[73] 4460 2-9-3 .... JosephO'Brien 4 108+
(A P O'Brien, Ire) *hld up in tch: 4th 1/2-way: tk clsr order in 3rd 2f out and qcknd to ld ent fnl f: sn edgd lft: kpt on wl towards fin: readily* **4/7**[1]

2 *1 1/4* **Oklahoma City**[71] 4547 2-9-3 **108**..........................(b) SeamieHeffernan 5 104
(A P O'Brien, Ire) *trckd ldrs: sltly hmpd early: cl 3rd 1/2-way: pushed along into st and sn rdn in 4th: swtchd rt ent fnl f and kpt on wl u.p into 2nd fnl 150yds: nt trble wnr* **5/1**[3]

3 *3/4* **Altruistic (IRE)**[55] 5076 2-9-3 .... JohnnyMurtagh 3 103
(J P Murtagh, Ire) *trckd ldr: edgd lft early: cl 2nd 1/2-way: pushed along into st and sn rdn: no imp on wnr ins fnl f and dropped to 3rd ins fnl 150yds: kpt on same pce* **3/1**[2]

4 *2* **All Set To Go (IRE)**[13] 6483 2-9-3 **94**............................ ChrisHayes 2 98
(A Oliver, Ire) *led: narrow advantage 1/2-way: pushed along into st and strly pressed 1 1/2f out: hdd u.p ent fnl f and sn no ex in 3rd: dropped to 4th fnl 150yds* **33/1**

5 *7* **Not To Yield (USA)**[22] 6221 2-9-3 ....(b[1]) PatSmullen 1 82
(D K Weld, Ire) *hld up in rr: rdn fr 2f out and no ex u.p: one pce fnl f* **33/1**

1m 42.7s (-3.30) **Going Correction** -0.50s/f (Hard) **5** Ran SP% **111.2**
Speed ratings: **96,94,94,92,85**
CSF £4.07 TOTE £1.90: £1.02, £2.10; DF 3.80 Trifecta £4.90.
Owner Mrs John Magnier & Michael Tabor & Derrick Smith **Bred** March Thoroughbreds **Trained** Ballydoyle, Co Tipperary

FOCUS
This race has gone to some top-class horses and, although it is hard to overstate the quality of this renewal, the winner looks every inch a Derby contender.

6885 - 6886a (Foreign Racing) - See Raceform Interactive

5576 HANOVER (L-H)
Sunday, September 29

OFFICIAL GOING: Turf: good to soft

6887a GROSSER PREIS VON GERMAN TOTE (GROUP 3) (3YO+ FILLIES & MARES) (TURF) 1m 3f
3:55 (12:00) 3-Y-O+
£26,016 (£8,943; £4,471; £2,439; £1,626; £1,219)

RPR

1 **Fitful Skies (IRE)**[29] 6010 4-9-5 0....................................... FabriceVeron 3 106
(H-A Pantall, France) *stdd and hld up: sn towards rr: rdn and hdwy fr 2f out: swtchd lft between rivals and chal over 1f out: led ins fnl f and readily asserted* **31/10**[1]

2 *1 1/2* **Night Power (FR)**[47] 3-8-11 0.. APietsch 1 102
(W Hickst, Germany) *dwlt sltly and pushed along to rcvr: trckd ldr on inner: rdn 3f out: led 2f out: strly pressed fr over 1f out: styd on but worn down and hdd ins fnl f: no ex* **63/10**[2]

3 *1/2* **Wilddrossel (GER)**[35] 4-9-5 0.. SHellyn 14 102
(Markus Klug, Germany) *got across fr wdst draw and led: rdn 3f out: hdd 2f out: nt qckn u.p but styd on wl for 3rd* **174/10**

4 *3 1/2* **Lady Of Budysin (GER)**[35] 4-9-5 0................................ AHelfenbein 4 96
(Markus Klug, Germany) *stdd and hld up in rr: hdwy into midfield on inner 1/2-way: rdn to chal and ev ch 2f out: no ex ins fnl f: jst hld on for 4th* **96/10**

5 *nk* **Daksha (FR)**[28] 3-8-11 0.. AndreBest 7 95
(W Hickst, Germany) *restrained in midfield: rdn 3f out: ev ch whn nt clr run as wnr swtchd lft over 1f out: sn outpcd by ldrs: styd on* **162/10**

6 *1 1/4* **Lalandia (IRE)**[85] 4-9-5 0.. AStarke 2 93
(P Schiergen, Germany) *midfield on inner: rdn 3f out: outpcd by ldrs ins fnl 2f: styd on* **36/5**[3]

7 *nse* **Daytona Bay**[56] 5044 3-8-11 0....................... LennartHammer-Hansen 12 92
(Ferdinand J Leve, Germany) *restrained fr wd draw and hld towards rr on outer: rdn 3f out: styd on u.p but nt pce to chal* **31/10**[1]

8 *1 1/4* **Thunderstruck (GER)**[35] 3-8-11 0................................ MaximPecheur 9 90
(R Dzubasz, Germany) *sn prom on outer: rdn and ev ch 3f out: outpcd ins fnl 2f: plugged on* **32/1**

9 *2* **Path Wind (FR)**[29] 6010 4-9-5 0... EPedroza 8 87
(A Wohler, Germany) *midfield: rdn 3f out: outpcd ins fnl 2f: eased whn btn fnl 100yds* **10/1**

10 *3 1/2* **Laviva**[85] 5-9-5 0... RobertHavlin 5 81
(Ferdinand J Leve, Germany) *dwlt and pushed along to rcvr: hld up on inner: rdn in rr 3f out: sn btn: nvr a factor* **109/10**

11 *1/2* **Lili Moon (GER)**[98] 4-9-5 0.. BClos 6 80
(Werner Glanz, Germany) *midfield: rdn 3f out: no ex and btn ent fnl f: fdd* **211/10**

12 *1* **Neckara (GER)**[28] 3-8-11 0... JBojko 10 77
(A Wohler, Germany) *hld up: rdn 3f out: no ex and btn ent fnl f: fdd* **25/1**

13 *1/2* **Leopardin (GER)**[35] 5-9-5 0... WPanov 11 77
(H J Groschel, Germany) *hld up in midfield: rdn 3f out: outpcd and btn over 1f out: n.d* **18/1**

14 *20* **Magali (GER)**[21] 3-8-11 0.. ADeVries 13 40
(W Giedt, Germany) *trckd ldr: rdn and wknd rapidly 4f out: last and btn over 2f out: eased and t.o* **28/1**

2m 23.46s (143.46)
WFA 3 from 4yo+ 7lb **14** Ran SP% **133.0**
WIN (incl. 10 euro stake): 41. PLACES: 17, 25, 65. SF: 284.
Owner Sheikh Mohammed **Bred** Darley **Trained** France

6888 - (Foreign Racing) - See Raceform Interactive

6679 SAN SIRO (R-H)
Sunday, September 29

OFFICIAL GOING: Turf: good to soft

6889a PREMIO VITTORIO DI CAPUA (GROUP 1) (3YO+) (TURF) 1m
3:10 (12:00) 3-Y-O+ **£77,235** (£33,983; £18,536; £9,268)

RPR

1 **Shamalgan (FR)**[36] 5739 6-9-2 0.. MaximeGuyon 6 110+
(X Thomas-Demeaulte, France) *chsd ldrs: 3rd and 5 l down over 2 1/2f out: shkn up and hdwy over 2f out: rdn to ld appr fnl f: sn drvn clr and in command: won easing down* **37/10**

2 *2 1/2* **Saint Bernard**[220] 744 4-9-2 0.. CColombi 3 104
(D Camuffo, Italy) *midfield: rdn and hdwy 2 1/2f out: chsd ldrs ins fnl 2f: hrd rdn 1f out: r.o fnl f: nt pce of wnr* **218/10**

3 *2* **Nabucco (GER)**[86] 4043 3-8-11 0.................................... CristianDemuro 9 98
(R Rohne, Germany) *chsd ldr: rdn to ld 2f out: hdd appr fnl f: one pce u.p: fdd and lost 2nd 75yds out* **19/10**[3]

4 *snk* **Samba Brazil (GER)**[14] 6451 4-8-13 0............................... AndreaAtzeni 4 96+
(J Hirschberger, Germany) *midfield: rdn and outpcd over 2f out: styd on wl u.p fnl f: jst missed 3rd* **9/5**[2]

5 *1* **Vedelago (IRE)**[140] 2295 4-9-2 0.. MEsposito 5 97
(S Botti, Italy) *dwlt: towards rr: laboured hdwy over 2f out: sn rdn and styd on fnl f: nt pce to chal: nvr on terms* **9/10**[1]

6 *1 3/4* **Storming Loose**[91] 3881 6-9-2 0.. DarioVargiu 7 93+
(B Grizzetti, Italy) *in rr: last and rdn over 2f out: hdwy 1 1/2f out: styd on ins fnl f: nvr in contention* **172/10**

7 *2 1/2* **Principe Adepto (USA)**[126] 2698 5-9-2 0..........................(b) CFiocchi 1 87
(E Botti, Italy) *hld up towards rr: rdn and no imp over 2f out: plugged on ins fnl f: nvr threatened ldrs* **54/10**

8 *nk* **Free Winner (IRE)**[735] 5-9-2 0........................ PierantonioConvertino 11 86
(M Tellini, Italy) *chsd ldrs: rdn 2f out: sn btn and wknd fnl f* **57/1**

9 *10* **Libano (IRE)**[126] 2698 7-9-2 0...................................... MarcoMonteriso 8 63
(L Polito, Italy) *broke wl and led: set decent gallop: shkn up and 4 l clr over 3f out: hdd 2f out: sn wknd* **25/1**

10 *8* **Douce Vie (IRE)**[126] 2698 7-9-2 0...................................... FabioBranca 10 45
(S Botti, Italy) *a bhd: nvr a factor* **159/10**

1m 35.1s (-7.00)
WFA 3 from 4yo+ 4lb **10** Ran SP% **181.1**
WIN (incl. 1 euro stake): 4.68. PLACES: 2.03, 3.36, 1.76. DF: 59.90.
Owner Ardak Amirkulov **Bred** Mathieu Daguzan-Garros & Rolling Hills Farm **Trained** France

6890a PREMIO SERGIO CUMANI (GROUP 3) (3YO+ FILLIES & MARES) (TURF) 1m
3:45 (12:00) 3-Y-O+ **£28,455** (£12,520; £6,829; £3,414)

RPR

1 **Killachy Loose**[105] 4-9-0 0.. DarioVargiu 9 101+
(B Grizzetti, Italy) *midfield: hdwy on outside over 2 1/2f out: sn rdn to chal 1 1/2f out: led ent fnl f: r.o wl: readily* **145/20**[3]

2 *2 1/4* **Kadabra (IRE)**[21] 6-9-0 0... FabioBranca 4 96
(E Botti, Italy) *midfield: hdwy on outside over 1 1/2f out: r.o u.p fnl f: nt pce to chal wnr* **37/10**[2]

3 *1/2* **Clorofilla (IRE)**[21] 3-8-9 0.. LManiezzi 5 94
(Marco Gasparini, Italy) *led after 1f: qcknd clr over 2f out: hdd ent fnl f: one pce u.p* **91/10**

4 *2 3/4* **Grand Treasure (IRE)**[66] 4700 3-8-9 0............................... MEsposito 8 88
(G Colella, Italy) *towards rr: hdwy on outside 2f out: styd on ins fnl f: nvr in contention* **94/10**

5 *1 1/2* **Baratella (FR)**[140] 4-9-0 0... CColombi 2 85
(L Racco, Italy) *towards rr: hdwy on ins over 1 1/2f out: kpt on ins fnl f: nvr threatened ldrs* **74/10**

6 *1 1/2* **Deflection (IRE)**[154] 1866 3-8-9 0................................ CristianDemuro 7 81
(S Botti, Italy) *settled in fnl trio: rdn over 2f out and no immediate imp: styd on fnl f: nrest at fin* **214/10**

7 *1 1/2* **Rosina Bella (IRE)**[21] 4-9-0 0.......................................(b) StefanoLandi 10 78
(P L Giannotti, Italy) *chsd ldrs: 2nd and hrd rdn 1 1/2f out: wknd appr fnl f* **206/10**

8 *1 1/2* **Gothic Dance (IRE)**[105] 4-9-0 0............................ PierantonioConvertino 1 75
(B Grizzetti, Italy) *midfield: 5th and rdn over 2f out: wknd on run to fnl f* **37/10**[2]

9 *2 3/4* **Avomcic (IRE)**[119] 3-8-9 0... FBossa 3 67
(M Maroni, Italy) *broke wl and led: hdd after 1f: chsd ldr: rdn and nt qckn over 2f out: wknd u.p appr fnl f* **33/1**

P Akemi (IRE)[25] 6124 3-8-9 0.. MaximeGuyon 6
(X Thomas-Demeaulte, France) *injured and p.u after 1f* 11/20[1]

1m 35.8s (-6.30)
WFA 3 from 4yo+ 4lb 10 Ran SP% **162.7**
WIN (incl. 1 euro stake): 8.22. PLACES: 3.26, 2.97, 4.10. DF: 70.11.
Owner Scuderia Blueberry **Bred** Scuderia Blueberry S R L **Trained** Italy

6423 BATH (L-H)

Monday, September 30

OFFICIAL GOING: Good to firm (8.8)
Wind: Moderate across Weather: Overcast

6895 M J CHURCH H'CAP (DIV I) 1m 5f 22y

2:00 (2:00) (Class 6) (0-60,60) 3-Y-O+ **£1,940** (£577; £288; £144) **Stalls High**

Form RPR
3103 1 **Cabuchon (GER)**[4] 6782 6-8-13 **54**........................(t) EoinWalsh(7) 4 61
(David Evans) *hld up in rr: hdwy on ins 3f out: led over 1f out: drvn out fnl f* 7/2[1]
5335 2 1 3/4 **Glens Wobbly**[2] 6853 5-8-7 **46** oh1........................ RyanTate(5) 8 51
(Jonathan Geake) *in tch: hdwy 6f out: pushed along 4f out: chal 2f out: sn led: hdd over 1f out: chsd wnr fnl f: no imp* 17/2
3 nk **Gung Ho (FR)**[29] 4-9-11 **59**........................ AdamKirby 3 63
(Tony Newcombe) *in tch: hdwy towards outer 3f out: styd on fr 2f out to take 3rd ins fnl f: clsng on 2nd nr fin but no imp on wnr* 18/1
3624 4 3/4 **Walter De La Mare (IRE)**[6] 6723 6-9-0 **48**........................ MartinHarley 12 51
(Anabel K Murphy) *in rr: hdwy over 2f out: styd on same pce u.p fnl f* 9/1
3235 5 2 **Eyeline**[14] 6479 3-8-7 **55**........................(p) JackDuern(5) 1 55
(Andrew Hollinshead) *led: jnd 2f out: sn hdd: wknd fnl f* 8/1[3]
1332 6 nk **Men Don't Cry (IRE)**[14] 6479 4-9-4 **55**........................(b) MarkCoumbe(3) 5 55
(Ed de Giles) *t.k.h: chsd ldrs: rdn 3f out: wknd over 1f out* 4/1[2]
0404 7 1/2 **Iguacu**[23] 5377 9-8-11 **48**........................ ThomasBrown(3) 11 47
(Richard Price) *in rr: hdwy and nt clr run 2f out: swtchd rt towards outer over 1f out: kpt on but nt trble ldrs* 14/1
0344 8 1 **Hero's Story**[15] 6435 3-9-3 **60**........................(p) PatDobbs 2 57
(Amanda Perrett) *chsd ldrs: rdn 3f out: wknd over 1f out* 7/2[1]
2000 9 nk **Jewelled Dagger (IRE)**[25] 4714 9-9-6 **54**........................(bt) JimCrowley 6 51
(Sharon Watt) *chsd ldr tl appr fnl 3f: wknd fr 2f out* 20/1
050 10 4 1/2 **Finalee**[18] 6319 3-8-4 **52**........................ JoeyHaynes(5) 9 42
(John Gallagher) *in tch: rdn 3f out: sn btn* 25/1
11 7 **Illegale (IRE)**[30] 7-9-9 **60**........................(t) WilliamTwiston-Davies(3) 14 40
(Nikki Evans) *chsd ldrs: wknd qckly 3f out: eased whn no ch* 66/1

2m 50.85s (-1.15) **Going Correction** -0.075s/f (Good)
WFA 3 from 4yo+ 9lb 11 Ran SP% **118.1**
Speed ratings (Par 101): **100,98,98,98,97 96,96,95,95,92 88**
toteswingers 1&2 £6.90, 1&3 £17.70, 2&3 £23.60 CSF £33.33 CT £475.68 TOTE £5.50: £1.80, £3.10, £5.90; EX 45.00 Trifecta £761.60 Pool: £2,606.41 - 2.56 winning units.
Owner Mrs E Evans **Bred** Gestut Schlenderhan **Trained** Pandy, Monmouths

FOCUS
Three non-runners left 11 to go to post for the first division of the 1m5f handicap.

6896 IRISH STALLION FARMS EBF MAIDEN STKS 1m 2f 46y

2:30 (2:30) (Class 5) 2-Y-O **£2,911** (£866; £432; £216) **Stalls Low**

Form RPR
50 1 **Notarised**[12] 6528 2-9-5 0........................ AdamKirby 3 75
(Mark Johnston) *mde virtually all: rdn and qcknd 3 out: edgd rt u.p fnl 75yds: hld on all out* 9/2[3]
04 2 nk **Dullingham**[16] 6378 2-9-5 0........................ SilvestreDeSousa 6 74
(Charlie Appleby) *sn chsng wnr: rdn 3f out: styd on wl fnl f: pushed rt fnl 75yds: no ex clsng stages* 11/4[2]
05 3 2 1/4 **Libeccio (FR)**[12] 6528 2-9-5 0........................ LiamKeniry 2 70+
(Andrew Balding) *chsd ldrs: rdn 3f out: one pce over 2f out: styd on again ins fnl f* 10/1
036 4 hd **Template (IRE)**[7] 6689 2-9-5 0........................ RichardHughes 8 70
(Richard Hannon) *chsd ldrs: rdn over 3f out and sn one pce: kpt on again ins fnl f* 9/4[1]
5 5 10 **Tioga Pass**[12] 6523 2-9-0 0........................ JimCrowley 7 46
(Paul Cole) *in tch: rdn over 3f out: wknd 2f out* 11/4[2]
52 6 7 **Arthur's Melody**[101] 3541 2-8-12 0........................ RyanWhile(7) 4 37
(Bill Turner) *in rr but in tch: rdn over 3f out: sn btn* 40/1
00 7 6 **Lord Lexington**[35] 5811 2-9-5 0........................ PatDobbs 5 26
(Richard Hannon) *s.i.s: in rr: rdn 4f out: sn no ch* 33/1
000 8 14 **Craftybird**[16] 6409 2-9-0 35........................ DavidProbert 1
(Brett Johnson) *in rr: rdn over 4f out and sn lost tch* 100/1

2m 10.36s (-0.64) **Going Correction** -0.075s/f (Good) 8 Ran SP% **117.7**
Speed ratings (Par 95): **99,98,96,96,88 83,78,67**
toteswingers 1&2 £2.90, 1&3 £5.80, 2&3 £3.80 CSF £17.78 TOTE £7.40: £1.70, £1.60, £1.60; EX 17.60 Trifecta £110.80 Pool: £2,666.18 - 18.04 winning units.
Owner Hugh Hart **Bred** Mrs P Hart **Trained** Middleham Moor, N Yorks

FOCUS
A stamina test for 2yos.

6897 SEDDON NURSERY H'CAP 1m 2f 46y

3:00 (3:00) (Class 5) (0-75,69) 2-Y-O **£2,587** (£770; £384; £192) **Stalls Low**

Form RPR
620 1 **Aristocracy**[16] 6401 2-8-12 **60**........................ MartinHarley 6 65
(Mick Channon) *trckd ldr: led 2f out: hrd drvn fr over 1f out: hld on wl* 10/1
6251 2 3/4 **Rising Dawn (IRE)**[18] 6322 2-9-7 **69**........................ RichardHughes 1 73
(Richard Hannon) *chsd ldrs: drvn along 4f out: chsd wnr u.p ins fnl 2f: styd on but a hld* 5/4[1]
466 3 2 1/4 **Samtu (IRE)**[19] 6314 2-9-6 **68**........................ LukeMorris 8 68
(Clive Brittain) *chsd ldrs: rdn over 3f out: kpt on u.p to take wl hld 3rd fnl 110yds* 9/2[2]
3664 4 2 1/4 **Power Up**[12] 6520 2-9-4 **66**........................ SilvestreDeSousa 3 61
(Mark Johnston) *led: rdn 3f out: hdd 2f out: wknd fnl f and dropped to 4th fnl 110yds* 5/1[3]
0023 5 4 1/2 **My Anchor**[14] 6460 2-9-3 **65**........................ LiamKeniry 4 52
(Sylvester Kirk) *chsd ldrs: rdn over 3f out: no ch fr over 2f out* 10/1
6046 6 11 **Maysville (IRE)**[15] 6426 2-8-6 **54**........................ JimmyQuinn 2 20
(Charles Hills) *in rr but in tch: rdn over 3f out and sn wknd* 16/1
5600 7 1/2 **Freddie Kilroy**[18] 6322 2-8-2 **50**........................ CathyGannon 5 15
(Ed Dunlop) *rdn over 3f out: a in rr* 20/1
6000 8 1 **Big Kenny**[33] 5893 2-7-11 **50**........................ NoelGarbutt(5) 10 13
(David Evans) *s.i.s: a in rr* 50/1
0040 9 shd **Kaizen Factor**[12] 6520 2-9-5 **67**........................ DavidProbert 7 30
(Rod Millman) *chsd ldrs: wknd 4f out* 20/1
0340 10 59 **Earl's Bridge**[10] 6605 2-8-1 **56** ow1........................ RyanWhile(7) 9
(Bill Turner) *in rr: awkward and hung rt bnd 5f out: sn wl bhd: t.o* 33/1

2m 10.24s (-0.76) **Going Correction** -0.075s/f (Good) 10 Ran SP% **117.8**
Speed ratings (Par 95): **100,99,97,95,92 83,83,82,82,34**
toteswingers 1&2 £2.40, 1&3 £6.50, 2&3 £2.30 CSF £22.32 CT £68.51 TOTE £10.10: £2.30, £1.70, £1.90; EX 26.60 Trifecta £138.50 Pool: £2,134.47 - 11.55 winning units.
Owner M Channon **Bred** R F And S D Knipe **Trained** West Ilsley, Berks

FOCUS
Plenty failed to land a blow in this staying nursery.

6898 A.DAVID.CO.UK FOOD WITH SERVICE "BE HOPEFUL" H'CAP 1m 2f 46y

3:30 (3:31) (Class 5) (0-75,74) 3-Y-O+ **£2,587** (£770; £384; £192) **Stalls Low**

Form RPR
2134 1 **Precision Five**[16] 6398 4-8-11 **66**........................(p) RyanTate(5) 3 76
(Jeremy Gask) *chsd ldrs: led u.p 1f out: edgd rt u.p fnl 75yds: hld on all out* 14/1
2-1 2 nse **Appease**[11] 6555 4-9-10 **74**........................ RichardHughes 9 84+
(Richard Hannon) *chsd ldrs: rdn 3f out: styd on u.p fr 2f out: pressed wnr and pushed rt fnl 75yds: jst failed* 2/1[1]
4021 3 1 1/2 **Excellent Puck (IRE)**[11] 6556 3-9-0 **70**........................ JimmyFortune 4 77
(Jamie Osborne) *chsd ldrs: chal 2f out: led sn after: hdd u.p 1f out: one pce into 3rd fnl 110yds* 5/1[2]
5050 4 2 **Kelpie Blitz (IRE)**[17] 6358 4-9-10 **74**........................(t) GeorgeBaker 8 77
(Seamus Durack) *chsd ldrs: chal 3f out: slt ld 2f out: sn hdd: no ex fnl f* 12/1
0056 5 1/2 **Gilded Frame**[12] 6522 3-8-7 **63**........................ HarryBentley 12 65
(Marcus Tregoning) *chsd ldrs: rdn 2f out: swtchd lft over 1f out: kpt on fnl f: nt pce to trble ldrs* 16/1
5126 6 3/4 **Jewelled**[21] 6258 7-9-10 **74**........................(v) SebSanders 10 75
(Lady Herries) *in rr: hdwy over 2f out: styd on ins fnl f: nt rch ldrs* 9/1[3]
4324 7 nk **Red Shuttle**[21] 6258 6-9-10 **74**........................ AdamKirby 14 74
(Andi Brown) *s.i.s: in rr: rdn over 2f out: hdwy over 1f out: kpt on clsng stages: nt rch ldrs* 12/1
6521 8 2 1/2 **Jan De Heem**[29] 6015 3-8-13 **69**........................(v) JimCrowley 11 65
(Ralph Beckett) *in rr: hdwy ins fnl f: kpt on wl cl home* 14/1
4106 9 nse **Silver Alliance**[42] 5587 5-9-4 **73**........................(p) ShelleyBirkett(5) 13 68
(Julia Feilden) *in tch: rdn 3f out: one pce fnl 2f* 25/1
2014 10 1/2 **Lady Sylvia**[19] 6315 4-9-6 **70**........................ PatDobbs 5 64
(Joseph Tuite) *chsd ldrs: wknd ins fnl 2f* 33/1
000- 11 hd **One Pursuit (IRE)**[467] 3274 5-9-3 **67**........................ JackMitchell 1 61
(Brendan Powell) *rrd stalls: s.i.s: and behiind: hdwy on outside over 1f out: sme late prog* 50/1
6642 12 2 **Woolston Ferry (IRE)**[16] 6398 7-9-7 **71**........................ FergusSweeney 7 61
(Henry Candy) *in tch: rdn over 2f out: wknd over 1f out* 10/1
4621 13 1 1/2 **Bold Cross (IRE)**[30] 5980 10-9-3 **70**........................ ThomasBrown(3) 2 57
(Edward Bevan) *towards rr most of way* 20/1
6051 14 nk **April Ciel**[13] 6491 4-9-5 **69**........................(p) LukeMorris 15 56
(Ronald Harris) *led: hdd 2f out and wknd qckly* 22/1

2m 9.11s (-1.89) **Going Correction** -0.075s/f (Good)
WFA 3 from 4yo+ 6lb 14 Ran SP% **121.5**
Speed ratings (Par 103): **104,103,102,101,100 100,99,97,97,97 97,95,94,94**
toteswingers 1&2 £9.00, 1&3 £10.70, 2&3 £4.20 CSF £39.97 CT £171.12 TOTE £12.60: £2.80, £1.50, £1.80; EX 51.60 Trifecta £327.10 Pool: £2,828.45 - 6.48 winning units.
Owner Calne Engineering Ltd **Bred** Edward J G Young **Trained** Sutton Veny, Wilts
■ Stewards' Enquiry : Ryan Tate caution: careless riding.

FOCUS
A strong handicap for the grade.

6899 M J CHURCH H'CAP (DIV II) 1m 5f 22y

4:00 (4:02) (Class 6) (0-60,60) 3-Y-O+ **£1,940** (£577; £288; £144) **Stalls High**

Form RPR
2502 1 **Grayswood**[7] 6693 3-9-0 **57**........................(p) MartinDwyer 4 67
(William Muir) *in rr: hdwy on outside over 3f out: drvn to challege 1f out: led fnl 110yds: drvn out* 7/2[2]
5-33 2 1 **Train Hard**[180] 1326 3-8-9 **52**........................ SilvestreDeSousa 3 60+
(Mark Johnston) *sn led: rdn to hold advantage and veered lft into rail wl over 1f out: sn jnd: hdd fnl 110yds: nt pce of wnr but hld on to 2nd cl home* 4/1[3]
6602 3 shd **Dumbfounded (FR)**[28] 6044 5-9-6 **54**........................ RichardHughes 7 62
(Lady Herries) *chsd ldr: rdn over 3f out: chal 1f out: styd disputing 2nd fnl 110yds: dropped to 3rd last strides* 5/2[1]
4115 4 3 1/4 **See And Be Seen**[9] 6629 3-9-2 **59**........................(p) LiamKeniry 9 62
(Sylvester Kirk) *in tch: hdwy on outside fr over 2f out: styd on same pce ins fnl f* 7/1
-442 5 1 **Manshoor (IRE)**[30] 5977 8-9-4 **52**........................ DougieCostello 2 53
(Lucy Wadham) *sn chsng ldrs: rdn and one pce over 2f out: kpt on same pce ins fnl f* 14/1
3-06 6 3/4 **Two Sugars**[40] 5633 5-9-2 **50**........................ AdamKirby 14 50
(Laura Mongan) *towards rr: hdwy over 3f out: sn drvn no imp on ldrs over 1f out: hung lft u.p and wknd ins fnl f* 12/1
-002 7 1 1/4 **Ocean Power (IRE)**[53] 5178 3-8-6 **49**........................ LukeMorris 13 47
(Richard Phillips) *in rr: rdn over 4f out: sme hdwy over 2f out: nvr rchd ldrs and kpt on same pce fnl f* 20/1
04 8 1 **Zaminate**[40] 5631 4-8-13 **47**........................ DavidProbert 5 44
(Patrick Chamings) *chsd ldrs: rdn over 2f out: wknd over 1f out* 33/1
0610 9 12 **Bondi Mist (IRE)**[46] 5434 4-9-7 **60**........................(v) RyanTate(5) 8 39
(Jonathan Geake) *a towards rr* 25/1
-660 10 nk **Ruff Luck**[22] 3014 3-8-9 **52**........................ CathyGannon 6 31
(Seamus Mullins) *chsd ldrs: rdn over 4f out: wknd 3f out* 80/1
000- 11 27 **Misteray**[334] 7492 3-8-3 **46** oh1........................(t) JimmyQuinn 12
(Bill Turner) *a in rr: no ch fnl 3f* 14/1
00-0 12 1 1/4 **Hal Of A Lover**[100] 3595 5-8-9 **46** oh1........................(tp) MarkCoumbe(3) 11
(Lisa Williamson) *a in rr* 80/1

2m 50.47s (-1.53) **Going Correction** -0.075s/f (Good)
WFA 3 from 4yo+ 9lb 12 Ran SP% **118.3**
Speed ratings (Par 101): **101,100,100,98,97 97,96,95,88,88 71,70**
toteswingers 1&2 £4.30, 1&3 £3.00, 2&3 £3.40 CSF £17.02 CT £40.80 TOTE £4.20: £1.80, £2.00, £1.80; EX 22.60 Trifecta £64.90 Pool: £4,068.19 - 46.99 winning units.
Owner C L A Edginton **Bred** Car Colston Hall Stud **Trained** Lambourn, Berks

FOCUS
The second and faster division of the 1m5f handicap in which the market principals came to the fore.

6900 BBC RADIO BRISTOL H'CAP 5f 11y
4:30 (4:32) (Class 4) (0-80,78) 3-Y-O £4,690 (£1,395; £697; £348) Stalls Centre

Form RPR
5211 1 **Marmalady (IRE)**[25] 6138 3-9-3 **74**.................... GeorgeBaker 10 83
(Gary Moore) *trckd ldrs: drvn to chal 1f out: rdn to ld fnl 110yds: styd on wl* **7/1**[3]
0632 2 1 ½ **Vallarta (IRE)**[9] 6647 3-9-4 **75**.................... MartinHarley 2 79+
(Mick Channon) *in rr: n.m.r on inner ins fnl 2f: hdwy appr fnl f: pushed along clsng stages to take 2nd last strides but no ch w wnr* **2/1**[1]
0124 3 nk **Edged Out**[28] 6045 3-8-11 **73**.................... OisinMurphy(5) 6 76
(Christopher Mason) *pressed ldr: led 2f out: hung lft appr fnl f and hrd pressed tl hdd fnl 110yds: sn outpcd by wnr: dropped to 3rd last strides* **10/1**
1353 4 1 ¼ **Daylight**[15] 6429 3-9-7 **78**....................(t) JimmyFortune 9 77
(Andrew Balding) *in tch: hdwy 2f out: styd on u.p fnl f: nt rch ldrs* **7/1**[3]
0505 5 2 ½ **Ask The Guru**[15] 6429 3-9-5 **76**....................(v) SebSanders 7 66
(Michael Attwater) *pressed ldr: rdn 2f out: wknd over 1f out* **33/1**
1400 6 hd **Lager Time (IRE)**[23] 6214 3-8-7 **67**.................... DeclanBates(3) 5 56
(David Evans) *in rr: sme hdwy fr 2f out: nvr gng pce to rch ldrs* **33/1**
556 7 ½ **Khefyn (IRE)**[50] 5300 3-8-7 **64** oh2.................... LukeMorris 8 51
(Ronald Harris) *in tch: sme hdwy whn n.m.r and stmbld 2f out: sme late progres* **40/1**
-444 8 hd **Somoud (IRE)**[27] 6077 3-8-11 **68**....................(v[1]) SilvestreDeSousa 4 54
(J R Jenkins) *in rr: pushed along over 1f out: styd on clsng stages: nvr any ch* **10/1**
411 9 hd **Emjayem**[26] 6100 3-9-3 **74**.................... RichardHughes 3 60
(Ed McMahon) *slt ld but hrd pressed tl hdd 2f out: btn whn hmpd on rail appr 1f out* **11/4**[2]
1-40 10 1 ½ **Cross My Heart**[17] 6362 3-8-9 **66**.................... LiamJones 1 46
(William Haggas) *chsd ldrs: rdn and nt much daylight 2f out: wknd over 1f out* **12/1**

1m 0.55s (-1.95) **Going Correction** -0.30s/f (Firm) **10** Ran SP% **119.2**
Speed ratings (Par 103): **103,100,100,98,94 93,93,92,92,89**
toteswingers 1&2 £3.80, 1&3 £9.60, 2&3 £5.30 CSF £21.62 CT £148.25 TOTE £7.50: £1.70, £1.40, £2.70; EX 26.40 Trifecta £216.90 Pool: £4,491.36 - 15.52 winning units.
Owner Heart Of The South Racing **Bred** Tribes Man Syndicate **Trained** Lower Beeding, W Sussex

FOCUS
The feature race on the card. The market got this wrong.

6901 BATH LUXURY TOILET HIRE H'CAP 5f 11y
5:00 (5:00) (Class 6) (0-60,60) 3-Y-O+ £1,940 (£577; £288; £144) Stalls Centre

Form RPR
050 1 **Compton Prince**[18] 6324 4-9-2 **55**....................(b) AdamKirby 3 63
(Milton Bradley) *chsd ldrs: rdn to chal fr 1f out: led fnl 75yds: a jst doing enough* **33/1**
5032 2 nk **Mossgo (IRE)**[6] 6732 3-9-4 **58**....................(t) GeorgeBaker 5 65
(John Best) *led: jnd 1f out: hdd fnl 75yds: nt pce of wnr but jst hld on for 2nd* **7/1**[3]
1040 3 nk **Spray Tan**[36] 5796 3-9-6 **60**.................... LiamKeniry 4 66
(Tony Carroll) *chsd ldrs: rdn over 1f out: styd on clsng stages to press for 2nd nr fin but nt quite pce of wnr* **18/1**
3621 4 1 ¼ **Burnt Cream**[30] 5982 6-9-2 **55**....................(t) RobertHavlin 6 57
(Martin Bosley) *chsd ldrs: rdn over 1f out: styd on same pce ins fnl f* **5/1**[2]
026 5 1 **Diamond Vine (IRE)**[6] 6732 5-9-3 **56**....................(v) LukeMorris 11 54
(Ronald Harris) *wnt rt s: in rr: rdn over 1f out: styd on wl fnl 110yds* **15/2**
0000 6 ½ **Cristaliyev**[28] 6038 5-8-4 **46** oh1....................(p) DeclanBates(3) 13 42
(David Evans) *bmpd s: in rr: hdwy fr 2f out: kpt on u.p ins fnl f* **12/1**
6403 7 hd **Brandywell Boy (IRE)**[26] 6101 10-8-7 **46** oh1............(b) CathyGannon 1 41
(Dominic Ffrench Davis) *chsd ldrs: rdn 2f out: wknd ins fnl f* **25/1**
4145 8 ¾ **Arch Walker (IRE)**[39] 5670 6-9-4 **57**....................(b) JimmyQuinn 8 50
(John Weymes) *chsd ldrs: hung lft over 1f out and sn wknd* **8/1**
6653 9 1 ¼ **Talqaa**[15] 6425 3-9-2 **56**.................... MartinHarley 10 44
(Mick Channon) *in tch: rdn 2f out: wknd appr fnl f* **10/1**
0323 10 shd **Little China**[9] 6652 4-8-11 **50**....................(b) FrederikTylicki 9 38
(William Muir) *chsd ldr: wkng whn bmpd over 1f out* **5/2**[1]
2440 11 5 **Scommettitrice (IRE)**[24] 6156 5-8-12 **54**..(b) WilliamTwiston-Davies(3) 7 24
(Mark Gillard) *outpcd* **33/1**
5600 12 1 ¼ **Fletcher Christian**[11] 6560 3-9-1 **60**....................(b[1]) JoeyHaynes(5) 12 25
(John Gallagher) *bmpd s: outpcd* **14/1**

1m 1.21s (-1.29) **Going Correction** -0.30s/f (Firm)
WFA 3 from 4yo+ 1lb **12** Ran SP% **119.1**
Speed ratings (Par 101): **98,97,97,95,93 92,92,91,89,88 80,78**
toteswingers 1&2 £26.20, 1&3 £58.70, 2&3 £19.30 CSF £248.04 CT £2697.87 TOTE £24.30: £9.60, £2.60, £5.00; EX 254.70 Trifecta £2238.10 Part won. Pool: £2,984.25 - 0.26 winning units.
Owner E A Hayward **Bred** Whitsbury Manor Stud **Trained** Sedbury, Gloucs

FOCUS
A low-grade handicap run over the minimum trip, in which it paid to be up with the pace.

6902 FRP ADVISORY "HANDS AND HEELS" APPRENTICE SERIES H'CAP (PART OF RACING EXCELLENCE INITIATIVE) 5f 161y
5:30 (5:33) (Class 6) (0-60,60) 3-Y-O £1,940 (£577; £288; £144) Stalls Centre

Form RPR
0430 1 **Tiger's Home**[13] 6502 3-9-0 **53**.................... ShelleyBirkett 11 59
(Julia Feilden) *in tch: hdwy 2f out: drvn to ld fnl 110yds: kpt on wl* **20/1**
3441 2 ½ **Imperial Spirit**[9] 6651 3-9-0 **53**....................(v) DanielCremin 1 57
(Mick Channon) *led: drvn 2f out: hdd fnl 110yds: no ex* **7/1**[3]
0010 3 ¾ **Scarlet Strand**[17] 6362 3-8-8 **52**.................... RobHornby(5) 12 54+
(Andrew Hollinshead) *in tch: hdwy over 1f out: styd on to take 3rd clsng stages: nt rch ldng duo* **14/1**
0230 4 ½ **Black Truffle (FR)**[19] 6316 3-8-9 **51**....................(v) CharlotteJenner(3) 3 51
(Mark Usher) *chsd ldrs: drvn in 3rd and no imp fnl f: dropped to 4th clsng stages* **9/2**[1]
004 5 ½ **Princess Sheila (IRE)**[2] 6849 3-8-10 **52**.................... DavidParkes(3) 14 50
(J S Moore) *in rr: drvn and gd hdwy appr fnl f: fin wl* **20/1**
56 6 ½ **Assertive Agent**[53] 5177 3-9-6 **59**....................[1] JoeyHaynes 2 56
(Tony Carroll) *in tch: chsd ldrs and drvn 2f out: styd on same pce ins fnl f* **5/1**[2]
-530 7 ¾ **Birdie Queen**[58] 4999 3-9-0 **58**.................... HectorCrouch(5) 8 52
(Gary Moore) *chsd ldrs: rdn 2f out: wknd ins fnl f* **14/1**
-055 8 3 ½ **Little Miss Zuri (IRE)**[28] 6033 3-8-7 **46** oh1.................... LouisSteward 4 29
(Sylvester Kirk) *chsd ldr: wknd over 1f out* **20/1**
4450 9 1 ¾ **Baltic Gin (IRE)**[35] 5817 3-8-13 **52**.................... EoinWalsh 7 29
(Malcolm Saunders) *chsd ldrs: wknd over 1f out* **12/1**
2033 10 ½ **Winnie Perry**[28] 6043 3-9-4 **57**....................(b) PatMillman 9 32
(Rod Millman) *chsd ldrs: wknd wl over 1f out* **8/1**
0130 11 hd **Blue Clumber**[24] 6156 3-8-7 **51**.................... JoshQuinn(5) 13 25
(Shaun Harris) *in rr: drvn over 2f out: sme hdwy fnl f* **18/1**
0053 12 1 ¼ **Chelsea Grey (IRE)**[24] 6157 3-8-4 **46** oh1....................(b) JackGarritty(3) 5 16
(Ronald Harris) *chsd ldrs 3f* **14/1**
6300 13 ¾ **Daisie Cutter**[125] 2762 3-8-2 **46** oh1.................... EilishMcCall(5) 16 14
(Graeme McPherson) *outpcd* **25/1**
0544 14 hd **Senora Lobo (IRE)**[32] 5916 3-8-9 **48**.................... RobJFitzpatrick 15 15
(Lisa Williamson) *outpcd* **25/1**
3203 15 ½ **Coconut Kisses**[15] 6436 3-9-4 **60**.................... OllieGarner(3) 10 26
(Bill Turner) *chsd ldrs to 1/2-way* **12/1**
5000 16 ¾ **Exit Clause**[119] 2919 3-8-6 **48**....................(tp) AaronJones(3) 6 11
(Mark Gillard) *outpcd* **66/1**

1m 10.93s (-0.27) **Going Correction** -0.30s/f (Firm) **16** Ran SP% **122.6**
Speed ratings (Par 99): **89,88,87,86,86 85,84,79,77,76 76,74,73,73,72 71**
toteswingers 1&2 £35.80, 1&3 £58.40, 2&3 £22.70 CSF £144.06 CT £2140.99 TOTE £30.80: £7.80, £1.50, £5.10, £1.60; EX 255.20 Trifecta £1980.60 Part won. Pool: £2,640.82 - 0.39 winning units.
Owner Miss J Feilden **Bred** East Burrow Farm **Trained** Exning, Suffolk

FOCUS
A wide-open apprentice handicap in which riders were unable to use their whips.
T/Jkpt: Not won. T/Plt: £28.30 to a £1 stake. Pool: £94,595.89 - 2,439.48 winning units T/Qpdt: £3.70 to a £1 stake. Pool: £8,268.47 - 1,630.13 winning units ST

6681 HAMILTON (R-H)
Monday, September 30

OFFICIAL GOING: Good (good to soft in places; 7.5)
Wind: Breezy, half behind Weather: Cloudy, bright

6903 FREE BINGO AT BINGO.FREEBETS.CO.UK H'CAP 5f 4y
2:10 (2:10) (Class 6) (0-65,62) 3-Y-O+ £2,045 (£603; £302) Stalls Centre

Form RPR
0060 1 **Fol Hollow (IRE)**[1] 6878 8-9-3 **55**.................... MichaelO'Connell 6 63
(Stuart Coltherd) *mde all: rdn over 1f out: edgd lft ins fnl f: kpt on* **12/1**
4040 2 ½ **Tuibama (IRE)**[5] 6757 4-9-8 **60**....................(p) JoeFanning 8 66
(Tracy Waggott) *pressed wnr: rdn 2f out: kpt on ins fnl f* **9/2**[3]
5651 3 1 ½ **Manatee Bay**[7] 6682 3-8-11 **57** 6ex.................... JordanNason(7) 4 58
(David Nicholls) *dwlt: t.k.h and sn in tch: effrt and rdn over 1f out: kpt on ins fnl f* **2/1**[1]
00 4 2 ½ **Red Roar (IRE)**[10] 6603 6-9-0 **52**....................(p) PatrickMathers 12 44
(Alan Berry) *taken early to post: hld up: rdn over 2f out: kpt on fnl f: nvr able to chal* **18/1**
025 5 hd **Rock Canyon (IRE)**[7] 6687 4-8-10 **48**....................(p) PJMcDonald 7 39
(Linda Perratt) *in tch: rdn and outpcd over 2f out: sme late hdwy: nvr on terms* **11/2**
002 6 hd **Hills Of Dakota**[7] 6687 5-9-7 **59**....................(b) TomEaves 10 49
(Keith Dalgleish) *taken early to post: in tch: effrt and rdn 2f out: outpcd fnl f* **4/1**[2]
0056 7 1 **Flow Chart (IRE)**[3] 6808 6-8-8 **49**.................... SladeO'Hara(3) 3 36
(Peter Grayson) *towards rr: drvn along 1/2-way: nvr able to chal* **16/1**
0000 8 nse **Musical Strike**[1] 6878 4-8-2 **45**....................(vt) ShirleyTeasdale(5) 2 31
(Shaun Harris) *chsd ldrs: rdn and edgd rt 1/2-way: wknd appr fnl f* **66/1**
4000 9 3 ½ **Pitt Rivers**[11] 6547 4-9-6 **58**.................... PhillipMakin 5 32
(Linda Perratt) *bhd: rdn and edgd rt over 2f out: nvr on terms* **22/1**

59.81s (-0.19) **Going Correction** +0.025s/f (Good)
WFA 3 from 4yo+ 1lb **9** Ran SP% **111.6**
Speed ratings (Par 101): **102,101,98,94,94 94,92,92,86**
toteswingers 1&2 £7.20, 2&3 £2.60, 1&3 £5.60 CSF £62.23 CT £152.35 TOTE £11.20: £2.40, £1.30, £1.30; EX 64.90 Trifecta £283.80 Pool: £2,274.16 - 6.00 winning units.
Owner Aidan Gunning **Bred** Dan O'Brien **Trained** Selkirk, Borders

FOCUS
Rail realignment around the loop reduced races on Round course by about 25 yards. The ground had continued to dry out and after the opener Joe Fanning reckoned it was "just on the easy side of good" on the straight track. A low-grade sprint handicap and they raced in one group mainly towards the centre. The first two home were one-two throughout.

6904 FREEBETS AT FREEBETS.CO.UK AUCTION NURSERY H'CAP 6f 5y
2:40 (2:40) (Class 5) 2-Y-O £2,587 (£770; £384; £192) Stalls Centre

Form RPR
2520 1 **Milly's Secret (IRE)**[34] 5858 2-9-7 **76**.................... PJMcDonald 6 79
(Ann Duffield) *chsd ldrs: rdn over 2f out: styd on strly fnl f to ld cl home* **4/1**[3]
0040 2 hd **Gym Shoes**[10] 6582 2-8-13 **68**.................... TonyHamilton 2 70
(Richard Fahey) *chsd ldrs: drvn over 2f out: edgd lft and led wl ins fnl f: ct cl home* **3/1**[2]
2160 3 ½ **Soul Instinct**[34] 5858 2-8-7 **69**....................(p) KevinStott(7) 4 70
(Kevin Ryan) *t.k.h: led: rdn and drifted lft over 1f out: hdd and no ex wl ins fnl f* **15/2**
4406 4 2 **Dry Your Eyes (IRE)**[23] 6206 2-8-10 **65**.................... JoeFanning 1 60
(Mark Johnston) *chsd ldrs: rdn and outpcd over 2f out: kpt on ins fnl f* **9/4**[1]
5054 5 1 ¼ **Red Forever**[20] 6286 2-8-2 **57**.................... PatrickMathers 5 48
(Alan Berry) *t.k.h in rr: rdn and outpcd over 2f out: rallied fnl f: nvr able to chal* **22/1**
2654 6 nk **Henke (IRE)**[19] 6295 2-8-2 **64**.................... DanielleMooney(7) 3 54
(Nigel Tinkler) *chsd ldrs: rdn and edgd rt wl over 1f out: outpcd fnl f* **9/2**

1m 13.15s (0.95) **Going Correction** +0.025s/f (Good) **6** Ran SP% **110.1**
Speed ratings (Par 95): **94,93,93,90,88 88**
toteswingers 1&2 £2.30, 1&3 £4.20, 2&3 £3.80 CSF £15.65 TOTE £6.50: £2.20, £2.30; EX 17.30 Trifecta £84.30 Pool: £2,074.71 - 18.44 winning units.
Owner Jimmy Kay **Bred** John B Hughes **Trained** Constable Burton, N Yorks
■ Stewards' Enquiry : P J McDonald two-day ban: used whip above permitted level (Oct 14-15)

The Form Book Flat, Raceform Ltd, Compton, RG20 6NL.

FOCUS
A tricky-looking if ordinary nursery and a tight three-way finish.

6905 MOBILE BETTING FREE BETS AT FREEBETS.CO.UK CLASSIFIED CLAIMING STKS 6f 5y
3:10 (3:10) (Class 6) 3-Y-0+ **£2,045** (£603; £302) **Stalls** Centre

Form RPR
3004 **1** **Bunce (IRE)**[10] 6606 5-9-4 62.....................(b) DanielTudhope 1 69
(David O'Meara) *hld up in tch: rdn over 2f out: hdwy to ld over 1f out: kpt on strly: eased cl home* **9/2**[2]
2263 **2** 2 **Hanalei Bay (IRE)**[10] 6587 3-9-4 63.....................(p) TomEaves 5 65
(Keith Dalgleish) *w ldrs: rdn over 2f out: kpt on fnl f: nt gng pce of wnr* **11/2**[3]
3325 **3** nk **Beckermet (IRE)**[20] 6291 11-8-6 68..................... PJMcDonald 7 50
(Ruth Carr) *led: rdn over 2f out: hdd over 1f out: kpt on same pce* **1/1**[1]
6054 **4** 1 ½ **Song Of Parkes**[19] 6310 6-8-12 66..................... SladeO'Hara(3) 3 54
(Peter Grayson) *prom: effrt and drvn wl over 1f out: kpt on same pce fnl f* **10/1**
350 **5** 7 **We Have A Dream**[10] 6606 8-8-10 67.....................(tp) CharlesBishop(3) 4 29
(Violet M Jordan) *cl up: rdn over 2f out: wknd wl over 1f out* **14/1**
-600 **6** 14 **Crown Choice**[174] 1442 8-8-8 68..................... GrahamGibbons 6
(Paul Midgley) *missed break: sn in tch: rdn over 2f out: sn wknd: eased whn no ch fnl f* **13/2**

1m 11.63s (-0.57) **Going Correction** +0.025s/f (Good)
WFA 3 from 5yo+ 2lb **6 Ran SP% 112.7**
Speed ratings (Par 101): **104,101,100,98,89 70**
toteswingers 1&2 £2.50, 2&3 £2.00, 1&3 £1.60 CSF £28.67 TOTE £3.80: £2.10, £2.20; EX 17.10 Trifecta £58.50 Pool: £1,926.53 - 24.67 winning units.
Owner Wildcard Racing Syndicate X1 & Partners **Bred** John Doyle **Trained** Nawton, N Yorks

FOCUS
A 6f claimer in which official ratings went out of the window.

6906 CASINO BETS AT BONUS.CO.UK H'CAP 1m 65y
3:40 (3:40) (Class 5) (0-75,74) 3-Y-0+ **£3,408** (£1,006; £503) **Stalls** Low

Form RPR
6620 **1** **Spes Nostra**[11] 6548 5-9-3 70.....................(b) GrahamGibbons 4 78
(David Barron) *chsd ldrs: hdwy to dispute ld after 2f: rdn 2f out: led wl ins fnl f: kpt on wl* **13/2**
6132 **2** ¾ **Tectonic (IRE)**[1] 6877 4-9-3 70.....................(p) TomEaves 9 76
(Keith Dalgleish) *trckd ldrs: rdn to chal over 1f out: edgd rt: kpt on fnl f: hld nr fin* **13/2**
1322 **3** hd **Ralphy Boy (IRE)**[11] 6562 4-9-2 69..................... MichaelO'Connell 1 75
(Alistair Whillans) *led: jnd after 2f: rdn over 2f out: hdd and no ex wl ins fnl f* **7/2**[2]
0612 **4** 2 **Pivotman**[47] 5383 5-9-5 72..................... DanielTudhope 8 73
(Michael Easterby) *prom: effrt and rdn 2f out: kpt on same pce fnl f* **11/4**[1]
504 **5** ½ **I'm Super Too (IRE)**[6] 6730 6-9-1 68..................... BenCurtis 2 68
(Alan Swinbank) *prom: rdn over 2f out: kpt on same pce appr fnl f* **8/1**
0-00 **6** 1 ¼ **Good Boy Jackson**[11] 6550 5-9-7 74..................... DavidAllan 3 71
(R Mike Smith) *hld up in tch: drvn and outpcd over 3f out: no imp fr over 1f out* **11/1**
0053 **7** 3 **Steer By The Stars (IRE)**[15] 6433 3-9-3 74.....................(b1) JoeFanning 5 64
(Mark Johnston) *s.i.s: hld up: rdn over 3f out: nvr able to chal* **6/1**[3]
5042 **8** 3 ½ **Konzert (ITY)**[9] 6657 3-8-4 64..................... RyanPowell(3) 6 46
(Ian Williams) *s.i.s: t.k.h in rr: rdn along over 3f out: wknd over 2f out* **12/1**

1m 46.27s (-2.13) **Going Correction** -0.15s/f (Firm)
WFA 3 from 4yo+ 4lb **8 Ran SP% 117.0**
Speed ratings (Par 103): **104,103,103,101,100 99,96,92**
toteswingers 1&2 £7.10, 1&3 £5.30, 2&3 £4.70 CSF £49.05 CT £174.19 TOTE £9.30: £2.90, £2.70, £1.20; EX 51.70 Trifecta £136.00 Pool: £1,845.03 - 10.17 winning units.
Owner J Cringan & D Pryde **Bred** James A Cringan **Trained** Maunby, N Yorks

FOCUS
An open-looking, soundly run extended mile handicap and three going head-to-head over the final quarter mile.

6907 WILLIAM HILL FREE BETS AT FREEBETS.CO.UK APPRENTICE H'CAP (HAMILTON PARK APPRENTICE SERIES FINAL) 1m 1f 36y
4:10 (4:11) (Class 6) (0-65,65) 3-Y-0+ **£1,940** (£577; £288; £144) **Stalls** Low

Form RPR
0-03 **1** **Camerooney**[28] 6053 10-9-5 58.....................(p) NathanAlison 3 69
(Marjorie Fife) *mde all: rdn over 2f out: hung lft 1f out: kpt on wl* **22/1**
6003 **2** 2 ¾ **High Resolution**[8] 6667 6-9-9 62..................... ConnorBeasley 9 67
(Linda Perratt) *t.k.h: hld up: hdwy on outside to chse wnr over 2f out: hung rt: kpt on fnl f* **11/2**[3]
5215 **3** 2 ¾ **Taxiformissbyron**[6] 6723 3-8-11 55..................... KevinStott 8 55
(Michael Herrington) *midfield on outside: effrt and hdwy over 2f out: kpt on same pce fnl f* **11/4**[1]
6-34 **4** nk **Watt Broderick (IRE)**[42] 1220 4-9-12 65..................... LeeTopliss 4 63
(Ian Williams) *prom: effrt and rdn over 2f out: one pce over 1f out* **9/2**[2]
620 **5** 3 ¼ **Politbureau**[46] 5420 6-8-12 51 oh2.....................(p) ShirleyTeasdale 5 42
(Michael Easterby) *midfield: rdn and outpcd over 3f out: styd on fnl f: nvr rchd ldrs* **22/1**
0-00 **6** 1 **Funky Munky**[54] 5143 8-8-12 51 oh3.....................(p) JulieBurke 7 40
(Alistair Whillans) *cl up tl rdn and wknd over 1f out* **22/1**
030 **7** 1 ¼ **Bitusa (USA)**[28] 6049 3-8-12 56.....................(b1) GemmaTutty 2 43
(Alan Swinbank) *midfield: rdn and outpcd whn n.m.r briefly over 2f out: sn btn* **14/1**
-060 **8** ½ **Inniscastle Boy**[35] 5833 4-8-5 51 oh4..................... SophieRobertson(7) 6 36
(Jim Goldie) *hld up: pushed along on outside 3f out: sme late hdwy: nvr on terms* **22/1**
1315 **9** shd **Mcconnell (USA)**[3] 6804 8-9-0 53.....................(b) CharlesBishop 12 38
(Violet M Jordan) *chsd ldrs: drvn over 3f out: wknd 2f out* **16/1**
6100 **10** 3 ½ **Lucy Bee**[10] 6588 3-9-2 60..................... IanBurns 10 38
(R Mike Smith) *in tch: rdn along over 3f out: wknd over 2f out* **40/1**
0-04 **11** 1 ¼ **Travel (USA)**[11] 6566 3-9-4 62..................... MichaelJMMurphy 11 37
(Mark Johnston) *towards rr: rdn and struggling whn and hung rt over 2f out: nvr on terms* **13/2**
0005 **12** nse **Ay Tay Tate (IRE)**[6] 6722 7-9-2 55.....................(p) JasonHart 13 29
(Noel Wilson) *midfield: drvn over 4f out: wknd wl over 2f out* **22/1**
020 **13** 7 **Dialogue**[9] 6634 7-9-12 65.....................(t) JordanNason 1 24
(Geoffrey Harker) *hld up in midfield on ins: stdy hdwy over 3f out: rdn and wknd over 2f out* **10/1**

1m 57.89s (-1.81) **Going Correction** -0.15s/f (Firm)
WFA 3 from 4yo+ 5lb **13 Ran SP% 119.4**
Speed ratings (Par 101): **102,99,97,96,93 93,91,91,91,88 87,87,80**
toteswingers 1&2 £29.80, 1&3 £20.10, 2&3 £3.80 CSF £128.60 CT £450.18 TOTE £28.50: £7.50, £2.20, £1.60; EX 147.80 Trifecta £658.80 Pool: £2,212.80 - 2.51 winning units.
Owner Mrs Jean Stapleton **Bred** Miss Dianne Hill **Trained** Stillington, N Yorks

FOCUS
The winner made all, with the second in last to halfway. The form looks ok for the grade.

6908 DOWNLOAD AT FREE BETS APP FREEBETS.CO.UK H'CAP 6f 5y
4:40 (4:41) (Class 4) (0-80,80) 3-Y-0+ **£5,175** (£1,540; £769; £384) **Stalls** Centre

Form RPR
6100 **1** **Barkston Ash**[2] 6822 5-9-5 78.....................(p) JasonHart(3) 11 86
(Eric Alston) *rrd s: sn in tch: rdn and hdwy over 1f out: styd on wl to ld nr fin* **16/1**
0020 **2** hd **Towbee**[35] 5832 4-9-7 77.....................(b) GrahamGibbons 9 84
(Michael Easterby) *led: rdn over 1f out: kpt on fnl f: hdd nr fin* **33/1**
1113 **3** ½ **Lothair (IRE)**[6] 6728 4-8-12 68..................... BenCurtis 2 74
(Alan Swinbank) *prom: effrt and rdn 2f out: kpt on ins fnl f: hld nr fin* **6/1**[3]
5033 **4** 1 ½ **Amenable (IRE)**[4] 6771 6-8-13 72.....................(p) CharlesBishop(3) 12 73
(Violet M Jordan) *hld up: rdn and hdwy over 1f out: kpt on fnl f: nrst fin* **20/1**
000 **5** nk **Jinky**[10] 6586 5-9-4 74..................... TomEaves 7 74
(Linda Perratt) *midfield: rdn over 2f out: kpt on fnl f: nvr able to chal* **20/1**
5410 **6** hd **Indego Blues**[10] 6586 4-9-0 77..................... JordanNason(7) 1 76+
(David Nicholls) *bhd: hdwy on far side over 2f out: kpt on same pce fnl f* **9/1**
2050 **7** nk **Sunraider (IRE)**[31] 5971 6-9-7 77..................... LeeTopliss 3 75
(Paul Midgley) *towards rr: rdn over 2f out: hdwy over 1f out: nrst fin* **12/1**
4020 **8** nk **Economic Crisis (IRE)**[8] 6665 4-8-13 69..................... PatrickMathers 6 66
(Alan Berry) *dwlt: sn pushed along towards rr: hdwy and prom over 2f out: one pce fnl f* **40/1**
0102 **9** 1 **Just The Tonic**[6] 6728 6-8-11 72..................... ShirleyTeasdale(5) 5 66
(Marjorie Fife) *chsd ldrs tl rdn and wknd over 1f out* **14/1**
4232 **10** nse **Tajneed (IRE)**[35] 5832 10-9-2 72..................... AdrianNicholls 13 66
(David Nicholls) *in tch: drvn over 2f out: no ex over 1f out* **14/1**
0000 **11** 1 ¼ **Klynch**[13] 6496 7-9-8 78.....................(b) PJMcDonald 10 68
(Ruth Carr) *towards rr: drvn along 1/2-way: nvr rchd ldrs* **20/1**
6435 **12** ½ **Bonnie Charlie**[10] 6583 7-9-5 75..................... PaulQuinn 8 63
(David Nicholls) *bhd: rdn over 2f out: nvr on terms* **11/1**
0U41 **13** ¾ **Master Bond**[12] 6515 4-9-10 80..................... DanielTudhope 4 66
(David O'Meara) *in tch: rdn over 2f out: wknd over 1f out* **11/2**[2]
6350 **14** 7 **The Nifty Fox**[10] 6583 9-9-5 75.....................(p) PhillipMakin 16 39
(Tim Easterby) *dwlt: hld up: pushed along over 2f out: sn btn* **25/1**
331 **15** 6 **Dawn Calling (IRE)**[9] 6630 3-9-6 78..................... JoeFanning 15 22
(Mark Johnston) *in tch tl rdn and wknd qckly fr 2f out* **3/1**[1]
05R3 **R** **Defence Council (IRE)**[4] 6774 5-9-5 75..................... TonyHamilton 14
(Mel Brittain) *ref to r* **16/1**

1m 11.57s (-0.63) **Going Correction** +0.025s/f (Good)
WFA 3 from 4yo+ 2lb **16 Ran SP% 129.3**
Speed ratings (Par 105): **105,104,104,102,101 101,101,100,99,99 97,96,95,86,78**
toteswingers 1&2 £105.60, 1&3 £34.80, 2&3 £97.50 CSF £492.80 CT £3652.38 TOTE £24.60: £4.50, £7.70, £1.80, £3.10; EX 791.50 Trifecta £1312.00 Part won. Pool: £1,749.38 - 0.08 winning units.
Owner The Selebians **Bred** Jonathan Shack **Trained** Longton, Lancs

FOCUS
A maximum field of 16 runners in this fiercely competitive sprint handicap. They raced middle-to-stands' side.

6909 FOOTBALL FREE BETS AT FREEBETS.CO.UK H'CAP 1m 4f 17y
5:10 (5:11) (Class 5) (0-70,76) 3-Y-0+ **£3,234** (£962; £481; £240) **Stalls** Low

Form RPR
1240 **1** **Vittachi**[11] 6552 6-8-8 53.....................(p) JasonHart(3) 5 64
(Alistair Whillans) *midfield: hdwy on outside to ld over 3f out: sn rdn: kpt on wl fr 2f out* **8/1**
5530 **2** 1 ¾ **Korngold**[10] 6598 5-8-9 51 oh1..................... JoeFanning 4 59
(Tracy Waggott) *t.k.h: hld up: stdy hdwy over 4f out: effrt and chsd wnr over 1f out: kpt on same pce wl ins fnl f* **4/1**[2]
4001 **3** 6 **Bling King**[7] 6700 4-9-13 76 6ex..................... JordanNason(7) 3 74
(Geoffrey Harker) *t.k.h: prom: effrt and chsd wnr over 3f out: hung lft and lost 2nd over 1f out: sn outpcd* **7/1**[3]
5440 **4** 4 ½ **Grandiloquent**[10] 6598 4-9-4 60.....................(p) PhillipMakin 11 51
(Kevin Ryan) *hld up: drvn and hdwy over 2f out: kpt on fnl f: no imp* **10/1**
3232 **5** 1 ½ **Geanie Mac (IRE)**[14] 6470 4-8-12 54.....................(p) PJMcDonald 2 43
(Linda Perratt) *w ldr to over 3f out: sn rdn: wknd wl over 1f out* **8/1**
0000 **6** 1 ¾ **Jawaab (IRE)**[14] 6470 9-8-13 55.....................(p) MichaelO'Connell 7 41
(Philip Kirby) *hld up: rdn and outpcd over 4f out: eased whn hld over 2f out: sme hdwy and shkn up fnl f: nvr nrr* **11/1**
2564 **7** 8 **Light The City (IRE)**[14] 6479 6-8-4 51 oh6..........(b1) ConnorBeasley(5) 1 24
(Ruth Carr) *slt ld to over 3f out: rdn and wknd over 2f out* **18/1**
2410 **8** 10 **Dean Iarracht (IRE)**[14] 6470 7-8-10 52.....................(p) GrahamGibbons 9 9
(Tracy Waggott) *in tch: drvn and outpcd over 3f out: sn btn* **20/1**
3051 **9** 17 **Naburn**[9] 6632 5-10-0 70..................... BenCurtis 8
(Alan Swinbank) *cl up on outside tl rdn and wknd over 3f out: eased whn no ch fnl f* **5/2**[1]
60 **10** 20 **Causeway Foot (USA)**[97] 3653 3-8-8 58 ow1.....................(t) TomEaves 6
(Jedd O'Keeffe) *in tch: struggling 1/2-way: lost tch fr 4f out: t.o* **20/1**

2m 37.03s (-1.57) **Going Correction** -0.15s/f (Firm)
WFA 3 from 4yo+ 8lb **10 Ran SP% 115.5**
Speed ratings (Par 103): **99,97,93,90,89 88,83,76,65,52**
toteswingers 1&2 £6.90, 1&3 £9.60, 2&3 £6.00 CSF £39.65 CT £234.02 TOTE £8.30: £3.00, £1.80, £2.20; EX 37.40 Trifecta £334.40 Pool: £1,176.38 - 2.63 winning units.
Owner Sutherland Five **Bred** London Thoroughbred Services Ltd **Trained** Newmill-On-Slitrig, Borders

FOCUS
An open-looking handicap run at a sound pace and in the end just the first three were seriously involved.
T/Plt: £348.60 to a £1 stake. Pool: £73,594.61 - 154.10 winning units T/Qpdt: £67.20 to a £1 stake. Pool: £4,659.91 - 51.30 winning units RY

6910 - 6913a (Foreign Racing) - See Raceform Interactive

6619 AYR (L-H)

Tuesday, October 1

OFFICIAL GOING: Good (good to firm in places; 9.0)

Wind: Fresh, half behind Weather: Overcast

6914 £25 FREE BET AT BETVICTOR.COM NURSERY H'CAP 7f 50y

2:10 (2:10) (Class 6) (0-65,64) 2-Y-O **£1,940** (£577; £288; £144) **Stalls** High

Form RPR

060 **1** **Marlismamma (FR)**[15] 6477 2-8-4 **50** JulieBurke(3) 3 56+
(David O'Meara) *trckd ldrs: shkn up to ld over 2f out: rdn and r.o wl fnl f* **16/1**

3205 **2** ½ **Sakhalin Star (IRE)**[46] 5467 2-9-0 **62** ConnorBeasley(5) 2 64
(Richard Guest) *hld up: effrt and hdwy on outside 2f out: chsd wnr ins fnl f: r.o* **13/2**

0045 **3** 2¾ **Two Shades Of Grey (IRE)**[9] 6663 2-9-7 **64** TonyHamilton 4 59
(Richard Fahey) *trckd ldrs: rdn over 2f out: edgd rt: kpt on ins fnl f* **10/3**[1]

400 **4** 1 **Alaskan Night (IRE)**[60] 4963 2-9-3 **60** GrahamLee 7 52
(Kevin Ryan) *t.k.h: led to over 2f out: rallied: outpcd ins fnl f* **8/1**

0000 **5** 3¾ **Bridge Of Avon**[35] 5865 2-8-2 **45** DuranFentiman 8 27
(Mel Brittain) *s.i.s: bhd: rdn over 2f out: hdwy over 1f out: nvr able to chal* **100/1**

006 **6** 2½ **Trinity Lorraine (IRE)**[27] 6112 2-7-11 **45** NoelGarbutt(5) 1 21
(Alan Bailey) *chsd ldng gp: effrt and rdn over 2f out: wknd over 1f out* **4/1**[2]

5103 **7** 1½ **Strictly Glitz (IRE)**[14] 6494 2-8-8 **58** JoeDoyle(7) 6 30
(John Quinn) *plld hrd: in tch tl rdn and wknd over 1f out* **9/1**

430 **8** 9 **Chookie's Lass**[36] 5826 2-9-7 **64** TomEaves 9 12
(Keith Dalgleish) *prom on outside: rdn over 2f out: wknd over 1f out* **6/1**[3]

5031 **9** 26 **Witchy Woman**[60] 4964 2-8-11 **59** JoeyHaynes(5) 5
(K R Burke) *in tch: rdn over 2f out: sn btn: t.o* **6/1**[3]

1m 34.11s (0.71) **Going Correction** -0.075s/f (Good) **9** Ran SP% **113.0**

Speed ratings (Par 93): **92,91,88,87,82 80,78,68,38**

toteswingers 1&2 £20.00, 2&3 £3.80, 1&3 £14.60 CSF £113.31 CT £433.98 TOTE £21.20: £5.60, £2.20, £3.00; EX 208.60 Trifecta £1584.20 Pool: £2499.67 - 1.18 winning units..

Owner Middleham Park Racing LXVI & Partners **Bred** Alain Fracas **Trained** Nawton, N Yorks

FOCUS

Bends and home straight moved out 8m, adding 24yds to races of 7f and 1m, and 38yds to 1m5f race. Moderate nursery form.

6915 BETVICTOR.COM MAIDEN AUCTION STKS 6f

2:40 (2:41) (Class 5) 2-Y-O **£2,911** (£866; £432) **Stalls** Low

Form RPR

220 **1** **Sandra's Diamond (IRE)**[10] 6622 2-8-4 77 BarryMcHugh 3 77
(Keith Dalgleish) *taken early to post: mde all: rdn and edgd lft over 1f out: kpt on wl: unchal* **4/5**[1]

3534 **2** 3½ **Missouri Spirit**[10] 6627 2-8-9 77 GrahamLee 2 72
(Kevin Ryan) *chsd wnr thrght: rdn along 2f out: kpt on same pce fnl f* **6/5**[2]

040 **3** 9 **Penny Pursuits**[7] 6718 2-8-4 0 PatrickMathers 4 40
(Alan Berry) *bhd and outpcd: drvn along 1/2-way: nvr able to chal* **25/1**[3]

1m 12.24s (-0.16) **Going Correction** -0.025s/f (Good) **3** Ran SP% **104.9**

Speed ratings (Par 95): **100,95,83**

CSF £1.99 TOTE £2.00; EX 2.60 Trifecta £2.20 Pool: £1735.48 - 587.26 winning units..

Owner Prestige Thoroughbred Racing **Bred** Robert Norton **Trained** Carluke, S Lanarks

FOCUS

Only two of the three runners looked to matter beforehand, but with the runner-up never really travelling the favourite Sandra's Diamond was left to score a ready success.

6916 RBS MENTOR H'CAP 6f

3:15 (3:17) (Class 5) (0-70,70) 3-Y-O+ **£2,911** (£866; £432; £216) **Stalls** Low

Form RPR

0242 **1** **Compton Heights**[2] 6878 4-8-10 **59** GrahamLee 6 68+
(Jim Goldie) *cl up: led over 1f out: drvn out fnl f* **9/1**

3042 **2** 1¼ **Khelman (IRE)**[9] 6664 3-9-1 **70** GeorgeChaloner(5) 9 75
(Richard Fahey) *in tch: drvn and outpcd over 2f out: rallied over 1f out: kpt on strly to take 2nd nr fin: nt rch wnr* **4/1**[2]

1230 **3** ¾ **Lucky Lodge**[5] 6771 3-9-1 **65** (b) DuranFentiman 5 68
(Mel Brittain) *prom: rdn over 2f out: effrt and hdwy over 1f out: kpt on fnl f: hld towards fin* **18/1**

1104 **4** 1 **Gran Canaria Queen**[12] 6547 4-9-7 **70** DavidAllan 4 70
(Tim Easterby) *w ldrs: ev ch over 1f out: no ex ins fnl f* **7/2**[1]

0064 **5** 2¾ **Meshardal (GER)**[10] 6634 3-8-6 **56** PJMcDonald 12 48
(Ruth Carr) *prom: rdn over 2f out: hung lft over 1f out: sn outpcd* **11/1**

603 **6** ¾ **Saxonette**[9] 6669 5-8-2 **56** oh4 ConnorBeasley(5) 11 46
(Linda Perratt) *hld up: rdn and hdwy over 1f out: nvr able to chal* **14/1**

1023 **7** ½ **Black Douglas**[6] 6761 4-8-2 **58** oh1 ow2 JordanNason(7) 7 46
(Jim Goldie) *bhd and sn outpcd: hung lft over 2f out: sn no imp* **8/1**

0002 **8** 2½ **Kuanyao (IRE)**[34] 5876 7-9-5 **68** AdrianNicholls 1 49
(David Nicholls) *led tl rdn and hdwy over 1f out: sn btn* **12/1**

4334 **9** 10 **Alexandrakollontai (IRE)**[9] 6664 3-9-0 **64** (b) MichaelO'Connell 8 15
(Alistair Whillans) *dwlt: bhd and sn rdn along: no ch fr 1/2-way* **11/2**[3]

4500 **10** ¾ **Secret City (IRE)**[60] 4970 7-9-2 **68** (b) JasonHart(3) 10 16
(Robin Bastiman) *sn drvn along towards rr: struggling fr 1/2-way: sn btn* **12/1**

1m 11.49s (-0.91) **Going Correction** -0.025s/f (Good)

WFA 3 from 4yo+ 1lb **10** Ran SP% **114.4**

Speed ratings (Par 103): **105,103,102,101,97 96,95,92,79,78**

toteswingers 1&2 £7.00, 2&3 £15.90, 1&3 £14.80 CSF £44.04 CT £637.91 TOTE £10.40: £2.90, £1.60, £3.90; EX 45.70 Trifecta £616.70 Pool: £3436.75 - 4.17 winning units..

Owner David McKenzie **Bred** Jim Goldie **Trained** Uplawmoor, E Renfrews

FOCUS

Fair form for the level.

6917 DEBRA CHARITY H'CAP (QUALIFIER FOR THE £15,000 BETFAIR SCOTTISH STAYERS' SERIES FINAL) 1m 5f 13y

3:50 (3:50) (Class 5) (0-75,73) 3-Y-O+ **£2,911** (£866; £432; £216) **Stalls** Low

Form RPR

3466 **1** **Grand Diamond (IRE)**[12] 6552 9-8-5 **59** oh3 JordanNason(7) 4 66
(Jim Goldie) *hld up bhd ldng gp: hdwy to chal over 2f out: led over 1f out: rdn and r.o wl* **12/1**

3334 **2** 1 **Arr' Kid (USA)**[11] 6601 3-9-2 **71** TomEaves 2 76
(Keith Dalgleish) *cl up: rdn and led over 2f out: hdd over 1f out: kpt on fnl f: hld towards fin* **7/2**[3]

3400 **3** nk **Forrest Flyer (IRE)**[12] 6552 9-8-13 **60** GrahamLee 7 65+
(Jim Goldie) *led: rdn and hdd over 2f out: sn outpcd: kpt on wl fnl f: hld towards fin* **8/1**

00/6 **4** 2¾ **Worth A King'S**[129] 430 7-8-10 **64** EvaMoscrop(7) 3 64
(Philip Kirby) *hld up: rdn and hdwy over 2f out: no imp fr over 1f out* **14/1**

613 **5** ¾ **Beat The Tide**[45] 5549 3-8-13 **73** ConnorBeasley(5) 8 72
(Michael Dods) *cl up: effrt and ev ch over 2f out: rdn and hung lft over 1f out: sn no ex* **11/5**[1]

0050 **6** 4½ **Key Gold**[12] 6552 4-8-12 **64** GeorgeChaloner(5) 5 57
(Richard Fahey) *hld up in tch: drvn and outpcd over 2f out: edgd lft and sn no imp* **3/1**[2]

1/6- **7** 1 **Golden Groom**[399] 5714 10-8-5 **59** oh6 JackGarritty(7) 1 50
(Patrick Holmes) *t.k.h: in tch tl rdn: edgd lft and wknd 2f out* **12/1**

2m 59.36s (5.36) **Going Correction** -0.075s/f (Good)

WFA 3 from 4yo+ 8lb **7** Ran SP% **111.6**

Speed ratings (Par 103): **80,79,79,77,77 74,73**

toteswingers 1&2 £3.90, 2&3 £3.60, 1&3 £6.40 CSF £50.97 CT £354.91 TOTE £12.60: £4.30, £1.90; EX 56.00 Trifecta £186.40 Pool: £3011.49 - 12.11 winning units..

Owner Caledonia Racing **Bred** Newberry Stud Company **Trained** Uplawmoor, E Renfrews

FOCUS

Another race on the round course in which the winner challenged against the far rail.

6918 DOWNLOAD THE BETVICTOR APP NOW H'CAP (DIV I) 7f 50y

4:25 (4:25) (Class 6) (0-60,59) 3-Y-O+ **£2,045** (£603; £302) **Stalls** High

Form RPR

003 **1** **Natures Law (IRE)**[11] 6588 3-9-5 **59** TomEaves 5 66+
(Keith Dalgleish) *taken early to post: t.k.h in midfield: hdwy to ld and hrd pressed over 1f out: styd on wl last 100yds* **11/2**[2]

3221 **2** ½ **Lil Sophella (IRE)**[10] 6633 4-8-11 **56** JackGarritty(7) 1 63+
(Patrick Holmes) *hld up: gd hdwy over 2f out: chal over 1f out to ins fnl f: hld nr fin* **11/4**[1]

1056 **3** 3 **Monel**[11] 6600 5-9-1 **53** GrahamLee 6 52
(Jim Goldie) *t.k.h: hld up: smooth hdwy over 2f out: effrt and prom over 1f out: one pce fnl f* **6/1**[3]

5220 **4** ¾ **Eilean Mor**[28] 6083 5-8-4 **47** NoelGarbutt(5) 9 44
(R Mike Smith) *hld up: rdn over 2f out: hdwy over 1f out: kpt on ins fnl f* **15/2**

0564 **5** 2½ **Loukoumi**[39] 5709 5-8-7 **45** (b) RobertHavlin 11 35
(Tim Easterby) *in tch on outside: rdn and outpcd over 2f out: edgd lft: styd on fnl f: no imp* **10/1**

050U **6** 1 **Stoneacre Oskar**[8] 6687 4-9-4 **59** SladeO'Hara(3) 3 47
(Peter Grayson) *bhd: rdn 3f out: hdwy over 1f out: nvr able to chal* **22/1**

3306 **7** 2¾ **Carrie's Magic**[8] 6687 6-8-5 **46** JasonHart(3) 10 27
(Alistair Whillans) *s.i.s: sn in tch on outside: hdwy to chse ldr over 3f out: rdn and wknd over 1f out* **12/1**

4000 **8** ½ **Fife Jo**[28] 6083 3-8-5 **45** (v[1]) BarryMcHugh 8 23
(Jim Goldie) *led: rdn over 2f out: hdd over 1f out: sn wknd* **16/1**

54 **9** 1½ **Dalandra**[13] 6518 3-8-8 **53** ConnorBeasley(5) 2 28
(Michael Dods) *taken early to post: trckd ldrs: rdn over 2f out: wkng whn hmpd wl over 1f out* **11/2**[2]

4003 **10** 3 **Poetic Belle**[18] 6362 3-8-8 **53** (t) ShirleyTeasdale(5) 14 20
(Shaun Harris) *t.k.h: chsd ldr to over 3f out: hung rt fr over 2f out: sn struggling* **33/1**

1m 32.94s (-0.46) **Going Correction** -0.075s/f (Good)

WFA 3 from 4yo+ 2lb **10** Ran SP% **113.4**

Speed ratings (Par 101): **99,98,95,94,91 90,87,86,84,81**

toteswingers 1&2 £4.20, 2&3 £4.30, 1&3 £5.30 CSF £20.34 CT £92.79 TOTE £6.60: £2.10, £1.40, £1.70; EX 22.70 Trifecta £110.70 Pool: £2969.37 - 20.10 winning units..

Owner Prestige Thoroughbred Racing **Bred** Paul Hensey **Trained** Carluke, S Lanarks

■ Stewards' Enquiry : Jack Garritty two-day ban: careless riding (Oct 15,16)

FOCUS

Reasonable form for the level, with an unexposed 3yo beating an in-form filly.

6919 CASINO ON YOUR MOBILE AT BETVICTOR.COM H'CAP (DIV II) 7f 50y

5:00 (5:01) (Class 6) (0-60,60) 3-Y-O+ **£2,045** (£603; £302) **Stalls** High

Form RPR

0340 **1** **Deliberation (IRE)**[10] 6634 5-8-9 **51** RaulDaSilva(3) 8 58
(John Quinn) *t.k.h: led 2f: cl up: led over 2f out: rdn over 1f out: hld on wl fnl f* **6/1**[2]

0040 **2** 1¼ **Maillot Jaune (IRE)**[28] 6083 3-8-0 **48** JackGarritty(7) 1 52+
(Patrick Holmes) *hld up: hdwy on ins 2f out: chsd wnr ins fnl f: r.o* **18/1**

1600 **3** 1¼ **Nonaynever**[11] 6600 5-8-9 **48** (b) PJMcDonald 10 49
(Ruth Carr) *prom: effrt and ev ch over 2f out: one pce fnl f* **16/1**

5000 **4** hd **Hellbender (IRE)**[33] 5921 7-8-6 **50** ShirleyTeasdale(5) 3 50
(Shaun Harris) *prom: rdn over 2f out: kpt on ins fnl f* **14/1**

00-2 **5** ¾ **Ad Vitam (IRE)**[6] 6760 5-8-8 **47** (p) DavidAllan 2 45
(Mel Brittain) *midfield on ins: rdn and hdwy 2f out: r.o ins fnl f* **11/2**[1]

0446 **6** nk **Flipping**[53] 5239 6-8-13 **52** TomEaves 6 49
(Nicky Richards) *hld up towards rr: rdn over 2f out: hdwy over 1f out: no imp ins fnl f* **10/1**

1000 **7** nk **Goninodaethat**[12] 6549 5-9-3 **56** GrahamLee 5 52
(Jim Goldie) *t.k.h in midfield: effrt over 2f out: edgd lft and no imp over 1f out* **12/1**

550 **8** 3½ **Amy Farah Fowler (IRE)**[4] 6804 4-8-7 **46** oh1 (v[1]) BarryMcHugh 9 33
(Ian Williams) *hld up: rdn and effrt on outside over 1f out: nvr able to chal* **10/1**

5000 **9** ½ **Viking Warrior (IRE)**[10] 6634 6-8-11 **55** (p) ConnorBeasley(5) 7 41
(Michael Dods) *plld hrd: in tch tl rdn and wknd wl over 1f out* **11/1**

-440 **10** 1¼ **Troy Boy**[48] 5407 3-8-4 **48** oh1 ow2 JasonHart(3) 11 30
(Robin Bastiman) *bhd: drvn over 2f out: nvr able to chal* **25/1**

412- **11** 8 **Cheeky Wee Red**[416] 5081 5-8-13 **59** LauraBarry(7) 14 21
(Alistair Whillans) *hld up: struggling over 2f out: sn btn* **9/1**[3]

00 **12** 5 **Drive Home (USA)**[15] 6464 6-8-10 **56** (p) BTTreanor(7) 13 5
(Noel Wilson) *led after 2f: hdd over 2f out: wknd over 1f out* **28/1**

0034 **13** 2 **Bapak Pesta (IRE)**[39] 5704 3-8-12 **60** KevinStott(7) 4 3
(Kevin Ryan) *in tch tl rdn and wknd over 2f out* **11/2**[1]

1m 32.6s (-0.80) **Going Correction** -0.075s/f (Good)

WFA 3 from 4yo+ 2lb **13** Ran SP% **114.4**

Speed ratings (Par 101): **101,99,98,97,97 96,96,92,91,90 81,75,73**

toteswingers 1&2 £18.70, 2&3 £41.40, 1&3 £20.30 CSF £104.34 CT £1684.66 TOTE £6.00: £2.20, £7.70, £5.90; EX 170.80 Trifecta £2326.40 Part won. Pool: £3101.87 - 0.41 winning units..

Owner Livvys Racing Group **Bred** Berkie Brown **Trained** Settrington, N Yorks

FOCUS
The weaker of the two divisions. The winner was finally taking advantage of a good mark.

6920 ALBA FACILITIES SERVICES 10TH ANNIVERSARY H'CAP 5f
5:30 (5:33) (Class 3) (0-95,92) 3-Y-O+ **£7,762** (£2,310; £1,154; £577) **Stalls** Low

Form RPR

0301 **1** **Equitania**[10] 6647 3-8-11 **82** ... RobertWinston 7 91
(Alan Bailey) *mde all centre: rdn over 1f out: hld on wl* **6/1**[2]

0633 **2** ½ **Fitz Flyer (IRE)**[8] 6699 7-8-10 **88** ...(v) JordanNason(7) 6 94
(David Nicholls) *t.k.h to post: trckd ldrs: effrt and ev ch over 1f out to ins fnl f: hld nr fin* **5/1**[1]

046 **3** 2 **Perfect Blossom**[3] 6848 6-8-2 **78** ... ConnorBeasley(5) 2 77
(Alan Berry) *in tch: effrt and rdn over 1f out: kpt on ins fnl f* **6/1**[2]

0003 **4** ¾ **Rasaman (IRE)**[10] 6648 9-8-8 **79** ... BarryMcHugh 10 75
(Jim Goldie) *hld up: rdn over 2f out: hdwy fnl f: nrst fin* **12/1**

6642 **5** *hd* **Go Go Green (IRE)**[12] 6547 7-8-0 **78** oh4 ... JackGarritty(7) 13 74
(Jim Goldie) *missed break: bhd tl hdwy 2f out: styd on fnl f: n.d* **9/1**[3]

2000 **6** *nse* **Tax Free (IRE)**[41] 5651 11-9-5 **90** ... AdrianNicholls 9 85
(David Nicholls) *chsd ldrs: rdn over 2f out: one pce fnl f* **20/1**

0000 **7** ¾ **Stonefield Flyer**[10] 6621 4-9-7 **92** ... TomEaves 5 85
(Keith Dalgleish) *racd far side: cl up tl rdn and no ex over 1f out* **10/1**

0000 **8** 1 **Lucky Numbers (IRE)**[21] 6273 7-9-1 **86** ...(p) DanielTudhope 8 75
(David O'Meara) *in tch: rdn over 2f out: no imp over 1f out* **11/1**

0001 **9** 3 ¼ **Hazelrigg (IRE)**[11] 6583 8-8-7 **78** oh1 ...(e) RobertHavlin 1 55
(Tim Easterby) *racd far side: in tch: swtchd rt 1/2-way: rdn and wknd over 1f out* **10/1**

6000 **10** *nse* **Bapak Chinta (USA)**[81] 4263 4-8-11 **87** ... ShaneGray(5) 3 64
(Kevin Ryan) *in tch far side: swtchd rt 1/2-way: rdn and wknd 2f out* **11/1**

2550 **11** 2 ½ **Moorhouse Lad**[8] 6699 10-8-9 **83** ... JasonHart(3) 11 51
(Garry Moss) *taken early to post: cl up nr side: rdn 2f out: sn btn* **10/1**

0500 **12** 1 **Lost In Paris (IRE)**[3] 6848 7-8-7 **78** oh1 ...(p) DavidAllan 12 43
(Tim Easterby) *hld up towards nr side: rdn over 2f out: sn btn* **16/1**

58.23s (-1.17) **Going Correction** -0.025s/f (Good) **12** Ran SP% **117.5**
Speed ratings (Par 107): **108,107,104,102,102 102,101,99,94,94 90,88**
toteswingers 1&2 £3.10, 2&3 £7.00, 1&3 £8.10 CSF £35.71 CT £190.11 TOTE £8.10: £2.90, £1.50, £2.50; EX 43.50 Trifecta £206.50 Pool: £2912.53 - 10.57 winning units..
Owner John Stocker **Bred** Longdon Stud **Trained** Newmarket, Suffolk

FOCUS
A decent sprint, but little got into it with the winner coming centre-field.

6921 TALK TO VICTOR RACING EXCELLENCE APPRENTICE TRAINING SERIES H'CAP 1m
6:00 (6:01) (Class 6) (0-65,63) 3-Y-O+ **£2,045** (£603; £302) **Stalls** Low

Form RPR

0005 **1** **Rasselas (IRE)**[10] 6634 6-9-2 **60** ... AnnaHesketh(5) 8 68
(David Nicholls) *chsd ldrs: led over 2f out: styd on wl fnl f* **12/1**

0032 **2** 3 **High Resolution**[1] 6907 6-9-4 **62** ... RossSmith(5) 2 63
(Linda Perratt) *s.i.s: hld up: hdwy on outside 2f out: chsd wnr ins fnl f: kpt on: no imp* **3/1**[1]

3306 **3** 1 ½ **Remember Rocky**[28] 6083 4-8-10 **49** oh2 ...(p) IanBurns 9 47
(Lucy Normile) *prom: effrt and chsd wnr over 1f out to ins fnl f: sn one pce* **9/1**

6000 **4** 6 **Schoolboy Champ**[8] 6687 6-8-10 **49** oh4 ...(tp) JacobButterfield 11 33
(Lisa Williamson) *led to over 2f out: rdn and wknd over 1f out* **50/1**

3-06 **5** 1 **Coax**[7] 6723 5-9-1 **59** ...(b[1]) JackGarritty(5) 5 41
(Patrick Holmes) *prom: rdn over 2f out: wknd over 1f out* **8/1**

2632 **6** 1 ¼ **Hanalei Bay (IRE)**[1] 6905 3-9-0 **63** ... GeorginaBaxter(7) 10 42
(Keith Dalgleish) *midfield: stdy hdwy over 2f out: wknd over 1f out* **7/2**[2]

-660 **7** 1 ½ **Windsor Secret**[29] 6049 3-8-7 **49** oh4 ...(p) NoelGarbutt 1 24
(Keith Dalgleish) *hld up towards rr: drvn over 2f out: no imp over 1f out* **28/1**

3010 **8** 1 ½ **Captain Baldwin**[33] 5921 4-8-12 **51** ...(v) JordanNason 4 23
(Jim Goldie) *bhd: rdn over 3f out: no imp fr 2f out* **5/1**[3]

3406 **9** 10 **Hazza The Jazza**[18] 6368 3-9-6 **62** ...(p) ConnorBeasley 3 11
(Richard Guest) *hld up: rdn over 2f out: sn btn* **5/1**[3]

0000 **10** 14 **Babushka's Girl**[50] 5354 4-8-10 **49** oh4 ...(vt[1]) KevinStott 7
(Lisa Williamson) *midfield: struggling over 2f out: sn btn* **66/1**

1m 42.63s (-1.17) **Going Correction** -0.075s/f (Good)
WFA 3 from 4yo+ 3lb **10** Ran SP% **116.3**
Speed ratings (Par 101): **102,99,97,91,90 89,87,86,76,62**
toteswingers 1&2 £7.60, 2&3 £8.90, 1&3 £13.90 CSF £47.55 CT £355.23 TOTE £12.30: £3.50, £2.30, £1.70; EX 46.00 Trifecta £284.40 Pool: £883.66 - 2.33 winning units..
Owner J P Honeyman **Bred** Lynch Bages Ltd **Trained** Sessay, N Yorks

FOCUS
Not the first race on the day to fall to a prominent racer who stuck towards the inside rail, but it's not hard to have reservations over the form.
T/Plt: £203.30 to a £1 stake. Pool of £64710.36 - 232.27 winning tickets. T/Qpdt: £51.00 to a £1 stake. Pool of £5360.50 - 77.70 winning tickets. RY

6746 KEMPTON (A.W) (R-H)
Tuesday, October 1

OFFICIAL GOING: Standard
Wind: Fresh, half behind Weather: Overcast

6922 KEMPTON PARK REINDEER RACING CHRISTMAS PARTIES MAIDEN AUCTION STKS (DIV I) 7f (P)
5:50 (5:59) (Class 6) 2-Y-O **£1,940** (£577; £288; £144) **Stalls** Low

Form RPR

1 **Champagne Sydney (IRE)** 2-9-1 0 ... RichardHughes 4 83+
(Richard Hannon) *led 2f: trckd ldr: led again jst over 2f out and kicked for home: pushed out and wl in command fnl f* **7/2**[2]

2 1 ¾ **Isabella Beeton** 2-8-1 0 ... JemmaMarshall(3) 12 68
(Pat Phelan) *prog fr wd draw to ld after 2f: hdd jst over 2f out: wl hld by wnr after but kpt on for clr 2nd* **25/1**

02 **3** 2 ½ **Tullia (IRE)**[17] 6409 2-8-10 0 ... NeilCallan 8 67
(William Knight) *t.k.h early: trckd ldng trio: nt qckn whn wnr kicked on 2f out: drvn and one pce after* **5/4**[1]

4 1 ¼ **Steppe Daughter (IRE)** 2-8-4 0 ... CathyGannon 3 58+
(Denis Coakley) *hld up in rr: pushed along over 2f out: styd on fnl 2f to take 4th ins fnl f* **33/1**

0302 **5** 2 ½ **Nice Arty (IRE)**[15] 6460 2-8-13 70 ... PatDobbs 10 60
(Jamie Osborne) *chsd ldng pair: shoved along over 2f out: steadily wknd over 1f out* **8/1**[3]

6 1 ½ **Swordbearer** 2-9-1 0 ... FrederikTylicki 9 58
(James Fanshawe) *racd on outer: wl in tch: pushed along 2f out: steadily wknd* **8/1**[3]

7 ½ **Sheer Poetry (IRE)** 2-8-8 0 ... ShaneKelly 7 49
(Mike Murphy) *s.s: wl in rr: pushed along over 2f out: nvr on terms but kpt on* **20/1**

60 **8** *nk* **Touche De Rouge (IRE)**[36] 5812 2-8-6 0 ...[1] JohnFahy 2 47
(Peter Makin) *dwlt: wl in rr: pushed along over 2f out: nvr on terms but kpt on* **33/1**

0000 **9** 3 ¼ **Astral Rose**[17] 6409 2-8-8 45 ... WilliamCarson 5 40
(Jonathan Portman) *t.k.h: hld up in midfield: outpcd over 2f out: steadily wknd* **50/1**

000 **10** 8 **No Second Thoughts (IRE)**[28] 6079 2-8-9 25 ow1 .. FergusSweeney 1 19
(Michael Blanshard) *dropped to last after 3f: sn struggling: t.o* **100/1**

0 **11** 1 ¼ **Macnamara**[17] 6409 2-8-10 0 ... DavidProbert 6 17
(Harry Dunlop) *chsd ldrs: rdn 3f out: sn lost pl and in rr: t.o* **25/1**

1m 26.22s (0.22) **Going Correction** -0.10s/f (Stan) **11** Ran SP% **110.2**
Speed ratings (Par 93): **94,92,89,87,84 83,82,82,78,69 67**
toteswingers 1&2 £14.00, 2&3 £10.40, 1&3 £1.50 CSF £64.11 TOTE £4.90: £1.40, £6.70, £1.10; EX 151.70 Trifecta £657.60 Pool: £2110.98 - 2.40 winning units..
Owner The Sydney Arms Racing Club **Bred** Thomas G Cooke **Trained** East Everleigh, Wilts

FOCUS
The principals were all handy throughout and it appeared a more truly-run race than some contests of this nature.

6923 KEMPTON PARK REINDEER RACING CHRISTMAS PARTIES MAIDEN AUCTION STKS (DIV II) 7f (P)
6:20 (6:25) (Class 6) 2-Y-O **£1,940** (£577; £288; £144) **Stalls** Low

Form RPR

23 **1** **Tides Reach (IRE)**[32] 5949 2-8-10 0 ... JamesDoyle 2 69+
(Roger Charlton) *trckd ldrs: prog on inner to chal 2f out: narrow ld over 1f out: edgd lft fnl f: rdn out* **1/1**[1]

646 **2** ½ **Moonspring (IRE)**[17] 6409 2-8-6 64 ... MartinLane 3 64
(Tobias B P Coles) *dwlt then squeezed out s: wl in rr: prog on inner over 2f out: clsd to chal over 1f out: hanging lft and nt qckn ins fnl f* **10/1**

06 **3** *shd* **Zugzwang (IRE)**[11] 6590 2-8-12 0 ... MarkCoumbe(3) 4 73
(Ed de Giles) *settled in midfield: rdn and prog fr jst over 2f out: clsd on ldrs 1f out: nvr quite able to chal* **3/1**[2]

55 **4** 2 ¼ **Royal River**[80] 4302 2-8-11 0 ... LiamKeniry 5 63
(J S Moore) *t.k.h early: trckd ldrs: brought to chal 2f out: nt qckn over 1f out: wknd ins fnl f* **20/1**

05 **5** 1 ¾ **Cadmium**[34] 5891 2-8-6 0 ... DavidProbert 10 53
(Harry Dunlop) *mde most to over 1f out: wknd fnl f* **6/1**[3]

0 **6** 2 ¼ **Fenella Foghorn**[17] 6409 2-8-7 0 ... MatthewLawson(3) 7 51+
(Jonathan Portman) *hld up and sn in last: prog on inner 2f out: rchd 6th fnl f but nvr any threat* **25/1**

6 **7** 3 **Divine Bay**[17] 6408 2-8-8 0 ... SamHitchcott 11 41
(Gary Moore) *racd wd in midfield: rdn and outpcd fr over 2f out: nvr on terms after* **33/1**

00 **8** *shd* **Lucky Dottie**[28] 6079 2-8-4 0 ... FrankieMcDonald 8 36
(Pat Phelan) *wl in rr: lft bhd by ldrs fr over 2f out: pushed along and nvr on terms after* **50/1**

064 **9** *shd* **Dream Impossible (IRE)**[11] 6589 2-8-6 58 ... JohnFahy 6 38
(Peter Makin) *sn in rr: rdn and struggling over 2f out: no ch after* **16/1**

00 **10** ½ **Coiste Bodhar (IRE)**[11] 6590 2-8-4 0 ... NoraLooby(7) 9 42
(Joseph Tuite) *plld hrd early: hld up in last pair: nudged along fr 2f out: nvr remotely involved* **20/1**

55 **11** 1 ½ **Solent Lad (USA)**[28] 6079 2-8-11 0 ... NickyMackay 1 38
(Robert Eddery) *w ldr tl wknd u.p over 2f out* **20/1**

0 **12** ½ **Topofthedrops (IRE)**[15] 6460 2-8-13 0 ... FergusSweeney 12 38
(Philip Hide) *chsd ldng pair to 3f out: sn lost pl and btn* **66/1**

1m 27.5s (1.50) **Going Correction** -0.10s/f (Stan) **12** Ran SP% **128.8**
Speed ratings (Par 93): **87,86,86,83,81 79,75,75,75,74 73,72**
toteswingers 1&2 £3.60, 2&3 £10.00, 1&3 £1.40 CSF £13.19 TOTE £2.20: £1.10, £2.90, £1.70; EX 20.80 Trifecta £41.00 Pool: £3406.16 - 62.21 winning units..
Owner D J Deer **Bred** D J And Mrs Deer **Trained** Beckhampton, Wilts
■ Stewards' Enquiry : Mark Coumbe two-day ban: used whip above permitted level (Oct 15-16)

FOCUS
Just an ordinary maiden. The gallop looked on the steady side until past halfway with plenty taking a while to settle.

6924 £25 FREE BET AT BETVICTOR.COM NURSERY H'CAP 1m (P)
6:50 (6:52) (Class 6) (0-65,66) 2-Y-O **£1,940** (£577; £288; £144) **Stalls** Low

Form RPR

1565 **1** **Hedge End (IRE)**[19] 6322 2-9-5 **63** ... RichardHughes 2 78+
(Richard Hannon) *trckd ldrs: clsd over 2f out: pushed into ld wl over 1f out: shkn up and drew clr: comf* **5/1**[2]

0035 **2** 5 **Island Remede**[47] 5424 2-9-7 **65** ... RyanMoore 7 68+
(Ed Dunlop) *chsd ldrs on outer: rdn in 5th 3f out: outpcd after: styd on fr over 1f out to take 2nd last strides* **4/1**[1]

000 **3** *nk* **Jarlath**[36] 5811 2-8-11 **55** ... SteveDrowne 4 57
(Seamus Mullins) *trckd ldng pair: clsd to chal 2f out: wnr sn wnt by and no ch w her after: lost 2nd last strides* **33/1**

000 **4** ¾ **Earthflight**[37] 5797 2-8-11 **55** ...(p) JimmyFortune 10 56
(Philip McBride) *hld up in rr: shkn up over 2f out: styd on fr over 1f out: nrst fin* **7/1**[3]

000 **5** 1 ½ **Cape Arrow**[88] 4026 2-9-4 **62** ... JimCrowley 11 59
(Paul Cole) *hld up and sn in last: shkn up and stl there jst over 2f out: pushed along after and kpt on steadily fr over 1f out* **4/1**[1]

000 **6** 1 ½ **Allergic Reaction (IRE)**[14] 6485 2-9-1 **59** ... AdamKirby 6 53
(William Knight) *towards rr: rdn into midfield 3f out: nvr pce to threaten ldrs after* **5/1**[2]

0042 **7** 1 **Starlight Princess (IRE)**[6] 6749 2-8-9 **53** ...(b[1]) LiamJones 1 44
(J S Moore) *led to over 2f out: wknd* **7/1**[3]

066 **8** 2 ¾ **Stagewise (IRE)**[25] 6152 2-8-6 **50** ... WilliamCarson 8 35
(Jonathan Portman) *chsd ldr to over 2f out: wknd* **16/1**

234 **9** 3 ¼ **Weisse Girl**[119] 2947 2-9-2 **60** ...(b) PatCosgrave 9 38
(Noel Quinlan) *sn restrained in rr: pushed along over 2f out: reminder over 1f out: nvr involved* **14/1**

0040 **10** 3 ¾ **St Vincent (IRE)**[11] 6605 2-9-7 **65** ...(p) TedDurcan 5 34
(David Lanigan) *hld up in midfield: u.p and struggling over 2f out: sn wknd* **16/1**

0451 **11** *3 ¼* **Diffident Beats**[10] 6654 2-9-5 **63**....................(v) SamHitchcott 13 24
(Mick Channon) *a in rr: drvn and no prog over 2f out: sn wknd* **14/1**

1m 40.25s (0.45) **Going Correction** -0.10s/f (Stan) **11** Ran SP% **126.4**
Speed ratings (Par 93): **93,88,87,86,85 83,82,80,76,73 69**
toteswingers 1&2 £7.90, 2&3 £31.40, 1&3 £30.00 CSF £27.63 CT £629.00 TOTE £6.30: £2.40, £1.70, £8.70; EX 30.70 Trifecta £994.40 Pool: £2233.93 - 1.68 winning units..
Owner Grimes, Ivory, Bull, Hannon **Bred** Airlie Stud **Trained** East Everleigh, Wilts

FOCUS
This ended up being a one-sided nursery.

6925 DOWNLOAD THE BETVICTOR APP H'CAP 1m (P)
7:20 (7:20) (Class 4) (0-85,85) 3-Y-0+ **£4,851** (£1,443; £721; £360) **Stalls** Low

Form RPR
6330 **1** **Defendant**[66] 4743 3-9-3 **84**.................... JamesDoyle 10 92
(Sir Michael Stoute) *trckd ldng pair: wnt 2nd over 2f out and sn clr of rest: rdn to ld 1f out: pushed out firmly* **9/2**[2]

4-20 **2** *1* **Dixie's Dream (IRE)**[18] 6359 4-9-2 **80**.................... RichardHughes 7 86
(William Jarvis) *sn hld up in 6th: prog to chse clr ldng pair over 1f out: clsd fnl f: tk 2nd but no imp on wnr nr fin* **10/1**

0216 **3** *½* **Bartack (IRE)**[18] 6356 3-9-1 **82**....................(b) KierenFallon 8 87
(Luca Cumani) *led after 2f: stdd pce 1/2-way: tried to kick on over 2f out: hdd 1f out: kpt on but lost 2nd nr fin* **7/1**

1236 **4** *1* **Ree's Rascal (IRE)**[38] 5742 5-9-7 **85**.................... PatCosgrave 6 87
(Jim Boyle) *hld up in 7th and nt on terms: rdn and prog jst over 2f out: tk 4th 1f out but nt on terms: kpt on: nrst fin* **5/1**[3]

0000 **5** *2 ¾* **Embankment**[8] 6701 4-8-8 **72**....................(p) JimmyQuinn 5 68
(William Jarvis) *s.v.s: ct up at bk of field after 2f: prog on inner 2f out: plugged on but nvr a threat* **25/1**

-060 **6** *nk* **Chelwood Gate (IRE)**[61] 4922 3-9-4 **85**.................... JamieSpencer 3 80
(Roger Varian) *hld up in last pair: rdn and no prog over 2f out: kpt on fr over 1f out: n.d* **8/1**

3041 **7** *½* **For Posterity**[27] 6106 3-8-10 **77**.................... MickaelBarzalona 9 71
(Charlie Appleby) *chsd ldng trio: rdn and nt qckn over 2f out: sn wknd* **11/4**[1]

0004 **8** *1* **Webbow (IRE)**[21] 6278 11-9-4 **82**.................... LiamKeniry 12 74
(Julie Camacho) *restrained into last quartet and t.k.h: shkn up over 2f out: no real prog* **16/1**

6665 **9** *2 ½* **Byroness**[12] 6556 3-8-0 **72**.................... RyanTate(5) 4 58
(Heather Main) *chsd ldrs in 5th: rdn over 2f out: wknd over 1f out* **20/1**

120- **10** *5* **Zaeem**[255] 291 4-9-3 **81**.................... AdamKirby 11 56
(Dean Ivory) *restrained s and t.k.h in last quartet: wknd over 2f out: sn bhd* **25/1**

21-0 **11** *¾* **Intiba (USA)**[36] 5847 3-8-10 **77**....................[1] SilvestreDeSousa 2 50
(Saeed bin Suroor) *led 2f: chsd ldr to over 2f out: wknd rapidly* **5/1**[3]

1m 38.51s (-1.29) **Going Correction** -0.10s/f (Stan)
WFA 3 from 4yo+ 3lb **11** Ran SP% **129.2**
Speed ratings (Par 105): **102,101,100,99,96 96,95,94,92,87 86**
toteswingers 1&2 £12.50, 2&3 £20.90, 1&3 £6.60 CSF £52.96 CT £323.35 TOTE £4.60: £1.80, £4.60, £2.10; EX 59.90 Trifecta £827.00 Pool: £3138.35 - 2.84 winning units..
Owner K Abdullah **Bred** Juddmonte Farms Ltd **Trained** Newmarket, Suffolk

FOCUS
A fairly useful handicap. The pace looked sound once Bartack got to the front early on.

6926 FOLLOW US ON TWITTER @BETVICTOR MAIDEN STKS 1m 3f (P)
7:50 (7:50) (Class 5) 3-Y-0+ **£2,587** (£770; £384; £192) **Stalls** Low

Form RPR
03 **1** **Diamond Mine**[17] 6402 3-9-5 0.................... KierenFallon 7 84+
(Luca Cumani) *trckd ldrs: shkn up to cl over 2f out: chal over 1f out: drvn and gd battle fnl f: edgd lft but led narrowly and decisively nr fin* **7/2**[1]

2 *hd* **Murasil (USA)** 3-9-5 0.................... MickaelBarzalona 5 84+
(Saeed bin Suroor) *dwlt: hld up wl in rr: gd prog fr 3f out: shkn up and clsd to ld over 1f out but jnd: edgd lft but fought on wl: hdd nr fin* **8/1**

5553 **3** *¾* **Near Time**[20] 6312 3-9-0 73.................... JimmyFortune 10 77
(Andrew Balding) *wl in tch: urged along over 2f out: wnt 3rd jst over 1f out: clsd on ldng pair but nvr quite pce to chal* **9/2**[3]

0 **4** *7* **Mrs Micawber**[13] 6532 3-9-0 0.................... JamieSpencer 4 66
(Michael Bell) *t.k.h early: prom: wnt 2nd 5f out: led over 2f out: hdd & wknd over 1f out* **33/1**

5 *1 ¼* **Aalim** 3-9-5 0.................... SilvestreDeSousa 1 69+
(Saeed bin Suroor) *hld up in rr: tried to make prog 3f out: shkn up over 2f out: no ch w ldrs and wl outpcd over 1f out* **7/2**[1]

3 **6** *2 ¾* **Quality Alliance**[33] 5925 3-9-0 0.................... FrederikTylicki 2 60
(James Fanshawe) *trckd ldrs: disp 3rd jst over 2f out: wknd over 1f out* **14/1**

7 *½* **Hope's Wishes** 3-9-0 0.................... DavidProbert 6 59
(Andrew Balding) *s.i.s: wl in rr: sme prog 2f out but sn wl outpcd* **33/1**

06- **8** *1 ¾* **Leo Luna**[157] 4542 4-9-11 0.................... RyanMoore 13 61
(Gary Moore) *sn in last and quite sluggish early on: stl wl in rr and urged along over 2f out: modest late prog* **4/1**[2]

000 **9** *½* **Up Tipp**[26] 6134 3-9-5 43.................... PatDobbs 9 60
(Mike Murphy) *mde most to over 2f out: sn wknd* **100/1**

0 **10** *2* **Sir Tyto (IRE)**[17] 6402 5-9-11 0.................... SteveDrowne 8 57
(Peter Makin) *dwlt: a in rr: rn wd bnd 3f out: no ch after* **100/1**

4-0 **11** *16* **Roaring Rocks (FR)**[262] 184 3-9-0 0.................... RyanTate(5) 12 32
(Heather Main) *pressed ldrs: rdn and wknd on outer over 3f out: t.o* **100/1**

12 *22* **Galeb Warrior** 3-9-5 0.................... RichardHughes 3
(William Haggas) *nvr bttr than midfield: wknd over 4f out: wl t.o* **7/1**

13 *19* **Private Jones**[22] 4-9-4 0.................... DanielCremin(7) 11
(Miss Imogen Pickard) *w ldr to 5f out: wknd rapidly: wl t.o* **100/1**

2m 20.35s (-1.55) **Going Correction** -0.10s/f (Stan)
WFA 3 from 4yo+ 6lb **13** Ran SP% **122.7**
Speed ratings (Par 103): **101,100,100,95,94 92,91,90,90,88 77,61,47**
toteswingers 1&2 £5.80, 2&3 £9.70, 1&3 £4.40 CSF £32.91 TOTE £4.80: £1.90, £2.90, £2.30; EX 27.00 Trifecta £163.10 Pool: £2365.49 - 10.87 winning units..
Owner Fittocks Stud **Bred** Fittocks Stud **Trained** Newmarket, Suffolk

FOCUS
Fair form from the first three home, who pulled clear.

6927 BETVICTOR.COM H'CAP (LONDON MIDDLE DISTANCE SERIES QUALIFIER) 1m 3f (P)
8:20 (8:20) (Class 3) (0-95,93) 3-Y-0+ **£7,439** (£2,213; £1,106; £553) **Stalls** Low

Form RPR
4010 **1** **Lowther**[19] 6336 8-8-12 **86**....................(v) OisinMurphy(5) 4 93
(Lee Carter) *w.w in tch: clsd on ldrs over 2f out: rdn to ld over 1f out: hld on wl fnl f* **20/1**

3121 **2** *hd* **Break Rank (USA)**[36] 5824 4-9-2 **85**.................... JamesDoyle 6 92
(Ed de Giles) *hld up in last pair: hrd rdn and prog over 2f out: tk 2nd 1f out and sn chalng: nt qckn last 100yds* **9/2**[3]

1000 **3** *2 ¼* **Expert Fighter (USA)**[25] 6172 4-9-8 **91**.................... KierenFallon 1 94
(Saeed bin Suroor) *dwlt: pushed up to ld after 1f: hdd 1/2-way: rdn to ld again over 2f out to over 1f out: one pce* **6/1**

0145 **4** *½* **Al Saham**[66] 4765 4-9-9 **92**.................... SilvestreDeSousa 3 94
(Saeed bin Suroor) *trckd ldrs: wnt 3rd 4f out: drvn to chal over 2f out to over 1f out: fdd fnl f* **6/4**[1]

11 **5** *11* **Classic Punch (IRE)**[48] 5382 10-9-10 **93**.................... RichardHughes 7 78
(Tim Etherington) *led 1f: chsd ldr to 1/2-way: urged along over 3f out: wknd 2f out* **16/1**

5220 **6** *1 ¾* **Come On Blue Chip (IRE)**[39] 5723 4-9-7 **90**....................(p) FrederikTylicki 2 72
(Paul D'Arcy) *hld up in last pair: rdn and no prog over 2f out: wknd over 1f out* **10/1**

4-05 **7** *21* **Anomaly**[25] 6163 4-9-8 **91**.................... MickaelBarzalona 5 39
(Charlie Appleby) *t.k.h: trckd ldrs on outer tl prog to ld 1/2-way: racd awkwardly bnd 3f out: sn hdd & wknd rapidly: t.o* **11/4**[2]

2m 18.13s (-3.77) **Going Correction** -0.10s/f (Stan) **7** Ran SP% **118.9**
Speed ratings (Par 107): **109,108,107,106,98 97,82**
toteswingers 1&2 £15.80, 2&3 £5.50, 1&3 £23.20 CSF £111.50 TOTE £17.80: £8.80, £2.50; EX 82.70 Trifecta £371.80 Pool: £4562.44 - 9.20 winning units..
Owner Miss Victoria Baalham **Bred** L J Barratt **Trained** Epsom, Surrey

FOCUS
A pretty useful handicap. The gallop didn't look overly strong until Anomaly went on around halfway.

6928 BETVICTOR CASINO ON YOUR MOBILE H'CAP (DIV I) 6f (P)
8:50 (8:50) (Class 5) (0-70,70) 3-Y-0+ **£2,587** (£770; £384; £192) **Stalls** Low

Form RPR
1-00 **1** **Pettochside**[120] 2918 4-9-7 **70**....................(t) DavidProbert 5 78+
(Stuart Williams) *trckd ldrs in 6th: rdn and prog jst over 2f out: clsd to ld ins fnl f: sn clr* **6/1**

-002 **2** *1 ¾* **Take The Lead**[22] 6255 3-9-1 **65**.................... RichardHughes 8 68
(Richard Hannon) *led to over 4f out: rdn to chal 2f out: led briefly jst ins fnl f: outpcd last 100yds* **4/1**[2]

06-4 **3** *nk* **Kylladdie**[10] 6648 6-9-7 **70**....................(b) MickaelBarzalona 10 72
(Steve Gollings) *chsd ldng pair: drvn over 2f out: clsd enough but nt qckn over 1f out: styd on* **7/1**

0400 **4** *nk* **Lujeanie**[67] 4707 7-9-7 **70**....................[1] ShaneKelly 7 71
(Peter Crate) *settled towards rr: urged along and prog fr 2f out: rdn and styd on fnl f: nt pce to chal* **14/1**

1215 **5** *nk* **Victorian Number (FR)**[20] 6315 5-9-2 **65**.................... GeorgeBaker 4 65
(Geoffrey Deacon) *trckd ldrs: rdn over 2f out: tried to cl on inner over 1f out: kpt on but nt pce to chal* **5/2**[1]

0204 **6** *1* **Only Ten Per Cent (IRE)**[20] 6317 5-9-7 **70**.......(v[1]) SilvestreDeSousa 12 67
(J R Jenkins) *spd fr wdst draw to ld over 4f out: drvn over 2f out: hdd & wknd jst ins fnl f* **14/1**

0205 **7** *1 ¾* **Jarrow (IRE)**[19] 6323 6-9-5 **68**....................(p) RichardKingscote 1 60
(Milton Bradley) *hld up in midfield: pushed along 2f out: one pce and nvr threatened ldrs* **8/1**

P350 **8** *½* **Bussa**[11] 6606 5-9-1 **67**.................... DeclanBates(3) 9 57
(David Evans) *mostly in last trio: pushed along and wl off the pce 2f out: modest late prog: nvr involved* **20/1**

2363 **9** *1* **Proper Charlie**[33] 5930 5-8-12 **61**....................(v) RyanMoore 3 48
(Lee Carter) *nvr on terms w ldrs: rdn over 2f out: no real prog* **5/1**[3]

-600 **10** *5* **Bobby Two Shoes**[17] 6412 3-9-1 **65**....................(v) WilliamCarson 2 37
(Brett Johnson) *a in rr: u.p and struggling bef 1/2-way* **33/1**

2313 **11** *nk* **Blessing Box**[37] 5800 3-9-6 **70**.................... SebSanders 11 42
(Chris Wall) *racd wd: chsd ldrs: edgd lft and wknd fr 2f out* **8/1**

0000 **12** *nk* **Pick A Little**[26] 6135 5-9-1 **64**.................... SteveDrowne 6 35
(Michael Blake) *a in last trio: struggling over 2f out* **33/1**

1m 11.68s (-1.42) **Going Correction** -0.10s/f (Stan)
WFA 3 from 4yo+ 1lb **12** Ran SP% **138.2**
Speed ratings (Par 103): **105,102,102,101,101 100,97,97,95,89 88,88**
toteswingers 1&2 £19.20, 2&3 £10.80, 1&3 £11.50 CSF £35.09 CT £188.87 TOTE £7.10: £2.30, £3.00, £3.10; EX 124.30 Trifecta £849.40 Pool: £2345.43 - 2.07 winning units..
Owner James Thom **Bred** New Hall Stud **Trained** Newmarket, Suffolk

FOCUS
A modest contest which was run at a good pace.

6929 BETVICTOR CASINO ON YOUR MOBILE H'CAP (DIV II) 6f (P)
9:20 (9:21) (Class 5) (0-70,70) 3-Y-0+ **£2,587** (£770; £384; £192) **Stalls** Low

Form RPR
5436 **1** **Gung Ho Jack**[45] 5522 4-8-13 **62**.................... RichardHughes 8 68
(John Best) *chsd ldrs: rdn and clsd fr over 1f out: sustained effrt fnl f to ld post* **10/1**

4624 **2** *nse* **Generalyse**[39] 5697 4-9-7 **70**....................(b) AdamKirby 4 76
(Ben De Haan) *trckd ldrs: drvn and clsd on inner fr 2f out: led last 100yds: hdd post* **9/2**[2]

2321 **3** *shd* **Rock Up (IRE)**[16] 6425 3-9-6 **70**....................(b) RyanMoore 9 76
(David Elsworth) *trckd ldng pair: rdn to ld wl over 1f out: drvn and hdd last 100yds: kpt on but jst hld* **5/2**[1]

1325 **4** *2 ¼* **Jay Bee Blue**[20] 6306 4-9-4 **67**....................(bt) JamesDoyle 7 66
(Sean Curran) *hld up in rr: prog over 1f out: styd on to take 4th ins fnl f: unable to threaten* **5/1**[3]

2045 **5** *2 ¼* **Haadeeth**[6] 6761 6-9-2 **68**.................... DeclanBates(3) 2 60
(David Evans) *trckd ldrs: n.m.r and lost pl fr 2f out: pushed along and kpt on again fnl f* **14/1**

6036 **6** *1 ½* **Commandingpresence (USA)**[17] 6412 7-8-10 **59**.................... KieranO'Neill 1 47
(John Bridger) *led 2f: pressed ldr: upsides 2f out to over 1f out: wknd fnl f* **25/1**

4331 **7** *hd* **Rambo Will**[33] 5931 5-9-2 **65**.................... CathyGannon 6 52
(J R Jenkins) *bmpd s: racd freely and rcvrd to ld after 2f: hdd wl over 1f out: wknd* **14/1**

4660 **8** *½* **The Wee Chief (IRE)**[32] 5956 7-8-8 **64**.................... CameronHardie(7) 11 49
(Jimmy Fox) *v awkward s: wl in rr: threatened briefly to cl over 1f out: sn no prog* **12/1**

0440 **9** *5* **Avonmore Star**[13] 6526 5-9-7 **70**.................... PatDobbs 5 40
(Mike Murphy) *v awkward s: a in rr: no ch fnl 2f* **16/1**

0030 **10** *1 ½* **Torres Del Paine**[13] 6527 6-9-1 **64**....................(v) WilliamCarson 10 30
(Brett Johnson) *nvr on terms w ldrs: no ch fnl 2f* **20/1**

10/0 **11** *8* **Alkhataaf (USA)**[20] 6310 6-9-0 **66**............................ SimonPearce(3) 12 8
(Lydia Pearce) *racd wd towards rr: wknd over 2f out: t.o* **50/1**
1m 12.22s (-0.88) **Going Correction** -0.10s/f (Stan)
WFA 3 from 4yo+ 1lb **11** Ran SP% **110.0**
Speed ratings (Par 103): **101,100,100,97,94 92,92,91,85,83 72**
toteswingers 1&2 £8.80, 2&3 £2.80, 1&3 £6.40 CSF £115.07 TOTE £11.80: £3.70, £1.40, £1.30; EX 51.30 Trifecta £51.40 Pool: £3126.04 - 45.57 winning units..
Owner John Best **Bred** D R Tucker **Trained** Hucking, Kent
■ Stewards' Enquiry : Adam Kirby two-day ban: used whip above permitted level (Oct 15-16)
FOCUS
The second division of this run-of-the-mill sprint.
T/Jkpt: Part won. £21168.70 to a £1 stake. Pool of £29815.12 - 0.50 winning tickets. T/Plt: £89.60 to a £1 stake. Pool of £85850.67 - 699.09 winning tickets. T/Qpdt: £55.30 to a £1 stake. Pool of £6667.30 - 89.20 winning tickets. JN

6922 KEMPTON (A.W) (R-H)
Wednesday, October 2

OFFICIAL GOING: Standard
Wind: Moderate, half behind Weather: Fine, warm

6930 DAY DELEGATE RATES FROM £39 H'CAP — 5f (P)
5:40 (5:40) (Class 7) (0-50,50) 3-Y-O+ **£1,617** (£481; £240; £120) **Stalls** Low

Form RPR
6106 **1** **Metropolitan Chief**[179] 1396 9-9-3 **49**........................(p) SamHitchcott 3 56
(Paul Burgoyne) *mistimed s and slowly away: sn chsd ldrs: urged along to take 2nd 1f out: grad clsd and led post* **20/1**
0534 **2** *nse* **Volcanic Dust (IRE)**[32] 5982 5-9-4 **50**...................(t) RichardKingscote 4 57
(Milton Bradley) *mde most: def advantage 1f out: drvn and kpt on: hdd post* **4/1**[2]
6400 **3** *1 ½* **Borough Boy (IRE)**[11] 6651 3-9-4 **50**...........................(v) DaneO'Neill 7 52
(Derek Shaw) *stdd s: hld up in 8th off the pce: rdn and prog over 1f out: styd on to take 3rd ins fnl f: unable to chal* **6/1**
4560 **4** *1 ¼* **Christopher Chua (IRE)**[11] 6651 4-8-13 **50**...............(v) JackDuern(5) 1 47
(Michael Scudamore) *chsd ldng pair: rdn and one pce over 1f out: fdd nr fin* **10/1**
4650 **5** *1* **Royal Caper**[13] 6553 3-9-4 **50**.....................................(vt) PatCosgrave 10 44
(John Ryan) *dwlt: chsd ldrs in 6th: rdn over 1f out: kpt on one pce: n.d* **11/4**[1]
00-0 **6** *2 ½* **Avonlini**[20] 6344 7-8-12 **49**...(v) NoelGarbutt(5) 2 33
(Richard Ford) *w ldr to over 1f out: wknd* **14/1**
2460 **7** *1 ¼* **Foie Gras**[56] 5128 3-9-0 **49**... RobertTart(3) 9 30
(Chris Dwyer) *nt on terms in 7th: pushed along 1/2-way: no real prog* **6/1**
3635 **8** *nk* **Rightcar**[179] 1395 6-8-13 **48**... SladeO'Hara(3) 5 27
(Peter Grayson) *rrd s and then nrly uns rdr: mostly in last: pumped along and no prog 2f out* **5/1**[3]
00-0 **9** *¾* **Jemimaville (IRE)**[21] 6310 6-9-2 **48**..................................(v) PatrickDonaghy 6 24
(Giles Bravery) *racd on outer: chsd ldrs: wd bnd 2f out: wknd* **14/1**
1m 0.65s (0.15) **Going Correction** -0.075s/f (Stan) **9** Ran SP% **119.1**
Speed ratings (Par 97): **95,94,92,90,88 84,82,82,81**
toteswingers 1&2 £4.00, 1&3 £22.70, 2&3 £2.90 CSF £101.45 CT £560.99 TOTE £13.50: £3.80, £1.60, £2.90; EX 64.90 Trifecta £296.40 Pool: £1899.57 - 4.80 winning units..
Owner Mrs C Leigh-Turner **Bred** J A Prescott And C M Oakshott **Trained** Shepton Montague, Somerset
FOCUS
A desperately poor handicap.

6931 WINNERS ARE WELCOME AT BETDAQ EBF MAIDEN STKS — 6f (P)
6:10 (6:10) (Class 5) 2-Y-O **£2,911** (£866; £432; £216) **Stalls** Low

Form RPR
1 **Our Generation (IRE)** 2-9-5 0.. NeilCallan 9 83+
(Marco Botti) *t.k.h early: mostly trckd ldr: hung lft fr over 2f out and ended against nr side rail: rdn to ld over 1f out: styd on wl* **12/1**
332 **2** *2 ½* **Pool House**[20] 6333 2-9-5 76.. RichardHughes 6 75
(Andrew Balding) *led at mod pce: kicked on over 2f out: hdd and one pce over 1f out* **9/4**[1]
45 **3** *2* **Quantum Dot (IRE)**[16] 6477 2-9-5 0....................... RichardKingscote 2 69
(Tom Dascombe) *chsd ldng pair: rdn over 2f out: hung lft wl over 1f out: nt qckn after* **5/1**
6 **4** *1 ¼* **Mutawathea**[95] 3833 2-9-5 0... DaneO'Neill 5 65+
(Richard Hannon) *chsd ldrs: shkn up and wl outpcd over 2f out: pushed along and styd on steadily fr over 1f out* **7/2**[3]
3 **5** *nk* **Almargo (IRE)**[28] 6110 2-9-5 0..................................... MickaelBarzalona 4 64
(Charlie Appleby) *chsd ldrs: shkn up and outpcd over 2f out: kpt on same pce after: n.d* **5/2**[2]
6 *3* **Alderley** 2-9-0 0.. JohnFahy 3 50
(Jamie Osborne) *slowly away: mostly in last pair and off the pce: sme prog on inner 2f out: no hdwy fnl f* **66/1**
7 *2* **Broadway Ranger (IRE)** 2-9-5 0.............................. WilliamCarson 1 49
(Charles Hills) *in tch: shkn up and outpcd over 2f out: no prog after* **25/1**
0 **8** *shd* **Caminel (IRE)**[16] 6477 2-9-0 0.. LiamKeniry 7 44
(Jeremy Gask) *in tch at rr of main gp: rdn and wandered lft and rt 2f out: sn btn* **50/1**
0 **9** *6* **Majestic Sun (IRE)**[25] 6184 2-9-5 0.............................. PatCosgrave 8 31
(Peter Chapple-Hyam) *prog on wd outside to press ldrs 4f out: wknd qckly 2f out* **16/1**
10 *10* **Henry Grace (IRE)** 2-9-5 0.. KieranO'Neill 11
(Jimmy Fox) *s.s: a in last pair: t.o* **66/1**
1m 12.2s (-0.90) **Going Correction** -0.075s/f (Stan) **10** Ran SP% **120.6**
Speed ratings (Par 95): **103,99,97,95,94 90,88,88,80,66**
toteswingers 1&2 £4.90, 1&3 £12.30, 2&3 £4.10 CSF £40.27 TOTE £13.40: £2.40, £1.20, £1.80; EX 81.60 Trifecta £352.50 Pool: £1321.38 - 2.81 winning units..
Owner Kai Fai Leung **Bred** Lynn Lodge Stud **Trained** Newmarket, Suffolk
FOCUS
Not a great deal of strength in depth to this juvenile maiden, but there was much to like about the performance of the winner.

6932 REINDEER RACING AT KEMPTON PARK 06.12.13 H'CAP (DIV I) — 1m (P)
6:40 (6:40) (Class 6) (0-60,60) 3-Y-O+ **£1,940** (£577; £288; £144) **Stalls** Low

Form RPR
3444 **1** **Tammuz (IRE)**[11] 6655 3-8-11 **56**.. RobertTart(3) 2 69
(Tony Carroll) *sn trckd ldrs: prog jst over 2f out: shkn up to ld over 1f out: pushed out fnl f: won decisively* **7/1**
0663 **2** *2* **Warbond**[28] 6105 5-9-4 **57**..(p) SamHitchcott 11 65
(Michael Madgwick) *s.i.s: wl in rr in main gp: rdn and gd prog on inner over 2f out: chsd wnr jst over 1f out: styd on but unable to chal* **20/1**
502 **3** *2 ½* **Knight Charm**[18] 6400 3-9-4 **60**.......................................(p) JohnFahy 10 62
(Eve Johnson Houghton) *hld up in rr: sme prog 1/2-way: shkn up 2f out: hdwy over 1f out: styd on to take 3rd nr fin* **9/2**[2]
5001 **4** *1* **Kielty's Folly**[13] 6553 9-9-0 **53**........................... RichardKingscote 7 53
(Brian Baugh) *led 2f: led again over 2f out gng strly: rdn and hdd over 1f out: immediately outpcd: fdd nr fin* **12/1**
4500 **5** *½* **Admiralofthesea (USA)**[13] 6560 3-8-11 **60**...........(p) LouisSteward(7) 8 59
(Robert Eddery) *trckd ldng pair: rdn and cl enough 2f out: steadily outpcd* **8/1**
0505 **6** *1 ¼* **Tenessee**[25] 6218 6-9-7 **60**... LukeMorris 6 56
(Jamie Osborne) *led after 2f to over 2f out: steadily fdd* **6/1**[3]
5405 **7** *1 ¼* **Snap Music (USA)**[22] 6276 3-9-4 **60**................................. LiamJones 1 53
(Mark Johnston) *nt gng wl in mdifield bef 1/2-way: lost pl over 3f out: tried to renew effrt u.p 2f out: no hdwy after* **10/1**
5000 **8** *shd* **Kindia (IRE)**[18] 6399 5-9-1 **54**.......................................(p) JimmyQuinn 13 47
(Michael Attwater) *racd wd thrght: nvr beyond midfield: outpcd over 2f out: nvr on terms after* **33/1**
024- **9** *1 ½* **Barista (IRE)**[181] 7437 5-8-9 **51**...................................... CharlesBishop(3) 9 40
(Brian Forsey) *chsd ldrs to 1/2-way: lost pl and wl in rr 3f out: pushed along after: passed a few late on* **16/1**
-500 **10** *3* **Tigerish**[16] 6459 3-8-11 **53**... NeilCallan 4 35
(Amanda Perrett) *chsd ldrs: hrd rdn over 2f out: sn wknd* **16/1**
0043 **11** *1 ¼* **Primo D'Oro (USA)**[7] 6752 3-9-4 **60**.......................... RichardHughes 12 40
(Richard Hannon) *hld up at bk of main gp: shkn up over 2f out: no prog and wl btn after* **3/1**[1]
64-0 **12** *1 ¾* **Straight Shot (IRE)**[12] 6612 4-9-7 **60**...............................(b[1]) LiamKeniry 5 36
(John Butler) *t.k.h early: chsd ldrs: drvn and wknd over 2f out* **20/1**
5-25 **13** *11* **Spymistress**[183] 1299 3-8-10 **52**.................................. RichardThomas 14
(Zoe Davison) *s.i.s: sn wl detached: t.o 1/2-way* **100/1**
1m 39.11s (-0.69) **Going Correction** -0.075s/f (Stan)
WFA 3 from 4yo+ 3lb **13** Ran SP% **123.1**
Speed ratings (Par 101): **100,98,95,94,94 92,91,91,89,86 85,83,72**
toteswingers 1&2 £12.20, 1&3 £6.50, 2&3 £24.40 CSF £147.01 CT £732.75 TOTE £11.10: £2.90, £4.70, £1.60; EX 167.20 Trifecta £608.00 Pool: £1857.40 - 2.29 winning units..
Owner Longview Stud & Bloodstock Ltd **Bred** Longview Stud & Bloodstock Ltd **Trained** Cropthorne, Worcs
FOCUS
Some disappointing individuals contested this handicap.

6933 REINDEER RACING AT KEMPTON PARK 06.12.13 H'CAP (DIV II) — 1m (P)
7:10 (7:10) (Class 6) (0-60,60) 3-Y-O+ **£1,940** (£577; £288; £144) **Stalls** Low

Form RPR
4154 **1** **Cape Crossing**[13] 6554 4-8-13 **52**.......................................(t) LiamKeniry 8 60
(Andrew Balding) *tk fierce hold: plld way through to ld after 2f: mde rest: kicked on over 2f out: hung lft after: clung on in desperate fin* **6/1**[2]
1064 **2** *hd* **Compton Bird**[5] 6802 4-9-1 **59**.................................. JoeyHaynes(5) 14 67+
(Hans Adielsson) *hld up in last pair: rdn and gd prog fr jst over 2f out: sustained effrt towards far side fnl f: tk 2nd last stride: jst failed* **12/1**
1P3 **3** *nse* **Santadelacruze**[8] 6737 4-9-7 **60**.......................................(b) RyanMoore 11 67
(Gary Moore) *prom: trckd wnr 1/2-way: drvn to chal fr 2f out: carried lft for rest of r and ended against nr side rail: kpt trying but jst hld and lost 2nd last stride* **5/2**[1]
0000 **4** *nse* **Diplomatic (IRE)**[21] 6315 8-9-7 **60**......................................(p) LiamJones 1 67
(Michael Squance) *wl in tch in midfield: prog towards inner fr 2f out: drvn to chal jst over 1f out: jst hld* **10/1**
3056 **5** *1 ½* **Welsh Inlet (IRE)**[13] 6553 5-9-1 **54**.............................. KieranO'Neill 10 58
(John Bridger) *hld up in last quartet: rdn over 2f out: prog wl over 1f out: styd on: nrst fin* **20/1**
0030 **6** *nk* **Uncle Fred**[93] 3901 8-9-4 **57**... GeorgeBaker 6 60
(Patrick Chamings) *hld up towards rr: gng strly over 2f out: tried to make prog over 1f out but hanging and nt qckn: styd on fnl f: nrst fin* **12/1**
0-04 **7** *½* **Polydamos**[15] 6492 4-8-10 **49**.. JimmyQuinn 5 51
(Tony Carroll) *awkward s: racd in last quartet: prog on inner over 2f out: chsd ldrs over 1f out: one pce after* **25/1**
0230 **8** *nk* **Strategic Action (IRE)**[93] 3901 4-9-4 **57**............................[1] PatDobbs 2 58
(Linda Jewell) *trckd ldrs: rdn and nt qckn 2f out: kpt on one pce after* **16/1**
0664 **9** *nk* **Tagalaka (IRE)**[5] 6805 3-9-4 **60**...(b[1]) JohnFahy 3 61
(Eve Johnson Houghton) *trckd ldrs: tried to chal but isolated in centre of crse over 1f out: wknd fnl f* **10/1**
5506 **10** *1 ¼* **Rock Anthem (IRE)**[18] 6400 9-9-0 **53**........................ RichardHughes 13 51
(Mike Murphy) *wl in tch in midfield: rdn and nt qckn 2f out: btn 1f out: eased* **8/1**[3]
0400 **11** *nk* **Evermore (IRE)**[15] 6491 3-9-4 **60**.............................. SilvestreDeSousa 9 57
(Mark Johnston) *hld up in last pair: rdn and tried to make prog on inner over 2f out: sn no hdwy and btn* **6/1**[2]
3046 **12** *1 ¾* **Exopuntia**[13] 6554 7-8-8 **47**.. AdamBeschizza 4 40
(Julia Feilden) *nvr beyond midfield: urged along furiously over 2f out: no prog* **25/1**
4005 **13** *1 ½* **Zaheeb**[18] 6400 5-9-2 **55**... WilliamCarson 12 45
(Dave Morris) *led at modest pce 2f: chsd ldr to 1/2-way: wknd u.p over 2f out* **16/1**
00-0 **14** *1 ¾* **Fitz**[18] 6399 7-8-11 **50**.. LukeMorris 7 36
(Martin Bosley) *racd wd in midfield: wknd over 2f out* **50/1**
1m 41.26s (1.46) **Going Correction** -0.075s/f (Stan)
WFA 3 from 4yo+ 3lb **14** Ran SP% **128.0**
Speed ratings (Par 101): **89,88,88,88,87 86,86,86,85,84 84,82,81,79**
toteswingers 1&2 £17.00, 1&3 £3.10, 2&3 £11.40 CSF £77.93 CT £239.91 TOTE £8.90: £2.60, £4.70, £1.40; EX 86.80 Trifecta £304.50 Pool: £2613.01 - 6.43 winning units..
Owner Mildmay Racing & D H Caslon **Bred** Jeremy Green & Sons & Brian McGrath **Trained** Kingsclere, Hants
■ Stewards' Enquiry : Liam Keniry two-day ban: careless riding (Oct 16-17)
FOCUS
Another modest event, but it produced a thrilling finish with a little over a head covering the first four home.

6934 COMMISSION FREE 1ST MONTH AT BETDAQ NOVICE STKS — 1m (P)
7:40 (7:40) (Class 5) 2-Y-O **£2,587** (£770; £384; £192) **Stalls** Low

Form RPR
222 **1** **Red Galileo**[12] 6593 2-9-0 91.. RyanMoore 2 82+
(Ed Dunlop) *mde all: 3 l clr and pushed along firmly 2f out: nvr in danger but rdn out fnl f* **1/5**[1]

61 **2** 4½ **Andy Dandy (IRE)**[41] 5675 2-9-2 76 RichardKingscote 1 73
(Tom Dascombe) *chsd wnr: pushed along over 3f out: no imp fnl 2f but won battle for 2nd* **14/1**[3]

51 **3** *nse* **Zumurudah (FR)**[21] 6298 2-9-0 0 SilvestreDeSousa 3 71
(Mark Johnston) *chsd wnr: pushed along over 3f out: no imp fnl 2f and jst lost out in battle for 2nd* **5/1**[2]

4 ¾ **Capers Royal Star (FR)** 2-9-0 0 FergusSweeney 4 69
(Alastair Lidderdale) *wl in tch in last: shkn up to chal for 2nd fr 2f out: no ex fnl f: shaped w sme promise* **100/1**

1m 39.54s (-0.26) **Going Correction** -0.075s/f (Stan) **4** Ran SP% **107.7**
Speed ratings (Par 95): **98,93,93,92**
CSF £4.07 TOTE £1.60; EX 4.40 Trifecta £5.70 Pool: £2613.01 - 162.06 winning units..
Owner The Hon R J Arculli **Bred** T R G Vestey **Trained** Newmarket, Suffolk

FOCUS
This looked a gilt-edged opportunity for the winner on paper.

6935 £200 FREE BETS AT BETDAQ NURSERY H'CAP 1m (P)
8:10 (8:10) (Class 3) (0-95,92) 2-Y-O **£6,469** (£1,925; £962; £481) **Stalls** Low

Form RPR

212 **1** **Extra Noble**[18] 6395 2-9-0 85 RichardKingscote 7 89+
(Ralph Beckett) *hld up in last pair: stdy prog jst over 2f out: pushed into ld jst over 1f out: drvn out last 150yds* **7/4**[1]

31 **2** ½ **Top Tug (IRE)**[34] 5922 2-8-10 81 RyanMoore 5 84+
(Sir Michael Stoute) *hld up in last pair: pushed along over 3f out: rdn whn carried wide over 2f out: styd on to take 2nd last 100yds: clsd on wnr but nvr able to threaten* **7/4**[1]

1410 **3** 2 **Fire Fighting (IRE)**[18] 6395 2-9-7 92 NeilCallan 2 89
(Mark Johnston) *led: lugging rt bnd 4f out to 3f out: hdd and one pce u.p jst over 1f out* **16/1**

641 **4** *nk* **Adventure Seeker (IRE)**[26] 6168 2-8-7 78 LukeMorris 6 75
(Ed Vaughan) *s.i.s and urged along early: t.k.h after 2f: wnt 3rd 1/2-way and rdn to chse ldr 2f out: chal over 1f out: nt qckn* **8/1**[3]

3621 **5** 1¼ **Art Wave (IRE)**[20] 6340 2-8-6 77 AndreaAtzeni 1 71
(Marco Botti) *t.k.h: chsd ldr to 2f out: steadily fdd* **5/1**[2]

4153 **6** 1 **Zampa Manos (USA)**[21] 6314 2-9-0 85 DavidProbert 3 76
(Andrew Balding) *chsd ldng pair to 1/2-way: sn pushed along: dropped to last 2f out and wl btn after* **14/1**

1m 39.24s (-0.56) **Going Correction** -0.075s/f (Stan) **6** Ran SP% **113.1**
Speed ratings (Par 99): **99,98,96,96,94 93**
toteswingers 1&2 £1.20, 1&3 £4.30, 2&3 £4.70 CSF £4.89 TOTE £3.00: £1.50, £1.10; EX 6.60 Trifecta £45.00 Pool: £1934.69 - 32.23 winning units..
Owner Ballymore Downunder Syndicate **Bred** Mr & Mrs A E Pakenham **Trained** Kimpton, Hants

FOCUS
A competitive feature, despite the small field, and much to like about the runs of the first two home, both of whom were set plenty to do in a steadily run race.

6936 BETDAQ 1ST UK RACE COMMISSION FREE H'CAP (LONDON MIDDLE DISTANCE SERIES QUALIFIER) 1m 3f (P)
8:40 (8:41) (Class 4) (0-85,85) 3-Y-O+ **£4,690** (£1,395; £697; £348) **Stalls** Low

Form RPR

023- **1** **Troopingthecolour**[401] 5664 7-9-10 85 (t) MickaelBarzalona 9 96
(Steve Gollings) *settled towards rr: brought wd in st: rdn over 2f out: gd prog fr 2f out to ld last 100yds: styd on wl* **14/1**

-413 **2** 1¼ **Glorious Protector (IRE)**[112] 3214 3-9-2 83 RichardHughes 3 92
(Ed Walker) *led briefly after 100yds: trckd ldr after: led 2f out and sent for home: hdd and outpcd last 100yds* **3/1**[2]

1315 **3** 1¾ **Curly Come Home**[31] 6016 4-9-6 81 (t) GeorgeBaker 10 87
(Chris Wall) *hld up in last trio: gng bttr than most whn sed to make prog jst over 2f out: clsd w wnr 1f out: one pce after* **20/1**

4100 **4** 2½ **Waverunner**[15] 6499 3-8-9 76 LiamJones 11 77
(Mark Johnston) *towards rr: rdn over 2f out: swtchd lft over 1f out: drvn and styd on fnl f to take 4th nr fin* **33/1**

621- **5** 1 **Fresa**[433] 4505 4-8-10 71 LukeMorris 1 70
(Sir Mark Prescott Bt) *wl in tch: rdn 3f out: wnt 3rd briefly 2f out: one pce after* **20/1**

02 **6** 1¼ **Rosaceous**[17] 6433 3-9-2 83 RyanMoore 2 80
(Daniel Kubler) *led 100yds: chsd ldrs: drvn in 3rd over 2f out: steadily fdd over 1f out* **12/1**

4212 **7** 2½ **Jazz Master**[13] 6559 3-9-1 82 (b) SilvestreDeSousa 8 75
(Luca Cumani) *led after 1f and set decent pce: hdd 2f out: wknd over 1f out* **9/4**[1]

1615 **8** 4½ **Mount Tiger**[15] 6495 3-9-0 81 NeilCallan 4 65
(James Tate) *t.k.h: trckd ldrs: rdn 3f out: wknd 2f out* **3/1**[2]

1220 **9** *nk* **Apache Glory (USA)**[112] 3204 5-9-2 77 (p) AndreaAtzeni 5 61
(John Stimpson) *hld up in last trio: pushed along and no prog over 2f out: wl btn after* **33/1**

2200 **10** ¾ **Reflect (IRE)**[9] 6694 5-9-3 78 (vt) DaneO'Neill 7 61
(Derek Shaw) *restrained into last sn after s: shkn up and no prog over 2f out: wl btn after* **33/1**

4300 **11** 1½ **Beaufort Twelve**[32] 6001 4-9-8 83 (p) TomQueally 12 63
(William Jarvis) *wl in tch: shkn up and nt qckn over 2f out: sn wknd* **10/1**[3]

2m 18.26s (-3.64) **Going Correction** -0.075s/f (Stan)
WFA 3 from 4yo+ 6lb **11** Ran SP% **122.6**
Speed ratings (Par 105): **110,109,107,106,105 104,102,99,99,98 97**
toteswingers 1&2 £10.70, 1&3 £34.80, 2&3 £11.00 CSF £55.01 CT £862.60 TOTE £21.70: £2.60, £1.40, £6.20; EX 86.10 Trifecta £940.60 Pool: £2970.12 - 2.36 winning units..
Owner Irvin S Naylor **Bred** Meon Valley Stud **Trained** Scamblesby, Lincs

FOCUS
As competitive a race as you'd expect for the grade and it saw a thoroughly likeable display from the winner on his belated return to action.

6937 BOOK YOUR CHRISTMAS PARTY ON 01932 753518 H'CAP 7f (P)
9:10 (9:11) (Class 6) (0-65,65) 3-Y-O+ **£1,940** (£577; £288; £144) **Stalls** Low

Form RPR

203 **1** **Bowstar**[21] 6315 4-9-6 65 (p) RobertHavlin 10 74
(Michael Attwater) *trckd ldrs: clsd on outer 2f out: rdn to ld jst over 1f out: r.o wl and sn clr* **5/1**[2]

2125 **2** 2 **Wordismybond**[16] 6459 4-9-6 65 RichardHughes 8 69
(Peter Makin) *chsd ldr: rdn over 2f out: kpt on fr over 1f out but nt pce to threaten wnr* **6/1**[3]

6050 **3** *shd* **Shifting Star (IRE)**[33] 5948 8-9-4 63 SeanLevey 4 67
(John Bridger) *led: rdn 2f out: hdd and one pce jst over 1f out: lost 2nd last stride* **20/1**

6451 **4** 1½ **Mrs Warren**[91] 3946 3-9-2 63 PatCosgrave 7 62
(George Baker) *chsd ldng pair: rdn to go 2nd 2f out: tried to chal over 1f out: one pce after* **14/1**

4660 **5** 1½ **Rondeau (GR)**[21] 6310 8-9-6 65 DavidProbert 6 61
(Patrick Chamings) *hld up towards rr: pushed along over 2f out: hanging briefly whn shkn up over 1f out: kpt on but no threat* **20/1**

-600 **6** *nse* **Catch The Cider**[35] 5892 3-9-2 63 (t) GeorgeBaker 11 58+
(Hans Adielsson) *dwlt: hld up in last trio: looking for room over 2f out: shkn up and styd on fr over 1f out: nvr any threat* **5/2**[1]

0000 **7** ½ **Sea Soldier (IRE)**[21] 6317 5-8-13 65 RobHornby(7) 2 59
(Andrew Balding) *dwlt: hld up in rr: tried to make prog on inner fr over 2f out: no hdwy fnl f* **10/1**

3410 **8** 1 **Red Tulip**[21] 6315 3-9-2 63 FrederikTylicki 9 54
(James Fanshawe) *wl in rr: stuck out wd and struggling over 2f out: sme hdwy over 1f out: no imp fnl f* **8/1**

0235 **9** *nk* **Annes Rocket (IRE)**[12] 6606 8-9-5 64 (p) PatDobbs 13 55
(Jimmy Fox) *t.k.h: hld up in last trio: stl there 2f out: pushed along and assed a few late on* **8/1**

0000 **10** ½ **Cocozza (USA)**[16] 6473 5-9-6 65 (b[1]) AdamBeschizza 3 55
(K F Clutterbuck) *t.k.h early: hld up in last trio: rdn on inner over 2f out: sn no real prog* **20/1**

6000 **11** *shd* **Orders From Rome (IRE)**[21] 6306 4-9-6 65 (t) JohnFahy 12 54
(Eve Johnson Houghton) *t.k.h: trckd ldrs: nt qckn 2f out: fdd fnl f* **20/1**

0066 **12** ½ **Caramelita**[14] 6535 6-9-4 63 (v) TomQueally 1 51
(J R Jenkins) *chsd ldrs on inner: rdn 2f out: wknd jst over 1f out* **20/1**

3440 **13** ½ **Ghostwing**[30] 6039 6-8-10 62 (v) SineadAlderman(7) 14 49
(Luke Dace) *plld hrd and racd wd: prog to chse ldrs 1/2-way: wknd over 2f out* **25/1**

0000 **14** 8 **Dark Ages (IRE)**[14] 6525 4-9-6 65 (tp) JimmyQuinn 5 31
(Paul Burgoyne) *nvr beyond midfield: no imp 2f out: wknd rapidly over 1f out* **25/1**

1m 26.12s (0.12) **Going Correction** -0.075s/f (Stan)
WFA 3 from 4yo+ 2lb **14** Ran SP% **129.0**
Speed ratings (Par 101): **96,93,93,91,90 90,89,88,88,87 87,86,86,77**
toteswingers 1&2 £2.50, 1&3 £21.90, 2&3 £17.80 CSF £33.44 CT £587.78 TOTE £3.80: £1.30, £2.90, £7.80; EX 18.20 Trifecta £718.10 Pool: £2275.75 - 2.37 winning units..
Owner Canisbay Bloodstock **Bred** Juddmonte Farms Ltd **Trained** Epsom, Surrey

FOCUS
A modest finale.
T/Plt: £29.80 to a £1 stake. Pool: £73168.12 - 1786.95 winning tickets T/Qpdt: £6.40 to a £1 stake. Pool: £7832.47 - 903.50 winning tickets JN

6597 NEWCASTLE (L-H)
Wednesday, October 2

OFFICIAL GOING: Good to firm (7.7)
Wind: Fresh, half behind Weather: Overcast, raining

6938 IRISH STALLION FARMS EBF MAIDEN STKS 1m 3y(S)
2:10 (2:10) (Class 4) 2-Y-O **£4,075** (£1,212; £606; £303) **Stalls** Centre

Form RPR

3 **1** **Raven Ridge (IRE)**[20] 6330 2-9-5 0 JamieSpencer 5 79+
(Michael Bell) *trckd ldrs: shkn up to ld over 2f out: rdn clr over 1f out: kpt on strly: eased nr fin* **10/11**[1]

4 **2** 4 **Mayfield Boy**[14] 6513 2-9-5 0 DavidAllan 10 67
(Mel Brittain) *chsd ldr: rdn and outpcd over 2f out: rallied to chse (clr) wnr ins fnl f: no imp* **12/1**

3 1 **Think Ahead** 2-9-5 0 KierenFallon 6 65
(Saeed bin Suroor) *dwlt: hld up: smooth hdwy over 3f out: rdn and edgd lft over 1f out: kpt on same pce ins fnl f* **9/4**[2]

0 **4** 3½ **Irene Hull (IRE)**[14] 6513 2-8-11 0 JasonHart(3) 9 52
(Garry Moss) *led: rdn and hdd over 2f out: rallied: faltered and wknd ins fnl f* **66/1**

0 **5** 7 **Uplifted (IRE)**[12] 6581 2-9-5 0 GrahamLee 3 41+
(Kevin Ryan) *in tch: hung lft and outpcd over 3f out: rallied over 1f out: sn n.d* **40/1**

0 **6** 1¼ **Enquiring**[32] 5995 2-9-5 0 JoeFanning 8 38
(Mark Johnston) *chsd ldrs tl rdn and wknd fr 2f out* **25/1**

66 **7** 6 **Little Bruv**[14] 6513 2-9-5 0 RobertWinston 2 24
(Tim Easterby) *plld hrd in midfield: struggling over 2f out: btn over 1f out* **25/1**

0 **8** ¾ **Hello Sweetness**[12] 6597 2-8-7 0 DanielleMooney(7) 7 17
(Jason Ward) *hld up towards rr: struggling 3f out: sn btn* **100/1**

9 5 **Worcharlie'Slass** 2-9-5 0 TomEaves 4 6
(Michael Herrington) *dwlt: hld up: rdn over 3f out: sn btn* **50/1**

10 ½ **Al Zaman Thaman (FR)** 2-9-5 0 (b[1]) SaleemGolam 1 10
(Marco Botti) *hld up: pushed along over 3f out: sn wknd* **10/1**[3]

1m 39.84s (-3.56) **Going Correction** -0.425s/f (Firm) **10** Ran SP% **114.5**
Speed ratings (Par 97): **100,96,95,91,84 83,77,76,71,71**
toteswingers 1&2 £3.30, 1&3 £1.40, 2&3 £4.80 CSF £12.55 TOTE £1.70: £1.10, £2.30, £2.00; EX 8.70 Trifecta £34.10 Pool: £3328.91 - 73.20 winning units..
Owner Saleh Al Homaizi & Imad Al Sagar **Bred** Stonethorn Stud Farms Ltd **Trained** Newmarket, Suffolk

FOCUS
Probably just a fair maiden, although a couple of decent performers have taken it down the years, namely Montaff in 2008 and Redford in 2007. The winning time was fairly slow compared to other races on the day.

6939 BARBOUR/BRITISH STALLION STUDS EBF MAIDEN STKS 7f
2:40 (2:41) (Class 4) 2-Y-O **£4,075** (£1,212; £606; £303) **Stalls** Centre

Form RPR

1 **Lat Hawill (IRE)** 2-9-5 0 JamieSpencer 3 90+
(Marco Botti) *trckd ldrs gng wl: led on bit appr 2f out: pushed along and qcknd clr over 1f out: kpt on strly: promising* **11/4**[2]

06 **2** 8 **Poetic Choice**[12] 6607 2-9-0 0 MartinLane 7 58
(Nick Littmoden) *hld up: effrt over 2f out: chsd (clr) wnr ent fnl f: kpt on: no imp* **100/1**

4 **3** *shd* **Scurr Mist (IRE)**[8] 6724 2-9-5 0 TomEaves 4 63
(Keith Dalgleish) *t.k.h: prom: effrt over 2f out: disp modest 2nd pl ins fnl f: kpt on: no imp* **16/1**

03 **4** 2½ **Upholland**[9] 6681 2-9-5 0 PaulHanagan 6 56
(Richard Fahey) *midfield: outpcd and hung lft wl over 2f out: plugged on fnl f: nvr able to chal* **5/2**[1]

5 *nk* **Branston De Soto** 2-9-5 0 JoeFanning 1 56
(Mark Johnston) *w ldrs: led over 3f out to appr 2f out: lost 2nd and outpcd fnl f: bttr for r* **7/1**

6 2 **Stanarley Pic** 2-9-5 0 BenCurtis 10 50
(Alan Swinbank) *chsd ldrs: rdn over 2f out: wknd over 1f out* **20/1**

The Form Book Flat, Raceform Ltd, Compton, RG20 6NL.

7 1 ½ **Nabeel (IRE)** 2-9-5 0 KierenFallon 2 46
(Saeed bin Suroor) *colty in preliminaries: dwlt: rn green towards rr: effrt and hdwy 3f out: wknd 1f out: bttr for r* **7/2**[3]

8 nse **Green Zone (IRE)** 2-9-2 0 DeclanCannon(3) 9 46
(Nigel Tinkler) *dwlt: hld up: rdn over 2f out: n.d* **50/1**

3560 9 shd **Nowinaminute (IRE)**[12] 6605 2-9-0 57 GrahamLee 5 41
(James Given) *cl up: ev ch and rdn over 3f out: wknd over 2f out* **18/1**

00 10 13 **Where's Tiger**[7] 6754 2-9-5 0 MichaelO'Connell 11 11
(Jedd O'Keeffe) *upset in stalls: bhd: struggling 1/2-way: nvr on terms: t.o* **20/1**

00 11 3 ½ **Take A Break**[11] 6627 2-8-9 0 ConnorBeasley(5) 8
(Robert Johnson) *t.k.h: led to over 3f out: rdn and wknd over 2f out* **100/1**

1m 25.0s (-2.80) **Going Correction** -0.425s/f (Firm) **11** Ran SP% **114.6**
Speed ratings (Par 97): **99,89,89,86,86 84,82,82,82,67 63**
toteswingers 1&2 £35.50, 1&3 £8.60, 2&3 £44.20 CSF £276.06 TOTE £4.40: £1.10, £13.70, £2.80; EX 241.10 Trifecta £2704.10 Part won. Pool: £3605.46 - 0.77 winning units..
Owner Qatar Racing & Essafinaat **Bred** Windymains Farm Ltd **Trained** Newmarket, Suffolk

FOCUS
Those who had raced already didn't seem to set a high level to overturn, so it was pleasing to see a newcomer win.

6940 S.V. RUTTER MAIDEN STKS 6f
3:10 (3:12) (Class 5) 3-Y-0+ **£2,587** (£770; £384; £192) **Stalls** Centre

Form RPR

063 1 **Intrinsic**[15] 6502 3-9-5 72 JamieSpencer 12 83+
(Sir Michael Stoute) *racd w one other stands' side: mde all and overall ldr: drvn over 2f out: kpt on wl fnl f* **15/8**[1]

442/ 2 3 ¼ **Fanoos**[709] 7056 4-9-1 66 (p) PaulHanagan 2 68
(William Haggas) *in tch centre: pushed along 2f out: kpt on to take 2nd that gp nr fin: nt rch stands' side wnr* **7/2**

5222 3 ¾ **Millkwood**[14] 6516 3-9-5 75 (bt[1]) PhillipMakin 6 70
(John Davies) *t.k.h: cl up centre: led that gp over 2f out: rdn and hung lft over 1f out: hdd and no ex that gp towards fin* **3/1**[2]

00 4 2 ¼ **Redalani (IRE)**[15] 6497 3-9-0 0 DaleSwift 7 58
(Alan Brown) *chsd ldrs centre: effrt over 2f out: one pce whn flashed tail ins fnl f* **66/1**

4/- 5 2 ¼ **Tarquin (IRE)**[743] 6232 4-9-1 0 JacobButterfield(5) 1 56
(Kristin Stubbs) *t.k.h: prom: effrt over 2f out: outpcd fnl f* **10/3**[3]

004 6 2 **Spring Bird**[11] 6630 4-8-8 45 JordanNason(7) 10 44
(David Nicholls) *led centre to over 2f out: wknd over 1f out* **80/1**

5650 7 ½ **Busy Bimbo (IRE)**[12] 6604 4-8-12 48 JasonHart(3) 5 43
(Alan Berry) *hld up bhd ldng gp centre: drvn over 2f out: sn btn* **33/1**

8 28 **Noble Maximus** 3-9-5 0 PatrickMathers 3
(Alan Berry) *missed break: a wl bhd centre: t.o* **100/1**

9 2 ¾ **Harpers Ruby** 3-9-0 0 MichaelStainton 9
(Simon Griffiths) *dwlt: sn struggling centre: t.o* **100/1**

00 10 25 **Ramata**[100] 3641 3-9-0 0 RobertWinston 11
(James Unett) *dwlt: chsd wnr stands' side tl wknd fr 3f out: virtually p.u fnl f* **80/1**

1m 11.6s (-3.00) **Going Correction** -0.425s/f (Firm)
WFA 3 from 4yo 1lb **10** Ran SP% **114.0**
Speed ratings (Par 103): **103,98,97,94,91 89,88,51,47,14**
toteswingers 1&2 £2.10, 1&3 £2.20, 2&3 £2.70 CSF £8.51 TOTE £2.90: £1.50, £1.40, £1.30; EX 9.10 Trifecta £27.30 Pool: £4880.85 - 134.07 winning units..
Owner Cheveley Park Stud **Bred** Cheveley Park Stud Ltd **Trained** Newmarket, Suffolk

FOCUS
Modest fare.

6941 S.T.P. CONSTRUCTION FILLIES' H'CAP 7f
3:45 (3:45) (Class 5) (0-70,70) 3-Y-0+ **£2,587** (£770; £384; £192) **Stalls** Centre

Form RPR

5321 1 **Rufoof**[34] 5932 3-9-5 70 PaulHanagan 13 82
(Charles Hills) *t.k.h early: cl up: rdn to ld over 2f out: qcknd ins fnl f: kpt on strly* **3/1**[1]

2630 2 2 ¾ **Blue Maisey**[21] 6301 5-8-9 65 KevinStott(7) 8 71
(Edwin Tuer) *chsd ldrs: effrt and edgd lft over 2f out: chsd (clr) wnr ins fnl f: kpt on: no imp* **11/2**[3]

015 3 ¾ **Fab Lolly (IRE)**[37] 5830 3-8-12 63 JamieSpencer 1 66
(James Bethell) *dwlt and swtchd rt s: hld up: rdn and hdwy 2f out: kpt on fnl f: nrst fin* **12/1**

4025 4 hd **Emerald Sea**[27] 6135 3-9-2 67 TomEaves 9 69
(Chris Wall) *cl up: effrt and rdn over 2f out: kpt on same pce ins fnl f* **14/1**

0130 5 shd **First Class Favour (IRE)**[11] 6634 5-8-11 60 DavidAllan 12 63
(Tim Easterby) *led: rdn over 2f out: hdd over 1f out: kpt on same pce fnl f* **10/1**

0616 6 2 **Diamond Blue**[45] 5564 5-9-4 67 PhillipMakin 7 65
(Richard Whitaker) *hld up: rdn over 2f out: hdwy over 1f out: kpt on fnl f: nvr able to chal* **25/1**

6243 7 ½ **Graceful Act**[11] 6634 5-8-2 56 oh4 (p) ConnorBeasley(5) 2 52
(Ron Barr) *hld up bhd ldng gp on outside: rdn over 2f out: no imp over 1f out* **10/1**

1213 8 hd **Imaginary World (IRE)**[20] 6341 5-9-4 70 (p) JasonHart(3) 15 66
(John Balding) *t.k.h: in tch: rdn over 2f out: outpcd fnl f* **4/1**[2]

2450 9 2 ¾ **My New Angel (IRE)**[11] 6633 4-8-7 61 GeorgeChaloner(5) 11 49
(Jason Ward) *t.k.h early in midfield: rdn and outpcd over 2f out: n.d after* **16/1**

3015 10 hd **Gift Of Silence**[14] 6535 4-9-5 68 DanielTudhope 14 56
(John Berry) *t.k.h: hld up: struggling over 2f out: sn btn* **8/1**

5460 11 nk **Jillywinks**[13] 6556 3-8-11 62 ow1 RobertWinston 3 48
(Scott Dixon) *t.k.h: hld up in midfield: rdn over 2f out: sn btn* **33/1**

1m 24.93s (-2.87) **Going Correction** -0.425s/f (Firm)
WFA 3 from 4yo+ 2lb **11** Ran SP% **116.7**
Speed ratings (Par 100): **99,95,95,94,94 92,91,91,88,88 87**
toteswingers 1&2 £5.40, 1&3 £2.80, 2&3 £11.90 CSF £19.11 CT £176.45 TOTE £3.10: £2.10, £1.80, £2.60; EX 23.20 Trifecta £145.20 Pool: £3704.49 - 19.13 winning units..
Owner Hamdan Al Maktoum **Bred** Shadwell Estate Company Limited **Trained** Lambourn, Berks

FOCUS
The early gallop was far from strong and the tempo only increased from around the 3f marker.

6942 NORTH SEA LOGISTICS H'CAP 2m 19y
4:20 (4:21) (Class 5) (0-75,75) 3-Y-0+ **£2,587** (£770; £384; £192) **Stalls** Low

Form RPR

63 1 **Bin Singspiel**[104] 3491 3-9-0 72 DavidAllan 5 84+
(James Tate) *trckd ldrs: shkn up to ld over 2f out: rdn and edgd lft over 1f out: kpt on wl fnl f* **3/1**[1]

2 1 ½ **Secret Seven (USA)**[13] 6577 3-8-0 58 oh6 MartinLane 9 66
(J L Hassett, Ire) *t.k.h: led after 2f: rdn and hdd over 2f out: checked over 1f out: kpt on ins fnl f: nt rch wnr* **28/1**

6044 3 6 **Hit The Jackpot (IRE)**[16] 6466 4-9-13 74 DanielTudhope 8 75+
(David O'Meara) *hld up and bhd: stdy hdwy over 2f out: rdn and chsd clr ldrs 1f out: no imp* **10/3**[2]

0440 4 2 ¾ **Authentication**[13] 6565 4-8-11 58 AndrewElliott 4 56
(Mel Brittain) *t.k.h: hld up in tch: rdn and outpcd over 2f out: rallied over 1f out: no imp* **16/1**

110 5 nk **Almost Gemini (IRE)**[34] 5933 4-9-7 68 (p) JamieSpencer 2 65
(Don Cantillon) *in tch: effrt and rdn 3f out: one pce whn hung lft over 1f out* **6/1**[3]

4250 6 ½ **Knightly Escapade**[36] 3345 5-10-0 75 (p) TomEaves 1 72
(Brian Ellison) *hld up: hdwy over 2f out: sn rdn: no imp over 1f out* **8/1**

0200 7 2 ½ **Tartan Jura**[24] 6237 5-9-11 72 (p) JoeFanning 10 66
(Mark Johnston) *trckd ldrs: drvn and outpcd 3f out: n.d after* **12/1**

06-3 8 nk **Hunters Belt (IRE)**[13] 6552 9-8-13 60 (vt) GrahamLee 6 53
(George Bewley) *hld up: rdn and outpcd over 3f out: sn n.d* **7/1**

3020 9 4 ½ **Petella**[13] 6565 7-8-13 60 (p) PJMcDonald 3 48
(George Moore) *hld up: niggled 1/2-way: drvn over 4f out: nvr on terms* **14/1**

50-0 10 24 **Spirit Of Adjisa (IRE)**[20] 6346 9-9-4 65 (b) RobertWinston 7 24
(David C Griffiths) *t.k.h: led 2f: cl up: rdn over 3f out: sn wknd: t.o* **25/1**

3m 34.15s (-5.25) **Going Correction** -0.25s/f (Firm)
WFA 3 from 4yo+ 11lb **10** Ran SP% **113.5**
Speed ratings (Par 103): **103,102,99,97,97 97,96,96,93,81**
toteswingers 1&2 £14.90, 1&3 £3.30, 2&3 £17.10 CSF £84.69 CT £293.46 TOTE £4.10: £2.30, £8.70, £1.60; EX 92.10 Trifecta £501.80 Pool: £3251.63 - 4.85 winning units..
Owner Saif Ali **Bred** The Lavington Stud **Trained** Newmarket, Suffolk

FOCUS
Not an easy race to assess because a few of these were unproven at the distance, but the pace set by the leader did seem generous.

6943 MALONE & SONS H'CAP 1m 3y(S)
4:50 (4:51) (Class 5) (0-70,74) 3-Y-0+ **£2,587** (£770; £384; £192) **Stalls** Centre

Form RPR

-016 1 **Cape Samba**[21] 6301 4-9-5 68 ThomasBrown(3) 3 79
(Ismail Mohammed) *cl up: led over 2f out: hrd pressed ins fnl f: edgd rt: drvn out* **9/2**[1]

4661 2 nk **The Blue Banana (IRE)**[14] 6518 4-8-7 60 (b) KevinStott(7) 8 70
(Edwin Tuer) *prom: effrt and chsd wnr over 1f out: ev ch ins fnl f: edgd lft: hld nr fin* **8/1**

0563 3 3 ¼ **Brockfield**[7] 6758 7-9-7 67 DavidAllan 10 70
(Mel Brittain) *chsd ldrs: swtchd to stands' rail after 2f: drvn and ev ch 2f out: one pce fnl f* **12/1**

0336 4 shd **Ted's Brother (IRE)**[13] 6548 5-9-5 70 (e) ConnorBeasley(5) 13 72+
(Richard Guest) *hld up: rdn and hdwy 2f out: kpt on fnl f: nrst fin* **10/1**

0251 5 1 ¼ **Chiswick Bey (IRE)**[8] 6727 5-9-7 74 6ex (p) SamanthaBell(7) 11 73
(Richard Fahey) *prom: rdn over 2f out: kpt on same pce fnl f* **7/1**[2]

3334 6 shd **McCool Bannanas**[30] 6042 5-9-1 61 RobertWinston 16 60
(James Unett) *racd stands' rail: towards rr: rdn over 2f out: hdwy over 1f out: nrst fin* **12/1**

4304 7 ¾ **Obboorr**[13] 6567 4-9-3 63 BarryMcHugh 9 60
(Brian Rothwell) *prom: effrt and rdn 2f out: kpt on same pce fnl f* **15/2**[3]

4443 8 6 **Broctune Papa Gio**[56] 5138 6-9-10 70 PhillipMakin 12 54
(Keith Reveley) *midfield: swtchd to stands' side after 2f: rdn over 2f out: wknd over 1f out* **12/1**

045 9 1 ½ **I'm Super Too (IRE)**[2] 6906 6-9-8 68 BenCurtis 14 48
(Alan Swinbank) *hld up: rdn along over 2f out: edgd lft and sn outpcd* **12/1**

3140 10 4 **Botteen (IRE)**[88] 4045 3-9-4 67 DanielTudhope 6 38
(David O'Meara) *hld up bhd ldng gp: rdn over 2f out: wknd over 1f out* **25/1**

0036 11 hd **Whispered Times (USA)**[26] 6181 6-9-2 62 (p) JoeFanning 2 33
(Tracy Waggott) *t.k.h: cl up tl rdn and wknd over 1f out* **16/1**

5201 12 1 **Jupiter Fidius**[26] 6181 6-9-1 68 GemmaTutty(7) 7 36
(Karen Tutty) *bhd: drvn along 3f out: nvr rchd ldrs* **12/1**

500- 13 ¾ **Charpoy (USA)**[19] 6374 5-9-3 63 (p) TomEaves 5 30
(Keith Dalgleish) *led to over 2f out: sn lost pl and struggling* **16/1**

0460 P **Living Leader**[12] 6609 4-9-9 69 (b[1]) MartinLane 15
(Nick Littmoden) *hld up: struggling 1/2-way: sn p.u and dismntd* **20/1**

1m 39.21s (-4.19) **Going Correction** -0.425s/f (Firm)
WFA 3 from 4yo+ 3lb **14** Ran SP% **121.5**
Speed ratings (Par 103): **103,102,99,99,98 98,97,91,89,85 85,84,83,**
toteswingers 1&2 £10.30, 1&3 £14.00, 2&3 £23.60 CSF £39.14 CT £425.75 TOTE £6.00: £3.10, £1.80, £5.40; EX 51.90 Trifecta £588.20 Pool: £3223.32 - 4.10 winning units..
Owner Ismail Mohammed **Bred** Jeremy Gompertz **Trained** Newmarket, Suffolk

FOCUS
Quite a clean race considering the field size, although the first two did come close late on, and they all ended up middle-to-stands' side in the final stages.

6944 BOOKER CASH & CARRY H'CAP (DIV I) 5f
5:20 (5:23) (Class 6) (0-60,60) 3-Y-0+ **£1,940** (£577; £288; £144) **Stalls** Centre

Form RPR

0031 1 **Windforpower (IRE)**[16] 6469 3-9-2 55 (p) JoeFanning 5 65
(Tracy Waggott) *prom: rdn to ld ins fnl f: hrd pressed last 100yds: jst hld on* **9/1**

2654 2 nse **Keep It Dark**[26] 6181 4-9-7 60 BarryMcHugh 9 69
(Tony Coyle) *in tch: rdn and hdwy over 1f out: chal last 100yds: jst failed* **3/1**[1]

6605 3 1 ½ **Myjestic Melody (IRE)**[77] 4398 5-8-7 46 oh1 MartinLane 6 49
(Brian Ellison) *cl up: led over 1f out to ins fnl f: kpt on same pce last 100yds* **8/1**

4 1 **Better Value (IRE)**[12] 6614 3-9-0 53 (p) BenCurtis 13 54
(J L Hassett, Ire) *chsd ldrs: effrt and rdn over 1f out: kpt on same pce fnl f* **10/1**

6650 5 1 ¾ **Lichen Angel**[22] 6289 3-8-1 47 ow1 [1] DanielleMooney(7) 7 42
(Richard Whitaker) *towards rr: rdn and outpcd 1/2-way: styd on fnl f: nrst fin* **25/1**

4303 6 shd **Balinka**[12] 6604 3-9-7 59 DavidAllan 11 54
(Mel Brittain) *unruly at s: chsd ldrs: effrt and ev ch over 1f out: no ex ins fnl f* **8/1**

-050 7 nk **Classy Anne**[3] 6879 3-8-0 46 oh1 JackGarritty(7) 8 39
(Jim Goldie) *in tch: rdn and outpcd 1/2-way: styd on fnl f: nrst fin* **50/1**

5050 8 ¾ **Amis Reunis**[7] 6761 4-9-4 57 (p) PatrickMathers 4 46
(Alan Berry) *bhd: drvn and struggling 1/2-way: kpt on fnl f: n.d* **16/1**

0036 **9** 2 1/4 **Lizzy's Dream**[42] 5639 5-9-4 **60**.. JasonHart(3) 3 41+
(Robin Bastiman) *missed break: hld up: hdwy and in tch 1/2-way: rdn and no ex over 1f out: wknd ins fnl f* **4/1**[2]

000 **10** 3/4 **Sharp Shoes**[12] 6603 6-8-4 **50** ow3.................................... KevinStott(7) 1 29
(Christopher Wilson) *racd away fr main gp: prom: drvn over 2f out: wknd over 1f out* **33/1**

0000 **11** 2 1/4 **Baybshambles (IRE)**[7] 6760 9-8-10 **49**..........................(p) TomEaves 12 19
(Tina Jackson) *chsd ldrs: rdn over 2f out: wknd over 1f out* **40/1**

0036 **12** 1/2 **Pearl Noir**[27] 6138 3-9-2 **55**...............................(b[1]) RobertWinston 2 25
(Scott Dixon) *racd away fr main gp: overall ldr at str gallop: hdd over 1f out: sn btn* **20/1**

0053 **13** 1 1/2 **Lord Buffhead**[9] 6687 4-8-12 **56**.........................(v) ConnorBeasley(5) 10 19
(Richard Guest) *dwlt: bhd and sn pushed along: no ch fr 1/2-way* **6/1**[3]

59.9s (-1.20) **Going Correction** -0.425s/f (Firm) **13** Ran SP% **122.4**
Speed ratings (Par 101): **92,91,89,87,85 84,84,83,79,78 74,74,71**
toteswingers 1&2 £9.40, 1&3 £8.20, 2&3 £9.90 CSF £35.19 CT £235.87 TOTE £7.70: £1.80, £1.60, £5.10; EX 47.00 Trifecta £781.60 Pool: £2247.42 - 2.15 winning units..
Owner David Tate **Bred** Tally-Ho Stud **Trained** Spennymoor, Co Durham
■ Stewards' Enquiry : Barry McHugh two-day ban: used whip above permitted level (Oct 16-17)

FOCUS
A narrow margin separated the first two.

6945 BOOKER CASH & CARRY H'CAP (DIV II) 5f
5:50 (5:52) (Class 6) (0-60,60) 3-Y-O+ **£1,940** (£577; £288; £144) **Stalls** Centre

Form RPR

4264 **1** **Thatcherite (IRE)**[7] 6760 5-9-5 **58**..............................(t) StephenCraine 10 69+
(Tony Coyle) *dwlt: hld up bhd ldng gp: smooth hdwy to ld over 1f out: pushed along and kpt on wl fnl f* **5/2**[1]

0230 **2** 1 1/4 **Black Douglas**[1] 6916 4-9-2 **55**.. TomEaves 1 61
(Jim Goldie) *hld up: rdn and hdwy over 1f out: chsd wnr fnl 100yds: r.o* **4/1**[3]

0000 **3** 1 3/4 **Fathom Five (IRE)**[7] 6760 9-9-1 **59**......................... ShirleyTeasdale(5) 12 59
(Shaun Harris) *prom: effrt and rdn 2f out: kpt on ins fnl f* **25/1**

0402 **4** shd **Tuibama (IRE)**[2] 6903 4-9-7 **60**..(p) DaleSwift 4 59
(Tracy Waggott) *dwlt: hld up in midfield: hdwy and ev ch over 1f out: one pce fnl 100yds* **7/2**[2]

0540 **5** 1 1/4 **Fleurtille**[11] 6634 4-8-11 **55**.................................... ConnorBeasley(5) 5 50
(Robert Johnson) *prom: hdwy to ld briefly over 1f out: outpcd ins fnl f* **16/1**

0360 **6** 1 1/4 **Mr Snooks**[3] 6879 3-8-7 **46**.. JoeFanning 2 37
(David Nicholls) *t.k.h: hld up in tch on outside: rdn over 1f out: sn outpcd* **9/1**

5005 **7** nk **Piste**[3] 6879 7-8-2 **46** oh1.......................................(be) ShaneGray(5) 6 35
(Tina Jackson) *hld up bhd ldng gp: rdn over 2f out: no imp over 1f out* **28/1**

0400 **8** 1 **China Excels**[13] 6568 6-9-3 **56**.................................... RussKennemore 11 42
(Sue Smith) *cl up: rdn over 2f out: wknd over 1f out* **10/1**

2350 **9** nse **Baker's Pursuit**[13] 6547 3-8-13 **52**................................ GrahamLee 8 38
(Jim Goldie) *reluctant to enter stalls: bhd: rdn over 2f out: sme late hdwy: nvr on terms* **14/1**

0063 **10** 1 3/4 **Wicked Wilma (IRE)**[3] 6878 9-8-7 **46** oh1...............(p) PatrickMathers 7 25
(Alan Berry) *cl up: led over 2f out to over 1f out: sn btn* **10/1**

0-00 **11** 6 **On The High Tops (IRE)**[7] 6757 5-9-1 **54**.................. BarryMcHugh 9 12
(Colin Teague) *led to over 2f out: sn rdn and wknd* **33/1**

59.9s (-1.20) **Going Correction** -0.425s/f (Firm) **11** Ran SP% **121.8**
Speed ratings (Par 101): **92,90,87,87,85 83,82,80,80,78 68**
toteswingers 1&2 £3.60, 1&3 £16.20, 2&3 £20.60 CSF £12.61 CT £211.95 TOTE £3.40: £1.50, £2.00, £9.30; EX 16.60 Trifecta £393.20 Pool: £2853.18 - 5.44 winning units..
Owner Brian Kerr **Bred** Taroka Equine Investments **Trained** Norton, N Yorks

FOCUS
A win for a horse who has won over much further in the past.
T/Jkpt: £649.40 to a £1 stake. Pool: £25000.00 - 27.33 winning tickets T/Plt: £17.10 to a £1 stake. Pool: £88691.02 - 3775.00 winning tickets T/Qpdt: £3.70 to a £1 stake. Pool: £6438.10 - 1283.30 winning tickets RY

[5494] NOTTINGHAM (L-H)
Wednesday, October 2

OFFICIAL GOING: Good (good to soft in places; 7.5)
Wind: Virtually nil Weather: Overcast and showers Rails: Outer track in use. Rail on innermost lines.

6946 £32 BONUS AT 32RED.COM NURSERY H'CAP 1m 2f 50y
2:00 (2:01) (Class 5) (0-75,74) 2-Y-O **£2,587** (£770; £384; £192) **Stalls** Low

Form RPR

0322 **1** **Fair Flutter (IRE)**[4] 6844 2-8-11 **64**............................ FrankieDettori 3 67
(Richard Fahey) *in tch: hdwy 3f out: rdn wl over 1f out: styd on to chse ldr ent fnl f: kpt on strly u.p towards fin to ld on line* **9/4**[1]

5034 **2** nse **Haayil**[18] 6401 2-9-3 **70**.. RobertHavlin 2 73
(John Gosden) *sn led: pushed along over 2f out: rdn clr appr fnl f: hdd and no ex on line* **9/4**[1]

0305 **3** 2 1/2 **Blue Talisman (IRE)**[7] 6755 2-8-4 **57**......................(b[1]) DuranFentiman 1 55
(Tim Easterby) *trckd ldrs on inner: swtchd rt and hdwy 3f out: sn cl up: rdn wl over 1f out: drvn and kpt on same pce fnl f* **20/1**

5633 **4** 2 3/4 **The Wallace Line (IRE)**[14] 6520 2-8-9 **62**.................... SamHitchcott 4 55
(Mick Channon) *dwlt and pushed along in rr: hdwy on inner over 3f out: rdn to chse ldrs wl over 1f out: sn no imp* **7/1**[3]

0520 **5** 1 1/4 **Ultimate Warrior (IRE)**[4] 6852 2-9-7 **74**...................... RyanMoore 7 65
(Richard Hannon) *cl up: rdn along over 3f out: wknd over 2f out* **4/1**[2]

6300 **6** 3/4 **Strassman**[18] 6401 2-8-3 **56**.................................... AdrianNicholls 8 45
(Mark Johnston) *prom on outer: rdn along over 3f out: wknd over 2f out* **25/1**

066 **7** 7 **Scottish Academy**[22] 6271 2-8-3 **59**........................ MichaelJMMurphy(3) 6 35
(Mark Johnston) *chsd ldrs: pushed along 1/2-way: rdn 4f out: sn outpcd and rr* **12/1**

2m 14.04s (-0.26) **Going Correction** -0.325s/f (Firm) 2y crse rec **7** Ran SP% **110.3**
Speed ratings (Par 95): **88,87,85,83,82 82,76**
toteswingers 1&2 £1.20, 1&3 £4.40, 2&3 £9.40 CSF £6.70 CT £67.63 TOTE £3.50: £1.90, £2.00; EX 8.40 Trifecta £48.80 Pool: £2019.66 - 31.00 winning units..
Owner Mr And Mrs J D Cotton **Bred** Thomas G Cooke **Trained** Musley Bank, N Yorks

FOCUS
All races on outer track and course at innermost configuration. A proper test of stamina for these 2yos, especially on the softening ground, and the time was slow. There was a nasty shock for some in-running punters as the second horse was matched at 1.01 to decent amounts.

6947 SIR HENRY CECIL SLIP ANCHOR EBF MAIDEN STKS 5f 13y
2:30 (2:32) (Class 5) 2-Y-O **£3,234** (£962; £481; £240) **Stalls** High

Form RPR

0 **1** **Amahoro**[13] 6561 2-9-0 0.................................... SilvestreDeSousa 10 80+
(Mick Channon) *in tch: hdwy over 2f out: led over 1f out: rdn clr ins fnl f: kpt on* **5/1**[3]

30 **2** 2 3/4 **Qatar Princess (IRE)**[28] 6107 2-9-0 0.......................... TedDurcan 14 70
(Olly Stevens) *prom on outer: cl up 1/2-way: rdn and ev ch over 1f out: drvn and kpt on same pce fnl f* **9/2**[2]

40 **3** 1 1/2 **By Rights**[44] 5593 2-8-11 0.................................... MarkCoumbe(3) 6 65
(Tony Carroll) *in tch: pushed along over 2f out: rdn over 1f out: kpt on fnl f: nrst fin* **25/1**

4 1 1/2 **Royal Brave (IRE)** 2-9-5 0.. DougieCostello 1 64
(William Muir) *in tch on wd outside: rdn along 2f out: styd on fnl f: nrst fin* **10/1**

03 **5** nse **Monarch Maid**[44] 5584 2-9-0 0.................................. WilliamCarson 7 59
(Peter Hiatt) *dwlt and towards rr: hdwy 1/2-way: sn chsng ldrs: rdn wl over 1f out: kpt on same pce* **5/1**[3]

6 shd **Foxtrot Pearl (IRE)** 2-8-11 0.................................. CharlesBishop(3) 5 59
(Olly Stevens) *dwlt and sltly hmpd s: towards rr tl styd on fnl 2f: nrst fin* **7/1**

00 **7** hd **Miss Tallulah (IRE)**[22] 6286 2-9-0 0.......................... JimmyFortune 4 58
(Mel Brittain) *wnt rt s: sn led: hdd 1/2-way and sn pushed along: cl up tl rdn wl over 1f out and grad wknd* **100/1**

0 **8** 3/4 **Warm Order**[98] 3694 2-9-0 0...................................... SeanLevey 3 55
(Tony Carroll) *cl up: slt ld 1/2-way: rdn wl over 1f out: sn hdd & wknd* **50/1**

9 1/2 **Gauchita** 2-9-0 0.. ChrisCatlin 8 53
(Michael Bell) *a towards rr* **10/1**

10 nk **Storyline (IRE)** 2-9-0 0.. DuranFentiman 2 52
(Tim Easterby) *midfield: swtchd rt and effrt 2f out: sn rdn and n.d* **16/1**

0 **11** 5 **Who Splashed Me**[127] 2744 2-9-0 0............................ AdrianNicholls 13 34
(J R Jenkins) *a towards rr* **50/1**

0 **12** 2 3/4 **Under The Moon (IRE)**[64] 4858 2-9-5 0........................ SebSanders 12 29
(Charles Hills) *trckd ldrs: pushed along bef 1/2-way: sn rdn and wknd over 2f out: sn in rr* **7/2**[1]

000 **13** 5 **Vadara**[7] 6754 2-9-5 0.. GrahamGibbons 9 11
(Michael Easterby) *chsd ldrs to 1/2-way: sn wknd* **50/1**

1m 0.55s (-0.95) **Going Correction** -0.25s/f (Firm) **13** Ran SP% **121.0**
Speed ratings (Par 95): **97,92,90,87,87 87,87,86,85,84 76,72,64**
toteswingers 1&2 £8.10, 1&3 £28.70, 2&3 £22.90 CSF £27.44 TOTE £5.70: £2.00, £1.80, £7.80; EX 21.80 Trifecta £489.20 Pool: £1183.49 - 1.81 winning units..
Owner Dave and Gill Hedley **Bred** G Hedley & Mike Channon Bloodstock Limited **Trained** West Ilsley, Berks

FOCUS
An ordinary maiden in which the runners raced up the centre. The winner was quite impressive.

6948 32RED.COM H'CAP 5f 13y
3:00 (3:04) (Class 5) (0-75,75) 3-Y-O+ **£2,587** (£770; £384; £192) **Stalls** High

Form RPR

3511 **1** **Perfect Pasture**[8] 6728 3-9-5 **73** 6ex......................(v) GrahamGibbons 12 86
(Michael Easterby) *sn led: rdn along wl over 1f out: drvn ins fnl f: hld on wl* **9/4**[1]

-060 **2** 1/2 **Willbeme**[14] 6515 5-8-10 **69**.. AdamCarter(5) 8 79
(Neville Bycroft) *prom: cl up 2f out: rdn over 1f out and ev ch tl drvn ins fnl f and no ex towards fin* **10/1**

6511 **3** nk **Ambitious Icarus**[4] 6848 4-9-6 **74** 6ex....................(e) RobbieFitzpatrick 4 83
(Richard Guest) *wnt lft s and towards rr: hdwy 2f out: swtchd lft and rdn to chal ent fnl f: ev ch tl drvn and nt qckn last 50yds* **4/1**[3]

-004 **4** 1/2 **Muhdiq (USA)**[69] 4675 4-9-7 **75**................................ RyanMoore 2 82
(Mike Murphy) *trckd ldrs: hdwy and cl up wl over 1f out: sn rdn and one pce ins fnl f* **7/2**[2]

2126 **5** 2 1/2 **Dodina (IRE)**[37] 5820 3-9-5 **73**................................ JimmyFortune 6 72
(Peter Chapple-Hyam) *towards rr: hdwy 2f out: swtchd rt to inner and rdn over 1f out: kpt on fnl f: nrst fin* **14/1**

4450 **6** 3/4 **Hot Sugar (USA)**[202] 998 4-8-8 **62**..............................(t) AndrewMullen 7 58
(Michael Appleby) *chsd ldrs: rdn wl over 1f out: sn drvn and no imp* **20/1**

000 **7** hd **Medici Time**[14] 6515 8-9-3 **71**.................................. TedDurcan 3 66
(Tim Easterby) *dwlt and sltly hmpd s: bhd: hdwy wl over 1f out: sn rdn and kpt on fnl f: nrst fin* **25/1**

6000 **8** nse **Taurus Twins**[4] 6850 7-9-7 **75**..................................(v) ShaneKelly 10 70
(Richard Price) *cl up: rdn along wl over 12f out: sn wknd* **11/1**

4-0 **9** 6 **Dreamy Ciara**[13] 6547 3-8-13 **67**................................ SeanLevey 13 41
(David Brown) *chsd ldrs: rdn along 2f out: sn wknd* **14/1**

59.75s (-1.75) **Going Correction** -0.25s/f (Firm) **9** Ran SP% **112.4**
Speed ratings (Par 103): **104,103,102,101,97 96,96,96,86**
toteswingers 1&2 £8.20, 1&3 £1.10, 2&3 £10.50 CSF £25.11 CT £84.05 TOTE £4.20: £1.50, £3.60, £1.70; EX 37.10 Trifecta £438.60 Pool: £1468.30 - 2.51 winning units..
Owner Mrs Jean Turpin **Bred** Mrs Jean Turpin **Trained** Sheriff Hutton, N Yorks

FOCUS
A sprint handicap weakened by four non-runners. This time the runners came stands' side.

6949 SIR HENRY CECIL OH SO SHARP EBF MAIDEN FILLIES' STKS 1m 75y
3:35 (3:36) (Class 5) 2-Y-O **£3,234** (£962; £481; £240) **Stalls** Centre

Form RPR

1 **Cambridge** 2-9-0 0.. TedDurcan 1 85+
(Charles Hills) *in tch on inner: smooth hdwy 3f out: chsd ldng pair over 1f out: rdn and styd on strly fnl f to ld last 50yds* **16/1**

02 **2** 3/4 **Regardez**[20] 6318 2-9-0 0.. SebSanders 8 83+
(Ralph Beckett) *trckd ldrs: hdwy 4f out: cl up 3f out: rdn to ld over 1f out: drvn ins fnl f: hdd and no ex last 50yds* **3/1**[3]

2 **3** 5 **Sweeping Up**[22] 6281 2-9-0 0.................................... JimmyFortune 2 72
(Hughie Morrison) *trckd ldng pair: hdwy 4f out: led wl over 2f out: sn jnd and rdn: hdd over 1f out: kpt on same pce fnl f* **11/4**[2]

02 **4** 2 1/2 **Adore**[14] 6512 2-9-0 0.. RyanMoore 13 66
(Sir Michael Stoute) *hld up towards rr: hdwy 4f out: chsd ldrs over 2f out: sn rdn and one pce* **5/2**[1]

6 **5** 3/4 **Chortle**[22] 6281 2-9-0 0.. SilvestreDeSousa 11 64
(Charlie Appleby) *hld up: hdwy on outer 4f out: rdn wl over 2f out: drvn and one pce fr wl over 1f out* **7/1**

The Form Book Flat, Raceform Ltd, Compton, RG20 6NL.

6 5 **Star Chart (IRE)** 2-9-0 0 RobertHavlin 3 53+
(John Gosden) *dwlt and towards rr: sme hdwy 4f out: n.d* **16/1**
7 1 **Shallow Lake (USA)** 2-9-0 0 AhmedAjtebi 10 50
(Charlie Appleby) *dwlt: a towards rr* **25/1**
8 ½ **Red Passiflora** 2-9-0 0 AndreaAtzeni 7 49
(Sir Mark Prescott Bt) *dwlt: a towards rr* **50/1**
0 9 1¼ **Hasta La Vista**46 5516 2-8-11 0 MichaelJMMurphy(3) 5 46
(Mark Johnston) *chsd ldrs: rdn along 3f out: sn wknd* **50/1**
10 3½ **Stream Of Light** 2-9-0 0 GrahamGibbons 4 38
(John Mackie) *sn led: rdn along over 4f out: hdd over 3f out and sn wknd* **100/1**
11 7 **Key To Your Heart** 2-9-0 0 SeanLevey 9 22
(Hughie Morrison) *trckd ldr: hdwy to ld over 3f out: rdn and hdd wl over 2f out: sn wknd* **50/1**

1m 46.87s (-2.13) **Going Correction** -0.325s/f (Firm) 2y crse rec **11 Ran SP% 115.2**
Speed ratings (Par 92): **97,96,91,88,88 83,82,81,80,76 69**
toteswingers 1&2 £11.40, 1&3 £3.30, 2&3 £1.20 CSF £61.32 TOTE £25.20: £4.90, £2.00, £1.10; EX 105.70 Trifecta £1136.20 Pool: £2205.18 - 1.49 winning units..
Owner K Abdullah **Bred** Juddmonte Farms Ltd **Trained** Lambourn, Berks

FOCUS
The three at the head of the market had all finished runner-up in their last starts but, in a race run at a decent pace, this went to a newcomer.

6950 32RED CASINO MAIDEN STKS 1m 75y
4:10 (4:11) (Class 5) 3-Y-0+ £2,587 (£770; £384; £192) **Stalls** Centre

Form RPR
0- 1 **Sensiz (IRE)**326 7686 3-9-0 0 AndreaAtzeni 8 85
(Roger Varian) *prom: trckd ldr after 3f: effrt over 2f out: rdn to chal wl over 1f out: drvn ins fnl f: styd on wl to ld last 50yds* **20/1**
4 2 ½ **Musaddas**8 6738 3-9-5 0 SilvestreDeSousa 10 88
(Saeed bin Suroor) *sn led: pushed along 4f out: rdn wl over 2f out: drvn over 1f out: hdd and no ex last 50yds* **3/1**2
3 2¼ **Desert Skies (IRE)** 3-9-0 0 RobertHavlin 4 78
(Saeed bin Suroor) *hld up in rr: hdwy over 3f out: effrt to chse ldrs 2f out: sn rdn: kpt on fnl f: nrst fin* **12/1**
243 4 2¼ **Vermont (IRE)**13 6566 3-9-5 85 RyanMoore 11 78
(Luca Cumani) *trckd ldrs: hdwy on outer 4f out: rdn over 2f out: sn chsng ldng pair and drvn: kpt on one pce* **5/4**1
62 5 8 **Aomen Rock**13 6555 3-9-5 0 FrederikTylicki 5 60
(James Fanshawe) *trckd ldrs: hdwy 4f out: rdn 3f out: sn drvn and one pce fnl 2f* **6/1**3
0-20 6 1¼ **Arms (IRE)**146 2192 3-9-5 78 SebSanders 3 57
(J W Hills) *trckd ldng pair: rdn along on inner wl over 2f out: grad wknd* **10/1**
0 7 5 **Stanlow**58 5069 3-9-5 0 ShaneKelly 1 45
(John Stimpson) *midfield: rdn along wl over 3f out: sn outpcd* **100/1**
0 8 nk **Zeteah**19 6366 3-9-0 0 TedDurcan 13 40
(David Lanigan) *a towards rr* **66/1**
9 2¼ **Deserving Honour** 3-9-5 0 AhmedAjtebi 6 39
(Charlie Appleby) *dwlt: t.k.h in rr: hdwy on outer and in tch 3f out: sn rdn and wknd* **10/1**
00 10 23 **Rowlestone Lass**49 5386 3-9-0 0 GrahamGibbons 12
(Richard Price) *dwlt: a in rr* **200/1**

1m 44.93s (-4.07) **Going Correction** -0.325s/f (Firm)
WFA 3 from 4yo 3lb **10 Ran SP% 117.3**
Speed ratings (Par 103): **107,106,104,102,94 92,87,87,85,62**
toteswingers 1&2 £7.70, 1&3 £24.80, 2&3 £2.30 CSF £79.62 TOTE £34.20: £5.40, £1.90, £3.50; EX 151.30 Trifecta £593.50 Pool: £2205.18 - 2.78 winning units..
Owner Saleh Al Homaizi & Imad Al Sagar **Bred** Grangecon Stud **Trained** Newmarket, Suffolk

FOCUS
A modest older-horse maiden.

6951 32RED H'CAP 1m 75y
4:40 (4:40) (Class 4) (0-85,85) 3-Y-0 £5,498 (£1,636; £817; £408) **Stalls** Centre

Form RPR
2661 1 **Saigon City**64 4865 3-8-9 **73** (b) AndreaAtzeni 7 86+
(Luca Cumani) *dwlt and hld up in rr: hdwy over 3f out: chsd ldrs 2f out: rdn ent fnl furlong: styd on wl to ld nr fin* **5/1**3
3163 2 nk **Magistral**45 5562 3-9-4 **82** RobertHavlin 12 92+
(John Gosden) *hld up towards rr: gd hdwy 1/2-way: trckd ldrs on outer over 2f out: rdn to ld ent fnl f: sn drvn: hdd and no ex towards fin* **9/2**2
2502 3 1¾ **Al Mukhdam**35 5886 3-9-6 **84** ChrisCatlin 1 90
(Peter Chapple-Hyam) *led: rdn along over 3f out: hdd over 2f out: drvn and kpt on fnl f* **6/1**
0120 4 ½ **Regal Silk**33 5958 3-9-4 **82** SebSanders 9 87
(Jeremy Noseda) *trckd ldrs: hdwy over 3f out: led over 2f out and sn rdn: drvn and hdd ent fnl f: kpt on same pce* **8/1**
2454 5 ½ **Freeport**18 6379 3-8-12 **76** JimmyFortune 11 80
(Brian Meehan) *hld up in rr: hdwy on outer 3f out: rdn wl over 1f out: styd on fnl f: nrst fin* **10/1**
1560 6 1¾ **Woody Bay**13 6563 3-8-13 **77** FrederikTylicki 5 77
(James Given) *trckd ldrs on inner: effrt over 3f out: rdn along 2f out: kpt on one pce* **16/1**
4612 7 ¾ **Loved One**39 5758 3-9-0 **78** ShaneKelly 6 76
(James Fanshawe) *midfield: hdwy to chse ldrs 3f out: rdn 2f out: sn no imp* **7/2**1
5052 8 ½ **Fraserburgh (IRE)**8 6730 3-8-4 **71** oh1 MichaelJMMurphy(3) 3 68
(Mark Johnston) *prom: pushed along over 4f out: chsd ldrs 3f out: rdn and hld whn n.m.r and sltly hmpd wl over 1f out: sn wknd* **12/1**
041 9 5 **Defiant Spirit**17 6431 3-8-9 **73** SeanLevey 4 58
(Roger Charlton) *dwlt: sn in midfield: effrt to chse ldrs 3f out: sn rdn and wknd* **10/1**
1004 10 3¼ **Mister Marcasite**12 6602 3-8-9 **73** DuranFentiman 2 51
(Mel Brittain) *cl up: rdn along 3f out: sn wknd* **33/1**

1m 45.42s (-3.58) **Going Correction** -0.325s/f (Firm) **10 Ran SP% 117.2**
Speed ratings (Par 103): **104,103,101,101,100 99,98,97,92,89**
toteswingers 1&2 £5.90, 1&3 £12.40, 2&3 £6.60 CSF £27.95 CT £142.47 TOTE £6.80: £2.50, £1.20, £2.30; EX 26.60 Trifecta £124.30 Pool: £966.52 - 5.82 winning units..
Owner Leonidas Marinopoulos **Bred** Martin Percival **Trained** Newmarket, Suffolk

FOCUS
A fair handicap and a race of changing fortunes, with four different leaders from over a furlong out. The first two came from well back.

6952 32REDPOKER.COM AJA LADY AMATEUR RIDERS' H'CAP 1m 2f 50y
5:10 (5:13) (Class 5) (0-70,75) 3-Y-0+ £2,495 (£774; £386; £193) **Stalls** Low

Form RPR
5402 1 **Valentine's Gift**8 6722 5-10-0 **55** oh8 MissCWalton 2 63
(Neville Bycroft) *trckd ldrs on inner: hdwy over 4f out: cl up 3f out: led wl over 1f out: rdn and kpt on wl fnl f* **20/1**
3305 2 1¾ **Batgirl**5 6794 6-10-7 **67** MissKMargarson(5) 8 72
(Martin Smith) *dwlt and in rr: stdy hdwy on inner 4f out: trckd ldrs 3f out: swtchd rt and effrt to chse wnr over 1f out: sn rdn and no imp towards fin* **8/1**
260 3 4½ **Outlaw Torn (IRE)**5 6794 4-10-0 **60** (e) MissBeckySmith(5) 7 56
(Richard Guest) *trckd ldrs on outer: pushed along and lost pl 1/2-way: hdwy 3f out: rdn wl over 1f out: kpt on same pce* **9/2**3
3233 4 nk **Thereabouts (USA)**9 6700 4-10-11 **66** MrsCBartley 11 62
(Michael Appleby) *prom: effrt over 3f out and sn cl up: rdn over 2f out: grad wknd appr fnl f* **5/1**
5553 5 hd **Having A Ball**22 6283 9-10-0 **55** oh5 MissRachelKing 9 50
(Geoffrey Deacon) *dwlt and towards rr: hdwy 3f out: chsd ldrs 2f out: sn rdn and kpt on same pce* **25/1**
1321 6 2½ **Absent Amy (IRE)**8 6730 4-11-3 **75** 6ex MissHayleyMoore(3) 5 65
(Amy Weaver) *trckd ldrs: hdwy 4f out: led 3f out: rdn and hdd wl over 1f out: wknd appr fnl f* **11/4**1
3045 7 ¾ **Astrosapphire**20 6335 3-9-6 **59** MissNMcCaffrey(7) 4 48
(Mark H Tompkins) *prom: led after 3f: rdn along 4f out: hdd 3f out: wknd wl over 1f out* **12/1**
-604 8 3¼ **Self Employed**21 6306 6-10-12 **67** MissSBrotherton 10 50
(Garry Woodward) *chsd ldrs: rdn along over 3f out: wknd 2f out* **7/2**2
0060 9 8 **Vogarth**12 6606 9-9-9 **55** oh10 (b) MissLWilson(5) 1 23
(Michael Chapman) *t.k.h: led 3f: prom tl rdn along over 2f out and sn wknd* **100/1**
06-0 10 23 **Orpen Wide (IRE)**7 6756 11-9-11 **55** oh10 (t) MissAliceMills(3) 6
(Michael Chapman) *chsd ldrs 3f: sn lost pl and bhd* **100/1**

2m 13.0s (-1.30) **Going Correction** -0.325s/f (Firm)
WFA 3 from 4yo+ 5lb **10 Ran SP% 113.1**
Speed ratings (Par 103): **92,90,87,86,86 84,84,81,75,56**
toteswingers 1&2 £8.40, 1&3 £14.60, 2&3 £9.60 CSF £162.43 CT £851.63 TOTE £19.40: £3.90, £2.80, £1.90; EX 104.50 Trifecta £1353.60 Part won. Pool: £1804.86 - 0.22 winning units..
Owner Hambleton Racing Partnership **Bred** N Bycroft **Trained** Brandsby, N Yorks

FOCUS
A moderate lady amateurs' handicap.
T/Plt: £35.30 to a £1 stake. Pool: £69869.04 - 1441.57 winning tickets T/Qpdt: £13.20 to a £1 stake. Pool: £4582.92 - 255.57 winning tickets JR

6139 SALISBURY (R-H)
Wednesday, October 2

OFFICIAL GOING: Heavy (soft in places; goingstick 6.9)
Wind: mild against Weather: overcast with rain at times

6953 FRANCIS CLARK BRITISH STALLION STUDS EBF MAIDEN STKS (DIV I) 1m
1:45 (1:46) (Class 4) 2-Y-0 £4,204 (£1,251; £625; £312) **Stalls** Low

Form RPR
1 **Field Of Fame** 2-9-5 0 DavidProbert 11 81+
(Andrew Balding) *leggy: athletic: disp ld: rdn into outrt ld 2f out: edgd lft jst over 1f out: kpt on strly: rdn out* **12/1**
2 1¼ **Black Schnapps (IRE)** 2-9-5 0 MartinDwyer 13 78+
(William Muir) *str: towards rr of midfield: pushed along over 3f out: hdwy jst over 2f out: styd on to chse wnr ent fnl f: a being hld* **25/1**
3 1¾ **Skilled** 2-9-5 0 GeorgeBaker 10 76+
(Roger Charlton) *lengthy: tall: lw: dwlt: bhd: pushed along and stdy hdwy fr wl over 2f out: styd on to chse ldrs ent fnl f: kpt on: snatched 3rd fnl stride* **9/1**
4 nse **Belrog** 2-9-5 0 HarryBentley 15 74
(Ralph Beckett) *lengthy: scope: mid-div: pushed along and hdwy 3f out: sn rdn: styd on to chse ldng pair jst over 1f out: kpt on same pce fnl f: lost 3rd fnl stride* **7/1**3
5 4 **Kisanji** 2-9-5 0 MartinHarley 6 65
(Mick Channon) *w'like: mid-div: rdn over 2f out: kpt on but nvr any real imp on ldrs* **10/1**
6 1¾ **Galizzi (USA)** 2-9-5 0 TomQueally 12 61
(Michael Bell) *lengthy: tall: towards rr: swtchd lft and stdy prog whn rdn 3f out: styd on fr over 1f out: nvr trbld ldrs* **25/1**
7 shd **Strait Run (IRE)** 2-9-5 0 DaneO'Neill 4 61
(Richard Hannon) *w'like: tall: in tch: trckd ldrs 4f out: rdn on far side wl over 2f out: no ex fr over 1f out* **16/1**
00 8 2¼ **Winter Spice (IRE)**47 5473 2-9-5 0 AdamKirby 5 56
(Clive Cox) *struggling in rr early: sme late prog: nvr a factor* **14/1**
4 9 ¾ **Manor Way (IRE)**15 6485 2-9-5 0 PatDobbs 7 54
(Richard Hannon) *neat: trckd ldrs: ev ch 3f out: sn rdn on far side rails: wknd over 1f out* **14/1**
6 10 1 **Gannicus**18 6378 2-9-0 0 RyanTate(5) 8 52
(Brendan Powell) *tall: strong: disp ld: rdn over 2f out: sn hdd: wknd over 1f out* **100/1**
0 11 ¾ **Arab Dawn**19 6355 2-9-5 0 LiamKeniry 16 51
(Hughie Morrison) *leggy: trckd ldrs: rdn over 2f out: sn wknd* **12/1**
3 12 2½ **Magnus Maximus**11 6635 2-9-5 0 RichardHughes 9 45
(Richard Hannon) *lengthy: trckd ldrs: effrt 2f out: wknd jst over 1f out* **3/1**1
13 11 **Orion's Bow** 2-9-5 0 WilliamBuick 14 21
(John Gosden) *str: lw: towards rr: effrt to cl jst over 3f out: nvr rchd ldrs: wknd over 1f out* **5/1**2

1m 49.97s (6.47) **Going Correction** +0.65s/f (Yiel) **13 Ran SP% 116.5**
Speed ratings (Par 97): **93,91,90,89,85 84,84,81,81,80 79,76,65**
toteswingers 1&2 £28.30, 1&3 £23.90, 2&3 £50.80 CSF £279.10 TOTE £12.80: £4.20, £9.40, £3.50; EX 410.50 Trifecta £2110.80 Part won. Pool: £2814.49 - 0.29 winning units..
Owner Thurloe Thoroughbreds XXXI **Bred** Mrs S A Hunt **Trained** Kingsclere, Hants

FOCUS
There was 5mm of rain overnight and in total the track had taken 25.5mm over the previous seven days, resulting in the ground being described as heavy, soft in places (GoingStick 6.9). David Probert said it was "very testing", and Pat Dobbs that it was "heavy and horrible". One or two interesting newcomers in this maiden.

6954 FRANCIS CLARK BRITISH STALLION STUDS EBF MAIDEN STKS (DIV II) 1m
2:20 (2:21) (Class 4) 2-Y-O **£4,204** (£1,251; £625; £312) **Stalls** Low

Form RPR
34 **1** **Snow Sky**[27] 6125 2-9-5 0 .... JamesDoyle 7 90+
(Sir Michael Stoute) *tall: cl-cpld: mid-div in centre gp: smooth hdwy fr 3f out: led 2f out: rdn clr ent fnl f: styd on strly* **7/2**[1]

3 **2** *11* **Ultimate Act**[17] 6430 2-9-5 0 .... LiamKeniry 12 66
(Seamus Mullins) *unf: racd on farside and overall ldr: rdn whn drifted to centre gp 3f out: hdd 2f out: kpt drifting lft but styd on depite being wl hld by wnr* **8/1**

3250 **3** *1 1/4* **Solo Hunter**[3] 6865 2-9-5 70 .... CathyGannon 6 63
(David Evans) *chsd ldrs in centre gp: rdn wl over 2f out: nt pce to get on terms: styd on ent fnl f: snatched 3rd fnl strides* **14/1**

04 **4** *hd* **Cosette (IRE)**[22] 6281 2-9-0 0 .... DaneO'Neill 3 58
(Henry Candy) *unf: racd far side: chsd ldr: rdn whn lft to r alone of far rails fr 3f out: ev ch 2f out: sn wl hld by wnr: kpt on: lost 3rd fnl strides* **14/1**

6 **5** *nse* **High Master (IRE)**[7] 6739 2-9-5 0 .... RichardHughes 9 62
(Richard Hannon) *led centre gp: overall chsd far side ldr: rdn and ch 2f out: sn disputing wl hld 3rd: lost 4th fnl strides* **9/2**[2]

6 *3/4* **Sea Goddess (IRE)** 2-9-0 0 .... RichardKingscote 1 56+
(Ralph Beckett) *tall: angular: in tch in centre gp: rdn 3f out: sn wl hld in midfield but styd on again fnl f* **5/1**[3]

55 **7** *1 1/2* **Mishko (IRE)**[40] 5698 2-9-5 0 .... AdamKirby 10 58
(Clive Cox) *w'like: chsd ldrs in centre gp: rdn wl over 2f out: wknd over 1f out* **10/1**

0 **8** *3/4* **Bold Runner**[47] 5473 2-9-5 0 .... FrankieMcDonald 11 56
(Sean Curran) *mid-div in centre gp tl rdn over 4f out: sn towards rr* **100/1**

4 **9** *nk* **Hands Up (IRE)**[40] 5718 2-9-5 0 .... NeilCallan 15 55
(William Knight) *cmpt: lw: racd stands' side tl swtchd to centre 4f out: chsd ldrs: rdn over 3f out: wknd over 1f out* **7/1**

0 **10** *20* **Intense Effort (IRE)**[22] 6277 2-9-5 0 .... MickaelBarzalona 4 11
(Charlie Appleby) *str: lengthy: lw: chsd ldrs in centre gp: rdn 3f out: wknd 2f out: t.o* **14/1**

11 *10* **Secure Cloud (IRE)** 2-9-5 0 .... GeorgeBaker 13
(J W Hills) *str: dwlt: racd centre: a struggling in rr: t.o* **20/1**

00 **12** *6* **Frosty The Snowman (IRE)**[14] 6528 2-9-5 0 .... TomQueally 5
(Charles Hills) *s.i.s: sn mid-div in centre gp: wknd 2f out: t.o* **40/1**

0 **13** *19* **Severn Crossing**[17] 6430 2-9-5 0 .... MartinDwyer 16
(William Muir) *w'like: racd stands' side: chsd ldrs: rdn over 3f out: sn wknd: t.o* **33/1**

1m 48.44s (4.94) **Going Correction** +0.65s/f (Yiel) **13** Ran SP% **120.9**
Speed ratings (Par 97): **101,90,88,88,88 87,86,85,85,65 55,49,30**
toteswingers 1&2 £7.60, 1&3 £13.10, 2&3 £20.00 CSF £31.23 TOTE £4.60: £1.50, £2.80, £3.70; EX 40.70 Trifecta £412.60 Pool: £3551.29 - 6.45 winning units..
Owner K Abdullah **Bred** Juddmonte Farms Ltd **Trained** Newmarket, Suffolk

FOCUS
Much the quicker of the two divisions, 1.53sec faster than the first race. This was all about the winner.

6955 BOOKER WHOLESALE BRITISH STALLION STUDS E B F NOVICE STKS 6f 212y
2:50 (2:50) (Class 4) 2-Y-O **£4,528** (£1,347; £673; £336) **Stalls** Low

Form RPR
1 **1** **Piping Rock**[66] 4795 2-9-3 0 .... RichardHughes 5 100+
(Richard Hannon) *str: lw: wnt lft s: trckd ldrs: shkn up to chal over 1f out: led jst ins fnl f: r.o wl to draw clr: readily* **5/2**[1]

021 **2** *4* **Hartnell**[17] 6430 2-9-3 0 .... LiamJones 3 90
(Mark Johnston) *w'like: str: led: rdn 3f out: edgd lft fr over 1f out: hdd hust ins fnl f: sn hld: kpt on for clr 2nd* **11/4**[2]

10 **3** *4 1/2* **Baby Bush (IRE)**[53] 5284 2-8-12 0 .... PatDobbs 1 73
(Richard Hannon) *unf: scope: trckd ldrs: rdn 2f out: nt pce to get on terms: kpt on to claim disp 3rd ins fnl f* **12/1**

4425 **4** *1* **Rosso Corsa**[20] 6328 2-9-3 93 .... MartinHarley 2 76
(Mick Channon) *stdd bhd ldng pair after breaking wl: racd keenly early: rdn 2f out: nt pce to chal: no ex whn lost disp 3rd fnl 75yds* **5/2**[1]

3653 **5** *8* **Lone Warrior (IRE)**[3] 6866 2-9-0 94 .... (v[1]) TomQueally 4 52
(David Evans) *pressed ldr tl rdn 3f out: hld fr 2f out: wknd ent fnl f* **9/2**[3]

1m 31.93s (3.33) **Going Correction** +0.65s/f (Yiel) **5** Ran SP% **109.7**
Speed ratings (Par 97): **106,101,96,95,86**
CSF £9.57 TOTE £2.70: £1.30, £2.40; EX 8.60 Trifecta £36.20 Pool: £3342.81 - 69.20 winning units..
Owner R J McCreery & Pall Mall Partners **Bred** Stowell Hill Ltd **Trained** East Everleigh, Wilts

FOCUS
Richard Hannon has dominated this race in recent years, sending out four of the last seven winners, and he enhanced that record further.

6956 HIGOS INSURANCE SERVICES SOUTHAMPTON CLAIMING STKS 1m 1f 198y
3:20 (3:20) (Class 5) 3-4-Y-O **£2,749** (£818; £408; £204) **Stalls** High

Form RPR
1100 **1** **Breaking The Bank**[12] 6596 4-9-8 80 .... MartinDwyer 4 86
(William Muir) *trckd ldr: kpt wd on bnd 6f out but sn led: racd centre over 4f out: rdn over 1f out: styd on wl to assert fnl 120yds* **13/8**[1]

3054 **2** *3* **Hipster**[20] 6335 3-8-12 73 .... (b) JamesDoyle 2 75
(Ralph Beckett) *led tl wl over 5f out: pressed wnr: racd clsr to far side than other 3: rdn 2f out: kpt on tl no ex fnl 120yds* **9/4**[3]

3450 **3** *18* **Lord Ofthe Shadows (IRE)**[62] 4923 4-9-8 84 .... RichardHughes 5 53
(Richard Hannon) *trckd ldrs: racd centre over 4f out: effrt over 3f out: wknd 2f out* **15/8**[2]

400 **4** *26* **Bustling Darcey**[15] 6486 3-8-2 42 .... (b[1]) JimmyQuinn 3
(Mark Gillard) *s.i.s: trckd ldrs: struggling over 5f out: racd in centre over 4f out but sn btn: t.o* **50/1**

2m 18.8s (8.90) **Going Correction** +0.725s/f (Yiel)
WFA 3 from 4yo 5lb **4** Ran SP% **105.6**
Speed ratings (Par 103): **93,90,76,55**
CSF £5.32 TOTE £2.80; EX 5.10 Trifecta £8.00 Pool: £3027.30 - 281.14 winning units..Breaking The Bank was subject of a Friendly claim of £26,000.
Owner R W Devlin **Bred** Cheveley Park Stud Ltd **Trained** Lambourn, Berks

FOCUS
There wasn't a great deal between the first three in the betting on ratings and this was all about who handled conditions best.

6957 WEATHERBYS BANK FOREIGN EXCHANGE H'CAP 1m 1f 198y
3:55 (3:55) (Class 2) (0-105,103) 3-Y-0+
£12,450 (£3,728; £1,864; £932; £466; £234) **Stalls** High

Form RPR
3212 **1** **Nabucco**[64] 4854 4-9-9 100 .... WilliamBuick 4 113
(John Gosden) *trckd ldrs: looked in trble briefly whn pushed along over 3f out: chal bk gng strly over 2f out: sn led: styd on strly to draw clr ent fnl f: comf* **7/4**[1]

40-5 **2** *6* **Open Water (FR)**[149] 2101 4-8-7 84 oh1 .... DavidProbert 5 86
(Andrew Balding) *lw: trckd ldr: chal 4f out: rdn over 2f out: dropped to hld 3rd sn after: kpt on ins fnl f to regain 2nd nring fin* **7/1**

1436 **3** *nk* **Noble Gift**[14] 6537 3-8-3 85 .... JimmyQuinn 9 86
(William Knight) *hld up bhd ldrs: swtchd rt over 2f out: sn rdn to chal: chsd wnr fr over 1f out but a readily hld: no ex whn lost 2nd nring fin* **7/1**

1360 **4** *2 1/2* **Viewpoint (IRE)**[11] 6638 4-9-4 95 .... RichardHughes 3 92
(Richard Hannon) *lw: led: jnd over 3f out: sn rdn: hdd 2f out: sn hld in disp 3rd: fdd ins fnl f* **9/1**

0002 **5** *1 1/2* **Mister Impatience**[7] 6741 3-8-12 94 .... LiamJones 10 88
(Mark Johnston) *cl up: swtchd out and pushed along over 3f out: sn chal: rdn wl over 2f out: hld fr 2f out* **10/3**[2]

1000 **6** *hd* **Resurge (IRE)**[20] 6332 8-9-5 96 .... (t) NeilCallan 6 89
(Stuart Kittow) *cl up: effrt 3f out: nvr really threatened: hld fr 2f out* **14/1**

400 **R** **King's Warrior (FR)**[81] 4310 6-9-2 98 .... OisinMurphy[(5)] 7
(Peter Chapple-Hyam) *ref to r: tk no part* **13/2**[3]

2m 14.76s (4.86) **Going Correction** +0.725s/f (Yiel)
WFA 3 from 4yo+ 5lb **7** Ran SP% **114.4**
Speed ratings (Par 109): **109,104,103,101,100 100,**
toteswingers 1&2 £3.80, 1&3 £3.50, 2&3 £7.00 CSF £14.75 CT £68.79 TOTE £2.60: £2.20, £4.10; EX 18.20 Trifecta £75.90 Pool: £37.20 - 3766.84 winning units..
Owner HRH Princess Haya Of Jordan **Bred** Darley **Trained** Newmarket, Suffolk

FOCUS
A decent handicap won by a colt with a progressive profile.

6958 HIGOS INSURANCE SERVICES CONDITIONS STKS 6f
4:30 (4:30) (Class 2) 2-Y-O **£9,703** (£2,887; £1,443; £721) **Stalls** Low

Form RPR
2052 **1** **Justice Day (IRE)**[21] 6304 2-9-4 101 .... WilliamBuick 4 104
(David Elsworth) *mde all: rdn clr ent fnl f: kpt on strly* **4/1**[3]

61 **2** *3* **Complicit (IRE)**[74] 4539 2-9-1 0 .... AshleyMorgan 5 92
(Paul Cole) *w'like: tall: dismntd to load in stalls: wnt sltly lft s: racd keenly: trckd ldrs: rdn 2f out: chsd wnr ent fnl f but a hld: kpt on to fin clr 2nd* **10/1**

51 **3** *5* **Desert Ace (IRE)**[19] 6354 2-9-1 0 .... AdamKirby 1 77
(Clive Cox) *w'like: racd keenly: trckd wnr: rdn 2f out: no ex whn lost 2nd ent fnl f* **8/1**

4024 **4** *3/4* **Figure Of Speech (IRE)**[11] 6637 2-9-1 107 .... (v[1]) MickaelBarzalona 6 75
(Charlie Appleby) *wnt sltly lft s: racd keenly: trckd ldrs: effrt 3f out: nvr threatened: sn one pce* **1/1**[1]

5423 **5** *2 1/4* **Expert (IRE)**[21] 6304 2-9-1 99 .... RichardHughes 3 68
(Richard Hannon) *settled last but wl in tch: pushed along 3f out: nvr threatened: fdd fnl f* **7/2**[2]

1m 18.63s (3.83) **Going Correction** +0.65s/f (Yiel) **5** Ran SP% **112.4**
Speed ratings (Par 101): **100,96,89,88,85**
CSF £37.49 TOTE £5.00: £2.00, £3.80; EX 39.70 Trifecta £103.10 Pool: £2998.21 - 21.80 winning units..
Owner Robert Ng **Bred** Gerry Kenny **Trained** Newmarket, Suffolk

FOCUS
The winner showed a good attitude after getting easy lead.

6959 HIGOS INSURANCE SERVICES BOURNEMOUTH H'CAP 6f
5:00 (5:00) (Class 4) (0-85,85) 3-Y-0+ **£4,851** (£1,443; £721; £360) **Stalls** Low

Form RPR
-000 **1** **Magic Secret**[11] 6647 5-9-2 80 .... MartinDwyer 1 93
(William Muir) *taken down early: mde all: jnd 3f out: rdn 2f out: edgd lft ent fnl f: r.o strly: rdn out* **14/1**

0100 **2** *1 3/4* **Pivotal Movement**[11] 6642 3-8-13 78 .... RichardHughes 2 85
(Richard Hannon) *lw: trckd wnr: chal travelling wl 3f out: rdn wl over 1f out: edgd lft: kpt on but nt pce of wnr fnl f* **9/2**[2]

6452 **3** *1 3/4* **Rocky Reef**[19] 6360 4-8-9 73 .... (b) JackMitchell 11 74+
(Philip Hide) *hld up towards rr: swtchd to centre 3f out: sn rdn and hdwy: kpt on ins fnl f: wnt 3rd towards fin* **15/2**[3]

1430 **4** *1 1/2* **Grand Denial (IRE)**[18] 6382 3-8-5 75 .... (b) RyanTate[(5)] 3 72
(Clive Cox) *trckd ldrs: rdn over 2f out: kpt on wout ever threatening* **8/1**

0053 **5** *2 1/2* **Accession (IRE)**[63] 4879 4-9-2 80 .... (b) AdamKirby 6 69
(Clive Cox) *little slowly away: sn mid-div: rdn whn swtchd rt to chse ldrs 2f out: one pce fnl f* **11/4**[1]

1004 **6** *nse* **Royal Reyah**[16] 6461 4-8-10 74 .... TomQueally 18 62
(Stuart Kittow) *hld up bhd: swtchd to centre and rdn wl over 2f out: styd on past wkng horses fnl f: nvr a threat* **10/1**

3114 **7** *4 1/2* **Tight Fit**[15] 6488 3-9-6 85 .... FergusSweeney 12 59
(Henry Candy) *lw: little slowly away: in rr: swtchd lft to centre 3f out: rdn and hdwy over 2f out: wknd ent fnl f* **15/2**[3]

5460 **8** *1* **Mister Musicmaster**[170] 1583 4-8-9 78 .... OisinMurphy[(5)] 14 49
(Ron Hodges) *mid-div: hdwy 3f out: sn rdn to chse ldrs: wknd jst over 1f out* **25/1**

3315 **9** *1 1/4* **Lucky Di**[20] 6338 3-8-8 73 .... KierenFox 10 40
(Peter Hedger) *mid-div: rdn over 2f out: wknd over 1f out* **22/1**

-020 **10** *3 3/4* **Miliika**[18] 6382 4-9-4 82 .... WilliamBuick 15 37
(Rae Guest) *mid-div: swtchd to centre 3f out: sn rdn: wknd over 1f out* **15/2**[3]

6/05 **11** *23* **Egotist (IRE)**[15] 6489 5-8-13 80 .... WilliamTwiston-Davies[(3)] 8
(Milton Bradley) *chsd ldrs: rdn 3f out: sn wknd: t.o* **40/1**

1m 17.68s (2.88) **Going Correction** +0.65s/f (Yiel)
WFA 3 from 4yo+ 1lb **11** Ran SP% **117.6**
Speed ratings (Par 105): **106,103,101,99,96 95,89,88,86,81 51**
toteswingers 1&2 £23.10, 1&3 £24.00, 2&3 £7.40 CSF £74.57 CT £528.04 TOTE £19.20: £4.30, £1.40, £2.90; EX 111.20 Trifecta £939.60 Pool: £2859.35 - 2.28 winning units..
Owner Carmel Stud **Bred** Carmel Stud **Trained** Lambourn, Berks

The Form Book Flat, Raceform Ltd, Compton, RG20 6NL.

FOCUS
Plenty of non-runners due to the ground so this was less competitive than it had promised to be. The far rail may have been an advantage as four of the first five raced there.

6960 **HIGOS INSURANCE SERVICES CHRISTCHURCH H'CAP** **1m 6f 21y**
5:30 (5:30) (Class 5) (0-75,75) 3-Y-O+ **£2,911** (£866; £432; £216)

Form RPR
4254 **1** **Opera Buff**[25] 6200 4-9-3 **67**.....(p) JamesDoyle 14 85
(Sean Curran) *mde all: kpt to far side rails over 4f out: drvn clr fr 2f out: styd on wl* **14/1**
4006 **2** *10* **Abundantly**[18] 6377 4-9-9 **73**..... WilliamBuick 5 78
(Hughie Morrison) *trckd ldrs: led gp of 4: swtchd to centre over 5f out but lost pl: rdn bk in to 3rd 3f out: wnt 2nd 2f out but nvr any ch w wnr: styd on same pce* **6/1**[3]
0/13 **3** *4 ½* **Highway Code (USA)**[5] 6788 7-9-3 **70**..... DeclanBates(3) 8 69
(Richard Lee) *mid-div: kpt nr far side over 4f out: rdn whn drifted lft over 2f out: styd on same pce to go 3rd ent fnl f* **7/2**[2]
6000 **4** *nk* **Shades Of Grey**[18] 6377 6-9-0 **69**..... RyanTate(5) 7 68
(Clive Cox) *hld up towards rr: swtchd to centre gp of 4 over 5f out: rdn and stdy prog fr over 3f out: styd on same pce fnl 2f* **13/2**
0335 **5** *2* **The Betchworth Kid**[20] 6336 8-9-11 **75**.....(v) TomQueally 13 71
(Michael Bell) *hld up towards rr: swtchd to centre gp of 4 over 5f out: rdn over 4f out: nvr any imp tl styd on fnl f* **3/1**[1]
1122 **6** *1* **Chapter Five**[17] 6424 6-9-1 **68**.....(b) RyanPowell(3) 11 63
(Ian Williams) *trckd ldr: kpt to far side over 4f out: rdn over 2f out: sn lost 2nd: wknd ins fnl f* **13/2**
0456 **7** *9* **Linkable**[94] 3865 4-9-2 **66**..... JackMitchell 6 49
(Brendan Powell) *mid-div: swtchd to centre gp of 4 over 5f out: rdn over 3f out: wknd over 1f out* **33/1**
0603 **8** *13* **Admirable Duque (IRE)**[5] 6809 7-8-9 **66**.....(b) JoshBaudains(7) 1 32
(Dominic Ffrench Davis) *mid-div: kpt to far side rails over 4f out: rdn over 3f out: wknd wl over 1f out* **12/1**
4250 **9** *9* **Tingo In The Tale (IRE)**[28] 6108 4-9-2 **69**. WilliamTwiston-Davies(3) 10 24
(David Arbuthnot) *hld up towards rr: rdn whn kpt to far side over 4f out: wknd over 3f out* **14/1**
560/ **10** *4* **Advisor (FR)**[62] 5440 7-9-10 **74**.....(b) LiamTreadwell 2 23
(Mark Gillard) *trckd ldr tl over 4f out: sn bhd on far side: t.o* **25/1**
3m 22.46s (15.06) **Going Correction** +0.725s/f (Yiel) **10** Ran SP% **116.0**
Speed ratings (Par 103): **85,79,76,76,75 74,69,62,57,54**
toteswingers 1&2 £14.20, 1&3 £12.30, 2&3 £6.00 CSF £95.15 CT £364.41 TOTE £14.50: £4.40, £2.00, £2.10; EX 83.50 Trifecta £783.90 Pool: £2033.89 - 1.94 winning units..
Owner Bob Cooper & Val Dean **Bred** Littleton Stud **Trained** Hatford, Oxon

FOCUS
An ordinary handicap that was all about the winner.
T/Plt: £1,108.00 to a £1 stake. Pool: £58816.44 - 38.75 winning tickets T/Qpdt: £23.10 to a £1 stake. Pool: £5047.75 - 161.30 winning tickets TM

6292 CHANTILLY (R-H)
Wednesday, October 2
OFFICIAL GOING: Turf: soft; polytrack: standard

6961a **PRIX DE L'ORME (MAIDEN) (2YO) (POLYTRACK)** **1m 1f**
2:35 (12:00) 2-Y-O **£9,756** (£3,902; £2,926; £1,951; £975)

RPR
1 **Tempo Royale (FR)**[39] 2-8-13 0..... TheoBachelot 16 81
(S Wattel, France) **136/10**
2 *½* **San Benedeto (FR)**[30] 2-9-2 0..... TonyPiccone 6 83
(C Lerner, France) **68/10**
3 *nk* **Zlatan In Paris (FR)** 2-9-2 0..... ChristopheSoumillon 7 82
(J-C Rouget, France) **9/5**[1]
4 *¾* **Downhill Only**[40] 2-9-2 0..... FabriceVeron 1 81
(H-A Pantall, France) **5/1**[2]
5 *shd* **Time For Mabel (FR)**[32] 2-9-2 0..... AntoineHamelin 8 81
(F-H Graffard, France) **30/1**
6 *2* **Uradel (GER)** 2-9-2 0..... Pierre-CharlesBoudot 2 77
(H Blume, Germany) **24/1**
7 *2 ½* **Azucardel (FR)**[69] 2-9-2 0..... Christophe-PatriceLemaire 3 72
(T Lallie, France) **119/1**
8 *1 ½* **Saint Clement (FR)** 2-8-8 0..... Georges-AntoineAnselin(8) 14 69
(N Clement, France) **52/1**
9 *½* **Sparkel D'Hermeray (FR)**[69] 2-8-13 0..... FabienLefebvre 5 65
(Mme C De La Soudiere-Niault, France) **132/1**
10 *1 ¼* **Encore Encore (FR)**[35] 5891 2-8-13 0..... OlivierPeslier 11 62
(Harry Dunlop) *t.k.h: trckd ldrs on outer: pushed along and outpcd by ldrs fr 2f out: one pce fnl f* **14/1**
11 *1 ¾* **Vamosalaplaya (FR)**[22] 2-9-2 0..... GeraldMosse 13 62
(F Doumen, France) **25/1**
12 *2* **Jazz Poem (FR)**[21] 2-9-2 0..... ThierryJarnet 12 58
(Mlle B Renk, France) **37/1**
13 *1* **Giny Queen (FR)**[30] 2-8-13 0..... DavidBreux 10 53
(Mlle V Dissaux, France) **104/1**
14 *1 ¼* **Viva Valaria**[15] 2-8-13 0..... MaximeGuyon 4 50
(A Fabre, France) **16/1**
15 *1 ¾* **Matorico (IRE)**[17] 2-9-2 0..... UmbertoRispoli 15 50
(M Delzangles, France) **63/10**[3]
16 *hd* **Le Valentino (FR)**[22] 2-9-2 0..... SebastienMaillot 9 49
(T Doumen, France) **102/1**
1m 53.97s (113.97) **16** Ran SP% **117.4**
WIN (incl. 1 euro stake): 14.60. PLACES: 3.30, 2.10, 1.70. DF: 42.90. SF: 113.90.
Owner Mme Magalen Bryant **Bred** Mme M Bryant **Trained** France

6962a **PRIX CHARLES LAFFITTE (LISTED RACE) (3YO FILLIES) (TURF)** **1m 2f**
4:05 (12:00) 3-Y-O **£22,357** (£8,943; £6,707; £4,471; £2,235)

RPR
1 **Narniyn (IRE)**[26] 3-8-13 0..... Christophe-PatriceLemaire 7 101
(A De Royer-Dupre, France) **11/1**
2 *1 ¾* **Nuit D'Amour (FR)**[28] 6124 3-8-13 0..... IoritzMendizabal 8 97
(Mme Pia Brandt, France) **58/10**[3]
3 *shd* **Permission Slip (IRE)**[30] 3-8-13 0..... MaximeGuyon 4 97
(A Fabre, France) *disp ld on outer: trckd ldr fr 3f out: shkn up to ld 1 1/2f out: sn rdn and hdd over 1f out: kpt on u.p but nt pce of wnr: lost 2nd fnl stride* **3/1**[1]
4 *1 ½* **More Than Sotka (FR)**[9] 6715 3-8-13 0..... AntoineHamelin 3 94
(Matthieu Palussiere, France) **15/1**
5 *1* **Soccer Mom (GER)**[16] 6484 3-8-13 0..... GregoryBenoist 5 92
(X Nakkachdji, France) **19/1**
6 *shd* **Dear Nofa (IRE)**[66] 3-8-13 0..... Pierre-CharlesBoudot 10 92?
(A Fabre, France) **47/1**
7 *hd* **Dakatari (FR)**[31] 6031 3-8-13 0..... FlavienPrat 1 91
(F Head, France) **24/1**
8 *snk* **Venturous Spirit (FR)**[76] 4468 3-8-13 0.....(b) UmbertoRispoli 13 91
(M Delzangles, France) **15/1**
9 *¾* **Alta Stima (IRE)**[16] 6484 3-8-13 0..... StephanePasquier 12 89
(E Lellouche, France) **20/1**
10 *3* **Indigo Lady**[104] 3482 3-8-13 0..... GeraldMosse 2 83
(Peter Chapple-Hyam) *disp ld on inner: wnt on 3f out: rdn 2f out: hdd appr 1 1/2f out: wknd fnl f* **13/1**
11 *2 ½* **Piana (FR)**[31] 6031 3-9-2 0..... RonanThomas 9 81
(A Bonin, France) **7/2**[2]
12 *2* **Indigo (FR)**[48] 5461 3-9-2 0.....(b) OlivierPeslier 11 77
(C Ferland, France) **12/1**
13 *3 ½* **Artemisia (IRE)**[32] 6010 3-9-2 0..... TheoBachelot 6 70
(P Schiergen, Germany) **28/1**
2m 3.83s (-0.97) **13** Ran SP% **116.9**
WIN (incl. 1 euro stake): 12.00. PLACES: 3.30, 2.30, 1.90. DF: 36.00. SF: 78.10.
Owner H H Aga Khan **Bred** His Highness The Aga Khan's Studs S C **Trained** Chantilly, France

5961 SOUTHWELL (L-H)
Thursday, October 3
OFFICIAL GOING: Standard
Wind: Moderate against Weather: Overcast

6963 **PLAY GOLF AT SOUTHWELL GOLF CLUB H'CAP (DIV I)** **1m (F)**
2:00 (2:00) (Class 5) (0-75,75) 3-Y-O+ **£2,587** (£770; £384; £192) **Stalls** Low

Form RPR
0433 **1** **Peter's Friend**[26] 6218 4-8-7 **61**..... PJMcDonald 2 72
(Michael Herrington) *trckd ldrs: hdwy on inner 3f out: rdn to chse ldr over 1f out: drvn and styd on wl fnl f: led nr fin* **12/1**
3436 **2** *hd* **Chrissycross (IRE)**[61] 5001 4-8-12 **66**.....(v) RobertWinston 8 77
(Roger Teal) *trckd ldrs: hdwy over 3f out: led over 2f out: rdn clr over 1f out: drvn and jnd ins fnl f: hdd and no ex nr fin* **10/1**
1302 **3** *5* **Royal Holiday (IRE)**[13] 6600 6-9-2 **70**.....(p) DanielTudhope 10 69
(Marjorie Fife) *prom: rdn along 3f out: drvn and hung lft wl over 1f out: sn one pce* **8/1**[3]
5152 **4** *2* **Soaring Spirits (IRE)**[10] 6701 3-9-3 **74**.....(b) AndreaAtzeni 7 68
(Roger Varian) *towards rr: rdn along 1/2-way: wd st: hdwy over 2f out: drvn and no imp appr fnl f* **7/2**[1]
5204 **5** *1 ¾* **Mingun Bell (USA)**[27] 6167 6-9-7 **75**.....(p) AdamKirby 4 65
(Ed de Giles) *towards rr: rdn along 1/2-way: hdwy over 2f out: chsd ldrs over 1f out: sn drvn and no imp* **7/2**[1]
2251 **6** *2 ¼* **Master Of Song**[36] 5903 6-8-7 **64**.....(p) MarkCoumbe(3) 5 49
(Roy Bowring) *s.i.s and bhd: wd st sn rdn and plugged on: nvr nr ldrs* **11/1**
0001 **7** *nse* **Monzino (USA)**[13] 6612 5-8-4 **65**..... PaulBooth(7) 9 50
(Michael Chapman) *s.i.s and bhd: rdn along and wd st: plugged on: nvr nr ldrs* **50/1**
6335 **8** *¾* **Putin (IRE)**[12] 6653 5-8-8 **62**.....(tp) DavidProbert 1 45
(Phil McEntee) *led 1 1/2f: cl up: rdn along wl over 2f out: wknd over 1f out* **25/1**
5210 **9** *5* **Piceno (IRE)**[22] 6306 5-9-2 **70**.....(p) JoeFanning 6 42
(Scott Dixon) *cl up: led over 6f out: rdn along and hdd over 2f out: sn drvn and wknd* **16/1**
4460 **10** *31* **Sharp And Smart (IRE)**[21] 6337 4-9-6 **74**..... NeilCallan 3
(Hughie Morrison) *trckd ldrs on inner: pushed along wl over 3f out: sn rdn and wknd qckly: bhd and eased fnl 2f* **9/2**[2]
1m 41.8s (-1.90) **Going Correction** -0.025s/f (Stan)
WFA 3 from 4yo+ 3lb **10** Ran SP% **110.5**
Speed ratings (Par 103): **108,107,102,100,99 96,96,96,91,60**
toteswingers 1&2 £16.90, 2&3 £16.20, 1&3 £11.60 CSF £118.22 CT £993.45 TOTE £9.30: £3.40, £3.00, £2.20; EX 104.40 Trifecta £743.80 Pool: £1900.52 - 1.91 winning units..
Owner Stuart Herrington **Bred** Norton Grove Stud Ltd **Trained** Cold Kirby, N Yorks

FOCUS
They seemed to go off at a good pace and they came home well strung out with the first two clear in the end. The first three raced middle to far side in the home straight.

6964 **CONNOLLY'S REDMILLS H'CAP** **1m 4f (F)**
2:30 (2:31) (Class 6) (0-60,60) 3-Y-O **£2,045** (£603; £302) **Stalls** Low

Form RPR
006 **1** **Mystery Drama**[60] 5038 3-9-4 **57**..... AdamKirby 2 74+
(Alan King) *prom: trckd ldr after 4f: led on bit over 3f out: rdn over 1f out: styd on* **9/2**[2]
0606 **2** *1 ½* **Hurricane John (IRE)**[57] 5143 3-8-7 **46** oh1..... AdrianNicholls 3 54
(David Nicholls) *prom: rdn along and lost pl over 4f out: hdwy 2f out: sn drvn and kpt on to chse wnr ins fnl f: no imp towards fin* **17/2**
0402 **3** *3 ¾* **Halfwaytocootehill (IRE)**[9] 6717 3-8-5 **49**.....(tp) JacobButterfield(5) 8 51
(Ollie Pears) *towards rr: hdwy 4f out: wd st and rdn to chse ldrs over 2f out: drvn and edgd lft ent fnl f: kpt on same pce* **7/1**
0434 **4** *½* **Point Of Control**[32] 6015 3-9-5 **58**.....(v[1]) AndreaAtzeni 1 60
(Michael Bell) *sn led: rdn along and hdd over 3f out: drvn 2f out: kpt on one pce appr fnl f* **13/2**
1203 **5** *2 ¾* **Helamis**[20] 6361 3-8-10 **54** ow1.....(v[1]) TobyAtkinson(5) 10 52
(Alison Hutchinson) *chsd ldrs: rdn along 3f out: drvn 2f out: wknd over 1f out* **8/1**
2024 **6** *11* **Aminah**[15] 6522 3-9-7 **60**..... NeilCallan 7 41
(Robert Cowell) *prom on outer: hdwy and cl up over 3f out: rdn over 2f out: sn wknd* **4/1**[1]
5-00 **7** *14* **Doctor's Gift**[119] 3013 3-9-4 **57**..... JoeFanning 6 17
(Pat Eddery) *chsd ldrs: rdn along wl over 3f out: drvn and wknd over 2f out* **20/1**
-000 **8** *17* **Platinum Proof (USA)**[12] 6657 3-8-13 **52**..... DanielTudhope 4
(David O'Meara) *in tch: rdn along over 4f out: sn outpcd and bhd* **6/1**[3]
-000 **9** *8* **Sweet Louise (IRE)**[15] 6522 3-8-10 **49**.....(t) KirstyMilczarek 5
(Barry Brennan) *a in rr: bhd fnl 4f* **40/1**

-666 **10** *26* **Santa Fe Stinger**[65] 4849 3-8-7 **46** oh1....................(e[1]) DuranFentiman 11
(Tim Easterby) *towards rr: rdn along 1/2-way: sn outpcd and bhd fnl 4f* **25/1**

2m 42.85s (1.85) **Going Correction** -0.025s/f (Stan) **10** Ran SP% **111.0**
Speed ratings (Par 99): **92,91,88,88,86 79,69,58,53,35**
toteswingers 1&2 £7.80, 2&3 £6.60, 1&3 £7.00 CSF £39.03 CT £251.91 TOTE £4.80: £1.50, £4.50, £2.30; EX 44.00 Trifecta £391.80 Pool: £3513.88 - 6.72 winning units..
Owner Barbury Castle Stud **Bred** Barbury Castle Stud **Trained** Barbury Castle, Wilts

FOCUS
A low-grade handicap and they came home well strung out. Every single runner in the line-up was having its first outing on Fibresand.

6965 MEMBERSHIP AVAILABLE AT SOUTHWELL GOLF CLUB MAIDEN STKS 5f (F)
3:00 (3:02) (Class 5) 3-4-Y-O **£2,587** (£770; £384; £192) **Stalls** High

Form RPR

5503 **1** **Max The Machine**[15] 6519 3-9-5 59.................... DaleSwift 3 60
(Derek Shaw) *dwlt and in rr: hdwy 2f out: chsd ldrs over 1f out: swtchd rt and rdn ent fnl f: kpt on wl to ld nr fin* **10/1**

6 **2** *½* **Jiminy**[36] 5884 3-9-5 0....................(b[1]) RobertWinston 6 58
(Scott Dixon) *led: rdn over 1f out: drvn ins fnl f: hdd and no ex towards fin* **20/1**

2- **3** *½* **Master Wizard**[295] 8068 3-9-5 0.................... DavidProbert 4 56
(David C Griffiths) *trckd ldrs: smooth hdwy 2f out and sn cl up: rdn to chal jst over 1f out and ev ch tl drvn and one pce wl ins fnl f* **6/4[1]**

5650 **4** *1* **Coire Gabhail**[14] 6560 3-9-0 57.................... AndreaAtzeni 10 48
(Hughie Morrison) *racd nr stands' rail: prom: effrt wl over 1f out: sn rdn and ev ch tl edgd lft and one pce ins fnl f* **8/1**

40 **5** *2 ¾* **Chessfield Park**[23] 6289 3-9-5 0.................... GrahamLee 8 43
(Bryan Smart) *chsd ldrs: rdn along 2f out: sn one pce* **20/1**

0065 **6** *½* **Kaahen (USA)**[31] 6043 3-9-5 34....................(b[1]) JoeFanning 7 41
(Pat Eddery) *dwlt and in rr whn hung bdly lft to far rails after 1f: wl bhd 1/2-way: styd on appr fnl f: nrst fin* **50/1**

0322 **7** *nk* **Shillito**[5] 6843 3-8-12 59....................(p) LauraBarry(7) 9 40
(Tony Coyle) *prom: rdn along 2f out: wknd over 1f out* **4/1[2]**

0063 **8** *3 ½* **Lily The Dragon (IRE)**[57] 5156 3-9-0 37.................... PaoloSirigu 11 22
(Mick Quinn) *racd nr stands' rail: sn rdn along and a outpcd in rr* **66/1**

0400 **9** *½* **Lady Cricketer**[16] 6502 4-9-0 43....................(b) CathyGannon 1 20
(Michael Squance) *a towards rr* **100/1**

0360 **10** *1 ½* **Pearl Noir**[1] 6944 3-9-5 55....................(b) AdamKirby 2 20
(Scott Dixon) *cl up: rdn along over 2f out: drvn and wknd wl over 1f out* **5/1[3]**

6656 **11** *2 ½* **Princess Bounty**[12] 6651 3-8-10 48 ow1....................[1] TobyAtkinson(5) 5 7
(Phil McEntee) *a towards rr: bhd fnl 2f* **40/1**

1m 1.61s (1.91) **Going Correction** +0.175s/f (Slow) **11** Ran SP% **113.3**
Speed ratings (Par 103): **91,90,89,87,83 82,82,76,75,73 69**
toteswingers 1&2 £30.50, 2&3 £7.50, 1&3 £5.00 CSF £185.48 TOTE £10.10: £3.80, £6.70, £1.10; EX 145.50 Trifecta £765.00 Pool: £5181.47 - 5.07 winning units..
Owner Brian Johnson (Northamptonshire) **Bred** Digamist Bloodstock **Trained** Sproxton, Leics

FOCUS
A poor sprint maiden and the first three finished towards the centre of the track.

6966 BRITISH STALLION STUDS E B F MEDIAN AUCTION MAIDEN STKS 5f (F)
3:30 (3:31) (Class 5) 2-Y-O **£2,911** (£866; £432; £216) **Stalls** High

Form RPR

26 **1** **Meadway**[15] 6517 2-9-5 0.................... GrahamLee 5 88
(Bryan Smart) *cl up: led 3f out: rdn and qcknd clr appr fnl f: readily* **3/1[1]**

2253 **2** *8* **Simply Black (IRE)**[37] 5857 2-9-0 72.................... DanielTudhope 7 54
(David O'Meara) *led 2f: cl up: effrt and ev ch 2f out: rdn over 1f out: kpt on: no ch w wnr* **3/1[1]**

035 **3** *2 ¼* **Chainsaw**[14] 6569 2-9-5 0.................... HarryBentley 9 51
(Stuart Williams) *trckd ldrs: hdwy 2f out: rdn to chse ldng pair whn edgd lft appr fnl f: sn one pce* **4/1[2]**

03 **4** *hd* **Brave Imp**[15] 6517 2-9-0 0.................... ShaneGray(5) 6 50
(Kevin Ryan) *trckd ldrs: rdn along and outpcd 2f out: styd on u.p fnl f* **7/1**

00 **5** *1* **Grande Mago (IRE)**[17] 6477 2-9-5 0....................[1] PJMcDonald 4 47
(Robert Cowell) *cl up: rdn along over 2f out: drvn and wknd over 1f out* **9/1**

0 **6** *½* **Kheleyf Diamond (IRE)**[14] 6561 2-9-0 0.................... BarryMcHugh 2 40
(Tony Coyle) *chsd ldrs: rdn along 2f out: sn wknd* **50/1**

0 **7** *¾* **Dont Tell Nan**[17] 6477 2-8-7 0.................... AdamMcLean(7) 1 37
(Derek Shaw) *rrd and dwlt s: sn hung lft and a in rr* **25/1**

0320 **8** *nk* **Black Vale (IRE)**[21] 6320 2-9-5 60....................(b[1]) NeilCallan 3 41
(James Tate) *chsd ldrs: cl up 1/2-way: sn rdn and wknd wl over 1f out* **6/1[3]**

9 *8* **Chennai Wind** 2-9-5 0.................... DaleSwift 8 12
(Derek Shaw) *sn outpcd and a bhd* **66/1**

1m 0.89s (1.19) **Going Correction** +0.175s/f (Slow) **9** Ran SP% **114.1**
Speed ratings (Par 95): **97,84,80,80,78 77,76,76,63**
toteswingers 1&2 £3.10, 2&3 £3.50, 1&3 £3.40 CSF £11.63 TOTE £4.60: £1.10, £1.50, £2.00; EX 16.00 Trifecta £88.00 Pool: £3939.32 - 33.53 winning units..
Owner Michael Moses & Terry Moses **Bred** Bond Thoroughbred Corporation **Trained** Hambleton, N Yorks

FOCUS
A one-sided maiden. There are the usual Fibresand concerns and the form is rated negatively, but the winner still showed useful form.

6967 GREEN FEE OFFERS AT SOUTHWELLGOLFCLUB.COM NURSERY H'CAP 5f (F)
4:00 (4:02) (Class 5) (0-75,73) 2-Y-O **£2,726** (£805; £402) **Stalls** High

Form RPR

2222 **1** **Genuine Quality (USA)**[17] 6477 2-9-7 73....................[1] HarryBentley 9 81
(Ed Vaughan) *trckd ldrs: hdwy to chse ldr over 2f out: rdn to ld over 1f out: clr ins fnl f: readily* **3/1[1]**

1002 **2** *2 ½* **Madagascar Moll (IRE)**[7] 6778 2-9-1 67.................... DanielTudhope 6 66
(David O'Meara) *prom: effrt 2f out: sn rdn and kpt on same pce fnl f* **5/1[2]**

25 **3** *½* **Lilo Lil**[19] 6386 2-9-0 66....................(p) DavidProbert 4 63
(David C Griffiths) *led 1f: cl up: rdn wl over 1f out: edgd rt and drvn ent fnl f: kpt on same pce* **8/1**

2236 **4** *1* **Anfield**[30] 6073 2-8-0 52 oh1.................... PaoloSirigu 10 46
(Mick Quinn) *racd nr stands' rail: cl up: led after 1f: rdn along and hdd over 1f out: sn drvn and edgd lft ent fnl f: sn wknd* **25/1**

0041 **5** *1 ½* **Scarborough (IRE)**[34] 5964 2-8-1 53....................(p) JimmyQuinn 1 41
(Paul Midgley) *prom on wd outside: rdn along wl over 1f out: sn one pce* **7/1**

425 **6** *3* **Dynamo Walt (IRE)**[26] 6213 2-8-0 56 ow2.................... NeilFarley(3) 3 32
(Derek Shaw) *cl up: rdn along 1/2-way: sn wknd* **14/1**

6355 **7** *½* **Red Biba (IRE)**[15] 6517 2-7-11 52 oh2.................... NataliaGemelova(3) 2 28
(Alan McCabe) *chsd ldrs: rdn along over 2f out: grad wknd* **50/1**

420 **8** *1 ¾* **Annie's Rose**[12] 6627 2-8-2 57.................... RaulDaSilva(3) 8 26
(Bryan Smart) *chsd ldrs: rdn along 2f out: sn wknd* **16/1**

2015 **9** *hd* **Anytimeatall (IRE)**[21] 6320 2-8-12 64.................... RobertWinston 5 33
(Alan Bailey) *in tch: rdn along 1/2-way: sn btn* **5/1[2]**

041 **10** *¾* **Britain (IRE)**[36] 5900 2-8-8 60.................... CathyGannon 7 26
(David C Griffiths) *in tch: rdn along 1/2-way: sn hung lft and wknd* **6/1[3]**

1m 1.1s (1.40) **Going Correction** +0.175s/f (Slow) **10** Ran SP% **114.6**
Speed ratings (Par 95): **95,91,90,88,86 81,80,77,77,76**
toteswingers 1&2 £3.30, 2&3 £8.60, 1&3 £4.90 CSF £17.29 CT £110.29 TOTE £3.00: £1.30, £2.00, £3.00; EX 18.20 Trifecta £81.90 Pool: £4278.13 - 39.17 winning units..
Owner Qatar Racing Limited **Bred** Summer Wind Farm **Trained** Newmarket, Suffolk

FOCUS
A fair sprint nursery, and straightforward form.

6968 LIKE US ON FACEBOOK SOUTHWELL RACECOURSE H'CAP 1m (F)
4:30 (4:36) (Class 6) (0-65,65) 3-Y-O **£2,045** (£603; £302) **Stalls** Low

Form RPR

1266 **1** **Bertie Moon**[29] 6109 3-9-0 63.................... ThomasGarner(5) 7 70
(Geoffrey Deacon) *cl up on outer: chal wl over 2f out: rdn wl over 1f out: drvn ent fnl f: kpt on gamely to ld nr line* **7/2[3]**

4045 **2** *hd* **Birdy Boy (USA)**[12] 6657 3-9-2 60.................... JoeFanning 5 67
(Mark Johnston) *slt ld: rdn along over 2f out: drvn ent fnl f: hdd and no ex nr line* **5/2[2]**

0300 **3** *3 ¾* **Minimee**[15] 6522 3-8-13 57....................(v) CathyGannon 8 55
(Phil McEntee) *trckd ldrs: hdwy to chse ldng pair wl over 2f out: rdn along wl over 1f out: kpt on same pce* **8/1**

-036 **4** *2 ¾* **Codebreaker**[30] 6081 3-9-7 65.................... AndreaAtzeni 3 57
(Hughie Morrison) *cl up on inner: rdn along over 3f out: sn drvn: wknd wl over 2f out* **7/4[1]**

0-00 **5** *2* **Spirit Man**[28] 6133 3-8-5 56.................... AdamMcLean(7) 4 43
(Derek Shaw) *chsd ldrs: rdn along 1/2-way: sn drvn and outpcd fnl 3f* **28/1**

1360 **6** *¾* **Mick Dundee (IRE)**[22] 6317 3-9-4 62....................(bt) FrankieMcDonald 6 47
(John Ryan) *dwlt: sn rdn along and a in rr* **16/1**

1m 43.7s **Going Correction** -0.025s/f (Stan) **6** Ran SP% **107.6**
Speed ratings (Par 99): **99,98,95,92,90 89**
toteswingers 1&2 £1.70, 2&3 £3.10, 1&3 £2.60 CSF £11.55 CT £52.64 TOTE £4.10: £1.50, £1.70; EX 11.40 Trifecta £63.10 Pool: £2627.07 - 31.17 winning units..
Owner Jim Kelly **Bred** M E Wates **Trained** Compton, Berks

FOCUS
A weak 3yo handicap and a two-horse war from early in the home straight.

6969 FOLLOW US ON TWITTER @SOUTHWELL_RACES H'CAP 6f (F)
5:00 (5:03) (Class 5) (0-75,75) 3-Y-O+ **£2,587** (£770; £384; £192) **Stalls** Low

Form RPR

0202 **1** **King Bertie (IRE)**[20] 6362 3-9-0 74.................... GeorgeChaloner(5) 10 86
(Michael Wigham) *cl up on outer: led wl over 2f out: rdn wl over 1f out: drvn out* **4/1[2]**

0000 **2** *2 ½* **Monnoyer**[14] 6547 4-8-9 63....................(p) PJMcDonald 11 67
(Scott Dixon) *cl up: effrt wl over 2f out and ev ch tl drvn and one pce fnl f* **28/1**

0225 **3** *½* **Ace Master**[8] 6757 5-9-4 75....................(b) MarkCoumbe(3) 1 77
(Roy Bowring) *in tch: rdn along and hdwy 1/2-way: chsd ldrs over 1f out: drvn and kpt on fnl f: nrst fin* **20/1**

4043 **4** *2* **Ray Of Joy**[15] 6535 7-9-4 72.................... DavidProbert 8 68
(J R Jenkins) *towards rr: hdwy wl over 2f out: rdn wl over 1f out: kpt on appr fnl f: nrst fin* **20/1**

1000 **5** *1* **Hannahs Turn**[86] 4145 3-8-12 70.................... RaulDaSilva(3) 7 63
(Chris Dwyer) *led: rdn along 1/2-way: sn hdd: cl up tl drvn and wknd over 1f out* **8/1**

00 **6** *2* **Fama Mac**[26] 6205 6-8-4 65.................... EvaMoscrop(7) 5 51
(Neville Bycroft) *in tch: hdwy to chse ldrs over 3f out: rdn over 2f out: sn one pce* **25/1**

066 **7** *2 ¼* **Mazovian (USA)**[184] 1309 5-8-0 61 oh1.................... DanielleMooney(7) 2 40
(Michael Chapman) *in rr tl sme hdwy fnl 2f: n.d* **33/1**

6-00 **8** *¾* **Izzy Boy (USA)**[132] 2624 3-8-6 61 oh1.................... JoeFanning 4 38
(Mark Johnston) *dwlt: a in rr* **13/2**

2300 **9** *hd* **Repetition**[23] 6291 3-9-2 71....................(p) NeilCallan 9 47
(Kevin Ryan) *cl up: rdn along over 2f out: swtchd lft and drvn over 1f out: grad wknd* **9/2[3]**

54-1 **10** *½* **Upper Grosvenor**[15] 6519 4-9-1 69....................[1] AndreaAtzeni 6 44
(Roger Varian) *dwlt: sn rdn along: a in rr* **11/4[1]**

0354 **11** *1 ¼* **Polish World (USA)**[9] 6720 9-8-9 63.................... BarryMcHugh 3 34
(Paul Midgley) *chsd ldrs: rdn along over 3f out: sn wknd* **10/1**

1m 16.52s (0.02) **Going Correction** -0.025s/f (Stan)
WFA 3 from 4yo+ 1lb **11** Ran SP% **118.1**
Speed ratings (Par 103): **98,94,94,91,90 87,84,83,83,82 80**
toteswingers 1&2 £20.20, 2&3 £33.60, 1&3 £6.60 CSF £118.26 CT £2048.07 TOTE £4.50: £1.50, £9.70, £2.90; EX 109.10 Trifecta £2284.60 Pool: £3999.52 - 1.31 winning units..
Owner Mrs Jo Brisland **Bred** P J Fahey **Trained** Newmarket, Suffolk

FOCUS
The four leaders went off very strongly, yet the first two home were two of the pacesetters.

6970 PLAY GOLF AT SOUTHWELL GOLF CLUB H'CAP (DIV II) 1m (F)
5:30 (5:31) (Class 5) (0-75,75) 3-Y-O+ **£2,587** (£770; £384; £192) **Stalls** Low

Form RPR

2025 **1** **Greyfriarschorista**[13] 6608 6-9-7 75.................... JimmyQuinn 6 86
(Tom Keddy) *trckd ldrs gng wl: smooth hdwy over 2f out: led over 1f out: sn rdn and kpt on wl* **11/1**

6500 **2** *2 ½* **Winged Icarus (USA)**[13] 6587 3-8-8 65.................... BarryMcHugh 8 70
(Brian Ellison) *hld up: hdwy over 3f out: wd st and rdn to ld wl over 1f out: hdd and drvn over 1f out: kpt on same pce* **8/1**

4523 **3** *4 ½* **Two No Bids (IRE)**[21] 6324 3-8-11 68....................(be) CathyGannon 9 63
(Phil McEntee) *trckd ldrs: hdwy on outer over 3f out: led wl over 2f out: sn rdn and hdd wl over 1f out: drvn and one pce appr fnl f* **20/1**

056 **4** *3* **Tribal Path (IRE)**[14] 6556 3-8-11 68.................... JoeFanning 4 56
(Mark Johnston) *cl up: rdn along over 3f out: drvn over 2f out: sn one pce* **9/2[3]**

5051 **5** *5* **Fluctuation (IRE)**[17] 6473 5-8-13 70....................(v) MichaelJMMurphy(3) 5 47
(Ian Williams) *a towards rr* **10/1**

The Form Book Flat, Raceform Ltd, Compton, RG20 6NL.

3004 **6** *1 3/4* **Eutropius (IRE)**[14] 6549 4-9-5 **73** NeilCallan 1 45
(Alan Swinbank) *cl up on inner: led 3f out: rdn and hdd over 2f out: sn drvn and wknd* **4/1**[2]
1652 **7** *5* **Final Delivery**[115] 3152 4-8-7 **61** AndreaAtzeni 7 22
(Jim Boyle) *a towards rr* **20/1**
6066 **8** *3/4* **Watts Up Son**[14] 6562 5-8-10 **67** (v) NeilFarley(3) 2 26
(Declan Carroll) *cl up: rdn along after 3f: sn lost pl and bhd* **10/1**
166 **9** *1 3/4* **Thistleandtworoses (USA)**[60] 5030 3-9-3 **74** DanielTudhope 3 29
(David O'Meara) *sn led: pushed along and hdd 3f out: sn rdn and wknd* **2/1**[1]

1m 41.52s (-2.18) **Going Correction** -0.025s/f (Stan)
WFA 3 from 4yo+ 3lb **9** Ran SP% **118.7**
Speed ratings (Par 103): **109,106,102,99,94 92,87,86,84**
toteswingers 1&2 £10.20, 2&3 £20.60, 1&3 £8.90 CSF £97.89 CT £1729.70 TOTE £11.50: £2.30, £3.10, £3.40; EX 110.60 Trifecta £3006.20 Part won. Pool: £4008.34 - 0.76 winning units..
Owner Hayley Keddy, Lynn Lambert, Val Beeson **Bred** Castlemartin Stud And Skymarc Farm **Trained** Newmarket, Suffolk

FOCUS
The pacesetters dropped away this time and the first two came from off the pace.
T/Plt: £128.00 to a £1 stake. Pool of £68272.70 - 389.10 winning tickets. T/Qpdt: £4.70 to a £1 stake. Pool of £7332.45 - 1142.40 winning tickets. JR

5841 WARWICK (L-H)
Thursday, October 3

OFFICIAL GOING: Good to firm (7.9)
Wind: light, across Weather: overcast, dry

6971 REWARDS4RACING.COM (S) STKS — 1m 2f 188y
2:10 (2:10) (Class 5) 3-Y-O **£2,587** (£770; £384; £192) **Stalls** Low

Form RPR
1455 **1** **Lady Lunchalot (USA)**[9] 6737 3-9-4 59 (p) LiamJones 2 60
(J S Moore) *trckd ldrs: rdn and effrt over 2f out: ev ch over 1f out: wandered rt u.p 1f out: led ins fnl f: styd on wl: rdn out* **5/1**
-064 **2** *1* **Zinnobar**[39] 5791 3-8-12 39 MartinHarley 8 52
(Jonathan Portman) *led: rdn and qcknd over 2f out: hrd pressed and edgd lft u.p over 1f out: kpt on wl tl hdd ins fnl f: one pce after* **33/1**
00-0 **3** *6* **Herbalist**[122] 2934 3-9-3 70 (p) DaneO'Neill 4 46
(Ben Pauling) *t.k.h: chsd ldr: rdn and pressed ldr 2f out: drvn and nt qckn over 1f out: sn btn in 3rd: wknd fnl f* **5/2**[1]
234 **4** *1 3/4* **Well Owd Mon**[17] 6473 3-8-12 60 JackDuern(5) 6 43
(Andrew Hollinshead) *stdd s: hld up wl in tch in last pair: swtchd rt and effrt u.p over 2f out: outpcd and btn over 1f out: wnt modest 4th 1f out* **7/2**[3]
4144 **5** *1 1/4* **Handsome Stranger (IRE)**[13] 6612 3-9-4 62 (b) TimClark(5) 7 47
(Alan Bailey) *t.k.h: chsd ldrs: rdn and nt qckn over 2f out: hung lft and btn over 1f out: wknd* **3/1**[2]
0340 **6** *3/4* **Florida Beat**[15] 6521 3-8-12 60 (p) DanielMuscutt(5) 3 40
(Andrew Balding) *wl in tch in midfield: rdn and immediately outpcd over 2f out: drvn and no hdwy over 1f out* **7/1**
-500 **7** *11* **Barbsiz (IRE)**[89] 4071 3-8-12 46 TedDurcan 1 15
(Mark H Tompkins) *dwlt: wl in tch in last pair: rdn over 2f out: sn btn: wknd wl over 1f out: bhd and eased ins fnl f* **25/1**

2m 23.21s (2.11) **Going Correction** -0.10s/f (Good) **7** Ran SP% **111.7**
Speed ratings (Par 101): **88,87,82,81,80 80,72**
toteswingers 1&2 £5.30, 2&3 £7.30, 1&3 £4.00 CSF £122.33 TOTE £6.00: £2.80, £4.80; EX 82.20 Trifecta £499.90 Pool: £1785.65 - 2.67 winning units..There was no bid for the winner.
Owner M Briddon **Bred** Fred W Hertrich III **Trained** Upper Lambourn, Berks

FOCUS
It was raining before this modest seller. Several of the runners raced keenly off the steady pace and the first two pulled clear.

6972 COLLIERS INTERNATIONAL BUSINESS RATES SERVICES NURSERY H'CAP — 7f 26y
2:40 (2:43) (Class 4) (0-85,80) 2-Y-O **£3,752** (£1,116; £557; £278) **Stalls** Low

Form RPR
562 **1** **Sahra Al Khadra**[32] 6014 2-8-7 **66** PaulHanagan 10 70+
(Charles Hills) *in tch in midfield: rdn over 2f out: hdwy u.p nrest stands' side over 1f out: drvn to ld ins fnl f: sustained duel w rival after: r.o wl* **5/1**[1]
2315 **2** *hd* **Finn Class (IRE)**[22] 6303 2-9-3 **79** WilliamTwiston-Davies(3) 2 82
(Michael Bell) *in tch in midfield: rdn over 2f out: hdwy and racing towards stands' rail over 1f out: ev ch jst ins fnl f: sustained duel u.p w wnr but a jst hld* **5/1**[1]
064 **3** *1 1/2* **Rathealy (IRE)**[14] 6569 2-8-4 **63** SilvestreDeSousa 6 63
(Alan Bailey) *chsd ldfing trio: rdn: rn green and hung lft ent fnl 2f: sn sltly outpcd and swtchd rt: rallied u.p 1f out: wnt 3rd fnl 100yds: kpt on* **14/1**
4221 **4** *hd* **Peak Royale**[32] 6014 2-9-4 **77** PatDobbs 7 76
(Richard Hannon) *stdd s: hld up wl in tch towards rr: hdwy u.p on inner over 1f out: pressed ldrs 1f out: styd on same pce ins fnl f* **5/1**[1]
5413 **5** *1 1/4* **Aspirant**[19] 6376 2-8-9 **68** JamesDoyle 11 64
(Roger Charlton) *stdd and dropped in bhd after s: t.k.h: hld up tch in rr: rdn and effrt over 2f out: swtchd lft and hdwy jst over 1f out: kpt on same pce ins fnl f* **5/1**[1]
3334 **6** *1/2* **Needless Shouting (IRE)**[12] 6628 2-8-9 **68** SamHitchcott 9 63
(Mick Channon) *chsd ldr: rdn and unable qck over 2f out: rallied u.p over 1f out: led 1f out: sn hdd: wknd fnl 100yds* **25/1**
402 **7** *1* **Flycatcher (IRE)**[38] 5827 2-8-13 **72** (t) TonyHamilton 12 64
(Richard Fahey) *in tch in rr: last and rdn jst over 2f out: hdwy u.p ent fnl f: kpt on but nvr gng pce to trble ldrs* **10/1**[3]
3304 **8** *1 1/4* **Major Crispies**[25] 6233 2-9-7 **80** (p) LukeMorris 4 69
(James Eustace) *chsd ldrs: rdn ent fnl 2f: hrd drvn and pressing ldrs ent fnl f: awkward hd carriage and no rspnse to str press 1f out: wknd ins fnl f* **5/1**[1]
4541 **9** *1 1/2* **Hulcolt (IRE)**[15] 6513 2-9-1 **77** JasonHart(3) 3 62
(Garry Moss) *led: fnd ex and wnt 3 l clr jst over 2f out: drvn over 1f out: hdd over 1f out: sn btn and wknd* **8/1**[2]
605 **10** *8* **Katja**[18] 6423 2-8-4 **63** LiamJones 1 27
(J W Hills) *in tch in midfield: drvn and no rspnse jst over 2f out: wknd and bhd 1f out* **25/1**

1m 23.94s (-0.66) **Going Correction** -0.10s/f (Good) **10** Ran SP% **117.9**
Speed ratings (Par 97): **99,98,97,96,95 94,93,92,90,81**
toteswingers 1&2 £6.60, 2&3 £15.70, 1&3 £11.90 CSF £29.57 CT £333.13 TOTE £6.40: £2.00, £2.20, £3.20; EX 33.80 Trifecta £417.30 Pool: £2431.10 - 4.36 winning units..
Owner Sheikh Hamdan Bin Maktoum Al Maktoum **Bred** Sheikh Hamdan Bin Maktoum Al Maktoum **Trained** Lambourn, Berks

FOCUS
A competitive nursery. The pace was strong and there was a tight finish.

6973 IRISH STALLION FARMS E B F MAIDEN FILLIES' STKS (DIV I) — 7f 26y
3:10 (3:11) (Class 5) 2-Y-O **£2,911** (£866; £432; £216) **Stalls** Low

Form RPR
64 **1** **Miss Buckshot (IRE)**[29] 6107 2-9-0 0 ChrisCatlin 2 79
(Rae Guest) *chsd ldrs: rdn and chsd wnr 2f out: chal and qcknd clr w wnr over 1f out: led ins fnl f: r.o wl: rdn out* **16/1**
42 **2** *hd* **Alys Love**[28] 6140 2-9-0 0 MartinDwyer 5 78
(William Muir) *t.k.h: led and set stdy gallop: rdn and qcknd ent fnl 2f: qcknd clr w wnr over 1f out: hdd ins fnl f: r.o u.p: a jst hld* **11/4**[2]
0 **3** *4* **Great Wave (IRE)**[54] 5282 2-9-0 0 WilliamBuick 4 67
(David Simcock) *chsd ldr tl 2f out: 3rd and outpcd by ldrs over 1f out: no threat to ldrs but hld on to 3rd u.p ins fnl f* **10/1**
60 **4** *1* **Yeah Baby (IRE)**[12] 6643 2-9-0 0 RichardKingscote 12 65
(Charles Hills) *in tch in midfield: rdn and sltly outpcd jst over 2f out: rallied u.p to go 4th 1f out: kpt on steadily but no threat to ldng pair* **6/1**[3]
4 **5** *1 3/4* **Maiden Approach**[22] 6298 2-9-0 0 TonyHamilton 9 60
(Richard Fahey) *chsd ldng trio: rdn and unable qck over 2f out: 4th and btn over 1f out: wknd fnl f* **25/1**
6 *nse* **Muhawalah (IRE)** 2-9-0 0 PaulHanagan 6 64+
(Roger Varian) *restless in stalls: dwlt: rn green: in tch towards rr: hdwy into midfield 4f out: outpcd and wnt rt over 1f out: sn swtchd lft and styd on same pce fnl f* **6/4**[1]
0 **7** *3* **Keep Close**[12] 6641 2-9-0 0 SamHitchcott 1 52
(Mick Channon) *s.i.s: in tch in rr: swtchd rt and rdn over 2f out: sn outpcd and n.d after* **50/1**
00 **8** *shd* **Dutch Lady**[21] 6342 2-9-0 0 RobertHavlin 10 51
(John Holt) *in tch towards rr: rdn over 2f out: sn struggling and outpcd: n.d but plugged on fnl f* **200/1**
03 **9** *1 1/4* **Arabian Sunset (IRE)**[19] 6408 2-9-0 0 KierenFallon 3 48
(Brendan Powell) *t.k.h: hld up in midfield on inner: rdn and outpcd jst over 2f out: sn btn: wknd over 1f out* **25/1**
304 **10** *4* **Dime Dancer (IRE)**[13] 6594 2-9-0 76 PatDobbs 8 37
(Richard Hannon) *wl in tch in midfield: rdn and unable qck ent fnl 2f: wknd u.p over 1f out: fdd fnl f* **8/1**
11 *9* **Lutra** 2-9-0 0 JimCrowley 13 13
(Paul Cole) *rn green: styd wd early: in tch in midfield tl bhd 4f out: rdn and struggling over 2f out: sn lost tch* **33/1**

1m 26.73s (2.13) **Going Correction** -0.10s/f (Good) **11** Ran SP% **120.1**
Speed ratings (Par 92): **83,82,78,77,75 75,71,71,70,65 55**
toteswingers 1&2 £11.30, 2&3 £5.30, 1&3 £21.50 CSF £59.47 TOTE £22.40: £5.00, £1.20, £3.00; EX 97.60 Trifecta £1347.70 Pool: £2150.39 - 1.19 winning units..
Owner Buckhurst Chevaliers **Bred** Mrs S M Rogers & Sir Thomas Pilkington **Trained** Newmarket, Suffolk

FOCUS
They went a steady pace in this fair maiden. One of the market leaders was just denied by a big-priced runner but the pair pulled clear.

6974 IRISH STALLION FARMS EBF MAIDEN FILLIES' STKS (DIV II) — 7f 26y
3:40 (3:43) (Class 5) 2-Y-O **£2,911** (£866; £432; £216) **Stalls** Low

Form RPR
23 **1** **Artistic Charm**[50] 5385 2-9-0 0 JamesDoyle 4 84
(David Simcock) *chsd ldr: rdn and effrt 2f out: drvn and str chal over 1f out: led ins fnl f: sn clr and styd on wl: eased nr fin* **2/1**[1]
2 *3 1/4* **Song Of Norway** 2-9-0 0 SebSanders 5 75+
(Peter Makin) *racd off the pce in midfield: effrt and modest 4th jst over 2f out: rn green: hung lft and chsd clr ldng pair over 1f out: r.o wl ins fnl f: snatched 2nd last stride* **33/1**
32 **3** *shd* **Mia San Triple**[10] 6691 2-9-0 0 MartinHarley 6 75
(Peter Chapple-Hyam) *led: rdn ent fnl 2f: drvn and hrd pressed over 1f out: hdd ins fnl f: sn btn: wknd and lost 2nd last stride* **9/2**[2]
4 *7* **This Is The Day** 2-9-0 0 PaulHanagan 7 56+
(William Haggas) *rn green: wl off the pce in rr: sme hdwy past btn horses 2f out: styd on fnl f to snatch 4th last stride: n.d* **12/1**
00 **5** *shd* **Ventura Ice (IRE)**[10] 6690 2-9-0 0 PatDobbs 2 56
(Richard Hannon) *bmpd s: sn rcvrd and chsd ldrs: 3rd and rdn 3f out: no imp and wl hld whn lost 3rd over 1f out: wknd ins fnl f* **25/1**
6 *2* **Super Moment (IRE)** 2-9-0 0 SilvestreDeSousa 8 50
(Saeed bin Suroor) *wl off the pce in rr of main gp: sme hdwy past btn horses 2f out: kpt on: n.d* **5/1**[3]
7 *7* **Mary Le Bow** 2-9-0 0 LukeMorris 9 31
(Lucy Wadham) *racd off the pce in midfield: drvn and no hdwy over 2f out: sn wknd and wl btn fnl 2f* **14/1**
5 **8** *3* **Little Tinka**[16] 6500 2-9-0 0 TedDurcan 12 23
(Mark H Tompkins) *racd off the pce in midfield: rdn and no hdwy over 2f out: sn wl btn and wknd 2f out* **25/1**
9 *10* **Liddle Dwiggs** 2-9-0 0 PatCosgrave 10
(Denis Coakley) *chsd ldrs early: steadily lost pl: bhd over 2f out: sn lost tch: t.o* **50/1**
0 **10** *5* **Heavenly**[61] 5003 2-9-0 0 WilliamBuick 11
(Jeremy Noseda) *chsd ldrs: 4th and btn over 2f out: wknd 2f out: wl btn and virtually p.u ins fnl f: t.o* **11/2**
11 *19* **First Experience** 2-9-0 0 (b[1]) ChrisCatlin 1
(Rae Guest) *wnt rt and bmpd rival s: immediately outpcd and t.o after 2f* **20/1**
00 **U** **Step Away**[29] 6112 2-9-0 0 RichardKingscote 3
(Charles Hills) *veered rt and uns rdr sn after s* **20/1**

1m 23.58s (-1.02) **Going Correction** -0.10s/f (Good) **12** Ran SP% **120.0**
Speed ratings (Par 92): **101,97,97,89,89 86,78,75,63,58 36,**
toteswingers 1&2 £20.00, 2&3 £16.70, 1&3 £2.80 CSF £93.27 TOTE £2.90: £1.20, £9.20, £1.80; EX 108.30 Trifecta £511.30 Pool: £4341.40 - 6.36 winning units..
Owner Mrs Barbara M Keller **Bred** T R Watson & Miss D S Peasley **Trained** Newmarket, Suffolk

FOCUS
They went a good pace in this maiden but the two market leaders dominated the race and the hold-up runners couldn't get involved.

6975 "BREEDERS BACKING RACING" E B F MAIDEN STKS — 7f 26y
4:10 (4:10) (Class 5) 2-Y-O **£2,911** (£866; £432; £216) **Stalls** Low

Form RPR
4235 **1** **Wickhambrook (IRE)**[8] 6747 2-9-0 75 WilliamBuick 14 81+
(Ismail Mohammed) *hld up in tch in midfield: swtchd rt and effrt ent fnl 2f: rdn to ld over 1f out: r.o wl to assert fnl 75yds* **7/1**[3]

0 **2** *1* **Maraayill (IRE)**[34] 5957 2-9-0 0..(t) MartinHarley 9 78+
(Marco Botti) *hld up in tch in midfield: rdn and effrt on inner 2f out: drvn and pressed wnr jst ins fnl f: no ex and btn fnl 75yds* **5/2**[1]

3 **3** *2 ¼* **Chatez (IRE)**[38] 5843 2-9-0 0.................................. FergusSweeney 2 72
(Alan King) *t.k.h early: chsd ldr after 1f tl 5f out: rdn and led wl over 1f out: sn hdd: 3rd and kpt on same pce ins fnl f* **11/4**[2]

0 **4** *2* **Despot (IRE)**[23] 6277 2-9-0 0.. JamesDoyle 13 67
(Charles Hills) *hld up in tch in midfield: rdn and effrt 2f out: edgd lft but hdwy u.p to chse ldrs jst over 1f out: no imp fnl f* **14/1**

0 **5** *4* **Etaad (USA)**[67] 4795 2-9-0 0.. PaulHanagan 8 56
(J W Hills) *t.k.h: chsd ldrs: rdn and unable qck over 2f out drvn and btn 2f out: wknd over 1f out* **7/1**[3]

30 **6** *½* **Passover**[10] 6689 2-9-0 0... LiamKeniry 7 55
(Andrew Balding) *t.k.h: chsd ldrs tl wnt 2nd 5f out: rdn and lost 2nd wl over 1f out: sn btn and wknd* **16/1**

6 **7** *nk* **Eugenic**[18] 6430 2-9-0 0... DougieCostello 11 54
(Rod Millman) *hld up towards rr: rdn over 2f out: swtchd lft and sme hdwy over 1f out: kpt on: n.d* **100/1**

0 **8** *4 ½* **Squaw King**[12] 6641 2-9-0 0.. ShaneKelly 6 42
(Eve Johnson Houghton) *s.i.s: hld up in tch in last quartet: effrt whn rn green and hung lft ent fnl 2f: sn btn and wknd over 1f out* **33/1**

9 *¾* **Classical Art (IRE)** 2-9-0 0... DaneO'Neill 4 40
(Roger Varian) *dwlt and short of room leaving stalls: rn green in rr and pushed along thrght: n.d but past btn horses fr over 1f out* **8/1**

6 **10** *1 ¾* **Samhain**[67] 4801 2-9-0 0.. SeanLevey 10 35
(David Brown) *stdd and dropped in bhd after s: t.k.h: hld up in tch in rr: rdn and no hdwy over 2f out: wknd 2f out* **50/1**

0 **11** *2 ¼* **Excedo Praecedo**[13] 6589 2-9-0 0..................................... PatDobbs 3 29
(Amanda Perrett) *t.k.h: led after 1f tl rdn and hdd wl over 1f out: sn wknd: bhd fnl f* **25/1**

12 *5* **Booloo (IRE)** 2-8-11 0.. JasonHart(3) 5 15
(Garry Moss) *t.k.h: w ldrs: stdd into midfield after 1f out: rdn and struggling over 2f out: wknd 2f out: bhd fnl f* **50/1**

0 **13** *4 ½* **Characterise**[12] 6635 2-9-0 0... SamHitchcott 1
(Mick Channon) *s.i.s: a in rr but in tch tl over 2f out: sn rdn and wknd: bhd fnl f* **50/1**

1m 24.64s (0.04) **Going Correction** -0.10s/f (Good) **13** Ran SP% **117.6**
Speed ratings (Par 95): **95,93,91,89,84 83,83,78,77,75 72,67,62**
toteswingers 1&2 £3.80, 2&3 £2.40, 1&3 £4.40 CSF £23.43 TOTE £7.40: £1.60, £1.40, £1.70; EX 21.10 Trifecta £74.90 Pool: £3074.11 - 30.76 winning units..
Owner Dr Ali Ridha **Bred** Rabbah Bloodstock Limited **Trained** Newmarket, Suffolk

FOCUS
They went a stop-start pace in this maiden and the most exposed runner in the line-up scored but the market leaders finished placed and the form looks solid.

6976 JOCKEY CLUB GRASSROOTS MIDDLE DISTANCE SERIES FINAL (H'CAP) 1m 2f 188y
4:40 (4:40) (Class 3) 3-Y-0+
£15,562 (£4,660; £2,330; £1,165; £582; £292) **Stalls** Low

Form RPR
1354 **1** **Cashpoint**[4] 6868 8-9-2 **80**.. RichardKingscote 11 90+
(Ian Williams) *hld up: wl in tch: smooth hdwy to join ldrs 1f out: pushed into ld ins fnl f comf* **5/1**[1]

6533 **2** *1* **Markttag**[9] 6738 3-8-2 **72**.. LukeMorris 10 79
(Luca Cumani) *in tch in midfield: rdn and effrt 2f out: drvn and hdwy to chse wnr ins fnl f: kpt on* **8/1**[3]

1304 **3** *½* **Theodore Gericault (IRE)**[49] 5436 3-8-13 **83**.................. PatDobbs 13 89+
(Sir Michael Stoute) *t.k.h: hld up in rr: hdwy whn nt clr run over 1f out: swtchd lft: r.o strly ins fnl f: nt rch ldrs* **7/1**[2]

4412 **4** *¾* **Manchestar**[46] 5562 3-8-2 **72**... PaulHanagan 9 77
(Richard Fahey) *chsd ldr: rdn to ld over 1f out: hdd ins fnl f: one pce* **8/1**[3]

4011 **5** *2* **Dolphin Village (IRE)**[12] 6631 3-8-4 **81**.................... SamanthaBell(7) 3 82
(Richard Fahey) *hld up in midfield: effrt on inner over 1f out: one pce fnl f* **10/1**

0010 **6** *shd* **Super Say (IRE)**[25] 6236 7-9-5 **83**..............................(t) AndrewMullen 7 84
(Michael Appleby) *t.k.h: chsd ldrs: rdn and n.m.r 2f out: styd on same pce fnl f* **16/1**

330 **7** *1 ½* **Hydrant**[23] 6288 7-8-11 **80**... ConnorBeasley(5) 4 78
(Richard Guest) *led tl rdn 2f out: hdd over 1f out: wknd ins fnl f* **16/1**

3334 **8** *½* **Penny Rose**[15] 6533 3-8-9 **79**.. KierenFallon 2 77
(Mark Johnston) *towards rr: rdn 4f out: sme hdwy whn jostled over 1f out: sn pushed lft and one pce after* **10/1**

1133 **9** *½* **Lyric Ballad**[15] 6533 3-8-7 **77**.................................... SilvestreDeSousa 5 74
(Hughie Morrison) *chsd ldrs: drvn and unable to quiicken 2f out: wknd ins fnl f* **7/1**[2]

2210 **10** *2 ¼* **Euston Square**[28] 6130 7-7-12 **65**...................................(v) JulieBurke(3) 1 58
(Alistair Whillans) *s.i.s: hld up bhd: hdwy 1/2-way: wknd u.p over 1f out* **20/1**

3202 **11** *1 ¼* **Candyman Can (IRE)**[18] 6435 3-8-0 **70**.............................. MartinLane 8 60
(Dominic Ffrench Davis) *in tch towards rr: effrt and sme hdwy whn jostled over 1f out: sn wknd* **20/1**

4014 **12** *½* **Thecornishcowboy**[6] 6794 4-8-2 **69**..........................(t) RyanPowell(3) 14 58
(John Ryan) *chsd ldrs: rdn over 2f out: unable qck: wknd 1f out* **10/1**

6430 **13** *16* **Claude Monet (BRZ)**[19] 6398 4-7-11 **66** oh3 ow2........ JoeyHaynes(5) 6 27
(Simon Dow) *t.k.h: hld up towards rr: dropped to last 4f out: wknd 2f out* **50/1**

1403 **14** *11* **Invincible Cara (IRE)**[19] 6387 3-8-7 **77** ow1..................[1] TedDurcan 12 18
(Ed Dunlop) *stdd s: hld up in rr: wknd 2f out: bhd and eased ins fnl f* **20/1**

2m 18.29s (-2.81) **Going Correction** -0.10s/f (Good)
WFA 3 from 4yo+ 6lb **14** Ran SP% **119.2**
Speed ratings (Par 107): **106,105,104,104,102 102,101,101,101,99 98,98,86,78**
toteswingers 1&2 £9.10, 2&3 £11.20, 1&3 £8.60 CSF £40.79 CT £284.65 TOTE £5.70: £1.80, £2.90, £2.70; EX 53.80 Trifecta £413.00 Pool: £1356.56 - 2.46 winning units..
Owner Macable Partnership **Bred** Stowell Park Stud **Trained** Portway, Worcs

FOCUS
The winner landed a gamble in smooth style in this highly competitive handicap.

6977 JOCKEY CLUB GRASSROOTS SPRINT SERIES FINAL (H'CAP) 6f
5:10 (5:11) (Class 3) 3-Y-0+
£15,562 (£4,660; £2,330; £1,165; £582; £292) **Stalls** Low

Form RPR
6212 **1** **Trinityelitedotcom (IRE)**[5] 6854 3-9-1 **78**............ RichardKingscote 12 88
(Tom Dascombe) *a.p: rdn and ev ch over 1f out: led and edgd rt ins fnl f: r.o wl* **8/1**

3016 **2** *1* **Ambitious Boy**[17] 6476 4-8-13 **75**.. ShaneKelly 5 82
(Andrew Hollinshead) *bmpd s: chsd ldrs: rdn and effrt to chal 1f out: styd on same pce fnl 75yds* **14/1**

4352 **3** *hd* **Mission Approved**[15] 6525 3-9-3 **80**................................ JamesDoyle 15 86
(Sir Michael Stoute) *wl in tch on outer: effrt u.p and edgd lft 2f out: led ent fnl f: hdd and carried rt ins fnl f: one pce fnl 75yds* **9/2**[1]

4025 **4** *½* **Captain Scooby**[14] 6547 7-8-1 **68**......................... ConnorBeasley(5) 10 73
(Richard Guest) *in tch in midfield: drvn and sltly outpcd over 1f out: rallied ins fnl f: styd on again fnl 100yds* **25/1**

3212 **5** *hd* **Lulu The Zulu (IRE)**[26] 6205 5-8-13 **75**......................... AndrewMullen 1 79
(Michael Appleby) *chsd ldrs on inner: rdn wl over 1f out: styd on same pce ins fnl f* **7/1**[3]

0023 **6** *hd* **Midnight Rider (IRE)**[12] 6647 5-9-9 **85**............................ TedDurcan 14 91+
(Chris Wall) *hld up in tch in rr: effrt and nt clr run jst over 1f out: swtchd rt and hdwy ins fnl f: runnung on whn nt clr run and eased towards fin* **6/1**[2]

0326 **7** *nk* **My Kingdom (IRE)**[4] 6871 7-9-1 **77**......................(t) SilvestreDeSousa 4 80
(Stuart Williams) *in tch in midfield: effrt u.p to chse ldrs 1f out: drvn and styd on same pce fnl f* **7/1**[3]

0511 **8** *hd* **Baron Run**[11] 6664 3-8-6 **74** 6ex.................................. JoeyHaynes(5) 6 76
(K R Burke) *led: rdn 2f out: drvn and hdd ent fnl f: no ex and one pce fnl 150yds* **16/1**

1305 **9** *2* **Bajan Bear**[12] 6648 5-8-8 **73**..................... WilliamTwiston-Davies(3) 7 68
(Michael Blanshard) *hld up in tch towards rr: rdn and effrt over 1f out: styng on same pce whn n.m.r ins fnl f: nvr able to chal* **25/1**

500 **10** *nk* **Mappin Time (IRE)**[5] 6822 5-9-1 **77**..............................(p) DavidAllan 13 72
(Tim Easterby) *in tch in midfield: rdn 2f out: outpcd and lost pl ent fnl f: wl hld and one pce fnl f* **20/1**

3212 **11** *shd* **Marjong**[21] 6338 3-9-0 **77**.. SebSanders 11 71
(Simon Dow) *stdd s: hld up in rr: rdn and hdwy on inner over 1f out: no imp 1f out: wknd ins fnl f* **20/1**

1310 **12** *¾* **Hadaj**[13] 6586 4-9-3 **86**.. KevinStott(7) 3 78
(Ruth Carr) *bmpd s: sn chsng ldrs: rdn and no ex over 1f out: wknd ins fnl f* **8/1**

3-42 **13** *nk* **Broughtons Charm (IRE)**[54] 5280 3-8-10 **73**................ WilliamBuick 2 64
(Willie Musson) *wnt rt s: in tch in midfield: rdn and effrt over 1f out: no imp: wknd ins fnl f* **16/1**

1001 **14** *½* **Barkston Ash**[3] 6908 5-9-5 **84** 6ex.............................(p) JasonHart(3) 16 73
(Eric Alston) *sn rdn in rr on outer: sme hdwy u.p 1/2-way: no ex jst over 1f out: wknd ins fnl f* **14/1**

1004 **15** *nk* **Mount Hollow**[27] 6161 8-8-10 **77**..............................(p) JackDuern(5) 8 65
(Andrew Hollinshead) *in tch towards rr: rdn and effrt over 1f out: no hdwy and sltky hmpd 1f out: sn wknd* **33/1**

4100 **16** *13* **Jontleman (IRE)**[12] 6648 3-8-12 **78**......................... CharlesBishop(3) 17 25
(Mick Channon) *in tch in midfield tl rdn and lost pl over 1f out: bhd whn sltly hmpd 1f out: wknd* **50/1**

1m 10.94s (-0.86) **Going Correction** +0.025s/f (Good)
WFA 3 from 4yo+ 1lb **16** Ran SP% **126.9**
Speed ratings (Par 107): **106,104,104,103,103 103,102,102,99,99 99,98,97,97,96 79**
toteswingers 1&2 £44.70, 2&3 £6.60, 1&3 £8.40 CSF £109.28 CT £600.57 TOTE £7.60: £3.10, £4.00, £1.60, £7.60; EX 136.50 Trifecta £791.70 Pool: £2839.49 - 2.68 winning units..
Owner Manor House Stables LLP **Bred** Natasha Newsome **Trained** Malpas, Cheshire

FOCUS
They went a solid pace in this good sprint handicap and were spread across the track in the straight.

6978 DINE IN THE 1707 RESTAURANT H'CAP 1m 6f 213y
5:45 (5:45) (Class 4) (0-85,84) 3-Y-O **£4,690** (£1,395; £697; £348) **Stalls** Low

Form RPR
1432 **1** **Nateeja (IRE)**[15] 6540 3-9-0 **77**....................................... PaulHanagan 5 88
(J W Hills) *hld up in tch in last trio: rdn and hdwy on inner jst over 2f out: led wl over 1f out: in command and styd on wl fnl f* **6/1**

2410 **2** *2 ¼* **Snowy Dawn**[40] 5764 3-9-1 **78**......................................(p) ShaneKelly 9 86
(Andrew Hollinshead) *hld up in tch in last trio: rdn and effrt 2f out: hdwy u.p over 1f out: chsd wnr ins fnl f: kpt on same pce fnl 100yds* **8/1**

4334 **3** *2 ½* **Candoluminescence**[30] 6081 3-8-8 **71** ow1...............(p) JamesDoyle 6 76
(Roger Charlton) *chsd ldrs: rdn and effrt nrest stands' rail jst over 2f out: chsd wnr over 1f out tl ins fnl f: plugged on same pce after* **10/1**

1023 **4** *3* **Lion Beacon**[22] 6302 3-9-7 **84**..(p) PatDobbs 1 85
(Amanda Perrett) *chsd ldr tl 12f out: rdn and wnt 2nd again over 2f out tl over 1f out: sn hrd drvn and no ex: 4th and outpcd fnl f* **5/1**[3]

3433 **5** *4* **The Welsh Wizard (IRE)**[14] 6557 3-8-12 **75**........(b) RichardKingscote 8 71
(Charles Hills) *t.k.h: hld up in midfield: effrt and rdn 2f out: drvn and btn over 1f out: wknd fnl f* **10/1**

5253 **6** *6* **Sweet Martoni**[30] 6081 3-8-1 **69**..................................... OisinMurphy(5) 10 57
(William Knight) *led: clr 8f out: rdn and hdd wl over 1f out: sn btn and wknd over 1f out* **10/1**

2232 **7** *1 ½* **Shalwa**[14] 6574 3-9-2 **79**..(p) MartinHarley 4 65
(Marco Botti) *dwlt: rcvrd to r in midfield: rdn 4f out: drvn and btn 2f out: wknd and hung rt 1f out: eased ins fnl f* **11/4**[1]

066 **8** *1 ½* **Russian Link**[108] 3402 3-8-2 **65** oh2................................... PatrickMathers 2 49
(John Berry) *hld up in rr: rdn and no hdwy over 2f out: wknd 2f out and sn bhd* **50/1**

3244 **9** *11* **Astorgs Galaxy**[22] 6313 3-8-8 **71**..........................(v[1]) SilvestreDeSousa 3 41
(Sir Michael Stoute) *chsd ldrs tl wnt 2nd 12f out tl over 2f out: sn rdn and btn: bhd and eased over 1f out: t.o* **4/1**[2]

3m 16.62s (-2.38) **Going Correction** -0.10s/f (Good) **9** Ran SP% **118.0**
Speed ratings (Par 103): **102,100,99,97,95 92,91,90,85**
toteswingers 1&2 £10.10, 2&3 £11.80, 1&3 £8.70 CSF £54.22 CT £476.99 TOTE £7.00: £1.80, £3.50, £2.20; EX 64.70 Trifecta £659.20 Pool: £1738.10 - 1.97 winning units..
Owner Hamdan Al Maktoum **Bred** Shadwell Estate Company Limited **Trained** Upper Lambourn, Berks

FOCUS
The winner scored in good style in this staying handicap for 3yos.

T/Jkpt: Not won. T/Plt: £153.30 to a £1 stake. Pool of £68,947.91 - 328.13 winning tickets. T/Qpdt: £4.80 to a £1 stake. Pool of £4,958.76 - 763.10 winning tickets. SP

The Form Book Flat, Raceform Ltd, Compton, RG20 6NL.

6849 WOLVERHAMPTON (A.W) (L-H)

Thursday, October 3

OFFICIAL GOING: Standard to slow

Wind: Fresh across changing to fresh half-behind Weather: Rain clearing

6979 BIDS 5 NURSERY H'CAP 5f 216y(P)

5:40 (5:41) (Class 6) (0-60,60) 2-Y-O **£1,940** (£577; £288; £144) **Stalls** Low

Form RPR

045 **1** **Shyron**[57] 5140 2-8-13 **59**........ JordanVaughan(7) 12 62+
(George Margarson) *s.i.s: sn pushed along in rr: hdwy and hung lft fr over 1f out: r.o to ld wl ins fnl f: readily* **5/1**[2]

0040 **2** ½ **Dancing Sal (IRE)**[5] 6821 2-9-4 **60**........ DeclanBates(3) 4 61
(David Evans) *led 1f: chsd ldrs: rdn over 1f out: r.o* **14/1**

000 **3** *hd* **Sweet Amaalie (IRE)**[15] 6517 2-9-1 **54**........ LiamJones 7 54
(William Haggas) *led 5f out: hdd over 3f out: pushed along to ld again 2f out: rdn and hdd wl ins fnl f* **7/1**[3]

4460 **4** 1 ¼ **Senorita Guest (IRE)**[16] 6487 2-9-6 **59**........ SamHitchcott 6 56
(Mick Channon) *mid-div: hdwy on outer over 2f out: rdn and ev ch ins fnl f: styng on same pce whn hmpd towards fin* **11/1**

0603 **5** 2 ¼ **Dandys Perier (IRE)**[16] 6487 2-9-0 **53**........ DaneO'Neill 8 43
(Ronald Harris) *pushed along in rr early: hmpd 4f out: hdwy over 1f out: rdn and edgd lft ins fnl f: r.o: nt rch ldrs* **9/2**[1]

0660 **6** 1 **Almost Famous (IRE)**[44] 5610 2-9-3 **56**........(b) AdamKirby 10 43
(Jamie Osborne) *trckd ldrs: plld hrd: led over 3f out: rdn and hdd 2f out: wknd ins fnl f* **5/1**[2]

000 **7** 1 ½ **Clear Focus (IRE)**[26] 6213 2-9-2 **55**........ JackMitchell 9 37
(Brendan Powell) *chsd ldrs: rdn over 1f out: no ex fnl f* **33/1**

5040 **8** 2 **Kopkap**[15] 6511 2-9-1 **54**........ GrahamGibbons 2 30
(Ed McMahon) *prom: rdn over 1f out: wknd fnl f* **16/1**

0300 **9** ¾ **Chance Of Romance (IRE)**[44] 5610 2-8-12 **56**........ RyanTate(5) 5 30
(Clive Cox) *prom: rdn over 1f out: wknd fnl f* **22/1**

040 **10** 1 **Polar Express**[39] 5790 2-9-2 **58**........ MatthewLawson(3) 3 29
(Jonathan Portman) *s.i.s: in rr: nt clr run over 1f out: n.d* **12/1**

3206 **11** *hd* **Emily Davison (IRE)**[37] 5857 2-9-0 **60**........ AliRawlinson(7) 13 31
(David C Griffiths) *trckd ldrs: plld hrd: hung lft and wknd over 1f out* **20/1**

006 **12** 3 ¾ **Blunos (IRE)**[53] 5307 2-9-6 **59**........ LiamKeniry 1 18
(Rod Millman) *prom tl rdn and wknd over 1f out* **14/1**

0604 **13** 1 **Society Diva (IRE)**[40] 5757 2-9-6 **59**........ PatCosgrave 11 15
(George Baker) *sn pushed along and a in rr* **11/1**

1m 16.25s (1.25) **Going Correction** +0.025s/f (Slow) **13** Ran SP% **119.6**
Speed ratings (Par 93): **92,91,91,89,86 85,83,80,79,78 77,72,71**
toteswingers 1&2 £28.60, 2&3 £73.20, 1&3 £12.80 CSF £71.39 CT £515.26 TOTE £9.60: £3.00, £6.00, £2.00; EX 107.10 Trifecta £1719.90 Part won. Pool: £2293.20 - 0.69 winning units..
Owner F Butler **Bred** F Butler **Trained** Newmarket, Suffolk

FOCUS
The surface, subject to more binding since the last meeting, was again criticised by riders after the opener with plenty of kickback still evident. This was an ordinary nursery and it was wide open.

6980 BETTING.CO.UK INAUGURAL H'CAP 5f 216y(P)

6:10 (6:10) (Class 6) (0-60,60) 3-Y-O+ **£1,940** (£577; £288; £144) **Stalls** Low

Form RPR

0453 **1** **Gregori (IRE)**[33] 5981 3-9-2 **56**........(t) DaneO'Neill 5 68
(Brian Meehan) *sn led: rdn clr over 1f out: kpt on* **6/1**[3]

000 **2** 1 ½ **Speightowns Kid (USA)**[12] 6652 5-9-7 **60**........(b[1]) RobertHavlin 6 67
(Richard Ford) *s.i.s: sn pushed along and prom: racing keenly whn nt clr run over 3f out: pushed along over 1f out: rdn and r.o ins fnl f: nt rch wnr* **7/1**

0524 **3** *nk* **Powerful Pierre**[52] 5354 6-9-2 **60**........(b) JacobButterfield(5) 11 66
(Ollie Pears) *s.i.s: sn pushed along in rr: hdwy u.p over 1f out: r.o* **7/2**[1]

0342 **4** 1 ¼ **Hoppy's Flyer (FR)**[13] 6610 5-9-7 **60**........ GrahamGibbons 7 62
(Mark Brisbourne) *chsd ldrs: rdn over 2f out: styd on same pce ins fnl f* **4/1**[2]

2630 **5** ¾ **One Last Dream**[27] 6156 4-9-2 **55**........(b) GrahamLee 2 55
(Ron Hodges) *mid-div: outpcd over 2f out: r.o ins fnl f* **16/1**

6054 **6** *hd* **Hamis Al Bin (IRE)**[8] 6753 4-8-10 **56**........(t) JordanVaughan(7) 8 55
(Milton Bradley) *hld up: hdwy over 2f out: edgd lft and nt clr run over 1f out: nt rch ldrs* **8/1**

6604 **7** 1 ¼ **Rise To Glory (IRE)**[6] 6808 5-8-12 **51**........ DuranFentiman 3 46
(Shaun Harris) *chsd ldrs: rdn over 2f out: no ex fnl f* **16/1**

0400 **8** 2 **Excellent Addition (IRE)**[12] 6655 3-8-12 **59**........ LukeLeadbitter(7) 1 48
(Declan Carroll) *prom: rdn over 2f out: wknd over 1f out* **10/1**

6004 **9** 1 ¾ **Camache Queen (IRE)**[18] 6436 5-9-5 **58**........(tp) KirstyMilczarek 12 41
(Joseph Tuite) *sn pushed along in rr: nvr on terms* **14/1**

0026 **10** ½ **Outbid**[8] 6753 3-9-0 **57**........ RobertTart(3) 10 38
(Tony Carroll) *led early: chsd ldr: pushed along over 2f out: wknd over 1f out* **33/1**

0030 **11** 1 ½ **Legal Bond**[12] 6633 4-9-0 **60**........(p) JoshDoyle(7) 9 37
(David O'Meara) *mid-div: wknd over 2f out: eased over 1f out* **16/1**

1m 14.84s (-0.16) **Going Correction** +0.025s/f (Slow)
WFA 3 from 4yo+ 1lb **11** Ran SP% **116.5**
Speed ratings (Par 101): **102,100,99,97,96 96,95,92,90,89 87**
toteswingers 1&2 £9.30, 2&3 £7.70, 1&3 £3.80 CSF £47.20 CT £173.58 TOTE £8.30: £2.80, £2.70, £1.90; EX 63.50 Trifecta £322.50 Pool: £2187.64 - 5.08 winning units..
Owner Stephen Tucker **Bred** Mrs James Wigan **Trained** Manton, Wilts

FOCUS
This weak sprint handicap was another wide-open event.

6981 BRITISH STALLION STUDS E B F MEDIAN AUCTION MAIDEN STKS 5f 216y(P)

6:40 (6:40) (Class 5) 2-Y-O **£2,911** (£866; £432; £216) **Stalls** Low

Form RPR

2 **1** **Miss Atomic Bomb**[18] 6423 2-9-0 0........ AdamKirby 5 77+
(Marco Botti) *s.i.s: racd keenly and sn trcking ldrs: shkn up to ld ins fnl f: flashed tail: r.o wl: comf* **4/6**[1]

02 **2** 3 ½ **Buy And Sell (IRE)**[12] 6654 2-9-5 0........ SeanLevey 4 68
(David Brown) *w ldr tl led over 2f out: rdn and hdd whn rdr dropped whip ins fnl f: styd on same pce* **10/1**[3]

55 **3** 4 **Baker Man (IRE)**[12] 6635 2-9-2 0........ WilliamTwiston-Davies(3) 3 56
(Sylvester Kirk) *trckd ldrs: racd keenly: pushed along over 2f out: rdn over 1f out: sn hung lft: styd on same pce* **9/4**[2]

60 **4** 4 **Man Of Law (USA)**[66] 4827 2-9-5 0........ JimCrowley 1 44
(Ralph Beckett) *led: pushed along and hdd over 2f out: wknd over 1f out* **14/1**

0 **5** 4 **Copper Cavalier**[7] 6776 2-9-5 0........ GrahamLee 6 32
(Robert Cowell) *sn outpcd: bhd whn hung lft over 1f out* **100/1**

40 **6** 22 **Captain Devious**[38] 5843 2-9-2 0........ DeclanBates(3) 2
(David Evans) *prom: lost pl 4f out: sn bhd* **66/1**

1m 15.57s (0.57) **Going Correction** +0.025s/f (Slow) **6** Ran SP% **109.0**
Speed ratings (Par 95): **97,92,87,81,76 47**
toteswingers 1&2 £1.40, 2&3 £1.60, 1&3 £1.10 CSF £8.18 TOTE £1.90: £1.10, £2.50; EX 8.50 Trifecta £10.90 Pool: £3268.20 - 224.17 winning units..
Owner Roldvale Limited **Bred** Tarworth Bloodstock Investments Ltd **Trained** Newmarket, Suffolk

FOCUS
Straightforward maiden form.

6982 MR GG FILLIES' H'CAP 5f 216y(P)

7:10 (7:10) (Class 5) (0-75,74) 3-Y-O+ **£2,911** (£866; £432; £216) **Stalls** Low

Form RPR

1412 **1** **Burren View Lady (IRE)**[12] 6655 3-8-12 **66**........(e[1]) DavidAllan 8 78
(Tim Easterby) *led early: chsd ldrs: led over 2f out: rdn: edgd rt and flashed tail fr over 1f out: styd on u.p* **3/1**[2]

4531 **2** 2 **Glastonberry**[12] 6653 5-9-3 **73**........ DeclanBates(3) 5 79
(Geoffrey Deacon) *a.p: chsd wnr over 1f out: sn rdn and edgd lft: no imp ins fnl f* **3/1**[2]

023 **3** 1 ¼ **Chasing Dreams**[11] 6664 3-9-6 **74**........ GrahamLee 4 76
(Kevin Ryan) *a.p: rdn over 2f out: styd on same pce ins fnl f* **5/1**[3]

0063 **4** 2 ¾ **Night Trade (IRE)**[7] 6777 6-8-6 **64**........(p) PhilipPrince(5) 7 57
(Ronald Harris) *broke wl: sn lost pl: bhd 4f out: hdwy over 1f out: sn rdn: no ex ins fnl f* **33/1**

2002 **5** 7 **Sakhee's Rose**[14] 6560 3-8-11 **65**........(b) GrahamGibbons 1 36
(Ed McMahon) *chsd ldrs: pushed along 1/2-way: wknd over 1f out* **16/1**

3320 **6** 2 **Mother Jones**[8] 6757 5-8-8 **61**........ SeanLevey 2 25
(David Brown) *sn w ldr: rdn and ev ch over 2f out: wknd fnl f* **20/1**

0121 **7** 3 ½ **Threave**[8] 6745 5-9-4 **71**........ JimCrowley 6 24
(Violet M Jordan) *sn led: pushed along and hdd over 2f out: wknd over 1f out* **9/4**[1]

1225 **8** 11 **Climaxfortackle (IRE)**[150] 2088 5-9-3 **70**........ DaneO'Neill 3
(Derek Shaw) *s.i.s: outpcd* **16/1**

1m 15.06s (0.06) **Going Correction** +0.025s/f (Slow)
WFA 3 from 5yo+ 1lb **8** Ran SP% **116.9**
Speed ratings (Par 100): **100,97,95,92,82 80,75,60**
toteswingers 1&2 £2.30, 2&3 £4.10, 1&3 £4.50 CSF £12.82 CT £43.60 TOTE £3.50: £1.40, £1.10, £1.90; EX 14.30 Trifecta £66.50 Pool: £2797.17 - 31.50 winning units..
Owner Habton Farms **Bred** L Mulryan **Trained** Great Habton, N Yorks

FOCUS
A moderate fillies' sprint handicap, run at a decent clip.

6983 ELITE DIGITAL SYSTEMS (S) STKS 7f 32y(P)

7:40 (7:41) (Class 6) 2-Y-O **£1,940** (£577; £288; £144) **Stalls** High

Form RPR

0623 **1** **Hickster (IRE)**[12] 6654 2-8-11 58........(v) RichardKingscote 6 69
(Tom Dascombe) *trckd ldr tl led 3f out: pushed clr fnl 2f* **11/8**[1]

0450 **2** 7 **Rural Affair**[17] 6460 2-8-6 53........ JohnFahy 8 47+
(Harry Dunlop) *hld up: hdwy u.p over 1f out: styd on to go 2nd wl ins fnl f: no ch w wnr* **12/1**

06 **3** ¾ **Jaeger Connoisseur (IRE)**[27] 6160 2-8-1 0........ JoeyHaynes(5) 3 45
(K R Burke) *prom: rdn to chse winjner over 2f out: sn outpcd: lost 2nd wl ins fnl f* **8/1**[3]

3035 **4** 4 **Princess Tamay (IRE)**[7] 6779 2-8-6 63........ DuranFentiman 12 35
(Mark Johnston) *chsd ldrs: rdn over 2f out: sn wknd* **11/1**

50 **5** ½ **Reflection**[14] 6546 2-8-6 0........(b[1]) PatrickMathers 1 34
(Richard Fahey) *sn drvn along in rr: nvr nrr* **20/1**

5630 **6** 2 ¼ **Severnwind (IRE)**[17] 6474 2-8-11 58........ LukeMorris 2 33
(Ronald Harris) *mid-div: rdn over 2f out: wknd over 1f out* **16/1**

2253 **7** *shd* **Chilly In Rio (IRE)**[7] 6779 2-8-6 59........(p) WilliamCarson 5 28
(William Muir) *led 4f: rdn and wknd over 1f out* **9/1**

06 **8** 3 ½ **Flower Arranger (IRE)**[23] 6279 2-8-1 0........ NoelGarbutt(5) 9 20
(David Evans) *sn pushed along and prom: rdn 1/2-way: wknd 2f out* **40/1**

0060 **9** *hd* **Monsieur Blanc (IRE)**[30] 6073 2-8-11 51........ PatCosgrave 10 24
(Denis Coakley) *mid-div: hdwy over 2f out: rdn and wknd over 1f out* **25/1**

5300 **10** 3 ½ **Ambria's Fury (IRE)**[8] 6749 2-8-11 63........(v) SamHitchcott 4 16
(Mick Channon) *s.i.s: outpcd* **7/1**[2]

526 **11** 13 **Arthur's Melody**[3] 6896 2-8-4 0........(p) RyanWhile(7) 7
(Bill Turner) *s.i.s: outpcd* **10/1**

1m 30.19s (0.59) **Going Correction** +0.025s/f (Slow) **11** Ran SP% **117.8**
Speed ratings (Par 93): **97,89,88,83,83 80,80,76,76,72 57**
toteswingers 1&2 £6.30, 2&3 £29.90, 1&3 £2.60 CSF £18.98 TOTE £2.50: £1.10, £4.20, £3.10; EX 25.80 Trifecta £199.50 Pool: £2214.36 - 8.32 winning units..The winner was bought by A Hutchinson for 5200gns.
Owner Edwards Hughes Jenkins Roberts **Bred** Me Surrender Syndicate **Trained** Malpas, Cheshire

FOCUS
This was a very weak affair.

6984 2DB DISPLAY SYSTEMS CLAIMING STKS 1m 4f 50y(P)

8:10 (8:10) (Class 5) 3-Y-O+ **£2,587** (£770; £384; £192) **Stalls** Low

Form RPR

0602 **1** **Perennial**[26] 6217 4-9-12 82........ DanielTudhope 4 91+
(David O'Meara) *chsd ldrs: led over 2f out: sn rdn clr* **10/11**[1]

-203 **2** 11 **Sherman McCoy**[114] 3180 7-9-4 67........ AndrewMullen 1 65
(Michael Appleby) *trckd ldr: chal over 4f out: rdn over 2f out: sn outpcd* **7/1**[3]

3043 **3** 10 **Incendo**[19] 6421 7-9-12 83........(v) StevieDonohoe 3 57
(Ian Williams) *hld up: shkn up over 2f out: sn hung lft and wknd* **15/8**[2]

0030 **4** 3 ½ **Arabian Star (IRE)**[23] 6288 5-9-9 80........(tp) WilliamTwiston-Davies(3) 7 51
(Alan McCabe) *led: clr 10f out tl 6f out: jnd over 4f out: rdn and hdd over 2f out: sn wknd* **14/1**

06 **5** 50 **Global Recovery (IRE)**[42] 5671 6-8-13 43........(v[1]) DeclanBates(3) 5
(David Evans) *hld up: rdn and wknd over 3f out* **100/1**

2m 39.21s (-1.89) **Going Correction** +0.025s/f (Slow) **5** Ran SP% **107.3**
Speed ratings (Par 103): **107,99,93,90,57**
CSF £7.46 TOTE £1.50: £1.30, £2.00; EX 6.70 Trifecta £10.00 Pool: £2137.38 - 159.56 winning units..Perennial was claimed by P. Rolls for £12000.
Owner Middleham Park Racing LXXV & Partner **Bred** Juddmonte Farms Ltd **Trained** Nawton, N Yorks

FOCUS
An easy win for Perennial.

6985 SIS LIVE H'CAP (DIV I) 1m 141y(P)
8:40 (8:41) (Class 6) (0-55,53) 3-Y-0+ **£1,940** (£577; £288; £144) **Stalls** Low

Form RPR
0551 **1** **Let Me In (IRE)**[21] 6321 3-9-2 **52**....(v) DavidProbert 2 65
(Patrick Chamings) *a.p: racd keenly: shkn up to ld wl ins fnl f: r.o wl* **9/2**[3]
4466 **2** *2 ¼* **Crucis Abbey (IRE)**[6] 6804 5-9-1 **47**....(p) TomMcLaughlin 7 54
(Mark Brisbourne) *trckd ldrs: racd keenly: led 6f out: rdn over 1f out: hdd and unable qck wl ins fnl f* **16/1**
1232 **3** *2* **Pour La Victoire (IRE)**[24] 6260 3-9-0 **53**.... RobertTart(3) 6 56
(Tony Carroll) *trckd ldrs: racd keenly: rdn and ev ch over 1f out: no ex ins fnl f* **11/4**[1]
0025 **4** *¾* **Baile Atha Cliath (IRE)**[17] 6472 4-9-0 **53**.... LukeLeadbitter(7) 12 54
(Declan Carroll) *hld up: hdwy over 1f out: r.o: nt rch ldrs* **6/1**
0064 **5** *2 ¼* **Justcallmehandsome**[17] 6472 11-8-8 **45**....(v) ShelleyBirkett(5) 11 41
(Dominic Ffrench Davis) *hld up: hdwy over 1f out: no ex ins fnl f* **16/1**
0213 **6** *4 ½* **I'm Harry**[14] 6553 4-9-6 **52**....(vt) PatCosgrave 9 37
(George Baker) *trckd ldrs: rdn over 2f out: wknd fnl f* **7/2**[2]
0 **7** *1 ½* **Strove For Gold (IRE)**[230] 672 8-9-0 **46**.... DaneO'Neill 8 28
(Thomas McLaughlin, Ire) *hld up: nt clr run over 2f out: nvr on terms* **20/1**
5043 **8** *2* **Stamp Duty (IRE)**[157] 1893 5-8-10 **47**....(p) JacobButterfield(5) 4 24
(Suzzanne France) *s.i.s: hld up: hdwy 1/2-way: rdn over 2f out: wknd over 1f out* **20/1**
000 **9** *12* **Tumbleweed Finale**[31] 6036 3-8-10 **46**.... GrahamGibbons 10
(Rae Guest) *led: hdd 6f out: rdn over 3f out: wknd over 1f out* **33/1**
-633 **10** *16* **Betzyoucan**[245] 447 3-9-2 **52**.... GrahamLee 13
(Robert Stephens) *trckd ldrs: plld hrd: rdn and wknd over 2f out* **40/1**
3006 **11** *3 ½* **Spinning Ridge (IRE)**[21] 6323 8-9-5 **51**....(v) LukeMorris 1
(Ronald Harris) *hld up: rdn over 2f out: eased over 1f out* **16/1**
6006 **12** *7* **Poetry Writer**[29] 6103 4-9-4 **50**....(b[1]) FergusSweeney 3
(Michael Blanshard) *hld up: rdn over 4f out: wknd wl over 2f out* **33/1**

1m 51.63s (1.13) **Going Correction** +0.025s/f (Slow)
WFA 3 from 4yo+ 4lb **12** Ran SP% **116.8**
Speed ratings (Par 101): **95,93,91,90,88 84,83,81,70,56 53,47**
toteswingers 1&2 £12.30, 2&3 £9.40, 1&3 £3.30 CSF £66.56 CT £234.91 TOTE £5.30: £2.20, £5.10, £1.60; EX 79.90 Trifecta £373.80 Pool: £1919.51 - 3.85 winning units..
Owner Select Racing Bloodstock Ltd **Bred** Epona Bloodstock Ltd **Trained** Baughurst, Hants

FOCUS
They went an average pace in this moderate handicap and most took a keen grip.

6986 SIS LIVE H'CAP (DIV II) 1m 141y(P)
9:10 (9:10) (Class 6) (0-55,55) 3-Y-0+ **£1,940** (£577; £288; £144) **Stalls** Low

Form RPR
4004 **1** **Schottische**[10] 6698 3-9-3 **55**....(v) DaneO'Neill 1 66
(Derek Haydn Jones) *a.p: rdn to ld ins fnl f: r.o* **12/1**
/606 **2** *¾* **Bond Artist (IRE)**[66] 4834 4-9-0 **48**.... GrahamLee 9 56
(Geoffrey Oldroyd) *dwlt: hld up: hdwy over 2f out: rdn over 1f out: r.o* **11/2**[3]
5006 **3** *3 ½* **Cheers Big Ears (IRE)**[21] 6324 7-8-7 **46** oh1....(t) DanielMuscutt(5) 7 46
(Richard Price) *hld up: hdwy over 3f out: rdn over 1f out: edgd lft ins fnl f: styd on* **10/1**
-000 **4** *1* **Nakuru Breeze (IRE)**[8] 6759 4-8-7 **46** oh1....(be) JacobButterfield(5) 4 44
(Suzzanne France) *led: rdn over 1f out: hdd and no ex ins fnl f* **50/1**
00 **5** *¾* **Gadobout Dancer**[64] 4893 6-9-1 **49**....(t[1]) LukeMorris 6 45
(Julie Camacho) *s.i.s: hld up: rdn over 3f out: hdwy u.p over 1f out: r.o: nt trble ldrs* **11/1**
/0-0 **6** *1* **Dance To Destiny**[14] 6554 5-8-13 **47**....[1] AdamBeschizza 11 41
(K F Clutterbuck) *w ldr tl pushed along over 3f out: rdn over 2f out: styd on same pce fr over 1f out* **25/1**
5253 **7** *¾* **Lambert Pen (USA)**[21] 6321 3-8-10 **55**.... DanielCremin(7) 8 48
(Mick Channon) *mid-div: pushed along and lost pl over 3f out: n.d after* **2/1**[1]
0000 **8** *2 ¾* **Rocky Couloir**[30] 6074 3-8-12 **50**.... GrahamGibbons 13 37
(Michael Easterby) *trckd ldrs: wnt 2nd over 3f out tl rdn over 1f out: wknd fnl f* **9/2**[2]
4530 **9** *11* **Hittin'The Skids (IRE)**[105] 3513 5-9-1 **49**.... JimmyQuinn 2 9
(Mandy Rowland) *s.i.s: a in rr* **16/1**
200- **10** *18* **Hardy Plume**[474] 3142 4-8-13 **47**.... PatCosgrave 3
(Denis Coakley) *hld up: rdn over 3f out: sn wknd* **9/1**
000/ **11** *shd* **Superior Duchess**[1053] 7461 8-8-12 **46** oh1.... FergusSweeney 10
(Michael Blanshard) *prom tl rdn and wknd over 2f out* **33/1**

1m 52.66s (2.16) **Going Correction** +0.025s/f (Slow)
WFA 3 from 4yo+ 4lb **11** Ran SP% **116.6**
Speed ratings (Par 101): **91,90,87,86,85 84,84,81,71,55 55**
toteswingers 1&2 £9.80, 2&3 £13.80, 1&3 £19.40 CSF £74.95 CT £709.56 TOTE £9.30: £1.70, £2.00, £3.60; EX 51.80 Trifecta £406.10 Pool: £1697.18 - 3.13 winning units..
Owner Mrs E M Haydn Jones **Bred** Mrs M L Parry & P M Steele-Mortimer **Trained** Efail Isaf, Rhondda C Taff

FOCUS
The second division of the extended 1m handicap. It was run at a brisk early pace but steadied after 2f.
T/Plt: £36.00 to a £1 stake. Pool of £87957.38 - 1780.22 winning tickets. T/Qpdt: £6.40 to a £1 stake. Pool of £9247.32 - 1061.0 winning tickets. CR

4571 HOPPEGARTEN (R-H)
Thursday, October 3

OFFICIAL GOING: Turf: good

6987a WESTMINSTER 23. PREIS DER DEUTSCHEN EINHEIT (GROUP 3) (3YO+) (TURF) 1m 2f
4:15 (12:00) 3-Y-0+
£40,650 (£13,821; £6,097; £4,065; £2,845; £1,626)

RPR
1 **Neatico (GER)**[40] 5778 6-9-4 0.... AStarke 1 107
(P Schiergen, Germany) *nvr far off pce on rail: 3rd and swtchd outside ldrs 2 1/2f out: shkn up to ld 1 1/2f out: sn clr: drvn out fnl f* **31/10**[2]
2 *5* **Destor (GER)**[90] 4042 3-9-0 0.... JBojko 10 98
(U Stech, Germany) *hld up in rr: hdwy over 1 1/2f out: styd on wl fnl f: wnt 2nd 50yds out: nvr on terms w wnr* **20/1**
3 *nk* **Vanishing Cupid (SWI)**[27] 6182 3-9-0 0....(p) FabriceVeron 6 97
(H-A Pantall, France) *midfield towards outside: sltly outpcd 3f out: hrd rdn over 2f out: styd on u.p fr over 1 1/2f out: wnt 2nd ins fnl f: kpt on wout ever getting nr wnr: rn flattened out and lost 2nd 50yds out* **27/10**[1]
4 *hd* **Ostinato (GER)**[215] 870 5-9-4 0....(b) KKerekes 9 96
(Sandor Kovacs, Hungary) *towards rr: pushed along and began to stay on over 1 1/2f out: kpt on wl ins fnl f: nt pce to chal* **193/10**
5 *½* **Dubday**[46] 5576 3-9-0 0.... AHelfenbein 7 96
(A Trybuhl, Germany) *midfield on inner: 5th and rdn 2f out: kpt on u.p and swtchd ins to chse plcd horses ins fnl f: one pce u.p fnl 100yds* **91/10**
6 *1 ¼* **Ars Nova (GER)**[33] 6010 3-8-10 0.... FrederikTylicki 5 90
(W Figge, Germany) *midfield: rdn and no immediate imp 2f out: effrt but nt clr run 1 1/2f out: styd on ins fnl f: nvr plcd to chal* **203/10**
7 *1* **Bermuda Reef (IRE)**[46] 5576 3-9-0 0.... MrDennisSchiergen 8 92
(P Schiergen, Germany) *midfield: rushed up to trck ldr after 3f: pressed ldr fr 3f out: cl 2nd and ev ch 2 1/2f out: hrd rdn to chse wnr fr 1 1/2f out: fdd and dropped five pls ins fnl f* **208/10**
8 *nk* **Polish Vulcano (GER)**[40] 5778 5-9-4 0.... WPanov 4 90
(H J Groschel, Germany) *towards rr: effrt u.p on rail to chse ldrs over 1 1/2f out: kpt on but nt pce to chal* **59/10**
9 *½* **Belango (GER)**[32] 6030 7-9-4 0.... EPedroza 3 89
(R Dzubasz, Germany) *trckd ldrs: rdn and nt qckn over 2f out: kpt on u.p to chse ldrs fr 1 1/2f out but readily outpcd ins fnl f* **57/10**
10 *6* **Limario (GER)**[46] 5576 3-9-0 0.... APietsch 2 78
(R Dzubasz, Germany) *led: pressed fr 3f out: hrd rdn and nt qckn 2f out: hdd 1 1/2f out: sn wknd* **9/2**[3]

2m 2.0s (-4.70)
WFA 3 from 5yo+ 5lb **10** Ran SP% **127.9**
WIN (incl. 10 euro stake): 41. PLACES: 18, 35, 15. SF: 983.
Owner Gestut Ittlingen **Bred** Gestut Hof Ittlingen **Trained** Germany

6183 ASCOT (R-H)
Friday, October 4

OFFICIAL GOING: Good to soft (good in places) changing to soft after race 1 (2:30).
Wind: Moderate, against Weather: Fine but cloudy

6988 NATIONAL RACECOURSE CATERING AWARDS H'CAP 7f
2:00 (2:02) (Class 4) (0-85,85) 3-Y-0+ **£6,469** (£1,925; £962; £481) **Stalls** High

Form RPR
0000 **1** **Common Touch (IRE)**[48] 5533 5-9-4 **82**....(b) KierenFallon 9 96
(Willie Musson) *trckd ldng quartet: prog to ld wl over 1f out: rdn and styd on strly* **16/1**
360 **2** *3 ¾* **Lutine Bell**[14] 6608 6-9-1 **79**....(b) ShaneKelly 13 83
(Mike Murphy) *dwlt: hld up towards rr: smooth prog fr 3f out: shkn up to chse wnr jst over 1f out: styd on but no imp* **14/1**
0055 **3** *3* **Alfred Hutchinson**[16] 6538 5-9-5 **83**.... GrahamLee 6 79
(Geoffrey Oldroyd) *w ldrs: led briefly 4f out: outpcd fr 2f out but kpt on* **10/1**
1334 **4** *1 ½* **Levi Draper**[20] 6403 4-9-2 **80**.... FrederikTylicki 2 72
(James Fanshawe) *w.w in midfield: rdn over 2f out: kpt on to take 4th fnl f: nvr gng pce to threaten* **8/1**[3]
-000 **5** *1 ½* **Myboyalfie (USA)**[13] 6650 6-9-1 **84**....(v) OisinMurphy(5) 5 72
(J R Jenkins) *w ldrs: led over 3f out: drvn and hdd wl over 1f out: steadily wknd* **6/1**[1]
05 **6** *¾* **Rebellious Guest**[15] 6571 4-9-7 **85**.... TomQueally 7 71
(George Margarson) *dwlt: towards rr: rdn on outer of gp 3f out: kpt on fnl 2f but wl outpcd by ldrs* **7/1**[2]
2221 **7** *nk* **Footstepsintherain (IRE)**[27] 6203 3-9-4 **84**.... TedDurcan 11 69
(David Lanigan) *settled in midfield on outer of gp: rdn over 2f out: sn outpcd but kpt on fr over 1f out* **7/1**[2]
0210 **8** *2 ½* **Brocklebank (IRE)**[5] 6871 4-9-5 **83**.... JamieSpencer 1 62
(Simon Dow) *sn toiling in last: u.p bef 1/2-way: kpt on to pass toiling rivals fr 2f out: nvr a factor* **14/1**
5000 **9** *½* **Personal Touch**[14] 6586 4-9-1 **79**.... PaulHanagan 18 57
(Richard Fahey) *racd alone on nr side and nt on terms: hung rt to join rest 2f out: no great prog* **12/1**
1140 **10** *nk* **Dashing David (IRE)**[42] 5721 3-9-5 **85**.... PatDobbs 15 61
(Richard Hannon) *hld up wl in rr: rdn over 2f out: plugged on past wkng rivals over 1f out* **20/1**
0664 **11** *4* **Poetic Dancer**[29] 6143 4-9-4 **82**.... AdamKirby 4 49
(Clive Cox) *trckd ldrs: rdn and cl enough over 2f out: hanging and wknd over 1f out* **16/1**
-000 **12** *nk* **Top Offer**[62] 5009 4-9-6 **84**.... SteveDrowne 12 50
(Peter Crate) *a wl in rr: rdn and no prog wl over 2f out: wknd* **40/1**
0146 **13** *2 ¾* **Illustrious Prince (IRE)**[8] 6774 6-8-9 **80**.... LukeLeadbitter(7) 3 39
(Declan Carroll) *w ldrs to 3f out: wknd qckly* **25/1**
1160 **14** *21* **Bassara (IRE)**[63] 4960 4-9-3 **84**.... AshleyMorgan(3) 16
(Chris Wall) *a in last quartet: wknd over 2f out: t.o* **16/1**
0-14 **15** *nk* **Bay Knight (IRE)**[41] 5759 7-9-5 **83**....(b[1]) JamesDoyle 8
(Sean Curran) *led to 4f out: wknd rapidly over 2f out: eased and t.o* **14/1**
0000 **16** *21* **Edge Closer**[34] 5998 9-9-3 **84**.... WilliamTwiston-Davies(3) 10
(Tony Carroll) *chsd ldrs to 1/2-way: wknd rapidly: wl t.o* **40/1**
1540 **17** *7* **Yourartisonfire**[21] 6356 3-9-5 **85**.... DanielTudhope 17
(K R Burke) *a in rr: wknd 3f out: wl t.o* **12/1**

1m 29.59s (1.99) **Going Correction** +0.45s/f (Yiel)
WFA 3 from 4yo+ 2lb **17** Ran SP% **126.0**
Speed ratings (Par 105): **106,101,98,96,94 94,93,90,90,89 85,84,81,57,57 33,25**
toteswingers 1&2 £61.80, 1&3 £58.70, 2&3 £46.10 CSF £221.71 CT £2447.87 TOTE £24.60: £4.80, £3.10, £2.90, £2.10; EX 308.30 Trifecta £2641.70 Part won..
Owner Broughton Thermal Insulation **Bred** Overbury Stallions Ltd And D Boocock **Trained** Newmarket, Suffolk

FOCUS
Straight course stands' rail positioned 7yds inside its normal position. Round course rail positioned 6yds inside from 1m4f, decreasing to 4yds at 1m2f start, continuing at 4yds to the home bend where it increased to 9yds up the far side of the straight. 1m4f race increased by 16yds, 1m6f & 2m increased by 22yds. There was a slight headwind up the straight and the ground was changed to soft following this opening contest. The winner is rated close to last year's form for a different yard.

6989 WILLIS GROUP EBF CLASSIFIED STKS 1m (S)
2:30 (2:33) (Class 3) 3-Y-0+

£9,337 (£2,796; £1,398; £699; £349; £175) **Stalls** High

Form RPR

1415 **1** **Tinghir (IRE)**[16] 6537 3-8-13 88 TedDurcan 5 101
(David Lanigan) *wl in tch: pushed along over 3f out: rdn and prog over 2f out: chsd ldr jst over 1f out: edgd rt but styd on u.p to ld last strides* **7/1**[3]

0015 **2** *nse* **Modern Tutor**[13] 6650 4-9-2 88 RyanMoore 6 100
(Sir Michael Stoute) *trckd ldrs: prog to ld wl over 1f out: hrd pressed and drvn fnl f: hdd last strides* **11/4**[1]

0142 **3** *2 1/2* **Gworn**[28] 6163 3-8-13 88 GrahamLee 1 94
(Ed Dunlop) *trckd ldrs: smooth prog to ld over 2f out: hdd and nt qckn wl over 1f out: one pce* **8/1**

2050 **4** *1 1/4* **Shahdaroba (IRE)**[23] 6308 3-8-13 90 AndreaAtzeni 2 91
(Rod Millman) *trckd ldrs: shkn up over 2f out: kpt on same pce fr over 1f out: nvr able to chal* **20/1**

0000 **5** *1 1/2* **Anton Chigurh**[39] 5838 4-9-2 86 RichardKingscote 9 88
(Tom Dascombe) *hld up in last trio: pushed along over 2f out: kpt on one pce: nvr posed a threat* **14/1**

202- **6** *hd* **Credit Swap**[335] 7556 8-9-2 90 JimCrowley 10 87
(Michael Wigham) *hld up in last trio: shkn up on outer over 2f out: kpt on steadily: nt pce to be involved* **9/1**

2203 **7** *2 1/4* **Jodies Jem**[21] 6356 3-8-13 87 PaulHanagan 11 82
(William Jarvis) *led at stdy pce to over 3f out: sn rdn: steadily fdd on outer of gp fr 2f out* **5/1**[2]

3025 **8** *6* **Princess Of Orange**[56] 5246 4-8-13 88 SilvestreDeSousa 3 65
(Rae Guest) *carried rt s: wl in rr: prog 1/2-way: rdn to chse ldrs over 2f out: wknd over 1f out* **20/1**

0060 **9** *3/4* **Emilio Largo**[27] 6199 5-9-2 90 (t) TomQueally 7 67
(James Fanshawe) *dwlt: a in last trio: struggling fr over 2f out* **8/1**

6040 **10** *27* **Born To Surprise**[27] 6183 4-9-2 90 (v[1]) JamieSpencer 4
(Michael Bell) *awkward s and wnt rt: plld hrd in rr: allowed his hd and prog to ld over 3f out: hdd over 2f out: wknd rapidly: t.o* **8/1**

0045 **11** *nk* **Baileys Jubilee**[11] 6685 3-8-10 90 JoeFanning 8
(Mark Johnston) *dwlt: sn pressed ldrs: wknd wl over 2f out: t.o* **33/1**

1m 46.48s (5.68) **Going Correction** +0.45s/f (Yiel)
WFA 3 from 4yo+ 3lb **11** Ran SP% **118.3**
Speed ratings (Par 107): **89,88,86,85,83 83,81,75,74,47 47**
toteswingers 1&2 £4.80, 1&3 £9.60, 2&3 £4.60 CSF £25.99 TOTE £7.90: £2.70, £1.30, £2.70; EX 31.50 Trifecta £191.90 Pool: £4,131.22 - 16.14 winning units..
Owner B E Nielsen **Bred** Bjorn Nielsen **Trained** Upper Lambourn, Berks

FOCUS
Solid form, despite the muddling pace, with three progressive types coming clear. They again raced centre-to-far side.

6990 WEAR IT PINK H'CAP 6f
3:05 (3:05) (Class 2) (0-105,103) 3-Y-0

£12,450 (£3,728; £1,864; £932; £466; £234) **Stalls** High

Form RPR

02 **1** **Intibaah**[20] 6411 3-9-4 100 PaulHanagan 6 113
(Brian Meehan) *trckd ldrs: smooth prog to go 2nd 2f out: shkn up to ld jst over 1f out: rdn and styd on strly* **16/1**

61- **2** *2 1/4* **Blessington (IRE)**[430] 4688 3-8-3 85 NickyMackay 4 91
(John Gosden) *dwlt: sn in tch: prog 2f out: drvn to take 2nd last 150yds: styd on but no ch w wnr* **7/1**[2]

-201 **3** *1 1/2* **Breton Rock (IRE)**[23] 6308 3-9-1 97 MartinLane 10 98+
(David Simcock) *hld up in rr: prog on outer of main gp 2f out: drvn and styd on to take 3rd last stride* **7/1**[2]

5305 **4** *nse* **Normal Equilibrium**[16] 6539 3-8-1 88 (p) OisinMurphy[(5)] 1 89
(Robert Cowell) *hld up in rr: rdn and prog 2f out: chal for a pl fnl f: hung lft briefly: kpt on* **14/1**

4402 **5** *hd* **Pearl Sea (IRE)**[12] 6665 3-8-9 91 JamieSpencer 9 91
(David Brown) *taken down early: led main gp: hdd and no ex jst over 1f out: lost 2 pls nr fin* **12/1**

1000 **6** *3/4* **Robot Boy (IRE)**[26] 6238 3-8-6 88 HarryBentley 8 86
(David Barron) *hld up in rr: waiting for room 2f out: rdn and styd on wl fnl f: nrst fin* **16/1**

1040 **7** *1* **Tamayuz Star (IRE)**[42] 5728 3-9-1 97 TomQueally 3 92
(George Margarson) *sn in last trio: rdn 3f out: styd on fr over 1f out: nrst fin* **25/1**

5320 **8** *1 3/4* **Secretinthepark**[23] 6308 3-8-13 95 SteveDrowne 14 84
(Ed McMahon) *trckd ldrs: cl up 2f out: sn rdn and grad wknd* **11/1**[3]

0450 **9** *1/2* **Ninjago**[48] 5538 3-9-6 102 RyanMoore 5 89+
(Richard Hannon) *mostly in last pair: rdn over 2f out: sme prog on outer of gp over 1f out: no hdwy fnl f* **7/2**[1]

0-33 **10** *2 1/4* **Master Of War**[17] 6505 3-9-6 102 SeanLevey 18 82
(Richard Hannon) *hld up in trio on nr side: chal 2f out: led gp over 1f out but wl off the pce of main gp* **20/1**

4015 **11** *shd* **Lucky Beggar (IRE)**[48] 5538 3-9-7 103 JamesDoyle 7 83
(Charles Hills) *chsd ldr to 2f out: sn wknd quite qckly* **14/1**

3-01 **12** *1 1/2* **Hoodna (IRE)**[11] 6692 3-9-2 98 6ex SilvestreDeSousa 12 73
(Saeed bin Suroor) *dwlt: prog fr rr and prom over 3f out: wknd over 1f out* **12/1**

1000 **13** *3/4* **Effie B**[91] 4024 3-8-8 90 AndreaAtzeni 16 63
(Mick Channon) *hld up in trio on nr side: chal over 2f out but nt on terms after* **25/1**

-635 **14** *1/2* **Birdman (IRE)**[126] 2843 3-9-4 100 JimCrowley 2 71
(David Simcock) *taken down early: nvr beyond midfield: shkn up over 2f out: sn wknd* **20/1**

0460 **15** *nk* **Chilworth Icon**[23] 6308 3-8-11 93 MartinHarley 11 63
(Mick Channon) *pressed ldrs: lost pl over 2f out: rdn and wknd over 1f out* **16/1**

2000 **16** *1 1/4* **Vincentti (IRE)**[55] 5260 3-8-5 87 (t) LukeMorris 13 53
(Ronald Harris) *nvr beyond midfield: wknd over 2f out* **33/1**

0510 **17** *2 3/4* **Storm Moon (USA)**[16] 6539 3-8-4 86 JoeFanning 15 43
(Mark Johnston) *led nr side trio: clr of other pair and on terms w main gp: wknd qckly and hdd over 1f out* **33/1**

1m 15.03s (0.53) **Going Correction** +0.45s/f (Yiel) **17** Ran SP% **125.0**
Speed ratings (Par 107): **114,111,109,108,108 107,106,104,103,100 100,98,97,96,96 94,90**
toteswingers 1&2 £21.50, 1&3 £17.90, 2&3 £8.80 CSF £114.96 CT £876.12 TOTE £19.20: £3.90, £2.90, £2.20, £3.40; EX 250.00 Trifecta £2353.90 Part won. Pool: £3,138.59 - 0.87 winning units..
Owner Hamdan Al Maktoum **Bred** Shadwell Estate Company Limited **Trained** Manton, Wilts

FOCUS
All bar three of the runners raced far side in what was a decent sprint handicap. A sizeable personal best from the winner.

6991 ASCOT UNDERWRITING NOEL MURLESS STKS (LISTED RACE) 1m 6f
3:40 (3:40) (Class 1) 3-Y-O

£20,982 (£7,955; £3,981; £1,983; £995; £499) **Stalls** Low

Form RPR

3260 **1** **Nichols Canyon**[44] 5653 3-9-0 97 WilliamBuick 4 108
(John Gosden) *led 5f: trckd ldr: drvn to ld again 2f out: edgd rt sn after: styd on wl* **5/1**[3]

2002 **2** *2* **Greatwood**[20] 6394 3-9-0 104 KierenFallon 5 105
(Luca Cumani) *stdd s: tk v t.k.h in 4th allowed to stride on and led after 5f: kicked on 3f out: hdd 2f out: tightened up sn after: styd on but readily hld* **7/2**[2]

231 **3** *2* **Refectory (IRE)**[28] 6166 3-9-0 85 JimCrowley 2 103
(Andrew Balding) *trckd ldr 5f: styd in tch: disp 3rd over 3f out: hanging and nt qckn over 2f out: kpt on same pce after* **20/1**

4202 **4** *nse* **Goodwood Mirage (IRE)**[14] 6591 3-9-0 96 RyanMoore 6 103
(William Knight) *stdd s and then v s.i.s: t.k.h in 5th: prog to dispute 3rd over 3f out: nt qckn over 2f out: kpt on same pce after* **10/1**

2312 **5** *2 1/2* **Shwaiman (IRE)**[21] 6348 3-9-0 97 JamesDoyle 7 99
(James Fanshawe) *stdd s: t.k.h in 5th: dropped to last 4f out: outpcd over 2f out: no ch after* **11/2**

1 **6** *2* **Dark Crusader (IRE)**[41] 5764 3-8-9 97 FMBerry 8 92
(A J Martin, Ire) *trckd ldng pair 5f: outpcd and rdn wl over 2f out: sn wl btn* **5/4**[1]

3m 9.68s (189.68) **6** Ran SP% **112.6**
toteswingers 1&2 £3.40, 1&3 £8.80, 2&3 £7.20 CSF £22.70 TOTE £6.30: £2.70, £2.00; EX 25.80 Trifecta £233.50 Pool £3,821.61 - 12.27 winning units..
Owner Rachel Hood & Elaine Lawlor **Bred** Rabbah Bloodstock Limited **Trained** Newmarket, Suffolk
■ Stewards' Enquiry : William Buick caution; careless riding.

FOCUS
They got racing a fair way out in what looked quite a good Listed event, but little got into it with the front pair kicking off the final bend. A personal best from the winner.

6992 MITIE EVENTS & LEISURE GORDON CARTER STKS (H'CAP) 2m
4:15 (4:15) (Class 3) (0-95,90) 3-Y-0+ **£7,439** (£2,213; £1,106; £553) **Stalls** Low

Form RPR

3321 **1** **Ballinderry Boy**[27] 6202 3-8-3 81 OisinMurphy[(5)] 5 91
(Andrew Balding) *trckd ldng pair to over 4f out: styd cl up on inner: clsd to ld over 1f out: rdn and styd on wl* **9/4**[1]

0161 **2** *2 1/4* **Man Of Plenty**[18] 6466 4-9-6 82 (p) WilliamBuick 7 89
(Ed Dunlop) *trckd ldrs: moved clsr over 4f out: drvn to ld jst over 2f out: edgd rt and hdd over 1f out: one pce* **10/1**

4110 **3** *1 1/4* **Argent Knight**[31] 6066 3-9-1 88 (v) SteveDrowne 8 94
(William Jarvis) *hld up in 7th: prog on inner fr 3f out: drvn to chse ldng pair over 1f out: kpt on same pce* **10/1**

0436 **4** *nk* **Arch Villain (IRE)**[13] 6646 4-9-13 89 (b) RyanMoore 3 94
(Amanda Perrett) *hld up in 10th: quick prog to press ldrs 5f out: lost pl on outer over 3f out: kpt on again u.p fnl 2f to take 4th nr fin* **8/1**

1001 **5** *3/4* **Sula Two**[14] 6591 6-9-10 86 GrahamLee 6 90
(Ron Hodges) *trckd ldng trio: pushed along over 3f out: nt qckn over 2f out: one pce after* **14/1**

46-2 **6** *1 1/4* **Perfect Heart**[17] 6498 4-9-4 80 [1] AndreaAtzeni 2 83
(Roger Varian) *slipped bdly leaving stalls: hld up in 11th: rdn and struggling over 3f out: rallied and styd on fnl 2f: nrst fin* **6/1**[3]

2243 **7** *3 1/4* **Presto Volante (IRE)**[19] 6424 5-9-5 81 (p) PatDobbs 10 80
(Amanda Perrett) *trckd ldrs in 6th: lost pl and rdn over 3f out: tried to make prog 2f out: fdd fnl f* **20/1**

5445 **8** *1 1/2* **Spice Fair**[37] 5895 6-9-4 80 JimmyFortune 11 77
(Mark Usher) *stdd s: hld up in detached last: crept clsr fr 4f out: shkn up and rchd 6th over 1f out: fdd fnl f* **16/1**

2021 **9** *13* **Linguine (FR)**[37] 5879 3-9-3 90 JamesDoyle 13 71
(Seamus Durack) *mostly trckd ldr: rdn to chal over 2f out: wknd rapidly over 1f out: eased* **11/2**[2]

1156 **10** *1 3/4* **Sunny Future (IRE)**[19] 6424 7-9-0 76 CathyGannon 12 55
(Malcolm Saunders) *led: edgd lft and hdd jst over 2f out: wknd qckly* **33/1**

532 **11** *15* **Luggers Hall (IRE)**[41] 5065 5-9-1 77 TomQueally 9 38
(Tony Carroll) *hld up in 8th and t.k.h on occasions: wknd 3f out: t.o* **20/1**

0652 **12** *4 1/2* **Mawaakef (IRE)**[17] 6504 5-9-11 87 KierenFallon 1 43
(J R Jenkins) *hld up in 9th: shkn up and no prog over 3f out: wknd and eased over 2f out: t.o2* **20/1**

103- **13** *64* **Asker (IRE)**[212] 6428 5-9-5 81 (b) RichardThomas 4
(Zoe Davison) *hld up in last pair: struggling after 6f: t.k.h v briefly 7f out: sn rel to r and wl t.o* **50/1**

3m 34.31s (5.31) **Going Correction** +0.55s/f (Yiel)
WFA 3 from 4yo+ 11lb **13** Ran SP% **121.5**
Speed ratings (Par 107): **108,106,106,106,105 105,103,102,96,95 87,85,53**
toteswingers 1&2 £6.80, 1&3 £6.80, 2&3 £11.70 CSF £24.22 CT £197.14 TOTE £3.00: £1.40, £3.10, £3.50; EX 34.00 Trifecta £244.40 Pool: £4,333.41 - 13.29 winning units..
Owner Rainbow Racing **Bred** Spring Bloodstock Ltd **Trained** Kingsclere, Hants

FOCUS
They were strung out from an early stage in this staying event, but it still paid to race in the first half of the field and it was no surprise to see the race go to one of the 3yos. The winner is rated in line with his Kempton form, bearing in mind the jockey's claim.

6993 TROY ASSET MANAGEMENT H'CAP 7f
4:50 (4:50) (Class 3) (0-95,94) 3-Y-0 **£8,409** (£2,502; £1,250; £625) **Stalls** High

Form RPR

5313 **1** **Consign**[13] 6650 3-9-1 88 (v) WilliamBuick 2 100
(Jeremy Noseda) *hld up in rr: smooth prog over 2f out: mostly on bridle tl cajoled into ld jst over 1f out: sn clr: rdn out* **8/1**[3]

2266 **2** *1 3/4* **Fils Anges (IRE)**[23] 6308 3-9-2 89 JamieSpencer 1 96
(Michael Bell) *hld up in last: stl there jst over 2f out: rapid prog over 1f out: chsd wnr last 120yds: r.o but no hope of chalng* **8/1**[3]

1453 **3** 2 ¼ **Gold Hunter (IRE)**[23] 6308 3-9-6 **93**.......................... SilvestreDeSousa 6 94
(Saeed bin Suroor) *trckd ldrs: clsd 1/2-way: led over 2f out gng strly: rdn and hdd jst over 1f out: outpcd* **9/2**[1]

13 **4** ½ **Purcell (IRE)**[11] 6692 3-8-10 **88**.......................... OisinMurphy(5) 3 88
(Andrew Balding) *pressed ldr: upsides 2f out: sn drvn: hld whn hung lft 1f out: one pce* **7/1**[2]

-111 **5** ½ **Brownsea Brink**[13] 6650 3-9-4 **91**.......................... RyanMoore 7 90
(Richard Hannon) *trckd ldrs: shkn up wl over 2f out: kpt on and stl chsng ldrs over 1f out: outpcd* **9/2**[1]

3041 **6** hd **Whipper Snapper (IRE)**[13] 6642 3-8-7 **80**.................. AndreaAtzeni 15 78
(William Knight) *hld up in rr: rdn over 2f out: kpt on u.p over 1f out: nvr able to threaten* **20/1**

3110 **7** 1 ½ **Life Partner (IRE)**[23] 6308 3-9-7 **94**.................. MickaelBarzalona 12 88
(Charlie Appleby) *hld up in last trio: shuffled along on outer of gp 2f out: kpt on one pce: nvr involved* **16/1**

5540 **8** ¾ **Tipping Over (IRE)**[49] 5493 3-8-10 **83**.......................... MartinDwyer 9 75
(Hugo Palmer) *trckd ldrs: cl up and rdn 2f out: steadily wknd* **25/1**

4055 **9** ½ **Sorella Bella (IRE)**[27] 6188 3-9-2 **89**.......................... MartinHarley 5 80
(Mick Channon) *led to over 2f out: sn rdn and wknd* **20/1**

2252 **10** 6 **Related**[17] 6488 3-8-10 **83**.......................... JamesDoyle 11 58
(Clive Cox) *nvr bttr than midfield: rdn over 2f out: sn wknd: bhd fnl f* **14/1**

2111 **11** 1 ¾ **Trucanini**[16] 6524 3-9-0 **87**.......................... TedDurcan 8 58
(Chris Wall) *w ldrs to 1/2-way: wknd over 2f out: bhd fnl f* **10/1**

6053 **12** ¾ **Flyman**[6] 6840 3-9-2 **89**..........................(p) PaulHanagan 14 58
(Richard Fahey) *nvr beyond midfield: wknd jst over 2f out: bhd fnl f* **8/1**[3]

12-6 **13** 1 ½ **Give Way Nelson (IRE)**[128] 2783 3-8-12 **85**.............. JimmyFortune 10 50
(Brian Meehan) *racd away fr rest down centre of crse: on terms 4f: struggling over 2f out: bhd fnl f* **50/1**

1m 29.66s (2.06) **Going Correction** +0.45s/f (Yiel) **13** Ran SP% **119.2**
Speed ratings (Par 105): **106,104,101,100,100 100,98,97,96,90 88,87,85**
toteswingers 1&2 £12.00, 1&3 £8.20, 2&3 £7.40 CSF £67.02 CT £266.46 TOTE £8.70: £2.90, £3.60, £2.60; EX 68.10 Trifecta £343.10 Pool: £4,772.98 - 10.43 winning units..
Owner Miss Yvonne Jacques **Bred** Natton House Thoroughbreds & Mark Woodall **Trained** Newmarket, Suffolk

FOCUS
They raced centre-field in what was a fair handicap and the front pair came clear. The winner continued his progress.
T/Jkpt: Not won. T/Plt: £120.00 to a £1 stake. Pool: £160271.31 - 974.30 winning tickets T/Qpdt: £22.50 to a £1 stake. Pool: £9645.94 - 316.10 winning tickets JN

6979 WOLVERHAMPTON (A.W) (L-H)

Friday, October 4

OFFICIAL GOING: Standard
Wind: Light behind Weather: Fine

6994 BETFRED "THE HOME OF GOALS GALORE" H'CAP 5f 20y(P)
5:55 (5:55) (Class 6) (0-60,57) 3-Y-O+ £1,940 (£577; £288; £144) Stalls Low

Form RPR

6040 **1** **Rise To Glory (IRE)**[1] 6980 5-9-1 **51**..........................(v) DuranFentiman 6 66
(Shaun Harris) *mde all: shkn up over 1f out: rdn and edgd lft ins fnl f: styd on* **4/1**[3]

6410 **2** 1 ¼ **Beach Rhythm (USA)**[19] 6436 6-8-12 **51**..........................(v) DeclanBates(3) 1 61
(Jim Allen) *a.p: chsd wnr over 3f out: rdn over 1f out: styd on* **5/1**

4531 **3** 3 **Beauty Pageant (IRE)**[5] 6879 6-9-0 **57**.......................... ClaireMurray(7) 2 56
(David Brown) *chsd wnr tl over 3f out: remained handy: pushed along over 1f out: styd on same pce fnl f* **11/4**[1]

4003 **4** 1 **Borough Boy (IRE)**[2] 6930 3-9-0 **50**..........................(v) PatrickMathers 7 47
(Derek Shaw) *prom: pushed along 1/2-way: rdn over 1f out: styd on same pce* **4/1**[3]

-000 **5** 6 **Cashel's Missile (IRE)**[19] 6436 3-8-5 **48**..........................(p) LouisSteward(7) 3 23
(John Spearing) *prom: pushed along 1/2-way: rdn over 1f out: wknd fnl f* **33/1**

0530 **6** 3 **Lord Buffhead**[2] 6944 4-9-0 **55**..........................(v) ConnorBeasley(5) 8 18
(Richard Guest) *s.i.s: outpcd* **7/2**[2]

0-60 **7** 7 **Mrs Medley**[14] 6611 7-8-7 **48** ow3..........................(be) AnnStokell(5) 9
(Ann Stokell) *prom: lost pl after 1f: sn bhd* **100/1**

1500 **8** 3 ½ **La Sylphe**[13] 6653 3-9-5 **55**.......................... DaneO'Neill 5
(Derek Shaw) *sn pushed along to chse ldrs: hmpd and lost pl over 3f out: rdn 1/2-way: sn wknd and eased* **16/1**

4205 **9** 2 ¼ **Gracie's Games**[19] 6436 7-8-9 **45**..........................(b) LiamJones 4
(John Spearing) *sn outpcd* **20/1**

1m 2.01s (-0.29) **Going Correction** 0.0s/f (Stan) **9** Ran SP% **120.1**
Speed ratings (Par 101): **102,100,95,93,84 79,68,62,58**
toteswingers 1&2 £4.30, 1&3 £3.90, 2&3 £3.60 CSF £25.03 CT £65.41 TOTE £6.00: £2.30, £1.60, £1.40; EX 31.10 Trifecta £80.30 Pool: £1803.35 - 16.83 winning units..
Owner N Blencowe,J Sunderland,M Lenton,CHarris **Bred** Bryan Ryan **Trained** Carburton, Notts

FOCUS
The winner landed a gamble under a front-running ride in this low-grade handicap. The second matched his August Southwell form.

6995 BETFRED MOBILE LOTTO CLAIMING STKS 5f 216y(P)
6:25 (6:26) (Class 6) 3-Y-O+ £1,940 (£577; £288; £144) Stalls Low

Form RPR

4114 **1** **George Fenton**[6] 6855 4-8-9 **73**..........................(e[1]) ConnorBeasley(5) 3 79
(Richard Guest) *sn pushed along in rr: nt clr run over 2f out: hdwy over 1f out: rdn to ld wl ins fnl f: r.o* **4/1**[3]

-505 **2** 1 ½ **Electric Qatar**[20] 6388 4-9-10 **78**.......................... RichardKingscote 2 84
(Tom Dascombe) *led 5f out: rdn over 1f out: hdd and unable qck ins wl ins fnl f* **7/1**

0455 **3** ¾ **Haadeeth**[3] 6929 6-8-7 **68**..........................(t) DeclanBates(3) 13 68
(David Evans) *a.p: rdn over 2f out: styd on* **20/1**

1306 **4** 1 **Fathsta (IRE)**[16] 6515 8-8-11 **79**.......................... NeilFarley(3) 6 69
(Declan Carroll) *prom: rdn over 2f out: styd on towards fin* **7/1**

6013 **5** nse **Dream Ally (IRE)**[13] 6653 3-9-1 **67**..........................(tp) MichaelO'Connell 7 70
(Jedd O'Keeffe) *chsd ldrs: rdn over 2f out: styd on same pce ins fnl f* **7/2**[2]

0045 **6** ½ **Red Cape (FR)**[35] 5973 10-8-10 **68**..........................(b) PJMcDonald 9 63
(Ruth Carr) *prom: chsd ldr over 3f out: rdn and ev ch over 1f out: no ex ins fnl f* **14/1**

0040 **7** 1 ½ **Seek The Fair Land**[27] 6215 7-8-7 **79**..........................(v) ThomasBrown(3) 8 58
(Jim Boyle) *hld up: rdn over 1f out: nt rch ldrs* **3/1**[1]

6005 **8** hd **Divine Call**[53] 5349 6-9-1 **70** ow1.......................... AdamKirby 4 62
(Milton Bradley) *prom: n.m.r over 2f out: rdn over 1f out: no ex ins fnl f* **12/1**

3006 **9** 8 **Portrush Storm**[14] 6606 8-8-0 **50**.......................... JoeyHaynes(5) 1 27
(Ray Peacock) *led 1f: chsd ldr tl over 3f out: sn rdn: wknd over 1f out* **100/1**

0-40 **10** 23 **Berrymead**[14] 6606 8-8-8 **43**.......................... AnnStokell(5) 11
(Ann Stokell) *s.i.s: outpcd* **100/1**

1m 14.52s (-0.48) **Going Correction** 0.0s/f (Stan)
WFA 3 from 4yo+ 1lb **10** Ran SP% **113.3**
Speed ratings (Par 101): **103,101,100,98,98 97,95,95,85,54**
toteswingers 1&2 £4.00, 1&3 £7.20, 2&3 £25.90 CSF £30.76 TOTE £3.70: £1.40, £2.60, £4.50; EX 33.10 Trifecta £365.30 Pool: £1632.06 - 3.35 winning units..
Owner Mrs Alison Guest **Bred** R P Williams **Trained** Wetherby, W Yorks

FOCUS
A competitive claimer. The pace was solid and the winner came from some way back. He confirmed his recent improvement.

6996 BETFRED MOBILE CASINO H'CAP 1m 5f 194y(P)
6:55 (6:56) (Class 6) (0-65,65) 3-Y-O+ £1,940 (£577; £288; £144) Stalls Low

Form RPR

260 **1** **Alpine Mysteries (IRE)**[30] 6109 3-9-0 **63**..............[1] ThomasBrown(3) 7 73
(Harry Dunlop) *hld up: hdwy to ld 5f out: rdn over 1f out: styd on wl* **11/2**

3105 **2** 3 ¼ **Nolecce**[13] 6658 6-9-3 **61**.......................... JackGarritty(7) 3 66
(Tony Forbes) *a.p: chsd wnr over 3f out: rdn over 1f out: styd on same pce ins fnl f* **10/1**

6502 **3** 1 ¾ **My Destination (IRE)**[13] 6658 4-9-8 **62**.......................... JasonHart(3) 1 68+
(Declan Carroll) *prom: lost pl over 4f out: hdwy u.p over 1f out: r.o wl towards fin* **9/2**[3]

4420 **4** 6 **Lucky Black Star (IRE)**[21] 6361 3-8-10 **56**.......................... PatCosgrave 5 50
(George Baker) *hld up: hdwy u.p over 3f out: wknd fnl f* **6/1**

0 **5** 4 ½ **Santayana (GER)**[11] 6696 4-8-9 **49**..........................(v[1]) DeclanBates(3) 6 37
(David Evans) *led after 1f: hdd over 9f out: rdn over 3f out: wknd 2f out* **25/1**

2364 **6** hd **Gods Gift (IRE)**[57] 5196 3-9-5 **65**.......................... ChrisCatlin 4 53
(Rae Guest) *hld up: pushed along and wknd wl over 2f out* **7/2**[2]

0-50 **7** 5 **Impertinent**[157] 1897 3-8-2 **48**.......................... PatrickMathers 2 29
(Jonathan Portman) *led 1f: chsd ldrs: rdn over 3f out: wknd over 2f out* **20/1**

522 **8** 2 **Jezza**[28] 6173 7-10-0 **65**..........................(bt) LukeMorris 8 43
(Karen George) *pushed along in rr early: hdwy over 11f out: led over 9f out: pushed along and hdd 5f out: rdn over 3f out: wknd 2f out* **11/4**[1]

3m 6.0s **Going Correction** 0.0s/f (Stan)
WFA 3 from 4yo+ 9lb **8** Ran SP% **114.4**
Speed ratings (Par 101): **100,98,97,93,91 91,88,87**
toteswingers 1&2 £8.40, 1&3 £5.10, 2&3 £5.20 CSF £58.12 CT £267.33 TOTE £5.10: £1.90, £3.30, £1.20; EX 62.90 Trifecta £706.90 Pool: £1390.96 - 1.47 winning units..George Fenton was claimed by Mr C. R. Dore £7000. Seek The Fair Land was claimed by Mr L. A. Carter £5000.
Owner Windflower Overseas Holdings Inc **Bred** Windflower Overseas Holdings Inc **Trained** Lambourn, Berks

FOCUS
They went a steady pace in this handicap but the winner scored in decent style and the third didn't get much luck. Improvement from the winner.

6997 BETFRED "CATCH FRED'S PUSHES ON BETFRED TV" MAIDEN STKS 1m 4f 50y(P)
7:25 (7:26) (Class 5) 3-Y-O+ £2,587 (£770; £384; £192) Stalls Low

Form RPR

1 **Silent Movie (IRE)** 3-9-5 **0**.......................... AdamKirby 6 82+
(Mark Johnston) *hld up: hdwy over 6f out: shkn up to ld over 2f out: rdn over 1f out: jst hld on* **7/2**[3]

6 **2** nk **Caterina De Medici (FR)**[23] 6312 4-9-7 **75**.............. TomMcLaughlin 4 76
(Ed Walker) *led: hdd over 10f out: remained handy: rdn to chse wnr and edgd rt over 1f out: r.o* **8/1**

5203 **3** 3 ¼ **Just Darcy**[51] 5410 3-8-11 **68**..........................[1] ThomasBrown(3) 3 71
(Sir Michael Stoute) *hld up: hdwy over 2f out: rdn and hmpd over 1f out: styd on same pce ins fnl f* **4/1**

4225 **4** 2 **Fatima's Gift**[19] 6433 3-9-0 **71**.......................... LukeMorris 1 68
(David Simcock) *prom: nt clr run over 2f out: rdn and swtchd rt over 1f out: edgd lft and no ex fnl f* **3/1**[2]

0 **5** 11 **Jowhara**[11] 6696 3-9-0 **0**.......................... FrederikTylicki 5 50
(Gerard Butler) *trckd ldrs: wnt 2nd over 9f out tl led over 3f out: pushed along and hdd over 2f out: wknd over 1f out* **25/1**

50-5 **6** 30 **Alnawiyah**[113] 3237 3-9-0 **71**.......................... DaneO'Neill 2
(Charles Hills) *plld hrd: led over 10f out: pushed along and hdd over 3f out: wknd over 2f out* **5/2**[1]

2m 42.98s (1.88) **Going Correction** 0.0s/f (Stan)
WFA 3 from 4yo 7lb **6** Ran SP% **110.8**
Speed ratings (Par 103): **93,92,90,89,81 61**
toteswingers 1&2 £6.30, 1&3 £3.20, 2&3 £7.10 CSF £29.02 TOTE £7.80: £2.90, £3.60; EX 32.30 Trifecta £64.90 Pool: £1050.09 - 12.12 winning units..
Owner Sheikh Hamdan Bin Mohammed Al Maktoum **Bred** Darley **Trained** Middleham Moor, N Yorks

FOCUS
Several of the runners were closely matched on form in this maiden but it was won by a Mark Johnston-trained newcomer. The form is not especially convincing but could be rated higher at face value.

6998 BETFRED MOBILE SPORTS H'CAP 7f 32y(P)
7:55 (7:58) (Class 5) (0-75,75) 3-Y-O £2,587 (£770; £384; £192) Stalls High

Form RPR

5012 **1** **Living The Life (IRE)**[6] 6856 3-9-2 **70**..........................(b) RichardKingscote 8 83
(Jamie Osborne) *s.i.s: hdwy to ld over 5f out: pushed clr over 1f out: comf* **10/11**[1]

3614 **2** 3 ¼ **Malaysian Boleh**[15] 6560 3-9-4 **72**.......................... HarryBentley 9 76
(Simon Dow) *hld up: hdwy over 1f out: rdn to go 2nd and hung lft ins fnl f: nt rch wnr* **8/1**[3]

632 **3** nk **Gabrial The Boss (USA)**[48] 5527 3-9-5 **73**..........................(t) AdamKirby 6 76
(David Simcock) *hld up: rdn over 1f out: r.o ins fnl f: nrst fin* **20/1**

-304 **4** 1 ¼ **Zain Spirit (USA)**[15] 6556 3-9-2 **70**..........................(p) NeilCallan 4 70
(Gerard Butler) *a.p: chsd wnr 4f out: rdn and hung lft over 1f out: no ex ins fnl f* **10/1**

2-06 **5** nk **Meet Me Halfway**[21] 6362 3-8-12 **69**.......................... AshleyMorgan(3) 7 68
(Chris Wall) *w ldrs tl over 5f out: remained handy: pushed along 1/2-way: styd on same pce fnl f* **25/1**

2063 **6** 3 ¼ **Reminisce (IRE)**[38] 5867 3-9-6 **74**..........................(bt) LukeMorris 3 64
(Marco Botti) *prom: rdn over 1f out: sn hung lft and wknd* **20/1**

The Form Book Flat, Raceform Ltd, Compton, RG20 6NL.

3331 7 hd **Fossa**[18] 6476 3-9-5 73 RobertWinston 1 63
(Dean Ivory) *plld hrd: led: hdd over 5f out: sn lost pl: n.d after: hung lft ins fnl f* **4/1**[2]
-446 8 ½ **Smart Eighteen**[29] 6134 3-8-12 66 FrederikTylicki 5 55
(Paul D'Arcy) *prom: rdn over 2f out: wknd over 1f out* **8/1**[3]
1m 29.31s (-0.29) **Going Correction** 0.0s/f (Stan) 8 Ran SP% **117.1**
Speed ratings (Par 101): **101,97,96,95,95 91,91,90**
toteswingers 1&2 £4.00, 1&3 £2.90, 2&3 £9.50 CSF £9.04 CT £91.22 TOTE £1.80: £1.10, £2.40, £3.30; EX 13.20 Trifecta £107.50 Pool: £1461.45 - 10.19 winning units..
Owner Michael Buckley **Bred** Michael Begley **Trained** Upper Lambourn, Berks
FOCUS
The hot favourite powered clear under a forcing ride in this handicap. The winner was 8lb well in and is rated to her Leicester form.

6999 BETFRED "RACING'S BIGGEST SUPPORTER" MAIDEN AUCTION STKS 1m 141y(P)
8:25 (8:25) (Class 5) 2-Y-O **£2,587** (£770; £384; £192) **Stalls** Low

Form RPR
04 1 **Aramadyh**[21] 6365 2-8-8 0 (p) LukeMorris 6 72+
(James Tate) *led over 7f out: shkn up over 1f out: hrd rdn ins fnl f: edgd lft: styd on* **12/1**
2 1½ **Hadya (IRE)** 2-8-9 0 NeilCallan 2 70+
(James Tate) *a.p: chsd wnr over 1f out: rdn ins fnl f: eased whn hld towards fin* **11/4**[2]
23 3 7 **Larsen Bay (IRE)**[153] 2011 2-8-12 0 RichardKingscote 4 58
(Tom Dascombe) *led: hdd over 7f out: chsd ldr to over 5f out: rdn over 2f out: wknd ins fnl f* **5/2**[1]
4 7 **Jayeff Herring (IRE)** 2-8-13 0 JamieSpencer 5 44
(Michael Bell) *prom: chsd ldr over 5f out tl pushed along over 1f out: wknd fnl f* **4/1**
3025 5 2½ **Nice Arty (IRE)**[3] 6922 2-8-8 70 WilliamTwiston-Davies(3) 1 37
(Jamie Osborne) *pushed along in rr early: tk clsr order over 5f out: rdn over 2f out: sn wknd* **3/1**[3]
00 6 15 **Paint It Red (IRE)**[125] 2883 2-8-0 0 ConnorBeasley(5) 3
(Richard Guest) *sn outpcd: bhd fnl 6f* **50/1**
1m 51.68s (1.18) **Going Correction** 0.0s/f (Stan) 6 Ran SP% **109.9**
Speed ratings (Par 95): **94,92,86,80,78 64**
toteswingers 1&2 £5.00, 1&3 £3.30, 2&3 £1.40 CSF £42.95 TOTE £14.00: £4.00, £1.80; EX 49.70 Trifecta £541.40 Pool: £1140.34 - 1.57 winning units..
Owner Saif Ali **Bred** Old Mill Stud **Trained** Newmarket, Suffolk
FOCUS
Two runners trained by James Tate pulled clear in this maiden, which lacked depth.

7000 BETFRED "STILL TREBLE ODDS ON LUCKY 15'S" H'CAP 1m 1f 103y(P)
8:55 (8:55) (Class 5) (0-75,75) 3-Y-O+ **£2,587** (£770; £384; £192) **Stalls** Low

Form RPR
1114 1 **Save The Bees**[26] 6236 5-9-5 73 JasonHart(3) 1 83
(Declan Carroll) *mde all: pushed along over 2f out: rdn over 1f out: styd on* **11/4**[2]
3162 2 1¼ **Golden Jubilee (USA)**[35] 5966 4-8-9 63 (v) WilliamTwiston-Davies(3) 5 70
(Nigel Twiston-Davies) *a.p: rdn over 2f out: r.o to go 2nd wl ins fnl f: nt rch wnr* **8/1**
-413 3 1¼ **Lyric Piece**[30] 6098 3-9-4 73 (p) MartinHarley 8 79
(Sir Mark Prescott Bt) *chsd ldrs: rdn over 3f out: r.o towards fin* **5/2**[1]
2303 4 ½ **Lean On Pete (IRE)**[22] 6346 4-9-10 75 ShaneKelly 3 79
(Ollie Pears) *dwlt: hld up: nt clr run over 1f out: swtchd rt: rdn and r.o ins fnl f: nt rch ldrs* **7/2**[3]
5-53 5 ½ **Ruwaiyan (USA)**[17] 6497 4-9-10 75 NeilCallan 9 78
(James Tate) *a.p: chsd wnr 3f out: rdn over 1f out: no ex ins fnl f* **6/1**
4063 6 ½ **Signature Dish (IRE)**[14] 6612 3-8-9 64 ow1 JamieSpencer 6 67
(Andrew Balding) *chsd wnr tl pushed along 3f out: rdn over 1f out: no ex fnl f* **8/1**
3653 7 1¼ **Prime Exhibit**[18] 6468 8-9-7 72 (t) LukeMorris 7 71
(John Stimpson) *hld up: hdwy over 4f out: rdn over 2f out: styd on same pce fr over 1f out* **16/1**
1015 8 5 **Attraction Ticket**[46] 5587 4-8-12 70 GeorgeBuckell(7) 4 58
(David Simcock) *pushed along early in rr: hld up: sme hdwy u.p over 1f out: rdr dropped reins and wknd ins fnl f* **16/1**
2m 1.29s (-0.41) **Going Correction** 0.0s/f (Stan)
WFA 3 from 4yo+ 4lb 8 Ran SP% **125.7**
Speed ratings (Par 103): **101,99,98,98,97 97,96,91**
toteswingers 1&2 £5.80, 1&3 £2.50, 2&3 £4.10 CSF £27.98 CT £65.09 TOTE £4.50: £1.30, £2.60, £1.50; EX 26.90 Trifecta £134.50 Pool: £1987.38 - 11.07 winning units..
Owner Steve Ryan **Bred** S P Ryan **Trained** Sledmere, E Yorks
FOCUS
A well-backed runner dominated this competitive handicap. He rates a small personal best.
T/Plt: £309.10 to a £1 stake. Pool: £92250.64 - 217.85 winning tickets T/Qpdt: £68.10 to a £1 stake. Pool: £7444.29 - 80.80 winning tickets CR

7001 - 7004a (Foreign Racing) - See Raceform Interactive

6811 DUNDALK (A.W) (L-H)
Friday, October 4

OFFICIAL GOING: Standard

7005a DIAMOND STKS (GROUP 3) 1m 2f 150y(P)
7:45 (7:46) 3-Y-O+ **£31,707** (£9,268; £4,390; £1,463)

RPR
1 **Parish Hall (IRE)**[27] 6226 4-9-8 113 KevinManning 7 108
(J S Bolger, Ire) *sn trckd ldr in 2nd: almost on terms under 2f out: led over 1f out: pushed clr: comf* **7/4**[2]
2 1¼ **Manalapan (IRE)**[27] 6225 3-9-3 96 ChrisHayes 1 107
(P J Prendergast, Ire) *w.w: niggled along in 6th under 3f out: prog on inner in 4th 1f out: kpt on strly into 2nd cl home: nt trble wnr* **40/1**
3 ½ **Afonso De Sousa (USA)**[7] 6818 3-9-3 105 JosephO'Brien 4 106+
(A P O'Brien, Ire) *led: clly pressed 2f out: hdd over 1f out: kpt on one pce and dropped to 3rd cl home* **5/4**[1]
4 1¼ **Captain Joy (IRE)**[37] 5907 4-9-8 107 RonanWhelan 6 103+
(Tracey Collins, Ire) *chsd ldrs: niggled along in 4th 3f out: nt qckn w ldrs in 3rd over 1f out: kpt on same pce and dropped to 4th clsng stages* **14/1**
5 3¾ **Certerach (IRE)**[19] 6441 5-9-8 108 ConorHoban 5 95
(M Halford, Ire) *hld up in rr: kpt on fr over 1f out: nvr nrr* **8/1**[3]
6 3¼ **Prince Alzain (USA)**[27] 6198 4-9-8 103 (p) WayneLordan 8 89
(Gerard Butler) *trckd ldrs in 3rd: pushed along and nt qckn under 2f out: sn no ex* **14/1**
7 2 **Opera Gloves (IRE)**[34] 6009 3-9-0 98 NGMcCullagh 2 83
(M Halford, Ire) *hld up towards rr: pushed along to chse ldrs in 5th under 3f out: sn no imp: wknd* **25/1**
8 37 **Levanto (IRE)**[16] 6543 3-9-0 104 PatSmullen 3 11
(W P Mullins, Ire) *chsd ldrs on inner tl wknd qckly 3f out: eased ins fnl 2f* **12/1**
2m 10.97s (130.97)
WFA 3 from 4yo+ 6lb 8 Ran SP% **119.2**
CSF £66.78 TOTE £2.40: £1.50, £6.00, £1.02; DF 61.40 Trifecta £340.10.
Owner Mrs J S Bolger **Bred** J S Bolger **Trained** Coolcullen, Co Carlow
FOCUS
The performance of the runner-up puts the form under question, but he's been rated to his best.

7006 - 7009a (Foreign Racing) - See Raceform Interactive

6988 ASCOT (R-H)
Saturday, October 5

OFFICIAL GOING: Good to soft (straight 7.6, round 7.7)
Wind: Light, against Weather: Fine but cloudy, mild

7010 MACQUARIE GROUP ROUS STKS (LISTED RACE) 5f
1:30 (1:30) (Class 1) 3-Y-O+
£20,982 (£7,955; £3,981; £1,983; £995; £499) **Stalls** High

Form RPR
2220 1 **Steps (IRE)**[14] 6639 5-8-12 104 (b) JamieSpencer 15 111
(Roger Varian) *dwlt: hld up in tch: prog 2f out: drvn to chal fnl f: styd on to ld nr fin* **11/2**[2]
311- 2 shd **Eton Rifles (IRE)**[317] 7829 8-8-12 108 GrahamGibbons 17 111
(Stuart Williams) *trckd ldrs: prog to ld gp in centre over 1f out: overall ldr ins fnl f: collared nr fin* **5/1**[1]
0500 3 nk **Medicean Man**[24] 6305 7-9-1 105 (tp) FergusSweeney 1 113
(Jeremy Gask) *trckd ldr far side: nt clr run fr 2f out to over 1f out: clsd u.p against far rail fnl f: jst hld* **16/1**
001 4 shd **Free Zone**[17] 6539 4-8-12 100 PaulHanagan 3 109
(Bryan Smart) *led far side trio and overall ldr: drvn and hdd ins fnl f: no ex* **10/1**
3300 5 1¼ **Dinkum Diamond (IRE)**[43] 5726 5-8-12 101 CathyGannon 5 105
(Henry Candy) *towards rr: rdn 2f out: kpt on fr over 1f out: nvr gng pce to rch ldrs* **14/1**
0061 6 shd **Doc Hay (USA)**[7] 6845 6-8-12 103 DavidNolan 2 104
(David O'Meara) *taken down early: hanging rt thrght: chsd ldr far side: nt qckn over 1f out: one pce after* **8/1**
3026 7 2 **Lady Gibraltar**[7] 6830 4-8-7 89 (v) MichaelJMMurphy 8 92
(Alan Jarvis) *w ldrs: led gp in centre over 2f out to over 1f out: wknd* **33/1**
0420 8 1 **Masamah (IRE)**[7] 6830 7-8-13 104 ow1 (p) AdamKirby 14 95
(Marco Botti) *racd alone against nr side rail: nvr on terms w ldrs* **6/1**[3]
0000 9 nk **Caledonia Lady**[14] 6639 4-8-7 99 SamHitchcott 6 87
(Jo Hughes) *t.k.h: hld up in last pair: stl wl in rr but gng strly whn nowhere to go over 1f out: swtchd lft and styd on fnl f: no ch to rcvr* **14/1**
0121 10 ½ **New Fforest**[12] 6699 3-8-7 93 LiamKeniry 7 87
(Andrew Balding) *trckd ldrs: cl up 2f out: rdn over 1f out: wknd* **16/1**
-502 11 ¾ **El Manati (IRE)**[12] 6685 3-8-7 95 (b[1]) SilvestreDeSousa 10 84
(James Tate) *dwlt: t.k.h: hld up in rr: hmpd after 1f: rdn bef 1/2-way and struggling: plugged on fnl f* **25/1**
0600 12 2 **Elusivity (IRE)**[7] 6830 5-8-12 96 (v[1]) KierenFallon 16 81
(David O'Meara) *chsd ldrs: cl up 2f out: wknd qckly over 1f out* **14/1**
0330 13 1½ **Judge 'n Jury**[14] 6639 9-8-12 100 (t) LukeMorris 11 75
(Ronald Harris) *led cntre gp to over 2f out: wknd qckly* **25/1**
0-00 14 1½ **Definightly**[21] 6391 7-8-12 100 (p) SteveDrowne 13 70
(Roger Charlton) *a in rr: rdn and wknd 2f out* **20/1**
3013 15 nk **Noble Storm (USA)**[7] 6830 7-8-12 100 GrahamLee 12 69
(Ed McMahon) *w ldrs tl wknd rapidly wl over 1f out* **12/1**
1m 0.7s (0.20) **Going Correction** +0.325s/f (Good) 15 Ran SP% **121.4**
Speed ratings (Par 111): **111,110,110,110,108 108,104,103,102,101 100,97,95,92,92**
toteswingers 1&2 £7.50, 1&3 £24.70, 2&3 £14.20 CSF £31.44 TOTE £5.10: £2.10, £2.30, £6.00; EX 32.90 TRIFECTA Pool: £2,688.79 - 1.90 winning units.
Owner Michael Hill **Bred** Eamon Beston **Trained** Newmarket, Suffolk
■ Stewards' Enquiry : Graham Gibbons four-day ban; used whip above permitted level (20th-23rd Oct).
FOCUS
Straight course stands' rail positioned 7yds inside its normal position. Round course rail positioned 6yds inside from 1m4f, decreasing to 4yds at 1m2f start, continuing at 4yds to the home bend where it increased to 9yds up the far side of the straight. 1m4f race increased by 16yds, 1m6f & 2m increased by 22yds. The jockeys in the first reported the ground to be riding good to soft to dead, and the official going description was amended after the opener. The times for the first two races suggested that conditions on the straight track were nearer to good. This was the third running of this event since it was transferred from Newmarket, and it was a competitive Listed sprint. The form makes sense. At first three raced in a cluster on the far rail with the remainder, apart from Masamah who soon went to race solo on the stands' side, racing nearer the centre. The groups merged and the first four all ended up near the far rail.

7011 BMW CORNWALLIS STKS (GROUP 3) 5f
2:05 (2:05) (Class 1) 2-Y-O
£22,684 (£8,600; £4,304; £2,144; £1,076; £540) **Stalls** High

Form RPR
1153 1 **Hot Streak (IRE)**[14] 6637 2-9-0 107 JamieSpencer 14 112+
(Kevin Ryan) *trckd clr ldr: clsd easily to ld over 1f out: sn clr: drvn out: impressive* **9/2**[2]
1 2 5 **Outer Space**[58] 5186 2-9-0 0 RyanMoore 10 94
(Richard Hannon) *towards rr: rdn over 2f out: prog over 1f out: chsd clr wnr jst ins fnl f: styd on but no imp* **3/1**[1]
2410 3 ½ **Kickboxer (IRE)**[15] 6582 2-9-0 79 SamHitchcott 5 92
(Mick Channon) *sn rdn and struggling in rr: prog 2f out: styd on to battle for 2nd fnl f: no ch w wnr* **50/1**
4103 4 4 **Extortionist (IRE)**[22] 6347 2-9-0 104 HarryBentley 12 78
(Olly Stevens) *stdd s: hld up in rr: rdn 2f out: hanging rt but kpt on fr over 1f out: nvr any threat* **9/2**[2]
024 5 1 **Excel's Beauty**[42] 5767 2-8-11 99 (b) GrahamLee 6 71
(James Tate) *led at str pce and sn clr: hdd over 1f out: no ch w wnr: lost 2nd jst ins fnl f and wknd* **16/1**
1304 6 1¾ **Oasis Town**[15] 6584 2-8-11 89 DeclanMcDonogh 13 65
(Kevin Ryan) *t.k.h: hld up in last pair: tried to make prog fr 2f out but no ch of getting involved* **22/1**

0614 **7** *hd* **Fast (IRE)**[22] 6347 2-8-11 99 PatDobbs 1 64
(Richard Hannon) *led to post early: outpcd and shoved along after 2f: nvr on terms after* **14/1**

261 **8** *nse* **Royal Mezyan (IRE)**[85] 4259 2-9-0 93 SilvestreDeSousa 2 67
(William Haggas) *chsd ldrs: struggling to stay in tch 2f out: sn wknd* **6/1**[3]

3211 **9** *¾* **Hay Chewed (IRE)**[64] 4965 2-8-11 93 RobertHavlin 8 61
(Peter Chapple-Hyam) *prom in chsng gp: wknd over 1f out* **12/1**

36 **10** *3* **Abbakova (IRE)**[50] 5476 2-8-11 0 GrahamGibbons 11 51
(David O'Meara) *chsd ldrs 3f: wknd* **25/1**

0450 **11** *4* **Lady Chantilly (IRE)**[14] 6622 2-8-11 94 KierenFallon 3 36
(Jo Hughes) *a wl in rr: shkn up and no prog 2f out* **25/1**

2113 **12** *3* **Umneyati**[15] 6584 2-8-11 96 PaulHanagan 7 25
(James Tate) *nvr on terms w ldrs: struggling 1/2-way: sn wknd* **11/1**

1m 0.24s (-0.26) **Going Correction** +0.325s/f (Good) 12 Ran SP% **118.2**
Speed ratings (Par 105): **115,107,106,99,98 95,95,95,93,89 82,77**
toteswingers 1&2 £3.40, 1&3 £27.30, 2&3 £30.10 CSF £17.48 TOTE £4.60: £1.90, £1.80, £8.90; EX 14.80 Trifecta £455.30 Pool: £4235.69 - 6.97 winning units..
Owner Qatar Racing Limited **Bred** Barry Noonan **Trained** Hambleton, N Yorks

FOCUS
Despite the absence of previous Group winners this looked a decent renewal of this event, which will switch to Newmarket next season. They raced down the centre and the impressive winner clocked a time 0.46sec quicker than the older sprinters in the first race. He rates as among the best recent winners of this event. The winner built on his debut and the third showed big improvement.

7012 GROSVENOR CASINOS CUMBERLAND LODGE STKS (GROUP 3) 1m 4f
2:40 (2:40) (Class 1) 3-Y-O+

£34,026 (£12,900; £6,456; £3,216; £1,614; £810) **Stalls** Low

Form RPR

4536 **1** **Secret Number**[21] 6393 3-8-7 111 SilvestreDeSousa 2 115
(Saeed bin Suroor) *trckd ldng pair: wnt 2nd over 2f out: drvn to ld over 1f out: edgd rt but styd on wl* **4/1**[2]

0112 **2** *2½* **Royal Empire (IRE)**[28] 6198 4-9-3 112 KierenFallon 6 114
(Saeed bin Suroor) *trckd ldrs: pushed along over 3f out: prog u.p on inner to take 2nd jst ins fnl f: kpt on but no imp on wnr* **4/1**[2]

16-2 **3** *2½* **Gatewood**[24] 6307 5-9-0 109 RobertHavlin 1 107
(John Gosden) *t.k.h: trckd ldr: led over 2f out to over 1f out: sn outpcd u.p* **3/1**[1]

4036 **4** *hd* **Repeater**[9] 6766 4-9-0 107 GrahamLee 3 107
(David O'Meara) *hld up in last: rdn over 2f out: kpt on one pce fr over 1f out: n.d* **20/1**

0-01 **5** *½* **Gospel Choir**[10] 6741 4-9-0 101 RyanMoore 5 106+
(Sir Michael Stoute) *hld up in last pair: taken to r against far side rail over 6f out to over 3f out: dropped to last and struggling sn after: plugged on fnl 2f* **3/1**[1]

-106 **6** *¾* **Mijhaar**[64] 4944 5-9-0 106 JamieSpencer 4 105
(Roger Varian) *led: steered wd into st and hdd: steadily wknd* **7/1**[3]

12-6 **7** *6* **Hajras (IRE)**[14] 6620 4-9-0 105 PaulHanagan 7 95
(Mark Johnston) *wl in tch: rdn and nt qckn over 2f out: wknd qckly fnl f* **14/1**

2m 35.03s (2.53) **Going Correction** +0.325s/f (Good)
WFA 3 from 4yo+ 7lb 7 Ran SP% **113.9**
Speed ratings (Par 113): **104,102,100,100,100 99,95**
toteswingers 1&2 £2.90, 1&3 £3.30, 2&3 £3.20 CSF £20.14 TOTE £4.10: £2.20, £2.10; EX 13.80 Trifecta £45.60 Pool: £4297.50 - 70.58 winning units..
Owner Godolphin **Bred** Darley **Trained** Newmarket, Suffolk

FOCUS
The actual race distance was 1m4f16yds. This was the first race on the round course, where the ground appeared to be riding easier than on the straight track. They went a fairly steady pace and avoided the rail in the back straight. It didn't look one of the better renewals but Secret Number more than backed up his St Leger run.

7013 JOHN GUEST BENGOUGH STKS (GROUP 3) 6f
3:15 (3:16) (Class 1) 3-Y-O+

£39,697 (£15,050; £7,532; £3,752; £1,883; £945) **Stalls** High

Form RPR

1610 **1** **Tropics (USA)**[14] 6623 5-9-1 107 RobertWinston 7 117
(Dean Ivory) *hld up towards far side: smooth prog 2f out: led 1f out: cajoled along and sn clr: rdn out nr fin* **9/1**

2520 **2** *3½* **Music Master**[42] 5738 3-9-0 103 (t) FergusSweeney 9 106
(Henry Candy) *prom in centre: overall ldr 2f out: hdd 1f out: no ch w wnr: kpt on* **8/1**

0030 **3** *1¾* **Hoof It**[14] 6623 6-9-1 109 KierenFallon 13 100
(Michael Easterby) *trckd ldrs towards nr side of gp: drvn to try to chal 2f out: outpcd fnl f: kpt on* **13/2**[2]

6210 **4** *shd* **Heeraat (IRE)**[28] 6193 4-9-5 112 PaulHanagan 2 104
(William Haggas) *overall ldr towards far side to 2f out: styd on terms tl outpcd fnl f* **10/1**

324 **5** *¾* **Free Wheeling (AUS)**[15] 6595 5-9-1 109 (vt[1]) RobertHavlin 17 98
(Saeed bin Suroor) *trckd ldrs towards nr side: prog over 2f out: tried to mount a chal wl over 1f out: sn outpcd* **14/1**

-055 **6** *1¾* **Soul (AUS)**[28] 6193 6-9-1 111 SilvestreDeSousa 14 92
(Saeed bin Suroor) *prom towards nr side of gp: rdn to try to chal 2f out: wknd fnl f* **4/1**[1]

150 **7** *hd* **Hitchens (IRE)**[21] 6414 8-9-5 108 GrahamGibbons 12 95
(David Barron) *towards rr: drvn and no prog 2f out: plugged on fnl f: no ch* **25/1**

3221 **8** *nk* **Intransigent**[30] 6129 4-9-1 105 LiamKeniry 8 90
(Andrew Balding) *t.k.h: hld up in tch: shkn up and nt qckn 2f out: no prog after* **15/2**[3]

1-52 **9** *1¾* **Fairway To Heaven (IRE)**[23] 6331 4-9-1 87 PatDobbs 5 85
(Michael Wigham) *dwlt: hld up in rr towards far side: rdn 2f out: no hdwy over 1f out* **20/1**

1660 **10** *¾* **Kavanagh (SAF)**[28] 6193 6-9-1 112 (t) PatCosgrave 11 82
(M F De Kock, South Africa) *nvr beyond midfield: rdn and struggling over 2f out* **16/1**

4000 **11** *1* **Prodigality**[21] 6391 5-9-1 97 GrahamLee 4 79
(Ronald Harris) *chsd ldng pair towards far side to 2f out: wknd* **25/1**

1601 **12** *1½* **Ladyship**[9] 6768 4-8-12 100 RyanMoore 16 71
(Sir Michael Stoute) *racd towards nr side: wl in rr: brief prog u.p over 1f out: fdd fnl f* **8/1**

0-20 **13** *2½* **Jimmy Styles**[133] 2676 9-9-1 105 (p) AdamKirby 3 66
(Clive Cox) *chsd overall ldr towards far side to 2f out: wknd* **28/1**

6302 **14** *2* **Morache Music**[18] 6505 5-9-1 104 SteveDrowne 18 60
(Peter Makin) *a wl in rr: bhd fnl 2f* **20/1**

0030 **15** *2¼* **Secret Witness**[7] 6830 7-9-1 100 (p) LukeMorris 15 53
(Ronald Harris) *nvr gng wl: a in rr* **33/1**

1m 14.55s (0.05) **Going Correction** +0.325s/f (Good)
WFA 3 from 4yo+ 1lb 15 Ran SP% **122.6**
Speed ratings (Par 113): **112,107,105,104,103 101,101,100,98,97 96,94,90,88,85**
toteswingers 1&2 £16.50, 1&3 £15.70, 2&3 £12.20 CSF £72.20 TOTE £11.90: £4.20, £3.30, £2.30; EX 100.70 Trifecta £1814.00 Pool: £5775.95 - 2.38 winning units..
Owner Dean Ivory **Bred** D Konecny, S Branch & A Branch **Trained** Radlett, Herts
■ A first Group winner for Dean Ivory, who also bred the horse.

FOCUS
The sixth running of this Group 3 sprint, and fair form for the grade. They raced in one group. Another personal best from Tropics, but not many showed their form.

7014 BETFRED "GOALS GALORE" CHALLENGE CUP (HERITAGE H'CAP) 7f
3:50 (3:52) (Class 2) 3-Y-O+

£93,375 (£27,960; £13,980; £6,990; £3,495; £1,755) **Stalls** High

Form RPR

1004 **1** **Heaven's Guest (IRE)**[14] 6623 3-8-13 100 RyanMoore 12 109
(Richard Fahey) *trckd ldrs: lost pl sltly over 2f out: rallied to chse ldr jst over 1f out: clsd to ld last 150yds: jst hld on* **9/1**

2002 **2** *nk* **Bertiewhittle**[22] 6352 5-9-0 99 JamieSpencer 11 108
(David Barron) *hld up in last pair: stl there wl over 1f out: rapid prog on outer after: hrd rdn and flew home to grab 2nd last strides but too late* **9/1**

6303 **3** *nk* **Loving Spirit**[28] 6199 5-8-10 98 RobertTart[(3)] 10 106
(James Toller) *blindfold off late and slowly away: hld up in last trio: prog on outer over 2f out: rdn over 1f out: r.o fnl f: clsd on wnr nr fin but lost 2nd last strides* **8/1**[3]

00 **4** *1¾* **Arnold Lane (IRE)**[15] 6595 4-9-9 108 SamHitchcott 6 111
(Mick Channon) *hld up wl in rr: shkn up over 2f out: prog on outer over 1f out: styd on fnl f but nvr gng pce to chal* **33/1**

0501 **5** *hd* **Redvers (IRE)**[28] 6183 5-8-13 98 (b) PatCosgrave 14 101
(Ed Vaughan) *awkward s: sn prom: chsd ldr over 2f out to jst over 1f out: one pce* **10/1**

2350 **6** *nse* **Shamaal Nibras (USA)**[70] 4744 4-8-13 98 HarryBentley 15 101
(Ismail Mohammed) *wl in tch: prog and prom over 2f out: rdn and kpt on same pce fr over 1f out* **12/1**

6523 **7** *shd* **Es Que Love (IRE)**[35] 5992 4-9-4 103 AdamKirby 18 105
(Mark Johnston) *led: clr 3f out: wandered sltly fr 2f out: hdd & wknd last 150yds* **20/1**

3110 **8** *1¼* **Pacific Heights (IRE)**[7] 6838 4-8-10 95 PaulHanagan 17 94
(Brian Ellison) *trckd ldrs: tightened up and lost pl over 2f out: styd on again fr over 1f out despite hanging rt* **20/1**

1115 **9** *nse* **Magic City (IRE)**[15] 6595 4-9-3 102 PatDobbs 16 101
(Richard Hannon) *awkward s: hld up towards rr: rdn 2f out: kpt on fr over 1f out: nt pce to threaten* **20/1**

0301 **10** *¾* **Royal Rock**[18] 6505 9-9-6 105 6ex GeorgeBaker 3 102
(Chris Wall) *taken down early: wl in tch: prog against far rail 2f out: tried to cl on ldrs 1f out: fdd* **33/1**

4100 **11** *½* **Glen Moss (IRE)**[28] 6183 4-8-12 97 SteveDrowne 7 92
(Charles Hills) *wl in tch: tried to cl on ldrs 2f out: no imp 1f out: fdd* **33/1**

1015 **12** *¾* **Sirius Prospect (USA)**[21] 6392 5-9-6 105 RobertWinston 1 98
(Dean Ivory) *towards rr: tried to make prog against far rail fr 2f out: no hdwy fnl f* **11/1**

0046 **13** *1¼* **Pastoral Player**[21] 6392 6-9-6 105 GrahamLee 13 95
(Hughie Morrison) *taken down early: t.k.h: hld up in midfield: shkn up and nt qckn 2f out: wl btn after* **14/1**

21 **14** *½* **Ascription (IRE)**[21] 6396 4-9-10 109 (t) KierenFallon 5 98
(Hugo Palmer) *t.k.h: hld up in rr: shkn up over 2f out: no prog and wl btn over 1f out* **7/2**[1]

0024 **15** *4½* **Pied A Terre (AUS)**[21] 6396 5-8-12 97 SilvestreDeSousa 4 74
(Saeed bin Suroor) *hld up in last pair: shkn up over 2f out: no prog* **25/1**

12-1 **16** *1½* **Anaconda (FR)**[252] 407 4-8-12 97 RichardKingscote 8 69
(Tom Dascombe) *t.k.h: prom 4f: sn lost pl and btn* **20/1**

3111 **17** *1¾* **Big Johnny D (IRE)**[29] 6164 4-8-12 97 GrahamGibbons 2 65
(David Barron) *restless in stalls: chsd ldr to over 2f out: wknd qckly* **6/1**[2]

1m 28.79s (1.19) **Going Correction** +0.325s/f (Good)
WFA 3 from 4yo+ 2lb 17 Ran SP% **131.1**
Speed ratings (Par 109): **106,105,105,103,103 103,102,101,101,100 100,99,97,97,92 90,88**
toteswingers 1&2 £25.90, 1&3 £19.10, 2&3 £18.40 CSF £82.87 CT £693.61 TOTE £11.00: £2.50, £2.30, £2.60, £9.60; EX 111.00 Trifecta £1170.90 Pool: £80549.49 - 51.59 winning units..

Owner J K Shannon & M A Scaife **Bred** Yeomanstown Stud **Trained** Musley Bank, N Yorks

FOCUS
A high-class and competitive handicap, but they didn't go a great pace. Despite that, the second, third and fourth all came from the rear. The runners initially formed two groups before coming together. A length personal best from the winner.

7015 EBF STALLIONS OCTOBER STKS (LISTED RACE) (F&M) 7f
4:25 (4:25) (Class 1) 3-Y-O+

£22,684 (£8,600; £4,304; £2,144; £1,076; £540) **Stalls** High

Form RPR

1261 **1** **Tantshi (IRE)**[30] 6143 3-8-11 94 JamieSpencer 9 104
(Roger Varian) *hld up in last pair: prog jst over 2f out: led 1f out: drvn and sn clr* **8/1**

1322 **2** *2¾* **Ghanaian (FR)**[30] 6143 3-8-11 93 SilvestreDeSousa 10 97
(Charlie Appleby) *trckd ldrs: clsd to ld jst ins fnl 2f: hdd 1f out: no ch w wnr and jst clung on for 2nd* **6/1**[3]

3223 **3** *shd* **Maid A Million**[49] 5538 3-8-11 90 WilliamCarson 5 97
(David Elsworth) *trckd ldrs: rdn over 2f out: no prog over 1f out: rallied fnl f: styd on and nrly snatched 2nd* **14/1**

6-50 **4** *nk* **Valais Girl**[119] 3103 3-8-11 92 (p) HarryBentley 3 96
(Marcus Tregoning) *prom: chal and upsides 2f out: one pce fnl f* **33/1**

0302 **5** *2* **Enrol**[15] 6595 4-8-13 100 RyanMoore 7 92
(Sir Michael Stoute) *hld up in last pair: effrt whn nt clr run 2f out and lost all ch: kpt on fnl f* **3/1**[1]

0001 **6** *nk* **Nargys (IRE)**[23] 6327 3-9-3 103 LukeMorris 2 96
(Luca Cumani) *hld up: rdn and prog to press ldrs 2f out: wknd fnl f* **7/2**[2]

-030 **7** *½* **Winter's Night (IRE)**[35] 6000 5-8-13 97 AdamKirby 11 90
(Clive Cox) *t.k.h: hld up in midfield: rdn wl over 2f out: sn in trble and btn: plugged on* **7/1**

655 **8** *shd* **I'm So Glad**[21] 6411 4-8-13 89 GrahamLee 4 89
(Mick Channon) *hld up in midfield: tried to make prog 2f out: nt clr run briefly ovet 1f out: wknd fnl f* **25/1**

3005 **9** *1½* **Melbourne Memories**[56] 5271 3-8-11 98 (b[1]) PaulHanagan 8 84
(Clive Cox) *trckd clr ldr: clsd and upsides 2f out: wknd qckly fnl f* **11/1**

6320 **10** 2 1/4 **Switcher (IRE)**[8] 6796 4-8-13 99 KierenFallon 1 80
(Richard Fahey) *led and clr: wknd and hdd jst ins fnl 2f* **8/1**
1m 28.94s (1.34) **Going Correction** +0.325s/f (Good)
WFA 3 from 4yo+ 2lb **10** Ran SP% **118.0**
Speed ratings (Par 111): **105,101,101,101,99 98,98,98,96,93**
toteswingers 1&2 £5.30, 1&3 £13.10, 2&3 £10.40 CSF £56.11 TOTE £8.70: £3.00, £2.20, £2.70; EX 48.10 Trifecta £324.10 Pool: £4373.94 - 10.11 winning units..
Owner Sheikh Ahmed Al Maktoum **Bred** Darley **Trained** Newmarket, Suffolk
■ Stewards' Enquiry : William Carson two-day ban; careless riding (20th-21st Oct).
FOCUS
They raced in one group towards the far side in this ordinary fillies' Listed race, which was run at a brisk gallop.
T/Jkpt: Not won. T/Plt: £1,692.70 to a £1 stake. Pool: £185813.05 - 80.13 winning tickets T/Qpdt: £219.40 to a £1 stake. Pool: £12424.94 - 41.90 winning tickets JN

6835 NEWMARKET (R-H)

Saturday, October 5

OFFICIAL GOING: Good to firm (good in places; 7.6)
Wind: light, half behind Weather: overcast, dry

7016 £300,000 TATTERSALLS MILLIONS 2YO FILLIES' TROPHY 7f
1:50 (1:51) (Class 2) 2-Y-O
£162,330 (£66,420; £29,550; £14,730; £7,380; £2,940) **Stalls** Low

Form RPR
5331 **1** **Wedding Ring (IRE)**[14] 6644 2-9-0 96 MartinLane 9 92
(Charlie Appleby) *hld up in last trio: swtchd lft wl over 1f out: rdn and str run over 1f out: led ins fnl f: r.o wl: rdn out* **11/4**[1]
030 **2** 3/4 **Manderley (IRE)**[14] 6644 2-9-0 76 SeanLevey 12 90
(Richard Hannon) *chsd ldrs: effrt u.p to ld over 1f out: drvn and hdd ins fnl f: styd on same pce fnl 100yds* **33/1**
033 **3** 1 1/2 **Fashion Fund**[14] 6644 2-9-0 87 KevinManning 1 86
(Brian Meehan) *wl in tch in midfield: effrt u.p to press ldrs over 1f out: no ex 1f out and one pce fnl 150yds* **10/1**[3]
012 **4** shd **Oxsana**[14] 6644 2-9-0 92 TomQueally 4 87+
(William Haggas) *hld up in last quartet: effrt whn n.m.r and swtchd lft over 1f out: hdwy n.m.r again 1f out: styd on u.p fnl 150yds* **5/1**[2]
04 **5** nk **Wedding Wish (IRE)**[30] 6140 2-9-0 0 JohnnyMurtagh 14 85
(Michael Bell) *wnt lft s: chsd ldrs tl led 3f out: drvn and hdd over 1f out: unable qck 1f out: styd on same pce after* **12/1**
0216 **6** 3/4 **Aqlaam Vision**[14] 6644 2-9-0 85 JimmyFortune 3 83
(Clive Brittain) *in tch in midfield: swtchd rt and effrt u.p wl over 1f out: one pce and no imp ins fnl f* **12/1**
0310 **7** hd **Amnesia (IRE)**[14] 6644 2-9-0 75 ShaneKelly 10 83
(William Haggas) *stdd s: t.k.h: hld up in rr: rdn and hdwy over 1f out: styd on same pce u.p ins fnl f: nvr trbld ldrs* **40/1**
0 **8** nk **Broughtons Secret**[14] 6644 2-9-0 0 JamieMackay 2 82
(Willie Musson) *in tch in midfield: effrt u.p over 1f out: kpt on ins fnl f but nvr gng pce to threaten ldrs* **66/1**
12 **9** 1/2 **Night Song**[29] 6171 2-9-0 0 WilliamBuick 8 81
(John Gosden) *hld up in last pair: swtchd lft and effrt wl over 1f out: sme hdwy ent fnl f: one pce fnl 100yds: nvr trbld ldrs* **11/4**[1]
6224 **10** shd **Zawiyah**[14] 6644 2-9-0 84 AndreaAtzeni 6 80
(Luca Cumani) *chsd ldrs: effrt u.p 2f out: pressing ldrs and drvn over 1f out: no ex 1f out: wknd fnl 100yds* **20/1**
60 **11** 1/2 **Two Smart (IRE)**[14] 6644 2-9-0 0 MartinHarley 13 79
(K R Burke) *stdd s: t.k.h: hld up in tch: rdn 2f out: styng on same pce whn sltly hmpd 1f out: no imp after* **25/1**
541 **12** 1 **Flippant (IRE)**[7] 6828 2-9-0 79 SebSanders 5 76
(William Haggas) *led tl hdd and rdn 3f out: drvn and btn over 1f out: wknd ins fnl f* **14/1**
066 **13** 8 **Modify**[11] 6716 2-9-0 57 (p) JoeFanning 11 56
(Bryan Smart) *chsd ldr tl 3f out: sn rdn: lost pl over 1f out: bhd and eased wl ins fnl f* **150/1**
1m 25.19s (-0.21) **Going Correction** -0.10s/f (Good) **13** Ran SP% **117.3**
Speed ratings (Par 98): **97,96,94,94,93 93,92,92,91,91 91,90,81**
Tote Swingers: 1&2 £28.40, 1&3 £5.40, 2&3 £38.60 CSF £115.77 TOTE £3.30: £1.50, £9.20, £2.90; EX 156.90 Trifecta £1250.30 Part won. Pool: £1,667.09 - 0.01 winning units..
Owner Godolphin **Bred** Swettenham Stud **Trained** Newmarket, Suffolk
FOCUS
Stalls: far side. Drying weather and the ground had quickened up to good to firm all round. There was a breeze behind them up the straight. The stalls were on the far side and in this valuable sales race for fillies they stayed mainly centre to far side.

7017 £500,000 TATTERSALLS MILLIONS 2YO TROPHY 7f
2:20 (2:24) (Class 2) 2-Y-O
£270,550 (£110,700; £49,250; £24,550; £12,300; £4,900) **Stalls** Low

Form RPR
22 **1** **Oklahoma City**[6] 6884 2-9-3 0 (b) JosephO'Brien 18 100+
(A P O'Brien, Ire) *chsd ldrs: clsd 1/2-way: led over 2f out: hrd pressed and rdn wl over 1f out: styd on wl and asserted ins fnl f* **3/1**[2]
51 **2** 1 1/2 **Postponed (IRE)**[52] 5405 2-9-3 85 AndreaAtzeni 10 96+
(Luca Cumani) *hld up in tch in midfield: rdn and effrt 2f out: hdwy to chse ldrs 1f out: swtchd rt ins fnl f: styd on wl to go 2nd last strides* **16/1**
234 **3** nk **Bon Voyage**[14] 6645 2-9-3 89 DaneO'Neill 1 95
(Richard Hannon) *hld up in tch in midfield: hdwy u.p wl over 1f out: chsd ldrs and swtchd rt ins fnl f: wnt 2nd towards fin: no imp on wnr and lost 2nd last strides* **25/1**
214 **4** hd **Hunters Creek (IRE)**[35] 6002 2-9-3 79 WilliamBuick 11 94
(John Gosden) *chsd ldrs: rdn and chsd ldng pair wl over 1f out: edgd rt u.p: kpt on but nt pce of wnr whn wnt 2nd wl ins fnl f: one pce and lost 2 pls towards fin* **25/1**
4542 **5** nk **Jallota**[14] 6645 2-9-3 112 MartinHarley 16 94
(Mick Channon) *hld up in tch in midfield: clsd to join ldrs 3f out: chsd wnr and drvn wl over 1f out: sn ev ch tl no ex and lost 2nd wl ins fnl f: one pce and lost 2 pls towards fin* **7/1**[3]
321 **6** 2 **Toofi (FR)**[14] 6645 2-9-3 98 JohnnyMurtagh 14 88
(Roger Varian) *hld up towards rr: rdn over 2f out: hdwy u.p but stl plenty to do over 1f out: kpt on steadily ins fnl f: nvr trbld ldrs* **5/2**[1]
1 **7** 3/4 **Ensuring**[36] 5957 2-9-3 0 ShaneKelly 6 86+
(James Fanshawe) *hld up towards rr: effrt and switching rt over 1f out: kpt on steadily ins fnl f: nvr trbld ldrs* **12/1**
26 **8** 3 1/2 **Quickaswecan**[14] 6645 2-9-3 0 JimmyFortune 13 77
(Mark Johnston) *towards rr: rdn and effrt over 2f out: sme hdwy over 1f out: styd on same pce fnl f: nvr trbld ldrs* **33/1**
511 **9** shd **Signposted (IRE)**[17] 6529 2-9-3 90 TomQueally 4 77
(Andrew Balding) *t.k.h: hld up in tch in midfield: short of room: hmpd and lost pl over 2f out: forced to switch rt and then pushed further rt over 1f out: sme hdwy 1f out: kpt on but no threat to ldrs* **9/1**
61 **10** 1/2 **Extremity (IRE)**[14] 6635 2-9-3 82 MartinDwyer 8 75
(Hugo Palmer) *wl in tch in midfield: clsd to chse ldrs 3f out: rdn and unable qck 2f out: wknd ent fnl f* **11/1**
20U0 **11** 2 3/4 **Regiment**[14] 6645 2-9-3 82 LeeTopliss 15 68
(Richard Fahey) *in tch in midfield: rdn and effrt over 2f out: sn drvn and outpcd 2f out: no threat to ldrs after* **100/1**
0 **12** 2 3/4 **Sir Guy Porteous (IRE)**[14] 6645 2-9-3 0 SebSanders 12 60
(Mark Johnston) *led tl over 2f out: sn rdn and struggling: lost pl wl over 1f out: sn wknd* **66/1**
0213 **13** 1/2 **Muir Lodge**[14] 6645 2-9-3 93 (t) JimCrowley 17 59
(Andrew Balding) *stdd s: hld up in rr: effrt 2f out: no imp over 1f out: wknd fnl f* **20/1**
2160 **14** 2 **Lanark (IRE)**[14] 6645 2-9-3 94 JoeFanning 9 54
(Mark Johnston) *chsd ldr tl 3f out: lost pl u.p and btn over 2f out: bhd over 1f out* **33/1**
0 **15** 2 3/4 **Newton's Law (IRE)**[14] 6645 2-9-3 0 (t) KevinManning 3 46
(Brian Meehan) *t.k.h: wl in tch in midfield: rdn and struggling over 2f out: wknd over 1f out: no ch and eased ins fnl f* **50/1**
0001 **16** 2 **Fiftyshadesfreed (IRE)**[10] 6749 2-9-3 65 SeanLevey 5 41
(George Baker) *wl in tch in midfield tl rdn and lost pl over 2f out: bhd over 1f out* **100/1**
052 **P** **Maxie T**[14] 6635 2-9-3 74 MartinLane 2
(Mark Johnston) *bhd: eased over 5f out: sn t.o: eventually p.u and dismntd over 2f out* **100/1**
1m 23.66s (-1.74) **Going Correction** -0.10s/f (Good) **17** Ran SP% **122.7**
Speed ratings (Par 101): **105,103,102,102,102 100,99,95,95,94 91,88,87,85,82 79,**
Tote Swingers: 1&2 £20.90, 1&3 £15.00, 2&3 £101.60 CSF £46.24 TOTE £3.60: £1.60, £5.10, £6.70; EX 57.40 Trifecta £1200.60 Part won. Pool: £1,600.83 - 0.03 winning units..
Owner Derrick Smith & Mrs John Magnier & Michael Tabor **Bred** Meon Valley Stud **Trained** Ballydoyle, Co Tipperary
FOCUS
This sales race was run in a time 1.53sec quicker than the fillies' one that opened the card.

7018 CHRIS BLACKWELL MEMORIAL H'CAP 1m
2:55 (2:57) (Class 2) (0-105,105) 3-Y-0+ **£12,291** (£3,657; £1,827; £913) **Stalls** Low

Form RPR
3541 **1** **Mabait**[9] 6767 7-8-2 91 oh2 ShelleyBirkett(5) 1 99
(David Simcock) *hld up in tch in midfield: effrt to chse ldrs 1f out: n.m.r ins fnl f: qcknd through narrow gap between rivals to ld fnl 50yds: r.o wl* **5/1**[3]
2004 **2** 1/2 **Validus**[17] 6530 4-9-2 100 AndreaAtzeni 6 107
(Luca Cumani) *chsd ldr: rdn to ld over 1f out: hrd pressed and drvn ins fnl f: r.o wl tl hdd and no ex fnl 50yds* **3/1**[1]
6210 **3** nk **Mister Music**[10] 6742 4-8-12 99 (b) WilliamTwiston-Davies(3) 3 105
(Richard Hannon) *chsd ldng pair: swtchd lft and effrt over 1f out: drvn to chse wnr 1f out: ev ch ins fnl f: carried lft and unable qck cl home* **10/1**
3040 **4** 3 **Trail Blaze (IRE)**[14] 6621 4-8-11 95 (p) JimmyFortune 7 94
(Kevin Ryan) *led: rdn and hdd over 1f out: no ex u.p 1f out: wknd ins fnl f* **10/3**[2]
1000 **5** 3/4 **Directorship**[56] 5255 7-8-13 97 DaneO'Neill 9 95
(Patrick Chamings) *stdd after s: hld up in last pair: rdn and no hdwy over 1f out: styd on ins fnl f: no threat to ldrs* **7/1**
2130 **6** 3/4 **Intrigo**[56] 5287 3-8-9 96 SeanLevey 8 92
(Richard Hannon) *in tch in midfield: effrt 2f out: no ex and outpcd over 1f out: wl hld and plugged on same pce fnl f* **7/1**
-0U0 **7** 1 1/4 **Fort Bastion (IRE)**[15] 6595 4-9-4 102 WilliamBuick 2 95
(Richard Fahey) *s.i.s: hld up in last pair: rdn and no hdwy over 1f out: n.d but kpt on again ins fnl f* **7/1**
1m 37.44s (-1.16) **Going Correction** -0.10s/f (Good)
WFA 3 from 4yo+ 3lb **7** Ran SP% **111.3**
Speed ratings (Par 109): **101,100,100,97,96 95,94**
Tote Swingers: 1&2 £2.50, 1&3 £11.90, 2&3 £5.80 CSF £19.25 CT £137.92 TOTE £5.70: £2.90, £2.40; EX 21.30 Trifecta £50.80 Pool: £1,253.17 - 18.48 winning units..
Owner Khalifa Dasmal **Bred** L A C Ashby Newhall Estate Farm **Trained** Newmarket, Suffolk
FOCUS
A really competitive little handicap, but the form is a bit muddling. The winner rates closer to last year's form.

7019 TBA NEXT GENERATION CLUB EBF MAIDEN STKS 1m
3:35 (3:35) (Class 4) 2-Y-O **£4,528** (£1,347; £673; £336) **Stalls** Low

Form RPR
1 **Seagull Star** 2-9-5 0 JoeFanning 3 82+
(William Haggas) *in tch in midfield: hdwy to chse ldrs 2f out: rdn and ev ch over 1f out: led jst ins fnl f: r.o wl: rdn out* **22/1**
50 **2** 1 1/4 **Rasameel (USA)**[36] 5941 2-9-5 0 DaneO'Neill 7 79
(J W Hills) *chsd ldr: rdn and ev ch wl over 1f out: drvn and led jst over 1f out: hdd jst ins fnl f: one pce fnl 100yds* **33/1**
4 **3** nk **Venezia (IRE)**[22] 6355 2-9-5 0 TomQueally 4 78
(Lady Cecil) *chsd ldrs: 5th and outpcd whn edgd rt over 1f out: rallied and swtchd lft ins fnl f: styd on wl towards fin* **15/8**[1]
4 3/4 **Johann Strauss** 2-9-5 0 JosephO'Brien 9 78+
(A P O'Brien, Ire) *hld up in tch in rr: stl last 2f out: shkn up and hdwy but stl plenty to do jst over 1f out: r.o strly under hands and heels ins fnl f: nt rch ldrs* **5/2**[2]
5 **5** 1/2 **Mountain Lion (IRE)**[36] 5941 2-9-5 0 ChrisCatlin 13 75
(Saeed bin Suroor) *led: rdn over 2f out: drvn and hdd jst over 1f out: styd on same pce ins fnl f: lost 2 pls towards fin* **8/1**
6 1 3/4 **Wannabe Yours (IRE)** 2-9-5 0 WilliamBuick 6 71
(John Gosden) *t.k.h: in tch in midfield: rdn 2f out: outpcd whn rn green and edgd rt over 1f out: no threat to ldrs but kpt on again ins fnl f* **12/1**
00 **7** 1 **Excellent Royale (IRE)**[15] 6581 2-9-5 0 MartinHarley 14 69
(Charles Hills) *t.k.h: hld up in tch in midfield: rdn and chal wl over 1f out: no ex over 1f out: wknd ins fnl f* **80/1**
8 1 1/2 **Dance Of Heroes** 2-9-5 0 JohnnyMurtagh 1 65
(Jeremy Noseda) *hld up wl in tch towards rr: rdn and outpcd ent fnl 2f: kpt on same pce fr over 1f out* **13/2**[3]
9 1 **Battersea** 2-9-5 0 AndreaAtzeni 2 63
(Roger Varian) *dwlt: hld up wl in tch towards rr: rdn over 2f out: outpcd and btn 2f out: n.d but plugged on ins fnl f* **16/1**

10 ½ **Indus River (IRE)** 2-9-5 0 .... MartinLane 12 62
(Charlie Appleby) *hld up in tch towards rr: rdn and effrt over 2f out: outpcd and wl hld whn rn green and edgd rt wl over 1f out: n.d* **16/1**

0 11 ½ **Clodoaldo (IRE)**[62] 5033 2-9-5 0 .... SeanLevey 11 61
(Brian Meehan) *in tch in midfield: rdn and unable qck 2f out: outpcd and btn over 1f out: wknd fnl f* **50/1**

12 7 **Protected** 2-9-5 0 .... JimmyFortune 10 45
(Richard Hannon) *in tch in midfield: rdn and lost pl over 2f out: bhd over 1f out* **33/1**

U **Worthy Spirit (GER)** 2-9-5 0 .... ShaneKelly 15
(Andrew Balding) *v free to post: v.s.a, veered lft and uns rdr leaving stalls* **66/1**

1m 39.24s (0.64) **Going Correction** -0.10s/f (Good) 13 Ran SP% **122.2**
Speed ratings (Par 97): **92,90,90,89,89 87,86,84,83,83 82,75,**
Tote Swingers: 1&2 £69.00, 1&3 £14.90, 2&3 £8.00 CSF £590.41 TOTE £22.70: £5.30, £6.20, £1.10; EX 913.60 Trifecta £749.60 Part won. Pool: £999.53 - 0.03 winning units..
Owner Tony Bloom **Bred** Meon Valley Stud **Trained** Newmarket, Suffolk

FOCUS
This looked an interesting maiden on paper, featuring several with eyecatching pedigrees.

7020 TRM PRIDE STKS (LISTED RACE) (F&M) 1m 2f
4:10 (4:13) (Class 1) 3-Y-O+

£20,982 (£7,955; £3,981; £1,983; £995; £499) **Stalls** Low

Form RPR

0230 1 **Sound Hearts (USA)**[77] 4532 4-9-2 95 .... AndreaAtzeni 14 104
(Roger Varian) *racd in centre: led gp and chsd overall ldr tl led overall 3f out: rdn 2f out: clr over 1f out: r.o wl* **12/1**

136 2 1¾ **Cushion**[19] 6484 3-8-11 97 .... WilliamBuick 1 103+
(John Gosden) *racd on far side: hld up in tch in midfield: rdn and swtchd lft over 1f out: styd on u.p to go 2nd towards fin: no ch w wnr* **3/1**[1]

6026 3 ½ **Reyaadah**[35] 6000 3-8-11 101 .... DaneO'Neill 15 100
(Charles Hills) *racd in centre: t.k.h: hld up in tch in midfield: rdn and effrt over 2f out: chsd wnr over 1f out: kpt on: lost 2nd towards fin* **18/1**

0005 4 4 **Agent Allison**[17] 6536 3-8-11 95 .... JimCrowley 10 92
(Peter Chapple-Hyam) *racd on far side: chsd ldrs: led gp and chsd wnr over 2f out: 3rd and btn wl over 1f out: wknd but hld on to 4th fnl f* **10/1**

1134 5 1 **Rock Choir**[17] 6536 3-8-11 94 .... SebSanders 8 90
(William Haggas) *racd on far side: hld up in tch in rr: rdn and effrt over 2f out: no imp over 1f out: nvr trbld ldrs* **4/1**[2]

241 6 2¾ **Tuscania**[17] 6537 5-9-2 88 .... SeanLevey 9 84
(Lucy Wadham) *racd in centre: hld up in rr: rdn and effrt over 2f out: no imp 2f out: sn wknd* **20/1**

0624 7 ½ **Gertrude Versed**[52] 5402 3-8-11 93 .... MarcHalford 11 83
(John Gosden) *racd in centre: hld up towards rr: rdn and no hdwy whn hung rt 2f out: sn wknd* **12/1**

2056 8 nk **Westwiththenight (IRE)**[17] 6530 4-9-2 92 .... JohnnyMurtagh 12 82
(William Haggas) *racd in centre: chsd ldrs: rdn and unable qck over 2f out: sn struggling: wknd wl over 1f out* **17/2**

2534 9 hd **Jathabah (IRE)**[23] 6329 3-8-11 97 .... JimmyFortune 4 82
(Clive Brittain) *racd on far side: overall ldr tl rdn and hdd 3f out: wknd wl over 1f out: bhd fnl f* **16/1**

1034 10 2½ **Great Timing (USA)**[28] 6188 3-8-11 94 .... MartinLane 3 77
(Charlie Appleby) *racd on far side: t.k.h: hld up in midfield: rdn and no hdwy over 2f out: wknd 2f out: bhd fnl f* **8/1**[3]

421 U **Bonanza Creek (IRE)**[50] 5478 3-8-11 89 .... JoeFanning 7
(Luca Cumani) *stmbld: uns rdr sn after leaving stalls* **8/1**[3]

2m 2.33s (-3.47) **Going Correction** -0.10s/f (Good)
WFA 3 from 4yo+ 5lb 11 Ran SP% **118.1**
Speed ratings (Par 111): **109,107,107,104,103 101,100,100,100,98**
Tote Swingers: 1&2 £11.60, 1&3 £72.60, 2&3 £14.20 CSF £48.18 TOTE £14.70: £3.70, £2.00, £3.30; EX 65.80 Trifecta £1298.00 Part won. Pool: £1,730.72 - 0.09 winning units..
Owner Y Masuda **Bred** M A Co , Ltd **Trained** Newmarket, Suffolk

FOCUS
Bonanza Creek unseated soon after the start and the ten who were left split into two groups of five, one racing on the far rail and the other up the centre. There was no pace on early. Ordinary form for the grade.

7021 EBF NATIONAL STUD BOADICEA FILLIES' STKS (LISTED RACE) 6f
4:45 (4:48) (Class 1) 3-Y-O+

£22,684 (£8,600; £4,304; £2,144; £1,076; £540) **Stalls** Low

Form RPR

3033 1 **Mince**[27] 6235 4-8-13 101 ....(p) JohnnyMurtagh 15 110
(Roger Charlton) *travelled wl: chsd ldrs: hdwy to join ldrs on bit 2f out: rdn to ld over 1f out: in command and r.o wl ins fnl f* **11/4**[1]

4123 2 1½ **Winning Express (IRE)**[23] 6327 3-9-1 105 .... SeanLevey 7 108
(Ed McMahon) *in tch in midfield: rdn and effrt wl over 1f out: swtchd rt and hdwy over 1f out: chsd wnr ins fnl f: r.o but no imp on wnr* **5/1**[2]

014 3 ¾ **The Gold Cheongsam (IRE)**[64] 4949 3-8-12 102 .....(t) WilliamBuick 10 103
(Jeremy Noseda) *hld up in tch towards rr: rdn and hdwy over 1f out: kpt on wl ins fnl f to go 3rd wl ins fnl f: no threat to wnr* **5/1**[2]

1225 4 1¼ **Minalisa**[35] 5984 4-8-13 101 .... ChrisCatlin 5 99
(Rae Guest) *chsd ldrs: rdn over 2f out: pressing ldrs and drvn over 1f out: no ex and outpcd ins fnl f* **12/1**

0010 5 nse **Angels Will Fall (IRE)**[14] 6639 4-8-13 100 .... DaneO'Neill 12 99
(Charles Hills) *stdd s: hld up in tch in rr: nt clr run 2f out: swtchd lft and effrt wl over 1f out: styd on wl ins fnl f: nt rch ldrs* **11/1**

1243 6 ½ **Midnight Flower (IRE)**[43] 5700 3-8-12 95 .... JoeFanning 9 97
(David Simcock) *chsd ldr tl 2f out: sn drvn: outpcd and losing pl whn sltly hmpd ent fnl f: styd on same pce after* **14/1**

1230 7 nk **La Fortunata**[9] 6768 6-8-13 93 .... AndreaAtzeni 8 96
(Mike Murphy) *led: rdn wl over 1f out: hdd over 1f out: lost 2nd and no ex jst ins fnl f: wknd wl ins fnl f* **40/1**

2010 8 1¼ **Miss Lahar**[14] 6639 4-9-2 102 .... MartinHarley 1 95
(Mick Channon) *hld up in tch in midfield: nt clr run wl over 1f out: hdwy u.p ins fnl f: kpt on fnl 100yds: nvr trbld ldrs* **25/1**

13 9 ¾ **Reqaaba**[9] 6768 3-8-12 85 .... MartinLane 3 90
(Robert Cowell) *hld up in tch towards rr: nt clr run and swtchd rt over 1f out: drvn and effrt 1f out: no imp* **16/1**

-222 10 ½ **Gracia Directa (GER)**[55] 5-8-13 101 .... TomQueally 6 88
(D Moser, Germany) *taken down early: chsd ldr tl 1/2-way: struggling to qckn u.p 2f out: btn ent fnl f: wknd ins fnl f* **13/2**[3]

2351 11 1 **Jubilante**[16] 6564 3-8-12 87 .... JimmyFortune 14 85
(Hughie Morrison) *stdd s: hld up in tch in rr: clsd over 2f out: rdn and no imp 2f out: nvr trbld ldrs* **33/1**

1011 12 4 **Hopes N Dreams (IRE)**[12] 6685 5-8-13 99 .... SeamieHeffernan 13 72
(Kevin Ryan) *chsd ldrs: rdn 3f out: lost pl and btn 2f out: bhd over 1f out* **20/1**

0461 13 ¾ **Finesse**[33] 6045 4-8-13 80 .... JimCrowley 2 70
(Ralph Beckett) *stdd s: hld up in tch in midfield: hdwy 3f out: rdn and no hdwy wl over 1f out: fdd ins fnl f* **66/1**

2020 14 nse **Links Drive Lady**[14] 6621 5-8-13 88 .... MartinDwyer 11 70
(Dean Ivory) *awkward leaving stalls and pushed along early: in tch towards rr: hdwy 3f out: no prog u.p wl over 1f out: fdd ins fnl f* **50/1**

1m 10.52s (-1.68) **Going Correction** -0.10s/f (Good)
WFA 3 from 4yo+ 1lb 14 Ran SP% **119.3**
Speed ratings (Par 108): **107,105,104,102,102 101,101,99,98,97 96,91,90,90**
Tote Swingers: 1&2 £4.00, 1&3 £3.90, 2&3 £6.40 CSF £14.33 TOTE £3.40: £1.40, £2.00, £2.40; EX 16.40 Trifecta £97.40 Pool: £3,098.14 - 23.85 winning units..
Owner Lady Rothschild **Bred** The Rt Hon Lord Rothschild **Trained** Beckhampton, Wilts

7022 FLUID POWER SERVICES LIVERPOOL 25TH ANNIVERSARY H'CAP 1m 2f
5:15 (5:19) (Class 2) (0-100,92) 3-Y-O

£12,450 (£3,728; £1,864; £932; £466; £234) **Stalls** Low

Form RPR

1145 1 **Breden (IRE)**[22] 6356 3-9-2 87 .... WilliamBuick 6 95
(John Gosden) *t.k.h: hld up in midfield tl hdwy to chse after 2f: led over 2f out and qcknd gallop: clr and in command fr over 1f out: r.o wl: eased nr fin* **11/4**[2]

1-1 2 1¾ **Ajman Bridge**[16] 6563 3-9-5 90 .... AndreaAtzeni 2 95
(Luca Cumani) *t.k.h: chsd ldrs: rdn whn gallop qcknd ent fnl 2f: chsd clr wnr ins fnl f: r.o but no threat to wnr* **2/1**[1]

5100 3 ¾ **Hunting Ground (USA)**[11] 6729 3-8-7 78 .... JoeFanning 1 82
(Mark Johnston) *led and set stdy gallop: hdd and rdn jst over 2f out: outpcd by wnr and 3 l 2nd over 1f out: kpt on same pce and lost 2nd ins fnl f* **20/1**

4061 4 nse **Miss Marjurie (IRE)**[45] 5632 3-8-10 81 .... MartinDwyer 5 84
(Denis Coakley) *t.k.h: hld up in tch in midfield: rdn and effrt whn gallop qcknd jst over 2f out: styd on ins fnl f: no threat to wnr* **20/1**

2203 5 ½ **Aussie Reigns (IRE)**[6] 6868 3-9-7 92 ....(v) JimCrowley 7 95
(William Knight) *stdd s: t.k.h: hld up in last pair: rdn and effrt wl over 1f out: kpt on ins fnl f: no threat to wnr* **8/1**

4052 6 ½ **Cruck Realta**[7] 6832 3-9-5 90 .... MartinHarley 4 92
(Mick Channon) *t.k.h: chsd ldr for 2f: 4th and rdn jst over 2f out: no imp and one pce fnl f* **10/1**

2112 7 ¾ **Mahican (IRE)**[17] 6537 3-9-5 90 .... JohnnyMurtagh 3 90
(Mark Johnston) *stdd s: hld up in last pair: rdn and effrt ent fnl 2f: styd on but n.d* **7/2**[3]

2m 8.94s (3.14) **Going Correction** -0.10s/f (Good) 7 Ran SP% **111.9**
Speed ratings (Par 107): **83,81,81,80,80 80,79**
Tote Swingers: 1&2 £1.90, 1&3 £10.70, 2&3 £7.70 CSF £8.28 TOTE £3.80: £2.10, £1.20; EX 11.30 Trifecta £88.70 Pool: £3,424.49 - 28.93 winning units..
Owner Lady Rothschild **Bred** Mrs C L Weld **Trained** Newmarket, Suffolk

FOCUS
The topweight was rated 8lb below the ceiling for the race. The early gallop was steady.
T/Plt: £79.20 to a £1 stake. Pool: £107,519.79 - 990.79 winning tickets. T/Qpdt: £6.50 to a £1 stake. Pool: £4,978.60 - 560.70 winning tickets. SP

6754 REDCAR (L-H)
Saturday, October 5

OFFICIAL GOING: Good to firm (good in places; 9.2)
Wind: Virtually nil Weather: Cloudy with sunny periods

7023 BRITISH STALLION STUDS SUPPORTING BRITISH RACING EBF MAIDEN STKS 7f
1:40 (1:40) (Class 5) 2-Y-O

£2,911 (£866; £432; £216) **Stalls** Centre

Form RPR

2 1 **Erroneous (IRE)**[71] 4731 2-9-5 0 .... FrederikTylicki 17 77+
(David Simcock) *sn led: mde most: jnd and rdn over 1f out: drvn and edgd lft last 100yds: hld on wl towards fin* **11/8**[1]

62 2 nk **Alisios (GR)**[25] 6277 2-9-5 0 .... KirstyMilczarek 5 76+
(Luca Cumani) *midfield: hdwy to trck ldrs wl over 2f out: effrt wl over 1f out: rdn to chal and ev ch appr fnl f: sn drvn and no ex towards fin* **3/1**[2]

0 3 1¼ **Mindblowing**[10] 6754 2-9-5 0 .... FMBerry 6 73+
(Kevin Ryan) *midfield: hdwy over 2f out: chsd ldrs and swtchd rt over 1f out: sn rdn and kpt on fnl f: nrst fin* **25/1**

4 ¾ **Saranta** 2-9-0 0 .... TonyHamilton 2 66+
(Richard Fahey) *towards rr: hdwy on outer over 2f out: chsd ldrs over 1f out: sn rdn and kpt on fnl f: nrst fin* **20/1**

04 5 1 **Pure Amber (IRE)**[12] 6681 2-9-5 0 .... AdrianNicholls 4 68+
(Mark Johnston) *cl up: ev ch whn rdn and hung rt wl over 1f out: sn drvn and one pce fnl f* **14/1**

6 2¼ **Ryeolliean** 2-9-0 0 .... DavidBergin[(5)] 9 62
(David O'Meara) *trckd ldrs: pushed along and sltly outpcd 1/2-way: hdwy wl over 1f out: rdn and kpt on fnl f* **33/1**

0 7 1¼ **Unfinishedbusiness**[12] 6681 2-8-12 0 .... EireannCagney[(7)] 13 59
(Richard Fahey) *dwlt and towards rr: stdy hdwy on wd outside 2f out: rdn over 1f out: kpt on ins fnl f: nrst fin* **40/1**

3 8 2¼ **Smart Alec (IRE)**[9] 6769 2-9-5 0 .... AndrewMullen 16 53
(Alan Swinbank) *cl up: ev ch 2f out: sn rdn and grad wknd* **11/1**[3]

5 9 hd **Mighty Missile (IRE)**[10] 6754 2-9-5 0 .... AndrewElliott 12 52
(Tom Tate) *towards rr: hdwy wl over 2f out: rdn along and kpt on appr fnl f: nvr nr ldrs* **16/1**

0 10 2¼ **Twenty Roses (IRE)**[43] 5716 2-9-0 0 .... TomMcLaughlin 8 41
(Ed Walker) *trckd ldrs: pushed along over 2f out: sn rdn: n.m.r and swtchd rt wl over 1f out: grad wknd appr fnl f* **16/1**

3 11 6 **Tears And Rain (IRE)**[148] 2238 2-9-0 0 .... DavidAllan 10 25
(Tim Easterby) *chsd ldrs: rdn along wl over 2f out: sn wknd* **25/1**

12 3¾ **Elle West** 2-8-11 0 .... JasonHart[(3)] 18 15
(Michael Easterby) *a towards rr* **80/1**

13 ¾ **Slingsby** 2-9-5 0 .... TomEaves 11 18
(Michael Easterby) *s.i.s: a in rr* **66/1**

00 14 4 **Oriental Dream (IRE)**[8] 6790 2-9-2 0 .... DeclanCannon[(3)] 19 7
(Nigel Tinkler) *chsd ldrs to 1/2-way: sn rdn along and wknd wl over 2f out* **100/1**

The Form Book Flat, Raceform Ltd, Compton, RG20 6NL.

00 **15** ½ **Garfunkel (IRE)**[14] 6627 2-9-5 0 BarryMcHugh 15 5
(Tony Coyle) *in tch: rdn along 1/2-way: sn wknd* **100/1**
16 ½ **Molly Molone** 2-9-0 0 RaulDaSilva 1
(David Brown) *in tch: rdn along 1/2-way: sn wknd* **22/1**
17 4½ **Tawan** 2-9-5 0 DaleSwift 3
(Brian Rothwell) *sn rdn along in rr: bhd fr 1/2-way* **200/1**

1m 26.81s (2.31) **Going Correction** +0.125s/f (Good) **17** Ran SP% **121.3**
Speed ratings (Par 95): **91,90,89,88,87 84,83,80,80,77 71,66,65,61,60 60,55**
Tote Swingers: 1&2 £1.20, 1&3 £28.10, 2&3 £24.10 CSF £4.27 TOTE £2.30: £1.20, £1.70, £7.00; EX 6.20 Trifecta £85.40 Pool: £732.44 - 6.42 winning units..
Owner Mrs Fitri Hay **Bred** Raffaele Nardi **Trained** Newmarket, Suffolk
■ Stewards' Enquiry : Frederik Tylicki two-day ban; used whip above permitted level (20th-21st Oct).
Kirsty Milczarek four-day ban; used whip above permitted level (20th-23rd Oct).

FOCUS
Straightforward enough maiden form. The front pair are nice prospects and should do better than the bare form.

7024 WATCH RACING UK ON SKY 432 STRAIGHT-MILE CHAMPIONSHIP FINAL (H'CAP) 1m
2:15 (2:16) (Class 2) 3-Y-0+
£12,450 (£3,728; £1,864; £932; £466; £234) **Stalls** Centre

Form RPR
4611 **1** **Ingleby Angel (IRE)**[8] 6792 4-9-5 **90** DavidBergin(5) 17 99
(David O'Meara) *hld up: swtchd rt over 2f out: sn drvn: kpt on wl: led post* **5/1**[1]
4103 **2** *shd* **Sound Advice**[16] 6550 4-9-0 **80** TomEaves 7 89
(Keith Dalgleish) *racd keenly: trckd ldrs: led gng wl over 2f out: rdn over 1f out: sn pressed: kpt on: hdd post* **8/1**[3]
3505 **3** 2¾ **Hakuna Matata**[16] 6562 6-8-9 **75** (b) BarryMcHugh 5 78
(Michael Dods) *stmbld s: sn midfield: rdn to chse ldrs 2f out: kpt on* **16/1**
2564 **4** *nk* **Lilac Lace (IRE)**[18] 6495 3-8-12 **81** DavidAllan 18 83
(Tim Easterby) *midfield: smooth hdwy over 2f out: rdn to press ldr over 1f out: no ex ins fnl f* **14/1**
4430 **5** *hd* **Broctune Papa Gio**[3] 6943 6-8-4 **70** WayneLordan 4 72
(Keith Reveley) *hld up: rdn over 3f out: hdwy to chse ldrs over 1f out: kpt on same pce* **9/1**
2023 **6** 1 **No Dominion (IRE)**[16] 6567 4-8-8 **77** JasonHart(3) 11 76
(James Given) *dwlt: hld up: rdn and hdwy 2f out: kpt on fnl f: nvr threatened* **9/1**
0543 **7** 1¾ **Jo'Burg (USA)**[10] 6756 9-9-1 **81** FrederikTylicki 12 76
(David O'Meara) *midfield: rdn over 2f out: one pce* **16/1**
0200 **8** 2½ **Kiwi Bay**[16] 6567 8-8-4 **75** ow2 (p) KevinStott(7) 19 66
(Michael Dods) *in tch on outer: rdn over 2f out: grad wknd fnl f* **7/1**[2]
2000 **9** 3¼ **Snooky**[30] 6126 4-8-10 **76** (b[1]) TonyHamilton 15 58
(Richard Fahey) *s.i.s: hld up in rr: nvr threatened* **20/1**
0420 **10** 2¼ **Victoire De Lyphar (IRE)**[25] 6288 6-9-0 **80** (e) PhillipMakin 2 57
(Ruth Carr) *prom: rdn 3f out: wknd over 1f out* **25/1**
1430 **11** *shd* **Toto Skyllachy**[16] 6550 8-9-7 **87** MichaelO'Connell 1 64
(David O'Meara) *dwlt: sn midfield: rdn over 2f out: wknd and eased fnl f* **20/1**
5000 **12** 1¾ **Copperwood**[8] 6801 8-8-5 **71** AdrianNicholls 3 44
(Mark Johnston) *trckd ldrs: rdn 3f out: wknd fnl 2f* **25/1**
6120 **13** 1¼ **Eeny Mac (IRE)**[28] 6211 6-8-7 **73** (p) AndrewElliott 9 43
(Neville Bycroft) *prom tl wknd over 2f out* **22/1**
1502 **14** 2¼ **Surround Sound**[100] 3730 3-8-1 **70** PaulQuinn 8 34
(Tim Easterby) *hld up: a towards rr* **18/1**
5600 **15** *hd* **Jonny Lesters Hair (IRE)**[24] 6297 8-8-0 **66** oh9 (p) RaulDaSilva 14 30
(Tim Easterby) *led: rdn whn hdd over 2f out: wknd* **50/1**
5606 **16** 7 **Steelriver (IRE)**[12] 6694 3-8-2 **75** ow1 (b[1]) OisinMurphy(5) 16 24
(James Bethell) *sn chsd ldrs: wknd over 2f out* **8/1**[3]
1345 **17** 4½ **Black Rider (IRE)**[15] 6602 3-8-2 **71** (p[1]) KieranO'Neill 13 9
(Julie Camacho) *chsd ldrs: wknd over 2f out* **25/1**

1m 37.76s (1.16) **Going Correction** +0.125s/f (Good)
WFA 3 from 4yo+ 3lb **17** Ran SP% **122.5**
Speed ratings (Par 109): **99,98,96,95,95 94,92,90,87,84 84,83,81,79,79 72,67**
Tote Swingers: 1&2 £5.90, 1&3 £21.80, 2&3 £36.70 CSF £38.21 CT £630.36 TOTE £4.00: £1.30, £2.80, £5.60, £3.40; EX 52.30 Trifecta £457.60 Part won. Pool: £610.19 - 0.03 winning units..
Owner Dave Scott **Bred** Dave Scott **Trained** Nawton, N Yorks
■ Stewards' Enquiry : David Bergin seven-day ban; used whip above permitted level (19th-25th Oct).

FOCUS
An ultra-competitive handicap and again the centre of the track was favoured. The winner continues to progress and the first pair were clear.

7025 TOTESCOOP6 EBF GUISBOROUGH STKS (LISTED RACE) 7f
2:50 (2:50) (Class 1) 3-Y-0+
£22,684 (£8,600; £4,304; £2,144; £1,076; £540) **Stalls** Centre

Form RPR
21 **1** **Top Notch Tonto (IRE)**[28] 6191 3-9-3 112 DaleSwift 5 117
(Brian Ellison) *cl up: led 2f out: rdn over 1f out: drvn and edgd lft fnl f: hld on gamely* **5/1**[2]
-244 **2** 1¼ **Caspar Netscher**[21] 6392 4-9-0 110 FrederikTylicki 8 110
(David Simcock) *trckd ldrs: hdwy 2f out: effrt and nt clr run over 1f out: sn swtchd lft and rdn to chal ent fnl f: sn drvn and ev ch tl n.m.r last 100yds and no ex towards fin* **2/1**[1]
3053 **3** 4 **You Da One (IRE)**[21] 6384 3-8-12 87 OisinMurphy 1 98
(Andrew Balding) *trckd ldng pair: effrt over 2f out: sn rdn and edgd rt: drvn and one pce appr fnl f* **20/1**
0040 **4** *hd* **Dandy Boy (ITY)**[21] 6414 7-9-0 103 WayneLordan 7 98
(David Marnane, Ire) *stdd s and hld up in rr: hdwy wl over 2f out: rdn to chse ldrs appr fnl f: kpt on same pce* **8/1**
4506 **5** 4 **Galician**[28] 6183 4-8-9 100 AdrianNicholls 2 82
(Mark Johnston) *prom: rdn along on outer 3f out: drvn and wknd 2f out* **10/1**
5212 **6** ½ **Dutch Rose (IRE)**[24] 6300 4-8-9 99 FMBerry 6 81
(David O'Meara) *chsd ldrs: rdn along 3f out: sn wknd* **6/1**[3]
3-10 **7** 5 **Taayel (IRE)**[42] 5747 3-8-12 105 NickyMackay 9 72
(John Gosden) *hld up in rr: effrt and sme hdwy on wd outside 3f out: sn rdn and n.d* **12/1**
0023 **8** 5 **Firebeam**[15] 6595 5-9-0 104 AhmedAjtebi 4 59
(Charlie Appleby) *led: rdn along 3f out: hdd 2f out and sn wknd* **7/1**
61-0 **9** 3½ **Royal Rascal**[143] 2368 3-8-7 100 DavidAllan 3 44
(Tim Easterby) *chsd ldrs: rdn along 1/2-way: sn wknd* **50/1**

1m 24.04s (-0.46) **Going Correction** +0.125s/f (Good)
WFA 3 from 4yo+ 2lb **9** Ran SP% **111.4**
Speed ratings (Par 111): **107,105,101,100,96 95,89,84,80**
Tote Swingers: 1&2 £2.90, 1&3 £5.50, 2&3 £5.20 CSF £14.56 TOTE £6.80: £1.80, £1.30, £3.80; EX 17.40 Trifecta £156.10 Pool: £1,920.20 - 9.22 winning units..
Owner Keith Brown **Bred** Seamus Finucane **Trained** Norton, N Yorks
■ Stewards' Enquiry : Dale Swift caution; careless riding.

FOCUS
An average Listed event.

7026 TOTEPOOL TWO-YEAR-OLD TROPHY (LISTED RACE) 6f
3:30 (3:31) (Class 1) 2-Y-0
£93,231 (£35,346; £17,689; £8,811; £4,422; £2,219) **Stalls** Centre

Form RPR
2033 **1** **Ventura Mist**[14] 6622 2-8-7 97 (p) DavidAllan 13 96
(Tim Easterby) *trckd ldrs: hdwy over 2f out: chal over 1f out: sn rdn and styd on to ld ins fnl f* **10/1**
5122 **2** *nk* **Emirates Flyer**[35] 5999 2-9-2 104 AhmedAjtebi 16 104
(Saeed bin Suroor) *trckd ldrs: hdwy 1/2-way: led 2f out: rdn over 1f out: drvn and hdd ins fnl f: kpt on* **5/1**[1]
5061 **3** *nk* **Morning Post**[23] 6328 2-9-2 104 (b) FMBerry 14 103
(Kevin Ryan) *hld up towards rr: hdwy over 2f out: rdn over 1f out: styd on strly fnl f* **20/1**
1122 **4** 2 **Mecca's Angel (IRE)**[15] 6584 2-8-9 97 TomEaves 6 90
(Michael Dods) *cl up: effrt 2f out: sn rdn and ev ch tl drvn and one pce ins fnl f* **12/1**
5262 **5** ¾ **The Hooded Claw (IRE)**[7] 6842 2-8-12 77 DaleSwift 1 91
(Tim Easterby) *hld up and bhd: hdwy 2f out: sn rdn: styd on wl fnl f: nrst fin* **100/1**
0620 **6** ½ **Azagal (IRE)**[14] 6622 2-8-4 91 BarryMcHugh 4 81
(Tim Easterby) *prom towards outer: effrt 2f out: sn rdn and one pce fnl f* **12/1**
5206 **7** *nk* **Anticipated (IRE)**[14] 6637 2-8-12 106 KieranO'Neill 12 89
(Richard Hannon) *trckd ldrs: effrt over 2f out: rdn wl over 1f out: kpt on same pce* **7/1**[3]
010 **8** *hd* **Trading Profit**[14] 6637 2-8-12 103 OisinMurphy 17 88
(Andrew Balding) *in tch: effrt over 2f out: sn rdn and kpt on same pce* **11/2**[2]
2221 **9** 2¾ **Lincoln (IRE)**[15] 6581 2-8-12 83 BenCurtis 7 80
(Mick Channon) *led: rdn along 1/2-way: hdd 2f out: grad wknd* **28/1**
3222 **10** *hd* **Urban Dreamer (IRE)**[8] 6791 2-8-9 77 (b) AndrewElliott 20 76
(Rod Millman) *racd nr stands' rail: dwlt and bhd: gd hdwy 2f out: sn rdn and kpt on u.p fnl f* **66/1**
0 **11** *nse* **Celtic Man (IRE)**[8] 6811 2-9-0 0 (b[1]) WayneLordan 10 81
(David Marnane, Ire) *chsd ldrs: rdn along over 2f out: wknd fnl f* **33/1**
1 **12** 1 **Comino (IRE)**[28] 6206 2-8-9 0 ChrisHayes 21 73
(Kevin Ryan) *racd towards stands' rail: chsd ldrs: rdn along 1/2-way: wknd over 2f out* **16/1**
5515 **13** *nk* **One Boy (IRE)**[8] 6791 2-8-6 76 JasonHart 9 69
(Michael Dods) *chsd ldrs: rdn along 1/2-way: sn wknd* **80/1**
1620 **14** ½ **Muspelheim**[8] 6791 2-8-6 78 RowanScott 8 68
(Ann Duffield) *chsd ldrs: rdn along 2f out: grad wknd* **125/1**
262 **15** ½ **Red Pike (IRE)**[12] 6681 2-8-12 77 (v) PhillipMakin 18 72
(Bryan Smart) *chsd ldrs: rdn along 1/2-way: wknd over 2f out* **100/1**
2106 **16** ½ **Lexington Rose**[8] 6791 2-8-1 77 RaulDaSilva 15 60
(Bryan Smart) *cl up: rdn along over 2f out: sn drvn and wknd* **66/1**
1060 **17** *shd* **Ben Hall (IRE)**[23] 6328 2-9-0 98 NickyMackay 5 72
(John Gosden) *in tch: rdn along over 2f out: sn wknd* **14/1**
4111 **18** ½ **Deeds Not Words (IRE)**[8] 6791 2-9-2 92 FrederikTylicki 22 73
(Mick Channon) *racd towards stands' rail: in tch: rdn along 1/2-way: sn wknd* **12/1**
0306 **19** *nk* **Foxy Clarets (IRE)**[15] 6582 2-8-9 79 TonyHamilton 23 65
(Richard Fahey) *prom: rdn along wl over 2f out: sn wknd* **80/1**
2231 **20** 3¾ **Omaha Gold (IRE)**[16] 6561 2-8-4 78 JimmyQuinn 19 49
(Bryan Smart) *prom: rdn along wl over 2f out: sn wknd* **20/1**
1110 **21** 4½ **Viva Verglas (IRE)**[44] 5679 2-8-12 94 AndrewMullen 2 43
(David Barron) *prom on wd outside: rdn along wl over 2f out: sn wknd* **33/1**
3320 **22** 4 **Atlantic Affair (IRE)**[23] 6326 2-8-7 80 AdrianNicholls 11 26
(Mark Johnston) *cl up: rdn along 1/2-way: sn wknd* **80/1**
5311 **23** ¾ **See The Sun**[18] 6493 2-8-9 88 MichaelO'Connell 3 26
(Tim Easterby) *chsd ldrs: rdn along wl over 2f out: sn wknd* **12/1**

1m 12.19s (0.39) **Going Correction** +0.125s/f (Good) **23** Ran SP% **125.3**
Speed ratings (Par 103): **102,101,101,98,97 96,96,96,92,92 92,90,90,89,89 88,88,87,87,82 76,70,69**
Tote Swingers: 1&2 £11.50, 1&3 £33.10, 2&3 £42.70 CSF £53.58 TOTE £13.20: £3.80, £2.00, £7.50; EX 83.50 Trifecta £1368.00 Pool: £2,006.47 - 1.10 winning units..
Owner Middleham Park Racing Xxiv **Bred** Bumble Bloodstock & C Liesack **Trained** Great Habton, N Yorks
■ Stewards' Enquiry : Barry McHugh two-day ban; used whip above permitted level (20th-21st Oct).
Jason Hart two-day ban; used whip above permitted level (20th-21st Oct).

FOCUS
A typically well-contested running of this 2-y-o Listed prize and it served up a thrilling finish.

7027 WIN A VIP DAY OUT @ REDCARRACING.CO.UK (S) STKS 1m 2f
4:00 (4:00) (Class 5) 3-5-Y-0 **£2,587** (£770; £384; £192) **Stalls** Low

Form RPR
0013 **1** **Bling King**[5] 6909 4-9-2 70 KevinStott(7) 9 79
(Geoffrey Harker) *trckd ldr: rdn over 2f out: led over 1f out: kpt on to go clr: eased towards fin* **5/2**[1]
0002 **2** 3 **Sunnybridge Boy (IRE)**[10] 6759 4-9-3 63 FMBerry 11 67
(K R Burke) *in tch: hdwy to ld narrowly over 2f out: sn rdn: hdd over 1f out: one pce and sn no ch w wnr* **10/3**[2]
0504 **3** 9 **Certral**[10] 6756 5-8-12 65 BarryMcHugh 5 45
(Mel Brittain) *trckd ldr: rdn over 2f out: sn one pce in poor 3rd* **7/1**[3]
3001 **4** 2¼ **Auto Mac**[10] 6759 5-9-6 62 JasonHart(3) 4 52
(Neville Bycroft) *s.i.s: hld up: rdn over 3f out: wnt remote 4th over 1f out: nvr threatened ldrs* **9/1**
6006 **5** *nk* **Waltz Darling (IRE)**[10] 6756 5-9-3 66 TomEaves 7 45
(Keith Reveley) *dwlt: hld up: rdn over 3f out: nvr threatened ldrs* **28/1**
1620 **6** 5 **Harbinger Lass**[14] 6657 3-8-13 62 FrederikTylicki 1 37
(Mick Channon) *led: rdn whn hdd over 2f out: wknd* **10/3**[2]

06 **7** ¾ **Hilda Ogden (IRE)**[10] 6759 3-8-7 0 PaulQuinn 3 29
(David Nicholls) *midfield: wknd over 2f out* **66/1**
300 **8** 2¼ **Bitusa (USA)**[5] 6907 3-8-12 56 (b) BenCurtis 6 30
(Alan Swinbank) *hld up: nvr threatened* **16/1**
4323 **9** 2¼ **Diddy Eric**[40] 5343 3-8-12 49 MichaelO'Connell 10 26
(Micky Hammond) *midfield: wknd over 2f out* **25/1**
/0-0 **10** 8 **Spokesperson (USA)**[10] 6759 5-9-3 45 (p) DavidAllan 2 11
(Frederick Watson) *midfield: wknd over 2f out* **150/1**
2m 7.48s (0.38) **Going Correction** +0.125s/f (Good)
WFA 3 from 4yo+ 5lb **10** Ran SP% **112.6**
Speed ratings (Par 103): **103,100,93,91,91 87,86,84,83,76**
Tote Swingers: 1&2 £2.20, 1&3 £3.90, 2&3 £3.70 CSF £10.13 TOTE £2.90: £1.30, £1.60, £2.20; EX 12.00 Trifecta £42.00 Pool: £1,335.45 - 23.83 winning units..Winner bought in for £6,500.
Owner P I Harker **Bred** Whitsbury Manor Stud And Mrs M E Slade **Trained** Thirkleby, N Yorks

FOCUS
Not a bad seller. The winner is rated back to this year's best.

7028 MARKET CROSS JEWELLERS H'CAP 1m 2f
4:35 (4:35) (Class 4) (0-85,85) 3-Y-0+ **£5,175** (£1,540; £769; £384) **Stalls** Low

Form RPR
4000 **1** **San Cassiano (IRE)**[7] 6846 6-9-0 **75** (b) DaleSwift 4 85
(Ruth Carr) *led 3f: cl up: led again over 3f out: rdn over 2f out: drvn ent fnl f: hld on gamely* **18/1**
2030 **2** hd **Gioia Di Vita**[12] 6701 3-8-5 **71** PaulQuinn 2 81
(David Nicholls) *t.k.h: trckd ldrs: hdwy and cl up 3f out: rdn to chal wl over 1f out: ev ch tl drvn ins fnl f and no ex towards fin* **12/1**
4005 **3** 4 **Barren Brook**[27] 6236 6-9-2 **77** FrederikTylicki 3 79
(Michael Easterby) *trckd ldrs: hdwy 4f out: rdn along to chse ldng pair wl over 1f out: drvn and no imp fnl f* **9/2**[1]
1164 **4** 6 **Morocco**[22] 6353 4-9-1 **81** DavidBergin(5) 5 71
(David O'Meara) *hld up in midfield: hdwy on outer over 3f out: rdn to chse ldrs 2f out: sn drvn and no imp appr fnl f* **13/2**[2]
1500 **5** nk **Arc Light (IRE)**[16] 6563 5-8-12 **73** DavidAllan 11 62
(Tim Easterby) *hld up towards rr: hdwy 3f out: rdn and n.m.r 2f out: kpt on one pce u.p fr over 1f out* **12/1**
1051 **6** hd **Fazza**[16] 6562 6-8-10 **78** KevinStott(7) 6 67
(Edwin Tuer) *hld up towards rr: hdwy on wd outside over 3f out: rdn to chse ldrs over 2f out: sn drvn and one pce* **11/1**
5502 **7** nk **Moccasin (FR)**[16] 6563 4-9-4 **79** AndrewMullen 7 67
(Geoffrey Harker) *hld up in rr: hdwy whn nt clr run and hmpd 2f out: effrt whn n.m.r jst over 1f out: rdn and no imp after* **16/1**
6402 **8** 1 **Presburg (IRE)**[15] 6596 4-8-13 **79** OisinMurphy(5) 15 65
(Joseph Tuite) *v.s.a: a in rr* **7/1**[3]
5005 **9** 1¾ **Love Marmalade (IRE)**[17] 6514 3-8-12 **78** AdrianNicholls 9 61
(Mark Johnston) *cl up: led after 3f: rdn along 4f out: sn hdd and grad wknd* **12/1**
3305 **10** 1¼ **Dubai Hills**[24] 6300 7-9-10 **85** TomEaves 8 65
(Bryan Smart) *midfield: hdwy 4f out: rdn along 3f out: sn drvn and wknd* **16/1**
1604 **11** nk **Never Forever**[16] 6563 4-8-7 **71** JasonHart(3) 1 50
(George Moore) *midfield: effrt on inner 4f out: rdn along over 3f out: sn btn* **9/1**
0-15 **12** 1½ **Returntobrecongill**[10] 6758 3-8-6 **72** BarryMcHugh 13 48
(Sally Hall) *in tch: rdn along over 3f out: wknd over 2f out* **25/1**
5321 **13** 2 **Dance King**[33] 6036 3-9-0 **80** FMBerry 10 52
(David Lanigan) *trckd ldrs: effrt to chse ldng pair over 3f out: rdn along wl over 2f out: sn wknd* **7/1**[3]
2m 6.82s (-0.28) **Going Correction** +0.125s/f (Good)
WFA 3 from 4yo+ 5lb **13** Ran SP% **118.8**
Speed ratings (Par 105): **106,105,102,97,97 97,97,96,95,94 93,92,90**
Tote Swingers: 1&2 £36.60, 1&3 £21.90, 2&3 £15.00 CSF £217.89 CT £1150.89 TOTE £24.90: £7.30, £4.90, £2.30; EX 304.90 Trifecta £1474.00 Pool: £1,965.43 - 0.59 winning units..
Owner Mitchell, Jackson and Shaw **Bred** Peter Savill **Trained** Huby, N Yorks

FOCUS
This looked wide open, but the principals dominated and again two came clear near the finish. The handicapper had given the winner a chance.

7029 RACING REPLAY, ALL TODAY'S RACING SKY432 H'CAP (DIV I) 5f
5:05 (5:05) (Class 5) (0-70,78) 3-Y-0+ **£2,587** (£770; £384; £192) **Stalls** Centre

Form RPR
5111 **1** **Perfect Pasture**[3] 6948 3-10-1 **78** 6ex (v) PhillipMakin 1 97
(Michael Easterby) *racd alone towards far side: mde most: qcknd clr over 1f out: easily* **11/4**[1]
6542 **2** 4 **Keep It Dark**[3] 6944 4-8-11 **60** BarryMcHugh 5 64
(Tony Coyle) *racd centre: cl up: rdn and ev ch 2f out: drvn and edgd rt over 1f out: kpt on fnl f: no ch w wnr* **10/3**[2]
0000 **3** 3 **Just Like Heaven (IRE)**[19] 6469 4-9-2 **65** (p) DavidAllan 2 58
(Tim Easterby) *cl up: rdn along 2f out: sn drvn and one pce* **50/1**
606 **4** nk **Foxy Music**[16] 6547 9-9-1 **67** JasonHart(3) 11 59
(Eric Alston) *racd towards stands' rail: cl up: rdn 2f out: sn drvn and one pce* **16/1**
1553 **5** nk **Ingenti**[17] 6516 5-8-13 **69** KevinStott(7) 4 60
(Christopher Wilson) *chsd ldrs: rdn 2f out: drvn and no imp fnl f* **14/1**
0602 **6** 2 **Willbeme**[3] 6948 5-9-6 **69** AndrewElliott 12 53
(Neville Bycroft) *in tch: hdwy to chse ldrs 2f out: sn rdn and no imp appr fnl f* **11/2**[3]
4503 **7** shd **Foreign Rhythm (IRE)**[15] 6603 8-8-8 **62** ShirleyTeasdale(5) 3 45
(Ron Barr) *chsd ldrs: rdn along 2f out: sn wknd* **22/1**
636 **8** ½ **Mr Mo Jo**[10] 6757 5-9-5 **68** (b) FrederikTylicki 7 50
(Lawrence Mullaney) *cl up: rdn along over 2f out: sn wknd* **14/1**
0254 **9** 1¾ **Captain Scooby**[2] 6977 7-8-11 **67** AnnaHesketh(7) 13 42
(Richard Guest) *a outpcd in rr* **11/2**[3]
0000 **10** hd **Mission Impossible**[16] 6547 8-9-1 **64** (p) PatrickMathers 10 39
(Tracy Waggott) *a towards rr* **28/1**
/006 **11** 3¾ **Your Gifted (IRE)**[21] 6388 6-9-7 **70** (e) TomEaves 9 31
(Lisa Williamson) *dwlt: a towards rr* **33/1**
1000 **12** 5 **Chosen One (IRE)**[9] 6771 8-9-2 **65** DaleSwift 6 8
(Ruth Carr) *in tch: rdn along and lost pl 1/2-way: sn bhd* **33/1**
0005 **13** 3 **Kyzer Chief**[6] 6878 8-8-7 **56** oh2 BenCurtis 14
(Tina Jackson) *racd towards stands' rail: a towards rr* **50/1**
58.12s (-0.48) **Going Correction** +0.125s/f (Good) **13** Ran SP% **117.3**
Speed ratings (Par 103): **108,101,96,96,95 92,92,91,88,88 82,74,69**
Tote Swingers: 1&2 £28.10, 1&3 £3.20, 2&3 £28.90 CSF £10.52 CT £333.20 TOTE £3.30: £1.60, £1.70, £9.90; EX 13.90 Trifecta £1584.60 Pool: £2,112.86 - 0.86 winning units..
Owner Mrs Jean Turpin **Bred** Mrs Jean Turpin **Trained** Sheriff Hutton, N Yorks

FOCUS
Few landed a serious blow in this moderate sprint handicap. It was 1.32sec faster than division II and the winner recorded a big figure for the grade.

7030 RACING REPLAY, ALL TODAY'S RACING SKY432 H'CAP (DIV II) 5f
5:35 (5:35) (Class 5) (0-70,73) 3-Y-0+ **£2,587** (£770; £384; £192) **Stalls** Centre

Form RPR
2641 **1** **Thatcherite (IRE)**[3] 6945 5-9-3 **66** 6ex (t) StephenCraine 1 75+
(Tony Coyle) *stdd s: hld up in rr: smooth hdwy over 1f out: led ins fnl f: rdn out* **9/4**[1]
6464 **2** 1¼ **Lady Poppy**[10] 6757 3-8-8 **60** DeclanCannon(3) 10 65
(George Moore) *chsd ldrs: rdn and ev ch over 1f out: kpt on* **22/1**
0502 **3** ½ **Cocktail Charlie**[14] 6653 5-8-13 **69** (p) GaryMahon(7) 7 71
(Tim Easterby) *midfield: rdn 1/2-way: chsd ldrs over 1f out: kpt on* **6/1**[3]
322 **4** ¾ **Modern Lady**[17] 6515 3-9-2 **68** JasonHart(3) 4 69
(Richard Guest) *led: hdd 3f out: led again over 1f out: hdd ins fnl f: no ex* **10/1**
0500 **5** hd **Elusive Bonus (IRE)**[16] 6547 4-8-8 **62** DavidBergin(5) 9 61
(David O'Meara) *chsd ldrs: rdn 1/2-way: one pce fnl f* **16/1**
1105 **6** shd **Captain Royale (IRE)**[9] 6771 8-9-1 **69** (p) JacobButterfield(5) 5 67
(Tracy Waggott) *dwlt: hld up: pushed along 1/2-way: kpt on fnl f: nvr threatened* **18/1**
02 **7** ¾ **Eland Ally**[10] 6757 5-9-10 **73** (p) AndrewMullen 3 69
(Tom Tate) *midfield: rdn 1/2-way: one pce* **9/1**
2050 **8** 1 **Commanche Raider (IRE)**[10] 6757 6-9-2 **65** (b) PhillipMakin 13 57
(Michael Dods) *hld up: rdn 1/2-way: minor late hdwy: nvr threatened* **22/1**
03-3 **9** nk **Marabout (IRE)**[10] 6757 3-8-7 **56** BarryMcHugh 2 48
(Mel Brittain) *midfield: rdn 1/2-way: no imp* **12/1**
1005 **10** nse **A J Cook (IRE)**[15] 6604 3-9-0 **63** (p) DaleSwift 11 55
(Ron Barr) *midfield: rdn 1/2-way: wknd fnl f* **40/1**
0000 **11** 1¼ **Master Rooney (IRE)**[17] 6516 7-9-4 **67** (p) TomEaves 8 53
(Geoffrey Harker) *dwlt: sn prom: led 3f out: hdd over 1f out: wknd* **33/1**
1133 **12** 1¾ **Lothair (IRE)**[5] 6908 4-9-5 **68** BenCurtis 12 48
(Alan Swinbank) *in tch: rdn 1/2-way: sn wknd* **7/2**[2]
59.44s (0.84) **Going Correction** +0.125s/f (Good) **12** Ran SP% **119.3**
Speed ratings (Par 103): **98,96,95,94,93 93,92,90,90,90 88,85**
Tote Swingers: 1&2 £17.70, 1&3 £5.70, 2&3 £25.90 CSF £62.06 CT £276.88 TOTE £4.20: £2.00, £7.00, £1.40; EX 81.30 Trifecta £620.70 Pool: £1,510.19 - 1.82 winning units..
Owner Brian Kerr **Bred** Taroka Equine Investments **Trained** Norton, N Yorks

FOCUS
The second division of the ordinary sprint handicap.
T/Plt: £27.10 to a £1 stake. Pool: £63,003.1 - 1,696.50 winning tickets. T/Qpdt: £15.20 to a £1 stake. Pool: £3,886.30 - 189.10 winning tickets. JR

6994 WOLVERHAMPTON (A.W) (L-H)
Saturday, October 5

OFFICIAL GOING: Standard
Wind: Light across Weather: Cloudy with sunny spells

7031 BETFRED "THE BONUS KING" CLAIMING STKS 7f 32y(P)
5:30 (5:31) (Class 6) 3-Y-0+ **£1,940** (£577; £288; £144) **Stalls** High

Form RPR
0000 **1** **Capaill Liath (IRE)**[14] 6625 5-9-5 83 (p) ShaneGray(5) 6 90
(Kevin Ryan) *sn trcking ldr: led over 1f out: sn rdn: edgd lft ins fnl f: idled towards fin* **8/1**
1464 **2** ½ **Ortac Rock (IRE)**[32] 6072 4-9-0 75 (t) LeeTopliss 2 78
(Richard Fahey) *sn led: shkn up over 2f out: hdd over 1f out: edgd lft and r.o u.p* **5/2**[1]
010 **3** ¾ **Mr David (USA)**[15] 6609 6-9-2 80 (b) KirstyMilczarek 3 78
(Jamie Osborne) *led early: racd keenly: sn stdd to trck ldrs: rdn and hung lft fr over 1f out: r.o* **7/2**[2]
1260 **4** 1¼ **Light From Mars**[14] 6648 8-9-0 81 JackDuern(5) 4 78
(Tom Dascombe) *prom: rdn over 1f out: r.o: nt rch ldrs* **4/1**[3]
5424 **5** 3¾ **Al Muheer (IRE)**[7] 6822 8-8-11 82 LMcNiff(3) 1 63
(Ruth Carr) *s.s: pushed along 1/2-way: hdwy u.p over 1f out: nvr nrr* **7/2**[2]
3000 **6** 7 **Jack My Boy (IRE)**[7] 6854 6-8-13 78 DeclanBates(3) 5 46
(David Evans) *hld up: a in rr: bhd fnl 3f* **22/1**
0000 **7** ½ **Bheleyf (IRE)**[29] 6157 3-7-9 49 NoraLooby(7) 7 31
(Joseph Tuite) *plld hrd and prom: rdn over 2f out: wknd over 1f out* **80/1**
1m 29.29s (-0.31) **Going Correction** +0.075s/f (Slow)
WFA 3 from 4yo+ 2lb **7** Ran SP% **109.7**
Speed ratings (Par 101): **104,103,102,101,96 88,88**
Tote Swingers: 1&2 £2.90, 1&3 £4.00, 2&3 £5.20 CSF £26.03 TOTE £9.30: £4.90, £1.80; EX 56.50 Trifecta £168.60 Pool: £1,973.62 - 8.77 winning units..
Owner T A Rahman **Bred** Stanley Estate & Stud Co & Mount Coote Stud **Trained** Hambleton, N Yorks

FOCUS
Two non-runners left seven for the opening claimer.

7032 BETFRED ON 0800 221 221 NURSERY H'CAP 1m 141y(P)
6:00 (6:01) (Class 6) (0-60,60) 2-Y-0 **£2,587** (£770; £384; £192) **Stalls** Low

Form RPR
0001 **1** **Emerahldz (IRE)**[11] 6726 2-9-7 **60** LeeTopliss 2 68+
(Richard Fahey) *chsd ldrs and pushed along at various stages: nt clr run over 2f out: swtchd rt and rdn to chse ldr over 1f out: sn hung lft: led ins fnl f: drvn out* **11/4**[2]
0000 **2** 2¾ **Assoluta (IRE)**[24] 6311 2-9-5 **58** LiamKeniry 8 57
(Sylvester Kirk) *chsd ldr tl led over 2f out: rdn clr over 1f out: hdd and unable qck ins fnl f* **33/1**
6500 **3** 1¼ **It's All A Game**[10] 6755 2-8-13 **52** (v) RobbieFitzpatrick 7 49
(Richard Guest) *prom: pushed along 5f out: outpcd over 2f out: r.o ins fnl f* **20/1**
0304 **4** nse **Mimbleberry**[11] 6726 2-9-0 **58** (v[1]) JackDuern(5) 1 54+
(Tom Dascombe) *s.i.s: outpcd: pushed along over 4f out: hung lft and r.o ins fnl f: nt trble ldrs* **8/1**[3]
6006 **5** 6 **Jana**[30] 6131 2-8-5 **51** ow2 JoshBaudains(7) 5 35
(Sylvester Kirk) *hld up: pushed along 1/2-way: nvr nrr* **20/1**
5003 **6** 1½ **Paddy's Bay**[11] 6725 2-8-11 **55** (b) ShaneGray(5) 4 36
(Kevin Ryan) *led: rdn and hdd over 2f out: hung lft and wknd over 1f out* **20/1**
50 **7** 1 **Aspenbreeze**[17] 6520 2-8-6 **50** TimClark(5) 6 29
(Alan Bailey) *sn outpcd: nvr nrr* **10/1**

The Form Book Flat, Raceform Ltd, Compton, RG20 6NL.

0002 **8** *hd* **Suni Dancer**[10] 6755 2-8-10 **49** .... KirstyMilczarek 3 27
(Paul Green) *mid-div: rdn over 3f out: hdwy over 2f out: wknd over 1f out* **16/1**

6565 **9** *2* **Mister Uno (IRE)**[11] 6726 2-8-12 **51** .... (p) RussKennemore 11 25
(Ann Duffield) *prom: drvn along over 5f out: wknd 3f out* **16/1**

6523 **10** *2 3/4* **Rockie Road (IRE)**[11] 6726 2-9-1 **57** .... MichaelJMMurphy(3) 10 25
(Paul Green) *chsd ldrs: rdn over 2f out: wknd over 1f out* **8/1**[3]

000 **11** *2* **Douman (USA)**[22] 6355 2-9-7 **60** .... (t) RobertHavlin 12 24
(Ed Dunlop) *dwlt: hdwy over 7f out: rdn over 2f out: sn wknd and eased* **7/4**[1]

444 **12** *31* **Doncaster Belle (IRE)**[114] 3255 2-9-0 **58** .... TobyAtkinson(5) 9
(Charles Smith) *mid-div: n.m.r and lost pl over 6f out: wknd 1/2-way* **80/1**

1m 52.5s (2.00) **Going Correction** +0.075s/f (Slow) **12** Ran SP% **124.6**
Speed ratings (Par 93): **94,91,90,90,85 83,82,82,80,78 76,49**
Tote Swingers: 1&2 £13.40, 1&3 £15.90, 2&3 £228.30 CSF £105.48 CT £1607.88 TOTE £4.10: £1.80, £6.90, £7.40; EX 84.40 Trifecta £1911.10 Pool: £4,259.64 - 1.67 winning units..
Owner Mrs H Steel **Bred** D G Iceton **Trained** Musley Bank, N Yorks

FOCUS
A low-grade nursery, but enough in-form or unexposed performers to provide some intrigue.

7033 BETFRED "HAT TRICK HEAVEN" H'CAP 1m 4f 50y(P)

6:30 (6:30) (Class 5) (0-70,75) 3-Y-O+ **£2,911** (£866; £432; £216) **Stalls** Low

Form RPR

4151 **1** **Mister Fizz**[8] 6787 5-9-10 **75** .... DanielCremin(7) 5 85
(Miss Imogen Pickard) *trckd ldr tl led over 2f out: rdn clr over 1f out: styd on: swvd rt after the line and uns rdr* **5/2**[2]

22R5 **2** *3 1/4* **Kittens**[16] 6574 4-9-10 **68** .... (p) DougieCostello 1 73
(William Muir) *led: shkn up and hdd over 2f out: rdn and edgd rt over 1f out: styd on same pce ins fnl f* **20/1**

-405 **3** *9* **Everlasting Light**[21] 6398 3-9-3 **68** .... KirstyMilczarek 2 59
(Luca Cumani) *wnt rt s: chsd ldrs: pushed along over 5f out: rdn over 3f out: wknd over 1f out: eased* **2/1**[1]

4424 **4** *2 3/4* **Mistral Wind (IRE)**[22] 6363 3-9-0 **65** .... RobertHavlin 6 51
(Ed Dunlop) *prom: rdn over 2f out: sn wknd* **3/1**[3]

0525 **5** *15* **Pencombe (FR)**[43] 5702 3-8-10 **68** .... LewisWalsh(7) 4 30
(David Simcock) *hld up: hmpd 7f out: rdn and wknd over 2f out* **8/1**

322 **6** *20* **Awattan**[207] 972 3-9-4 **69** .... LiamKeniry 3
(Ed Vaughan) *hmpd s: hld up: wknd 3f out* **11/1**

2m 41.49s (0.39) **Going Correction** +0.075s/f (Slow)
WFA 3 from 4yo+ 7lb **6** Ran SP% **111.1**
Speed ratings (Par 103): **101,98,92,91,81 67**
Tote Swingers: 1&2 £3.90, 1&3 £1.50, 2&3 £5.80 CSF £42.84 TOTE £3.10: £1.50, £4.30; EX 26.90 Trifecta £115.10 Pool: £1,215.36 - 79.00 winning units..
Owner Mrs Margaret J Wilson **Bred** Mrs Margaret J Wilson **Trained** Ullingswick, Herefordshire

FOCUS
This middle-distance handicap was one of the features on a poor card.

7034 STUART EVANS 50TH BIRTHDAY CELEBRATION H'CAP (DIV I) 1m 1f 103y(P)

7:00 (7:00) (Class 6) (0-55,58) 3-Y-O **£1,940** (£577; £288; £144) **Stalls** Low

Form RPR

0-05 **1** **Tracks Of My Tears**[52] 5393 3-8-9 **46** oh1 .... RyanPowell(3) 10 49
(Giles Bravery) *hld up: hdwy over 5f out: pushed along over 2f out: styd on u.p to ld and edgd lft wl ins fnl f* **50/1**

2035 **2** *1 1/2* **Ground Ginger**[9] 6782 3-8-12 **46** oh1 .... JimmyQuinn 8 46
(James Bethell) *chsd ldrs: rdn over 3f out: ev ch wl ins fnl f: styd on same pce* **8/1**

0004 **3** *1/2* **Switch On**[22] 6361 3-8-13 **47** .... (bt) SebSanders 7 46
(Chris Wall) *sn chsng ldr: led over 5f out: edgd lft over 4f out: rdn over 1f out: hdd wl ins fnl f* **3/1**[2]

060 **4** *13* **Hispania (IRE)**[50] 5495 3-9-7 **55** .... GeorgeBaker 5 27
(Michael Bell) *sn led: hdd over 5f out: rdn over 2f out: wknd over 1f out* **4/1**[3]

2323 **5** *2 1/4* **Pour La Victoire (IRE)**[2] 6985 3-9-0 **53** .... GeorgeDowning(5) 6 20
(Tony Carroll) *hld up: hdwy u.p over 2f out: wknd wl over 1f out* **7/4**[1]

0056 **6** *7* **Ella Motiva (IRE)**[17] 6518 3-8-7 **46** oh1 .... NoelGarbutt(5) 1
(Mark Brisbourne) *hld up: pushed along 1/2-way: drvn and wknd over 2f out* **10/1**

3400 **7** *5* **Duchess Of Dreams**[25] 6276 3-8-12 **46** oh1 .... RobbieFitzpatrick 4
(Richard Guest) *hld up: rdn over 3f out: wknd over 2f out* **33/1**

0003 **8** *45* **Holli Deya**[8] 6804 3-8-12 **46** oh1 .... (p) JohnFahy 3
(Andi Brown) *trckd ldrs: rdn over 4f out: wknd over 3f out* **16/1**

2m 2.24s (0.54) **Going Correction** +0.075s/f (Slow) **8** Ran SP% **112.3**
Speed ratings (Par 99): **100,98,98,86,84 78,74,34**
Tote Swingers: 1&2 £15.10, 1&3 £20.70, 2&3 £3.70 CSF £389.08 CT £1584.69 TOTE £30.40: £6.20, £2.30, £1.70; EX 171.80 Trifecta £1311.40 Pool: £6,067.99 - 3.47 winning units..
Owner D B Clark **Bred** The Policy Setters **Trained** Newmarket, Suffolk

FOCUS
The first division of the extended 1m1f handicap was severely weakened by the defection of Let Me In who had won at this venue the previous evening.

7035 STUART EVANS 50TH BIRTHDAY CELEBRATION H'CAP (DIV II) 1m 1f 103y(P)

7:30 (7:30) (Class 6) (0-55,55) 3-Y-O **£1,940** (£577; £288; £144) **Stalls** Low

Form RPR

4220 **1** **Scepticism (USA)**[13] 1879 3-9-0 **55** .... JoshBaudains(7) 3 63
(Charlie Mann) *led after 1f: rdn over 1f out: styd on* **4/1**[2]

050 **2** *nk* **My Claire**[81] 4391 3-8-12 **46** oh1 .... AdamBeschizza 8 53
(Nigel Tinkler) *hld up: hdwy over 1f out: rdn to chse wnr and edgd lft ins fnl f: r.o* **8/1**

0455 **3** *2 1/4* **Penang Power**[22] 6361 3-8-6 **47** .... LouisSteward(7) 9 50
(Michael Bell) *sn pushed along in to mid-div: hdwy over 2f out: rdn and nt clr run over 1f out: styd on* **7/2**[1]

5040 **4** *nk* **Entrapping**[37] 5935 3-9-5 **53** .... CathyGannon 5 55
(John E Long) *mid-div: hdwy over 1f out: styd on: nt rch ldrs* **4/1**[2]

6504 **5** *3* **Impeccability**[7] 6851 3-8-12 **46** .... LeeTopliss 1 42
(John Mackie) *led 1f: chsd wnr tl 5f out: remained handy: rdn over 2f out: wknd ins fnl f* **6/1**[3]

-506 **6** *nse* **Prairie Prince (IRE)**[14] 6657 3-8-7 **46** oh1 .... ShelleyBirkett(5) 4 42
(Gay Kelleway) *prom: chsd wnr 5f out: rdn over 2f out: wknd and lost 2nd ins fnl f* **13/2**

0005 **7** *3 1/2* **Terpsichore**[26] 6257 3-8-12 **46** oh1 .... LiamKeniry 10 34
(Sylvester Kirk) *prom: rdn over 2f out: hung lft and wknd over 1f out* **28/1**

0004 **8** *8* **Cool And Clear (IRE)**[33] 6043 3-8-12 **46** oh1 .... (b) JohnFahy 7 17
(Pat Eddery) *sn outpcd* **22/1**

4540 **9** *23* **Betty Boo (IRE)**[22] 6361 3-8-12 **46** oh1 .... JimmyQuinn 2
(Shaun Harris) *chsd ldrs tl rdn and wknd over 2f out* **25/1**

2m 2.54s (0.84) **Going Correction** +0.075s/f (Slow) **9** Ran SP% **112.6**
Speed ratings (Par 99): **99,98,96,96,93 93,90,83,63**
Tote Swingers: 1&2 £10.00, 2&3 £2.70 CSF £33.68 CT £120.47 TOTE £5.50: £1.80, £3.80, £1.60; EX 50.30 Trifecta £151.20 Pool: £3,876.59 - 19.22 winning units..
Owner S Beccle, P Cook & T Simmons **Bred** Darley **Trained** Upper Lambourn, Berks

FOCUS
The second division of the extended 1m1f handicap was a touch more competitive than the first.

7036 BETFRED "DOUBLE DELIGHT" (S) STKS 5f 20y(P)

8:05 (8:06) (Class 6) 2-Y-O **£1,940** (£577; £288; £144) **Stalls** Low

Form RPR

5365 **1** **Skinny Love**[11] 6731 2-8-6 65 .... AdamBeschizza 4 64
(Robert Cowell) *w ldr tl led 2f out: rdn and edgd rt ins fnl f: r.o* **6/4**[1]

U5 **2** *1* **Kodafine (IRE)**[14] 6654 2-8-11 63 .... CathyGannon 7 65
(David Evans) *sn led: hdd 2f out: rdn and edgd rt fnl f: r.o* **6/1**[3]

4502 **3** *3 3/4* **Little Big Man**[22] 6364 2-8-11 57 .... (b) LiamKeniry 2 52
(Sylvester Kirk) *trckd ldrs: hmpd 4f out: rdn over 1f out: no ex ins fnl f* **7/1**

4230 **4** *1/2* **Outback Lover (IRE)**[22] 6364 2-8-11 65 .... (b) LukeMorris 6 50
(J S Moore) *chsd ldrs: rdn over 1f out: styd on same pce* **9/2**[2]

2500 **5** *1* **Vodka Chaser (IRE)**[19] 6474 2-8-6 61 .... (p) JimmyQuinn 1 42
(J S Moore) *prom: n.m.r and lost pl sn after s: hdwy over 1f out: sn rdn: styd on same pce fnl f* **7/1**

000 **6** *2 1/2* **Sands Legends**[91] 4073 2-8-6 40 .... JohnFahy 3 33
(James Given) *in rr: sme hdwy and hung lft over 1f out: n.d* **66/1**

50 **7** *1/2* **Brean Splash Susie**[30] 6131 2-8-1 0 ow2 .... RyanWhile(7) 8 33
(Bill Turner) *awkward leaving stalls: sn pushed along towards rr wknd 2f out* **50/1**

0520 **8** *1 1/2* **Red Tiger Lily**[17] 6511 2-7-13 50 .... DanielleMooney(7) 10 25
(Nigel Tinkler) *racd wd: hdwy 1/2-way: wknd over 1f out* **20/1**

665 **9** *11* **Riley's Missile (IRE)**[106] 3541 2-8-11 50 .... RobbieFitzpatrick 9
(Charles Smith) *s.i.s: outpcd* **66/1**

0600 **10** *3/4* **Absconder (IRE)**[18] 6494 2-8-11 35 .... JoeFanning 5
(Mark Johnston) *sn prom: rdn 1/2-way: wknd over 1f out* **12/1**

1m 2.81s (0.51) **Going Correction** +0.075s/f (Slow) **10** Ran SP% **114.9**
Speed ratings (Par 93): **98,96,90,89,88 84,83,80,63,62**
Tote Swingers: 1&2 £4.60, 1&3 £2.80, 2&3 £7.20 CSF £10.32 TOTE £3.00: £1.20, £2.10, £2.60; EX 14.60 Trifecta £45.40 Pool: £2,605.16 - 42.97 winning units..The winner was bought in for 5,500gns.
Owner T W Morley & J Barton **Bred** Raffles Dancers **Trained** Six Mile Bottom, Cambs

FOCUS
Bits and pieces of form were brought to the table in this two-year-old seller run over the minimum trip.

7037 BETFRED TV MEDIAN AUCTION MAIDEN STKS 7f 32y(P)

8:40 (8:40) (Class 6) 3-4-Y-O **£1,940** (£577; £288; £144) **Stalls** High

Form RPR

03 **1** **You Look So Good**[10] 6748 3-9-0 0 .... AndreaAtzeni 7 66
(Roger Varian) *trckd ldr: shkn up to ld over 1f out: sn rdn: styd on u.p* **10/11**[1]

02- **2** *3/4* **Daring Dragon**[289] 8185 3-9-5 0 .... (b) GeorgeBaker 3 69
(Ed Walker) *trckd ldrs: shkn up to go 2nd over 1f out: rdn and hung lft ins fnl f: nt run on* **15/8**[2]

0000 **3** *6* **Shelling Peas**[16] 6554 4-8-9 45 .... (v[1]) AdamMcLean(7) 6 49
(Derek Shaw) *led: rdn and hdd over 1f out: hung rt and wknd ins fnl f* **66/1**

6 **4** *1* **Diva Delight (IRE)**[7] 6849 3-9-0 0 .... AdamBeschizza 5 45
(Robert Cowell) *s.i.s: sn in tch: rdn over 2f out: styd on same pce fr over 1f out* **33/1**

-254 **5** *1 3/4* **Messageinabottle (USA)**[25] 6291 3-9-0 62 .... JimmyQuinn 2 41
(James Bethell) *trckd ldrs: racd keenly: rdn over 2f out: wknd fnl f* **13/2**[3]

0-6 **6** *16* **Somerton Star**[103] 3641 3-9-5 0 .... JoeFanning 1 2
(Pat Eddery) *s.i.s: outpcd: sme hdwy 1/2-way: wknd over 2f out* **25/1**

1m 30.78s (1.18) **Going Correction** +0.075s/f (Slow)
WFA 3 from 4yo 2lb **6** Ran SP% **108.8**
Speed ratings (Par 101): **96,95,88,87,85 66**
Tote Swingers: 1&2 £1.02, 1&3 £10.60, 2&3 £36.90 CSF £2.58 TOTE £1.70: £2.30, £1.10; EX 2.90 Trifecta £101.80 Pool: £2,500.80 - 18.41 winning units..
Owner A D Spence **Bred** Exors Of The Late T E Pocock **Trained** Newmarket, Suffolk

FOCUS
The front three in the market brought reasonable form into this median auction maiden considering the time of the year and venue.

7038 BETFRED "BETTER ODDS ON GOALS GALORE" FILLIES' H'CAP 1m 141y(P)

9:15 (9:16) (Class 5) (0-75,76) 3-Y-O+ **£2,911** (£866; £432; £216) **Stalls** Low

Form RPR

105 **1** **Yojojo (IRE)**[15] 6599 4-9-5 **75** .... DanielMuscutt(5) 4 84
(Gay Kelleway) *trckd ldrs: rdn over 1f out: r.o to ld post* **7/1**[3]

4303 **2** *nk* **Elnadwa (USA)**[9] 6780 3-9-6 **75** .... DaneO'Neill 2 83
(Saeed bin Suroor) *led: rdn over 1f out: hung lft ins fnl f: hdd post* **11/4**[2]

4104 **3** *1 3/4* **Northern Meeting (IRE)**[50] 5496 3-9-6 **75** .... AndreaAtzeni 8 79
(Sir Michael Stoute) *hld up: hdwy over 2f out: rdn over 1f out: styd on same pce ins fnl f* **11/10**[1]

6301 **4** *1/2* **Madeira Girl (IRE)**[36] 5967 4-9-3 **68** .... GeorgeBaker 7 70
(Jonjo O'Neill) *chsd ldr: rdn and ev ch over 1f out: styd on same pce ins fnl f* **16/1**

0-34 **5** *4 1/2* **India's Song**[193] 1185 3-8-8 **63** .... MartinLane 5 56
(David Simcock) *hld up: rdn over 2f out: nvr trbld ldrs* **10/1**

3605 **6** *shd* **Ingleby Symphony (IRE)**[15] 6587 3-8-12 **67** .... LeeTopliss 3 59
(Richard Fahey) *prom: rdn over 2f out: wknd fnl f* **11/1**

0-00 **7** *7* **Majestic Zafeen**[75] 4593 4-9-10 **75** .... LiamKeniry 1 50
(Alastair Lidderdale) *chsd ldrs: rdn over 2f out: hung lft and wknd over 1f out* **25/1**

1m 52.61s (2.11) **Going Correction** +0.075s/f (Slow)
WFA 3 from 4yo 4lb **7** Ran SP% **113.9**
Speed ratings (Par 100): **93,92,91,90,86 86,80**
Tote Swingers 1&2 £3.00, 2&3 £1.80, 1&3 £3.30 CSF £26.37 CT £36.81 TOTE £5.60: £2.30, £2.40; EX 21.60 Trifecta £47.70 Pool: £2,174.52 - 34.15 winning units..
Owner Winterbeck Manor Stud **Bred** Rossenarra Bloodstock Limited **Trained** Exning, Suffolk

FOCUS
A fair fillies' handicap to close the card in which a couple of the top Newmarket yards were represented.
T/Plt: £397.20 to a £1 stake. Pool: £76,944.28 - 141.40 winning tickets. T/Qpdt: £31.00 to a £1 stake. Pool: £8,912.98 - 212.35 winning tickets. CR

7039 - 7042a (Foreign Racing) - See Raceform Interactive

1548 KEENELAND (L-H)

Saturday, October 5

OFFICIAL GOING: Polytrack: fast; turf: yielding

7043a FIRST LADY STKS (GRADE 1) (3YO+ FILLIES & MARES) (TURF) 1m

9:17 (12:00) 3-Y-0+

£147,239 (£49,079; £24,539; £12,269; £7,361; £1,636)

RPR

1 **Better Lucky (USA)**[21] 4-8-12 0 JRLeparoux 3 113
(Thomas Albertrani, U.S.A) *hdd main gp of five abt 10l off pce: stdy hdwy fr over 3 1/2f out: 3rd and clsng under 2f out: r.o to ld fnl 150yds: drvn out* **48/10**[3]

2 *hd* **Dayatthespa (USA)**[50] 4-8-12 0 JRVelazquez 6 113
(Chad C Brown, U.S.A) *w.w in 3rd bhd two clr ldrs: tk clsr order to chse ldr over 2f out: rdn and led 1 1/2f out: r.o u.p: hdd 150yds out: rallied gamely but nvr quite getting bk up* **27/10**[1]

3 *4* **Daisy Devine (USA)**[119] 5-8-12 0 (b) JamesGraham 4 104
(Andrew McKeever, U.S.A) *led: first two sn clr: 3l ld over 2f out: sn rdn: hdd 1 1/2f out: outpcd by first two but plugged on at one pce fnl f* **66/10**

4 *7 1/4* **Miz Ida (USA)**[42] 4-8-12 0 SXBridgmohan 7 87
(Steve Margolis, U.S.A) *trckd eventual wnr wl off pce: sme hdwy over 3 1/2f out but no real imp: kpt on u.p fr 2f out to go 4th ent fnl f: plugged on but nvr in contention* **41/5**

5 *4 1/4* **Hungry Island (USA)**[21] 5-8-12 0 GKGomez 2 77
(Claude McGaughey III, U.S.A) *settled one fr last wl off pce: sme mod late prog: nvr a factor* **48/10**[3]

6 *nse* **Say (IRE)**[28] 6224 3-8-9 0 JBravo 1 77
(A P O'Brien, Ire) *trckd eventual wnr wl off pce: rdn and sme hdwy over 3f out: wknd ins fnl 2f: nvr really figured* **14/5**[2]

7 *6 1/4* **Winding Way (USA)**[48] 4-8-12 0 RAlbarado 5 63
(Carla Gaines, U.S.A) *pressed ldr: outpcd 3f out: sn rdn: wknd ins fnl 1 1/2f* **29/1**

8 *nk* **Amazonas (IRE)**[56] 5271 3-8-9 0 JRoccoJr 8 62
(Ed Dunlop) *awkward leaving stalls: hld up in rr wl off pce: a bhd* **185/10**

1m 39.78s (99.78)
WFA 3 from 4yo+ 3lb 8 Ran SP% **120.3**
PARI-MUTUEL (all including 2 usd stake): WIN 11.60; PLACE (1-2) 5.00, 4.20; SHOW (1-2-3) 3.40, 3.20, 3.40; SF 50.60.
Owner Godolphin Racing LLC **Bred** Darley **Trained** USA

7044 - 7045a (Foreign Racing) - See Raceform Interactive

6710 LONGCHAMP (R-H)

Saturday, October 5

OFFICIAL GOING: Turf: soft

7046a QATAR PRIX CHAUDENAY (GROUP 2) (3YO) (TURF) 1m 7f

1:30 (12:00) 3-Y-0 £92,682 (£35,772; £17,073; £11,382; £5,691)

RPR

1 **Valirann (FR)**[27] 6250 3-9-2 0 ChristopheSoumillon 5 110+
(A De Royer-Dupre, France) *hld up in tch in midfield: rdn 2f out: styd on to chal ent fnl f: led ins fnl 120yds: a jst doing enough under firm hands and heels cl home: shade cosily* **7/4**[1]

2 *nk* **Montclair (IRE)**[27] 6250 3-9-2 0 Pierre-CharlesBoudot 2 109
(A Fabre, France) *prom on inner: angled off rail and rdn 2f out: chal ent fnl f: styd on and wnt 2nd towards fin: nt quite pce of wnr* **10/3**[2]

3 *shd* **Lucky Look (FR)**[27] 6250 3-8-13 0 GregoryBenoist 6 106
(D Smaga, France) *midfield in tch on outer: 4th 1/2-way: rdn to chal 2f out: led over 1f out: strly pressed ent fnl f: styd on but hdd ins fnl 120yds and dropped to 3rd towards fin* **6/1**[3]

4 *nse* **Darbadar (FR)**[35] 3-9-2 0 Christophe-PatriceLemaire 3 109
(M Delzangles, France) *hld up in last pair: pushed along 2f out: rdn ent fnl f: styd on steadily but nt quite pce to chal and edgd lft cl home* **6/1**[3]

5 *2* **Green Byron (FR)**[27] 6250 3-9-2 0 IoritzMendizabal 1 106
(J-M Lefebvre, France) *midfield in tch on inner: rdn over 2f out: styd on u.p and wnt 5th ins fnl 100yds: nt pce to chal* **33/1**

6 *1 3/4* **Nearly Caught (IRE)**[28] 6196 3-9-2 0 GeraldMosse 4 104
(Hughie Morrison) *led: rdn over 2f out: strly pressed and hdd over 1f out: no ex and fdd ins fnl f* **9/1**

7 *2 1/2* **Saratino (GER)**[27] 6248 3-9-2 0 OlivierPeslier 7 101
(Mario Hofer, Germany) *hld up in last: rdn 3f out: bhd and outpcd over 1f out: styd on under hands and heels ins fnl f and sme late hdwy but nvr a factor* **11/1**

8 *12* **Arkhip**[36] 3-9-2 0 UmbertoRispoli 8 85
(M Delzangles, France) *trckd ldr on outer: rdn and brief effrt over 2f out: sn no ex and btn: wknd: eased and dropped to last ins fnl f* **25/1**

3m 22.68s (6.68) **Going Correction** +0.40s/f (Good) 8 Ran SP% **113.1**
Speed ratings: **98,97,97,97,96 95,94,88**
WIN (incl. 1 euro stake): 1.90(Valirann coupled with Darbadar). Places: 1.20, 1.30, 1.50. DF: 4.00. SF: 7.20.
Owner H H Aga Khan **Bred** Haras De S.A. Aga Khan Scea **Trained** Chantilly, France

FOCUS
This was run at just an ordinary gallop and it produced a bunched finish. It's been rated around the averages for the race.

7047a QATAR PRIX DANIEL WILDENSTEIN (GROUP 2) (3YO+) (TURF) 1m

2:08 (12:00) 3-Y-0+ £92,682 (£35,772; £17,073; £11,382; £5,691)

RPR

1 **Pollyana (IRE)**[126] 2897 4-8-11 0 (p) FlavienPrat 11 110+
(D Prod'Homme, France) *midfield: pushed along 2 1/2f out: hdwy towards outside 2f out: sustained run u.p fnl 1 1/2f to ld cl home: all out* **20/1**

2 *snk* **Pinturicchio (IRE)**[41] 5808 5-9-1 0 AnthonyCrastus 6 114
(E Lellouche, France) *midfield wl in tch: effrt to chal ldrs over 2f out: led under 1 1/2f out: rdn 2 l clr appr 1f out: r.o u.p fnl f: hdd cl home: no ex* **32/1**

3 *shd* **Siyenica (FR)**[51] 5461 3-8-8 0 Christophe-PatriceLemaire 4 109+
(A De Royer-Dupre, France) *midfield: nowhere to go fr 2f out: bmpd between horses 1 1/2f out: in clr and rdn over 1f out: r.o u.p fnl f: nrest at fin: jst missed 2nd* **9/1**

4 *snk* **Yellow Rosebud (IRE)**[65] 4933 4-8-11 0 (b) PatSmullen 17 109+
(D K Weld, Ire) *hld up towards rr: gd hdwy towards outer over 1 1/2f out: r.o u.p fnl f: nvr nrr* **20/1**

5 *nk* **Topaze Blanche (IRE)**[14] 6714 3-8-8 0 ThierryThulliez 15 108+
(C Laffon-Parias, France) *hld up in rr: last nring 1 1/2f out: hdwy on outside sn after: rdn and hung rt over 1f out: styd on wl fnl f: nvr on terms* **12/1**

6 *2* **Peace Burg (FR)**[69] 4817 3-8-10 0 ChristopheSoumillon 8 106
(J-C Rouget, France) *midfield: bmpd 1 1/2f out and short of room: sn rdn and chsd ldrs: one pce u.p fnl f* **8/1**[3]

7 *1 1/4* **Mshawish (USA)**[60] 5120 3-8-11 0 OlivierPeslier 14 104
(M Delzangles, France) *hld in fnl 3rd: rdn 2f out: pluged on fr 1 1/2f out: nt pce to get involved* **6/1**[2]

8 *shd* **Gregorian (IRE)**[21] 6392 4-9-3 0 GeraldMosse 5 107
(John Gosden) *tk a t.k.h: chsd ldrs: rdn and led briefly bef 1 1/2f out: hdd sn after: fdd ins fnl f* **9/2**[1]

9 *nse* **Dastarhon (IRE)**[41] 5808 3-8-11 0 MaximeGuyon 10 104
(Mme Pia Brandt, France) *midfield: outpcd in fnl 3rd 2 1/2f out: sn rdn: kpt on wl u.p fnl f: nvr threatened ldrs* **20/1**

10 *1 1/4* **Don Bosco (FR)**[62] 5040 6-9-3 0 GregoryBenoist 1 104
(D Smaga, France) *broke wl and led taking a t.k.h: hdd after 1f: trckd ldng pair: rdn and chsd ldrs 1 1/2f out: wknd and eased ins fnl f* **14/1**

11 *snk* **Desert Blanc**[27] 6251 5-9-1 0 UmbertoRispoli 9 101
(C Baillet, France) *spread a plate and reshod at s: t.k.h in fnl 3rd: rdn and effrt over 1 1/2f out: sn no further imp: eased wl ins fnl f* **8/1**[3]

12 *1 1/4* **Mainsail**[41] 5808 4-9-1 0 JamesDoyle 16 98
(P Bary, France) *hld up towards rr: effrt on rail whn nt clr run over 1 1/2f out: swtchd outside and no real imp fnl f* **20/1**

13 *snk* **Amaron**[20] 6451 4-9-1 0 AHelfenbein 12 98
(Andreas Lowe, Germany) *pressed ldr: led over 2f out: rdn and hdd bef 1 1/2f out: wknd appr fnl f* **20/1**

14 *snk* **Fire Ship**[41] 5808 4-9-1 0 NeilCallan 2 98
(William Knight) *settled midfield wl in tch: hrd rdn and no imp 1 1/2f out: fdd fr over 1f out* **16/1**

15 *1 1/2* **Penitent**[8] 6797 7-9-1 0 DanielTudhope 13 94
(David O'Meara) *w ldng sextet: rdn and nt qckn over 1 1/2f out: wknd wl over 1f out* **14/1**

16 *7* **Gereon (GER)**[37] 5940 5-9-3 0 LiamJones 7 80
(C Zschache, Germany) *led after 1f: hdd 2f out: wkng on rail whn stmbld 1 1/2f out: sn bhd* **33/1**

17 *1 1/4* **Peace At Last (IRE)**[37] 5940 3-9-0 0 FabriceVeron 3 77
(H-A Pantall, France) *t.k.h in ldng sextet: rdn and nt qckn 2f out: in retreat whn bmpd 1 1/2f out and hmpd sn after: eased almost immediately* **40/1**

1m 40.24s (1.84) **Going Correction** +0.40s/f (Good)
WFA 3 from 4yo+ 3lb 17 Ran SP% **123.8**
Speed ratings: **106,105,105,105,105 103,102,101,101,100 100,99,99,98,97 90,89**
WIN (incl. 1 euro stake): 27.80. PLACES: 6.80, 6.10, 4.10. DF: 190.10. SF: 407.80.
Owner Bryan Lynam **Bred** Mesnil Investments Ltd & Carrigbeg Stud **Trained** France

FOCUS
Quite a messy race, with running room at a premium on the inside of the course, and it was no surprise to see the winner challenge wide. The runner-up limits the form in a tight finish.

7048a QATAR PRIX DE ROYALLIEU (GROUP 2) (3YO+ FILLIES & MARES) (TURF) 1m 4f 110y

2:40 (12:00) 3-Y-0+ £115,853 (£44,715; £21,341; £14,227; £7,113)

RPR

1 *hd* **Ebiyza (IRE)**[19] 6484 3-8-7 0 Christophe-PatriceLemaire 7 110+
(A De Royer-Dupre, France) *midfield in tch on outer: pushed along 2f out: rdn and wnt 2nd ent fnl f: chsd wnr: clsd rapidly and chal towards fin: bmpd by wnr cl home: jst failed: fin 2nd, hd: plcd 1st* **9/1**

2 **Chalnetta (FR)**[56] 5297 3-8-7 0 JulienAuge 9 110
(C Ferland, France) *trckd ldr: shkn up to chal 2f out: led over 1f out: sn rdn and qcknd clr: clsd down and strly pressed towards fin: edgd lft and bmpd runner-up cl home: jst hld on: fin 1st: disq & plcd 2nd* **6/1**[3]

3 *1* **Galvaun (IRE)**[20] 6448 4-9-1 0 Pierre-CharlesBoudot 10 108+
(A Fabre, France) *hld up in last trio on outer: pushed along 2f out: last 2f out: styd on steadily down wd outside and wnt 3rd post: nrst fin* **14/1**

4 *shd* **Baltic Baroness (GER)**[111] 3385 3-8-7 0 MaximeGuyon 3 108
(A Fabre, France) *midfield on inner: had to wait for run fr 3f out tl gap appeared on rail 2f out: swtchd lft for clr run again over 1f out: rdn and wnt 3rd ins fnl f: styd on but dropped to 4th post* **8/1**

5 *1* **Siljan's Saga (FR)**[19] 6484 3-8-7 0 AntoineHamelin 4 107
(J-P Gauvin, France) *prom on inner: 3rd 5f out: rdn 2f out: nt qckn over 1f out: styd on ins fnl f* **14/1**

6 *1/2* **Yellow And Green**[134] 2644 4-9-1 0 OlivierPeslier 2 106
(N Clement, France) *dwlt sltly and hld up in last trio on inner: nt clr run fr 3f out tl over 1f out: rdn and styd on steadily once in the clr but ch gone and nvr able to chal* **9/4**[1]

7 *1* **Riposte**[44] 5682 3-9-0 0 JamesDoyle 5 111
(Lady Cecil) *dwlt sltly and hld up in last: rn sltly wd off home bnd: pushed along and hdwy on outer over 2f out: rdn and nt qckn over 1f out: styd on ins fnl f but dropped to 7th* **5/1**[2]

8 *2* **Mila (FR)**[55] 5315 3-8-7 0 ThierryJarnet 8 101
(A De Royer-Dupre, France) *led: racd wd and alone early: cut across to join others after 3f: rdn 2f out: hdd over 1f out: sn no ex and btn: fdd bk through field on rail* **12/1**

9 *3 1/2* **Orion Love**[20] 6448 3-8-7 0 (p) FabriceVeron 6 95
(H-A Pantall, France) *dwlt sltly and pushed along to rcvr: restrained in midfield on outer: rdn over 2f out: dropped to last and btn over 1f out: eased ins fnl f* **9/1**

2m 44.17s (4.27) **Going Correction** +0.40s/f (Good)
WFA 3 from 4yo 7lb 9 Ran SP% **113.9**
Speed ratings: **101,102,101,101,100 100,99,98,96**
WIN (incl. 1 euro stake): 6.20 (Ebiyza coupled with Mila). PLACES: 3.60, 1.80, 2.40. DF: 28.30. SF: 68.40.
Owner H H Aga Khan **Bred** His Highness The Aga Khan's Studs S C **Trained** Chantilly, France

FOCUS
Ordinary form for the grade, with them going a steady gallop and finishing in a bit of a heap. The placings of the first two home were reversed after contact was made close home. The first past the post and the eighth were best placed turning in and have been rated to their previous best.

7049a QATAR PRIX DOLLAR (GROUP 2) (3YO+) (TURF) 1m 1f 165y
3:15 (12:00) 3-Y-0+ £92,682 (£35,772; £17,073; £11,382; £5,691)

RPR
1 **Cirrus Des Aigles (FR)**[15] 6618 7-9-0 0............ ChristopheSoumillon 7 123+
(Mme C Barande-Barbe, France) *midfield: 6th and travelling wl 3f out: smooth hdwy on outer to ld 1 1/2f out: pushed clr ins fnl f: comf* **7/4**[1]
2 1 ¾ **Mandour (USA)**[20] 6449 4-9-0 0................ Christophe-PatriceLemaire 2 118
(A De Royer-Dupre, France) *w.w in midfield on rail: effrt to trck eventual wnr 2f out: rdn to go 2nd over 1f out: r.o fnl f but a wl hld by wnr* **10/1**
3 4 **Petit Chevalier (FR)**[42] 5778 5-9-0 0.............................. GeraldMosse 5 110
(W Mongil, Germany) *midfield: 8th and pushed along over 2f out: rdn to chse ldrs over 1f out: kpt on u.p fnl f: readily outpcd by first two* **20/1**
4 1 ½ **Noble Mission**[56] 5270 4-9-0 0.. JamesDoyle 1 106
(Lady Cecil) *dwlt: in rr: effrt over 2 1/2f out: rdn and styng on whn swtchd outside 1 1/2f out: kpt on wl ins fnl f: nvr nrr* **14/1**
5 1 ¼ **Smoking Sun (USA)**[15] 6618 4-9-0 0.................... StephanePasquier 10 104
(P Bary, France) *towards rr: swtchd outside and hdwy 2f out: rdn 1 1/2f out: styd on u.p fnl f: nt pce to chal* **16/1**
6 hd **Fattsota**[14] 6636 5-9-0 0.. DanielTudhope 13 103
(David O'Meara) *trckd two ldrs: rdn to try and chal 1 1/2f out: wnt 2nd briefly but sn hrd rdn and nt qckn over 1f out: one pce fnl f and readily outpcd by ldrs* **50/1**
7 5 **Stellar Wind (JPN)**[20] 6449 4-9-0 0.................................. YutakaTake 4 93
(Tomohito Ozeki, Japan) *broke wl and led early: hdd bef the end of 1f: sn settled in midfield: rdn and no imp fr over 1 1/2f out* **14/1**
8 4 **Willie The Whipper**[14] 6620 3-8-9 0.............................. PJMcDonald 3 85
(Ann Duffield) *slow to stride: towards rr: rdn on outer and short-lived effrt under 2f out: no imp* **14/1**
9 5 **Al Waab (IRE)**[42] 5760 3-8-9 0.. NeilCallan 12 74
(Lady Cecil) *chsd ldr: led under 2f out: rdn over 1 1/2f out: sn hdd & wknd* **20/1**
10 2 ½ **Maputo**[55] 5317 3-8-9 0.. IoritzMendizabal 8 69
(Mark Johnston) *trckd two ldrs: 3rd and pushed along 3f out: sn rdn and no imp: grad wknd fnl 1 1/2f* **6/1**[3]
11 snk **Superplex (FR)**[20] 6451 3-8-9 0.................................... ThierryThulliez 6 68
(M Figge, Germany) *towards rr: rdn and no imp fr over 2f out* **40/1**
12 10 **Planteur (IRE)**[42] 5760 6-9-0 0...................................... OlivierPeslier 11 47
(Marco Botti) *led bef end of first 1f: set gd gallop: hdd under 2f out: sn wknd* **4/1**[2]
13 dist **Buckwheat**[51] 5462 3-8-9 0.. MaximeGuyon 9
(A Fabre, France) *towards rr: nvr in contention: bhd whn eased over 1f out: t.o* **16/1**

2m 2.83s (-0.07) **Going Correction** +0.40s/f (Good)
WFA 3 from 4yo+ 5lb **13** Ran SP% **125.4**
Speed ratings: **116,114,111,110,109 109,105,101,97,95 95,87,**
Win (incl. 1 euro stake): 2.40. PLACES: 1.40, 2.80, 2.70. DF: 14.10. SF: 18.00.
Owner Jean-Claude-Alain Dupouy **Bred** M Yvon Lelimouzin & M Benoit Deschamps **Trained** France

FOCUS
They went a good gallop here and the result fits the place averages. The runner-up has been rated to his best.

6703 TIPPERARY (L-H)
Sunday, October 6
OFFICIAL GOING: Flat course - yielding; jumps courses - good

7050a ATHASSEL HOUSE STUD EUROPEAN BREEDERS FUND MAIDEN 1m 1f
2:05 (2:07) 2-Y-0 £7,292 (£1,691; £739; £422)

RPR
1 **Buonarroti (IRE)**[27] 6262 2-9-5 .... JosephO'Brien 4 94+
(A P O'Brien, Ire) *sn led: narrow advantage 1/2-way: pushed along and extended advantage fr 2f out: clr ent fnl f: eased nr fin: easily* **7/4**[1]
2 8 ½ **Evason** 2-9-5 .... KevinManning 7 77+
(J S Bolger, Ire) *hld up towards rr: pushed along over 4f out and clsd into mod 5th ent fnl f: green: kpt on ins fnl f into nvr threatening 2nd fnl strides* **14/1**
3 nk **Abushamah (IRE)**[14] 6670 2-9-5 .... ChrisHayes 16 76
(Kevin Prendergast, Ire) *sn trckd ldrs on outer: cl 3rd 1/2-way: rdn in 2nd fr 2f out and no imp on easy wnr: dropped to mod 3rd fnl strides* **11/1**
4 nk **Whitey O' Gwaun (IRE)**[27] 6262 2-9-5 .... PatSmullen 13 76
(D K Weld, Ire) *chsd ldrs: 5th 1/2-way: rdn fr 3f out and sn no imp on easy wnr: kpt on same pce* **15/8**[2]
5 4 **Gentry (IRE)** 2-9-5 .... NGMcCullagh 9 68
(John M Oxx, Ire) *racd in rr of mid-div: tk clsr order fr after 1/2-way: hdwy fr 3f out: rdn in mod 7th 1 1/2f out and kpt on u.p ins fnl f* **20/1**
6 shd **Screenshot (IRE)**[18] 6541 2-9-5 .... WJLee 11 68
(W McCreery, Ire) *slowly away: sn pushed along to r in mid-div: 7th 1/2-way: no imp on easy wnr 2f out: kpt on same pce fnl f* **16/1**
7 1 ½ **Dai Bando (IRE)**[69] 4841 2-9-2 87.................................. ColinKeane(3) 6 65
(P J Prendergast, Ire) *trckd ldrs: cl 2nd 1/2-way: pushed along appr st and sn no imp on wnr: dropped to mod 4th ent fnl f: wknd towards fin* **12/1**
8 1 ¼ **Highly Toxic (IRE)**[22] 6413 2-9-5 .... DannyGrant 10 62
(Patrick J Flynn, Ire) *chsd ldrs: 6th 1/2-way: rdn and no imp on easy wnr fr 3f out: kpt on one pce fnl 2f* **7/1**[3]
9 2 ½ **Hatch Hall**[22] 6413 2-9-5 .... GaryCarroll 3 57
(Joseph G Murphy, Ire) *chsd ldrs: 4th 1/2-way: rdn and wknd fr 3f out* **28/1**
10 shd **Northern Surprise (IRE)**[6] 6910 2-9-0 .... MarcMonaghan(5) 8 57
(Timothy Doyle, Ire) *in rr of mid-div for most: rdn and no imp fr 3f out* **80/1**
11 2 ¼ **Mr Moondance (IRE)**[6] 6910 2-9-5 .... MichaelHussey 1 52
(Timothy Doyle, Ire) *racd in mid-div: rdn and no ex fr 3f out: one pce fnl 2f* **66/1**
12 ½ **Novel Approach (IRE)**[21] 6438 2-8-11 .... RonanWhelan(3) 15 46
(J S Bolger, Ire) *nvr bttr than mid-div: sme hdwy whn brought wd into st: one pce fnl 2f* **33/1**
13 4 ½ **Crecora (IRE)**[18] 6541 2-9-5 .... BenCurtis 12 42
(John Joseph Murphy, Ire) *towards rr: rdn and no imp fr 4f out* **66/1**
14 2 ¾ **Glance Of Doon (IRE)**[19] 6507 2-9-0 .... RoryCleary 14 32
(David Harry Kelly, Ire) *in rr of mid-div: rdn and no imp fr 3f out* **66/1**
15 2 **Shan Dun na nGall (IRE)**[27] 6262 2-9-5 74............ SeamieHeffernan 2 33
(John Joseph Murphy, Ire) *racd in mid-div: pushed along and no imp fr 3f out: wknd* **33/1**

2m 1.28s (121.28) **15** Ran SP% **132.0**
CSF £29.52 TOTE £4.00: £1.70, £2.80, £2.50; DF 34.70 Trifecta £171.70.
Owner Derrick Smith & Mrs John Magnier & Michael Tabor **Bred** Beauty Is Truth Syndicate **Trained** Ballydoyle, Co Tipperary

FOCUS
A thoroughly comprehensive victory for the Galileo colt Buonaroti.

7051a COOLMORE STUD HOME OF CHAMPIONS CONCORDE STKS (GROUP 3) 7f 100y
2:40 (2:45) 3-Y-0+ £34,349 (£10,040; £4,756; £1,585)

RPR
1 **Sruthan (IRE)**[21] 6440 3-9-3 107....................................... ChrisHayes 9 112
(P D Deegan, Ire) *chsd ldrs: 4th 1/2-way: hdwy to chal fr 2f out: rdn to ld narrowly ent fnl f: styd on wl u.p towards fin* **11/2**[2]
2 ¾ **Big Break**[107] 3524 3-9-0 106.. PatSmullen 5 107
(D K Weld, Ire) *settled bhd ldrs: clsr in 2nd after 1/2-way: hdwy gng wl to ld under 2f out: sn strly pressed and hdd narrowly u.p ent fnl f: kpt on wl towards fin wout matching wnr* **4/5**[1]
3 2 ¾ **Fort Knox**[21] 6440 3-9-3 104.. NGMcCullagh 8 103
(J P Murtagh, Ire) *hld up: niggled along in 6th 1/2-way: sn pushed along and clsd u.p into 3rd over 1f out: kpt on same pce: nt trble principals* **14/1**
4 nk **Wannabe Better (IRE)**[29] 6224 3-9-0 102.............................. WJLee 13 99
(T Stack, Ire) *w.w towards rr: hdwy into mod 5th over 1f out: kpt on same pce wout ever troubling principals* **14/1**
5 2 ¼ **Bold Thady Quill (IRE)**[21] 6440 6-9-5 102...................(v) GaryCarroll 11 98
(K J Condon, Ire) *slowly away and racd in rr: hdwy fr 3f out on outer into mod 6th over 1f out: kpt on same pce ins fnl f wout ever troubling principals* **33/1**
6 1 ¼ **Akira (IRE)**[61] 5114 3-9-0 94... DannyGrant 6 91
(Patrick J Flynn, Ire) *hld up in tch: 7th 1/2-way: sme hdwy over 2f out: rdn in mod 4th over 1f out and no ex u.p: wknd towards fin* **25/1**
7 4 ½ **Pop Art (IRE)**[153] 2107 3-9-0 95.. FMBerry 7 79
(Charles O'Brien, Ire) *slowly away and racd towards rr: niggled along 1/2-way: no imp on ldrs fr 2f out: kpt on one pce* **20/1**
8 nk **Lady Wingshot (IRE)**[182] 1413 4-9-2 102.................. KevinManning 2 80
(J S Bolger, Ire) *prom early: sn settled bhd ldrs: 5th 1/2-way: rdn and no imp fr 2f out: one pce fnl f* **14/1**
9 1 ¼ **Dont Bother Me (IRE)**[52] 5453 3-9-3 101........................ ColinKeane 3 79
(Niall Moran, Ire) *led early tl hdd after 1f: 3rd 1/2-way: pushed along and no imp on ldrs fr under 3f out: wknd fnl 2f* **16/1**
10 14 **Most Improved (IRE)**[100] 3798 4-9-5 110.................. JosephO'Brien 12 45
(A P O'Brien, Ire) *trckd ldr tl led after 1f: over 1 l clr at 1/2-way: pushed along bef st and hdd under 2f out: sn no ex u.p: wknd and eased fnl f* **6/1**[3]

1m 36.32s (96.32)
WFA 3 from 4yo+ 2lb **10** Ran SP% **122.7**
CSF £10.57 TOTE £7.10: £1.80, £1.02, £2.30; DF 16.90 Trifecta £259.80.
Owner Robert Ng **Bred** Messrs J , R & J Hyland **Trained** The Curragh, Co Kildare

FOCUS
A fascinating race, with two of the main players having a little bit to prove. The standard is set by the second, third, fourth and sixth.

7052 - (Foreign Racing) - See Raceform Interactive

5044 DUSSELDORF (R-H)
Sunday, October 6
OFFICIAL GOING: Turf: good to soft

7053a GROSSER PREIS DER LANDESHAUPTSTADT DUSSELDORF (GROUP 3) (3YO+) (TURF) 1m 110y
2:55 (12:00) 3-Y-0+
£26,016 (£8,943; £4,471; £2,439; £1,626; £1,219)

RPR
1 **Zazou (GER)**[150] 2202 6-9-2 0.. APietsch 5 112
(W Hickst, Germany) *hld up in rr: rdn and gd hdwy on wd outside over 1f out: r.o strly to ld post* **6/1**
2 nse **Calyxa**[14] 3-8-9 0.. LennartHammer-Hansen 1 110
(Ferdinand J Leve, Germany) *midfield on inner: n.m.r over 1f out: burst through gap to ld ins fnl f: kpt on: hdd post* **13/5**[1]
3 1 ¼ **Combat Zone (IRE)**[21] 6451 7-9-2 0...................................... NRichter 8 109
(Mario Hofer, Germany) *prom: rdn over 2f out: kpt on* **166/10**
4 ½ **Si Luna (GER)**[28] 4-8-13 0.. EddyHardouin 6 105
(W Mongil, Germany) *midfield: hdwy to trck ldrs 1/2-way: rdn and ev ch over 1f out: one pce fnl f* **42/10**[2]
5 shd **Empire Storm (GER)**[21] 6451 6-9-2 0...................................... AStarke 3 108
(A Wohler, Germany) *midfield: rdn over 2f out: kpt on* **57/10**
6 1 ½ **Global Thrill**[38] 5940 4-9-4 0.. SHellyn 4 106
(J Hirschberger, Germany) *led: rdn over 2f out: hdd ins fnl f: wknd* **58/10**
7 4 ½ **Akua'da (GER)**[21] 6451 3-9-0 0... JBojko 2 97
(A Wohler, Germany) *trckd ldrs: rdn over 2f out: sn wknd* **47/10**[3]
8 ½ **Point Blank (GER)**[21] 6451 5-9-2 0................................ StefanieHofer 9 93
(Mario Hofer, Germany) *hld up: rdn and sme hdwy over 2f out: wknd over 1f out: eased* **173/10**
9 8 **Flamingo Star (GER)**[91] 4103 3-8-13 0............................ TedDurcan 7 78
(R Dzubasz, Germany) *trckd ldrs: lost pl 1/2-way: bhd fnl 3f* **71/10**

1m 42.04s (-5.54)
WFA 3 from 4yo+ 3lb **9** Ran SP% **132.0**
WIN (incl. 10 euro stake): 70. PLACES: 22, 16, 33. SF: 590.
Owner Ramzan Kadyrov **Bred** Stiftung Gestt Fahrhof **Trained** Germany

[7046] LONGCHAMP (R-H)

Sunday, October 6

OFFICIAL GOING: Turf: soft

7054a QATAR PRIX DE L'ABBAYE DE LONGCHAMP (GROUP 1) (2YO+) (TURF) 5f (S)

12:45 (12:00) 2-Y-0+ **£162,593** (£65,048; £32,524; £16,247; £8,138)

RPR

1 **Maarek**[15] 6639 6-9-11 0 DeclanMcDonogh 7 118
(B Lalor, Ire) *hld up: sn pushed along: rdn and gd hdwy over 1f out: r.o strly to ld nr fin* 15/2[3]

2 snk **Catcall (FR)**[21] 6445 4-9-11 0 Francois-XavierBertras 10 117
(P Sogorb, France) *midfield: smooth hdwy over 1f out: qcknd to ld ins fnl f: idled: hdd nr fin* 10/1

3 1 1/2 **Hamza (IRE)**[15] 6623 4-9-11 0 (b) NeilCallan 2 112
(Kevin Ryan) *w ldr: rdn 1/2-way: kpt on* 20/1

4 shd **Jwala**[44] 5726 4-9-7 0 SteveDrowne 4 108
(Robert Cowell) *w ldr: rdn to ld over 1f out: hdd ins fnl f: one pce* 7/1[2]

5 1/2 **Reckless Abandon**[110] 3420 3-9-11 0 GeraldMosse 16 111
(Clive Cox) *prom towards outer: rdn 1/2-way: one pce fnl f* 9/1

6 1/2 **Sole Power**[44] 5726 6-9-11 0 JohnnyMurtagh 13 108
(Edward Lynam, Ire) *midfield: rdn 2f out: kpt on* 9/1

7 snk **Ladies Are Forever**[28] 6235 5-9-7 0 (b) GrahamLee 1 104
(Geoffrey Oldroyd) *chsd ldrs: rdn 1/2-way: kpt on one pce* 20/1

8 snk **Myasun (FR)**[42] 5806 6-9-11 0 OlivierPeslier 11 107
(C Baillet, France) *s.i.s: hld up in rr: stl plenty to do appr fnl f: r.o strly: nrst fin* 25/1

9 3/4 **Ballesteros**[15] 6639 4-9-11 0 JimmyFortune 14 104
(Brian Meehan) *midfield: rdn 1/2-way: one pce: nvr threatened* 25/1

10 shd **Dibajj (FR)**[21] 6445 3-9-7 0 AntoineHamelin 8 101
(A De Royer-Dupre, France) *dwlt: hld up: rdn 1/2-way: kpt on fnl f: nvr threatened* 16/1

11 snk **Justineo**[25] 6305 4-9-11 0 (b) WilliamBuick 15 103
(Roger Varian) *prom: rdn 1/2-way: grad wknd fnl f* 16/1

12 nk **Tickled Pink (IRE)**[15] 6639 4-9-7 0 TomQueally 12 98
(Lady Cecil) *chsd ldrs: rdn 1/2-way: grad wknd fnl f* 25/1

13 hd **Spirit Quartz (IRE)**[44] 5726 5-9-11 0 (p) JamieSpencer 3 102
(Robert Cowell) *led narrowly: rdn whn hdd over 1f out: wknd and btn whn short of room fnl 100yds* 20/1

14 3/4 **Kingsgate Choice (IRE)**[43] 5772 6-9-11 0 LiamKeniry 20 99
(Ed de Giles) *midfield on outer: rdn and hung rt 1/2-way: nvr threatened* 40/1

15 3/4 **Cape Of Approval (IRE)**[22] 6414 4-9-11 0 WayneLordan 18 96
(T Stack, Ire) *s.i.s: hld up on outer: nvr threatened* 25/1

16 1/2 **Kingsgate Native (IRE)**[15] 6639 8-9-11 0 ShaneKelly 9 94
(Robert Cowell) *hld up: sn pushed along: a towards rr* 25/1

17 nse **Dutch Masterpiece**[43] 5772 3-9-11 0 (b[1]) RyanMoore 6 95
(Gary Moore) *in tch: rdn 1/2-way: wknd and eased fnl f* 13/2[1]

18 1 3/4 **Gammarth (FR)**[42] 5804 5-9-11 0 FredericSpanu 19 88
(H-A Pantall, France) *midfield on outside: wknd 1/2-way* 66/1

19 1 **Mirza**[21] 6445 6-9-11 0 (p) RichardHughes 5 84
(Rae Guest) *s.i.s: hld up: a towards rr* 20/1

20 1 3/4 **Stepper Point**[15] 6639 4-9-11 0 (p) MartinDwyer 17 78
(William Muir) *prom on outside: wknd 1/2-way* 33/1

57.5s (1.20) **Going Correction** +0.625s/f (Yiel) 20 Ran SP% **123.6**
Speed ratings: **115,114,112,112,111 110,110,110,108,108 108,108,107,106,105 104,104,101,100,97**
WIN (incl. 1 euro stake): 11.20. PLACES: 4.00, 3.90, 10.70. DF: 85.60. SF: 160.80.
Owner Lisbunny Syndicate **Bred** New England Stud & P J & P M Vela **Trained** Fethard, Co Tipperary

FOCUS
The high-drawn runners were again seen at a disadvantage in a sprint that, although not always the classiest of the season, is certainly one of the more interesting. It was fast and furious stuff and the race set up for the closers. The winner is rated back to his best, with support from the third.

7055a TOTAL PRIX MARCEL BOUSSAC - CRITERIUM DES POULICHES (GROUP 1) (2YO FILLIES) (TURF) 1m

1:20 (12:00) 2-Y-0 **£139,365** (£55,756; £27,878; £13,926; £6,975)

RPR

1 **Indonesienne (IRE)**[36] 2-8-11 0 FlavienPrat 10 111
(C Ferland, France) *hld up towards rr: pushed along over 2f out: rdn and hdwy on outer fr over 1f out: wnt 2nd jst ins fnl f: r.o strly to reel in ldr: led towards fin and pushed out firmly* 16/1

2 3/4 **Lesstalk In Paris (IRE)**[26] 6292 2-8-11 0 IoritzMendizabal 11 109
(J-C Rouget, France) *qckly across fr wd draw and led: rdn 2f out: 2 l clr ent fnl f: r.o but reeled in and hdd towards fin: no ex* 3/1[1]

3 1 3/4 **Queen Catrine (IRE)**[45] 5680 2-8-11 0 JamieSpencer 1 106
(Charles Hills) *dwlt sltly: hld up in last trio on inner: pushed along 3f out: hdwy on rail fr over 2f out: swtchd lft and rdn over 1f out: r.o and wnt 3rd post* 16/1

4 nse **Royalmania**[26] 2-8-11 0 OlivierPeslier 8 105+
(F Head, France) *niggled along in last and nvr really travelling: rdn over 2f out: swtchd lft over 1f out: r.o u.p and wnt 4th post: nvr able to chal* 4/1[2]

5 shd **Stormyra (FR)**[28] 6249 2-8-11 0 UmbertoRispoli 4 105
(J-P Gallorini, France) *midfield on inner: rdn over 2f out: hdwy on rail and wnt 2nd over 1f out: dropped to 3rd jst ins fnl f: r.o but nt pce of front pair: lost 2 pls and dropped to 5th post* 50/1

6 nk **Wonderfully (IRE)**[9] 6798 2-8-11 0 (v) RyanMoore 5 105
(A P O'Brien, Ire) *restrained and hld up in midfield: rdn over 2f out: kpt on steadily and wnt 6th towards fin: nt pce to chal* 12/1

7 2 **Sandiva (IRE)**[50] 5555 2-8-11 0 RichardHughes 2 100
(Richard Fahey) *prom on inner: rdn over 2f out: 2nd and brief effrt 1 1/2f out: sn no imp on ldr: no ex and fdd ins fnl f* 9/2[3]

8 6 **Hoku (IRE)**[15] 6622 2-8-11 0 HarryBentley 13 87
(Olly Stevens) *sltly slow to stride fr wdst draw: hld up in last trio on outer: rdn 3f out: outpcd and hld over 1f out: kpt on and wnt 8th cl home* 33/1

9 1/2 **Majeyda (USA)**[23] 6350 2-8-11 0 MickaelBarzalona 9 86
(Charlie Appleby) *midfield on outer: rdn 3f out: kpt on tl no ex ins fnl f: eased whn btn and dropped to 9th cl home* 16/1

10 3 **Veda (FR)**[25] 2-8-11 0 Christophe-PatriceLemaire 12 79
(A De Royer-Dupre, France) *t.k.h early: prom on outer: rdn and ev ch 2f out: fnd little for press and sn btn: fdd and eased ins fnl f* 6/1

11 7 **Testina (IRE)**[34] 2-8-11 0 ChristopheSoumillon 6 64
(J-M Beguigne, France) *trckd ldr: rdn and brief effrt to chal over 2f out: no ex and btn over 1f out: fdd and eased ent fnl f* 20/1

12 4 **Princess Bavaroise (FR)**[43] 2-8-11 0 FabriceVeron 3 55
(H-A Pantall, France) *plld hrd early: prom in centre: rdn 3f out: sn lost pl and btn: dropped to last over 1f out: eased* 22/1

1m 38.74s (0.34) **Going Correction** +0.45s/f (Yiel) **12** Ran SP% **116.8**
Speed ratings: **116,115,113,113,113 113,111,105,104,101 94,90**
WIN (incl. 1 euro stake): 5.20 (Indonesienne coupled with Royalmania). PLACES: 4.90, 1.70, 3.30. DF: 39.80. SF: 138.50.
Owner Wertheimer & Frere **Bred** Wertheimer Et Frere **Trained** France

FOCUS
France's premier race for juvenile fillies, won during the past decade by luminaries such as Divine Proportions, Finsceal Beo, Zarkava, Misty For Me and Elusive Kate. This looked a modest renewal, with something of a compressed finish behind the first two. They went a fair gallop but it didn't prove easy to make ground from off the pace in the conditions.

7056a QATAR PRIX JEAN-LUC LAGARDERE (GRAND CRITERIUM) (GROUP 1) (2YO COLTS & FILLIES) (TURF) 7f

1:55 (12:00) 2-Y-0 **£162,593** (£65,048; £32,524; £16,247; £8,138)

RPR

1 **Karakontie (JPN)**[28] 6249 2-9-0 0 StephanePasquier 1 117+
(J E Pease, France) *trckd ldr: rdn to ld jst ins fnl f: kpt on* 11/4[1]

2 3/4 **Noozhoh Canarias (SPA)**[62] 5082 2-9-0 0 ChristopheSoumillon 5 115
(E Leon Penate, Spain) *racd keenly: led: rdn whn hdd jst ins fnl f: kpt on* 7/2[2]

3 1 1/4 **Charm Spirit (IRE)**[28] 2-9-0 0 OlivierPeslier 4 112
(F Head, France) *hld up in tch: hdwy into 3rd over 1f out: sn rdn: kpt on* 7/1

4 1/2 **Wilshire Boulevard (IRE)**[43] 5765 2-9-0 0 RyanMoore 2 110
(A P O'Brien, Ire) *midfield: rdn over 1f out: kpt on* 5/1[3]

5 1 **Barley Mow (IRE)**[23] 6351 2-9-0 0 RichardHughes 7 109
(Richard Hannon) *hld up in tch: stl gng wl whn n.m.r 2f out: swtchd rt to rail over 1f out: kpt on fnl f* 5/1[3]

6 1 1/2 **Baby Foot (IRE)**[47] 5628 2-9-0 0 FranckBlondel 6 104
(F Rossi, France) *hld up in rr: rdn 2f out: nvr threatened ldrs* 7/1

7 3 **Al Muthana (FR)**[26] 6293 2-9-0 0 JohnnyMurtagh 8 96
(F-H Graffard, France) *trckd ldrs: rdn 2f out: wknd over 1f out* 25/1

8 nse **Another Party (FR)**[26] 6293 2-9-0 0 AntoineHamelin 3 96
(Matthieu Palussiere, France) *midfield: wknd over 1f out* 33/1

1m 22.97s (2.27) **Going Correction** +0.45s/f (Yiel) **8** Ran SP% **114.0**
Speed ratings: **105,104,102,102,101 99,95,95**
win (incl. 1 euro stake): 2.70. PLACES: 1.20, 1.60, 1.70. DF: 4.80. SF: 9.40.
Owner Niarchos Family **Bred** Flaxman Holdings Limited **Trained** Chantilly, France

FOCUS
Not a particularly strong race for the level and those who raced on the pace were favoured. Karakontie could do better again and the fourth helps with the form.

7057a PRIX DE L'OPERA LONGINES (GROUP 1) (3YO+ FILLIES & MARES) (TURF) 1m 2f

2:30 (12:00) 3-Y-0+ **£185,821** (£74,341; £37,170; £18,569; £9,300)

RPR

1 **Dalkala (USA)**[49] 5574 4-9-2 0 ChristopheSoumillon 6 115
(A De Royer-Dupre, France) *dwlt sltly but qckly rcvrd: midfield in tch: gng best 2f out: rdn over 1f out: styd on to chal towards fin: drvn to ld post* **8/1**

2 nse **Tasaday (USA)**[21] 6448 3-8-11 0 MaximeGuyon 2 115
(A Fabre, France) *trckd ldr: cruised up to chal over 2f out: rdn and sn led: styd on but strly pressed towards fin and hdd post* 5/2[1]

3 nk **Thistle Bird**[43] 5739 5-9-2 0 JamesDoyle 5 114+
(Roger Charlton) *hld up in tch in last quartet on inner: pushed along over 2f out: angled lft and rdn over 1f out: styd on strly and wnt 3rd towards fin: nt quite rch ldrs* 12/1

4 1 1/4 **Red Lips (GER)**[63] 5044 3-8-11 0 FabriceVeron 1 112
(Andreas Lowe, Germany) *restrained early: prom on inner: pushed along 3f out: rdn 2f out: wnt 3rd ins fnl f: styd on same pce and dropped to 4th towards* 16/1

5 3/4 **Gifted Girl (IRE)**[15] 6636 4-9-2 0 TomQueally 7 110
(Paul Cole) *dwlt: hld up in last pair on inner: last 3f out: pushed along over 2f out: rdn over 1f out: styd on steadily: angled lft and wnt 5th cl home: nvr nrr* 10/1

6 1 1/4 **Silasol (IRE)**[21] 6448 3-8-11 0 OlivierPeslier 3 108
(C Laffon-Parias, France) *sn led: strly pressed over 2f out: sn rdn and hdd: kpt on tl no ex ins fnl f: fdd and dropped to 6th cl home* 5/1[3]

7 1 1/4 **Eleuthera (FR)**[47] 5629 3-8-11 0 CristianDemuro 4 105
(P Demercastel, France) *stdd and hld up in last pair on outer: rdn 2f out: outpcd over 1f out: styd on but nvr threatened* 33/1

8 1 **Sarkiyla (FR)**[49] 5574 4-9-2 0 Christophe-PatriceLemaire 8 103
(A De Royer-Dupre, France) *hld up in tch in last quartet on outer: pushed along over 2f out: rdn and outpcd over 1f out: styd on but nvr threatened* 9/1

9 nk **Secret Gesture**[45] 5682 3-8-11 0 JamieSpencer 9 103
(Ralph Beckett) *prom on outer: rdn and brief effrt 2f out: sn no ex and btn: fdd and dropped to last ins fnl f* 9/2[2]

2m 9.03s (5.03) **Going Correction** +0.625s/f (Yiel)
WFA 3 from 4yo+ 5lb **9** Ran SP% **110.1**
Speed ratings: **104,103,103,102,102 101,100,99,99**
WIN (incl. 1 euro stake): 4.70 (Dalkala coupled with Sarkiyla). PLACES: 2.70, 1.40, 4.40. DF: 10.20. SF: 28.20.
Owner H H Aga Khan **Bred** His Highness The Aga Khan Studs Sc **Trained** Chantilly, France

FOCUS
This event has held Group 1 status since 2000. It's proved a career peak for the majority of recent winners and this looked only a limited renewal. The second, third and fifth help with the standard. They didn't go much of a gallop and it turned into something of a sprint. Those attempting to come from the back were disadvantaged.

7058a QATAR PRIX DE L'ARC DE TRIOMPHE (GROUP 1) (3YO+ COLTS, FILLIES & MARES) (TURF) 1m 4f

3:15 (12:00) 3-Y-0**£2,229,853** (£892,097; £446,048; £222,829; £111,609)

RPR

1 **Treve (FR)**[21] 6448 3-8-8 0 ThierryJarnet 15 131+
(Mme C Head-Maarek, France) *dwlt sltly: t.k.h: hld up in midfield on outer: rapid hdwy and prom 3f out: chal gng strly 2f out: shkn up to ld and qcknd clr: rdn and styd on strly ins fnl f: v impressive* 9/2[2]

2 5 **Orfevre (JPN)**[21] 6449 5-9-5 0 ChristopheSoumillon 8 126
(Yasutoshi Ikee, Japan) *restrained in midfield: hdwy 3f out: rdn 2f out: wnt 2nd over 1f out: styd on and chsd wnr but absolutely no imp* 2/1[1]

The Form Book Flat, Raceform Ltd, Compton, RG20 6NL.

3 *nk* **Intello (GER)**[15] 6712 3-8-11 0 OlivierPeslier 9 125
(A Fabre, France) *prom on outer: rdn over 2f out: wnt 3rd over 1f out: styd on: pressed for 2nd and chsd wnr but absolutely no imp* **9/1**

4 *2* **Kizuna (JPN)**[21] 6446 3-8-11 0 YutakaTake 11 121
(Shozo Sasaki, Japan) *stdd and hld up in last trio: stdy hdwy on outer fr 5f out: rdn and ev ch 2f out: sn readily outpcd by wnr: styd on wl for 4th* **7/1**[3]

5 *2* **Penglai Pavilion (USA)**[17] 6580 3-8-11 0 MickaelBarzalona 10 118
(A Fabre, France) *trckd ldr on inner: cl 3rd 5f out: rdn over 2f out: shuffled bk whn short of room on rail and had to wait for run over 1f out: styd on strly once gap appeared but nvr able to chal* **40/1**

6 *2* **Al Kazeem**[29] 6226 5-9-5 0 JamesDoyle 18 116
(Roger Charlton) *t.k.h: dropped in fr wdst draw and hld up towards rr: stmbld 5f out: rdn and hdwy fr 3f out: styd on steadily for n.d 6th* **16/1**

7 *shd* **Ruler Of The World (IRE)**[21] 6446 3-8-11 0 (p) RyanMoore 6 115+
(A P O'Brien, Ire) *midfield on outer: shuffled bk and lost pl as pce qcknd 3f out: towards rr and rdn 2f out: rallied u.p and styd on wl for 7th* **7/1**[3]

8 *3/4* **Flintshire**[21] 6446 3-8-11 0 MaximeGuyon 7 114
(A Fabre, France) *midfield in tch on outer: shuffled bk and lost pl as pce qcknd 3f out: rdn over 2f out: styd on wout threatening* **12/1**

9 *nse* **Going Somewhere (BRZ)**[21] 6449 4-9-4 0 GregoryBenoist 4 115
(D Smaga, France) *prom on inner: shuffled bk on rail and lost pl as pce qcknd 3f out: rdn and swtchd lft 2f out: styd on wout threatening* **102/1**

10 *snk* **Meandre (FR)**[14] 6678 5-9-5 0 UmbertoRispoli 2 116+
(A Savujev, Czech Republic) *restrained in midfield on inner: shuffled bk on rail and in rr as pce qcknd 3f out: rdn over 2f out: nt clr run over 1f out: swtchd rt bk to rail and styd on but n.d* **50/1**

11 *nk* **Sahawar (FR)**[50] 3-8-11 0 ThierryThulliez 16 113
(C Ferland, France) *dropped in fr wd draw and hld up in last trio on inner: last 3f out: swtchd lft and rdn 2f out: sn outpcd: styd on but nvr a factor* **250/1**

12 *nse* **Leading Light (IRE)**[22] 6393 3-8-11 0 (p) GeraldMosse 5 113
(A P O'Brien, Ire) *racd awkwardly and appeared hrd to steer: sltly slow to stride and pushed along early: midfield: shuffled bk and lost pl as pce increased 3f out: rdn over 2f out: kpt on but n.d* **10/1**

13 *2* **Joshua Tree (IRE)**[49] 5575 6-9-5 0 RichardHughes 14 110
(Ed Dunlop) *sn led: rdn and strly pressed over 2f out: sn hdd: no ex and btn: steadily fdd* **100/1**

14 *3/4* **Ocovango**[21] 6446 3-8-11 0 StephanePasquier 13 108
(A Fabre, France) *trckd ldr on outer: cl 2nd 3f out: rdn to chal over 2f out: fnd little u.p and sn btn: steadily fdd* **28/1**

15 *snk* **Pirika (IRE)**[21] 6449 5-9-2 0 Pierre-CharlesBoudot 3 106
(A Fabre, France) *hld up in midfield on inner: dropped to rr as pce increased 3f out: rdn and btn over 1f out: nvr a factor* **40/1**

16 *2* **Very Nice Name (FR)**[21] 6449 4-9-5 0 PierantonioConvertino 1 106
(A De Mieulle, France) *dwlt sltly fr ins draw and pushed along to rcvr: midfield in tch on inner: lost pl as pce increased 3f out: sn rdn in rr: wl hld whn nt clr run ent fnl f* **100/1**

17 *3* **Haya Landa (FR)**[21] 6449 5-9-2 0 FranckBlondel 17 98
(Mme L Audon, France) *hld up in last: rdn and effrt to improve on outer 3f out: outpcd and btn over 1f out: sn dropped to last again: eased* **150/1**

2m 32.04s (1.64) **Going Correction** +0.625s/f (Yiel)
WFA 3 from 4yo+ 7lb **17 Ran SP% 123.5**
Speed ratings: **119,115,115,114,112 111,111,110,110,110 110,110,109,108,108 107,105**
WIN (incl. 1 euro stake): 5.80. PLACES: 1.70, 1.30, 2.20. DF: 5.20. SF: 14.40.
Owner HE Sh Joaan Bin Hamad Al Thani **Bred** Haras Du Quesnay **Trained** Chantilly, France
■ A second Arc for Criquette Head-Maarek, and a third for Thierry Jarnet.

FOCUS
Predictably run at a steady gallop, this was widely billed as a strong Arc de Triomphe, even in the absence of impressive King George winner Novellist, who defected the previous day on account of a fever. That impression was very much born out in the result, with the deeply impressive winner pulling clear of last year's runner-up and the French and Japanese Derby winners from this season. Treve has been rated as posting a big personal best, comparable to the best winners of recent years, with Orfevre to last year's Arc mark, and Kizuna to a small personal best.

7059a QATAR PRIX DE LA FORET (GROUP 1) (3YO+) (TURF) 7f
4:40 (12:00) 3-Y-0+ £139,365 (£55,756; £27,878; £13,926; £6,975)

RPR

1 **Moonlight Cloud**[56] 5314 5-8-13 0 ThierryJarnet 7 120+
(F Head, France) *stdd s and v confidently rdn: hld up in last: stl last but travelling wl 2f out: shkn up and qcknd v smartly over 1f out to sweep past rivals and ld ins fnl f: sn clr: easily* **4/7**[1]

2 *3* **Gordon Lord Byron (IRE)**[29] 6193 5-9-2 0 JohnnyMurtagh 6 114
(T Hogan, Ire) *t.k.h: sn led: rdn over 2f out: kpt on u.p tl hdd and brushed aside by wnr ins fnl f: kpt on to hold 2nd* **10/3**[2]

3 *snk* **Garswood**[29] 6193 3-9-0 0 RyanMoore 2 113
(Richard Fahey) *in tch in midfield: hdwy u.p on inner 2f out: chsd ldr jst ins fnl f: brushed aside by wnr ins fnl f but battled on and pressing for 2nd cl home* **12/1**

4 *snk* **Dux Scholar**[14] 5-9-2 0 UmbertoRispoli 9 114
(A Savujev, Czech Republic) *hld up in tch in last quartet: rdn and effrt wl over 1f out: 4th and r.o u.p fnl f: no ch w wnr* **50/1**

5 *1 1/4* **American Devil (FR)**[42] 5806 4-9-2 0 Pierre-CharlesBoudot 11 110
(J Van Handenhove, France) *hld up in tch in last trio: rdn and effrt wl over 2f out: styd on fnl f: no ch w wnr* **100/1**

6 *1/2* **Viztoria (IRE)**[22] 6392 3-8-10 0 WayneLordan 4 104
(Edward Lynam, Ire) *t.k.h: chsd ldrs: effrt u.p over 2f out: drvn to chse ldr 2f out tl jst ins fnl f: sn outpcd and wknd towards fin* **9/1**[3]

7 *1 1/4* **Anodin (IRE)**[21] 6450 3-9-0 0 (b) OlivierPeslier 1 104
(F Head, France) *t.k.h: led: sn hdd and trckd ldng trio: rdn and unable qck 2f out: no ex and swtchd lft over 1f out: wknd ins fnl f* **20/1**

8 *shd* **Blarney Stone (JPN)**[21] 6445 6-9-2 0 YusukeFujioka 3 105
(Yasutoshi Ikee, Japan) *hld up in tch in last trio: rdn and effrt whn swtchd rt over 1f out: kpt on but no threat to ldrs* **100/1**

9 *snk* **Sommerabend**[28] 6251 6-9-2 0 GeraldMosse 10 105
(M Rulec, Germany) *hld up in tch in midfield: rdn and effrt 2f out: no prog: wknd ins fnl f* **66/1**

10 *15* **Intense Pink**[29] 6193 4-8-13 0 SebSanders 8 61
(Chris Wall) *t.k.h: sn chsng ldr: jnd ldr 1/2-way tl rdn and unable qck ent fnl 2f: wknd over 1f out* **66/1**

11 *1 1/4* **Style Vendome (FR)**[21] 6450 3-9-0 0 (p) ThierryThulliez 5 60
(N Clement, France) *hld up in tch in midfield: rdn and no hdwy whn hmpd and lost pl qckly over 1f out: sn eased and lost tch* **20/1**

1m 21.08s (0.38) **Going Correction** +0.45s/f (Yiel)
WFA 3 from 4yo+ 2lb **11 Ran SP% 120.9**
Speed ratings: **115,111,111,111,109 109,107,107,107,90 88**
WIN (incl. 1 euro stake): 1.80. PLACES: 1.10, 1.30, 1.90. DF: 2.50. SF: 3.10.
Owner George Strawbridge **Bred** George Strawbridge **Trained** France

FOCUS
A decent edition of this event, the principal race in Europe for older horses over the trip, and a highly impressive performance from Moonlight Cloud. She didn't need to match her best, with the form rated around the third and fourth.

7060a QATAR PRIX DU CADRAN (GROUP 1) (4YO+) (TURF) 2m 4f
5:10 (12:00) 4-Y-0+ £139,365 (£55,756; £27,878; £13,926; £6,975)

RPR

1 **Altano (GER)**[28] 6248 7-9-2 0 EPedroza 10 116
(A Wohler, Germany) *hld up in tch in midfield: rdn and hdwy to chal 2f out: sn led but strly pressed: hdd over 1f out: drvn to ld again 1f out: styd on strly: drvn out* **9/1**

2 *2 1/2* **Tac De Boistron (FR)**[22] 6385 6-9-2 0 MartinHarley 8 113
(Marco Botti) *stdd s: t.k.h: hld up in midfield: hdwy on outer 4f out: chal 2f out: rdn and led over 1f out: drvn and hdd 1f out: kpt on but nt pce of wnr ins fnl f* **11/2**[2]

3 *6* **Times Up**[23] 6349 7-9-2 0 RyanMoore 7 107+
(Ed Dunlop) *stdd s: t.k.h: hld up in rr: effrt u.p on outer over 2f out: hung rt over 1f out but hdwy to chse ldng pair ins fnl f: styd on but no threat to ldrs* **4/1**[1]

4 *1 1/2* **Gloomy Sunday (FR)**[49] 5575 4-8-13 0 OlivierPeslier 4 103
(C Ferland, France) *chsd ldrs: wnt 2nd after 5f tl 8f out: rdn and effrt to chal ent fnl 2f: no ex and btn over 1f out: plugged on but lost 3rd ins fnl f* **13/2**[3]

5 *1* **High Jinx (IRE)**[23] 6349 5-9-2 0 JamesDoyle 6 105
(James Fanshawe) *hld up in midfield: rdn along 5f out: plenty to do but hdwy u.p 2f out: swtchd lft over 1f out: kpt on but no threat to ldrs* **4/1**[1]

6 *1 3/4* **Seismos (IRE)**[35] 6028 5-9-2 0 CristianDemuro 3 103
(A Wohler, Germany) *chsd ldrs: wnt 2nd 8f out tl ent fnl 2f: sn drvn and unable qck: btn over 1f out* **11/2**[2]

7 *10* **Chabal'Ozor (FR)**[49] 4-9-2 0 (b) ThierryThulliez 9 92
(Mlle C Cardenne, France) *hld up in rr: hdwy over 4f out: rdn and no hdwy jst over 2f out: sn wknd* **66/1**

8 *1/2* **Les Beaufs (FR)**[21] 6447 4-9-2 0 JulienGuillochon 1 93
(Mme V Seignoux, France) *led: rdn over 2f out: hdd wl over 1f out: no ex and btn over 1f out: sn wknd* **4/1**[1]

9 *snk* **Achtung (SPA)**[28] 6252 5-9-2 0 UmbertoRispoli 2 92
(J Lopez Sanchez, Spain) *in tch in midfield: rdn and struggling over 2f out: wknd wl over 1f out* **50/1**

10 *dist* **Coralhasi (FR)**[15] 11-9-2 0 Francois-XavierBertras 5
(Mlle I Gallorini, France) *chsd ldr for 5f: styd prom tl lost pl on inner 4f out: lost tch and virtually p.u fnl 2f: t.o* **66/1**

4m 24.38s (6.38) **Going Correction** +0.625s/f (Yiel) **10 Ran SP% 119.0**
Speed ratings: **112,111,108,108,107 106,102,102,102,**
WIN (incl. 1 euro stake): 11.60. PLACES: 2.90, 2.50, 2.50. DF: 25.10. SF: 59.30.
Owner Frau Dr I Hornig **Bred** Gestut Hof Ittlingen **Trained** Germany

FOCUS
A fair edition of this historic race. They took things pretty steadily, so that it wasn't the test of stamina it might have been. The first two finished clear and the winner posted a small personal best.

6769 PONTEFRACT (L-H)
Monday, October 7

OFFICIAL GOING: Good (good to soft in places; 7.0)
Wind: Light; behind Weather: Cloudy with sunny periods

7061 BRITISH STALLION STUDS EBF MAIDEN STKS 1m 2f 6y
2:10 (2:10) (Class 4) 2-Y-0 £4,528 (£1,347; £673; £336) Stalls Low

Form RPR

042 1 **Dullingham**[7] 6896 2-9-5 0 SilvestreDeSousa 5 79
(Charlie Appleby) *trckd ldr: cl up 1/2-way: led over 2f out and sn rdn clr: styd on wl fnl f* **2/1**[1]

42 2 *3* **Liberty Red (GER)**[54] 5379 2-9-5 0 GrahamLee 3 73
(Ed Dunlop) *trckd ldrs: hdwy 3f out: rdn 2f out: drvn over 1f out: kpt on one pce* **9/4**[2]

6 3 *nk* **Fun Mac (GER)**[43] 5790 2-9-5 0 RobertHavlin 2 72
(Hughie Morrison) *trckd ldrs on inner: effrt 3f out: rdn over 2f out: drvn wl over 1f out: kpt on one pce* **7/2**[3]

004 4 *14* **Slinky McVelvet**[69] 4848 2-8-11 47 BillyCray(3) 1 40
(Garry Moss) *led: rdn along over 3f out: hdd over 2f out and sn wknd* **100/1**

5 *9* **Mambo Rhythm** 2-9-0 0 LukeMorris 6 23
(Mark Johnston) *in tch: rdn along 1/2-way: sn drvn and outpcd fnl 3f* **18/1**

0562 6 *8* **Calrissian (IRE)**[57] 5309 2-9-5 76 DanielTudhope 10 13
(Alan Jarvis) *trckd ldng pair: pushed along 4f out: rdn 3f out: sn wknd* **8/1**

7 *1 1/4* **Petite Madame (IRE)** 2-9-0 0 PJMcDonald 7
(Ann Duffield) *green and sn pushed along in rr: rdn bef 1/2-way: sn outpcd and bhd* **40/1**

8 *17* **Walk Like A Giant** 2-9-5 0 AndrewElliott 8
(Tom Tate) *s.i.s: a in rr* **40/1**

0 9 *56* **Crafty Spell**[37] 5983 2-9-0 0 AdrianNicholls 9
(Mark Johnston) *towards rr: pushed along over 6f out: rdn 1/2-way: sn outpcd and bhd fnl 3f* **40/1**

2m 14.52s (0.82) **Going Correction** +0.05s/f (Good) **9 Ran SP% 111.0**
Speed ratings (Par 97): **98,95,95,84,76 70,69,55,11**
toteswingers 1&2 £1.30, 1&3 £1.70, 2&3 £1.90 CSF £6.21 TOTE £3.20: £1.20, £1.30, £1.60; EX 7.00 Trifecta £17.70 Pool: £3,848.31 - 162.81 winning units.
Owner Godolphin **Bred** Red House Stud **Trained** Newmarket, Suffolk

FOCUS
A stiff test for these juveniles, but no more than a fair maiden run at an even pace. The winner is progressing with each run.

7062 RACING UK ON SKY CHANNEL 432 NURSERY H'CAP 6f
2:40 (2:40) (Class 4) (0-85,84) 2-Y-0 £4,528 (£1,347; £673; £336) Stalls Low

Form RPR

31 1 **Focusofourthoughts (IRE)**[14] 6681 2-9-0 77 PJMcDonald 6 82
(Ann Duffield) *trckd ldng pair: swtchd rt and hdwy over 1f out: sn rdn: drvn ins fnl f: styd on to ld last 75yds* **11/1**

3520 2 *1/2* **Baars Causeway (IRE)**[9] 6821 2-8-7 70 LukeMorris 9 73
(Alan Jarvis) *cl up: rdn over 1f out: drvn to ld briefly ins fnl f: hdd and no ex last 75yds* **16/1**

3102 **3** *hd* **Instant Attraction (IRE)**[26] 6295 2-8-13 **76**............. MichaelO'Connell 8 78
(Jedd O'Keeffe) *slt ld: rdn wl over 1f out: drvn and hdd ins fnl f: kpt on u.p towards fin* **12/1**

3501 **4** *½* **Donny Rover (IRE)**[15] 6663 2-8-11 **74**..................(v) GrahamGibbons 13 75
(David C Griffiths) *dwlt: hdwy and in tch after 2f: chsd ldrs 2f out: rdn wl over 1f out: kpt on fnl f* **16/1**

643 **5** *½* **Breakable**[16] 6627 2-8-5 **68**.. BarryMcHugh 10 67+
(Tim Easterby) *dwlt and in rr: hdwy on outer 2f out: rdn over 1f out: styd on strly fnl f: nrst fin* **8/1**[3]

053 **6** *1 ¼* **Stomp**[17] 6589 2-8-13 **76**... DanielTudhope 4 72+
(Roger Charlton) *trckd ldrs whn n.m.r after 1f: t.k.h after: pushed along and lost pl 3f out: rdn 2f out: kpt on u.p fnl f* **15/8**[1]

5130 **7** *nk* **New Bidder**[29] 6233 2-9-4 **81**.. RussKennemore 7 76
(Jedd O'Keeffe) *trckd ldrs: hdwy over 2f out: rdn wl over 1f out: drvn and no imp fnl f* **8/1**[3]

1536 **8** *1 ¾* **Money Team (IRE)**[20] 6493 2-8-8 **78**............................ EvaMoscrop(7) 1 68+
(Philip Kirby) *trckd ldrs on inner whn bdly hmpd after 1f: towards rr tl hdwy on inner wl over 1f out: rdn and n.m.r ent fnl f: kpt on: nt rch ldrs* **16/1**

4241 **9** *hd* **Golden Spear**[20] 6487 2-9-1 **78**....................................(p) PatCosgrave 2 67
(Noel Quinlan) *trckd ldrs whn n.m.r and edgd lft after 1f: effrt and sme hdwy over 2f out: sn rdn and n.m.r over 1f out: one pce* **5/1**[2]

0430 **10** *¾* **Atheera (IRE)**[17] 6582 2-8-3 **66**...................................... PaulHanagan 5 53
(Mark Johnston) *trckd ldrs: pushed along 1/2-way: rdn over 2f out: sn wknd* **22/1**

5006 **11** *7* **Vine De Nada**[9] 6844 2-8-9 **72**................................. SilvestreDeSousa 3 38
(Mark Johnston) *a in rr* **14/1**

1m 18.38s (1.48) **Going Correction** +0.05s/f (Good) **11** Ran SP% **118.4**
Speed ratings (Par 97): **92,91,91,90,89 88,87,85,85,84 74**
toteswingers 1&2 £22.10, 1&3 £12.40, 2&3 £29.70 CSF £174.63 CT £2146.73 TOTE £11.70: £3.00, £5.00, £3.80; EX 161.80 Trifecta £1465.00 Pool: £2,889.60 - 1.47 winning units.
Owner Eshwin Racing, Hibbert & Starkie **Bred** James Hughes **Trained** Constable Burton, N Yorks
■ Stewards' Enquiry : Michael O'Connell one-day ban: careless riding (Oct 21); two-day ban: used whip above permitted level (Oct 22-23)

FOCUS
A fair nursery but it was a messy race, which favoured those ridden prominently. The form looks sound enough.

7063 £40 TOTEPOOL PACKAGE H'CAP — 1m 4y
3:10 (3:10) (Class 3) (0-95,85) 3-Y-O **£9,424** (£2,883; £1,485; £786) **Stalls** Low

Form RPR

1030 **1** **Party Royal**[11] 6767 3-9-5 **84**.................................. SilvestreDeSousa 2 93
(Mark Johnston) *mde most: rdn wl over 1f out: drvn ins fnl f: edgd rt and hld on wl towards fin* **11/2**

153 **2** *hd* **African Oil (FR)**[10] 6792 3-9-5 **84**.................................. GrahamLee 3 92
(Charles Hills) *t.k.h early: trckd ldng pair: hdwy to chse wnr 2f out: rdn to chal over 1f out: drvn and ev ch ins fnl f tl no ex nr fin* **15/8**[1]

230 **3** *21* **Veeraya**[51] 5510 3-9-6 **85**..(p) PaulHanagan 4 44
(William Haggas) *hld up in rr: pushed along over 3f out: rdn and outpcd over 2f out: plugged on u.p to take remote 3rd towards fin* **11/4**[2]

314 **4** *¾* **Bold Prediction (IRE)**[58] 5287 3-9-2 **81**...................... DanielTudhope 5 39
(K R Burke) *cl up: rdn along wl over 2f out: sn wknd: lost remote 3rd towards fin* **7/2**[3]

2010 **P** **Polar Chief**[18] 6550 3-9-5 **84**.. TonyHamilton 1
(Kristin Stubbs) *chsd ldrs whn lost action and qckly p.u after 1f: fatally injured* **10/1**

1m 45.36s (-0.54) **Going Correction** +0.05s/f (Good) **5** Ran SP% **108.1**
Speed ratings (Par 105): **104,103,82,82,**
CSF £15.66 TOTE £7.20: £2.60, £2.20; EX 16.60 Trifecta £48.10 Pool: £2,669.18 - 41.55 winning units.
Owner D & G Mercer 1 **Bred** Old Mill Stud & S Williams & J Parry **Trained** Middleham Moor, N Yorks

FOCUS
Not a strong handicap for the grade, with the front two pulling well clear. The race is rated around a better view of the winner's previous form.

7064 PHIL BULL TROPHY CONDITIONS STKS — 2m 1f 216y
3:40 (3:40) (Class 3) 3-Y-O+ **£7,762** (£2,310; £1,154; £577) **Stalls** Low

Form RPR

4142 **1** **Statutory (IRE)**[11] 6766 3-8-5 100.......................... SilvestreDeSousa 1 107+
(Mark Johnston) *mde all: rdn along over 2f out: styd on strly appr fnl f: sn clr: unchal* **4/9**[1]

4122 **2** *14* **Mutual Regard (IRE)**[34] 6066 4-9-3 95............................(p) LukeMorris 3 93
(Sir Mark Prescott Bt) *trckd ldng pair: chsd wnr fr 1/2-way: rdn 2f out: drvn and no imp over 1f out: eased fnl f* **3/1**[2]

6110 **3** *7* **Almagest**[17] 6585 5-9-3 88.. DanielTudhope 4 81
(David O'Meara) *hld up in rr: sme hdwy to chse ldng pair 6f out: rdn along 4f out: outpcd fnl 3f* **12/1**[3]

1001 **4** *6* **Riptide**[18] 6565 7-9-3 83..(v) GrahamLee 2 74
(Michael Scudamore) *chsd wnr: pushed along 1/2-way: grad lost pl and bhd fr 4f out* **14/1**

3m 58.89s (2.69) **Going Correction** +0.05s/f (Good)
WFA 3 from 4yo+ 12lb **4** Ran SP% **108.6**
Speed ratings (Par 107): **96,89,86,84**
CSF £2.06 TOTE £1.30; EX 2.20 Trifecta £3.90 Pool: £2,320.93 - 445.90 winning units.
Owner Sheikh Hamdan Bin Mohammed Al Maktoum **Bred** Darley **Trained** Middleham Moor, N Yorks

FOCUS
As is often the case this conditions event attracted a small field, and it was turned into a procession by very likeable winner. He rates a personal best.

7065 BOOK YOUR CHRISTMAS PARTY ON 0113 287 6387 CLAIMING STKS — 1m 4y
4:10 (4:10) (Class 5) 3-Y-O **£3,234** (£962; £481; £240) **Stalls** Low

Form RPR

330 **1** **Aglaophonos**[65] 5016 3-8-7 68..............................(p) SilvestreDeSousa 4 79
(Ian Williams) *trckd ldrs on inner: hdwy to chse clr ldr wl over 1f out: rdn to chal jst ins fnl f: led last 100yds: styd on strly* **6/1**[3]

1005 **2** *2 ½* **Unknown Villain (IRE)**[20] 6488 3-8-10 77................ RichardKingscote 1 76
(Tom Dascombe) *led: rdn clr 2f out: drvn and jnd ins fnl f: hdd and no ex last 100yds* **9/4**[1]

2666 **3** *8* **Rich Forever (IRE)**[13] 6720 3-8-7 67..........................(v) PaulHanagan 3 55
(James Bethell) *hld up in rr: hdwy on outer 2f out: sn rdn along to chse ldng pair: plugged on one pce* **7/2**[2]

4050 **4** *hd* **World Record (IRE)**[93] 4055 3-8-7 69.............................. RaulDaSilva 2 54
(Paul Green) *t.k.h early: sn trcking ldr: cl up 1/2-way: rdn along 3f out: wknd 2f out* **7/1**

0542 **5** *19* **Dark Ocean (IRE)**[17] 6587 3-8-9 66 ow1.................. MichaelO'Connell 5 12
(Jedd O'Keeffe) *chsd ldng pair: rdn along 3f out: drvn and wknd over 2f out* **9/4**[1]

1m 46.19s (0.29) **Going Correction** +0.05s/f (Good) **5** Ran SP% **110.5**
Speed ratings (Par 101): **100,97,89,89,70**
CSF £19.83 TOTE £5.00: £3.50, £1.70; EX 18.90 Trifecta £64.20 Pool: £2,131.75 - 24.89 winning units.
Owner Sir Alex Ferguson & Sotirios Hassiakos **Bred** Lady J Hayward **Trained** Portway, Worcs

FOCUS
A modest contest in which all five runners were dropping into claiming company for the first time. Not entirely convincing form.

7066 MANY THANKS TO DI PRICE H'CAP — 1m 4f 8y
4:40 (4:40) (Class 5) (0-70,70) 3-Y-O **£3,234** (£962; £481; £240) **Stalls** Low

Form RPR

0-25 **1** **Lady Of Yue**[102] 3735 3-8-7 **56** oh2.................................. PaulHanagan 3 70
(Eugene Stanford) *mde all: pushed along over 2f out: rdn clr wl over 1f out: styd on strly* **25/1**

3005 **2** *2 ¼* **Aiyana**[24] 6363 3-8-13 **62**... RobertHavlin 2 71
(Hughie Morrison) *trckd ldrs: hdwy 3f out: chsd wnr over 2f out: rdn wl over 1f out: drvn fnl f and no imp towards fin* **14/1**

5 **3** *6* **Lookbeforeyouleap**[11] 6780 3-9-7 **70**.......................... DanielTudhope 10 69
(David O'Meara) *hld up in midfield: hdwy 3f out: rdn to chse ldng pair wl over 1f out: drvn and no imp fnl f* **14/1**

-500 **4** *2* **Jackaddock**[125] 2957 3-8-10 **59**...................................... PJMcDonald 8 55
(James Bethell) *towards rr: hdwy over 2f out: rdn along wl over 1f out: kpt on u.p fnl f* **50/1**

5103 **5** *nk* **Nile Knight**[48] 5606 3-9-7 **70**...........................(b) RichardKingscote 9 66
(Marcus Tregoning) *trckd ldrs: hdwy over 3f out: rdn along over 2f out: drvn and one pce fnl 2f* **15/2**[3]

3032 **6** *2* **Polar Forest**[26] 6297 3-8-6 **58**...................................... JasonHart(3) 6 51
(Richard Guest) *dwlt and bhd: sme hdwy 3f out: rdn along wl over 1f out: nvr nr ldrs* **8/1**

1543 **7** *hd* **Nonotnow**[62] 5107 3-9-5 **68**.. DavidAllan 7 60
(Tim Easterby) *hld up towards rr: hdwy 3f out: pushed along and n.m.r 2f out: sn rdn and n.d* **7/1**[2]

05-3 **8** *¾* **Hurry Home Poppa (IRE)**[27] 6272 3-9-6 **69**..................... DaleSwift 4 60
(John Mackie) *trckd ldrs on inner: effrt 3f out: rdn along whn n.m.r and sltly hmpd 2f out: sn wknd* **7/1**[2]

6126 **9** *3 ¼* **First Secretary**[23] 6405 3-9-7 **70**.................................. GrahamLee 5 56
(Roger Charlton) *hld up in midfield: hdwy 4f out: rdn to chse ldrs 2f out: sn drvn and wknd* **3/1**[1]

0601 **10** *4* **El Massivo (IRE)**[11] 6782 3-9-2 **65**.............................. JimmyQuinn 1 44
(William Jarvis) *midfield: rdn along over 4f out: sn wknd* **8/1**

6013 **11** *25* **Darakti (IRE)**[60] 5197 3-9-0 **63**....................................(b) LukeMorris 12
(Alan McCabe) *dwlt: a in rr* **16/1**

6203 **12** *4* **Young Jay**[17] 6601 3-8-12 **61**.................................. SilvestreDeSousa 11
(Mark Johnston) *cl up: rdn along 3f out: wkng whn edgd lft 2f out: sn in rr* **12/1**

2m 39.46s (-1.34) **Going Correction** +0.05s/f (Good) **12** Ran SP% **116.7**
Speed ratings (Par 101): **106,104,100,99,98 97,97,97,94,92 75,72**
toteswingers 1&2 £61.50, 1&3 £50.80, 2&3 £42.00 CSF £334.16 CT £5019.02 TOTE £26.30: £8.20, £5.30, £4.50; EX 446.00 Trifecta £2036.10 Part won. Pool: £2,714.82 - 0.14 winning units..
Owner Mrs Janice Quy **Bred** Mrs J M Quy **Trained** Newmarket, Suffolk

FOCUS
Only a fair staying handicap for 3yos, but it looked competitive on paper. Big improvement from the winner, but no fluke and she could progress again.

7067 BUY YOUR 2014 ANNUAL BADGE TODAY MAIDEN STKS — 1m 4y
5:10 (5:17) (Class 5) 3-Y-O **£3,234** (£962; £481; £240) **Stalls** Low

Form RPR

5440 **1** **Duke Of Grazeon (IRE)**[34] 6071 3-9-5 62.......................... RaulDaSilva 3 70
(Mrs Ilka Gansera-Leveque) *trckd ldng pair on inner: hdwy 2f out: swtchd rt and rdn to ld over 1f out: clr ent fnl f: kpt on* **28/1**

6 **2** *½* **Bison Grass**[18] 6555 3-9-5 0..............................(b) PatrickDonaghy 2 69
(Giles Bravery) *trckd ldrs: hdwy over 2f out: rdn to chse wnr jst ins fnl f: kpt on* **8/1**[3]

6-2 **3** *5* **Thatchmaster (USA)**[168] 1713 3-9-5 0...................... SilvestreDeSousa 5 57
(Mark Johnston) *sn trcking ldr: effrt over 2f out: rdn along wl over 1f out: drvn ent fnl f and sn wknd* **8/13**[1]

-540 **4** *3* **Rust (IRE)**[13] 6728 3-9-5 65... PJMcDonald 9 50
(Ann Duffield) *hld up in rr: hdwy on inner 2f out: sn rdn: kpt on fnl f: nrst fin* **12/1**

4040 **5** *1 ½* **Tanawar (IRE)**[12] 6758 3-9-5 65....................................... GrahamLee 6 47
(Tim Etherington) *towards rr tl styd on fnl 2f: n.d* **16/1**

6 *1 ¼* **Frost Fire (USA)** 3-9-0 0.. AdrianNicholls 1 39
(Mark Johnston) *t.k.h: led: rdn along 2f out: hdd over 1f out and sn wknd* **10/1**

U00 **7** *9* **Top Line Banker**[31] 6178 3-9-5 0..................................... BarryMcHugh 7 23
(Brian Ellison) *a towards rr* **80/1**

43 **8** *1* **Artistical (IRE)**[20] 6486 3-9-5 0...................................... PaulHanagan 8 21
(William Haggas) *trckd ldrs: rdn along over 2f out: sn wknd* **4/1**[2]

9 *11* **Magical Mischief** 3-9-0 0.. MichaelStainton 10
(Chris Fairhurst) *wnt rt s: a in rr: rdn along 1/2-way: sn outpcd and bhd* **80/1**

10 *13* **Mrs Gorsky** 3-9-0 0.. RussKennemore 4
(Patrick Holmes) *dwlt: a towards rr: outpcd and bhd fnl 3f* **80/1**

1m 47.64s (1.74) **Going Correction** +0.05s/f (Good) **10** Ran SP% **122.8**
Speed ratings (Par 101): **93,92,87,84,83 81,72,71,60,47**
toteswingers 1&2 £25.30, 1&3 £8.10, 2&3 £2.20 CSF £245.57 TOTE £31.60: £6.10, £2.70, £1.10; EX 280.80 Trifecta £1398.60 Pool: £5,964.49 - 3.19 winning units.
Owner J R Rowbottom **Bred** Epona Bloodstock Ltd **Trained** Newmarket, Suffolk

FOCUS
An ordinary 3yo maiden, and much the slowest the three C&D races. Shaky form, rated a bit cautiously.

T/Plt: £1,317.90 to a £1 stake. Pool: £57,700.12 - 31.96 winning units T/Qpdt: £231.80 to a £1 stake. Pool: £3,227.08 - 10.30 winning units JR

5757 WINDSOR (R-H)

Monday, October 7

OFFICIAL GOING: Good (8.4)

Wind: Light; behind Weather: Fine but cloudy; mild

7068 THAMES MATERIALS FEGENTRI WORLD CUP OF NATIONS STKS (AN AMATEUR RIDERS' H'CAP) 5f 10y

1:50 (1:52) (Class 6) (0-65,65) 3-Y-0+ £1,871 (£435; £435; £145) Stalls Low

Form RPR

0600 **1** **Give Us A Belle (IRE)**[39] 5930 4-10-10 **51** oh6......(vt) MrAFerramosca 5 54
(Christine Dunnett) *pressed ldr after 1f: chal fr 2f out: upsides fnl f: won on the nod* **50/1**

5302 **2** *nse* **Madame Kintyre**[22] 6436 5-10-10 **51** oh1.............. MrYannickMergirie 3 54
(Rod Millman) *led after 1f: mde most after: hrd pressed fnl f: hdd post* **5/1**[3]

42U3 **2** *dht* **Griffin Point (IRE)**[12] 6745 6-11-8 **63**..........................(b) MrKevinTobin 4 66
(William Muir) *towards rr: clsd on outer fr 2f out: frnticaly rdn to chal fnl f: upsides last 100yds: jst pipped* **15/8**[1]

0430 **4** *¾* **Prince Of Passion (CAN)**[90] 4146 5-11-5 **60**............ MissEilidhGrant 7 60
(Derek Shaw) *towards rr: clsd on wd outside fr 1/2-way: nudged along and kpt on fr over 1f out: nvr quite able to chal* **12/1**

0601 **5** *2 ¼* **Gaelic Wizard (IRE)**[25] 6344 5-11-7 **62**......................(p) MrChrisMartin 8 54
(Dominic Ffrench Davis) *taken down early: pressed ldrs 2f: sn rdn: nt qckn 2f out: wl hld after* **11/4**[2]

4635 **6** *3* **Surrey Dream (IRE)**[21] 6462 4-10-10 **51** oh5.................(p) MrRDeegan 2 32
(John Bridger) *nvr on terms w ldrs: struggling fr 2f out* **7/1**

4600 **7** *8* **Marvelino**[25] 6345 3-11-0 **55**...(b) MissLMattes 1 9
(Pat Eddery) *led 1f: wknd 1/2-way: eased and wl bhd* **16/1**

060 **8** *35* **Laura's Bairn**[39] 5930 4-11-10 **65**..........................(v) MrFabrizioPerego 6
(J R Jenkins) *fractious bef ent stalls: dwlt: sn outpcd: wl t.o* **20/1**

1m 0.44s (0.14) **Going Correction** -0.225s/f (Firm) 8 Ran SP% **110.9**

Speed ratings (Par 101): **89,88,88,87,84 79,66,10**Places: Griffin Point £1.20; Madame Kintyre £1.30; CSF: GUAB, GP £67.68; AB, MK £133.54; Exacta: GUAB, GP £60.00; GUAB, MK £121.60; Tricast: GUAB, GP, MK £280.17; GUAB, MK, GP £348.47 toteswingers 1&GP £24.10, 1&MK £36.70, GP&MK £2.80 TOTE £34.50: £27, £Owner, £F Butler & Mrs C Dunnett, £BredAudrey Frances Stynes Trained Trifecta £Hingham, Norfolk n A first British success from Italian Antonio Ferramosca..

FOCUS

Inner of straight dolled out 2yds at 6f and at normal position at winning post. Top bend dolled out yards from inner configuration adding 3yds to race of 1m and beyond. The runners avoided the stands' rail in this amateur riders' handicap and it produced an incredibly tight finish. The form is just moderate, with a surprise personal best from the winner.

7069 IRISH STALLION FARMS EBF MAIDEN STKS (DIV I) 1m 67y

2:20 (2:21) (Class 5) 2-Y-0 £2,911 (£866; £432; £216) Stalls Low

Form RPR

44 **1** **Master Dancer**[61] 5122 2-9-5 0...................................... GeorgeBaker 10 74+
(Philip Hide) *taken down early: mde all: hanging lft bnd over 5f out to over 4f out: kicked on 3f out: hrd pressed fnl f: hld on wl* **8/1**[2]

4 **2** *nk* **Be Seeing You**[16] 6641 2-9-5 0...................................... JamesDoyle 1 74
(Roger Charlton) *trckd ldng pair: rdn over 2f out: wnt 2nd wl over 1f out: clsd to chal fnl f: jst hld nr fin* **11/10**[1]

0 **3** *3 ¾* **Honor Bound**[34] 6063 2-9-0 0.. JimCrowley 12 60
(Ralph Beckett) *chsd wnr: carried lft bnd 5f out: rdn over 2f out: lost 2nd wl over 1f out: steadily lft bhd* **8/1**[2]

045 **4** *2 ¼* **Jersey Royal**[16] 6641 2-9-5 63... SeanLevey 5 60
(Richard Hannon) *chsd ldrs in 5th: rdn over 2f out: sn outpcd: kpt on fnl f* **10/1**

0 **5** *hd* **Sweet Lily Pea (USA)**[14] 6690 2-9-0 0............................ HarryBentley 8 55
(Olly Stevens) *chsd ldng trio: shkn up over 2f out: nt qckn fr 2f out: one pce* **33/1**

00 **6** *2 ½* **Thunder Pass (IRE)**[45] 5698 2-9-5 0............................ JimmyFortune 7 54+
(Hughie Morrison) *s.i.s: sn in midfield: outpcd fr 3f out: no imp on ldrs after* **16/1**

7 *2 ¼* **Bountiful Sin** 2-9-5 0.. TomQueally 2 49+
(George Margarson) *mostly in last quartet: shkn up over 2f out: nvr on terms* **33/1**

0 **8** *½* **Gimme Five**[13] 6733 2-9-5 0.. FergusSweeney 3 47
(Alan King) *nvr beyond midfield: outpcd and shkn up over 2f out: nvr on terms* **50/1**

9 *nse* **Coastal Storm** 2-9-0 0.. AndreaAtzeni 11 42
(Hughie Morrison) *dwlt: a in last quartet: shkn up and no prog over 2f out* **33/1**

10 *1 ¾* **Solid Justice (IRE)** 2-9-5 0... DaneO'Neill 4 43
(Charles Hills) *dwlt: a in last quartet: rdn and no prog over 2f out* **9/1**[3]

0 **11** *4 ½* **Lochalsh (IRE)**[24] 6355 2-9-5 0.. AdamKirby 6 33
(William Knight) *hld up and mostly in last: shkn up 2f out: nvr a factor* **14/1**

0 **12** *2 ½* **With A Twist**[17] 6590 2-9-0 0...(t) LiamKeniry 9 22
(Andrew Balding) *in tch in midfield tl wknd 3f out* **25/1**

1m 44.95s (0.25) **Going Correction** -0.325s/f (Firm) 12 Ran SP% **116.1**

Speed ratings (Par 95): **85,84,80,78,78 76,73,73,73,71 66,64**

toteswingers 1&2 £3.00, 1&3 £11.00, 2&3 £1.40 CSF £15.98 TOTE £9.80: £2.50, £1.10, £2.00; EX 25.60 Trifecta £103.10 Pool: £1,798.03 - 13.06 winning units.

Owner S P C Woods **Bred** D J Bloodstock, G Roddick & Wrottesley Ltd **Trained** Findon, W Sussex

■ Stewards' Enquiry : George Baker Fine: £80, entered wrong stall.

FOCUS

The lesser of the two divisions, despite the time being fractionally the quicker. An 'old school' race for the track with the winner bagging the rail and the order barely changing. The bare form is nothing special.

7070 IRISH STALLION FARMS EBF MAIDEN STKS (DIV II) 1m 67y

2:50 (2:52) (Class 5) 2-Y-0 £2,911 (£866; £432; £216) Stalls Low

Form RPR

4 **1** **Oasis Fantasy (IRE)**[67] 4925 2-9-5 0............................ AndreaAtzeni 4 71+
(Ed Dunlop) *wl in tch in midfield: pushed along jst over 3f out: clsd on ldrs over 1f out: rdn and brought between rivals fnl f: led last 75yds: readily* **9/2**[3]

4 **2** *½* **Throne Room**[19] 6534 2-9-5 0.. WilliamBuick 9 70
(John Gosden) *prog out wd to chse ldr after 1f: rdn wl over 2f out: clsd to chal and upsides fnl f: outpcd last 75yds* **1/1**[1]

05 **3** *nk* **Glasgow Central**[22] 6430 2-9-5 0.................................... DaneO'Neill 5 69
(Charles Hills) *led: rdn over 2f out: jnd u.p ins fnl f: hdd last 75yds* **14/1**

4 **4** *½* **Elusive Guest (FR)** 2-9-5 0... TomQueally 6 68
(George Margarson) *wl in tch in midfield but rn green: prog 3f out: cl 3rd fr 2f out and tried to chal: no ex fnl f* **4/1**[2]

5 *nk* **Bury Pacer (IRE)** 2-9-5 0... SeanLevey 7 67+
(Richard Hannon) *s.i.s: sn in tch in midfield: shkn up over 2f out: clsd on ldrs and looked dangerous jst over 1f out: rn green and one pce after* **14/1**

00 **6** *nse* **Golden Journey (IRE)**[30] 6184 2-9-5 0............................ AdamKirby 3 67
(Clive Cox) *trckd ldr 1f: styd cl up: rdn over 2f out: hanging lft over 1f out: swtchd rt and kpt on fnl f* **20/1**

00 **7** *5* **Snow Conditions**[27] 6281 2-9-0 0.................................. LiamKeniry 11 51
(Philip Hide) *dwlt: mostly in 8th: nt on terms and shkn up wl over 2f out: kpt on fnl f* **100/1**

8 *¾* **Supachap** 2-9-5 0.. JimmyFortune 8 54+
(Hughie Morrison) *trckd ldrs: stl cl up 2f out: wkng whn short of room briefly jst over 1f out* **25/1**

66 **9** *hd* **Gavlar**[24] 6355 2-9-5 0.. JimCrowley 2 54
(William Knight) *s.i.s: mostly in last trio: pushed along 3f out: reminder 2f out: nvr on terms but nt totally disgracd* **33/1**

10 *4* **Gracie Hart** 2-9-0 0.. J-PGuillambert 10 39+
(Jo Hughes) *s.v.s: a in last trio: nvr a factor* **100/1**

11 *8* **Moscato** 2-9-5 0... ChrisCatlin 1 26
(Sir Mark Prescott Bt) *s.i.s: sn urged along in last trio and rn green: nvr a factor* **80/1**

1m 45.02s (0.32) **Going Correction** -0.325s/f (Firm) 11 Ran SP% **116.3**

Speed ratings (Par 95): **85,84,84,83,83 83,78,77,77,73 65**

toteswingers 1&2 £1.20, 1&3 £8.90, 2&3 £2.90 CSF £8.85 TOTE £6.20: £1.50, £1.40, £3.80; EX 12.50 Trifecta £58.00 Pool: £2,189.67 - 28.31 winning units.

Owner Windflower Overseas & J L Dunlop OBE **Bred** Windflower Overseas **Trained** Newmarket, Suffolk

FOCUS

This looked the better of the two divisions beforehand and, despite the time being a fraction slower, it should prove the stronger contest. The field finished compressed so it's hard to rate the form higher, but the race should produce winners.

7071 FRONTLINE SECURITY SOLUTIONS CLAIMING STKS 1m 2f 7y

3:20 (3:21) (Class 6) 3-4-Y-0 £1,940 (£577; £288; £144) Stalls Centre

Form RPR

0640 **1** **Well Painted (IRE)**[18] 6551 4-9-8 85............................(tp) WilliamBuick 1 82
(William Haggas) *trckd ldrs: prog and rdn over 2f out: chsd ldr over 1f out: drvn to ld ins fnl f: jst hld on* **13/8**[1]

1000 **2** *shd* **Stiff Upper Lip (IRE)**[12] 6743 3-8-11 73..........................(b) SeanLevey 3 76
(Richard Hannon) *trckd ldng pair: wnt 2nd 4f out: led over 2f out: hrd rdn and hdd ins fnl f: kpt on wl: jst failed* **6/1**

5662 **3** *4 ½* **Juvenal (IRE)**[14] 6700 4-9-4 73....................................(p) JimmyFortune 2 68
(Richard Hannon) *slowly away: hld up in last pair: prog fr 3f out: rdn to chse ldng pair and cl enough jst over 1f out: fdd* **7/2**[3]

2005 **4** *hd* **Fair Comment**[25] 6321 3-8-6 57.. HarryBentley 7 60
(Michael Blanshard) *hld up towards rr: tried to cl on ldrs on outer over 2f out: nt qckn wl over 1f out: outpcd* **33/1**

5200 **5** *3 ½* **Rock God (IRE)**[12] 6743 3-8-7 70.....................................(bt) JohnFahy 6 53
(Eve Johnson Houghton) *trckd ldrs: rdn and cl up 2f out: sn wknd* **11/1**

2440 **6** *2 ½* **Jack Who's He (IRE)**[8] 6869 4-9-4 74...........................[1] MartinDwyer 8 53
(William Muir) *mostly in last pair: urged along 3f out: no prog and btn 2f out* **3/1**[2]

03 **7** *3 ¼* **Violet Plum**[23] 6407 3-8-3 0.. SimonPearce(3) 5 39
(Laura Mongan) *trckd ldr: led over 4f out to over 2f out: wknd over 1f out* **66/1**

1000 **8** *1 ¾* **Halling Dancer**[42] 5825 4-9-2 71..................................... WilliamCarson 4 40
(Lee Carter) *gave problems in preliminaries: led and t.k.h: hdd and nt run on over 4f out: wknd over 2f out* **25/1**

000- **9** *58* **Noosa Boy**[340] 7499 4-9-1 41...(t) ChrisCatlin 9
(Luke Dace) *in tch to 4f out: wknd rapidly 3f out: t.o and virtually p.u* **125/1**

2m 5.95s (-2.75) **Going Correction** -0.325s/f (Firm)

WFA 3 from 4yo 5lb 9 Ran SP% **117.0**

Speed ratings (Par 101): **98,97,94,94,91 89,86,85,38**

toteswingers 1&2 £2.80, 1&3 £1.60, 2&3 £3.20 CSF £12.17 TOTE £2.90: £1.40, £1.40, £1.60; EX 15.90 Trifecta £47.20 Pool: £2,298.55 - 36.49 winning units.

Owner Options O Syndicate **Bred** Round Hill Stud **Trained** Newmarket, Suffolk

■ Stewards' Enquiry : Sean Levey one-day ban: careless riding (Oct 21)

FOCUS

The front pair drew clear in what was quite a decent claimer. The winner is rated a stone+ off his 3yo best, with the runner-up close to form.

7072 READING POST H'CAP 1m 3f 135y

3:50 (3:50) (Class 3) (0-90,90) 3-Y-0+ £7,439 (£2,213; £1,106; £553) Stalls Centre

Form RPR

4154 **1** **She's Late**[17] 6591 3-9-0 **85**..(p) WilliamBuick 4 95
(John Gosden) *mostly chsd ldr: taken to centre of crse in st: rdn to ld 2f out: in command fnl f: advantage dwindling at fin* **5/1**[3]

1213 **2** *½* **Bantam (IRE)**[43] 5795 3-9-3 **88**...................................... AndreaAtzeni 11 97+
(Ed Dunlop) *hld up in rr: rdn and prog fr 3f out: styd on to take 2nd ins fnl f: clsd on wnr fin* **4/1**[2]

2421 **3** *¾* **Hassle (IRE)**[14] 6696 4-9-1 **79**...(p) AdamKirby 5 87
(Clive Cox) *trckd ldrs: prog towards nr side rail to chal 2f out: chsd wnr over 1f out to ins fnl f: kpt on* **7/1**

3620 **4** *1 ¾* **Tinshu (IRE)**[17] 6596 7-9-2 **80**.......................................(p) DaneO'Neill 9 85
(Derek Haydn Jones) *hld up in midfield: gng wl enough on wd outside 3f out: rdn and nt qckn 2f out: one pce after* **16/1**

412 **5** *shd* **Alegra**[38] 5960 3-9-0 **85**... TomQueally 8 90
(Lady Cecil) *trckd ldrs: shkn up 3f out: nt qckn 2f out: one pce after* **11/4**[1]

4004 **6** *2 ½* **Pitchoun (IRE)**[22] 6434 3-8-11 **82**..................................... LiamJones 1 83
(Mark Johnston) *led: styd against nr side rail in st: drvn and hdd 2f out: wknd* **40/1**

1241 **7** *nse* **Rhombus (IRE)**[30] 6211 3-9-5 **90**...................................... ChrisCatlin 6 91
(Ismail Mohammed) *trckd ldrs: rdn wl over 2f out: steadily fdd fnl 2f* **11/2**

6006 **8** *nk* **Jupiter Storm**[18] 6559 4-9-1 **79**...................................... JimmyFortune 3 79
(Gary Moore) *stdd s: hld up in last: rdn 3f out: no great prog* **14/1**

3230 **9** *shd* **Starwatch**[17] 6596 6-8-10 **77**............................ MichaelJMMurphy(3) 10 77
(John Bridger) *a wl in rr: rdn and struggling 3f out* **50/1**

2630 **10** *¾* **Takeitfromalady (IRE)**[8] 6868 4-8-9 **78**...................(b) OisinMurphy(5) 2 77
(Lee Carter) *slowly away: prog to trck ldng pair after 3f: rdn 3f out: wknd jst over 2f out* **25/1**

5546 **11** 4 ½ **Aldwick Bay (IRE)**[51] 5535 5-8-12 **76** oh4 SeanLevey 7 67
(Richard Hannon) *hld up in last trio: jst pushed along fr 3f out: steadily wknd* **40/1**

2m 26.98s (-2.52) **Going Correction** -0.325s/f (Firm)
WFA 3 from 4yo+ 7lb 11 Ran SP% **114.5**
Speed ratings (Par 107): **95,94,94,93,92 91,91,91,90,90 87**
toteswingers 1&2 £4.20, 1&3 £6.90, 2&3 £4.60 CSF £23.85 CT £139.30 TOTE £6.30: £1.50, £1.50, £2.00; EX 21.50 Trifecta £186.40 Pool: £2,798.87 - 11.26 winning units.
Owner Martin Hughes & Michael Kerr-Dineen **Bred** Cheveley Park Stud Ltd **Trained** Newmarket, Suffolk

FOCUS
Run at just a fair gallop, the in-form, progressive types came to the fore and this looks decent form for the grade. The fourth sets the standard.

7073 JOE WARD HILL MEMORIAL MAIDEN STKS 6f
4:20 (4:22) (Class 5) 3-Y-O+ £2,587 (£770; £384; £192) Stalls Low

Form RPR
1 **Loud** 3-9-5 0 AdamKirby 13 79+
(Mark Johnston) *racd wd: prog to press ldng pair over 3f out: rdn to ld wl over 1f out: styd on wl fnl f* **7/2**[3]

23 **2** 1 **Pearl Angel (IRE)**[47] 5647 3-9-0 0 HarryBentley 2 71
(Olly Stevens) *trckd ldrs: rdn over 1f out: styd on to take 2nd ins fnl f: unable to threaten wnr* **5/1**

044 **3** 1 ¼ **Joyous**[47] 5647 3-9-0 58 FergusSweeney 11 67
(Dean Ivory) *pressed ldr after 2f: rdn and upsides 2f out: chsd wnr sn after tl ins fnl f: one pce* **16/1**

4 1 ½ **Poyle Vinnie** 3-9-5 0 TomQueally 10 67
(George Margarson) *s.i.s: in rr: prog towards outer fr 1/2-way: clsd on ldrs jst over 1f out: no ex* **25/1**

5 3 ¼ **Bookmaker** 3-9-5 0 JimCrowley 4 57
(Olly Stevens) *chsd ldrs: pushed along 1/2-way: outpcd fr 2f out* **10/3**[2]

2 **6** 2 **Pucker Up**[22] 6425 3-9-0 0 SeanLevey 9 45
(Ed McMahon) *led: styd against nr side rail in st: hdd & wknd wl over 1f out* **3/1**[1]

004 **7** ½ **Pashan Garh**[20] 6486 4-9-1 72 (p) ThomasGarner(5) 6 49
(Pat Eddery) *s.i.s: sn in tch: rdn on outer 1/2-way: steadily wknd fnl 2f* **13/2**

8 ¾ **Staines Massive** 3-9-5 0 KieranO'Neill 3 46
(Brett Johnson) *nvr beyond midfield: shkn up 1/2-way: nt on terms 2f out: no ch after* **50/1**

2-30 **9** 8 **Mosman**[13] 6735 3-9-5 65 MartinDwyer 12 21
(Dean Ivory) *pressed ldr 2f: sn lost pl and rdn: wknd rapidly over 1f out: eased* **25/1**

6 **10** 12 **Bossy Jane**[19] 6519 3-9-0 0 RichardThomas 7
(Zoe Davison) *slowly away: a struggling in last pair: t.o* **100/1**

0-0 **11** 2 ½ **Incognita**[25] 6319 3-9-0 0 ChrisCatlin 5
(Chris Down) *v.s.a: a struggling in last pair: t.o* **100/1**

1m 11.79s (-1.21) **Going Correction** -0.225s/f (Firm)
WFA 3 from 4yo 1lb 11 Ran SP% **117.8**
Speed ratings (Par 103): **99,97,96,94,89 87,86,85,74,58 55**
toteswingers 1&2 £4.00, 1&3 £12.40, 2&3 £10.30 CSF £20.71 TOTE £4.30: £1.20, £1.50, £4.70; EX 20.60 Trifecta £168.50 Pool: £3,695.30 - 16.44 winning units.
Owner Sheikh Hamdan Bin Mohammed Al Maktoum **Bred** P C Hunt **Trained** Middleham Moor, N Yorks

FOCUS
A typically modest late-season 3yo-plus sprint maiden, with the third carrying a BHA rating of just 58. A nice start to the winner, with the next two improving a little on their Warwick form.

7074 IVOR LAWS MEMORIAL NURSERY H'CAP 5f 10y
4:50 (4:50) (Class 4) (0-85,85) 2-Y-O £3,752 (£1,116; £557; £278) Stalls Low

Form RPR
1421 **1** **Bounty Hunter (IRE)**[22] 6432 2-9-2 **85** (p) JackDuern(5) 3 89
(Tom Dascombe) *disp ld: rdn over 1f out: kpt on wl to take narrow advantage last 50yds* **9/4**[1]

1053 **2** nk **Trinity River**[13] 6731 2-8-11 **75** JamesDoyle 2 78
(Daniel Kubler) *disp ld: rdn over 1f out: stl disputing ins fnl f: jst hld last 50yds* **6/1**

0610 **3** 1 **Finflash (IRE)**[25] 6328 2-9-1 **79** WilliamBuick 4 78
(Mick Channon) *w.w bhd ldrs: rdn to go 3rd jst over 1f out: tried to cl on ldng pair but no imp last 75yds* **5/2**[2]

1406 **4** 2 **Iseemist (IRE)**[94] 4025 2-8-6 **73** MichaelJMMurphy(3) 7 65
(John Gallagher) *racd on outer: cl up: on terms w ldng pair 2f out: fdd fnl f* **16/1**

1100 **5** ½ **Touch The Clouds**[17] 6582 2-8-12 **76** TomQueally 1 66
(Kevin Ryan) *racd against nr side rail: cl up: rdn 2f out: nt qckn over 1f out: outpcd after* **9/2**[3]

1345 **6** ½ **Captain Ryan**[33] 6111 2-8-0 **64** oh1 KieranO'Neill 6 53
(Peter Makin) *sn detached in last and struggling: nvr on terms but plugged on fr over 1f out* **12/1**

4000 **7** 4 **Overstep (IRE)**[15] 6663 2-8-1 **65** (b) NickyMackay 5 39
(Mark Johnston) *chsd ldrs but racd rather awkwardly: lost pl 2f out: wknd jst over 1f out* **12/1**

59.4s (-0.90) **Going Correction** -0.225s/f (Firm) 7 Ran SP% **113.1**
Speed ratings (Par 97): **98,97,95,92,91 91,84**
toteswingers 1&2 £3.80, 1&3 £1.90, 2&3 £2.60 CSF £15.83 TOTE £2.50: £1.80, £3.00; EX 12.10 Trifecta £46.00 Pool: £3,379.74 - 55.04 winning units.
Owner D Ward **Bred** B Holland, S Hillen & J Cullinan **Trained** Malpas, Cheshire

FOCUS
A decent nursery for the grade, and straightforward form.

7075 LADIES OF LEASING H'CAP 1m 67y
5:20 (5:21) (Class 4) (0-80,80) 3-Y-O+ £4,690 (£1,395; £697; £348) Stalls Low

Form RPR
0120 **1** **Investment Expert (IRE)**[32] 6126 3-9-0 **76** WilliamBuick 3 88+
(Jeremy Noseda) *hld up in last trio: prog on outer fr 3f out: drvn over 1f out: clsd fnl f: led post* **15/2**[3]

2233 **2** shd **Legal Waves (IRE)**[47] 5649 3-9-1 **77** JimmyFortune 13 88
(Brian Meehan) *trckd ldng pair: led against nr side rail 2f out: drvn over 1f out: edgd lft fnl f: hdd last stride* **8/1**

3562 **3** ¾ **Melvin The Grate (IRE)**[8] 6867 3-8-13 **80** OisinMurphy(5) 12 89
(Andrew Balding) *hld up in midfield: pushed along over 3f out: prog over 2f out: chsd ldrs over 1f out: clsd fnl f: nt quite pce to chal* **3/1**[1]

6015 **4** shd **Red Art (IRE)**[30] 6203 4-9-4 **77** JamesDoyle 1 86
(Charles Hills) *prom: rdn to chse ldr wl over 1f out: clsd fnl f but lost 2nd last 75yds* **8/1**

520 **5** 6 **Starlight Symphony (IRE)**[30] 6188 3-9-0 **76** (b) TomQueally 6 71
(Eve Johnson Houghton) *hld up in last: prog on wd outside fr 3f out: drvn and no hdwy over 1f out: edgd rt fnl f* **25/1**

4531 **6** ¾ **First Post (IRE)**[24] 6360 6-9-4 **77** DaneO'Neill 4 70
(Derek Haydn Jones) *t.k.h: trckd ldrs: rdn 3f out: nt qckn over 2f out: steadily lft bhd* **8/1**

5/34 **7** 2 ¾ **Life And Times (USA)**[22] 6431 5-9-5 **78** AdamKirby 11 65
(Mark Johnston) *s.i.s and urged along early: mostly in last trio tl sme prog on outer 3f out: wandered u.p 2f out: wknd* **20/1**

140 **8** ¾ **Order Of Service**[30] 6204 3-9-1 **77** SeanLevey 8 62
(David Brown) *led at gd pce: c away fr nr side rail in st: hdd 2f out: sn wknd* **25/1**

250 **9** 1 ¼ **Cruiser**[14] 6694 5-9-5 **78** (p) MartinDwyer 5 61
(William Muir) *hld up in rr: stl there 3f out: shkn up and no real prog 2f out* **6/1**[2]

3365 **10** hd **Choral Festival**[24] 6358 7-9-1 **74** KieranO'Neill 9 56
(John Bridger) *hld up in rr: shkn up over 3f out: no prog and wl btn fnl 2f* **25/1**

0 **11** ¾ **Collodi (GER)**[18] 6562 4-8-12 **74** JemmaMarshall(3) 10 54
(Roger Curtis) *w ldr to jst over 2f out: wknd qckly* **100/1**

313/ **12** 3 ¼ **Timothy T**[1147] 5184 5-9-7 **80** LiamKeniry 2 53
(Philip Hide) *nvr beyond midfield: wknd jst over 2f out* **25/1**

2263 **13** 1 ½ **Intomist (IRE)**[25] 6337 4-9-2 **75** (p) JimCrowley 7 44
(Jim Boyle) *nvr bttr than midfield: lost pl over 3f out: wl in rr fnl 2f* **16/1**

-130 **14** nse **Hilali (IRE)**[25] 6336 4-9-5 **78** (p) GeorgeBaker 14 47
(Gary Brown) *prom tl lost pl 3f out: wknd and eased* **8/1**

1m 41.1s (-3.60) **Going Correction** -0.325s/f (Firm)
WFA 3 from 4yo+ 3lb 14 Ran SP% **122.5**
Speed ratings (Par 105): **105,104,104,104,98 97,94,93,92,92 91,88,86,86**
toteswingers 1&2 £11.80, 1&3 £7.30, 2&3 £7.50 CSF £61.76 CT £229.53 TOTE £9.40: £2.90, £2.50, £1.60; EX 69.20 Trifecta £281.00 Pool: £1,662.55 - 4.43 winning units.
Owner Nigel O'Sullivan **Bred** Floors Farming **Trained** Newmarket, Suffolk

FOCUS
No hanging around here. The first four finished clear, three of them 3yos on good marks. The fourth looks the key.
T/Jkpt: Not won. T/Plt: £18.60 to a £1 stake. Pool: £89,772.83 - 3,515.83 winning units T/Qpdt: £8.30 to a £1 stake. Pool: £5,261.99 - 466.70 winning units JN

7031 WOLVERHAMPTON (A.W) (L-H)
Monday, October 7

OFFICIAL GOING: Standard
Wind: Light; behind Weather: Overcast

7076 BETFRED "THE HOME OF GOALS GALORE" H'CAP 7f 32y(P)
2:30 (2:30) (Class 5) (0-75,75) 3-Y-O+ £2,587 (£770; £384; £192) Stalls High

Form RPR
0003 **1** **Grilletto (USA)**[21] 6476 3-9-5 **75** (b) NeilCallan 1 85
(James Tate) *a.p: chsd ldr over 2f out: rdn to ld over 1f out: hung lft ins fnl f: styd on* **6/1**[3]

0015 **2** 1 **Evident (IRE)**[16] 6642 3-9-5 **75** RyanMoore 5 82
(Jeremy Noseda) *s.i.s: hdwy over 2f out: rdn to chse wnr fnl f: hung lft: styd on same pce towards fin* **15/8**[1]

0155 **3** 1 ¼ **The Great Gabrial**[9] 6856 4-8-13 **67** (v) CathyGannon 11 72
(Ian Williams) *hld up in tch: rdn over 1f out: styd on* **16/1**

4411 **4** 3 **Greensward**[9] 6856 7-9-6 **74** (b) ShaneKelly 7 71
(Mike Murphy) *s.i.s: hld up: pushed along 1/2-way: rdn over 1f out: r.o ins fnl f: nvr nrr* **5/1**[2]

3105 **5** ¾ **Smalljohn**[96] 3945 7-9-3 **71** (v) TomEaves 4 66
(Bryan Smart) *led: rdn and hdd over 1f out: wknd ins fnl f* **16/1**

2100 **6** 1 **Piceno (IRE)**[4] 6963 5-9-2 **70** (p) RobertWinston 12 62
(Scott Dixon) *prom: pushed along over 2f out: wknd fnl f* **33/1**

6315 **7** 3 ¼ **Declamation (IRE)**[58] 5291 3-9-4 **74** MartinLane 6 56
(Mark Johnston) *chsd ldr tl rdn over 2f out: wknd over 1f out* **12/1**

2464 **8** ½ **Amethyst Dawn (IRE)**[18] 6568 7-8-12 **69**(tp) WilliamTwiston-Davies(3) 3 51
(Alan McCabe) *s.i.s: rdn over 2f out: a in rr* **33/1**

0000 **9** ½ **President Lincoln (USA)**[14] 6701 5-8-13 **70** NeilFarley(3) 8 51
(Declan Carroll) *prom: rdn 3f out: wknd 2f out* **12/1**

0501 **10** 2 **Iceblast**[105] 3630 5-8-10 **64** (v) FrederikTylicki 10 39
(Michael Easterby) *hld up: pushed along 4f out: bhd fnl 3f* **33/1**

300 **11** 17 **Ewell Place (IRE)**[60] 5195 4-9-7 **75** JamieSpencer 9 4
(David Simcock) *prom: rdn over 2f out: wknd over 1f out: eased* **13/2**

1m 30.33s (0.73) **Going Correction** +0.275s/f (Slow)
WFA 3 from 4yo+ 2lb 11 Ran SP% **115.0**
Speed ratings (Par 103): **106,104,103,100,99 98,94,93,93,90 71**
toteswingers 1&2 £3.20, 1&3 £24.20, 2&3 £13.10 CSF £16.87 CT £170.63 TOTE £6.60: £1.50, £1.10, £7.30; EX 20.30 Trifecta £299.30 Pool: £2,410.51 - 6.03 winning units.
Owner Sheikh Juma Dalmook Al Maktoum **Bred** Respite Farm Inc **Trained** Newmarket, Suffolk

FOCUS
A modest handicap but a decent race for the grade. The winner got back to his best.

7077 BETFRED MOBILE LOTTO (S) STKS 5f 20y(P)
3:00 (3:00) (Class 6) 3-4-Y-O £1,940 (£577; £288; £144) Stalls Low

Form RPR
3230 **1** **Little China**[7] 6901 4-8-13 63 (b) FrederikTylicki 3 64
(William Muir) *trckd ldrs: racd keenly: rdn over 1f out: r.o to ld post* **2/1**[2]

401 **2** shd **Shamrocked (IRE)**[9] 6843 4-8-7 62 JacobButterfield(5) 5 63
(Ollie Pears) *trckd ldr tl shkn up to ld over 1f out: sn rdn: hdd post* **13/8**[1]

0500 **3** ¾ **Amis Reunis**[5] 6944 4-8-0 56 (p) JordanHibberd(7) 7 55
(Alan Berry) *hld up: shkn up and r.o ins fnl f: nt rch ldrs* **8/1**

0435 **4** 1 ½ **Cracking Choice (IRE)**[31] 6176 3-8-12 57 (b) TomEaves 4 56
(Michael Dods) *led: rdn and hdd over 1f out: styd on same pce ins fnl f* **7/1**[3]

5000 **5** ½ **Laudation**[15] 6664 3-8-12 57 NeilCallan 1 54
(Danielle McCormick) *chsd ldrs: rdn and ev ch over 1f out: no ex ins fnl f* **9/1**

0054 **6** ¾ **Stoneacre Hull (IRE)**[40] 5884 4-8-7 44 ow3 SladeO'Hara(3) 2 48?
(Peter Grayson) *sn pushed along in rr: rdn over 1f out: styng on same pce whn n.m.r towards fin* **66/1**

0000 **7** 5 **Code Six (IRE)**[41] 5864 4-8-7 47 (p) MartinLane 6 27
(Bryan Smart) *prom: rdn 1/2-way: wknd over 1f out* **20/1**

1m 3.69s (1.39) **Going Correction** +0.275s/f (Slow) 7 Ran SP% **111.3**
Speed ratings (Par 101): **99,98,97,95,94 93,85**
toteswingers 1&2 £1.10, 1&3 £4.50, 2&3 £2.80 CSF £5.29 TOTE £2.00: £1.40, £2.40; EX 6.90 Trifecta £25.20 Pool: £2,653.38 - 78.66 winning units. There was no bid for the winner.
Owner S Lamb **Bred** Stephen Lamb **Trained** Lambourn, Berks

■ Stewards' Enquiry : Jacob Butterfield two-day ban: used whip above permitted level (Oct 21-22)

FOCUS

A weak seller. The form is compromised by the proximity of the sixth.

7078 BETFRED MOBILE CASINO MAIDEN FILLIES' STKS — 5f 216y(P)

3:30 (3:30) (Class 5) 2-Y-O — £2,587 (£770; £384; £192) Stalls Low

Form — RPR

2 **1** **Expect**[20] 6500 2-9-0 0 ... RyanMoore 8 — 80+
(Jeremy Noseda) *led early: trckd ldrs: wnt 2nd over 3f out: shkn up to ld over 1f out: styd on* **1/1**[1]

2 2 ½ **Angel Flores (IRE)** 2-8-7 0 ... JoshQuinn(7) 3 — 73
(Richard Fahey) *a.p: racd keenly: chsd wnr fnl f: edgd lft and styd on same pce* **25/1**

5 **3** 6 **Big Boned (USA)**[14] 6691 2-9-0 0 ... JamieSpencer 5 — 55
(Ed Dunlop) *sn led: shkn up and hdd over 1f out: wknd ins fnl f* **2/1**[2]

400 **4** hd **Talent Spotter**[82] 4408 2-9-0 68 ... (p) AhmedAjtebi 2 — 54
(Charlie Appleby) *chsd ldr tl over 3f out: pushed along over 2f out: styd on same pce fr over 1f out* **11/1**

0265 **5** 3 **Gentle Breeze (IRE)**[53] 5421 2-9-0 70 ... MartinLane 6 — 45
(Charlie Appleby) *chsd ldrs: rdn over 2f out: wknd over 1f out* **6/1**[3]

6 9 **Zaria** 2-9-0 0 ... MartinHarley 7 — 18
(John Butler) *prom tl pushed along and wknd over 2f out* **40/1**

7 13 **Trefnant (IRE)** 2-8-11 0 ... RobertTart(3) 9
(Chris Dwyer) *sn outpcd* **50/1**

00 **8** 1 **Come On Lila**[17] 6589 2-9-0 0 ... CathyGannon 1
(Alex Hales) *prom: pushed along 1/2-way: wknd over 2f out* **66/1**

9 20 **Parisian Queen** 2-8-11 0 ... WilliamTwiston-Davies(3) 10
(Nikki Evans) *s.s: outpcd* **66/1**

1m 16.09s (1.09) **Going Correction** +0.275s/f (Slow) — **9** Ran SP% **117.2**
Speed ratings (Par 92): **103,99,91,91,87 75,58,56,30**
toteswingers 1&2 £4.50, 1&3 £1.10, 2&3 £4.70 CSF £34.26 TOTE £1.60: £1.10, £4.50, £1.20; EX 23.80 Trifecta £59.70 Pool: £2,931.99 - 36.78 winning units.
Owner Cheveley Park Stud **Bred** Cheveley Park Stud Ltd **Trained** Newmarket, Suffolk

FOCUS

Few got into this ordinary fillies' maiden in which they finished well spaced out. The winner could do little more than win this well.

7079 BETFRED MOBILE SPORTS H'CAP — 5f 216y(P)

4:00 (4:00) (Class 6) (0-55,55) 3-Y-O+ — £1,940 (£577; £288; £144) Stalls Low

Form — RPR

651- **1** **French Press (IRE)**[18] 6578 3-8-13 55 ... (bt[1]) CameronHardie(7) 8 — 64
(S Donohoe, Ire) *chsd ldrs: led over 1f out: sn rdn: jst hld on* **6/1**

0562 **2** hd **Presumido (IRE)**[19] 6519 3-9-6 55 ... SebSanders 6 — 63+
(Simon Dow) *hld up: hdwy over 1f out: rdn and edgd lft ins fnl f: r.o wl* **5/1**[2]

3345 **3** 3 ¾ **Sarah Berry**[12] 6752 4-9-6 54 ... (v) RyanMoore 5 — 50
(Chris Dwyer) *led 5f out: rdn and hdd over 1f out: no ex ins fnl f* **11/2**[3]

056 **4** 1 ½ **Fantasy Invader (IRE)**[25] 6343 3-9-2 51 ... (v) RobertWinston 1 — 42+
(John Quinn) *mid-div: nt clr run over 2f out: hdwy over 1f out: nt clr run ins fnl f: nt rch ldrs* **4/1**[1]

0621 **5** ½ **Euroquip Boy (IRE)**[31] 6156 6-8-11 50 ... IanBurns(5) 9 — 40
(Michael Scudamore) *prom: racd keenly: rdn over 1f out: sn edgd rt and no ex* **5/1**[2]

5603 **6** 2 **Steel City Boy (IRE)**[10] 6808 10-8-11 50 ... AnnStokell(5) 10 — 33
(Ann Stokell) *trckd ldrs: racd keenly: rdn over 2f out: edgd lft 1f out: wknd ins fnl f* **20/1**

0560 **7** ½ **Flow Chart (IRE)**[7] 6903 6-8-11 48 ... SladeO'Hara(3) 4 — 30
(Peter Grayson) *mid-div: sn pushed along: styd on same pce fnl 2f* **20/1**

1063 **8** hd **Amelia Jay**[14] 6682 3-9-1 50 ... TomEaves 11 — 31
(Danielle McCormick) *prom: rdn over 2f out: wknd over 1f out* **25/1**

0265 **9** 1 ½ **Monty Fay (IRE)**[21] 6478 4-9-0 48 ... (t) NeilCallan 12 — 24
(Derek Haydn Jones) *s.i.s: rdn over 2f out: n.d* **8/1**

060 **10** 1 ½ **Alberto**[42] 5845 3-8-9 51 ow1 ... [1] PaulNO'Brien(7) 13 — 22
(Paul Fitzsimons) *s.i.s: hld up: bhd fr 1/2-way* **66/1**

4060 **11** nse **Blue Noodles**[70] 4834 7-8-11 52 ... (v) KevinStott(7) 3 — 23
(John Wainwright) *sn pushed along and a in rr* **14/1**

6560 **12** 16 **Princess Bounty**[4] 6965 3-8-13 48 ... CathyGannon 2
(Phil McEntee) *sn led: hdd 5f out: rdn over 2f out: sn wknd* **28/1**

1m 17.35s (2.35) **Going Correction** +0.275s/f (Slow)
WFA 3 from 4yo+ 1lb — **12** Ran SP% **119.1**
Speed ratings (Par 101): **95,94,89,87,87 84,83,83,81,79 79,58**
toteswingers 1&2 £7.30, 1&3 £9.80, 2&3 £4.10 CSF £33.72 CT £177.70 TOTE £9.10: £2.80, £1.90, £1.90; EX 51.30 Trifecta £244.00 Pool: £2,161.85 - 6.64 winning units.
Owner Mrs Samantha Donohoe **Bred** A H And C E Robinson Partnership **Trained** Cootehill Road, Co Cavan
■ Cameron Hardie's first winner.

FOCUS

A moderate sprint handicap which wasn't strong run. The winner's best form since he was a 2yo.

7080 BETFRED "RACING'S BIGGEST SUPPORTER" H'CAP — 5f 216y(P)

4:30 (4:31) (Class 4) (0-85,85) 3-Y-O+ — £4,690 (£1,395; £697; £348) Stalls Low

Form — RPR

1005 **1** **Shafaani**[18] 6564 3-9-6 85 ... (bt) FrederikTylicki 10 — 98
(Clive Brittain) *mde virtually all: rdn over 1f out: styd on* **12/1**

3060 **2** 2 ¾ **Waking Warrior**[17] 6583 5-9-2 80 ... (bt[1]) NeilCallan 5 — 85
(Kevin Ryan) *a.p: chsd wnr 2f out: sn rdn: styd on same pce ins fnl f* **11/1**

4106 **3** 1 ½ **Excuse To Linger**[23] 6403 3-9-5 84 ... (v) RyanMoore 2 — 83+
(Jeremy Noseda) *prom: n.m.r and lost pl sn after s: rdn over 2f out: hdwy over 1f out: nt rch ldrs* **9/2**[2]

1030 **4** ½ **Half A Billion (IRE)**[17] 6586 4-9-1 79 ... TomEaves 3 — 77
(Michael Dods) *hld up: plld hrd: hdwy over 2f out: rdn over 1f out: kpt on towards fin* **25/1**

3525 **5** ½ **Commanche**[14] 6699 4-9-0 81 ... RobertTart(3) 8 — 77
(Chris Dwyer) *mid-div: rdn over 2f out: hdwy over 1f out: nvr nrr* **7/2**[1]

455 **6** shd **Piddie's Power**[53] 5437 6-8-13 80 ... RyanClark(3) 11 — 76
(Ed McMahon) *prom: rdn over 2f out: styd on same pce fnl f* **9/1**

1566 **7** ¾ **Sylvia Pankhurst (IRE)**[51] 5511 3-9-1 80 ... (v[1]) MartinHarley 4 — 73
(David C Griffiths) *sn pushed along in rr: rdn: hung lft and styd on ins fnl f: n.d* **16/1**

0005 **8** 1 ¼ **Al's Memory (IRE)**[9] 6822 4-9-3 84 ... DeclanBates(3) 9 — 73
(David Evans) *s.i.s: nvr on terms* **8/1**

20F **9** 1 ¼ **Arctic Lynx (IRE)**[30] 6189 6-9-2 80 ... MartinLane 1 — 65
(Robert Cowell) *chsd ldrs: rdn over 2f out: sn wknd* **16/1**

0120 **10** 1 **Clear Praise (USA)**[34] 6067 6-9-6 84 ... SebSanders 12 — 66
(Simon Dow) *prom: racd alone tl jnd main gp and chsd ldr 4f out: rdn over 1f out: wknd and eased fnl f* **16/1**

2253 **11** 3 **Howyadoingnotsobad (IRE)**[46] 5669 5-8-6 77 ... RyanWhile(7) 6 — 49
(Karen George) *chsd ldrs: rdn over 2f out: wknd over 1f out* **25/1**

3540 **12** 1 ½ **Signor Sassi**[19] 6525 4-9-4 82 ... ShaneKelly 7 — 50
(William Knight) *s.i.s: rdn over 2f out: a in rr* **6/1**[3]

1m 16.23s (1.23) **Going Correction** +0.275s/f (Slow)
WFA 3 from 4yo+ 1lb — **12** Ran SP% **117.2**
Speed ratings (Par 105): **102,98,96,95,95 94,93,92,90,89 85,83**
toteswingers 1&2 £26.30, 1&3 £11.20, 2&3 £13.10 CSF £135.87 CT £695.32 TOTE £11.50: £3.20, £4.00, £2.20; EX 191.00 Trifecta £2160.90 Pool: £2,893.88 - 1.00 winning unit.
Owner Saeed Manana **Bred** Rabbah Bloodstock Limited **Trained** Newmarket, Suffolk

FOCUS

A decent sprint handicap in which it was again crucial to race up with the pace. The form is rated around the second.

7081 BETFRED "THE BONUS KING" H'CAP — 1m 4f 50y(P)

5:00 (5:00) (Class 6) (0-60,60) 3-Y-O+ — £1,940 (£577; £288; £144) Stalls Low

Form — RPR

-003 **1** **Captain Caroline**[19] 6522 3-8-13 54 ... ShaneKelly 10 — 65
(Mike Murphy) *led after 1f: rdn over 1f out: edgd lft ins fnl f: styd on* **12/1**

-332 **2** 2 ½ **Train Hard**[7] 6899 3-8-11 52 ... NeilCallan 1 — 59
(Mark Johnston) *led 1f: chsd wnr tl over 9f out: wnt 2nd again 3f out: sn rdn: styd on same pce fnl f* **9/4**[2]

332 **3** nk **Inherited**[14] 6686 3-9-2 57 ... (b[1]) RyanMoore 3 — 64
(Sir Mark Prescott Bt) *chsd ldrs: rdn and hung lft fr over 1f out: nt run on* **15/8**[1]

3260 **4** 7 **Royal Etiquette (IRE)**[34] 6068 6-9-12 60 ... (vt) DougieCostello 7 — 56
(Lawney Hill) *hld up: hdwy over 2f out: sn rdn: wknd fnl f* **14/1**

4025 **5** 1 **Miss Ella Jade**[17] 6598 4-8-11 50 ... GeorgeChaloner(5) 6 — 44
(Richard Whitaker) *prom: racd keenly: trckd wnr over 9f out tl pushed along 3f out: sn rdn: wknd fnl f* **14/1**

4062 **6** hd **Brunello**[11] 6782 5-9-7 60 ... (b) AdamNicol(5) 11 — 54
(Philip Kirby) *hld up: hdwy over 5f out: rdn and nt clr run over 1f out: styd on same pce* **5/1**[3]

4050 **7** 6 **White Diamond**[147] 2311 6-9-9 57 ... AndrewMullen 4 — 41
(Michael Appleby) *chsd ldrs: rdn over 3f out: wknd over 1f out* **20/1**

000 **8** 29 **Addikt (IRE)**[11] 6782 8-9-1 54 ... TimClark(5) 8
(John Spearing) *hld up: a in rr: rdn and wknd over 4f out* **66/1**

4600 **9** 17 **Midnight Sequel**[61] 5123 4-9-2 50 ... MartinLane 5
(Michael Blake) *hld up: rdn over 4f out: wknd over 3f out* **20/1**

00-0 **10** 3 **Landaho**[13] 6730 4-8-12 46 oh1 ... TomEaves 2
(Alan Berry) *hld up: a in rr: rdn and wknd 5f out* **125/1**

2m 43.54s (2.44) **Going Correction** +0.275s/f (Slow)
WFA 3 from 4yo+ 7lb — **10** Ran SP% **115.1**
Speed ratings (Par 101): **102,100,100,95,94 94,90,71,60,58**
toteswingers 1&2 £5.90, 1&3 £5.40, 2&3 £1.30 CSF £37.74 CT £75.44 TOTE £9.70: £3.40, £1.90, £1.10; EX 49.70 Trifecta £264.50 Pool: £2,840.72 - 8.05 winning units.
Owner Mrs C J Barr **Bred** Mr And Mrs L Norris **Trained** Westoning, Beds

FOCUS

Few could be fancied according to the market in this moderate middle-distance handicap. They finished well spread out. The winner built on her kempton run, with the next two to form.

7082 BETFRED ON 0800 221 221 H'CAP (DIV I) — 1m 141y(P)

5:30 (5:30) (Class 6) (0-60,60) 3-Y-O+ — £1,940 (£577; £288; £144) Stalls Low

Form — RPR

4545 **1** **Icy Blue**[15] 6667 5-8-10 51 ... (p) GeorgeChaloner(5) 10 — 65
(Richard Whitaker) *prom: chsd ldr over 6f out: rdn to ld over 1f out: styd on u.p* **8/1**

031 **2** 1 ½ **Camerooney**[7] 6907 10-9-3 58 ... (p) NathanAlison(5) 12 — 69
(Marjorie Fife) *led: rdn and hdd over 1f out: styd on same pce towards fin* **5/2**[1]

0400 **3** 6 **Magic Lando (FR)**[17] 6612 3-9-6 60 ... (v[1]) JamieSpencer 5 — 58
(Ismail Mohammed) *trckd ldrs: rdn over 2f out: wknd ins fnl f* **3/1**[2]

0050 **4** 2 ¾ **Ajeeb (USA)**[21] 6473 5-9-10 60 ... (vt) LiamTreadwell 9 — 50
(Michael Scudamore) *mid-div: rdn over 3f out: sn outpcd: hung lft and styd on ins fnl f* **14/1**

5635 **5** 1 ½ **Buaiteoir (FR)**[63] 5073 7-9-4 57 ... WilliamTwiston-Davies(3) 3 — 44
(Nikki Evans) *hld up: hdwy over 2f out: sn rdn: wknd over 1f out* **10/1**

2650 **6** 3 **Lucky Mountain**[21] 6472 3-8-1 46 oh1 ... (p) TimClark(5) 6 — 27
(Scott Dixon) *prom: hmpd over 7f out: rdn over 2f out: sn wknd* **22/1**

1503 **7** 1 **King Of Wing (IRE)**[10] 6803 4-8-13 49 ... (be) CathyGannon 8 — 27
(Phil McEntee) *s.i.s and hmpd s: in rr: drvn along over 2f out: n.d* **7/1**[3]

0000 **8** 3 ¾ **Bankroll**[25] 6323 6-9-3 53 ... (p) DougieCostello 7 — 22
(Jonjo O'Neill) *mid-div: hdwy over 3f out: wknd over 2f out* **20/1**

9 30 **Erelight (IRE)**[45] 5732 5-8-10 46 oh1 ... (t) ShaneKelly 11
(R P O'Keeffe, Ire) *s.i.s: hdwy 7f out: wknd over 3f out* **66/1**

050 **10** 4 **Churt**[18] 6555 4-8-5 46 oh1 ... ShirleyTeasdale(5) 2
(Christopher Kellett) *hld up: a in rr: bhd fnl 3f* **125/1**

11 28 **Nine Bean Rows (IRE)**[35] 6055 4-8-10 46 oh1 ... (b) MartinHarley 1
(Niall Moran, Ire) *prom: plld hrd: n.m.r 7f out: lost pl 6f out: bhd fnl 4f* **8/1**

1m 52.84s (2.34) **Going Correction** +0.275s/f (Slow)
WFA 3 from 4yo+ 4lb — **11** Ran SP% **115.4**
Speed ratings (Par 101): **100,98,93,90,89 86,86,82,56,52 27**
toteswingers 1&2 £6.50, 1&3 £5.90, 2&3 £2.60 CSF £26.95 CT £75.86 TOTE £9.70: £2.90, £1.10, £1.70; EX 37.80 Trifecta £165.90 Pool: £2,521.32 - 11.39 winning units.
Owner Country Lane Partnership **Bred** Cheveley Park Stud Ltd **Trained** Scarcroft, W Yorks
■ Stewards' Enquiry : Nathan Alison two-day ban: careless riding (Oct 21-22)

FOCUS

A poor handicap and yet another race in which it proved impossible to make up ground from the rear. The front pair dominated throughout. The winner is rated close to this year's form.

7083 BETFRED ON 0800 221 221 H'CAP (DIV II) — 1m 141y(P)

6:00 (6:00) (Class 6) (0-60,60) 3-Y-O+ — £1,940 (£577; £288; £144) Stalls Low

Form — RPR

1333 **1** **Silly Billy (IRE)**[17] 6610 5-9-8 58 ... RyanMoore 1 — 72
(Brian Ellison) *trckd ldrs: led over 1f out: shkn up and styd on wl* **11/10**[1]

3060 **2** 3 ½ **Mudaawem (USA)**[15] 6667 3-9-0 54 ... NeilCallan 11 — 61
(Mark Johnston) *sn chsng ldr: rdn to ld wl over 1f out: sn edgd rt and hdd: styd on same pce fnl f* **5/1**[3]

0600 **3** 5 **Kingscombe (USA)**[40] 5899 4-9-10 60 ... SebSanders 10 — 54
(Linda Jewell) *prom: rdn over 1f out: wknd ins fnl f* **12/1**

0400 **4** 3 ½ **Direct Trade**[25] 6344 3-8-6 46 oh1 ... (e) MartinLane 9 — 33
(Mark Usher) *stdd s: hld up: racd keenly: hdwy u.p over 1f out: nvr nrr* **40/1**

	5	hd	**Eretara (IRE)**[17] 6616 4-9-1 **51**....(p) RobertWinston 7 (R P O'Keeffe, Ire) *s.i.s: hld up: hdwy over 2f out: sn rdn: wknd fnl f* **9/2**[2]	37
0645	6	½	**Justcallmehandsome**[4] 6985 11-8-5 **46** oh1....(be) ShelleyBirkett(5) 3 (Dominic Ffrench Davis) *s.i.s and hmpd s: hld up: styd on fr over 1f out: nvr nrr* **10/1**	31
000	7	5	**Refuse Colette (IRE)**[48] 5615 4-8-10 **46** oh1....(b) CathyGannon 5 (Paul Green) *hld up: hdwy 3f out: sn rdn and wknd* **40/1**	19
0050	8	2 ¾	**King Of Kudos (IRE)**[17] 6587 3-9-3 **57**....(p) FrederikTylicki 8 (Scott Dixon) *led: rdn and hdd wl over 1f out: sn wknd* **7/1**	25
0004	9	6	**Spoken Words**[10] 6806 4-8-10 **46** oh1....(b) TomEaves 6 (Alan Berry) *trckd ldrs: racd keenly: rdn and wknd over 2f out* **66/1**	
6606	10	12	**Benidorm**[10] 6806 5-8-3 **46** oh1.... KevinStott(7) 2 (John Wainwright) *hmpd s: chsd ldrs: rdn over 3f out: sn wknd* **66/1**	

1m 53.27s (2.77) **Going Correction** +0.275s/f (Slow)
WFA 3 from 4yo+ 4lb **10** Ran SP% **119.6**
Speed ratings (Par 101): **98,94,90,87,87 86,82,79,74,63**
toteswingers 1&2 £1.70, 1&3 £6.70, 2&3 £17.10 CSF £7.04 CT £45.46 TOTE £1.80: £1.10, £1.80, £3.10; EX 9.70 Trifecta £47.90 Pool: £3,767.30 - 58.95 winning units.
Owner L S Keys **Bred** Sir E J Loder **Trained** Norton, N Yorks

FOCUS
The winning time was 0.43 seconds slower than the first division. It took little winning and the form isn't particularly solid.
T/Plt: £15.00 to a £1 stake. Pool: £81,727.51 - 3,962.50 winning units T/Qpdt: £7.50 to a £1 stake. Pool: £6,250.41 - 612.30 winning units CR

6961 CHANTILLY (R-H)
Monday, October 7

OFFICIAL GOING: Turf: soft; polytrack: standard

7084a PRIX HEROD (LISTED RACE) (2YO) (TURF) 7f
12:00 (12:01) 2-Y-O £22,357 (£8,943; £6,707; £4,471; £2,235)

			RPR
1		**La Hoguette (FR)**[69] 2-8-13 0.... GregoryBenoist 2 (J-C Rouget, France) **8/5**[1]	99
2	2	**Petits Potins (IRE)**[18] 2-8-13 0.... StephanePasquier 4 (Rod Collet, France) **10/1**	94
3	hd	**Ascot Memory (IRE)**[11] 6786 2-8-13 0.... TheoBachelot 3 (S Wattel, France) **30/1**	93
4	1	**Stormy Paradise (IRE)**[25] 6328 2-9-2 0.... MaximeGuyon 8 (Brian Meehan) *wnt rt and bmpd rival s: midfield on outer: pushed along over 2f out: rdn over 1f out: kpt on same pce ins fnl f: wnt 4th post* **4/1**[2]	94
5	nse	**Rangali**[41] 5875 2-9-2 0.... FabriceVeron 7 (H-A Pantall, France) **73/10**	94
6	snk	**Ming Zhi Cosmos (FR)**[17] 2-8-13 0....(p) ThierryThulliez 9 (N Clement, France) **63/10**[3]	90
7	1 ½	**Ultradargent (FR)**[71] 2-8-13 0.... ThierryJarnet 5 (H-A Pantall, France) **44/5**	86
8	2 ½	**Najinska (GER)** 2-8-13 0.... TLukasek 1 (Z Koplik, Czech Republic) **18/1**	80
9	dist	**Mind That Girl (IRE)**[52] 2-8-13 0.... Pierre-CharlesBoudot 6 (Y Durepaire, France) **20/1**	

1m 26.6s (0.50) **9** Ran SP% **116.8**
WIN (incl. 1 euro stake): 2.60. PLACES: 1.40, 2.90, 5.20. DF: 14.20. SF: 22.60.
Owner Gerard Augustin-Normand **Bred** Franklin Finance **Trained** Pau, France

7085a PRIX DE BONNEVAL (LISTED RACE) (3YO+) (TURF) 5f 110y
1:35 (1:39) 3-Y-O+ £21,138 (£8,455; £6,341; £4,227; £2,113)

			RPR
1		**Wedge Trust (IRE)**[43] 5806 3-8-9 0.... IoritzMendizabal 6 (J-C Rouget, France) **31/10**[1]	100
2	snk	**A Huge Dream (IRE)**[22] 6445 4-8-9 0.... StephanePasquier 9 (F Rohaut, France) **5/1**[2]	99
3	2	**Lykea (IRE)**[27] 3-8-9 0.... JeromeClaudic 1 (C Laffon-Parias, France) **21/1**	93
4	½	**Mister Ryan (FR)**[50] 4-8-13 0.... ThierryJarnet 2 (H-A Pantall, France) **20/1**	95
5	nse	**Calrissian (GER)**[22] 9-8-13 0.... Pierre-CharlesBoudot 14 (Fredrik Reuterskiold, Sweden) **38/1**	95
6	¾	**Damsah (USA)**[27] 3-8-9 0.... Jean-BernardEyquem 4 (D De Watrigant, France) **17/2**[3]	89
7	¾	**Ghor (FR)**[33] 5-8-13 0....(b) Christophe-PatriceLemaire 7 (M Boutin, France) **20/1**	90
8	¾	**Maglietta Fina (IRE)**[23] 6381 4-8-9 0.... CristianDemuro 5 (Robert Cowell) *hld up in rr: pushed along 1/2-way: sn rdn: kpt on but nvr threatened* **38/1**	83
9	½	**Goldream**[19] 6539 4-8-13 0....(p) SteveDrowne 10 (Robert Cowell) *prom: rdn over 2f out: lost pl ent fnl f: no ex and btn: fdd* **12/1**	86
10	¾	**Lazzaz (FR)**[50] 4-8-13 0.... FranckBlondel 3 (D De Watrigant, France) **17/1**	83
11	2	**Xenophanes (IRE)**[41] 3-8-13 0.... UmbertoRispoli 8 (P Schiergen, Germany) **10/1**	77
12	nk	**Stark Danon (FR)**[19] 5-8-13 0.... EddyHardouin 12 (W Hickst, Germany) **10/1**	75
13	½	**Vital Spirit (FR)**[50] 4-8-13 0.... MaximeGuyon 13 (E J O'Neill, France) **10/1**	74
14	3 ½	**Swooning (IRE)**[22] 3-8-9 0.... FabriceVeron 11 (H-A Pantall, France) **12/1**	59

1m 3.19s (-1.31) **14** Ran SP% **119.0**
WIN (incl. 1 euro stake): 4.10. PLACES: 1.80, 2.30, 5.10. DF: 12.60. SF: 24.00.
Owner Ecurie I M Fares **Bred** Scea Haras De Manneville **Trained** Pau, France

6457 BRIGHTON (L-H)
Tuesday, October 8

OFFICIAL GOING: Good to soft (good in places; 6.5)
Wind: Almost nil Weather: Sunny and warm early, cloudy from race 6

7086 HARRINGTONS LETTINGS H'CAP 5f 213y
1:50 (1:50) (Class 6) (0-60,60) 3-Y-O+ £1,940 (£577; £288; £144) Stalls Low

Form				RPR
3155	1		**Koharu**[19] 6560 3-9-6 **60**....(t) SteveDrowne 12 (Peter Makin) *mid-div: hdwy 2f out: led 1f out: drvn clr: readily* **14/1**	72
2032	2	3 ¼	**Volito**[37] 6017 7-9-3 **56**.... GeorgeBaker 16 (Anabel K Murphy) *s.i.s: bhd: gd hdwy over 1f out: r.o to take 2nd fnl 100yds* **7/1**[2]	58
2330	3	1	**Speedfit Boy (IRE)**[22] 6462 3-9-6 **60**....(b) LukeMorris 8 (George Margarson) *chsd ldrs: rdn 2f out: styd on fnl f* **16/1**	59
3515	4	½	**Pharoh Jake**[14] 6732 5-8-12 **54**.... MichaelJMMurphy(3) 9 (John Bridger) *chsd ldrs: wnt 2nd 2f out: led briefly over 1f out: one pce* **12/1**	52
0006	5	½	**Skidby Mill (IRE)**[13] 6752 3-9-2 **56**.... FergusSweeney 11 (Laura Mongan) *in tch: rdn 2f out: styd on fnl f* **25/1**	52
6303	6	hd	**Ishi Honest**[19] 6560 3-9-6 **60**....(p) LiamKeniry 4 (Mark Usher) *chsd ldrs: led 3f out tl over 1f out: no ex* **16/1**	55
4040	7	1	**Perfect Pastime**[22] 6459 5-9-7 **60**....(p) WilliamCarson 3 (Jim Boyle) *rring s and missed break: hdwy into midfield after 2f: kpt on fnl 2f: nvr able to chal* **8/1**[3]	52+
2033	8	4 ½	**Chevise (IRE)**[37] 6019 5-9-3 **59**....(p) ThomasBrown(3) 13 (Steve Woodman) *mid-div: rdn 1/2-way: no hdwy fnl 2f* **10/1**	38
4040	9	1 ¼	**My Sweet Lord**[13] 6752 3-9-5 **59**....(v) HarryBentley 5 (Mark Usher) *s.s: bhd: mod effrt 2f out: n.d* **8/1**[3]	34
2050	10	1 ¼	**Gracie's Games**[4] 6994 7-8-7 **49**....(b) DeclanBates(3) 10 (John Spearing) *dwlt: a towards rr* **33/1**	20
50-0	11	shd	**Marygold**[13] 6745 4-9-2 **60**....(p) DannyBrock(5) 6 (Lee Carter) *in tch: outpcd 1/2-way: sn lost pl* **33/1**	31
00	12	4	**Ziefhd**[40] 5930 4-8-10 **52**....(p) WilliamTwiston-Davies(3) 1 (Tim McCarthy) *led 3f: wknd over 1f out* **25/1**	11
0-00	13	hd	**Fit For A King (IRE)**[43] 5818 3-8-6 **46**.... LiamJones 15 (John Best) *a towards rr: bhd fr 1/2-way* **66/1**	5
424	14	5	**Multitask**[14] 6732 3-9-2 **56**....(v1) AdamKirby 7 (Michael Madgwick) *prom over 3f: sn lost pl* **10/1**	
0001	U		**Bestfootforward**[22] 6462 4-8-12 **56**.... ShelleyBirkett(5) 14 (Julia Feilden) *anticipated s: hit sing stall gate and uns rdr* **5/2**[1]	

1m 11.54s (1.34) **Going Correction** +0.225s/f (Good)
WFA 3 from 4yo+ 1lb **15** Ran SP% **122.7**
Speed ratings (Par 101): **100,95,94,93,93 92,91,85,83,82 81,76,76,69,**
toteswingers 1&2 £20.50, 1&3 £23.40, 2&3 £19.00 CSF £105.16 CT £1644.86 TOTE £12.50: £5.10, £2.20, £5.40; EX 105.60 Trifecta £1554.40 Part won. Pool: £2072.61 - 0.92 winning units..
Owner Keith And Brian Brackpool **Bred** N E and Mrs Poole and Trickledown Stud **Trained** Ogbourne Maisey, Wilts

FOCUS
All races on inner line and distances as advertised. After riding in the opener the general opinion from jockeys was that the ground was riding "good or slightly easier", in keeping with the official going. A modest sprint handicap in which there was more drama at the start than at the finish. A step up from the winner, but a slightly negative view has been taken of the form.

7087 PAPA JOHN'S PIZZA MAIDEN AUCTION STKS 6f 209y
2:20 (2:20) (Class 5) 2-Y-O £2,587 (£770; £384; £192) Stalls Low

Form				RPR
3	1		**Manipulation (IRE)**[33] 6132 2-8-11 0.... FergusSweeney 6 (David Simcock) *stdd s: hld up in rr: hdwy on outer 2f out: led and hung bdly lft wl over 1f out: sn clr* **4/1**[3]	72+
64	2	2 ½	**Sweet P**[22] 6460 2-8-7 0.... MartinDwyer 5 (Marcus Tregoning) *in tch: effrt over 2f out: kpt on to take 2nd fnl 75yds* **5/2**[2]	61
2404	3	nk	**Stella Clavisque (IRE)**[12] 6786 2-9-0 72....(p) SeanLevey 4 (Brian Meehan) *prom on outer: led over 2f out tl wl over 1f out: carried lft: one pce* **6/1**	67
450	4	3 ½	**Ainmire**[28] 6271 2-8-10 62.... LiamKeniry 2 (John Quinn) *hld up in tch: shkn up 2f out: hung lft: sn btn* **7/1**	54
4320	5	1	**G Man (IRE)**[48] 5634 2-8-13 69.... HarryBentley 3 (Olly Stevens) *pressed ldr: rdn over 2f out: sn outpcd* **2/1**[1]	55
000	6	12	**Commanding Force**[22] 6460 2-8-9 45.... KieranO'Neill 1 (John Bridger) *led: rdn 3f out: hdd over 2f out: sn wknd* **66/1**	19

1m 24.77s (1.67) **Going Correction** +0.225s/f (Good) **6** Ran SP% **110.2**
Speed ratings (Par 95): **99,96,95,91,90 76**
toteswingers 1&2 £2.20, 1&3 £2.20, 2&3 £2.50 CSF £13.84 TOTE £5.20: £2.50, £1.20; EX 11.70 Trifecta £44.00 Pool: £1579.12 - 26.85 winning units..
Owner Mrs Z Wentworth **Bred** Intriguing Partners **Trained** Newmarket, Suffolk

FOCUS
No more than an ordinary maiden, as expected for the track and time of year.

7088 SMITH AND WESTERN RESTAURANTS NURSERY H'CAP 6f 209y
2:50 (2:50) (Class 5) (0-75,75) 2-Y-O £2,587 (£770; £384; £192) Stalls Low

Form				RPR
0204	1		**Know Your Name**[10] 6852 2-9-2 **73**....(v) DeclanBates(3) 5 (David Evans) *chsd ldr: led briefly 5f out: regained 2nd over 2f out: chal fnl f: drvn to ld fnl stride* **12/1**	77
3026	2	hd	**Jive**[24] 6401 2-9-1 **69**.... PatDobbs 6 (Richard Hannon) *prom: led over 4f out: hrd rdn and kpt on fnl f: hdd fnl stride* **8/1**[3]	73
005	3	1	**Sellingallthetime (IRE)**[29] 6256 2-8-13 **67**.... SteveDrowne 9 (Charles Hills) *t.k.h in rr: hdwy and squeezed for room wl over 1f out: rallied and r.o strly fnl f: clsng wl at fin* **6/1**[2]	68
2105	4	½	**Clever Miss**[43] 5829 2-9-4 **75**....(p) WilliamTwiston-Davies(3) 1 (Alan McCabe) *hld up towards rr: eased outside and hdwy over 2f out: hung lft wl over 1f out: kpt on* **10/1**	75
3010	5	½	**Ajig**[24] 6401 2-9-5 **73**.... JohnFahy 2 (Eve Johnson Houghton) *led 2f: sn lost pl: kpt on again fr over 1f out* **20/1**	71
6461	6	2 ¼	**Autopilot**[28] 6279 2-9-5 **73**....(b) GeorgeBaker 10 (Anabel K Murphy) *hld up in rr: rdn over 2f out: nvr able to chal* **10/1**	66
205	7	1 ¼	**After The Goldrush**[43] 5843 2-9-5 **73**.... SeanLevey 8 (Richard Hannon) *in tch on outer: effrt over 2f out: wknd over 1f out* **6/1**[2]	62

543 **8** *6* **Avocadeau (IRE)**[17] 6656 2-9-0 **68** .... MartinDwyer 3 42
(William Muir) *prom: rdn over 4f out: wknd 2f out* **8/1**[3]

433 **9** *2 ½* **Sullivan Street (IRE)**[29] 6256 2-9-1 **69** .... AhmedAjtebi 4 36
(Charlie Appleby) *hld up in 6th: effrt in centre and hung lft 2f out: unbalanced on camber: eased whn btn* **2/1**[1]

1m 25.59s (2.49) **Going Correction** +0.225s/f (Good) **9** Ran SP% **114.8**
Speed ratings (Par 95): **94,93,92,92,91 88,87,80,77**
toteswingers 1&2 £14.50, 1&3 £21.30, 2&3 £11.70 CSF £103.04 CT £637.25 TOTE £15.20: £3.40, £3.00, £2.80; EX 104.80 Trifecta £1240.60 Part won. Pool: £1654.25 - 0.96 winning units..
Owner David Lockwood & Fred Lockwood **Bred** Mill Farm Stud **Trained** Pandy, Monmouths

FOCUS
Just a fair nursery in which the pace was even. Routine form with a minor personal best from the winner.

7089 EBF STALLIONS/BRIGHTON & HOVE STREAMLINE TAXIS MAIDEN STKS — 7f 214y
3:20 (3:20) (Class 5) 2-Y-O **£2,911** (£866; £432; £216) **Stalls** Low

Form RPR

2 **1** **Desert Society (IRE)**[15] 6689 2-9-5 0 .... PatDobbs 1 77+
(Richard Hannon) *mde all: sn 3 l clr: in control fr over 1f out: pushed out* **11/4**[2]

4 **2** *1 ½* **Grand Meister**[19] 6570 2-9-5 0 .... AdamKirby 4 74
(Michael Bell) *chsd wnr most of way: edgd rt over 2f out: hung lft and hrd rdn over 1f out: kpt on same pce* **3/1**[3]

03 **3** *nk* **Caridadi (IRE)**[10] 6829 2-9-5 0 .... AhmedAjtebi 7 73
(Charlie Appleby) *trckd ldrs: disp 2nd over 2f out: hung lft and rt over 1f out: edgd lft fnl f: unable qck* **9/4**[1]

55 **4** *2 ½* **Castle Combe (IRE)**[18] 6593 2-9-5 0 .... MartinDwyer 5 68
(Marcus Tregoning) *plld hrd and bhd: hdwy and edgd rt 2f out: one pce* **8/1**

5 *2 ¾* **Mountain Kingdom (IRE)** 2-9-5 0 .... LukeMorris 2 61
(Sir Mark Prescott Bt) *hld up in 5th: rdn and wknd 2f out* **16/1**

6 *8* **Glorious Sinndar (FR)** 2-9-2 0 .... RyanPowell(3) 3 43
(George Margarson) *s.i.s: rdn along over 5f out: a bhd* **25/1**

7 *½* **Rookery (IRE)** 2-9-5 0 .... LiamJones 6 42
(Mark Johnston) *chsd ldrs: pushed along 4f out: wknd over 2f out* **12/1**

1m 38.87s (2.87) **Going Correction** +0.225s/f (Good) **7** Ran SP% **111.0**
Speed ratings (Par 95): **94,92,92,89,86 78,78**
toteswingers 1&2 £2.30, 1&3 £1.50, 2&3 £2.40 CSF £10.72 TOTE £3.50: £1.30, £1.70; EX 13.20 Trifecta £25.80 Pool: £2341.61 - 67.91 winning units.
Owner Chris Giles & Potensis Limited **Bred** Theo Waddington **Trained** East Everleigh, Wilts

FOCUS
Several ran green in this maiden but not the winner, who made all. The first two stepped forward.

7090 BECHUBE & SAM HARPER BRIGHOUSE MEMORIAL "HANDS AND HEELS" APPRENTICE SERIES H'CAP — 1m 3f 196y
3:50 (3:51) (Class 6) (0-55,60) 3-Y-O+ **£1,940** (£577; £288; £144) **Stalls** High

Form RPR

0446 **1** **Corn Maiden**[31] 6216 4-9-6 **54** .... LewisWalsh 11 62
(Lydia Pearce) *hld up in rr: hdwy in centre 2f out: edgd lft 1f out: led ins fnl f: pushed out* **14/1**

4400 **2** *1 ¾* **Like Clockwork**[19] 6558 4-9-4 **52** .... JackGarritty 6 57
(Mark H Tompkins) *hld up towards rr: hdwy over 2f out: unable qck fnl f: kpt on to take 2nd on line* **6/1**[3]

215 **3** *nse* **Sudden Wish (IRE)**[19] 6554 4-8-13 **55** .... HectorCrouch(8) 3 60+
(Gary Moore) *in tch: chsd ldrs 4f out: led over 2f out tl ins fnl f: one pce* **7/2**[1]

3460 **4** *4 ½* **Megalala (IRE)**[45] 5762 12-9-4 **52** .... CharlotteJenner 9 51
(John Bridger) *led tl over 2f out: no ex fnl f* **8/1**

4030 **5** *1* **Mariet**[40] 5934 4-8-12 **46** .... RobJFitzpatrick 2 43
(Suzy Smith) *s.s: bhd: rdn and styd on fnl 2f: nvr nrr* **10/1**

3531 **6** *1 ¼* **Gaelic Ice**[43] 5813 4-9-4 **55** ....(p) PatMillman(3) 4 50
(Rod Millman) *hld up towards rr: hdwy 5f out: wknd 1f out* **4/1**[2]

1005 **7** *5* **Frosty Secret**[22] 6457 4-9-1 **49** ....(p) JoeyHaynes 7 37
(Jane Chapple-Hyam) *prom tl wknd over 1f out* **8/1**

0-00 **8** *22* **Bennelong**[257] 361 7-9-7 **55** .... OllieGarner 1 10
(Richard Rowe) *in tch: wknd 3f out: sn bhd* **12/1**

005/ **9** *5* **Jody Bear**[759] 5912 5-8-12 **46** .... JohnLawson 12
(Jonathan Portman) *chsd ldrs: wknd 3f out: sn bhd* **16/1**

2260 **10** *44* **Red Mystique (IRE)**[146] 1175 4-9-4 **52** ....(b) ShelleyBirkett 5
(Philip Hide) *chsd ldr tl 1/2-way: rdn and qckly lost pl: wl bhd fnl 5f* **12/1**

2m 35.88s (3.18) **Going Correction** +0.225s/f (Good) **10** Ran SP% **115.8**
Speed ratings (Par 101): **98,96,96,93,93 92,88,74,70,41**
toteswingers 1&2 £18.20, 1&3 £10.10, 2&3 £6.50 CSF £94.96 CT £364.21 TOTE £14.90: £3.50, £2.10, £1.30; EX 114.90 Trifecta £1422.90 Part won. Pool: £1897.30 - 0.79 winning units..
Owner Ms Johanna McHugh **Bred** G B Turnbull Ltd **Trained** Newmarket, Suffolk

FOCUS
A low-grade handicap for apprentice riders. The form makes sense.

7091 3663 FIRST FOR CHRISTMAS SERVICE H'CAP — 1m 1f 209y
4:20 (4:20) (Class 6) (0-65,65) 3-Y-O+ **£1,940** (£577; £288; £144) **Stalls** High

Form RPR

0642 **1** **Compton Bird**[6] 6933 4-8-12 **58** .... JoeyHaynes(5) 7 69+
(Hans Adielsson) *hld up in rr: hdwy on inner and swtchd rt over 2f out: led over 1f out: styd on wl* **9/2**[1]

0430 **2** *2 ¾* **Grey Blue (IRE)**[22] 6470 3-9-4 **64** .... LiamJones 9 70
(Mark Johnston) *towards rr: hdwy 3f out: led in centre 2f out tl over 1f out: unable qck* **16/1**

0403 **3** *nk* **Santo Prince (USA)**[22] 6459 3-8-13 **62** ...... WilliamTwiston-Davies(3) 12 67
(Michael Bell) *mid-div: rdn and r.o fnl 2f: nrst at fin* **8/1**

0400 **4** *1 ¾* **Smokey Oakey (IRE)**[41] 5903 9-8-10 **54** .... SimonPearce(3) 6 55
(Mark H Tompkins) *bhd: rdn 3f out: r.o fr over 1f out: nvr nrr* **33/1**

3451 **5** *shd* **Sutton Sid**[24] 6406 3-8-12 **58** ....(p) SeanLevey 10 59
(Chris Gordon) *prom: rdn 3f out: one pce appr fnl f* **7/1**[3]

6212 **6** *1 ¼* **Mr Fickle (IRE)**[22] 6458 4-9-10 **65** ....(b) FergusSweeney 15 64
(Gary Moore) *in tch: rdn 3f out: no imp fnl 2f* **6/1**[2]

005- **7** *1 ¼* **Ninfea (IRE)**[66] 8170 5-9-8 **63** .... LiamKeniry 16 59
(Sylvester Kirk) *mid-div: rdn and lost pl 3f out: styd on same pce* **33/1**

-020 **8** *nk* **Syrenka**[17] 6658 3-9-1 **64** .... MichaelJMMurphy(3) 13 60
(Marcus Tregoning) *in tch: rdn and hung lft 2f out: sn btn* **14/1**

0500 **9** *12* **Watcheroftheskies**[21] 6492 3-8-9 **60** ....(b[1]) ShelleyBirkett(5) 3 32
(J W Hills) *led tl 2f out: sn wknd: eased when wl btn fnl f* **20/1**

3424 **10** *½* **Brown Pete (IRE)**[22] 6459 5-9-3 **61** .... DeclanBates(3) 4 32
(Violet M Jordan) *in tch tl wknd 2f out: eased whn wl btn fnl f* **8/1**

4044 **11** *2 ¼* **Hermosa Vaquera (IRE)**[48] 5650 3-9-0 **60** .... PatDobbs 14 26
(Anna Newton-Smith) *a towards rr: eased whn no ch fnl f* **20/1**

0010 **12** *nk* **Posh Boy (IRE)**[20] 6521 3-9-5 **65** .... GeorgeBaker 11 31
(Chris Wall) *prom tl wknd 2f out: eased whn no ch fnl f* **9/2**[1]

U340 **13** *nk* **Lady Barastar (IRE)**[33] 6137 5-8-10 **51** ....[1] SteveDrowne 1 16
(Amanda Perrett) *towards rr: rdn 5f out: eased whn no ch fnl f* **25/1**

0100 **14** *2 ¾* **Thewinningmachine**[28] 6283 4-8-12 **53** .... J-PGuillambert 2 12
(Jo Hughes) *prom tl wknd 2f out: eased whn no ch fnl f* **25/1**

2m 5.17s (1.57) **Going Correction** +0.225s/f (Good)
WFA 3 from 4yo+ 5lb **14** Ran SP% **121.0**
Speed ratings (Par 101): **102,99,99,98,98 97,96,95,86,85 84,83,83,81**
toteswingers 1&2 £16.80, 1&3 £11.40, 2&3 £19.50 CSF £71.78 CT £565.51 TOTE £5.80: £2.40, £4.20, £3.60; EX 99.70 Trifecta £1046.20 Pool: £2331.00 - 1.67 winning units.
Owner Erik Penser **Bred** Whitsbury Manor Stud **Trained** Kingston Lisle, Oxon
■ Stewards' Enquiry : William Twiston-Davies two-day ban: used whip above permitted level (Oct 22-23)

FOCUS
A modest handicap in which the pace was good, and this suited those ridden with restraint. The winner at least matched her previous form.

7092 UNION EVENTS H'CAP (DIV I) — 7f 214y
4:50 (4:50) (Class 6) (0-65,64) 3-Y-O+ **£1,940** (£577; £288; £144) **Stalls** Low

Form RPR

4000 **1** **Pat's Legacy (USA)**[27] 6315 7-8-12 **58** ....(p) JemmaMarshall(3) 14 67
(Pat Phelan) *mde all: hrd rdn over 1f out: hld on wl* **10/1**

0041 **2** *1 ¾* **Bloodsweatandtears**[22] 6459 5-9-6 **63** .... GeorgeBaker 6 68
(William Knight) *t.k.h in rr: hdwy and c alone to stands' side over 3f out: rdn and r.o fnl 2f: tk 2nd ins fnl f* **11/4**[1]

1360 **3** *¾* **Bold Ring**[15] 6702 7-8-10 **60** .... JenniferFerguson(7) 10 63
(Edward Creighton) *hld up in tch: effrt 2f out: r.o fnl f* **6/1**[3]

5400 **4** *1 ¼* **One Way Or Another (AUS)**[10] 6856 10-9-2 **62** ....(t) DeclanBates(3) 9 62
(David Evans) *chsd ldrs: disp 2nd over 2f out: one pce appr fnl f* **16/1**

2104 **5** *1* **Hawk Moth (IRE)**[49] 5607 5-9-3 **60** ....(b) LukeMorris 8 58
(John Spearing) *prom: rdn over 2f out: no ex appr fnl f* **20/1**

00-0 **6** *½* **Know No Fear**[27] 6316 8-9-7 **64** ....(p) FergusSweeney 11 61
(Alastair Lidderdale) *plld hrd towards rr: rdn and styd on fnl 2f: nrest at fin* **20/1**

3032 **7** *nk* **Copper Trade**[26] 6323 3-9-0 **60** .... JohnFahy 7 56
(Eve Johnson Houghton) *t.k.h in rr: gd hdwy on wd outside 5f out: no ex appr fnl f* **6/1**[3]

0516 **8** *hd* **All Right Now**[34] 6101 6-8-7 **50** ....(p) LiamKeniry 1 46
(Tony Newcombe) *prom on inner tl no ex over 1f out* **25/1**

4331 **9** *3 ¼* **Secret Success**[24] 6399 3-9-2 **62** ....(t) AdamKirby 3 50
(Paul Cole) *prom tl wknd over 1f out: eased whn btn ins fnl f* **5/1**[2]

050 **10** *2 ¼* **Polish Rider**[26] 6321 3-7-11 **50** oh5 .... CameronHardie(7) 2 33
(Richard Hannon) *mid-div on inner: n.m.r on rail 5f out: n.d fnl 3f* **25/1**

0000 **11** *2 ¼* **Waspy**[52] 5528 4-8-7 **50** oh2 .... RichardThomas 12 28
(Dr Jeremy Naylor) *mid-div: outpcd 3f out: sn struggling* **66/1**

642 **12** *1 ¼* **Silvee**[22] 6462 6-8-4 **50** oh2 .... MichaelJMMurphy(3) 5 25
(John Bridger) *mid-div tl outpcd 3f out* **16/1**

-315 **13** *1 ½* **Gypsy Rider**[73] 4752 4-8-6 **56** .... JoshBaudains(7) 13 28
(Roger Curtis) *t.k.h: mid-div on outer: rdn and wknd 3f out* **14/1**

1m 37.54s (1.54) **Going Correction** +0.225s/f (Good)
WFA 3 from 4yo+ 3lb **13** Ran SP% **118.1**
Speed ratings (Par 101): **101,99,98,97,96 95,95,95,92,89 87,86,84**
toteswingers 1&2 £9.00, 1&3 £17.00, 2&3 £4.90 CSF £34.63 CT £191.57 TOTE £13.70: £3.40, £1.10, £3.70; EX 62.80 Trifecta £404.00 Pool: £1899.72 - 3.52 winning units.
Owner Joe McCarthy **Bred** Brereton C Jones **Trained** Epsom, Surrey

FOCUS
A modest handicap, and another race on the card in which the winner made all. Straightforward form.

7093 UNION EVENTS H'CAP (DIV II) — 7f 214y
5:20 (5:20) (Class 6) (0-65,63) 3-Y-O+ **£1,940** (£577; £288; £144) **Stalls** Low

Form RPR

225 **1** **Sword Of The Lord**[32] 6153 3-8-11 **59** .... WilliamTwiston-Davies(3) 7 72+
(Michael Bell) *hld up in midfield: hdwy on bit fr 2f out and delayed chal: shkn up to ld ins fnl f: sn clr* **5/1**[2]

040 **2** *2 ¾* **Uncle Dermot (IRE)**[39] 5948 5-9-7 **63** .... JackMitchell 11 68
(Brendan Powell) *chsd ldrs: led 2f out tl ins fnl f: no ch w wnr* **5/1**[2]

6050 **3** *1 ¼* **Geeaitch**[31] 6218 4-9-2 **58** ....(p) WilliamCarson 8 60
(Anthony Carson) *chsd ldrs: rdn over 2f out: one pce appr fnl f* **10/1**

0246 **4** *nk* **Rioja Day (IRE)**[13] 6748 3-9-3 **62** ....(b) SebSanders 9 63
(J W Hills) *led 3f: pressed ldr after tl led again briefly over 2f out: one pce* **8/1**

441 **5** *¾* **Loraine**[24] 6400 3-9-4 **63** .... GeorgeBaker 13 62
(Jamie Osborne) *bhd: hdwy and hrd rdn 2f out: styd on* **6/1**[3]

330 **6** *hd* **St Georges Hill (IRE)**[19] 6555 3-9-3 **62** .... LukeMorris 3 61
(Michael Wigham) *chsd ldr: led 5f out tl over 2f out: no ex appr fnl f* **9/4**[1]

1601 **7** *1 ¾* **Just Isla**[26] 6323 3-9-0 **59** ....(p) SteveDrowne 4 54
(Peter Makin) *towards rr: effrt over 2f out: styd on same pce: nvr able to chal* **8/1**

0060 **8** *1 ¾* **Saint Irene**[22] 6459 4-8-9 **51** .... FergusSweeney 10 42
(Michael Blanshard) *towards rr: c alone to stands' side and effrt over 3f out: wl hld fnl 2f* **16/1**

-400 **9** *3 ¼* **Notabadgirl**[139] 2567 4-8-7 **49** oh1 .... LiamKeniry 12 32
(Simon Dow) *mid-div tl outpcd over 2f out* **33/1**

0000 **10** *11* **Baytown Bertie**[181] 1473 4-8-2 **49** oh4 .... ShelleyBirkett(5) 1 7
(Lydia Richards) *prom tl hrd rdn and wknd 3f out* **66/1**

1m 37.69s (1.69) **Going Correction** +0.225s/f (Good)
WFA 3 from 4yo+ 3lb **10** Ran SP% **120.0**
Speed ratings (Par 101): **100,97,96,95,94 94,93,91,88,77**
toteswingers 1&2 £6.70, 1&3 £11.20, 2&3 £10.60 CSF £31.25 CT £246.06 TOTE £4.60: £1.80, £2.30, £3.20; EX 38.70 Trifecta £367.90 Pool: £3337.59 - 6.80 winning units.
Owner Saleh Al Homaizi & Imad Al Sagar **Bred** Mrs Mary Taylor And James F Taylor **Trained** Newmarket, Suffolk

FOCUS
The second division of this modest handicap was run in a similar time to the first leg. The winner was value for extra and there's every chance of more to come.

T/Plt: £751.50 to a £1 stake. Pool: £61,103.47 - 59.35 winning units T/Qpdt: £82.40 to a £1 stake. Pool: £5435.02 - 48.80 winning units LM

[6627]CATTERICK (L-H)

Tuesday, October 8

OFFICIAL GOING: Good to soft (good in places; 7.2)

Wind: fresh 1/2 against Weather: fine but breezy

7094 YORKSHIRE-OUTDOORS.CO.UK ADVENTURE ACTIVITIES NURSERY H'CAP (DIV I) 5f 212y

2:00 (2:00) (Class 6) (0-65,65) 2-Y-O £2,385 (£704; £352) **Stalls** Low

Form RPR

403 **1** **Signore Piccolo**[24] 6383 2-9-3 **64** JasonHart(3) 6 70+
(Eric Alston) *hmpd s: t.k.h: hdwy to trck ldrs over 3f out: 2nd 1f out: hung lft and r.o to ld last 50yds* **2/1**[1]

5330 **2** 1/2 **Goadby**[35] 6073 2-8-13 **57** GrahamGibbons 12 58
(John Holt) *swtchd lft after s: led: hdd and no ex wl ins fnl f* **12/1**

01 **3** 1 3/4 **Lady Montenegro**[118] 3189 2-8-3 **54** RowanScott(7) 5 50
(Ann Duffield) *wnt rt s: in rr: hdwy over 1f out: styd on wl to take 3rd post* **14/1**

0006 **4** hd **Baileys Celebrate**[41] 5898 2-8-1 **45** NickyMackay 7 40
(Mark Johnston) *mid-div: hdwy over 2f out: kpt on ins fnl f* **33/1**

460 **5** nse **Raise A Billion**[15] 6681 2-8-1 **45** PatrickMathers 8 40
(Alan Berry) *wnt lft s: mid-div: hdwy to chse ldrs over 3f out: kpt on same pce fnl f* **100/1**

465 **6** 2 1/4 **Wadi Alamardi**[19] 6561 2-9-4 **62** StevieDonohoe 1 50
(Michael Bell) *towards rr: hdwy to chse ldrs 3f out: fdd ins fnl f* **7/1**[2]

040 **7** 1 1/4 **Tell Me When**[38] 5988 2-8-11 **55** BarryMcHugh 11 40
(Brian Rothwell) *dwlt: hdwy to chse ldrs over 3f out: lost pl over 1f out* **16/1**

026 **8** 1 1/4 **Scoreline**[19] 6561 2-9-7 **65** DavidNolan 9 46
(David O'Meara) *chsd ldr: j. path after 100yds: drvn over 2f out: wknd over 1f out* **8/1**[3]

6530 **9** 1/2 **Romantic Bliss (IRE)**[14] 6725 2-8-2 **46** (v[1]) CathyGannon 3 25
(K R Burke) *in rr: hung rt over 1f out: nvr a factor* **9/1**

5510 **10** 1 1/4 **White Flag**[9] 6872 2-9-3 **61** DavidAllan 4 37
(Tim Easterby) *hld up in rr: nt clr run 1f out: nvr on terms* **8/1**[3]

5400 **11** hd **Cheeky Peta'S**[15] 6695 2-9-1 **59** GrahamLee 2 34
(James Given) *chsd ldrs: drvn over 2f out: wknd over 1f out* **9/1**

1m 16.79s (3.19) **Going Correction** +0.175s/f (Good) **11 Ran SP% 112.2**

Speed ratings (Par 93): **85,84,82,81,81 78,77,75,74,73 72**

toteswingers 1&2 £3.80, 1&3 £6.90, 2&3 £20.60 CSF £26.19 CT £266.18 TOTE £3.30: £1.10, £4.30, £3.70; EX 29.40 Trifecta £298.10 Pool: £520.82 - 1.31 winning units.

Owner Lancashire Lads Partnership **Bred** Capt J H Wilson **Trained** Longton, Lancs

FOCUS

A moderate nursery lacking depth. The runner-up sets the opening level.

7095 IRISH STALLION FARMS EBF MAIDEN STKS 5f

2:30 (2:30) (Class 5) 2-Y-O £2,911 (£866; £432; £216) **Stalls** Low

Form RPR

2 **1** **Invoke (IRE)**[25] 6354 2-9-0 0 StevieDonohoe 5 73+
(Michael Bell) *chsd ldrs: drvn: outpcd and edgd rt over 2f out: hdwy over 1f out: styd on to ld last 30yds* **7/2**[3]

0420 **2** 3/4 **Bounty Girl (IRE)**[10] 6825 2-9-0 71 (e) DavidAllan 8 68
(Tim Easterby) *chsd ldr: styd on same pce clsng stages* **10/3**[2]

433 **3** 1 **Rock N Rouge (IRE)**[13] 6746 2-9-0 76 GrahamLee 6 64
(David Brown) *led: rdn over 1f out: wknd and hdd wl ins fnl f* **15/8**[1]

5222 **4** 2 1/2 **Fredricka**[14] 6718 2-8-11 65 JasonHart(3) 10 55
(Garry Moss) *s.i.s: sn chsng ldrs: drvn over 2f out: one pce fnl f* **11/2**

0545 **5** 1 1/4 **Red Forever**[8] 6904 2-9-5 57 PatrickMathers 4 56
(Alan Berry) *hld up towards rr: drvn over 2f out: kpt on one pce* **40/1**

50 **6** 1 1/2 **Orient Class**[17] 6627 2-9-5 0 LeeTopliss 1 51
(Paul Midgley) *dwlt: drvn to sn chse ldrs: wknd fnl 150yds* **50/1**

003 **7** 2 **Captain Gee**[19] 6561 2-9-5 66 MichaelO'Connell 7 43
(John Quinn) *chsd ldrs: drvn and outpcd over 2f out: no threat after* **10/1**

40 **8** 10 **Argent Touch**[67] 4963 2-8-12 0 AdamMcLean(7) 3 7
(Derek Shaw) *hld up in rr: lost pl over 2f out: bhd whn eased ins fnl f* **100/1**

6 **9** 15 **Etchy**[108] 3568 2-9-5 0 DuranFentiman 9
(Robin Bastiman) *sn outpcd and bhd: t.o over 1f out* **80/1**

1m 1.65s (1.85) **Going Correction** +0.275s/f (Good) **9 Ran SP% 111.2**

Speed ratings (Par 95): **96,94,93,89,87 84,81,65,41**

toteswingers 1&2 £3.20, 1&3 £2.20, 2&3 £2.10 CSF £14.60 TOTE £5.20: £1.70, £1.80, £1.10; EX 17.00 Trifecta £35.20 Pool: £1049.16 - 22.34 winning units.

Owner Highclere Thoroughbred Racing - Herbert Jones **Bred** J C Bloodstock **Trained** Newmarket, Suffolk

FOCUS

Just an ordinary maiden, the form rated around the second and fifth.

7096 YORKSHIRE-OUTDOORS.CO.UK ADVENTURE ACTIVITIES NURSERY H'CAP (DIV II) 5f 212y

3:00 (3:00) (Class 6) (0-65,65) 2-Y-O £2,385 (£704; £352) **Stalls** Low

Form RPR

3430 **1** **Heroique (IRE)**[17] 6628 2-9-4 **62** (e) DuranFentiman 11 67
(Tim Easterby) *swtchd lft after s: mde all: styd on wl fnl f: unchal* **12/1**

0020 **2** 2 1/2 **Sartori**[30] 6233 2-9-2 **65** ShirleyTeasdale(5) 9 63
(Marjorie Fife) *trckd ldrs: t.k.h: 2nd over 3f out: kpt on same pce fnl f* **5/1**[2]

6633 **3** nk **Another Royal**[28] 6285 2-8-13 **57** (b) DavidAllan 3 54
(Tim Easterby) *in rr: swtchd outside appr fnl f: fin strly to take 3rd nr fin* **3/1**[1]

0402 **4** 1 **Dancing Sal (IRE)**[5] 6979 2-9-0 **58** CathyGannon 7 52
(David Evans) *chsd ldrs: rdn over 2f out: kpt on same pce* **5/1**[2]

0601 **5** 1 **Marlismamma (FR)**[7] 6914 2-8-9 **56** 6ex JulieBurke(3) 8 47
(David O'Meara) *mid-div: hdwy to chse ldrs over 3f out: one pce fnl 2f* **7/1**[3]

000 **6** 1/2 **Hoof's So Lucky**[64] 5053 2-8-8 **52** GrahamGibbons 4 41
(Michael Easterby) *chsd ldrs: rdn over 2f out: one pce* **11/1**

4302 **7** 1/2 **Secret Applause**[35] 6082 2-9-0 **63** ConnorBeasley(5) 10 51
(Michael Dods) *hld up in rr: effrt outer over 2f out: kpt on: nvr a threat* **10/1**

050 **8** 3 **Pacquita**[10] 6821 2-8-11 **55** AdrianNicholls 2 34
(Mark Johnston) *mid-div: n.m.r on inner and lost pl bnd 4f out: sme hdwy 2f out: nvr a factor* **9/1**

000 **9** 1/2 **Poco Piccolo**[32] 6175 2-8-1 **45** (t) PatrickMathers 5 22
(Deborah Sanderson) *in rr: effrt on outer over 2f out: sltly hmpd 1f out: nvr a factor* **20/1**

0600 **10** 7 **Lady Dancer (IRE)**[21] 6494 2-7-12 **45** (b) DeclanCannon(3) 6 1
(George Moore) *mid-div: edgd rt over 1f out: sn lost pl: bhd whn eased ins fnl f* **80/1**

3066 **11** 14 **Reale Silenzio**[20] 6511 2-8-1 **45** (b) NickyMackay 1
(John Weymes) *sn outpcd and bhd: eased over 1f out: t.o* **33/1**

1m 15.77s (2.17) **Going Correction** +0.175s/f (Good) **11 Ran SP% 114.9**

Speed ratings (Par 93): **92,88,88,86,85 84,84,80,79,70 51**

toteswingers 1&2 £4.00, 1&3 £11.10, 2&3 £6.60 CSF £68.29 CT £232.82 TOTE £11.60: £4.00, £2.00, £1.10; EX 72.40 Trifecta £223.00 Pool: £959.00 - 3.22 winning units.

Owner K Nicholson **Bred** Paul McCarthy & Julie Carlton **Trained** Great Habton, N Yorks

■ Stewards' Enquiry : David Allan one-day ban: careless riding (Oct 22)

FOCUS

An ordinary nursery. The apce held up very well. The winner has slipped in the weights and is rated back to her best.

7097 TERRI AND DAVE'S 30TH WEDDING ANNIVERSARY NURSERY H'CAP 7f

3:30 (3:30) (Class 3) (0-95,85) 2-Y-O £6,792 (£2,021; £1,010; £505) **Stalls** Centre

Form RPR

310 **1** **Ventura Quest (USA)**[48] 5656 2-9-2 **80** TonyHamilton 1 84+
(Richard Fahey) *mde all: drvn over 2f out: hld on towards fin* **15/8**[2]

1 **2** 3/4 **King Of Macedon (IRE)**[10] 6842 2-9-1 **79** AdrianNicholls 5 81+
(Mark Johnston) *s.i.s: drvn 3f out: chsng ldng pair over 1f out: wnt 2nd last 75yds: styd on towards fin* **11/8**[1]

0620 **3** nk **Arrowzone**[39] 5941 2-8-2 **69** BillyCray(3) 7 70
(Garry Moss) *sn chsng ldrs on outer: drvn almost upsides 2f out: kpt on same pce last 100yds* **20/1**

433 **4** 9 **Intermath (IRE)**[9] 6865 2-9-7 **85** (p) CathyGannon 4 63
(David Evans) *chsd ldrs: drvn over 2f out: wknd over 1f out* **7/1**[3]

3100 **5** 4 **Sandsman's Girl (IRE)**[35] 6070 2-8-11 **75** GrahamLee 3 42
(James Given) *in rr: outpcd 4f out: sme hdwy over 2f out: sn wknd* **14/1**

0040 **6** 3 1/4 **Lady Liz**[53] 5468 2-7-12 **65** oh2 ow1 DeclanCannon(3) 2 24
(George Moore) *in rr: bhd fnl 3f* **50/1**

5012 **7** hd **Mount Cheiron (USA)**[28] 6284 2-7-12 **65** oh2 ow1 JulieBurke(3) 6 23
(Dianne Sayer) *chsd ldrs: outpcd over 3f out: wknd 2f out* **11/1**

1m 28.47s (1.47) **Going Correction** +0.175s/f (Good) **7 Ran SP% 111.1**

Speed ratings (Par 99): **98,97,96,86,81 78,78**

toteswingers 1&2 £1.30, 1&3 £5.40, 2&3 £23.00 CSF £4.49 CT £29.62 TOTE £2.70: £1.40, £1.50; EX 6.10 Trifecta £49.60 Pool: £1050.83 - 15.87 winning units.

Owner Middleham Park Racing LXIX **Bred** James T Gottwald **Trained** Musley Bank, N Yorks

FOCUS

A modest nursery. The winner did it quite well, with the third helping the level.

7098 SKYRAM H'CAP (DIV I) 1m 7f 177y

4:00 (4:00) (Class 6) (0-60,60) 3-Y-O+ £2,385 (£704; £352) **Stalls** Centre

Form RPR

006- **1** **Iron Butterfly**[196] 6948 4-9-6 **52** GrahamGibbons 3 64+
(James Eustace) *drvn to join ldrs after 1f: drvn to ld over 2f out: styd on strly: eased clsng stages* **15/2**[3]

-365 **2** 1 **Vandross (IRE)**[85] 4352 3-9-0 **57** (b) PJMcDonald 1 67
(Chris Wall) *hld up in rr: hdwy to trck ldrs over 6f out: chsd wnr over 1f out: kpt on: no imp* **9/4**[1]

0650 **3** 11 **Dubara Reef (IRE)**[10] 6853 6-9-0 **46** oh1 (p) TonyHamilton 10 43
(Paul Green) *drvn to ld 2f: chsd ldr: drvn over 4f out: led 3f out: sn hdd wknd over 1f out* **20/1**

0222 **4** nk **Danceintothelight**[17] 6632 6-9-8 **57** NeilFarley(3) 9 53
(Micky Hammond) *led after 2f: hdd 3f out: wknd over 1f out* **11/4**[2]

0/0- **5** 4 **Northern Acres**[165] 1240 7-9-4 **50** LucyAlexander 11 42
(N W Alexander) *sn detached in last: sme hdwy 3f out: modest 5th 1f out: nvr a factor* **14/1**

0-60 **6** 1 1/2 **Red Eyes**[13] 4435 5-10-0 **60** BrianHughes 4 50
(Chris Grant) *mid-div: chsd ldrs 7f out: drvn over 3f out: wknd 2f out* **17/2**

4650 **7** 12 **Ferney Boy**[42] 5863 7-9-0 **46** oh1 MichaelStainton 6 21
(Chris Fairhurst) *hld up in rr: hdwy 6f out: sn chsng ldrs: drvn over 4f out: lost pl over 2f out* **20/1**

0000 **8** 32 **Kingarrick**[19] 6552 5-9-6 **52** DuranFentiman 5
(Noel Wilson) *mid-div: drvn 7f out: lost pl over 3f out: wl bhd whn eased over 1f out: t.o* **12/1**

/6-0 **9** 45 **Golden Groom**[7] 6917 10-9-7 **53** RussKennemore 7
(Patrick Holmes) *t.k.h: hdwy to trck ldrs after 4f: reminders and lost pl over 7f out: hung rt and sn bhd: t.o 4f out: eased over 2f out: eventually completed* **11/1**

3m 36.37s (4.37) **Going Correction** +0.175s/f (Good)

WFA 3 from 4yo+ 11lb **9 Ran SP% 111.9**

Speed ratings (Par 101): **96,95,90,89,87 87,81,65,42**

toteswingers 1&2 £3.50, 1&3 £21.60, 2&3 £15.20 CSF £23.70 CT £321.07 TOTE £3.80: £1.10, £2.00, £7.10; EX 34.40 Trifecta £617.50 Part won. Pool: £823.46 - 0.83 winning units..

Owner Harold Nass **Bred** Rockville Pike Partnership **Trained** Newmarket, Suffolk

FOCUS

A weak staying handicap but there could be more to come from the winner.

7099 SKYRAM H'CAP (DIV II) 1m 7f 177y

4:30 (4:32) (Class 6) (0-60,59) 3-Y-O+ £2,385 (£704; £352) **Stalls** Centre

Form RPR

2262 **1** **Torero**[10] 6853 4-9-9 **54** (p) BrianHughes 4 64
(Kevin Ryan) *trckd ldrs: led 2f out: styd on strly to forge clr fnl f* **10/3**[2]

4045 **2** 5 **Beat The Shower**[17] 6632 7-9-11 **59** JasonHart(3) 11 63
(Peter Niven) *hld up towards rr: hdwy to trck ldrs 3f out: chsd wnr over 1f out: no imp* **5/2**[1]

-600 **3** 3/4 **Aegean Destiny**[11] 6787 6-9-8 **53** MichaelO'Connell 5 56
(John Mackie) *mid-div: effrt 3f out: kpt on same pce to take 3rd nr fin* **14/1**

40 **4** nk **Princeofthedesert**[21] 6498 7-9-8 **53** GrahamLee 7 56
(Garry Woodward) *trckd ldr: led over 3f out: hdd 2f out: one pce* **10/1**

2056 **5** 3 **Amir Pasha (UAE)**[76] 4622 8-9-6 **51** (p) PJMcDonald 10 50
(Micky Hammond) *trckd ldrs: t.k.h: effrt over 3f out: fdd last 150yds* **11/1**

6124 **6** 1 1/2 **Goodlukin Lucy**[96] 3467 6-9-7 **52** (t) LucyAlexander 6 49
(Dianne Sayer) *s.i.s: in rr: drvn over 3f out: kpt on fnl 2f: nvr a threat* **7/1**[3]

0006 **7** 1 1/2 **Erica Starprincess**[68] 4931 3-8-0 **45** DeclanCannon(3) 8 40
(George Moore) *mid-div: trckd ldrs after 5f: drvn over 3f out: wknd appr fnl f* **12/1**

0050 **8** 1/2 **Adili (IRE)**[17] 6632 4-9-11 **56** BarryMcHugh 1 51
(Brian Ellison) *hld up in rr: drvn over 5f out: reminders over 3f out: nvr a factor* **8/1**

00 **9** 3/4 **Dan's Heir**[32] 6177 11-8-7 **45** (p) SamanthaBell(7) 3 39
(Wilf Storey) *in rr: drvn over 3f out: nvr a factor* **16/1**

The Form Book Flat, Raceform Ltd, Compton, RG20 6NL.

0000 **10** *34* **Roc Fort**[59] 5295 4-9-0 **45**..............................(p) CathyGannon 2
(James Moffatt) *w ldrs: led over 12f out: hdd over 3f out: lost pl over 2f out: sn bhd: t.o* **66/1**

010P **P** **Mr Dream Maker (IRE)**[35] 6086 5-9-3 **48**.................... DuranFentiman 9
(Noel Wilson) *chsd ldrs: eased and p.u after 5f: b.b.v* **33/1**

3m 41.21s (9.21) **Going Correction** +0.175s/f (Good)
WFA 3 from 4yo+ 11lb **11** Ran SP% **117.4**
Speed ratings (Par 101): **83,80,80,79,78 77,76,76,76,59**
toteswingers 1&2 £2.40, 1&3 £11.20, 2&3 £6.10 CSF £12.02 CT £102.30 TOTE £5.60: £2.80, £1.02, £8.30; EX 10.50 Trifecta £122.70 Pool: £1691.05 - 10.33 winning units.
Owner Guy Reed Racing **Bred** G Reed **Trained** Hambleton, N Yorks

FOCUS
This looked stronger than the preceding division. The form is rated around the third.

7100 RACINGUK.COM H'CAP 1m 3f 214y
5:00 (5:00) (Class 5) (0-75,75) 3-Y-0+ **£2,911** (£866; £432; £216) **Stalls** Centre

Form RPR

1U10 **1** **Bayan Kasirga (IRE)**[17] 6631 3-8-12 **75**.................... SamanthaBell(7) 3 82+
(Richard Fahey) *hld up in mid-div: hdwy on ins over 2f out: swtchd rt and 4th appr fnl f: styd on wl to ld cl home* **7/1**[3]

0066 **2** *nk* **Mohawk Ridge**[39] 5966 7-9-5 **73**.............................. ConnorBeasley(5) 14 80
(Michael Dods) *led: drvn over 2f out: hdd and no ex nr fin* **16/1**

1302 **3** *1 1/2* **Rosie Rebel**[24] 6405 3-9-3 **73**.. ChrisCatlin 11 78
(Rae Guest) *s.i.s: hdwy to trck ldr after 4f: drvn over 2f out: kpt on same pce fnl f* **5/2**[1]

4034 **4** *hd* **Gran Maestro (USA)**[13] 6758 4-9-5 **71**.....................(p) JasonHart(3) 9 75
(Ruth Carr) *chsd ldrs: drvn over 2f out: kpt on same pce last 150yds* **9/2**[2]

5313 **5** *9* **Vicky Valentine**[10] 6827 3-8-7 **66**.................................... JulieBurke(3) 4 56
(Alistair Whillans) *chsd ldrs: drvn 3f out: wknd over 1f out* **15/2**

10-0 **6** *hd* **Dynastic**[13] 6758 4-9-2 **65**.. BarryMcHugh 6 55
(Tony Coyle) *in rr: hdwy 6f out: chsng ldrs over 3f out: wknd over 1f out: eased nr fin* **20/1**

1314 **7** *1 1/2* **Ailsa Craig (IRE)**[17] 6631 7-9-3 **73**.............................(p) KevinStott(7) 2 60
(Edwin Tuer) *chsd ldrs: drvn and outpcd over 3f out: wknd over 1f out* **8/1**

3124 **8** *11* **Dame Nellie Melba**[48] 5649 3-9-3 **73**........................ AdrianNicholls 12 43
(Mark Johnston) *sn chsng ldrs: drvn over 3f out: lost pl over 1f out: eased clsng stages* **9/1**

54-4 **9** *2 3/4* **How Fortunate**[21] 6497 5-9-2 **65**..................................... GrahamLee 5 30
(Tim Etherington) *hld up in rr: effrt 5f out: sn lost pl and bhd* **25/1**

340- **10** *nk* **Pinotage**[333] 5622 5-8-12 **61** oh4.............................. DuranFentiman 8 26
(Peter Niven) *hld up in rr: lost pl over 4f out: sn bhd* **33/1**

11 *9* **Peaks Of Fire (IRE)**[117] 5065 6-9-4 **67**..................... RussKennemore 10 17
(Joanne Foster) *mid-div: reminders over 6f out: lost pl 4f out: sn bhd* **50/1**

1405 **12** *21* **Underwritten**[12] 6775 4-9-3 **66**.....................................(b) NickyMackay 13
(John Weymes) *sn chsng ldrs: drvn over 6f out: lost pl over 4f out: sn bhd: eased ins fnl f: t.o* **50/1**

2m 42.41s (3.51) **Going Correction** +0.175s/f (Good)
WFA 3 from 4yo+ 7lb **12** Ran SP% **113.5**
Speed ratings (Par 103): **95,94,93,93,87 87,86,79,77,77 71,57**
toteswingers 1&2 £26.00, 1&3 £8.50, 2&3 £13.00 CSF £100.01 CT £353.06 TOTE £7.00: £1.80, £5.60, £1.60; EX 134.50 Trifecta £468.50 Pool: £1576.18 - 2.25 winning units.
Owner Stephen Humphreys **Bred** Lynn Lodge Stud **Trained** Musley Bank, N Yorks

FOCUS
A modest handicap in which the front four came clear. The winner looks progressive and the form is straightforward.

7101 RACING AGAIN SATURDAY 19TH OCTOBER AMATEUR RIDERS' H'CAP 5f
5:30 (5:31) (Class 6) (0-55,55) 3-Y-0+ **£2,305** (£709; £354) **Stalls** Low

Form RPR

5405 **1** **Fleurtille**[6] 6945 4-11-0 **55**.. MissCWalton 9 62
(Robert Johnson) *hmpd s: hdwy over 2f out: swtchd lft over 1f out: led jst ins fnl f: hld on nr fin* **18/1**

0566 **2** *nk* **Errigal Lad**[19] 6568 8-10-0 **46**.............................. MissBeckySmith(5) 8 52
(Garry Woodward) *wnt rt s: in rr: hdwy over 2f out: chsng ldrs and swtchd lft 1f out: styd on wl to take cl 2nd towards fin* **18/1**

6232 **3** *nk* **Prigsnov Dancer (IRE)**[11] 6808 8-10-7 **48**............(p) MissSBrotherton 5 53
(Deborah Sanderson) *in tch: hdwy 2f out: kpt on wl ins fnl f* **11/2**[2]

6140 **4** *nk* **Boy The Bell**[49] 5614 6-10-9 **55**..............................(be) MissHDukes(5) 14 59
(Ollie Pears) *dwlt and hmpd s: hdwy on outer 2f out: styd on wl ins fnl f* **14/1**

6500 **5** *1* **Busy Bimbo (IRE)**[6] 6940 4-10-4 **48**........................ MissJRRichards(3) 3 48
(Alan Berry) *chsd ldrs: led appr fnl f: hdd and one pce last 150yds* **25/1**

2431 **6** *hd* **Pull The Pin (IRE)**[16] 6669 4-10-13 **54**.............................(p) MrSWalker 11 54
(Paul Green) *w ldrs: kpt on same pce fnl 150yds* **7/4**[1]

5004 **7** *hd* **Ivestar (IRE)**[26] 6343 8-10-11 **52**...................................(v) MissJCoward 1 51
(Michael Easterby) *chsd ldrs: hdd appr fnl f: wknd last 50yds* **10/1**

0404 **8** *nse* **Headstight (IRE)**[9] 6878 4-10-7 **48**.................................(v[1]) MissADeniel 4 47
(Paul Midgley) *dwlt: hdwy 3f out: kpt on same pce appr fnl f* **14/1**

0441 **9** *4 1/2* **Irish Girls Spirit (IRE)**[9] 6878 4-10-4 **52**......................(p) MrAFrench(7) 12 35
(Paul Midgley) *wnt rt s: chsd ldrs: wknd fnl f* **6/1**[3]

0600 **10** *nk* **Boucher Garcon (IRE)**[22] 6469 5-10-7 **55**................ MrKyleWalker(7) 6 36
(Declan Carroll) *chsd ldrs: outpcd 3f out: wknd fnl f* **25/1**

0050 **11** *hd* **Piste**[6] 6945 7-10-5 **46** oh1...(be) MissHBethell 15 27
(Tina Jackson) *dwlt: mid-div: lost pl 2f out* **25/1**

0001 **12** *1* **Sophie's Beau (USA)**[63] 5085 6-10-10 **54**..............(b) MissAliceMills(3) 2 31
(Michael Chapman) *chsd ldr: rdn over 2f out: wknd over 1f out* **20/1**

-000 **13** *6* **On The High Tops (IRE)**[6] 6945 5-10-12 **53**......... ColmMcCormack 10 9
(Colin Teague) *in rr: bhd fnl 2f* **40/1**

0-40 **14** *3 3/4* **Hellolini**[79] 4558 3-10-9 **50**.. MrWHogg 13
(Robin Bastiman) *hmpd s: mid-div and sn drvn along: lost pl 2f out* **50/1**

1m 2.54s (2.74) **Going Correction** +0.275s/f (Good) **14** Ran SP% **119.7**
Speed ratings (Par 101): **89,88,88,87,85 85,85,85,78,77 77,75,66,60**
toteswingers 1&2 £74.00, 1&3 £21.50, 2&3 £25.80 CSF £279.22 CT £2026.57 TOTE £29.40: £7.00, £3.80, £2.00; EX 404.10 Trifecta £1354.70 Part won. Pool: £1806.33 - 0.03 winning units..
Owner Ray Craggs **Bred** Ray Craggs **Trained** Newburn, Tyne & Wear

FOCUS
A weak handicap, confined to amateur riders and run at what looked an overly strong pace. Straightforward, ordinary form.
T/Jkpt: Not won. T/Plt: £11.90 to a £1 stake. Pool: £62,205.63 - 3786.10 winning units T/Qpdt: £8.30 to a £1 stake. Pool: £3963.70 - 352.20 winning units WG

6695 LEICESTER (R-H)
Tuesday, October 8

OFFICIAL GOING: Good to firm (good in places; 8.2)
Wind: Light behind Weather: Cloudy with sunny spells

7102 BRITISH STALLION STUDS EBF MAIDEN FILLIES' STKS (DIV I) 7f 9y
2:10 (2:14) (Class 4) 2-Y-O **£5,175** (£1,540; £769; £384) **Stalls** High

Form RPR

1 **Bold Lass (IRE)** 2-9-0 0.. TedDurcan 8 80+
(David Lanigan) *a.p: shkn up over 1f out: r.o to ld wl ins fnl f: readily* **12/1**

4 **2** *1* **Amaseena (IRE)**[15] 6690 2-9-0 0... RyanMoore 6 77
(Roger Varian) *trckd ldrs: wnt 2nd 1/2-way: led 2f out: sn rdn and edgd rt: hdd and unable qck wl ins fnl f* **5/2**[1]

3 **3** *1 1/4* **Maria Bella (IRE)**[15] 6690 2-9-0 0............................... SilvestreDeSousa 5 74
(Charlie Appleby) *trckd ldrs: rdn over 1f out: styd on same pce ins fnl f* **3/1**[2]

4 *6* **Joys Of Spring (IRE)** 2-9-0 0... AndreaAtzeni 3 57
(Luca Cumani) *mid-div: pushed along 1/2-way: hdwy over 2f out: no ex fnl f* **16/1**

3 **5** *2 3/4* **Weekend Getaway (IRE)**[21] 6500 2-9-0 0................ DougieCostello 11 50
(Clive Brittain) *trckd ldr to 1/2-way: rdn over 2f out: wknd fnl f* **9/2**[3]

6 *2* **Wintour Leap** 2-9-0 0... JamesDoyle 2 45+
(Roger Charlton) *hld up: shkn up over 2f out: nvr trbld ldrs* **25/1**

00 **7** *nk* **Spring Lady**[15] 6691 2-9-0 0.. DavidProbert 4 44
(Alan Jarvis) *led: rdn and hdd 2f out: wknd fnl f* **200/1**

8 *3 3/4* **Dark Reality (IRE)** 2-9-0 0... JamieSpencer 1 34+
(Ralph Beckett) *wnt rt s: hld up: rdn over 2f out: sn wknd* **16/1**

0 **9** *shd* **Namely (IRE)**[15] 6690 2-9-0 0... DaneO'Neill 9 33
(Sir Mark Prescott Bt) *hld up: pushed along 1/2-way: wknd over 2f out* **100/1**

10 *4* **Song Beam** 2-9-0 0... TomQueally 7 23
(Michael Bell) *s.i.s: sn pushed along and a in rr: wknd over 2f out* **50/1**

1m 24.57s (-1.63) **Going Correction** -0.10s/f (Good) **10** Ran SP% **98.5**
Speed ratings (Par 94): **105,103,102,95,92 90,89,85,85,80**
toteswingers 1&2 £4.40, 1&3 £6.70, 2&3 £1.30 CSF £31.03 TOTE £15.40: £3.30, £1.10, £1.60; EX 36.90 Trifecta £126.30 Pool: £1703.28 - 10.10 winning units.
Owner B E Nielsen **Bred** Bjorn E Nielsen **Trained** Upper Lambourn, Berks
■ An Chulainn was withdrawn on vet's advice (6-1, deduct 10p in the £).

FOCUS
False rail from top of hill on back straight to winning post increased distances on Round course by 17m. Bends and home straight moved out 8m adding 24yds to races of 7f and 1m and 38yds to 1m5f race. An interesting maiden, though the late withdrawal of the 76-rated An Chulainn robbed the race of its main benchmark. The form could well rate higher in time.

7103 BRITISH STALLION STUDS EBF MAIDEN FILLIES' STKS (DIV II) 7f 9y
2:40 (2:41) (Class 4) 2-Y-O **£5,175** (£1,540; £769; £384) **Stalls** High

Form RPR

1 **Token Of Love** 2-9-0 0.. RyanMoore 7 80+
(William Haggas) *hld up: hdwy 1/2-way: shkn up to ld 1f out: r.o wl* **9/2**[2]

54 **2** *2 1/4* **Miss Brazil (IRE)**[11] 6789 2-9-0 0.................................. RichardHughes 3 74
(Richard Hannon) *led: hdd over 5f out: chsd ldr tl led again over 2f out: rdn and hdd 1f out: styd on same pce* **5/1**[3]

3 *2 3/4* **Sequester** 2-9-0 0.. TedDurcan 10 67+
(David Lanigan) *s.i.s: hld up: pushed along over 2f out: hdwy and nt clr run over 1f out: swtchd lft: r.o: nt rch ldrs* **20/1**

4 *3/4* **Alpine Storm (IRE)** 2-9-0 0.. MartinLane 12 65
(Charlie Appleby) *trckd ldrs: plld hrd: rdn over 1f out: no ex ins fnl f* **8/1**

5 *1 3/4* **Zanouska (USA)** 2-9-0 0.. KierenFallon 6 60
(Mark Johnston) *chsd ldrs: sn pushed along: rdn and edgd lft over 1f out: wknd ins fnl f* **20/1**

4 **6** *1 1/2* **Nibbling (IRE)**[20] 6523 2-9-0 0...................................... JimCrowley 1 56
(Paul Cole) *w ldr tl led over 5f out: rdn and hdd over 2f out: wknd ins fnl f* **3/1**[1]

7 *1 1/2* **Good Hope** 2-9-0 0... TomQueally 8 52
(Michael Bell) *chsd ldrs: rdn over 2f out: wknd fnl f* **16/1**

8 *3/4* **Arabian Beauty (IRE)** 2-9-0 0.................................. SilvestreDeSousa 2 50
(Saeed bin Suroor) *s.i.s: hdwy over 2f out: sn rdn and hung lft: wknd over 1f out: eased* **6/1**

0 **9** *nk* **Kelamita (IRE)**[13] 6739 2-9-0 0..................................... NeilCallan 9 49
(Hughie Morrison) *mid-div: pushed along 1/2-way: wknd over 1f out* **33/1**

10 *1* **Blossom Lane** 2-9-0 0.. WilliamBuick 11 46
(John Gosden) *s.i.s: hld up: pushed along and hdwy 3f out: wknd wl over 1f out* **7/1**

1m 25.52s (-0.68) **Going Correction** -0.10s/f (Good) **10** Ran SP% **116.1**
Speed ratings (Par 94): **99,96,93,92,90 88,87,86,85,84**
toteswingers 1&2 £4.40, 1&3 £14.60, 2&3 £12.10 CSF £26.37 TOTE £6.20: £1.90, £2.10, £6.00; EX 32.60 Trifecta £383.30 Pool: £3045.00 - 5.95 winning units.
Owner A E Oppenheimer **Bred** Hascombe And Valiant Studs **Trained** Newmarket, Suffolk

FOCUS
As with the first division, a nice winning debut performance. The winning time was nearly a second slower than the first leg. The opening level of the form is fluid.

7104 STOAT (S) STKS 1m 1f 218y
3:10 (3:10) (Class 6) 3-Y-O **£1,940** (£577; £288; £144) **Stalls** Low

Form RPR

4225 **1** **Banreenahreenkah (IRE)**[21] 6492 3-8-6 64.................. DavidProbert 1 51
(Denis Coakley) *trckd ldrs: plld hrd: rdn over 2f out: led 1f out: edgd lft: styd on* **5/4**[1]

0642 **2** *1 1/2* **Zinnobar**[5] 6971 3-8-6 39.. AndreaAtzeni 2 48
(Jonathan Portman) *trckd ldr tl rdn to ld 2f out: sn hung lft: hdd 1f out: styd on same pce* **8/1**

0600 **3** *3/4* **Lincolnrose (IRE)**[17] 6655 3-8-11 48.........................(p) AndrewMullen 6 52
(Michael Appleby) *led: stdd pce 5f out: qcknd over 3f out: rdn and hdd 2f out: styd on u.p* **33/1**

0035 **4** *nse* **Calon Lad (IRE)**[20] 6522 3-8-11 65................................ PatCosgrave 4 52
(George Baker) *slowly into strde and n.m.r s: hld up: hdwy u.p over 1f out: styd on: nt rch ldrs* **3/1**[2]

2344 **5** *3/4* **Well Owd Mon**[5] 6971 3-8-6 60.................................... JackDuern(5) 7 50
(Andrew Hollinshead) *hld up: hdwy over 3f out: rdn over 1f out: styd on same pce ins fnl f* **5/1**[3]

6605 **6** *1/2* **Dawn Beat**[68] 4931 3-8-6 50...................................... SilvestreDeSousa 9 44
(Jonathan Portman) *a.p: racd keenly: rdn over 3f out: no ex ins fnl f* **10/1**

6060 **7** 1/2 **The Ginger Berry**[67] 4961 3-8-11 45 TomQueally 3 48
(Dr Jon Scargill) *hld up: racd keenly: hdwy over 2f out: rdn and nt clr run 1f out: styd on same pce* **33/1**

0040 **8** 10 **Cool And Clear (IRE)**[3] 7035 3-8-8 43 (v) CharlesBishop(3) 5 29
(Pat Eddery) *hld up: rdn over 3f out: sn lost tch* **100/1**

4540 **P** **Aphrodite Spirit (IRE)**[21] 6491 3-8-6 45 JimmyQuinn 8
(Pat Eddery) *chsd ldrs tl rdn and lost pl over 3f out: sn bhd: wnt wrong over 1f out: sn p.u: fatally injured* **33/1**

2m 8.13s (0.23) **Going Correction** -0.10s/f (Good) 9 Ran SP% **116.1**
Speed ratings (Par 99): **95,93,93,93,92 92,91,83,**
toteswingers 1&2 £3.00, 1&3 £9.70, 2&3 £19.00 CSF £12.23 TOTE £2.00: £1.20, £1.40, £3.40; EX 12.40 Trifecta £142.30 Pool: £3168.54 - 16.69 winning units.Banreenahreenkah was bought by Jenny Candlish for 6500 guineas.
Owner Chris Van Hoorn **Bred** Edmund Power **Trained** West Ilsley, Berks

FOCUS
A poor seller and form to be negative about.

7105 VADERSTAD DEALER H'CAP 1m 3f 183y
3:40 (3:43) (Class 4) (0-85,85) 3-Y-0 **£5,175** (£1,540; £769; £384) **Stalls** Low

Form RPR

051 **1** **Hamelin (IRE)**[24] 6402 3-9-7 **85** RichardHughes 8 100+
(Lady Cecil) *hld up in tch: t.k.h: chsd ldr over 2f out: shkn up to ld over 1f out: styd on wl: eased nr fin* **2/1**[1]

-303 **2** 1 1/2 **Ice Pie**[13] 6743 3-8-9 **73** RichardKingscote 7 83
(Tom Dascombe) *led: rdn and hdd over 1f out: styd on same pce ins fnl f* **5/1**[3]

4432 **3** nk **Sunblazer (IRE)**[17] 6629 3-8-10 **74** DougieCostello 2 83
(William Muir) *trckd ldrs: rdn over 2f out: hung rt fr over 1f out: styd on* **20/1**

2523 **4** 6 **Pompeia**[19] 6559 3-9-0 **78** (p) JimCrowley 6 77
(Ralph Beckett) *prom: rdn over 3f out: edgd rt and wknd ins fnl f* **6/1**

6313 **5** 2 **Don Padeja**[39] 5954 3-8-13 **77** AndreaAtzeni 4 73
(Luca Cumani) *hld up: hdwy u.p 2f out: wknd ins fnl f* **3/1**[2]

6310 **6** 1 1/4 **Shamaheart (IRE)**[67] 4950 3-9-1 **79** RyanMoore 3 73
(Richard Hannon) *s.i.s: hld up: hdwy u.p over 1f out: nt trble ldrs* **10/1**

41 **7** 5 **Lineman**[12] 6781 3-8-8 **72** ShaneKelly 10 58
(Andrew Hollinshead) *hld up: rdn over 2f out: wknd over 1f out* **33/1**

21 **8** 9 **My History (IRE)**[26] 6272 3-9-1 **79** KierenFallon 1 50
(Mark Johnston) *chsd ldr tl rdn over 2f out: wknd over 1f out: eased* **12/1**

2m 31.5s (-2.40) **Going Correction** -0.10s/f (Good) 8 Ran SP% **113.8**
Speed ratings (Par 103): **104,103,102,98,97 96,93,87**
toteswingers 1&2 £3.00, 1&3 £8.20, 2&3 £17.90 CSF £12.24 CT £149.74 TOTE £2.50: £1.10, £1.70, £3.70; EX 16.20 Trifecta £158.10 Pool: £3851.68 - 18.26 winning units.
Owner Lordship Stud **Bred** Lordship Stud **Trained** Newmarket, Suffolk

FOCUS
Not a bad handicap featuring some progressive 3yos, and one of them proved successful. The second and third help with the level.

7106 RED DEER H'CAP 5f 218y
4:10 (4:11) (Class 5) (0-70,70) 3-Y-0+ **£2,587** (£770; £384; £192) **Stalls** High

Form RPR

6242 **1** **Generalyse**[7] 6929 4-9-7 **70** (b) JimCrowley 1 82
(Ben De Haan) *trckd ldrs: a gng wl: led over 1f out: sn edgd lft: rdn clr* **11/4**[1]

5450 **2** 3 3/4 **Another Try (IRE)**[40] 5928 8-9-6 **69** JamesDoyle 8 69
(Alan Jarvis) *a.p: rdn to chse wnr ins fnl f: styd on same pce* **8/1**[2]

2230 **3** 3/4 **Maria Montez**[46] 5697 4-9-5 **68** KierenFallon 12 66
(J W Hills) *chsd ldrs: rdn and ev ch over 1f out: no ex ins fnl f* **10/1**[3]

6623 **4** hd **Billyrayvalentine (CAN)**[21] 6489 4-9-7 **70** PatCosgrave 2 67
(George Baker) *mid-div: hdwy over 1f out: sn rdn: styd on same pce ins fnl f* **16/1**

-516 **5** 3 1/2 **Tychaios**[67] 4962 3-8-10 **60** AndreaAtzeni 16 46
(Stuart Williams) *hld up: shkn up over 2f out: rdn over 1f out: r.o ins fnl f: nvr nrr* **8/1**[2]

6630 **6** 1/2 **Charlemagne Diva**[11] 6808 3-8-12 **62** (t) SilvestreDeSousa 10 46
(Richard Guest) *led: rdn and hdd over 1f out: wknd ins fnl f* **20/1**

5036 **7** 1 1/2 **Methaaly (IRE)**[26] 6344 10-8-7 **59** oh2 ow3 (be) RobertTart(3) 15 38
(Michael Mullineaux) *hld up: pushed along over 2f out: edgd rt fnl f: nvr nrr* **20/1**

5056 **8** 3/4 **Deepest Blue**[41] 5886 3-9-2 **66** RaulDaSilva 4 43
(Michael Wigham) *hld up: rdn over 3f out: nvr on terms* **33/1**

4440 **9** 1 1/4 **Somoud (IRE)**[8] 6900 3-9-4 **68** (p) JimmyFortune 6 41
(J R Jenkins) *chsd ldrs: rdn over 1f out: wknd and eased ins fnl f* **33/1**

0230 **10** 3 1/2 **Emiratesdotcom**[27] 6316 7-9-2 **65** (tp) RyanMoore 9 27
(Milton Bradley) *s.v.s: a bhd* **8/1**[2]

2151 **11** hd **Batchworth Lady**[19] 6560 3-9-2 **66** JimmyQuinn 7 27
(Dean Ivory) *chsd ldrs: rdn over 2f out: wknd fnl f* **16/1**

4005 **12** 2 1/2 **Valdaw**[55] 5406 5-9-0 **63** ShaneKelly 13 16
(Mike Murphy) *hld up: pushed along over 3f out: n.d* **8/1**[2]

303 **13** 2 1/2 **Spiraea**[33] 6145 3-9-3 **67** JamieSpencer 11 12
(Mark Rimell) *hld up: pushed along and swtchd rt over 2f out: hrd rdn over 1f out: sn wknd and eased* **16/1**

2000 **14** 3 1/2 **Irish Boy (IRE)**[14] 6732 5-9-5 **68** (vt) TomMcLaughlin 5
(Christine Dunnett) *chsd ldrs: rdn over 2f out: wknd over 1f out* **33/1**

0421 **15** 6 **Solarmaite**[39] 5965 4-8-9 **61** (b) RyanClark(3) 3
(Roy Bowring) *chsd ldrs: rdn 1/2-way: wknd over 2f out* **16/1**

1m 11.88s (-1.12) **Going Correction** -0.10s/f (Good)
WFA 3 from 4yo+ 1lb 15 Ran SP% **122.1**
Speed ratings (Par 103): **103,98,97,96,92 91,89,88,86,82 81,78,75,70,62**
toteswingers 1&2 £5.70, 1&3 £6.30, 2&3 £7.90 CSF £21.97 CT £196.74 TOTE £3.80: £1.70, £2.40, £2.90; EX 30.80 Trifecta £182.50 Pool: £2913.51 - 11.97 winning units.
Owner Mrs D Vaughan **Bred** Mrs D Vaughan **Trained** Lambourn, Berks

FOCUS
A big field for this modest sprint handicap and there was no advantage in the draw. The front four were clear and the form could have been 4-6lb higher.

7107 SQUIRREL CONDITIONS STKS 1m 1f 218y
4:40 (4:40) (Class 3) 2-Y-0 **£7,762** (£2,310; £1,154; £577) **Stalls** Low

Form RPR

41 **1** **Miner's Lamp (IRE)**[20] 6528 2-8-13 0 SilvestreDeSousa 2 86+
(Charlie Appleby) *hld up: plld hrd: hdwy to trck ldr over 7f out: led over 3f out: rdn over 1f out: styd on: comf* **4/11**[1]

1304 **2** 1 1/4 **Gold Top (IRE)**[12] 6763 2-8-8 80 TedDurcan 1 79
(Richard Hannon) *hld up: hdwy over 2f out: rdn and edgd rt over 1f out: styd on to go 2nd wl ins fnl f: nt rch wnr* **8/1**[3]

100 **3** 3 **Recanted (USA)**[69] 4876 2-8-13 90 JimmyFortune 3 78
(Brian Meehan) *trckd ldrs: wnt 2nd over 2f out: rdn over 1f out: no ex wl ins fnl f* **5/1**[2]

201 **4** 1 3/4 **Aristocracy**[8] 6897 2-8-8 60 CharlesBishop(3) 4 73
(Mick Channon) *led: pushed along and hdd over 3f out: rdn over 2f out: no ex fnl f* **20/1**

2m 8.4s (0.50) **Going Correction** -0.10s/f (Good) 4 Ran SP% **105.9**
Speed ratings (Par 99): **94,93,90,89**
CSF £3.57 TOTE £2.00; EX 2.90 Trifecta £4.50 Pool: £1550.44 - 254.33 winning units.
Owner Godolphin **Bred** Mrs C L Weld **Trained** Newmarket, Suffolk

FOCUS
Despite just the four runners the pace looked solid enough in this stamina test for 2yos. The winner was just workmanlike, and the runer-up is rated to his recent nursery form.

7108 DORMOUSE MAIDEN STKS 7f 9y
5:10 (5:10) (Class 5) 3-Y-0 **£2,587** (£770; £384; £192) **Stalls** High

Form RPR

222 **1** **Endless Light**[21] 6486 3-9-0 69 RyanMoore 1 80+
(Jeremy Noseda) *mde all: rdn over 1f out: r.o wl* **11/10**[1]

0- **2** 3 3/4 **Interception (IRE)**[385] 6343 3-9-0 0 TedDurcan 10 70+
(David Lanigan) *a.p: rdn to chse wnr over 1f out: styd on same pce fnl f* **7/1**

2625 **3** 1 1/4 **Disco Inferno (IRE)**[21] 6486 3-9-5 72 (bt) JimmyFortune 8 72
(Brian Meehan) *chsd wnr tl rdn over 1f out: no ex ins fnl f* **3/1**[2]

4-0 **4** 1 3/4 **Marishi Ten (IRE)**[161] 1896 3-9-0 0 DavidProbert 4 62
(Andrew Balding) *hld up in tch: rdn over 1f out: no ex fnl f* **6/1**[3]

3504 **5** 1/2 **Persian Patriot**[40] 5932 3-9-0 64 RobertHavlin 6 60
(William Jarvis) *chsd ldrs: rdn over 1f out: no ex* **7/1**

0-0 **6** 11 **Mill I Am (USA)**[122] 3116 3-9-0 0 SaleemGolam 9 31
(Stuart Williams) *s.i.s: hdwy 1/2-way: rdn over 2f out: sn hung rt and wknd* **33/1**

7 6 **Port Lairge** 3-9-5 0 PatCosgrave 11 20
(Jonjo O'Neill) *hld up: t.k.h: rdn and wknd over 2f out* **33/1**

0-6 **8** 1 3/4 **Cote Reveur**[10] 6824 3-8-11 0 RobertTart(3) 2 10
(Michael Mullineaux) *chsd ldrs: pushed along over 4f out: rdn and wknd over 2f out* **100/1**

00 **9** 1 1/4 **Ismaali**[18] 6611 3-8-9 0 DavidBergin(5) 3 6
(James Given) *hld up: a in rr: wknd over 2f out* **100/1**

00 **10** 12 **Bahama Bay**[90] 4182 3-9-0 0 AdamBeschizza 7
(Stuart Williams) *hld up: a in rr: rdn and wknd over 2f out* **100/1**

00 **11** 7 **Miss Rebero**[17] 6630 3-9-0 0 AndrewMullen 5
(Tim Fitzgerald) *s.i.s: hdwy over 5f out: wknd 3f out* **100/1**

1m 24.52s (-1.68) **Going Correction** -0.10s/f (Good) 11 Ran SP% **121.7**
Speed ratings (Par 101): **105,100,99,97,96 84,77,75,73,60 52**
toteswingers 1&2 £3.10, 1&3 £1.60, 2&3 £4.30 CSF £10.33 TOTE £1.90: £1.10, £2.00, £1.40; EX 12.80 Trifecta £46.60 Pool: £3883.09 - 62.48 winning units.
Owner Cheveley Park Stud **Bred** Cheveley Park Stud Ltd **Trained** Newmarket, Suffolk

FOCUS
Not many could be seriously fancied in this modest 3yo maiden and several of these needed the run to qualify for a mark. The form has been given a bit of a chance.

7109 LEVERET APPRENTICE H'CAP 7f 9y
5:45 (5:45) (Class 6) (0-60,60) 3-Y-0+ **£1,940** (£577; £288; £144) **Stalls** High

Form RPR

24-0 **1** **Barista (IRE)**[6] 6932 5-9-4 **60** DanielCremin(5) 8 70
(Brian Forsey) *a.p: rdn to ld ins fnl f: r.o* **16/1**

5005 **2** 2 **Admiralofthesea (USA)**[6] 6932 3-9-2 **60** (p) LouisSteward(5) 10 64
(Robert Eddery) *hld up: pushed along and hdwy 1/2-way: rdn to ld over 1f out: hdd ins fnl f: styd on same pce* **6/1**[3]

00 **3** 2 **Tee It Up Tommo (IRE)**[63] 5100 4-9-9 **60** GeorgeChaloner 16 59
(Michael Wigham) *a.p: rdn over 2f out: styd on same pce ins fnl f* **4/1**[1]

056 **4** 3/4 **Admirable Art (IRE)**[18] 6587 3-9-4 **57** (p) GeorgeDowning 2 53
(Tony Carroll) *hld up: hdwy over 1f out: styd on: nt rch ldrs* **9/1**

5540 **5** 3/4 **True Spirit**[15] 6702 3-8-11 **57** StaceyKidd(7) 3 51
(Paul D'Arcy) *hld up: hdwy over 1f out: nt rch ldrs* **33/1**

2050 **6** 4 1/2 **Jarrow (IRE)**[7] 6928 6-9-2 **58** (p[1]) JordanVaughan(5) 7 41
(Milton Bradley) *w ldrs tl led over 5f out: rdn and hdd over 1f out: wknd ins fnl f* **16/1**

-000 **7** shd **Percythepinto (IRE)**[29] 6261 4-9-2 **56** (t) TimClark(3) 9 39
(George Baker) *s.i.s: hld up: pushed along and swtchd lft 3f out: rdn over 2f out: nvr nrr* **33/1**

5050 **8** 2 **Maakirr (IRE)**[13] 6760 4-9-0 **54** (t) IanBurns(3) 14 31
(Roy Bowring) *hld up: hdwy over 2f out: rdn over 1f out: wknd fnl f* **16/1**

64-2 **9** 2 **Byron's Dream**[166] 1772 3-9-7 **60** JacobButterfield 13 31
(Jedd O'Keeffe) *prom: rdn over 2f out: wknd fnl f* **5/1**[2]

0-00 **10** 1 3/4 **Courtland Avenue (IRE)**[23] 6436 4-9-5 **56** MatthewLawson 11 23
(Jonathan Portman) *chsd ldrs: hmpd and lost pl over 4f out: n.d after* **50/1**

5340 **11** nk **Shaunas Spirit (IRE)**[27] 6316 5-8-13 **55** (p) PaulBooth(5) 12 21
(Dean Ivory) *s.i.s: hdwy over 3f out: outpcd over 2f out: n.d after* **10/1**

0450 **12** nk **Rough Rock (IRE)**[15] 6702 8-9-7 **58** (v) JackDuern 17 24
(Chris Dwyer) *led: hdd over 5f out: chsd ldrs tl wknd over 1f out* **16/1**

6504 **13** 2 3/4 **My Learned Friend (IRE)**[32] 6154 9-9-2 **58** (p) JonathanWilletts(5) 1 16
(Andrew Balding) *hld up: rdn over 2f out: wknd over 1f out* **16/1**

3102 **13** dht **Sweet Talking Guy (IRE)**[33] 6138 3-9-2 **55** (t) TobyAtkinson 6 12
(Lydia Pearce) *plld hrd and prom: rdn over 2f out: wknd over 1f out* **14/1**

4550 **15** 16 **Exclusive Predator**[91] 4144 4-9-4 **58** (t) ThomasGarner(3) 15
(Bryan Smart) *chsd ldrs tl wknd over 2f out* **12/1**

0002 **16** 26 **Dancing Maite**[15] 6702 8-9-1 **59** (b) JoshQuinn(7) 5
(Roy Bowring) *s.i.s: hdwy over 5f out: pushed along whn lost action and eased wl over 1f out* **10/1**

1m 25.76s (-0.44) **Going Correction** -0.10s/f (Good)
WFA 3 from 4yo+ 2lb 16 Ran SP% **130.7**
Speed ratings (Par 101): **98,95,93,92,91 86,86,84,81,79 79,79,76,76,57 28**
toteswingers 1&2 £20.90, 1&3 £12.70, 2&3 £5.20 CSF £115.53 CT £496.38 TOTE £21.10: £3.60, £2.40, £1.60, £3.50; EX 165.50 Trifecta £609.50 Part won. Pool: £812.67 - 0.92 winning units..
Owner K Jago **Bred** Rathasker Stud **Trained** Ash Priors, Somerset
■ Stewards' Enquiry : Jacob Butterfield two-day ban: careless riding (Oct 23-24)

FOCUS
A competitive, if moderate apprentice handicap. The form seems straightforward.
T/Plt: £22.40 to a £1 stake. Pool: £75,621.43 - 2460.24 winning units T/Qpdt: £5.60 to a £1 stake. Pool: £4682.63 - 608.95 winning units CR

The Form Book Flat, Raceform Ltd, Compton, RG20 6NL.

[7076]WOLVERHAMPTON (A.W) (L-H)

Tuesday, October 8

OFFICIAL GOING: Standard

Wind: light, behind Weather: dry

7110 QUICKSILVERSLOTS ON THE HIGH STREET NURSERY H'CAP 1m 141y(P)

5:40 (6:15) (Class 5) (0-70,69) 2-Y-O **£2,587** (£770; £384; £192) **Stalls** Low

Form RPR

5651 **1** **Hedge End (IRE)**[7] 6924 2-9-8 **69** 6ex........................ RichardHughes 1 73+
(Richard Hannon) *chsd ldr: rdn and chalng whn carried rt over 1f out: sn ld: r.o wl to assert ins fnl f: comf* **1/1**[1]

6644 **2** *1 1/4* **Power Up**[8] 6897 2-9-5 **66**........................ NeilCallan 4 67
(Mark Johnston) *sn led: rdn and hung rt over 1f out: sn hdd and styd on same pce fnl f* **7/2**[3]

3035 **3** *5* **Ding Ding**[14] 6725 2-8-9 **56**........................ SamHitchcott 3 47
(Mick Channon) *stdd s: t.k.h: hld up in last: rdn and effrt to chse ldng pair 3f out: sn struggling and wknd over 1f out* **16/1**

1 **4** *5* **Improvized**[22] 6460 2-9-7 **68**........................ FrederikTylicki 2 48
(William Muir) *stdd s: hld up in 3rd: rdn 1/2-way: dropped to last 3f out and sn struggling: wl btn over 1f out* **11/4**[2]

1m 52.84s (2.34) **Going Correction** +0.10s/f (Slow) **4** Ran SP% **104.8**

Speed ratings (Par 95): **93,91,87,83**

CSF £4.41 TOTE £1.40; EX 3.60 Trifecta £11.90 Pool: £2519.25 - 157.72 winning units..

Owner Grimes, Ivory, Bull, Hannon **Bred** Airlie Stud **Trained** East Everleigh, Wilts

FOCUS

Effectively a fillies-only nursery but not a competitive event and, although the gallop was no more than fair, the official time suggests the Polytrack remains on the slow side. The winning rider described the surface as "horrible". The runner-up sets the level.

7111 QUICKSILVERSLOTS PLAY £500 ROULETTE MAIDEN AUCTION STKS 7f 32y(P)

6:10 (6:15) (Class 6) 2-Y-O **£1,940** (£577; £288; £144) **Stalls** High

Form RPR

5 **1** **Kalon Brama (IRE)**[11] 6807 2-8-1 0........................ RosieJessop(3) 4 63
(Peter Charalambous) *wnt rt s: t.k.h: chsd ldrs: effrt to chse ldr over 2f out: rdn and unable qck over 1f out: 2 l down and hld whn lft in ld ins fnl f: pushed out* **3/1**[2]

2 *3/4* **Passionate Affair (IRE)** 2-8-13 0........................ RichardKingscote 6 70
(Tom Dascombe) *s.i.s: in tch in last pair: rdn and effrt 3f out: hdwy over 1f out: lft chsng wnr ins fnl f: styd on steadily but nvr quite getting to wnr* **5/2**[1]

0 **3** *2 1/2* **Sky Ranger (IRE)**[18] 6607 2-8-10 0........................ NeilCallan 3 61
(James Tate) *chsd ldrs: wnt 2nd 5f out tl over 2f out: sn drvn and flashed tail u.p: lft 3rd ins fnl f: styd on same pce* **6/1**

46 **4** *3 1/4* **Winter Picnic (IRE)**[35] 6079 2-8-6 0........................ MartinLane 1 49
(Tobias B P Coles) *chsd ldr tl 5f out: drvn and outpcd 3f out: wknd over 1f out: lft modest 4th ins fnl f* **7/1**

5 *11* **Bow Quarter** 2-8-4 0........................ AndreaAtzeni 7 20
(J S Moore) *s.i.s: sn pushed along in rr: drvn and struggling over 3f out: sn wknd and bhd fnl 2f* **8/1**

0 **U** **Pendo**[18] 6589 2-8-9 0........................ MartinHarley 2 67+
(Alastair Lidderdale) *t.k.h: led: rdn over 1f out: 2 l clr and looking wnr whn cocked jaw: hung bdly rt: uns rdr and crashed into rail ins fnl f* **4/1**[3]

1m 32.26s (2.66) **Going Correction** +0.10s/f (Slow) **6** Ran SP% **111.5**

Speed ratings (Par 93): **88,87,84,80,68**

toteswingers 1&2 £3.90, 1&3 £1.90, 2&3 £1.90 CSF £10.76 TOTE £4.10: £2.10, £1.20; EX 14.90 Trifecta £60.30 Pool: £2098.19 - 26.08 winning units..

Owner P Charalambous **Bred** Tally-Ho Stud **Trained** Newmarket, Suffolk

FOCUS

A modest and uncompetitive maiden in which the gallop was just an ordinary one. There was plenty of late drama as the well-backed Pendo looked sure to win before veering markedly right and unseating his rider late on.

7112 QUICKSILVERSLOTS PLAY £500 RAINBOW RICHES H'CAP 5f 20y(P)

6:40 (6:15) (Class 4) (0-85,84) 3-Y-O+ **£4,851** (£1,443; £721; £360) **Stalls** Low

Form RPR

6311 **1** **Dangerous Age**[10] 6854 3-8-12 **75**........................ DaneO'Neill 7 84
(J W Hills) *chsd ldng trio: rdn and effrt to chal over 1f out: led ins fnl f: r.o wl* **11/4**[1]

6310 **2** *3/4* **Triple Dream**[32] 6159 8-9-3 **80**........................(tp) RichardKingscote 6 85
(Milton Bradley) *wl in tch in midfield: effrt u.p 2f out: styd on wl ins fnl f: snatched 2nd last stride* **33/1**

060 **3** *shd* **Rylee Mooch**[18] 6583 5-9-1 **78**........................(e) NeilCallan 11 83
(Richard Guest) *led: rdn over 1f out: hdd and edgd lft ins fnl f: kpt on same pce fnl 100yds: lost 2nd last stride* **16/1**

1420 **4** *3/4* **Port Alfred**[31] 6189 3-9-6 **83**........................ SilvestreDeSousa 2 86
(Charlie Appleby) *chsd ldrs: wnt 2nd 1/2-way: rdn and ev ch over 1f out: styd on same pce ins fnl f* **11/4**[1]

3454 **5** *1* **Agerzam**[10] 6854 3-9-7 **84**........................ AndreaAtzeni 1 86
(Roger Varian) *in tch in midfield: rdn and effrt on inner over 1f out: chsng ldrs and keeping on same pce whn jostling match w rival ins fnl f: wknd towards fin* **4/1**[2]

1100 **6** *3/4* **Royal Bajan (USA)**[10] 6854 5-9-4 **81**........................ FrederikTylicki 10 77
(James Given) *taken down early: in tch towards rr of main gp: rdn and hdwy over 1f out: styd on ins fnl f: nvr gng pce to chal* **25/1**

000 **7** *nk* **Cadeaux Pearl**[63] 5108 5-8-11 **74**........................(b) RobertWinston 4 69
(Scott Dixon) *taken down early: sn bustled along: chsd ldr tl 1/2-way: drvn and unable qck over 1f out: keeping on same pce and btn whn hmpd and swtchd rt ins fnl f* **33/1**

2324 **8** *1/2* **Dusty Storm (IRE)**[57] 5340 3-9-2 **79**........................ RichardHughes 5 73
(Ed McMahon) *t.k.h: hld up in tch in midfield: rdn and unable qck over 1f out: no imp fnl f* **6/1**[3]

0060 **9** *1 3/4* **Top Boy**[20] 6539 3-9-3 **80**........................(v[1]) DaleSwift 12 67
(Derek Shaw) *hld up in rr of main gp: wd bnd 1/2-way: rdn and effrt over 1f out: kpt on but n.d* **12/1**

5101 **10** *1 3/4* **Secret Missile**[23] 6429 3-9-4 **81**........................(p) DougieCostello 3 62
(William Muir) *v.s.a: detached in last: sme hdwy ins fnl f: n.d* **10/1**

2600 **11** *3/4* **Satsuma**[10] 6848 3-9-2 **79**........................(e[1]) KierenFallon 9 57
(David Brown) *dwlt and hmpd sn after s: a in rr: n.d* **33/1**

0130 **12** *nk* **First In Command (IRE)**[20] 6539 8-9-5 **82**........................(t) ShaneKelly 8 58
(John Stimpson) *toward rr of main gp: rdn and struggling over 2f out: wknd over 1f out* **33/1**

1m 2.22s (-0.08) **Going Correction** +0.10s/f (Slow) **12** Ran SP% **125.9**

Speed ratings (Par 105): **104,102,102,101,99 98,98,97,94,91 90,90**

toteswingers 1&2 £13.30, 1&3 £34.90, 2&3 £77.30 CSF £115.97 CT £1261.04 TOTE £4.40: £1.10, £8.40, £6.20; EX 124.30 Trifecta £1524.60 Part won. Pool: £2032.88 - 0.27 winning units..

Owner R Hunter, D Klein, M Hoodless **Bred** Mrs T Brudenell **Trained** Upper Lambourn, Berks

FOCUS

A useful handicap in which the gallop was decent throughout. The winner came down the centre in the straight and the kickback looked particularly severe. The winner is progressive and the second and third set the level.

7113 QUICKSILVERSLOTS GET UP TO £200 FREEPLAYS MAIDEN STKS 1m 141y(P)

7:10 (7:10) (Class 5) 2-Y-O **£2,587** (£770; £384; £192) **Stalls** Low

Form RPR

3246 **1** **Istimraar (IRE)**[19] 6572 2-9-5 78........................(p) DaneO'Neill 7 77
(Saeed bin Suroor) *chsd ldrs tl hdwy to chse ldr over 6f out: rdn to ld over 1f out: awkward hd carriage and edgd lft ins fnl f: styd on: rdn out* **5/2**[2]

0404 **2** *2* **Heska (IRE)**[17] 6656 2-9-5 67........................ SamHitchcott 3 72
(Mick Channon) *chsd ldrs tl led 7f out: rdn and drew clr w wnr 2f out: hdd over 1f out: styd on same pce ins fnl f* **20/1**

62 **3** *10* **Byron Gala**[25] 6365 2-9-5 0........................ AndreaAtzeni 2 51
(Marco Botti) *led tl 7f out: chsd ldng pair fr over 6f out: rdn and btn ent fnl 2f: sn wknd* **3/1**[3]

4 *5* **Francistown (IRE)** 2-9-5 0........................ SilvestreDeSousa 4 40
(Charlie Appleby) *s.i.s: rn v green and rdn along in rr: clsd and in tch 5f out: struggling u.p and btn over 3f out: wnt modest 4th and eased ins fnl f* **2/1**[1]

5 *3 1/2* **Modern Art** 2-9-0 0........................ NeilCallan 6 28
(Mark Johnston) *dwlt: in tch towards rr: hdwy to chse ldng trio 5f out: rdn and btn over 1f out: wknd qckly 2f out: wl bhd and eased ins fnl f* **7/1**

0 **6** *6* **Palace Dragon (IRE)**[14] 6733 2-9-2 0........................ RosieJessop(3) 5 20
(Sir Mark Prescott Bt) *t.k.h: chsd ldrs tl stdd bk into midfield 5f out: rdn and btn 3f out: lost tch 2f out* **66/1**

0 **7** *1* **Right Behind You**[39] 5941 2-9-5 0........................(v[1]) RichardKingscote 1 18
(Tom Dascombe) *sn pushed along in last pair and nvr travelling: rdn and dropped to last 4f out: sn lost tch* **50/1**

1m 52.2s (1.70) **Going Correction** +0.10s/f (Slow) **7** Ran SP% **107.6**

Speed ratings (Par 95): **96,94,85,80,77 72,71**

toteswingers 1&2 £5.50, 1&3 £1.60, 2&3 £6.70 CSF £40.08 TOTE £2.00: £1.10, £21.80; EX 40.10 Trifecta £89.60 Pool: £2249.95 - 18.82 winning units..

Owner Godolphin **Bred** Shadwell Estate Company Limited **Trained** Newmarket, Suffolk

FOCUS

Fair form from the winner but an uncompetitive maiden in which the first two pulled clear. The gallop was only fair and the winner edged towards the far rail in the closing stages. The winner is rated back to his best form.

7114 QUICKSILVERSLOTS £1 TO WIN £500 MAIDEN FILLIES' STKS 1m 1f 103y(P)

7:40 (7:40) (Class 5) 3-Y-O+ **£2,587** (£770; £384; £192) **Stalls** Low

Form RPR

602 **1** **Fossola (USA)**[18] 6611 3-9-0 78........................ SilvestreDeSousa 2 77+
(Charlie Appleby) *led tl 8f out: chsd ldr after tl led again on bit over 2f out: sn cruised clr and in command: idling and pushed along ins fnl f* **1/1**[1]

2 *2 3/4* **Wilhana (IRE)** 3-9-0 0........................ AndreaAtzeni 4 74+
(Roger Varian) *dwlt: rdn along in rr: clsd and in tch 5f out: 3rd and outpcd 3f out: chsd clr wnr jst over 1f out: kpt on but nvr a threat to wnr* **11/4**[2]

0-44 **3** *12* **Funky Cold Medina**[14] 6735 3-9-0 70........................ RobertWinston 1 47
(Charles Hills) *bustled along leaving stalls: led 8f out tl rdn and hdd over 2f out: sn btn: 3rd and fdd fnl f* **11/2**[3]

2644 **4** *35* **Heroine Required (FR)**[21] 6498 3-9-0 73........................(t) RichardHughes 3
(William Haggas) *chsd ldng pair: rdn over 3f out: dropped to last 3f out and sn lost tch: eased fnl 2f: t.o* **6/1**

2m 1.91s (0.21) **Going Correction** +0.10s/f (Slow) **4** Ran SP% **106.3**

Speed ratings (Par 100): **103,100,89,58**

CSF £3.82 TOTE £1.30; EX 2.80 Trifecta £6.70 Pool: £1038.80 - 114.78 winning units..

Owner Godolphin **Bred** Darley **Trained** Newmarket, Suffolk

FOCUS

Fair form from the winner but not a competitive event, especially with two of the four runners under-performing. The gallop was on the steady side and the winner came down the far side in the straight. The winner's pre-race mark dictates the level of this form.

7115 QUICKSILVERSLOTS PLAY YOUR FAVOURITE £500 JACKPOT H'CAP 1m 4f 50y(P)

8:10 (8:10) (Class 4) (0-85,85) 4-Y-O+ **£4,851** (£1,443; £721; £360) **Stalls** Low

Form RPR

-120 **1** **Azrag (USA)**[26] 6336 5-9-2 **80**........................(vt) FrederikTylicki 7 90
(Gerard Butler) *hld up in last trio: clsd and swtchd rt 4f out: rdn and effrt over 1f out: chsd wnr ins fnl f: styd on to ld towards fin* **8/1**

1230 **2** *1/2* **Fennell Bay (IRE)**[17] 6638 4-9-6 **84**........................ NeilCallan 5 93
(Mark Johnston) *wnt rt s: led: rdn ent fnl 2f: forged ahd gamely over 1f out: kpt on u.p tl hdd and no ex towards fin* **4/1**[2]

1132 **3** *5* **Royal Alcor (IRE)**[11] 6809 6-8-13 **77**........................ RichardHughes 10 79
(Gay Kelleway) *hld up in tch in midfield: rdn and effrt to chse ldr over 2f out: no ex u.p over 1f out: lost 2nd ins fnl f: wknd towards fin* **2/1**[1]

0050 **4** *1 1/2* **Sir Boss (IRE)**[13] 6750 8-8-10 **77**........................ SladeO'Hara(3) 3 76
(Michael Mullineaux) *hld up in tch in midfield: nt clr run over 2f out: swtchd rt and rdn over 1f out: plugged on ins fnl f but no threat to ldrs* **33/1**

0660 **5** *1 1/4* **Maria's Choice (IRE)**[19] 6562 4-8-11 **75**........................(p) SilvestreDeSousa 8 72
(Alan McCabe) *chsd ldr for 1f: styd chsng ldrs: wnt 2nd again over 4f out tl over 2f out: 3rd and no ex 2f out: wknd ins fnl f* **14/1**

-043 **6** *1 3/4* **Lyric Street (IRE)**[19] 6573 5-9-7 **85**........................(p) AndreaAtzeni 2 80
(Jeremy Noseda) *chsd ldrs: rdn 3f out: no ex u.p 2f out: wknd 1f out* **7/1**

5043 **7** *3 1/4* **Wyborne**[17] 6626 4-9-2 **80**........................(p) DaleSwift 1 70
(Brian Ellison) *hld up in last pair: clsd and wl in tch 4f out: rdn over 3f out: struggling u.p 3f out: sn wknd* **5/1**[3]

3162 **8** *30* **Colinca's Lad (IRE)**[19] 6573 11-8-4 **71** oh1........................ RosieJessop(3) 6 16
(Peter Charalambous) *bmpd s and towards rr: stdy hdwy 8f out to chse ldrs 6f out: rdn and dropped out qckly over 3f out: t.o and eased fnl f* **12/1**

0-64 **9** *32* **Ultimate**[121] 2579 7-8-10 **77**........................ PaulPickard(3) 9
(Brian Ellison) *rdn along leaving stalls: chsd ldr after 1f out: rdn 5f out: lost pl qckly 4f out and sn bhd: t.o fnl 2f* **33/1**

P214 **10** *10* **All The Winds (GER)**[195] 1212 8-9-2 **80**.......................(t) KierenFallon 4
(Shaun Lycett) *s.i.s: a bhd: rdn and btn over 3f out: lost tch 3f out: sn eased and t.o* **25/1**

2m 40.11s (-0.99) **Going Correction** +0.10s/f (Slow) **10** Ran SP% **117.7**
Speed ratings (Par 105): **107,106,103,102,101 100,98,78,56,50**
toteswingers 1&2 £7.20, 1&3 £4.10, 2&3 £2.20 CSF £39.74 CT £88.85 TOTE £5.00: £3.00, £3.30, £1.10; EX 56.70 Trifecta £176.60 Pool: £2055.90 - 8.73 winning units..
Owner Beetle N Wedge Partnership **Bred** Aislabie Bloodstock **Trained** Newmarket, Suffolk

FOCUS
A useful handicap run at just a reasonable gallop. The first two, who pulled clear, came down the centre. It's probably wise to take the margins too literally.
T/Plt: £86.40 to a £1 stake. Pool: £62,195.07 - 525.19 winning units T/Qpdt: £37.60 to a £1 stake. Pool: £7984.64 - 157.05 winning units SP

6786 MAISONS-LAFFITTE (R-H)
Tuesday, October 8

OFFICIAL GOING: Turf: good to soft

7116a PRIX LE FABULEUX (LISTED RACE) (3YO) (TURF) 1m 1f
2:20 (12:00) 3-Y-O £22,357 (£8,943; £6,707; £4,471; £2,235)

RPR
1 **Nocturnal Secret**[30] 3-9-0 0.................................... StephanePasquier 7 105
(J E Pease, France) **19/10**[1]
2 *2 ½* **Kokaltash (FR)**[20] 3-9-0 0........................ Christophe-PatriceLemaire 11 100
(M Delzangles, France) **7/1**[3]
3 *1* **Hay Dude**[31] 6191 3-9-3 0.................................... DanielTudhope 2 101
(K R Burke) *hld up towards rr of gp on ins rail: hdwy over 2f out: rdn to chal ldrs 1 1/2f out: one pce u.p fnl f* **44/5**
4 *½* **Abilene**[101] 3834 3-8-10 0.. UmbertoRispoli 9 93
(F-H Graffard, France) **33/1**
5 *snk* **Zamaam**[32] 6182 3-9-0 0... ThierryJarnet 5 96
(F Rohaut, France) **6/1**[2]
6 *1 ¼* **Tecla (IRE)**[90] 3-8-10 0...(b) BriceRaballand 6 90?
(Mme C Head-Maarek, France) **24/1**
7 *3* **Intimhir (IRE)**[100] 3877 3-8-10 0.. OlivierPeslier 4 83
(F Head, France) **11/1**
8 *1 ¼* **Auditor (USA)**[31] 6230 3-9-0 0.. JulienAuge 10 85
(C Ferland, France) **78/10**
9 *nse* **Boomshackerlacker (IRE)**[20] 6530 3-9-0 0...............(p) MaximeGuyon 8 85
(George Baker) *t.k.h: w ldrs tl allowed to stride on and ld gp of five in centre of trck after 2 1/2f: sn had overall ld: rdn and hdd 1 1/2f out: wknd appr fnl f* **73/10**
10 *dist* **Nervi (FR)**[95] 3-9-0 0.. ChristopheSoumillon 1
(P Bary, France) **13/1**

1m 50.82s (-3.88) **10** Ran SP% **117.3**
PARI-MUTUEL (all including 1 euro stakes): WIN 2.90; PLACE 1.40, 2.30, 2.80; DF 9.50; SF 12.60.
Owner George Strawbridge **Bred** George Strawbridge **Trained** Chantilly, France

6930 KEMPTON (A.W) (R-H)
Wednesday, October 9

OFFICIAL GOING: Standard
Wind: Brisk across Weather: Overcast early, getting dark

7117 BOOK NOW FOR JUMP RACING 20.10.13 CLAIMING STKS 6f (P)
5:40 (5:40) (Class 6) 2-Y-O £1,940 (£577; £288; £144) Stalls Low

Form RPR
214 **1** **Hipz (IRE)**[16] 6695 2-8-10 71.. PatCosgrave 8 70
(George Baker) *in rr: hdwy on outside over 2f out: str run u.p to ld fnl 150yds: edgd rt cl home: hld on all out* **4/1**[3]
2405 **2** *shd* **Princess Rose**[36] 6070 2-8-6 70.................................(b[1]) LiamJones 5 66
(William Haggas) *chsd ldrs: rdn and one pce over 2f out: rallied and edgd lft over 1f out: styd on wl to chal whn pushed rt in clsng stages: jst failed* **8/1**
1023 **3** *1 ¼* **Party Ruler (IRE)**[18] 6628 2-9-5 84.......................... RichardKingscote 3 75
(Tom Dascombe) *chsd ldr: led ins fnl 2f: hdd u.p fnl 150yds: outpcd into 3rd fnl 30yds* **5/4**[1]
0600 **4** *1 ¼* **My My My Diliza**[27] 6322 2-8-3 51..........................(b) AndreaAtzeni 10 55
(J S Moore) *in tch: rdn and outpcd ins fnl 3f: rallied fnl f: fin wl in clsng stages* **50/1**
3265 **5** *½* **Sleepy Joe (IRE)**[29] 6279 2-8-6 59.......................... CharlesBishop(3) 9 60
(Mick Channon) *chsd ldrs: drvn 3f out: one pce whn n.m.r over 1f out: kpt on again cl home* **33/1**
1315 **6** *½* **Limegrove**[13] 6778 2-7-12 62.................................... NoelGarbutt(5) 6 52
(David Evans) *in tch: rdn and outpcd over 2f out: kpt on again fnl f* **14/1**
3113 **7** *2 ¾* **Fine Art Fair (IRE)**[35] 6104 2-9-5 71.............................. RyanMoore 2 60
(Gary Moore) *awkward fr stalls: chsd ldrs: rdn and ev ch over 2f out: wknd 1f out* **3/1**[2]
3645 **8** *½* **Aweebitowinker**[99] 3914 2-8-7 55................................. DavidProbert 11 46
(J S Moore) *in rr: rdn over 2f out: sme hdwy sn after: nvr nr ldrs and sn wknd* **33/1**
606 **9** *1 ¼* **Dancing Juice**[88] 4282 2-8-11 56.. MartinLane 1 47
(Alan Jarvis) *led tl hdd ins fnl 2f: sn wknd* **33/1**
0600 **10** *2 ¾* **Monsieur Blanc (IRE)**[6] 6983 2-8-6 51............................ JohnFahy 7 33
(Denis Coakley) *stdd s: sme hdwy on ins over 2f out: nvr nr ldrs and sn wknd* **66/1**

1m 13.76s (0.66) **Going Correction** 0.0s/f (Stan) **10** Ran SP% **119.5**
Speed ratings (Par 93): **95,94,93,91,90 90,86,85,84,80**
toteswingers 1&2 £5.90, 2&3 £2.80, 1&3 £2.40 CSF £34.88 TOTE £9.70: £2.40, £2.40, £1.02; EX 48.50 Trifecta £162.60 Pool: £1265.97 - 5.83 winning units..
Owner George Baker & Partners **Bred** Mrs Noelle Walsh **Trained** Manton, Wilts

FOCUS
This modest 2yo claimer proved a bit of a rough race early, but the form looks okay for the class. The winner was entitled to win at these weights.

7118 DDR FROM £39/HEAD CLAIMING STKS 1m 3f (P)
6:10 (6:10) (Class 6) 3-4-Y-O £1,940 (£577; £288; £144) Stalls Low

Form RPR
5522 **1** **Checkpoint**[14] 6748 4-9-2 67......................................(p) RyanMoore 3 74
(Gary Moore) *travelling wl: led 2f out: drvn clr fnl f: readily* **1/1**[1]
5400 **2** *7* **Knight's Parade (IRE)**[14] 6743 3-9-6 65.......................... RichardHughes 6 71
(Amanda Perrett) *led: drvn and qcknd 3f out: hdd 2f out: sn no ch w wnr but styd on wl for 2nd* **6/1**[3]
3664 **3** *3* **Poetic Verse**[34] 6136 3-9-1 73... AndreaAtzeni 4 61
(Rod Millman) *in rr: hdwy to take 3rd 2f out: no further prog u.p* **2/1**[2]
4400 **4** *1 ½* **Run It Twice (IRE)**[13] 6777 3-8-10 70.........................(b) DeclanBates(3) 1 56
(David Evans) *in rr: styd on fnl 2f: nvr any ch w ldrs* **14/1**
040 **5** *2 ½* **Zaminate**[9] 6899 4-8-9 47.. DavidProbert 5 42
(Patrick Chamings) *chsd ldrs: wknd appr fnl 2f* **50/1**
604 **6** *7* **Bell'Arte (IRE)**[30] 6257 3-8-4 50.................................(p) SimonPearce(3) 7 33
(Laura Mongan) *chsd ldr: wknd 3f out* **33/1**
0-00 **7** *2 ¾* **Valley Dreamer**[12] 6803 3-8-2 44 ow1.................................... MartinLane 2 23
(Robert Stephens) *in tch: wknd ins fnl 3f* **66/1**

2m 20.01s (-1.89) **Going Correction** 0.0s/f (Stan)
WFA 3 from 4yo 6lb **7** Ran SP% **110.7**
Speed ratings (Par 101): **106,100,98,97,95 90,88**
toteswingers 1&2 £1.30, 2&3 £1.60, 1&3 £1.10 CSF £7.17 TOTE £1.80: £1.10, £3.00; EX 7.00 Trifecta £9.20 Pool: £2602.73 - 211.34 winning units..Checkpoint was claimed by T Coyle for £8000.
Owner B Siddle & B D Haynes **Bred** Juddmonte Farms Ltd **Trained** Lower Beeding, W Sussex

FOCUS
A weak claimer, run at a fair enough pace. The winner may be back to his best, but it's hard to rate the form at that level.

7119 COMMISSION FREE 1ST MONTH AT BETDAQ MAIDEN STKS (DIV I) 7f (P)
6:40 (6:44) (Class 5) 2-Y-O £2,587 (£770; £384; £192) Stalls Low

Form RPR
23 **1** **Pearl Spectre (USA)**[77] 4640 2-9-5 0............................ JamieSpencer 5 79+
(Andrew Balding) *sn led: rdn over 1f out: styd on strly ins fnl f* **2/1**[1]
2 *1 ¾* **Cannock Chase (USA)** 2-9-5 0...................................... RyanMoore 2 74+
(Sir Michael Stoute) *s.i.s and drvn along: stl pushed along and hdwy fr over 2f out: chsd wnr fnl f but no imp* **3/1**[2]
3 *nk* **Ghosting (IRE)** 2-9-5 0.. RichardKingscote 7 74+
(Tom Dascombe) *chsd ldrs: disp 2nd fr over 2f out: styd on same pce into 3rd fnl f* **7/1**[3]
4 *hd* **Three Cliffs** 2-9-5 0.. AndreaAtzeni 14 73+
(Roger Varian) *s.i.s: in rr: hdwy on outside over 2f out: styd on wl in clsng stages* **16/1**
5 *½* **Sea Defence (USA)** 2-9-5 0... GeorgeBaker 11 74+
(Roger Charlton) *s.i.s: in rr: pushed along and green fr over 2f out: hdwy appr fnl f: stl green and n.m.r but styd on encouragingly fnl f: fin wl* **9/1**
6 *¾* **Maghaanem (IRE)** 2-9-5 0.. PaulHanagan 4 70
(Ed Dunlop) *chsd ldrs: drvn to dispute 2nd fr 2f out: styd on same pce ins fnl f* **33/1**
35 **7** *½* **Almargo (IRE)**[7] 6931 2-9-5 0.. MartinLane 6 69
(Charlie Appleby) *chsd ldrs: drvn over 2f out: styd on one pce fnl f* **7/1**[3]
0 **8** *2 ½* **Sweetheart Abbey**[25] 6378 2-9-0 0.................................... TedDurcan 13 57
(William Knight) *s.i.s: in rr: sme hdwy fnl f* **100/1**
304 **9** *hd* **Souville**[22] 6500 2-9-0 72... SebSanders 8 57
(Chris Wall) *in rr: hdwy over 2f out: nvr rchd ldrs and wknd fnl f* **33/1**
066 **10** *3 ¾* **Hostile Fire (IRE)**[18] 6635 2-9-5 67.................................... AdamKirby 3 52
(Ed de Giles) *t.k.h: chsd ldrs: rdn 3f out: wknd over 2f out* **33/1**
00 **11** *14* **Dover The Moon (IRE)**[33] 6168 2-9-5 0....................... RichardHughes 12 15
(Richard Hannon) *chsd ldrs: wknd ins fnl 3f* **25/1**
12 *nk* **Scrutiny** 2-9-5 0.. LiamJones 1 15
(William Haggas) *chsd ldrs: rdn 4f out: wknd ins fnl 3f* **33/1**

1m 26.08s (0.08) **Going Correction** 0.0s/f (Stan) **12** Ran SP% **115.8**
Speed ratings (Par 95): **99,97,96,96,95 95,94,91,91,87 71,70**
toteswingers 1&2 £1.70, 2&3 £4.90, 1&3 £3.50 CSF £6.97 TOTE £2.10: £1.10, £1.40, £2.90; EX 9.90 Trifecta £33.80 Pool: £1943.46 - 43.07 winning units..
Owner Pearl Bloodstock Ltd **Bred** Estate Of Edward P Evans **Trained** Kingsclere, Hants

FOCUS
Potentially a good maiden with plenty of well-bred, sizeable 2yos in attendance. A number should prove better than the bare form.

7120 COMMISSION FREE 1ST MONTH AT BETDAQ MAIDEN STKS (DIV II) 7f (P)
7:10 (7:11) (Class 5) 2-Y-O £2,587 (£770; £384; £192) Stalls Low

Form RPR
0 **1** **Best Kept**[14] 6739 2-9-5 0... AndreaAtzeni 9 78+
(Amanda Perrett) *in tch: gd hdwy and drvn 2f out: chsd ldr appr fnl f: r.o strly to ld fnl 40yds: kpt on wl* **25/1**
2 *1* **Potentate (IRE)** 2-9-5 0... RichardHughes 13 76+
(Richard Hannon) *led: drvn 3 l clr over 2f out: hdd and no ex fnl 40yds* **15/2**
00 **3** *3 ½* **Filament Of Gold (USA)**[15] 6716 2-9-5 0............................ AdamKirby 11 67
(Mark Johnston) *chsd ldrs: drvn and hung rt 2f out: styd on same pce for 3rd fnl f* **20/1**
42 **4** *nk* **Hesbaan (IRE)**[19] 6589 2-9-5 0....................................... PaulHanagan 8 66
(Marcus Tregoning) *chsd ldrs: rdn over 2f out: one pce fnl f* **11/4**[1]
0 **5** *½* **Si Senor (IRE)**[41] 5924 2-9-5 0.................................. FrederikTylicki 1 65+
(Ed Vaughan) *in rr: hdwy fr 2f out: kpt on ins fnl f: nt rch ldrs* **20/1**
6 *3* **Sahara Desert (IRE)** 2-9-5 0... RyanMoore 5 57+
(Sir Michael Stoute) *sn towards rr: shkn up 2f out: r.o fr over 1f out: kpt on in clsng stages* **6/1**
02 **7** *3* **Wilde Inspiration (IRE)**[14] 6739 2-9-5 0............................... JimCrowley 10 49
(Ralph Beckett) *chsd ldrs: wknd over 1f out* **11/2**[3]
3 **8** *nk* **Wellesbourne**[12] 6807 2-9-5 0.. KierenFallon 6 48
(Charlie Appleby) *chsd ldrs: rdn over 2f out: wknd over 1f out* **7/2**[2]
0 **9** *nse* **Like A Prayer**[21] 6534 2-9-5 0.. MartinHarley 4 48
(Marco Botti) *s.i.s: in rr: sme hdwy fr over 1f out* **20/1**
03 **10** *nk* **Berrahri (IRE)**[18] 6641 2-9-5 0..................................... SteveDrowne 12 47
(John Best) *chsd ldr: outpcd wl over 2f out: wknd over 1f out* **20/1**
11 *nk* **Sharp Lookout** 2-9-5 0... GeorgeBaker 3 47
(Roger Charlton) *t.k.h: in rr: sme hdwy 2f out* **12/1**
12 *½* **Vied (USA)** 2-9-0 0... MartinLane 7 40
(Robert Cowell) *s.i.s: a towards rr* **33/1**
13 *1 ¾* **Emerald Gg (IRE)** 2-9-5 0... LiamJones 2 41
(J S Moore) *bhd most of way* **66/1**

1m 26.74s (0.74) **Going Correction** 0.0s/f (Stan) **13** Ran SP% **125.3**
Speed ratings (Par 95): **95,93,89,89,88 85,82,81,81,81 81,80,78**
toteswingers 1&2 £53.00, 2&3 £9.70, 1&3 £121.90 CSF £196.55 TOTE £39.20: £5.00, £3.10, £6.80; EX 247.40 Trifecta £960.20 Part won. Pool: £1280.27 - 0.01 winning units..
Owner Coombelands Racing Syndicate 3 **Bred** Wayne And Hilary Thornton **Trained** Pulborough, W Sussex

The Form Book Flat, Raceform Ltd, Compton, RG20 6NL.

FOCUS
This wasn't as strong as the opening division and few got involved. The winner left his debut effort behind.

7121 WINNERS ARE WELCOME AT BETDAQ H'CAP (LONDON MIDDLE DISTANCE SERIES QUALIFIER) 1m 3f (P)
7:40 (7:41) (Class 4) (0-85,85) 3-Y-O+ **£4,690** (£1,395; £697; £348) **Stalls** Low

Form RPR
3314 **1** **I'm Fraam Govan**[39] [6004] 5-9-8 **83**.................................(t) PatCosgrave 6 94
(George Baker) *in rr: hdwy on outer 3f out: str run to ld over 1f out: strly chal ins fnl f but a jst doing enough* **2/1**[1]
-125 **2** *hd* **Saoi (USA)**[215] [926] 6-9-8 **83**.................................. JimCrowley 12 93
(William Knight) *in rr: hdwy fr 2f out: chsd wnr 1f out: chal fnl 150yds but a jst hld* **16/1**
0332 **3** *1 1/2* **Cosmic Sun**[10] [6876] 7-8-12 **73**.................................(t) PaulHanagan 7 80
(Richard Fahey) *in tch: rdn 3f out: styd on to take 3rd fnl 75yds but no imp on ldng duo* **8/1**[3]
3104 **4** *hd* **Sinaadi (IRE)**[25] [6387] 3-8-8 **75**.................................. LukeMorris 3 82
(Clive Brittain) *in tch: drvn over 2f out: chsd ldrs over 1f out: styd on same pce ins fnl f* **33/1**
1223 **5** *1 1/2* **Duke Of Perth**[40] [5953] 3-9-4 **85**.................................. KierenFallon 9 89
(Luca Cumani) *chsd ldr: rdn 2f out: wknd fnl 110yds* **7/1**[2]
2216 **6** *1* **Qanan**[14] [6750] 4-8-11 **75**.................................. AshleyMorgan(3) 4 77
(Chris Wall) *in rr: drvn over 2f out: sme hdwy fnl f* **20/1**
6141 **7** *1/2* **Uphold**[14] [6750] 6-9-10 **85**.................................(v) AdamKirby 5 86
(Gay Kelleway) *chsd ldrs: rdn over 2f out: styd on same pce* **7/1**[2]
16 **8** *4* **Warrigal (IRE)**[166] [1803] 3-8-6 **73**.................................. AndreaAtzeni 2 67
(Jeremy Noseda) *led: hdd & wknd over 1f out* **8/1**[3]
0465 **9** *3* **Red Runaway**[22] [6503] 3-8-11 **78**.................................. RichardHughes 10 67
(Ed Dunlop) *in rr: rapid hdwy to chse ldrs 7f out: wknd qckly over 2f out* **7/1**[2]
0443 **10** *1/2* **Purple 'n Gold (IRE)**[9] [6004] 4-9-3 **78**.................................(p) RyanMoore 1 66
(David Pipe) *chsd ldrs: wknd qckly ins fnl 2f* **12/1**

2m 21.99s (0.09) **Going Correction** 0.0s/f (Stan)
WFA 3 from 4yo+ 6lb **10** Ran SP% **114.3**
Speed ratings (Par 105): **99,98,97,97,96 95,95,92,90,89**
toteswingers 1&2 £9.20, 2&3 £24.90, 1&3 £4.60 CSF £37.21 CT £213.50 TOTE £2.80: £1.30, £4.50, £2.70; EX 39.80 Trifecta £165.20 Pool: £1625.00 - 7.37 winning units..
Owner Sir Alex Ferguson **Bred** M Kehoe **Trained** Manton, Wilts

FOCUS
A modest handicap, run at an ordinary pace, but the form is rated slightly positively.

7122 £200 FREE BETS AT BETDAQ NURSERY H'CAP 7f (P)
8:10 (8:10) (Class 2) 2-Y-O **£8,715** (£2,609; £1,304; £652) **Stalls** Low

Form RPR
3152 **1** **Finn Class (IRE)**[6] [6972] 2-8-12 **79**.................................. LukeMorris 3 83
(Michael Bell) *chsd ldrs in 3rd: rdn fr 3f out: styd on u.p to chse ldr fnl f: led fnl 50yds: drvn out* **11/4**[3]
161 **2** *3/4* **Claim The Roses (USA)**[41] [5927] 2-9-7 **88**.................................. RyanMoore 4 90+
(Ed Vaughan) *rced in 4th: drvn over 2f out: styd on ins fnl f to take 2nd last stride: nt rch wnr* **7/4**[1]
0032 **3** *nse* **Beau Nash (IRE)**[34] [6132] 2-9-4 **85**.................................. RichardHughes 1 87
(Richard Hannon) *led: rdn 3f clr over 2f out: hdd and no ex fnl 50yds: lost 2nd last stride* **8/1**
3512 **4** *1 3/4* **Mime Dance**[10] [6865] 2-8-4 **76** ow2.................................. OisinMurphy(5) 5 71
(Andrew Balding) *chsd ldr: rdn and one pce 2f out: wknd ins fnl f* **2/1**[2]

1m 27.93s (1.93) **Going Correction** 0.0s/f (Stan) **4** Ran SP% **107.5**
Speed ratings (Par 101): **88,87,87,85**
CSF £7.82 TOTE £3.90; EX 8.50 Trifecta £23.10 Pool: £1022.12 - 33.10 winning units..
Owner Saif Ali **Bred** Rabbah Bloodstock Limited **Trained** Newmarket, Suffolk
■ Stewards' Enquiry : Oisin Murphy three-day ban: weighed-in 2lb heavy (Oct 23-25)

FOCUS
A fair little nursery which was predictably tactical. The winner basically ran to his latest Warwick form.

7123 BETDAQ 1ST UK RACE COMMISSION FREE H'CAP 7f (P)
8:40 (8:40) (Class 4) (0-80,80) 3-Y-O+ **£4,690** (£1,395; £697; £348) **Stalls** Low

Form RPR
0103 **1** **Mr David (USA)**[4] [7031] 6-9-7 **80**.................................(b) DavidProbert 5 91
(Jamie Osborne) *in tch: hdwy on outside wl over 1f out: kpt on to ld ins fnl f: r.o strly* **16/1**
2123 **2** *2* **Secret Beau**[22] [6488] 3-9-3 **78**.................................(t) AdamKirby 6 83
(David Evans) *chsd ldr: led over 1f out: hdd and outpcd ins fnl f* **10/1**
0050 **3** *nse* **Restaurateur (IRE)**[19] [6608] 4-9-5 **78**.................................(b) KierenFallon 14 84
(Andrew Balding) *stdd s: in rr: hdwy on ins over 2f out: too 3rd u.p ins fnl f and pressed for 2nd last strides but no ch w wnr* **9/1**
000 **4** *3/4* **Scottish Glen**[76] [4685] 7-9-3 **76**.................................. JimCrowley 8 80
(Patrick Chamings) *in rr: hdwy 2f out: sn hung lft kpt on ins fnl f* **25/1**
1106 **5** *shd* **Duke Cosimo**[46] [5748] 3-9-5 **80**.................................. RyanMoore 9 83
(Sir Michael Stoute) *chsd ldrs: rdn over 2f out: one pce fr over 1f out* **10/3**[2]
4614 **6** *nk* **Glanely (IRE)**[18] [6642] 3-9-3 **78**.................................. ShaneKelly 11 80
(James Fanshawe) *in rr: drvn over 2f out: hdwy over 1f out: styd on in clsng stages* **11/4**[1]
3602 **7** *1* **Lutine Bell**[5] [6988] 6-9-6 **79**.................................(b) RichardHughes 7 79
(Mike Murphy) *in rr: hdwy fr 2f out: n.m.r and no prog ins fnl f* **4/1**[3]
463 **8** *hd* **Queen Aggie (IRE)**[37] [6045] 3-8-13 **77**.................................. DeclanBates(3) 3 76
(David Evans) *in tch: drvn to chse ldrs ins fnl 2f: no ex fnl f* **25/1**
0353 **9** *nk* **Comrade Bond**[20] [6571] 5-9-1 **74**.................................. TedDurcan 2 73
(Mark H Tompkins) *chsd ldrs: wkng whn n.m.r ins fnl f* **25/1**
0060 **10** *3* **Fanrouge (IRE)**[25] [6381] 4-9-5 **78**.................................(b[1]) AndreaAtzeni 13 69
(Rod Millman) *s.i.s: in rr: rdn 2f out: nvr gng pce to rch ldrs* **25/1**
5006 **11** *1* **Compton**[21] [6526] 4-9-5 **78**.................................(e[1]) LiamJones 4 66
(Robert Cowell) *led: t.k.h: hdd over 1f out: sn wknd* **16/1**
2026 **12** *6* **Kung Hei Fat Choy (USA)**[19] [6609] 4-9-4 **77**..........(b) FrederikTylicki 12 49
(James Given) *in tch on outside: rdn over 2f out: sn wknd* **33/1**
0030 **13** *7* **Bayleyf (IRE)**[21] [6525] 4-9-2 **75**.................................(t) GeorgeBaker 1 28
(John Best) *chsd ldrs: wknd qckly fr 2f out* **33/1**

1m 25.37s (-0.63) **Going Correction** 0.0s/f (Stan)
WFA 3 from 4yo+ 2lb **13** Ran SP% **121.9**
Speed ratings (Par 105): **103,100,100,99,99 99,98,97,97,94 93,86,78**
toteswingers 1&2 £9.30, 2&3 £19.80, 1&3 £31.60 CSF £155.49 CT £1592.80 TOTE £15.70: £4.40, £3.00, £4.50; EX 158.10 Trifecta £1169.70 Part won. Pool: £1559.60 - 0.15 winning units..
Owner Steve Jakes & S J Piper Partnership **Bred** Mr & Mrs R David Randal **Trained** Upper Lambourn, Berks

FOCUS
This was competitive and it was run at a decent pace. The winner's best run since last summer. The winner gave the second a bigger beating than he had in a Worcester claimer last month.

7124 BOOK YOUR CHRISTMAS PARTY ON 01932 753518 H'CAP 7f (P)
9:10 (9:11) (Class 6) (0-55,55) 3-Y-O+ **£1,940** (£577; £288; £144) **Stalls** Low

Form RPR
0205 **1** **Arabian Flight**[20] [6553] 4-9-4 **54**.................................. AndrewMullen 12 67
(Michael Appleby) *mde all: drvn clr over 2f out: unchal* **16/1**
0565 **2** *3 1/2* **Welsh Inlet (IRE)**[7] [6933] 5-9-4 **54**.................................. RichardHughes 5 58
(John Bridger) *in tch: hdwy 2f out: chsd wnr inder press fnl f but no imp* **6/1**[3]
2530 **3** *3/4* **Lambert Pen (USA)**[6] [6986] 3-9-0 **55**.................................. CharlesBishop(3) 1 56
(Mick Channon) *in rr: hdwy over 2f out: styd on u.p to take 3rd in clsng stages but no ch w wnr* **16/1**
0505 **4** *1 1/4* **Bladewood Girl**[40] [5961] 5-9-4 **54**.................................. FrederikTylicki 6 52
(J R Jenkins) *chsd ldrs: rdn over 2f out: wknd ins fnl f* **13/2**
2400 **5** *hd* **Arachnophobia (IRE)**[77] [4623] 7-9-5 **55**.................................(b) GeorgeBaker 8 53
(Martin Bosley) *in rr: drvn and hdwy on outside over 2f out: styd on wl in clsng stages: nt rch ldrs* **12/1**
0233 **6** *1* **Hail Promenader (IRE)**[20] [6554] 7-8-12 **55**............(bt) LouisSteward(7) 9 50
(Anthony Carson) *chsd ldrs: rdn over 2f out: wknd ins fnl f* **4/1**[1]
3604 **7** *1/2* **Archelao (IRE)**[15] [6737] 5-9-4 **54**.................................. KierenFox 4 48
(Richard Rowe) *chsd ldrs: wknd over 1f out* **20/1**
0300 **8** *1 1/2* **Bajan Story**[15] [6737] 4-9-2 **52**.................................(p) FergusSweeney 7 42
(Michael Blanshard) *in rr: drvn and hdwy over 1f out: kpt on in clsng stages* **16/1**
2662 **9** *1 3/4* **Sunny Hollow**[11] [6849] 3-8-12 **55**.................................(v) DanielMuscutt(5) 3 39
(James Toller) *mid-div: rdn 3f out: wknd ins fnl 2f* **33/1**
0621 **10** *1* **Moment In The Sun**[12] [6805] 4-9-5 **55**.................................(v) KierenFallon 10 37
(David Flood) *in tch rdn and hld whn hmpd over 2f out* **5/1**[2]
5600 **11** *2* **Compton Silver**[19] [6610] 3-9-3 **55**.................................(b) LukeMorris 14 31
(Hans Adielsson) *chsd ldrs: wknd and btn whn hmpd over 2f out* **25/1**
-606 **12** *1/2* **Comadoir (IRE)**[124] [3051] 7-9-5 **55**.................................(p) LiamKeniry 2 30
(Jo Crowley) *chsd ldrs: wknd 2f out* **33/1**
0050 **13** *3 1/4* **Zaheeb**[7] [6933] 5-9-5 **55**.................................. WilliamCarson 11 22
(Dave Morris) *chsd ldrs: wknd over 2f out* **20/1**
000 **14** *3 1/4* **First Peninsular**[41] [5932] 3-9-2 **54**.................................. TedDurcan 13 11
(Chris Wall) *stdd s: rdn 4f out and no rspnse* **8/1**

1m 26.09s (0.09) **Going Correction** 0.0s/f (Stan)
WFA 3 from 4yo+ 2lb **14** Ran SP% **121.1**
Speed ratings (Par 101): **99,95,94,92,92 91,90,89,87,85 83,83,79,75**
toteswingers 1&2 £16.50, 2&3 £13.10, 1&3 £28.40 CSF £105.43 CT £1626.93 TOTE £9.70: £1.80, £2.40, £6.10; EX 45.80 Trifecta £641.70 Pool: £1306.46 - 1.52 winning units..
Owner Dallas Racing **Bred** Mr & Mrs A E Pakenham **Trained** Danethorpe, Notts

FOCUS
This weak handicap was wide open. There was a sound early pace on, but still few got seriously involved. The winner is rated back to something like his best, with the runner-up to recent form.
T/Plt: £290.60 to a £1 stake. Pool of £84337.99 - 211.80 winning tickets. T/Qpdt: £86.40 to a £1 stake. Pool of £8808.65 - 75.40 winning tickets. ST

6946 NOTTINGHAM (L-H)
Wednesday, October 9

OFFICIAL GOING: Good (7.9)
Wind: Moderate half against Weather: Overcast

7125 BRITISH STALLION STUDS/32REDPOKER.COM EBF MAIDEN STKS (DIV I) 6f 15y
2:00 (2:01) (Class 5) 2-Y-O **£3,234** (£962; £481; £240) **Stalls** High

Form RPR
45 **1** **Lexington Abbey**[20] [6546] 2-9-5 0.................................. NeilCallan 4 84
(Kevin Ryan) *mde all: rdn over 1f out: clr ins fnl f: kpt on* **6/1**[3]
2 *1 3/4* **Conflicting** 2-9-5 0.................................. PatDobbs 1 79+
(Richard Hannon) *in rr: hdwy wl over 2f out: effrt to chse wnr ent fnl f: sn rdn and kpt on* **5/1**[2]
055 **3** *2 3/4* **Highland Acclaim (IRE)**[18] [6645] 2-9-5 89.................................. DavidProbert 7 70
(Andrew Balding) *wnt lft s: t.k.h and sn cl up on inner: effrt 2f out: sn rdn and wknd ent fnl f* **4/5**[1]
4 *3 1/2* **Baltic Brave (IRE)** 2-9-5 0.................................. JimmyFortune 8 60
(Hughie Morrison) *dwlt and in rr: hdwy 1/2-way chsd ldrs 2f out: sn rdn: green and one pce* **20/1**
0206 **5** *1 1/4* **Miss Acclaimed (IRE)**[27] [6330] 2-9-0 72.................................. TomQueally 6 51
(Brian Ellison) *chsd ldng pair: rdn along over 2f out: wknd over 1f out* **8/1**
6 *1* **Strike A Light** 2-9-0 0.................................. ChrisCatlin 5 48
(Rae Guest) *sltly hmpd s and towards rr: hdwy 1/2-way: rdn along to chse ldrs over 2f out: sn wknd* **25/1**
06 **7** *1 1/4* **Geniusinrhyme**[72] [4820] 2-9-2 0.................................. DeclanCannon(3) 9 49
(Nigel Tinkler) *trckd ldrs on inner: rdn along over 2f out: grad wknd* **100/1**
0 **8** *4* **Urban Sanctuary**[18] [6635] 2-9-5 0.................................. TomMcLaughlin 3 37
(Ed Walker) *a towards rr* **50/1**
2062 **9** *3/4* **Llyrical**[22] [6487] 2-9-5 68.................................. DaneO'Neill 2 35
(Derek Haydn Jones) *chsd ldrs on outer: rdn along 1/2-way: sn wknd* **12/1**

1m 14.83s (0.13) **Going Correction** -0.15s/f (Firm) **9** Ran SP% **116.9**
Speed ratings (Par 95): **93,90,87,82,80 79,77,72,71**
toteswingers 1&2 £2.50, 2&3 £2.10, 1&3 £1.70 CSF £35.10 TOTE £5.10: £1.60, £2.10, £1.10; EX 48.30 Trifecta £78.10 Pool: £1634.35 - 15.68 winning units..
Owner Middleham Park Racing Xix **Bred** D R Tucker **Trained** Hambleton, N Yorks

FOCUS
All races on Outer track and home bend moved out 2m adding 6yds to races on Round course. Not much depth to this opening maiden where the 89-rated Highland Acclaim was turned over at odds-on and not many got into it. However the first two showed decent form.

7126 BRITISH STALLION STUDS/32REDPOKER.COM EBF MAIDEN STKS (DIV II) 6f 15y
2:30 (2:31) (Class 5) 2-Y-O **£3,234** (£962; £481; £240) **Stalls** High

Form RPR
1 **Argot** 2-9-5 0.................................. WilliamCarson 3 74+
(Anthony Carson) *dwlt and in rr: hdwy 2f out: swtchd lft to outer over 1f out: rdn and styd on wl to ld last 50yds* **16/1**
30 **2** *3/4* **Dandana (IRE)**[47] [5727] 2-9-5 0.................................. JamesDoyle 7 72
(Clive Brittain) *led: rdn along 2f out: drvn ent fnl f: hdd and no ex last 50yds* **10/11**[1]

0 **3** *nk* **Sweet Angelica**[19] 6607 2-9-0 0........ GrahamLee 5 66
(James Given) *prom on outer: cl up 2f out: sn rdn and ev ch tl drvn and no ex last 100yds* **33/1**

4 *3/4* **Twin Appeal (IRE)** 2-9-5 0........ GrahamGibbons 2 69+
(David Barron) *trckd ldrs: effrt whn n.m.r and sltly hmpd wl over 1f out: swtchd lft and rdn ent fnl f: styng on whn n.m.r last 100yds* **7/1**

550 **5** *2 1/4* **Offshore Bond**[73] 4808 2-9-5 0........(b[1]) MichaelO'Connell 6 62
(Jedd O'Keeffe) *cl up: rdn to chal 2f out: sn rdn and ev ch tl drvn and wknd ins fnl f* **16/1**

236 **6** *2 1/4* **Margrets Gift**[56] 5380 2-9-0 72........ DavidAllan 8 50
(Tim Easterby) *trckd ldrs: rdn along wl over 1f out: drvn and wknd appr fnl f* **4/1**[2]

065 **7** *nk* **Fisher Lane**[23] 6460 2-9-5 67........ HarryBentley 9 54
(Olly Stevens) *trckd ldrs on inner: pushed along 1/2-way: rdn over 2f out: sn btn* **13/2**[3]

40 **8** *1 1/2* **Kingsway Lad (IRE)**[20] 6570 2-9-5 0........ DaleSwift 4 50
(Derek Shaw) *dwlt and wnt rt s: a in rr* **50/1**

1m 15.46s (0.76) **Going Correction** -0.15s/f (Firm) **8** Ran SP% **114.9**
Speed ratings (Par 95): **88,87,86,85,82 79,79,77**
toteswingers 1&2 £7.40, 2&3 £19.40, 1&3 £12.50 CSF £31.41 TOTE £34.00: £5.10, £1.10, £10.30; EX 83.10 Trifecta £1302.00 Part won. Pool: £1736.11 - 0.01 winning units..
Owner Alderson Carson Francis **Bred** Millsec Limited **Trained** Newmarket, Suffolk

FOCUS
Those that brought form into this race looked no great shakes and this is probably just a modest maiden. The time was over half a second slower than the first division. The runner-up is rated back to his debut form.

7127 32RED CASINO NURSERY H'CAP 5f 13y
3:00 (3:00) (Class 4) (0-80,80) 2-Y-O **£3,881** (£1,155; £577; £288) **Stalls** High

Form RPR

1000 **1** **Hopefilly (IRE)**[12] 6791 2-9-3 **76**........ GrahamLee 5 80
(Ed Walker) *prom: hdwy and cl up 2f out: led over 1f out: rdn ins fnl f: kpt on wl* **7/1**

6006 **2** *nk* **Corncockle**[25] 6376 2-9-5 **78**........ PatDobbs 7 81
(Richard Hannon) *in tch: hdwy 2f out: rdn to chal ent fnl f: ev ch tl drvn and no ex towards fin* **14/1**

2310 **3** *shd* **Sleepy Sioux**[12] 6795 2-9-6 **79**........[1] LiamKeniry 11 83+
(David Elsworth) *towards rr: pushed along and hdwy to trck ldrs on inner 1/2-way: effrt and n.m.r wl over 1f out: sn rdn and hung lft: styd on wl fnl f* **5/1**[3]

0215 **4** *3* **Tinsill**[10] 6872 2-8-8 **70**........(v) DeclanCannon(3) 6 62
(Nigel Tinkler) *in tch: hdwy 2f out: sn rdn: kpt on same pce fnl f* **20/1**

2342 **5** *nse* **Searchlight**[22] 6493 2-9-3 **76**........ NeilCallan 12 68
(Kevin Ryan) *led: rdn along 2f out: sn hdd and grad wknd* **11/4**[1]

2224 **6** *1/2* **Exceeder**[62] 5186 2-9-2 **75**........ MartinHarley 2 65+
(Marco Botti) *in rr and swtchd rt s: hdwy 2f out: chsd ldrs whn hmpd over 1f out: sn rdn and one pce after* **7/2**[2]

4256 **7** *nk* **Dynamo Walt (IRE)**[6] 6967 2-8-0 **59** oh6........(v[1]) RaulDaSilva 8 48
(Derek Shaw) *wnt lft and sltly hamperred s: in rr: hdwy wl over 1f out: styng on whn n.m.r and hmpd over 1f out: one pce after* **50/1**

6200 **8** *3/4* **Dream Sika (IRE)**[13] 6778 2-8-0 **59** oh4........(e[1]) LukeMorris 1 45
(Clive Cox) *prom on outer: hdwy and cl up 1/2-way: rdn wl over 1f out: ev ch tl drvn and wknd appr fnl f* **25/1**

2010 **9** *1 1/2* **De Repente (IRE)**[11] 6825 2-9-2 **75**........ TomQueally 10 59
(Paul Green) *cl up: rdn along over 2f out: wkng whn hmpd over 1f out* **11/2**

0503 **10** *4* **Classical Diva**[23] 6467 2-8-5 **67**........(b) NeilFarley(3) 4 33
(Declan Carroll) *chsd ldrs: rdn along over 2f out: wkng whn hmpd over 1f out* **20/1**

1m 1.03s (-0.47) **Going Correction** -0.15s/f (Firm) **10** Ran SP% **115.4**
Speed ratings (Par 97): **97,96,96,91,91 90,90,89,86,80**
toteswingers 1&2 £16.40, 2&3 £39.50, 1&3 £8.00 CSF £91.32 CT £544.39 TOTE £7.60: £2.00, £4.40, £1.60; EX 111.20 Trifecta £621.30 Pool: £1381.00 - 1.66 winning units..
Owner Laurence A Bellman **Bred** Mount Coote Stud & M & W Bell Racing **Trained** Newmarket, Suffolk

FOCUS
A fair nursery where not a lot covered the first three fillies home and there was a bit of trouble in behind. Routine form, the second helping with the level.

7128 EBF STALLIONS/£32 BONUS AT 32RED.COM MAIDEN STKS 1m 75y
3:30 (3:31) (Class 5) 2-Y-O **£3,234** (£962; £481; £240) **Stalls** Centre

Form RPR

23 **1** **Torrid**[59] 5299 2-9-5 0........ JamesDoyle 8 90+
(Amanda Perrett) *trckd ldng pair: hdwy 3f out: led wl over 1f out: sn clr: styd on strly* **5/2**[1]

2 *8* **Saab Almanal** 2-9-5 0........ ShaneKelly 10 72+
(James Fanshawe) *towards rr: hdwy and in tch 5f out: effrt to chse wnr wl over 1f out: sn rdn and no imp* **9/2**[3]

3 *2 1/2* **Melrose Abbey (IRE)** 2-9-0 0........ JimCrowley 5 61+
(Ralph Beckett) *trckd ldrs: pushed along over 3f out: rdn and sltgly outpcd 2f out: styd on appr fnl f* **3/1**[2]

4 *nk* **Tucson Arizona** 2-9-5 0........ WilliamCarson 7 65+
(Anthony Carson) *towards rr: hdwy on outer 4f out: chsd ldrs over 2f out: sn rdn and kpt on same pce* **50/1**

0 **5** *3 3/4* **Captain Swift (IRE)**[12] 6799 2-9-5 0........ JimmyFortune 1 57
(Brian Meehan) *led: rdn along and jnd 3f out: drvn and hdd wl over 1f out: sn wknd* **20/1**

0 **6** *1 3/4* **Mustadrik (USA)**[13] 6762 2-9-5 0........ DaneO'Neill 4 53
(J W Hills) *chsd ldrs on inner: rdn along over 2f out: sn one pce* **12/1**

7 *1/2* **Sworn Vow (IRE)** 2-9-5 0........ WilliamBuick 13 51+
(John Gosden) *a towards rr* **9/1**

8 *1/2* **Sarpech (IRE)** 2-9-5 0........ HarryBentley 2 50
(Sir Mark Prescott Bt) *dwlt and a towards rr* **7/1**

00 **9** *1 1/4* **Mukhtazel (IRE)**[44] 5826 2-9-5 0........ GrahamLee 6 47
(Mark Johnston) *chsd ldr: cl up 3f out: sn disputing ld and rdn: wknd wl over 1f out* **25/1**

0 **10** *9* **Vaguely Spanish**[18] 6641 2-9-5 0........ PatDobbs 9 27
(Tony Carroll) *a in rr* **100/1**

11 *4 1/2* **Cape Parade (IRE)** 2-9-5 0........ AdamKirby 12 16
(Clive Cox) *dwlt: a in rr* **33/1**

12 *63* **Faisal Lion (IRE)** 2-9-5 0........ LiamKeniry 3
(J S Moore) *towards rr: effrt and sme hdwy 5f out: rdn along 4f out: sn wknd and bhd: eased fr over 2f out* **100/1**

1m 46.2s (-2.80) **Going Correction** -0.30s/f (Firm) 2y crse rec **12** Ran SP% **117.4**
Speed ratings (Par 95): **102,94,91,91,87 85,85,84,83,74 69,6**
toteswingers 1&2 £2.20, 2&3 £5.20, 1&3 £2.60 CSF £12.97 TOTE £3.90: £1.20, £1.70, £1.30; EX 17.70 Trifecta £40.90 Pool: £1188.48 - 21.74 winning units..
Owner K Abdullah **Bred** Juddmonte Farms Ltd **Trained** Pulborough, W Sussex

FOCUS
Some good types have taken this maiden down the years, with the majority of winners able to subsequently record RPRs in excess of 100. However, out of those with previous form only one had shown any real ability and he took this in style. He was arguably value for a few lengths extra, but this isn't easy form to pin down.

7129 32RED NURSERY H'CAP 1m 1f
4:00 (4:01) (Class 3) (0-90,88) 2-Y-O **£9,703** (£2,887; £1,443; £721) **Stalls** Low

Form RPR

31 **1** **Volume**[19] 6597 2-8-13 **80**........ WilliamBuick 5 88+
(Luca Cumani) *trckd ldrs on inner: hdwy 3f out: cl up 2f out: rdn to chal over 1f out: drvn ins fnl f: styd on wl to ld last 100yds* **9/4**[1]

01 **2** *1 1/4* **Gold Trail (IRE)**[34] 6125 2-9-4 **85**........ MickaelBarzalona 2 90+
(Charlie Appleby) *cl up: led after 1f and set gd pce: rdn along over 2f out and sn jnd: drvn and edgd lft ins fnl f: hdd and no ex last 100yds* **5/2**[2]

1205 **3** *3 1/2* **Malachim Mist (IRE)**[18] 6640 2-9-7 **88**........ SeanLevey 3 86
(Richard Hannon) *trckd ldrs: hdwy 3f out: rdn 2f out: chsd ldng pair and kpt on u.p fnl f* **14/1**

4516 **4** *5* **Photography (IRE)**[13] 6763 2-8-8 **75**........ PatrickMathers 6 63
(Hugo Palmer) *sn rdn along and towards rr: hdwy wl over 2f out: sn drvn and kpt on same pce* **9/1**[3]

2134 **5** *3/4* **If (GER)**[22] 6501 2-8-7 **79**........ OisinMurphy(5) 1 66
(Andrew Balding) *in tch: hdwy 3f out: chsd ldrs over 2f out: sn rdn and one pce* **20/1**

341 **6** *shd* **Top Of The Glas (IRE)**[62] 5180 2-8-11 **81**........ MichaelJMMurphy(3) 4 67
(Alan Jarvis) *towards rr: hdwy 3f out: rdn to chse ldrs 2f out: sn one pce* **9/1**[3]

5425 **7** *4* **Crakehall Lad (IRE)**[18] 6628 2-8-3 **70**........ JimmyQuinn 8 48
(Alan Swinbank) *a outpcd in rr* **12/1**

2100 **8** *6* **Fair Ranger**[28] 6303 2-9-4 **85**........ PatDobbs 9 51
(Richard Hannon) *in tch: rdn along over 3f out: sn wknd* **20/1**

1010 **9** *1 1/2* **Bureau (IRE)**[11] 6839 2-8-13 **80**........ AdrianNicholls 7 43
(Mark Johnston) *cl up: rdn along 3f out: drvn 2f out and sn wknd* **25/1**

0242 **10** *3 1/4* **All Talk N No Do (IRE)**[28] 6299 2-8-11 **78**........ GrahamLee 10 35
(Seamus Durack) *led 1f: cl up: rdn along 3f out: grad wknd* **10/1**

1m 53.94s (113.94) **10** Ran SP% **116.2**
toteswingers 1&2 £1.10, 2&3 £7.00, 1&3 £19.50 CSF £7.62 CT £61.34 TOTE £3.40: £1.10, £1.20, £4.10; EX 9.40 Trifecta £85.90 Pool: £1799.50 - 15.70 winning units..
Owner S Stuckey **Bred** Stuart Stuckey **Trained** Newmarket, Suffolk

FOCUS
This looked to be a decent nursery with eight of the ten boasting previous winning form. They were all going beyond 1m for the first time and, off a good pace, they finished strung out. The front pair were both ahead of their marks.

7130 32REDBET.COM H'CAP 1m 75y
4:30 (4:37) (Class 5) (0-73,79) 3-Y-O+ **£2,587** (£770; £384; £192) **Stalls** Centre

Form RPR

-012 **1** **Amulet**[15] 6735 3-8-12 67........ ShaneKelly 7 76
(Eve Johnson Houghton) *mde all: rdn clr wl over 1f out: drvn ins fnl f: styd on strly* **10/1**

2612 **2** *1 1/2* **Extraterrestrial**[23] 6468 9-9-2 73........ GeorgeChaloner(5) 8 79
(Richard Fahey) *chsd ldrs: hdwy on outer to trck ldng pair after 3f: effrt over 2f out and sn rdn: drvn to chse wnr ins fnl f: no imp towards fin* **11/1**

1060 **3** *1* **Silver Alliance**[9] 6898 5-9-2 73........(p) ShelleyBirkett(5) 4 77
(Julia Feilden) *midfield: stdy hdwy 4f out: chsd ldrs over 2f out: rdn wl over 1f out: drvn and kpt on fnl f* **25/1**

1141 **4** *1/2* **Save The Bees**[5] 7000 5-9-10 79 6ex........ JasonHart(3) 14 82
(Declan Carroll) *sn chsng wnr: rdn over 2f out: drvn over 1f out: kpt on same pce* **5/1**[1]

0006 **5** *1/2* **Mr Spiggott (IRE)**[28] 6306 4-9-2 68........(v) TomQueally 9 69
(Gary Moore) *hld up towards rr: hdwy 3f out: rdn over 2f out: styd on fnl f: nrst fin* **10/1**

2514 **6** *1* **Storming (IRE)**[34] 6126 3-9-4 73........(p) CathyGannon 3 72
(Andrew Balding) *trckd ldrs: hdwy 3f out: rdn 2f out: sn drvn and no imp fnl f* **11/2**[2]

2522 **7** *1/2* **Fantasy Gladiator**[28] 6316 7-9-7 73........(p) WilliamBuick 11 71
(John Quinn) *hld up: hdwy on outer wl over 2f out: rdn wl over 1f out: kpt on fnl f: nrst fin* **8/1**[3]

6000 **8** *1* **Great Expectations**[20] 6571 5-9-6 72........ NeilCallan 6 68
(J R Jenkins) *hld up in midfield: hdwy 3f out: rdn to chse ldrs 2f out: sn no imp* **25/1**

3500 **9** *1 1/4* **Rock Supreme (IRE)**[14] 6758 4-8-13 70........(b[1]) ConnorBeasley(5) 15 63
(Michael Dods) *in tch: hdwy on outer to chse ldrs over 3f out: rdn over 2f out: sn drvn and gradiually wknd* **20/1**

1330 **10** *2 1/4* **Aerodynamic (IRE)**[31] 6236 6-9-5 71........(b) GrahamGibbons 5 59
(Michael Easterby) *in tch on inner: hdwy over 3f out: rdn along over 2f out: sn wknd* **8/1**[3]

0502 **11** *1/2* **Poetic Lord**[23] 6459 4-9-2 68........ JamesDoyle 17 54
(Sylvester Kirk) *hld up: a towards rr* **20/1**

6335 **12** *5* **Medici Dancer**[19] 6588 3-9-0 69........(b[1]) DavidAllan 16 44
(Tim Easterby) *n.m.r after s: a towards rr* **20/1**

0262 **13** *shd* **Charitable Act (FR)**[30] 6259 4-9-7 73........ JimmyFortune 1 48
(Gary Moore) *trckd ldng pair on inner whn n.m.r bnd after 2 1/2f: rdn along wl over 2f out: drvn and wknd wl over 1f out* **11/1**

2116 **14** *7* **Tenbridge**[16] 6702 4-8-9 64........(v) RosieJessop(3) 13 23
(Derek Haydn Jones) *dwlt and in rr: sme hdwy on outer and in tch 3f out: sn rdn and wknd* **20/1**

0000 **15** *3 1/4* **Ferdy (IRE)**[40] 5947 4-9-1 67........ RaulDaSilva 10 18
(Paul Green) *a towards rr* **50/1**

2516 **16** *47* **Master Of Song**[6] 6963 6-8-9 64........(p) RyanClark(3) 2
(Roy Bowring) *galloped a circ en route to s: dwlt: a in rr: bhd and eased fnl 2f* **25/1**

1m 45.74s (-3.26) **Going Correction** -0.30s/f (Firm)
WFA 3 from 4yo+ 3lb **16** Ran SP% **121.7**
Speed ratings (Par 103): **104,102,101,101,100 99,99,98,96,94 94,89,88,81,78 31**
toteswingers 1&2 £22.40, 2&3 £37.20, 1&3 £46.70 CSF £99.85 CT £2684.13 TOTE £14.80: £2.80, £2.80, £6.40, £1.80; EX 116.80 Trifecta £2034.40 Part won. Pool: £2712.61 - 0.26 winning units..
Owner Mrs Virginia Neale **Bred** Cherry Park Stud **Trained** Blewbury, Oxon

FOCUS
Just a fair race. It looked competitive on paper, but nothing really could get into from off the pace and the winner made all. The time was half a second quicker than the earlier juvenile maiden over the same distance. A clear personal best from the winner, with the second rated to his more recent claimer form.

7131 32RED.COM H'CAP 1m 2f 50y
5:00 (5:01) (Class 4) (0-85,85) 3-Y-O+ **£5,175** (£1,540; £769; £384) **Stalls** Low

Form				RPR
-003	1		**Border Legend**[33] 6167 4-9-9 **84** ... JimmyFortune 9 (Roger Charlton) *stdd s: hld up in rr: gd hdwy over 2f out: led 1f out: drvn out* **6/1**[2]	93+
3060	2	¾	**Amaze**[65] 5055 5-9-6 **81** ... BarryMcHugh 12 (Brian Ellison) *in rr: gd hdwy on outer over 2f out: chsng ldrs and hung lft ins fnl f: kpt on* **33/1**	89
2350	3	1 ¾	**Villoresi (IRE)**[33] 6172 4-9-10 **85** ... ShaneKelly 15 (James Fanshawe) *in tch: effrt 3f out: sn chsng ldrs: keeping on same pce whn hmpd wl ins fnl f* **11/1**[3]	89
4360	4	nse	**Invincible Hero (IRE)**[31] 6236 6-9-0 **78** ... JasonHart(3) 2 (Declan Carroll) *led: hdd 3f out: hung rt and kpt on same pce fnl f* **20/1**	82
1235	5	1 ¾	**Stellar Express (IRE)**[26] 6353 4-9-5 **85** ... TobyAtkinson(5) 1 (Michael Appleby) *sn chsng ldrs: led 3f out: hdd 1f out: sn wknd* **11/1**[3]	86
4-34	6	1 ¾	**Demonic**[146] 2384 3-9-5 **85** ... JamesDoyle 5 (Lady Cecil) *s.i.s: in rr: effrt over 3f out: hung lft over 2f out: kpt on fnl f: nvr a threat* **9/4**[1]	83
3124	7	3 ½	**Angelic Upstart (IRE)**[16] 6694 5-9-2 **77** ... LiamKeniry 4 (Andrew Balding) *in rr: sme hdwy over 3f out: nvr nr ldrs* **14/1**	68
3404	8	1 ¾	**Harry Buckle**[21] 6537 4-8-11 **79** ...(t) LouisSteward(7) 6 (Philip McBride) *mid-div: hdwy over 4f out: chsng ldrs3f out: wknd fnl f* **16/1**	67
0050	9	2 ½	**Memory Cloth**[18] 6626 6-8-13 **74** ... TomQueally 16 (Brian Ellison) *mid-div: lost pl after 2f: sme hdwy on outer over 3f out: nvr a factor* **16/1**	57
3300	10	1 ½	**Hydrant**[6] 6976 7-9-0 **80** ... ConnorBeasley(5) 3 (Richard Guest) *chsd ldr: wknd over 1f out* **20/1**	60
0000	11	7	**King Of Jazz (IRE)**[29] 6278 5-9-5 **80** ...(v) GrahamLee 8 (Peter Bowen) *trckd ldrs: effrt over 3f out: lost pl over 2f out* **40/1**	47
02-2	12	9	**Personable**[20] 6566 3-9-4 **84** ... MickaelBarzalona 7 (Charlie Appleby) *mid-div: effrt 3f out: sn wknd* **6/1**[2]	34
0042	13	18	**Amoya (GER)**[103] 3785 6-8-13 **74** ... AdamBeschizza 10 (Philip McBride) *chsd ldrs: drvn over 4f out: lost pl over 3f out: wl bhd and eased 2f out: t.o* **25/1**	
1100	14	3 ¼	**Tapis Libre**[15] 6729 5-9-2 **77** ... GrahamGibbons 11 (Michael Easterby) *sn chsng ldrs: drvn 6f out: lost pl over 3f out: wl bhd and eased 2f out: t.o* **50/1**	

2m 10.49s (-3.81) **Going Correction** -0.30s/f (Firm)
WFA 3 from 4yo+ 5lb **14** Ran SP% **115.1**
Speed ratings (Par 105): **103,102,101,100,99 98,95,93,91,90 85,77,63,60**
toteswingers 1&2 £57.90, 2&3 £60.80, 1&3 £8.90 CSF £199.30 CT £2107.33 TOTE £7.50: £2.00, £9.00, £3.70; EX 257.40 Trifecta £1394.30 Part won. Pool: £1859.11 - 0.37 winning units..
Owner The Queen **Bred** The Queen **Trained** Beckhampton, Wilts
■ Stewards' Enquiry : Barry McHugh two-day ban: careless riding (Oct 23-24)

FOCUS
An above-average race of its type for this time of the year and, with just 11lb covering all 14 runners, it was a hotly contested. With prominent racers doing well all afternoon, there was a solid pace here and the winner came all the way from the back to win a shade comfortably. The winner is rated back to his best.

7132 32REDBINGO.COM APPRENTICE H'CAP 1m 2f 50y
5:30 (5:31) (Class 5) (0-70,70) 3-Y-O+ **£2,587** (£770; £384; £192) **Stalls** Low

Form				RPR
3410	1		**Handheld**[110] 3534 6-9-1 **66** ...(p) ShelleyBirkett(5) 2 (Julia Feilden) *mde all: rdn over 2f out: drvn and edgd rt appr fnl f: kpt on wl* **9/1**	76
3650	2	2	**Mcbirney (USA)**[54] 5492 6-8-13 **66** ... StaceyKidd(7) 11 (Paul D'Arcy) *in rr: hdwy on outer 3f out: rdn to chse ldrs and hung lft 2f out: styd on to chse wnr whn swtchd lft ent fnl f: kpt on* **33/1**	72
2210	3	1 ¼	**Whinging Willie (IRE)**[45] 5793 4-9-1 **68** ... HectorCrouch(7) 3 (Gary Moore) *dwlt and in rr: hdwy over 3f out: chsd ldrs 2f out: sn rdn: styd on fnl f: nrst fin* **16/1**	72
2120	4	5	**Unex Michelangelo (IRE)**[14] 6758 4-9-7 **70** ... ShirleyTeasdale(3) 8 (Michael Easterby) *trckd ldrs: hdwy 3f out: rdn whn n.m.r and hmpd 2f out: styd on fnl f: nrst fin* **14/1**	64
0316	5	nk	**Flash Crash**[33] 6158 4-9-1 **66** ...(tp) LouisSteward(5) 16 (Anthony Carson) *midfield: hdwy 4f out: rdn to chse ldrs whn n.m.r and hmpd 2f out: sn drvn and one pce* **16/1**	60
4500	6	1 ¼	**Buster Brown (IRE)**[15] 6730 4-8-11 **60** ... ConnorBeasley(3) 5 (James Given) *in tch: hdwy to chse ldrs whn n.m.r and stmbld 3f out: rdn over 2f out: kpt on one pce* **12/1**	51
1404	7	1 ¼	**Hernando Torres**[15] 6721 5-8-9 **62** ... AnnaHesketh(7) 12 (Michael Easterby) *hld up: hdwy 3f out: rdn over 2f out: sn no imp* **12/1**	51
-366	8	½	**Hot Spice**[13] 6775 5-9-1 **68** ... JoshQuinn(7) 7 (Michael Easterby) *chsd ldrs on inner: rdn along 3f out: grad wknd* **20/1**	56
3614	9	1 ½	**Panettone (IRE)**[13] 6782 4-9-7 **67** ... RossAtkinson 6 (Roger Varian) *cl up: rdn along over 3f out: drvn over 2f out and sn wknd* **7/1**[2]	52
4603	10	hd	**Maybeagrey**[19] 6599 4-8-7 **60** ...(t) GaryMahon(7) 9 (Tim Easterby) *prom: rdn along over 3f out: drvn over 2f out and grad wknd* **10/1**	45
3132	11	shd	**Hector's Chance**[26] 6359 4-9-7 **67** ... ThomasBrown 4 (Heather Main) *dwlt and in rr effrt over 3f out: sn rdn and nvr a factor* **7/2**[1]	52
26-6	12	¾	**Only You Maggie (IRE)**[84] 4403 6-8-9 **62** ...(v) JohnLawson(7) 10 (Gary Harrison) *a towards rr* **28/1**	45
1650	13	3	**West End Lad**[16] 6701 10-9-10 **70** ...(b) RyanClark 15 (Roy Bowring) *dwlt: a bhd* **20/1**	48
0-55	14	5	**Witch Way Went**[22] 6497 3-9-3 **68** ... RobertTart 13 (Brian Ellison) *chsd ldrs: rdn along over 4f out: sn wknd* **10/1**	36
-353	15	10	**Raamz (IRE)**[77] 4638 6-9-0 **63** ... GeorgeChaloner(3) 1 (Kevin Morgan) *trckd ldrs on inner: chsd ldng pair 1/2-way: rdn along over 3f out: sn wknd* **8/1**[3]	12

2m 11.36s (-2.94) **Going Correction** -0.30s/f (Firm)
WFA 3 from 4yo+ 5lb **15** Ran SP% **123.7**
Speed ratings (Par 103): **99,97,96,92,92 91,90,89,88,88 88,87,85,81,73**
toteswingers 1&2 £39.50, 2&3 £59.20, 1&3 £28.50 CSF £291.58 CT £4641.45 TOTE £11.40: £5.40, £8.30, £4.40; EX 491.10 Trifecta £1069.10 Part won. Pool: £1425.57 - 0.04 winning units..
Owner Hoofbeats Ltd Racing Club **Bred** Juddmonte Farms Ltd **Trained** Exning, Suffolk

FOCUS
A modest apprentice handicap to end the card. It was nearly a second slower than the preceding race but there's a chance this form is worth a bit more than this.
T/Jkpt: Not won T/Plt: £20.60 to a £1 stake. Pool of £69394.56 - 2448.75 winning tickets T/Qpdt: £16.10 to a £1 stake. Pool of £4555.38 - 208.82 winning tickets. JR

BORDEAUX LE BOUSCAT (R-H)
Wednesday, October 9
OFFICIAL GOING: Turf: good to soft

7142a PRIX ANDRE BABOIN (GRAND PRIX DES PROVINCES) (GROUP 3) (3YO+) (TURF) 1m 1f 110y
2:35 (12:00) 3-Y-O+ **£32,520** (£13,008; £9,756; £6,504; £3,252)

			RPR
1		**Celtic Rock**[55] 5465 4-8-13 0 ... J-LMartinez 11 (J C Fernandez, Spain) *mde all: grad increased tempo fr 2 1/2f out: rdn and qcknd nrly 2 l clr over 1 1/2f out: r.o willingly u.p fnl f: nvr really chal* **178/10**	106
2	1 ½	**Bonfire**[19] 6592 4-9-2 0 ... MaximeGuyon 1 (Andrew Balding) *trckd ldng trio: scrubbed along whn outpcd fr 2 1/2f out: kpt on u.p fnl 1 1/2f: nvr on terms w wnr* **14/1**	106
3	shd	**Glowing Cloud**[18] 6714 4-8-9 0 ... JulienAuge 7 (C Ferland, France) *hld up towards rr: rdn 2f out: hdwy over 1 1/2f out: styd on wl fnl f: nrest at fin* **57/10**[3]	99
4	shd	**Kapour (IRE)**[45] 5807 3-8-13 0 ... Francois-XavierBertras 9 (F Rohaut, France) *trckd ldrs: 3rd and rdn 1 1/2f out: one pce u.p fnl f* **9/1**	108
5	¾	**Agent Secret (IRE)**[38] 6030 7-8-13 0 ... ChristopheSoumillon 10 (F Rohaut, France) *midfield: rdn and no immediate imp 2f out: styd on u.p fnl f: nt pce to chal* **19/10**[1]	101
6	shd	**Abdel (FR)**[55] 5465 5-8-13 0 ... VJanacek 6 (J-M Osorio, Spain) *trckd ldr: rdn and no imp on wnr fr over 1 1/2f out: kpt on at one pce fnl f* **12/1**	101
7	snk	**Bravodino (USA)**[20] 6580 3-8-13 0 ... StephanePasquier 2 (J E Pease, France) *midfield: outpcd over 2f out: kpt on u.p fnl f: nvr on terms w ldrs* **39/10**[2]	106
8	½	**Tharsis (IRE)**[170] 3-8-6 0 ... AnthonyCrastus 8 (C Laffon-Parias, France) *towards rr: rdn and prog 1 1/2f out: keeping on whn sltly hmpd ins fnl f: nvr plcd to chal* **13/1**	98
9	1 ½	**Zagros (FR)**[10] 6894 4-8-13 0 ... AlexisBadel 4 (J Heloury, France) *towards rr: rdn and plugged on fnl 1 1/2f: nt pce to trble ldrs* **25/1**	97
10	1 ½	**Hectomare (IRE)**[207] 4-8-13 0 ... Jean-BernardEyquem 3 (J-C Rouget, France) *hld up towards rr: rdn and no imp fr 2f out: nvr in contention* **25/1**	94
11	dist	**Espero (FR)**[158] 4-9-2 0 ... ThomasHenderson 5 (J-C Rouget, France) *towards rr thrght: nvr a factor* **28/1**	

2m 6.66s (126.66)
WFA 3 from 4yo+ 4lb **11** Ran SP% **117.8**
WIN (incl. 1 euro stake): 18.80. PLACES: 4.00, 4.90, 2.50. DF: 107.50. SF: 284.50.
Owner Mme Maria De Los Angeles Maestre Torres **Bred** E Puerari, F Mc Nulty & Oceanic Bloodstock **Trained** Spain

5327 LES LANDES
Monday, August 26
OFFICIAL GOING: Good (good to firm in places)

7143a PRIORY DEVIL'S HOLE H'CAP 5f 100y
3:05 (3:09) 3-Y-O+ **£1,460** (£525; £315)

			RPR
1		**Novabridge**[56] 3887 5-10-2 ...(b) GerardTumelty 4 (Neil Mulholland) *chsd ldrs: drvn and 3 l down 1f out: led nr fin* **1/1**[1]	
2	nk	**Fast Freddie**[15] 5328 9-9-3 ...(p) JoshBaudains 1 (Mrs A Corson, Jersey) *broke wl: chsd ldr: ev ch fnl f: tk 2nd on line* **4/1**	
3	hd	**Country Blue (FR)**[15] 5327 4-9-6 ...(p) ThomasGarner 3 (Mrs A Malzard, Jersey) *broke best: led: sn clr: 3 l ahd 1f out: hdd and no ex nr fin* **4/1**	
4	2	**Kersivay**[29] 7-8-5 ... JemmaMarshall 6 (Mrs A Malzard, Jersey) *chsd ldrs tl over 1f out: one pce* **11/2**	
5	4	**Spanish Bounty**[15] 5327 8-10-12 ... MattieBatchelor 2 (Mrs A Malzard, Jersey) *outpcd: unable to chal fr 2f out* **9/4**[2]	
6	1 ½	**First Cat**[15] 5327 6-9-13 ... AntonyProcter 7 (S Arthur, Jersey) *s.s: a bhd* **3/1**[3]	
7	12	**Nordic Light (USA)**[29] 9-8-5 ... MissJenniferPowell 5 (Mrs A Malzard, Jersey) *sn bhd: t.o* **16/1**	

1m 7.0s (-2.00) **7** Ran SP% **167.0**
Owner Dajam Ltd **Bred** Bishopswood Bloodstock & Trickledown Stud **Trained** Limpley Stoke, Wilts

7144a HATSTONE LAWYERS' CLARENDON H'CAP 1m 4f
3:40 (3:42) 3-Y-O+ **£1,905** (£684; £411)

			RPR
1		**River Du Nord (FR)**[15] 5329 6-8-5 ... JemmaMarshall 8 (Susan Gardner) *set sedate pce: mde virtually all: qcknd tempo fr 1/2-way: all out fnl f: jst hld on* **13/2**	
2	shd	**Garden Party**[15] 5329 9-9-8 ...(b) JenniferFerguson 2 (T J Bougourd, Guernsey) *hld up: hdwy fr 2f out: stl 6th 1f out: styd on strly: jst failed* **10/3**[3]	
3	2	**Neuilly**[15] 6-10-10 ... MattieBatchelor 5 (Mrs A Malzard, Jersey) *trckd ldr: rdn to chal 2f out: ev ch 1f out: one pce* **3/1**[2]	
4	3	**Major Maximus**[15] 6-10-12 ... DavidCuthbert 3 (Mrs C Gilbert, Jersey) *hld up: hdwy 3f out: nt pce to rch ldrs* **4/6**[1]	
5	½	**Sissi Guihen (FR)**[15] 5329 7-9-4 ... ThomasGarner 6 (Mrs A Malzard, Jersey) *prom: pressed ldr after 3f tl outpcd fr 4f out* **8/1**	
6	2	**Moose Moran (USA)**[15] 6-10-12 ...(b) AntonyProcter 1 (Mrs J L Le Brocq, Jersey) *hld up: nvr able to chal* **9/2**	

7 4 1/2 **King Kenny**[15] 5329 8-9-4 ....(v) JoshBaudains 4
(Mrs A Corson, Jersey) *trckd ldrs tl over 3f out: sn wknd* **5/1**
8 10 **Bollin Fergus**[15] 5329 9-9-0 ow9.................... MrPCollington 7
(Mrs J L Le Brocq, Jersey) *trckd ldrs: outpcd 4f out: t.o* **18/1**
2m 53.0s (3.00) **8** Ran SP% **172.6**

Owner J Mercier & Miss J Edgar **Bred** Mrs Jane Edgar & John Mercier **Trained** Longdown, Devon

7145a ANIMAL HEALTH TRUST CORONATION MILE (H'CAP) 1m 100y
4:50 (4:50) 3-Y-0+ **£1,460** (£525; £315)

RPR

1 **I'm Harry**[15] 5329 4-10-12 ....(vt[1]) MattieBatchelor 2
(George Baker) **2/1**[1]
2 4 **Pas D'Action**[15] 5327 5-10-5 .... JemmaMarshall 9
(Mrs A Malzard, Jersey) **2/1**[1]
3 1 1/2 **Mr Opulence**[15] 5327 4-10-6 ....(b) MrFTett 6
(T Le Brocq, Jersey) **10/1**
4 2 **Lucifers Shadow (IRE)**[15] 5328 4-9-13 .... DavidCuthbert 7
(Mrs C Gilbert, Jersey) **9/2**[3]
5 shd **Athania (IRE)**[15] 7-9-8 .... MrPCollington 8
(S Arthur, Jersey) **11/2**
6 2 **Beck's Bolero (IRE)**[15] 7-10-11 ....(p) JoshBaudains 5
(Mrs A Corson, Jersey) **9/2**[3]
7 2 **Jackpot**[15] 5328 3-8-13 .... MissJenniferPowell 4
(Mrs A Malzard, Jersey) **9/4**[2]
8 3 **Lady Petrus**[15] 5328 8-8-5 .... TimClark 3
(S Arthur, Jersey) **13/2**
9 dist **Rebel Woman**[15] 5328 7-9-7 .... JenniferFerguson 1
(Mrs A Corson, Jersey) **6/1**
1m 52.0s (112.00)
WFA 3 from 4yo+ 6lb **9** Ran SP% **185.9**

Owner Wickfield Stud And Hartshill Stud **Bred** Wickfield Stud And Hartshill Stud **Trained** Manton, Wilts

6914 AYR (L-H)
Thursday, October 10

OFFICIAL GOING: Soft (8.4)
Wind: Fresh, across Weather: Cloudy, bright

7146 EBF STALLIONS MAIDEN STKS 1m
1:40 (1:40) (Class 4) 2-Y-0 **£4,204** (£1,251; £625; £312) **Stalls** Low

Form RPR

2022 1 **El Beau (IRE)**[19] 6619 2-9-5 76.................... MichaelO'Connell 2 74+
(John Quinn) *prom: rdn to ld over 1f out: edgd lft: kpt on strly to draw clr fnl f* **5/4**[1]
5 2 3 **Thorntoun Care**[21] 6545 2-9-5 0.................... GrahamLee 5 67
(Jim Goldie) *hld up in tch: effrt and pushed along 2f out: edgd lft and styd on fnl f: tk 2nd cl home: no ch w wnr* **25/1**
43 3 nk **Scurr Mist (IRE)**[8] 6939 2-9-5 0.................... TomEaves 1 67
(Keith Dalgleish) *chsd ldrs: rdn and outpcd 2f out: styd on fnl f: no imp* **11/1**
0563 4 nk **The Grumpy Gnome (IRE)**[20] 6605 2-9-5 65............(p) TonyHamilton 4 66
(Richard Fahey) *led at ordinary gallop: rdn and hdd over 2f out: kpt on same pce fnl f* **8/1**[3]
60 5 shd **Rainbow Rock (IRE)**[14] 6762 2-9-5 0.................... AdrianNicholls 6 66
(Mark Johnston) *t.k.h early: pressed ldr: rdn to ld over 2f out: edgd lft and hdd over 1f out: wknd and lost several pls towards fin* **13/8**[2]
00 6 11 **Greenbury (IRE)**[113] 3461 2-9-5 0.................... PJMcDonald 3 42
(Ann Duffield) *hld up in tch: rdn over 2f out: lost tch over 1f out: t.o* **80/1**
1m 48.7s (4.90) **Going Correction** +0.475s/f (Yiel) **6** Ran SP% **107.1**
Speed ratings (Par 97): **94,91,90,90,90 79**
toteswingers 1&2 £2.90, 2&3 £7.10, 1&3 £1.90 CSF £27.86 TOTE £2.30: £1.70, £9.50; EX 32.80 Trifecta £69.60 Pool: £2971.71 - 32.00 winning units..
Owner Highfield Racing (Camacho) **Bred** Bayview Properties Ltd **Trained** Settrington, N Yorks

FOCUS
Bends out 8m, home straight moved out 12m adding 24yds to races of 7f and 1m and 38yds to 1m5f race. An uncompetitive maiden run at an honest pace. After riding in the opener Michael O'Connell said: "It is quite tacky ground". Straightforward form.

7147 RACINGUK PROFITS ALL RETURNED TO RACING NURSERY H'CAP 6f
2:10 (2:10) (Class 5) (0-75,75) 2-Y-0 **£2,911** (£866; £432; £216) **Stalls** Low

Form RPR

2014 1 **Kenny The Captain (IRE)**[20] 6582 2-9-7 75.................... DuranFentiman 2 81
(Tim Easterby) *chsd ldrs: rdn to ld over 1f out: kpt on wl fnl f* **12/5**[1]
0500 2 1 1/2 **Neighbother**[32] 6233 2-9-1 69.................... TonyHamilton 4 70
(Richard Fahey) *in tch: hdwy to chse wnr over 1f out: kpt on fnl f* **6/1**[3]
5130 3 2 3/4 **Straits Of Malacca**[33] 6187 2-9-5 73.................... TomEaves 8 66
(Kevin Ryan) *led tl rdn and hdd over 1f out: kpt on same pce fnl f* **9/1**
2514 4 4 **Pensax Lad (IRE)**[26] 6376 2-9-6 74.................... RobertWinston 6 55
(Ronald Harris) *t.k.h early: cl up: effrt and rdn 2f out: wknd ins fnl f* **6/1**[3]
523 5 3 1/4 **Pennine Warrior**[52] 5577 2-9-5 73.................... TomQueally 7 44
(Scott Dixon) *dwlt: sn pushed along in rr: hung lft over 2f out: sme late hdwy: nvr on terms* **9/2**[2]
000 6 9 **Bashiba (IRE)**[13] 6790 2-8-0 54 oh4....................(v[1]) AndrewMullen 3
(Nigel Tinkler) *t.k.h early: in tch: drvn along 1/2-way: wknd 2f out* **22/1**
104 7 4 **Arabda**[93] 4134 2-9-1 69.................... GrahamLee 11 1
(Mark Johnston) *hld up towards rr: struggling over 2f out: sn btn* **7/1**
055 8 6 **False Witness (IRE)**[19] 6627 2-9-3 71.................... AdrianNicholls 5
(David Nicholls) *in tch: drvn along over 2f out: sn btn* **14/1**
1m 15.45s (3.05) **Going Correction** +0.475s/f (Yiel) **8** Ran SP% **109.7**
Speed ratings (Par 95): **98,96,92,87,82 70,65,57**
toteswingers 1&2 £3.00, 2&3 £8.10, 1&3 £5.80 CSF £15.47 CT £99.04 TOTE £3.40: £1.10, £1.80, £3.30; EX 17.40 Trifecta £148.50 Pool: £3187.40 - 16.09 winning units..
Owner Reality Partnerships V **Bred** Joe Foley & John Grimes **Trained** Great Habton, N Yorks

FOCUS
A fair pace for this nursery with the field strung out at the line. It paid to race handy. The form is taken at face value around the first two.

7148 GBI RACING SERVICE LIVE IN ISRAEL H'CAP (DIV I) 6f
2:40 (2:41) (Class 6) (0-65,65) 3-Y-0+ **£2,385** (£704; £352) **Stalls** Low

Form RPR

0401 1 **Rise To Glory (IRE)**[6] 6994 5-9-0 57 6ex.................... DuranFentiman 8 67
(Shaun Harris) *mde all stands' side: rdn over 1f out: hld on wl fnl f: 1st of 8 in gp* **14/1**
0600 2 1 1/2 **Royal Duchess**[37] 6088 3-8-1 50 oh4.................... IanBurns[(5)] 14 55
(Lucy Normile) *hld up stands' side: rdn and hdwy over 2f out: chsd wnr appr fnl f: kpt on: no imp: 2nd of 8 in gp* **50/1**
0002 3 3/4 **Red Cobra (IRE)**[19] 6633 3-9-0 58.................... DavidAllan 16 61
(Tim Easterby) *chsd ldrs: drvn over 2f out: rallied over 1f out: kpt on ins fnl f: 3rd of 8 in gp* **4/1**[1]
0000 4 3/4 **Pitt Rivers**[10] 6903 4-8-10 58.................... ConnorBeasley[(5)] 15 58
(Linda Perratt) *hld up stands' side: rdn and hdwy over 1f out: kpt on fnl f: nrst fin: 4th of 8 in gp* **40/1**
2163 5 1/2 **Angels Calling**[17] 6698 3-8-11 60.................... JoeyHaynes[(5)] 13 59
(K R Burke) *prom stands' side: effrt and rdn over 2f out: no ex ins fnl f: 5th of 8 in gp* **8/1**
3/5- 6 nk **Cookie Crumbles (IRE)**[50] 5662 6-8-11 54............(t) RobertWinston 10 52
(Adrian McGuinness, Ire) *hld up stands' side: pushed along over 2f out: hdwy over 1f out: kpt on: 6th of 8 in gp* **12/1**
2421 7 nk **Compton Heights**[9] 6916 4-9-8 65 6ex.................... GrahamLee 1 62
(Jim Goldie) *cl up far side: led that gp over 2f out: kpt on fnl f: no ch w stands' side gp: 1st of 4 in gp* **9/2**[2]
032- 8 2 3/4 **Drinmoy Lad (IRE)**[25] 6439 4-9-4 64.................... LMcNiff[(3)] 12 52
(Michael McElhone, Ire) *chsd wnr stands' side tl rdn and wknd over 1f out: 7th of 8 in gp* **15/2**
0563 9 hd **Monel**[9] 6918 5-8-10 53.................... TomEaves 3 40
(Jim Goldie) *chsd far side ldrs: effrt and wnt 2nd that gp over 1f out: kpt on fnl f: no imp: 2nd of 4 in gp* **6/1**[3]
0634 10 3/4 **Night Trade (IRE)**[7] 6982 6-9-6 63....................(p) RaulDaSilva 9 48
(Ronald Harris) *chsd stands' side ldrs tl rdn and wknd appr fnl f: last of 8 in gp* **18/1**
-004 11 1 1/2 **Tadalavil**[11] 6879 8-8-12 55.................... PJMcDonald 7 35
(Linda Perratt) *led far side to over 1f out: wknd ins fnl f: 3rd of 4 in gp* **16/1**
031/ 12 21 **Newbury Street**[801] 4600 6-9-3 60.................... RussKennemore 2
(Patrick Holmes) *chsd far side ldrs tl wknd 2f out: sn lost tch: t.o: last of 4 in gp* **40/1**
4420 U **Layla's Hero (IRE)**[69] 4970 6-9-2 59.................... AdrianNicholls 4
(David Nicholls) *rrd and uns rdr as stall opened* **17/2**
1m 14.83s (2.43) **Going Correction** +0.475s/f (Yiel)
WFA 3 from 4yo+ 1lb **13** Ran SP% **118.2**
Speed ratings (Par 101): **102,100,99,98,97 96,96,92,92,91 89,61,**
toteswingers 1&2 £70.40, 2&3 £47.80, 1&3 £14.10 CSF £581.11 CT £3394.71 TOTE £20.20: £7.90, £13.20, £2.10; EX 946.20 Trifecta £2115.50 Part won. Pool: £2820.77 - 0.26 winning units..
Owner N Blencowe,J Sunderland,M Lenton,CHarris **Bred** Bryan Ryan **Trained** Carburton, Notts

FOCUS
This moderate handicap was run at a fair pace, with the field splitting into two groups. The first six home race stands' side and the time was a bit quicker than division II. The winner rates back to his old best.

7149 GBI RACING SERVICE LIVE IN ISRAEL H'CAP (DIV II) 6f
3:10 (3:12) (Class 6) (0-65,64) 3-Y-0+ **£2,385** (£704; £352) **Stalls** Low

Form RPR

3340 1 **Alexandrakollontai (IRE)**[9] 6916 3-9-3 64............(b) JulieBurke[(3)] 14 76+
(Alistair Whillans) *trckd ldrs stands' side: n.m.r fr 1/2-way tl gap appeared and qcknd to ld ins fnl f: pushed out: 1st of 10 in gp* **10/1**
1460 2 1 1/4 **Little Jimmy Odsox (IRE)**[15] 6760 5-9-7 64............(b) DuranFentiman 15 71
(Tim Easterby) *led stands' rail: rdn over 2f out: hdd ins fnl f: kpt on: nt pce of wnr: 2nd of 10 in gp* **8/1**
0-35 3 1 **My Boy Bill**[27] 6362 3-9-6 64.................... GrahamGibbons 13 68
(Michael Easterby) *cl up stands' side: ev ch and rdn over 1f out to ins fnl f: hld nr fin: 3rd of 10 in gp* **5/1**[2]
0255 4 1 1/4 **Rock Canyon (IRE)**[10] 6903 4-8-2 50............(p) ConnorBeasley[(5)] 7 50
(Linda Perratt) *hld up stands' side: pushed along over 2f out: hdwy over 1f out: kpt on fnl f: 4th of 10 in gp* **16/1**
561 5 1 **Mysterious Wonder**[17] 6687 3-8-7 58............(b) EvaMoscrop[(7)] 11 55
(Philip Kirby) *prom stands' side: rdn over 1f out: kpt on fnl f: 5th of 10 in gp* **8/1**
6036 6 hd **Saxonette**[9] 6916 5-8-10 53.................... PJMcDonald 8 49
(Linda Perratt) *prom stands' side: rdn over 2f out: one pce appr fnl f: 6th of 10 in gp* **12/1**
2302 7 1 **Black Douglas**[8] 6945 4-8-12 55.................... GrahamLee 5 48
(Jim Goldie) *hld up stands' side: rdn and hdwy over 1f out: edgd lft: no imp: 7th of 10 in gp* **9/2**[1]
043 8 3/4 **Music Festival (USA)**[15] 6760 6-8-2 52.................... JackGarritty[(7)] 9 42
(Jim Goldie) *s.i.s: hld up stands' side: rdn and hdwy over 1f out: nvr able to chal: 8th of 10 in gp* **11/2**[3]
600 9 2 **Military Call**[14] 6083 6-8-8 51 oh5 ow1....................(p) DavidAllan 3 35
(R Mike Smith) *led centre: rdn over 2f out: outpcd fr over 1f out: sn btn: 1st of 3 in gp* **80/1**
0545 10 1/2 **Distant Sun (USA)**[18] 6669 9-8-7 50 oh2............(p) BarryMcHugh 4 32
(Linda Perratt) *t.k.h: hld up stands' side: rdn over 2f out: nvr on terms: 9th of 10 in gp* **40/1**
0355 11 nk **Done Dreaming (IRE)**[15] 6760 3-8-4 55.................... SamanthaBell[(7)] 6 36
(Richard Fahey) *chsd stands' side ldrs tl edgd rt and wknd over 1f out: last of 10 in gp* **10/1**
50U6 12 1 3/4 **Stoneacre Oskar**[9] 6918 4-8-13 59.................... SladeO'Hara[(3)] 1 35
(Peter Grayson) *sn outpcd centre: no ch fr 1/2-way: 2nd of 3 in gp* **50/1**
26 13 nse **Hills Of Dakota**[10] 6903 5-9-3 60....................(b) TomEaves 2 36
(Keith Dalgleish) *chsd centre ldr: rdn over 2f out: wknd over 1f out: last of 3 in gp* **11/1**
1m 15.06s (2.66) **Going Correction** +0.475s/f (Yiel)
WFA 3 from 4yo+ 1lb **13** Ran SP% **118.2**
Speed ratings (Par 101): **101,99,98,96,95 94,93,92,89,89 88,86,86**
toteswingers 1&2 £15.50, 2&3 £10.40, 1&3 £11.00 CSF £86.29 CT £352.98 TOTE £13.20: £3.70, £3.90, £2.90; EX 97.50 Trifecta £196.20 Pool: £1584.32 - 6.05 winning units..
Owner Chris Spark & William Orr **Bred** Sean O'Sullivan **Trained** Newmill-On-Slitrig, Borders
■ Beau Satchel was withdrawn on vet's advice (7-2, deduct 20p in the £ under R4).

FOCUS
The pace was sound for this modest handicap but the time was a bit slower than division I. Again those racing stands' side were favoured. The form makes sense.

7150 J H COMMERCIALS H'CAP 5f
3:40 (3:43) (Class 5) (0-70,67) 3-Y-O £2,911 (£866; £432; £216) Stalls Low

Form RPR
4430 1 Dark Opal (IRE)[16] 6728 3-9-2 67 JoeyHaynes(5) 4 74
(John Weymes) *cl up on outside: effrt over 1f out: led ins fnl f: rdn out* 5/1[3]
5362 2 *nk* Starlight Angel (IRE)[50] 5644 3-9-5 65 RobertWinston 5 71
(Ronald Harris) *sn crossed to stands' rail: t.k.h: led: rdn 2f out: hdd ins fnl f: kpt on fin* 6/1
5560 3 *1* Khefyn (IRE)[10] 6900 3-9-2 62 RaulDaSilva 7 64
(Ronald Harris) *chsd ldrs: effrt and ev ch over 1f out: one pce ins fnl f* 5/1[3]
0500 4 *1* Classy Anne[8] 6944 3-8-2 48 oh3 DuranFentiman 3 47
(Jim Goldie) *bhd: rdn over 2f out: hdwy over 1f out: kpt on: nrst fin* 28/1
0601 5 *nk* Opt Out[24] 6471 3-9-6 66 PJMcDonald 1 64
(Alistair Whillans) *hld up bhd ldng gp: effrt and rdn over 1f out: edgd lft: kpt on fnl f* 4/1[2]
0000 6 *¾* Fife Jo[9] 6918 3-8-4 50 oh3 ow2 (v) BarryMcHugh 8 45
(Jim Goldie) *hld up: rdn over 2f out: r.o fnl f: no imp* 20/1
0253 7 *nse* Our Diane (IRE)[21] 6547 3-9-1 61 TonyHamilton 6 56
(Richard Fahey) *cl up: rdn and outpcd over 1f out: n.d after* 5/2[1]
0050 8 *nk* Red Star Lady (IRE)[44] 5864 3-7-11 48 oh3 ShirleyTeasdale(5) 2 42
(Shaun Harris) *in tch on outside: rdn over 2f out: wknd over 1f out* 80/1
1000 9 *3 ½* Lucy Bee[10] 6907 3-8-9 60 NoelGarbutt(5) 9 41
(R Mike Smith) *chsd ldrs: sn rdn along: wknd wl over 1f out* 14/1

1m 1.75s (2.35) **Going Correction** +0.475s/f (Yiel) 9 Ran SP% **112.3**
Speed ratings (Par 101): **100,99,97,96,95 94,94,94,88**
toteswingers 1&2 £4.70, 2&3 £5.50, 1&3 £4.60 CSF £33.16 CT £155.37 TOTE £5.60: £1.70, £1.60, £1.80; EX 27.30 Trifecta £267.20 Pool: £3138.91 - 8.80 winning units..
Owner Scothern,Leadbetter,Heaton & Partners **Bred** M S And C S Griffiths **Trained** Middleham Moor, N Yorks
■ Stewards' Enquiry : Noel Garbutt one-day ban: did not keep straight from stalls

FOCUS
A moderate sprint handicap run at a steady pace, and again the prominent runners dominated. Straightforward form, rated around the second.

7151 100% RACINGUK PROFITS RETURNED TO RACING H'CAP 1m 5f 13y
4:10 (4:10) (Class 6) (0-65,64) 3-Y-O+ £2,385 (£704; £352) Stalls Low

Form RPR
0065 1 Forced Family Fun[115] 3394 3-9-4 64 TomQueally 4 76+
(Michael Bell) *t.k.h: hld up: smooth hdwy on outside to ld over 2f out: sn clr: pushed along and styd on wl fnl f* 7/2[3]
0011 2 *5* Blue Top[30] 6290 4-9-6 61 (p) JasonHart(3) 3 65
(Tim Walford) *hld up: hdwy to chse wnr over 2f out: sn rdn: kpt on fnl f: no imp* 5/2[1]
0452 3 *4 ½* Latin Rebel (IRE)[21] 6552 6-9-7 59 GrahamLee 2 56
(Jim Goldie) *hld up in tch: effrt and chsd ldr over 3f out to over 2f out: sn one pce* 3/1[2]
006 4 *4* Funky Munky[10] 6907 8-8-12 50 oh2 (p) BarryMcHugh 7 41
(Alistair Whillans) *chsd ldrs: drvn over 3f out: outpcd fnl 2f* 14/1
2/ 5 *1 ¾* Hide The Evidence (IRE)[15] 1440 12-9-5 60 (t) LMcNiff(3) 12 49
(Michael McElhone, Ire) *s.i.s: hld up: hdwy on outside over 3f out: rdn and no imp over 2f out* 16/1
5640 6 *2 ¾* Light The City (IRE)[10] 6909 6-8-7 50 oh5 (b) ConnorBeasley(5) 11 35
(Ruth Carr) *cl up: led 5f out to over 2f out: sn rdn and wknd* 20/1
0310 7 *9* Lady Gargoyle[14] 6177 5-8-5 50 oh3 SophieRobertson(7) 8 21
(Jim Goldie) *led to 5f out: sn rdn: wknd over 2f out* 40/1
560 8 *19* Swift Encounter (IRE)[68] 4995 4-9-0 52 PJMcDonald 9
(Ann Duffield) *prom: rdn over 4f out: wknd 3f out* 7/1
9 *¾* Harbin (IRE)[143] 2522 3-8-7 53 (b[1]) PatrickMathers 5
(Adrian McGuinness, Ire) *cl up tl rdn and wknd over 2f out* 16/1

3m 3.39s (9.39) **Going Correction** +0.475s/f (Yiel)
WFA 3 from 4yo+ 8lb 9 Ran SP% **113.9**
Speed ratings (Par 101): **90,86,84,81,80 78,73,61,61**
toteswingers 1&2 £2.80, 2&3 £1.80, 1&3 £3.60 CSF £12.47 CT £28.10 TOTE £7.70: £1.90, £1.10, £1.60; EX 14.40 Trifecta £29.20 Pool: £2256.69 - 57.80 winning units..
Owner M B Hawtin **Bred** M B Hawtin **Trained** Newmarket, Suffolk

FOCUS
A modest staying handicap run at a steady pace. The first two home came from the rear.

7152 BETFAIR SCOTTISH RACING MILE SERIES FINAL H'CAP 1m
4:40 (4:44) (Class 3) 3-Y-O+ £9,703 (£2,887; £1,443; £721) Stalls Low

Form RPR
6056 1 Ingleby Symphony (IRE)[5] 7038 3-8-0 69 oh2 PatrickMathers 8 76
(Richard Fahey) *hld up towards rr: rdn over 2f out: hdwy over 1f out: led wl ins fnl f: r.o* 16/1
1314 2 *½* True Pleasure (IRE)[43] 5881 6-7-9 66 oh5 ShirleyTeasdale(5) 7 72
(James Bethell) *chsd ldrs: rdn over 2f out: ch ins fnl f: kpt on to take 2nd nr fin* 18/1
00-6 3 *shd* Toufan Express[6] 7002 11-7-12 69 (b) JoeyHaynes(5) 13 75
(Adrian McGuinness, Ire) *t.k.h: hld up on outside: rdn and hdwy 2f out: kpt on wl fnl f* 14/1
050 4 *hd* Dubious Escapade (IRE)[68] 4994 4-8-1 67 ow1 (p) DuranFentiman 1 72
(Ann Duffield) *t.k.h: cl up: led wl over 1f out: sn rdn: hdd and no ex wl ins fnl f* 40/1
0322 5 *1 ¼* High Resolution[9] 6921 6-7-7 66 oh5 SamanthaBell(7) 12 68
(Linda Perratt) *hld up: stdy hdwy over 2f out: rdn whn n.m.r over 1f out: kpt on ins fnl f* 10/1
3364 6 *1* Ted's Brother (IRE)[8] 6943 5-7-13 70 (e) ConnorBeasley(5) 3 70
(Richard Guest) *hld up in midfield: hdwy and cl up over 2f out: kpt on same pce ins fnl f* 8/1[3]
1322 7 *nk* Tectonic (IRE)[10] 6906 4-8-7 73 ow2 (p) TomEaves 2 72
(Keith Dalgleish) *in tch: effrt 2f out: one pce fnl f* 7/1[2]
6111 8 *nk* Ingleby Angel (IRE)[7] 7024 4-9-11 96 6ex DavidBergin(5) 14 95
(David O'Meara) *dwlt: bhd on outside: rdn and hdwy over 1f out: kpt on: nvr able to chal* 7/2[1]
3223 9 *¾* Ralphy Boy (IRE)[10] 6906 4-8-0 69 JulieBurke(3) 9 66
(Alistair Whillans) *led tl rdn and hdd wl over 1f out: outpcd fnl f* 10/1
1201 10 *¾* Silver Rime (FR)[19] 6625 8-9-2 87 OisinMurphy(5) 5 82
(Linda Perratt) *s.i.s: hld up on ins: rdn and outpcd over 2f out: n.d after* 10/1
2120 11 *1* Violent Velocity (IRE)[20] 6600 10-8-0 66 oh2 RaulDaSilva 10 59
(John Quinn) *midfield: effrt on outside over 2f out: no ex over 1f out* 33/1
0464 12 *1* Another For Joe[21] 6548 5-8-4 70 BarryMcHugh 4 61
(Jim Goldie) *in tch: stdy hdwy over 2f out: edgd lft and wknd wl over 1f out* 8/1[3]
1000 13 *14* Cono Zur (FR)[21] 6562 6-7-10 67 NoelGarbutt(5) 11 25
(Ruth Carr) *chsd ldr tl rdn and wknd over 2f out: t.o* 40/1

1m 46.5s (2.70) **Going Correction** +0.475s/f (Yiel)
WFA 3 from 4yo+ 3lb 13 Ran SP% **109.8**
Speed ratings (Par 107): **105,104,104,104,102 101,101,101,100,99 98,97,83**
toteswingers 1&2 £46.20, 2&3 £39.00, 1&3 £32.40 CSF £239.08 CT £3601.19 TOTE £17.20: £5.30, £5.30, £3.80; EX 359.70 Trifecta £2436.70 Part won. Pool: £3249.04 - 0.11 winning units..
Owner Percy Green Racing 4 & Partner **Bred** Sunderland Holdings Inc **Trained** Musley Bank, N Yorks
■ Star Links was withdrawn (14-1, ref to ent stalls). Deduct 5p in the £ under R4.
■ Stewards' Enquiry : Patrick Mathers two-day ban: careless riding (24-25 Oct)

FOCUS
A decent contest run at a fair pace.

7153 RACING UK H'CAP 7f 50y
5:10 (5:12) (Class 6) (0-60,60) 3-Y-O+ £2,264 (£673; £336; £168) Stalls High

Form RPR
4300 1 Baraboy (IRE)[20] 6600 3-8-6 50 (p) JulieBurke(3) 8 64
(Barry Murtagh) *hld up: rdn and hdwy to ld over 1f out: kpt on strly fnl f* 16/1
0000 2 *3 ¼* Viking Warrior (IRE)[9] 6919 6-8-11 55 (b[1]) ConnorBeasley(5) 5 62
(Michael Dods) *hld up on ins: rdn over 2f out: chsd (clr) wnr over 1f out: kpt on: no imp* 16/1
2212 3 *1 ¾* Lil Sophella (IRE)[9] 6918 4-9-3 56 RussKennemore 4 58
(Patrick Holmes) *hld up: hdwy and swtchd rt 2f out: kpt on fnl f: nvr able to chal* 4/1[1]
0051 4 *1 ¼* Rasselas (IRE)[9] 6921 6-9-0 60 AnnaHesketh(7) 3 59
(David Nicholls) *hld up in midfield: effrt on outside 2f out: kpt on fnl f: no imp* 9/2[2]
5562 5 *1* Monsieur Pontaven[28] 6324 6-8-8 50 (b) JasonHart(3) 1 46
(Robin Bastiman) *hld up: rdn and swtchd rt 2f out: styd on fnl f: nt pce to rch ldrs* 8/1
0000 6 *1* Goninodaethat[9] 6919 5-8-10 56 JordanNason(7) 9 50
(Jim Goldie) *t.k.h in midfield: hdwy to ld over 2f out: edgd lft and hdd over 1f out: sn outpcd* 16/1
0502 7 *nk* Imperial Bond[19] 6630 4-8-11 55 (t) KevinStott(5) 12 48
(Jason Ward) *prom: effrt and ev ch over 2f out: no ex over 1f out* 28/1
3401 8 *1 ¼* Deliberation (IRE)[9] 6919 5-8-13 57 6ex DarylByrne(5) 10 47
(John Quinn) *t.k.h: cl up: rdn and ev ch over 2f out: wknd over 1f out* 7/1[3]
0004 9 *nk* Hellbender (IRE)[9] 6919 7-8-6 50 ShirleyTeasdale(5) 14 39
(Shaun Harris) *led tl rdn and hdd over 1f out: sn btn* 14/1
044 10 *2 ¼* Last Supper[43] 5899 4-9-0 58 (p) JoeyHaynes(5) 7 41
(James Bethell) *in tch: rdn and outpcd over 2f out: n.d after* 20/1
4305 11 *1 ½* Clumber Place[19] 6633 7-9-2 55 GrahamLee 6 34
(James Given) *t.k.h: cl up: rdn over 2f out: wknd over 1f out* 15/2
0-00 12 *3 ¾* Galilee Chapel (IRE)[127] 2972 4-8-4 50 RowanScott(7) 11 19
(Alistair Whillans) *hld up: rdn over 2f out: nvr on terms* 28/1
2204 13 *1 ¼* Eilean Mor[9] 6918 5-8-3 47 NoelGarbutt(5) 13 13
(R Mike Smith) *midfield on outside: rdn over 2f out: edgd lft and sn wknd* 12/1

1m 36.48s (3.08) **Going Correction** +0.475s/f (Yiel)
WFA 3 from 4yo+ 2lb 13 Ran SP% **117.2**
Speed ratings (Par 101): **101,97,95,93,92 91,91,89,89,86 85,80,79**
toteswingers 1&2 £42.30, 2&3 £14.90, 1&3 £18.30 CSF £239.38 CT £1222.44 TOTE £26.30: £6.10, £4.20, £1.90; EX 341.50 Trifecta £1269.00 Pool: £3350.41 - 1.98 winning units..
Owner Anthony White **Bred** Holborn Trust Co **Trained** Low Braithwaite, Cumbria
■ Stewards' Enquiry : Shirley Teasdale two-day ban: careless riding (24-25 Oct)

FOCUS
Plenty of pace on for this moderate handicap.
T/Jkpt: Not won. T/Plt: £170.60 to a £1 stake. Pool of £72053.38 - 308.29 winning tickets. T/Qpdt: £49.60 to a £1 stake. Pool of £5706.15 - 85.0 winning tickets. RY

7117 KEMPTON (A.W) (R-H)
Thursday, October 10

OFFICIAL GOING: Standard
Wind: Moderate ahead Weather: Overcast

7154 DOWNLOAD THE BETVICTOR APP MAIDEN STKS 7f (P)
5:40 (5:44) (Class 5) 3-4-Y-O £2,587 (£770; £384; £192) Stalls Low

Form RPR
302 1 Desert Wings (IRE)[45] 5845 3-9-5 80 MickaelBarzalona 10 93
(Charlie Appleby) *trckd ldr: led over 2f out: pushed clr over 1f out: easily* 5/4[1]
0 2 *8* Tasrih (USA)[30] 6289 4-9-7 0 MartinHarley 4 72
(Alan McCabe) *led: hdd over 2f out: easily outpcd over 1f out but kpt on wl for 2nd* 50/1
6-4 3 *1 ¼* Takaathur (USA)[27] 6366 3-9-5 0 DaneO'Neill 2 68
(Saeed bin Suroor) *chsd ldes: rdn and styd on same pce fnl 2f* 7/2[3]
4 4 *nk* Zuhd (IRE)[21] 6555 3-9-5 0 PaulHanagan 6 67
(William Haggas) *chsd ldrs: rdn and styd on same pce fnl 2f* 7/4[2]
0656 5 *17* Kaahen (USA)[7] 6965 3-9-2 34 (b) CharlesBishop(3) 3 21
(Pat Eddery) *a in rr* 66/1
6 *¾* Allegra Clairmont 4-9-2 0 CathyGannon 8 15
(John Best) *rdn 4f out: a in rr* 25/1
00-6 7 *3 ¼* Gold Weight[274] 123 3-9-5 47 AdamKirby 9 10
(Michael Madgwick) *a wl bhd* 66/1
8 *½* Puteri Kash 3-9-0 0 SamHitchcott 5
(Gary Moore) *a wl bhd* 25/1
0 9 *5* Summer In February[57] 5386 3-8-11 0 WilliamTwiston-Davies(3) 1
(Nikki Evans) *chsd ldrs to 1/2-way: sn wknd* 50/1
10 *37* Breezealong Riley 4-9-2 0[1] RichardThomas 7
(Zoe Davison) *slowly away: a wl bhd* 66/1

1m 23.85s (-2.15) **Going Correction** -0.05s/f (Stan)
WFA 3 from 4yo 2lb 10 Ran SP% **119.1**
Speed ratings (Par 103): **110,100,99,99,79 78,75,74,68,26**
toteswingers 1&2 £13.00, 2&3 £20.40, 1&3 £1.20 CSF £79.82 TOTE £2.10: £1.10, £10.30, £1.30; EX 58.60 Trifecta £175.90 Pool: £3713.17 - 15.83 winning units..
Owner Godolphin **Bred** Corduff Stud Ltd & T J Rooney **Trained** Newmarket, Suffolk

FOCUS
There was not much strength in depth in this maiden but the favourite was an easy winner and the next three home finished a long way clear of the rest.

7155 BETVICTOR CASINO ON YOUR MOBILE/E.B.F. STALLIONS MAIDEN STKS 6f (P)
6:10 (6:15) (Class 5) 2-Y-O **£2,911** (£866; £432; £216) **Stalls** Low

Form RPR
30 1 **Magnus Maximus**[8] 6953 2-9-5 0 RichardHughes 12 84+
(Richard Hannon) *chsd ldrs: drvn over 2f out: led 1f out: hrd pressed fnl 110yds: a jst doing enough* **10/1**
20 2 *hd* **Much Promise**[71] 4877 2-9-0 0 WilliamBuick 7 78+
(John Gosden) *chsd ldrs: drvn 2f out: led briefly appr fnl f: sn hdd: rallied fnl 110yds but a jst hld* **7/4**[1]
3 *2 ¾* **Secret Hint** 2-9-0 0 DavidProbert 5 69+
(Andrew Balding) *chsd ldrs: rdn and one pce appr fnl 2f: kpt on wl fnl f to take 3rd clsng stages: no imp on ldng duo* **20/1**
4 4 *1 ¾* **Pushkin Museum (IRE)**[15] 6747 2-9-5 0 JamesDoyle 6 69
(Gary Moore) *led: rdn over 2f out: hdd appr fnl f: sn btn* **20/1**
4 5 *¾* **Isabella Bird**[83] 4484 2-9-0 0 MartinHarley 9 61
(Mick Channon) *chsd ldr: rdn over 2f out: wknd fnl f* **2/1**[2]
6 6 *3 ¼* **Mr Win (IRE)**[21] 6569 2-9-5 0 GeorgeBaker 4 56
(Chris Wall) *in rr: hdwy 2f out: kpt on same pce fnl f* **16/1**
5 7 *nse* **Reaffirmed (IRE)**[74] 4795 2-9-5 0 JimmyFortune 8 59
(Ed Vaughan) *reluctant to load: in rr: hdwy 3f out: chsd ldrs ins fnl 2f: wknd fnl f* **5/1**[3]
00 8 *½* **Kopenhagen (IRE)**[34] 6169 2-9-2 0 MarkCoumbe(3) 11 54
(Ed de Giles) *towards rr: sme late hdwy* **66/1**
0 9 *1* **Strategic Force (IRE)**[20] 6589 2-9-5 0 AdamKirby 10 51
(Clive Cox) *a towards rr* **33/1**
00 10 *4 ½* **Razin' Hell**[28] 6340 2-9-2 0 WilliamTwiston-Davies(3) 3 36
(Alan McCabe) *chsd ldrs over 3f* **66/1**
0 11 *6* **Twelve Bore**[28] 6342 2-9-5 0 JamieMackay 1 17
(Willie Musson) *s.i.s: in rr: wd bnd 3f out: no ch after* **66/1**
12 *2 ¼* **One Picture** 2-9-5 0 PatDobbs 2 10
(Richard Hannon) *s.i.s: outpcd* **25/1**

1m 12.94s (-0.16) **Going Correction** -0.05s/f (Stan) **12 Ran SP% 122.1**
Speed ratings (Par 95): **99,98,95,92,91 87,87,86,85,79 71,68**
toteswingers 1&2 £3.30, 2&3 £9.20, 1&3 £23.60 CSF £27.20 TOTE £9.80: £1.90, £1.10, £5.00; EX 30.40 Trifecta £542.20 Pool: £2700.86 - 3.73 winning units..
Owner Carmichael Humber **Bred** St Albans Bloodstock Llp **Trained** East Everleigh, Wilts

FOCUS
The wind had picked up and it was raining before this interesting maiden. They went a decent pace and the favourite was denied in a tight finish. There was no fluke about this.

7156 COME JUMP RACING AT KEMPTON 20.10.13 CLAIMING STKS 1m (P)
6:40 (6:42) (Class 6) 2-Y-O **£1,940** (£577; £288; £144) **Stalls** Low

Form RPR
056 1 **Sydney James (IRE)**[15] 6747 2-8-10 54 ow1 RichardHughes 4 60
(Richard Hannon) *in tch: pushed along over 2f out: chal over 1f out: sn led: edgd lft u.p ins fnl f: styd on wl* **3/1**[1]
4502 2 *2* **Rural Affair**[7] 6983 2-8-7 53 JohnFahy 6 52
(Harry Dunlop) *chsd ldrs: drvn to take brief ld over 1f out: hdd sn after: styd on same pce to hold 2nd* **3/1**[1]
06 3 *nk* **Dark Crystal**[28] 6334 2-8-8 0 MichaelJMMurphy(3) 3 56
(John Gallagher) *led: hdd over 1f out: styd on same pce fnl f* **9/2**[2]
0354 4 *4 ½* **Princess Tamay (IRE)**[7] 6983 2-8-7 60 LiamJones 7 41
(Mark Johnston) *chsd ldr tl rdn over 2f out: wknd over 1f out* **9/2**[2]
4510 5 *13* **Diffident Beats**[9] 6924 2-8-11 63 SamHitchcott 1 15
(Mick Channon) *slowly away: rcvrd and in tch 4f out: wknd 3f out* **3/1**[1]
00 6 *4 ½* **Topofthedrops (IRE)**[9] 6923 2-8-12 0 (b[1]) LiamKeniry 2
(Philip Hide) *rdn 4 out: sn lost tch* **25/1**[3]

1m 41.14s (1.34) **Going Correction** -0.05s/f (Stan) **6 Ran SP% 115.2**
Speed ratings (Par 93): **91,89,88,84,71 66**
toteswingers 1&2 £2.00, 2&3 £3.20, 1&3 £2.10 CSF £12.67 TOTE £4.20: £3.00, £2.20; EX 13.50 Trifecta £68.70 Pool: £1527.96 - 16.66 winning units..Sydney James was claimed by L. A. Carter for £3000.
Owner The Sydney Arms Racing Club I **Bred** John Fielding **Trained** East Everleigh, Wilts

FOCUS
There was a tight market for this weak claimer. The pace was fair and the winner scored with something in hand. Not form to dwell on.

7157 BETVICTOR.COM/BRITISH STALLION STUDS EBF CONDITIONS STKS 1m (P)
7:10 (7:11) (Class 4) 3-Y-O+ **£6,225** (£1,864; £932; £466) **Stalls** Low

Form RPR
11-0 1 **Tamarkuz (USA)**[19] 6650 3-8-13 96 DaneO'Neill 5 107
(Saeed bin Suroor) *racd in 4th tl drvn and qcknd smartly over 1f out to ld ins fnl f: easily* **6/1**[3]
1616 2 *2* **Ehtedaam (USA)**[33] 6199 4-9-2 100 PaulHanagan 4 102
(Saeed bin Suroor) *sn led: rdn over 1f out: hdd ins fnl f: no ch w wnr but kpt on for 2nd* **11/8**[2]
4136 3 *1 ½* **Snowboarder (USA)**[56] 5446 3-8-13 107 MickaelBarzalona 2 99
(Charlie Appleby) *trckd ldrs in 3rd tl wnt 2nd 2f out: drvn and hdwy to cl on ldr over 1f out but nvr on terms and btn into 3rd ins fnl f* **1/1**[1]
-300 4 *7* **Shamir**[43] 5894 6-9-2 86 LiamKeniry 3 83
(Jo Crowley) *chsd ldr: tl rdn over 2f out: wknd wl over 1f out* **50/1**

1m 38.43s (-1.37) **Going Correction** -0.05s/f (Stan)
WFA 3 from 4yo+ 3lb **4 Ran SP% 108.4**
Speed ratings (Par 105): **104,102,100,93**
CSF £14.68 TOTE £5.70; EX 14.10 Trifecta £19.90 Pool: £2203.48 - 82.90 winning units..
Owner Godolphin **Bred** John D Gunther **Trained** Newmarket, Suffolk

FOCUS
A useful conditions event. Godolphin runners filled the first three places but in reverse order of how they figured in the betting.

7158 £25 FREE BET AT BETVICTOR.COM MEDIAN AUCTION MAIDEN STKS 1m 4f (P)
7:40 (7:41) (Class 5) 3-5-Y-O **£2,587** (£770; £384; £192) **Stalls** Centre

Form RPR
02 1 **First Warning**[21] 6557 3-9-5 0 JamesDoyle 7 80
(Amanda Perrett) *trckd ldr: rdn 3f out and u.p fr 2f out: chal jst ins fnl f: led fnl 110yds: styd on* **6/4**[2]
2 *¾* **Devon Drum**[544] 5-9-12 0 RichardHughes 4 79
(Paul Webber) *s.i.s: sn trcking ldrs: led over 2f out: sn pushed along: jnd ins fnl f: hdd and no ex fnl 110yds* **6/1**[3]
23 3 *8* **Mahdiyah**[43] 5892 3-9-0 0 PaulHanagan 6 61
(Saeed bin Suroor) *led: t.k.h: hdd over 2f out: wknd wl over 1f out* **1/1**[1]
26 4 *2 ¾* **Chattanooga Line**[21] 6557 3-9-0 0 (t) DaneO'Neill 1 57
(George Baker) *in tch tl outpcd wl over 2f out* **16/1**
50 5 *1 ¼* **Seabougg**[17] 6696 5-9-7 0 RyanTate(5) 3 60
(James Eustace) *a towards rr* **50/1**
6 *8* **Share The Dosh**[58] 5-9-7 0 JamieMackay 5 42
(J R Jenkins) *bhd most of way* **66/1**

2m 36.59s (2.09) **Going Correction** -0.05s/f (Stan)
WFA 3 from 5yo 7lb **6 Ran SP% 113.6**
Speed ratings (Par 103): **91,90,85,83,82 77**
toteswingers 1&2 £1.10, 2&3 £1.40, 1&3 £1.10 CSF £11.19 TOTE £2.60: £1.40, £2.40; EX 13.30 Trifecta £20.30 Pool: £2753.25 - 101.30 winning units..
Owner K Abdullah **Bred** Millsec Limited **Trained** Pulborough, W Sussex

FOCUS
The favourite was disappointing in this maiden but the first two pulled a long way clear and the form could work out.

7159 FOLLOW US ON TWITTER @BETVICTOR H'CAP 2m (P)
8:10 (8:10) (Class 6) (0-65,65) 4-Y-O+ **£1,940** (£577; £288; £144) **Stalls** Low

Form RPR
5225 1 **Bramshill Lass**[117] 3328 4-9-6 **64** JimCrowley 11 74
(Amanda Perrett) *hld up in rr: stdy hdwy fr 3f out to led 2f out: clr over 1f out: comf* **7/1**
220 2 *3 ¼* **Jezza**[6] 6996 7-9-7 **65** (bt) RichardHughes 4 71
(Karen George) *rr: drvn 3f out: hdwy over 2f out: styd o to chse wnr ins fnl f but nvr any ch* **7/2**[1]
62P0 3 *3 ½* **Ice Apple**[21] 6558 5-8-3 **47** CathyGannon 6 49
(John E Long) *in tch: drvn to chse ldrs over 2f out: sn chsng wnr but no imp: one pave into 3rd ins fnl f* **20/1**
134 4 *2 ½* **Neighbourhood (USA)**[26] 6404 5-8-12 **61** (b) RyanTate(5) 8 60
(James Evans) *sn led: hdd after 3f: chal 5f out tl slt ld fr 4f out: hdd 2f out: wknd over 1f out* **9/2**[2]
6322 5 *nk* **Capriska**[46] 5801 4-8-6 **50** JamieMackay 2 49
(Willie Musson) *rr: stl bhd 2f out: hdwy over 1f out: fin wl: nt rch ldrs* **14/1**
00-5 6 *4 ½* **Minty Fox**[37] 6068 4-8-7 **58** DanielCremin(7) 1 51
(Eve Johnson Houghton) *chsd ldrs: wknd wl over 1f out* **7/1**
1545 7 *1 ¾* **Proud Times (USA)**[16] 6736 7-9-5 **63** (b) AdamKirby 7 54
(Ali Brewer) *in tch: sme hdwy 3f out: wknd ins fnl 2f* **8/1**
66-0 8 *1 ½* **Mohair**[16] 6737 4-8-8 **55** (p[1]) MarkCoumbe(3) 9 44
(Luke Dace) *chsd ldrs: wknd 2f out* **16/1**
4400 9 *8* **Ctappers**[101] 3884 4-8-9 **53** SamHitchcott 12 33
(Mick Channon) *chsd ldrs: wknd fr 3f out* **16/1**
000/ 10 *3 ½* **Graylyn Ruby (FR)**[1050] 5382 8-8-6 **50** WilliamCarson 5 25
(Robin Dickin) *chsd ldrs: wknd 3f out* **14/1**
3062 11 *½* **Rock Of Ages**[127] 2991 4-8-12 **56** (b) LiamJones 3 31
(Michael Murphy) *led after 3f: jnd 5f out: hdd 4f out: wknd fr 3f out* **6/1**[3]
20-0 12 *17* **Filun**[42] 5168 8-9-4 **62** (t) LiamKeniry 13 16
(Anthony Middleton) *slowly away: a bhd* **50/1**

3m 30.37s (0.27) **Going Correction** -0.05s/f (Stan) **12 Ran SP% 122.6**
Speed ratings (Par 101): **97,95,93,92,92 89,89,88,84,82 82,73**
toteswingers 1&2 £7.20, 2&3 £18.70, 1&3 £25.30 CSF £32.80 CT £485.70 TOTE £8.50: £2.60, £2.20, £3.50; EX 35.70 Trifecta £608.90 Pool: £2176.04 - 2.68 winning units..
Owner Mrs Karen Hancock **Bred** Bloomsbury Stud **Trained** Pulborough, W Sussex

FOCUS
They were tightly bunched for a long way in this steadily-run staying handicap but the winner powered clear from the staying-on favourite.
T/Plt: £273.50 to a £1 stake. Pool of £77580.90 - 207.07 winning tickets. T/Qpdt: £90.80 to a £1 stake. Pool of £7139.00 - 58.17 winning tickets. ST

7009 SAINT-CLOUD (L-H)
Thursday, October 10

OFFICIAL GOING: Turf: very soft

7160a PRIX THOMAS BRYON (GROUP 3) (2YO) (TURF) 1m
12:15 (12:15) 2-Y-O **£32,520** (£13,008; £9,756; £6,504; £3,252)

RPR
1 **Earnshaw (USA)**[36] 2-8-11 0 MaximeGuyon 3 109+
(A Fabre, France) *hld up in tch: 4th 1/2-way: shkn up and hdwy on outer to chal 2f out: rdn over 1f out: led jst ins fnl f and qcknd clr: pushed out: readily* **13/10**[1]
2 *1 ¾* **Stillman (FR)**[32] 6249 2-8-11 0 ChristopheSoumillon 7 105
(Mario Hofer, Germany) *trckd ldr: shkn up to chal 2f out: rdn to ld over 1f out: hdd jst ins fnl f: readily outpcd by wnr but kpt on wl for 2nd* **33/10**[2]
3 *2* **Marbre Rose (IRE)**[30] 6292 2-8-8 0 ThierryJarnet 4 98
(F Head, France) *midfield in tch: 3rd 1/2-way: clsd 2f out: ev ch whn rdn over 1f out: nt qckn and outpcd by front pair ins fnl f: kpt on and jst hld on for 3rd* **5/1**[3]
4 *shd* **Dylan Boy (IRE)**[40] 2-8-11 0 ThierryThulliez 5 100
(E Lellouche, France) *led: 3 l clr 1/2-way: clsd down and strly pressed fr 2f out: rdn and hdd over 1f out: sn outpcd by front pair and dropped to 4th: kpt on u.p and almost got bk up for 3rd* **66/10**
5 *snk* **Aventador (FR)**[17] 2-8-11 0 RaphaelMarchelli 2 100?
(T Castanheira, France) *t.k.h under restraint: hld up in last trio: pushed along over 2f out: rdn and outpcd over 1f out: kpt on and fin strly but nvr threatened* **20/1**
6 *3* **Soresca (IRE)**[14] 6785 2-8-8 0 GregoryBenoist 1 90
(X Nakkachdji, France) *t.k.h under restraint: hld up in last trio on inner: rdn 2f out: outpcd in rr ent fnl f: kpt on but n.d* **8/1**
7 *hd* **Galinea (IRE)**[7] 2-8-8 0 StephanePasquier 6 90
(M Boutin, France) *hld up and last thrght: rdn over 2f out: sn outpcd: kpt on but nvr a factor* **23/1**

1m 47.7s (0.20) **7 Ran SP% 116.6**
WIN (incl. 1 euro stake): 2.30. PLACES: 1.50, 1.80. SF: 6.20.
Owner Godolphin SNC **Bred** Darley **Trained** Chantilly, France

FOCUS
The form is rated in line with the race average.

7161 - (Foreign Racing) - See Raceform Interactive

[7110]WOLVERHAMPTON (A.W) (L-H)

Friday, October 11

OFFICIAL GOING: Standard

Wind: Fresh against Weather: Cloudy

7162 BETFRED 3X THE ODDS ON LUCKY 15'S MEDIAN AUCTION MAIDEN STKS 7f 32y(P)

5:40 (5:41) (Class 6) 2-Y-O £1,940 (£577; £288; £144) Stalls High

Form				RPR
4320	1		**Salford Secret (IRE)**[23] 6513 2-9-5 75 LukeMorris 5 (Marco Botti) *a.p: rdn to ld ins fnl f: r.o* 7/2[3]	80
023	2	1 1/4	**Arantes**[15] 6773 2-9-5 75 MartinHarley 8 (Mick Channon) *a.p: chsd ldr 3f out: rdn to ld over 1f out: hdd and unable qck ins fnl f* 11/4[1]	77
5	3	4 1/2	**Go Sakhee**[23] 6534 2-9-5 0 DaneO'Neill 4 (Roger Varian) *w ldr tl led over 5f out: rdn and hdd over 1f out: hung rt and no ex ins fnl f* 3/1[2]	66
3	4	3	**Space Walker (IRE)**[18] 6689 2-9-5 0 JohnFahy 3 (Harry Dunlop) *led: hdd over 5f out: chse ldr tl 3f out: sn rdn: wknd over 1f out* 5/1	59
0	5	3	**Kaheyll**[14] 6790 2-9-0 0 NathanAlison(5) 1 (William Haggas) *trckd ldrs: nt clr run 3f out: sn lost pl: rdn and swtchd rt wl over 1f out: n.d after* 8/1	51
4	6	2	**Dazza**[43] 5929 2-9-0 0 RichardHughes 7 (Gary Moore) *prom: lost pl over 5f out: pushed along over 2f out: wknd over 1f out* 5/1	41
	7	2 3/4	**Febrayer Star (IRE)** 2-9-5 0 ShaneKelly 2 (Robert Cowell) *s.i.s: sn pushed along in rr: wknd over 2f out* 50/1	40
B	8	2	**Synonym (ITY)**[18] 6689 2-9-0 0 FergusSweeney 9 (J W Hills) *hdwy over 5f out: rdn over 2f out: sn wknd* 66/1	30
	9	10	**Molly Ahoy** 2-8-7 0 AaronJones(7) 6 (Alan McCabe) *s.s: outpcd* 100/1	5

1m 29.67s (0.07) **Going Correction** +0.075s/f (Slow) 9 Ran SP% 122.8

Speed ratings (Par 93): **102,100,95,92,88 86,83,80,69**

toteswingers 1&2 £2.60, 1&3 £3.30, 2&3 £2.50 CSF £14.60 TOTE £4.40: £1.40, £1.10, £2.30; EX 13.80 Trifecta £56.10 Pool: £2306.43 - 30.79 winning units..

Owner Exors of the Late A J Thompson **Bred** Hyphen Bloodstock **Trained** Newmarket, Suffolk

FOCUS

The two most experienced runners in the field pulled clear.

7163 BETFRED RACING FOLLOW US ON TWITTER H'CAP 7f 32y(P)

6:10 (6:11) (Class 6) (0-65,65) 3-Y-O+ £1,940 (£577; £288; £144) Stalls High

Form				RPR
0311	1		**Viennese Verse**[20] 6655 3-9-2 62 DaneO'Neill 7 (Henry Candy) *s.i.s: hdwy over 4f out: chsd ldr over 2f out: rdn to ld ins fnl f: edgd lft: r.o* 6/4[1]	71
0050	2	1 1/2	**Available (IRE)**[31] 6274 4-9-4 62 (tp) StephenCraine 5 (John Mackie) *w ldr tl led 3f out: rdn over 1f out: hdd and unable qck ins fnl f* 20/1	68
4245	3	nk	**Orpsie Boy (IRE)**[13] 6855 10-9-3 61 LukeMorris 4 (Ruth Carr) *hld up: hdwy over 2f out: rdn over 1f out: r.o* 14/1	66
0000	4	1/2	**Cocozza (USA)**[9] 6937 5-9-7 65 (p) DougieCostello 10 (K F Clutterbuck) *sn pushed along and prom: rdn over 1f out: r.o* 25/1	69
1453	5	5	**Makinson Lane (IRE)**[22] 6548 3-9-5 65 TonyHamilton 6 (Richard Fahey) *chsd ldrs: rdn over 1f out: wknd ins fnl f* 6/1[3]	54
310	6	2 1/2	**Arcadian Legend (USA)**[30] 6315 3-9-4 64 SebSanders 8 (Jeremy Noseda) *hld up: pushed along over 2f out: sme hdwy u.p over 1f out: wknd fnl f* 10/1	47
00	7	1/2	**Ferryview Place**[13] 6855 4-9-1 62 MichaelJMMurphy(3) 2 (Ian Williams) *sn outpcd: nvr nrr* 33/1	44
5410	8	2 1/4	**Basle**[87] 4385 6-9-4 62 (t) RichardKingscote 3 (Roy Brotherton) *prom: nt clr run and lost pl over 2f out: rdn over 1f out: wknd fnl f* 25/1	38
1-00	9	18	**Beam Of Light**[30] 6316 3-9-5 65 (b[1]) FergusSweeney 1 (Jamie Osborne) *sn led: hdd 4f out: rdn and wknd 2f out* 20/1	
600-	10	38	**Berengar (IRE)**[349] 7415 4-9-7 65 RichardHughes 9 (John Butler) *chsd ldrs tl pushed along and wknd over 2f out: eased* 7/2[2]	

1m 29.93s (0.33) **Going Correction** +0.075s/f (Slow)

WFA 3 from 4yo+ 2lb 10 Ran SP% 112.4

Speed ratings (Par 101): **101,99,98,98,92 89,89,86,66,22**

toteswingers 1&2 £10.80, 1&3 £5.40, 2&3 £36.20 CSF £39.17 CT £305.04 TOTE £1.90: £1.20, £5.00, £2.60; EX 34.50 Trifecta £237.70 Pool: £1729.21 - 5.45 winning units..

Owner The Chevaliers **Bred** Tony Hirschfeld & L K Piggott **Trained** Kingston Warren, Oxon

FOCUS

An ordinary handicap. The winner's previous win here has been franked and the second was on a good mark.

7164 BETFRED RACING'S BIGGEST SUPPORTER H'CAP (DIV I) 5f 216y(P)

6:40 (6:41) (Class 5) (0-75,75) 3-Y-O+ £2,587 (£770; £384; £192) Stalls Low

Form				RPR
-000	1		**Fat Gary**[16] 6744 3-9-6 75 (p) RichardKingscote 10 (Tom Dascombe) *mde virtually all: rdn over 1f out: edgd lft ins fnl f: jst hld on* 9/4[1]	84
6200	2	hd	**Bogsnog (IRE)**[19] 6664 3-8-12 72 JacobButterfield(5) 9 (Kristin Stubbs) *a.p: rdn to chse wnr fnl f: hung lft: styd on* 20/1	80
0434	3	2 1/2	**Ray Of Joy**[8] 6969 7-9-4 72 RichardHughes 8 (J R Jenkins) *hld up: pushed along and hdwy over 2f out: rdn over 1f out: styd on to go 3rd post: nt rch ldrs* 5/1[2]	72
0005	4	nk	**Hannahs Turn**[8] 6969 3-9-1 70 RaulDaSilva 5 (Chris Dwyer) *hld up: hdwy and nt clr run over 1f out: nt rch ldrs* 16/1	69
2401	5	nse	**Little Choosey**[13] 6849 3-8-8 63 LukeMorris 7 (Anabel K Murphy) *led early: chsd ldrs: rdn over 1f out: styd on same pce ins fnl f* 8/1[3]	62
4632	6	1	**Dark Lane**[37] 6096 7-8-6 67 EoinWalsh(7) 3 (David Evans) *prom: pushed along over 2f out: rdn over 1f out: styd on same pce fnl f* 8/1[3]	63
0500	7	1	**Sewn Up**[20] 6653 3-9-1 70 (e[1]) ShaneKelly 4 (Andrew Hollinshead) *hld up: r.o ins fnl f: nvr nrr* 12/1	63
3035	8	3 3/4	**Going French (IRE)**[20] 6652 6-8-13 67 (p) DaneO'Neill 2 (Dai Burchell) *s.i.s: hdwy over 4f out: rdn over 2f out: wknd over 1f out* 12/1	48
3101	9	1 1/2	**Excellent Jem**[20] 6652 4-8-13 72 (b) IanBurns(5) 1 (Jane Chapple-Hyam) *sn chsng ldr: chal 3f out tl rdn over 1f out: wknd fnl f* 5/1[2]	48
2250	10	8	**Climaxfortackle (IRE)**[8] 6982 5-8-9 70 (v) AdamMcLean(7) 6 (Derek Shaw) *s.s: outpcd* 25/1	20

1m 14.78s (-0.22) **Going Correction** +0.075s/f (Slow)

WFA 3 from 4yo+ 1lb 10 Ran SP% 116.2

Speed ratings (Par 103): **104,103,100,100,99 98,97,92,90,79**

toteswingers 1&2 £10.80, 1&3 £5.40, 2&3 £36.20 CSF £53.73 CT £194.20 TOTE £2.60: £1.10, £8.30, £2.00; EX 71.30 Trifecta £597.10 Pool: £1307.54 - 1.64 winning units..

Owner Manor House Stables LLP **Bred** J M Beever **Trained** Malpas, Cheshire

FOCUS

A modest sprint handicap run in a similar time to division II. The winner is rated close to his 2yo best.

7165 BETFRED RACING'S BIGGEST SUPPORTER H'CAP (DIV II) 5f 216y(P)

7:10 (7:11) (Class 5) (0-75,74) 3-Y-O+ £2,587 (£770; £384; £192) Stalls Low

Form				RPR
2212	1		**Hi Filwah (USA)**[15] 6777 3-9-5 73 (p) SebSanders 7 (Jeremy Noseda) *hld up: hdwy over 1f out: rdn to ld ins fnl f: r.o wl* 7/4[1]	91
0100	2	3	**You're The Boss**[22] 6575 3-9-6 74 LukeMorris 9 (Ed Walker) *a.p: pushed along over 2f out: rdn and ev ch ins fnl f: edgd lft: styd on same pce* 11/4[2]	82
0002	3	2 1/4	**Live Dangerously**[22] 6549 3-8-13 67 (tp) TomEaves 5 (Keith Dalgleish) *hld up: hdwy over 2f out: rdn over 1f out: styd on same pce* 8/1	68
4005	4	1/2	**Alnoomaas (IRE)**[20] 6647 4-9-5 72 JimmyQuinn 1 (Luke Dace) *sn led: rdn over 1f out: hdd and no ex ins fnl f* 7/1[3]	71
0500	5	1 1/2	**Monsieur Royale**[84] 4499 3-8-13 70 (p) WilliamTwiston-Davies(3) 8 (Geoffrey Oldroyd) *chsd ldrs: rdn and edgd lft over 1f out: no ex fnl f* 10/1	64
0000	6	1	**Exceedexpectations (IRE)**[25] 6476 4-9-4 71 LiamKeniry 6 (Conor Dore) *led early: chsd ldr tl rdn over 1f out: wknd ins fnl f* 25/1	62
0316	7	3/4	**Invigilator**[15] 6777 5-8-7 67 (t) AdamMcLean(7) 4 (Derek Shaw) *broke wl: sn stdd to trck ldrs: rdn over 1f out: wknd ins fnl f* 20/1	56
4000	8	6	**Prince Of Burma (IRE)**[16] 6744 5-8-10 70 (b) EoinWalsh(7) 2 (David Evans) *s.s: a bhd* 16/1	40
4666	9	nk	**Frognal (IRE)**[20] 6652 7-9-1 68 (bt) MartinHarley 3 (Violet M Jordan) *chsd ldrs: pushed along over 2f out: wknd over 1f out* 20/1	37

1m 14.76s (-0.24) **Going Correction** +0.075s/f (Slow)

WFA 3 from 4yo+ 1lb 9 Ran SP% 115.0

Speed ratings (Par 103): **104,100,97,96,94 93,92,84,83**

toteswingers 1&2 £1.70, 1&3 £5.10, 2&3 £3.70 CSF £6.21 CT £28.82 TOTE £2.40: £1.10, £1.70, £2.90; EX 10.00 Trifecta £41.70 Pool: £1766.66 - 31.73 winning units..

Owner Faisal Alsheikh **Bred** Peter Redekop Bc Limited **Trained** Newmarket, Suffolk

FOCUS

There was virtually no difference in the times of the two divisions. The winner seems to be getting his act together and the form is arguably worth a bit more.

7166 BETFRED NEW ROOSTER BOOSTER LOTTO BET H'CAP 1m 5f 194y(P)

7:40 (7:40) (Class 5) (0-75,75) 3-Y-O+ £2,587 (£770; £384; £192) Stalls Low

Form				RPR
3416	1		**Getaway Car**[12] 6869 3-9-5 75 (b) NeilCallan 4 (Gerard Butler) *hld up: hdwy over 2f out: shkn up to ld over 1f out: hung lft ins fnl f: idled towards fin: comf* 2/1[1]	88+
601	2	3/4	**Alpine Mysteries (IRE)**[7] 6996 3-8-10 69 6ex ThomasBrown(3) 7 (Harry Dunlop) *a.p: chsd ldr over 9f out: led over 2f out: rdn and hdd over 1f out: kpt on* 9/2[3]	79
1052	3	6	**Nolecce**[7] 6996 6-8-7 61 AdamMcLean(7) 2 (Tony Forbes) *trckd ldrs: led over 5f out: rdn and hdd over 2f out: no ex fnl f* 14/1	63
6030	4	3/4	**Admirable Duque (IRE)**[9] 6960 7-9-5 71 (be) JoshBaudains(5) 5 (Dominic Ffrench Davis) *hld up: hdwy 5f out: rdn over 2f out: styd on same pce fr over 1f out* 14/1	72
022	5	5	**Toughness Danon**[19] 4838 7-9-6 67 RobbieFitzpatrick 3 (Ian Williams) *prom: pushed along and lost pl over 4f out: rallied over 2f out: wknd over 1f out* 7/1	61
0644	6	15	**Oscilate Wildly (IRE)**[14] 6788 3-9-0 70 RichardHughes 1 (Peter Chapple-Hyam) *led: hdd over 10f out: chsd ldrs: pushed along over 4f out: wknd over 2f out* 11/4[2]	43
5220	7	10	**Scribe (IRE)**[126] 3065 5-9-6 70 (vt) DeclanBates(3) 6 (David Evans) *w ldr tl led over 10f out: hdd over 5f out: sn pushed along: wknd over 2f out* 16/1	29

3m 6.69s (0.69) **Going Correction** +0.075s/f (Slow)

WFA 3 from 5yo+ 9lb 7 Ran SP% 109.9

Speed ratings (Par 103): **101,100,97,96,93 85,79**

toteswingers 1&2 £1.20, 1&3 £4.40, 2&3 £10.20 CSF £10.37 TOTE £2.30: £1.60, £1.80; EX 11.70 Trifecta £59.20 Pool: £1193.83 - 15.10 winning units..

Owner A D Spence **Bred** Mascalls Stud **Trained** Newmarket, Suffolk

FOCUS

This was run in a slow time. The winner was well on top and the second improved again.

7167 BETFRED CALL CENTRE ON 0800 221 221 MEDIAN AUCTION MAIDEN STKS 1m 141y(P)

8:10 (8:10) (Class 5) 3-5-Y-O £2,587 (£770; £384; £192) Stalls Low

Form				RPR
040-	1		**Miguel Grau (USA)**[364] 7020 3-9-2 63 (b[1]) DaneO'Neill 3 (Roger Varian) *sn pushed along to chse ldrs: shkn up to ld over 1f out: sn rdn clr* 5/2[2]	67
	2	8	**Memphis Magic (GER)** 3-9-2 0 (t) NeilCallan 6 (Ed Walker) *s.i.s: hdwy to chse ldr 7f out: led 2f out: rdn: hung lft and hdd over 1f out: hung lft and wknd ins fnl f* 9/2[3]	48
00	3	1	**The Bay Tigress**[88] 4356 3-8-8 0 MarkCoumbe(3) 1 (Lisa Williamson) *sn pushed along in rr: hdwy over 1f out: styd on to go 3rd towards fin: nvr nrr* 66/1	41
432	4	1	**Icon Dance**[76] 4750 3-8-11 70 RichardHughes 7 (Ben De Haan) *led: rdn and hdd 2f out: wknd ins fnl f* 11/10[1]	39
0000	5	3/4	**Thecornishwren (IRE)**[5] 6700 4-9-1 31 (vt) KirstyMilczarek 5 (John Ryan) *prom: rdn over 3f out: wknd fnl f* 66/1	36
0000	6	15	**Green Mitas (ITY)**[118] 3326 4-9-6 55 LukeMorris 2 (Frank Sheridan) *prom: rdn over 2f out: sn wknd* 12/1	7
0546	7	10	**Vermeyen**[66] 5091 4-9-3 41 DeclanBates(3) 8 (Geoffrey Deacon) *s.s: a in rr: rdn and wknd over 2f out* 33/1	

-6 **8** *3* **Truth Hurts**[42] 5962 3-9-2 0........ TomEaves 4
(Violet M Jordan) *prom: drvn along over 5f out: wknd over 3f out* **12/1**

1m 51.68s (1.18) **Going Correction** +0.075s/f (Slow)
WFA 3 from 4yo 4lb **8** Ran SP% **115.7**
Speed ratings (Par 103): **97,89,89,88,87 74,65,62**
toteswingers 1&2 £2.70, 1&3 £24.70, 2&3 £63.90 CSF £14.32 TOTE £3.20: £1.10, £2.00, £11.40; EX 13.20 Trifecta £386.60 Pool: £1527.61 - 2.96 winning units..

Owner J Barton & C Pizarro **Bred** Sea Horse Breeders **Trained** Newmarket, Suffolk

FOCUS
A poor maiden run in a slow time. The third and fifth were close enough and the favourite was way below form.

7168 BETFRED "CATCH FRED'S PUSHES ON BETFRED TV" NURSERY H'CAP 1m 141y(P)

8:40 (8:41) (Class 6) (0-65,63) 2-Y-O £1,940 (£577; £288; £144) Stalls Low

Form RPR

0004 **1** **Earthflight**[10] 6924 2-8-6 **55**........ LouisSteward(7) 9 60
(Philip McBride) *hld up: hdwy over 2f out: rdn to chse ldr over 1f out: styd on u.p to ld wl ins fnl f* **7/1**

0643 **2** *1* **Rathealy (IRE)**[8] 6972 2-9-7 **63**........ SebSanders 4 66
(Alan Bailey) *trckd ldrs: racd keenly: shkn up to ld 2f out: edgd lft over 1f out: rdn and hdd wl ins fnl f* **9/2**[2]

4463 **3** *2* **By The Light (IRE)**[13] 6852 2-9-4 **60**........ AdamKirby 8 59
(Mark Johnston) *hld up: hdwy over 5f out: drvn along over 2f out: styd on u.p* **9/2**[2]

0036 **4** *¾* **Paddy's Bay**[6] 7032 2-8-13 **55**........(p) NeilCallan 3 52
(Kevin Ryan) *chsd ldr tl led over 2f out: sn rdn and hdd: styd on same pce fnl f* **20/1**

000 **5** *3½* **La Faisan Blanche (USA)**[18] 6690 2-8-11 **53**........(b) LukeMorris 7 43
(Luca Cumani) *prom: rdn over 2f out: styd on same pce* **20/1**

2052 **6** *3¾* **Sakhalin Star (IRE)**[10] 6914 2-9-1 **62**........(e[1]) ConnorBeasley(5) 10 44
(Richard Guest) *hld up: pushed along over 2f out: nvr on terms* **6/1**[3]

0002 **7** *½* **Assoluta (IRE)**[6] 7032 2-9-2 **58**........ RichardHughes 1 39
(Sylvester Kirk) *s.i.s: sn prom: rdn over 2f out: wknd fnl f* **3/1**[1]

253 **8** *5* **Evacusafe Lady**[45] 5865 2-9-3 **59**........(p) KirstyMilczarek 2 29
(John Ryan) *led: rdn and hdd over 2f out: wknd over 1f out* **33/1**

506 **9** *47* **Pacarama**[23] 6512 2-8-3 **48**........ BillyCray(3) 5
(Jason Ward) *dwlt: outpcd* **100/1**

3044 **P** **Mimbleberry**[6] 7032 2-9-2 **58**........(v) RichardKingscote 6
(Tom Dascombe) *hld up: rdn 1/2-way: wknd over 2f out: p.u and dismntd wl over 1f out* **7/1**

1m 52.02s (1.52) **Going Correction** +0.075s/f (Slow) **10** Ran SP% **114.1**
Speed ratings (Par 93): **96,95,93,92,89 86,85,81,39,**
toteswingers 1&2 £6.90, 1&3 £7.00, 2&3 £5.10 CSF £36.08 CT £160.62 TOTE £11.60: £3.30, £2.30, £1.70; EX 48.90 Trifecta £323.70 Pool: £1964.07 - 4.54 winning units..

Owner Four Winds Racing Partnership **Bred** Wood Farm Stud (Waresley) **Trained** Newmarket, Suffolk

FOCUS
Modest nursery form.

7169 BETFRED "YOU'LL LOVE A BIT OF BETFRED" H'CAP 1m 1f 103y(P)

9:10 (9:10) (Class 5) (0-70,70) 3-Y-O+ £2,587 (£770; £384; £192) Stalls Low

Form RPR

3101 **1** **Tatting**[14] 6804 4-9-3 **63**........ RaulDaSilva 4 76+
(Chris Dwyer) *hld up: hdwy 1/2-way: led on bit wl ins fnl f: shkn up and r.o* **3/1**[2]

1622 **2** *1½* **Golden Jubilee (USA)**[7] 7000 4-9-0 **63**....(v) WilliamTwiston-Davies(3) 3 71
(Nigel Twiston-Davies) *pushed along in rr early: hld up: drvn along over 3f out: hdwy over 2f out: rdn to ld over 1f out: hdd and unable qck wl ins fnl f* **5/1**[3]

4024 **3** *4* **It's My Time**[69] 5006 4-9-8 **68**........ TonyHamilton 12 67
(Richard Fahey) *s.i.s: hld up: hdwy over 2f out: rdn over 1f out: styd on same pce ins fnl f* **12/1**

1550 **4** *3* **Yasir (USA)**[20] 6631 5-9-7 **67**........(p) LiamKeniry 5 60
(Conor Dore) *s.i.s: hld up: rdn over 1f out: swtchd rt and r.o ins fnl f: nvr nrr* **20/1**

2132 **5** *¾* **Mizyen (IRE)**[14] 6810 3-9-6 **70**........ NeilCallan 13 63
(James Tate) *chsd ldrs: rdn over 2f out: edgd rt and wknd fnl f* **11/4**[1]

4-25 **6** *2¼* **Gravitate**[60] 5356 4-9-9 **69**........(p) AdamKirby 9 56
(Paul Webber) *led over 6f: led again 3f out: rdn and hdd over 1f out: wknd ins fnl f* **10/1**

603 **7** *¾* **Outlaw Torn (IRE)**[9] 6952 4-9-2 **62**........(e) RobbieFitzpatrick 11 47
(Richard Guest) *trckd ldr: plld hrd: led 6f out tl 3f out: rdn over 1f out: wknd fnl f* **20/1**

1404 **8** *2¾* **Barton Bounty**[17] 6722 6-8-11 **57**........ DaleSwift 6 37
(Peter Niven) *sn pushed along and a in rr* **25/1**

2360 **9** *2¼* **Spieta (IRE)**[30] 6313 3-9-1 **65**........(b[1]) LukeMorris 2 41
(Luca Cumani) *prom: rdn over 4f out: wknd over 1f out* **14/1**

1445 **10** *10* **Handsome Stranger (IRE)**[8] 6971 3-8-12 **62**........(b) RobertWinston 10 17
(Alan Bailey) *prom: rdn over 2f out: wknd over 1f out* **20/1**

-344 **11** *12* **Watt Broderick (IRE)**[11] 6907 4-9-5 **65**........(p) MichaelO'Connell 8
(Ian Williams) *prom: racd keenly: rdn over 3f out: sn wknd* **8/1**

5233 **12** *12* **Gabrial The Thug (FR)**[13] 6824 3-9-2 **66**........(t) TomEaves 1
(Richard Fahey) *prom: rdn over 5f out: wknd 4f out* **16/1**

2m 2.6s (0.90) **Going Correction** +0.075s/f (Slow)
WFA 3 from 4yo+ 4lb **12** Ran SP% **126.9**
Speed ratings (Par 103): **99,97,94,91,90 88,88,85,83,74 64,53**
toteswingers 1&2 £4.30, 1&3 £6.70, 2&3 £10.90 CSF £18.83 CT £168.17 TOTE £5.90: £2.30, £1.70, £3.10; EX 17.40 Trifecta £208.90 Pool: £1396.99 - 5.01 winning units..

Owner Mrs K W Sneath **Bred** Darley **Trained** Newmarket, Suffolk

FOCUS
A modest handicap and another personal best from the winner, who was value for a bit extra.

T/Plt: £24.10 to a £1 stake. Pool: £94692.44 - 2863.23 winning tickets T/Qpdt: £10.50 to a £1 stake. Pool: £9295.31 - 653.10 winning tickets CR

6233 YORK (L-H)

Friday, October 11

OFFICIAL GOING: Good (good to soft in places; overall 6.3; home straight: far side 6.0; centre 5.9; stands' side 6.0)
Wind: fresh 1/2 against Weather: overcast, very breezy

7170 TSG STKS (NURSERY H'CAP) 6f

2:00 (2:02) (Class 3) (0-95,87) 2-Y-O £7,762 (£2,310; £1,154; £577) Stalls Centre

Form RPR

51 **1** **Aeolus**[27] 6383 2-9-5 **85**........ GrahamGibbons 16 99+
(Ed McMahon) *mid-div: hdwy over 2f out: led appr fnl f: styd on strly* **9/1**

012 **2** *3½* **Musical Comedy**[34] 6194 2-9-5 **85**........ RichardHughes 5 88
(Richard Hannon) *chsd ldr: styd on same pce fnl f* **11/2**[1]

533 **3** *nk* **Sherston**[14] 6790 2-8-7 **73**........ SilvestreDeSousa 2 75
(Mark Johnston) *chsd ldrs far side: kpt on same pce fnl f* **20/1**

01 **4** *hd* **Penina (IRE)**[177] 1605 2-8-0 **66**........ RaulDaSilva 8 68+
(Brian Ellison) *t.k.h in rr far side: hdwy swtchd lft and nt clr run 2f out: edgd lft and styd on wl ins fnl f* **33/1**

630 **5** *½* **Tancred (IRE)**[46] 5843 2-8-6 **72**........ MartinLane 1 72
(Peter Chapple-Hyam) *s.i.s: swtchd rt after s: hdwy far side over 2f out: swtchd lft: keeping on same pce whn crowded wl ins fnl f* **25/1**

5002 **6** *½* **Neighbother**[1] 7147 2-8-3 **69**........ PatrickMathers 19 68
(Richard Fahey) *in rr stands' side: hdwy over 2f out: kpt on wl ins fnl f* **25/1**

210 **7** *nk* **Disclosure**[24] 6493 2-8-10 **76**........(p) DavidAllan 3 74
(Bryan Smart) *led: hdd appr fnl f: wknd last 100yds* **66/1**

431 **8** *1* **Spiceupyourlife (IRE)**[113] 3500 2-8-10 **76**........ LeeTopliss 6 71
(Richard Fahey) *mid-div: hdwy far side to chse ldrs 2f out: one pce* **22/1**

620 **9** *1¼* **Iftaar (IRE)**[14] 6799 2-8-13 **79**........ PaulHanagan 14 70
(Charles Hills) *wnt lft s: chsd ldrs towards stands' side: wknd over 1f out* **10/1**

4103 **10** *hd* **Kickboxer (IRE)**[6] 7011 2-8-13 **79**........ SamHitchcott 18 69
(Mick Channon) *hld up in rr stands' side: effrt over 2f out: kpt on fnl f* **6/1**[2]

2625 **11** *1* **The Hooded Claw (IRE)**[6] 7026 2-8-11 **77**........ DuranFentiman 9 64
(Tim Easterby) *mid-div: hdwy 3f out: sn drvn: wknd fnl f* **8/1**[3]

1 **12** *shd* **Rozene (IRE)**[23] 6517 2-8-4 **70**........ AndrewMullen 10 57
(David Barron) *chsd ldrs: wknd over 1f out* **18/1**

4122 **13** *3¼* **Makin The Rules (IRE)**[21] 6582 2-8-6 **77**........ OisinMurphy(5) 15 54
(John Quinn) *in rr: hdwy over 2f out: sn rdn: wknd over 1f out* **11/2**[1]

315 **14** *1¼* **Storm Trooper (IRE)**[18] 6697 2-9-7 **87**........ RyanMoore 20 60
(Richard Hannon) *hld up in rr stands' side: sme hdwy over 2f out: lost pl over 1f out* **14/1**

215 **15** *hd* **Smart Salute**[41] 6002 2-8-13 **79**........ TomMcLaughlin 12 52
(Ed Walker) *squeezed out sn after s: in rr: sme hdwy over 2f out: sn wknd* **14/1**

35U **16** *2* **Mr Matthews (IRE)**[21] 6582 2-9-4 **84**........ DanielTudhope 13 51
(K R Burke) *carried lft s: a towards rr* **20/1**

2550 **17** *9* **Bahamian C**[33] 6234 2-8-6 **72**........ BarryMcHugh 17 12
(Richard Fahey) *in rr stands' side: bhd and eased fnl f* **20/1**

1m 13.22s (1.32) **Going Correction** +0.20s/f (Good) **17** Ran SP% **124.6**
Speed ratings (Par 99): **99,94,93,93,93 92,91,90,88,88 87,87,82,81,80 78,66**
toteswingers 1&2 £5.00, 1&3 £31.80, 2&3 £13.40 CSF £51.65 CT £1026.85 TOTE £11.40: £2.90, £1.50, £4.40, £5.90; EX 45.50 Trifecta £868.90 Pool: £2714.37 - 2.34 winning units..

Owner A Buxton **Bred** Andrew Buxton **Trained** Lichfield, Staffs

FOCUS
Racing on inside line and races of 1m and over decreased in distance by 24yds. A good, competitive nursery that was won in impression fashion by Aeolus, who looks a Listed winner in waiting.

7171 NOVUS STKS (H'CAP) 5f

2:30 (2:31) (Class 3) (0-95,95) 3-Y-O+ £12,291 (£3,657; £1,827; £913) Stalls Centre

Form RPR

2-20 **1** **Take Cover**[20] 6621 6-9-4 **92**........ DavidProbert 16 105
(David C Griffiths) *mde all: rdn over 1f out: drvn and hld on wl fnl f* **5/1**[1]

0042 **2** *1¼* **Kyleakin Lass**[18] 6699 4-9-3 **91**........ RichardHughes 15 99
(Jonathan Portman) *trckd ldrs: hdwy wl over 1f out: rdn to chse wnr ins fnl f: drvn and no imp towards fin* **16/1**

-004 **3** *1¼* **Pearl Blue (IRE)**[18] 6699 5-9-4 **92**........ HarryBentley 9 96
(Chris Wall) *trckd ldrs: hdwy 2f out: rdn over 1f out: kpt on fnl f* **12/1**

4660 **4** *nk* **Above Standard (IRE)**[13] 6845 5-8-13 **87**........ GrahamGibbons 18 89
(Michael Easterby) *chsd ldrs: hdwy 2f out: rdn and ch over 1f out: drvn ent fnl f: kpt on same pce* **12/1**

0000 **5** *1¼* **Cheviot (USA)**[13] 6830 7-9-3 **94**........(b) JasonHart(3) 13 92
(Ian Semple) *prom: chsd wnr 1/2-way: rdn along wl over 1f out: drvn and one pce ent fnl f* **16/1**

3012 **6** *hd* **Imperial Legend (IRE)**[21] 6583 4-8-13 **87**........(p) TomQueally 12 84
(David Nicholls) *dwlt and towards rr: hdwy and in tch 1/2-way: rdn over 1f out: kpt on towards fin* **16/1**

3 **7** *¾* **Jamaican Bolt (IRE)**[23] 6539 5-9-7 **95**........(b[1]) GrahamLee 19 90
(Geoffrey Oldroyd) *in tch: pushed along over 2f out: rdn wl over 1f out: no imp* **8/1**[2]

6620 **8** *½* **Singeur (IRE)**[20] 6621 6-9-2 **90**........ AdamBeschizza 11 83
(Robin Bastiman) *towards rr and sn pushed along: rdn 1/2-way: swtchd rt and drvn wl over 1f out: styd on fnl f: nrst fin* **33/1**

3310 **9** *shd* **Bop It**[21] 6586 4-9-0 **88**........ DanielTudhope 8 80
(David O'Meara) *chsd ldrs: rdn along 2f out: sn one pce* **16/1**

0000 **10** *shd* **Doctor Parkes**[13] 6830 7-9-7 **95**........ J-PGuillambert 10 87
(Stuart Williams) *trckd ldrs: pushed along 1/2-way: sn rdn and one pce* **50/1**

0411 **11** *shd* **Dungannon**[13] 6831 6-9-1 **94**........(b) OisinMurphy(5) 3 86
(Andrew Balding) *trckd ldrs: effrt 2f out: sn rdn and wknd appr fnl f* **5/1**[1]

6332 **12** *2* **Fitz Flyer (IRE)**[10] 6920 7-8-7 **88**........(v) JordanNason(7) 5 72
(David Nicholls) *prom: rdn along 2f out: grad wknd* **16/1**

0000 **13** *½* **Polski Max**[20] 6621 3-9-6 **94**........ PaulHanagan 7 78
(Richard Fahey) *a towards rr* **20/1**

0050 **14** *nk* **Pabusar**[69] 4986 5-9-4 **92**........[1] JamieSpencer 6 74
(Jamie Osborne) *dwlt and in rr: swtchd lft to outer and rdn along over 2f out: nvr a factor* **16/1**

0002 **15** *1¼* **Dick Bos**[13] 6850 4-8-9 **88**........ DavidBergin(5) 1 65
(David O'Meara) *prom: rdn along 2f out: sn drvn and wknd* **20/1**

0000 **16** *1¼* **Bapak Chinta (USA)**[10] 6920 4-8-13 **87**........ RyanMoore 17 60
(Kevin Ryan) *a towards rr* **20/1**

3 6 **Banu (GER)**[81] 3-9-0 0 ChristopheSoumillon 3 76
(J-P Carvalho, France) **6/1**[2]
4 nse **Fair Moon (FR)**[9] 3-9-1 0 GregoryBenoist 17 77
(D Smaga, France) **15/1**
5 ¾ **Toni Fortebracci (FR)**[33] 3-9-3 0 UmbertoRispoli 9 77
(G Botti, France) **14/1**
6 ¾ **Manamerican (FR)**[15] 3-8-5 0 (p) AlexisBadel 5 63
(J Heloury, France) **45/1**
7 nk **Le Deluge (FR)**[33] 3-9-3 0 CathyGannon 14 75
(John Best) *t.k.h: towards rr: stdy prog on outer fr 3f out: rdn 1 1/2f out: kpt on ins fnl f: nvr on terms w ldrs* **39/1**
8 2 **Hernan Cortez (FR)**[33] 3-9-2 0 ThierryJarnet 11 69
(G Botti, France) **19/1**
9 nse **Gorki Park (FR)**[33] 3-8-6 0 FabienLefebvre 15 59
(Mme G Rarick, France) **83/10**
10 1 ½ **Excellent Touch (IRE)**[22] 3-8-3 0 MarcLerner 7 53
(C Lerner, France) **44/1**
11 3 ½ **Cassini (FR)**[18] 3-9-0 0 (p) MaximeGuyon 8 56
(Mme Pia Brandt, France) **83/10**
12 nk **Just One Wish (IRE)**[112] 3-8-10 0 (p) Pierre-CharlesBoudot 1 51
(H De Nicolay, France) **10/1**
13 1 ¼ **Ver Coquin (FR)**[11] 3-8-13 0 (p) TheoBachelot 4 51
(J-P Carvalho, France) **22/1**
14 2 **Zaafran (FR)**[81] 3-9-3 0 StephanePasquier 12 50
(N Bertran De Balanda, France) **7/1**[3]
15 2 **So Much**[20] 3-8-13 0 (b) SylvainRuis 6 42
(B Dutruel, France) **27/1**
16 nk **Secret Taboo (FR)**[20] 6713 3-8-3 0 (p) AntoineCoutier 18 31
(A Lyon, France) **37/1**
17 3 ½ **Lucax (FR)**[20] 6713 3-8-7 0 ValentinGambart(3) 2 30
(Mlle V Dissaux, France) **85/1**
18 1 ¼ **Angry Kitten (USA)**[24] 3-9-7 0 ThierryThulliez 16 38
(Gianluca Bietolini, Italy) **66/1**

1m 39.63s (1.63) **18 Ran SP% 117.5**
WIN (incl. 1 euro stake): 6.50. Places: 2.30, 4.80, 2.70. DF: 47.80. SF: 107.70..
Owner Mme Marlene Henkel **Bred** Mme Marlene Henkel **Trained** France

TOULOUSE
Friday, October 11
OFFICIAL GOING: Turf: good to soft

7189a PRIX PANACEE (LISTED RACE) (3YO+ FILLIES & MARES) (TURF) 1m 4f
8:05 (12:00) 3-Y-0+ **£21,138** (£8,455; £6,341; £4,227; £2,113)

RPR
1 **Pearls Or Passion (FR)**[41] 6010 4-9-1 0 Francois-XavierBertras 11 101
(F Rohaut, France) **92/10**
2 1 ¼ **Oriental Wind**[25] 6484 3-8-8 0 RonanThomas 4 99+
(Rod Collet, France) **13/1**
3 ¼ **Aquilla (IRE)**[24] 6498 4-9-1 0 Jean-BernardEyquem 3 99
(David Simcock) **16/1**
4 nk **Frine (IRE)**[19] 3-8-8 0 JeremyCrocquevieille 1 98
(J-M Osorio, Spain) **78/10**
5 1 ½ **Incroyable (USA)**[11] 4-9-1 0 FlavienPrat 5 96
(C Laffon-Parias, France) **51/10**[2]
6 2 ½ **Holly Polly (GER)**[26] 6447 4-9-1 0 FabriceVeron 10 92
(H-A Pantall, France) **17/1**
7 nse **Yorkshire Lass (IRE)**[47] 5-9-1 0 (p) JulienAuge 7 92
(H-A Pantall, France) **32/1**
8 5 **Shindigger (IRE)**[63] 5-9-1 0 MickaelForest 12 84
(J Merienne, France) **24/1**
9 ¼ **Zamfara**[20] 6711 3-8-8 0 AurelienLemaitre 2 83
(H-A Pantall, France) **46/1**
10 2 ½ **Encore Merci (IRE)**[37] 3-8-8 0 (p) FabriceBillieres 6 79
(F Rohaut, France) **80/1**
11 3 **Two Days In Paris (FR)**[32] 6270 4-9-1 0 ChristopheSoumillon 8 74
(J-C Rouget, France) **17/10**[1]
12 2 ½ **Modern Eagle (GER)**[19] 3-8-8 0 AntoineHamelin 9 70
(A De Royer-Dupre, France) **57/10**[3]

2m 29.86s (-2.44)
WFA 3 from 4yo+ 7lb **12 Ran SP% 118.5**
WIN (incl. 1 euro stake): 10.20 (Pearls Or Passion coupled with Encore Merci). PLACES: 3.50, 3.90, 5.20. DF: 46.00. SF: 171.10.
Owner Scea Haras De Saint Pair **Bred** 6 C Racing Ltd **Trained** Sauvagnon, France

7016 NEWMARKET (R-H)
Saturday, October 12
OFFICIAL GOING: Good to soft (good in places; 7.0)
Wind: Light against Weather: Cloudy

7190 DUBAI CHALLENGE STKS (GROUP 2) 7f
2:05 (2:05) (Class 1) 3-Y-0+
£51,039 (£19,350; £9,684; £4,824; £2,421; £1,215) **Stalls** High

Form RPR
1615 1 **Fiesolana (IRE)**[35] 6224 4-9-0 110 WJLee 3 116
(W McCreery, Ire) *lengthy; str: trckd ldrs: shkn up to ld ins fnl f: r.o wl* **3/1**[1]
4124 2 2 **Amarillo (IRE)**[27] 4-9-3 112 MartinHarley 1 114
(P Schiergen, Germany) *str: lw: chsd ldrs: led over 1f out: rdn and hdd ins fnl f: styd on same pce* **8/1**
4505 3 2 ½ **Libranno**[34] 6254 5-9-3 107 RichardHughes 5 108
(Richard Hannon) *w ldr: rdn and ev ch over 1f out: no ex ins fnl f* **20/1**
6311 4 1 **Highland Colori (IRE)**[21] 6623 5-9-3 111 DavidProbert 9 105
(Andrew Balding) *chsd ldrs: rdn over 1f out: styd on same pce fnl f* **9/2**[3]
0120 5 nk **Gabriel's Lad (IRE)**[21] 6623 4-9-3 101 PaulHanagan 2 104
(Denis Coakley) *hld up: rdn over 1f out: styd on ins fnl f: nt trble ldrs* **9/1**
1006 6 1 ½ **Trumpet Major (IRE)**[91] 4276 4-9-7 113 RyanMoore 7 104
(Richard Hannon) *hld up: pushed along 1/2-way: rdn over 1f out: n.d* **9/1**
0242 7 1 ¼ **Ansgar (IRE)**[27] 6440 5-9-3 110 (t) RoryCleary 8 97
(Sabrina J Harty, Ire) *s.i.s: sn rcvrd to ld: rdn over 2f out: hdd over 1f out: wknd ins fnl f* **12/1**
004 8 shd **Arnold Lane (IRE)**[7] 7014 4-9-3 107 SamHitchcott 10 97
(Mick Channon) *hld up: racd keenly: rdn over 2f out: wknd fnl f* **25/1**
3112 9 ¾ **Lockwood**[28] 6392 4-9-3 113 SilvestreDeSousa 4 95
(Saeed bin Suroor) *hld up: pushed along 1/2-way: rdn over 2f out: wknd over 1f out* **7/2**[2]

1m 24.24s (-1.16) **Going Correction** +0.275s/f (Good)
WFA 3 from 4yo+ 2lb **9 Ran SP% 112.8**
Speed ratings (Par 115): **117,114,111,110,110 108,107,107,106**
toteswingers 1&2 £4.70, 2&3 £17.10, 1&3 £10.70 CSF £26.75 TOTE £3.30: £1.30, £1.90, £3.60; EX 27.00 Trifecta £381.30 Pool: £3800.00 - 7.47 winning units..
Owner K Leavy/L Cribben/Mrs A McCreery **Bred** Robert De Vere Hunt **Trained** The Curragh, Co.Kildare

FOCUS
Stands' side track used. Stalls: stands' side except 2m2f: far side. The third running of Dubai Future Champions Day, for which the stands'-side track was in use. The stands'-side 20 metres of the Rowley Mile was used for the first time since May. Following 3.5mm of rain overnight, the ground had eased slightly and was officially described as Good to soft, good in places (from Good). After the opener the jockeys reported the ground just on the easy side of good, but not as soft as they had expected after the rain. The winning time was only 1.74 seconds outside standard. The 3yo generation had taken five of the last six runnings of this race, but that sequence was never going to be extended once the only 3yo Darwin had been withdrawn. The finish was fought out between two of the overseas raiders. Straightforward form, ordinary for the grade.

7191 VISION.AE MIDDLE PARK STKS (GROUP 1) (ENTIRE COLTS) 6f
2:35 (2:36) (Class 1) 2-Y-O
£119,034 (£45,128; £22,585; £11,250; £5,646; £2,833) **Stalls** High

Form RPR
1611 1 **Astaire (IRE)**[49] 5765 2-9-0 111 NeilCallan 13 116
(Kevin Ryan) *mde all: qcknd and hung rt over 1f out: sn rdn: styd on gamely* **8/1**
1531 2 ½ **Hot Streak (IRE)**[7] 7011 2-9-0 112 JamieSpencer 12 115
(Kevin Ryan) *trckd ldrs: wnt 2nd over 1f out: rdn and ev ch ins fnl f: unable qck towards fin* **5/1**[3]
0521 3 1 ½ **Justice Day (IRE)**[10] 6958 2-9-0 103 WilliamBuick 11 110
(David Elsworth) *a.p: rdn and edgd rt over 1f out: styd on* **22/1**
0422 4 1 ¼ **Speedfiend**[17] 6747 2-9-0 84 PatCosgrave 2 106
(Noel Quinlan) *awkward leaving stalls: hld up: hdwy over 1f out: styd on: nt rch ldrs* **100/1**
112 5 nk **Sudirman (USA)**[27] 6442 2-9-0 0 WayneLordan 6 105
(David Wachman, Ire) *str: chsd ldrs: rdn over 1f out: styd on same pce ins fnl f* **4/1**[2]
5111 6 2 **Supplicant**[21] 6637 2-9-0 110 RyanMoore 8 99
(Richard Fahey) *athletic: chsd ldrs: rdn over 2f out: styd on same pce fnl f* **13/2**
5425 7 1 ¼ **Jallota**[7] 7017 2-9-0 108 MartinHarley 10 96
(Mick Channon) *chsd wnr: pushed along over 2f out: rdn and lost 2nd over 1f out: sn hung rt and no ex* **25/1**
1 8 ½ **Great White Eagle (USA)**[41] 6021 2-9-0 0 JosephO'Brien 9 94
(A P O'Brien, Ire) *lengthy: s.i.s: hld up: effrt and edgd rt wl over 1f out: nvr on terms* **2/1**[1]
0151 9 5 **Brown Sugar (IRE)**[35] 6201 2-9-0 111 PatDobbs 1 79
(Richard Hannon) *hld up: racd keenly: rdn and edgd lft wl over 1f out: sn wknd* **14/1**
3101 10 13 **Green Door (IRE)**[29] 6347 2-9-0 109 (b) JimCrowley 7 40
(Olly Stevens) *hld up: racd keenly: hmpd and wknd wl over 1f out* **20/1**

1m 12.33s (0.13) **Going Correction** +0.275s/f (Good) **10 Ran SP% 115.1**
Speed ratings (Par 109): **110,109,107,105,105 102,100,100,93,76**
toteswingers 1&2 £6.60, 2&3 £13.10, 1&3 £8.40 CSF £44.99 TOTE £8.30: £2.30, £2.00, £5.20; EX 44.10 Trifecta £547.80 Pool: £7213.65 - 9.87 winning units..
Owner Mrs Angie Bailey **Bred** John O'Connor **Trained** Hambleton, N Yorks

■ Stewards' Enquiry : Neil Callan six-day ban: used whip above permitted level, down the shoulder in the forehand (Oct 26,Oct 28-Nov 1)

FOCUS
An ordinary-looking edition of this juvenile Group 1, with some of the fancied runners performing below expectations, and few got involved. They raced stands' side. The race saw a terrific training performance from Kevin Ryan, who saddled the one-two. The form could possibly be rated a shade higher than it has, the first two both credited with finding two lengths' improvement.

7192 DUBAI DEWHURST STKS (GROUP 1) (ENTIRE COLTS & FILLIES) 7f
3:10 (3:12) (Class 1) 2-Y-O
£228,541 (£86,645; £43,362; £21,600; £10,840; £5,440) **Stalls** High

Form RPR
131 1 **War Command (USA)**[49] 5774 2-9-1 0 JosephO'Brien 5 118
(A P O'Brien, Ire) *lw: trckd ldrs: rdn to ld 1f out: styd on u.p* **10/11**[1]
2432 2 1 ¼ **Cable Bay (IRE)**[16] 6765 2-9-1 108 JamieSpencer 4 115
(Charles Hills) *trckd ldrs: led over 1f out: sn rdn and hdd: unable qck wl ins fnl f* **20/1**
121 3 1 ½ **Outstrip**[28] 6390 2-9-1 114 MickaelBarzalona 6 111
(Charlie Appleby) *hld up: rdn over 1f out: styd on ins fnl f: nt rch ldrs* **15/8**[2]
011 4 nk **Anjaal**[93] 4212 2-9-1 107 PaulHanagan 3 110
(Richard Hannon) *hld up: pushed along 1/2-way: rdn over 1f out: styd on: nt trble ldrs* **10/1**[3]
4213 5 3 ¾ **Stormardal (IRE)**[16] 6763 2-9-1 88 NeilCallan 2 100
(Ismail Mohammed) *str: w ldr tl led 2f out: sn rdn and hdd: wknd ins fnl f* **50/1**
044 6 5 **Friendship (IRE)**[27] 6442 2-9-1 0 (p) SeamieHeffernan 1 87
(A P O'Brien, Ire) *led: rdn and hdd 2f out: wknd fnl f* **20/1**

1m 25.06s (-0.34) **Going Correction** +0.275s/f (Good) **6 Ran SP% 107.7**
Speed ratings (Par 109): **112,110,108,108,104 98**
toteswingers 1&2 £3.50, 2&3 £3.90, 1&3 £1.10 CSF £19.77 TOTE £1.60: £1.10, £5.20; EX 14.40 Trifecta £26.60 Pool: £10083.65 - 284.21 winning units..
Owner J Allen/Mrs J Magnier/M Tabor/D Smith **Bred** Joseph Allen **Trained** Ballydoyle, Co Tipperary

■ Stewards' Enquiry : Mickael Barzalona two-day ban: used whip above permitted level (Oct 28-29)

FOCUS
Hardly the most memorable of Dewhursts, with the form nothing special and the winner only workmanlike, but it's probably worth being positive about War Command who can better this figure. Surprise but believable improvement from Cable Bay. They raced stands' side and Stormardal and Friendship, who both had plenty to find, ruined their chances by taking each other on up front.

7193 BETFRED CESAREWITCH (HERITAGE H'CAP) 2m 2f
3:50 (3:53) (Class 2) 3-Y-O+

£155,625 (£46,600; £23,300; £11,650; £5,825; £2,925) **Stalls** High

Form | | | | RPR
5604 **1** **Scatter Dice (IRE)**[13] 6876 4-8-8 **88**..................(v[1]) SilvestreDeSousa 18 99
(Mark Johnston) *s.v.s: hld up: nt clr run: hdwy and swtchd lft over 2f out: rdn and edgd rt over 1f out: led ins fnl f: styd on wl* **66/1**
0324 **2** *3* **Waterclock (IRE)**[39] 6066 4-8-3 **88**..........................(p) JoeyHaynes(5) 6 96
(Roger Charlton) *lw a.p: rdn over 3f out: styd on* **20/1**
2132 **3** *1/2* **Lieutenant Miller**[73] 4873 7-8-11 **91**.................................. RyanMoore 32 98
(Nicky Henderson) *hld up: hdwy over 4f out: led 2f out: rdn and hdd ins fnl f: styd on same pce* **10/1**
5136 **4** *3/4* **Chiberta King**[29] 6349 7-9-3 **102**..............................(p) OisinMurphy(5) 1 108
(Andrew Balding) *hld up: hdwy over 4f out: rdn over 2f out: styd on* **20/1**
11-3 **5** *nk* **Pallasator**[35] 6192 4-9-6 **100**.. LukeMorris 7 106
(Sir Mark Prescott Bt) *swtg: hld up: hdwy over 5f out: rdn and ev ch over 2f out: styd on same pce fnl f* **8/1[2]**
4501 **6** *1/2* **Oriental Fox (GER)**[21] 6646 5-9-10 **104** 4ex............ JohnnyMurtagh 20 109
(Mark Johnston) *hld up: hdwy over 3f out: rdn and hmpd over 1f out: sn hung rt: eased whn hld towards fin* **8/1[2]**
4023 **7** *1* **Jonny Delta**[14] 6833 6-7-7 **80** oh3................................ JackGarritty(7) 23 84
(Jim Goldie) *hld up: nt clr run over 2f out: sn rdn: styd on appr fnl f: nvr nrr* **50/1**
-121 **8** *1* **Tiger Cliff (IRE)**[49] 5766 4-9-10 **104**.......................... TomQueally 30 107
(Lady Cecil) *lw: hld up: hdwy over 4f out: led 3f out: rdn and hdd 2f out: no ex fnl f* **7/1[1]**
3503 **9** *1 1/4* **Brockwell**[21] 6646 4-8-8 **91**...[1] JasonHart(3) 17 93
(Tom Dascombe) *prom: rdn and ev ch 3f out: no ex fnl f* **20/1**
6624 **10** *3/4* **Moidore**[22] 6585 4-8-5 **90**.. DarylByrne(5) 15 91
(John Quinn) *hld up: rdn over 2f out: hdwy and hung lft over 1f out: nt rch ldrs* **33/1**
5110 **11** *nk* **Poyle Thomas**[35] 6192 4-8-4 **84**..................................(p) MartinLane 4 85
(Ralph Beckett) *prom: rdn over 2f out: wknd over 1f out* **66/1**
0455 **12** *1* **Sign Manual**[25] 6504 4-8-0 **80** oh2............................... JimmyQuinn 12 80
(Michael Bell) *hld up: hdwy u.p over 2f out: wknd ins fnl f* **66/1**
6040 **13** *hd* **High Office**[21] 6626 7-8-0 **80** oh3.................................... KieranO'Neill 9 79
(Richard Fahey) *prom: racd keenly: rdn over 3f out: wknd over 1f out* **50/1**
3632 **14** *nk* **Clowance Estate (IRE)**[35] 6192 4-8-13 **93**..................... GrahamLee 2 92
(Roger Charlton) *chsd ldrs: rdn over 3f out: wknd fnl f* **12/1**
0431 **15** *shd* **Swinging Hawk (GER)**[14] 6833 7-7-11 **80** 4ex........... RyanPowell(3) 25 79
(Ian Williams) *hld up: hmpd over 3f out: rdn over 2f out: nt trble ldrs* **66/1**
1604 **16** *shd* **Taglietelle**[81] 4606 4-8-0 **80**..................................... DavidProbert 28 79
(Andrew Balding) *hld up: hdwy 5f out: rdn and wknd fnl f* **66/1**
0-4 **17** *1 3/4* **Smoky Hill (IRE)**[27] 6447 4-8-11 **91**.......................... UmbertoRispoli 14 88
(M Delzangles, France) *str: hld up: hdwy over 4f out: ev ch over 2f out: sn rdn: wknd fnl f* **9/1[3]**
1020 **18** *6* **Flashman**[22] 6585 4-8-0 **80** oh1.................................. DuranFentiman 26 70
(Richard Fahey) *prom: pushed along over 6f out: wknd over 2f out* **100/1**
3614 **19** *1 1/4* **Cosimo de Medici**[21] 6646 6-8-7 **87**............................ PaulHanagan 19 76
(Hughie Morrison) *hld up: nvr nrr* **50/1**
0025 **20** *1/2* **Albert Bridge**[21] 6626 5-8-7 **87**...................................... WayneLordan 8 75
(Ralph Beckett) *chsd ldr tl led 6f out: hdd 4f out: rdn and wknd 2f out* **25/1**
0 **21** *3* **Big Easy (GER)**[116] 3423 6-8-10 **90**............................ JamieSpencer 36 75
(Philip Hobbs) *hld up: pushed along over 5f out: rdn over 2f out: n.d: eased ins fnl f* **20/1**
1600 **22** *3 3/4* **Nanton (USA)**[21] 6646 11-8-5 **85**................................ BarryMcHugh 31 66
(Jim Goldie) *hld up: rdn over 2f out: n.d* **100/1**
3510 **23** *hd* **Eagle Rock (IRE)**[21] 6646 5-8-4 **84** 4ex...................(p) AndrewMullen 33 65
(Tom Tate) *prom: rdn over 3f out: wknd 2f out* **80/1**
6-05 **24** *3* **Los Nadis (GER)**[22] 6585 9-7-7 **80** oh1........................ JoeDoyle(7) 13 57
(Jim Goldie) *hld up: wknd over 3f out* **100/1**
/01- **25** *5* **Domination**[48] 4842 6-9-1 **95**.. FMBerry 16 67
(C Byrnes, Ire) *hld up: hdwy over 6f out: wknd over 2f out* **8/1[2]**
5000 **26** *3 1/4* **Sohar**[45] 5895 5-8-0 **80**.. CathyGannon 24 48
(James Toller) *chsd ldr: led over 4f out: hdd 3f out: sn wknd* **33/1**
00/0 **27** *1* **Recession Proof (FR)**[34] 6237 7-7-11 **82**...................(p) ConnorKing(5) 3 49
(John Quinn) *hld up: rdn over 3f out: sn wknd* **18/1**
2111 **28** *4 1/2* **Platinum (IRE)**[35] 6192 6-9-0 **94** 4ex.....................(p) RussKennemore 21 56
(Philip Kirby) *hld up: hdwy 11f out: rdn along over 5f out: hung rt and wknd over 3f out* **25/1**
3020 **29** *1 1/4* **Cousin Khee**[35] 6192 6-8-7 **87**................................... AndreaAtzeni 27 48
(Hughie Morrison) *prom: racd keenly: rdn over 2f out: sn wknd and eased* **40/1**
2666 **30** *11* **Merchant Of Dubai**[13] 6876 8-7-11 **82** oh3 ow2....... ShelleyBirkett(5) 11 31
(Jim Goldie) *led: hdd 6f out: wknd over 3f out* **100/1**
6160 **31** *16* **Broxbourne (IRE)**[21] 6646 4-9-0 **94**............................. WilliamBuick 22 25
(Mark Johnston) *hld up: bhd fnl 4f* **33/1**
20 **32** *5* **Earth Amber**[164] 1920 4-9-0 **94**................................... RichardHughes 5 20
(Nicky Henderson) *hld up: hdwy over 5f out: wknd and eased over 2f out* **16/1**
4333 **33** *42* **Seaside Sizzler**[34] 6252 6-8-8 **88**...............................(vt) JimCrowley 35
(Ralph Beckett) *hld up: pushed along over 7f out: wknd and eased over 4f out* **40/1**

3m 52.75s (0.75) **Going Correction** +0.275s/f (Good) **33 Ran SP% 142.7**
Speed ratings (Par 109): **109,107,107,107,106 106,106,105,105,104 104,104,104,104,104 104,103,100,100,99 98,96,95,93**
toteswingers 1&2 £283.20, 2&3 £67.40, 1&3 £283.20 CSF £1145.46 CT £13406.61 TOTE £73.40: £14.20, £7.40, £3.10, £4.80; EX 1542.50 Trifecta £6822.20 Part won. Pool: £9096.39 - 0.10 winning units..
Owner Sheikh Hamdan Bin Mohammed Al Maktoum **Bred** Darley **Trained** Middleham Moor, N Yorks

FOCUS
A typically competitive Cesarewitch with a 66-1 winner for the second year in a row. The pace set by the freely sweating Merchant Of Dubai, Albert Bridge and Sohar seemed solid enough and there looked to be few hard-luck stories. The runners stayed on the inside on reaching the straight. The surprise winner had dropped to a good mark, and the form nakes plenty of sense.

7194 VISION.AE ROCKFEL STKS (GROUP 2) 7f
4:25 (4:29) (Class 1) 2-Y-O

£39,697 (£15,050; £7,532; £3,752; £1,883; £945) **Stalls** High

Form | | | | RPR
1 **1** **Al Thakhira**[25] 6500 2-8-12 0.. MartinHarley 8 110+
(Marco Botti) *neat: hld up: hdwy over 2f out: led over 1f out: shkn up and r.o wl* **5/1[2]**
0110 **2** *3 1/4* **Blockade (IRE)**[21] 6622 2-8-12 93.................................. NeilCallan 6 99
(James Tate) *chsd ldr over led over 1f out: sn rdn and hdd: styd on same pce ins fnl f* **33/1**
214 **3** *3/4* **Valonia**[21] 6622 2-8-12 96.. JamieSpencer 3 97
(Henry Candy) *lw: racd alone tl jnd main gp 1/2-way: chsd ldrs: rdn over 1f out: styd on same pce ins fnl f* **7/1[3]**
112 **4** *hd* **Lightning Thunder**[15] 6795 2-8-12 110......................... HarryBentley 4 96+
(Olly Stevens) *prom: rdn over 2f out: sn outpcd: rallied ins fnl f: r.o* **8/11[1]**
1222 **5** *nk* **Thewandaofu (IRE)**[14] 6839 2-8-12 77........................... RyanMoore 9 96
(Jamie Osborne) *ang: led: rdn and hdd over 1f out: no ex ins fnl f* **25/1**
1420 **6** *6* **Hoku (IRE)**[6] 7055 2-8-12 98.. JimCrowley 5 80
(Olly Stevens) *hld up: rdn: hung rt and wknd over 1f out* **16/1**
0331 **7** *3* **Ventura Mist**[7] 7026 2-8-12 97................................(p) DuranFentiman 2 72
(Tim Easterby) *swtchd to join main gp 6f out: chsd ldrs: rdn over 2f out: wknd over 1f out* **14/1**
14 **8** *1 3/4* **Lustrous**[29] 6350 2-8-12 0.. RichardHughes 7 68
(Richard Hannon) *lw: hld up: rdn over 2f out: wknd over 1f out* **12/1**

1m 25.54s (0.14) **Going Correction** +0.275s/f (Good) **8 Ran SP% 114.1**
Speed ratings (Par 107): **110,106,105,105,104 98,94,92**
toteswingers 1&2 £16.80, 2&3 £18.50, 1&3 £3.70 CSF £138.01 TOTE £6.00: £1.60, £5.70, £1.60; EX 165.40 Trifecta £1248.60 Pool: £19081.89 - 11.46 winning units..
Owner HE Sh Joaan Bin Hamad Al Thani **Bred** Qatar Bloodstock Ltd **Trained** Newmarket, Suffolk

FOCUS
The Rockfel is often a good pointer to the 1000 Guineas and last year's winner of this, Just The Judge, finished second in the fillies' Classic back here before taking the Irish equivalent. This year's race saw an impressive winner in Al Thakhira, who looks a smart filly. Lightning Thunder was below par, but the rest of the form fits. The field raced stands' side, although Valonia was alone towards the middle early on.

7195 AUTUMN STKS (GROUP 3) 1m
4:55 (4:56) (Class 1) 2-Y-O

£22,684 (£8,600; £4,304; £2,144; £1,076; £540) **Stalls** High

Form | | | | RPR
1 **1** **Kingston Hill**[21] 6641 2-9-0 0.. AndreaAtzeni 5 109+
(Roger Varian) *str: lw: hld up: hdwy over 1f out: shkn up to ld ins fnl f: r.o wl* **15/2[3]**
221 **2** *2* **Oklahoma City**[7] 7017 2-9-0 0..................................(b) JosephO'Brien 9 104
(A P O'Brien, Ire) *overall ldr to 1/2-way: rdn to ld again over 1f out: hdd and unable qck ins fnl f* **6/5[1]**
6211 **3** *1* **Truth Or Dare**[59] 5400 2-9-0 91.. RyanMoore 7 102
(Richard Hannon) *trckd ldrs: rdn over 1f out: styd on same pce ins fnl f* **16/1**
15 **4** *3/4* **God Willing**[16] 6765 2-9-0 0.. JamieSpencer 2 100
(Ed Dunlop) *lw: trckd ldr in centre: rdn: edgd lft and ev ch over 1f out: no ex ins fnl f* **17/2**
2121 **5** *4 1/2* **Safety Check (IRE)**[16] 6763 2-9-0 99.................... MickaelBarzalona 3 91
(Charlie Appleby) *led pair in centre tl overall ldr 1/2-way: rdn: edgd lft and hdd over 1f out: wknd ins fnl f* **7/1[2]**
013 **6** *1 3/4* **Pupil (IRE)**[22] 6593 2-9-0 92.. RichardHughes 6 86
(Richard Hannon) *hld up: hdwy over 2f out: rdn over 1f out: wknd fnl f* **8/1**
41 **7** *3 3/4* **Mount Logan (IRE)**[23] 6570 2-9-0 85.............................. JamesDoyle 4 77
(Luca Cumani) *cmpt: str: hld up: hdwy 1/2-way: rdn over 2f out: sn wknd* **14/1**
2313 **8** *22* **Nezar (IRE)**[16] 6765 2-9-0 96.......................................(p) WilliamBuick 8 26
(William Haggas) *trckd ldrs: pushed along over 3f out: rdn and wknd over 1f out* **14/1**

1m 39.07s (0.47) **Going Correction** +0.275s/f (Good) **8 Ran SP% 110.6**
Speed ratings (Par 105): **108,106,105,104,99 98,94,72**
toteswingers 1&2 £5.20, 2&3 £6.40, 1&3 £8.00 CSF £15.80 TOTE £8.30: £2.00, £1.10, £3.60; EX 20.60 Trifecta £360.40 Pool: £3611.43 - 7.51 winning units..
Owner Paul Smith **Bred** Ridgecourt Stud **Trained** Newmarket, Suffolk

FOCUS
Last year's Autumn Stakes went to subsequent Irish Derby hero Trading Leather. The main action was stands' side, but God Willing and Safety Check raced wide of the others early on. This form is well up to the recent average for the race, Kingston Hill doing it in the style of a horse with more to offer.

7196 DARLEY STKS (GROUP 3) 1m 1f
5:25 (5:28) (Class 1) 3-Y-O+

£34,026 (£12,900; £6,456; £3,216; £1,614; £810) **Stalls** High

Form | | | | RPR
2465 **1** **Highland Knight (IRE)**[27] 6427 6-9-3 104..................(t) DavidProbert 17 113
(Andrew Balding) *mde all: rdn over 1f out: jst hld on* **25/1**
4-51 **2** *shd* **Tales Of Grimm (USA)**[22] 6592 4-9-3 105......................... RyanMoore 13 113
(Richard Fahey) *hld up in tch: shkn up over 1f out: rdn and ev ch ins fnl f: r.o* **16/1**
4002 **3** *1* **Chapter Seven**[21] 6638 4-9-3 103................................... JamieSpencer 7 111
(Stuart Williams) *hld up: rdn over 2f out: hdwy over 1f out: r.o: nt rch ldrs* **14/1**
1-12 **4** *1 1/4* **French Navy**[22] 6592 5-9-3 110.............................. MickaelBarzalona 10 108
(Charlie Appleby) *trckd wnr tl rdn over 2f out: styd on same pce ins fnl f* **5/1[2]**
3111 **5** *1 1/2* **Short Squeeze (IRE)**[14] 6834 3-8-13 106........................ MartinDwyer 18 106+
(Hugo Palmer) *trckd ldrs: racd keenly: chsd wnr over 2f out: rdn and ev ch 1f out: no ex ins fnl f* **9/4[1]**
2334 **6** *nk* **Gabrial (IRE)**[17] 6742 4-9-3 106...................................... PaulHanagan 2 104
(Richard Fahey) *trckd ldr in centre: rdn over 2f out: edgd lft over 1f out: styd on same pce fnl f* **16/1**
2016 **7** *2 1/4* **Kassiano (GER)**[21] 6636 4-9-3 113........................... SilvestreDeSousa 15 99
(Saeed bin Suroor) *swtg: s.i.s: sn prom: rdn over 2f out: eased whn btn wl ins fnl f* **7/1**

15-0 **8** 1¾ **Bronze Angel (IRE)**[14] 6838 4-9-3 100 ....(p) JimCrowley 6 95
(Marcus Tregoning) *hld up: swtchd rt over 3f out: rdn over 1f out: n.d* **16/1**

-321 **9** nk **Amralah (IRE)**[14] 6841 3-8-13 89 .... TomQueally 11 95
(Mick Channon) *hld up: rdn over 3f out: n.d* **25/1**

131- **10** 1 **Tullius (IRE)**[422] 5278 5-9-3 112 .... RichardHughes 1 92
(Andrew Balding) *hld up: swtchd rt over 3f out: rdn over 1f out: wknd ins fnl f* **13/2**[3]

1054 **11** 3¾ **Pavlosk (USA)**[50] 5725 3-8-10 103 .... JamesDoyle 5 82
(Sir Michael Stoute) *hld up in tch: racd keenly: rdn over 2f out: n.m.r and wknd over 1f out* **14/1**

4350 **12** 2¼ **Proud Chieftain**[14] 6838 5-9-3 95 ....(p) GrahamLee 9 79
(Clifford Lines) *chsd ldrs tl rdn and wknd over 2f out* **50/1**

0143 **13** 18 **Premio Loco (USA)**[15] 6797 9-9-3 111 .... GeorgeBaker 3 39
(Chris Wall) *led centre pair tl pushed along over 3f out: wknd over 2f out* **20/1**

1m 51.21s (-0.49) **Going Correction** +0.275s/f (Good)
WFA 3 from 4yo+ 4lb **13 Ran SP% 118.7**
Speed ratings (Par 113): **113,112,112,110,109 109,107,105,105,104 101,99,83**
toteswingers 1&2 £42.50, 2&3 £17.20, 1&3 £45.10 CSF £364.70 TOTE £38.90: £9.70, £3.80, £4.90; EX 1166.80 Trifecta £2182.80 Part won. Pool: £2910.41 - 0.26 winning units..
Owner J C Smith **Bred** Littleton Stud **Trained** Kingsclere, Hants

FOCUS
A race hit by five non-runners, but it still served up a stirring finish. The first five raced nearest the stands' rail, which seemed an advantage on the day. The winner is rated back to something like his best.

T/Jkpt: Not won. T/Plt: £906.80 to a £1 stake. Pool of £166313.95 - 133.88 winning tickets. T/Qpdt: £87.40 to a £1 stake. Pool of £10010.69 - 84.75 winning tickets. CR

7162 WOLVERHAMPTON (A.W) (L-H)
Saturday, October 12

OFFICIAL GOING: Standard
Wind: Almost nil Weather: Cloudy, some rain

7197 £32 BONUS AT 32RED.COM H'CAP — 5f 216y(P)
5:50 (5:55) (Class 6) (0-60,60) 3-Y-O+ **£1,940** (£577; £288; £144) **Stalls** Low

Form RPR

555 **1** **Greek Spirit (IRE)**[117] 3401 3-9-3 57 .... SebSanders 11 69+
(Jeremy Noseda) *hld up towards rr: smooth hdwy on outer 2f out: led 1f out: rdn out: readily* **7/2**[1]

0530 **2** 1½ **Logans Lad (IRE)**[29] 6368 3-9-6 60 ....(t) StephenCraine 6 67
(John Stimpson) *hld up in midfield: rdn to chse ldrs over 2f out: r.o to take 2nd ins fnl f* **4/1**[2]

3602 **3** ¾ **Whipphound**[30] 6344 5-9-4 60 .... RyanClark(3) 12 65
(Mark Brisbourne) *trckd ldrs gng wl: wnt 2nd 2f out: jnd ldrs and hrd rdn over 1f out: unable qck* **15/2**[3]

6050 **4** 2½ **Bitaphon (IRE)**[15] 6803 4-8-10 54 ....(t) TobyAtkinson(5) 7 51
(Michael Appleby) *chsd ldrs: rdn over 2f out: one pce appr fnl f* **10/1**

0400 **5** 1¼ **Red Shadow**[203] 1147 4-8-9 51 .... PaulPickard(3) 9 44
(Alan Brown) *led: rdn over 2f out: hdd & wknd 1f out* **33/1**

01 **6** hd **Game All (IRE)**[17] 6752 4-9-7 60 ....(b) PatCosgrave 1 52
(Hugo Palmer) *mid-div: outpcd over 2f out: styd on same pce fnl f* **4/1**[2]

-000 **7** 2½ **Izzy Boy (USA)**[9] 6969 3-9-3 57 .... AdrianNicholls 10 41
(Mark Johnston) *a wd: in tch: rdn along over 3f out: btn over 2f out* **12/1**

6001 **8** 3½ **Give Us A Belle (IRE)**[5] 7068 4-8-12 51 6ex ....(vt) AdamBeschizza 5 24
(Christine Dunnett) *towards rr: rdn over 3f out: nvr able to chal* **14/1**

6036 **9** ¾ **Steel City Boy (IRE)**[5] 7079 10-8-6 50 .... AnnStokell(5) 8 21
(Ann Stokell) *pressed ldr for 4f: wknd over 1f out* **33/1**

4030 **10** ½ **Steelcut**[17] 6752 9-9-2 60 ....(p) JacobButterfield(5) 3 29
(Mark Buckley) *dwlt: in rr: drvn along on outer 3f out: nvr nr ldrs* **20/1**

6305 **11** 1 **One Last Dream**[9] 6980 4-9-1 54 ....(b) SteveDrowne 2 20
(Ron Hodges) *chsd ldrs on rail tl wknd over 2f out* **10/1**

0-06 **12** 9 **Red Bay**[33] 6259 4-8-13 57 .... IanBurns(5) 4
(Jane Chapple-Hyam) *a outpcd in rr: no ch fnl 2f* **25/1**

1m 14.78s (-0.22) **Going Correction** +0.075s/f (Slow)
WFA 3 from 4yo+ 1lb **12 Ran SP% 121.0**
Speed ratings (Par 101): **104,102,101,97,96 95,92,87,86,86 84,72**
toteswingers 1&2 £8.70, 1&3 £9.00, 2&3 £7.20 CSF £16.85 CT £101.01 TOTE £4.40: £2.40, £2.50, £2.60; EX 26.50 Trifecta £98.30 Pool: £779.43 - 5.94 winning units..
Owner A Ferguson **Bred** Maddenstown Equine Enterprise Ltd **Trained** Newmarket, Suffolk

FOCUS
A competitive, low-grade sprint handicap which was sound run. The winner can do better still.

7198 32REDPOKER.COM NURSERY H'CAP (DIV I) — 5f 216y(P)
6:20 (6:21) (Class 6) (0-65,64) 2-Y-O **£1,940** (£433; £433; £144) **Stalls** Low

Form RPR

2556 **1** **Tautira (IRE)**[50] 5693 2-9-3 63 .... WilliamTwiston-Davies(3) 7 68
(Michael Bell) *sn prom on outer: led after 2f: rdn and over 2 l ahd 2f out: drvn along fnl f: a in control* **18/1**

406 **2** 1¼ **Tanojin (IRE)**[17] 6746 2-9-0 60 .... CharlesBishop(3) 3 61+
(Mick Channon) *s.i.s: hld up in rr: rdn and hdwy 2f out: hung lft: r.o u.p to dead-heat for 2nd on line* **5/1**[2]

4000 **2** dht **Black Geronimo**[31] 6311 2-8-11 57 ....(v[1]) DeclanBates(3) 9 58
(David Evans) *led for 2f: chsd wnr after: unable qck fnl f: a hld* **20/1**

4233 **4** ½ **The Dukkerer (IRE)**[16] 6778 2-9-2 62 .... JulieBurke(3) 10 62
(David O'Meara) *broke wl: settled in 5th: rdn and one pce fnl 2f* **5/1**[2]

5430 **5** 1¼ **Exceed Areeda (IRE)**[22] 6605 2-9-7 64 .... LukeMorris 1 60+
(James Tate) *hld up in rr: hdwy in centre and hrd rdn over 1f out: styd on* **13/2**[3]

6606 **6** 1¾ **Almost Famous (IRE)**[9] 6979 2-8-10 53 .... SteveDrowne 2 44
(Jamie Osborne) *hld up in rr: rdn and sme hdwy over 1f out: nt rch ldrs* **10/1**

5032 **7** 2½ **Sukari Gold (IRE)**[25] 6494 2-9-1 58 ....(b) RichardKingscote 4 41
(Tom Dascombe) *chsd ldrs on rail: lost pl 3f out: sn rdn and btn* **7/2**[1]

0660 **8** 2¾ **Reale Silenzio**[4] 7096 2-8-2 45 ....(v[1]) CathyGannon 5 20
(John Weymes) *prom: outpcd by ldng pair over 2f out: sn lost pl* **66/1**

553 **9** ½ **Paradise Child**[68] 5066 2-8-7 50 .... JimmyQuinn 6 24
(Bill Turner) *hld up in midfield: outpcd over 2f out: sn rdn and n.d* **22/1**

04 **10** 6 **Tez**[65] 5194 2-9-1 63 .... TobyAtkinson(5) 8 19
(Marco Botti) *s.i.s: t.k.h towards rr: bhd fnl 2f* **7/2**[1]

1m 16.56s (1.56) **Going Correction** +0.075s/f (Slow) **10 Ran SP% 116.1**
Speed ratings (Par 93): **92,90,90,89,88 85,82,78,78,70**
PLACE: Tanojin £1.60, Black Geronimo £7.00. F/C: TAU&TAN £51.54, TAU&BG £161.73. EX: TAU&TAN £53.50, TAU&BG £251.90. T/C: TAU&TAN&BG £934.64, TAU&BG&TAN £1051.75. CSF £161.73 CT £1051.75 TOTE £14.70: £4.30, £7.00; EX 251.90 Trifecta £309.20 Part won..
Owner Sheikh Marwan Al Maktoum **Bred** Darley **Trained** Newmarket, Suffolk
■ Stewards' Enquiry : Declan Bates five-day ban: failed to ride out for 2nd (Oct 26,28-31)

FOCUS
The first division of a modest nursery with most of the runners looking exposed.

7199 32REDPOKER.COM NURSERY H'CAP (DIV II) — 5f 216y(P)
6:50 (6:51) (Class 6) (0-65,64) 2-Y-O **£1,940** (£577; £288; £144) **Stalls** Low

Form RPR

0451 **1** **Shyron**[9] 6979 2-9-0 64 .... JordanVaughan(7) 8 73+
(George Margarson) *s.s and wl bhd: 7 l detached at 1/2-way: rapid hdwy on inner to ld 1f out: sn clr: comf* **4/6**[1]

3430 **2** 2 **Stoney Quine (IRE)**[22] 6582 2-9-1 58 .... TomEaves 4 57
(Keith Dalgleish) *chsd ldrs: rdn 2f out: kpt on to take 2nd ins fnl f: no ch w wnr* **25/1**

564 **3** ½ **Clapperboard**[30] 6342 2-9-6 63 .... RichardKingscote 9 61
(Paul Fitzsimons) *chsd ldr: rdn 2f out: one pce appr fnl f* **9/1**[3]

2050 **4** 2 **Where The Boys Are (IRE)**[19] 6695 2-9-4 61 .... SebSanders 7 53
(Ed McMahon) *led: rdn over 2f out: hdd & wknd 1f out* **11/1**

0003 **5** 2 **Sweet Amaalie (IRE)**[9] 6979 2-8-12 55 .... JohnFahy 2 41
(William Haggas) *towards rr: outpcd and struggling 1/2-way: wd st: sme late hdwy* **11/2**[2]

640 **6** 2 **Shirley Vanessa (IRE)**[19] 6689 2-8-8 51 .... SamHitchcott 1 31
(Luke Dace) *dwlt: towards rr: rdn over 3f out: nvr able to chal* **28/1**

3156 **7** 3¼ **Limegrove**[3] 7117 2-9-0 62 .... NoelGarbutt(5) 6 32
(David Evans) *dwlt: towards rr: rdn 4f out: n.d* **10/1**

2060 **8** ¾ **Emily Davison (IRE)**[9] 6979 2-8-12 58 .... LMcNiff(3) 3 26
(David C Griffiths) *prom on rail: rdn over 2f out: wknd over 1f out* **33/1**

6304 **9** 2½ **Ibecke**[18] 6725 2-8-4 47 .... AdrianNicholls 5 7
(Mark Johnston) *sltly hmpd s and swtchd to outer: t.k.h early: chsd ldrs: wd and rdn on bnd over 3f out: wknd 2f out* **25/1**

1m 15.79s (0.79) **Going Correction** +0.075s/f (Slow) **9 Ran SP% 116.9**
Speed ratings (Par 93): **97,94,93,91,88 85,81,80,77**
toteswingers 1&2 £3.90, 1&3 £5.40, 2&3 £12.50 CSF £27.48 CT £96.18 TOTE £1.90: £1.10, £4.20, £2.50; EX 24.50 Trifecta £101.60 Pool: £1886.86 - 13.92 winning units..
Owner F Butler **Bred** F Butler **Trained** Newmarket, Suffolk

FOCUS
A similarly modest bunch to the first division with the exception of the winner.

7200 32RED EBF MAIDEN STKS — 5f 216y(P)
7:20 (7:22) (Class 5) 2-Y-O **£2,911** (£866; £432; £216) **Stalls** Low

Form RPR

43 **1** **Look Here's Al**[30] 6342 2-9-5 0 .... SebSanders 3 71
(Ed McMahon) *trckd ldrs gng wl: rdn to ld over 1f out: drvn out* **13/8**[1]

6 **2** 1¼ **Jolly Red Jeanz (IRE)**[15] 6789 2-9-0 0 .... MartinLane 10 62
(J W Hills) *prom: rdn and wd into st: hung lft and wnt 2nd 1f out: r.o* **12/1**

0 **3** 1½ **Aurelia Cotta (IRE)**[15] 6789 2-9-0 0 .... SteveDrowne 9 58
(Charles Hills) *pressed ldr: led 3f out tl over 1f out: one pce* **3/1**[2]

00 **4** nk **Exceeding Power**[15] 6790 2-9-5 0 .... LukeMorris 5 62
(Michael Bell) *mid-div on outer: effrt and wd into st: hmpd and swtchd lft over 1f out: styd on* **17/2**

55 **5** 1¼ **Caesars Gift (IRE)**[159] 2082 2-8-12 0 .... AdamMcLean(7) 8 58
(Derek Shaw) *towards rr: shkn up and sme hdwy over 1f out: no imp* **66/1**

4004 **6** nk **Alaskan Night (IRE)**[11] 6914 2-9-0 57 .... ShaneGray(5) 7 57
(Kevin Ryan) *led tl 3f out: wknd over 1f out* **11/1**

7 16 **Secret Suspect** 2-9-0 0 ....[1] TomMcLaughlin 2 4
(Ed Walker) *midfield to rr: rdn 3f out: effrt on inner ent st: eased whn no imp over 1f out* **4/1**[3]

8 8 **Minnyvinny** 2-9-0 0 .... CathyGannon 1
(Frank Sheridan) *missed break and lost 10 l: a wl bhd* **66/1**

1m 16.1s (1.10) **Going Correction** +0.075s/f (Slow) **8 Ran SP% 112.6**
Speed ratings (Par 95): **95,93,91,90,89 88,67,56**
toteswingers 1&2 £3.20, 1&3 £2.40, 2&3 £19.20 CSF £22.56 TOTE £2.70: £1.40, £3.10, £1.30; EX 15.70 Trifecta £39.20 Pool: £2084.77 - 39.78 winning units..
Owner S L Edwards **Bred** S L Edwards **Trained** Lichfield, Staffs

FOCUS
An ordinary maiden.

7201 32REDBET.COM H'CAP — 1m 1f 103y(P)
7:50 (7:50) (Class 6) (0-55,58) 3-Y-O+ **£1,940** (£577; £288; £144) **Stalls** Low

Form RPR

0-62 **1** **Cantor**[14] 6851 5-9-7 55 .... PatrickDonaghy 3 66
(Giles Bravery) *rdn to chse ldr leaving stalls: led 3f out: rdn and wd into st: drvn clr 1f out: styd on wl* **3/1**[1]

0615 **2** 2¾ **Kyle Of Bute**[14] 6851 7-8-12 51 .... NoelGarbutt(5) 2 56
(Richard Ford) *prom: chsd wnr over 2f out: hrd rdn over 1f out: kpt on same pce* **25/1**

5064 **3** 1¼ **Count Ceprano (IRE)**[204] 1120 9-8-10 47 .... SimonPearce(3) 7 49
(Lydia Pearce) *hld up towards rr: sme hdwy and rdn 3f out: styd on wl fnl f: tk 3rd on line* **28/1**

2203 **4** hd **Greyemkay**[14] 6851 5-8-12 51 .... DanielMuscutt(5) 5 53
(Richard Price) *in tch: effrt over 2f out: wnt 3rd and hung lft over 1f out: one pce* **8/1**

2444 **5** nk **Chasin' Rainbows**[37] 6137 5-9-3 51 .... CathyGannon 4 52
(Sylvester Kirk) *dwlt: sn in midfield: wnt 5th 6f out: hung rt on bnd into st: rdn and styd on same pce* **8/1**

6062 **6** 1½ **Bond Artist (IRE)**[9] 6986 4-9-2 50 .... TomEaves 11 48
(Geoffrey Oldroyd) *hld up in rr: sme hdwy in centre and hrd rdn over 1f out: nvr nrr* **7/1**[3]

05 **7** 3½ **Gadobout Dancer**[9] 6986 6-8-13 47 ....(t) LukeMorris 12 38
(Julie Camacho) *towards rr: rdn 3f out: modest effrt over 1f out: nt trble ldrs* **33/1**

2201 **8** 3¼ **Scepticism (USA)**[7] 7035 3-9-1 58 .... JoshBaudains(5) 1 43
(Charlie Mann) *led tl 3f out: wknd wl over 1f out* **7/2**[2]

004 **9** 1¾ **Operettist**[67] 5091 4-8-11 48 .... MarkCoumbe(3) 9 28
(Tony Carroll) *bhd: pushed along over 3f out: nvr nr ldrs* **25/1**

3536 **10** 4 **Elizabeth Coffee (IRE)**[26] 6479 5-8-13 52 ....(t) JoeyHaynes(5) 10 24
(John Weymes) *rdn to post: t.k.h towards rr: rdn and n.d fnl 3f* **11/1**

6-00 **11** ¾ **Hartlebury**[79] 4667 3-9-3 55 .... JimmyQuinn 8 26
(James Bethell) *mid-div: sn pushed along: lost pl and struggling over 3f out: bhd and eased over 1f out* **8/1**

200 **12** *9* **Willow Island (IRE)**[29] 6366 4-8-11 **48**........................ DeclanBates(3) 13
(David Evans) *chsd ldrs on outer: rdn 5f out: wknd 4f out: bhd and eased fnl 3f* **22/1**

2m 3.16s (1.46) **Going Correction** +0.075s/f (Slow)
WFA 3 from 4yo+ 4lb **12** Ran SP% **119.8**
Speed ratings (Par 101): **96,93,92,92,92 90,87,84,83,79 78,70**
toteswingers 1&2 £6.50, 1&3 £42.50, 2&3 £65.50 CSF £88.58 CT £1797.86 TOTE £3.40: £1.70, £4.80, £3.70; EX 60.90 Trifecta £1154.00 Part won. Pool: £1538.70 - 0.12 winning units..
Owner Jim Tew **Bred** Cheveley Park Stud Ltd **Trained** Newmarket, Suffolk

FOCUS
Quite a competitive handicap. The winner is rated back to his best and the runner-up to his recent C&D win.

7202 32RED.COM NURSERY H'CAP 7f 32y(P)
8:20 (8:20) (Class 5) (0-75,75) 2-Y-O **£2,911** (£866; £432; £216) **Stalls** High

Form RPR
0601 **1** **Lawyer (IRE)**[16] 6778 2-9-7 **75**.. AdamKirby 4 79+
(Luca Cumani) *hld up in midfield: hdwy and swtchd ins ent st: drvn to ld ins fnl f* **5/6**[1]

5551 **2** *1/2* **More Aspen (USA)**[22] 6605 2-9-5 **73**.............................. MartinHarley 2 76
(Marco Botti) *chsd ldrs: effrt 2f out: drvn to chal over 1f out: r.o: jst hld* **7/2**[2]

4330 **3** *1 3/4* **Sullivan Street (IRE)**[4] 7088 2-9-4 **72**............................... MartinLane 7 70
(Charlie Appleby) *chsd ldr: led 3f out: rdn 2 l ahd 2f out: hdd ins fnl f: one pce* **12/1**[3]

4244 **4** *1 1/4* **Boogangoo (IRE)**[21] 6619 2-9-5 **73**............................... TomEaves 11 68
(Keith Dalgleish) *hld up in midfield: rdn over 2f out: styd on fnl f* **20/1**

3124 **5** *3/4* **Pyjama Day**[23] 6572 2-9-6 **74**...(b) PatCosgrave 8 68
(Hugo Palmer) *prom on outer: wd on bnd and rdn over 2f out: no ex over 1f out* **14/1**

0236 **6** *nse* **China In My Hands**[17] 6749 2-8-7 **64**........................ CharlesBishop(3) 3 57
(Mick Channon) *dwlt: sn trcking ldrs: rdn over 2f out: edgd lft and btn over 1f out* **50/1**

3166 **7** *1 1/4* **Yajamila**[32] 6284 2-9-5 **73**...(p) LukeMorris 9 63
(James Tate) *towards rr: drvn along over 2f out: sme hdwy on inner over 1f out: nt rch ldrs* **33/1**

434 **8** *2* **Sound Of Summer (IRE)**[30] 6318 2-9-5 **73**................. SteveDrowne 10 59
(Charles Hills) *stdd s: hld up towards rr: rdn over 3f out: nvr able to chal* **14/1**

4322 **9** *9* **Amadaffair**[22] 6605 2-8-9 **63**...................................... RichardKingscote 6 26
(Tom Dascombe) *led tl 3f out: wknd 2f out* **20/1**

1512 **10** *2* **Lady Captain (IRE)**[54] 5591 2-9-0 **68**.......................... StephenCraine 5 27
(Kevin Ryan) *dwlt: a bhd* **66/1**

542 **11** *35* **Monte Viso**[16] 6776 2-9-2 **70**.. ShaneKelly 1
(Stuart Kittow) *in tch: wknd 4f out: bhd whn virtually p.u ins fnl 2f* **25/1**

1m 30.03s (0.43) **Going Correction** +0.075s/f (Slow) **11** Ran SP% **117.6**
Speed ratings (Par 95): **100,99,97,96,95 95,93,91,81,78 38**
toteswingers 1&2 £2.50, 1&3 £4.30, 2&3 £3.70 CSF £3.19 CT £20.27 TOTE £2.20: £1.10, £1.30, £3.70; EX 4.20 Trifecta £27.60 Pool: £2091.24 - 56.74 winning units..
Owner Sheikh Mohammed Obaid Al Maktoum **Bred** Drumlin Bloodstock **Trained** Newmarket, Suffolk

FOCUS
A fair 7f nursery run at a decent pace.

7203 32RED CASINO MAIDEN STKS 5f 20y(P)
8:50 (8:50) (Class 5) 3-Y-O+ **£2,587** (£770; £384; £192) **Stalls** Low

Form RPR
6530 **1** **Talqaa**[12] 6901 3-8-11 54.. CharlesBishop(3) 7 55
(Mick Channon) *towards rr: hdwy in centre over 1f out: slt ld jst ins fnl f: drvn ahd fnl 75yds* **11/4**[2]

0034 **2** *1* **Borough Boy (IRE)**[8] 6994 3-9-5 49..................................(v) TomEaves 8 56
(Derek Shaw) *patiently rdn in 5th: hdwy 2f out: rdn to join ldrs 1f out: jst outpcd fnl 75yds* **10/3**[3]

5005 **3** *1 1/2* **Busy Bimbo (IRE)**[4] 7101 4-8-11 47............................... MarkCoumbe(3) 1 45
(Alan Berry) *chsd ldrs: effrt on inner and clsd ent st: one pce fnl f* **15/2**

0-50 **4** *1/2* **Mid Yorkshire Golf**[157] 2169 4-8-11 45.......................... SladeO'Hara(3) 3 43
(Peter Grayson) *s.s: outpcd and bhd: wd into st: edgd lft fr over 1f out: 5th and styng on whn nt clr run ins fnl f: gng on at fin* **33/1**

053 **5** *1 1/2* **Daneglow (IRE)**[14] 6849 3-9-0 48.. ShaneKelly 6 38
(Mike Murphy) *sn led and set fast pce: 4 l clr after 1f: hdd & wknd jst ins fnl f* **5/1**

00- **6** *2 1/4* **Stoneacre Thirsk (IRE)**[388] 6362 4-9-0 .... StephenCraine 4 29
(Peter Grayson) *dwlt: outpcd and bhd: nvr nr ldrs* **40/1**

004 **7** *1/2* **Redalani (IRE)**[10] 6940 3-8-11 58.................................. PaulPickard(3) 2 29
(Alan Brown) *prom: chsd clr ldr after 1f tl hrd rdn and wknd over 1f out* **5/2**[1]

-600 **8** *7* **Mrs Medley**[8] 6994 7-8-9 27...(be) AnnStokell(5) 5
(Ann Stokell) *chsd ldr for 1f: prom in chsng gp tl wknd over 2f out* **80/1**

1m 3.42s (1.12) **Going Correction** +0.075s/f (Slow) **8** Ran SP% **113.4**
Speed ratings (Par 103): **94,92,90,89,86 83,82,71**
toteswingers 1&2 £2.80, 1&3 £5.90, 2&3 £2.10 CSF £12.10 TOTE £4.30: £1.10, £1.80, £3.00; EX 11.90 Trifecta £98.80 Pool: £1956.85 - 14.85 winning units..
Owner Sheikh Mohammed Bin Khalifa Al Maktoum **Bred** Card Bloodstock **Trained** West Ilsley, Berks

FOCUS
A weak maiden sprint with little strength in depth where the strong pace panned out nicely for the winner. The first two both had a regressive profile.

7204 32REDBINGO.COM H'CAP 1m 4f 50y(P)
9:20 (9:20) (Class 6) (0-60,60) 3-Y-O **£1,940** (£577; £288; £144) **Stalls** Low

Form RPR
6062 **1** **Hurricane John (IRE)**[9] 6964 3-8-12 **51**........................ AdrianNicholls 8 57
(David Nicholls) *pressed ldr: drvn along fr 1/2-way: slt ld ins fnl f: all out* **5/1**[3]

0052 **2** *nk* **Our Golden Girl**[29] 6361 3-8-13 **55**..................................(b) RobertTart(3) 5 60
(Shaun Lycett) *hld up in 6th: rdn and hdwy over 1f out: jnd ldrs ent fnl f: r.o* **6/1**

1154 **3** *shd* **See And Be Seen**[12] 6899 3-9-6 **59**...................................(p) AdamKirby 7 64
(Sylvester Kirk) *chsd ldrs on outer: led 3f out and sn kicked on: edgd rt and hdd ins fnl f: kpt on* **2/1**[2]

-412 **4** *1/2* **Ana Shababiya (IRE)**[28] 6406 3-9-7 **60**.......................... HarryBentley 4 64
(Ismail Mohammed) *plld hrd: cl up: rdn 3f out: pressed ldrs fnl f: kpt on* **7/4**[1]

406 **5** *17* **Bullseye Babe**[29] 6361 3-8-7 **51**.....................................(e) JoeyHaynes(5) 3 28
(Mark Usher) *chsd ldrs tl wknd over 2f out* **14/1**

-005 **6** *13* **Spirit Man**[9] 6968 3-8-13 **52**... KierenFox 1 8
(Derek Shaw) *led tl 3f out: wknd 2f out* **28/1**

300- **7** *7* **Vegas Belle**[411] 5675 3-8-12 **51**... TomEaves 6
(Geoffrey Oldroyd) *dwlt: a bhd: no ch fnl 3f* **20/1**

6050 **8** *1* **Lady Margaeux (IRE)**[105] 3809 3-9-2 **58**........................ PaulPickard(3) 2 1
(Alan Brown) *dwlt: a bhd: no ch fnl 3f* **33/1**

2m 43.59s (2.49) **Going Correction** +0.075s/f (Slow) **8** Ran SP% **118.5**
Speed ratings (Par 99): **94,93,93,93,82 73,68,68**
toteswingers 1&2 £6.40, 1&3 £16.80, 2&3 £6.40 CSF £35.06 CT £79.97 TOTE £5.10: £2.00, £2.40, £1.10; EX 28.00 Trifecta £81.10 Pool: £1841.62 - 17.01 winning units..
Owner John Nicholls (Trading) Ltd **Bred** Michael O'Rahilly **Trained** Sessay, N Yorks

FOCUS
A low-grade middle-distance handicap with little strength in depth but a thrilling finish in which four of the runners had every chance inside the final furlong. The time was slow and the winner built on his latest form.

T/Plt: £77.20 to a £1 stake. Pool: £97043.22 - 916.84 winning tickets T/Qpdt: £3.40 to a £1 stake. Pool: £11579.97 - 2479.25 winning tickets LM

7170 YORK (L-H)
Saturday, October 12

OFFICIAL GOING: Good (good to soft in places; 6.4)
Wind: moderate 1/2 against Weather: overcast, damp, light rain

7205 CORAL MOBILE THREE CLICKS TO BET STKS (H'CAP) 1m 208y
1:50 (1:51) (Class 2) (0-100,99) 3-Y-O **£16,172** (£4,812; £2,405; £1,202) **Stalls** Low

Form RPR
1245 **1** **Seek Again (USA)**[14] 6838 3-9-5 **97**............................... RobertHavlin 7 109
(John Gosden) *trckd ldrs: chal stands' side over 1f out: led last 100yds: styd on wl* **3/1**[1]

3125 **2** *1 3/4* **Gabrial's Kaka (IRE)**[14] 6823 3-9-2 **94**........................ TomEaves 11 102
(Richard Fahey) *led 2f: hung lft and led over 3f out: hdd and no ex ins fnl f* **16/1**

3635 **3** *3/4* **Centurius**[14] 6834 3-9-2 **94**.. AdamKirby 2 100
(Marco Botti) *in rr: effrt over 3f out: chsng ldrs over 1f out: kpt on same pce* **12/1**

5043 **4** *2 1/4* **Romantic Settings**[14] 6823 3-9-1 **93**.......................... TonyHamilton 5 94
(Richard Fahey) *chsd ldrs: outpcd and lost pl 6f out: kpt on fnl 2f* **10/1**

6104 **5** *1/2* **Jeeraan (USA)**[16] 6767 3-8-9 **87**..................................... DaneO'Neill 10 87
(Ed Dunlop) *stdd s: hld up in rr: hdwy stands' side over 2f out: kpt on* **16/1**

6 *nk* **Lillebonne (FR)**[106] 3-8-10 **88**................................... DanielTudhope 4 88
(David O'Meara) *trckd ldrs: effrt over 3f out: chsng ldrs over 2f out: wknd appr fnl f* **25/1**

3020 **7** *2 1/4* **Beedee**[13] 6868 3-8-8 **86**.. SeanLevey 8 81
(Richard Hannon) *mid-div: effrt 3f out: wknd over 1f out* **33/1**

0152 **8** *nk* **Butterfly McQueen (USA)**[38] 6124 3-9-2 **97**........... ThomasBrown(3) 3 91
(Andrew Balding) *chsd ldrs: drvn over 3f out: wknd over 1f out* **5/1**[3]

2114 **9** *1 3/4* **King Of The Danes**[14] 6823 3-8-11 **89**............................ LiamJones 6 79
(Mark Johnston) *w ldr: led after 2f: hdd over 3f out: lost pl 2f out* **10/1**

6030 **10** *5* **King George River (IRE)**[14] 6838 3-9-7 **99**............. RobertWinston 1 78
(Alan Bailey) *hld up in mid-div: eddort over 3f out: hung rt and lost pl 2f out* **7/1**

1211 **P** **Thouwra (IRE)**[13] 6867 3-9-2 **94**....................................(p) KierenFallon 9
(Saeed bin Suroor) *hld up in rr: p.u over 7f out: lame* **4/1**[2]

1m 50.08s (-1.92) **Going Correction** -0.05s/f (Good) **11** Ran SP% **118.6**
Speed ratings (Par 107): **106,104,103,101,101 101,99,98,97,92**
toteswingers 1&2 £6.90, 2&3 £65.20, 1&3 £5.80 CSF £54.58 CT £525.02 TOTE £4.00: £1.90, £3.50, £5.70; EX 31.50 Trifecta £114.40 Pool: £1659.01 - 10.86 winning units..
Owner K Abdullah **Bred** Juddmonte Farms Inc **Trained** Newmarket, Suffolk

FOCUS
Racing on inside line and races of 1m and over decreased in distance by 24yds. Just 0.5mm of rain the previous day and dry overnight, so the going was left as good, good to soft in places, and jockeys returning after the first concurred. A strong 3yo handicap and solid form, the winner progressing again.

7206 CORAL APP DOWNLOAD FROM THE APP STORE STKS (H'CAP) 1m 2f 88y
2:20 (2:26) (Class 2) (0-112,110) 3-Y-O+**£19,407** (£5,775; £2,886; £1,443) **Stalls** Low

Form RPR
1 **Seussical (IRE)**[127] 3074 3-9-0 **103**................................. AdamKirby 11 116
(Luca Cumani) *hld up towards rr: hdwy 3f out: trckd ldrs 2f out: swtchd lft and rdn to ld jst over 1f out: styd on strly* **6/1**[3]

4450 **2** *4* **Area Fifty One**[14] 6838 5-9-0 **103**........................ GeorgeChaloner(5) 4 108
(Richard Fahey) *led 2f: cl up: rdn and ev ch 2f out: drvn and kpt on same pce fnl f* **16/1**

6140 **3** *1/2* **Strictly Silver (IRE)**[14] 6838 4-9-1 **102**.......................(p) RobertTart(3) 7 106
(Alan Bailey) *hld up: hdwy 3f out: rdn along whn n.m.r wl over 1f out: swtchd lft and drvn ent fnl f: kpt on wl towards fin* **8/1**

0101 **4** *1 1/2* **Excellent Result (IRE)**[35] 6186 3-8-10 **99**.................. RobertWinston 5 100
(Saeed bin Suroor) *in tch: hdwy 4f out: led 3f out: rdn along and hdd over 2f out: cl up tl drvn and one pce ent fnl f* **9/2**[2]

1305 **5** *hd* **First Mohican**[21] 6620 5-9-10 **108**................................ JimmyFortune 1 109
(Lady Cecil) *trckd ldrs: effrt wl over 2f out: rdn wl over 1f out: drvn and one pce appr fnl f* **4/1**[1]

6 **6** *1/2* **Charles Camoin (IRE)**[17] 6741 5-9-0 **93**........................... LiamKeniry 14 98
(Sylvester Kirk) *hld up in rr: hdwy wl over 2f out: swtchd rt and rdn over 1f out: styd on fnl f: nrst fin* **25/1**

2610 **7** *3/4* **Sam Sharp (USA)**[14] 6838 7-9-0 **97**...................... RichardKingscote 12 96
(Ian Williams) *s.i.s and in rr: hdwy wl over 2f out: sn rdn and n.d* **15/2**

0U00 **8** *1* **Fort Bastion (IRE)**[7] 7018 4-9-0 **98**.................................... LeeTopliss 2 95
(Richard Fahey) *s.i.s and in rr: sme hdwy over 3f out: rdn along over 2f out: n.d* **33/1**

4202 **9** *shd* **Benzanno (IRE)**[13] 6868 4-8-11 **93**.......................... ThomasBrown(3) 10 94
(Andrew Balding) *trckd ldrs: smooth hdwy 4f out: led over 2f out: sn rdn and hdd over 1f out: wknd* **16/1**

1000 **10** *2 1/2* **Prince Of Johanne (IRE)**[14] 6838 7-9-4 **102**................(p) DavidNolan 3 94
(Tom Tate) *hld up: rdn along wl over 3f out: sn btn* **28/1**

4040 **11** *1 1/2* **Black Spirit (USA)**[21] 6638 6-8-11 **100**........................(tp) RyanTate(5) 9 89
(Clive Cox) *prom: trckd ldr 1/2-way: rdn along 3f out: sn wknd* **16/1**

1666 **12** *11* **Broughton (GER)**[13] 6868 3-8-9 **91**.................................... LiamJones 8 66
(Mark Johnston) *chsd ldrs: rdn along over 3f out: sn wknd* **28/1**

2031 **13** *8* **Out Of Bounds (USA)**[31] 6307 4-9-12 **110**........................ KierenFallon 6 63
(Saeed bin Suroor) *cl up: led after 2f: rdn along over 3f out: sn hdd & wknd fnl 2f* **7/1**

2m 9.03s (-3.47) **Going Correction** -0.05s/f (Good)
WFA 3 from 4yo+ 5lb **13** Ran SP% **119.2**
Speed ratings (Par 109): **111,107,107,106,106 105,105,104,104,102 100,92,85**
toteswingers 1&2 £16.20, 2&3 £25.60, 1&3 £8.60 CSF £93.28 CT £780.41 TOTE £7.10: £2.80, £4.20, £3.00; EX 117.00 Trifecta £1526.50 Pool: £2438.32 - 1.19 winning units..
Owner O T I Racing **Bred** Danehill Music Syndicate **Trained** Newmarket, Suffolk

FOCUS
A decent handicap, but there weren't too many progressive, well-handicapped types in attendance. Sound if exposed form, the winner the exception.

7207 CORAL.CO.UK ROCKINGHAM STKS (LISTED RACE) 6f
2:55 (2:55) (Class 1) 2-Y-O
£25,519 (£9,675; £4,842; £2,412; £1,210; £607) **Stalls** Centre

Form RPR

1 **1** **Mushir**[17] 6747 2-9-0 0.. DaneO'Neill 9 103+
(Roger Varian) *hld up in rr: nt clr run and swtchd to wd outside 2f out: r.o to ld last 100yds: hld on nr fin* **11/2**[3]

213 **2** *hd* **No Leaf Clover (IRE)**[22] 6582 2-9-0 80.................... RobertWinston 8 103
(Ollie Pears) *hld up in rr: hdwy over 2f out: led over 1f out: hdd ins fnl f: rallied nr fin: jst hld* **20/1**

3116 **3** *4 ½* **Brave Boy (IRE)**[35] 6201 2-9-0 103.............................. KierenFallon 10 89
(Saeed bin Suroor) *in rr: hdwy over 2f out: upsides over 1f out: kpt on same pce* **7/1**

6023 **4** *½* **Blurred Vision**[52] 5656 2-9-0 82................................ GrahamGibbons 4 88
(William Jarvis) *hmpd s: sn chsng ldrs: edgd rt over 1f out: kpt on same pce* **20/1**

1352 **5** *1* **Rufford (IRE)**[21] 6637 2-9-0 108...................................... TonyHamilton 6 85
(Richard Fahey) *trckd ldrs: outpcd over 2f out: kpt on fnl f* **9/2**[2]

1210 **6** *3 ¾* **Northern Water**[35] 6201 2-9-0 89.............................. DanielTudhope 3 73
(K R Burke) *chsd ldrs: wknd over 1f out* **28/1**

0413 **7** *4 ½* **Haikbidiac (IRE)**[32] 6293 2-9-0 102.................................(p) LiamJones 1 60
(William Haggas) *led: crossed stands' side rail over 4f out: hdd over 2f out: lost pl over 1f out* **6/1**

0244 **8** *nk* **Figure Of Speech (IRE)**[10] 6958 2-9-0 107....................(v) AdamKirby 5 59
(Charlie Appleby) *wnt lft s: hdwy to chse ldrs over 2f out: upsides over 1f out: sn wknd* **8/1**

31 **9** *2 ¼* **Online Alexander (IRE)**[58] 5421 2-8-9 82.......................... TomEaves 2 47
(Kevin Ryan) *trckd ldrs: edgd rt and led stands' side rail over 2f out: hdd & wknd over 1f out* **14/1**

12 **10** *3* **Outer Space**[7] 7011 2-9-0 0... JimmyFortune 7 49
(Richard Hannon) *chsd ldrs: lost pl over 2f out: sn bhd* **7/2**[1]

1m 12.92s (1.02) **Going Correction** +0.275s/f (Good) **10** Ran SP% **113.3**
Speed ratings (Par 103): **104,103,97,97,95 90,84,84,81,77**
toteswingers 1&2 £29.00, 2&3 £33.30, 1&3 £8.30 CSF £108.32 TOTE £6.00: £2.00, £4.90, £2.80; EX 155.60 Trifecta £861.60 Pool: £2334.57 - 2.03 winning units..
Owner Hamdan Al Maktoum **Bred** Shadwell Estate Company Limited **Trained** Newmarket, Suffolk

FOCUS
Despite no real evidence that the stands' rail was a big advantage in the earlier races the whole field edged over to race on the rail in this Listed 2yo event. The early pace didn't appear that strong, but the pace picked up some way out and the first two came from the back, and out wide. This is usually a strong Listed race, and that looks the case again. This could underestimate the bare form with the first two clear.

7208 CORAL SPRINT TROPHY (H'CAP) 6f
3:30 (3:30) (Class 2) (0-105,105) 3-Y-O+
£46,687 (£13,980; £6,990; £3,495; £1,747; £877) **Stalls** Centre

Form RPR

2500 **1** **Mass Rally (IRE)**[21] 6623 6-9-7 **103**.............................(b) PJMcDonald 4 113
(Michael Dods) *dwlt and in rr: pushed along 1/2-way: swtchd lft to outer and gd hdwy 2f out: rdn over 1f out: chal ent fnl f: led last 100yds* **14/1**

3313 **2** *1 ½* **Seeking Magic**[14] 6845 5-8-11 **98**..................................(t) RyanTate[(5)] 13 103
(Clive Cox) *trckd ldrs: effrt 2f out and sn n.m.r: nt clr run over 1f out: swtchd lft and rdn ins fnl f: kpt on wl towards fin* **10/1**

1431 **3** *nse* **Hallelujah**[34] 6235 5-9-6 **102**..(t) FrederikTylicki 3 107
(James Fanshawe) *trckd ldrs: hdwy and cl up 1/2-way: rdn to ld ent fnl f: drvn and hdd last 100yds* **7/1**[2]

200 **4** *¾* **Jimmy Styles**[7] 7013 9-9-7 **103**.....................................(p) AdamKirby 14 106
(Clive Cox) *in tch: effrt and n.m.r 2f out: swtchd lft and hdwy over 1f out: nt clr run and swtchd rt ins fnl f: styd on wl towards fin* **33/1**

1202 **5** *½* **Spinatrix**[14] 6845 5-9-4 **105**.....................................(p) ConnorBeasley[(5)] 10 106
(Michael Dods) *sn led: rdn over 2f out: hdd wl over 1f out: sn drvn and grad wknd fnl f* **16/1**

-240 **6** *½* **Valbchek (IRE)**[18] 6719 4-9-6 **102**...................................(p) TedDurcan 7 101
(Jeremy Noseda) *hld up towards rr: hdwy and n.m.r 2f out: chsd ldrs whn nt clr run over 1f out and again ent fnl f: swtchd rt and kpt on wl towards fin* **20/1**

0001 **7** *½* **Ancient Cross**[21] 6621 9-9-5 **101**...............................(tp) GrahamGibbons 2 99
(Michael Easterby) *hld up: hdwy 2f out: rdn to chse ldrs over 1f out: drvn and one pce fnl f* **20/1**

4030 **8** *¾* **Humidor (IRE)**[21] 6623 6-9-0 **99**..............................(t) ThomasBrown[(3)] 20 94
(George Baker) *in rr whn hmpd after 1f: bhd after tl hdwy over 2f out: swtchd lft over 1f out: kpt on: nrst fin* **16/1**

3460 **9** *¾* **Khubala (IRE)**[21] 6623 4-9-2 **98**....................................(b) ChrisHayes 16 91
(Hugo Palmer) *hld up towards rr: hdwy 2f out: rdn whn n.m.r over 1f out: no imp after* **8/1**[3]

1002 **10** *1 ¾* **Louis The Pious**[21] 6623 5-9-3 **99**.............................. DanielTudhope 1 86
(David O'Meara) *trckd ldrs: hdwy on outer and cl up over 2f out: ev ch tl rdn and wknd appr fnl f* **7/1**[2]

0460 **11** *shd* **Pastoral Player**[7] 7014 6-9-8 **104**................................ JimmyFortune 5 91
(Hughie Morrison) *hld up towards rr: hdwy 1/2-way: rdn over 2f out: sn no imp* **25/1**

6043 **12** *nse* **An Saighdiur (IRE)**[21] 6621 6-9-3 **99**..................... DeclanMcDonogh 12 86
(Andrew Slattery, Ire) *trckd ldrs: pushed along and sltly outpcd 2f out: sn n.m.r and one pce* **12/1**

120 **13** *½* **Harrison George (IRE)**[21] 6621 8-8-11 **98**...........(bt) NatashaEaton[(5)] 8 83
(P J O'Gorman) *chsd ldrs: rdn along over 2f out: hld whn n.m.r over 1f out* **33/1**

0615 **14** *1 ¼* **Baccarat (IRE)**[21] 6623 4-9-5 **101**................................. TonyHamilton 17 82
(Richard Fahey) *a towards rr* **9/2**[1]

U100 **15** *2 ¾* **Bogart**[21] 6623 4-9-0 **101**... KevinStott[(5)] 11 74
(Kevin Ryan) *led: rdn along 2f out: sn hdd & wknd* **16/1**

0300 **16** *1* **Secret Witness**[7] 7013 7-9-3 **99**....................................(b) ShaneKelly 18 68
(Ronald Harris) *in rr whn hmpd after 1f: bhd after* **25/1**

0354 **17** *4* **Borderlescott**[18] 6719 11-9-7 **103**................................ TomEaves 15 60
(Robin Bastiman) *chsd ldrs on inner: rdn along wl over 2f out: sn wknd* **25/1**

0104 **18** *1* **Confessional**[14] 6830 6-9-4 **100**......................................(e) DavidAllan 9 53
(Tim Easterby) *prom: rdn along 2f out: sn wknd* **33/1**

0616 **19** *38* **Doc Hay (USA)**[7] 7010 6-9-7 **103**...................................... DavidNolan 19
(David O'Meara) *dwlt and in rr whn hmpd and stmbld after 1f: wl bhd after* **16/1**

1m 11.92s (0.02) **Going Correction** +0.275s/f (Good)
WFA 3 from 4yo+ 1lb **19** Ran SP% **131.2**
Speed ratings (Par 109): **110,108,107,106,106 105,104,103,102,100 100,100,99,98,94 93,87,86,35**
toteswingers 1&2 £72.30, 2&3 £16.10, 1&3 £71.80 CSF £139.38 CT £1109.14 TOTE £18.40: £3.90, £3.50, £1.90, £7.70; EX 326.60 Trifecta £2292.60 Pool: £102594.31 - 33.56 winning units..
Owner Business Development Consultants Limited **Bred** Round Hill Stud **Trained** Denton, Co Durham

FOCUS
Once again, for no obvious reason, they congregated stands' side, and several were denied a clear run. The winner came down the centre of the track and is rated as running a length personal best in a messy race.

7209 JOIN CORAL.CO.UK FOR A £50 FREE BET EBF MAIDEN STKS 7f
4:10 (4:12) (Class 3) 2-Y-O **£7,439** (£2,213; £1,106; £553) **Stalls** Low

Form RPR

1 **Patentar (FR)** 2-9-5 0...(t) AdamKirby 6 82+
(Marco Botti) *trckd ldrs: led over 1f out: styd on strly ins fnl f: readily* **3/1**[2]

4364 **2** *2 ¾* **Supersta**[31] 6303 2-9-5 72.. ShaneKelly 12 75
(Ronald Harris) *t.k.h: trckd ldrs: led over 3f out: hdd over 1f out: edgd lft and kpt on same pce ins fnl f* **7/1**

3 *shd* **Premium Pressure (USA)** 2-9-5 0.......................... GrahamGibbons 5 75+
(David Barron) *trckd ldrs: effrt and green over 1f out: styd on towards fin: will improve* **5/2**[1]

4 *¾* **Kafeel (USA)** 2-9-5 0.. DaneO'Neill 2 73+
(Roger Varian) *s.i.s: in rr: hdwy 3f out: chsng ldrs over 1f out: kpt on same pce* **8/1**

5 **5** *6* **Soviet Courage (IRE)**[16] 6769 2-9-5 0.............................. TedDurcan 9 57
(William Haggas) *mid-div: outpcd over 2f out: kpt on fnl f* **6/1**[3]

6 *2 ¾* **Saythatagain (IRE)** 2-9-0 0... DavidAllan 10 45
(Tim Easterby) *in rr: kpt on fnl 2f: nvr a factor* **33/1**

7 *¾* **Tuddenham (USA)** 2-9-5 0...................................... RobertWinston 4 48+
(Charles Hills) *dwlt: in rr: hdwy over 2f out: wknd over 1f out* **16/1**

0060 **8** *2 ¾* **Nu Form Fire (IRE)**[24] 6517 2-9-5 55................................ LeeTopliss 1 41
(Nigel Tinkler) *trckd ldrs: t.k.h: lost pl over 1f out* **66/1**

0 **9** *1* **Elle West**[7] 7023 2-9-0 0.. FrederikTylicki 13 33
(Michael Easterby) *dwlt: hld up towards rr: effrt over 2f out: nvr a factor* **66/1**

0 **10** *nk* **Cahal (IRE)**[14] 6842 2-9-5 0.. PaulQuinn 3 38
(David Nicholls) *chsd ldrs: drvn over 3f out: sn lost pl* **66/1**

0 **11** *nk* **Slingsby**[7] 7023 2-9-5 0.. DanielTudhope 7 37
(Michael Easterby) *in rr: drvn over 2f out: nvr a factor* **50/1**

0 **12** *nk* **Sooqaan**[32] 6286 2-9-5 0.. JimmyFortune 8 36
(Mel Brittain) *led: hdd over 3f out: wknd over 1f out* **50/1**

5 **13** *6* **Branston De Soto**[10] 6939 2-9-5 0.................................. LiamJones 14 20
(Mark Johnston) *mid-div: drvn to chse ldrs over 3f out: lost pl over 2f out: sn bhd* **16/1**

4 **14** *1* **Shore Patrol (IRE)**[44] 5915 2-9-5 0............................. TonyHamilton 11 18
(Richard Fahey) *in rr: sn pushed along: bhd fnl 2f* **10/1**

1m 27.68s (2.38) **Going Correction** +0.275s/f (Good) **14** Ran SP% **123.7**
Speed ratings (Par 99): **97,93,93,92,86 82,82,78,77,77 77,76,69,68**
toteswingers 1&2 £5.00, 2&3 £2.70, 1&3 £2.00 CSF £24.59 TOTE £4.80: £1.90, £2.30, £1.80; EX 28.10 Trifecta £86.30 Pool: £2020.87 - 17.55 winning units..
Owner Saleh Al Homaizi & Imad Al Sagar **Bred** Peter Dane Player **Trained** Newmarket, Suffolk

FOCUS
No more than a fair maiden using the rather exposed runner-up as a guide, but this was still a nice debut performance from the winner, who along with the third will rate higher.

7210 CORAL BACKING MACMILLAN CANCER SUPPORT STKS (H'CAP) 2m 2f
4:40 (4:43) (Class 4) (0-85,88) 3-Y-O+ **£7,439** (£2,213; £1,106; £553) **Stalls** Low

Form RPR

6303 **1** **Be Perfect (USA)**[14] 6846 4-9-9 **80**................................. ChrisHayes 7 89
(David Nicholls) *hld up towards rr: hdwy over 4f out: effrt to chse wnr 2f out: rdn and styd on wl to ld ins fnl f: kpt on* **20/1**

0034 **2** *1 ½* **Theology**[14] 6833 6-10-0 **85**....................................... JimmyFortune 16 92
(Steve Gollings) *led: pushed clr over 3f out: rdn wl over 1f out: hdd ins fnl f: drvn and rallied towards fin* **20/1**

0000 **3** *1 ¼* **Valid Reason**[21] 6646 6-8-9 **66** oh1.........................(p) FrankieMcDonald 15 72
(Dean Ivory) *prom: trckd ldr after 6f: pushed along over 3f out: rdn and outpcd over 2f out: sn drvn and rallied fnl f: kpt on* **9/1**[3]

3035 **4** *nse* **Caledonia**[20] 6668 6-8-9 **66** oh1................................ GrahamGibbons 10 72
(Jim Goldie) *trckd ldrs: pushed along over 3f out: rdn and outpcd over 2f out: drvn and kpt on fnl f* **9/1**[3]

0443 **5** *1* **Hit The Jackpot (IRE)**[10] 6942 4-9-3 **74**.......................... DanielTudhope 5 78
(David O'Meara) *hld up in rr: hdwy 4f out: rdn along 2f out: styd on fnl f: nrst fin* **14/1**

631 **6** *hd* **Bin Singspiel**[10] 6942 3-8-11 **80**...................................... DavidAllan 13 85
(James Tate) *in tch: hdwy 3f out: rdn along over 2f out: drvn and one pce fnl f* **13/2**[2]

2330 **7** *1 ¼* **Twelve Strings (IRE)**[22] 6585 4-9-7 **81**............................ RobertTart[(3)] 1 84
(Brian Ellison) *hld up in rr: hdwy wl over 2f out: rdn and kpt on fnl f: nrst fin* **14/1**

1513 **8** *1 ½* **Dr Irv**[26] 6466 4-9-2 **78**.. ConnorBeasley[(5)] 2 79
(Philip Kirby) *hld up towards rr: hdwy 4f out: rdn along 2f out: styd on fnl f: nrst fin* **12/1**

0500 **9** *1* **Desert Recluse (IRE)**[29] 6349 6-9-9 **80**........................ RobertWinston 9 80
(Brendan Powell) *midfield: hdwy and in tch 5f out: rdn to chse ldrs 3f out: sn drvn and no imp* **25/1**

0/4- **10** *nk* **Scots Gaelic (IRE)**[315] 7280 6-10-0 **85**........................ MichaelO'Connell 14 85
(John Quinn) *hld up: hdwy on wd outside 4f out: rdn to chse ldrs over 2f out: sn wknd* **20/1**

1256 **11** *shd* **Hawk Mountain (UAE)**[22] 6585 8-9-4 **75**............................ LiamKeniry 4 75
(John Quinn) *nvr bttr than midfield* **16/1**

6511 **12** *4* **Kelvingrove (IRE)**[24] 6540 3-9-5 **88**............................ FrederikTylicki 8 84
(Ed Vaughan) *midfield: pushed along over 7f out: nvr a factor* **3/1**[1]

0022 **13** 3 1/4 **Bowdler's Magic**[26] 6466 6-9-9 **80**....................(t) PJMcDonald 3 72
(David Thompson) *nvr nr ldrs* **14/1**
4221 **14** hd **Gabrial The Master (IRE)**[14] 6827 3-8-12 **81**............ TonyHamilton 12 73
(Richard Fahey) *prom: pushed along 4f out: rdn 3f out: sn drvn and grad wknd* **12/1**
4612 **15** 1 1/2 **Duke Of Yorkshire**[14] 6827 3-8-0 **72**.................... NeilFarley(3) 11 63
(Declan Carroll) *chsd ldrs: rdn along over 4f out: sn wknd* **20/1**
1422 **16** nk **King Kurt (IRE)**[33] 5786 5-8-13 **75**.................... KevinStott(5) 17 65
(Kevin Ryan) *chsd ldrs: rdn along 4f out: sn wknd* **28/1**
0500 **17** 4 1/2 **Aleksandar**[21] 6626 4-8-11 **68**.................... ShaneKelly 6 53
(Jim Goldie) *in tch: rdn along over 4f out: sn wknd* **33/1**

3m 57.85s (2.45) **Going Correction** -0.05s/f (Good)
WFA 3 from 4yo+ 12lb **17 Ran SP% 128.9**
Speed ratings (Par 105): **92,91,90,90,90 90,89,89,88,88 88,86,85,85,84 84,82**
toteswingers 1&2 £87.00, 2&3 £38.80, 1&3 £41.50 CSF £363.33 CT £3850.42 TOTE £25.70: £4.90, £5.30, £2.40, £2.80; EX 431.60 Trifecta £1225.70 Part won. Pool: £1634.38 - 0.01 winning units..
Owner Lady O'Reilly **Bred** Joseph Allen **Trained** Sessay, N Yorks

FOCUS
Few got into this, with a prominent position turning in the key. The winner is rated to this year's form.

7211 COLDSTREAM GUARDS ASSOCIATION CUP (H'CAP) 1m 2f 88y
5:10 (5:15) (Class 4) (0-85,84) 3-Y-O+ **£8,086** (£2,406; £1,202; £601) **Stalls** Low

Form RPR
0244 **1** **Running Deer (IRE)**[22] 6611 4-8-8 **75**.................... LouisSteward(7) 5 84
(Lady Cecil) *w ldrs: led over 6f out: drifted lft fnl f: hld on nr fin* **16/1**
1-35 **2** hd **Flow (USA)**[22] 6596 3-9-4 **83**.................... JimmyFortune 6 92
(Lady Cecil) *trckd ldrs: effrt over 2f out: styd on ins fnl f: no ex nr fin* **11/4**[1]
0523 **3** 1 **War Poet**[25] 6499 6-9-5 **82**....................(t) RobertTart(3) 8 89
(Brian Ellison) *in tch: effrt and chsng ldrs over 2f out: kpt on same pce ins fnl f* **9/1**[3]
5050 **4** nk **Hefner (IRE)**[15] 6801 4-9-7 **84**.................... MichaelJMMurphy(3) 4 90
(William Jarvis) *trckd ldrs: drvn over 3f out: rdr dropped reigns over 2f out: kpt on same pce fnl f* **14/1**
5606 **5** 2 1/4 **Christmas Light**[15] 6801 6-9-3 **77**.................... FrederikTylicki 11 79
(Brian Ellison) *hld up in rr: hdwy over 2f out: styd on fnl f* **25/1**
5350 **6** 1 1/4 **Asgardella (IRE)**[14] 6823 3-9-0 **79**.................... TonyHamilton 18 79
(Richard Fahey) *mid-div: hdwy to chse ldrs over 3f out: kpt on same pce over 1f out* **20/1**
4550 **7** nk **Karaka Jack**[15] 6792 6-9-3 **82**.................... ConnorBeasley(5) 17 81
(David Nicholls) *dwlt: swtchd lft after s: in rr: gd hdwy on outside over 1f out: styng on wl at fin* **20/1**
1260 **8** nse **Triple Eight (IRE)**[23] 6563 5-9-2 **76**....................(b) MichaelO'Connell 9 75
(Philip Kirby) *mid-div: hdwy 3f out: kpt on same pce* **33/1**
4001 **9** 2 1/2 **Berlusca (IRE)**[13] 6877 4-9-3 **77**.................... DavidNolan 12 71
(David O'Meara) *hld up in mid-div: hdwy to chse ldrs over 2f out: wknd over 1f out* **25/1**
0000 **10** hd **St Moritz (IRE)**[46] 5860 7-9-7 **81**....................[1] DanielTudhope 16 75
(David O'Meara) *mid-div: reminders over 5f out: sme hdwy over 3f out: nvr a threat* **16/1**
032 **11** 1/2 **Sheila's Buddy**[15] 6801 4-9-3 **77**.................... LiamKeniry 13 70
(J S Moore) *hld up in mid-div: effrt 3f out: nvr a factor* **16/1**
0053 **12** 3/4 **Barren Brook**[7] 7028 6-9-2 **76**....................(b[1]) GrahamGibbons 7 68
(Michael Easterby) *t.k.h in mid-div: sme hdwy over 3f out: wknd over 1f out* **8/1**[2]
0001 **13** 1/2 **San Cassiano (IRE)**[7] 7028 6-9-6 **80**....................(b) DaleSwift 2 71
(Ruth Carr) *led tl over 6f out: wknd over 1f out* **25/1**
1100 **14** hd **Rocket Ronnie (IRE)**[13] 6874 3-9-3 **82**.................... PaulQuinn 20 72
(David Nicholls) *mid-div: effrt over 3f out: sn chsng ldrs: wknd fnl 2f* **33/1**
5262 **15** hd **Prophesy (IRE)**[17] 6758 4-9-1 **78**.................... NeilFarley(3) 15 68
(Declan Carroll) *chsd ldrs: wknd 2f out* **16/1**
000 **16** 3/4 **Stevie Thunder**[15] 6801 8-9-1 **80**.................... GeorgeChaloner(5) 1 68
(Ian Williams) *a towards rr* **20/1**
17 3 1/2 **Cloud Monkey (IRE)**[38] 6121 3-9-3 **82**.................... PJMcDonald 19 64
(Martin Todhunter) *chsd ldrs: lost pl over 3f out* **40/1**
4311 **18** 3/4 **Bold Duke**[15] 6794 5-8-13 **80**.................... EoinWalsh(7) 3 60
(Edward Bevan) *trckd ldrs: hmpd and lost pl 9f out: bhd fnl 2f* **10/1**
5430 **19** 11 **Jo'Burg (USA)**[7] 7024 9-9-0 **79**.................... DavidBergin(5) 14 39
(David O'Meara) *in rr: bhd fnl 2f: eased in clsng stages* **25/1**
1003 **20** 7 **Hunting Ground (USA)**[7] 7022 3-8-13 **78**.................... LiamJones 10 24
(Mark Johnston) *chsd ldrs: lost pl over 2f out: sn bhd: eased in clsng stages* **20/1**

2m 10.36s (-2.14) **Going Correction** -0.05s/f (Good)
WFA 3 from 4yo+ 5lb **20 Ran SP% 129.8**
Speed ratings (Par 105): **106,105,105,104,103 102,101,101,99,99 99,98,98,98,97 97,94,93,85,79**
toteswingers 1&2 £11.00, 2&3 £7.20, 1&3 £20.70 CSF £51.90 CT £455.11 TOTE £22.60: £4.80, £1.50, £2.50, £3.90; EX 104.70 Trifecta £1112.00 Part won. Pool: £1482.68 - 0.60 winning units..
Owner W H Ponsonby **Bred** Mrs E Henry **Trained** Newmarket, Suffolk
■ Stewards' Enquiry : Louis Steward two-day ban: used whip above permitted level (Oct 28-29)
Jimmy Fortune two-day ban: used whip above permitted level ()ct 28-29)

FOCUS
They didn't go that quick early and it paid to race fairly handily. The form makes sense.
T/Plt: £2,468.70 to a £1 stake. Pool of £179617.52 - 53.11 winning tickets. T/Qpdt: £128.30 to a £1 stake. Pool of £8497.0 - 49.0 winning tickets. JR

7212 - 7216a (Foreign Racing) - See Raceform Interactive

6739 GOODWOOD (R-H)
Sunday, October 13

OFFICIAL GOING: Soft (5.9)
Wind: Moderate, half against Weather: Dank, light rain

7217 ALDERBROOK STKS (H'CAP) (TO BE RIDDEN BY PROFESSIONAL NATIONAL HUNT JOCKEYS) 2m
2:00 (2:00) (Class 4) (0-80,80) 4-Y-O+ **£6,469** (£1,925; £962; £481) **Stalls** Low

Form RPR
21/3 **1** **Harry Hunt**[133] 40 6-11-12 **80**.................... WayneHutchinson 1 91
(Graeme McPherson) *trckd ldng pair after 5f: clsd to chal over 3f out: narrow ld over 2f out: drifted bk to far rail after: hld on gamely fnl f* **14/1**
2541 **2** nk **Opera Buff**[11] 6960 4-11-8 **76**....................(p) MarkGrant 13 87
(Sean Curran) *trckd ldr: led after 5f: brought field down centre in st: rdn and hdd over 2f out: drifted bk to far rail w wnr sn after: fought on wl: jst hld* **7/1**
4450 **3** 9 **Spice Fair**[9] 6992 6-11-11 **79**.................... TimmyMurphy 16 79
(Mark Usher) *stdd s: hld up in last pair: stl covered up 3f out as ldrs wnt for home: rdn and prog fr 2f out to take modest 3rd jst ins fnl f* **6/1**[3]
06-2 **4** 2 **Four Nations (USA)**[16] 6787 5-11-3 **71**.................... AndrewTinkler 4 69
(George Baker) *hld up in midfield: rdn 3f out: plugged on to chal for 3rd 1f out: one pce* **8/1**
2204 **5** 3 **Our Folly**[28] 6424 5-11-6 **74**....................(t) ConorO'Farrell 14 68
(Stuart Kittow) *hld up in last pair: rdn and sme prog fr 3f out: pressed for a pl 1f out but no ch w ldng pair: fdd* **10/3**[1]
4045 **6** 2 **Freddy Q (IRE)**[14] 6869 4-11-0 **68**.................... TomCannon 10 60
(Roger Teal) *chsd ldng pair 5f: styd prom: tried to chal 3f out: wknd 2f out* **10/1**
125 **7** 3/4 **Ampleforth**[28] 6424 5-11-2 **70**....................(v) RobertMcCarth 8 61
(Ian Williams) *chsd ldrs: rdn 3f out: no prog and wl btn 2f out* **5/1**[2]
3514 **8** 1 3/4 **Mediterranean Sea (IRE)**[80] 4692 7-11-7 **75**.................... AidanColeman 5 64
(J R Jenkins) *t.k.h: hld up in last quartet: rdn 3f out: no real prog* **25/1**
1560 **9** 4 **Sunny Future (IRE)**[9] 6992 7-11-7 **75**.................... HaddenFrost 12 59
(Malcolm Saunders) *led 5f: chsd ldr to 3f out: wknd* **16/1**
2345 **10** 9 **Guards Chapel**[21] 5954 5-11-0 **68**....................(v) JamieMoore 7 41
(Gary Moore) *hld up in midfield: rdn and lost pl 3f out: swtchd to r alone nr side 2f out: wknd* **10/1**
0/0- **11** 11 **Minneapolis**[524] 1939 8-11-2 **70**.................... LeightonAspell 9 30
(Alison Batchelor) *slowly away: a in rr: rdn and wknd jst over 4f out: t.o* **40/1**

3m 50.1s (21.10) **Going Correction** +0.85s/f (Soft) **11 Ran SP% 114.7**
Speed ratings (Par 105): **81,80,76,75,73 72,72,71,69,65 59**
toteswingers 1&2 £7.60, 1&3 £13.90, 2&3 £10.40 CSF £106.03 CT £657.15 TOTE £12.10: £3.00, £2.00, £2.30; EX 58.60 Trifecta £217.50 Pool: £1,566.50 - 5.40 winning units..
Owner Arion Racing **Bred** Darley **Trained** Upper Oddington, Gloucs
■ Stewards' Enquiry : Mark Grant seven-day ban: used whip above permitted level (Oct 28-Nov 2,3)

FOCUS
On a wet and miserable day, conditions were testing. It was proved hard to make up ground in this staying handicap for professional jump jockeys. The field headed middle-to-stands' side early in the straight, but the front two drifted back towards the far side in the closing stages and ended up well away from the others.

7218 GREENE KING IPA MAIDEN AUCTION STKS 6f
2:30 (2:31) (Class 5) 2-Y-O **£3,234** (£962; £481; £240) **Stalls** High

Form RPR
1 **Night Of Thunder (IRE)** 2-9-0 0.................... RichardHughes 4 92+
(Richard Hannon) *a gng wl: trckd ldrs: led jst over 2f out: pushed along and drew rt away jst over 1f out: impressive* **9/2**[1]
0020 **2** 6 **Nakuti (IRE)**[31] 6326 2-8-7 74.................... LiamKeniry 8 65
(Sylvester Kirk) *hld up in tch: gng strly jst over 2f out: swtchd to outer sn after: rdn to take 2nd jst over 1f out: edgd lft and no ch w wnr but kpt on wl* **11/2**[2]
3 2 **Penny Drops** 2-8-8 0.................... RyanMoore 12 63+
(William Haggas) *slowly away: mostly in last pair tl prog against rail over 2f out: nowhere to go whn trying to force way through over 1f out: styd on to take 3rd fnl f* **13/2**
045 **4** 1 1/2 **Johara (IRE)**[22] 6644 2-8-8 73.................... TedDurcan 9 56
(Chris Wall) *trckd ldrs: waiting for room over 2f out: nt clr run over 1f out: kpt on same pce fnl f* **7/1**
3346 **5** 1/2 **Needless Shouting (IRE)**[10] 6972 2-8-6 65.................... CharlesBishop(3) 5 55
(Mick Channon) *mde most to jst over 2f out: wknd fnl f* **7/1**
46 **6** 1/2 **Hoon (IRE)**[33] 6277 2-8-12 0.................... MartinLane 1 57
(Rae Guest) *prom on outer: upsides over 2f out but drvn: wknd fnl f* **6/1**[3]
0 **7** 2 1/4 **Stan Nineteen (IRE)**[23] 6590 2-9-0 0.................... PatCosgrave 13 52
(George Baker) *racd against nr side rail: w ldrs: rdn over 2f out: bmpd by rival fr bhd over 1f out: wknd* **6/1**[3]
06 **8** 1 1/4 **Seven Lucky Seven**[27] 6460 2-8-10 0.................... J-PGuillambert 10 44
(Gary Harrison) *pushed along in last pair: sme prog 2f out: no hdwy 1f out: fdd* **33/1**
9 2 1/4 **Plauseabella** 2-8-3 0.................... MichaelJMMurphy(3) 3 33
(Stuart Kittow) *prom on outer to over 2f out: wknd over 1f out* **50/1**
3043 **10** 7 **Island Kingdom (IRE)**[19] 6724 2-8-9 63....................(b[1]) LukeMorris 11 15
(J S Moore) *w ldrs to over 2f out: wknd qckly: wl bhd ins fnl f* **33/1**
02 **11** 6 **Concrete Mac**[79] 4708 2-8-13 0.................... JimmyFortune 7
(Hughie Morrison) *trckd ldrs to 1/2-way: hanging and wknd qckly: t.o* **10/1**
000 **12** 1 **Khloe**[44] 5950 2-8-6 45.................... DavidProbert 2
(Michael Blanshard) *hld up in rr: hanging and wknd over 2f out: t.o* **66/1**

1m 16.2s (4.00) **Going Correction** +0.725s/f (Yiel) **12 Ran SP% 118.9**
Speed ratings (Par 95): **102,94,91,89,88 88,85,83,80,71 63,61**
toteswingers 1&2 £7.70, 1&3 £6.90, 2&3 £9.30 CSF £28.35 TOTE £4.40: £2.40, £2.00, £2.50; EX 35.10 Trifecta £221.60 Pool: £1941.12 - 6.56 winning units..
Owner Saeed Manana **Bred** Frank Dunne **Trained** East Everleigh, Wilts

FOCUS
A race that ought to produce winners. The action unfolded stands' side.

7219 IRISH STALLION FARMS EBF MAIDEN STKS 1m 1f
3:05 (3:06) (Class 4) 2-Y-O **£5,175** (£1,540; £769; £384) **Stalls** Low

Form RPR
2 **1** **Laugharne**[37] 6168 2-9-5 0.................... GeorgeBaker 12 86+
(Roger Charlton) *mostly trckd ldng pair: clsd to ld jst over 2f out: pushed along and wl in command after: v comf* **5/2**[2]
6 **2** 2 **Carthage (IRE)**[17] 6762 2-9-5 0.................... RichardHughes 2 82+
(Richard Hannon) *trckd ldrs: rdn over 2f out: wnt 2nd over 1f out: styd on but unavailing chse of wnr* **13/8**[1]
5 **3** 9 **Vent De Force**[18] 6740 2-9-5 0.................... JimmyFortune 11 63+
(Hughie Morrison) *wl in tch: pushed along over 3f out: outpcd over 2f out: stl pushed and kpt on fr over 1f out to take 3rd nr fin* **12/1**
4 1/2 **Big Orange** 2-9-5 0.................... JamieSpencer 6 62+
(Michael Bell) *hld up in last trio: outpcd over 2f out: nudged along and kpt on encouragingly fr over 1f out: tk 4th last strides* **25/1**
005 **5** nk **State Law (IRE)**[17] 6773 2-9-5 0.................... MickaelBarzalona 13 61
(Charlie Appleby) *led 2f: led again over 3f out to jst over 2f out: wknd over 1f out: lost 2 pls nr fin* **25/1**
6 5 **Authorized Too** 2-9-5 0.................... RyanMoore 3 51
(William Haggas) *c out of the stalls 20 l bhd rest: rcvrd and in tch at bk of field after 4f: effrt 3f out: disp wl btn 4th 2f out: sn wknd* **9/2**[3]
0 **7** 1 1/2 **Nos Galan (IRE)**[29] 6378 2-9-5 0.................... SeanLevey 10 48
(Richard Hannon) *free to post: trckd ldrs: shkn up over 2f out: wknd over 1f out: eased* **50/1**

0 **8** *15* **Norse Star (IRE)**[17] 6762 2-9-5 0 LiamKeniry 4 18
(Sylvester Kirk) *in tch tl wknd 3f out: t.o* **20/1**
06 **9** *3/4* **Enquiring**[11] 6938 2-9-5 0 SilvestreDeSousa 1 17
(Mark Johnston) *led after 2f to over 3f out: sn wknd u.p: t.o* **25/1**
10 *2* **Lord Brantwood** 2-9-5 0 SamHitchcott 7 13
(Mick Channon) *s.s: in tch in rr tl wknd 3f out: t.o* **40/1**
11 *17* **Burmese Breeze** 2-9-5 0 TedDurcan 14
(Chris Wall) *a in rr: wknd over 3f out: wl t.o* **25/1**
2m 2.85s (6.55) **Going Correction** +0.85s/f (Soft) **11** Ran SP% **117.1**
Speed ratings (Par 97): **104,102,94,93,93 89,87,74,73,71 56**
toteswingers 1&2 £1.60, 1&3 £5.90, 2&3 £4.90 CSF £6.20 TOTE £4.00: £1.50, £1.20, £2.80; EX 8.60 Trifecta £59.30 Pool: £2948.00 - 37.28 winning units..
Owner Seasons Holidays **Bred** Seasons Holidays **Trained** Beckhampton, Wilts
FOCUS
They raced up the middle of the track in the straight in what was probably just a fair maiden.

7220 JRL GROUP GENTLEMAN AMATEUR H'CAP (FOR GENTLEMAN AMATEUR RIDERS) 1m 4f
3:40 (3:43) (Class 5) (0-75,75) 3-Y-O+ **£3,119** (£967; £483; £242) **Stalls** High

Form RPR
5300 **1** **Cuckoo Rock (IRE)**[31] 6325 6-10-5 **61** oh7 (p) MrJHarding(5) 10 67
(Jonathan Portman) *trckd ldr after 2f: led after 5f to over 4f out: c towards nr side fr 3f out and on terms: narrow ld fnl 2f: jst hld on* **20/1**
0304 **2** *hd* **Admirable Duque (IRE)**[2] 7166 7-10-8 **64**..(p) MrBenFfrenchDavis(5) 11 70
(Dominic Ffrench Davis) *wl in tch: prog to ld main gp in centre jst over 2f out: edgd rt fr over 1f out: jst hld* **20/1**
420 **3** *nk* **Frosty Berry**[48] 5840 4-10-3 **61** oh4 MrAFrench(7) 3 66
(John Wainwright) *hld up in rr: prog towards far side to press ldrs fr 2f out: kpt on but jst hld nr fin* **50/1**
3354 **4** *1 3/4* **No Such Number**[29] 6377 5-11-6 **71** (p) MrRossBirkett 4 74
(Julia Feilden) *trckd ldr 2f: styd cl up: chal over 2f out: nt qckn fnl f* **9/1**
0400 **5** *nk* **The Quarterjack**[37] 6158 4-10-6 **64** MrCBarber(7) 12 66
(Ron Hodges) *hld up in detached last: prog to cl on ldrs over 2f out: nt qckn and hld in 5th whn swtchd lft 150yds out: racd sideways after but kpt on* **8/1**[3]
0363 **6** *5* **Saint Helena (IRE)**[14] 6869 5-11-1 **71** MrDLevey(5) 5 66
(Harry Dunlop) *dwlt: in tch in rr: rdn and struggling 3f out: passed wkng rivals fr over 1f out* **9/1**
5530 **7** *2 3/4* **Nordic Quest (IRE)**[18] 6758 4-11-7 **72** (b[1]) MrSWalker 13 64
(Gerard Butler) *restless stalls and slowly away: in tch in rr: clsd on ldrs fr 3f out: rdn over 2f out: wknd wl over 1f out* **7/2**[2]
040 **8** *nse* **Star Date (IRE)**[22] 6658 4-10-7 **61** (p) MrChrisMartin(3) 8 53
(Michael Attwater) *t.k.h: cl up: led over 4f out to jst over 2f out: hanging and wknd: eased* **20/1**
-022 **9** *1/2* **While You Wait (IRE)**[45] 5933 4-11-10 **75** MrPWMullins 1 66
(Gary Moore) *trckd ldrs: shkn up over 2f out: nt qckn and sn wknd* **7/4**[1]
566 **10** *4* **Advisory**[26] 6498 3-10-7 **70** MrAlexFerguson(5) 2 55
(Mark Johnston) *led 5f: wknd over 3f out* **9/1**
046- **11** *6* **Royal Trooper (IRE)**[32] 6626 7-10-6 **64** (t) MrTAddis(7) 7 41
(Jim Best) *in tch tl wknd fr 3f out* **20/1**
2m 55.05s (16.65) **Going Correction** +0.85s/f (Soft)
WFA 3 from 4yo+ 7lb **11** Ran SP% **120.7**
Speed ratings (Par 103): **78,77,77,76,76 72,71,71,70,68 64**
toteswingers 1&2 £55.60, 1&3 £28.80, 2&3 £44.70 CSF £350.26 CT £17948.67 TOTE £23.80: £4.10, £4.60, £5.50; EX 611.50 Trifecta £1182.10 Pool: £3052.50 - 1.93 winning units..
Owner Prof C D Green **Bred** Prof C Green **Trained** Upper Lambourn, Berks
FOCUS
A modest contest in which some of the fancied runners underperformed. The field raced middle-to-stands' side in the straight, with the winner closer to the near rail than the other principals.

7221 IRISH STALLION FARMS EBF NURSERY STKS (H'CAP) (THE SUNDAY £5K BONUS RACE) 7f
4:15 (4:15) (Class 4) (0-85,84) 2-Y-O **£6,469** (£1,925; £962; £481) **Stalls** Low

Form RPR
632 **1** **Pretty Flemingo (IRE)**[29] 6408 2-8-7 **70** KieranO'Neill 7 89+
(Richard Hannon) *hld up in last trio: smooth prog over 2f out to ld wl over 1f out: shkn up and sn wl clr: eased w jockey looking arnd last 150yds* **7/1**
022 **2** *7* **Nova Champ (IRE)**[59] 5428 2-8-9 **72** JamieSpencer 6 70
(Stuart Williams) *hld up in midfield: shkn up over 2f out: kpt on fr over 1f out to take 2nd jst ins fnl f: no ch w wnr* **8/1**
01 **3** *1 1/2* **Black Caesar (IRE)**[23] 6589 2-9-7 **84** RichardHughes 8 78
(Richard Hannon) *chsd ldng pair to over 2f out: kpt on u.p to dispute 2nd over 1f out: one pce after* **7/2**[2]
3412 **4** *2* **Gender Agenda**[24] 6572 2-8-13 **83** LouisSteward(7) 11 72
(Michael Bell) *nt gng wl in last early: stl last and shkn up wl over 2f out: kpt on over 1f out to take 4th nr fin* **9/2**[3]
61 **5** *2 3/4* **Never To Be (USA)**[71] 4997 2-8-11 **74** (t) WilliamBuick 4 56
(John Gosden) *dwlt: sn chsd ldrs: rdn over 2f out: disp 2nd over 1f out but no ch: wknd ins fnl f* **5/2**[1]
2116 **6** *5* **Dovil's Duel (IRE)**[31] 6320 2-8-11 **74** DavidProbert 5 43
(Rod Millman) *t.k.h: chsd ldr to 2f out: wknd qckly* **14/1**
4104 **7** *nse* **Mops Angel**[40] 6070 2-8-7 **70** AndrewMullen 10 39
(Michael Appleby) *mostly in last trio: effrt u.p over 2f out: sn wknd* **16/1**
5001 **8** *1 1/2* **Maid In Rio (IRE)**[27] 6465 2-8-8 **71** SilvestreDeSousa 3 37
(Mark Johnston) *led at str pce to wl over 1f out: wknd rapidly* **8/1**
1m 32.96s (5.96) **Going Correction** +0.85s/f (Soft) **8** Ran SP% **116.2**
Speed ratings (Par 97): **99,91,89,87,83 78,78,76**
toteswingers 1&2 £11.50, 1&3 £7.20, 2&3 £4.40 CSF £61.96 CT £230.24 TOTE £8.70: £2.40, £3.00, £1.90; EX 43.80 Trifecta £319.10 Pool: £2522.95 - 5.92 winning units..
Owner Thurloe Thoroughbreds XXXIII **Bred** Lynch Bages Ltd **Trained** East Everleigh, Wilts
FOCUS
They raced middle-to-stands' side in what looked a fair enough nursery.

7222 STUDENT RACEDAY STKS (H'CAP) 6f
4:45 (4:47) (Class 3) (0-95,98) 3-Y-O+ **£9,703** (£2,887; £1,443; £721) **Stalls** High

Form RPR
2116 **1** **Ashpan Sam**[23] 6586 4-9-5 **90** RichardHughes 5 102
(John Spearing) *led after 2f: mde rest: rdn clr fnl f: readily* **9/2**[1]
6062 **2** *3 1/4* **Naabegha**[15] 6822 6-9-4 **89** PatCosgrave 10 91
(Ed de Giles) *dwlt: in tch: rdn and prog 2f out: wnt 2nd jst ins fnl f: kpt on but no ch w wnr* **14/1**
4052 **3** *shd* **Joe Packet**[15] 6831 6-9-5 **90** RyanMoore 2 92
(Jonathan Portman) *sltly awkward s: outpcd and wl adrift in last pair: rdn and prog on outer over 1f out: styd on and nrly snatched 2nd* **9/2**[1]
0040 **4** *1* **The Confessor**[22] 6621 6-9-5 **90** CathyGannon 3 89
(Henry Candy) *chsd ldrs on outer: rdn over 2f out: prog to dispute 2nd and edgd lft 1f out: no ex last 100yds* **8/1**
2604 **5** *2 1/4* **Tarooq (USA)**[15] 6831 7-8-10 **81** (t) AdamBeschizza 12 73
(Stuart Williams) *chsd ldrs: rdn and hld whn checked 1f out: swtchd rt: drvn and one pce* **16/1**
-253 **6** *nk* **Athenian (IRE)**[21] 6665 4-9-1 **86** LukeMorris 9 77
(Sir Mark Prescott Bt) *prom: chsd wnr over 2f out to jst ins fnl f: wknd* **6/1**[3]
41- **7** *1* **Don Marco**[364] 7078 3-9-2 **88** GeorgeBaker 13 76
(Roger Charlton) *prom: nt qckn 2f out: hld whn short of room briefly 1f out: fdd* **5/1**[2]
3054 **8** *1* **Normal Equilibrium**[9] 6990 3-8-11 **88** (p) OisinMurphy(5) 16 73
(Robert Cowell) *in tch: rdn 2f out: fdd jst over 1f out* **11/1**
2001 **9** *8* **Cruise Tothelimit (IRE)**[15] 6822 5-8-12 **83** MickaelBarzalona 6 44
(Ian Williams) *led 2f: chsd wnr to over 2f out: wknd* **16/1**
0200 **10** *8* **Links Drive Lady**[8] 7021 5-9-3 **88** SilvestreDeSousa 11 25
(Dean Ivory) *dwlt: nvr on terms w ldrs: struggling 2f out: t.o* **14/1**
0000 **11** *11* **Effie B**[9] 6990 3-9-2 **88** WilliamBuick 14
(Mick Channon) *nvr gng wl: a bhd: wl t.o* **20/1**
0300 **P** **Thunderball**[15] 6845 7-9-3 **88** (p) FrederikTylicki 19
(Scott Dixon) *burst out of stalls bef they opened: swvd rt and p.u* **14/1**
1m 15.47s (3.27) **Going Correction** +0.725s/f (Yiel)
WFA 3 from 4yo+ 1lb **12** Ran SP% **123.3**
Speed ratings (Par 107): **107,102,102,101,98 97,96,95,84,73 59,**
toteswingers 1&2 £7.80, 1&3 £3.30, 2&3 £11.30 CSF £71.38 CT £312.12 TOTE £5.80: £1.70, £5.20, £2.10; EX 71.60 Trifecta £352.80 Pool: £1893.05 - 4.02 winning units..
Owner Advantage Chemicals Holdings Ltd **Bred** Advantage Chemicals Holdings Ltd **Trained** Kinnersley, Worcs
FOCUS
Loads of non-runners, but still a fair sprint handicap. The race unfolded middle-to-stands' side.

7223 GOODWOOD RACEHORSE OWNERS GROUP STKS (H'CAP) 1m 4f
5:15 (5:19) (Class 3) (0-95,92) 3-Y-O **£9,703** (£2,887; £1,443; £721) **Stalls** High

Form RPR
0112 **1** **Thomas Hobson**[26] 6503 3-9-6 **91** WilliamBuick 7 105
(John Gosden) *hld up in 6th: prog over 4f out: led over 2f out: wandered rt and lft but drvn and styd on wl fnl f* **7/2**[1]
4132 **2** *3 1/4* **Glorious Protector (IRE)**[11] 6936 3-9-1 **86** RichardHughes 11 95
(Ed Walker) *led: stdd pce bef 1/2-way: hdd 5f out: styd cl up: chsd wnr 2f out: one pce over 1f out* **9/2**[3]
521 **3** *hd* **Empress Adelaide**[25] 6532 3-8-13 **84** RyanMoore 8 93
(William Haggas) *hld up in last pair: pushed along 3f out but in tch: rdn and styd on fr over 1f out: pressed runner-up nr fin* **7/2**[1]
3104 **4** *4 1/2* **Chesterfield (IRE)**[29] 6380 3-9-2 **87** MickaelBarzalona 2 89
(Charlie Appleby) *hld up in last trio: in tch 3f out: drvn to chse ldng pair wl over 1f out: wknd fnl f* **11/1**
500 **5** *hd* **Hollowina**[36] 6196 3-8-11 **82** SeanLevey 5 84
(David Brown) *wl in tch: pushed along and lft bhd fr over 2f out: kpt on ins fnl f* **16/1**
3560 **6** *1/2* **Salutation (IRE)**[22] 6638 3-9-6 **91** SilvestreDeSousa 10 92
(Mark Johnston) *mostly chsd ldr: led 5f out to over 2f out: hanging rt and wknd over 1f out* **14/1**
2521 **7** *13* **Lady Pimpernel**[25] 6533 3-9-2 **87** DaneO'Neill 6 69
(Henry Candy) *mostly trckd ldng pair tl wknd over 2f out: eased fnl f* **4/1**[2]
2544 **8** *67* **Mujazif (IRE)**[23] 6592 3-9-6 **91** (t) JimmyFortune 9
(Brian Meehan) *in tch: wknd 3f out: already t.o whn virtually p.u over 1f out* **8/1**
2m 47.97s (9.57) **Going Correction** +0.85s/f (Soft) **8** Ran SP% **114.6**
Speed ratings (Par 105): **102,99,99,96,96 96,87,42**
toteswingers 1&2 £2.80, 1&3 £2.30, 2&3 £2.70 CSF £19.50 CT £58.12 TOTE £4.50: £1.80, £1.60, £1.60; EX 20.90 Trifecta £32.80 Pool: £2042.20 - 46.58 winning units..
Owner Bailey, Hall & Hood **Bred** Mount Coote Stud And M H Dixon **Trained** Newmarket, Suffolk
FOCUS
A decent 3yo handicap. The runners were all over the place in the straight.

7224 GWA CARS AND FINANCE STKS (H'CAP) 1m
5:45 (5:50) (Class 4) (0-85,86) 3-Y-O+ **£6,469** (£1,925; £962; £481) **Stalls** Low

Form RPR
5316 **1** **First Post (IRE)**[6] 7075 6-8-13 **77** [1] DaneO'Neill 3 87
(Derek Haydn Jones) *trckd ldrs: rdn over 2f out: clsd u.p to ld 1f out: sn hdd: rallied to ld last 75yds* **5/1**[2]
0005 **2** *hd* **Myboyalfie (USA)**[9] 6988 6-9-4 **82** (v) DavidProbert 20 91
(J R Jenkins) *towards rr: rdn 3f out: prog u.p on outer 2f out: led jst ins fnl f: styd on but hdd and hld last 75yds* **5/1**[2]
P155 **3** *4* **Ogbourne Downs**[74] 4897 3-9-0 **81** WilliamCarson 1 81
(Charles Hills) *pressed ldr: drvn to ld 2f out: hdd 1f out: sn lft bhd by ldng pair* **10/1**
0315 **4** *4 1/2* **Sir Mike**[20] 6694 4-9-6 **84** GeorgeBaker 16 73
(Amanda Perrett) *pressed ldng pair: rdn over 2f out: wknd jst over 1f out* **12/1**
3412 **5** *2 1/4* **Naaz (IRE)**[22] 6642 3-9-3 **84** (b) RyanMoore 10 68
(Ed Dunlop) *hld up in last: racd alone against far side in st: sme prog over 2f out: no hdwy and btn jst over 1f out* **9/2**[1]
5545 **6** *shd* **Master Ming (IRE)**[80] 4683 3-8-11 **78** (b) SeanLevey 14 62
(Brian Meehan) *n.m.r s: towards rr: shkn up and no prog wl over 2f out: passed wkng rivals fnl f* **14/1**
5320 **7** *nk* **Corn Snow (USA)**[127] 3117 3-8-8 **75** SilvestreDeSousa 12 58
(Mark Johnston) *led to 2f out: wknd fnl f* **20/1**
5004 **8** *1/2* **Mr Red Clubs (IRE)**[23] 6609 4-8-10 **74** AndrewMullen 15 56
(Michael Appleby) *wl in tch: rdn over 2f out: tried to cl wl over 1f out: nt qckn and sn wknd* **8/1**[3]
6314 **9** *1* **Tobacco Road (IRE)**[14] 6867 3-9-4 **85** RichardHughes 13 65
(Richard Hannon) *taken down early: trckd ldrs: shkn up over 2f out: sn no prog: wknd over 1f out* **5/1**[2]
6100 **10** *2 1/4* **Messila Star**[36] 6204 3-8-13 **80** (vt[1]) JimmyFortune 8 55
(Jeremy Noseda) *nvr beyond midfield: rdn and nt qckn over 2f out: hung rt and wknd over 1f out* **33/1**
1050 **11** *nk* **Caldercruix (USA)**[16] 6792 6-8-9 **78** (p) RyanTate(5) 11 52
(James Evans) *nvr beyond midfield: u.p and struggling wl over 2f out* **66/1**
-140 **12** *12* **Bay Knight (IRE)**[9] 6988 7-9-4 **82** LiamKeniry 17 28
(Sean Curran) *a wl in rr: struggling 3f out: wl bhd over 1f out* **33/1**
100- **13** *24* **Galatian**[347] 7485 6-8-8 **72** MartinDwyer 5
(Rod Millman) *a wl in rr: wknd over 2f out: t.o* **33/1**

050 **14** *7* **Boom To Bust (IRE)**[102] 3951 5-8-8 **72**..........................(v[1]) TedDurcan 2
(Barry Brennan) *a wl in rr: wknd over 2f out: t.o* **33/1**
3350 **15** *16* **Al Raqeeb (IRE)**[22] 6642 3-8-9 **76**.................................. J-PGuillambert 7
(Gary Harrison) *trckd ldrs: wknd rapidly over 2f out: sn eased and t.o* **66/1**

1m 45.43s (5.53) **Going Correction** +0.85s/f (Soft)
WFA 3 from 4yo+ 3lb **15** Ran SP% **122.3**
Speed ratings (Par 105): **106,105,101,97,95 94,94,94,93,90 90,78,54,47,31**
toteswingers 1&2 £6.70, 1&3 £11.00, 2&3 £12.50 CSF £28.60 CT £252.12 TOTE £6.20: £2.40, £2.60, £3.60; EX 34.10 Trifecta £445.20 Pool: £3474.61 - 5.85 winning units..
Owner Llewelyn, Runeckles **Bred** D Llewelyn & J Runeckles **Trained** Efail Isaf, Rhondda C Taff
■ Stewards' Enquiry : Dane O'Neill two-day ban: used whip above permitted level (Oct 28-29)
David Probert two-day ban: used whip above permitted level (Oct 28-29)
FOCUS
A fair, competitive handicap and the main action was up the middle in the straight.
T/Jkpt: Not won. T/Plt: £1,598.10 to a £1 stake. Pool: £122,858.80 - 56.12 winning tickets
T/Qpdt: £303.60 to a £1 stake. Pool: £9141.87 - 22.27 winning tickets JN

6880 CURRAGH (R-H)
Sunday, October 13

OFFICIAL GOING: Good (good to yielding in places on straight course)

7227a JOHNNY O'SULLIVAN LIFETIME IN RACING ACHIEVEMENT WATERFORD TESTIMONIAL STKS (LISTED RACE) 6f
2:55 (2:57) 3-Y-0+ **£21,138** (£6,178; £2,926; £975)

RPR
1 **Balmont Mast (IRE)**[29] 6414 5-9-6 112........................ JohnnyMurtagh 2 108+
(Edward Lynam, Ire) *w.w on far side: t.k.h: 9th 1/2-way: hdwy on outer fr 2f out: edgd lft and rdn in 3rd ent fnl f: qcknd wl ins fnl 150yds to ld cl home: readily* **5/2**[1]
2 *3/4* **Angels Will Fall (IRE)**[8] 7021 4-9-1 100.................. RobertWinston 8 101
(Charles Hills) *trckd ldrs: t.k.h: clsr in 2nd at 1/2-way: clsd travelling wl to get on terms ent fnl f: sn led narrowly and rdn: hdd fnl 50yds: no ex* **7/1**[3]
3 *1 1/2* **Red Dubawi (IRE)**[22] 6623 5-9-6 98.................................... WJLee 4 101
(David Marnane, Ire) *w.w in rr: swtchd to outer 2f out and kpt on wl into nvr nrr 3rd on line: nt trble principals* **25/1**
4 *nse* **Boston Rocker (IRE)**[65] 5249 3-9-0 100..............(v[1]) DeclanMcDonogh 9 96
(Edward Lynam, Ire) *prom on nrside: led bef 1/2-way: rdn fr 2f out and jnd ent fnl f: sn hdd and no ex in 3rd nr fin: dropped to 4th on line* **14/1**
5 *1/2* **Liberating**[59] 5454 3-9-0 95...(p) FMBerry 12 94
(Mrs John Harrington, Ire) *w.w on nrside: 10th 1/2-way: sme hdwy into mod 5th ins fnl f: kpt on same pce* **25/1**
6 *nk* **Arctic (IRE)**[29] 6415 6-9-6 102.. PatSmullen 11 98
(Tracey Collins, Ire) *loaded wout rdr: trckd ldrs on nrside: 6th 1/2-way: rdn fr 2f out and no imp on ldrs u.p ent fnl f: kpt on same pce* **16/1**
7 *1* **Cristoforo Colombo (USA)**[9] 7004 3-9-5 109............. JosephO'Brien 5 95
(A P O'Brien, Ire) *chsd ldrs: 8th 1/2-way: n.m.r bhd horse ent fnl f: kpt on towards fin wout ever threatening* **5/2**[1]
8 *1/2* **Burn The Boats (IRE)**[92] 4297 4-9-6 95.................. GaryCarroll 7 94
(G M Lyons, Ire) *chsd ldrs: 7th 1/2-way: sme hdwy u.p to chse ldrs in 4th over 1f out: sn no ex and dropped to 7th wl ins fnl f: one pce towards fin* **10/1**
9 *3* **Joe Eile (IRE)**[14] 6883 5-9-6 97................................ EmmetMcNamara 1 84
(G M Lyons, Ire) *prom on far side: 4th 1/2-way: pushed along and no imp 2f out: dropped towards rr: ent fnl f* **25/1**
10 *1 1/2* **Scream Blue Murder (IRE)**[29] 6414 3-9-3 105............ WayneLordan 6 77
(T Stack, Ire) *trckd ldrs: 3rd 1/2-way: rdn and no imp fr 2f out: dropped towards rr ins fnl f* **8/1**
11 *3/4* **Leitir Mor (IRE)**[59] 5453 3-9-10 109............................(t) KevinManning 3 82
(J S Bolger, Ire) *prom on far side early: niggled along in 5th bef 1/2-way and sn no ex: dropped towards rr 2f out: one pce fnl f* **13/2**[2]

1m 12.27s (-3.23) **Going Correction** -0.25s/f (Firm)
WFA 3 from 4yo+ 1lb **11** Ran SP% **127.3**
Speed ratings: **111,110,108,107,107 106,105,104,100,98 97**
CSF £22.52 TOTE £3.20: £1.20, £2.70, £8.20; DF 32.90 Trifecta £390.60.
Owner Derek Iceton **Bred** Limestone And Tara Studs **Trained** Dunshaughlin, Co Meath
FOCUS
A solid event. The third, fifth and eighth set the standard, with the winner rated to his recent form.

7230a TOTE SUPER TRIFECTA IRISH CESAREWITCH (PREMIER H'CAP) 2m
4:40 (4:40) 3-Y-0+
£48,780 (£15,447; £7,317; £2,439; £1,626; £813) **Stalls** Far side

RPR
1 **Montefeltro**[24] 6573 5-9-4 **89**.. RobertTart[(3)] 94+
(Brian Ellison) *hld up in mid-div: hdwy in 15th over 2f out to chal ent fnl f: led ins fnl 100yds where wnt lft: kpt on wl* **8/1**[3]
2 *1 1/2* **Marchese Marconi (IRE)**[22] 6659 4-9-7 **89**.................... JosephO'Brien 92
(A P O'Brien, Ire) *w.w in rr of mid-div: hdwy fr 4f out to chse ldrs on outer 1 1/2f out: rdn to chal ins fnl f: kpt on wl towards fin wout matching wnr* **12/1**
3 *nse* **Call Me Bubbles (FR)**[26] 6227 4-9-5 **87**..............................(t) WJLee 90
(W P Mullins, Ire) *hld up in tch: hdwy fr over 3f out to chse ldrs in 7th into st: rdn fr 2f out and clsd u.p to chal ins fnl f: no ex between horses whn sltly hmpd nr fin: dropped to 3rd* **14/1**
4 *nk* **Majenta (IRE)**[14] 6886 3-9-3 **96**.. ChrisHayes 99
(Kevin Prendergast, Ire) *hld up in tch: hdwy over 2f out to ld 1 1/2f out: sn strly pressed and hdd ins fnl 100yds: no ex nr fin* **14/1**
5 *1/2* **Truthwillsetufree (IRE)**[42] 6022 4-9-7 **89**............................ PatSmullen 91
(D K Weld, Ire) *in tch: prog in 10th under 3f out: swtchd rt over 1f out to sn chal: no ex u.p ins fnl 100yds* **14/1**
6 *shd* **Giant's Quest (AUS)**[33] 5212 7-8-11 **79**.......................... DannyGrant 81
(H Rogers, Ire) *trckd ldrs: 6th 1/2-way: rdn over 2f out and sn swtchd rt: kpt on u.p towards fin wout troubling principals* **20/1**
7 *1 3/4* **Time For Action (IRE)**[20] 6708 3-9-8 **101**....................... WayneLordan 101
(David Wachman, Ire) *hld up in tch: rdn in 7th over 1f out and sn no imp on ldrs whn n.m.r: kpt on same pce towards fin* **15/2**[2]
8 *hd* **Spacious Sky (USA)**[22] 4-9-3 **85**.................................... JohnnyMurtagh 85
(A J Martin, Ire) *hld up in tch: gd hdwy over 2f out to chal: sn rdn in 2nd and no ex u.p ent fnl f: wknd towards fin* **16/1**
9 *hd* **Rossvoss**[33] 4842 5-8-3 **78**..(t) RayDawson[(7)] 78
(T M Walsh, Ire) *hld up in rr of mid-div: hdwy fr 4f out to chse ldrs on outer over 1f out: no ex u.p in 9th ins fnl f: kpt on same pce* **16/1**
10 *shd* **Mourani (IRE)**[36] 6227 3-8-12 **91**..............................(p) DeclanMcDonogh 91
(John M Oxx, Ire) *racd in mid-div: tk clsr order u.p 2f out: kpt on fnl f* **20/1**
11 *1 1/4* **Maxim Gorky (IRE)**[24] 5908 6-9-1 **86**................................ ColinKeane[(3)] 84
(Noel Meade, Ire) *racd in mid-div: tk clsr order 2f out: sn rdn and no imp ent fnl f: kpt on same pce* **20/1**
12 *2* **Cebuano**[36] 6227 8-8-10 **81**..(p) ConorHoban[(3)] 77
(M Halford, Ire) *racd in mid-div: rdn and no imp fr over 2f out: kpt on* **50/1**
13 *3/4* **Crystal Earth (IRE)**[30] 6375 6-8-12 **83**.......................... RonanWhelan[(3)] 78
(Peter Fahey, Ire) *chsd ldrs: 8th 1/2-way: tk clsr order 3f out: sn rdn and no ex u.p fr 2f out: wknd* **25/1**
14 *nk* **Hisaabaat (IRE)**[25] 6544 5-8-12 **80**.....................................(b) GaryCarroll 75
(D K Weld, Ire) *hld up in mid-div: rdn and no imp fr 2f out: kpt on one pce* **20/1**
15 *nk* **Weather Watch (IRE)**[36] 6227 3-9-0 **98**............................ ConnorKing[(5)] 93
(Mrs John Harrington, Ire) *hld up in mid-div: rdn into st and sn no imp u.p: kpt on same pce ins fnl f* **13/2**[1]
16 *5 1/2* **Paddy The Celeb (IRE)**[43] 5414 7-9-12 **94**......................(p) ShaneFoley 83
(M Halford, Ire) *chsd ldrs: 7th 1/2-way: pushed along into 3rd over 3f out: sn clsd to ld briefly tl hdd under 2f out: no ex u.p: wknd fnl f* **33/1**
17 *3/4* **Celestial Prospect (AUS)**[15] 5734 7-8-6 **74**....................(tp) RoryCleary 62
(Martin Brassil, Ire) *hld up in tch: 9th 1/2-way: rdn and no imp on ldrs fr 2f out: wknd ins fnl f* **20/1**
18 *shd* **Victory Song (IRE)**[9] 7006 3-8-13 **92**............................ SeamieHeffernan 80
(A P O'Brien, Ire) *nvr bttr than mid-div: pushed along and no imp over 2f out: wknd nr fin* **8/1**[3]
19 *nk* **Flameseeker (USA)**[25] 6544 3-8-4 **83** oh5............................... BenCurtis 70
(P J Prendergast, Ire) *in rr of mid-div: rdn and no imp into st: one pce fnl 2f* **66/1**
20 *2 1/4* **Jack Daddy**[36] 6227 4-8-13 **84**.. IJBrennan[(3)] 69
(Joseph G Murphy, Ire) *nvr bttr than mid-div: rdn and no imp fr over 2f out* **25/1**
21 *1/2* **Egyptian Warrior (IRE)**[23] 6615 4-8-12 **87**.......................(b) AnaO'Brien[(7)] 71
(A P O'Brien, Ire) *towards rr: sme modest hdwy fr 2f out: nvr a factor* **25/1**
22 *1 3/4* **Shamiran (IRE)**[22] 4271 8-8-5 **73**.......................................(p) TadhgO'Shea 56
(Rodger Sweeney, Ire) *trckd ldr tl led after 1f: pushed along over 4f out and hdd over 2f out: sn wknd* **33/1**
23 *1/2* **Caim Hill (IRE)**[22] 6659 10-9-10 **92**.. FMBerry 74
(Philip Fenton, Ire) *chsd ldrs: pushed along into st and sn no imp on ldrs: wknd and eased over 1f out* **25/1**
24 *nk* **Cullentry Royal**[53] 5663 5-9-4 **93**....................................(p) LukeDempsey[(7)] 75
(Gordon Elliott, Ire) *hld up in tch: pushed along fr 6f out: sn wknd* **20/1**
25 *6 1/2* **Alhellal (IRE)**[36] 6227 7-9-3 **85**................................(v[1]) EmmetMcNamara 60
(M Phelan, Ire) *trckd ldrs: 4th 1/2-way: rdn and wknd over 2f out* **33/1**
26 *1 3/4* **Becausewecan (USA)**[352] 7377 7-8-5 **72** oh8 ow1.......... BarryMcHugh 45
(Brian Ellison) *led tl hdd after 1f: 3rd 1/2-way: rdn and wknd 3f out* **16/1**
27 *10* **Abou Ben (IRE)**[24] 6579 11-8-7 **75**.................................... NGMcCullagh 37
(A Oliver, Ire) *sn trckd ldrs: t.k.h: 2nd 1/2-way rdn and wknd over 3f out* **33/1**
28 *2 1/2* **Olympiad (IRE)**[158] 2149 5-9-8 **93**.. ShaneGorey[(3)] 52
(D K Weld, Ire) *in rr of mid-div: rdn and no imp fr 4f out* **25/1**
29 *1/2* **Clara Bel La (IRE)**[24] 6579 7-9-4 **86**................................ KevinManning 44
(John E Kiely, Ire) *in rr of mid-div: tk clsr order fr 4f out: sn pushed along and no imp 2f out: wknd and eased* **25/1**
30 *18* **Splendid Light**[163] 2001 5-9-0 **82**.. FergalLynch 20
(A Oliver, Ire) *hld up in tch: clsr in 5th at 1/2-way: pushed along in 2nd over 3f out and sn no ex u.p: wknd into st: eased fnl 2f* **66/1**

3m 25.8s (-7.20) **Going Correction** -0.225s/f (Firm)
WFA 3 from 4yo+ 11lb **30** Ran SP% **161.0**
Speed ratings: **109,108,108,108,107 107,106,106,106,106 106,105,104,104,104 101,101,101,101,99 99,98,98,98,95**
CSF £97.49 CT £1426.54 TOTE £8.60: £2.60, £4.10, £4.40, £3.50; DF 129.90 Trifecta £2627.80.
Owner D Gilbert, M Lawrence, A Bruce **Bred** Darley **Trained** Norton, N Yorks
■ Stewards' Enquiry : Robert Tart three-day ban: careless riding (Nov 1,3,8)
FOCUS
Plenty of these finished close up.

6451 MUNICH (L-H)
Sunday, October 13

OFFICIAL GOING: Turf: soft

7232a PREIS DES WINTERFAVORITEN (GROUP 3) (2YO) (TURF) 1m
4:00 (12:00) 2-Y-0
£69,105 (£25,203; £16,666; £8,373; £4,471; £2,195)

RPR
1 **Born To Run (GER)** 2-9-2 0..(b[1]) SHellyn 10 102
(R Dzubasz, Germany) *dwlt and pushed along in sltly detached last early: tacked on to main body of field 3f out: rapid hdwy on inner and rdn to chal 2f out: led over 1f out and sn asserted: pushed out firmly towards fin* **43/1**
2 *2* **Nadelwald** 2-9-2 0.. AStarke 4 97
(P Schiergen, Germany) *midfield: rdn and hdwy into 3rd over 1f out: kpt on wout matching wnr and wnt 2nd cl home* **42/10**[3]
3 *1/2* **Madurai (GER)**[28] 2-9-2 0.. APietsch 5 96
(W Hickst, Germany) *stdd and hld up towards rr: rdn over 2f out: kpt on steadily and wnt 3rd fnl strides: nvr able to chal* **48/10**
4 *1/2* **Magic Artist (IRE)**[46] 5911 2-9-2 0.................................... ADeVries 2 95
(W Figge, Germany) *hld up in rr: rdn and hdwy fr 2f out: wnt 2nd ins fnl f: kpt on same pce and no imp on wnr: no ex and lost 2 pls cl home* **17/5**[2]
5 *1 1/4* **Oil Of England (GER)**[80] 2-9-2 0...................................... GregoryBenoist 12 92
(M Figge, Germany) *sent forward fr wdst draw and led: rdn and strly pressed fr 2f out: hdd over 1f out: edgd lft u.p ent fnl f: kpt on same pce and dropped to 5th* **216/10**
6 *2* **Mac Moneysac (GER)** 2-9-2 0... JBojko 1 87
(A Wohler, Germany) *midfield on inner: rdn over 2f out: kpt on same pce and nvr threatened* **73/10**
7 *6* **Simba** 2-9-2 0.. EPedroza 6 74
(A Wohler, Germany) *dwlt: steadily rcvrd into midfield on outer: rdn over 2f out: sn outpcd and dropped towards rr: btn ent fnl f* **29/10**[1]
8 *1/2* **Rock Of Cashel (GER)** 2-9-2 0... FabriceVeron 9 72
(R Dzubasz, Germany) *trckd ldr: rdn over 2f out: outpcd and lost pl over 1f out: steadily fdd* **47/10**

9 1 1/2 **Bear Power (GER)**[28] 2-9-2 0 MrDennisSchiergen 8 69
(C Sprengel, Germany) *trckd ldr on inner: rdn and brief effrt over 2f out: sn no ex and btn: steadily fdd* **26/1**

10 32 **Lady Love (GER)** 2-8-11 0 BClos 11
(M Angermann, Germany) *t.k.h: broke wl and trckd ldr on outer: rn v wd on home bnd and lost all ch: sn in rr and btn: t.o* **122/1**

1m 43.28s (103.28) **10** Ran SP% **125.6**
WIN (incl. 10 euro stake): 438. PLACES: 61, 17, 23. SF: 1,719.
Owner Stall Carolus **Bred** Gestut Gorlsdorf **Trained** Germany

6678 COLOGNE (R-H)
Sunday, October 13

OFFICIAL GOING: Turf: soft

7233a STUTENPREIS DER ILSE UND HEINZ RAMM-STIFTUNG (LISTED RACE) (F&M) (TURF) 1m
3:45 (12:00) 3-Y-0+ **£10,569** (£3,252; £1,626; £813)

RPR

1 **Koffi Angel (GER)**[21] 4-9-2 0 WPanov 11 95
(H J Groschel, Germany) **23/10**[1]

2 1/2 **Nevada (GER)**[35] 4-9-2 0 EddyHardouin 3 94
(P Harley, Germany) **104/10**

3 2 1/2 **Molly Amour (GER)**[43] 6010 4-9-2 0 LennartHammer-Hansen 1 88
(M Rulec, Germany) **116/10**

4 1 3/4 **Galician**[8] 7025 4-9-2 0 LiamJones 7 84
(Mark Johnston) *pressed ldr: lost pl and pushed along 4f out: rdn over 2f out: outpcd by ldng trio but kpt on wl u.p and wnt 4th toward fin* **13/5**[2]

5 1 **Julissima**[21] 3-8-13 0 DPorcu 10 82
(P Schiergen, Germany) **42/10**[3]

6 2 **Eleona (GER)**[21] 6-9-2 0 StefanieHofer 2 77
(Frau E Mader, Germany) **233/10**

7 3/4 **Foreign Princess (GER)**[35] 4-9-2 0 NRichter 4 75
(H J Groschel, Germany) **102/10**

8 3/4 **Patuca**[56] 3-8-13 0 MaximPecheur 5 74
(A Wohler, Germany) **175/10**

9 2 1/2 **Savannah Blue (GER)**[364] 5-9-2 0 MartinSeidl 8 68
(Markus Klug, Germany) **243/10**

10 hd **Not Expected (GER)**[21] 3-8-13 0 SteveDrowne 9 68
(A Trybuhl, Germany) **99/10**

11 3 1/2 **Anaita (GER)**[35] 4-9-2 0 AndreBest 6 59
(P Harley, Germany) **217/10**

1m 39.13s (0.74)
WFA 3 from 4yo+ 3lb **11** Ran SP% **130.0**
WIN (incl. 1 euro stake): 33. PLACES: 13, 27, 25. SF: 340.
Owner Rennstall Darboven **Bred** Gestut Idee **Trained** Germany

6889 SAN SIRO (R-H)
Sunday, October 13

OFFICIAL GOING: Turf: heavy

7234a PREMIO VERZIERE (GROUP 3) (3YO+ FILLIES & MARES) (TURF) 1m 2f
3:20 (12:00) 3-Y-0+ **£25,868** (£11,382; £6,208; £3,104)

RPR

1 **Quaduna**[42] 3-8-9 0 FabioBranca 7 102
(A Wohler, Germany) *tk v t.k.h: prom: allowed to stride on and ld after 1 1/2f: mde rest: shkn up and qcknd 2f out: hrd rdn over 1f out: r.o ins fnl f: drvn out: jst hld on* **604/100**[3]

2 snk **La Banderilla (FR)**[36] 6229 3-8-9 0 Francois-XavierBertras 1 102
(F Rohaut, France) *led: hdd after 1 1/2f and settled in 3rd: rdn to chse ldr over 1 1/2f out: r.o u.p fnl f: nt quite get up* **2/5**[1]

3 4 **Summer Fall (USA)**[112] 4-9-0 0 PierantonioConvertino 4 94
(B Grizzetti, Italy) *racd in fnl pair: hdwy 2 1/2f out: wnt 3rd appr fnl f: kpt on u.p: nvr on terms w first two* **98/10**

4 3/4 **Licia (ITY)**[14] 3-8-11 0 UmbertoRispoli 2 95
(S Botti, Italy) *trckd ldr: rdn and nt qckn 2f out: one pce fnl f* **21/10**[2]

5 nk **Danspi**[112] 3616 3-8-9 0 DarioVargiu 5 92
(B Grizzetti, Italy) *midfield: 4th and rdn over 2 1/2f out: no imp: kpt on fnl 100yds* **173/10**

6 1 **Linarda (DEN)**[14] 3-8-9 0 MEsposito 6 90
(M Rulec, Germany) *t.k.h: hld up in fnl pair: rdn and short-lived effrt over 2f out: one pce fnl f* **159/10**

7 4 **Sciolina (IRE)**[35] 4-9-0 0 SUrru 3 82
(Cristiana Signorelli, Italy) *midfield: pushed along 3f out: outpcd 2 1/2f out: sn wl btn* **7/1**

2m 9.2s (2.50)
WFA 3 from 4yo 5lb **7** Ran SP% **151.0**
WIN (incl. 1 euro stake): 7.03. PLACES: 2.17, 1.36. DF: 4.51.
Owner Stiftung Gestut Fahrhof **Bred** Stiftung Gestut Fahrhof **Trained** Germany

7235a GRAN CRITERIUM (GROUP 1) (2YO COLTS & FILLIES) (TURF) 7f 110y
4:00 (12:00) 2-Y-0 **£97,560** (£42,926; £23,414; £11,707)

RPR

1 **Priore Philip (ITY)**[22] 2-8-11 0 UmbertoRispoli 4 108
(S Botti, Italy) *w.w towards rr: 6th and swtchd outside under 2f out: sustained run to ld ins fnl f: sn clr: comf* **17/4**[3]

2 3 **Grey Greezly (FR)**[21] 2-8-11 0 FabioBranca 2 101
(B Grizzetti, Italy) *trckd ldr of main gp: rdn to chse ldr 2f out: r.o to ld appr 1f out: hdd ins fnl f: no ex but wl in control of 2nd* **61/10**

3 1 3/4 **Arpinati**[33] 2-8-11 0 MEsposito 5 96
(S Botti, Italy) *midfield: prog to chse ldrs 2f out: cl 3rd and rdn 1 1/2f out: kpt on wout qckning fnl f* **11/10**[2]

4 1 1/2 **Fanoulpifer**[105] 2-8-11 0 DarioVargiu 6 93
(B Grizzetti, Italy) *hdd main gp bhd two clr ldrs: tk clsr order 2 1/2f out: 3rd and niggled along over 2f out: sn hrd rdn and outpcd 1 1/2f out: edgd sharply rt then lft over 1f out: kpt on u.p fnl f: tk 4th cl home* **4/5**[1]

5 hd **Filou (SWI)** 2-8-11 0 RaphaelLingg 3 92
(Th Von Ballmoos, Switzerland) *disp ld early taking a t.k.h: sn wnt on and set gd gallop: pressed fr 3f out but rallied gamely: hrd rdn and hdd appr 1f out: grad fdd ins fnl f: hung sharply rt 100yds out: lost 4th cl home* **73/10**

6 dist **Sentimentodarcadia (ITY)**[105] 2-8-11 0 IRossi 1
(B Grizzetti, Italy) *disp ld early: sn chsng ldr: pressed ldr fr 3f out: wknd ins fnl 2f: eased fnl f* **4/5**[1]

7 2 1/2 **Crissolo (ITY)**[141] 2-8-11 0 PierantonioConvertino 7
(B Grizzetti, Italy) *in rr: rdn and no imp 2 1/2f out: sn wl bhd: eased ins fnl f* **61/10**

1m 36.6s (1.10) **7** Ran SP% **218.0**
WIN (incl. 1 euro stake): 5.27. PLACES: 2.67, 4.33. DF: 22.17.
Owner Scuderia Ste Ma **Bred** Azienda Agricola Luciani Loreto **Trained** Italy

6872 MUSSELBURGH (R-H)
Monday, October 14

OFFICIAL GOING: Round course - good to firm (good in places); straight course - good (good to firm in places) (7.9)
Wind: Moderate; half behind Weather: Overcast and showers

7236 32RED.COM APPRENTICE RIDERS' H'CAP 5f
2:10 (2:10) (Class 6) (0-60,60) 3-Y-0+ **£2,385** (£704; £352) **Stalls** High

Form RPR

0040 1 **Tadalavil**[4] 7148 8-8-9 **53** SamanthaBell(5) 13 61
(Linda Perratt) *trckd ldrs: hdwy 2f out: chal over 1f out: rdn to ld ent fnl f: kpt on* **14/1**

5313 2 3/4 **Beauty Pageant (IRE)**[10] 6994 6-9-0 **60** ClaireMurray(7) 14 65
(David Brown) *qckly away: led: rdn along over 1f out: hdd ent fnl f: sn drvn and kpt on* **5/1**[2]

2233 3 hd **Here Now And Why (IRE)**[15] 6879 6-9-5 **58** (b) NeilFarley 11 62
(Iain Jardine) *trckd ldrs: hdwy wl over 1f out: rdn ent fnl f: kpt on same pce* **6/1**[3]

5003 4 1 **Amis Reunis**[7] 7077 4-8-9 **55** (p) JordanHibberd(7) 3 56+
(Alan Berry) *in rr: rdn along over 1f out: styd on strly fnl f: nrst fin* **18/1**

4642 5 nse **Lady Poppy**[9] 7030 3-9-4 **60** ConnorBeasley(3) 10 62
(George Moore) *cl up: rdn along 2f out: drvn and one pce appr fnl f* **9/2**[1]

0360 6 3/4 **Lizzy's Dream**[12] 6944 5-9-5 **58** JasonHart 6 56
(Robin Bastiman) *dwlt and in rr tl styd on appr fnl f: nrst fin* **7/1**

6053 7 1 1/4 **Myjestic Melody (IRE)**[12] 6944 5-8-5 **47** ow1 JacobButterfield(3) 7 40
(Brian Ellison) *chsd ldrs: rdn along 2f out: grad wknd* **6/1**[3]

5450 8 1 **Distant Sun (USA)**[4] 7149 9-8-7 **49** ow1 (p) DavidBergin(3) 4 39
(Linda Perratt) *a towards rr* **16/1**

0202 9 1 1/2 **Cheyenne Red (IRE)**[15] 6879 7-8-2 **48** PaulMcGiff(7) 1 32
(Michael Herrington) *chsd ldrs: rdn along 2f out: sn wknd* **12/1**

0-06 10 1 1/4 **Chorister Choir (IRE)**[44] 5989 3-8-9 **55** GaryMahon(7) 12 36
(Tim Easterby) *in tch: swtchd lft and rdn 2f out: n.d* **33/1**

-400 11 3/4 **Hellolini**[6] 7101 3-8-6 **50** (p) KevinStott(5) 8 28
(Robin Bastiman) *a towards rr* **66/1**

1253 12 1 1/4 **Megaleka**[32] 6345 3-9-1 **59** TimClark(5) 2 33
(Alan Bailey) *in tch on outer: effrt to chse ldrs 2f out: sn rdn and wknd* **10/1**

58.99s (-1.41) **Going Correction** -0.225s/f (Firm) **12** Ran SP% **114.9**
Speed ratings (Par 101): **102,100,100,98,98 97,95,94,91,89 88,86**
toteswingers 1&2 £16.80, 1&3 £18.50, 2&3 £2.50 CSF £80.07 CT £372.80 TOTE £14.10: £6.10, £2.80, £1.90; EX 155.30 Trifecta £708.70 Pool: £1,338.92 - 1.41 winning units..
Owner Ken McGarrity **Bred** Theakston Stud **Trained** East Kilbride, S Lanarks

FOCUS
A moderate apprentice handicap in which those drawn nearside held sway, with the first three starting from stalls 13, 14 and 11. Ordinary form.

7237 IRISH STALLION FARMS EBF MAIDEN STKS 1m
2:40 (2:40) (Class 4) 2-Y-0 **£4,204** (£1,251; £625; £312) **Stalls** Low

Form RPR

03 1 **Mindblowing**[9] 7023 2-9-5 0 DanielTudhope 5 79+
(Kevin Ryan) *cl up: led wl over 2f out: rdn wl over 1f out: clr ins fnl f: kpt on* **11/4**[2]

5 2 3/4 **Mambo Rhythm**[7] 7061 2-9-0 0 AdrianNicholls 3 70+
(Mark Johnston) *dwlt and hld up in rr: swtchd wd and hdwy wl over 2f out: rdn wl over 1f out: styd on strly fnl f* **40/1**

6 3 1 3/4 **Layla's Red Devil (IRE)**[16] 6821 2-9-0 0 BarryMcHugh 8 66
(Richard Fahey) *prom: effrt to chal 2f out: sn rdn and ev ch tl drvn and one pce fnl f* **5/2**[1]

2 4 1 1/4 **Art Obsession (IRE)**[24] 6581 2-9-5 0 RobertWinston 7 68
(David Barron) *trckd ldrs: n.m.r and sltly hmpd after 2f: pushed along and lost pl 1/2-way: gd hdwy and cl up over 2f out: sn rdn and ch tl drvn and one pce appr fnl f* **3/1**[3]

0 5 nk **Insaany**[24] 6581 2-9-5 0 GrahamLee 2 68+
(Mark Johnston) *hld up: hdwy over 2f out: nt clr run and swtchd lft wl over 1f out: effrt and n.m.r appr fnl f: no imp* **28/1**

6232 6 2 **Porthos Du Vallon**[15] 6873 2-9-5 72 TomEaves 4 63
(Keith Dalgleish) *trckd ldrs: hdwy wl over 2f out: swtchd lft and rdn wl over 1f out: sn drvn and wknd appr fnl f* **8/1**

56 7 3/4 **Ice Mayden**[33] 6299 2-9-0 0 DuranFentiman 1 56
(Bryan Smart) *hld up in rr: effrt and sme hdwy on outer 3f out: rdn along over 2f out: n.d* **25/1**

00 8 18 **Mariners Moon (IRE)**[50] 5790 2-9-5 0 JoeFanning 6 20
(Mark Johnston) *led: rdn along 3f out: sn hdd & wknd over 2f out* **6/1**

1m 41.54s (0.34) **Going Correction** -0.125s/f (Firm) **8** Ran SP% **115.4**
Speed ratings (Par 97): **93,92,90,89,88 86,86,68**
toteswingers 1&2 £22.00, 1&3 £2.90, 2&3 £17.60 CSF £105.15 TOTE £3.80: £1.10, £5.40, £2.00; EX 144.70 Trifecta £1063.70 Pool: £2,540.26 - 1.79 winning units..
Owner T G & Mrs M E Holdcroft, K MacPherson **Bred** Bearstone Stud **Trained** Hambleton, N Yorks

FOCUS
An ordinary maiden run at a steady tempo. The winner was value for a bit extra.

7238 GBI RACING WELCOMES NICOSIA RACE CLUB (S) H'CAP 1m 1f
3:15 (3:15) (Class 6) (0-65,64) 3-Y-0+ **£2,264** (£673; £336; £168) **Stalls** Low

Form RPR

0312 1 **Camerooney**[7] 7082 10-9-3 **62** (p) NathanAlison(5) 11 72
(Marjorie Fife) *mde all: pushed clr 3f out: rdn wl over 1f out: sn edgd lft: drvn and edgd lft ins fnl f: hld on wl* **13/2**[3]

3331 **2** ½ **Silly Billy (IRE)**[7] 7083 5-8-12 **57** 6ex........................ JacobButterfield(5) 7 66
(Brian Ellison) *trckd ldrs: hdwy 3f out: chal over 1f out: sn rdn and ev ch: kpt on same pce towards fin* **3/1**[1]

0543 **3** ¾ **Royal Straight**[15] 6877 8-9-3 **64**..............................(t) SamanthaBell(7) 13 71
(Linda Perratt) *dwlt and hld up in rr: hdwy over 2f out: chsd ldrs over 1f out: sn rdn and kpt on fnl f: nrst fin* **14/1**

1200 **4** ¾ **Violent Velocity (IRE)**[4] 7152 10-9-3 **64**........................... JoeDoyle(7) 2 69
(John Quinn) *in tch: hdwy to chse ldrs wl over 2f out: sn rdn swtchd lft and drvn over 1f out: one pce* **10/1**

0300 **5** 3 **Monthly Medal**[24] 6598 10-8-12 **52**..................................(t) GrahamLee 6 51
(Wilf Storey) *hld up in rr: swtchd to outer and hdwy over 2f out: rdn to chse ldrs and hung rt over 1f out: no imp fnl f* **16/1**

0044 **6** 1¾ **Assizes**[19] 6759 4-9-8 **62**... LukeMorris 5 57
(Ruth Carr) *dwlt: t.k.h in rr: hdwy over 3f out: rdn to chse ldrs over 2f out: drvn: edgd rt and no imp appr fnl f* **8/1**

00-0 **7** ¾ **Charpoy (USA)**[12] 6943 5-9-6 **60**..(p) TomEaves 1 53
(Keith Dalgleish) *chsd ldrs on inner: rdn along 3f out: drvn and wknd wl over 1f out* **18/1**

4030 **8** 6 **Meglio Ancora**[28] 6472 6-8-7 **52**.............................. ConnorBeasley(5) 9 32
(Richard Ford) *midfield: effrt on outer 3f out: sn rdn along and n.d* **20/1**

0600 **9** hd **Inniscastle Boy**[14] 6907 4-8-3 **50** oh5........................(v[1]) JackGarritty(7) 4 30
(Jim Goldie) *nvr bttr than midfield* **25/1**

0003 **10** 1 **Elspeth's Boy (USA)**[16] 6856 6-9-9 **63**...................... RussKennemore 3 40
(Philip Kirby) *in tch: hdwy over 3f out: chsd ldrs over 2f out: sn rdn: drvn wl over 1f out and sn wknd* **5/1**[2]

4400 **11** 4½ **Mujarrad (USA)**[24] 6588 3-9-3 **64**.................................... JasonHart(3) 14 33
(Ian Semple) *trckd ldng pair: effrt on outer 3f out: rdn over 2f out: sn wknd* **20/1**

3500 **12** ½ **Samoan (IRE)**[33] 6315 4-9-2 **59**................................ SladeO'Hara(3) 8 25
(Alan Berry) *a in rr* **50/1**

0602 **13** 7 **Mudaawem (USA)**[7] 7083 3-8-10 **54**................................... JoeFanning 12 6
(Mark Johnston) *chsd ldrs: rdn along 3f out: sn wknd* **14/1**

6000 **14** 1¼ **Jonny Lesters Hair (IRE)**[9] 7024 8-9-3 **57**...........(p) DuranFentiman 10 5
(Tim Easterby) *in tch on outer: rdn along over 3f out: sn wknd* **14/1**

1m 52.15s (-1.75) **Going Correction** -0.125s/f (Firm)
WFA 3 from 4yo+ 4lb **14 Ran SP% 121.7**
Speed ratings (Par 101): **102,101,100,100,97 96,95,90,89,88 84,84,78,77**
toteswingers 1&2 £3.20, 1&3 £6.70, 2&3 £6.30 CSF £25.19 CT £281.25 TOTE £6.50: £3.20, £1.80, £4.40; EX 16.60 Trifecta £118.80 Pool: £2,072.78 - 13.07 winning units..There was no bid for the winner.
Owner Mrs Jean Stapleton **Bred** Miss Dianne Hill **Trained** Stillington, N Yorks

FOCUS
A competitive, if moderate selling handicap and not many got into it.

7239 BETFAIR SCOTTISH STAYERS' FINAL (H'CAP) 1m 5f
3:45 (3:45) (Class 3) 3-Y-0+ **£9,703** (£2,887; £1,443; £721) **Stalls** Low

Form RPR

U101 **1** **Bayan Kasirga (IRE)**[6] 7100 3-8-5 **81** 6ex.................. SamanthaBell(7) 8 89+
(Richard Fahey) *hld up towards rr: hdwy wl over 2f out: chsd ldrs whn n.m.r and sltly hmpd ent fnl f: sn rdn and styd on strly to ld last 50yds* **6/1**[3]

5043 **2** 1¼ **Hawdyerwheesht**[15] 6876 5-9-4 **79**.. GrahamLee 1 85
(Jim Goldie) *trckd ldrs on inner: smooth hdwy over 2f out: led over 1f out: rdn ins fnl f: hdd and no ex last 50yds* **7/1**

5130 **3** ¾ **Corton Lad**[23] 6626 3-8-8 **77**...(tp) TomEaves 9 82
(Keith Dalgleish) *hld up towards rr: hdwy on wd outside 3f out: chsd ldrs wl over 1f out: rdn and edgd rt ent fnl f: sn drvn and kpt on* **8/1**

2401 **4** nk **Vittachi**[14] 6909 6-7-11 **61** oh2...(p) JulieBurke(3) 2 66
(Alistair Whillans) *hld up in midfield: hdwy 3f out: chsd ldrs 2f out: rdn to chal and ev ch ent fnl f: sn drvn and kpt on same pce* **20/1**

2325 **5** 1 **Geanie Mac (IRE)**[14] 6909 4-7-9 **61** oh8.............(p) ShirleyTeasdale(5) 12 64?
(Linda Perratt) *prom: effrt to chal 3f out: rdn along 2f out: drvn and hld whn n.m.r and sltly hmpd ent fnl f: one pce after* **66/1**

3-61 **6** ½ **Calculated Risk**[25] 6552 4-8-12 **73**............................ MichaelO'Connell 4 75
(John Quinn) *trckd ldrs: hdwy wl over 2f out: rdn and ch wl over 1f out: sn drvn and one pce* **11/4**[1]

4661 **7** 1½ **Grand Diamond (IRE)**[13] 6917 9-7-8 **62**........................ JackGarritty(7) 10 62
(Jim Goldie) *hld up in rr: hdwy on inner 3f out: rdn to chse ldrs 2f out: drvn and one pce appr fnl f* **33/1**

05-3 **8** 2¾ **Burns Night**[17] 6470 7-7-10 **62**.....................................(p) JoeyHaynes(5) 14 58
(Philip Kirby) *hld up towards rr: hdwy 3f out: rdn along 2f out: n.d* **10/1**

1321 **9** shd **Discay**[16] 6846 4-9-10 **85**.. JoeFanning 11 81
(Mark Johnston) *trckd ldrs on outer: hdwy 3f out: rdn 2f out: sn wknd* **4/1**[2]

0/64 **10** 1½ **Worth A King'S**[13] 6917 7-8-1 **62**...(p) LukeMorris 7 55
(Philip Kirby) *towards rr: rdn along 1/2-way: nvr a factor* **33/1**

246 **11** ¾ **Goodlukin Lucy**[6] 7099 6-8-0 **61** oh9......................................(t) RaulDaSilva 3 53
(Dianne Sayer) *a towards rr* **28/1**

4300 **12** nk **Titus Bolt (IRE)**[15] 6877 4-7-9 **63**................................... JoeDoyle(7) 6 55
(Jim Goldie) *sn led tl rn wd bnd after 4f: cl up and led again 1/2-way: rdn along 3f out: sn hdd & wknd* **25/1**

3120 **13** ½ **St Ignatius**[25] 6552 6-8-11 **72**...(v) RobertWinston 5 63
(Alan Bailey) *cl up: led after 4f: hdd 1/2-way: cl up tl rdn to ld again wl over 2f out: sn drvn: hdd & wknd over 1f out* **18/1**

2m 48.06s (-3.94) **Going Correction** -0.125s/f (Firm)
WFA 3 from 4yo+ 8lb **13 Ran SP% 118.3**
Speed ratings (Par 107): **107,106,105,105,104 104,103,102,101,101 100,100,100**
toteswingers 1&2 £9.90, 1&3 £13.80, 2&3 £14.00 CSF £43.30 CT £342.39 TOTE £7.00: £3.20, £2.70, £3.40; EX 46.30 Trifecta £352.00 Pool: £2,239.02 - 4.77 winning units..
Owner Stephen Humphreys **Bred** Lynn Lodge Stud **Trained** Musley Bank, N Yorks

FOCUS
A modest staying handicap. They finished well bunched and the fifth casts doubts on the form. The winner looks to have more to offer.

7240 32RED CASINO H'CAP 5f
4:20 (4:22) (Class 5) (0-75,75) 3-Y-0+ **£2,587** (£770; £384; £192) **Stalls** High

Form RPR

3040 **1** **Layla's Oasis**[25] 6547 3-8-10 **64**.. BarryMcHugh 8 73
(Richard Fahey) *trckd ldrs: hdwy 2f out: sn cl up: rdn to chal appr fnl f: kpt on wl u.p to ld last 40yds* **22/1**

1100 **2** ½ **Gottcher**[24] 6583 5-9-4 **72**.. TomEaves 7 78
(Keith Dalgleish) *cl up: rdn to ld over 1f out: drvn ins fnl f: hdd and no ex last 40yds* **18/1**

0000 **3** ½ **Rothesay Chancer**[24] 6583 5-9-4 **72**.. JoeFanning 2 76
(Jim Goldie) *in tch: hdwy on outer 2f out: rdn to chal ent fnl f: drvn and ev ch tl nt qckn towards fin* **10/1**

6015 **4** nk **Opt Out**[4] 7150 3-8-9 **66**.. JulieBurke(3) 1 70+
(Alistair Whillans) *dwlt and in rr: swtchd to outer and hdwy over 1f out: sn rdn and styd on strly towards fin* **7/1**[2]

212 **5** nk **Tom Sawyer**[28] 6471 5-8-12 **71**..................................(b) ConnorBeasley(5) 10 73
(Julie Camacho) *led: rdn along 2f out: hdd over 1f out: sn drvn and kpt on same pce fnl f* **4/1**[1]

410 **6** nk **Algar Lad**[24] 6586 3-9-7 **75**.. GrahamLee 5 77
(Jim Goldie) *hld up: rdn along 2f out: rdn and kpt on fnl f* **4/1**[1]

3500 **7** hd **The Nifty Fox**[14] 6908 9-9-5 **73**...(p) DuranFentiman 11 73
(Tim Easterby) *hld up in tch: hdwy 2f out: sn swtchd rt and rdn: n.m.r ent fnl f: kpt on same pce* **14/1**

005 **8** ½ **Jinky**[14] 6908 5-9-5 **73**.. DaleSwift 3 72
(Linda Perratt) *hld up in rr: hdwy over 1f out: nt clr run ent fnl f: no ch after* **15/2**[3]

0060 **9** nse **Your Gifted (IRE)**[9] 7029 6-8-7 **66**...........................(e) JacobButterfield(5) 9 64
(Lisa Williamson) *in tch: hdwy to chse ldrs 2f out: swtchd rt and rdn over 1f out: n.m.r ent fnl f: kpt on towards fin* **50/1**

0000 **10** 1 **Master Rooney (IRE)**[9] 7030 7-8-4 **65** ow1.............(p) JordanNason(7) 4 60
(Geoffrey Harker) *cl up: rdn along wl over 1f out: drvn and grad wknd appr fnl f* **22/1**

-55 **11** shd **Million Faces**[41] 6077 4-9-3 **71**... LukeMorris 13 66
(Rae Guest) *chsd ldrs: rdn along wl over 1f out: grad wknd* **10/1**

3100 **12** hd **Someone's Darling**[15] 6874 3-9-4 **72**.................................. DanielTudhope 6 67+
(Jim Goldie) *trckd ldrs: effrt whn nt clr run over 1f out: sn one pce* **12/1**

0200 **13** ½ **Economic Crisis (IRE)**[14] 6908 4-8-11 **68**.................. SladeO'Hara(3) 12 60
(Alan Berry) *a in rr* **12/1**

58.74s (-1.66) **Going Correction** -0.225s/f (Firm) **13 Ran SP% 120.4**
Speed ratings (Par 103): **104,103,102,101,101 100,100,99,99,98 98,97,96**
toteswingers 1&2 £62.20, 1&3 £24.40, 2&3 £34.40 CSF £368.85 CT £4291.95 TOTE £22.70: £6.00, £5.50, £2.90; EX 621.00 Trifecta £2261.60 Part won. Pool: £3,015.49 - 0.17 winning units..
Owner Dr Marwan Koukash **Bred** P T Tellwright **Trained** Musley Bank, N Yorks

FOCUS
A modest but competitive sprint handicap. The form looks sound with the winner rated back to his best.

7241 MCEWAN FRASER H'CAP 7f 30y
4:50 (4:53) (Class 3) (0-95,90) 3-Y-0+ **£7,762** (£2,310; £1,154; £577) **Stalls** Low

Form RPR

0200 **1** **Chookie Royale**[23] 6625 5-8-8 **80**.......................................(p) JasonHart(3) 1 93
(Keith Dalgleish) *chsd ldrs: hdwy and cl up 3f out: led over 2f out: rdn and hung bdly lft over 1f out: styd on wl towards fin* **9/1**

2010 **2** 2¾ **Silver Rime (FR)**[4] 7152 8-8-13 **87**.................................. ConnorBeasley(5) 2 93
(Linda Perratt) *s.i.s and in rr: hdwy 3f out: rdn to chse ldrs wl over 1f out: drvn and kpt on fnl f* **16/1**

1600 **3** nk **Wannabe King**[16] 6826 7-8-13 **89**.................................(v) JordanNason(7) 6 94
(Geoffrey Harker) *chsd ldrs: hdwy 3f out: rdn 2f out: drvn over 1f out: kpt on same pce fnl f* **22/1**

1040 **4** 1 **Alejandro (IRE)**[16] 6826 4-9-1 **89**............................... GeorgeChaloner(5) 7 91
(Richard Fahey) *hld up in midfield: hdwy 3f out: rdn to chse ldrs 2f out: drvn and one pce ent fnl f* **9/2**[2]

4000 **5** 3¼ **Gandalak (FR)**[23] 6621 4-9-1 **89**.. DavidBergin(5) 4 83
(David O'Meara) *cl up: led after 1 1/2f and set str pce: rdn along 3f out: sn hdd and drvn: grad wknd* **12/1**

2350 **6** 3 **Frontier Fighter**[16] 6840 5-9-7 **90**.. DanielTudhope 8 76
(David O'Meara) *towards rr: hdwy 2f out: sn rdn and plugged on: nvr nr ldrs* **7/1**

1032 **7** 2¾ **Sound Advice**[9] 7024 4-9-2 **85**... TomEaves 3 64
(Keith Dalgleish) *chsd ldrs: rdn along over 2f out: n.m.r wl over 1f out: sn wknd* **11/2**[3]

2211 **8** nk **Iptisam**[15] 6871 4-9-1 **84**.. GrahamLee 12 62
(James Tate) *t.k.h: chsd ldng pair: hdwy 3f out: rdn 2f out: sn wknd* **10/3**[1]

0542 **9** 1½ **Misplaced Fortune**[18] 6768 8-9-1 **89**.............................. KevinStott(5) 10 63
(Nigel Tinkler) *chsd ldrs on outer: rdn along over 2f out: sn wknd* **16/1**

/506 **10** 1¾ **Enderby Spirit (GR)**[58] 5537 7-8-13 **82**...........................(t) DuranFentiman 9 52
(Bryan Smart) *s.i.s: a in rr* **33/1**

3000 **11** 3½ **Zacynthus (IRE)**[16] 6826 5-9-3 **86**....................................... RobertWinston 11 47
(Kevin Ryan) *a towards rr* **20/1**

1145 **12** 5 **Skytrain**[20] 6727 3-8-11 **82**... JoeFanning 5 29
(Mark Johnston) *led 1 1/2f: chsd ldr: rdn along 3f out: wknd 2f out* **11/1**

1m 26.89s (-2.11) **Going Correction** -0.125s/f (Firm)
WFA 3 from 4yo+ 2lb **12 Ran SP% 119.0**
Speed ratings (Par 107): **107,103,103,102,98 95,92,91,90,88 84,78**
toteswingers 1&2 £36.30, 1&3 £44.20, 2&3 £30.40 CSF £140.51 CT £3099.79 TOTE £13.10: £3.10, £4.50, £7.00; EX 203.80 Trifecta £2511.10 Part won. Pool: £3,348.14 - 0.23 winning units..
Owner Raeburn Brick Limited **Bred** D And J Raeburn **Trained** Carluke, S Lanarks

FOCUS
A fair handicap which was strongly run. The winner had the best draw and this rates a small turf personal best.

7242 WILLIE PARK TROPHY (H'CAP) 1m 6f
5:20 (5:20) (Class 2) (0-100,94) 3-Y-O **£12,938** (£3,850; £1,924; £962) **Stalls** Centre

Form RPR

21 **1** **Commissioned (IRE)**[59] 5469 3-9-7 **94**................................ JoeFanning 3 104+
(Mark Johnston) *trckd ldng pair: hdwy 3f out: sn pushed along rdn to chal over 1f out: drvn ent fnl f: styd on gamely u.p to ld on line* **6/5**[1]

1522 **2** nse **Deficit (IRE)**[17] 6793 3-8-8 **81**.. TomEaves 5 90
(Michael Bell) *led after 1f: pushed along and qcknd over 3f out: rdn 2f out: drvn ent fnl f: hdd on line* **7/2**[2]

1113 **3** 1¾ **Slip Of The Tongue**[48] 5868 3-8-7 **80**................................ LukeMorris 1 86
(Sir Mark Prescott Bt) *led 1f: trckd ldr: pushed along over 4f out: rdn to chal wl over 2f out: ev ch tl drvn appr fnl f and kpt on same pce* **5/1**[3]

4441 **4** 2¼ **Aramist (IRE)**[21] 6686 3-8-2 **75** oh2...................................... BenCurtis 4 78
(Alan Swinbank) *in tch: pushed along 3f out: rdn over 2f out: sn drvn and kpt on one pce* **8/1**

1 **5** hd **Silent Movie (IRE)**[10] 6997 3-8-9 **82**.................................. GrahamLee 7 85
(Mark Johnston) *in tch: rdn along 3f out: drvn wl over 1f out and kpt on one pce* **5/1**[3]

3m 2.73s (-2.57) **Going Correction** -0.125s/f (Firm) **5 Ran SP% 112.1**
Speed ratings (Par 107): **102,101,100,99,99**
CSF £5.81 TOTE £2.70: £1.50, £1.90; EX 6.10 Trifecta £19.00 Pool: £2,163.57 - 85.01 winning units..
Owner Sheikh Hamdan Bin Mohammed Al Maktoum **Bred** Kilfrush Stud **Trained** Middleham Moor, N Yorks

■ Stewards' Enquiry : Tom Eaves one-day ban: careless riding (Oct 28)

The Form Book Flat, Raceform Ltd, Compton, RG20 6NL.

FOCUS
A muddling affair and the progressive winner is value for further. The form is rated around the third and fourth.
T/Plt: £2,367.20 to a £1 stake. Pool: £54,317.50 - 16.75 winning units T/Qpdt: £1,039.40 to a £1 stake. Pool: £6,320.76 - 4.50 winning units JR

6953 SALISBURY (R-H)

Monday, October 14

OFFICIAL GOING: Soft (heavy in places; 7.2) changing to heavy after race 1 (1.50)
Wind: Mild breeze; against Weather: Overcast with showers

7243 BATHWICK TYRES REDUCED ADMISSION RACE DAY MAIDEN AUCTION STKS 6f 212y
1:50 (1:53) (Class 5) 2-Y-O **£2,911** (£866; £432; £216) **Stalls** Low

Form RPR
023 **1** **Tullia (IRE)**[13] [6922] 2-8-9 74 .... NeilCallan 2 76
(William Knight) *mde all: drifted lft ins fnl f: kpt on wl: rdn out* **9/4**[1]
65 **2** *1 ½* **Rolling Dice**[17] [6790] 2-8-13 0 .... LiamKeniry 11 76+
(Dominic Ffrench Davis) *mid-div: rdn over 2f out: stdy prog over 1f out: styd on to chse wnr ins fnl f* **20/1**
2503 **3** *2 ¾* **Solo Hunter**[12] [6954] 2-9-1 67 .... RyanMoore 10 72
(David Evans) *trckd ldrs: rdn over 2f out: chsd wnr over 1f out tl ins fnl f: kpt on same pce* **3/1**[2]
3 **4** *3* **Marmarus**[45] [5950] 2-8-13 0 .... SteveDrowne 5 62
(Clive Cox) *trckd ldrs: rdn over 2f out: kpt on same pce tl no ex ins fnl f* **6/1**
5 *¾* **Rapunzal** 2-8-6 0 .... CathyGannon 1 53
(Henry Candy) *mid-div: pushed along early: rdn over 2f out: styd on but nvr any real imp on ldrs* **10/1**
553 **6** *3 ¼* **Baker Man (IRE)**[11] [6981] 2-9-1 68 ....(t) RichardHughes 3 54
(Sylvester Kirk) *mid-div: trckd ldrs 4f out: rdn over 2f out: wknd fnl f* **4/1**[3]
06 **7** *1 ¼* **Fenella Foghorn**[13] [6923] 2-8-7 0 .... MatthewLawson(3) 13 46
(Jonathan Portman) *hld up towards rr: rdn over 2f out: nvr any imp* **40/1**
8 *15* **Janet's Legacy** 2-8-9 0 .... DavidProbert 7 7
(Harry Dunlop) *pressed wnr tl rdn over 3f out: sn edgd lft and wknd* **20/1**
9 *9* **Norse Legend** 2-8-11 0 .... MickaelBarzalona 12
(Daniel Kubler) *dwlt: a bhd* **33/1**
10 *nk* **Thylyer (IRE)** 2-8-9 0 .... SimonPearce(3) 9
(Peter Makin) *s.i.s: a towards rr* **50/1**

1m 35.73s (7.13) **Going Correction** +1.025s/f (Soft) **10** Ran SP% **116.0**
Speed ratings (Par 95): **100,98,95,91,90 87,85,68,58,57**
toteswingers 1&2 £5.00, 1&3 £2.50, 2&3 £9.90 CSF £53.25 TOTE £2.90: £1.20, £6.70, £1.40; EX 44.30 Trifecta £147.40 Pool: £725.67 - 3.69 winning units..
Owner P Winkworth **Bred** Sc Archi Romani **Trained** Patching, W Sussex

FOCUS
Richard Hughes said of the ground "it's about as heavy as you can get". The runners stayed far side, which isn't always the case here when the ground is testing. The winner had the run of things and is rated to his Lingfield form.

7244 BATHWICK TYRES EBF STALLIONS MAIDEN FILLIES' STKS (DIV I) 6f 212y
2:20 (2:24) (Class 5) 2-Y-O **£3,234** (£962; £481; £240) **Stalls** Low

Form RPR
4223 **1** **Tea In Transvaal (IRE)**[23] [6643] 2-9-0 79 .... RichardHughes 9 80
(Richard Hannon) *mde all: kpt on strly to assert ent fnl f: pushed out* **1/1**[1]
0 **2** *6* **White Russian**[23] [6635] 2-9-0 0 .... CathyGannon 2 65
(Henry Candy) *trckd wnr: rdn over 2f out: kpt on but readily hld by wnr fr over 1f out* **6/1**[3]
3 *2 ¾* **Lobster Pot** 2-9-0 0 .... SteveDrowne 8 58+
(Hugo Palmer) *hld up bhd ldrs: swtchd lft and hdwy 3f out: sn rdn into 3rd: styd on same pce fnl 2f* **20/1**
3 **4** *9* **Nissaki Kasta**[24] [6590] 2-9-0 0 .... RyanMoore 11 36
(Hughie Morrison) *wnt lft s: hld up last but in tch: pushed along and hdwy 3f out: sn rdn: disp wl hld 4th over 1f out: fdd fnl f* **5/2**[2]
0 **5** *4 ½* **Just Rubie**[106] [3853] 2-9-0 0 .... HarryBentley 5 24
(Michael Blanshard) *trckd wnr tl rdn over 2f out: wknd ent fnl f* **100/1**
6 *3 ¾* **Darting** 2-9-0 0 .... DavidProbert 10 15
(Andrew Balding) *wnt lft s: sn trcking wnr: rdn over 2f out: sn wknd* **17/2**
7 *1* **Bertie Baby** 2-8-7 0 .... DanielCremin(7) 6 13
(Ralph Smith) *awkward leaving stalls: hld up bhd ldrs: rdn over 2f out: sn wknd* **100/1**

1m 35.05s (6.45) **Going Correction** +1.025s/f (Soft) **7** Ran SP% **110.1**
Speed ratings (Par 92): **104,97,94,83,78 74,73**
toteswingers 1&2 £1.90, 1&3 £9.60, 2&3 £1.80 CSF £7.02 TOTE £1.60: £1.10, £2.80; EX 6.00 Trifecta £40.20 Pool: £1,551.59 - 28.89 winning units..
Owner Sheikh Juma Dalmook Al Maktoum **Bred** Summerville Bloodstock **Trained** East Everleigh, Wilts

FOCUS
The runners came home at fairly wide margins in what was an ordinary maiden. The winner's pre-race mark sets the level.

7245 BATHWICK TYRES EBF STALLIONS MAIDEN FILLIES' STKS (DIV II) 6f 212y
2:50 (2:54) (Class 5) 2-Y-O **£3,234** (£962; £481; £240) **Stalls** Low

Form RPR
4 **1** **Dutch Romance**[23] [6635] 2-9-0 0 .... RyanMoore 5 85+
(Charles Hills) *hld up: hdwy over 2f out: swtchd to far side rails sn after: led over 1f out: r.o wl: rdn out* **11/8**[1]
2 *2* **Miniskirt** 2-9-0 0 .... WilliamBuick 4 80+
(Rae Guest) *in tch: rdn and hdwy 2f out: wnt clr 2nd ent fnl f: kpt on same pce* **14/1**
4 **3** *3 ½* **Joohaina (IRE)**[117] [3471] 2-9-0 0 .... PaulHanagan 6 71
(Marco Botti) *trckd ldrs: chal 3f out: sn rdn: hld over 1f out: no ex ins fnl f* **10/3**[2]
0 **4** *¾* **Aertex (IRE)**[19] [6739] 2-9-0 0 .... RichardHughes 1 69
(Richard Hannon) *led: rdn whn jnd over 2f out: hdd over 1f out: no ex ins fnl f* **5/1**[3]
0 **5** *10* **Be My Icon**[26] [6523] 2-9-0 0 .... NeilCallan 8 44
(Roger Charlton) *wnt lft s: towards rr: effrt over 2f out: wknd jst over 1f out* **8/1**
6 *½* **Vera Lou (IRE)** 2-9-0 0 .... RobertHavlin 10 43
(Pat Eddery) *s.i.s: towards rr: rdn 3f out: wknd over 1f out* **40/1**
0 **7** *2* **Trillian Astra (IRE)**[21] [6691] 2-9-0 0 .... SteveDrowne 7 38
(Clive Cox) *hld up: rdn wl over 2f out: wknd over 1f out* **50/1**
8 *1 ¾* **Alumina (IRE)** 2-9-0 0 .... DavidProbert 3 34
(Andrew Balding) *trckd ldrs: rdn wl over 2f out: wknd over 1f out* **10/1**
0 **9** *4 ½* **Liddle Dwiggs**[11] [6974] 2-9-0 0 .... CathyGannon 2 23
(Denis Coakley) *trckd ldr: rdn 3f out: sn hld: wknd over 1f out* **100/1**

1m 35.42s (6.82) **Going Correction** +1.025s/f (Soft) **9** Ran SP% **114.1**
Speed ratings (Par 92): **102,99,95,94,83 82,80,78,73**
toteswingers 1&2 £6.80, 1&3 £2.10, 2&3 £9.10 CSF £23.27 TOTE £2.90: £1.60, £3.20, £1.50; EX 27.10 Trifecta £80.10 Pool: £1,011.49 - 9.46 winning units..
Owner Mrs Susan Roy **Bred** Mrs S M Roy **Trained** Lambourn, Berks

FOCUS
There was little between this and the first division, and as in the previous race, it went to the favourite. A fluid opening form to the level.

7246 BATHWICK TYRES BOURNEMOUTH H'CAP 6f 212y
3:25 (3:27) (Class 6) (0-60,60) 3-Y-O+ **£2,587** (£770; £384; £192) **Stalls** Low

Form RPR
564 **1** **Admirable Art (IRE)**[6] [7109] 3-8-11 57 ....(p) RyanTate(5) 8 65
(Tony Carroll) *hld up in tch: squeezed through gap and hdwy over 2f out: sn pushed along: led fnl 120yds: r.o* **5/2**[1]
0310 **2** *2* **Who's That Chick (IRE)**[20] [6737] 4-8-11 57 .... DanielCremin(7) 2 61
(Ralph Smith) *led: rdn over 2f out: kpt on tl hdd fnl 120yds: no ex* **11/4**[2]
6400 **3** *3 ¼* **Delightful Sleep**[38] [6153] 5-8-12 58 .... EoinWalsh(7) 4 54
(David Evans) *hld up in tch: hdwy over 3f out to dispute 2nd: sn rdn: one pce fnl f* **7/1**
0040 **4** *1 ¼* **Camache Queen (IRE)**[11] [6980] 5-9-2 55 ....(tp) SteveDrowne 1 47
(Joseph Tuite) *trckd ldr: rdn over 2f out: no ex fnl 120yds* **10/1**
5 *6* **Bigger Picture (IRE)**[118] 3-9-5 60 .... NeilCallan 5 36
(John Butler) *stdd s: nt clr run on rails over 3f out: rdn to chse ldrs 2f out: wknd ent fnl f* **4/1**[3]
2300 **6** *12* **Strategic Action (IRE)**[12] [6933] 4-9-3 56 .... SaleemGolam 9 2
(Linda Jewell) *trckd ldrs: rdn wl over 2f out: wknd wl over 1f out* **8/1**
/40- **7** *1 ¾* **Hooligan Sean**[350] [7436] 6-9-4 57 ....[1] DavidProbert 12
(Mark Usher) *pressed ldr: rdn over 2f out: wknd wl over 1f out* **12/1**

1m 35.53s (6.93) **Going Correction** +1.025s/f (Soft)
WFA 3 from 4yo+ 2lb **7** Ran SP% **115.6**
Speed ratings (Par 101): **101,98,95,93,86 73,71**
toteswingers 1&2 £2.00, 1&3 £2.90, 2&3 £6.50 CSF £9.90 CT £41.29 TOTE £3.80: £2.00, £2.00; EX 11.10 Trifecta £68.20 Pool: £1,017.84 - 11.18 winning units..
Owner Longview Stud & Bloodstock Ltd **Bred** Longview Stud & Bloodstock Ltd **Trained** Cropthorne, Worcs

FOCUS
A weak handicap, in which more than half of those originally declared came out. The form is rated around the runner-up to his latest form.

7247 EBF STALLIONS BATHWICK TYRES CONDITIONS STKS 6f 212y
4:00 (4:01) (Class 3) 3-Y-O+ **£9,056** (£2,695; £1,346; £673) **Stalls** Low

Form RPR
6030 **1** **Hasopop (IRE)**[23] [6623] 3-9-0 104 .... PaulHanagan 4 106
(Marco Botti) *hld up bhd ldrs: hdwy on rails fr 2f out: sn rdn: swtchd off rails to chse wnr ent fnl f: kpt on wl to ld nr fin* **7/2**[3]
3434 **2** *¾* **Mar Mar (IRE)**[30] [6411] 3-8-9 96 ....(b) MickaelBarzalona 5 99
(Saeed bin Suroor) *racd keenly: sn led: rdn over 1f out: no ex whn hdd nring fin* **7/1**
3506 **3** *2 ½* **Shamaal Nibras (USA)**[9] [7014] 4-9-2 98 .... NeilCallan 1 99
(Ismail Mohammed) *cl up: rdn wl over 2f out: nt pce to get on terms: styd on to go 3rd fnl stride* **9/4**[1]
-266 **4** *nse* **I'm Back (IRE)**[219] [953] 3-9-0 96 .... WilliamBuick 2 97
(Saeed bin Suroor) *broke wl: led early: trckd ldr: rdn over 2f out: nt pce to chal: lost 2nd ent fnl f: no ex whn lost 3rd fnl stride* **10/1**
1000 **5** *3 ¾* **Anna's Pearl**[23] [6624] 3-9-0 95 .... HarryBentley 7 88
(Ralph Beckett) *awkward leaving stalls: sn rcvrd to trck ldrs: effrt over 2f out: fdd fnl f* **18/1**
0336 **6** *¾* **The Cheka (IRE)**[30] [6411] 7-9-7 98 ....(p) RyanMoore 3 92
(Eve Johnson Houghton) *hld up bhd ldrs: rdn over 2f out: nvr threatened: fdd fnl f* **12/1**
1150 **7** *1 ¼* **Magic City (IRE)**[9] [7014] 4-9-2 101 .... RichardHughes 6 83
(Richard Hannon) *cl up: effrt to cl over 2f out: nvr threatened: wknd ent fnl f* **10/3**[2]

1m 34.31s (5.71) **Going Correction** +1.025s/f (Soft)
WFA 3 from 4yo+ 2lb **7** Ran SP% **110.6**
Speed ratings (Par 107): **108,107,104,104,99 99,97**
toteswingers 1&2 £2.90, 1&3 £2.20, 2&3 £3.60 CSF £25.79 TOTE £4.70: £2.70, £3.70; EX 28.40 Trifecta £106.30 Pool: £2,496.10 - 17.60 winning units..
Owner Giuliano Manfredini **Bred** B Kennedy **Trained** Newmarket, Suffolk

FOCUS
Not form to put much faith in, with it looking an ordinary race by Listed standards anyway, but it was run at a fair gallop. The bare time was the fastest of the five C&D races. The form is rated around the runner-up and the fourth.

7248 BATHWICK TYRES SALISBURY H'CAP (DIV I) 1m 1f 198y
4:30 (4:31) (Class 5) (0-70,70) 3-Y-O **£2,749** (£818; £408; £204) **Stalls** Low

Form RPR
0660 **1** **Ronaldinho (IRE)**[31] [6358] 3-9-7 70 ....(b[1]) RichardHughes 2 85
(Richard Hannon) *mde all: swtchd to nrside rails over 4f out: pushed wl clr fr 2f out: eased fnl 100yds* **7/2**[2]
3440 **2** *15* **Hero's Story**[14] [6895] 3-8-10 59 .... WilliamBuick 5 47
(Amanda Perrett) *trckd ldrs: wnt prom in centre gp 4f out overall pressing wnr: rdn 3f out: wl-hld by wnr and one pce fnl 2f* **11/4**[1]
3460 **3** *2 ¼* **Munhamer (IRE)**[31] [6358] 3-9-4 67 .... PaulHanagan 8 51
(John Gosden) *trckd ldrs: led centre gp 4f out overall pressing wnr tl rdn 3f out: wl hld and one pce fnl 2f* **11/4**[1]
0-00 **4** *¾* **Newtown Cross (IRE)**[51] [5762] 3-8-5 57 oh4 ow1. MatthewLawson(3) 9 40
(Jimmy Fox) *sn pushed along in rr: travelling bttr whn racing in centre gp 4f out: rdn 3f out: nvr threatened: one pce fnl 2f* **33/1**
3660 **5** *2 ¼* **Squeeze My Brain (IRE)**[33] [6313] 3-9-6 69 ....(t) HarryBentley 11 48
(Ralph Beckett) *in tch: pressed ldrs between the 2 gps 4f out: rdn 3f out: one pce fnl 2f* **9/1**
6605 **6** *1* **Hallingham**[27] [6491] 3-9-0 63 .... SamHitchcott 12 40
(Jonathan Portman) *hld up: swtchd to nrside gp 4f out: rdn 3f out: nvr threatened* **14/1**
5023 **7** *6* **Knight Charm**[12] [6932] 3-8-11 60 ....(p) JohnFahy 10 26
(Eve Johnson Houghton) *racd keenly: nvr settled: in tch: swtchd to nrside gp 4f out: rdn 3f out: nvr threatened: wknd fnl f* **8/1**[3]

40-0 **8** *4* **Night's Watch**[21] 6696 3-9-2 **65**.. SteveDrowne 4 24
(William Jarvis) *awkward leaving stalls: towards rr: centre gp 4f out: sn rdn: drifted lft fr 2f out: wknd over 1f out* **14/1**

2m 16.33s (6.43) **Going Correction** +0.675s/f (Yiel) **8** Ran SP% **112.9**
Speed ratings (Par 101): **101,89,87,86,84 84,79,76**
toteswingers 1&2 £4.30, 1&3 £2.80, 2&3 £3.10 CSF £13.21 CT £28.83 TOTE £5.20: £1.40, £1.50, £1.30; EX 18.30 Trifecta £46.00 Pool: £1,751.76 - 28.51 winning units..
Owner Macdonald,Wright,Creed,Smith & Jiggins **Bred** J Fallon **Trained** East Everleigh, Wilts

FOCUS
A number of these didn't handle the ground and for the first time on the day they came centre-to-stands' side. Much the winner's best run of the year but the form is not that convincing.

7249 BATHWICK TYRES SALISBURY H'CAP (DIV II) 1m 1f 198y
5:00 (5:00) (Class 5) (0-70,70) 3-Y-O **£2,749** (£818; £408; £204) **Stalls** Low

Form RPR
035 **1** **Stomachion (IRE)**[31] 6366 3-9-5 **68**.. RyanMoore 8 81
(Sir Michael Stoute) *trckd ldr: rdn 3f out: disp ld 2f out: led narrowly but tended to lean on runner up thrght fnl f: asserted fnl 50yds: drvn out* **9/4**[1]

3143 **2** *1* **Kastini**[33] 6313 3-9-2 **65**.. RichardHughes 5 76
(Denis Coakley) *trckd ldrs: disp ld 2f out tl rdn and narrowly hdd ent fnl f: tended to lean on wnr: no ex fnl 50yds* **9/4**[1]

0636 **3** *12* **Signature Dish (IRE)**[10] 7000 3-8-13 **62**.. DavidProbert 6 51
(Andrew Balding) *trckd ldrs: rdn 3f out: nvr threatened: styd on to go 3rd ins fnl f: no ch w ldng pair* **7/1**[3]

0060 **4** *4 ½* **Harwoods Star (IRE)**[19] 6743 3-9-4 **67**........................(p) WilliamBuick 7 48
(Amanda Perrett) *led: rdn and hdd 2f out: kpt chsng ldng pair tl no ex ins fnl f* **7/1**[3]

0365 **5** *10* **Mesmerized (IRE)**[26] 6521 3-9-3 **66**.. PaulHanagan 1 29
(Marco Botti) *hld up in tch: rdn over 2f out: wknd over 1f out* **9/2**[2]

4350 **6** *1 ¼* **Carrera**[16] 6851 3-8-2 **56**.. ShelleyBirkett(5) 9 17
(J W Hills) *hld up in tch: rdn 3f out: nvr threatened: wknd over 1f out* **10/1**

0000 **7** *65* **Exit Clause**[14] 6902 3-8-7 **56** oh10........................(tp) FrankieMcDonald 10
(Mark Gillard) *hld up in tch: rdn over 4f out: sn wknd: t.o* **100/1**

2m 15.87s (5.97) **Going Correction** +0.675s/f (Yiel) **7** Ran SP% **114.8**
Speed ratings (Par 101): **103,102,92,89,81 80,28**
toteswingers 1&2 £2.10, 1&3 £3.90, 2&3 £3.80 CSF £7.33 CT £28.70 TOTE £3.30: £1.20, £2.00; EX 8.10 Trifecta £36.10 Pool: £1,584.24 - 32.90 winning units..
Owner Niarchos Family **Bred** Niarchos Family **Trained** Newmarket, Suffolk

FOCUS
The front pair drew right away and the form looks sound, with the time quicker than division I. They came stands' side.

7250 BATHWICK TYRES "SEASON FINALE" H'CAP 1m 6f 21y
5:30 (5:31) (Class 3) (0-95,94) 3-Y-O+ **£7,762** (£2,310; £1,154; £577) **Stalls** Low

Form RPR
3041 **1** **Sizzler**[60] 5448 3-8-13 **88**.. PaulHanagan 3 100
(Ralph Beckett) *mde all: hung off rails fr 4f out: rdn and drifted rt fr 2f out: fin in centre of crse: styd on wl* **10/1**

131 **2** *2 ¼* **Chocala (IRE)**[30] 6389 3-8-7 **82**.. DavidProbert 13 91
(Alan King) *trckd wnr: nt best of runs on rails fr 4f out tl 2f out whn rdn: styd on but a being hld fnl f* **9/4**[1]

1503 **3** *3 ¼* **Duke Of Clarence (IRE)**[19] 6741 4-10-0 **94**...........(p) RichardHughes 8 99
(Richard Hannon) *hld up towards rr: midfield 6f out: rdn to chse ldrs 3f out: styd on same pce fnl 2f* **9/1**

-121 **4** *2 ½* **Centred (IRE)**[105] 3891 3-9-0 **89**.. RyanMoore 7 91
(Sir Michael Stoute) *trckd ldrs: rdn 3f out: one pce fnl 2f* **5/1**[2]

1130 **5** *2* **Silver Samba**[23] 6646 4-8-9 **80**.. OisinMurphy(5) 10 79
(Andrew Balding) *mid-div: trckd ldrs 4f out: rdn over 2f out: fdd fnl f* **16/1**

12 **6** *6* **Buchanan**[68] 5146 3-8-7 **82**.. CathyGannon 12 73
(Henry Candy) *mid-div: hdwy 4f out to trck ldrs: rdn over 2f out: wknd jst over 1f out* **7/1**[3]

-505 **7** *3 ½* **Signed Up**[24] 6591 4-9-8 **88**.. SteveDrowne 4 75
(Amanda Perrett) *trckd ldrs tl lost pl over 4f out: sn rdn: nvr bk on terms* **11/1**

1140 **8** *11* **Beacon Lady**[23] 6646 4-9-5 **85**.. NeilCallan 14 57
(William Knight) *rdn over 4f out: a towards rr* **25/1**

2410 **9** *2 ¾* **Princess Caetani (IRE)**[16] 6832 4-9-9 **89**.. SamHitchcott 1 58
(David Dennis) *swtchd rt and rdn over 3f out: a towards rr* **14/1**

-500 **10** *4* **Saytara (IRE)**[23] 6649 4-9-12 **92**.. WilliamBuick 6 56
(Saeed bin Suroor) *mid-div: rdn 3f out: no imp: wknd over 1f out* **16/1**

04-0 **11** *44* **Samba King**[24] 6591 4-9-8 **88**.. MickaelBarzalona 5
(Charlie Appleby) *in tch: rdn 3f out: wknd 2f out* **9/1**

3m 16.16s (8.76) **Going Correction** +0.675s/f (Yiel)
WFA 3 from 4yo+ 9lb **11** Ran SP% **119.6**
Speed ratings (Par 107): **101,99,97,96,95 91,89,83,82,79 54**
toteswingers 1&2 £5.00, 1&3 £8.90, 2&3 £7.80 CSF £33.29 CT £220.11 TOTE £8.10: £3.10, £1.50, £2.80; EX 38.10 Trifecta £312.60 Pool: £1,606.48 - 3.85 winning units..
Owner Heseltine, Henley & Jones **Bred** Newsells Park Stud **Trained** Kimpton, Hants

FOCUS
A good-quality staying handicap in which the runners again headed stands' side. The first pair were 1-2 virtually throughout. Solid form, the winner showing his previous C&D win didn't flatter.
T/Plt: £9.70 to a £1 stake. Pool: £57,543.45 - 4,296.78 winning units T/Qpdt: £4.30 to a £1 stake. Pool: £3,734.73 - 633.36 winning units TM

7068 WINDSOR (R-H)
Monday, October 14

OFFICIAL GOING: Soft (7.1)
Inner of straight out 8yds at 6f to intersection and 3yds at WP. Top bend out 6yards from inner configuration, adding 24yds to race of 1m-plus.
Wind: Light; behind Weather: Overcast with frequent showers

7251 BRITISH STALLION STUDS EBF MAIDEN STKS 6f
2:00 (2:01) (Class 5) 2-Y-O **£2,911** (£866; £432; £216) **Stalls** Low

Form RPR
U **1** **Idea (USA)**[19] 6739 2-9-5 0.. JamesDoyle 8 82+
(Sir Michael Stoute) *trckd ldrs: shkn up over 2f out: checked briefly over 1f out: sn chsd ldr: rdn and styd on wl to ld last 50yds: shade cleverly* **9/2**[3]

42 **2** *½* **Exchequer (IRE)**[23] 6641 2-9-5 0.. PatDobbs 7 80+
(Richard Hannon) *trckd ldng pair: shkn up and clsd to ld wl over 1f out: edgd lft sn after: drvn fnl f: hdd and hld last 50yds* **5/4**[1]

02 **3** *3 ¾* **Smidgen (IRE)**[18] 6769 2-9-5 0.. AdamKirby 11 69
(Ed de Giles) *led: tk field to far side fr 1f 1/2-way: hdd wl over 1f out: steadily outpcd* **20/1**

06 **4** *½* **Faure Island**[51] 5744 2-9-5 0.. DaneO'Neill 3 67+
(Henry Candy) *trckd ldrs: hanging whn rdn fr jst over 2f out: nt qckn wl over 1f out: one pce* **9/4**[2]

5 *8* **Bon Port** 2-9-0 0.. SilvestreDeSousa 4 38+
(Hughie Morrison) *dwlt: hld up in last pair: nudged along and wl adrift over 2f out: kpt on fnl f: nt wout sme promise* **33/1**

4 **6** *hd* **Roring Samson (IRE)**[32] 6333 2-9-5 0.. PatCosgrave 13 43
(George Baker) *chsd ldr to jst over 2f out: wknd rapidly* **33/1**

7 *3 ¼* **Tahchee** 2-9-5 0.. FrederikTylicki 5 33
(James Fanshawe) *in tch: pushed along 3f out: sn struggling* **40/1**

8 *3 ¼* **Suitsus** 2-9-5 0.. SebSanders 9 23
(Peter Makin) *nvr on terms: struggling 1/2-way: wknd 2f out* **50/1**

9 *6* **Comanchero (IRE)** 2-9-5 0.. JimmyFortune 1 5
(Andrew Balding) *dwlt: a in last pair: shkn up and struggling by 1/2-way: sn wl bhd* **14/1**

1m 12.99s (-0.01) **Going Correction** -0.10s/f (Good) **9** Ran SP% **115.1**
Speed ratings (Par 95): **96,95,90,89,79 78,74,70,62**
toteswingers 1&2 £1.90, 1&3 £4.20, 2&3 £3.80 CSF £10.07 TOTE £6.00: £1.60, £1.10, £2.00; EX 12.60 Trifecta £57.60 Pool: £2,617.27 - 34.05 winning units..
Owner K Abdullah **Bred** Juddmonte Farms Inc **Trained** Newmarket, Suffolk
■ Stewards' Enquiry : Pat Dobbs one-day ban: careless riding (Oct 28)

FOCUS
Following 10mm of rain the previous day and 1mm overnight the going was changed to soft. Stands' side rail dolled out 2yds at 6f, reducing to 0yds at winning post. Top bend dolled out 11yds from the normal inner configuration, adding 38yds to race distances of 1m plus. An ordinary maiden in which they came up the far rail. Quite a taking effort from the winner.

7252 LADBROKES NURSERY H'CAP 1m 67y
2:30 (2:31) (Class 5) (0-75,75) 2-Y-O **£2,587** (£770; £384; £192) **Stalls** Low

Form RPR
4432 **1** **Killing Time (IRE)**[30] 6401 2-9-3 **71**........................(b) SebSanders 3 77
(Ralph Beckett) *hld up in last trio: prog and taken to far rail 3f out: clsd 2f out: drvn to ld 1f out: styd on* **7/2**[1]

3100 **2** *1 ½* **The Alamo (IRE)**[18] 6763 2-9-7 **75**.. PatDobbs 4 78
(Richard Hannon) *trckd ldrs: styd centre in st: rdn to chal 2f out: upsides 1f out: one pce* **12/1**

5304 **3** *hd* **Shimba Hills**[16] 6844 2-8-10 **64**.. SilvestreDeSousa 13 66
(Mick Channon) *w ldr after 1f: styd centre in st: rdn to ld over 2f out: hdd and one pce 1f out* **12/1**

604 **4** *2 ½* **Inevitable**[22] 6666 2-9-7 **75**.. AdamKirby 14 72
(Mark Johnston) *prog into midfield after 3f: rdn over 3f out: taken to far rail sn after: no imp u.p 2f out: styd on ins fnl f* **5/1**[3]

051 **5** *nk* **Madame Mirasol (IRE)**[48] 5865 2-9-5 **73**.. JamesDoyle 7 69
(Kevin Ryan) *mde most: styd centre in st: hdd over 2f out: one pce* **14/1**

063 **6** *1 ¼* **Zugzwang (IRE)**[13] 6923 2-9-4 **75**.. MarkCoumbe(3) 12 68
(Ed de Giles) *trckd ldrs: styd centre in st: rdn and tried to chal wl over 1f out: wknd fnl f* **11/1**

2142 **7** *½* **Lucky Visione**[16] 6852 2-9-1 **74**..[1] DanielMuscutt(5) 1 66
(Gay Kelleway) *hld up in tch: styd centre in st: urged along and no imp on ldrs over 2f out* **10/1**

0454 **8** *15* **Jersey Royal**[7] 7069 2-8-9 **63**.. SeanLevey 5 22
(Richard Hannon) *a in rr: struggling over 3f out: sn bhd* **7/1**

005 **9** *1 ¼* **Enfys Hud**[16] 6821 2-8-10 **67**.. DeclanBates(3) 9 24
(David Evans) *a in rr: struggling over 3f out: sn wl bhd* **20/1**

31 **10** *56* **Howz The Family (IRE)**[131] 2985 2-9-7 **75**.........(t) RichardKingscote 10
(Tom Dascombe) *lost tch u.p bef 1/2-way: t.o and virtually p.u 2f out* **9/2**[2]

1m 45.22s (0.52) **Going Correction** -0.025s/f (Good) **10** Ran SP% **113.8**
Speed ratings (Par 95): **96,94,94,91,91 90,89,74,73,17**
toteswingers 1&2 £6.00, 1&3 £8.60, 2&3 £23.30 CSF £45.39 CT £459.12 TOTE £3.50: £1.40, £4.00, £4.80; EX 40.70 Trifecta £475.10 Pool: £1,643.26 - 2.59 winning units..
Owner Kennet Valley Thoroughbreds VIII **Bred** Kilfrush Stud **Trained** Kimpton, Hants

FOCUS
A fair nursery, run at an even pace .in pretty testing ground. Pretty straightforward, ordinary form.

7253 LADBROKES GAME ON! MAIDEN STKS 1m 67y
3:05 (3:06) (Class 5) 3-Y-O+ **£2,587** (£770; £384; £192) **Stalls** Low

Form RPR
0- **1** **Modernstone**[362] 7159 3-9-0 0..[1] ShaneKelly 8 77
(William Knight) *towards rr: shkn up and stl there over 2f out: str run on outer fr wl over 1f out to ld nr fin* **33/1**

42 **2** *1* **Musaddas**[12] 6950 3-9-5 0.. SilvestreDeSousa 9 79
(Saeed bin Suroor) *t.k.h: prom: pressed ldr over 3f out: rdn to ld against far rail over 1f out: 2 l clr ins fnl f: collared nr fin* **11/8**[1]

-206 **3** *2 ¾* **Arms (IRE)**[12] 6950 3-9-5 68.. DaneO'Neill 14 73
(J W Hills) *trckd ldrs and travelled wl: wnt 3rd over 2f out: nt qckn but kpt on fnl f* **14/1**

6-60 **4** *1 ½* **The Best Doctor (IRE)**[39] 6133 3-9-5 75.. SebSanders 12 70
(Jeremy Noseda) *in tch in midfield: shkn up over 2f out: nvr on terms w ldrs but kpt on steadily fr over 1f out* **11/2**[3]

3 **5** *hd* **Modem**[29] 6431 3-9-5 0.. MartinDwyer 4 69
(Rod Millman) *towards rr: pushed along 3f out: no imp whn rdn 2f out: kpt on fr over 1f out* **25/1**

64 **6** *1* **Wandsworth (IRE)**[16] 6824 3-9-5 0.. AndreaAtzeni 10 67
(Roger Varian) *led: hdd towards far side in st but unable to grab the rail: hdd over 1f out: wknd fnl f* **9/2**[2]

66 **7** *2 ¼* **Bethan**[26] 6532 4-9-3 0.. AdamBeschizza 11 57
(Julia Feilden) *nvr beyond midfield: rdn over 2f out: no prog* **50/1**

8 *2* **Ittijah (USA)** 3-9-0 0.. AdamKirby 2 52
(Mark Johnston) *wl in rr: prog into midfield 1/2-way: rdn over 2f out: steadily fdd* **7/1**

9 *½* **Exotic Lady (IRE)** 3-9-0 0.. PatDobbs 7 51
(Sylvester Kirk) *mostly in last pair: struggling bef 1/2-way: pushed along and passed a few late on* **100/1**

0-2 **10** *7* **Red Invader (IRE)**[17] 6806 3-9-5 0.. RichardKingscote 5 40
(Charles Hills) *trckd ldrs: rdn over 2f out: wknd qckly wl over 1f out* **14/1**

0 **11** *7* **Deserving Honour**[12] 6950 3-9-5 0.. MartinLane 13 24
(Charlie Appleby) *chsd ldr to over 3f out: wknd qckly over 2f out* **20/1**

00 **12** *23* **Donard Lass**[25] 6555 3-9-0 0.. KieranO'Neill 3
(Jimmy Fox) *a in last pair: t.o fnl 3f* **100/1**

1m 45.36s (0.66) **Going Correction** -0.025s/f (Good)
WFA 3 from 4yo 3lb **12** Ran SP% **117.0**
Speed ratings (Par 103): **95,94,91,89,89 88,86,84,83,76 69,46**
toteswingers 1&2 £15.40, 1&3 £42.90, 2&3 £4.50 CSF £75.87 TOTE £44.20: £10.10, £1.30, £3.70; EX 127.00 Trifecta £1524.70 Pool: £4,050.68 - 1.99 winning units..

Owner Biddestone Racing Club **Bred** Oscar Stud **Trained** Patching, W Sussex

FOCUS

No more than a fair 3yo maiden and the bare time was slower than the previous 2yo race. There are doubts over the bare form with the second a stone off his Nottingham run.

7254 LADBROKES MOBILE H'CAP (DIV I) 6f

3:35 (3:36) (Class 4) (0-80,80) 3-Y-0+ £4,690 (£1,395; £697; £348) **Stalls** Low

Form RPR

0515 **1** **Prince Regal**[15] 6871 3-8-12 **75**........ RobertTart(3) 5 84
(Alan Jarvis) *trckd ldrs: rdn to chal on outer over 1f out: kpt on wl to ld nr fin* **5/1**[2]

060 **2** ½ **Church Music (IRE)**[37] 6189 4-9-1 **77**.....(v) WilliamTwiston-Davies(3) 12 84
(Michael Scudamore) *led: rdn over 1f out: hrd pressed on both sides fnl f: hdd nr fin* **9/1**

2130 **3** *nse* **Sarangoo**[32] 6337 5-9-4 **77**........ TomMcLaughlin 14 84
(Malcolm Saunders) *trckd ldr: chal fr over 1f out and grabbed pl against far side rail: upsides ins fnl f: nt qckn nr fin* **12/1**

0006 **4** 2¼ **Jack My Boy (IRE)**[9] 7031 6-8-13 **75**........(b) DeclanBates(3) 15 75
(David Evans) *trckd ldrs: rdn against far side rail 2f out: one pce fr over 1f out* **20/1**

3211 **5** *shd* **The Strig**[26] 6527 6-9-3 **76**........(v) JamesDoyle 9 76
(Stuart Williams) *trckd ldrs: rdn 2f out: one pce and no imp fnl f* **11/2**[3]

1203 **6** 1¼ **Tidal's Baby**[19] 6744 4-9-1 **79**........ GeorgeDowning(5) 3 75
(Tony Carroll) *hld up towards rr: rdn to chse ldrs on outer 2f out: no imp over 1f out* **5/1**[2]

0000 **7** 1¾ **Top Offer**[10] 6988 4-9-7 **80**........ ShaneKelly 7 71
(Peter Crate) *hld up in last pair: nudged along over 2f out: kpt on to pass wkng rivals fr over 1f out: nvr involved* **12/1**

1000 **8** 1¼ **Upavon**[21] 6692 3-9-6 **80**........ LiamKeniry 2 67
(David Elsworth) *hld up in last pair: pushed along 2f out: passed a few wkng rivals fnl f: nvr involved* **16/1**

3660 **9** *1* **Ertikaan**[52] 5735 6-9-3 **76**........(tp) DaneO'Neill 10 60
(Harry Whittington) *nvr beyond midfield: rdn and no prog over 2f out: one pce after* **12/1**

340 **10** *7* **Miss Diva**[72] 4989 3-9-6 **80**........ PatDobbs 11 43
(Richard Hannon) *restless stalls: chsd ldrs to over 2f out: wknd qckly* **12/1**

4031 **11** *1* **Oh So Spicy**[26] 6535 6-9-1 **74**........ TedDurcan 6 34
(Chris Wall) *chsd ldrs to 1/2-way: wknd 2f out: eased fnl f* **9/2**[1]

1m 14.0s (1.00) **Going Correction** +0.30s/f (Good)
WFA 3 from 4yo+ 1lb **11** Ran SP% **118.3**
Speed ratings (Par 105): **105,104,104,101,101 99,97,95,94,84 83**
toteswingers 1&2 £14.00, 1&3 £9.70, 2&3 £15.40 CSF £49.93 CT £526.66 TOTE £5.40: £1.50, £3.00, £3.50; EX 58.30 Trifecta £1623.80 Pool: £2,332.91 - 1.07 winning units..
Owner T&J Partnership **Bred** Mrs Ann Jarvis **Trained** Twyford, Bucks

FOCUS

An open sprint handicap in which the pace was solid. A similar time to division II. The winner rates back to his 2yo best.

7255 LADBROKES MOBILE H'CAP (DIV II) 6f

4:10 (4:10) (Class 4) (0-80,80) 3-Y-0+ £4,690 (£1,395; £697; £348) **Stalls** Low

Form RPR

4560 **1** **Gatepost (IRE)**[16] 6822 4-9-4 **77**........ PatDobbs 11 88
(Richard Fahey) *led 2f: styd prom: chal over 1f out: led last 150yds: forged clr* **9/2**[2]

2336 **2** 2¾ **Tagula Night (IRE)**[26] 6525 7-9-5 **78**........(bt) AdamKirby 7 81
(Dean Ivory) *chsd ldrs: drvn over 2f out: nt qckn over 1f out: kpt on to take 2nd last strides* **10/1**

6611 **3** *nse* **Joey's Destiny (IRE)**[19] 6744 3-9-3 **80**........ ThomasBrown(3) 8 85
(George Baker) *hld up in last pair: taken to far rail and rdn 2f out: hld whn nt clr run ins fnl f: kpt on to take 3rd last stride* **3/1**[1]

1514 **4** *hd* **The Dark Wizard (IRE)**[26] 6526 3-9-3 **77**........(b) JamesDoyle 10 79
(Roger Charlton) *chsd ldrs: grabbed far side rail in st: drvn to ld over 1f out: edgd rt sn after: hdd last 150yds: wknd and lost 2 pls last strides* **15/2**

0530 **5** ½ **The Tichborne (IRE)**[37] 6203 5-9-2 **75**........(v) AndreaAtzeni 4 76
(Roger Teal) *chsd ldrs: rdn bef 1/2-way: nvr able to chal but kpt on one pce u.p* **10/1**

2261 **6** *nk* **Gravitational (IRE)**[27] 6502 3-9-6 **80**........ SebSanders 5 80
(Chris Wall) *dwlt: hld up in last pair: rdn 2f out: kpt on one pce after: nvr able to threaten* **3/1**[1]

540 **7** *3* **Strictly Silca**[23] 6642 3-9-4 **78**........ SilvestreDeSousa 12 74
(Mick Channon) *led after 2f: drvn and hdd over 1f out: hld whn squeezed out sn after: eased* **7/1**[3]

1m 13.93s (0.93) **Going Correction** +0.30s/f (Good)
WFA 3 from 4yo+ 1lb **7** Ran SP% **110.6**
Speed ratings (Par 105): **105,101,101,101,100 99,95**
toteswingers 1&2 £8.40, 1&3 £4.10, 2&3 £5.40 CSF £43.72 CT £146.78 TOTE £6.90: £2.60, £3.90; EX 49.50 Trifecta £161.90 Pool: £2,360.12 - 10.93 winning units..
Owner Dr Marwan Koukash **Bred** Michael Doyle **Trained** Musley Bank, N Yorks
■ Stewards' Enquiry : James Doyle two-day ban: careless riding (Oct 28-29)

FOCUS

The second division of this sprint handicap was run was run in a time marginally quicker than the first leg. The winner is rated to this year's best.

7256 LADBROKES ODDS ON! FILLIES' H'CAP 1m 67y

4:40 (4:40) (Class 4) (0-80,79) 3-Y-0+ £4,690 (£1,395; £697; £348) **Stalls** Low

Form RPR

2240 **1** **Magique (IRE)**[26] 6531 3-8-11 **72**........ JimmyFortune 3 81
(Jeremy Noseda) *dwlt: hld up in last trio: prog against far rail over 2f out: hrd drvn over 1f out: r.o to ld last 100yds* **4/1**[2]

13 **2** 1¼ **Rainbow Beauty**[21] 6701 3-9-1 **76**........(p) JamesDoyle 8 82
(Gerard Butler) *hld up in last trio: rdn and prog on outer over 2f out: chsd ldr over 1f out to ins fnl f: outpcd but kpt on to take 2nd again last stride* **11/4**[1]

5022 **3** *shd* **Light Rose (IRE)**[15] 6875 3-8-12 **73**........ LiamJones 13 79
(Mark Johnston) *led: skipped at least 3 l clr over 3f out: hrd rdn over 1f out: hdd 100yds out: lost 2nd post* **7/1**[3]

2124 **4** *1* **Lady Bayside**[60] 5430 5-9-1 **73**........ TomMcLaughlin 2 77
(Malcolm Saunders) *hld up and sn in last trio: rdn and prog on wd outside over 2f out: disp 2nd over 1f out: kpt on one pce after* **14/1**

6261 **5** 2¾ **Madame Elizabeth**[30] 6379 3-8-9 **75**........ JackDuern(5) 12 72
(Andrew Hollinshead) *chsd ldrs: rdn over 2f out: nt qckn and no imp sn after: one pce* **8/1**

-256 **6** *2* **Abigails Angel**[32] 6337 6-8-10 **68**........ PatCosgrave 10 61
(Brett Johnson) *t.k.h: chsd ldr 1f and again over 3f out: sn rdn: wknd over 1f out* **7/1**[3]

1005 **7** ¾ **Hill Of Dreams (IRE)**[56] 5589 4-9-0 **72**........(b) AdamKirby 4 63
(Dean Ivory) *awkward s: prog fr rr over 4f out: disp 2nd 2f out: pushed along and sn wknd* **20/1**

0340 **8** *hd* **Califante**[26] 6524 3-9-4 **79**........(b[1]) DougieCostello 5 69
(William Muir) *hld up in tch: gng strly over 2f out: shkn up and no rspnse wl over 1f out: wknd* **10/1**

6526 **9** *10* **Russian Royale**[18] 6780 3-8-10 **71**........ ShaneKelly 9 38
(Stuart Kittow) *dwlt: rcvrd to chse ldr after 1f: rdn and lost 2nd over 3f out: sn btn* **8/1**

1m 47.3s (2.60) **Going Correction** +0.375s/f (Good)
WFA 3 from 4yo+ 3lb **9** Ran SP% **114.4**
Speed ratings (Par 102): **102,100,100,99,96 94,94,93,83**
toteswingers 1&2 £3.80, 1&3 £8.10, 2&3 £3.60 CSF £15.26 CT £73.80 TOTE £4.50: £1.20, £1.90, £3.10; EX 20.40 Trifecta £128.00 Pool: £2,676.27 - 15.67 winning units..
Owner Miss Yvonne Jacques **Bred** Mrs Cherry Faeste **Trained** Newmarket, Suffolk

FOCUS

A fair fillies' handicap. The pace was solid and once again they headed over to the far side in the straight. The form makes sense among the front four.

7257 BET IN PLAY WITH LADBROKES H'CAP 1m 2f 7y

5:10 (5:13) (Class 4) (0-85,82) 3-Y-0 £4,690 (£1,395; £697; £348) **Stalls** Centre

Form RPR

5416 **1** **Eric The Grey (IRE)**[23] 6626 3-8-13 **74**........(p) FrederikTylicki 13 86
(Richard Fahey) *s.s: hld up in last: gd prog on wd outside fr over 2f out: led jst over 1f out: rdn clr* **11/1**

3416 **2** 2¼ **Raskova (USA)**[51] 5743 3-8-11 **72**........ TedDurcan 3 79
(William Jarvis) *hld up in rr: gng easily 3f out: prog on outer over 2f out: brought to chal over 1f out: kpt on but outpcd by wnr* **25/1**

2552 **3** 1¼ **Nickels And Dimes (IRE)**[41] 6062 3-8-13 **74**........ RobertHavlin 8 80
(John Gosden) *settled in midfield: lost pl and short of room 2f out: styd on again fr over 1f out to take 3rd nr fin* **9/1**[2]

5345 **4** *hd* **Angus Glens**[19] 6743 3-9-1 **76**........ RichardKingscote 4 80
(David Dennis) *pushed along towards rr: rdn 3f out: styd on fr wl over 1f out: nrly tk 3rd* **14/1**

00 **5** *nk* **Mr Fitzroy (IRE)**[20] 6734 3-8-12 **73**........ LiamKeniry 9 77
(Andrew Balding) *trckd ldrs: cl up fr 3f out: rdn over 2f out: stl chsng over 1f out: no ex* **20/1**

31-4 **6** *2* **Lilac Tree**[177] 1683 3-9-4 **79**........ AdamKirby 10 79
(Mark Johnston) *led 1f: styd prom: rdn to ld again 3f out: hdd & wknd jst over 1f out* **10/1**[3]

0-1 **7** *hd* **Jakey (IRE)**[15] 6870 3-9-2 **77**........ FergusSweeney 16 76
(Pat Phelan) *racd wd in midfield: rdn against far rail and prog 2f out: chsd ldrs over 1f out: wknd fnl f* **14/1**

1- **8** 2¼ **Muhtaris (IRE)**[341] 7637 3-9-0 **75**........ SilvestreDeSousa 14 70
(Saeed bin Suroor) *t.k.h: prom: upsides 3f out: wknd over 1f out* **11/4**[1]

0002 **9** *nse* **Stiff Upper Lip (IRE)**[7] 7071 3-8-12 **73**........(b) PatDobbs 12 68
(Richard Hannon) *towards rr: rdn 3f out: slt prog over 1f out but nvr on terms* **12/1**

2215 **10** 1¼ **Blighty (IRE)**[25] 6563 3-9-7 **82**........ JamesDoyle 1 75
(Lady Cecil) *trckd ldrs: shkn up on outer over 2f out: lost pl sn after: wl btn over 1f out* **11/4**[1]

062 **11** *8* **Ocean Applause**[5] 6823 3-8-13 **77**........(t) RyanPowell(3) 11 55
(John Ryan) *in tch: rdn to chse ldrs over 2f out: wknd over 1f out: eased* **20/1**

0315 **12** 4½ **Dragon City**[17] 6809 3-9-3 **78**........ DaneO'Neill 2 47
(Harry Dunlop) *pressed ldrs: upsides and rdn 3f out: losing pl whn short of room 2f out: wknd qckly* **16/1**

3U56 **13** *17* **Martinas Delight (USA)**[71] 5037 3-8-12 **73**........ MartinLane 15 10
(Alan Jarvis) *restless stalls: drvn to ld after 1f: hdd & wknd rapidly 3f out: t.o* **66/1**

2m 11.32s (2.62) **Going Correction** +0.375s/f (Good) **13** Ran SP% **122.5**
Speed ratings (Par 103): **104,102,101,101,100 99,99,97,97,96 89,86,72**
toteswingers 1&2 £32.90, 1&3 £11.80, 2&3 £32.60 CSF £269.74 CT £2584.80 TOTE £11.00: £3.20, £9.40, £3.70; EX 316.70 Trifecta £2114.10 Part won. Pool: £2,818.89 - 0.38 winning units..
Owner The Clynes & Knaggs Partnership **Bred** David Carey **Trained** Musley Bank, N Yorks

FOCUS

This competitive 3yo handicap was run at a good pace on the worst of the ground. Three of the first four home raced in the last trio.

7258 LADBROKES H'CAP 1m 3f 135y

5:40 (5:44) (Class 5) (0-70,69) 3-Y-0 £2,587 (£770; £384; £192) **Stalls** Centre

Form RPR

4342 **1** **Magika**[68] 5130 3-9-6 **68**........(t) AndreaAtzeni 12 77
(Marco Botti) *wl in tch: prog 4f out to ld wl over 2f out gng strly: drvn over 1f out: a in command* **7/2**[1]

4244 **2** 1¼ **Mistral Wind (IRE)**[9] 7033 3-9-1 **63**........ AdamKirby 11 69
(Ed Dunlop) *hld up in rr: prog fr over 3f out: drvn over 2f out: kpt on to take 2nd ins fnl f: nvr able to chal* **7/1**[2]

4304 **3** 1½ **Silk Route**[25] 6557 3-9-3 **65**........ DaneO'Neill 9 69
(Henry Candy) *trckd ldrs: cl up 3f out: drvn to chse wnr over 2f out: no imp over 1f out: lost 2nd ins fnl f* **14/1**

4010 **4** *1* **Jacobella**[40] 6109 3-9-2 **64**........ RichardKingscote 7 66
(Jonathan Portman) *hld up in rr: rdn and prog fr over 2f out: kpt on one pce to take 4th fnl f: n.d* **9/1**

5-06 **5** ½ **Red Four**[154] 2331 3-8-11 **59**........ PatCosgrave 5 60
(George Baker) *slowly away: wl in rr: pushed along 5f out: prog on wd outside over 2f out: kpt on one pce fr over 1f out* **25/1**

24 **6** 3¼ **Landau (IRE)**[19] 6743 3-9-4 **66**........ LiamKeniry 1 62
(Sylvester Kirk) *trckd ldrs: rdn over 2f out: hanging and nt qckn after: steadily lft bhd* **9/1**

0-66 **7** *5* **King's Request (IRE)**[136] 2833 3-9-4 **69**........ ThomasBrown(3) 14 57
(Laura Mongan) *restless stalls: hd over the side whn they opened and v.s.a: nvr on terms: struggling 3f out: modest late prog* **33/1**

0044 **8** ¾ **Strategic Strike (IRE)**[26] 6521 3-9-1 **63**........(t) SilvestreDeSousa 8 50
(Paul Cole) *pressed ldr: led 7f out to over 3f out: steadily fdd fnl 2f* **7/1**[2]

6415 **9** 2½ **Chocolate Block (IRE)**[58] 5535 3-9-1 **63**........ FergusSweeney 2 46
(Pat Phelan) *in tch towards rr: rdn and struggling over 3f out: sn btn* **8/1**[3]

3655 **10** *1* **Perfect Calm (USA)**[24] 6601 3-9-3 **65**........ FrederikTylicki 4 46
(Julie Camacho) *in tch in midfield: rdn and struggling over 3f out: sn btn* **25/1**

0141 **11** *7* **Ebony Roc (IRE)**[26] 6522 3-9-5 **67**................................ JamesDoyle 13 37
(Amanda Perrett) *prom: led over 3f out to wl over 2f out: wknd rapidly and eased* **8/1**[3]

4056 **12** *36* **Miss Mitigate**[82] 4634 3-8-9 **57**...................................... MartinDwyer 10
(Andrew Balding) *led to 7f out: drvn over 4f out: sn wknd: t.o* **8/1**[3]

2m 35.22s (5.72) **Going Correction** +0.375s/f (Good) **12** Ran SP% **117.9**
Speed ratings (Par 101): **95,94,93,92,92 90,86,86,84,83 79,55**
toteswingers 1&2 £5.60, 1&3 £12.00, 2&3 £18.50 CSF £26.34 CT £308.72 TOTE £5.70: £1.80, £2.30, £4.90; EX 38.10 Trifecta £616.20 Pool: £2,436.69 - 2.96 winning units..
Owner Marco & Sara Moretti & Partner **Bred** Immobiliare Casa Paola SRL **Trained** Newmarket, Suffolk

FOCUS
A modest staying handicap for 3yos. This rates a small personal best from the winner.
T/Jkpt: Not won. T/Plt: £110.00 to a £1 stake. Pool: £96,028.03 - 637.06 winning units T/Qpdt: £30.70 to a £1 stake. Pool: £6,949.88 - 167.50 winning units JN

7154 KEMPTON (A.W) (R-H)
Tuesday, October 15

OFFICIAL GOING: Standard
Wind: virtually nil Weather: dry

7260 REINDEER RACING AT KEMPTON PARK 06.12.13 MAIDEN FILLIES' STKS 1m (P)
5:40 (5:41) (Class 5) 2-Y-O **£2,587** (£770; £384; £192) **Stalls** Low

Form RPR

3 **1** **Sequined (USA)**[27] 6523 2-9-0 0.............................. MickaelBarzalona 5 80+
(Charlie Appleby) *chsd ldng trio: rdn and effrt to ld 2f out: qcknd clr over 1f out: r.o wl: comf* **10/11**[1]

2 *1 1/4* **Swan Lakes (IRE)** 2-9-0 0.. FergusSweeney 2 77+
(David Simcock) *chsd ldrs: rdn and effrt on inner 2f out: chsd wnr over 1f out: a hld by wnr but r.o wl for clr 2nd* **20/1**

05 **3** *4 1/2* **Lunar Spirit**[39] 6168 2-9-0 0... JimCrowley 8 67
(Ralph Beckett) *chsd ldr after 1f out: rdn and chsd wnr 2f out tl over 1f out: sn outpcd and btn 1f out: kpt on to hold 2nd* **7/1**[3]

4 *1/2* **Award (IRE)** 2-9-0 0.. NickyMackay 4 66+
(John Gosden) *s.i.s: hld up in tch towards rr: rdn and hdwy over 1f out: no threat to ldrs but kpt on wl fnl f* **14/1**

5 *2 3/4* **Loch Ma Naire (IRE)** 2-9-0 0... PatDobbs 9 59
(Ed Dunlop) *wl in tch in midfield: rdn and effrt over 2f out: wknd over 1f out* **33/1**

6 *2* **Broadway Musical (IRE)** 2-9-0 0.............................. RichardHughes 7 55+
(Richard Hannon) *s.i.s: hld up in tch towards rr: rdn and effrt over 2f out: unable qck and wknd over 1f out* **12/1**

0 **7** *3/4* **Shallow Lake (USA)**[13] 6949 2-9-0 0...................... SilvestreDeSousa 6 53+
(Charlie Appleby) *s.i.s: t.k.h: hld up in rr: rdn over 2f out: modest hdwy ins fnl f: nvr trbld ldrs* **20/1**

53 **8** *3/4* **Testing (FR)**[17] 6828 2-9-0 0... NeilCallan 10 51
(Mark Johnston) *led and crossed to inner: rdn and hdd 2f out: wknd over 1f out: fdd ins fnl f* **3/1**[2]

0 **9** *1 3/4* **La Grassetta (GER)**[50] 5819 2-9-0 0..................................... JimmyQuinn 3 47
(Tobias B P Coles) *in tch in midfield: rdn and struggling over 2f out: wknd over 1f out* **66/1**

10 *1 3/4* **Rio Yuma (ITY)** 2-8-9 0.. JacobButterfield[(5)] 1 43
(Kristin Stubbs) *t.k.h: hld up in last pair: rdn and struggling over 2f out: sn wknd* **66/1**

1m 39.97s (0.17) **Going Correction** -0.025s/f (Stan) **10** Ran SP% **119.7**
Speed ratings (Par 92): **98,96,92,91,89 87,86,85,83,82**
CSF £28.87 TOTE £1.70: £1.10, £5.60, £2.00; EX 31.80 Trifecta £165.40 Pool: £2916.29 - 13.22 winning units..
Owner Godolphin **Bred** Darley **Trained** Newmarket, Suffolk

FOCUS
Probably not a strong maiden overall but the leading pair, who pulled clear off what looked a pretty steady pace until halfway, are probably both pretty useful. They can better this form.

7261 BOOK NOW FOR JUMP RACING 20.10.13 MAIDEN AUCTION STKS 6f (P)
6:10 (6:10) (Class 5) 2-Y-O **£2,587** (£770; £384; £192) **Stalls** Low

Form RPR

0 **1** **You're Fired (IRE)**[65] 5307 2-9-1 0.. JimCrowley 1 76+
(Alan Jarvis) *s.i.s: rdn along in rr: stl plenty to do and hdwy over 1f out: str run ins fnl f to ld on post* **9/2**[3]

5342 **2** *nse* **Missouri Spirit**[14] 6915 2-8-11 75.. NeilCallan 4 72
(Kevin Ryan) *t.k.h: led for 1f: chsd ldr after tl rdn to ld over 1f out: drvn fnl f: kpt on but hrd pressed towards fin: hdd on post* **2/1**[1]

3 *hd* **Cincuenta Pasos (IRE)** 2-9-3 0................................ SteveDrowne 5 77
(Joseph Tuite) *in tch in midfield: hmpd bnd over 4f out: swtchd lft and effrt to chse ldrs 2f out: chsd wnr fnl 100yds: str chal towards fin: jst hld* **25/1**

0 **4** *2 3/4* **Thundering Cloud (IRE)**[30] 6423 2-8-12 0................... JackMitchell 12 64
(Brendan Powell) *s.i.s and swtchd rt after s: hld up towards rr: rdn and hdwy over 1f out: styd on wl to go 4th towards fin* **33/1**

345 **5** *nk* **Elsie Partridge (IRE)**[25] 6607 2-8-10 67................................ JimmyQuinn 2 61
(Noel Quinlan) *chsd ldrs: rdn and effrt 2f out: no ex jst ins fnl f: wknd fnl 100yds* **8/1**

04 **5** *dht* **Groundworker (IRE)**[20] 6746 2-9-1 0................................ RichardHughes 6 66
(Sylvester Kirk) *t.k.h: chsd ldr tl led after 1f out: rdn and hdd over 1f out: no ex: wknd ins fnl f* **5/1**

303 **7** *2* **Too Elusive**[21] 6718 2-8-10 70................................ JacobButterfield[(5)] 7 60
(Kristin Stubbs) *chsd ldrs: rdn and outpcd ent fnl 2f: styd on same pce after* **12/1**

2520 **8** *3/4* **Secret Kode (IRE)**[22] 6695 2-8-12 68........................ SilvestreDeSousa 3 57
(Brendan Powell) *stdd s: hld up towards rr: hdwy on inner over 1f out: nt clr run ins fnl f: swtchd lft fnl 100yds and nt pushed after* **4/1**[2]

00 **9** *3* **Charleys Angel**[42] 6079 2-8-3 0................................ JemmaMarshall[(3)] 10 40
(Pat Phelan) *in tch in midfield on outer: rdn and no hdwy over 2f out: wknd over 1f out* **66/1**

00 **10** *1 3/4* **Sutton Sioux**[20] 6746 2-8-10 0.. FergusSweeney 9 39
(Jeremy Gask) *t.k.h: hld up in midfield: rdn and struggling over 2f out: wknd 2f out* **66/1**

0 **11** *3* **Trefnant (IRE)**[8] 7078 2-8-5 0.. RobertTart[(3)] 8 28
(Chris Dwyer) *hld up towards rr: rdn and struggling over 2f out: wknd 2f out* **100/1**

1m 13.67s (0.57) **Going Correction** -0.025s/f (Stan) **11** Ran SP% **117.7**
Speed ratings (Par 95): **95,94,94,91,90 90,87,86,82,80 76**
toteswingers 1&2 £3.10, 1&3 £26.10, 2&3 £12.10 CSF £13.59 TOTE £6.20: £1.90, £1.50, £6.80; EX 19.20 Trifecta £349.50 Pool: £2258.19 - 4.84 winning units..
Owner Market Avenue Racing Club & Partners **Bred** Shefford Valley Stud **Trained** Twyford, Bucks

FOCUS
The bare result doesn't tell the full story in this maiden auction, which was run at a good pace. The form, though, is largely straightforward.

7262 REWARDS4RACING.COM H'CAP (DIV I) 6f (P)
6:40 (6:40) (Class 5) (0-70,70) 3-Y-O+ **£2,587** (£770; £384; £192) **Stalls** Low

Form RPR

6-43 **1** **Kylladdie**[14] 6928 6-9-7 70...............................(b) MickaelBarzalona 5 78
(Steve Gollings) *chsd ldrs: effrt 2f out: drvn to ld jst ins fnl f: hld on towards fin* **9/2**[2]

3254 **2** *nk* **Jay Bee Blue**[14] 6929 4-9-3 66...............................(bt) FrankieMcDonald 9 73
(Sean Curran) *hld up in tch in last quartet: rdn and effrt over 1f out: r.o wl ins fnl f: pressing wnr towards fin: jst hld* **10/1**

2540 **3** *1* **Captain Scooby**[10] 7029 7-9-3 66...............................(e) RobbieFitzpatrick 6 70
(Richard Guest) *chsd ldrs: drvn and effrt over 1f out: pressing wnr jst ins fnl f: no ex and one pce fnl 100yds* **16/1**

0022 **4** *1/2* **Take The Lead**[14] 6928 3-9-1 65.................................... RichardHughes 4 68
(Richard Hannon) *chsd ldr: rdn and chal ent fnl 2f: unable qck 1f out: kpt on same pce ins fnl f* **5/1**[3]

0400 **5** *1/2* **Perfect Pastime**[7] 7086 5-8-11 60...............................(p) WilliamCarson 10 61
(Jim Boyle) *hld up in tch: hdwy u.p whn nt clr run and swtchd rt 1f out: styd on u.p fnl 100yds* **14/1**

0503 **6** *1/2* **Shifting Star (IRE)**[13] 6937 8-9-0 63.................................. SeanLevey 11 63
(John Bridger) *chsd ldrs: rdn and outpcd ent fnl 2f: rallied and styd on again ins fnl f* **14/1**

3350 **7** *3/4* **Putin (IRE)**[12] 6963 5-8-11 60...............................(bt) NeilCallan 7 57
(Phil McEntee) *led: rdn and hrd pressed ent fnl 2f: hdd jst ins fnl f: no ex and wknd towards fin* **12/1**

6551 **8** *shd* **Athletic**[62] 5398 4-9-2 65...............................(v) JimCrowley 3 62
(Andrew Reid) *s.i.s: hld up in tch in rr: effrt but forced to switch lft arnd many rivals over 1f out: styd on ins fnl f: nvr able to chal* **3/1**[1]

4504 **9** *1/2* **Ada Lovelace**[41] 6100 3-9-4 68.. JimmyQuinn 12 64
(Dean Ivory) *t.k.h: chsd ldrs: drvn and effrt over 1f out: no ex 1f out: wknd ins fnl f* **33/1**

5446 **10** *1 1/2* **Ryan Style (IRE)**[43] 6040 7-8-13 62...............................(v) SamHitchcott 1 53
(Lisa Williamson) *hld up in tch towards rr: effrt u.p on inner over 1f out: no imp ins fnl f* **25/1**

6460 **11** *2 1/2* **Street Power (USA)**[27] 6526 8-9-0 70............................. DavidParkes[(7)] 8 54
(Jeremy Gask) *stdd s: hld up in rr: rdn and no hdwy over 1f out: n.d* **5/1**[3]

1m 12.65s (-0.45) **Going Correction** -0.025s/f (Stan)
WFA 3 from 4yo+ 1lb **11** Ran SP% **119.3**
Speed ratings (Par 103): **102,101,100,99,98 98,97,97,96,94 91**
toteswingers 1&2 £7.60, 1&3 £7.80, 2&3 £17.20 CSF £49.92 CT £670.53 TOTE £5.20: £1.70, £3.50, £5.10; EX 52.10 Trifecta £566.40 Pool: £1942.79 - 2.57 winning units..
Owner C Johnstone **Bred** Horizon Bloodstock Limited **Trained** Scamblesby, Lincs

FOCUS
A fair sprint run at a sound pace, and straightforward form rated around the principals.

7263 REWARDS4RACING.COM H'CAP (DIV II) 6f (P)
7:10 (7:10) (Class 5) (0-70,70) 3-Y-O+ **£2,587** (£770; £288; £288) **Stalls** Low

Form RPR

452 **1** **Harrogate Fair**[20] 6753 3-8-13 63...................................... LiamJones 9 70
(Michael Squance) *stdd after s: hld up in rr: rdn over 2f out: hdwy on outer jst over 1f out: led ins fnl f: r.o wl* **12/1**

2/00 **2** *3/4* **Alis Aquilae (IRE)**[20] 6757 7-8-11 60............................ AdamBeschizza 7 65
(Tim Etherington) *chsd ldrs: effrt u.p to chal over 1f out: led 1f out: hdd ins fnl f: kpt on* **14/1**

0306 **3** *nk* **Uprise**[56] 5607 4-8-11 63.. RyanPowell[(3)] 8 67
(George Margarson) *hld up in last quartet: swtchd rt 2f out: gd hdwy over 1f out: ev ch ins fnl f: unable qck fnl 100yds* **8/1**

4531 **3** *dht* **First Class**[34] 6317 5-9-1 64...............................(p) MickaelBarzalona 11 68
(Rae Guest) *hld up in last quartet: rdn and hdwy over 1f out: pressing ldrs ins fnl f: kpt on* **2/1**[1]

1230 **5** *1* **Perfect Venture**[33] 6341 3-8-12 67.................................. RyanTate[(5)] 2 68
(Clive Cox) *chsd ldrs: effrt u.p to chal 1f out: unable qck fnl 100yds* **7/1**[3]

-054 **6** *hd* **Dear Maurice**[131] 3010 9-9-3 66...............................(t) JimmyQuinn 6 66
(Tobias B P Coles) *swtchd rt and bmpd sn after s: hld up in last quartet: rdn and hdwy on inner over 1f out: pressing ldrs ins fnl f: no ex fnl 75yds* **25/1**

4361 **7** *nse* **Gung Ho Jack**[14] 6929 4-9-2 65.................................... SteveDrowne 10 68
(John Best) *hld up in midfield: nt clr run over 1f out: swtchd lft and r.o ins fnl f: unable to chal* **5/1**[2]

4600 **8** *3* **Jillywinks**[13] 6941 3-8-10 60...................................... SilvestreDeSousa 1 51
(Scott Dixon) *led: rdn wl over 1f out: hdd 1f out: wknd ins fnl f* **14/1**

2046 **9** *1 1/2* **Only Ten Per Cent (IRE)**[14] 6928 5-9-6 69.............(v) RichardHughes 4 56
(J R Jenkins) *in tch in midfield: rdn and effrt 2f out: unable qck whn squeezed for room ent fnl f: wknd ins fnl f* **5/1**[2]

2210 **10** *4 1/2* **Gebayl**[32] 6367 3-8-12 62...............................(p) NeilCallan 3 35
(Olivia Maylam) *chsd ldrs: rdn and unable qck ent fnl 2f: wknd 1f out* **25/1**

3505 **11** *2* **We Have A Dream**[15] 6905 8-9-3 66...............................(tp) MartinHarley 12 33
(Violet M Jordan) *taken down early: pressed ldr tl no ex u.p wl over 1f out: wknd jst over 1f out* **33/1**

1m 12.41s (-0.69) **Going Correction** -0.025s/f (Stan)
WFA 3 from 4yo+ 1lb **11** Ran SP% **121.9**
Speed ratings (Par 103): **103,102,101,101,100 100,99,95,93,87 85**PL:Uprise £1.90, First Class £0.60; TRICAST: HF/AA/FC £241.34, HF/AA/U £720.29; TRIFECTA: HF/AA/FC £604.70, HF/AA/U £654.10; toteswingers 1&2 £61.60, 1&FC £1.80, 2&FC £4.90, 1&U £30.70, 2&U #20.50 CSF £169.72 TOTE £10.30: £5.10, £6.50; EX 212.30 TRIFECTA Pool: £17427 Owner.

■ Stewards' Enquiry : Liam Jones four-day ban: careless riding (Oct 29-Nov 1)

FOCUS
The leaders went hard in the second division of this 0-70 sprint, setting it up for those coming from behind. The form is rated at the mid point of the possibilities.

7264 BOOK YOUR CHRISTMAS PARTY ON 01932 753518 H'CAP 6f (P)
7:40 (7:40) (Class 4) (0-85,85) 3-Y-0+ **£4,851** (£1,443; £721; £360) **Stalls** Low

Form RPR

2146 **1** **Dominium (USA)**[20] 6744 6-8-4 71....(b) RobertTart(3) 6 83+
(Jeremy Gask) *s.i.s: hld up in rr: swtchd lft and hdwy over 1f out: str run to ld fnl 100yds: sn clr and r.o wl: readily* **7/1**

1002 **2** *3* **Pivotal Movement**[13] 6959 3-9-0 79....(p) RichardHughes 4 83
(Richard Hannon) *chsd ldrs: rdn and qcknd to ld over 1f out: hdd fnl 100yds and sn brushed aside by wnr: kpt on to hold 2nd* **5/2**[1]

2235 **3** *3/4* **Panther Patrol (IRE)**[22] 6692 3-8-11 76.... NeilCallan 2 77
(Eve Johnson Houghton) *chsd ldrs: rdn and chal over 1f out: drew clr w ldr ent fnl f: outpcd by wnr fnl 100yds* **6/1**

3430 **4** *1 1/4* **Apollo D'Negro (IRE)**[73] 4983 5-8-9 78....(v) RyanTate(5) 3 75
(Clive Cox) *hld up in last trio: switching lft and effrt wl over 1f out: styd on fnl f but no ch w wnr* **8/1**

500 **5** *1 1/4* **Banovallum**[62] 5401 3-8-10 75.... LiamKeniry 7 68
(Sylvester Kirk) *chsd ldr: rdn and ev ch 2f out: unable qck and btn ent fnl f: wknd ins fnl f* **8/1**

5110 **6** *1* **Gabrial's Gift (IRE)**[17] 6822 4-9-2 80.... SilvestreDeSousa 1 70
(Scott Dixon) *hld up in last trio: effrt and hdwy on inner over 1f out: no imp 1f out: sn wknd* **5/1**[3]

-001 **7** *hd* **Pettochside**[14] 6928 4-8-11 75....(t) DavidProbert 9 65
(Stuart Williams) *in tch in midfield: rdn and unable qck 2f out: wknd ent fnl f* **4/1**[2]

5055 **8** *3 1/4* **Ask The Guru**[15] 6900 3-8-9 74....(v) RobertHavlin 11 54
(Michael Attwater) *led: rdn 2f out: drvn and hdd over 1f out: wknd fnl f* **33/1**

1m 11.59s (-1.51) **Going Correction** -0.025s/f (Stan)
WFA 3 from 4yo+ 1lb **8** Ran SP% **117.2**
Speed ratings (Par 105): **109,105,104,102,100 99,99,94**
toteswingers 1&2 £5.70, 1&3 £7.90, 2&3 £4.30 CSF £25.57 CT £113.69 TOTE £8.10: £3.00, £1.30, £2.00; EX 31.80 Trifecta £255.30 Pool: £1732.11 - 5.08 winning units..
Owner Horses First Racing Limited **Bred** Corbett Farm **Trained** Sutton Veny, Wilts

FOCUS
A fairly useful handicap which was soundly run, although it wasn't a particularly competitive race for the level. Another race where the front runners came back.

7265 DAY DELEGATE RATES FROM £39 H'CAP (DIV I) 7f (P)
8:10 (8:10) (Class 6) (0-52,52) 3-Y-0+ **£1,940** (£577; £288; £144) **Stalls** Low

Form RPR

2-30 **1** **Dustland Fairytale (IRE)**[162] 2072 5-9-5 50.... SilvestreDeSousa 8 60+
(Ian Williams) *chsd ldng trio: rdn and qckrnd to ld over 1f out: sn clr: r.o wl* **11/4**[1]

4300 **2** *1 3/4* **Chez Vrony**[31] 6399 7-9-1 46 oh1.... WilliamCarson 4 51
(Dave Morris) *hld up in midfield: swtchd lft and effrt 2f out: hdwy and edging rt over 1f out: chsd clr wnr 1f out: kpt on* **14/1**

6306 **3** *2 3/4* **Charlemagne Diva**[7] 7106 3-9-0 52....(t) RyanTate(5) 13 49
(Richard Guest) *chsd ldrs: rdn and ev ch over 1f out: unable qck w wnr jst over 1f out: 3rd and one pce fnl f* **8/1**

4600 **4** *1 1/2* **Foie Gras**[13] 6930 3-8-12 48.... RobertTart(3) 11 41
(Chris Dwyer) *hld up in last trio: sme hdwy over 1f out: swtchd rt 1f out: styd on wl fnl f: nvr trbld ldrs* **16/1**

045 **5** *1/2* **Princess Sheila (IRE)**[15] 6902 3-8-11 51.... DavidParkes(7) 9 43
(J S Moore) *in tch in midfield: effrt and hung rt over 2f out: no threat to ldrs but kpt on fnl f* **16/1**

3245 **6** *hd* **Sally Bruce**[48] 5890 3-8-12 52.... JenniferFerguson(7) 7 44
(Edward Creighton) *in tch in midfield on outer: rdn and effrt over 2f out: no imp and one pce fnl 2f* **16/1**

0000 **7** *shd* **World Freight Girl**[22] 6698 3-9-0 47....(p) JimmyQuinn 10 38
(Dean Ivory) *in tch in midfield: rdn and effrt over 2f out: styd on same pce and no imp fnl 2f* **25/1**

00-0 **8** *2 1/2* **Royal Intruder**[63] 5373 8-9-5 50....(t) MartinHarley 12 36
(Violet M Jordan) *stdd s: t.k.h: hld up in last pair: hdwy on inner 2f out: no hdwy over 1f out: wknd fnl f* **12/1**

6330 **9** *nk* **Do More Business (IRE)**[31] 6400 6-9-0 50....(bt) PhilipPrince(5) 5 35
(Liam Corcoran) *hld up in tch: rdn and hdwy over 2f out: no hdwy u.p over 1f out: sn wknd* **7/1**[3]

420 **10** *1 1/4* **Silvee**[7] 7092 6-9-3 48.... SeanLevey 1 30
(John Bridger) *led tl rdn and hdd over 1f out: sn btn: fdd fnl f* **8/1**

6-34 **11** *10* **Lilly White (USA)**[49] 5869 3-9-4 51.... MickaelBarzalona 2 6
(John Butler) *chsd ldrs: rdn and no ex ent fnl 2f: wknd over 1f out* **5/1**[2]

664 **12** *4* **Wishformore (IRE)**[29] 6462 6-9-7 52....(p) RichardThomas 6
(Zoe Davison) *stdd s: t.k.h: hld up towards rr: eased wl over 1f out: sddle slipped* **20/1**

006 **13** *1 1/2* **Majnon Fajer (IRE)**[43] 6036 3-9-3 50....(b[1]) RobertHavlin 3
(Roger Ingram) *s.i.s: sn rdn along in rr: n.d* **10/1**

1m 25.9s (-0.10) **Going Correction** -0.025s/f (Stan)
WFA 3 from 5yo+ 2lb **13** Ran SP% **127.8**
Speed ratings (Par 101): **99,97,93,92,91 91,91,88,88,86 75,70,68**
toteswingers 1&2 £5.80, 1&3 £19.50, 2&3 £66.70 CSF £48.22 CT £305.22 TOTE £5.60: £1.70, £6.80, £2.40; EX 64.00 Trifecta £721.30 Pool: £961.84 - 0.64 winning units..
Owner Ian Williams **Bred** Liam Cashman And M Fahy **Trained** Portway, Worcs

FOCUS
A low-grade affair but the winner is one to keep on side. The runner-up helps with the standard.

7266 DAY DELEGATE RATES FROM £39 H'CAP (DIV II) 7f (P)
8:40 (8:40) (Class 6) (0-52,52) 3-Y-0+ **£1,940** (£577; £288; £144) **Stalls** Low

Form RPR

050 **1** **Kindlelight Storm (USA)**[26] 6555 3-9-5 52.... RobertHavlin 7 58+
(Nick Littmoden) *dwlt and rdn along early: hdwy into midfield after 2f: weaved way through fr over 2f out: chal ent fnl f: led ins fnl f: r.o wl* **7/2**[1]

3535 **2** *1/2* **Chester Deelyte (IRE)**[41] 6101 5-9-1 46 oh1....(v) SamHitchcott 5 52
(Lisa Williamson) *in tch in midfield: rdn and hdwy over 1f out: led ins fnl f: sn hdd: kpt on but a hld* **16/1**

500 **3** *1 3/4* **Up In Flames (IRE)**[50] 5816 4-9-2 50....(b) WilliamTwiston-Davies(3) 14 51+
(Martin Keighley) *chsd ldr tl led over 2f: rdn clr 2f out: drvn and hdd ins fnl f: no ex and one pce after* **10/1**

3244 **4** *hd* **Sakhee's Alround**[31] 6400 3-9-3 50....(p) AdamBeschizza 11 52
(K F Clutterbuck) *taken down early: pushed along in midfield: lost pl and rdn over 2f out: n.m.r 2f out: hdwy u.p over 1f out: kpt on wl fnl f* **7/2**[1]

4520 **5** *1 1/2* **Fairy Mist (IRE)**[36] 6261 6-9-1 46 oh1.... KieranO'Neill 10 43
(John Bridger) *chsd ldrs: effrt but unable qck 2f out: styd on same pce fr over 1f out* **8/1**[3]

6000 **6** *1/2* **Man In The Arena**[48] 5890 3-8-11 47....[1] RobertTart(3) 8 42
(Dr Jon Scargill) *hld up in tch: switching lft and effrt 2f out: styd on ins fnl f* **16/1**

0206 **7** *1 1/2* **Blue Deer (IRE)**[41] 6105 5-9-7 52....(p) KierenFox 1 44
(Lee Carter) *hld up in rr: swtchd rt 2f out: hdwy u.p over 1f out: styd on same pce fnl f* **8/1**[3]

/000 **8** *1/2* **Storey Hill (USA)**[17] 4892 8-9-1 46.... RobbieFitzpatrick 6 37
(Richard Guest) *chsd ldrs: drvn and unable qck ent fnl 2f: styd on same pce and no imp over 1f out* **20/1**

0600 **9** *1 1/2* **Alberto**[8] 7079 3-9-3 50.... JohnFahy 13 36
(Paul Fitzsimons) *taken down early: stdd s: t.k.h: hld up in midfield: rdn and no hdwy jst over 2f out: wknd over 1f out* **25/1**

0605 **10** *5* **Otto The First**[66] 5275 3-8-13 46.... SteveDrowne 9 19
(John Best) *hld up in tch towards rr: rdn and no hdwy ent fnl 2f: wknd wl over 1f out* **16/1**

4640 **11** *2* **Princess Cammie (IRE)**[20] 6745 3-9-5 52....(p) SeanLevey 2 19
(John Bridger) *t.k.h: hld up in tch in midfield: rdn and no hdwy ent fnl 2f: wknd over 1f out* **20/1**

5030 **12** *1 1/2* **King Of Wing (IRE)**[8] 7082 4-9-4 49....(v) DavidProbert 12 14
(Phil McEntee) *wl in tch in midfield: rdn and no ex 2f out: sn wknd* **10/1**

00-0 **13** *1 1/2* **Rose Madder**[236] 733 4-8-12 50.... NedCurtis(7) 3 11
(Roger Curtis) *led tl over 2f out: rdn and struggling ent fnl 2f: wknd over 1f out* **66/1**

554- **14** *5* **Onertother**[405] 5939 4-9-4 49.... LiamKeniry 4
(Joseph Tuite) *chsd ldrs: rdn over 2f out: lost pl qckly 1f out: bhd fnl f* **7/1**[2]

1m 25.93s (-0.07) **Going Correction** -0.025s/f (Stan)
WFA 3 from 4yo+ 2lb **14** Ran SP% **129.9**
Speed ratings (Par 101): **99,98,96,96,94 93,92,91,89,84 81,80,78,72**
toteswingers 1&2 £15.80, 1&3 £15.50, 2&3 £30.50 CSF £69.60 CT £558.38 TOTE £6.80: £2.50, £8.50, £5.40; EX 78.70 Trifecta £673.30 Pool: £897.76 - 0.53 winning units..
Owner Kindlelight Ltd, N Shields & N Littmoden **Bred** Kirsten Rausing **Trained** Newmarket, Suffolk
■ Stewards' Enquiry : Kieran O'Neill one-day ban: careless riding (Oct 29)

FOCUS
More basement-level stuff, although the winner is at least unexposed. The pace was good.

7267 BOOK NOW FOR CHRISTMAS FESTIVAL H'CAP 1m 4f (P)
9:10 (9:10) (Class 4) (0-80,79) 3-Y-0+ **£4,851** (£1,443; £721; £360) **Stalls** Centre

Form RPR

1423 **1** **Grendisar (IRE)**[22] 6693 3-9-4 78....(p) MartinHarley 7 86+
(Marco Botti) *stdd s: hld up in tch in rr: effrt 2f out: hdwy to chal 1f out: led ins fnl f: r.o wl* **7/4**[1]

2066 **2** *nk* **Where's Susie**[39] 6173 8-8-13 66.... RobertHavlin 9 74
(Michael Madgwick) *stdd s: hld up in last pair: swtchd lft and effrt over 2f out: hdwy u.p over 1f out: chal 1f out: ev ch and r.o fnl 150yds: a jst hld* **33/1**

65-1 **3** *2 1/2* **Little Buxted (USA)**[283] 74 3-9-1 75.... KierenFox 4 79
(Robert Mills) *in tch in midfield: effrt u.p over 2f out: kpt on same pce fnl f: wnt 3rd fnl 100yds* **12/1**

2113 **4** *1 3/4* **Thwart**[92] 4349 3-9-1 75.... JimCrowley 5 76
(Ralph Beckett) *t.k.h: chsd ldr after 2f tl rdn to ld wl over 1f out: hdd ins fnl f: sn outpcd: wknd fnl 100yds* **4/1**[3]

451 **5** *2 3/4* **Wizara (IRE)**[17] 6847 3-9-5 79.... SilvestreDeSousa 1 76
(Saeed bin Suroor) *t.k.h: chsd ldr for 2f: chsd ldrs after: rdn and effrt over 2f out: no ex and btn 1f out: wknd ins fnl f* **2/1**[2]

1004 **6** *2 3/4* **Waverunner**[13] 6936 3-9-0 74.... LiamJones 6 67
(Mark Johnston) *led and set stdy gallop: rdn and qcknd wl over 2f out: hdd wl over 1f out: btn jst over 1f out: sn wknd* **8/1**

3650 **7** *1 1/2* **Choral Festival**[8] 7075 7-9-7 74.... KieranO'Neill 8 65
(John Bridger) *in tch in midfield: effrt u.p over 2f out: outpcd and btn over 1f out: sn wknd* **25/1**

2m 33.4s (-1.10) **Going Correction** -0.025s/f (Stan)
WFA 3 from 4yo+ 7lb **7** Ran SP% **115.3**
Speed ratings (Par 105): **102,101,100,98,97 95,94**
toteswingers 1&2 £15.30, 1&3 £7.50, 2&3 £34.90 CSF £55.52 CT £547.40 TOTE £2.90: £1.50, £6.30; EX 43.40 Trifecta £354.00 Pool: £1678.63 - 3.55 winning units..
Owner Mohamed Albousi Alghufli **Bred** Old Carhue & Graeng Bloodstock **Trained** Newmarket, Suffolk

FOCUS
A fair handicap. The pace didn't look overly strong in the first half of the contest but it was another race where the principals came from the rear. The form is rated around the runner-up.
T/Jkpt: £111,697.40. Pool: £1,022,582.23 - 6.50 winning units. T/Plt: £58.70. Pool: £106,610.49 - 1325.57 winning units. T/Qpdt: £30.20. Pool: £8760.86 - 214.59 winning units. SP

7102 LEICESTER (R-H)
Tuesday, October 15

OFFICIAL GOING: Soft (heavy in places; 5.7)
False rail from top of hill on back straight to Winning Post increased distances on Round course by 17m.
Wind: Light across Weather: Overcast

7268 WYMESWOLD CONDITIONS STKS 7f 9y
2:10 (2:12) (Class 3) 2-Y-0 **£6,469** (£1,925) **Stalls** High

Form RPR

0100 **1** **Trading Profit**[10] 7026 2-9-2 102.... RyanMoore 4 103
(Andrew Balding) *mde all: shkn up and c clr fr over 1f out: easily* **4/7**[1]

311 **2** *14* **Focusofourthoughts (IRE)**[8] 7062 2-9-2 77.... PaulHanagan 1 71
(Ann Duffield) *chsd wnr: pushed along 1/2-way: sn hung rt: wknd over 1f out* **6/1**[2]

1m 30.4s (4.20) **Going Correction** +0.45s/f (Yiel) **2** Ran SP% **77.9**
Speed ratings (Par 99): **94,78**
TOTE £1.30.
Owner Another Bottle Racing 2 **Bred** D J And Mrs Deer **Trained** Kingsclere, Hants

FOCUS
Conditions were quite testing after 9mm of rain overnight. Paul Hanagan described the ground as "hard work and very soft". Due to a false rail all races run on the round course were increased by 17m. A one-sided match after the bad-tempered Complicit misbehaved and, not for the first time, refused to enter the stalls (withdrawn, 7-4, deduct 35p in the £ under R4). The winner has been given a token rating.

7269 WHISSENDINE (S) STKS 7f 9y
2:40 (2:40) (Class 6) 3-4-Y-O £1,940 (£577; £288; £144) Stalls High

Form				RPR
4-	1		**Collingbourneducis (IRE)**[104] 3967 3-8-5 60 ConnorBeasley(5) 7 (Michael Dods) *sn pushed along in rr: hdwy over 2f out: rdn to ld 1f out: styd on* **16/1**	72
0154	2	1 ¾	**Red Art (IRE)**[8] 7075 4-9-3 77 JamesDoyle 8 (Charles Hills) *trckd ldrs: shkn up to ld over 2f out: rdn and hdd 1f out: styd on same pce* **2/7**[1]	74
03-3	3	3	**Global Icon**[24] 6630 3-8-10 70 (p) PaulHanagan 4 (Michael Dods) *trckd ldrs: rdn over 2f out: no ex ins fnl f* **10/1**[3]	60
0353	4	3 ½	**Thomasina**[36] 6260 3-8-5 45 DavidProbert 1 (Denis Coakley) *s.i.s: sn pushed along in rr: rdn over 2f out: nvr trbld ldrs* **25/1**	46
4514	5	5	**Mrs Warren**[13] 6937 3-8-10 62 PatCosgrave 3 (George Baker) *trckd ldrs: rdn over 2f out: wknd over 1f out* **8/1**[2]	39
0-00	6	11	**Misty Eyes**[27] 6518 4-8-7 37 ChrisCatlin 5 (Geoffrey Harker) *w ldr tl led over 5f out: rdn and hdd over 2f out: wknd over 1f out* **100/1**	7
4060	7	60	**Roland**[26] 6547 3-9-1 66 (b) LukeMorris 6 (Kevin Ryan) *led: hdd over 5f out: drvn along 1/2-way: sn hung rt and wknd* **20/1**	

1m 29.25s (3.05) **Going Correction** +0.45s/f (Yiel)
WFA 3 from 4yo 2lb 7 Ran SP% **113.4**
Speed ratings (Par 101): **100,98,94,90,84 72,3**
toteswingers 1&2 £3.20, 1&3 £6.80, 2&3 £1.70 CSF £21.28 TOTE £16.50: £7.10, £1.10; EX 34.00 Trifecta £151.40 Pool: £2418.80 - 11.97 winning units..Collingbourneducis was bought by M Gates for 6200gns. Red Art was claimed by Tony Newcombe for £6000.
Owner Andrew Tinkler **Bred** J Breslin **Trained** Denton, Co Durham

FOCUS
A shock result to this 7f selling race. The runner-up was a bit below form, and the fourth offers perspective.

7270 EBF REFERENCE POINT MAIDEN STKS (C&G) (DIV I) 7f 9y
3:10 (3:13) (Class 4) 2-Y-O £5,175 (£1,540; £769; £384) Stalls High

Form				RPR
203	1		**Rock Of Dreams (IRE)**[20] 6739 2-9-0 75 JamesDoyle 10 (Charles Hills) *s.i.s: hld up: pushed along and swtchd rt 3f out: hdwy over 2f out: rdn to ld and hung rt fr over 1f out: styd on* **4/1**[2]	75
	2	1 ¼	**Takreym (IRE)** 2-9-0 0 DaneO'Neill 7 (Roger Varian) *s.s: hdwy 2f out: rdn over 1f out: r.o* **7/1**[3]	72+
	3	¾	**Majorities** 2-9-0 0 RyanMoore 8 (Brian Meehan) *hld up: t.k.h: hdwy over 1f out: edgd rt ins fnl f: r.o* **16/1**	70+
0	4	1 ¼	**Bilimbi (IRE)**[38] 6184 2-9-0 0 ShaneKelly 4 (William Haggas) *hmpd s: hld up: hdwy over 1f out: r.o: nt trble ldrs* **20/1**	67+
	5	½	**Ashkari (IRE)** 2-9-0 0 PaulHanagan 2 (Clive Cox) *prom: pushed along over 2f out: ev ch over 1f out: no ex ins fnl f* **16/1**	66+
00	6	4 ½	**Sir Guy Porteous (IRE)**[10] 7017 2-9-0 0 KierenFallon 6 (Mark Johnston) *edgd rt s: led: shkn up over 2f out: rdn: hung rt and hdd over 1f out: wknd and eased ins fnl f* **7/2**[1]	56
	7	3 ¼	**Hopeigetlucky** 2-9-0 0 PatCosgrave 9 (Stuart Kittow) *chsd ldrs: pushed along 1/2-way: wknd 2f out* **100/1**	46
0	8	8	**Royal Preserve**[18] 6799 2-9-0 0 DavidProbert 1 (Andrew Balding) *trckd ldr tl rdn wl over 1f out: sn wknd* **7/1**[3]	26
4	9	2 ½	**Pipe Dream**[25] 6590 2-9-0 0 JimmyFortune 5 (Brian Meehan) *hmpd s: chsd ldrs: shkn up 1/2-way: wknd over 2f out* **10/1**	20

1m 29.9s (3.70) **Going Correction** +0.45s/f (Yiel) 9 Ran SP% **93.8**
Speed ratings (Par 97): **96,94,93,92,91 86,82,73,70**
toteswingers 1&2 £3.80, 1&3 £6.30, 2&3 £10.50 CSF £21.05 TOTE £3.90: £1.50, £2.20, £2.70; EX 18.00 Trifecta £101.00 Pool: £1714.85 - 12.73 winning units..
Owner Marston Stud & Arthur Mitchell **Bred** Lady Richard Wellesley **Trained** Lambourn, Berks
■ Salmon Sushi was withdrawn (4-1, bolted to post). Deduct 20p in the £ under R4.

FOCUS
It paid to sit off the pace in this 7f 2yo maiden race, in which previous form was thin on the ground. A fluid level to the form, and not a race to be confident about.

7271 EBF REFERENCE POINT MAIDEN STKS (C&G) (DIV II) 7f 9y
3:40 (3:40) (Class 4) 2-Y-O £5,175 (£1,540; £769; £384) Stalls High

Form				RPR
02	1		**Cordite (IRE)**[27] 6517 2-9-0 0 PaulHanagan 5 (Michael Appleby) *mde all: shkn up over 1f out: edgd rt and rdn clr fnl f: easily* **9/4**[1]	88+
64	2	7	**Lacock**[18] 6790 2-9-0 0 DaneO'Neill 4 (Henry Candy) *trckd wnr: rdn over 1f out: no ex ins fnl f: eased towards fin* **3/1**[2]	71
04	3	3	**Despot (IRE)**[12] 6975 2-9-0 0 JamesDoyle 3 (Charles Hills) *hld up: hdwy over 2f out: rdn over 1f out: wknd fnl f* **9/2**[3]	63+
00	4	¾	**Majestic Sun (IRE)**[13] 6931 2-9-0 0 ShaneKelly 1 (Peter Chapple-Hyam) *hld up: hdwy over 2f out: wknd over 1f out* **14/1**	61+
	5	6	**Piton** 2-9-0 0 KierenFallon 6 (Mark Johnston) *s.i.s: sn pushed along and prom: rdn over 2f out: sn wknd* **16/1**	46
60	6	¾	**Samhain**[12] 6975 2-9-0 0 SeanLevey 7 (David Brown) *trckd ldrs: rdn over 2f out: wknd over 1f out* **100/1**	44
	7	2 ¼	**Rapid Advance** 2-9-0 0 RyanMoore 2 (Roger Varian) *s.s: sn pushed along in rr: drvn along 1/2-way: wknd 2f out* **3/1**[2]	39+

1m 28.83s (2.63) **Going Correction** +0.45s/f (Yiel) 7 Ran SP% **112.5**
Speed ratings (Par 97): **102,94,90,89,82 82,79**
toteswingers 1&2 £2.30, 1&3 £2.30, 2&3 £3.30 CSF £8.94 TOTE £3.60: £2.10, £2.10; EX 10.10 Trifecta £23.30 Pool: £1537.73 - 49.36 winning units..
Owner Shaw Greaves Gamble **Bred** Raymond Sutton **Trained** Danethorpe, Notts

FOCUS
Part two of this maiden and again previous form was thin on the ground. This time they raced in one group middle-to-far side. Improvement from the winner, but it would be dangerous to take the form too literally.

7272 WREAKE FILLIES' CONDITIONS STKS 1m 60y
4:10 (4:10) (Class 3) 3-Y-O+ £7,561 (£2,263; £1,131; £566) Stalls Low

Form				RPR
451	1		**Princess Loulou (IRE)**[28] 6497 3-8-12 85 DaneO'Neill 3 (Roger Varian) *mde all: shkn up over 2f out: rdn over 1f out: styd on: comf* **5/6**[1]	93+
-060	2	1 ½	**Beautiful View**[95] 4252 3-8-9 85 RyanMoore 4 (Richard Hannon) *trckd wnr: pushed along over 2f out: rdn over 1f out: styd on same pce ins fnl f* **3/1**[2]	86
6250	3	2 ¼	**Trapeze**[118] 3460 3-8-9 85 RobertHavlin 1 (John Gosden) *chsd ldrs: swtchd lft over 3f out: rdn over 1f out: no ex ins fnl f* **4/1**[3]	81
0250	4	6	**Princess Of Orange**[11] 6989 4-8-12 86 TedDurcan 2 (Rae Guest) *dwlt: hld up: rdn 2f out: wknd fnl f: eased* **10/1**	68

1m 49.31s (4.21) **Going Correction** +0.55s/f (Yiel)
WFA 3 from 4yo 3lb 4 Ran SP% **108.6**
Speed ratings (Par 104): **100,98,96,90**
CSF £3.61 TOTE £1.90; EX 3.80 Trifecta £6.70 Pool: £1303.57 - 144.36 winning units..
Owner Saleh Al Homaizi & Imad Al Sagar **Bred** David John Brown **Trained** Newmarket, Suffolk

FOCUS
Just 4lb between the four fillies and they raced in their finishing position throughout. The form is rated around the second and third.

7273 FOSSE WAY CLASSIFIED CLAIMING STKS 1m 3f 183y
4:40 (4:41) (Class 6) 3-5-Y-O £2,587 (£770; £384; £192) Stalls Low

Form				RPR
5504	1		**Yasir (USA)**[4] 7169 5-9-4 67 (p) LiamKeniry 5 (Conor Dore) *s.i.s: sn prom: chsd ldr 10f out: rdn over 2f out: styd on u.p to ld wl ins fnl f: edgd rt nr fin* **5/4**[1]	68
032	2	1 ¾	**Flamingo Beat**[33] 6325 3-9-3 70 ChrisCatlin 4 (Rae Guest) *led: rdn over 1f out: hdd and unable qck wl ins fnl f: n.m.r nr fin* **7/2**[3]	71
521-	3	3 ¾	**Vexillum (IRE)**[48] 6838 4-8-12 66 (t) LukeMorris 2 (Simon Hodgson) *prom: t.k.h: rdn over 2f out: styd on same pce fnl f* **8/1**	53
0354	4	½	**Calon Lad (IRE)**[7] 7104 3-8-9 65 PatCosgrave 1 (George Baker) *w ldr 2f: remained handy: rdn over 2f out: styd on same pce fr over 1f out* **5/2**[2]	57
0500	5	47	**Churt**[8] 7082 4-8-12 35 KirstyMilczarek 6 (Christopher Kellett) *hld up: pushed along 1/2-way: wknd over 3f out* **200/1**	

2m 42.22s (8.32) **Going Correction** +0.55s/f (Yiel)
WFA 3 from 4yo+ 7lb 5 Ran SP% **106.8**
Speed ratings (Par 101): **94,92,90,90,58**
CSF £5.57 TOTE £2.30: £1.30, £1.70; EX 5.30 Trifecta £13.10 Pool: £2140.12 - 122.24 winning units..
Owner Mrs Louise Marsh **Bred** Shadwell Farm LLC **Trained** Hubbert's Bridge, Lincs

FOCUS
A classified claimer and the pace was steady until the final 4f. Ordinary form with the winner almost certainly a few pounds below their best. The form is rated on the negative side.

7274 IRISH STALLION FARMS EBF MAIDEN STKS 1m 60y
5:10 (5:10) (Class 4) 2-Y-O £5,175 (£1,540; £769; £384) Stalls Low

Form				RPR
6	1		**Gothic**[18] 6799 2-9-5 0 RyanMoore 2 (Sir Michael Stoute) *mde all: shkn up over 1f out: rdn ins fnl f: styd on* **4/11**[1]	79+
	2	2 ¼	**Alex My Boy (IRE)** 2-9-5 0 KierenFallon 6 (Mark Johnston) *sn chsng ldr: pushed along and lost 2nd over 2f out: rdn to go 2nd again 1f out: styd on* **6/1**[2]	73+
	3	½	**Seek A Star (USA)** 2-9-0 0 KirstyMilczarek 4 (Luca Cumani) *chsd ldrs: wnt 2nd over 2f out: pushed along and hung rt fr over 1f out: sn lost 2nd: styd on same pce ins fnl f* **8/1**[3]	67+
	4	7	**Intense Tango** 2-9-0 0 PaulHanagan 1 (Alan Jarvis) *s.s: hld up: shkn up over 1f out: nvr nrr* **33/1**	51+
06	5	½	**Palace Dragon (IRE)**[7] 7113 2-9-5 0 LukeMorris 5 (Sir Mark Prescott Bt) *prom: pushed along over 3f out: wknd 2f out* **100/1**	55
	6	15	**Opera Duke (IRE)** 2-9-5 0 DavidProbert 3 (Andrew Balding) *chsd ldrs tl rdn and wknd over 2f out* **14/1**	

1m 53.2s (8.10) **Going Correction** +0.55s/f (Yiel) 6 Ran SP% **109.3**
Speed ratings (Par 97): **81,78,78,71,70 55**
toteswingers 1&2 £1.20, 1&3 £1.30, 2&3 £1.70 CSF £2.81 TOTE £1.50: £1.10, £2.60; EX 3.90 Trifecta £7.10 Pool: £3166.28 - 330.30 winning units..
Owner Highclere Thoroughbred Racing -Petrushka **Bred** Mr & Mrs G Middlebrook **Trained** Newmarket, Suffolk

FOCUS
Not easy to assess the form, but the winner almost certainly built on his pleasing debut.

7275 STEWARDS H'CAP 1m 1f 218y
5:45 (5:46) (Class 5) (0-75,75) 3-Y-O+ £3,234 (£962; £481; £240) Stalls Low

Form				RPR
-263	1		**Ty Gwr**[21] 6721 4-9-7 72 DaneO'Neill 17 (Brian Ellison) *dwlt: hld up: hdwy over 3f out: led on bit over 1f out: shkn up and sn clr* **12/1**	90+
-540	2	7	**Mystery Bet (IRE)**[80] 4777 3-9-0 75 GeorgeChaloner(5) 13 (Richard Fahey) *chsd ldrs: led 2f out: rdn and hdd over 1f out: styd on same pce* **5/1**[2]	80
3212	3	4	**Mash Potato (IRE)**[25] 6588 3-8-10 71 (p) ConnorBeasley(5) 11 (Michael Dods) *trckd ldrs: t.k.h: rdn over 2f out: no ex fnl f* **4/1**[1]	69
4545	4	¾	**Freeport**[13] 6951 3-9-5 75 JimmyFortune 3 (Brian Meehan) *hld up: hdwy u.p over 2f out: no ex fnl f* **16/1**	71
0530	5	2 ½	**Steer By The Stars (IRE)**[15] 6906 3-9-0 70 KierenFallon 2 (Mark Johnston) *hld up: hdwy 2f out: sn rdn: wknd ins fnl f* **14/1**	62
5332	6	¾	**Markttag**[12] 6976 3-9-4 74 RyanMoore 14 (Luca Cumani) *prom: chsd ldr over 7f out: led 3f out: rdn and hdd 2f out: wknd fnl f* **4/1**[1]	64
0014	7	1 ½	**Guilded Spirit**[32] 6358 3-9-2 72 ShaneKelly 4 (Stuart Kittow) *hld up: hdwy over 2f out: sn rdn: wknd over 1f out* **16/1**	59
-525	8	6	**Ever Fortune (USA)**[81] 4718 4-9-10 75 LukeMorris 10 (Rae Guest) *prom: pushed along whn hmpd over 2f out: sn wknd* **16/1**	51
3300	9	¾	**Aerodynamic (IRE)**[6] 7130 6-9-6 71 (b) PatCosgrave 9 (Michael Easterby) *s.i.s: hld up: rdn over 2f out: n.d* **25/1**	46

The Form Book Flat, Raceform Ltd, Compton, RG20 6NL.

2334 **10** *1 ¼* **Thereabouts (USA)**[13] 6952 4-8-9 **65**........................ TobyAtkinson(5) 5 38
(Michael Appleby) *mid-div: hmpd over 3f out: sn rdn: swtchd lft over 2f out: sn wknd* **25/1**

1266 **11** *6* **Mazaaher**[32] 6358 3-9-5 **75**........................ PaulHanagan 1 37
(J W Hills) *hld up: sme hdwy on outer 2f out: sn wknd* **14/1**

2066 **12** *4 ½* **Mombasa**[31] 6389 3-9-3 **73**........................ JamesDoyle 7 26
(Ralph Beckett) *led: rdn and hdd 3f out: wknd and eased over 1f out* **10/1**[3]

0660 **13** *½* **Watts Up Son**[12] 6970 5-8-12 **70**........................(v) LukeLeadbitter(7) 8 22
(Declan Carroll) *sn pushed along to chse ldrs: rdn over 4f out: wknd over 2f out* **20/1**

15-0 **14** *3 ¾* **King Zeal (IRE)**[142] 144 9-9-4 **69**........................(t) KirstyMilczarek 15 14
(Barry Leavy) *chsd ldrs: rdn over 3f out: wknd over 2f out* **20/1**

2m 12.33s (4.43) **Going Correction** +0.55s/f (Yiel)
WFA 3 from 4yo+ 5lb **14** Ran SP% **121.6**
Speed ratings (Par 103): **104,98,95,94,92 92,90,86,85,84 79,76,75,72**
toteswingers 1&2 £20.40, 1&3 £11.00, 2&3 £5.90 CSF £67.91 CT £288.85 TOTE £14.20: £2.70, £2.80, £3.00; EX 144.60 Trifecta £617.60 Pool: £1280.25 - 3.00 winning units..
Owner Kevin Corcoran Aaron Pierce Chris Weare **Bred** Mrs A E Simcock **Trained** Norton, N Yorks

FOCUS
The gallop was sound and they came home well strung out behind a wide-margin winner. This rates much-imroved form from him.
T/Plt: £11.10. Pool £54,972.00 - 3604.49 winning units. T/Qpdt: £5.70. Pool £3111.20 - 399.85 winning units. CR

6938 NEWCASTLE (L-H)

Tuesday, October 15

OFFICIAL GOING: Soft (heavy in places; 5.3)
Wind: Light, half behind Weather: Overcast

7276 BETFRED 4X THE ODDS ON LUCKY 31'S EBF MAIDEN STKS (THE £5K BONUS RACE) 1m 3y(S)

2:00 (2:00) (Class 5) 2-Y-O **£2,911** (£866; £432; £216) **Stalls** Centre

Form RPR

6 **1** **Ryeollean**[10] 7023 2-9-0 0........................ DanielTudhope 2 75+
(David O'Meara) *cl up: led appr fnl f: pushed clr: comf* **5/1**[2]

4 **2** *4 ½* **Beyond Smart (USA)**[17] 6829 2-9-0 0........................ WilliamBuick 6 63
(John Gosden) *plld hrd early: in tch: hdwy 3f out: rdn and hung lft over 1f out: chsd (clr) wnr ins fnl f: no imp* **1/2**[1]

6 **3** *1 ¼* **Stanarley Pic**[13] 6939 2-9-0 0........................ AndrewMullen 5 60
(Alan Swinbank) *prom: effrt and chsd wnr fr 2f out to ins fnl f: rdn and kpt on same pce* **20/1**

4 *3 ¼* **Medicine Hat** 2-9-0 0........................ TomEaves 9 53+
(George Moore) *s.i.s: hld up: rdn and outpcd 3f out: styd on fnl f: nvr able to chal* **100/1**

04 **5** *½* **Tizlove Regardless (USA)**[19] 6773 2-9-0 0........................ JoeFanning 3 52
(Mark Johnston) *led: pushed along and hdd appr 2f out: wknd over 1f out* **16/1**

53 **6** *4* **Blazers Rock (IRE)**[21] 6716 2-9-0 0........................ BarryMcHugh 4 43
(Kevin Ryan) *t.k.h: trckd ldrs tl rdn and wknd fr 2f out* **6/1**[3]

0 **7** *2 ¼* **Highway Pursuit**[46] 5969 2-9-0 0........................ RaulDaSilva 1 38
(George Moore) *prom: drvn along fr 1/2-way: wknd over 2f out* **100/1**

1m 46.39s (2.99) **Going Correction** +0.425s/f (Yiel) **7** Ran SP% **110.2**
Speed ratings (Par 95): **102,97,96,93,92 88,86**
toteswingers 1&2 £1.40, 1&3 £7.50, 2&3 £4.30 CSF £7.35 TOTE £7.70: £2.20, £1.10; EX 9.40 Trifecta £51.10 Pool: £2638.52 - 38.65 winning units..
Owner Direct Racing Partnership **Bred** Dale Ablitt **Trained** Nawton, N Yorks

FOCUS
An uncompetitive maiden that was run at a steady pace in the bad ground, with the field racing up the centre. The form is rated on the negative side.

7277 BETFRED RACING FOLLOW US ON FACEBOOK/EBF MAIDEN FILLIES' STKS 1m 3y(S)

2:30 (2:32) (Class 5) 2-Y-O **£2,911** (£866; £432; £216) **Stalls** Centre

Form RPR

0 **1** **Jordan Princess**[27] 6523 2-9-0 0........................ AndreaAtzeni 4 75+
(Luca Cumani) *dwlt: hld up in tch: smooth hdwy to ld over 2f out: rdn and r.o strly fnl f* **5/2**[2]

02 **2** *2 ¾* **Empress Ali (IRE)**[25] 6597 2-9-0 0........................ AndrewMullen 1 69
(Tom Tate) *cl up: rdn and ev ch over 2f out: sn chsng wnr: kpt on fnl f: nt pce to chal* **7/1**

3 *¾* **Momentus (IRE)** 2-9-0 0........................ MartinLane 9 67+
(David Simcock) *missed break: hld up: smooth hdwy 3f out: pushed along and kpt on fnl f: no imp* **20/1**

35 **4** *1 ½* **Lady Yeats**[25] 6597 2-9-0 0........................ RaulDaSilva 2 64
(George Moore) *cl up: rdn and ev ch over 2f out: hung lft appr fnl f: sn no ex* **20/1**

64 **5** *8* **Lovelocks (IRE)**[64] 5330 2-9-0 0........................ RobertWinston 6 46
(Charles Hills) *led: rdn and hdd appr 2f out: wknd over 1f out* **2/1**[1]

03 **6** *3* **Great Wave (IRE)**[12] 6973 2-9-0 0........................ TomQueally 7 40
(David Simcock) *led to over 2f out: sn rdn and wknd* **12/1**

00 **7** *1 ½* **Mrs Pat**[17] 6828 2-9-0 0........................ TonyHamilton 13 37
(Richard Fahey) *bhd: rdn over 4f out: sme hdwy over 1f out: nvr on terms* **50/1**

0 **8** *2* **Wannabe Magic**[34] 6298 2-9-0 0........................ MichaelO'Connell 10 32
(Jedd O'Keeffe) *towards rr: drvn and struggling over 3f out: sn btn* **66/1**

9 *7* **Oxbow Lake (USA)** 2-9-0 0........................ JoeFanning 12 17
(Roger Varian) *in tch tl rdn and wknd fr 3f out* **5/1**[3]

1m 46.02s (2.62) **Going Correction** +0.425s/f (Yiel) **9** Ran SP% **111.7**
Speed ratings (Par 92): **103,100,99,98,90 87,85,83,76**
toteswingers 1&2 £3.90, 1&3 £10.70, 2&3 £15.40 CSF £18.50 TOTE £4.00: £1.80, £1.90, £6.60; EX 17.20 Trifecta £236.50 Pool: £1545.02 - 4.89 winning units..
Owner Sheikh Mohammed Obaid Al Maktoum **Bred** Darley **Trained** Newmarket, Suffolk

FOCUS
A steadily run fillies' maiden with the front four pulling clear. Probably just ordinary form.

7278 BETFRED NEW ROOSTER BOOSTER LOTTO BET H'CAP 1m 4f 93y

3:00 (3:00) (Class 6) (0-65,65) 3-Y-O+ **£1,940** (£577; £288; £144) **Stalls** Low

Form RPR

433 **1** **Pereira**[209] 1089 3-9-2 **65**........................ MartinLane 9 74+
(David Simcock) *t.k.h: trckd ldrs: effrt and swtchd rt over 1f out: sn rdn: kpt on wl fnl f: led nr fin* **5/1**[2]

-250 **2** *nk* **Alborz (IRE)**[42] 6071 4-9-9 **65**........................ LeeTopliss 8 74
(Tim Vaughan) *led: jnd 1/2-way: rdn over 2f out: kpt on wl fnl f: hdd nr fin* **8/1**[3]

-556 **3** *2 ¾* **Gosforth Park**[51] 5786 7-9-8 **64**........................ DavidAllan 1 69
(Mel Brittain) *t.k.h: cl up: effrt and chal over 1f out to ins fnl f: one pce last 75yds* **11/4**[1]

2242 **4** *1 ½* **Handiwork**[141] 2716 3-9-2 **65**........................ TomQueally 12 68
(Michael Bell) *t.k.h: cl up: chal 1/2-way: rdn over 2f out: kpt on same pce fnl f* **11/4**[1]

620 **5** *2 ¼* **Ravi River (IRE)**[24] 6632 9-8-13 **58**........................ JasonHart(3) 10 57
(Alistair Whillans) *taken early to post: hld up in tch: effrt and rdn over 2f out: no imp fr over 1f out* **25/1**

-600 **6** *hd* **Isdaal**[33] 6346 6-9-7 **63**........................(p) GrahamLee 11 62
(Kevin Morgan) *hld up towards rr: effrt whn n.m.r briefly over 2f out: rdn and no imp fr over 1f out* **20/1**

5-45 **7** *9* **Frank's Folly (IRE)**[75] 4927 4-9-9 **65**........................ DuranFentiman 7 50
(Tim Walford) *s.i.s: hld up: rdn and shortlived effrt over 2f out: btn over 1f out* **8/1**[3]

33-0 **8** *3 ½* **Queen Of Skies (IRE)**[260] 429 4-9-5 **61**........................ AndrewMullen 6 41
(Michael Appleby) *hld up in tch: drvn and outpcd over 2f out: n.d after* **10/1**

2m 54.61s (9.01) **Going Correction** +0.60s/f (Yiel)
WFA 3 from 4yo+ 7lb **8** Ran SP% **109.9**
Speed ratings (Par 101): **93,92,90,89,88 88,82,80**
toteswingers 1&2 £10.40, 1&3 £3.40, 2&3 £4.20 CSF £40.57 CT £121.32 TOTE £7.40: £2.30, £2.70, £1.60; EX 40.80 Trifecta £159.00 Pool: £1906.40 - 8.98 winning units..
Owner St Albans Bloodstock I **Bred** St Albans Bloodstock Llp **Trained** Newmarket, Suffolk
■ Stewards' Enquiry : Lee Topliss two-day ban: used whip above permitted level (Oct 29-30)

FOCUS
A moderate handicap run at a steady pace. It paid to race handy and produced a thorough test in the ground. There could be more to come from the winner.

7279 BETFRED/R F HENDERSON LTD MEDIAN AUCTION MAIDEN STKS 1m 4f 93y

3:30 (3:31) (Class 6) 3-4-Y-O **£1,940** (£577; £288; £144) **Stalls** Low

Form RPR

1 **Tweed** 3-9-0 0........................ GrahamLee 7 72+
(William Haggas) *t.k.h: in tch: stdy hdwy 1/2-way: effrt and led appr fnl f: pushed clr: readily* **7/2**[3]

60 **2** *4 ½* **Arty Campbell (IRE)**[26] 6557 3-9-5 0........................ MartinLane 4 70
(David Simcock) *led: rdn over 2f out: hdd appr fnl f: kpt on same pce* **8/1**

25 **3** *nk* **Obstacle**[22] 6696 3-9-5 0........................ WilliamBuick 3 70
(John Gosden) *trckd ldr: drvn along over 2f out: sn outpcd: plugged on fnl f* **5/4**[1]

035 **4** *5* **Mount Macedon**[48] 5892 3-9-5 76........................ AndreaAtzeni 6 62
(Luca Cumani) *t.k.h: in tch: stdy hdwy on outside over 3f out: drvn and outpcd over 2f out: n.d after* **5/2**[2]

00 **5** *3* **Generous George (IRE)**[28] 6498 4-9-12 0........................ DavidAllan 8 58?
(Mel Brittain) *hld up: rdn and outpcd over 4f out: n.d after* **100/1**

6 *3 ½* **Cedar Glory** 4-9-7 0........................ DuranFentiman 2 48
(Tim Walford) *hld up in tch: drvn along over 3f out: sn drvn and wknd* **50/1**

00 **7** *37* **Nowcando**[17] 6847 3-9-0 0........................ DanielTudhope 5
(K R Burke) *prom tl rdn and wknd over 2f out* **50/1**

2m 56.56s (10.96) **Going Correction** +0.60s/f (Yiel)
WFA 3 from 4yo 7lb **7** Ran SP% **111.3**
Speed ratings (Par 101): **87,84,83,80,78 76,51**
toteswingers 1&2 £2.20, 1&3 £1.80, 2&3 £2.20 CSF £28.21 TOTE £6.00: £1.60, £3.10; EX 25.90 Trifecta £83.60 Pool: £2208.42 - 19.79 winning units..
Owner B Haggas **Bred** J B Haggas **Trained** Newmarket, Suffolk

FOCUS
Not much pace on for this maiden with the field well strung out at the line. The winner looked an above-average type but the bare form is limited by the fifth.

7280 BETFRED CALL CENTRE ON 0800 221 221 H'CAP 2m 19y

4:00 (4:00) (Class 5) (0-75,75) 3-Y-O+ **£2,587** (£770; £384; £192) **Stalls** Low

Form RPR

3154 **1** **Embsay Crag**[26] 6565 7-9-11 **72**........................ GrahamLee 7 80
(Philip Kirby) *hld up in tch: hdwy to ld over 1f out: rdn out fnl f* **10/1**

0220 **2** *1 ¼* **Rosairlie (IRE)**[37] 6237 5-9-10 **74**........................ JasonHart(3) 9 80
(Micky Hammond) *hld up: rdn over 2f out: gd hdwy over 1f out: chsd wnr last 100yds: r.o* **8/1**

-063 **3** *2* **Generous Dream**[49] 5862 5-8-12 **59**........................ DavidAllan 4 62
(Mel Brittain) *cl up: rdn to ld over 2f out: hdd over 1f out: one pce ins fnl f* **7/2**[1]

105 **4** *1 ¾* **Almost Gemini (IRE)**[13] 6942 4-9-6 **67**........................(p) JamieSpencer 3 68
(Don Cantillon) *hld up: stdy hdwy 3f out: rdn and hung lft wl over 1f out: kpt on same pce fnl f* **10/1**

0/0- **5** *hd* **Wayward Glance**[14] 3502 5-10-0 **75**........................(p) TomEaves 11 76
(Keith Dalgleish) *chsd ldrs: effrt and ev ch over 2f out: sn rdn and edgd lft: no ex over 1f out* **16/1**

0631 **6** *1 ¾* **Cowslip**[49] 5862 4-8-9 **56**........................ RaulDaSilva 6 55
(George Moore) *in tch: rdn over 2f out: no imp fr wl over 1f out* **7/1**[3]

3512 **7** *1 ½* **Kodicil (IRE)**[11] 6565 5-9-9 **70**........................ GrahamGibbons 2 67
(Tim Walford) *led 6f: cl up: led over 3f out to over 2f out: sn outpcd* **5/1**[2]

0506 **8** *2* **Key Gold**[14] 6917 4-8-13 **60**........................ TonyHamilton 1 54
(Richard Fahey) *trckd ldrs on ins: rdn over 2f out: wknd wl over 1f out* **18/1**

4404 **9** *8* **Authentication**[13] 6942 4-8-10 **57**........................ DuranFentiman 5 42
(Mel Brittain) *hld up in tch on ins: struggling over 2f out: sn btn* **16/1**

0054 **10** *17* **Harrison's Cave**[14] 5640 5-9-11 **72**........................ TomQueally 10 36
(Chris Grant) *t.k.h: in tch: hdwy to ld after 6f: rdn and hdd over 3f out: sn lost pl* **12/1**

5036 **11** *11* **Zarosa (IRE)**[24] 6632 4-8-11 **63**........................ NoelGarbutt(5) 8 14
(John Berry) *hld up: rdn and outpcd over 4f out: sn struggling: t.o* **8/1**

3m 47.02s (7.62) **Going Correction** +0.60s/f (Yiel) **11** Ran SP% **116.5**
Speed ratings (Par 103): **104,103,102,101,101 100,99,98,94,86 80**
toteswingers 1&2 £7.50, 1&3 £9.90, 2&3 £8.80 CSF £86.82 CT £339.10 TOTE £10.20: £3.10, £2.90, £1.80; EX 76.10 Trifecta £292.90 Pool: £1494.07 - 3.82 winning units..
Owner Grange Park Racing IV & Partner **Bred** Mrs Glenda Swinglehurst **Trained** Middleham, N Yorks

FOCUS
This open handicap was run at a honest pace in the testing ground. Easy form to assess.

7281 BETFRED "CALL CENTRE CASH BACK OFFERS" H'CAP (DIV I) 6f

4:30 (4:30) (Class 5) (0-75,75) 3-Y-0+ **£2,587** (£770; £384; £192) **Stalls** Centre

Form RPR
5422 **1** **Keep It Dark**[10] 7029 4-8-10 **64** BarryMcHugh 4 74
(Tony Coyle) *cl up: led 2f out: pushed out fnl f* **9/2**[3]
5040 **2** 1 ¾ **Delores Rocket**[26] 6548 3-8-12 **67** (b) JamieSpencer 10 72
(Kevin Ryan) *in tch: rdn and swtchd rt over 2f out: styd on wl fnl f to take 2nd cl home: no ch w wnr* **4/1**[2]
0040 **3** nk **Sunny Side Up (IRE)**[17] 6848 4-9-2 **70** TonyHamilton 11 74
(Richard Fahey) *led tl rdn and hdd 2f out: edgd lft: kpt on same pce fnl f: lost 2nd cl home* **14/1**
1056 **4** 1 ¾ **Captain Royale (IRE)**[10] 7030 8-9-1 **69** (p) RobertWinston 3 68
(Tracy Waggott) *t.k.h: stdd in tch: stdy hdwy over 2f out: effrt over 1f out: kpt on same pce ins fnl f* **25/1**
3253 **5** 2 ½ **Beckermet (IRE)**[15] 6905 11-8-13 **67** DaleSwift 13 58
(Ruth Carr) *in tch: rdn over 2f out: no imp fr over 1f out* **9/1**
5005 **6** 1 ¾ **Staff Sergeant**[20] 6756 6-9-3 **71** DavidAllan 8 57
(Iain Jardine) *prom: rdn and outpcd over 2f out: rallied appr fnl f: no imp* **25/1**
2500 **7** ½ **Roker Park (IRE)**[21] 6728 8-9-4 **72** (v) DanielTudhope 14 56
(David O'Meara) *hld up: stdy hdwy over 2f out: rdn and hung lft wl over 1f out: sn btn* **6/1**
0/1 **8** 3 ¾ **Brother Tiger**[35] 6289 4-9-0 **68** MartinLane 5 41
(David C Griffiths) *chsd ldrs: rdn along 1/2-way: wknd over 1f out* **5/2**[1]
006 **9** 7 **Fama Mac**[12] 6969 6-8-8 **62** AndreaAtzeni 7 14
(Neville Bycroft) *prom: drvn and outpcd 1/2-way: nvr on terms after* **12/1**

1m 16.62s (2.02) **Going Correction** +0.425s/f (Yiel)
WFA 3 from 4yo+ 1lb **9** Ran SP% **113.1**
Speed ratings (Par 103): **103,100,100,97,94 92,91,86,77**
toteswingers 1&2 £3.50, 1&3 £8.50, 2&3 £14.30 CSF £22.33 CT £228.75 TOTE £4.40: £1.50, £2.10, £2.80; EX 21.60 Trifecta £321.30 Pool: £2536.34 - 5.91 winning units..
Owner N Hetherton **Bred** Heather Raw **Trained** Norton, N Yorks

FOCUS
A wide-open handicap run at a fair pace. The winner is rated back to his April course win.

7282 BETFRED "CALL CENTRE CASH BACK OFFERS" H'CAP (DIV II) 6f

5:00 (5:00) (Class 5) (0-75,75) 3-Y-0+ **£2,587** (£770; £384; £192) **Stalls** Centre

Form RPR
2320 **1** **Tajneed (IRE)**[15] 6908 10-9-4 **72** AdrianNicholls 10 81
(David Nicholls) *mde virtually all: rdn 2f out: kpt on gamely fnl f* **5/1**[2]
2303 **2** 2 ½ **Lucky Lodge**[14] 6916 3-8-10 **65** (b) DuranFentiman 12 67
(Mel Brittain) *t.k.h: prom: drvn along 2f out: chsd wnr ins fnl f: kpt on* **7/1**[3]
0041 **3** ½ **Bunce (IRE)**[15] 6905 5-8-12 **66** (b) DanielTudhope 5 66
(David O'Meara) *in tch: smooth hdwy 1/2-way: effrt and ev ch over 1f out: nt qckn fnl f* **15/2**
3000 **4** nk **Meandmyshadow**[16] 6871 5-9-3 **71** DaleSwift 11 70
(Alan Brown) *racd alone stands' rail: drvn over 3f out: drifted lft and hdwy over 1f out: kpt on fnl f: nrst fin* **12/1**
2213 **5** 1 ¼ **Rigolleto (IRE)**[29] 6463 5-9-0 **68** GrahamLee 7 63
(Anabel K Murphy) *trckd ldrs: effrt and rdn 2f out: kpt on same pce fnl f* **5/1**[2]
1300 **6** 1 ¾ **Flighty Clarets (IRE)**[26] 6568 3-8-10 **65** TonyHamilton 9 55
(Richard Fahey) *hld up: rdn and outpcd over 2f out: edgd lft: rallied over 1f out: no imp* **12/1**
0000 **7** 1 ½ **Mission Impossible**[10] 7029 8-8-7 **61** (p) PatrickMathers 13 47
(Tracy Waggott) *hld up in tch: drvn along over 2f out: no imp over 1f out* **12/1**
0206 **8** nse **Red Gift (IRE)**[26] 6575 3-8-13 **68** (p) TomEaves 1 53
(Brian Ellison) *in tch: drvn over 2f out: wknd over 1f out* **16/1**
233 **9** 2 ¾ **Chasing Dreams**[12] 6982 3-9-4 **73** JamieSpencer 6 53
(Kevin Ryan) *disp ld to over 1f out: drvn and wknd ins fnl f* **3/1**[1]

1m 17.05s (2.45) **Going Correction** +0.425s/f (Yiel)
WFA 3 from 5yo+ 1lb **9** Ran SP% **111.6**
Speed ratings (Par 103): **100,96,96,95,93 91,89,89,85**
toteswingers 1&2 £5.50, 1&3 £5.70, 2&3 £8.00 CSF £37.80 CT £254.75 TOTE £5.90: £1.90, £2.50, £2.10; EX 28.30 Trifecta £247.10 Pool: £1874.26 - 5.68 winning units..
Owner Mrs Alex Nicholls **Bred** R Hodgins **Trained** Sessay, N Yorks
■ Stewards' Enquiry : Dale Swift caution: careless riding; one-day ban: failed to ride to draw (Oct 29)

FOCUS
This competitive handicap was run at a sound pace. Ordinary form, with a step up from the winner on his recent efforts.

7283 BETFRED RACING'S BIGGEST SUPPORTER H'CAP 7f

5:30 (5:30) (Class 6) (0-65,65) 3-Y-0+ **£1,940** (£577; £288; £144) **Stalls** Centre

Form RPR
3023 **1** **Royal Holiday (IRE)**[12] 6963 6-9-6 **64** (p) RussKennemore 3 75
(Marjorie Fife) *mde all: pushed along fr 1/2-way: drvn 2f out: styd on gamely fnl f* **8/1**
0621 **2** 1 ¾ **Trixie Malone**[25] 6588 3-8-11 **62** JoeyHaynes[(5)] 8 68
(K R Burke) *t.k.h early: chsd ldrs: effrt and wnt 2nd over 2f out: rdn and clsd over 1f out: one pce ins fnl f* **4/1**[1]
6302 **3** 2 ¾ **Blue Maisey**[13] 6941 5-9-2 **65** KevinStott[(5)] 11 65
(Edwin Tuer) *hld up: rdn over 2f out: hdwy over 1f out: kpt on ins fnl f: nrst fin* **10/1**
031 **4** ½ **Uncle Brit**[25] 6600 7-9-5 **63** TonyHamilton 1 62
(Malcolm Jefferson) *prom: rdn over 2f out: rallied over 1f out: kpt on same pce fnl f* **7/1**[3]
0514 **5** 1 **Rasselas (IRE)**[5] 7153 6-9-0 **65** AnnaHesketh[(7)] 5 61
(David Nicholls) *hld up in tch: shkn up and hdwy over 1f out: no imp fnl f* **11/1**
0060 **6** ½ **Ellaal**[136] 2889 4-9-4 **62** DaleSwift 4 57
(Ruth Carr) *hld up: rdn and hdwy on outside 2f out: no imp fnl f* **40/1**
6040 **7** ¾ **Self Employed**[13] 6952 6-9-7 **65** GrahamLee 2 58
(Garry Woodward) *chsd ldrs: rdn over 2f out: no ex ent fnl f* **7/1**[3]
2221 **8** ½ **Border Bandit (USA)**[21] 6721 5-9-7 **65** (p) RobertWinston 12 57+
(Tracy Waggott) *hld up: effrt whn repeatedly denied room over 2f out: hdwy over 1f out: r.o: nvr able to chal* **5/1**[2]
000 **9** 5 **Mitchum**[27] 6515 4-9-1 **64** ShirleyTeasdale[(5)] 13 44
(Ron Barr) *chsd wnr to over 2f out: rdn and wknd over 1f out* **40/1**
4-40 **10** 2 **How Fortunate**[7] 7100 5-9-7 **65** BarryMcHugh 6 40
(Tim Etherington) *hld up towards rr: drvn and outpcd over 2f out: sn btn* **25/1**
0162 **11** 3 **John Coffey (IRE)**[26] 6568 4-9-6 **64** AndrewMullen 14 31
(Michael Appleby) *hld up: pushed along over 2f out: sn btn* **10/1**
1400 **12** 2 ¼ **Botteen (IRE)**[13] 6943 3-9-5 **65** DanielTudhope 9 25
(David O'Meara) *hld up in midfield: pushed along over 2f out: wknd wl over 1f out* **25/1**
4500 **13** 7 **My New Angel (IRE)**[13] 6941 4-9-2 **60** (p) DuranFentiman 16 4
(Jason Ward) *hld up: rdn along wl over 2f out: sn btn* **25/1**

1m 31.36s (3.56) **Going Correction** +0.425s/f (Yiel)
WFA 3 from 4yo+ 2lb **13** Ran SP% **115.7**
Speed ratings (Par 101): **96,94,90,90,89 88,87,87,81,79 75,73,65**
toteswingers 1&2 £9.60, 1&3 £10.40, 2&3 £12.30 CSF £36.35 CT £334.08 TOTE £7.40: £2.20, £3.70, £4.20; EX 46.20 Trifecta £319.10 Pool: £1280.25 - 3.00 winning units..
Owner Mrs Marion Turner **Bred** E Tynan **Trained** Stillington, N Yorks

FOCUS
A tight contest with only 5lb covering the 13 runners. It was run at a fair pace with the winner making all under a fine ride. Modest form which could be rated a little higher or lower.
T/Plt: £72.10. Pool £74,423.49 - 752.80 winning units. T/Qpdt: £33.10. Pool £5423.60 - 121.10 winning units. RY

7284 - 7291a (Foreign Racing) - See Raceform Interactive

7260 KEMPTON (A.W) (R-H)

Wednesday, October 16

OFFICIAL GOING: Standard
Wind: Brisk, across (away fron stands) Weather: Fine, mild

7292 COME JUMP RACING HERE ON SUNDAY H'CAP 5f (P)

5:40 (5:40) (Class 6) (0-55,55) 3-Y-0+ **£1,940** (£577; £288; £144) **Stalls** Low

Form RPR
3453 **1** **Sarah Berry**[9] 7079 4-9-6 **54** (v) LukeMorris 1 64
(Chris Dwyer) *cl up on inner: chsd ldr 1/2-way: rdn to ld over 1f out: drvn out* **8/1**
1061 **2** 1 ¼ **Metropolitan Chief**[14] 6930 9-9-5 **53** (p) SamHitchcott 3 59
(Paul Burgoyne) *hld up in 8th: rdn and prog over 1f out: r.o fnl f to take 2nd last 50yds* **12/1**
5342 **3** ¾ **Volcanic Dust (IRE)**[14] 6930 5-9-5 **53** (t) RichardKingscote 7 56
(Milton Bradley) *forced to racd quite wd: pressed ldrs: rdn over 1f out: wnt 2nd briefly ins fnl f: kpt on* **10/1**
0260 **4** ½ **Outbid**[13] 6980 3-9-2 **55** GeorgeDowning[(5)] 5 57
(Tony Carroll) *led: drvn and hdd over 1f out: one pce* **14/1**
2420 **5** ½ **Exkaliber**[25] 6651 4-8-13 **50** (bt) RobertTart[(3)] 8 49
(Jeremy Gask) *trapped out quite wd towards rr: rdn over 1f out: styd on ins fnl f: n.d* **11/2**[2]
6214 **6** 1 **Burnt Cream**[16] 6901 6-9-7 **55** (t) RobertHavlin 4 51
(Martin Bosley) *chsd ldng quartet: urged along over 1f out: one pce and no imp* **6/1**[3]
2030 **7** 1 ¼ **Coconut Kisses**[16] 6902 3-9-7 **55** RichardHughes 2 47
(Bill Turner) *chsd ldrs in 6th: shkn up and nt qckn on inner over 1f out: fdd fnl f* **6/1**[3]
4412 **8** ½ **Imperial Spirit**[16] 6902 3-9-4 **55** (v) CharlesBishop[(3)] 6 45
(Mick Channon) *chsd ldr to 1/2-way: sn lost pl: toiling towards rr over 1f out* **4/1**[1]
060- **9** shd **Salford Prince (IRE)**[509] 2464 5-9-2 **50** WilliamCarson 11 39
(David Elsworth) *trapped out wd and lost grnd bnd after 1f: a in last pair: no ch over 1f out: kpt on* **25/1**
6406 **10** 2 **South Kenter (USA)**[35] 6317 4-9-1 **49** KierenFallon 9 31
(Heather Main) *trapped out wd and lost grnd after 1f: a in last pair: eased whn no ch ins fnl f* **13/2**

1m 0.07s (-0.43) **Going Correction** -0.05s/f (Stan) **10** Ran SP% **115.7**
Speed ratings (Par 101): **101,99,97,97,96 94,92,91,91,88**
toteswingers 1&2 £21.00, 1&3 £5.90, 2&3 £13.50 CSF £98.56 CT £993.41 TOTE £9.60: £2.70, £3.70, £3.10; EX 49.90 Trifecta £241.90 Pool: £1659.10 - 5.14 winning units..
Owner Miss Lilo Blum **Bred** F B B White **Trained** Newmarket, Suffolk

FOCUS
Predictably there was no hanging about in this weak sprint handicap.

7293 BOOK YOUR CHRISTMAS PARTY ON 01932 753518 NURSERY H'CAP 5f (P)

6:10 (6:11) (Class 6) (0-60,60) 2-Y-0 **£1,940** (£577; £288; £144) **Stalls** Low

Form RPR
053 **1** **Gower Princess**[42] 6095 2-9-6 **59** LukeMorris 2 64
(Ronald Harris) *chsd ldr: rdn over 1f out: clsd to chal new ldr last 100yds: drvn to ld post* **10/1**
0334 **2** hd **Debt Settler (IRE)**[42] 6104 2-9-3 **56** JimmyQuinn 10 60
(Luke Dace) *trapped out wd bnd after 1f: sn in midfield: pushed along and prog over 1f out: clsd to ld last 100yds: styd on but hdd post* **11/2**[2]
000 **3** ¾ **Back On Baileys**[21] 6746 2-9-0 **53** RichardHughes 5 54
(Chris Dwyer) *bmpd s: towards rr: rdn and prog over 1f out: styd on to take 3rd nr fin* **7/1**[3]
6060 **4** 1 **Dancing Juice**[7] 7117 2-9-0 **56** RobertTart[(3)] 7 54+
(Alan Jarvis) *led: swung quite wd bnd after 1f: drvn 2 l clr over 1f out: hdd & wknd last 10yds* **8/1**
5023 **5** ½ **Little Big Man**[11] 7036 2-9-4 **57** (b) SeanLevey 1 53
(Sylvester Kirk) *chsd ldrs: shkn up 1/2-way: nt qckn over 1f out: no imp after* **11/2**[2]
2560 **6** nse **Dynamo Walt (IRE)**[7] 7127 2-9-0 **53** (v) RaulDaSilva 4 49
(Derek Shaw) *bmpd s: t.k.h in midfield: nt clr run over 1f out: swtchd lft and lost grnd: styd on ins fnl f: no ch* **9/2**[1]
060 **7** 1 ½ **Golly Miss Molly**[34] 6342 2-9-2 **55** FergusSweeney 6 45
(Jeremy Gask) *sltly bmpd s: sn in last: jst pushed along fr over 1f out: sme prog on inner but nvr involved* **16/1**
000 **8** ½ **Prim And Proper**[26] 6607 2-9-2 **60** RyanTate[(5)] 8 49
(Brendan Powell) *lost midfield pl after 2f and sn struggling towards rr: shkn up over 1f out: no real prog* **7/1**[3]
000 **9** shd **Lady Emmuska**[23] 6690 2-9-6 **59** KieranO'Neill 11 47
(Richard Hannon) *trapped out wd bnd after 1f: a wl in rr* **16/1**
000 **10** hd **My Secret Dream (FR)**[72] 5061 2-8-13 **52** WilliamCarson 9 39
(Ron Hodges) *chsd ldrs to over 1f out: wknd fnl f* **25/1**
2340 **11** 1 ¾ **Weisse Girl**[15] 6924 2-9-4 **57** (b) MartinLane 3 38
(Noel Quinlan) *wnt lft s then squeezed out: a in rr after* **10/1**

1m 0.62s (0.12) **Going Correction** -0.05s/f (Stan) **11** Ran SP% **118.9**
Speed ratings (Par 93): **97,96,95,93,93 93,90,89,89,89 86**
toteswingers 1&2 £8.70, 1&3 £22.50, 2&3 £7.00 CSF £64.89 CT £425.61 TOTE £9.60: £3.60, £2.70, £2.40; EX 60.70 Trifecta £201.00 Pool: £1555.15 - 201.00 winning units..
Owner David & Gwyn Joseph **Bred** Willoxton Farm Stud **Trained** Earlswood, Monmouths

FOCUS
This moderate nursery was wide open. It proved rough from the gates and again they went hard early. A compressed finish and ordinary form.

7294 COMMISSION FREE 1ST MONTH AT BETDAQ MAIDEN FILLIES' STKS 6f (P)
6:40 (6:40) (Class 5) 2-Y-O £2,587 (£770; £384; £192) **Stalls** Low

Form RPR
1 **Continental Drift (USA)** 2-9-0 0 MartinLane 9 76+
(Roger Charlton) *hld up in rr: pushed along and gd prog fr 2f out: wnt 2nd 1f out: clsd to ld last 75yds: promising debut* **16/1**
36 2 ½ **Minnalouse (IRE)**[18] 6828 2-9-0 0 WilliamBuick 7 74
(John Gosden) *trckd ldng pair: led 2f out and sent for home: styd on but hdd and readily hld last 75yds* **6/1**[3]
06 3 2 **Goodwood Storm**[34] 6318 2-9-0 0 LukeMorris 6 68
(William Knight) *trckd ldrs: cl up whn stmbld over 2f out: renewed effrt over 1f out: styd on same pce fnl f* **12/1**
4 1 **Anna's Vision (IRE)** 2-9-0 0 RyanMoore 8 65+
(Jeremy Noseda) *in tch: shkn up over 2f out: prog and rn green over 1f out: kpt on same pce fnl f* **6/1**[3]
5 1 ½ **Frangipanni (IRE)** 2-9-0 0 RichardKingscote 11 61+
(Roger Charlton) *hld up and sn in last: nudged along 2f out: reminder jst over 1f out: styd on quite takingly ins fnl f* **16/1**
3 6 ¾ **Perfect Pursuit**[31] 6423 2-8-9 0 RyanTate(5) 5 58
(Clive Cox) *trckd ldrs on inner: rdn 2f out: nt qckn and no prog over 1f out* **3/1**[1]
7 ¾ **Sultanty** 2-9-0 0 MartinHarley 3 56+
(Kevin Ryan) *squeezed out s: towards rr: sme prog 2f out: shkn up and no hdwy over 1f out* **25/1**
05 8 ½ **Setai**[91] 4408 2-9-0 0 JimmyFortune 2 56
(Brian Meehan) *awkward s but led: hdd & wknd 2f out* **7/1**
9 1 **Renaissance Rio (IRE)** 2-9-0 0 SteveDrowne 10 52
(Ed McMahon) *rn v green in rr: nvr a threat: kpt on last 100yds* **16/1**
3 10 nk **Previous Acclaim (IRE)**[53] 5740 2-9-0 0 RichardHughes 4 51
(Richard Hannon) *wnt rt s: t.k.h: w ldr to jst over 2f out: wknd qckly* **7/2**[2]
11 15 **Stage Girl** 2-8-7 0 JenniferFerguson(7) 1
(Chris Dwyer) *bmpd s: a bhd: t.o* **100/1**

1m 14.27s (1.17) **Going Correction** -0.05s/f (Stan) 11 Ran SP% 118.5
Speed ratings (Par 92): **90,89,86,85,83 82,81,80,79,78 58**
toteswingers 1&2 £9.80, 1&3 £15.50, 2&3 £10.50 CSF £109.94 TOTE £16.90: £6.20, £2.50, £4.50; EX 135.10 Trifecta £233.70 Pool: £1610.38 - 5.16 winning units..
Owner K Abdullah **Bred** Juddmonte Farms Inc **Trained** Beckhampton, Wilts

FOCUS
A fair fillies' maiden, run at an average pace and in a slow time. Not the easiest form to pin down but the winner impressed.

7295 £200 FREE BETS AT BETDAQ MAIDEN FILLIES' STKS (DIV I) 7f (P)
7:10 (7:10) (Class 5) 2-Y-O £2,587 (£770; £384; £192) **Stalls** Low

Form RPR
1 **Pelerin (IRE)** 2-9-0 0 MartinHarley 10 85+
(Marco Botti) *trckd ldrs in 6th: pushed along and prog over 2f out: led over 1f out: shkn up and drew clr: promising* **7/2**[2]
6 2 3 **A Legacy Of Love (IRE)**[23] 6691 2-9-0 0 JimCrowley 5 77
(Amanda Perrett) *trckd ldrs: pushed along and clsd fr over 2f out: inclined to hang sltly lft but styd on to take 2nd nr fin* **4/1**[3]
542 3 1 ¼ **Miss Brazil (IRE)**[8] 7103 2-9-0 0 RichardHughes 3 74
(Richard Hannon) *led to over 5f out: trckd ldr to over 3f out: wnt 2nd again over 2f out: clsd to chal over 1f out: one pce fnl f* **2/1**[1]
0 4 2 **Silver Mirage**[19] 6789 2-9-0 0 RyanMoore 12 69
(Michael Bell) *racd freely: led over 5f out: hdd & wknd over 1f out* **8/1**
5 4 **Baynunah (USA)** 2-9-0 0 ShaneKelly 7 58+
(James Fanshawe) *towards rr: shkn up and rn green fr over 2f out: kpt on fr over 1f out: nt disgracd* **25/1**
00 6 2 ¾ **Rehanaat (USA)**[48] 5924 2-9-0 0 DaneO'Neill 9 51
(Ed Dunlop) *prom: chsd ldr over 3f out to over 2f out: wknd* **33/1**
7 10 **The Silver Kebaya (FR)** 2-9-0 0 SebSanders 8 25
(Jeremy Noseda) *in tch in rr to 3f out: sn wknd: t.o* **25/1**
8 ¾ **Stars Aligned (IRE)** 2-9-0 0 JimmyQuinn 11 23
(Richard Hannon) *slowly away: v green and detached in last: nvr a factor: t.o* **25/1**
9 2 ¾ **Quoth** 2-9-0 0 MickaelBarzalona 4 16
(Charlie Appleby) *in tch in rr to 3f out: wknd and eased: t.o* **13/2**

1m 25.14s (-0.86) **Going Correction** -0.05s/f (Stan) 9 Ran SP% 114.5
Speed ratings (Par 92): **102,98,97,94,90 87,75,74,71**
toteswingers 1&2 £3.50, 1&3 £2.10, 2&3 £2.20 CSF £16.83 TOTE £5.70: £2.20, £1.30, £1.20; EX 20.40 Trifecta £58.60 Pool: £1498.65 - 19.14 winning units..
Owner Mr Bruni & Mr Somma **Bred** Rabbah Bloodstock Limited **Trained** Newmarket, Suffolk

FOCUS
The first four dominated the finish of this fillies' maiden, which was run at average pace. The winner impressed and the form is rated around the second and third.

7296 £200 FREE BETS AT BETDAQ MAIDEN FILLIES' STKS (DIV II) 7f (P)
7:40 (7:41) (Class 5) 2-Y-O £2,587 (£770; £384; £192) **Stalls** Low

Form RPR
1 **Don'T** 2-9-0 0 AndreaAtzeni 4 74+
(Luca Cumani) *in tch in midfield: pushed along and sltly outpcd whn pce lifted 2f out: gd prog on outer over 1f out: r.o to ld last 50yds* **25/1**
2 nk **Billowing (IRE)** 2-9-0 0 WilliamBuick 10 73+
(John Gosden) *sn in last: gd prog on inner fr wl over 1f out: clsd to chal last 50yds: jst hld* **8/1**
3 nk **Cameo Tiara (IRE)** 2-9-0 0 PatDobbs 7 72+
(Richard Hannon) *dwlt: t.k.h and hld up in 10th: gd prog between rivals over 1f out: r.o fnl f: nrst fin* **33/1**
622 4 nk **Dancing Sands (IRE)**[18] 6828 2-9-0 78 MickaelBarzalona 3 71
(Charlie Appleby) *trckd ldng pair: led jst over 2f out: 2 l clr over 1f out: drvn fnl f: swamped last 50yds* **10/11**[1]
2 5 1 ½ **Acclio (IRE)**[42] 6107 2-9-0 0 FrederikTylicki 5 67
(Clive Brittain) *trckd ldng trio: tried to cl fr 2f out: kpt on same pce fnl f* **4/1**[2]
55 6 ½ **Persian Bolt (USA)**[26] 6594 2-9-0 0 JohnFahy 8 66
(Eve Johnson Houghton) *wl in tch on outer: tried to cl on ldrs 2f out: one pce fr over 1f out* **13/2**[3]
043 7 ½ **Kinloss**[18] 6821 2-9-0 70 RichardHughes 9 64
(Richard Hannon) *led: set v stdy pce: tried to kick on over 2f out: sn hdd: nudged along and fdd ins fnl f* **16/1**

05 8 nse **Mahatta (IRE)**[41] 6141 2-9-0 0 DaneO'Neill 1 64
(Charles Hills) *trckd ldrs: sltly outpcd 2f out: shkn up and one pce over 1f out* **33/1**
9 ½ **Gracious Lady** 2-9-0 0 JimmyFortune 12 63
(Andrew Balding) *trckd ldr: tried to chal over 2f out: stl disputing 2nd over 1f out: fdd fnl f* **50/1**
10 ½ **Spirit Raiser (IRE)** 2-9-0 0 ShaneKelly 11 61
(James Fanshawe) *s.s: wl in rr: rn green and outpcd 2f out: kpt on one pce after* **20/1**
11 shd **Gift Of Rain (IRE)** 2-9-0 0 RyanMoore 6 61
(Ed Dunlop) *towards rr but wl in tch: sltly outpcd 2f out: jst pushed along and one pce after* **20/1**

1m 28.03s (2.03) **Going Correction** -0.05s/f (Stan) 11 Ran SP% 123.9
Speed ratings (Par 92): **86,85,85,84,83 82,82,82,81,80 80**
toteswingers 1&2 £31.60, 1&3 £55.60, 2&3 £105.30 CSF £206.56 TOTE £18.80: £9.90, £2.60, £14.20; EX 143.10 Trifecta £1253.00 Part won. Pool: £1670.68 - 0.39 winning units..
Owner Fittocks Stud **Bred** Fittocks Stud **Trained** Newmarket, Suffolk

FOCUS
The second division of the 7f fillies' maiden and it was run at a very slow pace. They finished compressed and a negative view of the bare form has been taken, but there were plenty of promising performances.

7297 WINNERS ARE WELCOME AT BETDAQ/CHOOSE EBF FILLIES' H'CAP 7f (P)
8:10 (8:10) (Class 4) (0-85,84) 3-Y-O+
£6,225 (£1,864; £932; £466; £233; £117) **Stalls** Low

Form RPR
-130 1 **Mystical Sapphire**[179] 1676 3-9-5 **84** RyanMoore 8 95+
(Jo Crowley) *hld up towards rr: shkn up and prog over 2f out: led over 1f out: drvn and styd on wl* **5/2**[1]
1654 2 2 **Oasis Spirit**[41] 6135 3-8-5 **70** oh1 (v[1]) DavidProbert 2 75
(Andrew Balding) *trckd ldng pair: tried to chal w others wl over 1f out: chsd wnr fnl f: styd on but no imp* **12/1**
-121 3 nk **Lunette (IRE)**[82] 4709 3-8-8 **73** JimCrowley 5 77
(Ralph Beckett) *trckd ldrs: rdn and clsd w other to chal over 1f out: styd on same pce after* **4/1**[2]
1210 4 2 ¼ **Combustible (IRE)**[25] 6642 3-8-13 **78** RichardHughes 4 76
(John Stimpson) *stdd s: plld hrd and hld up in last pair: clsd on ldng gp over 2f out but shifted markedly lft fr over 1f out and lost all ch: light reminder and kpt on to take 4th nr fin* **14/1**
3623 5 1 **Diamond Belle**[26] 6609 4-9-4 **81** PatCosgrave 6 77
(Noel Quinlan) *t.k.h: pressed ldr: led jst over 2f out: rdn and hdd over 1f out: wknd fnl f* **14/1**
3032 6 1 ¾ **Elnadwa (USA)**[11] 7038 3-8-12 **77** SilvestreDeSousa 9 67
(Saeed bin Suroor) *hld up in tch: pushed along 1/2-way: hrd rdn and no rspnse over 2f out: no ch after* **6/1**
3603 7 1 ¼ **Bold Ring**[8] 7092 7-8-7 **70** oh3 JimmyQuinn 10 58
(Edward Creighton) *trckd ldrs: effrt on inner jst over 2f out: wknd over 1f out* **20/1**
1034 8 ½ **Moma Lee**[42] 6106 3-8-6 **71** WilliamBuick 1 57
(John Gosden) *led to jst over 2f out: wknd qckly over 1f out* **9/1**
3211 9 3 **Rufoof**[14] 6941 3-8-12 **77** DaneO'Neill 7 54
(Charles Hills) *plld hrd: hld up: last after 3f: struggling bdly over 2f out* **9/2**[3]
2-60 10 10 **Give Way Nelson (IRE)**[12] 6993 3-9-1 **80** JimmyFortune 3 30
(Brian Meehan) *plld hrd: trckd ldrs tl wknd rapidly over 2f out: t.o* **16/1**

1m 24.75s (-1.25) **Going Correction** -0.05s/f (Stan)
WFA 3 from 4yo+ 2lb 10 Ran SP% 122.7
Speed ratings (Par 102): **105,102,102,99,98 96,95,94,91,79**
toteswingers 1&2 £11.00, 1&3 £3.10, 2&3 £11.10 CSF £37.08 CT £125.57 TOTE £6.20: £1.70, £5.10, £1.90; EX 43.80 Trifecta £297.10 Pool: £1824.07 - 4.60 winning units..
Owner Mrs Liz Nelson **Bred** Mrs R I Nelson **Trained** Whitcombe, Dorset

FOCUS
A modest fillies' handicap, run at an ordinary early pace.

7298 BETDAQ 1ST UK RACE COMMISSION FREE MAIDEN STKS 1m 4f (P)
8:40 (8:42) (Class 5) 3-5-Y-O £2,587 (£770; £384; £192) **Stalls** Centre

Form RPR
62 1 **Okavango**[142] 2713 3-9-0 0 FrederikTylicki 12 79
(James Fanshawe) *trckd ldng trio: rdn and prog to ld jst over 2f out: drvn and kpt on wl fr over 1f out* **13/2**
020 2 1 ¼ **Sharareh**[47] 5942 3-9-0 0 AndreaAtzeni 9 77
(Luca Cumani) *hld up in 6th: drvn and prog to chal over 2f out: nt qckn over 1f out: kpt on fnl f* **8/1**
4235 3 1 ½ **Kingston Eucalypt**[61] 5492 3-9-0 67 DaneO'Neill 8 75
(David Elsworth) *hld up in 8th: drvn and prog fr over 2f out: kpt on to take 3rd nr fin* **25/1**
2220 4 1 **Saddaqa (USA)**[23] 6696 3-9-0 81 (p) MickaelBarzalona 1 73
(Saeed bin Suroor) *trckd ldng quartet: clsd to chal on inner over 2f out: nt qckn over 1f out: one pce after* **7/2**[3]
45- 5 5 **Layl (USA)**[357] 7324 3-9-5 0 JoeFanning 11 70
(Mark Johnston) *t.k.h: trckd ldr: led briefly over 2f out: sn fnd nil and btn* **3/1**[2]
6 4 ½ **Shalianzi (IRE)**[109] 3-9-5 0 RyanMoore 3 63
(Gary Moore) *racd in 9th: nt gng wl fr 1/2-way: dropped away 3f out: rdr persisted and kpt on fnl 2f though wandered* **20/1**
2 7 ¾ **Murasil (USA)**[15] 6926 3-9-5 0 (t) SilvestreDeSousa 7 62
(Saeed bin Suroor) *stdd s: hld up in 12th: long way off the pce whn drvn over 2f out: modest prog and nvr any ch* **7/4**[1]
0500 8 3 ½ **Himalayan Peak**[30] 6458 3-9-5 58 (b[1]) LukeMorris 14 56
(James Eustace) *hld up in 10th: hrd rdn wl over 2f out: no real prog and sn btn* **66/1**
0 9 3 ¾ **Hope's Wishes**[15] 6926 3-9-0 0 DavidProbert 10 45
(Andrew Balding) *chsd ldng pair: tried to chal over 2f out: sn wknd qckly* **50/1**
10 2 ½ **Give Us A Reason** 3-9-0 0 WilliamCarson 4 41
(James Toller) *led to over 2f out: wknd qckly* **66/1**
-046 11 25 **Atmanna**[120] 3437 4-9-7 44 (p[1]) RichardThomas 2
(Zoe Davison) *hld up in 7th: rdn and wknd rapidly 3f out: t.o* **66/1**
332 12 6 **Alshan Fajer**[93] 4352 3-9-5 70 RobertHavlin 5
(Roger Ingram) *hld up in 11th: wknd rapidly over 3f out: eased and t.o* **20/1**

13 46 **Little Windsor**[19] 4-9-7 0 .... GeorgeBaker 13
(Peter Hiatt) *s.s: immediately t.o: trailed arnd long way bhd* **66/1**

2m 31.9s (-2.60) **Going Correction** -0.05s/f (Stan)
WFA 3 from 4yo 7lb 13 Ran SP% **129.3**
Speed ratings (Par 103): **106,105,104,103,100 97,96,94,91,90 73,69,38**
toteswingers 1&2 £6.80, 1&3 £13.50, 2&3 £16.10 CSF £58.18 TOTE £9.80: £1.50, £3.50, £6.10; EX 64.30 Trifecta £1513.50 Part won. Pool: £2018.09 - 0.73 winning units..
Owner T R G Vestey **Bred** T R G Vestey & Partners **Trained** Newmarket, Suffolk

FOCUS
A typical middle-distance maiden for the time of year.

7299 BOOK YOUR CHRISTMAS PARTY AT KEMPTON CLASSIFIED STKS 1m (P)

9:10 (9:10) (Class 6) 3-Y-0+ **£1,940** (£577; £288; £144) **Stalls** Low

Form RPR

3331 **1** **Princess Spirit**[27] 6554 4-8-12 55 .... (p) JenniferFerguson(7) 6 61
(Edward Creighton) *trckd ldrs: prog to ld wl over 1f out: shkn up and hld on wl fnl f* **3/1**[2]

634 **2** *nk* **Pretty Bubbles**[21] 6748 4-9-5 55 .... RichardHughes 8 60
(J R Jenkins) *trckd ldrs: clsd to chal 2f out: pressed wnr wl over 1f out: nt qckn u.p: kpt on* **6/4**[1]

5004 **3** *3/4* **La Rosiere (USA)**[27] 6553 4-9-5 55 .... (p) JackMitchell 10 59+
(Pat Murphy) *hld up in 9th: rdn and prog over 2f out: styd on to take 3rd 1f out: clsd on ldng pair but jst unable to chal* **8/1**

0000 **4** *3 1/2* **Up Tipp**[15] 6926 3-9-2 55 .... PatDobbs 5 50
(Mike Murphy) *t.k.h: prom: rdn and nt qckn over 2f out: kpt on same pce after* **10/1**

4-00 **5** *nk* **Roaring Rocks (FR)**[15] 6926 3-9-2 52 .... AndreaAtzeni 13 49
(Heather Main) *chsd ldr to 2f out: fdd over 1f out* **40/1**

000 **6** *3/4* **Mignonne**[41] 6134 3-9-2 55 .... (b[1]) JimCrowley 3 47
(Hans Adielsson) *hld up in last pair: pushed along over 2f out: nt clr run briefly over 1f out: reminder and kpt on: nvr involved* **6/1**[3]

3420 **7** *1/2* **Minstrel Lad**[105] 3953 5-9-2 54 .... SimonPearce(3) 14 47
(Lydia Pearce) *hld up in last: jst nudged along fr over 2f out: styd on steadily fnl 2f: nvr remotely competitive* **14/1**

0650 **8** *2 1/2* **Thewestwalian (USA)**[34] 6323 5-9-5 48 .... WilliamCarson 1 41
(Peter Hiatt) *stdd into 8th after 1f: rdn over 2f out: no real prog* **25/1**

005 **9** *9* **Tarmo (IRE)**[47] 5962 3-9-2 41 .... MartinHarley 7 20
(Marco Botti) *led to wl over 1f out: wknd qckly* **20/1**

-000 **10** *2* **Doctor's Gift**[13] 6964 3-8-13 52 .... CharlesBishop(3) 11 15
(Pat Eddery) *hld up in last trio: rdn and no prog wl over 2f out* **50/1**

6600 **11** *2 1/4* **Ruff Luck**[16] 6899 3-9-2 46 .... SteveDrowne 2 10
(Seamus Mullins) *gave trble to post: prom: rdn wl over 3f out: sn lost pl and btn* **33/1**

000/ **12** *3 3/4* **Demolition Blue (IRE)**[746] 6532 4-8-12 25 .... RyanWhile(7) 4 2
(Bill Turner) *in tch in midfield: furiously drvn over 3f out: wknd and stl drvn over 2f out* **66/1**

1m 40.07s (0.27) **Going Correction** -0.05s/f (Stan)
WFA 3 from 4yo+ 3lb 12 Ran SP% **123.6**
Speed ratings (Par 101): **96,95,94,91,91 90,89,87,78,76 74,70**
toteswingers 1&2 £1.70, 1&3 £3.00, 2&3 £1.70 CSF £7.73 TOTE £4.00: £1.90, £1.60, £2.50; EX 10.10 Trifecta £47.60 Pool: £1494.89 - 23.50 winning units..
Owner N Dyshaev **Bred** Harton Limited **Trained** Wormshill, Kent

FOCUS
This weak classified event was run at a fair pace and the form is straightforward.
T/Plt: £3,522.00 to a £1 stake. Pool: £80573.39 - 16.70 winning tickets T/Qpdt: £536.50 to a £1 stake. Pool: £12182.22 - 16.80 winning tickets JN

6731 LINGFIELD (L-H)

Wednesday, October 16

OFFICIAL GOING: Standard
Wind: light, half behind Weather: rain, clearing

7300 YOUNG EPILEPSY NURSERY H'CAP 6f (P)

2:00 (2:00) (Class 4) (0-85,85) 2-Y-0 **£3,752** (£1,116; £557; £278) **Stalls** Low

Form RPR

41 **1** **Outback Traveller (IRE)**[42] 6110 2-8-11 75 .... RyanMoore 4 80+
(Jeremy Noseda) *chsd ldr tl rdn to ld over 1f out: clr ins fnl f: kpt on and a holding rivals: rdn out* **5/4**[1]

521 **2** *3/4* **Pound Piece (IRE)**[132] 3009 2-8-6 70 .... LiamJones 5 73
(J S Moore) *t.k.h: hld up in tch in last quartet: clsd whn nt clr run over 1f out: swtchd lft and hdwy 1f out: chsd wnr fnl 75yds: r.o wl* **20/1**

6220 **3** *1/2* **Handwoven (IRE)**[25] 6628 2-8-8 72 .... JoeFanning 1 73
(Mark Johnston) *led: rdn 2f out: hdd over 1f out: styd on same pce u.p and lost 2nd fnl 75yds* **12/1**

1004 **4** *3/4* **Lady In Blue (IRE)**[22] 6731 2-8-5 69 .... (b) KirstyMilczarek 2 68
(William Haggas) *t.k.h: chsd ldrs: effrt and unable qck over 1f out: drvn and edgd rt ins fnl f: one pce* **14/1**

6245 **5** *1/2* **Chord Chart (IRE)**[29] 6493 2-9-2 80 .... MickaelBarzalona 3 78
(Charlie Appleby) *hld up wl in tch in midfield: travelling wl in 4th 2f out: rdn and fnd little over 1f out: styd on same pce ins fnl f* **4/1**[2]

6145 **6** *nse* **Penny's Boy**[18] 6825 2-8-6 70 .... (t) CathyGannon 9 67
(Sylvester Kirk) *hld up in tch in last quartet: rdn and over 1f out: hdwy 1f out: r.o ins fnl f: nt rch ldrs* **33/1**

554 **7** *1 3/4* **Royal River**[15] 6923 2-8-2 66 .... JimmyQuinn 10 58
(J S Moore) *stdd s and dropped in bhd: hld up in rr: rdn and effrt on inner over 1f out: kpt on but no real imp* **25/1**

1510 **8** *11* **La Tinta Bay**[18] 6825 2-9-7 85 .... RichardHughes 6 44
(Richard Hannon) *chsd ldrs on outer: rdn and lost pl 2f out: wknd over 1f out: bhd and eased wl ins fnl f* **5/1**[3]

0402 **9** *6* **Gym Shoes**[16] 6904 2-8-6 70 .... PatrickMathers 7 11
(Richard Fahey) *sn dropped to rr and rdn along: drvn and struggling 1/2-way: wknd 2f out: sn lost tch* **14/1**

1m 11.59s (-0.31) **Going Correction** -0.10s/f (Stan) 9 Ran SP% **113.7**
Speed ratings (Par 97): **98,97,96,95,94 94,92,77,69**
toteswingers 1&2 £5.00, 1&3 £5.20, 2&3 £31.10 CSF £32.61 CT £214.13 TOTE £1.80: £1.20, £4.10, £3.30; EX 29.00 Trifecta £102.80 Pool: £1129.17 - 8.23 winning units..
Owner Saeed Suhail **Bred** Tally-Ho Stud **Trained** Newmarket, Suffolk

FOCUS
The heavily backed winner should improve again, and the second and third help with the opening level.

7301 WILL YOU MARRY ME LISA WESTWORTH MAIDEN AUCTION STKS 1m (P)

2:30 (2:33) (Class 6) 2-Y-0 **£2,045** (£603; £302) **Stalls** High

Form RPR

2 **1** **Black Schnapps (IRE)**[14] 6953 2-9-2 0 .... MartinDwyer 6 80
(William Muir) *chsd ldr tl led over 2f out: rdn and qcknd wl clr over 1f out: r.o wl: comf* **6/4**[1]

0 **2** *4 1/2* **Ujagar (IRE)**[18] 6829 2-9-0 0 .... RichardKingscote 10 68+
(Tom Dascombe) *chsd ldng trio: rdn and effrt in 3rd ent fnl 2f: no ch w wnr but styd on to go 2nd ins fnl f: kpt on* **11/4**[2]

0 **3** *3 1/4* **Bountiful Sin**[9] 7069 2-9-1 0 .... NeilCallan 8 61
(George Margarson) *hld up in midfield: outpcd over 2f out: no ch w wnr but hdwy over 1f out: wnt 3rd ins fnl f* **7/1**

4 *2 1/2* **Lifejacket (IRE)** 2-9-0 0 .... RyanMoore 9 54
(Ed Dunlop) *in tch in midfield on outer: rdn and outpcd over 2f out: n.d but plugged on fnl f to go 4th nr fin* **5/1**[3]

50 **5** *3/4* **Lawman's Lady (IRE)**[20] 6776 2-8-11 0 .... JoeFanning 5 50
(Mark Johnston) *led tl over 2f out: rdn and outpcd by wnr over 1f out: wknd and lost 3 pls ins fnl f* **16/1**

6 *3 3/4* **Llandanwg** 2-8-7 0 .... JohnFahy 3 37
(Jamie Osborne) *s.i.s: racd in last pair: rdn and outpcd over 2f out: no ch but kpt on ins fnl f* **25/1**

6000 **7** *1 3/4* **Indie Star**[34] 6322 2-8-7 52 .... (v[1]) SamHitchcott 11 33
(Harry Dunlop) *s.i.s: bhd and rdn along early: outpcd u.p and btn over 2f out: no ch but plugged on past btn horses over 1f out* **50/1**

5 **8** *3* **Bow Quarter**[8] 7111 2-8-7 0 .... LiamJones 4 26
(J S Moore) *chsd ldrs: 4th and wkng jst over 2f out: fdd over 1f out* **33/1**

00 **9** *2 3/4* **Lingfield Lupus (IRE)**[23] 6688 2-9-0 0 .... SteveDrowne 7 27
(John Best) *sn rdn along in midfield: wknd u.p over 2f out: bhd over 1f out* **50/1**

10 *3/4* **Foxie Girl** 2-8-6 0 .... CathyGannon 2 17
(John Best) *in tch towards rr: rdn and struggling wl over 2f out: sn wknd and bhd* **16/1**

0 **11** *4 1/2* **Princess Florentia**[137] 2856 2-8-7 0 .... JimmyQuinn 1 8
(John Gallagher) *in tch in midfield: rdn and lost pl 4f out: bhd fnl 2f* **66/1**

1m 38.88s (0.68) **Going Correction** -0.10s/f (Stan) 11 Ran SP% **119.8**
Speed ratings (Par 93): **92,87,84,81,81 77,75,72,69,69 64**
toteswingers 1&2 £1.80, 1&3 £3.30, 2&3 £5.90 CSF £5.47 TOTE £2.40: £1.20, £1.10, £2.40; EX 6.80 Trifecta £33.30 Pool: £3174.28 - 71.28 winning units..
Owner O'Mulloy, Collenette, Quaintance, Clark **Bred** J & J Waldron **Trained** Lambourn, Berks

FOCUS
It's unlikely there was a great deal of strength-in-depth to this maiden auction contest, but the winner impressed, building on his recent debut.

7302 IRISH STALLION FARMS EBF MAIDEN STKS 7f (P)

3:00 (3:01) (Class 5) 2-Y-0 **£3,067** (£905; £453) **Stalls** Low

Form RPR

1 **Tree Of Grace (FR)** 2-9-5 0 .... RichardHughes 9 75+
(Richard Hannon) *chsd ldrs: rdn and effrt to chse clr ldr jst over 1f out: rdn and qcknd smartly ins fnl f to ld fnl 50yds: immediately in command and pricked ears in front: comf* **9/2**[2]

03 **2** *1/2* **Syros (IRE)**[21] 6754 2-9-5 0 .... JimmyFortune 8 74
(Brian Meehan) *hld up in tch in midfield: rdn and effrt 2f out: no imp tl str run ins fnl f to snatch 2nd last strides* **8/1**

6 **3** *hd* **My Target (IRE)**[20] 6769 2-9-5 0 .... MickaelBarzalona 12 73
(Saeed bin Suroor) *pressed ldr tl led travelling wl ent fnl 2f: rdn and qcknd 3 l clr ent fnl f: hdd and no ex fnl 50yds: lost 2nd last strides* **5/1**[3]

4 *1* **Nigel's Destiny (USA)** 2-9-5 0 .... RyanMoore 10 71+
(Jeremy Noseda) *hld up in midfield: rdn 2f out: no imp tl styd on wl ins fnl f: wnt 4th cl home* **6/1**

5 *shd* **Zee Zeely** 2-9-5 0 .... JoeFanning 3 70+
(William Haggas) *s.i.s: bhd: rdn and hdwy whn switchd rt over 1f out: r.o strly ins fnl f: nt rch ldrs* **25/1**

6 *nk* **Black Shadow** 2-9-5 0 .... NeilCallan 11 70
(Amanda Perrett) *chsd ldrs: rdn and effrt to chse clr ldr briefly over 1f out: 3rd and one pce 1f out: kpt on but lost 3 pls cl home* **20/1**

7 *4* **Third Strike** 2-9-5 0 .... GeorgeBaker 4 59
(Gary Moore) *hld up in tch towards rr: hdwy over 2f out: rn green and hung lft over 1f out: swtchd rt and styd on same pce fnl f* **66/1**

0 **8** *3/4* **Mind**[47] 5957 2-9-5 0 .... DaneO'Neill 6 57
(Henry Candy) *squeezed for room sn after s: hld up in tch in midfield: rdn and unable qck 2f out: outpcd and btn 1f out: plugged on* **20/1**

40 **9** *3/4* **Hands Up (IRE)**[14] 6954 2-9-5 0 .... MartinHarley 14 55
(William Knight) *in tch towards rr: dropped to last over 3f out: effrt on inner 2f out: kpt on but no threat to ldrs* **8/1**

03 **10** *2* **Irish Tears**[47] 5957 2-9-5 0 .... WilliamBuick 2 49
(John Gosden) *led tl rdn and hdd ent fnl 2f: sn outpcd and btn: fdd fnl f* **7/2**[1]

40 **11** *3/4* **Manor Way (IRE)**[14] 6953 2-9-5 0 .... SeanLevey 7 47
(Richard Hannon) *in tch in midfield: rdn and struggling over 2f out: wknd wl over 1f out* **50/1**

5 **12** *1* **Master Of Alkmaar**[65] 5344 2-9-5 0 .... JamieSpencer 1 45
(Roger Varian) *s.i.s: a towards rr: rdn and no hdwy whn rn green and hung rt bnd 2f out: n.d* **8/1**

50 **13** *3 3/4* **Berkeley Vale**[21] 6739 2-9-5 0 .... SebSanders 5 35
(Roger Teal) *in tch towards rr: rdn and struggling over 2f out: wknd wl over 1f out* **33/1**

1m 24.86s (0.06) **Going Correction** -0.10s/f (Stan) 13 Ran SP% **124.5**
Speed ratings (Par 95): **95,94,94,93,92 92,88,87,86,84 83,82,77**
toteswingers 1&2 £4.70, 1&3 £6.00, 2&3 £8.20 CSF £38.85 TOTE £5.80: £2.20, £2.40, £2.20; EX 39.20 Trifecta £325.40 Pool: £2410.30 - 5.55 winning units..
Owner HE Sh Joaan Bin Hamad Al Thani **Bred** E A R L Haras Du Taillis **Trained** East Everleigh, Wilts

The Form Book Flat, Raceform Ltd, Compton, RG20 6NL.

FOCUS
There were plenty of big yards represented and the potential of plenty of future winners in what may prove a well above-average juvenile contest. The first six finished compressed and it's hard to rate the bare form higher.

7303 ST PIERS SCHOOL CLASSIFIED CLAIMING STKS 7f (P)
3:35 (3:35) (Class 6) 3-Y-0+ **£2,045** (£603; £302) **Stalls** Low

Form RPR
441 **1** **Four Winds**[42] 6105 7-8-8 70..............................(v) RichardKingscote 6 78
(Tom Dascombe) *t.k.h: hld up towards rr: hdwy whn bmpd and pushed rt over 1f out: rdn and qcknd to ld ins fnl f: hanging lft and bmpd runner-up ins fnl f: a doing enough to hold rival* **11/10**[1]
3503 **2** *hd* **Kimbali (IRE)**[26] 6606 4-8-2 65.................................. PatrickMathers 8 71
(Richard Fahey) *taken down early: hld up wl in tch in midfield: swtchd rt bmpd wnr and hdwy over 1f out: ev ch but carried lft and bmpd ins fnl f: r.o but a hld* **12/1**
0515 **3** *2¼* **Fluctuation (IRE)**[13] 6970 5-8-1 70..............................(v) RyanPowell(3) 4 67
(Ian Williams) *in tch in midfield: rdn and hdwy over 1f out: kpt on to go 3rd ins fnl f: no threat to ldng pair* **12/1**
6200 **4** *1* **Fever Few**[28] 6535 4-8-12 68..............................(p) MickaelBarzalona 11 73
(Jane Chapple-Hyam) *in tch in midfield: effrt on outer over 1f out: kpt on u.p ins fnl f: no threat to ldng pair* **20/1**
0456 **5** *1½* **The Mongoose**[30] 6475 5-8-3 67..............................(t) DeclanBates(3) 7 63
(David Evans) *chsd ldr tl drvn to ld jst over 1f out: hdd jst ins fnl f: sn no ex and one pce fnl 100yds* **16/1**
4400 **6** *1¾* **Avonmore Star**[15] 6929 5-8-6 67.................................. MartinDwyer 5 58
(Mike Murphy) *chsd ldrs: effrt u.p and ev ch over 1f out: no ex 1f out: wknd ins fnl f* **20/1**
0333 **7** *hd* **Golden Desert (IRE)**[35] 6317 9-8-10 66..................... RichardHughes 3 62
(Simon Dow) *stdd s: hld up in tch in last trio: hdwy jst over 1f out: kpt on: nvr threatened ldrs* **7/1**[3]
3400 **8** *hd* **Olympic Jule**[43] 6080 3-8-10 65.................................. CathyGannon 2 62
(Harry Dunlop) *led: rdn ent fnl 2f: hdd and no ex jst over 1f out: wknd ins fnl f* **25/1**
0000 **9** *2* **Orders From Rome (IRE)**[14] 6937 4-8-2 62.............(tp) RaulDaSilva 12 48
(Eve Johnson Houghton) *t.k.h: hld up in tch towards rr: effrt whn nt clr run wl over 1f out: rdn and styd on same pce fr over 1f out* **33/1**
0506 **10** *nk* **Jarrow (IRE)**[8] 7109 6-8-8 66..............................(p) JoeFanning 13 53
(Milton Bradley) *stdd s: t.k.h: hld up in tch in rr: swtchd rt and effrt wl over 1f out: kpt on but no real imp* **25/1**
5106 **11** *2¾* **Hornboy**[50] 5853 3-8-13 70..............................(p) RyanMoore 9 52
(Jeremy Noseda) *chsd ldrs: rdn and unable qck ent fnl 2f: wknd over 1f out* **9/2**[2]
6534 **12** *6* **Maypole Joe (IRE)**[12] 684 3-7-12 62 ow1................ SimonPearce(3) 1 24
(Raymond York) *a towards rr: last and struggling u.p 3f out: bhd fnl 2f* **66/1**

1m 23.74s (-1.06) **Going Correction** -0.10s/f (Stan)
WFA 3 from 4yo+ 2lb **12** Ran SP% **121.2**
Speed ratings (Par 101): **102,101,99,98,96 94,94,93,91,91 88,81**
toteswingers 1&2 £4.50, 1&3 £3.60, 2&3 £20.70 CSF £14.66 TOTE £2.00: £1.10, £3.10, £3.80; EX 22.80 Trifecta £150.20 Pool: £2762.49 - 13.78 winning units..Kimbali was claimed by Mr P. D. Evans for £5,000.
Owner T Dascombe **Bred** The Queen **Trained** Malpas, Cheshire
■ Stewards' Enquiry : Richard Kingscote one-day ban: careless riding (Oct 30)

FOCUS
It's hard to know what ability the winner retains, but this had more depth than most claimers.

7304 NEVILLE CHILDHOOD EPILEPSY CENTRE H'CAP 1m 4f (P)
4:05 (4:08) (Class 2) (0-100,96) 3-Y-0 **£12,291** (£3,657; £1,827; £913) **Stalls** Low

Form RPR
-110 **1** **Winterlude (IRE)**[54] 5723 3-9-7 96..................... MickaelBarzalona 10 108
(Charlie Appleby) *hld up in tch in midfield: rdn and hdwy to ld 3f out: drvn over 1f out: forged ahd ins fnl f: sn clr and r.o wl* **9/2**[3]
3125 **2** *2¾* **Cafe Society (FR)**[39] 6186 3-9-1 90.................................. JamieSpencer 6 98
(David Simcock) *stdd s: hld up in rr: pushed rt wl over 1f out: swtchd rt and hdwy 3f out: drvn and hung lft over 1f out: swtchd rt and styd on fnl 100yds to snatch 2nd last stride* **7/4**[1]
1411 **3** *shd* **Evangelist**[32] 6380 3-8-10 85..............................(p) RyanMoore 3 93
(Sir Michael Stoute) *led tl 6f out: chsd ldr after: rdn and ev ch 2f out tl no ex and btn ins fnl f: wknd and lost 2nd last stride* **6/1**
1120 **4** *½* **Mahican (IRE)**[11] 7022 3-9-0 89.................................. JoeFanning 7 96
(Mark Johnston) *t.k.h: chsd ldrs for 2f: chsd ldrs after: 3rd and drvn 2f out: styd on same pce ins fnl f* **12/1**
2121 **5** *1* **Nautilus**[36] 6280 3-9-6 95.................................. RobertHavlin 8 100
(John Gosden) *s.i.s: hld up in last pair: swtchd rt and hdwy wl over 3f out: hung rt and lost pl bnd 2f out: edging lft but rallied fnl f: kpt on* **12/1**
1620 **6** *2½* **Space Ship**[97] 4214 3-9-5 94.................................. WilliamBuick 2 95
(John Gosden) *hld up in tch in midfield: rdn and effrt over 2f out: no ex 1f out: wknd ins fnl f* **4/1**[2]
6500 **7** *4* **King Muro**[23] 6693 3-8-2 77 oh6.................................. CathyGannon 5 72
(Andrew Balding) *t.k.h: chsd ldrs: struggling u.p ent fnl 2f: wknd over 1f out* **33/1**
3434 **8** *25* **Edwyn Ralph**[18] 6827 3-8-2 77 oh1.................................. NickyMackay 9 32
(David Simcock) *hdwy to chse ldr after 2f: led 6f out: rdn and hdd 3f out: sn dropped out: lost tch 2f out: t.o* **12/1**

2m 28.24s (-4.76) **Going Correction** -0.10s/f (Stan) **8** Ran SP% **114.8**
Speed ratings (Par 107): **111,109,109,108,108 106,103,87**
toteswingers 1&2 £2.70, 1&3 £5.50, 2&3 £2.80 CSF £12.86 CT £46.79 TOTE £6.60: £2.50, £1.20, £1.20; EX 20.00 Trifecta £122.70 Pool: £3853.14 - 23.54 winning units..
Owner Godolphin **Bred** Darley **Trained** Newmarket, Suffolk

FOCUS
This had looked a very competitive renewal on paper, but it was turned into something of a procession by the winner who produced a smart effort. A personal best from the winner too.

7305 YOUNG EPILEPSY'S PURPLE DAY H'CAP 2m (P)
4:40 (4:41) (Class 6) (0-65,65) 3-Y-0+ **£2,045** (£603; £302) **Stalls** Low

Form RPR
0052 **1** **Aiyana**[9] 7066 3-9-1 62.................................. RyanMoore 10 70
(Hughie Morrison) *led after 1f: mde rest and set stdy gallop: drvn and fnd ex ent fnl 2f: kpt on u.p fnl f* **3/1**[1]
4404 **2** *1½* **Grandiloquent**[16] 6909 4-9-6 57..............................(p) JamieSpencer 6 63
(Kevin Ryan) *stdd s: hld up in rr: hdwy into midfield 7f out: rdn to chse wnr 2f out: styd on same pce ins fnl f* **5/1**[2]
5265 **3** *½* **Happy Families**[27] 6557 3-9-4 65.................................. MartinDwyer 9 70
(Heather Main) *t.k.h: hld up in midfield: rdn and hdwy 3f out: styd on to chse ldng pair 1f out: one pce ins fnl f* **12/1**[3]
-360 **4** *1½* **It's A Girl Thing (IRE)**[30] 6457 4-9-9 60.................................. GeorgeBaker 2 63
(Gary Moore) *hld up in last pair: effrt on outer jst over 2f out: hdwy 1f out: styd on fnl f: nt rch ldrs* **25/1**
1031 **5** *hd* **Cabuchon (GER)**[16] 6895 6-9-0 58..............................(t) EoinWalsh(7) 8 61
(David Evans) *hld up in midfield: nt clr run and shuffled bk to rr over 2f out: swtchd rt and effrt bnd 2f out: styd on ins fnl f* **5/1**[2]
551 **6** *2* **Superciliary**[15] 6404 4-9-10 61.................................. DaneO'Neill 7 62
(Chris Gordon) *chsd wnr tl drvn and unable qck 2f out: wknd ins fnl f* **5/1**[2]
600 **7** *1½* **Bold Citizen (IRE)**[43] 6062 3-9-4 65.................................. JoeFanning 1 64
(Ed Dunlop) *in tch in midfield: nt clr run and shuffled bk over 2f out: drvn and rallied over 1f out: sn no imp and one pce fnl f* **3/1**[1]
6100 **8** *½* **Bondi Mist (IRE)**[16] 6899 4-9-2 58..............................(v) RyanTate(5) 5 56
(Jonathan Geake) *chsd ldrs: rdn and unable qck over 2f out: lost pl u.p wl over 1f out: wknd ins fnl f* **33/1**
6060 **9** *½* **Parsons Green**[32] 6404 4-8-9 46 oh1.................................. LiamJones 4 44?
(Michael Attwater) *hld up in tch in midfield: n.m.r over 2f out: rdn and outpcd 2f out: wknd over 1f out* **50/1**
00-0 **10** *4½* **Shot In The Dark (IRE)**[47] 5954 4-9-2 53.............(tp) HarryBentley 3 45
(Jonathan Geake) *chsd ldrs tl lost pl u.p jst over 2f out: wknd and bhd over 1f out* **33/1**

3m 27.1s (1.40) **Going Correction** -0.10s/f (Stan)
WFA 3 from 4yo+ 10lb **10** Ran SP% **119.4**
Speed ratings (Par 101): **92,91,91,90,90 89,88,88,87,85**
toteswingers 1&2 £2.70, 1&3 £7.50, 2&3 £8.80 CSF £18.24 CT £160.48 TOTE £4.20: £1.50, £1.80, £2.60; EX 12.90 Trifecta £149.80 Pool: £2825.21 - 14.14 winning units..
Owner The End-R-Ways Partnership & Partners **Bred** The Lavington Stud **Trained** East Ilsley, Berks

FOCUS
A modest staying handicap in which the winner had an easy lead. The form makes sense among the front three.

7306 VINES BMW H'CAP (DIV I) 1m (P)
5:10 (5:11) (Class 5) (0-75,75) 3-Y-0+ **£2,726** (£805; £402) **Stalls** High

Form RPR
1553 **1** **The Great Gabrial**[9] 7076 4-8-13 67..............................(v) JamieSpencer 5 79
(Ian Williams) *hld up in tch in midfield: rdn and effrt ent fnl 2f: rdn and str chal fnl 75yds: r.o to ld cl home* **5/1**[1]
6510 **2** *shd* **Duke Of Destiny (IRE)**[19] 6794 4-9-2 70..............................(p) GeorgeBaker 6 81
(Ed Walker) *hld up wl in tch in midfield: rdn and effrt 1f out: led ins fnl f: hrd pressed and drvn fnl 75yds: r.o but hdd and no ex last strides* **5/1**[1]
0000 **3** *3¾* **Copperwood**[11] 7024 8-9-1 69.................................. JoeFanning 7 71
(Mark Johnston) *t.k.h: chsd ldrs: nt clr run ent fnl 2f: swtchd rt and effrt wl over 1f out: styd on same pce ins fnl f* **10/1**
0006 **4** *½* **Midnight Feast**[40] 6167 5-8-13 70..............................(v) ThomasBrown(3) 12 71
(Lee Carter) *bustled along early: chsd ldrs: drvn and ev ch over 1f out: styd on same pce ins fnl f* **16/1**
5020 **5** *1¼* **Poetic Lord**[7] 7130 4-9-5 73.................................. TedDurcan 2 71
(Sylvester Kirk) *in midfield: drvn and no hdwy 2f out: no threat to ldrs but plugged on same pce ins fnl f* **10/1**
4412 **6** *1* **Perfect Mission**[57] 5607 5-9-1 74..............................(v) DanielMuscutt(5) 8 70
(Andrew Balding) *led: drvn and hrd pressed over 1f out: hdd ins fnl f: sn wknd* **10/1**
6623 **7** *½* **Juvenal (IRE)**[9] 7071 4-9-2 73..................... WilliamTwiston-Davies(3) 3 68
(Richard Hannon) *hld up in midfield: drvn and no hdwy wl over 1f out: plugged on but nvr threatened ldrs* **7/1**[2]
0001 **8** *2½* **Dimitar (USA)**[18] 6855 4-8-12 69.................................. ShaneGorey(3) 4 58
(Brendan Powell) *taken down early: t.k.h: hld up towards rr: swtchd rt and hdwy into midfield on outer 5f out: rdn and no hdwy 2f out: wknd 1f out* **8/1**[3]
1500 **9** *5* **Standpoint**[42] 6108 7-9-7 75.................................. DaneO'Neill 9 52
(Conor Dore) *stdd and dropped in bhd after s: hld up in last trio: n.d* **33/1**
1261 **10** *4* **Dana's Present**[35] 6306 4-9-3 71.................................. PatCosgrave 10 39
(George Baker) *chsd ldr tl 2f out: sn struggling and btn over 1f out: fdd qckly fnl f* **5/1**[1]
0563 **11** *5* **Scottish Lake**[35] 6316 5-9-2 70.................................. CathyGannon 1 27
(Olivia Maylam) *hld up towards rr: rdn and struggling over 2f out: bhd over 1f out* **14/1**
1150 **12** *18* **Siouxperhero (IRE)**[23] 6701 4-9-0 68..............................(p) SteveDrowne 11
(William Muir) *a in rr and nvr gng wl: lost tch and eased wl over 1f out: t.o* **16/1**

1m 36.46s (-1.74) **Going Correction** -0.10s/f (Stan) **12** Ran SP% **122.3**
Speed ratings (Par 103): **104,103,100,99,98 97,96,94,89,85 80,62**
toteswingers 1&2 £5.10, 1&3 £11.20, 2&3 £8.60 CSF £29.53 CT £248.52 TOTE £10.40: £2.60, £2.50, £4.60; EX 36.40 Trifecta £544.50 Pool: £1916.48 - 2.63 winning units..
Owner Dr Marwan Koukash **Bred** Juddmonte Farms Ltd **Trained** Portway, Worcs

FOCUS
A fair race for the grade and it served up a thrilling finish. The time was decent and the form has been given a bit of a chance, with the first two clear.

7307 VINES BMW H'CAP (DIV II) 1m (P)
5:45 (5:47) (Class 5) (0-75,74) 3-Y-0+ **£2,726** (£805; £402) **Stalls** High

Form RPR
0000 **1** **Johnno**[26] 6596 4-9-6 73..............................(bt[1]) SebSanders 10 82
(J W Hills) *styd wd early: w ldr: rdn and qcknd clr w ldr wl over 1f out: led 1f out: styd on: drvn out* **8/1**[3]
4366 **2** *1½* **Wilfred Pickles (IRE)**[43] 6080 7-9-3 70.................................. PatCosgrave 3 76
(Jo Crowley) *hld up in tch in midfield: effrt and swtchd rt over 1f out: kpt on u.p ins fnl f: wnt 2nd last strides* **8/1**[3]
5505 **3** *nse* **Flamborough Breeze**[66] 5310 4-9-7 74..............................(t) GeorgeBaker 6 79
(Ed Vaughan) *stdd s: hld up in last pair: switching lft and hdwy over 1f out: r.o wl ins fnl f: wnt 3rd last strides* **10/1**
301 **4** *nse* **Aglaophonos**[9] 7065 3-9-4 74 6ex..............................(p) JoeFanning 1 78
(Ian Williams) *t.k.h: chsd ldrss: rdn and sltly outpcd wl over 1f out: rallied and styd on again ins fnl f* **6/1**[2]
2000 **5** *½* **Fulney**[49] 5896 4-9-7 74.................................. HarryBentley 2 78
(James Eustace) *led: rdn and qcknd clr w wnr wl over 1f out: hdd 1f out: no ex and one pce after: lost 3 pls cl home* **20/1**
0002 **6** *1* **Kyllachy Star**[27] 6567 7-9-3 70.................................. JamieSpencer 5 72
(Richard Fahey) *hld up in tch in midfield: effrt on outer over 1f out: kpt on u.p fnl f* **9/2**[1]
4220 **7** *nk* **Ssafa**[26] 6609 5-9-2 72..............................(p) ThomasBrown(3) 7 73
(Alastair Lidderdale) *chsd ldrs: rdn and outpcd wl over 1f out: plugged on same pce ins fnl f* **20/1**
2243 **8** *3* **Martial Art (IRE)**[51] 5845 3-9-0 70..............................(p) CathyGannon 12 63
(Andrew Balding) *hld up in tch in last quartet: rdn and hdwy on inner over 1f out: no ex and wknd ins fnl f* **14/1**

4266 **9** *6* **Club House (IRE)**[57] 5604 3-8-13 **69**................................ KierenFox 11 48
(Robert Mills) *stdd and dropped in bhd after s: hld up in last pair: rdn and effrt ent fnl 2f: sn btn: wknd over 1f out* **20/1**

0000 **10** *3/4* **Lastkingofscotland (IRE)**[30] 6475 7-8-13 **69**...........(b) RyanPowell(3) 4 48
(Conor Dore) *hld up in tch in last quartet: rdn and no hdwy 2f out: sn wknd* **50/1**

2500 **11** *1 1/2* **Darnathean**[57] 5621 4-8-13 **69**..................(p) WilliamTwiston-Davies(3) 8 44
(Paul D'Arcy) *taken down early: t.k.h: chsd ldrs: rdn and lost pl over 2f out: bhd 1f out* **25/1**

1m 37.09s (-1.11) **Going Correction** -0.10s/f (Stan)
WFA 3 from 4yo+ 3lb **11 Ran SP% 90.5**
Speed ratings (Par 103): **101,99,99,99,98 97,97,94,88,87 86**
toteswingers 1&2 £20.60, 1&3 £9.30, 2&3 £8.40 CSF £34.23 CT £234.82 TOTE £9.30: £1.80, £2.70, £2.20; EX 49.70 Trifecta £567.20 Part won. Pool: £756.32 - 0.49 winning units..
Owner Gary And Linnet Woodward **Bred** Gestut Sohrenhof **Trained** Upper Lambourn, Berks

FOCUS
There was suspicion that this was the much weaker of the two divisions and, with That's Plenty being withdrawn at the start on veterinary advice, it remains to be seen what was required. Slower than division I and a little bit less solid. The runner-up is a fair guide.
T/Plt: £13.40 to a £1 stake. Pool: £74744.23 - 4048.11 winning tickets T/Qpdt: £7.70 to a £1 stake. Pool: £4924.00 - 471.60 winning tickets SP

7125 NOTTINGHAM (L-H)
Wednesday, October 16

OFFICIAL GOING: Soft changing to heavy after race 2 (2:40)
All races on Outer track and home bend moved out 6m from inside line, adding 24yds to races on Round course.

7308 EBF STALLIONS NEXT GENERATION SECURITY MAIDEN STKS 1m 75y
2:10 (2:11) (Class 5) 2-Y-O **£3,234** (£962; £481; £240) **Stalls** Centre

Form RPR

5 **1** **Montaly**[22] 6733 2-9-5 0................................ DavidProbert 4 83
(Andrew Balding) *prom: trckd ldr after 2f: effrt 2f out: rdn to chal over 1f out: styd on fnl f to ld nr fin* **5/1**[3]

52 **2** *nk* **Istikshaf (IRE)**[27] 6570 2-9-5 0.............................. SilvestreDeSousa 9 82
(Saeed bin Suroor) *led: pushed along 3f out: rdn 2f out: drvn ent fnl f: hdd and no ex nr fin* **7/4**[1]

6 **3** *1 1/4* **Donncha (IRE)**[49] 5891 2-9-5 0.............................. TomQueally 12 80
(Robert Eddery) *in tch on outer: gd hdwy over 3f out: cl up 2f out: rdn over 1f out: ev ch tl kpt on same pce ins fnl f* **10/1**

4 *4* **Idder (IRE)** 2-9-5 0................................ AndreaAtzeni 6 71+
(Roger Varian) *in tch: hdwy to chse ldrs 4f out: effrt over 2f out: sn rdn and ev ch tl wknd appr fnl f* **6/1**

0 **5** *2 1/4* **Deauville Dancer (IRE)**[19] 6799 2-9-5 0.................... RobertWinston 3 66
(Lady Herries) *trckd ldrs: pushed along over 3f out: rdn wl over 2f out: grad wknd* **50/1**

6 *9* **Sea Here** 2-9-5 0................................ JimCrowley 10 46+
(Ralph Beckett) *chsd ldng pair: pushed along 3f out: rdn over 2f out: sn wknd* **17/2**

7 *3/4* **Dragoon Guard (IRE)** 2-9-5 0.............................. JamesDoyle 13 44
(Marco Botti) *dwlt: a towards rr* **14/1**

00 **8** *1 1/4* **Gimme Five**[9] 7069 2-9-5 0.............................. FergusSweeney 2 42
(Alan King) *a towards rr* **100/1**

36 **9** *2 1/2* **Amood (IRE)**[39] 6184 2-9-5 0.............................. PaulHanagan 1 36
(Charles Hills) *trckd ldrs on inner: rdn along over 3f out: sn wknd* **4/1**[2]

0 **10** *3/4* **Masterpaver**[20] 6762 2-9-5 0.............................. GrahamLee 11 34
(Alan Bailey) *a towards rr* **50/1**

0 **11** *12* **Mighty Force (IRE)**[20] 6769 2-9-5 0.......................... MartinLane 5 8
(Nick Littmoden) *dwlt: a in rr* **100/1**

0 **12** *5* **Moscato**[9] 7070 2-9-5 0................................ ChrisCatlin 8
(Sir Mark Prescott Bt) *a towards rr* **100/1**

1m 52.72s (3.72) **Going Correction** +0.475s/f (Yiel) **12 Ran SP% 120.5**
Speed ratings (Par 95): **100,99,98,94,92 83,82,81,78,77 65,60**
toteswingers 1&2 £2.80, 1&3 £9.70, 2&3 £4.60 CSF £14.35 TOTE £7.70: £1.60, £1.30, £2.40; EX 20.60 Trifecta £183.00 Pool: £1710.25 - 7.00 winning units..
Owner The Farleigh Court Racing Partnership **Bred** Farleigh Court Racing Partnership **Trained** Kingsclere, Hants

FOCUS
The outer track was in use and with the rail being 6m from the inside line, race distances were increased by 24yds. General consensus amongst riders was that the ground was 'heavy' and it was officially changed to that, from Soft, after the second race. Fair maiden form, with little getting into it from off the pace, something which would be a continuing theme throughout the day. The first five were clear.

7309 EXCLUSIVE NETWORKS NURSERY H'CAP 1m 75y
2:40 (2:41) (Class 5) (0-70,70) 2-Y-O **£2,587** (£770; £384; £192) **Stalls** Centre

Form RPR

0466 **1** **Ahoy There (IRE)**[36] 6275 2-8-13 **62**.......................... AndrewMullen 9 66
(Tom Tate) *mde most: rdn over 2f out: drvn over 1f out: styd on gamely towards fin* **10/1**[3]

0352 **2** *nk* **Island Remede**[15] 6924 2-9-3 **66**.............................. JamesDoyle 17 69+
(Ed Dunlop) *hld up towards rr: gd hdwy on wd outside over 3f out: rdn to chse ldrs and edgd lft wl over 1f out: styd on u.p fnl f: jst failed* **6/1**[1]

6203 **3** *hd* **Arrowzone**[8] 7097 2-9-3 **66**................................ BillyCray(3) 11 72
(Garry Moss) *cl up: rdn along wl over 2f out: drvn over 1f out: kpt on wl u.p fnl f* **10/1**[3]

0235 **4** *1* **My Anchor**[16] 6897 2-9-0 **63**.............................. AndreaAtzeni 4 63
(Sylvester Kirk) *trckd ldrs: hdwy over 3f out: rdn along 2f out: drvn over 1f out: kpt on wl towards fin* **6/1**[1]

000 **5** *2* **Nyanza (GER)**[43] 6063 2-8-11 **60**.............................. FergusSweeney 10 56
(Alan King) *hld up: hdwy 1/2-way: rdn to chse ldrs 2f out: drvn over 1f out: no imp fnl f* **16/1**

360 **6** *9* **Darling Boyz**[65] 5338 2-8-11 **60**.......................... MichaelO'Connell 16 35
(John Quinn) *midfield: hdwy on outer and in tch 1/2-way: rdn along 3f out: plugged on fnl 2f: n.d* **14/1**

062 **7** *3 1/4* **Poetic Choice**[14] 6939 2-9-0 **63**.............................. MartinLane 2 30
(Nick Littmoden) *in tch on inner: hdwy to chse ldrs over 3f out: rdn over 2f out: drvn and wknd wl over 1f out* **16/1**

0534 **8** *3/4* **Habdab**[31] 6426 2-8-13 **69**.............................. CameronHardie(7) 1 35
(Richard Hannon) *hld up: hmpd and lost pl after 2f: sn in rr: hdwy 3f out: rdn over 2f out: nvr nr ldrs* **25/1**

0000 **9** *2 1/4* **All Yours (IRE)**[19] 6807 2-9-7 **70**..............................(v[1]) JimCrowley 3 31
(William Knight) *chsd ldrs on inner: rdn along wl over 2f out: grad wknd* **16/1**

0001 **10** *4 1/2* **Roving Bunny**[22] 6725 2-9-6 **69**.............................. GrahamLee 14 19
(James Given) *prom: effrt and ev ch 3f out: rdn over 2f out: sn wknd* **14/1**

233 **11** *4* **Larsen Bay (IRE)**[12] 6999 2-8-11 **60**.......................(v[1]) StephenCraine 8
(Tom Dascombe) *in midfield: awkward and hung lft on bnd after 2f: t.k.h after: chsd ldrs tl wknd 3f out* **16/1**

603 **12** *19* **Gold Class**[28] 6513 2-8-13 **62**.............................. GrahamGibbons 13
(Ed McMahon) *chsd ldrs: rdn along wl over 3f out: sn wknd* **10/1**[3]

56U1 **13** *3/4* **Cascadia (IRE)**[47] 5963 2-8-7 **61**.............................. JoeyHaynes(5) 7
(K R Burke) *a in rr: bhd fr 1/2-way* **33/1**

504 **14** *1 1/4* **Prostate Awareness (IRE)**[51] 5827 2-9-3 **66**........(p) RussKennemore 6
(Patrick Holmes) *a towards rr: rdn along 1/2-way: sn bhd* **25/1**

0032 **15** *1* **Acquaint (IRE)**[35] 6311 2-9-3 **66**.............................. PatDobbs 12
(Richard Hannon) *midfield: pushed along and lost pl 1/2-way: sn rdn and bhd* **8/1**[2]

3240 **16** *19* **Emaad (USA)**[35] 6303 2-9-7 **70**.............................. PaulHanagan 15
(Mark Johnston) *in tch on outer: hdwy 1/2-way: rdn along over 3f out: sn wknd* **10/1**[3]

1m 53.75s (4.75) **Going Correction** +0.475s/f (Yiel) **16 Ran SP% 123.5**
Speed ratings (Par 95): **95,94,94,93,91 82,79,78,76,71 67,48,48,46,45 26**
toteswingers 1&2 £16.70, 1&3 £35.60, 2&3 £17.10 CSF £68.18 CT £658.65 TOTE £16.20: £3.90, £2.10, £3.50, £2.10; EX 132.50 Trifecta £444.40 Part won. Pool: £592.56 - 0.01 winning units..
Owner Ms Fionnuala Cassidy **Bred** Kildaragh Stud **Trained** Tadcaster, N Yorks
■ Stewards' Enquiry : Billy Cray two-day ban plus eight-day deffered; used whip above permitted level (Oct 30-Nov 2, 4-9)

FOCUS
It proved an advantage to race prominently in what had looked an open nursery beforehand. Ordinary form.

7310 FORTINET MEDIAN AUCTION MAIDEN FILLIES' STKS 1m 75y
3:15 (3:16) (Class 5) 2-Y-O **£2,587** (£770; £384; £192) **Stalls** Centre

Form RPR

60 **1** **Ejadah (IRE)**[76] 4921 2-9-0 0.............................. PaulHanagan 6 76
(Roger Varian) *t.k.h: trckd ldrs: hdwy over 2f out: rdn to chse ldng pair over 1f out: drvn ent fnl f: styd on gamely to ld nr fin* **7/2**[2]

0 **2** *shd* **Stereo Love (FR)**[28] 6523 2-9-0 0.............................. PatDobbs 10 76
(Clive Cox) *in tch on outer: hdwy over 3f out: cl up 2f out: rdn to chal over 1f out: drvn and slt ld ins fnl f: hdd and no ex nr fin* **7/1**

3065 **3** *1 1/4* **Full Day**[18] 6852 2-9-0 73.............................. JimCrowley 7 73
(Ralph Beckett) *trckd ldng pair: hdwy to ld over 2f out: rdn wl over 1f out: drvn and hdd ins fnl f: kpt on same pce last 100yds* **9/4**[1]

0 **4** *hd* **Groovejet**[25] 6643 2-9-0 0.............................. AndreaAtzeni 5 73+
(Peter Chapple-Hyam) *in tch: pushed along and outpcd over 3f out: swtchd rt toi outer and rdn over 1f out: styd on strly fnl f: nrst fin* **4/1**[3]

06 **5** *14* **Three Heart's**[26] 6597 2-9-0 0.............................. RobertWinston 3 42
(Hugo Palmer) *chsd ldr: rdn along 3f out: wknd over 2f out* **12/1**

04 **6** *5* **Irene Hull (IRE)**[14] 6938 2-8-11 0.............................. JasonHart(3) 2 31
(Garry Moss) *set gd pce: rdn along 3f out: sn hdd and grad wknd* **8/1**

7 *7* **Chesil Beach** 2-9-0 0.............................. DavidProbert 4 15
(Andrew Balding) *dwlt and a outpcd in rr* **14/1**

0 **8** *7* **Key To Your Heart**[14] 6949 2-9-0 0.............................. GrahamLee 8
(Hughie Morrison) *a towards rr* **33/1**

0 **9** *11* **Petale Noir**[41] 6141 2-9-0 0.............................. StephenCraine 1
(Jonathan Portman) *chsd ldrs on inner: rdn along over 3f out: sn wknd* **100/1**

1m 53.84s (4.84) **Going Correction** +0.475s/f (Yiel) **9 Ran SP% 114.9**
Speed ratings (Par 92): **94,93,92,92,78 73,66,59,48**
toteswingers 1&2 £5.40, 1&3 £2.20, 2&3 £3.60 CSF £28.10 TOTE £4.00: £1.80, £3.80, £1.02; EX 31.30 Trifecta £115.30 Pool: £1969.36 - 12.79 winning units..
Owner Hamdan Al Maktoum **Bred** Herbertstown House Stud **Trained** Newmarket, Suffolk

FOCUS
Another race in which those who raced up with the pace were favoured. The form looks just ordinary, the third's pre-race form setting the standard.

7311 FORTIGUARD MAIDEN STKS 1m 2f 50y
3:45 (3:48) (Class 5) 3-Y-O **£3,234** (£962; £481; £240) **Stalls** Low

Form RPR

2534 **1** **Thorpe (IRE)**[39] 6202 3-9-5 75..............................(p) JimCrowley 11 81
(Ralph Beckett) *cl up: led after 2f: wd st and pushed along over 3f out: rdn 2f out: sn drvn and edgd lft: drvn out* **11/4**[2]

23 **2** *4* **Lady Guinevere**[228] 864 3-9-0 0.............................. DavidProbert 3 69
(Stuart Williams) *trckd ldrs: hdwy over 3f out: rdn to chse wnr over 2f out: sn ev ch tl drvn and one pce fnl f* **7/1**[3]

332 **3** *8* **Proximate**[23] 6684 3-9-5 82.............................. JamesDoyle 6 59
(Sir Michael Stoute) *trckd ldrs: hdwy 4f out: pushed along 3f out: sn rdn and one pce* **11/10**[1]

0 **4** *6* **Perivale (USA)**[110] 3764 3-9-0 0.............................. GrahamLee 10 44
(Mark Johnston) *trckd ldrs: hdwy to chse wnr over 3f out: sn rdn: drvn wl over 2f out and plugged on one pce* **20/1**

0 **5** *9* **Summerfree (USA)**[23] 6696 3-9-5 0.............................. AdrianNicholls 7 32
(Mark Johnston) *led 2f: cl up: rdn along over 4f out: sn wknd* **10/1**

0 **6** *hd* **Thomas Blossom (IRE)**[21] 6748 3-9-5 0.............................. AndrewMullen 1 32
(Nigel Tinkler) *in tch: rdn along 4f out: sn outpcd* **100/1**

0 **7** *21* **Magical Mischief**[9] 7067 3-9-0 0.............................. MichaelStainton 5
(Chris Fairhurst) *chsd ldrs: rdn along over 4f out: wknd qckly* **100/1**

8 *27* **Maya De Ventura** 3-9-0 0.............................. TomEaves 9
(Alison Hutchinson) *s.i.s: a towards rr: t.o fnl 3f* **100/1**

0 **9** *12* **Boboli Gardens**[41] 6133 3-9-5 0..............................(t) PatDobbs 4
(Mrs Ilka Gansera-Leveque) *towards rr: rdn along 1/2-way: sn outpcd and bhd: t.o fnl 3f* **16/1**

10 *5* **Mutashabek (USA)** 3-9-5 0.............................. PaulHanagan 2
(Brian Meehan) *s.i.s: a in rr: outpcd and bhd fnl 3f: eased and t.o fnl 3f* **16/1**

11 *62* **Spessartine (IRE)** 3-9-5 0.............................. AndreaAtzeni 12
(Robert Eddery) *s.i.s and bhd: t.o and eased fnl 3f* **50/1**

2m 20.86s (6.56) **Going Correction** +0.675s/f (Yiel) **11 Ran SP% 117.3**
Speed ratings (Par 101): **100,96,90,85,78 78,61,39,30,26**
toteswingers 1&2 £2.40, 1&3 £1.40, 2&3 £2.20 CSF £21.79 TOTE £3.40: £1.20, £2.00, £1.10; EX 16.50 Trifecta £25.80 Pool: £2502.48 - 72.55 winning units..
Owner Mr and Mrs David Aykroyd **Bred** Mr & Mrs David Aykroyd **Trained** Kimpton, Hants

The Form Book Flat, Raceform Ltd, Compton, RG20 6NL.

FOCUS
This seemed to develop into a right old slog and is not form to put much faith in. The winner is rated just to his best. For the first time on the day they headed centre-to-stands' side in the straight.

7312 FORTINET GOLD PARTNER H'CAP 1m 2f 50y
4:20 (4:20) (Class 3) (0-95,93) 3-Y-O+
£7,470 (£2,236; £1,118; £559; £279; £140) Stalls Low

Form RPR
5563 **1** **Tahaamah**[53] 5749 5-9-7 **90**.......... JamesDoyle 4 100
(Saeed bin Suroor) *hld up towards rr: stdy hdwy 3f out: chsd ldrs 2f out: sn chal on inner: rdn to ld appr fnl f: drvn and kpt on wl towards fin* **6/1**[2]
2334 **2** ½ **Las Verglas Star (IRE)**[20] 6772 5-8-9 **83**.......... GeorgeChaloner(5) 2 92
(Richard Fahey) *hld up in tch: hdwy 3f out: chsd ldrs 2f out: rdn to chal over 1f out: ev ch tl drvn: edgd lft and no ex last 50yds* **5/1**[1]
4006 **3** ½ **Awake My Soul (IRE)**[20] 6772 4-9-10 **93**.......... DanielTudhope 5 101
(David O'Meara) *trckd ldrs on inner: hdwy 3f out: led 2f out: sn rdn and hdd appr fnl f: drvn and hung rt ins fnl f: kpt on same pce* **20/1**
0-52 **4** 4 ½ **Open Water (FR)**[14] 6957 4-9-0 **83**.......... DavidProbert 10 83
(Andrew Balding) *trckd ldrs: hdwy over 3f out: rdn along 2f out: sn drvn and one pce* **15/2**
0602 **5** 2 ½ **Amaze**[7] 7131 5-8-12 **81**.......... TomEaves 3 77
(Brian Ellison) *dwlt and hld up towards rr: hdwy 3f out: chsd ldrs 2f out: sn rdn and one pce appr fnl f* **6/1**[2]
2302 **6** 1 ¼ **Fennell Bay (IRE)**[8] 7115 4-9-9 **92**.......... GrahamLee 7 85
(Mark Johnston) *cl up: led 3f out: rdn and hdd 2f out: sn drvn and wknd over 1f out* **16/1**
100 **7** 2 ½ **Snow Trooper**[28] 6537 5-9-1 **84**.......... RobertWinston 14 73
(Dean Ivory) *hld up in rr: hdwy on wd outside over 3f out: rdn to chse ldrs over 2f out: sn drvn and one pce* **16/1**
2500 **8** 6 **Carry On Sydney**[102] 4084 3-8-10 **84**.......... PatDobbs 12 62
(Richard Hannon) *cl up on outer: effrt to dispute ld 3f out: rdn along over 2f out: sn drvn and wknd* **10/1**
0040 **9** 4 ½ **Prompter**[18] 5894 6-9-5 **88**.......... PaulHanagan 13 58
(Jonjo O'Neill) *in tch: hdwy and cl up 3f out: rdn over 2f out: sn drvn and btn* **20/1**
0001 **10** 7 **Weapon Of Choice (IRE)**[17] 6868 5-9-5 **88**.......... TomQueally 1 45
(Stuart Kittow) *hld up: a towards rr* **12/1**
0504 **11** 7 **Zafisio (IRE)**[26] 6596 7-8-11 **80**.......... GrahamGibbons 8 25
(Jo Hughes) *sn led: rdn along 4f out: hdd 3f out and sn wknd* **10/1**
6010 **12** 9 **Hunting Rights (USA)**[26] 6596 3-8-7 **81**.......... AdrianNicholls 9 9
(Mark Johnston) *midfierld: pushed along bef 1/2-way: sn lost pl and bhd* **25/1**
1125 **13** 1 ½ **Sadiq**[47] 5944 3-8-12 **86**..........(p) SilvestreDeSousa 11 12
(Saeed bin Suroor) *prom: effrt and cl up 4f out: rdn along 3f out: drvn 2f out and sn wknd* **7/1**[3]

2m 18.94s (4.64) **Going Correction** +0.675s/f (Yiel)
WFA 3 from 4yo+ 5lb **13** Ran SP% **120.5**
Speed ratings (Par 107): **108,107,107,103,101 100,98,93,90,84 79,71,70**
toteswingers 1&2 £6.70, 1&3 £29.70, 2&3 £44.00 CSF £35.29 CT £576.35 TOTE £7.00: £2.10, £1.40, £13.20; EX 46.50 Trifecta £1110.20 Part won. Pool: £1480.33 - 0.90 winning units..
Owner Godolphin **Bred** Darley **Trained** Newmarket, Suffolk

FOCUS
A good-quality handicap in which the runners headed centre-field in the straight. A small personal best from the winner.

7313 FORTINET SILVER PARTNER H'CAP (DIV I) 5f 13y
4:50 (4:51) (Class 4) (0-85,85) 3-Y-O+ £4,851 (£1,443; £721; £360) Stalls High

Form RPR
2321 **1** **Da'Quonde (IRE)**[32] 6388 5-9-1 **79**.......... GrahamLee 5 93
(Bryan Smart) *w ldr centre: led over 1f out: hld on wl clsng stages* **6/1**[2]
4006 **2** 1 **Even Stevens**[26] 6583 5-9-6 **84**..........(p) RobertWinston 4 94
(Scott Dixon) *chsd ldrs: wnt 2nd appr fnl f: styd on same pce* **10/1**
1461 **3** 2 ½ **Monsieur Jamie**[32] 6412 5-8-12 **76**..........(v) MichaelO'Connell 16 77+
(J R Jenkins) *chsd ldrs: swtchd lft over 1f out: kpt on same pce: tk 3rd post* **5/1**[1]
2-00 **4** shd **Senator Bong**[28] 6527 3-8-9 **73**.......... ChrisCatlin 12 75
(David Elsworth) *w ldrs stands' side: kpt on same pce appr fnl f* **10/1**
U410 **5** 2 **Master Bond**[16] 6908 4-9-1 **79**.......... DanielTudhope 13 72
(David O'Meara) *chsd ldrs: drvn over 2f out: wknd appr fnl f* **5/1**[1]
3000 **6** nk **Lupo D'Oro (IRE)**[34] 6331 4-9-6 **84**.......... JamesDoyle 11 76
(John Best) *in rr: hdwy 2f out: nvr nr ldrs* **12/1**
0060 **7** 1 ¼ **Compton**[7] 7123 4-9-0 **78**..........(v) PJMcDonald 6 66
(Robert Cowell) *led towards centre: hdd over 1f out: sn wknd* **7/1**[3]
0000 **8** nse **West Leake Diman (IRE)**[34] 6331 4-9-5 **83**.......... TomQueally 14 71
(Charles Hills) *stmbld s: in rr: sme hdwy 2f out: nvr a factor* **16/1**
0-04 **9** ½ **Ruby's Day**[18] 6848 4-9-1 **79**.......... PaulHanagan 17 65
(David Brown) *in rr: sme hdwy 2f out: nvr on terms* **6/1**[2]
0010 **10** nk **Hazelrigg (IRE)**[15] 6920 8-8-13 **77**..........(e) DavidAllan 3 62
(Tim Easterby) *chsd ldrs outer: lost pl over 1f out* **14/1**
3000 **11** 2 ¾ **Aubrietia**[24] 6665 4-9-7 **85**..........(v) AndrewMullen 7 60
(Alan McCabe) *mid-div: drvn 3f out: wknd 2f out* **16/1**
0000 **12** 4 **Strange Magic (IRE)**[26] 6583 3-9-1 **79**.......... TonyHamilton 2 41
(Richard Fahey) *mid-div on outer: drvn over 2f out: sn lost pl* **33/1**

1m 2.26s (0.76) **Going Correction** +0.325s/f (Good) **12** Ran SP% **121.7**
Speed ratings (Par 105): **106,104,100,100,97 96,94,94,93,93 88,82**
toteswingers 1&2 £8.20, 1&3 £4.40, 2&3 £11.90 CSF £66.70 CT £333.01 TOTE £5.00: £1.50, £3.60, £1.50; EX 54.90 Trifecta £225.40 Pool: £2086.30 - 6.94 winning units..
Owner The Barber Girls **Bred** Gestut Sohrenhof **Trained** Hambleton, N Yorks

FOCUS
The runners came centre-to-stands' side in what was a fair sprint. The time was good compared with division II.

7314 FORTINET SILVER PARTNER H'CAP (DIV II) 5f 13y
5:20 (5:21) (Class 4) (0-85,85) 3-Y-O+ £4,851 (£1,443; £721; £360) Stalls High

Form RPR
5000 **1** **Cheveton**[18] 6831 9-9-0 **78**.......... SaleemGolam 17 88
(Richard Price) *in tch: hdwy 2f out: rdn and qcknd to ld ins fnl f: sn edgd lft and kpt on wl towards fin* **5/1**[2]
5113 **2** ½ **Ambitious Icarus**[14] 6948 4-8-13 **77**..........(e) RobbieFitzpatrick 9 85
(Richard Guest) *in rr: hdwy 2f out: rdn over 1f out: str run ent fnl f: kpt on* **14/1**
2223 **3** 1 **Millkwood**[14] 6940 3-8-11 **75**..........(tp) PJMcDonald 13 81
(John Davies) *towards rr: hdwy wl over 1f out: rdn and styd on fnl f: nrst fin* **14/1**
5254 **4** 1 ½ **Gowanharry (IRE)**[26] 6583 4-8-8 **77**.......... ConnorBeasley(5) 14 76
(Michael Dods) *trckd ldrs: hdwy to ld over 1f out: rdn and hdd ins fnl f: sn drvn and one pce* **9/2**[1]
1600 **5** 1 **Noodles Blue Boy**[23] 6699 7-9-1 **79**..........(p) TomEaves 10 75
(Ollie Pears) *in tch: hdwy to chse ldrs wl over 1f out: sn rdn and one pce fnl f* **33/1**
4100 **6** ½ **Threes Grand**[26] 6583 3-9-5 **83**.......... TomQueally 12 78
(Scott Dixon) *cl up: rdn wl over 1f out and ev ch tl drvn and wknd ent fnl f* **14/1**
0100 **7** hd **Bronze Beau**[18] 6848 6-8-10 **79**..........(tp) JacobButterfield(5) 6 72
(Kristin Stubbs) *led: rdn along 2f out: hdd over 1f out: kpt on same pce fnl f* **33/1**
0040 **8** 2 **Mary's Daughter**[26] 6586 3-8-11 **80**.......... GeorgeChaloner(5) 11 67
(Richard Fahey) *in rr and rdn along bef 1/2-way: hdwy over 1f out: kpt on fnl f: nvr nr ldrs* **6/1**[3]
0200 **9** ½ **Rusty Rocket (IRE)**[18] 6826 4-9-7 **85**.......... TonyHamilton 16 69
(Paul Green) *chsd ldrs: rdn along 2f out: sn wknd* **16/1**
5204 **10** 2 ¼ **Flash City (ITY)**[62] 5441 5-9-1 **79**..........(vt) GrahamLee 5 55
(Bryan Smart) *chsd ldrs: rdn along wl over 1f out: sn btn* **25/1**
6051 **11** ¾ **R Woody**[18] 6850 6-8-9 **73**..........(v[1]) AdamBeschizza 8 46
(Robert Cowell) *chsd ldrs: rdn along 2f out: sn wknd* **16/1**
0202 **12** ½ **Towbee**[16] 6908 4-9-1 **79**..........(b) GrahamGibbons 2 50
(Michael Easterby) *cl up: rdn 2f out: wknd over 1f out* **10/1**
4435 **13** 1 ¼ **Silvanus (IRE)**[18] 6848 8-8-13 **77**.......... PaulHanagan 7 44
(Paul Midgley) *hld up in rr: swtchd lft and hdwy wl over 1f out: rdn appr fnl f: n.d* **8/1**
6000 **14** 2 ¼ **Chester Aristocrat**[18] 6831 4-9-2 **83**.......... JasonHart(3) 1 42
(Eric Alston) *dwlt and a bhd* **16/1**
3-00 **15** 4 ½ **Spokeswoman (IRE)**[23] 6692 3-9-0 **78**..........[1] JamesDoyle 3 22
(Saeed bin Suroor) *chsd ldrs: rdn along 2f out: sn wknd* **16/1**

1m 3.63s (2.13) **Going Correction** +0.525s/f (Yiel) **15** Ran SP% **122.6**
Speed ratings (Par 105): **103,102,100,98,96 95,95,92,91,87 86,85,83,80,73**
toteswingers 1&2 £27.40, 1&3 £20.60, 2&3 £22.40 CSF £73.02 CT £950.62 TOTE £6.10: £1.30, £4.60, £3.70; EX 87.00 Trifecta £1508.10 Part won. Pool: £2010.83 - 0.48 winning units..
Owner Mrs K Oseman **Bred** Miss K Rausing **Trained** Ullingswick, H'fords

FOCUS
Probably the lesser of the two divisions, and the time was slower. The winner is rated close to his form from this time last year.

7315 FORTINET BRONZE PARTNER H'CAP 5f 13y
5:50 (5:52) (Class 6) (0-65,65) 3-Y-O+ £1,940 (£577; £288; £144) Stalls High

Form RPR
2253 **1** **Ace Master**[13] 6969 5-8-11 **60**..........(b) IanBurns(5) 13 71
(Roy Bowring) *prom: hdwy over 2f out: chsd ldr over 1f out: styd on to ld towards fin* **8/1**
050 **2** ½ **New Decade**[33] 6368 4-9-5 **63**.......... RobertWinston 3 72
(Milton Bradley) *chsd ldrs: led over 2f out: hdd and no ex clsng stages* **16/1**
0000 **3** 2 **Mission Impossible**[1] 7282 8-9-3 **61**..........(p) DaleSwift 14 63
(Tracy Waggott) *in rr: hdwy over 2f out: kpt on same pce fnl f* **7/1**[3]
4004 **4** 1 ½ **Passionada**[68] 5227 4-9-7 **65**.......... GrahamLee 7 61
(Ed McMahon) *chsd ldrs: kpt on one pce over 1f out* **10/1**
006 **5** nse **Breezolini**[74] 4993 5-9-2 **65**.......... JacobButterfield(5) 4 61
(Ollie Pears) *mid-divfar side: hdwy far side over 2f out: kpt on same pce over 1f out* **10/1**
0440 **6** ½ **Danzoe (IRE)**[25] 6652 6-9-7 **65**..........(v) TomMcLaughlin 15 59
(Christine Dunnett) *in rr: hdwy over 2f out: swtchd stands' side over 1f out: styd on wl* **25/1**
3036 **7** 1 ¾ **Ishi Honest**[8] 7086 3-9-2 **60**..........(p) PaulHanagan 8 49
(Mark Usher) *towards rr: sme hdwy over 2f out: nvr nr ldrs* **12/1**
5005 **8** shd **Elusive Bonus (IRE)**[11] 7030 4-8-12 **61**.......... DavidBergin(5) 17 49
(David O'Meara) *chsd ldrs stands' side: drvn over 2f out: one pce* **4/1**[1]
4304 **9** nk **Prince Of Passion (CAN)**[9] 7068 5-9-2 **60**.......... RobbieFitzpatrick 6 47
(Derek Shaw) *chsd ldrs: wknd over 1f out* **25/1**
0002 **10** 1 **Monnoyer**[13] 6969 4-9-5 **63**..........(p) PJMcDonald 5 46
(Scott Dixon) *chsd ldrs: wknd over 1f out* **14/1**
2530 **11** 1 ¼ **Our Diane (IRE)**[6] 7150 3-9-3 **61**.......... TonyHamilton 16 41
(Richard Fahey) *chsd ldrs towards stands' side: drvn over 2f out: wknd over 1f out* **5/1**[2]
4024 **12** 1 ½ **Tuibama (IRE)**[14] 6945 4-9-2 **63**..........(p) JasonHart(3) 11 36
(Tracy Waggott) *chsd ldrs: wknd over 1f out* **16/1**
210 **13** 3 ¼ **Pastureyes**[43] 6075 3-9-6 **64**..........(p) TomQueally 9 26
(Scott Dixon) *a towards rr* **25/1**
0040 **14** 1 **El McGlynn (IRE)**[36] 6287 4-8-11 **62**.......... RachelRichardson(7) 1 20
(Eric Alston) *led: hdd over 2f out: sn lost pl and bhd* **16/1**
5046 **15** 4 ½ **Royal Award**[28] 6527 4-9-4 **65**.......... MatthewLawson(3) 12 7
(Jonathan Portman) *a towards rr* **25/1**

1m 4.03s (2.53) **Going Correction** +0.525s/f (Yiel) **15** Ran SP% **125.9**
Speed ratings (Par 101): **100,99,96,93,93 92,89,89,89,87 85,83,78,76,69**
toteswingers 1&2 £31.80, 1&3 £7.90, 2&3 £33.10 CSF £128.49 CT £954.05 TOTE £13.20: £3.10, £11.60, £3.20; EX 303.10 Trifecta £1253.10 Part won. Pool: £1670.84 - 0.02 winning units..
Owner S R Bowring **Bred** S R Bowring **Trained** Edwinstowe, Notts

FOCUS
They got racing a fair way out here although the first two were always prominent. A turf personal best from the winner.
T/Jkpt: Not won. T/Plt: £37.90 to a £1 stake. Pool: £75602.93 - 1454.37 winning tickets T/Qpdt: £9.00 to a £1 stake. Pool: £4528.61 - 368.52 winning tickets JR

7054 LONGCHAMP (R-H)
Wednesday, October 16

OFFICIAL GOING: Turf: soft

7316a PRIX DE SAINT-CYR (LISTED RACE) (3YO FILLIES) (TURF) 7f
1:05 (12:00) 3-Y-O £22,357 (£8,943; £6,707; £4,471; £2,235)

RPR
1 **Anazone (IRE)**[35] 3-8-9 0.......... FranckBlondel 7 106
(F Rossi, France) **3/1**[1]
2 nk **Key To Peace (IRE)**[35] 3-8-9 0.......... MaximeGuyon 3 105+
(A Fabre, France) *prom on outer: 4th 1/2-way: rdn to improve over 1f out: wnt 2nd ins fnl f: r.o and pressed wnr but a jst being hld* **63/10**
3 1 ¼ **Zejel**[60] 3-8-9 0.......... Pierre-CharlesBoudot 4 102
(C Ferland, France) **6/1**[3]

4 snk **Arch Duchess (FR)**[24] 3-8-9 0 AntoineHamelin 9 101
(A De Royer-Dupre, France) 13/1

5 3/4 **Penmaen (IRE)**[36] 3-8-9 0 FabienLefebvre 8 99+
(J E Hammond, France) 19/5[2]

6 1 3/4 **Morning Frost (IRE)**[52] 5806 3-8-13 0 JulienAuge 5 98
(C Ferland, France) 68/10

7 1 1/2 **Single (FR)**[25] 3-8-9 0 OlivierPeslier 2 90
(C Laffon-Parias, France) 12/1

8 1 1/2 **Dream Can True (IRE)**[22] 3-8-9 0 CristianDemuro 6 86
(L Riccardi, Italy) 36/1

9 1 1/4 **Snow Bell (FR)**[42] 6124 3-8-13 0 GregoryBenoist 10 87
(N Clement, France) 73/10

10 1 1/4 **Flawless Beauty**[19] 6819 3-8-9 0 (b) Christophe-PatriceLemaire 1 80
(Hugo Palmer) *trckd ldr on inner: 3rd 1/2-way: rdn 2f out: lost pl over 1f out: no ex and btn: eased and dropped to last towards fin* 67/1

1m 24.36s (3.66) 10 Ran SP% 117.7
WIN (incl. 1 euro stake): 4.00. PLACES: 1.50, 2.00, 2.00. DF: 13.20. SF: 27.30.
Owner Jean-Claude Seroul **Bred** Jean Claude Seroul **Trained** France

7086 BRIGHTON (L-H)

Thursday, October 17

OFFICIAL GOING: Soft (5.8)
Rail dolled out 3yds between 4.5f and 3f adding 4yds to race distances.
Wind: light to medium, across Weather: dry, sunny spells

7317 IRISH STALLION FARMS E B F MAIDEN STKS 5f 213y
1:40 (1:40) (Class 5) 2-Y-O £2,911 (£866; £432; £216) **Stalls** Centre

Form RPR

260 1 **Quickaswecan**[12] 7017 2-9-5 85 SilvestreDeSousa 1 82+
(Mark Johnston) *chsd ldr tl pushed into ld over 1f out: sn edgd rt to stands' rail: kpt on: eased towards fin* 1/7[1]

000 2 1 1/2 **Black Rodded**[26] 6644 2-9-0 62 PatDobbs 3 70
(Hughie Morrison) *dwlt: hld up in rr: rdn and effrt 2f out: chsd wnr over 1f out: kpt on but no real imp* 20/1[3]

3334 3 8 **Flicksta (USA)**[21] 6778 2-9-5 69 LukeMorris 4 51
(Ronald Harris) *led: rdn over 2f out: hdd over 1f out and sn btn: wknd 1f out* 8/1[2]

0 4 11 **Aussie Sky (IRE)**[41] 6160 2-9-0 0 ShaneKelly 2 13
(John Stimpson) *chsd ldrs: effrt to press ldr and racd nrest stands' rail 3f out: sn rdn and struggling: bhd over 1f out* 100/1

1m 14.24s (4.04) **Going Correction** +0.60s/f (Yiel) 4 Ran SP% 104.4
Speed ratings (Par 95): **97,95,84,69**
CSF £3.66 TOTE £1.10; EX 2.80 Trifecta £11.20 Pool: £1,157.27 - 77.39 winning units..
Owner Douglas Livingston **Bred** Mrs R D Peacock **Trained** Middleham Moor, N Yorks

FOCUS
A weak and uncompetitive maiden to start the card and the quartet predictably made for the traditional stands' rail route on the testing ground. Improved form from the second and the form could feasibly be worth another 5lb.

7318 32RED H'CAP (DIV I) 6f 209y
2:10 (2:10) (Class 5) (0-75,75) 3-Y-O+ £2,587 (£770; £384; £192) **Stalls** Centre

Form RPR

2620 1 **Charitable Act (FR)**[8] 7130 4-9-5 73 (b[1]) GeorgeBaker 6 83
(Gary Moore) *mde virtually: c to r against stands' rail over 3f out: hrd pressed and rdn over 1f out: edgd lft u.p ins fnl f: hld on wl: all out* 5/1[3]

0000 2 shd **Great Expectations**[8] 7130 5-9-4 72 NeilCallan 1 81
(J R Jenkins) *chsd ldrs: wnt 2nd 4f out: rdn and ev ch over 1f out: sustained duel w wnr and kpt on wl u.p fnl f: jst hld* 3/1[1]

1410 3 3 1/4 **Olney Lass**[18] 6871 6-9-1 72 SimonPearce(3) 4 72
(Lydia Pearce) *hld up in tch in last trio: effrt to chse ldng pair 2f out: drvn and styd on same pce fr over 1f out* 5/1[3]

1551 4 1 3/4 **Koharu**[9] 7086 3-8-10 66 6ex (t) SteveDrowne 8 61
(Peter Makin) *broke wl: sn stdd and hld up in rr: effrt to go 4th wl over 1f out: styd on same pce u.p fr over 1f out* 4/1[2]

4600 5 6 **Mister Musicmaster**[15] 6959 4-9-7 75 WilliamCarson 5 55
(Ron Hodges) *hld up in tch in midfield: effrt u.p over 2f out: struggling 2f out: sn wknd* 20/1

1420 6 3 1/2 **All Or Nothin (IRE)**[53] 5793 4-9-1 74 JoeyHaynes(5) 3 45
(Paddy Butler) *chsd ldrs: rdn and effrt over 2f out: sn struggling and btn wl over 1f out: sn wknd* 25/1

1200 7 15 **Rezwaan**[111] 3780 6-9-2 70 ShaneKelly 7
(Murty McGrath) *dwlt: hld up in rr: rdn and struggling 3f out: sn wknd: wl bhd and virtually p.u ins fnl f* 50/1

0412 8 3/4 **Bloodsweatandtears**[9] 7092 5-8-9 63 JimmyQuinn 9
(William Knight) *rdn along leaving stalls: chsd ldr tl 4f out: sn rdn and dropped to rr 3f out: lost tch 2f out and virtually p.u ins fnl f: t.o* 3/1[1]

1m 26.78s (3.68) **Going Correction** +0.60s/f (Yiel)
WFA 3 from 4yo+ 2lb 8 Ran SP% 113.9
Speed ratings (Par 103): **102,101,98,96,89 85,68,67**
toteswingers 1&2 £3.20, 2&3 £4.60, 1&3 £5.70 CSF £19.88 CT £78.40 TOTE £6.00: £1.50, £1.60, £2.40; EX 22.80 Trifecta £112.80 Pool: £1778.04 - 11.82 winning units..
Owner G A Jackman **Bred** Aleyrion Bloodstock Ltd **Trained** Lower Beeding, W Sussex

FOCUS
A modest handicap run in a length slower time than division II. The winner is rated back to his best.

7319 32RED H'CAP (DIV II) 6f 209y
2:40 (2:40) (Class 5) (0-75,75) 3-Y-O+ £2,587 (£770; £384; £192) **Stalls** Centre

Form RPR

4523 1 **Rocky Reef**[15] 6959 4-9-4 72 (b) PatDobbs 4 83
(Philip Hide) *in tch in midfield: hdwy and led racing against stands' rail over 2f out: rdn clr 2f out: styd on wl: comf* 5/2[1]

0040 2 3 3/4 **Sword In Hand**[36] 6306 4-9-2 70 LukeMorris 8 71
(Alan Jarvis) *hld up in last trio: rdn and hdwy to chse ldrs over 2f out: chsd clr wnr over 1f out: no imp: kpt on* 5/1

0402 3 5 **Uncle Dermot (IRE)**[9] 7093 5-8-9 63 JackMitchell 7 51
(Brendan Powell) *hld up in tch in last trio: rdn and hdwy in center 3f out: chsd clr wnr 2f out: outpcd and hung lft over 1f out: in 3rd and wknd fnl f* 4/1[2]

001U 4 2 **Bestfootforward**[9] 7086 4-8-2 61 oh5 ShelleyBirkett(5) 2 44
(Julia Feilden) *chsd ldrs: styd on ins 3f out: rdn and no ex over 2f out: 4th and wknd over 1f out* 7/1

/050 5 6 **Egotist (IRE)**[15] 6959 5-9-7 75 (t) AdamKirby 9 42
(Milton Bradley) *in tch in midfield: rdn and effrt 3f out: struggling u.p over 2f out: sn wknd* 50/1

135 6 15 **Decent Fella (IRE)**[90] 4496 7-9-5 73 (tp) GeorgeBaker 5
(Violet M Jordan) *pressed ldr tl led 3f out: sn hdd and btn: wl bhd over 1f out: eased ins fnl f* 8/1

6214 7 21 **Jimmy Elder**[82] 4772 3-9-2 72 DaneO'Neill 3
(Richard Hannon) *s.i.s: detached in last: clsd and effrt in centre 3f out: sn btn: t.o and virtually p.u after* 20/1

6100 8 28 **Orbison (IRE)**[47] 6003 3-9-4 74 NeilCallan 1
(Roger Varian) *dwlt: sn rcvrd to ld: rdn and hdd 3f out: sn dropped out: t.o and virtually plld fr over 1f out* 9/2[3]

1m 26.58s (3.48) **Going Correction** +0.60s/f (Yiel)
WFA 3 from 4yo+ 2lb 8 Ran SP% 113.8
Speed ratings (Par 103): **104,99,94,91,84 67,43,11**
toteswingers 1&2 £3.20, 2&3 £4.90, 1&3 £2.70 CSF £15.10 CT £47.35 TOTE £3.40: £1.70, £1.80, £1.50; EX 16.70 Trifecta £66.90 Pool: £2678.30 - 30.00 winning units..
Owner Mrs L E Ramsden & Richard Morecombe **Bred** Gary Sanderson **Trained** Findon, W Sussex

FOCUS
They finished well spread out in this division, for which the winning time was 0.2sec faster than the first leg. Little depth to the race but the winner looks back to his best.

7320 E B F STALLIONS/32RED.COM MEDIAN AUCTION MAIDEN STKS 7f 214y
3:10 (3:10) (Class 5) 2-Y-O £2,911 (£866; £432; £216) **Stalls** Centre

Form RPR

00 1 **Collaboration**[97] 4256 2-9-5 0 (t) DavidProbert 2 75
(Andrew Balding) *chsd ldrs: rdn to ld over 1f out: edgd lft u.p fnl f: hld on wl* 6/1

0 2 nk **Classical Art (IRE)**[14] 6975 2-9-5 0 AndreaAtzeni 11 74
(Roger Varian) *chsd ldrs: rdn and effrt 2f out: pressed ldrs over 1f out: ev ch and carried lft ins fnl f: r.o but jst hld* 11/4[1]

3 3 1 3/4 **Stosur (IRE)**[33] 6409 2-9-0 0 LukeMorris 10 65
(Gay Kelleway) *chsd ldrs: effrt u.p to chal over 1f out: stl pressing ldrs whn pushed lft wl ins fnl f: wknd towards fin* 7/2[2]

4 2 **Spectator** 2-9-2 0 ThomasBrown(3) 6 66+
(Andrew Balding) *s.i.s: pushed along in rr: hdwy against stands' rail 3f out: chsng ldrs whn nt clr run and swtchd lft over 1f out: no ex and one pce ins fnl f* 10/1

5 6 **Bishop Wulstan (IRE)** 2-9-5 0 PatDobbs 9 52
(Richard Hannon) *in tch in midfield: rdn and effrt over 2f out: outpcd and btn 2f out: plugged on but wl hld after* 5/1[3]

6 4 **Armourer (IRE)** 2-9-5 0 MartinDwyer 3 43
(William Muir) *s.i.s: hld up in rr: sme hdwy 3f out: no imp fnl 2f: plugged on* 12/1

5524 7 nk **Nakeeta**[46] 6014 2-9-5 69 SamHitchcott 4 42
(Mick Channon) *taken down early: led and racd keenly: wnt clr 1/2-way: rdn and hdd over 1f out: sn btn: fdd fnl f* 7/1

8 11 **Confucius Legend (IRE)** 2-9-5 0 NeilCallan 1 17
(Jim Boyle) *s.i.s: a bhd: lost tch 3f out* 50/1

0 9 1 3/4 **One Picture**[7] 7155 2-9-5 0 DaneO'Neill 8 13
(Richard Hannon) *chsd ldr tl 2f out: sn btn: eased ent fnl f* 33/1

3400 10 18 **Earl's Bridge**[17] 6897 2-9-5 50 (p) CathyGannon 7
(Bill Turner) *s.i.s: a bhd: lost tch 3f: t.o and eased over 1f out* 66/1

00 11 41 **Wildling**[29] 6528 2-9-0 0 PatCosgrave 5
(Jim Boyle) *in tch in midfield: rdn and dropped to rr 3f out: sn lost tch: t.o and virtually p.u over 1f out* 100/1

1m 41.52s (5.52) **Going Correction** +0.60s/f (Yiel) 11 Ran SP% 116.5
Speed ratings (Par 95): **96,95,93,91,85 81,81,70,68,50 9**
toteswingers 1&2 £4.70, 2&3 £3.00, 1&3 £5.70 CSF £22.39 TOTE £7.80: £2.20, £1.20, £2.80; EX 27.90 Trifecta £151.00 Pool: £2870.49 - 14.25 winning units..
Owner Another Bottle Racing 2 **Bred** Shareef Racing & Redmyre Bloodstock **Trained** Kingsclere, Hants

FOCUS
An ordinary maiden and quite a test in the ground. Improvement from the first two.

7321 MADISONSOLUTIONS.CO.UK H'CAP 1m 1f 209y
3:40 (3:41) (Class 6) (0-60,66) 3-Y-O+ £1,940 (£577; £288; £144) **Stalls** High

Form RPR

4004 1 **Smokey Oakey (IRE)**[9] 7091 9-9-1 54 SimonPearce(3) 16 62
(Mark H Tompkins) *hld up in tch in midfield: hdwy to chse ldrs and racing against stands' rail 3f out: led over 2f out: styd on wl fnl f: rdn out* 12/1

4515 2 1 1/2 **Sutton Sid**[9] 7091 3-9-3 58 (p) PatCosgrave 1 63
(Chris Gordon) *in tch in midfield: effrt u.p over 2f out: chsd ldrs and drvn over 1f out: kpt on: snatched 2nd on post* 7/1

4445 3 nse **Chasin' Rainbows**[5] 7201 5-9-1 51 DaneO'Neill 10 56
(Sylvester Kirk) *dwlt: hld up towards rr: hdwy against stands' rail over 3f out: rdn and chal over 1f out: no ex and one pce ins fnl f: lost 2nd on post* 6/1[3]

4602 4 1 1/4 **Attain**[29] 6518 4-8-10 51 (p) ShelleyBirkett(5) 11 54
(Julia Feilden) *chsd ldrs: rdn over 1f out: no ex and one pce fnl f* 10/1

6421 5 3 3/4 **Compton Bird**[9] 7091 4-9-11 66 6ex JoeyHaynes(5) 2 61+
(Hans Adielsson) *hld up in rr: hdwy in centre 3f out: drvn to chse ldrs over 1f out: no ex 1f out: wknd ins fnl f* 4/1[1]

500- 6 1/2 **Red Catkin**[388] 6534 3-9-3 58 TomQueally 8 52
(George Margarson) *hld up in last quartet: rdn and hdwy past btn horses in centre over 1f out: kpt on fnl f: nvr trbld ldrs* 5/1[2]

4604 7 2 **Megalala (IRE)**[9] 7090 12-9-2 52 KieranO'Neill 7 43
(John Bridger) *led: rdn and hdd over 2f out: no ex and btn over 1f out: wknd fnl f* 12/1

3150 8 3 3/4 **Mcconnell (USA)**[17] 6907 8-9-2 52 (b) GeorgeBaker 3 36
(Violet M Jordan) *hld up in midfield: rdn and effrt over 2f out: no ex and btn over 1f out: wknd fnl f* 25/1

4300 9 1 3/4 **Finlodex**[128] 3169 6-9-3 53 (v[1]) ShaneKelly 5 33
(Murty McGrath) *t.k.h: chsd ldrs: rdn and struggling over 2f out: wknd wl over 1f out* 33/1

000 10 2 3/4 **Ferryview Place**[6] 7163 4-9-3 56 MichaelJMMurphy(3) 4 31
(Ian Williams) *hld up in rr: rdn along over 5f out: wknd over 2f out: n.d* 12/1

1045 11 3 1/4 **Hawk Moth (IRE)**[9] 7092 5-9-10 60 (b) ChrisCatlin 6 29
(John Spearing) *hld up in last quartet: rdn and no hdwy over 2f out: sn wknd* 33/1

-000 12 3 1/2 **Bennelong**[9] 7090 7-9-5 55 (p) WilliamCarson 9 17
(Richard Rowe) *in tch in midfield: rdn and btn over 2f out: wknd and bhd whn swtchd rt over 1f out* 33/1

3000 13 nse **Salient**[23] 6737 9-9-1 51 SebSanders 12 13
(Michael Attwater) *chsd ldr tl 3f out: wknd u.p 2f out: bhd fnl f* 33/1

The Form Book Flat, Raceform Ltd, Compton, RG20 6NL.

0105 **14** *15* **Szabo's Art**[49] 5935 3-9-1 **56**...(p) LukeMorris 14
(Sir Mark Prescott Bt) *in tch in midfield: rdn and no hdwy over 2f out: wl btn whn hung lft over 1f out: bhd and eased ins fnl f* **6/1**[3]

2m 9.56s (5.96) **Going Correction** +0.60s/f (Yiel)
WFA 3 from 4yo+ 5lb **14** Ran SP% **125.5**
Speed ratings (Par 101): **100,98,98,97,94 94,92,89,88,86 83,80,80,68**
toteswingers 1&2 £10.80, 2&3 £8.60, 1&3 £14.50 CSF £93.10 CT £561.05 TOTE £14.80: £3.90, £1.70, £2.90; EX 113.30 Trifecta £391.50 Pool: £2954.09 - 5.64 winning units..
Owner Judi Dench and Bryan Agar **Bred** Hyde Park Stud **Trained** Newmarket, Suffolk

FOCUS
A moderate handicap and another indication of just how big an advantage getting the stands' rail was. The first two both improved a bit on their recent C&D efforts.

7322 32RED CASINO H'CAP 7f 214y
4:10 (4:11) (Class 6) (0-60,65) 3-Y-0 **£1,940** (£577; £288; £144) **Stalls** Centre

Form RPR

2251 **1** **Sword Of The Lord**[9] 7093 3-9-9 **65** 6ex.... WilliamTwiston-Davies(3) 10 76
(Michael Bell) *s.i.s: hld up in rr main gp: clsd and nt clr run 3f out: trcking ldrs and swtchd sharply rt 2f out: swtchd lft over 1f out: chal and awkward hd carriage ins fnl f: led and lft clr fnl 100yds* **10/11**[1]

4400 **2** *1 3/4* **Khelac**[37] 6276 3-9-7 **60**...(be) PatDobbs 6 68
(Philip Hide) *sn bustled along to ld: c to r against stands' rail 3f out: drvn over 1f out: hrd pressed ins fnl f: hdd whn hit rail and unbalanced fnl 100yds: nt rcvr* **7/1**[3]

3003 **3** *7* **Minimee**[11] 6968 3-9-2 **55**..(v) LukeMorris 12 46
(Phil McEntee) *chsd ldrs: wnt 2nd 4f out tl ent fnl f: sn wknd* **16/1**

-060 **4** *2* **Norphin**[35] 6321 3-9-4 **57**.. PatCosgrave 8 43
(Denis Coakley) *dwlt: hld up in rr: rdn and effrt over 2f out: chsd ldrs over 1f out: wknd fnl f* **10/1**

3606 **5** *1/2* **Mick Dundee (IRE)**[14] 6968 3-9-5 **58**...........................(bt) AdamKirby 11 43
(John Ryan) *in tch in midfield: hdwy to chse ldrs over 2f out: stl travelling wl enough whn bdly hmpd and pushed into rail 2f out: nt rcvr and wl hld after* **25/1**

-060 **6** *1 1/4* **Birdie King**[58] 5602 3-9-4 **57**... GeorgeBaker 7 39
(Gary Moore) *taken down early: s.i.s: bhd: rdn 3f out: no real imp: n.d* **16/1**

4003 **7** *3/4* **Magic Lando (FR)**[10] 7082 3-9-7 **60**...............................(v) DavidProbert 3 41
(Ismail Mohammed) *in tch in midfield: hdwy u.p to chse ldrs 2f out: no ex and btn jst over 1f out: sn wknd* **4/1**[2]

0606 **8** *2 1/2* **Shikamoo**[97] 4240 3-8-8 **47**.. RichardThomas 2 22
(Dr Jeremy Naylor) *in tch in midfield: rdn and struggling 3f out: wknd 2f out* **66/1**

0034 **9** *10* **Perseverent Pete (USA)**[20] 6804 3-8-7 **46** oh1.................. KierenFox 1
(Christine Dunnett) *taken down early: chsd ldr tl 4f out: wknd u.p over 2f out* **20/1**

1330 **10** *80* **Actonetaketwo**[155] 2362 3-9-0 **53**................................ WilliamCarson 5
(Ron Hodges) *in tch in midfield: rdn and struggling over 3f out: sn wknd: wl t.o and virtually p.u over 1f out* **33/1**

1m 41.06s (5.06) **Going Correction** +0.60s/f (Yiel) **10** Ran SP% **118.8**
Speed ratings (Par 99): **98,96,89,87,86 85,84,82,72,**
toteswingers 1&2 £2.70, 2&3 £14.10, 1&3 £6.00 CSF £7.69 CT £67.28 TOTE £2.00: £1.30, £2.20, £2.50; EX 8.00 Trifecta £78.80 Pool: £2978.64 - 28.34 winning units..
Owner Saleh Al Homaizi & Imad Al Sagar **Bred** Mrs Mary Taylor And James F Taylor **Trained** Newmarket, Suffolk
■ Stewards' Enquiry : William Twiston-Davies seven-day ban: careless riding (Oct 31-Nov 2,4,5-7)

FOCUS
A moderate handicap, but not without incident. The winner is open to improvement and the second is rated back to soemthing like his best.

7323 32RED ON APP STORE H'CAP 5f 213y
4:40 (4:40) (Class 6) (0-55,55) 3-Y-0+ **£2,045** (£603; £302) **Stalls** Centre

Form RPR

6036 **1** **Ficelle (IRE)**[32] 6436 4-8-12 **46**...................................(p) CathyGannon 8 56+
(Ronald Harris) *towards rr: rdn over 2f out: hdwy u.p in centre over 1f out: str chal u.p and edging rt ins fnl f: led cl home* **14/1**

4663 **2** *nk* **Ishiamiracle**[35] 6323 4-8-12 **46**...................................(p) DavidProbert 14 55
(Phil McEntee) *led: c to r against stands' rail 3f out: forged ahd u.p 1f out: hrd pressed and battled on wl ins fnl f: hdd and no ex cl home* **9/2**[1]

0006 **3** *1 1/4* **Cristaliyev**[17] 6901 5-8-9 **46** oh1..........................(p) DeclanBates(3) 15 51
(David Evans) *in tch in midfield: effrt u.p to chse ldrs over 1f out: kpt on same pce ins fnl f* **14/1**

/541 **4** *2 1/2* **Coalburn**[32] 6436 5-9-0 **51**...(v) SimonPearce(3) 1 49
(Gary Harrison) *broke fast to press ldr: c across towards stands' rail: ev ch and wandered u.p over 1f out: no ex 1f out: wknd ins fnl f* **6/1**[2]

65 **5** *1/2* **Diamond Vine (IRE)**[17] 6901 5-9-7 **55**............................(v) LukeMorris 4 51
(Ronald Harris) *in tch in midfield: rdn 1/2-way: hdwy to chse ldrs over 1f out: no ex and edgd lft 1f out: wknd fnl 100yds* **8/1**

0546 **6** *1 1/4* **Hamis Al Bin (IRE)**[14] 6980 4-9-7 **55**.............................(t) AdamKirby 10 48
(Milton Bradley) *hld up in midfield: rdn and hdwy wl over 1f out: n.m.r 1f out: no hdwy ins fnl f* **7/1**[3]

5604 **7** *1 1/2* **Christopher Chua (IRE)**[15] 6930 4-8-12 **49** WilliamTwiston-Davies(3) 13 37
(Michael Scudamore) *stdd after s: hld up towards rr: rdn and hdwy over 1f out: nt clr run 1f out: no ex 1f out: wknd and eased towards fin* **16/1**

2456 **8** *nk* **Sally Bruce**[2] 7265 3-8-10 **52**................................. JenniferFerguson(7) 9 39
(Edward Creighton) *dwlt: sn pushed up into midfield: rdn and hdwy to chse ldrs over 1f out: no ex 1f out: wknd ins fnl f* **10/1**

4340 **9** *nk* **Microlight**[124] 3325 5-8-12 **46** oh1..............................(b) KirstyMilczarek 5 32
(John E Long) *s.i.s: bhd: sme hdwy u.p 2f out: no imp fnl f* **14/1**

0-00 **10** *hd* **Zed Candy Girl**[61] 5517 3-8-12 **47**.................................. ShaneKelly 2 33
(John Stimpson) *in tch in midfield: effrt 2f out: chsd ldrs over 1f out: no ex and btn 1f out: wknd ins fnl f* **16/1**

6356 **11** *1* **Surrey Dream (IRE)**[10] 7068 4-8-12 **46**.....................(p) SamHitchcott 16 29
(John Bridger) *chsd ldrs: rdn and no ex 2f out: lost pl over 1f out: wknd fnl f* **25/1**

0530 **12** *3/4* **Chelsea Grey (IRE)**[17] 6902 3-8-6 **46** oh1.................(b) PhilipPrince(5) 6 26
(Ronald Harris) *racd in midfield: rdn and no hdwy over 2f out: wknd over 1f out* **25/1**

3660 **13** *1 1/4* **Flaxen Lake**[45] 6033 6-8-12 **46** oh1...............................(p) ChrisCatlin 11 23
(Milton Bradley) *a bhd* **33/1**

-000 **14** *1/2* **Fit For A King (IRE)**[9] 7086 3-8-11 **46**........................ WilliamCarson 12 21
(John Best) *in tch in midfield: rdn and effrt 3f out: wknd wl over 1f out* **33/1**

1300 **15** *4 1/2* **Blue Clumber**[17] 6902 3-9-1 **50**.. JimmyQuinn 7 12
(Shaun Harris) *chsd ldrs tl 2f out: sn btn and wknd over 1f out* **20/1**

0035 **16** *3 1/4* **Coach Montana (IRE)**[51] 5869 4-8-12 **46** oh1...........(b) FrederikTylicki 3
(Jane Chapple-Hyam) *chsd ldrs: rdn over 2f out: unable qck and wandered u.p over 1f out: fdd fnl f* **8/1**

1m 15.23s (5.03) **Going Correction** +0.60s/f (Yiel)
WFA 3 from 4yo+ 1lb **16** Ran SP% **126.4**
Speed ratings (Par 101): **90,89,87,84,83 82,80,79,79,79 77,76,75,74,68 64**
toteswingers 1&2 £22.00, 2&3 £15.10, 1&3 £44.40 CSF £73.76 CT £966.72 TOTE £22.90: £5.10, £1.80, £5.30, £1.20; EX 132.20 Trifecta £1189.20 Part won. Pool: £1585.62 - 0.17 winning units..
Owner Brian Hicks **Bred** Tally-Ho Stud **Trained** Earlswood, Monmouths
■ Stewards' Enquiry : Cathy Gannon two-day ban: used whip above permitted level (Oct 31-Nov 1)

FOCUS
A big field for this moderate sprint handicap, but competitive enough. The form is rated as straightforward but the winner is perhaps worth extra credit.

7324 £32 FREE AT 32RED.COM H'CAP 5f 59y
5:10 (5:11) (Class 5) (0-75,74) 3-Y-0+ **£2,587** (£770; £384; £192) **Stalls** Centre

Form RPR

6026 **1** **Waseem Faris (IRE)**[22] 6745 4-9-7 **74**............................ GeorgeBaker 3 82
(Mick Channon) *hld up in tch in midfield: clsd to press ldr and shkn up 1f out: rdn to ld wl ins fnl f: fnd enough to hold rival cl home: rdn out* **7/2**[1]

4145 **2** *hd* **Ladweb**[33] 6412 3-8-8 **66**.. JoeyHaynes(5) 1 74
(John Gallagher) *chsd ldr tl led over 2f out: rdn over 2f out: drvn and hdd wl ins fnl f: r.o but hld cl home* **10/1**

0002 **3** *2 1/2* **Cardinal**[31] 6461 8-9-2 **69**.. PatDobbs 2 68
(Robert Cowell) *hld up towards rr: hdwy u.p over 1f out: kpt on to go 3rd towards fin* **5/1**

1210 **4** *1/2* **Threave**[14] 6982 5-9-7 **74**..(t) AdamKirby 7 71
(Violet M Jordan) *led tl over 2f out: sn rdn and unable qck over 1f out: wknd ins fnl f* **4/1**[2]

4065 **5** *1* **Whitecrest**[33] 6381 5-9-7 **74**.. ChrisCatlin 9 67
(John Spearing) *broke fast but stmbld leaving stalls: chsd ldrs tl lost pl u.p ent fnl 2f: swtchd lft 1f out: one pce after* **9/2**[3]

2U32 **6** *1/2* **Griffin Point (IRE)**[10] 7068 6-8-10 **63**.........................(b) WilliamCarson 4 55
(William Muir) *chsd ldrs: rdn and unable qck 2f out: no ex ent fnl f: wknd fnl 150yds* **5/1**

4006 **7** *hd* **Lager Time (IRE)**[17] 6900 3-8-10 **66**............................... DeclanBates(3) 5 58
(David Evans) *hld up in rr: swtchd lft and sme hdwy: rdr dislocated shoulder and unable to offer much assistance fr over 1f out: no ex and btn ins fnl f* **20/1**

0150 **8** *1 1/4* **Exotic Guest**[30] 6506 3-9-4 **71**.. TomQueally 8 58
(George Margarson) *in tch in last pair: effrt u.p wl over 1f out: no imp* **8/1**

1m 6.18s (3.88) **Going Correction** +0.60s/f (Yiel) **8** Ran SP% **118.7**
Speed ratings (Par 103): **92,91,87,86,85 84,84,82**
toteswingers 1&2 £4.90, 2&3 £8.40, 1&3 £3.80 CSF £40.45 CT £159.25 TOTE £3.30: £1.30, £2.10, £2.00; EX 33.50 Trifecta £291.20 Pool: £2866.35 - 7.38 inning units..
Owner Living Legend Racing Partnership 1 **Bred** Rabbah Bloodstock Limited **Trained** West Ilsley, Berks

FOCUS
An ordinary sprint handicap which saw a cool piece of riding from George Baker aboard the winner. Ordinary form, the winner to this year's best.
T/Plt: £24.50 to a £1 stake. Pool of £60471.21 - 1797.54 winning tickets. T/Qpdt: £8.80 to a £1 stake. Pool of £5206.32 - 434.80 winning tickets. SP

[7292] KEMPTON (A.W) (R-H)
Thursday, October 17

OFFICIAL GOING: Standard
Wind: Nil Weather: Bright early, getting dark

7325 JUMP RACING HERE ON SUNDAY CLAIMING STKS 1m (P)
5:20 (5:22) (Class 6) 3-Y-0 **£1,940** (£577; £288; £144) **Stalls** Low

Form RPR

3341 **1** **Poitin**[43] 6113 3-9-0 62.. JamesDoyle 5 74
(Harry Dunlop) *trckd ldrs: led ins fnl 2f: drvn out* **16/1**

35 **2** *1* **Caerwyn**[52] 5845 3-8-11 0.. MartinDwyer 9 69
(Marcus Tregoning) *in rr: rdn over 2f out: styd on u.p fnl f to take 2nd in clsng stages: no imp on wnr* **10/1**

2153 **3** *1* **Taxiformissbyron**[17] 6907 3-8-12 67................................. JoeFanning 4 67
(Michael Herrington) *chsd ldrs: chal ins fnl 2f: chsd wnr fnl f but no imp: lost 2nd in clsng stages* **8/1**[3]

323 **4** *1 1/2* **Gabrial The Boss (USA)**[13] 6998 3-9-1 73................(t) JamieSpencer 3 67
(David Simcock) *towards rr: hdwy fr 3f out: styd on to chse ldrs over 1f out: sn no ex* **5/2**[2]

0600 **5** *2* **Operation Chariot (IRE)**[18] 6871 3-9-4 75.............. ThomasBrown(3) 1 68
(Andrew Balding) *in rr: hdwy and rdn 2f out: nvr rchd ldrs and wl hld fnl f* **9/4**[1]

600 **6** *7* **Continental Divide (IRE)**[26] 6657 3-8-11 65.........(b[1]) FergusSweeney 7 42
(Jamie Osborne) *led after 1f: hdd & wknd ins fnl 2f* **16/1**

6640 **7** *2* **Tagalaka (IRE)**[15] 6933 3-8-8 58.......................................(b) JohnFahy 8 35
(Eve Johnson Houghton) *towards rr most of way* **25/1**

3100 **8** *3/4* **Jadesnumberone (IRE)**[28] 6556 3-9-0 69................... RichardHughes 6 39
(Michael Bell) *a in rr* **10/1**

3044 **9** *2* **Zain Spirit (USA)**[13] 6998 3-9-7 69..................................(p) NeilCallan 2 41
(Gerard Butler) *led 1f: chsd ldr: chal 2f out: wknd qckly wl over 1f out* **8/1**[3]

1m 38.56s (-1.24) **Going Correction** -0.10s/f (Stan) **9** Ran SP% **115.4**
Speed ratings (Par 99): **102,101,100,98,96 89,87,86,84**
toteswingers 1&2 £16.40, 2&3 £12.70, 1&3 £10.70 CSF £164.20 TOTE £27.00: £5.80, £4.10, £1.70; EX 124.80 Trifecta £1034.70 Pool: £1937.86 - 1.40 winning units..Caerwyn was claimed by A. W. Carroll £6000.
Owner David & Paul Hearson **Bred** David & Paul Hearson **Trained** Lambourn, Berks

FOCUS
A modest claimer in which they were soon strung out. The time was good compared with the following nursery. Modest improvement from the winner.

7326 DOWNLOAD BETVICTOR APP NURSERY H'CAP 1m (P)
5:50 (5:51) (Class 4) (0-85,83) 2-Y-0 **£3,752** (£1,116; £557; £278) **Stalls** Low

Form RPR

031 **1** **Spiritual Flame**[24] 6690 2-8-11 **73**...................................... RyanMoore 8 78+
(William Haggas) *hld up in rr: hdwy 2f out: drvn and qckcnd fnl f to take slt ld fnl 110yds: hld on all out* **5/1**[2]

11 **2** *shd* **Hiking (USA)**[61] 5524 2-9-4 **80**... JamesDoyle 6 84
(Roger Charlton) *trckd ldrs: drvn over 2f out: kpt on to ld 1f out: hdd fnl 110yds: styd chalng: no ex last strides* **6/4**[1]

024 **3** 1 ½ **Adore**[15] 6949 2-8-5 **67** .... AndreaAtzeni 2 67
(Sir Michael Stoute) *chsd ldrs: drvn to chal 1f out: nt gng pce of ldng duo fnl 150yds* **6/1**[3]

4042 **4** 1 ½ **Heska (IRE)**[9] 7113 2-8-5 **67** .... JoeFanning 3 64
(Mick Channon) *led after 1f: rdn over 2f out: hdd 1f out: wknd ins fnl f* **8/1**

3361 **5** 2 ½ **Edge (IRE)**[47] 5995 2-9-5 **81** .... RichardHughes 7 72
(Richard Hannon) *in tch: rdn and hdwy to chse ldrs appr fnl f wknd fnl 150yds* **6/1**[3]

541 **6** ¾ **Ninety Minutes (IRE)**[24] 6689 2-9-0 **76** .... SteveDrowne 5 65
(John Best) *in rr but in tch: rdn over 3f out: nvr gng pce to rch ldrs* **14/1**

1023 **7** 2 **Xanthos**[19] 6844 2-9-7 **83** .... TomMcLaughlin 4 68
(Ed Walker) *t.k.h: led 1f: chsd ldrs: wknd over 1f out* **12/1**

1m 39.61s (-0.19) **Going Correction** -0.10s/f (Stan) 7 Ran SP% **110.7**
Speed ratings (Par 97): **96,95,94,92,90 89,87**
toteswingers 1&2 £1.80, 2&3 £2.20, 1&3 £3.40 CSF £12.09 CT £42.05 TOTE £4.90: £2.10, £1.40; EX 11.90 Trifecta £66.20 Pool: £2535.80 - 28.69 winning units..
Owner Cheveley Park Stud **Bred** Cheveley Park Stud Ltd **Trained** Newmarket, Suffolk

FOCUS
A good little nursery dominated by fillies from good stables. The first two looked nicely treated and both improved.

7327 £25 FREE BET AT BETVICTOR.COM MAIDEN AUCTION STKS 7f (P)
6:20 (6:21) (Class 5) 2-Y-O **£2,587** (£770; £384; £192) **Stalls** Low

Form RPR

0 **1** **New Row**[30] 6500 2-8-11 0 .... RobertHavlin 2 74+
(William Jarvis) *s.i.s: sn trcking ldrs: wnt 2nd 2f out: drvn to ld fnl 150yds: kpt on wl* **15/2**

04 **2** 1 **Red Cossack (CAN)**[24] 6689 2-9-2 0 .... JimmyFortune 5 76
(Paul Webber) *sn led: drvn over 1f out: hdd fnl 150yds: kpt on: nt gng pce of wnr* **7/2**[1]

2440 **3** 3 ½ **Bonjour Steve**[89] 4519 2-8-12 66 .... LiamJones 3 63
(J S Moore) *chsd ldrs: rdn to go 2nd over 3f out tl 2f out: outpcd fnl f* **7/1**

6045 **4** shd **Christmas Wish**[23] 6724 2-8-10 58 .... MartinHarley 7 61
(Mick Channon) *in tch: on outer: drvn and outpcd 3f out: kpt on again fr over 1f out* **6/1**[3]

4 **5** shd **Softly She Treads (IRE)**[53] 5790 2-8-6 0 .... JemmaMarshall(3) 4 59
(Pat Phelan) *sn pushed along in rr: styd on fr over 1f out: kpt on fnl f* **6/1**[3]

6462 **6** 3 **Moonspring (IRE)**[16] 6923 2-8-9 66 .... MartinLane 6 52
(Tobias B P Coles) *in tch: pushed along and styd on same pce fnl 2f* **4/1**[2]

7 1 ¼ **Beakers N Num Nums (IRE)** 2-9-0 0 .... JoeFanning 9 53
(William Jarvis) *s.i.s: in rr: pushed along fr 3f out: a outpcd* **12/1**

8 9 **Amadiva (IRE)** 2-8-8 0 .... AndreaAtzeni 10 24
(Dean Ivory) *sn rdn and a wl bhd* **10/1**

05 **9** 6 **Copper Cavalier**[14] 6981 2-9-1 0 .... JamieSpencer 1 15
(Robert Cowell) *chsd ldrs: wknd ins fnl 3f* **33/1**

1m 26.06s (0.06) **Going Correction** -0.10s/f (Stan) 9 Ran SP% **114.8**
Speed ratings (Par 95): **95,93,89,89,89 86,84,74,67**
toteswingers 1&2 £5.70, 2&3 £6.00, 1&3 £12.60 CSF £33.73 TOTE £7.90: £1.90, £2.20, £2.40; EX 39.20 Trifecta £307.70 Pool: £1632.90 - 3.98 winning units..
Owner The New Row Partnership **Bred** Genesis Green Stud Ltd **Trained** Newmarket, Suffolk

FOCUS
A modest maiden rated around the third and fourth. The pace was sound and the winner has the scope to do better.

7328 BETVICTOR BACK OF THE NET OFFER MAIDEN STKS 6f (P)
6:50 (6:50) (Class 5) 2-Y-O **£2,587** (£770; £384; £192) **Stalls** Low

Form RPR

442 **1** **Merletta**[41] 6160 2-9-0 97 .... RyanMoore 4 78
(Jeremy Noseda) *led 1f: trckd ldr: led 2f out: kpt on wl fnl f and a doing enough* **11/8**[2]

2 **2** ¾ **Potentate (IRE)**[8] 7120 2-9-5 0 .... RichardHughes 7 81+
(Richard Hannon) *chsd ldrs: drvn over 2f out: chsd wnr over 1f out: kpt on u.p fnl 150yds but a hld* **4/5**[1]

3 4 **Celestial Knight** 2-9-5 0 .... ShaneKelly 3 69+
(James Fanshawe) *chsd ldr: drvn and outpcd over 2f out: styd on again over 1f out and kpt on to take 3rd fnl 110yds: no ch w ldng duo* **20/1**[3]

4 1 **Monsieur Lavene (IRE)** 2-9-5 0 .... KierenFox 2 66
(Robert Mills) *plld hrd early: in rr but in tch: drvn and hdwy over 1f out: kpt on fnl f: nvr a threat* **66/1**

00 **5** 1 **Excedo Praecedo**[14] 6975 2-9-5 0 .... JimCrowley 6 63
(Amanda Perrett) *led after 1f: hdd 2f out: wknd appr fnl f* **50/1**

6 7 **Crafted (IRE)** 2-9-5 0 .... JoeFanning 5 42
(Mark Johnston) *slowly away: sn rcvrd and in tch: rdn over 3f out: wknd over 2f out* **20/1**[3]

1m 13.03s (-0.07) **Going Correction** -0.10s/f (Stan) 6 Ran SP% **110.6**
Speed ratings (Par 95): **96,95,89,88,87 77**
toteswingers 1&2 £1.02, 2&3 £3.70, 1&3 £4.00 CSF £2.66 TOTE £2.70: £1.40, £1.10; EX 2.70 Trifecta £9.80 Pool: £2300.27 - 175.86 winning units..
Owner Cheveley Park Stud **Bred** Cheveley Park Stud Ltd **Trained** Newmarket, Suffolk

FOCUS
An interesting contest. The winner was fully entitled to win a race like this and the second should do better again from here.

7329 £25 FREE BET #BACKOFTHENET NURSERY H'CAP 6f (P)
7:20 (7:20) (Class 3) (0-95,89) 2-Y-O
£6,225 (£1,864; £932; £466; £233; £117) **Stalls** Low

Form RPR

2100 **1** **Meritocracy (IRE)**[79] 4855 2-9-3 **85** .... JamieSpencer 7 90
(Paul Cole) *in rr: hdwy on outer fr 2f out: str run u.p to ld fnl 110yds: kpt on wl* **10/1**

2101 **2** ½ **Musicora**[44] 6070 2-9-5 **87** .... RichardHughes 2 91
(Richard Hannon) *led: hdd over 3f out: drvn to ld again over 1f out: hdd and nt qckne fnl 110yds* **3/1**[1]

41 **3** ¾ **Dutch Interior**[22] 6746 2-8-12 **80** .... RyanMoore 6 81
(Gary Moore) *n.m.r and hmpd s: in rr: pushed along 2f out: stl last over 1f out: styd on wl fnl f to take 3rd in clsng stages and gaining on ldng duo nr fin but a jst hld* **3/1**[1]

045 **4** ¾ **Pure Amber (IRE)**[12] 7023 2-8-4 **72** .... JoeFanning 1 71
(Mark Johnston) *chsd ldrs: drvn over 2f out: one pce over 1f out: styd on again in clsng stages* **16/1**

144 **5** nk **Montaigne**[20] 6791 2-9-2 **84** .... JimCrowley 4 82
(Ralph Beckett) *chsd ldr: led over 3f out: drvn over 2f out: hdd over 1f out: outpcd ins fnl f* **7/2**[2]

4254 **6** 1 ¾ **Rosso Corsa**[15] 6955 2-9-7 **89** .... MartinHarley 5 82
(Mick Channon) *chsd ldrs: chal over 2f out: wknd fnl f* **6/1**

010 **7** 2 ¾ **Red Lady (IRE)**[118] 3522 2-9-6 **88** .... JimmyFortune 3 73
(Brian Meehan) *t.k.h: chsd ldrs: wknd fr 1f out* **4/1**[3]

1m 12.68s (-0.42) **Going Correction** -0.10s/f (Stan) 7 Ran SP% **121.5**
Speed ratings (Par 99): **98,97,96,95,94 92,88**
toteswingers 1&2 £5.50, 2&3 £2.30, 1&3 £5.50 CSF £43.15 CT £117.09 TOTE £9.70: £3.90, £2.10; EX 32.00 Trifecta £153.50 Pool: £2196.92 - 10.73 winning units..
Owner Mrs Fitri Hay **Bred** Oghill House Stud **Trained** Whatcombe, Oxon

FOCUS
Not that strong a contest for the grade with the top weight rated 6lb below the race ceiling. The winner had been given a real chance by the handicapper and did not need to quite replicate his 5f form. The second and third are rated as improvers.

7330 FOLLOW US ON TWITTER @BETVICTOR H'CAP (LONDON MIDDLE DISTANCE SERIES QUALIFIER) 1m 3f (P)
7:50 (7:54) (Class 3) (0-90,90) 3-Y-O
£7,158 (£2,143; £1,071; £535; £267; £134) **Stalls** Low

Form RPR

1501 **1** **Gone Dutch**[20] 6802 3-8-10 **79** .... FrederikTylicki 11 88
(James Fanshawe) *chsd ldrs: drvn on inner over 2f out: led over 1f out: drvn fnl f: in command in clsng stages* **14/1**

1-41 **2** nk **Sweet Deal (IRE)**[22] 6743 3-8-12 **81** .... WilliamBuick 7 89
(Jeremy Noseda) *in rr but in tch: rdn on outside over 2f out: hdwy over 1f out: qcknd u.p fnl f to chse wnr in clsng stages but a hld* **4/1**[2]

-143 **3** ¾ **Majeed**[125] 3277 3-8-10 **79** .... JamieSpencer 2 86
(David Simcock) *in rr and sn pushed along: drvn over 4f out: gd hdwy on outside fr 2f out: kpt on fnl f to take 3rd: nt quite gng pce of ldng duo* **16/1**

131 **4** hd **Soryah (IRE)**[46] 6016 3-9-5 **88** .... RichardHughes 3 94
(Luca Cumani) *chsd ldr tl rdn over 2f out: sn one pce: kpt on again ins fnl* **12/1**

4133 **5** nse **Lyric Piece**[13] 7000 3-8-7 **76** oh3 .... (p) CathyGannon 6 82
(Sir Mark Prescott Bt) *led: rdn ins fnl 3f: hdd over 1f out: one pce ins fnl f* **25/1**

331 **6** 1 **Duchess Of Seville**[34] 6366 3-8-13 **82** .... MartinHarley 5 86
(Marco Botti) *chsd ldrs: rdn over 2f out: styd on same pce fnl f* **9/2**[3]

1260 **7** hd **One Pekan (IRE)**[82] 4765 3-9-0 **83** .... AndreaAtzeni 4 87
(Roger Varian) *chsd ldrs: rdn over 2f out: styd on same pce fr over 1f out* **10/1**

3043 **8** nk **Theodore Gericault (IRE)**[14] 6976 3-9-2 **85** .... RyanMoore 8 89
(Sir Michael Stoute) *in rr: pushed along: sme hdwy and n.m.r over 2f out: drvn and kpt on fnl f but nvr gng pce to rch ldrs* **11/4**[1]

400 **9** 8 **Granell (IRE)**[27] 6596 3-8-10 **79** .... (b) JimmyFortune 9 68
(Brian Meehan) *in rr rdn 3f out: wknd over 1f out: eased in clsng stages* **33/1**

2m 20.13s (-1.77) **Going Correction** -0.10s/f (Stan) 9 Ran SP% **101.0**
Speed ratings (Par 105): **102,101,101,101,101 100,100,99,94**
toteswingers 1&2 £6.30, 2&3 £5.90, 1&3 £9.60 CSF £49.48 CT £484.22 TOTE £13.50: £3.50, £1.80, £4.30; EX 61.60 Trifecta £451.90 Pool: £1495.02 - 2.48 winning units..
Owner The Ice Syndicate **Bred** Cheveley Park Stud Ltd **Trained** Newmarket, Suffolk

FOCUS
A good handicap, but one of the fancied runners, Autun, was withdrawn at the start (and now needs to pass a stalls test), and Lyric Piece set a muddling gallop. A bunch finish and some may be flattered, but a personal best from the winner.

7331 BOOK NOW FOR CHRISTMAS FESTIVAL H'CAP 2m (P)
8:20 (8:23) (Class 6) (0-60,60) 3-Y-O **£1,940** (£577; £288; £144) **Stalls** Low

Form RPR

0-42 **1** **Luckster**[34] 6363 3-8-13 **52** .... CathyGannon 4 57
(David Evans) *chsd ldrs: rdn over 2f out: styd on u.p to ld fnl 110yds: hld on wl* **11/2**[3]

046 **2** ½ **Bell'Arte (IRE)**[8] 7118 3-8-11 **50** .... (p) FergusSweeney 5 55
(Laura Mongan) *in rr but in tch: drvn and hdwy 2f out: styd on wl fnl f to chse wnr fnl 75yds but a hld* **50/1**

-503 **3** 1 ½ **Likelikelikelikeit**[23] 6717 3-8-9 **48** .... (b) LiamJones 1 51
(Mark H Tompkins) *chsd ldrs: led u.p ins fnl 2f: hdd and outpcd fnl 110yds* **33/1**

4344 **4** 1 **Point Of Control**[14] 6964 3-9-4 **57** .... (v) JamieSpencer 3 59
(Michael Bell) *in tch: hdwy 4f out: chsd ldrs u.p 2f out: styd on same pce fnl f* **8/1**

323 **5** 1 ¾ **Inherited**[10] 7081 3-9-4 **57** .... (p) LukeMorris 9 57
(Sir Mark Prescott Bt) *chsd ldr: u.p fr 3f out: styd on same pce fnl 2f* **4/1**[2]

0020 **6** ½ **Pink Mischief**[29] 6522 3-8-11 **50** .... JoeFanning 7 49
(Harry Dunlop) *s.i.s: in rr: pushed along over 2f out: kpt on fnl f* **20/1**

1325 **7** hd **Noor Al Haya (IRE)**[52] 5846 3-9-6 **59** .... KieranO'Neill 12 58
(Mark Usher) *in rr: hdwy over 2f out: nt clr run over 1f out: kpt on: nt rch ldrs* **16/1**

000 **8** 1 **Double Accord**[143] 2713 3-8-9 **48** .... SteveDrowne 6 46
(Anthony Honeyball) *chsd ldrs: rdn 3f out: wknd over 1f out* **14/1**

3000 **9** 2 ½ **Hanga Roa (IRE)**[11] 1879 3-8-8 **47** .... AndreaAtzeni 10 42
(Gary Moore) *led: hdd ins fnl 2f: btn sn after* **13/2**

5040 **10** 1 **Bold Assertion**[20] 6787 3-9-6 **59** .... (v) JamesDoyle 11 52
(John Best) *in rr: sme hdwy fr 2f out: styd on u.p fnl f: nvr rchd ldrs* **14/1**

3600 **11** 7 **Zhuba (IRE)**[20] 6788 3-9-7 **60** .... GeorgeBaker 2 45
(John Best) *chsd ldrs: wknd qckly wl over 1f out* **12/1**

-054 **12** 50 **Sweeping Rock (IRE)**[28] 6558 3-9-3 **56** .... WilliamBuick 8
(Marcus Tregoning) *chsd ldrs: wknd 3f out: eased whn no ch fnl 2f* **11/4**[1]

3m 29.73s (-0.37) **Going Correction** -0.10s/f (Stan) 12 Ran SP% **123.1**
Speed ratings (Par 99): **96,95,95,94,93 93,93,92,91,91 87,62**
toteswingers 1&2 £47.40, 2&3 £200.50, 1&3 £25.50 CSF £268.93 CT £8118.58 TOTE £8.60: £3.20, £10.20, £10.10; EX 361.60 Trifecta £1724.40 Pool: £2496.41 - 1.08 winning units..
Owner Miss E J Tanner **Bred** D J Weston **Trained** Pandy, Monmouths

FOCUS
A poor staying handicap in which loads were unproven over this trip. The form is rated on the negative side.

T/Plt: £155.10 to a £1 stake. Pool of £80920.0, - 380.76 winning tickets. T/Qpdt: £29.30 to a £1 stake. Pool of £12309.05 - 309.94 winning tickets. ST

[6828] HAYDOCK (L-H)

Friday, October 18

OFFICIAL GOING: Good to soft (soft in places) changing to soft after race 1 (2.20)

All races on Stands side Home straight. Races on Round course increased by 57yds except and 2m 45y race which increased by 63yds.

Wind: Moderate; half behind Weather: Overcast, light rain

7332 APOLLOBET ONLINE CASINO MAIDEN STKS — 1m 2f 95y

2:20 (2:21) (Class 5) 2-Y-O — £2,587 (£770; £384; £192) Stalls High

Form — RPR

63 **1** **Fun Mac (GER)**[11] 7061 2-9-5 0 .... RichardHughes 8 — 81
(Hughie Morrison) *hld up in rr: hdwy on outer 3f out: chal over 1f out: hung bdly rt and led jst ins fnl f: styd on wl* — 10/3[2]

5 **2** 2¾ **Personal Opinion**[20] 6829 2-9-5 0 .... MickaelBarzalona 3 — 76
(Charlie Appleby) *hld up in rr: hdwy over 3f out: led 2f out: hdd and no ex jst ins fnl f* — 7/2[3]

0 **3** ½ **Battersea**[13] 7019 2-9-5 0 .... AndreaAtzeni 1 — 75
(Roger Varian) *chsd ldrs: upsides over 1f out: kpt on same pce last 150yds* — 9/2

00 **4** 3½ **Come On Sunshine**[20] 6829 2-9-5 0 .... TonyHamilton 10 — 68
(Richard Fahey) *hld up: drvn 4f out: sn outpcd: kpt on fnl 2f: tk modest 4th last 100yds* — 100/1

3622 **5** 1¾ **Newmarket Warrior (IRE)**[22] 6763 2-9-5 80 .... RyanMoore 4 — 65
(Michael Bell) *hld up in rr: hdwy 3f out: upsides over 1f out: wknd last 150yds* — 11/4[1]

32 **6** 7 **Ultimate Act**[16] 6954 2-9-5 0 .... LiamKeniry 9 — 52
(Seamus Mullins) *dwlt: t.k.h in rr: gd hdwy and 2nd over 6f out: led 3f out: hdd 2f out: sn wknd* — 12/1

5 **7** hd **Deadly Approach**[29] 6570 2-9-5 0 .... SilvestreDeSousa 2 — 55+
(Charlie Appleby) *t.k.h in rr: gd hdwy to ld 7f out: hdd 3f out: lost pl and eased over 1f out* — 8/1

00 **8** 4½ **Hasta La Vista**[16] 6949 2-9-0 0 .... LukeMorris 6 — 42+
(Mark Johnston) *led: hdd 7f out: drvn over 4f out: wknd over 2f out* — 66/1

5 **9** nk **Modern Art**[10] 7113 2-9-0 0 .... JoeFanning 7 — 37+
(Mark Johnston) *trckd ldrs: lost pl over 2f out* — 40/1

0 **10** 30 **Al Zaman Thaman (FR)**[16] 6938 2-9-5 0 .... (b) MartinHarley 5
(Marco Botti) *mid-div: lost pl over 3f out: sn bhd: t.o* — 50/1

2m 19.51s (4.01) **Going Correction** +0.175s/f (Good) — **10** Ran SP% **115.8**
Speed ratings (Par 95): **90,87,87,84,83 77,77,73,73,49**
toteswingers 1&2 £3.10, 1&3 £3.90, 2&3 £3.90 CSF £15.20 TOTE £4.20: £1.50, £1.80, £2.80; EX 14.90 Trifecta £84.30 Pool: £2,964.31 - 26.35 winning units..
Owner Mrs Angela McAlpine & Partners **Bred** Gestut Gorlsdorf **Trained** East Ilsley, Berks
■ Richard Hughes's 200th winner of the calendar year, the first time he's reached the landmark.

FOCUS
It was dry overnight and the ground was given as good to soft, soft in places (GoingStick 7.6). All races were run on the stands' side home straight. Actual race distances: 5f, 6f, 7f57yds, 1m57yds, 1m2f152yds, 2m108yds. A real test for these 2yos. The early pace wasn't great but things picked up once Deadly Approach went to the front, and those who were held up out the back eventually came through to dominate. The runner-up helps with the opening level.

7333 APOLLOBET MOBILE GAMES NURSERY H'CAP — 5f

2:55 (2:55) (Class 2) 2-Y-O — £9,056 (£2,695; £1,346; £673) Stalls Centre

Form — RPR

3103 **1** **Sleepy Sioux**[9] 7127 2-8-3 79 .... SilvestreDeSousa 11 — 84
(David Elsworth) *chsd ldrs stands' side: styd on fnl f: led nr fin* — 7/2[1]

1100 **2** nk **Viva Verglas (IRE)**[13] 7026 2-9-2 92 .... (b[1]) GrahamGibbons 8 — 96
(David Barron) *racd centre: w ldrs: led over 3f out: hdd and no ex nr fin* — 11/1

2220 **3** ½ **Urban Dreamer (IRE)**[13] 7026 2-8-2 78 ow1 .... (b) AndreaAtzeni 9 — 80
(Rod Millman) *led towards stands' side: hdd over 3f out: styd on last 75yds: no ex clsng stages* — 15/2

261 **4** ½ **Meadway**[15] 6966 2-8-9 85 .... PaulHanagan 1 — 85
(Bryan Smart) *chsd ldrs centre: kpt on same pce fnl f* — 9/2[2]

0420 **5** 1¼ **Tableforten**[20] 6825 2-8-0 76 oh1 .... (b[1]) LukeMorris 4 — 72
(J S Moore) *mid-div centre: outpcd over 2f out: kpt on fnl f* — 20/1

2313 **6** 1 **Jamboree Girl**[21] 6791 2-8-0 76 oh1 .... DuranFentiman 7 — 68
(Tim Easterby) *mid-div centre: hdwy over 2f out: chsng ldrs over 1f out: sn wknd* — 11/1

513 **7** hd **Desert Ace (IRE)**[16] 6958 2-8-4 85 .... RyanTate(5) 2 — 77
(Clive Cox) *mid-div centre: hdwy to chse ldrs over 2f out: wknd fnl f* — 7/1[3]

2010 **8** 2¾ **Suzi's Connoisseur**[36] 6328 2-9-7 97 .... JoeFanning 6 — 79
(Mark Johnston) *dwlt: sn mid-div stands' side: hdwy to chse ldrs over 2f out: wknd over 1f out* — 11/1

5014 **9** 2 **Donny Rover (IRE)**[11] 7062 2-8-0 76 oh2 .... (b[1]) JimmyQuinn 10 — 50
(David C Griffiths) *slipped s and slowly away: reminders after s stands' side: nvr on terms* — 25/1

2120 **10** 1¼ **Back Lane**[28] 6584 2-8-9 85 .... RyanMoore 5 — 55
(Richard Fahey) *mid-div: lost pl over 2f out: sn bhd* — 7/1[3]

2516 **11** ½ **Skye's The Limit**[34] 6386 2-8-0 76 oh2 .... PatrickMathers 3 — 44
(Richard Fahey) *mid-div: towards far side: outpcd over 3f out: sme hdwy over 2f out: sn lost pl* — 25/1

1m 0.04s (-0.76) **Going Correction** -0.125s/f (Firm) — **11** Ran SP% **114.6**
Speed ratings (Par 101): **101,100,99,98,96 95,95,90,87,85 84**
toteswingers 1&2 £10.40, 1&3 £4.40, 2&3 £19.30 CSF £40.36 CT £223.82 TOTE £4.60: £2.10, £3.30, £2.40; EX 46.50 Trifecta £288.80 Pool: £2,988.58 - 7.75 winning units..
Owner D R C Elsworth **Bred** New Hall Stud **Trained** Newmarket, Suffolk

FOCUS
The going was changed to soft all round before this race. A decent nursery, won last year by subsequent Group 3 winner Dutch Masterpiece, and the previous year by smart performer Ballesteros, from Mince, who has since won at Group 3 level, so perhaps a result to note. The winner rates up a fraction, while the second showed very useful form.

7334 APOLLOBET BEST ODDS GUARANTEED CONDITIONS STKS — 6f

3:30 (3:30) (Class 3) 2-Y-O — £8,086 (£2,406; £1,202) Stalls Centre

Form — RPR

122 **1** **Musical Comedy**[7] 7170 2-9-0 85 .... RichardHughes 1 — 100
(Richard Hannon) *mde all: pushed along over 2f out: drew clr fnl f: eased nr fin* — 5/4[2]

3110 **2** 6 **See The Sun**[13] 7026 2-9-0 88 .... DuranFentiman 3 — 82
(Tim Easterby) *trckd wnr: effrt over 2f out: rdn over 1f out: sn btn* — 8/1[3]

1 **3** 5 **Red Stargazer (IRE)**[29] 6546 2-9-0 0 .... GrahamGibbons 4 — 73
(David Barron) *a last: sn pushed along: drvn over 3f out: wknd over 1f out: eased ins fnl f* — 1/1[1]

1m 14.16s (0.36) **Going Correction** +0.025s/f (Good) — **3** Ran SP% **105.6**
Speed ratings (Par 99): **98,90,83**
CSF £7.43 TOTE £1.90; EX 4.40 Trifecta £5.20 Pool: £1,406.43 - 199.52 winning units..
Owner The Queen **Bred** The Queen **Trained** East Everleigh, Wilts
■ Richard Hannon's 219th winner of the calendar year, breaking the record held by himself.

FOCUS
Just the three runners for this conditions race, run on softening ground. The useful winner is rated as a minor improver.

7335 APOLLOBET FREE DOWNLOAD APP EBF MAIDEN STKS — 7f

4:05 (4:06) (Class 5) 2-Y-O — £2,911 (£866; £432; £216) Stalls Centre

Form — RPR

2 **1** **Baarez (USA)**[21] 6799 2-9-5 0 .... [1] PaulHanagan 12 — 82
(Roger Varian) *swtchd lft after s: trckd ldrs: 2nd over 3f out: led 1f out: styd on* — 1/2[1]

2026 **2** 2 **Rogue Wave (IRE)**[20] 6829 2-9-2 80 .... RobertTart(3) 6 — 77
(Alan Jarvis) *trckd ldrs: chal over 2f out: kpt on to take 2nd last 100yds* — 20/1

5 **3** hd **Three Peaks**[114] 3695 2-9-5 0 .... JamesDoyle 4 — 77+
(Charles Hills) *hld up in mid-div: hdwy over 3f out: styd on to take 3rd last 75yds* — 33/1

033 **4** 4½ **Caridadi (IRE)**[10] 7089 2-9-5 0 .... MickaelBarzalona 9 — 65
(Charlie Appleby) *led: swtchd lft after s: hdd 1f out: wknd fnl 120yds* — 10/1[3]

5 ½ **Framed Masterpiece** 2-9-5 0 .... (p) RichardKingscote 5 — 64+
(Paul Fitzsimons) *w ldr: wknd appr fnl f* — 66/1

0 **6** 2¼ **Tall Ship (IRE)**[21] 6799 2-9-5 0 .... RyanMoore 11 — 58
(Sir Michael Stoute) *in rr: outpcd and drvn 4f out: kpt on fnl 2f: nvr a factor* — 3/1[2]

05 **7** hd **Etaad (USA)**[15] 6975 2-9-5 0 .... RichardHughes 7 — 58
(J W Hills) *chsd ldrs: outpcd over 2f out: wknd over 1f out* — 33/1

8 ½ **Attenzione (IRE)** 2-9-5 0 .... (t) NeilCallan 1 — 57
(Marco Botti) *mid-div: effrt over 3f out: nvr a factor* — 16/1

9 2¼ **Rochelle (IRE)** 2-9-0 0 .... MartinDwyer 3 — 46
(William Muir) *dwlt: in rr: sme hdwy 3f out: wknd over 1f out* — 66/1

00 **10** 1½ **McCarthy Mor (IRE)**[28] 6581 2-9-5 0 .... TonyHamilton 8 — 47
(Richard Fahey) *in rr-div: sme hdwy over 2f out: sn lost pl* — 66/1

11 14 **Essanar** 2-9-0 0 .... JackDuern(5) 2 — 12
(Andrew Hollinshead) *in rr and sn drvn along: wl bhd fnl 2f* — 100/1

12 27 **Oly'Roccs (IRE)** 2-9-5 0 .... JoeFanning 10
(David Nicholls) *s.s: bhd and drvn along: t.o 3f out: virtually p.u* — 66/1

1m 33.34s (2.64) **Going Correction** +0.325s/f (Good) — **12** Ran SP% **124.2**
Speed ratings (Par 95): **97,94,94,89,88 86,85,85,82,81 65,34**
toteswingers 1&2 £5.10, 1&3 £9.70, 2&3 £23.90 CSF £19.96 TOTE £1.60: £1.10, £3.60, £5.50; EX 14.10 Trifecta £185.50 Pool: £5,562.08 - 22.47 winning units..
Owner Hamdan Al Maktoum **Bred** Shadwell Farm LLC **Trained** Newmarket, Suffolk

FOCUS
The market told the story here. The runner-up guides a pretty solid level to the form.

7336 APOLLOBET £50 MATCH BET NURSERY H'CAP — 1m

4:40 (4:40) (Class 2) 2-Y-O — £9,056 (£2,695; £1,346; £673) Stalls Centre

Form — RPR

1061 **1** **Latenightrequest**[27] 6619 2-8-7 75 .... PaulHanagan 4 — 78
(Richard Fahey) *trckd ldrs: pushed along over 4f out: swtchd wd 2f out: led jst ins fnl f: edgd rt: styd on* — 9/4[1]

31 **2** 1¼ **Emef Diamond**[49] 5969 2-8-11 79 .... SilvestreDeSousa 3 — 79
(Mick Channon) *t.k.h: trckd ldr: led narrowly 3f out: hung lft and hdd appr fnl f: rallied to take 2nd nr fin* — 9/4[1]

513 **3** ½ **Zumurudah (FR)**[16] 6934 2-8-13 81 .... JoeFanning 2 — 80
(Mark Johnston) *led: narrowly hdd 3f out: styd on same pce fnl f* — 6/1[2]

2110 **4** nk **Art Official (IRE)**[36] 6328 2-9-7 89 .... RichardHughes 1 — 87
(Richard Hannon) *dwlt: hld up in rr: hdwy to trck ldrs over 4f out: rdn to ld narrowly appr fnl f: hdd and no ex last 150yds* — 9/4[1]

1m 48.14s (4.44) **Going Correction** +0.475s/f (Yiel) — **4** Ran SP% **106.6**
Speed ratings (Par 101): **96,94,94,93**
CSF £7.26 TOTE £3.10; EX 8.30 Trifecta £12.20 Pool: £2,119.01 - 130.08 winning units..
Owner Middleham Park Racing XVI & Partner **Bred** Mrs S J Walker **Trained** Musley Bank, N Yorks

FOCUS
Despite the small field they went a fair gallop in the ground. The winner found plenty to build on her Ayr win.

7337 CJM MAINTENANCE SOLUTIONS H'CAP — 1m

5:10 (5:12) (Class 3) (0-95,95) 3-Y-O+ — £8,086 (£2,406; £1,202; £601) Stalls Centre

Form — RPR

1423 **1** **Gworn**[14] 6989 3-8-11 88 .... AndreaAtzeni 10 — 97
(Ed Dunlop) *hld up in rr: gd hdwy stands' side over 2f out: styd on wl to ld nr fin* — 17/2[3]

0152 **2** hd **Modern Tutor**[14] 6989 4-9-4 92 .... RyanMoore 12 — 101
(Sir Michael Stoute) *trckd ldrs: drvn over 3f out: led stands' side appr fnl f: idled and ct fnl strides* — 7/2[1]

2030 **3** hd **Chosen Character (IRE)**[20] 6826 5-9-0 93 .... (vt) NatashaEaton(5) 4 — 101
(Tom Dascombe) *sn led: hdd appr fnl f: rallied post* — 22/1

1002 **4** 1½ **Sea Shanty (USA)**[79] 4897 3-9-1 92 .... (p) RichardHughes 7 — 97
(Richard Hannon) *chsd ldrs: drvn and outpcd over 3f out: styd on fnl 2f* — 17/2[3]

0005 **5** ½ **Anton Chigurh**[14] 6989 4-8-11 85 .... RichardKingscote 11 — 88
(Tom Dascombe) *mid-div: lost pl over 3f out: hdwy 2f out: nt clr run and swtchd rt appr fnl f: styng on fin* — 12/1

0140 **6** nk **Swiftly Done (IRE)**[7] 7172 6-8-13 90 .... JasonHart(3) 6 — 93
(Declan Carroll) *in rr: hdwy on outer over 2f out: kpt on same pce appr fnl f* — 12/1

0100 **7** nse **Osteopathic Remedy (IRE)**[7] 7172 9-9-2 95 .... ConnorBeasley(5) 5 — 98
(Michael Dods) *chsd ldrs: drvn over 3f out: kpt on one pce over 1f out* — 20/1

2066 **8** nse **Number One London (IRE)**[90] 4542 3-8-4 81 oh3 .... MartinDwyer 15 — 83
(Brian Meehan) *chsd ldrs on outer: one pce fnl 2f* — 11/1

1640 **8** dht **George Cinq**[21] 6801 3-8-10 87 .... JamesDoyle 9 — 89
(Michael Bell) *s.i.s: towards rr: sme hdwy over 2f out: nvr trbld ldrs* — 12/1

13 **10** 1¼ **Joe Sugden**[30] 6538 4-8-8 82 .... (t) MartinLane 14 — 82
(Mrs Ilka Gansera-Leveque) *chsd ldrs: outpcd and lost pl over 2f out: kpt on fnl f* — 11/1

5016 **11** 1 **Maven**[29] 6551 5-8-13 87 .... DuranFentiman 8 — 84
(Tim Easterby) *led early: chsd ldrs: lost pl over 2f out* — 50/1

3050 **12** *9* **Dubai Hills**[13] 7028 7-8-9 **83**............ PaulHanagan 2 60
(Bryan Smart) *s.i.s: sme hdwy over 3f out: wknd 2f out: eased clsng stages* **22/1**

4533 **13** *4 1/2* **Gold Hunter (IRE)**[14] 6993 3-9-2 **93**............ SilvestreDeSousa 3 58
(Saeed bin Suroor) *in rr: hdwy on outer 3f out: wknd whn n.m.r over 1f out: eased clsng stages* **9/2**[2]

0433 **14** *3 3/4* **Dubai Dynamo**[24] 6727 8-8-10 **84**............(p) DaleSwift 13 42
(Ruth Carr) *in rr: bhd fnl 3f: eased* **33/1**

0030 **15** *nk* **Lord Of The Dance (IRE)**[21] 6792 7-8-11 **88**............ RobertTart(3) 1 45
(Michael Mullineaux) *hld up in rr: effrt wd outside over 2f out: sn wknd: eased fnl f* **28/1**

1m 46.95s (3.25) **Going Correction** +0.625s/f (Yiel)
WFA 3 from 4yo+ 3lb **15** Ran SP% **123.0**
Speed ratings (Par 107): **108,107,107,106,105 105,105,105,105,103 102,93,89,85,85**
toteswingers 1&2 £7.30, 1&3 £39.40, 2&3 £18.50 CSF £35.44 CT £671.08 TOTE £7.60: £2.10, £2.30, £5.10; EX 36.70 Trifecta £1702.80 Part won. Pool: £2,270.45 - 0.80 winning units..
Owner N Martin **Bred** Azienda Agricola F Lli Nencini **Trained** Newmarket, Suffolk
■ A 100th winner of the calendar year, his first century, for Andrea Atzeni.

FOCUS
A competitive handicap run at a good gallop. The first three were among the few to stick to the favoured stands' side. The third sets the standard.

7338 APOLLOBET IN-PLAY BETTING H'CAP 2m 45y
5:40 (5:43) (Class 4) (0-85,89) 3-Y-O+ **£5,175** (£1,540; £769; £384) **Stalls** Low

Form RPR

6-26 **1** **Perfect Heart**[14] 6992 4-9-9 **80**............ AndreaAtzeni 12 90
(Roger Varian) *sn trcking ldr: styd on stands' side to ld last 100yds* **10/3**[1]

205 **2** *1 3/4* **Stopped Out**[20] 6847 8-9-7 **78**............(p) RussKennemore 9 86
(Philip Kirby) *led: forged clr over 3f out: edgd lft and hdd ins fnl f: no ex* **16/1**

1414 **3** *2 1/4* **Rutherglen**[31] 6490 3-8-10 **77**............ PatCosgrave 3 82
(George Baker) *mid-div: drvn over 3f out: kpt on same pce to take 3rd ins fnl f* **14/1**

4126 **4** *nk* **Wadaa (USA)**[36] 6329 3-9-8 **89**............ JoeFanning 10 94
(James Tate) *hld up in mid-div: hdwy 10f out: chsng ldrs 6f out: kpt on same pce over 1f out* **20/1**

1166 **5** *3/4* **Zenafire**[20] 6833 4-9-0 **76**............(p) JackDuern(5) 8 80
(Andrew Hollinshead) *hld up in mid-div: hdwy 10f out: one pce fnl 2f* **28/1**

0651 **6** *shd* **Forced Family Fun**[8] 7151 3-8-3 **70** 6ex............ MartinLane 11 74
(Michael Bell) *hld up in rr: hdwy over 2f out: kpt on: nt rch ldrs* **7/2**[2]

1612 **7** *4* **Man Of Plenty**[14] 6992 4-10-0 **85**............(p) RyanMoore 6 84
(Ed Dunlop) *hld up in rr: hdwy 7f out: chsng ldrs 5f out: wknd over 1f out* **7/1**[3]

3-00 **8** *hd* **New Youmzain (FR)**[20] 6846 4-9-6 **77**............ SilvestreDeSousa 7 76
(Mick Channon) *n.m.r sn after s: hld up in rr: hdwy on outer over 3f out: wknd over 1f out* **11/1**

1323 **9** *2 1/2* **Alwilda**[30] 6540 3-9-3 **84**............ LukeMorris 2 80
(Sir Mark Prescott Bt) *chsd ldrs: drvn over 3f out: wknd over 1f out* **15/2**

4321 **10** *3* **Nateeja (IRE)**[15] 6978 3-9-2 **83**............ PaulHanagan 5 75
(J W Hills) *hld up in rr: hdwy 5f out: wknd over 1f out: eased* **9/1**

2033 **11** *3 1/4* **Rocktherunway (IRE)**[28] 6585 4-9-6 **82**............(p) ConnorBeasley(5) 1 70
(Michael Dods) *mid-div: effrt over 3f out: lost pl over 2f out* **12/1**

1100 **12** *shd* **Nashville (IRE)**[27] 6646 4-9-6 **77**............ JamesDoyle 4 65
(Richard Fahey) *chsd ldrs: drvn over 3f out: wknd 2f out* **25/1**

3m 44.66s (10.36) **Going Correction** +0.775s/f (Yiel)
WFA 3 from 4yo+ 10lb **12** Ran SP% **120.2**
Speed ratings (Par 105): **105,104,103,102,102 102,100,100,99,97 95,95**
toteswingers 1&2 £14.60, 1&3 £11.50, 2&3 £36.00 CSF £56.67 CT £675.79 TOTE £4.70: £2.60, £5.40, £3.90; EX 89.90 Trifecta £1163.50 Part won. Pool: £1,551.39 - 0.82 winning units..
Owner Normandie Stud Ltd **Bred** Normandie Stud Ltd **Trained** Newmarket, Suffolk
■ Stewards' Enquiry : Jack Duern One-day ban: careless riding (Nov 1)

FOCUS
An ordinary pace and two of the three greys in the race dominated this race throughout. Improvement from the winner, and the third fits.
T/Plt: £110.40 to a £1 stake. Pool: £63,628.91 - 420.68 winning units. T/Qpdt: £21.10 to a £1 stake. Pool: £3,781.77 - 132.54 winning units. WG

7023 REDCAR (L-H)
Friday, October 18
OFFICIAL GOING: Soft (good to soft in places; 6.8)
Wind: Light half behind Weather: Overcast

7339 BRITISH STALLION STUDS SUPPORTING BRITISH RACING EBF MAIDEN STKS 1m
1:30 (1:30) (Class 5) 2-Y-O **£3,067** (£905; £453) **Stalls** Centre

Form RPR

3 **1** **Latin Charm (IRE)**[29] 6570 2-9-5 0............ PaoloSirigu 4 74+
(Marco Botti) *in tch: pushed along 3f out: rdn 2f out: styd on appr fnl f: led last 50yds* **11/4**[2]

26 **2** *1/2* **Bold Captain (IRE)**[7] 7175 2-9-5 0............ MichaelO'Connell 2 73
(John Quinn) *cl up: led 2f out: rdn clr ent fnl f: drvn and hdd last 50yds: no ex* **8/1**

0 **3** *1 1/2* **Arbaab**[23] 6739 2-9-5 0............ DaneO'Neill 8 70
(Sir Michael Stoute) *trckd ldrs: hdwy and cl up 1/2-way: rdn 2f out: drvn to chse ldr ent fnl f: sn edgd lft and one pce* **13/8**[1]

4 *nk* **Ruwasi** 2-9-5 0............ DavidAllan 5 69+
(James Tate) *s.i.s and pushed along in rr: swtchd rt to outer and hdwy over 3f out: rdn to chse ldrs wl over 1f out: styd on fnl f: nrst fin* **14/1**

5 *7* **Odeon** 2-9-5 0............ GrahamLee 9 54
(James Given) *cl up on outer: effrt and ev ch over 2f out: sn rdn and grad wknd* **16/1**

6 *1 1/4* **Conquerant** 2-9-5 0............ TomEaves 3 51
(Charlie Appleby) *hld up in rr tl sme late hdwy* **11/1**

7 *1/2* **Sr Swing** 2-9-0 0............ RussKennemore 6 45
(Philip Kirby) *chsd ldrs: rdn along over 3f out: sn wknd* **66/1**

0 **8** *1/2* **Indus River (IRE)**[13] 7019 2-9-5 0............ TomQueally 7 49
(Charlie Appleby) *t.k.h: slt ld: pushed along 3f out: rdn and hdd 2f out: sn wknd* **7/1**[3]

0 **9** *12* **Tawan**[13] 7023 2-9-5 0............ BarryMcHugh 1 22
(Brian Rothwell) *towards rr: rdn along bef 1/2-way: sn outpcd* **100/1**

00 **10** *12* **Gravy Dipper (IRE)**[42] 6174 2-9-5 0............ RobertWinston 10
(John Quinn) *towards rr: rdn along 1/2-way: sn outpcd and bhd* **100/1**

1m 44.04s (7.44) **Going Correction** +0.575s/f (Yiel) **10** Ran SP% **112.7**
Speed ratings (Par 95): **85,84,83,82,75 74,73,73,61,49**
toteswingers 1&2 £4.50, 1&3 £1.10, 2&3 £3.70 CSF £24.17 TOTE £3.30: £1.10, £1.50, £1.30; EX 23.30 Trifecta £52.90 Pool: £1,286.02 - 18.22 winning units..
Owner Grundy Bloodstock Limited **Bred** Grundy Bloodstock Srl **Trained** Newmarket, Suffolk

FOCUS
A dry night but, although the pace was no more than fair, the time of the opener suggested the ground was very much on the slow side (over 9secs above standard). A fair maiden in which the first four pulled clear, and a creditable effort from the winner.

7340 MARKET CROSS JEWELLERS CLAIMING STKS 7f
2:00 (2:00) (Class 6) 2-Y-O **£2,045** (£603; £302) **Stalls** Centre

Form RPR

063 **1** **Dark Crystal**[8] 7156 2-7-13 0............ JulieBurke(3) 13 58
(John Gallagher) *cl up: led wl over 2f out: rdn clr ent fnl f: sn hung lft: drvn out* **14/1**

0400 **2** *1 1/2* **Mr Carbonfootprint**[21] 6791 2-8-7 66............ BarryMcHugh 12 60
(Richard Fahey) *trckd ldrs: hdwy wl over 2f out: rdn to chse wnr over 1f out: drvn and edgd lft ent fnl f: kpt on* **7/2**[1]

040 **3** *1* **Pure Impressions**[23] 6754 2-8-2 62............(v1) JoeyHaynes(5) 8 57
(K R Burke) *in tch: hdwy to trck ldrs 3f out: n.m.r and swtchd rt over 1f out: sn rdn and styd on fnl f* **6/1**

006 **4** *3* **Greenbury (IRE)**[8] 7146 2-8-7 0............(p) PJMcDonald 7 50
(Ann Duffield) *slt ld: rdn along over 3f out: hdd wl over 2f out: grad wknd appr fnl f* **50/1**

6 **5** *1/2* **Ivory**[27] 6654 2-8-2 0............ PaoloSirigu 11 43
(Garry Moss) *towards rr: swtchd to wd outside and hdwy over 2f out: sn rdn and no imp fnl f* **66/1**

013 **6** *shd* **Lady Montenegro**[10] 7094 2-7-11 54 ow2............ RowanScott(7) 4 45
(Ann Duffield) *trckd ldrs: cl up 1/2-way: rdn along over 2f out: sn one pce* **7/1**

000 **7** *3* **Miss Lawlass (IRE)**[28] 6607 2-7-7 35............ SamanthaBell(7) 6 34
(James Given) *dwlt and in rr: sme hdwy over 2f out: sn rdn along and n.d* **100/1**

0120 **8** *nk* **Mount Cheiron (USA)**[10] 7097 2-9-1 62............ GrahamLee 9 48
(Dianne Sayer) *towards rr: rdn along wl over 2f out: sn outpcd* **9/2**[3]

4016 **9** *2 3/4* **Casper Lee (IRE)**[24] 6725 2-9-1 65............(v) AndrewMullen 5 41
(Nigel Tinkler) *dwlt and sn pushed along: hdwy on wd outside and cl up 1/2-way: rdn along over 2f out: sn wknd* **8/1**

5120 **10** *shd* **Lady Captain (IRE)**[6] 7202 2-8-2 65............ RaulDaSilva 3 28
(Kevin Ryan) *cl up: disp ld 1/2-way: rdn along wl over 2f out: sn wknd* **4/1**[2]

000 **11** *1 1/4* **Mavree (IRE)**[29] 6546 2-8-4 46............(b1) PaulQuinn 10 27
(Tim Easterby) *chsd ldrs: rdn along wl over 2f out: sn wknd* **66/1**

5440 **12** *34* **Camatini (IRE)**[23] 6755 2-8-8 58............(b1) TomEaves 2
(Michael Dods) *virtually ref to r: a t.o* **14/1**

1m 29.85s (5.35) **Going Correction** +0.575s/f (Yiel) **12** Ran SP% **117.6**
Speed ratings (Par 93): **92,90,89,85,85 85,81,81,78,78 76,37**
toteswingers 1&2 £13.90, 1&3 £12.80, 2&3 £6.50 CSF £61.98 TOTE £11.50: £5.00, £1.80, £3.00; EX 95.00 Trifecta £565.70 Pool: £1,573.53 - 2.08 winning units..Dark Crystal was claimed by Miss L A Perratt for £6,000.
Owner R Biggs **Bred** R Biggs **Trained** Chastleton, Oxon

FOCUS
Not much to dwell on in a modest claimer, which has been rated conservatively. The gallop was reasonable.

7341 BRITISH STALLION STUDS E B F MAIDEN STKS 6f
2:30 (2:32) (Class 5) 2-Y-O **£2,911** (£866; £432; £216) **Stalls** Centre

Form RPR

0 **1** **Danzeno**[27] 6635 2-9-5 0............ AndrewMullen 6 86
(Michael Appleby) *dwlt and in rr: hdwy over 3f out: trckd ldrs over 2f out: rdn to chse wnr appr fnl f: styd on wl to ld last 100yds* **10/1**[3]

22 **2** *1 1/4* **Kommander Kirkup**[29] 6546 2-9-5 0............ PJMcDonald 9 82
(Michael Dods) *prom: led 2f out: rdn and jnd over 1f out: drvn and hdd last 100yds* **4/6**[1]

0 **3** *8* **Sleeper Class**[20] 6842 2-9-0 0............ GrahamLee 2 53
(Jim Goldie) *midfield: hdwy over 2f out: chsd ldrs and n.m.r over 1f out: sn swtchd lft and rdn: kpt on fnl f* **66/1**

35 **4** *3/4* **Beautiful Stranger (IRE)**[28] 6581 2-9-5 0............ TomEaves 1 56
(Keith Dalgleish) *cl up: led after 2f: rdn along and hdd 2f out: drvn and wkng whn edgd rt ent fnl f* **16/1**

0 **5** *3 1/2* **Ty Cobb (IRE)**[42] 6174 2-9-5 0............ MichaelO'Connell 12 45+
(John Quinn) *in tch: pushed along over 2f out: swtchd rt and rdn wl over 1f out: kpt on fnl f: n.d* **16/1**

600 **6** *3/4* **Wolfwood**[63] 5482 2-9-0 50............ KevinStott(5) 11 43
(John Davies) *chsd ldrs: rdn along over 2f out: grad wknd* **66/1**

0 **7** *shd* **Booloo (IRE)**[15] 6975 2-9-2 0............ BillyCray(3) 10 43
(Garry Moss) *led 2f: prom tl rdn along over 2f out and grad wknd* **50/1**

8 *6* **Locky Taylor (IRE)** 2-9-5 0............ TomQueally 14 25
(Kevin Ryan) *racd wd: prom: pushed along 1/2-way: sn rdn and wknd 2f out* **3/1**[2]

06 **9** *3/4* **First Commandment**[20] 6842 2-9-5 0............(e1) DavidAllan 4 22
(Tim Easterby) *chsd ldrs on outer: rdn along wl over 2f out: sn wknd* **33/1**

00 **10** *3/4* **Slingsby**[6] 7209 2-8-12 0............ AnnaHesketh(7) 7 20
(Michael Easterby) *a towards rr* **100/1**

11 *3/4* **Three Pips** 2-9-5 0............ SebSanders 5 18
(Ed McMahon) *chsd ldrs: rdn along 1/2-way: sn wknd* **14/1**

12 *7* **Major Rowan** 2-9-2 0............ MarkCoumbe(3) 3
(Bryan Smart) *s.i.s: a bhd* **50/1**

13 *4 1/2* **Gee Sharp** 2-9-5 0............ BarryMcHugh 15
(Julie Camacho) *dwlt: a in rr* **50/1**

0 **14** *30* **Molly Molone**[13] 7023 2-9-0 0............ RobertWinston 13
(David Brown) *a towards rr: bhd fr 1/2-way* **66/1**

1m 14.35s (2.55) **Going Correction** +0.575s/f (Yiel) **14** Ran SP% **126.8**
Speed ratings (Par 95): **106,104,93,92,88 87,86,78,77,76 75,66,60,20**
toteswingers 1&2 £3.60, 1&3 £36.50, 2&3 £42.60 CSF £17.68 TOTE £10.30: £3.20, £1.10, £21.30; EX 25.60 Trifecta £1353.70 Pool: £1,805.00 - 0.74 winning units..
Owner Goldform Racing **Bred** A M Wragg **Trained** Danethorpe, Notts

FOCUS
An uncompetitive maiden run at a reasonable gallop. The first two, who showed useful form, pulled clear.

7342 SAM HALL MEMORIAL H'CAP 1m 6f 19y
3:05 (3:05) (Class 5) (0-75,75) 3-Y-O+ £2,911 (£866; £432; £216) Stalls Low

Form RPR
1113 **1** **Duchess Of Gazeley (IRE)**[55] 5743 3-9-4 **74**............... SebSanders 10 89+
(Gary Harrison) *trckd ldrs: hdwy 4f out: led 3f out: rdn clr wl over 1f out: styd on: readily* **4/1[2]**

6402 **2** 4 1/2 **Perfect Summer (IRE)**[21] 6788 3-8-12 **68**......................... TomQueally 2 75
(Lady Cecil) *hld up in midfield: hdwy over 3f out: n.m.r and pushed along 2f out: swtchd lft and rdn over 1f out: styd on to chse wnr ins fnl f: no imp* **7/2[1]**

5023 **3** 1/2 **My Destination (IRE)**[14] 6996 4-8-12 **62**.......................... NeilFarley(3) 9 68
(Declan Carroll) *hld up in midfield: hdwy over 4f out: prom 3f out: rdn to chse wnr 2f out: drvn and one pce appr fnl f* **11/1**

1-30 **4** 2 1/2 **Tobrata**[72] 5137 7-8-10 **57**.. DavidAllan 5 60
(Mel Brittain) *chsd ldrs: hdwy over 4f out: rdn along wl over 2f out: drvn wl over 1f out: one pce* **25/1**

2406 **5** 3 1/4 **Zaplamation (IRE)**[29] 6565 8-9-0 **66**.............................. KevinStott(5) 16 64
(John Quinn) *hld up and bhd: hdwy 3f out: rdn 2f out: styd on fnl f: nrst fin* **16/1**

5302 **6** nse **Korngold**[18] 6909 5-8-9 **56** oh2... BarryMcHugh 4 54
(Tracy Waggott) *trckd ldrs on inner: effrt whn nt clr run wl over 2f out: swtchd rt and rdn 2f out: plugged on one pce* **9/1**

21-0 **7** 1 3/4 **Categorical**[156] 1805 10-9-11 **72**.................................... PJMcDonald 15 67
(Keith Reveley) *hld up and bhd: stdy hdwy 3f out: rdn wl over 1f out: swtchd rt and kpt on fnl f: nvr nr ldrs* **12/1**

4003 **8** 5 **Forrest Flyer (IRE)**[17] 6917 9-8-13 **60**............................... GrahamLee 7 48
(Jim Goldie) *chsd ldng pair: rdn along 4f out: drvn 3f out and sn wknd* **28/1**

2-11 **9** shd **Sporting Gold (IRE)**[21] 6788 4-10-0 **75**............................. DaneO'Neill 8 63
(Roger Varian) *hld up towards rr: hdwy over 3f out: chsd ldrs 2f out: sn rdn and wknd* **9/2[3]**

0-00 **10** 1 1/4 **Spirit Of Adjisa (IRE)**[16] 6942 9-8-12 **59**.............(b) MichaelO'Connell 14 46
(David C Griffiths) *led: rdn along 4f out: drvn and hdd 3f out: sn wknd* **66/1**

2506 **11** shd **Knightly Escapade**[16] 6942 5-9-9 **73**.........................(p) PaulPickard(3) 1 59
(Brian Ellison) *hld up: a towards rr* **14/1**

0065 **12** nk **Waltz Darling (IRE)**[13] 7027 5-9-1 **62**............................ TomEaves 3 48
(Keith Reveley) *hld up: a bhd* **33/1**

205 **13** 7 **Dewala**[147] 2619 4-9-12 **73**.. AndrewMullen 11 49
(Michael Appleby) *trckd ldr: pushed along over 4f out: rdn over 3f out: sn wknd* **14/1**

0400 **14** 36 **Persian Peril**[37] 6302 9-9-9 **70**....................................... RobertWinston 6
(Alan Swinbank) *hld up: a towards rr* **33/1**

3m 8.13s (3.43) **Going Correction** +0.35s/f (Good)
WFA 3 from 4yo+ 9lb **14 Ran SP% 120.3**
Speed ratings (Par 103): **104,101,101,99,97 97,96,93,93,93 93,92,88,68**
toteswingers 1&2 £7.60, 1&3 £9.50, 2&3 £11.90 CSF £17.38 CT £146.04 TOTE £4.40: £1.60, £3.30, £4.60; EX 22.30 Trifecta £156.10 Pool: £1,423.42 - 6.83 winning units..
Owner Franconson Partners **Bred** Overbury Stallions Ltd And D Boocock **Trained** Newmarket, Suffolk

FOCUS
A couple of progressive sorts in a fair handicap but the wide-margin winner turned in a useful effort. The gallop was fair.

7343 DOWNLOAD THE FREE RACING UK APP H'CAP (DIV I) 7f
3:40 (3:42) (Class 5) (0-70,70) 3-Y-O+ £2,911 (£866; £432; £216) Stalls Centre

Form RPR
42/2 **1** **Fanoos**[16] 6940 4-9-3 **66**..(p) DaneO'Neill 1 83+
(William Haggas) *hld up towards rr: gd hdwy on outer wl over 2f out: hld wl over 1f out: rdn appr fnl f: kpt on strly* **4/1[1]**

0023 **2** 3 **Red Cobra (IRE)**[8] 7148 3-8-7 **58**.................................... DavidAllan 7 66
(Tim Easterby) *trckd ldrs: hdwy and cl up 2f out: rdn to chse wnr over 1f out: drvn and no imp fnl f* **11/2[2]**

-405 **3** 1 3/4 **Bond Club**[26] 6664 3-9-1 **66**..(p) GrahamLee 14 69
(Geoffrey Oldroyd) *towards rr: gd hdwy on outer 3f out: rdn to chse ldrs wl over 1f out: edgd lft and kpt on same pce fnl f* **10/1**

5040 **4** 2 1/4 **Space War**[24] 6720 6-8-11 **67**...................................... AnnaHesketh(7) 8 66
(Michael Easterby) *dwlt and towards rr: hdwy over 2f out: rdn over 1f out: kpt on fnl f: nrst fin* **12/1**

5025 **5** 3 **Beau Amadeus (IRE)**[24] 6728 4-9-4 **67**.........................(b) TomQueally 6 58
(David Nicholls) *t.k.h: cl up: led 3f out: rdn over 2f out: hdd wl over 1f out: sn drvn and grad wknd* **4/1[1]**

5006 **6** 3/4 **Pivotal Prospect**[28] 6603 5-8-7 **56**................................ BarryMcHugh 5 45
(Tracy Waggott) *prom: rdn along 2f out: sn drvn and wknd* **10/1**

0343 **7** 1 3/4 **Perfect Words (IRE)**[27] 6633 3-8-10 **61**......................... RaulDaSilva 10 44
(Marjorie Fife) *trckd ldrs: cl up and ev ch over 2f out: sn rdn and wknd* **8/1[3]**

3000 **8** 3 1/2 **Cinderslipper (IRE)**[101] 4143 3-8-9 **60**........................(p) PJMcDonald 2 34
(Ann Duffield) *chsd ldrs: rdn along over 2f out: sn wknd* **14/1**

5000 **9** 1 1/2 **Secret City (IRE)**[17] 6916 7-8-13 **65**...........................(b) NeilFarley(3) 12 36
(Robin Bastiman) *prom: rdn along over 2f out: sn wknd* **25/1**

4-10 **10** 2 1/4 **Upper Grosvenor**[15] 6969 4-9-1 **67**............................. RossAtkinson(3) 9 32
(Roger Varian) *t.k.h: slt ld: hdd 3f out and sn rdn: wknd fnl 2f* **11/1**

5006 **11** shd **Eastlands Lad (IRE)**[93] 4400 4-8-7 **56** oh2......................(p) TomEaves 3 21
(Micky Hammond) *in rr: swtchd rt to outer 3f out: sn rdn along and nvr a factor* **33/1**

6650 **12** 2 1/4 **Don't Tell**[25] 6687 3-8-5 **56** oh11..................................[1] AndrewMullen 13 14
(George Moore) *in tch: rdn along wl over 2f out: sn wknd* **100/1**

1m 27.99s (3.49) **Going Correction** +0.575s/f (Yiel)
WFA 3 from 4yo+ 2lb **12 Ran SP% 115.1**
Speed ratings (Par 103): **103,99,97,95,91 90,88,84,83,80 80,77**
CSF £24.09 CT £207.78 TOTE £4.30: £1.30, £2.20, £4.70; EX 23.00 Trifecta £158.10 Pool: £2,217.67 - 10.51 winning units..
Owner Hamdan Al Maktoum **Bred** Miss Otis Partnership **Trained** Newmarket, Suffolk

FOCUS
A modest handicap in which the gallop was a reasonable one. The winner was well on top and the second set the standard on recent form.

7344 DOWNLOAD THE FREE RACING UK APP H'CAP (DIV II) 7f
4:15 (4:20) (Class 5) (0-70,69) 3-Y-O+ £2,911 (£866; £432; £216) Stalls Centre

Form RPR
2535 **1** **Beckermet (IRE)**[3] 7281 11-9-5 **67**.................................... PJMcDonald 1 78
(Ruth Carr) *cl up: led after 1f: jnd and rdn 2f out: drvn ent fnl f: styd on strly* **11/1**

3000 **2** 2 1/2 **Bassett Road (IRE)**[95] 4338 5-8-9 **57**.............................(p) TomEaves 6 62
(Keith Dalgleish) *trckd ldrs: hdwy 2f out: rdn over 1f out: styd on wl fnl f* **7/1[3]**

6000 **3** 1/2 **Hidden Talent**[62] 5527 3-9-3 **67**.................................... MichaelStainton 8 69
(David Brown) *in tch: hdwy to chse ldrs 3f out: rdn wl over 1f out: drvn and edgd lft fnl f: kpt on same pce* **25/1**

3401 **4** hd **Alexandrakollontai (IRE)**[8] 7149 3-9-1 **68** 6ex..........(b) JulieBurke(3) 13 70
(Alistair Whillans) *hld up: hdwy over 2f out: rdn to chse ldrs over 1f out: drvn and edgd lft ins fnl f: styd on: nrst fin* **10/1**

4305 **5** 1/2 **Broctune Papa Gio**[13] 7024 6-9-2 **69**.......................... DavidBergin(5) 11 70
(Keith Reveley) *wnt lft s: in rr: hdwy on outer wl over 2f out: rdn along wl over 1f out: kpt on fnl f: nrst fin* **8/1**

0606 **6** 3/4 **Orwellian**[23] 6761 4-8-11 **59**... GrahamLee 12 58
(Bryan Smart) *hld up in rr: hdwy over 2f out: rdn to chse ldrs whn n.m.r ins fnl f: kpt on towards fin* **10/1**

3023 **7** 1 1/2 **Blue Maisey**[3] 7283 5-8-12 **65**.. KevinStott(5) 2 61
(Edwin Tuer) *trckd ldrs: cl up 1/2-way: effrt to chal 2f out: sn rdn and ev ch tl drvn ent fnl f and sn wknd* **7/2[1]**

0543 **8** 1/2 **Tukitinyasok (IRE)**[50] 5921 6-8-0 **55** oh6.................... SamanthaBell(7) 4 49
(Clive Mulhall) *chsd ldrs: rdn along over 2f out: sn drvn and wknd* **16/1**

0001 **9** 5 **Mercers Row**[23] 6760 6-8-12 **67**................................... GemmaTutty(7) 7 48
(Karen Tutty) *prom: pushed along 3f out: rdn 2f out: sn wknd* **22/1**

6000 **10** 1 **Liliargh (IRE)**[28] 6599 4-8-0 **55**...............................(p) AnnaHesketh(7) 10 34
(Ben Haslam) *a towards rr* **33/1**

0321 **11** nk **Lees Anthem**[23] 6761 6-8-8 **56**... DavidAllan 3 34
(Mel Brittain) *trckd ldrs: hdwy 3f out: cl up and ev ch 2f out: sn rdn and grad wknd* **10/1**

3142 **12** hd **True Pleasure (IRE)**[8] 7152 6-8-13 **61**......................... TomQueally 9 38
(James Bethell) *hld up: swtchd rt and rdn wl over 2f out: nvr a factor* **9/2[2]**

3540 **13** hd **Polish World (USA)**[15] 6969 9-9-6 **68**........................... BarryMcHugh 5 45
(Paul Midgley) *led 1f: cl up: rdn along over 3f out: sn wknd* **25/1**

1m 28.7s (4.20) **Going Correction** +0.575s/f (Yiel)
WFA 3 from 4yo+ 2lb **13 Ran SP% 120.5**
Speed ratings (Par 103): **99,96,95,95,94 93,92,91,85,84 84,84,83**
toteswingers 1&2 £15.60, 1&3 £32.30, 2&3 £40.20 CSF £82.91 CT £1960.17 TOTE £11.50: £3.40, £3.00, £8.80; EX 112.80 Trifecta £1707.40 Part won. Pool: £2,276.61 - 0.07 winning units..
Owner Mrs Marion Chapman **Bred** Fritz Von Ball Moss **Trained** Huby, N Yorks
■ A win for Beckermet on his 150th career start.

FOCUS
A modest handicap run at a decent pace, but the time was slower than division I. The winner's best effort this year.

7345 BET AND WATCH RACINGUK'S APP MAIDEN STKS 6f
4:50 (4:52) (Class 5) 3-Y-O+ £2,911 (£866; £432; £216) Stalls Centre

Form RPR
2045 **1** **Adiator**[51] 5876 5-8-10 58.. AdamCarter(5) 11 67
(Neville Bycroft) *a.p: cl up 1/2-way: led 2f out: rdn over 1f out: jnd and drvn ins fnl f: kpt on gamely towards fin* **10/1[3]**

2 nk **Great Minds (IRE)**[9] 7133 3-9-5 0.................................. WayneLordan 9 71
(T Stack, Ire) *hld up towards rr: hdwy whn n.m.r 2f out: sn chsng ldrs: rdn to chal ins fnl f and ev ch tl drvn: edgd lft and no ex last 75yds* **1/1[1]**

3 2 3/4 **Watchable** 3-9-5 0... RobertWinston 6 63
(Tobias B P Coles) *trckd ldrs: hdwy over 2f out: rdn over 1f out: ev ch tl one pce ins fnl f* **22/1**

5020 **4** 2 1/2 **Imperial Bond**[8] 7153 4-9-1 55.................................(t) KevinStott(5) 4 55
(Jason Ward) *chsd ldrs: rdn along 2f out: drvn over 1f out: kpt on same pce* **33/1**

5-2 **5** 3 1/4 **Dutiful Son (IRE)**[38] 6289 3-9-5 0................................... SebSanders 10 46
(Jeremy Noseda) *dwlt: trckd ldrs: hdwy 2f out: rdn over 1f out: drvn ent fnl f: sn wknd* **2/1[2]**

0-30 **6** 2 **Ri Na Si**[45] 6074 3-9-5 57.. AndrewMullen 7 40
(Michael Appleby) *led 1f: cl up: rdn over 2f out: grad wknd* **20/1**

2530 **7** 3/4 **Gambino (IRE)**[25] 6687 3-9-5 46.. TomEaves 1 37
(Alan Berry) *led after 1f: rdn along over 2f out: sn hdd and drvn: grad wknd* **100/1**

2430 **8** 1 **Graceful Act**[16] 6941 5-9-1 52......................................(p) DavidAllan 13 29
(Ron Barr) *cl up: rdn along bef 1/2-way: sn outpcd* **14/1**

9 2 1/4 **Cumberworth** 3-9-5 0.. GrahamLee 3 28
(Michael Easterby) *dwlt: a in rr* **50/1**

00- **10** 2 **Cottam Stella**[454] 4348 5-8-12 45..................................[1] NeilFarley(3) 8 17
(John Wainwright) *a in rr* **100/1**

3220 **11** 8 **Shillito**[15] 6965 3-9-5 59... BarryMcHugh 12
(Tony Coyle) *racd wd: cl up: pushed along bef 1/2-way: sn rdn and outpcd* **16/1**

0 **12** 15 **Noble Maximus**[16] 6940 3-9-2 0...................................... PaulPickard(3) 2
(Alan Berry) *s.i.s: a in rr* **100/1**

1m 15.09s (3.29) **Going Correction** +0.575s/f (Yiel)
WFA 3 from 4yo+ 1lb **12 Ran SP% 122.0**
Speed ratings (Par 103): **101,100,96,93,89 86,85,84,81,78 67,47**
toteswingers 1&2 £3.50, 1&3 £35.00, 2&3 £8.70 CSF £20.33 TOTE £10.70: £2.20, £1.30, £6.30; EX 29.30 Trifecta £725.20 Pool: £4,274.80 - 4.42 winning units..
Owner N Bycroft **Bred** Mickley Stud & C J Whiston **Trained** Brandsby, N Yorks

FOCUS
No strength to this very ordinary maiden. The gallop was sound. The winner is a more likely guide than the runner-up.

7346 READ HAYLEY TURNER EVERY FRIDAY RACINGUK.COM LADIES' H'CAP (FOR LADY AMATEUR RIDERS) 1m 2f
5:20 (5:22) (Class 6) (0-65,65) 3-Y-O+ £1,975 (£607; £303) Stalls Low

Form RPR
4021 **1** **Valentine's Gift**[16] 6952 5-10-0 **58**...................................... MissCWalton 5 67
(Neville Bycroft) *hld up towards rr: stdy hdwy 3f out: chsd ldrs over 1f out: rdn to chal ent fnl f: styd on to ld last 100yds* **14/1**

000 **2** *nk* **Top Diktat**[50] 5928 5-10-4 **65**.................................. MissHayleyMoore(3) 8 74
(Gary Moore) *hld up in tch: smooth hdwy to trck ldrs over 3f out: led 2f out: sn rdn: drvn and hdd last 100yds: no ex nr fin* **7/1**[3]

3406 **3** *2* **Gold Show**[28] 6599 4-10-7 **65**.................................. MissJCoward 3 70
(Edwin Tuer) *trckd ldng pair: hdwy on inner 3f out: cl up 2f out: sn rdn and ev ch tl one pce wl ins fnl f* **8/1**

6302 **4** *¾* **Pertuis (IRE)**[22] 6775 7-10-2 **65**.............................. MissBeckySmith(5) 10 69
(Micky Hammond) *in tch: hdwy to chse ldrs 3f out: effrt 2f out: sn rdn and ev ch ent fnl f: wknd last 100yds* **9/1**

3040 **5** *1 ½* **Obboorr**[16] 6943 4-10-4 **62**.................................. MissHBethell 14 63
(Brian Rothwell) *hld up in rr: hdwy 3f out: rdn along to chse ldrs over 1f out: kpt on fnl f: nrst fin* **12/1**

5025 **6** *5* **Nezami (IRE)**[21] 6803 8-10-2 **60**.................................. MissSBrotherton 15 51
(Patrick Clinton) *in tch: hdwy to chse ldrs 4f out: rdn along wl over 2f out: sn no imp* **14/1**

5316 **7** *2* **Woodacre**[37] 6297 6-10-3 **64**..............................(p) MissJRRichards(3) 7 51
(Richard Whitaker) *trckd ldrs: hdwy 4f out: led 3f out: rdn and hdd 2f out: wknd over 1f out* **6/1**[2]

4033 **8** *nk* **Santo Prince (USA)**[10] 7091 3-9-13 **62**.................. MissRachelKing 12 49
(Michael Bell) *chsd ldrs: rdn along over 3f out: sn wknd* **5/1**[1]

4011 **9** *nk* **Rise To Glory (IRE)**[8] 7148 5-9-12 **63** 6ex........... MissMeganHarris(7) 2 49
(Shaun Harris) *led: rdn along 4f out: hdd 3f out: cl up tl rdn and wknd over 1f out* **16/1**

6612 **10** *2* **The Blue Banana (IRE)**[16] 6943 4-10-4 **65**....(b) MissJoannaMason(3) 9 47
(Edwin Tuer) *midfield: rdn along 4f out: n.d* **10/1**

3100 **11** *20* **Yorksters Prince (IRE)**[19] 6877 6-9-10 **59**..............(b) MissNHayes(5) 4 3
(Marjorie Fife) *chsd ldr: rdn along 4f out: sn wknd* **11/1**

6000 **12** *10* **Millies Quest**[28] 6612 4-9-11 **60**.............................. MissKMargarson(5) 1
(Martin Smith) *dwlt: a bhd* **40/1**

0153 **13** *1 ½* **Conducting**[23] 6759 5-9-13 **64**................ MissAnne-SophieCrombez(7) 13
(Gay Kelleway) *chsd ldrs: rdn along 4f out: sn wknd* **12/1**

5000 **14** *2 ½* **Samoan (IRE)**[4] 7238 4-10-1 **59**.................................. MissADeniel 11
(Alan Berry) *a in rr: bhd fnl 4f* **40/1**

2m 13.3s (6.20) **Going Correction** +0.35s/f (Good)
WFA 3 from 4yo+ 5lb **14** Ran SP% **121.5**
Speed ratings (Par 101): **89,88,87,86,85 81,79,79,79,77 61,53,52,50**
toteswingers 1&2 £17.30, 1&3 £26.90, 2&3 £12.70 CSF £109.82 CT £852.11 TOTE £9.20: £3.50, £2.80, £3.40; EX 122.50 Trifecta £537.80 Pool: £1,502.90 - 2.09 winning units..
Owner Hambleton Racing Partnership **Bred** N Bycroft **Trained** Brandsby, N Yorks
■ Stewards' Enquiry : Miss Hayley Moore four-day ban: used whip above permitted level (Nov 20,26,Dec 2,4)

FOCUS
A modest handicap run at a decent gallop. The first five finished clear. The winner more than confirmed his latet form, with the second and fourth helping with the standard.
T/Plt: £96.70 to a £1 stake. Pool: £54,801.35 - 413.39 winning units. T/Qpdt: £37.10 to a £1 stake. Pool: £4,902.70 - 97.75 winning units. JR

7197 WOLVERHAMPTON (A.W) (L-H)

Friday, October 18

OFFICIAL GOING: Standard
Wind: Fresh half-against Weather: Overcast

7347 32RED CASINO APPRENTICE H'CAP 5f 216y(P)
5:25 (5:25) (Class 6) (0-65,63) 3-Y-0+ **£1,940** (£577; £288; £144) **Stalls** Low

Form RPR

5243 **1** **Powerful Pierre**[15] 6980 6-9-5 **60**..............................(b) JacobButterfield 1 70
(Ollie Pears) *sn pushed along towards rr: r.o u.p ins fnl f to ld towards fin* **4/1**[1]

0610 **2** *nk* **Trending (IRE)**[22] 6771 4-9-1 **61**..............................(bt) DavidParkes(5) 2 70
(Jeremy Gask) *hld up: hdwy over 1f out: rdn: edgd lft ins fnl f: sn ev ch: r.o* **8/1**

4506 **3** *½* **Hot Sugar (USA)**[16] 6948 4-9-2 **60**..............................(p) DanielMuscutt(3) 12 67
(Michael Appleby) *chsd ldrs: rdn to ld over 1f out: hdd towards fin* **12/1**

51-1 **4** *1* **French Press (IRE)**[11] 7079 3-9-0 **61** 6ex...........(bt) CameronHardie(5) 3 65
(S Donohoe, Ire) *prom: nt clr run and lost pl over 3f out: hdwy over 1f out: rdn and edgd lft ins fnl f: styd on* **9/2**[2]

6015 **5** *½* **Gaelic Wizard (IRE)**[11] 7068 5-9-4 **62**....................(p) JoshBaudains(3) 10 65
(Dominic Ffrench Davis) *w ldr tl led over 2f out: rdn and hdd over 1f out: styd on same pce ins fnl f* **6/1**[3]

0034 **6** *2* **Amis Reunis**[4] 7236 4-8-9 **55**.................................. JordanHibberd(5) 7 51
(Alan Berry) *prom: rdn and hung rt over 2f out: no ex ins fnl f* **10/1**

0030 **7** *¾* **Divertimenti (IRE)**[85] 4669 9-8-12 **58**..............................(b) AdamMcLean(5) 8 52
(Roy Bowring) *chsd ldrs: rdn over 1f out: no ex ins fnl f* **16/1**

1010 **8** *1 ¼* **Artful Lady (IRE)**[45] 6075 4-9-3 **63**.............................. JordanVaughan(5) 4 53+
(George Margarson) *s.i.s: sn outpcd: rdn over 2f out: nvr trbld ldrs* **8/1**

0606 **9** *½* **Seamster**[28] 6610 6-8-9 **53**..............................(tp) NoelGarbutt(3) 6 41
(Richard Ford) *prom: rdn over 3f out: wknd ins fnl f* **25/1**

6224 **10** *6* **One Kool Dude**[28] 6603 4-8-10 **56**..............................(b) LouisSteward(5) 9 25
(Neville Bycroft) *prom: drvn along 1/2-way: wknd over 1f out* **12/1**

0500 **11** *2 ¼* **Red Star Lady (IRE)**[8] 7150 3-8-7 **49** oh4............(e[1]) ShirleyTeasdale 11 11
(Shaun Harris) *led over 3f: wknd fnl f* **50/1**

0000 **12** *8* **Major Muscari (IRE)**[178] 1748 5-8-3 **49** oh4................ JackGarritty(5) 13
(Shaun Harris) *hood removed late and s v slowly: a bhd* **20/1**

1m 14.84s (-0.16) **Going Correction** -0.05s/f (Stan)
WFA 3 from 4yo+ 1lb **12** Ran SP% **115.6**
Speed ratings (Par 101): **99,98,97,96,95 93,92,90,89,81 78,68**
toteswingers 1&2 £13.50, 1&3 £12.80, 2&3 £8.70 CSF £34.14 CT £357.34 TOTE £2.00: £1.10, £4.60, £4.40; EX 54.70 Trifecta £366.40 Pool: £512.40 - 1.04 winning units..
Owner Terence Elsey **Bred** Hedsor Stud **Trained** Norton, N Yorks
■ Stewards' Enquiry : Jack Garritty five-day ban: used whip when out of contention (Nov 1,2,4,5,6)

FOCUS
More wax had been added to the surface since the previous meeting five days earlier in an attempt to address the prevailing kickback issues. All change late on in this moderate affair, as both the first two were produced from off the pace to swamp those played sooner. The winner is rated to form.

7348 32RED.COM E B F MEDIAN AUCTION MAIDEN STKS 5f 216y(P)
5:55 (5:59) (Class 5) 2-Y-0 **£2,911** (£866; £432; £216) **Stalls** Low

Form RPR

6 **1** **Alderley**[16] 6931 2-9-0 0.................................. JohnFahy 6 65+
(Jamie Osborne) *sn outpcd: rdn and str run fnl f to ld nr fin* **6/1**

022 **2** *¾* **Buy And Sell (IRE)**[15] 6981 2-9-5 72.................................. SeanLevey 7 68
(David Brown) *chsd ldr tl shkn up to ld over 1f out: rdn and edgd lft ins fnl f: hdd nr fin* **9/4**[1]

3 *2 ¼* **Definite Secret** 2-9-0 0.................................. GrahamGibbons 5 56
(James Tate) *sn led: rdn: hung lft and hdd over 1f out: styd on same pce ins fnl f* **5/1**[3]

05 **4** *1* **Kaheyll**[7] 7162 2-9-5 0..............................(b[1]) LiamJones 8 58
(William Haggas) *prom and sn pushed along: rdn and hung lft over 1f out: styd on same pce fnl f* **4/1**[2]

24 **5** *4 ½* **Hot Amber (USA)**[85] 4686 2-9-0 0.................................. ShaneKelly 4 40
(Robert Cowell) *prom: drvn along 1/2-way: wknd fnl f* **4/1**[2]

05 **6** *1 ¼* **Injaz**[25] 6681 2-9-5 0.................................. MartinHarley 1 41
(Kevin Ryan) *s.i.s: hld up: pushed along over 2f out: rdn over 1f out: wknd fnl f* **4/1**[2]

00 **7** *6* **Who Splashed Me**[16] 6947 2-9-0 0.................................. FrederikTylicki 2 18
(J R Jenkins) *chsd ldrs: pushed along over 2f out: wknd over 1f out* **100/1**

8 *30* **Skinny Latte** 2-9-5 0.................................. LiamKeniry 3
(Deborah Sanderson) *s.i.s: outpcd* **66/1**

1m 15.25s (0.25) **Going Correction** -0.05s/f (Stan) **8** Ran SP% **124.2**
Speed ratings (Par 95): **96,95,92,90,84 83,75,35**
toteswingers 1&2 £4.80, 1&3 £7.30, 2&3 £4.10 CSF £21.83 TOTE £5.40: £2.30, £1.40, £2.30; EX 27.40 Trifecta £186.10 Pool: £2890.83 - 11.64 winning units..
Owner Ladyswood Stud **Bred** Ladyswood Stud **Trained** Upper Lambourn, Berks

FOCUS
A moderate-looking maiden. The second, fourth and the time suggest the bare form can rate no higher.

7349 32RED NURSERY H'CAP 5f 20y(P)
6:25 (6:25) (Class 4) (0-85,81) 2-Y-0 **£3,752** (£1,116; £557; £278) **Stalls** Low

Form RPR

2246 **1** **Exceeder**[9] 7127 2-9-1 **75**.................................. MartinHarley 4 77
(Marco Botti) *chsd ldrs: rdn to ld ins fnl f: r.o* **9/4**[2]

223 **2** *nk* **Sunset Shore**[48] 5976 2-9-3 **77**.................................. ChrisCatlin 1 78
(Sir Mark Prescott Bt) *led: rdn and hdd ins fnl f: r.o* **12/1**

1060 **3** *2 ¼* **Lexington Rose**[13] 7026 2-8-10 **75**.................................. GeorgeChaloner(5) 6 68
(Bryan Smart) *w ldr: rdn and ev ch over 1f out: styd on same pce ins fnl f* **9/2**[3]

323 **4** *2* **Gilmer (IRE)**[42] 6169 2-9-7 **81**.................................. AdamKirby 5 67+
(Charlie Appleby) *sn drvn along in rr: hdwy u.p over 1f out: styd on same pce fnl f* **2/1**[1]

U52 **5** *nk* **Kodafine (IRE)**[13] 7036 2-8-1 **66**.................................. NoelGarbutt(5) 7 51
(David Evans) *prom: rdn over 1f out: styd on same pce fnl f* **33/1**

2532 **6** *5* **Simply Black (IRE)**[15] 6966 2-8-9 **69**.................................. GrahamGibbons 8 36
(David O'Meara) *chsd ldrs: rdn over 1f out: wknd fnl f* **16/1**

1130 **7** *9* **Fine Art Fair (IRE)**[9] 7117 2-8-11 **71**.................................. SeanLevey 2 5
(Gary Moore) *s.i.s: outpcd: rdn 1/2-way: sn wknd* **7/1**

1m 1.69s (-0.61) **Going Correction** -0.05s/f (Stan) **7** Ran SP% **111.3**
Speed ratings (Par 97): **102,101,97,94,94 86,71**
toteswingers 1&2 £13.70, 1&3 £3.50, 2&3 £9.80 CSF £26.83 CT £107.95 TOTE £3.90: £2.00, £5.50; EX 23.30 Trifecta £129.20 Pool: £1559.76 - 9.05 winning units..
Owner Sheikh Mohammed Bin Khalifa Al Maktoum **Bred** Martin Percival **Trained** Newmarket, Suffolk

FOCUS
Not the deepest nursery for the grade, and not the most watertight of form with the favourite running well below expectations. The pace was good, however.

7350 £32 BONUS AT 32RED.COM (S) STKS 1m 141y(P)
7:00 (7:00) (Class 6) 3-5-Y-0 **£1,940** (£577; £288; £144) **Stalls** Low

Form RPR

0-1 **1** **That's Plenty (IRE)**[21] 6806 4-9-6 70.................................. TadhgO'Shea 5 77
(John Patrick Shanahan, Ire) *chsd ldrs tl led over 6f out: hdd 5f out: led again over 2f out: rdn clr fnl f* **6/5**[1]

5153 **2** *7* **Fluctuation (IRE)**[2] 7303 5-9-6 70..............................(v) NeilCallan 3 61
(Ian Williams) *chsd ldrs: rdn over 2f out: styd on same pce fr over 1f out: wnt 2nd wl ins fnl f* **3/1**[2]

0625 **3** *nk* **Honey Of A Kitten (USA)**[23] 6759 5-8-13 69..............(v) EoinWalsh(7) 1 60
(David Evans) *led: hdd over 6f out: led again 5f out: rdn and hdd over 2f out: no ex ins fnl f* **7/1**

0005 **4** *nk* **Dansili Dutch (IRE)**[21] 6805 4-8-9 33.................................. GrahamGibbons 2 49
(David O'Meara) *t.k.h: w ldr tl over 6f out: remained handy: rdn over 3f out: styd on same pce fr over 1f out* **33/1**

3350 **5** *60* **Medici Dancer**[9] 7130 3-8-6 69 ow1.................................. ChrisCatlin 4
(Tim Easterby) *sn outpcd: bhd fnl 6f* **7/2**[3]

1m 48.83s (-1.67) **Going Correction** -0.05s/f (Stan)
WFA 3 from 4yo+ 4lb **5** Ran SP% **108.1**
Speed ratings (Par 101): **105,98,98,98,44**
CSF £4.83 TOTE £1.70: £1.50, £1.30; EX 6.20 Trifecta £13.00 Pool: £1053.39 - 60.47 winning units..There was no bid for the winner.
Owner Thistle Bloodstock Limited **Bred** Denis Brosnan **Trained** Danesfort, Co. Kilkenny

FOCUS
Straightforward for the winner, who's rated back to his early-season form.

7351 32REDPOKER.COM CLASSIFIED STKS 1m 1f 103y(P)
7:30 (7:30) (Class 6) 3-Y-0+ **£1,940** (£577; £288; £144) **Stalls** Low

Form RPR

022 **1** **Poppy Bond**[21] 6803 3-8-7 50.................................. TimClark(5) 2 56
(Alan Bailey) *mde all: plld hrd: rdn over 2f out: jst hld on* **9/4**[1]

502 **2** *nk* **My Claire**[13] 7035 3-8-12 48.................................. AdamBeschizza 9 55
(Nigel Tinkler) *hld up in tch: pushed along over 3f out: rdn over 1f out: r.o u.p* **7/1**[3]

5054 **3** *¾* **Bladewood Girl**[9] 7124 5-9-2 51.................................. FrederikTylicki 6 54
(J R Jenkins) *trckd ldrs: rdn over 2f out: styd on* **4/1**[2]

0000 **4** *1* **Platinum Proof (USA)**[15] 6964 3-8-12 47..............(v[1]) GrahamGibbons 7 52
(David O'Meara) *trckd wnr: rdn over 2f out: styd on same pce ins fnl f* **10/1**

255 **5** *¾* **Phils Wish (IRE)**[45] 6092 4-8-13 55.............. WilliamTwiston-Davies(3) 8 50
(John C McConnell, Ire) *hld up: hdwy 5f out: rdn over 1f out: styd on same pce ins fnl f* **4/1**[2]

0546 **6** *3 ¼* **Hawaiian Freeze**[22] 6782 4-9-2 44.................................. ShaneKelly 10 43
(John Stimpson) *s.i.s: hld up: hdwy over 2f out: rdn over 1f out: no ex fnl f* **33/1**

0063 **7** *9* **Cheers Big Ears (IRE)**[15] 6986 7-8-11 43..............(t) DanielMuscutt(5) 4 24
(Richard Price) *hld up: hmpd over 3f out: sn rdn and wknd* **16/1**

8 *4* **Marvelous James (IRE)**[24] 3303 3-8-12 52.................................. MartinHarley 3 16
(Paul W Flynn, Ire) *s.s: hld up: hmpd over 3f out: sn wknd* **7/1**[3]

5220 **9** *3 3/4* **Saint Boniface**[29] 6553 4-9-2 53 .... SteveDrowne 5 8
(Peter Makin) *plld hrd and prom: pushed along and lost pl 4f out: hmpd over 3f out: sn wknd* **12/1**

0-06 **10** *9* **Dance To Destiny**[15] 6986 5-9-2 44 .... DougieCostello 1
(K F Clutterbuck) *trckd ldrs: rdn over 3f out: wknd wl over 2f out* **66/1**

2m 1.65s (-0.05) **Going Correction** -0.05s/f (Stan)
WFA 3 from 4yo+ 4lb **10** Ran SP% **122.9**
Speed ratings (Par 101): **98,97,97,96,95 92,84,81,77,69**
toteswingers 1&2 £9.10, 1&3 £4.00, 2&3 £6.80 CSF £20.09 TOTE £4.50: £1.10, £2.00, £2.20; EX 30.50 Trifecta £112.80 Pool: £1533.93 - 10.19 winning units..
Owner North Cheshire Trading & Storage Ltd **Bred** North Cheshire Trading And Storage Ltd **Trained** Newmarket, Suffolk

FOCUS
Few got into this poor classified contest, the winner given an easy lead. He's rated to his latest effort here.

7352 32REDBET.COM NURSERY H'CAP 7f 32y(P)
8:00 (8:01) (Class 6) (0-65,70) 2-Y-O **£1,940** (£577; £288; £144) **Stalls** High

Form RPR

033 **1** **Rayoumti (IRE)**[30] 6512 2-9-7 65 .... MartinHarley 8 70
(Marco Botti) *chsd ldrs: shkn up to ld over 1f out: r.o: comf* **3/1**[2]

0330 **2** *2* **Tyrsal (IRE)**[23] 6749 2-8-11 55 .... AndreaAtzeni 5 55
(Robert Eddery) *a.p: rdn to chse wnr over 1f out: r.o* **14/1**

4511 **3** *1/2* **Shyron**[6] 7199 2-9-5 70 6ex .... JordanVaughan(7) 9 71+
(George Margarson) *s.i.s: outpcd: nt clr run over 2f out: hdwy over 1f out: r.o: nt rch ldrs* **6/4**[1]

000 **4** *1* **Barbary (IRE)**[53] 5843 2-9-1 59 ....[1] ShaneKelly 11 55
(James Fanshawe) *hld up: hdwy over 3f out: rdn over 1f out: r.o* **14/1**

0036 **5** *2* **Sheacheval (IRE)**[28] 6605 2-9-7 65 .... LiamJones 4 57
(J S Moore) *hld up: drvn along over 3f out: hdwy over 1f out: styd on same pce fnl f* **50/1**

0561 **6** *1* **Sydney James (IRE)**[8] 7156 2-9-1 59 6ex .... WilliamCarson 2 48
(Lee Carter) *chsd ldrs: rdn over 2f out: wknd ins fnl f* **25/1**

4024 **7** *nk* **Dancing Sal (IRE)**[10] 7096 2-9-4 62 .... AdamKirby 10 50
(David Evans) *hld up: rdn over 2f out: n.d* **20/1**

504 **8** *nse* **Miguela McGuire**[34] 6383 2-8-6 53 .... JasonHart(3) 6 41
(Eric Alston) *s.i.s: sn pushed along and prom: nt clr run over 2f out: rdn and swtchd lft over 1f out: no ex fnl f* **8/1**[3]

0432 **9** *5* **Tunnel Tiger (IRE)**[77] 4964 2-9-0 58 .... RichardKingscote 7 34
(William Knight) *w ldr tl led over 2f out: rdn and hdd over 1f out: wknd fnl f* **14/1**

4305 **10** *1* **Exceed Areeda (IRE)**[6] 7198 2-9-6 64 .... NeilCallan 1 38
(James Tate) *led: rdn and hdd over 2f out: wknd fnl f* **16/1**

5000 **11** *3 1/2* **Red Oasis**[22] 6778 2-8-6 50 .... JimmyQuinn 3 15
(Robert Eddery) *prom: pushed along 1/2-way: wknd over 1f out* **100/1**

1m 29.95s (0.35) **Going Correction** -0.05s/f (Stan) **11** Ran SP% **113.6**
Speed ratings (Par 93): **96,93,93,92,89 88,88,88,82,81 77**
toteswingers 1&2 £5.40, 1&3 £1.40, 2&3 £16.90 CSF £40.86 CT £84.34 TOTE £4.20: £1.10, £3.80, £1.40; EX 35.30 Trifecta £142.80 Pool: £1504.95 - 7.90 winning units..
Owner Saleh Al Homaizi & Imad Al Sagar **Bred** Denis & David McDonnell **Trained** Newmarket, Suffolk

■ Stewards' Enquiry : Liam Jones three-day ban: used whip without giving filly time to respond (Nov 2,4,5)

FOCUS
A moderate nursery. The runner-up helps with the opening level.

7353 32REDBINGO.COM H'CAP (DIV I) 7f 32y(P)
8:30 (8:30) (Class 6) (0-60,60) 3-Y-O+ **£1,940** (£577; £288; £144) **Stalls** High

Form RPR

5254 **1** **Harvest Mist (IRE)**[157] 2345 5-8-12 54 .... WilliamTwiston-Davies(3) 8 62
(Shaun Lycett) *a.p: rdn to chse ldr over 1f out: styd on u.p to ld wl ins fnl f* **14/1**

0030 **2** *1* **Poetic Belle**[17] 6918 3-8-7 53 ....(t) ShirleyTeasdale(5) 4 57
(Shaun Harris) *chsd ldr tl led wl over 1f out: sn rdn: hdd wl ins fnl f* **25/1**

4606 **3** *3* **No Win No Fee**[147] 2624 3-9-5 60 .... AndrewMullen 11 56
(Michael Appleby) *hld up: rdn 1/2-way: hdwy u.p over 1f out: nt rch ldrs* **2/1**[1]

6060 **4** *1* **True Prince (USA)**[35] 6367 4-8-13 52 ....(b) FergusSweeney 5 47
(Alastair Lidderdale) *mid-div: pushed along over 4f out: hdwy over 2f out: sn rdn: styd on same pce fnl f* **25/1**

5352 **5** *hd* **Chester Deelyte (IRE)**[3] 7266 5-8-7 46 oh1 ....(v) SamHitchcott 7 40
(Lisa Williamson) *hld up in tch: rdn over 2f out: styd on same pce fnl f* **7/1**

0005 **6** *2* **Laudation**[11] 7077 3-8-13 57 .... SladeO'Hara(3) 9 45
(Danielle McCormick) *sn outpcd: styd on fr over 1f out: nvr nrr* **33/1**

0244 **7** *1/2* **Piccolo Express**[28] 6610 7-9-6 59 .... ShaneKelly 6 46
(Brian Baugh) *hld up: nt clr run wl over 1f out: nvr on terms* **8/1**

3424 **8** *9* **Hoppy's Flyer (FR)**[15] 6980 5-9-7 60 .... GrahamGibbons 2 23+
(Mark Brisbourne) *prom: pushed along whn hmpd wl over 1f out: sn wknd* **6/1**[3]

002 **9** *4* **Speightowns Kid (USA)**[15] 6980 5-9-7 60 ....(b) RobertHavlin 3 12
(Richard Ford) *led: rdn over 2f out: hdd & wknd wl over 1f out* **5/1**[2]

U034 **10** *13* **Vitznau (IRE)**[199] 1310 9-9-4 57 .... AdamBeschizza 12
(K F Clutterbuck) *prom tl rdn and wknd over 2f out* **14/1**

5300 **11** *2 1/4* **Hittin'The Skids (IRE)**[15] 6986 5-8-8 47 .... JimmyQuinn 1
(Mandy Rowland) *sn pushed along in rr: rdn 4f out: wknd 3f out* **33/1**

500 **12** *13* **Immediately**[100] 4176 3-8-5 46 oh1 .... LiamJones 10
(Robert Cowell) *s.i.s: outpcd* **33/1**

1m 29.67s (0.07) **Going Correction** -0.05s/f (Stan)
WFA 3 from 4yo+ 2lb **12** Ran SP% **117.7**
Speed ratings (Par 101): **97,95,92,91,91 88,88,77,73,58 55,41**
toteswingers 1&2 £16.50, 1&3 £4.40, 2&3 £19.60 CSF £325.42 CT £1006.44 TOTE £8.20: £2.10, £10.10, £1.70; EX 161.60 Trifecta £660.80 Part won. Pool: £881.16 - 0.13 winning units..
Owner Chris Buckingham **Bred** Mrs Amanda Brudenell **Trained** Clapton-on-the-Hill, Gloucs

FOCUS
Division one of a low-grade 7f handicaP was run 0.44sec faster than division II. A small personal best from the winner.

7354 32REDBINGO.COM H'CAP (DIV II) 7f 32y(P)
9:00 (9:01) (Class 6) (0-60,60) 3-Y-O+ **£1,940** (£577; £288; £144) **Stalls** High

Form RPR

32-4 **1** **Monte Cassino (IRE)**[163] 2171 8-8-10 54 ....(e) GeorgeChaloner(5) 10 64
(Bryan Smart) *chsd ldr tl led over 5f out: rdn over 1f out: styd on* **14/1**

0500 **2** *nk* **Maakirr (IRE)**[10] 7109 4-9-4 60 ....(t) MarkCoumbe(3) 11 69
(Roy Bowring) *s.i.s: hdwy over 4f out: rdn and ev ch fr over 1f out: r.o* **5/1**[2]

2054 **3** *1 1/4* **Annie Gogh**[20] 6843 3-8-8 56 .... RachelRichardson(7) 6 61+
(Tim Easterby) *hld up: hdwy on outer 2f out: rdn and hung lft fr over 1f out: r.o* **12/1**[3]

2051 **4** *1 1/4* **Arabian Flight**[9] 7124 4-9-7 60 6ex .... AndrewMullen 5 62
(Michael Appleby) *led: hdd over 5f out: chsd ldr: rdn over 2f out: styd on same pce ins fnl f* **9/4**[1]

-650 **5** *4 1/2* **Mon Chic**[38] 6289 3-8-5 46 oh1 .... JimmyQuinn 4 35
(Geoffrey Oldroyd) *trckd ldrs: plld hrd: lost pl over 5f out: rallied over 1f out: wknd fnl f* **20/1**

5302 **6** *5* **Logans Lad (IRE)**[6] 7197 3-9-5 60 ....(t) ShaneKelly 2 36
(John Stimpson) *chsd ldrs: rdn over 2f out: wknd fnl f* **9/4**[1]

5600 **7** *3/4* **Frosted Off**[42] 6154 3-8-7 48 ow1 .... SamHitchcott 9 22
(John Spearing) *prom: drvn along 1/2-way: wknd over 1f out* **33/1**

6010 **8** *1 3/4* **Just Isla**[10] 7093 3-9-4 59 ....(p) SteveDrowne 1 28
(Peter Makin) *sn pushed along in rr: nvr nrr* **12/1**[3]

440 **9** *2 1/2* **Senora Lobo (IRE)**[18] 6902 3-8-2 46 oh1 ....(p) RyanPowell(3) 7 8
(Lisa Williamson) *s.i.s: outpcd* **50/1**

0000 **10** *1 1/2* **High On The Hog (IRE)**[28] 6610 5-8-13 52 ....(p) TomMcLaughlin 12 11
(Mark Brisbourne) *chsd ldrs tl rdn and wknd over 2f out* **33/1**

0-06 **11** *1 3/4* **Avonlini**[16] 6930 7-8-4 48 ....(p) NoelGarbutt(5) 8
(Richard Ford) *prom: rdn over 2f out: sn wknd* **50/1**

1m 30.11s (0.51) **Going Correction** -0.05s/f (Stan)
WFA 3 from 4yo+ 2lb **11** Ran SP% **114.8**
Speed ratings (Par 101): **95,94,93,91,86 80,80,78,75,73 71**
toteswingers 1&2 £9.70, 1&3 £11.20, 2&3 £9.80 CSF £76.83 CT £882.68 TOTE £12.60: £4.30, £2.20, £3.50; EX 99.60 Trifecta £796.00 Part won. Pool: £1061.40 - 0.42 winning units..
Owner Woodcock Electrical Limited **Bred** R N Auld **Trained** Hambleton, N Yorks

FOCUS
Despite the generous-looking early pace, the winning time was 0.44sec slower than the first division. The winner rates close to his old best.
T/Plt: £25.30. Pool: £62,211.64 - 1792.14 wining units. T/Qpdt: £6.10. Pool: £9575.09 - 1160.34 CR

7355 - 7360a (Foreign Racing) - See Raceform Interactive

7177 DUNDALK (A.W) (L-H)
Friday, October 18

OFFICIAL GOING: Standard

7361a CARLINGFORD STKS (LISTED RACE) 1m 2f 150y(P)
8:45 (8:53) 3-Y-O+ **£21,138** (£6,178; £2,926; £975)

RPR

1 **Paene Magnus (IRE)**[14] 7006 4-9-7 99 ....(tp) KevinManning 6 106
(J S Bolger, Ire) *sn led: strly pressed fr 2f out: rallied wl to hold on fnl 50yds* **7/1**[3]

2 *hd* **Manalapan (IRE)**[14] 7005 3-9-2 110 .... ChrisHayes 7 107+
(P J Prendergast, Ire) *trckd ldrs: 2nd after 4f: almost on terms fr 2f out: kpt on wl: jst hld* **6/1**[2]

3 *1/2* **Afonso De Sousa (USA)**[14] 7005 3-9-2 110 .... JosephO'Brien 3 106
(A P O'Brien, Ire) *chsd ldrs: pushed along in 3rd over 1f out: kpt on wl wout getting on terms w principals* **4/7**[1]

4 *2 1/4* **Sweet Lightning**[47] 6025 8-9-7 106 ....(t) FergalLynch 1 101
(J P Murtagh, Ire) *chsd ldrs on inner: nt qckn over 1f out: kpt on same pce* **12/1**

5 *2* **Love And Cherish (IRE)**[39] 6266 3-8-11 92 ....(p) WJLee 9 93
(David Wachman, Ire) *racd in mid-div tl prog to chse ldrs in 3rd 1/2-way: pushed along and nt qckn over 1f out: kpt on one pce* **50/1**

6 *1 3/4* **Cardinal Palace (IRE)**[14] 7006 3-9-2 100 .... SeamieHeffernan 5 94
(John Joseph Murphy, Ire) *racd in mid-div: strly rdn 2f out: sn no imp* **7/1**[3]

7 *nse* **Opera Gloves (IRE)**[14] 7005 3-8-11 97 .... ShaneFoley 8 89
(M Halford, Ire) *hld up towards rr: kpt on one pce fnl f: nvr on terms* **20/1**

8 *nse* **Majestic Jasmine (IRE)**[41] 6222 3-8-11 94 ....(tp) DeclanMcDonogh 2 89
(John M Oxx, Ire) *hld up towards rr: t.k.h: sme hdwy under 2f out: no imp ent fnl f* **33/1**

9 *1 1/4* **Magnolia Ridge (IRE)**[26] 6676 3-9-2 77 .... PatSmullen 4 92?
(D K Weld, Ire) *a in rr: nvr a factor* **50/1**

2m 14.8s (134.80)
WFA 3 from 4yo+ 6lb **9** Ran SP% **122.3**
CSF £49.30 TOTE £7.80: £1.60, £2.30, £1.10; DF 38.50 Trifecta £101.40.
Owner Mrs J S Bolger **Bred** J S Bolger **Trained** Coolcullen, Co Carlow

FOCUS
A thoroughly game effort by the winner, who also won this race last year. The form looks sound enough rated around the placed horses to their C&D latest.

7362 - (Foreign Racing) - See Raceform Interactive

7010 ASCOT (R-H)
Saturday, October 19

OFFICIAL GOING: Soft (stands' side 7.2, centre 7.9, far side 7.6, round 6.4)
Wind: Light, across Weather: Overcast, drizzly, mild, becoming brighter

7363 QIPCO BRITISH CHAMPIONS LONG DISTANCE CUP (GROUP 3) 2m
1:45 (1:45) (Class 1) 3-Y-O+
£113,420 (£43,000; £21,520; £10,720; £5,380; £2,700) **Stalls** Low

Form RPR

2215 **1** **Royal Diamond (IRE)**[34] 6441 7-9-7 112 .... JohnnyMurtagh 4 115
(J P Murtagh, Ire) *lw: t.k.h: sn hld up in 7th: rdn and prog over 2f out: hanging sltly over 1f out: r.o fnl f to ld last stride* **20/1**

2311 **2** *nse* **Harris Tweed**[56] 5741 6-9-7 115 ....(p) GeorgeBaker 7 115
(William Haggas) *lw: prog on outer to ld after 2f: kicked on 4f out: hrd pressed over 1f out and battled on wl: edgd lft nr fin: hdd last stride* **8/1**

3-2 **3** *3/4* **Eye Of The Storm (IRE)**[20] 6886 3-8-11 112 .... WJLee 10 114
(A P O'Brien, Ire) *racd on outer in 6th: prog 4f out: chsd ldr over 2f out: rdn and tried to chal wl over 1f out: hld and lost 2nd last 75yds* **13/2**[2]

5-10 **4** *1* **Pale Mimosa (IRE)**[34] 6441 4-9-4 109 .... PatSmullen 12 110
(D K Weld, Ire) *hld up in last: same pl 3f out but gng bttr than many: rdn and prog over 2f out: styd on to take 4th nr fin: no ch to threaten* **14/1**

0003 **5** *nk* **Saddler's Rock (IRE)**[34] 6441 5-9-7 112 .... DeclanMcDonogh 8 112
(John M Oxx, Ire) *hld up in last trio: rdn over 3f out: styd on fr 2f out on outer: nvr gng pce to chal* **25/1**

4204 **6** *nk* **Biographer**[36] 6349 4-9-7 109 ....(p) TedDurcan 9 112
(David Lanigan) *hld up in last trio: rdn over 3f out: no prog over 2f out: r.o over 1f out: nrst fin* **16/1**

3-11 **7** ½ **Estimate (IRE)**[121] 3483 4-9-4 114.................................... RyanMoore 3 108
(Sir Michael Stoute) *hld up in 9th: pushed along over 4f out: tried to make prog on outer fr over 2f out: kpt on one pce* **2/1**[1]

0313 **8** ¾ **Times Up**[13] 7060 7-9-7 112.................................. ChristopheSoumillon 1 111
(Ed Dunlop) *prom: chsd ldr over 3f out to over 2f out: steadily fdd* **20/1**

2212 **9** 4 ½ **Ahzeemah (IRE)**[34] 6441 4-9-7 113........................(p) SilvestreDeSousa 5 105
(Saeed bin Suroor) *led 2f: sn settled in 4th: rdn to dispute 2nd over 3f out to over 2f out: wknd over 1f out* **15/2**[3]

-425 **10** 4 ½ **High Jinx (IRE)**[13] 7060 5-9-7 110................................(t) JamesDoyle 11 100
(James Fanshawe) *lw: chsd ldr after 3f tl wknd u.p over 3f out* **16/1**

1041 **11** 7 **Caucus**[23] 6766 6-9-7 110.. WilliamBuick 6 91
(John Gosden) *hld up disputing 7th: pushed along 5f out: wknd 3f out: sn bhd* **14/1**

2-60 **12** 11 **Aiken**[34] 6447 5-9-7 107.....................................(p) RichardHughes 2 78
(John Gosden) *trckd ldrs in 5th: lost pl 4f out: rdn 3f out: wknd rapidly 2f out: eased* **12/1**

3m 38.09s (9.09) **Going Correction** +0.725s/f (Yiel)
WFA 3 from 4yo+ 10lb **12** Ran SP% **115.7**
Speed ratings (Par 113): **106,105,105,105,104 104,104,104,101,99 96,90**
toteswingers 1&2 £12.30, 1&3 £18.90, 2&3 £9.70 CSF £164.23 CT £1166.78 TOTE £16.50: £4.00, £2.90, £2.10; EX 231.50 Trifecta £1809.90 Pool: £6,766.46 - 2.80 winning units..
Owner Andrew Tinkler **Bred** Moyglare Stud Farm Ltd **Trained** Coolaghknock Glebe,Co Kildare
■ Stewards' Enquiry : Johnny Murtagh seven-day ban: used whip above permitted level (Nov 2,4-9)
Pat Smullen seven-day ban: used whip above permitted level (Nov 2,4-9)
W J Lee nine-day ban: used whip above permitted level (Nov 2,4-9,11-12); Fine: £350.

FOCUS
There was minimal rain overnight but the ground still looked testing, an impression confirmed by those who rode in the opener, with Richard Hughes describing it as "heavy" and William Buick feeling it was "bottomless". The going in the straight certainly seemed better than on the Round course, confirmed by the GoingStick readings. The third running of this race since it was renamed and moved to Ascot, somewhat predictably, given the conditions, just slow fractions were set and a couple of the main contenders failed to give their running.Royal Diamond rates a small personal best, with Harris Tweed close to his form over shorter.

7364 QIPCO BRITISH CHAMPIONS SPRINT STKS (GROUP 2) 6f
2:20 (2:20) (Class 1) 3-Y-0+
£207,856 (£78,802; £39,438; £19,645; £9,859; £4,948) **Stalls** High

Form RPR
3102 **1** **Slade Power (IRE)**[42] 6193 4-9-0 115............................ WayneLordan 6 119
(Edward Lynam, Ire) *trckd ldr in gp towards centre: overall ldr 2f out: hrd pressed and edgd lft 1f out: r.o wl and hld on* **7/1**[3]

6413 **2** nk **Jack Dexter**[28] 6623 4-9-0 110................................... GrahamLee 13 118
(Jim Goldie) *lw: led quartet against nr side rail: rdn to take 2nd overall over 1f out: str chal after: r.o but jst hld* **5/1**[2]

1616 **3** 3 ¼ **Viztoria (IRE)**[13] 7059 3-8-10 112.. PatSmullen 14 105
(Edward Lynam, Ire) *chsd ldr nr side: rdn and cl enough wl over 1f out: outpcd fnl f* **5/1**[2]

0303 **4** hd **Hoof It**[14] 7013 6-9-0 107.. KierenFallon 11 108
(Michael Easterby) *overall ldr in gp towards centre: drvn and hdd 2f out: no ch w ldng pair fnl f: jst lost out in battle for 3rd* **20/1**

0150 **5** 2 ½ **Sirius Prospect (USA)**[14] 7014 5-9-0 105.................. RobertWinston 4 100
(Dean Ivory) *led pair in centre: rdn and struggling to stay on terms over 2f out: outpcd after* **20/1**

5001 **6** ¾ **Mass Rally (IRE)**[7] 7208 6-9-0 108..................................(b) PJMcDonald 12 98
(Michael Dods) *hld up in gp towards centre: outpcd over 2f out: wnt 3rd in gp over 1f out but no ch* **16/1**

0041 **7** ½ **Heaven's Guest (IRE)**[14] 7014 3-8-13 104..................... RyanMoore 2 97
(Richard Fahey) *lw: chsd rival in centre pair: nt on terms fr 1/2-way: n.d* **11/1**

0040 **8** ¾ **Hawkeyethenoo (IRE)**[28] 6623 7-9-0 106.................. RichardHughes 1 94
(Jim Goldie) *swtchd sharply fr wd draw and hld up at bk of nr side quartet: outpcd 2f out: no ch after* **16/1**

5542 **9** ½ **Racy**[21] 6830 6-9-0 101... FrederikTylicki 5 93
(Brian Ellison) *prom in gp towards centre: chsd ldng pair after 2f: rdn over 2f out: fdd over 1f out* **33/1**

0000 **10** nk **Excellent Guest**[42] 6183 6-9-0 95............................... TomQueally 3 92
(George Margarson) *hld up in rr of gp towards centre: rdn and edgd rt 2f out: no real prog* **66/1**

3251 **11** nk **Balmont Mast (IRE)**[6] 7227 5-9-0 112..................... JohnnyMurtagh 7 91
(Edward Lynam, Ire) *hld up in rr of gp towards centre: shkn up and no prog 2f out: nvr on terms* **8/1**

0011 **12** 1 **Maarek**[13] 7054 6-9-0 114... DeclanMcDonogh 10 88
(B Lalor, Ire) *restless in stalls and slowly away: hld up in 3rd of nr side gp: rdn and no prog 2f out* **7/2**[1]

2060 **13** hd **Cape Of Approval (IRE)**[13] 7054 4-9-0 107............................ WJLee 9 87
(T Stack, Ire) *chsd ldng pair in gp towards centre for 2f: lost pl 1/2-way: wl btn 2f out* **12/1**

0300 **14** 14 **Humidor (IRE)**[7] 7208 6-9-0 98..................................(tp) PatCosgrave 8 45
(George Baker) *taken down early: rel to r: a wl bhd* **66/1**

1m 15.79s (1.29) **Going Correction** +0.60s/f (Yiel)
WFA 3 from 4yo+ 1lb **14** Ran SP% **122.4**
Speed ratings (Par 115): **115,114,110,110,106 105,105,104,103,102 102,101,100,82**
toteswingers 1&2 £9.60, 1&3 £8.50, 2&3 £7.30 CSF £40.48 CT £200.61 TOTE £7.40: £2.40, £2.40, £2.40; EX 39.60 Trifecta £246.00 Pool: £8.823.72 - 26.89 winning units..
Owner Mrs S Power **Bred** Mrs S Power **Trained** Dunshaughlin, Co Meath

FOCUS
With just one Group 1 winner in action, and only four individual Group winners in total, this was perhaps not the strongest line-up for the money on offer. Lethal Force, Sole Power, Gordon Lord Byron and Society Rock were all missing for a variety of reasons. The field soon separated into three separate groups, with four runners close to the stands' side, eight a little further out, and a couple down the middle. The gallop was by no means a strong one and not many got into the race, the first two finishing clear. Given the state of the ground it's not form to treat too positively, but the first pair both rate personal bests.

7365 QIPCO BRITISH CHAMPIONS FILLIES & MARES STKS (GROUP 1) 1m 4f
2:55 (2:55) (Class 1) 3-Y-0+
£300,563 (£113,950; £57,028; £28,408; £14,257; £7,155) **Stalls** Low

Form RPR
-11F **1** **Seal Of Approval**[37] 6329 4-9-3 99................................... GeorgeBaker 2 118
(James Fanshawe) *lw: hld up in 5th: cl up whn nt clr run 2f out and swtchd lft: rdn and prog to ld jst over 1f out: r.o wl and sn clr* **16/1**

2-41 **2** 4 **Belle De Crecy (IRE)**[35] 6416 4-9-3 110......................... JohnnyMurtagh 7 112
(J P Murtagh, Ire) *lengthy: strong: lw: t.k.h: trckd ldr 4f: styd cl up: drvn to ld 2f out: hdd jst over 1f out and sn outpcd: kpt on to hold on for 2nd* **10/1**

1102 **3** nk **Talent**[35] 6393 3-8-10 114... JimCrowley 4 112
(Ralph Beckett) *hld up in last pair: prog fr 4f out to chse ldrs 3f: sn u.p: clsd to try to chal over 1f out: sn outpcd: kpt on to press runner-up nr fin* **7/2**[1]

1031 **4** ¾ **Dalkala (USA)**[13] 7057 4-9-3 115......................... ChristopheSoumillon 9 110
(A De Royer-Dupre, France) *lw: hld up in last pair: prog on outer over 2f out: drvn and tried to chal over 1f out: sn outpcd: kpt on* **7/2**[1]

1032 **5** 1 ¼ **Hot Snap**[35] 6416 3-8-10 111.. JamesDoyle 5 109
(Lady Cecil) *hld up in last trio: pushed along bef 1/2-way and nt gng wl after: drvn in last 2f out: kpt on fnl f* **7/2**[1]

-213 **6** 2 ¾ **Nymphea (IRE)**[41] 6253 4-9-3 115.. AStarke 8 104
(P Schiergen, Germany) *w'like: trckd ldng pair tl allowed to stride on in front after 4f: drvn and hdd 2f out: wknd 1f out* **8/1**[3]

-151 **7** 2 ¾ **Waila**[91] 4532 3-8-10 110.. RyanMoore 1 100
(Sir Michael Stoute) *trckd ldng trio: lost pl on inner over 3f out: wknd 2f out* **13/2**[2]

6502 **8** 2 ½ **Igugu (AUS)**[22] 6796 6-9-3 109.. PatCosgrave 6 97
(M F De Kock, South Africa) *t.k.h: led at mod pce for 4f: trckd ldr after: rdn to chal jst over 2f out: wknd qckly over 1f out* **10/1**

2m 39.09s (6.59) **Going Correction** +0.90s/f (Soft)
WFA 3 from 4yo+ 7lb **8** Ran SP% **115.2**
Speed ratings (Par 117): **114,111,111,110,109 107,106,104**
CSF £163.00 CT £692.83 TOTE £19.20: £3.60, £2.30, £1.60; EX 145.70 Trifecta £258.70 Pool: £7,299.78 - 21.15 winning units..
Owner T R G Vestey **Bred** T R G Vestey **Trained** Newmarket, Suffolk
■ This race had Group 1 status for the first time. George Baker's first Group 1 winner.
■ Stewards' Enquiry : Jim Crowley two-day ban: used whip above permitted level (Nov 2,4)

FOCUS
This turned into a proper test at the distance, despite them appearing to go just a fair gallop, and it produced a surprise winner in Seal Of Approval. It appears no fluke, though. Belle De Crecy backed up her recent clear best in Ireland, and Taalent was close to her St Leger mark.

7366 QUEEN ELIZABETH II STKS (SPONSORED BY QIPCO) (BRITISH CHAMPIONS MILE) (GROUP 1) 1m (S)
3:30 (3:34) (Class 1) 3-Y-0+
£601,126 (£227,900; £114,056; £56,816; £28,514; £14,310) **Stalls** High

Form RPR
1022 **1** **Olympic Glory (IRE)**[34] 6450 3-9-0 124..................(b[1]) RichardHughes 7 127
(Richard Hannon) *hld up in rr: prog 3f out: forced way through over 2f out: drvn to ld over 1f out: sn clr: r.o wl and pushed out nr fin* **11/2**[3]

211 **2** 3 ¼ **Top Notch Tonto (IRE)**[14] 7025 3-9-0 115.......................... DaleSwift 4 120
(Brian Ellison) *trckd ldng trio: prog to ld over 2f out: drvn and hdd over 1f out: no ch w wnr but kpt on wl for 2nd* **14/1**

1-6 **3** ¾ **Kingsbarns (IRE)**[42] 6226 3-9-0 116............................ JosephO'Brien 12 118
(A P O'Brien, Ire) *trckd ldng trio: clsd to take 2nd jst over 2f out and sn chalng: edgd lft and nt qckn over 1f out: kpt on* **14/1**

0125 **4** 2 **Dawn Approach (IRE)**[69] 5314 3-9-0 125...................... KevinManning 5 113
(J S Bolger, Ire) *lw: hld up in midfield: pushed along over 3f out: clsd and wl in tch over 2f out: sn rdn and nt qckn: one pce after* **2/1**[1]

1104 **5** hd **Elusive Kate (USA)**[21] 6837 4-9-0 117.......................... WilliamBuick 11 111
(John Gosden) *w.w in midfled: pushed along 3f out: tried to cl on ldrs over 2f out: one pce after* **16/1**

5130 **6** 3 **Gregorian (IRE)**[14] 7047 4-9-3 116.. RyanMoore 6 107
(John Gosden) *settled in last trio: rdn and outpcd over 3f out: kpt on fnl 2f: nt pce to threaten* **20/1**

3112 **7** 3 ¾ **Gordon Lord Byron (IRE)**[13] 7059 5-9-3 118............ JohnnyMurtagh 2 98
(T Hogan, Ire) *hld up towards rr: urged along and in tch 3f out: nt qckn over 2f out: wknd over 1f out* **8/1**

2161 **8** 13 **Maxios**[34] 6450 5-9-3 123..................................... StephanePasquier 8 68
(J E Pease, France) *hld up in rr: brief effrt over 3f out: wknd over 2f out: eased and t.o* **4/1**[2]

6630 **9** ½ **Leitir Mor (IRE)**[6] 7227 3-9-0 109..................................(tp) RonanWhelan 3 66
(J S Bolger, Ire) *dwlt: rcvrd to chse clr ldr: cl enough 3f out: losing pl whn bmpd jst over 2f out: t.o and eased* **100/1**

2442 **10** 2 **Caspar Netscher**[14] 7025 4-9-3 108.................................... MartinLane 9 63
(David Simcock) *a wl in rr: struggling 3f out: sn wknd: t.o* **50/1**

1121 **11** 4 ½ **Soft Falling Rain (SAF)**[22] 6797 4-9-3 122................. PaulHanagan 10 52
(M F De Kock, South Africa) *chsd ldng pair to 3f out: wknd qckly: t.o and eased* **7/1**

0300 **12** 15 **Burwaaz**[35] 6391 4-9-3 95.. DaneO'Neill 1 18
(Ed Dunlop) *led at str pce to over 2f out: wkng whn squeezed out sn after: eased and wl t.o* **100/1**

1m 44.18s (3.38) **Going Correction** +0.775s/f (Yiel)
WFA 3 from 4yo+ 3lb **12** Ran SP% **120.2**
Speed ratings (Par 117): **114,110,110,108,107 104,101,88,87,85 81,66**
CSF £79.11 CT £1053.08 TOTE £6.20: £2.30, £4.90, £4.20; EX 104.20 Trifecta £1622.70 Pool: £16,094.83 - 7.43 winning units..
Owner HE Sh Joaan Bin Hamad Al Thani **Bred** Denis McDonnell **Trained** East Everleigh, Wilts
■ Stewards' Enquiry : Richard Hughes two-day ban: careless riding (Nov 2,4)

FOCUS
The third running of this event since it was switched from the round mile. With seven previous winners at the highest level the field was well up to scratch, but the testing ground prevented a number of runners from showing their form. The field raced in one group down the centre of the track, Kingsbarns and Elusive Kate tacking over from the stands' side to join the main body after a furlong. The pace was strong with pacemakers Burwaaz, and to a lesser extent Leitir Mor doing their jobs, and not many saw it out. Olymoic Glory is rated back to his Deauville figure, which places him just behind Toronado and Dawn Approach. Top Notch Tonto backed up his recent efforts and Kingsbarns got back to his Racing Post Trophy form.

7367 QIPCO CHAMPION STKS (BRITISH CHAMPIONS MIDDLE DISTANCE) (GROUP 1) 1m 2f
4:05 (4:12) (Class 1) 3-Y-0+
£737,230 (£279,500; £139,880; £69,680; £34,970; £17,550) **Stalls** Low

Form RPR
22-1 **1** **Farhh**[154] 2446 5-9-3 124.. SilvestreDeSousa 5 128
(Saeed bin Suroor) *lw: t.k.h: trckd ldr: led wl over 1f out: hrd pressed and drvn fnl f: hld on wl* **11/4**[2]

2511 **2** nk **Cirrus Des Aigles (FR)**[14] 7049 7-9-3 123.......... ChristopheSoumillon 3 127
(Mme C Barande-Barbe, France) *lw: hld up in midfield: prog over 2f out: drvn to press wnr over 1f out: persistent chal after: jst hld* **6/4**[1]

1520 **3** ½ **Ruler Of The World (IRE)**[13] 7058 3-8-12 120..............(p) RyanMoore 9 126
(A P O'Brien, Ire) *trapped out wd thrght: in rr: drvn and prog over 2f out: pressed ldng pair jst over 1f out: styd on but a jst hld* **13/2**[3]

0630 **4** 6 **Hunter's Light (IRE)**[63] 5553 5-9-3 113................(v[1]) MickaelBarzalona 2 115
(Saeed bin Suroor) *pushed up to ld: drvn and hdd wl over 1f out: sn btn but hld on for 4th* **25/1**

1231 **5** ½ **Mukhadram**[84] 4779 4-9-3 123.. PaulHanagan 4 114
(William Haggas) *hld up in last pair: shkn up over 2f out: sn outpcd: kpt on same pce over 1f out* **14/1**

2134 **6** nk **Hillstar**[59] 5654 3-8-12 119... RichardHughes 6 114
(Sir Michael Stoute) *tk fierce hold early: hld up and sn in last pair: rdn on outer over 2f out: kpt on same pce fr over 1f out* **14/1**

6202 **7** 1 **Morandi (FR)**[28] 6712 3-8-12 116............... Christophe-PatriceLemaire 7 112
(J-C Rouget, France) *mostly chsd ldng pair to 3f out: steadily wknd* **10/1**

2433 **8** 4½ **Main Sequence (USA)**[28] 6636 4-9-3 111....................(p) TedDurcan 10 103
(David Lanigan) *dwlt: hld up in rr: rdn over 2f out: sn wknd* **66/1**

1341 **9** nk **Parish Hall (IRE)**[15] 7005 4-9-3 113.............................. KevinManning 8 103
(J S Bolger, Ire) *lw: cl up: drvn to chse ldng pair 3f out to over 2f out: wknd qckly* **50/1**

1310 **10** 7 **Triple Threat (FR)**[34] 6446 3-8-12 114.......................... MaximeGuyon 1 89
(A Fabre, France) *w'like: trckd ldrs tl wknd wl over 2f out: eased* **20/1**

2m 12.02s (4.62) **Going Correction** +0.90s/f (Soft)
WFA 3 from 4yo+ 5lb **10** Ran SP% **114.5**
Speed ratings (Par 117): **117,116,116,111,111 110,110,106,106,100**
CSF £6.79 CT £22.53 TOTE £4.40: £2.00, £1.10, £2.50; EX 7.70 Trifecta £46.40 Pool: £170,594 - 2,751.71 winning units..
Owner Godolphin **Bred** Darley **Trained** Newmarket, Suffolk

FOCUS
Every reason to believe this was a strong edition of the race, with the two genuine top-class older horses pulling clear with this year's Derby winner, who ran a career-best effort in defeat. It was run at a steady gallop, with Mickael Barzalona, aboard Godolphin pacemaker Hunter's Light, doing a good job at seeing it didn't turn into too much of a test at the distance for his winning stablemate Farhh. The winner rates alongside Novellist as the season's best older horse, while Cirrus Des Aigles posted his best form of the year.

7368 QIPCO FUTURE STARS APPRENTICE H'CAP 7f
4:45 (4:48) (Class 2) (0-100,98) 3-Y-O+ **£32,345** (£9,625; £4,810; £2,405) **Stalls** High

Form RPR

2013 **1** **Breton Rock (IRE)**[15] 6990 3-9-4 97.............................. LewisWalsh(5) 8 108
(David Simcock) *hld up in last pair of far side gp: stdy prog fr 3f out: rdn 2f out: styd on wl to ld last 100yds* **12/1**

1306 **2** 1 **Intrigo**[14] 7018 3-9-7 95........................ WilliamTwiston-Davies 4 103
(Richard Hannon) *hld up in last trio far side: stdy prog over 3f out: rdn to ld overall over 1f out: hdd and one pce last 100yds* **20/1**

3160 **3** 1¼ **Gramercy (IRE)**[28] 6621 6-9-2 93.........................(be) ShelleyBirkett(5) 28 99
(David Simcock) *trckd ldr nr side: led gp over 2f out: styd on wl but nt quite on terms w far side ldrs* **50/1**

0431 **4** ½ **Levitate**[28] 6624 5-9-12 98..(v) CharlesBishop 13 102
(John Quinn) *prom in far side gp: drvn to chal wl over 1f out: styd on same pce* **16/1**

2143 **5** shd **Kinglami**[46] 6067 4-8-5 80...(p) PhilipPrince(3) 2 84
(Brian Gubby) *pressed far side ldrs: lost pl 1/2-way: swtchd rt over 2f out: prog wl over 1f out: kpt on but unable to chal* **25/1**

035 **6** hd **Boots And Spurs**[28] 6621 4-9-2 91..............................(v) JoeyHaynes(3) 7 95
(K R Burke) *w far side ldrs: overall ldr 4f out: drvn over 2f out: hdd and fdd over 1f out* **12/1**

1164 **7** 1 **Majestic Moon (IRE)**[21] 6840 3-9-3 91.............................. LeeTopliss 29 91
(Richard Fahey) *led nr side gp to over 2f out: chsd ldr after: kpt on fnl f* **25/1**

400 **8** nse **Fury**[21] 6838 5-9-7 96...(b) NathanAlison(3) 15 97+
(William Haggas) *racd on outer of nr side gp: hld up: prog over 2f out: styd on fr over 1f out: nvr able to rch ldrs* **9/1**[2]

0006 **9** 2 **Tartiflette**[27] 6665 4-9-1 87..(b) RyanClark 3 83
(Ed McMahon) *trckd ldrs far side: gng strly 3f out: rdn 2f out: one pce after* **25/1**

0404 **10** nk **Trail Blaze (IRE)**[14] 7018 4-9-2 93..............................(b) KevinStott(5) 20 88
(Kevin Ryan) *racd alone in centre: wl on terms w ldrs: edgd across to far side 2f out and chsng ldrs: wknd fnl f* **20/1**

0600 **11** 1¼ **Our Jonathan**[28] 6623 6-9-4 95.................................. GeorgeBuckell(5) 5 87
(David Simcock) *taken down early: hld up on far side: sme prog over 2f out: no hdwy over 1f out* **11/1**

0466 **12** 1¼ **Regal Parade**[28] 6623 9-9-8 97............................(t) MatthewLawson(3) 26 85
(Milton Bradley) *wl in rr nr side: rdn over 2f out: kpt on fr over 1f out: nvr on terms* **16/1**

2405 **13** ¾ **George Guru**[23] 6767 6-9-3 92..................................... RyanTate(3) 6 79
(Michael Attwater) *in tch far side: lost pl and in rr 3f out: plugged on one pce fnl 2f* **40/1**

2122 **14** ¾ **Balty Boys (IRE)**[21] 6834 4-9-9 95.................................. RobertTart 9 80
(Brian Ellison) *prom in far side gp tl steadily wknd fr 2f out* **10/1**[3]

3402 **15** nk **Jack's Revenge (IRE)**[8] 7172 5-9-9 95...................(bt) ThomasBrown 12 79
(George Baker) *sn last of far side gp and nt gng wl: drvn and edgd lft fr 3f out: kpt on but no ch* **8/1**[1]

6100 **16** 1½ **Askaud (IRE)**[8] 7172 5-9-1 92...(p) TimClark(5) 10 72
(Scott Dixon) *overall ldr far side to 4f out: wknd over 2f out* **66/1**

0002 **17** 2 **One Word More (IRE)**[38] 6308 3-9-4 97................. DanielMuscutt(5) 25 71
(Charles Hills) *hld up in midfield nr side: no prog over 2f out: wknd over 1f out* **20/1**

0510 **18** nk **Crew Cut (IRE)**[28] 6621 5-8-7 86............................(bt) DavidParkes(7) 22 60
(Jeremy Gask) *hld up in rr nr side: no real prog over 2f out: wl btn after* **66/1**

0001 **19** 1 **Common Touch (IRE)**[15] 6988 5-9-4 90...........(b) MichaelJMMurphy 18 61
(Willie Musson) *hld up in tch nr side: no prog over 2f out: wknd over 1f out* **14/1**

0504 **20** ½ **Shahdaroba (IRE)**[15] 6989 3-8-10 89 ow1..................... PatMillman(5) 14 58
(Rod Millman) *towards rr far side: tried to make prog on outer of gp over 2f out: wknd over 1f out* **50/1**

2010 **21** shd **Pearl Ice**[28] 6621 5-9-8 94.. LMcNiff 11 64
(David Barron) *nvr beyond midfield on far side: no prog 2f out: wknd over 1f out* **50/1**

2662 **22** nk **Fils Anges (IRE)**[15] 6993 3-9-0 93................................ LouisSteward(5) 27 61
(Michael Bell) *s.s: hld up in rr nr side: no prog whn drifted across towards far side 2f out* **14/1**

0400 **23** ¾ **Dubawi Sound**[28] 6623 5-9-7 96...................................... OisinMurphy(3) 1 63
(David Brown) *taken down early: pressed ldrs far side to 3f out: wknd rapidly* **20/1**

56 **24** 1¾ **Rebellious Guest**[15] 6988 4-8-6 83.......................... JordanVaughan(5) 23 45
(George Margarson) *a wl in rr nr side: drifted across towards far side 2f out* **25/1**

0000 **25** 2¼ **Bubbly Bellini (IRE)**[13] 7052 6-9-9 95......................(p) RonanWhelan 19 52
(Adrian McGuinness, Ire) *hld up in midfield on nr side: no prog over 2f out: sn bhd* **33/1**

0216 **26** 16 **Sir Reginald**[28] 6621 5-9-4 93.............................. GeorgeChaloner(3) 16 8
(Richard Fahey) *awkward s: chsd nr side ldrs: rdn 1/2-way: sn wknd* **10/1**[3]

1006 **27** 28 **Silverheels (IRE)**[23] 6767 4-8-13 85.........................(t) AshleyMorgan 17
(Paul Cole) *chsd nr side ldrs 4f: wknd rapidly: eased and wl t.o* **50/1**

1m 31.43s (3.83) **Going Correction** +0.775s/f (Yiel)
WFA 3 from 4yo+ 2lb **27** Ran SP% **138.7**
Speed ratings (Par 109): **109,107,106,105,105 105,104,104,102,101 100,98,97,97,96 95,92,92,91,90 90,90,89,87,84 66,34**
CSF £243.25 CT £11217.35 TOTE £13.80: £3.60, £6.70, £12.10, £5.30; EX 240.40 TRIFECTA Not won..
Owner John Cook **Bred** George Kent **Trained** Newmarket, Suffolk

FOCUS
The third running of this event, and good handicap form even if the race was short on progressive types. They split into two similar sized groups, with tenth home Trail Blaze racing on his own between them, and it was the far side who held the advantage. The finish was fought out by a pair of 3-y-os, both of whom came from the rear of the far-side group, and showed improvement. The fourth and fifth help with the level.
T/Jkpt: Not won. T/Plt: £469.30 to a £1 stake. Pool: £264167.90 - 410.91 winning tickets T/Qpdt: £38.60 to a £1 stake. Pool: £15839.53 - 303.39 winning tickets JN

7094 CATTERICK (L-H)
Saturday, October 19

OFFICIAL GOING: Soft (6.6) changing to heavy after race 3 (3.30)
3m of fresh ground on bend turning into straight and up the home straight.
Wind: Moderate behind Weather: Heavy cloud and showers

7369 WIN BIG WITH THE TOTEJACKPOT H'CAP 1m 3f 214y
1:20 (1:20) (Class 4) (0-80,80) 3-Y-O+ **£4,690** (£1,395; £697; £348) **Stalls** Low

Form RPR

-640 **1** **Ultimate**[11] 7115 7-8-13 70... PaulPickard(3) 1 82
(Brian Ellison) *mde all: rdn clr wl over 2f out: drvn and kpt on wl fnl f* **16/1**

3342 **2** 5 **Arr' Kid (USA)**[18] 6917 3-8-11 72... TomEaves 2 77
(Keith Dalgleish) *chsd wnr to 1/2-way: rdn along over 3f out: drvn and styd on to chse wnr over 1f out: no imp* **12/1**

5050 **3** 1½ **Villa Royale**[21] 6846 4-9-12 80....................................... DanielTudhope 5 83
(David O'Meara) *trckd ldrs on inner: hdwy 3f out: rdn to chse ldng pair 2f out: sn drvn and kpt on one pce* **12/1**

5404 **4** nse **Mutanaweb (IRE)**[32] 6504 3-9-2 77...........................(p) RobertHavlin 11 80
(John Gosden) *sn prom: trckd wnr fr 1/2-way: rdn along 3f out: drvn 2f out: sn one pce* **11/2**[2]

2015 **5** 8 **Fly Solo**[145] 2706 4-9-8 76.. LukeMorris 13 68
(Alan Swinbank) *t.k.h in midfield: hdwy over 3f out: rdn along 2f out: sn drvn and no further prog* **9/1**

2531 **6** 2 **Pravda Street**[102] 4153 8-8-11 72................................ RichardOliver(7) 12 61
(Brian Ellison) *hld up in rr: hdwy over 3f out: rdn along over 2f out: plugged on: nvr a factor* **33/1**

-130 **7** 5 **Discovery Bay**[143] 2369 5-9-3 71................................ GrahamGibbons 10 53
(Brian Ellison) *hld up towards rr: sme hdwy 3f out: rdn along over 2f out: nvr a factor* **4/1**[1]

5000 **8** ½ **Rock Supreme (IRE)**[10] 7130 4-8-8 67......................... ConnorBeasley(5) 9 48
(Michael Dods) *hld up: a towards rr* **20/1**

4356 **9** 2¼ **Now My Sun**[25] 6729 4-9-8 76.. DavidAllan 6 54
(K R Burke) *hld up towards rr: hdwy on outer 5f out: chsd ldng pair 3f out: rdn along over 2f out: sn drvn and wknd* **14/1**

20-0 **10** 3 **Song Of The Siren**[127] 3301 5-8-10 71............................... JoshDoyle(7) 4 45
(David O'Meara) *a towards rr* **50/1**

0415 **11** ½ **Judicious**[25] 6730 6-9-0 68... AndrewMullen 3 41
(Geoffrey Harker) *hld up in midfield: pushed along 4f out: sn outpcd* **33/1**

4P2 **12** 2 **Allnecessaryforce (FR)**[61] 5582 3-9-2 77.................(p) TonyHamilton 7 47
(Richard Fahey) *trckd ldrs: pushed along over 4f out: rdn over 3f out and sn wknd* **4/1**[1]

5221 **13** 48 **Checkpoint**[10] 7118 4-8-13 67..(p) BarryMcHugh 8
(Tony Coyle) *t.k.h: chsd ldrs: rdn along over 4f out: sn wknd and bhd* **8/1**[3]

2m 47.45s (8.55) **Going Correction** +0.85s/f (Soft)
WFA 3 from 4yo+ 7lb **13** Ran SP% **117.0**
Speed ratings (Par 105): **105,101,100,100,95 93,90,90,88,86 86,85,53**
Tote Swingers: 1&2 £13.60, 1&3 £32.20, 2&3 £73.10 CSF £184.57 CT £2384.57 TOTE £32.20: £9.10, £2.30, £6.50; EX 427.00 Trifecta £485.60 Part won. Pool: £647.53 - 0.20 winning units..
Owner Dan Gilbert **Bred** Avington Manor Stud **Trained** Norton, N Yorks

FOCUS
Following 2mm of overnight rain the going remained as soft. There was a three-metre strip of fresh ground on the turn into the home straight. The pace was sound for this competitive handicap with the winner making all under a fine ride. It paid to race handy. The form is rated around the second and third to their recent marks.

7370 TOTESCOOP6 NOVICE STKS 5f
1:55 (1:55) (Class 5) 2-Y-O **£3,622** (£1,078; £538; £269) **Stalls** Low

Form RPR

2201 **1** **Sandra's Diamond (IRE)**[18] 6915 2-8-11 79....................... TomEaves 4 77
(Keith Dalgleish) *cl up: led after 1f: pushed clr over 1f out: rdn out* **1/3**[1]

6 **2** 8 **Captain Joe**[8] 7173 2-9-0 0..[1] GrahamGibbons 5 56
(Michael Easterby) *trckd ldrs: hdwy to chse wnr 1/2-way: rdn along wl over 1f out: sn one pce* **11/4**[2]

0 **3** 4½ **Chennai Wind**[16] 6966 2-9-0 0... JoeFanning 2 35
(Derek Shaw) *prom: rdn along over 2f out: sn one pce* **40/1**

6000 **4** 1¼ **Lady Dancer (IRE)**[11] 7096 2-8-9 30.............................(b) RaulDaSilva 6 26
(George Moore) *qckly away and led 1f: sn rdn along and outpcd fr 1/2-way* **80/1**

5 11 **Diamondsinthesky (IRE)** 2-8-2 0.............................. AdamMcLean(7) 1
(Derek Shaw) *green: sn outpcd and bhd* **16/1**[3]

1m 2.24s (2.44) **Going Correction** +0.40s/f (Good) **5** Ran SP% **111.2**
Speed ratings (Par 95): **96,83,76,74,56**
CSF £1.58 TOTE £1.20: £1.02, £1.20; EX 1.70 Trifecta £6.70 Pool: £916.40 - 102.54 winning units..
Owner Prestige Thoroughbred Racing **Bred** Robert Norton **Trained** Carluke, S Lanarks

FOCUS
A desperately uncompetitive contest run at a fair pace. The runners came stands' side and the winner was entitled to win well..

7371 TOTEQUADPOT FOUR PLACES IN FOUR RACES MEDIAN AUCTION MAIDEN STKS 7f
2:30 (2:35) (Class 5) 2-Y-O £3,817 (£1,127; £563) Stalls Centre

Form RPR
530 1 **Gilbey's Mate**[22] 6799 2-9-5 79 RobertHavlin 4 78+
(John Gosden) *hld up in tch: hdwy to trck ldrs 1/2-way: wd st to stands' rail and led 2f out: sn rdn clr: readily* 7/4[1]
355 2 6 **Lendal Bridge**[39] 6285 2-9-5 55 BarryMcHugh 1 59
(Tony Coyle) *trckd ldrs: hdwy on inner 4f out: led 1/2-way: wd st to stands' rail: rdn and hdd 2f out: sn drvn and kpt on: no ch w wnr* 25/1
00 3 2 ½ **Namely (IRE)**[11] 7102 2-9-0 0 LukeMorris 2 48
(Sir Mark Prescott Bt) *cl up: rdn along 3f out: drvn over 2f out and sn wknd* 28/1
63 4 ½ **Ronya (IRE)**[29] 6581 2-9-0 0 DanielTudhope 3 47+
(K R Burke) *led 1f: cl up on inner: rdn along 3f out: sn drvn and wknd over 2f out* 9/2[3]
06 5 1 **Kalahari Kingdom (IRE)**[24] 6754 2-9-5 0 TonyHamilton 8 49
(Richard Fahey) *trckd ldrs: pushed along 3f out: hdwy 2f out: sn rdn and one pce* 9/2[3]
6 12 **Bint Malyana (IRE)** 2-9-0 0 DavidAllan 7 14
(James Tate) *cl up on outer: slt ld after 1f: hdd 4f out: rdn along wl over 2f out: sn wknd* 8/1
06 7 1 ¾ **Vosne Romanee**[26] 6681 2-9-5 0 TomEaves 9 15
(Keith Dalgleish) *a in rr: outpcd and bhd fr 1/2-way* 66/1
6 8 8 **Giant Samurai (USA)**[85] 4731 2-9-5 0 (b[1]) MichaelO'Connell 5
(John Quinn) *in tch: rdn along 1/2-way: sn outpcd and bhd* 4/1[2]
0 9 55 **Stream Of Light**[17] 6949 2-9-0 0 GrahamGibbons 6
(John Mackie) *cl up: rdn along and wknd qckly bef 1/2-way: sn bhd* 50/1

1m 33.23s (6.23) **Going Correction** +0.85s/f (Soft) 9 Ran SP% 114.6
Speed ratings (Par 95): **98,91,88,87,86 72,70,61,**
Tote Swingers: 1&2 £13.60, 1&3 £32.20, 2&3 £73.10 CSF £53.06 TOTE £2.70: £1.40, £5.00, £4.90; EX 33.60 Trifecta £234.60 Pool: £1,957.26 - 6.25 winning units..
Owner C J Murfitt **Bred** Pantile Stud **Trained** Newmarket, Suffolk

FOCUS
A moderate maiden run at a fair pace. Improvement from the runner-up, who the form is rated around.

7372 LIVE SCOOP6 INFORMATION AT TOTEPOOL.COM CLAIMING STKS 1m 3f 214y
3:05 (3:05) (Class 6) 3-Y-O+ £2,726 (£805; £402) Stalls Low

Form RPR
2032 1 **Sherman McCoy**[16] 6984 7-9-1 67 AndrewMullen 2 83
(Michael Appleby) *trckd ldr: cl up after 4f: chal 4f out: rdn to ld wl over 2f out: drvn clr wl over 1f out: kpt on strly* 11/4[2]
0662 2 13 **Mohawk Ridge**[11] 7100 7-9-1 76 ConnorBeasley(5) 10 70
(Michael Dods) *led: pushed along 4f out: rdn 3f out: sn hdd and drvn: one pce* 11/10[1]
3000 3 19 **Joe The Coat**[25] 6736 4-9-6 57 (b[1]) JoeFanning 9 43
(Mark H Tompkins) *hmpd s and sn rdn along: hdwy to trck ldrs after 2f: riddn along to chse ldng pair 5f out: drvn 3f out: plugged on: n.d* 17/2[3]
4300 4 8 **Silver Tigress**[28] 6632 5-8-12 53 [1] RaulDaSilva 4 24
(George Moore) *hld up in tch: sme hdwy 4f out: rdn along over 3f out: sn drvn and nvr a factor* 14/1
0003 5 nk **Kathlatino**[75] 5050 6-8-10 55 MichaelStainton 3 22
(Micky Hammond) *chsd ldrs: rdn along 1/2-way: sn outpcd and bhd fnl 3f* 16/1
4000 6 shd **Eijaaz (IRE)**[80] 4888 12-9-1 52 (p) DuranFentiman 11 26
(Geoffrey Harker) *in tch: rdn along 5f out: sn outpcd and bhd fnl 3f* 25/1
6203 7 4 **Madame Blavatsky (FR)**[84] 4763 5-8-3 47 [1] EvaMoscrop(7) 8 16
(Simon West) *wnt rt s: chsd ldng pair: rdn along over 4f out: drvn over 3f out: sn outpcd* 33/1
0000 8 26 **Roc Fort**[11] 7099 4-9-1 40 TomEaves 7
(James Moffatt) *a in rr: bhd fr 1/2-way* 100/1
03 9 65 **Iktiview**[154] 2462 5-9-8 0 RussKennemore 1
(Philip Kirby) *in rr: rdn along after 4f: bhd fr 1/2-way: t.o fnl 3f* 12/1

2m 49.11s (10.21) **Going Correction** +0.95s/f (Soft) 9 Ran SP% 112.8
Speed ratings (Par 101): **103,94,81,76,76 76,73,56,12**
Tote Swingers: 1&2 £1.02, 1&3 £7.40, 2&3 £3.50 CSF £5.83 TOTE £3.50: £1.70, £1.02, £2.20; EX 7.90 Trifecta £40.20 Pool: £1,796.04 - 33.44 winning units..Sherman McCoy claimed by Mr Brian Ellison for £5,000.
Owner Mick Appleby Racing **Bred** Horizon Bloodstock Limited **Trained** Danethorpe, Notts

FOCUS
The pace was solid for this moderate claimer, with the front two in command throughout. The field finished very well strung out and it's tricky to pin down what the winner achieved.

7373 TOTEPOOL MOBILE CATTERICK DASH (HANDICAP STKS) 5f
3:40 (3:43) (Class 2) (0-100,100) 3-Y-O+ £16,172 (£4,812; £2,405; £1,202) Stalls Low

Form RPR
0062 1 **Even Stevens**[3] 7313 5-8-7 86 oh2 (p) TomEaves 6 96
(Scott Dixon) *slt ld: pushed along and edgd rt to stands' rail 1/2-way: rdn over 1f out: c;lear ent fnl f: styd on* 17/2
3415 2 1 ½ **Bondesire**[41] 6238 3-8-4 86 JulieBurke(3) 4 92
(David O'Meara) *cl up: rdn and ev ch wl over 1f out: sn drvn and kpt on same pce fnl f* 10/1
0123 3 shd **Aetna**[29] 6583 3-8-7 86 GrahamGibbons 3 91+
(Michael Easterby) *sltly hmpd s: in tch: hdwy 2f out: rdn to chse ldrs over 1f out: drvn and kpt on fnl f* 5/2[1]
6200 4 1 ½ **Singeur (IRE)**[8] 7171 6-8-7 89 JasonHart(3) 2 88
(Robin Bastiman) *in tch: hdwy on outer to chse ldrs 2f out: sn rdn and no imp fnl f* 10/1
1040 5 nk **Confessional**[7] 7208 6-9-7 100 (e) DavidAllan 12 98
(Tim Easterby) *cl up: rdn along 1/2-way: sn drvn and wknd appr fnl f* 12/1
310 6 ¾ **Angus Og**[29] 6583 3-8-0 86 oh2 RobJFitzpatrick(7) 15 82
(K R Burke) *cl up: rdn along and lost pl on stands' rail after 1 1/2f: swtchd lft and drvn wl over 1f out: sn no imp* 22/1
3010 7 3 **Maglietta Fina (IRE)**[12] 7085 4-8-7 86 RobertHavlin 10 70
(Robert Cowell) *hld up in rr: swtchd lft: rdn and sme hdwy 2f out: sn drvn and nvr nr ldrs* 18/1
0126 8 2 ¾ **Imperial Legend (IRE)**[8] 7171 4-8-3 89 ow2 (p) JordanNason(7) 13 63
(David Nicholls) *chsd ldrs: rdn along over 2f out: sn wknd* 15/2[3]
0106 9 nse **El Viento (FR)**[21] 6845 5-8-11 97 (v) SamanthaBell(7) 5 71
(Richard Fahey) *wnt lft s: in tch: rdn along 1/2-way: sn btn* 10/1
0622 10 ¾ **Naabegha**[6] 7222 6-8-10 89 LiamKeniry 1 60
(Ed de Giles) *a in rr* 5/1[2]
0000 11 6 **Doctor Parkes**[8] 7171 7-9-1 94 AdamBeschizza 9 44
(Stuart Williams) *a in rr* 40/1

1m 0.58s (0.78) **Going Correction** +0.40s/f (Good) 11 Ran SP% 114.5
Speed ratings (Par 109): **109,106,106,104,103 102,97,93,93,91 82**
Tote Swingers: 1&2 £6.00, 1&3 £6.20, 2&3 £7.60 CSF £88.14 CT £275.00 TOTE £8.00: £2.60, £2.30, £1.50; EX 142.70 Trifecta £1014.60 Pool: £1,479.76 - 1.09 winning units..
Owner Paul J Dixon **Bred** Mrs Yvette Dixon **Trained** Babworth, Notts

FOCUS
A typically competitive renewal of the Catterick Dash which was run at a fierce pace. Surprisingly with the field racing stands' side, the first three home were drawn 6,4,3. The winner rates a small turf best.

7374 YOUR FAVOURITE POOL BETS AT TOTEPOOL.COM H'CAP 7f
4:15 (4:17) (Class 4) (0-80,80) 3-Y-O+ £6,469 (£1,925; £962; £481) Stalls Centre

Form RPR
6252 1 **Showboating (IRE)**[23] 6774 5-9-4 77 (tp) DanielTudhope 9 86
(Alan McCabe) *hld up: hdwy over 2f out: chsd ldrs whn n.m.r and swtchd lft jst over 1f out: rdn and styd on wl to ld last 75yds* 12/1
0000 2 ¾ **Personal Touch**[15] 6988 4-9-5 78 TonyHamilton 4 85
(Richard Fahey) *led to 1/2-way: cl up: rdn to chal over 1f out and ev ch tl drvn ins fnl f and no ex last 75yds* 7/1[3]
3231 3 nk **Llewellyn**[30] 6549 5-8-8 74 JordanNason(7) 13 80
(David Nicholls) *trckd ldrs: cl up after 2f: slt ld 1/2-way: rdn 2f out: hrd pressed and drvn ent fnl f: hdd and no ex last 100yds* 13/2[2]
0260 4 nk **Kung Hei Fat Choy (USA)**[10] 7123 4-9-0 73 (b) TomEaves 6 78
(James Given) *chsd ldrs: wd st to stands' rail: rdn 2f out and ev ch tl drvn ent fnl f and no ex last 100yds* 22/1
4106 5 1 ¾ **Indego Blues**[19] 6908 4-9-3 76 AdrianNicholls 2 77
(David Nicholls) *trckd ldrs on inner: rdn along 2f out: drvn over 1f out: kpt on same pce* 12/1
3310 6 nk **Dawn Calling (IRE)**[19] 6908 3-9-3 78 JoeFanning 5 77
(Mark Johnston) *cl up: rdn over 2f out: drvn over 1f out: one pce fnl f* 9/1
0260 7 1 ¼ **Green Park (IRE)**[21] 6822 10-8-9 75 (b) LukeLeadbitter(7) 11 72
(Declan Carroll) *t.k.h: in tch: hdwy to chse ldrs 2f out: rdn over 1f out: sn one pce* 16/1
6030 8 ¾ **West Leake Hare (IRE)**[29] 6586 4-9-4 77 PaulQuinn 1 72
(David Nicholls) *hld up towards rr on inner: effrt over 2f out: sn rdn and n.d* 8/1
5230 9 shd **Hot Rod Mamma (IRE)**[20] 6875 6-9-5 78 BarryMcHugh 10 73
(Dianne Sayer) *hld up towards rr: hdwy over 2f out: rdn to chse ldrs over 1f out: sn drvn and no imp fnl f* 10/1
4200 10 hd **Victoire De Lyphar (IRE)**[14] 7024 6-9-2 78 (e) JasonHart(3) 15 72
(Ruth Carr) *midfield: rdn along and hdwy on outer 1/2-way: drvn 2f out and one pce* 14/1
2515 11 6 **Chiswick Bey (IRE)**[17] 6943 5-8-9 75 (p) SamanthaBell(7) 8 54
(Richard Fahey) *a towards rr* 10/1
4050 12 ¾ **Shrimper Roo**[57] 5728 3-9-4 79 (b) DuranFentiman 3 55
(Tim Easterby) *dwlt: a in rr* 33/1
5121 13 5 **Just Paul (IRE)**[20] 6874 3-8-9 77 EvaMoscrop(7) 14 40
(Philip Kirby) *a towards rr* 6/1[1]
-120 14 3 ¾ **Sherzam**[20] 6874 3-9-0 80 ConnorBeasley(5) 12 33
(Michael Dods) *a in rr: c wd to stands' side and bhd fnl 2f* 16/1

1m 32.69s (5.69) **Going Correction** +0.95s/f (Soft)
WFA 3 from 4yo+ 2lb 14 Ran SP% 120.5
Speed ratings (Par 105): **105,104,103,103,101 101,99,98,98,98 91,90,85,80**
Tote Swingers: 1&2 £15.00, 1&3 £10.90, 2&3 £8.90 CSF £93.73 CT £621.08 TOTE £15.40: £5.90, £3.60, £1.60; EX 127.10 Trifecta £441.80 Part won. Pool: £589.14 - 0.01 winning units..
Owner Mr & Mrs L Cooke A Pierce A McCabe **Bred** Crone Stud Farms Ltd **Trained** Averham Park, Notts

FOCUS
A wide-open contest run at a fair pace. The field was spread across the track near the line with the first two home racing nearer the far side. The form makes sense.

7375 COLLECT TOTEPOOL WINNINGS AT BETFRED SHOPS APPRENTICE H'CAP (DIV I) 1m 5f 175y
4:50 (4:51) (Class 6) (0-60,60) 3-Y-O+ £2,726 (£805; £402) Stalls Low

Form RPR
064 1 **Funky Munky**[9] 7151 8-9-1 47 (p) ConnorBeasley 12 55
(Alistair Whillans) *prom: chsd ldrs and wd st to stands' rail: rdn 2f out: drvn over 1f out and styd on wl to ld last 100yds* 7/1[3]
6503 2 1 ¼ **Dubara Reef (IRE)**[11] 7098 6-8-11 46 oh1 (p) JordanNason(3) 5 52
(Paul Green) *led: pushed along and hdd 4f out: wd st to stands' side and rdn over 2f out: drvn wl over 1f out: ev ch tl drvn and one pce wl ins fnl f* 8/1
4006 3 1 ¼ **Father Shine (IRE)**[27] 1721 10-8-10 49 AlexHopkinson(7) 1 53
(Shaun Harris) *prom: hdwy on inner to ld 4f out: styd far rail in st: rdn 2f out: drvn over 1f out: hdd and no ex ins fnl f* 16/1
6003 4 ¾ **Aegean Destiny**[11] 7099 6-9-6 52 GeorgeDowning 3 55
(John Mackie) *in tch on inner: hdwy over 3f out: styd inner rail in home st and sn rdn: ev ch over 1f out tl drvn ent fnl f and kpt on same pce* 6/1[2]
0565 5 5 **Amir Pasha (UAE)**[11] 7099 8-8-13 50 (p) RobJFitzpatrick(5) 10 46
(Micky Hammond) *hld up towards rr: hdwy over 3f out: rdn over 2f out: styd on u.p fr over 1f out: n.d* 11/1
04- 6 1 ½ **Denison Flyer**[347] 7603 6-8-9 46 oh1 (p) JoeDoyle(5) 9 40
(Lawrence Mullaney) *hld up: hdwy to chse ldrs 5f out: rdn along 3f out: drvn and one pce fnl 2f* 18/1
3 7 6 **Gung Ho (FR)**[19] 6895 4-9-11 60 EoinWalsh(3) 2 46
(Tony Newcombe) *midfield: rdn along 4f out: wd st to stands' side: sn drvn and outpcd* 6/1[2]
3043 8 2 ¼ **Operateur (IRE)**[117] 3625 5-9-4 55 AnnaHesketh(5) 4 38
(Ben Haslam) *trckd ldrs: effrt 4f out and sn rdn: drvn over 2f out and sn wknd* 8/1
000 9 5 **Dan's Heir**[11] 7099 11-8-11 46 oh1 (p) SamanthaBell(3) 11 22
(Wilf Storey) *a in rr* 16/1
4023 10 1 ½ **Halfwaytocootehill (IRE)**[16] 6964 3-8-8 49 (tp) JacobButterfield 8 22
(Ollie Pears) *in tch: pushed along on inner over 5f out: rdn along 4f out: sn wknd* 7/2[1]
-000 11 59 **Rahy's Promise (USA)**[215] 1060 4-8-12 51 RobHornby(7) 7
(David O'Meara) *hld up: a bhd: t.o fnl 4f* 10/1

3m 19.16s (15.56) **Going Correction** +1.05s/f (Soft)
WFA 3 from 4yo+ 9lb 11 Ran SP% 120.0
Speed ratings (Par 101): **97,96,95,95,92 91,88,86,83,83 49**
Tote Swingers: 1&2 £15.10, 1&3 £30.50, 2&3 £24.90 CSF £63.34 CT £877.17 TOTE £6.60: £2.80, £2.90, £6.90; EX 70.60 Trifecta £695.20 Pool: £1,069.89 - 1.15 winning units..
Owner The Twelve Munkys **Bred** Mrs S Corbett **Trained** Newmill-On-Slitrig, Borders

The Form Book Flat, Raceform Ltd, Compton, RG20 6NL.

FOCUS
A desperately weak handicap confined to apprentice riders, run at an honest pace with the prominent runners again dominating. The first two home came stands' side.

7376 COLLECT TOTEPOOL WINNINGS AT BETFRED SHOPS APPRENTICE H'CAP (DIV II) 1m 5f 175y
5:20 (5:20) (Class 6) (0-60,60) 3-Y-O+ **£2,726** (£805; £402) **Stalls** Low

Form RPR
5020 **1** **Wee Giant (USA)**[39] 6290 7-9-5 **54** LauraBarry(3) 5 62
(Tony Coyle) *hld up in rr: stdy hdwy over 3f out: wd to stands' rail in home st: rdn to ld jst over 1f out: edgd lft and kpt on wl fnl f* **5/1[3]**
4014 **2** *3* **Vittachi**[5] 7239 6-9-8 **59** (p) RowanScott(5) 6 63
(Alistair Whillans) *hld up: hdwy over 3f out: styd towards far side in home st and sn rdn to chse ldr: swtchd grad rt towards stands' side gp over 1f out and kpt on wl towards fin* **5/1[3]**
63- **3** *nk* **Think**[142] 7248 6-8-11 **46** oh1 (t) SamanthaBell(3) 11 50
(Clive Mulhall) *trckd ldrs: hdwy 4f out: swtchd rt towards stands' side and rdn to ld wl over 1f out: sn drvn and hdd appr fnl f: one pce* **14/1**
4002 **4** *4* **Like Clockwork**[11] 7090 4-9-1 **52** JackGarritty(5) 3 50
(Mark H Tompkins) *hld up in rr: hdwy over 3f out: wd st to stands' rail and sn rdn: chsd ldrs over 1f out: no imp fnl f* **7/2[1]**
205 **5** *1* **Politbureau**[19] 6907 6-9-0 **49** NoelGarbutt(3) 1 46
(Michael Easterby) *trckd ldrs: hdwy over 3f out: wd st and sn rdn: drvn and no imp fr wl over 1f out* **14/1**
0621 **6** *4* **Hurricane John (IRE)**[7] 7204 3-8-8 **52** JordanNason(3) 2 44
(David Nicholls) *chsd ldrs: rdn along and wd st: drvn and btn over 1f out* **4/1[2]**
006 **7** *1 1/2* **Anne's Valentino**[30] 6566 3-8-0 **46** oh1 AaronJones(5) 9 36
(Malcolm Jefferson) *t.k.h: prom: led over 5f out: rdn 3f out: styd far side in home st: drvn and hdd wl over 1f: sn wknd* **33/1**
6500 **8** *3* **Ferney Boy**[11] 7098 7-8-9 **46** oh1 LukeLeadbitter(5) 10 32
(Chris Fairhurst) *trckd ldrs: hdwy and cl up 6f out: rdn along over 3f out: sn wknd* **20/1**
0-00 **9** *50* **Speedy Star (IRE)**[70] 5295 4-9-0 **46** oh1 (p) ConnorBeasley 8
(Tina Jackson) *a towards rr: bhd fnl 3f* **50/1**
-020 **10** *10* **Berkeley Street (USA)**[22] 6787 3-9-2 **60** IanBurns(3) 7
(Jane Chapple-Hyam) *trckd ldrs: hdwy over 4f out: rdn along over 3f out: sn wknd and bhd* **9/1**
-045 **11** *hd* **Margo Channing**[92] 4509 4-8-11 **48** RobJFitzpatrick(5) 12
(Micky Hammond) *a in rr: bhd fnl 3f* **14/1**
0204 **12** *14* **Lea Valley**[60] 5619 4-9-0 **46** oh1 (p) ShirleyTeasdale 4
(Julia Feilden) *led: hdd and rdn over 5f out: sn wknd* **40/1**

3m 21.58s (17.98) **Going Correction** +1.05s/f (Soft)
WFA 3 from 4yo+ 9lb **12** Ran SP% **117.7**
Speed ratings (Par 101): **90,88,88,85,85 82,82,80,51,46 46,38**
Tote Swingers: 1&2 £6.10, 1&3 £18.00, 2&3 £10.70 CSF £28.91 CT £331.77 TOTE £4.50: £1.60, £4.60, £4.20; EX 31.40 Trifecta £420.80 Pool: £2,395.18 - 4.26 winning units..
Owner Gap Personnel **Bred** Barnett Enterprises **Trained** Norton, N Yorks

FOCUS
The second division of this weak apprentice handicap was run steady pace. Again the runners spread across the track with the stands' side dominating. It was slower than division I and similarly weak. The winner was helped by getting the rail.
T/Plt: £89.60 to a £1 stake. Pool: £52,389.59 - 426.41 winning tickets. T/Qpdt: £9.10 to a £1 stake. Pool: £3,993.79 - 321.40 winning tickets. JR

7347 WOLVERHAMPTON (A.W) (L-H)
Saturday, October 19

OFFICIAL GOING: Standard
Wind: Fresh behind Weather: Overcast

7377 32RED.COM MEDIAN AUCTION MAIDEN STKS 1m 141y(P)
5:50 (5:55) (Class 5) 3-Y-O **£2,587** (£770; £384; £192) **Stalls** Low

Form RPR
2623 **1** **Candy Kitten**[25] 6734 3-9-0 67 (p) LukeMorris 2 69
(Alastair Lidderdale) *trckd ldr tl shkn up to ld over 2f out: rdn ins fnl f: jst hld on* **4/1[2]**
2 **2** *nk* **Wilhana (IRE)**[11] 7114 3-9-0 0 (b[1]) AndreaAtzeni 1 68
(Roger Varian) *led: rdn and hdd over 2f out: r.o u.p* **1/7[1]**
3 *11* **Boom** 3-9-0 0 ChrisCatlin 5 43
(Olivia Maylam) *s.s: hdwy over 4f out: pushed along over 2f out: sn outpcd* **25/1[3]**
4 *2 1/2* **Izzy Too** 3-8-9 0 JackDuern(5) 3 37
(Alison Hutchinson) *s.i.s: sn chsng ldrs: rdn over 2f out: wknd over 1f out* **80/1**
00 **5** *20* **Bridge To My Heart**[24] 6748 3-9-0 0 [1] CathyGannon 4
(Olivia Maylam) *chsd ldrs tl rdn and wknd over 3f out* **100/1**

1m 51.45s (0.95) **Going Correction** +0.05s/f (Slow) **5** Ran SP% **113.6**
Speed ratings (Par 101): **97,96,86,84,66**
CSF £5.34 TOTE £6.10: £1.20, £1.10; EX 6.80 Trifecta £13.40 Pool: £3,830.64 - 213.78 winning units..
Owner Andy Weller **Bred** Raffin Bloodstock **Trained** Lambourn, Berks
■ Stewards' Enquiry : Andrea Atzeni two-day ban: used whip above permitted level (Nov 2,4)

FOCUS
A weak maiden, the only two with any previous worthwhile form predictably dominating, though not in the order the betting suggested. The time was slow and the winner is a better guide than the favourite.

7378 £32 BONUS AT 32RED.COM H'CAP 1m 1f 103y(P)
6:20 (6:20) (Class 6) (0-60,60) 3-Y-O+ **£1,940** (£577; £288; £144) **Stalls** Low

Form RPR
060 **1** **Olivers Mount**[35] 6399 3-8-6 **46** oh1 (t) JimmyQuinn 3 55
(Ed Vaughan) *s.i.s: hld up: hdwy over 2f out: r.o u.p to ld towards fin* **28/1**
0326 **2** *1* **Polar Forest**[12] 7066 3-9-3 **57** (e[1]) RobertWinston 11 64
(Richard Guest) *a.p: chsd ldr over 1f out: shkn up to ld ins fnl f: sn rdn and edgd lft: hdd towards fin* **9/1**
5006 **3** *1* **Buster Brown (IRE)**[10] 7132 4-9-8 **58** GrahamLee 6 63
(James Given) *hld up: hdwy and nt clr run over 1f out: rdn and r.o ins fnl f: nt rch ldrs* **9/2[2]**
4 *1* **La Oliva (IRE)**[22] 6672 4-9-10 **60** (p) LukeMorris 7 63
(Paul W Flynn, Ire) *a.p: chsd ldr 3f out tl rdn over 1f out: styd on same pce ins fnl f* **16/1**
5511 **5** *nse* **Let Me In (IRE)**[16] 6985 3-9-4 **58** (v) DavidProbert 10 61
(Patrick Chamings) *hld up: nt clr run over 2f out: hdwy over 1f out: sn rdn: r.o: nt trble ldrs* **5/4[1]**
460 **6** *2* **Dandarrell**[29] 6600 6-9-10 **60** FrederikTylicki 9 58
(Julie Camacho) *trckd ldr tl led over 6f out: rdn over 1f out: hdd & wknd ins fnl f* **14/1**
5166 **7** *4* **Safwaan**[75] 5073 6-9-8 **58** ShaneKelly 5 48
(Gary Harrison) *s.i.s: hld up: hdwy over 2f out: rdn over 1f out: wknd fnl f* **20/1**
4500 **8** *1/2* **Flying Applause**[60] 5612 8-9-1 **54** (b) MarkCoumbe(3) 4 43
(Roy Bowring) *prom: rdn over 3f out: wknd 2f out* **40/1**
3412 **9** *3 3/4* **Napinda**[22] 6804 3-9-4 **58** WilliamCarson 8 39
(Philip McBride) *prom: pushed along and lost pl over 6f out: rdn 3f out: wknd 2f out* **15/2[3]**
0504 **10** *11* **Ajeeb (USA)**[12] 7082 5-9-8 **58** (vt) LiamTreadwell 1 16
(Michael Scudamore) *led: hdd over 6f out: chsd ldr tl rdn 3f out: wknd over 1f out* **20/1**
4050 **11** *68* **Snap Music (USA)**[17] 6932 3-9-3 **57** KierenFallon 2
(Mark Johnston) *sn pushed along and prom: lost pl 1/2-way: wknd 3f out: virtually p.u fnl 2f* **16/1**

2m 0.86s (-0.84) **Going Correction** +0.05s/f (Slow)
WFA 3 from 4yo+ 4lb **11** Ran SP% **118.2**
Speed ratings (Par 101): **105,104,103,102,102 100,96,96,93,83 22**
Tote Swingers: 1&2 £19.00, 1&3 £20.10, 2&3 £7.70 CSF £252.53 CT £1364.25 TOTE £38.20: £6.90, £3.00, £1.50; EX 555.70 Trifecta £1456.30 Part won. Pool: £1,941.79 - 0.57 winning units..
Owner A M Pickering **Bred** Mrs A D Bourne **Trained** Newmarket, Suffolk

FOCUS
A modest contest which was soundly run. The winner had had fewer chances than most and this rates a clear best.

7379 32REDPOKER.COM H'CAP 1m 4f 50y(P)
6:50 (6:50) (Class 6) (0-60,60) 3-Y-O+ **£1,940** (£577; £288; £144) **Stalls** Low

Form RPR
-604 **1** **Absolutely Me (IRE)**[128] 3256 4-8-12 **46** RobertWinston 7 55
(Willie Musson) *hld up: hdwy over 3f out: chsd ldr over 1f out: rdn to ld wl ins fnl f: styd on* **18/1**
-213 **2** *1/2* **Amantius**[9] 6558 4-9-7 **55** (b) CathyGannon 8 65+
(Johnny Farrelly) *hld up: hdwy and nt clr run over 2f out: rdn over 1f out: r.o wl: nt rch wnr* **11/4[1]**
3326 **3** *1 3/4* **Men Don't Cry (IRE)**[19] 6895 4-9-9 **60** (b) MarkCoumbe(3) 9 65
(Ed de Giles) *led: clr over 5f out: rdn over 1f out: hdd and unable qck wl ins fnl f* **4/1[2]**
00/2 **4** *1 1/2* **Poncho**[23] 6783 4-8-13 **47** (p) LukeMorris 11 50
(Mark Rimell) *chsd ldr: rdn over 2f out: lost 2nd over 1f out: styd on same pce ins fnl f* **16/1**
-040 **5** *2 3/4* **Travel (USA)**[19] 6907 3-9-5 **60** KierenFallon 5 59
(Mark Johnston) *hld up: pushed along over 4f out: hdwy over 1f out: nt rch ldrs* **6/1[3]**
1030 **6** *1 3/4* **Royal Sea (IRE)**[22] 6787 4-9-11 **59** GrahamLee 3 55
(Michael Mullineaux) *prom: pushed along over 3f out: rdn and wknd over 1f out* **7/1**
0/6- **7** *3 1/2* **Ghufa (IRE)**[652] 63 9-9-4 **55** SimonPearce(3) 10 45
(Lydia Pearce) *hld up: hdwy u.p 3f out: wknd 2f out* **25/1**
2006 **8** *1/2* **Uncle Bernie (IRE)**[21] 6827 3-9-1 **56** (e[1]) ShaneKelly 6 45
(Andrew Hollinshead) *dwlt: hld up: shkn up over 1f out: n.d* **8/1**
006 **9** *10* **Indian Giver**[25] 6730 5-9-8 **56** DaleSwift 2 29
(Alan Berry) *prom: rdn over 3f out: wknd over 2f out* **50/1**
5052 **10** *3* **Marina Ballerina**[50] 5961 5-8-12 **46** JimmyQuinn 1 15
(Roy Bowring) *chsd ldrs tl rdn and wknd over 2f out* **22/1**
0/ **11** *3/4* **City Line (IRE)**[15] 7007 6-8-9 **46** oh1 (bt) IJBrennan(3) 12 13
(Karl Thornton, Ire) *s.i.s: hld up and a in rr: wknd over 3f out* **17/2**

2m 41.7s (0.60) **Going Correction** +0.05s/f (Slow)
WFA 3 from 4yo+ 7lb **11** Ran SP% **116.4**
Speed ratings (Par 101): **100,99,98,97,95 94,92,91,85,83 82**
Tote Swingers: 1&2 £14.70, 1&3 £11.60, 2&3 £2.70 CSF £65.47 CT £246.63 TOTE £16.10: £4.30, £1.60, £1.90; EX 103.40 Trifecta £576.30 Pool: £1,808.48 - 2.35 winning units..
Owner Miss A Jones **Bred** Kilco Builders **Trained** Newmarket, Suffolk

FOCUS
Another low-grade affair, though it probably represents solid enough form for the level, with the leading pair lightly-raced sorts who look worth keeping on side. The third helps with the standard. A steady pace increased from halfway.

7380 32RED CASINO MAIDEN STKS 5f 20y(P)
7:20 (7:20) (Class 5) 3-Y-O+ **£2,587** (£770; £384; £192) **Stalls** Low

Form RPR
0342 **1** **Borough Boy (IRE)**[7] 7203 3-9-5 52 (v) DaleSwift 9 57
(Derek Shaw) *hld up: hdwy 1/2-way: rdn to ld wl ins fnl f: r.o* **13/8[1]**
0053 **2** *1 1/4* **Busy Bimbo (IRE)**[7] 7203 4-8-11 47 MarkCoumbe(3) 3 46
(Alan Berry) *chsd ldrs: rdn to ld 1f out: hdd and unable qck wl ins fnl f* **15/2[3]**
0040 **3** *nk* **Spoken Words**[12] 7083 4-9-0 36 (b) GrahamLee 7 45
(Alan Berry) *chsd ldrs: pushed along 1/2-way: rdn over 1f out: r.o* **33/1**
-504 **4** *1/2* **Mid Yorkshire Golf**[7] 7203 4-8-11 46 SladeO'Hara(3) 8 43
(Peter Grayson) *sn pushed along in rr: rdn over 1f out: r.o: nt rch ldrs* **16/1**
4-50 **5** *nk* **Kerfuffle (IRE)**[231] 863 4-8-9 44 (b) JackDuern(5) 4 44+
(Simon Dow) *chsd ldrs: running on whn hmpd and lost pl over 1f out: r.o wl towards fin* **8/1**
0546 **6** *nk* **Stoneacre Hull (IRE)**[12] 7077 4-9-0 50 StephenCraine 2 41
(Peter Grayson) *led: hdd over 3f out: rdn and ev ch 1f out: styd on same pce* **12/1**
0000 **7** *1/2* **Artillery Train (IRE)**[46] 6084 4-9-5 38 AdamBeschizza 5 44
(Tim Etherington) *prom: sn pushed along: lost pl over 3f out: rdn over 1f out: r.o ins fnl f* **40/1**
300 **8** *1* **Ishisoba**[47] 6038 3-9-0 49 LukeMorris 1 37
(Ronald Harris) *w ldr tl led over 3f out: rdn and hdd 1f out: no ex ins fnl f* **10/3[2]**
9 *20* **Lieutenant Nelson** 3-9-5 0 DavidAllan 6
(Kevin Tork) *sn outpcd* **10/1**

1m 2.97s (0.67) **Going Correction** +0.05s/f (Slow) **9** Ran SP% **112.1**
Speed ratings (Par 103): **96,94,93,92,92 91,90,89,57**
Tote Swingers: 1&2 £1.40, 1&3 £16.50, 2&3 £13.20 CSF £13.87 TOTE £2.00: £1.30, £2.90, £8.10; EX 11.60 Trifecta £154.90 Pool: £1,937.32 - 9.37 winning units..
Owner Brian Johnson (Northamptonshire) **Bred** E Kopica And M Rosenfeld **Trained** Sproxton, Leics

FOCUS
Weak form. The winner, second and fourth ran similarly to how thay had in another bad race last Saturday.

7381 32RED FILLIES' H'CAP 5f 216y(P)
7:50 (7:50) (Class 5) (0-75,73) 3-Y-O+ £3,234 (£962; £481; £240) Stalls Low

Form RPR
212 1 **Dilgura**24 6744 3-9-7 **73** ShaneKelly 1 86
(Stuart Kittow) *chsd ldr: shkn up over 1f out: rdn to ld ins fnl f: r.o* **7/2**2
4121 2 nk **Burren View Lady (IRE)**16 6982 3-9-6 **72** (e) DavidAllan 9 84
(Tim Easterby) *sn led: rdn over 1f out: hdd ins fnl f: r.o* **2/1**1
0502 3 3 ¾ **Available (IRE)**8 7163 4-8-12 **63** (tp) StephenCraine 6 63
(John Mackie) *s.i.s: hdwy over 3f out: rdn over 1f out: styd on same pce fnl f* **8/1**
4343 4 nk **Ray Of Joy**8 7164 7-9-5 **70** KierenFallon 2 69
(J R Jenkins) *prom: rdn over 1f out: styd on same pce* **8/1**
4430 5 nk **Alluring Star**24 6761 5-8-11 **62** FrederikTylicki 8 60
(Michael Easterby) *led early: chsd ldrs: rdn over 2f out: styd on* **11/2**3
0054 6 1 ½ **Hannahs Turn**8 7164 3-9-2 **68** RaulDaSilva 7 61
(Chris Dwyer) *prom: lost pl after 1f: plld hrd in rr: sme hdwy over 1f out: nt trble ldrs* **11/1**
-00 7 nk **Dreamy Ciara**17 6948 3-8-12 **64** CathyGannon 4 56
(David Brown) *s.i.s: nvr nrr* **33/1**
0200 8 1 ½ **Mey Blossom**23 6771 8-8-7 **63** (p) GeorgeChaloner(5) 3 51
(Richard Whitaker) *chsd ldrs: pushed along over 3f out: outpcd fnl 2f* **25/1**
4015 9 7 **Little Choosey**8 7164 3-8-9 **61** LukeMorris 5 26
(Anabel K Murphy) *sn pushed along in rr: drvn over 2f out: sn wknd* **14/1**
1m 13.88s (-1.12) **Going Correction** +0.05s/f (Slow)
WFA 3 from 4yo+ 1lb 9 Ran SP% **114.9**
Speed ratings (Par 100): **109,108,103,103,102 100,100,98,89**
Tote Swingers: 1&2 £2.20, 1&3 £5.60, 2&3 £2.80 CSF £10.83 CT £50.81 TOTE £3.70: £1.60, £1.10, £2.80; EX 7.90 Trifecta £41.60 Pool: £1,978.11 - 35.61 winning units..
Owner S Kittow, R Perry, B Hopkins **Bred** Hopkins, Kittow & Mrs Perry **Trained** Blackborough, Devon
FOCUS
Form to view positively from the leading pair, who are both going the right way and pulled nicely clear of the rest. The form could conceivably be rated higher.

7382 32REDBET.COM H'CAP 2m 119y(P)
8:20 (8:23) (Class 6) (0-60,58) 3-Y-O+ £1,940 (£577; £288; £144) Stalls Low

Form RPR
3225 1 **Capriska**9 7159 4-9-6 **50** RobertWinston 4 56
(Willie Musson) *s.i.s: hld up: hdwy over 2f out: rdn to ld ins fnl f: styd on* **10/1**3
466/ 2 nk **Street Runner**5 4328 7-9-6 **53** (p) IJBrennan(3) 10 59
(Karl Thornton, Ire) *chsd ldrs: pushed along over 3f out: led 2f out: sn rdn: hdd ins fnl f: styd on* **15/2**1
403 3 nk **Mr Burbidge**23 6781 5-9-10 **54** (b) LiamKeniry 8 59
(Neil Mulholland) *hld up: hdwy over 3f out: rdn and ev ch fr 2f out: styd on* **10/1**3
-044 4 7 **Maoi Chinn Tire (IRE)**13 6658 6-10-0 **58** StephenCraine 5 55
(Jennie Candlish) *hld up: pushed along over 3f out: nt clr run over 2f out: hdwy over 1f out: sn rdn: no ex fnl f* **18/1**
/131 5 hd **River Du Nord (FR)**54 7144 6-8-12 **45** JemmaMarshall(3) 1 42
(Susan Gardner) *hld up: hdwy over 2f out: rdn over 1f out: styd on same pce* **16/1**
5004 6 4 ½ **Kayef (GER)**21 6853 6-10-0 **58** (v) LiamTreadwell 7 49
(Michael Scudamore) *chsd ldr tl led wl over 2f out: rdn and hdd 2f out: wknd over 1f out* **14/1**
2035 7 10 **Helamis**16 6964 3-8-12 **52** (p) LukeMorris 2 31
(Alison Hutchinson) *led: rdn and hdd wl over 2f out: wknd and eased over 1f out* **16/1**
55-0 8 12 **Cloudy Start**21 6853 7-9-9 **53** JimmyQuinn 3 18
(Violet M Jordan) *mid-div: rdn over 4f out: wknd wl over 3f out* **28/1**
-400 9 42 **Spanish Legacy**39 6290 4-9-4 **48** FrederikTylicki 9
(Julie Camacho) *chsd ldrs: pushed along over 4f out: wknd 3f out* **8/1**2
3m 44.59s (2.79) **Going Correction** +0.05s/f (Slow)
WFA 3 from 4yo+ 10lb 9 Ran SP% **68.2**
Speed ratings (Par 101): **95,94,94,91,91 89,84,78,59**
Tote Swingers: 1&2 £1.90, 1&3 £6.50, 2&3 £1.70 CSF £28.59 CT £131.24 TOTE £4.60: £1.20, £1.20, £2.80; EX 16.70 Trifecta £218.50 Pool: £625.46 - 2.14 winning units..
Owner Laurence Mann **Bred** Mr & Mrs J T Thomas **Trained** Newmarket, Suffolk
FOCUS
A modest staying event which was steadily run for a long way, with the front three coming clear. The form is rated cautiously.

7383 32REDBINGO.COM H'CAP 1m 141y(P)
8:50 (8:51) (Class 6) (0-65,71) 3-Y-O+ £1,940 (£577; £288; £144) Stalls Low

Form RPR
551 1 **Dancing Cosmos (IRE)**22 6803 3-9-3 **62** LiamKeniry 3 71
(John Patrick Shanahan, Ire) *a.p: rdn over 1f out: r.o u.p to ld wl ins fnl f* **9/2**3
5451 2 ½ **Icy Blue**12 7082 5-8-12 **58** (p) GeorgeChaloner(5) 4 66
(Richard Whitaker) *awkward leaving stalls: sn pushed along and prom: chsd ldr 7f out tl led over 2f out: rdn and hdd wl ins fnl f* **9/1**
0504 3 nk **Bitaphon (IRE)**7 7197 4-8-12 **53** (t) LukeMorris 11 61+
(Michael Appleby) *hld up: hdwy over 1f out: rdn and r.o wl: nt rch ldrs* **25/1**
4360 4 ½ **Petrify**35 6400 3-8-12 **57** AndreaAtzeni 5 63
(Luca Cumani) *chsd ldrs: rdn over 1f out: r.o* **9/1**
1011 5 ¾ **Tatting**8 7169 4-10-0 **69** RaulDaSilva 8 74+
(Chris Dwyer) *hld up: hdwy and nt clr run over 1f out: r.o: nt rch ldrs* **5/2**1
-141 6 1 **Goal (IRE)**5 7259 5-10-2 **71** 6ex (t) RobertWinston 6 73
(Gordon Elliott, Ire) *a.p: rdn over 2f out: styd on same pce ins fnl f* **7/2**2
6030 7 1 ½ **Outlaw Torn (IRE)**8 7169 4-9-6 **61** (e) RobbieFitzpatrick 12 60
(Richard Guest) *led: rdn and hdd over 2f out: no ex ins fnl f* **16/1**
1500 8 ½ **Angel Cake (IRE)**26 6702 4-9-10 **65** AndrewMullen 1 63
(Michael Appleby) *s.i.s: sn pushed along and prom: rdn over 2f out: no ex fnl f* **16/1**
0420 9 4 ½ **Konzert (ITY)**19 6906 3-9-3 **62** KierenFallon 7 50
(Ian Williams) *hld up: pushed along over 2f out: sme hdwy and edgd lft over 1f out: wknd ins fnl f* **5/1**
2530 10 2 ¾ **Action Front (USA)**67 5377 5-8-10 **51** (v) FrederikTylicki 10 32
(Derek Shaw) *hld up: rdn over 2f out: a in rr* **40/1**
0616 11 2 ¼ **Larghetto (USA)**180 1734 5-9-7 **62** ShaneKelly 9 38
(John Stimpson) *hld up: pushed along over 2f out: wknd over 1f out* **33/1**
1m 49.89s (-0.61) **Going Correction** +0.05s/f (Slow)
WFA 3 from 4yo+ 4lb 11 Ran SP% **126.6**
Speed ratings (Par 101): **104,103,103,102,102 101,99,99,95,93 91**
Tote Swingers: 1&2 £11.40, 1&3 £47.20, 2&3 £69.20 CSF £47.76 CT £970.03 TOTE £4.40: £2.20, £1.70, £5.80; EX 41.90 Trifecta £1268.70 Part won. Pool: £1,691.60 - 0.33 winning units..
Owner Thistle Bloodstock Limited **Bred** Thistle Bloodstock Ltd **Trained** Danesfort, Co. Kilkenny
FOCUS
A good handicap for the grade and the form is rated on the positive side. The gallop didn't appear overly strong, while the performance of the third, who came from a long way back, is worth marking up slightly.
T/Plt: £21.20 to a £1 stake. Pool: £66,274.27 - 2,274 winning tickets. T/Qpdt: £1.90 to a £1 stake. Pool: £7,269.03 - 2,799.33 winning tickets. CR

5111 CORK (R-H)
Saturday, October 19
OFFICIAL GOING: Yielding to soft (soft in places)

7388a CORKRACECOURSE.IE NAVIGATION STKS (LISTED RACE) 1m 100y
4:20 (4:22) 3-Y-O+ £21,138 (£6,178; £2,926; £975)

RPR
1 **Rich Coast**29 6617 5-9-7 105 NGMcCullagh 6 109
(J P Murtagh, Ire) *prom: settled bhd ldr: cl 2nd 1/2-way: got on terms over 2f out and rdn to ld narrowly 1 1/2f out: kpt on best ins fnl f to assert cl home* **5/1**3
2 1 ¼ **Brendan Brackan (IRE)**34 6440 4-9-12 117 ColinKeane 1 111
(G M Lyons, Ire) *led: narrow advantage 1/2-way: jnd over 2f out: sn rdn and hdd narrowly 1 1/2f out: kpt on wl ins fnl f wout matching wnr* **6/5**1
3 3 **Beacon Lodge (IRE)**13 7052 8-9-7 102 ShaneFoley 3 100+
(T Stack, Ire) *w.w: 6th 1/2-way: hdwy over 2f out to chse ldrs in 3rd 1 1/2f out: no ex u.p ins fnl f: kpt on same pce* **12/1**
4 1 **Croi An Or (IRE)**52 5907 4-9-7 98 FergalLynch 7 97+
(T Stack, Ire) *chsd ldrs: 5th 1/2-way: pushed along into st and sn no imp on ldrs: kpt on u.p into mod 4th ins fnl f: nt trble principals* **25/1**
5 ½ **Line Drummer (FR)**20 6885 3-9-4 101 SeamieHeffernan 5 95+
(A P O'Brien, Ire) *chsd ldrs: 4th 1/2-way: rdn over 2f out and sn no imp on ldrs: kpt on same pce ins fnl f* **9/2**2
6 3 ¼ **Pop Art (IRE)**13 7051 3-8-13 93 GaryCarroll 4 83+
(Charles O'Brien, Ire) *dwlt sltly and racd in rr: niggled along fr 1/2-way: rdn under 3f out and no imp: kpt on one pce ins fnl f* **33/1**
7 4 ¾ **Tandem**42 6225 4-9-7 105 (v) FMBerry 2 79+
(D K Weld, Ire) *trckd ldrs: 3rd 1/2-way: rdn over 2f out and no ex u.p: sn wknd into 5th: eased ins fnl f* **9/2**2
1m 48.87s (108.87)
WFA 3 from 4yo+ 3lb 7 Ran SP% **113.0**
CSF £11.15 TOTE £4.90: £2.60, £1.50; DF 11.20 Trifecta £101.00.
Owner Andrew Tinkler **Bred** Millsec Limited **Trained** Coolaghknock Glebe,Co Kildare
FOCUS
The progressive winner looked impressive and he may well try and follow up at Leopardstown next Saturday. The third has been rated to his latest effort, with those behind off their best.

7389 - 7391a (Foreign Racing) - See Raceform Interactive

7417 CAULFIELD (R-H)
Saturday, October 19
OFFICIAL GOING: Turf: good

7392a BMW CAULFIELD CUP (GROUP 1 H'CAP) (3YO+) (TURF) 1m 4f
7:45 (12:00) 3-Y-O+
£1,057,692 (£240,384; £128,205; £70,512; £57,692; £48,076)

RPR
1 **Fawkner (AUS)**14 7042 6-8-9 **0** (b) NicholasHall 10 115
(Robert Hickmott, Australia) *midfield on inner: angled off rail over 2f out: rdn and hdwy on outer fr over 1f out: styd on strly and led ins fnl 100yds: drvn clr* **10/1**
2 1 ¼ **Dandino**63 5550 6-8-13 **0** CraigAWilliams 16 117+
(Marco Botti) *stdd fr wd draw and hld up towards rr: fanned wd and rdn on turn into st: styd on strly ins fnl f and wnt 2nd post: nvr nrr* **10/1**
3 nse **Dear Demi (AUS)**14 7042 4-8-5 **0** (b) JamesMcDonald 18 111
(Clarry Conners, Australia) *immediately dropped in fr wdst draw and hld up towards rr on inner: rdn and hdwy fr over 2f out: styd on against rail in st and wnt 2nd 50yds out: no imp on wnr and dropped to 3rd post* **25/1**
4 ½ **Jet Away**14 7042 6-8-9 **0** DamienOliver 11 112
(David Hayes, Australia) *t.k.h in midfield: hdwy on outer and w ldrs over 3f out: rdn to ld over 1f out: kpt on but hdd ins fnl 100yds and dropped to 4th cl home* **9/1**
5 shd **Royal Descent (AUS)**14 7042 4-8-7 **0** NashRawiller 3 112
(Chris Waller, Australia) *w ldrs early: sn restrained and racd in midfield: rdn and hdwy 2f out: styd on wl but nt quite pce to chal* **6/1**2
6 ½ **Mr Moet (AUS)**22 6-8-10 **0** HughBowman 8 112
(Adam Durrant, Australia) *sn prom on inner: rdn and ev ch 2f out: outpcd by wnr ins fnl f: styd on steadily* **20/1**
7 shd **Hawkspur (AUS)**14 7042 4-8-8 **0** (bt) JimCassidy 14 112
(Chris Waller, Australia) *stdd and hld up in last pair: rdn on rail 2f out: styd on wl and wnt 7th cl home but nvr able to chal* **16/5**1
8 shd **Silent Achiever (NZ)**14 7042 5-8-8 **0** GlenBoss 5 110
(Roger James, New Zealand) *stdd and settled in midfield: rdn and fanned wd on turn into st: styd on steadily but nvr able to chal* **7/1**3
9 hd **Kelinni (IRE)**14 5-8-9 **0** (p) StevenArnold 1 111
(Chris Waller, Australia) *midfield in tch on inner: rdn over 1f out: styd on but nt pce to chal* **40/1**
10 shd **Moriarty (IRE)**14 5-8-9 **0** (t) CraigNewitt 15 110
(Chris Waller, Australia) *dropped in fr wd draw and hld up in last: stl in rr whn rdn 2f out: swtchd rt over 1f out: hung in u.p but styd on steadily: fin wl but n.d* **25/1**
11 1 ¼ **Mr O'Ceirin (NZ)**14 7042 6-8-8 **0** (vt) DwayneDunn 17 107
(Ciaron Maher, Australia) *sent forward fr wd draw and sn trcking ldr: w ldrs over 3f out: rdn and hdd over 1f out: sn no ex and btn: steadily fdd* **50/1**

12 2 1/4 **Tuscan Fire (AUS)**[14] 7042 7-8-6 0 (t) MichaelWalker 2 102
(Dan O'Sullivan, Australia) *led 2f: in tch on inner once hdd: lost pl 3f out: rdn 2f out: plugged on but n.d ins fnl f* **70/1**
13 3 1/4 **Ethiopia (AUS)**[28] 5-8-13 0 (v1) RhysMcLeod 12 104
(Pat Carey, Australia) *hld up in rr: rdn 3f out: fanned wd on turn into st: readily outpcd ins fnl f: plugged on but nvr a factor* **40/1**
14 1 3/4 **Glencadam Gold (IRE)**[14] 7042 5-8-10 0 TommyBerry 6 98
(Gai Waterhouse, Australia) *dwlt sltly: snatched up whn short of room on rail on run to first bnd: midfield on inner: towards rr fr 1/2-way: rdn over 2f out: outpcd ent fnl f: nt given hrd time once btn* **40/1**
15 3/4 **Manighar (FR)**[14] 7042 7-9-2 0 LukeNolen 9 103
(Peter G Moody, Australia) *prom on outer: rdn over 2f out: lost pl and btn over 1f out: fdd and eased ins fnl f* **60/1**
16 2 **My Quest For Peace (IRE)**[28] 5-8-9 0 (b) CoreyBrown 4 92
(Peter G Moody, Australia) *settled in midfield: pushed along whn nt clr run and shuffled bk on turn into st: in rr ent fnl f and n.d after* **30/1**
17 7 **Waldpark (GER)**[13] 5-8-11 0 (t) BrentonAvdulla 7 83
(Anthony Freedman, Australia) *prom early: stdd after 2f but remained in tch: rdn over 2f out: lost pl and btn over 1f out: in rr whn eased ins fnl f* **40/1**
18 7 **Julienas (IRE)**[14] 6-8-8 0 KerrinMcEvoy 13 69
(Gai Waterhouse, Australia) *sent forward and led after 2f: jnd over 3f out: rdn and hdd over 2f out: sn no ex and btn: fdd and dropped to last ent fnl f: eased* **17/1**

2m 29.1s (149.10) **18 Ran SP% 114.8**
PARI-MUTUEL (NSW TAB - all including 1 aud stake): WIN 9.90; PLACE 3.30, 3.70, 6.20; DF 48.10; SF 93.50.
Owner N C Williams & Mr & Mrs L J Williams **Bred** S Bennetts **Trained** Australia

FOCUS
A strong-looking renewal of a famous race. Nicky Henderson's Forgotten Voice was a reserve but didn't get a run. The pace set by the leaders seemed respectable and the majority of these are engaged in the Melbourne Cup.

6895 BATH (L-H)
Sunday, October 20

OFFICIAL GOING: Soft (racing abandoned after race 4 (3.05) due to sewage in the jockeys' changing room)
Wind: quite strong behind Weather: overcast with showers

7393 IRISH STALLION FARMS EBF MAIDEN STKS 5f 161y
1:30 (1:30) (Class 5) 2-Y-O £2,911 (£866; £432; £216) **Stalls** Centre

Form RPR
0002 1 **Black Rodded**[3] 7317 2-9-0 62 RichardHughes 3 70
(Hughie Morrison) *a.p: led 2f out: strly pressed fr over 1f out: shkn up and kpt on wl: asserting towards fin* **11/8**[1]
3343 2 1 3/4 **Flicksta (USA)**[3] 7317 2-9-5 69 LukeMorris 1 70
(Ronald Harris) *trckd ldrs: rdn to chal over 1f out: ev ch ins fnl f: no ex and hld towards fin* **6/1**
3465 3 2 **Needless Shouting (IRE)**[7] 7218 2-9-5 65 GeorgeBaker 7 63
(Mick Channon) *prom: rdn over 2f out: one pce fr over 1f out* **3/1**[2]
4 1 1/4 **Byron's Gold** 2-8-9 0 RyanTate(5) 2 54
(Ben De Haan) *s.i.s: racd green in rr: hdwy over 1f out: styd on fnl f* **33/1**
0665 5 2 1/2 **Thrtypointstothree (IRE)**[33] 6487 2-9-2 61 WilliamTwiston-Davies(3) 4 51
(Nikki Evans) *trckd ldrs: rdn over 2f out: wknd ent fnl f* **20/1**
00 6 4 1/2 **Picanight**[83] 4828 2-9-0 0 JimCrowley 6 31
(Eve Johnson Houghton) *chsd ldrs: rdn over 2f out: wknd over 1f out* **33/1**
6 7 3 **Foxtrot Pearl (IRE)**[18] 6947 2-8-11 0 CharlesBishop(3) 8 21
(Olly Stevens) *unsettled stalls: trckd ldrs: rdn and ch wl over 2f out: wknd over 1f out* **5/1**[3]
8 2 1/4 **Wedgewood Estates** 2-9-0 0 JimmyFortune 5 13
(Tony Carroll) *s.i.s: racd green: a towards rr* **33/1**
00 9 1 3/4 **Warm Order**[18] 6947 2-9-0 0 SeanLevey 9 8
(Tony Carroll) *sn led: rdn and hdd 2f out: sn wknd* **50/1**

1m 14.16s (2.96) **Going Correction** +0.15s/f (Good) **9 Ran SP% 113.6**
Speed ratings (Par 95): **86,83,81,79,76 70,66,63,60**
toteswingers 1&2 £2.00, 1&3 £1.60, 2&3 £2.40 CSF £9.32 TOTE £2.30: £1.20, £1.60, £1.30; EX 10.50 Trifecta £23.00 Pool: £2046.88 - 66.72 winning units..
Owner Michael Kerr-Dineen **Bred** G B Balding **Trained** East Ilsley, Berks

FOCUS
Despite the soft ground, it was an advantage not to come too wide, which helped two of the form horses contest the finish from stalls 3 and 1. The first two had been second and third at Brighton three days earlier. Ordinary form.

7394 EBF STALLIONS IRISH EBF MAIDEN STKS (THE SUNDAY £5K BONUS RACE) 5f 11y
2:00 (2:00) (Class 5) 2-Y-O £2,911 (£866; £432; £216) **Stalls** Centre

Form RPR
62 1 **Charles Molson**[44] 6169 2-9-5 0 DaneO'Neill 4 85+
(Henry Candy) *trckd ldrs: led over 1f out: rdn clr: eased nr fin: readily* **1/2**[1]
2626 2 3 1/2 **Flashy Queen (IRE)**[24] 6778 2-9-0 66 CathyGannon 6 67
(Joseph Tuite) *led: rdn whn hdd over 1f out: sn outpcd by wnr* **5/1**[2]
00 3 6 **Bazooka (IRE)**[25] 6746 2-9-5 0 PatCosgrave 5 51
(Ed de Giles) *little slowly away: last but wl in tch: rdn over 2f out: styd on same pce to go 3rd ins fnl f: no ch w ldng pair* **25/1**
4 4 1 1/2 **Royal Brave (IRE)**[18] 6947 2-9-5 0 DougieCostello 2 45
(William Muir) *prom: rdn over 2f out: sn hld: fdd ins fnl f* **6/1**[3]
5320 5 2 1/4 **Zafraaj**[46] 6111 2-9-5 65 LukeMorris 1 37
(Ronald Harris) *chsd ldrs: sn pushed along: wknd over 1f out* **18/1**
030 6 15 **Arabian Sunset (IRE)**[17] 6973 2-9-0 58 JackMitchell 8
(Brendan Powell) *trckd ldrs: rdn 3f out: hung lft and wknd over 1f out: t.o* **12/1**

1m 3.16s (0.66) **Going Correction** +0.15s/f (Good) **6 Ran SP% 114.4**
Speed ratings (Par 95): **100,94,84,82,78 54**
toteswingers 1&2 £1.40, 1&3 £2.90, 2&3 £4.90 CSF £3.64 TOTE £1.50: £1.10, £2.30; EX 3.70 Trifecta £30.40 Pool: £3135.04 - 77.19 winning units..
Owner Simon Broke And Partners **Bred** Mrs Sheila Oakes **Trained** Kingston Warren, Oxon

FOCUS
This became a procession, with the winner comfortably outspeeding the runner-up, who in turn was well ahead of the rest. The runner-up and the time offer a fair guide.

7395 GRAZE ALE AND CHOP HOUSE STEAKS H'CAP 2m 1f 34y
2:30 (2:30) (Class 5) (0-75,73) 3-Y-O £2,587 (£770; £384; £192) **Stalls** Centre

Form RPR
3123 1 **Fitzwilly**[36] 6389 3-8-8 60 LiamJones 2 71
(Mick Channon) *mde all: pushed clr 5f out: unchal and styd on wl fnl 2f: rdn out* **7/2**[2]
421 2 4 1/2 **Luckster**[3] 7331 3-8-2 54 6ex CathyGannon 5 60
(David Evans) *trckd ldrs: rdn to chse wnr wl over 2f out: styd on for clr 2nd but nvr able to get on terms w wnr* **9/2**[3]
5510 3 12 **Hattie Jacques**[37] 6363 3-8-9 61 SamHitchcott 1 54
(Mick Channon) *hld up last: rdn over 3f out: styd on steadily to go 3rd 2f out: nvr threatened ldrs* **10/1**
1440 4 4 **Miss Tiger Lily**[29] 6646 3-9-7 73 LukeMorris 7 61
(Harry Dunlop) *trckd ldrs: rdn over 3f out: nvr threatened: wknd 2f out* **5/1**
3646 5 11 **Gods Gift (IRE)**[16] 6996 3-8-10 62 ChrisCatlin 6 38
(Rae Guest) *trckd ldrs: chsd wnr over 4f out tl rdn wl over 2f out: sn wknd* **10/1**
3343 6 62 **Candoluminescence**[17] 6978 3-9-4 70 (p) RichardHughes 3
(Roger Charlton) *hld up in last pair: struggling over 3f out: sn btn and eased: virtually p.u* **5/2**[1]
4010 7 31 **Cherry Princess**[43] 6202 3-8-4 56 DavidProbert 4
(Stuart Williams) *w wnr tl 5f out: rdn and lost 2nd over 3f out: sn wknd: virtually p.u* **12/1**

4m 3.16s (11.26) **Going Correction** +0.725s/f (Yiel) **7 Ran SP% 111.5**
Speed ratings (Par 101): **102,99,94,92,87 58,43**
toteswingers 1&2 £3.00, 1&3 £7.60, 2&3 £8.40 CSF £18.51 TOTE £5.10: £1.80, £2.40; EX 18.60 Trifecta £128.90 Pool: £1985.88 - 11.54 winning units..
Owner Peter Taplin **Bred** Imperial & Mike Channon Bloodstock Ltd **Trained** West Ilsley, Berks

FOCUS
There was a heavy shower before this race, which made this stiff test of stamina even more demanding, especially given the solid gallop. The result looks hollow because most of them were floundering in the mud in the last 4f.

7396 BAVARIAN BEERHOUSE BRISTOL H'CAP 1m 5f 22y
3:05 (3:05) (Class 5) (0-75,75) 3-Y-O+ £2,587 (£770; £384; £192) **Stalls** High

Form RPR
00-0 1 **One Pursuit (IRE)**[20] 6898 5-8-13 62 JackMitchell 8 75
(Brendan Powell) *cl up: rdn to chal wl over 2f out: sn led: styd on strly to draw clr ent fnl f: rdn out* **25/1**
0062 2 4 **Abundantly**[18] 6960 4-9-10 73 JimmyFortune 14 80
(Hughie Morrison) *trckd ldr: rdn to ld 3f out tl jst over 2f out: hld by wnr fr over 1f out: styd on same pce* **7/2**[1]
2020 3 9 **Candyman Can (IRE)**[17] 6976 3-8-12 69 DaneO'Neill 5 63
(Dominic Ffrench Davis) *cl up: rdn 3f out: sn chsd ldng pair but nvr threatened to get on terms: hld on wl for 3rd fnl f* **4/1**[2]
4010 4 nk **Laser Blazer**[35] 6424 5-9-12 75 (p) JimCrowley 4 68
(Jeremy Gask) *hld up bhd: racd wd: stdy prog on outer fr 3f out: disp 3rd over 1f out: styd on same pce: nvr any ch w ldng pair* **10/1**
40-0 5 11 **Whipcrackaway (IRE)**[176] 639 4-9-6 69 (p) JohnFahy 6 46
(Peter Hedger) *hld up in last pair: rdn 3f out: nvr any real imp on ldrs* **12/1**
2406 6 nk **Paloma's Prince (IRE)**[55] 5823 4-9-9 72 GeorgeBaker 2 48
(Jim Boyle) *trckd ldr tl rdn 3f out: wknd over 1f out* **8/1**
5600 7 2 **Sunny Future (IRE)**[7] 7217 7-9-12 75 TomMcLaughlin 11 48
(Malcolm Saunders) *mid-div: rdn and sme prog over 3f out: no further imp fr over 2f out: wknd over 1f out* **16/1**
054 8 28 **Gerrards Cross (IRE)**[168] 2055 3-8-12 69 RichardHughes 9
(Richard Hannon) *cl up: wnt 3rd briefly over 3f out: sn rdn and btn: eased: t.o* **11/2**
214- 9 2 3/4 **Cottesmore (USA)**[140] 6193 4-9-11 74 LiamJones 13
(Richard Ford) *led tl rdn 3f out: sn wknd: eased over 1f out: t.o* **20/1**
1045 10 1 1/2 **Kashgar**[36] 6377 4-9-7 75 RobertWilliams(5) 1
(Bernard Llewellyn) *mid-div: rdn 3f out: sn btn: eased over 1f out: t.o* **5/1**[3]

3m 2.19s (10.19) **Going Correction** +0.725s/f (Yiel)
WFA 3 from 4yo+ 8lb **10 Ran SP% 116.7**
Speed ratings (Par 103): **97,94,89,88,82 81,80,63,61,60**
toteswingers 1&2 £18.20, 1&3 £21.20, 2&3 £4.30 CSF £111.13 CT £438.62 TOTE £25.20: £7.50, £1.90, £1.30; EX 181.90 Trifecta £2313.80 Part won. Pool: £3085.16 - 0.94 winning units..
Owner Nicholas J E Maher **Bred** Clougher Partnership **Trained** Upper Lambourn, Berks

FOCUS
The soft ground really sorted them out over this trip, and there were only two in contention in the home straight.

7397 32RED FILLIES' H'CAP 1m 2f 46y
() (Class 5) (0-70,) 3-Y-O+ £

7398 32RED.COM H'CAP (DIV I) 5f 161y
() (Class 5) (0-75,) 3-Y-O+ £

7399 32RED.COM H'CAP (DIV II) 5f 161y
() (Class 5) (0-75,) 3-Y-O+ £

7400 32RED CASINO H'CAP 5f 161y
() (Class 6) (0-58,) 3-Y-O+ £

T/Jkpt: £3294.00. Pool: £90,470.75 - 19.50 winning units. T/Plt: £4.80. Pool: £108,504.00 - 16,475.10 winning units. T/Qpdt: £4.00. Pool: £6855.54 - 1266.54 winning units. TM

7401 - 7403a (Foreign Racing) - See Raceform Interactive

5074 NAAS (L-H)

Sunday, October 20

OFFICIAL GOING: Flat course - soft; hurdle course - yielding

7404a CLODOVIL EUROPEAN BREEDERS FUND GARNET STKS (LISTED RACE) (F&M) — 1m

3:15 (3:16) 3-Y-O+ **£27,743** (£8,109; £3,841; £1,280)

RPR

1 **Wannabe Better (IRE)**[14] 7051 3-9-3 101 .... WayneLordan 8 109
(T Stack, Ire) *squeezed for room s: hld up in tch: 8th 1/2-way: brought wd into st and hdwy on nrside to ld 1f out: kpt on wl u.p and extended advantage nr fin* **10/1**

2 2 ½ **Mizzava (IRE)**[67] 5415 3-9-0 106 .... ShaneFoley 10 100
(M Halford, Ire) *hld up in tch: clipped heels and stmbld sn after s: pushed along in 9th after 1/2-way: clsd between horses 2f out into nvr threatening 2nd ins fnl f: kpt on wl u.p: nt trble wnr* **7/1**

3 nse **Uleavemebreathless**[28] 6674 3-9-0 102 .... SeamieHeffernan 1 100
(A Oliver, Ire) *sn trckd ldrs: cl 3rd 1/2-way: effrt under 2f out: no imp on wnr ins fnl f: kpt on same pce* **7/1**

4 nk **Euphrasia (IRE)**[35] 6441 4-9-8 104 .... GaryCarroll 11 105+
(Joseph G Murphy, Ire) *wnt sltly lft s: sn chsd ldrs: clsr in 5th bef 1/2-way: sn pushed along and brought wd into st where lost pl: rdn in 8th 2f out and kpt on wl u.p ins fnl f: nt trble wnr* **25/1**

5 1 ½ **Rasmeyaa (IRE)**[59] 5688 3-9-0 101 .... PatSmullen 4 96
(D K Weld, Ire) *chsd ldrs: 4th 1/2-way: hdwy under 3f out to dispute 2f out: sn no ex u.p and dropped to 5th wl ins fnl f* **7/4**[1]

6 2 **Romantic Stroll (IRE)**[33] 6510 4-9-3 97 ....(t) WJLee 7 92
(T Stack, Ire) *in rr of mid-div: pushed along into st and wnt 7th u.p over 1f out: kpt on u.p towards fin: nvr on terms* **16/1**

7 ½ **Tobann (IRE)**[9] 7181 3-9-0 105 ....(t) KevinManning 5 90+
(J S Bolger, Ire) *sn trckd ldrs: 3rd 1/2-way: effrt under 2f out: rdn and no ex u.p ins fnl f: wknd towards fin* **9/2**[2]

8 1 ¼ **Spinacre (IRE)**[66] 5461 3-9-0 104 .... JosephO'Brien 6 87
(Roger Varian) *hld up in mid-div: tk clsr order bhd ldrs over 2f out: sn rdn and no imp on ldrs ent fnl f: kpt on one pce* **6/1**[3]

9 ½ **Salhooda (IRE)**[63] 5572 3-9-0 95 .... LeighRoche 13 86
(D K Weld, Ire) *led early tl jnd at 1/2-way: brought wd into st: hung under 3f out and rdn: sn no ex: wknd* **20/1**

10 1 ½ **Audacia (IRE)**[32] 6536 3-9-0 84 .... DeclanMcDonogh 12 83
(Hugo Palmer) *tacked over to nrside to trck ldr: disp 1/2-way: rdn to ld under 3f out: sn hdd and no ex u.p 2f out: wknd* **12/1**

11 ½ **Coolibah (IRE)**[14] 7052 3-9-0 88 .... FMBerry 9 81
(Charles O'Brien, Ire) *in rr thrght: rdn into st and no imp: kpt on one pce fnl 2f* **33/1**

12 ½ **Starbright (IRE)**[41] 6266 3-9-0 96 .... ChrisHayes 3 80
(Kevin Prendergast, Ire) *w.w in rr of mid-div: tk clsr order under 3f out: no ex fr 2f out: wknd and eased ins fnl f* **33/1**

1m 40.49s (0.49)
WFA 3 from 4yo 3lb **12 Ran SP% 131.0**
CSF £83.41 TOTE £9.50: £3.10, £2.80, £2.70; DF 74.60 Trifecta £1080.80.
Owner Mrs T Gaffney **Bred** Churchtown House Stud **Trained** Golden, Co Tipperary

FOCUS
They neglected the inside rail in the home straight and it's worth noting that the winner came widest of all. There were plenty of disappointing displays, none more than that of the favourite, who found very little off the bridle. The gallop was good given the conditions. The third and sixth help set the standard.

7405 - (Foreign Racing) - See Raceform Interactive

6028 BADEN-BADEN (L-H)

Sunday, October 20

OFFICIAL GOING: Turf: heavy

7406a MEHL MULHENS STIFTUNG - PREIS DER WINTERKONIGIN (GROUP 3) (2YO FILLIES) (TURF) — 1m

3:35 (12:00) 2-Y-O

£48,780 (£18,699; £8,943; £4,878; £2,439; £1,626)

RPR

1 **Diamond Dove (GER)** 2-9-2 0 .... AndreBest 4 104
(Andreas Lowe, Germany) *w ldrs early: sn hdd and trckd ldr on inner: swtchd out and rdn 2f out: clsd on ldr fr over 1f out and led ent fnl f: r.o strly and forged clr: v readily* **158/10**

2 3 **Feodora (GER)**[28] 2-9-2 0 .... ADeVries 1 97
(Frau Agnieszka Klus, Germany) *hld up towards rr on inner: pushed along over 2f out: rdn and hdwy on rail fr over 1f out: styd on and wnt 2nd towards fin: no ch w wnr* **7/2**[1]

3 1 ¼ **Filaga (FR)**[121] 2-9-2 0 .... JBojko 10 94
(M Figge, Germany) *w ldrs early: sn restrained and trckd ldr on outer: chal 3f out: rdn to ld over 2f out and sn 2 l clr: reeled in and hdd ent fnl f: no ex: fdd and dropped to 3rd towards fin* **186/10**

4 1 ¼ **Turmalina (GER)** 2-9-2 0 .... EddyHardouin 11 92
(J Hirschberger, Germany) *w ldrs early: sn led and crossed to rail: strly pressed fr 3f out: rdn and hdd over 2f out: kpt on same pce and sn hld: dropped to 4th ins fnl f* **113/10**

5 ½ **Indian Rainbow (IRE)** 2-9-2 0 .... FabienLefebvre 6 90
(Andreas Lowe, Germany) *dwlt sltly: t.k.h: hld up in tch: clsd over 2f out: rdn and kpt on same pce fr over 1f out: wnt 5th fnl strides: nvr able to chal* **32/5**

6 nk **Danza Classica (GER)** 2-9-2 0 .... TedDurcan 8 90
(W Hickst, Germany) *prom on outer: rdn over 2f out and sn outpcd by ldrs: kpt on steadily but dropped to 6th fnl strides* **49/10**[2]

7 2 **Wild Step (GER)**[17] 2-9-2 0 .... MartinSeidl 3 85
(Markus Klug, Germany) *midfield in tch on inner: rdn over 2f out: kpt on same pce and nvr threatened* **31/1**

8 shd **Weltklasse (GER)** 2-9-2 0 .... AHelfenbein 7 85
(Markus Klug, Germany) *midfield in tch: pushed along over 3f out: rdn 2f out and sn outpcd: plugged on but nvr threatened* **99/10**

9 ¾ **Veligandu (GER)** 2-9-2 0 .... APietsch 2 83
(R Dzubasz, Germany) *sltly slow to stride and pushed along early: a toward rr: rdn over 2f out: plugged on but nvr a factor* **11/2**[3]

10 13 **Perfect Mood (IRE)**[28] 2-9-2 0 .... DPorcu 12 55
(W Hickst, Germany) *a toward rr: rdn over 2f out: sn no imp and btn: eased ins fnl f: nvr a factor* **206/10**

11 3 **Turfmaid (GER)** 2-9-2 0 .... SHellyn 9 48
(J Hirschberger, Germany) *dwlt sltly: midfield on outer: rdn over 2f out: sn outpcd and dropped to rr: eased whn btn ent fnl f* **94/10**

12 ¾ **Girl On Fire (IRE)** 2-9-2 0 .... AStarke 5 47
(P Schiergen, Germany) *a in rr and mostly last: rdn over 2f out: sn no imp and btn: eased ins fnl f: nvr a factor* **11/2**[3]

1m 49.72s (10.61) **12 Ran SP% 129.2**
WIN (incl. 10 euro stake): 168. PLACES: 45, 23, 39. SF: 1,191.
Owner Gestut Wiesengrund **Bred** Meadow Land Stud **Trained** Germany

7407a HUBERTUS-LIEBRECHT-GEDACHTNISPREIS (GROUP 3) (3YO+) (TURF) — 1m 4f

4:40 (12:00) 3-Y-O+

£26,016 (£8,943; £4,471; £2,439; £1,626; £1,219)

RPR

1 **Vif Monsieur (GER)**[28] 6678 3-8-10 0 .... KClijmans 1 108+
(S Smrczek, Germany) *mde all: rdn 2f out: over 2 l clr ent fnl f: styd on strly: grad diminishing advantage towards fin but a doing enough* **3/1**[1]

2 1 ¼ **Slowfoot (GER)**[42] 6248 5-9-0 0 .... LennartHammer-Hansen 10 103
(Markus Klug, Germany) *wnt rt s: hld up towards rr: rdn and hdwy on outer over 2f out: wnt 2nd and chsd wnr fr over 1f out: styd on wl but no real imp tl wl ins fnl f and a being hld* **141/10**

3 6 **Wilddrossel (GER)**[21] 6887 4-8-10 0 .... SHellyn 3 89
(Markus Klug, Germany) *trckd ldr on inner: rdn over 3f out: styd on steadily in st but readily outpcd by front pair* **36/5**

4 1 ¾ **Salut (GER)**[56] 5-9-2 0 .... AStarke 4 93
(P Schiergen, Germany) *midfield on inner: rdn over 2f out: styd on steadily in st but readily outpcd by front pair* **3/1**[1]

5 2 ½ **Saltanat (IRE)** 3-8-3 0 .... JBojko 7 83
(Artut Resulov, Czech Republic) *trckd ldr on outer: rdn over 3f out: outpcd and lost pl 2f out: plugged on wout threatening after* **228/10**

6 nk **Lady Of Budysin (GER)**[21] 6887 4-8-10 0 .... AHelfenbein 5 82
(Markus Klug, Germany) *hld up in last pair on inner: rdn 3f out: swtchd to outer on turn into st: plugged on but nvr threatened* **98/10**

7 10 **Rawaki (IRE)**[71] 5256 5-9-2 0 .... LiamKeniry 6 72
(Andrew Balding) *midfield in tch: rdn 3f out: outpcd and dropped to rr over 1f out: btn ent fnl f* **18/5**[2]

8 11 **Silvaner (GER)**[17] 5-9-0 0 .... DPorcu 9 53
(P Schiergen, Germany) *hld up and a in rr: rdn over 2f out: outpcd and btn over 1f out: eased ins fnl f and t.o: nvr a factor* **103/10**

9 15 **See The Rock (IRE)**[28] 6678 3-8-8 0 .... EddyHardouin 8 30
(A Wohler, Germany) *midfield in tch on outer: rdn and lost pl over 3f out: detached in last and btn 2f out: sn eased and t.o* **53/10**[3]

2m 46.15s (12.69)
WFA 3 from 4yo+ 7lb **9 Ran SP% 128.7**
WIN (incl. 10 euro stake): 39. PLACES: 20, 45, 25. SF: 429.
Owner F Van Gorp **Bred** Frau Ursula Herberts **Trained** Germany

CHOLET (R-H)

Sunday, October 20

OFFICIAL GOING: Turf: soft

7408a GRAND PRIX DE CHOLET (CONDITIONS) (3YO+) (TURF) — 6f 165y

11:15 (12:00) 3-Y-O+ **£13,008** (£5,203; £3,902; £2,601; £1,300)

RPR

1 **Bilge Kagan (IRE)**[18] 3-8-4 0 .... ValentinSeguy(7) 3 88
(X Thomas-Demeaulte, France) **23/5**[3]

2 ½ **Wingate**[131] 3186 3-8-13 0 .... SebastienMartino(7) 5 96
(H-A Pantall, France) **7/5**[1]

3 2 **Tariq Too**[22] 6840 6-9-5 0 .... StephaneBreux 4 88
(Amy Weaver) *dwlt sltly: hld up in last but wl in tch: rdn and hdwy fr 2f out: swtchd lft over 1f out: wnt 3rd ins fnl f: kpt on wout matching front pair* **10/1**

4 2 **Besito (IRE)**[98] 4-8-6 0 .... JulienGuillochon(3) 6 72
(H-F Devin, France) **10/1**

5 nse **Zenji (USA)**[82] 3-9-8 0 .... AlexandreRoussel 2 86
(G Henrot, France) **22/5**[2]

6 shd **Uldiko (FR)**[45] 5-8-9 0 .... JulienMagniez(8) 7 80
(Mme C Barande-Barbe, France) **10/1**

7 10 **Fontaine Margot (FR)**[332] 7830 4-8-13 0 .... CesarPasserat(3) 1 51
(M Cesandri, France) **32/5**

1m 27.11s (87.11)
WFA 3 from 4yo+ 2lb **7 Ran SP% 118.8**
WIN (incl. 1 euro stake): 5.60. PLACES: 2.40, 1.40. SF: 19.70.
Owner Artur Adilgaliyev **Bred** Iona Equine **Trained** France

7316 LONGCHAMP (R-H)

Sunday, October 20

OFFICIAL GOING: Turf: very soft

7409a PRIX DE CONDE (GROUP 3) (2YO) (TURF) — 1m 1f

1:35 (12:00) 2-Y-O **£32,520** (£13,008; £9,756; £6,504; £3,252)

RPR

1 **Elliptique (IRE)**[29] 6710 2-8-11 0 .... MaximeGuyon 6 105
(A Fabre, France) *hld up and sn last: hdwy on outer fr 3f out: pushed along over 2f out: rdn over 1f out: edgd rt u.p but led ent fnl f: styd on strly and asserted towards fin* **5/4**[1]

2 1 **Diaghan (FR)**[33] 2-8-11 0 .... ChristopheSoumillon 2 103
(M Delzangles, France) *dwlt sltly and hld up in last trio on inner: last 3f out: pushed along and stdy hdwy on rail fr over 2f out: swtchd lft and rdn to chal ent fnl f: sn wnt 2nd: styd on and pressed wnr but hld towards fin* **4/1**[3]

3 ½ **Salai (FR)**[41] 6269 2-8-11 0 Christophe-PatriceLemaire 4 102
(J-C Rouget, France) *t.k.h: hld up in last trio on outer: in rr whn rdn 2f out: swtchd lft and hdwy fr over 1f out: wnt 3rd jst ins fnl f: styd on wl but no imp on wnr* **7/2**[2]

4 3 **Landym (FR)**[40] 2-8-11 0 FabriceVeron 5 96
(H-A Pantall, France) *midfield in tch on outer: clsd 3f out: rdn 2f out: styd on steadily but nt pce of ldng trio* **11/1**

5 3 **Bondi (GER)**[21] 2-8-8 0 AntoineCoutier 7 87
(Frau J Mayer, Germany) *worked across fr wdst draw and sn led: jnd over 3f out: pushed along and wnt on again over 2f out: rdn and 2 l clr over 1f out: reeled in and hdd ent fnl f: no ex and fdd* **50/1**

6 6 **Double Bluff (IRE)**[25] 6740 2-8-11 0 JoeFanning 3 78
(Mark Johnston) *led early: sn hdd and trckd ldr: jnd ldr on outer over 3f out: rdn and dropped to 2nd again over 2f out: sn no ex and btn: fdd* **9/2**

7 2 ½ **Rising Breeze (FR)**[29] 6710 2-8-11 0 AntoineHamelin 1 73
(K R Burke) *prom on inner: rdn and lost pl over 2f out: last and btn over 1f out* **20/1**

1m 58.01s (6.41) 7 Ran SP% **119.9**
WIN (incl. 1 euro stake): 2.00. PLACES: 1.30, 1.80. SF: 6.10.
Owner Rothschild Family **Bred** Famille Rothschild **Trained** Chantilly, France

FOCUS
An average renewal, rated around the winenr and third.

7410a PRIX DU CONSEIL DE PARIS (GROUP 2) (3YO+) (TURF) 1m 4f
2:40 (12:00) 3-Y-0+ **£60,243** (£23,252; £11,097; £7,398; £3,699)

RPR

1 **Norse King (FR)**[16] 7009 4-9-2 0 AlexisBadel 6 116
(Mme M Bollack-Badel, France) *led early: sn hdd and trckd ldr: shkn up to chal 2f out: rdn to ld over 1f out: styd on strly and asserted ins fnl f: readily* **11/4**[3]

2 2 ½ **Dupontal (IRE)**[31] 6580 3-8-9 0 DavidMorisson 2 112
(C Gourdain, France) *sn led: rdn and strly pressed 2f out: hdd over 1f out: styd on but readily outpcd by wnr ins fnl f* **7/4**[1]

3 nk **Childa (IRE)**[34] 6484 3-8-6 0 StephanePasquier 3 109+
(S Wattel, France) *hld up in tch: clsd on inner and prom in 3rd 1/2-way: ev ch whn rdn 2f out: sn outpcd by wnr: styd on steadily and pressed for 2nd cl home* **8/1**

4 2 ½ **Gentle Storm (FR)**[16] 7009 4-9-2 0 (p) ChristopheSoumillon 5 108+
(Y Barberot, France) *hld up and sn last: pushed along over 2f out: rdn and outpcd by ldrs over 1f out: styd on and tk n.d 4th ins fnl f* **14/1**

5 ¾ **Darbadar (FR)**[15] 7046 3-8-9 0 Christophe-PatriceLemaire 4 108+
(M Delzangles, France) *t.k.h: in tch on outer: 4th 1/2-way: rdn and brief effrt 2f out: outpcd by ldrs over 1f out: no ex and dropped to last ins fnl f* **5/2**[2]

2m 44.81s (14.41)
WFA 3 from 4yo 7lb 5 Ran SP% **109.4**
WIN (incl. 1 euro stake): 3.90. PLACES: 1.70, 1.50. SF: 8.30.
Owner J C Smith **Bred** Littleton Stud **Trained** Lamorlaye, France

FOCUS
The time was slow and the winner, who was well placed for the sprint in the straight, has been rated as running a personal best.

7412a PRIX DE CLIGNANCOURT (CLAIMER) (3YO) (TURF) 1m 4f
3:45 (12:00) 3-Y-0 **£10,975** (£4,390; £3,292; £2,195; £1,097)

RPR

1 **Eurato (FR)**[23] 3-9-1 0 (p) FlavienPrat 2 86
(C Laffon-Parias, France) **43/10**[3]

2 1 **Aouasif (IRE)**[27] 3-8-8 0 SoufyaneMoulin(3) 4 80
(E Lellouche, France) **23/10**[1]

3 ¾ **Agent Mimi (FR)**[33] 3-8-8 0 MaximeGuyon 6 76
(J-P Carvalho, France) **44/5**

4 nse **Sevros (FR)**[152] 3-8-9 0 RudyPimbonnet(6) 1 83
(C Laffon-Parias, France) **83/10**

5 2 ½ **Niente Paura (IRE)**[23] 3-8-11 0 MarcLerner 3 75
(C Lerner, France) **9/1**

6 1 **Kahdian (IRE)**[27] 3-9-1 0 (b) Christophe-PatriceLemaire 7 77
(M Delzangles, France) **11/1**

7 4 ½ **Aussie Lyrics (FR)**[25] 6743 3-9-1 0 (p) ChristopheSoumillon 5 70
(George Baker) **5/2**[2]

2m 45.91s (15.51) 7 Ran SP% **117.0**
WIN (incl. 1 euro stake): 5.30. Places: 2.20, 1.80. SF: 14.20..
Owner Wertheimer & Frere **Bred** Wertheimer & Frere **Trained** Chantilly, France

7234 SAN SIRO (R-H)
Sunday, October 20

OFFICIAL GOING: Turf: heavy

7413a PREMIO DEL PIAZZALE (GROUP 3) (3YO+) (TURF) 1m
2:30 (12:00) 3-Y-0+ **£22,764** (£10,016; £5,463; £2,731)

RPR

1 **Nabucco (GER)**[21] 6889 3-8-9 0 CristianDemuro 7 101
(R Rohne, Germany) *mde all: rdn fr 1 1/2f out: forged clr appr 1f out: drvn out fnl f: a in control* **29/20**[2]

2 ¾ **Porsenna (IRE)**[133] 3-8-9 0 FabioBranca 1 99+
(S Botti, Italy) *hld up towards rr: rdn and hdwy on inner 2f out: swtchd outside ldr and chal between horses over 1f out: styd on ins fnl f: a hld by wnr* **22/5**

3 1 ¼ **Killachy Loose**[21] 6890 4-8-10 0 DarioVargiu 4 95+
(B Grizzetti, Italy) *t.k.h: trckd ldr: rdn and effrt over 1 1/2f out: kpt on wout qckning ins fnl f* **77/20**[3]

4 2 ½ **Passaggio (ITY)**[175] 5-8-11 0 CFiocchi 6 90+
(A Cascio, Italy) *tk a t.k.h: trckd ldng trio: rdn and effrt over 1 1/2f out: one pce fnl f* **228/10**

5 nk **Storming Loose**[21] 6889 6-8-11 0 EPedroza 3 90+
(B Grizzetti, Italy) *in rr: short-lived effrt and hung rt 1 1/2f out: no further imp* **77/20**[3]

6 2 ¾ **Saint Bernard**[21] 6889 4-8-11 0 CColombi 2 83+
(D Camuffo, Italy) *tk a v t.k.h: restrained in 3rd: rdn and no imp fr 2f out: sn btn* **6/5**[1]

1m 42.5s (0.40)
WFA 3 from 4yo+ 3lb 6 Ran SP% **150.2**
WIN (incl. 1 euro stake): 2.45. PLACES: 1.66, 2.28. DF: 11.36.
Owner Gestut Graditz **Bred** Gestut Graditz **Trained** Germany

7414a GRAN PREMIO DEL JOCKEY CLUB (GROUP 1) (3YO+) (TURF) 1m 4f
3:10 (12:00) 3-Y-0+ **£77,235** (£33,983; £18,536; £9,268)

RPR

1 **Earl Of Tinsdal (GER)**[28] 6678 5-9-4 0 EPedroza 5 110
(A Wohler, Germany) *trckd ldr gng wl: pushed along and qcknd to ld under 1 1/2f out: r.o fnl f: readily* **11/10**[1]

2 ¾ **Biz The Nurse (IRE)**[28] 6679 3-8-13 0 CristianDemuro 4 111
(S Botti, Italy) *racd in 5th: pushed along 2 1/2f out: sn rdn and 5 l 3rd under 2f out: styd on u.p fr 1 1/2f out: nvr on terms w wnr* **6/5**[2]

3 snk **Orsino (GER)**[28] 6679 6-9-4 0 AndreaAtzeni 6 109
(R Rohne, Germany) *led: set decent gallop: shkn up and qcknd over 2f out: hdd under 1 1/2f out: kpt on gamely u.p fnl f* **19/4**[3]

4 9 **Jehannedarc (IRE)**[38] 6329 5-9-1 0 GBietolini 1 91
(Ed Dunlop) *hld up in rr: effrt 2f out: nvr in contention* **136/10**

5 2 ½ **Summer Fall (USA)**[7] 7234 4-9-1 0 DarioVargiu 2 87
(B Grizzetti, Italy) *a towards rr: nvr a factor* **53/1**

6 3 **Duca Di Mantova**[14] 4-9-4 0 PierantonioConvertino 7 86
(R Biondi, Italy) *chsd ldng pair on outer: rdn and no imp over 2 1/2f out: sn wknd* **59/1**

7 dist **Wild Wolf (IRE)**[28] 6679 4-9-4 0 (b) FabioBranca 3
(S Botti, Italy) *chsd ldng pair on inner: lost pl over 3f out: sn wl bhd and virtually p.u* **91/10**

2m 31.1s (-0.40)
WFA 3 from 4yo+ 7lb 7 Ran SP% **130.7**
WIN (incl. 1 euro stake): 2.10. PLACES: 1.24, 1.33. DF: 2.09.
Owner Sunrace Stables **Bred** Hannes K Gutschow **Trained** Germany

7415a PREMIO DORMELLO (GROUP 3) (2YO FILLIES) (TURF) 1m
3:55 (12:00) 2-Y-0 **£36,585** (£16,097; £8,780; £4,390)

RPR

1 **Ombrage (FR)** 2-8-11 0 DarioVargiu 1 105+
(B Grizzetti, Italy) *a handy: led over 2f out: qcknd clr appr 1f out: pushed out fnl f: impressive* **43/20**[2]

2 1 **Vague Nouvelle (IRE)**[21] 2-8-11 0 PierantonioConvertino 4 95
(R Biondi, Italy) *midfield: rdn to chse ldrs 2 1/2f out: hrd rdn to dispute 2nd 1 1/2f out: kpt on at same pce fnl f: fin 3rd: plcd 2nd* **9/2**[3]

3 ½ **Finidaprest (IRE)** 2-8-11 0 FabioBranca 8 94
(B Grizzetti, Italy) *settled in midfield wl in tch: rdn and outpcd 4f out: sn dropped towards rr: styd on fr 2f out: 4th and hrd rdn over 1f out: kpt on at same pce u.p: fin 4th: plcd 3rd* **58/10**

4 nse **Lady Penko (ITY)**[35] 2-8-11 0 CColombi 10 94
(M Guarnieri, Italy) *in rr: hdwy 2f out: styd on ins fnl f: nvr on terms: fin 5th: plcd 4th* **144/10**

5 2 ½ **Sognando La Cometa (IRE)**[21] 2-8-11 0 LManiezzi 11 89
(P L Giannotti, Italy) *towards rr: rdn and sme hdwy 1 1/2f out: run flattening out whn short of room and snatched up fnl 100yds: fin 6th: plcd 5th* **25/1**

6 2 **Tucci (ITY)**[112] 2-8-11 0 AndreaAtzeni 5 85
(M Guarnieri, Italy) *tk a t.k.h: chsd ldr: rdn and grad wknd ins fnl 2f: fin 7th: plcd 6th* **31/5**

7 1 ½ **Denusa (IRE)**[21] 2-8-11 0 GBietolini 9 84
(Laura Grizzetti, Italy) *chsd ldng pair: rdn and outpcd 2f out: sn wknd: fin 8th: plcd 7th* **48/1**

8 8 **Carmagnola (ITY)**[35] 2-8-11 0 SDiana 6 66
(F Camici, Italy) *burst out of stalls bef s: towards rr: gd hdwy on rail 3f out: chsd ldrs over 2f out: sn rdn and no further imp: wknd fnl 1 1/2f: fin 9th: plcd 8th* **29/4**

9 4 **Musa D'Oriente**[21] 2-8-11 0 SUrru 2 57
(B Grizzetti, Italy) *led: hdd over 2f out: sn wknd: eased ins fnl f: fin 10th: plcd 9th* **43/20**[2]

10 3 ¼ **Donna Prassede (ITY)**[21] 2-8-11 0 CristianDemuro 3 97
(S Botti, Italy) *hld up towards rr: hdwy 3f out: rdn to chse ldr whn edgd rt and hmpd salar art 2f out: sn outpcd by ldr: styd on fnl f: no ch w wnr: fin 2nd: disqualified and plcd last* **13/8**[1]

F **Salar Art**[21] 2-8-11 0 EPedroza 7
(B Grizzetti, Italy) *towards rr: plld herself to chse ldng gp bef 1/2-way: rdn and nt qckn whn and hmpd and fell 2f out* **43/20**[2]

1m 42.4s (0.30) 11 Ran SP% **204.6**
WIN (incl. 1 euro stake): 3.15. PLACES: 1.94, 2.19, 2.31. DF: 25.35.
Owner Scuderia Diamante **Bred** Edy S R L **Trained** Italy

7416a PREMIO OMENONI (GROUP 3) (3YO+) (TURF) 5f
5:10 (12:00) 3-Y-0+ **£22,764** (£10,016; £5,463; £2,731)

RPR

1 **Clorofilla (IRE)**[21] 6890 3-8-10 0 LManiezzi 5 97
(Marco Gasparini, Italy) *chsd ldrs: disp ld over 1f out: shkn up and qcknd clr ins fnl f: comf* **9/2**[3]

2 1 ½ **Kramulkie (IRE)**[14] 3-9-0 0 PierantonioConvertino 6 96
(A Marcialis, Italy) *towards rr: hdwy on outside over 1 1/2f out: styd on ins fnl f: nvr on terms w wnr* **57/10**

3 ¾ **Art Of Dreams (FR)**[14] 4-9-0 0 DarioVargiu 3 92
(B Grizzetti, Italy) *a.p: disp ld over 1f out: sn rdn and nt qckn: one pce fnl f* **69/20**[2]

4 2 ½ **Elettrotreno (IRE)**[14] 3-9-0 0 CristianDemuro 4 84
(A Giorgi, Italy) *broke wl and led: jnd over 1f out: sn rdn and no ex: wknd ins fnl f* **76/100**[1]

5 nk **Guagliona**[140] 4-8-10 0 CFiocchi 1 78
(Patrizia Giorgi, Italy) *towards rr: rdn and no imp fr 2f out* **25/1**

6 3 ½ **Virgin Queen (IRE)**[350] 7585 3-8-10 0 MEsposito 2 66
(S Botti, Italy) *a.p on rail: disp ld and ev ch 1 1/2f out: sn rdn and wknd* **128/10**

1m 1.6s (2.40) 6 Ran SP% **133.4**
WIN (incl. 1 euro stake): 5.52. PLACES: 3.72, 3.68. DF: 42.98.
Owner Vincenzo Caldarola **Bred** Francesca Turri **Trained** Italy

[7212]CAULFIELD (R-H)
Wednesday, October 16

OFFICIAL GOING: Turf: good

7417a BIRETTA & BUSBY HATMAKER CO. H'CAP (3YO+) (TURF) 1m 2f
5:00 (12:00) 3-Y-O+

£30,769 (£9,230; £4,615; £2,307; £1,282; £615)

RPR

1 **Backbone (AUS)**[529] 1874 5-9-6 0 (b) JamesMcDonald 8 101
(Michael Kent, Australia) 11/1

2 *shd* **Ruscello (IRE)**[40] 6172 4-9-2 0 KerrinMcEvoy 16 97
(Ed Walker) *sent forward fr wdst draw and sn trcking ldr on outer: rdn to chal 2f out: sn disputing ld: styd on wl and sustained battle w eventual wnr: jst denied* 11/2[2]

3 *1* **Fabriano (AUS)**[10] 7-9-2 0 (b) JyeMcNeil 10 95
(Peter Donnelly, Australia) 20/1

4 *½* **Hannaford (AUS)** 4-8-10 0 DwayneDunn 12 88+
(Robbie Laing, Australia) 9/1

5 *1 ¾* **Dylanson (AUS)** 4-9-2 0 DominicTourneur 13 91
(Phillip Stokes, Australia) 15/2[3]

6 *hd* **Supreme Warrior (NZ)** 5-9-3 0 (t) MichaelRodd 2 91
(Leon Corstens, Australia) 16/1

7 *shd* **Angola (AUS)** 5-8-11 0 (tp) RhysMcLeod 4 85
(Pat Carey, Australia) 16/1

8 *shd* **Kinesthetic (AUS)** 6-8-11 0 (p) JakeNoonan 3 85
(Leon Corstens, Australia) 10/1

9 *shd* **Phantom Brew (NZ)** 6-9-6 0 DamienOliver 14 94
(Colin Little, Australia) 16/1

10 *2* **Hunger (AUS)**[333] 4-9-2 0 (t) GlenBoss 9 86
(Mick Price, Australia) 11/1

11 *nk* **Altonio (NZ)** 7-9-2 0 (v) BradRawiller 1 85
(Pat Carey, Australia) 30/1

12 *shd* **Final Folly (AUS)** 7-9-6 0 (t) BillyEgan 11 89
(Barbara Marshman, Australia) 50/1

13 *hd* **Electric Fusion (AUS)**[130] 3130 4-9-6 0 (t) BenMelham 7 88
(Robert Smerdon, Australia) 5/1[1]

14 *8* **Tycoon Rob (NZ)** 6-8-11 0 (t) BenKnobel 6 63
(Doug Harrison, Australia) 60/1

15 *2* **Ominous**[454] 4281 4-9-0 0 MichaelWalker 15 62
(Nigel Blackiston, Australia) 8/1

16 *1 ¾* **Purettan (AUS)**[1243] 7-9-0 0 (bt) LukeNolen 5 59
(John Leek Jr, Australia) 60/1

2m 3.66s (123.66) **16 Ran SP% 121.6**
PARI-MUTUEL (NSW TAB - all including 1 aud stake): WIN 13.30; PLACE 4.00, 2.80, 8.30; DF 61.20; SF 136.40.
Owner M J Casey, Mrs J Casey Et Al **Bred** D Guihot **Trained** Australia

[7061]PONTEFRACT (L-H)
Monday, October 21

OFFICIAL GOING: Heavy (5.8)
Wind: Light across Weather: Heavy rain clearing, now bright and dry

7418 WIN BIG WITH THE TOTEJACKPOT NURSERY H'CAP 1m 4y
2:10 (2:30) (Class 5) (0-75,75) 2-Y-O £3,234 (£962; £481; £240) Stalls Low

Form RPR

004 1 **Firecruise**[32] 6546 2-9-0 68 (b[1]) RobertWinston 7 80
(David Barron) *hld up: gd hdwy over 3f out: led over 2f out and sn rdn clr: kpt on strly* 8/1[3]

013 2 *6* **Solidarity**[34] 6501 2-9-7 75 MickaelBarzalona 5 75
(Charlie Appleby) *in tch: hdwy 2f out: rdn to chse wnr appr fnl f: sn no imp* 4/1[1]

6334 3 *2 ¾* **The Wallace Line (IRE)**[19] 6946 2-8-6 60 PaulHanagan 4 53
(Mick Channon) *prom: rdn 2f out: drvn and kpt on same pce appr fnl f* 7/1[2]

000 4 *3 ¾* **Kashstaree**[40] 6298 2-8-1 55 JamieMackay 16 40
(David Barron) *bhd and drvn along after 2f: hdwy over 2f out: sn rdn: styd on fnl f: nrst fin* 66/1

6435 5 *2 ¾* **Breakable**[14] 7062 2-8-13 67 DuranFentiman 2 46
(Tim Easterby) *midfield: rdn along over 2f out: kpt on u.p appr fnl f: nrst fin* 17/2

5022 6 *½* **Supa U**[27] 6724 2-8-13 67 (e) DavidAllan 9 45
(Tim Easterby) *towards rr: hdwy wl over 2f out: sn rdn to chse ldrs: drvn and btn over 1f out* 7/1[2]

044 7 *4* **Native Falls (IRE)**[27] 6716 2-9-0 68 AndrewMullen 12 37
(Alan Swinbank) *prom: rdn along over 2f out: grad wknd* 28/1

005 8 *½* **Victory Danz (IRE)**[27] 6716 2-8-1 58 JulieBurke(3) 1 26
(David O'Meara) *cl up: rdn along over 2f out: grad wknd* 8/1[3]

2014 9 *hd* **Musical Molly (IRE)**[95] 4431 2-8-9 63 SilvestreDeSousa 17 30
(Brian Ellison) *cl up: rdn along over 2f out: grad wknd* 22/1

000 10 *6* **Bentons Lad**[81] 4925 2-8-1 55 PaulQuinn 13 9
(George Moore) *stmbld sn after s and a towards rr* 50/1

0262 11 *8* **Jive**[13] 7088 2-9-3 71 PatDobbs 10 7
(Richard Hannon) *midfield: rdn along over 3f out: sn wknd: bhd and eased wl over 1f out* 10/1

360 12 *6* **Astrowolf**[32] 6570 2-8-10 64 JoeFanning 14
(Mark H Tompkins) *a in rr: bhd and eased fr wl over 1f out* 25/1

001 13 *2 ¼* **Running Wolf (IRE)**[27] 6724 2-9-0 73 ConnorBeasley(5) 6
(Michael Dods) *chsd ldrs: rdn along 3f out: sn wknd and bhd: eased over 1f out* 16/1

515 14 *21* **Madame Mirasol (IRE)**[7] 7252 2-9-3 71 (p) TomEaves 3
(Kevin Ryan) *mde most tl rdn along over 2f out and sn wknd: bhd and eased fr wl over 1f out* 10/1

1m 54.72s (8.82) **Going Correction** +1.075s/f (Soft) **14 Ran SP% 116.9**
Speed ratings (Par 95): **98,92,89,85,82 82,78,77,77,71 63,57,55,34**
toteswingers 1&2 £1.80, 1&3 £6.20, 2&3 £7.40 CSF £36.72 CT £238.88 TOTE £9.00: £3.50, £1.50, £3.30; EX 46.20 Trifecta £351.40 Pool: £2361.93 - 5.03 winning units..
Owner Profile Storage Ltd **Bred** Fifehead Farms M C Denning **Trained** Maunby, N Yorks
■ Stewards' Enquiry : Paul Quinn two-day ban: improper riding (Nov 4-5)

FOCUS
After 11mm of morning rain the ground was eased to Heavy. The course had to pass a 1.30 inspection with racing delayed 15 minutes, as the home bend was moved out. Plenty of unexposed types in this nursery, which was run at a fair pace with the field racing wide into the straight. A big step forward from the winner.

7419 TOTEPOOL.COM HOME OF POOL BETTING MAIDEN AUCTION STKS 6f
2:40 (2:57) (Class 5) 2-Y-O £3,234 (£962; £481; £240) Stalls Low

Form RPR

233 1 **Ribbleton**[32] 6546 2-8-11 73 PaulHanagan 4 77+
(Richard Fahey) *chsd ldrs: drvn and lost pl over 4f out: hdwy over 2f out: led ins fnl f: kpt on* 7/4[2]

62 2 *½* **Percy's Gal**[26] 6754 2-8-7 0 JoeFanning 5 72+
(Karen Tutty) *treackjed ldrs: led over 1f out: edgd lft and hdd ins fnl f: no ex towards fin* 6/4[1]

6 3 *6* **Wilberfoss (IRE)**[54] 5900 2-8-11 0 DavidAllan 3 58
(Mel Brittain) *w ldrs: outpcd over 1f out: kpt on to take modest 3rd clsng stages* 28/1

03 4 *1 ½* **Sweet Angelica**[12] 7126 2-8-7 0 TomEaves 1 49
(James Given) *led tl over 4f out: led over 2f out: hdd over 1f out: swtchd rt: kpt on one pce* 9/1

04 5 *2* **Bearskin (IRE)**[25] 6769 2-9-2 0 (p) PJMcDonald 6 52
(Ann Duffield) *chsd ldrs: drvn over 2f out: grad wknd* 7/1[3]

00 6 *1* **Tinchy Ryder**[26] 6754 2-8-11 0 GrahamLee 9 44
(Bryan Smart) *t.k.h: w ldrs: led over 4f out: hdd over 2f out: grad wknd* 22/1

00 7 *½* **Hello Sweetness**[19] 6938 2-8-6 0 DuranFentiman 2 38
(Jason Ward) *in rr: sme hdwy over 2f out: nvr on terms* 100/1

00 8 *3 ½* **Shikari**[10] 7173 2-8-13 0 NeilFarley(3) 8 37
(Robin Bastiman) *in rr: bhd fnl 2f* 33/1

060 9 *8* **Geniusinrhyme**[12] 7125 2-8-13 55 SilvestreDeSousa 7 10
(Nigel Tinkler) *hood removed late: s.s: sme hdwy whn swtchd v wd over 2f out: sn wknd: eased clsng stages* 40/1

10 *12* **Takemybreathaway** 2-8-1 0 ConnorBeasley(5) 10
(Brian Rothwell) *s.i.s: sn mid-div: lost pl over 2f out: bhd whn eased clsng stages* 40/1

1m 24.7s (7.80) **Going Correction** +1.075s/f (Soft) **10 Ran SP% 115.5**
Speed ratings (Par 95): **91,90,82,80,77 76,75,71,60,44**
toteswingers 1&2 £1.20, 1&3 £14.00, 2&3 £12.60 CSF £4.33 TOTE £2.80: £1.10, £1.10, £7.90; EX 5.30 Trifecta £79.40 Pool: £2804.92 - 26.47 winning units..
Owner David W Armstrong **Bred** Highfield Farm Llp **Trained** Musley Bank, N Yorks

FOCUS
An honest pace for this modest maiden with the market leaders fighting out an exciting finish, clear of the rest. The winner is rated a minor improver.

7420 TOTEQUADPOT FOUR PLACES IN FOUR RACES H'CAP 5f
3:10 (3:22) (Class 4) (0-85,84) 3-Y-O+ £5,175 (£1,540; £769; £384) Stalls Low

Form RPR

0000 1 **Arctic Feeling (IRE)**[23] 6831 5-8-10 80 SamanthaBell(7) 2 92
(Richard Fahey) *midfield: hdwy over 2f out: chal over 1f out: rdn to ld ins fnl f: styd on wl* 7/1[2]

0001 2 *2 ¼* **Oldjoesaid**[25] 6771 9-9-0 77 PJMcDonald 14 81
(Paul Midgley) *towards rr: gd hdwy on wd outside 2f out: rdn to chse ldrs 1f out: sn drvn and kpt on same towards fin* 14/1

1000 3 *hd* **Cheworee**[135] 3114 4-9-7 84 WilliamBuick 5 87
(Tom Dascombe) *in tch: hdwy over 2f out: rdn to chal over 1f out: led briefly ent fnl f: sn drvn and hdd: kpt on same pce* 11/1

0261 4 *2* **Waseem Faris (IRE)**[4] 7324 4-9-3 80 6ex GeorgeBaker 9 76
(Mick Channon) *towards rr: hdwy wl over 1f out: sn rdn and styd on fnl f: nrst fin* 8/1[3]

603 5 *1 ¾* **Rylee Mooch**[13] 7112 5-8-10 78 (e) ConnorBeasley(5) 10 68
(Richard Guest) *led to 1/2-way: chsd ldrs: rdn and edgd rt over 1f out: sn drvn and one pce* 9/1

3314 6 *1* **Wild Sauce**[44] 6205 4-9-0 77 (bt) TomEaves 3 64
(Bryan Smart) *chsd ldrs: led 1/2-way: rdn and jnd over 1f out: drvn and hdd ent fnl f: sn wknd* 10/1

0001 7 *¾* **Cheveton**[5] 7314 9-9-0 84 6ex LouisSteward(7) 17 68
(Richard Price) *chsd ldrs: rdn along whn carried rt over 1f out: sn one pce* 7/2[1]

2450 8 *2 ¾* **Mon Brav**[10] 7176 6-9-3 80 MichaelO'Connell 4 55
(Brian Ellison) *bhd and rdn along: drvn 2f out and sme late hdwy* 16/1

2660 9 *1 ¾* **Lastchancelucas**[23] 6822 3-9-2 82 NeilFarley(3) 16 51
(Declan Carroll) *hld up: gd hdwy 2f out: rdn to chse ldrs whn hmpd over 1f out: nt rcvr* 17/2

0600 10 *1 ½* **Top Boy**[13] 7112 3-9-0 77 (v) DaleSwift 11 41
(Derek Shaw) *a in rr* 14/1

4355 11 *nk* **Avon Breeze**[29] 6665 4-9-0 82 GeorgeChaloner(5) 12 44
(Richard Whitaker) *chsd ldrs to 1/2-way: sn wknd* 8/1[3]

000 12 *4* **Oil Strike**[34] 6496 6-9-0 77 DuranFentiman 7 25
(Michael Easterby) *chsd ldrs: rdn along over 2f out: sn drvn and wknd* 40/1

463 13 *1 ½* **Perfect Blossom**[20] 6920 6-8-13 76 PaulHanagan 6 19
(Alan Berry) *chsd ldrs: rdn along bef 1/2-way: sn lost pl and bhd* 14/1

1m 7.84s (4.54) **Going Correction** +1.075s/f (Soft) **13 Ran SP% 123.2**
Speed ratings (Par 105): **106,102,102,98,96 94,93,88,86,83 83,76,74**
toteswingers 1&2 £36.20, 1&3 £17.40, 2&3 £18.30 CSF £104.58 CT £1119.01 TOTE £8.30: £2.60, £4.60, £4.00; EX 143.30 Trifecta £1369.80 Part won. Pool: £1826.46 - 0.06 winning units..
Owner Percy / Green Racing 2 **Bred** John McEnery **Trained** Musley Bank, N Yorks
■ Stewards' Enquiry : Tom Eaves two-day ban: careless riding (Nov 4-5)

FOCUS
A competitive sprint handicap, run at a fair pace in the conditions. Few showed their form but the winner is rated back to the past year's best.

7421 EBF STALLIONS/TOTEPOOL MOBILE SILVER TANKARD STKS (LISTED RACE) 1m 4y
3:40 (3:46) (Class 1) 2-Y-O £22,684 (£8,600; £4,304; £2,144; £1,076) Stalls Low

Form RPR

43 1 **Lady Heidi**[31] 6597 2-8-11 0 SilvestreDeSousa 6 97
(Philip Kirby) *hld up in rr: hdwy over 2f out and sn pushed along: rdn to chse ldng pair over 1f out: styd on and cl up ent fnl f: led last 100yds: drvn out* 20/1

1215 2 *2 ¾* **Safety Check (IRE)**[9] 7195 2-9-2 99 MickaelBarzalona 1 96
(Charlie Appleby) *trckd ldng pair: smooth hdwy 2f out and cl up tl rdn to take slt ld 1f out: sn drvn: hdd and one pce last 100yds* 7/4[2]

0245 **3** *6*	**Riverboat Springs (IRE)**[22] 6866 2-9-2 95 WilliamBuick 3 *(Mick Channon) in rr: pushed along 3f out: rdn over 2f out: styd on u.p fnl f: n.d* **8/1**	83
3101 **4** *2 ¼*	**Bow Creek (IRE)**[30] 6640 2-9-2 98 JoeFanning 5 *(Mark Johnston) led: pushed along 2f out: sn rdn and hdd 1f out: sn drvn and wknd* **6/4**[1]	78
2141 **5** *19*	**Greed Is Good**[23] 6844 2-9-2 90 DanielTudhope 2 *(K R Burke) trckd ldr: rdn along wl over 2f out: sn wknd and bhd whn eased over 1f out* **11/2**[3]	36

1m 53.52s (7.62) **Going Correction** +1.15s/f (Soft) **5** Ran SP% **107.6**
Speed ratings (Par 103): **107,104,98,96,77**
CSF £52.97 TOTE £12.30: £3.20, £1.60; EX 55.20 Trifecta £115.30 Pool: £ 2969.77 - 377.03 winning units..
Owner Hardisty Rolls II **Bred** Laundry Cottage Stud Farm **Trained** Middleham, N Yorks

FOCUS
Willie The Whipper landed this Listed prize in 2012 and went on to finish fifth in the French Derby, while third placed Top Notch Tonto chased home Olympic Glory in the Group 1 Queen Elizabeth II Stakes. The heavy ground meant this contest was a real test for these juveniles. A shock winner, but no fluke. It's hard to rate the form higher in the conditions.

7422 RUGBY LEAGUE WORLD CUP AT TOTEPOOL.COM MAIDEN STKS 1m 4f 8y
4:10 (4:11) (Class 5) 3-Y-0+ **£3,234** (£962; £481; £240) **Stalls** Low

Form			RPR
2 **1**		**Norway Cross**[33] 6532 3-9-0 0 WilliamBuick 8 *(Luca Cumani) in tch: hdwy to trck ldrs 1/2-way: cl up 4f out: led wl over 2f out: sn rdn clr: styd on* **7/4**[1]	85
5 **2**	*9*	**Aalim**[20] 6926 3-9-5 0 (p) SilvestreDeSousa 1 *(Saeed bin Suroor) dwlt and sn pushed along in rr: hdwy on inner: rdn along to chse ldrs whn n.m.r and swtchd rt to outer wl over 2f out: sn chsng wnr: drvn over 1f out and no imp* **5/1**[3]	77
0 **3**	*15*	**Wannabe Your Man**[28] 6696 3-9-5 0 AndreaAtzeni 4 *(Roger Varian) prom: chsd clr ldr after 3f: rdn along over 3f out: drvn over 2f out: plugged on to hold distant 3rd* **5/1**[3]	56
4600 **4**	*2 ¾*	**Rancho Montoya (IRE)**[36] 6435 3-9-0 62 (v[1]) TedDurcan 2 *(Andrew Balding) trckd ldrs on inner: hdwy 1/2-way: led wl over 3f out: sn rdn and hdd wl over 2f out: immediately drvn and plugged on one pce* **22/1**	48
6- **5**	*19*	**After The Storm**[520] 2266 4-9-5 0 CiaranMckee(7) 11 *(John O'Shea) in tch: rdn along over 4f out: sn outpcd* **50/1**	26
3- **6**	*4 ½*	**Newsreader (USA)**[385] 6733 3-9-5 0 JoeFanning 5 *(Mark Johnston) trckd ldrs: effrt 4f out: rdn along over 3f out: sn wknd and bhd* **4/1**[2]	20
0 **7**	*14*	**Rhinestone Rebel (IRE)**[37] 6402 7-9-7 0 ThomasGarner(5) 7 *(Peter Hiatt) dwlt: hdwy and in tch: after 3f: rdn along 5f out: sn outpcd and t.o fnl 3f* **80/1**	
/ **8**	*11*	**Eton Dorney (USA)**[47] 4-9-12 0 GrahamLee 10 *(Mark Johnston) chsd ldrs to 1/2-way: sn outpcd and bhd: t.o fnl 3f* **25/1**	
0000 **9**	*19*	**Penderyn**[27] 6723 6-9-7 34 (p) RobbieFitzpatrick 6 *(Charles Smith) led and sn clr: rdn along over 4f out: hdd wl over 3f out and wknd qckly: sn t.o: sddle slipped* **150/1**	
0042 **10**	*7*	**Maraweh (IRE)**[28] 6696 3-9-5 75 PaulHanagan 3 *(J W Hills) dwlt: sn in tch: rdn along 5f out: wknd 4f out: t.o fnl 3f* **8/1**	
11	*26*	**Mykia**[608] 5-9-12 0 BrianHughes 9 *(Ollie Pears) a in rr: t.o fnl 4f* **100/1**	

2m 55.14s (14.34) **Going Correction** +1.15s/f (Soft)
WFA 3 from 4yo+ 7lb **11** Ran SP% **113.8**
Speed ratings (Par 103): **98,92,82,80,67 64,55,47,35,30 13**
toteswingers 1&2 £2.70, 1&3 £2.80, 2&3 £4.80 CSF £9.83 TOTE £2.40: £1.10, £2.00, £3.00; EX 12.50 Trifecta £47.00 Pool: £3451.58 - 55.02 winning units..
Owner Bartisan Racing Ltd **Bred** Tsega Mares Sarl **Trained** Newmarket, Suffolk

FOCUS
Some big stables lined up for this maiden which was run at a fair pace. The field was very well strung out at the line and there's little to pin the form around. The easy winner built on her debut.

7423 TOTEPOOL MOBILE BLUFF COVE H'CAP 2m 1f 216y
4:40 (4:40) (Class 5) (0-75,75) 3-Y-0+ **£3,234** (£962; £481; £240) **Stalls** Low

Form			RPR
23-1 **1**		**Madam Lilibet (IRE)**[45] 6177 4-9-0 61 PaulQuinn 5 *(Sharon Watt) hld up in rr: stdy hdwy over 3f out: rdn to ld wl over 1f out: drvn and kpt on wl fnl f* **3/1**[1]	68
6316 **2**	*1 ¼*	**Cowslip**[6] 7280 4-8-9 56 PJMcDonald 10 *(George Moore) trckd ldrs: hdwy 4f out: effrt on inner to ld over 2f out: sn rdn and hdd wl over 1f out: drvn ins fnl f: no ex fnl 150yds* **8/1**	61
/0-5 **3**	*1*	**Wayward Glance**[6] 7280 5-10-0 75 (p) WilsonRenwick 8 *(Keith Dalgleish) trckd ldrs: hdwy over 4f out: rdn along 3f out: drvn 2f out and kpt on same pce fnl f* **5/1**[3]	79
4040 **4**	*hd*	**Authentication**[6] 7280 4-8-10 57 DavidAllan 7 *(Mel Brittain) trckd ldrs on inner: hdwy 4f out: cl up 3f out: rdn wl over 1f out: kpt on same pce* **8/1**	61
0500 **5**	*3*	**Adili (IRE)**[13] 7099 4-8-9 56 oh3 (p) SilvestreDeSousa 1 *(Brian Ellison) led 3f: chsd ldr: rdn along over 3f out: drvn 2f out: sn one pce* **10/1**	56
3/ **6**	*50*	**Rockawango (FR)**[215] 7-9-5 66 (t) GrahamLee 9 *(James Ewart) cl up: led after 3f: rdn along and hdd over 2f out: wknd qckly and eased in rr* **4/1**[2]	11
0063 **7**	*71*	**Mr Crystal (FR)**[32] 6565 9-8-10 57 (p) WilliamBuick 6 *(Micky Hammond) hld up in rr: hdwy over 6f out: rdn along on outer 4f out: sn wknd and t.o fr over 2f out* **4/1**[2]	

4m 26.08s (29.88) **Going Correction** +1.15s/f (Soft) **7** Ran SP% **113.0**
Speed ratings (Par 103): **79,78,78,77,76 54,22**
toteswingers 1&2 £5.30, 1&3 £2.80, 2&3 £2.90 CSF £26.60 CT £114.40 TOTE £3.50: £1.40, £4.30; EX 27.00 Trifecta £56.60 Pool: £2358.33 - 31.22 winning units..
Owner D H Montgomerie **Bred** Mrs Clodagh McStay **Trained** Brompton-on-Swale, N Yorks

FOCUS
A real staying test in this heavy ground. The winner liked the ground and this rates a small personal best.

7424 COLLECT TOTEPOOL WINNINGS AT BETFRED SHOPS H'CAP (DIV I) 1m 2f 6y
5:10 (5:11) (Class 4) (0-85,85) 3-Y-0+ **£5,175** (£1,540; £769; £384) **Stalls** Low

Form			RPR
3506 **1**		**Asgardella (IRE)**[9] 7211 3-8-10 76 PaulHanagan 4 *(Richard Fahey) hld up in rr: effrt over 3f out: hdwy on ins to chse ldrs over 2f out: led over 1f out: edgd rt styd on wl* **9/2**[2]	87
3000 **2**	*3*	**Hydrant**[12] 7131 7-8-12 78 ConnorBeasley(5) 2 *(Richard Guest) led: hdd over 1f out: kpt on same pce last 100yds* **12/1**	84
-500 **3**	*2 ½*	**Musnad (USA)**[149] 1237 5-8-10 71 oh1 SilvestreDeSousa 7 *(Brian Ellison) mid-div: drvn over 4f out: chsng ldng pair over 2f out: kpt on same pce* **20/1**	72
15-1 **4**	*2 ¼*	**Headline News (IRE)**[38] 6358 4-9-10 85 ChrisCatlin 5 *(Rae Guest) s.i.s: in rr: effrt over 3f out: outpcd over 2f out: kpt on to take n.d 4th ins fnl f* **13/8**[1]	82
0060 **5**	*4*	**Venutius**[32] 6550 6-8-13 74 RussKennemore 6 *(Philip Kirby) trckd ldrs: outpcd over 2f out: wknd over 1f out* **25/1**	64
5005 **6**	*4 ½*	**Arc Light (IRE)**[16] 7028 5-8-10 71 (t) DavidAllan 12 *(Tim Easterby) t.k.h in rr: effrt over 3f out: wknd over 1f out* **13/2**[3]	53
0010 **7**	*9*	**San Cassiano (IRE)**[9] 7211 6-9-5 80 (b) DaleSwift 8 *(Ruth Carr) chsd ldrs: lost pl over 2f out: bhd whn swtchd rt to stands' side rail over 1f out* **20/1**	46
4300 **8**	*7*	**Toto Skyllachy**[16] 7024 8-9-10 85 DanielTudhope 10 *(David O'Meara) trckd ldrs: wknd over 1f out: heavily eased last 100yds* **25/1**	38
2116 **9**	*9*	**Artful Prince**[24] 6788 3-8-12 78 (b) GrahamLee 13 *(James Given) trckd ldrs on outer: lost pl after 2f: sme hdwy over 4f out: lost pl 3f out: sn bhd: eased clsng stages* **9/2**[2]	15
/340 **10**	*9*	**Life And Times (USA)**[14] 7075 5-9-0 75 JoeFanning 9 *(Mark Johnston) dwlt: sn mid-div: lost pl 3f out: sn bhd: eased ins fnl f* **20/1**	

2m 24.36s (10.66) **Going Correction** +1.225s/f (Soft)
WFA 3 from 4yo+ 5lb **10** Ran SP% **117.5**
Speed ratings (Par 105): **106,103,101,99,96 93,85,80,73,65**
toteswingers 1&2 £13.10, 1&3 £13.80, 2&3 £35.30 CSF £50.07 CT £970.08 TOTE £5.60: £1.50, £3.10, £4.70; EX 68.40 Trifecta £2537.50 Part won. Pool: £3384.43 - 0.77 winning units..
Owner Middleham Park Racing XLVII **Bred** Ruskerne Ltd **Trained** Musley Bank, N Yorks

FOCUS
A sound pace for this competitive handicap, run in the same time as division II. The winner rates up a length on his form this year but a standout run in a Listed race.

7425 COLLECT TOTEPOOL WINNINGS AT BETFRED SHOPS H'CAP (DIV II) 1m 2f 6y
5:40 (5:40) (Class 4) (0-85,85) 3-Y-0+ **£5,175** (£1,540; £769; £384) **Stalls** Low

Form			RPR
10-0 **1**		**Totalize**[10] 7174 4-9-7 82 TomEaves 11 *(Brian Ellison) hld up towards rr: gd hdwy over 2f out: str run over 1f out: rdn to ld ins fnl f: sn drvn and kpt on strly* **9/1**	93
5020 **2**	*2 ¼*	**Moccasin (FR)**[16] 7028 4-9-4 79 SilvestreDeSousa 3 *(Geoffrey Harker) in tch: hdwy to trck ldrs 2f out: effrt and n.m.r over 1f out: rdn to chal ent fnl f: sn drvn and ev ch tl no ex last 75yds* **9/2**[2]	86
-002 **3**	*2 ¼*	**Dark Ruler (IRE)**[31] 6598 4-8-10 71 oh1 AndrewMullen 9 *(Alan Swinbank) trckd ldrs on outer: hdwy 3f out: cl up 2f out: sn rdn and sltly outpcd over 1f out: drvn and kpt on fnl f* **8/1**	74+
000 **4**	*nk*	**Ardmay (IRE)**[24] 6792 4-9-10 85 (p) BrianHughes 6 *(Kevin Ryan) a.p: cl up 4f out: led over 2f out: rdn wl over 1f out: drvn and hdd ins fnl f: wknd* **25/1**	87
51 **5**	*9*	**Tabaayun (IRE)**[28] 6683 3-8-11 77 (v) DanielTudhope 4 *(David O'Meara) trckd ldrs: pushed along on inner over 3f out: rdn over 2f out: sn drvn and btn* **14/1**	63
1414 **6**	*nk*	**Save The Bees**[12] 7130 5-8-10 78 LukeLeadbitter(7) 5 *(Declan Carroll) led 2f: cl up: rdn along over 2f out: sn wknd* **6/1**[3]	64
4231 **7**	*3 ¼*	**Jordaura**[29] 6667 7-8-9 73 SladeO'Hara(3) 12 *(Alan Berry) a towards rr* **20/1**	53
6-23 **8**	*20*	**Thatchmaster (USA)**[14] 7067 3-9-0 80 JoeFanning 2 *(Mark Johnston) cl up: led after 2f: rdn along 3f out: hdd and drvn over 2f out: sn wknd* **16/1**	24
5633 **9**	*nk*	**Brockfield**[19] 6943 7-8-10 71 oh4 DavidAllan 7 *(Mel Brittain) hld up in tch: hdwy and wd st to stands rail: sn rdn and btn* **9/1**	14
4161 **10**	*2 ¾*	**Eric The Grey (IRE)**[7] 7257 3-9-0 80 6ex (p) PaulHanagan 10 *(Richard Fahey) rrd s and s.i.s: sme hdwy and in tch 1/2-way: rdn along over 3f out: sn btn* **2/1**[1]	18

2m 24.35s (10.65) **Going Correction** +1.225s/f (Soft)
WFA 3 from 4yo+ 5lb **10** Ran SP% **118.1**
Speed ratings (Par 105): **106,104,102,102,94 94,92,76,75,73**
toteswingers 1&2 £10.10, 1&3 £18.70, 2&3 £7.10 CSF £49.93 CT £344.46 TOTE £14.10: £3.40, £2.20, £3.40; EX 56.20 Trifecta £448.70 Pool: £2842.36 - 4.75 winning units..
Owner D Gilbert, M Lawrence, A Bruce **Bred** Meon Valley Stud **Trained** Norton, N Yorks

FOCUS
Division two of this handicap was run at a fair pace, and in the same time as division I. The runner-up sets the standard.
T/Jkpt: Not won. T/Plt: £91.90 to a £1 stake. Pool: £84544.38 - 671.05 winning tickets T/Qpdt: £59.50 to a £1 stake. Pool: £3798.53 - 47.17 winning tickets JR

7251 WINDSOR (R-H)
Monday, October 21

OFFICIAL GOING: Heavy (6.3)
Wind: Moderate, half behind Weather: Mostly overcast

7426 WORLD HORSE WELFARE MEDIAN AUCTION MAIDEN STKS 5f 10y
2:00 (2:01) (Class 5) 2-Y-0 **£2,587** (£770; £384; £192) **Stalls** Low

Form			RPR
46 **1**		**Dazza**[10] 7162 2-9-0 0 FergusSweeney 8 *(Gary Moore) mde all: tk field to far side and grabbed position against rail: shkn up over 1f out: sn asserted: rdn out* **8/1**	68+
403 **2**	*3*	**By Rights**[19] 6947 2-8-11 65 MarkCoumbe(3) 2 *(Tony Carroll) t.k.h: cl up: rdn to chal over 1f out: one pce fnl f* **9/2**[3]	57
005 **3**	*½*	**Little Briar Rose**[53] 5929 2-9-0 50 LiamJones 5 *(John Spearing) t.k.h: pressed wnr to over 1f out: one pce fnl f* **16/1**	55
4 **4**	*shd*	**Baltic Brave (IRE)**[12] 7125 2-9-5 0 JimmyFortune 3 *(Hughie Morrison) dwlt sltly: mostly in last tl pushed along and tried to make prog 1/2-way: plugged on same pce* **7/4**[1]	60
005 **5**	*6*	**Cueca (FR)**[31] 6590 2-9-0 68 RichardHughes 7 *(Jonathan Portman) chsd ldrs to 1/2-way: sn wknd: eased fnl f* **2/1**[2]	33
0000 **6**	*½*	**Astral Rose**[20] 6922 2-8-11 45 (b[1]) MatthewLawson(3) 6 *(Jonathan Portman) s.i.s: nvr on terms w ldrs: struggling over 2f out: sn bhd* **33/1**	31

1m 3.94s (3.64) **Going Correction** +0.475s/f (Yiel) **6** Ran SP% **107.8**
Speed ratings (Par 95): **89,84,83,83,73 72**
toteswingers 1&2 £5.00, 1&3 £6.70, 2&3 £8.10 CSF £39.38 TOTE £8.90: £3.40, £2.00; EX 19.60 Trifecta £1272.80 Part won. Pool: £1697.12 - 0.52 winning units..
Owner Galloping On The South Downs Partnership **Bred** Jeremy Hinds **Trained** Lower Beeding, W Sussex

FOCUS
Inner of straight dolled out 8yds at 6f to the intersection and 3yds at the winning post. Top bend dolled out 6yds from normal inner configuration, adding 24yds to race distances of 1m and over. As is often the case here when the ground is testing, the runners headed across to the far side in the straight. Modest maiden form, with an improved effort from the winner.

7427 BHEST RACING TO SCHOOL CLAIMING STKS 6f
2:30 (2:34) (Class 6) 3-Y-O+ **£1,940** (£577; £288; £144) **Stalls** Low

Form RPR

5255 **1** **Commanche**[14] 7080 4-9-2 81 .... AdamKirby 12 78
(Chris Dwyer) *trckd ldrs: clsd 2f out: drvn to ld jst over 1f out: styd on wl* **11/4**[1]

4642 **2** *1* **Ortac Rock (IRE)**[16] 7031 4-8-10 75 .... (t) KierenFallon 6 69
(Richard Fahey) *chsd ldrs: pushed along bef 1/2-way: prog 2f out: drvn to chse wnr ins fnl f: nt qckn and no imp last 100yds* **11/4**[1]

3660 **3** *½* **Fortrose Academy (IRE)**[94] 4494 4-8-10 62 .... DavidProbert 3 67
(Andrew Balding) *pressed ldr: led over 2f out: drvn and hdd jst over 1f out: one pce* **10/1**

0404 **4** *nk* **Camache Queen (IRE)**[7] 7246 5-8-1 55 .... (vt) KieranO'Neill 8 57
(Joseph Tuite) *pressed ldrs: rdn to chal over 2f out: kpt on same pce fr over 1f out* **25/1**

2-00 **5** *4½* **Beachwood Bay**[54] 5876 5-7-13 49 .... JosephineGordon(7) 2 49
(Jo Hughes) *pressed ldrs: pushed along 1/2-way: nt qckn 2f out: one pce fr over 1f out* **66/1**

0046 **6** *1¼* **Royal Reyah**[19] 6959 4-8-11 72 .... ShaneKelly 5 50
(Stuart Kittow) *in tch: outpcd and rdn over 2f out: neveer on terms w ldrs after* **6/1**[2]

-000 **7** *¾* **Mac's Power (IRE)**[38] 6352 7-9-7 88 .... JimmyFortune 11 58
(Willie Musson) *hld up in last trio: sme prog 1/2-way: outpcd and shkn up wl over 1f out: no hdwy after* **8/1**[3]

0000 **8** *5* **Kings 'n Dreams**[35] 6462 6-8-7 52 .... (p) JimmyQuinn 4 29
(Dean Ivory) *s.s: mostly in last trio: struggling u.p 1/2-way* **66/1**

0000 **9** *4½* **Taurus Twins**[19] 6948 7-8-8 72 .... (b) FergusSweeney 10 16
(Richard Price) *led to over 2f out: lost pl qckly* **16/1**

0064 **10** *nk* **Jack My Boy (IRE)**[7] 7254 6-8-9 75 .... (b) CathyGannon 1 16
(David Evans) *chsd ldrs: rdn by 1/2-way: sn wknd* **10/1**

0430 **11** *15* **Primo D'Oro (USA)**[19] 6932 3-8-10 61 .... RichardHughes 9
(Richard Hannon) *stdd s: hld up in last trio: pushed along and struggling 1/2-way: sn bhd: eased and t.o* **20/1**

1m 15.98s (2.98) **Going Correction** +0.475s/f (Yiel)
WFA 3 from 4yo+ 1lb 11 Ran SP% **114.4**
Speed ratings (Par 101): **99,97,97,96,90 88,87,81,75,74 54**
toteswingers 1&2 £1.80, 1&3 £6.20, 2&3 £7.40 CSF £8.73 TOTE £3.50: £1.70, £1.30, £2.80; EX 10.80 Trifecta £102.30 Pool: £1643.43 - 12.04 winning units..
Owner M M Foulger **Bred** Paramount Bloodstock **Trained** Newmarket, Suffolk

FOCUS
The far rail was again in popular demand in what was a fair claimer. The form of the first two is limited by lesser rivals.

7428 R J CLYDE BUILDERS NURSERY H'CAP 1m 67y
3:00 (3:00) (Class 4) (0-85,79) 2-Y-O **£3,752** (£1,116; £557; £278) **Stalls** Low

Form RPR

1002 **1** **The Alamo (IRE)**[7] 7252 2-9-2 74 .... RichardHughes 3 78
(Richard Hannon) *hld up: rdn over 2f out: sn chsd ldng pair: responded 1f out to cl: led last 100yds: styd on* **2/1**[1]

0650 **2** *1½* **Midnight Rambler (IRE)**[26] 6749 2-8-0 58 oh1 .... KieranO'Neill 8 59
(Richard Hannon) *led: hanging lft bnd fr 6f out: hdd 5f out to 4f out: drvn 3f out: hdd briefly over 1f out: battled on wl but hdd and btn last 100yds* **20/1**

0005 **3** *½* **Cape Arrow**[20] 6924 2-8-1 59 .... JimmyQuinn 1 59
(Paul Cole) *s.i.s: mostly in last: pushed along 1/2-way: sme prog u.p 2f out but nt on terms: styd on fnl f to take 3rd cl home* **8/1**

2351 **4** *¾* **Wickhambrook (IRE)**[18] 6975 2-9-7 79 .... TomQueally 2 77
(Ismail Mohammed) *cl up: led 5f out to 4f out: drvn over 2f out: led again briefly over 1f out: no ex fnl f* **7/2**[3]

033 **5** *2½* **Storm Force Ten**[28] 6688 2-9-2 74 .... DavidProbert 5 66
(Andrew Balding) *hld up in last pair: shkn up wl over 1f out: nvr involved but kpt on steadily fnl f* **5/2**[2]

3304 **6** *3¼* **Left Defender (IRE)**[29] 6663 2-8-10 68 .... (p) JohnFahy 10 53
(Jo Hughes) *prom: drvn wl over 2f out: wknd wl over 1f out* **20/1**

6236 **7** *23* **Ellalan**[56] 5819 2-9-0 72 .... JimCrowley 7 7
(David Simcock) *prom: hanging lft bnd over 5f out: wknd rapidly over 2f out: t.o* **10/1**

1m 48.59s (3.89) **Going Correction** +0.25s/f (Good) 7 Ran SP% **113.9**
Speed ratings (Par 97): **90,88,88,87,84 81,58**
toteswingers 1&2 £7.60, 1&3 £3.60, 2&3 £16.00 CSF £41.12 CT £262.57 TOTE £2.20: £1.10, £6.90; EX 22.00 Trifecta £208.10 Pool: £1126.18 - 4.05 winning units..
Owner Ivory, Woodcock, Bull, Hannon **Bred** Tommy James **Trained** East Everleigh, Wilts

FOCUS
Ordinary nursery form. Straightforward form which could possibly be rated a bit better.

7429 CELEBRATING GIBBO'S STAG H'CAP (DIV I) 1m 67y
3:30 (3:30) (Class 5) (0-70,70) 3-Y-O+ **£2,587** (£770; £384; £192) **Stalls** Low

Form RPR

2464 **1** **Rioja Day (IRE)**[13] 7093 3-8-9 61 .... (b) MartinLane 1 69
(J W Hills) *mde all: gng strly and 3 l clr 3f out: rdn 2f out: styd on wl: unchal* **6/1**

3010 **2** *2* **The Scuttler (IRE)**[24] 6794 3-9-1 70 .... CharlesBishop(3) 10 73
(Mick Channon) *in tch: rdn over 2f out: prog against far rail to take 2nd 1f out: styd on but no imp on wnr* **9/2**[3]

6530 **3** *1¾* **Prime Exhibit**[17] 7000 8-9-7 70 .... (t) ShaneKelly 8 70
(John Stimpson) *hld up in last pair: gng smoothly over 2f out but stl in rr: pushed along and prog over 1f out: reminders and r.o to take 3rd ins fnl f: no ch to threaten* **10/1**

5606 **4** *1½* **Authoritarian**[74] 5181 4-9-4 67 .... (b[1]) RichardHughes 11 64
(Richard Hannon) *prom: rdn to dispute 2nd fr over 2f out to 1f out: no imp on wnr: fdd last 100yds* **7/2**[2]

0006 **5** *nk* **Empiricist (IRE)**[37] 6379 3-8-13 65 .... (p) JimCrowley 2 60
(Amanda Perrett) *prom: chsd wnr fr 3f out: no imp u.p 2f out: fdd fnl f* **3/1**[1]

0-06 **6** *2* **Know No Fear**[13] 7092 8-8-13 62 .... (p) FergusSweeney 5 54
(Alastair Lidderdale) *heavily restrained s: hld up in last: urged along and sme prog over 2f out: no hdwy fr over 1f out* **14/1**

-666 **7** *6* **Croeso Mawr**[36] 6433 7-9-2 65 .... SteveDrowne 4 43
(John Spearing) *pressed wnr to 3f out: wknd qckly* **8/1**

-535 **8** *1* **Ivor's Princess**[56] 5816 4-9-1 64 .... (b) SeanLevey 6 40
(Rod Millman) *s.i.s: in tch: rdn 3f out: sn struggling* **20/1**

0000 **9** *1¼* **Kindia (IRE)**[19] 6932 5-8-2 56 oh5 .... (p) RyanTate(5) 7 29
(Michael Attwater) *chsd ldrs tl wknd over 3f out* **33/1**

1m 47.52s (2.82) **Going Correction** +0.25s/f (Good)
WFA 3 from 4yo+ 3lb 9 Ran SP% **114.3**
Speed ratings (Par 103): **95,93,91,89,89 87,81,80,79**
toteswingers 1&2 £4.30, 1&3 £9.20, 2&3 £8.10 CSF £32.77 CT £265.72 TOTE £8.60: £2.10, £2.10, £2.40; EX 36.10 Trifecta £268.40 Pool: £2435.65 - 6.80 winning units..
Owner Neil Ledger And Gary Woodward **Bred** Mrs Eleanor Commins **Trained** Upper Lambourn, Berks

FOCUS
Modest handicap form with doubts over the field. The winner is rated back to his best.

7430 CELEBRATING GIBBO'S STAG H'CAP (DIV II) 1m 67y
4:00 (4:01) (Class 5) (0-70,70) 3-Y-O+ **£2,587** (£770; £384; £192) **Stalls** Low

Form RPR

00 **1** **Collodi (GER)**[14] 7075 4-9-0 70 .... NedCurtis(7) 2 81
(Roger Curtis) *hld up in tch: smooth prog to trck ldr over 2f out: rdn to ld over 1f out: drvn clr* **16/1**

4023 **2** *3* **Uncle Dermot (IRE)**[4] 7319 5-9-1 64 .... KierenFallon 3 68
(Brendan Powell) *trckd ldng pair: led over 3f out: drvn over 2f out: hdd over 1f out: one pce and no ch w wnr fnl f* **5/2**[1]

5641 **3** *½* **Admirable Art (IRE)**[7] 7246 3-8-5 62 6ex .... (p) RyanTate(5) 8 64
(Tony Carroll) *hld up: prog over 2f out: rdn to chse ldng pair over 1f out: kpt on to press runner-up nr fin* **7/2**[2]

4-01 **4** *2½* **Barista (IRE)**[13] 7109 5-8-10 66 .... DanielCremin(7) 6 63
(Brian Forsey) *led at gd pce to over 4f out: rdn 3f out: steadily lft bhd fr over 2f out* **8/1**

0303 **5** *6* **Balmoral Castle**[24] 6794 4-9-1 67 .... MatthewLawson(3) 10 50
(Jonathan Portman) *in tch: rdn over 3f out: sn struggling: bhd fnl 2f* **4/1**[3]

10 **6** *1* **Welsh Sunrise**[27] 6735 3-8-13 65 .... TomMcLaughlin 7 45
(Ed Walker) *chsd ldr: led over 4f out to over 3f out: wknd wl over 2f out* **33/1**

400 **7** *nk* **Star Date (IRE)**[8] 7220 4-8-11 60 .... (p) RobertHavlin 9 40
(Michael Attwater) *s.i.s: urged along and bhd early: gng bttr and in tch after 3f: sn drvn and lost tch again 3f out: nvr on terms after* **11/1**

0430 **8** *50* **Moortahan**[28] 6702 3-8-11 63 .... RichardHughes 4
(Richard Hannon) *in tch: rdn 1/2-way: sn wknd and eased: wl t.o* **7/1**

1m 46.09s (1.39) **Going Correction** +0.25s/f (Good)
WFA 3 from 4yo+ 3lb 8 Ran SP% **111.6**
Speed ratings (Par 103): **103,100,99,97,91 90,89,39**
toteswingers 1&2 £7.90, 1&3 £8.20, 2&3 £2.60 CSF £53.46 CT £174.01 TOTE £12.90: £3.70, £1.30, £1.70; EX 52.60 Trifecta £250.60 Pool: £2879.22 - 8.61 winning units..
Owner Stocky And Gunny **Bred** Stiftung Gestut Fahrhof **Trained** Lambourn, Berks

FOCUS
As was the case in the first division, we saw a fairly clear-cut winner. The slightly faster division, and form rated around the runner-up.

7431 ARC SUPPORTS RETRAINING OF RACEHORSES H'CAP 1m 2f 7y
4:30 (4:30) (Class 4) (0-85,85) 3-Y-O+ **£4,690** (£1,395; £697; £348) **Stalls** Centre

Form RPR

1354 **1** **Vital Evidence (USA)**[26] 6751 3-8-13 79 .... (p) JamesDoyle 9 95
(Sir Michael Stoute) *mde all: a gng strly: rdn wl clr fr 2f out* **7/2**[1]

5460 **2** *8* **Aldwick Bay (IRE)**[14] 7072 5-8-10 71 oh1 .... (b[1]) RichardHughes 7 73
(Richard Hannon) *t.k.h: hld up in rr: rchd midfield 3f out: rdn and taken out wd fr 2f out: prog to take 2nd 1f out: no ch w wnr* **6/1**

5000 **3** *1½* **Carry On Sydney**[5] 7312 3-9-4 84 .... SeanLevey 1 83
(Richard Hannon) *t.k.h: prom: rdn to chse wnr 3f out: no imp: lost 2nd and one pce 1f out* **5/1**[2]

5521 **4** *2* **Lybica (IRE)**[33] 6521 3-8-5 71 .... SamHitchcott 10 66
(Gary Moore) *prom: rdn over 4f out: kpt on u.p but nt pce to threaten after* **8/1**

4020 **5** *nk* **Presburg (IRE)**[16] 7028 4-9-4 79 .... LiamKeniry 12 74
(Joseph Tuite) *hld up in tch: rdn 3f out: no prog and btn 2f out: plugged on* **12/1**

1001 **6** *1¾* **Breaking The Bank**[19] 6956 4-9-5 80 .... MartinDwyer 11 72
(William Muir) *mostly chsd wnr to 3f out: steadily fdd* **5/1**[2]

2300 **7** *3* **Starwatch**[14] 7072 6-8-11 75 .... MichaelJMMurphy(3) 5 61
(John Bridger) *chsd ldrs: rdn over 4f out: sn struggling* **16/1**

14-0 **8** *nk* **Ex Oriente (IRE)**[22] 6868 4-9-10 85 .... AdamBeschizza 8 71
(Stuart Williams) *lft 10 l s: ct up at bk of field after 3f: rdn and lost tch over 4f out: nvr on terms after* **16/1**

6300 **9** *½* **Takeitfromalady (IRE)**[14] 7072 4-8-11 75 .... (v) ThomasBrown(3) 6 60
(Lee Carter) *hld up in rr: rdn and no prog 3f out: sn btn* **11/2**[3]

2m 11.23s (2.53) **Going Correction** +0.25s/f (Good)
WFA 3 from 4yo+ 5lb 9 Ran SP% **115.8**
Speed ratings (Par 105): **99,92,91,89,89 88,85,85,85**
toteswingers 1&2 £4.70, 1&3 £4.00, 2&3 £6.90 CSF £24.65 CT £104.54 TOTE £5.30: £1.50, £2.30, £3.20; EX 23.20 Trifecta £213.10 Pool: £1661.73 - 5.84 winning units..
Owner K Abdullah **Bred** Juddmonte Farms Inc **Trained** Newmarket, Suffolk

FOCUS
Slightly suspect form with a few of these failing to give their running. Not form to get carried away with, but there's a chance the winner is better than this.

7432 BEN WOOLLACOTT MEMORIAL H'CAP 5f 10y
5:00 (5:00) (Class 5) (0-70,70) 3-Y-O+ **£2,587** (£770; £384; £192) **Stalls** Low

Form RPR

3310 **1** **Rambo Will**[20] 6929 5-9-1 64 .... CathyGannon 5 76
(J R Jenkins) *mde all: led field to nr side fr 3f out: drvn 2f out: clr over 1f out: styd on wl* **8/1**[3]

3042 **2** *2¼* **Indian Tinker**[37] 6412 4-9-4 67 .... SteveDrowne 10 71
(Robert Cowell) *prom: rdn over 2f out: chsd wnr over 1f out: kpt on same pce* **8/1**[3]

5165 **3** *½* **Tychaios**[13] 7106 3-8-10 59 .... AdamBeschizza 9 63
(Stuart Williams) *chsd ldrs: rdn over 2f out: kpt on u.p to take 3rd ins fnl f* **8/1**[3]

0401 **4** *½* **Layla's Oasis**[7] 7240 3-9-7 70 6ex .... RichardHughes 1 72
(Richard Fahey) *chsd ldrs against rail: shkn up 2f out: kpt on but nt pce to threaten* **6/1**[2]

440 **5** *nk* **Solemn**[26] 6745 8-9-7 70 .... (b) AdamKirby 4 70
(Milton Bradley) *mostly chsd wnr to over 1f out: one pce* **8/1**[3]

3060 **6** *¾* **Shawkantango**[33] 6516 6-9-3 66 .... (v) HarryBentley 8 63
(Derek Shaw) *mostly in last trio: shkn up wl over 1f out: kpt on after: nrst fin* **16/1**

0006 **7** *1¼* **Heartsong (IRE)**[37] 6381 4-9-4 70 .... MichaelJMMurphy(3) 11 63
(John Gallagher) *prom: racd alone in centre fr 3f out: nt on terms w ldrs fr over 1f out* **10/1**

5403 **8** 3/4 **Captain Scooby**[6] 7262 7-8-12 **68**....(e) PatMillman(7) 7 59
(Richard Guest) *nvr bttr than midfield: struggling in rr over 1f out* **6/1**[2]
3160 **9** 2 **Invigilator**[10] 7165 5-8-5 **61**....(t) AdamMcLean(7) 2 45
(Derek Shaw) *mostly in last trio: pumped along and no real prog fnl 2f* **20/1**
0444 **10** 1/2 **Indian Affair**[38] 6362 3-9-5 **68**.... JimmyQuinn 6 51
(Milton Bradley) *chsd ldrs: lost pl 1/2-way: struggling in rr over 1f out* **16/1**
366 **11** 1 3/4 **Commandingpresence (USA)**[20] 6929 7-9-4 **67**.... KieranO'Neill 3 43
(John Bridger) *dwlt: a in last trio: shkn up and no prog over 2f out* **33/1**
521 **12** 18 **Harrogate Fair**[6] 7263 3-9-2 **65** 6ex.... LiamJones 12
(Michael Squance) *chsd ldrs: rdn 2f out: wknd rapidly over 1f out: t.o: b.b.v* **5/1**[1]

1m 2.29s (1.99) **Going Correction** +0.475s/f (Yiel) 12 Ran SP% **118.2**
Speed ratings (Par 103): **103,99,98,97,97 96,94,92,89,88 86,57**
toteswingers 1&2 £15.80, 1&3 £6.10, 2&3 £9.40 CSF £70.46 CT £542.23 TOTE £6.90: £2.60, £2.20, £2.90; EX 88.80 Trifecta £291.60 Pool: £2616.36 - 6.72 winning units..
Owner Mrs S Bambridge **Bred** T H Bambridge **Trained** Royston, Herts

FOCUS
This had looked an open sprint, but for the first time on the day the runners came stands' side, with the ground on the far side looking chewed up at this stage. The winner made all and is rated close to last year's best.

7433 JRL GROUP AMATEUR H'CAP (FOR GENTLEMAN AMATEUR RIDERS) 1m 3f 135y
5:30 (5:30) (Class 5) (0-70,69) 3-Y-O+ **£2,495** (£774; £386; £193) **Stalls** Centre

Form RPR
3431 **1** **Ebony Express**[26] 6758 4-11-5 **69**.... MrORJSangster(5) 5 78
(Alan Swinbank) *cl up: styd nr side fr 3f out: rdn to ld overall over 1f out: styd on* **5/2**[1]
-556 **2** 2 1/4 **Hyperlink (IRE)**[46] 6130 4-11-4 **68**.... MrAlexFerguson(5) 8 74
(Michael Bell) *racd freely: sn led: 4 l clr 1/2-way: wnt to far side 3f out and sn lost overall ld: styd at hd of gp and kpt on* **8/1**
0065 **3** 3/4 **Mr Spiggott (IRE)**[12] 7130 4-11-8 **67**....(v) MrFMitchell 9 72
(Gary Moore) *mostly trckd ldr: styd nr side in st and sn overall ldr: hdd and one pce over 1f out* **7/2**[2]
3001 **4** nse **Cuckoo Rock (IRE)**[8] 7220 6-10-10 **60** 6ex....(p) MrJHarding(5) 4 64
(Jonathan Portman) *wl in rr: lost tch 1/2-way and nrly t.o: wnt far side 3f out: kpt on after: nrst fin* **8/1**
2150 **5** 1 1/2 **On Stage**[39] 6325 4-11-0 **59**.... MrSWalker 3 61
(Stuart Kittow) *w.w off the pce: clsd 5f out: styd nr side fr 3f out and chsd ldr to wl over 1f out: fdd* **7/1**[3]
3665 **6** 3/4 **Tawseef (IRE)**[24] 6788 5-11-9 **68**.... MrJHamilton 2 69
(Roy Brotherton) *w.w off the pce: clsd 5f out: wnt to far side 3f out and chsd ldr: no imp 2f out: fdd fnl f* **7/1**[3]
0656 **7** 18 **Wordiness**[24] 6787 5-11-4 **68**.... MrMatthewStanley(5) 1 42
(Brendan Powell) *prom: rdn and styd nr side fr 3f out: sn wknd: t.o* **12/1**
000/ **8** 3 **Drussell (IRE)**[148] 1372 7-10-13 **65**.... MrZBaker(7) 6 35
(Martin Bosley) *a wl in rr: t.o sn after 1/2-way* **33/1**
0030 **9** 5 **Urban Space**[30] 6658 7-10-7 **55**.... MrChrisMartin(3) 7 17
(Tony Carroll) *in tch: lost pl bef 1/2-way: wnt far side 3f out: wknd over 2f out: eased: t.o* **20/1**

2m 37.2s (7.70) **Going Correction** +0.25s/f (Good) 9 Ran SP% **113.4**
Speed ratings (Par 103): **84,82,82,81,80 80,68,66,63**
toteswingers 1&2 £4.40, 1&3 £2.40, 2&3 £6.90 CSF £22.71 CT £68.92 TOTE £2.50: £1.10, £2.90, £2.30; EX 24.00 Trifecta £99.80 Pool: £2092.42 - 15.71 winning units..
Owner Mrs T Blackett **Bred** Miss E J Wright **Trained** Melsonby, N Yorks

FOCUS
There was a difference in opinion in this amateur riders' handicap, with three heading far side in the straight, but the winner came from the stands' side group. The form is rated around the runner-up.
T/Plt: £131.90 to a £1 stake. Pool: £80140.57 - 443.52 winning tickets T/Qpdt: £24.40 to a £1 stake. Pool: £6738.39 - 203.77 winning tickets JN

7325 KEMPTON (A.W) (R-H)
Tuesday, October 22

OFFICIAL GOING: Standard
Wind: Fresh across Weather: Fine

7434 DAY DELEGATE RATES FROM £39 H'CAP 1m 3f (P)
5:40 (5:40) (Class 6) (0-65,65) 3-Y-O **£1,940** (£577; £288; £144) **Stalls** Low

Form RPR
0100 **1** **Posh Boy (IRE)**[14] 7091 3-9-5 63.... JimCrowley 6 69+
(Chris Wall) *dwlt: hld up in rr: pushed along and hdwy on outside 2f out: rdn and qcknd to ld ent fnl f: kpt on wl* **5/1**[3]
4402 **2** 2 3/4 **Hero's Story**[8] 7248 3-9-1 59....(v[1]) RichardHughes 4 61
(Amanda Perrett) *midfield: hdwy to trck ldrs 3f out: rdn over 1f out: wnt 2nd jst ins fnl f: kpt on but no ch w wnr* **11/2**
503 **3** 1 3/4 **Estibdaad (IRE)**[38] 6399 3-9-2 60....(t) SteveDrowne 9 59
(Anthony Honeyball) *hld up in tch: rdn over 2f out: kpt on: wnt 3rd ins fnl f* **5/1**[3]
4001 **4** 3 3/4 **Solvanna**[28] 6737 3-9-7 65.... TomQueally 3 58
(Heather Main) *trckd ldr: rdn to ld over 2f out: hdd ent fnl f: wknd* **12/1**
6000 **5** 1 3/4 **Quadriga (IRE)**[29] 6702 3-9-1 59.... JimmyQuinn 7 49
(Robert Eddery) *hld up in tch: rdn over 2f out: nvr threatened* **16/1**
5255 **6** nk **Pencombe (FR)**[17] 7033 3-9-0 65.... GeorgeBuckell(7) 5 55
(David Simcock) *midfield on inner: rdn over 2f out: sn btn* **11/1**
0200 **7** nse **Syrenka**[14] 7091 3-9-1 62.... MichaelJMMurphy(3) 8 51
(Marcus Tregoning) *sn trckd ldr on outer: pushed along 4f out: wknd fnl 2f* **14/1**
2446 **8** 1 **Bejeweled (IRE)**[25] 6794 3-9-2 65.... TimClark(5) 1 53
(Lady Cecil) *trckd ldr: rdn over 3f out: wknd over 2f out* **9/2**[2]
000 **9** 3 **Achtung**[103] 4223 3-9-6 64....(v[1]) WilliamBuick 2 47
(Jeremy Noseda) *s.i.s: sn rcvrd to ld: rdn whn hdd over 2f out: wknd* **4/1**[1]

2m 22.4s (0.50) **Going Correction** +0.10s/f (Slow) 9 Ran SP% **115.5**
Speed ratings (Par 99): **102,100,98,96,94 94,94,93,91**
toteswingers 1&2 £3.90, 2&3 £3.70, 1&3 £5.80 CSF £32.62 CT £144.58 TOTE £4.60: £1.70, £1.60, £1.80; EX 20.00 Trifecta £115.80 Pool: £1652.52 - 10.69 winning units..
Owner Des Thurlby **Bred** Deerfield Farm **Trained** Newmarket, Suffolk

FOCUS
A modest but open handicap run in which the gallop soon steadied. The winner, who made his ground in the centre, edged towards the far rail late on. The winner is rated up a fraction with the runner-up fitting in.

7435 REWARDS4RACING.COM MAIDEN FILLIES' STKS 7f (P)
6:10 (6:11) (Class 5) 2-Y-O **£2,587** (£770; £384; £192) **Stalls** Low

Form RPR
04 **1** **Aertex (IRE)**[8] 7245 2-9-0 0.... RichardHughes 7 73
(Richard Hannon) *t.k.h early: in tch: rdn and hdwy to chse ldr over 1f out: kpt on wl to ld fnl 50yds* **8/1**[3]
45 **2** 1 1/4 **Alfaayza (IRE)**[25] 6789 2-9-0 65.... DaneO'Neill 3 70
(Brian Meehan) *led: rdn 2f out: kpt on: hdd fnl 50yds* **14/1**
3 3 1/2 **Lady Horatia** 2-9-0 0.... MartinDwyer 12 61
(William Muir) *trckd ldr: rdn over 2f out: kpt on one pce* **33/1**
4400 **4** 3/4 **Starlit Cantata**[42] 6275 2-9-0 67.... JohnFahy 2 59
(Eve Johnson Houghton) *trckd ldr: rdn over 2f out: one pce* **25/1**
6 **5** 3/4 **Penny Sixpence (FR)**[88] 4716 2-9-0 0.... WilliamBuick 4 57+
(John Gosden) *dwlt: hld up: rdn and sme hdwy over 1f out: one pce fnl f: nvr threatened ldrs* **2/1**[1]
6 3/4 **Gay Marriage (IRE)** 2-9-0 0.... RobertHavlin 6 55+
(John Gosden) *s.i.s: hld up in rr: pushed along over 2f out: kpt on fnl f: nrst fin* **16/1**
7 1/2 **Kalifi (USA)** 2-9-0 0.... PatDobbs 1 54+
(Amanda Perrett) *dwlt: sn midfield: rdn over 2f out: one pce* **16/1**
3 **8** 1 1/4 **Sequester**[14] 7103 2-9-0 0.... TedDurcan 8 51
(David Lanigan) *midfield: rdn and outpcd 1/2-way: no threat after* **9/4**[2]
53 **9** 2 1/4 **Big Boned (USA)**[15] 7078 2-9-0 0.... JamieSpencer 10 45
(Ed Dunlop) *dwlt: hld up: pushed along over 2f out: sn no imp: eased nr fin* **8/1**[3]
10 3 1/2 **Synaesthesia (FR)** 2-9-0 0.... TomQueally 13 36
(Lady Cecil) *sn chsd ldr on outer: wknd over 2f out* **10/1**
5 **11** 4 **Zanouska (USA)**[14] 7103 2-9-0 0.... JoeFanning 11 25
(Mark Johnston) *slowly away: sn midfield on outer: rdn over 2f out: wknd* **20/1**
000 **12** 3 3/4 **Wildling**[5] 7320 2-8-9 0.... NathanAlison(5) 5 15
(Jim Boyle) *sn pushed along towards rr: a bhd* **100/1**
13 1 1/2 **Gracefilly** 2-9-0 0.... TomMcLaughlin 9 12
(Ed Walker) *racd keenly in tch: settled into midfield 1/2-way: wknd fnl 2f* **33/1**

1m 27.45s (1.45) **Going Correction** +0.10s/f (Slow) 13 Ran SP% **129.3**
Speed ratings (Par 92): **95,93,89,88,87 87,86,85,82,78 73,69,67**
toteswingers 1&2 £12.20, 2&3 £144.00, 1&3 £46.70 CSF £117.42 TOTE £7.60: £2.10, £4.70, £7.30; EX 96.20 Trifecta £1778.30 Part won. Pool: £2371.07 - 0.43 winning units..
Owner Mrs James Wigan **Bred** Mrs James Wigan **Trained** East Everleigh, Wilts
■ Richard Hughes's 200th winner of the turf season. He's the seventh post-war jockey to achieve this feat.

FOCUS
Little strength in depth but fair form from the principals in a race in which the gallop was on the steady side to halfway. The first two, who came down the centre, pulled clear of the rest. Ordinary form at first glance, the race averages suggesting it won't rate much better.

7436 REINDEER RACING AT KEMPTON PARK 06.12.13 H'CAP 7f (P)
6:40 (6:41) (Class 4) (0-82,82) 3-Y-O+ **£4,851** (£1,443; £721; £360) **Stalls** Low

Form RPR
5-00 **1** **Apostle (IRE)**[24] 6826 4-9-7 82.... JamieSpencer 4 91
(David Simcock) *mde all: rdn 2f out: briefly jnd over 1f out: drvn and kpt on fnl f* **11/2**[3]
0410 **2** 1 1/4 **Ocean Legend (IRE)**[38] 6403 8-9-4 79.... TomQueally 9 85
(Tony Carroll) *midfield: rdn and hdwy over 1f out: chsd wnr ins fnl f: kpt on but a hld* **16/1**
1461 **3** 1 **Dominium (USA)**[7] 7264 6-9-2 77 6ex....(b) DaneO'Neill 14 80+
(Jeremy Gask) *racd keenly: hld up in rr: rdn and stl plenty to do over 1f out: kpt on fnl f: wnt 3rd post* **13/2**
1 **4** shd **Loud**[15] 7073 3-8-9 72.... JoeFanning 3 74
(Mark Johnston) *trckd ldr: rdn over 2f out: one pce: lost 3rd post* **7/2**[2]
4114 **5** 3/4 **Greensward**[15] 7076 7-8-13 74....(b) ShaneKelly 8 75
(Mike Murphy) *slowly away: hld up: rdn over 2f out: kpt on ins fnl f: nvr threatened* **16/1**
6020 **6** 1 **Lutine Bell**[13] 7123 6-9-4 79....(b) PatDobbs 11 77
(Mike Murphy) *dwlt: hld up in midfield: rdn over 2f out: nvr threatened* **8/1**
6253 **7** nse **Disco Inferno (IRE)**[14] 7108 3-8-2 70....(bt) TimClark(5) 6 67
(Brian Meehan) *trckd ldr: rdn and briefly upsides over 1f out: wknd fnl f* **20/1**
2630 **8** 1/2 **Intomist (IRE)**[15] 7075 4-8-8 74....(p) NathanAlison(5) 2 71
(Jim Boyle) *in tch: rdn over 2f out: grad wknd fnl f* **20/1**
0152 **9** 1 1/4 **Evident (IRE)**[15] 7076 3-9-1 78.... WilliamBuick 7 71
(Jeremy Noseda) *hld up: rdn over 2f out: nvr threatened* **5/2**[1]
1002 **10** 1 1/4 **Sheikh The Reins (IRE)**[41] 6317 4-8-11 72....(v) SteveDrowne 5 62
(John Best) *chsd ldrs: rdn over 2f out: sn wknd* **16/1**
0400 **11** 4 **Seek The Fair Land**[18] 6995 7-9-1 76....(v) WilliamCarson 12 56
(Lee Carter) *in tch on outer: rdn 3f out: wknd over 1f out* **33/1**

1m 26.22s (0.22) **Going Correction** +0.10s/f (Slow)
WFA 3 from 4yo+ 2lb 11 Ran SP% **120.7**
Speed ratings (Par 105): **102,100,99,99,98 97,97,96,95,93 89**
toteswingers 1&2 £6.20, 2&3 £18.80, 1&3 £5.70 CSF £89.10 CT £605.06 TOTE £6.40: £2.20, £3.90, £2.30; EX 87.60 Trifecta £573.00 Pool: £1873.41 - 2.45 winning units..
Owner Dr Marwan Koukash **Bred** Mrs Eleanor Kent **Trained** Newmarket, Suffolk

FOCUS
A couple of unexposed performers in a fair handicap in which the winner, who came down the centre, was able to dictate his own tempo. It proved difficult to come from off the pace. Straightforward form, with the winner entitled to rate this high.

7437 BOOK YOUR CHRISTMAS PARTY ON 01932 753518 H'CAP 1m (P)
7:10 (7:10) (Class 5) (0-68,73) 3-Y-O+ **£2,587** (£770; £384; £192) **Stalls** Low

Form RPR
0004 **1** **Diplomatic (IRE)**[20] 6933 8-9-1 61....(p) AdamKirby 7 79
(Michael Squance) *hld up: pushed along and rapid hdwy 2f out: led appr fnl f: rdn clr* **8/1**
1 **2** 3 **Havelovewilltravel (IRE)**[27] 6748 3-9-2 65.... WilliamBuick 8 75+
(Jeremy Noseda) *dwlt and sltly hmpd s: hld up: rdn and stl in rr over 2f out: r.o fnl f: wnt 2nd fnl 75yds: no ch w wnr* **2/1**[1]
5531 **3** 1 3/4 **The Great Gabrial**[6] 7306 4-9-13 73 6ex....(v) JamieSpencer 5 80
(Ian Williams) *midfield: hdwy and ev ch over 1f out: sn rdn and one pce* **7/2**[2]

5600 **4** 2 ½ **Derfenna Art (IRE)**[122] 3580 4-9-2 62..........................(t) GeorgeBaker 11 63
(Seamus Durack) *hld up: rdn over 2f out: sme hdwy over 1f out: kpt on one pce: nvr threatened ldrs* **25/1**

4441 **5** 1 ¼ **Tammuz (IRE)**[20] 6932 3-9-0 63.................................. RichardHughes 10 60
(Tony Carroll) *midfield: rdn over 2f out: one pce and nvr threatened ldrs* **6/1**[3]

2100 **6** 2 **Super Cookie**[67] 5492 3-9-3 66...................................... WilliamCarson 2 59
(Philip McBride) *prom: rdn to ld 2f out: hdd appr fnl f: wknd* **11/1**

6520 **7** nk **Final Delivery**[19] 6970 4-9-0 60.......................................(b) PatCosgrave 6 54
(Jim Boyle) *sltly hmpd s: hld up in rr: rdn over 2f out: nvr threatened* **25/1**

0200 **8** ½ **Emman Bee (IRE)**[25] 6794 4-9-7 67..........................(v[1]) SteveDrowne 12 59
(Luke Dace) *chsd ldrs: rdn over 2f out: wknd fnl f* **20/1**

-300 **9** 5 **Mosman**[15] 7073 3-8-13 62..(t) MartinDwyer 13 42
(Dean Ivory) *midfield on outer: rdn over 3f out: wknd over 1f out* **50/1**

0230 **10** 4 **Knight Charm**[8] 7248 3-8-11 60.......................................(p) JimCrowley 3 30
(Eve Johnson Houghton) *in tch: rdn over 2f out: wknd over 1f out* **8/1**

2661 **11** 3 ¼ **Bertie Moon**[19] 6968 3-8-13 67.............................. ThomasGarner[(5)] 1 30
(Geoffrey Deacon) *led narrowly: hdd over 3f out: sn btn* **14/1**

4400 **12** 1 ¼ **Ghostwing**[20] 6937 6-8-6 59..................................(b) JoshQuinn[(7)] 9 20
(Luke Dace) *w ldr: led over 3f out: hdd 2f out: wknd* **50/1**

1m 39.66s (-0.14) **Going Correction** +0.10s/f (Slow)
WFA 3 from 4yo+ 3lb **12** Ran SP% **123.4**
Speed ratings (Par 103): **104,101,99,96,95 93,93,92,87,83 80,79**
toteswingers 1&2 £4.70, 2&3 £2.70, 1&3 £5.00 CSF £24.11 CT £69.99 TOTE £11.70: £2.20, £1.70, £2.30; EX 25.00 Trifecta £156.70 Pool: £2105.96 - 10.07 winning units..
Owner Miss K Squance **Bred** Darley **Trained** Newmarket, Suffolk

FOCUS
A modest handicap in which unexposed sorts were in a minority. The gallop was reasonable and the winner came down the centre. A step back to last season's form here from the winner.

7438 BOOK NOW FOR THE CHRISTMAS FESTIVAL H'CAP 1m (P)
7:40 (7:42) (Class 4) (0-80,80) 3-Y-0+ **£4,851** (£1,443; £721; £360) **Stalls** Low

Form RPR

5305 **1** **Cayuga**[23] 6868 4-9-5 78...(p) JimCrowley 4 86
(Brett Johnson) *hld up in midfield: rdn and hdwy 2f out: led ins fnl f: kpt on* **10/1**[3]

1232 **2** ¾ **Secret Beau**[13] 7123 3-9-2 78...(t) TomQueally 11 83
(David Evans) *hld up in rr: rdn and gd hdwy 2f out: chsd wnr ins fnl f: kpt on but a jst hld* **12/1**

5606 **3** 1 ¼ **Woody Bay**[20] 6951 3-9-0 76.. FrederikTylicki 5 78
(James Given) *in tch: rdn over 2f out: kpt on one pce* **20/1**

1143 **4** 1 ½ **Pleasure Bent**[29] 6694 3-9-4 80................................ RichardHughes 9 79
(Luca Cumani) *midfield: rdn and hdwy to chse ldr appr fnl f: no ex ins fnl f* **5/6**[1]

0223 **5** hd **Light Rose (IRE)**[8] 7256 3-8-11 73....................................... JoeFanning 1 71
(Mark Johnston) *trckd ldr: led 2f out: sn rdn: hdd ins fnl f: wknd fnl 100yds* **10/1**[3]

1660 **6** nk **Thistleandtworoses (USA)**[19] 6970 3-8-12 74.......... DanielTudhope 3 72
(David O'Meara) *slowly away: hld up: racd keenly: rdn 2f out: kpt on ins fnl f* **20/1**

2000 **7** 1 ¾ **Bank On Me**[25] 6801 4-9-6 79..................................(v[1]) WilliamCarson 8 74
(Philip McBride) *t.k.h early: midfield: rdn and lost pl over 3f out: no threat after* **11/2**[2]

2460 **8** nk **Emmuska**[29] 6694 4-9-7 80.. AdamKirby 7 74
(Clive Cox) *in tch: rdn over 2f out: wknd fnl f* **33/1**

0005 **9** 10 **Embankment**[21] 6925 4-8-13 72.......................................(p) JimmyQuinn 10 43
(William Jarvis) *reluctant to s: a bhd* **25/1**

010- **10** 3 **Munsarim (IRE)**[378] 6969 6-9-4 80..........................(b) ThomasBrown[(3)] 6 44
(Lee Carter) *led: clr 5f out tl 3f out: hdd 2f out: wknd* **33/1**

2000 **11** shd **Rezwaan**[5] 7318 6-9-4 77...(p) ShaneKelly 2 41
(Murty McGrath) *dwlt: hld up in midfield: rdn over 2f out: sn wknd* **33/1**

20-0 **12** 24 **Zaeem**[21] 6925 4-9-4 77...[1] GeorgeBaker 12
(Dean Ivory) *midfield on outer: wknd over 2f out: eased* **33/1**

1m 39.49s (-0.31) **Going Correction** +0.10s/f (Slow)
WFA 3 from 4yo+ 3lb **12** Ran SP% **120.9**
Speed ratings (Par 105): **105,104,103,101,101 101,99,98,88,85 85,61**
toteswingers 1&2 £8.70, 2&3 £48.10, 1&3 £22.10 CSF £112.75 CT £2348.75 TOTE £14.20: £3.80, £2.90, £6.50; EX 107.00 Trifecta £1770.90 Part won. Pool: £2361.24 - 0.18 winning units..
Owner J Daniels **Bred** Juddmonte Farms Ltd **Trained** Epsom, Surrey

FOCUS
A fair handicap in which the gallop was reasonable throughout. The winner came down the centre in the straight and is rated back to his Polytrack best.

7439 BOOK NOW FOR JUMP RACING ON 04.11.13 H'CAP 1m 4f (P)
8:10 (8:11) (Class 5) (0-70,70) 3-Y-0+ **£2,587** (£770; £384; £192) **Stalls** Centre

Form RPR

306 **1** **Commissar**[30] 6667 4-9-10 68...(t) JimCrowley 2 77+
(Ian Williams) *hld up in midfield: smooth hdwy over 2f out: qcknd to ld over 1f out: rdn out fnl f: comf* **5/1**[3]

5021 **2** 1 ½ **Grayswood**[22] 6899 3-9-5 70.......................................(p) MartinDwyer 8 77
(William Muir) *hld up in rr: rdn over 2f out: hdwy over 1f out: kpt on to go 2nd fnl 100yds: no ch w wnr* **11/4**[1]

4053 **3** 1 ¾ **Everlasting Light**[17] 7033 3-9-2 67............................... WilliamBuick 11 71
(Luca Cumani) *prom: rdn to ld 2f out: hdd over 1f out: sn no ch w wnr: one pce and lost 2nd fnl 100yds* **7/2**[2]

2604 **4** 2 ¼ **Royal Etiquette (IRE)**[15] 7081 6-9-0 58.......................(vt) DaneO'Neill 5 59
(Lawney Hill) *hld up in rr: rdn over 2f out: kpt on fnl f: nvr threatened ldrs* **16/1**

1040 **5** nk **Super Duplex**[22] 4679 6-8-13 60........................... JemmaMarshall[(3)] 7 60
(Pat Phelan) *trckd ldrs: rdn over 1f out: sn one pce: grad wknd fnl f* **33/1**

1410 **6** 2 ½ **Ebony Roc (IRE)**[8] 7258 3-9-2 67.. PatDobbs 4 64
(Amanda Perrett) *trckd ldrs: rdn over 2f out: sn outpcd and btn* **7/1**

1224 **7** 1 ¼ **Shahrazad (IRE)**[47] 6130 4-9-0 63..........................(t) NoelGarbutt[(5)] 10 58
(Patrick Gilligan) *led: hdd 8f out: trckd ldr: briefly n.m.r over 2f out: rdn 2f out: grad wknd* **12/1**

4004 **8** 1 ¼ **Run It Twice (IRE)**[13] 7118 3-9-3 68..............................(b) TomQueally 3 61
(David Evans) *midfield: rdn and outpcd 3f out: no threat after* **25/1**

2536 **9** 2 **Sweet Martoni**[19] 6978 3-9-3 68..................................... AdamKirby 9 58
(William Knight) *in tch: hdwy to ld 8f out: sn stdd pce: qcknd pce 3f out: hdd 2f out: wknd* **6/1**

2m 35.87s (1.37) **Going Correction** +0.10s/f (Slow)
WFA 3 from 4yo+ 7lb **9** Ran SP% **112.7**
Speed ratings (Par 103): **99,98,96,95,95 93,92,91,90**
toteswingers 1&2 £3.80, 2&3 £3.60, 1&3 £4.30 CSF £18.58 CT £53.10 TOTE £6.20: £2.30, £1.10, £2.10; EX 23.00 Trifecta £101.30 Pool: £1919.09 - 14.20 winning units..
Owner S Hassiakos **Bred** R A Instone **Trained** Portway, Worcs

FOCUS
A modest handicap run at a steady gallop to the home turn and this bare form isn't reliable. The winner came down the centre and should be able to progress on this surface.
T/Jkpt: Not won. T/Plt: £1119.40 to a £1 stake. Pool of £80892.76 - 52.75 winning units. T/Qpdt: £56.50 to a £1 stake. Pool of £9223.82 - 120.70 winning tickets. AS

7300 LINGFIELD (L-H)
Tuesday, October 22

OFFICIAL GOING: Standard
Wind: Moderate, behind; becoming fresh, behind by race 4 Weather: Heavy rain before racing, then cloudy, fine from race 4

7440 BAKER TILLY APPRENTICE H'CAP 1m 4f (P)
2:00 (2:01) (Class 6) (0-55,55) 3-Y-0+ **£2,045** (£603; £302) **Stalls** Low

Form RPR

-500 **1** **Impertinent**[18] 6996 3-8-7 46 oh1................................. DannyBrock 16 53
(Jonathan Portman) *mid-div: swtchd wd and hdwy 3f out: pressed ldrs fnl f: r.o to ld fnl strides* **20/1**

630 **2** hd **El Libertador (USA)**[28] 6737 7-9-7 53...............................(b) JoeyHaynes 5 60
(Eric Wheeler) *hld up in tch: effrt and gng wl 3f out: led over 2f out: jnd ins fnl f: hdd fnl strides* **7/1**[1]

3006 **3** ¾ **Lord Golan**[175] 1916 5-9-5 51....................................(b) GeorgeChaloner 1 57
(Violet M Jordan) *trckd ldrs: rdn to chal over 2f out: jnd ldr ins fnl f: no ex nr fin* **10/1**[3]

05/0 **4** 1 ¾ **Jody Bear**[14] 7090 5-9-0 46.. MatthewLawson 4 49
(Jonathan Portman) *hld up towards rr: rdn and r.o fnl 2f: nrest at fin* **50/1**

00-0 **5** 1 ¾ **Stadium Of Light (IRE)**[16] 5521 6-8-8 47 oh1 ow1 AlexHopkinson[(7)] 10 48
(Shaun Harris) *prom: chal on bit 3f out: rdn over 2f out: unable qck* **16/1**

40-3 **6** 1 ½ **Opus (IRE)**[147] 2764 4-9-0 49.................................... ThomasGarner[(3)] 2 47
(Lucy Wadham) *mde most tl over 2f out: wknd over 1f out* **10/1**[3]

6-00 **7** 2 ¾ **Mohair**[12] 7159 4-9-6 52..(b[1]) GeorgeDowning 11 46
(Luke Dace) *mid-div: rdn and no hdwy fnl 3f* **14/1**

2000 **8** 2 ¼ **Willow Island (IRE)**[10] 7201 4-8-11 46 oh1.................(v[1]) EoinWalsh[(3)] 9 37
(David Evans) *in tch: rdn 5f out: btn over 3f out* **14/1**

5466 **9** nse **Hawaiian Freeze**[4] 7351 4-8-9 46 oh1....................... JordanVaughan[(5)] 3 37
(John Stimpson) *in tch on rail: outpcd over 2f out: sn hrd rdn and btn* **10/1**[3]

-000 **10** 1 ¾ **Nandura**[57] 5816 3-8-7 46 oh1.. NathanAlison 12 34
(Harry Dunlop) *sn bhd: rdn 8f out: carried hd high: nvr nr ldrs* **10/1**[3]

-050 **11** shd **Awesome Rock (IRE)**[54] 5934 4-9-0 46............................ PhilipPrince 15 34
(Roger Ingram) *hld up in midfield: hdwy towards outer 3f out: wknd 2f out* **8/1**[2]

00-0 **12** 13 **Misteray**[22] 6899 3-8-4 46 oh1....................................(t) RyanWhile[(3)] 13 15
(Bill Turner) *in tch on outer: rdn 5f out: wknd 3f out* **50/1**

0-00 **13** nk **Filun**[12] 7159 8-9-6 55...(tp) TimClark[(3)] 6 23
(Anthony Middleton) *s.s: rdn 7f out: a bhd* **25/1**

4030 **14** ½ **Devon Diva**[36] 6472 7-8-9 46............................. JeanVanOvermeire[(5)] 8 13
(John Gallagher) *pressed ldr tl wknd over 3f out* **16/1**

2600 **15** 1 ¼ **Red Mystique (IRE)**[14] 7090 4-9-0 51.........................(b) JackGarritty[(5)] 7 16
(Philip Hide) *sn wl bhd* **8/1**[2]

6056 **16** 46 **Dawn Beat**[14] 7104 3-8-3 47.. JohnLawson[(5)] 14
(Jonathan Portman) *s.s: a towards rr: wl bhd fnl 3f: fin lame* **8/1**[2]

2m 33.89s (0.89) **Going Correction** +0.05s/f (Slow)
WFA 3 from 4yo+ 7lb **16** Ran SP% **119.8**
Speed ratings (Par 101): **99,98,98,97,96 95,93,91,91,90 90,81,81,81,80 49**
toteswingers 1&2 £29.90, 2&3 £9.50, 1&3 £35.50 CSF £147.66 CT £1503.21 TOTE £21.80: £4.00, £1.60, £2.90, £13.70; EX 285.10 Trifecta £1258.20 Part won. Pool: £1677.66 - 0.43 winning units..
Owner Paul Moulton **Bred** Paul Moulton **Trained** Upper Lambourn, Berks
■ Stewards' Enquiry : Danny Brock four-day ban: used whip above permitted level (Nov 5-7 & tbn)

FOCUS
A moderate 0-55 apprentice handicap and wide open, as 7-1 the field would suggest. Despite a disputed lead, the pace seemed ordinary. Straightforward form.

7441 H&V SERVICEPLAN MAIDEN AUCTION STKS 7f (P)
2:30 (2:31) (Class 6) 2-Y-0 **£2,045** (£603; £302) **Stalls** Low

Form RPR

642 **1** **Sweet P**[14] 7087 2-8-8 65... MartinDwyer 1 68
(Marcus Tregoning) *swtchd outside after 1f and sn pressing ldr: led 2f out: pushed clr 1f out: comf* **3/1**[2]

2 2 ¼ **Mr Wickfield** 2-8-13 .... SteveDrowne 3 66+
(John Best) *dwlt: sn in tch: rn green thrght: r.o fr over 1f out: tk 2nd nr fin* **20/1**

60 **3** nk **Bognor (USA)**[97] 4414 2-8-8 .... PhilipPrince[(5)] 9 65
(Jo Hughes) *chsd ldng pair: pushed along over 3f out: styd on to chse wnr ins fnl f: jst lost 2nd* **7/1**[3]

5202 **4** 1 ¼ **Baars Causeway (IRE)**[15] 7062 2-8-6 72.............................. LukeMorris 2 55
(Alan Jarvis) *led tl 2f out: no ex appr fnl f* **4/7**[1]

5 2 **Lady Knight (IRE)** 2-8-4 .... JimmyQuinn 8 48
(J S Moore) *dwlt: in last pair most of way: shkn up and styd on fnl 2f* **33/1**

6 8 **Charlies Mate** 2-8-9 .... JohnFahy 4 32
(John Best) *hld up in last pair: n.d fnl 3f* **25/1**

60 **7** 2 ¼ **Divine Bay**[21] 6923 2-8-6 .... SamHitchcott 7 23
(Gary Moore) *in tch: pushed wd after 1f: rdn along 5f out and awkward on bnds: wknd over 3f out* **50/1**

1m 26.47s (1.67) **Going Correction** +0.05s/f (Slow) **7** Ran SP% **114.7**
Speed ratings (Par 93): **92,89,89,87,85 76,73**
toteswingers 1&2 £5.00, 2&3 £12.90, 1&3 £2.70 CSF £51.92 TOTE £3.90: £1.50, £7.20; EX 57.90 Trifecta £193.00 Pool: £2737.46 - 10.63 winning units..
Owner M P N Tregoning **Bred** W & T Barrons And Mr & Mrs A Pakenham **Trained** Whitsbury, Hants
■ Stewards' Enquiry : Martin Dwyer two-day ban: careless riding (Nov 5-6)

FOCUS
An uncompetitive maiden auction event and the form looks modest with the odds-on favourite running so poorly. The winner is rated as an improver and the runner-up shaped well.

7442 R P METAL/IRISH STALLION FARMS EBF MEDIAN AUCTION MAIDEN STKS 1m (P)
3:00 (3:01) (Class 5) 2-Y-0 **£3,067** (£905; £453) **Stalls** High

Form RPR

1 **Tanqeya (IRE)** 2-9-5 0.. DaneO'Neill 9 80+
(Richard Hannon) *mid-div: hdwy 3f out: swtchd rt over 1f out: r.o to ld nr fin* **5/1**[3]

The Form Book Flat, Raceform Ltd, Compton, RG20 6NL.

2 nk **Invasor Luck (USA)** 2-9-5 0 .... FrederikTylicki 2 79+
(James Fanshawe) *chsd ldrs: led jst ins fnl f: kpt on u.p: ct nr fin* **8/1**

05 3 1 1/2 **Captain Swift (IRE)**[13] 7128 2-9-5 0 .... SeanLevey 11 76
(Brian Meehan) *prom on outer: pressed ldrs fnl f: kpt on* **14/1**

5 4 nk **Courageous Rock (USA)**[40] 6330 2-9-5 0 .... JimmyFortune 7 75
(Ed Vaughan) *pressed ldr: rdn to ld briefly 1f out: unable qck* **7/4**[1]

5626 5 5 **Calrissian (IRE)**[15] 7061 2-9-5 73 .... JimCrowley 5 63
(Alan Jarvis) *sn led: rdn and hdd 1f out: wknd fnl f* **7/2**[2]

6 2 1/4 **Artistic Flame** 2-9-5 0 .... (b[1]) PatDobbs 3 58
(Amanda Perrett) *s.i.s: bhd: rdn 3f out: nvr rchd ldrs* **16/1**

0 7 2 1/2 **Coastal Storm**[15] 7069 2-9-0 0 .... RobertHavlin 6 47
(Hughie Morrison) *hld up in rr: rdn 3f out: nvr nr to chal* **25/1**

00 8 nk **Squaw King**[19] 6975 2-9-5 0 .... JohnFahy 1 52
(Eve Johnson Houghton) *broke wl: settled in tch on rail: outpcd and btn 3f out* **33/1**

9 3/4 **Spiritoftheunion** 2-9-0 0 .... JamieSpencer 12 45
(Michael Bell) *a bhd* **7/1**

10 1 1/2 **Jolie Blonde** 2-9-0 0 .... LukeMorris 4 42
(Sir Mark Prescott Bt) *rn green: a towards rr: bhd fnl 4f* **33/1**

0006 11 12 **Commanding Force**[14] 7087 2-9-5 40 .... KieranO'Neill 8 19
(John Bridger) *plld hrd: in tch: rdn over 3f out: sn wknd* **200/1**

1m 39.88s (1.68) **Going Correction** +0.05s/f (Slow) 11 Ran SP% **121.6**
Speed ratings (Par 95): **93,92,91,90,85 83,81,80,80,78 66**
toteswingers 1&2 £10.70, 2&3 £21.60, 1&3 £16.40 CSF £45.10 TOTE £7.10: £3.30, £3.80, £4.80; EX 55.80 Trifecta £644.20 Pool: £2786.10 - 3.24 inning units..
Owner Hamdan Al Maktoum **Bred** Ballylinch Stud **Trained** East Everleigh, Wilts

FOCUS
A modest median auction event, but the finish was fought out by a pair of newcomers who both seem likely to progress. The first four were clear.

7443 P&M ELECTRICAL (S) STKS 6f (P)
3:30 (3:30) (Class 6) 3-Y-O **£2,045** (£603; £302) **Stalls** Low

Form RPR

5526 1 **Hartwright**[23] 6867 3-9-5 74 .... (v) JamieSpencer 5 74+
(Michael Bell) *wnt lft and bmpd s: hld up in tch: effrt 2f out: drvn to ld ins fnl f* **4/9**[1]

000 2 2 **Dreamy Ciara**[3] 7381 3-8-9 64 .... SteveDrowne 1 56
(David Brown) *trckd ldr: jnd ldr on inner ent st: one pce ins fnl f* **4/1**[2]

6504 3 3/4 **Coire Gabhail**[19] 6965 3-8-9 55 .... RobertHavlin 9 54
(Hughie Morrison) *sn led: jnd by runner-up ent st: hdd and one pce ins fnl f* **8/1**[3]

6505 4 2 3/4 **Lichen Angel**[20] 6944 3-8-5 46 ow1 .... GeorgeChaloner(5) 7 47
(Richard Whitaker) *hld up in 6th: rdn over 2f out: styd on same pce* **25/1**

0000 5 6 **Whitford (IRE)**[39] 6368 3-9-0 47 .... LukeMorris 4 33
(Chris Dwyer) *wnt rt and bmpd s: bhd: sme hdwy on rail ent st: hrd rdn and wknd over 1f out* **25/1**

0-60 6 5 **Gold Weight**[12] 7154 3-8-9 46 .... PhilipPrince(5) 10 18
(Michael Madgwick) *stdd s and swtchd lft: hld up in rr: rdn 3f out: outpcd and rn wd on home turn* **66/1**

6400 7 2 1/2 **Princess Cammie (IRE)**[7] 7266 3-8-9 52 .... (p) JoeyHaynes(5) 8 10
(John Bridger) *stmbld s: chsd ldrs on outer: wknd 2f out* **20/1**

0600 8 3 **Roland**[7] 7269 3-9-5 66 .... (p) JimmyQuinn 3 6
(Kevin Ryan) *prom: sn pushed along: wknd 2f out* **8/1**[3]

1m 11.73s (-0.17) **Going Correction** +0.05s/f (Slow) 8 Ran SP% **125.4**
Speed ratings (Par 99): **103,100,99,95,87 81,77,73**
toteswingers 1&2 £1.30, 2&3 £6.60, 1&3 £2.40 CSF £2.95 TOTE £1.40: £1.02, £1.80, £2.50; EX 3.90 Trifecta £11.90 Pool: £3179.77 - 199.98 winning units..The winner was bought in for 14,600gns.
Owner Mrs L J Garton **Bred** New England Stud And Partners **Trained** Newmarket, Suffolk

FOCUS
An uncompetitive seller in which the pair joint best in at the weights finished 1-2. Straightforward low-grade form.

7444 CHARTPLAN H'CAP 6f (P)
4:00 (4:04) (Class 5) (0-70,70) 3-Y-O+ **£2,726** (£805; £402) **Stalls** Low

Form RPR

2542 1 **Jay Bee Blue**[7] 7262 4-9-2 66 .... (bt) AdamKirby 3 75
(Sean Curran) *hld up in tch: smooth hdwy over 1f out: r.o to ld fnl 75yds* **3/1**[1]

2300 2 1/2 **Emiratesdotcom**[14] 7106 7-9-4 68 .... (tp) DavidProbert 2 76
(Milton Bradley) *prom on rail: led 1f out: kpt on u.p: hdd fnl 75yds* **20/1**

5000 3 hd **Sewn Up**[11] 7164 3-9-3 68 .... (p) JimCrowley 6 75
(Andrew Hollinshead) *hld up towards rr: gd hdwy over 1f out: pressed ldrs ins fnl f: hrd rdn: r.o* **12/1**

4502 4 1 **Another Try (IRE)**[14] 7106 8-9-5 69 .... LukeMorris 5 73
(Alan Jarvis) *chsd ldrs: rdn 2f out: styd on fnl f* **4/1**[2]

5200 5 1 1/4 **Meridius (IRE)**[36] 6476 3-9-5 70 .... (b[1]) ShaneKelly 7 70
(Gary Harrison) *prom: chal 2f out: no ex fnl f* **6/1**[3]

4553 6 2 1/4 **Haadeeth**[18] 6995 6-8-9 66 .... (t) EoinWalsh(7) 1 59
(David Evans) *led: rdn and hdd 1f out: wknd fnl f* **12/1**

0000 7 1 3/4 **Billy Red**[35] 6506 9-9-5 69 .... (b) FergusSweeney 4 57
(J R Jenkins) *dwlt: bhd: sme hdwy on inner ent st: no imp* **20/1**

644 8 1 3/4 **Ceelo**[31] 6657 3-9-4 69 .... DaneO'Neill 8 52
(Sylvester Kirk) *chsd ldrs on outer: wknd 2f out* **6/1**[3]

0054 9 1/2 **Alnoomaas (IRE)**[11] 7165 4-9-6 70 .... SteveDrowne 9 51
(Luke Dace) *dwlt: nvr trbld ldrs* **10/1**

6660 10 nk **Frognal (IRE)**[11] 7165 7-9-2 66 .... (bt) GeorgeBaker 12 47
(Violet M Jordan) *a bhd* **20/1**

3330 11 3 **Bapak Bangsawan**[140] 2959 3-9-5 70 .... JimmyQuinn 11 42
(Kevin Ryan) *mid-div on outer: wknd 2f out* **16/1**

0006 12 4 1/2 **Exceedexpectations (IRE)**[11] 7165 4-9-4 68 .... LiamKeniry 10 26
(Conor Dore) *chsd ldrs 4f* **33/1**

1m 11.65s (-0.25) **Going Correction** +0.05s/f (Slow)
WFA 3 from 4yo+ 1lb 12 Ran SP% **121.2**
Speed ratings (Par 103): **103,102,102,100,99 96,93,91,90,90 86,80**
toteswingers 1&2 £15.10, 2&3 £39.90, 1&3 £7.90 CSF £72.09 CT £651.99 TOTE £3.30: £1.40, £7.30, £4.50; EX 76.40 Trifecta £751.60 Pool: £2904.31 - 2.89 winning units..
Owner Scuderia Vita Bella **Bred** L A C Ashby Newhall Estate Farm **Trained** Hatford, Oxon

FOCUS
There was plenty of pace on here with a few who like to force it. The form could possibly be rated a shade lower.

7445 CATLIN HOWARD GLOBAL H'CAP 5f (P)
4:30 (4:32) (Class 5) (0-75,75) 3-Y-O+ **£2,726** (£805; £402) **Stalls** High

Form RPR

4231 1 **Oh So Sassy**[38] 6397 3-9-6 74 .... GeorgeBaker 2 88+
(Chris Wall) *trckd ldrs on rail: rdn to ld ins fnl f: hld on wl* **7/2**[2]

632 2 shd **Desert Command**[57] 5820 3-9-7 75 .... DavidProbert 1 89
(Andrew Balding) *chsd ldr: led 2f out tl ins fnl f: r.o wl* **6/4**[1]

3120 3 4 **Pucon**[38] 6412 4-9-1 69 .... LiamKeniry 7 67
(Roger Teal) *chsd ldrs: one pce fnl 2f* **16/1**

3213 4 3/4 **Rock Up (IRE)**[21] 6929 3-9-4 72 .... (b) DaneO'Neill 10 69
(David Elsworth) *in tch: rdn over 2f out: one pce* **4/1**[3]

6326 5 1 **Dark Lane**[11] 7164 7-8-4 65 .... EoinWalsh(7) 6 57
(David Evans) *towards rr: rdn 2f out: styd on* **12/1**

530 6 hd **Howyadoingnotsobad (IRE)**[15] 7080 5-9-0 75 .... RyanWhile(7) 4 66
(Karen George) *led tl 2f out: no ex appr fnl f* **20/1**

0550 7 hd **Ask The Guru**[7] 7264 3-9-6 74 .... (b) RobertHavlin 5 66
(Michael Attwater) *mid-div: rdn over 2f out: sn outpcd* **25/1**

000 8 3/4 **Burnhope**[33] 6547 4-9-6 74 .... (p) LukeMorris 8 62
(Scott Dixon) *s.s: a wd and towards rr* **12/1**

1500 9 3 3/4 **Exotic Guest**[5] 7324 3-9-0 71 .... RyanPowell(3) 9 46
(George Margarson) *a bhd* **20/1**

0400 10 8 **Appointee (IRE)**[47] 6135 4-9-2 70 .... (v) ShaneKelly 3 16
(Robert Cowell) *towards rr on rail: n.d fnl 2f* **33/1**

57.94s (-0.86) **Going Correction** +0.05s/f (Slow) 10 Ran SP% **119.8**
Speed ratings (Par 103): **108,107,101,100,98 98,98,96,90,78**
toteswingers 1&2 £1.70, 2&3 £7.90, 1&3 £9.10 CSF £8.91 CT £76.26 TOTE £4.20: £1.30, £1.20, £3.40; EX 10.80 Trifecta £83.30 Pool: £3287.71 - 29.57 winning units..
Owner The Eight Of Diamonds **Bred** Mrs C J Walker **Trained** Newmarket, Suffolk

FOCUS
A couple of the 3yos came right away from the others in this sprint handicap and both look better than this grade. The pair were well clear.

7446 CRYSTAL PALACE FOOTBALL CLUB H'CAP (DIV I) 1m 2f (P)
5:00 (5:01) (Class 5) (0-70,70) 3-Y-O+ **£2,726** (£805; £402) **Stalls** Low

Form RPR

46 1 **Landau (IRE)**[8] 7258 3-9-1 66 .... LiamKeniry 3 75
(Sylvester Kirk) *prom on rail: rdn along fr 3f out: led 1f out: hld on gamely* **9/2**[3]

5000 2 nk **Shirataki (IRE)**[26] 6775 5-9-5 65 .... PatCosgrave 7 73
(Peter Hiatt) *mid-div: effrt on outer 2f out: r.o to press wnr fnl 100yds: jst hld* **16/1**

40-1 3 hd **Miguel Grau (USA)**[11] 7167 3-9-2 67 .... (b) JimmyFortune 8 75
(Roger Varian) *trckd ldrs: effrt 2f out: chal over 1f out: r.o* **6/4**[1]

0501 4 3 1/2 **Silver Lace (IRE)**[41] 6315 4-9-7 67 .... GeorgeBaker 10 68
(Chris Wall) *trckd ldr: rdn over 2f out: no ex fnl f* **4/1**[2]

3165 5 1/2 **Flash Crash**[13] 7132 4-9-5 65 .... (t) WilliamCarson 6 65
(Anthony Carson) *in tch: rdn 5f out: outpcd over 2f out: kpt on fnl f* **14/1**

6144 6 1 1/4 **Understory (USA)**[72] 5311 6-9-9 69 .... LukeMorris 9 67
(Tim McCarthy) *led: set modest pce: qcknd over 2f out: hdd & wknd 1f out* **10/1**

4362 7 7 **Chrissycross (IRE)**[19] 6963 4-9-10 70 .... (v) AdamKirby 5 54
(Roger Teal) *dwlt: towards rr on outer: mod effrt over 2f out: sn btn* **5/1**

3050 8 nk **Star Of Mayfair (USA)**[40] 6325 3-8-8 59 .... DavidProbert 4 43
(Alan Jarvis) *bhd: hrd rdn 3f out: nvr trbld ldrs* **16/1**

2300 9 3/4 **Fearless Lad (IRE)**[60] 5694 3-9-2 67 .... FrederikTylicki 2 49
(John Best) *hld up towards rr: pushed along and n.d fnl 3f* **16/1**

-000 10 3/4 **Anjuna Beach (USA)**[123] 3528 3-9-4 69 .... SeanLevey 1 50
(Gary Moore) *s.s: plld hrd in rr: rdn and n.d fnl 3f* **25/1**

2m 6.46s (-0.14) **Going Correction** +0.05s/f (Slow)
WFA 3 from 4yo+ 5lb 10 Ran SP% **132.1**
Speed ratings (Par 103): **102,101,101,98,98 97,91,91,90,90**
toteswingers 1&2 £16.90, 2&3 £12.00, 1&3 £3.00 CSF £84.05 CT £164.76 TOTE £4.50: £1.10, £5.70, £1.70; EX 96.50 Trifecta £240.50 Pool: £2973.97 - 9.27 winning units..
Owner Mrs Barbara Facchino **Bred** Barouche Stud (IRE) Ltd **Trained** Upper Lambourn, Berks
■ Stewards' Enquiry : Luke Morris two-day ban: careless riding (Nov 5-6)
Liam Keniry two-day ban: careless riding (Nov 5-6)

FOCUS
An ordinary handicap run at a crawl, and something of a messy race. The form is rated around the second.

7447 CRYSTAL PALACE FOOTBALL CLUB H'CAP (DIV II) 1m 2f (P)
5:30 (5:30) (Class 5) (0-70,70) 3-Y-O+ **£2,726** (£805; £402) **Stalls** Low

Form RPR

3500 1 **Typhon (USA)**[34] 6521 3-9-2 67 .... FrederikTylicki 5 75
(David Lanigan) *in tch: effrt 2f out: r.o wl fnl f: led fnl strides* **8/1**

1432 2 hd **Kastini**[8] 7249 3-9-0 65 .... PatCosgrave 7 73
(Denis Coakley) *cl up: jnd ldr 2f out: sn outpcd: rallied fnl f: narrow ld nr fin: jst ct* **7/4**[1]

1410 3 1/2 **Winslow Arizona (IRE)**[41] 6306 3-9-4 69 .... LukeMorris 1 76
(Michael Bell) *in tch: rdn to chse ldrs 2f out: r.o fnl f* **7/1**

2050 4 nk **Whitby Jet (IRE)**[38] 6398 5-9-7 67 .... JimmyFortune 4 73
(Ed Vaughan) *hld up in rr: rdn over 1f out: str run fnl f: fin wl* **8/1**

1265 5 hd **Enriching (USA)**[67] 5491 5-9-2 69 .... (t) JordanVaughan(7) 9 75
(Gary Harrison) *chsd ldr: led over 2f out: qcknd 3 l clr whn rdr dropped whip over 1f out: hdd and no ex nr fin* **14/1**

1341 6 1 1/4 **Precision Five**[22] 6898 4-9-10 70 .... (p) GeorgeBaker 8 74
(Jeremy Gask) *stdd s: hld up in rr: eased outside 3f out: stuck wd home turn: r.o fnl f* **9/2**[2]

4405 7 shd **Echo Brava**[28] 6735 3-9-1 66 .... FergusSweeney 2 69
(Luke Dace) *hld up towards rr: rdn and sme hdwy over 1f out: styd on same pce* **20/1**

31-5 8 4 1/2 **Absolutely Right (IRE)**[28] 6734 3-9-2 70 .... RyanPowell(3) 3 64
(George Margarson) *prom: rdn whn n.m.r over 2f out: sn lost pl* **6/1**[3]

65-0 9 14 **Danehill Dante (IRE)**[28] 5403 5-9-2 62 .... (tp) SamHitchcott 6 28
(Chris Gordon) *led tl wknd over 2f out* **50/1**

2m 8.0s (1.40) **Going Correction** +0.05s/f (Slow)
WFA 3 from 4yo+ 5lb 9 Ran SP% **116.9**
Speed ratings (Par 103): **96,95,95,95,95 94,93,90,79**
toteswingers 1&2 £4.10, 2&3 £3.40, 1&3 £12.80 CSF £22.70 CT £106.41 TOTE £12.30: £3.10, £1.10, £1.80; EX 29.60 Trifecta £200.50 Pool: £2474.40 - 9.26 winning units..
Owner Niarchos Family **Bred** Flaxman Holdings Limited **Trained** Upper Lambourn, Berks

FOCUS
A typical Lingfield finish with a few looking likely to win at one stage or another in the home straight. The pace looked modest and the winning time was 1.54 seconds slower than the first division. It's hard to rate the form any higher.
T/Plt: £175.90 to a £1 stake. Pool of £67756.82 - 281.10 winning tickets. T/Qpdt: £22.20 to a £1 stake. Pool of £6045.10 - 201.30 winning tickets LM

6569 YARMOUTH (L-H)
Tuesday, October 22

OFFICIAL GOING: Soft (6.8)
Wind: Fresh half-against Weather: Overcast

7448 BRITISH STALLION STUDS EBF MAIDEN STKS — 6f 3y
1:50 (1:50) (Class 5) 2-Y-O — **£2,911** (£866; £432; £216) **Stalls** Centre

Form — RPR
0 **1** **Kaab (IRE)**[148] 2712 2-9-5 0 ... PaulHanagan 8 — 82
(Ed Dunlop) *trckd ldr tl led over 2f out: rdn over 1f out: r.o* **5/1**[3]
2 2 1/4 **Resolute** 2-9-5 0 ... SebSanders 9 — 75+
(William Haggas) *s.i.s: hdwy 1/2-way: rdn and edgd lft over 1f out: r.o to go 2nd wl ins fnl f: nt rch wnr* **8/1**
3 1 3/4 **Sir Robert Cheval** 2-9-5 0 ... MartinHarley 2 — 70+
(Marco Botti) *hld up in tch: shkn up and ev ch fr 2f out tl no ex wl ins fnl f* **7/4**[1]
4 2 3/4 **Ametrine (IRE)** 2-9-0 0 ... CathyGannon 5 — 56+
(William Jarvis) *s.i.s: sn pushed along and rn green in rr: r.o wl ins fnl f: nvr trbld ldrs* **28/1**
5 3 **High Stand** 2-9-5 0 ... (p) RyanMoore 6 — 52
(Sir Michael Stoute) *prom: rdn over 2f out: wknd over 1f out* **17/2**
6 **6** 3 3/4 **Strike A Light**[13] 7125 2-9-0 0 ... ChrisCatlin 7 — 36+
(Rae Guest) *prom: racd keenly: lost pl 4f out: wknd over 2f out* **20/1**
34 **7** 1/2 **Sunningdale Rose (IRE)**[165] 2230 2-9-0 0 ... RobertWinston 3 — 35
(Gay Kelleway) *chsd ldrs: rdn over 2f out: wknd over 1f out* **20/1**
0 **8** 1/2 **Right Of Appeal**[129] 3350 2-9-5 0 ... SilvestreDeSousa 4 — 38
(Mark Johnston) *led: rdn and hdd over 2f out: wknd over 1f out* **10/3**[2]
9 1/2 **Sybilicious** 2-9-0 0 ... AdamBeschizza 1 — 32
(Stuart Williams) *s.i.s: sn pushed along and a in rr: wknd over 2f out* **66/1**

1m 18.28s (3.88) **Going Correction** +0.575s/f (Yiel) — **9** Ran SP% **112.2**
Speed ratings (Par 95): **97,94,91,88,84 79,78,77,77**
toteswingers 1&2 £7.50, 2&3 £4.60, 1&3 £3.10 CSF £40.16 TOTE £5.60: £1.30, £2.70, £1.60; EX 42.50 Trifecta £167.60 Pool: £2672.46 - 11.95 winning units..
Owner Hamdan Al Maktoum **Bred** Victor Stud Bloodstock Ltd **Trained** Newmarket, Suffolk
FOCUS
A fair 2-y-o maiden.

7449 BREEDERS BACKING RACING EBF MAIDEN FILLIES' STKS (DIV I) — 1m 3y
2:20 (2:22) (Class 5) 2-Y-O — **£2,911** (£866; £432; £216) **Stalls** Centre

Form — RPR
1 **Madame Chiang** 2-9-0 0 ... ChrisCatlin 10 — 77+
(David Simcock) *s.i.s: sn pushed along in rr: nt clr run over 2f out: gd hdwy over 1f out: led wl ins fnl f: sn clr: readily* **33/1**
5 **2** 4 **Dorset Cream**[42] 6281 2-9-0 0 ... JamesDoyle 9 — 68
(Lady Cecil) *a.p: pushed along over 3f out: rdn over 1f out: styd on same pce ins fnl f* **4/1**[2]
0 **3** 1/2 **Gracie Hart**[15] 7070 2-8-7 0 ... JosephineGordon[(7)] 5 — 67
(Jo Hughes) *w ldr: plld hrd: ev ch fr 2f out tl no ex wl ins fnl f* **100/1**
6 **4** 1 1/4 **Gold Approach**[31] 6643 2-9-0 0 ... GrahamLee 8 — 64
(William Haggas) *trckd ldrs: pushed along over 3f out: rdn over 1f out: styd on same pce* **6/4**[1]
65 **5** nk **Chortle**[20] 6949 2-9-0 0 ... MickaelBarzalona 7 — 63
(Charlie Appleby) *prom: hmpd over 6f out: led over 2f out: rdn: hdd & wknd wl ins fnl f* **17/2**[3]
0 **6** 6 **Blossom Lane**[14] 7103 2-9-0 0 ... NickyMackay 11 — 50
(John Gosden) *hld up: hdwy over 2f out: rdn and wknd over 1f out* **14/1**
7 3 1/4 **Across The Cape** 2-9-0 0 ... AndreaAtzeni 6 — 43
(Michael Bell) *mid-div: pushed along over 2f out: sn wknd* **10/1**
8 3 **Wulfthryth** 2-9-0 0 ... RobertWinston 4 — 36
(Tobias B P Coles) *s.i.s: hdwy over 2f out: rdn and wknd over 1f out* **100/1**
0 **9** 4 **Pearlofthequarter**[34] 6523 2-9-0 0 ... MartinHarley 3 — 27
(Marco Botti) *led: racd keenly: pushed along and hdd over 2f out: wknd over 1f out* **4/1**[2]
10 1 3/4 **Al Shoogh** 2-9-0 0 ... MartinLane 2 — 24
(David Simcock) *s.i.s: hld up: hung lft 1/2-way: wknd over 2f out* **22/1**

1m 46.47s (5.87) **Going Correction** +0.575s/f (Yiel) — **10** Ran SP% **115.6**
Speed ratings (Par 92): **93,89,88,87,86 80,77,74,70,68**
toteswingers 1&2 £30.60, 2&3 £37.80, 1&3 £113.50 CSF £157.80 TOTE £47.30: £9.20, £1.60, £17.50; EX 315.20 Trifecta £2100.00 Part won. Pool: £2800.03 - 0.20 winning units..
Owner Miss K Rausing **Bred** Miss K Rausing **Trained** Newmarket, Suffolk
FOCUS
A modest 2-y-o maiden but hard to fault the performance of the winner.

7450 BREEDERS BACKING RACING EBF MAIDEN FILLIES' STKS (DIV II) — 1m 3y
2:50 (2:51) (Class 5) 2-Y-O — **£2,911** (£866; £432; £216) **Stalls** Centre

Form — RPR
4 **1** **Asyad (IRE)**[47] 6141 2-9-0 0 ... RyanMoore 4 — 80+
(Sir Michael Stoute) *mde all: rdn and edgd lft ins fnl f: styd on* **8/11**[1]
2 1 **Madame Mere (IRE)** 2-9-0 0 ... AndreaAtzeni 10 — 78+
(Roger Varian) *chsd ldrs: wnt 2f out: shkn up over 1f out: edgd lft ins fnl f: styd on* **12/1**
3 1/2 **She's Gorgeous (IRE)** 2-9-0 0 ... MickaelBarzalona 6 — 77+
(Lady Cecil) *chsd ldrs: pushed along over 2f out: styd on* **9/1**[3]
4 1 3/4 **Prestige Roses (IRE)** 2-9-0 0 ... MartinHarley 2 — 73+
(Marco Botti) *hld up: hdwy over 3f out: shkn up over 1f out: n.m.r ins fnl f: styd on same pce* **16/1**
5 2 1/4 **Promise You** 2-9-0 0 ... SilvestreDeSousa 8 — 68+
(Saeed bin Suroor) *hld up in tch: effrt over 2f out: styd on same pce fr over 1f out* **5/1**[2]
6 nk **Some Site (IRE)** 2-9-0 0 ... MartinLane 9 — 67+
(David Simcock) *s.i.s: hld up: pushed along over 2f out: nt trble ldrs* **20/1**
0 **7** 1 3/4 **Red Passiflora**[20] 6949 2-9-0 0 ... CathyGannon 7 — 63
(Sir Mark Prescott Bt) *hld up: pushed along over 2f out: nvr on terms* **28/1**
0 **8** 3 **Mary Le Bow**[19] 6974 2-9-0 0 ... RaulDaSilva 1 — 57
(Lucy Wadham) *chsd wnr tl rdn 2f out: wknd over 1f out* **25/1**
9 31 **Bed Bed** 2-8-7 0 ... ThomasHemsley[(7)] 3
(Michael Bell) *chsd ldrs: pushed along over 3f out: wknd over 2f out* **33/1**

1m 46.65s (6.05) **Going Correction** +0.575s/f (Yiel) — **9** Ran SP% **113.1**
Speed ratings (Par 92): **92,91,90,88,86 86,84,81,50**
toteswingers 1&2 £3.30, 2&3 £8.70, 1&3 £2.40 CSF £9.58 TOTE £1.50: £1.02, £2.90, £1.80; EX 10.00 Trifecta £31.30 Pool: £3207.24 - 76.75 winning units..
Owner HE Sh Joaan Bin Hamad Al Thani **Bred** Gestut Wittekindshof **Trained** Newmarket, Suffolk
FOCUS
Another fair maiden.

7451 £25 FREE BET AT BETVICTOR NURSERY H'CAP — 6f 3y
3:20 (3:21) (Class 5) (0-75,74) 2-Y-O — **£2,587** (£770; £384; £192) **Stalls** Centre

Form — RPR
114 **1** **Cape Factor (IRE)**[49] 6076 2-9-1 **68** ... ChrisCatlin 15 — 83+
(Rae Guest) *mde virtually all: shkn up to go clr fr over 1f out: easily* **15/2**
030 **2** 5 **Berrahri (IRE)**[13] 7120 2-9-1 **68** ... GrahamLee 16 — 66
(John Best) *prom: rdn over 2f out: nt clr run and lost pl over 1f out: swtchd lft and r.o to go 2nd nr fin: no ch w wnr* **11/2**[3]
004 **3** nk **Exceeding Power**[10] 7200 2-8-10 **63** ... JamesDoyle 14 — 60
(Michael Bell) *chsd ldrs: rdn over 2f out: styd on same pce fr over 1f out* **9/1**
4064 **4** shd **Iseemist (IRE)**[15] 7074 2-9-2 **69** ... PaulHanagan 5 — 66
(John Gallagher) *prom: chsd wnr 2f out: sn rdn: no ex fnl f* **18/1**
5036 **5** 4 1/2 **Craftsmanship (FR)**[54] 5926 2-9-5 **72** ... NickyMackay 3 — 55
(Robert Eddery) *hmpd sn after s: hld up: styd on fr over 1f out: nvr on terms* **22/1**
2350 **6** 3/4 **George The First**[24] 6852 2-9-1 **68** ... AndrewMullen 2 — 49
(Alan Swinbank) *sn pushed along in rr: hdwy u.p over 1f out: wknd fnl f* **25/1**
240 **7** nk **Blue Bounty**[70] 5364 2-8-12 **65** ... RobertWinston 1 — 45
(Mark H Tompkins) *hld up: hdwy and hung lft fr over 2f out: rdn over 1f out: sn wknd* **16/1**
1603 **8** 2 **Soul Instinct**[22] 6904 2-8-12 **70** ... (p) KevinStott[(5)] 12 — 44
(Kevin Ryan) *w wnr tl rdn 2f out: wknd over 1f out* **14/1**
5333 **9** 1 1/2 **Sherston**[11] 7170 2-9-6 **73** ... SilvestreDeSousa 11 — 43
(Mark Johnston) *prom: lost pl over 4f out: rdn and hung lft over 2f out: n.d after* **3/1**[1]
003 **10** nk **Nick The Odds (IRE)**[35] 6485 2-8-7 **67** ... JosephineGordon[(7)] 13 — 36
(Jo Hughes) *racd keenly: w wnr tl rdn 2f out: wknd over 1f out* **33/1**
0340 **11** 1/2 **Honey Meadow**[29] 6695 2-8-11 **64** ... AndreaAtzeni 8 — 31
(Robert Eddery) *mid-div: rdn over 2f out: hmpd and wknd over 1f out* **16/1**
050 **12** nk **Green Music**[68] 5435 2-8-7 **65** ... RyanTate[(5)] 6 — 31
(James Eustace) *prom: rdn over 2f out: wknd over 1f out* **25/1**
0500 **13** 3 1/4 **Caledonia Laird**[70] 5371 2-8-9 **62** ... (p) LiamJones 9 — 19
(Jo Hughes) *hld up: hdwy over 2f out: rdn: edgd rt and wknd over 1f out* **66/1**
3642 **14** 4 1/2 **Supersta**[10] 7209 2-9-7 **74** ... (b[1]) MartinHarley 10 — 17
(Ronald Harris) *s.i.s: hdwy over 4f out: rdn and lost pl 1/2-way: sn wknd* **5/1**[2]

1m 16.7s (2.30) **Going Correction** +0.575s/f (Yiel) — **14** Ran SP% **119.0**
Speed ratings (Par 95): **107,100,99,99,93 92,92,89,87,87 86,86,81,75**
toteswingers 1&2 £12.60, 2&3 £13.10, 1&3 £10.00 CSF £45.02 CT £297.75 TOTE £6.00: £1.80, £2.50, £5.60; EX 65.10 Trifecta £535.40 Pool: £2726.24 - 3.81 winning units..
Owner Derek J Willis **Bred** Nanallac Stud **Trained** Newmarket, Suffolk
FOCUS
A competitive, if only modest nursery.

7452 DOWNLOAD THE BETVICTOR APP H'CAP — 6f 3y
3:50 (3:53) (Class 4) (0-85,84) 3-Y-O+ — **£4,690** (£1,395; £697; £348) **Stalls** Centre

Form — RPR
3400 **1** **Chooseday (IRE)**[24] 6845 4-9-7 **84** ... (p) GrahamLee 9 — 93
(Kevin Ryan) *mde virtually all: rdn over 1f out: styd on u.p* **7/1**
6003 **2** shd **Italian Tom (IRE)**[34] 6527 6-8-10 **73** ... LiamJones 4 — 82
(Ronald Harris) *hld up: hdwy over 2f out: rdn over 1f out: ev ch ins fnl f: styd on* **16/1**
4613 **3** 1/2 **Monsieur Jamie**[6] 7313 5-8-13 **76** ... (v) SilvestreDeSousa 1 — 83
(J R Jenkins) *w ldrs: rdn and ev ch ins fnl f: styd on same pce towards fin* **8/1**
3530 **4** 5 **Comrade Bond**[13] 7123 5-8-10 **73** ... RobertWinston 11 — 65
(Mark H Tompkins) *hld up: hdwy and nt clr run over 2f out: rdn over 1f out: styd on same pce fnl f* **11/1**
2125 **5** 1/2 **Lulu The Zulu (IRE)**[19] 6977 5-8-12 **75** ... AndrewMullen 8 — 66
(Michael Appleby) *s.i.s: plld hrd: hdwy over 4f out: rdn over 1f out: no ex ins fnl f* **6/1**[3]
5601 **6** 1 **Gatepost (IRE)**[8] 7255 4-9-6 **83** 6ex ... PaulHanagan 12 — 71
(Richard Fahey) *prom: rdn over 2f out: sn hung lft: styd on same pce* **9/2**[2]
1024 **7** shd **Green Howard**[11] 7176 5-9-4 **84** ... JasonHart[(3)] 13 — 71
(Robin Bastiman) *s.i.s: hdwy over 2f out: rdn over 1f out: no ex fnl f* **7/2**[1]
2115 **8** 8 **The Strig**[8] 7254 6-8-13 **76** ... (v) JamesDoyle 5 — 39
(Stuart Williams) *chsd ldrs: rdn over 2f out: wknd over 1f out* **18/1**
2021 **9** 6 **King Bertie (IRE)**[19] 6969 3-8-11 **80** ... OisinMurphy[(5)] 6 — 25
(Michael Wigham) *trckd ldrs: plld hrd: rdn 1/2-way: wknd over 2f out* **16/1**
3266 **10** 3/4 **Exzachary**[30] 6664 3-8-2 **73** ... JosephineGordon[(7)] 7 — 16
(Jo Hughes) *trckd ldrs: plld hrd: rdn over 2f out: sn wknd* **40/1**
5423 **11** nse **Front Page News**[31] 6642 3-8-10 **74** ... AndreaAtzeni 10 — 17
(Robert Eddery) *s.i.s: a in rr: wknd over 2f out* **9/1**

1m 16.81s (2.41) **Going Correction** +0.575s/f (Yiel)
WFA 3 from 4yo+ 1lb — **11** Ran SP% **116.1**
Speed ratings (Par 105): **106,105,105,98,97 96,96,85,77,76 76**
totewingers 1&2 £22.50, 2&3 £28.20, 1&3 £13.00 CSF £111.42 CT £931.17 TOTE £8.80: £2.80, £3.80, £3.40; EX 134.30 Trifecta £2116.60 Part won. Pool: £2822.21 - 0.45 winning units..
Owner Mrs S J Barker **Bred** Jerry O'Sullivan **Trained** Hambleton, N Yorks
FOCUS
A modest sprint handicap.

7453 BET VICTOR BACK OF THE NET OFFER H'CAP — 1m 3f 101y
4:20 (4:21) (Class 5) (0-75,74) 3-Y-O+ — **£2,587** (£770; £384; £192) **Stalls** Low

Form — RPR
0351 **1** **Stomachion (IRE)**[8] 7249 3-9-4 **74** 6ex ... RyanMoore 8 — 89+
(Sir Michael Stoute) *sn led: hdd 7f out: led again over 3f out: shkn up over 1f out: sn clr: eased nr fin* **10/11**[1]
1551 **2** nk **The Ducking Stool**[33] 6574 6-9-0 **69** ... ShelleyBirkett[(5)] 5 — 74
(Julia Feilden) *chsd ldrs: rdn over 2f out: n.m.r fr over 1f out: styd on same pce: fin 3rd: plcd 2nd* **12/1**

-663 **3** *4 ½* **Red Pilgrim (IRE)**[29] 6696 3-9-1 **74**...............................(t) RobertTart(3) 7 78
(James Toller) *s.i.s and hmpd s: hdwy 7f out: rdn to chse wnr over 2f out: hung lft fr over 1f out: styd on same pce: fin 2nd: plcd 3rd* **12/1**
2442 **4** *2* **Mistral Wind (IRE)**[8] 7258 3-8-7 **63**................................. AndreaAtzeni 4 64
(Ed Dunlop) *prom: lost pl 7f out: pushed along and hdwy over 2f out: sn rdn: styd on same pce fr over 1f out* **5/1[2]**
1034 **5** *1* **Size (IRE)**[30] 6667 4-9-4 **68**................................. PaulHanagan 9 67
(Richard Fahey) *hld up: hdwy over 2f out: rdn and edgd lft over 1f out: no ex* **8/1[3]**
0140 **6** *¾* **Thecornishcowboy**[19] 6976 4-9-8 **72**...............................(t) GrahamLee 11 70
(John Ryan) *hld up: hdwy 2f out: sn rdn: no ex fr over 1f out* **20/1**
3530 **7** *5* **Raamz (IRE)**[13] 7132 6-8-9 **62**... DarrenEgan(3) 2 52
(Kevin Morgan) *hld up: rdn over 2f out: wknd over 1f out* **40/1**
3014 **8** *½* **Layline (IRE)**[33] 6552 6-9-3 **72**..................................... DanielMuscutt(5) 6 61
(Gay Kelleway) *chsd ldrs: rdn over 2f out: wknd over 1f out* **10/1**
61-6 **9** *33* **Zenarinda**[25] 6802 6-9-4 **68**... RobertWinston 13 4+
(Mark H Tompkins) *hld up: plld hrd: sddle slipped after 3f: hdwy to ld 7f out: c towards centre turning for home: hdd over 3f out: sn bhd* **33/1**

2m 33.41s (4.71) **Going Correction** +0.575s/f (Yiel)
WFA 3 from 4yo+ 6lb **9** Ran SP% **114.8**
Speed ratings (Par 103): **105,101,101,100,99 98,95,94,70**
toteswingers 1&3 £3.30, 3&2 £19.10, 1&2 £3.40 CSF £12.98 CT £83.58 TOTE £2.30: £1.10, £3.70, £3.20; EX 14.20 Trifecta £98.80 Pool: £2221.37 - 16.85 winning units..
Owner Niarchos Family **Bred** Niarchos Family **Trained** Newmarket, Suffolk

FOCUS
A fair race for the grade.

7454 FOLLOW US ON TWITTER @BETVICTORRACING H'CAP 6f 3y

4:50 (4:52) (Class 6) (0-60,60) 3-Y-O+ **£1,940** (£577; £288; £144) **Stalls** Centre

Form RPR
5160 **1** **All Right Now**[14] 7092 6-8-10 **49**...................................(p) MartinHarley 3 58
(Tony Newcombe) *a.p: rdn to ld ins fnl f: r.o* **9/1[3]**
0000 **2** *2* **First Peninsular**[13] 7124 3-8-8 **51**............................ AshleyMorgan(3) 1 54
(Chris Wall) *hld up: hdwy over 2f out: rdn and ev ch over 1f out: styd on same pce ins fnl f* **25/1**
-114 **3** *1 ¼* **Resonare**[80] 4996 4-9-5 **58**... RyanMoore 7 57
(Stuart Williams) *led early: chsd ldrs: rdn over 2f out: styd on same pce ins fnl f* **9/4[1]**
0010 **4** *½* **Give Us A Belle (IRE)**[10] 7197 4-9-0 **53**..............(vt) AdamBeschizza 13 51
(Christine Dunnett) *a.p: chsd ldr 1/2-way: led over 1f out: sn rdn: hdd and no ex ins fnl f* **33/1**
5233 **5** *¾* **Two No Bids (IRE)**[19] 6970 3-9-1 **55**...........................(be) PaddyAspell 6 51
(Phil McEntee) *sn pushed along in rr: nt clr run over 2f out: hdwy over 1f out: nt rch ldrs* **12/1**
4304 **6** *1 ¼* **Copper To Gold**[40] 6323 4-8-4 **46**..................................... JasonHart(3) 4 38
(Robin Bastiman) *awkward leaving stalls: hdwy 1/2-way: rdn over 1f out: no ex fnl f* **10/1**
0000 **7** *¾* **Carlarajah**[27] 6752 3-9-1 **58**.........................(v) WilliamTwiston-Davies(3) 5 48
(Michael Bell) *broke wl: n.m.r and lost pl after 1f: rdn and styd on fnl f: nt trble ldrs* **10/1**
6130 **8** *1 ¼* **Clock Opera (IRE)**[34] 6535 3-9-1 **60**............................ LauraPike(5) 10 46
(William Stone) *sn led: hdd over 2f out: wknd fnl f* **10/1**
4500 **9** *5* **Rough Rock (IRE)**[14] 7109 8-9-2 **55**............................ CathyGannon 15 26
(Chris Dwyer) *mid-div: rdn 1/2-way: hung lft and wknd over 2f out* **13/2[2]**
10 *2* **Iffranesia (FR)**[44] 3-8-13 **53**.. TomEaves 9 18
(Robert Cowell) *mid-div: rdn 1/2-way: wknd over 2f out* **20/1**
-042 **11** *1 ¾* **College Doll**[31] 6651 4-8-5 **47**.......................................(t) DarrenEgan(3) 8 7
(Christine Dunnett) *hld up: hdwy over 2f out: sn rdn and wknd* **20/1**
3000 **12** *nse* **Blue Clumber**[5] 7323 3-8-10 **50**..............................(be) DuranFentiman 11 9
(Shaun Harris) *chsd ldr 5f out tl rdn 1/2-way: wknd over 2f out* **20/1**
0500 **13** *7* **Gracie's Games**[14] 7086 7-8-8 **47**.................................. LiamJones 12
(John Spearing) *s.i.s: sn pushed along in rr: wknd over 2f out* **16/1**
0/00 **14** *1 ¼* **Alkhataaf (USA)**[21] 6929 6-9-7 **60**................................ SaleemGolam 2
(Lydia Pearce) *sn pushed along towards rr: rdn and wknd over 2f out* **33/1**

1m 18.26s (3.86) **Going Correction** +0.575s/f (Yiel)
WFA 3 from 4yo+ 1lb **14** Ran SP% **119.0**
Speed ratings (Par 101): **97,94,92,92,91 89,88,86,80,77 75,74,65,63**
toteswingers 1&2 £45.60, 2&3 £18.50, 1&3 £6.60 CSF £223.60 CT £697.87 TOTE £10.10: £2.40, £10.20, £1.30; EX 279.90 Trifecta £2245.10 Part won. Pool: £2993.58 - 0.69 winning units..
Owner Justin Hay **Bred** Rolyon Stud **Trained** Yarnscombe, Devon

FOCUS
A competitive handicap for the class.

7455 £25 FREE BET #BACKOFTHENET H'CAP 7f 3y

5:20 (5:22) (Class 6) (0-65,65) 3-Y-O+ **£1,940** (£577; £288; £144) **Stalls** Centre

Form RPR
0033 **1** **Minimee**[5] 7322 3-8-6 **55**..(v) RobertTart(3) 15 62
(Phil McEntee) *mid-div: hdwy over 1f out: r.o to ld nr fin* **10/1**
3050 **2** *½* **Clumber Place**[12] 7153 7-8-9 **53** ow1............................. GrahamLee 8 60
(James Given) *chsd ldrs: led over 1f out: sn rdn: hdd nr fin* **12/1**
0004 **3** *¾* **Cocozza (USA)**[11] 7163 5-9-6 **64**..............................(p) AdamBeschizza 1 69
(K F Clutterbuck) *sn pushed along towards rr: hdwy 1/2-way: rdn over 1f out: r.o* **16/1**
5625 **4** *½* **Monsieur Pontaven**[12] 7153 6-8-4 **51** oh1.................(b) JasonHart(3) 10 55
(Robin Bastiman) *s.i.s: sn pushed along in rr: hdwy u.p over 1f out: nt clr run ins fnl f: r.o: nt rch ldrs* **12/1**
0500 **5** *½* **Royal Marskell**[71] 5346 4-9-4 **65**............(p) WilliamTwiston-Davies(3) 14 68
(K F Clutterbuck) *s.s: bhd: hdwy over 1f out: r.o: nt rch ldrs* **16/1**
1634 **6** *nk* **Hamble**[29] 6702 4-8-6 **55**...(t) ShelleyBirkett(5) 4 57
(Julia Feilden) *mid-div: hdwy 1/2-way: rdn over 1f out: styd on same pce ins fnl f* **5/1[1]**
0660 **7** *hd* **Caramelita**[20] 6937 6-9-7 **65**.......................................(v) SilvestreDeSousa 2 66
(J R Jenkins) *hld up: hdwy 1/2-way: rdn over 2f out: styd on same pce wl ins fnl f* **7/1[2]**
2300 **8** *2 ½* **Mucky Molly**[32] 6610 5-8-11 **55**......................................(vt) TomEaves 3 50
(Alison Hutchinson) *chsd ldrs: rdn and ev ch over 1f out: no ex ins fnl f* **25/1**
0110 **9** *hd* **Rise To Glory (IRE)**[4] 7346 5-9-4 **62**........................... DuranFentiman 16 57
(Shaun Harris) *chsd ldr tl led 1/2-way: rdn and hdd over 1f out: no ex ins fnl f* **8/1[3]**
0251 **10** *2 ¼* **Marsh Dragon**[29] 6698 3-8-12 **58**................................... RobertWinston 5 46
(Mark H Tompkins) *hld up: hdwy over 1f out: sn rdn: eased whn btn wl ins fnl f* **12/1**

6632 **11** *2 ½* **Ishiamiracle**[5] 7323 4-8-0 **51** oh5...........................(p) DonnaCaldwell(7) 11 34
(Phil McEntee) *led to 1/2-way: sn rdn: wknd fnl f* **8/1[3]**
2-53 **12** *4 ½* **Nelina**[24] 6855 3-9-0 **60**.. LiamJones 7 31
(Robert Cowell) *mid-div: rdn 1/2-way: wknd over 2f out* **8/1[3]**
500 **13** *10* **Jack Barker**[71] 5341 4-8-7 **51** oh5................................ CathyGannon 12
(Robin Bastiman) *prom over 4f* **50/1**
2545 **14** *15* **Messageinabottle (USA)**[17] 7037 3-8-7 **60**.............. LouisSteward(7) 6
(James Bethell) *prom: reminder and lost pl over 5f out: wknd over 2f out* **16/1**
5 **15** *14* **Bigger Picture (IRE)**[8] 7246 3-9-0 **60**...............................(t) JamesDoyle 9
(John Butler) *chsd ldrs tl rdn and wknd over 2f out* **25/1**

1m 32.42s (5.82) **Going Correction** +0.575s/f (Yiel)
WFA 3 from 4yo+ 2lb **15** Ran SP% **122.0**
Speed ratings (Par 101): **89,88,87,87,86 86,85,83,82,80 77,72,60,43,27**
toteswingers 1&2 £26.50, 2&3 £46.00, 1&3 £36.00 CSF £123.33 CT £1959.90 TOTE £13.30: £3.80, £4.60, £5.30; EX 136.10 Trifecta £654.90 Pool: £1964.66 - 2.24 winning units..
Owner Eventmaker Racehorses **Bred** M A Jarvis **Trained** Newmarket, Suffolk

FOCUS
Another trappy, low-grade handicap but it served up a tremendous finish.
T/Plt: £201.90 to a £1 stake. Pool of £66441.58 - 240.14 winning tickets. T/Qpdt: £40.80 to a £1 stake. Pool of £6637.15 - 120.30 winning tickets. CR

7434 KEMPTON (A.W) (R-H)

Wednesday, October 23

OFFICIAL GOING: Standard
Wind: light, across Weather: Fine

7458 BOOK NOW FOR BOXING DAY H'CAP 1m 2f (P)

5:50 (5:50) (Class 6) (0-55,58) 3-Y-O+ **£1,940** (£577; £288; £144) **Stalls** Low

Form RPR
2136 **1** **I'm Harry**[20] 6985 4-9-4 **52**...(vt) PatCosgrave 5 60
(George Baker) *trckd ldr: rdn over 2f out: kpt on: led 50yds out* **8/1[3]**
050 **2** *½* **Legal Legacy**[189] 1617 7-9-1 **52**............................... ThomasBrown(3) 4 59
(Lee Carter) *dwlt: sn midfield on inner: rdn over 2f out: kpt on wl fnl f: wnt 2nd post* **12/1**
0043 **3** *shd* **La Rosiere (USA)**[7] 7299 4-9-7 **55**...............................(p) KierenFallon 10 62
(Pat Murphy) *trckd ldr: rdn over 2f out: kpt on* **10/1**
6342 **4** *nk* **Pretty Bubbles**[7] 7299 4-9-7 **55**.................................... RyanMoore 1 61
(J R Jenkins) *led: rdn over 2f out: hdd 50yds out: no ex* **9/2[2]**
0000 **5** *1 ½* **Kindia (IRE)**[2] 7429 5-8-12 **51**.......................................(p) RyanTate(5) 8 54
(Michael Attwater) *t.k.h: hld up: rdn over 2f out: kpt on fnl f: nvr threatened ldrs* **20/1**
4453 **6** *1 ¼* **Chasin' Rainbows**[6] 7321 5-9-2 **50**................................ LiamKeniry 12 51
(Sylvester Kirk) *chsd ldrs: rdn over 2f out: grad wknd fnl f* **8/1[3]**
5-00 **7** *hd* **Red Willow**[67] 5528 7-9-2 **50**.. CathyGannon 3 51
(John E Long) *in tch: rdn over 2f out: sn no imp* **50/1**
3432 **8** *¾* **Fonterutoli (IRE)**[146] 2787 6-9-6 **54**.............................(e) JimCrowley 14 53
(Roger Ingram) *hld up: rdn over 2f out: nvr threatened* **20/1**
0501 **9** *1 ¼* **Kindlelight Storm (USA)**[8] 7266 3-9-5 **58** 6ex.............. RobertHavlin 11 55
(Nick Littmoden) *sn trckd ldrs: pushed along 4f out: wknd over 2f out* **4/1[1]**
0326 **10** *nse* **Belle Park**[36] 6492 6-9-6 **54**... AdamKirby 9 50
(Karen George) *midfield: rdn over 2f out: sn btn* **10/1**
3340 **11** *shd* **Rockweiller**[29] 6722 6-9-6 **54**....................................(v) FrederikTylicki 7 50
(Steve Gollings) *midfield: rdn over 2f out: sn btn* **9/2[2]**
0000 **12** *2 ½* **Percythepinto (IRE)**[15] 7109 4-9-6 **54**..........................(t) TedDurcan 13 45
(George Baker) *s.i.s: hld up in rr: a bhd* **25/1**

2m 9.28s (1.28) **Going Correction** +0.05s/f (Slow)
WFA 3 from 4yo+ 5lb **12** Ran SP% **119.8**
Speed ratings (Par 101): **96,95,95,95,94 93,92,92,91,91 91,89**
toteswingers 1&2 £20.00, 1&3 £8.10, 2&3 £25.70 CSF £95.85 CT £979.91 TOTE £6.30: £3.30, £7.10, £4.10; EX 141.20 Trifecta £764.70 Part won. Pool: £1019.63 - 0.44 winning units..
Owner Wickfield Stud And Hartshill Stud **Bred** Wickfield Stud And Hartshill Stud **Trained** Manton, Wilts

FOCUS
A rock-bottom handicap with just a 5lb weight range. The pace was steady until turning in. Three of the first four home raced up with the pace but the form makes a fair bit of sense.

7459 £500 FREE BETS AT BETDAQ MEDIAN AUCTION MAIDEN STKS 6f (P)

6:20 (6:20) (Class 5) 3-4-Y-O **£2,587** (£770; £384; £192) **Stalls** Low

Form RPR
2430 **1** **Martial Art (IRE)**[7] 7307 3-9-5 70....................................(v[1]) LiamKeniry 5 71
(Andrew Balding) *trckd ldr: rdn to ld narrowly 1f out: strly pressed whn bmpd by 2nd ins fnl f: asserted nr fin* **5/2[1]**
4 **2** *nk* **Poyle Vinnie**[16] 7073 3-9-2 0.................................... RyanPowell(3) 4 70
(George Margarson) *led: rdn and wandered over 1f out: hdd narrowly 1f out: edgd lft and sltly bmpd wnr 100yds out: hld nr fin* **5/1[3]**
5622 **3** *2* **Presumido (IRE)**[16] 7079 3-9-5 60................................. HarryBentley 10 64
(Simon Dow) *dwlt: hld up in rr: rdn and sme hdwy over 1f out: kpt on fnl f: wnt 3rd post* **5/1[3]**
3- **4** *nk* **Ostralegus**[435] 5213 3-9-5 0.. RichardHughes 1 63
(John Gallagher) *in tch: rdn to chse ldng pair appr fnl f: one pce: lost 3rd post* **3/1[2]**
2-3 **5** *2 ¼* **Master Wizard**[20] 6965 3-9-5 0......................................(p) CathyGannon 8 55
(David C Griffiths) *midfield: rdn over 2f out: one pce and nvr threatened* **6/1**
6 *½* **Ellen May** 3-9-0 0.. ShaneKelly 12 49
(Gary Harrison) *hld up: pushed along over 1f out: nvr threatened ldrs* **20/1**
-000 **7** *½* **Seraphiel**[41] 6324 4-9-6 46.. SteveDrowne 2 52?
(Chris Down) *midfield: rdn over 2f out: nvr threatened* **66/1**
0005 **8** *½* **Robyn**[59] 5788 3-9-0 45..[1] LukeMorris 3 46?
(Scott Dixon) *trckd ldr: rdn over 2f out: wknd fnl f* **33/1**
6565 **9** *22* **Kaahen (USA)**[13] 7154 3-9-5 47...................................(b) RobertHavlin 9
(Pat Eddery) *slowly away: sn reminders in rr: a wl bhd* **50/1**
64 **10** *1 ¼* **Diva Delight (IRE)**[18] 7037 3-9-0 0............................. FrederikTylicki 7
(Robert Cowell) *in tch on inner: rn wd on bnd 3f out: sn wknd* **33/1**
0-00 **11** *17* **Incognita**[16] 7073 3-9-0 29... ChrisCatlin 6
(Chris Down) *a wl bhd* **100/1**

1m 13.36s (0.26) **Going Correction** +0.05s/f (Slow)
WFA 3 from 4yo 1lb **11** Ran SP% **116.3**
Speed ratings (Par 103): **100,99,96,96,93 92,92,91,62,60 37**
toteswingers 1&2 £3.40, 1&3 £2.80, 2&3 £7.80 CSF £14.33 TOTE £3.40: £1.70, £2.00, £1.20; EX 13.60 Trifecta £85.80 Pool: £1874.26 - 16.37 winning units..
Owner Jackie & George Smith **Bred** G A E & J Smith Bloodstock Ltd **Trained** Kingsclere, Hants
■ Stewards' Enquiry : Liam Keniry caution: careless riding

Ryan Powell caution: careless riding

FOCUS

A modest maiden rated around the winner, though the poor 7th and 8th were not beaten far and, given recent runs, some doubt over form.

7460 BRITISH STALLION STUDS EBF MAIDEN STKS (DIV I) 1m (P)
6:50 (6:51) (Class 5) 2-Y-O £2,911 (£866; £432; £216) Stalls Low

Form RPR

1 **Marzocco (USA)** 2-9-5 0 WilliamBuick 9 81+
(John Gosden) *dwlt: sn rcvrd to trck ldrs: pushed along over 2f out: rdn to ld jst ins fnl f: kpt on wl* **7/1[2]**

00 2 1 ¾ **Roskilly (IRE)**[27] 6762 2-9-5 0 LiamKeniry 1 77
(Andrew Balding) *prom: rdn to ld 2f out: hdd jst ins fnl f: kpt on but sn no ch w wnr* **25/1**

2 3 ¾ **Moonfaarid**[60] 5744 2-9-5 0 PatCosgrave 2 75
(M F De Kock, South Africa) *trckd ldng pair: pushed along and briefly short of room over 1f out: drvn and one pce ins fnl f* **1/1[1]**

2420 4 2 ¼ **All Talk N No Do (IRE)**[14] 7129 2-9-5 78 (t) GeorgeBaker 7 70
(Seamus Durack) *led: rdn whn hdd 2f out: sn one pce in 4th* **10/1[3]**

5 nse **Cry Joy (USA)** 2-9-5 0 AdamKirby 6 70+
(Charlie Appleby) *hld up in rr: pushed along 3f out: rdn and hdwy over 1f out: kpt on fnl f* **7/1[2]**

6 ½ **Warrior Of Light (IRE)** 2-9-5 0 TedDurcan 4 69+
(David Lanigan) *hld up: rdn and hdwy over 1f out: one pce fnl f* **12/1**

00 7 2 ¼ **Arab Dawn**[21] 6953 2-9-5 0 JimCrowley 11 64
(Hughie Morrison) *midfield on outer: pushed along over 2f out: nvr threatened* **50/1**

8 1 ¾ **Steve Rogers (IRE)** 2-9-5 0 RyanMoore 5 60
(Sir Michael Stoute) *s.i.s: hld up: pushed along over 2f out: nvr threatened* **16/1**

9 ½ **Moontown** 2-9-5 0 RichardKingscote 8 58
(Charles Hills) *hld up: nvr threatened* **25/1**

00 10 1 ¾ **Moscato**[7] 7308 2-9-5 0 LukeMorris 3 54
(Sir Mark Prescott Bt) *in tch: pushed along 1/2-way: wknd over 2f out* **100/1**

11 11 **Mutamakkin (IRE)** 2-9-5 0 DaneO'Neill 10 29
(Richard Hannon) *midfield: pushed along 1/2-way: wknd over 2f out* **12/1**

1m 41.12s (1.32) **Going Correction** +0.05s/f (Slow) 11 Ran SP% **116.0**
Speed ratings (Par 95): **95,93,92,90,90 89,87,85,85,83 72**
toteswingers 1&2 £29.50, 1&3 £3.40, 2&3 £8.90 CSF £169.12 TOTE £7.90: £2.30, £5.60, £1.10; EX 188.20 Trifecta £640.70 Pool: £2215.49 - 2.59 winning units..
Owner HRH Princess Haya Of Jordan **Bred** Dr John A Chandler **Trained** Newmarket, Suffolk

FOCUS

Some choicely bred and expensive juveniles racing for a first-prize of just £2,911. The pace was not strong but there should be plenty of future winners coming out of this.

7461 BRITISH STALLION STUDS EBF MAIDEN STKS (DIV II) 1m (P)
7:20 (7:22) (Class 5) 2-Y-O £2,911 (£866; £432; £216) Stalls Low

Form RPR

1 **Billingsgate (IRE)** 2-9-5 0 KierenFallon 5 74
(Charlie Appleby) *s.i.s: sn midfield: pushed along 3f out: rdn to chse clr ldr over 1f out: kpt on to ld fnl strides* **20/1**

5 2 hd **Bury Pacer (IRE)**[16] 7070 2-9-5 0 RichardHughes 4 73
(Richard Hannon) *hld up in midfield on inner: rdn and hdwy over 1f out: kpt on wl: jst failed* **13/2[3]**

3 hd **Pretend (IRE)** 2-9-5 0 JamieSpencer 9 73+
(Charlie Appleby) *t.k.h: trckd ldrs on outer: pushed along to ld 2f out: sn qcknd 4 l clr: drvn appr fnl f: wknd fnl 100yds and hdd fnl strides* **4/1[2]**

4 4 ¾ **Ian's Memory (USA)**[29] 6733 2-9-5 0 JimmyFortune 3 71
(Jeremy Noseda) *trckd ldrs: rdn 2f out: kpt on* **7/4[1]**

5 3 **D'Avignon (USA)** 2-9-5 0 WilliamBuick 11 64+
(John Gosden) *s.i.s: hld up: pushed along 1/2-way kpt on fr over 1f out: nvr threatened ldrs* **11/1**

6 1 ¼ **Late Shipment** 2-9-5 0 AdamKirby 10 61+
(Mark Johnston) *hld up in rr: rn green: bhd tl kpt on fnl f* **33/1**

0 7 2 ¼ **Supachap**[16] 7070 2-9-5 0 JimCrowley 7 56
(Hughie Morrison) *midfield: pushed along over 2f out: nvr threatened* **33/1**

6 8 ¾ **Sahara Desert (IRE)**[14] 7120 2-9-5 0 RyanMoore 8 54
(Sir Michael Stoute) *in tch: rdn 2f out: sn wknd* **4/1[2]**

0000 9 2 ½ **Douman (USA)**[18] 7032 2-9-5 60 (t) GeorgeBaker 1 49
(Ed Dunlop) *led: rdn whn hdd 2f out: wknd* **66/1**

05 10 ½ **Sweet Lily Pea (USA)**[16] 7069 2-9-0 0 HarryBentley 6 42
(Olly Stevens) *prom: wknd fnl 2f* **66/1**

11 12 **Ragged Robbin (FR)** 2-9-5 0 TedDurcan 2 20
(David Lanigan) *slowly away: sn pushed along in rr: a bhd* **20/1**

1m 40.18s (0.38) **Going Correction** +0.05s/f (Slow) 11 Ran SP% **116.4**
Speed ratings (Par 95): **100,99,99,98,95 94,92,91,89,88 76**
toteswingers 1&2 £24.90, 1&3 £17.50, 2&3 £7.10 CSF £135.22 TOTE £21.00: £5.90, £3.00, £1.10; EX 93.40 Trifecta £850.50 Pool: £2398.87 - 2.11 winning units..
Owner Godolphin **Bred** Darley **Trained** Newmarket, Suffolk

FOCUS

They did not impress as much as a bunch in the paddock, but the time was nearly one second quicker thanks to a more even gallop.

7462 BETDAQ - THE SPORTS BETTING EXCHANGE H'CAP 1m (P)
7:50 (7:50) (Class 5) (0-75,75) 3-Y-O+ £2,587 (£770; £384; £192) Stalls Low

Form RPR

0161 1 **Cape Samba**[21] 6943 4-9-3 74 ThomasBrown(3) 5 83
(Ismail Mohammed) *prom: rdn over 2f out: led narrowly over 1f out: a strly pressed: hld on wl* **3/1[1]**

2031 2 nk **Bowstar**[21] 6937 4-9-2 70 (p) RobertHavlin 6 78
(Michael Attwater) *in tch: stl gng wl 2f out: rdn to chal over 1f out: upsides ins fnl f: kpt on: jst hld* **7/1[3]**

6142 3 nse **Malaysian Boleh**[19] 6998 3-9-1 72 HarryBentley 11 79
(Simon Dow) *hld up in midfield: rdn and gd hdwy on outside over 1f out: ev ch jst ins fnl f: kpt on* **16/1**

2244 4 1 **Syncopate**[133] 3218 4-9-2 70 DaneO'Neill 7 76
(Pam Sly) *s.i.s: sn midfield: briefly n.m.r and shuffled bk 2f out: kpt on wl fnl f: nrst fin* **12/1**

500 5 nse **Savanna Days (IRE)**[47] 6167 4-9-5 73 MartinHarley 8 79
(Mick Channon) *in tch: rdn 2f out: kpt on* **6/1[2]**

6420 6 ½ **Woolston Ferry (IRE)**[23] 6898 7-9-3 71 FergusSweeney 12 76
(Henry Candy) *hld up: rdn and hdwy over 1f out: kpt on fnl f* **8/1**

0406 7 3 ¾ **Everleigh**[60] 5758 3-9-0 71 RichardHughes 4 66
(Richard Hannon) *led narrowly: rdn whn hdd over 1f out: wknd* **12/1**

0205 8 3 ½ **Poetic Lord**[7] 7306 4-9-4 72 PatDobbs 14 60
(Sylvester Kirk) *hld up: nvr threatened* **20/1**

-000 9 2 ½ **Majestic Zafeen**[18] 7038 4-9-2 70 (p) LukeMorris 2 52
(Alastair Lidderdale) *t.k.h: trckd ldrs: rdn over 2f out: wknd over 1f out* **33/1**

U560 10 3 ¾ **Martinas Delight (USA)**[9] 7257 3-9-2 73 KierenFallon 9 46
(Alan Jarvis) *chsd ldrs on outside: rdn over 3f out: wkng whn sltly hmpd 2f out* **25/1**

1350 11 ¾ **Russian Ice**[203] 1318 5-9-7 75 (p) JimCrowley 3 47
(Dean Ivory) *dwlt: hld up: nvr threatened* **16/1**

0003 12 2 **Copperwood**[7] 7306 8-9-1 69 AdamKirby 10 36
(Mark Johnston) *trckd ldrs: rdn over 2f out: wknd over 1f out* **10/1**

0300 13 ¾ **Bayleyf (IRE)**[14] 7123 4-9-4 72 GeorgeBaker 13 38
(John Best) *v.s.a: a bhd* **50/1**

3534 14 3 ¼ **George Baker (IRE)**[64] 5621 6-9-4 72 PatCosgrave 1 30
(George Baker) *midfield on inner: rdn over 2f out: sn wknd* **10/1**

1m 39.1s (-0.70) **Going Correction** +0.05s/f (Slow)
WFA 3 from 4yo+ 3lb 14 Ran SP% **121.7**
Speed ratings (Par 103): **105,104,104,103,103 103,99,95,93,89 88,86,86,82**
toteswingers 1&2 £3.50, 1&3 £15.30, 2&3 £23.40 CSF £22.19 CT £306.53 TOTE £4.40: £1.60, £1.90, £5.20; EX 20.40 Trifecta £85.30 Pool: £1469.83 - 12.82 winning units..
Owner Ismail Mohammed **Bred** Jeremy Gompertz **Trained** Newmarket, Suffolk
■ Stewards' Enquiry : Robert Havlin caution: careless riding

FOCUS

A tight 1m handicap with no fewer than seven previous course winners in the line-up. A three-way photo and there was not a lot between the first six home at the line. Personal bests from the first three.

7463 WINNERS ARE WELCOME AT BETDAQ NURSERY H'CAP 7f (P)
8:20 (8:20) (Class 4) (0-85,82) 2-Y-O £3,752 (£1,116; £557; £278) Stalls Low

Form RPR

615 1 **Never To Be (USA)**[10] 7221 2-8-13 74 (t) WilliamBuick 5 79+
(John Gosden) *dwlt: hld up in midfield: smooth hdwy over 1f out: swtchd lft into clr appr fnl f: qcknd to ld 110yds out: kpt on: comf* **11/2[3]**

200 2 1 ½ **Man Amongst Men (IRE)**[26] 6799 2-9-7 82 (t) JamieSpencer 1 84
(Brian Meehan) *hld up in rr: rdn and gd hdwy over 1f out: upsides jst ins fnl f: kpt on but no match wnr fnl 110yds* **12/1**

12 3 hd **King Of Macedon (IRE)**[15] 7097 2-9-6 81 AdamKirby 8 82
(Mark Johnston) *pressed ldr: rdn to ld 2f out: hdd 110yds out: one pce* **11/4[2]**

1 4 1 ½ **Bold Lass (IRE)**[15] 7102 2-9-1 76 TedDurcan 6 73
(David Lanigan) *in tch: rdn over 2f out: one pce* **7/4[1]**

2444 5 hd **Boogangoo (IRE)**[11] 7202 2-8-10 71 TomEaves 13 68
(Keith Dalgleish) *s.i.s: hld up in rr: rdn and sme hdwy over 1f out: kpt on fnl f: nrst fin* **25/1**

3421 6 ½ **Archibald Thorburn (IRE)**[26] 6807 2-8-12 73 SteveDrowne 4 68
(Ed McMahon) *t.k.h: trckd ldrs: rdn 2f out: no ex fnl f* **12/1**

4130 7 1 **Constantine**[32] 6645 2-9-2 77 RichardHughes 3 71
(Richard Hannon) *t.k.h: trckd ldrs: rdn 2f out: no ex fnl f* **12/1**

3516 8 2 **Basil Berry**[29] 6731 2-8-10 71 LukeMorris 7 58
(Chris Dwyer) *midfield: wknd over 1f out* **16/1**

1005 9 1 **Sandsman's Girl (IRE)**[15] 7097 2-8-7 72 JasonHart(3) 9 57
(James Given) *hld up in midfield on outside: rdn over 2f out: sn btn* **50/1**

1054 10 shd **Clever Miss**[15] 7088 2-9-3 78 (p) SeanLevey 10 63
(Alan McCabe) *chsd ldrs on outer: wknd over 1f out* **33/1**

3020 11 nk **Misty Sparkler**[30] 6695 2-9-0 75 JimmyFortune 2 59
(Brian Meehan) *led narrowly: rdn whn hdd 2f out: wknd fnl f* **25/1**

1m 27.26s (1.26) **Going Correction** +0.05s/f (Slow) 11 Ran SP% **120.0**
Speed ratings (Par 97): **94,92,92,90,90 89,88,86,84,84 84**
toteswingers 1&2 £8.90, 1&3 £5.20, 2&3 £9.90 CSF £67.80 CT £227.98 TOTE £6.20: £1.90, £3.30, £2.00; EX 93.30 Trifecta £301.90 Pool: £1196.25 - 2.97 winning units..
Owner M Al-Qatami, K Al-Mudhaf & Mrs G Voute **Bred** John Griggs & Linda Griggs **Trained** Newmarket, Suffolk

FOCUS

A competitive 7f nursery and the winner was impressive. The pace was even.

7464 BETDAQ 1ST UK RACE COMMISSION FREE H'CAP 7f (P)
8:50 (8:50) (Class 4) (0-85,91) 3-Y-O+ £4,690 (£1,395; £697; £348) Stalls Low

Form RPR

2001 1 **Chookie Royale**[9] 7241 5-9-8 91 6ex (p) JasonHart(3) 8 100
(Keith Dalgleish) *midfield on outer: rdn over 2f out: gd hdwy appr fnl f: led narrowly 75yds out: hld on wl* **9/1**

4040 2 nk **Head Of Steam (USA)**[25] 6840 6-9-5 85 (p) PatDobbs 3 93
(Amanda Perrett) *midfield: hdwy to chse ldrs 2f out: rdn and upsides ins fnl f: kpt on: hld nr fin* **7/1[3]**

3154 3 ¾ **Sir Mike**[10] 7224 4-9-4 84 AdamKirby 6 90
(Amanda Perrett) *prom: rdn to ld 2f out: hdd 75yds out: no ex* **8/1**

2210 4 ¾ **Footstepsintherain (IRE)**[19] 6988 3-9-2 84 TedDurcan 7 87
(David Lanigan) *hld up in midfield: rdn 2f out: kpt on fnl f* **11/2[2]**

1206 5 shd **Corporal Maddox**[25] 6831 6-9-5 85 (p) LukeMorris 10 89
(Ronald Harris) *hld up: rdn 2f out: briefly n.m.r appr fnl f: kpt on ins fnl f* **33/1**

2223 6 shd **Future Reference (IRE)**[24] 6874 3-9-3 85 (t) SilvestreDeSousa 12 87+
(Saeed bin Suroor) *hld up on outer: rdn 2f out: kpt on fnl f: nvr threatened* **5/1[1]**

0560 7 nse **Nassau Storm**[25] 6831 4-9-3 83 ShaneKelly 2 86
(William Knight) *trckd ldrs: rdn and ev ch over 1f out: no ex ins fnl f* **10/1**

-000 8 ½ **Janoub Nibras (IRE)**[40] 6356 3-9-3 85 (p) TomQueally 13 86+
(Ismail Mohammed) *swtchd rt s: hld up in rr: pushed along and sme hdwy over 1f out: kpt on ins fnl f* **10/1**

4225 9 2 ½ **Kakatosi**[82] 4960 6-9-4 84 RichardHughes 4 79
(Mike Murphy) *s.i.s: hld up: rdn 2f out: nvr threatened* **16/1**

0054 10 ¾ **Palace Moon**[61] 5696 8-9-5 85 (t) JimmyQuinn 5 78
(William Knight) *dwlt: sn midfield: rdn over 2f out: wknd fnl f* **12/1**

0236 11 nk **Midnight Rider (IRE)**[20] 6977 5-9-5 85 GeorgeBaker 14 77
(Chris Wall) *hld up in rr: rdn over 2f out: nvr threatened* **9/1**

124 12 1 ½ **Lunar Deity**[24] 6871 4-9-3 83 JimmyFortune 1 71
(Eve Johnson Houghton) *led: rdn whn hdd 2f out: sn wknd* **25/1**

1031 13 shd **Mr David (USA)**[14] 7123 6-9-5 85 (b) DavidProbert 11 73
(Jamie Osborne) *chsd ldrs on outer: wknd over 1f out* **14/1**

1m 24.98s (-1.02) **Going Correction** +0.05s/f (Slow)
WFA 3 from 4yo+ 2lb 13 Ran SP% **120.9**
Speed ratings (Par 105): **107,106,105,104,104 104,104,104,101,100 100,98,98**
toteswingers 1&2 £17.80, 1&3 £12.90, 2&3 £17.20 CSF £71.59 CT £536.24 TOTE £12.70: £4.30, £3.40, £2.50; EX 98.70 Trifecta £856.20 Part won. Pool: £1,141.72 - 0.52 winning units..
Owner Raeburn Brick Limited **Bred** D And J Raeburn **Trained** Carluke, S Lanarks

FOCUS
A wide-open 84-91 handicap with eight previous course winners in the line-up and the pace was strong. Many still in with a chance in the final furlong, and a step up from the winner on his best form.

7465 BOOK CHRISTMAS FESTIVAL TICKETS NOW CLASSIFIED STKS 7f (P)
9:20 (9:20) (Class 6) 3-Y-O+ **£1,940** (£577; £288; £144) **Stalls** Low

Form RPR

240 **1** **Multitask**[15] 7086 3-9-5 55 ...[1] GeorgeBaker 6 68
(Michael Madgwick) *hld up in midfield: smooth hdwy over 1f out: led jst ins fnl f: pushed clr: comf* **11/2**[1]

2640 **2** *2* **Squirrel Wood (IRE)**[39] 6399 5-9-7 53 ... PatCosgrave 2 64
(George Baker) *midfield: rdn and hdwy over 1f out: kpt on to go 2nd 75yds out: no ch w wnr* **6/1**[2]

0-30 **3** *1 ¼* **Be Royale**[78] 5091 3-9-5 45 ... AndrewMullen 1 60
(Michael Appleby) *led: rdn whn hdd jst ins fnl f: no ex* **8/1**

0065 **4** *½* **Skidby Mill (IRE)**[15] 7086 3-9-5 55 ... DaneO'Neill 13 58
(Laura Mongan) *chsd ldrs on outer: rdn over 2f out: one pce fnl f* **8/1**

440 **5** *1 ¼* **Another Name (IRE)**[40] 6366 3-9-5 48 ... JimCrowley 9 55
(Paul Cole) *sltly hmpd s: hld up in rr: angled lft to outer over 1f out: sn hdwy: one pce ins fnl f* **8/1**

0302 **6** *1 ¾* **Poetic Belle**[5] 7353 3-9-0 53 ...(t) ShirleyTeasdale(5) 3 50
(Shaun Harris) *chsd ldrs on inner: rdn over 2f out: wknd ins fnl f* **7/1**[3]

0500 **7** *2 ¼* **King Of Kudos (IRE)**[16] 7083 3-9-5 53 ...(p) TomQueally 4 44
(Scott Dixon) *in tch: rdn over 2f out: wknd fnl f* **8/1**

0200 **8** *5* **Our Sweet Art**[28] 6752 3-9-5 53 ... SteveDrowne 7 31
(John Best) *hld up: rdn 3f out: sn btn* **33/1**

60-0 **9** *nse* **Salford Prince (IRE)**[7] 7292 5-9-0 50 ... HayleyBurton(7) 10 31
(David Elsworth) *wnt rt s: hld up in rr: a bhd* **33/1**

0604 **10** *½* **True Prince (USA)**[5] 7353 4-9-7 52 ...(b) FergusSweeney 12 30
(Alastair Lidderdale) *pressed ldr: rdn over 2f out: sn wknd* **8/1**

0000 **11** *3 ½* **Tumbleweed Finale**[20] 6985 3-9-5 44 ...(b[1]) DavidProbert 14 20
(Rae Guest) *midfield on outer: rdn over 2f out: sn wknd* **33/1**

000/ **12** *54* **Midnight Pearl (USA)**[176] 3759 10-9-4 50 ... MichaelJMMurphy(3) 11
(John Gallagher) *hld up on outside: sn pushed along: bhd fr 1/2-way* **66/1**

1m 26.07s (0.07) **Going Correction** +0.05s/f (Slow)
WFA 3 from 4yo+ 2lb 12 Ran SP% **108.0**
Speed ratings (Par 101): **101,98,97,96,95 93,90,85,84,84 80,18**
toteswingers 1&2 £9.40, 1&3 £12.00, 2&3 £5.80 CSF £28.98 TOTE £5.80: £2.00, £2.10, £3.60; EX 46.40 Trifecta £252.50 Pool: £966.04 - 2.86 winning units..
Owner Mrs L N Harmes **Bred** Mrs L N Harmes **Trained** Denmead, Hants

FOCUS
A weak 0-55 classified stakes, but the pace and time weren't bad and the form is rated through the runner-up.
T/Jkpt: Not won. T/Plt: £238.90. Pool: £80,019.01 - 244.47 winning units. T/Qpdt: £20.70. Pool: £8971.17 - 320.70 winning units. AS

7190 NEWMARKET (R-H)
Wednesday, October 23

OFFICIAL GOING: Soft (5.8)
Wind: fresh to strong, across Weather: dry and windy

7466 THOROUGHBRED BREEDERS' ASSOCIATION MEDIAN AUCTION MAIDEN FILLIES' STKS 7f
2:30 (2:31) (Class 5) 2-Y-O **£3,234** (£962; £481; £240) **Stalls** Low

Form RPR

0 **1** **Fray**[32] 6643 2-9-0 0 ... JamesDoyle 7 74+
(Roger Charlton) *strong: close-coupled: in tch in midfield: rdn and effrt 2f out: hdwy to chse clr ldr over 1f out: styd on wl u.p to ld fnl 100yds: rdn out* **7/4**[1]

530 **2** *1 ½* **Evacusafe Lady**[12] 7168 2-9-0 57 ...(p) MichaelO'Connell 10 70
(John Ryan) *led: rdn and 3 l clr over 1f out: drvn and hdd fnl 100yds: no ex* **66/1**

3 *1* **Eastern Belle** 2-9-0 0 ... WilliamBuick 2 68
(John Gosden) *athletic: in tch in midfield: rdn and effrt over 2f out: 6th and hdwy over 1f out: styd on wl ins fnl f: wnt 3rd towards fin: no threat to wnr* **9/2**[2]

0 **4** *1 ¼* **Dark Reality (IRE)**[15] 7102 2-9-0 0 ... HarryBentley 6 64
(Ralph Beckett) *strong: lengthy: in tch: rdn and effrt over 2f out: chsd clr ldr wl over 1f out tl over 1f out: no imp and one pce fnl f* **12/1**

00 **5** *4* **Stybba**[25] 6821 2-9-0 0 ... JamieSpencer 13 54
(Andrew Balding) *chsd ldr tl wl over 1f out: no ex over 1f out: edgd rt and wknd ins fnl f* **14/1**

5 **6** *nk* **Maracuja**[24] 6873 2-9-0 0 ... JoeFanning 9 54
(Mark Johnston) *w'like: bit bkwd: chsd ldrs: rdn and unable qck 2f out: 5th and no hdwy over 1f out: wknd ins fnl f* **25/1**

7 *1* **Postal Order** 2-9-0 0 ...[1] GrahamLee 8 51
(James Eustace) *lengthy: s.i.s: rn green towards rr: rdn and wandered 2f out: sme hdwy over 1f out: no threat to ldrs but kpt on steadily fnl f* **20/1**

8 *2 ¼* **Windy Citi** 2-9-0 0 ... TedDurcan 3 46
(Chris Wall) *tall: scope: bit bkwd: stdd s: t.k.h: hld up in rr: pushed along and hdwy ent fnl 2f: no hdwy over 1f out: wknd ins fnl f* **33/1**

9 *1 ¾* **Saltwater Creek (IRE)** 2-9-0 0 ... TomQueally 14 41
(Michael Bell) *leggy: unf: bit bkwd: chsd ldrs: rdn 1/2-way: sn struggling and lost pl over 2f out: wknd over 1f out* **20/1**

6 **10** *shd* **Wunderkind (USA)**[26] 6807 2-9-0 0 ... LukeMorris 1 41
(Sir Mark Prescott Bt) *neat: towards rr: rdn and sme hdwy wl over 1f out: plugged on same pce fnl f: nvr trbld ldrs* **10/1**[3]

11 *shd* **Crystal Pearl** 2-9-0 0 ... LiamJones 12 41
(Mark H Tompkins) *lengthy: tall: bit bkwd: s.i.s: sn rcvrd and in midfield after 2f: rdn and no ex ent fnl 2f: wknd over 1f out* **66/1**

12 *1* **Three Quid (IRE)** 2-9-0 0 ... JimmyQuinn 4 38
(Gary Harrison) *unf: bit bkwd: hld up towards rr: rdn and no hdwy ent fnl 2f: plugged on fnl f: nvr trbld ldrs* **50/1**

13 *1 ¼* **Tipsy Star** 2-9-0 0 ... SilvestreDeSousa 11 35
(Daniel Kubler) *leggy: s.i.s: sn rcvrd and hld up in midfield: rdn and effrt ent fnl 2f: no hdwy and sn btn: bhd and eased wl ins fnl f* **10/1**[3]

14 *½* **Tete Orange** 2-9-0 0 ... AndreaAtzeni 15 34
(Stuart Williams) *tall: lengthy: in tch towards rr: effrt and no hdwy over 2f out: wknd and bhd over 1f out* **20/1**

15 *4 ½* **Archduchess** 2-9-1 0 ow1 ... SebSanders 5 24
(Rae Guest) *tall: lengthy: edgy: sweating: bit bkwd: in tch in midfield: rdn 1/2-way: sn struggling: wknd and bhd over 1f out: eased ins fnl f* **12/1**

1m 27.45s (2.05) **Going Correction** +0.175s/f (Good) 15 Ran SP% **120.8**
Speed ratings (Par 92): **95,93,92,90,86 85,84,82,80,79 79,78,77,76,71**
toteswingers 1&2 £8.60, 1&3 £2.60, 2&3 £21.00 CSF £188.27 TOTE £2.90: £1.20, £6.30, £2.10; EX 59.30 Trifecta £456.40 Pool: £2117.54 - 3.47 winning units..
Owner K Abdullah **Bred** Juddmonte Farms Ltd **Trained** Beckhampton, Wilts

FOCUS
The stalls were on the far side of the far side track for a card with five races for 2yos. There was a strong wind which wouldn't have been ideal conditions for those on the card making their debut. They came down the middle to near side in the first maiden for fillies' where the 57-rated second nearly caused a shock from the front.

7467 THOROUGHBRED BREEDERS' ASSOCIATION MAIDEN STKS (C&G) 7f
3:05 (3:08) (Class 4) 2-Y-O **£3,881** (£1,155; £577; £288) **Stalls** Low

Form RPR

1 **Pretzel (IRE)** 2-9-0 0 ... AndreaAtzeni 4 81+
(Roger Varian) *cmpt: chsd ldrs: rdn and ev ch wl over 1f out: led 1f out: kpt on wl: rdn out* **5/1**[2]

2 *1 ½* **Mutakayyef** 2-9-0 0 ... PaulHanagan 9 77+
(William Haggas) *tall: lengthy: scope: lw: s.i.s: in rr: hdwy and travelling wl 1/2-way: rdn to chse ldrs wl over 1f out: sltly hmpd over 1f out: wnt 2nd and kpt on same pce ins fnl f* **9/2**[1]

3 *1 ¼* **Stetchworth (IRE)** 2-9-0 0 ... JoeFanning 12 74
(Mark Johnston) *lengthy: lw: narrow: sn chsd ldr: rdn to ld and rn green wl over 1f out: hdd 1f out: edgd rt and no ex ins fnl f* **13/2**[3]

503 **4** *3 ¼* **Headlong (IRE)**[89] 4716 2-9-0 70 ... JimmyFortune 10 66
(Brian Meehan) *w'like: wl in tch in midfield: rdn and effrt over 2f out: unable qck and sltly outpcd wl over 1f out: ralied 1f out: kpt on same pce fnl 150yds* **9/1**

60 **5** *nk* **Gannicus**[21] 6953 2-9-0 0 ... JackMitchell 2 65
(Brendan Powell) *chsd ldrs: rdn and unable qck wl over 1f out: plugged on same pce fnl f* **50/1**

4 **6** *¾* **Capers Royal Star (FR)**[21] 6934 2-9-0 0 ... FergusSweeney 8 63
(Alastair Lidderdale) *unf: led: rdn and hdd wl over 1f out: 4th and btn ent fnl f: wknd fnl 150yds* **10/1**

7 *nk* **Daydreamer** 2-9-0 0 ... RyanMoore 11 63
(William Haggas) *str: scope: wl in tch in midfield: rdn and outpcd wl over 1f out: no threat to ldrs and plugged on same pce after* **9/2**[1]

0 **8** *nse* **Applejack Lad**[183] 1749 2-9-0 0 ...(t) MichaelO'Connell 3 63
(John Ryan) *w'like: in tch in midfield: rdn and unable qck 3f out: no threat to ldrs and plugged on same pce u.p fnl 2f* **66/1**

9 *1 ¾* **Naadirr (IRE)** 2-9-0 0 ... MartinHarley 6 58+
(Marco Botti) *str: bit bkwd: in tch in rr: rdn and effrt over 2f out: rn green and no imp wl over 1f out: nvr trbld ldrs* **5/1**[2]

10 *1* **Battle Command (USA)** 2-9-0 0 ... JamieSpencer 7 56
(Peter Chapple-Hyam) *leggy: scope: lengthy: hld up in tch in rr: rdn and no hdwy 2f out: nvr trbld ldrs* **11/1**

00 **11** *3* **Moxey**[27] 6762 2-9-0 0 ... DaneO'Neill 1 48
(Henry Candy) *w'like: close-coupled: in tch in midfield: rdn and no hdwy over 2f out: wknd wl over 1f out* **28/1**

12 *17* **Rock Charm** 2-8-7 0 ... JeanVanOvermeire(7) 5 6
(Stuart Williams) *leggy: scope: bit bkwd: s.i.s: in tch in rr: rdn and struggling ent fnl 2f: sn wknd: t.o* **66/1**

1m 27.41s (2.01) **Going Correction** +0.175s/f (Good) 12 Ran SP% **118.8**
Speed ratings (Par 97): **95,93,91,88,87 86,86,86,84,83 79,60**
toteswingers 1&2 £4.60, 1&3 £9.30, 2&3 £5.60 CSF £27.40 TOTE £6.30: £2.00, £2.30, £2.70; EX 23.50 Trifecta £180.10 Pool: £2767.99 - 11.52 winning units..
Owner Normandie Stud Ltd **Bred** Normandie Stud Ltd **Trained** Newmarket, Suffolk

FOCUS
This modest maiden was left to the newcomers to front the market and to fill the places. They came down the centre and the time was almost the same as the opener.

7468 THOROUGHBRED BREEDERS' ASSOCIATION HOUGHTON CONDITIONS STKS 1m
3:40 (3:41) (Class 2) 2-Y-O **£8,715** (£2,609; £1,304; £652) **Stalls** Low

Form RPR

42 **1** **Sudden Wonder (IRE)**[68] 5490 2-8-12 0 ... MickaelBarzalona 2 95+
(Charlie Appleby) *str: gd-bodied: lw: led for 2f: styd pressing ldr tl led again ent fnl 2f: rdn and qcknd clr ent fnl f: r.o strly: readily* **8/11**[1]

105 **2** *8* **Noble Metal**[67] 5530 2-9-3 85 ... ShaneKelly 3 82
(Peter Chapple-Hyam) *neat: taken down early: stdd s: hld up in tch in last: rdn and effrt to chse wnr over 1f out: outpcd and btn ent fnl f: wknd fnl 150yds* **7/1**[3]

1 **3** *2 ¼* **Cape Wrath**[33] 6590 2-9-3 0 ... RichardHughes 5 79
(Richard Hannon) *lw: stdd s: in tch in 3rd: rdn 3f out: chsd wnr briefly u.p wl over 1f out: 3rd and outpcd ent fnl f: wknd* **15/8**[2]

51 **4** *4 ½* **Kalon Brama (IRE)**[15] 7111 2-8-7 65 ... RosieJessop 1 57
(Peter Charalambous) *close-coupled: t.k.h: chsd ldr tl led 6f out: edgd lft and hdd ent fnl 2f: dropped to last and btn over 1f out: wknd fnl f* **50/1**

1m 40.63s (2.03) **Going Correction** +0.175s/f (Good) 4 Ran SP% **107.1**
Speed ratings (Par 101): **96,88,85,81**
CSF £6.11 TOTE £1.70; EX 5.00 Trifecta £6.60 Pool: £3214.85 - 364.67 winning units..
Owner Godolphin **Bred** Rabbah Bloodstock Limited **Trained** Newmarket, Suffolk

FOCUS
Just the four went to post for this 2yo conditions race. It was the first race they stuck to the far rail and the winner took it easily.

7469 BRITISH STALLION STUDS EBF TBA MAIDEN STKS 1m
4:10 (4:12) (Class 4) 2-Y-O **£4,528** (£1,347; £673; £336) **Stalls** Low

Form RPR

1 **Moontime** 2-9-5 0 ... MickaelBarzalona 8 80+
(Charlie Appleby) *athletic: mde most tl hdd 3f out: styd upsides ldr: rdn and ev ch over 1f out: led 1f out: kpt on gamely u.p: hld on wl* **14/1**

3 **2** *nse* **Munjaz**[68] 5490 2-9-5 0 ... PaulHanagan 13 80
(John Gosden) *str: scope: lw: bmpd and pushed lft s: sn rcvrd to chse ldrs and travelled wl: led 3f out: rdn over 1f out: hdd 1f out: kpt on wl u.p after: jst hld* **5/4**[1]

3 *shd* **Mange All** 2-9-5 0 ... LiamJones 7 80+
(William Haggas) *str: gd-bodied: bit bkwd: in tch in last quartet: rdn and effrt wl over 1f out: hdwy to chse ldng pair fnl 100yds: styd on wl and clsng towards fin* **20/1**

4 2 1/2 **Reedcutter** 2-9-2 0 .... RobertTart[3] 9 74
(James Toller) *leggy: in tch in midfield: rdn and effrt ent fnl 2f: hdwy to chse ldng pair 1f out: no imp and lost 3rd fnl 100yds: wknd towards fin* **100/1**

4 5 1/2 **Touch The Sky**[27] 6762 2-9-5 0 .... TomQueally 12 73
(Lady Cecil) *str: wnt sharply lft s: sn in tch in midfield: rdn and outpcd wl over 1f out: rallied and kpt on again ins fnl f* **3/1**[2]

4 6 1/2 **Big Orange**[10] 7219 2-9-5 0 .... JamieSpencer 4 72
(Michael Bell) *rangy: scope: lw: chsd ldrs: rdn and effrt wl over 1f out: no ex u.p ent fnl f: wknd fnl 150yds* **12/1**

7 2 **Danjeu (IRE)** 2-9-5 0 .... WilliamBuick 3 68
(John Gosden) *str: s.i.s: rn green in rr: rdn and no hdwy 2f out: hdwy 1f out: styd on wl ins fnl f: nvr trbld ldrs* **7/1**[3]

8 3/4 **Mutaraadif (USA)** 2-9-5 0 .... DaneO'Neill 5 66
(Roger Varian) *tall: str: scope: dwlt: sn rcvrd and chsd ldr tl 3f out: rdn and unable qck over 2f out: wknd over 1f out* **14/1**

9 hd **Lucky Jim** 2-9-5 0 .... GeorgeBaker 2 66
(Chris Wall) *w'like: str: bit bkwd: chsd ldrs: rdn and unable qck over 1f out: btn 1f out: wknd ins fnl f* **100/1**

0 10 hd **Dalarosso**[27] 6762 2-9-5 0 .... GrahamLee 6 65
(Ed Dunlop) *w'like: close-coupled: in tch in midfield: rdn and unable qck 2f out: outpcd and btn over 1f out: wknd fnl f* **66/1**

11 3 **Purple Lane (IRE)** 2-9-5 0 .... FergusSweeney 11 59
(David Simcock) *athletic: hld up in tch in last quartet: rdn and effrt on far side wl over 1f out: no hdwy over 1f out: wknd fnl f* **33/1**

12 8 **Alzammaar (USA)** 2-9-5 0 .... JamesDoyle 10 41
(Charles Hills) *athletic: lw: in tch in rr: rdn ent fnl 2f: sn struggling: wknd over 1f out* **33/1**

1m 41.97s (3.37) **Going Correction** +0.175s/f (Good) 12 Ran SP% **117.1**
Speed ratings (Par 97): **90,89,89,87,86 86,84,83,83,83 80,72**
toteswingers 1&2 £4.20, 1&3 £32.10, 2&3 £10.50 CSF £30.56 TOTE £13.00: £3.50, £1.10, £6.60; EX 54.10 Trifecta £582.10 Pool: £2277.21 - 2.93 winning units..
Owner Godolphin **Bred** W And R Barnett Ltd **Trained** Newmarket, Suffolk

FOCUS
No fewer than five Derby entries in this field. They tended to keep towards the far side and little got into it from off the pace. The principals fought out a close finish which resulted in a one-two for sire Sea The Stars.

7470 THOROUGHBRED BREEDERS' ASSOCIATION FILLIES' H'CAP 1m
4:45 (4:46) (Class 2) (0-100,99) 3-Y-O+ £12,938 (£3,850; £1,924; £962) Stalls Low

Form RPR
1051 1 **Yojojo (IRE)**[18] 7038 4-8-5 80 oh2 .... DavidProbert 2 91
(Gay Kelleway) *racd far side: chsd ldr tl led over 2f out: rdn and clr over 1f out: r.o wl: rdn out* **20/1**

0654 2 3 1/2 **Galician**[10] 7233 4-9-10 99 .... JoeFanning 7 102
(Mark Johnston) *racd in centre: midfield overall: hdwy u.p and chsd ldr over 1f out: unable qck and btn 1f out: plugged on to hold 2nd fnl f* **9/1**

13 3 1 3/4 **Deglet Noor**[35] 6531 3-8-6 84 ....[1] PaulHanagan 4 82
(Roger Varian) *lw: racd far side: hld up in midfield overall: rdn and effrt 2f out: wnt 3rd 1f out: kpt on but no threat to wnr* **3/1**[1]

2312 4 1/2 **Cosseted**[35] 6531 3-8-2 80 oh5 .... AndreaAtzeni 8 77
(James Fanshawe) *racd in centre: hld up in last trio: rdn 3f out: hdwy past btn horses over 1f out: styd on: no threat to wnr* **3/1**[1]

203 5 1 3/4 **Trulee Scrumptious**[26] 6805 4-8-5 80 oh29 ....(be) JimmyQuinn 1 74?
(Peter Charalambous) *racd far side: led tl over 2f out: sn rdn: outpcd and lost 2nd over 1f out: wknd ins fnl f* **100/1**

32 6 3 1/4 **Rainbow Beauty**[9] 7256 3-7-11 80 oh4 ....(p) JoeyHaynes[5] 3 65
(Gerard Butler) *racd far side: chsd ldng pair tl no ex u.p over 1f out: wknd fnl f* **7/1**[3]

2233 7 5 **Maid A Million**[18] 7015 3-9-1 93 .... WilliamCarson 6 67
(David Elsworth) *lw: racd in centre: hld up in last trio: rdn over 2f out: drvn and no hdwy 2f out: wknd over 1f out* **7/1**[3]

3114 8 8 **Narmin (IRE)**[35] 6531 3-8-2 80 .... NickyMackay 9 35
(John Gosden) *racd in centre: hld up in last pair: rdn and effrt over 2f out: drvn and wknd wl over 1f out: bhd fnl f* **5/1**[2]

0550 9 3/4 **Sorella Bella (IRE)**[19] 6993 3-8-9 87 .... TomQueally 5 41
(Mick Channon) *racd in centre: midfield overall: rdn and lost pl wl over 2f out: bhd over 1f out* **11/1**

1m 38.74s (0.14) **Going Correction** +0.175s/f (Good)
WFA 3 from 4yo 3lb 9 Ran SP% **115.8**
Speed ratings (Par 96): **106,102,100,100,98 95,90,82,81**
toteswingers 1&2 £20.20, 1&3 £9.70, 2&3 £5.60 CSF £187.33 CT £705.61 TOTE £8.10: £3.10, £2.90, £2.00; EX 122.30 Trifecta £469.10 Pool: £2813.10 - 4.49 winning units..
Owner Winterbeck Manor Stud **Bred** Rossenarra Bloodstock Limited **Trained** Exning, Suffolk

FOCUS
The only non-juvenile race on the card was a decent fillies' handicap which subsequent Listed scorer Hippy Hippy Shake took last year. The presence of the 99-rated Galician meant a few went from out of the handicap. They roughly split into two groups, and the four coming up the far side seemed to hold the advantage over the with the rest. The time compared favourably to the other 1m races on the card. The winner been progressing, but may not be as good as a literal reading of this form suggests, with the fifth an obvious doubt.

7471 THOROUGHBRED BREEDERS' ASSOCIATION NURSERY H'CAP 1m 1f
5:20 (5:20) (Class 4) (0-85,81) 2-Y-O £3,881 (£1,155; £577; £288) Stalls Low

Form RPR
3522 1 **Island Remede**[7] 7309 2-8-6 66 .... PaulHanagan 4 79+
(Ed Dunlop) *lengthy: w ldr tl led ent fnl 2f: rdn and readily wnt clr over 1f out: r.o strly: easily* **9/2**[3]

421 2 7 **Devilment**[30] 6688 2-9-7 81 .... SilvestreDeSousa 1 80
(Charlie Appleby) *athletic: lw: hld up in last pair: rdn and hdwy to go 3rd and edgd rt over 1f out: kpt on u.p fnl f: wnt 2nd last stride: no ch w wnr* **4/1**[2]

501 3 shd **Notarised**[23] 6896 2-9-2 76 .... JoeFanning 6 75
(Mark Johnston) *led tl rdn and hdd ent fnl 2f: outpcd and btn over 1f out: kpt on: lost 2nd fnl stride* **8/1**

0211 4 2 1/4 **Anglophile**[54] 5951 2-9-6 80 .... MickaelBarzalona 2 74
(Charlie Appleby) *cmpt: stdd s: hld up in tch in last pair: rdn and effrt over 2f out: no real hdwy: plugged on ins fnl f: no ch w wnr* **3/1**[1]

311 5 3 1/2 **Jelly Fish**[35] 6520 2-9-4 78 .... JamesDoyle 3 65
(Amanda Perrett) *str: close coupled: in tch in midfield: rdn and effrt over 2f out: no ex and btn over 1f out: wknd fnl f* **11/2**

5164 6 1 3/4 **Photography (IRE)**[14] 7129 2-9-1 75 .... MartinDwyer 8 59
(Hugo Palmer) *chsd ldng pair: rdn: racd awkwardly and outpcd wl over 1f out: wknd over 1f out* **10/1**

622 7 12 **Alisios (GR)**[18] 7023 2-9-5 79 .... AndreaAtzeni 7 39
(Luca Cumani) *w'like: tall: t.k.h early: in tch in midfield: short-lived effrt jst over 2f out: sn btn and wknd wl over 1f out: eased wl ins fnl f* **6/1**

540 8 25 **Plucky Dip**[123] 3574 2-8-2 62 .... JimmyQuinn 5
(John Ryan) *in tch in midfield: rdn and lost pl wl over 2f out: lost tch 2f out: t.o fnl f* **66/1**

1m 53.25s (1.55) **Going Correction** +0.175s/f (Good) 8 Ran SP% **114.5**
Speed ratings (Par 97): **100,93,93,91,88 87,76,54**
toteswingers 1&2 £4.80, 1&3 £7.40, 2&3 £9.40 CSF £22.89 CT £139.51 TOTE £4.40: £2.00, £1.90, £2.60; EX 23.70 Trifecta £223.10 Pool: £2277.16 - 7.65 winning units..
Owner Mrs Janice Quy **Bred** Mrs J M Quy **Trained** Newmarket, Suffolk

FOCUS
A fair nursery won by Derby runner-up Main Sequence in 2011 and, while there was nothing near the same quality here, some of these should be able to improve on this bare form as they step up in trip next year.
T/Plt: £36.60. Pool:£71,875.09 - 1430.44 winning units. T/Qpdt: £12.80. Pool: £4042.38 - 233.64 winning units. SP

7472 - 7482a (Foreign Racing) - See Raceform Interactive

GEELONG (L-H)
Wednesday, October 23

OFFICIAL GOING: Turf: heavy

7483a SPORTINGBET GEELONG CUP (GROUP 3 H'CAP) (3YO+) (TURF) 1m 4f
6:00 (12:00) 3-Y-O+
£125,000 (£34,615; £17,307; £8,653; £4,807; £3,846)

RPR
1 **Ibicenco (GER)**[18] 5-8-13 0 ....(b) BradRawiller 7 113+
(Peter G Moody, Australia) *midfield early: hdwy to trck ldr on outer bef 1/2-way: rdn over 2f out: styd on steadily and grad wore down eventual runner-up: led cl home* **9/2**[2]

2 nk **Verdant**[11] 7213 6-8-8 0 ....(tp) BenMelham 9 108
(Robert Smerdon, Australia) *worked across fr wdst draw and sn led: pushed along on turn into st: 1 l clr and rdn ent fnl f: styd on but grad worn down and hdd cl home* **7/1**

3 4 1/4 **Moudre (AUS)**[11] 7213 8-8-13 0 ....(b) CraigAWilliams 1 106
(Ciaron Maher, Australia) *hld up in midfield: pushed along and hdwy on outer over 2f out: rdn and styd on steadily: wnt 3rd fnl strides: nt pce to chal* **11/2**[3]

4 shd **Crafty Cruiser (AUS)**[18] 6-8-8 0 .... MichaelWalker 2 101
(Bryce Stanaway, Australia) *midfield on inner: rdn 2f out: hdwy on rail and wnt 3rd on turn into st: styd on but sn outpcd by front pair: dropped to 4th fnl strides* **8/1**

5 3/4 **Forgotten Voice (IRE)**[82] 4944 8-9-2 0 .... BrettPrebble 5 107
(Nicky Henderson) *midfield in tch on outer: clsd 3f out: rdn in 3rd and ev ch 2f out: styd on but outpcd by ldng pair in st and dropped to 5th ent fnl f: nt given hrd time once hld towards fin* **5/2**[1]

6 hd **Warwarick (AUS)**[12] 7-8-8 0 ....(b) KerrinMcEvoy 3 99+
(David Hayes, Australia) *w ldr early: sn stdd and hld up in last trio on outer: rdn and fanned wd on turn into st: styd on steadily but n.d* **30/1**

7 1 1/4 **Brigantin (USA)**[18] 6-8-11 0 .... MarkZahra 4 100
(Pat Carey, Australia) *stdd and hld up in rr: sn last: rdn 2f out: plugged on in st but no imp: nvr a factor* **20/1**

8 1 1/4 **Polish Knight (NZ)**[18] 5-8-8 0 ....(v) DwayneDunn 8 95
(Michael, Wayne & John Hawkes, Australia) *dwlt sltly and dropped in fr wd draw: hld up: last early and a towards rr: rdn 2f out: outpcd and btn in st: nvr a factor* **11/2**[3]

9 20 **Goldoni (IRE)**[11] 7213 4-8-8 0 .... ChadSchofield 6 63
(David Hayes, Australia) *led early: sn hdd and trckd ldr on inner: rdn and lost pl 2f out: dropped to last and btn over 1f out: eased and t.o* **13/1**

2m 35.17s (155.17) 9 Ran SP% **116.3**
PARI-MUTUEL (NSW TAB - all including 1 aud stake): WIN 5.10; PLACE 2.10, 2.30, 2.30; DF 18.40; SF 36.20.
Owner Oti Racing, J Higgins Et Al **Bred** Gestut Schlenderhan **Trained** Australia

7377 WOLVERHAMPTON (A.W) (L-H)
Thursday, October 24

OFFICIAL GOING: Standard
Wind: Light across Weather: Cloudy

7484 32REDPOKER.COM MEDIAN AUCTION MAIDEN STKS 7f 32y(P)
5:40 (5:41) (Class 6) 3-5-Y-O £1,940 (£577; £288; £144) Stalls High

Form RPR
02-2 1 **Daring Dragon**[19] 7037 3-9-5 67 ....(b) GeorgeBaker 1 67+
(Ed Walker) *wnt lft s: sn trcking ldrs: led on bit ins fnl f: shkn up and r.o: comf* **4/5**[1]

4 2 1 1/2 **Tiger Jim**[128] 3435 3-9-5 0 .... TedDurcan 3 63
(Chris Wall) *sn pushed along to chse ldr: rdn to ld over 1f out: hdd and unable qck ins fnl f* **3/1**[2]

3303 3 3 **Speedfit Boy (IRE)**[16] 7086 3-9-5 59 ....(b) TomQueally 5 55
(George Margarson) *a.p: rdn over 1f out: styd on same pce fnl f* **7/2**[3]

0004 4 6 **Nakuru Breeze (IRE)**[21] 6986 4-8-11 43 ....(bt) JacobButterfield[5] 2 35
(Suzzanne France) *led: rdn and hdd over 1f out: wknd ins fnl f* **33/1**

00-6 5 hd **Stoneacre Thirsk (IRE)**[12] 7203 4-8-13 35 .... SladeO'Hara[3] 9 34
(Peter Grayson) *hld up: drvn along over 2f out: wknd fnl f* **50/1**

0340 6 2 3/4 **Lady Calantha**[33] 6630 3-9-0 45 .... PaddyAspell 4 26
(Alan Berry) *chsd ldrs: pushed along 1/2-way: rdn and wknd over 1f out* **66/1**

0005 7 16 **Thecornishwren (IRE)**[13] 7167 4-8-9 41 ....(vt) JordonMcMurray[7] 7
(John Ryan) *sn outpcd* **100/1**

1m 30.21s (0.61) **Going Correction** +0.05s/f (Slow)
WFA 3 from 4yo 2lb 7 Ran SP% **110.2**
Speed ratings (Par 101): **98,96,92,86,85 82,64**
toteswingers 1&2 £1.20, 2&3 £1.50, 1&3 £1.40 CSF £3.16 TOTE £1.70: £1.10, £1.80; EX 4.20 Trifecta £6.00 Pool: £2967.44 - 370.47 winning units..
Owner Ms A A Yap **Bred** Reid & Shriver **Trained** Newmarket, Suffolk

The Form Book Flat, Raceform Ltd, Compton, RG20 6NL.

FOCUS
A typically weak back-end maiden for older horses, run at a routine pace.

7485 32REDBET.COM H'CAP 7f 32y(P)
6:10 (6:12) (Class 7) (0-50,56) 3-Y-O+ **£1,940** (£577; £288; £144) **Stalls** High

Form RPR
2323 **1** **Prigsnov Dancer (IRE)**[16] 7101 8-8-10 **49**...............(p) DavidParkes(7) 4 61
(Deborah Sanderson) *trckd ldr tl led over 2f out: rdn clr fr over 1f out* **10/1**[3]
6500 **2** *6* **Thewestwalian (USA)**[8] 7299 5-9-2 **48**...................... WilliamCarson 12 44
(Peter Hiatt) *led: rdn and hdd over 2f out: wknd fnl f* **10/1**[3]
0000 **3** *1 1/4* **George Benjamin**[42] 6324 6-9-3 **49**..............................(t) JoeFanning 6 42
(Christopher Kellett) *s.i.s: in rr: pushed along over 2f out: hdwy over 1f out: wnt 3rd ins fnl f: nrst fin* **14/1**
/5-0 **4** *1 3/4* **Interchoice Star**[48] 6156 8-9-4 **50**................................(p) GeorgeBaker 2 38
(Ray Peacock) *chsd ldrs tl rdn and wknd over 1f out* **14/1**
-301 **5** *1/2* **Dustland Fairytale (IRE)**[9] 7265 5-9-10 **56** 6ex....... SilvestreDeSousa 3 43
(Ian Williams) *mid-div: drvn along 1/2-way: nvr trbld ldrs* **5/4**[1]
564 **6** *2 1/4* **Fantasy Invader (IRE)**[17] 7079 3-9-2 **50**.................(e[1]) RobertWinston 7 30
(John Quinn) *hld up: pushed along over 2f out: nvr on terms* **3/1**[2]
0003 **7** *1/2* **Shelling Peas**[19] 7037 4-8-9 **48**................................(v) AdamMcLean(7) 9 28
(Derek Shaw) *s.i.s: in rr: rdn 1/2-way: nvr on terms* **33/1**
4060 **8** *1 1/4* **Marshall Art**[27] 6808 4-9-3 **49**......................................(tp) CathyGannon 8 26
(Ken Wingrove) *chsd ldrs: drvn along 1/2-way: wknd over 2f out* **16/1**
0360 **9** *1* **Steel City Boy (IRE)**[12] 7197 10-8-12 **49**...................... AnnStokell(5) 1 23
(Ann Stokell) *chsd ldrs tl rdn and wknd over 2f out* **50/1**
060 **10** *9* **Bix (IRE)**[26] 6843 3-9-2 **50**.. TomEaves 5
(Alan Berry) *in rr: bhd fnl 4f* **33/1**

1m 30.21s (0.61) **Going Correction** +0.05s/f (Slow)
WFA 3 from 4yo+ 2lb **10** Ran SP% **114.7**
Speed ratings (Par 97): **98,91,89,87,87 84,84,82,81,71**
toteswingers 1&2 £10.10, 2&3 £27.70, 1&3 £20.00 CSF £101.76 CT £1423.30 TOTE £9.00: £2.40, £4.10, £3.10; EX 152.90 Trifecta £2107.60 Part won. Pool: £2810.16 - 0.91 winning units..
Owner J M Lacey **Bred** Tom Radley **Trained** Tickhill, S Yorks

FOCUS
It paid to race handily in this bottom-drawer handicap.

7486 32RED H'CAP (DIV I) 7f 32y(P)
6:40 (6:40) (Class 5) (0-75,75) 3-Y-O+ **£2,587** (£770; £384; £192) **Stalls** High

Form RPR
2002 **1** **Bogsnog (IRE)**[13] 7164 3-8-13 **74**.......................... JacobButterfield(5) 9 81
(Kristin Stubbs) *hld up: hdwy over 2f out: rdn to ld and hung lft fr over 1f out: jst hld on* **10/1**
2453 **2** *shd* **Orpsie Boy (IRE)**[13] 7163 10-8-7 **61**.............................. LukeMorris 6 69
(Ruth Carr) *hld up: hdwy over 2f out: rdn over 1f out: r.o wl* **8/1**
1123 **3** *1/2* **Cape Of Hope (IRE)**[71] 5406 3-9-5 **75**........................... ShaneKelly 5 80+
(Peter Chapple-Hyam) *s.i.s: hld up: hdwy over 1f out: sn rdn: edgd lft and r.o wl towards fin: nt quite rch ldrs* **3/1**[1]
4410 **4** *2 1/2* **Celtic Sixpence (IRE)**[37] 6496 5-9-2 **75**.................(p) ShelleyBirkett(5) 8 75
(Nick Kent) *w ldr tl led 2f out: rdn and hdd over 1f out: styd on same pce ins fnl f* **16/1**
1055 **5** *nse* **Smalljohn**[17] 7076 7-9-2 **70**..(v) TomEaves 4 69
(Bryan Smart) *led: rdn and hdd 2f out: styd on same pce ins fnl f* **7/1**
1100 **6** *1 1/2* **Pilates (IRE)**[30] 6720 3-9-0 **70**.............................. SilvestreDeSousa 7 64
(Mark Johnston) *s.i.s: outpcd: hdwy and nt clr run over 1f out: swtchd rt ins fnl f: r.o: nt rch ldrs* **4/1**[2]
3340 **7** *1* **Summer Dream (IRE)**[30] 6734 3-9-3 **73**......................... MartinHarley 1 65
(Marco Botti) *chsd ldrs: rdn over 2f out: no ex fnl f* **9/2**[3]
-600 **8** *5* **Sky Crossing**[134] 3192 4-9-4 **72**................................ AndrewMullen 3 51
(Tom Tate) *chsd ldrs: rdn over 2f out: wknd over 1f out* **10/1**
0000 **9** *3 3/4* **Lastkingofscotland (IRE)**[8] 7307 7-9-1 **69**....................(b) LiamKeniry 2 38
(Conor Dore) *s.i.s: sn pushed along in rr: wknd over 2f out* **25/1**

1m 29.27s (-0.33) **Going Correction** +0.05s/f (Slow)
WFA 3 from 4yo+ 2lb **9** Ran SP% **114.7**
Speed ratings (Par 103): **103,102,102,99,99 97,96,90,86**
toteswingers 1&2 £11.00, 2&3 £4.30, 1&3 £6.00 CSF £86.29 CT £302.27 TOTE £16.00: £3.40, £3.10, £1.40; EX 63.00 Trifecta £406.30 Pool: £2201.37 - 4.06 winning units..
Owner Facts & Figures **Bred** J R Weston **Trained** Norton, N Yorks
■ Stewards' Enquiry : Luke Morris two-day ban: used whip above shoulder height (Nov 7-8)

FOCUS
This modest handicap was run at a sound enough pace.

7487 32RED H'CAP (DIV II) 7f 32y(P)
7:10 (7:11) (Class 5) (0-75,75) 3-Y-O+ **£2,587** (£770; £384; £192) **Stalls** High

Form RPR
3620 **1** **Benoni**[33] 6642 3-9-5 **75**.. DaneO'Neill 2 83
(Henry Candy) *trckd ldrs: nt clr run over 1f out: rdn to ld ins fnl f: r.o* **6/4**[1]
5020 **2** *1/2* **Relight My Fire**[30] 6720 3-8-13 **74**.............................(e[1]) DarylByrne(5) 5 81
(Tim Easterby) *a.p: rdn to ld 1f out: sn hdd: r.o* **25/1**
1265 **3** *1 1/4* **Dodina (IRE)**[22] 6948 3-9-1 **71**.. ShaneKelly 8 74
(Peter Chapple-Hyam) *hld up: nt clr run over 1f out: hdwy sn after: rdn and r.o: nt rch ldrs* **12/1**
0010 **4** *shd* **Dimitar (USA)**[8] 7306 4-9-1 **69**...................................... JimmyFortune 9 73
(Brendan Powell) *hld up: racd keenly: hdwy over 1f out: sn rdn: r.o* **12/1**
4200 **5** *1 1/2* **Lovesome**[42] 6341 3-8-11 **74**.. LouisSteward(7) 3 73
(Michael Bell) *w ldr: pushed along over 2f out: rdn and ev ch whn edgd lft over 1f out: no ex ins fnl f* **25/1**
3150 **6** *2* **Declamation (IRE)**[17] 7076 3-9-2 **72**................................ JoeFanning 6 66
(Mark Johnston) *chsd ldrs: rdn over 1f out: no ex fnl f* **8/1**
0003 **7** *1/2* **Sewn Up**[2] 7444 3-8-12 **68**..(e) TomQueally 7 60
(Andrew Hollinshead) *hld up: pushed along 1/2-way: nvr trbld ldrs* **7/1**[3]
0052 **8** *2 1/2* **Unknown Villain (IRE)**[17] 7065 3-9-4 **74**.................... RichardKingscote 1 59
(Tom Dascombe) *led: rdn and hdd 1f out: wknd and eased wl ins fnl f* **11/4**[2]

1m 29.05s (-0.55) **Going Correction** +0.05s/f (Slow)
WFA 3 from 4yo 2lb **8** Ran SP% **114.3**
Speed ratings (Par 103): **105,104,103,102,101 98,98,95**
toteswingers 1&2 £14.90, 2&3 £113.30, 1&3 £8.30 CSF £43.07 CT £340.45 TOTE £2.70: £1.60, £4.50, £2.70; EX 44.40 Trifecta £169.90 Pool: £2538.72 - 11.20 winning units..
Owner Clayton, Frost, Kebell & Candy **Bred** New Hall Farms Estate **Trained** Kingston Warren, Oxon

FOCUS
The second division of the modest 7f handicap.

7488 32RED.COM MAIDEN STKS 1m 5f 194y(P)
7:40 (7:42) (Class 5) 3-Y-O+ **£2,587** (£770; £384; £192) **Stalls** Low

Form
6 **1** **Great Fighter**[31] 6696 3-9-5 0...................... SilvestreDeSousa 9 91+
(Saeed bin Suroor) *s.i.s: hld up: hdwy on outer to ld over 2f out: rdn clr fr over 1f out* **2/1**[2]
332 **2** *2 3/4* **Flemish School**[26] 6847 3-9-0 75....................................(p) LukeMorris 3 82
(Gerard Butler) *s.i.s: hld up: hdwy over 3f out: rdn and ev ch 2f out: sn outpcd* **7/4**[1]
05 **3** *13* **Summerfree (USA)**[8] 7311 3-9-5 0................................ JoeFanning 1 69
(Mark Johnston) *led: rdn and hdd over 2f out: wknd over 1f out* **10/1**
3433 **4** *7* **Fantasy In Blue**[26] 6847 3-8-11 72........................... ThomasBrown(3) 6 54
(Sir Michael Stoute) *chsd ldrs: rdn over 2f out: sn wknd* **4/1**[3]
0 **5** *hd* **Coconell**[35] 6557 3-9-0 0.. SebSanders 7 54
(Jeremy Noseda) *prom tl rdn and wknd over 2f out* **33/1**
04 **6** *1* **Mrs Micawber**[23] 6926 3-9-0 0...................................... TomQueally 10 52
(Michael Bell) *hld up: racd keenly: hdwy over 2f out: rdn and wknd over 1f out* **6/1**
36 **7** *44* **Quality Alliance**[23] 6926 3-9-0 0............................. FrederikTylicki 5
(James Fanshawe) *prom: rdn over 3f out: sn wknd* **25/1**
05 **8** *8* **Jowhara**[20] 6997 3-9-0 0..[1] DaneO'Neill 2
(Gerard Butler) *sn pushed along to chse ldr: reminders over 6f out: rdn and wknd over 3f out* **66/1**
0 **9** *99* **Lady Faye**[26] 6824 4-9-9 0..[1] RobertWinston 8
(Alan Bailey) *prom: lost pl after 2f: bhd fnl 6f: virtually p.u fnl 3f* **100/1**

3m 2.57s (-3.43) **Going Correction** +0.05s/f (Slow)
WFA 3 from 4yo 9lb **9** Ran SP% **122.3**
Speed ratings (Par 103): **111,109,102,98,97 97,72,67,11**
toteswingers 1&2 £2.10, 2&3 £4.70, 1&3 £4.70 CSF £6.25 TOTE £2.80: £1.50, £1.40, £3.10; EX 9.20 Trifecta £73.30 Pool: £2154.69 - 22.01 winning units..
Owner Godolphin **Bred** Darley **Trained** Newmarket, Suffolk

FOCUS
Straightforward maiden form.

7489 32RED CASINO FILLIES' H'CAP 1m 141y(P)
8:10 (8:11) (Class 5) (0-75,74) 3-Y-O+ **£2,587** (£770; £384; £192) **Stalls** Low

Form RPR
4330 **1** **Capella's Song (IRE)**[28] 6780 3-8-10 **71**.................... LouisSteward(7) 8 79
(Michael Bell) *trckd ldr tl led 3f out: pushed clr and hung rt over 2f out: rdn over 1f out: jst hld on* **8/1**[3]
2136 **2** *nk* **Wakeup Little Suzy (IRE)**[36] 6524 3-9-6 **74**................(t) MartinHarley 1 81
(Marco Botti) *a.p: rdn over 2f out: chsd wnr fnl f: r.o* **8/1**[3]
1565 **3** *1 1/4* **Whispering Lady (IRE)**[77] 5181 3-9-2 **70**........................ TedDurcan 6 74+
(David Simcock) *hld up: drvn along 5f out: nt clr run wl over 1f out: rdn and r.o ins fnl f: nt rch ldrs* **11/4**[2]
1244 **4** *1/2* **Lady Bayside**[10] 7256 5-9-9 **73**................................ TomMcLaughlin 7 76
(Malcolm Saunders) *a.p: rdn over 2f out: sn chsng wnr: styd on same pce fnl f* **20/1**
1533 **5** *nk* **Taxiformissbyron**[7] 7325 3-8-13 **67**.............................. PaulHanagan 3 69
(Michael Herrington) *s.i.s: hld up: rdn over 3f out: r.o ins fnl f: nvr nrr* **8/1**[3]
4600 **6** *4* **Sharp And Smart (IRE)**[21] 6963 4-9-10 **74**.................... JimmyFortune 4 67
(Hughie Morrison) *prom: rdn over 2f out: wknd fnl f* **8/1**[3]
1305 **7** *3 1/4* **First Class Favour (IRE)**[22] 6941 5-8-10 **60**.................(e[1]) DavidAllan 9 45
(Tim Easterby) *hld up: hdwy u.p over 3f out: wknd 2f out* **16/1**
0031 **8** *1* **Natures Law (IRE)**[23] 6918 3-8-9 **63**................................ TomEaves 2 46
(Keith Dalgleish) *trckd ldrs: rdn over 2f out: hmpd and wknd wl over 1f out* **10/1**
031 **9** *11* **You Look So Good**[19] 7037 3-8-10 **64**.............................. AndreaAtzeni 5 22
(Roger Varian) *led: hdd 3f out: sn rdn: wknd over 1f out* **5/2**[1]

1m 50.73s (0.23) **Going Correction** +0.05s/f (Slow)
WFA 3 from 4yo+ 4lb **9** Ran SP% **119.4**
Speed ratings (Par 100): **100,99,98,98,97 94,91,90,80**
toteswingers 1&2 £7.40, 2&3 £16.20, 1&3 £3.00 CSF £72.44 CT £226.08 TOTE £10.70: £2.50, £2.50, £1.20; EX 82.90 Trifecta £366.20 Pool: £2257.14 - 4.62 winning units..
Owner P A Philipps & C E L Philipps **Bred** Churchtown, Lane & Orpendale Bloodstock **Trained** Newmarket, Suffolk

FOCUS
Not a bad fillies' handicap for the class, run at an average pace.

7490 32REDBINGO.COM MEDIAN AUCTION MAIDEN STKS 1m 1f 103y(P)
8:40 (8:41) (Class 6) 3-5-Y-O **£1,940** (£577; £288; £144) **Stalls** Low

Form RPR
233 **1** **Mahdiyah**[14] 7158 3-9-0 72.. PaulHanagan 5 77+
(Saeed bin Suroor) *mde all: rdn clr fr over 1f out: styd on wl* **4/6**[1]
2 **2** *7* **Memphis Magic (GER)**[13] 7167 3-9-5 0.......................(t) GeorgeBaker 3 67
(Ed Walker) *chsd wnr tl over 6f out: wnt 2nd again over 2f out: rdn and hung lft fr over 1f out: no ex fnl f* **12/1**
64 **3** *4 1/2* **Wall Street Boss (USA)**[50] 6116 3-9-5 0..................... FrederikTylicki 7 58
(James Fanshawe) *hld up: pushed along over 2f out: hung lft and styd on ins fnl f: nvr nrr* **4/1**[3]
50 **4** *1 1/4* **Lalinde**[112] 3989 3-9-0 0...[1] RichardKingscote 8 50
(Daniel Kubler) *trckd ldrs: racd keenly: rdn over 2f out: hung lft and wknd over 1f out* **66/1**
0 **5** *1 3/4* **Exotic Lady (IRE)**[10] 7253 3-9-0 0.................................. LiamKeniry 2 47
(Sylvester Kirk) *prom: rdn over 3f out: wknd over 1f out* **25/1**
060- **6** *2* **Ossie's Dancer**[457] 4440 4-9-9 41................................... JoeFanning 9 47
(Martin Smith) *s.s: rdn over 3f out: a in rr* **100/1**
62 **7** *1/2* **Bison Grass**[17] 7067 3-9-5 0....................................(b) SebSanders 6 46
(Giles Bravery) *s.i.s: hld up: plld hrd: hdwy over 2f out: wknd over 1f out* **11/4**[2]
0-0 **8** *1 1/4* **Granule**[167] 2206 3-9-0 0... ShaneKelly 10 39
(Peter Chapple-Hyam) *hld up: a in rr: drvn along over 3f out: no ch whn hung lft over 1f out* **16/1**
4 **9** *12* **Ghetto Diva**[131] 3327 3-9-0 0.. LukeMorris 4 13
(Daniel Kubler) *chsd ldrs: wnt 2nd over 6f out tl rdn over 2f out: hung lft and wknd over 1f out* **50/1**

2m 2.55s (0.85) **Going Correction** +0.05s/f (Slow)
WFA 3 from 4yo 4lb **9** Ran SP% **128.5**
Speed ratings (Par 101): **98,91,87,86,85 83,82,81,71**
toteswingers 1&2 £2.60, 2&3 £4.50, 1&3 £2.10 CSF £13.44 TOTE £1.70: £1.10, £2.70, £2.00; EX 15.20 Trifecta £36.50 Pool: £2688.28 - 55.14 winning units..
Owner Godolphin **Bred** Shadwell Estate Company Limited **Trained** Newmarket, Suffolk

FOCUS
One-way traffic for the well-backed winner.

7491 £32 BONUS AT 32RED.COM H'CAP 1m 1f 103y(P)
9:10 (9:11) (Class 5) (0-75,75) 3-Y-O £2,587 (£770; £384; £192) Stalls Low

Form RPR
-410 **1** **Soul Intent (IRE)**[132] 3294 3-9-4 **72**................................ GeorgeBaker 4 86+
(J W Hills) *hld up: hdwy over 1f out: rdn and r.o to ld nr fin* **5/1**[2]
1466 **2** ½ **Off The Pulse**[37] 6495 3-9-7 **75**................................ GrahamGibbons 9 88
(John Mackie) *hld up: hdwy on outer over 2f out: rdn to ld over 1f out: edgd lft ins fnl f: hdd nr fin* **11/2**[3]
0-32 **3** 2 ½ **Muthafar (IRE)**[41] 6366 3-9-2 **70**................................ PaulHanagan 5 78
(William Haggas) *trckd ldrs: rdn over 1f out: styd on same pce fnl f: wnt 3rd post* **3/1**[1]
1335 **4** *nk* **Lyric Piece**[7] 7330 3-9-5 **73**................................(p) CathyGannon 7 80
(Sir Mark Prescott Bt) *sn pushed along to chse ldrs: rdn to ld 2f out: hdd over 1f out: edgd lft and no ex ins fnl f: lost 3rd post* **3/1**[1]
305 **5** *7* **Arlecchino (IRE)**[45] 6258 3-9-3 **71**................................(b) SeanLevey 1 64
(Ed McMahon) *mid-div: rdn and nt clr run over 2f out: n.d* **16/1**
564 **6** 1 ¼ **Tribal Path (IRE)**[21] 6970 3-8-12 **66**................................ JoeFanning 3 56
(Mark Johnston) *trckd ldrs: rdn over 2f out: wknd fnl f* **12/1**
2615 **7** *9* **Madame Elizabeth**[10] 7256 3-9-7 **75**................................ LiamKeniry 6 46
(Andrew Hollinshead) *trckd ldr: rdn over 2f out: wknd over 1f out* **16/1**
12-0 **8** *nk* **Seaside Rock (IRE)**[133] 3241 3-9-2 **70**................................ TomEaves 2 41
(Keith Dalgleish) *hld up: drvn along over 5f out: wknd over 2f out* **16/1**
3200 **9** *11* **Corn Snow (USA)**[11] 7224 3-9-7 **75**................................ SilvestreDeSousa 8 22
(Mark Johnston) *led: rdn and hdd 2f out: eased fnl f* **6/1**

2m 1.32s (-0.38) **Going Correction** +0.05s/f (Slow) **9 Ran SP% 121.7**
Speed ratings (Par 101): **103,102,100,100,93 92,84,84,74**
toteswingers 1&2 £8.10, 2&3 £6.50, 1&3 £3.00 CSF £34.57 CT £99.14 TOTE £6.40: £2.00, £2.40, £1.30; EX 34.20 Trifecta £190.80 Pool: £2728.51 - 10.72 winning units..
Owner Andy Weller & Gary Styles **Bred** Flamingo Guitar Syndicate **Trained** Upper Lambourn, Berks

FOCUS
Fair AW form.
T/Jkpt: Part won. £39,096.90 to a £1 stake. Pool of £55066.15 - 0.50 winning tickets. T/Plt: £173.20 to a £1 stake. Pool of £109051.90 - 459.48 winning tickets. T/Qpdt: £9.10 to a £1 stake. Pool of £11864.60 - 956.38 winning tickets. CR

6390 DONCASTER (L-H)
Friday, October 25

OFFICIAL GOING: Soft (good to soft in places) changing to soft after race 1 (1:40)
Wind: fresh 1/2 against Weather: fine but becoming breezy

7492 RACING POST WEEKENDER NURSERY H'CAP 1m (S)
1:40 (1:42) (Class 3) (0-95,88) 2-Y-O £6,469 (£1,925; £962; £481) Stalls High

Form RPR
0212 **1** **Hartnell**[23] 6955 2-9-7 **88**................................ JoeFanning 3 94
(Mark Johnston) *racd towards centre: cl up: led 1/2-way: rdn clr wl over 1f out: edgd lft and styd on strly fnl f* **4/1**[1]
5223 **2** *4* **Our Gabrial (IRE)**[56] 5945 2-8-7 **74**................................ PaulHanagan 1 71
(Richard Fahey) *racd centre: trckd wnr: effrt 3f out and sn rdn: drvn over 1f out: no imp fnl f* **9/1**
41 **3** ¾ **Mr Gallivanter (IRE)**[33] 6666 2-9-0 **81**................................ MichaelO'Connell 2 77
(John Quinn) *racd towards centre: trckd ldrs: hdwy wl over 3f out: rdn along wl over 2f out: drvn wl over 1f out and kpt on same pce* **16/1**
621 **4** *7* **Act Of Charity (IRE)**[29] 6773 2-9-2 **83**................................ MartinHarley 5 63+
(Marco Botti) *hld up: hdwy over 3f out: chsd ldrs 2f out: sn rdn and one pce* **11/2**[2]
0420 **5** *shd* **Dalaki (IRE)**[29] 6763 2-8-2 **69**................................(b) MartinLane 6 49+
(Clive Brittain) *dwlt and in rr: hdwy 1/2-way: rdn along over 3f out: chsd ldrs over 2f out: sn drvn and no imp* **33/1**
443 **6** *7* **Rock 'N' Roll Star**[56] 5968 2-8-10 **77**................................ LukeMorris 9 42
(Charles Hills) *a towards rr* **11/2**[2]
21 **7** *nk* **Desert Society (IRE)**[17] 7089 2-8-12 **79**................................ PatDobbs 8 43
(Richard Hannon) *in tch: rdn along wl over 3f out: wknd over 2f out* **13/2**[3]
103 **8** 2 ¾ **Belayer (IRE)**[48] 6194 2-8-10 **77**................................ TomEaves 4 35
(Kevin Ryan) *prom towards stands' rail: rdn along over 3f out: sn wknd* **11/1**
421 **9** *3* **Mayfield Boy**[14] 7175 2-8-11 **78**................................ DavidAllan 7 29
(Mel Brittain) *racd nr stands' rail: sn led: pushed along over 4f out: hdd 1/2-way and sn: rdn: wknd 3f out* **13/2**[3]
4661 **10** 2 ¼ **Ahoy There (IRE)**[9] 7309 2-8-1 **68** 6ex................................ AndrewMullen 10 14
(Tom Tate) *racd nr stands' rail: cl up: rdn along 1/2-way: sn wknd* **8/1**

1m 45.48s (6.18) **Going Correction** +0.75s/f (Yiel) **10 Ran SP% 115.7**
Speed ratings (Par 99): **99,95,94,87,87 80,79,77,74,71**
toteswingers 1&2 £8.10, 1&3 £11.90, 2&3 £26.50 CSF £40.22 CT £406.89 TOTE £4.40: £2.00, £3.20, £6.30; EX 42.90 Trifecta £524.10 Pool: £2,451.25 - 3.50 winning units..
Owner Sheikh Hamdan Bin Mohammed Al Maktoum **Bred** Darley **Trained** Middleham Moor, N Yorks

FOCUS
With five last-time-out winners in attendance this was a highly competitive nursery on paper. There was a difference of opinion as to the best ground, but it was the trio that kept towards the centre who dominated.

7493 PIONEERFURNITURE.CO.UK LEISURE AND HOSPITALITY MANUFACTURERS EBF MAIDEN FILLIES' STKS 1m (S)
2:10 (2:14) (Class 5) 2-Y-O £2,911 (£866; £432; £216) Stalls High

Form RPR
022 **1** **Regardez**[23] 6949 2-9-0 **79**................................ RichardKingscote 5 83+
(Ralph Beckett) *w ldr: led over 2f out: styd on strly to forge clr fnl f* **6/4**[1]
0 **2** *4* **Arabian Beauty (IRE)**[17] 7103 2-9-0 **0**................................ MickaelBarzalona 15 73
(Saeed bin Suroor) *hld up in rr: hdwy and swtchd rt over 2f out: hung lft and styd on to take 2nd clsng stages* **14/1**
00 **3** 1 ¼ **Broughtons Secret**[20] 7016 2-9-0 **0**................................ RobertWinston 6 70
(Willie Musson) *trckd ldrs: upsides over 2f out: chsd wnr over 1f out: styd on same pce* **13/2**
4 ¾ **Natural Choice** 2-9-0 **0**................................ KierenFallon 4 69+
(Saeed bin Suroor) *mid-div: hdwy over 3f out: 3rd over 1f out: kpt on same pce* **6/1**[3]
5 1 ¼ **Micras** 2-9-0 **0**................................ LiamKeniry 11 66+
(Andrew Balding) *chsd ldrs: drvn over 2f out: one pce* **66/1**
63 **6** *hd* **Layla's Red Devil (IRE)**[11] 7237 2-9-0 **0**................................ PaulHanagan 10 66
(Richard Fahey) *chsd ldrs: drvn over 2f out: one pce* **11/1**
7 1 ½ **Aurora Borealis (IRE)** 2-9-0 **0**................................ MartinHarley 9 62+
(Ed Dunlop) *in rr: hdwy over 2f out: kpt on fnl f* **25/1**
6 **8** 1 ¼ **Saythatagain (IRE)**[13] 7209 2-9-0 **0**................................ DavidAllan 14 60
(Tim Easterby) *in rr: hdwy over 2f out: wknd over 1f out* **33/1**
9 ½ **Telegraphy (USA)** 2-9-0 **0**................................ TedDurcan 7 58
(Ed Dunlop) *dwlt: in rr: hdwy to chse ldrs over 3f out: wknd over 1f out* **33/1**
4 **10** *nk* **Joys Of Spring (IRE)**[17] 7102 2-9-0 **0**................................ AndreaAtzeni 1 58
(Luca Cumani) *chsd ldrs: upsides over 2f out: wknd fnl f* **11/2**[2]
11 *11* **Alps** 2-9-0 **0**................................ MartinLane 8 34
(David Simcock) *s.i.s: in rr: hung rt over 2f out: sn bhd* **40/1**
12 2 ¾ **Minionette (IRE)** 2-9-0 **0**................................ AndrewMullen 12 28
(Alan Swinbank) *dwlt: sn mid-div: drvn over 3f out: lost pl over 2f out: sn bhd* **100/1**
0 **13** *14* **Sultanty**[9] 7294 2-9-0 **0**................................ TomEaves 2
(Kevin Ryan) *led: hdd over 2f out: hung rt and lost pl over 1f out: sn bhd: eased ins fnl f* **33/1**

1m 46.79s (7.49) **Going Correction** +0.75s/f (Yiel) **13 Ran SP% 115.6**
Speed ratings (Par 92): **92,88,86,86,84 84,83,81,81,81 70,67,53**
toteswingers 1&2 £6.20, 1&3 £3.20, 2&3 £12.70 CSF £23.00 TOTE £2.30: £1.40, £4.00, £1.80; EX 24.10 Trifecta £140.60 Pool: £3354.41 - 17.88 winning units..
Owner J H Richmond-Watson **Bred** Lawn Stud **Trained** Kimpton, Hants

FOCUS
An average fillies' maiden. The winner probably only needed replicate her previous run to win.

7494 INITIATEC CCTV EBF MAIDEN STKS 7f
2:40 (2:43) (Class 5) 2-Y-O £2,911 (£866; £432; £216) Stalls High

Form RPR
1 **End Of Line** 2-9-5 **0**................................ HarryBentley 11 90+
(Andrew Balding) *dwlt and hld up towards rr: smooth hdwy on outer over 2f out: chal over 1f out: led ent fnl f: sn rdn clr: readily* **25/1**
2 *6* **Yagheer (IRE)** 2-9-5 **0**................................ AndreaAtzeni 15 75
(Roger Varian) *hld up in tch: hdwy wl over 2f out: chsd ldrs whn n.m.r over 1f out: rdn and styd on to chse wnr ins fnl f: sn no imp* **15/2**[3]
6 **3** 2 ¼ **Wannabe Yours (IRE)**[20] 7019 2-9-5 **0**................................ RobertHavlin 3 69
(John Gosden) *led: rdn along 2f out: jnd over 1f out: edgd lft and hdd ent fnl f: sn one pce* **5/2**[2]
2343 **4** ¾ **Bon Voyage**[20] 7017 2-9-5 **98**................................ PatDobbs 12 67
(Richard Hannon) *prom: cl up 1/2-way: rdn along over 2f out: wknd wl over 1f out* **6/5**[1]
5 *nk* **Racing's Dream** 2-9-5 **0**................................ MartinLane 16 66+
(Brian Meehan) *trckd ldrs: hdwy on outer 3f out: effrt 2f out: sn rdn and one pce* **50/1**
6 ¾ **Zilber (GER)** 2-9-5 **0**................................ GrahamLee 8 65
(Ed Dunlop) *hld up: hdwy and in tch: 3f: pushed along over 2f out: sn no imp* **12/1**
6000 **7** 3 ½ **Petergate**[14] 7175 2-9-5 **58**................................ BarryMcHugh 10 56
(Brian Rothwell) *in rr tl styd on fr over 2f out: nvr nr ldrs* **100/1**
05 **8** *7* **Green Zone (IRE)**[14] 7175 2-9-5 **0**................................ AndrewMullen 9 38
(Nigel Tinkler) *trckd ldrs: pushed along 4f out: rdn 3f out: grad wknd* **20/1**
9 3 ¼ **High Secret (IRE)** 2-9-5 **0**................................ LukeMorris 1 30
(Sir Mark Prescott Bt) *s.i.s and wnt lft s: a bhd* **66/1**
50 **10** *7* **Mighty Missile (IRE)**[20] 7023 2-9-5 **0**................................ RobertWinston 7 13
(Tom Tate) *prom: rdn along 1/2-way: sn wknd* **66/1**
11 *shd* **Fennann** 2-9-5 **0**................................ DominicFox 4 12
(Roger Varian) *dwlt and green: a outpcd and wl bhd fr 1/2-way* **16/1**
00 **12** *8* **Elle West**[13] 7209 2-9-0 **0**................................ GrahamGibbons 14
(Michael Easterby) *cl up: rdn along 1/2-way: sn wknd* **100/1**
440 **13** *19* **Doncaster Belle (IRE)**[20] 7032 2-9-0 **54**................................ RobbieFitzpatrick 5
(Charles Smith) *chsd ldrs: rdn along 4f out: sn lost pl and bhd* **100/1**
5 **14** 2 ½ **Piton**[10] 7271 2-9-5 **0**................................ JoeFanning 2
(Mark Johnston) *chsd ldrs: rdn along bef 1/2-way: sn wknd and bhd* **40/1**

1m 32.2s (5.90) **Going Correction** +0.75s/f (Yiel) **14 Ran SP% 118.3**
Speed ratings (Par 95): **96,89,86,85,85 84,80,72,68,60 60,51,29,26**
toteswingers 1&2 £36.70, 1&3 £13.20, 2&3 £3.60 CSF £192.48 TOTE £38.60: £7.20, £1.90, £2.30; EX 312.20 Trifecta £2552.50 Pool: £4380.18 - 1.28 winning units..
Owner Qatar Racing Limited **Bred** Carmel Stud **Trained** Kingsclere, Hants

FOCUS
A fair maiden and an impressive winner.

7495 RACING POST/SIS BETTING SHOP MANAGER H'CAP 6f
3:10 (3:15) (Class 2) (0-105,105) 3-Y-O+£12,291 (£3,657; £1,370; £1,370) Stalls High

Form RPR
3020 **1** **Morache Music**[20] 7013 5-9-7 **102**................................ AndrewMullen 22 110
(Peter Makin) *towards rr: hdwy stands' side over 2f out: swtchd lft and chsd ldr over 1f out: styd on to ld last 50yds* **25/1**
2025 **2** *nk* **Spinatrix**[13] 7208 5-9-5 **105**................................(p) ConnorBeasley[(5)] 4 112
(Michael Dods) *led: edgd rt to stands' side over 2f out: hdd and no ex wl ins fnl f* **14/1**
5420 **3** *1* **Misplaced Fortune**[11] 7241 8-8-5 **89**................................(v) JasonHart[(3)] 20 93
(Nigel Tinkler) *chsd ldrs stands' side: kpt on same pce fnl f* **25/1**
0530 **3** *dht* **Flyman**[21] 6993 3-8-8 **90**................................(b[1]) PaulHanagan 6 94
(Richard Fahey) *mid-div: hdwy far side to chse ldrs over 2f out: kpt on same pce ins fnl f* **16/1**
0000 **5** ½ **Prodigality**[20] 7013 5-9-0 **95**................................ LukeMorris 18 98
(Ronald Harris) *in rr-div: swtchd rt over 4f out: hdwy towards stands' side 2f out: styd on fnl f* **16/1**
0020 **6** 1 ½ **Fast Shot**[27] 6845 5-8-9 **90**................................ DavidAllan 9 88
(Tim Easterby) *mid-div: hdwy over 2f out: n.m.r jst ins fnl f: kpt on* **16/1**
0411 **7** *nk* **Lancelot Du Lac (ITY)**[47] 6238 3-9-2 **98**................................ RobertWinston 19 95+
(Dean Ivory) *hld up in rr: hdwy over 2f out: chsng ldrs 1f out: kpt on same pce* **8/1**[2]
6000 **8** *hd* **Our Jonathan**[6] 7368 6-9-0 **95**................................ HarryBentley 7 92
(David Simcock) *prom: drvn over 2f out: kpt on same pce over 1f out* **6/1**[1]
0020 **9** ¾ **Louis The Pious**[13] 7208 5-9-4 **99**................................ DanielTudhope 13 93
(David O'Meara) *mid-div: effrt over 2f out: kpt on fnl f* **10/1**[3]
0630 **10** *nse* **Yeeoow (IRE)**[34] 6621 4-8-11 **92**................................ MartinHarley 14 86
(K R Burke) *in rr: hdwy over 1f out: keeping on at fin* **11/1**
1603 **11** ¾ **Gramercy (IRE)**[6] 7368 6-8-9 **93**................................(be) DarrenEgan[(3)] 17 85
(David Simcock) *in rr: swtchd centre 3f out: edgd lft and sme hdwy over 1f out: nvr a factor* **8/1**[2]
3000 **12** *nk* **Secret Witness**[13] 7208 7-9-3 **98**................................(b) AndreaAtzeni 16 89
(Ronald Harris) *swtchd lft after s: t.k.h in rr: kpt on fnl 2f: nvr a factor* **33/1**

The Form Book Flat, Raceform Ltd, Compton, RG20 6NL.

3010 **13** *nse* **Royal Rock**[20] 7014 9-9-9 **104** .... TedDurcan 21 95
(Chris Wall) *hld up in rr: sme hdwy stands' side over 1f out: nvr a factor* **33/1**

1320 **14** *hd* **Clear Spring (IRE)**[34] 6621 5-8-9 **93** .... WilliamTwiston-Davies(3) 8 83
(John Spearing) *mid-div: effrt over 2f out: kpt on fnl f* **25/1**

0100 **15** *1* **Pearl Ice**[6] 7368 5-8-13 **94** .... GrahamGibbons 15 81
(David Barron) *chsd ldrs: drvn over 2f out: wknd over 1f out* **14/1**

3164 **16** *hd* **Secret Look**[32] 6685 3-8-9 **91** .... GrahamLee 3 78
(Ed McMahon) *chsd ldrs: drvn over 2f out: wknd appr fnl f* **25/1**

3100 **17** *2* **Bop It**[14] 7171 4-8-6 **87** .... JoeFanning 1 68
(David O'Meara) *w ldrs far side: wknd over 1f out* **20/1**

6350 **18** *6* **Birdman (IRE)**[21] 6990 3-9-1 **97** .... MartinLane 5 60
(David Simcock) *chsd ldrs: wkng whn hmpd over 1f out* **40/1**

0300 **19** *3* **Rodrigo De Torres**[27] 6845 6-8-10 **91** .... TonyHamilton 11 45
(David Nicholls) *chsd ldrs stands' side: wknd 2f out* **50/1**

0010 **20** *3 ¾* **Ancient Cross**[13] 7208 9-9-6 **101** .... (tp) PatCosgrave 10 43
(Michael Easterby) *dwlt: a in rr* **25/1**

4213 **21** *2* **Kyllachy Rise**[26] 6871 3-8-10 **92** .... PatDobbs 12 28
(Richard Hannon) *mid-div: effrt over 2f out: sn lost pl* **10/1**[3]

1m 16.52s (2.92) **Going Correction** +0.75s/f (Yiel)
WFA 3 from 4yo+ 1lb **21** Ran SP% **128.3**
Speed ratings (Par 109): **110,109,107,107,107 105,104,104,103,103 102,102,102,101,100 100,97,89,85,80 77**
PL: £5.30 Flyman, £4.80 Misplaced Fortune EX: £456.60; CSF: £319.06; TC: MM&SP&MF£4362.62, MM&SP&FL £2903.30; toteswingers 1&2 £37.00, 2&MF £74.10, 1&F £54.80, 2&F £25.50, 1&MF £74.10 TOTE £22.10: £5.20, £3.20 TRIFECTA Not won..
Owner R P Marchant D M Ahier Mrs E Lee **Bred** Michael E Broughton **Trained** Ogbourne Maisey, Wilts
■ Stewards' Enquiry : Andrew Mullen four-day ban: use of whi[(8, 9, 11, 12 Nov)

FOCUS
This was ultra-competitive. They went a solid early pace and once more the centre of the straight was favoured, but the first pair were stands' side in the final furlong.

7496 DONCASTER MINI H'CAP — 1m 6f 132y
3:45 (3:46) (Class 3) (0-95,96) 3-Y-0+ **£7,439** (£2,213; £1,106; £553) **Stalls** Low

Form RPR

2-44 **1** **White Nile (IRE)**[38] 6499 4-9-1 **82** .... MartinHarley 2 92
(David Simcock) *a.p: hdwy to chal over 2f out: rdn to ld wl over 1f out: drvn ins fnl f: hld on gamely towards fin* **5/1**[2]

0215 **2** *shd* **Zipp (IRE)**[34] 6649 3-8-4 **80** .... AndreaAtzeni 12 90
(Charles Hills) *hld up in midfield: hdwy on outer over 3f out: chsd ldrs and swtchd lft over 1f out: sn rdn: n.m.r ins fnl f: drvn and styd on wl towards fin: jst failed* **4/1**[1]

0025 **3** *hd* **Mister Impatience**[23] 6957 3-9-3 **96** .... MichaelJMMurphy(3) 3 105
(Mark Johnston) *led 1 1/2f: trckd ldrs: hdwy on outer 4f out: rdn along wl over 2f out: chal over 1f out and ev ch tl drvn ins fnl f and no ex towards fin* **13/2**[3]

0400 **4** *2 ½* **High Office**[13] 7193 7-8-9 **76** oh1 .... PaulHanagan 7 81
(Richard Fahey) *prom: hdwy to chal 4f out: rdn along over 2f out: drvn and ev ch over 1f out: hld and one pce whn n.m.r jst ins fnl f* **14/1**

0210 **5** *1* **Linguine (FR)**[21] 6992 3-9-0 **90** .... AdamKirby 11 94
(Seamus Durack) *cl up: led after 1 1/2f: rdn along over 4f out: drvn and hdd wl over 1f out: grad wknd* **12/1**

5030 **6** *2* **Brockwell**[13] 7193 4-9-10 **91** .... RichardKingscote 4 92
(Tom Dascombe) *hld up: hdwy to chses 5f out: rdn along 3f out: sn drvn and one pce* **9/1**

3210 **7** *2 ¼* **Discay**[11] 7239 4-9-4 **85** .... JoeFanning 14 84
(Mark Johnston) *hld up towards rr: hdwy 5f out: rdn to chse ldrs wl over 2f out: sn drvn and one pce* **20/1**

0230 **8** *1 ½* **Jonny Delta**[13] 7193 6-8-13 **80** .... GrahamLee 10 77
(Jim Goldie) *hld up in rr: sme hdwy 4f out: rdn along 3f out: sn one pce* **10/1**

3300 **9** *1 ½* **Twelve Strings (IRE)**[13] 7210 4-8-11 **81** .... (v[1]) RobertTart(3) 1 76
(Brian Ellison) *hld up towards rr: sme hdwy 5f out: rdn along 4f out: sn one pce* **15/2**

5010 **10** *10* **Sirvino**[34] 6626 8-9-7 **91** .... LMcNiff(3) 9 73
(David Barron) *hld up: a towards rr* **20/1**

6340 **11** *16* **All The Aces (IRE)**[35] 6591 8-9-9 **90** .... TomQueally 6 51
(Nicky Henderson) *hld up in rr: rdn along over 4f out: nvr a factor* **16/1**

1130 **12** *1 ¾* **Kiwayu**[14] 7174 4-9-6 **87** .... (p) MichaelO'Connell 5 46
(Philip Kirby) *trckd ldrs on inner: rdn along 4f out: sn wknd* **12/1**

1103 **13** *3 ¼* **Almagest**[18] 7064 5-9-6 **87** .... DanielTudhope 8 41
(David O'Meara) *a in rr: rdn along over 4f out: sn outpcd* **33/1**

3m 19.05s (11.65) **Going Correction** +1.00s/f (Soft)
WFA 3 from 4yo+ 9lb **13** Ran SP% **121.3**
Speed ratings (Par 107): **108,107,107,106,105 104,103,102,102,96 88,87,85**
toteswingers 1&2 £4.90, 1&3 £7.20, 2&3 £5.20 CSF £24.97 CT £135.32 TOTE £6.50: £2.60, £2.10, £3.30; EX 40.20 Trifecta £225.10 Pool: £3387.07 - 11.28 winning units..
Owner Sir Robert Ogden **Bred** Super Gift Syndicate **Trained** Newmarket, Suffolk
■ Stewards' Enquiry : Michael J M Murphy 11-day ban: use of whip (8, 9, 11 - 16, 18-20 Nov)

FOCUS
A fair staying handicap which served up a real test and it saw a cracking three-way finish.

7497 ARTSIGN H'CAP — 1m 2f 60y
4:20 (4:20) (Class 3) (0-95,95) 3-Y-O **£7,439** (£2,213; £1,106; £553) **Stalls** Low

Form RPR

440 **1** **Stepping Ahead (FR)**[41] 6396 3-9-1 **89** .... DanielTudhope 5 98
(K R Burke) *trckd ldrs: led after 2f: stepped up pce 6f out: edgd rt fnl f: hld on wl* **25/1**

1335 **2** *1 ½* **Madame Vestris (IRE)**[32] 6693 3-8-7 **81** oh1 .... JimmyQuinn 9 87
(Sir Michael Stoute) *chsd ldrs: 2nd over 7f out: drvn 3f out: rallied to chse wnr last 75yds* **16/1**

1-12 **3** *1* **Ajman Bridge**[20] 7022 3-9-3 **91** .... AndreaAtzeni 1 95
(Luca Cumani) *led 2f: chsd ldrs: end over 1f out: kpt on same pce* **7/2**[2]

4135 **4** *4* **Matrooh (USA)**[106] 4214 3-8-13 **87** .... PaulHanagan 6 84
(William Haggas) *trckd ldrs: drvn 3f out: one pce: wknd last 100yds* **3/1**[1]

0526 **5** *2 ¾* **Cruck Realta**[20] 7022 3-9-2 **90** .... MartinHarley 3 81
(Mick Channon) *trckd ldrs: effrt 3f out: wknd fnl f* **11/1**

-510 **6** *6* **Spirit Of Rio (IRE)**[59] 5860 3-8-7 **81** oh1 .... GrahamGibbons 4 61
(David Barron) *hld up in rr: drvn over 5f out: sme hdwy over 3f out: wknd over 2f out* **20/1**

-116 **7** *nk* **Zain Eagle**[27] 6823 3-9-7 **95** .... AdamKirby 7 74
(Gerard Butler) *hld up in rr: rffort over 4f out: hung lft and wknd over 2f out* **7/2**[2]

15 **8** *1 ¼* **Groundbreaking**[61] 5792 3-9-1 **89** .... MickaelBarzalona 8 66
(Charlie Appleby) *hld up in rr: drvn over 3f out: hung lft: wknd 2f out* **4/1**[3]

2m 17.93s (8.53) **Going Correction** +1.00s/f (Soft) **8** Ran SP% **112.3**
Speed ratings (Par 105): **105,103,103,99,97 92,92,91**
toteswingers 1&2 £17.40, 1&3 £15.10, 2&3 £6.00 CSF £344.02 CT £1742.13 TOTE £26.20: £5.80, £2.70, £1.40; EX 313.30 Trifecta £2242.70 Part won. Pool: £2990.64 - 0.72 winning units..
Owner Mark James & Mrs Elaine Burke **Bred** S C E A Haras De Manneville **Trained** Middleham Moor, N Yorks

FOCUS
A decent handicap.

7498 AMATEUR JOCKEYS ASSOCIATION AMATEUR RIDERS' H'CAP — 1m 2f 60y
4:50 (4:51) (Class 5) (0-75,78) 3-Y-O+ **£2,495** (£774; £386; £193) **Stalls** Low

Form RPR

0023 **1** **Dark Ruler (IRE)**[4] 7425 4-10-5 **70** .... MrORJSangster(5) 19 83
(Alan Swinbank) *in tch: gd hdwy on outer to ld over 4f out: rdn 2f out: sn jnd and hdd appr fnl f: cl up whn bmpd jst ins fnl f: rallied gamely to ld last 75yds* **9/2**[2]

2631 **2** *½* **Ty Gwr**[10] 7275 4-11-4 **78** 6ex .... MrSWalker 14 90
(Brian Ellison) *dwlt and hld up towards rr: stdy hdwy 4f out: trckd ldrs over 2f out: effrt to ld jst over 1f out: rdn and hung lft ins fnl f: hdd and no ex last 75yds* **5/4**[1]

1-0 **3** *1 ¾* **Muhtaris (IRE)**[11] 7257 3-10-5 **75** .... MrAlexFerguson(5) 10 84
(Saeed bin Suroor) *hld up: hdwy 3f out: rdn to chse ldrs 2f out: styd on fnl f: nrst fin* **13/2**[3]

0000 **4** *7* **Choisan (IRE)**[27] 6846 4-10-9 **74** .... MrWEasterby(5) 3 70
(Tim Easterby) *in tch: hdwy over 4f out: sn chsng ldrs: rdn along over 2f out: kpt on one pce* **25/1**

410 **5** *7* **Skyfire**[35] 6600 6-10-1 **64** .... (p) MissAliceMills(3) 12 48
(Nick Kent) *led 1f: prom: effrt and cl up over 4f out: rdn along whn n.m.r over 2f out: sn drvn and wknd* **20/1**

2310 **6** *nk* **Jordaura**[4] 7425 7-10-10 **73** .... MissJRRichards(3) 4 56
(Alan Berry) *hld up and bhd: hdwy over 3f out: kpt on fnl 2f: nvr nr ldrs* **20/1**

1200 **7** *1 ¼* **Eeny Mac (IRE)**[20] 7024 6-10-12 **72** .... MissCWalton 18 53
(Neville Bycroft) *dwlt and bhd tl styd on fr wl over 2f out: nvr nr ldrs* **25/1**

600 **8** *3 ½* **Zainda (IRE)**[79] 5144 3-9-2 **60** oh8 .... MrAFrench(7) 1 35
(John Wainwright) *nvr bttr than midfield* **100/1**

0-05 **9** *9* **Stadium Of Light (IRE)**[3] 7440 6-9-7 **60** oh15 ... MissMeganHarris(7) 15 18
(Shaun Harris) *midfield: hdwy to join ldrs 1/2-way: cl up over 4f out: sn rdn along and wknd 3f out* **50/1**

4640 **10** *nk* **Another For Joe**[15] 7152 5-10-8 **68** .... MrsCBartley 13 26
(Jim Goldie) *in tch: hdwy to chse ldrs 1/2-way: rdn along 3f out: sn drvn and wknd over 2f out* **16/1**

3140 **11** *2 ½* **Ailsa Craig (IRE)**[17] 7100 7-10-12 **72** .... (p) MrJHamilton 8 25
(Edwin Tuer) *midfield: hdwy 1/2-way: rdn along over 3f out: sn btn* **25/1**

265- **12** *1* **Travis County (IRE)**[153] 8142 4-9-12 **63** .... [1] MrJohnWilley(5) 11 15
(Brian Ellison) *a towards rr* **16/1**

6200 **13** *2 ¾* **Singzak**[104] 4313 5-10-11 **74** .... MissJoannaMason(3) 7 21
(Michael Easterby) *nvr bttr than midfield* **33/1**

3005 **14** *5* **Monthly Medal**[11] 7238 10-9-13 **62** oh8 ow2 .... (t) MissSMDoolan(3) 20
(Wilf Storey) *a towards rr* **50/1**

2600 **15** *3 ¼* **Triple Eight (IRE)**[13] 7211 5-10-9 **74** .... (b) MrPDennis(5) 6 6
(Philip Kirby) *midfield: rdn along over 4f out: sn wknd* **20/1**

3240 **16** *23* **Munaawib**[116] 3909 5-9-9 **60** oh6 .... MrBenFfrenchDavis(5) 16
(Charles Smith) *cl up: rdn along 4f out: wknd over 3f out* **66/1**

0103 **17** *7* **City Ground (USA)**[48] 6217 6-10-5 **65** .... (v[1]) MissSBrotherton 9
(Michael Easterby) *chsd ldrs: rdn along over 4f out: sn wknd* **25/1**

-006 **18** *13* **Narcissist (IRE)**[80] 5086 4-10-9 **74** .... MrHAABannister(5) 17
(Michael Easterby) *cl up: slt ld after 1f: rdn along and hdd 1/2-way: sn wknd* **33/1**

2m 18.5s (9.10) **Going Correction** +1.00s/f (Soft)
WFA 3 from 4yo+ 5lb **18** Ran SP% **129.7**
Speed ratings (Par 103): **103,102,101,95,90 89,88,85,78,78 76,75,73,69,66 48,42,32**
toteswingers 1&2 £2.80, 1&3 £5.80, 2&3 £4.10 CSF £9.25 CT £41.26 TOTE £5.40: £1.60, £1.30, £1.90, £5.40; EX 15.00 Trifecta £88.00 Pool: £3971.93 - 33.82 winning units..
Owner Kenneth Walters **Bred** John Thompson **Trained** Melsonby, N Yorks
■ Stewards' Enquiry : Mr H A A Bannister five-day ban: use of whip (TBC)

FOCUS
There was no hanging about in this handicap for amateur riders and the form looks straightforward.

7499 EUROPEAN ASSOCIATION OF RACING SCHOOLS APPRENTICE H'CAP — 1m (S)
5:20 (5:22) (Class 4) (0-85,85) 3-Y-O+ **£6,469** (£1,925; £962; £481) **Stalls** High

Form RPR

0504 **1** **Hefner (IRE)**[13] 7211 4-9-8 **85** .... LukeLeadbitter 2 95
(William Jarvis) *trckd ldrs: effrt over 2f out: cl 2nd 1f out: led jst ins fnl f: edgd lft: kpt on wl* **11/2**[3]

4403 **2** *1 ½* **Kalk Bay (IRE)**[14] 7176 6-9-3 **80** .... (t) SoufianeSaadi 9 87
(Michael Easterby) *trckd ldrs: chal over 2f out: led appr fnl f: sn hdd and edgd lft: no ex* **9/1**

5623 **3** *4 ½* **Melvin The Grate (IRE)**[18] 7075 3-9-0 **80** .... GaryHalpin 8 76
(Andrew Balding) *led: hdd appr fnl f: one pce* **7/2**[2]

0320 **4** *1 ¼* **Sound Advice**[11] 7241 4-9-8 **85** .... RowanScott 4 79
(Keith Dalgleish) *trckd ldrs: t.k.h: drvn over 2f out: sn outpcd: kpt on ins fnl f* **12/1**

5500 **5** *nk* **Karaka Jack**[13] 7211 6-9-3 **80** .... JeremyMoisan 3 73
(David Nicholls) *trckd ldrs: drvn and outpcd over 2f out: kpt on ins fnl f* **9/1**

0516 **6** *hd* **Fazza**[20] 7028 6-9-1 **78** .... AlexandraVilmar 10 71
(Edwin Tuer) *mid-div: drvn 3f out: sn outpcd: kpt on ins fnl f* **16/1**

5233 **7** *½* **War Poet**[13] 7211 6-9-6 **83** .... (t) DylanRobinson 11 74
(Brian Ellison) *hld up towards rr: hdwy over 4f out: drvn and outpcd over 2f out: kpt on ins fnl f* **3/1**[1]

0561 **8** *4 ½* **Ingleby Symphony (IRE)**[15] 7152 3-8-5 **71** .... BrunoPanicucci 1 51
(Richard Fahey) *swtchd rt s: hdwy over 2f out: lost pl over 1f out* **10/1**

4125 **9** *2* **Naaz (IRE)**[12] 7224 3-9-4 **84** .... (b) EstherRuthWeissmeier 6 60
(Ed Dunlop) *hld up in rr: effrt over 3f out: edgd lft: wknd over 1f out* **10/1**

0/0 **10** *11* **Printmaker (IRE)**[14] 7176 5-9-1 **78** .... JordanVaughan 12 29
(Tim Easterby) *hld up in rr: wknd over 2f out: sn bhd* **33/1**

1m 46.1s (6.80) **Going Correction** +1.00s/f (Soft)
WFA 3 from 4yo+ 3lb **10** Ran SP% **117.3**
Speed ratings (Par 105): **106,104,100,98,98 98,97,93,91,80**
toteswingers 1&2 £7.60, 1&3 £4.70, 2&3 £8.40 CSF £54.53 CT £203.98 TOTE £6.80: £2.30, £3.10, £1.70; EX 52.20 Trifecta £345.10 Pool: £2457.55 - 5.34 winning units..
Owner Clive Washbourn **Bred** Denis A McCarthy **Trained** Newmarket, Suffolk

■ Stewards' Enquiry : Alexandra Vilmar two-day ban: use of whip (TBC)

FOCUS

A modest handicap, confined to apprentice riders.

T/Jkpt: Not won. T/Plt: £1,581.10 to a £1 stake. Pool: £95538.99 - 44.11 winning tickets T/Qpdt: £166.50 to a £1 stake. Pool: £9318.51 - 41.40 winning tickets JR

6635 NEWBURY (L-H)

Friday, October 25

OFFICIAL GOING: Soft (heavy in places) changing to heavy after race 7 (4:40)

Wind: Brisk across Weather: Overcast

7500 FREE BETS FREEBETS.CO.UK MAIDEN STKS (DIV I) 1m (S)

1:30 (1:33) (Class 4) 2-Y-O **£3,881** (£1,155; £577; £288) **Stalls** Centre

Form RPR

0 **1** **Strait Run (IRE)**[23] 6953 2-9-5 0 RichardHughes 6 80+
(Richard Hannon) *trckd ldrs: chal fr 3f out tl slt ld ins fnl f: drvn out* **7/2**[2]

2 ½ **Flight Officer** 2-9-5 0 SilvestreDeSousa 4 79+
(Saeed bin Suroor) *str: chsd ldrs: rdn 2f out: styd on and edgd rt fnl f: chsd wnr fnl 110yds: no imp* **3/1**[1]

00 **3** 1¼ **Ravenous**[28] 6799 2-9-5 0 JimCrowley 2 76
(Ralph Beckett) *str: chsd ldrs: chal 2f out: slt ld 1f out: sn hdd: no ex and one pce into 3rd fnl 110yds* **8/1**

4 4 **Canova (IRE)** 2-9-5 0 GeorgeBaker 3 67+
(Roger Charlton) *cmpt: chsd ldrs: slt ld but hrd pressed fr over 3f out: hdd u.p 1f out: wknd fnl f* **7/1**[3]

5 1 **Impulsive Moment (IRE)** 2-9-5 0 RyanMoore 7 65+
(Andrew Balding) *lengthy: str: lw: sn in tch: pushed along to chse ldrs over 2f out: one pce over 1f out* **3/1**[1]

6 6 **Cinnamon Spice** 2-9-5 0 [1] JamesDoyle 1 52
(Harry Dunlop) *unf: in tch and pushed along 3f out: no ch w ldrs after* **16/1**

7 2 **Swanwick Shore (IRE)** 2-9-5 0 SeanLevey 9 48
(Richard Hannon) *str: bit bkwd: chsd ldrs over 4f* **16/1**

0 **8** hd **Norse Legend**[11] 7243 2-9-2 0 ThomasBrown(3) 8 47
(Daniel Kubler) *str: slt ld but hrd pressed tl over 3f out: wknd over 2f out* **100/1**

9 2½ **Rowlestone Express** 2-8-11 0 MarkCoumbe(3) 5 37
(Tony Carroll) *unf: tall: s.i.s: a in rr* **100/1**

10 19 **Desert Island Dusk** 2-9-5 0 SamHitchcott 11
(John Bridger) *w'like: bit bkwd: bhd fr 1/2-way* **200/1**

11 10 **Bon A Savoir** 2-9-5 0 JamieSpencer 10
(Peter Chapple-Hyam) *athletic: slowly away: sn rdn: a in rr* **12/1**

1m 47.89s (8.19) **Going Correction** +0.875s/f (Soft) **11 Ran SP% 117.8**
Speed ratings (Par 97): **94,93,92,88,87 81,79,79,76,57 47**
toteswingers 1&2 £1.90, 1&3 £2.60, 2&3 £5.90 CSF £14.52 TOTE £5.70: £2.00, £1.80, £1.50; EX 19.20 Trifecta £122.90 Pool: £1624.69 - 9.91 winning units..
Owner Noodles Racing **Bred** Pat Grogan **Trained** East Everleigh, Wilts

FOCUS

Inside rail moved out from 5f and there was a cut-off at 2.5f. Rail on Round course moved in. The first three pulled clear late on in the first division of what was a fair maiden, run in a time 0.53secs quicker than the second leg.

7501 JOIN HOT TO TROT FOR 2014 EBF MAIDEN STKS 6f 110y

2:00 (2:06) (Class 4) 2-Y-O **£4,075** (£1,212; £606; £303) **Stalls** Centre

Form RPR

0 **1** **Scrutiny**[16] 7119 2-9-5 0 SilvestreDeSousa 3 87+
(William Haggas) *lengthy: unf: pressed ldrs: rdn and one pce 2f out but styd chsng ldr: kpt on gamely u.p to ld fnl 50yds* **20/1**

2 1¼ **G Force (IRE)** 2-9-5 0 JamieSpencer 12 84+
(Richard Hannon) *w'like: leggy: s.i.s: sn chsng ldrs: led gng smoothly over 2f out: stl travelling wl fnl f: began to fade fnl 110yds: hdd and no ex fnl 50yds* **12/1**

2 **3** 7 **Dark Leopard**[35] 6590 2-9-5 0 JamesDoyle 8 64
(Roger Charlton) *lw: led: shkn up and hdd over 2f out: wknd appr fnl f* **11/8**[1]

3 **4** ½ **Master Of Suspense**[126] 3536 2-9-5 0 WilliamBuick 7 63
(Peter Chapple-Hyam) *str: lw: chsd ldrs: drvn over 2f out: wknd appr fnl f* **9/4**[2]

5 8 **Dutchartcollector** 2-9-5 0 RyanMoore 9 41+
(Gary Moore) *tall: in tch: rdn 3f out: wknd ins fnl 2f* **6/1**[3]

6 1 **Columbian Roulette (IRE)** 2-9-5 0 [1] SteveDrowne 2 38
(Charles Hills) *tall: str: s.i.s: rdn 3f out: mod hdwy fnl 2f* **33/1**

7 nk **Willy Brennan (IRE)** 2-9-5 0 DavidProbert 11 37
(Andrew Balding) *leggy: bit bkwd: chsd ldrs: wknd over 2f out* **20/1**

8 2½ **Treasure Cay (IRE)** 2-9-5 0 JimCrowley 6 30
(Paul Cole) *w'like: sn rdn: sme hdwy u.p 3f out but nver any ch and wknd ins fnl 2f* **16/1**

00 **9** 16 **Kelamita (IRE)**[17] 7103 2-9-0 0 JimmyFortune 10
(Hughie Morrison) *a in rr* **50/1**

10 shd **Sweet Cherry (IRE)** 2-9-0 0 JackMitchell 4
(Pat Murphy) *w'like: cl cpld: chsd ldrs over 3f* **50/1**

0 **11** 1¾ **Henry Grace (IRE)**[23] 6931 2-9-5 0 KieranO'Neill 1
(Jimmy Fox) *unf: in tch: rdn 3f out: sn wknd* **200/1**

1m 25.1s (5.80) **Going Correction** +0.875s/f (Soft) **11 Ran SP% 117.6**
Speed ratings (Par 97): **101,99,91,91,81 80,80,77,59,59 57**
toteswingers 1&2 £33.30, 1&3 £6.60, 2&3 £2.90 CSF £223.57 TOTE £25.20: £5.00, £2.50, £1.10; EX 157.50 Trifecta £1405.90 Pool: £2548.64 - 1.35 winning units..
Owner HighclereThoroughbredRacing-LakeConiston **Bred** Qatar Bloodstock Ltd **Trained** Newmarket, Suffolk

FOCUS

An ordinary maiden, with neither of the big two in the market looking entirely happy on the ground.

7502 FREE BETS FREEBETS.CO.UK MAIDEN STKS (DIV II) 1m (S)

2:30 (2:36) (Class 4) 2-Y-O **£3,881** (£1,155; £577; £288) **Stalls** Centre

Form RPR

33 **1** **Chatez (IRE)**[22] 6975 2-9-5 0 FergusSweeney 6 80+
(Alan King) *str: t.k.h: stdd towards rr: stdy hdwy over 2f out: led appr fnl f: drvn and styd on wl and a doing enough* **8/1**

2 nk **Observational** 2-9-5 0 GeorgeBaker 4 79+
(Roger Charlton) *tall: leggy: chsd ldrs: drvn to ld 2f out: hddappr fnl f: styd on u.p but a jst hld by wnr* **9/2**[3]

62 **3** 2 **Carthage (IRE)**[12] 7219 2-9-5 0 RichardHughes 8 75
(Richard Hannon) *str: trckd ldrs: drvn and styd on to chse ldng duo over 1f out: one pce ins fnl f* **5/4**[1]

0 **4** shd **Express Himself (IRE)**[27] 6829 2-9-5 0 SteveDrowne 1 75
(Ed McMahon) *w'like: t.k.h chsd ldrs: drvn to chal 2f out: styd on same pce fnl f* **11/1**

5 4½ **Jefferson City (IRE)** 2-9-5 0 WilliamBuick 7 65+
(John Gosden) *tall: s.i.s: sn in tch: chsd ldrs and rdn 2f out: wknd appr fnl f* **4/1**[2]

6 ½ **Moshe (IRE)** 2-9-5 0 JimmyFortune 3 64+
(Hughie Morrison) *w'like: cl cpld: in rr: hdwy to cl on ldrs over 2f out: wknd wl over 1f out* **33/1**

00 **7** 2 **Vaguely Spanish**[16] 7128 2-9-5 0 DaneO'Neill 2 59
(Tony Carroll) *str: led: drvn and hdd 2f out: wknd over 1f out* **100/1**

8 ¾ **Epsom Hill (SWE)** 2-9-5 0 JimCrowley 5 58
(Tobias B P Coles) *neat: chsd ldrs: wknd qckly 2f out* **50/1**

00 **9** 1¾ **Bold Runner**[23] 6954 2-9-5 0 FrankieMcDonald 10 54
(Sean Curran) *w'like: in rr: sme hdwy to cl on ldrs over 2f out: sn wknd* **100/1**

10 2½ **Nabatean (IRE)** 2-9-5 0 DavidProbert 9 48
(Andrew Balding) *leggy: tall: unf: in rr: sme hdwy over 2f out: sn wknd* **16/1**

1m 48.42s (8.72) **Going Correction** +0.875s/f (Soft) **10 Ran SP% 114.8**
Speed ratings (Par 97): **91,90,88,88,84 83,81,80,79,76**
toteswingers 1&2 £6.20, 1&3 £2.10, 2&3 £2.10 CSF £42.79 TOTE £9.90: £2.50, £1.60, £1.10; EX 41.70 Trifecta £140.20 Pool: £2495.92 - 13.35 winning units..
Owner Mrs Peter Andrews **Bred** Colin Kennedy **Trained** Barbury Castle, Wilts

FOCUS

The runners raced across the track in division two of the maiden, which was run in a time 0.53secs slower than the first leg.

7503 SIR GERALD WHENT MEMORIAL NURSERY H'CAP 6f 8y

3:00 (3:04) (Class 3) (0-95,92) 2-Y-O **£6,469** (£1,925; £962; £481) **Stalls** Centre

Form RPR

1221 **1** **Musical Comedy**[7] 7334 2-9-13 **92** 6ex RichardHughes 3 104+
(Richard Hannon) *bmpd s: sn in tch: hdwy over 2f out: led over 1f out: drvn clr fnl 150yds* **11/8**[1]

4301 **2** 5 **Heroique (IRE)**[17] 7096 2-8-5 **70** (e) DuranFentiman 5 67
(Tim Easterby) *led: rdn over 2f out: hdd over 1f out: no ch w wnr fnl f but hld on wl for 2nd* **20/1**

1 **3** nk **Dutch S**[28] 6789 2-8-11 **76** JohnFahy 8 72+
(Clive Cox) *unf: scope: tall: s.i.s: in rr but in tch: hdwy fr 2f out: styd on fnl f to take 3rd cl home but no ch w wnr* **4/1**[2]

2203 **4** ¾ **Urban Dreamer (IRE)**[7] 7333 2-8-12 **77** (b) DavidProbert 4 71
(Rod Millman) *wnt lft s: chsd ldr: rdn and ev ch 2f out: outpcd by wnr fnl f and lost 3rd cl home* **5/1**[3]

6103 **5** 6 **Finflash (IRE)**[18] 7074 2-9-0 **79** WilliamBuick 1 55
(Mick Channon) *lw: in tch: rdn and no imp over 2f out: no ch after* **5/1**[3]

31 **6** ¾ **Mitchelton (FR)**[120] 3710 2-9-4 **83** AdrianNicholls 2 57
(Mark Johnston) *chsd ldrs: wknd over 2f out* **14/1**

2100 **7** 2 **Kanz**[27] 6839 2-8-10 **75** SilvestreDeSousa 7 43
(Mick Channon) *chsd ldrs: wknd qukickly over 1f out* **16/1**

1140 **8** 9 **Diamond Lady**[83] 5005 2-9-6 **85** DaneO'Neill 6 26
(Jo Hughes) *rdn bef1/2-way: a bhd* **33/1**

1m 18.19s (5.19) **Going Correction** +0.875s/f (Soft) **8 Ran SP% 115.7**
Speed ratings (Par 99): **100,93,92,91,83 82,80,68**
toteswingers 1&2 £9.60, 1&3 £1.60, 2&3 £11.50 CSF £34.47 CT £94.97 TOTE £2.30: £1.30, £3.80, £1.90; EX 29.70 Trifecta £117.80 Pool: £2174.06 - 13.84 winning units..
Owner The Queen **Bred** The Queen **Trained** East Everleigh, Wilts

FOCUS

No great depth to this nursery, but the winner is clearly thriving.

7504 SMITH & WILLIAMSON FILLIES' H'CAP 1m 2f 6y

3:35 (3:36) (Class 4) (0-85,85) 3-Y-O+ **£4,851** (£1,443; £721; £360) **Stalls** Centre

Form RPR

52-5 **1** **Kalispell (IRE)**[37] 6532 3-8-9 **75** SilvestreDeSousa 4 92
(Charlie Appleby) *chsd ldrs: led over 2f out: drvn clr fnl f* **8/1**

4102 **2** 5 **Astra Hall**[38] 6490 4-9-5 **80** JimCrowley 10 87
(Ralph Beckett) *lw: chsd ldrs: rdn over 2f out: styd on to go 2nd fnl f but nvr any ch w wnr* **8/1**

4162 **3** 2 **Raskova (USA)**[11] 7257 3-8-6 **72** DavidProbert 11 75
(William Jarvis) *in tch: hdwy and rdn over 2f out: kpt on wl to take 3rd clsng stages but no ch w ldng duo* **7/1**[2]

2441 **4** nk **Running Deer (IRE)**[13] 7211 4-8-11 **79** LouisSteward(7) 5 82
(Lady Cecil) *chsd ldrs: drvn to chal over 2f out: no ex wl over 1f out: wknd ins fnl f* **15/2**[3]

21 **5** nse **Storm (IRE)**[218] 1095 3-8-0 **71** oh5 RyanTate(5) 3 74
(Charles Hills) *tall: unf: chsd ldrs: rdn fr over 2f out: styd on same pce fr over 1f out* **20/1**

-222 **6** ¾ **Puligny (IRE)**[27] 6824 3-8-9 **75** JamieSpencer 15 76
(Charles Hills) *in tch: hdwy fr 2f out: chsd ldrs over 1f out: styd on same pce fnl frlong* **16/1**

26 **7** ¾ **Rosaceous**[23] 6936 3-9-2 **82** GeorgeBaker 9 82
(Daniel Kubler) *sn led: hdd over 2f out: wknd fnl f* **8/1**

3023 **8** ½ **Rosie Rebel**[17] 7100 3-8-8 **74** ChrisCatlin 13 73
(Rae Guest) *lw: chsd ldrs: rdn over 2f out: styd on same pce fnl furkong* **8/1**

5-15 **9** 8 **Our Phylli Vera (IRE)**[139] 3095 4-8-13 **74** FergusSweeney 8 58
(Alan King) *rdn 3f out: sme prog over 2f out: sn wknd* **16/1**

2503 **10** 1 **Trapeze**[10] 7272 3-9-5 **85** RichardHughes 6 67
(John Gosden) *rdn along 3f out: a towards rr* **16/1**

62 **11** 1¾ **Caterina De Medici (FR)**[21] 6997 4-9-0 **75** TomMcLaughlin 2 53
(Ed Walker) *lw: chsd ldrs: drvn fr 4f out: wknd u.p wl over 1f out* **50/1**

603 **12** 5 **Martagon Lily**[37] 6532 3-8-11 **77** WilliamBuick 1 46
(John Gosden) *in rr: rdn and hdwy to cl on ldrs over 2f out: sn wknd* **9/2**[1]

0331 **13** ½ **Bohemian Dance (IRE)**[53] 6046 3-8-12 **78** RyanMoore 14 46
(Sir Michael Stoute) *lw: rdn wl over 2f out: a towards rr* **12/1**

225- **14** 5 **Altaria**[385] 6839 4-9-0 **75** (t) DaneO'Neill 12 33
(Seamus Durack) *in tch: rdn and wknd ins fnl 3f* **33/1**

2m 13.17s (4.37) **Going Correction** +0.60s/f (Yiel)
WFA 3 from 4yo 5lb **14 Ran SP% 121.9**
Speed ratings (Par 102): **106,102,100,100,100 99,98,98,92,91 89,85,85,81**
toteswingers 1&2 £19.20, 1&3 £5.90, 2&3 £21.60 CSF £70.33 CT £480.56 TOTE £9.40: £4.30, £2.60, £2.50; EX 82.70 Trifecta £491.00 Part won Pool: £654.74 - 0.13 winning units..
Owner Godolphin **Bred** Darley **Trained** Newmarket, Suffolk

The Form Book Flat, Raceform Ltd, Compton, RG20 6NL.

FOCUS
The first race of the day on the round course and the entire field headed centre-field in the straight. What had looked a wide-open handicap was taken in ready fashion by the winner.

7505 CSP H'CAP 1m 7y(R)
4:10 (4:10) (Class 5) (0-75,74) 3-Y-O **£3,234** (£962; £481; £240) **Stalls** Centre

Form RPR
0121 **1** **Amulet**[16] 7130 3-9-5 **72** ShaneKelly 7 89
(Eve Johnson Houghton) *mde all: c clr fnl 2f: unchal* **4/1**[1]
4401 **2** *9* **Duke Of Grazeon (IRE)**[18] 7067 3-9-3 **70** RaulDaSilva 10 66
(Mrs Ilka Gansera-Leveque) *chsd ldrs: wnt 2nd over 2f out and nvr any ch w unchal wnr but kpt on wl to hold 2nd fnl f* **14/1**
0213 **3** *½* **Excellent Puck (IRE)**[25] 6898 3-9-4 **71** JimmyFortune 2 66
(Jamie Osborne) *t.k.h towards rr: hdwy fr 3f out: styd on to press for 2nd fnl f but nvr any ch w unchal wnr* **9/2**[2]
2030 **4** *½* **Red Dragon (IRE)**[134] 3241 3-9-7 **74** FergusSweeney 4 68
(Michael Blanshard) *chsd ldrs: rdn 3f out: styd on same pce fnl 2f* **40/1**
210 **5** *6* **Unison (IRE)**[41] 6379 3-9-3 **70** SteveDrowne 3 50
(Peter Makin) *towards rr: hdwy 3f out: nvr nr unchal wnr and looked btn ins fnl 2f: kpt on again clsng stages* **14/1**
6520 **6** *1 ¼* **Mystical Moment**[40] 6433 3-9-4 **71** RichardHughes 9 48
(Richard Hannon) *in rr: c to stands' side and rdn over 2f out and no prog* **16/1**
430 **7** *1 ¼* **Artistical (IRE)**[18] 7067 3-9-2 **69** (t) GeorgeBaker 12 43
(William Haggas) *lw: in rr: rdn over 2f out: mod prog fr over 1f out* **12/1**
0542 **8** *2 ¾* **Hipster**[23] 6956 3-9-4 **71** (v) JimCrowley 8 39
(Ralph Beckett) *chsd wnr to 3f out: wknd fr 2f out* **5/1**[3]
2430 **9** *1 ½* **Tilstarr (IRE)**[31] 6734 3-9-4 **71** DaneO'Neill 5 36
(Roger Teal) *chsd ldrs: rdn and wknd ins fnl 3f* **10/1**
0102 **10** *nse* **The Scuttler (IRE)**[4] 7429 3-9-0 **70** CharlesBishop(3) 11 35
(Mick Channon) *lw: in rr: sme hdwy 3f out: nvr nr ldrs and wknd over 2f out* **5/1**[3]
0000 **11** *2* **Kazak**[125] 3585 3-9-3 **70** JamesDoyle 6 30
(Roger Charlton) *rdn 3f out: a bhd* **12/1**
0310 **12** *1* **Equitissa (IRE)**[82] 5037 3-8-11 **71** CameronHardie(7) 1 29
(Richard Hannon) *in rr early: hdwy to cl on ldng gp 3f out: wknd qckly over 2f out* **28/1**

1m 43.81s (5.11) **Going Correction** +0.60s/f (Yiel) **12 Ran SP% 121.1**
Speed ratings (Par 101): **98,89,88,88,82 80,79,76,75,75 73,72**
toteswingers 1&2 £14.90, 1&3 £4.70, 2&3 £7.40 CSF £62.79 CT £272.42 TOTE £4.40: £1.50, £4.60, £1.90; EX 64.90 Trifecta £263.60 Pool: £1212.76 - 3.44 winning units..
Owner Mrs Virginia Neale **Bred** Cherry Park Stud **Trained** Blewbury, Oxon

FOCUS
A modest handicap that was taken in dominant fashion by the highly progressive winner.

7506 CSP "HANDS AND HEELS" APPRENTICE SERIES FINAL H'CAP (PART OF THE RACING EXCELLENCE INITIATIVE) 2m
4:40 (4:40) (Class 5) (0-75,75) 4-Y-O+ **£2,587** (£770; £384; £192) **Stalls** High

Form RPR
213/ **1** **Secret Edge**[169] 6057 5-9-2 **67** RobJFitzpatrick 6 76
(Alan King) *trckd ldr: led 3f out: drvn and styd on wl fr over 1f out* **10/1**
2360 **2** *3 ½* **Filatore (IRE)**[19] 6424 4-9-5 **70** (b[1]) LouisSteward 11 75
(Bernard Llewellyn) *in tch: chsd ldrs fr 5f out: drvn to chse wnr* **14/1**
1054 **3** *2* **Almost Gemini (IRE)**[10] 7280 4-9-2 **67** (v[1]) JoeDoyle 10 70
(Don Cantillon) *in rr whn stmbld bnd over 5f out: styd on wl to fr over 1f out to take 3rd clsng stages but nt rch ldng duo* **7/1**
3544 **4** *1 ¼* **No Such Number**[12] 7220 5-9-6 **71** (p) ShelleyBirkett 9 72
(Julia Feilden) *sn led: hdd 3f out and sn drive: styd chsng ldrs but one pce fnl 2f* **8/1**
1344 **5** *nk* **Decana**[56] 5966 5-8-3 **57** CharlieBennett(3) 4 58
(Hughie Morrison) *chsd ldrs: drvn 3f out: styd on same pce fr over 2f out* **11/2**
2/3 **6** *hd* **Pateese (FR)**[38] 1670 8-9-5 **75** (b) JonathanMoore(5) 3 76
(Philip Hobbs) *in tch: pushed along and hdwy 3f out: styd on same pce fnl 2f* **4/1**[2]
15-6 **7** *1 ¼* **Mcvicar**[181] 639 4-8-13 **67** ThomasHemsley(3) 8 66+
(Alan King) *lw: in rr hmpd and lost further grnd ins fnl 5f: styd on fnl 2f: nvr rchd ldrs* **3/1**[1]
1150 **8** *¾* **Tijori (IRE)**[13] 6424 5-9-0 **65** (p) JoeyHaynes 5 63
(Bernard Llewellyn) *towards rr but in tch: chsd ldrs over 2f out: wknd wl over 1f out* **5/1**[3]
130- **9** *99* **Reillys Daughter**[317] 8073 5-8-9 **60** DanielCremin 1
(Richard Mitchell) *chsd ldrs tl wknd rapidly over 5f out* **50/1**

3m 50.78s (18.78) **Going Correction** +0.60s/f (Yiel) **9 Ran SP% 118.4**
Speed ratings (Par 103): **77,75,74,73,73 73,72,72,22**
toteswingers 1&2 £9.10, 1&3 £12.20, 2&3 £15.00 CSF £141.67 CT £1051.42 TOTE £12.50: £2.90, £4.40, £2.00; EX 112.70 Trifecta £1637.40 Part won. Pool: £2183.32 - 0.97 winning units..
Owner Nigel Bunter & David Anderson **Bred** Mrs S M Lee **Trained** Barbury Castle, Wilts

FOCUS
It proved difficult to make up ground in this staying handicap.

7507 HENNESSY HERITAGE FESTIVAL H'CAP 6f 110y
5:10 (5:15) (Class 3) (0-90,90) 3-Y-O+ **£7,439** (£2,213; £1,106; £553) **Stalls** Centre

Form RPR
0053 **1** **Tariq Too**[5] 7408 6-9-2 **90** ShelleyBirkett(5) 4 105
(Amy Weaver) *s.i.s: hld up in rr: stdy hdwy fr 2f out: trckd ldrs on bit and waited for a run over 1f out: led sn after: pushed clr: easily* **8/1**
2322 **2** *8* **Secret Beau**[3] 7438 3-8-7 **78** SilvestreDeSousa 1 70
(David Evans) *chsd ldrs: chal on outer fr 3f out: chsd thrght fnl f but nvr any ch* **6/1**[2]
1600 **3** *shd* **Fortinbrass (IRE)**[41] 6382 3-8-10 **81** (p) JimCrowley 8 73
(Ralph Beckett) *chsd ldrs: rdn and effrt to press ldr over 2f out: outpcd appr fnl f: kpt on again clsng stages to press for 2nd cl home but no ch w wnr* **33/1**
5305 **4** *½* **The Tichborne (IRE)**[11] 7255 5-8-2 **76** oh1 (p[1]) JoeyHaynes(5) 7 68
(Roger Teal) *chsd ldrs: led 3f out but sn hrd pressed: hdd 1f out and sn no ch w wnr: styd on same pce and dropped to 4th cl home* **50/1**
0416 **5** *5* **Whipper Snapper (IRE)**[21] 6993 3-8-9 **80** JamieSpencer 5 57
(William Knight) *in tch: rdn 2f out: no prog fr over 1f out* **7/1**[3]
04 **6** *5* **Jack Luey**[43] 6331 6-9-3 **86** DuranFentiman 2 51
(Lawrence Mullaney) *chsd ldrs: wknd qckly 2f out* **20/1**
200 **7** *17* **Freddy With A Y (IRE)**[32] 6692 3-8-13 **84** RichardHughes 6
(Gary Moore) *sn led: hdd 3f out: wknd qckly wl over 1f out: eased whn no ch* **16/1**
61-2 **8** *42* **Blessington (IRE)**[21] 6990 3-9-3 **88** WilliamBuick 3
(John Gosden) *chsd ldrs: wknd over 2f out: eased fr over 1f out* **8/11**[1]

1m 25.1s (5.80) **Going Correction** +1.025s/f (Soft)
WFA 3 from 4yo+ 1lb **8 Ran SP% 111.3**
Speed ratings (Par 107): **107,97,97,97,91 85,66,18**
toteswingers 1&2 £7.60, 1&3 £4.70, 2&3 £8.40 CSF £51.30 CT £1468.66 TOTE £7.70: £1.90, £1.40, £6.00; EX 44.50 Trifecta £650.30 Pool: £2926.93 - 3.37 winning units..
Owner Bringloe Clarke Spain Hensby Partridge **Bred** D R Botterill **Trained** Newmarket, Suffolk

FOCUS
The runners came stands' side for this sprint handicap, the form of which looks a bit suspect with the red-hot favourite running a shocker and very few appearing to handle the ground.
T/Plt: £22.20 to a £1 stake. Pool: £68516.24 - 2245.33 winning tickets T/Qpdt: £7.90 to a £1 stake. Pool: £5330.39 - 493.30 winning tickets ST

7484 WOLVERHAMPTON (A.W) (L-H)
Friday, October 25

OFFICIAL GOING: Standard
Wind: Fresh behind Weather: Showers

7508 LADBROKES CLASSIFIED STKS 5f 216y(P)
5:30 (5:30) (Class 6) 3-Y-O+ **£1,940** (£577; £288; £144) **Stalls** Low

Form RPR
0000 **1** **Izzy Boy (USA)**[13] 7197 3-9-0 **54** LiamJones 4 57
(Mark Johnston) *s.i.s: hdwy over 4f out: rdn to ld over 1f out: styd on u.p* **7/1**
0630 **2** *1* **Amelia Jay**[18] 7079 3-8-11 **48** SladeO'Hara(3) 7 54
(Danielle McCormick) *hld up: hdwy 1/2-way: nt clr run and swtchd rt over 1f out: rdn and r.o ins fnl f: nt rch wnr* **20/1**
0000 **3** *1 ½* **Major Muscari (IRE)**[7] 7347 5-8-12 **43** BillyCray(3) 10 49
(Shaun Harris) *s.s: hld up: hdwy and n.m.r over 1f out: sn rdn: styd on same pce ins fnl f* **25/1**
4005 **4** *¾* **Red Shadow**[13] 7197 4-8-12 **50** (b) PaulPickard(3) 12 47
(Alan Brown) *chsd ldrs: rdn over 1f out: styd on same pce fnl f* **8/1**
4102 **5** *1* **Beach Rhythm (USA)**[21] 6994 6-8-8 **53** (v) DavidParkes(7) 1 44
(Jim Allen) *led: rdn and hdd over 1f out: no ex ins fnl f* **15/8**[1]
3000 **6** *1 ½* **Ishisoba**[6] 7380 3-9-0 **49** CathyGannon 11 39
(Ronald Harris) *prom: lost pl after 1f: drvn along 1/2-way: styd on ins fnl f* **20/1**
0560 **7** *nk* **Kasbhom**[30] 6752 3-9-0 **55** WilliamCarson 13 38
(Anthony Carson) *trckd ldrs: plld hrd: lost pl wl over 3f out: sn drvn along: n.d after* **5/1**[2]
6620 **8** *5* **Sunny Hollow**[16] 7124 3-8-9 **53** (b[1]) DanielMuscutt(5) 6 22
(James Toller) *chsd ldrs tl rdn and wknd over 1f out* **6/1**[3]
0430 **9** *nk* **Kwanto**[34] 6651 3-8-9 **46** TimClark(5) 8 21
(Ken Wingrove) *prom: drvn along 1/2-way: wknd 2f out* **25/1**
5305 **10** *7* **Kaylee**[212] 1195 4-9-1 **47** LiamKeniry 3
(Brett Johnson) *w ldr tl rdn over 2f out: wknd over 1f out* **14/1**
40-4 **11** *13* **Gypsy Jazz (IRE)**[192] 1596 6-8-10 **47** (p) AnnStokell(5) 5
(Ann Stokell) *sn outpcd* **66/1**

1m 16.36s (1.36) **Going Correction** +0.15s/f (Slow)
WFA 3 from 4yo+ 1lb **11 Ran SP% 114.7**
Speed ratings (Par 101): **96,94,92,91,90 88,87,81,80,71 54**
toteswingers 1&2 £32.90, 1&3 £41.80, 2&3 £58.60 CSF £139.21 TOTE £7.20: £2.70, £6.70, £9.70; EX 125.30 Trifecta £1929.90 Pool: £2652.89 - 1.03 winning units..
Owner Frank Bird **Bred** Pollock Farms & Darley **Trained** Middleham Moor, N Yorks

FOCUS
Moderate stuff, but the winner probably isn't a bad type for the level.

7509 LADBROKES (S) STKS 5f 216y(P)
6:00 (6:01) (Class 6) 2-Y-O **£1,940** (£577; £288; £144) **Stalls** Low

Form RPR
525 **1** **Kodafine (IRE)**[7] 7349 2-8-4 **66** EoinWalsh(7) 4 65
(David Evans) *chsd ldrs: led over 3f out: rdn clr over 1f out: hung rt ins fnl f: kpt on* **11/4**[2]
4302 **2** *1 ¼* **Stoney Quine (IRE)**[13] 7199 2-8-7 **59** ow1 TomEaves 9 57
(Keith Dalgleish) *a.p: rdn to chse wnr over 1f out: flashed tail ins fnl f: styd on u.p* **6/4**[1]
3 *1 ¾* **Armelle (FR)** 2-8-1 **0** TimClark(5) 3 51
(Scott Dixon) *s.i.s: in rr and drvn along 4f out: hdwy u.p over 1f out: edgd rt ins fnl f: nt rch ldrs* **33/1**
6306 **4** *2* **Severnwind (IRE)**[22] 6983 2-8-11 **54** (b[1]) CathyGannon 5 50
(Ronald Harris) *prom: rdn whn nt clr run and outpcd over 2f out: rallied over 1f out: styng on same pce whn hmpd ins fnl f* **12/1**
0640 **5** *hd* **Hija**[95] 4583 2-8-1 **48** ow2 (b[1]) RyanWhile(7) 8 46
(Bill Turner) *s.i.s: outpcd: drvn along 1/2-way: r.o wl ins fnl f: nvr nrr* **33/1**
06 **6** *1 ½* **Without Truth (IRE)**[108] 4142 2-8-12 **0** ow1 SeanLevey 10 46
(David Brown) *hld up: rdn over 2f out: styd on same pce appr fnl f* **16/1**
0046 **7** *5* **Alaskan Night (IRE)**[13] 7200 2-8-11 **57** (p) StephenCraine 11 30
(Kevin Ryan) *led 1f: chsd ldrs: rdn over 2f out: wknd fnl f* **5/1**[3]
4000 **8** *½* **Cheeky Peta'S**[17] 7094 2-8-6 **62** (b[1]) JamesSullivan 2 23
(James Given) *led 5f out tl over 3f out: rdn and ev ch over 2f out: wknd fnl f* **11/1**
0 **9** *19* **Parisian Queen**[18] 7078 2-8-1 **0** [1] PhilipPrince(5) 12
(Nikki Evans) *s.i.s: bhd fr 1/2-way* **100/1**

1m 16.39s (1.39) **Going Correction** +0.15s/f (Slow) **9 Ran SP% 112.1**
Speed ratings (Par 93): **96,94,92,89,89 87,80,79,54**
toteswingers 1&2 £1.40, 1&3 £12.80, 2&3 £10.50 CSF £6.89 TOTE £3.60: £1.10, £2.00, £7.10; EX 6.80 Trifecta £150.60 Pool: £2669.29 - 13.28 winning units..There was no bid for the winner.
Owner J A Wilcox & P D Evans **Bred** Tally-Ho Stud **Trained** Pandy, Monmouths
■ Stewards' Enquiry : Stephen Craine one-day ban: careless riding (8 Nov)

FOCUS
Despite being taken on for the lead on both sides (by the well-beaten Alaskan Night and Cheeky Peta's), Kodafine went clear at the top of the straight and was never in danger thereafter, despite hanging right late on.

7510 LADBROKES H'CAP 1m 5f 194y(P)
6:30 (6:30) (Class 5) (0-75,75) 3-Y-O+ **£3,234** (£962; £481; £240) **Stalls** Low

Form RPR
4323 **1** **Sunblazer (IRE)**[17] 7105 3-9-5 **75** MartinDwyer 9 84
(William Muir) *s.i.s: hdwy 10f out: chsd ldr 4f out: led over 2f out: rdn over 1f out: styd on u.p* **7/2**[2]
012 **2** *2 ¼* **Alpine Mysteries (IRE)**[14] 7166 3-8-13 **72** ThomasBrown(3) 2 79
(Harry Dunlop) *s.i.s: hld up: hdwy over 2f out: rdn to chse wnr over 1f out: hung lft ins fnl f: no imp* **4/1**[3]

0 3 1 ½ **Meetings Man (IRE)**[30] 6750 6-9-9 **75**............................(p) TimClark(5) 6 79
(Ali Brewer) *broke wl: sn stdd and lost pl: plld hrd in rr: drvn along over 3f out: hdwy u.p over 1f out: nt rch ldrs* **12/1**

130 4 nk **Bridgehampton**[41] 6377 4-9-11 **75**............... WilliamTwiston-Davies(3) 5 78
(Michael Bell) *chsd ldrs: rdn whn nt clr run and lost pl over 2f out: rallied over 1f out: styd on same pce ins fnl f* **10/3**[1]

0523 5 7 **Nolecce**[14] 7166 6-8-8 **62**............................ JackGarritty(7) 4 56
(Tony Forbes) *chsd ldr 10f: rdn over 2f out: wknd over 1f out* **20/1**

326 6 7 **Copybook**[27] 6847 3-8-9 **65**.. JoeFanning 3 49
(Mark Johnston) *led: rdn and hdd over 2f out: wknd over 1f out* **15/2**

3422 7 2 ¾ **Arr' Kid (USA)**[6] 7369 3-9-2 **72**.............................. TomEaves 1 52
(Keith Dalgleish) *chsd ldrs: rdn over 4f out: wknd 3f out* **9/2**

410 8 shd **Lineman**[17] 7105 3-9-2 **72**.. LiamKeniry 8 52
(Andrew Hollinshead) *hld up: pushed along and hdwy over 3f out: rdn and wknd over 2f out* **16/1**

3m 5.36s (-0.64) **Going Correction** +0.15s/f (Slow)
WFA 3 from 4yo+ 9lb 8 Ran SP% **113.6**
Speed ratings (Par 103): **107,105,104,104,100 96,95,95**
toteswingers 1&2 £2.30, 1&3 £8.40, 2&3 £10.80 CSF £17.67 CT £147.74 TOTE £4.70: £1.70, £1.20, £4.50; EX 20.90 Trifecta £101.40 Pool: £2152.57 - 15.90 winning units..
Owner Mrs D Edginton **Bred** Michael G Daly **Trained** Lambourn, Berks

FOCUS
Not bad form for the grade, with a few to consider beforehand, and a couple of improving 3yos filling the first two positions.

7511 DOWNLOAD THE LADBROKES APP H'CAP (DIV I) 7f 32y(P)

7:00 (7:01) (Class 6) (0-60,60) 3-Y-0+ **£2,102** (£625; £312; £156) **Stalls** High

Form RPR

2336 1 **Hail Promenader (IRE)**[16] 7124 7-9-2 **55**.................(tp) WilliamCarson 1 65
(Anthony Carson) *mde all: rdn over 1f out: styd on u.p* **3/1**[1]

3200 2 1 ¾ **Just A Pound (IRE)**[35] 6588 3-8-10 **58**......................... HarryBurns(7) 8 62
(Jo Hughes) *trckd wnr: rdn and hung lft over 1f out: styd on* **8/1**

424 3 nk **Loyal N Trusted**[29] 6777 5-9-0 **60**.............................. GemmaTutty(7) 2 64
(Karen Tutty) *hld up: hdwy over 2f out: nt clr run over 1f out: rdn and r.o: nvr able to chal* **4/1**[2]

5030 4 1 ¼ **Jackie Love (IRE)**[26] 6871 5-8-7 **46** oh1...................(v) CathyGannon 11 47
(Olivia Maylam) *hld up: rdn over 1f out: r.o ins fnl f: nvr nrr* **20/1**

2041 5 1 ¾ **Admirals Walk (IRE)**[32] 6698 3-9-5 **60**.........................(tp) LiamKeniry 4 55
(Sylvester Kirk) *chsd ldrs: rdn over 1f out: no ex ins fnl f* **7/1**[3]

0542 6 1 ¾ **Hinton Admiral**[77] 5230 9-9-0 **53**... JoeFanning 5 44
(Pat Eddery) *racd promly: rdn over 1f out: no ex ins fnl f* **7/1**[3]

05 7 2 ½ **The Which Doctor**[148] 2787 8-8-7 **46** oh1......................(bt) LukeMorris 3 31
(Violet M Jordan) *s.i.s: outpcd* **14/1**

3000 8 nse **Daisie Cutter**[25] 6902 3-7-12 **46** oh1.............................. EilishMcCall(7) 7 29
(Graeme McPherson) *trckd ldrs: racd keenly: wknd 2f out* **40/1**

1m 30.97s (1.37) **Going Correction** +0.15s/f (Slow)
WFA 3 from 4yo+ 2lb 8 Ran SP% **95.0**
Speed ratings (Par 101): **98,96,95,94,92 90,87,87**
toteswingers 1&2 £3.50, 1&3 £2.90, 2&3 £5.50 CSF £18.25 CT £49.33 TOTE £2.30: £1.30, £1.90, £1.20; EX 25.50 Trifecta £133.00 Pool: £1171.00 - 6.60 winning units..
Owner David J Newman & Ross Bennett **Bred** Rathbarry Stud **Trained** Newmarket, Suffolk

FOCUS
Solid-looking form for the level, despite the late withdrawal of Game All.

7512 DOWNLOAD THE LADBROKES APP H'CAP (DIV II) 7f 32y(P)

7:30 (7:31) (Class 6) (0-60,60) 3-Y-0+ **£2,102** (£625; £312; £156) **Stalls** High

Form RPR

2431 1 **Powerful Pierre**[7] 7347 6-9-2 **60**..........................(b) JacobButterfield(5) 6 74
(Ollie Pears) *hld up: hdwy over 1f out: rdn to ld ins fnl f: r.o* **2/1**[2]

5002 2 1 **Maakirr (IRE)**[7] 7354 4-9-4 **60**....................................(t) MarkCoumbe(3) 2 71
(Roy Bowring) *trckd ldr tl led 4f out: rdn over 1f out: hdd ins fnl f: styd on* **7/4**[1]

U000 3 4 **Lucy Minaj**[30] 6760 3-8-6 **47**..(p) JoeFanning 10 47
(Bryan Smart) *s.i.s: racd keenly and hdwy 6f out: nt clr run fr over 2f out tl wl over 1f out: styd on same pce fnl f* **33/1**

2650 4 ¾ **Monty Fay (IRE)**[18] 7079 4-8-8 **47**..................................(tp) LukeMorris 5 45
(Derek Haydn Jones) *a.p: rdn to chse ldr over 2f out: no ex fnl f* **20/1**

0360 5 1 ½ **Methaaly (IRE)**[17] 7106 10-9-1 **57**..............................(be) RobertTart(3) 3 51
(Michael Mullineaux) *sn outpcd: hdwy u.p over 1f out: nt trble ldrs* **14/1**

4405 6 ½ **Wotalad**[27] 6849 3-8-8 **54**.. GeorgeChaloner(5) 1 46
(Richard Whitaker) *led 3f: rdn over 2f out: wknd ins fnl f* **25/1**

0000 7 ½ **Mataajir (USA)**[113] 3977 5-9-2 **55**..(t) DaleSwift 4 47
(Derek Shaw) *hld up: hdwy u.p over 1f out: wknd ins fnl f* **20/1**

0340 8 3 ½ **Bapak Pesta (IRE)**[24] 6919 3-9-3 **58**............................... TomEaves 7 39
(Kevin Ryan) *chsd ldrs: rdn 1/2-way: wknd fnl f* **8/1**[3]

0004 9 2 ¼ **Schoolboy Champ**[24] 6921 6-8-7 **46** oh1...................(tp) CathyGannon 9 22
(Lisa Williamson) *in rr: pushed along 1/2-way: sn wknd* **33/1**

1635 10 3 **Angels Calling**[15] 7148 3-8-10 **58**.................................... BTTreanor(7) 8 25
(K R Burke) *hld up: rdn and wknd over 2f out* **14/1**

1m 30.26s (0.66) **Going Correction** +0.15s/f (Slow)
WFA 3 from 4yo+ 2lb 10 Ran SP% **113.4**
Speed ratings (Par 101): **102,100,96,95,93 93,92,88,86,82**
toteswingers 1&2 £1.50, 1&3 £32.30, 2&3 £20.00 CSF £5.11 CT £76.53 TOTE £3.40: £1.30, £1.10, £7.80; EX 7.80 Trifecta £138.70 Pool: £1644.70 - 8.88 winning units..
Owner Terence Elsey **Bred** Hedsor Stud **Trained** Norton, N Yorks

FOCUS
The front two were well handicapped and pulled clear of some moderate rivals in a quicker time than the first division.

7513 LADBROKES BRITISH STALLION STUDS EBF MEDIAN AUCTION MAIDEN STKS 1m 1f 103y(P)

8:00 (8:00) (Class 5) 2-Y-0 **£2,911** (£866; £432; £216) **Stalls** Low

Form RPR

44 1 **Sbraase**[118] 3810 2-9-5 0.. LukeMorris 6 79
(James Tate) *a.p: chsd ldr over 5f out: rdn over 2f out: edgd lft and styd on u.p to ld wl ins fnl f* **5/1**[2]

0232 2 1 ½ **Arantes**[14] 7162 2-9-5 78.. MartinHarley 3 76
(Mick Channon) *led: rdn over 1f out: edgd lft: hdd and unable qck wl ins fnl f* **4/5**[1]

3 2 ¼ **Al Busayyir (IRE)** 2-9-5 0...................................... SaleemGolam 2 72
(Marco Botti) *s.i.s: sn prom: rdn over 1f out: styd on same pce fnl f* **7/1**

4 2 ¾ **Can't Change It (IRE)** 2-9-5 0.. MartinLane 8 67
(David Simcock) *hld up: pushed along over 2f out: r.o ins fnl f: nvr nrr* **12/1**

6 5 ½ **Glorious Sinndar (FR)**[17] 7089 2-9-5 0......................... BarryMcHugh 7 66
(George Margarson) *hld up: hmpd after 1f: pushed along 1/2-way: hdwy u.p over 2f out: hung lft and wknd fnl f* **40/1**

6 nk **Hallouella** 2-9-0 0.. JoeFanning 1 60
(James Tate) *trckd ldr tl over 5f out: remained handy tl rdn over 2f out: wknd over 1f out* **14/1**

7 68 **Rite To Reign** 2-9-5 0... WilliamCarson 5 +
(Philip McBride) *dwlt: hmpd after 1f: a in rr: drvn along 4f out: wknd 3f out* **33/1**

0 P **Sworn Vow (IRE)**[16] 7128 2-9-5 0................................... RobertHavlin 4
(John Gosden) *prom tl wnt wrong and p.u after 1f: fatally injured* **11/2**[3]

2m 4.7s (3.00) **Going Correction** +0.15s/f (Slow) 8 Ran SP% **119.8**
Speed ratings (Par 95): **92,90,88,86,85 85,25,**
toteswingers 1&2 £1.50, 1&3 £6.10, 2&3 £4.30 CSF £9.87 TOTE £3.80: £1.30, £1.10, £2.90; EX 9.80 Trifecta £59.80 Pool: £2146.23 - 26.89 winning units..
Owner Saeed Manana **Bred** Miss K Rausing **Trained** Newmarket, Suffolk

FOCUS
An interesting little maiden, but unfortunately Sworn Vow went badly wrong on the first circuit and had to be put down.

7514 LADBROKES MOBILE H'CAP 1m 1f 103y(P)

8:30 (8:33) (Class 6) (0-60,60) 3-Y-0+ **£2,102** (£625; £312; £156) **Stalls** Low

Form RPR

0063 1 **Buster Brown (IRE)**[6] 7378 4-9-8 **58**.............................. GrahamLee 11 72
(James Given) *hld up: hdwy over 2f out: led over 1f out: rdn clr: eased nr fin* **7/4**[1]

6600 2 4 **Windsor Secret**[24] 6921 3-8-7 **47** oh1 ow1.....................(p) TomEaves 10 53
(Keith Dalgleish) *chsd ldrs: n.m.r over 3f out: nt clr run 2f out: sn lost pl: hung lft and styd on ins fnl f* **50/1**

3026 3 hd **Dubai Celebration**[35] 6598 5-9-6 **56**.............................. BarryMcHugh 5 61
(Julie Camacho) *mid-div: nt clr run over 2f out: hdwy u.p over 1f out: styd on* **4/1**[3]

3260 4 1 ¾ **Xpres Maite**[149] 2785 10-9-7 **60**..............................(v) MarkCoumbe(3) 12 62
(Roy Bowring) *s.s: hdwy over 4f out: rdn and ev ch over 2f out: hmpd over 1f out: no ex fnl f* **20/1**

-621 5 ½ **Cantor**[13] 7201 5-9-10 **60**... PatrickDonaghy 3 60
(Giles Bravery) *s.i.s: sn pushed along in rr: r.o ins fnl f: nvr nrr* **11/4**[2]

000 6 2 ¾ **Inigo Montoya**[32] 6700 3-8-4 **49**........................... ShirleyTeasdale(5) 13 44
(Alan McCabe) *mid-div: hdwy over 3f out: rdn to ld wl over 1f out: sn hung lft and hdd: wknd ins fnl f* **100/1**

0000 7 3 **Silver Fawn (IRE)**[116] 3909 3-8-1 **46**......................(be) JoeyHaynes(5) 9 34
(John Weymes) *hld up: hdwy on outer over 2f out: rdn and ev ch whn hung lft over 1f out: wknd ins fnl f* **33/1**

3000 8 2 ¾ **Smirfy's Silver**[48] 6216 9-8-8 **47**............................... RobertTart(3) 6 30
(Michael Mullineaux) *trckd ldr tl led 4f out: rdn and hdd wl over 1f out: hmpd sn after and wknd* **16/1**

9 2 ½ **Aaronkayzo (IRE)**[142] 3005 4-8-10 **46** oh1...................... KieranO'Neill 1 23
(Peter McCreery, Ire) *prom: racd keenly: rdn over 2f out: wknd over 1f out* **33/1**

6506 10 ¾ **Lucky Mountain**[18] 7082 3-8-6 **46** oh1...........................[1] LukeMorris 2 22
(Scott Dixon) *sn led: hdd 4f out: sn drvn along: wknd over 1f out* **20/1**

0000 11 11 **Doctor's Gift**[9] 7299 3-8-12 **52**.....................................(p) LiamKeniry 4 5
(Pat Eddery) *chsd ldrs: pushed along over 4f out: wknd over 2f out* **66/1**

6020 12 7 **Mudaawem (USA)**[11] 7238 3-9-0 **54**.................................... JoeFanning 8
(Mark Johnston) *mid-div: pushed along and lost pl over 6f out: sn bhd* **7/1**

2m 3.34s (1.64) **Going Correction** +0.15s/f (Slow)
WFA 3 from 4yo+ 4lb 12 Ran SP% **121.3**
Speed ratings (Par 101): **98,94,94,92,92 89,87,84,82,81 72,65**
toteswingers 1&2 £26.90, 1&3 £2.10, 2&3 £50.10 CSF £121.36 CT £335.44 TOTE £3.70: £1.80, £10.70, £1.10; EX 134.30 Trifecta £1515.70 Pool: £2686.78 - 1.32 winning units..
Owner Mrs Linda P Fish **Bred** Yeguada De Milagro Sa **Trained** Willoughton, Lincs

FOCUS
A moderate handicap.

7515 FOLLOW US ON TWITTER @LADBROKES H'CAP 1m 141y(P)

9:00 (9:02) (Class 6) (0-65,65) 3-Y-0+ **£1,940** (£577; £288; £144) **Stalls** Low

Form RPR

4000 1 **Punditry**[37] 6521 3-8-12 **60**..(v) RobertTart(3) 11 71
(James Toller) *hld up: nt clr run over 2f out: hdwy over 1f out: r.o to ld wl ins fnl f* **8/1**[3]

6326 2 2 ¼ **Hanalei Bay (IRE)**[24] 6921 3-9-4 **63**................................... TomEaves 8 69
(Keith Dalgleish) *a.p: rdn over 3f out: hung lft and styd on ins fnl f* **7/1**[2]

045 3 hd **Testa Rossa (IRE)**[35] 6612 3-9-4 **63**.................................. SebSanders 9 68
(J W Hills) *hld upm: pushed along 1/2-way: hdwy on outer over 2f out: rdn to ld over 1f out: hdd and no ex wl ins fnl f* **4/1**[1]

0001 4 1 ¾ **Pat's Legacy (USA)**[17] 7092 7-9-5 **63**...............(p) JemmaMarshall(3) 12 64
(Pat Phelan) *led: rdn and hdd over 1f out: no ex ins fnl f* **16/1**

4512 5 ¾ **Icy Blue**[6] 7383 5-8-12 **58**...(p) GeorgeChaloner(5) 6 58
(Richard Whitaker) *chsd ldrs: rdn over 2f out: styd on same pce fr over 1f out* **4/1**[1]

4003 6 3 ½ **Delightful Sleep**[11] 7246 5-8-10 **58**................................. EoinWalsh(7) 3 50
(David Evans) *hld up: nt clr run fr over 2f out tl swtchd rt ins fnl f: nvr trbld ldrs* **16/1**

0316 7 ½ **Warden Bond**[48] 6218 5-9-10 **65**....................................(p) LukeMorris 5 55
(William Stone) *prom: rdn over 3f out: wknd ins fnl f* **14/1**

0452 8 3 **Birdy Boy (USA)**[22] 6968 3-9-4 **63**.................................. JoeFanning 7 47
(Mark Johnston) *chsd ldrs: rdn over 2f out: wknd and eased fnl f* **7/1**[2]

4240 9 ½ **Brown Pete (IRE)**[17] 7091 5-9-4 **59**................................ MartinHarley 1 41
(Violet M Jordan) *s.i.s: a in rr* **10/1**

0503 10 6 **Geeaitch**[17] 7093 4-9-2 **57**.. WilliamCarson 2 26
(Anthony Carson) *chsd ldrs: hmpd and eased over 2f out* **8/1**[3]

5160 11 hd **Master Of Song**[16] 7130 6-9-6 **64**...........................(p) MarkCoumbe(3) 10 32
(Roy Bowring) *hld up: hdwy 1/2-way: rdn and wknd over 1f out: eased* **40/1**

6260 12 22 **Silvas Romana (IRE)**[29] 6780 4-9-6 **61**......................... TomMcLaughlin 4
(Mark Brisbourne) *s.i.s: sn drvn along into mid-div: wknd over 3f out* **33/1**

1m 50.32s (-0.18) **Going Correction** +0.15s/f (Slow)
WFA 3 from 4yo+ 4lb 12 Ran SP% **120.1**
Speed ratings (Par 101): **106,104,103,102,101 98,98,95,94,89 89,69**
toteswingers 1&2 £24.90, 1&3 £19.40, 2&3 £9.90 CSF £63.96 CT £262.22 TOTE £13.10: £4.10, £2.70, £1.10; EX 79.50 Trifecta £658.30 Pool: £2013.13 - 2.29 winning units..
Owner P C J Dalby **Bred** George Strawbridge **Trained** Newmarket, Suffolk

FOCUS
Another moderate handicap, but truly run.

T/Plt: £45.90 to a £1 stake. Pool: £91429.34 - 1452.43 winning tickets T/Qpdt: £2.50 to a £1 stake. Pool: £14924.10 - 4392.90 winning tickets CR

7516 - 7520a (Foreign Racing) - See Raceform Interactive

[7355]DUNDALK (A.W) (L-H)

Friday, October 25

OFFICIAL GOING: Standard

7521a MERCURY STKS (LISTED RACE) 5f (P)

8:15 (8:18) 2-Y-O+ **£21,138** (£6,178; £2,926; £975)

RPR

1 **Timeless Call (IRE)**[41] 6415 5-9-8 100 PatSmullen 3 98
(Reginald Roberts, Ire) *trckd ldr: cl 2nd 1/2-way: got on terms fr 2f out gng best: rdn to ld ent fnl f and kpt on wl towards fin* **6/1**

2 *3/4* **Monsieur Joe (IRE)**[31] 6719 6-9-13 98 JosephO'Brien 2 101+
(Robert Cowell) *chsd ldrs: 4th 1/2-way: hdwy bhd horses fr 2f out: n.m.r ent fnl f: sn rdn and wnt 2nd cl home: hld* **14/1**

3 *3/4* **Angels Will Fall (IRE)**[12] 7227 4-9-8 100 WayneLordan 4 93+
(Charles Hills) *trckd ldrs: cl 3rd 1/2-way: rdn fr 2f on outer and wnt 2nd ins fnl f: sn no ex and edgd lft u.p: dropped to 3rd cl home* **6/4**[1]

4 *1/2* **Almadaa**[7] 7355 6-9-13 86 FergalLynch 5 96
(David Marnane, Ire) *broke wl to ld: narrow advantage 1/2-way: rdn and strly pressed fr 2f out: no imp u.p on wnr whn sltly hmpd ins fnl f: kpt on same pce* **33/1**

5 *1/2* **Fast In The Wind (IRE)**[153] 2675 2-8-9 94 ChrisHayes 7 88+
(P D Deegan, Ire) *w.w: 6th 1/2-way: stl gng wl bhd horses over 1f out: sn swtchd and rdn in 5th: kpt on same pce wout ever threatening* **10/1**

6 *nse* **Yulong Baoju (IRE)**[21] 7004 3-9-8 97 (tp) JohnnyMurtagh 1 90+
(Edward Lynam, Ire) *w.w: tk clsr order fr under 2f out: nt clr run on inner ent fnl f: sn rdn and kpt on towards fin wout ever threatening* **9/2**[3]

7 *nk* **Nocturnal Affair (SAF)**[21] 7004 7-9-13 103 WJLee 6 93+
(David Marnane, Ire) *in tch: 5th 1/2-way: rdn 1 1/2f out and kpt on u.p towards fin wout troubling principals* **3/1**[2]

58.85s (58.85)
WFA 2 from 3yo+ 18lb **7 Ran SP% 116.2**
CSF £82.41 TOTE £6.90: £3.00, £3.10; DF 109.30 Trifecta £441.20.
Owner Reginald Roberts **Bred** John Quinn **Trained** Rathangan, Co Kildare

FOCUS
Not the strongest of Listed sprints. The fourth, who has a good record here, has been rated to the best view of his C&D form.

7522 - 7524a (Foreign Racing) - See Raceform Interactive

[7492]DONCASTER (L-H)

Saturday, October 26

OFFICIAL GOING: Soft (6.0)

Wind: Fresh; half against Weather: Mostly fine but breezy

7525 SCOTT DOBSON MEMORIAL DONCASTER STKS (LISTED RACE) 6f

2:05 (2:05) (Class 1) 2-Y-O **£15,835** (£5,989; £2,993; £1,495) **Stalls** High

Form RPR

1 **1** **Night Of Thunder (IRE)**[13] 7218 2-9-1 0 RichardHughes 6 108+
(Richard Hannon) *trckd ldrs: led over 1f out: qcknd clr ins fnl f: v readily* **6/4**[1]

511 **2** *3* **Aeolus**[15] 7170 2-9-1 96 GrahamGibbons 5 99
(Ed McMahon) *trckd ldrs: swtchd rt over 1f out: styd on to take 2nd last 50yds* **10/3**[2]

16 **3** *hd* **Stubbs (IRE)**[130] 3422 2-9-4 0 JosephO'Brien 1 101
(A P O'Brien, Ire) *stdd s: hld up: hdwy on outside over 2f out: upsides over 1f out: kpt on same pce* **9/2**[3]

3525 **4** *3* **Rufford (IRE)**[14] 7207 2-9-1 107 RyanMoore 4 89
(Richard Fahey) *trckd ldr: led after 1f: hdd over 1f out: wknd last 150yds* **6/1**

1163 **5** *3 1/4* **Brave Boy (IRE)**[14] 7207 2-9-1 99 (v[1]) MickaelBarzalona 3 80
(Saeed bin Suroor) *t.k.h: led 1f: trckd ldrs: drvn over 2f out: wknd fnl f* **8/1**

1m 16.91s (3.31) **Going Correction** +0.50s/f (Yiel) **5 Ran SP% 106.7**
Speed ratings (Par 103): **97,93,92,88,84**
CSF £6.19 TOTE £2.20: £1.30, £2.10; EX 6.50 Trifecta £15.40 Pool: £2,129.81 - 103.33 winning units..
Owner Saeed Manana **Bred** Frank Dunne **Trained** East Everleigh, Wilts

FOCUS
An interesting Listed race to start proceedings, in which the quintet raced centre-to-stands' side, and it saw a hugely impressive performance from the winner.

7526 DOWNLOAD THE RACING POST MOBILE APP H'CAP 1m 4f

2:40 (2:40) (Class 2) (0-100,100) 3-Y-O+ **£12,938** (£3,850; £1,924; £962) **Stalls** Low

Form RPR

1121 **1** **Thomas Hobson**[13] 7223 3-9-2 97 RobertHavlin 2 106
(John Gosden) *trckd ldrs: led 2f out: edgd lft ins fnl f: jst hld on* **9/2**[2]

230 **2** *hd* **Kashmir Peak (IRE)**[15] 7174 4-8-7 86 ow1 OisinMurphy[(5)] 9 94
(John Quinn) *mid-div: hdwy and upsides over 2f out: hung rt ins fnl f: styd on wl towards fin: jst hld* **11/1**

4330 **3** *1/2* **Highland Castle**[63] 5766 5-9-5 93 JohnnyMurtagh 13 100
(David Elsworth) *t.k.h towards rr: hdwy on outside 3f out: hung bdly rt to stands' side over 1f out: styd on wl ins fnl f* **16/1**

5433 **4** *1/2* **Voodoo Prince**[35] 6638 5-9-6 94 (p) GrahamLee 8 101
(Ed Dunlop) *trckd ldrs: upsides over 1f out: kpt on same pce* **8/1**

4635 **5** *2 3/4* **Van Percy**[15] 7174 3-8-7 88 CathyGannon 10 90
(Andrew Balding) *t.k.h: trckd ldrs: hung rt ins fnl f: one pce* **11/2**[3]

-502 **6** *1 3/4* **Nicholascopernicus (IRE)**[15] 7174 4-9-5 93 TomMcLaughlin 6 93
(Ed Walker) *hld up towards rr: effrt over 3f out: styd on fnl f* **13/2**

1511 **7** *1 1/4* **Ennistown**[30] 6772 3-9-5 100 MickaelBarzalona 1 98
(Charlie Appleby) *t.k.h in mid-div: hdwy on ins over 4f out: led over 3f out: hdd 2f out: sn wknd* **4/1**[1]

1660 **8** *1* **O Ma Lad (IRE)**[35] 6631 5-9-0 88 (p) MichaelO'Connell 12 84
(John Quinn) *in rr: sme hdwy over 2f out: kpt on fnl f: nvr a factor* **33/1**

2420 **9** *1 1/4* **Rio's Rosanna (IRE)**[15] 7174 6-8-13 87 RussKennemore 7 82
(Richard Whitaker) *t.k.h in mid-div: hdwy and upsides over 3f out: wknd over 1f out* **16/1**

1000 **10** *9* **Warlu Way**[15] 7174 6-9-0 88 (t) JamesSullivan 11 69
(Michael Easterby) *t.k.h in rr: effrt over 3f out: sn lost pl* **66/1**

1214 **11** *3 1/2* **Centred (IRE)**[12] 7250 3-8-8 89 RyanMoore 3 65
(Sir Michael Stoute) *set stdy pce: hdd over 3f out: sn lost pl: eased over 1f out* **7/1**

0060 **12** *10* **Itlaaq**[15] 7174 7-8-12 86 (tp) GrahamGibbons 14 47
(Michael Easterby) *trckd ldrs: drvn over 2f out: sn lost pl: eased whn bhd ins fnl f* **28/1**

2m 41.65s (6.75) **Going Correction** +0.50s/f (Yiel)
WFA 3 from 4yo+ 7lb **12 Ran SP% 118.5**
Speed ratings (Par 109): **97,96,96,96,94 93,92,91,90,84 82,75**
toteswingers 1&2 £7.70, 1&3 £11.10, 2&3 £18.00 CSF £52.61 CT £734.95 TOTE £5.00: £1.70, £4.40, £4.40; EX 52.90 Trifecta £1160.40 Pool: £99,341.63 - 64.20 winning units..
Owner Bailey, Hall & Hood **Bred** Mount Coote Stud And M H Dixon **Trained** Newmarket, Suffolk

FOCUS
A decent middle-distance handicap, but they went no pace early which caused a few to take a hold and a couple, including the winner, showed some wayward tendencies late on. The runners came off the inside rail on reaching the straight.

7527 BET THROUGH THE RACING POST MOBILE APP H'CAP 5f

3:15 (3:17) (Class 2) 3-Y-O+

£31,125 (£9,320; £4,660; £2,330; £1,165; £585) **Stalls** High

Form RPR

4110 **1** **Dungannon**[15] 7171 6-8-7 95 ow1 (b) OisinMurphy[(5)] 16 106
(Andrew Balding) *chsd ldrs stands' side: led 1f out: hld on towards fin* **16/1**

0400 **2** *1/2* **Hawkeyethenoo (IRE)**[7] 7364 7-9-8 105 GrahamLee 3 114
(Jim Goldie) *hld up towards far side: effrt over 1f out: sn w ldrs: styd on take 2nd clsng stages* **16/1**

200 **3** *nk* **Harrison George (IRE)**[14] 7208 8-9-0 97 (t) GrahamGibbons 12 105
(P J O'Gorman) *mid-div stands' side: hdwy 2f out: chsng ldrs 1f out: kpt on same pce clsng stages* **33/1**

0043 **4** *1 1/2* **Pearl Blue (IRE)**[15] 7171 5-8-9 92 TedDurcan 17 95
(Chris Wall) *in rr stands' side: hdwy 2f out: styd on same pce ins fnl f* **10/1**

0060 **5** *nk* **Tangerine Trees**[45] 6305 8-9-5 102 (v) JoeFanning 14 104
(Bryan Smart) *led overall stands' side gp: hdd 1f out: no ex* **25/1**

30 **6** *nk* **Jamaican Bolt (IRE)**[15] 7171 5-8-11 94 JamesDoyle 18 95
(Geoffrey Oldroyd) *chsd ldrs stands' side: kpt on same pce appr fnl f* **6/1**[2]

2201 **7** *1/2* **Steps (IRE)**[21] 7010 5-9-9 106 (b) AndreaAtzeni 20 105
(Roger Varian) *hld up in mid-div stands' side: effrt over 1f out: kpt on same pce* **7/1**[3]

0050 **8** *1/2* **Ballesteros**[20] 7054 4-9-8 105 MartinLane 22 102
(Brian Meehan) *hld up stands' side: effrt 2f out: kpt on: nvr a factor* **14/1**

0430 **9** *nk* **An Saighdiur (IRE)**[14] 7208 6-9-2 99 JosephO'Brien 1 95
(Andrew Slattery, Ire) *trckd ldrs far side: kpt on same pce appr fnl f* **9/1**

0422 **10** *1 1/2* **Kyleakin Lass**[15] 7171 4-8-11 94 (p) RichardHughes 2 84
(Jonathan Portman) *prom far side: effrt over 2f out: one pce over 1f out* **14/1**

0405 **11** *hd* **Confessional**[7] 7373 6-9-2 99 (e) DavidAllan 9 89
(Tim Easterby) *chsd ldrs stands' side: one pce over 1f out* **25/1**

0000 **12** *shd* **Secret Witness**[1] 7495 7-9-1 98 (b) ShaneKelly 11 87
(Ronald Harris) *s.i.s: in rr stands' side: swtchd lft over 1f out: nvr a factor* **25/1**

2406 **13** *shd* **Valbchek (IRE)**[14] 7208 4-9-4 101 (b[1]) RyanMoore 10 90
(Jeremy Noseda) *in rr stands' side: effrt over 2f out: kpt on fnl f* **11/1**

50 **14** *1/2* **Forest Edge (IRE)**[33] 6699 4-8-4 92 (b) NoelGarbutt[(5)] 6 79
(David Evans) *mid-div far side: effrt over 2f out: one pce* **50/1**

01 **15** *1 1/4* **Take Cover**[15] 7171 6-9-2 99 JohnnyMurtagh 5 82
(David C Griffiths) *led far side gp: wknd appr fnl f* **9/2**[1]

6160 **16** *3/4* **Doc Hay (USA)**[14] 7208 6-9-6 103 DanielTudhope 8 83
(David O'Meara) *strated slowly: swtchd rt to stands' side rail after 1f: rdn over 2f out: nvr on terms* **22/1**

014 **17** *1/2* **Free Zone**[21] 7010 4-9-7 104 PaulHanagan 4 82
(Bryan Smart) *w ldrs towards far side: wknd over 1f out* **20/1**

4562 **18** *1 3/4* **Addictive Dream (IRE)**[32] 6719 6-9-1 98 TonyHamilton 19 70
(David Nicholls) *chsd ldrs stands' side: lost pl over 1f out* **25/1**

300 **19** *11* **Judge 'n Jury**[21] 7010 9-8-8 98 (t) RossCoakley[(7)] 7 30
(Ronald Harris) *s.i.s: sn trcking ldrs far side: lost pl over 2f out: edgd rt and bhd whn rdr dropped reins over 1f out: eased* **25/1**

1m 1.7s (1.20) **Going Correction** +0.50s/f (Yiel) **19 Ran SP% 130.7**
Speed ratings (Par 109): **110,109,108,106,105 105,104,103,103,100 100,100,100,99,97 96,95,92,75**
toteswingers 1&2 £72.90, 1&3 £126.90, 2&3 £126.90 CSF £231.82 CT £8296.79 TOTE £24.80: £4.60, £3.70, £7.50, £2.70; EX 413.40 Trifecta £3814.60 Part won. Pool: £5,086.15 - 0.30 winning units..
Owner DR E Harris **Bred** J A E Hobby **Trained** Kingsclere, Hants

FOCUS
A red-hot sprint handicap in which the field split into two early, with the smaller group of seven coming up the centre and the larger group of 12 racing nearer the stands' rail. The two groups had merged by the time they reached the furlong pole.

7528 RACING POST TROPHY (GROUP 1) (ENTIRE COLTS & FILLIES) 1m (S)

3:50 (3:52) (Class 1) 2-Y-O

£149,714 (£56,760; £28,406; £14,150; £7,101; £3,564) **Stalls** High

Form RPR

11 **1** **Kingston Hill**[14] 7195 2-9-0 0 AndreaAtzeni 8 119+
(Roger Varian) *trckd ldrs: chsd ldr over 2f out: led over 1f out: drvn clr: styd on strly* **7/2**[1]

4 **2** *4 1/2* **Johann Strauss**[6] 7401 2-9-0 0 RyanMoore 6 110
(A P O'Brien, Ire) *hld up in rr t.k.h early: hdwy over 2f out: chsd wnr 1f out: styd on: no imp* **9/1**

3 **3** *2 1/2* **Altruistic (IRE)**[27] 6884 2-9-0 0 JohnnyMurtagh 9 104
(J P Murtagh, Ire) *in rr: effrt over 3f out: styd on fnl f: tk 3rd nr fin* **14/1**

4 **4** *nk* **Dolce N Karama (IRE)**[29] 6807 2-9-0 0 TadhgO'Shea 10 103
(John Patrick Shanahan, Ire) *stdd s: hld up in rr: hdwy over 3f out: sn drvn: chsng ldrs over 1f out: kpt on same pce* **200/1**

1 **5** *3/4* **Buonarroti (IRE)**[20] 7050 2-9-0 0 PaulHanagan 11 102
(A P O'Brien, Ire) *led: drvn over 3f out: hdd over 1f out: one pce* **14/1**

111 **6** *3 1/4* **Chief Barker (IRE)**[49] 6195 2-9-0 103 RichardHughes 2 95
(Richard Hannon) *hld up in rr: hdwy over 3f out: sn drvn: wknd jst ins fnl f* **8/1**

122 **7** *1/2* **The Grey Gatsby (IRE)**[42] 6390 2-9-0 108 GrahamLee 7 93
(Kevin Ryan) *chsd ldrs: drvn over 3f out: wknd jst ins fnl f* **16/1**

341 **8** *shd* **Snow Sky**[24] 6954 2-9-0 89 JamesDoyle 3 93
(Sir Michael Stoute) *trckd ldrs: drvn 3f out: sn lost pl: edgd rt over 1f out: kpt on towards fin* **15/2**

4212 **9** *2* **Somewhat (USA)**[28] 6835 2-9-0 112 JoeFanning 4 89
(Mark Johnston) *chsd ldrs: drvn over 2f out: wknd over 1f out* **9/1**

11 **10** *nk* **Pinzolo**[36] 6593 2-9-0 0 .... MickaelBarzalona 5 88
(Charlie Appleby) *hld up in mid-div: hdwy 3f out: sn drvn: hung lft and lost pl over 1f out* **4/1**[2]

11 *32* **Century (IRE)**[13] 7225 2-9-0 0 .... JosephO'Brien 1 18
(A P O'Brien, Ire) *dwlt: in rr: drvn over 4f out: reminder over 3f out: sn lost pl: bhd whn eased fnl f: t.o* **6/1**[3]

1m 44.83s (5.53) **Going Correction** +0.85s/f (Soft) **11 Ran SP% 119.1**
Speed ratings (Par 109): **106,101,99,98,97 94,94,94,92,91 59**
toteswingers 1&2 £6.90, 1&3 £8.60, 2&3 £23.00 CSF £36.14 TOTE £4.00: £1.60, £4.00, £4.50; EX 35.80 Trifecta £316.80 Pool: £9,797.52 - 23.18 winning units..
Owner Paul Smith **Bred** Ridgecourt Stud **Trained** Newmarket, Suffolk

FOCUS
The final domestic Group 1 contest of the season and the 25th running of the race as the Racing Post Trophy. The withdrawal of Toormore earlier in the week due to the prospect of soft ground had robbed the race of an established Group 1 performer. None of the 11 runners who eventually went to post (four of them supplementary entries) had won at above Group 3 level, but class eventually came to the fore with the only previous Group-race winner coming out on top. The field race up the centre and the pace looked solid enough.

7529 CROWNHOTEL-BAWTRY.COM NURSERY H'CAP 7f
4:25 (4:27) (Class 3) (0-95,86) 2-Y-O £6,469 (£1,925; £962; £481) **Stalls High**

Form RPR

313 **1** **Roachdale House (IRE)**[37] 6545 2-9-6 **85** .... RyanMoore 7 92+
(Richard Fahey) *hld up in rr: hdwy over 2f out: led over 1f out: edgd rt: drvn out* **5/2**[1]

6305 **2** *2 1/4* **Tancred (IRE)**[15] 7170 2-8-6 **71** .... BarryMcHugh 10 72
(Tony Coyle) *hld up in rr: hdwy stands' side to ld over 2f out: hdd over 1f out: kpt on to take 2nd nr fin* **11/2**[3]

0140 **3** *hd* **Donny Rover (IRE)**[8] 7333 2-8-9 **74** ....(v) RobbieFitzpatrick 8 75
(David C Griffiths) *drvn to chse ldrs: hmpd over 2f out: kpt on to chse wnr jst ins fnl f: one pce* **25/1**

2053 **4** *2* **Malachim Mist (IRE)**[17] 7129 2-9-7 **86** .... RichardHughes 5 82
(Richard Hannon) *chsd ldrs: drvn over 2f out: kpt on fnl f* **6/1**

302 **5** *1* **Dandana (IRE)**[17] 7126 2-8-10 **75** .... MartinLane 9 68
(Clive Brittain) *chsd ldrs: upsides over 2f out: one pce fnl f* **14/1**

021 **6** *6* **Torchlighter (IRE)**[30] 6769 2-9-6 **85** .... JoeFanning 11 63
(Mark Johnston) *led: hung lft thrght: hdd over 1f out: lost pl over 1f out* **4/1**[2]

10 **7** *nk* **Comino (IRE)**[21] 7026 2-9-6 **85** .... JamesDoyle 4 62
(Kevin Ryan) *w ldrs: drvn over 2f out: wknd fnl f* **11/2**[3]

0U00 **8** *8* **Regiment**[21] 7017 2-8-11 **76** .... PaulHanagan 3 33
(Richard Fahey) *chsd ldrs: drvn over 4f out: lost pl appr fnl f: heavily eased clsng stages* **14/1**

2033 **9** *2 1/4* **Arrowzone**[10] 7309 2-8-3 **71** .... BillyCray[(3)] 2 23
(Garry Moss) *drvn to chse ldrs: lost pl after 2f: chsd ldrs 3f out: sn lost pl and bhd* **16/1**

1m 32.32s (6.02) **Going Correction** +0.85s/f (Soft) **9 Ran SP% 116.7**
Speed ratings (Par 99): **99,96,96,93,92 85,85,76,73**
toteswingers 1&2 £4.50, 1&3 £25.50, 2&3 £18.30 CSF £16.67 CT £278.14 TOTE £3.70: £1.70, £2.10, £5.50; EX 21.50 Trifecta £510.00 Pool: £2,179.38 - 3.20 winning units..
Owner G Devlin **Bred** G Devlin **Trained** Musley Bank, N Yorks

FOCUS
A decent nursery.

7530 RACING POST IPAD APP CONDITIONS STKS 7f
5:00 (5:00) (Class 3) 3-Y-0+ £8,092 (£2,423; £1,211; £605; £302) **Stalls High**

Form RPR

3114 **1** **Highland Colori (IRE)**[14] 7190 5-8-13 111 .... OisinMurphy[(5)] 2 116
(Andrew Balding) *led one other towards centre: edgd rt and styd on wl fnl f: readily* **15/8**[1]

0020 **2** *3* **Sovereign Debt (IRE)**[42] 6392 4-8-11 108 .... RyanMoore 3 101
(Michael Bell) *trckd wnr centre: effrt over 1f out: kpt on: no imp* **9/4**[2]

3600 **3** *7* **Stand My Ground (IRE)**[42] 6396 6-8-11 97 .... DanielTudhope 1 83
(David O'Meara) *s.s: swtchd to stands' side after 100yds: effrt 3f out: kpt on to take modest 3rd 1f out* **20/1**

3245 **4** *5* **Free Wheeling (AUS)**[21] 7013 5-8-11 107 ....(p) PaulHanagan 5 70
(Saeed bin Suroor) *trckd ldr stands' side: drvn 3f out: wknd fnl f* **7/2**[3]

0230 **5** *15* **Firebeam**[21] 7025 5-8-11 102 .... MickaelBarzalona 4 31
(Charlie Appleby) *led 2 others to stands' side: drvn over 2f out: lost pl over 1f out: eased whn bhd* **9/2**

1m 30.97s (4.67) **Going Correction** +0.85s/f (Soft) **5 Ran SP% 110.7**
Speed ratings (Par 107): **107,103,95,89,72**
CSF £6.46 TOTE £2.90: £1.50, £1.60; EX 6.10 Trifecta £49.40 Pool: £1,532.06 - 23.23 winning units..
Owner Evan M Sutherland **Bred** Rathbarry Stud **Trained** Kingsclere, Hants

FOCUS
A strange conditions event as, despite there only being five runners, they split into two groups and it was the pair who raced up the centre who dominated, beating the trio who came up the stands' rail out of sight.

7531 UNIVERSAL RECYCLING APPRENTICE H'CAP 7f
5:30 (5:30) (Class 4) (0-85,84) 3-Y-O £5,175 (£1,540; £769; £384) **Stalls High**

Form RPR

1524 **1** **Soaring Spirits (IRE)**[23] 6963 3-9-0 **77** ....(b) OisinMurphy 3 86
(Roger Varian) *trckd ldrs: led over 2f out: hung rt and lft ins fnl f: hld on nr fin* **7/1**

3004 **2** *1/2* **Lazarus Bell**[27] 6874 3-9-3 **80** .... JacobButterfield 11 87
(Alan Brown) *mid-div: hdwy over 2f out: chsd wnr ins fnl f: no ex* **16/1**

4133 **3** *1 1/4* **Tatlisu (IRE)**[36] 6586 3-9-7 **84** .... GeorgeChaloner 2 88
(Richard Fahey) *hld up in mid-div: hdwy over 2f out: chal 1f out: fnd little* **5/1**[2]

4355 **4** *1 1/4* **George Rooke (IRE)**[72] 5440 3-9-0 **80** .... KevinStott[(3)] 6 81
(Kevin Ryan) *hld up: hdwy over 2f out: kpt on fnl f* **11/2**[3]

0620 **5** *1* **Ocean Applause**[12] 7257 3-8-8 **76** ....(tp) JordonMcMurray[(5)] 5 74
(John Ryan) *outpcd and in rr after 2f: hdwy over 2f out: edgd rt over 1f out: one pce* **25/1**

3012 **6** *1 1/2* **Teetotal (IRE)**[33] 6682 3-8-9 **75** .... LauraBarry[(3)] 4 69
(Nigel Tinkler) *t.k.h: led: hdd over 2f out: one pce* **16/1**

2560 **7** *nk* **Entwined (IRE)**[59] 5896 3-8-7 **70** oh1 .... RyanTate 8 63
(Clive Cox) *trckd ldrs: upsides over 2f out: wknd last 100yds* **20/1**

6146 **8** *6* **Glanely (IRE)**[17] 7123 3-8-10 **78** .... LewisWalsh[(5)] 13 56
(James Fanshawe) *s.i.s: sme hdwy over 2f out: wknd over 1f out* **4/1**[1]

1-46 **9** *1/2* **Lilac Tree**[12] 7257 3-9-1 **78** .... ConnorBeasley 14 54
(Mark Johnston) *chsd ldrs: lost pl 3f out* **4/1**[1]

0500 **10** *6* **Shrimper Roo**[7] 7374 3-9-0 **77** ....(b) DarylByrne 7 38
(Tim Easterby) *strated v slowly: nvr on terms* **25/1**

2303 **11** *1 1/2* **Huntsmans Close**[37] 6575 3-9-2 **84** .... LouisSteward[(5)] 12 41
(Michael Bell) *t.k.h: trckd ldrs: lost pl over 2f out: eased ins fnl f* **9/1**

1m 31.47s (5.17) **Going Correction** +0.85s/f (Soft) **11 Ran SP% 118.8**
Speed ratings (Par 103): **104,103,102,100,99 97,97,90,89,83 81**
toteswingers 1&2 £20.70, 1&3 £4.70, 2&3 £13.60 CSF £110.14 CT £618.65 TOTE £7.30: £2.30, £3.70, £2.00; EX 117.90 Trifecta £1411.80 Pool: £2,478.36 - 1.31 winning units..
Owner J Collins, N Horsfall & N O'Sullivan **Bred** Kevin & Meta Cullen **Trained** Newmarket, Suffolk
■ Stewards' Enquiry : Jacob Butterfield four-day ban: use of whip (9, 11 -13 Nov)

FOCUS
Quite a competitive apprentice handicap.
T/Jkpt: £18,280.20 to a £1 stake. Pool: £51,493.57 - 2.00 winning units T/Plt: £195.80 to a £1 stake. Pool: £175,583.00 - 654.60 winning units T/Qpdt: £50.20 to a £1 stake. Pool: £9,228.64 - 135.94 winning units WG

7500 NEWBURY (L-H)
Saturday, October 26

OFFICIAL GOING: Heavy (5.1)
Wind: Brisk across Weather: Overcast Rails: Rail has been moved in on the Round course. Rail has been moved out from the 5f and there is a cut off at 2 1/2f on the inside rail

7532 CRACKED 80 EBF MAIDEN FILLIES' STKS (DIV I) 1m (S)
1:15 (1:16) (Class 4) 2-Y-O £4,075 (£1,212; £606; £303) **Stalls Centre**

Form RPR

1 **Wylye** 2-9-0 0 .... DavidProbert 4 75+
(Andrew Balding) *led 2f: styd trcking ldr: led again appr fnl 2f: hrd drvn whn pressed thrght fnl f: hld on wl in clsng stages* **8/1**

2 *nk* **Dogaressa (IRE)** 2-9-0 0 .... JamieSpencer 6 75+
(Peter Chapple-Hyam) *hld up towards rr: stdy hdwy to trck ldrs over 2f out: drvn to chal ins fnl f: kpt on but no ex in clsng stages* **10/1**

4 **3** *2 1/2* **Cascading**[28] 6828 2-9-0 0 .... JimmyFortune 7 69
(Hughie Morrison) *chsd ldrs: drvn to chal 2f out: styd on same pce u.p ins fnl f* **11/2**[2]

504 **4** *shd* **Crystal Nymph (IRE)**[15] 7175 2-9-0 69 .... DaneO'Neill 3 69
(Richard Hannon) *chsd ldrs: drvn to chal fr over 1f out tl ins fnl f: kpt on same pce* **13/2**

0 **5** *2* **Isabella Liberty (FR)**[86] 4921 2-9-0 0 .... JimmyQuinn 2 65+
(Robert Eddery) *in rr: hdwy ins fnl 2f: kpt on fnl f but nvr gng pce to rch ldrs* **20/1**

0 **6** *1 3/4* **Cradle Of Life (IRE)**[28] 6828 2-9-0 0 .... WilliamBuick 10 61+
(Ed Dunlop) *in rr: pushed along and hdwy fr 2f out: kpt on same pce ins fnl f* **13/2**

3 **7** *4 1/2* **Cameo Tiara (IRE)**[10] 7296 2-9-0 0 .... PatDobbs 11 51+
(Richard Hannon) *in rr whn stmbld after 1f: t.k.h: after: in tch fr 1/2-way: rdn 2f out: wknd fnl f* **6/1**[3]

8 *3 1/2* **Cinnilla** 2-9-0 0 .... JimCrowley 5 43+
(Ralph Beckett) *chsd ldrs: drvn over 2f out: wknd wl over 1f out* **4/1**[1]

0 **9** *11* **Good Hope**[18] 7103 2-9-0 0 .... TomQueally 12 19
(Michael Bell) *towards rr early: hdwy 1/2-way: wknd over 2f out* **12/1**

00U **10** *1 1/2* **Step Away**[23] 6974 2-9-0 0 .... SteveDrowne 1 16
(Charles Hills) *veered bdly lft s and lost many l: rcvrd to take slt ld after 2f: hdd appr fnl 2f: wknd qckly* **50/1**

0 **11** *32* **Secret Suspect**[14] 7200 2-9-0 0 .... PatCosgrave 9
(Ed Walker) *in tch: wknd ins fnl 3f* **20/1**

1m 48.2s (8.50) **Going Correction** +0.975s/f (Soft) **11 Ran SP% 115.7**
Speed ratings (Par 94): **96,95,93,93,91 89,84,81,70,68 36**
toteswingers 1&2 £16.30, 1&3 £10.40, 2&3 £11.00 CSF £81.67 TOTE £10.20: £3.20, £3.70, £2.10; EX 110.20 Trifecta £300.90 Pool: £924.91 - 2.30 winning units..
Owner Mrs James Wigan **Bred** Mrs James Wigan **Trained** Kingsclere, Hants

FOCUS
Inside rail moved out from 5f and there was a cut off at 2.5f. Rail on round course moved out between 8f and 5f which increased distances on round course by 22m.There'd been further rain since the previous day's meeting and the ground was really testing. In 2011 a division of this maiden went to subsequent Oaks runner-up Shirocco Star, while last year's race was won by Secret Gesture, who also ran second in the fillies' Classic at Epsom. There were some nice types amongst this lot, but few would have really liked the ground. They raced middle-to-stands' side.

7533 CRACKED 80 EBF MAIDEN FILLIES' STKS (DIV II) 1m (S)
1:45 (1:48) (Class 4) 2-Y-O £4,075 (£1,212; £606; £303) **Stalls Centre**

Form RPR

5 **1** **Lady Tyne**[58] 5922 2-9-0 0 .... MartinHarley 6 84+
(Roger Charlton) *chsd ldrs: led ins fnl 2f: pushed clr fnl f* **8/1**

55 **2** *8* **Tioga Pass**[26] 6896 2-9-0 0 .... TomQueally 5 66+
(Paul Cole) *wnt lft s: in rr: hdwy 2f out and sn swtchd rt: stayig on whn hmpd 1f out: styd on again to take 2nd in clsng stages but no ch w wnr* **20/1**

25 **3** *1/2* **Acclio (IRE)**[10] 7296 2-9-0 0 .... MartinDwyer 3 65
(Clive Brittain) *in tch: hdwy whn bmpd over 2f out: kpt on to chse ldrs fnl f and styd on for 3rd but nvr any ch w wnr* **16/1**

604 **4** *nk* **Yeah Baby (IRE)**[23] 6973 2-9-0 72 .... SteveDrowne 7 65
(Charles Hills) *chsd ldrs: rdn and kpt on fr over 1f out to chse wnr ins fnl f: no imp and one pce into 4th in clsng stages* **12/1**

6 **5** *1/2* **Super Moment (IRE)**[23] 6974 2-9-0 0 .... SilvestreDeSousa 12 64
(Saeed bin Suroor) *chsd ldrs: rdn and edgd rt u.p 1f out: dispured 2nd ins fnl f: styd on same pce into 5th in clsng stages* **4/1**[2]

0333 **6** *5* **Royal Connection**[15] 7175 2-8-7 73 .... CameronHardie[(7)] 1 53
(Richard Hannon) *led: hdd ins fnl 2f: edgd rt and wknd fnl f* **8/1**

633 **7** *1* **Cay Dancer**[44] 6318 2-9-0 75 .... JimmyFortune 8 54
(Richard Hannon) *in tch hdwy to chse ldrs u.p whn wnt lft over 2f out: wknd wl over 1f out* **7/1**[3]

8 *3* **What A Scorcher** 2-9-0 0 .... AdamKirby 9 44
(Clive Cox) *in tch: hdwy to cl on ldrs 3f out: wknd over 2f out* **10/1**

0 **9** *1/2* **Olymnia**[93] 4668 2-9-0 0 .... JimmyQuinn 2 43
(Robert Eddery) *in rr: sme hdwy over 2f out whn bmpd and sn wknd* **66/1**

10 *8* **Female Strategy (IRE)** 2-9-0 0 .... JamieSpencer 4 25
(Peter Chapple-Hyam) *hmpd s: a towards rr* **12/1**

6 **11** *2 1/2* **Sea Goddess (IRE)**[24] 6954 2-9-0 0 .... JimCrowley 11 20
(Ralph Beckett) *chsd ldrs: wknd qckly 3f out* **3/1**[1]

50 **12** *nk* **Modern Art**[8] 7332 2-9-0 0 .... AdrianNicholls 10 19
(Mark Johnston) *chsd ldr tl over 3f out: sn btn* **33/1**

1m 47.69s (7.99) **Going Correction** +0.975s/f (Soft) **12 Ran SP% 119.3**
Speed ratings (Par 94): **99,91,90,90,89 84,83,80,80,72 69,69**
toteswingers 1&2 £16.20, 1&3 £27.60, 2&3 £28.00 CSF £159.29 TOTE £10.80: £3.60, £6.10, £4.50; EX 260.30 Trifecta £689.00 Part won. Pool: £978.78 - 0.02 winning units..

The Form Book Flat, Raceform Ltd, Compton, RG20 6NL.

Owner Paul Hearson **Bred** Paul Hearson Bloodstock **Trained** Beckhampton, Wilts

FOCUS

Hard to know what to make of this form, but the time was just over half a second quicker than the first leg, and they again raced middle-to-stands' side. The winner was impressive and looks a decent prospect.

7534 WORTHINGTON'S WHIZZ KIDS STKS (REGISTERED AS THE HORRIS HILL STAKES) (GROUP 3) (C&G) 7f (S)

2:20 (2:21) (Class 1) 2-Y-O

£22,684 (£8,600; £4,304; £2,144; £1,076; £540) **Stalls** Centre

Form RPR

11 **1** **Piping Rock**[24] 6955 2-8-12 0 PatDobbs 7 107+
(Richard Hannon) *in tch: hdwy to trck ldr and hung lft over 2f out: qcknd to ld over 1f out: styd on strly* **3/1**[2]

2 *2 ¾* **Galiway**[29] 2-8-12 0 OlivierPeslier 3 100+
(A Fabre, France) *in tch: drvn 2f out: hdwy over 1f out: kpt on fnl f to take 2nd fnl 50yds but no imp on wnr* **5/2**[1]

3112 **3** *¾* **Day Of Conquest**[27] 6866 2-8-12 97 JimmyFortune 8 98
(Richard Hannon) *chsd ldrs: drvn to chal 2f out: chsd wnr over 1f out: no imp fnl f and one pce into 3rd fnl 50yds* **25/1**

021 **4** *1 ¾* **Cordite (IRE)**[11] 7271 2-8-12 85 AndrewMullen 11 94
(Michael Appleby) *sn led: rdn and hdd 2f out: rallied and kpt on to take 4th ins fnl f but no imp on ldng trio* **11/1**

1001 **5** *1* **Trading Profit**[11] 7268 2-8-12 100 DavidProbert 1 91
(Andrew Balding) *chsd ldrs: led 2f out: hdd over 1f out: wknd ins fnl f* **9/1**[3]

2121 **6** *¾* **Extra Noble**[24] 6935 2-8-12 90 JimCrowley 10 89
(Ralph Beckett) *stdd s: in rr: hdwy fr 2f out: styd on fnl f nt rch ldrs* **12/1**

1030 **7** *4* **Kickboxer (IRE)**[15] 7170 2-8-12 86 SamHitchcott 2 79
(Mick Channon) *in tch: drvn and hdwy to chse ldrs wl over 2f out: wknd wl over 1f out* **40/1**

12 **8** *6* **Invincible Strike (IRE)**[33] 6697 2-8-12 0 MartinHarley 5 64
(James Tate) *rdn over 2f out: a towards rr* **16/1**

0613 **9** *4* **Morning Post**[21] 7026 2-8-12 103 (b) JamieSpencer 9 54
(Kevin Ryan) *stdd s: hrd drvn over 2f out: a towards rr* **10/1**

2110 **10** *4* **Lyn Valley**[35] 6645 2-8-12 94 SilvestreDeSousa 4 44
(Mark Johnston) *t.k.h: chsd ldrs to 3f out* **20/1**

2060 **11** *½* **Anticipated (IRE)**[21] 7026 2-8-12 106 DaneO'Neill 6 43
(Richard Hannon) *rdn ins fnl 3f: a towards rr* **9/1**[3]

1m 30.84s (5.14) **Going Correction** +0.975s/f (Soft) **11** Ran SP% **115.6**

Speed ratings (Par 105): **109,105,105,103,101 101,96,89,85,80 79**

toteswingers 1&2 £1.40, 1&3 £14.70, 2&3 £18.70 CSF £10.39 TOTE £4.40: £1.80, £1.40, £6.00; EX 7.20 Trifecta £133.10 Pool: £ 2223.14- 12.51 winning units..

Owner R J McCreery & Pall Mall Partners **Bred** Stowell Hill Ltd **Trained** East Everleigh, Wilts

FOCUS

Usually just an ordinary Group 3, but the front two both look quite smart. They raced up the middle.

7535 WORTHINGTON'S CHAMPION SHIELD & VICTORIA CLUB STKS (REGISTERED AS THE ST SIMON STAKES) (GROUP 3) 1m 4f 5y

2:55 (2:55) (Class 1) 3-Y-O+

£34,026 (£12,900; £6,456; £3,216; £1,614; £810) **Stalls** Centre

Form RPR

-532 **1** **Cubanita**[42] 6385 4-9-0 102 JimCrowley 3 109
(Ralph Beckett) *trckd ldrs: drvn to go 2nd appr fnl f: carried rt sn after but kpt on wl to ld fnl 150yds* **9/2**[2]

2601 **2** *1 ¾* **Nichols Canyon**[22] 6991 3-8-10 104 WilliamBuick 8 110
(John Gosden) *trckd ldrs: led appr fnl 2f: hung rt u.p fnl f: hdd and no ex fnl 150yds* **7/4**[1]

2-40 **3** *5* **Cocktail Queen (IRE)**[167] 2299 3-8-7 97 WilliamCarson 5 100
(David Elsworth) *sn trcking ldr: chal over 2f out tl outpcd over 1f out* **25/1**

5601 **4** *5* **Quiz Mistress**[46] 6294 5-9-0 106 PatDobbs 2 93
(Hughie Morrison) *in rr: drvn 3f out: hdwy ins fnl 2f sn no prog u.p* **17/2**

2100 **5** *2 ¾* **Sugar Boy (IRE)**[31] 6742 3-8-13 109 (b[1]) MartinHarley 7 95
(Marco Botti) *in rr: rdn and styd on fr 3f out but nvr nr ldrs and wknd over 2f out* **12/1**

5054 **6** *5* **Model Pupil**[30] 6766 4-9-3 100 TomQueally 6 85
(Charles Hills) *rdn over 3f out: a towards rr* **10/1**

3-50 **7** *½* **Masterstroke (USA)**[49] 6198 4-9-3 114 AdamKirby 4 84
(Charlie Appleby) *led: hdd & wknd over 2f out* **8/1**

3301 **8** *56* **Prince Bishop (IRE)**[49] 6198 6-9-6 112 (v) SilvestreDeSousa 1
(Saeed bin Suroor) *chsd ldrs: rdn and btn 3f out* **5/1**[3]

2m 43.62s (8.12) **Going Correction** +0.975s/f (Soft)

WFA 3 from 4yo+ 7lb **8** Ran SP% **113.5**

Speed ratings (Par 113): **111,109,106,103,101 98,97,60**

toteswingers 1&2 £3.90, 1&3 £26.90, 2&3 £10.60 CSF £12.58 TOTE £5.90: £1.90, £1.10, £3.90; EX 14.90 Trifecta £348.70 Pool: £2191.41 - 4.71 winning units..

Owner Miss K Rausing **Bred** Miss K Rausing **Trained** Kimpton, Hants

FOCUS

An ordinary Group 3 and the front two travelled best before drawing clear.

7536 BATHWICK TYRES H'CAP 1m 2f 6y

3:30 (3:30) (Class 2) (0-105,100) 3-Y-O+

£12,450 (£3,728; £1,864; £932; £466; £234) **Stalls** Centre

Form RPR

6031 **1** **Hi There (IRE)**[37] 6551 4-8-10 **91** SamanthaBell(7) 8 104
(Richard Fahey) *in tch: stdy hdwy over 2f out: led appr fnl f: pushed clr* **13/2**[2]

0020 **2** *3 ½* **Beaumont's Party (IRE)**[29] 6801 6-9-7 **95** JamieSpencer 12 101
(Brian Ellison) *sn stdd in rr: hdwy over 2f out: sn rdn: styd on fnl f to chse wnr fnl 110yds but nvr any ch* **8/1**

3541 **3** *¾* **Cashpoint**[23] 6976 8-8-11 **85** WilliamBuick 4 90
(Ian Williams) *trckd ldrs: led appr fnl 2f and sn rdn: hdd appr fnl f: sn outpcd by wnr: styd on same pce for 3rd fnl 110yds* **8/1**

0055 **4** *½* **Anton Chigurh**[8] 7337 4-8-10 **84** RichardKingscote 10 88
(Tom Dascombe) *in rr: hdwy 3f out: styd on u.p fr over 1f out: kpt on one pce fnl f* **15/2**[3]

1100 **5** *2 ¾* **Soviet Rock (IRE)**[107] 4214 3-9-0 **93** DavidProbert 2 91
(Andrew Balding) *led: hdd 2f out: wknd 1f out* **7/2**[1]

0R **6** *1 ¾* **King's Warrior (FR)**[24] 6957 6-9-10 **98** JimmyFortune 1 93
(Peter Chapple-Hyam) *stdd s: in rr: rdn and hdwy over 2f out: sn one pce* **25/1**

0006 **7** *5* **Resurge (IRE)**[24] 6957 8-9-6 **94** (t) TomQueally 7 80
(Stuart Kittow) *in rr: hdwy 3f out: sn drvn: wknd fr 2f out* **20/1**

1212 **8** *4 ½* **Break Rank (USA)**[25] 6927 4-9-0 **88** PatCosgrave 6 65
(Ed de Giles) *chsd ldrs: wknd over 2f out* **8/1**

5606 **9** *2 ¾* **Salutation (IRE)**[13] 7223 3-8-10 **89** AdrianNicholls 5 61
(Mark Johnston) *chsd ldr: rdn 3f out: wknd sn after* **18/1**

6100 **10** *5* **Sam Sharp (USA)**[14] 7206 7-9-8 **96** JimCrowley 11 58
(Ian Williams) *a towards rr* **8/1**

2203 **11** *2 ½* **Tigers Tale (IRE)**[29] 6801 4-9-0 **88** (v) DaneO'Neill 3 46
(Roger Teal) *in tch: trckd ldrs fr 4f out: wknd wl over 2f out* **14/1**

2103 **12** *16* **Mister Music**[21] 7018 4-9-9 **100** (b) WilliamTwiston-Davies(3) 9 27
(Richard Hannon) *chsd ldrs tl wknd rapidly ins fnl 3f* **18/1**

2m 18.14s (9.34) **Going Correction** +1.175s/f (Soft)

WFA 3 from 4yo+ 5lb **12** Ran SP% **117.6**

Speed ratings (Par 109): **109,106,105,105,103 101,97,94,91,87 85,73**

toteswingers 1&2 £14.90, 1&3 £3.80, 2&3 £19.80 CSF £57.26 CT £425.87 TOTE £7.40: £2.60, £2.90, £2.40; EX 71.00 Trifecta £583.80 Pool: £2602.62 - 3.34 winning units..

Owner Market Avenue Racing Club Ltd **Bred** J & J Waldron **Trained** Musley Bank, N Yorks

FOCUS

It was raining and conditions were gloomy, but a decent enough handicap which went to an improving sort. The action unfolded up the middle of the track in the straight.

7537 FREE BETS FREEBETS.CO.UK STKS (REGISTERED AS THE RADLEY STAKES) (LISTED RACE) (FILLIES) 7f (S)

4:05 (4:07) (Class 1) 2-Y-O

£14,461 (£5,482; £2,743; £1,366; £685; £344) **Stalls** Centre

Form RPR

2166 **1** **Aqlaam Vision**[21] 7016 2-8-12 85 WilliamBuick 4 95
(Clive Brittain) *hld up in rr: hdwy over 1f out: styd on gamely u.p fnl 150yds to ld cl home* **7/1**

0124 **2** *nk* **Oxsana**[21] 7016 2-8-12 92 TomQueally 9 94
(William Haggas) *hld up in rr: drvn and hdwy fr 2f out: styd on wl fnl f: tk 2nd last stride but nt rch wnr* **5/1**[3]

41 **3** *nse* **Dutch Romance**[12] 7245 2-8-12 0 JamieSpencer 1 94+
(Charles Hills) *t.k.h: trckd ldrs: led 2f out: rdn fnl f: hdd cl home and ct for 2nd last stride* **3/1**[1]

33 **4** *2 ½* **Stosur (IRE)**[9] 7320 2-8-12 0 (p) DavidProbert 8 88
(Gay Kelleway) *in tch: rdn and outpcd over 2f out: styd on again u.p fnl f* **25/1**

2116 **5** *2 ½* **Ligeia**[93] 4682 2-8-12 85 PatDobbs 10 82
(Richard Hannon) *led: hdd 2f out: wknd ins fnl f* **20/1**

416 **6** *nk* **Veiled Intrigue**[35] 6622 2-8-12 94 DaneO'Neill 3 81
(Henry Candy) *chsd ldr: rdn over 2f out: wknd wl over 1f out* **6/1**

6321 **7** *2* **Pretty Flemingo (IRE)**[13] 7221 2-8-12 87 JimmyFortune 7 76
(Richard Hannon) *chsd ldrs: wknd ins fnl 2f* **7/2**[2]

6206 **8** *4* **Azagal (IRE)**[21] 7026 2-8-12 89 DuranFentiman 5 66
(Tim Easterby) *in tch: chsd ldrs and rdn over 2f out: wknd wl over 1f out* **8/1**

6140 **9** *10* **Gown (IRE)**[29] 6795 2-8-12 76 KierenFallon 2 41
(Charles Hills) *t.k.h: chsd ldrs: rdn over 2f out: wknd rapidly over 1f out* **20/1**

1m 34.23s (8.53) **Going Correction** +1.175s/f (Soft) **9** Ran SP% **115.2**

Speed ratings (Par 100): **98,97,97,94,91 91,89,84,73**

toteswingers 1&2 £9.00, 1&3 £5.60, 2&3 £3.30 CSF £40.39 TOTE £7.30: £2.00, £2.00, £1.70; EX 44.40 Trifecta £246.50 Pool: £2548.44 - 7.75 winning units..

Owner Saeed Manana **Bred** Mrs T Brudenell & Trickledown Stud **Trained** Newmarket, Suffolk

FOCUS

A really weak fillies' Listed event. They raced middle-to-stands' side.

7538 WORTHINGTON'S & AYLESBURY EX SERVICEMEN'S CLUB EBF FILLIES' H'CAP 7f (S)

4:40 (4:41) (Class 3) (0-95,93) 3-Y-O+ **£8,733** (£2,598; £1,298; £649) **Stalls** Centre

Form RPR

5644 **1** **Lilac Lace (IRE)**[21] 7024 3-8-7 **81** DuranFentiman 3 90
(Tim Easterby) *mde all: rdn fr over 1f out: styd on wl fnl f: unchal* **10/1**

3510 **2** *2 ½* **Jubilante**[21] 7021 3-8-13 **87** JimmyFortune 5 90
(Hughie Morrison) *hld up in rr: hdwy on stands' rail over 1f out: styd on wl to chse wnr fnl 110yds but no imp* **10/1**

2330 **3** *2 ¼* **Maid A Million**[3] 7470 3-9-5 **93** WilliamCarson 2 90
(David Elsworth) *chsd ldrs: styd on u.p to dispute 2nd ins fnl f but nvr any ch w wnr* **9/2**[3]

2402 **4** *nk* **Magic Destiny**[35] 6625 4-8-11 **88** JoeyHaynes(5) 7 85
(K R Burke) *in tch: rdn over 2f out: styd on to dispute 2nd ins fnl f but nvr any ch w wnr* **10/3**[1]

2041 **5** *½* **Dusky Queen (IRE)**[15] 7176 3-8-7 **88** SamanthaBell(7) 6 83
(Richard Fahey) *in tch: hdwy and hung lft ins fnl 2f: chsd wnr over 1f out but no imp: wknd fnl 110yds* **7/2**[2]

000 **6** *1 ½* **Radio Gaga**[35] 6625 4-9-3 **89** (b[1]) SebSanders 8 81
(Ed McMahon) *chsd ldrs: rdn 2f out: wknd fnl f* **8/1**

0602 **7** *9* **Beautiful View**[11] 7272 3-8-11 **85** TomQueally 1 52
(Richard Hannon) *chsd ldrs: pushed lft ins fnl 2f and sn wknd* **9/2**[3]

1m 32.94s (7.24) **Going Correction** +1.175s/f (Soft)

WFA 3 from 4yo 2lb **7** Ran SP% **111.0**

Speed ratings (Par 104): **105,102,99,99,98 96,86**

toteswingers 1&2 £11.30, 1&3 £8.20, 2&3 £5.90 CSF £94.55 CT £495.77 TOTE £13.10: £3.80, £3.80; EX 98.30 Trifecta £468.30 Pool: £3172.49 - 5.07 winning units..

Owner S A Heley **Bred** Robert Ryan, Brendan Quinn & Joan Quinn **Trained** Great Habton, N Yorks

FOCUS

Again, they raced middle-to-stands' side and the winner had an easy time in front, so not form to take literally.

7539 FREE BETS FREEBETS.CO.UK H'CAP (FOR LADY AMATEUR RIDERS) 1m 4f 5y

5:10 (5:10) (Class 5) (0-75,75) 4-Y-O+ **£2,807** (£870; £435; £217) **Stalls** Centre

Form RPR

0-01 **1** **One Pursuit (IRE)**[6] 7396 5-9-9 **68** 6ex MissJenniferPowell(5) 7 85
(Brendan Powell) *in rr: hdwy over 5f out: led over 3f out: sn drvn clr: easily* **3/1**[1]

/133 **2** *11* **Highway Code (USA)**[24] 6960 7-10-4 **72** MissSBrotherton 14 74
(Richard Lee) *in rr but in tch: hdwy 3f out: chsd easy wnr appr fnl 2f but nvr any ch* **9/2**[2]

5041 **3** *1 ¾* **Yasir (USA)**[11] 7273 5-9-13 **67** (p) MissEJJones 15 66
(Conor Dore) *in rr: hdwy 3f out: styd on to take 3rd fr 2f out: styd on u.p but nvr any ch w easy wnner* **9/1**

5113 **4** *7* **Foxhaven**[126] 3579 11-10-3 **74** (v) MissHayleyMoore(3) 1 63
(Patrick Chamings) *in rr: hdwy fr 2f out: styd on for wl hld 4th fnl f* **14/1**

004 **5** *1 ¾* **Shades Of Grey**[24] 6960 6-10-0 **68** MissRachelKing 16 55
(Clive Cox) *in tch: hdwy to chse ldrs fr 3f out: nvr any ch w easy wnr: wknd fr 2f out* **6/1**[3]

1000 **6** *9* **Tapis Libre**[17] 7131 5-10-4 **75**............................ MissJoannaMason(3) 9 49
(Michael Easterby) *chsd ldrs: wknd 3f out* **25/1**

6500 **7** *1 1/4* **Choral Festival**[11] 7267 7-10-3 **71**............................ MissADeniel 10 44
(John Bridger) *in rr: hdwy over 3f out: sn rdn and nvr rchd ldrs: btn sn after* **16/1**

0-01 **8** *1 3/4* **Spin Cast**[22] 5052 5-10-4 **72**............................(p) MissHBethell 13 42
(Philip Kirby) *chsd ldrs to 3f out* **7/1**

256/ **9** *11* **Compassion**[155] 6891 5-9-0 **61** oh1............................ MsPFeld(7) 4 16
(Emma Lavelle) *bhd most of way* **25/1**

516 **10** *1 1/2* **Superciliary**[10] 7305 4-9-0 **61**............................ MissMNicholls(7) 11 14
(Chris Gordon) *chsd ldrs: sn wknd* **25/1**

1323 **11** *36* **Royal Alcor (IRE)**[18] 7115 6-9-9 **70**........ MissAnne-SophieCrombez(7) 8
(Gay Kelleway) *led tl hdd over 3f out: sn wknd* **7/1**

0-56 **12** *11* **Minty Fox**[16] 7159 4-9-4 **61** oh5............................ MissAliceMills(3) 2
(Noel Williams) *chsd ldrs 7f* **25/1**

2m 47.97s (12.47) **Going Correction** +1.175s/f (Soft) **12** Ran SP% **120.4**
Speed ratings (Par 103): **105,97,96,91,90 84,83,82,75,74 50,43**
toteswingers 1&2 £3.50, 2&3 £9.30, 1&3 £7.60 CSF £15.31 CT £104.97 TOTE £4.10: £2.10, £2.20, £2.80; EX 21.10 Trifecta £112.30 Pool: £1612.64 - 10.76 winning units..
Owner Nicholas J E Maher **Bred** Clougher Partnership **Trained** Upper Lambourn, Berks

FOCUS
A lady amateur riders' contest run in desperate ground, so not the most reliable form.
T/Plt: £386.20 to a £1 stake. Pool of £87455.79 - 165.28 winning tickets. T/Qpdt: £9.30 to a £1 stake. Pool of £7790.20 - 618.50 winning tickets. ST

7508 WOLVERHAMPTON (A.W) (L-H)

Saturday, October 26

OFFICIAL GOING: Standard
Wind: Fresh; behind Weather: Showery

7540 LADBROKES H'CAP — 7f 32y(P)
5:45 (5:46) (Class 2) (0-105,103) 3-Y-O+ **£12,291** (£3,657; £1,827; £913) **Stalls** Low

Form RPR

4010 **1** **My Freedom (IRE)**[105] 4297 5-9-5 **98**.................. SilvestreDeSousa 10 110
(Saeed bin Suroor) *trckd ldrs: wnt 2nd over 2f out: rdn to ld over 1f out: r.o* **2/1**[1]

1305 **2** *1 1/2* **Solar Deity (IRE)**[49] 6199 4-9-2 **95**............................ LukeMorris 9 103
(Marco Botti) *mid-div: hdwy over 2f out: sn rdn: r.o* **7/2**[2]

103 **3** *1/2* **Grey Mirage**[42] 6411 4-9-3 **96**............................(p) MartinHarley 8 103
(Marco Botti) *led 1f: trckd ldr tl led again 1/2-way: rdn and hdd over 1f out: styd on same pce ins fnl f* **6/1**[3]

5136 **4** *1* **Laffan (IRE)**[28] 6826 4-8-13 **92**............................(e[1]) DavidAllan 6 96
(Tim Easterby) *a.p: racd keenly: rdn over 2f out: hung lft and styd on same pce ins fnl f* **16/1**

6045 **5** *3/4* **Tarooq (USA)**[13] 7222 7-9-7 **100**............................(t) AdamBeschizza 5 102
(Stuart Williams) *trckd ldrs: shkn up over 2f out: no ex ins fnl f* **10/1**

0021 **6** *4* **Free Spin (IRE)**[36] 6609 4-8-12 **91**............................ GrahamGibbons 12 82
(David Barron) *s.i.s: hld up: hdwy over 1f out: nt rch ldrs* **8/1**

2-10 **7** *1/2* **Anaconda (FR)**[21] 7014 4-9-4 **97**............................ StephenCraine 1 87
(Tom Dascombe) *hld up: racd keenly: hdwy over 2f out: rdn and wknd over 1f out* **12/1**

0000 **8** *9* **Aubrietia**[10] 7313 4-9-2 **95**............................(b) AndrewMullen 11 60
(Alan McCabe) *hld up: sme hdwy on outer over 2f out: sn wknd* **66/1**

4600 **9** *nk* **Pastoral Player**[14] 7208 6-9-9 **102**............................ TomEaves 3 67
(Hughie Morrison) *s.i.s: a in rr* **14/1**

000 **10** *1 3/4* **Piscean (USA)**[35] 6648 8-9-4 **97**............................ GeorgeBaker 7 57
(Tom Keddy) *hld up: hdwy over 2f out: wknd over 1f out* **22/1**

0100 **11** *6* **Clockmaker (IRE)**[35] 6650 7-9-3 **96**............................ LiamKeniry 4 40
(Conor Dore) *led 6f out: hdd 1/2-way: rdn and wknd over 2f out* **20/1**

5206 **12** *2 3/4* **Pintura**[35] 6624 6-9-5 **103**............................(b) ShaneGray(5) 2 39
(Kevin Ryan) *mid-div: rdn 1/2-way: wknd over 2f out* **25/1**

1m 27.71s (-1.89) **Going Correction** +0.05s/f (Slow) **12** Ran SP% **124.7**
Speed ratings (Par 109): **112,110,109,108,107 103,102,92,91,89 83,79**
toteswingers 1&2 £2.90, 1&3 £3.90, 2&3 £4.30 CSF £8.68 CT £38.40 TOTE £3.10: £1.40, £1.40, £2.70; EX 14.70 Trifecta £60.00 Pool: £2,250.96 - 28.10 winning units..
Owner Godolphin **Bred** Skymarc Farm **Trained** Newmarket, Suffolk

FOCUS
A cracking start to the new British All-Weather Championships with a good quality and valuable handicap. The gallop was just an ordinary one and the winner came down the in the straight. The first five pulled clear.

7541 32RED CASINO BRITISH STALLION STUDS EBF MAIDEN STKS — 5f 20y(P)
6:15 (6:15) (Class 5) 2-Y-O **£2,911** (£866; £432; £216) **Stalls** Low

Form RPR

45 **1** **Maiden Approach**[23] 6973 2-9-0 0............................ TonyHamilton 5 70+
(Richard Fahey) *s.i.s and hmpd s: hdwy over 1f out: shkn up: hung rt and r.o to ld wl ins fnl f: comf* **10/3**[2]

5326 **2** *1* **Simply Black (IRE)**[8] 7349 2-9-0 66............................ DavidNolan 4 64
(David O'Meara) *chsd ldrs: lft in ld 1/2-way: rdn and hung rt fr over 1f out: hdd wl ins fnl f* **9/2**[3]

4202 **3** *shd* **Bounty Girl (IRE)**[18] 7095 2-9-0 71............................(e) DavidAllan 8 64
(Tim Easterby) *chsd ldrs: hmpd 1/2-way: rdn to chse ldr over 1f out: styd on* **6/4**[1]

4 *1* **Random** 2-9-0 0............................ ShaneKelly 9 60
(John Stimpson) *s.i.s: hdwy over 1f out: sn rdn: r.o* **9/1**

5 **5** *1/2* **Diamondsinthesky (IRE)**[7] 7370 2-9-0 0............................ DaleSwift 6 58
(Derek Shaw) *hld up: hdwy 1/2-way: rdn over 1f out: edgd rt: styd on same pce ins fnl f* **66/1**

00 **6** *4 1/2* **Dont Tell Nan**[23] 6966 2-8-7 0............................ AdamMcLean(7) 3 42
(Derek Shaw) *sn led: hung rt over 3f out: hdd and lost pl 1/2-way: sn rdn: wknd fnl f* **16/1**

04 **7** *2* **Aussie Sky (IRE)**[9] 7317 2-9-0 0............................ StephenCraine 2 35
(John Stimpson) *chsd ldr: rdn over 1f out: wknd fnl f* **40/1**

0 **8** *3 3/4* **Minnyvinny**[14] 7200 2-9-0 0............................ LukeMorris 10 21
(Frank Sheridan) *prom: rdn 1/2-way: wknd over 1f out* **66/1**

6305 **9** *3* **Our Sherona**[42] 6408 2-9-0 56............................ JimmyQuinn 1 11
(Gary Harrison) *sn pushed along in rr: hdwy 1/2-way: rdn and wknd over 1f out* **7/1**

03 **10** *7* **Chennai Wind**[7] 7370 2-9-5 0............................ TomEaves 7
(Derek Shaw) *chsd ldrs: hung rt over 3f out: sn lost pl and bhd* **25/1**

1m 3.79s (1.49) **Going Correction** +0.05s/f (Slow) **10** Ran SP% **118.9**
Speed ratings (Par 95): **90,88,88,86,85 78,75,69,64,53**
toteswingers 1&2 £3.10, 1&3 £1.70, 2&3 £1.40 CSF £18.82 TOTE £3.50: £1.80, £1.50, £1.30; EX 24.60 Trifecta £30.70 Pool: £2,697.40 - 65.88 winning units..
Owner Middleham Park Racing LXVII **Bred** Westminster Race Horses Gmbh **Trained** Musley Bank, N Yorks

FOCUS
An uncompetitive maiden, but the winner looks the sort to make further improvement. The gallop was sound and the winner made his ground against the far rail in the home straight.

7542 32RED H'CAP — 1m 5f 194y(P)
6:45 (6:46) (Class 2) (0-105,92) 3-Y-O+ **£12,291** (£3,657; £1,827; £913) **Stalls** Low

Form RPR

6316 **1** **Bin Singspiel**[14] 7210 3-8-7 **80**............................ LukeMorris 8 96+
(James Tate) *a.p: chsd ldr over 3f out: shkn up to ld over 2f out: rdn and hung lft over 1f out: styd on wl: readily* **7/2**[2]

0003 **2** *4* **Expert Fighter (USA)**[25] 6927 4-9-13 **91**.................. SilvestreDeSousa 9 98
(Saeed bin Suroor) *a.p: trckd ldr 11f out: led 4f out: rdn and hdd over 2f out: styd on same pce fr over 1f out* **3/1**[1]

3500 **3** *4 1/2* **Kiama Bay (IRE)**[15] 7174 7-9-12 **90**............................ TomEaves 5 91
(Richard Fahey) *hld up: hdwy 5f out: rdn over 2f out: wknd over 1f out* **16/1**

6010 **4** *8* **Aegaeus**[29] 6802 4-9-12 **90**............................ GrahamLee 4 80
(Ed Dunlop) *racd keenly: trckd ldr 3f: remained handy: shkn up over 2f out: sn wknd* **16/1**

0101 **5** *8* **Lowther**[25] 6927 8-9-9 **90**............................(v) ThomasBrown(3) 7 68
(Lee Carter) *broke wl: sn stdd and lost pl: racd keenly: rdn over 3f out: wknd over 2f out* **14/1**

1201 **6** *2 1/2* **Azrag (USA)**[18] 7115 5-9-8 **86**............................(vt) FrederikTylicki 1 61
(Gerard Butler) *hld up: rdn over 3f out: sn wknd* **9/2**[3]

600 **7** *11* **Masterful Act (USA)**[58] 3765 6-9-3 **84**........ WilliamTwiston-Davies(3) 10 43
(Alan McCabe) *sn led: hdd 4f out: sn hung lft: wknd over 2f out* **20/1**

4231 **8** *47* **Grendisar (IRE)**[11] 7267 3-8-10 **83**............................(p) MartinHarley 3
(Marco Botti) *s.i.s: hld up: rdn over 3f out: sn wknd* **7/1**

4040 **9** *7* **Cavaleiro (IRE)**[30] 6766 4-10-0 **92**............................(p) MartinDwyer 6
(Marcus Tregoning) *s.i.s: racd keenly: hdwy 12f out: rdn and wknd over 3f out* **5/1**

0200 **10** *9* **Sadler's Risk (IRE)**[36] 6591 5-9-12 **90**............................ AdamKirby 2
(Mark Johnston) *prom: pushed along over 6f out: wknd 5f out* **28/1**

3m 1.72s (-4.28) **Going Correction** +0.05s/f (Slow)
WFA 3 from 4yo+ 9lb **10** Ran SP% **121.2**
Speed ratings (Par 109): **114,111,109,104,100 98,92,65,61,56**
toteswingers 1&2 £3.20, 1&3 £13.90, 2&3 £12.00 CSF £15.12 CT £152.46 TOTE £3.60: £2.00, £2.00, £6.20; EX 18.30 Trifecta £247.70 Pool: £2,315.52 - 7.00 winning units..
Owner Saif Ali **Bred** The Lavington Stud **Trained** Newmarket, Suffolk

FOCUS
A very useful handicap but, although a steady gallop only picked up leaving the back straight, the field finished well strung out. The winner raced against the far rail in the straight.

7543 CORAL MOBILE "JUST THREE CLICKS TO BET" H'CAP — 1m 4f 50y(P)
7:15 (7:15) (Class 6) (0-65,65) 3-Y-O **£1,940** (£577; £288; £144) **Stalls** Low

Form RPR

0061 **1** **Mystery Drama**[23] 6964 3-9-7 **65**............................ AdamKirby 5 81+
(Alan King) *hld up: hdwy on bit over 2f out: stl travelling all over rivals whn led wl ins fnl f: easily* **13/8**[1]

-051 **2** *3/4* **Tracks Of My Tears**[21] 7034 3-8-4 **51** oh2............................ RyanPowell(3) 8 57
(Giles Bravery) *hld up: hdwy 1/2-way: rdn to ld over 1f out: sn hung lft: hdd wl ins fnl f: no ch w wnr* **10/1**

3322 **3** *1 3/4* **Train Hard**[19] 7081 3-8-12 **56**............................ SilvestreDeSousa 7 59
(Mark Johnston) *chsd ldrs: pushed along over 3f out: rdn over 2f out: styd on* **11/4**[2]

0600 **4** *3 1/4* **Rocky Two (IRE)**[71] 5497 3-8-10 **54**............................ GrahamGibbons 4 52
(David O'Meara) *trckd ldr: plld hrd: led wl over 1f out: sn rdn and hdd: no ex ins fnl f* **20/1**

0522 **5** *3/4* **Our Golden Girl**[14] 7204 3-8-8 **55**............................(b) RobertTart(3) 9 52
(Shaun Lycett) *hld up: rdn over 3f out: hdwy u.p over 1f out: nt trble ldrs* **8/1**

4615 **6** *4 1/2* **Precision Strike**[20] 6787 3-9-0 **61**............................(v) JasonHart(3) 3 51
(Richard Guest) *led: rdn over 2f out: hdd wl over 1f out: wknd fnl f* **10/1**

0004 **7** *4 1/2* **Platinum Proof (USA)**[8] 7351 3-8-4 **51** oh3............................(v) JulieBurke(3) 1 33
(David O'Meara) *chsd ldrs: rdn over 2f out: wknd over 1f out* **25/1**

6000 **8** *26* **Bold Citizen (IRE)**[10] 7305 3-9-6 **64**............................ GrahamLee 2 5
(Ed Dunlop) *hld up: rdn over 3f out: wknd over 2f out* **15/2**[3]

2m 42.31s (1.21) **Going Correction** +0.05s/f (Slow) **8** Ran SP% **114.4**
Speed ratings (Par 99): **97,96,95,93,92 89,86,69**
toteswingers 1&2 £4.00, 1&3 £1.10, 2&3 £4.80 CSF £19.32 CT £42.44 TOTE £3.10: £1.40, £1.50, £1.60; EX 21.70 Trifecta £60.10 Pool: £2,486.58 - 30.99 winning units..
Owner Incipe Partnership **Bred** Barbury Castle Stud **Trained** Barbury Castle, Wilts

FOCUS
A modest handicap, but a ready and impressive winner. The gallop was an ordinary one and the winner raced centre-to-far side in the straight.

7544 DOWNLOAD THE LADBROKES APP CLAIMING STKS — 1m 141y(P)
7:45 (7:45) (Class 6) 3-Y-O+ **£1,940** (£577; £288; £144) **Stalls** Low

Form RPR

001 **1** **Alakhan (IRE)**[31] 6756 7-9-13 77............................(p) SilvestreDeSousa 9 79
(Ian Williams) *unruly in stalls: s.i.s: rcvrd to trck ldr 7f out: led 3f out: rdn over 1f out: styd on u.p* **2/1**[1]

050 **2** *1/2* **Not Rigg (USA)**[32] 6735 3-9-1 70............................(t) ShaneKelly 3 70
(Gary Harrison) *led 1f: chsd ldrs: rdn over 2f out: styd on* **16/1**

3034 **3** *nk* **Lean On Pete (IRE)**[22] 7000 4-9-8 75.................. JacobButterfield(5) 1 77
(Ollie Pears) *a.p: pushed along over 2f out: rdn and nt clr run ins fnl f: styd on* **11/4**[2]

0505 **4** *1/2* **Egotist (IRE)**[9] 7319 5-9-9 70............................(t) AdamKirby 4 72
(Milton Bradley) *hld up: pushed along over 3f out: hdwy u.p over 1f out: styd on* **11/1**

0500 **5** *3 1/4* **Boom To Bust (IRE)**[13] 7224 5-9-9 69............................(b) SebSanders 7 65
(Barry Brennan) *sn drvn along: led over 7f out: rdn and hdd 3f out: ev ch over 1f out: no ex ins fnl f* **16/1**

1520 **6** *4 1/2* **Officer In Command (USA)**[49] 6215 7-9-9 72............................ LiamKeniry 2 54
(John Butler) *s.i.s: hld up: rdn over 2f out: n.d* **16/1**

110- **7** *14* **A Little Bit Dusty**[354] 7617 5-9-7 80............................(b) FergusSweeney 11 20
(Conor Dore) *chsd ldrs tl rdn and wknd over 2f out* **7/1**

3234 **8** *10* **Gabrial The Boss (USA)**[9] 7325 3-8-10 72.................. DarrenEgan(3) 6
(David Simcock) *hld up: rdn over 2f out: sn wknd* **7/2**[3]

1m 51.97s (1.47) **Going Correction** +0.05s/f (Slow)
WFA 3 from 4yo+ 4lb **8** Ran SP% **120.7**
Speed ratings (Par 101): **95,94,94,93,90 86,74,65**
toteswingers 1&2 £9.00, 1&3 £1.50, 2&3 £16.00 CSF £38.54 TOTE £3.50: £1.10, £4.80, £1.50; EX 40.30 Trifecta £80.20 Pool: £2,301.78 - 21.50 winning units..
Owner Patrick Kelly **Bred** Juergen Imm **Trained** Portway, Worcs

FOCUS
A fair claimer in which the gallop was an ordinary one. The winner came down the centre in the straight.

7545 32RED.COM NURSERY H'CAP 5f 20y(P)
8:15 (8:15) (Class 2) 2-Y-0 £9,056 (£2,695; £1,346; £673) Stalls Low

Form RPR
1002 1 **Viva Verglas (IRE)**[8] 7333 2-9-7 **94**..........................(b) GrahamGibbons 2 97
(David Barron) *mde all: rdn over 1f out: styd on u.p* **11/4**[2]
415 2 ½ **Captain Midnight (IRE)**[53] 6065 2-8-12 **85**.................... GrahamLee 9 86
(David Brown) *sn pushed along in rr: hdwy u.p over 1f out: edgd lft ins fnl f: r.o* **6/1**
1530 3 *shd* **Zalzilah**[29] 6791 2-9-2 **89**..(p) MartinHarley 8 90
(James Tate) *chsd wnr: rdn 1/2-way: hung lft ins fnl f: r.o* **15/2**
0130 4 *nse* **Peterkin (IRE)**[130] 3424 2-8-11 **84**............................ SilvestreDeSousa 5 85
(Mark Johnston) *chsd ldrs: pushed along and edgd lft 1/2-way: rdn over 1f out: r.o* **5/2**[1]
0603 5 1 ¼ **Lexington Rose**[8] 7349 2-8-0 **73**...................................... JimmyQuinn 6 69
(Bryan Smart) *a.p: rdn over 1f out: r.o* **9/2**[3]
5360 6 ¾ **Money Team (IRE)**[19] 7062 2-8-4 **77**.......................... AdamBeschizza 7 70
(Philip Kirby) *sn pushed along in rr: rdn over 1f out: r.o ins fnl f: nt trble ldrs* **22/1**
1006 7 1 ¾ **Champagne Babe**[133] 3332 2-8-2 **75**.............................. LukeMorris 4 62
(Keith Dalgleish) *edgd lft s: mid-div: drvn along 1/2-way: sme hdwy over 1f out: no ex ins fnl f* **22/1**
4305 8 2 ¼ **Orton Park (IRE)**[83] 5029 2-8-3 **76**.................................... MartinLane 1 55
(Tobias B P Coles) *chsd ldrs: rdn whn hmpd 1/2-way: wknd over 1f out* **18/1**
53 9 3 ¼ **Lilo Lil**[23] 6967 2-7-11 **73** oh7...(v[1]) DarrenEgan(3) 3 40
(David C Griffiths) *s.i.s and hmpd s: outpcd* **16/1**

1m 2.6s (0.30) **Going Correction** +0.05s/f (Slow) **9** Ran SP% **119.3**
Speed ratings (Par 101): **99,98,98,97,95 94,91,88,83**
toteswingers 1&2 £2.70, 1&3 £4.10, 2&3 £14.90 CSF £20.59 CT £111.06 TOTE £3.10: £1.20, £2.40, £1.50; EX 25.80 Trifecta £128.80 Pool: £1,527.10 - 8.88 winning units..
Owner Raymond Miquel **Bred** Mrs Mary Coonan **Trained** Maunby, N Yorks
FOCUS
A very useful nursery in which the pace was sound throughout and the principals finished in a bit of a heap. The winner came down the centre in the straight.

7546 32RED ON THE APP STORE FILLIES' H'CAP 1m 1f 103y(P)
8:45 (8:46) (Class 5) (0-75,75) 3-Y-0+ £2,911 (£866; £432; £216) Stalls Low

Form RPR
21-5 1 **Fresa**[24] 6936 4-9-4 **69**.. LukeMorris 8 76
(Sir Mark Prescott Bt) *trckd ldr tl led over 2f out: rdn and hung lft fr over 1f out: styd on* **11/4**[2]
3410 2 1 ¼ **Oratorio's Joy (IRE)**[76] 5304 3-9-3 **72**........................ FergusSweeney 3 77
(Jamie Osborne) *hld up: hdwy over 3f out: rdn over 1f out: styd on* **16/1**
0243 3 *nk* **It's My Time**[15] 7169 4-9-2 **67**.. TonyHamilton 9 71
(Richard Fahey) *hld up: hdwy over 1f out: rdn and r.o wl towards fin* **7/1**[3]
-225 4 2 **Conserve (IRE)**[57] 5942 3-9-6 **75**...................................... TomQueally 11 75
(Lady Cecil) *s.i.s: hld up: hdwy over 3f out: rdn over 1f out: no ex ins fnl f* **5/4**[1]
0420 5 11 **Amoya (GER)**[17] 7131 6-9-8 **73**.................................. AdamBeschizza 12 50
(Philip McBride) *sn led: rdn and hdd over 2f out: wknd over 1f out* **7/1**[3]
2254 6 *nk* **Fatima's Gift**[22] 6997 3-8-11 **69**.................................... DarrenEgan(3) 1 45
(David Simcock) *hld up: rdn over 2f out: sn wknd* **11/1**
3114 7 15 **Remix (IRE)**[59] 5882 4-9-4 **69**.................................... SilvestreDeSousa 6 14
(Ian Williams) *chsd ldrs: pushed along over 3f out: wknd over 2f out* **11/1**

2m 0.99s (-0.71) **Going Correction** +0.05s/f (Slow)
WFA 3 from 4yo+ 4lb **7** Ran SP% **118.7**
Speed ratings (Par 100): **105,103,103,101,92 91,78**
toteswingers 1&2 £15.80, 1&3 £3.60, 2&3 £4.90 CSF £45.55 CT £286.63 TOTE £3.40: £3.00, £4.60; EX 46.30 Trifecta £220.20 Pool: £1,636.40 - 5.57 winning units..
Owner Miss K Rausing **Bred** Miss K Rausing **Trained** Newmarket, Suffolk
FOCUS
A fair fillies' handicap in which the gallop was just an ordinary one. The winner hung towards the far side in the closing stages and the first four pulled clear.
T/Plt: £7.90 to a £1 stake. Pool: £96,660.33 - 8,883.84 winning units T/Qpdt: £6.00 to a £1 stake. Pool: £8,256.88 - 1,010.97 winning units CR

6220 LEOPARDSTOWN (L-H)
Saturday, October 26

OFFICIAL GOING: Soft changing to soft (soft to heavy in places) after race 1 (2.00) changing to soft to heavy after race 3 (3.10)

7548a JRA KILLAVULLAN STKS (GROUP 3) 7f
2:35 (2:36) 2-Y-0 £31,707 (£9,268; £4,390; £1,463)

RPR
1 **Craftsman (IRE)**[6] 7403 2-9-3 **95**.................................. MichaelHussey 6 104
(A P O'Brien, Ire) *mde virtually all: pushed along over 2 l clr into st: reduced advantage nr fin: all out* **7/1**[3]
2 1 **Michaelmas (USA)**[173] 2103 2-9-3 **96**......................... SeamieHeffernan 7 101
(A P O'Brien, Ire) *chsd ldrs on outer: 4th 1/2-way: pushed along into 3rd 2f out: clsd u.p to dispute 2nd ins fnl f and kpt on wl towards fin wout rching wnr* **3/1**[2]
3 *shd* **Shining Emerald**[27] 6882 2-9-3 **112**................................ ChrisHayes 4 101
(P D Deegan, Ire) *trckd ldr: t.k.h: 2nd 1/2-way: rdn and little imp on wnr u.p ins fnl f: dropped to 3rd cl home and kpt on wl wout rching wnr* **4/5**[1]
4 4 ¾ **All Set To Go (IRE)**[27] 6884 2-9-3 **98**.................................. GaryCarroll 5 89
(A Oliver, Ire) *chsd ldrs: 6th 1/2-way: pushed along into st and sn no imp on ldrs: wnt mod 4th ins fnl f: kpt on same pce* **25/1**
5 ½ **Intensical (IRE)**[6] 7403 2-9-3 **85**.................................... KevinManning 2 88
(J S Bolger, Ire) *w.w: tk clsr order in 5th 1/2-way: rdn fr 2f out and sn no imp on ldrs: wnt mod 4th briefly over 1f out: kpt on same pce* **33/1**
6 ½ **Davids Park**[39] 6485 2-9-3 .... WJLee 3 87
(John Joseph Murphy, Ire) *s.i.s and racd in rr: rdn 2f out and kpt on u.p ins fnl f: nvr a threat* **14/1**
7 5 **Lanyard (USA)**[39] 6509 2-9-0 .... PatSmullen 1 71
(D K Weld, Ire) *settled bhd ldr: 3rd 1/2-way: pushed along into st and sn lost pl: no ex u.p: wknd and eased fnl f* **9/1**

1m 33.18s (4.48) **Going Correction** +0.80s/f (Soft) **7** Ran SP% **116.5**
Speed ratings: **106,104,104,99,98 98,92**
CSF £29.20 TOTE £6.30: £3.00, £2.40; DF 29.60 Trifecta £64.70.
Owner Derrick Smith & Mrs John Magnier & Michael Tabor **Bred** Epona Bloodstock Ltd **Trained** Ballydoyle, Co Tipperary
FOCUS
This looked a decent renewal.

7524 MOONEE VALLEY (L-H)
Saturday, October 26

OFFICIAL GOING: Turf: good

7556a SPORTINGBET COX PLATE (GROUP 1) (3YO+) (TURF) 1m 2f 44y
7:40 (12:00) 3-Y-0+
£1,185,897 (£282,051; £141,025; £83,333; £70,512; £64,102)

RPR
1 **Shamus Award (AUS)**[14] 7215 3-7-11 0.....................(t) ChadSchofield 3 112
(Danny O'Brien, Australia) *broke wl and mde virtually all: rdn 2f out: styd on: rapidly diminishing advantage cl home: jst hld on: all out* **20/1**
2 *shd* **Happy Trails (AUS)**[21] 7042 6-9-4 0.............................. DwayneDunn 2 117+
(Byron Cozamanis, Australia) *midfield on inner: rdn and hdwy fr 2f out: str late run and wnt 2nd cl home: clsng rapidly on wnr: jst failed* **11/1**
3 ½ **Fiorente (IRE)**[21] 7042 5-9-4 0...(b) BlakeShinn 14 116
(Gai Waterhouse, Australia) *midfield early: sn trcking ldr on outer: rdn to chal and ev ch 2f out: styd on and chsd wnr but a being hld: dropped to 3rd cl home* **7/1**
4 ¾ **Foreteller**[14] 7212 6-9-4 0...(b) CraigNewitt 8 115+
(Chris Waller, Australia) *hld up towards rr on inner: rdn and hdwy over 1f out: swtchd rt ent fnl f and styd on to go 4th ins fnl 75yds: clsng on ldrs: nrst fin* **20/1**
5 2 **Super Cool (AUS)**[14] 7212 4-9-1 0................................(b) CoreyBrown 13 108
(Mark Kavanagh, Australia) *sn prom: w ldr on outer after 2f and then trckd ldr: 4th 1/2-way: rdn over 2f out: 3rd ent fnl f: styd on but no imp and dropped to 5th ins fnl 75yds* **17/1**
6 ¾ **Side Glance**[70] 5553 6-9-4 0.. CraigAWilliams 1 109
(Andrew Balding) *t.k.h: prom on inner: rdn and styd on steadily against rail in st but nt pce to chal* **40/1**
7 1 ½ **Seville (GER)**[21] 5-9-4 0...(b) HughBowman 9 106
(Robert Hickmott, Australia) *hld up towards rr on outer: hdwy fr 3f out: rdn 2f out: styd on steadily in st but nvr threatened* **30/1**
8 *hd* **It's A Dundeel (NZ)**[35] 4-9-1 0..................................(b) JamesMcDonald 12 103
(Murray Baker, New Zealand) *midfield on outer: rdn over 2f out: styd on steadily but n.d* **3/1**[1]
9 1 ¾ **Green Moon (IRE)**[35] 6-9-4 0.. BrettPrebble 11 102
(Robert Hickmott, Australia) *t.k.h and prom early: sn restrained in tch bhd ldrs: rdn and lost pl over 2f out: outpcd and btn ins fnl f: jnd for 9th post* **11/1**
9 *dht* **Long John (AUS)**[14] 7215 3-7-11 0..............................(b) KerrinMcEvoy 10 97
(Peter Snowden, Australia) *dropped in and hld up in last: rdn and hdwy on wd outside fr over 1f out: styd on steadily in st and dead-heated for 9th post but nvr a factor* **6/1**[3]
11 *shd* **Mull Of Killough (IRE)**[70] 5553 7-9-4 0............................ StevenArnold 4 102
(Jane Chapple-Hyam) *restrained and settled in midfield: rdn over 2f out: sn outpcd: plugged on but nvr a factor* **40/1**
12 3 **Puissance De Lune (IRE)**[21] 7042 5-9-4 0....................(tp) BenMelham 7 96+
(Darren Weir, Australia) *plld hrd and w ldr early: sn restrained in midfield in tch: rdn over 2f out: lost pl and btn over 1f out: fdd and eased towards fin* **9/2**[2]
13 ¾ **Masked Marvel**[21] 5-9-4 0.. MichaelRodd 5 94
(Robert Hickmott, Australia) *hld up in rr: rdn over 2f out: no imp and btn ins fnl f: nvr a factor* **30/1**
14 2 **Rekindled Interest (AUS)**[21] 6-9-4 0...............................(bt) MarkZahra 6 90
(Jim Conlan, Australia) *hld up and sn towards rr: rdn in last over 1f out: sn btn: eased towards fin: nvr a factor* **50/1**

2m 5.27s (125.27)
WFA 3 from 4yo+ 5lb **14** Ran SP% **115.0**
PARI-MUTUEL (NSW TAB - all including 1 aud stake): WIN 21.40; PLACE 5.40, 3.50, 2.80; DF 126.10; SF 261.50.
Owner P S Buckley & G & C Pastoral Co Pty Ltd **Bred** R D Hannon **Trained** Australia
FOCUS
This had looked a competitive renewal of a prestigious race, but plenty of the fancied horses ran poorly and nearly half the field swept wide on the final bend. The winner and third were in the first two positions from an early stage and being drawn low, plus having the patience to hug the inside rail, proved beneficial.

2489 CAPANNELLE (R-H)
Sunday, October 27

OFFICIAL GOING: Turf: good

7558a PREMIO LYDIA TESIO LONGINES (GROUP 1) (3YO+ FILLIES & MARES) (TURF) 1m 2f
3:35 (12:00) 3-Y-0+ £89,430 (£39,349; £21,463; £10,731)

RPR
1 **Charity Line (IRE)**[154] 2697 3-8-10 0................................ FabioBranca 6 106+
(S Botti, Italy) *racd in 4th: tk clsr order on outer over 2f out: qcknd to ld 1 1/2f out: sn hrd pressed by eventual 2nd: hdd 1f out: rallied to regain narrow ld sn after: r.o gamely u.p: asserted cl home* **11/10**[1]
2 *nk* **Path Wind (FR)**[28] 6887 4-9-0 0.................................... CristianDemuro 2 104
(A Wohler, Germany) *midfield: chsd ldrs over 2f out: rdn to press ldr 1 1/2f out: led briefly 1f out: sn hdd: r.o gamely u.p: edgd rt and c cl to wnr: hld cl home* **67/10**[3]
3 2 ½ **Red Lips (GER)**[21] 7057 3-8-10 0.. DarioVargiu 5 100
(Andreas Lowe, Germany) *broke wl and led: hdd after 1f: trckd ldrs: cl 3rd on inner and scrubbed along 2f out: nt pce to go w first two 1 1/2f out: kpt on at same pce fnl f* **6/5**[2]
4 4 **Adriana (GER)**[28] 6894 5-9-0 0.. HarryBentley 8 91
(M Rulec, Germany) *led after 1f: rdn 2 1/2f out: hdd 1 1/2f out: wandered u.p and outpcd by ldrs over 1f out: one pce ins fnl f and jst hld on for 4th* **68/10**
5 *nse* **Valvibrata (ITY)**[28] 4-9-0 0.. MPasquale 1 91
(C Felaco, Italy) *towards rr: rdn 3f out and no immediate imp: disputing last and hrd rdn over 1 1/2f out: styd on fnl f: nrest at fin* **212/10**

6 nk **Kadabra (IRE)**[28] 6890 6-9-0 0.. CFiocchi 3 90
(E Botti, Italy) *midfield on inner: 6th and outpcd over 2 1/2f out: kpt on u.p fnl f: nvr on terms w ldrs* **45/1**

7 hd **Lucky Serena (IRE)**[28] 3-8-10 0......................................(b) MEsposito 4 91
(Agostino Affe', Italy) *hld up towards rr: hdwy u.p over 1 1/2f out: nvr threatened ldrs* **38/1**

8 5 **Licia (ITY)**[14] 7234 3-8-10 0................................ PierantonioConvertino 7 81
(S Botti, Italy) *prom: rdn and wknd over 2f out: eased ins fnl f* **29/1**

9 5 **Shirley's Kitten (USA)**[50] 6229 3-8-10 0................................ GBietolini 9 71
(Gianluca Bietolini, Italy) *hld up towards rr: nvr in contention* **63/1**

2m 3.06s (-0.24)
WFA 3 from 4yo+ 5lb **9** Ran SP% **133.0**
WIN (incl. 1 euro stake): 2.10. PLACES: 1.14, 1.41, 1.14. DF: 12.44.
Owner Effevi **Bred** Razza Del Velino Srl **Trained** Italy

7559 - 7561a (Foreign Racing) - See Raceform Interactive

6454WOODBINE (R-H)

Sunday, October 27

OFFICIAL GOING: Turf: yielding

7562a E P TAYLOR STKS (GRADE 1) (3YO+ FILLIES & MARES) (TURF) 1m 2f (T)

8:38 (12:00) 3-Y-O+

£186,335 (£62,111; £31,055; £15,527; £6,211; £3,105)

RPR

1 **Tannery (IRE)**[29] 6860 4-8-12 0.. JRosario 10 108
(Alan E Goldberg, U.S.A) *hld up in rr: hdwy on outside 2 1/2f out: led 1 1/2f out and r.o u.p: drvn out ins fnl f: hld on gamely* **2/1**[1]

2 hd **Fitful Skies (IRE)**[28] 6887 4-8-12 0................................ FabriceVeron 7 108
(H-A Pantall, France) *midfield: gd prog to trck ldng trio gng wl 2 1/2f out: nt clr run fr 2f out: swtchd ins and chal between horses: rdn to chse ldr 1f out: r.o u.p fnl f: jst failed* **8/1**

3 2 **Moment In Time (IRE)**[66] 5682 4-8-12 0.......................... RyanMoore 5 104
(David Simcock) *dwlt: settled towards rr: last turning fr home over 2f out: sn pushed along and angled out: prog on outsdie 1 1/2f out: styd on u.p fnl f: tk 3rd cl home: nvr on terms w ldrs* **98/10**

4 1/2 **Minakshi (FR)**[42] 6454 5-8-12 0.. LContreras 4 103
(Michael Matz, U.S.A) *chsd ldng pair: cl 3rd and rdn 2f out: ev ch 1 1/2f out: r.o u.p: outpcd by front two ins fnl f: fdd fnl 75yds: lost 3rd cl home* **23/4**[2]

5 1 3/4 **Samba Brazil (GER)**[28] 6889 4-8-12 0........................ AndreaAtzeni 8 100
(J Hirschberger, Germany) *keen in midfield: rdn to chse ldng gp 1 1/2f out: styd on u.p fnl f: nt pce to get on terms* **206/10**

6 3 **No Explaining (IRE)**[42] 6454 6-8-12 0................................ MESmith 1 94
(Roger L Attfield, Canada) *led: hdd 2f out: remained prom tl wknd appr fnl f* **9/1**

7 hd **Irish Mission (CAN)**[42] 6455 4-8-12 0.............................. GBoulanger 3 93
(Mark Frostad, Canada) *4th on inner: lost pl over 3f out: last 2f out: rdn and plugged on ins fnl 1 1/2f: nvr in contention* **107/10**

8 1 1/4 **Moment Of Majesty (CAN)**[42] 6454 6-8-12 0................ JRVelazquez 9 91
(Roger L Attfield, Canada) *towards rr: rdn and short-lived effrt 2f out: nvr threatened ldrs* **141/10**

9 3/4 **Colonial Flag (USA)**[42] 6454 4-8-12 0............................ JRLeparoux 2 89
(Michael Matz, U.S.A) *pressed ldr: led 2f out: hdd 1 1/2f out: sn wknd* **59/10**[3]

10 dist **Nancy O (IRE)**[15] 3-8-7 0.. DJMoran 6
(Carolyn M Costigan, U.S.A) *midfield on outer: rdn to hold pl over 3f out: sn wknd and lost tch over 1 1/2f out: eased ins fnl f* **194/10**

2m 7.13s (3.11)
WFA 3 from 4yo+ 5lb **10** Ran SP% **117.7**
PARI-MUTUEL (all including 2 usd stake): WIN 6.00; PLACE (1-2) 3.80, 6.90; SHOW (1-2-3) 3.10, 4.30, 5.00; SF 48.50.
Owner Richard Santulli **Bred** Grange Stud **Trained** North America

7563a PATTISON CANADIAN INTERNATIONAL STKS (GRADE 1) (3YO+) (TURF) 1m 4f (T)

9:44 (12:00) 3-Y-O+

£372,670 (£124,223; £62,111; £31,055; £12,422; £6,211)

RPR

1 **Joshua Tree (IRE)**[21] 7058 6-9-0 0.................................. RyanMoore 5 114
(Ed Dunlop) **67/10**[3]

2 3/4 **Hyper (USA)**[50] 6-9-0 0..(b) JRosario 1 113
(Chad C Brown, U.S.A) **29/4**

3 3/4 **Seismos (IRE)**[21] 7060 5-9-0 0.................................... AndreaAtzeni 9 112
(A Wohler, Germany) **103/10**

4 nk **Now We Can**[42] 6449 4-9-0 0................................ ThierryThulliez 7 111
(N Clement, France) **14/1**

5 3 **Temeraine (USA)**[43] 4-9-0 0.. LContreras 2 107
(Thomas F Proctor, U.S.A) **211/10**

6 2 1/4 **Slumber**[29] 6861 5-9-0 0.. MESmith 11 103
(William Mott, U.S.A) **7/4**[1]

7 3 1/2 **Forte Dei Marmi**[42] 6455 7-9-0 0.............................. ERosaDaSilva 8 97
(Roger L Attfield, Canada) **103/20**[2]

8 hd **Stormy Len (USA)**[22] 7039 3-8-7 0.. EPrado 6 97
(David Donk, U.S.A) **31/1**

9 1 3/4 **Lucayan (FR)**[27] 4-9-0 0.................................. StephanePasquier 3 94
(Neil Drysdale, U.S.A) **115/10**

10 nk **Perfect Timber (CAN)**[42] 6455 4-9-0 0............................ JRVelazquez 4 94
(Roger L Attfield, Canada) **98/10**

2m 35.45s (5.85)
WFA 3 from 4yo+ 7lb **10** Ran SP% **118.2**
PARI-MUTUEL (all including 2 usd stake): WIN 15.30; PLACE (1-2) 7.20, 6.90; SHOW (1-2-3) 4.50, 4.60, 6.00; SF 92.90.
Owner K K Al Nabooda & K Albahou **Bred** Castlemartin Stud And Skymarc Farm **Trained** Newmarket, Suffolk

7565 - (Foreign Racing) - See Raceform Interactive

7409LONGCHAMP (R-H)

Sunday, October 27

OFFICIAL GOING: Turf: very soft

7566a PRIX ROYAL-OAK (GROUP 1) (3YO+) (TURF) 1m 7f 110y

2:40 (12:00) 3-Y-O+ **£116,138** (£46,463; £23,231; £11,605; £5,813)

RPR

1 **Tac De Boistron (FR)**[21] 7060 6-9-4 0.............................. MartinHarley 8 119+
(Marco Botti) *hld up and sn towards rr: hdwy whn nt clr run fr 3f out tl rdn and swtchd lft over 1f out: styd on strly and led ent fnl f: forged clr: comf* **4/1**[1]

2 5 **Going Somewhere (BRZ)**[21] 7058 4-9-2 0.............. GregoryBenoist 15 116
(D Smaga, France) *hld up towards rr: rdn and hdwy on outer 3f out: drifted rt u.p: chal and ev ch ent fnl f: styd on wl for 2nd but readily outpcd by wnr* **10/1**

3 3/4 **Missunited (IRE)**[28] 6886 6-9-1 0........................... SeamieHeffernan 6 109
(Michael Winters, Ire) *dwlt sltly but qckly rcvrd: midfield: dropped to rr 1/2-way: pushed along in last 5f out: rdn over 2f out: edgd rt ent fnl f: styd on wl and wnt 3rd towards fin: no ch w wnr* **14/1**

4 1 3/4 **Goldtara (FR)**[23] 7009 5-9-1 0.. ThierryJarnet 5 107
(A Lyon, France) *midfield in tch: rdn over 2f out: styd on steadily but nt pce to chal* **20/1**

5 1 **Ebiyza (IRE)**[22] 7048 3-8-6 0.......................... Christophe-PatriceLemaire 4 107
(A De Royer-Dupre, France) *midfield: pushed along 2f out: short of room and shuffled bk over 1f out: carried rt by eventual 3rd ent fnl f: nt rcvr but r.o strly under hands and heels towards fin and wnt 5th fnl strides* **6/1**[2]

6 snk **Tres Rock Danon (FR)**[23] 7009 7-9-4 0........... ChristopheSoumillon 10 109
(Gerald Geisler, Germany) *sn led: rdn 3f out: hung lft and hdd ent fnl f: no ex and fdd: dropped to 6th fnl strides* **16/1**

7 1 1/4 **The Lark**[45] 6329 3-8-6 0.. JamieSpencer 11 105
(Michael Bell) *dwlt sltly and hld up in rr: rdn 2f out: kpt on same pce fr over 1f out and wnt 7th post: nvr able to chal* **6/1**[2]

8 nse **Altano (GER)**[21] 7060 7-9-4 0.. EPedroza 3 107
(A Wohler, Germany) *t.k.h: in rr early but sn hdwy into midfield: prom on outer whn rdn 3f out: hung rt u.p: plugged on but outpcd and hld ent fnl f* **4/1**[1]

9 hd **Green Byron (FR)**[22] 7046 3-8-9 0.................... Pierre-CharlesBoudot 13 108
(J-M Lefebvre, France) *prom: rdn whn shuffled bk 3f out: styd on steadily u.p but nvr able to chal: no ex and lost multiple pls towards fin* **25/1**

10 3 1/2 **Les Beaufs (FR)**[21] 7060 4-9-4 0.............................. JulienGuillochon 14 103
(Mme V Seignoux, France) *dwlt and in rr early: t.k.h: stdy hdwy and prom 1/2-way: cl 2nd 3f out: rdn and effrt to chal over 2f out: sn outpcd: no ex and btn ent fnl f: fdd and eased* **8/1**[3]

11 6 **Donn Halling (IRE)**[35] 6678 5-9-4 0.................................. TheoBachelot 9 95
(V Luka Jr, Czech Republic) *t.k.h: midfield: rdn and effrt over 2f out: bmpd over 1f out: sn lost pl and btn: fdd and eased* **33/1**

12 3 **Quinzieme Monarque (USA)**[56] 6028 3-8-9 0............ FranckBlondel 7 93
(J Hirschberger, Germany) *trckd ldr: rdn and effrt over 2f out: outpcd whn sltly short of room between rivals over 1f out: sn btn and wknd: eased* **20/1**

13 10 **Silver Valny (FR)**[7] 7-9-4 0.. ThomasMessina 1 80
(Mlle M-L Mortier, France) *stdd and hld up towards rr: rdn and effrt to improve over 2f out: no imp and btn ent fnl f: eased and t.o* **40/1**

14 12 **Lucarelli (GER)**[63] 7-9-4 0..........................(b) LennartHammer-Hansen 12 65
(Ferdinand J Leve, Germany) *s.i.s and pushed along early: stdy hdwy and sn trcking ldr: rdn and lost pl rapidly 3f out: sn in rr and btn: eased and t.o* **40/1**

15 20 **Da Capo (IRE)**[19] 7-9-4 0.. MaximeGuyon 2 41
(Mme Pia Brandt, France) *hld up and a in rr: rdn over 2f out: no ex and btn over 1f out: heavily eased and tailed rt off* **33/1**

3m 38.12s (16.62) **Going Correction** +1.35s/f (Soft)
WFA 3 from 4yo+ 9lb **15** Ran SP% **125.5**
Speed ratings: **112,109,109,108,107 107,107,107,106,105 102,100,95,89,79**
WIN (incl. 1 euro stake): 4.60. PLACES: 2.20, 3.30, 4.80. DF: 25.20. SF: 39.80.
Owner Australian Thoroughbred Bloodstock **Bred** Mme Isabelle Reverseau **Trained** Newmarket, Suffolk

FOCUS
A strong-looking field lined up for this staying event. The winner has been rated to the better view of his Chester win.

5875DEAUVILLE (R-H)

Tuesday, October 22

OFFICIAL GOING: Fibresand: standard; turf: heavy

7567a PRIX DU JOURNAL LE PAYS D'AUGE - PRIX DE VARAVILLE (CONDITIONS) (2YO) (TURF) 5f 110y

2:20 (2:23) 2-Y-O **£11,788** (£4,715; £3,536; £2,357; £1,178)

RPR

1 **Passing Burg (FR)**[95] 2-8-10 0.................................... ThierryThulliez 6 83
(L A Urbano-Grajales, France) **32/5**

2 1/2 **Laia Chope (FR)**[15] 2-9-1 0.. ThomasMessina 5 86
(X Nakkachdji, France) **68/10**

3 1 3/4 **Pound Piece (IRE)**[6] 7300 2-9-4 0.......................... ChristopheSoumillon 1 83
(J S Moore) *dwlt: sn trcking ldrs on rail: cl 4th and waiting for gap 2f out: chal between horses 1 1/2f out: sn rdn and nt qckn appr 1f out: kpt on ins fnl f but nt pce of first two* **33/10**[2]

4 nk **Winshine (FR)**[42] 6293 2-9-1 0............................ Pierre-CharlesBoudot 7 79
(J-M Capitte, France) **44/5**

5 3 **Honeysuckle Rose (FR)**[20] 2-8-10 0................................ ThierryJarnet 9 64
(P Bary, France) **2/1**[1]

6 5 **Easy Risk (FR)**[35] 2-8-10 0.. MaximeGuyon 2 48
(F Chappet, France) **43/10**[3]

7 3 1/2 **Just Divine (FR)** 2-8-7 0.. RonanThomas 3 33
(J Heloury, France) **39/1**

8 2 **New Elite (FR)**[12] 2-8-10 0.......................................(b) TonyPiccone 4 30
(C Boutin, France) **34/1**

1m 7.69s (67.69) **8** Ran SP% **117.4**
PARI-MUTUEL (all including 1 euro stake): 7.40. PLACES: 2.30, 2.20, 1.90. DF: 20.50. SF: 42.70.
Owner Ecurie D Primes **Bred** Sarl Ecurie D **Trained** Pau, France

7568a PRIX DE LA BANCHE (CLAIMER) (2YO) (TURF) 6f
2:55 (2:57) 2-Y-0 £9,349 (£3,739; £2,804; £1,869; £934)

RPR

1 Atlantic City (FR)[22] 2-9-2 0 FabriceVeron 14 75
(H-A Pantall, France) **14/1**
2 1 Bonjour Steve[5] 7327 2-8-8 0 (p) SoufyaneMoulin(3) 15 67
(J S Moore) *led: jnd over 3f out: hdd but cl 2nd whn rdn over 1f out: kpt on wl but nt pce of wnr* **12/1**
3 snk Madoka (FR) 2-8-11 0 (b) FranckBlondel 13 67
(L A Urbano-Grajales, France) **40/1**
4 3/4 Cafetiere[65] 2-9-5 0 Christophe-PatriceLemaire 12 72
(Paul Cole) *chsd ldrs: rdn 2f out: kpt on wl u.p but nt pce to chal* **10/1**
5 3/4 Color Code (FR)[22] 2-8-11 0 (b) ChristopheSoumillon 16 62
(S Wattel, France) **5/1[2]**
6 3 Easy De Glanville (FR)[58] 2-8-8 0 (b) MaximeGuyon 6 50
(C Baillet, France) **13/2**
7 3/4 Jack Beauregard (IRE)[26] 6786 2-8-11 0 CristianDemuro 11 51
(Gianluca Bietolini, Italy) **35/1**
8 3 1/2 Golden Surprise (FR)[12] 2-8-11 0 FlavienPrat 7 40
(D Windrif, France) **6/1[3]**
9 1 1/4 Pengabelot (FR)[12] 2-8-11 0 TonyPiccone 3 37
(C Boutin, France) **51/1**
10 10 Emerald Gg (IRE)[13] 7120 2-8-11 0 ThierryThulliez 17 7
(J S Moore) *in rr: last 1/2-way: no imp whn rdn and sn btn: eased: nvr a factor* **75/1**
11 1 1/4 Royal River[6] 7300 2-9-1 0 StephanePasquier 8 7
(J S Moore) *midfield in tch: rdn over 2f out: outpcd and btn ent fnl f: eased and fdd* **27/1**
12 nk Ahouva (FR)[29] 2-8-11 0 (p) AnthonyCrastus 5
(F Chappet, France) **19/1**
13 4 Shepherd Gate (USA)[57] 5848 2-9-1 0 (b) ThierryJarnet 1
(J S Moore) *midfield in tch on inner: rdn 2f out: no ex and btn ent fnl f: eased and fdd* **3/1[1]**
14 nk Blue Chocolate (IRE)[11] 7185 2-8-8 0 (b) GregoryBenoist 4
(D Prod'Homme, France) **41/1**
15 1/2 Hornblower (FR)[73] 2-8-11 0 CesarPasserat(4) 2
(Mme C Head-Maarek, France) **36/1**
16 1 1/4 Its My Life (FR) 2-8-8 0 SylvainRuis 9
(J Reynier, France) **88/1**

1m 13.35s (2.35) **16** Ran SP% **116.0**
PARI-MUTUEL (all including 1 euro stake): 15.00. PLACES: 4.80, 4.00, 11.20. DF: 62.00. SF: 113.00.
Owner Jacques Herold **Bred** Ecurie Haras Du Cadran & A Gilbert **Trained** France

7569a PRIX DE L'ORBIQUET (CLAIMER) (3YO) (TURF) 1m 7f
3:55 (3:59) 3-Y-0 £9,349 (£3,739; £2,804; £1,869; £934)

RPR

1 Faerie Reel (FR)[12] 3-8-11 0 VincentVion 1 72
(C Ferland, France) **7/5[1]**
2 1 1/2 Montesquieu (FR)[29] 3-8-11 0 (p) Georges-AntoineAnselin 3 70
(C Boutin, France) **5/1[2]**
3 3 1/2 Star Of Namibia (IRE)[31] 6711 3-8-11 0 (b) GaetanFaucon 5 65
(J S Moore) *t.k.h in midfield: hdwy on outside 2 1/2f out: 6th and hrd rdn under 2f out: styd on fr 1 1/2f out and wnt 3rd 1f out: kpt on fnl f but nvr on terms w front two* **10/1[3]**
4 1/2 Churada (IRE)[61] 5692 3-8-8 0 NicolasLarenaudie 9 62
(J-M Lefebvre, France) **5/1[2]**
5 1/2 Allez Viv (FR)[116] 3-9-4 0 KarlMartin 4 71
(P Van De Poele, France) **11/1**
6 3 Go On (FR)[12] 3-8-11 0 MlleAudeDuporte 6 60
(C Boillot, France) **80/1**
7 3 Adriano (FR) 3-9-1 0 (p) RaphaelDesanti 10 60
(M Delzangles, France) **10/1[3]**
8 2 1/2 Karitza (FR)[54] 5925 3-9-1 0 DavidParkes 11 57
(Jeremy Gask) *w ldrs: 2nd and pushed along to hold pl 2 1/2f out: sn rdn and wknd over 1 1/2f out* **45/1**
9 snk River Prince (FR)[81] 3-9-2 0 (p) YannickLetondeur 2 58
(P Adda, France) **10/1[3]**
10 dist Lets Rock Malcolm (FR) 3-8-8 0 YoannRousset 7
(H Billot, France) **72/1**
11 dist Voce Della Note (FR) 3-8-8 0 (p) YannickFournand 8
(Mme A Soulat, France) **78/1**

3m 30.96s (11.86) **11** Ran SP% **116.7**
PARI-MUTUEL (all including 1 euro stake): WIN 2.40; PLACE 1.20, 1.60, 2.20; DF 5.80; SF 7.70.
Owner Gerard Augustin-Normand **Bred** E.A.R.L. Elevage Des Loges **Trained** France

7567 DEAUVILLE (R-H)
Wednesday, October 23

OFFICIAL GOING: Turf: very soft: fibresand: standard

7570a PRIX DU PIN AU HARAS (CONDITIONS) (2YO) (FIBRESAND) 6f 110y
1:20 (12:00) 2-Y-0 £13,821 (£5,528; £4,146; £2,764; £1,382)

RPR

1 Imperiator[56] 5911 2-9-0 0 FranckBlondel 5 97
(P Decouz, France) **3/1[2]**
2 snk Trophee (FR)[12] 2-8-7 0 ThierryJarnet 8 90
(Mme C Head-Maarek, France) **69/10**
3 2 1/2 Al Muthana (FR)[17] 7056 2-9-1 0 CesarPasserat(3) 6 94
(F-H Graffard, France) **47/10[3]**
4 1 1/4 Gone With The Wind (FR) 2-8-10 0 TheoBachelot 7 82
(Y Barberot, France) **26/1**
5 1/2 Caja (FR)[44] 6269 2-8-10 0 FabriceVeron 3 81
(H-A Pantall, France) **9/1**
6 snk Talksalot (IRE)[75] 5362 2-9-0 0 ThierryThulliez 1 84
(J S Moore) *t.k.h: sn led: set a gd gallop and established a 3 l ld: rdn over 1 1/2f out: hdd ins fnl f: grad lft bhd* **12/1**
7 4 Battlefront (USA)[21] 2-9-0 0 ChristopheSoumillon 4 73
(J-C Rouget, France) **19/10[1]**
8 9 Zylpha (IRE)[43] 2-8-10 0 (b) MaximeGuyon 2 44
(H-A Pantall, France) **19/1**
9 hd Vanvidd (FR)[47] 6169 2-8-10 0 (p) TonyPiccone 9 43
(C Boutin, France) **49/1**

1m 19.0s (79.00) **9** Ran SP% **118.1**
WIN (incl. 1 euro stake): 4.00. PLACES: 1.70, 2.30, 2.00. DF: 16.20. SF: 27.20.
Owner Arnaud De Seyssel **Bred** Haras De La Perelle **Trained** France

7571a PRIX DES RESERVOIRS (GROUP 3) (2YO FILLIES) (TURF) 1m (R)
1:50 (12:00) 2-Y-0 £32,520 (£13,008; £9,756; £6,504; £3,252)

RPR

1 Stellar Path (FR)[14] 7141 2-8-9 0 GregoryBenoist 10 106
(X Thomas-Demeaulte, France) *towards rr on outer: shkn up and hdwy over 1 1/2f out: 5 l 3rd and styng on over 1f out: r.o wl to ld 50yds out: comf* **9/2[2]**
2 3/4 Kenzadargent (FR)[43] 6292 2-8-9 0 Christophe-PatriceLemaire 9 104
(J-C Rouget, France) *midfield on outer: prog to trck ldr 1/2-way: 2 l 2nd and rdn 1 1/2f out: r.o u.p fnl f: collared long-time ldr cl home to claim 2nd after wnr had gone past* **32/5**
3 1/2 Waikika (FR)[31] 2-8-9 0 StephanePasquier 3 103
(Y Barberot, France) *tk a t.k.h: pressed ldr: led bef 1/2-way: rdn and wnt 2 l clr under 2f out: kpt on u.p fnl f: hdd 50yds out: no ex and lost 2nd cl home* **5/1[3]**
4 1 3/4 Bereni Ka (FR)[19] 2-8-9 0 TonyPiccone 2 99
(Y Gourraud, France) *midfield on inner: shkn up but nt clr run under 2f out: sn in clr but no immediate imp: styd on on u.p fnl f: nt pce to chal* **16/1**
5 1 1/4 So In Love[33] 2-8-9 0 MaximeGuyon 1 97
(A Fabre, France) *t.k.h: led on rail: hdd bef 1/2-way: remained prom: rdn to hold pl over 2 1/2f out: rallied u.p 1 1/2f out: kpt on ins fnl f* **31/10[1]**
6 2 1/2 Stormyra (FR)[17] 7055 2-8-9 0 ThierryJarnet 7 91
(J-P Gallorini, France) *trckd ldrs: rdn over 2f out: kpt on at same pce u.p fnl 1 1/2f* **31/5**
7 2 1/2 Waris (FR)[27] 2-8-9 0 RonanThomas 6 86
(R Chotard, France) *midfield: rdn and short-lived effrt over 2f out: sn rdn and no further imp: kpt on at same pce fnl f* **28/1**
8 1 1/2 Konkan (IRE)[33] 2-8-9 0 CristianDemuro 5 82
(L Riccardi, Italy) *midfield: rdn and nt qckn 2f out: one pce fnl f* **19/1**
9 2 Volkovkha[30] 2-8-9 0 ChristopheSoumillon 8 78
(J-C Rouget, France) *dwlt: towards rr: rdn and tk clsr order 2f out: nt clr run 1 1/2f out: sn btn* **66/10**
10 6 Ascot Memory (IRE)[16] 7084 2-8-9 0 TheoBachelot 4 65
(S Wattel, France) *hld up in rr: rdn and no imp fr 2f out: nvr in contention* **27/1**

1m 48.02s (7.22) **10** Ran SP% **117.7**
WIN (incl. 1 euro stake): 5.50. PLACES: 2.10, 2.70, 2.20. DF: 16.00. SF: 32.20.
Owner Alidar Utemuratov **Bred** S.F. Bloodstock Llc **Trained** France

7573a PRIX DU TERROIR NORMAND (H'CAP) (3YO+ FILLIES & MARES) (FIBRESAND) 1m 1f 110y
4:55 (12:00) 3-Y-0+ £7,317 (£2,926; £2,195; £1,463; £731)

RPR

1 Mrs Dubawi (IRE)[80] 4-9-4 0 (p) Francois-XavierBertras 8 78
(F Rohaut, France) **47/10[2]**
2 1 1/2 Redondelle (FR)[73] 6-8-13 0 ChristopheSoumillon 6 70
(M Maillard, France) **11/1**
3 1 Money Time (IRE)[61] 3-9-3 0 (p) TheoBachelot 11 77
(S Wattel, France) **87/10**
4 snk Yadelarumbadanlair (FR)[12] 7187 3-8-6 0 MorganDelalande 2 66
(G Pannier, France) **35/1**
5 nse Bella Sheba (FR)[36] 4-8-11 0 StephaneLaurent(4) 9 69
(Mme L Poulain de la Fontaine, France) **16/1**
6 1 1/2 Marmaris (FR)[16] 4-8-9 0 (b) MarcLerner 16 60
(C Lerner, France) **14/1**
7 snk Susukino (FR)[16] 4-8-13 0 Christophe-PatriceLemaire 3 64
(S Kobayashi, France) **12/1**
8 nse Pixie Cut (IRE)[56] 5913 3-9-4 0 SoufyaneMoulin 4 74
(J S Moore) *led: rdn and hdd 2f out: sn outpcd by ldrs: one pce fnl f* **13/1**
9 nk Line Et Bleu (FR)[16] 5-9-5 0 FabienLefebvre 12 69
(F Vermeulen, France) **84/10[3]**
10 3/4 Double Mast (FR)[216] 5-9-2 0 AdrienFouassier 15 65
(A Vetault, France) **23/1**
11 snk Remember Salsa (FR)[58] 4-9-4 0 FrankieLeroy 10 67
(R Le Gal, France) **46/1**
12 1 Seven Seas (FR)[78] 3-9-6 0 GregoryBenoist 5 71
(M Delzangles, France) **21/1**
13 2 Belle Aumone (FR)[19] 5-7-9 0 (b) NathanKasztelan(5) 14 42
(S Jesus, France) **45/1**
14 nk Mahajanga (FR)[30] 3-8-10 0 (p) AntoineHamelin 13 57
(C Boutin, France) **18/1**
15 3/4 No More Tears (FR)[67] 4-9-2 0 (p) TonyPiccone 1 56
(E Lellouche, France) **4/1[1]**
16 7 Lucax (FR)[12] 7188 3-9-4 0 AlexisBadel 7 49
(Mlle V Dissaux, France) **36/1**

2m 1.92s (121.92)
WFA 3 from 4yo+ 4lb **16** Ran SP% **118.0**
WIN (incl. 1 euro stake): 5.70. PLACES: 2.20, 3.70, 3.40. DF: 39.90. SF: 57.50.
Owner Gerard Laboureau **Bred** Skymarc Farm **Trained** Sauvagnon, France

7268 LEICESTER (R-H)
Monday, October 28

7574 Meeting Abandoned - Waterlogged

7339 REDCAR (L-H)
Monday, October 28

7581 Meeting Abandoned - Waterlogged

[3912]NANTES (R-H)
Saturday, October 26

OFFICIAL GOING: Turf: heavy

7590a GRAND PRIX DE NANTES (LISTED RACE) (3YO+) (TURF) 1m 4f
12:45 (12:00) 3-Y-0+ **£24,390** (£9,756; £7,317; £4,878; £2,439)

RPR
1 **Tunkwa (FR)**[40] 6484 3-8-5 0 TheoBachelot 7 106+
(D Sepulchre, France) **194/10**
2 1 1/2 **Usuelo (FR)**[22] 7009 5-9-1 0 AntoineHamelin 2 106
(J-L Guillochon, France) **9/2**[2]
3 1 1/2 **Gentle Storm (FR)**[6] 7410 4-9-1 0 (b) ChristopheSoumillon 3 104
(Y Barberot, France) **14/5**[1]
4 3/4 **Griraz (FR)**[133] 3362 8-9-1 0 Roberto-CarlosMontenegro 4 103
(P Sogorb, France) **5/1**[3]
5 1 **Opera Vert (FR)**[142] 5-9-1 0 (p) ArnaudBourgeais 10 101
(D Sepulchre, France) **21/1**
6 1 **Vasias (FR)**[18] 5-9-1 0 AlexandreRoussel 1 100
(C Lotoux, France) **57/10**
7 15 **Tigre D'Or (FR)**[47] 6270 7-9-1 0 (b) AdrienFouassier 9 76
(A Couetil, France) **13/1**
8 2 **Zagros (FR)**[17] 7142 4-9-1 0 AlexisBadel 5 72
(J Heloury, France) **17/1**
9 dist **Miss Cap Estel**[41] 6434 4-8-11 0 MaximeGuyon 6
(Andrew Balding) *dwlt sltly: t.k.h in midfield early: clsd and prom 1/2-way: steadily lost pl fr over 3f out: rdn in last 2f out: sn no ex and btn: eased over 1f out and tailed rt off* **9/2**[2]

2m 42.81s (7.81)
WFA 3 from 4yo+ 7lb **9** Ran SP% **116.4**
WIN (incl. 1 euro stake): 20.40. PLACES: 4.40, 2.10, 1.70. DF: 50.40. SF: 166.80.
Owner Wildenstein Stables Limited **Bred** Dayton Investments Limited **Trained** France

[7413]SAN SIRO (R-H)
Saturday, October 26

OFFICIAL GOING: Turf: heavy

7591a ST LEGER ITALIANO (GROUP 3) (3YO+) (TURF) 1m 6f
3:15 (12:00) 3-Y-0+ **£22,764** (£10,016; £5,463; £2,731)

RPR
1 **Parivash**[112] 4-8-9 0 DarioVargiu 1 98+
(W Hickst, Germany) *chsd ldrs: scrubbed along to chal fr 2f out: r.o u.p fnl f: led cl home* **23/5**
2 hd **Rock Of Romance (IRE)**[139] 3-8-5 0 EPedroza 2 103
(A Wohler, Germany) *led: hdd bef 1/2-way: trckd ldrs: regained ld 2 1/2f out: sn rdn: strly pressed by eventual wnr and r.o u.p fnl f: hdd cl home: no ex* **11/10**[1]
3 15 **Saratoga Black (IRE)**[41] 6-8-13 0 PierantonioConvertino 4 81
(B Grizzetti, Italy) *settled in 4th: rapid hdwy on outside to ld bef 1/2-way: hdd 2 1/2f out: hrd rdn and drifted rt on to ins rail: outpcd by front two over 1 1/2f out* **126/10**
4 2 **Shisun (IRE)**[87] 4-8-13 0 OlivierPlacais 3 78
(M Weiss, Switzerland) *trckd ldr: rdn and outpcd 3f out: sn wknd and wl bhd* **21/10**[2]
5 snk **Bacchelli**[286] 5-8-13 0 CFiocchi 5 78
(S Botti, Italy) *w.w in rr: short-lived effrt 4f out: sn rdn and no further imp: wknd* **37/10**[3]

3m 7.7s (187.70)
WFA 3 from 4yo+ 9lb **5** Ran SP% **126.4**
WIN (incl. 1 euro stake): 5.65. PLACES: 2.08, 1.36. DF: 10.56.
Owner Frau Shahpar & Dr Stefan Oschmann **Bred** Brundeanlaws Stud **Trained** Germany

[7369]CATTERICK (L-H)
Tuesday, October 29

OFFICIAL GOING: Heavy (5.8)
Wind: Fresh across Weather: Sunny but cold

7592 RACING POST WEEKENDER OUT TOMORROW MEDIAN AUCTION MAIDEN STKS 5f 212y
12:50 (12:50) (Class 6) 2-Y-O **£2,385** (£704; £352) **Stalls** Low

Form RPR
6250 1 **The Hooded Claw (IRE)**[18] 7170 2-9-5 85 DuranFentiman 10 77
(Tim Easterby) *cl up on outer: led over 2f out and c wd st: rdn and edgd rt to stands' rail over 1f out: kpt on wl fnl f* **15/8**[2]
2 2 2 **Angel Flores (IRE)**[22] 7078 2-9-0 0 TonyHamilton 6 66
(Richard Fahey) *trckd ldng pair: effrt on outer and wd st: rdn whn n.m.r over 1f out: sn swtchd lft and rdn: kpt on same pce fnl f* **11/8**[1]
2055 3 nse **Brownsville (USA)**[76] 5400 2-9-5 67 JoeFanning 4 71
(Mark Johnston) *slt ld: rdn along and hdd over 2f out: drvn over 1f out: kpt on same pce* **5/1**[3]
00 4 7 **Cahal (IRE)**[17] 7209 2-9-5 0 AdrianNicholls 2 50
(David Nicholls) *chsd ldng pair: rdn along over 2f out: sn drvn and wknd over 1f out* **66/1**
5 2 3/4 **Vale Mentor (IRE)** 2-9-5 0 DavidAllan 9 42
(Tim Easterby) *in tch: pushed along 1/2-way: sn rdn and n.d* **14/1**
62 6 2 **Captain Joe**[10] 7370 2-9-5 0 JamesSullivan 7 36
(Michael Easterby) *t.k.h: hld up: a in rr* **14/1**

1m 19.1s (5.50) **Going Correction** +0.90s/f (Soft) **6** Ran SP% **108.4**
Speed ratings (Par 93): **99,96,96,86,83 80**
toteswingers 1&2 £1.10, 1&3 £1.80, 2&3 £1.60 CSF £4.43 TOTE £2.70: £1.20, £1.90; EX 4.00 Trifecta £11.90 Pool: £1667.16 - 104.68 winning units..
Owner April Fools **Bred** Newlands House Stud **Trained** Great Habton, N Yorks

FOCUS
Bend into home straight moved in to give 2yds of fresh ground. Underfoot conditions were very testing and there was a brisk, almost head-on, wind in the home straight.

7593 RACING POST WEEKENDER OUT EVERY WEDNESDAY H'CAP (DIV I) 5f 212y
1:20 (1:20) (Class 4) (0-80,80) 3-Y-0+ **£5,175** (£1,540; £769; £384) **Stalls** Low

Form RPR
0001 1 **Fat Gary**[18] 7164 3-9-4 78 (p) StephenCraine 8 89
(Tom Dascombe) *cl up: led over 2f out: jnd and rdn over 1f out: drvn and kpt on wl fnl f* **15/2**
0403 2 1/2 **Sunny Side Up (IRE)**[14] 7281 4-8-11 70 TonyHamilton 3 80
(Richard Fahey) *trckd ldng pair: hdwy and cl up 2f out: chal wl over 1f out: sn rdn and ev ch tl drvn ins fnl f and no ex towards fin* **7/1**[3]
5660 3 1 3/4 **Sylvia Pankhurst (IRE)**[22] 7080 3-8-13 76 (p) LMcNiff[(3)] 5 80
(David C Griffiths) *towards rr: pushed along over 2f out: hdwy wl over 1f out: sn rdn and kpt on fnl f: nrst fin* **18/1**
0032 4 1 **Italian Tom (IRE)**[7] 7452 6-9-0 73 LukeMorris 6 74
(Ronald Harris) *dwlt and towards rr: hdwy wl over 2f out: rdn to chse ldng pair over 1f out: sn drvn and one pce* **9/4**[1]
0020 5 3 3/4 **Kuanyao (IRE)**[28] 6916 7-8-9 68 (v[1]) JoeFanning 10 58
(David Nicholls) *chsd ldrs: rdn along wl over 2f out: sn edgd lft and no imp* **12/1**
0/00 6 2 1/4 **Son Du Silence (IRE)**[39] 6583 4-9-7 80 (t) GrahamLee 1 63
(James Ewart) *in tch on inner: pushed along over 2f out: sn rdn and no imp* **4/1**[2]
5000 7 shd **The Nifty Fox**[15] 7240 9-8-13 72 (p) DuranFentiman 7 55
(Tim Easterby) *trckd ldrs: hdwy on outer and wd st: swtchd lft and rdn 2f out: drvn over 1f out and sn wknd* **16/1**
0004 8 2 3/4 **Meandmyshadow**[14] 7282 5-8-11 70 PJMcDonald 2 45
(Alan Brown) *towards rr: pushed along 1/2-way: rdn over 2f out: n.d* **17/2**
2020 9 9 **Majestic Manannan (IRE)**[41] 6515 4-9-1 74 AdrianNicholls 9 22
(David Nicholls) *slt ld: wd st to stands' rail: sn rdn and hdd over 2f out: drvn wl over 1f out: sn wknd and eased* **25/1**
6005 10 2 1/4 **Noodles Blue Boy**[13] 7314 7-9-5 78 TomEaves 4 19
(Ollie Pears) *a in rr* **33/1**

1m 19.41s (5.81) **Going Correction** +1.00s/f (Soft)
WFA 3 from 4yo+ 1lb **10** Ran SP% **111.2**
Speed ratings (Par 105): **101,100,98,96,91 88,88,84,72,69**
toteswingers 1&2 £3.30, 1&3 £11.00, 2&3 £17.60 CSF £56.03 CT £905.61 TOTE £7.90: £2.40, £1.90, £5.00; EX 58.40 Trifecta £967.50 Pool: £1636.09 - 1.26 winning units..
Owner Manor House Stables LLP **Bred** J M Beever **Trained** Malpas, Cheshire

FOCUS
It paid to race up with the pace in this competitive sprint handicap. The first two home were in the first three throughout.

7594 RACING POST WEEKENDER OUT EVERY WEDNESDAY H'CAP (DIV II) 5f 212y
1:50 (1:50) (Class 4) (0-80,79) 3-Y-0+ **£5,175** (£1,540; £769; £384) **Stalls** Low

Form RPR
1020 1 **Just The Tonic**[29] 6908 6-8-9 72 NathanAlison[(5)] 4 81
(Marjorie Fife) *dwlt: gd hdwy on inner after 2f: sn trcking ldrs: hdwy wl over 1f out: sn rdn and styd on to ld ins fnl f* **13/2**
0564 2 2 1/4 **Captain Royale (IRE)**[14] 7281 8-8-10 68 (p) BarryMcHugh 8 70
(Tracy Waggott) *led: wd st to stands' rail: hdd over 2f out: cl up and rdn to ld again jst over 1f out: drvn and hdd ins fnl f: one pce* **11/1**
3014 3 3/4 **Holy Angel (IRE)**[33] 6771 4-9-3 75 (e) DanielTudhope 6 75
(Tim Easterby) *prom: hdwy and wd st: slt ld over 2f out: rdn wl over 1f out: hdd appr fnl f: sn drvn and one pce* **10/1**
-000 4 2 **Chellalla**[54] 6126 4-8-9 70 (t) RyanPowell[(3)] 5 64
(Ian Williams) *dwlt: t.k.h and hld up in rr: hdwy over 2f out: rdn to chse ldrs whn hung lft over 1f out: kpt on same pce fnl f* **18/1**
1065 5 3/4 **Indego Blues**[10] 7374 4-9-3 75 PaulQuinn 7 67
(David Nicholls) *chsd ldrs: hdwy wl over 2f out: rdn along wl over 1f out: sn one pce* **7/2**[1]
4030 6 1 1/4 **Captain Scooby**[8] 7432 7-8-10 68 (e) GrahamLee 9 56
(Richard Guest) *chsd ldrs: rdn along wl over 2f out: sn drvn and no imp* **6/1**
0422 7 nse **Khelman (IRE)**[28] 6916 3-8-13 72 TonyHamilton 3 60
(Richard Fahey) *a towards rr* **9/2**[2]
3201 8 1 3/4 **Tajneed (IRE)**[14] 7282 10-9-5 77 AdrianNicholls 1 60
(David Nicholls) *chsd ldrs: pushed along 1/2-way: rdn 2f out and sn btn* **5/1**[3]
0360 9 15 **Sunrise Dance**[37] 6665 4-9-2 74 AndrewMullen 10 12
(Robert Johnson) *chsd ldng pair on outer: rdn along 1/2-way: sn wknd and bhd* **16/1**

1m 19.68s (6.08) **Going Correction** +1.10s/f (Soft)
WFA 3 from 4yo+ 1lb **9** Ran SP% **113.3**
Speed ratings (Par 105): **103,100,99,96,95 93,93,91,71**
toteswingers 1&2 £13.30, 1&3 £17.50, 2&3 £13.70 CSF £73.36 CT £708.44 TOTE £10.50: £2.70, £4.10, £2.70; EX 105.00 Trifecta £1232.50 Part won. Pool: £1643.41 - 0.84 winning units..
Owner R W Fife **Bred** West Dereham Abbey Stud **Trained** Stillington, N Yorks

FOCUS
The first three home were the first three turning for home.

7595 HAPPY 90TH BIRTHDAY JOHN GAWTHORPE H'CAP 7f
2:20 (2:21) (Class 4) (0-85,85) 3-Y-0+ **£6,469** (£1,925; £962; £240; £240) **Stalls** Centre

Form RPR
2521 1 **Showboating (IRE)**[10] 7374 5-9-3 81 (tp) SeanLevey 8 92
(Alan McCabe) *towards rr: hdwy over 2f out: sn rdn: styd on wl appr fnl f: led last 100yds* **5/1**[1]
1006 2 3 **Piceno (IRE)**[22] 7076 5-8-7 71 oh3 (p) TomEaves 13 75
(Scott Dixon) *prom: cl up 2f out: sn rdn and ev ch tl drvn ent fnl f and kpt on same pce* **16/1**
2313 3 1/2 **Llewellyn**[10] 7374 5-8-11 75 AdrianNicholls 7 77
(David Nicholls) *prom: led 3f out and wd st towards stands' rail: rdn over 2f out: sn hdd and edgd rt: drvn and ev ch ent fnl f: one pce* **5/1**[1]
5351 4 3/4 **Beckermet (IRE)**[11] 7344 11-8-8 72 PJMcDonald 9 72
(Ruth Carr) *led: hdd and rdn along 3f out: wd st: drvn and one pce fr over 1f out* **15/2**[3]
2300 4 dht **Hot Rod Mamma (IRE)**[10] 7374 6-8-13 77 DuranFentiman 2 77
(Dianne Sayer) *midfield: hdwy to trck ldrs 1/2-way: led 2f out: rdn over 1f out: drvn ent fnl f: hdd & wknd last 100yds* **11/1**

1000 **6** 1/2 **Nasharra (IRE)**[39] 6586 5-8-12 **81**....(tp) KevinStott(5) 4 80
(Kevin Ryan) *s.i.s and wl bhd: hdwy 2f out: rdn to chse ldrs over 1f out: drvn and no imp fnl f* **20/1**

0300 **7** 1 1/2 **West Leake Hare (IRE)**[10] 7374 4-8-6 **77** ow2.... JordanNason(7) 12 72
(David Nicholls) *in rr tl styd on fnl 2f: n.d* **15/2**[3]

1102 **8** 2 1/2 **Monakova (IRE)**[18] 7176 3-9-5 **85**.... DanielTudhope 10 73
(David O'Meara) *chsd ldrs: rdn along over 2f out: sn drvn and wknd* **11/2**[2]

2600 **9** 1/2 **Green Park (IRE)**[10] 7374 10-8-7 **74**....(b) NeilFarley(3) 11 62
(Declan Carroll) *in tch: rdn along to chse ldrs wl over 2f out: sn drvn and wknd* **14/1**

2126 **10** 5 **Maggie Pink**[150] 2884 4-8-7 **71** oh2.... AndrewMullen 1 46
(Michael Appleby) *cl up: wd st to stands' rail: rdn along whn hmpd and almost fell 2f out: bhd and eased after* **8/1**

6002 **11** 17 **Majestic Dream (IRE)**[35] 6720 5-8-9 **73**.... JamesSullivan 5 6
(Michael Easterby) *broke wl: sn pushed along: rdn and lost pl after 1 1/2f: bhd fr 1/2-way* **25/1**

0030 **12** 1 3/4 **New Leyf (IRE)**[40] 6549 7-8-7 **71**....(e[1]) PaulQuinn 6
(David Nicholls) *chsd ldrs: pushed along and lost pl 4f out: sn bhd* **33/1**

1m 34.14s (7.14) **Going Correction** +1.20s/f (Soft)
WFA 3 from 4yo+ 2lb **12** Ran SP% **115.8**
Speed ratings (Par 105): **107,103,103,102,102 101,99,97,96,90 71,69**
toteswingers 1&2 £17.50, 1&3 £3.70, 2&3 £18.50 CSF £80.81 CT £427.72 TOTE £5.60: £1.70, £5.40, £1.90; EX 83.90 Trifecta £700.80 Pool: £2635.00 - 2.81 winning units..
Owner Mr & Mrs L Cooke A Pierce A McCabe **Bred** Crone Stud Farms Ltd **Trained** Averham Park, Notts
■ Stewards' Enquiry : Adrian Nicholls seven-day ban: careless riding (12-16 Nov, 18-19 Nov)

FOCUS
A wide open 7f handicap. The winner deserves extra credit having been plum last at halfway.

7596 RACING UK ON SKY 432 H'CAP — 1m 3f 214y
2:50 (2:50) (Class 4) (0-85,80) 3-Y-O+ **£5,453** (£1,610; £805) **Stalls** Centre

Form RPR

0260 **1** **Calaf**[32] 6801 5-9-9 **80**.... PaulPickard(3) 7 89
(Brian Ellison) *t.k.h early: chsd ldng pair: hdwy and cl up 1/2-way: led 3f out: rdn and hdd 2f out: rallied to ld again over 1f out: drvn and kpt on gamely fnl f* **9/1**

-133 **2** 3/4 **Sioux Chieftain (IRE)**[123] 3783 3-9-1 **76**.... AndrewMullen 6 84
(Michael Appleby) *t.k.h early: cl up: led over 5f out: hdd 3f out: cl up and rdn to ld again 2f out: drvn and hdd over 1f out: no ex ins fnl f* **5/2**[1]

0302 **3** 6 **Gioia Di Vita**[24] 7028 3-9-0 **75**.... PaulQuinn 4 74
(David Nicholls) *trckd ldrs: hdwy to chse ldng pair 3f out: rdn along over 2f out: sn drvn and one pce* **9/1**

0503 **4** hd **Villa Royale**[10] 7369 4-9-11 **79**.... DanielTudhope 3 78
(David O'Meara) *trckd ldrs: effrt 4f out: rdn along 3f out: drvn and one pce fnl 2f* **9/2**[3]

005 **5** 12 **Hollowina**[16] 7223 3-9-4 **79**.... GrahamLee 1 60
(David Brown) *hld up: a towards rr: outpcd and bhd fnl 3f* **10/3**[2]

6622 **6** 5 **Mohawk Ridge**[10] 7372 7-9-3 **76**.... ConnorBeasley(5) 5 49
(Michael Dods) *slt ld: rdn along and hdd 1/2-way: drvn over 3f out and sn wknd* **16/1**

2005 **7** 2 **Entihaa**[35] 6729 5-9-9 **77**.... BenCurtis 8 47
(Alan Swinbank) *hld up towards rr: effrt over 4f out: sn rdn along and outpcd: nvr a factor* **12/1**

2202 **8** 94 **Rosairlie (IRE)**[14] 7280 5-9-7 **75**.... PJMcDonald 2
(Micky Hammond) *hld up: a in rr: rdn along and lost tch over 5f out: sn t.o* **8/1**

2m 52.89s (13.99) **Going Correction** +1.30s/f (Soft)
WFA 3 from 4yo+ 7lb **8** Ran SP% **114.5**
Speed ratings (Par 105): **105,104,100,100,92 89,87,25**
toteswingers 1&2 £4.90, 1&3 £10.60, 2&3 £5.00 CSF £31.92 CT £211.70 TOTE £13.40: £3.60, £1.30, £1.90; EX 36.50 Trifecta £269.30 Pool: £2922.15 - 8.13 winning units..
Owner Prism Bloodstock **Bred** Norcroft Park Stud **Trained** Norton, N Yorks

FOCUS
A sound gallop on here and the first four home finished well clear.

7597 BOOK NOW FOR NEW YEAR'S DAY H'CAP — 1m 7f 177y
3:20 (3:20) (Class 5) (0-70,70) 3-Y-O+ **£2,911** (£866; £432; £216) **Stalls** Centre

Form RPR

225 **1** **Toughness Danon**[18] 7166 7-9-9 **65**.... TonyHamilton 4 75
(Ian Williams) *hld up in midfield: smooth hdwy to trck ldrs over 6f out: cl up over 3f out: wd st and led on bit over 2f out: sn swtchd rt to stands' rail and pushed clr: easily* **12/1**

5032 **2** 3 **Dubara Reef (IRE)**[10] 7375 6-8-6 **55** oh5 ow3....(p) JordanNason(7) 9 59
(Paul Green) *led: rdn along over 5f out: hdd 4f out: wd st and rdn over 2f out: sn drvn and kpt on same pce* **20/1**

0201 **3** 1 1/4 **Wee Giant (USA)**[10] 7376 7-8-10 **59**.... LauraBarry(7) 5 62
(Tony Coyle) *hld up and bhd: stdy hdwy 4f out: effrt to chse ldrs 3f out: rdn to chse wnr over 1f out: sn no imp* **4/1**[2]

06-1 **4** 6 **Iron Butterfly**[21] 7098 4-9-2 **58**.... GrahamLee 11 53
(James Eustace) *trckd ldrs: hdwy 5f out: rdn along over 2f out: sn drvn and one pce* **3/1**[1]

0-00 **5** 3 **Song Of The Siren**[10] 7369 5-9-12 **68**.... DanielTudhope 2 59
(David O'Meara) *chsd ldrs: hdwy to ld 4f out: rdn along and hdd over 2f out: sn drvn and wknd* **22/1**

2-32 **6** 9 **Stickleback**[190] 1721 4-9-1 **57**.... PJMcDonald 1 37
(Micky Hammond) *midfield: rdn along and sme hdwy over 5f out: drvn over 3f out: n.d* **8/1**

0540 **7** 18 **Harrison's Cave**[14] 7280 5-9-13 **69**....(t) BrianHughes 7 28
(Chris Grant) *midfield: rdn along 6f out: drvn over 3f out and sn bhd* **25/1**

0204 **8** 70 **Joyful Motive**[78] 5337 4-8-10 **52** oh3....(p) JamesSullivan 3
(Tom Tate) *chsd ldrs 7f: sn rdn along and lost pl 6f out: t.o fnl 3f* **33/1**

04-0 **9** 1 1/4 **Becausewecan (USA)**[16] 7230 7-9-9 **65**.... BarryMcHugh 8
(Brian Ellison) *prom: rdn along over 5f out: sn wknd and t.o fnl 3f* **6/1**[3]

0510 **10** 13 **Naburn**[29] 6909 5-10-0 **70**.... BenCurtis 10
(Alan Swinbank) *a towards rr: rdn along over 6f out: sn bhd: t.o fnl 3f* **16/1**

0633 **11** 6 **Generous Dream**[14] 7280 5-9-3 **59**.... DavidAllan 6
(Mel Brittain) *a towards rr: t.o fnl 3f* **7/1**

4050 **12** 7 **Underwritten**[21] 7100 4-9-7 **63**....(b) TomEaves 12
(John Weymes) *chsd ldrs: rdn along 7f out: wknd 6f out: sn bhd and t.o fnl 3f* **40/1**

3m 54.42s (22.42) **Going Correction** +1.40s/f (Soft) **12** Ran SP% **114.8**
Speed ratings (Par 103): **99,97,96,93,92 87,78,43,43,36 33,30**
toteswingers 1&2 £14.30, 1&3 £7.50, 2&3 £13.40 CSF £230.21 CT £1130.11 TOTE £14.90: £4.30, £4.20, £1.70; EX 210.00 Trifecta £1388.00 Pool: £2627.38 - 1.41 winning units..
Owner Paul Frank Barry **Bred** Stiftung Gestut Fahrhof **Trained** Portway, Worcs

FOCUS
A sound gallop and a severe test of stamina in the testing conditions. Very few were in serious contention from some way out.

7598 JUMP SEASON NEXT ON DECEMBER 4TH H'CAP (DIV I) — 5f
3:50 (3:50) (Class 6) (0-65,65) 3-Y-O+ **£2,385** (£704; £352) **Stalls** Low

Form RPR

4051 **1** **Fleurtille**[21] 7101 4-9-1 **59**.... PJMcDonald 10 67
(Robert Johnson) *trckd ldrs: swtchd rt to stands' rail and hdwy wl over 1f out: rdn to chal ent fnl f: sn led: edgd lft and kpt on wl towards fin* **13/2**[3]

5414 **2** 3/4 **Coalburn**[12] 7323 5-8-4 **51**....(v) RyanPowell(3) 1 56
(Gary Harrison) *chsd ldrs: hdwy 2f out: rdn to chal ent fnl f and ev ch tl drvn and kpt on same pce last 100yds* **4/1**[2]

0346 **3** 1/2 **Amis Reunis**[11] 7347 4-8-7 **54**....(p) PaulQuinn(3) 2 57
(Alan Berry) *hld up in rr: hdwy 1/2-way: swtchd rt and rdn over 1f out: styd on fnl f: nrst fin* **11/1**

0003 **4** 1/2 **Fathom Five (IRE)**[27] 6945 9-9-0 **58**.... RaulDaSilva 11 59
(Shaun Harris) *prom: hdwy 2f out: rdn to ld wl over 1f out: drvn and hdd ins fnl f: wknd last 75yds* **18/1**

502 **5** 1/2 **New Decade**[13] 7315 4-9-7 **65**.... GrahamLee 8 65
(Milton Bradley) *chsd ldrs: hdwy and cl up 2f out: rdn over 1f out and ev ch tl drvn and one pce fnl f* **7/2**[1]

0066 **6** 2 3/4 **Pivotal Prospect**[11] 7343 5-8-10 **54**.... BarryMcHugh 7 44
(Tracy Waggott) *cl up: rdn along 2f out: grad wknd appr fnl f* **4/1**[2]

1340 **7** 1 1/2 **Quality Art (USA)**[56] 6088 5-8-11 **60**.... ConnorBeasley(5) 9 44
(Richard Guest) *prom: cl up 2f out: sn rdn and ev ch tl drvn and wknd appr fnl f* **9/1**

0050 **8** 4 **A J Cook (IRE)**[24] 7030 3-9-3 **61**....(p) DavidAllan 5 32
(Ron Barr) *slt ld: rdn along 2f out: sn hdd & wknd over 1f out* **16/1**

400 **9** 1 3/4 **Senora Lobo (IRE)**[11] 7354 3-8-7 **51** oh5....(p) TomEaves 3 16
(Lisa Williamson) *cl up: rdn along over 2f out: sn wknd* **66/1**

0000 **10** 3 3/4 **Master Rooney (IRE)**[15] 7240 7-8-11 **62**....(p) JordanNason(7) 6 12
(Geoffrey Harker) *cl up: rdn along over 2f out: sn drvn and wknd* **10/1**

1m 5.05s (5.25) **Going Correction** +0.90s/f (Soft) **10** Ran SP% **115.6**
Speed ratings (Par 101): **94,92,92,91,90 86,83,77,74,68**
toteswingers 1&2 £5.10, 1&3 £13.40, 2&3 £9.10 CSF £32.40 CT £290.05 TOTE £5.40: £2.10, £1.70, £2.70; EX 42.50 Trifecta £346.00 Pool: £3251.76 - 7.04 winning units..
Owner Ray Craggs **Bred** Ray Craggs **Trained** Newburn, Tyne & Wear

FOCUS
They raced right across the track in this moderate sprint handicap. The winner ended up under the stands' rail and the runner-up, who was drawn in stall one, raced nearest the far rail.

7599 JUMP SEASON NEXT ON DECEMBER 4TH H'CAP (DIV II) — 5f
4:20 (4:20) (Class 6) (0-65,63) 3-Y-O+ **£2,385** (£704; £352) **Stalls** Low

Form RPR

4316 **1** **Pull The Pin (IRE)**[21] 7101 4-8-12 **54**....(b) RaulDaSilva 9 69
(Paul Green) *swtchd rt s and racd alone stands' rail: cl up: led 1/2-way: pushed clr on bit wl over 1f out: readily* **5/2**[1]

5000 **2** 3 **Tongalooma**[37] 6669 7-8-9 **51**....(p) PJMcDonald 7 55
(James Moffatt) *racd towards centre: led: hdd 1/2-way: sn swtchd rt towards stands' rail and rdn along: drvn over 1f out: kpt on: no ch w wnr* **12/1**

0500 **3** 3/4 **Commanche Raider (IRE)**[24] 7030 6-9-2 **63**....(b) ConnorBeasley(5) 6 64
(Michael Dods) *hld up in centre: hdwy wl over 1f out: n.m.r and swtchd rt ent fnl f: sn rdn and kpt on: nrst fin* **8/1**[3]

0050 **4** 1 1/4 **Elusive Bonus (IRE)**[13] 7315 4-9-3 **59**.... DanielTudhope 3 56
(David O'Meara) *racd centre: chsd ldr: rdn along wl over 1f out: drvn over 1f out and sn one pce* **5/1**[2]

0003 **5** 1 3/4 **Mission Impossible**[13] 7315 8-9-4 **60**....(p) BarryMcHugh 4 51
(Tracy Waggott) *chsd ldrs centre: rdn along wl over 1f out: sn edgd rt and drvn: wknd fnl f* **5/1**[2]

5030 **6** nk **Foreign Rhythm (IRE)**[24] 7029 8-9-5 **61**.... DavidAllan 2 50
(Ron Barr) *hld up: hdwy wl over 1f out: sn rdn and no imp fnl f* **10/1**

55 **7** 2 1/4 **Diamond Vine (IRE)**[12] 7323 5-8-7 **54**....(p) PhilipPrince(5) 10 35
(Ronald Harris) *towards rr and swtchd lft to r centre sn after s: sme hdwy over 2f out: sn rdn and nvr a factor* **8/1**[3]

6000 **8** 2 **Boucher Garcon (IRE)**[21] 7101 5-8-7 **52**.... NeilFarley(3) 8 26
(Declan Carroll) *racd towards centre: cl up: rdn 1/2-way and sn wknd* **12/1**

0600 **9** hd **Your Gifted (IRE)**[15] 7240 6-9-7 **63**....(e) TomEaves 5 36
(Lisa Williamson) *trckd ldrs: effrt and n.m.r wl over 1f out: sn swtchd rt and rdn: wknd ent fnl f* **25/1**

04 **10** 3 1/4 **Red Roar (IRE)**[29] 6903 6-8-8 **50**....(p) JamesSullivan 1 12
(Alan Berry) *hld up: hdwy to chse ldrs over 2f out: sn rdn and wknd* **28/1**

1m 4.6s (4.80) **Going Correction** +1.00s/f (Soft) **10** Ran SP% **115.9**
Speed ratings (Par 101): **101,96,95,93,90 89,86,82,82,77**
toteswingers 1&2 £8.30, 1&3 £4.30, 2&3 £18.10 CSF £34.63 CT £211.85 TOTE £3.20: £1.90, £4.40, £2.30; EX 44.60 Trifecta £310.60 Pool: £2554.41 - 6.16 winning units..
Owner Paddy Mason **Bred** T J Ryan **Trained** Lydiate, Merseyside

FOCUS
The winner raced virtually alone against the stands' rail.
T/Jkpt: Not won. T/Plt: £278.40. Pool: £60,489.37 - 158.61 winning units. T/Qpdt: £73.70. Pool: £5995.81 - 60.16 winning units. JR

7540 WOLVERHAMPTON (A.W) (L-H)
Tuesday, October 29

OFFICIAL GOING: Standard
Wind: Fresh behind Weather: Fine

7600 32RED CASINO MAIDEN FILLIES' STKS — 5f 216y(P)
4:40 (4:40) (Class 5) 3-Y-O+ **£2,587** (£770; £384; £192) **Stalls** Low

Form RPR

0-2 **1** **Interception (IRE)**[21] 7108 3-9-0 0.... TedDurcan 4 72+
(David Lanigan) *hld up in tch: shkn up to ld and edgd lft ins fnl f: sn clr: eased towards fin* **4/5**[1]

020- **2** 1 1/2 **Shy Rosa (USA)**[449] 4876 4-9-1 70.... JimCrowley 3 64
(Marcus Tregoning) *s.i.s: t.k.h: hdwy to trck ldr 4f out: rdn over 1f out: nt clr run ins fnl f: styd on same pce* **11/2**[3]

34- **3** nk **My Trust (IRE)**[377] 7161 3-9-0 0.... HarryBentley 5 63
(Saeed bin Suroor) *trckd ldrs: led over 4f out: rdn over 1f out: hdd and no ex ins fnl f* **2/1**[2]

455 **4** 2 1/2 **Princess Sheila (IRE)**[14] 7265 3-8-7 50.... DavidParkes(7) 2 55
(J S Moore) *led 1f: t.k.h: hung rt fr over 3f out: rdn over 1f out: styd on same pce* **28/1**

0532 **5** 3 ¾ **Busy Bimbo (IRE)**[10] 7380 4-8-12 45......................... MarkCoumbe(3) 1 44
(Alan Berry) *chsd ldr 1f: sn lost pl: n.d after* **50/1**

1m 15.6s (0.60) **Going Correction** +0.025s/f (Slow)
WFA 3 from 4yo 1lb **5** Ran SP% **109.7**
Speed ratings (Par 100): **97,95,94,91,86**
CSF £5.81 TOTE £1.80: £1.10, £1.90; EX 4.20 Trifecta £7.60 Pool: £2625.85 - 256.48 winning units..
Owner B E Nielsen **Bred** Corduff Bloodstock Ltd & David Egan **Trained** Upper Lambourn, Berks

FOCUS
Clearly a weak maiden overall but the well-bred winner has potential. The pace was steady.

7601 BEST ODDS AT BOOKMAKERS.CO.UK H'CAP 5f 216y(P)
5:10 (5:10) (Class 4) (0-78,78) 3-Y-0+ **£4,851** (£1,443; £721; £360) **Stalls** Low

Form RPR

1002 **1** **You're The Boss**[18] 7165 3-9-2 74.................... LukeMorris 4 90+
(Ed Walker) *s.i.s: hdwy over 2f out: nt clr run over 1f out: shkn up to ld ins fnl f: qcknd clr* **9/4**[1]

-123 **2** 3 **Jinker Noble**[31] 6848 4-9-6 77.................... PatCosgrave 3 80
(Ed de Giles) *chsd ldrs: hmpd over 1f out: rdn and ev ch ins fnl f: styd on same pce* **9/2**[3]

6150 **3** 1 **Jungle Bay**[34] 6744 6-9-5 76....................(p) TedDurcan 7 76
(Jane Chapple-Hyam) *hld up: hdwy over 2f out: rdn and hung lft over 1f out: styd on same pce ins fnl f* **9/1**

0 **4** nk **Rowe Park**[31] 6854 10-9-6 77....................(p) LiamKeniry 9 76
(Linda Jewell) *hld up: hdwy over 1f out: sn rdn: styd on same pce ins fnl f* **16/1**

5050 **5** nk **We Have A Dream**[14] 7263 8-8-0 64 oh1....................(p) NoraLooby(7) 8 62
(Violet M Jordan) *sn pushed along to join ldr: led over 3f out: rdn and hdd over 1f out: no ex wl ins fnl f* **66/1**

5052 **6** ½ **Electric Qatar**[25] 6995 4-9-7 78.................... GeorgeBaker 10 75
(Tom Dascombe) *led: hdd over 3f out: remained w ldr: rdn and ev ch over 1f out: no ex wl ins fnl f* **11/4**[2]

000F **7** hd **Boxing Shadows**[36] 6682 3-8-9 72.................... GeorgeChaloner(5) 5 68
(Bryan Smart) *chsd ldrs: led over 1f out: sn rdn: hdd and no ex ins fnl f* **14/1**

0000 **8** 2 ½ **Prince Of Burma (IRE)**[18] 7165 5-8-4 68.................... EoinWalsh(7) 1 56
(David Evans) *s.s: outpcd* **28/1**

4306 **9** 5 **Alpha Tauri (USA)**[126] 3660 7-9-2 73....................(t) RobbieFitzpatrick 6 45
(Charles Smith) *rn wout declared tongue strap: prom tl wknd wl over 1f out* **40/1**

6050 **10** 2 ¾ **Midnight Dream (FR)**[146] 2983 3-9-0 77.................... JacobButterfield(5) 2 40
(Kristin Stubbs) *chsd ldrs: rdn over 2f out: wknd fnl f* **8/1**

1m 14.05s (-0.95) **Going Correction** +0.025s/f (Slow)
WFA 3 from 4yo+ 1lb **10** Ran SP% **116.7**
Speed ratings (Par 105): **107,103,101,101,100 100,99,96,89,86**
toteswingers 1&2 £3.00, 1&3 £5.10, 2&3 £7.20 CSF £12.52 CT £76.36 TOTE £3.10: £1.10, £2.70, £3.00; EX 13.70 Trifecta £102.70 Pool: £3654.93 - 26.88 winning units..
Owner Laurence A Bellman **Bred** Mrs Fiona Denniff **Trained** Newmarket, Suffolk
■ Stewards' Enquiry : Pat CosgraveM two-day ban: careless riding (12-13 Nov)

FOCUS
A fair handicap which was soundly run.

7602 32RED.COM MAIDEN AUCTION STKS 7f 32y(P)
5:40 (5:40) (Class 5) 2-Y-0 **£2,587** (£770; £384; £192) **Stalls** High

Form RPR

24 **1** **Art Obsession (IRE)**[15] 7237 2-8-11 0.................... GrahamGibbons 2 76
(David Barron) *trckd ldr over 5f out: shkn up to ld over 1f out: clr fnl f: eased towards fin* **11/10**[1]

6 **2** 3 ¼ **Crystal Lake (IRE)**[53] 6169 2-9-1 0.................... JimCrowley 1 70
(Ralph Beckett) *chsd ldrs: rdn over 2f out: styd on same pce fr over 1f out: wnt 2nd wl ins fnl f* **11/8**[2]

3 **3** 2 ¼ **Definite Secret**[11] 7348 2-8-10 0.................... LukeMorris 4 60
(James Tate) *sn led: pushed along over 2f out: hdd over 1f out: no ex ins fnl f* **5/1**[3]

0 **4** 6 **Tortoise**[60] 5968 2-8-3 0.................... BillyCray(3) 3 41
(Richard Guest) *s.i.s: a in rr: drvn along over 2f out: sn wknd* **100/1**

1m 31.13s (1.53) **Going Correction** +0.025s/f (Slow) **4** Ran SP% **107.4**
Speed ratings (Par 95): **92,88,85,78**
CSF £2.88 TOTE £2.10; EX 3.10 Trifecta £3.30 Pool: £2006.64 - 450.56 winning units..
Owner D Pryde & J Cringan **Bred** Lynch Bages Ltd & Camas Park Stud **Trained** Maunby, N Yorks

FOCUS
The market got it right here.

7603 LADBROKES H'CAP 7f 32y(P)
6:10 (6:10) (Class 4) (0-78,78) 3-Y-0+ **£4,851** (£1,443; £721; £360) **Stalls** High

Form RPR

-535 **1** **Ruwaiyan (USA)**[25] 7000 4-9-2 73....................(p) LukeMorris 3 90+
(James Tate) *s.i.s and hmpd s: pushed along in rr early: gd hdwy over 1f out: shkn up to ld ins fnl f: sn clr: easily* **8/1**

0500 **2** 4 ½ **Caldercruix (USA)**[16] 7224 6-9-2 78....................(v) RyanTate(5) 6 82
(James Evans) *a.p: chsd ldr 1/2-way: rdn over 2f out: styd on same pce ins fnl f* **22/1**

0121 **3** 1 **Living The Life (IRE)**[25] 6998 3-9-5 78....................(b) TedDurcan 4 79
(Jamie Osborne) *hmpd s: hdwy to ld over 5f out: rdn over 1f out: hdd and no ex ins fnl f* **7/4**[1]

4314 **4** nse **Breccbennach**[38] 6647 3-9-5 78....................(tp) GeorgeBaker 7 78
(Seamus Durack) *hld up: hdwy over 2f out: rdn over 1f out: styd on same pce fnl f* **11/2**[3]

3106 **5** 1 **Dawn Calling (IRE)**[10] 7374 3-9-4 77.................... JoeFanning 5 77
(Mark Johnston) *edgd lft s: sn led: hdd over 5f out: chsd ldr to 1/2-way: rdn over 2f out: nt clr run over 1f out and ins fnl f: styd on same pce* **3/1**[2]

0030 **6** 2 **Patrona Ciana (FR)**[30] 6874 3-9-3 76.................... DavidNolan 2 69
(David O'Meara) *sn prom: rdn over 2f out: wknd ins fnl f* **25/1**

4630 **7** ½ **Queen Aggie (IRE)**[20] 7123 3-8-10 76.................... EoinWalsh(7) 1 68
(David Evans) *chsd ldrs: lost pl over 5f out: drvn along over 2f out: wknd over 1f out* **14/1**

2136 **8** 4 **Funding Deficit (IRE)**[30] 6874 3-8-11 70.................... GrahamGibbons 8 52
(David Barron) *towards rr: hdwy over 4f out: rdn over 2f out: wknd over 1f out* **8/1**

1m 28.46s (-1.14) **Going Correction** +0.025s/f (Slow)
WFA 3 from 4yo+ 2lb **8** Ran SP% **113.8**
Speed ratings (Par 105): **107,101,100,100,99 97,96,92**
toteswingers 1&2 £12.30, 1&3 £3.20, 2&3 £5.50 CSF £155.52 CT £443.31 TOTE £10.70: £1.60, £4.00, £1.40; EX 150.70 Trifecta £362.60 Pool: £2909.90 - 6.01 winning units..
Owner Saeed Manana **Bred** Rabbah Bloodstock Llc **Trained** Newmarket, Suffolk

FOCUS
This ended up being a very one-sided handicap.

7604 32RED NURSERY H'CAP 1m 141y(P)
6:40 (6:41) (Class 6) (0-65,65) 2-Y-0 **£1,940** (£577; £288; £144) **Stalls** Low

Form RPR

6206 **1** **Jazzy Lady (IRE)**[34] 6755 2-8-1 50.................... NoelGarbutt(5) 2 57
(David Evans) *hld up: hdwy over 2f out: hmpd over 1f out: led and hung lft ins fnl f: pushed out* **22/1**

623 **2** 1 ½ **Byron Gala**[21] 7113 2-8-10 54.................... LukeMorris 5 58
(Marco Botti) *a.p: chsd ldr over 5f out tl led 4f out: rdn and hung rt over 1f out: hdd and carried lft ins fnl f: styd on same pce* **5/4**[1]

0041 **3** 1 **Earthflight**[18] 7168 2-9-2 60.................... WilliamCarson 7 64
(Philip McBride) *hld up: hdwy over 5f out: cl up whn hmpd over 1f out: rdn and nt clr run ins fnl f: r.o* **9/2**[3]

045 **4** 3 ½ **Tizlove Regardless (USA)**[14] 7276 2-9-4 62.................... JoeFanning 1 56
(Mark Johnston) *chsd ldrs: pushed along over 3f out: rdn over 1f out: styd on same pce* **7/2**[2]

5003 **5** 1 ½ **It's All A Game**[24] 7032 2-8-3 50....................(be[1]) BillyCray(3) 6 41
(Richard Guest) *chsd ldrs: led over 6f out: hdd 4f out: rdn over 2f out: styd on same pce* **14/1**

5441 **6** 1 ¼ **May Whi (IRE)**[33] 6779 2-9-7 65....................(v) MichaelO'Connell 4 54
(John Quinn) *t.k.h: led: hdd over 6f out: trckd ldrs: rdn and ev ch over 2f out: wknd fnl f* **7/1**

0320 **7** 33 **Sukari Gold (IRE)**[17] 7198 2-8-11 55....................(b) GrahamGibbons 3
(Tom Dascombe) *hld up: pushed along over 4f out: wknd 3f out* **20/1**

0500 **8** 6 **Kitty Brown (IRE)**[41] 6520 2-8-1 50....................(b[1]) JoeyHaynes(5) 8
(David Evans) *s.s and rel to r: a bhd* **50/1**

1m 51.61s (1.11) **Going Correction** +0.025s/f (Slow) **8** Ran SP% **115.1**
Speed ratings (Par 93): **96,94,93,90,89 88,58,53**
toteswingers 1&2 £9.00, 1&3 £23.90, 2&3 £1.70 CSF £49.76 CT £159.80 TOTE £21.10: £3.80, £1.10, £1.60; EX 84.80 Trifecta £162.30 Pool: £2312.14 - 10.67 winning units..
Owner Will Dawson **Bred** Limestone And Tara Studs **Trained** Pandy, Monmouths
■ Stewards' Enquiry : Luke Morris three-day ban: careless riding (12-14 Nov)

FOCUS
Just a modest nursery. The gallop didn't look particularly strong but the field were still quite well strung out.

7605 CORAL APP DOWNLOAD FROM THE APP STORE H'CAP 1m 1f 103y(P)
7:10 (7:10) (Class 5) (0-70,71) 3-Y-0+ **£2,587** (£770; £384; £192) **Stalls** Low

Form RPR

461 **1** **Landau (IRE)**[7] 7446 3-9-7 71 6ex....................(p) LiamKeniry 6 79
(Sylvester Kirk) *chsd ldrs: led over 1f out: sn rdn and hung lft: styd on* **4/1**[2]

0115 **2** 1 **Tatting**[10] 7383 4-9-2 69.................... JenniferFerguson(7) 4 75
(Chris Dwyer) *fly-leapt s: hld up: hdwy over 1f out: hung lft and r.o to go 2nd wl ins fnl f: nt rch wnr* **9/2**[3]

0300 **3** ½ **Outlaw Torn (IRE)**[10] 7383 4-9-0 60....................(e) RobbieFitzpatrick 3 65
(Richard Guest) *trckd ldr: plld hrd: rdn over 2f out: ev ch over 1f out: styd on* **25/1**

3445 **4** 2 **On With The Dance (IRE)**[52] 6214 3-9-6 70.................... LukeMorris 7 71
(Ed Vaughan) *a.p: rdn over 2f out: styd on same pce ins fnl f* **9/2**[3]

6063 **5** 1 ¾ **No Win No Fee**[11] 7353 3-8-10 60.................... AndrewMullen 2 58
(Michael Appleby) *hld up: hdwy 1/2-way: rdn over 2f out: no ex fnl f* **9/2**[3]

0000 **6** ¾ **Knowe Head (NZ)**[108] 4287 6-9-7 67....................(v) GeorgeBaker 8 66
(James Unett) *hld up: hdwy over 2f out: rdn and hung lft over 1f out: no ex* **5/2**[1]

0056 **7** shd **Staff Sergeant**[14] 7281 6-9-3 70....................(p) JackGarritty(7) 9 66
(Iain Jardine) *led: rdn and hdd over 1f out: wknd ins fnl f* **28/1**

3020 **8** 7 **Elsie Bay**[65] 5793 4-8-4 57.................... DavidParkes(7) 5 40
(J S Moore) *hld up: rdn over 2f out: sn wknd* **16/1**

2m 1.66s (-0.04) **Going Correction** +0.025s/f (Slow)
WFA 3 from 4yo+ 4lb **8** Ran SP% **116.3**
Speed ratings (Par 103): **101,100,99,97,96 95,95,89**
toteswingers 1&2 £9.00, 1&3 £23.90, 2&3 £1.70 CSF £22.79 CT £397.07 TOTE £4.80: £1.30, £1.50, £3.90; EX 19.40 Trifecta £740.40 Pool: £2140.59 - 2.16 winning units..
Owner Mrs Barbara Facchino **Bred** Barouche Stud (IRE) Ltd **Trained** Upper Lambourn, Berks

FOCUS
Another modest heat. The gallop didn't look particularly strong, the performance of the runner-up, who came from well back, is worth marking up slightly.
T/Plt: £23.50. Pool: £74,582.60 - 2308.75 winning units. T/Qpdt: £9.00. Pool: £8559.36 - 703.29 winning units. CR

7448 YARMOUTH (L-H)
Tuesday, October 29

OFFICIAL GOING: Soft (heavy in places; 5.7)
Wind: fresh, across Weather: mainly dry, blustery showers

7606 IRISH STALLION FARMS EBF MAIDEN STKS 7f 3y
1:10 (1:11) (Class 5) 2-Y-0 **£2,911** (£866; £432; £216) **Stalls** Centre

Form RPR

04 **1** **Bilimbi (IRE)**[14] 7270 2-9-5 0.................... ShaneKelly 3 79+
(William Haggas) *chsd ldr tl led ent fnl 2f: rdn and gng clr whn edgd lft 1f out: r.o wl: comf* **5/1**[2]

0 **2** 4 **Gift Of Rain (IRE)**[13] 7296 2-9-0 0.................... KierenFallon 4 64
(Ed Dunlop) *in tch in midfield: clsd and pressed ldrs 1/2-way: rdn and unable qck w wnr over 1f out: chsd clr wnr ins fnl f: no imp* **10/1**[3]

522 **3** 3 **Istikshaf (IRE)**[13] 7308 2-9-5 78.................... SilvestreDeSousa 6 62
(Saeed bin Suroor) *chsd ldrs: clsd and ev ch ent fnl 2f: wnt 2nd but unable qck whn swtchd rt over 1f out: wknd ins fnl f* **4/11**[1]

400 **4** 1 ½ **Hands Up (IRE)**[13] 7302 2-9-5 75.................... AdamKirby 1 58
(William Knight) *sn led: hdd and rdn ent fnl 2f: dropped to 4th and btn ent fnl f: wknd* **14/1**

00 **5** 6 **Urban Sanctuary**[20] 7125 2-9-5 0.................... TomMcLaughlin 5 43
(Ed Walker) *stdd s: hld up in last pair: rdn and struggling 1/2-way: n.d* **100/1**

6 23 **Swilken** 2-9-5 0.................... TomQueally 7
(Mark H Tompkins) *a in rr: rdn along over 4f out: lost tch over 2f out: t.o and eased ins fnl f* **40/1**

1m 30.19s (3.59) **Going Correction** +0.525s/f (Yiel) **6** Ran SP% **109.2**
Speed ratings (Par 95): **100,95,92,90,83 57**
toteswingers 1&2 £1.10, 1&3 £1.20, 2&3 £1.40 CSF £46.80 TOTE £5.30: £1.70, £3.30; EX 40.20 Trifecta £51.10 Pool: £2321.12 - 34.04 winning units..
Owner The Starship Partnership **Bred** T Hirschfeld **Trained** Newmarket, Suffolk

FOCUS
Shane Kelly felt the ground was "soft", while Kieren Fallon described it as "heavy". Questionable maiden form, with the red-hot favourite failing to give his running.

7607 EBFSTALLIONS.COM IRISH EBF MAIDEN STKS 1m 3y
1:40 (1:40) (Class 5) 2-Y-O £2,911 (£866; £432; £216) Stalls Centre

Form RPR
1 **Mannaro (IRE)** 2-9-5 0 SilvestreDeSousa 2 80+
(Marco Botti) *wnt rt s: hld up in tch towards rr: stdy prog 1/2-way: rdn to ld over 1f out: styd on wl ins fnl f: rdn out* 9/2[1]
2 nk **Second Step (IRE)** 2-9-5 0 AdamKirby 3 79+
(Luca Cumani) *hld up in tch towards rr: hdwy 1/2-way: chsd ldrs ent fnl 2f: rdn over 1f out: pressed wnr and rn green jst ins fnl f: ev ch fnl f: styd on wl* 6/1[3]
3 2 **Wrangler** 2-9-5 0 KierenFallon 11 75+
(William Haggas) *hld up in tch in midfield: hdwy over 3f out: ev ch and rdn over 1f out: styd on same pce ins fnl f* 8/1
4 3 1/2 **Sternrubin (GER)** 2-9-5 0 ShaneKelly 5 67+
(Peter Chapple-Hyam) *t.k.h: hld up in tch in midfield: effrt to chse ldrs 2f out: sn rdn: no ex and wknd ins fnl f* 8/1
5 3/4 **Stout Cortez** 2-9-5 0 FrederikTylicki 6 66+
(Mark Johnston) *led: rdn ent fnl 2f: hdd over 1f out: no ex and btn 1f out: wknd* 14/1
6 8 **Itsnowcato** 2-9-5 0 TomMcLaughlin 9 48
(Ed Walker) *hld up in tch towards rr: rdn and effrt over 2f out: no imp u.p 2f out: wknd over 1f out* 8/1
7 hd **Alexanor (IRE)** 2-9-5 0 (t) PaoloSirigu 7 48
(Marco Botti) *sltly hmpd s: t.k.h and sn rcvrd to r in midfield: rdn and effrt over 2f out: wknd over 1f out* 11/1
8 nk **Tactical Strike** 2-9-5 0 (t) SebSanders 12 47
(Hugo Palmer) *hld up in tch in midfield: rdn and effrt over 2f out: 6th and btn over 1f out: sn wknd* 5/1[2]
9 10 **Rock Of Leon** 2-9-5 0 PaulHanagan 4 25
(Michael Bell) *a towards rr: rdn 1/2-way: bhd fnl 2f* 12/1
10 1/2 **Bourbon Prince** 2-9-5 0 MartinLane 1 24
(Michael Bell) *chsd ldrs: rdn 1/2-way: wknd qckly over 2f out: bhd fnl f* 22/1
11 13 **Astrovirtue** 2-9-5 0 TomQueally 10
(Mark H Tompkins) *a in rr: rdn 1/2-way: sn struggling: bhd fnl 2f: t.o* 66/1
00 12 10 **Masterpaver**[13] 7308 2-9-5 0 RobertWinston 8
(Alan Bailey) *wnt rt s: chsd ldr: rdn 1/2-way: lost pl over 2f out: t.o and eased ins fnl f* 20/1
1m 45.25s (4.65) **Going Correction** +0.525s/f (Yiel) 12 Ran SP% 115.8
Speed ratings (Par 95): **97,96,94,91,90 82,82,81,71,71 58,48**
toteswingers 1&2 £5.40, 1&3 £3.00, 2&3 £9.90 CSF £29.53 TOTE £5.20: £2.20, £1.60, £1.90; EX 26.50 Trifecta £331.60 Pool: £1803.10 - 4.07 winning units..
Owner La Tesa Spa **Bred** La Tesa Spa **Trained** Newmarket, Suffolk
FOCUS
It's unlikely this was anything more than a fair maiden. Those coming from off the pace dominated.

7608 BETVICTOR NEW LIVE CASINO H'CAP 1m 3y
2:10 (2:10) (Class 5) (0-75,76) 3-Y-O+ £2,587 (£770; £384; £192) Stalls Centre

Form RPR
0232 1 **Uncle Dermot (IRE)**[8] 7430 5-8-9 63 KierenFallon 4 72
(Brendan Powell) *mde virtually all: rdn ent fnl 2f: clr over 1f out: styd on wl: rdn out* 6/1[2]
3646 2 1 3/4 **Ted's Brother (IRE)**[19] 7152 5-8-12 69 (e) JasonHart(3) 5 74
(Richard Guest) *chsd ldrs: rdn over 2f out: drvn to chse clr wnr over 1f out: kpt on u.p but a hld* 16/1
2214 3 1 3/4 **Al Freej (IRE)**[35] 6727 4-9-7 75 DaleSwift 1 76
(Brian Ellison) *stdd s: t.k.h: chsd ldrs: effrt u.p to chse ldng pair over 1f out: kpt on same pce ins fnl f* 16/1
1220 4 hd **Pelmanism**[32] 6801 6-9-2 70 AdamKirby 6 71
(Brian Ellison) *hld up in midfield: rdn and effrt over 2f out: no real imp tl styd on ins fnl f: nvr trbld ldrs* 17/2
0603 5 nk **Silver Alliance**[20] 7130 5-9-0 73 (p) ShelleyBirkett(5) 8 73
(Julia Feilden) *hld up in tch towards rr: rdn and effrt ent fnl 2f: styd on steadily ins fnl f: nvr trbld ldrs* 14/1
001 6 1/2 **Collodi (GER)**[8] 7430 4-9-1 76 6ex NedCurtis(7) 10 75
(Roger Curtis) *hld up in tch towards rr: rdn and effrt 2f out: plugged on ins fnl f: nvr trbld ldrs* 5/1[1]
2401 7 1 1/4 **Magique (IRE)**[15] 7256 3-9-4 75 SebSanders 3 70
(Jeremy Noseda) *stdd s: t.k.h: hld up towards rr: hdwy 1/2-way: chsd ldrs and drvn over 1f out: no ex 1f out: wknd fnl 100yds* 7/1[3]
0026 8 1 1/4 **Kyllachy Star**[13] 7307 7-9-2 70 PaulHanagan 7 64
(Richard Fahey) *in tch in midfield: effrt u.p over 1f out: no real imp and plugged on same pce fr over 1f out* 8/1
0432 9 2 **Ela Goog La Mou**[50] 6261 4-8-4 61 oh8 RosieJessop(3) 2 50
(Peter Charalambous) *sn pressing wnr: rdn over 2f out: lost pl and btn over 1f out: wknd fnl f* 16/1
0334 10 9 **Barwick**[41] 6538 5-9-7 75 TomQueally 9 44
(Mark H Tompkins) *stdd s: hld up in tch in rr: rdn 3f out: drvn and no hdwy over 2f out: wknd wl over 1f out* 5/1[1]
0003 11 6 **Hidden Talent**[11] 7344 3-8-10 67 SteveDrowne 12 22
(David Brown) *racd against stands' rail: hld up towards rr overall: rdn and effrt 2f out: no hdwy and sn btn: wl bhd fnl f* 25/1
2604 12 22 **Kung Hei Fat Choy (USA)**[10] 7374 4-9-5 73 (b) FrederikTylicki 13
(James Given) *racd against stands' rail: midfield overall: rdn and btn over 2f out: t.o and heavily eased fnl f* 14/1
1m 43.94s (3.34) **Going Correction** +0.525s/f (Yiel)
WFA 3 from 4yo+ 3lb 12 Ran SP% 116.6
Speed ratings (Par 103): **104,102,100,100,100 99,98,97,95,86 80,58**
toteswingers 1&2 £19.20, 1&3 £22.50, 2&3 £60.50 CSF £96.33 CT £1458.34 TOTE £5.30: £1.90, £6.00, £3.00; EX 91.40 Trifecta £1583.50 Pool: £2427.16 - 1.14 winning units..
Owner K Rhatigan **Bred** Ballyhane Stud **Trained** Upper Lambourn, Berks
FOCUS
Little got into this.

7609 BETVICTOR LIVE CASINO £175 CASH BONUS NURSERY H'CAP 7f 3y
2:40 (2:40) (Class 5) (0-75,75) 2-Y-O £2,587 (£770; £384; £192) Stalls Centre

Form RPR
0041 1 **Firecruise**[8] 7418 2-9-4 72 6ex (b) RobertWinston 8 77+
(David Barron) *in tch towards rr: rdn 1/2-way: hdwy u.p to chal ent fnl f: led ins fnl f: r.o strly and gng away fin* 5/4[1]
4143 2 1 **Intense Feeling (IRE)**[44] 6432 2-9-4 72 SilvestreDeSousa 3 75
(David Evans) *hld up in tch in midfield: rdn and hdwy betwen rivals to ld over 1f out: hdd jst ins fnl f: kpt on wl tl no ex and btn fnl 50yds* 20/1
0203 3 5 **Oriental Relation (IRE)**[42] 6493 2-9-5 73 DaleSwift 4 63
(James Given) *led: rdn ent fnl 2f: hdd and unable qck over 1f out: wknd ins fnl f* 15/2[3]
5113 4 2 3/4 **Shyron**[11] 7352 2-9-7 75 TomQueally 5 59
(George Margarson) *squeezed for room leaving stalls: hld up in tch in rr: hdwy and swtchd rt over 2f out: rdn to chal and wandered u.p over 1f out: wknd fnl 150yds* 14/1
0000 5 2 1/4 **Syrian Pearl**[34] 6749 2-8-7 64 ow1 AshleyMorgan(3) 2 42
(Chris Wall) *t.k.h: chsd ldrs: rdn and unable qck ent fnl 2f: wknd u.p 1f out* 12/1
302 6 nk **Evacusafe Lady**[6] 7466 2-8-2 56 (p) MartinLane 6 33
(John Ryan) *pressed ldr: rdn and ev ch ent fnl 2f: no ex and btn over 1f out: wknd 1f out* 4/1[2]
602 7 10 **Palace Princess (FR)**[78] 5352 2-9-0 68 AdamKirby 7 21
(Ed Dunlop) *hld up in tch in midfield: rdn and effrt over 2f out: struggling 2f out and sn wknd: bhd and eased ins fnl f* 8/1
31 8 5 **Baileys Forever**[78] 5338 2-9-3 71 FrederikTylicki 1 12
(James Given) *chsd ldrs: rdn 3f out: lost pl u.p over 2f out: bhd and eased ins fnl f* 14/1
1m 31.13s (4.53) **Going Correction** +0.525s/f (Yiel) 8 Ran SP% 113.1
Speed ratings (Par 95): **95,93,88,85,82 82,70,64**
toteswingers 1&2 £5.80, 1&3 £3.80, 2&3 £10.40 CSF £29.66 CT £138.90 TOTE £2.70: £1.70, £2.50, £1.80; EX 29.40 Trifecta £155.50 Pool: £4019.98 - 19.38 winning units..
Owner Profile Storage Ltd **Bred** Fifehead Farms M C Denning **Trained** Maunby, N Yorks
FOCUS
A race that revolved around the favourite.

7610 PLAY ROULETTE AT VICTOR'S LIVE CASINO H'CAP 1m 1f
3:10 (3:10) (Class 6) (0-60,60) 3-Y-O £1,940 (£577; £288; £144) Stalls Low

Form RPR
0404 1 **Entrapping**[24] 7035 3-9-0 51 JimmyQuinn 5 61
(John E Long) *hld up in rr of main gp: rdn and effrt over 2f out: hdd to ld over 1f out: drvn clr 1f out: in command after: rdn out* 8/1
00-6 2 1 1/2 **Red Catkin**[12] 7321 3-9-6 57 TomQueally 2 66+
(George Margarson) *hld up in tch in midfield: clsng on ldrs whn hmpd 2f out: swtchd rt over 1f out and rallied u.p 1f out: chsd clr wnr fnl 100yds: r.o but nvr a threat* 3/1[1]
5006 3 4 1/2 **Cherry Tiger**[35] 6737 3-9-4 58 [1] RobertTart(3) 9 56
(James Toller) *chsd ldrs: rdn and ev ch ent fnl 2f: led over 1f out: sn hdd and unable qck: outpcd and lost 2nd fnl 100yds* 9/2[2]
0331 4 3/4 **Minimee**[7] 7455 3-9-9 60 6ex (v) PaddyAspell 10 57
(Phil McEntee) *wnt rt s: in tch in midfield: clsng on ldrs whn nt clr run and swtchd sharply rt 2f out: drvn and ev ch over 1f out: no ex and btn 1f out: plugged on* 9/2[2]
0006 5 2 **Mrs Mann (USA)**[33] 6783 3-9-0 51 RobertWinston 7 44
(Willie Musson) *chsd ldrs: effrt on inner but n.m.r over 2f out: btn whn swtchd rt over 1f out: wknd* 16/1
5400 6 2 3/4 **Betty Boo (IRE)**[24] 7035 3-8-3 45 ShirleyTeasdale(5) 12 32
(Shaun Harris) *chsd ldrs: wnt 2nd over 7f out tl led over 2f out: hdd over 1f out: sn wknd* 25/1
-360 7 3 **Prom Dress**[182] 1906 3-9-6 57 FrederikTylicki 6 38
(J R Jenkins) *t.k.h: hld up in midfield: effrt whn hmpd and swtchd rt ent fnl 2f: sn btn* 16/1
5040 8 1/2 **Azabitmour (FR)**[32] 6788 3-9-7 58 SteveDrowne 3 38
(John Best) *hld up in detached last: rdn and effrt over 3f out: no prog: n.d* 16/1
04-0 9 4 **Believe In Me**[145] 3013 3-8-4 46 ShelleyBirkett(5) 8 18
(Julia Feilden) *led for over 1f: chsd ldrs: rdn and effrt over 2f out: drvn to press ldrs briefly over 1f out: sn btn: wknd fnl f* 22/1
0556 10 3 3/4 **East Texas Red (IRE)**[45] 6406 3-8-8 45 PaoloSirigu 11 10
(Mick Quinn) *pushed rt s: rcvrd to ld over 7f out: rdn and hdd over 2f out: lost pl 2f out: bhd fnl f* 6/1[3]
2m 2.4s (6.60) **Going Correction** +0.45s/f (Yiel) 10 Ran SP% 112.6
Speed ratings (Par 99): **88,86,82,82,80 77,75,74,71,67**
toteswingers 1&2 £5.60, 1&3 £5.70, 2&3 £3.40 CSF £31.05 CT £123.54 TOTE £9.60: £2.50, £1.50, £1.60; EX 33.20 Trifecta £136.20 Pool: £2260.27 - 12.44 winning units..
Owner M Fernandes E Cooper V Fox F Collyer **Bred** K Snell **Trained** Caterham, Surrey
■ Stewards' Enquiry : Paddy Aspell one-day ban: careless riding (12 Nov)
FOCUS
A moderate handicap, but one that should produce winners at a similar level.

7611 PLAY BLACKJACK AT VICTOR'S LIVE CASINO H'CAP 1m 2f 21y
3:40 (3:41) (Class 4) (0-80,80) 3-Y-O+ £4,690 (£1,395; £697; £348) Stalls Low

Form RPR
51 1 **Martian (IRE)**[56] 6062 3-9-5 80 ShaneKelly 8 93+
(William Haggas) *hld up in midfield: hdwy to chse ldng pair over 2f out: steadily clsd and pushed along to chse ldr over 1f out: led fnl 100yds: pushed out: cleverly* 7/2[2]
5402 2 1/2 **Mystery Bet (IRE)**[14] 7275 3-9-0 75 PaulHanagan 7 84
(Richard Fahey) *chsd ldr: steadily clsd over 2f out: rdn to ld over 1f out: drvn and hdd fnl 100yds: kpt on but comf hld* 3/1[1]
5513 3 1 1/2 **The Ducking Stool**[7] 7453 6-8-8 69 ShelleyBirkett(5) 3 75
(Julia Feilden) *hld up in midfield: effrt u.p over 2f out: hdwy to chse clr ldng trio 2f out: wnt 3rd ins fnl f: styd on* 6/1
6611 4 1 1/4 **Saigon City**[27] 6951 3-9-3 78 (b) AdamKirby 2 82
(Luca Cumani) *dwlt: hld up off the pce in rr: hdwy u.p over 2f out: 5th over 1f out: styd on u.p fnl f: nvr trbld ldrs* 9/2[3]
4444 5 2 1/4 **Perfect Delight**[45] 6405 4-8-10 66 oh1 (p) MartinLane 9 66
(Ralph Beckett) *hld up off the pce in midfield: effrt u.p over 2f out: plugged on ins fnl f: nvr trbld ldrs* 10/1
1620 6 3/4 **Colinca's Lad (IRE)**[21] 7115 11-9-7 80 RosieJessop(3) 12 79
(Peter Charalambous) *led: wnt clr 7f out: rdn over 2f out: hdd and no ex over 1f out: wknd and lost 3 pls ins fnl f* 16/1
6140 7 14 **Panettone (IRE)**[20] 7132 4-8-10 66 oh1 DominicFox 4 40
(Roger Varian) *chsd ldrs: rdn and no imp over 3f out: 7th and wl btn over 1f out* 20/1
13/0 8 1 1/2 **Timothy T**[22] 7075 5-9-7 77 TomQueally 13 48
(Philip Hide) *chsd ldrs: rdn and no imp over 2f out: wl btn over 1f out: eased ins fnl f* 33/1
0316 9 2 1/2 **Mountain Range (IRE)**[125] 3692 5-9-0 70 JamieMackay 10 36
(Willie Musson) *stdd s: t.k.h: hld up wl off the pce in rr: n.d* 25/1

5316 **10** *nse* **Pravda Street**[10] 7369 8-9-1 **71** DaleSwift 1 37
(Brian Ellison) *pushed along leaving stalls: racd off the pce in midfield: rdn and no hdwy 3f out: no ch fnl 2f* **25/1**

000- **11** *12* **Paddyfrommenlo (IRE)**[386] 6933 4-9-2 **72** KierenFallon 5 17
(Gary Harrison) *racd off the pce in midfield: dropped to rr 4f out: lost tch 3f out: t.o* **25/1**

05 **12** *1 3/4* **Mespone (FR)**[131] 3503 4-9-5 **75** RobertWinston 11 17
(Alan Bailey) *hld up off the pce in last trio: lost tch 3f out: sn wl bhd: t.o* **50/1**

0100 **13** *13* **Hunting Rights (USA)**[13] 7312 3-9-4 **79** SilvestreDeSousa 6
(Mark Johnston) *racd in midfield: rdn and no rspnse 4f out: bhd over 2f out: t.o* **16/1**

2m 13.69s (3.19) **Going Correction** +0.45s/f (Yiel)
WFA 3 from 4yo+ 5lb **13** Ran SP% **121.7**
Speed ratings (Par 105): **105,104,103,102,100 100,88,87,85,85 75,74,64**
toteswingers 1&2 £3.10, 1&3 £7.30, 2&3 £4.80 CSF £13.35 CT £63.04 TOTE £5.40: £2.80, £1.20, £2.50; EX 17.90 Trifecta £84.80 Pool: £1968.18 - 17.39 winning units..
Owner The Starship Partnership **Bred** T Hirschfeld **Trained** Newmarket, Suffolk

FOCUS
No surprise to see this dominated by 3yos.

7612 FOLLOW LIVE CASINO @VICTORCASINO H'CAP 1m 6f 17y
4:10 (4:10) (Class 6) (0-55,55) 4-Y-0+ **£1,940** (£577; £288; £144) **Stalls** Centre

Form RPR

2P03 **1** **Ice Apple**[19] 7159 5-8-12 **46** JimmyQuinn 5 52
(John E Long) *hld up in last quartet: hdwy into midfield but stl plenty to do 3f out: styd on and clsng whn swtchd rt 1f out: kpt on to ld wl ins fnl f: rdn out* **28/1**

460 **2** *1* **Goodlukin Lucy**[15] 7239 6-9-0 **51** JasonHart(3) 10 56
(Keith Dalgleish) *led: rdn clr 3f out: drvn and 2 l clr 1f out: kpt on tl hdd and no ex wl ins fnl f* **7/1**[3]

64 **3** *1/2* **Omega Omega**[55] 6097 4-8-12 **46** oh1 (p) AdamBeschizza 1 50
(Julia Feilden) *chsd ldrs: rdn and effrt 3f out: 4th and hrd drvn 2f out: kpt on and clsd on ldr 1f out: wnt 3rd towards fin* **28/1**

0655 **4** *3/4* **Reach The Beach**[84] 5093 4-9-1 **49** KierenFallon 9 52
(Brendan Powell) *chsd ldrs: wnt 2nd 5f out: rdn and outpcd 3f out: rallied and 2 l down 1f out: kpt on same pce after and lost 2 pls fnl 100yds* **9/2**[2]

0244 **5** *hd* **Royal Defence (IRE)**[14] 6458 7-8-10 **47** RobertTart(3) 7 50+
(Mick Quinn) *racd in midfield: effrt u.p over 2f out: 6th and styng on whn nt clr run and swtchd lft 1f out: kpt on: n.m.r and swtchd rt towards fin* **14/1**

0063 **6** *1/2* **Father Shine (IRE)**[10] 7375 10-8-10 **49** ShirleyTeasdale(5) 13 51
(Shaun Harris) *chsd ldrs: effrt to chse ldng pair and rdn 3f out: kpt on u.p: styd on same pce ins fnl f* **12/1**

/6-0 **7** *11* **Ghufa (IRE)**[10] 7379 9-9-2 **53** RosieJessop(3) 6 41
(Lydia Pearce) *hld up in rr: effrt in centre 3f out: plugged on past btn horses fnl 2f: n.d* **33/1**

6205 **8** *6* **Soweto Star (IRE)**[40] 6558 5-9-1 **49** SteveDrowne 3 29
(John Best) *racd in midfield: rdn and no hdwy 3f out: wknd 2f out* **25/1**

/ **9** *9* **Ticoz (USA)**[67] 8-8-13 **47** (t) PaulHanagan 2 15
(Marco Botti) *hld up in midfield: clsd 5f out: rdn over 2f out: sn btn: wl bhd over 1f out* **11/8**[1]

0003 **10** *10* **Joe The Coat**[10] 7372 4-9-7 **55** (b) TomQueally 8 10
(Mark H Tompkins) *hld up in last quartet: n.d: wl bhd and eased ins fnl f: t.o* **14/1**

0620 **11** *37* **Rock Of Ages**[19] 7159 4-9-7 **55** (b) AdamKirby 4
(Michael Murphy) *hld up in last quartet: lost tch over 3f out: eased fnl 2f: t.o* **20/1**

0000 **12** *nk* **Willow Island (IRE)**[7] 7440 4-8-12 **46** oh1 (v) SilvestreDeSousa 11
(David Evans) *chsd ldr tl 5f out: sn dropped out: t.o and eased fnl 2f* **22/1**

3m 15.7s (8.10) **Going Correction** +0.45s/f (Yiel) **12** Ran SP% **116.6**
Speed ratings (Par 101): **94,93,93,92,92 92,86,82,77,71 50,50**
toteswingers 1&2 £30.80, 1&3 £32.90, 2&3 £21.10 CSF £195.12 CT £5485.78 TOTE £21.20: £5.00, £1.70, £4.10; EX 261.60 Trifecta £1187.60 Pool: £2926.70 - 1.84 winning units..
Owner Mr & Mrs K G Newland **Bred** Arches Hall Stud **Trained** Caterham, Surrey

FOCUS
Weak handicap form.
T/Plt: £302.70. Pool: £65,151.09 - 157.12 winning units. T/Qpdt: £16.20. Pool: £8143.95 - 371.75 winning units. SP

7160 SAINT-CLOUD (L-H)
Tuesday, October 29

OFFICIAL GOING: Turf: very soft

7613a PRIX DE FLORE (GROUP 3) (3YO+ FILLIES & MARES) (TURF) 1m 2f 110y
1:50 (12:00) 3-Y-0+ **£32,520** (£13,008; £9,756; £6,504; £3,252)

RPR

1 **Narniyn (IRE)**[27] 6962 3-8-7 0 Christophe-PatriceLemaire 3 111+
(A De Royer-Dupre, France) *restrained and trckd ldr early: chsd clr ldrs 1/2-way: clsd fr 3f out: led gng strly over 2f out: rdn whn jnd over 1f out: styd on strly and asserted ins fnl f: pushed out towards fin* **15/2**[2]

2 *1 3/4* **Gaga A (URU)**[22] 4-8-10 0 GregoryBenoist 6 106
(D Smaga, France) *wnt rt s: restrained and hld up in last pair: rdn and hdwy fr 3f out: crossed to nr side rail in st and jnd ldr over 1f out: styd on wout matching wnr and hld ins fnl f* **26/1**

3 *5* **Vally Jem (FR)**[39] 6618 4-8-11 0 (p) AntoineHamelin 7 96
(D Sepulchre, France) *squeezed s: hld up in last pair: last 1/2-way: stdy hdwy on turn into st: rdn 2f out: wnt 3rd over 1f out: styd on but readily outpcd by front pair ins fnl f* **13/2**[3]

4 *7* **Kyurem (IRE)**[32] 6819 3-8-7 0 FlavienPrat 2 84
(T Clout, France) *midfield: rdn over 3f out: outpcd by ldrs in st: plugged on for mod 4th* **13/2**[3]

5 *3* **Galvaun (IRE)**[24] 7048 4-8-11 0 MaximeGuyon 5 76
(A Fabre, France) *trckd ldr early: sn midfield: rdn over 3f out: outpcd and no imp fr over 1f out* **9/5**[1]

6 *12* **Miss You Too**[41] 6536 3-8-7 0 ChrisCatlin 4 55
(David Simcock) *led: clr of remainder whn jnd bef 1/2-way: rdn 3f out: clsd down rapidly and hdd over 2f out: no ex and btn: steadily fdd* **78/10**

7 *3 1/2* **Orion Love**[24] 7048 3-8-7 0 (b[1]) FabriceVeron 8 48
(H-A Pantall, France) *wnt lft s: t.k.h: trckd ldr: clr of remainder whn jnd ldr bef 1/2-way: clsd down rapidly and hdd over 2f out: hung lft whn rdn and sn btn: dropped to last and eased over 1f out* **9/1**

2m 21.34s (1.74)
WFA 3 from 4yo 5lb **7** Ran SP% **116.9**
WIN (incl. 1 euro stake): 3.40. PLACES: 1.60, 4.20, 2.20. DF: 36.90. SF: 55.20.
Owner H H Aga Khan **Bred** His Highness The Aga Khan's Studs S C **Trained** Chantilly, France

7146 AYR (L-H)
Wednesday, October 30

7614 Meeting Abandoned - Waterlogged

7458 KEMPTON (A.W) (R-H)
Wednesday, October 30

OFFICIAL GOING: Standard
Wind: Brisk, across (away from stands) Weather: Fine

7622 BOOK CHRISTMAS FESTIVAL TICKETS NOW H'CAP 1m 2f (P)
4:35 (4:38) (Class 6) (0-65,65) 3-Y-0+ **£1,940** (£577; £288; £144) **Stalls** Low

Form RPR

3542 **1** **Bobs Her Uncle**[40] 6599 4-9-9 **64** TedDurcan 11 73
(James Bethell) *trckd ldr 1f: styd prom: gng best whn wnt 2nd again wl over 1f out: clsd to ld jst ins fnl f: rdn out* **9/2**[2]

1124 **2** *1/2* **Mr Lando**[15] 5694 4-9-8 **63** JimmyQuinn 4 71
(Tony Carroll) *trckd ldrs: prog over 2f out: rdn to chse wnr ins fnl f: sn clsd: nt qckn last 75yds* **7/1**

4415 **3** *2 1/4* **Loraine**[22] 7093 3-9-3 **63** GeorgeBaker 6 67+
(Jamie Osborne) *hld up wl in rr: stl in last trio 3f out but gng wl: rapid prog fr 2f out: r.o to take 3rd nr fin: hopeless task* **4/1**[1]

-400 **4** *3/4* **How Fortunate**[15] 7283 5-9-6 **61** PaulHanagan 7 63
(Tim Etherington) *off the pce in midfield: rdn 3f out: styd on fr wl over 1f out to take 4th nr fin* **16/1**

0014 **5** *1/2* **Solvanna**[8] 7434 3-9-5 **65** AndreaAtzeni 10 66
(Heather Main) *led: kicked on fr over 2f out: hdd & wknd jst ins fnl f* **10/1**

0-00 **6** *1/2* **Night's Watch**[16] 7248 3-9-0 **60** MartinDwyer 14 60
(William Jarvis) *hld up in last trio fr wd draw: plld out and prog fr 3f out: wd bnd 2f out: kpt on fr over 1f out: no ch* **11/1**

6003 **7** *3* **Kingscombe (USA)**[23] 7083 4-9-3 **58** SebSanders 2 52
(Linda Jewell) *trckd ldrs: rdn over 2f out: no imp over 1f out: wknd fnl f* **20/1**

4320 **8** *1* **Fonterutoli (IRE)**[7] 7458 6-8-13 **54** (b) RobertHavlin 8 46
(Roger Ingram) *s.i.s: rousted to chse ldr after 1f to wl over 1f out: wknd* **10/1**

3003 **9** *5* **Bert The Alert**[56] 6114 5-9-10 **65** FergusSweeney 9 47
(Laura Mongan) *settled wl in rr: rdn 3f out: plugged on one pce fnl 2f: no ch* **25/1**

05-0 **10** *4* **Ninfea (IRE)**[22] 7091 5-9-6 **61** (b[1]) LiamKeniry 5 35
(Sylvester Kirk) *s.i.s: nvr gng wl: a in rr* **10/1**

00-0 **11** *13* **Berengar (IRE)**[19] 7163 4-9-10 **65** AdamKirby 1 13
(John Butler) *nvr bttr than midfield: drvn and no prog over 3f out: wknd 2f out: t.o* **20/1**

0055 **12** *nk* **Scamperdale**[82] 5234 11-9-8 **63** JackMitchell 12 10
(Brian Baugh) *settled in last trio: prog u.p over 3f out: chsd ldrs briefly over 2f out: wknd qckly over 1f out: t.o* **20/1**

0050 **13** *26* **Pearl Street (USA)**[42] 6521 3-9-5 **65** HarryBentley 13
(Henry Candy) *chsd ldrs: shoved along 1/2-way: sn wknd: eased over 1f out: wl t.o* **11/2**[3]

2m 5.76s (-2.24) **Going Correction** +0.025s/f (Slow)
WFA 3 from 4yo+ 5lb **13** Ran SP% **125.7**
Speed ratings (Par 101): **109,108,106,106,105 105,103,102,98,95 84,84,63**
toteswingers 1&2 £4.80, 1&3 £4.50, 2&3 £6.90 CSF £35.91 CT £142.16 TOTE £4.40: £1.60, £1.90, £1.80; EX 25.70 Trifecta £105.60 Pool: £3689.82 - 26.19 winning units..
Owner Robert Gibbons **Bred** Robert Gibbons **Trained** Middleham Moor, N Yorks

FOCUS
They raced on the inner loop and it paid to be up with the pace in this weak, but competitive handicap for the grade. The pace was true and the time good for the grade. Length personal bests from the first two.

7623 JEWSON NURSERY H'CAP 6f (P)
5:10 (5:11) (Class 6) (0-65,65) 2-Y-0 **£1,940** (£577; £288; £144) **Stalls** Low

Form RPR

0531 **1** **Gower Princess**[14] 7293 2-9-5 **63** LukeMorris 9 66
(Ronald Harris) *reluctant to enter stalls: chsd ldr: shkn up to ld over 1f out: hrd pressed fnl f: kpt on wl* **5/1**[2]

3400 **2** *3/4* **Honey Meadow**[8] 7451 2-9-6 **64** AndreaAtzeni 7 65
(Robert Eddery) *chsd ldrs disputing 5th: shkn up wl over 2f out: prog over 1f out: styd on to take 2nd nr fin: unable to chal* **10/1**

555 **3** *nk* **Caesars Gift (IRE)**[18] 7200 2-9-0 **58** HarryBentley 2 58
(Derek Shaw) *chsd ldrs: clsd over 2f out: drvn to press wnr ins fnl f: no imp and lost 2nd nr fin* **16/1**

400 **4** *shd* **Manor Way (IRE)**[14] 7302 2-9-4 **62** SeanLevey 6 62
(Richard Hannon) *settled in rr: rdn 3f out: prog 2f out: forced to switch lft 1f out: styd on: nrst fin* **6/1**[3]

4466 **5** *1 3/4* **Elite Freedom (IRE)**[38] 6663 2-9-2 **60** SamHitchcott 8 54
(Jo Hughes) *hld up in last pair: shkn up over 2f out: styd on u.p fr over 1f out: nrst fin* **10/1**

6061 **6** *1/2* **Gulland Rock**[31] 6872 2-9-3 **61** MartinDwyer 11 54
(William Muir) *chsd ldng pair: rdn over 2f out: nt qckn over 1f out: fdd nr fin: lame* **7/2**[1]

002 **7** *1/2* **Black Geronimo**[18] 7198 2-9-1 **59** (v) TomQueally 4 50
(David Evans) *chsd ldng pair: rdn over 2f out: nt qckn wl over 1f out: fdd fnl f* **14/1**

035 **8** *hd* **Monarch Maid**[28] 6947 2-9-7 **65** WilliamCarson 1 56
(Peter Hiatt) *nt that wl away but sn led: rdn 2f out: hdd over 1f out: wknd ins fnl f* **5/1**[2]

055 **9** *1* **Trigger Park (IRE)**[43] 6485 2-9-4 **62** ShaneKelly 5 50
(Ronald Harris) *t.k.h: hld up in last pair: prog on inner 2f out: wknd fnl f* **16/1**

5643 **10** *9* **Clapperboard**[18] 7199 2-9-5 **63**.....................(p) AdamKirby 10 24
(Paul Fitzsimons) *racd wd towards rr: rdn and no prog wl over 2f out: sn wknd* **8/1**

1m 13.82s (0.72) **Going Correction** +0.025s/f (Slow) **10** Ran SP% **117.6**
Speed ratings (Par 93): **96,95,94,94,92 91,90,90,89,77**
toteswingers 1&2 £7.40, 1&3 £11.70, 2&3 £1.02 CSF £54.61 CT £766.20 TOTE £4.00: £1.40, £3.60, £6.40; EX 37.10 Trifecta £1352.80 Pool: £5701.90 - 3.16 winning units..
Owner David & Gwyn Joseph **Bred** Willoxton Farm Stud **Trained** Earlswood, Monmouths

FOCUS
An ordinary sprint nursery and the winner came up the centre of the track.

7624 BETDAQ - THE SPORTS BETTING EXCHANGE MAIDEN STKS (DIV I) 7f (P)

5:40 (5:45) (Class 5) 3-Y-0+ **£2,587** (£770; £384; £192) **Stalls** Low

Form RPR

1 **Triple Chocolate** 3-9-5 0..................... JimmyQuinn 7 74+
(Roger Ingram) *difficult to load into stalls: slowly away: racd in last pair tl prog 2f out: rdn over 1f out: sustained run to ld last 75yds: won gng away* **50/1**

3 **2** *1 ¼* **Desert Skies (IRE)**[28] 6950 3-9-0 0..................... SilvestreDeSousa 6 66
(Saeed bin Suroor) *reluctant to enter stalls: pressed ldr: upsides fr 1/2-way: cajoled into ld over 1f out: hdd and outpcd last 75yds* **4/5**[1]

3 **3** *1 ¼* **Enfijaar (IRE)**[90] 4911 3-9-0 0..................... PaulHanagan 4 62
(William Haggas) *led: shkn up 2f out: hdd over 1f out: one pce fnl f* **11/4**[2]

4/-5 **4** *¾* **Tarquin (IRE)**[28] 6940 4-9-2 0..................... JacobButterfield[(5)] 9 66
(Kristin Stubbs) *reluctant to enter stalls: t.k.h: trckd ldng trio: shkn up to take 3rd briefly 1f out: one pce after* **8/1**[3]

0 **5** *½* **Clear Loch**[125] 3739 3-9-5 60..................... NickyMackay 5 64
(John Spearing) *chsd ldng pair: shkn up 2f out: lost 3rd 1f out: one pce after* **25/1**

00 **6** *10* **Stanlow**[28] 6950 3-9-5 0..................... ShaneKelly 3 37
(John Stimpson) *hld up: nudged along and wknd fr 2f out* **66/1**

60 **7** *2* **Pastoral Dancer**[35] 6748 4-9-7 0..................... LukeMorris 8 33
(Richard Rowe) *t.k.h: hld up: shkn up over 2f out: sn wknd* **66/1**

8 *½* **She Wont Tell** 4-9-2 0..................... SamHitchcott 2 26
(John Bridger) *last after 2f: shkn up over 2f out: sn wknd* **66/1**

1m 26.75s (0.75) **Going Correction** +0.025s/f (Slow)
WFA 3 from 4yo 2lb **8** Ran SP% **103.6**
Speed ratings (Par 103): **96,94,93,92,91 80,78,77**
toteswingers 1&2 £7.40, 1&3 £11.70, 2&3 £1.02 CSF £69.29 TOTE £10.90: £2.90, £1.10, £1.10; EX 34.10 Trifecta £93.00 Pool: £9071.93 - 73.09 winning units..
Owner Fahed Al Dabbous **Bred** Lael Stables **Trained** Epsom, Surrey

FOCUS
Division 1 of the 7f maiden was a race of changing fortunes, with the unbacked winner coming from last to first. The form looked nothing out of the ordinary and the contest was less competitive after the withdrawal of Discussiontofollow who refused to enter the stalls, got loose near the entrance to the parade ring and almost caused carnage as the field went past the winning post. The time was quicker than division I and the form is rated around the fifth.

7625 BETDAQ - THE SPORTS BETTING EXCHANGE MAIDEN STKS (DIV II) 7f (P)

6:10 (6:13) (Class 5) 3-Y-0+ **£2,587** (£770; £384; £192) **Stalls** Low

Form RPR

1 **Leonard Thomas** 3-9-5 0..................... TedDurcan 8 72+
(David Lanigan) *dwlt: mostly in last tl gd prog on inner fr 2f out: rdn to ld 100yds out: styd on wl* **5/2**[2]

26 **2** *1* **Pucker Up**[23] 7073 3-9-0 0..................... SeanLevey 9 64+
(David Brown) *towards rr: clsd on ldrs 2f out: hanging over 1f out: rdn and styd on to take 2nd nr fin* **10/1**

23 **3** *½* **Dark Amber**[31] 6870 3-9-0 0..................... SebSanders 3 63
(Brendan Powell) *led 1f: styd cl up: shkn up to ld 2f out: hdd and nt qckn last 100yds* **11/8**[1]

0 **4** *1 ¼* **Port Lairge**[22] 7108 3-9-5 0..................... PatCosgrave 4 65
(Jonjo O'Neill) *prom: rdn to chal wl over 1f out: one pce fnl f* **33/1**

06 **5** *2 ½* **White Peak (USA)**[31] 6870 3-9-5 0..................... AdamKirby 6 58
(Mark Johnston) *led after 1f: rdn and hdd 2f out: wknd fnl f* **5/1**[3]

6 *1 ¼* **Vermuyden** 4-9-7 0..................... LiamKeniry 1 56
(Pam Sly) *dwlt: t.k.h and in tch: nt qckn 2f out: rdn over 1f out: steadily fdd* **20/1**

6 **7** *3 ¾* **Allegra Clairmont**[20] 7154 4-9-2 0..................... LukeMorris 2 40
(John Best) *in tch to over 2f out: steadily wknd* **50/1**

8 *6* **Little Pudding**[15] 5-9-2 0.....................(t) GeorgeBaker 5 24
(Mary Hambro) *wl in tch tl wknd qckly jst over 2f out* **25/1**

1m 27.91s (1.91) **Going Correction** +0.025s/f (Slow)
WFA 3 from 4yo+ 2lb **8** Ran SP% **109.9**
Speed ratings (Par 103): **90,88,88,86,84 82,78,71**
toteswingers 1&2 £5.10, 1&3 £1.10, 2&3 £3.10 CSF £23.58 TOTE £3.60: £1.50, £2.30, £1.10; EX 27.40 Trifecta £67.70 Pool: £9180.78 - 101.58 winning units..
Owner Wedgewood Estates **Bred** Wedgewood Estates **Trained** Upper Lambourn, Berks

FOCUS
The second division of the 7f maiden was run almost a second slower than the first division, although they went off a shade too quickly in front. The winner and runner-up were the last two two and half furlongs out and are probably better than the bare form.

7626 £500 FREE BETS AT BETDAQ NURSERY H'CAP 7f (P)

6:40 (6:41) (Class 3) (0-95,85) 2-Y-0 **£6,469** (£1,925; £962; £481) **Stalls** Low

Form RPR

421 **1** **Monsea (IRE)**[32] 6829 2-9-7 **85**..................... GeorgeBaker 7 92
(Richard Hannon) *prom: trckd ldr 3f out: shkn up and clsd to ld over 1f out: decisive move and rdn out fnl f* **11/2**[2]

6151 **2** *1* **Never To Be (USA)**[7] 7463 2-9-0 **78** 6ex.....................(t) PaulHanagan 5 82
(John Gosden) *t.k.h: hld up in last trio: prog fr 2f out: rdn and r.o fnl f to take 2nd last 75yds: too much to do* **6/5**[1]

2203 **3** *1 ¼* **Handwoven (IRE)**[14] 7300 2-8-8 **72**..................... SilvestreDeSousa 9 73
(Mark Johnston) *led after 2f: drvn and hdd over 1f out: wl hld after: fdd nr fin* **20/1**

641 **4** *shd* **Miss Buckshot (IRE)**[27] 6973 2-9-2 **80**..................... ChrisCatlin 3 81
(Rae Guest) *hld up in last trio: rdn 2f out: styd on fr jst over 1f out: nrly snatched 3rd* **25/1**

01 **5** *¾* **New Row**[13] 7327 2-8-8 **72**..................... RobertHavlin 8 71
(William Jarvis) *t.k.h: hld up in tch: rdn 2f out: nt qckn over 1f out: kpt on same pce after* **20/1**

232 **6** *¾* **Sunset Shore**[12] 7349 2-9-3 **81**..................... LukeMorris 2 78
(Sir Mark Prescott Bt) *led 2f: chsd ldr to 3f out: drvn to chal wl over 1f out: fdd fnl f* **14/1**

413 **7** *hd* **Dutch Interior**[13] 7329 2-9-3 **81**..................... JimmyFortune 6 77
(Gary Moore) *dwlt: hld up in last: rdn over 1f out: kpt on but nvr gng pce to threaten* **6/1**[3]

045 **8** *2* **Dream And Search (GER)**[54] 6174 2-8-11 **75**..................... HarryBentley 4 66
(Charles Hills) *chsd ldrs: nt qckn 2f out: wknd jst over 1f out* **8/1**

1000 **9** *shd* **Fair Ranger**[21] 7129 2-9-5 **83**..................... SeanLevey 1 74
(Richard Hannon) *trckd ldrs: rdn and wknd 2f out* **33/1**

1m 25.94s (-0.06) **Going Correction** +0.025s/f (Slow) **9** Ran SP% **113.5**
Speed ratings (Par 99): **101,99,98,98,97 96,96,94,93**
toteswingers 1&2 £2.60, 1&3 £8.70, 2&3 £9.90 CSF £11.96 CT £121.73 TOTE £5.10: £1.50, £1.10, £5.20; EX 14.80 Trifecta £228.00 Pool: £9726.17 - 31.98 winning units..
Owner Saeed Manana **Bred** Timmy & Michael Hillman **Trained** East Everleigh, Wilts

FOCUS
The pace was ordinary for this decent nursery and although the runner-up found his path blocked when the leaders were making decisive moves, it could not be deemed an unsatisfactory race.

7627 BETDAQ 1ST UK RACE COMMISSION FREE H'CAP (LONDON MIDDLE DISTANCE SERIES QUALIFIER) 1m 3f (P)

7:10 (7:10) (Class 4) (0-85,82) 3-Y-0 **£4,690** (£1,395; £697; £348) **Stalls** Low

Form RPR

2120 **1** **Jazz Master**[28] 6936 3-9-7 **82**.....................(b) AndreaAtzeni 5 92
(Luca Cumani) *trckd ldng trio: shkn up and prog to ld jst over 2f out: edgd lft fr over 1f out: styd on wl* **7/2**[2]

216 **2** *1 ¼* **Noble Protector**[47] 6359 3-9-4 **79**..................... TomQueally 6 87
(Stuart Kittow) *hld up in last: off the bridle over 4f out: urged along and prog jst over 2f out: chsd wnr over 1f out: styd on but no real imp* **11/4**[1]

1013 **3** *1 ½* **Quest For More (IRE)**[46] 6380 3-9-5 **80**..................... GeorgeBaker 2 85
(Roger Charlton) *hld up in 5th: waiting for room over 2f out: nt qckn wl over 1f out: prog to take 3rd ins fnl f: hung lft but styd on* **4/1**[3]

1303 **4** *2* **Corton Lad**[16] 7239 3-9-2 **77**.....................(tp) TomEaves 1 78
(Keith Dalgleish) *led 1f: trckd ldng pair after: rdn over 3f out: rallied to chal jst over 2f out: sn outpcd* **9/1**

210 **5** *3 ¾* **My History (IRE)**[22] 7105 3-9-2 **77**..................... AdamKirby 4 72
(Mark Johnston) *trckd ldr after 1f: rdn to chal and upsides over 2f out: wknd over 1f out* **8/1**

-441 **6** *9* **Singersongwriter**[45] 6433 3-9-2 **77**..................... MartinLane 3 56
(Ed Dunlop) *prog to ld after 1f: rdn over 2f out: sn hdd & wknd qckly* **4/1**[3]

2m 19.48s (-2.42) **Going Correction** +0.025s/f (Slow) **6** Ran SP% **110.0**
Speed ratings (Par 103): **109,108,107,105,102 96**
toteswingers 1&2 £2.50, 1&3 £2.40, 2&3 £2.90 CSF £12.93 TOTE £3.30: £1.50, £3.00; EX 10.60 Trifecta £31.00 Pool: £10535.87 - 254.74 winning units..
Owner Castle Down Racing **Bred** Meon Valley Stud **Trained** Newmarket, Suffolk

FOCUS
A paucity of runners for this fair handicap, run at a reasonable pace. They finished quite strung out. The winner resumed his progress and the next two may have more to offer aswell.

7628 BOOK THE RESTAURANT FOR BOXING DAY H'CAP 1m 4f (P)

7:40 (7:43) (Class 6) (0-60,60) 3-Y-0+ **£1,940** (£577; £288; £144) **Stalls** Centre

Form RPR

3360 **1** **Asia Minor (IRE)**[134] 3437 4-9-9 **59**.....................(t) MartinLane 8 74
(Dr Jon Scargill) *hld up towards rr: rdn over 2f out: gd prog on outer to ld jst over 1f out: swept clr* **10/1**

3263 **2** *6* **Men Don't Cry (IRE)**[11] 7379 4-9-7 **60**.....................(b) MarkCoumbe[(3)] 14 65
(Ed de Giles) *t.k.h: prom: plld way into ld 1/2-way and sn 4 l clr: kicked for home 3f out: hdd jst over 1f out: no ch w wnr but clung on for 2nd* **15/2**[2]

000- **3** *½* **Yes Chef**[359] 4504 6-9-10 **60**..................... PatCosgrave 3 64
(Chris Gordon) *trckd ldrs in 5th: drvn over 2f out: kpt on fr over 1f out to take 3rd nr fin* **20/1**

6243 **4** *¾* **Princess Willow**[55] 6137 5-9-2 **55**..................... JemmaMarshall[(3)] 9 58
(John E Long) *t.k.h: led to 1/2-way: chsd ldr to over 1f out: fdd ins fnl f* **15/2**[2]

3462 **5** *½* **My Manekineko**[41] 6558 4-9-10 **60**..................... JimmyFortune 4 62
(J R Jenkins) *hld up in rr: shkn up over 2f out: kpt on fr wl over 1f out but nvr gng pce to threaten* **3/1**[1]

5450 **6** *¾* **Proud Times (USA)**[20] 7159 7-9-10 **60**.....................(b) AdamKirby 5 61
(Ali Brewer) *s.s: hld up in last trio: rdn and no prog over 2f out: styd on fr jst over 1f out: nrst fin* **14/1**

3300 **7** *hd* **Thane Of Cawdor (IRE)**[141] 3168 4-9-6 **56**..................... SteveDrowne 2 57
(Joseph Tuite) *hld up in midfield on inner: rdn over 2f out: one pce and no imp on ldrs* **8/1**[3]

4461 **8** *1 ½* **Corn Maiden**[22] 7090 4-9-0 **57**..................... LewisWalsh[(7)] 7 55
(Lydia Pearce) *chsd ldrs: rdn and no imp 2f out: fdd fnl f* **14/1**

4-36 **9** *hd* **Ice Nelly (IRE)**[93] 4832 5-9-8 **58**.....................(t) TomQueally 12 56
(Stuart Kittow) *s.v.s: in tch in last pair: rdn and no prog over 2f out: modest late hdwy* **16/1**

6044 **10** *1 ¼* **Royal Etiquette (IRE)**[8] 7439 6-9-8 **58**.....................(vt) LukeMorris 10 54
(Lawney Hill) *wl in tch: rdn over 2f out: no imp over 1f out: wknd fnl f* **10/1**

0005 **11** *hd* **Quadriga (IRE)**[8] 7434 3-9-2 **59**..................... JimmyQuinn 1 55
(Robert Eddery) *prom tl wknd 2f out* **14/1**

46-0 **12** *nk* **Royal Trooper (IRE)**[9] 7220 7-9-10 **60**.....................(vt) FergusSweeney 13 55
(Jim Best) *rel to r: ct up at bk after 3f: no prog over 2f out: wl btn after* **50/1**

3604 **13** *14* **It's A Girl Thing (IRE)**[14] 7305 4-9-10 **60**..................... GeorgeBaker 11 33
(Gary Moore) *hld up towards rr on outer: pushed along and no prog over 2f out: sn wknd: t.o* **12/1**

0440 **14** *8* **Hermosa Vaquera (IRE)**[22] 7091 3-9-2 **59**.....................(p) TedDurcan 6 19
(Anna Newton-Smith) *prom tl wknd rapidly over 2f out: t.o* **33/1**

2m 36.64s (2.14) **Going Correction** +0.025s/f (Slow)
WFA 3 from 4yo+ 7lb **14** Ran SP% **121.1**
Speed ratings (Par 101): **93,89,88,88,87 87,87,86,86,85 85,84,75,70**
toteswingers 1&2 £20.20, 1&3 £33.30, 2&3 £26.50 CSF £82.12 CT £1492.49 TOTE £12.50: £4.20, £3.00, £7.00; EX 119.50 Trifecta £1560.90 Part won. Pool: £2081.32 - 0.03 winning units..
Owner Strawberry Fields Stud **Bred** Darley **Trained** Newmarket, Suffolk

FOCUS
Plenty of runners for this poor handicap which was run at an unsatisfactory pace. Few got into it and it would not pay to put too much truck on the form. A big step up from the winner, with the runer-up the most obvious guide.

7629 WINNERS ARE WELCOME AT BETDAQ H'CAP 1m (P)

8:10 (8:11) (Class 5) (0-70,76) 3-Y-0+ **£2,587** (£770; £384; £192) **Stalls** Low

Form RPR

0041 **1** **Diplomatic (IRE)**[8] 7437 8-9-4 **67** 6ex.....................(p) AdamKirby 14 77+
(Michael Squance) *stdd s and dropped out in last fr wdst draw: prog fr 2f out: clsng whn nt clr run 1f out: fnd way through ins fnl f: r.o determinedly to ld last strides* **6/1**

0140 **2** *hd* **Lady Sylvia**[30] 6898 4-9-5 **68** .... SilvestreDeSousa 4 76
(Joseph Tuite) *w.w in midfield: drvn on outer over 2f out: prog over 1f out: str run to ld ins fnl f: hdd last strides* **10/1**

2444 **3** *1 ½* **Syncopate**[7] 7462 4-9-7 **70** .... LiamKeniry 8 75
(Pam Sly) *trckd ldng pair: rdn over 2f out: prog to ld over 1f out: hdd and outpcd ins fnl f* **11/2**[3]

5303 **4** *1 ¼* **Prime Exhibit**[9] 7429 8-9-7 **70** ....(t) PaulHanagan 7 72
(John Stimpson) *dwlt: hld up in last pair: pushed along on outer over 2f out: drvn and prog over 1f out: styd on fnl f: no ch to chal* **16/1**

625 **5** *hd* **Aomen Rock**[28] 6950 3-9-2 **68** .... FrederikTylicki 1 73+
(James Fanshawe) *w.w in midfield: clsd on ldrs 2f out: nt clr run over 1f out and checked: effrt and nt clr run ins fnl f: styd on nr fin* **9/4**[1]

2655 **6** *nk* **Enriching (USA)**[8] 7447 5-9-6 **69** .... ShaneKelly 5 70
(Gary Harrison) *prom on inner: rdn to chal fr 2f out: stl cl up 1f out: fdd last 100yds* **16/1**

0040 **7** *shd* **Mr Red Clubs (IRE)**[17] 7224 4-9-7 **70** .... AndrewMullen 13 70
(Michael Appleby) *trckd ldrs on outer: rdn over 2f out: tried to chal over 1f out: fdd ins fnl f* **9/2**[2]

6650 **8** *1* **Byroness**[29] 6925 3-9-4 **70** .... AndreaAtzeni 11 67
(Heather Main) *trckd ldr: rdn to ld briefly wl over 1f out: wknd ins fnl f* **25/1**

0636 **9** *1* **Poor Duke (IRE)**[36] 6735 3-9-4 **70** ....(b[1]) JamesDoyle 6 65
(Jamie Osborne) *mde most to wl over 1f out: wknd last 150yds* **9/1**

00-0 **10** *¾* **Galatian**[17] 7224 6-9-7 **70** .... MartinDwyer 3 64
(Rod Millman) *hld up in rr: rdn over 2f out: prog over 1f out: nt clr run sn after: fdd fnl f* **33/1**

0064 **11** *hd* **Midnight Feast**[14] 7306 5-9-6 **69** ....(v) LukeMorris 2 63
(Lee Carter) *slowly away: wl in rr: tried to make prog on inner fr 2f out: no hdwy 1f out: wknd* **14/1**

2200 **12** *nk* **Ssafa**[14] 7307 5-9-7 **70** ....(p) SteveDrowne 10 63
(Alastair Lidderdale) *a in rr: rdn and no prog over 2f out* **33/1**

000 **13** *3 ¼* **Dellbuoy**[47] 6360 4-9-4 **67** ....(p) FergusSweeney 9 52
(Pat Phelan) *chsd ldrs: rdn over 2f out: sn lost pl and struggling* **20/1**

1m 39.24s (-0.56) **Going Correction** +0.025s/f (Slow)
WFA 3 from 4yo+ 3lb **13** Ran SP% **130.6**
Speed ratings (Par 103): **103,102,101,100,99 99,99,98,97,96 96,96,92**
toteswingers 1&2 £14.70, 1&3 £6.80, 2&3 £9.30 CSF £68.40 CT £373.27 TOTE £7.90: £1.50, £3.90, £2.30; EX 91.50 Trifecta £600.80 Pool: £2060.62 - 2.57 winning units..
Owner Miss K Squance **Bred** Darley **Trained** Newmarket, Suffolk

FOCUS
A typical Kempton finish with a few looking likely to win at one stage or another in the home straight. The pace was modest and there were a few hard-luck stories. They finished in a heap and the winner is rated a bit better than the bare form.
T/Plt: £12.00 to a £1 stake. Pool: £81600.72 - 4952.52 winning tickets T/Qpdt: £2.40 to a £1 stake. Pool: £10114.36 - 3038.16 winning tickets JN

7308 NOTTINGHAM (L-H)
Wednesday, October 30

OFFICIAL GOING: Soft (6.5)
Wind: Moderate against Weather: Bright & dry

7630 32REDBINGO.COM (S) STKS — 1m 75y
1:00 (1:01) (Class 6) 2-Y-O — **£1,940** (£577; £288; £144) **Stalls** Centre

Form RPR

5022 **1** **Rural Affair**[20] 7156 2-8-6 55 .... LukeMorris 8 55
(Harry Dunlop) *trckd ldng pair: hdwy 3f out: chal 2f out and sn rdn: drvn ent fnl f: styd on gamely to ld last 50yds* **4/1**[2]

0255 **2** *nk* **Nice Arty (IRE)**[26] 6999 2-8-11 66 .... JamesDoyle 4 60
(Jamie Osborne) *led: rdn along 2f out: drvn ent fnl f: edgd rt: hdd and no ex last 50yds* **7/4**[1]

0044 **3** *¾* **Slinky McVelvet**[23] 7061 2-8-6 47 .... AndrewMullen 5 53
(Garry Moss) *chsd ldng pair on inner: rdn along wl over 2f out: sltly outpcd over 1f out: drvn and styd on fnl f* **6/1**[3]

0000 **4** *4 ½* **Miss Lawlass (IRE)**[12] 7340 2-8-6 35 .... JoeFanning 6 43
(James Given) *cl up: rdn along over 3f out: grad wknd fnl 2f* **50/1**

65 **5** *1 ¼* **Ivory**[12] 7340 2-8-6 0 .... PaoloSirigu 9 40
(Garry Moss) *in tch: rdn along and sme hdwy wl over 2f out: sn no imp* **12/1**

3000 **6** *1 ½* **Ambria's Fury (IRE)**[27] 6983 2-8-11 57 .... KierenFallon 7 42
(Mick Channon) *hld up in tch: rdn along 3f out: sn one pce* **4/1**[2]

5000 **7** *9* **Kitty Brown (IRE)**[1] 7604 2-8-3 50 ....(b) DarrenEgan(3) 2 17
(David Evans) *chsd ldrs on outer: rdn along wl over 3f out: sn wknd* **25/1**

8 *49* **Zigzag Hill** 2-8-2 0 ow3 ....(t) RyanWhile(7) 1
(Bill Turner) *s.i.s: green and a bhd* **25/1**

1m 50.97s (1.97) **Going Correction** +0.025s/f (Good) **8** Ran SP% **108.0**
Speed ratings (Par 93): **91,90,89,85,84 82,73,24**
toteswingers 1&2 £1.70, 1&3 £3.50, 2&3 £2.90 CSF £10.03 TOTE £4.00: £1.10, £1.90, £1.30; EX 11.80 Trifecta £46.10 Pool: £1956.31 - 31.77 winning units..The winner was sold to Michael Appleby for 4,000gns.
Owner Love Lambourn **Bred** Stowell Hill Ltd **Trained** Lambourn, Berks

FOCUS
All races on Inner track. It was dry overnight and the going was given as Soft (GoingStick 6.5). Luke Morris, returning after the first, described it as very soft and very holding. The inner track, not raced on since April, was in use. None of these had won a race before.

7631 EBF STALLIONS/32RED.COM OATH MAIDEN STKS (C&G) — 1m 75y
1:30 (1:30) (Class 4) 2-Y-O — **£5,175** (£1,540; £769; £384) **Stalls** Centre

Form RPR

1 **Farquhar (IRE)** 2-9-0 0 .... ShaneKelly 4 80+
(Peter Chapple-Hyam) *trckd ldrs: hdwy on outer to trck ldng pair 2f out: rdn and qcknd to ld appr fnl f: sn clr* **4/1**[2]

50 **2** *3 ½* **Branston De Soto**[18] 7209 2-9-0 0 .... JoeFanning 6 70
(Mark Johnston) *led: pushed along over 2f out: rdn wl over 1f out: hdd appr fnl f: drvn and kpt on same pce fnl f* **8/1**

3 *¾* **Bishop Of Ruscombe** 2-9-0 0 .... DavidProbert 2 68+
(Andrew Balding) *trckd ldrs: hdwy over 2f out and sn chsng ldr: rdn and ev ch over 1f out: kpt on same pce fnl f* **5/4**[1]

4 *2 ½* **Spanish Artist** 2-9-0 0 .... JamesDoyle 1 63
(Harry Dunlop) *trckd ldng pair on inner: pushed along over 3f out: rdn and outpcd wl over 1f out: kpt on fnl f* **6/1**[3]

065 **5** *nse* **Palace Dragon (IRE)**[15] 7274 2-9-0 0 .... LukeMorris 5 63
(Sir Mark Prescott Bt) *trckd ldr: cl up 1/2-way: rdn along 3f out: drvn and wknd 2f out* **16/1**

6 *4 ½* **Kashmiri Sunset** 2-9-0 0 .... ChrisCatlin 3 53+
(Ed de Giles) *s.i.s: green and a bhd* **7/1**

1m 51.32s (2.32) **Going Correction** +0.025s/f (Good) **6** Ran SP% **108.2**
Speed ratings (Par 97): **89,85,84,82,82 77**
toteswingers 1&2 £2.10, 1&3 £1.30, 2&3 £1.90 CSF £31.39 TOTE £5.10: £2.20, £3.90; EX 21.20 Trifecta £58.90 Pool: £1025.66 - 13.05 winning units..
Owner P W Chapple-Hyam **Bred** D G Iceton **Trained** Newmarket, Suffolk

FOCUS
Every winner of this maiden since 2007 (two divisions in 2007 and 2010) has, with the exception of one who didn't race again, gone on to record an RPR of at least 98 in its career.

7632 32RED H'CAP — 1m 75y
2:00 (2:00) (Class 4) (0-85,83) 3-Y-O+ — **£5,498** (£1,636; £817; £408) **Stalls** Centre

Form RPR

3604 **1** **Invincible Hero (IRE)**[21] 7131 6-8-13 **78** .... JasonHart(3) 8 86
(Declan Carroll) *slt ld: hdd 3f out: rdn along and cl up tl drvn to ld again appr fnl f: styd on wl towards fin* **12/1**

6035 **2** *1 ¼* **Eurystheus (IRE)**[37] 6701 4-8-10 **72** .... AndrewMullen 3 77
(Michael Appleby) *s.i.s and bhd: hdwy 3f out: rdn to chse ldrs over 1f out: swtchd lft wl ins fnl f and kpt on strly towards fin* **12/1**

4106 **3** *shd* **Le Chat D'Or**[41] 6550 5-9-6 **82** ....(bt) JamesDoyle 10 87
(Michael Dods) *hld up towards rr: hdwy on wd outside 3f out: rdn over 1f out: drvn and styd on fnl f: nrst fin* **7/1**[2]

1211 **4** *shd* **Amulet**[5] 7505 3-8-13 **78** 6ex .... ShaneKelly 9 82
(Eve Johnson Houghton) *cl up: slt ld 3f out and sn rdn: drvn and hdd appr fnl f: wknd last 100yds* **5/4**[1]

3161 **5** *1 ¼* **First Post (IRE)**[17] 7224 6-9-2 **83** .... OisinMurphy(5) 6 85
(Derek Haydn Jones) *in tch: hdwy 3f out: rdn wl over 1f out: chsd ldng pair ent fnl f: wknd last 100yds* **7/1**[2]

0040 **6** *4 ½* **Mister Marcasite**[28] 6951 3-8-5 **70** .... JoeFanning 7 60
(Mel Brittain) *chsd ldng pair: rdn along over 2f out: drvn wl over 1f out: grad wknd* **33/1**

6350 **7** *2 ¼* **Dolphin Rock**[33] 6801 6-9-1 **77** .... DaleSwift 4 63
(Brian Ellison) *chsd ldrs on inner: rdn along 3f out: sn wknd* **20/1**

0236 **8** *1* **No Dominion (IRE)**[25] 7024 4-9-0 **76** .... FrederikTylicki 1 60
(James Given) *in tch: rdn along 3f out: sn wknd* **10/1**

1022 **9** *14* **Topamichi**[42] 6533 3-9-1 **80** .... KierenFallon 2 31
(Mark H Tompkins) *t.k.h: in tch: rdn along over 3f out: sn wknd* **8/1**[3]

5000 **10** *19* **Day Of The Eagle (IRE)**[36] 6727 7-8-10 **72** .... GrahamGibbons 5
(Michael Easterby) *hld up: a in rr: bhd fr wl over 2f out* **50/1**

1m 47.88s (-1.12) **Going Correction** +0.025s/f (Good)
WFA 3 from 4yo+ 3lb **10** Ran SP% **114.7**
Speed ratings (Par 105): **106,104,104,104,103 98,96,95,81,62**
toteswingers 1&2 £34.20, 1&3 £19.60, 2&3 £16.40 CSF £140.47 CT £1109.48 TOTE £16.40: £3.00, £3.60, £3.30; EX 178.00 Trifecta £1207.80 Part won. Pool: £1610.52 - 0.01 winning units..
Owner Mrs Sarah Bryan **Bred** Fortbarrington Stud **Trained** Sledmere, E Yorks

FOCUS
They went a decent pace here.

7633 £32 BONUS AT 32RED.COM H'CAP (DIV I) — 5f 13y
2:30 (2:31) (Class 5) (0-75,75) 3-Y-O+ — **£2,587** (£770; £384; £192) **Stalls** High

Form RPR

3123 **1** **Steel Rain**[77] 5389 5-8-13 **72** .... RyanTate(5) 12 81
(Nikki Evans) *chsd ldrs: hdwy wl over 1f out: rdn to ld ins fnl f: sn drvn and jst hld on* **8/1**[3]

2531 **2** *nse* **Ace Master**[14] 7315 5-8-5 **64** ....(b) IanBurns(5) 9 73
(Roy Bowring) *led: rdn along over 1f out: hdd ins fnl f: drvn and rallied wl towards fin: jst hld* **9/2**[2]

2233 **3** *1* **Millkwood**[14] 7314 3-9-7 **75** ....(p) PJMcDonald 10 81
(John Davies) *hld up: hdwy 2f out: rdn over 1f out: styd on fnl f: nrst fin* **3/1**[1]

2050 **4** *½* **Foxtrot Jubilee (IRE)**[32] 6854 3-9-7 **75** .... JamesDoyle 2 79
(Ralph Beckett) *in tch: hdwy on wd outside 2f out: rdn to chse ldrs over 1f out: drvn and ch ent fnl f: kpt on same pce* **25/1**

0023 **5** *¾* **Cardinal**[13] 7324 8-9-0 **68** .... SteveDrowne 13 69
(Robert Cowell) *dwlt and towards rr: hdwy wl over 1f out: sn rdn and kpt on fnl f: nrst fin* **10/1**

101 **6** *shd* **Rock On Candy**[85] 5094 4-9-5 **73** .... ChrisCatlin 3 73
(John Spearing) *chsd ldr: rdn along wl over 1f out: drvn ent fnl f and one pce* **8/1**[3]

0002 **7** *1* **Time Medicean**[42] 6527 7-9-4 **72** .... RobertWinston 11 69
(Tony Carroll) *chsd ldrs: rdn wl over 1f out: wknd ent fnl f* **8/1**[3]

0606 **8** *½* **Shawkantango**[9] 7432 6-8-12 **66** ....(v) DaleSwift 14 61
(Derek Shaw) *chsd ldrs: rdn wl over 1f out: grad wknd* **16/1**

2104 **9** *½* **Threave**[13] 7324 5-9-2 **73** ....(t) CharlesBishop(3) 7 66
(Violet M Jordan) *dwlt: a towards rr* **12/1**

0-00 **10** *nk* **Invincible Lad (IRE)**[35] 6745 9-9-2 **70** .... GrahamGibbons 1 62
(Ed McMahon) *hld up: hdwy 2f out: sn rdn and kpt on fnl f: n.d* **50/1**

0045 **11** *nse* **Lucky Dan (IRE)**[32] 6850 7-8-13 **67** .... RaulDaSilva 4 59
(Paul Green) *midfield: rdn along wl over 1f out: sn no imp* **25/1**

1141 **12** *½* **George Fenton**[26] 6995 4-9-2 **73** ....(e) RyanPowell(3) 15 63
(Conor Dore) *a towards rr* **10/1**

0622 **13** *13* **Saga Lout**[121] 3904 3-9-2 **70** .... JohnFahy 8 14
(Ray Peacock) *a towards rr* **25/1**

1m 2.64s (1.14) **Going Correction** +0.225s/f (Good) **13** Ran SP% **121.8**
Speed ratings (Par 103): **99,98,97,96,95 95,93,92,91,91 91,90,69**
toteswingers 1&2 £6.80, 1&3 £8.20, 2&3 £3.60 CSF £43.06 CT £136.59 TOTE £8.80: £2.30, £1.70, £1.90; EX 66.90 Trifecta £276.10 Pool: £1496.17 - 4.06 winning units..
Owner John Berry (Gwent) **Bred** L T Roberts **Trained** Pandy, Monmouths

7634 £32 BONUS AT 32RED.COM H'CAP (DIV II) — 5f 13y
3:05 (3:08) (Class 5) (0-75,75) 3-Y-O+ — **£2,587** (£770; £384; £192) **Stalls** High

Form RPR

6064 **1** **Foxy Music**[25] 7029 9-8-9 **66** .... JasonHart(3) 3 79
(Eric Alston) *qckly away: mde all: rdn clr wl over 1f out: kpt on strly* **10/1**

252 **2** *3* **Perfect Muse**[55] 6145 3-8-2 **61** oh3 .... RyanTate(5) 7 64
(Clive Cox) *towards rr: gd hdwy 1/2-way: rdn to chse wnr over 1f out: drvn and no imp ins fnl f* **20/1**

4221 **3** *hd* **Keep It Dark**[15] 7281 4-9-1 **69** .... BarryMcHugh 6 70
(Tony Coyle) *trckd ldrs: hdwy 2f out: rdn over 1f out: drvn and kpt on same pce fnl f* **3/1**[1]

3064 **4** *¾* **Fathsta (IRE)**[26] 6995 8-9-2 **73** .... NeilFarley(3) 8 72
(Declan Carroll) *towards rr: pushed along over 2f out: sn rdn and styd on wl fnl f: nrst fin* **25/1**

0334 **5** ½ **Amenable (IRE)**30 6908 6-9-6 **74**....(p) PJMcDonald 5 71
(Violet M Jordan) *chsd ldrs: rdn along 2f out: kpt on same pce fnl f* **20/1**
-431 **6** ½ **Kylladdie**15 7262 6-9-6 **74**....(b) JoeFanning 12 69
(Steve Gollings) *towards rr: hdwy wl over 1f out: sn rdn and kpt on fnl f: nrst fin* **10/1**
3065 **7** 1 **West Coast Dream**32 6854 6-9-4 **75**.... MarkCoumbe(3) 9 67
(Roy Brotherton) *fly-jmpd s and s.i.s: bhd tl styd on fnl 2f: nrst fin* **8/1**
0140 **8** nse **Storm Lightning**42 6527 4-9-5 **73**....(b) TomMcLaughlin 4 64
(Mark Brisbourne) *prom: chsd wnr after 2f: rdn wl over 1f out: wknd appr fnl f* **25/1**
0422 **9** nk **Indian Tinker**9 7432 4-8-13 **67**.... SteveDrowne 1 57
(Robert Cowell) *prom: rdn along 2f out: grad wknd appr fnl f* **12/1**
0060 **10** 2¼ **Lager Time (IRE)**13 7324 3-8-5 **66**.... EoinWalsh(7) 2 49
(David Evans) *in tch: hdwy to chse ldrs 1/2-way: rdn wl over 1f out: sn wknd* **33/1**
6351 **11** ½ **Beau Mistral (IRE)**35 6757 4-9-5 **73**.... RaulDaSilva 14 53
(Paul Green) *a towards rr* **6/1**2
6031 **12** 1½ **Barbs Princess**131 3533 3-9-3 **71**.... KierenFallon 11 47
(Charles Hills) *midfield: hdwy on outer to chse ldrs 1/2-way: sn rdn and wknd wl over 1f out* **7/1**3
3130 **13** 3 **Flirtinaskirt**111 4203 3-9-4 **72**.... GrahamGibbons 10 37
(Ed McMahon) *in tch: hdwy to chse ldrs 1/2-way: rdn wl over 1f out: sn wknd* **16/1**
5015 **14** 7 **Alpha Delta Whisky**35 6745 5-9-2 **70**....(v) JamesDoyle 15 9
(John Gallagher) *a towards rr* **16/1**

1m 2.08s (0.58) **Going Correction** +0.225s/f (Good) **14** Ran SP% **120.7**
Speed ratings (Par 103): **104,99,98,97,96 96,94,94,93,90 89,87,82,71**
toteswingers 1&2 £37.70, 1&3 £9.00, 2&3 £10.40 CSF £202.25 CT £754.00 TOTE £12.70: £5.20, £7.20, £1.40; EX 238.70 Trifecta £1681.50 Part won. Pool: £2242.05 - 0.56 winning units..
Owner G M & Mrs C Baillie **Bred** G M & C Baillie & Springs Equestrian **Trained** Longton, Lancs

FOCUS
The quicker of the two divisions by 0.56sec.

7635 32RED CASINO H'CAP 1m 6f 15y
3:40 (3:41) (Class 4) (0-85,89) 3-Y-O+ **£5,175** (£1,540; £769; £384) **Stalls** Low

Form RPR
3000 **1** **Twelve Strings (IRE)**5 7496 4-9-7 **81**.... RobertTart(3) 8 90
(Brian Ellison) *dwlt: hld up in rr: stdy hdwy 4f out: chsd ldrs 2f out: sn swtchd rt and rdn to ld jst ins fnl f: kpt on strly* **7/2**1
0321 **2** 2¼ **Sherman McCoy**11 7372 7-9-6 **77**.... DaleSwift 4 83
(Brian Ellison) *trckd ldrs: hdwy to ld 3f out: sn rdn: drvn over 1f out: hdd jst ins fnl f: kpt on* **5/1**2
5000 **3** 1¾ **Desert Recluse (IRE)**18 7210 6-9-8 **79**.... KierenFallon 9 83
(Brendan Powell) *trckd ldrs: hdwy 4f out: chal 3f out: ev ch whn rdn and hung lft wl over 1f out: sn drvn and one pce* **10/1**
U03- **4** 2¼ **Allied Answer**318 7294 5-9-7 **78**.... RobertWinston 3 79
(Steve Gollings) *hld up in rr: stdy hdwy on inner 4f out: cl up over 2f out: sn rdn to chal and ev ch tl drvn and one pce appr fnl f* **7/1**3
100/ **5** 5 **Mamlook (IRE)**801 1808 9-10-4 **89**.... ConorO'Farrell 5 83
(David Pipe) *trckd ldrs: effrt 4f out: rdn along wl over 2f out: sn drvn and no imp* **16/1**
5412 **6** 2 **Opera Buff**17 7217 4-9-9 **80**....(p) JamesDoyle 10 72
(Sean Curran) *cl up: rdn along 3f out: drvn 2f out and sn wknd* **7/2**1
5000 **7** shd **Blue Wave (IRE)**109 4301 3-9-2 **82**....(b) JoeFanning 6 74
(Mark Johnston) *prom: pushed along over 4f out: rdn over 3f out: sn wknd* **10/1**
3660 **8** 2½ **Hot Spice**21 7132 5-8-9 **66**.... GrahamGibbons 1 54
(Michael Easterby) *led: rdn along over 4f out: hdd 3f out and sn wknd* **20/1**
061 **9** 8 **Jimmy Sewell (IRE)**147 2995 4-8-13 **70**.... AndrewMullen 2 48
(Michael Appleby) *hld up: pushed along 4f out: rdn over 3f out: sn wknd* **8/1**

3m 11.41s (4.41) **Going Correction** +0.025s/f (Good)
WFA 3 from 4yo+ 9lb **9** Ran SP% **113.5**
Speed ratings (Par 105): **88,86,85,84,81 80,80,78,74**
toteswingers 1&2 £4.30, 1&3 £6.60, 2&3 £10.50 CSF £20.44 CT £156.98 TOTE £3.80: £1.10, £1.70, £3.00; EX 25.00 Trifecta £100.70 Pool: £4100.23 - 12.76 winning units..
Owner M Khan X2 **Bred** John & Anne-Marie O'Connor **Trained** Norton, N Yorks

FOCUS
There was a decent gallop on here.

7636 AJA 32REDPOKER.COM FEGENTRI GENTLEMEN AMATEUR RIDERS' H'CAP 1m 2f 50y
4:10 (4:10) (Class 6) (0-60,60) 3-Y-O+ **£1,871** (£580; £290; £145) **Stalls** Low

Form RPR
-065 **1** **Red Four**16 7258 3-11-0 **58**....(p) MrSWalker 5 67
(George Baker) *trckd ldrs: hdwy 3f out: led wl over 1f out: rdn clr fnl f* **5/2**1
6422 **2** 2¼ **Zinnobar**22 7104 3-10-6 **50**.... MrJHamilton 6 55
(Jonathan Portman) *trckd ldng pair on inner: hdwy 3f out: rdn 2f out: swtchd rt and drvn to chse wnr ent fnl f: sn no imp* **8/1**
4000 **3** nk **Star Date (IRE)**9 7430 4-11-6 **59**....(p) MrFabrizioPerego 3 63
(Michael Attwater) *s.i.s and in rr: hdwy on wd outside over 3f out: rdn wl over 1f out: kpt on appr fnl f: nrst fin* **16/1**
-005 **4** 2½ **Lordship (IRE)**4 5091 9-10-7 **46** oh1.... MrWHogg 1 46
(Tom Gretton) *t.k.h: in tch: hdwy 4f out: rdn to chse ldrs over 2f out: drvn and one pce fr over 1f out* **7/1**3
3303 **5** ¾ **Supa Seeker (USA)**44 6472 7-10-10 **49**.... MrFMitchell 9 48
(Tony Carroll) *hld up towards rr: hdwy 4f out: rdn to chse ldrs over 2f out: drvn and no imp appr fnl f* **10/1**
0024 **6** 1¾ **Noosa Sound**40 6598 3-10-8 **52**....(t) MrAlexandreLemarie 4 47
(John Davies) *led: rdn along over 3f out: drvn over 2f out: hdd wl over 1f out: grad wknd* **8/1**
5000 **7** 6 **Flying Applause**11 7378 8-11-5 **58**....(b) MrKevinTobin 12 43
(Roy Bowring) *t.k.h: hld up: a towards rr* **8/1**
0 **8** 4½ **Illegale (IRE)**30 6895 7-11-1 **54**....(t) MrMPrice 2 31
(Nikki Evans) *cl up: rdn along wl over 3f out: sn wknd* **33/1**
6/- **9** 2¾ **Forgiving Light**371 7336 4-10-11 **50**.... MrWEasterby 10 22
(John Berry) *a towards rr* **12/1**
3200 **10** 3½ **Rosie's Lady (IRE)**74 5514 4-11-7 **60**.... MrDavidTurner 11 25
(Paul Green) *cl up: rdn along over 3f out: sn wknd* **25/1**
6210 **11** 19 **Ivy Port**203 1486 3-11-0 **58**.... MrHAABannister 14
(Michael Appleby) *a in rr: bhd fr 1/2-way* **6/1**2

2m 18.96s (4.66) **Going Correction** +0.025s/f (Good)
WFA 3 from 4yo+ 5lb **11** Ran SP% **118.1**
Speed ratings (Par 101): **82,80,79,77,77 75,71,67,65,62 47**
toteswingers 1&2 £5.00, 1&3 £10.60, 2&3 £27.10 CSF £22.79 CT £269.36 TOTE £3.90: £1.60, £2.90, £5.00; EX 29.50 Trifecta £411.50 Part won. Pool: £3227.01 - 34.80 winning units..
Owner Lady Cobham **Bred** Lady Cobham **Trained** Manton, Wilts
■ Stewards' Enquiry : Mr David Turner three-day ban: careless riding (Nov 20,26,Dec 2)

FOCUS
The early gallop wasn't strong and it paid to race handily.
T/Jkpt: Not won. T/Plt: £526.70 to a £1 stake. Pool: £59794.71 - 82.87 winning tickets T/Qpdt: £90.40 to a stake. Pool: £7015.17 - 57.40 winning tickets JR

7622 KEMPTON (A.W) (R-H)
Thursday, October 31

OFFICIAL GOING: Standard
Wind: Moderate across (away from stands) Weather: Overcast

7637 COME JUMP RACING AT KEMPTON 04.11.13 (S) STKS 1m 3f (P)
4:30 (4:30) (Class 6) 3-Y-O **£1,940** (£577; £288; £144) **Stalls** Low

Form RPR
2000 **1** **Syrenka**9 7434 3-8-9 **62**....(v1) MartinDwyer 9 62
(Marcus Tregoning) *dwlt: hld up in last pair: rdn over 2f out: prog wl over 1f out: styd on u.p fnl f: led post* **6/1**
5033 **2** nse **Estibdaad (IRE)**9 7434 3-9-0 **60**....(t) SteveDrowne 11 67
(Anthony Honeyball) *hld up in 6th: prog over 2f out: drvn to ld jst over 1f out: kpt on but hdd post* **7/4**1
50- **3** 1¼ **Wrecking Ball (IRE)**398 6645 3-9-0 **0**.... KierenFallon 10 65
(Amy Weaver) *dwlt: sn trckd ldrs: rdn to go 2nd wl over 2f out: led over 1f out: sn hdd and nt qckn* **8/1**
6003 **4** 6 **Lincolnrose (IRE)**23 7104 3-9-0 **53**....(p) FrederikTylicki 7 54
(Michael Appleby) *led at fair pce: drvn and hdd over 1f out: wknd fnl f* **12/1**
4551 **5** ¾ **Lady Lunchalot (USA)**28 6971 3-8-7 **58**....(p) DavidParkes(7) 1 53
(J S Moore) *chsd ldrs: rdn on inner over 2f out: nt qckn wl over 1f out: sn wknd* **4/1**2
2556 **6** 7 **Pencombe (FR)**9 7434 3-9-0 **65**.... MartinLane 3 40
(David Simcock) *trckd ldng pair: wnt 2nd briefly 3f out: rdn over 2f out: wknd qckly over 1f out* **5/1**3
0206 **7** 2½ **Pink Mischief**14 7331 3-9-0 **49**.... DavidProbert 4 36
(Harry Dunlop) *awkward s: a towards rr: wknd over 2f out* **12/1**
0060 **8** ¾ **Sings Poet**33 6853 3-9-0 **38**....(b1) WilliamCarson 2 34
(Peter Hiatt) *dwlt: a in last pair: struggling over 2f out* **50/1**
0060 **9** 16 **Sporting Club Girl**75 5528 3-8-9 **20**....(b1) JimmyQuinn 8
(Jim Best) *chsd ldr to 3f out: wknd rapidly: t.o* **50/1**

2m 20.83s (-1.07) **Going Correction** 0.0s/f (Stan) **9** Ran SP% **117.7**
Speed ratings (Par 99): **103,102,102,97,97 92,90,89,78**
toteswingers 1&2 £3.60, 2&3 £4.90, 1&3 £10.50 CSF £17.25 TOTE £11.50: £2.20, £1.40, £2.40; EX 25.50 Trifecta £157.50 Pool: £2523.06 - 12.00 winning units..There was no bid for the winner. Estibdaad was claimed by P. Butler for £6000. Lady Lunchalot was claimed by A Bain for £6000.
Owner Sarah Lady Allendale & Partners **Bred** Miss K Rausing **Trained** Whitsbury, Hants

FOCUS
Two of the three with the highest BHA ratings came to the fore in this seller. The runner-up is the bset guide to this very limited form.

7638 BETVICTOR NEW LIVE CASINO MAIDEN STKS 6f (P)
5:00 (5:00) (Class 5) 2-Y-O **£2,587** (£770; £384; £192) **Stalls** Low

Form RPR
06 **1** **Terhaab (USA)**38 6690 2-9-0 **0**.... PaulHanagan 9 75
(John Gosden) *trckd ldrs: pushed along and prog 2f out: led jst over 1f out: drvn and asserted fnl f* **8/1**3
23 **2** 1¼ **Jacob's Pillow**33 6842 2-9-5 **0**.... JoeFanning 3 76
(William Haggas) *trckd ldr 2f: styd prom: rdn to chal and upsides jst over 1f out: styd on one pce* **11/8**1
3 ½ **Speed Hawk (USA)** 2-9-5 **0**.... ShaneKelly 1 75+
(Robert Cowell) *s.s: hld up in last: stl there wl over 1f out: gd prog on wd outside after: shkn up and fin wl* **50/1**
0 **4** 1½ **He's My Boy (IRE)**42 6569 2-9-5 **0**.... FrederikTylicki 2 70
(James Fanshawe) *wl in tch: prog on inner 2f out: led briefly over 1f out: sn outpcd: fdd nr fin* **14/1**
04 **5** hd **Thundering Cloud (IRE)**16 7261 2-9-0 **0**.... JackMitchell 5 64
(Brendan Powell) *in tch: rdn over 2f out: styd on fr over 1f out: nrst fin* **20/1**
6 1 **For Ayman** 2-9-5 **0**.... SteveDrowne 11 66
(Seamus Durack) *s.s: racd in last pair: shkn up and sme prog on inner fr 2f out: one pce over 1f out* **50/1**
7 1 **Shaft Of Light** 2-9-5 **0**.... LukeMorris 6 63
(Sir Mark Prescott Bt) *dwlt: rn green towards rr: shkn up over 2f out: kpt on one pce: n.d* **25/1**
0 **8** 3 **Alumina (IRE)**17 7245 2-9-0 **0**.... JimmyFortune 12 49
(Andrew Balding) *t.k.h: hld up in rr: shkn up over 2f out: no prog and sn btn* **25/1**
0 **9** hd **Broadway Ranger (IRE)**29 6931 2-9-5 **0**.... RobertWinston 4 54
(Charles Hills) *mde most to over 1f out: sn wknd* **25/1**
4 **10** 1¾ **Monsieur Lavene (IRE)**14 7328 2-9-5 **0**.... KierenFox 10 49
(Robert Mills) *t.k.h: racd wd: prom tl wknd 2f out* **14/1**
11 12 **Rochester** 2-9-5 **0**.... SilvestreDeSousa 8 13
(Saeed bin Suroor) *free to post: t.k.h: trckd ldr after 2f tl wknd rapidly 2f out: t.o* **9/4**2

1m 13.29s (0.19) **Going Correction** 0.0s/f (Stan) **11** Ran SP% **117.5**
Speed ratings (Par 95): **98,96,95,93,93 92,90,86,86,84 68**
toteswingers 1&2 £2.20, 2&3 £23.80, 1&3 £44.30 CSF £18.04 TOTE £7.20: £2.30, £1.10, £7.70; EX 20.00 Trifecta £254.60 Pool: £4522.73 - 13.32 winning units..
Owner Hamdan Al Maktoum **Bred** Grousemont Farm **Trained** Newmarket, Suffolk

FOCUS
Ordinary maiden form.

7639 BETVICTOR LIVE CASINO £175 CASH BONUS H'CAP 1m (P)
5:30 (5:31) (Class 6) (0-55,61) 3-Y-O+ **£1,940** (£577; £288; £144) **Stalls** Low

Form RPR
1322 **1** **Sonnetation (IRE)**42 6553 3-9-2 **53**.... PatCosgrave 14 66
(Jim Boyle) *trckd ldrs: pushed along and prog to ld 2f out: drvn and styd on wl fnl f* **9/2**2

0502 **2** ¾ **Legal Legacy**[8] 7458 7-9-4 **52** LukeMorris 12 63
(Lee Carter) *hld up towards rr: gd prog fr 2f out to chse wnr jst over 1f out: styd on but no imp last 75yds* **5/1**[3]

4200 **3** 2¾ **Minstrel Lad**[15] 7299 5-9-6 **54** DavidProbert 6 59
(Lydia Pearce) *sn in last trio: pushed along and stl there 2f out: drvn and styd on fr over 1f out to take 3rd nr fin* **8/1**

5060 **4** 1 **Rock Anthem (IRE)**[29] 6933 9-9-3 **51** ShaneKelly 10 53
(Mike Murphy) *s.i.s: racd in last trio tl prog on inner over 2f out: dispputed 2nd briefly over 1f out: one pce after* **10/1**

0U60 **5** nk **Stoneacre Oskar**[21] 7149 4-8-13 **50** SladeO'Hara(3) 3 52
(Peter Grayson) *in tch in midfield: urged along and prog over 2f out: pressed for a pl over 1f out: one pce after* **33/1**

3361 **6** 1½ **Hail Promenader (IRE)**[6] 7511 7-9-13 **61** 6ex (tp) WilliamCarson 9 59
(Anthony Carson) *racd wd thrght: mostly in midfield: shkn up over 2f out: kpt on one pce fr over 1f out: nvr able to threaten* **4/1**[1]

034- **7** 1¾ **Cativo Cavallino**[344] 7815 10-9-1 **52** NataliaGemelova(3) 2 46
(John E Long) *t.k.h in midfield: rdn to chse ldrs 2f out: nt qckn over 1f out: fdd* **16/1**

3314 **8** 1½ **Minimee**[2] 7610 3-9-2 **60** 6ex (v) DonnaCaldwell(7) 8 50
(Phil McEntee) *sn in last pair: stl there wl over 1f out: reminders and passed wkng rivals fnl f* **9/1**

0014 **9** 1¼ **Kielty's Folly**[29] 6932 9-9-5 **53** TomEaves 4 41
(Brian Baugh) *t.k.h: prom: waiting for room jst over 2f out: tried to mount an effrt over 1f out: wknd fnl f* **8/1**

0000 **10** 1¼ **Percythepinto (IRE)**[8] 7458 4-9-6 **54** (tp) TedDurcan 11 39
(George Baker) *s.i.s: rapid prog to chse ldr after 3f to jst over 2f out: wknd over 1f out* **16/1**

300 **11** 1¾ **Lightning Spirit**[42] 6553 5-9-1 **49** (p) SeanLevey 13 30
(Gary Moore) *wl in tch: rdn over 3f out: lost pl and struggling 2f out: eased whn btn* **16/1**

440 **12** ¾ **Last Supper**[21] 7153 4-9-7 **55** (p) JimmyQuinn 5 34
(James Bethell) *t.k.h: wl in tch: lost pl over 2f out: rdn and wknd wl over 1f out* **33/1**

3300 **13** 12 **Actonetaketwo**[14] 7322 3-8-11 **53** PhilipPrince(5) 1
(Ron Hodges) *led to 2f out: wknd rapidly: t.o* **33/1**

1m 39.8s **Going Correction** 0.0s/f (Stan)
WFA 3 from 4yo+ 3lb **13** Ran SP% **122.6**
Speed ratings (Par 101): **100,99,96,95,95 93,91,90,89,87 86,85,73**
toteswingers 1&2 £5.50, 2&3 £9.40, 1&3 £7.40 CSF £27.65 CT £181.91 TOTE £4.50: £1.60, £2.10, £3.30; EX 31.10 Trifecta £253.50 Pool: £2819.50 - 8.33 winning units..
Owner The 'In Recovery' Partnership **Bred** Dr Dean Harron **Trained** Epsom, Surrey

FOCUS
This appeared to be run at a good gallop and the front pair drew a little way clear late on. The second and third are perhaps a little better than the bare form.

7640 PLAY ROULETTE @ VICTORS LIVE CASINO NURSERY H'CAP 1m (P)
6:00 (6:00) (Class 4) (0-85,78) 2-Y-O **£3,752** (£1,116; £557; £278) **Stalls** Low

Form RPR

4321 **1** **Killing Time (IRE)**[17] 7252 2-9-4 **75** (b) JimCrowley 7 79+
(Ralph Beckett) *hld up in 6th in slowly run event: wound up over 2f out and drvn to cl over 1f out: led jst ins fnl f: styd on wl* **5/2**[2]

0311 **2** 1½ **Spiritual Flame**[14] 7326 2-9-6 **77** SebSanders 8 78+
(William Haggas) *hld up in last in slowly run event: pushed along over 2f out: stl in last and drvn over 1f out: r.o to take 2nd post: no ch to chal* **9/4**[1]

5512 **3** nse **More Aspen (USA)**[19] 7202 2-9-6 **77** MartinHarley 5 78
(Marco Botti) *trckd ldr: rdn to chal 2f out: led over 1f out to jst ins fnl f: one pce* **4/1**[3]

31 **4** shd **Star Code (IRE)**[49] 6333 2-9-7 **78** SeanLevey 1 79
(Richard Hannon) *t.k.h in 5th: clsd on ldrs over 2f out: drvn to chal and upsides jst over 1f out: one pce* **8/1**

003 **5** 2 **Filament Of Gold (USA)**[22] 7120 2-8-12 **69** JoeFanning 6 65
(Mark Johnston) *trckd ldng trio: shkn up and nt qckn 2f out: one pce and no imp after* **7/1**

4204 **6** ½ **All Talk N No Do (IRE)**[8] 7460 2-9-7 **78** (t) GeorgeBaker 3 73
(Seamus Durack) *led at v stdy pce: tried to kick on over 2f out: hdd & wknd over 1f out* **16/1**

0053 **7** 3½ **Cape Arrow**[10] 7428 2-8-2 **59** JimmyQuinn 2 46
(Paul Cole) *trckd ldng pair to jst over 2f out: wknd over 1f out* **12/1**

1m 41.24s (1.44) **Going Correction** 0.0s/f (Stan) **7** Ran SP% **116.5**
Speed ratings (Par 97): **92,90,90,90,88 87,84**
toteswingers 1&2 £1.40, 2&3 £2.00, 1&3 £2.20 CSF £8.91 CT £21.07 TOTE £3.50: £1.90, £1.70; EX 10.30 Trifecta £31.90 Pool: £3314.09 - 77.73 winning units..
Owner Kennet Valley Thoroughbreds VIII **Bred** Kilfrush Stud **Trained** Kimpton, Hants

FOCUS
This turned into a dash for the line.

7641 PLAY BLACKJACK @ VICTORS LIVE CASINO H'CAP 1m (P)
6:30 (6:34) (Class 3) (0-95,95) 3-Y-O+
£7,158 (£2,143; £1,071; £535; £267; £134) **Stalls** Low

Form RPR

2-00 **1** **Captain Cat (IRE)**[68] 5749 4-8-12 **86** JamesDoyle 3 100
(Roger Charlton) *a gng wl: trckd ldr: prog to ld wl over 1f out: hd quite high but sn drvn clr: in command after* **7/1**

0011 **2** 1¼ **Chookie Royale**[8] 7464 5-9-1 **92** 6ex (p) JasonHart(3) 7 103
(Keith Dalgleish) *hld up in midfield: lost pl 3f out and sn rdn in rr: prog 2f out: chsd wnr jst over 1f out: r.o but nvr able to chal* **6/1**[3]

4050 **3** 3 **George Guru**[12] 7368 6-9-4 **92** KierenFallon 13 96
(Michael Attwater) *wl in rr early: prog on outer 1/2-way to chse ldrs: rdn over 2f out: disp 2nd 1f out: one pce after* **16/1**

0024 **4** ¾ **Sea Shanty (USA)**[13] 7337 3-9-1 **92** (p) SeanLevey 2 94
(Richard Hannon) *wl in tch in midfield: rdn over 2f out and nt qckn: struggling over 1f out: styd on after to take 4th nr fin* **12/1**

360- **5** ½ **Marshgate Lane (USA)**[369] 7396 4-9-3 **91** JoeFanning 12 92
(Mark Johnston) *hld up in rr fr wd draw: effrt on outer over 2f out: prog over 1f out: one pce fnl f* **14/1**

2206 **6** 1¼ **Come On Blue Chip (IRE)**[30] 6927 4-9-0 **88** (p) RobertWinston 14 86
(Paul D'Arcy) *hld up in last pair fr wdst draw: jst shuffled along on outer fr over 2f out: styd on steadily: nvr involved* **33/1**

0036 **7** hd **Monsieur Chevalier (IRE)**[20] 7172 6-9-6 **94** AdamKirby 8 92
(P J O'Gorman) *hld up in last pair: prog on inner jst over 2f out: tried to cl on ldrs over 1f out: one pce after* **10/1**

0512 **8** ¾ **Uppercut**[35] 6767 5-8-8 **85** RobertTart(3) 9 81
(Stuart Kittow) *racd wd: chsd ldrs: lost pl and drvn over 2f out: in rr over 1f out: plugged on nr fin* **11/2**[2]

1/5- **9** nse **Mighty Ambition (USA)**[560] 1470 4-9-4 **92** SilvestreDeSousa 11 88
(Charlie Appleby) *t.k.h: trckd ldr over 6f out: chal and upsides 2f out: wknd fnl f* **3/1**[1]

-064 **10** nk **True To Form (IRE)**[68] 5749 6-9-7 **95** (p) MartinDwyer 6 90
(Alan McCabe) *led after 1f to wl over 1f out: wknd* **14/1**

0030 **11** 1 **Maverik**[54] 6199 5-8-13 **87** JimCrowley 4 80
(William Knight) *led 1f: stdd: shkn up 2f out: no prog and n.m.r over 1f out: wknd* **20/1**

51 **12** 1 **Atlantis Crossing (IRE)**[227] 1061 4-9-2 **90** PatCosgrave 10 81
(Jim Boyle) *hld up in rr: effrt over 2f out: no prog over 1f out: wknd* **20/1**

3540 **13** ½ **Verse Of Love**[32] 6868 4-9-1 **89** MartinHarley 5 79
(David Evans) *sn trckd ldng pair: reminders and nt qckn over 2f out: wknd over 1f out: eased* **50/1**

4600 **14** 2¼ **Chapter And Verse (IRE)**[38] 6701 7-8-12 **86** ShaneKelly 1 71
(Mike Murphy) *towards rr: brief effrt 2f out: sn wknd* **25/1**

1m 37.28s (-2.52) **Going Correction** 0.0s/f (Stan)
WFA 3 from 4yo+ 3lb **14** Ran SP% **121.4**
Speed ratings (Par 107): **112,110,107,107,106 105,105,104,104,103 102,101,101,99**
toteswingers 1&2 £10.30, 2&3 £16.90, 1&3 £35.60 CSF £45.80 CT £682.01 TOTE £13.60: £4.60, £2.60, £6.80; EX 74.30 Trifecta £1266.50 Pool: £2850.18 - 1.68 winning units..
Owner Seasons Holidays **Bred** Azienda Agricola Mediterranea **Trained** Beckhampton, Wilts

FOCUS
Quite an interesting handicap, featuring several with the potential to be a good bit better than their current marks. The form is rated on the positive side around the first two.

7642 FOLLOW LIVE CASINO @ VICTORS CASINO H'CAP 6f (P)
7:00 (7:01) (Class 3) (0-95,94) 3-Y-O+
£7,158 (£2,143; £1,071; £535; £267; £134) **Stalls** Low

Form RPR

00 **1** **Forest Edge (IRE)**[5] 7527 4-9-5 **92** (b) AdamKirby 10 104
(David Evans) *gd spd to ld fr wd draw: drvn over 2f out: a abt 2 l clr after: styd on wl* **20/1**

0103 **2** 1¼ **If So**[33] 6831 4-9-1 **88** FrederikTylicki 1 96+
(James Fanshawe) *in tch in midfield: prog jst over 2f out: rdn to chse wnr over 1f out: styd on but nvr able to chal* **5/2**[1]

11 **3** 1 **Peace Seeker**[44] 6506 5-8-12 **85** WilliamCarson 9 90
(Anthony Carson) *chsd wnr to over 4f out: styd prom: rdn and kpt on same pce fnl 2f* **10/1**

4244 **4** ½ **Exceptionelle**[35] 6768 3-8-13 **87** AndreaAtzeni 5 90
(Roger Varian) *hld up towards rr: sme prog fr 2f out: kpt on fnl f: nt gng pce to threaten* **4/1**[2]

0000 **5** ½ **Stonefield Flyer**[30] 6920 4-9-3 **90** TomEaves 2 92
(Keith Dalgleish) *a in midfield: hrd rdn and nt qckn 2f out: no imp tl kpt on nr fin* **16/1**

0500 **6** nse **Pabusar**[20] 7171 5-9-3 **90** JamesDoyle 4 91
(Jamie Osborne) *settled in last pair: rdn and sme prog on inner fr 2f out: kpt on one pce fnl f: n.d* **16/1**

204 **7** 2 **Bern Me Baby (USA)**[51] 6282 3-9-6 **94** (t) MartinHarley 8 89
(Marco Botti) *chsd wnr over 4f out: rdn and no imp over 2f out: lost 2nd and wknd over 1f out: eased* **12/1**

0260 **8** ½ **Goldream**[24] 7085 4-9-0 **92** (p) OisinMurphy(5) 11 85
(Robert Cowell) *chsd ldrs: rdn and fnd nil jst over 2f out: sn struggling* **6/1**[3]

024 **9** shd **Love Island**[33] 6845 4-9-0 **92** GeorgeChaloner(5) 6 85
(Richard Whitaker) *towards rr: rdn and no prog over 2f out: no ch after* **8/1**

4046 **10** 1¾ **Diamond Charlie (IRE)**[54] 6189 5-9-1 **88** SebSanders 7 76
(Simon Dow) *dwlt: tk fierce hold in last pair early: rdn and no prog over 2f out: wl btn after* **10/1**

1m 11.6s (-1.50) **Going Correction** 0.0s/f (Stan)
WFA 3 from 4yo+ 1lb **10** Ran SP% **116.4**
Speed ratings (Par 107): **110,108,107,106,105 105,102,102,102,99**
toteswingers 1&2 £22.80, 2&3 £3.50, 1&3 £37.20 CSF £69.82 CT £564.07 TOTE £19.00: £4.60, £1.30, £2.60; EX 86.40 Trifecta £459.90 Pool: £2267.03 - 3.69 winning units..
Owner P & K Swinnerton **Bred** Alberto Panetta **Trained** Pandy, Monmouths

FOCUS
A decent sprint handicap and aggressive tactics worked a treat on the winner, who looks better than ever. The form is taken at face value.

7643 BOOK CHRISTMAS FESTIVAL TICKETS NOW H'CAP (DIV I) 7f (P)
7:30 (7:30) (Class 6) (0-55,55) 3-Y-O+ **£1,940** (£577; £288; £144) **Stalls** Low

Form RPR

3050 **1** **One Last Dream**[19] 7197 4-9-4 **52** (b) DavidProbert 3 61
(Ron Hodges) *mde vritually all: drvn and jnd fnl f: kpt on wl nr fin* **16/1**

5426 **2** nk **Hinton Admiral**[6] 7511 9-9-5 **53** JoeFanning 2 61
(Pat Eddery) *wl in tch: prog 3f out: chsd wnr 2f out: drvn to chal and upsides fnl f: nt qckn nr fin* **9/1**

3150 **3** 1¾ **Gypsy Rider**[23] 7092 4-9-0 **55** NedCurtis(7) 5 58
(Roger Curtis) *hld up towards rr: urged along and prog fr over 2f out: chsd ldng pair fnl f: no imp after* **16/1**

5666 **4** ½ **Elle Rebelle**[52] 6260 3-8-13 **49** KierenFallon 1 50
(Mark Brisbourne) *awkward s: sn prom: chsd ldng pair 1/2-way: drvn over 2f out: kpt on same pce* **10/1**

640 **5** 1¼ **Wishformore (IRE)**[16] 7265 6-9-4 **52** (p) RichardThomas 9 51
(Zoe Davison) *t.k.h: hld up in rr: shkn up and prog 2f out: kpt on fnl f: nvr rchd ldrs* **25/1**

4005 **6** ½ **Arachnophobia (IRE)**[22] 7124 7-9-5 **53** (v) GeorgeBaker 7 50
(Martin Bosley) *mostly chsd wnr to 2f out: nt qckn and hld after: fdd and eased last 100yds* **4/1**[1]

6004 **7** shd **Foie Gras**[16] 7265 3-8-8 **47** RobertTart(3) 4 43
(Chris Dwyer) *dwlt: hld up towards rr: prog on inner over 2f out: chsd ldrs over 1f out: no hdwy after* **7/1**[3]

0606 **8** ½ **Medam**[89] 4982 4-8-10 **49** ShirleyTeasdale(5) 14 45
(Shaun Harris) *dwlt: hld up in last pair fr wdst draw: pushed along and sme prog 2f out: nt clr run briefly over 1f out: kpt on same pce after* **33/1**

5652 **9** 3 **Welsh Inlet (IRE)**[22] 7124 5-9-6 **54** SeanLevey 12 42
(John Bridger) *nvr beyond midfield: rdn and no prog over 2f out: n.d after* **5/1**[2]

0000 **10** nk **Mataajir (USA)**[6] 7512 5-9-7 **55** (t) DaleSwift 6 42
(Derek Shaw) *prom: rdn over 2f out: steadily wknd* **12/1**

6330 **11** 1½ **Betzyoucan**[28] 6985 3-9-0 **50** JamesDoyle 8 32
(Robert Stephens) *stdd s: t.k.h in midfield: rdn and no prog 2f out: wknd* **25/1**

-306 **12** 1¼ **Ri Na Si**[13] 7345 3-9-2 **52** AndrewMullen 11 30
(Michael Appleby) *hld up in last pair: rdn and no prog over 2f out* **7/1**[3]

4200 **13** 2 ¼ **Silvee**[16] 7265 6-8-13 **47**........ SamHitchcott 10 20
(John Bridger) *chsd ldrs tl wknd 2f out* **25/1**

040 **14** 3 ¼ **Operettist**[19] 7201 4-8-12 **46**........ LukeMorris 13 11
(Tony Carroll) *racd wd: nvr beyond midfield: wknd over 2f out* **14/1**

1m 26.59s (0.59) **Going Correction** 0.0s/f (Stan)
WFA 3 from 4yo+ 2lb **14** Ran SP% **121.4**
Speed ratings (Par 101): **96,95,93,93,91 91,90,90,86,86 84,83,80,77**
toteswingers 1&2 £16.00, 2&3 £58.30, 1&3 £55.40 CSF £148.19 CT £1476.90 TOTE £21.10: £7.20, £3.20, £6.60; EX 245.60 Trifecta £1282.00 Part won. Pool: £1709.41 - 0.3 winning units..
Owner Mrs L Sharpe & Mrs S G Clapp **Bred** P E Axon **Trained** Charlton Mackrell, Somerset

FOCUS
Moderate handicap form, although the time was 0.36secs quicker than division two. The all-the-way winner is rated back to his best.

7644 BOOK CHRISTMAS FESTIVAL TICKETS NOW H'CAP (DIV II) 7f (P)
8:00 (8:01) (Class 6) (0-55,55) 3-Y-O+ **£1,940** (£577; £288; £144) **Stalls** Low

Form RPR

0035 **1** **Sweet Vintage (IRE)**[40] 6630 3-9-1 **51**........ KierenFallon 3 59
(Mark Brisbourne) *prom: pushed into ld wl over 1f out: sn drvn clr: in n.d fnl f* **12/1**

6402 **2** 1 ¾ **Squirrel Wood (IRE)**[8] 7465 5-9-5 **53**........ GeorgeBaker 6 57
(George Baker) *hld up in last trio: prog on inner over 2f out: rdn and styd on to take 2nd ins fnl f: no ch w wnr* **15/8**[1]

0640 **3** nk **Appyjack**[33] 6851 5-8-12 **46**........(t) LukeMorris 8 49+
(Tony Carroll) *towards rr: rdn over 2f out: prog on outer over 1f out: styd on wl to take 3rd nr fin* **7/1**

4056 **4** nk **Wotalad**[6] 7512 3-8-13 **54**........(p) GeorgeChaloner(5) 14 56
(Richard Whitaker) *pressed ldr: led 1/2-way: rdn and hdd wl over 1f out: one pce and lost 2 pls ins fnl f* **16/1**

0612 **5** hd **Metropolitan Chief**[15] 7292 9-9-6 **54**........(p) SamHitchcott 2 55
(Paul Burgoyne) *wl in tch on inner: prog 2f out: chsd ldrs over 1f out: kpt on same pce after* **12/1**

0-00 **6** 3 ¼ **Salford Prince (IRE)**[8] 7465 5-8-13 **47**........ WilliamCarson 9 40
(David Elsworth) *t.k.h: cl up: impeded after 2f: rdn and nt qckn in midfield over 2f out: n.d after: kpt on nr fin* **33/1**

3350 **7** shd **Purley Queen (IRE)**[75] 5522 4-9-7 **55**........ LiamKeniry 1 47
(Sylvester Kirk) *towards rr: rdn and prog into midfield 2f out: no hdwy after* **25/1**

4004 **8** ¾ **Spellmaker**[89] 4999 4-9-3 **51**........(e) AdamKirby 11 41
(Tony Newcombe) *t.k.h: prom: rdn and cl enough 2f out: wknd over 1f out* **6/1**[3]

3560 **9** 1 ¼ **Surrey Dream (IRE)**[14] 7323 4-8-12 **46** oh1........ SeanLevey 10 33
(John Bridger) *led to 1/2-way: cl up tl wknd over 1f out* **25/1**

0005 **10** ½ **Whitford (IRE)**[9] 7443 3-8-11 **47**........ JimmyQuinn 7 32
(Chris Dwyer) *a towards rr: no prog over 2f out: n.d after* **25/1**

4500 **11** ½ **Puteri Nur Laila (IRE)**[103] 4544 3-9-5 **55**........(t) JimCrowley 4 38
(Paul Cole) *a wl in rr: struggling in last trio over 2f out* **12/1**

2444 **12** shd **Sakhee's Alround**[16] 7266 3-9-0 **50**........(p) AdamBeschizza 13 33
(K F Clutterbuck) *v.s.a: t.k.h and prom on outer after 2f: wknd 2f out* **11/2**[2]

-000 **13** 2 ½ **Courtland Avenue (IRE)**[23] 7109 4-9-2 **53**........ MatthewLawson(3) 5 30
(Jonathan Portman) *slowly away: a in last trio: struggling over 2f out* **33/1**

1m 26.95s (0.95) **Going Correction** 0.0s/f (Stan)
WFA 3 from 4yo+ 2lb **13** Ran SP% **123.3**
Speed ratings (Par 101): **94,92,91,91,91 87,87,86,84,84 83,83,80**
toteswingers 1&2 £8.10, 2&3 £3.50, 1&3 £15.90 CSF £33.90 CT £181.04 TOTE £16.00: £3.20, £1.40, £2.90; EX 30.10 Trifecta £469.90 Pool: £2234.51 - 3.56 winning units..
Owner Derek & Mrs Marie Dean **Bred** Watership Down Stud **Trained** Great Ness, Shropshire

FOCUS
This was run in a time 0.36secs slower than the first division, and rates similar form. The winner is rated back to something like his best.
T/Jkpt: Not won. T/Plt: £57.10 to a £1 stake. Pool of £84735.68 - 1082.40 winning tickets. T/Qpdt: £20.50 to a £1 stake. Pool of £10550.50 - 380.30 winning tickets. JN

7440 LINGFIELD (L-H)
Thursday, October 31

OFFICIAL GOING: Standard
Wind: virtually nil Weather: overcast

7645 32RED CASINO/BRITISH STALLION STUDS EBF MAIDEN FILLIES' STKS 7f (P)
12:50 (12:52) (Class 5) 2-Y-O **£3,067** (£905; £453) **Stalls** Low

Form RPR

1 **Muteela** 2-9-0 0........ PaulHanagan 3 75+
(Mark Johnston) *led after 2f tl 4f out: chsd ldr tl rdn 2f out: chsd wnr again but sltly outpcd over 1f out: rallied u.p ins fnl f: edgd rt but r.o to ld wl ins fnl f* **12/1**

2 **2** nse **Song Of Norway**[28] 6974 2-9-0 0........ LukeMorris 11 75
(Peter Makin) *t.k.h early: chsd ldrs: wnt 2nd and rdn 2f out: outpcd and dropped to 4th 1f out: drvn and rallied strly ins fnl f: ev ch towards fin: jst hld* **4/1**[1]

3 shd **Shasta Daisy** 2-9-0 0........ JamesDoyle 6 75+
(Lady Cecil) *chsd ldrs: effrt and rdn whn rn green and wnt wd bnd 2f out: 5th and looked hld 1f out: rallied and str run fnl 100yds: clsng qckly on ldrs towards fin: nt quite get up* **10/1**

4 1 **Nice Life (IRE)** 2-9-0 0........ SilvestreDeSousa 8 72
(Saeed bin Suroor) *t.k.h: w ldr tl led 4f out: rdn and qcknd wl over 1f out: over 1 l clr and looked wnr ins fnl f: drvn and tiring fnl 100yds: hdd wl ins fnl f: fdd cl home* **4/1**[1]

4 **5** shd **This Is The Day**[28] 6974 2-9-0 0........ JoeFanning 1 72
(William Haggas) *chsd ldrs: effrt u.p and sltly outpcd over 1f out: rallied u.p ins fnl f: pressing ldrs wl ins fnl f: keeping on whn hmpd and snatched up cl home* **6/1**[3]

6 2 **Shama's Song (IRE)** 2-9-0 0........ JimmyFortune 12 66+
(Sir Michael Stoute) *s.i.s: hld up in tch in last trio: hdwy into midfield and rdn 2f out: styd on steadily ins fnl f: nvr trbld ldrs* **5/1**[2]

7 1 **Trust The Wind** 2-9-0 0........ NickyMackay 10 64
(John Gosden) *hld up in tch towards rr: rdn and hdwy wl over 1f out: kpt on ins fnl f: nvr trbld ldrs* **20/1**

8 ¾ **Popping Candy** 2-9-0 0........ AndreaAtzeni 2 62
(Roger Varian) *rn green and pushed along at times: in tch in midfield: rdn and unable qck 2f out: kpt on same pce fr over 1f out* **7/1**

9 2 **Her Honour (IRE)** 2-9-0 0........[1] RobertHavlin 7 56
(John Gosden) *s.i.s: hld up in tch in rr: rdn and effrt wl over 1f out: kpt on fnl f: nvr trbld ldrs* **12/1**

10 shd **Magic Shoes (IRE)** 2-9-0 0........[1] MartinLane 5 56
(Roger Charlton) *in tch in midfield: sltly outpcd and lost pl over 2f out: towards rr whn swtchd lft wl over 1f out: one pce after* **33/1**

11 6 **Secret Keeper** 2-9-0 0........ MartinHarley 13 40
(Sir Mark Prescott Bt) *s.i.s: sn rcvrd and in tch in midfield: rdn and struggling ent fnl 2f: wknd over 1f out* **66/1**

0 **12** 4 **Bed Bed**[9] 7450 2-9-0 0........ TomQueally 4 29
(Michael Bell) *in tch in midfield: rdn and no hdwy wl over 1f out: sn wknd* **66/1**

1m 25.18s (0.38) **Going Correction** -0.075s/f (Stan) **12** Ran SP% **118.6**
Speed ratings (Par 92): **94,93,93,92,92 90,89,88,86,85 79,74**
toteswingers 1&2 £7.10, 2&3 £8.90, 1&3 £20.60 CSF £58.18 TOTE £13.50: £3.10, £1.70, £2.40; EX 66.40 Trifecta £715.40 Pool: £2804.19 - 2.93 winning units..
Owner Hamdan Al Maktoum **Bred** Shadwell Estate Company Limited **Trained** Middleham Moor, N Yorks

■ Stewards' Enquiry : Paul Hanagan two-day ban: careless riding (Nov 14-15)

FOCUS
This looked a fair fillies' maiden, with some nicely bred newcomers up against a couple who had already shown ability, and it provided a thrilling finish.

7646 32RED ON THE APP STORE/IRISH EBF MAIDEN STKS (DIV I) 7f (P)
1:20 (1:22) (Class 5) 2-Y-O **£3,067** (£905; £453) **Stalls** Low

Form RPR

63 **1** **My Target (IRE)**[15] 7302 2-9-5 0........ SilvestreDeSousa 9 78
(Saeed bin Suroor) *t.k.h: chsd ldr tl led 4f out: rdn and qcknd clr wl over 1f out: r.o wl: rdn out* **2/1**[2]

55 **2** 2 ½ **Soviet Courage (IRE)**[19] 7209 2-9-5 0........ JoeFanning 6 71+
(William Haggas) *chsd ldrs: sltly hmpd and swtchd rt ent fnl 2f: chsd clr ldng trio 2f out: styd on wl under hands and heels riding ins fnl f: snatched 2nd on post: no threat to wnr* **10/1**

0 **3** shd **Dance Of Heroes**[26] 7019 2-9-5 0........ JimmyFortune 4 71
(Jeremy Noseda) *chsd ldrs: pushed along and hdwy to chse ldr jst over 2f out: drvn and outpcd by wnr wl over 1f out: kpt on same pce after: lost 2nd on post* **8/1**[3]

4 **4** ¾ **Three Cliffs**[22] 7119 2-9-5 0........ AndreaAtzeni 2 69
(Roger Varian) *chsd ldrs: rdn and outpcd in 3rd wl over 1f out: kpt on same pce u.p fr over 1f out* **5/4**[1]

65 **5** 1 ¾ **High Master (IRE)**[29] 6954 2-9-5 0........ SeanLevey 5 64
(Richard Hannon) *stdd s: hld up in tch towards rr: clsd and wl in tch in midfield over 2f out: nt clr run and shuffled bk wl over 1f out: rallied fnl f: no threat to wnr* **10/1**

64 **6** 1 **Mersad (IRE)**[120] 3948 2-9-5 0........ MartinHarley 10 62
(James Tate) *in tch in midfield: pushed along to cl on outer over 2f out: rdn and outpcd bnd 2f out: kpt on but no threat to wnr fnl f* **50/1**

05 **7** 5 **Deauville Dancer (IRE)**[15] 7308 2-9-5 0........ SebSanders 3 48
(Lady Herries) *dwlt: in tch towards rr: rdn over 4f out: struggling 3f out: wknd 2f out* **25/1**

0 **8** 1 ¾ **High Secret (IRE)**[6] 7494 2-9-5 0........ LukeMorris 7 43
(Sir Mark Prescott Bt) *stdd s: t.k.h early: hld up in rr: rdn over 4f out: wknd 2f out* **66/1**

0 **9** 3 ¼ **Tuddenham (USA)**[19] 7209 2-9-5 0........ JamesDoyle 1 35+
(Charles Hills) *t.k.h: led tl 4f out: hung rt and lost pl qckly bnd ent fnl 2f: eased and plld out rt over 1f out: virtually p.u fnl f* **16/1**

1m 24.53s (-0.27) **Going Correction** -0.075s/f (Stan) **9** Ran SP% **120.3**
Speed ratings (Par 95): **98,95,95,94,92 91,85,83,79**
toteswingers 1&2 £7.10, 2&3 £8.90, 1&3 £20.60 CSF £23.35 TOTE £2.90: £1.30, £3.00, £2.10; EX 28.10 Trifecta £170.20 Pool: £2238.30 - 9.86 winning units..
Owner Godolphin **Bred** Darley **Trained** Newmarket, Suffolk

FOCUS
This was probably just an ordinary maiden and weakened further when the fancied Zerfaal had to be withdrawn after taking a hefty kick at the start (4-1, deduct 20p in the £ under R4).

7647 32RED ON THE APP STORE/IRISH EBF MAIDEN STKS (DIV II) 7f (P)
1:50 (1:50) (Class 5) 2-Y-O **£3,067** (£905; £453) **Stalls** Low

Form RPR

4 **1** **Kafeel (USA)**[19] 7209 2-9-5 0........ PaulHanagan 7 78+
(Roger Varian) *chsd ldrs: rdn and ev ch over 1f out: edgd lft briefly ins fnl f: led fnl 50yds: styd on strly* **5/2**[2]

02 **2** ¾ **Maraayill (IRE)**[28] 6975 2-9-5 0........(t) MartinHarley 1 76
(Marco Botti) *chsd ldrs: effrt u.p to chal over 1f out: drvn to ld fnl 150yds: hdd and no ex fnl 50yds* **9/4**[1]

0454 **3** nse **Pure Amber (IRE)**[14] 7329 2-9-5 71........ JoeFanning 3 76
(Mark Johnston) *led: rdn and hrd pressed wl over 1f out: hdd fnl 150yds: no ex and one pce after* **8/1**

05 **4** 6 **Si Senor (IRE)**[22] 7120 2-9-5 0........ FrederikTylicki 4 60
(Ed Vaughan) *wnt sharply rt s: rn green: in tch in midfield: nt clr run and swtchd rt jst over 2f out: modest 5th over 1f out: kpt on to go 4th towards fin* **16/1**

5 **5** 1 ¼ **Ganges (IRE)**[34] 6799 2-9-2 0........ RobertTart(3) 6 56
(James Toller) *bmpd and pushed rt s: hld up in last pair: pushed along and effrt whn hmpd jst over 2f out: n.d after: kpt on ins fnl f* **7/2**[3]

0 **6** nk **Suitsus**[17] 7251 2-9-5 0........ SebSanders 8 55
(Peter Makin) *t.k.h: chsd ldrs: rdn and wnt clr in ldng quartet 2f out: btn jst over 1f out: fdd ins fnl f* **50/1**

7 1 ¼ **Westminster (IRE)** 2-9-5 0........ RobertHavlin 5 52
(John Gosden) *short of room and hmpd leaving stalls: hld up in tch in rr: outpcd 2f out: rdn and sme modest hdwy over 1f out: nvr trbld ldrs* **10/1**

5 **8** 1 **Bishop Wulstan (IRE)**[14] 7320 2-9-5 0........ SeanLevey 2 49
(Richard Hannon) *pushed along early and reminder sn after s: in tch in midfield: rdn and struggling 1/2-way: wknd ent fnl 2f* **25/1**

9 2 ½ **Dynamic Ranger (USA)** 2-9-5 0........ GeorgeBaker 9 43
(Gary Moore) *t.k.h: hld up in tch in midfield: rdn and struggling whn wd bnd 2f out: sn wknd* **33/1**

00 **10** 6 **One Picture**[14] 7320 2-9-5 0........ KieranO'Neill 10 26
(Richard Hannon) *chsd ldrs: rdn 1/2-way: lost pl over 2f out: bhd fnl f* **66/1**

1m 24.84s (0.04) **Going Correction** -0.075s/f (Stan) **10** Ran SP% **117.9**
Speed ratings (Par 95): **96,95,95,88,86 86,85,83,81,74**
toteswingers 1&2 £2.00, 2&3 £3.20, 1&3 £3.60 CSF £8.44 TOTE £3.50: £1.20, £1.30, £2.90; EX 9.60 Trifecta £36.60 Pool: £3648.69 - 74.66 winning units..
Owner Hamdan Al Maktoum **Bred** Shadwell Farm LLC **Trained** Newmarket, Suffolk

FOCUS
The front three came clear in the second division of this ordinary maiden in which the winning time was 0.31sec slower than the first leg.

7648 DOWNLOAD THE LADBROKES APP H'CAP 7f (P)
2:20 (2:21) (Class 3) (0-95,94) 3-Y-O+ **£7,439** (£2,213; £1,106; £553) **Stalls** Low

Form RPR

21-1 **1** **Horsted Keynes (FR)**[41] 6608 3-8-8 **83**........ AndreaAtzeni 9 94+
(Roger Varian) *chsd ldrs: rdn and effrt over 1f out: chsd ldr 1f out: led wl ins fnl f: r.o wl and gng away at fin* **5/6**[1]

41 **2** ½ **Favourite Treat (USA)**[44] 6486 3-9-1 **90**........ JoeFanning 4 99
(Mark Johnston) *chsd ldr tl led over 2f out: rdn ent fnl 2f: drvn and hrd pressed ins fnl f: hdd and no ex wl ins fnl f* **8/1**[2]

300- **3** ¾ **Indian Jack (IRE)**[418] 6036 5-8-11 **84**........ LukeMorris 5 92
(Ed Walker) *chsd ldrs: effrt u.p over 1f out: chsd ldng pair fnl 100yds: kpt on* **10/1**[3]

6220 **4** ½ **Naabegha**[12] 7373 6-9-2 **89**........ PatCosgrave 11 96
(Ed de Giles) *t.k.h: hld up in tch towards rr: rdn and effrt whn swtchd rt wl over 1f out: kpt on wl ins fnl f* **16/1**

4200 **5** nk **Democretes**[54] 6183 4-9-5 **92**........ SeanLevey 7 98
(Richard Hannon) *in tch in midfield: effrt u.p over 1f out: hrd drvn and styd on same pce fnl 100yds* **14/1**

0035 **6** 1 **Capo Rosso (IRE)**[32] 6874 3-8-9 **84**........(v[1]) MartinDwyer 12 86
(Tom Dascombe) *dwlt and sn bustled along in midfield: rdn and hdwy to join ldrs 1/2-way: ev ch and drvn 2f out: no ex 1f out: wknd ins fnl f* **8/1**[2]

032 **7** hd **Noble Citizen (USA)**[63] 5928 8-8-10 **83**........(be) JimCrowley 8 86
(David Simcock) *s.i.s: hld up in rr: clsng whn nt clr run and hmpd 1f out: swtchd lft ins fnl f: r.o: nvr able to chal* **12/1**

3310 **8** ¾ **Mia's Boy**[161] 2592 9-9-4 **94**........ RobertTart[(3)] 6 95
(Chris Dwyer) *hld up in tch towards rr: rdn and hdwy whn edgd lft 1f out: kpt on same pce ins fnl f* **14/1**

0000 **9** ¾ **Loyalty**[54] 6199 6-8-9 **89**........(v) AdamMcLean[(7)] 10 88
(Derek Shaw) *t.k.h: hld up in midfield: dropped bk to last quartet but stl in tch 4f out: rdn over 1f out: kpt on: nvr trbld ldrs* **25/1**

2000 **10** 1 ¼ **Docofthebay (IRE)**[127] 3684 9-9-0 **87**........(b) TomQueally 3 82
(Scott Dixon) *s.i.s: in tch in last trio: effrt on inner over 1f out: hmpd jst ins fnl f: wl hld after* **50/1**

0050 **11** nse **Al's Memory (IRE)**[24] 7080 4-8-9 **82**........ MartinHarley 1 77
(David Evans) *led tl over 2f out: sn rdn and lost pl: wknd over 1f out* **25/1**

1m 23.28s (-1.52) **Going Correction** -0.075s/f (Stan)
WFA 3 from 4yo+ 2lb **11** Ran SP% **122.4**
Speed ratings (Par 107): **105,104,103,103,102 101,101,100,99,98 98**
toteswingers 1&2 £2.60, 2&3 £9.50, 1&3 £3.40 CSF £8.36 CT £47.38 TOTE £1.60: £1.10, £2.60, £2.90; EX 11.50 Trifecta £79.10 Pool: £5012.63 - 47.48 winning units..
Owner Mrs Fitri Hay **Bred** Oceanic Bloodstock & Mme A Gravereaux **Trained** Newmarket, Suffolk

FOCUS
A decent handicap, run at a good pace. With the finish being fought out between a couple of unexposed 3yos, this is form to take a positive view of. The race is rated around the fourth and fifth.

7649 32RED/EBFSTALLIONS.COM FLEUR DE LYS FILLIES' STKS (LISTED RACE) 1m (P)
2:50 (2:52) (Class 1) 3-Y-O+
£22,684 (£8,600; £4,304; £2,144; £1,076; £540) **Stalls** High

Form RPR

3120 **1** **Forgive**[33] 6838 4-9-0 99........ SilvestreDeSousa 1 101
(Richard Hannon) *mounted on crse: led for 1f: chsd ldrs after: effrt u.p over 1f out: drvn to ld fnl 100yds: hld on wl cl home* **7/1**[3]

6542 **2** hd **Galician**[8] 7470 4-9-0 97........ JoeFanning 3 101
(Mark Johnston) *bustled along leaving stalls: chsd ldrs: rdn and effrt over 1f out: drvn and ev ch ins fnl f: str chal but hld towards fin* **5/1**[1]

0000 **3** nk **Masarah (IRE)**[50] 6308 3-8-11 89........ FrederikTylicki 2 99
(Clive Brittain) *led after 1f: rdn and qcknd ent fnl 2f: drvn and hrd pressed 1f out: hdd fnl 100yds: no ex* **25/1**

3025 **4** ½ **Enrol**[26] 7015 4-9-0 100........ JamesDoyle 4 99
(Sir Michael Stoute) *wl in tch in midfield: effrt to chse ldng trio and rdn wl over 1f out: kpt on u.p ins fnl f* **5/1**[1]

1301 **5** 2 ¼ **Mystical Sapphire**[15] 7297 3-8-11 90........ LiamKeniry 11 93
(Jo Crowley) *hld up in tch in midfield: n.m.r bnd 2f out: swtchd rt and effrt u.p to chse ldng quartet jst over 1f out: kpt on same pce after* **6/1**[2]

1200 **6** ½ **Spicy Dal**[43] 6536 3-8-11 88........ TomQueally 5 91
(Hughie Morrison) *dwlt: sn rcvrd and in tch in midfield: rdn over 2f out: outpcd u.p 2f out: kpt on same pce after* **33/1**

1020 **7** nk **Rhagori**[78] 5402 4-9-0 88........ JimCrowley 6 92
(Ralph Beckett) *stdd s: t.k.h: hld up in tch in last trio: rdn and hdwy whn hmpd jst over 1f out: kpt on but nvr threatened ldrs* **10/1**

0400 **8** hd **Spinacre (IRE)**[11] 7404 3-8-11 0........(p) AndreaAtzeni 9 90
(Roger Varian) *s.i.s: hld up in tch in rr: effrt and hdwy on inner over 1f out: kpt on: nvr trbld ldrs* **8/1**

102 **9** 3 ¼ **Indignant**[70] 5684 3-8-11 98........ SeanLevey 7 83
(Richard Hannon) *chsd ldrs: rdn jst over 2f out: drvn and outpcd wl over 1f out: wknd fnl f* **5/1**[1]

-504 **10** nk **Valais Girl**[26] 7015 3-8-11 92........(p) HarryBentley 10 82
(Marcus Tregoning) *in tch in midfield: rdn and unable qck wl over 1f out: wknd 1f out* **25/1**

40 **11** 1 **Collusiva (IRE)**[11] 7411 3-8-11 0........ MartinHarley 12 80
(G Botti, France) *hld up in tch in last quartet: rdn and no hdwy wl over 1f out: bhd fnl f* **14/1**

12 4 ½ **Moi Lolita**[60] 4-9-0 0........ AHelfenbein 8 70
(Markus Klug, Germany) *s.i.s: in tch towards rr: pushed along and hdwy into midfield over 3f out: rdn and lost pl over 2f out: bhd over 1f out* **20/1**

1m 35.48s (-2.72) **Going Correction** -0.075s/f (Stan)
WFA 3 from 4yo 3lb **12** Ran SP% **119.0**
Speed ratings (Par 108): **110,109,109,109,106 106,105,105,102,102 101,96**
toteswingers 1&2 £4.80, 2&3 £24.50, 1&3 £33.30 CSF £40.06 TOTE £6.70: £2.60, £2.10, £7.40; EX 30.90 Trifecta £967.00 Pool: £4574.09 - 3.54 winning units..
Owner Highclere Thoroughbred Racing-Spearmint **Bred** The Athenians And Cheveley Park Stud Ltd **Trained** East Everleigh, Wilts

FOCUS
The first of the "win and you're in" qualifiers for the All-Weather Championships Finals Day and the only one specifically for the £150,000 32Red Fillies & Mares Stakes over 7f back here next April. An interesting Listed event, featuring challengers from France and Germany, in which the 3yos had taken seven of the previous ten runnings, but the older fillies held the edge this time. The pace held up well and the third is the key to the form.

7650 32RED.COM/CHOOSE EBF NOMINATED RIVER EDEN FILLIES' STKS (LISTED RACE) 1m 5f (P)
3:20 (3:21) (Class 1) 3-Y-O+
£22,684 (£8,600; £4,304; £2,144; £1,076; £540) **Stalls** Low

Form RPR

31 **1** **Speckled (USA)**[50] 6312 3-8-8 85........ SilvestreDeSousa 12 96+
(Charlie Appleby) *t.k.h: chsd ldr tl led after 2f: mde rest: rdn and qcknd clr 2f out: in command and r.o wl fnl f* **10/1**

1256 **2** 1 ¾ **Livia's Dream (IRE)**[35] 6764 4-9-2 82........ TomMcLaughlin 2 93
(Ed Walker) *t.k.h: led for 2f: chsd wnr tl 10f out: chsd ldrs after: effrt u.p ent fnl 2f: chsd clr wnr 1f out: kpt on but a hld* **100/1**

6120 **3** hd **Phiz (GER)**[35] 6764 3-8-8 103........ RobertHavlin 9 93
(John Gosden) *wl in tch in midfield: hdwy on outer 3f out: drvn and disputing 2nd over 1f out: kpt on but no imp on wnr* **8/1**[3]

1050 **4** ¾ **Banoffee (IRE)**[89] 4985 3-8-11 103........ JimmyFortune 10 95+
(Hughie Morrison) *stdd and dropped in bhd after s: t.k.h: hld up in tch towards rr: clsd and nt clr run jst over 2f out: swtchd rt over 1f out: r.o wl fnl f: nt rch ldrs* **10/1**

2132 **5** nk **Bantam (IRE)**[24] 7072 3-8-8 90........ AndreaAtzeni 8 91
(Ed Dunlop) *hld up in tch towards rr: rdn and hdwy into midfield 2f out: styd on wl u.p fnl f: nt rch ldrs* **8/1**[3]

2155 **6** ½ **Kikonga**[35] 6764 3-8-8 92........ JamesDoyle 5 90
(Luca Cumani) *wl in tch in midfield: n.m.r briefly jst over 2f out: sn rdn: kpt on same pce fr over 1f out* **10/1**

5131 **7** 1 **Phaenomena (IRE)**[40] 6649 3-8-8 89........ PaulHanagan 1 89
(Lady Cecil) *dwlt: in tch towards rr: rdn and effrt on outer wl over 2f out: styd on ins fnl f: nvr trbld ldrs* **11/4**[1]

3230 **8** nk **Alwilda**[13] 7338 3-8-8 83........(p) LukeMorris 6 88
(Sir Mark Prescott Bt) *chsd ldrs: rdn 4f out: drvn and unable qck over 2f out: keeping on same pce and hld whn swtchd rt ins fnl f* **33/1**

51-4 **9** ½ **Tempest Fugit (IRE)**[61] 5993 4-9-2 98........ NickyMackay 13 88
(John Gosden) *stdd and dropped in bhd after s: t.k.h: hld up in tch: nt clr run and shuffled bk over 2f out: rallied ent fnl f: styd on: nvr trbld ldrs* **5/1**[2]

6 **10** 1 ¼ **Lalandia (IRE)**[18] 4-9-2 0........ AStarke 7 86
(P Schiergen, Germany) *hld up in tch in midfield: rdn and effrt on inner wl over 1f out: no imp* **8/1**[3]

3115 **11** nk **Lemon Pearl**[54] 6196 3-8-8 85........ JimCrowley 14 85
(Ralph Beckett) *chsd ldrs: wnt 2nd 10f out tl jst over 1f out: wknd ins fnl f* **20/1**

6002 **12** ½ **Bite Of The Cherry**[61] 5993 4-9-2 97........(v) TomQueally 3 85
(Michael Bell) *stdd s: hld up in rr: rdn and effrt over 1f out: no imp: n.d* **20/1**

1411 **13** 2 **Prospera (IRE)**[38] 6693 3-8-8 84........(b) JohnFahy 11 82
(Ralph Beckett) *hld up in last pair: rdn and effrt on outer over 2f out: no hdwy: n.d* **20/1**

2m 44.03s (-1.97) **Going Correction** -0.075s/f (Stan)
WFA 3 from 4yo 8lb **13** Ran SP% **122.2**
Speed ratings (Par 108): **103,101,101,101,101 100,100,100,99,98 98,98,97**
toteswingers 1&2 £54.30, 2&3 £118.20, 1&3 £12.60 CSF £802.59 TOTE £11.80: £3.40, £14.20, £1.90; EX 960.60 Trifecta £2519.50 Pool: £4135.95 - 1.23 winning units..
Owner Godolphin **Bred** Darley **Trained** Newmarket, Suffolk

FOCUS
Another Listed race for fillies and mares, this time for stayers, but they went no pace and it was a big advantage to be up there early. The runner-up is the key and the winner is capable of better than the bare form.

7651 CORAL APP DOWNLOAD FROM THE APP STORE H'CAP 1m 2f (P)
3:50 (3:50) (Class 5) (0-75,75) 3-Y-O+ **£2,726** (£805; £402) **Stalls** Low

Form RPR

0035 **1** **Modernism**[36] 6750 4-9-10 **75**........ JimCrowley 12 84
(David Simcock) *led tl hdd over 8f out and stdd to chse ldrs: rdn to chal 1f out: led ins fnl f: r.o wl: drvn out* **3/1**[1]

5240 **2** nk **Red Warrior (IRE)**[40] 6630 3-9-5 **75**........ TomQueally 5 83
(Ismail Mohammed) *t.k.h: hld up towards rr: hmpd over 8f out: rdn and hdwy over 1f out: led jst over 1f out: hdd ins fnl f: r.o wl but a hld* **10/1**

1320 **3** 1 **Hector's Chance**[22] 7132 4-9-7 **72**........ AndreaAtzeni 1 78
(Heather Main) *broke wl: sn stdd and hld up in tch towards rr: stuck bhd horses 2f out: swtchd lft and hdwy over 1f out: kpt on wl ins fnl f* **8/1**

0504 **4** hd **Kelpie Blitz (IRE)**[31] 6898 4-9-7 **72**........(t) GeorgeBaker 6 78
(Seamus Durack) *broke wl: stdd and hld up wl in tch: trckd ldrs over 2f out: rdn and chal over 1f out: no ex and btn wl ins fnl f* **9/2**[2]

-423 **5** 1 ½ **Fairyinthewind (IRE)**[31] 421 4-9-9 **74**........ FergusSweeney 10 77
(Alan King) *dwlt: pushed along and sn rcvrd to r in midfield: rdn and effrt over 2f out: kpt on same pce u.p fnl f* **8/1**

050 **6** ½ **Xinbama (IRE)**[32] 6869 4-9-5 **75**........(t) ShelleyBirkett[(5)] 2 77
(J W Hills) *hld up in tch towards rr: n.m.r jst over 2f out: hdwy jst over 1f out: kpt on wl* **10/1**

5524 **7** 1 ¼ **Spring Tonic**[32] 6869 4-9-7 **72**........ SebSanders 14 71
(Simon Dow) *chsd ldrs: rdn and ev ch wl over 1f out: no ex 1f out: wknd ins fnl f* **5/1**[3]

-150 **8** hd **Unmoothaj**[25] 6533 3-9-5 **75**........ AdamKirby 13 74
(Pam Sly) *hld up in tch in last pair: hdwy on outer 3f out: drvn and edgd rt 1f out: styd on same pce fnl f* **20/1**

2355 **9** nk **Stellar Express (IRE)**[22] 7131 4-9-9 **74**........ AndrewMullen 7 72
(Michael Appleby) *chsd ldrs: wnt 2nd over 8f out tl rdn to ld over 2f out: hdd jst over 1f out: sn wknd* **7/1**

5000 **10** 6 **Standpoint**[15] 7306 7-9-9 **74**........ LiamKeniry 8 60
(Conor Dore) *hld up in rr: n.d* **50/1**

0304 **11** nk **Arabian Star (IRE)**[28] 6984 5-9-10 **75**........(t) MartinHarley 11 61
(Alan McCabe) *chsd ldr tl led over 8f out: rdn and hdd over 2f out: btn over 1f out: wknd fnl f* **25/1**

2m 4.39s (-2.21) **Going Correction** -0.075s/f (Stan)
WFA 3 from 4yo+ 5lb **11** Ran SP% **123.3**
Speed ratings (Par 103): **105,104,103,103,102 102,101,101,100,96 95**
toteswingers 1&2 £10.50, 2&3 £18.40, 1&3 £7.50 CSF £35.67 CT £228.24 TOTE £3.80: £1.50, £3.80, £2.90; EX 51.30 Trifecta £394.60 Pool: £3841.85 - 7.30 winning units..
Owner Dr Marwan Koukash **Bred** Darley **Trained** Newmarket, Suffolk

The Form Book Flat, Raceform Ltd, Compton, RG20 6NL.

FOCUS
An ordinary handicap run in a fair time. The winner produced a personal best on this Polytrack debut.

7652 LADBROKES MOBILE APPRENTICE H'CAP 7f (P)
4:20 (4:23) (Class 6) (0-65,65) 3-Y-O+ £2,045 (£603; £302) Stalls Low

Form RPR
4004 1 One Way Or Another (AUS)[23] 7092 10-9-0 61..........(t) EoinWalsh(3) 3 73
(David Evans) stdd s: hld up in rr: hdwy 3f out: 5th and rdn 2f out: straong run over 1f out: led fnl 100yds: sn clr 6/1[2]
0002 2 3 ¾ Bassett Road (IRE)[13] 7344 5-9-5 63....................(p) GeorgeChaloner 11 65
(Keith Dalgleish) t.k.h: chsd ldr: rdn and ev ch 2f out: styd on same pce ins fnl f 3/1[1]
0025 3 1 Homeboy (IRE)[149] 2949 5-9-2 60.. RyanTate 7 59
(Marcus Tregoning) racd keenly: led: rdn 2f out: hrd drvn and kpt on over 1f out: hdd fnl 100yds: no ex and sn outpcd 8/1[3]
2350 4 ¾ Annes Rocket (IRE)[29] 6937 8-9-0 63.................(p) CameronHardie(5) 6 60
(Jimmy Fox) stdd s: hld up in tch in midfield: stdd bk to last pair 4f out: rdn and hdwy over 1f out: styd on: no threat to wnr 16/1
0546 5 ½ Baby Dottie[60] 6019 6-8-9 58.....................................(t) SophieRalston(5) 9 54
(Pat Phelan) in tch in midfield: pushed along and hdwy to chse ldrs over 4f out: 3rd and rdn over 2f out: kpt on tl no ex and wknd ins fnl f 14/1
6605 6 nk Rondeau (GR)[29] 6937 8-9-3 64................................ DanielMuscutt(3) 2 59
(Patrick Chamings) taken down early: stdd s: hld up in rr: rdn and hdwy over 1f out: kpt on fnl f: nvr trbld ldrs 12/1
1252 7 ¾ Wordismybond[29] 6937 4-9-7 65..................................... JoeyHaynes 12 58
(Peter Makin) chsd ldrs: 4th and unable qck u.p ent fnl 2f: plugged on same pce fr over 1f out 3/1[1]
0330 8 1 ¾ Chevise (IRE)[23] 7086 5-9-0 61..(p) IanBurns(3) 5 49
(Steve Woodman) in tch in midfield: rdn along over 4f out: rdn and outpcd ent fnl 2f: wknd jst over 1f out 10/1
6600 9 1 ¾ The Wee Chief (IRE)[30] 6929 7-9-4 62..................... MatthewLawson 8 46
(Jimmy Fox) stdd s: hld up towards rr: hdwy on outer 3f out: no imp wl over 1f out: sn wknd 10/1
0000 10 3 ½ Lastkingofscotland (IRE)[7] 7486 7-9-3 64...............(b) NoraLooby(3) 13 38
(Conor Dore) stdd s: hld up in rr: n.d 20/1
0050 11 6 Interakt[43] 6535 6-8-13 60.. NedCurtis(3) 10 18
(Joseph Tuite) a towards rr: rdn wl over 3f out: wknd 2f out 50/1
2100 12 3 ½ Gebayl[16] 7263 3-8-11 60..(p) ShelleyBirkett(3) 4 7
(Olivia Maylam) chsd ldrs: rdn and lost pl over 2f out: bhd fnl f 33/1

1m 23.95s (-0.85) **Going Correction** -0.075s/f (Stan)
WFA 3 from 4yo+ 2lb 12 Ran SP% **123.5**
Speed ratings (Par 101): **101,96,95,94,94 93,92,90,88,84 78,74**
toteswingers 1&2 £4.30, 2&3 £6.30, 1&3 £8.50 CSF £24.94 CT £153.63 TOTE £8.50: £2.50, £1.80, £2.80; EX 32.90 Trifecta £220.40 Pool: £4118.74 - 14.01 winning units..
Owner Mrs E Evans **Bred** Segenho Stud **Trained** Pandy, Monmouths

FOCUS
A moderate apprentice handicap. The winner is rated back to his best form of the past year, but the form isn't that solid.
T/Plt: £139.80 to a £1 stake. Pool of £63728.84 - 332.67 winning tickets. T/Qpdt: £24.50 to a £1 stake. Pool of £6728.18 - 202.70 winning tickets. SP

7184 CHANTILLY (R-H)
Thursday, October 31
OFFICIAL GOING: Turf: heavy; polytrack: standard

7653a PRIX DE WELLS (MAIDEN) (2YO) (TURF) 6f
1:20 (12:00) 2-Y-O £9,756 (£3,902; £2,926; £1,951; £975)

RPR
1 Orangefield (FR) 2-9-2 0.................................. ChristopheSoumillon 12 80+
(J-C Rouget, France) 27/10[2]
2 3 Silver Treasure (FR)[20] 7185 2-9-2 0........................... MaximeGuyon 9 71
(Amy Weaver) t.k.h: trckd ldrs: shkn up and effrt whn nt clr run, bmpd and squeezed out ins last 2f: sn rdn and swtchd to outside: r.o ins fnl f to go 2nd 100yds out: no ch w wnr 19/10[1]
3 2 Elliot Carver (FR)[115] 2-9-2 0.. FranckBlondel 7 65
(M Munch, Germany) 67/1
4 snk Little Cupcake[24] 2-8-13 0... JulienAuge 5 62
(E J O'Neill, France) 74/10
5 2 ½ Square Lamartine (FR)[45] 2-9-2 0.......... Christophe-PatriceLemaire 11 57
(M Boutin, France) 36/1
6 2 Molesne Chop (FR)[20] 7185 2-9-2 0......................(b) ThomasMessina 6 51
(Mlle C Cardenne, France) 34/1
7 1 ½ Neuf Histoire (FR)[13] 2-8-13 0................................. FrankieLeroy(3) 4 47
(R Le Gal, France) 93/1
8 ¾ Pretty Pearl (FR)[93] 2-8-13 0.. TonyPiccone 3 41
(N Caullery, France) 22/1
9 7 Ameli (FR)[35] 6786 2-8-13 0... ThierryJarnet 14 20
(J Heloury, France) 18/1
10 20 Nougaboo (USA)[100] 2-8-13 0.. FlavienPrat 1
(F Head, France) 31/5[3]
11 snk Glory Traou Land (FR) 2-8-9 0........................... MatthiasLauron(4) 13
(P Sogorb, France) 30/1
12 1 ¼ Kokoumin (FR)[124] 2-8-5 0.................................. MlleJeanneCotta(8) 8
(M Boutin, France) 85/1
13 20 Zafeen Style (FR) 2-9-2 0.. FabriceVeron 10
(H-A Pantall, France) 11/1

1m 14.93s (3.53) 13 Ran SP% **117.7**
WIN (incl. 1 euro stake): 3.70. PLACES: 1.60, 1.40, 8.50. DF:3.50. SF: 6.50.
Owner Mme Beatrice Hermelin **Bred** A Chopard **Trained** Pau, France

7466 NEWMARKET (R-H)
Friday, November 1
OFFICIAL GOING: Soft (6.0)
Wind: light, across Weather: dry

7654 EBF EXPRESS COFFEE MAIDEN STKS (DIV I) 7f
12:30 (12:33) (Class 4) 2-Y-O £4,528 (£1,347; £673; £336) Stalls High

Form RPR
5 1 Sea Defence (USA)[23] 7119 2-9-0 0................................ JamesDoyle 2 85+
(Roger Charlton) lengthy: str: unf: pressed ldrs: chsd wnr over 2f out: pushed along to ld wl over 1f out: rdn ent fnl f: styd on wl: eased towards fin 5/4[1]
3 2 1 ½ Think Ahead[30] 6938 2-9-0 0.................................... SilvestreDeSousa 11 81+
(Saeed bin Suroor) str: athletic: stdd s: t.k.h: hld up in tch towards rr: hdwy 3f out: rdn to chse ldng pair and edgd rt wl over 1f out: chsd wnr over 1f out: kpt on same pce fnl f 7/2[2]
3 10 Loving Home 2-9-0 0.. RobertHavlin 4 56+
(John Gosden) leggy: t.k.h: led tl rdn and hdd wl over 1f out: 3rd and btn over 1f out: wknd fnl f 8/1
4 3 Tara's Treasure (IRE) 2-9-0 0................................. FergusSweeney 6 49
(Gary Moore) lengthy: tall: in tch in midfield: rdn and outpcd 2f out: n.d after: styd on past btn horses fnl f 66/1
6 5 2 ½ Columbian Roulette (IRE)[7] 7501 2-9-0 0.................... SteveDrowne 8 43
(Charles Hills) w ldr tl rdn and struggling ent fnl 2f: 4th and wl btn over 1f out: wknd 33/1
0 6 hd Rock Charm[9] 7467 2-9-0 0... AdamBeschizza 10 42
(Stuart Williams) in tch in midfield: rdn and outpcd ent fnl 2f: 5th and wl btn over 1f out: wknd 100/1
7 2 ½ Certificate 2-9-0 0.. AndreaAtzeni 3 36+
(Roger Varian) tall: athletic: s.i.s: sn rcvrd and in tch in midfield: rdn over 2f out: sn btn and wknd 2f out 4/1[3]
8 1 ¾ Authenticity 2-9-0 0... PatCosgrave 1 31
(John Butler) str: bit bkwd: in tch in midfield: rdn and btn over 2f out: sn wknd 33/1
9 hd Mr Greenspan (USA) 2-9-0 0.. SeanLevey 5 31
(Richard Hannon) leggy: scope: v.s.a: a in rr: rdn and losing tch whn swtchd rt 2f out 20/1
10 3 ¾ Born To Reign 2-9-0 0... TomQueally 7 22
(Michael Bell) cmpct: s.i.s: sn pushed along in rr: lost tch over 2f out 50/1
11 12 Archambo 2-9-0 0... JoeFanning 9
(Mark Johnston) tall: awkward leaving stalls: sn rcvrd and chsd ldrs tl rdn and lost pl qckly over 2f out: t.o and eased ins fnl f 28/1

1m 29.42s (4.02) **Going Correction** +0.65s/f (Yiel) 11 Ran SP% **116.3**
Speed ratings (Par 98): **103,101,89,86,83 83,80,78,78,73 60**
toteswingers 1&2 £1.60, 2&3 £6.40, 1&3 £4.10 CSF £5.13 TOTE £2.30: £1.10, £1.50, £2.50; EX 7.70 Trifecta £34.30 Pool: £2414.60 - 52.67 winning units..
Owner K Abdullah **Bred** Juddmonte Farms Inc **Trained** Beckhampton, Wilts

FOCUS
Stands' side track used with stalls on far side, except 1m4f & 2m: centre. There was 1.5mm of rain overnight and the going was given as soft (GoingStick 6.0). Jockeys returning after the first generally reported that it was soft, bordering on heavy. The market got this right with the first two in the betting pulling clear in the closing stages.

7655 EBF EXPRESS COFFEE MAIDEN STKS (DIV II) 7f
1:00 (1:06) (Class 4) 2-Y-O £4,528 (£1,347; £673; £336) Stalls High

Form RPR
4 1 Idder (IRE)[16] 7308 2-9-0 0.. AndreaAtzeni 4 80
(Roger Varian) angular: chsd ldrs: pushed along to chse ldr over 2f out: drvn ent fnl f: sustained effrt to ld wl ins fnl f: hld on cl home 3/1[2]
5 2 nse Zee Zeely[16] 7302 2-9-0 0... JamesDoyle 10 80
(William Haggas) lengthy: lw: in tch in midfield: effrt ent fnl 2f: rdn to chse ldrs and wandered lft u.p 1f out: styd on and str chal fnl 50yds: jst hld 3/1[2]
3 3 ¾ Stetchworth (IRE)[9] 7467 2-9-0 0...................................... JoeFanning 3 78
(Mark Johnston) lw: led: rdn over 1f out: drvn ins fnl f: hdd and no ex wl ins fnl f 9/4[1]
4 1 ½ Warbrook (IRE) 2-9-0 0.. RobertHavlin 6 75+
(John Gosden) str: attractive: in tch: effrt to chse ldrs and rdn 2f out: styd on same pce ins fnl f: eased cl home 14/1
5 5 9 Framed Masterpiece[14] 7335 2-9-0 0.....................(p) PatCosgrave 2 52
(Paul Fitzsimons) lengthy: str: chsd ldr tl over 2f out: 5th and btn over 1f out: fdd fnl f 25/1
6 ½ Final Countdown 2-9-0 0.. MartinLane 8 51
(Anthony Carson) w'like: in tch in last trio: rdn and rn green over 2f out: sn outpcd and btn: no ch but plugged on fnl f 50/1
0 7 shd Ragged Robbin (FR)[9] 7461 2-9-0 0.................................. TedDurcan 9 50
(David Lanigan) str: in tch in midfield: rdn and lost pl over 2f out: n.d after 40/1
8 1 ½ Brigliadoro (IRE) 2-9-0 0.. WilliamCarson 11 47
(Philip McBride) leggy: unf: wnt lft s: hld up in tch in last trio: rdn and effrt into midfield 3f out: sn struggling: wknd 2f out 20/1
9 11 Stapleford Lad 2-9-0 0... KierenFox 7 19
(Stuart Williams) str: s.i.s: in tch in last trio: rdn and struggling over 2f out: sn dropped out and bhd 50/1
10 7 Pantoloni 2-9-0 0.. SilvestreDeSousa 1
(Charlie Appleby) unf: scope: in tch in midfield: rdn and lost pl 3f out: bhd over 2f out: eased fnl f: t.o 7/1[3]

1m 30.17s (4.77) **Going Correction** +0.65s/f (Yiel) 10 Ran SP% **114.9**
Speed ratings (Par 98): **98,97,97,95,85 84,84,82,70,62**
toteswingers 1&2 £3.70, 1&3 £1.40, 2&3 £1.90 CSF £11.55 TOTE £3.50: £1.40, £1.80, £1.10; EX 14.30 Trifecta £47.20 Pool: £2851.58 - 45.27 winning units..
Owner Saleh Al Homaizi & Imad Al Sagar **Bred** Saleh Al Homaizi & Imad Al Sagar **Trained** Newmarket, Suffolk

FOCUS
The early pace didn't look as strong in this division and the final time was slower by 0.75sec.

7656 THAI STREET CAFE & CROWN ROOMS NEWMARKET H'CAP 1m 2f
1:30 (1:34) (Class 4) (0-85,85) 3-Y-O+ £4,690 (£1,395; £697; £348) Stalls High

Form RPR
0000 1 Creme Anglaise[47] 6433 5-9-1 76.. TomQueally 9 85
(Michael Bell) swtg: t.k.h: hld up in tch in midfield: hdwy 3f out: rdn to chal wl over 1f out: clr w rival 1f out: led ins fnl f: styd on 20/1

1623 **2** ½ **Raskova (USA)**[7] 7504 3-8-8 **73** TedDurcan 2 81
(William Jarvis) *racd on far side: trckd ldrs: rdn and effrt ent fnl 2f: drvn to ld over 1f out: forged clr w wnr 1f out: hdd and one pce ins fnl f* **6/1**

000 **3** 5 **Stevie Thunder**[20] 7211 8-9-0 **75** (p) SilvestreDeSousa 10 74
(Ian Williams) *hld up in tch in rr: hdwy u.p over 2f out: chsd clr ldng pair and edgd rt 1f out: no imp fnl f* **11/2**[3]

0200 **4** 1¼ **Beedee**[20] 7205 3-9-5 **84** SeanLevey 5 80
(Richard Hannon) *in tch in midfield: rdn and effrt ent fnl 2f: 5th and no threat to ldng pair whn nt clr run ent fnl f: plugged on* **20/1**

441 **5** ½ **Squire Osbaldeston (IRE)**[38] 6738 3-9-6 **85** JamesDoyle 1 80
(Lady Cecil) *lw: racd on far side: led tl rdn and hdd over 1f out: no ex and sn btn: wknd ins fnl f* **3/1**[1]

105 **6** 2 **Unison (IRE)**[7] 7505 3-8-6 **71** oh1 AndrewMullen 11 62
(Peter Makin) *stdd and dropped in bhd after s: hld up in tch in last trio: rdn and effrt jst over 2f out: 6th and no hdwy over 1f out: wknd fnl f* **8/1**

1410 **7** *hd* **Uphold**[23] 7121 6-9-3 **85** (v) CameronHardie(7) 4 76
(Gay Kelleway) *dwlt: t.k.h: sn rcvrd to chse ldrs: rdn and lost pl wl over 2f out: bhd whn swtchd rt over 1f out* **8/1**

3342 **8** 6 **Las Verglas Star (IRE)**[16] 7312 5-9-5 **85** GeorgeChaloner(5) 3 65
(Richard Fahey) *in tch in midfield: rdn and effrt over 2f out: sn struggling: wknd wl over 1f out* **10/3**[2]

1-05 **9** 14 **King Of The Celts (IRE)**[38] 6721 5-8-10 **71** PaulHanagan 7 24
(Tim Easterby) *t.k.h: led main gp and chsd overall ldr tl over 2f out: sn dropped out: wl bhd and eased ins fnl f* **14/1**

2m 11.18s (5.38) **Going Correction** +0.65s/f (Yiel)
WFA 3 from 4yo+ 4lb 9 Ran SP% **116.2**
Speed ratings (Par 105): **104,103,99,98,98 96,96,91,80**
toteswingers 1&2 £19.20, 1&3 £13.70, 2&3 £6.10 CSF £135.70 CT £757.05 TOTE £28.60: £6.40, £1.80, £2.30; EX 228.90 Trifecta £524.00 Pool: £3856.61 - 5.51 winning units..

Owner Mrs G Rowland-Clark **Bred** Newsells Park Stud **Trained** Newmarket, Suffolk

FOCUS
They split into two groups here, with Squire Osbaldeston and Raskova heading over to the far side rail and the rest racing a little apart, more towards the centre. The first two were clear, but the form isn't rated too positively.

7657 IRISH STALLION FARMS EBF BOSRA SHAM FILLIES' STKS (LISTED RACE) 6f
2:00 (2:03) (Class 1) 2-Y-O

£17,013 (£6,450; £3,228; £1,608; £807; £405) **Stalls** High

Form RPR

1141 **1** **Cape Factor (IRE)**[10] 7451 2-8-12 68 ChrisCatlin 8 91
(Rae Guest) *lengthy: lw: chsd ldrs: rdn and effrt to ld wl over 1f out: in command and styd on wl fnl f: rdn out* **7/2**[1]

3 **2** 1½ **Penny Drops**[19] 7218 2-8-12 0 JoeFanning 1 87
(William Haggas) *unf: scope: hld up in tch in midfield: rdn and effrt whn nt clr run over 1f out: hdwy u.p 1f out: r.o wl to go 2nd wl ins fnl f: no threat to wnr* **5/1**[3]

2221 **3** *nk* **Genuine Quality (USA)**[29] 6967 2-8-12 82 HarryBentley 3 86
(Ed Vaughan) *neat: hld up in tch in last trio: rdn and hdwy wl over 1f out: chsd clr wnr 1f out: kpt on but no real imp: lost 2nd wl ins fnl f* **12/1**

516 **4** 2¼ **Valen (IRE)**[69] 5737 2-8-12 89 TomQueally 4 79
(Michael Bell) *stdd and wnt lft s: hld up in tch in last trio: rdn and hdwy over 1f out: kpt on steadily ins fnl f: nvr trbld ldrs* **5/1**[3]

6636 **5** 2 **Mendacious Harpy (IRE)**[47] 6452 2-8-12 67 PatCosgrave 5 73
(George Baker) *dwlt and sltly hmpd leaving stalls: in rr: rdn: flashed tail and wnt lft 2f out: wandered bk rt over 1f out: kpt on past btn horses fnl f: nvr trbld ldrs* **66/1**

4140 **6** ½ **Fig Roll**[97] 4742 2-9-1 98 SeanLevey 6 74
(Richard Hannon) *chsd ldr: rdn and chsd wnr wl over 1f out tl 1f out: sn btn: fdd fnl 100yds* **5/1**[3]

21 **7** 3 **Expect**[25] 7078 2-8-12 0 JamesDoyle 2 62
(Jeremy Noseda) *leggy: chsd ldrs: rdn and unable qck wl over 1f out: btn over 1f out: wknd fnl f* **4/1**[2]

1012 **8** 3½ **Musicora**[15] 7329 2-8-12 90 JimCrowley 7 52
(Richard Hannon) *t.k.h: led tl rdn and hdd wl over 1f out: losing pl whn hung rt over 1f out: sn wknd* **7/1**

1m 15.26s (3.06) **Going Correction** +0.65s/f (Yiel) 8 Ran SP% **113.9**
Speed ratings (Par 101): **105,103,102,99,96 96,92,87**
toteswingers 1&2 £4.50, 1&3 £6.80, 2&3 £7.20 CSF £21.06 TOTE £4.20: £1.40, £1.80, £2.60; EX 26.50 Trifecta £289.20 Pool: £3950.56 - 10.24 winning units..

Owner Derek J Willis **Bred** Nanallac Stud **Trained** Newmarket, Suffolk

FOCUS
An ordinary Listed race on paper, with not a single runner rated in three figures.

7658 EXPRESS CAFES CONDITIONS STKS 6f
2:30 (2:30) (Class 3) 2-3-Y-O **£7,158** (£2,143; £1,071; £535) **Stalls** High

Form RPR

4235 **1** **Expert (IRE)**[30] 6958 2-8-8 99 SeanLevey 2 90
(Richard Hannon) *chsd ldr: pushed along to chal over 1f out: rdn to ld jst ins fnl f: sn in command and styd on: rdn out* **7/2**[3]

4342 **2** 1¾ **Mar Mar (IRE)**[18] 7247 3-9-8 96 (b) SilvestreDeSousa 5 85
(Saeed bin Suroor) *led: rdn over 1f out: drvn and hdd jst ins fnl f: no ex: wknd towards fin and jst hld 2nd* **6/4**[1]

621 **3** *hd* **Charles Molson**[12] 7394 2-8-8 0 FergusSweeney 1 84
(Henry Candy) *t.k.h: hld up in tch in 3rd: rdn and swtchd out lft over 1f out: kpt on u.p ins fnl f: pressing for 2nd cl home* **13/8**[2]

1403 **4** ½ **Donny Rover (IRE)**[6] 7529 2-8-5 74 (v) AndrewMullen 3 80
(David C Griffiths) *in tch in rr: rdn over 2f out: no imp and edgd rt over 1f out: kpt on u.p ins fnl f: no threat to wnr* **12/1**

1m 15.91s (3.71) **Going Correction** +0.65s/f (Yiel) 4 Ran SP% **108.0**
Speed ratings: **101,98,98,97**
CSF £9.11 TOTE £4.10; EX 8.40 Trifecta £12.70 Pool: £2072.20 - 121.89 winning units..

Owner Mrs J Wood **Bred** Edgeridge Ltd **Trained** East Everleigh, Wilts

■ Stewards' Enquiry : Fergus Sweeney caution: careless riding.

FOCUS
Despite the poor record of 3yos in this race Mar Mar was sent off a solid favourite. She isn't the first to find the concession of so much weight to the juveniles beyond her, though, and the race went the way of a Richard Hannon-trained juvenile for the fourth time in the last seven years.

7659 EBF WARRENS OF WARWICK & MOBILE PIMMS BAR FILLIES' H'CAP 1m 4f
3:05 (3:07) (Class 3) (0-90,88) 3-Y-O+

£8,092 (£2,423; £1,211; £605; £302; £152) **Stalls** Centre

Form RPR

1 **1** **Tweed**[17] 7279 3-8-4 **74** oh3 JoeFanning 1 94
(William Haggas) *str: bit on the leg: chsd ldrs: wnt 2nd 8f out tl led 4f out: rdn and gng clr whn edgd lft to stands' rail over 1f out: styd on wl: readily* **3/1**[1]

1131 **2** 7 **Duchess Of Gazeley (IRE)**[14] 7342 3-9-1 **85** SebSanders 7 94
(Dean Ivory) *pushed along leaving stalls: chsd ldrs: hdwy to chse wnr ent fnl 3f: rdn and no ex 2f out: no ch w wnr but plugged on to hold 2nd fnl f* **8/1**

014 **3** ¾ **Silk Sari**[41] 6649 3-9-1 **85** AndreaAtzeni 11 93
(Luca Cumani) *in tch towards rr: rdn and hdwy over 3rd: wnt 3rd wl over 1f out: no ch w wnr but plugged on fnl f* **11/2**[3]

3132 **4** 2¼ **Hold On Tight (IRE)**[76] 5542 3-8-10 **80** JimCrowley 10 84
(Ralph Beckett) *in tch in midfield: rdn and effrt ent fnl 3f: no ch w wnr and plugged on same pce fr over 1f out* **8/1**

5-14 **5** 2¾ **Headline News (IRE)**[11] 7424 4-9-7 **85** ChrisCatlin 12 85
(Rae Guest) *stdd s: t.k.h: hld up in tch in rr: hdwy 3f out: sn rdn: plugged on same pce and no imp over 1f out* **12/1**

5234 **6** 1¾ **Pompeia**[24] 7105 3-8-8 **78** (p) JimmyQuinn 3 75
(Ralph Beckett) *in tch in midfield: rdn and effrt over 3f out: drvn and outpcd ent fnl 2f: n.d and plugged on same pce after* **25/1**

123 **7** 1 **Willow Beck**[41] 6649 4-9-5 **88** OisinMurphy(5) 8 83
(John Gosden) *in tch in midfield: hdwy 4f out: drvn and effrt wl over 2f out: 3rd and no ex 2f out: sn btn and wknd over 1f out* **5/1**[2]

5533 **8** 27 **Near Time**[31] 6926 3-8-4 **74** oh2 DavidProbert 5 26
(Andrew Balding) *stdd s: hld up in tch towards rr: rdn 4f out: sn btn: t.o over 1f out: eased ins fnl f* **16/1**

4515 **9** 4 **Wizara (IRE)**[17] 7267 3-8-6 **76** SilvestreDeSousa 9 22
(Saeed bin Suroor) *stdd s: t.k.h: hld up in tch in rr: rdn and short-lived effrt over 3f out: sn lost tch: t.o over 1f out: eased ins fnl f* **20/1**

3032 **10** 1¾ **Ice Pie**[24] 7105 3-8-5 **75** PaulHanagan 4 18
(Tom Dascombe) *lw: led tl 4f out: sn rdn and dropped out: wl btn 2f out: t.o and eased ins fnl f* **8/1**

166 **11** 4 **Premium**[120] 3990 3-9-0 **84** JamesDoyle 6 21
(Charles Hills) *chsd ldr tl 8f out: styd chsng ldrs tl rdn and dropped out over 3f out: t.o and eased ins fnl f* **20/1**

451 **12** 3 **Silk Train**[64] 5925 3-8-4 **74** oh1 MartinLane 2 6
(David Simcock) *lengthy: lw: in tch in midfield: rdn and lost pl 4f out: lost tch 3f out: t.o and eased ins fnl f* **50/1**

2m 36.37s (4.37) **Going Correction** +0.325s/f (Good)
WFA 3 from 4yo 6lb 12 Ran SP% **119.3**
Speed ratings (Par 104): **98,93,92,91,89 88,87,69,67,65 63,61**
toteswingers 1&2 £5.00, 1&3 £6.40, 2&3 £11.10 CSF £26.06 CT £128.91 TOTE £3.50: £1.60, £2.30, £2.40; EX 25.50 Trifecta £219.20 Pool: £4614.00 - 15.78 winning units..

Owner B Haggas **Bred** J B Haggas **Trained** Newmarket, Suffolk

FOCUS
A good end-of-season handicap and quite competitive on paper. The easy winner is bred to be lot better than her mark and stepped up on her debut win.

7660 MILOS SEAFOOD & NORFOLK COUNTY ICE CREAM H'CAP 2m
3:40 (3:43) (Class 3) (0-90,87) 3-Y-O+ **£7,439** (£2,213; £1,106; £553) **Stalls** Centre

Form RPR

0000 **1** **Sohar**[20] 7193 5-9-4 **77** TomQueally 9 91
(James Toller) *dwlt: in tch in rr: clsd to trck ldrs 4f out: clr w rival and led on bit 2f out: rdn hands and heels and fnd enough to assert ins fnl f: eased last strides* **7/1**[3]

3211 **2** ½ **Ballinderry Boy**[28] 6992 3-9-0 **87** OisinMurphy(5) 1 100
(Andrew Balding) *chsd ldrs: led wl over 3f out and sn clr w 2 rivals: clr w wnr whn hdd and drvn 2f out: styd upsides cruising wnr: unable qck ins fnl f* **11/8**[1]

0-01 **3** 10 **Shelford (IRE)**[45] 6504 4-10-0 **87** AndrewMullen 10 88
(Michael Appleby) *in tch in midfield: hdwy to chse ldrs 4f out: 4th and outpcd u.p over 3f out: no ch w ldng pair 2f out: plugged on to go modest 3rd ins fnl f* **8/1**

2045 **4** 8 **Our Folly**[19] 7217 5-9-0 **73** (tp) SilvestreDeSousa 5 65
(Stuart Kittow) *hld up in last pair: hdwy to chse ldrs 5f out: rdn to chal and drew clr w 2 rivals 3f out: 3rd and btn 2f out: wknd and lost 3rd ins fnl f* **20/1**

13/1 **5** 12 **Secret Edge**[7] 7506 5-8-2 **68** oh1 RobJFitzpatrick(7) 6 45
(Alan King) *lw: in tch in midfield: rdn and struggling over 4f out: 5th and wknd 3f out: t.o fnl 2f* **6/1**[2]

2430 **6** 30 **Presto Volante (IRE)**[28] 6992 5-9-7 **80** (p) JimCrowley 8 21
(Amanda Perrett) *in tch in last trio: rdn and effrt over 5f out: 6th and wl btn 3f out: t.o fnl 2f* **14/1**

303- **7** 32 **Pistol (IRE)**[20] 4294 4-9-2 **75** (v) ChrisCatlin 3
(Philip Hobbs) *chsd ldr tl 5f out: sn dropped out: wl t.o fnl 3f* **20/1**

0342 **8** *nse* **Theology**[20] 7210 6-10-0 **87** PaulHanagan 2
(Steve Gollings) *led tl wl over 3f out: sn dropped out and wl btn: t.o and eased fnl 2f* **16/1**

6120 **9** 7 **Man Of Plenty**[14] 7338 4-9-12 **85** (p) JamesDoyle 7
(Ed Dunlop) *in tch in midfield: rdn and lost pl 5f out: wl t.o fnl 3f* **14/1**

15 **10** ¾ **Silent Movie (IRE)**[18] 7242 3-9-0 **82** JoeFanning 4
(Mark Johnston) *chsd ldrs tl rdn and dropped to rr over 5f out: wl t.o fnl 3f* **14/1**

3m 32.87s (2.37) **Going Correction** +0.325s/f (Good)
WFA 3 from 4yo+ 9lb 10 Ran SP% **115.4**
Speed ratings (Par 107): **107,106,101,97,91 76,60,60,57,56**
toteswingers 1&2 £3.20, 1&3 £9.30, 2&3 £3.60 CSF £16.76 CT £77.84 TOTE £8.20: £3.20, £1.30, £2.90; EX 21.50 Trifecta £145.10 Pool: £5460.82 - 28.22 winning units..

Owner G B Partnership **Bred** G B Partnership **Trained** Newmarket, Suffolk

FOCUS
They went a good gallop in the conditions and just two mattered from some way out. The winner is rated back to her previous best, which came in this race last year.

7661 YACHTIES CARIBBEAN & FIRESIDE BARS APPRENTICE JOCKEYS' TRAINING SERIES FINAL (H'CAP) 1m
4:15 (4:15) (Class 4) (0-85,80) 3-Y-0+ **£4,690** (£1,395; £697; £348) **Stalls** High

Form RPR
504 **1** **Falcon's Reign (FR)**[153] 2889 4-8-8 **67**.......................... DanielMuscutt 9 77
(Michael Appleby) *t.k.h: hld up in tch in midfield: rdn to chse ldr over 1f out: edgd lft ins fnl f: styd on to ld wl ins fnl f: gng away at fin* **13/2**[3]
4101 **2** *1* **Handheld**[23] 7132 6-8-13 **72**..(p) ShelleyBirkett 4 80
(Julia Feilden) *chsd ldr tl led 2f out: sn rdn: drvn ins fnl f: hdd and no ex wl ins fnl f* **3/1**[1]
0-1 **3** *6* **Modernstone**[18] 7253 3-9-5 **80**.. OisinMurphy 8 74
(William Knight) *str: in tch in last trio: rdn 1/2-way: outpcd and btn wl over 1f out: n.d but kpt on to go 3rd ins fnl f* **7/2**[2]
0251 **4** *1* **Greyfriarschorista**[29] 6970 6-8-13 **72**.................................... TimClark 6 64
(Tom Keddy) *hld up in tch in last trio: rdn and effrt wl over 1f out: no ch w ldng pair but modest 3rd 1f out: no imp and lost 3rd ins fnl f* **11/1**
1444 **5** *2 1/4* **Gabrial's Wawa**[126] 3756 3-8-8 **76**................................ RhiainIngram(7) 2 63
(Roger Ingram) *b: led tl 2f out: sn rdn and unable qck: 3rd and btn over 1f out: wknd fnl f* **14/1**
4032 **6** *7* **Kalk Bay (IRE)**[7] 7499 6-9-7 **80**......................................(bt[1]) NoelGarbutt 3 51
(Michael Easterby) *hld up in tch: hdwy to chse ldrs 3f out: rdn and unable qck 2f out: sn wknd* **7/2**[2]
6205 **7** *nse* **Ocean Applause**[6] 7531 3-8-10 **76**.......................(t) JordonMcMurray(5) 1 47
(John Ryan) *in tch in midfield: rdn and unable qck ent fnl 2f: sn wknd* **10/1**
1010 **8** *17* **Excellent Jem**[21] 7164 4-8-13 **72**..(p) IanBurns 7
(Jane Chapple-Hyam) *a in rr: rdn and struggling 3f out: wknd over 2f out: t.o and eased ins fnl f* **16/1**

1m 42.57s (3.97) **Going Correction** +0.65s/f (Yiel)
WFA 3 from 4yo+ 2lb **8** Ran SP% **112.8**
Speed ratings (Par 105): **106,105,99,98,95 88,88,71**
toteswingers 1&2 £5.80, 1&3 £5.70, 2&3 £4.20 CSF £25.58 CT £79.23 TOTE £6.70: £2.20, £1.50, £2.00; EX 36.40 Trifecta £149.00 Pool: £3453.29 - 17.37 winning units..
Owner Michael Appleby **Bred** Rabbah Bloodstock Ltd **Trained** Danethorpe, Notts

FOCUS
Once again two came clear in this handicap. The first two look better than ever.
T/Plt: £109.00. Pool: £64,903.90 - 434.33 winning units. T/Qpdt: £88.30. Pool: £5604.46 - 46.95 winning units. SP

[7600]WOLVERHAMPTON (A.W) (L-H)
Friday, November 1

OFFICIAL GOING: Standard
Wind: Light behind until easing later on Weather: Rain clearing

7662 32RED.COM NOVICE STKS 7f 32y(P)
4:25 (4:25) (Class 5) 2-Y-0 **£2,587** (£770; £384; £192) **Stalls** High

Form RPR
521 **1** **Toast Of New York (USA)**[49] 6365 2-9-2 78.................... AdamKirby 6 99
(Jamie Osborne) *mde all: qcknd clr 2f out: rdn out* **10/11**[1]
2105 **2** *16* **Inyordreams**[39] 6695 2-9-0 74.. DaleSwift 3 58
(James Given) *chsd ldrs: rdn over 2f out: sn outpcd: wnt remote 2nd wl ins fnl f* **10/1**
21 **3** *1 1/2* **Miss Atomic Bomb**[29] 6981 2-8-11 78.............................. MartinHarley 5 51
(Marco Botti) *sn trcking wnr: shkn up over 2f out: outpcd fr wl over 1f out* **11/4**[2]
000 **4** *7* **Slingsby**[14] 7341 2-9-0 0... GrahamGibbons 4 37
(Michael Easterby) *chsd ldrs: rdn 3f out: wknd 2f out* **100/1**
21 **5** *8* **Black Schnapps (IRE)**[16] 7301 2-9-2 0............................ MartinDwyer 2 19
(William Muir) *chsd ldrs: rdn 1/2-way: wknd over 2f out* **7/2**[3]
0 **6** *14* **The Cat**[39] 6681 2-8-4 0..[1] ConnorBeasley(5) 1
(Linda Perratt) *s.i.s: sn outpcd* **100/1**

1m 28.38s (-1.22) **Going Correction** +0.15s/f (Slow) **6** Ran SP% **112.3**
Speed ratings (Par 96): **112,93,92,84,74 58**
toteswingers 1&2 £3.10, 1&3 £1.20, 2&3 £3.50 CSF £11.73 TOTE £1.80: £1.10, £5.70; EX 8.10 Trifecta £25.50 Pool: £3120.25 - 91.66 winning units..
Owner Michael Buckley **Bred** Ashleigh Stud, F Ramos And J Ramos **Trained** Upper Lambourn, Berks
■ Stewards' Enquiry : Adam Kirby 18-day ban (6-days deferred until Jan 28) - hitting a horse when clearly winning (5th offence in 6 months) (Nov 15-28)

FOCUS
This was a decent novice race for the surface, and they finished at long intervals.

7663 32RED FILLIES' H'CAP 7f 32y(P)
4:55 (4:55) (Class 5) (0-75,74) 3-Y-0+ **£3,234** (£962; £481; £240) **Stalls** High

Form RPR
1043 **1** **Amosite**[68] 5798 7-9-2 **69**..(v) MartinHarley 2 78
(J R Jenkins) *mde all: clr 5f out: rdn over 1f out: edgd rt ins fnl f: styd on: unchal* **10/1**
-221 **2** *1 3/4* **Bouyrin (IRE)**[246] 821 3-9-6 **74**.. AdamKirby 5 77
(Michael Bell) *prom: rdn to chse wnr over 1f out: edgd lft ins fnl f: styd on* **4/1**[2]
0546 **3** *1 1/4* **Hannahs Turn**[13] 7381 3-8-12 **66**.. LukeMorris 7 66
(Chris Dwyer) *s.i.s: hld up: nt clr run over 1f out: r.o ins fnl f: nvr trbld ldrs* **12/1**
420 **4** *1/2* **Broughtons Charm (IRE)**[29] 6977 3-9-4 **72**.................... GrahamLee 6 70
(Willie Musson) *hld up: rdn over 1f out: r.o ins fnl f: nvr nrr* **2/1**[1]
4305 **5** *1* **Alluring Star**[13] 7381 5-8-7 **60**.. JamesSullivan 4 57
(Michael Easterby) *chsd wnr: rdn over 2f out: lost 2nd over 1f out: styd on same pce fnl f* **7/1**[3]
3434 **6** *5* **Ray Of Joy**[13] 7381 7-9-2 **69**.. GrahamGibbons 1 52
(J R Jenkins) *chsd ldrs: rdn over 2f out: wknd fnl f* **9/1**
3-55 **7** *24* **La Belle Epoque (USA)**[42] 6611 3-8-6 **65**.................(b) JoeyHaynes(5) 3
(Gerard Butler) *s.i.s: hdwy over 5f out: rdn and wknd 1/2-way* **4/1**[2]

1m 30.03s (0.43) **Going Correction** +0.15s/f (Slow)
WFA 3 from 5yo+ 1lb **7** Ran SP% **112.6**
Speed ratings (Par 100): **103,101,99,99,97 92,64**
toteswingers 1&2 £3.10, 1&3 £23.90, 2&3 £7.50 CSF £47.87 TOTE £7.60: £4.80, £1.90; EX 47.00 Trifecta £283.00 Pool: £3556.90 - 9.42 winning units..
Owner Mrs Claire Goddard **Bred** Richard Kent **Trained** Royston, Herts

FOCUS
This was a middling race, but several of these fillies haven't been at their peak in recent races. The time was modest and the form may not prove solid.

7664 32RED CASINO MEDIAN AUCTION MAIDEN STKS 7f 32y(P)
5:25 (5:25) (Class 6) 2-Y-0 **£1,940** (£577; £288; £144) **Stalls** High

Form RPR
05 **1** **Just Rubie**[18] 7244 2-9-0 0.. MartinHarley 6 65
(Michael Blanshard) *chsd ldr tl led wl over 1f out: sn rdn: edgd rt u.p ins fnl f: jst hld on* **50/1**
2 *hd* **Choice Of Destiny** 2-9-0 0.. WilliamCarson 8 64
(Philip McBride) *hld up: hdwy over 2f out: nt clr run over 1f out: rdn and r.o wl towards fin* **7/1**
000 **3** *1/2* **Star Anise (FR)**[44] 6523 2-9-0 62.................................... SamHitchcott 1 63
(Harry Dunlop) *a.p: rdn over 2f out: edgd rt ins fnl f: r.o u.p* **12/1**
4 **4** *4* **Twin Appeal (IRE)**[23] 7126 2-9-5 0........................... GrahamGibbons 10 58
(David Barron) *chsd ldrs: rdn and hung rt 1/2-way: no ex ins fnl f* **10/11**[1]
0 **5** *2 1/2* **Tahchee**[18] 7251 2-9-5 0... LukeMorris 9 52
(James Fanshawe) *s.i.s: sn prom: rdn over 1f out: n.m.r and wknd ins fnl f* **9/2**[2]
6 *1/2* **Frankthetank (IRE)** 2-9-5 0... TomEaves 5 51
(Keith Dalgleish) *led: pushed along over 2f out: rdn and hdd wl over 1f out: wknd fnl f* **13/2**[3]
60 **7** *1 1/2* **Lady Bubbles**[34] 6821 2-9-0 0... JamesSullivan 7 42
(Michael Easterby) *hld up: rdn over 2f out: n.d* **20/1**
50 **8** *13* **Crazy Dancer**[57] 5827 2-9-0 0.............................. RobbieFitzpatrick 3 10
(Richard Guest) *s.i.s: in rr: rdn and wknd 1/2-way* **50/1**
9 *1* **Rose Boeuf (FR)** 2-9-0 0.. DavidNolan 2 8
(David O'Meara) *sn pushed along in rr: wknd over 2f out* **14/1**

1m 32.45s (2.85) **Going Correction** +0.15s/f (Slow) **9** Ran SP% **119.4**
Speed ratings (Par 94): **89,88,88,83,80 80,78,63,62**
toteswingers 1&2 £31.70, 1&3 £22.90, 2&3 £16.30 CSF £374.46 TOTE £17.50: £4.40, £3.00, £3.00; EX 496.30 Trifecta £2139.70 Part won. Pool: £2853.06 - 0.97 winning units..
Owner D A Poole **Bred** David Poole **Trained** Upper Lambourn, Berks

FOCUS
This looked a winnable race, but the favourite didn't live up to expectations.

7665 32RED ON THE APP STORE NURSERY H'CAP 5f 20y(P)
5:55 (5:56) (Class 6) (0-60,59) 2-Y-0 **£1,940** (£577; £288; £144) **Stalls** Low

Form RPR
5606 **1** **Dynamo Walt (IRE)**[16] 7293 2-9-1 **53**.............................(v) RaulDaSilva 9 65+
(Derek Shaw) *hld up: hdwy 1/2-way: shkn up to ld ins fnl f: r.o wl* **11/2**[2]
0504 **2** *2 1/2* **Where The Boys Are (IRE)**[20] 7199 2-9-6 **58**.......... GrahamGibbons 7 59
(Ed McMahon) *chsd ldr: rdn and ev ch ins fnl f: styd on same pce* **8/1**
2364 **3** *2 1/4* **Anfield**[29] 6967 2-8-13 **51**... PatCosgrave 6 44
(Mick Quinn) *led: rdn over 1f out: hdd and no ex ins fnl f* **7/1**[3]
0000 **4** *1 1/4* **Clear Focus (IRE)**[29] 6979 2-8-12 **50**...............................(p) JackMitchell 8 38
(Brendan Powell) *prom: rdn 1/2-way: edgd lft over 1f out: styd on same pce* **20/1**
0003 **5** *nk* **Back On Baileys**[16] 7293 2-9-2 **54**.. LukeMorris 1 41
(Chris Dwyer) *edgd rt s: prom: hmpd and lost pl over 4f out: styd on u.p fr over 1f out: nt trble ldrs* **7/2**[1]
6066 **6** *1 3/4* **Almost Famous (IRE)**[20] 7198 2-8-11 **49**..........................(b) JohnFahy 2 30
(Jamie Osborne) *hmpd s: pushed along in rr early: rdn over 1f out: nvr on terms* **8/1**
633 **7** *1/2* **Rebel Code (USA)**[74] 5590 2-9-3 **55**................................... GrahamLee 5 34
(James Given) *trckd ldrs: t.k.h: rdn and hung lft over 1f out: wknd fnl f* **7/2**[1]
1560 **8** *3 3/4* **Limegrove**[20] 7199 2-9-5 **57**.. AdamKirby 3 23
(David Evans) *sn pushed along in rr: nvr on terms* **11/2**[2]
5433 **9** *4* **Resist**[92] 4910 2-9-7 **59**..(t) HarryBentley 10 10
(Tobias B P Coles) *mid-div: pushed along over 3f out: sme hdwy u.p wl over 1f out: sn wknd* **14/1**
4400 **10** *2 1/4* **Doncaster Belle (IRE)**[7] 7494 2-9-2 **54**..............(e[1]) RobbieFitzpatrick 12
(Charles Smith) *prom: sn pushed along: lost pl wl over 3f out: sn bhd* **50/1**
0540 **11** *5* **Boston Alex (IRE)**[41] 6654 2-8-12 **50**..............................(p) LiamKeniry 4
(Conor Dore) *chsd ldrs: edgd lft over 4f out: rdn 1/2-way: sn wknd* **40/1**
530 **12** *1/2* **Paradise Child**[20] 7198 2-8-3 **48**.. RyanWhile(7) 11
(Bill Turner) *sn pushed along and prom: rdn 1/2-way: sn wknd* **40/1**

1m 2.95s (0.65) **Going Correction** +0.15s/f (Slow) **12** Ran SP% **128.2**
Speed ratings (Par 94): **100,96,92,90,89 87,86,80,73,70 62,61**
toteswingers 1&2 £9.10, 1&3 £9.30, 2&3 £11.20 CSF £51.87 CT £326.25 TOTE £8.20: £2.80, £3.40, £2.60; EX 68.10 Trifecta £472.00 Pool: £2203.88 - 3.50 winning units..
Owner Brian Johnson (Northamptonshire) **Bred** Dan Major **Trained** Sproxton, Leics

FOCUS
This was a modest nursery, but the winner is progressive at a realistic level.

7666 CORAL APP DOWNLOAD FROM THE APP STORE H'CAP (DIV I) 1m 1f 103y(P)
6:25 (6:25) (Class 6) (0-60,60) 3-Y-0 **£1,940** (£577; £288; £144) **Stalls** Low

Form RPR
5115 **1** **Let Me In (IRE)**[13] 7378 3-9-5 **58**..................................(v) DavidProbert 4 71+
(Patrick Chamings) *a.p: rdn to ld 1f out: r.o wl* **11/8**[1]
0040 **2** *3* **Platinum Proof (USA)**[6] 7543 3-8-9 **48**................(bt[1]) GrahamGibbons 8 52
(David O'Meara) *trckd ldr: rdn over 2f out: ev ch over 1f out: styd on same pce ins fnl f* **10/1**
6006 **3** *1 3/4* **Continental Divide (IRE)**[15] 7325 3-9-7 **60**....................(p) AdamKirby 1 60
(Jamie Osborne) *led: pushed along and qcknd over 2f out: rdn and hdd 1f out: no ex ins fnl f* **8/1**
3262 **4** *3/4* **Polar Forest**[13] 7378 3-9-0 **58**.................................(e) ConnorBeasley(5) 2 57
(Richard Guest) *hmpd s: sn mid-div: hdwy over 3f out: rdn and ev ch over 1f out: edgd lft and no ex ins fnl f* **11/4**[2]
0060 **5** *1* **Uncle Bernie (IRE)**[13] 7379 3-9-0 **53**................................(p) ShaneKelly 9 50
(Andrew Hollinshead) *hld up: t.k.h: hdwy wl over 1f out: n.m.r sn after: rdn and wknd wl ins fnl f* **16/1**
5022 **6** *3* **My Claire**[14] 7351 3-8-12 **51**.. AdamBeschizza 3 41
(Nigel Tinkler) *chsd ldrs: rdn over 2f out: ev ch over 1f out: wknd ins fnl f* **15/2**[3]
0000 **7** *1/2* **Silver Fawn (IRE)**[7] 7514 3-8-2 **46**..........................(be) JoeyHaynes(5) 7 35
(John Weymes) *mid-div: rdn over 2f out: carried wd wl over 1f out: hung lft and wknd fnl f* **16/1**
0-00 **8** *3 1/2* **Last Chance Ranch**[291] 212 3-8-7 **46** oh1...................[1] RaulDaSilva 6 28
(Derek Shaw) *s.i.s: a in rr* **100/1**

006 9 3 1/2 **Inigo Montoya**[7] 7514 3-8-5 49 ShirleyTeasdale(5) 5 24
(Alan McCabe) *s.i.s: a in rr* 33/1

2m 3.95s (2.25) **Going Correction** +0.15s/f (Slow) 9 Ran SP% **116.4**
Speed ratings (Par 98): **96,93,91,91,90 87,87,84,80**
toteswingers 1&2 £3.70, 1&3 £5.60, 2&3 £13.90 CSF £17.10 CT £84.08 TOTE £2.80: £1.20, £2.70, £2.70; EX 18.30 Trifecta £155.20 Pool: £1894.05 - 9.14 winning units..
Owner Select Racing Bloodstock Ltd **Bred** Epona Bloodstock Ltd **Trained** Baughurst, Hants

FOCUS
With the exception of the winner, these were either out of form or generally hard to win with. Muddling form, rated a bit cautiously around the winner.

7667 CORAL APP DOWNLOAD FROM THE APP STORE H'CAP (DIV II) 1m 1f 103y(P)
6:55 (6:56) (Class 6) (0-60,60) 3-Y-O £1,940 (£577; £288; £144) Stalls Low

Form RPR
4124 1 **Ana Shababiya (IRE)**[20] 7204 3-9-7 60 HarryBentley 7 74
(Ismail Mohammed) *led: hdd 8f out: trckd ldr tl led again over 2f out: rdn clr fnl f* 4/1[2]
221 2 3 1/4 **Poppy Bond**[14] 7351 3-8-13 52 LiamKeniry 9 59
(Alan Bailey) *hld up: t.k.h: hdwy over 6f out: pushed along over 2f out: styd on to go 2nd towards fin: no ch w wnr* 4/1[2]
601 3 1 1/4 **Olivers Mount**[13] 7378 3-8-11 50 (t) JimmyQuinn 8 54
(Ed Vaughan) *trckd ldrs: jnd wnr over 2f out: rdn over 1f out: no ex ins fnl f* 9/4[1]
6002 4 6 **Windsor Secret**[7] 7514 3-8-7 46 oh1 (p) TomEaves 3 38
(Keith Dalgleish) *led over 8f out: rdn and hdd over 2f out: hung rt and wknd over 1f out* 10/1
6004 5 1 1/2 **Rocky Two (IRE)**[6] 7543 3-9-1 54 DavidNolan 1 43
(David O'Meara) *trckd ldrs: t.k.h: rdn over 3f out: wknd 2f out* 8/1[3]
003 6 3/4 **The Bay Tigress**[21] 7167 3-8-6 48 oh1 ow2 MarkCoumbe(3) 4 35
(Lisa Williamson) *hld up: rdn over 3f out: a in rr* 25/1
4553 7 4 **Penang Power**[27] 7035 3-8-1 47 LouisSteward(7) 6 26
(Michael Bell) *n.m.r after s: pushed along early towards rr: rdn and wknd over 2f out* 12/1
5640 8 2 **Sakhees Romance**[57] 5016 3-8-9 48 [1] LukeMorris 2 22
(Philip Kirby) *prom: pushed along over 4f out: rdn and wknd over 2f out* 20/1
2010 9 53 **Scepticism (USA)**[20] 7201 3-9-0 58 JoshBaudains(5) 5
(Charlie Mann) *prom: hmpd and lost pl after 1f: last and rdn over 3f out: sn wknd and eased* 11/1

2m 3.25s (1.55) **Going Correction** +0.15s/f (Slow) 9 Ran SP% **115.6**
Speed ratings (Par 98): **99,96,95,89,88 87,84,82,35**
toteswingers 1&2 £3.00, 1&3 £2.10, 2&3 £1.20 CSF £20.44 CT £43.94 TOTE £5.40: £1.40, £1.60, £1.30; EX 17.20 Trifecta £61.50 Pool: £1621.82 - 19.76 winning units..
Owner Ahmad Abdulla Al Shaikh **Bred** Thomas Hassett **Trained** Newmarket, Suffolk
■ Stewards' Enquiry : Jimmy Quinn three-day ban: careless riding (Nov 15,16,18)

FOCUS
There was a bit more depth here than in the first division, but yet again the winner was by far the best. This rates a clear personal best.

7668 32RED.COM H'CAP 2m 119y(P)
7:25 (7:26) (Class 6) (0-60,60) 3-Y-O+ £1,940 (£577; £288; £144) Stalls Low

Form RPR
4033 1 **Mr Burbidge**[13] 7382 5-9-8 56 (b) LiamKeniry 11 72
(Neil Mulholland) *hld up: hdwy over 3f out: shkn up to ld over 1f out: sn rdn: styd on wl: eased towards fin* 9/1
0055 2 3 1/2 **High On A Hill (IRE)**[23] 6470 6-9-9 57 (v) PatCosgrave 8 68
(Iain Jardine) *hld up in tch: led over 2f out: rdn: hung lft and hdd over 1f out: no ex ins fnl f* 16/1
3223 3 3 3/4 **Train Hard**[6] 7543 3-8-13 56 JoeFanning 6 63
(Mark Johnston) *a.p: chsd ldr 12f out tl led over 3f out: pushed along and hdd over 2f out: styd on same pce fr over 1f out* 2/1[2]
0006 4 10 **Jawaab (IRE)**[32] 6909 9-9-4 52 (v) MichaelO'Connell 1 47
(Philip Kirby) *hld up: rdn over 3f out: nvr nrr* 8/1[3]
4212 5 3/4 **Luckster**[12] 7395 3-9-0 57 AdamKirby 4 51
(David Evans) *chsd ldrs: rn in snatches: drvn along over 6f out: outpcd over 5f out: wknd over 2f out* 7/4[1]
3255 6 2 3/4 **Geanie Mac (IRE)**[18] 7239 4-9-7 60 (p) SamanthaBell(5) 10 50
(Linda Perratt) *prom tl rdn and wknd over 2f out* 20/1
U54/ 7 2 1/2 **Pearl (IRE)**[640] 7704 9-8-12 46 DavidProbert 5 33
(Ron Hodges) *hld up: rdn and wknd over 3f out* 40/1
040/ 8 6 **Highland River**[35] 1983 7-8-11 48 CharlesBishop(3) 2 28
(Dave Roberts) *hld up: rdn over 4f out: sn wknd* 40/1
0030 9 1 3/4 **Forrest Flyer (IRE)**[14] 7342 9-9-11 59 GrahamLee 7 37
(Jim Goldie) *prom: led 14f out: rdn and hdd over 3f out: wknd over 2f out* 12/1
406/ 10 55 **Miles Of Sunshine**[833] 4274 8-8-9 48 PhilipPrince(5) 3
(Ron Hodges) *led: hdd 14f out: chsd ldrs: rdn over 5f out: wknd over 3f out* 50/1

3m 44.16s (2.36) **Going Correction** +0.15s/f (Slow)
WFA 3 from 4yo+ 9lb 10 Ran SP% **116.0**
Speed ratings (Par 101): **100,98,96,91,91 90,89,86,85,59**
toteswingers 1&2 £64.40, 1&3 £7.40, 2&3 £15.80 CSF £132.30 CT £401.67 TOTE £9.00: £2.20, £5.60, £1.10; EX 79.10 Trifecta £1119.00 Pool: £1820.36 - 1.22 winning units..
Owner Dajam Ltd **Bred** M Burbidge **Trained** Limpley Stoke, Wilts

FOCUS
The gallop was just a solid medium for these stayers, but only three were in contention in the last 3f. Modest form, with improvement from the winner.

7669 LADBROKES MOBILE H'CAP 1m 141y(P)
7:55 (7:55) (Class 5) (0-70,70) 3-Y-O+ £2,587 (£770; £384; £192) Stalls Low

Form RPR
0030 1 **Elspeth's Boy (USA)**[18] 7238 6-8-7 63 EvaMoscrop(7) 6 78
(Philip Kirby) *s.i.s: hld up: hdwy 1/2-way: led over 1f out: r.o wl* 10/1
3262 2 3 3/4 **Hanalei Bay (IRE)**[7] 7515 3-8-10 62 TomEaves 8 69
(Keith Dalgleish) *s.i.s: hdwy over 6f out: rdn and ev ch over 1f out: styd on same pce ins fnl f* 5/2[1]
0425 3 5 **Oilinda**[78] 5430 3-8-10 69 LouisSteward(7) 3 65
(Michael Bell) *led: hdd over 3f out: led again over 2f out: rdn and hdd over 1f out: hung lft and wknd ins fnl f* 10/1
6231 4 1 **Candy Kitten**[13] 7377 3-9-1 67 (p) LukeMorris 2 61
(Alastair Lidderdale) *hld up: plld hrd: hdwy over 5f out: rdn and wknd over 1f out* 13/2[3]
4032 5 3/4 **Fame Again**[94] 4850 5-9-7 70 [1] GrahamGibbons 4 61
(Michael Easterby) *rrd s: hld up: drvn along over 3f out: nvr nrr* 7/2[2]
5433 6 3 **Royal Straight**[18] 7238 8-8-10 64 (t) SamanthaBell(5) 10 48
(Linda Perratt) *hld up: rdn over 2f out: n.d* 7/1
062 7 3 3/4 **Glenridding**[34] 6855 9-9-0 63 (p) DaleSwift 5 38
(James Given) *chsd ldr tl rdn over 3f out: wknd over 1f out* 20/1
200- 8 23 **Ebony Clarets**[377] 7256 4-8-11 60 GrahamLee 1
(Linda Perratt) *chsd ldrs: rdn 1/2-way: sn wknd* 25/1
3500 9 1 3/4 **Bussa**[31] 6928 5-9-2 65 AdamKirby 7
(David Evans) *chsd ldrs: led over 3f out: rdn: hdd & wknd over 2f out* 7/1

1m 51.0s (0.50) **Going Correction** +0.15s/f (Slow)
WFA 3 from 4yo+ 3lb 9 Ran SP% **115.9**
Speed ratings (Par 103): **103,99,95,94,93 91,87,67,65**
toteswingers 1&2 £5.30, 1&3 £47.50, 2&3 £13.00 CSF £35.43 CT £264.67 TOTE £13.80: £3.90, £1.20, £4.40; EX 44.50 Trifecta £622.70 Pool: £1946.10 - 2.34 winning units..
Owner Preesall Garage **Bred** S M D Ltd **Trained** Middleham, N Yorks

FOCUS
This was a routine Polytrack handicap, and a number of these will have their day some time during the winter. The winner's best run since early last year.
T/Plt: £372.90. Pool: £80,448.05 - 157.47 winning units. T/Qpdt: £208.20. Pool: £12,560.82 - 44.64 winning units. CR

7670 - 7677a (Foreign Racing) - See Raceform Interactive

7558 CAPANNELLE (R-H)
Friday, November 1

OFFICIAL GOING: Turf: good

7678a PREMIO GUIDO BERARDELLI (GROUP 3) (2YO) (TURF) 1m 1f
3:10 (12:00) 2-Y-O £28,455 (£12,520; £6,829; £3,414)

RPR
1 **Gentleman Only (IRE)** 2-8-11 0 FabioBranca 1 105
(S Botti, Italy) *trckd ldr: shkn up to ld 2 1/2f out: rdn clr fr over 1 1/2f out: wl clr ent fnl f: won easing down* 6/5[1]
2 4 **Bertinoro (IRE)** 2-8-11 0 CFiocchi 4 97
(S Botti, Italy) *dwlt: settled in rr: hdwy on outer over 2 1/2f out: sn rdn: styd on wl fnl f: no ch w wnr* 9/2
3 1/2 **Vallecupa (ITY)**[124] 2-8-8 0 DPerovic 2 93
(D Zarroli, Italy) *towards rr: hdwy over 2f out: styd on u.p fnl f: nrest at fin* 216/10
4 3 1/2 **Ratmansky (ITY)** 2-8-11 0 (b) SDiana 7 89
(F Camici, Italy) *trckd ldr: rdn and nt qckn 2 1/2f out: one pce fnl f* 26/5
5 hd **Windfinder**[40] 2-8-11 0 CColombi 3 89
(M Guarnieri, Italy) *midfield: rdn and no imp over 2f out: kpt on at same pce fnl f* 37/10[3]
6 8 **Cospirator (IRE)** 2-8-11 0 DarioVargiu 6 73
(S Botti, Italy) *led: hdd over 2f out: sn rdn and nt qckn: wknd fnl f* 21/10[2]
7 10 **Bridge Orteip (IRE)** 2-8-11 0 PBorrelli 5 53
(Filippo Sbariggia, Italy) *tk v t.k.h in midfield: rdn and wknd fr over 2f out* 77/1

1m 48.86s (-5.84) 7 Ran SP% **139.0**
WIN (incl. 1 euro stake): 2.20. PLACES: 1.45, 1.96. DF: 6.66.
Owner Effevi **Bred** Massimo Parri **Trained** Italy

1131 JEBEL ALI (L-H)
Friday, November 1

OFFICIAL GOING: Dirt: fast

7679a AL SHAFAR INVESTMENT (H'CAP) (DIRT) 1m 1f
10:15 (10:15) (60-75,75) 3-Y-O+ £6,532 (£2,177; £1,197; £653; £326)

RPR
1 **Street Act (USA)**[258] 697 6-9-3 72 (bt) RoystonFfrench 7 82
(A Al Raihe, UAE) *mid-div: smooth prog 3f out: led 1 1/2f out: comf* 9/2[2]
2 7 1/4 **Muhamee (IRE)**[236] 4-8-10 65 (b) CSandoval 8 60
(A bin Huzaim, UAE) *s.i.s: chsd ldrs 3f out: kpt on same pce fnl 2f* 20/1
3 hd **Mark To Market (IRE)**[232] 1003 6-9-3 72 PatDobbs 9 66
(Doug Watson, UAE) *trckd ldng pair: smooth prog to ld 2 1/2f out: hdd 1 1/2f out: kpt on same pce* 5/1[3]
4 7 1/2 **Mr Churchill (IRE)**[224] 1132 4-8-5 60 (b) AdrianNicholls 3 39
(Ismail Mohammed) *sn rdn in rr: kpt on* 12/1
5 3 1/2 **Hazaz (IRE)**[272] 499 4-9-3 72 (t) WayneSmith 1 43
(M Al Muhairi, UAE) *mid-div: rdn 3f out: nvr able to chal* 2/1[1]
6 12 1/2 **Futurist**[979] 6-8-7 62 (b) JRosales 2 7
(A bin Huzaim, UAE) *trckd ldng pair: rdn 3f out: no ex* 16/1
7 nk **Calabash Cove (USA)**[1694] 9-9-6 75 (bt) ADeVries 6 19
(E Charpy, UAE) *trckd ldrs: led 4f out: hdd & wknd 3f out* 8/1
8 3 1/4 **Spanish Wedding**[224] 1131 4-9-0 72 ThomasBrown(3) 4 10
(D Selvaratnam, UAE) *nvr bttr than mid-div* 12/1
P **Kala Kanta (IRE)**[280] 391 7-8-10 65 (bt) RichardMullen 5
(M Ramadan, UAE) *sn led: hdd: wknd and p.u 4f out* 5/1[3]

1m 52.36s (112.36) 9 Ran SP% **122.0**
CSF: 92.70; EX: 95.60; TRIFECTA: 731.70; TRICAST: 477.86; WIN: 7.50; PL: 2.30, 4.70, 3.00.
Owner Sheikh Ahmed Bin Mohammed Al Maktoum **Bred** Larry W Baker Jr & Darley **Trained** UAE

7683a COMMERCIAL BANK OF DUBAI (H'CAP) (DIRT) 6f (D)
12:45 (12:45) (65-80,80) 3-Y-O+ £7,035 (£2,345; £1,289; £703; £351)

RPR
1 **Latkhaf (USA)**[224] 1134 5-9-4 78 RoystonFfrench 5 80
(A Al Raihe, UAE) *chsd ldrs: led 100yds out: r.o gamely* 11/4[1]
2 hd **Journalistic (USA)**[224] 1136 4-9-4 78 PatDobbs 7 79
(M Ibrahim, UAE) *in rr: chsd ldrs 2 1/2f out: r.o fnl 1 1/2f: jst failed* 6/1[3]
3 1 1/2 **Bircham (IRE)**[230] 3-9-3 77 ADeVries 4 74
(Ismail Mohammed) *led in centre: kicked clr 2f out: hdd 100yds out: kpt on same pce* 3/1[2]
4 6 **Firstknight**[238] 941 5-8-5 65 (t) RichardMullen 3 42
(Doug Watson, UAE) *settled in rr: rdn 3 1/2f out: nvr nr to chal* 6/1[3]
5 1 **Backstage Tour**[232] 1003 3-9-6 80 TadhgO'Shea 2 54
(A bin Huzaim, UAE) *s.i.s: a in rr* 13/2
6 8 1/2 **Penniston Line (IRE)**[238] 939 4-9-2 79 ThomasBrown(3) 1 26
(D Selvaratnam, UAE) *slowly away: a in rr* 9/1

1m 12.46s (-0.95) 6 Ran SP% **103.6**
CSF: 16.14; EX: 30.50; TRIFECTA: 102.20; WIN: 4.00; PL: 1.10, 2.20, 1.40.
Owner Khalid Khalifa Al Nabooda **Bred** Darley **Trained** UAE

The Form Book Flat, Raceform Ltd, Compton, RG20 6NL.

7684 - (Foreign Racing) - See Raceform Interactive

7613 SAINT-CLOUD (L-H)

Friday, November 1

OFFICIAL GOING: Turf: very soft

7685a PRIX PERTH (GROUP 3) (3YO+) (TURF) 1m

12:50 (12:00) 3-Y-O+ **£32,520** (£13,008; £9,756; £6,504; £3,252)

RPR

1 **Amaron**[27] [7047] 4-9-0 0 .... FabienLefebvre 5 116
(Andreas Lowe, Germany) *trckd ldrs on inner: rdn to chal over 2f out: led over 1f out: kpt on wl u.p and in control towards fin* **216/10**

2 ¾ **Sommerabend**[26] [7059] 6-9-0 0 .... TheoBachelot 8 114
(M Rulec, Germany) *led: rdn and strly pressed fr over 2f out: hdd over 1f out: kpt on wl u.p but hld towards fin* **27/1**

3 1 ¾ **Sarkiyla (FR)**[26] [7057] 4-8-10 0 .... Christophe-PatriceLemaire 13 110+
(A De Royer-Dupre, France) *hld up towards rr: gng wl whn nt clr run fr over 2f out tl rdn and swtchd lft over 1f out: r.o and wnt 3rd cl home: nvr nrr* **9/1**

4 nk **Pinturicchio (IRE)**[27] [7047] 5-9-0 0 .... AnthonyCrastus 10 109
(E Lellouche, France) *trckd ldrs: rdn over 2f out: wnt 3rd over 1f out: kpt on same pce ins fnl f and dropped to 4th cl home* **63/10[3]**

5 1 ½ **Peace Burg (FR)**[27] [7047] 3-9-0 0 .... ChristopheSoumillon 6 108
(J-C Rouget, France) *midfield: rdn over 2f out: kpt on same pce fr over 1f out and nvr able to chal* **10/1**

6 ½ **Hay Dude**[24] [7116] 3-8-11 0 .... DanielTudhope 9 104
(K R Burke) *midfield: rdn 2f out: kpt on but no threat to ldrs* **19/1**

7 nk **Yellow Rosebud (IRE)**[27] [7047] 4-8-10 0 .... (b) PatSmullen 16 100
(D K Weld, Ire) *trckd ldrs on outer: rdn and effrt to chal over 2f out: sn outpcd by ldrs: kpt on* **11/2[2]**

8 1 ½ **Gris De Reve (FR)**[26] 4-9-0 0 .... CristianDemuro 4 101
(A Lyon, France) *hld up towards rr: rdn and hdwy 2f out: kpt on tl no ex and btn ins fnl f* **14/1**

9 hd **Kokaltash (FR)**[24] [7116] 3-8-11 0 .... ThierryThulliez 3 99
(M Delzangles, France) *midfield on inner: rdn over 2f out: kpt on tl no ex and btn ins fnl f* **14/1**

10 1 ½ **Grand Vintage (FR)**[21] [7186] 4-9-0 0 .... EddyHardouin 15 97
(W Mongil, Germany) *midfield on outer: rdn over 2f out: outpcd and btn ins fnl f* **43/1**

11 1 ½ **Zinabaa (FR)**[21] [7186] 8-9-0 0 .... ThierryJarnet 12 93
(Mlle T Puitg, France) *midfield: pushed along 3f out: nt clr run and dropped to rr over 1f out: kpt on under hands and heels ins fnl f but nt rcvr and nvr threatened* **14/1**

12 ½ **Peace At Last (IRE)**[27] [7047] 3-9-3 0 .... FabriceVeron 2 97
(H-A Pantall, France) *hld up in rr on inner: rdn over 2f out: kpt on but sn outpcd: eased fnl 100yds: nvr threatened* **48/1**

13 1 ¾ **Zack Hope**[39] [6715] 5-9-0 0 .... TonyPiccone 7 88
(N Caullery, France) *dwlt sltly and hld up in rr: rdn over 2f out: short of room on rail fr over 1f out: eased whn ch gone ins fnl f: nvr threatened* **34/1**

14 12 **Topaze Blanche (IRE)**[27] [7047] 3-8-8 0 .... MaximeGuyon 1 56
(C Laffon-Parias, France) *hld up towards rr on inner: rdn over 2f out: no ex and btn over 1f out: sn eased* **5/1[1]**

15 3 ½ **Gengis (FR)**[54] [6251] 3-9-1 0 .... StephanePasquier 11 55
(G Doleuze, France) *t.k.h: prom: rdn and lost pl over 2f out: in rr and btn over 1f out: eased* **16/1**

16 ¾ **Desert Blanc**[27] [7047] 5-9-3 0 .... GregoryBenoist 14 54
(C Baillet, France) *sn w ldr on outer: rdn and lost pl over 2f out: in rr and btn ent fnl f: eased* **17/1**

1m 50.59s (3.09)
WFA 3 from 4yo+ 2lb **16** Ran SP% **116.4**
WIN (incl. 1 euro stake): 22.60. PLACES: 6.90, 7.70, 3.60. DF: 137.40. SF: 248.50.
Owner Gestut Winterhauch **Bred** Genesis Green Stud Ltd **Trained** Germany

FOCUS
The order didn't change that month and the winner, second and ninth set the standard.

7686a CRITERIUM INTERNATIONAL (GROUP 1) (2YO COLTS & FILLIES) (TURF) 1m

1:50 (12:00) 2-Y-O **£116,138** (£46,463; £23,231; £11,605)

RPR

1 **Ectot**[41] [6710] 2-9-0 0 .... GregoryBenoist 4 114
(E Lellouche, France) *t.k.h under restraint early and sn allowed to stride on: led after 2f and mde rest: strly pressed fr 2f out: rdn over 1f out: r.o and asserted under firm hands and heels towards fin: shade cosily* **7/10[1]**

2 ¾ **Earnshaw (USA)**[22] [7160] 2-9-0 0 .... MaximeGuyon 3 112
(A Fabre, France) *cl up: trckd ldr after 2f: rdn to chal 2f out: kpt on wl u.p but nt quite pce of wnr* **23/10[2]**

3 snk **Prestige Vendome (FR)**[36] [6785] 2-9-0 0 .... (p) ThierryThulliez 1 112
(N Clement, France) *trckd early ldr: hld up in rr after 2f out: pushed along to cl over 2f out: rdn to chal and ev ch ent fnl f: kpt on wl but nt quite pce of wnr* **53/10[3]**

4 1 ¾ **Stillman (FR)**[22] [7160] 2-9-0 0 .... (p) ChristopheSoumillon 2 108
(Mario Hofer, Germany) *led 2f: hld up in 3rd once hdd: rdn over 1f out: nt qckn and dropped to last: kpt on but hld ins fnl f* **13/2**

1m 50.93s (3.43) **4** Ran SP% **118.3**
WIN (incl. 1 euro stake): 1.70. PLACES: 1.10, 1.10. SF: 2.50.
Owner G Augustin-Normand & Mme E Vidal **Bred** Ecurie Des Monceaux & Skymarc Farm **Trained** Lamorlaye, France

■ Gregory Benoist's first Group 1 win.

6891 SANTA ANITA (L-H)

Friday, November 1

OFFICIAL GOING: Dirt: fast; turf: firm

7687a BREEDERS' CUP MARATHON (GRADE 2) (3YO+) (DIRT) 1m 6f

8:45 (12:00) 3-Y-O+ **£168,711** (£55,214; £30,674; £18,404; £9,202)

RPR

1 **London Bridge (USA)**[78] [5463] 3-8-10 0 .... (p) MESmith 7 108
(Jo Hughes) *midfield: rdn over 4f out: kpt responding to press and hdwy on outer over 1f out: styd on dourly and led towards fin* **8/1**

2 1 **Blueskiesnrainbows (USA)**[18] 4-9-0 0 .... MartinAPedroza 8 103+
(Jerry Hollendorfer, U.S.A) *trckd ldrs on inner: w ldrs over 4f out: rdn and ev ch 2f out: led ent fnl f: styd on but hdd towards fin and no ex* **8/1**

3 nk **Worldly (USA)**[33] 6-9-0 0 .... DFlores 10 103+
(Brendan P Walsh, U.S.A) *midfield on outer: clsd and w ldrs over 4f out: rdn and ev ch 2f out: styd on but dropped to 3rd and hld towards fin* **13/2[3]**

4 1 ¼ **Suns Out Guns Out (USA)**[41] 4-9-0 0 .... (b) JRLeparoux 5 101+
(Dale Romans, U.S.A) *trckd ldrs on outer: w over ldrs 4f out: rdn and ev ch 2f out: styd on but no ex toward fin: jst hld on for 4th* **12/1**

5 hd **Indian Jones (USA)**[36] 6-9-0 0 .... (b) ACastillo 6 101
(Philip T Aristone, U.S.A) *hld up in detached last: hdwy fr 4f out: rdn over 2f out: styd on wl in st and almost snatched 4th but nvr able to chal* **5/1[2]**

6 3 ¼ **Old Time Hockey (USA)**[32] 4-9-0 0 .... JLezcano 1 96+
(Thomas F Proctor, U.S.A) *t.k.h: midfield on inner: swtchd to outer and clsd on ldrs over 4f out: rdn to chal and ev ch 3f out: outpcd in st: plugged on* **8/1**

7 13 ½ **Pool Play (CAN)**[33] 8-9-0 0 .... ERosaDaSilva 9 77
(Mark Casse, Canada) *hld up last in main body of field: rdn 4f out: no ex and btn ent fnl f: eased* **9/1**

8 2 ¼ **Commander (USA)**[17] 5-9-0 0 .... AGryder 3 74
(Troy Taylor, Canada) *led: hdd over 4f out: lost pl and sn rdn: steadily fdd: in rr and btn ent fnl f: eased* **11/1**

9 4 ¼ **Cease (USA)**[22] 6-9-0 0 .... (b) DCohen 2 68
(David Jacobson, U.S.A) *midfield in tch on inner: rdn and lost pl over 3f out: in rr and btn over 1f out: eased ins fnl f* **12/1**

P **Ever Rider (ARG)**[133] 5-9-0 0 .... GaryStevens 4
(Maria Cristina Munoz, Argentina) *pressed ldr on outer tl wknd rapidly 5f out: eased and p.u* **9/2[1]**

2m 58.32s (178.32)
WFA 3 from 4yo+ 8lb **10** Ran SP% **115.2**
PARI-MUTUEL (all including 2 usd stake): WIN 20.00; PLACE (1-2) 10.20, 9.00; SHOW (1-2-3) 6.40, 6.20, 4.80; SF 192.40.
Owner Waratah Thoroughbreds Pty Ltd **Bred** Patricia S Purdy **Trained** Lambourn, Berks

FOCUS
All credit to the connections of London Bridge, whose enterprise in taking this previously unheralded colt to the States was greatly rewarded, but a staying race on a dirt surface just doesn't work as so few horses are bred for the job. Plus, with the Juvenile Sprint having been scrapped since last year, this is now the only race at the meeting without top-level status. They went quite quick but were slowing up at the finish. The progressive winner is rated to a best view of his latest run.

7688a BREEDERS' CUP JUVENILE TURF (GRADE 1) (2YO COLTS & GELDINGS) (TURF) 1m (T)

9:25 (12:00) 2-Y-O **£337,423** (£110,429; £61,349; £36,809; £18,404)

RPR

1 **Outstrip**[20] [7192] 2-8-10 0 .... MESmith 4 116
(Charlie Appleby) *dwlt: hld up: gd hdwy and weaved through over 2f out: effrt and drvn over 1f out: styd on strly fnl f to ld nr fin* **6/1[3]**

2 ½ **Giovanni Boldini (USA)**[21] [7180] 2-8-10 0 .... RyanMoore 2 115+
(A P O'Brien, Ire) *in tch on ins: smooth hdwy to chse ldr over 2f out: rdn to ld over 1f out: kpt on wl u.p: hdd and no ex towards fin* **3/1[2]**

3 1 ¼ **Bobby's Kitten (USA)**[26] 2-8-10 0 .... JJCastellano 5 112
(Chad C Brown, U.S.A) *t.k.h: led at decent gallop: rdn and hdd over 1f out: rallied: no ex wl ins fnl f* **9/4[1]**

4 3 ¾ **Bon Accord (USA)**[26] 2-8-10 0 .... JRosario 8 103
(Antonio Sano, U.S.A) *prom on outside: rdn along over 2f out: outpcd over 1f out* **25/1**

5 2 ¼ **Got Shades (USA)**[26] 2-8-10 0 .... GaryStevens 3 98
(Danny Pish, U.S.A) *hld up on ins: plenty to do whn n.m.r briefly ent st: styd on wl fnl f: nvr able to chal* **40/1**

6 ½ **Bashart (USA)**[26] 2-8-10 0 .... JRVelazquez 13 97
(Todd Pletcher, U.S.A) *hld up jst bhd midfield: effrt and rdn over 2f out: no imp fr over 1f out* **14/1**

7 ½ **Aotearoa (USA)**[26] 2-8-10 0 .... CNakatani 7 96
(Leonard Powell, U.S.A) *in tch: rdn along over 2f out: wknd over 1f out* **18/1**

8 1 ¼ **Poker Player (USA)**[26] 2-8-10 0 .... CHill 11 93
(Wayne Catalano, U.S.A) *hld up: rdn and c wdst of all ent st: kpt on fnl f: nvr rchd ldrs* **14/1**

9 ¾ **Wilshire Boulevard (IRE)**[26] [7056] 2-8-10 0 .... WilliamBuick 9 91
(A P O'Brien, Ire) *midfield on ins: effrt and rdn whn hmpd and lost pl over 2f out: sme late hdwy: nvr able to chal* **8/1**

10 nse **Ontology (USA)**[33] [6891] 2-8-10 0 .... (b) MGutierrez 10 91
(Simon Callaghan, U.S.A) *midfield on outside: rdn and outpcd over 2f out: btn over 1f out* **66/1**

11 2 ¼ **Shamshon (IRE)**[41] [6637] 2-8-10 0 .... RichardHughes 12 86
(Richard Hannon) *stdd and swtchd lft s: hld up: angled towards outside and drvn along over 2f out: sn btn* **20/1**

12 11 ¾ **Home School (IRE)**[26] 2-8-10 0 .... (b[1]) RBejarano 6 59
(Doug O'Neill, U.S.A) *t.k.h: chsd ldrs tl rdn and wknd over 2f out: eased whn no ch fr over 1f out* **40/1**

13 4 ¼ **All Cash (USA)**[26] 2-8-10 0 .... (b) LSaez 1 49
(D Wayne Lukas, U.S.A) *chsd ldr to over 2f out: sn lost pl: eased whn no ch fr over 1f out* **40/1**

1m 33.2s (-0.67) **13** Ran SP% **117.2**
PARI-MUTUEL (all including 2 usd stake): WIN 14.00; PLACE (1-2) 6.80, 6.40; SHOW (1-2-3) 3.60, 3.40, 2.40; SF 46.20.
Owner Godolphin Racing LLC, Lessee **Bred** Darley **Trained** Newmarket, Suffolk

■ Like last year, Lasix was forbidden in all 2yo races at the Breeders' Cup. Charlie Appleby's first G1 winner.

FOCUS
While the Marathon has no place at this meeting, there can be no doubt the Juvenile Turf races have proved worthy additions to the schedule and this was a cracking running of the colts/geldings version. However, while the best three horses pulled well clear, the order in which they finished might not want taking literally. The pace was fast.

7689a BREEDERS' CUP DIRT MILE (GRADE 1) (3YO+) (DIRT) 1m

10:05 (12:00) 3-Y-O+ **£337,423** (£110,429; £61,349; £36,809; £18,404)

RPR

1 **Goldencents (USA)**[26] 3-8-11 0 .... RBejarano 11 123+
(Doug O'Neill, U.S.A) *broke wl fr wd draw and made all: set v.fast pace: prssd from hlfwy tl rdn clr 2f out: lugged rt ent fnl f but in control and r.o strongly: impressive* **5/1[2]**

2 2 ¾ **Golden Ticket (USA)**33 6893 4-9-0 0 JRosario 1 118
(Kenneth McPeek, U.S.A) *hld up towards rr on inner: rdn and hdwy on rail fr over 2f out: wnt 2nd over 1f out, r.o and chasd wnr but no real imp* **8/1**

3 3 ½ **Brujo De Olleros (BRZ)**34 6858 5-9-0 0 AGarcia 3 110
(Richard C Mettee, U.S.A) *hld up towards rr: rdn over 3f out, kpt on and tk nvr dangerous 3rd ins fnl f* **7/1**3

4 1 ½ **Verrazano (USA)**69 5782 3-8-11 0 JRVelazquez 9 105
(Todd Pletcher, U.S.A) *pushed along but unable to go early pace: midfield, rdn 3f out: kpt on and tk wl hld 4th ins fnl f* **11/4**1

5 ½ **Hymn Book (USA)**34 6858 7-9-0 0 (b) JJCastellano 2 105
(Claude McGaughey III, U.S.A) *hld up towards rr: rdn over 2f out, kpt on in str but nvr a factor* **14/1**

6 3 ¼ **Fed Biz (USA)**67 4-9-0 0 MGarcia 4 98
(Bob Baffert, U.S.A) *midfield: rdn over 2f out: plugged on wthout threatening in str* **10/1**

7 ½ **Pants On Fire (USA)**54 5-9-0 0 PLopez 10 96
(Kelly Breen, U.S.A) *chsd ldrs: rdn over 2f out: kpt on tl no ex and btn ins fnl f: faded* **9/1**

8 1 ¼ **Alpha (USA)**34 6862 4-9-0 0 (b) JBravo 6 94
(Kiaran McLaughlin, U.S.A) *dwlt slightly and in rr: last halfway: rdn over 2f out: plugged on but nvr a factor* **16/1**

9 1 **Broadway Empire (USA)**33 3-8-11 0 RicoWWalcott 5 90
(Robertino Diodoro, U.S.A) *pressed ldr: rdn over 2f out: no ex and btn over 1f out: tired and faded* **12/1**

10 2 ¾ **Holy Lute (USA)**27 3-8-11 0 MESmith 7 84
(James Cassidy, U.S.A) *midfield on outer: rdn over 2f out: in rr and btn ent fnl f: eased* **14/1**

11 dist **Centralinteligence (USA)**26 5-9-0 0 VEspinoza 8
(Ronald W Ellis, U.S.A) *prom early: checked on run to first turn and hmpd on rail soon after: towards rr: rdn in last 3f out: btn and eased over 2f out: tailed off* **20/1**

1m 35.12s (95.12)
WFA 3 from 4yo+ 2lb **11** Ran SP% **117.7**
PARI-MUTUEL (all including 2 usd stake): WIN 9.60; PLACE (1-2) 5.00, 6.40; SHOW (1-2-3) 4.00, 4.60, 4.60; SF 69.80.
Owner W C Racing, Dave Kenney & RAP Racing **Bred** Rosecrest Farm & Karyn Pirrello **Trained** USA

FOCUS
Evidence of just how quick the dirt surface was riding as Goldencents set strong fractions of 22.12, 44.75, 1:08.64 but still won decisively.

7690a BREEDERS' CUP JUVENILE FILLIES TURF (GRADE 1) (2YO FILLIES) (TURF) 1m (T)
10:50 (12:00) 2-Y-0 **£337,423** (£110,429; £61,349; £36,809; £18,404)

RPR

1 **Chriselliam (IRE)**35 6798 2-8-10 0 RichardHughes 8 114+
(Charles Hills) *dwlt: t.k.h and sn in midfield: smooth hdwy to chase ldrs over 2f out: rdn to ld ins fnl f: edged lft and qcknd clr: readily* **5/1**2

2 2 ½ **Testa Rossi (FR)**26 2-8-10 0 JLezcano 12 108
(Chad C Brown, U.S.A) *bhd: effrt but plenty to do whn short of room briefly on ins bend ent str: weaved through over 1f out: styd on strongly to tk second towards fin: no ch with wnr* **12/1**

3 ½ **Colonel Joan (USA)**25 2-8-10 0 JTalamo 3 107
(Eoin Harty, U.S.A) *hld up in midfield on ins: effort and rdn 2f out: kpt on fnl f: nrst fin* **33/1**

4 hd **My Conquestadory (USA)**28 2-8-10 0 ERosaDaSilva 14 107
(Mark Casse, Canada) *chasd ldrs on outside: rdn to ld over 1f out: hdd ins fnl f: edged lft, no ex and lost two places towards fin* **7/1**3

5 1 ¼ **Dancing House (USA)**26 2-8-10 0 MESmith 9 104
(Kiaran McLaughlin, U.S.A) *hld up on ins: rdn over 2f out: hdwy over 1f out: kpt on fnl f: not pace to chal* **33/1**

6 hd **Ready To Act (USA)**48 2-8-10 0 JRosario 11 103
(Chad C Brown, U.S.A) *chsd ldr: rdn and led briefly wl over 1f out: hung left: wknd ins fnl f* **12/1**

7 1 ¼ **Vorda (FR)**34 6836 2-8-10 0 OlivierPeslier 6 100
(P Sogorb, France) *hld up on outside: steady hdwy over 3f out: drvn and outpaced wl over 1f out: sn no imp* **11/4**1

8 nse **Clenor (IRE)**25 2-8-10 0 RBejarano 10 100
(Doug O'Neill, U.S.A) *hld up: rdn over 2f out: hdwy on outside over 1f out: kpt on fnl f: nvr able to chal* **14/1**

9 1 **Sky Painter (USA)**26 2-8-10 0 LSaez 13 98
(Kiaran McLaughlin, U.S.A) *prom on outside: effort and rdn when edged rt off home bend over 1f out: wknd ins fnl f* **14/1**

10 ½ **Nesso (USA)**25 2-8-10 0 (b) MGarcia 1 97
(Vann Belvoir, U.S.A) *made most to wl over 1f out: sn rdn: wknd ins fnl f* **33/1**

11 1 **Kitten Kaboodle (USA)**23 2-8-10 0 JRVelazquez 4 95
(Chad C Brown, U.S.A) *t.k.h: prom: rdn along over 2f out: wknd wl over 1f out* **14/1**

12 1 ¼ **Granny Mc's Kitten (USA)**26 2-8-10 0 JJCastellano 5 92
(Chad C Brown, U.S.A) *towards rr: hdwy on outside after 3f: rdn and wknd fr over 2f out* **33/1**

13 7 ½ **Street Sailing (USA)**23 2-8-10 0 AGarcia 7 74
(Richard C Mettee, U.S.A) *unruly before start and in stalls: pulled hard in midfield: hmpd and lost place bend after 2f: a.bhd thereafter: struggling fnl 3f* **33/1**

14 11 ¼ **Al Thakhira**20 7194 2-8-10 0 RyanMoore 2 49
(Marco Botti) *t.k.h: prom on ins tl rdn and wknd quickly 2f out: sn eased whn no ch* **5/1**2

1m 33.72s (-0.15) **14** Ran SP% **122.6**
PARI-MUTUEL (all including 2 usd stake): WIN 15.80; PLACE (1-2) 7.80, 11.20; SHOW (1-2-3) 6.20, 9.00, 16.60; SF 158.40.
Owner W Carson, Miss E Asprey, C Wright **Bred** Ballylinch Stud **Trained** Lambourn, Berks

FOCUS
Not as fast a pace as in Outstrip's race, but still a good gallop. Chriselliam only ran to her British form, with her fellow raiders below par.

7691a BREEDERS' CUP DISTAFF (GRADE 1) (3YO+ FILLIES & MARES) (DIRT) 1m 1f (D)
11:35 (12:00) 3-Y-0+ **£674,846** (£220,858; £122,699; £73,619; £36,809)

RPR

1 **Beholder (USA)**33 6892 3-8-9 0 GaryStevens 5 123+
(Richard E Mandella, U.S.A) *trckd ldrs gng wl: wnt second over 4f out: led on bit over 2f out: rdn clr fr over 1f out: readily* **11/4**2

2 4 ¼ **Close Hatches (USA)**41 3-8-9 0 JRosario 3 114
(William Mott, U.S.A) *t.k.h early: prom: effort over 2f out: chsd (clr) wnr over 1f out: kpt on fnl f: no imp* **15/2**3

3 1 ¾ **Authenticity (USA)**33 6892 6-8-12 0 JRVelazquez 2 109
(Todd Pletcher, U.S.A) *led at ordinary gallop: rdn and hdd over 2f out: lost second over 1f out: kpt on same pace* **8/1**

4 2 ¼ **Royal Delta (USA)**34 6857 5-8-12 0 MESmith 4 105
(William Mott, U.S.A) *pressed ldr to ovr 4f out: sn pushed along: outpcd wl ovr 2f out: 4th and btn over 1f out* **15/8**1

5 4 ¾ **Street Girl (USA)**41 3-8-9 0 ACastillo 1 96
(Manuel J Azpurua, U.S.A) *hld up: pushed along and outpcd ovr 3f out: btn fnl 2f* **50/1**

6 3 ¼ **Princess Of Sylmar (USA)**34 6857 3-8-9 0 JJCastellano 6 89
(Todd Pletcher, U.S.A) *steadied start: hld up bhd ldng quartet: stdy hdwy over 4f out: outpcd wl ovr 2f out: sn btn* **11/4**2

1m 47.77s (-1.13)
WFA 3 from 5yo+ 3lb **6** Ran SP% **113.0**
PARI-MUTUEL (all including 2 usd stake): WIN 7.60; PLACE (1-2) 4.20, 6.60; SHOW (1-2-3) 3.20, 4.80, 4.20; SF 42.60.
Owner Spendthrift Farm LLC **Bred** Clarkland Farm **Trained** USA

FOCUS
A small but select field for a race that again carries its original title, having spent the previous five years as the Ladies Classic, and it was eagerly anticipated, especially with Gary Stevens and Mike Smith, two of the best and most experienced jockeys around, seemingly holding the key to the pace set-up. As it turned out, both riders were happy enough to forgo the early lead and, with a couple of the big guns disappointing, we didn't get the sort of clash we were hoping for. It was, however, still a gripping contest and Stevens, not that long out of a seven-year retirement, was brilliant aboard the winner.

7654 NEWMARKET (R-H)
Saturday, November 2

OFFICIAL GOING: Soft (6.0)
Wind: light, across Weather: dry

7692 FINJAAN STANDING AT GAZELEY STUD EBF MAIDEN FILLIES' STKS (DIV I) 7f
12:10 (12:12) (Class 4) 2-Y-0 **£4,528** (£1,347; £673; £336) **Stalls** Low

Form RPR

1 **Queen Of Ice** 2-9-0 0 SebSanders 2 77+
(William Haggas) *lengthy: bit on the leg: in tch in midfield: rdn and effrt 2f out: swtchd rt and hdwy 1f out: rn green and edgd lft ins fnl f: str run u.p to ld wl ins fnl f: styd on* **8/1**

35 2 nk **Makruma**91 5003 2-9-0 0 PaulHanagan 4 76
(J W Hills) *neat: lw: chsd ldr: rdn to ld over 1f out: hrd pressed but battled on wl fnl f tl hdd and one pce fnl wl ins fnl f* **5/2**1

3 hd **Angelic Air** 2-9-0 0 JamesDoyle 8 76+
(John Gosden) *leggy: athletic: lw: s.i.s: in rr: hdwy 1/2-way: rdn and chsd ldrs wl over 1f out: wnt 2nd over 1f out: styd on and str chal ins fnl f: one pce fnl 75yds* **6/1**3

4 3 ¼ **Sea The Bloom** 2-9-0 0 JimmyFortune 11 67+
(Sir Michael Stoute) *lengthy: scope: t.k.h: chsd ldrs: rdn over 1f out: no ex ent fnl f: wknd ins fnl f* **6/1**3

5 ¾ **Cadeaux Power** 2-9-0 0 TomQueally 12 66+
(Clive Brittain) *leggy: scope: attractive: chsd ldrs: rdn and effrt 2f out: no ex u.p ent fnl f: wknd ins fnl f* **20/1**

6 2 ¾ **Excellent View** 2-9-0 0 SilvestreDeSousa 7 59+
(Saeed bin Suroor) *str: lw: racd keenly: led: rdn: hdd and wandered u.p over 1f out: btn 1f out: fdd ins fnl f* **3/1**2

6 7 13 **Vera Lou (IRE)**19 7245 2-9-0 0 JoeFanning 6 26
(Pat Eddery) *leggy: lengthy: dwlt: sn in tch in midfield: lost pl and bhd 1/2-way: lost tch over 2f out* **50/1**

0 8 11 **Tete Orange**10 7466 2-9-0 0 DavidProbert 9
(Stuart Williams) *in tch towards rr: rdn and struggling over 2f out: lost tch 2f out: eased fnl f: t.o* **80/1**

0 9 13 **Katawi**69 5797 2-9-0 0 ShaneKelly 5
(Peter Chapple-Hyam) *leggy: hld up in tch in last trio: rdn over 2f out: sn lost tch: eased over 1f out: t.o* **10/1**

1m 29.86s (4.46) **Going Correction** +0.625s/f (Yiel) **9** Ran SP% **110.3**
Speed ratings (Par 95): **99,98,98,94,93 90,75,63,48**
Tote Swingers: 1&2 £5.00, 1&3 £10.50, 2&3 £2.60 CSF £26.29 TOTE £7.40: £2.50, £1.30, £1.90; EX 31.40 Trifecta £177.60 Pool: £1,513.82 - 6.39 winning units..
Owner Cheveley Park Stud **Bred** Cheveley Park Stud Ltd **Trained** Newmarket, Suffolk

FOCUS
Stands' side track used with stalls on stands' side. Just 0.2mm of rain overnight and the going remained soft, with an identical GoingStick reading (6.0) to the previous day. This maiden has been won by some smart sorts in recent years, including future Group 1 winners Sariska and The Fugue, and both divisions look sure to produce a number of future winners.

7693 FINJAAN STANDING AT GAZELEY STUD EBF MAIDEN FILLIES' STKS (DIV II) 7f
12:40 (12:42) (Class 4) 2-Y-0 **£4,528** (£1,347; £673; £336) **Stalls** Low

Form RPR

5220 1 **Miss Lillie**70 5737 2-9-0 79 AndreaAtzeni 5 81
(Roger Teal) *chsd ldr: rdn to chal wl over 1f out: sustained duel w rival u.p fr over 1f out: led last stride: gamely* **9/2**3

3 2 shd **Eastern Belle**10 7466 2-9-0 0 RobertHavlin 11 81
(John Gosden) *lw: led: rdn and pressed wl over 1f out: sustained duel w wnr fr over 1f out: battled on wl and maintained narrow ld tl hdd last stride* **2/1**1

5 3 3 ½ **Loch Ma Naire (IRE)**18 7260 2-9-0 0 AdamKirby 10 72
(Ed Dunlop) *cmpct: chsd ldng pair: rdn and outpcd whn edgd rt over 1f out: styd on same pce fr over 1f out* **8/1**

4 2 **True Match (IRE)** 2-9-0 0 SilvestreDeSousa 2 67+
(Saeed bin Suroor) *str: lw: stdd s: t.k.h: hld up in tch in midfield: rdn and effrt to chse ldng trio wl over 1f out: one pce and no imp fr over 1f out* **10/3**2

4 5 2 **Ametrine (IRE)**11 7448 2-9-0 0 GrahamLee 12 62
(William Jarvis) *w'like: wl in tch in midfield: rdn and effrt 2f out: outpcd and btn whn edgd rt ent fnl f: wknd* **14/1**

6 1 ¼ **Inheritance** 2-9-0 0 JimmyFortune 6 59
(Sir Michael Stoute) *leggy: wnt lft: hld up in tch in rr of main gp: rdn and hdwy ent fnl 2f: outpcd and rn green wl over 1f out: wknd over 1f out* **10/1**

7 2 ¾ **Venus Marina** 2-9-0 0...[1] TedDurcan 8 52
(Chris Wall) *lengthy: str: bit bkwd: stdd s: hld up in tch in midfield: rdn ent fnl 2f: sn outpcd and btn: wknd over 1f out* **50/1**

8 1 ¼ **Gracesome (IRE)** 2-9-0 0... AdamBeschizza 9 49
(Stuart Williams) *str: gd bodied: hld up in tch in rr of main gp: rdn over 2f out: sn struggling: wknd wl over 1f out* **40/1**

0 9 5 **Wulfthryth**[11] 7449 2-9-0 0... MartinLane 4 36
(Tobias B P Coles) *lengthy: hld up in tch in rr of main gp: rdn over 2f out: sn struggling: edgd rt and wknd wl over 1f out* **100/1**

10 9 **Cape Castle (IRE)** 2-9-0 0... FrederikTylicki 7 14
(Clive Brittain) *tall: s.i.s: rn green and a bhd* **12/1**

4 11 7 **Classic Princess**[57] 6171 2-9-0 0... DavidProbert 1 11
(Gay Kelleway) *leggy: unf: chsd ldrs: rdn and struggling 3f out: sn lost pl: bhd and eased ins fnl f* **40/1**

1m 31.05s (5.65) **Going Correction** +0.625s/f (Yiel) **11** Ran SP% **117.0**
Speed ratings (Par 95): **92,91,87,85,83 81,78,77,71,61 60**
Tote Swingers: 1&2 £2.70, 1&3 £7.30, 2&3 £4.40 CSF £13.61 TOTE £5.50: £1.70, £1.10, £2.70; EX 17.20 Trifecta £136.10 Pool: £3,630.36 - 19.99 winning units..
Owner M Vickers **Bred** Newsells Park Stud & Cannon Bloodstock **Trained** Ashtead, Surrey

FOCUS
They came over to race stands' side this time, went steadier early on (final time was 1.19sec slower than the first division), and the front two were in those positions throughout.

7694 LAUNDRY COTTAGE STUD FARM ZETLAND CONDITIONS STKS 1m 2f
1:10 (1:11) (Class 3) 2-Y-O **£6,225** (£1,864; £932; £466) **Stalls** Low

Form RPR

2121 1 **Hartnell**[8] 7492 2-9-0 97... JoeFanning 2 101
(Mark Johnston) *lw: chsd ldr tl led 3f out: c clr on bit ent fnl 2f: in n.d after: eased towards fin: v easily* **30/100**[1]

51 2 10 **Montaly**[17] 7308 2-9-0 79... DavidProbert 1 81
(Andrew Balding) *leggy: cl cpld: dwlt and pushed along leaving stalls: hld up in tch: chsd ldr wl over 2f out: sn rdn and no hdwy: wknd over 1f out* **4/1**[2]

6 3 15 **Automated**[43] 6581 2-9-0 0... JamesDoyle 3 54
(Clive Brittain) *cmpct: hld up in tch: rdn over 3f out: sn struggling: no ch fnl 2f: wnt modest 3rd 1f out* **16/1**[3]

4663 4 6 **Samtu (IRE)**[33] 6897 2-9-0 67... FrederikTylicki 5 43
(Clive Brittain) *lengthy: ld tl 3f out: sn rdn and struggling: no ch fnl 2f: t.o* **25/1**

2m 12.26s (6.46) **Going Correction** +0.625s/f (Yiel) **4** Ran SP% **106.7**
Speed ratings (Par 100): **99,91,79,74**
CSF £1.73 TOTE £1.20; EX 1.80 Trifecta £2.90 Pool: £2,849.61 - 725.25 winning units..
Owner Sheikh Hamdan Bin Mohammed Al Maktoum **Bred** Darley **Trained** Middleham Moor, N Yorks

FOCUS
As the figures suggested this proved an uncompetitive race.

7695 EBF STALLIONS/LANWADES MONTROSE FILLIES' STKS (LISTED RACE) 1m
1:45 (2:08) (Class 1) 2-Y-O
£17,013 (£6,450; £3,228; £1,608; £807; £405) **Stalls** Low

Form RPR

5120 1 **Majeyda (USA)**[27] 7055 2-9-1 99... SilvestreDeSousa 9 101
(Charlie Appleby) *racd in centre: hld up in midfield overall: hdwy to join ldrs and drew clr w 2 rivals 2f out: led over 1f out: edgd rt and forged clr 1f out: styd on wl* **7/2**[1]

2142 2 2 ½ **Adhwaa**[56] 6185 2-8-12 92... PaulHanagan 12 93
(J W Hills) *racd on stands' side: hld up in midfield: swtchd to join centre gp 1/2-way: hdwy to join ldng trio and wnt clr 2f out: drvn and outpcd over 1f out: chsd wnr 1f out: kpt on same pce: 2nd of 10 in gp* **12/1**

5221 3 ¾ **Island Remede**[10] 7471 2-8-12 78... GrahamLee 6 91
(Ed Dunlop) *racd in centre gp: chsd ldrs: rdn to ld wl over 2f out: clr w 2 rivals 2f out: drvn and hdd over 1f out: lost 2nd and plugged on same pce fnl f: 3rd of 10 in gp* **13/2**

6212 4 7 **Rosehill Artist (IRE)**[43] 6594 2-8-12 85... TomQueally 4 75
(Charles Hills) *racd in centre: hld up in tch in rr: rdn and effrt over 2f out: no ch w ldng trio but plugged to go modest 4th 1f out: no imp: 4th of 10 in gp* **16/1**

012 5 3 ¾ **Mutatis Mutandis (IRE)**[37] 6770 2-8-12 79... JimCrowley 2 67
(Ed Walker) *leggy: racd in centre: in tch in midfield: rdn and effrt over 2f out: outpcd and wl btn 4th over 1f out: wknd fnl f: 5th of 10 in gp* **14/1**

311 6 2 ¼ **Top Dollar**[35] 6852 2-8-12 82... MartinHarley 7 62
(James Tate) *leggy: racd in centre: hld up in midfield: rdn and effrt over 2f out: sn outpcd: battling for modest 4th over 1f out: wknd fnl f: 6th of 10 in gp* **16/1**

1 7 3 **Surcingle (USA)**[53] 6281 2-8-12 77... JamesDoyle 11 56
(Sir Michael Stoute) *lengthy: s.i.s: bhd and racd on stands' side tl swtchd to join centre gp 1/2-way: rdn and hdwy over 3f out: no ex and btn 2f out: sn wknd: 7th of 10 in gp* **11/2**[2]

42 8 shd **Amaseena (IRE)**[25] 7102 2-8-12 0... AndreaAtzeni 10 55
(Roger Varian) *str: racd on stands' side: in tch in midfield: rdn and effrt over 2f out: no threat to ldrs but battling for modest 4th 2f out tl over 1f out: fdd fnl f: 1st of 4 in gp* **8/1**

334 9 1 ¼ **Stosur (IRE)**[7] 7537 2-8-12 90...(p) DavidProbert 14 53
(Gay Kelleway) *racd on stands' side: t.k.h: hld up in rr overall: rdn and effrt over 3f out: sn struggling: wl btn fnl 2f: 2nd of 4 in gp* **20/1**

4305 10 5 **Les Gar Gan (IRE)**[42] 6619 2-8-12 73... DanielTudhope 3 42
(Keith Dalgleish) *racd in centre: in tch in midfield: rdn and effrt 3f out: sn struggling and btn: wknd 2f out: 8th of 10 in gp* **25/1**

015 11 19 **Stealth Missile (IRE)**[36] 6795 2-8-12 88... MartinDwyer 15
(Clive Brittain) *racd on stands' side: bustled along leaving stalls: midfield overall: rdn and struggling over 3f out: sn wknd: t.o and eased fnl f: 3rd of 4 in gp* **12/1**

54 12 hd **Crown Pleasure (IRE)**[87] 5131 2-8-12 0... FrederikTylicki 13
(Clive Brittain) *leggy: unf: racd on stands' side: midfield overall: rdn and btn 1/2-way: sn lost tch: t.o over 1f out: 4th of 4 in gp* **66/1**

3026 13 17 **Evacusafe Lady**[4] 7609 2-8-12 70...(p) PatCosgrave 1
(John Ryan) *racd in centre: overall ldr tl hdd 3f out: sn dropped out: t.o and eased fnl f: 9th of 10 in gp* **200/1**

0114 14 44 **Remember**[35] 6839 2-8-12 90... JimmyFortune 5
(Richard Hannon) *racd in centre: chsd ldrs tl rdn to ld 3f out: sn drvn and hdd: wkng and eased wl over 1f out: t.o and virtually p.u ins fnl f: 10th of 10 in gp* **6/1**[3]

1m 42.3s (3.70) **Going Correction** +0.625s/f (Yiel) **14** Ran SP% **120.8**
Speed ratings (Par 101): **106,103,102,95,92 89,86,86,85,80 61,61,44,**
Tote Swingers: 1&2 £9.00, 1&3 £5.20, 2&3 £11.90 CSF £46.19 TOTE £4.20: £2.00, £3.90, £2.70; EX 44.70 Trifecta £325.60 Pool: £5,538.96 - 12.75 winning units..
Owner Godolphin **Bred** Darley **Trained** Newmarket, Suffolk

FOCUS
This looked a weak Listed race on paper.

7696 FINJAAN STANDING AT GAZELEY STUD H'CAP 1m
2:20 (2:44) (Class 3) (0-95,95) 3-Y-O+
£7,158 (£2,143; £1,071; £535; £267; £134) **Stalls** Low

Form RPR

3100 1 **Haaf A Sixpence**[42] 6625 4-9-2 **90**... JimCrowley 1 100
(Ralph Beckett) *racd in centre tl swtchd to join stands' side gp after 2f: chsd ldrs: drvn to chal over 1f out: led ins fnl f: styd on wl: rdn out* **10/1**

632 2 1 ½ **Magistral**[31] 6951 3-8-10 **86**...(p) RobertHavlin 5 93
(John Gosden) *lw: racd in centre tl swtchd to stands' side after 2f: in tch in midfield: hdwy u.p over 1f out: styd on to snatch 2nd on post* **12/1**

2032 3 nse **Buckstay (IRE)**[45] 6538 3-8-9 **85**... AndreaAtzeni 10 92
(Peter Chapple-Hyam) *racd on stands' side: chsd ldr: rdn to ld and edgd lft over 1f out: drvn and hdd ins fnl f: styd on same pce: lost 2nd on post* **8/1**

1406 4 ½ **Swiftly Done (IRE)**[15] 7337 6-8-12 **89**...(b) JasonHart[(3)] 17 95
(Declan Carroll) *racd on stands' side: chsd ldrs: rdn whn short of room and hmpd over 1f out: rallied and chsd ldrs 1f out: one pce fnl 100yds* **20/1**

2030 5 ½ **Jodies Jem**[29] 6989 3-8-11 **87**... GrahamLee 14 92
(William Jarvis) *racd on stands' side: wnt rt s: t.k.h: hld up wl in tch: rdn and chsd ldrs over 1f out: styd on same pce ins fnl f* **16/1**

4151 6 1 **Tinghir (IRE)**[29] 6989 3-9-4 **94**... MartinDwyer 15 96
(David Lanigan) *racd on stands' side: in tch in midfield: rdn and effrt whn nt clr run and swtchd rt arnd many rivals 1f out: styd on same pce fnl 100yds* **6/1**[1]

0060 7 1 ¼ **Justonefortheroad**[22] 7172 7-8-10 **84**... TonyHamilton 9 83
(Richard Fahey) *racd in centre: swtchd to r stands' side after 2f: in tch towards rr: rdn and hdwy 2f out: styd on same pce ins fnl f* **20/1**

0052 8 1 ½ **Myboyalfie (USA)**[20] 7224 6-8-13 **87**...(v) MartinHarley 16 83
(J R Jenkins) *racd on stands' side: overall ldr: rdn and hdd over 1f out: wknd ins fnl f* **7/1**[3]

3131 9 3 ¼ **Consign**[29] 6993 3-9-5 **95**...(v) JamesDoyle 8 83
(Jeremy Noseda) *lw: racd in centre tl swtchd to stands' side after 2f: t.k.h: hld up in tch in midfield: rdn and effrt 2f out: no ex ent fnl f: wknd ins fnl f* **13/2**[2]

02-6 10 2 ½ **Credit Swap**[29] 6989 8-9-0 **88**... TomQueally 7 71
(Michael Wigham) *racd in centre tl swtchd to stands' side after 2f: hld up in rr: rdn 3f out: plugged on past btn horses fnl f: nvr trbld ldrs* **15/2**

1553 11 ½ **Ogbourne Downs**[20] 7224 3-8-5 **81**... DavidProbert 4 63
(Charles Hills) *lw: racd in centre tl swtchd to stands' side after 2f: hld up in tch: rdn and effrt over 2f out: wknd over 1f out* **16/1**

0206 12 ½ **Dance And Dance (IRE)**[35] 6838 7-9-5 **93**... JimmyFortune 11 73
(Ed Vaughan) *hmpd s and slowly away: swtchd to r stands' side after 2f: hld up in midfield: rdn and no hdwy 2f out: wknd ent fnl f* **8/1**

6003 13 7 **Wannabe King**[19] 7241 7-9-1 **89**...(v) SilvestreDeSousa 13 53
(Geoffrey Harker) *racd on stands' side: t.k.h: hld up in tch in midfield: rdn and no hdwy 2f out: btn over 1f out: fdd fnl f* **16/1**

0400 14 3 ¾ **Prompter**[17] 7312 6-8-12 **86**... PaulHanagan 2 42
(Jonjo O'Neill) *racd in centre tl swtchd to racd stands' side after 2f: hld up in tch towards rr: rdn over 2f out: sn btn and bhd* **33/1**

0301 15 1 ¼ **Party Royal**[26] 7063 3-8-10 **86**... JoeFanning 3 39
(Mark Johnston) *racd solo on far side: chsd ldrs overall: rdn over 2f out: sn struggling: wknd wl over 1f out* **20/1**

3051 16 8 **Cayuga**[11] 7438 4-8-8 **82**...(p) JimmyQuinn 6 16
(Brett Johnson) *racd in centre tl swtchd to stands' side after 2f: in tch: rdn and struggling over 2f out: sn wknd: bhd fnl f* **33/1**

1m 42.6s (4.00) **Going Correction** +0.625s/f (Yiel)
WFA 3 from 4yo+ 2lb **16** Ran SP% **128.7**
Speed ratings (Par 107): **105,103,103,102,102 101,100,98,95,92 92,91,84,81,79 71**
Tote Swingers: 1&2 £41.20, 1&3 £28.50, 2&3 £15.70 CSF £122.29 CT £1070.42 TOTE £14.10: £3.00, £2.50, £2.70, £4.20; EX 254.70 Trifecta £2453.50 Part won. Pool: £3,271.39 - 0.72 winning units..
Owner Melody Racing **Bred** Melody Bloodstock **Trained** Kimpton, Hants

FOCUS
A competitive handicap. The early pace was stronger on the stands' side than the far side, which prompted the riders of those drawn low to ditch their leader Party Royal and edge over to join the bunch headed by Myboyalfie. The right horses were involved and the form makes sense.

7697 FASTTRACKTOSUCCESS FINJAAN JAMES SEYMOUR STKS (LISTED RACE) 1m 2f
2:55 (3:15) (Class 1) 3-Y-O+ **£20,982** (£7,955; £3,981; £1,983; £995) **Stalls** Low

Form RPR

2121 1 **Nabucco**[31] 6957 4-9-2 109... RobertHavlin 4 105
(John Gosden) *chsd ldng pair: swtchd out rt and effrt over 1f out: drvn and str chal ins fnl f: styd on gamely u.p to ld towards fin* **10/11**[1]

3500 2 nk **Proud Chieftain**[21] 7196 5-9-2 94...(p) JamesDoyle 1 104
(Clifford Lines) *chsd ldr tl rdn to ld over 1f out: hrd pressed and drvn 1f out: battled on gamely tl hdd and no ex towards fin* **20/1**

0156 3 1 ½ **Fattsota**[28] 7049 5-9-2 103... DanielTudhope 2 101
(David O'Meara) *led tl rdn and hdd over 1f out: styd on same pce u.p ins fnl f* **9/2**[3]

4353 4 ¾ **Bana Wu**[45] 6530 4-8-11 102... DavidProbert 5 95
(Andrew Balding) *s.i.s and rdn along leaving stalls: in tch in rr: switching rt and n.m.r over 1f out: drvn and effrt 1f out: styd on same pce fnl f* **7/1**

0023 5 7 **Chapter Seven**[21] 7196 4-9-2 106... HarryBentley 3 86
(Stuart Williams) *in tch in last pair: rdn and effrt to press ldrs 2f out: no ex and btn whn edgd lft 1f out: sn wknd* **7/2**[2]

2m 8.88s (3.08) **Going Correction** +0.625s/f (Yiel) **5** Ran SP% **110.0**
Speed ratings (Par 111): **112,111,110,109,104**
CSF £19.01 TOTE £1.50: £1.20, £4.20; EX 23.80 Trifecta £72.40 Pool: £2,877.93 - 29.77 winning units..
Owner HRH Princess Haya Of Jordan **Bred** Darley **Trained** Newmarket, Suffolk

FOCUS
The least exposed and most progressive of these also happened to be best in at the weights, and the winner didn't run to his best. The runner-up is the obvious key to the form.

7698 FASTTRACKTOSUCCESS FINJAAN AT GAZELEY STUD BEN MARSHALL STKS (LISTED RACE) 1m
3:30 (3:45) (Class 1) 3-Y-O+

£20,982 (£7,955; £3,981; £1,983; £995; £499) **Stalls** Low

Form RPR
6140 1 **Penitent**[28] 7047 7-9-3 113 DanielTudhope 6 115
(David O'Meara) *lw: chsd ldr: rdn and upsides 2f out: drvn to ld over 1f out: hrd pressed and battled on v gamely ins fnl f: all out* **13/2**

-124 2 *nk* **French Navy**[21] 7196 5-9-3 110 SilvestreDeSousa 4 114
(Charlie Appleby) *hld up in tch in last pair: rdn and effrt 2f: hdwy u.p to chse wnr 1f out: str chal and ev ch ins fnl f: styd on wl: jst hld* **9/4**[2]

31-0 3 *hd* **Tullius (IRE)**[21] 7196 5-9-0 111 JimmyFortune 2 111
(Andrew Balding) *lw: hld up in tch in last pair: rdn and effrt wl over 1f out: hdwy u.p 1f out: pressing ldrs wl ins fnl f: styd on wl* **7/2**[3]

6620 4 *2* **Boomshackerlacker (IRE)**[25] 7116 3-8-12 108 (p) PatCosgrave 3 106
(George Baker) *t.k.h: hld up in tch in midfield: rdn and unable qck over 1f out: styd on same pce ins fnl f* **16/1**

-040 5 *½* **Daddy Long Legs (USA)**[238] 958 4-9-0 112 RobertHavlin 5 105
(M F De Kock, South Africa) *led: rdn 2f out: hdd over 1f out: no ex 1f out: wknd ins fnl f* **16/1**

5-13 6 *1 ¾* **Lanansaak (IRE)**[36] 6796 3-8-7 104 PaulHanagan 1 96
(Roger Varian) *chsd ldng pair: rdn and effrt 2f: styng on same pce whn sltly hmpd ent fnl f: wknd ins fnl f* **2/1**[1]

1m 41.65s (3.05) **Going Correction** +0.625s/f (Yiel)
WFA 3 from 4yo+ 2lb 6 Ran SP% **111.4**
Speed ratings (Par 111): **109,108,108,106,106 104**
Tote Swingers: 1&2 £2.90, 1&3 £3.80, 2&3 £3.30 CSF £21.20 TOTE £8.40: £3.20, £1.50; EX 16.00 Trifecta £100.40 Pool: £3,305.51 - 24.68 winning units..

Owner Middleham Park Racing XVII **Bred** Cheveley Park Stud Ltd **Trained** Nawton, N Yorks

FOCUS
A very tight Listed race with just 5lb covering the whole field on adjusted official ratings. They didn't go that quick early. The winner seemed back to something like his best at face value.

7699 FINJAAN SON OF ROYAL APPLAUSE H'CAP 7f
4:00 (4:14) (Class 4) (0-85,85) 3-Y-O+ **£4,690** (£1,395; £697; £348) **Stalls** Low

Form RPR
0062 1 **Piceno (IRE)**[4] 7595 5-8-2 71 oh3 (p) TimClark(5) 13 81
(Scott Dixon) *sn led and mde rest: rdn and 3 l clr ent fnl f: styd on wl* **9/1**

040 2 *3* **Pashan Garh**[26] 7073 4-8-7 71 oh3 JoeFanning 4 73
(Pat Eddery) *chsd ldrs: rdn and effrt ent fnl 2f: kpt on to chse clr wnr ins fnl f: no imp* **12/1**

-060 3 *1* **Conry (IRE)**[34] 6871 7-9-2 80 JamesDoyle 5 80
(Ian Williams) *hld up in last trio: hdwy u.p over 1f out: styd on wl u.p ins fnl f: wnt 3rd last strides: no threat to wnr* **16/1**

0140 4 *hd* **Tellovoi (IRE)**[35] 6840 5-9-7 85 (v) TomQueally 10 84
(Ian Williams) *t.k.h: hld up in tch in midfield: rdn and effrt over 2f out: styd on u.p ins fnl f: wnt 4th on post: no threat to wnr* **12/1**

0002 5 *nse* **Personal Touch**[14] 7374 4-9-2 80 PaulHanagan 11 79
(Richard Fahey) *chsd ldrs: wnt 2nd over 3f out: rdn and unable qck w wnr over 1f out: styd on same pce after: lost 3 pls fnl 100yds* **5/1**[1]

11 6 *½* **Four Winds**[17] 7303 7-8-8 72 (v) ShaneKelly 12 70+
(Tom Dascombe) *stdd s: t.k.h: hld up in rr: swtchd lft to r against stands' rail 4f out: repeatedly denied a run fr wl over 1f out tl swtchd rt ins fnl f: styd on but nvr able to chal* **5/1**[1]

1-00 7 *nk* **Annina (IRE)**[37] 6767 3-9-6 85 FergusSweeney 14 81
(Henry Candy) *led briefly early: sn stdd and hld up in midfield: effrt and unable qck wl over 1f out: kpt on same pce ins fnl f* **8/1**[3]

3260 8 *1 ¼* **My Kingdom (IRE)**[30] 6977 7-8-12 76 (t) AdamBeschizza 15 70
(Stuart Williams) *hld up in tch in midfield: effrt 2f out: keeping on whn n.m.r and swtchd rt ins fnl f: styd on same pce after* **14/1**

4230 9 *6* **Front Page News**[11] 7452 3-8-8 73 AndreaAtzeni 9 50
(Robert Eddery) *in tch in midfield: rdn and effrt ent fnl 2f: no imp over 1f out: swtchd rt and wknd ins fnl f* **20/1**

0002 10 *nk* **Great Expectations**[16] 7318 5-8-11 75 SilvestreDeSousa 3 52
(J R Jenkins) *stdd s: hld up in tch in last trio: effrt and hdwy 2f out: no imp over 1f out: wknd fnl f* **13/2**[2]

4103 11 *2 ¼* **Olney Lass**[16] 7318 6-8-2 71 oh1 JoeyHaynes(5) 2 42
(Lydia Pearce) *hld up in tch in midfield: rdn and effrt over 2f out: no prog and struggling wl over 1f out: wknd 1f out* **16/1**

4610 12 *shd* **Finesse**[28] 7021 4-9-2 80 JimCrowley 1 51
(Ralph Beckett) *stdd and swtchd lft s: in tch: rdn to chse ldrs 2f out: btn over 1f out: fdd ins fnl f* **16/1**

5150 13 *½* **Chiswick Bey (IRE)**[14] 7374 5-8-4 73 (t) SamanthaBell(5) 7 43
(Richard Fahey) *in tch towards rr: rdn and struggling over 2f out: bhd over 1f out* **20/1**

5100 14 *½* **Jonnie Skull (IRE)**[8] 6809 7-8-4 75 (t) DonnaCaldwell(7) 6 44
(Phil McEntee) *chsd ldr tl over 3f out: lost pl over 2f out: bhd over 1f out* **40/1**

1m 28.58s (3.18) **Going Correction** +0.625s/f (Yiel)
WFA 3 from 4yo+ 1lb 14 Ran SP% **119.4**
Speed ratings (Par 105): **106,102,101,101,101 100,100,98,91,91 89,88,88,87**
Tote Swingers: 1&2 £28.80, 1&3 £33.00, 2&3 £45.70 CSF £108.92 CT £1749.05 TOTE £12.40: £3.90, £4.50, £4.80; EX 114.50 Trifecta £1837.40 Part won. Pool: £2,449.92 - 0.50 winning units..

Owner Ontoawinner 4 **Bred** Miss Wendy Fox **Trained** Babworth, Notts

FOCUS
An ordinary handicap for the track. The front-running winner seemed to match his Southwell best.

T/Plt: £32.50 to a £1 stake. Pool: £47,996.19 - 27.87 winning tickets. T/Qpdt: £227.00 to a £1 stake. Pool: £5,061.50 - 16.50 winning tickets. SP

7042 FLEMINGTON (L-H)
Saturday, November 2

OFFICIAL GOING: Turf: good

7700a LEXUS STKS (GROUP 3 QUALITY H'CAP) (3YO+) (TURF) 1m 4f 110y
1:45 (12:00) 3-Y-O+

£116,346 (£34,615; £17,307; £8,653; £4,807; £3,846)

RPR
1 **Ruscello (IRE)**[17] 7417 4-8-7 0 KerrinMcEvoy 12 103
(Ed Walker) *sn led on rail and mde rest: rdn 2f out: strly pressed and jnd ent fnl f: styd on and edgd ahd again ins fnl 120yds: drvn out* **10/1**

2 *hd* **Let's Make Adeal (AUS)**[21] 7213 4-8-7 0 MichaelWalker 13 104
(Nigel Blackiston, Australia) **17/2**[3]

3 *1 ½* **Araldo**[28] 5-8-7 0 GlenBoss 6 101+
(Michael Moroney, Australia) **16/5**[1]

4 *1* **Ethiopia (AUS)**[14] 7392 5-9-2 0 (v) HughBowman 9 108
(Pat Carey, Australia) **25/1**

5 *½* **Garud (IRE)**[14] 5-8-7 0 (b) CraigAWilliams 1 98
(Michael Moroney, Australia) **13/1**

6 *shd* **Ironstein (AUS)**[28] 8-8-7 0 (b) BrentonAvdulla 2 98
(Gerald Ryan, Australia) **11/1**

7 *shd* **Kingdoms (NZ)**[28] 4-8-7 0 (t) JamesMcDonald 5 99
(J O'Shea, Australia) **13/1**

8 *½* **Moudre (AUS)**[10] 7483 8-8-8 0 (b) MichellePayne 7 98
(Ciaron Maher, Australia) **60/1**

9 *2 ¼* **Motivado**[175] 5-8-7 0 CraigNewitt 4 93
(David Hayes, Australia) **30/1**

10 *1 ¾* **Kelinni (IRE)**[14] 7392 5-9-0 0 (p) NashRawiller 3 98
(Chris Waller, Australia) **9/2**[2]

11 *1 ¼* **Julienas (IRE)**[14] 7392 6-8-13 0 DamienOliver 11 95
(Gai Waterhouse, Australia) **13/1**

12 *nk* **Bass Strait (NZ)**[14] 4-8-7 0 (b) DwayneDunn 10 89
(David Hayes, Australia) **11/1**

13 *shd* **Vaquera (NZ)**[28] 4-8-7 0 TommyBerry 8 89
(Gai Waterhouse, Australia) **25/1**

14 *6 ¼* **My Quest For Peace (IRE)**[14] 7392 5-8-13 0 (b) LukeNolen 14 84
(Peter G Moody, Australia) **30/1**

2m 39.87s (159.87) 14 Ran SP% **115.5**
PARI-MUTUEL (NSW TAB - all including 1 aud stake): WIN 11.20; PLACE 3.50, 3.00, 1.90; DF 62.10; SF 137.00.

Owner L Bellman, Uthmeyer Racing Syndicate Et Al **Bred** Ballymacoll Stud Farm Ltd **Trained** Newmarket, Suffolk

■ Ed Walker's first Group winner.

FOCUS
This was run at a steady pace, with a bunch finish.

7702a LONGINES MACKINNON STKS (GROUP 1) (3YO+) (TURF) 1m 2f
3:15 (12:00) 3-Y-O+

£386,217 (£115,384; £57,692; £28,846; £16,025; £12,820)

RPR
1 **Side Glance**[7] 7556 6-9-4 0 JamieSpencer 6 114
(Andrew Balding) *t.k.h under restraint and towards rr early: hdwy on outer and sn led: set slow pce and mde rest: rdn 2f out: qcknd clr over 1f out: kpt on wl: diminishing advantage towards fin but in control: gd ride* **11/1**

2 *¾* **Dear Demi (AUS)**[14] 7392 4-8-13 0 (b) ChrisMunce 8 107+
(Clarry Conners, Australia) *t.k.h: hld up towards rr on inner: last 3f out: pushed along whn nt clr run briefly 2f out: swtchd lft and rdn over 1f out: kpt on wl and wnt 2nd towards fin: clsd on wnr but a being hld* **10/1**

3 *shd* **Moriarty (IRE)**[14] 7392 5-9-4 0 (t) CraigNewitt 9 112+
(Chris Waller, Australia) *hld up in rr: rdn and hdwy on outer fr 2f out: wnt 2nd ent fnl f: kpt on and clsd on wnr but nt pce to chal and dropped to 3rd towards fin* **16/1**

4 *½* **Mr Moet (AUS)**[14] 7392 6-9-4 0 DamienOliver 5 111
(Adam Durrant, Australia) *hld up towards rr on outer: pushed along over 3f out: rdn and hdwy 2f out: kpt on same pce fr over 1f out and nvr quite able to chal* **12/1**

5 *shd* **Pakal (GER)**[20] 4-9-4 0 (t) HughBowman 3 111
(Mick Price, Australia) *midfield in tch: rdn over 2f out: sltly outpcd as pce increased over 1f out: styd on and fin wl but nvr able to chal* **16/5**[2]

6 *3 ¼* **Jet Away**[14] 7392 6-9-4 0 GlenBoss 1 104
(David Hayes, Australia) *t.k.h: midfield on inner: rdn and effrt 2f out: outpcd by wnr over 1f out: no ex and fdd ins fnl 150yds: eased fnl 75yds* **2/1**[1]

7 *3 ¼* **Mourayan (IRE)**[28] 7-9-4 0 (b) StevenArnold 4 98
(Robert Hickmott, Australia) *trckd ldr on outer: rdn to chal and ev ch over 2f out: no ex and btn over 1f out: fdd: eased towards fin* **20/1**

8 *1 ¼* **Hvasstan (AUS)**[7] 4-9-3 0 (b) BrettPrebble 7 94
(Peter Gelagotis, Australia) *midfield in tch on outer: clsd and prom over 3f out: rdn to chal and ev ch 2f out: no ex and btn ent fnl f: fdd and eased towards fin* **40/1**

9 *14* **Solzhenitsyn (NZ)**[21] 7214 7-9-4 0 (p) NashRawiller 2 67
(Robert Heathcote, Australia) *broke wl and led early: t.k.h: trckd ldr on inner once hdd: lost pl over 2f out and sn rdn: dropped to last and btn over 1f out: eased and sn bhd* **11/2**[3]

2m 3.59s (123.59) 9 Ran SP% **110.7**
PARI-MUTUEL (NSW TAB - all including 1 aud stake): WIN 12.80; PLACE 3.30, 1.90, 3.80; DF 58.70; SF 111.90.

Owner Pearl Bloodstock Ltd **Bred** Kingsclere Stud **Trained** Kingsclere, Hants

7703 - 7704a (Foreign Racing) - See Raceform Interactive

2403 LE CROISE-LAROCHE

Saturday, November 2

OFFICIAL GOING: Turf: heavy

7705a GRAND PRIX DU NORD (LISTED RACE) (3YO) (TURF) 1m 2f 110y

4:35 (12:00) 3-Y-O £22,357 (£8,943; £6,707; £4,471; £2,235)

RPR

1 **Nicolosio (IRE)**34 6894 3-9-2 0 EddyHardouin 4 113+
(W Hickst, Germany) 11/5[2]

2 5 **Vanishing Cupid (SWI)**30 6987 3-9-2 0 (p) FabriceVeron 2 103
(H-A Pantall, France) 9/5[1]

3 1 1/4 **Battalion (IRE)**46 6503 3-9-2 0 Pierre-CharlesBoudot 5 101
(William Haggas) *led: shkn up and 1 l clr 2f out: hdd 1 1/2f out: kpt on at one pce u.p fnl f* 37/10[3]

4 4 **Perfect Queen (FR)**47 6484 3-8-13 0 AurelienLemaitre 6 90
(F Head, France) 78/10

5 3 1/2 **As Des Flandres (FR)**57 6182 3-9-2 0 StephanePasquier 3 86
(Y Barberot, France) 69/10

6 dist **Tokum (FR)**136 3-9-2 0 CesarPasserat 1
(N Bertran De Balanda, France) 20/1

2m 23.4s (143.40) 6 Ran SP% 117.0
WIN (incl. 1 euro stake): 3.20. PLACES: 1.60, 1.40. SF: 9.90.
Owner Stall Nizza **Bred** Juergen Imm **Trained** Germany

7591 SAN SIRO (R-H)

Saturday, November 2

OFFICIAL GOING: Turf: heavy

7706a PREMIO CHIUSURA (GROUP 3) (2YO+) (TURF) 7f

2:35 (12:00) 2-Y-O+ £22,764 (£10,016; £5,463; £2,731)

RPR

1 **Regarde Moi**160 2698 5-9-4 0 FabioBranca 7 106+
(S Botti, Italy) *trckd ldrs on outer: shkn up to ld 1 1/2f out: rdn 1f out and rn: hung lft on to stands' rail: rdn out* 19/5[2]

2 1 1/2 **Pearl Flute (IRE)**125 3876 3-9-8 0 PierantonioConvertino 2 106
(F-H Graffard, France) *trckd ldng trio: rdn to chse eventual wnr appr fnl f: r.o u.p: no imp fnl 75yds* 4/5[1]

3 2 **Mr Muzzare (USA)**174 4-9-4 0 DPerovic 6 97
(M Massimi Jr, Italy) *trckd ldng trio towards out: rdn and ldrs fr 1 1/2f out: kpt on at one pce fnl f* 92/10

4 2 1/2 **Killachy Loose**13 7413 4-9-5 0 DarioVargiu 4 91
(B Grizzetti, Italy) *towards rr: prog to chse ldrs 1/2-way: sltly outpcd 2f out: kpt on at one pce u.p ins fnl f* 77/20[3]

5 3 **Majestic Power (GER)**58 3-9-4 0 MEsposito 5 82
(M Rulec, Germany) *led: hdd after 1 1/2f by free-running Carnoustie but stl led main pack: hdd and rdn 1 1/2f out: grad wknd* 134/10

6 2 1/2 **Art Of Dreams (FR)**13 7416 4-9-4 0 CColombi 3 75
(B Grizzetti, Italy) *w.w towards rr: rdn and short-lived effrt over 1 1/2f: eased whn wl hld fnl f* 29/1

7 9 **Carnoustie (FR)**40 6715 4-9-1 0 (b) CristianDemuro 1 48+
(X Thomas-Demeaulte, France) *tk v t.k.h: trckd ldrs on inner: sddle slipped forward and rdr kicked out irons after 1 1/2f and led under no control: wknd qckly fr over 1 1/2f out* 66/10

1m 29.5s (1.30)
WFA 3 from 4yo+ 1lb 7 Ran SP% 130.2
WIN (incl. 1 euro stake): 4.82. PLACES: 1.71, 1.30. DF: 3.94.
Owner Dioscuri Srl **Bred** Finanza Locale Consulting **Trained** Italy

7687 SANTA ANITA (L-H)

Saturday, November 2

OFFICIAL GOING: Dirt: fast; turf: firm

7707a BREEDERS' CUP JUVENILE FILLIES (GRADE 1) (2YO FILLIES) (DIRT) 1m 110y(D)

7:05 (12:00) 2-Y-O £674,846 (£220,858; £122,699; £73,619; £36,809)

RPR

1 nse **Ria Antonia (USA)**28 7040 2-8-10 0 (b[1]) JJCastellano 5 110+
(Jeremiah C Englehart, U.S.A) *midfield: hdwy to chse clr ldr over 2f out: hrd rdn and pressed ldr fr 1f out: virtually on level terms whn bmpd 50yds out: jst failed: fin 2nd, nse: awrdd r* 40/1

2 **She's A Tiger (USA)**35 6863 2-8-10 0 (b) GaryStevens 10 110
(Jeff Bonde, U.S.A) *broke wl and led: kicked 4 l clr over 2f out: hrd pressed over 1f out: r.o gamely ins fnl f: edgd rt under rt-hand drive and bmpd Ria Antonia fnl 50yds: jst hld on: fin 1st: disqualified and plcd 2nd* 4/1[2]

3 1/2 **Rosalind (USA)**29 2-8-10 0 JRosario 2 109+
(Kenneth McPeek, U.S.A) *w.w in rr wl adrift: last and hdwy on outside over 3f out: 10 l 5th and clsng 2f out: hrd rdn 1 1/2f out: styd on wl ins fnl f: nt quite get up* 10/1

4 1 1/2 **Sweet Reason (USA)**28 7040 2-8-10 0 ASolis 9 105
(Leah Gyarmati, U.S.A) *hld up towards rr: rdn and hdwy 3f out: 3rd and jinked lft and hmpd Artemis Agrotera 1 1/2f out: one pce u.p fnl f* 4/1[2]

5 9 1/4 **Artemis Agrotera (USA)**28 7040 2-8-10 0 JLezcano 1 85
(Michael Hushion, U.S.A) *trckd ldr: shkn up and no imp over 2f out: 3rd and wkng whn hmpd 1 1/2f out: plugged on fnl f* 7/2[1]

6 30 **Scandalous Act (USA)**21 2-8-10 0 (b) EduardoONunez 8 85
(Kathleen O'Connell, U.S.A) *chsd ldrs: lost pl bef 1/2-way: sn wl btn* 14/1

7 9 1/4 **Designer Legs (USA)**29 2-8-10 0 JTalamo 3 65
(Dallas Stewart, U.S.A) *hld up towards rr: rdn and effrt 3f out: hmpd by faller and rdr lost irons 3f out: nt persevered w fnl 2f* 40/1

8 18 1/4 **Untapable (USA)**55 2-8-10 0 RosieNapravnik 7 25
(Steven Asmussen, U.S.A) *midfield: wkng whn sltly hmpd by faller 3f out: nt persevered w* 11/2[3]

9 4 1/4 **Concave (CAN)**62 6029 2-8-10 0 MGutierrez 6 15
(Doug O'Neill, U.S.A) *midfield: 5th and styng on whn hmpd by faller 3f out: nt rcvr and eased* 12/1

F **Secret Compass (USA)**35 6863 2-8-10 0 (b) JRVelazquez 4
(Bob Baffert, U.S.A) *settled in 3rd on inner: shkn up and chsng ldr whn fell under 3f out: fatally injured* 8/1

1m 43.02s (0.60) 10 Ran SP% 117.0
PARI-MUTUEL (all including 2 usd stake): WIN 66.60; PLACE (1-2) 29.80, 6.40; SHOW (1-2-3) 17.40, 4.80, 6.80; SF 739.20.
Owner Loooch Racing Stable Inc & Christopher T Dunn **Bred** Lynn B Schiff **Trained** USA

FOCUS
Like last year, Lasix was forbidden in all 2yo races at the Breeders' Cup. This was a dramatic race as Secret Compass sadly took a fatal fall around the final bend, hampering the last three finishers, and a separate incident led to the result being reversed. Considering the strict interference rules in the States, there can be no real complaints about the decision to demote the first-past-the-post. The dirt surface didn't look to be favouring speed as much as the previous day. A tighter finish than typical for the race, which has been rated at the low end of the win averages.

7708a BREEDERS' CUP FILLY & MARE TURF (GRADE 1) (3YO+ FILLIES & MARES) (TURF) 1m 2f

7:43 (12:00) 3-Y-O+ £674,846 (£220,858; £122,699; £73,619; £36,809)

RPR

1 **Dank**77 5552 4-8-12 0 RyanMoore 1 115+
(Sir Michael Stoute) *broke wl and led early: sn restrained and trckd ldr: rdn to chal 2f out: led over 1f out: styd on wl and a doing enough* 6/4[1]

2 1/2 **Romantica**48 6448 4-8-12 0 MaximeGuyon 2 114+
(A Fabre, France) *prom on inner: rdn 3f out: styd on and wnt 2nd towards fin: nt quite pce of wnr* 4/1[2]

3 1/2 **Alterite (FR)**21 7216 3-8-8 0 JJCastellano 4 113+
(Chad C Brown, U.S.A) *midfield in tch: rdn 2f out: styd on and wnt 3rd post: nt pce to chal* 16/1

4 nse **Emollient (USA)**27 3-8-8 0 MESmith 8 113
(William Mott, U.S.A) *hdwy on outer and led after 2f: rdn and strly pressed fr 2f out: hdd over 1f out: styd on but nt pce of wnr and dropped to 4th post* 16/1

5 1/2 **Marketing Mix (CAN)**35 6864 5-8-12 0 GaryStevens 6 112
(Thomas F Proctor, U.S.A) *sn led: hdd after 2f and trckd ldrs: rdn over 2f out: styd on but nt pce to chal and dropped to 5th towards fin* 8/1

6 1/2 **Tiz Flirtatious (USA)**35 6864 5-8-12 0 JRLeparoux 3 111+
(Martin F Jones, U.S.A) *hld up in midfield: rdn over 2f out: kpt on and wnt 6th cl home: nvr threatened* 7/1[3]

7 3/4 **Laughing (IRE)**35 6860 5-8-12 0 JLezcano 7 109
(Alan E Goldberg, U.S.A) *stdd after 2f and settled in midfield on inner: rdn over 2f out: kpt on same pce and nvr threatened: dropped to 7th cl home* 8/1

8 3/4 **Lady Of Shamrock (USA)**35 6864 4-8-12 0 VEspinoza 5 108
(John W Sadler, U.S.A) *stdd and hld up in rr: sn last: rdn 2f out: styd on and sme late hdwy but nvr a factor* 33/1

9 3 3/4 **Kitten's Dumplings (USA)**21 7216 3-8-8 0 JRosario 10 100
(Michael J Maker, U.S.A) *dropped in fr wdst draw and hld up in last trio: rdn to try and improve on outer 2f out: no imp and btn ins fnl f* 16/1

10 2 3/4 **Qushchi**35 6860 5-8-12 0 EPrado 9 95
(H Graham Motion, U.S.A) *dropped in fr wd draw and hld up in last trio: hdwy into midfield on outer 4f out: rdn and lost pl again over 2f out: last and btn ent fnl f* 40/1

1m 58.73s (118.73)
WFA 3 from 4yo+ 4lb 10 Ran SP% 117.7
PARI-MUTUEL (all including 2 usd stake): WIN 5.00; PLACE (1-2) 3.40, 5.20; SHOW (1-2-3) 2.80, 4.00, 7.00; SF 23.20.
Owner James Wigan **Bred** London Thoroughbred Services Ltd **Trained** Newmarket, Suffolk

FOCUS
The early pace wasn't that strong (24.02, 47.50, 1:11.52, and 1:35.26) given the firm ground, and it was an advantage to race handily. The fourth and sixth help with the standard.

7709a BREEDERS' CUP FILLY & MARE SPRINT (GRADE 1) (3YO+ FILLIES & MARES) (DIRT) 7f

8:21 (12:00) 3-Y-O+ £337,423 (£110,429; £61,349; £36,809; £18,404)

RPR

1 **Groupie Doll (USA)**28 5-8-12 0 (b) RMaragh 11 116
(William Bradley, U.S.A) *trckd ldng trio: cl 3rd and gng wl 3f out: shkn up to ld 1 1/2f out: rdn and r.o fnl f: hld on gamely* 7/2[1]

2 1/2 **Judy The Beauty (CAN)**28 4-8-12 0 LSaez 9 115
(Wesley A Ward, U.S.A) *chsd front two: outpcd 3f out: 4th and rdn over 1 1/2f out: r.o u.p fnl f: nvr quite on terms w wnr* 13/2[3]

3 1/2 **Dance Card (USA)**42 4-8-12 0 JRosario 4 114
(Kiaran McLaughlin, U.S.A) *towards rr: pushed along and hdwy 2 1/2f out: 5th and styng on 1 1/2f out: r.o fnl f: nvr quite on terms* 6/1[2]

4 3 1/2 **Summer Applause (USA)**27 4-8-12 0 JJCastellano 7 104
(Chad C Brown, U.S.A) *towards rr: rdn and prog 2 1/2f out: styd on wl ins fnl f: nvr on terms w ldrs* 20/1

5 3/4 **Sweet Lulu (USA)**42 3-8-10 0 JRLeparoux 12 100
(Jerry Hollendorfer, U.S.A) *wnt rt s: sn led fr wd draw and moved on to rail: jnd 3f out: rdn and hdd 2f out: wknd appr fnl f* 6/1[2]

6 1 1/2 **Dance To Bristol (USA)**42 4-8-12 0 XPerez 8 98
(Ollie Figgins III, U.S.A) *midfield: 5th and rdn 3f out: nt qckn u.p 2f out: one pce fnl f* 6/1[2]

7 1/2 **Great Hot (BRZ)**27 5-8-12 0 (b) ChantalSutherland-Kruse 10 97
(A C Avila, U.S.A) *trckd ldng trio between horses: lost pl 3 1/2f out: 7th and hrd rdn over 2f out: no imp: one pce fnl f* 33/1

8 nk **Teddy's Promise (USA)**27 5-8-12 0 VEspinoza 5 96
(Ronald W Ellis, U.S.A) *chsd ldr: disp ld 3f out: led 2f out: sn rdn and hdd 1 1/2f out: wknd fnl f* 9/1

9 3 1/4 **Book Review (USA)**71 5736 4-8-12 0 RBejarano 2 87
(Bob Baffert, U.S.A) *towards rr: hdwy 2 1/2f out: run flattened out fnl 1 1/2f: n.d* 8/1

10 1 3/4 **Renee's Titan (USA)**22 3-8-10 0 MGutierrez 1 80
(Doug O'Neill, U.S.A) *in rr: rdn and shortlived effrt over 1 1/2f out: nvr in contention* 50/1

11 2 1/4 **Ismene (USA)**20 4-8-12 0 MESmith 6 76
(Bill Spawr, U.S.A) *midfield: lost pl 1/2-way: sn wknd and btn* 20/1

12 3 1/4 **Starship Truffles (USA)**42 4-8-12 0 (b) GaryStevens 3 68
(Martin D Wolfson, U.S.A) *chsd ldng trio on inner: lost pl over 3f out: sn rdn and btn* 18/1

1m 20.75s (80.75)
WFA 3 from 4yo+ 1lb 12 Ran SP% 119.2
PARI-MUTUEL (all including 2 usd stake): WIN 8.00; PLACE (1-2) 4.60, 9.20; SHOW (1-2-3) 3.40, 5.40, 4.80; SF 58.00.

Owner Fred F & William B Bradley et al **Bred** Fred & William Bradley **Trained** USA

FOCUS

Sweet Lulu, closely pursued by Teddy's Promise, took them through splits of 22.19 and 44.19. The winner didn't have to be in the same form as when wining a stronger renewal last year.

7710a GEICO BREEDERS' CUP TURF SPRINT (GRADE 1) (3YO+) (TURF) 6f 110y

9:05 (12:00) 3-Y-0+ **£337,423** (£85,889; £85,889; £36,809; £18,404)

RPR

1 **Mizdirection (USA)**[147] 5-8-11 0 .... MESmith 12 111+
(Mike Puype, U.S.A) *in tch on outside: effrt and rdn over 1f out: gd hdwy to ld last 50yds: kpt on wl* **3/1**[1]

2 1/2 **Reneesgotzip (USA)**[76] 4-8-11 0 .... (b) EMaldonado 4 110
(Peter Miller, U.S.A) *led at str pce: qcknd 3 l clr ent st: sn rdn: edgd rt and hdd last 50yds: kpt on: jnd for 2nd on line* **5/1**[2]

2 dht **Tightend Touchdown (USA)**[61] 4-9-0 0 .... (b) JJCastellano 7 113
(Jason Servis, U.S.A) *chsd ldr: rdn over 2f out: rallied and ev ch last 75yds: kpt on to dead-heat for 2nd on line* **14/1**

4 1 1/4 **Unbridled's Note (USA)**[35] 4-9-0 0 .... CNakatani 14 109+
(Steven Asmussen, U.S.A) *midfield on outside: effrt and drvn wl over 1f out: kpt on ins fnl f: nt pce to rch first three* **6/1**[3]

5 1 1/4 **Dimension**[48] 6456 5-9-0 0 .... DJMoran 13 105+
(Conor Murphy, U.S.A) *midfield: drvn and hdwy over 1f out: kpt on ins fnl f: nrst fin* **16/1**

6 nse **Rock Me Baby (USA)**[35] 4-9-0 0 .... JTalamo 2 105+
(Craig Dollase, U.S.A) *midfield on ins: drvn along and outpcd 2f out: no imp ins fnl f* **20/1**

7 1/2 **Jeranimo (USA)**[34] 6893 7-9-0 0 .... VEspinoza 1 104+
(Michael Pender, U.S.A) *bhd and outpcd: hdwy on wd outside over 1f out: kpt on fnl f: nvr able to chal* **20/1**

8 nse **Handsome Mike (USA)**[28] 7045 4-9-0 0 .... MGutierrez 8 104+
(Doug O'Neill, U.S.A) *bhd and sn outpcd: hdwy over 1f out: kpt on ins fnl f: nt pce to chal* **33/1**

9 nk **Chips All In (USA)**[35] 4-9-0 0 .... (b) JRLeparoux 3 103+
(Jeff Mullins, U.S.A) *prom on ins: drvn along over 2f out: no ex fr over 1f out* **6/1**[3]

10 nk **Havelock (USA)**[28] 6-9-0 0 .... JamesGraham 10 102+
(Darrin Miller, U.S.A) *s.i.s: bhd and outpcd: rdn and hdwy over 1f out: nvr rchd ldrs* **14/1**

11 1/2 **Spring To The Sky (USA)**[28] 4-9-0 0 .... RMaragh 11 100
(Bruce R Brown, U.S.A) *chsd ldrs tl rdn and wknd over 1f out* **33/1**

12 1/2 **Boat Trip (USA)**[35] 4-9-0 0 .... RBejarano 6 99
(Michael Pender, U.S.A) *bhd and sn outpcd: plenty to do ent st: nvr on terms* **12/1**

13 1 **Capo Bastone (USA)**[70] 5781 3-8-12 0 .... JRosario 9 94
(Todd Pletcher, U.S.A) *towards rr: drvn along over 2f out: nvr on terms* **10/1**

1m 12.25s (72.25) **13** Ran SP% **121.6**

PARI-MUTUEL (all including 2 usd stake): WIN 7.40; PLACE (1-2) 4.40, 6.80 Tightend Touchdown, 3.60 Reneesgotzip; SHOW (1-2-3) 3.40, 8.60 Tightend Touchdown, 4.80 Reneesgotzip; SF 66.60 Tightend Touchdown, 19.40 Reneesgotzip.

Owner Jungle Racing Llc, Strauss Et Al **Bred** Joseph J Perrotta **Trained** USA

FOCUS

The first three from this race last year returned, and this time they filled three of the first four places.

7711a BREEDERS' CUP JUVENILE (GRADE 1) (2YO COLTS & GELDINGS) (DIRT) 1m 110y(D)

9:43 (12:00) 2-Y-0 **£674,846** (£220,858; £122,699; £73,619; £36,809)

RPR

1 **New Year's Day (USA)**[63] 2-8-10 0 .... (b) MGarcia 4 118+
(Bob Baffert, U.S.A) *midfield: rdn 3f out: styd on strly against rail in st and led towards fin: won gng away* **8/1**[3]

2 1 1/4 **Havana (USA)**[28] 7041 2-8-10 0 .... GaryStevens 12 115
(Todd Pletcher, U.S.A) *chsd ldrs: wnt 2nd 3f out: rdn to ld over 1f out: clr ent fnl f and looked in control: clsd down and hdd towards fin: no ex* **3/1**[1]

3 3/4 **Strong Mandate (USA)**[28] 7041 2-8-10 0 .... (b) JRosario 13 114
(D Wayne Lukas, U.S.A) *stdy hdwy on outer and w ldrs after 2f: led after 4f out: strly pressed fr 2f out: rdn and hdd over 1f out: kpt on same pce ins fnl f* **9/1**

4 1 1/4 **Bond Holder (USA)**[34] 6891 2-8-10 0 .... MGutierrez 5 111
(Doug O'Neill, U.S.A) *sn towards rr: rdn and hdwy fr 3f out: styd on steadily in st and wnt 4th towards fin* **8/1**[3]

5 hd **Tap It Rich (USA)**[21] 2-8-10 0 .... MESmith 6 110
(Bob Baffert, U.S.A) *in tch on wd outside: rdn over 2f out: kpt on same pce in st and nvr able to chal* **4/1**[2]

6 1/2 **Mexikoma (USA)**[51] 2-8-10 0 .... (b) AGarcia 3 109
(Richard C Mettee, U.S.A) *pushed along in rr: last 1/2-way: rdn and hdwy fr 3f out: swtchd rt whn briefly short of room over 1f out: styd on and wnt 6th post: nvr nrr* **12/1**

7 hd **We Miss Artie (CAN)**[28] 7044 2-8-10 0 .... JJCastellano 9 109
(Todd Pletcher, U.S.A) *chsd ldrs: rdn over 2f out: kpt on tl no ex and lost multiple pls towards fin* **10/1**

8 5 1/4 **Dance With Fate (USA)**[34] 6891 2-8-10 0 .... RBejarano 2 97
(Peter Eurton, U.S.A) *dwlt sltly and towards rr: rdn and hdwy into midfield over 3f out: plugged on u.p in st but no imp* **10/1**

9 nk **Diamond Bachelor (USA)**[27] 2-8-10 0 .... JRLeparoux 11 97
(Patrick L Biancone, U.S.A) *sn towards rr: rdn in last 2f out: kpt on and sme hdwy in st but nvr a factor* **10/1**

10 7 1/4 **Smarty's Echo (USA)**[28] 7044 2-8-10 0 .... EBaird 1 81
(Anne P Smith, U.S.A) *dwlt sltly and a in rr: rdn over 3f out: no imp and btn over 1f out: nvr a factor* **20/1**

11 nk **Medal Count (USA)**[27] 2-8-10 0 .... RAlbarado 10 80
(Dale Romans, U.S.A) *chsd ldrs early: midfield fr bef 1/2-way: rdn 3f out: sn dropped to rr and btn* **50/1**

12 1 1/4 **Rum Point (USA)**[28] 7044 2-8-10 0 .... (b) EMaldonado 8 77
(Doug O'Neill, U.S.A) *pressed ldr: w ldrs after 2f: hdd after 4f: rdn and lost pl over 2f out: btn and eased ent fnl f* **40/1**

13 8 1/2 **Conquest Titan (USA)**[28] 7044 2-8-10 0 .... ERosaDaSilva 7 59
(Mark Casse, Canada) *led: jnd after 2f: hdd after 4f: rdn and wknd on rail over 2f out: sn in rr and btn: eased* **40/1**

1m 43.52s (1.10) **13** Ran SP% **123.8**

PARI-MUTUEL (all including 2 usd stake): WIN 23.00; PLACE (1-2) 9.20, 4.60; SHOW (1-2-3) 6.60, 3.40, 6.00; SF 107.80.

Owner Gary L & Mary E West **Bred** Clearsky Farms **Trained** USA

FOCUS

Like in the Juvenile Fillies, they went fast and came home slowly, and the overall time was 0.50secs off the earlier contest. Here are the splits with other race in brackets: 22.66 (22.55), 45.38 (45.31), 1:09.79 (1:09.30), 1:36.66 (1:36.03). The firt two improved, with the next pair setting the standard.

7712a BREEDERS' CUP TURF (GRADE 1) (3YO+) (TURF) 1m 4f (T)

10:22 (12:00) 3-Y-0£**1,012,269** (£331,288; £184,049; £110,429; £55,214)

RPR

1 **Magician (IRE)**[137] 3421 3-8-10 0 .... RyanMoore 11 123+
(A P O'Brien, Ire) *hld up and bhd: rdn over 2f out: gd hdwy on outside over 1f out: styd on strly u.p to ld towards fin* **7/1**[3]

2 1/2 **The Fugue**[56] 6226 4-8-11 0 .... WilliamBuick 7 117
(John Gosden) *in tch: smooth hdwy over 4f out: rdn to ld over 1f out: kpt on wl fnl f: hdd towards fin* **1/1**[1]

3 3/4 **Indy Point (ARG)**[33] 4-9-0 0 .... GaryStevens 9 119
(Richard E Mandella, U.S.A) *hld up towards rr: hdwy to chse ldrs over 1f out: rdn and styd on fnl f to take 3rd last 50yds: r.o* **12/1**

4 1/2 **Point Of Entry (USA)**[147] 3126 5-9-0 0 .... (b) JRosario 8 118
(Claude McGaughey III, U.S.A) *hld up: rdn and hdwy over 2f out: kpt on fnl f: nvr able to chal* **5/1**[2]

5 1/2 **Vagabond Shoes (IRE)**[33] 6-9-0 0 .... VEspinoza 1 117
(John W Sadler, U.S.A) *chsd ldrs: rdn and ev ch ent st: kpt on: no ex last 50yds* **33/1**

6 nse **Twilight Eclipse (USA)**[35] 6861 4-9-0 0 .... JRLeparoux 3 117?
(Thomas Albertrani, U.S.A) *hld up: effrt whn n.m.r briefly bnd ent st: rdn and styd on wl fnl f: nvr able to chal* **40/1**

7 1 1/4 **Little Mike (USA)**[35] 6861 6-9-0 0 .... MESmith 4 115
(Dale Romans, U.S.A) *chsd ldr: led over 3f out: rdn and hdd over 1f out: rallied: fdd last 100yds* **8/1**

8 1 1/4 **Big Blue Kitten (USA)**[35] 6861 5-9-0 0 .... JBravo 10 113
(Chad C Brown, U.S.A) *s.i.s: bhd: plenty to do appr st: hdwy and edgd lft over 1f out: kpt on: n.d* **8/1**

9 hd **Real Solution (USA)**[35] 6861 4-9-0 0 .... JJCastellano 12 113
(Chad C Brown, U.S.A) *prom: effrt and drvn over 2f out: wknd appr fnl f* **20/1**

10 9 1/4 **Skyring (USA)**[28] 7045 4-9-0 0 .... (b) LSaez 5 98
(Jose Fernandez, U.S.A) *hld up in midfield on ins: rdn and outpcd over 2f out: wknd over 1f out* **66/1**

11 2 1/2 **Teaks North (USA)**[33] 6-9-0 0 .... (b) MGarcia 2 94
(Eric J Guillot, U.S.A) *t.k.h early: led: rdn and hdd over 3f out: wknd over 2f out* **66/1**

12 18 1/4 **Tale Of A Champion (USA)**[33] 5-9-0 0 .... JTalamo 6 65
(Kristin Mulhall, U.S.A) *trckd ldrs tl wknd qckly fr 3f out: virtually p.u ent st* **66/1**

2m 23.23s (-3.42)

WFA 3 from 4yo+ 6lb **12** Ran SP% **123.7**

PARI-MUTUEL (all including 2 usd stake): WIN 27.00; PLACE (1-2) 11.80, 4.40; SHOW (1-2-3) 7.00, 3.00, 5.40; SF 73.40.

Owner Michael Tabor & Derrick Smith & Mrs John Magnier **Bred** Absolutelyfabulous Syndicate **Trained** Ballydoyle, Co Tipperary

FOCUS

European-trained horses have now won this race in 12 of the last 15 years. Teaks North took them along at a good gallop (24.02, 46.94, and 1:10.67), and they were well strung out until beginning to bunch up rounding the turn into the straight. This wan't a strong renewal and form pick The Fugue was below her best.

7713a XPRESSBET BREEDERS' CUP SPRINT (GRADE 1) (3YO+) (DIRT) 6f (D)

11:01 (12:00) 3-Y-0+ **£506,134** (£165,644; £92,024; £55,214; £27,607)

RPR

1 **Secret Circle (USA)**[19] 4-9-0 0 .... MGarcia 9 119
(Bob Baffert, U.S.A) *in tch gng wl: effrt and rdn on wd outside bnd appr st: hdwy to ld ins fnl f: edgd lft: hld on wl* **3/1**[1]

2 nk **Laugh Track (USA)**[29] 4-9-0 0 .... (b) MESmith 12 118
(Mark Casse, Canada) *racd wd: hld up: pushed along over 2f out: gd hdwy over 1f out: chsd wnr last 50yds: kpt on wl* **20/1**

3 1 1/4 **Gentlemen's Bet (USA)**[29] 4-9-0 0 .... (b) JJCastellano 3 114
(Ronald Moquett, U.S.A) *cl up: led against ins rail and maintained str pce 1/2-way: rdn over 1f out: hdd ins fnl f: no ex towards fin* **11/1**

4 hd **Majestic Stride (USA)**[27] 4-9-0 0 .... (b) EMaldonado 4 113
(Jeff Bonde, U.S.A) *hld up bhd ldng gp: effrt and rdn 2f out: kpt on ins fnl f: nt pce to chal* **28/1**

5 3/4 **Justin Phillip (USA)**[35] 6859 5-9-0 0 .... (b) GaryStevens 1 111
(Steven Asmussen, U.S.A) *bhd and outpcd: hdwy whn n.m.r bnd appr st: gd hdwy over 1f out: fin wl* **6/1**[3]

6 1/2 **Bahamian Squall (USA)**[35] 6859 4-9-0 0 .... (b) LSaez 6 109
(David Fawkes, U.S.A) *sn outpcd and drvn along: hdwy on outside over 1f out: kpt on fnl f: nrst fin* **12/1**

7 1 1/2 **Fast Bullet (USA)**[63] 5-9-0 0 .... (b) JRosario 8 104
(D Wayne Lukas, U.S.A) *chsd ldrs on outside: drvn over 2f out: wknd ent fnl f* **7/1**

8 1/2 **Wine Police (USA)**[34] 5-9-0 0 .... EPGomez 10 103
(Henry Dominguez, U.S.A) *chsd ldrs: rdn over 2f out: wknd ent fnl f* **33/1**

9 nk **Trinniberg (USA)**[27] 4-9-0 0 .... (b) RMaragh 11 102
(Shivananda Parbhoo, U.S.A) *hld up on outside: rdn and outpcd wl over 2f out: n.d after* **10/1**

10 1 1/4 **Private Zone (CAN)**[35] 6859 4-9-0 0 .... (b) MartinAPedroza 7 98
(Doug O'Neill, U.S.A) *chsd ldrs: drvn along over 2f out: wknd qckly over 1f out* **4/1**[2]

11 2 1/4 **The Lumber Guy (USA)**[35] 6859 4-9-0 0 .... MLuzzi 2 90
(Michael Hushion, U.S.A) *bhd: hdwy 1/2-way: rdn over 2f out: sn btn* **16/1**

12 1/2 **Sum Of The Parts (USA)**[29] 4-9-0 0 .... LRGoncalves 5 89
(Thomas Amoss, U.S.A) *led at str gallop to 1/2-way: rallied: rdn and wknd over 1f out* **12/1**

1m 8.73s (0.47) **12** Ran SP% **121.6**

PARI-MUTUEL (all including 2 usd stake): WIN 7.00; PLACE (1-2) 4.80, 13.40; SHOW (1-2-3) 3.60, 8.60, 7.00; SF 100.80.

Owner Karl Watson, Michael E Pegram & Paul Weitman **Bred** Willmott Stables **Trained** USA

FOCUS
The pace was predictably furious - 21.34, 43.72 and 55.97 - and this set up for the sensibly ridden winner.

7714a BREEDERS' CUP MILE (GRADE 1) (3YO+) (TURF) 1m (T)
11:40 (12:00) 3-Y-O+ £674,846 (£220,858; £122,699; £73,619; £36,809)

RPR

1 **Wise Dan (USA)**28 7045 6-9-0 0 JLezcano 8 121+
(Charles LoPresti, U.S.A) *stmbld s but qckly rcvrd: t.k.h: midfield on outer: rdn 2f out: r.o and chal wl ins fnl f: led towards fin: drvn out* **4/5**1

2 ¾ **Za Approval (USA)**21 5-9-0 0 JRosario 10 119
(Christophe Clement, U.S.A) *midfield in tch: rdn and hdwy on outer 2f out: led over 1f out: r.o wl but hdd towards fin and no ex* **33/1**

3 ¾ **Silentio (USA)**69 4-9-0 0 RBejarano 2 118
(Gary Mandella, U.S.A) *midfield on inner: swtchd off rail and rdn 2f out: hdwy and wnt 3rd ins fnl f: swtchd bk to rail and kpt on wl wout matching front pair towards fin* **50/1**

4 4 ¼ **Silver Max (USA)**28 7045 4-9-0 0 RAlbarado 3 108+
(Dale Romans, U.S.A) *broke wl and led early: sn hdd and trckd ldr: rdn to chal over 2f out: outpcd by ldrs and lost pl over 1f out: kpt on again towards fin and tk mod 4th cl home* **10/1**

5 nk **Obviously (IRE)**28 5-9-0 0 JTalamo 4 107+
(Mike Mitchell, U.S.A) *dwlt sltly but qckly rcvrd: sn led and set v fast pce: rdn 2f out: hdd over 1f out: no ex and btn: fdd* **16/1**

6 nse **No Jet Lag (USA)**28 3-8-11 0 MESmith 1 106+
(Simon Callaghan, U.S.A) *chsd ldrs on inner: rdn and ev ch 2f out: kpt on same pce fr over 1f out* **9/1**3

7 ½ **Cristoforo Colombo (USA)**20 7227 3-8-11 0 RyanMoore 9 105
(A P O'Brien, Ire) *dwlt sltly and hld up last in detached fnl pair: rdn over 2f out: kpt on against rail in st but nvr a factor* **12/1**

8 ½ **He Be Fire N Ice (USA)**28 5-9-0 0 VEspinoza 7 105
(John W Sadler, U.S.A) *stdd and hld up in detached fnl pair: tacked onto main body of field 1/2-way: rdn over 2f out: no imp in st: nvr a factor* **33/1**

9 ½ **Olympic Glory (IRE)**14 7366 3-8-11 0 (b) RichardHughes 5 103
(Richard Hannon) *dwlt sltly: hld up in midfield: rdn over 2f out: drvn in rr and toiling over 1f out: plugged on but nvr threatened* **9/2**2

10 12 **Bright Thought (USA)**231 4-9-0 0 (b) JRLeparoux 6 76+
(Jorge Gutierrez, U.S.A) *chsd ldrs on outer: rdn and lost pl over 2f out: last and btn over 1f out: eased* **33/1**

1m 32.47s (-1.40)
WFA 3 from 4yo+ 2lb **10** Ran SP% **117.2**
PARI-MUTUEL (all including 2 usd stake): WIN 3.60; PLACE (1-2) 2.80, 8.40; SHOW (1-2-3) 2.20, 5.80, 9.00; SF 33.60.
Owner Morton Fink **Bred** Mort Fink **Trained** USA

FOCUS
This race was set up nicely for the winner, the leaders going fast in front, setting fractions of 21.94 for the opening 2f and 44.47 for the half-mile.

7707 SANTA ANITA (L-H)
Sunday, November 3

OFFICIAL GOING: Dirt: fast

7715a BREEDERS' CUP CLASSIC (GRADE 1) (3YO+) (DIRT) 1m 2f (D)
12:35 (12:00) 3-Y-O£41,687,116 (£552,147; £306,748; £184,049; £92,024)

RPR

1 **Mucho Macho Man (USA)**35 6893 5-9-0 0 GaryStevens 6 125+
(Kathy Ritvo, U.S.A) *disp ld 1f: sn stdd bhd ldrs on outside: hdwy to ld over 2f out: drvn over 1f out: kpt on wl fnl f: jst hld on* **4/1**2

2 nse **Will Take Charge (USA)**43 3-8-10 0 LSaez 10 124
(D Wayne Lukas, U.S.A) *hld up bhd ldng gp: pushed along after 3f: stdy hdwy 1/2-way: drvn and outpcd over 2f out: rallied and edgd lft over 1f out: kpt on strly fnl f: jst hld* **12/1**

3 hd **Declaration Of War (USA)**74 5654 4-9-0 0 JosephO'Brien 5 124
(A P O'Brien, Ire) *trckd ldrs: effrt and pressed wnr over 1f out: sn hrd rdn: kpt on u.p ins fnl f: hld nr fin* **9/2**3

4 3 ¼ **Fort Larned (USA)**35 5-9-0 0 (b) BHernandezJr 7 117
(Ian Wilkes, U.S.A) *w ldrs: led after 4f: rdn and hdd over 2f out: rallied and ev ch ent st: outpcd by first three fnl f* **8/1**

5 1 ¼ **Last Gunfighter (USA)**36 6862 4-9-0 0 (b) JJCastellano 1 115
(Chad C Brown, U.S.A) *broke wl but sn bhd: detached 1/2-way: gd hdwy over 1f out: fin strly but nvr any ch of rching ldrs* **50/1**

6 2 ½ **Palace Malice (USA)**36 6862 3-8-10 0 RBejarano 8 110
(Todd Pletcher, U.S.A) *s.i.s: hld up: hdwy on outside and prom wl over 2f out: sn rdn: wknd over 1f out* **9/1**

7 1 ¾ **Paynter (USA)**35 6893 4-9-0 0 MGarcia 2 106
(Bob Baffert, U.S.A) *chsd ldng gp on ins: drvn and outpcd 3f out: no imp tl styd on fnl f: nvr able to chal* **16/1**

8 1 **Flat Out (USA)**36 6862 7-9-0 0 JRosario 12 104
(William Mott, U.S.A) *hld up in rr: rdn along and shortlived effrt over 2f out: wknd over 1f out* **20/1**

9 1 ¼ **Game On Dude (USA)**69 5849 6-9-0 0 (b) MESmith 9 102
(Bob Baffert, U.S.A) *w ldrs on outside: ev ch tl rdn and wknd over 1f out: eased whn btn fnl f* **5/2**1

10 8 ¼ **Moreno (USA)**43 3-8-10 0 (b) JTalamo 4 85
(Eric J Guillot, U.S.A) *led 4f: w ldrs on ins tl wknd wl over 2f out* **25/1**

11 ½ **Planteur (IRE)**29 7049 6-9-0 0 1 RyanMoore 3 84
(Marco Botti) *sweating and edgy in preliminaries: in tch: drvn and outpcd over 3f out: btn fnl 2f* **33/1**

2m 0.72s (0.84)
WFA 3 from 4yo+ 4lb **11** Ran SP% **114.9**
PARI-MUTUEL (all including 2 usd stake): WIN 10.00; PLACE (1-2) 4.60, 7.20; SHOW (1-2-3) 3.60, 4.80, 4.80; SF 73.00.
Owner Reeves Thoroughbred Racing **Bred** John D Rio & Carole A Rio **Trained** USA

FOCUS
Strictly from a form standpoint this was not a vintage Breeders' Cup Classic, even with the one-two from last year back for more, but there was also a legitimate European-trained contender, and the competitive nature of the race made for a truly thrilling spectacle. As expected, there was a contested pace with 2012 winner Fort Larned, favourite Game On Dude, and Moreno taking each other on for much of the way, and that trio were easily picked off. The early pace was solid before the tempo gradually slowed: 23.20, 46.50, 1:10.12, 1:34.84. The second and third set the standard.

7716 - 7718a (Foreign Racing) - See Raceform Interactive

7547 LEOPARDSTOWN (L-H)
Sunday, November 3

OFFICIAL GOING: Soft

7719a KNOCKAIRE STKS (LISTED RACE) 7f
2:00 (2:02) 3-Y-O+ £21,138 (£6,178; £2,926; £975)

RPR

1 **Francis Of Assisi (IRE)**63 6025 3-9-5 104 (p) SeamieHeffernan 1 109+
(A P O'Brien, Ire) *hld up in mid-div: 7th 1/2-way: rdn fr 2f out and hdwy u.p to ld ins fnl 100yds: styd on wl* **9/2**2

2 1 ½ **Big Break**28 7051 3-9-0 106 PatSmullen 14 100
(D K Weld, Ire) *hld up in tch: 6th 1/2-way: hdwy on outer fr 2f out to ld 1 1/2f out: sn strly pressed and hdd ins fnl 100yds: no ex* **2/1**1

3 2 ¼ **Pop Art (IRE)**15 7388 3-9-0 91 NGMcCullagh 4 94
(Charles O'Brien, Ire) *chsd ldrs: 5th 1/2-way: tk clsr order into st: rdn in 3rd fr 2f out and no imp on ldrs ins fnl f: kpt on same pce* **33/1**

4 ½ **Mizzava (IRE)**14 7404 3-9-0 106 ShaneFoley 5 93
(M Halford, Ire) *chsd ldrs: 4th 1/2-way: lost pl into st: rdn in 6th fr 2f out and sn n.m.r between horses: kpt on same pce in 4th towards fin* **5/1**3

5 hd **Boston Rocker (IRE)**21 7227 3-9-0 100 (v) DeclanMcDonogh 7 92
(Edward Lynam, Ire) *s.i.s: racd towards rr: rdn in 11th 1 1/2f out and kpt on wl ins fnl f wout ever threatening principals: nrst fin* **12/1**

6 nk **Bubbly Bellini (IRE)**11 7474 6-9-6 95 (p) FergalLynch 10 97
(Adrian McGuinness, Ire) *in rr of mid-div: 10th 1/2-way: tk clsr order on inner into st: short of room u.p over 1f out: kpt on towards fin* **33/1**

7 1 **Romantic Stroll (IRE)**14 7404 4-9-1 96 WayneLordan 16 90
(T Stack, Ire) *in rr of mid-div: 9th 1/2-way: rdn into st and sn no imp on ldrs: kpt on one pce* **20/1**

8 ½ **Bold Thady Quill (IRE)**8 7550 6-9-9 101 (v) GaryCarroll 11 96
(K J Condon, Ire) *s.i.s and racd towards rr: kpt on wl u.p fr under 2f out: nrst fin* **33/1**

9 nk **Ondeafears (IRE)**46 6542 6-9-1 95 ConorHoban 13 87
(M Halford, Ire) *dwlt and racd towards rr: tk clsr order on inner into st: n.m.r fr 2f out: kpt on ins fnl f* **14/1**

10 nk **Red Dubawi (IRE)**21 7227 5-9-6 101 JohnnyMurtagh 15 92
(David Marnane, Ire) *sn trckd ldrs: 3rd 1/2-way: pushed along fr 2f out and sn no imp on ldrs u.p: wknd fnl f* **8/1**

11 1 **Arctic (IRE)**21 7227 6-9-6 100 (t) RonanWhelan 2 89
(Tracey Collins, Ire) *in rr of mid-div: rdn and no imp fr over 2f out: kpt on one pce* **16/1**

12 3 ½ **Northern Rocked (IRE)**63 6025 7-9-6 90 LeighRoche 6 79
(D K Weld, Ire) *trckd ldr: 2nd 1/2-way: rdn and wknd over 1 1/2f out: eased fnl f* **40/1**

13 hd **Beacon Lodge (IRE)**15 7388 8-9-6 102 FMBerry 12 79
(T Stack, Ire) *towards rr: pushed along into st and sn no ex u.p: one pce fnl f* **8/1**

14 1 **Allegra Tak (ITY)**11 7474 7-9-1 88 (t) ChrisHayes 3 71
(H Rogers, Ire) *led: narrow advantage 1/2-way: rdn into st and hdd 1 1/2f out: wknd* **50/1**

15 ½ **Ballyorban (IRE)**28 7052 3-9-5 87 (t) WJLee 9 74
(K J Condon, Ire) *in rr of mid-div: rdn and wknd over 2f out* **50/1**

16 shd **Einsteins Folly (IRE)**161 2687 3-9-5 93 KevinManning 8 74
(J S Bolger, Ire) *hld up in tch: 8th 1/2-way: rdn and no imp fr 2f out: wknd and eased fnl f* **25/1**

1m 28.15s (-0.55)
WFA 3 from 4yo+ 1lb **16** Ran SP% **134.4**
CSF £14.23 TOTE £5.20: £2.00, £1.60, £16.00; DF 15.70 Trifecta £1326.30.
Owner Mrs John Magnier **Bred** Queen Cleopatra Syndicate **Trained** Ballydoyle, Co Tipperary

FOCUS
This is rated through the sicxth and the seventh - the winner won with something to spare after coming under pressure turning in.

7720a EYREFIELD STKS (LISTED RACE) 1m 1f
2:35 (2:35) 2-Y-O £21,138 (£6,178; £2,926; £975)

RPR

1 **Mekong River (IRE)**48 6483 2-9-3 104 (b1) SeamieHeffernan 2 104+
(A P O'Brien, Ire) *sn led: over 1 l clr at 1/2-way: pushed along into st and sn rdn clr: styd on wl ins fnl f: easily* **4/6**1

2 6 ½ **Achnaha (IRE)**19 7284 2-8-12 (p) WayneLordan 5 86
(P D Deegan, Ire) *w.w: cl 4th 1/2-way: prog between horses into 2nd 2f out: sn no imp on easy wnr: kpt on same pce* **20/1**

3 5 ½ **Mandatario**23 7180 2-9-3 104 (t) KevinManning 4 80
(J S Bolger, Ire) *trckd ldrs: cl 2nd 1/2-way: pushed along into st and sn no imp on easy wnr in 3rd: kpt on one pce* **5/2**2

4 3 ¼ **Ubiquitous Mantle (IRE)**8 7549 2-8-12 86 ColinKeane 6 69
(G M Lyons, Ire) *trckd ldr: cl 3rd 1/2-way: pushed along on outer into st and sn no ex u.p in 4th: one pce fnl 2f* **7/1**3

5 9 ½ **Leafcutter (IRE)**50 6413 2-9-3 (b) PatSmullen 3 55
(D K Weld, Ire) *w.w: cl up in rr after 1/2-way: pushed along 3f out and sn no ex u.p: wknd* **14/1**

1m 54.43s (0.33) **5** Ran SP% **112.5**
CSF £15.81 TOTE £1.40: £1.02, £7.70; DF 14.00 Trifecta £26.50.
Owner Mrs John Magnier & Michael Tabor & Derrick Smith **Bred** Roncon, Wynatt & Chelston **Trained** Ballydoyle, Co Tipperary

FOCUS
Mekong River made it four wins from four starts with his best performance to date.

7723a MOVEMBER H'CAP (PREMIER HANDICAP) 1m 6f
4:10 (4:12) 3-Y-O+
£48,780 (£15,447; £7,317; £2,439; £1,626; £813)

RPR

1 **Sir Ector (USA)**35 6886 6-9-7 100 (b) JohnnyMurtagh 3 107
(J J Lambe, Ire) *chsd ldrs: 7th 1/2-way: hdwy into st and clsd to chal 1 1/2f out: sn led and kpt on wl u.p ins fnl f* **14/1**

2 ½ **Quick Jack (IRE)**11 7479 4-8-4 83 5ex oh3 WayneLordan 13 89+
(A J Martin, Ire) *w.w in rr of mid-div: prog gng wl fr 3f out: hdwy between horses to chal in 2nd 1f out: kpt on wl ins fnl f wout matching wnr* **10/1**

3 2 ½ **Bayan (IRE)**15 4974 4-8-4 83 (tp) SilvestreDeSousa 10 86+
(Gordon Elliott, Ire) *settled in mid-div: hdwy u.p fr 2f out on outer to chse ldrs in 3rd ins fnl f: kpt on wl towards fin: nt trble principals* **6/1**2

4 *1/2* **Saptapadi (IRE)**[23] 7174 7-8-11 **90**........................(t) FMBerry 6 92
(Brian Ellison) *w.w towards rr: tk clsr order over 2f out: sn swtchd rt in 9th and kpt on wl u.p towards fin: nvr nrr* **10/1**

5 *nk* **Rawnaq (IRE)**[11] 7479 6-8-4 **83** oh5........................ DannyGrant 8 85
(Matthew J Smith, Ire) *chsd ldrs: 5th 1/2-way: rdn and no imp on ldrs in 4th fr under 2f out: kpt on same pce fnl f and dropped to 5th fnl strides* **25/1**

6 *1 1/4* **Totalize**[13] 7425 4-8-8 **87** 5ex........................ TomEaves 18 87
(Brian Ellison) *w.w towards rr: hdwy on inner into st to sn chse ldrs: rdn in 7th ins fnl f and kpt on u.p towards fin: nt trble principals* **11/2**[1]

7 *3/4* **Ancient Sands (IRE)**[14] 7405 5-8-13 **97**....................(tp) ConnorKing(5) 5 96
(Ms Joanna Morgan, Ire) *chsd ldr in 2nd tl led 2f out: sn strly pressed and hdd over 1f out: wknd ins fnl f* **14/1**

8 *1 1/4* **Call Me Bubbles (FR)**[21] 7230 4-8-10 **89**........................(t) WJLee 4 86
(W P Mullins, Ire) *hld up: pushed along and no imp towards rr 4f out: kpt on wl u.p in 15th fr over 1f out: nrst fin* **7/1**[3]

9 *nk* **Majenta (IRE)**[21] 7230 3-8-6 **98**........................ OisinMurphy(5) 7 94
(Kevin Prendergast, Ire) *in rr of mid-div: sme hdwy 3f out: rdn and no imp on ldrs fr 2f out: kpt on same pce* **10/1**

10 *nk* **Be Perfect (USA)**[22] 7210 4-8-8 **87**........................ ChrisHayes 15 83
(David Nicholls) *hld up in tch: sltly hmpd after 1f: 8th 1/2-way: tk clsr order appr st: rdn in cl 5th and sn no ex u.p: one pce fnl f* **16/1**

11 *1 3/4* **Certerach (IRE)**[30] 7005 5-9-13 **106**........................ ShaneFoley 19 100
(M Halford, Ire) *w.w towards rr: sme hdwy fr 3f out: rdn into st and sn no imp u.p: kpt on same pce* **25/1**

12 *1 1/4* **Face Value**[11] 7479 5-7-8 **83** oh9........................(p) TomMadden(10) 1 75
(Adrian McGuinness, Ire) *led and sn clr: reduced advantage and rdn into st: hdd 2f out and sn wknd* **16/1**

13 *7 1/2* **Stony Grey (IRE)**[14] 7405 3-8-5 **92**........................(p) NGMcCullagh 17 73
(A Oliver, Ire) *chsd ldrs: 6th 1/2-way: pushed along fr 3f out and sn no ex u.p: wknd fnl 2f* **7/1**[3]

14 *1/2* **Paddy The Celeb (IRE)**[21] 7230 7-8-11 **93**...........(p) ConorHoban(3) 14 74
(M Halford, Ire) *chsd ldrs: 4th 1/2-way: pushed along into st and sn no ex u.p: wknd fr under 2f out* **33/1**

15 *1 3/4* **Jack Daddy**[21] 7230 4-7-8 **83**........................ IanQueally(10) 2 61
(Joseph G Murphy, Ire) *chsd ldrs: 3rd 1/2-way: rdn and wknd fr 4f out* **16/1**

16 *9 1/2* **Sho Girl (IRE)**[45] 6579 4-8-5 **84**........................ RoryCleary 16 49
(P J Prendergast, Ire) *racd in mid-div: sltly hmpd after 1f: rdn and no imp 4f out: wknd and eased st* **25/1**

17 *1 1/4* **Truthwillsetufree (IRE)**[21] 7230 4-8-11 **90**........................ PatSmullen 12 53
(D K Weld, Ire) *chsd ldrs early: sltly hmpd after 1f and settled in mid-div: rdn and no imp into st: wknd and eased* **8/1**

U **Tantalising (IRE)**[35] 6886 5-8-5 **84**........................(p) BenCurtis 9
(P J Prendergast, Ire) *chsd ldrs early: wnt rt after 1f and uns rdr* **40/1**

2m 59.46s (-1.54)
WFA 3 from 4yo+ 8lb **18** Ran SP% **141.0**
CSF £159.93 CT £972.09 TOTE £21.00: £3.80, £2.70, £1.50, £3.00; DF 319.90 Trifecta £1153.30.
Owner Mrs L Carr **Bred** George Strawbridge Jnr **Trained** Kilmore, Co Armagh
■ This race is registered as the Leopardstown November Handicap.

FOCUS
This brought the curtain down on the Flat turf season.This was fiercely competitive, as you would expect for the lucrative pot on offer. There didn't appear to be too many hard-luck stories and the gallop was generous. The winner is gradually progressive.
T/Jkpt: Not won. T/Plt: @28.60. Pool of @23497.55 - 573.78 winning units BF

7721 - 7723a (Foreign Racing) - See Raceform Interactive

7678 CAPANNELLE (R-H)
Sunday, November 3

OFFICIAL GOING: Turf: good to soft

7724a PREMIO ROMA GBI RACING (GROUP 1) (3YO+) (TURF) 1m 2f
2:35 (12:00) 3-Y-O+ **£77,235** (£33,983; £18,536; £9,268)

RPR

1 **Feuerblitz (GER)**[35] 6894 4-9-2 0........................ ThierryThulliez 7 113+
(M Figge, Germany) *t.k.h: hld up in midfield on outer: wl in tch fr 1/2-way: eased into narrow ld under 3f out: shkn up over 1f out: pushed clr fnl f: comf* **5/3**[1]

2 *3 1/2* **Shamalgan (FR)**[35] 6889 6-9-2 0........................ CristianDemuro 5 106
(X Thomas-Demeaulte, France) *towards rr but wl in tch: hdwy to trck ldng trio over 3f out: rdn to chse eventual wnr 1 1/2f out: readily outpcd but kpt on for 2nd* **7/4**[2]

3 *2 1/2* **Dogma Noir (IRE)**[35] 4-9-2 0........................ SDiana 2 101
(F Camici, Italy) *hld up towards rr: rdn and effrt 2f out: styd on at same pce 3rd 50yds out: nvr on terms* **135/10**

4 *1 1/2* **Vedelago (IRE)**[35] 6889 4-9-2 0........................ MEsposito 1 98
(S Botti, Italy) *midfield on inner: rdn and no real imp over 2f out: kpt on at one pce fnl f: nvr threatened ldrs* **42/10**

5 *nse* **Lodovico Il Moro (IRE)**[168] 2490 3-9-0 0........................ DarioVargiu 3 100
(L Riccardi, Italy) *t.k.h: led: hdd after 1f: chsd clr ldr and wnt on w eventual wnr under 3f out: sn hrd rdn: outpcd and rdn fr 1 1/2f out: fdd ins fnl f* **232/10**

6 *2 1/2* **Orsino (GER)**[14] 7414 6-9-2 0........................ AndreaAtzeni 8 93
(R Rohne, Germany) *led after 1f: sn clr: hdd under 3f out: grad dropped away u.p* **11/4**[3]

7 *7* **Fancy Beat**[35] 6-9-2 0........................ GBietolini 6 79
(Gianluca Bietolini, Italy) *a among bkmarkers: no ch whn eased ins fnl f* **95/1**

8 *12* **Refuse To Bobbin (IRE)**[35] 3-9-0 0........................(b) AFresu 4 57
(A Giorgi, Italy) *chsd clr ldr: rdn and no imp over 2 1/2f out: wl btn whn eased ins fnl f* **86/1**

1m 59.14s (-4.16)
WFA 3 from 4yo+ 4lb **8** Ran SP% **133.0**
WIN (incl. 1 euro stake): 2.66. PLACES: 1.23, 1.24, 2.16. DF: 2.94.
Owner Stall Eivissa **Bred** Gestut Park Wiedingen **Trained** Germany

7725a PREMIO RIBOT (GROUP 2) (3YO+) (TURF) 1m
3:45 (12:00) 3-Y-O+ **£38,617** (£16,991; £9,268; £4,634)

RPR

1 **Saint Bernard**[14] 7413 4-9-2 0........................ GBietolini 6 105
(D Camuffo, Italy) *midfield: hdwy 2 1/2f out: qcknd to ld ent fnl f: drvn clr* **58/10**

2 *2 1/2* **Libano (IRE)**[35] 6889 7-9-2 0........................ AFresu 5 99
(L Polito, Italy) *led: set decent gallop: rdn and nrly 3 l clr 2f out: hdd ent fnl f: kpt on at one pce u.p: hld on gamely for 2nd* **35/1**

3 *hd* **Porsenna (IRE)**[14] 7413 3-9-1 0........................ CFiocchi 2 100
(S Botti, Italy) *midfield on outer: rdn and prog over 1 1/2f out: styd on u.p fnl f: jst missed 2nd* **14/5**[2]

4 *3/4* **Delrock (GER)**[546] 6-9-2 0........................ DarioVargiu 1 97
(S Bazzani, Italy) *chsd ldrs: 4th and hrd rdn over 2f out: kpt on u.p fnl f: nt pce to chal* **91/10**

5 *3/4* **Nabucco (GER)**[14] 7413 3-9-1 0........................ CristianDemuro 10 96
(R Rohne, Germany) *hld up towards rr: rdn and no immediate rspnse over 2f out: styd on fr over 1f out: nvr on terms* **11/10**[1]

6 *nk* **Sciolina (IRE)**[21] 7234 4-8-13 0........................ DPerovic 8 92
(Cristiana Signorelli, Italy) *towards rr: rdn and outpcd over 3f out: styd on u.p fr over 1f out: nrest at fin* **217/10**

7 *2 1/2* **Passaggio (ITY)**[14] 7413 5-9-2 0........................ GMarcelli 7 89
(A Cascio, Italy) *towards rr: rdn and no imp fr over 2f out* **46/1**

8 *nse* **Bastiani (IRE)**[168] 3-9-1 0........................ AndreaAtzeni 4 90
(L Racco, Italy) *settled in midfield: rdn and no imp fnl 2f: eased whn btn fnl f* **97/10**

9 *1/2* **Super Test (ITY)**[161] 2698 4-9-2 0........................ SDiana 9 88
(M Oppo, Italy) *chsd ldr: rdn and nt qckn over 2f out: sn wknd* **38/1**

10 *3* **Principe Adepto (USA)**[35] 6889 5-9-4 0........................(b) FabioBranca 3 83
(E Botti, Italy) *midfield: hdwy on inner to chse clr ldr 2f out: sn rdn and nt qckn: wkng whn eased ins fnl f* **37/10**[3]

1m 35.17s (-4.63)
WFA 3 from 4yo+ 2lb **10** Ran SP% **141.0**
WIN (incl. 1 euro stake): 6.82. PLACES: 2.25, 6.86, 1.95. DF: 172.76.
Owner Scuderia Colle Papa **Bred** Grundy Bloodstock Slr **Trained** Italy

4333 KREFELD (R-H)
Sunday, November 3

OFFICIAL GOING: Turf: soft

7726a HERZOG VON RATIBOR-RENNEN (GROUP 3) (2YO) (TURF) 1m 110y
1:55 (12:00) 2-Y-O **£26,016** (£8,943; £4,471; £2,439; £1,626)

RPR

1 **Nordico (GER)** 2-9-2 0........................ DPorcu 3 101
(Mario Hofer, Germany) *mde all: rdn over 2f out: r.o strly and a doing enough: pushed out firmly towards fin* **47/10**

2 *3/4* **Madurai (GER)**[21] 7232 2-9-2 0........................ APietsch 5 99
(W Hickst, Germany) *dwlt sltly: in rr and nvr really travelling: rdn and hdwy on outer 2f out: wnt 2nd over 1f out: hung rt u.p but kpt on and chsd wnr: clsd but a being hld* **6/5**[1]

3 *5* **Nightdance Dream (GER)** 2-8-13 0........................ AStarke 6 85
(P Schiergen, Germany) *trckd ldr: rdn to chal over 2f out: outpcd by ldrs and dropped to 3rd over 1f out: kpt on* **33/10**[3]

4 *1* **Simba**[21] 7232 2-8-13 0........................ EPedroza 4 83
(A Wohler, Germany) *in tch on inner: rdn over 2f out: outpcd over 1f out: kpt on* **19/10**[2]

5 *4* **Force Aliee (FR)** 2-8-13 0........................ AHelfenbein 7 74
(P Harley, Germany) *in tch on outer: rdn over 3f out: outpcd in rr and btn over 1f out* **76/10**

1m 52.89s (6.29) **5** Ran SP% **132.4**
WIN (incl. 10 euro stake): 57. PLACES: 18, 13. SF: 95.
Owner Eckhard Sauren **Bred** Gestut Brummerhof **Trained** Germany

7727 - (Foreign Racing) - See Raceform Interactive

7662 WOLVERHAMPTON (A.W) (L-H)
Monday, November 4

OFFICIAL GOING: Standard
Wind: Fresh across Weather: Sunny spells

7728 COMPARE BOOKMAKERS AT BOOKMAKERS.CO.UK H'CAP (DIV I) 5f 216y(P)
2:15 (2:17) (Class 6) (0-65,65) 3-Y-O+ **£1,940** (£577; £288; £144) **Stalls** Low

Form RPR

5536 **1** **Haadeeth**[13] 7444 6-9-7 **65**........................(t) AdamKirby 7 75
(David Evans) *broke wl: stdd and lost pl after 1f: hdwy and nt clr run over 1f out: shkn up and r.o to ld nr fin* **4/1**[1]

1100 **2** *nk* **Rise To Glory (IRE)**[13] 7466 5-9-4 **62**........................ DuranFentiman 11 71
(Shaun Harris) *sn led: shkn up and edgd rt over 1f out: rdn ins fnl f: hdd nr fin* **15/2**[2]

2340 **3** *1/2* **Elusive Gold (IRE)**[37] 6856 3-9-7 **65**........................ MartinLane 1 72
(J W Hills) *s.i.s: hdwy over 3f out: rdn over 1f out: r.o* **16/1**

5063 **4** *2* **Hot Sugar (USA)**[17] 7347 4-9-4 **62**........................(p) AndrewMullen 13 63
(Michael Appleby) *a.p: chsd ldr 4f out: rdn and hung lft over 1f out: styd on same pce ins fnl f* **4/1**[1]

3342 **5** *2* **Verus Delicia (IRE)**[40] 6761 4-9-1 **59**........................ ShaneKelly 3 54
(John Stimpson) *chsd ldrs: rdn over 1f out: no ex ins fnl f* **15/2**[2]

0400 **6** *3/4* **El McGlynn (IRE)**[19] 7315 4-8-13 **60**........................ JasonHart(3) 2 52
(Eric Alston) *prom: racd keenly: rdn over 1f out: no ex fnl f* **20/1**

2333 **7** *1 1/2* **Here Now And Why (IRE)**[21] 7236 6-9-0 **58**................(b) GrahamLee 8 45
(Iain Jardine) *mid-div: hdwy over 3f out: rdn over 1f out: styd on same pce* **4/1**[1]

0000 **8** *1 1/2* **Lastkingofscotland (IRE)**[4] 7652 7-9-3 **64**............(b) RyanPowell(3) 12 47
(Conor Dore) *sn outpcd: styd on ins fnl f: nvr nrr* **16/1**

3040 **9** *5* **Prince Of Passion (CAN)**[19] 7315 5-9-5 **63**........................ JoeFanning 4 30
(Derek Shaw) *s.i.s: hld up: pushed along 1/2-way: nvr on terms* **8/1**[3]

3500 **10** *2 3/4* **Baker's Pursuit**[33] 6945 3-8-7 **51** oh1........................ BarryMcHugh 6 9
(Jim Goldie) *a in rr* **40/1**

006 **11** *1 1/2* **Pavers Star**[36] 6878 4-8-12 **56**........................ RobertWinston 9 9
(Noel Wilson) *chsd ldrs: rdn over 2f out: hung lft and eased over 1f out* **20/1**

00/0 **12** *2 3/4* **Superior Duchess**[32] 6986 8-8-2 **51** oh6........................ DanielMuscutt(5) 5
(Michael Blanshard) *chsd ldrs: lost pl 4f out: sn rdn: wknd 1/2-way* **100/1**

000 **13** *nse* **Evens And Odds (IRE)**[44] 6653 9-9-3 **64**........................ SladeO'Hara(3) 10 8
(Peter Grayson) *sn outpcd* **25/1**

1m 15.29s (0.29) **Going Correction** +0.075s/f (Slow) **13** Ran SP% **123.2**
Speed ratings (Par 101): **101,100,99,97,94 93,91,89,82,79 77,73,73**
toteswingers 1&2 £10.90, 1&3 £12.00, 2&3 £29.20 CSF £33.70 CT £464.03 TOTE £5.10: £2.10, £2.00, £4.00; EX 42.70 Trifecta £565.20 Pool: £2677.56 - 3.55 winning units..

Owner Mrs I M Folkes **Bred** Bolton Grange **Trained** Pandy, Monmouths
■ Stewards' Enquiry : Adam Kirby caution: entered the wrong stall

FOCUS
The first of eight races on a dry, breezy day at Dunstall Park and it was one for David Evans and Adam Kirby, who seem likely to prove as potent as ever on the AW this winter. The pace was sound and the form is rated slightly positively.

7729 COMPARE BOOKMAKERS AT BOOKMAKERS.CO.UK H'CAP (DIV II) 5f 216y(P)
2:50 (2:50) (Class 6) (0-65,65) 3-Y-O+ **£1,940** (£577; £288; £144) **Stalls** Low

Form				RPR
3265	1		**Dark Lane**[13] 7445 7-9-5 **63** AdamKirby 4 (David Evans) *trckd ldrs: shkn up to go 2nd over 1f out: sn rdn: r.o to ld nr fin* **4/1**[2]	72
0040	2	½	**Ivestar (IRE)**[27] 7101 8-8-11 **55** (v) GrahamGibbons 12 (Michael Easterby) *chsd ldr: led over 4f out: rdn over 1f out: hdd nr fin* **10/1**	63
1600	3	½	**Invigilator**[14] 7432 5-9-6 **64** (t) RaulDaSilva 10 (Derek Shaw) *s.s: bhd: hdwy over 1f out: rdn: hung rt and r.o ins fnl f: nt rch ldrs* **6/1**[3]	70
0546	4	¾	**Dear Maurice**[20] 7263 9-9-0 **65** (t) AlfieWarwick(7) 5 (Tobias B P Coles) *hld up: rdn over 1f out: r.o ins fnl f: nt rch ldrs* **16/1**	69
0060	5	¾	**Exceedexpectations (IRE)**[13] 7444 4-9-7 **65** LiamKeniry 2 (Conor Dore) *a.p: puished along over 3f out: rdn over 1f out: styd on* **20/1**	66
1-14	6	¾	**French Press (IRE)**[17] 7347 3-9-3 **61** (bt) ShaneKelly 7 (John Stimpson) *prom: rdn over 2f out: styd on same pce fnl f* **7/2**[1]	60
3400	7	¾	**Bapak Pesta (IRE)**[10] 7512 3-8-13 **57** (b[1]) TonyHamilton 11 (Kevin Ryan) *trckd ldrs: racd keenly: rdn over 2f out: no ex fnl f* **14/1**	53
000-	8	3 ¼	**Befortyfour**[336] 7970 8-9-0 **58** RobbieFitzpatrick 6 (Charles Smith) *s.i.s: sme hdwy over 1f out: wknd ins fnl f* **25/1**	44
012	9	1 ¼	**Shamrocked (IRE)**[28] 7077 4-8-13 **62** JacobButterfield(5) 9 (Ollie Pears) *prom: rdn over 2f out: wknd fnl f* **4/1**[2]	44
0000	10	1	**Pick A Little**[34] 6928 5-9-1 **59** SteveDrowne 8 (Michael Blake) *sn outpcd* **25/1**	38
6504	11	1	**Monty Fay (IRE)**[10] 7512 4-8-7 **51** oh5 (vt[1]) LukeMorris 3 (Derek Haydn Jones) *led: hdd over 4f out: rdn over 2f out: wknd over 1f out* **20/1**	27
4001	12	¾	**Katy Spirit (IRE)**[82] 5397 3-9-5 **63** FergusSweeney 1 (Michael Blanshard) *hld up: rdn over 2f out: wknd over 1f out* **20/1**	36

1m 15.86s (0.86) **Going Correction** +0.075s/f (Slow) 12 Ran SP% **120.1**
Speed ratings (Par 101): **97,96,95,94,93 92,91,87,85,84 83,82**
toteswingers 1&2 £7.20, 1&3 £6.80, 2&3 £11.40 CSF £39.95 CT £241.85 TOTE £5.30: £1.70, £3.40, £2.10; EX 50.10 Trifecta £265.30 Pool: £3069.51 - 8.67 winning units..
Owner Mrs E Evans **Bred** David Jamison Bloodstock **Trained** Pandy, Monmouths

FOCUS
The second division of the 6f handicap went the same way as the first with the lethal Evans/Kirby partnership striking again. It was the slower division and the winner showed similar form as when taking this race last year.

7730 BEST ODDS AT BOOKMAKERS.CO.UK (S) STKS 5f 20y(P)
3:20 (3:20) (Class 6) 3-5-Y-O **£1,940** (£577; £288; £144) **Stalls** Low

Form				RPR
0206	1		**Decision By One**[37] 6850 4-9-3 78 (t) StephenCraine 2 (Tom Dascombe) *trckd ldr: shkn up to ld 1f out: rdn clr* **11/10**[1]	79
0003	2	5	**Rothesay Chancer**[21] 7240 5-9-9 73 GrahamLee 7 (Jim Goldie) *in rr: pushed along 3f out: rdn and r.o ins fnl f: wnt 2nd nr fin: no ch w wnr* **11/4**[2]	67
5466	3	¾	**Stoneacre Hull (IRE)**[16] 7380 4-8-9 47 SladeO'Hara(3) 3 (Peter Grayson) *outpcd: r.o ins fnl f: wnt 3rd nr fin* **66/1**	53?
0410	4	shd	**Novabridge**[51] 6412 5-9-9 68 (b) AdamKirby 8 (Neil Mulholland) *pushed along to ld 4f out: rdn and hdd 1f out: wknd ins fnl f* **7/2**[3]	64
0244	5	3 ¾	**Above The Stars**[49] 6463 5-9-4 62 (p) LiamKeniry 1 (Conor Dore) *sn pushed along and prom: rdn over 1f out: wknd ins fnl f* **14/1**	45
0300	6	2 ¾	**Coconut Kisses**[19] 7292 3-8-5 53 RyanWhile(7) 5 (Bill Turner) *led 1f: chsd ldrs: rdn 1/2-way: wknd over 1f out* **22/1**	29
5000	7	5	**La Sylphe**[31] 6994 3-9-1 52 RosieJessop(3) 6 (Derek Shaw) *chsd ldrs tl rdn and wknd 1/2-way* **40/1**	17

1m 2.47s (0.17) **Going Correction** +0.075s/f (Slow) 7 Ran SP% **111.5**
Speed ratings (Par 101): **101,93,91,91,85 81,73**
toteswingers 1&2 £1.30, 1&3 £6.90, 2&3 £7.30 CSF £4.04 TOTE £2.10: £1.30, £2.00; EX 5.70 Trifecta £111.90 Pool: £3377.58 - 22.63 winning units..The winner was sold to David Evans for 9,000gns.
Owner Manor House Racing Club **Bred** G E Amey **Trained** Malpas, Cheshire

FOCUS
This was all about the winner, who did not need to be at his best with the runner-up below form.

7731 BEST ODDS AT BOOKMAKERS.CO.UK H'CAP 5f 216y(P)
3:55 (3:55) (Class 4) (0-85,85) 3-Y-O+ **£4,690** (£1,395; £697; £348) **Stalls** Low

Form				RPR
2536	1		**Athenian (IRE)**[22] 7222 4-9-7 **85** (p) LukeMorris 2 (Sir Mark Prescott Bt) *s.i.s: sn pushed along into mid-div: hdwy over 2f out: rdn over 1f out: r.o to ld wl ins fnl f* **3/1**[1]	97
1212	2	nk	**Burren View Lady (IRE)**[16] 7381 3-8-13 **77** (e) DavidAllan 9 (Tim Easterby) *chsd ldr 5f out: rdn to ld 1f out: hdd wl ins fnl f: styd on* **3/1**[1]	88
0014	3	3	**Space Artist (IRE)**[50] 6429 3-9-3 **81** JoeFanning 7 (Bryan Smart) *led: rdn and hdd 1f out: edgd rt and no ex ins fnl f* **9/1**	82
0250	4	nk	**Rio's Pearl**[45] 6583 3-8-13 **77** (p) HarryBentley 5 (Ralph Beckett) *chsd ldrs: shkn up over 1f out: cl up whn hmpd ins fnl f: styd on same pce* **8/1**[2]	77
2503	5	1 ½	**Angelito**[37] 6822 4-9-1 **79** SeanLevey 10 (Ed McMahon) *hld up in tch: rdn over 1f out: styd on same pce fnl f* **17/2**[3]	75
0034	6	1	**Rasaman (IRE)**[34] 6920 9-9-1 **79** GrahamLee 4 (Jim Goldie) *broke wl: n.m.r and lost pl over 5f out: r.o ins fnl f* **8/1**[2]	71
0424	7	½	**Rhagori Aur**[91] 5057 3-8-11 **80** (b) GeorgeChaloner(5) 3 (Bryan Smart) *s.s: outpcd: rdn over 1f out: n.d* **16/1**	71
5064	8	½	**Johnny Cavagin**[39] 6774 4-8-13 **77** (t) RobertWinston 6 (Richard Guest) *mid-div: rdn over 1f out: n.d* **9/1**	66
000	9	2	**Mappin Time (IRE)**[32] 6977 5-8-11 **75** (p) DuranFentiman 12 (Tim Easterby) *hld up: pushed along over 3f out: nvr on terms* **20/1**	58
1000	10	nk	**Bronze Beau**[19] 7314 6-8-8 **77** (tp) JacobButterfield(5) 1 (Kristin Stubbs) *chsd ldrs: rdn over 2f out: wknd over 1f out* **40/1**	59
040	11	4	**Ruby's Day**[19] 7313 4-9-0 **78** SilvestreDeSousa 8 (David Brown) *prom: n.m.r and lost pl wl over 3f: in rr whn nt clr run over 2f out* **12/1**	47
1400	12	8	**Desert Strike**[37] 6854 7-8-13 **77** (p) LiamKeniry 11 (Conor Dore) *chsd ldrs tl wknd wl over 1f out* **50/1**	21

1m 14.64s (-0.36) **Going Correction** +0.075s/f (Slow) 12 Ran SP% **125.5**
Speed ratings (Par 105): **105,104,100,100,98 96,96,95,92,92 87,76**
toteswingers 1&2 £2.60, 1&3 £7.50, 2&3 £5.10 CSF £11.06 CT £78.00 TOTE £3.20: £1.30, £1.70, £2.50; EX 14.20 Trifecta £93.50 Pool: £3207.14 - 25.71 winning units..
Owner Axom (XXXI) **Bred** Keatly Overseas Ltd **Trained** Newmarket, Suffolk

FOCUS
The best race on the card and by far the fastest of the three 6f contests. Two fillies pulled clear and the form looks sound.

7732 32RED MAIDEN AUCTION STKS 1m 141y(P)
4:25 (4:25) (Class 6) 2-Y-O **£1,940** (£577; £288; £144) **Stalls** Low

Form				RPR
040	1		**Encore Encore (FR)**[33] 6961 2-8-7 0 SilvestreDeSousa 6 (Harry Dunlop) *led: hdd over 7f out: led again over 5f out: rdn over 1f out: hung rt ins fnl f: kpt on* **6/1**	69
02	2	½	**Ujagar (IRE)**[19] 7301 2-9-0 0 StephenCraine 2 (Tom Dascombe) *w wnr tl led over 7f out: hdd over 5f out: chsd wnr: rdn over 3f out: r.o* **3/1**[2]	75
3	3	7	**Lady Horatia**[13] 7435 2-8-10 0 MartinDwyer 4 (William Muir) *trckd ldrs: racd keenly: rdn over 2f out: edgd lft and styd on same pce fr over 1f out* **7/2**[3]	56
4	4	2 ¾	**Ruwasi**[17] 7339 2-9-3 0 LukeMorris 3 (James Tate) *hld up: pushed along over 5f out: nt clr run wl over 1f out: nvr nrr* **11/8**[1]	57
04	5	2	**Tortoise**[6] 7602 2-8-6 0 AndrewMullen 5 (Richard Guest) *hld up: effrt over 2f out: n.d* **100/1**	42
0	6	2	**Gee Sharp**[17] 7341 2-8-13 0 BarryMcHugh 1 (Julie Camacho) *trckd ldrs: rdn over 3f out: wknd over 1f out* **66/1**	45
505	7	8	**Reflection**[32] 6983 2-8-11 54 (v[1]) GrahamGibbons 8 (Brian Baugh) *chsd ldrs: rdn over 3f out: wknd over 2f out* **40/1**	26
05	8	8	**Uplifted (IRE)**[33] 6938 2-9-4 0 TonyHamilton 7 (Kevin Ryan) *hld up: rdn: hung lft and wknd over 3f out* **25/1**	16

1m 52.45s (1.95) **Going Correction** +0.075s/f (Slow) 8 Ran SP% **112.4**
Speed ratings (Par 94): **94,93,87,84,83 81,74,67**
toteswingers 1&2 £3.40, 1&3 £3.10, 2&3 £1.90 CSF £23.30 TOTE £6.70: £1.70, £1.10, £1.60; EX 19.70 Trifecta £57.70 Pool: £4489.46 - 58.30 winning units..
Owner Pam & Peter Deal & Jeni & David Sieff **Bred** Team Hogdala A B **Trained** Lambourn, Berks

FOCUS
The two form principals fought out the finish, clear of the rest. Routine maiden form.

7733 CORAL APP DOWNLOAD FROM THE APP STORE H'CAP 1m 1f 103y(P)
4:55 (4:55) (Class 6) (0-60,60) 3-Y-O+ **£1,940** (£577; £288; £144) **Stalls** Low

Form				RPR
0036	1		**Delightful Sleep**[10] 7515 5-9-4 **57** AdamKirby 8 (David Evans) *hld up: hdwy over 3f out: swtchd lft over 1f out: shkn up to ld ins fnl f: r.o wl* **7/2**[1]	67
6152	2	2 ¼	**Kyle Of Bute**[23] 7201 7-8-7 **51** JoshBaudains(5) 2 (Richard Ford) *trckd ldrs: led 1f out: sn rdn and hdd: styd on same pce* **8/1**	56
3003	3	½	**Outlaw Torn (IRE)**[6] 7605 4-9-7 **60** (e) RobbieFitzpatrick 13 (Richard Guest) *hld up: hdwy on outer over 1f out: r.o to go 3rd nr fin: nt rch ldrs* **4/1**[2]	64
2034	4	½	**Greyemkay**[23] 7201 5-8-7 **51** JacobButterfield(5) 9 (Richard Price) *chsd ldrs: rdn over 2f out: edgd lft and styd on ins fnl f* **9/1**	54
4606	5	nk	**Dandarrell**[16] 7378 6-9-5 **58** FrederikTylicki 6 (Julie Camacho) *trckd ldr tl led over 2f out: rdn and hdd 1f out: no ex ins fnl f* **5/1**[3]	61
6300	6	½	**Joshua The First**[46] 6548 4-9-3 **59** (p) JasonHart(3) 12 (Ian Semple) *s.s: swtchd lft sn after s: hld up and bhd: hdwy over 1f out: rdn and r.o: nt rch ldrs* **9/1**	60
0256	7	3 ¾	**Nezami (IRE)**[17] 7346 8-8-13 **57** JackDuern(5) 3 (Patrick Clinton) *prom: rdn over 2f out: wknd fnl f* **16/1**	51
6160	8	7	**Larghetto (USA)**[16] 7383 5-9-7 **60** ShaneKelly 4 (John Stimpson) *hld up: hdwy over 1f out: nt trble ldrs* **33/1**	39
0500	9	8	**Sondeduro**[44] 6658 4-9-7 **60** FergusSweeney 10 (Jamie Osborne) *prom: rdn over 3f out: wknd over 2f out* **16/1**	22
4200	10	nk	**Konzert (ITY)**[16] 7383 3-9-4 **60** SilvestreDeSousa 1 (Ian Williams) *led: rdn and hdd over 2f out: wknd and eased over 1f out* **5/1**[3]	22
40-0	11	15	**Seraphima**[250] 817 3-9-4 **60** DavidProbert 11 (James Unett) *hld up: racd keenly: rdn over 3f out: wknd over 2f out* **40/1**	

2m 2.47s (0.77) **Going Correction** +0.075s/f (Slow)
WFA 3 from 4yo+ 3lb 11 Ran SP% **123.8**
Speed ratings (Par 101): **99,97,96,96,95 95,92,85,78,78 65**
toteswingers 1&2 £6.30, 1&3 £4.80, 2&3 £4.40 CSF £34.06 CT £121.37 TOTE £5.60: £2.40, £3.00, £2.00; EX 27.50 Trifecta £61.70 Pool: £3946.49 - 47.92 winning units..
Owner Mrs E Evans **Bred** Theresa Fitsall **Trained** Pandy, Monmouths

FOCUS
Another Class 6 handicap and another success for the Evans/Kirby combination. The pace was muddling and the form is modest.

7734 CORAL MOBILE "JUST THREE CLICKS TO BET" MAIDEN STKS 1m 4f 50y(P)
5:25 (5:25) (Class 5) 3-Y-O+ **£2,587** (£770; £384; £192) **Stalls** Low

Form				RPR
52	1		**Aalim**[14] 7422 3-9-4 0 (p) SilvestreDeSousa 7 (Saeed bin Suroor) *hld up: hdwy to chse ldr over 6f out: led over 4f out: rdn and hdd over 2f out: rallied to ld ins fnl f: r.o u.p* **8/11**[1]	77
/0	2	shd	**Eton Dorney (USA)**[14] 7422 4-9-10 0 JoeFanning 3 (Mark Johnston) *led 2f: chsd ldrs: led again over 2f out: rdn and hdd ins fnl f: r.o* **14/1**[3]	77
3332	3	5	**Rex Whistler (IRE)**[38] 6794 3-9-4 73 BarryMcHugh 1 (Julie Camacho) *hld up: nt clr run over 3f out: hdwy over 2f out: rdn over 1f out: styd on same pce fnl f* **7/4**[2]	69
00	4	18	**Rhinestone Rebel (IRE)**[14] 7422 7-9-10 0 WilliamCarson 4 (Peter Hiatt) *chsd ldrs: lost pl over 5f out: rallied over 3f out: wknd 2f out* **80/1**	40
	5	1	**Sonny Jim**[29] 5-9-10 0 (p) StephenCraine 6 (John Mackie) *hdwy 10f out: rdn to chse wnr over 3f out tl over 2f out: sn wknd* **125/1**	38

303/ **6** *11* **Argaum (IRE)**[41] 7045 6-9-10 70....................................(tp) AdamKirby 5 21
(Richard Price) *w ldr tl led 10f out: rdn and hdd over 4f out: nt clr run over 3f out: sn wknd* **14/1**[3]

50 **7** *25* **Ginjo**[54] 6312 3-8-13 0.. SeanLevey 8
(Nigel Twiston-Davies) *trckd ldrs: racd keenly: rdn over 3f out: wknd over 2f out* **50/1**

2m 41.58s (0.48) **Going Correction** +0.075s/f (Slow)
WFA 3 from 4yo+ 6lb 7 Ran SP% **111.6**
Speed ratings (Par 103): **101,100,97,85,84 77,60**
toteswingers 1&2 £2.20, 1&3 £1.02, 2&3 £4.20 CSF £12.41 TOTE £1.40: £1.10, £9.40; EX 12.90 Trifecta £27.70 Pool: £3543.75 - 95.67 winning units..
Owner Godolphin **Bred** Darley **Trained** Newmarket, Suffolk

FOCUS
A modest maiden for older horses. The front two raced towards the centre of the track in the home straight and were able to pull clear. The winner rates similar to his Pontefract form, with the runner-up a big improver.

7735 CORAL.CO.UK BEST ODDS GUARANTEED ON RACING H'CAP 1m 4f 50y(P)
5:55 (5:55) (Class 6) (0-65,65) 3-Y-O+ **£1,940** (£577; £288; £144) **Stalls** Low

Form RPR
2132 **1** **Amantius**[16] 7379 4-9-3 **58**.......................................(b) GrahamLee 4 77+
(Johnny Farrelly) *sn pushed along in rr: hdwy to trck ldr over 3f out: led on bit wl over 1f out: sn clr: easily* **11/8**[1]

4602 **2** *9* **Goodlukin Lucy**[6] 7612 6-8-10 **51**........................ JoeFanning 7 53
(Keith Dalgleish) *trckd ldrs tl led over 4f out: rdn and hdd wl over 1f out: sn outpcd* **6/1**[3]

4-00 **3** *6* **Becausewecan (USA)**[6] 7597 7-9-7 **65**...................... RobertTart(3) 6 57
(Brian Ellison) *prom: rdn over 2f out: sn wknd* **7/2**[2]

1150 **4** *9* **Lochiel**[46] 6552 9-9-8 **63**.. PJMcDonald 5 41
(Ian Semple) *hld up: hdwy over 2f out: sn rdn and wknd* **8/1**

0-36 **5** *2 ¾* **Opus (IRE)**[13] 7440 4-8-10 **51** oh2...........................(p) MartinDwyer 1 24
(Lucy Wadham) *hld up in tch: chsd ldr over 4f out tl over 3f out: rdn and wknd over 2f out* **20/1**

0444 **6** *43* **Maoi Chinn Tire (IRE)**[16] 7382 6-9-1 **56**.................(b[1]) StephenCraine 2
(Jennie Candlish) *racd keenly: led: rdn and hdd over 4f out: wknd over 3f out* **20/1**

4560 **7** *99* **Linkable**[33] 6960 4-9-9 **64**...(t) SebSanders 3
(Brendan Powell) *chsd ldrs: rdn over 3f out: wknd and eased over 2f out: virtually p.u* **7/1**

2m 41.58s (0.48) **Going Correction** +0.075s/f (Slow) 7 Ran SP% **111.7**
Speed ratings (Par 101): **101,95,91,85,83 54,**
toteswingers 1&2 £3.10, 1&3 £1.20, 2&3 £5.90 CSF £9.64 CT £22.94 TOTE £2.50: £1.70, £2.70; EX 8.00 Trifecta £35.70 Pool: £3395.87 - 71.32 winning units..
Owner Wayne Clifford **Bred** Mickley Stud **Trained** Bridgwater, Somerset

FOCUS
This was turned into a rout by the winner, who rates a clear personal best, but there was little depth.
T/Jkpt: £17,750.00 to a £1 stake. Pool: £25,000.00 - 1.00 winning ticket T/Plt: £37.60 to a £1 stake. Pool: £100737.47 - 1952.39 winning tickets T/Qpdt: £4.00 to a £1 stake. Pool: £8863.58 - 1632.44 winning tickets CR

7653 CHANTILLY (R-H)
Monday, November 4

OFFICIAL GOING: Polytrack: standard; turf: heavy

7736a PRIX DU BOIS DE LA TUILERIE (CLAIMER) (3YO) (POLYTRACK) 1m 2f 110y
1:35 (1:35) 3-Y-O **£9,349** (£3,739; £2,804; £1,869; £934)

RPR
1 **Leo El Toro (GER)**[187] 3-9-2 0.................................(b) MaximeGuyon 12 77
(A Wohler, Germany) **19/1**

2 *nk* **Laquiella (FR)** 3-9-2 0.. Pierre-CharlesBoudot 4 76
(A Wohler, Germany) **68/10**[3]

3 *1 ¼* **Be A Flirt (IRE)**[33] 3-8-8 0.. FabienLefebvre 16 66
(J E Hammond, France) **42/1**

4 *2 ½* **Beroye (FR)**[63] 3-9-2 0.. GregoryBenoist 14 69
(Mme Pia Brandt, France) **33/10**[1]

5 *1* **Paddy's Saltantes (IRE)**[53] 6325 3-8-11 0..............(b) IoritzMendizabal 9 62
(J S Moore) *t.k.h: midfield: swtchd lft for clr run and rdn over 1f out: kpt on and wnt 5th cl home: nvr threatened ldrs* **24/1**

6 *snk* **Teolagi (IRE)**[44] 6713 3-9-6 0...................................... SoufyaneMoulin(4) 1 75
(J S Moore) *took keen hold, midfield, switched left for clear run and ridden over 1f out, kept on and went 5th close home, never threatened leaders* **26/1**

7 *snk* **Nam June Paik (FR)**[81] 3-8-13 0............................(p) CesarPasserat(3) 3 66
(S Wattel, France) **6/1**[2]

8 *nk* **Jupiter (FR)**[39] 3-8-11 0.. AntoineHamelin 10 61
(E Leenders, France) **31/1**

9 *½* **Hernan Cortez (FR)**[24] 7188 3-9-4 0............................. CristianDemuro 6 67
(G Botti, France) **10/1**

10 *½* **Bibactic (IRE)**[68] 5914 3-8-11 0................................... ThomasMessina 5 59
(J E Pease, France) **16/1**

11 *1 ½* **Carlton Blue (IRE)**[4] 3-8-8 0.............................(p) MatthiasLauron(3) 8 56
(D Windrif, France) **19/1**

12 *shd* **Aussie Lyrics (FR)**[15] 7412 3-9-4 0...............(p) ChristopheSoumillon 15 63
(F Chappet, France) **44/5**

13 *nk* **Skyfall (IRE)**[148] 3-9-4 0.. FlavienPrat 7 62
(Mlle B Renk, France) **50/1**

14 *5* **Keen Glance (IRE)**[15] 7411 3-8-13 0.............................. NicolasPerret 11 47
(Y Gourraud, France) **18/1**

15 *4* **Taboule**[104] 3-9-1 0.. StephanePasquier 13 42
(G Martin, Austria) **18/1**

16 *1 ½* **Prairie Sunset (FR)**[17] 3-8-13 0.................................... TheoBachelot 2 37
(S Wattel, France) **18/1**

2m 15.75s (135.75) 16 Ran SP% **116.4**
WIN (incl. 1 euro stake): 19.90. Places: 6.50, 2.90, 11.60. DF: 44.80. SF: 50.30..
Owner Rennstall Wohler **Bred** Rennstall Wohler **Trained** Germany

7637 KEMPTON (A.W) (R-H)
Tuesday, November 5

OFFICIAL GOING: Standard
Wind: medium, across Weather: dry

7737 REWARDS4RACING.COM MAIDEN FILLIES' STKS 6f (P)
4:30 (4:35) (Class 5) 2-Y-O **£2,587** (£770; £384; £192) **Stalls** Low

Form RPR
202 **1** **Much Promise**[26] 7155 2-9-0 77.................................... WilliamBuick 2 79+
(John Gosden) *taken down early: t.k.h: chsd ldng pair: nt clr run ent fnl 2f: swtchd lft and rdn over 1f out: qcknd to ld 1f out: r.o strly: readily* **2/5**[1]

5423 **2** *3 ¼* **Miss Brazil (IRE)**[20] 7295 2-9-0 71.................................... SeanLevey 6 66
(Richard Hannon) *chsd ldr: clsd and jnd ldr 2f out: sn rdn and led over 1f out: hdd 1f out and immediately outpcd by wnr: kpt on same pce to hold 2nd* **11/4**[2]

3 *nk* **Majestic Song** 2-8-11 0...................................... RobertTart(3) 5 65
(James Toller) *uns rdr and galloped loose to s: dwlt: t.k.h: hld up wl in tch in last pair: rdn and effrt to press ldrs 2f out: one pce fnl f* **14/1**[3]

4 **4** *½* **Byron's Gold**[16] 7393 2-8-9 0...................................... RyanTate(5) 4 64
(Ben De Haan) *led: rdn ent fnl 2f: hdd over 1f out and outpcd 1f out: kpt on same pce fnl f* **25/1**

5 *15* **Sylvan Spirit (IRE)** 2-9-0 0...................................... LiamKeniry 3 19
(Roger Teal) *s.i.s: t.k.h: hld up in tch in rr: rdn and struggling ent fnl 2f: wknd over 1f out* **33/1**

1m 14.05s (0.95) **Going Correction** +0.025s/f (Slow) 5 Ran SP% **111.5**
Speed ratings (Par 93): **94,89,89,88,68**
CSF £1.83 TOTE £1.50: £1.10, £1.20; EX 1.70 Trifecta £4.20 Pool: £3558.73 - 624.64 winning units..
Owner Mark Dixon & J L Rowsell **Bred** Ashbrittle Stud & M H Dixon **Trained** Newmarket, Suffolk

FOCUS
An uncompetitive maiden but fair form from the cosy winner. The runner-up is rated below his best. The gallop was steady to the intersection and the winner came down the centre.

7738 BOOK YOUR CHRISTMAS PARTY ON 01932 753518 MAIDEN STKS 1m 3f (P)
5:00 (5:05) (Class 5) 3-Y-O+ **£2,587** (£770; £384; £192) **Stalls** Low

Form RPR
1 **Kindu** 3-9-0 0.. AdamKirby 3 87+
(Luca Cumani) *hld up in tch in midfield: rdn and hdwy to chse ldrs over 2f out: led wl over 1f out: r.o strly and drew clr fnl f: readily* **16/1**

5 **2** *4* **Freedom's Light**[42] 6738 3-9-0 0................................ WilliamBuick 5 81+
(John Gosden) *t.k.h: hld up wl in tch in midfield: hdwy to chse ldrs 1/2-way: rdn to ld 2f out: sn hdd and outpcd by wnr over 1f out: kpt on for clr 2nd* **2/1**[1]

2204 **3** *6* **Saddaqa (USA)**[20] 7298 3-9-0 77..................(v[1]) SilvestreDeSousa 10 74
(Saeed bin Suroor) *t.k.h: chsd ldr for 3f: styd chsng ldrs: swtchd lft and sltly hmpd over 2f out: 3rd and btn over 1f out: wknd fnl f* **3/1**[3]

/502 **4** *2 ¼* **Fragonard**[58] 6236 4-9-5 78.. MartinHarley 2 67
(Lady Cecil) *hld up in tch in midfield: rdn and effrt over 2f out: sn btn and wknd 2f out: wnt modest 4th and hung rt 1f out* **5/2**[2]

00 **5** *8* **Sir Tyto (IRE)**[35] 6926 5-9-10 0................................. SteveDrowne 11 60
(Peter Makin) *stdd and dropped in bhd after s: wl off the pce in last trio: clsd 4f out: swtchd rt and sme hdwy 2f out: kpt on but nvr any ch* **100/1**

0- **6** *2 ¾* **Jaladee**[377] 7323 3-9-5 0.. AndreaAtzeni 9 55
(Roger Varian) *chsd ldrs: wnt 2nd 8f out tl over 2f out: rdn and hdd 2f out: wknd over 1f out: fdd qckly fnl f* **8/1**

3-6 **7** *16* **Newsreader (USA)**[15] 7422 3-9-5 0................................. JimCrowley 1 30
(Mark Johnston) *led tl over 2f out: sn lost pl and btn 2f out: fdd qckly ent fnl 2f: t.o* **10/1**

4 **8** *6* **Tamaletta (IRE)**[159] 2804 3-9-0 0................................. JimmyQuinn 6 15
(Paul Burgoyne) *pushed along in midfield: rdn and struggling over 3f out: lost tch over 2f out: t.o* **66/1**

3 **9** *5* **Boom**[17] 7377 3-9-0 0.. ChrisCatlin 12 7
(Olivia Maylam) *stdd and dropped in bhd after s: hld up in rr of main gp: wknd over 2f out: t.o* **50/1**

000 **10** *13* **Rowlestone Lass**[34] 6950 3-9-0 40.............................. ShaneKelly 7
(Richard Price) *v s.i.s: a wl off the pce in rr: lost tch 4f out: t.o* **100/1**

2520 **11** *1 ¼* **Keep Kicking (IRE)**[52] 6404 6-9-10 62.............................. SebSanders 8
(Simon Dow) *wl in tch in midfield: hdwy to chse ldrs 1/2-way: rdn and lost pl over 3f out: bhd 2f out: t.o* **33/1**

12 *12* **Keckerrockernixes (IRE)**[766] 7-9-10 0.................... TomMcLaughlin 4
(Paul Burgoyne) *s.i.s: a wl bhd: t.o fr 1/2-way* **100/1**

2m 18.95s (-2.95) **Going Correction** +0.025s/f (Slow)
WFA 3 from 4yo+ 5lb 12 Ran SP% **122.4**
Speed ratings (Par 103): **111,108,103,102,96 94,82,78,74,65 64,55**
toteswingers 1&2 £10.70, 1&3 £11.80, 2&3 £2.60 CSF £49.87 TOTE £23.70: £5.80, £1.50, £1.20; EX 77.80 Trifecta £452.30 Pool: £4932.32 - 8.17 winning units..
Owner Fittocks Stud **Bred** Fittocks Stud **Trained** Newmarket, Suffolk

FOCUS
A fair maiden on paper and a pleasing performance from the winner. The gallop was no more than fair to the home straight and the winner came down the centre. The time was reasonable and this was a nice start from the winner.

7739 REINDEER RACING AT KEMPTON PARK 06.12.13 H'CAP 1m 3f (P)
5:30 (5:35) (Class 4) (0-80,80) 3-Y-O+ **£4,851** (£1,443; £721; £360) **Stalls** Low

Form RPR
031 **1** **Diamond Mine**[35] 6926 3-9-4 79.................................... KierenFallon 9 87+
(Luca Cumani) *in tch in midfield: rdn over 3f out: hdwy to chse ldr ent fnl 2f: led over 1f out: a doing enough and holding runner-up ins fnl f: styd on* **11/8**[1]

2220 **2** *¾* **Scottish Star**[39] 6801 5-9-5 80...................................... RyanTate(5) 4 86
(James Eustace) *led: rdn and fnd ex ent fnl 2f: drvn and hdd over 1f out: kpt on gamely but a hld by wnr fnl f* **7/2**[2]

0205 **3** *nse* **Presburg (IRE)**[15] 7431 4-9-8 78.................................... LiamKeniry 8 84
(Joseph Tuite) *stdd s: hld up in tch in midfield: swtchd lft and effrt over 2f out: hdwy to chse ldrs over 1f out: styd on wl ins fnl f* **16/1**

3-32 **4** *½* **Emperical**[167] 2568 3-9-2 77.. TomQueally 3 82
(Lady Cecil) *hld up in tch in midfield: clsd and n.m.r on inner over 2f out: swtchd rt and effrt 2f out: styd on ins fnl f* **4/1**[3]

1511 **5** *7* **Mister Fizz**[31] 7033 5-9-3 80.................................... DanielCremin(7) 5 74
(Miss Imogen Pickard) *chsd ldr tl unable qck over 2f out: wknd u.p over 1f out* **8/1**

/50- **6** *5* **Planetoid (IRE)**[27] 3502 5-9-8 78 AmirQuinn 7 64
(Jim Best) *stdd s: hld up in last pair: rdn over 3f out: struggling and rn wd bnd 3f out: n.d after* **20/1**

1240 **7** *3 ½* **Dame Nellie Melba**[28] 7100 3-8-11 72 RobertHavlin 6 52
(Mark Johnston) *chsd ldrs: looked to be travelling wl over 2f out: rdn and no rspnse ent fnl 2f: sn btn and wknd over 1f out* **16/1**

21-0 **8** *10* **Peachez**[200] 1670 5-9-6 76 AdamKirby 1 40
(Seamus Durack) *stdd s: t.k.h: hld up in last pair: rdn over 3f out: sn struggling: lost tch over 2f out* **25/1**

2m 20.63s (-1.27) **Going Correction** +0.025s/f (Slow)
WFA 3 from 4yo+ 5lb **8** Ran SP% **115.8**
Speed ratings (Par 105): **105,104,104,104,98 95,92,85**
toteswingers 1&2 £2.30, 1&3 £7.90, 2&3 £11.50 CSF £6.34 CT £51.40 TOTE £2.60: £1.10, £2.00, £4.10; EX 9.70 Trifecta £82.50 Pool: £3564.46 - 32.37 winning units..
Owner Fittocks Stud **Bred** Fittocks Stud **Trained** Newmarket, Suffolk

FOCUS
A couple of unexposed sorts in a fair handicap. The gallop was on the steady side to the home straight and the winner came down the centre. The first four, who finished in a heap, pulled clear of the rest, and the form is solid.

7740 DAY DELEGATE RATES FROM £39 H'CAP (DIV I) 1m (P)
6:00 (6:07) (Class 6) (0-65,65) 3-Y-O+ **£1,940** (£577; £288; £144) **Stalls** Low

Form RPR

3400 **1** **Shaunas Spirit (IRE)**[28] 7109 5-9-7 65 (p) AdamKirby 10 75
(Dean Ivory) *stdd s: hld up in tch in rr: clsd and travelling wl whn nt clr run 2f out: gap opened and hdwy over 1f out: rdn to ld fnl 150yds: hld on wl fnl 50yds* **8/1**

0004 **2** *hd* **Up Tipp**[20] 7299 3-8-6 52 AndreaAtzeni 4 62
(Mike Murphy) *chsd ldrs: wnt 2nd over 3f out: rdn to ld 2f out: hdd fnl 150yds: rallied gamely and pressing wnr strly fnl 50yds: a jst hld* **15/2**[3]

265 **3** *2 ¼* **Lutine Charlie (IRE)**[67] 5948 6-9-0 61 RobertTart(3) 3 66
(Pat Eddery) *chsd ldr tl over 3f out: chsd ldrs after: sltly outpcd and n.m.r wl over 1f out: rallied and hdwy to chse ldrs ins fnl f: one pce* **8/1**

00 **4** *2 ½* **Mojo Bear**[112] 4385 3-9-0 60 LiamKeniry 1 59
(Sylvester Kirk) *in tch in midfield: rdn and effrt to chse ldrs 2f out: no ex 1f out: wknd fnl 100yds* **20/1**

0005 **5** *1 ¾* **The Wonga Coup (IRE)**[88] 5216 6-9-0 58 FergusSweeney 9 53
(Pat Phelan) *dwlt: racd in last trio: rdn and effrt over 2f out: edgd rt and styd on ins fnl f: nvr trbld ldrs* **20/1**

0-20 **6** *1* **Cool Hand Jake**[52] 6398 7-9-7 65 JimCrowley 6 58
(Ben De Haan) *s.i.s: hld up in last trio: clsd and swtchd rt ent fnl 2f: hdwy to chse ldrs over 1f out: no ex 1f out: wknd ins fnl f* **3/1**[2]

0052 **7** *½* **Habeshia**[25] 7187 3-9-2 62 (v) SteveDrowne 2 54
(John Best) *in tch in midfield: rdn and unable qck over 2f out: lost pl and dropped to rr 2f out: kpt on but n.d after* **8/1**

5036 **8** *nk* **Shifting Star (IRE)**[21] 7262 8-9-5 63 SeanLevey 5 54
(John Bridger) *led tl rdn and hdd ent fnl 2f: btn ent fnl f: wknd fnl 150yds* **11/1**

352 **9** *8* **Caerwyn**[19] 7325 3-9-5 65 KierenFallon 8 38
(Tony Carroll) *chsd ldrs: rdn over 2f out: unable qck ent fnl 2f: dropped to rr and btn 1f out: heavily eased towards fin* **9/4**[1]

1m 39.66s (-0.14) **Going Correction** +0.025s/f (Slow)
WFA 3 from 5yo+ 2lb **9** Ran SP% **118.7**
Speed ratings (Par 101): **101,100,98,96,94 93,92,92,84**
toteswingers 1&2 £9.50, 1&3 £10.50, 2&3 £10.10 CSF £68.26 CT £495.66 TOTE £10.40: £2.50, £3.20, £3.10; EX 58.80 Trifecta £668.50 Pool: £2599.45 - 2.91 winning units..
Owner Cynthia Smith & Dean Ivory **Bred** Miss Breda Wright **Trained** Radlett, Herts
■ Stewards' Enquiry : Andrea Atzeni two-day ban: used whip above permitted level (Nov 19-20)

FOCUS
A modest handicap in which the two market leaders disappointed. The pace was fair and the winner came down the centre. A race lacking depth.

7741 DAY DELEGATE RATES FROM £39 H'CAP (DIV II) 1m (P)
6:30 (6:36) (Class 6) (0-65,65) 3-Y-O+ **£1,940** (£577; £288; £144) **Stalls** Low

Form RPR

12 **1** **Havelovewilltravel (IRE)**[14] 7437 3-9-5 65 WilliamBuick 8 83+
(Jeremy Noseda) *stdd bk sn after s: hld up in tch in rr: rdn and gd hdwy 2f out: led over 1f out: r.o strly and drew clr fnl f: readily* **1/1**[1]

460- **2** *6* **Pearl Ransom (IRE)**[383] 7199 3-9-2 62 SebSanders 2 65
(Lady Herries) *led: drvn ent fnl 2f: hdd over 1f out and immediately outpcd by wnr: battled on gamely to hold 2nd fnl f* **25/1**

2346 **3** *shd* **Malih**[46] 6612 4-9-4 62 FergusSweeney 6 65
(Jamie Osborne) *chsd ldrs: rdn and ev ch wl over 1f out: outpcd by wnr and btn jst over 1f out: battling for 2nd and kpt on fnl f* **7/1**[3]

5404 **4** *¾* **Rust (IRE)**[29] 7067 3-9-2 62 PJMcDonald 9 63
(Ann Duffield) *in tch in midfield: swtchd rt and effrt u.p to chse ldrs 2f out: no ch w wnr and styd on same pce fnl f* **6/1**[2]

6064 **5** *¾* **Authoritarian**[15] 7429 4-9-7 65 SeanLevey 7 64
(Richard Hannon) *hld up in tch in last trio: rdn and effrt ent fnl 2f: no ex u.p over 1f out: no ch w wnr and one pce fnl f* **12/1**

4004 **6** *3 ¾* **Day In Day Out**[32] 4345 3-8-9 55 (p) LiamKeniry 1 46
(Seamus Mullins) *dwlt: sn rcvrd and in tch in midfield: rdn and outpcd ent fnl 2f: wknd over 1f out* **33/1**

0504 **7** *1 ¼* **Rapid Water**[49] 6489 7-8-7 51 oh6 (p) RobertHavlin 3 39
(Pat Eddery) *s.i.s: in tch in last trio: effrt u.p ent fnl 2f: no ex and btn over 1f out: wknd fnl f* **25/1**

03 **8** *1 ¼* **Natalia**[80] 5512 4-8-11 60 JackDuern(5) 10 45
(Andrew Hollinshead) *chsd ldrs tl no ex u.p ent fnl 2f: lost pl and btn over 1f out: wknd fnl f* **14/1**

1m 39.8s **Going Correction** +0.025s/f (Slow)
WFA 3 from 4yo+ 2lb **8** Ran SP% **101.8**
Speed ratings (Par 101): **101,95,94,94,93 89,88,87**
toteswingers 1&2 £5.20, 1&3 £1.90, 2&3 £16.40 CSF £25.18 CT £73.10 TOTE £1.60: £1.10, £5.60, £1.50; EX 21.20 Trifecta £124.40 Pool: £1577.63 - 9.50 winning units..
Owner Joseph Barton **Bred** Lynch Bages Ltd **Trained** Newmarket, Suffolk

FOCUS
Division two of a modest handicap but a wide-margin winner. The gallop was fair and the winner came down the straight. She's a lot better than this grade.

7742 BOOK NOW FOR CHRISTMAS FESTIVAL H'CAP 7f (P)
7:00 (7:06) (Class 4) (0-80,80) 3-Y-O+ **£4,851** (£1,443; £721; £360) **Stalls** Low

Form RPR

4304 **1** **Apollo D'Negro (IRE)**[21] 7264 5-9-3 76 (v) AdamKirby 2 84
(Clive Cox) *hld up in midfield: rdn and hdwy over 1f out: chsd ldng pair ins fnl f: str run fnl 100yds to go between rivals and ld on post* **10/1**

0312 **2** *nse* **Bowstar**[13] 7462 4-8-13 72 (p) RobertHavlin 14 80
(Michael Attwater) *chsd ldrs: effrt to chal 2f out: rdn to ld over 1f out: 2 l clr jst ins fnl f: wknd u.p cl home and hdd on post* **12/1**

4031 **3** *nk* **Big Whiskey (IRE)**[42] 6735 3-8-12 79 JenniferFerguson(7) 7 85
(Edward Creighton) *squeezed for room leaving stalls: rcvrd and sn in tch in midfield on outer: hdwy to chse wnr jst over 1f out: kpt on wl fnl 100yds* **6/1**[3]

5313 **4** *1 ½* **The Great Gabrial**[14] 7437 4-9-0 73 (v) JimCrowley 13 76
(Ian Williams) *hld up in tch in midfield: effrt u.p on outer 2f out: chsd ldrs 1f out: kpt on same pce ins fnl f* **15/2**

5220 **5** *nk* **Fantasy Gladiator**[27] 7130 7-9-0 73 (p) JimmyQuinn 4 77
(John Quinn) *squeezed for room and hmpd s: in rr: stl last pair 2f out: swtchd rt and hdd over 1f out: clsng whn nt clr run and swtchd lft jst ins fnl f: r.o wl: nvr able to chal* **10/1**

4613 **6** *1 ¼* **Dominium (USA)**[14] 7436 6-9-3 79 (b) RobertTart(3) 9 78
(Jeremy Gask) *hld up towards rr: rdn and effrt on outer 2f out: styd on ins fnl f: nvr trbld ldrs* **4/1**[2]

3222 **7** *1 ½* **Secret Beau**[11] 7507 3-9-6 80 (t) TomQueally 5 74
(David Evans) *squeezed for room s: hld up in last trio: effrt ent fnl 2f: no imp tl styd on ins fnl f: nvr trbld ldrs* **7/1**

14 **8** *2 ¼* **Loud**[14] 7436 3-8-12 72 SilvestreDeSousa 8 60
(Mark Johnston) *wnt rt s: in tch in midfield: effrt u.p ent fnl 2f: drvn and no hdwy jst over 1f out: btn whn eased wl ins fnl f* **7/2**[1]

0040 **9** *½* **Mount Hollow**[33] 6977 8-8-12 76 (p) JackDuern(5) 3 64
(Andrew Hollinshead) *hld up in midfield: effrt but stl plenty to do whn pushed rt and n.m.r over 1f out: rdn ins fnl f: kpt on: nvr trbld ldrs* **50/1**

6235 **10** *½* **Diamond Belle**[20] 7297 4-9-7 80 PJMcDonald 11 67
(Noel Quinlan) *t.k.h: pressed ldrs: rdn and ev ch 2f out: no ex and btn jst over 1f out: wknd ins fnl f* **20/1**

0146 **11** *1 ½* **Aye Aye Skipper (IRE)**[50] 6461 3-8-12 79 PaulBooth(7) 10 61
(Dean Ivory) *led: rdn and hrd pressed ent fnl 2f: hdd over 1f out: wknd ins fnl f* **33/1**

3050 **12** *1* **Bajan Bear**[33] 6977 5-8-13 72 KierenFallon 1 52
(Michael Blanshard) *hld up in tch in midfield: effrt and no imp 2f out: edgd rt and wknd 1f out* **20/1**

0050 **13** *12* **Valdaw**[28] 7106 5-8-13 72 ShaneKelly 6 21
(Mike Murphy) *wnt lft s: chsd ldrs tl lost pl 2f out: bhd over 1f out* **33/1**

1m 25.6s (-0.40) **Going Correction** +0.025s/f (Slow)
WFA 3 from 4yo+ 1lb **13** Ran SP% **124.0**
Speed ratings (Par 105): **103,102,102,100,100 99,97,94,94,93 91,90,77**
toteswingers 1&2 £13.90, 1&3 £16.80, 2&3 £15.90 CSF £120.74 CT £799.10 TOTE £9.90: £2.70, £3.60, £2.50; EX 169.20 Trifecta £783.60 Pool: £2868.63 - 2.74 winning units..
Owner Gwyn Powell and Peter Ridgers **Bred** Patrick Cummins **Trained** Lambourn, Berks

FOCUS
A fair handicap in which the gallop seemed reasonable throughout. The winner came down the centre.

7743 BOOK NOW FOR JUMP RACING ON 25.11.13 H'CAP 6f (P)
7:30 (7:38) (Class 5) (0-72,72) 3-Y-O+ **£2,587** (£770; £384; £192) **Stalls** Low

Form RPR

5421 **1** **Jay Bee Blue**[14] 7444 4-9-5 70 (bt) AdamKirby 4 83
(Sean Curran) *hld up in tch in midfield: hdwy and rdn to ld over 1f out: clr and r.o strly fnl f: readily* **6/4**[1]

02U0 **2** *2 ¾* **Emkanaat**[63] 6089 5-9-5 70 RobertHavlin 10 75
(Amy Weaver) *swtchd sharply rt s: hld up in rr: gd hdwy on inner 2f out: chsd clr wnr 1f out: kpt on but no imp* **9/2**[2]

0020 **3** *1 ¾* **Sheikh The Reins (IRE)**[14] 7436 4-9-7 72 (v) SteveDrowne 6 72
(John Best) *chsd ldrs: rdn and effrt 2f out: unable qck ent fnl f: styd on same pce after* **8/1**[3]

1510 **4** *hd* **Batchworth Lady**[28] 7106 3-9-1 66 JimmyQuinn 5 65
(Dean Ivory) *taken down early: t.k.h: hld up wl in tch: effrt u.p to chse ldrs over 1f out: styd on same pce fnl f* **12/1**

3020 **5** *1 ½* **Dream Catcher (FR)**[45] 6652 5-9-4 69 (b) FergusSweeney 7 63
(Henry Candy) *led: rdn ent fnl 2f: hdd and outpcd by wnr over 1f out: lost 2nd 1f out and wknd ins fnl f* **8/1**[3]

4210 **6** *½* **Saskia's Dream**[41] 6744 5-8-13 64 (p) MartinHarley 1 57
(Jane Chapple-Hyam) *hld up in midfield: rdn and hdwy over 1f out: kpt on same pce and no imp fnl f* **16/1**

0031 **7** *nk* **Black Dave (IRE)**[146] 3221 3-9-4 69 TomQueally 8 61
(David Evans) *in tch in last quartet: rdn wl over 2f out: no imp tl styd on ins fnl f: nvr trbld ldrs* **9/1**

0030 **8** *¾* **Sewn Up**[12] 7487 3-9-5 70 (p) JimCrowley 9 60
(Andrew Hollinshead) *t.k.h: hld up in tch in midfield: drvn and no imp ent fnl 2f: wl hld and one pce fr over 1f out* **12/1**

4055 **9** *½* **Piazza San Pietro**[74] 5722 7-9-5 70 (p) AndreaAtzeni 11 58
(Zoe Davison) *stdd and swtchd rt after s: hld up in rr: effrt on outer over 2f out: no imp: nvr trbld ldrs* **10/1**

0050 **10** *½* **Belinsky (IRE)**[41] 6761 6-8-12 63 KieranO'Neill 2 50
(Julie Camacho) *rrd as stalls opened and s.i.s: hld up towards rr: rdn and hdwy over 2f out: no imp over 1f out: wknd fnl f* **16/1**

0000 **11** *1 ¾* **Taurus Twins**[15] 7427 7-9-3 68 (v) ShaneKelly 3 50
(Richard Price) *in tch in midfield: rdn and unable qck ent fnl 2f: wknd fnl f* **33/1**

-514 **12** *11* **Girl At The Sands (IRE)**[231] 1075 3-8-11 69 JenniferFerguson(7) 12 18
(Edward Creighton) *chsd ldr tl 2f out: sn lost pl: bhd fnl f* **50/1**

1m 12.65s (-0.45) **Going Correction** +0.025s/f (Slow) **12** Ran SP% **131.5**
Speed ratings (Par 103): **104,100,98,97,95 95,94,93,93,92 90,75**
toteswingers 1&2 £3.00, 1&3 £5.00, 2&3 £8.00 CSF £9.01 CT £48.02 TOTE £2.80: £1.30, £2.80, £3.30; EX 15.50 Trifecta £116.10 Pool: £2991.72 - 19.31 winning units..
Owner Scuderia Vita Bella **Bred** L A C Ashby Newhall Estate Farm **Trained** Hatford, Oxon

FOCUS
A fair handicap run at a reasonable gallop throughout. The ready winner came down the centre and this is rather out of line with his profile.
T/Plt: £76.80. Pool: £86,597.26 - 822.70 winning units. T/Qpdt: £27.50. Pool: £8933.30 - 240.04 winning units. SP

7339 **REDCAR** (L-H)
Tuesday, November 5
7744 Meeting Abandoned - Waterlogged

[6963] SOUTHWELL (L-H)

Tuesday, November 5

OFFICIAL GOING: Standard

Wind: Moderate half behind Weather: Sunny periods

7752 LADBROKES H'CAP (DIV I) 1m (F)

12:40 (12:42) (Class 6) (0-52,52) 3-Y-0+ £1,940 (£577; £288; £144) Stalls Low

Form RPR

2006 1 **On The Cusp (IRE)**[39] 6803 6-9-5 **50**..........(b) MartinHarley 5 60
(Violet M Jordan) *trckd ldrs: hdwy 3f out: cl up 2f out: led over 1f out: rdn clr ent fnl f: styd on* **4/1**[1]

0543 2 2 3/4 **Bladewood Girl**[18] 7351 5-9-6 **51**.......... FrederikTylicki 10 54
(J R Jenkins) *chsd ldrs: pushed along over 3f out: hdwy to ld over 2f out: sn rdn and hdd over 1f out: drvn and one pce fnl f* **4/1**[1]

5300 3 6 **Action Front (USA)**[17] 7383 5-9-4 **49**..........(v) GeorgeBaker 8 38+
(Derek Shaw) *midfield: hdwy wl over 2f out: rdn wl over 1f out: styd on* **11/2**[3]

-000 4 2 3/4 **Galilee Chapel (IRE)**[26] 7153 4-9-2 **50**..........(v[1]) JasonHart(3) 2 33
(Alistair Whillans) *slt ld: rdn along over 3f out: hdd and drvn over 2 out: grad wknd* **9/1**

000 5 nk **Just Five (IRE)**[50] 6472 7-9-3 **48**..........(be) MartinLane 1 30+
(John Weymes) *towards rr: hdwy wl over 2f out: sn rdn and kpt on: nvr nr ldrs* **10/1**

6540 6 6 **Coastal Passage**[103] 4660 5-9-6 **51**..........(t[1]) RobbieFitzpatrick 11 19
(Charles Smith) *midfield: hdwy wl over 2f out: sn rdn and no imp* **16/1**

050 7 5 **Gadobout Dancer**[24] 7201 6-9-1 **46**.......... JamesSullivan 6
(Julie Camacho) *in tch: rdn along over 3f out: sn outpcd* **20/1**

230 8 1/2 **Blackamoor Harry**[54] 6323 4-8-10 **46** oh1..........(t) NoelGarbutt(5) 7
(Richard Ford) *dwlt: a towards rr* **14/1**

5000 9 1 **Red Star Lady (IRE)**[18] 7347 3-8-13 **46** oh1.......... JimmyQuinn 9
(Shaun Harris) *chsd ldng pair: rdn along 3f out: sn drvn and wknd over 2f out* **50/1**

000 10 2 3/4 **Satwa Laird**[39] 6804 7-9-2 **52**..........(p) AnnStokell(5) 13
(Ann Stokell) *a towards rr* **33/1**

0-00 11 hd **Rose Madder**[21] 7266 4-8-10 **48** ow1..........(p) NedCurtis(7) 3
(Roger Curtis) *a towards rr* **33/1**

6060 12 1 3/4 **Seamster**[18] 7347 6-9-7 **52**..........(vt) GrahamLee 4
(Richard Ford) *cl up: rdn along 3f out: sn wknd* **5/1**[2]

5060 13 1 1/2 **Lucky Mountain**[11] 7514 3-8-13 **46** oh1..........(p) TomEaves 12
(Scott Dixon) *a towards rr: bhd fnl 3f* **16/1**

4000 14 8 **Notabadgirl**[28] 7093 4-9-1 **46**..........(b[1]) ChrisCatlin 14
(Simon Dow) *s.i.s: racd wd and sn rdn along: a bhd: t.o fr over 2f out* **16/1**

1m 44.22s (0.52) **Going Correction** -0.025s/f (Stan)
WFA 3 from 4yo+ 2lb **14** Ran SP% **128.1**
Speed ratings (Par 101): **96,93,87,84,84 78,73,72,71,68 68,67,65,57**
toteswingers 1&2 £5.10, 1&3 £5.60, 2&3 £6.00 CSF £19.78 CT £94.26 TOTE £5.30: £2.00, £1.20, £2.10; EX 23.20 Trifecta £143.40 Pool: £2410.34 - 12.60 winning units..
Owner Rakebackmypoker.com **Bred** J Stan Cosgrove **Trained** Moreton Morrell, Warwicks

FOCUS
The first division of this moderate handicap and very few got into it. The winner is rated just below his best 2013 run, with the first two clear.

7753 LADBROKES H'CAP (DIV II) 1m (F)

1:10 (1:11) (Class 6) (0-52,52) 3-Y-0+ £1,940 (£577; £288; £144) Stalls Low

Form RPR

0540 1 **Frosty Friday**[102] 4715 5-9-1 **46**..........(v[1]) FrederikTylicki 1 59
(J R Jenkins) *trckd ldrs on inner: hdwy over 2f out: swtchd rt and rdn to chal over 1f out: led ent fnl f: kpt on wl* **14/1**

0061 2 2 1/4 **Elusive Warrior (USA)**[70] 5869 10-8-12 **50**..........(p) AaronJones(7) 11 58
(Alan McCabe) *sn cl up: rdn to ld wl over 1f out: hdd ent fnl f: kpt on same pce* **8/1**

0254 3 2 **Baile Atha Cliath (IRE)**[33] 6985 4-9-4 **52**.......... JasonHart(3) 7 55
(Declan Carroll) *midfield: hdwy 3f out: rdn along over 2f out: styd on fnl f: nrst fin* **11/4**[1]

6000 4 1 **Frosted Off**[18] 7354 3-8-13 **46**.......... NickyMackay 12 47
(John Spearing) *led: rdn along and jnd over 2f out: hdd wl over 1f out: sn drvn and gradually wknd* **40/1**

60 5 3 **Xclusive**[40] 6782 3-9-0 **52**.......... PhilipPrince(5) 6 46
(Ronald Harris) *hld up in rr: hdwy 2f out: styd on appr fnl f: nrst fin* **20/1**

0030 6 nk **Holli Deya**[31] 7034 3-8-13 **46** oh1..........(p) ChrisCatlin 2 39
(Andi Brown) *towards rr: hdwy on inner wl over 2f out: sn rdn and kpt on appr fnl f: nrst fin* **33/1**

4662 7 1 3/4 **Crucis Abbey (IRE)**[33] 6985 5-9-2 **47**..........(p) TomMcLaughlin 10 36
(Mark Brisbourne) *chsd ldrs on outer: rdn along over 2f out: sn drvn and no imp* **7/1**[3]

3002 8 3 1/2 **Chez Vrony**[21] 7265 7-9-1 **46**.......... WilliamCarson 14 27
(Dave Morris) *in tch: hdwy on wd outside 3f out: rdn to chse ldrs over 2f out: sn drvn and wknd* **6/1**[2]

3000 9 2 1/4 **Mucky Molly**[14] 7455 5-9-6 **51**..........(vt) TomEaves 4 27
(Alison Hutchinson) *trckd ldrs: rdn along wl over 2f out: sn drvn and wknd* **12/1**

0300 10 3 **Meglio Ancora**[22] 7238 6-9-5 **50**.......... GrahamLee 9 19
(Richard Ford) *in tch: rdn along over 3f out: sn wknd* **7/1**[3]

-040 11 4 1/2 **Secret Lodge**[94] 4982 5-9-1 **46** oh1.......... AndrewMullen 8 5
(Garry Woodward) *midfield: rdn along wl over 3f out: sn outpcd* **33/1**

0560 12 1 **Abanoas (USA)**[146] 3219 3-8-13 **46** oh1.......... JohnFahy 13 2
(Alan Coogan) *s.i.s: a in rr* **18/1**

5360 13 1/2 **Elizabeth Coffee (IRE)**[24] 7201 5-9-7 **52**..........(bt[1]) JimmyQuinn 5 7
(John Weymes) *sn rdn along and a outpcd in rr* **16/1**

0003 14 13 **George Benjamin**[12] 7485 6-9-3 **48**.......... GeorgeBaker 3
(Christopher Kellett) *chsd ldrs on inner: rdn along over 3f out: sn wknd* **8/1**

1m 43.74s (0.04) **Going Correction** -0.025s/f (Stan)
WFA 3 from 4yo+ 2lb **14** Ran SP% **126.8**
Speed ratings (Par 101): **98,95,93,92,89 89,87,84,81,78 74,73,72,59**
toteswingers 1&2 £14.40, 1&3 £9.90, 2&3 £4.10 CSF £124.04 CT £422.67 TOTE £17.30: £4.40, £2.90, £1.30; EX 213.20 Trifecta £1265.90 Pool: £2714.29 - 1.60 winning units..
Owner T J Turner **Bred** Dullingham Park **Trained** Royston, Herts

FOCUS
The second leg of this handicap was run 0.48secs faster than the first. A weak race, and the winner's best effort of the year.

7754 DOWNLOAD THE LADBROKES APP H'CAP 7f (F)

1:40 (1:40) (Class 5) (0-70,74) 3-Y-0+ £2,587 (£770; £384; £192) Stalls Low

Form RPR

0040 1 **Hellbender (IRE)**[26] 7153 7-9-5 **66**..........(t) JimmyQuinn 14 76
(Shaun Harris) *in tch on wd outside: hdwy wl over 2f out: rdn and edgd lft over 1f out: led jst ins fnl f: drvn out* **8/1**

0022 2 nk **Bassett Road (IRE)**[5] 7652 5-8-13 **63**..........(b[1]) JasonHart(3) 4 72
(Keith Dalgleish) *trckd ldrs: smooth hdwy over 2f out and sn cl up: rdn and ev ch whn hung bdly lft to ins rail ent fnl f: sn drvn and kpt on* **11/4**[1]

3312 3 1 1/4 **Silly Billy (IRE)**[22] 7238 5-9-4 **65**.......... PaulPickard 2 71
(Brian Ellison) *cl up: led 1/2-way: rdn 2f out: drvn over 1f out: hdd jst ins fnl f: kpt on same pce* **7/2**[2]

4532 4 2 1/4 **Khajaaly (IRE)**[46] 6606 6-9-6 **67**..........(tp) AndrewMullen 12 67
(Michael Appleby) *chsd ldrs on outer: cl up 3f out: sn rdn and ev ch tl drvn and one pce fr wl over 1f out* **5/1**

2220 5 1/2 **Emperatriz**[46] 6587 3-9-3 **65**.......... RobertHavlin 7 62
(John Holt) *cl up: rdn along 3f out: sn wknd* **4/1**[3]

3540 6 hd **Speronella**[41] 6753 3-8-9 **57**..........(b[1]) JohnFahy 6 54
(Hughie Morrison) *dwlt and towards rr: gd hdwy wl over 2f out: swtchd lft and rdn to chal wl over 1f out: sn drvn and btn appr fnl f* **14/1**

0040 7 1/2 **Run It Twice (IRE)**[14] 7439 3-9-0 **67**..........(b) NoelGarbutt(5) 5 63
(David Evans) *chsd ldrs: rdn along 3f out: sn drvn and grad wknd* **25/1**

0606 8 20 **Ellaal**[21] 7283 4-8-13 **60**.......... JamesSullivan 11 3
(Ruth Carr) *chsd ldrs: rdn along and lost pl bef 1/2-way: sn bhd* **12/1**

-000 9 1 3/4 **Half A Crown (IRE)**[67] 5974 8-9-2 **68**..........(vt) ShelleyBirkett(5) 1 6
(Nick Kent) *slt ld: rdn along and hdd 1/2-way: sn wknd and bhd fnl 2f* **40/1**

1m 29.88s (-0.42) **Going Correction** -0.025s/f (Stan)
WFA 3 from 4yo+ 1lb **9** Ran SP% **117.3**
Speed ratings (Par 103): **101,100,99,96,96 95,95,72,70**
toteswingers 1&2 £8.00, 1&3 £7.90, 2&3 £2.10 CSF £30.82 CT £93.61 TOTE £8.30: £3.00, £1.40, £1.20; EX 44.70 Trifecta £113.50 Pool: £2298.05 - 15.18 winning units..
Owner Southwell Racecourse Owners Group **Bred** James Lombard **Trained** Carburton, Notts
■ Stewards' Enquiry : Paul Pickard two-day ban: used whip above permitted level (Nov 19-20)

FOCUS
A race which suffered from five withdrawals, but the time was decent and this is fair form for the grade. The winner was firmly entitled to rate this high.

7755 32RED CASINO NURSERY H'CAP 7f (F)

2:10 (2:11) (Class 6) (0-60,59) 2-Y-0 £1,940 (£577; £288; £144) Stalls Low

Form RPR

3022 1 **Stoney Quine (IRE)**[11] 7509 2-9-7 **59**.......... TomEaves 7 65
(Keith Dalgleish) *cl up: led wl over 2f out: rdn wl over 1f out: edgd rt ent fnl f: drvn out* **6/1**

5310 2 3/4 **Chanceuse**[64] 6059 2-8-7 **50**.......... DanielMuscutt(5) 8 54
(Gay Kelleway) *in tch: hdwy on outer 3f out: chal 2f out: sn rdn and ev ch tl drvn and one pce ins fnl f* **14/1**

6035 3 3 **Dandys Perier (IRE)**[33] 6979 2-8-7 **50**.......... PhilipPrince(5) 12 46
(Ronald Harris) *towards rr and rdn along after 2f: swtchd rt and wd st: hdwy 2f out: chsd ldng pair whn rdn and edgd lft over 1f out: sn drvn and one pce* **11/4**[1]

560 4 2 1/4 **Ice Mayden**[22] 7237 2-9-7 **59**.......... GrahamLee 2 49
(Bryan Smart) *slt ld on inner: hdd and rdn wl over 2f out: drvn over 1f out and one pce* **5/1**[3]

060 5 1 1/4 **Vosne Romanee**[17] 7371 2-8-9 **50**..........(p) JasonHart(3) 9 36
(Keith Dalgleish) *dwlt and in rr: hdwy on inner over 2f out: sn rdn and kpt on fnl f* **16/1**

6006 6 2 **Wolfwood**[18] 7341 2-8-12 **50**.......... MartinLane 5 31
(John Davies) *prom: rdn along wl over 2f out: drvn wl over 1f out and grad wknd* **20/1**

565 7 shd **Different Scenario**[38] 6842 2-8-9 **47**.......... JimmyQuinn 4 28
(Mel Brittain) *in rr tl styd on fnl 2f: n.d* **14/1**

000 8 1/2 **Penara**[48] 6523 2-9-5 **57**.......... GeorgeBaker 11 36
(Philip Hide) *hld up: a towards rr* **9/1**

5100 9 1 1/4 **White Flag**[28] 7094 2-9-5 **57**..........(b[1]) DuranFentiman 13 33
(Tim Easterby) *qckly away and cl up: rdn along over 2f out: drvn and wknd wl over 1f out* **20/1**

3550 10 1 1/2 **Red Biba (IRE)**[33] 6967 2-8-6 **47**.......... NataliaGemelova(3) 6 19
(Alan McCabe) *chsd ldrs: rdn along wl over 2f out: sn wknd* **20/1**

0000 11 5 **Kitty Brown (IRE)**[6] 7630 2-8-7 **50**.......... NoelGarbutt(5) 10 8
(David Evans) *sn rdn along and a in rr* **25/1**

000 12 nse **Hasta La Vista**[18] 7332 2-8-12 **50**.......... FrederikTylicki 3 8
(Mark Johnston) *in tch on inner: rdn along 3f out: sn wknd* **4/1**[2]

650 13 9 **Riley's Missile (IRE)**[31] 7036 2-8-8 **46**..........(vt[1]) WilliamCarson 1
(Charles Smith) *chsd ldrs on inner: rdn along over 3f out: sn wknd* **50/1**

1m 31.9s (1.60) **Going Correction** -0.025s/f (Stan) **13** Ran SP% **126.9**
Speed ratings (Par 94): **89,88,84,82,80 78,78,77,76,74 68,68,58**
toteswingers 1&2 £6.80, 1&3 £4.10, 2&3 £10.60 CSF £85.24 CT £291.41 TOTE £3.70: £2.40, £3.70, £1.40; EX 45.70 Trifecta £160.30 Pool: £3232.81 - 15.11 winning units..
Owner Middleham Park racing XXII **Bred** T Monaghan **Trained** Carluke, S Lanarks

FOCUS
This low-grade nursery was run just over 2secs slower than the preceding handicap. A weak race, but the in-form winner is credited with a step up along with the second.

7756 32RED.COM BRITISH STALLION STUDS EBF MAIDEN STKS 5f (F)

2:40 (2:41) (Class 5) 2-Y-0 £2,911 (£866; £432; £216) Stalls High

Form RPR

5235 1 **Pennine Warrior**[26] 7147 2-9-5 68..........(p) TomEaves 1 68
(Scott Dixon) *mde all: rdn clr over 1f out: kpt on strly* **4/5**[1]

2 2 1/2 **Misstemper (IRE)** 2-9-0 0.......... JackMitchell 5 54+
(Sean Curran) *a chsng wnr: rdn wl over 1f out: kpt on same pce fnl f* **20/1**

000 3 4 **Biscuiteer**[77] 5609 2-9-0 0..........(p) FrederikTylicki 2 40
(Scott Dixon) *chsd ldrs: rdn along over 2f out: sn one pce* **20/1**

0660 4 2 1/4 **Modify**[31] 7016 2-9-0 57..........(p) GrahamLee 7 32+
(Bryan Smart) *in tch: rdn along and outpcd 1/2-way: plugged on u.p appr fnl f: n.d* **7/2**[2]

0 5 2 **Motamayezah**[129] 3833 2-9-0 0.......... NickyMackay 4 24
(Ismail Mohammed) *dwlt: swtchd lft sn after s and chsd ldrs: rdn along 2f out: grad wknd* **5/1**[3]

6 3 **Kinkohyo** 2-8-11 0.......... MarkCoumbe(3) 3 14
(Bryan Smart) *dwlt: a bhd* **10/1**

00 **7** *1 1/4* **Molly Molone**[18] 7341 2-8-7 0 ClaireMurray(7) 6 9
(David Brown) *chsd ldrs: rdn along bef 1/2-way: sn outpcd* **33/1**
4000 **8** *4* **Doncaster Belle (IRE)**[4] 7665 2-9-0 50 RobbieFitzpatrick 8
(Charles Smith) *sn outpcd and bhd fr 1/2-way* **33/1**
58.73s (-0.97) **Going Correction** -0.20s/f (Stan) **8** Ran SP% **118.9**
Speed ratings (Par 96): **99,95,88,85,81 77,75,68**
toteswingers 1&2 £8.40, 1&3 £5.20, 2&3 £27.90 CSF £24.86 TOTE £1.70: £1.10, £5.50, £5.30; EX 24.00 Trifecta £231.80 Pool: £5289.21 - 17.10 winning units..
Owner Yorkshire Exiles **Bred** Mrs Yvette Dixon **Trained** Babworth, Notts
FOCUS
A weak juvenile sprint maiden and only two had any chance from halfway. The winner already had form on this surface.

7757 32RED H'CAP 2m (F)
3:10 (3:10) (Class 4) (0-85,85) 3-Y-0+ **£4,690** (£1,395; £697; £348) **Stalls** Low

Form RPR
000 **1** **Masterful Act (USA)**[10] 7542 6-9-9 **83** JasonHart(3) 4 100+
(Alan McCabe) *led: clr 1/2-way: rdn along over 2f out: kpt on strly: unchal* **4/1**[3]
6140 **2** *17* **Cosimo de Medici**[24] 7193 6-10-0 **85** GeorgeBaker 7 82
(Hughie Morrison) *chsd wnr: rdn along wl over 3f out: drvn over 2f out: no imp* **5/4**[1]
-011 **3** *21* **One Pursuit (IRE)**[10] 7539 5-9-7 **78** JackMitchell 1 49
(Brendan Powell) *trckd ldng pair: pushed along 5f out: rdn 4f out: plugged on one pce* **5/2**[2]
0-53 **4** *5* **Wayward Glance**[15] 7423 5-9-3 **74** (v) TomEaves 5 39
(Keith Dalgleish) *chsd ldrs: rdn along on outer after 3f: sn lost pl and bhd 1/2-way: sme hdwy fnl 3f: nvr a factor* **14/1**
2200 **5** *28* **Scribe (IRE)**[25] 7166 5-8-7 **69** (vt) NoelGarbutt(5) 6
(David Evans) *in tch: rdn along over 5f out: sn outpcd and wl bhd fnl 3f* **20/1**
6520 **6** *16* **Mawaakef (IRE)**[32] 6992 5-10-0 **85** AndrewMullen 3
(J R Jenkins) *hld up in rr: sme hdwy 1/2-way: rdn along over 5f out: sn outpcd and bhd* **12/1**
3135 **7** *46* **Vicky Valentine**[28] 7100 3-8-0 **69** oh1 ow3 JulieBurke(3) 2
(Alistair Whillans) *chsd ldrs: rdn along 6f out: sn outpcd and bhd fnl 3f* **33/1**
3m 39.31s (-6.19) **Going Correction** -0.025s/f (Stan)
WFA 3 from 5yo+ 9lb **7** Ran SP% **115.1**
Speed ratings (Par 105): **114,105,95,92,78 70,47**
toteswingers 1&2 £1.80, 1&3 £2.20, 2&3 £1.20 CSF £9.55 TOTE £6.10: £2.90, £1.50; EX 12.70 Trifecta £27.20 Pool: £3826.70 - 105.30 winning units..
Owner Universal Recycling Company **Bred** Fiona Craig & Dermot Cantillon **Trained** Averham Park, Notts
FOCUS
The feature race and a decent staying handicap, but turned into a real stamina test by the winner and the field finished well strung out. The winner thrashed these and this rating might underplay his superiority.

7758 CORAL APP DOWNLOAD FROM THE APP STORE CLAIMING STKS 1m 3f (F)
3:40 (3:40) (Class 6) 3-Y-0+ **£2,045** (£603; £302) **Stalls** Low

Form RPR
2100 **1** **Honoured (IRE)**[92] 5059 6-9-0 64 (t) AndrewMullen 8 70
(Michael Appleby) *mde all: pushed along over 3f out: rdn 2f out: drvn and kpt on gamely fnl f* **6/1**
3230 **2** *1 1/4* **Royal Alcor (IRE)**[10] 7539 6-9-7 75 (t) DanielMuscutt(5) 3 80
(Gay Kelleway) *trckd ldng pair: tk clsr order over 3f out: effrt on bit and cl up 2f out: shkn up and edgd lft over 1f out: sn rdn and ev ch tl one pce last 100yds* **15/8**[1]
3340 **3** *1 1/4* **Thereabouts (USA)**[21] 7275 4-8-8 63 PhilipPrince(5) 1 65
(Michael Appleby) *t.k.h: chsd wnr: pushed along 3f out: rdn 2f out and ev ch tl drvn and one pce ent fnl f* **7/2**[3]
0433 **4** *3 3/4* **Incendo**[33] 6984 7-9-6 80 (v) StevieDonohoe 6 66
(Ian Williams) *hld up: smooth hdwy to join ldrs 4f out: rdn along over 2f out: rdn wl over 1f out and sn btn* **5/2**[2]
0000 **5** *16* **Follow The Flag (IRE)**[122] 4071 9-8-10 55(be) NatalieHambling-Yates(7) 9 37
(Alan McCabe) *chsd ldrs: rdn along over 4f out: sn outpcd and bhd* **33/1**
-403 **6** *2 1/2* **Epic Storm (IRE)**[98] 562 5-8-12 0 (t) JasonHart(3) 7 31
(Paul Morgan) *hld up in rr: smooth hdwy 4f out: cl up on outer 3f out: rdn over 2f out: sn edgd rt and wknd: eased fnl f* **8/1**
2m 29.58s (1.58) **Going Correction** -0.025s/f (Stan) **6** Ran SP% **113.9**
Speed ratings (Par 101): **93,92,91,88,76 75**
toteswingers 1&2 £3.80, 1&3 £4.70, 2&3 £1.70 CSF £18.15 TOTE £5.80: £3.20, £1.90; EX 19.10 Trifecta £80.60 Pool: £3115.80 - 28.97 winning units..
Owner Dallas Racing **Bred** Kilfrush Stud **Trained** Danethorpe, Notts
FOCUS
Typically mixed levels of ability in this claimer, although the weights brought them closer together. The pace did not appear that strong and it produced a decent finish. Pretty straightforward form.

7759 COMPARE BOOKMAKERS AT BOOKMAKERS.CO.UK MAIDEN STKS 5f (F)
4:10 (4:10) (Class 5) 3-Y-0+ **£2,587** (£770; £384; £192) **Stalls** High

Form RPR
0444 **1** **Beacon Tarn**[134] 3626 3-8-11 53 JasonHart(3) 4 60
(Eric Alston) *cl up: led wl over 1f out: rdn clr ent fnl f: styd on* **10/1**
2333 **2** *3 3/4* **Millkwood**[6] 7633 3-9-5 75 (p) MartinLane 8 52
(John Davies) *sn rdn along and towards rr: hdwy wl over 1f out: styd on u.p fnl f to take 2nd nr line* **4/5**[1]
0050 **3** *hd* **Robyn**[13] 7459 3-8-9 45 TimClark(5) 1 46
(Scott Dixon) *racd wd: prom: rdn wl over 1f out: styd on to chse wnr ins fnl f: lost 2nd nr line* **50/1**
62 **4** *1 1/2* **Jiminy**[33] 6965 3-9-5 0 (b) FrederikTylicki 3 45
(Scott Dixon) *led: rdn along 2f out: sn hdd and drvn: wknd ent fnl f* **4/1**[2]
3600 **5** *1/2* **Pearl Noir**[33] 6965 3-9-5 53 [1] TomEaves 10 44
(Scott Dixon) *in tch: rdn along 2f out: sn no imp* **20/1**
4-06 **6** *3 1/4* **Knockamany Bends (IRE)**[162] 2719 3-9-0 58 AdamCarter(5) 9 32
(John Wainwright) *chsd ldrs: rdn along 2f out: sn one pce* **25/1**
405 **7** *7* **Chessfield Park**[33] 6965 3-9-2 48 MarkCoumbe(3) 7 7
(Bryan Smart) *chsd ldrs: rdn along over 2f out: sn wknd* **25/1**
3600 **8** *1/2* **Prom Dress**[7] 7610 3-9-0 57 AndrewMullen 2
(J R Jenkins) *dwlt: a in rr* **25/1**
6000 **9** *3* **Mrs Medley**[24] 7203 7-8-9 20 AnnStokell(5) 6
(Ann Stokell) *sn outpcd and a in rr* **100/1**

-326 **10** *2 1/2* **Scent Of Roses (IRE)**[199] 1682 3-9-0 64 (b[1]) JohnFahy 5
(Clive Cox) *trckd ldrs: pushed along over 3f out: rdn 1/2-way: sn wknd and bhd* **6/1**[3]
58.71s (-0.99) **Going Correction** -0.20s/f (Stan) **10** Ran SP% **118.2**
Speed ratings (Par 103): **99,93,92,90,89 84,73,72,67,63**
toteswingers 1&2 £3.10, 1&3 £20.00, 2&3 £13.90 CSF £17.83 TOTE £12.20: £3.10, £1.10, £7.10; EX 27.80 Trifecta £320.50 Pool: £4663.23 - 10.91 winning units..
Owner Mr & Mrs G Middlebrook **Bred** Mr & Mrs G Middlebrook **Trained** Longton, Lancs
FOCUS
The winner and third set a straightforward, poor level of form, although the race could be rated up to 7lb higher.
T/Jkpt: Not won. T/Plt: £13.70. Pool: £79,038.29 - 4188.94 winning units. T/Qpdt: £5.00. Pool: £8189.55 - 1211.08 winning units. JR

7700 FLEMINGTON (L-H)
Tuesday, November 5

OFFICIAL GOING: Turf: good

7760a CARNIVAL H'CAP (3YO+) (TURF) 1m 6f
12:45 (12:00) 3-Y-0+
£39,423 (£11,538; £5,769; £2,884; £1,602; £769)

RPR
1 **Mujadale (AUS)**[10] 7555 6-8-7 0 StephenBaster 3 100
(Paul A Jones, Australia) **14/1**
2 *2 1/2* **Like A Carousel (AUS)**[185] 4-8-7 0 (b) LukeNolen 12 99
(Ken Keys, Australia) **20/1**
3 *1* **Caravan Rolls On**[73] 5766 5-8-13 0 JamieSpencer 14 101+
(Peter Chapple-Hyam) *dwlt sltly and hld up in rr: rdn and hdwy 2f out: wnt 3rd jst ins fnl f: styd on wl and clsd on ldng pair but nvr able to chal* **7/1**[2]
4 *1 1/4* **Planet Purple (AUS)**[31] 7-8-10 0 MichaelRodd 7 96+
(Kerry Parker, Australia) **16/1**
5 *1 1/4* **Thubiaan (USA)**[782] 6103 5-8-10 0 (t) GlynSchofield 6 94
(Chris Waller, Australia) **20/1**
6 *1* **Rowland (AUS)**[1105] 8-8-7 0 RichardKingscote 9 90
(Robbie Laing, Australia) **80/1**
6 *dht* **North Lodge (AUS)** 8-8-7 0 (t) DwayneDunn 13 90
(John Blacker, Australia) **40/1**
8 *1 1/2* **Raki (AUS)** 6-8-8 0 ow1 (p) NicholasHall 17 89
(Tony McEvoy, Australia) **13/1**
9 *1/2* **Junoob**[535] 2267 5-8-7 0 (b) CraigNewitt 16 87
(Chris Waller, Australia) **17/2**[3]
10 *3/4* **Why Not (GER)**[31] 5-8-7 0 ChadSchofield 2 86
(David Hayes, Australia) **40/1**
11 *shd* **Brayroan (NZ)** 7-8-7 0 (b) CraigAWilliams 5 86
(Anthony Cummings, Australia) **19/1**
12 *6* **Raeburn (AUS)**[10] 7555 9-8-10 0 (bt) ChrisMunce 15 80
(Brian Smith, Australia) **50/1**
13 *hd* **Crafty Cruiser (AUS)**[13] 7483 6-9-3 0 BenMelham 18 87
(Bryce Stanaway, Australia) **12/1**
14 *2* **Trajet (AUS)**[136] 8-8-7 0 (bt) JamesMcDonald 1 74
(Liam Birchley, Australia) **17/1**
15 *4 1/4* **Caroun (IRE)**[742] 5-8-7 0 (t) PeterMertens 4 68
(Patrick F Ryan, Australia) **30/1**
16 *2* **Sacred Dream (AUS)** 5-8-7 0 GlenBoss 10 65
(Robbie Griffiths, Australia) **50/1**
17 *1* **Fabriano (AUS)**[20] 7417 7-8-7 0 (b) JyeMcNeil 11 64
(Peter Donnelly, Australia) **30/1**
18 *50* **Opinion (IRE)**[73] 5766 4-9-4 0 (t) NashRawiller 8 5
(Chris Waller, Australia) **11/5**[1]
2m 55.4s (175.40) **18** Ran SP% **118.2**
PARI-MUTUEL (NSW TAB - all including 1 aud stake): WIN 16.50; PLACE 4.70, 6.80, 3.20; DF 204.50; SF 426.00.
Owner M J Noske, Ms J A Nichols, T N & Mrs J M Chamberla **Bred** M Noske **Trained** Australia

7761a EMIRATES MELBOURNE CUP (GROUP 1 H'CAP) (3YO+) (TURF) 2m
4:00 (12:00) 3-Y-0+
£2,435,897 (£576,923; £288,461; £160,256; £112,179; £80,128)

RPR
1 **Fiorente (IRE)**[10] 7556 5-8-9 0 (b) DamienOliver 5 116+
(Gai Waterhouse, Australia) *midfield: swtchd out and hdwy on turn into st: rdn to chal 2f out: led over 1f out: styd on strly: drvn and asserted towards fin* **6/1**[1]
2 *3/4* **Red Cadeaux**[51] 6441 7-8-13 0 GeraldMosse 23 119
(Ed Dunlop) *midfield: stdy hdwy on outer to trck ldr 3f out: rdn to chal and led over 2f out: hdd over 1f out: styd on wl and continued to press wnr tl hld towards fin* **60/1**
3 *1 1/2* **Mount Athos (IRE)**[73] 5741 6-8-7 0 CraigAWilliams 22 111
(Luca Cumani) *midfield in tch: hdwy and prom bef 1/2-way: ct in pocket briefly whn looking to switch rt 3f out: rdn to chal on inner and ev ch over 2f out: styd on wl but nt pce to chal front pair ins fnl f* **12/1**
4 *hd* **Simenon (IRE)**[24] 7213 6-8-6 0 RichardHughes 12 110
(W P Mullins, Ire) *broke wl but stdd and racd in midfield: gd hdwy and prom 3f out: rdn to chal and ev ch 2f out: styd on wl but nt pce for front pair fr over 1f out* **19/1**
5 *1* **Dandino**[17] 7392 6-8-8 0 RyanMoore 4 111+
(Marco Botti) *broke wl but stdd and racd in midfield on inner: shuffled bk and towards rr 3f out: fanned out and rdn on turn into st: wnt 5th ent fnl f: styd on but nvr able to chal* **9/1**[2]
6 *2 1/2* **Fawkner (AUS)**[17] 7392 6-8-8 0 (b) NicholasHall 8 108
(Robert Hickmott, Australia) *broke wl but wnt sltly rt sn after s and bmpd rival: stdd and hld up in last: rdn and hdwy on wd outside on turn into st: drifted lft u.p: styd on but nvr able to chal* **15/1**
7 *1* **Ethiopia (AUS)**[3] 7700 5-8-8 0 (v) RhysMcLeod 14 107
(Pat Carey, Australia) *hld up towards rr: hdwy on outer over 3f out: rdn and effrt over 2f out: sn outpcd by ldrs: styd on* **80/1**
8 *nk* **Brown Panther**[41] 6742 5-8-9 0 RichardKingscote 6 108
(Tom Dascombe) *w ldrs on inner early: trckd ldr once hdd: rdn 3f out: effrt to chal and ev ch 2f out: sn outpcd by ldrs: kpt on tl no ex and fdd towards fin* **19/1**

9 ½ **Super Cool (AUS)**[10] 7556 4-8-8 0 (b) CoreyBrown 13 110
(Mark Kavanagh, Australia) *broke wl but sn settled in midfield: clsd over 3f out: rdn over 2f out: chsd ldrs but sn outpcd and hld* **40/1**

10 nk **Voleuse De Coeurs (IRE)**[51] 6441 4-8-7 0 JamesMcDonald 21 105
(Michael Moroney, Australia) *dropped in fr wd draw and hld up in rr of midfield: rdn over 2f out: kpt on same pce fr over 1f out and nvr able to chal* **17/1**

11 ¾ **Dunaden (FR)**[51] 6449 7-9-3 0 JamieSpencer 1 114
(M Delzangles, France) *midfield on inner: pushed along over 3f out: nt clr run and dropped to rr over 2f out: rdn and kpt on steadily in st but nvr threatened* **60/1**

12 hd **Seville (GER)**[10] 7556 5-8-8 0 (b) HughBowman 9 105
(Robert Hickmott, Australia) *bmpd sn after s: midfield in tch on inner: shuffled bk as pce qcknd on turn into st: sn rdn: kpt on same pce and n.d* **17/1**

13 ½ **Sea Moon**[24] 7213 5-8-13 0 StevenArnold 7 109
(Robert Hickmott, Australia) *hld up towards rr: effrt to improve on outer whn bmpd 3f out: rdn over 2f out: outpcd and btn over 1f out: nvr a factor* **10/1**[3]

14 1 **Royal Empire (IRE)**[31] 7012 4-8-7 0 KerrinMcEvoy 11 102
(Saeed bin Suroor) *sltly slow to stride and hld up towards rr: swtchd rt and bmpd rival 3f out: rdn over 2f out: outpcd and btn over 1f out: nvr a factor* **20/1**

15 1 ¼ **Mourayan (IRE)**[3] 7702 7-8-8 0 BrentonAvdulla 19 102
(Robert Hickmott, Australia) *midfield on outer: clsd and prom 1/2-way: led over 3f out: rdn and hdd over 2f out: sn no ex and btn: steadily fdd* **150/1**

16 ½ **Ibicenco (GER)**[13] 7483 5-8-5 0 (b) LukeNolen 17 98
(Peter G Moody, Australia) *sn midfield: rdn 3f out: outpcd and btn over 1f out: nvr threatened* **70/1**

17 ¾ **Foreteller**[10] 7556 6-8-9 0 (b) CraigNewitt 15 102
(Chris Waller, Australia) *dropped in and hld up in rr on inner: last whn swtchd off rail and rdn on turn into st: outpcd and btn over 1f out: nvr a factor* **30/1**

18 2 ¼ **Masked Marvel**[10] 7556 5-8-8 0 ow1 MichaelRodd 2 98
(Robert Hickmott, Australia) *hld up in rr of midfield on inner: taken bk and swtchd to outer over 3f out: rdn over 2f out: outpcd and btn ent fnl f: nvr a factor* **40/1**

19 ¾ **Dear Demi (AUS)**[3] 7702 4-8-0 0 (b) ChrisMunce 16 93
(Clarry Conners, Australia) *t.k.h: w ldrs early: chsd ldrs on inner once hdd: rdn over 2f out: no ex and lost pl over 1f out: fdd* **20/1**

20 4 ¼ **Hawkspur (AUS)**[17] 7392 4-8-6 0 (bt) JimCassidy 18 95
(Chris Waller, Australia) *w ldrs early: prom in midfield once hdd: rdn and brief effrt over 2f out: swtchd lft to rail over 1f out: no ex and btn ent fnl f: fdd* **15/1**

21 25 **Green Moon (IRE)**[10] 7556 6-9-1 0 (b[1]) BrettPrebble 10 72
(Robert Hickmott, Australia) *bmpd sn after s: prom in midfield on inner: reminders and lost pl rapidly over 2f out: sn drvn in rr and btn: eased as if smething amiss and t.o* **30/1**

22 10 **Tres Blue (IRE)**[72] 5807 3-8-0 0 TommyBerry 20 55
(Gai Waterhouse, Australia) *w ldrs early: trckd ldr on outer once hdd: rdn and brief effrt over 3f out: wknd rapidly over 2f out: sn in rr and btn: eased and t.o* **25/1**

23 2 ¼ **Ruscello (IRE)**[3] 7700 4-7-12 0 ChadSchofield 24 42
(Ed Walker) *w ldrs early: worked across fr wdst draw and sn led: rdn and hdd over 3f out: wknd qckly on rail and dropped to last over 2f out: eased and t.o* **50/1**

P **Verema (FR)**[79] 5575 4-8-5 0 (t) Christophe-PatriceLemaire 3
(A De Royer-Dupre, France) *midfield on outer: broke down bdly and dropped to rr exiting first turn: p.u: fatally injured* **16/1**

3m 20.3s (0.66)
WFA 3 from 4yo+ 9lb **24** Ran SP% **113.8**
PARI-MUTUEL (NSW TAB - all including 1 aud stake): WIN 7.00; PLACE 2.60, 11.10, 5.00; DF 171.00; SF 300.00.
Owner A T Roberts, McClure Ferguson Oman Et Al **Bred** Ballymacoll Stud Farm Ltd **Trained** Australia

FOCUS
This looked a really competitive renewal of one of the most famous contests in the world and, apart from the fatal injury that Verema sadly suffered quite early, it was a great spectacle. The pace, which had been missing from a couple of Australia's big races recently, was sound and nothing seemed to suffer any obvious interference. It worth noting that once again the winner had run in a local trial before taking the big prize (Vintage Crop in 1993 was the last to head straight from Europe and triumph), plus it appears ideal these days to have a horse who has the speed to hold their own at 1m4f rather than a recognised stayer.

7762a VISIT VICTORIA PLATE (LISTED H'CAP) (3YO+) (TURF) 1m 1f
4:55 (12:00) 3-Y-O+
£58,653 (£17,307; £8,653; £4,326; £2,403; £1,923)

RPR

1 **Salon Soldier (GER)**[177] 2294 4-8-8 0 JimCassidy 3 105
(Kris Lees, Australia) **9/5**[1]

2 1 **Midsummer Sun**[150] 5-8-7 0 DamienOliver 8 102+
(Sam Kavanagh, Australia) **15/1**

3 ¾ **Mull Of Killough (IRE)**[10] 7556 7-9-10 0 JamieSpencer 6 117
(Jane Chapple-Hyam) *pushed along early and sn trcking ldr on outer: rdn to chal on turn into st: w ldr 2f out: narrow advantage ent fnl f: sn hdd and readily outpcd by wnr: kpt on but dropped to 3rd cl home* **9/1**

4 ½ **Rain Drum (AUS)**[10] 6-8-13 0 (b) NashRawiller 1 105
(Gai Waterhouse, Australia) **3/1**[2]

5 ¾ **Durnford (AUS)**[17] 5-8-7 0 KerrinMcEvoy 2 98
(Pat Carey, Australia) **60/1**

6 ½ **Pelicano (AUS)**[45] 5-9-1 0 (b) MatthewNeilson 4 105
(Tony McEvoy, Australia) **9/1**

7 shd **Sheer Talent (AUS)**[17] 4-8-8 0 ow1 (t) MichaelRodd 10 98
(Mark Kavanagh, Australia) **13/1**

8 5 ½ **Gris Caro**[39] 4-8-9 0 DominicTourneur 9 87
(Jake Stephens, Australia) **5/1**[3]

9 1 **Langridge Street (AUS)**[308] 6-8-7 0 (b[1]) MarkZahra 7 83
(Michael Hibbs, Australia) **70/1**

1m 48.63s (108.63) **9** Ran SP% **113.8**
PARI-MUTUEL (NSW TAB - all including 1 aud stake): WIN 2.70; PLACE 1.40, 3.30, 2.90; DF 24.50; SF 30.80.
Owner Australian Bloodstock No 2 Syndicate, R Kaljo Et A **Bred** Gestt Wittekindshof **Trained** Australia

[7737] KEMPTON (A.W) (R-H)
Wednesday, November 6

OFFICIAL GOING: Standard
Wind: Fresh, across (away from stands) Weather: Murky, drizzly

7763 BETDAQ - SPORTS BETTING EXCHANGE MAIDEN FILLIES' STKS (DIV I) 1m (P)
4:30 (4:32) (Class 5) 2-Y-O **£2,587** (£770; £384; £192) **Stalls** Low

Form RPR

33 1 **Maria Bella (IRE)**[29] 7102 2-9-0 0 SilvestreDeSousa 2 75
(Charlie Appleby) *prom: shkn up and clsd on inner to ld wl over 1f out: clr fnl f: rdn out* **11/10**[1]

6 2 2 ¾ **Gay Marriage (IRE)**[15] 7435 2-9-0 0 WilliamBuick 3 69
(John Gosden) *wl in tch: shkn up over 2f out: prog on inner wl over 1f out: styd on to take 2nd last strides* **5/1**[3]

0 3 hd **Lady Crossmar (IRE)**[44] 6691 2-9-0 0 KieranO'Neill 7 68
(Richard Hannon) *led: rdn and hdd wl over 1f out: no ch w wnr fnl f: lost 2nd last strides* **50/1**

4 2 **Pink And Black (IRE)** 2-9-0 0 SteveDrowne 9 64+
(William Muir) *chsd ldrs: rdn over 2f out: wnt 4th over 1f out: one pce after* **50/1**

5 ¾ **Aristocratic Duty** 2-9-0 0 FergusSweeney 11 62
(Sylvester Kirk) *pressed ldr to 2f out: steadily fdd* **50/1**

0 6 1 ¼ **Song Beam**[29] 7102 2-9-0 0 TomQueally 4 59+
(Michael Bell) *sn in last trio: pushed along and prog on inner over 2f out: shkn up over 1f out: kpt on same pce after* **66/1**

7 nk **Button Down** 2-9-0 0 PaulHanagan 14 58+
(Lady Cecil) *hld up in rr: pushed along over 2f out: kpt on wout threatening fr over 1f out: reminder fnl f* **16/1**

30 8 1 **Sequester**[15] 7435 2-9-0 0 ShaneKelly 10 56
(David Lanigan) *stdd s: hld up in last trio: jst pushed along fr over 2f out: modest late prog: probable improver* **16/1**

9 ¾ **Talmada (USA)** 2-9-0 0 AndreaAtzeni 5 54+
(Roger Varian) *s.s: mostly in last: pushed along over 2f out: passed a few rivals fnl f* **7/2**[2]

10 ½ **Easton Arch (USA)** 2-9-0 0 KierenFallon 8 53
(Brian Meehan) *prom: pushed along over 3f out: steadily wknd fr over 2f out* **14/1**

0 11 nse **Jolie Blonde**[15] 7442 2-8-11 0 RosieJessop(3) 6 53
(Sir Mark Prescott Bt) *rousted along in rr at various stages: nvr on terms* **100/1**

0 12 2 **Vied (USA)**[28] 7120 2-9-0 0 AdamKirby 1 48
(Robert Cowell) *a towards rr: rdn and no prog over 2f out* **50/1**

03 13 hd **Aurelia Cotta (IRE)**[25] 7200 2-9-0 0 WilliamCarson 13 48
(Charles Hills) *racd wd: prom: lost grnd bnd 3f out: sn wknd* **16/1**

1m 41.78s (1.98) **Going Correction** +0.05s/f (Slow) **13** Ran SP% **121.1**
Speed ratings (Par 93): **92,89,89,87,86 85,84,83,83,82 82,80,80**
toteswingers 1&2 £2.10, 1&3 £19.60, 2&3 £32.70 CSF £6.70 TOTE £1.90: £1.10, £2.20, £12.30; EX 7.20 Trifecta £264.20 Pool: £2960.41 - 8.40 winning units..
Owner Godolphin **Bred** Darley **Trained** Newmarket, Suffolk

FOCUS
They went steady and it was tough to make up ground. The winner was the form pick but the field finished quite compressed.

7764 BETDAQ - SPORTS BETTING EXCHANGE MAIDEN FILLIES' STKS (DIV II) 1m (P)
5:00 (5:03) (Class 5) 2-Y-O **£2,587** (£770; £384; £192) **Stalls** Low

Form RPR

4 1 **Natural Choice**[12] 7493 2-9-0 0 SilvestreDeSousa 14 80+
(Saeed bin Suroor) *pressed ldr after 2f: drvn to ld jst over 2f out: clr over 1f out: styd on wl* **3/1**[2]

2 5 **Sibling Honour** 2-9-0 0 AdamKirby 4 70+
(Charlie Appleby) *v.s.i.s: in last pair to 1/2-way: gd prog fr over 2f out: styd on wl to take 2nd last 50yds* **8/1**

2 3 ¾ **Billowing (IRE)**[21] 7296 2-9-0 0 WilliamBuick 13 67
(John Gosden) *led over 6f out: rdn and hdd jst over 2f out: no ch w wnr over 1f out: fdd and lost 2nd last 50yds* **7/4**[1]

5 4 nk **Baynunah (USA)**[21] 7295 2-9-0 0 ShaneKelly 1 66
(James Fanshawe) *trckd ldrs in 5th: shkn up over 2f out: styd on same pce fr over 1f out* **12/1**

5 nk **Almashooqa (USA)** 2-9-0 0 PaulHanagan 6 66+
(Roger Varian) *chsd ldrs in 6th: shkn up and no prog over 2f out: styd on fnl f* **8/1**

0 6 ½ **By Jupiter**[46] 6643 2-9-0 0 TomQueally 9 64+
(Michael Bell) *towards rr: pushed along over 2f out: prog and reminder over 1f out: styd on quite wl fnl f* **25/1**

6 7 2 ½ **Broadway Musical (IRE)**[22] 7260 2-9-0 0 SeanLevey 2 59
(Richard Hannon) *led to over 6f out: chsd ldng pair: no ch fr wl over 1f out: wknd fnl f* **33/1**

6 8 1 ½ **Wintour Leap**[29] 7102 2-9-0 0 FrederikTylicki 5 55
(Roger Charlton) *nvr beyond midfield: shkn up and no prog over 2f out* **25/1**

9 hd **Interject (USA)** 2-9-0 0 SteveDrowne 7 55
(Charles Hills) *slowly away: wl in rr: shkn up over 2f out: no prog tl styd on last 100yds* **25/1**

3 10 hd **Seek A Star (USA)**[22] 7274 2-9-0 0 KierenFallon 10 54
(Luca Cumani) *chsd ldng trio: rdn and hanging over 2f out: losing pl whn short of room jst ins fnl f: eased* **5/1**[3]

11 ¾ **Next Stop** 2-9-0 0 KierenFox 3 53
(Lee Carter) *dropped to last after 2f and scrubbed along: struggling after: styd on ins fnl f* **100/1**

00 12 nk **Coastal Storm**[15] 7442 2-9-0 0 RobertHavlin 12 52
(Hughie Morrison) *a in rr: no ch fnl 2f* **100/1**

00 13 2 ¾ **Sweetheart Abbey**[28] 7119 2-9-0 0 HarryBentley 11 46
(William Knight) *struggling in rr on outer 1/2-way: no ch fnl 2f* **25/1**

0 14 ½ **Rochelle (IRE)**[19] 7335 2-9-0 0 AndreaAtzeni 8 44
(William Muir) *nvr beyond midfield: shkn up over 2f out: sn wknd* **66/1**

1m 40.16s (0.36) **Going Correction** +0.05s/f (Slow) **14** Ran SP% **129.7**
Speed ratings (Par 93): **100,95,94,93,93 93,90,89,88,88 88,87,84,84**
toteswingers 1&2 £5.20, 1&3 £2.00, 2&3 £4.50 CSF £27.76 TOTE £3.60: £1.10, £3.20, £1.50; EX 40.20 Trifecta £139.60 Pool: £3379.66 - 18.15 winning units..
Owner Godolphin **Bred** Darley **Trained** Newmarket, Suffolk

FOCUS
They went a better pace in this race and it was much the quicker of the two divisions, by 1.62sec. The winner was value for extra but there's a degree of suspicion as to what the form's worth.

7765 £500 FREE BETS AT BETDAQ H'CAP (LONDON MIDDLE DISTANCE SERIES QUALIFIER) 1m 3f (P)
5:30 (5:33) (Class 4) (0-85,85) 3-Y-0+ **£4,690** (£1,395; £697; £348) **Stalls** Low

Form RPR
0003 **1** **Stevie Thunder**[5] 7656 8-9-0 **75**....(p) SilvestreDeSousa 12 86
(Ian Williams) *mostly pressed ldr: led over 2f out and sent for home: drvn clr over 1f out: styd on wl* **7/1**[3]
0434 **2** *3 ½* **Karam Albaari (IRE)**[87] 5302 5-9-8 **83**.... FrederikTylicki 2 88
(J R Jenkins) *sn trckd ldng pair: drvn on inner to try to chal 2f out: no ch w wnr over 1f out: clung on for 2nd* **25/1**
3416 **3** *nse* **Deserted**[42] 6743 3-8-10 **76**.... AndreaAtzeni 3 83+
(Luca Cumani) *hld up in tch: hmpd over 2f out: swtchd and prog over 1f out: styd on wl fnl f and nrly snatched 2nd* **4/1**[1]
3625 **4** *½* **Burnham**[46] 6646 4-9-3 **78**....(p) GeorgeBaker 6 82
(Hughie Morrison) *wl in tch on outer: rdn over 2f out: styd on fr over 1f out: pressed for a pl nr fin* **4/1**[1]
5265 **5** *3* **Greylami (IRE)**[48] 6559 8-9-4 **84**.... RyanTate(5) 11 83
(Clive Cox) *anticipated s and stmbld leaving stalls: hld up towards rr: shkn up over 2f out: nt qckn and outpcd: kpt on fr over 1f out to take 5th ins fnl f* **10/1**
000 **6** *¾* **Granell (IRE)**[20] 7330 3-8-9 **75**.... SeanLevey 4 72
(Brian Meehan) *in tch: drvn to chse ldrs over 2f out: no prog or imp over 1f out* **33/1**
6440 **7** *hd* **Nave (USA)**[26] 7174 6-9-6 **81**.... JimCrowley 1 78
(David Simcock) *mde most to over 2f out: sn lost pl and btn* **8/1**
0546 **8** *½* **Forget Me Not Lane (IRE)**[48] 6563 4-8-10 **71**.... KierenFallon 10 67
(Kevin Ryan) *w ldng pair 2f: sn settled in 4th: rdn and no rspnse jst over 2f out: steadily fdd* **7/1**[3]
063- **9** *½* **Franco Is My Name**[364] 7626 7-9-7 **85**.... CharlesBishop(3) 9 80
(Peter Hedger) *hld up in last pair: rdn over 2f out: keeping on and may have fin 6th whn sltly hmpd last 75yds and eased* **16/1**
0545 **10** *½* **John Biscuit (IRE)**[143] 3370 5-9-8 **83**.... WilliamBuick 8 77
(Andrew Balding) *hld up in rr: shkn up and no prog over 2f out: no ch after* **11/2**[2]
146 **11** *1 ¼* **Song Light**[131] 3783 3-8-10 **76**.... WilliamCarson 5 68
(David Elsworth) *stdd s: plld hrd and hld up in rr: nt clr run over 2f out: no prog after* **33/1**
0010 **12** *1* **Cosmic Halo**[39] 6832 4-9-5 **80**.... PaulHanagan 7 70
(Richard Fahey) *dwlt: hld up in detached last: urged along 3f out: no prog* **16/1**

2m 21.8s (-0.10) **Going Correction** +0.05s/f (Slow)
WFA 3 from 4yo+ 5lb **12** Ran SP% **122.1**
Speed ratings (Par 105): **102,99,99,99,96 96,96,95,95,95 94,93**
toteswingers 1&2 £19.70, 1&3 £11.50, 2&3 £33.80 CSF £176.06 CT £800.50 TOTE £7.20: £2.40, £7.20, £1.60; EX 224.90 Trifecta £548.00 Pool: £2373.25 - 3.24 winning units..
Owner Steve Gray **Bred** Sir Eric Parker **Trained** Portway, Worcs

FOCUS
No great early gallop and once again the pace held up. The form is taken at face value.

7766 BRITISH STALLION STUDS EBF MAIDEN STKS 7f (P)
6:00 (6:03) (Class 5) 2-Y-0 **£2,911** (£866; £432; £216) **Stalls** Low

Form RPR
3 **1** **Pretend (IRE)**[14] 7461 2-9-5 0.... SilvestreDeSousa 13 90+
(Charlie Appleby) *mde virtually all: skipped clr over 2f out: in n.d after: pushed out and styd on strly* **4/5**[1]
42 **2** *7* **Beyond Smart (USA)**[22] 7276 2-9-5 0.... WilliamBuick 5 71
(John Gosden) *t.k.h early: trckd ldrs: drvn and outpcd over 2f out: prog to go 2nd jst over 1f out: styd on but no ch w wnr* **4/1**[2]
3 *2 ¼* **Twin Point** 2-9-5 0.... NickyMackay 8 66+
(John Gosden) *sn in midfield: prog whn nt clr run over 2f out: hdwy over 1f out: tk 3rd jst ins fnl f: styd on* **33/1**
4 *3* **Venus Grace** 2-9-0 0.... RichardThomas 4 52+
(Ralph Beckett) *towards rr: shkn up and prog over 2f out: kpt on to take 4th ins fnl f: nvr on terms* **50/1**
0 **5** *¾* **Salmon Sushi**[40] 6799 2-9-5 0.... ShaneKelly 6 55
(David Lanigan) *hld up towards rr: rdn and high quite high fr over 2f out: late prog: n.d* **15/2**[3]
43 **6** *1 ¼* **Wealth (IRE)**[38] 6873 2-9-5 0.... PaulHanagan 11 52
(Richard Fahey) *in tch: effrt whn outpcd over 2f out: shkn up and one pce after* **9/1**
0 **7** *nse* **Sharp Lookout**[28] 7120 2-9-5 0....[1] GeorgeBaker 2 51
(Roger Charlton) *wl in tch: shkn up and prog into 5th 2f out but wl outpcd: one pce and n.d after* **25/1**
6 **8** *hd* **Kantara Castle (IRE)**[57] 6279 2-9-5 0.... SeanLevey 10 51
(Richard Hannon) *t.k.h early: hld up wl in rr: shkn up over 2f out: kpt on fr over 1f out: n.d* **66/1**
4 **9** *hd* **Quinta Feira (IRE)**[195] 1778 2-9-2 0.... MarkCoumbe(3) 7 50
(Ed de Giles) *dwlt: hld up in last: jst pushed along fr 2f out: swtchd to inner over 1f out: kpt on quite takingly fnl f* **80/1**
10 *4 ½* **Secret Archive (USA)** 2-9-5 0.... JimCrowley 3 38
(Ralph Beckett) *dwlt: rn green and pushed along in last trio: prog on inner 2f out: pushed along and wknd fnl f* **20/1**
6 **11** *2 ¼* **Crafted (IRE)**[20] 7328 2-9-5 0.... AdamKirby 12 32
(Mark Johnston) *chsd wnr: clr of rest 2f out: hanging after: lost 2nd and wknd rapidly jst over 1f out* **50/1**
0 **12** *3 ¾* **Comanchero (IRE)**[23] 7251 2-9-5 0.... KierenFallon 9 22
(Andrew Balding) *t.k.h early: hld up in midfield: rdn and no prog over 2f out: sn bhd* **50/1**
0 **13** *17* **Gauchita**[35] 6947 2-9-0 0.... TomQueally 1
(Michael Bell) *chsd ldng pair to 3f out: wknd rapidly: t.o* **50/1**
00 **14** *7* **Henry Grace (IRE)**[12] 7501 2-9-5 0.... KieranO'Neill 14
(Jimmy Fox) *chsd ldrs 4f: wknd qckly: t.o* **100/1**

1m 25.34s (-0.66) **Going Correction** +0.05s/f (Slow) **14** Ran SP% **120.4**
Speed ratings (Par 96): **105,97,94,91,90 88,88,88,88,83 80,76,56,48**
toteswingers 1&2 £1.10, 1&3 £12.20, 2&3 £20.70 CSF £3.53 TOTE £1.80: £1.10, £1.40, £6.30; EX 4.90 Trifecta £72.90 Pool: £3454.25 - 35.49 winning units..
Owner Godolphin **Bred** Azienda Agricola Loreto Luciani **Trained** Newmarket, Suffolk

FOCUS
This proved very straightforward for the favourite, who stood out after his promising debut.

7767 BOOK CHRISTMAS FESTIVAL TICKETS NOW H'CAP 2m (P)
6:30 (6:32) (Class 6) (0-60,62) 3-Y-0+ **£1,940** (£577; £288; £144) **Stalls** Low

Form RPR
0331 **1** **Mr Burbidge**[5] 7668 5-10-0 **62** 6ex....(b) TomQueally 11 74
(Neil Mulholland) *hld up disputing 7th: rdn and prog over 2f out to ld over 1f out: drvn and styd on wl fnl f* **7/2**[2]
2 *1 ¼* **Echua (IRE)**[1194] 4610 7-9-6 **54**.... MartinHarley 4 64
(Emmet Michael Butterly, Ire) *trckd ldng pair: effrt over 2f out to ld wl over 1f out: sn hdd: kpt on wl u.p but hld fnl f* **3/1**[1]
6023 **3** *¾* **Dumbfounded (FR)**[37] 6899 5-9-10 **58**.... MartinLane 7 67
(Lady Herries) *trckd ldng pair: effrt to led over 2f out: hdd wl over 1f out: battled on tl no ex fnl f* **5/1**[3]
-166 **4** *7* **Entitlement**[53] 6404 4-9-12 **60**....(t[1]) ShaneKelly 1 61
(James Fanshawe) *trckd ldrs disputing 5th: rdn over 2f out: hanging and sn wl outpcd: kpt on to take modest 4th fnl f* **14/1**
5006 **5** *hd* **Dr Finley (IRE)**[43] 6736 6-9-6 **59**....(v) JoeyHaynes(5) 9 59
(Lydia Pearce) *hld up disputing 9th: hrd rdn over 2f out: prog over 1f out: kpt on to press for modest 4th fnl f* **25/1**
0315 **6** *7* **Cabuchon (GER)**[21] 7305 6-9-10 **58**....(t) AdamKirby 6 50
(David Evans) *trckd ldrs disputing 5th: drvn and cl up over 2f out: wknd over 1f out* **6/1**
0450 **7** *1 ½* **Epsom Salts**[53] 6404 8-9-4 **59**....(p) SophieRalston(7) 12 49
(Pat Phelan) *pressed ldr: led 7f out to over 2f out: wknd qckly over 1f out* **33/1**
3250 **8** *2 ¼* **Noor Al Haya (IRE)**[20] 7331 3-9-1 **58**.... KieranO'Neill 2 46
(Mark Usher) *in tch disputing 7th: outpcd over 2f out: wknd over 1f out* **14/1**
/03- **9** *16* **Sarando**[183] 7528 8-9-9 **57**....(t) PaulHanagan 5 25
(Alex Hales) *led to 7f out: pressed ldr to over 2f out: wknd qckly and eased over 1f out: t.o* **33/1**
6244 **10** *½* **Walter De La Mare (IRE)**[37] 6895 6-9-0 **48**.... SilvestreDeSousa 14 16
(Anabel K Murphy) *hld up in last trio: no prog 3f out: wknd and t.o* **8/1**
4042 **11** *8* **Grandiloquent**[21] 7305 4-9-11 **59**....(p) KierenFallon 10 17
(Kevin Ryan) *s.s: a towards rr: no prog 3f out: sn bhd: t.o* **12/1**
0134 **12** *32* **Boston Blue**[140] 3473 6-9-9 **57**.... JimCrowley 13
(Tony Carroll) *a in last trio: wl t.o* **14/1**
30-0 **13** *7* **Reillys Daughter**[12] 7506 5-9-6 **59**.... NatashaEaton(5) 3
(Richard Mitchell) *hld up in rr: brief effrt 4f out: sn wknd: wl t.o* **66/1**

3m 33.16s (3.06) **Going Correction** +0.05s/f (Slow)
WFA 3 from 4yo+ 9lb **13** Ran SP% **128.2**
Speed ratings (Par 101): **94,93,93,89,89 85,85,84,76,75 71,55,52**
toteswingers 1&2 £3.90, 1&3 £4.80, 2&3 £4.60 CSF £15.20 CT £56.38 TOTE £6.10: £1.60, £2.50, £2.30; EX 25.60 Trifecta £108.00 Pool: £1924.60 - 13.35 winning units..
Owner Dajam Ltd **Bred** M Burbidge **Trained** Limpley Stoke, Wilts

FOCUS
Not a bad race for the grade and the first three all look ahead of their marks. Pace had held up well in the previous races on the card and the second and third were always prominent in this race as well.

7768 WINNERS ARE WELCOME AT BETDAQ FLOODLIT STKS (LISTED RACE) 1m 4f (P)
7:00 (7:03) (Class 1) 3-Y-0+
£20,982 (£7,955; £3,981; £1,983; £995; £499) **Stalls** Centre

Form RPR
0213 **1** **Pether's Moon (IRE)**[54] 6348 3-8-11 101.... SeanLevey 2 112
(Richard Hannon) *mde all: set stdy pce: wound it up fr 4f out: kicked for home over 2f out: clr over 1f out: styd on wl* **7/2**[3]
6-23 **2** *3 ¾* **Gatewood**[32] 7012 5-9-3 109.... WilliamBuick 5 106
(John Gosden) *trckd wnr after 3f tl after 5f: rdn to go 2nd again over 2f out: nt qckn and no imp fr over 1f out: kpt on* **15/8**[1]
2035 **3** *3 ¼* **Aussie Reigns (IRE)**[32] 7022 3-8-11 94....(v) AndreaAtzeni 6 101
(William Knight) *hld up in last pair: rdn wl over 2f out: prog over 1f out to take 3rd fnl f: n.d* **33/1**
2010 **4** *¾* **Opera Box**[46] 6649 5-8-12 87.... HarryBentley 3 95
(Marcus Tregoning) *trckd wnr 3f: grad shuffled bk to rr: rdn wl over 2f out: kpt on one pce to take 4th nr fin* **50/1**
110 **5** *4* **Great Hall**[53] 6393 3-8-11 99....(b[1]) KierenFallon 1 93
(Brian Meehan) *trckd ldrs: rdn to dispute 2nd over 2f out: wknd over 1f out* **13/2**
112 **6** *5* **Urban Dance (IRE)**[39] 6841 3-8-11 99.... SilvestreDeSousa 4 85
(Charlie Appleby) *t.k.h: hld up and dropped to last pair after 3f: shkn up and effrt over 2f out: wknd wl over 1f out* **9/4**[2]
6654 **7** *7* **Jehannedarc (IRE)**[17] 7414 5-8-12 95....(t) PaulHanagan 7 69
(Ed Dunlop) *hld up tl prog to trck wnr after 5f: wknd qckly over 2f out* **25/1**

2m 32.01s (-2.49) **Going Correction** +0.05s/f (Slow)
WFA 3 from 5yo 6lb **7** Ran SP% **109.9**
Speed ratings (Par 111): **110,107,105,104,102 98,94**
toteswingers 1&2 £1.50, 1&3 £19.20, 2&3 £10.40 CSF £9.60 TOTE £4.60: £1.90, £1.50; EX 10.50 Trifecta £55.20 Pool: £2938.30 - 39.86 winning units..
Owner John Manley **Bred** Michael G Daly **Trained** East Everleigh, Wilts

FOCUS
An interesting Listed race and again there was an advantage to being ridden handily. The early pace wasn't strong. Another personal best from the winner but a bit of doubt over what the runner-up retains.

7769 BETDAQ 1ST UK RACE COMMISSION FREE H'CAP 7f (P)
7:30 (7:30) (Class 3) (0-95,94) 3-Y-0+
£7,158 (£2,143; £1,071; £535; £267; £134) **Stalls** Low

Form RPR
0010 **1** **Common Touch (IRE)**[18] 7368 5-9-3 **90**.... KierenFallon 3 101
(Willie Musson) *hld up in rr: rdn and prog fr 2f out to press ldr jst over 1f out: sustained effrt to ld last 50yds* **16/1**
0112 **2** *nk* **Chookie Royale**[6] 7641 5-9-4 **94**....(p) JasonHart(3) 10 104
(Keith Dalgleish) *t.k.h: hld up in tch on outer: prog to ld jst over 2f out: awkward hd carriage after but kpt on wl whn pressed 1f out: worn down last 50yds* **3/1**[2]
1-11 **3** *2 ½* **Horsted Keynes (FR)**[6] 7648 3-9-1 **89** 6ex.... AndreaAtzeni 1 91
(Roger Varian) *trckd ldrs on inner: shkn up to chal jst over 2f out: nt qckn over 1f out: one pce after* **13/8**[1]
0346 **4** *1 ½* **Regal Dan (IRE)**[39] 6840 3-8-13 **87**.... TomQueally 7 85
(Charles Hills) *hld up in rr on outer: drvn and sme prog 2f out: hanging and nt qckn over 1f out: kpt on same pce* **4/1**[3]

6005 **5** 1 ¼ **Mister Musicmaster**[20] 7318 4-8-7 80 WilliamCarson 8 76
(Ron Hodges) *hld up in last: prog towards innner 2f out: hanging whn rdn over 1f out: no hdwy fnl f* **66/1**
4102 **6** 2 ¾ **Ocean Legend (IRE)**[15] 7436 8-8-8 81 LukeMorris 5 69
(Tony Carroll) *trckd ldrs: tried to cl over 2f out: nt qckn wl over 1f out: fdd* **20/1**
-001 **7** 1 ¼ **Apostle (IRE)**[15] 7436 4-9-0 87 JimCrowley 6 72
(David Simcock) *mostly pressed ldr to over 2f out: lost pl and btn wl over 1f out* **13/2**
0540 **8** 4 ½ **Palace Moon**[14] 7464 8-8-10 83 (t) JimmyQuinn 4 56
(William Knight) *dwlt: hld up in rr: effrt over 2f out: no prog and btn over 1f out* **25/1**
0- **9** 10 **Suehail**[165] 2679 4-8-9 82 ShaneKelly 11 28
(Robert Cowell) *dwlt: rcvrd on outer to press ldng pair: wknd qckly over 2f out* **33/1**
60 **10** 7 **Lady Of The House (IRE)**[76] 5684 3-8-8 82 (p) PaulHanagan 2 8
(Kevin Ryan) *led to over 2f out: wknd rapidly* **33/1**

1m 24.82s (-1.18) **Going Correction** +0.05s/f (Slow)
WFA 3 from 4yo+ 1lb **10** Ran SP% **118.3**
Speed ratings (Par 107): **108,107,104,103,101 98,97,91,80,72**
toteswingers 1&2 £16.10, 1&3 £11.70, 2&3 £1.40 CSF £61.77 CT £127.83 TOTE £15.90: £4.10, £1.10, £1.40; EX 104.90 Trifecta £186.00 Pool: £2802.13 - 11.29 winning units..
Owner Broughton Thermal Insulation **Bred** Overbury Stallions Ltd And D Boocock **Trained** Newmarket, Suffolk

FOCUS
A good handicap, if lacking a bit of depth. There was plenty of competition for the lead here, with Lady Of The House taken on by Apostle and Suehail up front. All three paid for their efforts and set things up for those ridden with a bit more patience.

7770 BOOK RESTAURANT FOR CHRISTMAS FESTIVAL H'CAP 1m 4f (P)
8:00 (8:01) (Class 6) (0-55,55) 3-Y-O **£1,940** (£577; £288; £144) **Stalls** Centre

Form RPR
00-5 **1** **Atalanta Bay (IRE)**[210] 1487 3-9-6 54 HarryBentley 7 68
(Marcus Tregoning) *trckd ldng pair: pushed along to ld 2f out: shkn up and drew rt away fr over 1f out* **11/2**[3]
0020 **2** 8 **Ocean Power (IRE)**[37] 6899 3-9-0 48 LukeMorris 8 49
(Richard Phillips) *hld up in midfield: prog 3f out: rdn to go 2nd wl over 1f out: sn no ch w wnr: fdd fnl f* **16/1**
0006 **3** ½ **Mignonne**[21] 7299 3-8-13 52 (b) JoeyHaynes(5) 4 52
(Hans Adielsson) *taken down early: pressed ldr: led over 3f out gng easily: shkn up and no rspnse over 2f out: sn hdd and btn* **5/1**[2]
4204 **4** 8 **Lucky Black Star (IRE)**[33] 6996 3-9-7 55 AdamKirby 10 43
(George Baker) *hld up in last trio: rdn and outpcd fr 4f out: kpt on fr 3f out to take modest 4th jst over 1f out: no ch and eased last 100yds* **11/4**[1]
2300 **5** 6 **Mr Vendman (IRE)**[39] 6853 3-8-12 46 oh1 (b) SilvestreDeSousa 2 24
(Ian Williams) *mde most: rdn over 4f out: hdd over 3f out: wknd over 2f out* **6/1**
0-06 **6** 3 ½ **Mill I Am (USA)**[29] 7108 3-9-7 55 AndreaAtzeni 1 27
(Stuart Williams) *chsd ldng pair: rdn 4f out: wknd wl over 2f out* **14/1**
0402 **7** 4 **Platinum Proof (USA)**[5] 7666 3-8-8 47 (bt) DavidBergin(5) 3 13
(David O'Meara) *wl in tch tl wknd wl over 2f out* **13/2**
0500 **8** hd **Finalee**[37] 6895 3-9-1 49 TomQueally 9 15
(John Gallagher) *sn in last and urged along: nvr a factor* **33/1**
0600 **9** 14 **Sings Poet**[6] 7637 3-8-12 46 oh1 (p) WilliamCarson 6
(Peter Hiatt) *dwlt and urged along early: sn chsd ldrs: urged along again 5f out: sn wknd: t.o* **25/1**
0022 **10** 3 ¼ **Nepalese Pearl**[63] 6102 3-9-3 51 RobertHavlin 11
(Pat Eddery) *in tch to over 3f out: wknd rapidly: t.o* **15/2**

2m 34.81s (0.31) **Going Correction** +0.05s/f (Slow) **10** Ran SP% **117.4**
Speed ratings (Par 98): **100,94,94,89,85 82,80,79,70,68**
toteswingers 1&2 £21.10, 1&3 £6.30, 2&3 £17.00 CSF £89.63 CT £470.93 TOTE £6.60: £2.30, £3.70, £2.00; EX 110.10 Trifecta £321.80 Pool: £1998.82 - 4.65 winning units..
Owner Miss S Sharp **Bred** Manister House Stud **Trained** Whitsbury, Hants

FOCUS
A pretty weak handicap and few got involved. The form is rated around the second and third and it's hard to be positive about the form.
T/Plt: £7.90 to a £1 stake. Pool: £83554.85 - 7669.50 winning tickets T/Qpdt: £8.60 to a £1 stake. Pool: £8311.64 - 709.48 winning tickets JN

7630 NOTTINGHAM (L-H)
Wednesday, November 6

OFFICIAL GOING: Soft (6.1)
Wind: light 1/2 against Weather: overcast, light rain

7771 PHS GROUP NURSERY H'CAP 5f 13y
12:30 (12:31) (Class 4) (0-85,85) 2-Y-O **£3,881** (£1,155; £577; £288) **Stalls** High

Form RPR
1005 **1** **Touch The Clouds**[30] 7074 2-8-6 75 (p) KevinStott(5) 8 80
(Kevin Ryan) *chsd ldrs: effrt over 2f out: led appr fnl f: drvn out* **10/1**
1445 **2** 1 ¼ **Montaigne**[20] 7329 2-9-5 83 JimCrowley 3 83
(Ralph Beckett) *hmpd s: hld up: effrt over 2f out: styd on to chse wnr last 100yds* **5/2**[1]
5553 **3** nk **Caesars Gift (IRE)**[7] 7623 2-7-9 64 oh6 NoelGarbutt(5) 10 63+
(Derek Shaw) *sn outpcd and in rr: hdwy over 1f out: styd on wl ins fnl f* **16/1**
0150 **4** 1 ¼ **Anytimeatall (IRE)**[34] 6967 2-7-12 67 ow3 NatashaEaton(5) 12 61
(Alan Bailey) *chsd ldrs: kpt on same pce appr fnl f* **16/1**
4205 **5** ¾ **Tableforten**[19] 7333 2-8-10 74 (b) LiamJones 2 66
(J S Moore) *wnt rt s: chsd ldrs: swtchd lft over 1f out: one pce* **4/1**[2]
0001 **6** ¾ **Hopefilly (IRE)**[28] 7127 2-9-2 80 JimmyFortune 7 69
(Ed Walker) *led tl over 2f out: wknd fnl f* **4/1**[2]
5030 **7** 3 ½ **Classical Diva**[28] 7127 2-8-0 64 LukeMorris 6 40
(Declan Carroll) *chsd ldrs: wknd over 1f out* **33/1**
006 **8** ¾ **Dont Tell Nan**[11] 7541 2-8-0 64 oh7 RaulDaSilva 9 38
(Derek Shaw) *sn outpcd and in rr: nvr on terms* **50/1**
2304 **9** hd **Outback Lover (IRE)**[32] 7036 2-7-12 67 ow3 (b) ShirleyTeasdale(5) 5 40
(J S Moore) *chsd ldrs: drvn 3f out: lost pl over 1f out* **25/1**
1304 **10** ½ **Peterkin (IRE)**[11] 7545 2-9-7 85 GrahamLee 1 56
(Mark Johnston) *w ldrs: led over 2f out: hdd appr fnl f: sn wknd* **8/1**[3]
514 **11** 5 **Kalon Brama (IRE)**[14] 7468 2-8-1 65 JimmyQuinn 4 18
(Peter Charalambous) *chsd ldrs: lost pl over 1f out* **20/1**

1m 2.86s (1.36) **Going Correction** +0.375s/f (Good) **11** Ran SP% **114.0**
Speed ratings (Par 98): **104,102,101,99,98 97,91,90,90,89 81**
toteswingers 1&2 £7.30, 1&3 £24.30, 2&3 £11.80 CSF £32.82 CT £409.64 TOTE £10.30: £3.60, £1.50, £4.70; EX 42.50 Trifecta £942.00 Pool: £2236.97 - 1.78 winning units..
Owner Matt & Lauren Morgan 1 **Bred** Stuart McPhee Bloodstock Ltd **Trained** Hambleton, N Yorks

FOCUS
All races on inner track and home bend out 5m, increasing races on Round course by 13yds. An ordinary late-season nursery. They initially split into two groups but pretty much spread out across the track in the closing stages. There didn't look to be much bias wherever they raced.

7772 TREND MICRO VMWARE ARROW BUNDLE H'CAP 5f 13y
1:00 (1:01) (Class 6) (0-65,65) 3-Y-O+ **£1,940** (£577; £288; £144) **Stalls** High

Form RPR
2530 **1** **Megaleka**[23] 7236 3-8-10 57 RobertTart(3) 15 68+
(Alan Bailey) *chsd ldrs: led over 1f out: sn clr: hung bdly lft and ended up far side rail: hld on nr fin* **10/1**[3]
0065 **2** nk **Breezolini**[21] 7315 5-9-5 63 RobertWinston 16 71
(Ollie Pears) *in rr: hdwy over 2f out: chsd clr ldr 1f out: styd on* **5/1**[1]
3400 **3** ½ **Quality Art (USA)**[8] 7598 5-8-11 60 ConnorBeasley(5) 17 66
(Richard Guest) *in rr: hdwy over 2f out: chsd ldng pair 1f out: kpt on same pce* **16/1**
0034 **4** 1 **Fathom Five (IRE)**[8] 7598 9-8-9 58 ShirleyTeasdale(5) 10 61
(Shaun Harris) *chsd ldrs: kpt on one pce over 1f out* **14/1**
6060 **5** 2 ½ **Shawkantango**[7] 7633 6-9-6 64 (v) DaleSwift 14 58
(Derek Shaw) *dwlt: in rr: kpt on fnl 2f: nvr nrr* **14/1**
025 **6** nk **New Decade**[8] 7598 4-9-7 65 LukeMorris 9 58
(Milton Bradley) *chsd ldrs: one pce over 1f out* **6/1**[2]
3161 **7** shd **Pull The Pin (IRE)**[8] 7599 4-8-13 60 6ex (b) ThomasBrown(3) 6 53
(Paul Green) *led: hdd over 1f out: kpt on same pce* **5/1**[1]
060- **8** ¾ **Henry Morgan**[455] 4954 6-8-11 55 GrahamLee 11 45
(Bryan Smart) *in rr: kpt on over 1f out: nvr a factor* **25/1**
3421 **9** 1 ½ **Borough Boy (IRE)**[18] 7380 3-8-10 54 (v) RaulDaSilva 13 39
(Derek Shaw) *s.i.s: in rr: kpt on fnl 2f: nvr a factor* **20/1**
0000 **10** ¾ **Stonecrabstomorrow (IRE)**[55] 6343 10-8-10 57 MarkCoumbe(3) 8 39
(Roy Brotherton) *mid-div: effrt over 2f out: nvr a factor* **33/1**
-000 **11** 1 ½ **Risky Rizkova**[49] 6527 3-8-11 58 MatthewLawson(3) 1 35
(Jonathan Portman) *chsd ldrs: wknd over 1f out* **33/1**
0006 **12** 1 ¼ **See Clearly**[43] 6728 4-9-2 60 (b) DuranFentiman 2 32
(Tim Easterby) *chsd ldrs: wknd over 1f out* **25/1**
00-0 **13** hd **Befortyfour**[2] 7729 8-9-0 58 RobbieFitzpatrick 4 30
(Charles Smith) *chsd ldrs: wknd over 1f out* **40/1**
4406 **14** ¾ **Danzoe (IRE)**[21] 7315 6-9-5 63 TomMcLaughlin 12 32
(Christine Dunnett) *a towards rr* **16/1**
3036 **15** 3 ¾ **Balinka**[35] 6944 3-9-0 58 (v) DavidAllan 7 14
(Mel Brittain) *chsd ldrs: wknd over 1f out: eased clsng stages* **16/1**
4120 **16** ½ **Imperial Spirit**[21] 7292 3-8-8 55 (v) CharlesBishop(3) 3 9
(Mick Channon) *chsd ldrs: lost pl 2f out: sn eased* **25/1**
260 **17** 14 **Rex Romanorum (IRE)**[56] 6301 5-9-7 65 RussKennemore 5
(Patrick Holmes) *chsd ldrs: wknd 2f out: sn heavily eased* **10/1**[3]

1m 2.91s (1.41) **Going Correction** +0.375s/f (Good) **17** Ran SP% **121.4**
Speed ratings (Par 101): **103,102,101,100,96 95,95,94,91,90 88,86,85,84,78 77,55**
toteswingers 1&2 £13.60, 1&3 £53.80, 2&3 £22.40 CSF £53.51 CT £574.46 TOTE £9.40: £2.60, £1.70, £6.10, £3.90; EX 64.00 Trifecta £842.70 Part won. Pool: £1123.70 - 0.15 winning units..
Owner North Cheshire Trading & Storage Ltd **Bred** North Cheshire Trading And Storage Ltd **Trained** Newmarket, Suffolk

FOCUS
Question marks over a lot of these and this looked a moderate contest. They spread right across the track and, although the winner ended up on the far side rail, the first three home were drawn in 15,16 and 17. The time was only just slower than the opening Class 4 nursery. The winner looked a bit better than the bare form.

7773 TREND MICRO SECURING CLOUD MAIDEN STKS (DIV I) 1m 75y
1:30 (1:33) (Class 5) 2-Y-O **£2,587** (£770; £384; £192) **Stalls** Centre

Form RPR
0 **1** **Love Tangle (IRE)**[41] 6762 2-9-5 0 MartinLane 7 75+
(Brian Meehan) *trckd ldr: led appr fnl f: drvn out* **7/2**[1]
5 **2** 1 **Stout Cortez**[8] 7607 2-9-5 0 GrahamLee 2 73
(Mark Johnston) *led: green bnd over 4f out: hdd appr fnl f: styd on same pce* **5/1**[2]
00 **3** 1 ¼ **Supachap**[14] 7461 2-9-5 0 RobertHavlin 12 72+
(Hughie Morrison) *trckd ldrs: hung bdly lft and kpt on same pce fnl f* **10/1**
4 1 ¼ **Norab (GER)** 2-9-5 0 MartinHarley 5 67+
(Marco Botti) *s.i.s: hdwy over 5f out: sn chsng ldrs: drvn over 2f out: outpcd over 1f out: kpt on towards fin: will improve* **7/2**[1]
60 **5** nse **Sahara Desert (IRE)**[14] 7461 2-9-5 0 JimmyFortune 4 69
(Sir Michael Stoute) *trckd ldrs: t.k.h: swtchd rt 2f out: one pce whn hung lft fnl f: eased nr fin: bit slipped* **12/1**
00 **6** 7 **Derbyshire (IRE)**[47] 6581 2-9-5 0 TomEaves 8 52
(Kevin Ryan) *in rr: sme hdwy and swtchd rt over 3f out: wknd 2f out* **6/1**[3]
6 **7** nk **Kashmiri Sunset**[7] 7631 2-9-5 0 ChrisCatlin 11 51
(Ed de Giles) *mid-div: lost pl over 6f out* **50/1**
0 **8** 3 ½ **Rock Of Leon**[8] 7607 2-9-5 0 StevieDonohoe 6 43
(Michael Bell) *s.i.s: drvn 4f out: nvr on terms* **25/1**
6 **9** 17 **D'Arcy Indiana**[43] 6724 2-9-5 0 SebSanders 10 6
(Amy Weaver) *swtchd lft after s: in rr: sme hdwy on ins over 3f out: sn lost pl: eased whn bhd clsng stages* **40/1**

1m 54.56s (5.56) **Going Correction** +0.375s/f (Good) **9** Ran SP% **100.4**
Speed ratings (Par 96): **87,86,84,83,83 76,76,72,55**
toteswingers 1&2 £4.00, 1&3 £5.80, 2&3 £6.90 CSF £14.66 TOTE £3.80: £1.80, £1.30, £2.80; EX 22.40 Trifecta £162.00 Pool: £1043.48 - 4.82 winning units..
Owner Ballymacoll Stud **Bred** Ballymacoll Stud Farm Ltd **Trained** Manton, Wilts

FOCUS
A division of this maiden was won by recent Group 3 scorer Cubanita in 2011 but this didn't look the most competitive and it spoke volumes that the sole newcomer was so prominent in the market. It was further weakened by the withdrawal of Honor Bound, who refused to load. They went no sort of pace it paid to be prominent. The form is rated at the lower end of the race averages.

7774 TREND MICRO SECURING CLOUD MAIDEN STKS (DIV II) 1m 75y
2:00 (2:04) (Class 5) 2-Y-O **£2,587** (£770; £384; £192) **Stalls** Centre

Form RPR
3043 **1** **Shimba Hills**[23] 7252 2-9-2 65 CharlesBishop(3) 11 74
(Mick Channon) *led after 1f: kpt on fnl f: jst hld on* **6/1**[3]
0 **2** shd **Mountain Fighter**[39] 6829 2-9-5 0 (p) ChrisCatlin 9 74
(Saeed bin Suroor) *trckd ldrs: 2nd over 4f out: chal 1f out: sn rdn and kpt on: jst denied* **3/1**[1]
5 **3** 1 **Jefferson City (IRE)**[12] 7502 2-9-5 0 RobertHavlin 6 72+
(John Gosden) *mid-div: drvn over 3f out: hdwy 2f out: styd on wl fnl f: tk 3rd last 50yds* **7/2**[2]

4 2 **Sayed Youmzain** 2-9-5 0 .... MartinHarley 1 67+
(Marco Botti) *s.i.s: sn mid-div: hdwy over 2f out: 3rd 1f out: kpt on same pce* **14/1**

52 5 1 **Mambo Rhythm**[23] 7237 2-9-0 0 .... GrahamLee 8 60
(Mark Johnston) *led 1f: chsd wnr: drvn over 4f out: one pce fnl 2f* **7/2**[2]

6 6 **Norse Light** 2-9-5 0 .... JimCrowley 4 52+
(Ralph Beckett) *in tch: drvn over 4f out: lost pl over 2f out* **8/1**

0 7 ¾ **Steve Rogers (IRE)**[14] 7460 2-9-5 0 .... JimmyFortune 3 50
(Sir Michael Stoute) *chsd ldrs: drvn 4f out: wknd over 2f out* **16/1**

00 8 1¼ **High Secret (IRE)**[6] 7646 2-9-5 0 .... LukeMorris 7 47+
(Sir Mark Prescott Bt) *mid-div: drvn over 4f out: sn outpcd* **50/1**

00 9 11 **Norse Legend**[12] 7500 2-9-2 0 .... ThomasBrown(3) 10 23
(Daniel Kubler) *in rr: drvn 4f out: sn lost pl and bhd: eased ins fnl f* **100/1**

0 10 6 **Bourbon Prince**[8] 7607 2-9-5 0 .... StevieDonohoe 2 10
(Michael Bell) *in rr: sme hdwy 3f out: sn wknd: eased whn bhd ins fnl f* **33/1**

11 15 **Master Dan** 2-9-5 0 .... DaleSwift 5
(James Given) *strated slowly: detached last and drvn along: bhd fnl 4f: eased ins fnl f: t.o* **33/1**

1m 53.32s (4.32) **Going Correction** +0.375s/f (Good) **11 Ran SP% 116.2**
Speed ratings (Par 96): **93,92,91,89,88 82,82,80,69,63 48**
toteswingers 1&2 £4.50, 1&3 £4.30, 2&3 £3.00 CSF £23.60 TOTE £5.90: £2.10, £2.00, £1.20; EX 31.10 Trifecta £108.80 Pool: £2233.31 - 15.39 winning units..
Owner Dave and Gill Hedley **Bred** G Hedley & Mike Channon Bloodstock Limited **Trained** West Ilsley, Berks

FOCUS
Much like the preceding division this didn't look the strongest. They went over a second quicker than that race, courtesy of a better pace, but they were still over ten seconds over standard. Again the form is rated at the lower end of the race averages, but improved form from the winner.

7775 TREND MICRO SMART PROTECTION NETWORK H'CAP 1m 75y
2:30 (2:30) (Class 2) (100-112,107) 3-Y-0+ £19,407 (£5,775; £2,886; £1,443) **Stalls Centre**

Form RPR

1141 1 **Graphic (IRE)**[26] 7172 4-9-4 102 ....(p) SebSanders 3 112
(William Haggas) *led: swung wd bnd over 4f out: shkn up over 1f out: forged clr ins fnl f: readily* **7/4**[1]

0131 2 4 **Breton Rock (IRE)**[18] 7368 3-9-3 103 .... MartinLane 1 104
(David Simcock) *detached in 4th: drvn over 3f out: styd on to go 2nd 2f out: kpt on same pce* **7/4**[1]

0202 3 10 **Beaumont's Party (IRE)**[11] 7536 6-8-11 95 .... OisinMurphy(5) 2 78
(Brian Ellison) *chsd ldrs: drvn over 2f out: hung rt and one pce* **4/1**[2]

6003 4 2½ **Stand My Ground (IRE)**[11] 7530 6-9-2 95 .... DanielTudhope 5 72
(David O'Meara) *fly-jmpd and s.v.s: detached in last: racd wd: sme hdwy 4f out: sn drvn: tk modest 4th ins fnl f* **16/1**

3035 5 5 **Fulbright**[83] 5446 4-9-9 107 .... GrahamLee 4 68
(Charlie Appleby) *trckd ldrs: chsd wnr over 2f out: fnd nthing and sn wknd* **14/1**[3]

1m 49.44s (0.44) **Going Correction** +0.375s/f (Good)
WFA 3 from 4yo+ 2lb **5 Ran SP% 105.3**
Speed ratings (Par 109): **112,108,98,95,90**
CSF £4.44 TOTE £2.00: £1.10, £1.20; EX 4.90 Trifecta £9.20 Pool: £1146.73 - 93.39 winning units..
Owner The Royal Ascot Racing Club **Bred** Kevin & Meta Cullen **Trained** Newmarket, Suffolk

FOCUS
A slightly disappointing turnout to the feature race on the card, however, those declared were all useful horses and it looked to be a good race run at a sound pace. They came down the centre of the straight and the time was much quicker than the preceding 2yo maidens and just seven seconds outside of standard. Another personal best from the winner.

7776 TREND MICRO DEEP SECURITY H'CAP (DIV I) 5f 13y
3:05 (3:06) (Class 4) (0-85,85) 3-Y-0+ £5,175 (£1,540; £769; £384) **Stalls High**

Form RPR

5445 1 **Best Trip (IRE)**[26] 7176 6-9-5 83 .... BarryMcHugh 8 93
(Brian Ellison) *chsd ldrs: led over 1f out: styd on wl* **11/4**[1]

0400 2 1 **Lasilia (IRE)**[45] 6665 3-8-11 80 .... ShaneGray(5) 12 86
(Kevin Ryan) *chsd ldrs: 2nd over 2f out: edgd rt ins fnl f: styd on same pce* **25/1**

0010 3 shd **Cheveton**[16] 7420 9-9-1 82 .... ThomasBrown(3) 4 88
(Richard Price) *rrd s: in rr: hdwy over 2f out: chsng ldrs 1f out: kpt on same pce last 100yds* **8/1**[3]

0100 4 hd **Maglietta Fina (IRE)**[18] 7373 4-9-2 85 .... OisinMurphy(5) 10 90
(Robert Cowell) *mid-div: hdwy over 2f out: chsng ldrs over 1f out: styd on same pce last 100yds* **10/1**

2551 5 1 **Commanche**[16] 7427 4-9-0 81 .... RobertTart(3) 9 83+
(Chris Dwyer) *in rr: hdwy over 2f out: styd on ins fnl f* **8/1**[3]

1026 6 ¾ **Point North (IRE)**[46] 6653 6-8-7 74 ....(b) JasonHart(3) 11 79+
(John Balding) *hld up towards rr: hdwy 2f out: styng on whn nt clr run ins fnl f: nt rcvr* **6/1**[2]

1231 7 2½ **Steel Rain**[7] 7633 5-9-0 78 6ex .... RobertWinston 6 68
(Nikki Evans) *mid-div: drvn 3f out: nvr a threat* **8/1**[3]

3101 8 ¾ **Rambo Will**[16] 7432 5-8-7 71 .... JimmyQuinn 5 58
(J R Jenkins) *led 2f out: wknd appr fnl f* **10/1**

0650 9 1¼ **West Coast Dream**[7] 7634 6-8-6 75 .... GeorgeChaloner(5) 7 58
(Roy Brotherton) *dwlt: hdwy to chse ldrs 3f out: lost pl over 1f out* **8/1**[3]

000 10 ½ **Oil Strike**[16] 7420 6-8-12 76 .... GrahamGibbons 1 57
(Michael Easterby) *sn trcking ldrs: led over 3f out: hdd over 1f out: sn lost pl* **33/1**

34 11 7 **Sharaarah (IRE)**[60] 6212 3-9-6 84 .... DanielTudhope 2 40
(David O'Meara) *chsd ldrs: lost pl 2f out: bhd whn eased clsng stages* **12/1**

0050 12 hd **Verinco**[144] 3331 7-8-13 77 ....(vt) GrahamLee 3 32
(Bryan Smart) *chsd ldrs: lost pl over 1f out: eased whn bhd ins fnl f* **33/1**

1m 2.28s (0.78) **Going Correction** +0.375s/f (Good) **12 Ran SP% 121.0**
Speed ratings (Par 105): **108,106,106,105,104 103,99,97,95,95 83,83**
toteswingers 1&2 £22.40, 1&3 £7.20, 2&3 £50.00 CSF £86.07 CT £510.94 TOTE £4.40: £1.50, £6.30, £4.50; EX 97.30 Trifecta £1481.70 Pool: £2520.79 - 1.27 winning units..
Owner Koo's Racing Club **Bred** Limetree Stud **Trained** Norton, N Yorks
■ Stewards' Enquiry : Shane Gray three-day ban: careless riding (Nov 20-22)

FOCUS
No more than a fair race but it was competitive enough and they tended to come towards the near-side rail. The winner rates better than ever, with the second close to her 2yo best.

7777 TREND MICRO DEEP SECURITY H'CAP (DIV II) 5f 13y
3:40 (3:43) (Class 4) (0-85,84) 3-Y-0+ £5,175 (£1,540; £769; £384) **Stalls High**

Form RPR

2000 1 **Rusty Rocket (IRE)**[21] 7314 4-9-6 83 .... RaulDaSilva 12 93
(Paul Green) *mde all: jst hld on* **8/1**

1132 2 hd **Ambitious Icarus**[21] 7314 4-9-2 79 ....(e) RobbieFitzpatrick 10 88
(Richard Guest) *hld up in rr: hdwy 2f out: styd on to take 2nd last 50yds: jst hld* **6/1**[3]

6425 3 1¾ **Go Go Green (IRE)**[36] 6920 7-8-11 74 .... GrahamLee 9 77
(Jim Goldie) *s.s and wnt rt s: in rr: hdwy over 1f out: styd on to take 3rd last strides* **8/1**

3146 4 nk **Wild Sauce**[16] 7420 4-8-8 76 ....(bt) GeorgeChaloner(5) 11 78
(Bryan Smart) *s.s: hdwy over 2f out: chsng ldrs over 1f out: kpt on same pce* **5/1**[2]

6133 5 1 **Monsieur Jamie**[15] 7452 5-9-0 77 ....(v) JimmyFortune 5 75
(J R Jenkins) *hld up in mid-div: effrt 2f out: sn drvn and edgd rt: edgd lft and styd on clsng stages* **7/2**[1]

2500 6 1¼ **Climaxfortackle (IRE)**[26] 7164 5-8-7 70 oh2 .... LiamJones 2 64
(Derek Shaw) *chsd ldrs: sn drvn along: fdd appr fnl f* **50/1**

1300 7 1¾ **First In Command (IRE)**[29] 7112 8-9-4 81 ....(t) StephenCraine 8 69
(John Stimpson) *mid-div: effrt over 2f out: sn chsng ldrs: wknd fnl f* **25/1**

016 8 nk **Rock On Candy**[7] 7633 4-8-10 73 .... ChrisCatlin 4 59
(John Spearing) *chsd ldrs: wknd fnl f* **8/1**

4500 9 ½ **Mon Brav**[16] 7420 6-9-1 78 .... PaulPickard 3 63
(Brian Ellison) *in rr and sn drvn along: kpt on fnl f: nvr a factor* **16/1**

0000 10 ¾ **Vincentti (IRE)**[33] 6990 3-9-7 84 .... LukeMorris 1 66
(Ronald Harris) *chsd ldrs: lost pl over 1f out* **14/1**

1006 11 2 **Threes Grand**[21] 7314 3-9-5 82 .... TomEaves 6 57
(Scott Dixon) *trckd ldrs: t.k.h: lost pl over 1f out* **12/1**

/006 12 ½ **Son Du Silence (IRE)**[8] 7593 4-9-3 80 ....(t) TonyHamilton 7 53
(James Ewart) *in rr: sn drvn along: nvr on terms* **10/1**

1m 2.43s (0.93) **Going Correction** +0.375s/f (Good) **12 Ran SP% 121.6**
Speed ratings (Par 105): **107,106,103,103,101 99,97,96,95,94 91,90**
toteswingers 1&2 £10.50, 1&3 £15.90, 2&3 £6.10 CSF £56.97 CT £317.08 TOTE £11.10: £3.50, £1.30, £2.30; EX 66.10 Trifecta £373.10 Pool: £2498.04 - 5.02 winning units..
Owner Seven Stars Racing **Bred** Mike Hyde **Trained** Lydiate, Merseyside

FOCUS
Probably the weaker of the two divisions and fractionally slower. The first four home were drawn 12,10, 9 and 11. The winner was back to his September Haydock form.

7778 PHS DO MORE THAN YOU THINK! AJA GENTLEMEN AMATEUR RIDERS' H'CAP 1m 2f 50y
4:10 (4:14) (Class 5) (0-75,73) 3-Y-0+ £2,495 (£774; £386; £193) **Stalls Low**

Form RPR

4311 1 **Ebony Express**[16] 7433 4-11-2 73 .... MrORJSangster(5) 8 93
(Alan Swinbank) *mde all: rdn clr over 1f out: styd on strly: unchal* **9/2**[1]

0004 2 14 **Choisan (IRE)**[12] 7498 4-11-1 72 .... MrWEasterby(5) 15 65
(Tim Easterby) *prom: 3rd over 4f out: 2nd over 2f out: kpt on: no ch w wnr* **10/1**

5005 3 1¼ **Royal Marskell**[15] 7455 4-10-13 65 .... MrPCollington 14 56
(K F Clutterbuck) *racd wd: rr-div: hdwy over 3f out: kpt on to take 3rd last 100yds* **20/1**

0314 4 4½ **Uncle Brit**[22] 7283 7-10-4 63 .... MrJTeal(7) 9 45
(Malcolm Jefferson) *chsd ldrs: 3rd 1f out: one pce* **7/1**[3]

0014 5 1½ **Cuckoo Rock (IRE)**[16] 7433 6-10-5 62 ....(p) MrJHarding(5) 1 42
(Jonathan Portman) *sn detached in last: kpt on fnl 2f: nrst fin* **14/1**

6156 6 2 **Precision Strike**[11] 7543 3-9-12 59 oh1 ....(v) MrSBushby(5) 13 35
(Richard Guest) *racd wd: prom: effrt over 3f out: one pce fnl 2f* **33/1**

2350 7 ½ **May Be Some Time**[38] 6869 5-10-12 64 ....(bt[1]) MrSWalker 2 39
(Stuart Kittow) *hld up in mid-div: hdwy over 3f out: one pce fnl 2f* **10/1**

6124 8 ¾ **Pivotman**[37] 6906 5-11-1 72 .... MrHAABannister(5) 7 45
(Michael Easterby) *trckd ldrs: 2nd 4f out: wknd fnl f* **5/1**[2]

0-50 9 11 **Thackeray**[47] 6600 6-10-3 60 .... MrPDennis(5) 16 13
(Chris Fairhurst) *mid-div: wknd over 3f out* **50/1**

2100 10 13 **Euston Square**[34] 6976 7-10-11 63 ....(v) ColmMcCormack 6
(Alistair Whillans) *s.s: in rr: bhd fnl 3f* **25/1**

5562 11 10 **Hyperlink (IRE)**[16] 7433 4-10-11 68 .... MrAlexFerguson(5) 5
(Michael Bell) *chsd ldrs: lost pl 3f out: bhd whn eased over 1f out* **7/1**[3]

14-0 12 35 **Cottesmore (USA)**[17] 7396 4-11-6 72 ....(t) MrJHamilton 3
(Richard Ford) *s.i.s: sn chsng ldrs: lost pl over 6f out: t.o 4f out: virtually p.u* **50/1**

2m 20.9s (6.60) **Going Correction** +0.375s/f (Good)
WFA 3 from 4yo+ 4lb **12 Ran SP% 100.2**
Speed ratings (Par 103): **88,76,75,72,71 69,69,68,59,49 41,13**
toteswingers 1&2 £8.50, 1&3 £12.90, 2&3 £17.00 CSF £32.74 CT £486.89 TOTE £3.70: £1.40, £3.80, £5.10; EX 34.40 Trifecta £265.40 Pool: £1427.43 - 4.03 winning units..
Owner Mrs T Blackett **Bred** Miss E J Wright **Trained** Melsonby, N Yorks

FOCUS
This didn't look to be a bad race of its type but it was turned into an absolute procession. Tricky form to pin down, rated around the runner-up.
T/Jkpt: Not won. T/Plt: £33.30 to a £1 stake. Pool: £60954.25 - 1332.32 winning tickets T/Qpdt: £6.20 to a £1 stake. Pool: £4961.95 - 591.32 winning tickets WG

7645 LINGFIELD (L-H)
Thursday, November 7

OFFICIAL GOING: Standard
Wind: Almost nil Weather: Mainly cloudy

7779 32RED CASINO MAIDEN AUCTION STKS (DIV I) 1m (P)
12:20 (12:21) (Class 6) 2-Y-0 £2,215 (£654; £327) **Stalls High**

Form RPR

05 1 **Beach Bar (IRE)**[58] 6277 2-9-1 .... AndreaAtzeni 5 77
(William Knight) *hld up towards rr: hdwy and c wd 2f out: str run to ld jst ins fnl f: rdn clr* **7/2**[2]

2 2 **Billy Blue (IRE)** 2-9-2 .... WilliamBuick 8 73
(John Gosden) *dwlt: hld up towards rr: rdn and hdwy over 2f out: chal 1f out: unable qck* **8/1**

554 3 nk **Castle Combe (IRE)**[30] 7089 2-9-0 69 ....(v[1]) MartinDwyer 10 70
(Marcus Tregoning) *led after 1f: rdn and hdd jst ins fnl f: one pce* **6/1**[3]

2 4 4 **Hadya (IRE)**[34] 6999 2-8-11 .... MartinHarley 6 57
(James Tate) *prom: rdn to chal over 1f out: wknd ins fnl f* **11/4**[1]

2 5 ½ **Mr Wickfield**[16] 7441 2-8-13 .... SteveDrowne 4 58
(John Best) *in tch: rdn 3f out: wknd over 1f out* **12/1**

0 6 3 **Treasure Cay (IRE)**[13] 7501 2-9-1 .... JimCrowley 1 53
(Paul Cole) *led 1f: prom tl wknd over 1f out* **12/1**

6 7 shd **Late Shipment**[15] 7461 2-9-1 .... JoeFanning 3 53+
(Mark Johnston) *in tch on rail tl wknd jst over 2f out* **7/2**[2]

6 8 4 **Llandanwg**[22] 7301 2-8-7 .... JohnFahy 9 35
(Jamie Osborne) *a bhd* **50/1**

9 5 **Ede's The Business** 2-8-0 .... SophieRalston(7) 2 23
(Pat Phelan) *s.s: a wl bhd* **100/1**

6 10 3 **Charlies Mate**[16] 7441 2-8-11 .... KierenFallon 7 20
(John Best) *n.m.r after s and swtchd outside: chsd ldrs: rdn 4f out: wknd over 2f out* **66/1**

1m 38.04s (-0.16) **Going Correction** -0.075s/f (Stan) **10** Ran SP% **116.3**
Speed ratings (Par 94): **97,95,94,90,90 87,87,83,78,75**
toteswingers 1&2 £5.30, 2&3 £10.30, 1&3 £5.60 CSF £31.49 TOTE £4.20: £1.10, £3.40, £3.10; EX 29.90 Trifecta £178.70 Pool: £2431.21 - 10.19 winning units..
Owner P Winkworth & Mrs Bex Seabrook **Bred** Iona Equine **Trained** Patching, W Sussex

FOCUS
Not a strong maiden. It was run at a steady pace and surprisingly the first two came from the rear.

7780 32RED CASINO MAIDEN AUCTION STKS (DIV II) 1m (P)
12:50 (12:50) (Class 6) 2-Y-O **£2,215** (£654; £327) **Stalls High**

Form RPR

00 1 **Applejack Lad**[15] 7467 2-8-13 .... (t) SeanLevey 2 72
(John Ryan) *led 1f: trckd ldr after: rdn to ld jst over 1f out: drvn out* **16/1**

45 2 1 ¾ **Rudi Five One (FR)**[42] 6763 2-9-0 73 .... AndreaAtzeni 1 69
(Robert Eddery) *s.i.s: hdwy to ld on rail after 1f: rdn and hdd jst over 1f out: unable qck fnl 100yds* **6/4**[1]

5 3 1 **Lady Knight (IRE)**[16] 7441 2-8-7 .... LiamJones 5 59
(J S Moore) *chsd ldrs: pushed along over 4f out: wnt 3rd 2f out: kpt on fnl f* **25/1**

0 4 ½ **Percybelle**[76] 5716 2-8-8 .... ShaneKelly 4 59
(William Knight) *chsd ldrs: hrd rdn and hld over 1f out: styng on at fin* **11/4**[2]

5 ½ **Foxford** 2-8-2 .... DanielMuscutt(5) 3 57
(Patrick Chamings) *prom: rdn and one pce fnl 2f* **33/1**

0 6 1 ¾ **Scoppio Del Carro**[27] 7175 2-9-1 .... (t) DavidProbert 8 62
(Andrew Balding) *chsd ldrs on outer: rdn and btn over 2f out* **9/2**[3]

0 7 8 **Oracle Boy**[42] 6762 2-8-13 .... MartinDwyer 10 40
(William Muir) *a outpcd in rr* **33/1**

0 8 nk **Foxie Girl**[22] 7301 2-8-6 .... CathyGannon 9 32
(John Best) *in tch tl wknd over 3f out* **100/1**

9 9 **Lisamour (IRE)** 2-8-9 .... [1] JimCrowley 7 13
(Paul Cole) *s.s: outpcd: a bhd* **10/1**

40 10 11 **Think Again**[153] 3049 2-8-11 .... KierenFallon 6
(Kevin Ryan) *rrd s and s.i.s: a bhd* **12/1**

1m 38.79s (0.59) **Going Correction** -0.075s/f (Stan) **10** Ran SP% **118.2**
Speed ratings (Par 94): **94,92,91,90,90 88,80,80,71,60**
toteswingers 1&2 £6.10, 2&3 £7.10, 1&3 £31.90 CSF £40.34 TOTE £30.30: £5.10, £1.40, £5.30; EX 104.80 Trifecta £1682.60 Pool: £2260.39 - 1.00 winning units..
Owner Gerry McGladery **Bred** J C S Wilson Bloodstock **Trained** Newmarket, Suffolk

FOCUS
The second division of this maiden was run at a fair pace, with the front two always in command.

7781 DOWNLOAD THE LADBROKES APP MAIDEN STKS 1m (P)
1:20 (1:20) (Class 5) 3-4-Y-0 **£2,726** (£805; £402) **Stalls High**

Form RPR

02 1 **Tasrih (USA)**[28] 7154 4-9-7 .... MartinHarley 10 87
(Alan McCabe) *broke wl fr wd stall and swtchd to rail: mde all: rdn and r.o wl fnl 2f: readily* **4/1**[2]

2 3 ¾ **Bouclier (IRE)** 3-9-5 .... AndreaAtzeni 8 78+
(Luca Cumani) *hld up in midfield: outpcd 3f out: styd on to take 2nd 1f out: bttr for r* **7/4**[1]

20 3 2 ¾ **Swehan (IRE)**[51] 6498 3-9-5 .... KierenFallon 6 72
(Kevin Ryan) *chsd ldrs: rdn 3f out: one pce* **10/1**

6 4 3 ¾ **Ellen May**[15] 7459 3-9-0 .... ShaneKelly 2 58
(Gary Harrison) *prom: chsd wnr 4f out tl wknd 1f out* **10/1**

5 2 ¾ **Aeolian Blue** 3-9-0 .... JoeFanning 5 52
(William Knight) *chsd ldrs: effrt 3f out: wknd over 1f out* **16/1**

60 6 1 ¼ **Ovatory**[186] 2051 3-9-5 .... JimCrowley 11 54
(Amanda Perrett) *wd thrght: mid-div: rdn and no hdwy fnl 2f* **5/1**[3]

35 7 1 ½ **Modem**[24] 7253 3-9-5 .... MartinDwyer 7 51
(Rod Millman) *sn stdd towards rr: pushed along 6f out: n.d fnl 3f* **6/1**

0 8 8 **Broon Troot (IRE)**[43] 6748 3-9-5 .... HarryBentley 9 32
(Marcus Tregoning) *a towards rr* **33/1**

9 3 ¾ **Comfort And Joy (IRE)** 3-9-0 .... TomQueally 3 19
(Lee Carter) *dwlt: a bhd* **25/1**

10 12 **Be A Rebel** 3-9-0 .... JimmyQuinn 1
(John E Long) *dwlt: a wl bhd* **66/1**

0 11 21 **Lieutenant Nelson**[19] 7380 3-8-12 .... (b[1]) JordanVaughan(7) 4
(Kevin Tork) *chsd wnr 4f: wknd rapidly: sn bhd* **100/1**

1m 36.4s (-1.80) **Going Correction** -0.075s/f (Stan)
WFA 3 from 4yo 2lb **11** Ran SP% **120.7**
Speed ratings (Par 103): **106,102,99,95,93 91,90,82,78,66 45**
toteswingers 1&2 £2.40, 2&3 £5.70, 1&3 £5.20 CSF £11.49 TOTE £4.20: £1.70, £1.70, £2.80; EX 12.60 Trifecta £82.70 Pool: £2059.07 - 18.65 winning units..
Owner Craig and Maureen Buckingham **Bred** G Bolton, D Dipietro & R W Honour **Trained** Averham Park, Notts

FOCUS
Little pace on for this modest contest, with the winner making all and proving far too good for his rivals.

7782 32RED.COM NURSERY H'CAP 7f (P)
1:50 (1:51) (Class 5) (0-75,75) 2-Y-O **£2,726** (£805; £402) **Stalls Low**

Form RPR

0636 1 **Zugzwang (IRE)**[24] 7252 2-9-1 69 .... AndreaAtzeni 8 73
(Ed de Giles) *hld up towards rr: hdwy 2f out: str run to ld nr fin* **6/1**[2]

150 2 nk **Madame Mirasol (IRE)**[17] 7418 2-9-1 69 .... KierenFallon 12 72
(Kevin Ryan) *led 1f: prom: drvn to ld ins fnl f: hdd nr fin* **33/1**

31 3 ½ **Dutch Art Dealer**[80] 5584 2-9-7 75 .... JimCrowley 10 79+
(Paul Cole) *hld up in rr: rapid hdwy ins fnl f: fin wl* **7/2**[1]

5503 4 1 ½ **Queenie's Home**[43] 6755 2-9-5 73 .... TomQueally 4 71
(James Given) *trckd ldrs: rdn over 1f out: unable qck* **16/1**

4445 5 nse **Boogangoo (IRE)**[15] 7463 2-9-2 70 .... JoeFanning 5 68
(Keith Dalgleish) *chsd ldr: led 1f out: hrd rdn and hdd ins fnl f: no ex* **7/1**[3]

053 6 ¾ **Captain Swift (IRE)**[16] 7442 2-9-3 74 .... ThomasBrown(3) 9 70
(Brian Meehan) *mid-div: rdn over 2f out: styd on fr over 1f out* **8/1**

1432 7 2 ¾ **Intense Feeling (IRE)**[9] 7609 2-9-4 72 .... AdamKirby 3 65
(David Evans) *mid-div: effrt over 2f out: wl btn whn n.m.r ins fnl f* **7/1**[3]

6511 8 nk **Hedge End (IRE)**[30] 7110 2-9-6 74 .... SeanLevey 2 61
(Richard Hannon) *led after 1f tl wknd 1f out* **8/1**

4330 9 nk **Red Tide (IRE)**[58] 6284 2-9-3 71 .... MartinHarley 1 58
(Alan McCabe) *dwlt: sn chsng ldrs on rail: wknd jst over 1f out* **33/1**

5416 10 1 ¼ **Ninety Minutes (IRE)**[21] 7326 2-9-5 73 .... SteveDrowne 7 56
(John Best) *rdn s: nvr nr ldrs* **16/1**

2141 11 ½ **Hipz (IRE)**[29] 7117 2-9-3 71 .... WilliamBuick 11 53
(George Baker) *a bhd: no ch over 2f out* **10/1**

4032 12 2 ½ **Bonjour Steve**[16] 7568 2-9-0 68 .... (p) LiamJones 6 43
(J S Moore) *in tch tl wknd over 2f out* **25/1**

5634 13 1 ¼ **The Grumpy Gnome (IRE)**[28] 7146 2-9-0 68 .... (p) TonyHamilton 13 40
(Richard Fahey) *mid-div on outer: wknd 3f out* **20/1**

1m 24.68s (-0.12) **Going Correction** -0.075s/f (Stan) **13** Ran SP% **119.1**
Speed ratings (Par 96): **97,96,96,94,94 93,90,89,89,88 87,84,83**
toteswingers 1&2 £49.40, 2&3 £28.10, 1&3 £8.50 CSF £198.87 CT £797.49 TOTE £9.80: £2.80, £7.80, £1.70; EX 203.00 Trifecta £1817.20 Part won. Pool of £2422.97 - 0.70 winning units..
Owner Simon Treacher **Bred** Mrs C E Norton **Trained** Ledbury, H'fords

FOCUS
The pace was steady for this competitive nursery.

7783 COMPARE BOOKMAKERS AT BOOKMAKERS.CO.UK H'CAP 5f (P)
2:20 (2:24) (Class 5) (0-75,75) 3-Y-0+ **£2,726** (£805; £402) **Stalls High**

Form RPR

0000 1 **Billy Red**[16] 7444 9-8-13 67 .... (b) JoeFanning 7 76
(J R Jenkins) *chsd ldrs: rdn 2f out: r.o to ld ins fnl f* **8/1**

4004 2 1 ½ **Lujeanie**[37] 6928 7-9-1 69 .... ShaneKelly 1 73
(Peter Crate) *mid-div: rdn and r.o fnl 2f: jst snatched 2nd* **6/1**[3]

3300 3 nse **Bapak Bangsawan**[16] 7444 3-9-0 68 .... (p) KierenFallon 8 71
(Kevin Ryan) *pressed ldrs: led over 2f out tl ins fnl f: one pce* **6/1**[3]

5500 4 1 **Ask The Guru**[16] 7445 3-9-2 70 .... (b) RobertHavlin 2 70
(Michael Attwater) *chsd ldrs: rdn 2f out: one pce fnl f* **8/1**

0602 5 hd **Valmina**[43] 6745 6-9-2 75 .... (t) GeorgeDowning(5) 5 74+
(Tony Carroll) *towards rr tl styd on fr over 1f out: nvr nrr* **3/1**[1]

5040 6 nse **Ada Lovelace**[23] 7262 3-8-13 67 .... JimmyQuinn 3 66
(Dean Ivory) *led over 2f: prom tl edgd lft and no ex wl ins fnl f* **5/1**[2]

1242 7 2 ½ **Wooden King (IRE)**[54] 6382 8-9-5 73 .... TomMcLaughlin 9 63
(Malcolm Saunders) *mid-div on outer: rdn 3f out: sn btn* **10/1**

2310 8 ½ **Speedyfix**[140] 3498 6-8-3 62 .... (t) DanielMuscutt(5) 4 50
(Christine Dunnett) *a abt same pl* **16/1**

1034 9 nk **Catflap (IRE)**[54] 6412 4-8-4 61 oh1 .... (p) RosieJessop(3) 10 48
(Derek Haydn Jones) *w ldrs 3f* **16/1**

1250 10 11 **Studfarmer**[68] 2737 3-8-11 65 .... (b[1]) JimCrowley 6 12
(John Panvert) *outpcd: sn wl bhd* **50/1**

58.53s (-0.27) **Going Correction** -0.075s/f (Stan) **10** Ran SP% **115.3**
Speed ratings (Par 103): **99,96,96,94,94 94,90,89,89,71**
toteswingers 1&2 £9.00, 2&3 £9.40, 1&3 £11.90 CSF £54.74 CT £317.84 TOTE £13.30: £4.20, £1.70, £2.70; EX 36.60 Trifecta £389.80 Pool: £2890.47 - 5.56 winning units..
Owner Mrs Irene Hampson **Bred** D R Tucker **Trained** Royston, Herts

FOCUS
There was plenty of pace on.

7784 BET ON YOUR MOBILE H'CAP 1m (P)
2:50 (3:00) (Class 6) (0-60,60) 3-Y-0+ **£2,045** (£603; £302) **Stalls High**

Form RPR

3221 1 **Sonnetation (IRE)**[7] 7639 3-9-4 59 6ex .... AdamKirby 10 67
(Jim Boyle) *towards rr: rdn 3f out: hdwy over 1f out: r.o to ld nr fin* **5/2**[1]

003 2 ½ **Tee It Up Tommo (IRE)**[30] 7109 4-9-7 60 .... JimCrowley 7 67
(Michael Wigham) *towards rr: hdwy 2f out: led and hung lft 1f out: kpt on u.p: hdd nr fin* **4/1**[2]

0041 3 1 **Schottische**[35] 6986 3-9-1 59 .... (v) RosieJessop(3) 2 64
(Derek Haydn Jones) *rdn s and sn prom: rdn 2f out: unable qck ins fnl f* **25/1**

0430 4 nse **Nifty Kier**[76] 5697 4-9-6 59 .... JohnFahy 5 64
(Martin Bosley) *bhd: rdn and hdwy over 1f out: styd on* **100/1**

3006 5 ¾ **Strategic Action (IRE)**[24] 7246 4-9-2 55 .... RobertHavlin 1 58
(Linda Jewell) *chsd ldrs: led 2f out tl 1f out: no ex ins fnl f* **33/1**

0306 6 ½ **Uncle Fred**[36] 6933 8-8-12 56 .... DanielMuscutt(5) 12 58
(Patrick Chamings) *s.s: bhd: styd on fnl 2f: nvr nrr* **16/1**

6004 7 1 **Derfenna Art (IRE)**[16] 7437 4-9-7 60 .... (t) GeorgeBaker 6 60
(Seamus Durack) *led 2f: prom tl wknd over 1f out* **9/2**[3]

3000 8 1 **Mosman**[16] 7437 3-9-4 59 .... (tp) JimmyQuinn 3 56
(Dean Ivory) *t.k.h: in tch tl outpcd 2f out* **33/1**

0523 9 2 **Hot Mustard**[163] 2762 3-9-5 60 .... TomQueally 11 53
(Michael Bell) *t.k.h: stdd to trck ldrs: rdn and wknd jst over 2f out* **6/1**

0060 10 5 **Kilburn**[48] 6612 9-9-7 60 .... (b) SteveDrowne 8 41
(Alastair Lidderdale) *bolted 5f after false s: t.k.h: prom: led after 2f and set gd pce: hdd 2f out: wknd qckly over 1f out* **16/1**

1m 37.63s (-0.57) **Going Correction** -0.075s/f (Stan)
WFA 3 from 4yo+ 2lb **10** Ran SP% **103.5**
Speed ratings (Par 101): **99,98,97,97,96 96,95,94,92,87**
toteswingers 1&2 £3.30, 2&3 £10.90, 1&3 £7.70 CSF £9.44 CT £140.58 TOTE £3.10: £1.10, £1.10, £5.60; EX 10.70 Trifecta £101.50 Pool: £3216.53 - 23.75 winning units..
Owner The 'In Recovery' Partnership **Bred** Dr Dean Harron **Trained** Epsom, Surrey

FOCUS
There was drama at the start as the inside stall failed to open. The starter immediately raised his flag although a number of the runners ran nearly 3f before returning to the gates. Kilburn was the most inconvenienced while Claude Monet was withdrawn at the trainer's request. This was not a strong handicap, but it was run at a sound pace.

7785 LADBROKES H'CAP 1m (P)
3:20 (3:27) (Class 5) (0-75,75) 3-Y-0+ **£2,726** (£805; £402) **Stalls High**

Form RPR

004 1 **Scottish Glen**[29] 7123 7-9-7 75 .... DavidProbert 8 85
(Patrick Chamings) *mid-div: pushed along 3f out: hdwy over 1f out: styd on to ld ins fnl f* **5/1**[3]

6605 2 1 ¾ **Maria's Choice (IRE)**[30] 7115 4-9-5 73 .... (p) MartinHarley 10 79
(Alan McCabe) *led 2f: remained prom: drvn to chal ins fnl f: unable qck* **8/1**

3500 3 1 **Al Raqeeb (IRE)**[25] 7224 3-9-4 74 .... ShaneKelly 12 78
(Gary Harrison) *prom: led after 2f tl ins fnl f: no ex* **14/1**

The Form Book Flat, Raceform Ltd, Compton, RG20 6NL.

5102 **4** 1/2 **Duke Of Destiny (IRE)**[22] 7306 4-9-7 **75**.....................(p) GeorgeBaker 2 78+
(Ed Walker) *s.s: hld up in rr: rdn and hdwy fnl 2f: r.o* **5/2**[1]
2444 **5** 3/4 **Lady Bayside**[14] 7489 5-9-4 **72**........................... TomMcLaughlin 7 73
(Malcolm Saunders) *mid-div: rdn and styd on same pce fnl 2f: no imp* **25/1**
3205 **6** *nk* **Simply Shining (IRE)**[39] 6875 3-9-3 **73**.....................(p) TonyHamilton 6 73
(Richard Fahey) *chsd ldrs: rdn and one pce fnl 2f* **20/1**
0046 **7** 2 **Waverunner**[23] 7267 3-9-2 **72**... JoeFanning 11 68
(Mark Johnston) *prom tl wknd jst over 1f out* **14/1**
1213 **8** 3/4 **Lunette (IRE)**[22] 7297 3-9-3 **73**.. JimCrowley 1 67
(Ralph Beckett) *towards rr: modest effrt over 1f out: sn wknd* **7/2**[2]
460P **9** 3/4 **Living Leader**[36] 6943 4-9-6 **74**....................................(b) SteveDrowne 5 66
(Nick Littmoden) *bhd: last and struggling 3f out: nvr trbld ldrs* **16/1**
260 **10** 1 1/4 **Storm Runner (IRE)**[186] 2057 5-9-1 **72**......................... RyanPowell(3) 4 61
(George Margarson) *a towards rr: rdn and n.d fnl 2f* **25/1**
0120 **11** 3/4 **Young Dottie**[39] 6869 7-9-0 **75**.................................. SophieRalston(7) 9 62
(Pat Phelan) *prom tl wknd over 1f out* **16/1**
0000 **12** 6 **Rezwaan**[16] 7438 6-9-7 **75**...(b) AdamKirby 3 49
(Murty McGrath) *mid-div: rdn 3f out: sn outpcd* **33/1**

1m 37.42s (-0.78) **Going Correction** -0.075s/f (Stan)
WFA 3 from 4yo+ 2lb **12** Ran SP% **119.1**
Speed ratings (Par 103): **100,98,97,96,96 95,93,92,92,90 90,84**
toteswingers 1&2 £8.10, 2&3 £12.30, 1&3 £14.50 CSF £42.64 CT £532.89 TOTE £6.20: £1.90, £2.30, £5.50; EX 44.20 Trifecta £564.50 Pool: £3270.40 - 4.34 winning units..
Owner The Foxford House Partnership **Bred** Mrs Ann Jenkins **Trained** Baughurst, Hants

FOCUS
A tight handicap with only 3lb covering the 12 runners.

7786 CORAL APP DOWNLOAD FROM THE APP STORE H'CAP 1m 2f (P)
3:50 (3:53) (Class 5) (0-75,75) 3-Y-O **£2,726** (£805; £402) **Stalls** Low

Form RPR
031- **1** **Epic Battle (IRE)**[425] 6043 3-9-7 **75**.................................. LiamJones 7 83+
(William Haggas) *rring in stalls bef s: dwlt: towards rr: reminder 4f out: rdn 3f out: hdwy on inner over 1f out: styd on to ld ins fnl f* **9/2**[2]
4022 **2** 1/2 **Mystery Bet (IRE)**[9] 7611 3-9-2 **75**......................... GeorgeChaloner(5) 6 82
(Richard Fahey) *chsd ldrs: rdn over 2f out: kpt on wl fnl f* **7/2**[1]
326 **3** *shd* **Rainbow Beauty**[15] 7470 3-9-7 **75**.......................................(p) AdamKirby 11 82+
(Gerard Butler) *s.s: hld up in rr: wd into st: rdn and r.o wl fr over 1f out: nrest at fin* **6/1**[3]
1324 **4** 1/2 **Thankyou Very Much**[48] 6588 3-8-8 **62**........................... JimmyQuinn 1 68
(James Bethell) *prom: rdn over 2f out: kpt on fnl f* **25/1**
0145 **5** *nk* **Solvanna**[8] 7622 3-8-11 **65**.. AndreaAtzeni 12 70
(Heather Main) *sn led: hrd rdn and hdd ins fnl f: no ex* **10/1**
5045 **6** *shd* **Persian Patriot**[30] 7108 3-8-8 **62**... CathyGannon 5 67
(William Jarvis) *t.k.h: hld up in rr: rdn and hdwy on inner over 1f out: r.o* **25/1**
5214 **7** 1/2 **Lybica (IRE)**[17] 7431 3-9-3 **71**.. GeorgeBaker 13 75
(Gary Moore) *broke wl: awkward on 1st bnd: prom: hrd rdn over 1f out: one pce fnl f* **7/1**
1-50 **8** 1/2 **Absolutely Right (IRE)**[16] 7447 3-8-13 **67**........................ TomQueally 4 70
(George Margarson) *t.k.h: in tch: rdn over 2f out: sn outpcd* **25/1**
343 **9** 2 3/4 **Lady Who**[210] 1499 3-9-0 **68**... MartinDwyer 2 66
(William Muir) *t.k.h: settled in midfield: rdn 3f out: sn outpcd* **20/1**
050 **10** 3 1/4 **Barnaby Brook (CAN)**[32] 5960 3-9-0 **75**...............(p) JordanVaughan(7) 8 66
(Nick Littmoden) *a towards rr* **50/1**
4432 **11** 1/2 **Ruffled**[85] 5410 3-9-3 **71**... WilliamBuick 9 61
(John Gosden) *in tch on outer: rdn and bmpd 3f out: btn whn c wd into st* **9/2**[2]
2330 **12** 2 1/2 **Gabrial The Thug (FR)**[27] 7169 3-8-10 **64**.................(t) TonyHamilton 10 49
(Richard Fahey) *towards rr on outer: rdn and n.d fnl 3f* **16/1**

2m 5.03s (-1.57) **Going Correction** -0.075s/f (Stan) **12** Ran SP% **118.6**
Speed ratings (Par 102): **103,102,102,102,101 101,101,101,98,96 95,93**
toteswingers 1&2 £3.10, 2&3 £5.50, 1&3 £6.90 CSF £19.14 CT £96.69 TOTE £7.10: £2.70, £1.60, £2.40; EX 24.30 Trifecta £182.20 Pool: £3698.19 - 15.21 winning units..
Owner Saleh Al Homaizi & Imad Al Sagar **Bred** Castlemartin Sky & Skymarc Farm **Trained** Newmarket, Suffolk

FOCUS
Quite a competitive-looking handicap.
T/Plt: £67.60 to a £1 stake. Pool of £56900.17 - 613.83 winning tickets. T/Qpdt: £12.70 to a £1 stake. Pool of £6377.99 - 370.98 winning tickets. LM

7728 WOLVERHAMPTON (A.W) (L-H)

Thursday, November 7

OFFICIAL GOING: Standard
Wind: Fine Weather: Fresh behind

7787 LADBROKES MAIDEN STKS 7f 32y(P)
4:20 (4:22) (Class 5) 3-Y-O+ **£2,587** (£770; £384; £192) **Stalls** High

Form RPR
2063 **1** **Arms (IRE)**[24] 7253 3-9-5 75.. MartinLane 7 81
(J W Hills) *led: hdd over 5f out: trckd ldrs: wnt 2nd 2f out: sn rdn: led ins fnl f: r.o u.p* **11/2**[3]
422 **2** 1 1/4 **Musaddas**[24] 7253 3-9-5 85.. SilvestreDeSousa 4 78
(Saeed bin Suroor) *s.i.s: racd keenly and hdwy over 5f out: rdn and hung lft over 1f out: r.o to go 2nd towards fin: nt rch wnr* **4/11**[1]
022 **3** 1 1/2 **It Must Be Faith**[51] 6502 3-9-5 73...................................... AndrewMullen 6 74
(Michael Appleby) *trckd ldr: plld hrd: led over 5f out: rdn over 1f out: hdd and no ex ins fnl f* **4/1**[2]
560 **4** 10 **Medecis Mountain**[41] 6803 4-9-1 43.........................(v[1]) AdamCarter(5) 5 48
(John Wainwright) *prom: chsd ldr 5f out tl rdn 2f out: wknd over 1f out* **100/1**
04 **5** 8 **Port Lairge**[8] 7625 3-9-5 0.. FergusSweeney 1 25
(Jonjo O'Neill) *hld up: rdn over 2f out: sn wknd* **33/1**
000 **6** 1 1/4 **Ismaali**[30] 7108 3-8-9 30.. DavidBergin(5) 3 17
(James Given) *prom: pushed along 3f out: rdn and wknd 2f out* **100/1**
00 **7** 41 **Noble Maximus**[20] 7345 3-9-2 0.. SladeO'Hara(3) 8
(Alan Berry) *s.i.s: a in rr: wknd 3f out* **200/1**

1m 29.88s (0.28) **Going Correction** +0.05s/f (Slow)
WFA 3 from 4yo 1lb **7** Ran SP% **114.1**
Speed ratings (Par 103): **100,98,96,85,76 74,28**
toteswingers 1&2 £1.10, 2&3 £1.10, 1&3 £1.50 CSF £8.09 TOTE £5.10: £2.00, £1.10; EX 12.80 Trifecta £17.10 Pool: £4848.88 - 211.57 winning units..
Owner Ming Ho Lui **Bred** Austin Curran **Trained** Upper Lambourn, Berks

FOCUS
Modest form.

7788 32RED.COM NURSERY H'CAP (DIV I) 5f 216y(P)
4:50 (4:55) (Class 6) (0-65,65) 2-Y-O **£1,940** (£577; £288; £144) **Stalls** Low

Form RPR
0620 **1** **Poetic Choice**[22] 7309 2-9-5 **63**... MartinLane 10 77
(Nick Littmoden) *led 5f out: rdn clr fnl f* **12/1**
003 **2** 3 1/2 **Bazooka (IRE)**[18] 7394 2-8-13 **60**.................................. RobertTart(3) 6 64
(Ed de Giles) *sn pushed along in rr: rdn over 2f out: r.o ins fnl f: wnt 2nd towards fin: nt trble wnr* **3/1**[2]
0066 **3** 1 1/2 **Trinity Lorraine (IRE)**[37] 6914 2-8-1 **45**........................(p) NickyMackay 7 45
(Alan Bailey) *sn outpcd: hdwy u.p over 1f out: nt clr run and swtchd rt ins fnl f: r.o to go 3rd nr fin* **20/1**
3302 **4** *hd* **Goadby**[30] 7094 2-9-2 **60**.. GrahamGibbons 9 58
(John Holt) *led 1f: chsd wnr: rdn over 1f out: hung lft and no ex ins fnl f* **16/1**
354 **5** *nk* **Beautiful Stranger (IRE)**[20] 7341 2-9-7 **65**................(p) JimmyFortune 3 63
(Keith Dalgleish) *chsd ldrs: rdn over 2f out: hung lft over 1f out: styd on same pce fnl f* **3/1**[2]
63 **6** 1 1/2 **Jaeger Connoisseur (IRE)**[35] 6983 2-8-3 **52**............. JoeyHaynes(5) 2 45
(K R Burke) *hld up: r.o ins fnl f: nvr nrr* **8/1**[3]
136 **7** *nk* **Lady Montenegro**[20] 7340 2-8-9 **53**................................... PJMcDonald 1 45
(Ann Duffield) *prom: nt clr run and lost pl 5f out: rdn over 1f out: nt trble ldrs* **25/1**
0221 **8** 1 1/2 **Stoney Quine (IRE)**[2] 7755 2-9-7 **65** 6ex.............................. TomEaves 8 53
(Keith Dalgleish) *chsd ldrs: rdn over 2f out: wknd fnl f* **5/2**[1]
0060 **9** 5 **Blunos (IRE)**[35] 6979 2-8-12 **56**.................................... DanielTudhope 5 29
(Rod Millman) *chsd ldrs: rdn over 2f out: wknd over 1f out* **33/1**

1m 15.89s (0.89) **Going Correction** +0.05s/f (Slow) **9** Ran SP% **114.8**
Speed ratings (Par 94): **96,91,89,89,88 86,86,84,77**
toteswingers 1&2 £8.10, 2&3 £15.20, 1&3 £55.60 CSF £46.74 CT £730.39 TOTE £14.50: £3.50, £1.60, £5.00; EX 71.40 Trifecta £1202.80 Pool: £4048.69 - 2.52 winning units..
Owner A A Goodman, L Stratton, N Littmoden **Bred** Larry Stratton **Trained** Newmarket, Suffolk

7789 32RED.COM NURSERY H'CAP (DIV II) 5f 216y(P)
5:20 (5:23) (Class 6) (0-65,65) 2-Y-O **£1,940** (£577; £288; £144) **Stalls** Low

Form RPR
4300 **1** **Chookie's Lass**[37] 6914 2-8-13 **60**..................................... JasonHart(3) 9 65
(Keith Dalgleish) *mde all: rdn over 1f out: edgd lft: styd on* **4/1**[2]
0240 **2** 1 1/4 **Dancing Sal (IRE)**[20] 7352 2-9-4 **62**.......................... SilvestreDeSousa 1 63
(David Evans) *a.p: rdn to chse wnr fnl f: r.o* **4/1**[2]
0420 **3** 2 **Starlight Princess (IRE)**[37] 6924 2-8-10 **54**.................(b) LiamKeniry 8 49
(J S Moore) *prom: chsd wnr over 2f out tl rdn 1f out: styd on same pce* **13/2**[3]
056 **4** 5 **Injaz**[20] 7348 2-9-7 **65**.. DanielTudhope 5 45
(Kevin Ryan) *hld up: rdn over 2f out: nvr trbld ldrs* **11/4**[1]
540 **5** 3/4 **Royal Bushida**[62] 6169 2-8-9 **53**.. DaleSwift 2 31
(Derek Shaw) *hld up: rdn over 1f out: nvr on terms* **20/1**
0064 **6** 1 1/2 **Baileys Celebrate**[30] 7094 2-8-1 **45**................................. NickyMackay 7 18
(Mark Johnston) *prom: chsd wnr 4f out tl rdn over 2f out: wknd over 1f out* **14/1**
000 **7** 3 **Dutch Lady**[35] 6973 2-9-0 **58**.. GrahamGibbons 4 22
(John Holt) *sn pushed along in mid-div: drvn along 1/2-way: wknd over 2f out* **33/1**
5455 **8** 3/4 **Red Forever**[30] 7095 2-8-10 **57**..................................... SladeO'Hara(3) 6 19
(Alan Berry) *hood removed late and s.s: hld up: rdn over 2f out: sn wknd* **12/1**
005 **9** 2 3/4 **Grande Mago (IRE)**[35] 6966 2-9-2 **60**................................. GrahamLee 3 14
(Robert Cowell) *chsd ldrs: rdn over 2f out: sn wknd* **13/2**[3]

1m 16.52s (1.52) **Going Correction** +0.05s/f (Slow) **9** Ran SP% **115.4**
Speed ratings (Par 94): **91,89,86,80,79 77,73,72,68**
toteswingers 1&2 £4.30, 2&3 £5.00, 1&3 £5.40 CSF £20.40 CT £101.82 TOTE £5.90: £1.60, £1.80, £1.60; EX 23.10 Trifecta £123.90 Pool: £2622.29 - 15.86 winning units..
Owner Raeburn Brick Limited **Bred** D And J Raeburn **Trained** Carluke, S Lanarks

7790 32RED CASINO MAIDEN AUCTION STKS 5f 216y(P)
5:50 (5:51) (Class 6) 2-Y-O **£1,940** (£577; £288; £144) **Stalls** Low

Form RPR
4334 **1** **An Chulainn (IRE)**[48] 6581 2-8-11 75....................... SilvestreDeSousa 6 71
(Mark Johnston) *trckd ldr tl led 2f out: rdn and edgd rt over 1f out: styd on u.p* **13/8**[1]
0 **2** 2 1/4 **Three Pips**[20] 7341 2-8-12 0.. GrahamGibbons 7 65+
(Ed McMahon) *hld up: hdwy u.p over 1f out: r.o: nt rch wnr* **28/1**
44 **3** 1/2 **Baltic Brave (IRE)**[17] 7426 2-9-1 0...................................... JimmyFortune 5 67
(Hughie Morrison) *sn prom: rdn and ev ch over 1f out: hung rt and no ex ins fnl f* **5/1**[3]
62 **4** 4 **Jolly Red Jeanz (IRE)**[26] 7200 2-8-7 0.............................. MartinLane 3 47
(J W Hills) *chsd ldrs: rdn over 2f out: styd on same pce fr over 1f out* **11/4**[2]
0 **5** *hd* **Rose Buck**[64] 6107 2-8-10 0... RaulDaSilva 2 49
(Paul Cole) *led: rdn and hdd 2f out: no ex fnl f* **9/1**
06 **6** 4 **Mishnah**[49] 6546 2-8-6 0.. DuranFentiman 4 33
(John Holt) *sn pushed along in rr: rdn over 1f out: n.d* **25/1**
0 **7** 1 1/2 **Febrayer Star (IRE)**[27] 7162 2-8-13 0................................. GrahamLee 1 36
(Robert Cowell) *trckd ldrs tl rdn and wknd over 1f out* **14/1**
6 **8** 11 **Frankthetank (IRE)**[6] 7664 2-9-3 0.. TomEaves 8 7
(Keith Dalgleish) *chsd ldrs tl pushed along and wknd over 2f out* **10/1**

1m 16.09s (1.09) **Going Correction** +0.05s/f (Slow) **8** Ran SP% **114.5**
Speed ratings (Par 94): **94,91,90,85,84 79,77,62**
toteswingers 1&2 £8.80, 2&3 £13.70, 1&3 £1.90 CSF £51.13 TOTE £2.30: £1.10, £4.60, £1.60; EX 44.20 Trifecta £410.00 Pool: £2576.68 - 4.71 winning units..
Owner T J Monaghan **Bred** Robert Berns **Trained** Middleham Moor, N Yorks

7791 32RED MAIDEN FILLIES' STKS 1m 141y(P)
6:20 (6:22) (Class 5) 3-Y-O+ **£2,587** (£770; £384; £192) **Stalls** Low

Form RPR
1 **History Book (IRE)** 3-8-12 0... SilvestreDeSousa 4 84
(Charlie Appleby) *s.i.s: hdwy over 7f out: shkn up to ld and hung lft over 1f out: rdn and edgd rt ins fnl f: r.o wl* **6/4**[1]
22 **2** 4 1/2 **Wilhana (IRE)**[19] 7377 3-8-12 0... LiamKeniry 3 74
(Pam Sly) *chsd ldrs: pushed along to go 2nd over 3f out: rdn over 2f out: styd on same pce fnl f* **4/1**[3]

53 **3** 3/4 **Lookbeforeyouleap**[31] 7066 3-8-12 69 .... DanielTudhope 1 72
(David O'Meara) *led: rdn and hdd over 1f out: no ex ins fnl f* **5/2**[2]

55 **4** 4 1/2 **Meet Marhaba (IRE)**[94] 5071 3-8-12 0 .... PaulHanagan 9 62
(J W Hills) *prom: forced to r wd tl lost pl 7f out: hdwy over 3f out: rdn and edgd lft over 1f out: wknd fnl f* **10/1**

5 6 **Cassie Jem** 3-8-12 0 .... WilliamCarson 8 48
(David C Griffiths) *dwlt: sn pushed along in rr: hdwy over 2f out: wknd wl over 1f out* **40/1**

26 **6** 7 **Abbotsfield (IRE)**[51] 6497 3-8-12 0 .... GrahamLee 6 32
(Ben Haslam) *prom: pushed along over 3f out: wknd over 2f out* **8/1**

6 **7** 1 **Felice (IRE)**[56] 6319 3-8-12 0 .... TomEaves 5 29
(Scott Dixon) *prom: rdn over 4f out: wknd over 3f out* **33/1**

00 **8** 3 **Summer In February**[28] 7154 3-8-7 0 .... PhilipPrince(5) 2 23
(Nikki Evans) *chsd ldr tl rdn over 3f out: wknd 2f out* **80/1**

3000 **9** 2 3/4 **Queen's Princess**[135] 3654 5-8-10 45 ....[1] AdamCarter(5) 7 15
(John Wainwright) *hld up: rdn over 3f out: sn wknd* **80/1**

1m 50.75s (0.25) **Going Correction** +0.05s/f (Slow)
WFA 3 from 5yo 3lb **9** Ran SP% **116.6**
Speed ratings (Par 100): **100,96,95,91,86 79,78,76,73**
toteswingers 1&2 £1.90, 2&3 £1.80, 1&3 £1.50 CSF £7.90 TOTE £2.70: £1.10, £1.60, £1.30; EX 8.70 Trifecta £22.30 Pool: £3626.78 - 121.75 winning units..
Owner Godolphin **Bred** Darley **Trained** Newmarket, Suffolk

FOCUS
A fair maiden fillies' race.

7792 BEST ODDS AT BOOKMAKERS.CO.UK CLAIMING STKS 5f 216y(P)
6:50 (6:52) (Class 6) 3-Y-O+ **£1,940** (£577; £288; £144) **Stalls** Low

Form RPR

6003 **1** **Fortinbrass (IRE)**[13] 7507 3-9-2 79 .... FergusSweeney 9 85
(Amy Weaver) *a.p: rdn over 2f out: led over 1f out: styd on u.p* **13/2**

2604 **2** 3/4 **Light From Mars**[33] 7031 8-9-0 80 ....(p) StephenCraine 11 81
(Tom Dascombe) *hld up: hdwy over 2f out: rdn to chse wnr fnl f: edgd lft: styd on* **7/2**[2]

1410 **3** 3/4 **George Fenton**[8] 7633 4-9-2 73 ....(e) LiamKeniry 10 80
(Conor Dore) *sn pushed along in mid-div: hdwy over 3f out: rdn over 1f out: styd on* **14/1**

0001 **4** 1/2 **Capail Liath (IRE)**[33] 7031 5-9-2 87 ....(p) ShaneGray(5) 6 84
(Kevin Ryan) *chsd ldrs: rdn over 1f out: styd on* **3/1**[1]

3060 **5** 2 **Alpha Tauri (USA)**[9] 7601 7-9-4 73 ....(t) RobbieFitzpatrick 1 74
(Charles Smith) *hld up: swtchd rt over 2f out: hdwy and shkn up over 1f out: nvr nr to chal* **100/1**

0413 **6** hd **Bunce (IRE)**[23] 7282 5-8-12 65 ....(b) DanielTudhope 13 68
(David O'Meara) *hld up: hdwy u.p over 1f out: nt rch ldrs* **12/1**

4512 **7** 1 1/2 **Countryman**[96] 4998 3-8-9 74 .... LouisSteward(7) 3 67
(Amy Weaver) *chsd ldrs: rdn over 2f out: styd on same pce fr over 1f out* **8/1**

-004 **8** 1/2 **Rosa Lockwood**[73] 5817 4-8-8 42 .... GrahamGibbons 8 57?
(Ed McMahon) *chsd ldr: rdn and ev ch over 1f out: no ex ins fnl f* **150/1**

0361 **9** 3/4 **Ficelle (IRE)**[21] 7323 4-8-1 47 .... PhilipPrince(5) 12 53?
(Nikki Evans) *sn pushed along in rr: rdn over 2f out: n.d* **150/1**

6254 **10** 1 **Titus Gent**[40] 6850 8-8-9 84 .... DavidParkes(7) 4 60
(Jeremy Gask) *prom tl lost pl over 2f out* **7/1**

0000 **11** 1 1/2 **West Leake Diman (IRE)**[22] 7313 4-8-12 80 ....(p) TomEaves 7 51
(Keith Dalgleish) *led: rdn and hdd over 1f out: wknd fnl f* **11/2**[3]

1m 15.26s (0.26) **Going Correction** +0.05s/f (Slow) **11** Ran SP% **116.2**
Speed ratings (Par 101): **100,99,98,97,94 94,92,91,90,89 87**
toteswingers 1&2 £6.20, 2&3 £12.50, 1&3 £24.60 CSF £29.27 TOTE £11.10: £2.80, £2.30, £3.50; EX 47.40 Trifecta £631.30 Pool: £2591.88 - 3.07 winning units..Fortinbrass was claimed by D. O'Meara for £10000. Light From Mars was claimed by R. A. Harris for £8000.
Owner North Star Racing **Bred** Tom Wallace **Trained** Newmarket, Suffolk

FOCUS
A competitive claimer with no fewer than six of the runners having either their first of second outing for a new handler.

7793 CORAL APP DOWNLOAD FROM THE APP STORE H'CAP 1m 1f 103y(P)
7:20 (7:21) (Class 2) (0-105,103) 3-Y-**£01,971** (£3,583; £1,791; £896; £446) **Stalls** Low

Form RPR

-346 **1** **Prince Alzain (USA)**[34] 7005 4-9-5 103 ....(p) OisinMurphy(5) 7 114
(Gerard Butler) *pushed along in rr early: hdwy over 4f out: led 2f out: sn rdn: edgd rt ins fnl f: r.o wl* **4/1**[3]

1122 **2** 7 **Chookie Royale**[1] 7769 5-8-12 94 ....(p) JasonHart(3) 3 90
(Keith Dalgleish) *plld hrd and prom: lost pl over 6f out: hdwy over 1f out: sn rdn: styd on same pce ins fnl f* **2/1**[2]

3204 **3** 1 1/4 **Sound Advice**[13] 7499 4-8-5 84 .... JoeFanning 4 78
(Keith Dalgleish) *led: rdn and hdd 2f out: no ex fnl f* **33/1**

0106 **4** 3/4 **Super Say (IRE)**[35] 6976 7-8-5 84 oh2 ....(t) AndrewMullen 1 76
(Michael Appleby) *racd keenly: trckd ldr tl over 6f out: remained handy: pushed along and nt clr run over 2f out: sn rdn: no ex fnl f* **20/1**

5534 **5** 1 1/2 **Alfred Hutchinson**[27] 7172 5-8-13 92 .... GrahamLee 5 81
(Geoffrey Oldroyd) *prom: racd keenly: chsd ldr 5f out: rdn and hung lft over 1f out: wknd ins fnl f* **7/1**

1403 **6** 1/2 **Strictly Silver (IRE)**[26] 7206 4-9-5 101 ....(p) RobertTart(3) 6 89
(Alan Bailey) *hld up: pushed along over 3f out: rdn over 1f out: nvr on terms* **7/4**[1]

3010 **7** 2 1/2 **Party Royal**[5] 7696 3-8-4 86 .... SilvestreDeSousa 2 70
(Mark Johnston) *prom: chsd ldr over 6f out tl 5f out: rdn over 2f out: wknd fnl f* **14/1**

1m 59.09s (-2.61) **Going Correction** +0.05s/f (Slow)
WFA 3 from 4yo+ 3lb **7** Ran SP% **116.6**
Speed ratings (Par 109): **113,106,105,105,103 103,101**
toteswingers 1&2 £1.90, 2&3 £7.30, 1&3 £20.00 CSF £12.91 TOTE £5.30: £2.20, £1.70; EX 18.00 Trifecta £218.60 Pool: £2806.14 - 9.62 winning units..
Owner Asaad Al Banwan **Bred** Dermot Cantillon & Patrick Hayes **Trained** Newmarket, Suffolk

FOCUS
A competitive Class 2 handicap with £19,000 prize-money. The first two home were both unbeaten round here.

7794 CORAL MOBILE "JUST THREE CLICKS TO BET" H'CAP 1m 4f 50y(P)
7:50 (7:50) (Class 4) (0-85,80) 3-Y-O **£4,690** (£1,395; £697) **Stalls** Low

Form RPR

45-5 **1** **Layl (USA)**[22] 7298 3-9-5 80 .... SilvestreDeSousa 2 94
(Mark Johnston) *hld up in tch: rdn over 2f out: led ins fnl f: rn green: drvn out* **15/2**[2]

11 **2** nk **Tweed**[6] 7659 3-9-2 77 6ex .... JoeFanning 1 91
(William Haggas) *trckd ldr tl led over 2f out: rdn and hung lft over 1f out: hdd ins fnl f: styd on* **2/13**[1]

3034 **3** 10 **Corton Lad**[8] 7627 3-9-2 77 ....(tp) TomEaves 3 75
(Keith Dalgleish) *led: rdr lost iron briefly 4f out: rdn and hdd over 2f out: wknd fnl f* **16/1**[3]

2m 39.47s (-1.63) **Going Correction** +0.05s/f (Slow) **3** Ran SP% **104.3**
Speed ratings (Par 104): **107,106,100**
CSF £9.71 TOTE £3.60; EX 9.90 Trifecta £2.90 Pool: £1717.83 - 430.65 winning units..
Owner Sheikh Hamdan Bin Mohammed Al Maktoum **Bred** Darley **Trained** Middleham Moor, N Yorks

T/Plt: £34.60 to a £1 stake. Pool of £87184.66 - 1839.11 winning tickets. T/Qpdt: £9.70 to a £1 stake. Pool of £11767.29 - 895.90 winning tickets. CR

7787 WOLVERHAMPTON (A.W) (L-H)
Friday, November 8

OFFICIAL GOING: Standard
Wind: Light behind Weather: Raining

7801 COMPARE BOOKMAKERS AT BOOKMAKERS.CO.UK APPRENTICE H'CAP 5f 216y(P)
4:15 (4:15) (Class 5) (0-70,70) 3-Y-O+ **£2,587** (£770; £384; £192) **Stalls** Low

Form RPR

4311 **1** **Powerful Pierre**[14] 7512 6-9-0 66 ....(b) JacobButterfield(3) 2 76
(Ollie Pears) *prom: lost pl after 1f: pushed along 1/2-way: swtchd rt and hdwy over 1f out: rdn to ld ins fnl f: r.o* **5/1**[2]

6102 **2** 1/2 **Trending (IRE)**[21] 7347 4-8-8 64 ....(bt) DavidParkes(7) 8 72
(Jeremy Gask) *s.i.s: hdwy 1/2-way: rdn and ev ch ins fnl f: edgd lft: styd on* **17/2**

0200 **3** 1 3/4 **Lexi's Hero (IRE)**[92] 5183 5-9-6 69 .... WilliamTwiston-Davies 9 72
(Patrick Morris) *led: hdd over 3f out: sn rdn: ev ch ins fnl f: styd on same pce* **16/1**

5010 **4** nse **Iceblast**[32] 7076 5-8-8 62 ....(b) DanielMuscutt(5) 4 65
(Michael Easterby) *sn pushed along in rr: rdn over 1f out: r.o ins fnl f: nt rch ldrs* **12/1**

3002 **5** 1/2 **Emiratesdotcom**[17] 7444 7-9-7 70 ....(tp) ThomasBrown 11 71
(Milton Bradley) *hld up: rdn over 2f out: hdwy over 1f out: r.o: nt trble ldrs* **7/1**[3]

0222 **6** nk **Bassett Road (IRE)**[3] 7754 5-9-0 63 ....(b) JasonHart 5 63
(Keith Dalgleish) *trckd ldrs: plld hrd: rdn and ev ch ins fnl f: n.m.r sn after: styd on same pce* **2/1**[1]

5005 **7** 1/2 **Monsieur Royale**[28] 7165 3-8-11 67 ....(b) JackGarritty(7) 7 65
(Geoffrey Oldroyd) *prom: rdn over 2f out: styd on* **12/1**

0006 **8** 3/4 **Colourbearer (IRE)**[74] 5817 6-9-3 69 ....(t) GeorgeChaloner(3) 3 65
(Milton Bradley) *w ldr tl led over 3f out: rdn over 1f out: hdd and no ex ins fnl f* **28/1**

6166 **9** 3/4 **Diamond Blue**[37] 6941 5-8-12 66 .... SamanthaBell(5) 10 60
(Richard Fahey) *broke wl: sn lost pl: pushed along 1/2-way: nvr trbld ldrs* **10/1**

5256 **10** nk **Belle Bayardo (IRE)**[65] 6096 5-8-13 65 .... PhilipPrince(3) 6 58
(Ronald Harris) *chsd ldrs: rdn over 2f out: styd on same pce fr over 1f out* **14/1**

6600 **11** 2 1/4 **Frognal (IRE)**[17] 7444 7-8-10 64 ....(bt) EoinWalsh(5) 1 50
(Violet M Jordan) *s.i.s: hld up: shkn up over 2f out: nvr on terms* **33/1**

1m 15.31s (0.31) **Going Correction** +0.10s/f (Slow) **11** Ran SP% **116.4**
Speed ratings (Par 103): **101,100,98,97,97 96,96,95,94,93 90**
toteswingers 1&2 £4.60, 1&3 £9.90, 2&3 £18.30 CSF £46.70 CT £648.15 TOTE £4.30: £1.80, £2.50, £4.40; EX 32.60 Trifecta £262.70 Pool: £2726.93 - 7.78 winning units..
Owner Terence Elsey **Bred** Hedsor Stud **Trained** Norton, N Yorks
■ Stewards' Enquiry : Samantha Bell caution: entered wrong stall.

FOCUS
Plenty of rain during the day and traditionally a deluge quickens the surface, but the ground remained officially Standard. The rain eased before this weak apprentices' handicap and the breeze picked behind them in the home straight.

7802 BEST ODDS AT BOOKMAKERS.CO.UK MAIDEN STKS 5f 216y(P)
4:45 (4:46) (Class 5) 3-Y-O **£2,587** (£770; £384; £192) **Stalls** Low

Form RPR

0223 **1** **It Must Be Faith**[1] 7787 3-9-5 73 .... SilvestreDeSousa 1 78
(Michael Appleby) *s.i.s: plld hrd and sn prom: hung rt and led over 2f out: shkn up over 1f out: r.o* **5/6**[1]

4 **2** 3 1/4 **Random Success (IRE)**[107] 4627 3-9-0 0 ....[1] MartinLane 6 63
(Roger Charlton) *stdd s: hld up and bhd: hdwy over 2f out: rdn over 1f out: edgd lft ins fnl f: styd on same pce* **11/2**[3]

42 **3** 4 **Poyle Vinnie**[16] 7459 3-9-5 0 .... TomQueally 2 55
(George Margarson) *trckd ldrs: ev ch over 2f out: rdn and edgd rt over 1f out: hung lft and wknd ins fnl f* **5/2**[2]

4 5 **Fitrah (IRE)**[14] 7516 3-9-0 63 .... KieranO'Neill 4 34
(W McCreery, Ire) *led: hdd over 3f out: rdn and wknd over 1f out* **12/1**

0030 **5** 7 **Cape Appeal**[44] 6753 3-8-11 58 .... WilliamTwiston-Davies(3) 5 11
(Richard Hannon) *chsd ldr tl led over 3f out: rdn and hdd over 2f out: wknd wl over 1f out* **40/1**

6 1 3/4 **Global Leader (IRE)** 3-9-5 0 .... FrederikTylicki 3 11
(Paul D'Arcy) *s.i.s: sn pushed along in rr: wknd over 2f out* **33/1**

1m 15.51s (0.51) **Going Correction** +0.10s/f (Slow) **6** Ran SP% **111.6**
Speed ratings (Par 102): **100,95,90,83,74 72**
toteswingers 1&2 £1.90, 1&3 £1.10, 2&3 £2.50 CSF £6.02 TOTE £1.70: £1.10, £2.90; EX 6.40 Trifecta £17.50 Pool: £3264.38 - 139.41 winning units..
Owner Michael Appleby **Bred** Matthew Sharkey & Newsells Park Stud Ltd **Trained** Danethorpe, Notts

FOCUS
They went a decent clip and it was all-change with 2f to run in this modest sprint maiden.

7803 BOOKMAKERS.CO.UK H'CAP 5f 216y(P)
5:20 (5:20) (Class 2) (0-105,98) 3-Y-**£11,971** (£3,583; £1,791; £896; £446) **Stalls** Low

Form RPR

001 **1** **Forest Edge (IRE)**[8] 7642 4-9-5 96 6ex ....(b) AdamKirby 5 105
(David Evans) *sn pushed along in rr: hdwy over 1f out: sn rdn: r.o u.p to ld post* **9/2**[1]

13 **2** nse **Peace Seeker**[8] 7642 5-8-8 85 .... WilliamCarson 4 94
(Anthony Carson) *chsd ldrs: rdn over 2f out: led ins fnl f: hdd post* **8/1**

0001 **3** 1 3/4 **Arctic Feeling (IRE)**[18] 7420 5-8-4 86 .... SamanthaBell(5) 2 89
(Richard Fahey) *hld up: rdn and r.o ins fnl f: wnt 3rd post: nt rch ldrs* **15/2**

0005 **4** 1/2 **Stonefield Flyer**[8] 7642 4-8-13 90 .... TomEaves 10 92
(Keith Dalgleish) *chsd ldr: rdn over 1f out: styd on* **9/1**

The Form Book Flat, Raceform Ltd, Compton, RG20 6NL.

5620 **5** *nk* **Addictive Dream (IRE)**[13] 7527 6-9-5 **96** TonyHamilton 11 97
(David Nicholls) *led 5f out: rdn and hdd ins fnl f: styd on same pce* **7/1**

2204 **6** *hd* **Naabegha**[8] 7648 6-8-12 **89** LiamKeniry 1 89
(Ed de Giles) *s.i.s: hld up: hdwy over 1f out: sn rdn: r.o: nt rch ldrs* **6/1[2]**

3011 **7** *1 3/4* **Equitania**[38] 6920 3-8-9 **86** SilvestreDeSousa 8 80
(Alan Bailey) *led 1f: chsd ldrs: rdn over 2f out: no ex ins fnl f* **13/2[3]**

0600 **8** *1/2* **Woolfall Sovereign (IRE)**[134] 3741 7-9-7 **98** TomQueally 7 91
(George Margarson) *s.i.s: in rr and pushed along 1/2-way: rdn over 1f out: edgd lft and r.o ins fnl f: nvr nrr* **12/1**

0400 **9** *1* **Ruby's Day**[4] 7731 4-8-2 **79** oh1 NickyMackay 3 69
(David Brown) *sn pushed along in rr: nvr on terms* **33/1**

0000 **10** *3/4* **Aubrietia**[13] 7540 4-8-13 **93** (be) WilliamTwiston-Davies(3) 9 80
(Alan McCabe) *prom: pushed along over 3f out: wknd over 1f out* **33/1**

0621 **11** *3/4* **Even Stevens**[20] 7373 5-9-2 **93** (p) PJMcDonald 12 78
(Scott Dixon) *prom: chsd ldr over 3f out tl rdn over 1f out: wknd fnl f* **10/1**

10 **12** *10* **Burning Thread (IRE)**[41] 6830 6-9-2 **93** (b) JamesSullivan 6 46
(Tim Etherington) *chsd ldrs: rdn 1/2-way: wknd over 1f out* **40/1**

1m 14.46s (-0.54) **Going Correction** +0.10s/f (Slow) **12** Ran SP% **116.3**
Speed ratings (Par 109): **107,106,104,103,103 103,100,100,98,97 96,83**
toteswingers 1&2 £5.00, 1&3 £10.70, 2&3 £15.40 CSF £38.78 CT £265.28 TOTE £5.30: £2.20, £2.40, £2.50; EX 28.00 Trifecta £318.80 Pool: £1790.86 - 4.21 winning units..
Owner P & K Swinnerton **Bred** Alberto Panetta **Trained** Pandy, Monmouths

FOCUS
A decent and tight-knit sprint handicap, although the kickback was dreadful and the early pace merciless. The first three home were drawn low.

7804 32RED MAIDEN AUCTION STKS 5f 20y(P)
5:55 (5:55) (Class 6) 2-Y-O **£1,940** (£577; £288; £144) **Stalls** Low

Form RPR

1 **Distant Past** 2-8-13 0 GrahamLee 6 79+
(Kevin Ryan) *trckd ldrs: wnt 2nd 1/2-way: shkn up to ld over 1f out: c clr ins fnl f* **15/8[1]**

0006 **2** *5* **Astral Rose**[18] 7426 2-8-11 45 (b) ShaneKelly 7 59
(Jonathan Portman) *hld up: pushed along 1/2-way: hdwy u.p over 1f out: styd on to go 2nd nr fin: no ch w wnr* **66/1**

045 **3** *1/2* **Groundworker (IRE)**[24] 7261 2-9-2 72 LiamKeniry 5 62
(Sylvester Kirk) *trckd ldr: plld hrd: led 4f out: rdn and hdd over 1f out: no ex ins fnl f* **5/2[2]**

0 **4** *3/4* **Camanche Grey (IRE)**[51] 6517 2-8-13 0 JoeFanning 4 57
(Ben Haslam) *chsd ldrs: rdn 1/2-way: styd on same pce fr over 1f out* **9/1**

3262 **5** *3/4* **Simply Black (IRE)**[13] 7541 2-8-7 68 DavidBergin(5) 3 53
(David O'Meara) *hld up: nt clr run over 2f out: rdn over 1f out: nvr on terms* **3/1[3]**

55 **6** *3 1/2* **Diamondsinthesky (IRE)**[13] 7541 2-8-9 0 DaleSwift 2 37
(Derek Shaw) *s.i.s: a in rr* **12/1**

0000 **7** *hd* **Cheeky Peta'S**[14] 7509 2-8-6 55 ConnorBeasley(5) 1 38
(James Given) *led 1f: chsd ldr tl rdn 1/2-way: wknd over 1f out* **20/1**

1m 2.66s (0.36) **Going Correction** +0.10s/f (Slow) **7** Ran SP% **112.3**
Speed ratings (Par 94): **101,93,92,91,89 84,83**
toteswingers 1&2 £21.90, 1&3 £2.90, 2&3 £19.80 CSF £94.23 TOTE £3.60: £1.90, £10.70; EX 95.60 Trifecta £376.30 Pool: £2213.58 - 4.41 winning units..
Owner M Wynne **Bred** J E Rose **Trained** Hambleton, N Yorks

FOCUS
A weak sprint maiden and the winner looked a class or two above his rivals.

7805 CORAL APP DOWNLOAD FROM THE APP STORE H'CAP 1m 4f 50y(P)
6:30 (6:30) (Class 4) (0-85,85) 3-Y-O+ **£4,690** (£1,395; £697; £348) **Stalls** Low

Form RPR

1-03 **1** **Muhtaris (IRE)**[14] 7498 3-8-10 **77** SilvestreDeSousa 5 89+
(Saeed bin Suroor) *hld up in tch: nt clr run fr over 2f out tl swtchd lft over 1f out: sn rdn: r.o to ld towards fin* **10/11[1]**

2140 **2** *3/4* **All The Winds (GER)**[31] 7115 8-8-13 **77** (t) WilliamTwiston-Davies(3) 8 86
(Shaun Lycett) *dwlt: hld up: hdwy 2f out: rdn to ld 1f out: hdd towards fin* **50/1**

0155 **3** *6* **Fly Solo**[20] 7369 4-9-0 **75** MartinDwyer 10 74
(Alan Swinbank) *a.p: rdn and ev ch over 1f out: no ins ex fnl f* **10/1[3]**

0200 **4** *3/4* **Guising**[40] 6876 4-9-8 **83** TomQueally 4 81
(David Brown) *trckd ldr tl led 2f out: rdn and hung lft over 1f out: sn hdd: no ex ins fnl f* **14/1**

0360 **5** *hd* **Noble Alan (GER)**[48] 6626 10-9-10 **85** GrahamLee 7 83
(Nicky Richards) *trckd ldrs: pushed along and n.m.r over 1f out: styd on same pce* **11/2[2]**

0343 **6** *2 1/4* **Lean On Pete (IRE)**[13] 7544 4-8-9 **75** JacobButterfield(5) 2 69
(Ollie Pears) *hld up: hdwy over 2f out: rdn and nt clr run over 1f out: no ex* **16/1**

4100 **7** *1 1/4* **Uphold**[7] 7656 6-9-5 **85** (e) DanielMuscutt(5) 3 77
(Gay Kelleway) *led: rdn and hdd 2f out: hmpd over 1f out: wknd fnl f* **12/1**

4004 **8** *14* **High Office**[14] 7496 7-9-0 **75** TonyHamilton 6 45
(Richard Fahey) *stmbld s: hld up: rdn over 3f out: wknd over 2f out* **11/1**

6360 **9** *61* **Tartan Gigha (IRE)**[136] 3651 8-9-3 **78** JoeFanning 1
(Geoffrey Harker) *chsd ldrs: pushed along over 5f out: sn lost pl: wknd over 4f out* **66/1**

221- **P** **Chookie Hamilton**[326] 8149 9-9-1 **76** TomEaves 9
(Keith Dalgleish) *hld up: rdn and wknd over 2f out: bhd whn p.u and dismntd wl over 1f out* **12/1**

2m 38.9s (-2.20) **Going Correction** +0.10s/f (Slow)
WFA 3 from 4yo+ 6lb **10** Ran SP% **116.6**
Speed ratings (Par 105): **111,110,106,106,105 104,103,94,53,**
toteswingers 1&2 £5.30, 1&3 £4.70, 2&3 £27.80 CSF £62.73 CT £314.59 TOTE £2.00: £1.10, £6.40, £3.50; EX 36.60 Trifecta £554.60 Pool: £2190.89 - 2.96 winning units..
Owner Godolphin **Bred** Rabbah Bloodstock Limited **Trained** Newmarket, Suffolk

FOCUS
The pace was reasonable for this ordinary handicap and the winner might be better value than the margin suggests.

7806 LADBROKES CLASSIFIED STKS 1m 141y(P)
7:00 (7:01) (Class 6) 3-Y-O+ **£1,940** (£577; £288; £144) **Stalls** Low

Form RPR

0050 **1** **Quadriga (IRE)**[9] 7628 3-9-0 55 JimmyQuinn 9 60
(Robert Eddery) *mid-div: hdwy over 2f out: shkn up to ld over 1f out: sn hrd rdn: edgd lft ins fnl f: jst hld on* **11/2[3]**

-330 **2** *shd* **Reggie Bond**[126] 4008 3-8-11 54 (p) WilliamTwiston-Davies(3) 3 60
(Geoffrey Oldroyd) *hld up: hdwy over 2f out: nt clr run over 1f out: rdn to chse wnr ins fnl f: r.o: jst failed* **7/2[1]**

-303 **3** *2 1/4* **Be Royale**[16] 7465 3-9-0 45 TomQueally 5 55
(Michael Appleby) *hld up: nt clr run wl over 1f out: rdn and r.o ins fnl f: nt rch ldrs* **11/2[3]**

6460 **4** *2 1/4* **Shamiana**[125] 4064 3-9-0 55 SilvestreDeSousa 7 50
(Daniel Kubler) *sn led: rdn and hdd over 1f out: no ex ins fnl f* **8/1**

0-00 **5** *3/4* **Zaroud (IRE)**[246] 917 4-9-3 40 (t) AdamKirby 1 47
(Emmet Michael Butterly, Ire) *hld up in tch: rdn over 1f out: no ex ins fnl f* **5/1[2]**

-000 **6** *1/2* **Zed Candy Girl**[22] 7323 3-9-0 45 ShaneKelly 6 47
(John Stimpson) *hld up: styd on u.p fr over 1f out: nt trble ldrs* **66/1**

3026 **7** *3 1/4* **Poetic Belle**[16] 7465 3-8-9 55 (t) ShirleyTeasdale(5) 11 39
(Shaun Harris) *hld up: rdn over 1f out: nvr on terms* **16/1**

504 **8** *1/2* **Lalinde**[15] 7490 3-9-0 48 JoeFanning 13 38
(Daniel Kubler) *prom: chsd ldr 6f out tl rdn wl over 1f out: sn hung lft and wknd* **16/1**

3015 **9** *1/2* **Dustland Fairytale (IRE)**[15] 7485 5-9-3 55 JimCrowley 2 36
(Ian Williams) *chsd ldrs: rdn over 2f out: wknd fnl f* **5/1[2]**

-300 **10** *1/2* **Pink Cadillac (IRE)**[172] 2501 3-9-0 43 GrahamLee 8 36
(Ben Haslam) *prom: rdn over 2f out: wknd fnl f* **66/1**

2400 **11** *3* **Munaawib**[14] 7498 5-9-3 53 (t[1]) TomEaves 12 28
(Charles Smith) *mid-div: hdwy over 3f out: rdn and wknd over 2f out* **12/1**

1m 52.04s (1.54) **Going Correction** +0.10s/f (Slow)
WFA 3 from 4yo+ 3lb **11** Ran SP% **119.9**
Speed ratings (Par 101): **97,96,94,92,92 91,88,88,88,87 84**
toteswingers 1&2 £7.20, 1&3 £19.10, 2&3 £3.60 CSF £25.58 TOTE £8.10: £2.40, £1.60, £2.20; EX 30.50 Trifecta £218.60 Pool: £1546.07 - 5.30 winning units..
Owner Owen O'Brien **Bred** Anima Negra Gmbh & Co Kg **Trained** Newmarket, Suffolk

FOCUS
The pace held up in this moderate contest.

7807 DOWNLOAD THE LADBROKES APP H'CAP (DIV I) 7f 32y(P)
7:30 (7:30) (Class 6) (0-62,62) 3-Y-O+ **£1,940** (£577; £288; £144) **Stalls** High

Form RPR

4532 **1** **Orpsie Boy (IRE)**[15] 7486 10-9-4 **62** JasonHart(3) 2 69
(Ruth Carr) *hld up: hdwy over 2f out: pushed along and rdr lost iron over 1f out: r.o to ld post* **4/1[2]**

2-41 **2** *nk* **Monte Cassino (IRE)**[21] 7354 8-8-12 **58** (e) GeorgeChaloner(5) 6 64
(Bryan Smart) *chsd ldrs: rdn over 1f out: led ins fnl f: hdd post* **9/2[3]**

2440 **3** *shd* **Piccolo Express**[21] 7353 7-9-3 **58** ShaneKelly 7 64
(Brian Baugh) *chsd ldr: rdn over 1f out: ev ch ins fnl f: r.o* **8/1**

-006 **4** *1 1/4* **Misty Eyes**[24] 7269 4-8-10 **51** oh6 (v[1]) JoeFanning 3 54
(Geoffrey Harker) *led: rdn over 1f out: hdd ins fnl f: styd on same pce* **80/1**

0232 **5** *hd* **Red Cobra (IRE)**[21] 7343 3-9-2 **58** DavidAllan 11 59
(Tim Easterby) *chsd ldrs: rdn over 2f out: styd on* **5/2[1]**

3500 **6** *hd* **Purley Queen (IRE)**[8] 7644 4-9-0 **55** LiamKeniry 4 56
(Sylvester Kirk) *hld up: hdwy u.p over 1f out: r.o* **20/1**

0260 **7** *2 3/4* **Penbryn (USA)**[102] 4840 6-8-9 **57** JordanVaughan(7) 9 51
(Nick Littmoden) *s.i.s: sn prom: rdn over 1f out: no ex ins fnl f* **12/1**

4300 **8** *10* **Moortahan**[18] 7430 3-9-4 **60** GrahamLee 1 26
(Richard Hannon) *hld up: pushed along 1/2-way: wknd over 2f out* **4/1[2]**

4100 **9** *11* **Basle**[28] 7163 6-9-6 **61** (t) GeorgeBaker 10
(Roy Brotherton) *hld up: pushed along over 2f out: sn wknd* **25/1**

1m 30.42s (0.82) **Going Correction** +0.10s/f (Slow)
WFA 3 from 4yo+ 1lb **9** Ran SP% **115.4**
Speed ratings (Par 101): **99,98,98,97,96 96,93,82,69**
toteswingers 1&2 £3.60, 1&3 £9.30, 2&3 £6.80 CSF £21.88 CT £137.56 TOTE £3.70: £1.90, £1.60, £3.20; EX 17.00 Trifecta £120.30 Pool: £1596.19 - 9.95 winning units..
Owner Miss Vanessa Church **Bred** Minch Bloodstock **Trained** Huby, N Yorks

FOCUS
A poor handicap that produced a tight finish. The pace was reasonable for the grade.

7808 DOWNLOAD THE LADBROKES APP H'CAP (DIV II) 7f 32y(P)
8:00 (8:01) (Class 6) (0-62,61) 3-Y-O+ **£1,940** (£577; £288; £144) **Stalls** High

Form RPR

0041 **1** **One Way Or Another (AUS)**[8] 7652 10-9-0 **61** (t) EoinWalsh(7) 5 73
(David Evans) *hld up: hdwy over 2f out: rdn to ld ins fnl f: edgd lft: r.o wl* **5/4[1]**

400 **2** *3 1/4* **Triple Aitch (USA)**[105] 4721 3-8-10 **58** JordanVaughan(7) 7 60
(Giles Bravery) *trckd ldrs: rdn to ld over 1f out: hdd and unable qck ins fnl f* **25/1**

0054 **3** *1 3/4* **Red Shadow**[14] 7508 4-8-10 **50** (p) SilvestreDeSousa 6 49
(Alan Brown) *chsd ldrs: rdn over 1f out: styd on same pce fnl f* **14/1**

243 **4** *1* **Loyal N Trusted**[14] 7511 5-8-13 **60** (p) GemmaTutty(7) 10 56
(Karen Tutty) *hld up: pushed along over 2f out: rdn and r.o ins fnl f: nvr nrr* **6/1[3]**

0502 **5** *3 1/2* **Clumber Place**[17] 7455 7-9-1 **55** GrahamLee 8 41
(James Given) *led: hdd over 5f out: chsd ldr: rdn and ev ch over 1f out: wknd ins fnl f* **12/1**

2541 **6** *nse* **Harvest Mist (IRE)**[21] 7353 5-9-2 **59** WilliamTwiston-Davies(3) 2 45
(Shaun Lycett) *w ldr tl led over 5f out: rdn and hdd over 1f out: wknd ins fnl f* **13/2**

6065 **7** *3 1/2* **Mick Dundee (IRE)**[22] 7322 3-9-3 **58** (bt) AdamKirby 1 34
(John Ryan) *hld up: rdn over 2f out: nvr on terms* **11/2[2]**

40-0 **8** *3* **Hooligan Sean**[25] 7246 6-9-0 **54** DavidProbert 9 23
(Mark Usher) *prom: rdn over 2f out: wknd over 1f out* **25/1**

3231 **9** *3 1/4* **Prigsnov Dancer (IRE)**[15] 7485 8-8-11 **58** (p) DavidParkes(7) 3 18
(Deborah Sanderson) *s.i.s: hld up: plld hrd: rdn over 2f out: sn wknd* **14/1**

1m 30.17s (0.57) **Going Correction** +0.10s/f (Slow)
WFA 3 from 4yo+ 1lb **9** Ran SP% **116.2**
Speed ratings (Par 101): **100,96,94,93,89 89,85,81,77**
toteswingers 1&2 £11.70, 1&3 £6.50, 2&3 £67.50 CSF £39.68 CT £302.03 TOTE £1.90: £1.10, £5.80, £2.90; EX 67.40 Trifecta £385.10 Pool: £2091.03 - 4.07 winning units..
Owner Mrs E Evans **Bred** Segenho Stud **Trained** Pandy, Monmouths

FOCUS
The weaker, second division of the 7f handicap, was run at a true pace.

T/Jkpt: £4,571.30 to a £1 stake. Pool: £25754.00 - 4.00 winning tickets T/Plt: £125.00 to a £1 stake. Pool: £101100.76 - 590.18 winning tickets T/Qpdt: £17.90 to a £1 stake. Pool: £13302.29 - 547.60 winning tickets CR

7809 - 7816a (Foreign Racing) - See Raceform Interactive

[7525]DONCASTER (L-H)

Saturday, November 9

OFFICIAL GOING: Soft (6.0)

Wind: moderate 1/2 against Weather: raining after race 1

7817 BETFRED COCK O'THE NORTH EBF MAIDEN STKS (DIV I) 6f

12:05 (12:10) (Class 5) 2-Y-O **£2,911** (£866; £432; £216) **Stalls** High

Form RPR

3633 **1** **Jazz (IRE)**[45] 6747 2-9-5 83 .... JimCrowley 10 85
(Charles Hills) *mde all: rdn clr wl over 1f out: kpt on strly* **5/2**[2]

2 **2** 3 **Resolute**[18] 7448 2-9-5 0 .... SebSanders 14 76
(William Haggas) *in tch: hdwy to chse ldrs wl over 2f out: rdn to chse wnr wl over 1f out: drvn and no imp fnl f* **9/4**[1]

3 2 1/4 **Direct Times (IRE)** 2-9-5 0 .... WilliamBuick 8 69+
(Peter Chapple-Hyam) *hld up: swtchd lft and hdwy over 2f out: rdn to chse ldrs over 1f out: kpt on same pce* **16/1**

622 **4** 6 **Percy's Gal**[19] 7419 2-8-7 72 .... GemmaTutty(7) 1 46
(Karen Tutty) *prom on wd outside: rdn along over 2f out: sn one pce* **8/1**[3]

5 2 3/4 **Singing Star (IRE)** 2-9-0 0 .... DavidAllan 12 38+
(Mel Brittain) *towards rr: hdwy wl over 2f out: rdn and kpt on fr over 1f out: nvr nr ldrs* **100/1**

5 **6** 1/2 **Vale Mentor (IRE)**[11] 7592 2-9-5 0 .... DuranFentiman 13 42+
(Tim Easterby) *chsd ldrs: rdn along wl over 2f out: sn one pce* **100/1**

7 2 1/2 **Borough Belle** 2-9-0 0 .... FergusSweeney 2 29
(Henry Candy) *chsd ldrs: rdn along and lost pl 1/2-way: kpt on fr over 1f out: n.d* **50/1**

0222 **8** 1 1/4 **Nova Champ (IRE)**[27] 7221 2-9-5 73 .... HarryBentley 5 30
(Stuart Williams) *chsd ldrs: rdn along wl over 2f out: sn wknd* **8/1**[3]

4 **9** nk **Aran Sky (IRE)**[45] 6754 2-9-5 0 .... DanielTudhope 4 29
(K R Burke) *in tch: rdn along 1/2-way: sn wknd* **8/1**[3]

10 1 **Findhorn Magic** 2-9-0 0 .... SteveDrowne 9 21
(Peter Makin) *chsd wnr to 1/2-way: sn wknd* **50/1**

2305 **11** 1 **Jacquotte Delahaye**[87] 5380 2-9-0 74 ....(b[1]) GrahamLee 6 18
(Bryan Smart) *swtchd lft s and sn prom: rdn along wl over 2f out: sn wknd* **25/1**

0 **12** 1 1/4 **Roman Royal**[103] 4828 2-9-0 0 ....(e) KieranO'Neill 11 15
(Richard Hannon) *chsd ldrs: rdn along 1/2-way: sn wknd* **50/1**

13 6 **Almax** 2-9-5 0 .... TomQueally 15 2
(Michael Bell) *a towards rr: bhd fnl 2f* **33/1**

00 **14** 1 **Right Of Appeal**[18] 7448 2-9-5 0 .... SilvestreDeSousa 7
(Mark Johnston) *a towards rr: bhd fr 1/2-way* **25/1**

50 **15** 23 **Reaffirmed (IRE)**[30] 7155 2-9-5 0 .... GeorgeBaker 3
(Ed Vaughan) *green and a in rr: wl bhd fr 1/2-way* **20/1**

1m 17.56s (3.96) **Going Correction** +0.60s/f (Yiel) **15 Ran SP% 121.8**
Speed ratings (Par 96): **97,93,90,82,78 77,74,72,72,70 69,67,59,58,27**
toteswingers 1&2 £2.20, 1&3 £9.10, 2&3 £8.00 CSF £7.75 TOTE £3.50: £1.70, £1.40, £4.30; EX 8.60 Trifecta £148.90 Pool: £3001.14 - 15.10 winning units..
Owner N Browne,P McNamara,J Napier,J Powell **Bred** Minch Bloodstock **Trained** Lambourn, Berks

FOCUS
The ground was riding as advertised at this stage and the opener was run in a time 6.56sec outside standard, marginally slower than the second division. Just a fair maiden, in which the field raced down the centre and the winner made all. They finished well strung out. Straightforward form, with the runner-up matching his debut level.

7818 BETFRED COCK O'THE NORTH EBF MAIDEN STKS (DIV II) 6f

12:40 (12:42) (Class 5) 2-Y-O **£2,911** (£866; £432; £216) **Stalls** High

Form RPR

1 **Indy (IRE)** 2-9-5 0 .... GrahamGibbons 6 85+
(David Barron) *mid-div: hdwy over 2f out: led last 150yds: styd on strly* **14/1**

32 **2** 4 **Penny Drops**[8] 7657 2-9-0 0 .... PaulHanagan 2 68
(William Haggas) *trckd ldrs: led over 1f out: hdd ins fnl f: no ex* **8/15**[1]

00 **3** 3 3/4 **Broadway Ranger (IRE)**[9] 7638 2-9-5 0 .... JimCrowley 13 62
(Charles Hills) *led: hdd over 1f out: kpt on same pce* **33/1**

3 **4** 2 1/4 **Majorities**[25] 7270 2-9-5 0 .... JimmyFortune 14 55
(Brian Meehan) *dwlt: sn mid-div: effrt over 2f out: sn chsng ldrs: one pce* **4/1**[2]

3 **5** 1 1/2 **Armelle (FR)**[15] 7509 2-9-0 0 .... TomEaves 9 46
(Scott Dixon) *w ldrs: drvn over 2f out: sn fdd* **40/1**

6 3/4 **White Rose Runner** 2-9-0 0 .... DavidAllan 3 43+
(Mel Brittain) *s.i.s: hdwy and swtchd lft 2f out: kpt on: nvr nr ldrs* **50/1**

7 1/2 **Hank Schrader** 2-9-5 0 .... PJMcDonald 12 47+
(John Davies) *dwlt: in rr: kpt on fnl 2f: nvr a factor* **66/1**

8 nk **Roomie** 2-9-0 0 .... DuranFentiman 5 41+
(Tim Easterby) *dwlt: in rr: sme hdwy 2f out: nvr a factor* **33/1**

50 **9** 3/4 **Daisy Boy (IRE)**[52] 6534 2-9-5 0 .... AdamBeschizza 4 44+
(Stuart Williams) *swtchd rt after s: hld up in rr: kpt on fnl 2f: nvr a factor* **50/1**

65 **10** 7 **Columbian Roulette (IRE)**[8] 7654 2-9-5 0 .... SteveDrowne 11 23
(Charles Hills) *chsd ldrs: wknd 2f out* **33/1**

53 **11** 1 **Go Sakhee**[29] 7162 2-9-5 0 .... AndreaAtzeni 8 20
(Roger Varian) *w ldrs: wkng whn sltly hmpd 2f out* **7/1**[3]

0 **12** 1/2 **Major Rowan**[22] 7341 2-9-2 0 .... MarkCoumbe(3) 7 18
(Bryan Smart) *in rr and drvn along: nvr on terms* **80/1**

00 **13** 4 1/2 **Queen Of Arts**[44] 6769 2-9-0 0 .... TonyHamilton 15
(Richard Fahey) *mid-div: lost pl over 2f out: sn bhd* **66/1**

00 **14** 1/2 **San Remo Rose (IRE)**[166] 2715 2-9-0 0 .... SilvestreDeSousa 10
(Nigel Tinkler) *chsd ldrs: lost pl over 2f out: eased whn bhd ins fnl f* **50/1**

1m 17.49s (3.89) **Going Correction** +0.725s/f (Yiel) **14 Ran SP% 125.8**
Speed ratings (Par 96): **103,97,92,89,87 86,86,85,84,75 73,73,67,66**
toteswingers 1&2 £4.40, 1&3 £51.90, 2&3 £5.80 CSF £22.19 TOTE £16.20: £3.10, £1.10, £7.00; EX 44.20 Trifecta £1346.60 Pool: £3387.96 - 1.88 winning units..
Owner Mrs K Milne **Bred** Maurice Burns **Trained** Maunby, N Yorks

FOCUS
An ordinary maiden. The form can only be better than rated, and the winner did it well.

7819 BETFRED.COM NURSERY H'CAP 6f

1:15 (1:15) (Class 4) (0-85,83) 2-Y-O **£3,752** (£1,116; £557; £278) **Stalls** High

Form RPR

0141 **1** **Kenny The Captain (IRE)**[30] 7147 2-9-5 81 .... DuranFentiman 1 89
(Tim Easterby) *trckd ldrs: hdwy over 2f out: sn cl up: rdn and slt ld over 1f out: drvn ins fnl f: hld on gamely towards fin* **5/1**[2]

0216 **2** nk **Torchlighter (IRE)**[14] 7529 2-9-7 83 .... SilvestreDeSousa 5 90
(Mark Johnston) *trckd ldrs: hdwy on outer over 2f out: sn cl up: rdn to chal over 1f out: ev ch ins fnl f tl drvn and no ex towards fin* **8/1**

1023 **3** 4 **Instant Attraction (IRE)**[33] 7062 2-9-1 77 .... MichaelO'Connell 4 72
(Jedd O'Keeffe) *prom: led after 2f: rdn along 2f out: drvn and hdd over 1f out: kpt on same pce u.p fnl f* **20/1**

013 **4** 1 **Black Caesar (IRE)**[27] 7221 2-9-6 82 .... RichardHughes 8 74
(Richard Hannon) *a.p: cl up 1/2-way: rdn and ev ch over 1f out tl drvn and wknd jst ins fnl f* **4/1**[1]

034 **5** nk **Upholland**[38] 6939 2-8-10 72 .... PaulHanagan 6 63
(Richard Fahey) *chsd ldrs: rdn along over 2f out: sn one pce* **7/1**

2041 **6** 3/4 **Know Your Name**[32] 7088 2-9-0 76 ....(v) AdamKirby 7 65
(David Evans) *towards rr: hdwy over 2f out: rdn wl over 1f out: kpt on fnl f: nrst fin* **12/1**

2055 **7** 5 **Tableforten**[3] 7771 2-8-12 74 ....(b) LiamJones 13 48
(J S Moore) *swtchd lft s and towards rr: sme late hdwy* **12/1**

4034 **8** 2 **Donny Rover (IRE)**[8] 7658 2-9-3 79 ....(v) JFEgan 2 47
(David C Griffiths) *dwlt: sn chsng ldrs: rdn along wl over 2f out and sn wknd* **12/1**

0053 **9** 1 1/4 **Sellingallthetime (IRE)**[32] 7088 2-8-5 67 .... JimmyQuinn 3 31
(Philip Kirby) *s.i.s: a in rr* **16/1**

5160 **10** 6 **Basil Berry**[17] 7463 2-8-7 69 ....(p) LukeMorris 9 15
(Chris Dwyer) *dwlt: a towards rr* **25/1**

6030 **11** 1 1/4 **Soul Instinct**[18] 7451 2-8-7 69 .... TomEaves 12 11
(Kevin Ryan) *led 2f: cl up: rdn along 1/2-way: sn wknd* **33/1**

014 **12** 6 **Penina (IRE)**[29] 7170 2-8-4 66 .... ChrisHayes 11
(Brian Ellison) *towards rr: sme hdwy 1/2-way: sn rdn along and nvr a factor* **11/2**[3]

1m 18.77s (5.17) **Going Correction** +0.85s/f (Soft) **12 Ran SP% 116.2**
Speed ratings (Par 98): **99,98,93,91,91 90,83,81,79,71 69,61**
toteswingers 1&2 £5.40, 1&3 £8.30, 2&3 £21.20 CSF £42.65 CT £736.78 TOTE £5.80: £2.00, £2.90, £3.60; EX 51.00 Trifecta £348.30 Pool: £2473.69 - 5.32 winning units..
Owner Reality Partnerships V **Bred** Joe Foley & John Grimes **Trained** Great Habton, N Yorks

■ Stewards' Enquiry : Silvestre De Sousa used whip above permitted level: 14-day ban for fifth offence of mis-use of the whip within the last six months

FOCUS
An ordinary end-of-season nursery run in driving rain, and around a second slower than the two C&D maidens. The field went centre to stands' side, with the first two home racing down the outer of the group before edging over to their right to battle it out, clear of the rest. The likeable winner continues to progress.

7820 BETFRED FUN AND FRIENDLY H'CAP 7f

1:50 (1:51) (Class 2) (0-105,102) 3-Y-**£12,938** (£3,850; £1,924; £481; £481) **Stalls** High

Form RPR

4314 **1** **Levitate**[21] 7368 5-9-1 98 ....(v) OisinMurphy(5) 12 110
(John Quinn) *trckd ldrs: led over 1f out: forged clr ins fnl f* **6/1**[1]

0531 **2** 3 **Tariq Too**[15] 7507 6-9-3 102 .... LouisSteward(7) 8 106
(Amy Weaver) *hld up in rr: hdwy over 2f out: upsides 1f out: styd on same pce* **12/1**

1364 **3** 2 1/4 **Laffan (IRE)**[14] 7540 4-9-0 92 .... DavidAllan 18 90
(Tim Easterby) *in rr: hdwy over 2f out: kpt on fnl f: tk 3rd last 50yds* **25/1**

0060 **4** 2 1/4 **Tartiflette**[21] 7368 4-8-7 85 ....(b) GrahamGibbons 14 77
(Ed McMahon) *mid-div: hdwy over 2f out: kpt on same pce fnl f* **10/1**[3]

0415 **4** dht **Dusky Queen (IRE)**[14] 7538 3-8-2 86 .... SamanthaBell(5) 4 77
(Richard Fahey) *chsd ldrs on outer: hdwy over 2f out: edgd rt over 1f out: styd on same pce* **25/1**

0520 **6** 3/4 **Myboyalfie (USA)**[7] 7696 6-8-7 85 ....(v) PaulHanagan 9 75
(J R Jenkins) *led tl over 2f out: one pce over 1f out* **10/1**[3]

5211 **7** 1 **Showboating (IRE)**[11] 7595 5-8-10 88 ....(tp) MartinHarley 19 76
(Alan McCabe) *mid-div: effrt over 2f out: kpt on fnl f* **14/1**

162- **8** 3/4 **Rhamnus**[381] 7331 3-8-6 85 .... KieranO'Neill 13 70
(Richard Hannon) *s.i.s: hld up in rr: hdwy and wl in tch whn hmpd over 2f out: hmpd over 1f out: nvr rchd ldrs* **22/1**

506 **9** 1 **Frontier Fighter**[26] 7241 5-8-10 88 .... GrahamLee 3 71
(David O'Meara) *chsd ldrs on outside: edgd rt and fdd over 1f out* **22/1**

6441 **10** 1 1/2 **Lilac Lace (IRE)**[14] 7538 3-8-7 86 .... DuranFentiman 16 64
(Tim Easterby) *chsd ldrs: led over 2f out: hdd over 1f out: wknd fnl 75yds* **16/1**

0603 **11** 1 **Conry (IRE)**[7] 7699 7-8-5 83 oh3 .... LukeMorris 17 60
(Ian Williams) *in rr: kpt on fnl 2f: nvr a factor* **25/1**

322 **12** 1/2 **Magistral**[7] 7696 3-8-8 87 ....(b[1]) WilliamBuick 7 61
(John Gosden) *mid-div: swtchd lft over 2f out: wknd over 1f out* **8/1**[2]

1404 **13** 3 **Tellovoi (IRE)**[7] 7699 5-8-7 85 ....(b[1]) JimCrowley 1 53
(Ian Williams) *w ldrs on outer: wknd over 1f out* **25/1**

0360 **14** shd **Monsieur Chevalier (IRE)**[9] 7641 6-9-0 92 .... AdamKirby 2 59
(P J O'Gorman) *hld up in rr on outside: hdwy over 2f out: sn chsng ldrs: lost pl over 1f out* **14/1**

4064 **15** hd **Swiftly Done (IRE)**[7] 7696 6-8-8 89 ....(b) JasonHart(3) 15 56
(Declan Carroll) *chsd ldrs: hmpd and lost pl over 2f out: hung bdly rt over 1f out* **14/1**

0303 **16** 6 **Chosen Character (IRE)**[22] 7337 5-8-11 94 ....(vt) NatashaEaton(5) 10 45
(Tom Dascombe) *chsd ldrs: edgd rt and lost pl over 2f out* **25/1**

4203 **17** 2 **Misplaced Fortune**[15] 7495 8-8-11 89 .... TomQueally 5 35
(Nigel Tinkler) *hld up in rr: bhd fnl 2f* **22/1**

0200 **18** 16 **Sam Nombulist**[49] 6625 5-8-0 83 oh3 ....(p) ConnorBeasley(5) 20
(Ian Semple) *chsd ldrs: rdn and lost pl over 3f out: sn bhd: eased in clsng stages* **22/1**

412 **19** 11 **Favourite Treat (USA)**[9] 7648 3-8-13 92 .... SilvestreDeSousa 6
(Mark Johnston) *chsd ldrs: lost pl over 2f out: eased over 1f out* **10/1**[3]

2130 **20** 10 **Kyllachy Rise**[15] 7495 3-8-13 92 .... RichardHughes 21
(Richard Hannon) *prom: lost pl over 2f out: eased whn bhd ins fnl f* **20/1**

1m 32.23s (5.93) **Going Correction** +0.975s/f (Soft)
WFA 3 from 4yo+ 1lb **20 Ran SP% 127.6**
Speed ratings (Par 109): **105,101,99,96,96 95,94,93,92,90 89,89,85,85,85 78,76,57,45,33**WIN: 4.90 Levitate; PL: 1.80 Levitate, 7.30 Laffan, 3.40 Tariq Too, 3.80 Dusky Queen, 1.40 Tartiflette; EX: 62.80; CSF: 64.38; TC: 1683.01; TF: 1722.90; toteswingers 1&2 £29.50, 1&3 £107.10, 2&3 £107.10 TRIFECTA Part won. Pool: £2297.25 - 0.7827 Owner.

FOCUS
What had looked a wide-open handicap was won readily by the favourite.

7821 BETFRED GOALS GALORE WENTWORTH STKS (LISTED RACE) 6f
2:25 (2:28) (Class 1) 3-Y-O+ £21,904 (£8,284; £4,140; £2,068) Stalls High

Form RPR
4132 **1** **Jack Dexter**[21] 7364 4-9-9 114 GrahamLee 5 119
(Jim Goldie) *hld up in midfield: hdwy over 2f out: chsd ldrs whn nt clr run and hmpd over 1f out: sn swtchd lft and rdn: styd on wl to ld last 100yds* **10/3**[1]

1141 **2** ¾ **Highland Colori (IRE)**[14] 7530 5-9-3 111 DavidProbert 10 111
(Andrew Balding) *a.p: effrt 2f out: sn rdn and ev ch whn edgd rt over 1f out: drvn ent fnl f: kpt on same pce towards fin* **5/1**[2]

0252 **3** 1 ½ **Spinatrix**[15] 7495 5-8-12 108 (p) ConnorBeasley 18 101
(Michael Dods) *led: jnd and rdn along 2f out: drvn over 1f out: hdd and no ex last 100yds* **9/1**[3]

3034 **4** ¾ **Hoof It**[21] 7364 6-9-3 107 SilvestreDeSousa 16 104
(Michael Easterby) *prom: cl up over 2f out: sn rdn and ev ch tl drvn and one pce ins fnl f* **10/1**

0000 **5** 1 ½ **Caledonia Lady**[35] 7010 4-8-12 99 LiamJones 8 95
(Jo Hughes) *trckd ldrs: hdwy over 2f out: rdn wl over 1f out: drvn and kpt on same pce fnl f* **33/1**

3005 **6** ¾ **Dinkum Diamond (IRE)**[35] 7010 5-9-3 101 CathyGannon 4 97
(Henry Candy) *chsd ldrs: rdn along and sltly outpcd over 2f out: swtchd rt and drvn wl over 1f out: kpt on fnl f* **33/1**

11-2 **7** ½ **Eton Rifles (IRE)**[35] 7010 8-9-3 108 AndreaAtzeni 2 96
(Stuart Williams) *trckd ldrs: hdwy over 2f out: rdn whn nt clr run and hmpd over 1f out: wknd fnl f* **5/1**[2]

0040 **8** 1 ½ **Arnold Lane (IRE)**[28] 7190 4-9-9 107 MartinHarley 7 97
(Mick Channon) *towards rr: rdn along and hdwy 2f out: styd on fnl f: nrst fin* **40/1**

0201 **9** 1 **Morache Music**[15] 7495 5-9-3 106 SebSanders 3 88
(Peter Makin) *towards rr: rdn along over 2f out: sn no imp* **16/1**

4313 **10** 6 **Hallelujah**[28] 7208 5-9-1 103 (t) FrederikTylicki 11 68
(James Fanshawe) *chsd ldrs: rdn along wl over 2f out: sn wknd* **14/1**

0500 **11** hd **Ballesteros**[14] 7527 4-9-3 103 PaulHanagan 1 70
(Richard Fahey) *chsd ldrs: rdn along over 2f out: grad wknd* **14/1**

16-0 **12** ¾ **Malilla (IRE)**[44] 6768 3-8-12 90 JohnFahy 6 62
(Clive Cox) *a towards rr* **66/1**

0016 **13** 3 ¼ **Mass Rally (IRE)**[21] 7364 6-9-3 108 (b) PJMcDonald 17 58
(Michael Dods) *dwlt: a towards rr* **12/1**

3342 **14** 4 **Azenzar**[52] 6535 3-8-12 72 (b[1]) WilliamBuick 13 41
(Roger Varian) *chsd ldrs: rdn along 1/2-way: sn wknd* **50/1**

0106 **15** 1 ¼ **City Girl (IRE)**[83] 5561 3-8-12 100 JimCrowley 12 37
(Ralph Beckett) *chsd ldrs: rdn along wl over 2f out: sn drvn and wknd* **50/1**

140 **16** 2 **Free Zone**[14] 7527 4-9-3 103 RichardHughes 9 36
(Bryan Smart) *a in rr* **40/1**

17 2 ¼ **Amelie Beat (GER)**[22] 4-8-12 63 (b[1]) TomQueally 19 24
(D Moser, Germany) *a in rr: bhd fr 1/2-way* **100/1**

2220 **18** ½ **Gracia Directa (GER)**[35] 7021 5-8-12 101 RobertWinston 15 23
(D Moser, Germany) *a in rr: bhd fr 1/2-way* **25/1**

1m 18.44s (4.84) **Going Correction** +1.10s/f (Soft) **18 Ran SP% 123.4**
Speed ratings (Par 111): **111,110,108,107,105 104,103,101,100,92 91,90,86,81,79 76,73,73**
toteswingers 1&2 £4.60, 2&3 £10.50, 1&3 £6.60 CSF £17.34 TOTE £4.00: £2.10, £2.00, £2.60; EX 21.40 Trifecta £117.20 Pool: £7160.56 - 45.80 winning units..
Owner Johnnie Delta Racing **Bred** Jim Goldie **Trained** Uplawmoor, E Renfrews
■ Stewards' Enquiry : David Probert two-day ban: used whip above permitted level (Nov 23,25)

FOCUS
A good-quality Listed race, and solid form with the market principals to the fore. They raced in one group, with the third and fourth putting the pace to the race on the stands' side.

7822 BETFRED MOBILE/EBF STALLIONS GILLIES FILLIES' STKS (LISTED RACE) 1m 2f 60y
3:00 (3:01) (Class 1) 3-Y-O+ £23,680 (£8,956; £4,476; £2,236) Stalls Low

Form RPR
0010 **1** **Miss Cap Estel**[14] 7590 4-9-0 89 DavidProbert 18 103
(Andrew Balding) *hld up in rr: hdwy 5f out: effrt over 2f out: styd on to ld last 100yds* **25/1**

403 **2** 1 ¾ **Cocktail Queen (IRE)**[14] 7535 3-8-10 97 RichardHughes 6 100
(David Elsworth) *led 1f: trckd ldrs: styd on and upside 100yds out: hld whn eased nr fin* **9/2**[1]

362 **3** ¾ **Cushion**[35] 7020 3-8-10 102 WilliamBuick 7 99
(John Gosden) *hld up in mid-div: hdwy over 3f out: styd on to take 3rd nr fin* **9/2**[1]

4511 **4** 1 ¼ **Princess Loulou (IRE)**[25] 7272 3-8-10 93 AndreaAtzeni 16 96
(Roger Varian) *trckd ldrs: led 2f out: hdd ins fnl f: wknd towards fin* **7/1**[2]

0434 **5** 1 **Romantic Settings**[28] 7205 3-8-10 92 TonyHamilton 3 94
(Richard Fahey) *hld up in mid-div: hdwy over 3f out: kpt on one pce fnl 2f* **14/1**

2114 **6** 2 ¼ **Amulet**[10] 7632 3-8-10 85 ShaneKelly 17 90
(Eve Johnson Houghton) *chsd ldr: led after 1f: hdd 2f out: wknd ins fnl f* **33/1**

5-10 **7** hd **Lady Loch**[199] 1768 4-9-0 87 BarryMcHugh 15 90
(Richard Fahey) *chsd ldrs: effrt over 3f out: one pce fnl 2f* **33/1**

3422 **8** hd **Jabhaat (USA)**[52] 6536 3-8-10 94 PaulHanagan 8 90
(Ed Dunlop) *chsd ldrs: effrt over 2f out: one pce* **14/1**

5325 **9** 3 ½ **Reckoning (IRE)**[106] 4732 4-9-0 98 (p) GeorgeBaker 11 83
(Jeremy Noseda) *dwlt: in rr: hdwy 3f out: wknd 1f out* **12/1**

0054 **10** ½ **Agent Allison**[35] 7020 3-8-10 95 TomQueally 4 82
(Peter Chapple-Hyam) *hld up in rr: hdwy over 3f out: wknd 1f out* **14/1**

1022 **11** ¾ **Astra Hall**[15] 7504 4-9-0 82 JimCrowley 14 81
(Ralph Beckett) *hld up in rr: effrt over 3f out: wknd over 1f out* **20/1**

6 **12** 1 ¼ **Lillebonne (FR)**[28] 7205 3-8-10 86 [1] GrahamGibbons 20 79
(David O'Meara) *stdd and swtchd lft s: hld up in rr: hdwy over 3f out: wknd 2f out* **33/1**

53 **13** hd **Making Eyes (IRE)**[45] 6742 5-9-3 100 MartinDwyer 13 82
(Hugo Palmer) *t.k.h in midfield: effrt over 3f out: wknd 2f out* **7/1**[2]

110 **14** 7 **Miss Dashwood**[44] 6764 4-9-0 92 FrederikTylicki 5 66
(James Fanshawe) *trckd ldrs: lost pl over 2f out* **20/1**

421U **15** 3 ¼ **Bonanza Creek (IRE)**[35] 7020 3-8-10 89 MartinHarley 9 60
(Luca Cumani) *trckd ldrs: lost pl over 2f out* **16/1**

1405 **16** 2 ¼ **Contradict**[112] 4541 3-8-10 85 TomEaves 1 56
(Mick Channon) *t.k.h in rr: nvr on terms* **100/1**

-255 **17** 17 **Prussian**[134] 3775 4-9-0 102 SilvestreDeSousa 10 25
(Charlie Appleby) *trckd ldrs: brought wd 4f out: drvn and lost pl 3f out: eased whn bhd ins fnl f* **8/1**[3]

2m 19.43s (10.03) **Going Correction** +0.975s/f (Soft)
WFA 3 from 4yo+ 4lb **17 Ran SP% 129.2**
Speed ratings (Par 108): **98,96,96,95,94 92,92,92,89,88 88,87,87,81,78 77,63**
toteswingers 1&2 £34.30, 2&3 £4.70, 1&3 £40.20 CSF £133.55 TOTE £49.30: £12.10, £2.20, £2.10; EX 286.50 Trifecta £2199.10 Pool: £52805.21 - 18.00 winning units..
Owner J L C Pearce **Bred** J L C Pearce **Trained** Kingsclere, Hants
■ Stewards' Enquiry : William Buick one-day ban: careless riding (Nov 23)

FOCUS
This was run at just a steady gallop, given the conditions, and the form is unreliable. They split into two groups down the straight. It went to one of the older performers.

7823 BETFRED NOVEMBER H'CAP 1m 4f
3:35 (3:36) (Class 2) 3-Y-O+
£40,462 (£12,116; £6,058; £3,029; £1,514; £760) Stalls Low

Form RPR
2-53 **1** **Conduct (IRE)**[58] 6332 6-9-2 **96** SebSanders 21 111
(William Haggas) *in tch on outer: smooth hdwy 4f out: trckd ldrs 3f out: rdn to ld over 1f out: and sn edgd lft: clr ent fnl f: styd on strly* **8/1**[2]

4200 **2** 5 **Rio's Rosanna (IRE)**[14] 7526 6-8-0 **85** ConnorBeasley[(5)] 18 92
(Richard Whitaker) *hld up: stdy hdwy 5f out: chsd ldrs over 3f out: rdn to ld briefly 2f out: sn hdd and drvn: kpt on u.p fnl f* **33/1**

1 **3** 2 ½ **Open Eagle (IRE)**[46] 6729 4-9-1 **95** DanielTudhope 9 98
(David O'Meara) *a.p: cl up 4f out: led 3f out and sn rdn: hdd 2f out: cl up and ev ch tl drvn appr fnl f and kpt on same pce* **20/1**

1113 **4** 2 ¾ **Bohemian Rhapsody (IRE)**[78] 5719 4-8-8 **88** MartinHarley 8 87
(Seamus Durack) *hld up in midfield: hdwy over 4f out: chsd ldrs 3f out: rdn 2f out and sn no imp* **25/1**

3004 **5** 1 ½ **Communicator**[84] 5513 5-8-11 **91** DavidProbert 17 88
(Andrew Balding) *hld up in rr: hdwy 5f out: effrt to chse ldrs 3f out: rdn over 2f out: kpt on fnl f: nrst fin* **16/1**

023- **6** 5 **Swnymor (IRE)**[28] 7175 4-8-5 **85** JohnFahy 5 74
(Rebecca Curtis) *hld up in rr: hdwy wl over 3f out: swtchd rt and rdn over 2f out: kpt on u.p fnl 2f: nt rch ldrs* **20/1**

5026 **7** ½ **Nicholascopernicus (IRE)**[14] 7526 4-8-13 **93** AndreaAtzeni 23 82
(Ed Walker) *hld up: rdn along and sme hdwy wl over 2f out: nvr a factor* **10/1**

0063 **8** 2 ¼ **Awake My Soul (IRE)**[24] 7312 4-9-0 **94** GrahamGibbons 20 79
(David O'Meara) *sn led: clr after 3f: rdn along 4f out: hdd 3f out and grad wknd fr over 2f out* **33/1**

0001 **9** 2 ½ **Twelve Strings (IRE)**[10] 7635 4-8-4 **84** ChrisHayes 13 66
(Brian Ellison) *hld up in rr: sme hdwy fnl 3f: nvr a factor* **20/1**

0311 **10** ¾ **Hi There (IRE)**[14] 7536 4-8-13 **98** SamanthaBell[(5)] 10 78
(Richard Fahey) *midfield: hdwy over 4f out: chsd ldrs over 3 out: sn rdn and grad wknd* **14/1**

600 **11** 6 **Aiken**[21] 7363 5-9-10 **104** (b[1]) WilliamBuick 7 75
(John Gosden) *nvr bttr than midfield* **14/1**

5003 **12** 1 ½ **Kiama Bay (IRE)**[14] 7542 7-8-9 **89** TomEaves 1 58
(Richard Fahey) *prom: chsd clr ldr after 4f: rdn along 4f out: wknd over 3f out* **40/1**

5413 **13** 11 **Cashpoint**[14] 7536 8-8-0 **85** JoeyHaynes[(5)] 15 38
(Ian Williams) *trckd ldrs: hdwy over 4f out: rdn along over 3f out: sn drvn and wknd* **40/1**

4-00 **14** ¾ **Ex Oriente (IRE)**[19] 7431 4-8-2 **82** NickyMackay 22 34
(Stuart Williams) *dwlt: a towards rr* **100/1**

3303 **15** ½ **Highland Castle**[14] 7526 5-9-1 **95** TomQueally 16 46
(David Elsworth) *a towards rr* **16/1**

0031 **16** ¾ **Border Legend**[31] 7131 4-8-9 **89** GrahamLee 14 39
(Roger Charlton) *a towards rr* **12/1**

0200 **17** 5 **Cousin Khee**[28] 7193 6-8-5 **85** MartinLane 4 27
(Hughie Morrison) *midfield: hdwy on inner to chse ldrs 4f out: rdn along over 3f out: sn wknd* **50/1**

2410 **18** 4 ½ **Rhombus (IRE)**[33] 7072 3-8-4 **90** SilvestreDeSousa 12 25
(Ismail Mohammed) *towards rr: rdn along 5f out: nvr a factor* **13/2**[1]

0461 **19** 5 **Forgotten Hero (IRE)**[56] 6394 4-8-12 **92** JimCrowley 6 20
(Charles Hills) *a towards rr* **16/1**

0600 **20** 4 ½ **Itlaaq**[14] 7526 7-8-5 **85** (t) JamesSullivan 3 6
(Michael Easterby) *chsd ldrs: rdn along over 4f out: sn wknd* **100/1**

2551 **21** 25 **Lahaag**[29] 7174 4-9-7 **101** PaulHanagan 2
(John Gosden) *trckd ldrs: hdwy 4f out: rdn along 3f out: sn wknd* **9/1**[3]

3116 **22** 27 **Nearly Caught (IRE)**[35] 7046 3-9-2 **102** RichardHughes 11
(Hughie Morrison) *chsd ldrs: reminders after 4f: rdn along 1/2-way: wknd over 4f out: bhd and eased fnl 2f* **12/1**

3604 **23** 51 **Shrewd**[53] 6503 3-8-4 **90** LukeMorris 19
(Michael Bell) *towards rr: rdn along 1/2-way: sn wknd and bhd whn eased fnl 3f* **14/1**

2m 44.95s (10.05) **Going Correction** +1.10s/f (Soft)
WFA 3 from 4yo+ 6lb **23 Ran SP% 129.4**
Speed ratings (Par 109): **110,106,105,103,102 98,98,97,95,94 90,89,82,82,81 81,77,74,71,68 51,33,**
toteswingers 1&2 £139.00, 1&3 £139.00, 2&3 not won CSF £265.22 CT £5082.02 TOTE £7.60: £2.70, £10.10, £5.90, £5.20; EX 509.90 Trifecta £5091.20 Part won. Pool: £6788.37 - 0.10 winning units..
Owner Highclere T'bred Racing Royal Palace **Bred** The Lavington Stud **Trained** Newmarket, Suffolk

FOCUS
An open if not especially classy edition of this historic handicap, which proved a real stamina test in the deteriorating ground. Plenty of these can be forgiven for not handling the conditions. The runners came up the centre in the home straight.

7824 BETFRED HAT TRICK HEAVEN APPRENTICE H'CAP (FINAL ROUND GO RACING IN YORKSHIRE APPRENTICE SERIES) 7f
4:05 (4:09) (Class 5) (0-75,77) 3-Y-O+ £2,911 (£866; £432; £216) Stalls High

Form RPR
116 **1** **Four Winds**[7] 7699 7-9-5 **72** (v) RossAtkinson 16 88
(Tom Dascombe) *w ldr: hung bdly lft over 1f out: led 1f out: forged clr: eased nr fin* **5/1**[2]

1260 **2** 4 ½ **Maggie Pink**[11] 7595 4-8-13 **69** JoeyHaynes[(3)] 12 73
(Michael Appleby) *w ldrs: led over 3f out: hdd appr fnl f: kpt on same pce* **25/1**

0412 **3** nk **Raging Bear (USA)**[53] 6489 3-9-2 **73** RyanTate[(3)] 3 76
(James Evans) *s.i.s: detached in last: gd hdwy over 1f out: styd on wl to take 3rd nr line* **33/1**

0231 **4** ¾ **Royal Holiday (IRE)**[25] 7283 6-9-0 **70** (p) NathanAlison[(3)] 1 72
(Marjorie Fife) *led: hdd over 3f out: kpt on same pce appr fnl f* **10/1**

2000 **5** 1 1/2 **Kiwi Bay**[35] 7024 8-9-4 **74**.........................(p) ConnorBeasley(3) 15 72
(Michael Dods) *mid-div: hdwy to chse ldrs over 3f out: one pce over 1f out* **18/1**
4220 **6** 1/2 **Khelman (IRE)**[11] 7594 3-9-1 **72**......................... GeorgeChaloner(3) 9 67
(Richard Fahey) *mid-div: hdwy over 3f out: one pce over 1f out* **14/1**
04 **7** 5 **Orbit The Moon (IRE)**[78] 5711 5-9-1 **73**.................(bt[1]) KevinStott(5) 18 56
(Michael Dods) *chsd ldrs 2nd 3f out: wknd fnl 100yds* **33/1**
5500 **8** 1 **Steel Stockholder**[71] 5974 7-8-12 **72**.................. RobertDodsworth(7) 14 53
(Mel Brittain) *mid-div: effrt over 2f out: one pce* **28/1**
3034 **9** 3/4 **Prime Exhibit**[10] 7629 8-9-0 **70**.........................(t) PhilipPrince(3) 20 49
(John Stimpson) *in rr: kpt on fnl 2f: nvr a factor* **16/1**
0621 **10** 1 1/2 **Piceno (IRE)**[7] 7699 5-9-5 **77**.........................(p) TimClark(5) 8 52
(Scott Dixon) *dwlt: in rr: sme hdwy 2f out: nvr on terms* **8/1**[3]
4104 **11** 1 **Celtic Sixpence (IRE)**[16] 7486 5-9-3 **75**.................(p) AdamMcLean(5) 4 47
(Nick Kent) *chsd ldrs: lost pl over 1f out* **40/1**
0402 **12** 1 1/2 **Pashan Garh**[7] 7699 4-8-11 **71**......................... CameronHardie(7) 5 39
(Pat Eddery) *s.i.s: in rr: sme hdwy over 2f out: nvr a factor* **14/1**
3514 **13** 2 1/4 **Beckermet (IRE)**[11] 7595 11-9-5 **72**......................... JasonHart 6 35
(Ruth Carr) *trckd ldrs: effrt over 2f out: sn wknd* **14/1**
1205 **14** 1/2 **Strong Man**[51] 6548 5-9-2 **72**.........................(b) ShirleyTeasdale(3) 10 33
(Michael Easterby) *chsd ldrs: wknd 2f out* **33/1**
041 **15** 3/4 **Falcon's Reign (FR)**[8] 7661 4-9-1 **73**......................... DanielMuscutt(5) 2 32
(Michael Appleby) *mid-div: drvn to chse ldrs over 3f out: wknd over 2f out* **7/2**[1]
6462 **16** 3 1/4 **Ted's Brother (IRE)**[11] 7608 5-8-11 **69**.................(e) LukeLeadbitter(5) 17 20
(Richard Guest) *mid-div: sme hdwy over 2f out: sn wknd* **10/1**
6040 **17** nk **Kung Hei Fat Choy (USA)**[11] 7608 4-9-3 **73**.............(b) DavidBergin(3) 7 23
(James Given) *mid-div: drvn over 2f out: sn lost pl* **25/1**
0/00 **18** 9 **Printmaker (IRE)**[15] 7499 5-8-12 **72**.................. RachelRichardson(7) 21
(Tim Easterby) *a in rr: bhd fnl 2f* **66/1**
0000 **19** 2 3/4 **Day Of The Eagle (IRE)**[10] 7632 7-8-10 **70**.................. JoshQuinn(7) 19
(Michael Easterby) *s.i.s: in rr: bhd fnl 3f* **40/1**
0020 **20** 14 **Majestic Dream (IRE)**[11] 7595 5-9-6 **73**......................... RobertTart 13
(Michael Easterby) *in rr: bhd fnl 3f: eased fnl f* **33/1**
2041 **21** dist **Bountybeamadam**[58] 6319 3-9-4 **72**.........................(p) ThomasBrown 11
(George Baker) *chsd ldrs: lost pl 4f out: sn bhd and heavily eased: t.o 2f out: virtually p.u* **33/1**

1m 34.81s (8.51) **Going Correction** +1.225s/f (Soft)
WFA 3 from 4yo+ 1lb **21** Ran SP% **131.5**
Speed ratings (Par 103): **100,94,94,93,91 91,85,84,83,81 80,79,76,75,75 71,71,60,57,41**
toteswingers 1&2 £28.90, 1&3 £63.20, 2&3 £63.20 CSF £61.30 CT £3885.43 TOTE £6.70: £2.70, £4.90, £3.50, £2.50; EX 216.90 Trifecta £2550.10 Part won. Pool: £3400.14 - 0.42 winning units..
Owner T Dascombe **Bred** The Queen **Trained** Malpas, Cheshire
■ Stewards' Enquiry : Nathan Alison two-day ban: careless riding (Nov 23,25); seven-day ban: used whip above permitted level (Nov 26-30, Dec 2-3)

FOCUS
The runners were spread centre-to-stands' side in this modest handicap.
T/Jkpt: Not won. T/Plt: £32.20 to a £1 stake. Pool of £157,866.46 - 3577.36 winning units T/Qpdt: £21.30 to a £1 stake. Pool of £12,397.88 - 429.70 winning units JR

7825 - (Foreign Racing) - See Raceform Interactive

7760 FLEMINGTON (L-H)
Saturday, November 9

OFFICIAL GOING: Turf: good

7826a EMIRATES STKS (GROUP 1 QUALITY H'CAP) (3YO+) (TURF) 1m
4:45 (12:00) 3-Y-0+
£387,820 (£115,384; £57,692; £28,846; £16,025; £12,820)

RPR
1 **Boban (AUS)**[21] 4-9-0 **0**.........................(t) GlynSchofield 3 115
(Chris Waller, Australia) **18/5**[1]
2 hd **Smokin' Joey (AUS)**[7] 6-8-4 **0**.........................(tp) JasonBenbow 6 105
(Wez Hunter, Australia) **20/1**
3 shd **Speediness (AUS)**[14] 6-8-9 **0**.........................(b) CraigAWilliams 1 110
(Colin Scott, Australia) **8/1**
4 nk **Mull Of Killough (IRE)**[4] 7762 7-8-11 **0**......................... DamienOliver 11 111
(Jane Chapple-Hyam) *trckd ldr: rdn to chal and w ldr 2f out: r.o wl but hdd ins fnl f and dropped to 4th cl home* **17/1**
5 hd **Sacred Falls (NZ)**[14] 4-8-13 **0**.........................(b) GlenBoss 5 113
(Chris Waller, Australia) **13/2**[3]
6 nk **Toydini (AUS)**[14] 4-8-13 **0**......................... BlakeShinn 10 112
(Guy Walter, Australia) **8/1**
7 3/4 **Rhythm To Spare (NZ)**[154] 3130 4-8-3 **0**.................(b) KerrinMcEvoy 7 100
(Michael Moroney, Australia) **14/1**
8 hd **Strike The Stars (NZ)**[7] 5-8-3 **0**......................... ChadSchofield 12 100
(Anthony Cummings, Australia) **17/1**
9 hd **Spurtonic (AUS)**[21] 4-8-4 **0**.........................(b) TommyBerry 9 100
(Gai Waterhouse, Australia) **6/1**[2]
10 nk **Nashville (NZ)**[35] 5-8-10 **0**.........................(b[1]) StevenArnold 13 106
(Adrian Bull, New Zealand) **30/1**
11 1 1/4 **Blackie (NZ)**[14] 6-8-4 **0**.........................(t) ChrisSymons 2 97
(Jarrod McLean, Australia) **20/1**
12 1/2 **Stipulate**[77] 5739 4-8-5 **0**......................... DwayneDunn 8 97
(David Hayes, Australia) **25/1**
13 15 **Solzhenitsyn (NZ)**[7] 7702 7-9-2 **0**.........................(bt) NashRawiller 4 73
(Robert Heathcote, Australia) **16/1**

1m 36.58s (96.58)
WFA 3 from 4yo+ 2lb **13** Ran SP% **111.8**
PARI-MUTUEL (NSW TAB - all including 1 aud stake): WIN 3.50; PLACE 1.90, 5.30, 2.60; DF 59.70; SF 104.10.
Owner J A O'Neill, M Pejic Et Al **Bred** A B Thomas, R R Thomas **Trained** Australia

7827a QUEEN ELIZABETH STKS (GROUP 3 QUALITY H'CAP) (3YO+) (TURF) 1m 5f
5:30 (5:30) 3-Y-0+
£116,346 (£34,615; £17,307; £8,653; £4,807; £3,846)

RPR
1 **Precedence (NZ)**[14] 7555 8-9-2 **0**.........................(t) CraigAWilliams 8 110
(Bart & James Cummings, Australia) **11/2**[2]
2 shd **Sertorius (AUS)**[27] 6-8-10 **0**......................... RyanMaloney 5 104
(Jamie Edwards & Bruce Elkington, Australia) **16/5**[1]
3 2 1/4 **Let's Make Adeal (AUS)**[7] 7700 4-8-9 **0**......................... ChadSchofield 2 101+
(Nigel Blackiston, Australia) **7/1**[3]
4 nk **Forgotten Voice (IRE)**[17] 7483 8-9-0 **0**......................... BrettPrebble 12 104
(Nicky Henderson) *prom: trckd ldr after 3f: w ldrs and ev ch whn rdn 2f out: styd on but outpcd by front pair fr over 1f out: dropped to 4th cl home* **17/2**
5 2 **Ironstein (AUS)**[7] 7700 8-8-8 **0**......................... KerrinMcEvoy 4 95
(Gerald Ryan, Australia) **18/1**
6 shd **Garud (IRE)**[7] 7700 5-8-8 **0**.........................(b) DamienOliver 1 95
(Michael Moroney, Australia) **12/1**
7 hd **Moudre (AUS)**[7] 7700 8-8-9 **0**.........................(b) MichellePayne 13 96
(Ciaron Maher, Australia) **30/1**
8 3/4 **La Amistad (AUS)** 4-8-8 **0**......................... DwayneDunn 6 95
(Michael, Wayne & John Hawkes, Australia) **10/1**
9 1 1/4 **Kelinni (IRE)**[7] 7700 5-9-2 **0**.........................(tp) NashRawiller 9 100
(Chris Waller, Australia) **13/1**
10 hd **Verdant**[17] 7483 6-8-8 **0**.........................(tp) BenMelham 7 91
(Robert Smerdon, Australia) **30/1**
11 2 1/4 **Mourinho (AUS)**[14] 7555 6-8-9 **0** ow1.........................(b) HughBowman 10 89
(Peter Gelagotis, Australia) **17/1**
12 2 1/4 **Angola (AUS)**[24] 7417 5-8-8 **0**.........................(tp) JamesWinks 3 85
(Pat Carey, Australia) **25/1**
13 2 1/2 **Rothera (AUS)**[140] 8-8-9 **0** ow1.........................(t) JamesMcDonald 11 82
(Brian Smith, Australia) **19/1**

2m 46.45s (166.45) **13** Ran SP% **112.3**
PARI-MUTUEL (NSW TAB - all including 1 aud stake): WIN 4.70; PLACE 2.10, 1.80, 2.60; DF 9.70; SF 22.60.
Owner Dato Tan Chin Nam, Sir Patrick Hogan et al **Bred** Bloomsbury Stud & Sir Patrick & Lady Hogan **Trained** Australia

7685 SAINT-CLOUD (L-H)
Saturday, November 9

OFFICIAL GOING: Turf: heavy

7828a CRITERIUM DE SAINT-CLOUD (GROUP 1) (2YO COLTS & FILLIES) (TURF) 1m 2f
12:30 (12:00) 2-Y-0 **£116,138** (£46,463; £23,231; £11,605; £5,813)

RPR
1 **Prince Gibraltar (FR)**[44] 2-9-0 0......................... ChristopheSoumillon 5 114
(J-C Rouget, France) *hld up in rr: last 1/2-way: c across and racd alone against nr side' rail in st: rdn and hdwy fr over 2f out: styd on strly and led ins fnl f: forged clr towards fin: v readily* **33/10**[2]
2 5 **Bereni Ka (FR)**[17] 7571 2-8-10 0......................... TonyPiccone 1 101
(Y Gourraud, France) *stdd and hld up towards rr on inner: rdn and hdwy over 2f out: styd on wl and wnt 2nd ins fnl f: 1st in gp but wl hld by wnr who racd alone nr side* **21/1**
3 1 3/4 **Hartnell**[7] 7694 2-9-0 0......................... JoeFanning 3 102
(Mark Johnston) *sn trcking ldr on inner: rdn to ld over 2f out: styd on but hdd ins fnl f and sn dropped to 3rd: no ex* **73/10**
4 5 **Mekong River (IRE)**[6] 7720 2-9-0 0.........................(b) SeamieHeffernan 11 93
(A P O'Brien, Ire) *worked across fr wd draw and sn led: rdn and hdd over 2f out: kpt on same pce and hld in 4th fr over 1f out* **2/1**[1]
5 2 **King Rubi**[14] 7589 2-9-0 0......................... AntoineHamelin 2 89
(Matthieu Palussiere, France) *midfield on inner: rdn over 2f out: sn outpcd by ldrs: plugged on for wl hld 5th* **58/1**
6 2 **Laugharne**[27] 7219 2-9-0 0......................... MaximeGuyon 10 86
(Roger Charlton) *dwlt sltly but qckly rcvrd: midfield in tch: pushed along over 3f out: rdn over 2f out: sn outpcd by ldrs: plugged on for wl hld 6th* **23/1**
7 2 1/2 **Bal De France (FR)**[25] 2-9-0 0......................... GregoryBenoist 9 81
(S Kobayashi, France) *prom: rdn over 2f out: outpcd by ldrs over 1f out: plugged on but nvr threatened* **42/1**
8 4 **Dylan Boy (IRE)**[30] 7160 2-9-0 0......................... OlivierPeslier 7 74
(E Lellouche, France) *hld up in midfield: rdn over 2f out: outpcd and btn over 1f out: eased ins fnl f: n.d* **15/1**
9 4 1/2 **Free Port Lux**[24] 2-9-0 0......................... ThierryJarnet 6 66
(F Head, France) *hld up towards rr: rdn over 2f out: outpcd and btn over 1f out: eased ins fnl f: nvr a factor* **5/1**[3]
10 4 **Surspenders (FR)**[20] 2-9-0 0......................... TheoBachelot 4 59
(S Wattel, France) *hld up: in rr and rdn over 2f out: btn and eased ent fnl f: nvr a factor* **34/1**
11 3/4 **Shankly**[65] 6139 2-9-0 0......................... JamieSpencer 12 57
(Clive Cox) *hld up in midfield: sme hdwy on outer 3f out: rdn over 2f out: sn no ex and btn: fdd and dropped to rr: eased ent fnl f* **23/1**
12 6 **Rapido (GER)**[34] 2-9-0 0......................... FabienLefebvre 8 47
(Andreas Lowe, Germany) *sn trcking ldr on outer: rdn and brief effrt to chal 3f out: no ex and wknd qckly over 2f out: dropped to last and eased over 1f out* **16/1**

2m 26.25s (10.25) **12** Ran SP% **117.2**
WIN (incl. 1 euro stake): 4.30. PLACES: 2.00, 4.50, 2.80. DF: 48.60. SF: 71.80.
Owner Jean-Francois Gribomont **Bred** J-F Gribomont **Trained** Pau, France

FOCUS
A race with a mixed record at producing high class performers, it was again run on testing ground. An average renewal.

7724 CAPANNELLE (R-H)
Sunday, November 10

OFFICIAL GOING: Turf: heavy

7830a PREMIO CARLO E FRANCESCO ALOISI (GROUP 3) (2YO+) (TURF) 6f
3:10 (12:00) 2-Y-0+ **£22,764** (£10,016; £5,463; £2,731)

RPR
1 **Rosendhal (IRE)**[25] 6-9-4 0......................... SSulas 5 107
(G Botti, France) *trckd ldng gp: shkn up 2f out: qcknd to ld 1 1/2f: r.o wl u.p: drvn out fnl f* **97/20**[3]
2 2 **Elettrotreno (IRE)**[21] 7416 3-9-4 0......................... DarioVargiu 7 101
(A Giorgi, Italy) *pressed ldr: led over 2f out: hdd 1 1/2f out: r.o u.p fnl f: a hld by wnr* **19/2**

3 2 1/2 **Pride And Joy (IRE)**[154] 4-9-4 0 .... DPerovic 11 93
(Riccardo Santini, Italy) *towards rr: gd hdwy over 2f out: chsd ldrs fr 1 1/2f out: kpt on u.p fnl f: readily outpcd by first two* **213/10**

4 1 1/2 **Traditional Chic (IRE)**[154] 5-9-4 0 .... AndreaMezzatesta 2 88
(L Riccardi, Italy) *in rr: hdwy on wd outside over 2f out: 3rd and hrd rdn over 1f out: one pce u.p fnl f* **9/5[2]**

5 2 **Noble Hachy**[210] 1563 4-9-1 0 .... FabioBranca 3 79
(L Riccardi, Italy) *hld up towards rr: gd hdwy over 2 1/2f out: chsd ldrs fr 1 1/2f out: one pce fnl f* **9/5[2]**

6 2 **Chiara Wells (IRE)**[35] 4-9-1 0 .... SBasile 12 72
(A Floris, Italy) *prom on outer: rdn and nt qckn over 1 1/2f out: grad fdd fr over 1f out* **34/1**

7 hd **Bettolle (ITY)**[35] 4-9-5 0 .... GVirdis 6 76
(Jessica Lari, Italy) *towards rr: rdn and outpcd over 2f out: styd on u.p fnl f: nvr on terms* **124/10**

8 1 **Nuracale** 3-9-4 0 .... LManiezzi 9 72
(Marco Gasparini, Italy) *chsd ldrs: rdn and wknd fr over 1 1/2f out* **38/1**

9 nk **Omaticaya (IRE)**[14] 2-7-13 0 .... CristianDemuro 8 66
(Manila Illuminati, Italy) *chsd ldrs: w ldr 2f out: sn rdn and nt qckn: wknd ins fnl 1 1/2f* **23/20[1]**

10 1 **Onlyyouknowme (IRE)**[154] 5-9-1 0 .... MSanna 10 64
(E Botti, Italy) *midfield: rdn and outpcd over 2f out: sn fdd* **105/10**

11 4 **Guagliona**[21] 7416 4-9-1 0 .... CFiocchi 4 52
(Patrizia Giorgi, Italy) *a towards rr: rdn and btn over 1 1/2f out* **192/10**

12 6 **Guinnes Will (IRE)**[476] 3-9-4 0 .... MEsposito 1 35
(Agostino Affe', Italy) *led on rail: hdd over 2f out: sn wknd: eased fnl f* **61/1**

1m 9.62s (-0.68) **12 Ran SP% 177.2**
WIN (incl. 1 euro stake): 5.85. PLACES: 2.91, 3.69, 5.91. DF: 58.55.
Owner Allevamento Pian Di Neve SRL **Bred** Allevamento Pian Di Neve Srl **Trained** France

1867 FRANKFURT (L-H)
Sunday, November 10

OFFICIAL GOING: Turf: soft

7831a HESSEN-POKAL (GROUP 3) (3YO+) (TURF) 1m 2f
2:30 (12:00) 3-Y-O+
£26,016 (£8,943; £4,471; £2,439; £1,626; £1,219)

RPR

1 **Adriana (GER)**[14] 7558 5-8-11 0 .... LennartHammer-Hansen 4 109
(M Rulec, Germany) *mde all: set decent gallop: drvn clr fnl f: a in command* **152/10**

2 4 **Petit Chevalier (FR)**[36] 7049 5-9-3 0 .... AStarke 2 107
(W Mongil, Germany) *settled in fnl trio: hdwy on inner over 2 1/2f out: cl 3rd and ev ch 2f out: sn rdn and nt qckn: styd on at one pce u.p fnl f: tk 2nd cl home: wl hld by wnr* **6/5[1]**

3 nk **Polish Vulcano (GER)**[38] 6987 5-9-3 0 .... WPanov 5 106
(H J Groschel, Germany) *in rr but in tch: hdwy 2f out: hrd rdn and styd on ins fnl f: tk 3rd cl home: nvr on terms* **19/2**

4 nk **Zazou (GER)**[35] 7053 6-9-3 0 .... APietsch 1 106
(W Hickst, Germany) *t.k.h early: trckd ldng pair on inner: shkn up to chse ldr 2f out: rdn and no imp over 1f out: one pce u.p fnl f: lost two pls cl home* **19/10[2]**

5 5 **Swordhalf**[8] 3-8-6 0 .... JBojko 3 89
(A Wohler, Germany) *trckd ldng pair on outer: dropped towards rr 3f out: kpt on u.p fnl f to go 5th cl home but nvr trbld ldrs* **107/10**

6 1/2 **Belango (GER)**[21] 7-9-1 0 .... SHellyn 7 93
(R Dzubasz, Germany) *midfield: chsd ldrs 3f out: sn rdn and lft bhd by ldrs: plugged on at one pce fnl 1 1/2f* **96/10**

7 3/4 **Windsor (GER)**[84] 5576 3-8-9 0 .... AHelfenbein 6 89
(Markus Klug, Germany) *t.k.h: trckd ldr: rdn and outpcd over 2f out: wknd fnl f* **31/5[3]**

8 28 **Ostinato (GER)**[38] 6987 5-9-1 0 ....(b) EPedroza 8 35
(Sandor Kovacs, Hungary) *towards rr: lost tch over 2f out: nvr figured* **131/10**

2m 20.8s (12.23) **8 Ran SP% 134.6**
WFA 3 from 5yo+ 4lb
WIN (incl. 10 euro stake): 162. PLACES: 26, 14, 26. SF: 337.
Owner August Fockler **Bred** Gestut Sommerberg **Trained** Germany

7763 KEMPTON (A.W) (R-H)
Monday, November 11

OFFICIAL GOING: Standard
Wind: virtually nil Weather: light rain

7834 BRITISH STALLION STUDS EBF MAIDEN STKS (DIV I) 1m (P)
2:15 (2:18) (Class 5) 2-Y-O **£2,911** (£866; £432; £216) **Stalls Low**

Form RPR

6 1 **Warrior Of Light (IRE)**[19] 7460 2-9-5 0 .... TedDurcan 6 77+
(David Lanigan) *chsd ldrs: rdn and effrt in centre 2f out: str run to ld over 1f out: gng clr whn edgd rt ins fnl f: r.o wl* **9/2[2]**

0 2 1 **Rapid Advance**[27] 7271 2-9-5 0 .... TomQueally 13 75+
(Roger Varian) *hld up in tch in midfield: rdn over 3f out: rn green and stl midfield whn swtchd lft over 1f out: str run ins fnl f: to go 2nd fnl 50yds: clsng on wnr at fin* **50/1**

4 3 1 1/4 **Canova (IRE)**[17] 7500 2-9-5 0 .... FrederikTylicki 3 72
(Roger Charlton) *bustled along early: wl in tch in midfield: swtchd ins and effrt to press ldrs 2f out: chsd clr wnr fnl 100yds: kpt on same pce and lost 2nd fnl 50yds* **8/1[3]**

4 4 shd **Belrog**[40] 6953 2-9-5 0 .... JamieSpencer 1 72
(Ralph Beckett) *chsd ldrs: rdn and ev ch wl over 1f out: unable qck w wnr ent fnl f: one pce after* **9/4[1]**

55 5 1 **Mountain Lion (IRE)**[37] 7019 2-9-5 0 ....(p) SilvestreDeSousa 5 70
(Saeed bin Suroor) *chsd ldrs: rdn and everty ch wl over 1f out: outpcd by wnr ent fnl f: lost 2nd fnl 100yds and wknd fnl 50yds* **9/4[1]**

6 3/4 **Rydan (IRE)** 2-9-5 0 .... KierenFox 4 68
(Robert Mills) *chsd ldrs: rdn over 3f out: kpt on and stl chsng ldrs whn swtchd rt over 1f out: one pce ins fnl f* **33/1**

7 2 1/2 **Hooded (USA)** 2-9-5 0 .... SteveDrowne 11 62
(Roger Charlton) *dwlt: sn pushed along in last quartet: rdn and no imp over 2f out: hdwy 1f out: kpt on steadily ins fnl f: nvr trbld ldrs* **20/1**

8 3/4 **Forever Now** 2-9-5 0 .... WilliamBuick 10 61
(John Gosden) *dwlt: sn niggled along in last trio: rdn and no imp over 2f out: hdwy 1f out: styd on: nvr trbld ldrs* **14/1**

9 nk **Classic Devotion (USA)** 2-9-5 0 .... AdamKirby 14 60
(Charlie Appleby) *s.i.s: racd in last trio: rdn over 2f out: hdwy ent fnl f: styd on: nvr trbld ldrs* **8/1[3]**

10 shd **Captain Morley** 2-9-5 0 .... MartinLane 12 60
(David Simcock) *v.s.a: racd in rr: rdn over 2f out: hdwy ent fnl f: styd on but nvr trbld ldrs* **50/1**

0 11 1 1/4 **Chinotto (IRE)**[46] 6762 2-9-5 0 .... DavidProbert 9 57
(Andrew Balding) *led: rdn ent fnl 2f: hdd over 1f out: sn btn and wknd fnl f* **25/1**

6 12 3 1/4 **Artistic Flame**[20] 7442 2-9-5 0 ....(b) RobertHavlin 2 49
(Amanda Perrett) *rdn along leaving stalls: settled in tch in midfield after 2f out: rdn and effrt ent fnl 2f: no ex and wknd 1f out* **33/1**

1m 39.88s (0.08) **Going Correction** -0.05s/f (Stan) **12 Ran SP% 127.0**
Speed ratings (Par 96): **97,96,94,94,93 92,90,89,89,89 88,84**
toteswingers 1&2 £25.10, 1&3 £8.10, 2&3 £40.10 CSF £233.08 TOTE £6.10: £1.90, £9.50, £2.40; EX 285.80 Trifecta £2498.70 Part won. Pool: £3331.67 - 0.19 winning units..
Owner Niarchos Family **Bred** Peter Anastasiou **Trained** Upper Lambourn, Berks

FOCUS
There were probably some fair long-term prospects among this lot. The pace was just modest and the field finished compressed. The third to fifth help with the opening level of the form.

7835 BRITISH STALLION STUDS EBF MAIDEN STKS (DIV II) 1m (P)
2:50 (2:52) (Class 5) 2-Y-O **£2,911** (£866; £432; £216) **Stalls Low**

Form RPR

1 **Elite Army** 2-9-5 0 .... SilvestreDeSousa 5 83+
(Saeed bin Suroor) *t.k.h: chsd ldrs tl wnt 2nd 6f out: rdn and ev ch wl over 1f out: led ins fnl f: styd on wl and gng away at fin* **5/1[3]**

263 2 1 1/4 **Intermedium**[74] 5924 2-9-5 84 .... AdamKirby 12 80
(Charlie Appleby) *chsd ldr tl led after 2f out: rdn ent fnl 2f: hrd pressed wl over 1f out: hdd ins fnl f: no ex and one pce after* **7/2[2]**

3 2 1/4 **Arod (IRE)** 2-9-5 0 .... JamieSpencer 7 75
(Peter Chapple-Hyam) *chsd ldrs: 3rd and effrt ent fnl 2f: kpt on same pce and no imp fnl f* **7/4[1]**

42 4 2 1/2 **Be Seeing You**[35] 7069 2-9-5 0 .... FrederikTylicki 14 69+
(Roger Charlton) *t.k.h: in tch in midfield: effrt but outpcd ent fnl 2f: no threat to ldrs and kpt on same pce after* **14/1**

6225 5 1/2 **Newmarket Warrior (IRE)**[24] 7332 2-9-5 80 ....(p) TomQueally 3 68
(Michael Bell) *t.k.h: chsd ldrs: effrt u.p ent fnl 2f: hung lft and no hdwy over 1f out: one pce and wl hld fnl f* **12/1**

0 6 1 1/2 **Cape Summit**[73] 5957 2-9-5 0 .... MartinHarley 11 64+
(Ed Dunlop) *in tch in midfield: rdn and no imp over 2f out: one pce and no threat to ldrs fr over 1f out* **66/1**

7 1 **Mairise** 2-9-5 0 .... SebSanders 8 62+
(Sir Michael Stoute) *racd off the pce in midfield: rdn and effrt over 2f out: hdwy jst over 1f out: kpt on fnl f: nvr trbld ldrs* **25/1**

8 nk **Lil Rockerfeller (USA)** 2-9-5 0 .... SeanLevey 2 61
(Richard Hannon) *restless in stalls: s.i.s: sn pushed along and rcvrd to r in midfield: rdn and outpcd ent fnl 2f: wl hld and one pce fnl 2f* **25/1**

9 shd **Fractal** 2-9-5 0 .... MartinLane 6 61
(David Simcock) *s.i.s: racd off the pce in last quartet: sme hdwy past btn horses over 1f out: kpt on fnl f: nvr trbld ldrs* **33/1**

10 1 **Curbyourenthusiasm (IRE)** 2-9-5 0 .... FergusSweeney 1 59
(David Simcock) *s.i.s: sn pushed along and racd off the pce in last quartet: swtchd lft over 2f out: sme hdwy ent fnl f: styd on: nvr trbld ldrs* **66/1**

11 1 1/4 **Dumfries House** 2-9-5 0 .... SteveDrowne 13 56+
(Roger Charlton) *racd off the pce in midfield: rdn and no hdwy over 2f out: nvr trbld ldrs* **40/1**

12 9 **Wiggins (IRE)** 2-9-5 0 .... JimCrowley 9 35
(Ralph Beckett) *racd off the pce in last quartet: lost tch over 2f out: n.d* **20/1**

13 3/4 **Mr Smith** 2-9-5 0 .... WilliamBuick 10 34
(John Gosden) *s.i.s: sn rdn along and a bhd* **8/1**

50 14 12 **Bishop Wulstan (IRE)**[11] 7647 2-9-2 0 .... WilliamTwiston-Davies(3) 4 6
(Richard Hannon) *led tl over 6f out: lost pl wl over 2f out: bhd and eased ins fnl f: t.o* **66/1**

1m 39.41s (-0.39) **Going Correction** -0.05s/f (Stan) **14 Ran SP% 123.0**
Speed ratings (Par 96): **99,97,95,93,92 91,90,89,89,88 87,78,77,65**
toteswingers 1&2 £3.40, 1&3 £3.00, 2&3 £2.40 CSF £21.66 TOTE £7.10: £2.70, £1.50, £1.30; EX 24.10 Trifecta £96.20 Pool: £3293.34 - 25.67 winning units..
Owner Godolphin **Bred** Darley **Trained** Newmarket, Suffolk

FOCUS
A more even pace than in the first division and the overall time was quicker. Little got involved and the second seemed to run to his pre-race level.

7836 BETVICTOR'S NEW LIVE CASINO H'CAP 1m (P)
3:20 (3:20) (Class 5) (0-70,70) 3-Y-O+ **£2,587** (£770; £384; £192) **Stalls Low**

Form RPR

35-4 1 **Sugarformyhoney (IRE)**[287] 421 4-9-6 69 .... JackMitchell 10 79
(Brendan Powell) *chsd ldr: rdn to ld over 1f out and qcknd clr 1f out: in command and r.o wl fnl f: rdn out* **33/1**

0411 2 1 1/2 **Diplomatic (IRE)**[12] 7629 8-9-7 70 ....(p) AdamKirby 4 77+
(Michael Squance) *stdd after s: hld up in tch in rr: rdn and hdwy over 1f out: swtchd lft jst ins fnl f: r.o wl to go 2nd last strides* **9/4[1]**

0-00 3 nk **Galatian**[12] 7629 6-9-5 68 .... MartinDwyer 3 74
(Rod Millman) *t.k.h: hld up wl in tch in midfield: rdn and effrt ent fnl 2f: chsd wnr ins fnl f: kpt on but lost 2nd last strides* **33/1**

1420 4 1/2 **True Pleasure (IRE)**[24] 7344 6-9-4 67 .... TedDurcan 1 72
(James Bethell) *chsd ldrs: rdn and ev ch 2f out: outpcd by wnr over 1f out: styd on same pce and lost 2 pls ins fnl f* **25/1**

3662 5 hd **Wilfred Pickles (IRE)**[26] 7307 7-9-7 70 ....(p) JamieSpencer 7 75
(Jo Crowley) *hld up wl in tch in midfield: rdn and effrt 2f out: nt clr ent fnl f tl swtchd lft ins fnl f: kpt on but nvr able to chal* **5/1[3]**

5005 6 3 **Boom To Bust (IRE)**[16] 7544 5-9-4 67 ....(b) SebSanders 6 65
(Barry Brennan) *t.k.h: hld up wl in tch in midfield: rdn and effrt ent fnl 2f: no ex 1f out: wknd ins fnl f* **25/1**

4206 7 1/2 **Woolston Ferry (IRE)**[19] 7462 7-9-7 70 .... FergusSweeney 8 67
(Henry Candy) *stdd after s: hld up in tch in last quartet: rdn and effrt over 2f out: styd on ins fnl f: nvr trbld ldrs* **8/1**

2566 **8** ½ **Abigails Angel**[28] 7256 6-9-4 **70**... WilliamTwiston-Davies(3) 2 66
(Brett Johnson) *led and set stdy gallop: rdn ent fnl 2f: hdd and outpcd over 1f out: wknd ins fnl f* **14/1**

6030 **9** ¾ **Bold Ring**[26] 7297 7-8-11 **67**... JenniferFerguson(7) 9 61
(Edward Creighton) *in tch in midfield: rdn and unable qck ent fnl 2f: outpcd and btn over 1f out: wknd fnl f* **33/1**

6006 **10** 1¾ **Catch The Cider**[40] 6937 3-8-7 **63**...(t) JoeyHaynes(5) 12 53
(Hans Adielsson) *taken down early: in tch in midfield: rdn and no rspnse over 2f out: drvn and wknd 2f out* **7/2**[2]

130/ **11** ½ **Auden (USA)**[67] 6147 5-9-2 **65**... FrederikTylicki 5 54
(J R Jenkins) *stdd after s: hld up in tch in last quartet: rdn and no imp ent fnl 2f: nvr trbld ldrs* **10/1**

5350 **12** 1½ **Ivor's Princess**[21] 7429 4-8-13 **62**...(b) SeanLevey 13 47
(Rod Millman) *t.k.h: hld up in tch in rr: rdn and no hdwy over 2f out: n.d* **25/1**

6536 **13** 6 **Ogaritmo**[108] 4711 4-9-4 **67**...(p) MartinHarley 11 38
(Seamus Durack) *in tch in midfield: rdn and struggling ent fnl 2f: wknd and bhd ins fnl f* **33/1**

1m 40.13s (0.33) **Going Correction** -0.05s/f (Stan)
WFA 3 from 4yo+ 2lb **13** Ran SP% **119.8**
Speed ratings (Par 103): **96,94,94,93,93 90,90,89,88,87 86,85,79**
toteswingers 1&2 £17.20, 1&3 £97.90, 2&3 £15.40 CSF £101.70 CT £2635.66 TOTE £39.90: £6.90, £1.30, £7.50; EX 176.80 Trifecta £2060.30 Part won. Pool: £2747.19 - 0.29 winning units..
Owner W A Harrison-Allan **Bred** Mrs S M Roy **Trained** Upper Lambourn, Berks

FOCUS
They went steady in this modest handicap. The winner may get a bit closer to her 2yo level.

7837 DOWNLOAD THE BETVICTOR APP NURSERY H'CAP 6f (P)

3:50 (3:52) (Class 5) (0-70,70) 2-Y-O **£2,587** (£770; £384; £192) **Stalls** Low

Form RPR

3040 **1** **Souville**[33] 7119 2-9-5 **68**... SebSanders 4 77+
(Chris Wall) *in tch in midfield: swtchd lft and effrt wl over 1f out: drvn to ld 1f out: styd on wl and asserted fnl 75yds* **4/1**[1]

5144 **2** 1¾ **Pensax Lad (IRE)**[32] 7147 2-9-6 **69**... RobertWinston 10 71
(Ronald Harris) *hld up in tch in last quartet: swtchd lft and effrt ent fnl 2f: chal ent fnl f: drew clr w wnr ins fnl f: no ex and btn fnl 75yds* **10/1**

3510 **3** 2¼ **Alfie Lunete (IRE)**[49] 6695 2-9-5 **68**... LiamJones 6 63
(J S Moore) *in tch in midfield: hdwy u.p over 1f out: kpt on u.p to go 3rd last strides but no threat to ldng pair* **25/1**

0644 **4** hd **Iseemist (IRE)**[20] 7451 2-9-6 **69**... TomQueally 12 63
(John Gallagher) *hld up in tch in last quartet: hdwy u.p on inner 2f out: chsd ldng pair jst ins fnl f: no imp and lost 3rd last strides* **20/1**

341 **5** 3¼ **Kiss From A Rose**[46] 6776 2-9-2 **65**... ChrisCatlin 7 50
(Rae Guest) *chsd ldr: rdn and effrt ent fnl 2f: no ex and btn 1f out: wknd ins fnl f* **6/1**[2]

4323 **6** shd **Le Laitier (FR)**[78] 5787 2-9-4 **67**... FrederikTylicki 11 51
(Scott Dixon) *hld up in last trio: rdn and effrt on outer 2f out: styd on wl fnl f: nvr trbld ldrs* **14/1**

5561 **7** 1 **Tautira (IRE)**[30] 7198 2-9-4 **67**... JamieSpencer 2 48
(Michael Bell) *led: rdn and hrd pressed 2f out: hdd 1f out: wknd ins fnl f* **15/2**[3]

654 **8** 2½ **Rosita**[95] 5174 2-8-8 **60**...[1] MatthewLawson(3) 9 34
(Jonathan Portman) *s.i.s: hld up in tch in rr: effrt u.p over 2f out: no real imp: nvr trbld ldrs* **25/1**

41 **9** shd **Go For Broke**[73] 5950 2-9-6 **69**... TedDurcan 3 43
(Richard Hannon) *in tch in midfield: effrt ent fnl 2f: keeping on same pce whn n.m.r and hmpd jst over 1f out: no hdwy after and btn 1f out: wknd ins fnl f* **4/1**[1]

0430 **10** 2¼ **Kinloss**[26] 7296 2-9-7 **70**... SteveDrowne 1 37
(Richard Hannon) *pushed along leaving stalls: chsd ldrs: no ex u.p over 2f out: btn over 1f out and wknd fnl f* **20/1**

0050 **11** 2¼ **Sandsman's Girl (IRE)**[19] 7463 2-9-7 **70**... JimCrowley 5 30
(James Given) *in tch in midfield: rdn and hdwy over 2f out: lost pl over 1f out: wknd fnl f* **20/1**

5311 **12** nse **Gower Princess**[12] 7623 2-9-3 **66**... LukeMorris 8 26
(Ronald Harris) *wnt rt s: chsd ldrs but stuck wd: rdn and unable qck ent fnl 2f: wknd over 1f out* **6/1**[2]

1m 12.33s (-0.77) **Going Correction** -0.05s/f (Stan) **12** Ran SP% **118.1**
Speed ratings (Par 96): **103,100,97,97,93 92,91,88,88,85 82,82**
toteswingers 1&2 £9.40, 1&3 £22.30, 2&3 £41.00 CSF £40.65 CT £887.70 TOTE £3.90: £2.10, £3.10, £7.90; EX 41.90 Trifecta £1110.60 Pool: £3029.98 - 2.04 winning units..
Owner Hughes & Scott **Bred** Stowell Park Stud **Trained** Newmarket, Suffolk

FOCUS
Just an ordinary nursery. The runner-up is the best guide.

7838 BOOK CHRISTMAS FESTIVAL TICKETS NOW MEDIAN AUCTION MAIDEN STKS 1m 3f (P)

4:20 (4:21) (Class 6) 3-4-Y-O **£1,940** (£577; £288; £144) **Stalls** Low

Form RPR

0202 **1** **Sharareh**[26] 7298 3-9-0 75... AdamKirby 6 74
(Luca Cumani) *in tch in midfield: rdn hands and heels and effrt to chal 2f out: led over 1f out: clr 1f out: styd on wl: comf* **1/6**[1]

05 **2** 4½ **Coconell**[18] 7488 3-9-0 0... SebSanders 5 66
(Jeremy Noseda) *chsd ldr tl drvn to ld over 2f out: hdd over 1f out: no ex and btn 1f out: kpt on same pce: eased towards fin* **8/1**[2]

3 5 **Resourceful Miss**[36] 4-9-2 0... WilliamTwiston-Davies(3) 3 57
(Paul Webber) *in tch in last pair: clsd 3f out: effrt u.p ent fnl 2f: 3rd and btn over 1f out: wknd ins fnl f* **12/1**[3]

643 **4** 5 **Omega Omega**[13] 7612 4-9-5 46...(b) AdamBeschizza 1 48
(Julia Feilden) *rdn along leaving stalls to ld: drvn and hdd over 2f out: 4th and btn over 1f out: sn wknd* **20/1**

0660 **5** 2¼ **Russian Link**[39] 6978 3-9-0 60... MartinLane 4 44
(John Berry) *hld up in tch in last pair: rdn 5f out: sn struggling: lost tch 3f out: no ch but plugged on fnl f* **16/1**

3 **6** 24 **She's A Honey**[137] 3743 3-9-0 0... JimmyQuinn 2
(Kevin Morgan) *chsd ldng pair: rdn and struggling over 3f out: bhd and lost tch over 2f out: t.o fnl f* **33/1**

2m 20.33s (-1.57) **Going Correction** -0.05s/f (Stan)
WFA 3 from 4yo 5lb **6** Ran SP% **118.1**
Speed ratings (Par 101): **103,99,96,92,90 73**
toteswingers 1&2 £1.20, 1&3 £1.70, 2&3 £3.10 CSF £2.84 TOTE £1.10: £1.10, £2.60; EX 2.80 Trifecta £7.60 Pool: £4137.37 - 408.22 winning units..
Owner Sheikh Mohammed Obaid Al Maktoum **Bred** Meon Valley Stud **Trained** Newmarket, Suffolk

FOCUS
A weak maiden in which the fourth sets the level.

7839 £175 CASH BONUS AT VICTOR'S LIVE CASINO H'CAP 1m 3f (P)

4:50 (4:50) (Class 5) (0-70,70) 3-Y-O **£2,587** (£770; £384; £192) **Stalls** Low

Form RPR

643 **1** **Wall Street Boss (USA)**[18] 7490 3-9-0 **63**... FrederikTylicki 7 74+
(James Fanshawe) *niggled along early: in tch in rr: c wd and effrt over 2f out: hdwy to ld over 1f out: forged clr and in command whn rn green fnl 100yds: kpt on* **3/1**[2]

4050 **2** 1¼ **Echo Brava**[20] 7447 3-9-1 **64**... SteveDrowne 1 70
(Luke Dace) *chsd ldng pair: n.m.r on inner over 2f out: effrt u.p to chal 2f out: styd on same pce ins fnl f: wnt 2nd on post* **10/1**

0031 **3** nse **Captain Caroline**[35] 7081 3-8-10 **59**... ShaneKelly 4 65
(Mike Murphy) *wl in tch in midfield: rdn and effrt to ld 2f out: hdd over 1f out: no ex and styd on same pce ins fnl f: lost 2nd on post* **3/1**[2]

-660 **4** 1¼ **King's Request (IRE)**[28] 7258 3-9-4 **67**... FergusSweeney 6 71
(Laura Mongan) *wl in tch in last pair: rdn and effrt whn sltly outpcd 2f out: kpt on u.p ins fnl f* **16/1**

6354 **5** 6 **Gamble**[44] 6847 3-9-7 **70**... JamieSpencer 3 63
(Michael Bell) *led: hung lft bnd 8f out: rdn and qcknd over 2f out: hdd 2f out and unable qck: wknd 1f out* **11/4**[1]

00-6 **6** 2¾ **Ravens Nest**[26] 1367 3-8-8 **57**... JackMitchell 2 45
(Ben Pauling) *wl in tch in last trio: rdn and effrt whn n.m.r and outpcd 2f out: n.d after* **33/1**

0020 **7** 4½ **Stiff Upper Lip (IRE)**[28] 7257 3-9-7 **70**...(b) SeanLevey 5 50
(Richard Hannon) *chsd ldr: hmpd bnd 8f out: rdn over 3f out: lost pl u.p ent fnl f: wknd over 1f out: bhd fnl f* **7/2**[3]

2m 20.38s (-1.52) **Going Correction** -0.05s/f (Stan) **7** Ran SP% **116.8**
Speed ratings (Par 102): **103,102,102,101,96 94,91**
toteswingers 1&2 £6.90, 1&3 £2.20, 2&3 £6.90 CSF £33.20 TOTE £4.10: £1.80, £4.70; EX 28.70 Trifecta £124.20 Pool: £3623.75 - 21.87 winning units..
Owner Axom XXXIV **Bred** Peter E Clinton **Trained** Newmarket, Suffolk

FOCUS
An ordinary contest run a bit slower than the previous modest maiden. The form is rated around the second and third.

7840 BACK OF THE NET AT BETVICTOR H'CAP 1m 4f (P)

5:20 (5:24) (Class 5) (0-75,75) 3-Y-O+ **£2,587** (£770; £384; £192) **Stalls** Low

Form RPR

1432 **1** **Certavi (IRE)**[43] 6869 4-9-6 **74**... WilliamTwiston-Davies(3) 9 85
(Brendan Powell) *wl in tch in midfield: swtchd lft and effrt to ld over 1f out: r.o wl ins fnl f* **8/1**

4015 **2** 1¼ **Mallory Heights (IRE)**[65] 6202 3-9-4 **75**... SilvestreDeSousa 5 84
(Luca Cumani) *in tch in midfield: rdn over 3f out: hdwy u.p 1f out: chsd wnr ins fnl f: no imp* **9/2**[2]

-110 **3** ½ **Sporting Gold (IRE)**[24] 7342 4-9-10 **75**... TomQueally 14 83
(Roger Varian) *t.k.h: hld up in tch towards rr: rdn and hdwy on outer over 1f out: kpt on ins fnl f* **6/1**[3]

3203 **4** 1 **Hector's Chance**[11] 7651 4-9-2 **72**... RyanTate(5) 3 79
(Heather Main) *hld up in tch in midfield: clsd to trck ldrs and travelling wl 2f out: rdn and effrt over 1f out: kpt on same pce ins fnl f* **6/1**[3]

061 **5** 1¼ **Commissar**[20] 7439 4-9-9 **74**...(t) JimCrowley 2 79
(Ian Williams) *in tch in midfield: rdn and effrt to chal 2f out: chsd wnr 1f out tl ins fnl f: wknd towards fin* **4/1**[1]

-256 **6** 1¾ **Gravitate**[31] 7169 4-9-2 **67**...(t) FrederikTylicki 4 69
(Paul Webber) *chsd ldrs: effrt on inner to chal 2f out: unable qck 1f out: wknd ins fnl f* **33/1**

0104 **7** 1¼ **Laser Blazer**[22] 7396 5-9-6 **74**...(p) RobertTart(3) 13 74
(Jeremy Gask) *detached in last: hdwy u.p on outer over 1f out: kpt on fnl f: nvr trbld ldrs* **25/1**

5-13 **8** nk **Little Buxted (USA)**[27] 7267 3-9-4 **75**... KierenFox 12 74
(Robert Mills) *chsd ldrs: rdn and unable qck over 2f out: outpcd and btn over 1f out: one pce fnl f* **10/1**

5240 **9** shd **Spring Tonic**[11] 7651 4-9-6 **71**... SebSanders 1 70
(Simon Dow) *in tch in midfield: effrt but unable qck 2f out: styd on same pce u.p fr over 1f out* **25/1**

0220 **10** nk **While You Wait (IRE)**[29] 7220 4-9-10 **75**... FergusSweeney 6 74
(Gary Moore) *hld up in tch in midfield: effrt over 1f out: kpt on same pce fnl f: nvr trbld ldrs* **33/1**

4066 **11** 1 **Paloma's Prince (IRE)**[22] 7396 4-9-5 **70**... StephenCraine 7 67
(Jim Boyle) *led and set stdy gallop: rdn and hrd pressed ent fnl f: wknd 1f out* **16/1**

5044 **12** 2¾ **Kelpie Blitz (IRE)**[11] 7651 4-9-7 **72**...(t) MartinHarley 8 65
(Seamus Durack) *stdd s: hld up in tch in rr: rdn and effrt over 1f out: no hdwy: wknd fnl f* **16/1**

120 **13** 3 **Kent Ragstone (USA)**[55] 6504 4-9-9 **74**... ShaneKelly 11 62
(William Haggas) *chsd ldr: rdn 3f out: unable qck and lost pl over 2f out: short of room and wknd over 1f out* **8/1**

2m 34.34s (-0.16) **Going Correction** -0.05s/f (Stan)
WFA 3 from 4yo+ 6lb **13** Ran SP% **123.4**
Speed ratings (Par 103): **98,97,96,96,95 94,93,93,93,92 92,90,88**
CSF £43.69 CT £237.84 TOTE £8.40: £2.80, £1.90, £2.80; EX 51.40 Trifecta £368.50 Pool: £3386.47 - 6.89 winning units..
Owner Nigel M Davies **Bred** Anthony Jones **Trained** Upper Lambourn, Berks

FOCUS
They went steady in this modest handicap but the form is rated slightly positively.

7841 £25 FREE BET AT BETVICTOR.COM H'CAP 7f (P)

5:50 (5:50) (Class 5) (0-75,74) 3-Y-O **£2,587** (£770; £384; £192) **Stalls** Low

Form RPR

153 **1** **Fab Lolly (IRE)**[40] 6941 3-8-10 **63**... TedDurcan 5 70
(James Bethell) *stdd s: t.k.h: hld up in last pair: rdn and effrt on outer over 1f out: chal ins fnl f: r.o wl to ld cl home* **8/1**

6542 **2** hd **Oasis Spirit**[26] 7297 3-9-4 **71**...(v) DavidProbert 4 77
(Andrew Balding) *t.k.h: wl in tch in midfield: rdn and effrt jst over 1f out: chal ins fnl f: led fnl 75yds: hdd and no ex cl home* **2/1**[1]

0011 **3** ½ **Little Indian**[93] 5275 3-8-9 **62**... SilvestreDeSousa 6 67
(J R Jenkins) *t.k.h: chsd ldr: rdn over 2f out: drvn to ld ins fnl f: battled on tl hdd fnl 75yds: no ex* **4/1**[3]

2050 **4** 1¼ **Ocean Applause**[10] 7661 3-9-7 **74**...(t) AdamKirby 1 76
(John Ryan) *led and dictated stdy gallop: rdn ent fnl 2f: drvn and hdd jst ins fnl f: no ex fnl 100yds* **3/1**[2]

6500 **5** ¾ **Byroness**[12] 7629 3-9-1 **68**... TomQueally 3 68
(Heather Main) *t.k.h: hld up in tch in last pair: rdn and effrt on inner 2f out: pressed ldrs 1f out: one pce ins fnl f* **15/2**

The Form Book Flat, Raceform Ltd, Compton, RG20 6NL.

6241 **6** 1 1/4 **New Rich**[47] 6753 3-8-7 **60**......(p) JohnFahy 7 56
(Eve Johnson Houghton) *t.k.h: chsd ldrs on outer: rdn and effrt ent fnl 2f: no ex 1f out: wknd ins fnl f* **8/1**
5140 **7** 6 **Girl At The Sands (IRE)**[6] 7743 3-8-9 **69**...... JenniferFerguson(7) 2 49
(Edward Creighton) *stdd after s: t.k.h: chsd ldrs: rdn 2f out: lost pl over 1f out: wknd fnl f* **66/1**

1m 27.37s (1.37) **Going Correction** -0.05s/f (Stan) **7** Ran SP% **113.8**
Speed ratings (Par 102): **90,89,89,87,86 85,78**
CSF £24.23 TOTE £9.90: £4.00, £1.40; EX 23.90 Trifecta £131.60 Pool: £3313.21 - 18.86 winning units..
Owner James Lambert **Bred** James F Hanly **Trained** Middleham Moor, N Yorks

FOCUS
The early pace was slow and this was a burn-up in the straight. The form is rated as standard but may not be that good.
T/Jkpt: Not won. T/Plt: £1,308.50 to a £1 stake. Pool: £93696.43 - 52.27 winning tickets T/Qpdt: £82.40 to a £1 stake. Pool: £8364.47 - 75.10 winning tickets SP

7189 TOULOUSE
Monday, November 11
OFFICIAL GOING: Turf: very soft

7843a PRIX FILLE DE L'AIR (GROUP 3) (3YO+) (F&M) (TURF) 1m 2f 110y
2:20 (12:00) 3-Y-O+ **£32,520** (£13,008; £9,756; £6,504; £3,252)

RPR
1 **Frine (IRE)**[31] 7189 3-8-8 0...... JeremyCrocquevieille 9 108
(J-M Osorio, Spain) *midfield: tk clsr order over 3f out: rdn to chal 1 1/2f out: r.o to ld ent fnl f: drvn out* **191/10**
2 1 3/4 **Glowing Cloud**[33] 7142 4-8-11 0...... ThierryThulliez 6 103
(C Ferland, France) *t.k.h: midfield on inner: nt clr run fr 2f out: swtchd outside and hdwy ent fnl f: r.o to take 2nd: nt rch wnr* **7/1**[2]
3 1/4 **Gaga A (URU)**[13] 7613 4-8-11 0...... GregoryBenoist 2 103+
(D Smaga, France) *midfield: nt clr run and swtchd outside 1 1/2f out: styd on wl fnl f: tk 3rd cl home: nvr plcd to chal* **78/10**
4 1/2 **Odeliz (IRE)**[51] 6714 3-8-8 0...... AntoineHamelin 1 104
(K R Burke) *t.k.h: trckd ldr on inner: ev ch appr fnl f: sn rdn: one pce last 100yds* **12/1**
5 snk **Kenbella (FR)**[22] 7411 3-8-8 0...... FabriceVeron 5 103
(H-A Pantall, France) *t.k.h in midfield: kpt on wl u.p fr over 1f out: nrest at fin* **22/1**
6 hd **Chalnetta (FR)**[37] 7048 3-8-8 0...... JulienAuge 4 103
(C Ferland, France) *led: rdn 1 1/2f out: hdd ent fnl f: no ex and dropped to 6th last 75yds* **6/4**[1]
7 1/2 **Keegsquaw (IRE)**[32] 7161 4-8-11 0...... Pierre-CharlesBoudot 10 100
(Mme A Fabre, France) *hld up towards rr: hrd rdn and effrt on outer 1 1/2f out: styd on ins fnl f: nvr on terms* **21/1**
8 1 1/4 **Incroyable (USA)**[31] 7189 4-8-11 0...... OlivierPeslier 11 97
(C Laffon-Parias, France) *restrained towards rr on outer: prog to trck ldr 1/2-way: rdn to chal over 1 1/2f out: wknd appr fnl f* **13/1**
9 1/4 **Childa (IRE)**[22] 7410 3-8-8 0...... StephanePasquier 7 99
(S Wattel, France) *towards rr on inner: nt clr run over 1 1/2f out: plugged on u.p fnl f: nvr threatened ldrs* **15/2**[3]
10 1/2 **Dance In The Park (FR)**[65] 6229 3-8-8 0...... Jean-BaptisteHamel 3 98
(D Guillemin, France) *towards rr: rdn and no imp fnl 2f: nvr a factor* **14/1**
11 2 **Baino Rock (FR)**[32] 7161 4-8-11 0...... ChristopheSoumillon 8 92
(J-C Rouget, France) *trckd ldr on outer: midfield fr 1/2-way: rdn and no imp 1 1/2f out: outpcd ins fnl f and eased whn wl hld* **11/1**

2m 19.49s (139.49)
WFA 3 from 4yo 4lb **11** Ran SP% **119.3**
WIN (incl. 1 euro stake): 20.10. PLACES: 5.70, 2.80, 2.90. DF: 63.20. SF: 113.20..
Owner Duke Of Alburquerque **Bred** Duc D'Alburquerque **Trained** Spain

7801 WOLVERHAMPTON (A.W) (L-H)
Tuesday, November 12
OFFICIAL GOING: Standard
Wind: Light, across towards stand Weather: Clear

7844 32RED.COM MEDIAN AUCTION MAIDEN STKS 5f 216y(P)
4:15 (4:15) (Class 5) 2-Y-O **£2,911** (£866; £432; £216) **Stalls** Low

Form RPR
3 **1** **Speed Hawk (USA)**[12] 7638 2-9-5...... ShaneKelly 4 83
(Robert Cowell) *prom: led 2f out: pushed along and in control fnl f: comf* **11/10**[1]
362 **2** 1 1/4 **Minnaloushe (IRE)**[27] 7294 2-9-0 74...... RobertHavlin 3 74
(John Gosden) *prom: sltly outpcd over 2f out: rallied and chsd wnr over 1f out: kpt on: a hld* **6/4**[2]
3 3/4 **Dreese (IRE)** 2-9-5...... MartinHarley 8 77+
(James Tate) *in tch: effrt and hung lft over 1f out: styd on* **6/1**[3]
340 **4** 6 **Sunningdale Rose (IRE)**[21] 7448 2-9-0 62......(v[1]) RobertWinston 1 54
(Gay Kelleway) *led tl 2f out: wknd over 1f out* **16/1**
00 **5** 14 **Minnyvinny**[17] 7541 2-9-0...... CathyGannon 5 12
(Dave Roberts) *towards rr: rdn over 2f out: no ch after* **100/1**
6 1 **Alba Verde** 2-9-0...... ChrisCatlin 7 9
(Sir Mark Prescott Bt) *sn outpcd and rdn along: a bhd* **33/1**
0 **7** 12 **Stage Girl**[27] 7294 2-0-9...... NathanAlison(5) 2
(Chris Dwyer) *plld hrd early: chsd ldrs 3f: sn rdn and wknd* **100/1**

1m 15.17s (0.17) **Going Correction** 0.0s/f (Stan) **7** Ran SP% **112.7**
Speed ratings (Par 96): **98,96,95,87,68 67,51**
toteswingers 1&2 £1.10, 1&3 £1.90, 2&3 £1.70 CSF £2.87 TOTE £2.20: £1.40, £1.10; EX 4.20 Trifecta £8.90 Pool: £2585.09 - 217.76 winning units..
Owner Khalifa Dasmal **Bred** Santa Rosa Partners **Trained** Six Mile Bottom, Cambs

FOCUS
A fairly decent maiden in which the front three, who represent good trainers, pulled clear. The runner-up is rated to his mark.

7845 32RED CASINO FILLIES' H'CAP 5f 216y(P)
4:50 (4:50) (Class 5) (0-70,70) 3-Y-O+ **£2,911** (£866; £432; £216) **Stalls** Low

Form RPR
0-21 **1** **Interception (IRE)**[14] 7600 3-9-7 **70**...... TedDurcan 5 86+
(David Lanigan) *stdd s: hld up in rr: swtchd wd and smooth hdwy 2f out: led 1f out: pushed clr: comf* **4/6**[1]
4301 **2** 3 1/4 **Tiger's Home**[43] 6902 3-8-3 **57**...... ShelleyBirkett(5) 3 59
(Julia Feilden) *prom: rdn over 2f out: kpt on to take 2nd ins fnl f: no ch w wnr* **14/1**
5023 **3** 1/2 **Available (IRE)**[24] 7381 4-9-0 **63**......(tp) StephenCraine 6 64
(John Mackie) *chsd ldr on outer: led 2f out tl 1f out: easily outpcd by wnr* **4/1**[2]
2000 **4** 1 1/2 **Economic Crisis (IRE)**[29] 7240 4-9-4 **67**...... PaddyAspell 4 63
(Alan Berry) *chsd ldrs: rdn over 2f out: btn over 1f out* **25/1**
1550 **5** 2 1/2 **Alhaarth Beauty (IRE)**[60] 6362 3-9-3 **66**...... LiamJones 7 55
(Ismail Mohammed) *wd and towards rr: rdn 3f out: n.d after* **10/1**[3]
4044 **6** 1 1/4 **Camache Queen (IRE)**[22] 7427 5-8-7 **56** oh1......(bt) KieranO'Neill 2 41
(Joseph Tuite) *led: hrd rdn and hdd 2f out: wknd over 1f out* **12/1**
0544 **7** 2 3/4 **Song Of Parkes**[43] 6905 6-9-4 **70**......(p) SladeO'Hara(3) 8 47
(Peter Grayson) *in tch tl rdn and wknd 2f out* **12/1**
1536 **8** 11 **Balatina**[141] 3638 3-8-3 **57** ow1...... NathanAlison(5) 1 1
(Chris Dwyer) *fly-jmpd s: plld hrd: sn in tch on rail: wknd over 2f out: sn bhd* **33/1**

1m 14.89s (-0.11) **Going Correction** 0.0s/f (Stan) **8** Ran SP% **117.9**
Speed ratings (Par 100): **100,95,95,93,89 88,84,69**
toteswingers 1&2 £3.10, 1&3 £1.10, 2&3 £5.80 CSF £13.06 CT £26.69 TOTE £1.40: £1.10, £4.10, £1.70; EX 14.20 Trifecta £37.20 Pool: £3798.34 - 76.57 winning units..
Owner B E Nielsen **Bred** Corduff Bloodstock Ltd & David Egan **Trained** Upper Lambourn, Berks

FOCUS
Not a bad event of its type. The winner proved she was a good deal better than this mark.

7846 32RED NURSERY H'CAP 1m 141y(P)
5:20 (5:20) (Class 4) (0-85,80) 2-Y-O **£4,528** (£1,347; £673; £336) **Stalls** Low

Form RPR
0413 **1** **Earthflight**[14] 7604 2-8-3 **62**...... WilliamCarson 3 71
(Philip McBride) *fly-jmpd s and dwlt: sn led: mde rest: rdn and qcknd over 2f out: clr over 1f out: comf* **9/4**[2]
414 **2** 5 **Master Of Finance (IRE)**[66] 6207 2-9-7 **80**...... JoeFanning 5 79
(Mark Johnston) *chsd wnr: rdn over 2f out: comf outpcd over 1f out* **1/1**[1]
3102 **3** 2 1/4 **Chanceuse**[7] 7755 2-7-7 **59** oh9...... JoeDoyle(7) 4 53
(Gay Kelleway) *in tch: rdn over 2f out: sn btn: wnt modest 3rd ins fnl f* **16/1**
4320 **4** 1 1/4 **Intense Feeling (IRE)**[5] 7782 2-8-13 **77**...... NoelGarbutt(5) 2 68
(David Evans) *chsd ldrs tl outpcd 2f out* **6/1**[3]
3606 **5** 1/2 **Money Team (IRE)**[17] 7545 2-9-2 **75**...... GrahamLee 1 65
(Philip Kirby) *a last: rdn 3f out: n.d fnl 2f* **10/1**

1m 50.72s (0.22) **Going Correction** 0.0s/f (Stan) **5** Ran SP% **110.0**
Speed ratings (Par 98): **99,94,92,91,91**
CSF £4.89 TOTE £3.10: £1.30, £1.10; EX 5.10 Trifecta £21.90 Pool: £2407.18 - 82.36 winning units..
Owner Four Winds Racing Partnership **Bred** Wood Farm Stud (Waresley) **Trained** Newmarket, Suffolk

FOCUS
A disappointing turnout for this Class 4 nursery, just five runners and the top weight rated 5lb below the race ceiling. A notable step up from the winner.

7847 CORAL APP DOWNLOAD FROM THE APP STORE H'CAP 1m 4f 50y(P)
5:50 (5:52) (Class 6) (0-60,64) 3-Y-O+ **£1,940** (£577; £288; £144) **Stalls** Low

Form RPR
2 **1** **Echua (IRE)**[6] 7767 7-9-4 **54**...... MartinHarley 1 64+
(Emmet Michael Butterly, Ire) *prom: led over 2f out: drvn along and jnd over 1f out: hld on wl* **3/1**[2]
4000 **2** 1 3/4 **Evermore (IRE)**[41] 6933 3-9-1 **57**...... JoeFanning 4 63
(Mark Johnston) *dwlt and bmpd s: hld up in rr: hdwy on outer 3f out: jnd wnr over 1f out: unable qck ins fnl f* **20/1**
3444 **3** 2 1/4 **Point Of Control**[26] 7331 3-8-11 **58**......(v) JoeyHaynes(5) 6 61
(Michael Bell) *s.i.s: sn trcking ldrs: rdn over 2f out: one pce appr fnl f* **16/1**
1321 **4** 1/2 **Amantius**[8] 7735 4-10-0 **64** 6ex......(b) GrahamLee 2 66
(Johnny Farrelly) *s.i.s: rdn and sn in tch on rail: drvn along over 2f out: styd on same pce* **11/10**[1]
0030 **5** 1/2 **Kingscombe (USA)**[13] 7622 4-9-6 **56**...... RobertHavlin 9 58
(Linda Jewell) *chsd ldr: led 6f out tl over 2f out: wknd wl over 1f out* **25/1**
660 **6** shd **Bethan**[29] 7253 4-9-5 **60**...... ShelleyBirkett(5) 10 61
(Julia Feilden) *chsd ldrs on outer: wnt cl 2nd 4f out: hrd rdn and wknd over 1f out* **25/1**
5045 **7** nk **Impeccability**[38] 7035 3-8-4 **46** oh1...... RaulDaSilva 8 47
(John Mackie) *mid-div on outer: effrt over 2f out: no imp* **12/1**
5004 **8** 1 **Jackaddock**[36] 7066 3-9-1 **57**...... PJMcDonald 5 56
(James Bethell) *wnt lft and bmpd s: hld up in rr: rdn over 2f out: n.d* **12/1**
/ **9** 5 **Indian Scout**[340] 8031 5-9-7 **57**......(p) BenCurtis 3 49
(Eoin Doyle, Ire) *t.k.h towards rr: n.m.r after 2f: rdn 3f out: sn struggling* **10/1**[3]
0322 **10** 19 **Dubara Reef (IRE)**[14] 7597 6-9-3 **53**......(p) TonyHamilton 7 16
(Paul Green) *led tl 6f out: wknd qckly over 3f out: sn wl bhd* **25/1**

2m 41.45s (0.35) **Going Correction** 0.0s/f (Stan)
WFA 3 from 4yo+ 6lb **10** Ran SP% **114.5**
Speed ratings (Par 101): **98,96,95,95,94 94,94,93,90,77**
toteswingers 1&2 £10.40, 1&3 £8.70, 2&3 £39.20 CSF £64.96 CT £823.51 TOTE £3.60: £1.60, £5.20, £4.30; EX 60.90 Trifecta £733.60 Pool: £3762.81 - 3.84 winning units..
Owner D J Dolan **Bred** Newberry Stud Farm Ltd **Trained** Letterkenny, Co Donegal

FOCUS
The early pace was steady. A repeat of the winner's good recent return was enough wth the favourite below form.

7848 COMPARE BOOKMAKERS AT BOOKMAKERS.CO.UK H'CAP 5f 20y(P)
6:20 (6:24) (Class 6) (0-65,65) 3-Y-O+ **£1,940** (£577; £288; £144) **Stalls** Low

Form RPR
020 **1** **Speightowns Kid (USA)**[25] 7353 5-9-2 **60**......(b) RobertHavlin 1 68
(Alan Berry) *mid-div: hdwy and eased to outside over 1f out: str run in centre to ld fnl 50yds: won gng away* **8/1**[3]
1035 **2** 1 1/4 **Thorpe Bay**[153] 3196 4-9-1 **59**...... FrederikTylicki 11 63
(Michael Appleby) *w ldrs: drvn to ld ins fnl f: hdd and outpcd fnl 50yds* **8/1**[3]
1002 **3** 1 1/4 **Rise To Glory (IRE)**[8] 7728 5-9-4 **62**...... DuranFentiman 12 61
(Shaun Harris) *w ldrs: led over 3f out tl ins fnl f: no ex* **2/1**[1]
0600 **4** 1 **Lager Time (IRE)**[13] 7634 3-9-1 **64**...... NoelGarbutt(5) 10 59+
(David Evans) *dwlt: sn wl bhd: shkn up over 2f out: gd late hdwy* **10/1**
5031 **5** shd **Max The Machine**[40] 6965 3-9-3 **61**...... DaleSwift 9 56
(Derek Shaw) *s.i.s: wl bhd tl rdn and r.o fnl 2f: nrest at fin* **14/1**

6000 **6** 1 1/4 **Your Gifted (IRE)**[14] 7599 6-9-2 **60** .... TomEaves 5 51
(Lisa Williamson) *dwlt: towards rr: hdwy on outer 2f out: hrd rdn over 1f out: one pce* **33/1**

2445 **7** 1/2 **Above The Stars**[8] 7730 5-9-1 **62** .... (p) RyanPowell[(3)] 2 51
(Conor Dore) *outpcd and bhd: effrt on inner and drvn along 2f out: nvr able to chal* **33/1**

3100 **8** 1 **Speedyfix**[5] 7783 6-8-13 **62** .... (t) DanielMuscutt[(5)] 7 47
(Christine Dunnett) *chsd ldrs: hrd rdn over 1f out: sn wknd* **10/1**

0505 **9** 3 1/2 **We Have A Dream**[14] 7601 8-9-4 **62** .... (p) BenCurtis 3 35
(Violet M Jordan) *chsd ldrs over 2f* **20/1**

4133 **10** 3 1/4 **Confidential Creek**[114] 4558 3-9-4 **62** .... (p) GrahamLee 4 23
(Ollie Pears) *mid-div tl wknd 2f out* **4/1**[2]

4006 **11** 3/4 **El McGlynn (IRE)**[8] 7728 4-8-13 **60** .... (b[1]) NeilFarley[(3)] 13 18
(Eric Alston) *led over 1f: w ldrs tl wknd 2f out* **14/1**

1m 2.07s (-0.23) **Going Correction** 0.0s/f (Stan) **11** Ran SP% **117.7**
Speed ratings (Par 101): **101,99,97,95,95 93,92,90,85,80 78**
toteswingers 1&2 £8.80, 1&3 £4.80, 2&3 £4.60 CSF £69.01 CT £179.39 TOTE £9.90: £2.90, £2.10, £1.30; EX 94.20 Trifecta £245.80 Pool: £3297.99 - 10.06 winning units..
Owner Ged & Daz **Bred** Sandyview Farm **Trained** Cockerham, Lancs

FOCUS
A moderate sprint handicap run at an overly fast pace. Things set up well for the winner.

7849 LADBROKES H'CAP — 1m 141y(P)
6:50 (6:50) (Class 4) (0-85,83) 3-Y-O+ **£5,175** (£1,540; £769; £384) **Stalls** Low

Form RPR

0142 **1** **Silverware (USA)**[49] 6721 5-9-1 **77** .... TomEaves 8 85
(Kristin Stubbs) *mde all: rdn clr over 1f out: gamely* **7/1**

0010 **2** 3 **Berlusca (IRE)**[31] 7211 4-9-1 **77** .... DanielTudhope 4 79
(David O'Meara) *in tch on rail: sltly lost pl 4f out: rallied and nt clr run 2f out: chsd wnr jst ins fnl f: no imp* **11/2**

0301 **3** 1 1/4 **Elspeth's Boy (USA)**[11] 7669 6-8-4 **71** .... JoeyHaynes[(5)] 6 70
(Philip Kirby) *mid-div: hdwy over 2f out: chsd wnr over 1f out tl jst ins fnl f: no ex* **9/2**[2]

2124 **4** 1 1/4 **Ishikawa (IRE)**[60] 6360 5-8-9 **78** .... RobJFitzpatrick[(7)] 10 74
(K R Burke) *mid-div and wd: effrt and hrd rdn 2f out: hung lft: one pce* **5/1**[3]

4000 **5** 2 **Prompter**[10] 7696 6-9-6 **82** .... GrahamLee 2 74+
(Jonjo O'Neill) *towards rr: rdn and hmpd over 1f out: styng on at fin* **14/1**

-460 **6** nk **Lilac Tree**[17] 7531 3-8-12 **77** .... JoeFanning 1 70
(Mark Johnston) *chsd wnr tl wknd over 1f out* **10/3**[1]

0231 **7** 3/4 **Dark Ruler (IRE)**[18] 7498 4-9-0 **76** .... BenCurtis 9 66
(Alan Swinbank) *chsd ldrs over 5f* **6/1**

0263 **8** 4 1/2 **The Cayterers**[58] 6428 11-8-12 **79** .... DanielMuscutt[(5)] 7 60
(Ronald Harris) *dwlt: towards rr: drvn along and struggling over 2f out* **33/1**

0042 **9** 1 1/2 **Lazarus Bell**[17] 7531 3-9-4 **83** .... PaulPickard 5 61
(Alan Brown) *prom tl wknd 2f out: wkng whn edgd lft over 1f out* **14/1**

/-30 **10** 8 **Destiny Blue (IRE)**[211] 1576 6-9-2 **78** .... DaleSwift 3 39
(Brian Ellison) *s.s and rdn early: a bhd: hrd rdn and no ch 3f out* **25/1**

1m 48.83s (-1.67) **Going Correction** 0.0s/f (Stan)
WFA 3 from 4yo+ 3lb **10** Ran SP% **120.2**
Speed ratings (Par 105): **107,104,103,102,100 100,99,95,94,86**
toteswingers 1&2 £6.20, 1&3 £7.60, 2&3 £5.70 CSF £46.81 CT £196.68 TOTE £10.00: £3.70, £2.70, £1.60; EX 41.60 Trifecta £532.10 Pool: £2999.94 - 4.22 winning units..
Owner Paul & Linda Dixon **Bred** Alliand Equine **Trained** Norton, N Yorks

FOCUS
At least a return to his previous best from the winner and the form could be rated 3-4l higher.
T/Plt: £16.40. Pool: £84,795.38 - 3761.63 winning units. T/Qpdt: £14.80. Pool: £9391.48 - 469.34 winning units. LM

7834 KEMPTON (A.W) (R-H)
Wednesday, November 13

OFFICIAL GOING: Standard
Wind: Light, across Weather: Fine

7850 MIX BUSINESS AND PLEASURE AT KEMPTON H'CAP — 5f (P)
4:20 (4:20) (Class 7) (0-50,50) 3-Y-O+ **£1,617** (£481; £240; £120) **Stalls** Low

Form RPR

0 **1** **Iffranesia (FR)**[22] 7454 3-9-4 **50** .... (p) GrahamLee 2 60
(Robert Cowell) *nt that wl away: in tch in rr: prog on inner 2f out: rdn to chse ldng pair fnl f: brought between them to ld last 50yds* **20/1**

4205 **2** nk **Exkaliber**[28] 7292 4-8-10 **49** .... (bt) DavidParkes[(7)] 6 58
(Jeremy Gask) *t.k.h: trckd ldrs: nipped through on inner to ld wl over 1f out: urged along fnl f: hdd last 50yds* **9/2**[3]

0060 **3** nk **Demoiselle Bond**[205] 1717 5-9-3 **49** .... RobertHavlin 1 57
(Lydia Richards) *takwn down early: led: sltly wd bnd 2f out and sn hdd: rallied fnl f: kpt on but lost 2nd last 50yds* **14/1**

3063 **4** 1 1/4 **Charlemagne Diva**[29] 7265 3-9-4 **50** .... (t) GrahamGibbons 5 53
(Richard Guest) *chsd ldr on outer to 2f out: nt qckn over 1f out: one pce after* **3/1**[2]

050 **5** nk **Imjin River (IRE)**[62] 6343 6-9-4 **50** .... (t) RaulDaSilva 4 52
(William Stone) *taken down early: nt that wl away: hld up in rr: shkn up over 1f out: kpt on same pce fnl f: no threat* **7/1**

4560 **6** 1 1/2 **Chateau Lola**[184] 2326 4-9-3 **49** .... (v) JoeFanning 7 46
(Derek Shaw) *trckd ldrs: rdn and nt qckn over 1f out: fdd* **16/1**

6040 **7** hd **Christopher Chua (IRE)**[27] 7323 4-8-13 **48** WilliamTwiston-Davies[(3)] 9 44
(Michael Scudamore) *a in rr: rdn and struggling 2f out* **14/1**

0104 **8** 1 3/4 **Give Us A Belle (IRE)**[22] 7454 4-9-3 **49** .... (vt) AdamBeschizza 8 39
(Christine Dunnett) *chsd ldrs on outer: lost grnd bnd 2f out: rdn and fnd nil over 1f out* **12/1**

5060 **9** nse **Daneside (IRE)**[58] 6472 6-9-1 **50** .... MatthewLawson[(3)] 3 40
(P J O'Gorman) *v s.i.s: detached in last: drvn and one pce fnl 2f* **5/2**[1]

1m 0.09s (-0.41) **Going Correction** -0.15s/f (Stan) **9** Ran SP% **115.9**
Speed ratings (Par 97): **97,96,96,94,93 91,90,88,87**
toteswingers 1&2 £19.20, 2&3 £18.10, 1&3 £19.60 CSF £108.11 CT £1335.62 TOTE £19.60: £6.10, £2.40, £5.60; EX 120.20 Trifecta £1551.90 Part won. Pool: £2069.31 - 0.35 winning units..
Owner Cyril Humphris **Bred** Cyril Humphris **Trained** Six Mile Bottom, Cambs

FOCUS
A poor race, and trip and track position gave the first three the edge. Fair form for the grade.

7851 BETDAQ - THE SPORTS BETTING EXCHANGE H'CAP — 5f (P)
4:50 (4:50) (Class 3) (0-95,94) 3-Y-O+
£7,158 (£2,143; £1,071; £535; £267; £134) **Stalls** Low

Form RPR

1111 **1** **Perfect Pasture**[39] 7029 3-9-1 **88** .... (v) GrahamGibbons 9 98
(Michael Easterby) *v wd bnd over 3f out: prog to chse ldrs 1/2-way: clsd to ld jst over 1f out but jnd: r.o wl to assert last 75yds* **3/1**[1]

240 **2** nk **Love Island**[13] 7642 4-8-11 **89** .... GeorgeChaloner[(5)] 6 98
(Richard Whitaker) *sn chsd ldrs: squeezed through to chal jst over 1f out: w wnr and gd battle tl no ex last 75yds* **9/1**

-160 **3** 2 **Silken Express (IRE)**[144] 3561 4-9-2 **89** ....[1] SeanLevey 4 91
(Robert Cowell) *cl up on inner: nt clr run over 1f out: squeezed through to take 3rd jst ins fnl f: styd on but no imp on ldng pair* **8/1**

0300 **4** 1 **Prohibit**[56] 6539 8-9-7 **94** .... (p) GrahamLee 2 92
(Robert Cowell) *hld up in tch: nt clr run over 1f out: squeezed through jst ins fnl f to press for 3rd: effrt petered out nr fin* **10/1**

0000 **5** 1/2 **Ubetterbegood (ARG)**[124] 4263 5-9-2 **94** .... OisinMurphy[(5)] 5 90+
(Robert Cowell) *awkward s: wl in rr: nt clr run over 1f out: barged way through jst ins fnl f: kpt on but no ch to threaten* **9/2**[2]

2040 **6** 1 1/4 **Bern Me Baby (USA)**[13] 7642 3-9-3 **90** .... (bt) MartinHarley 3 82
(Marco Botti) *trckd ldrs: rdn over 1f out: one pce and no prog fnl f* **7/1**[3]

0006 **7** 1 1/4 **Tax Free (IRE)**[43] 6920 11-9-1 **88** .... RobertHavlin 1 75
(David Nicholls) *led fr ins draw: hdd & wknd jst over 1f out* **16/1**

1640 **8** shd **Secret Look**[19] 7495 3-9-3 **90** .... SteveDrowne 7 77
(Ed McMahon) *a towards rr and quite wd: no ch whn bmpd ins fnl f* **16/1**

6210 **9** nk **Even Stevens**[5] 7803 5-9-6 **93** .... (p) TomEaves 10 79
(Scott Dixon) *pressed ldr to over 1f out: wknd* **12/1**

3320 **10** 2 **Fitz Flyer (IRE)**[33] 7171 7-9-3 **90** .... (v) JoeFanning 8 69
(David Nicholls) *stdd s: t.k.h: hld up in last but stl wd bnd over 3f out: pushed along and no prog over 1f out: nvr involved* **7/1**[3]

59.09s (-1.41) **Going Correction** -0.15s/f (Stan) **10** Ran SP% **117.8**
Speed ratings (Par 107): **105,104,101,99,98 96,94,94,94,91**
toteswingers 1&2 £6.50, 2&3 £16.00, 1&3 £5.10 CSF £31.15 CT £203.97 TOTE £2.40: £1.20, £3.60, £2.30; EX 29.20 Trifecta £132.60 Pool: £3207.47 - 18.13 winning units..
Owner Mrs Jean Turpin **Bred** Mrs Jean Turpin **Trained** Sheriff Hutton, N Yorks
■ Stewards' Enquiry : Oisin Murphy two-day ban: careless riding (Nov 27-28)

FOCUS
This looked quite competitive beforehand, but the first two drew nicely clear. race. The winner confrmed the good impression from his Redcar win.

7852 WINNERS ARE WELCOME AT BETDAQ/E.B.F. STALLIONS MAIDEN STKS — 6f (P)
5:20 (5:22) (Class 5) 2-Y-O **£2,911** (£866; £432; £216) **Stalls** Low

Form RPR

1 **Furas (IRE)** 2-9-5 0 .... SilvestreDeSousa 7 87+
(Saeed bin Suroor) *edgy preliminaries and free to post: chsd ldng trio: shkn up and clsd to ld over 1f out: readily drew clr* **7/2**[2]

3 **2** 3 3/4 **Cincuenta Pasos (IRE)**[29] 7261 2-9-5 0 .... SteveDrowne 2 76
(Joseph Tuite) *trckd ldr 2f: styd prom: chal on ins and upsides over 1f out: styd on but no ch w wnr fnl f* **7/2**[2]

0 **3** 2 1/4 **Rush**[208] 1659 2-9-0 0 .... GrahamLee 3 64+
(Paul Cole) *chsd ldrs in 5th: shkn up jst over 2f out: outpcd over 1f out: kpt on to take 3rd ins fnl f* **10/1**

5 **4** hd **Frangipanni (IRE)**[28] 7294 2-9-0 0 .... MartinLane 10 64+
(Roger Charlton) *sn chsd ldrs disputing 6th: shkn up 2f out: outpcd over 1f out: kpt on to press for 3rd nr fin* **13/2**[3]

2 **5** 1 1/2 **Conflicting**[35] 7125 2-9-5 0 .... JimCrowley 12 64
(Richard Hannon) *spd fr wd draw and pressed ldr after 2f: led 2f out: rdn and hdd over 1f out: wknd* **13/8**[1]

0 **6** nk **Wedgewood Estates**[24] 7393 2-9-0 0 .... DavidProbert 6 58
(Tony Carroll) *towards rr and off the pce: pushed along and sme prog fr 2f out: kpt on same pce fnl f* **100/1**

30 **7** 1 3/4 **Previous Acclaim (IRE)**[28] 7294 2-8-11 0. WilliamTwiston-Davies[(3)] 11 53
(Richard Hannon) *sn off the pce in rr: pushed along on outer over 2f out: kpt on same pce: n.d* **25/1**

8 hd **Vision Of Rome** 2-9-0 0 .... MartinHarley 4 52
(Mick Channon) *sn wl off the pce in 10th: sme prog over 1f out: n.d* **50/1**

9 2 **Gentlemen** 2-9-5 0 .... (t[1]) GrahamGibbons 9 51
(P J O'Gorman) *sltly awkward s: sn in midfield disputing 6th: urged along and effrt on inner over 2f out: wknd jst over 1f out* **50/1**

10 2 1/2 **Gobertier** 2-9-5 0 .... SeanLevey 5 44
(Richard Hannon) *sn virtually t.o in last pair and pushed along: nvr a factor* **16/1**

00 **11** 1 1/4 **Gauchita**[7] 7766 2-9-0 0 .... ChrisCatlin 8 35
(Michael Bell) *led: appeared to be gng wl enough 1/2-way: hdd & wknd rapidly 2f out* **66/1**

12 15 **Acertainplace** 2-9-0 0 .... WilliamCarson 1
(David Elsworth) *sn t.o* **33/1**

1m 12.77s (-0.33) **Going Correction** -0.15s/f (Stan) **12** Ran SP% **124.0**
Speed ratings (Par 96): **96,91,88,87,85 85,83,82,80,76 75,55**
toteswingers 1&2 £3.10, 2&3 £7.90, 1&3 £8.00 CSF £16.48 TOTE £4.60: £1.50, £1.90, £3.70, EX 21.80 Trifecta £170.40 Pool: £3137.98 - 13.80 winning units..
Owner Godolphin **Bred** Shadwell Estate Company Limited **Trained** Newmarket, Suffolk

FOCUS
No more than a fair maiden, but a taking performance from the winner. The form is taken at face value.

7853 REWARDS4RACING.COM MEDIAN AUCTION MAIDEN STKS (DIV I) — 1m (P)
5:55 (5:58) (Class 6) 2-Y-O **£1,940** (£577; £288; £144) **Stalls** Low

Form RPR

63 **1** **Donncha (IRE)**[28] 7308 2-9-5 0 .... AndreaAtzeni 7 79
(Robert Eddery) *t.k.h: trckd ldr: led and hung lft 2f out: continued to hang but in command fnl f: rdn out* **1/1**[1]

6 **2** 1 **Itsnowcato**[15] 7607 2-9-5 0 .... JimCrowley 2 76+
(Ed Walker) *hld up disputing 7th: rdn and prog fr over 2f out: styd on to take 2nd fnl f: unable to chal* **8/1**

60 **3** 3 1/2 **Kantara Castle (IRE)**[7] 7766 2-9-5 0 .... SeanLevey 11 68
(Richard Hannon) *chsd ldng pair: hrd rdn fr 2f out: kpt on same pce* **25/1**

2033 **4** 1/2 **Oriental Relation (IRE)**[15] 7609 2-9-5 73 .... GrahamLee 3 67
(James Given) *led: hdd and veered lft 2f out: lost 2nd and fdd fnl f* **9/2**[2]

The Form Book Flat, Raceform Ltd, Compton, RG20 6NL.

03 **5** 4 1/2 **Bountiful Sin**[28] 7301 2-9-5 0 SilvestreDeSousa 4 56
(George Margarson) *chsd ldng pair: rdn wl over 2f out: steadily fdd fnl 2f* **7/1**[3]

0 **6** 2 **Tipsy Star**[21] 7466 2-9-0 0 SteveDrowne 9 46
(Daniel Kubler) *sn in tch disputing 5th: shkn up and outpcd over 2f out: no hdwy after* **20/1**

4 **7** 1 1/4 **Tara's Treasure (IRE)**[12] 7654 2-9-5 0 FergusSweeney 8 48
(Gary Moore) *hld up disputing 7th: shkn up over 2f out: no hdwy* **8/1**

0 **8** 20 **Amadiva (IRE)**[27] 7327 2-9-0 0 RobertWinston 10
(Dean Ivory) *chsd ldrs disputing 5th: rdn bef 1/2-way: wknd rapidly over 2f out: eased and t.o* **66/1**

9 5 **Deavin** 2-9-5 0 MartinLane 6
(Nick Littmoden) *stdd s: sn in trble: t.o sn after 1/2-way* **33/1**

00 **10** 1 1/2 **Jolie Blonde**[7] 7763 2-9-0 0 ChrisCatlin 5
(Sir Mark Prescott Bt) *immediately drvn in frntic style in last pair and stl looked clueless: t.o fr 1/2-way* **66/1**

0 **11** 3 3/4 **Oly'Roccs (IRE)**[26] 7335 2-9-5 0 JoeFanning 1
(David Nicholls) *t.k.h early and rn errntly in rr: lost tch after 3f: t.o* **50/1**

1m 39.01s (-0.79) **Going Correction** -0.15s/f (Stan) **11** Ran SP% **119.4**
Speed ratings (Par 94): **97,96,92,92,87 85,84,64,59,57 54**
toteswingers 1&2 £2.90, 2&3 £16.80, 1&3 £9.00 CSF £9.32 TOTE £1.90: £1.10, £2.60, £7.00; EX 12.70 Trifecta £180.10 Pool: £2864.20 - 11.92 winning units..
Owner David Bannon & Robert Eddery **Bred** Ballyhane Stud **Trained** Newmarket, Suffolk

FOCUS
Not a particularly strong maiden, and there wasn't much pace on. The winner is rated to the level of his recent turf run.

7854 REWARDS4RACING.COM MEDIAN AUCTION MAIDEN STKS (DIV II) 1m (P)
6:30 (6:30) (Class 6) 2-Y-O **£1,940** (£577; £288; £144) **Stalls** Low

Form RPR

04 **1** **Groovejet**[28] 7310 2-9-0 0 MartinHarley 7 73+
(Peter Chapple-Hyam) *trckd ldr: rdn to ld 2f out: clr fnl f: pushed out* **7/2**[2]

65 **2** 3/4 **Glorious Sinndar (FR)**[19] 7513 2-9-5 0 SilvestreDeSousa 2 74+
(George Margarson) *sn in last quartet: shkn up over 2f out: rdn and gd prog on inner over 1f out: wnt 2nd last 150yds: clsd on wnr fin* **12/1**

3 2 3/4 **Morning Watch (IRE)** 2-9-5 0 FrederikTylicki 6 68+
(Lady Cecil) *dwlt and pushed along in rr early: prog on outer over 3f out: rdn and kpt on to take 3rd fnl f: n.d* **9/2**[3]

0 **4** 1 1/2 **Turnbury**[140] 3689 2-9-5 0 KierenFox 4 64
(Robert Mills) *led to 2f out: wknd and lost 2nd ins fnl f* **33/1**

0 **5** nk **Lucky Jim**[21] 7469 2-9-5 0 TedDurcan 10 63+
(Chris Wall) *chsd ldrs: u.p fr 1/2-way: one pce fnl 2f* **7/2**[2]

4 **6** 3/4 **Spectator**[27] 7320 2-9-5 0 DavidProbert 9 61+
(Andrew Balding) *dwlt: in tch in last quartet: dropped to last 1/2-way: rdn and no prog over 2f out: styd on fnl f: nrst fin* **15/8**[1]

0 **7** nk **Dynamic Ranger (USA)**[13] 7647 2-9-5 0 AdamKirby 5 61
(Gary Moore) *chsd ldng pair: shkn up and nt qckn 2f out: hld together and fdd fnl f* **20/1**

0 **8** 6 **Rite To Reign**[19] 7513 2-9-5 0 WilliamCarson 8 46
(Philip McBride) *s.i.s: a in rr: lost tch over 2f out* **33/1**

00 **9** 28 **Liddle Dwiggs**[30] 7245 2-9-0 0 JohnFahy 1
(Denis Coakley) *chsd ldrs to 1/2-way: wknd rapidly: t.o* **66/1**

1m 39.98s (0.18) **Going Correction** -0.15s/f (Stan) **9** Ran SP% **117.2**
Speed ratings (Par 94): **93,92,89,88,87 86,86,80,52**
toteswingers 1&2 £8.40, 2&3 £9.70, 1&3 £2.00 CSF £42.19 TOTE £3.90: £1.60, £3.00, £1.90; EX 23.60 Trifecta £173.30 Pool: £2850.73 - 12.33 winning units..
Owner Phil Cunningham **Bred** P M Cunningham **Trained** Newmarket, Suffolk

FOCUS
The slower of the two divisions by 0.97sec. The winner was the pick of these pre-race and is rated to form.

7855 BETDAQ 1ST UK RACE COMMISSION FREE NURSERY H'CAP 1m (P)
7:00 (7:00) (Class 6) (0-60,60) 2-Y-O **£1,940** (£577; £288; £144) **Stalls** Low

Form RPR

061 **1** **Jazzy Lady (IRE)**[15] 7604 2-9-2 55 AdamKirby 3 64
(David Evans) *hld up in rr: gd prog against ins rail fr over 2f out: pushed into ld 1f out: edgd lft but drew clr: readily* **9/2**[1]

0020 **2** 2 1/2 **Choral Clan (IRE)**[49] 6749 2-9-4 57 JackMitchell 2 60
(Philip Mitchell) *prom on inner: rdn and prog to ld wl over 1f out: hdd 1f out whn clr of rest: kpt on but no ch w wnr last 100yds* **25/1**

0003 **3** 2 **Jarlath**[43] 6924 2-9-2 55 SteveDrowne 14 53
(Seamus Mullins) *pressed ldr to 2f out: outpcd sn after: kpt on same pce and jst hld on for 3rd* **14/1**

060 **4** shd **Frederic Chopin**[64] 6277 2-9-3 56 SeanLevey 1 54
(Stuart Williams) *t.k.h and sn trckd ldrs: outpcd fr 2f out: kpt on fnl f: nrly snatched 3rd* **16/1**

3302 **5** 1/2 **Tyrsal (IRE)**[26] 7352 2-9-3 56 AndreaAtzeni 9 55
(Robert Eddery) *hld up in rr: gng wl whn nt clr run over 2f out: prog wl over 1f out: styd on but unable to threaten* **9/2**[1]

0000 **6** 1 1/2 **Prim And Proper**[28] 7293 2-9-3 56 (p) GrahamLee 6 49
(Brendan Powell) *wl in tch in midfield: shkn up 2f out and sn outpcd: kpt on same pce after* **12/1**

6502 **7** 3/4 **Bajan Rebel**[50] 6726 2-9-3 56 GrahamGibbons 8 47
(Michael Easterby) *led: shkn up 2f out: sn hdd: wknd jst over 1f out* **8/1**

600 **8** 2 1/4 **Touche De Rouge (IRE)**[43] 6922 2-9-1 54 AndrewMullen 4 40
(Peter Makin) *stdd after s: tk fierce hold in last pair: trying to make prog whn chopped off on inner over 2f out: modest hdwy over 1f out: no ch* **33/1**

3343 **9** nk **The Wallace Line (IRE)**[23] 7418 2-9-5 58 MartinHarley 7 43
(Mick Channon) *wl in tch in midfield: rdn over 2f out: sn outpcd: no imp on ldrs after* **5/1**[2]

0550 **10** 1 3/4 **Trigger Park (IRE)**[14] 7623 2-9-7 60 ShaneKelly 12 41
(Ronald Harris) *a wl in rr: pushed along and lost grnd over 2f out: no ch whn shkn up over 1f out* **14/1**

3064 **11** 3/4 **Severnwind (IRE)**[19] 7509 2-9-1 54 (be) CathyGannon 5 33
(Ronald Harris) *racd wd towards rr: rdn over 2f out: no prog u.p over 1f out: wknd fnl f* **33/1**

200 **12** 5 **Water For Life**[53] 6643 2-9-4 57 WilliamCarson 11 24
(Dave Morris) *hld up in last pair: t.k.h after 2f: rdn on wd outside over 2f out: wknd* **16/1**

3200 **13** 5 **Black Vale (IRE)**[41] 6966 2-9-6 59 PaddyAspell 13 14
(Phil McEntee) *in tch in midfield: rdn over 2f out: sn wknd* **33/1**

0454 **14** 2 1/2 **Tizlove Regardless (USA)**[15] 7604 2-9-7 60 SilvestreDeSousa 10 9
(Mark Johnston) *wl in rr: prog on wd outside 5f out to go prom over 3f out: wknd rapidly 2f out: eased* **7/1**[3]

1m 40.43s (0.63) **Going Correction** -0.15s/f (Stan) **14** Ran SP% **122.1**
Speed ratings (Par 94): **90,87,85,85,84 83,82,80,80,78 77,72,67,65**
toteswingers 1&2 £21.30, 2&3 £55.40, 1&3 £22.80 CSF £125.66 CT £1499.81 TOTE £4.10: £1.70, £4.00, £4.80; EX 118.30 Trifecta £1314.30 Pool: £1762.65 - 1.00 winning units..
Owner Will Dawson **Bred** Limestone And Tara Studs **Trained** Pandy, Monmouths

FOCUS
An ordinary handicap, and not much pace on early. The winner is progressing.

7856 £500 FREE BETS AT BETDAQ CONDITIONS STKS 7f (P)
7:30 (7:31) (Class 2) 3-Y-O+ **£11,827** (£3,541; £1,770; £885; £442) **Stalls** Low

Form RPR

1033 **1** **Grey Mirage**[18] 7540 4-8-11 96 MartinHarley 3 105
(Marco Botti) *mde all: rdn clr fr 2f out: in n.d after: drvn out and styd on strly* **2/1**[1]

1500 **2** 6 **Magic City (IRE)**[30] 7247 4-8-11 100 WilliamTwiston-Davies 4 89
(Richard Hannon) *awkward s: hld up in last: effrt to chse wnr jst over 2f out: hd to one side and no imp* **4/1**[2]

1435 **3** 1 1/4 **Kinglami**[25] 7368 4-8-11 80 (p) OisinMurphy 5 85
(Brian Gubby) *cl up: rdn to dispute 2nd fr over 2f out: no ch w wnr and one pce fnl f* **12/1**

2003 **4** 6 **Harrison George (IRE)**[18] 7527 8-8-11 100 (t) GrahamGibbons 2 69
(P J O'Gorman) *cl up: rdn to chse wnr briefly over 2f out: sn btn: eased ins fnl f* **8/1**[3]

2005 **5** 6 **Democretes**[13] 7648 4-8-11 91 (b) SeanLevey 6 53
(Richard Hannon) *chsd wnr: pushed along 1/2-way: lost 2nd and wknd over 2f out* **14/1**

1m 23.82s (-2.18) **Going Correction** -0.15s/f (Stan)
WFA 3 from 4yo+ 1lb **5** Ran SP% **78.8**
Speed ratings (Par 109): **106,99,97,90,84**
CSF £4.62 TOTE £1.70: £1.10, £2.30; EX 4.70 Trifecta £31.60 Pool: £665.77 - 15.79 winning units..
Owner Giuliano Manfredini **Bred** Grundy Bloodstock Srl **Trained** Newmarket, Suffolk
■ I'm Back was withdrawn (6-4F, burst out of stalls). Deduct 40p in the £ under R4.

FOCUS
This was turned into a procession by the winner, but there are doubts over the other form horses on this surface. The third looks the best guide.

7857 BOOK NOW FOR BOXING DAY H'CAP 1m 3f (P)
8:00 (8:00) (Class 6) (0-65,65) 3-Y-O+ **£1,940** (£577; £288; £144) **Stalls** Low

Form RPR

6222 **1** **Golden Jubilee (USA)**[33] 7169 4-9-6 64 (v) WilliamTwiston-Davies(3) 5 76
(Nigel Twiston-Davies) *trckd ldrs in 4th: rdn and clsd to ld on outer jst over 2f out: kpt on wl and in command fnl f* **2/1**[1]

2632 **2** 2 **Men Don't Cry (IRE)**[14] 7628 4-9-1 59 (b) MarkCoumbe(3) 2 67
(Ed de Giles) *trckd ldrs in 5th: clsd to chal 2f out: drvn and nt qckn over 1f out: kpt on against far rail to take 2nd nr fin* **7/1**

046 **3** nk **Mrs Micawber**[20] 7488 3-9-1 61 AndreaAtzeni 4 69
(Michael Bell) *trckd ldng pair: clsd to chal and upsides over 2f out: one pce fr over 1f out: lost 2nd nr fin* **11/2**[3]

0133 **4** 6 **Jamaica Grande**[47] 6787 5-9-1 56 WilliamCarson 12 53
(Dave Morris) *hld up wl in rr gng wl: prog to take 6th wl over 2f out: wnt 4th over 1f out but disappointing rspnse to press and no imp* **9/2**[2]

0000 **5** 4 1/2 **Capetown Kid**[70] 6109 3-8-13 59 CathyGannon 10 48
(Sylvester Kirk) *wl in rr: rdn 3f out: plugged on fr over 2f out: n.d* **25/1**

6206 **6** 2 **Colinca's Lad (IRE)**[15] 7611 11-9-6 64 RosieJessop(3) 11 49
(Peter Charalambous) *dashed up fr wdst draw: sn led and set str pce: hdd & wknd jst over 2f out* **12/1**

0000 **7** nk **Anjuna Beach (USA)**[22] 7446 3-9-4 64 SeanLevey 14 49
(Gary Moore) *pushed up fr wd draw but unable to ld: chsd ldr to over 2f out: sn btn* **33/1**

4004 **8** 2 **How Fortunate**[14] 7622 5-9-4 59 GrahamLee 13 40
(Tim Etherington) *hld up in last pair: rdn 3f out: nvr a factor* **8/1**

6123 **9** 2 1/2 **Exclusion (USA)**[35] 5966 3-9-0 60 (b) AdamBeschizza 1 37
(Noel Quinlan) *a wl in rr: rdn over 3f out: sn struggling* **20/1**

120- **10** 1/2 **Tuxedo**[582] 1269 8-9-5 60 ChrisCatlin 9 36
(Peter Hiatt) *chsd ldrs in 6th: rdn and lost pl wl over 2f out: sn btn* **25/1**

3160 **11** 3/4 **Warden Bond**[19] 7515 5-9-3 63 LauraPike(5) 7 37
(William Stone) *nvr bttr than midfield: u.p and struggling over 3f out: wknd* **25/1**

0030 **12** 10 **Bert The Alert**[14] 7622 5-9-7 62 FergusSweeney 6 18
(Laura Mongan) *nvr bttr than midfield: wknd qckly u.p jst over 3f out: t.o* **33/1**

2m 18.96s (-2.94) **Going Correction** -0.15s/f (Stan)
WFA 3 from 4yo+ 5lb **12** Ran SP% **120.4**
Speed ratings (Par 101): **104,102,102,97,94 93,93,91,89,89 88,81**
toteswingers 1&2 £3.20, 2&3 £4.20, 1&3 £3.20 CSF £14.88 CT £68.11 TOTE £2.50: £1.50, £2.80, £2.70; EX 15.20 Trifecta £67.30 Pool: £2024.96 - 22.55 winning units..
Owner Mrs J K Powell **Bred** Dixiana Farms Llc **Trained** Naunton, Gloucs

FOCUS
A modest race, but there was a fair pace on early. This rates the winner's best Polytrack run.
T/Jkpt: Not won. T/Plt: £129.20 to a £1 stake. Pool of £83902.81 - 473.80 winning tickets.
T/Qpdt: £22.90, to a £1 stake. Pool of £11423.25 - 368.75 winning tickets. JN

7779 LINGFIELD (L-H)
Wednesday, November 13

OFFICIAL GOING: Standard
Wind: virtually nil Weather: dry and sunny

7858 LADBROKES H'CAP 1m (P)
12:30 (12:30) (Class 6) (0-65,65) 4-Y-O+ **£2,045** (£603; £302) **Stalls** High

Form RPR

0032 **1** nse **Tee It Up Tommo (IRE)**[6] 7784 4-9-2 60 JimCrowley 7 69+
(Michael Wigham) *hld up towards rr: clsd and gng wl but stuck bhd horses wl over 1f out: swtchd rt and gng for narrow gap whn hmpd ins fnl f: sn swtchd rt and str run fnl 100yds: jst hld: fin 2nd, nse: plcd 1st* **5/4**[1]

4120 **2** **Bloodsweatandtears**[27] 7318 5-9-7 65 AndreaAtzeni 6 72
(William Knight) *stdd s: hld up in tch: rdn and hdwy on outer over 1f out: edgd sltly lft jst ins fnl f: r.o strly to ld on post: fin 1st: plcd 2nd* **10/1**

0501 **3** nk **One Last Dream**[13] 7643 4-8-13 57 (b) DavidProbert 9 63
(Ron Hodges) *led: rdn and clr jst over 2f out: hrd pressed and battled on gamely u.p fnl f: hdd and lost 2 pls last strides* **33/1**

2320 **4** *hd* **Mishrif (USA)**[38] 6315 7-9-7 **65**..............(v) SilvestreDeSousa 2 71
(J R Jenkins) *chsd ldr: rdn over 2f out: styd on u.p and ev ch ins fnl f: no ex cl home* **12/1**

1P33 **4** *dht* **Santadelacruze**[42] 6933 4-9-5 **63**..............(b) AdamKirby 8 69
(Gary Moore) *in tch in midfield: rdn and effrt to chse ldrs 2f out: ev ch ins fnl f: no ex cl home* **4/1**[2]

0405 **6** *1 1/2* **Super Duplex**[22] 7439 6-9-0 **58**..............(t) FrankieMcDonald 10 60
(Roger Teal) *chsd ldrs: rdn and effrt 2f out: n.m.r and styd on same pce ins fnl f* **14/1**

3504 **7** *1/2* **Annes Rocket (IRE)**[13] 7652 8-9-1 **62**.....(p) WilliamTwiston-Davies(3) 1 63
(Jimmy Fox) *hld up in tch in last quartet: effrt over 1f out: n.m.r 1f out: styd on same pce fnl f* **25/1**

0400 **8** *3/4* **Benandonner (USA)**[58] 6457 10-8-11 **55**.............. ShaneKelly 4 55
(Mike Murphy) *chsd ldrs: effrt u.p on inner wl over 1f out: styd on same pce ins fnl f* **14/1**

2653 **9** *hd* **Lutine Charlie (IRE)**[8] 7740 6-9-0 **61**.............. RobertTart(3) 5 60
(Pat Eddery) *chsd ldrs: rdn and effrt 2f out: unable qck u.p 1f out: wknd ins fnl f* **8/1**[3]

0000 **10** *nk* **Lastkingofscotland (IRE)**[9] 7728 7-9-1 **62**..............(b) RyanPowell(3) 3 60
(Conor Dore) *dwlt and rdn along leaving stalls: sn rcvrd and in tch in midfield: effrt but n.m.r jst over 1f out: nvr enough room and no hdwy ins fnl f* **50/1**

5464 **11** *2 3/4* **Dear Maurice**[9] 7729 9-9-0 **65**..............(t) AlfieWarwick(7) 12 57
(Tobias B P Coles) *awkward leaving stalls and s.i.s: in tch in last pair: rdn and no imp over 1f out* **25/1**

1m 36.59s (-1.61) **Going Correction** -0.125s/f (Stan) 11 Ran SP% **118.3**
Speed ratings (Par 101): **102,103,102,102,102 100,100,99,99,99 96**
toteswingers 1&2 £4.80, 2&3 £21.70, 1&3 £14.30 CSF £14.50 CT £287.24 TOTE £1.70: £1.10, £4.80, £8.70; EX 15.80 Trifecta £315.10 Pool: £2582.43 - 6.14 winning units..
Owner Palatinate Thoroughbred Racing Limited **Bred** Oghill House Stud **Trained** Newmarket, Suffolk

FOCUS
A modest handicap in which they went an honest gallop. A bunched and messy finish. Tee It Up Tommo rates a bit better than the bare form.

7859 32RED CASINO MAIDEN STKS (DIV I) 7f (P)
1:00 (1:00) (Class 5) 2-Y-O **£2,726** (£805; £402) **Stalls** Low

Form RPR

00 **1** **Royal Preserve**[29] 7270 2-9-5 0.............. DavidProbert 9 70+
(Andrew Balding) *hld up in tch in last trio: swtchd lft and hdwy over 2f out: rdn to chal between horses 1f out: led fnl 75yds: r.o wl: rdn out* **6/1**[2]

2002 **2** *hd* **Man Amongst Men (IRE)**[21] 7463 2-9-5 84..............(t) JimCrowley 2 69
(Brian Meehan) *chsd ldng pair: effrt u.p over 1f out: hrd drvn to ld but flashed tail u.p 1f out: hdd fnl 75yds: r.o same pce after* **1/3**[1]

00 **3** *3 1/4* **Trillian Astra (IRE)**[30] 7245 2-9-0 0.............. AdamKirby 3 55
(Clive Cox) *chsd ldr: rdn and pressing ldr whn flashed tail u.p ent fnl f: outpcd by ldng pair and btn ins fnl f* **20/1**

00 **4** *1 1/4* **Ragged Robbin (FR)**[12] 7655 2-9-5 0.............. TedDurcan 1 57
(David Lanigan) *led: rdn over 1f out: drvn and hdd 1f out: no ex and wknd ins fnl f* **10/1**[3]

5 *1/2* **Tower Power** 2-9-5 0.............. LiamJones 8 56+
(Ismail Mohammed) *s.i.s and swtchd lft after s: hld up in tch in last trio: hdwy to chse ldrs over 2f out: rdn and wd bnd wl over 1f out: wknd 1f out* **6/1**[2]

00 **6** *8* **Booloo (IRE)**[26] 7341 2-9-2 0.............. BillyCray(3) 5 34
(Garry Moss) *in tch in rr: rdn over 4f out: effrt and struggling over 2f out: wknd u.p over 1f out* **50/1**

0 **7** *9* **Desert Island Dusk**[19] 7500 2-9-5 0.............. SeanLevey 4 10
(John Bridger) *in tch in midfield: rdn and wkng whn edgd rt bnd wl over 1f out: sn wknd* **200/1**

60 **8** *nse* **Wunderkind (USA)**[21] 7466 2-9-0 0.............. ChrisCatlin 7
(Sir Mark Prescott Bt) *in tch in midfield on outer: rdn and losing pl whn rn wd bnd wl over 1f out: sn bhd* **20/1**

0 **9** *37* **Janet's Legacy**[30] 7243 2-9-0 0.............. AndreaAtzeni 6
(Harry Dunlop) *in tch in midfield: rdn and dropped to rr 3f out: sn lost tch: t.o* **25/1**

1m 25.61s (0.81) **Going Correction** -0.125s/f (Stan) 9 Ran SP% **128.5**
Speed ratings (Par 96): **90,89,86,84,84 74,64,64,22**
toteswingers 1&2 £1.50, 2&3 £4.60, 1&3 £12.10 CSF £9.16 TOTE £6.10: £1.60, £1.02, £5.40; EX 17.80 Trifecta £169.50 Pool: £1535.64 - 6.79 winning units..
Owner Mick and Janice Mariscotti **Bred** Horizon Bloodstock Limited **Trained** Kingsclere, Hants

FOCUS
An ordinary maiden with the long odds-on favourite disappointing, and they didn't go much of a gallop. The winner was entitled to rate this high and the form has been given a bit of a chance.

7860 32RED CASINO MAIDEN STKS (DIV II) 7f (P)
1:30 (1:30) (Class 5) 2-Y-O **£2,726** (£805; £402) **Stalls** Low

Form RPR

3 **1** **Sir Robert Cheval**[22] 7448 2-9-5 0.............. MartinHarley 1 82+
(Marco Botti) *mde all: gng best ent fnl 2f: rdn and readily qcknd clr over 1f out: r.o strly: easily* **4/9**[1]

6 **2** *3 1/4* **Swilken**[15] 7606 2-9-5 0.............. LiamJones 2 73+
(Mark H Tompkins) *chsd ldrs: rdn and effrt ent fnl 2f: chsd clr wnr wl over 1f out: no ch w wnr but r.o for clr 2nd* **50/1**

3 *4* **Jalingo (IRE)** 2-9-5 0.............. JoeFanning 4 62
(Mark Johnston) *chsd wnr: rdn ent fnl 2f: 3rd and outpcd over 1f out: wknd fnl f* **5/1**[2]

5 **4** *3/4* **Dutchartcollector**[19] 7501 2-9-5 0.............. AdamKirby 6 60
(Gary Moore) *chsd ldng trio: shkn up over 4f out: rdn and unable qck ent fnl 2f: sn outpcd and wl hld over 1f out* **6/1**[3]

5 *3/4* **Ayers Rock (IRE)** 2-9-5 0.............. ShaneKelly 7 58+
(Marcus Tregoning) *rn green: v.s.a and slow to find stride: clsd and tagged on bk of field after 2f: rdn and outpcd over 2f out: no ch but kpt on fnl f* **12/1**

6 *3 3/4* **Queen Cee** 2-9-0 0.............. SeanLevey 5 44
(Simon Hodgson) *hld up in tch in midfield: rdn and ent fnl 2f: sn outpcd and wknd wl over 1f out* **33/1**

50 **7** *4* **Master Of Alkmaar**[28] 7302 2-9-5 0.............. AndreaAtzeni 9 38
(Roger Varian) *t.k.h early: hld up in tch towards rr: rdn over 2f out: sn btn and wknd over 1f out* **10/1**

8 *47* **Lena Player (SWE)** 2-9-0 0.............. SteveDrowne 8
(Linda Jewell) *in tch in rr tl lost tch rapidly over 3f out: wl t.o over 2f out* **66/1**

1m 24.47s (-0.33) **Going Correction** -0.125s/f (Stan) 8 Ran SP% **123.4**
Speed ratings (Par 96): **96,92,87,86,86 81,77,23**
toteswingers 1&2 £5.40, 2&3 £14.20, 1&3 £1.60 CSF £44.78 TOTE £2.00: £1.10, £8.80, £1.60; EX 44.70 Trifecta £190.90 Pool: £1522.62 - 5.98 winning units..
Owner Heart Of The South Racing **Bred** John And Caroline Penny **Trained** Newmarket, Suffolk

FOCUS
Another ordinary juvenile maiden, but they appeared to go a decent enough pace, and the winning time backs that up compared to the slower tempo of the first division. The easy winner is likely to rate higher.

7861 32RED FILLIES' H'CAP 7f (P)
2:00 (2:00) (Class 5) (0-75,75) 3-Y-0+ **£2,897** (£855; £427) **Stalls** Low

Form RPR

4204 **1** **Broughtons Charm (IRE)**[12] 7663 3-9-0 **71**.............. RobertWinston 10 80
(Willie Musson) *hld up in last trio: hdwy over 2f out: rdn and effrt wl over 1f out: chsd clr ldr 1f out: r.o u.p to ld fnl 50yds: hld on wl: rdn out* **5/1**[2]

0066 **2** *hd* **Balti's Sister (IRE)**[54] 6608 4-9-5 **75**.............. MartinLane 8 84
(Martin Smith) *s.i.s: hld up in last trio: hdwy u.p on outer over 1f out: str chal fnl 50yds: r.o but hld towards fin* **8/1**

2602 **3** *1 3/4* **Maggie Pink**[4] 7824 4-8-13 **69**.............. AndrewMullen 9 74
(Michael Appleby) *taken down early: chsd ldrs: rdn to ld wl over 1f out: drvn and clr 1f out: hdd fnl 50yds and wknd towards fin* **9/2**[1]

3150 **4** *2* **Lucky Di**[42] 6959 3-9-1 **72**.............. JimCrowley 11 70
(Peter Hedger) *stdd s: hld up in rr: effrt on inner and stl plenty to do whn nt clr run over 1f out: hdwy 1f out: r.o wl fnl f: nvr trbld ldrs* **6/1**[3]

0254 **5** *1* **Emerald Sea**[42] 6941 3-8-10 **67**.............. TedDurcan 5 63
(Chris Wall) *trckd ldrs: looked to be travelling wl 2f out: rdn and effrt to press ldr wl over 1f out: drvn and no ex ent fnl f: wknd ins fnl f* **5/1**[2]

5514 **6** *4* **Koharu**[27] 7318 3-8-11 **68**..............(t) SteveDrowne 1 53
(Peter Makin) *hld up in midfield: effrt towards inner wl over 1f out: sn no imp: wknd fnl f* **25/1**

0004 **7** *4 1/2* **Chellalla**[15] 7594 4-8-12 **68**..............(t) SilvestreDeSousa 7 42
(Ian Williams) *chsd ldr after over 5f out tl rdn and outpcd 2f out: wknd wl over 1f out* **10/1**

300- **8** *1/2* **Specialty (IRE)**[439] 5786 3-8-12 **69**.............. FergusSweeney 3 40
(Pam Sly) *chsd ldr tl over 5f out: sn hmpd and dropped to midfield: nvr travelling after: wknd 2f out* **20/1**

2212 **9** *3 3/4* **Bouyrin (IRE)**[12] 7663 3-9-1 **75**.............. WilliamTwiston-Davies(3) 6 36
(Michael Bell) *chsd ldrs: rdn and unable qck jst over 2f out: sn struggling and wknd wl over 1f out* **6/1**[3]

0431 **10** *1* **Amosite**[12] 7663 7-9-4 **74**..............(v) MartinHarley 2 34
(J R Jenkins) *led: rdn ent fnl 2f: hdd wl over 1f out: sn btn and fdd over 1f out* **8/1**

1m 23.26s (-1.54) **Going Correction** -0.125s/f (Stan)
WFA 3 from 4yo+ 1lb 10 Ran SP% **120.0**
Speed ratings (Par 100): **103,102,100,98,97 92,87,87,82,81**
toteswingers 1&2 £10.30, 2&3 £9.00, 1&3 £4.70 CSF £46.16 CT £171.59 TOTE £7.10: £2.00, £2.70, £1.60; EX 54.70 Trifecta £338.50 Pool: £1290.77 - 2.85 winning units..
Owner Broughton Thermal Insulation **Bred** West Dereham Abbey Stud **Trained** Newmarket, Suffolk

FOCUS
A fair fillies' handicap in which there was a contested pace. The form is rated around the second and third.

7862 COMPARE BOOKMAKERS AT BOOKMAKERS.CO.UK H'CAP 6f (P)
2:30 (2:32) (Class 6) (0-60,60) 3-Y-0+ **£2,045** (£603; £302) **Stalls** Low

Form RPR

6223 **1** **Presumido (IRE)**[21] 7459 3-8-12 **60**.............. JackDuern(5) 4 74
(Simon Dow) *stdd after s: hld up in last quartet: clsd and travelling wl ent fnl 2f: rdn and hdwy on inner over 1f out: r.o wl to ld wl ins fnl f: gng away at fin* **5/1**[2]

4531 **2** *1* **Gregori (IRE)**[41] 6980 3-9-3 **60**..............(t) MartinLane 7 71
(Brian Meehan) *w ldr and clr tl 1/2-way: led 4f out: rdn and edgd rt wl over 1f out: wnt rt again u.p 1f out: wnt bk lft u.p ins fnl f: hdd wl ins fnl f: no ex* **11/4**[1]

0253 **3** *1* **Homeboy (IRE)**[13] 7652 5-9-2 **59**.............. MartinDwyer 2 67
(Marcus Tregoning) *chsd ldrs: rdn and carried rt wl over 1f out: keeping on same pce whn n.m.r and swtchd lft wl ins fnl f* **7/1**[3]

6000 **4** *1 1/2* **The Wee Chief (IRE)**[13] 7652 7-9-3 **60**..............(b[1]) SeanLevey 3 63
(Jimmy Fox) *t.k.h: hld up in tch in midfield: clsd and gng wl whn pushed rt and hmpd wl over 1f out: sn rdn and limited rspnse: one pce fnl f* **12/1**

0300 **5** *3/4* **Dishy Guru**[133] 3949 4-9-2 **59**.............. FergusSweeney 5 60
(Michael Blanshard) *racd in midfield: clsd and chsng ldrs whn rn wd bnd 2f out: one pce fr over 1f out* **8/1**

005 **6** *3/4* **Perfect Pastime**[29] 7262 5-9-2 **59**..............(p) WilliamCarson 9 57
(Jim Boyle) *midfield: clsd over 2f out: rdn and unable qck wl over 1f out: one pce after* **5/1**[2]

0352 **7** *nse* **Thorpe Bay**[1] 7848 4-9-2 **59**.............. AndrewMullen 11 57
(Michael Appleby) *awkward as stalls opened and s.i.s: in rr: hdwy and in tch over 2f out: rdn and unable qck over 1f out: one pce and wl hld after* **10/1**

6340 **8** *1 1/4* **Night Trade (IRE)**[34] 7148 6-9-3 **60**..............(p) GrahamLee 6 54
(Ronald Harris) *a towards rr: rdn 1/2-way: kpt on fr over 1f out: nvr trbld ldrs* **16/1**

6006 **9** *5* **Lucky Mark (IRE)**[162] 2949 4-9-0 **60**..............(p) BillyCray(3) 1 38
(Garry Moss) *taken down early: led and clr w rival tl 1/2-way: rdn and nt clr run jst over 2f out: wknd over 1f out* **33/1**

501 **10** *1/2* **Compton Prince**[44] 6901 4-9-3 **60**..............(b) AdamKirby 10 36
(Milton Bradley) *chsd ldrs: rdn and struggling over 2f out: wknd over 1f out* **16/1**

1m 10.87s (-1.03) **Going Correction** -0.125s/f (Stan) 10 Ran SP% **115.1**
Speed ratings (Par 101): **101,99,98,96,95 94,94,92,85,85**
toteswingers 1&2 £3.10, 2&3 £4.50, 1&3 £5.60 CSF £18.84 CT £97.96 TOTE £5.40: £2.90, £1.10, £2.90; EX 15.90 Trifecta £104.20 Pool: £2015.68 - 14.49 winning units..
Owner R Moss & J Page **Bred** Lynn Lodge Stud **Trained** Epsom, Surrey

FOCUS
A modest handicap in which they went a strong gallop. The least exposed pair finished 1-2 and both improved.

7863 32RED.COM H'CAP 2m (P)
3:00 (3:00) (Class 5) (0-70,70) 3-Y-0+ **£2,726** (£805; £402) **Stalls** Low

Form RPR

2251 **1** **Bramshill Lass**[34] 7159 4-9-13 **70**.............. JimCrowley 8 78
(Amanda Perrett) *in tch in midfield: clsd and n.m.r ent fnl 2f: rdn and hdwy to chal 1f out: led fnl 100yds: styd on wl: drvn out* **5/1**[1]

6-24 **2** *1/2* **Four Nations (USA)**[31] 7217 5-9-13 **70**.............. MartinLane 6 77
(George Baker) *chsd ldrs: rdn and effrt to chse ldr wl over 1f out: ev ch fnl f: styd on same pce towards fin* **6/1**[2]

36 **3** *shd* **Swift Blade (IRE)**[71] 6068 5-9-11 **68**..............[1] RobertWinston 5 75
(Lady Herries) *t.k.h: hld up in tch in midfield: clsd and travelling wl 2f out: swtchd rt and effrt ent fnl f: racd awkwardly but r.o strly fnl 100yds* **7/1**[3]

The Form Book Flat, Raceform Ltd, Compton, RG20 6NL.

3436 **4** *nk* **Candoluminescence**[24] 7395 3-9-3 **69**......................(b[1]) SteveDrowne 3 76
(Roger Charlton) *led: rdn wl over 1f out: kpt on u.p tl hdd fnl 100yds: styd on same pce after* **6/1**[2]

0662 **5** *1 1/4* **Where's Susie**[29] 7267 8-9-12 **69**.................................. RobertHavlin 13 74
(Michael Madgwick) *hld up in last quartet: effrt on outer and wd bnd 2f out: hdwy u.p over 1f out: styd on same pce ins fnlf* **10/1**

3450 **6** *1/2* **Guards Chapel**[31] 7217 5-9-2 **66**..............................(v) NedCurtis(7) 7 70+
(Gary Moore) *hld up in last quartet: clsd and n.m.r over 2f out: swtchd lft and hdwy ent fnl f: styd on wl ins fnl f: nvr trbld ldrs* **5/1**[1]

00-3 **7** *3/4* **Yes Chef**[14] 7628 6-9-2 **59**.. LiamJones 1 63
(Chris Gordon) *t.k.h: chsd ldrs: effrt and swtchd rt over 1f out: n.m.r tl 1f out: styd on same pce u.p fnl f* **16/1**

0413 **8** *2 1/4* **Yasir (USA)**[18] 7539 5-9-6 **66**......................................(p) RyanPowell(3) 11 67
(Conor Dore) *chsd ldrs: rdn and effrt over 2f out: keeping on same pce whn pushed rt 1f out: wknd ins fnl f* **10/1**

-600 **9** *3/4* **Natural High (IRE)**[41] 6173 8-9-9 **66**......................(t) SilvestreDeSousa 4 66
(Sean Curran) *chsd ldr: rdn 3f out: lost 2nd and unable qck wl over 1f out: keeping on same pce and hld whn pushed rt and hmpd 1f out: wl hld and eased ins fnl f* **14/1**

/0-5 **10** *hd* **Brabazon (IRE)**[60] 6404 10-9-5 **62**...............................(bt) MartinHarley 10 62
(Emmet Michael Butterly, Ire) *stdd s: hld up in rr: clsd 3f out: effrt u.p on inner wl over 1f out: no real imp: n.d* **20/1**

2202 **11** *2 3/4* **Jezza**[34] 7159 7-9-11 **68**..(bt) AdamKirby 9 64
(Karen George) *dwlt: racd in last quartet: effrt over 2f out: no imp: n.d* **8/1**

12 *3/4* **Shadarpour (IRE)**[35] 4-9-9 **66**.. SeanLevey 14 61
(Gary Moore) *stdd after s: hld up in last quartet: rdn and no hdwy over 2f out: n.d* **20/1**

3m 23.52s (-2.18) **Going Correction** -0.125s/f (Stan)
WFA 3 from 4yo+ 9lb **12** Ran SP% **125.8**
Speed ratings (Par 103): **100,99,99,99,98 98,98,97,96,96 95,94**
toteswingers 1&2 £8.20, 2&3 £12.40, 1&3 £8.10 CSF £36.60 CT £215.44 TOTE £5.50: £2.90, £1.50, £2.90; EX 27.70 Trifecta £245.20 Pool: £1873.19 - 5.72 winning units..
Owner Mrs Karen Hancock **Bred** Bloomsbury Stud **Trained** Pulborough, W Sussex
■ Stewards' Enquiry : Robert Winston caution: careless riding.

FOCUS
A modest staying handicap in which the gallop appeared to be gradually wound up from the front. The winning time was relatively slow but the form is taken at face value.

7864 CORAL APP DOWNLOAD FROM THE APP STORE MAIDEN STKS 1m 2f (P)
3:30 (3:32) (Class 5) 3-Y-O **£2,726** (£805; £402) **Stalls** Low

Form RPR

32 **1** **Hawker**[50] 6738 3-9-5 0.. MartinLane 3 88
(Charlie Appleby) *stdd s: hld up in tch in last trio: swtchd rt and drvn to chal 1f out: led ins fnl f: sustained duel w rival fnl 100yds: hld on wl towards fin* **6/1**

2434 **2** *shd* **Vermont (IRE)**[42] 6950 3-9-5 80.. AndreaAtzeni 6 88
(Luca Cumani) *t.k.h early: in tch in midfield: drvn and str run to ld jst ins fnl f: hdd jst ins fnl f: r.o wl sustained duel w wnr fnl 100yds: jst hld* **3/1**[2]

2402 **3** *3* **Red Warrior (IRE)**[13] 7651 3-9-5 77.................................... AdamKirby 1 82
(Ismail Mohammed) *chsd ldrs: n.m.r bnd 2f out: drvn and ev ch jst over 1f out: no ex and outpcd fnl 100yds* **4/1**[3]

0660 **4** *1 3/4* **Number One London (IRE)**[26] 7337 3-9-5 78................ MartinDwyer 7 79
(Brian Meehan) *chsd ldr led over 7f out: rdn 2f out: drvn and hrd pressed ent fnl f: hdd jst ins fnl f: wknd fnl 100yds* **3/1**[2]

00 **5** *2 3/4* **Ballyshonagh**[63] 6312 3-9-0 0.. TedDurcan 4 68
(Chris Wall) *stdd s: hld up in tch in rr: rdn and effrt over 1f out: no imp: wknd ins fnl f* **100/1**

32 **6** *1* **Desert Skies (IRE)**[14] 7624 3-9-0 0........................... SilvestreDeSousa 2 66
(Saeed bin Suroor) *led tl over 7f out: rdn and ev ch 2f out: drvn and btn over 1f out: sn wknd: eased wl ins fnl f* **11/4**[1]

0 **7** *62* **Puteri Kash**[34] 7154 3-9-0 0.. ChrisCatlin 5
(Gary Moore) *dropped to rr and rdn after 1f: lost tch 6f out: t.o fnl 4f* **100/1**

2m 4.54s (-2.06) **Going Correction** -0.125s/f (Stan) **7** Ran SP% **112.9**
Speed ratings (Par 102): **103,102,100,99,96 96,46**
toteswingers 1&2 £4.40, 2&3 £2.70, 1&3 £2.50 CSF £23.69 TOTE £6.90: £2.00, £2.50; EX 29.60 Trifecta £75.80 Pool: £3889.87 - 38.46 winning units..
Owner Godolphin **Bred** Darley **Trained** Newmarket, Suffolk

FOCUS
A fair maiden. The pace was muddling and there were doubts over most of the field, but the winner built on his C&D latest.

7865 CORAL MOBILE "JUST THREE CLICKS TO BET" H'CAP 1m 2f (P)
4:00 (4:00) (Class 5) (0-70,70) 3-Y-O+ **£2,726** (£805; £402) **Stalls** Low

Form RPR

4320 **1** **Gaelic Silver (FR)**[183] 2348 7-9-4 **69**................................ AndreaAtzeni 7 78
(Gary Moore) *hld up off the pce in midfield: clsd to chse ldrs over 2f out: rdn and effrt ent fnl f: led fnl 75yds: r.o wl* **6/1**[2]

1446 **2** *1* **Understory (USA)**[22] 7446 6-9-3 **68**.............................. MartinDwyer 3 75
(Tim McCarthy) *chsd ldr for 2f: chsd ldrs after: clsd and wnt 2nd again over 2f out: rdn and led wl over 1f out: hdd and no ex fnl 75yds* **10/1**

0-00 **3** *1* **Zaeem**[22] 7438 4-9-5 **70**... RobertWinston 9 75
(Dean Ivory) *chsd ldrs: clsd over 2f out: ev ch u.p ent fnl f: styd on same pce ins fnl f* **25/1**

6502 **4** *3/4* **Mcbirney (USA)**[35] 7132 6-8-10 **68**................................ StaceyKidd(7) 1 72
(Paul D'Arcy) *hld up off the pce in rr: clsd 3f out: hdwy 2f out: chsd ldng trio and rdn ent fnl f: kpt on* **10/1**

0504 **5** *7* **Whitby Jet (IRE)**[22] 7447 5-9-2 **67**.................................. WilliamCarson 5 57
(Ed Vaughan) *hld up off the pce in midfield: clsd but hanging rt 3f out: rdn whn hmpd wl over 1f out: n.d after. kpt on ins fnl f* **11/4**[1]

1140 **6** *1/2* **Remix (IRE)**[18] 7546 4-8-11 **67**.. GeorgeDowning(5) 8 56
(Ian Williams) *racd off the pce in midfield: clsd to chse ldrs over 2f out: drvn and no ex over 1f out: wknd fnl f* **25/1**

5014 **7** *3 3/4* **Silver Lace (IRE)**[22] 7446 4-9-2 **67**................................... TedDurcan 4 48
(Chris Wall) *hld up off the pce in rr of main gp: pushed along and clsd over 2f out: rdn and no ex wl over 1f out: sn wknd* **7/1**[3]

5000 **8** *hd* **Choral Festival**[18] 7539 7-9-4 **69**.................................... KieranO'Neill 11 50
(John Bridger) *racd off the pce in last trio: clsd and in tch over 2f out: rdn and no hdwy wl over 1f out: wknd u.p over 1f out* **25/1**

0002 **9** *3 1/4* **Shirataki (IRE)**[22] 7446 5-9-3 **68**..................................... ChrisCatlin 12 42
(Peter Hiatt) *t.k.h: chsd ldrs tl jnd ldr and wnt clr over 6f out: led over 3f out: rdn and hdd wl over 1f out: sn wknd* **7/1**[3]

050 **10** *6* **Mespone (FR)**[15] 7611 4-8-13 **69**..................................... TimClark(5) 10 31
(Alan Bailey) *led: wnt clr w rival over 6f out tl hdd over 3f out: rdn and lost pl over 2f out: bhd over 1f out* **25/1**

25-0 **11** *31* **Altaria**[19] 7504 4-9-5 **70**... AdamKirby 13
(Seamus Durack) *racd in midfield: rdn and lost pl but stl in tch 4f out: rdn and btn 2f out: sn bhd: virtually p.u ins fnl f: t.o* **8/1**

0114 **12** *41* **Scary Movie (IRE)**[113] 1228 8-9-5 **70**................................ ShaneKelly 2
(Emmet Michael Butterly, Ire) *a wl off the pce in rr and nvr gng wl: lost tch over 4f out: t.o and eased fnl 2f* **14/1**

2m 3.48s (-3.12) **Going Correction** -0.125s/f (Stan) **12** Ran SP% **117.3**
Speed ratings (Par 103): **107,106,105,104,99 98,95,95,93,88 63,30**
toteswingers 1&2 £10.80, 2&3 £28.80, 1&3 £37.40 CSF £60.55 CT £1374.03 TOTE £9.40: £1.80, £2.60, £10.60; EX 43.30 Trifecta £2052.00 Part won. Pool: £2736.04 - 0.88 winning units..
Owner The Winning Hand **Bred** Earl Haras Du Camp Bernard Et Al **Trained** Lower Beeding, W Sussex

FOCUS
A modest handicap in which they went a strong gallop. The first four finished clear and the second sets the standard.
T/Plt: £9.40 to a £1 stake. Pool of £61159.05 - 4699.89 winning tickets. T/Qpdt: £4.70 to a £1 stake. Pool of £6276.73 - 983.90 winning tickets. SP

7866 - 7872a (Foreign Racing) - See Raceform Interactive

7850 KEMPTON (A.W) (R-H)
Thursday, November 14

OFFICIAL GOING: Standard
Wind: Fresh, against Weather: Fine but cloudy

7873 £25 FREE BET AT BETVICTOR MEDIAN AUCTION MAIDEN STKS 7f (P)
4:20 (4:20) (Class 6) 3-5-Y-O **£1,940** (£577; £288; £144) **Stalls** Low

Form RPR

3633 **1** **My Gigi**[100] 5098 3-9-0 63..(p) AdamKirby 4 61
(Gary Moore) *trckd ldr: led wl over 2f out: sn pushed wl clr: unchal* **11/10**[1]

05 **2** *6* **Clear Loch**[15] 7624 3-9-5 60.. NickyMackay 3 50
(John Spearing) *trckd ldng pair: swtchd lft and rdn to chse wnr over 2f out: sn lft bhd: plugged on* **7/2**[3]

006- **3** *1/2* **Fen Flyer**[503] 3591 4-9-6 30.. PaddyAspell 6 50?
(John Berry) *in tch: drvn over 2f out: kpt on to press for 2nd fnl f: one pce* **50/1**

00 **4** *1* **Zeteah**[43] 6950 3-9-0 0.. TedDurcan 5 42
(David Lanigan) *t.k.h: trckd ldrs: drvn to dispute 2nd over 2f out to 1f out: no ex* **9/4**[2]

600 **5** *3/4* **Pastoral Dancer**[15] 7624 4-9-6 39.. ChrisCatlin 1 46?
(Richard Rowe) *dwlt: hld up in last: nt clr run jst over 2f out: pushed along and prog wl over 1f out: stl pushed along and no hdwy fnl f* **50/1**

00 **6** *6* **Broon Troot (IRE)**[7] 7781 3-9-5 0..................................... MartinDwyer 2 29
(Marcus Tregoning) *t.k.h: hld up in tch: rdn over 2f out: no prog: wknd fnl f* **12/1**

0 **7** *30* **She Wont Tell**[15] 7624 4-9-1 0... SeanLevey 7
(John Bridger) *led to wl over 2f out: wknd rapidly: t.o* **33/1**

1m 27.04s (1.04) **Going Correction** 0.0s/f (Stan)
WFA 3 from 4yo 1lb **7** Ran SP% **115.2**
Speed ratings (Par 101): **94,87,86,85,84 77,43**
toteswingers 1&2 £2.10, 2&3 £7.20, 1&3 £10.20 CSF £5.49 TOTE £1.90: £1.40, £2.50; EX 4.60 Trifecta £38.10 Pool: £3078.02 - 60.57 winning units..
Owner Mrs H J Moorhead **Bred** Arabian Bloodstock **Trained** Lower Beeding, W Sussex

FOCUS
One of the weakest maiden races you're ever likely to witness and an effortless success from the very easy-to-back favourite. The time was slow and the winner didn't need to improve.

7874 BRITISH STALLION STUDS EBF MAIDEN FILLIES' STKS (DIV I) 1m (P)
4:50 (4:51) (Class 5) 2-Y-O **£2,911** (£866; £432; £216) **Stalls** Low

Form RPR

0 **1** **Crystal Pearl**[22] 7466 2-9-0 0... LiamJones 6 73
(Mark H Tompkins) *t.k.h: trckd ldrs: wnt 3rd over 2f out and sn rdn: clsd over 1f out: drvn to ld last 120yds: styd on* **33/1**

0 **2** *1 1/4* **Lisamour (IRE)**[7] 7780 2-9-0 0... RaulDaSilva 8 70
(Paul Cole) *mde most to 3f out: sn rdn: rallied to press ldr over 1f out: wnr wnt past ins fnl f: kpt on* **50/1**

3 *3/4* **Special Miss** 2-9-0 0.. MartinHarley 13 68+
(Marco Botti) *wl in rr early: stl towards rr 1/2-way: pushed along and prog 2f out: stl pushed along and fin wl to take 3rd last strides* **7/1**[3]

6224 **4** *nse* **Dancing Sands (IRE)**[29] 7296 2-9-0 78........................ SilvestreDeSousa 2 68
(Charlie Appleby) *pressed ldr: led 3f out: gng strly over 2f out: drvn over 1f out: wilted and hdd last 120yds: wl hld whn n.m.r nr fin and lost 3rd* **1/1**[1]

5 *1/2* **Sotise (IRE)** 2-9-0 0.. PaddyAspell 9 68+
(Marco Botti) *hld up in 9th: rdn over 2f out: prog wl over 1f out: styd on wl fnl f: nrst fin* **25/1**

00 **6** *5* **Wulfthryth**[12] 7693 2-8-8 0 ow1....................................... AlfieWarwick(7) 5 56
(Tobias B P Coles) *wl in rr early: prog into midfield over 2f out: no hdwy and lft bhd jst over 1f out* **66/1**

02 **7** *2* **Gift Of Rain (IRE)**[16] 7606 2-9-0 0..................................... AdamKirby 11 51
(Ed Dunlop) *racd wd: trckd ldng pair: shkn up and lost pl over 2f out: sn btn* **7/2**[2]

8 *1/2* **Saint's Victory** 2-9-0 0... ShaneKelly 1 50
(Sir Michael Stoute) *chsd ldrs: shkn up over 2f out: sn wknd* **12/1**

06 **9** *1* **Blossom Lane**[23] 7449 2-9-0 0.. NickyMackay 10 47
(John Gosden) *settled in last pair: pushed along over 2f out: no real prog* **16/1**

0 **10** *5* **Secret Keeper**[14] 7645 2-9-0 0... CathyGannon 12 36
(Sir Mark Prescott Bt) *t.k.h early: hld up: last and rdn bef 1/2-way: sn btn* **66/1**

05 **11** *shd* **Prize**[55] 6589 2-9-0 0.. KieranO'Neill 7 36
(Richard Hannon) *tok t.k.h: trckd ldrs: rdn and wknd over 2f out* **12/1**

1m 39.87s (0.07) **Going Correction** 0.0s/f (Stan) **11** Ran SP% **117.7**
Speed ratings (Par 93): **99,97,97,96,96 91,89,88,87,82 82**
toteswingers 1&2 £41.00, 2&3 £53.00, 1&3 £46.40 CSF £1092.10 TOTE £44.20: £7.80, £8.50, £2.70; EX 892.20 Trifecta £2845.00 Part won. Pool: £3793.38 - 0.03 winning units..
Owner John Brenchley **Bred** John Brenchley & Dullingham Park **Trained** Newmarket, Suffolk

FOCUS
Something of a shock result and a rare maiden success for trainer Mark Tompkins. Ordinary form.

7875 BRITISH STALLION STUDS EBF MAIDEN FILLIES' STKS (DIV II) 1m (P)
5:20 (5:22) (Class 5) 2-Y-O £2,911 (£866; £432; £216) Stalls Low

Form RPR
1 **Kind Invitation** 2-9-0 0 SilvestreDeSousa 7 79+
(Charlie Appleby) *mde most: shkn up and wnt for home jst over 2f out: pressed and drvn fnl f: styd on wl* **9/4**[1]
2 ½ **Water Hole (IRE)** 2-9-0 0 RobertHavlin 3 78+
(John Gosden) *dwlt: sn wl in tch: prog over 2f out: shkn up to chse wnr over 1f out: clsd to chal ins fnl f: styd on but hld nr fin* **10/1**
3 2 ¼ **Shama (IRE)** 2-9-0 0 ShaneKelly 2 72+
(Sir Michael Stoute) *w.w in midfield: pushed along quite firmly fr over 2f out: prog over 1f out: chsd ldng pair ins fnl f: kpt on but no imp* **6/1**[3]
4 1 **Windlass (IRE)** 2-9-0 0 NickyMackay 8 70+
(John Gosden) *racd on outer in midfield: pushed along fr over 2f out: nvr really on terms but kpt on steadily* **25/1**
05 5 hd **Isabella Liberty (FR)**[19] 7532 2-9-0 0 MartinDwyer 11 70+
(Robert Eddery) *broke smartly but sn restrained into last pair: pushed along over 2f out: reminder over 1f out: styd on in encouraging style fnl f* **20/1**
6 hd **Carnevale** 2-9-0 0 JimCrowley 1 69
(Ralph Beckett) *dwlt: in rr: pushed along and prog on inner 2f out: nvr on terms but kpt on steadily* **7/1**
43 7 1 ¼ **Joohaina (IRE)**[31] 7245 2-9-0 0 MartinHarley 5 66
(Marco Botti) *w wnr to 1/2-way: chsd after tl wknd over 1f out* **11/4**[2]
00 8 1 ¼ **Red Passiflora**[23] 7450 2-9-0 0 CathyGannon 10 63+
(Sir Mark Prescott Bt) *dwlt: rn green in last: pushed along and no prog over 2f out: fnlly sed to run on ins fnl f: fin quite takingly* **50/1**
9 1 **Blue Oyster** 2-9-0 0 WilliamCarson 6 61
(Philip McBride) *prom tl shkn up and wknd jst over 2f out* **33/1**
00 10 nk **La Grassetta (GER)**[30] 7260 2-9-0 0 MartinLane 4 60
(Tobias B P Coles) *prom tl wknd over 2f out* **66/1**
11 9 **Raphinae** 2-9-0 0 AdamKirby 9 38
(Charlie Appleby) *dwlt and stdd s: rn green towards rr: wknd qckly 2f out: t.o* **8/1**

1m 41.22s (1.42) **Going Correction** 0.0s/f (Stan) **11 Ran SP% 119.4**
Speed ratings (Par 93): **92,91,89,88,88 87,86,85,84,84 75**
toteswingers 1&2 £7.40, 2&3 £11.90, 1&3 £3.10 CSF £24.90 TOTE £3.30: £1.10, £3.50, £2.40; EX 29.80 Trifecta £121.60 Pool: £2643.38 - 16.29 winning units..
Owner Godolphin **Bred** Darley **Trained** Newmarket, Suffolk

FOCUS
A race packed full of unexposed fillies and much to the like about the performances of a number of these, including the well supported winner. Lots of promise on show but the bare form is probably as good as rated.

7876 BETVICTOR'S NEW LIVE CASINO FILLIES' H'CAP 1m (P)
5:50 (5:53) (Class 5) (0-75,75) 3-Y-O+ £2,587 (£770; £384; £192) Stalls Low

Form RPR
123 1 **Araqella (IRE)**[54] 6657 3-9-0 **70** LiamJones 11 81
(William Haggas) *chsd ldrs in 6th: rdn over 2f out: styd on fr over 1f out: clsd to ld last 100yds: drvn out* **8/1**[2]
106 2 ¾ **Welsh Sunrise**[24] 7430 3-8-6 **62** (v[1]) MartinLane 8 71
(Ed Walker) *chsd ldrs in 5th: drvn over 2f out: clsd to ld over 1f out: hdd and no ex last 100yds* **25/1**
3216 3 1 ¼ **Absent Amy (IRE)**[43] 6952 4-9-6 **74** RobertHavlin 5 80
(Amy Weaver) *sn in last quartet: rdn wl over 2f out: prog over 1f out: styd on past tiring rivals fnl f: tk 3rd post* **9/1**[3]
121 4 nse **Havelovewilltravel (IRE)**[9] 7741 3-9-1 **71** 6ex ShaneKelly 3 77
(Jeremy Noseda) *hld up in 8th and sme way off the pce: shkn up 3f out: prog u.p 2f out: clsd on ldrs fnl f: chsd ldng pair nr fin but unable to chal: lost 3rd post* **11/10**[1]
5053 5 ½ **Flamborough Breeze**[29] 7307 4-9-6 **74** (t) SeanLevey 14 79
(Ed Vaughan) *stdd s and dropped in fr wdst draw: hld up in last: gd prog over 2f out: weaved through and clsd on ldrs fnl f: wnt 3rd briefly but effrt flattened out last 75yds* **8/1**[2]
334 6 1 ¼ **Waveguide (IRE)**[55] 6599 4-9-0 **68** (p) FergusSweeney 9 70
(David Simcock) *trckd ldr at str pce: drvn ahd 2f out: hdd over 1f out: fdd fnl f* **25/1**
1362 7 ¾ **Wakeup Little Suzy (IRE)**[21] 7489 3-9-5 **75** (t) MartinHarley 12 75
(Marco Botti) *chsd ldng trio: drvn over 2f out: kpt on to press ldrs over 1f out: fdd fnl f* **8/1**[2]
5000 8 ¾ **Angel Cake (IRE)**[26] 7383 4-8-9 **63** AndrewMullen 4 61
(Michael Appleby) *chsd ldng pair: drvn and on terms 2f out: wknd fnl f* **33/1**
1402 9 nk **Lady Sylvia**[15] 7629 4-9-2 **70** SilvestreDeSousa 10 68
(Joseph Tuite) *settled in 7th and sme way off the pce: drvn over 2f out: tried to cl on ldrs over 1f out: fdd fnl f* **8/1**[2]
2000 10 3 **Emman Bee (IRE)**[23] 7437 4-8-12 **66** (bt[1]) CathyGannon 1 57
(Luke Dace) *led at str pce: hdd 2f out: sn wknd* **50/1**
3500 11 2 ¾ **Russian Ice**[22] 7462 5-9-6 **74** (p) JimCrowley 13 58
(Dean Ivory) *dropped in fr wd draw: pushed along in last pair: no prog and struggling over 2f out* **33/1**
34 12 1 ¼ **Push Me (IRE)**[26] 6048 6-9-3 **71** AdamKirby 2 53
(Iain Jardine) *a in rr and u.p sn after 1/2-way: no prog* **20/1**
4415 13 ¾ **Tammuz (IRE)**[23] 7437 3-7-13 **62** CameronHardie(7) 7 42
(Tony Carroll) *racd wd: a in rr: struggling over 2f out* **20/1**

1m 38.47s (-1.33) **Going Correction** 0.0s/f (Stan)
WFA 3 from 4yo+ 2lb **13 Ran SP% 127.1**
Speed ratings (Par 100): **106,105,104,103,103 102,101,100,100,97 94,93,92**
toteswingers 1&2 £61.70, 2&3 £125.60, 1&3 £30.20 CSF £201.02 CT £1866.25 TOTE £12.80: £4.10, £9.00, £3.80; EX 691.70 Trifecta £2266.70 Part won. Pool: £3022.36 - 0.03 winning units..
Owner Mr & Mrs D Hearson **Bred** Granham Farm Partnership **Trained** Newmarket, Suffolk

FOCUS
An above-average race for the grade and hard to fault the effort of the lightly raced winner. The form is rated slightly positively.

7877 REINDEER RACING CHRISTMAS PARTIES AT KEMPTON CLAIMING STKS 1m 4f (P)
6:20 (6:21) (Class 6) 3-Y-O £1,940 (£577; £288; £144) Stalls Centre

Form RPR
4300 1 **Artistical (IRE)**[20] 7505 3-8-12 67 DannyBrock(5) 3 76
(Lee Carter) *hld up in 5th: prog on outer and sweeping move to ld jst over 2f out: drvn over 1f out: kpt on wl enough fnl f* **12/1**
0001 2 1 ¼ **Syrenka**[14] 7637 3-8-3 57 (v) MartinDwyer 6 60
(Marcus Tregoning) *hld up in last: nudged along 1/2-way: clsd on ldrs over 2f out: nt clr run and eased out wd: rdn to chse wnr over 1f out: clsd grad but edgd lft and nvr looked like chalng properly* **7/4**[1]
203 3 6 **Star Of Namibia (IRE)**[23] 7569 3-8-12 67 (b) TedDurcan 2 59
(J S Moore) *trckd ldr: clsd to chal as wnr wnt by jst over 2f out: lost 2nd and wknd over 1f out* **7/2**[3]
0500 4 2 **Barnaby Brook (CAN)**[7] 7786 3-8-10 75 (p) MartinLane 4 54
(Nick Littmoden) *chsd ldng trio: hrd rdn 4f out and dropped to last 3f out: no ch after* **10/3**[2]
50-3 5 ¾ **Wrecking Ball (IRE)**[14] 7637 3-8-10 60 RobertHavlin 1 53
(Amy Weaver) *restless in stalls: rring as they opened but led: hdd jst over 2f out: wknd over 1f out* **9/2**
5566 6 ¾ **Pencombe (FR)**[14] 7637 3-8-5 58 ow1 (t) RobertTart(3) 5 50
(David Simcock) *chsd ldng pair to over 2f out: wknd* **8/1**

2m 33.69s (-0.81) **Going Correction** 0.0s/f (Stan) **6 Ran SP% 118.6**
Speed ratings (Par 98): **102,101,97,95,95 94**
toteswingers 1&2 £7.20, 2&3 £1.80, 1&3 £10.50 CSF £35.75 TOTE £13.30: £3.30, £1.40; EX 49.80 Trifecta £249.20 Pool: £1649.09 - 4.96 winning units..
Owner Miss Victoria Baalham **Bred** D I Scott **Trained** Epsom, Surrey

FOCUS
The absence of likely favourite Pixie Cut meant this was significantly weaker than it otherwise would have been but it produced a fair performance from the winner. The overall form is a bit shaky.

7878 £175 CASH BONUS AT VICTOR'S LIVE CASINO NURSERY H'CAP 7f (P)
6:50 (6:52) (Class 6) (0-65,65) 2-Y-O £1,940 (£577; £288; £144) Stalls Low

Form RPR
4203 1 **Starlight Princess (IRE)**[7] 7789 2-8-10 **54** (b) JohnFahy 11 61+
(J S Moore) *awkward s: hld up in last: prog towards inner 2f out: forced way through over 1f out and bmpd rival: drvn to ld ins fnl f: styd on wl* **16/1**
004 2 1 **Plough Boy (IRE)**[70] 6131 2-8-9 **53** TedDurcan 7 57
(Willie Musson) *trckd ldrs: clsd 2f out: rdn to ld jst over 1f out to ins fnl f: one pce* **4/1**[2]
6004 3 ¾ **My My My Diliza**[36] 7117 2-8-11 **55** (b) DavidProbert 12 57
(J S Moore) *in tch in midfield: rdn over 2f out: prog to chal and upsides over 1f out: nt qckn ins fnl f* **20/1**
0260 4 ½ **Evacusafe Lady**[12] 7695 2-9-7 **65** (tp) AdamKirby 5 66
(John Ryan) *awkward s: hld up in last trio: prog whn nt clr run over 1f out: drvn and hdwy to take 4th last 100yds: styd on but unable to chal* **12/1**
0010 5 ¾ **Fiftyshadesfreed (IRE)**[40] 7017 2-9-6 **64** JimCrowley 8 63
(George Baker) *w.w towards rr: rdn over 2f out: prog on outer over 1f out: kpt on but nt pce to threaten* **5/2**[1]
0500 6 ¾ **Green Music**[23] 7451 2-9-1 **59** CathyGannon 2 56
(James Eustace) *awkward s: hld up in midfield: swtchd to inner and prog 2f out: chal and upsides over 1f out: bmpd sn after: fdd* **16/1**
5405 7 ½ **Royal Bushida**[7] 7789 2-8-9 **53** RaulDaSilva 9 49
(Derek Shaw) *wl in rr: rdn over 2f out: styd on fnl f: no ch to threaten* **20/1**
4002 8 nk **Honey Meadow**[15] 7623 2-9-7 **65** MartinHarley 4 60
(Robert Eddery) *trckd ldrs: cl up gng strly over 2f out: got through to ld v briefly over 1f out: wknd fnl f* **9/2**[3]
000 9 1 ¾ **Charleys Angel**[30] 7261 2-8-1 **48** JemmaMarshall(3) 14 38
(Pat Phelan) *w ldr: led after 2f: mde most tl hdd over 1f out: wknd fnl f* **25/1**
0400 10 hd **Polar Express**[42] 6979 2-8-10 **57** MatthewLawson(3) 10 47
(Jonathan Portman) *racd wdst of ldng quartet: drvn over 2f out: wknd over 1f out* **25/1**
0320 11 1 **Acquaint (IRE)**[29] 7309 2-9-7 **65** (b[1]) SeanLevey 1 52
(Richard Hannon) *led 2f: pressed ldr: drvn and upsides over 2f out: wknd over 1f out* **4/1**[2]
6450 12 4 **Aweebitowinker**[36] 7117 2-8-10 **54** LiamJones 6 30
(J S Moore) *awkward s: nvr gng wl: drvn in rr 1/2-way and no prog* **33/1**
051 13 2 ½ **Just Rubie**[13] 7664 2-9-7 **65** FergusSweeney 13 34
(Michael Blanshard) *w ldng pair: stl upsides 2f out u.p: wknd qckly over 1f out* **16/1**

1m 26.93s (0.93) **Going Correction** 0.0s/f (Stan) **13 Ran SP% 132.2**
Speed ratings (Par 94): **94,92,92,91,90 89,89,88,86,86 85,80,78**
toteswingers 1&2 £14.50, 1&3 £24.20, 2&3 £18.00 CSF £82.12 CT £1362.31 TOTE £22.90: £3.90, £2.80, £4.80; EX 117.70 Trifecta £1640.00 Part won. Pool: £2186.72 - 0.05 winning units..
Owner J S Moore **Bred** Coleman Bloodstock Limited **Trained** Upper Lambourn, Berks
■ Stewards' Enquiry : John Fahy two-day ban: careless riding (Nov 28-29)

FOCUS
There was plenty of competition for the early lead in this low-grade nursery and that appeared to play into the hands of the confidently ridden winner. They finished compressed and the form looks limited.

7879 DOWNLOAD THE BETVICTOR APP NOW NURSERY H'CAP 6f (P)
7:20 (7:20) (Class 4) (0-85,81) 2-Y-O £3,752 (£1,116; £557; £278) Stalls Low

Form RPR
651 1 **Nova Princesse (GER)**[55] 6607 2-8-11 **71** (t) MartinHarley 1 77+
(Marco Botti) *hld up bhd ldng trio and a gng wl: smooth prog to ld over 1f out: pushed along and in command: cosily* **5/1**[3]
6201 2 ¾ **Poetic Choice**[7] 7700 2-8-9 **69** 6ex MartinLane 3 71
(Nick Littmoden) *trckd ldng trio: rdn and nt qckn over 2f out: styd on fr over 1f out to take 2nd last stride* **3/1**[2]
0536 3 shd **Stomp**[38] 7062 2-9-0 **74** JimCrowley 2 75
(Roger Charlton) *disp ld on inner: kicked on jst over 2f out: drvn over 1f out: sn hdd and nt qckn: lost 2nd post* **5/4**[1]
413 4 1 ¼ **Djinni (IRE)**[83] 5699 2-9-4 **78** SeanLevey 6 76
(Richard Hannon) *hld up in last: plenty to do once ldrs kicked on 2f out: shkn up and limited prog on inner over 1f out: nvr involved* **5/1**[3]
020 5 2 ¾ **Concrete Mac**[32] 7218 2-8-8 **75** CharlieBennett(7) 5 64
(Hughie Morrison) *racd on outer of ldng trio: drvn over 2f out: stl cl enough over 1f out: fdd fnl f* **16/1**
0000 6 shd **Fair Ranger**[15] 7626 2-8-12 **79** CameronHardie(7) 4 68
(Richard Hannon) *disp ld to over 2f out: lost pl and struggling after* **12/1**

1m 14.04s (0.94) **Going Correction** 0.0s/f (Stan) **6 Ran SP% 116.4**
Speed ratings (Par 98): **93,92,91,90,86 86**
toteswingers 1&2 £2.00, 1&3 £2.30, 2&3 £1.10 CSF £21.19 TOTE £7.10: £3.80, £2.00; EX 21.60 Trifecta £62.60 Pool: £1491.76 - 17.85 winning units..
Owner Scuderia Blueberry **Bred** Gestut Isarland **Trained** Newmarket, Suffolk

The Form Book Flat, Raceform Ltd, Compton, RG20 6NL.

FOCUS
An ordinary nursery. Improvement from the winner with the second not far her improved Wolverhampton level.

7880 BACK OF THE NET AT BETVICTOR H'CAP 7f (P)
7:50 (7:50) (Class 5) (0-70,70) 3-Y-0+ £2,587 (£770; £384; £192) Stalls Low

Form RPR
2U02 1 **Emkanaat**[9] 7743 5-9-7 **70** RobertHavlin 6 84
(Amy Weaver) *trckd ldrs gng wl: clsd 2f out: led over 1f out: strode clr last 150yds: v readily* **5/2**[1]
2-21 2 3 1/2 **Daring Dragon**[21] 7484 3-9-6 **70** (b) JimCrowley 5 74
(Ed Walker) *sltly awkward s: hld up towards rr: rdn 2f out: prog over 1f out: styd on to take 2nd last strides* **4/1**[2]
5313 3 hd **First Class**[30] 7263 5-9-1 **64** DavidProbert 14 68+
(Rae Guest) *hld up towards rr: rdn on outer jst over 2f out: prog over 1f out: styd on fnl f to take 3rd last strides* **6/1**[3]
3330 4 hd **Golden Desert (IRE)**[29] 7303 9-9-2 **65** MartinHarley 12 69+
(Simon Dow) *dwlt: hld up in last: prog whn nt clr run over 1f out to jst ins fnl f: cajoled along and r.o: no ch* **20/1**
4600 5 1/2 **Street Power (USA)**[30] 7262 8-9-2 **65** FergusSweeney 1 68
(Jeremy Gask) *awkward s: hld up in midfield: prog on inner 2f out: chal and w wnr over 1f out: lft bhd last 150yds: wknd fnl strides* **16/1**
2004 6 nk **Fever Few**[29] 7303 4-9-5 **68** (p) SilvestreDeSousa 3 70
(Jane Chapple-Hyam) *led to over 1f out: no ch w wnr fnl f: lost pls nr fin* **8/1**
3040 7 1/2 **The Happy Hammer (IRE)**[64] 6317 7-9-3 **66** MartinDwyer 2 66
(Eugene Stanford) *awkward s: hld up towards rr: pushed along and prog to chse ldrs jst over 1f out: shkn up and one pce after* **20/1**
4305 8 nse **Eager To Bow (IRE)**[64] 6316 7-9-2 **70** DanielMuscutt(5) 13 70
(Patrick Chamings) *hld up wl in rr: nudged along on outer over 2f out: sme prog and shkn up fnl f: styd on but nvr involved* **12/1**
5510 9 3/4 **Athletic**[30] 7262 4-9-2 **65** (v) MartinLane 7 63
(Andrew Reid) *hld up in midfield: tried to make prog over 1f out: rdn and nt qckn fnl f* **12/1**
5324 10 hd **Khajaaly (IRE)**[9] 7754 6-9-4 **67** (tp) AndrewMullen 4 65
(Michael Appleby) *prom: rdn and cl up 2f out: wknd fnl f* **12/1**
5000 11 3/4 **Darnathean**[29] 7307 4-9-2 **65** (p) FrederikTylicki 8 61
(Paul D'Arcy) *prom: rdn over 2f out: fdd over 1f out* **33/1**
6400 12 1 **Tiger Reigns**[67] 6236 7-9-5 **68** (t) SeanLevey 9 61
(John Butler) *a towards rr: shuffled along and no prog fnl 2f* **40/1**
4006 13 1 1/4 **Avonmore Star**[29] 7303 5-9-2 **65** ShaneKelly 10 55
(Mike Murphy) *hld up in rr: trying to make prog whn nowhere to go jst over 1f out: no hdwy fnl f* **33/1**
0605 14 3 **Exceedexpectations (IRE)**[10] 7729 4-8-13 **65** RyanPowell(3) 11 47
(Conor Dore) *pressed ldr: rdn over 2f out: wknd over 1f out* **33/1**

1m 25.39s (-0.61) **Going Correction** 0.0s/f (Stan)
WFA 3 from 4yo+ 1lb **14** Ran SP% **123.7**
Speed ratings (Par 103): **103,99,98,98,97 97,97,97,96,95 95,93,92,89**
toteswingers 1&2 £2.60, 1&3 £4.30, 2&3 £1.80 CSF £10.99 CT £58.71 TOTE £3.70: £2.00, £1.70, £2.10; EX 19.10 Trifecta £46.90 Pool: £2259.54 - 36.12 winning units..
Owner Bringloe, Powell & Executive Bloodlines **Bred** C J Mills **Trained** Newmarket, Suffolk

FOCUS
A competitive race was turned into a mere procession by the heavily backed winner, who is rated back to his old non-claiming form.
T/Plt: £3697.20. Pool: £77,490.20 - 15.3 winning units. T/Qpdt: £144.80. Pool: £13,100.26 - 66.94 winning units. JN

7752 SOUTHWELL (L-H)
Thursday, November 14

OFFICIAL GOING: Standard
Wind: fresh 1/2 behind Weather: fine and sunny but very windy

7881 CORAL MOBILE JUST THREE CLICKS TO BET H'CAP 1m 4f (F)
12:20 (12:21) (Class 5) (0-70,69) 3-Y-0+ £2,587 (£770; £384; £192) Stalls Low

Form RPR
0-06 1 **Dynastic**[37] 7100 4-8-10 **62** LauraBarry(7) 3 70
(Tony Coyle) *dwlt: in rr: hdwy 3f out: chsng ldrs over 1f out: styd on to ld last 50yds* **10/1**
533 2 1 1/4 **Lookbeforeyouleap**[7] 7791 3-9-4 **69** DanielTudhope 13 75
(David O'Meara) *chsd ldrs: led 3f out: hdd and no ex wl ins fnl f* **7/1**
0233 3 shd **My Destination (IRE)**[27] 7342 4-9-0 **62** NeilFarley(3) 4 68
(Declan Carroll) *mid-div: drvn over 5f out: kpt on to chse ldrs 1f out: styd on same pce* **11/2**[2]
1566 4 shd **Precision Strike**[8] 7778 3-8-6 **60** (v) BillyCray(3) 12 66
(Richard Guest) *mid-div: hdwy over 7f out: upsides over 4f out: kpt on same pce last 100yds* **33/1**
3230 5 1 1/2 **Bavarian Nordic (USA)**[65] 6290 8-8-7 **57** (v) GeorgeChaloner(5) 8 60
(Richard Whitaker) *chsd ldrs: drvn over 4f out: one pce fnl f* **16/1**
3031 6 1/2 **Bold And Free**[51] 6717 3-8-12 **63** GrahamLee 7 66
(David Thompson) *w ldrs: led over 5f out: hdd 3f out: kpt on one pce fnl f* **12/1**
1242 7 2 3/4 **Mr Lando**[15] 7622 4-9-7 **66** JimmyQuinn 10 64
(Tony Carroll) *mid-div: hdwy 7f out: chsd ldrs over 1f out: one pce* **11/2**[2]
2604 8 1/2 **Xpres Maite**[20] 7514 10-9-0 **59** (v) RobertWinston 11 56
(Roy Bowring) *s.i.s: in rr: hdwy over 2f out: nvr a factor* **16/1**
5000 9 1 1/4 **Mitchell**[50] 6757 3-8-10 **61** RaulDaSilva 9 56
(David Thompson) *in rr: hdwy over 5f out: wknd appr fnl f* **66/1**
2245 10 1 3/4 **Easydoesit (IRE)**[144] 2739 5-9-6 **68** WilliamTwiston-Davies(3) 1 61
(Tony Carroll) *drvn along: lost pl and bhd after 1f: sme hdwy over 2f out: nvr on terms* **25/1**
2246 11 2 1/4 **Amtired**[153] 3301 7-9-3 **62** (p) RussKennemore 5 51
(Marjorie Fife) *mid-div: hdwy on ins over 3f out: sn chsng ldrs: hung lft and wknd appr fnl f* **9/2**[1]
6500 12 12 **West End Lad**[36] 7132 10-9-6 **68** (b) MarkCoumbe(3) 14 38
(Roy Bowring) *chsd ldrs: led over 8f out: hdd over 5f out: sn lost pl* **33/1**
-005 13 3/4 **Song Of The Siren**[16] 7597 5-9-0 **66** JoshDoyle(7) 6 35
(David O'Meara) *chsd ldrs: lost pl 5f out: sn bhd* **25/1**
3014 14 8 **Madeira Girl (IRE)**[40] 7038 4-9-8 **67** DougieCostello 2 23
(Jonjo O'Neill) *led tl over 8f out: drvn and lost pl over 4f out: bhd whn eased fnl f* **6/1**[3]

2m 40.06s (-0.94) **Going Correction** +0.025s/f (Slow)
WFA 3 from 4yo+ 6lb **14** Ran SP% **119.4**
Speed ratings (Par 103): **104,103,103,103,102 101,99,99,98,97 96,88,87,82**
toteswingers 1&2 £14.30, 2&3 £8.10, 1&3 £12.80 CSF £73.88 CT £432.07 TOTE £13.70: £4.80, £2.90, £2.60; EX 100.90 Trifecta £806.30 Pool: £2672.68 - 2.48 winning units..
Owner Michael Anthony O'Donnell **Bred** Castleton Lyons & Kilboy Estate **Trained** Norton, N Yorks

FOCUS
A modest middle-distance handicap, but run at a fair pace with a few keen to get on with it. The winner rated similar to last winter's Dundalk form.

7882 32RED.COM CLAIMING STKS 6f (F)
12:50 (12:51) (Class 6) 2-Y-0 £1,940 (£577; £288; £144) Stalls Low

Form RPR
020 1 **Black Geronimo**[15] 7623 2-8-6 59 (v) DavidProbert 7 67
(David Evans) *mde all: drvn over 2f out: styd on strly fnl f: readily* **5/1**[3]
0300 2 3 **Soul Instinct**[5] 7819 2-8-8 69 (p) KevinStott(5) 12 65
(Kevin Ryan) *chsd ldrs: 2nd over 4f out: hung lft over 1f out: kpt on same pce* **11/2**
3220 3 2 1/2 **Amadaffair**[33] 7202 2-8-4 62 JimmyQuinn 10 49
(Tom Dascombe) *mid-div: hdwy over 3f out: 4th over 2f out: kpt on to take 3rd towards fin* **9/2**[2]
2210 4 1 **Stoney Quine (IRE)**[7] 7788 2-8-5 59 JoeFanning 11 47
(Keith Dalgleish) *chsd ldrs: 3rd over 3f out: one pce fnl 2f* **2/1**[1]
5 2 1/4 **Techtycoon** 2-8-8 0 ShirleyTeasdale(5) 6 48
(Michael Easterby) *s.i.s: hdwy over 2f out: kpt on fnl f* **50/1**
105 6 1 1/2 **Bird Of Light (IRE)**[98] 5175 2-8-8 70 JohnFahy 1 38
(Jamie Osborne) *chsd ldrs: wknd over 1f out* **11/2**
0 7 5 **Princess Tilly**[137] 3853 2-8-4 0 DuranFentiman 8 19
(Bill Turner) *s.i.s: hung rt and sn bhd: sme hdwy 2f out: nvr on terms* **66/1**
0 8 1 3/4 **Rievaulx Ranger (IRE)**[76] 5970 2-8-6 0 ShaneGray(5) 2 21
(Kevin Ryan) *s.i.s: sme hdwy over 3f out: wknd 2f out* **16/1**
0 9 8 **Two Tykes**[182] 2401 2-8-11 0 GrahamGibbons 4
(Michael Easterby) *s.i.s: sme hdwy over 1f out: sn wknd: eased ins fnl f* **25/1**
0006 10 1 3/4 **Sands Legends**[40] 7036 2-8-2 40 JamesSullivan 5
(James Given) *mid-div: lost pl3f out: bhd fnl 2f* **66/1**
000 11 7 **Molly Molone**[9] 7756 2-8-2 0 ow1 RaulDaSilva 3
(David Brown) *chsd ldrs: lost pl over 2f out: sn bhd and heavily eased: virtually p.u* **66/1**

1m 16.33s (-0.17) **Going Correction** +0.025s/f (Slow) **11** Ran SP% **115.1**
Speed ratings (Par 94): **102,98,94,93,90 88,81,79,68,66 57**
toteswingers 1&2 £7.30, 2&3 £4.70, 1&3 £5.70 CSF £30.99 TOTE £6.20: £1.20, £3.10, £1.80; EX 39.30 Trifecta £159.90 Pool: £1708.13 - 8.01 winning units..Black Geronimo was claimed by K Nicholls for £3000.
Owner Dukes Head Racing 1 **Bred** Azienda Agricola Mediterranea **Trained** Pandy, Monmouths

FOCUS
This modest juvenile claimer was won at the gates. A step back in the right direction by the winner.

7883 32RED MAIDEN AUCTION STKS 7f (F)
1:20 (1:22) (Class 5) 2-Y-0 £2,587 (£770; £384; £192) Stalls Low

Form RPR
5 1 **Bousfield**[84] 5675 2-8-10 0 NeilFarley(3) 8 73+
(Declan Carroll) *trckd ldrs: led over 1f out: sn rdn: styd on wl towards fin* **9/4**[2]
0226 2 1 1/4 **Supa U**[24] 7418 2-8-8 65 (e) DuranFentiman 7 65
(Tim Easterby) *trckd ldrs: effrt 2f out: rdn and almost upsides ins fnl f: no ex* **11/8**[1]
03 3 3 **Sky Ranger (IRE)**[37] 7111 2-9-0 0 JoeFanning 5 63
(James Tate) *mde most: hdd over 1f out: edgd rt and one pce* **4/1**[3]
0004 4 7 **Miss Lawlass (IRE)**[15] 7630 2-8-8 44 JamesSullivan 3 39
(James Given) *w ldrs: rdn over 2f out: wknd appr fnl f* **40/1**
63 5 4 **Wilberfoss (IRE)**[24] 7419 2-8-11 0 JimmyQuinn 1 32
(Mel Brittain) *chsd ldrs: drvn and lost pl over 3f out* **7/1**
00 6 4 1/2 **Black Tie Dancer (IRE)**[56] 6546 2-9-1 0 (t) RobertWinston 6 24
(Gay Kelleway) *dwlt: reminders sn after s: hdwy to chse ldrs over 4f out: lost pl 3f out* **20/1**
6 7 24 **L'Es Fremantle (FR)**[107] 4848 2-8-4 0 PaulBooth(7) 4
(Michael Chapman) *s.i.s: in rr and sn drvn along: bhd over 4f out: t.o 3f out* **100/1**

1m 31.66s (1.36) **Going Correction** +0.025s/f (Slow) **7** Ran SP% **113.6**
Speed ratings (Par 96): **93,91,88,80,75 70,43**
toteswingers 1&2 £1.30, 2&3 £1.70, 1&3 £2.50 CSF £5.63 TOTE £3.10: £1.40, £1.20; EX 8.30 Trifecta £18.90 Pool: £2187.67 - 86.74 winning units..
Owner Bousfield Boys **Bred** D Curran **Trained** Sledmere, E Yorks

FOCUS
A maiden auction lacking much strength in depth. Straightforward form.

7884 LADBROKES MAIDEN STKS 7f (F)
1:50 (1:50) (Class 5) 3-Y-0 £2,587 (£770; £384; £192) Stalls Low

Form RPR
1 **Barbados Bob (USA)**[26] 7391 3-9-0 67 GeorgeChaloner(5) 5 73
(Michael Wigham) *chsd ldrs: drvn and outpcd over 4f out: hdwy over 2f out: chal over 1f out: hung lft: led fnl strides* **13/8**[1]
2 hd **Shamassiba (IRE)** 3-9-0 0 (t) DavidProbert 8 67
(Andrew Balding) *w ldr: led over 4f out: jnd over 1f out: edgd lft ins fnl f: rdr dropped whip: hdd nr fin* **7/4**[2]
3 4 1/2 **Sugar Town** 3-9-0 0 GrahamLee 4 56
(Peter Niven) *strated slowly: wnt rt and wd after 1f: hdwy over 3f out: kpt on to take modest 3rd jst ins fnl f* **4/1**[3]
0 4 10 **Cumberworth**[27] 7345 3-9-5 0 GrahamGibbons 6 35
(Michael Easterby) *led tl over 4f out: wknd over 1f out: eased ins fnl f* **8/1**
0 5 18 **Harpers Ruby**[43] 6940 3-8-9 0 ShirleyTeasdale(5) 1
(Simon Griffiths) *w ldrs: lost pl over 2f out: bhd whn edgd rt over 1f out: eased* **66/1**
6 19 **Ash Cape** 3-9-5 0 AndrewMullen 3
(Brian Rothwell) *s.i.s: sn drvn along and hung rt: lost pl over 4f out: t.o 3f out* **33/1**

1m 30.77s (0.47) **Going Correction** +0.025s/f (Slow) **6** Ran SP% **110.0**
Speed ratings (Par 102): **98,97,92,81,60 38**
toteswingers 1&2 £1.20, 2&3 £1.60, 1&3 £1.50 CSF £4.55 TOTE £2.00: £1.10, £1.80; EX 5.70 Trifecta £9.30 Pool: £2697.25 - 216.50 winning units..
Owner D Hassan **Bred** Merrydale Farm Partners 2003 Llc **Trained** Newmarket, Suffolk

FOCUS
A desperately weak maiden, with the first pair doing their best to avoid winning. The winner is rated a bit closer to his 2yo form.

7885 LADBROKES MOBILE CLAIMING STKS 7f (F)
2:20 (2:21) (Class 6) 3-Y-0+ £1,940 (£577; £288; £144) Stalls Low

Form RPR
3123 1 **Silly Billy (IRE)**[9] 7754 5-9-0 65 (p) PaulPickard 12 76
(Brian Ellison) *trckd ldr: led appr 2f out: drvn clr jst ins fnl f* **11/2**

0030 **2** 4 1/2 **George Benjamin**[9] 7753 6-8-5 48 ow2.........................(t) JackDuern(5) 4 60
(Christopher Kellett) *in rr: hdwy over 2f out: styd on to take 2nd fnl strides* **100/1**
1400 **3** nk **Bay Knight (IRE)**[32] 7224 7-10-0 80................................ JoeFanning 11 77
(Sean Curran) *chsd ldrs: kpt on one pce over 1f out* **16/1**
1460 **4** 1 1/4 **Illustrious Prince (IRE)**[41] 6988 6-8-11 73...................... NeilFarley(3) 9 60
(Declan Carroll) *mid-div: drvn over 3f out: kpt on same pce fnl 2f* **9/2**[3]
3133 **5** 3 1/4 **Llewellyn**[16] 7595 5-9-5 75....................................... GeorgeChaloner(5) 13 61
(David Nicholls) *s.i.s: sn trcking ldrs: edgd lft over 4f out: led wl over 2f out: hdd appr fnl 2f: wknd jst ins fnl f* **3/1**[1]
6 3/4 **Strandfield Bay (IRE)**[14] 7-9-9 0.. PaulQuinn 7 58
(Sharon Watt) *s.s: in rr: kpt on fnl 2f: styd on fnl f: nvr a factor* **100/1**
0014 **7** 1/2 **Capaill Liath (IRE)**[7] 7792 5-9-9 87.............................(p) ShaneGray(5) 10 62
(Kevin Ryan) *chsd ldrs: drvn over 3f out: wknd over 1f out* **5/1**
0020 **8** 1/2 **Dancing Maite**[37] 7109 8-9-3 70...............................(b) MarkCoumbe(3) 6 52
(Roy Bowring) *sn chsng ldrs: wknd over 1f out* **25/1**
0644 **9** 3 1/2 **Fathsta (IRE)**[15] 7634 8-9-0 76.................................... GrahamGibbons 5 37
(Declan Carroll) *led: hdd wl over 2f out: lost pl over 1f out* **12/1**
4440 **10** 4 1/2 **Sakhee's Alround**[14] 7644 3-8-10 50............................(p) AdamBeschizza 3 21
(K F Clutterbuck) *s.s: a in rr* **100/1**
0600 **11** 4 **Justonefortheroad**[12] 7696 7-9-4 75................................. LeeTopliss 1 18
(Richard Fahey) *chsd ldrs: sn drvn along: lost pl over 3f out: hung rt over 2f out: bhd whn eased towards fin* **4/1**[2]
-146 **12** 9 **French Press (IRE)**[10] 7729 3-9-1 61........................(bt) StephenCraine 2
(John Stimpson) *chsd ldrs: wknd 2f out: bhd whn eased ins fnl f* **50/1**

1m 29.57s (-0.73) **Going Correction** +0.025s/f (Slow)
WFA 3 from 4yo+ 1lb 12 Ran SP% **117.6**
Speed ratings (Par 101): **105,99,99,98,94 93,92,92,88,83 78,68**
toteswingers 1&2 £1.20, 2&3 £1.60, 1&3 £1.50 CSF £479.77 TOTE £5.80: £1.80, £16.80, £4.50; EX 196.10 Trifecta £2176.60 Part won. Pool: £2902.16 - 0.99 winning units..George Benjamin was claimed by M Appleby for £2000. Silly Billy was subject to a friendly claim.
Owner L S Keys **Bred** Sir E J Loder **Trained** Norton, N Yorks

FOCUS
An ordinary claimer. The winner was more solid than most and is rated back to his old best. The runner-up further complicates the form.

7886 LADBROKES ALL-WEATHER "HANDS AND HEELS" APPRENTICE SERIES H'CAP (RACING EXCELLENCE INITIATIVE) 7f (F)
2:50 (2:52) (Class 6) (0-60,60) 3-Y-0+ **£2,045** (£603; £302) **Stalls** Low

Form RPR
5043 **1** **Bitaphon (IRE)**[26] 7383 4-9-1 53................................(t) GeorgeBuckell 3 67
(Michael Appleby) *w ldrs: led over 4f out: styd on wl to draw clr ins fnl f* **9/4**[1]
320/ **2** 3 **Fast On (IRE)**[56] 6578 4-8-9 50................................(e[1]) DavidParkes(3) 11 56
(Seamus Fahey, Ire) *in rr: hdwy 2f out: styd on wl to take 2nd nr fin* **9/1**
6005 **3** 3/4 **Pearl Noir**[9] 7759 3-8-9 53....................................... ThomasHemsley(5) 1 56
(Scott Dixon) *chsd ldrs: kpt on to take 2nd ins fnl f: styd on same pce* **33/1**
4 **4** 1 **Masked Dance (IRE)**[226] 1309 6-9-1 58............(p) JonathanWilletts(5) 5 60
(Scott Dixon) *led tl over 4f out: one pce fnl 2f* **12/1**
0612 **5** hd **Elusive Warrior (USA)**[9] 7753 10-8-9 50..................(p) AaronJones(3) 7 51
(Alan McCabe) *mid-div: hdwy to chse ldrs over 3f out: kpt on one pce fnl 2f* **4/1**[2]
0000 **6** nk **Mataajir (USA)**[14] 7643 5-9-1 53.............................(v[1]) AdamMcLean 14 53
(Derek Shaw) *s.i.s: hdwy over 4f out: one pce fnl 2f* **5/1**[3]
0340 **7** 1 1/4 **Vitznau (IRE)**[27] 7353 9-9-4 56.. LewisWalsh 6 53
(K F Clutterbuck) *s.i.s: hdwy over 4f out: upside over 2f out: one pce* **25/1**
0260 **8** 2 **Poetic Belle**[6] 7806 3-8-9 55..................................(t) AlexHopkinson(7) 12 46
(Shaun Harris) *chsd ldrs: wd bnd over 3f out: one pce* **20/1**
4060 **9** nk **Hazza The Jazza**[13] 6921 3-9-0 60................(e) MelissaThompson(7) 13 50
(Richard Guest) *s.s: outpcd over 2f out: hung rt and kpt on fnl f* **12/1**
0030 **10** 3/4 **Shelling Peas**[21] 7485 4-8-10 48..................................(v) DanielCremin 2 37
(Derek Shaw) *mid-div: effrt over 3f out: nvr a threat* **66/1**
0002 **11** nk **Upper Lambourn (IRE)**[162] 2998 5-9-3 55.........................(t) JoeDoyle 9 43
(Christopher Kellett) *mid-div: outpcd and reminder over 3f out: nvr a factor after* **16/1**
0-60 **12** 2 **Vale Of Clara (IRE)**[167] 2837 5-8-11 56........................ JoshQuinn(7) 10 39
(Peter Niven) *in rr and sn drvn along: nvr on terms* **50/1**
60 **13** 10 **Mazovian (USA)**[42] 6969 5-9-1 58.................................. PaulBooth(5) 8 15
(Michael Chapman) *sn bhd: detached fnl 2f* **14/1**
00 **14** 10 **Drive Home (USA)**[44] 6919 6-8-11 52..........................(p) BTTreanor(3) 4
(Noel Wilson) *chsd ldrs: wknd over 2f out: bhd whn eased ins fnl f* **25/1**

1m 31.37s (1.07) **Going Correction** +0.025s/f (Slow)
WFA 3 from 4yo+ 1lb 14 Ran SP% **121.3**
Speed ratings (Par 101): **94,90,89,88,88 88,86,84,83,83 82,80,69,57**
toteswingers 1&2 £6.40, 2&3 £56.50, 1&3 £23.00 CSF £21.40 CT £560.32 TOTE £3.40: £1.20, £4.60, £8.10; EX 32.90 Trifecta £1009.90 Pool: £3686.23 - 2.73 winning units..
Owner Dallas Racing **Bred** Pitrizzia Partnership **Trained** Danethorpe, Notts
■ Stewards' Enquiry : Joe Doyle seven-day ban: used whip contrary to race conditions (Nov 28, Dec 3,5,6,11,13,18)

FOCUS
A moderate "hands and heels" apprentice handicap and one-way traffic at the end. The winner's best run of the year but not a race to be positive about.

7887 COMPARE BOOKMAKERS AT BOOKMAKERS.CO.UK H'CAP (DIV I) 5f (F)
3:20 (3:20) (Class 4) (0-85,84) 3-Y-0+ **£4,690** (£1,395; £697; £348) **Stalls** High

Form RPR
2125 **1** **Tom Sawyer**[31] 7240 5-8-3 71.................................(b) ConnorBeasley(5) 3 81
(Julie Camacho) *w ldrs: upsides 1f out: kpt on to ld fnl strides* **10/1**
1335 **2** hd **Monsieur Jamie**[8] 7777 5-9-0 77..................................(v) JoeFanning 2 86
(J R Jenkins) *dwlt: sn w ldrs: narrow ld 1f out: edgd lft and hdd towards fin* **2/1**[1]
5500 **3** 1/2 **Moorhouse Lad**[44] 6920 10-9-3 80............................ GrahamGibbons 6 87
(Garry Moss) *led: hdd 1f out: kpt on towards fin* **12/1**
1006 **4** 1/2 **Royal Bajan (USA)**[37] 7112 5-9-2 79............................(p) GrahamLee 7 84
(James Given) *sn outpcd in rr: hdwy over 2f out: styd on fnl f* **9/2**[2]
4105 **5** 1/2 **Master Bond**[29] 7313 4-9-1 78.. DanielTudhope 4 82
(David O'Meara) *mid-div: outpcd over 3f out: hdwy 2f out: kpt on fnl f* **7/1**
000 **6** 3 1/2 **Cadeaux Pearl**[37] 7112 5-8-9 72..............................(p) JamesSullivan 9 63
(Scott Dixon) *sn outpcd: sme hdwy over 2f out: wknd over 1f out* **10/1**
3020 **7** 3/4 **The Art Of Racing (IRE)**[47] 6848 3-9-4 84(p) WilliamTwiston-Davies(3) 1 72
(Alan McCabe) *dwlt: sn w ldrs: drvn over 2f out: wknd over 1f out* **20/1**
4000 **8** 6 **Ruby's Day**[6] 7803 4-8-8 78... ClaireMurray(7) 5 45
(David Brown) *sn outpcd in rr: hung lft over 2f out: sn bhd* **20/1**
2352 **9** 2 **Ypres**[49] 6771 4-8-12 75..(b[1]) RobertWinston 8 35
(Jason Ward) *dwlt: in rr: drvn over 2f out: nvr on terms: eased ins fnl f* **5/1**[3]

58.08s (-1.62) **Going Correction** -0.15s/f (Stan) 9 Ran SP% **116.1**
Speed ratings (Par 105): **106,105,104,104,103 97,96,86,83**
toteswingers 1&2 £3.80, 2&3 £10.50, 1&3 £16.40 CSF £30.54 CT £245.64 TOTE £14.90: £2.00, £1.40, £3.20; EX 37.60 Trifecta £446.90 Pool: £2772.76 - 4.65 winning units..
Owner Bolingbroke J Howard FAO Mersey R & Ptns **Bred** Newsells Park Stud **Trained** Norton, N Yorks

FOCUS
The first division of a fair sprint handicap. As is usually the case, those that raced up the centre of the track were favoured. Pretty solid, straightforward form.

7888 COMPARE BOOKMAKERS AT BOOKMAKERS.CO.UK H'CAP (DIV II) 5f (F)
3:50 (3:50) (Class 4) (0-85,84) 3-Y-0+ **£4,690** (£1,395; £697; £348) **Stalls** High

Form RPR
40 **1** **Sharaarah (IRE)**[8] 7776 3-9-2 84..............................(b[1]) DavidBergin(5) 8 94
(David O'Meara) *trckd ldrs: led 1f out: pushed out* **6/1**[3]
1010 **2** 1 **Rambo Will**[8] 7776 5-8-3 71.. ShelleyBirkett(5) 1 77
(J R Jenkins) *w ldrs: styd on same pce ins fnl f* **8/1**
2121 **3** 3/4 **Hi Filwah (USA)**[34] 7165 3-9-3 80..............................(p) JoeFanning 3 83+
(Jeremy Noseda) *s.i.s: chsd ldrs after 1f: rdn over 1f out: kpt on same pce ins fnl f* **5/2**[1]
2421 **4** hd **Generalyse**[37] 7106 4-8-11 79................................(b) OisinMurphy(5) 4 82
(Ben De Haan) *w ldrs: kpt on same pce fnl f* **7/2**[2]
2506 **5** 3/4 **Bapak Sayang (USA)**[101] 5057 3-9-0 77.......................... GrahamLee 7 77
(Kevin Ryan) *led: hdd 1f out: one pce* **16/1**
5002 **6** 2 1/4 **Caldercruix (USA)**[16] 7603 6-8-10 78..........................(v) RyanTate(5) 5 70
(James Evans) *sn outpcd and in rr: kpt on fnl f: nvr a factor* **7/1**
0266 **7** 1/2 **Point North (IRE)**[8] 7776 6-8-11 74.........................(b) JamesSullivan 2 64
(John Balding) *chsd ldrs: wknd over 1f out* **10/1**
0300 **8** 1 1/2 **Sewn Up**[9] 7743 3-8-7 70..(p) PaulQuinn 6 55
(Andrew Hollinshead) *sn outpcd and bhd: kpt on over 1f out: nvr on terms* **16/1**
2040 **9** 3 1/4 **Flash City (ITY)**[29] 7314 5-8-9 77.......................(p) GeorgeChaloner(5) 9 50
(Bryan Smart) *s.i.s: sn drvn along: wknd over 1f out* **14/1**

58.4s (-1.30) **Going Correction** -0.15s/f (Stan) 9 Ran SP% **116.2**
Speed ratings (Par 105): **104,102,101,100,99 96,95,92,87**
CSF £53.37 CT £151.97 TOTE £9.40: £2.40, £2.70, £2.10; EX 75.20 Trifecta £408.50 Pool: £3442.00 - 6.31 winning units..
Owner Middleham Park Racing XXXVII & C Tasker **Bred** Shadwell Estate Company Limited **Trained** Nawton, N Yorks

FOCUS
The winning time was 0.32sec slower than the first division but the form looks similar. A personal best from the winner.
T/Plt: 149.10 to a £1 stake. Pool of £55638.51 - 272.26 winning tickets. T/Qpdt: £20.60 to a £1 stake. Pool of £5788.47 - 207.20 winning tickets. WG

7828 SAINT-CLOUD (L-H)
Thursday, November 14

OFFICIAL GOING: Turf: heavy

7889a PRIX TANERKO (CONDITIONS) (2YO COLTS & GELDINGS) (TURF) 7f
11:25 (12:00) 2-Y-0 **£13,821** (£5,528; £4,146; £2,764; £1,382)

RPR
1 **Mr Lucas (FR)** 2-8-6 0.. MlleZoePfeil(8) 2 90
(M Le Forestier, France) **12/5**[2]
2 6 **Le Baron Rouge (FR)** 2-9-0 0.. IoritzMendizabal 3 75
(J Heloury, France) **16/1**
3 1/2 **Cagoule**[21] 2-8-10 0.. ThierryThulliez 6 70
(P Bary, France) **1/1**[1]
4 shd **Berrahri (IRE)**[23] 7451 2-8-11 0 ow1.................. Pierre-CharlesBoudot 4 71
(John Best) *midfield in tch: rdn 3f out: sn outpcd by wnr: kpt on* **16/1**
5 2 **Star Dolois (FR)**[101] 2-9-0 0... RonanThomas 5 69
(A Bonin, France) **19/5**[3]
6 20 **Gone With The Wind (FR)**[22] 7570 2-8-10 0............... TheoBachelot 1 15
(Y Barberot, France) **15/1**

1m 40.17s (7.97) 6 Ran SP% **118.3**
WIN (incl. 1 euro stake): 3.40. Places: 1.80, 5.10. SF: 51.70..
Owner Mme Anja Wilde **Bred** Mme A Wilde **Trained** France

7890a PRIX DENISY (LISTED RACE) (3YO+) (TURF) 1m 7f 110y
2:05 (12:00) 3-Y-0+ **£21,138** (£8,455; £6,341; £4,227; £2,113)

RPR
1 **Nichols Canyon**[19] 7535 3-8-10 0.................................... OlivierPeslier 3 113+
(John Gosden) *in tch on inner: trckd ldr fr 1/2-way: swtchd off rail and rdn to chal over 2f out: led over 1f out: styd on strly and forged clr ins fnl f: pushed out: comf* **47/10**[3]
2 4 **Inis Meain (USA)**[57] 6543 6-9-4 0........................... StephanePasquier 1 107
(Denis Gerard Hogan, Ire) *led: rdn and strly pressed over 2f out: hdd over 1f out: readily outpcd by wnr ins fnl f but styd on for clr 2nd* **11/1**
3 6 **Tres Rock Danon (FR)**[18] 7566 7-9-1 0.............. ChristopheSoumillon 8 97
(Gerald Geisler, Germany) **9/2**[2]
4 1 1/2 **Gaterie (USA)**[60] 6447 4-9-1 0.. MaximeGuyon 6 95
(A Fabre, France) *midfield in tch on settling: pushed along over 3f out: rdn and wnt 4th over 2f out: plugged on but n.d to front pair* **73/10**
5 10 **Quidamo**[46] 6894 6-9-1 0...................................... Pierre-CharlesBoudot 10 83
(Frau J Mayer, Germany) **41/1**
6 1 **Blue Planet (GER)**[46] 4-9-1 0...................................... AurelienLemaitre 13 82
(Christina Bucher, Switzerland) **62/1**
7 8 **Smoky Hill (IRE)**[33] 7193 4-9-1 0.................................... ThierryThulliez 7 72
(M Delzangles, France) **83/10**
8 snk **Zipp (IRE)**[20] 7496 3-8-4 0.. AndreaAtzeni 9 70
(Charles Hills) *prom early: sn settled in midfield: rdn over 3f out: outpcd and no imp fr over 2f out* **44/1**
9 15 **Yorkshire Lass (IRE)**[34] 7189 5-8-11 0......................(p) FabriceVeron 5 50
(H-A Pantall, France) **30/1**
10 10 **Rollex Borget (FR)**[12] 4-9-1 0... ThierryJarnet 12 42
(J Bertran De Balanda, France) **20/1**

The Form Book Flat, Raceform Ltd, Compton, RG20 6NL.

11 *12* **Lucky Look (FR)**[40] 7046 3-8-4 0 .... FlavienPrat 2 26
(D Smaga, France) **7/2**[1]
12 *20* **Aloha Iwanaga (GER)**[19] 4-8-11 0 .... (p) CristianDemuro 11
(R Dzubasz, Germany) **39/1**
13 *20* **Usuelo (FR)**[19] 7590 5-9-1 0 .... AntoineHamelin 4
(J-L Guillochon, France) **9/1**

3m 53.62s (14.92)
WFA 3 from 4yo+ 8lb **13** Ran SP% **115.8**
WIN (incl. 1 euro stake): 5.70. PLACES: 2.10, 3.40, 1.70. DF: 26.40. SF: 32.70.
Owner Rachel Hood & Elaine Lawlor **Bred** Rabbah Bloodstock Limited **Trained** Newmarket, Suffolk

7891a PRIX BELLE DE NUIT (LISTED RACE) (3YO+ FILLIES & MARES) (TURF) 1m 4f 110y
2:40 (12:00) 3-Y-O+ **£21,138** (£8,455; £6,341; £4,227; £2,113)

RPR
1 **Modern Eagle (GER)**[34] 7189 3-8-7 0 .... AntoineHamelin 3 102+
(A De Royer-Dupre, France) **26/1**
2 *2 ½* **Mahnaz**[41] 7009 4-9-0 0 .... Pierre-CharlesBoudot 11 98
(A Fabre, France) **34/1**
3 *shd* **Wilddrossel (GER)**[25] 7407 4-9-4 0 .... SHellyn 1 102+
(Markus Klug, Germany) **19/1**
4 *hd* **Phiz (GER)**[14] 7650 3-8-11 0 .... OlivierPeslier 12 102+
(John Gosden) *hld up towards rr: hdwy fr over 3f out: rdn over 2f out: styd on steadily and wnt 4th towards fin but nvr able to chal* **14/1**
5 *4* **Shada (IRE)**[12] 4-9-0 0 .... MaximeGuyon 4 91
(F-H Graffard, France) **9/2**[2]
6 *snk* **Harbour Of Hope (GER)**[45] 3-8-7 0 .... (p) FabriceVeron 14 91
(H-A Pantall, France) **16/1**
7 *¾* **Night Power (FR)**[46] 6887 3-8-11 0 .... APietsch 13 94
(W Hickst, Germany) **7/2**[1]
8 *5* **Hikari (IRE)**[32] 7229 3-8-7 0 .... ChrisHayes 15 82
(D K Weld, Ire) *midfield: rdn over 3f out: c nr side in st: plugged on but sn no imp: eased towards fin* **20/1**
9 *4 ½* **Rosaceous**[20] 7504 3-8-7 0 .... (b[1]) SteveDrowne 5 74
(Daniel Kubler) *led: rdn and strly pressed over 2f out: sn hdd: no ex and fdd: eased ent fnl f* **86/1**
10 *7* **Tempest Fugit (IRE)**[14] 7650 4-9-0 0 .... ThierryJarnet 2 63
(John Gosden) *trckd ldr: pushed along 4f out: rdn and lost pl over 2f out: no ex and btn over 1f out: eased ent fnl f* **33/1**
11 *9* **Commute**[74] 6031 3-8-7 0 .... ThierryThulliez 10 49
(D Smaga, France) **10/1**
12 *¾* **Infinity One (SPA)**[18] 4-9-0 0 .... Jean-BaptisteHamel 16 48
(Barbara Valenti, Spain) **16/1**
13 *1 ½* **Lady Of Budysin (GER)**[25] 7407 4-9-0 0 .... AnthonyCrastus 6 45
(Markus Klug, Germany) **52/1**
14 *7* **Divergence (IRE)**[60] 6434 3-8-7 0 .... IoritzMendizabal 17 34
(Michael Bell) *hld up: hdwy on outer over 4f out: rdn 3f out: no ex and btn 2f out: eased and t.o* **29/1**
15 *20* **Elle Same**[18] 7561 3-8-7 0 .... TheoBachelot 8 2
(P Schiergen, Germany) **22/1**
16 *dist* **Two Days In Paris (FR)**[34] 7189 4-9-0 0 .... ChristopheSoumillon 7
(J-C Rouget, France) **83/10**[3]
17 *dist* **Songbird (IRE)**[49] 6764 4-9-0 0 .... AndreaAtzeni 18
(Lady Cecil) *hld up and a towards rr: detached in last and btn over 3f out: eased and tailed rt off* **14/1**

3m 6.65s (186.65)
WFA 3 from 4yo 6lb **17** Ran SP% **115.3**
WIN (incl. 1 euro stake): 27.10. PLACES: 8.40, 11.00, 5.70. DF: 204.90. SF: 266.70.
Owner Ballymore Thoroughbred Ltd **Bred** Dayton Investments Ltd **Trained** Chantilly, France

7858 LINGFIELD (L-H)
Friday, November 15

OFFICIAL GOING: Standard
Wind: light, half against Weather: dry and sunny

7892 32RED CASINO NURSERY H'CAP 7f (P)
11:55 (11:55) (Class 5) (0-75,75) 2-Y-O **£2,587** (£770; £384; £192) **Stalls** Low

Form RPR
1300 1 **Constantine**[23] 7463 2-9-7 **75** .... SeanLevey 3 81
(Richard Hannon) *t.k.h: hld up wl in tch in midfield: rdn and effrt to chal over 1f out: hrd drvn and edgd rt after: led ins fnl f: forged ahd fnl 75yds: drvn out* **14/1**
1502 2 *1* **Madame Mirasol (IRE)**[8] 7782 2-9-1 **69** .... RobertWinston 2 72
(Kevin Ryan) *led: hung rt bnd 4f out and again bnd 2f out: sn drvn and hrd pressed: battled on gamely tl hdd ins fnl f: no ex and wknd towards fin* **4/1**[2]
1456 3 *nk* **Penny's Boy**[30] 7300 2-8-13 **67** .... (t) SilvestreDeSousa 7 70
(Sylvester Kirk) *t.k.h: hld up wl in tch in midfield: effrt and unable qck wl over 1f out: rallied and styd on wl u.p fnl 100yds* **5/1**[3]
055 4 *2 ½* **Jeremos (IRE)**[97] 5279 2-8-12 **69** .... WilliamTwiston-Davies[(3)] 8 65
(Richard Hannon) *s.i.s and rdn along early: in tch in last trio: swtchd lft and hdwy to chse ldrs on inner over 1f out: no ex ins fnl f: wknd fnl 100yds* **8/1**
000 5 *shd* **Excellent Royale (IRE)**[41] 7019 2-9-0 **68** .... JimCrowley 5 64+
(Charles Hills) *wl in tch in midfield: wdst bnd 2f out and sn lost pl u.p: rallied and kpt on fnl f: no threat to ldrs* **5/2**[1]
045 6 *nk* **Thundering Cloud (IRE)**[15] 7638 2-8-11 **68** .... MatthewLawson[(3)] 4 63
(Brendan Powell) *sn detached in rr: bhd and rdn alon thrght: drvn over 4f out: styd on ins fnl f: nvr trbld ldrs* **20/1**
6421 7 *1 ¼* **Sweet P**[24] 7441 2-9-3 **71** .... MartinDwyer 6 63
(Marcus Tregoning) *w ldr: rdn and ev ch 2f out: sn outpcd and struggling: wknd ent fnl f* **8/1**
3110 8 *3* **Captain Secret**[48] 6839 2-9-7 **75** .... MartinHarley 9 59
(Marco Botti) *chsd ldrs on outer: rdn ent fnl 2f: sn outpcd and btn: wknd over 1f out* **6/1**
310 9 *4 ½* **Baileys Forever**[17] 7609 2-9-3 **71** .... FrederikTylicki 1 43
(James Given) *a towards rr: dropped to last and rdn 3f out: lost tch over 2f out* **25/1**

1m 24.26s (-0.54) **Going Correction** -0.075s/f (Stan) **9** Ran SP% **117.0**
Speed ratings (Par 96): **100,98,98,95,95 95,93,90,85**
toteswingers 1&2 £4.90, 1&3 £15.90, 2&3 £3.40 CSF £70.25 CT £329.37 TOTE £19.80: £4.00, £1.50, £2.00; EX 77.80 Trifecta £1167.70 Part won. Pool: £1556.94 - 0.98 winning units..
Owner The Royal Ascot Racing Club **Bred** D J & Mrs Brown **Trained** East Everleigh, Wilts

■ Stewards' Enquiry : Sean Levey two-day ban: used whip above permitted level (Nov 29-30)

FOCUS
This looked an interesting little nursery beforehand with a couple of potential improvers, but the three horses with the most experience filled the first three places. Straightforward, solid form.

7893 32RED.COM/EBF MAIDEN STKS 5f (P)
12:25 (12:25) (Class 5) 2-Y-O **£2,911** (£866; £432; £216) **Stalls** High

Form RPR
44 1 **Pushkin Museum (IRE)**[36] 7155 2-9-5 0 .... GeorgeBaker 10 72
(Gary Moore) *racd freely: led: rdn and wnt clr over 1f out: 3 l clr 1f out: tiring towards fin but a holding on* **8/1**[3]
3322 2 *nk* **Pool House**[44] 6931 2-9-5 76 .... DavidProbert 8 71
(Andrew Balding) *chsd ldrs: chsd wnr 1/2-way: rdn and unable qck wl over 1f out: 3 l down and drvn ent fnl f: styd on u.p fnl 100yds: nvr quite getting to wnr* **4/5**[1]
40 3 *2 ¾* **Monsieur Lavene (IRE)**[15] 7638 2-9-5 0 .... KierenFox 1 61
(Robert Mills) *t.k.h: chsd wnr tl 1/2-way: 3rd and unable qck over 1f out: kpt on same pce fnl f* **50/1**
0235 4 *¾* **Little Big Man**[30] 7293 2-9-0 55 .... (b) JoshBaudains[(5)] 9 58
(Sylvester Kirk) *wl in tch in midfield: effrt u.p and edgd lft over 1f out: styd on same pce fnl f: wnt 4th last strides* **66/1**
0 5 *hd* **Rochester**[15] 7638 2-9-5 0 ....[1] SilvestreDeSousa 2 58
(Saeed bin Suroor) *wnt rt s: t.k.h: hld up wl in tch in midfield: rdn and no rspnse over 1f out: kpt on same pce fnl f* **7/2**[2]
44 6 *3 ¼* **Royal Brave (IRE)**[26] 7394 2-9-5 0 .... MartinDwyer 4 46+
(William Muir) *hld up in last trio: rdn and effrt over 2f out: no prog 2f out: nvr trbld ldrs* **14/1**
00 7 *¾* **Stan Nineteen (IRE)**[33] 7218 2-9-5 0 .... RobertHavlin 6 43+
(George Baker) *s.i.s: hld up in rr: hung rt and wd bnd 2f out: sme modest hdwy fnl f: nvr trbld ldrs* **14/1**
0 8 *1 ½* **Shaft Of Light**[15] 7638 2-9-5 0 .... LukeMorris 7 38
(Sir Mark Prescott Bt) *in tch in midfield but sn rdn along: lost pl ent fnl 2f: n.d after* **16/1**
005 9 *2 ¾* **Excedo Praecedo**[29] 7328 2-9-5 60 .... JimCrowley 3 28+
(Amanda Perrett) *hmpd s: a in rr: n.d* **25/1**
10 *hd* **Ma Bella Paola (FR)** 2-9-0 0 .... (t) MartinLane 5 22
(Paul Cole) *hld up towards rr: rdn and no hdwy ent fnl 2f: wknd over 1f out* **25/1**

58.82s (0.02) **Going Correction** -0.075s/f (Stan) **10** Ran SP% **119.3**
Speed ratings (Par 96): **96,95,91,89,89 84,83,80,76,76**
toteswingers 1&2 £3.10, 1&3 £12.20, 2&3 £24.40 CSF £14.82 TOTE £9.30: £2.20, £1.10, £7.90; EX 21.40 Trifecta £583.10 Pool: £2321.50 - 2.98 winning units..
Owner R A Green **Bred** Miss Nicola Cullen **Trained** Lower Beeding, W Sussex

FOCUS
A modest juvenile sprint maiden in which the winner made all. The fourth looks the key to the form.

7894 CORAL APP DOWNLOAD FROM THE APP STORE MAIDEN STKS 1m 4f (P)
12:55 (12:56) (Class 5) 3-Y-O+ **£2,726** (£805; £402) **Stalls** Low

Form RPR
52 1 **Freedom's Light**[10] 7738 3-9-0 0 .... RobertHavlin 3 79+
(John Gosden) *t.k.h: w ldr tl settled in 3rd over 10f out: wnt 2nd 6f out: rdn and effrt ent fnl 2f: led over 1f out and edgd lft u.p: kpt wanting to edge lft ins fnl f: rdn out* **1/1**[1]
3322 2 *1 ½* **Flemish School**[22] 7488 3-8-11 75 .... (b[1]) WilliamTwiston-Davies[(3)] 11 77
(Gerard Butler) *hld up in tch in midfield: hdwy on outer to ld over 2f out: hrd drvn and hdd over 1f out: kpt on same pce u.p fnl f* **4/1**[2]
2353 3 *½* **Kingston Eucalypt**[30] 7298 3-9-0 73 .... SilvestreDeSousa 6 76
(David Elsworth) *in tch in midfield: 3rd and effrt 2f out: kpt on u.p ins fnl f* **7/1**
0354 4 *5* **Mount Macedon**[31] 7279 3-9-5 72 .... AndreaAtzeni 2 73
(Luca Cumani) *in tch in midfield: rdn and effrt to chse clr ldng trio 2f out: no imp and one pce after* **8/1**
5 *6* **Molly Hayes** 3-9-0 0 .... MartinLane 4 59
(David Simcock) *hld up in tch in midfield: rdn and outpcd over 2f out: no threat to ldrs but kpt on ins fnl f* **50/1**
/02 6 *1 ¼* **Eton Dorney (USA)**[11] 7734 4-9-11 0 .... JoeFanning 7 62
(Mark Johnston) *chsd ldrs tl led over 10f out: rdn an dhdd over 2f out: sn outpcd and wl btn 2f out: wknd* **9/2**[3]
60-6 7 *5* **Ossie's Dancer**[22] 7490 4-9-11 41 .... RobertWinston 8 54?
(Martin Smith) *stdd s and v.s.a: t.k.h: hld up off the pce in rr: clsd and in tch 6f out: rdn over 2f out: sn wknd and wl btn* **100/1**
54-0 8 *1 ¼* **Onertother**[31] 7266 4-9-11 46 .... SteveDrowne 1 52?
(Joseph Tuite) *led tl over 10f out: chsd ldr tl 6f out: chsd ldrs after tl rdn and wknd 2f out: fdd fnl f* **66/1**
40 9 *¾* **Tamaletta (IRE)**[10] 7738 3-9-0 0 .... TomMcLaughlin 9 45
(Paul Burgoyne) *hmpd s and v.s.a: wl off the pce in last quartet: clsd and in tch 5f out: rdn 3f out: sn toiling and bhd fnl 2f* **100/1**
10 *28* **Amberjam (IRE)** 3-8-12 0 .... GeorgeBuckell[(7)] 5
(Martin Smith) *v.s.a: a detached last and rdn along thrght: lost tch 4f out: t.o* **66/1**
0 11 *5* **Be A Rebel**[8] 7781 3-8-11 0 .... NataliaGemelova[(3)] 10
(John E Long) *wnt lft and bmpd rival s: rn green and rdn along in rr: clsd and in tch 1/2-way: rdn and struggling over 3f out: t.o fnl 2f* **66/1**

2m 30.13s (-2.87) **Going Correction** -0.075s/f (Stan)
WFA 3 from 4yo 6lb **11** Ran SP% **120.2**
Speed ratings (Par 103): **106,105,104,101,97 96,93,92,91,73 69**
toteswingers 1&2 £2.90, 1&3 £2.80, 2&3 £3.60 CSF £5.39 TOTE £2.20: £1.30, £1.70, £1.80; EX 7.80 Trifecta £22.40 Pool: £3554.49 - 118.83 winning units..
Owner George Strawbridge **Bred** George Strawbridge **Trained** Newmarket, Suffolk

FOCUS
A reasonable maiden, run at a sound pace, and he form has a solid enough feel with a pair of 70-rated fillies filling the places. However the seventh and eighth were not beaten far.

7895 32RED/EBF FILLIES' H'CAP 1m 2f (P)
1:25 (1:26) (Class 3) (0-90,84) 3-Y-O **£9,056** (£2,695; £1,346; £673) **Stalls** Low

Form RPR
146 1 **Paris Rose**[55] 6649 3-9-5 **82** .... SilvestreDeSousa 4 91
(William Haggas) *t.k.h: pressed ldr: drvn over 1f out: led 1f out: battled on gamely and forged ahd ins fnl f: hrd pressed towards fin: hld on: all out* **11/4**[2]
0-13 2 *hd* **Modernstone**[14] 7661 3-9-3 **80** .... ShaneKelly 7 89
(William Knight) *wnt lft s: in tch in last pair: rdn and effrt on outer over 1f out: hdwy and str chal ins fnl f: hld towards fin* **16/1**
5030 3 *1 ¼* **Trapeze**[21] 7504 3-9-3 **80** .... RobertHavlin 5 86
(John Gosden) *hld up wl in tch in last trio: effrt and chse ldrs but nt clr run over 1f out: gap opened ins fnl f: r.o u.p to go 2rd last strides* **20/1**

263 **4** *hd* **Rainbow Beauty**[8] 7786 3-8-7 **75**................................(p) OisinMurphy(5) 2 81
(Gerard Butler) *t.k.h: chsd ldrs: effrt and rdn to chal over 1f out: ev ch tl no ex fnl 100yds: wknd towards fin* **4/1**[3]

0222 **5** *nse* **Mystery Bet (IRE)**[8] 7786 3-9-0 **77**........................... LeeTopliss 8 83
(Richard Fahey) *wl in tch in midfield: effrt u.p to chse ldrs 2f out: styd on same pce ins fnl f* **10/1**

5653 **6** *1* **Whispering Lady (IRE)**[22] 7489 3-8-4 **70** oh1................ RobertTart(3) 3 74
(David Simcock) *chsd ldrs: rdn and effrt on inner over 1f out: ev ch 1f tl no ex ins fnl f: wknd fnl 50yds* **16/1**

3316 **7** *¾* **Duchess Of Seville**[29] 7330 3-9-3 **80**................................ MartinHarley 1 82
(Marco Botti) *led: rdn and hrd pressed over 1f out: hdd 1f out: wknd fnl 100yds* **6/1**

133 **8** *3 ¼* **Deglet Noor**[23] 7470 3-9-7 **84**.. AndreaAtzeni 6 80
(Roger Varian) *hmpd s: hld up in last pair: rdn and hdwy on outer to chse ldrs over 2f out: wd and lost pl bnd 2f out: wknd ent fnl f* **5/2**[1]

2m 4.28s (-2.32) **Going Correction** -0.075s/f (Stan) **8** Ran SP% **115.1**
Speed ratings (Par 103): **106,105,104,104,104 103,103,100**
toteswingers 1&2 £10.30, 1&3 £7.10, 2&3 £24.60 CSF £45.16 CT £735.78 TOTE £3.50: £1.30, £3.50, £3.40; EX 60.50 Trifecta £1545.20 Part won. Pool: £2060.38 - 0.48 winning units..
Owner Jaber Abdullah **Bred** Rabbah Bloodstock Limited **Trained** Newmarket, Suffolk

FOCUS
An interesting fillies' handicap where some sort of case could be made for all of these prior to the race. In the end it was a bit of a messy affair and seven of them still had a chance approaching the final half-furlong. The winner resumed her summer progress.

7896 BEST ODDS AT BOOKMAKERS.CO.UK H'CAP (DIV I) 6f (P)
1:55 (1:56) (Class 5) (0-75,76) 3-Y-0+ **£2,726** (£805; £402) **Stalls** Low

Form RPR

0/10 **1** **Brother Tiger**[31] 7281 4-9-0 **68**.. DavidProbert 4 79
(David C Griffiths) *taken down early: mde all: rdn over 1f out: hld on gamely u.p fnl f* **7/1**

3111 **2** *½* **Powerful Pierre**[7] 7801 6-8-7 **66**..........................(b) JacobButterfield(5) 5 75
(Ollie Pears) *hld up in tch in midfield: rdn and effrt over 1f out: drvn 1f out: styd on wl ins fnl f: wnt 2nd last strides* **6/1**[3]

U021 **3** *nk* **Emkanaat**[1] 7880 5-9-8 **76** 6ex.. RobertHavlin 1 84
(Amy Weaver) *chsd ldr on inner: rdn and effrt to press wnr over 1f out: kpt on but unable qck wl ins fnl f* **2/1**[1]

1503 **4** *1 ¾* **Jungle Bay**[17] 7601 6-9-7 **75**..(b) TedDurcan 12 77
(Jane Chapple-Hyam) *hld up in tch towards rr: hdwy on outer and v wd bnd 2f out: edgd lft u.p over 1f out: kpt on same pce ins fnl f* **16/1**

4211 **5** *nk* **Jay Bee Blue**[10] 7743 4-9-8 **76** 6ex..........................(bt) SilvestreDeSousa 11 77
(Sean Curran) *stdd and dropped in bhd after s: hld up in tch in rr: swtchd lft and hdwy over 1f out: kpt on same pce ins fnl f* **7/2**[2]

4000 **6** *1 ½* **Seek The Fair Land**[24] 7436 7-9-6 **74**..............................(v) AmirQuinn 7 71
(Lee Carter) *heavily restrained after s and hld up in detached last: rdn and hdwy on inner jst over 1f out: kpt on: nvr trbld ldrs* **33/1**

0500 **7** *½* **Bajan Bear**[10] 7742 5-9-1 **72**........................... WilliamTwiston-Davies(3) 2 67
(Michael Blanshard) *dwlt: in tch towards rr: rdn and gd hdwy on inner to chse ldrs over 1f out: no ex jst ins fnl f: wknd fnl 100yds* **25/1**

5024 **8** *nk* **Another Try (IRE)**[24] 7444 8-8-12 **69**.................................. RobertTart(3) 9 63
(Alan Jarvis) *in tch in midfield: rdn ent fnl 2f: edgd lft and no imp over 1f out: hld and one pce fnl f* **8/1**

0500 **9** *1 ½* **Belinsky (IRE)**[10] 7743 6-8-9 **63**.. KieranO'Neill 3 52
(Julie Camacho) *chsd ldrs: rdn and struggling 2f out: outpcd and lost pl over 1f out: wknd ins fnl f* **33/1**

4103 **10** *nk* **George Fenton**[8] 7792 4-9-2 **73**..................................(e) RyanPowell(3) 6 61
(Conor Dore) *chsd ldrs: rdn over 2f out: struggling 2f out and wknd over 1f out* **16/1**

0235 **11** *hd* **Cardinal**[16] 7633 8-9-4 **72**.. SteveDrowne 8 60
(Robert Cowell) *in tch towards rr: drvn and no hdwy wl over 1f out: nvr trbld ldrs* **25/1**

1m 11.25s (-0.65) **Going Correction** -0.075s/f (Stan) **11** Ran SP% **118.8**
Speed ratings (Par 103): **101,100,99,97,97 95,94,94,92,91 91**
toteswingers 1&2 £9.30, 1&3 £5.70, 2&3 £3.30 CSF £47.15 CT £115.18 TOTE £9.50: £2.50, £2.80, £1.40; EX 62.00 Trifecta £187.50 Pool: £2891.08 - 11.56 winning units..
Owner Norcroft Park Stud **Bred** Norcroft Park Stud **Trained** Bawtry, S Yorks

FOCUS
A reasonable sprint handicap for the grade, featuring several who came here in good form and the winning time was fractionally quicker than the second division. Solid form.

7897 BEST ODDS AT BOOKMAKERS.CO.UK H'CAP (DIV II) 6f (P)
2:30 (2:30) (Class 5) (0-75,75) 3-Y-0+ **£2,726** (£805; £402) **Stalls** Low

Form RPR

502 **1** **Novellen Lad (IRE)**[55] 6648 8-9-6 **74**................................ RobertWinston 7 85
(Willie Musson) *hld up in tch in rr: switching out rt and hdwy over 1f out: str run and qcknd to ld ins fnl f: sn in command: comf* **3/1**[1]

5312 **2** *1 ¼* **Glastonberry**[43] 6982 5-9-6 **74**...................................... GeorgeBaker 11 81
(Geoffrey Deacon) *in tch in midfield: clsd to trck ldrs 2f out: rdn and effrt over 1f out: ev ch ins fnl f: kpt on but outpcd by wnr fnl 50yds* **5/1**[3]

-004 **3** *¾* **Senator Bong**[30] 7313 3-9-4 **72**................................. SilvestreDeSousa 4 77
(David Elsworth) *led: drvn over 1f out: hdd ins fnl f: no ex and outpcd fnl 75yds* **4/1**[2]

2135 **4** *hd* **Rigolleto (IRE)**[31] 7282 5-9-0 **68**...................................... MartinHarley 9 72
(Anabel K Murphy) *chsd ldrs: shuffled bk and n.m.r over 1f out tl ins fnl f: styd on u.p fnl 100yds* **16/1**

2305 **5** *1* **Perfect Venture**[31] 7263 3-8-7 **66**.. RyanTate(5) 5 67
(Clive Cox) *w ldr: ev ch and drvn over 1f out: no ex ins fnl f: wknd fnl 100yds* **8/1**

04 **6** *nk* **Rowe Park**[17] 7601 10-9-7 **75**...(p) RobertHavlin 3 75
(Linda Jewell) *wnt lft and stdd s: hld up in tch towards rr: clsd but stuck bhd a wall of horses ent fnl f: nvr enough room ins fnl f: nvr able to chal* **14/1**

0042 **7** *shd* **Lujeanie**[8] 7783 7-9-1 **69**.. ShaneKelly 2 68
(Peter Crate) *pushed lft s: sn rcvrd to chse ldrs: rdn and effrt over 1f out: hrd drvn and no ex 1f out: wknd ins fnl f* **6/1**

0010 **8** *hd* **Katy Spirit (IRE)**[11] 7729 3-8-9 **63**................................... DavidProbert 6 62
(Michael Blanshard) *in tch in last trio: effrt u.p wl over 1f out: kpt on fnl f but nvr a threat to ldrs* **50/1**

000 **9** *½* **Burnhope**[24] 7445 4-9-3 **71**..(p) FrederikTylicki 1 68
(Scott Dixon) *pushed lft s: hld up in tch towards rr: rdn and hdwy on inner over 1f out: no ex ins fnl f: wknd fnl 100yds* **14/1**

4156 **10** *4* **Captain Kendall (IRE)**[179] 2516 4-9-4 **72**............................ JimCrowley 8 56
(Harry Chisman) *in tch towards rr: effrt and wdst bnd 2f out: sn wknd* **16/1**

1m 11.36s (-0.54) **Going Correction** -0.075s/f (Stan) **10** Ran SP% **114.1**
Speed ratings (Par 103): **100,98,97,97,95 95,95,94,94,88**
toteswingers 1&2 £2.40, 1&3 £4.60, 2&3 £3.40 CSF £17.45 CT £60.67 TOTE £3.90: £1.40, £2.00, £2.60; EX 18.60 Trifecta £88.20 Pool: £2240.58 - 19.04 winning units..
Owner Johnson & Broughton **Bred** Mrs Chris Harrington **Trained** Newmarket, Suffolk

FOCUS
A competitive sprint handicap, but the winner came from last to first to win a shade cosily in the end in a time fractionally slower than that of the first division. The form is taken at face value around the runner-up.

7898 DOWNLOAD THE LADBROKES APP H'CAP 1m (P)
3:05 (3:06) (Class 5) (0-75,74) 3-Y-0+ **£2,726** (£805; £402) **Stalls** High

Form RPR

3134 **1** **The Great Gabrial**[10] 7742 4-9-6 **73**.....................(v) SilvestreDeSousa 10 84
(Ian Williams) *t.k.h early: hld up wl in tch: hdwy to trck ldrs 2f out: rdn and qcknd to ld 1f out: sn edgd lft but wnt clr: r.o wl* **7/4**[1]

1 **2** *1 ¾* **Leonard Thomas**[16] 7625 3-9-3 **72**...................................... TedDurcan 9 79
(David Lanigan) *in tch in midfield: rdn and effrt over 1f out: hdwy to chse wnr wl ins fnl f: edgd lft but r.o* **3/1**[2]

1500 **3** *1* **Chiswick Bey (IRE)**[13] 7699 5-8-8 **68**..........................(p) JoshQuinn(7) 1 73
(Richard Fahey) *in tch in midfield: rdn and hdwy on inner over 1f out: chsd ldrs and kpt on same pce ins fnl f* **20/1**

6210 **4** *1 ¼* **Piceno (IRE)**[6] 7824 5-9-2 **74**...(p) TimClark(5) 3 76
(Scott Dixon) *t.k.h: w ldr: rdn wl over 1f out: led ent fnl f: sn hdd: no ex and wknd fnl 100yds* **6/1**[3]

000 **4** *dht* **Ewell Place (IRE)**[39] 7076 4-9-3 **70**.................................. MartinHarley 4 72
(David Simcock) *chsd ldrs: nt clr run over 1f out and forced to switch rt arnd rivals 1f out: kpt on same pce ins fnl f* **20/1**

3/00 **6** *1 ¼* **Timothy T**[17] 7611 5-9-3 **70**.. JimCrowley 2 69
(Philip Hide) *hld up in tch in last trio: drvn and effrt wl over 1f out: kpt on ins fnl f: nvr trbld ldrs* **10/1**

2-00 **7** *nk* **Rugosa**[96] 5310 4-9-6 **73**.. RobertWinston 5 72
(Charles Hills) *in tch in midfield: effrt but nt qckning whn sltly hmpd over 1f out: kpt on same pce ins fnl f* **8/1**

1030 **8** *2 ¼* **Kakapuka**[72] 6096 6-9-5 **72**.. GeorgeBaker 6 65
(Anabel K Murphy) *led: rdn wl over 1f out: drvn and hdd ent fnl f: sn btn and wknd ins fnl f* **16/1**

2660 **9** *½* **Club House (IRE)**[30] 7307 3-8-10 **65**..................................... KierenFox 7 57
(Robert Mills) *v.s.a: detached in last tl clsd on to bk of field 4f out: pushed along and no hdwy on inner over 1f out: n.d* **20/1**

-100 **10** *2 ¼* **Striking Echo**[193] 2094 3-9-1 **70**.. ShaneKelly 8 57
(Andrew Hollinshead) *in tch towards rr: rdn 4f out: edgd rt and dropped to rr bnd 2f out: wknd over 1f out* **66/1**

1m 36.61s (-1.59) **Going Correction** -0.075s/f (Stan)
WFA 3 from 4yo+ 2lb **10** Ran SP% **117.5**
Speed ratings (Par 103): **104,102,101,100,100 98,98,96,95,93**
toteswingers 1&2 £2.00, 1&3 £10.70, 2&3 £11.50 CSF £6.50 CT £77.81 TOTE £2.20: £1.10, £1.60, £6.60; EX 7.70 Trifecta £67.40 Pool: £3429.60 - 38.15 winning units..
Owner Tariq Al Nisf **Bred** Juddmonte Farms Ltd **Trained** Portway, Worcs

FOCUS
A moderate handicap, lacking much depth, but the first two were the most interesting.

7899 32RED ON THE APP STORE APPRENTICE H'CAP 1m 5f (P)
3:40 (3:40) (Class 6) (0-65,62) 3-Y-0+ **£2,045** (£603; £302) **Stalls** Low

Form RPR

0063 **1** **Lacey**[79] 5897 4-8-7 **48**.. RobHornby(7) 8 56
(Andrew Hollinshead) *chsd ldrs: cl 5th and nt clr run bnd wl over 1f out: rdn and hdwy on inner ent fnl f: led fnl 100yds: edgd rt but hld on gamely fnl 50ydss* **14/1**

6000 **2** *nse* **Hazzaat (IRE)**[58] 6522 3-9-2 **57**.. JoeDoyle 2 65
(Gary Harrison) *restless in stalls: s.i.s: sn rcvrd and in midfield: trcking ldrs and nt clr run 2f out: swtchd rt 1f out: str run u.p and ev ch fnl 75yds: r.o but jst hld* **25/1**

0-51 **3** *2 ¼* **Atalanta Bay (IRE)**[9] 7770 3-9-0 **60** 6ex.................... CharlieBennett(5) 5 65
(Marcus Tregoning) *stuck wd: in tch in midfield: hdwy to chse ldrs 5f out: rdn and effrt wl over 1f out: led jst over 1f out: hdd fnl 100yds: no ex* **8/13**[1]

5-30 **4** *6* **Galiotto (IRE)**[210] 1664 7-9-3 **58**.................................(v) HectorCrouch(7) 6 54
(Gary Moore) *s.i.s: hld up in tch in rr: 6th and pushed along over 2f out: clsd 2f out: rdn and btn over 1f out: wknd fnl f* **7/1**[3]

5200 **5** *nk* **Keep Kicking (IRE)**[10] 7738 6-10-0 **62**................................ DanielCremin 3 57
(Simon Dow) *in tch in midfield: hdwy to chse ldr 5f out tl led 2f out: sn rdn: hdd ent fnl f: wknd fnl 100yds* **20/1**

302 **6** *3 ¾* **El Libertador (USA)**[24] 7440 7-9-2 **55**....................(b) CameronHardie(5) 1 44
(Eric Wheeler) *mde most: rdn and hdd 2f out: drvn and btn ent fnl f: wknd* **5/1**[2]

00-0 **7** *25* **Nowdoro**[240] 94 4-8-11 **48** oh3.. JackGarritty(3) 7
(Julie Camacho) *in tch in last pair: rdn and lost tch over 4f out: t.o over 2f out* **20/1**

5/04 **8** *77* **Jody Bear**[24] 7440 5-8-11 **48** oh2.. DavidParkes(3) 4
(Jonathan Portman) *t.k.h: w ldr tl rdn and dropped to rr 5f out: lost tch 4f out: t.o fnl 3f* **12/1**

2m 45.5s (-0.50) **Going Correction** -0.075s/f (Stan)
WFA 3 from 4yo+ 7lb **8** Ran SP% **118.8**
Speed ratings (Par 101): **98,97,96,92,92 90,75,27**
toteswingers 1&2 £22.60, 1&3 £4.70, 2&3 £6.00 CSF £304.27 CT £541.34 TOTE £14.50: £4.20, £4.50, £1.10; EX 305.70 Trifecta £497.00 Pool: £3109.87 - 4.69 winning units..
Owner N S Sweeney **Bred** Millsec Limited **Trained** Upper Longdon, Staffs
■ Rob Hornby's first winner.

FOCUS
A weak apprentice handicap and not form to get carried away with. The winner is rated back to his early-season form.
T/Plt: £61.90 to a £1 stake. Pool: £40668.13 - 478.90 winning tickets T/Qpdt: £11.30 to a £1 stake. Pool: £5931.70 - 385.84 winning tickets SP

7844 WOLVERHAMPTON (A.W) (L-H)
Friday, November 15

OFFICIAL GOING: Standard
Wind: Fresh behind Weather: Fine

7900 32RED CASINO NURSERY H'CAP 5f 20y(P)
4:00 (4:01) (Class 5) (0-75,67) 2-Y-0 **£2,587** (£770; £384; £192) **Stalls** Low

Form RPR

3342 **1** **Debt Settler (IRE)**[30] 7293 2-8-13 **59**.................................. LukeMorris 6 63
(Luke Dace) *trckd ldr tl shkn up to ld over 1f out: edgd lft ins fnl f: drvn out* **9/4**[1]

5251 **2** *¾* **Kodafine (IRE)**[21] 7509 2-9-0 **67**...................................... EoinWalsh(7) 1 68
(David Evans) *hld up: hdwy over 1f out: rdn to chse wnr fnl f: r.o* **9/2**[2]

The Form Book Flat, Raceform Ltd, Compton, RG20 6NL.

3651 **3** 3 ½ **Skinny Love**[41] 7036 2-9-4 **64** .... AdamBeschizza 2 53
(Robert Cowell) *chsd ldrs: rdn over 1f out: no ex ins fnl f* **6/1**[3]
6061 **4** 1 ¾ **Dynamo Walt (IRE)**[14] 7665 2-9-2 **62** ....(v) RaulDaSilva 3 44
(Derek Shaw) *plld hrd and prom: shkn up 1/2-way: styd on same pce fr over 1f out* **9/4**[1]
1504 **5** ½ **Anytimeatall (IRE)**[9] 7771 2-8-13 **64** .... NatashaEaton(5) 4 45
(Alan Bailey) *led: rdn and hdd over 1f out: wknd ins fnl f* **8/1**
0060 **6** 2 **Dont Tell Nan**[9] 7771 2-8-11 **57** .... LiamJones 5 30
(Derek Shaw) *hld up in tch: plld hrd: hung rt over 3f out: lost tch 1/2-way* **25/1**

1m 3.13s (0.83) **Going Correction** +0.15s/f (Slow) **6** Ran SP% **109.0**
Speed ratings (Par 96): **99,97,92,89,88 85**
toteswingers 1&2 £2.70, 1&3 £1.90, 2&3 £2.20 CSF £11.91 TOTE £2.80: £1.80, £3.30; EX 11.90 Trifecta £34.30 Pool: £3429.22 - 74.92 winning units..
Owner Mark Benton **Bred** Patrick Monahan **Trained** Five Oaks, W Sussex

FOCUS
Although the top-weight was 2lb well in, that still left her rated 6lb below the ceiling for the race. Ordinary nursery form, the winner posting a personal best.

7901 32RED MAIDEN STKS 7f 32y(P)
4:30 (4:31) (Class 5) 2-Y-O **£2,587** (£770; £384; £192) **Stalls** High

Form RPR
0 **1** **Orange Grove**[61] 6430 2-8-12 0........ AlfieWarwick(7) 5 80+
(Tobias B P Coles) *mde virtually all: clr fr over 1f out: easily* **33/1**
46 **2** 7 **Capers Royal Star (FR)**[23] 7467 2-9-5 0........ FergusSweeney 4 63
(Alastair Lidderdale) *chsd ldrs: shkn up over 2f out: styd on same pce fr over 1f out: wnt 2nd post* **2/1**[2]
3 shd **Rocked The Boat** 2-9-5 0........ AdamBeschizza 2 63+
(Tobias B P Coles) *prom: rdn over 1f out: styd on same pce* **10/1**
40 **4** ¾ **Shore Patrol (IRE)**[34] 7209 2-9-5 0........ DavidNolan 8 61
(Richard Fahey) *chsd ldrs: rdn over 2f out: styd on same pce appr fnl f* **7/1**
5 2 ¾ **Chatsworth Express** 2-9-0 0........ GeorgeChaloner(5) 7 54
(Richard Whitaker) *w wnr to 1/2-way: sn pushed along: wknd fnl f* **33/1**
6 3 ½ **Excel Best** 2-9-5 0........ LukeMorris 1 46+
(James Tate) *swvd lft sn after s: sn pushed along and rn green in rr: rdn and wknd 2f out* **7/4**[1]
36 **7** 5 **Rostrum Farewell**[89] 5558 2-9-5 0........ SeanLevey 3 33
(David Brown) *hld up: rdn: hung lft and wknd over 1f out* **5/1**[3]
8 54 **Milo D'Acampo** 2-9-5 0........ JamesSullivan 6
(Tim Etherington) *rn green in rr: drvn along over 5f out: sn lost tch* **50/1**

1m 32.72s (3.12) **Going Correction** +0.15s/f (Slow) **8** Ran SP% **115.8**
Speed ratings (Par 96): **88,80,79,79,75 71,66,4**
toteswingers 1&2 £10.30, 1&3 £18.90, 2&3 £5.70 CSF £99.63 TOTE £16.00: £4.90, £2.00, £2.60; EX 132.90 Trifecta £1004.70 Pool: £4486.92 - 3.34 winning units..
Owner The Walled Garden Partnership **Bred** Miss K Rausing **Trained** Newmarket, Suffolk
■ Alfie Warwick's first winner.

FOCUS
A modest maiden in which the winner routed them. The form is rated around the second and fourth.

7902 32RED.COM MAIDEN STKS 1m 141y(P)
5:00 (5:01) (Class 5) 2-Y-O **£2,587** (£770; £384; £192) **Stalls** Low

Form RPR
60 **1** **Giant Samurai (USA)**[27] 7371 2-9-5 0........ RaulDaSilva 10 69
(John Quinn) *led: hdd over 6f out: chsd ldrs: shkn up to ld ins fnl f: edgd rt towards fin: styd on* **20/1**
0 **2** shd **Alexanor (IRE)**[17] 7607 2-9-5 0........(t) LukeMorris 6 68
(Marco Botti) *a.p: chsd ldr 6f out: rdn to ld over 1f out: hdd ins fnl f: styd on: bmpd nr fin* **8/1**[3]
6 **3** 2 **Authorized Too**[33] 7219 2-9-5 0........ LiamJones 7 64+
(William Haggas) *s.s: sn pushed along and rn green in rr: hdwy and nt clr run over 1f out: r.o to go 3rd post: nvr nrr* **5/4**[1]
2232 **4** shd **Our Gabrial (IRE)**[21] 7492 2-9-5 75........ DavidNolan 2 64
(Richard Fahey) *prom: rdn over 2f out: hung lft ins fnl f: nt run on* **5/2**[2]
00 **5** ½ **Vied (USA)**[9] 7763 2-9-0 0........ RichardKingscote 11 58
(Robert Cowell) *prom: rdn and nt clr run over 1f out: styd on same pce ins fnl f* **66/1**
6 2 **Old Town Boy** 2-9-5 0........ WilliamCarson 8 59
(Philip McBride) *s.s: hdwy over 3f out: rdn over 1f out: styd on same pce fnl f* **25/1**
06 **7** ½ **Mustadrik (USA)**[37] 7128 2-9-5 0........ GrahamLee 9 58
(J W Hills) *chsd ldrs: rdn over 2f out: sn outpcd: rallied over 1f out: no ex ins fnl f* **8/1**[3]
0403 **8** 5 **Chamberlain**[69] 6206 2-9-5 70........(p) SeanLevey 3 47
(Alan McCabe) *s.i.s: hdwy to ld over 6f out: rdn over 2f out: hdd over 1f out: wknd fnl f* **16/1**
9 15 **Aptitude** 2-9-0 0........ AdamBeschizza 5 15+
(Tobias B P Coles) *sn outpcd* **50/1**
10 ¾ **Cresta Rise** 2-8-9 0........ NatashaEaton(5) 4 9
(Alan Bailey) *s.i.s: sn outpcd* **50/1**
0 **11** 21 **Rose Boeuf (FR)**[14] 7664 2-9-0 0........ DanielTudhope 1
(David O'Meara) *prom: hmpd over 7f out: sn lost pl: rdn and wknd over 4f out* **100/1**

1m 53.38s (2.88) **Going Correction** +0.15s/f (Slow) **11** Ran SP% **116.1**
Speed ratings (Par 96): **93,92,91,91,90 88,88,83,70,69 51**
toteswingers 1&2 £12.80, 1&3 £8.50, 2&3 £3.40 CSF £161.68 TOTE £25.30: £4.80, £2.60, £1.40; EX 243.90 Trifecta £648.10 Pool: £4155.91 - 4.80 winning units..
Owner Mr & Mrs Paul Gaffney **Bred** Bill Justice & Ted Taylor **Trained** Settrington, N Yorks
■ Stewards' Enquiry : Raul Da Silva 1st incident: caution: careless riding. (2nd) three-day ban: careless riding (Nov 29,30,Dec 2)

FOCUS
The pace slowed right down once they got to the first bend and it paid to race handily. The bare form looks modest.

7903 BEST ODDS AT BOOKMAKERS.CO.UK H'CAP 5f 20y(P)
5:30 (5:30) (Class 6) (0-55,59) 3-Y-O+ **£1,940** (£577; £288; £144) **Stalls** Low

Form RPR
1025 **1** **Beach Rhythm (USA)**[21] 7508 6-9-6 **53**........(b) CathyGannon 7 62
(Jim Allen) *mde all: clr 1/2-way: rdn and edgd lft fr over 1f out: jst hld on* **2/1**[1]
4441 **2** nk **Beacon Tarn**[10] 7759 3-9-9 **59** 6ex........ NeilFarley(3) 6 67
(Eric Alston) *trckd wnr: pushed along 2f out: rdn over 1f out: r.o* **9/2**[2]
0003 **3** ¾ **Major Muscari (IRE)**[21] 7508 5-8-12 **48**........ BillyCray(3) 4 53
(Shaun Harris) *s.s: hdwy over 1f out: rdn and hung lft ins fnl f: r.o: nt rch ldrs* **12/1**
4000 **4** 1 ½ **Munaawib**[7] 7806 5-9-6 **53**........(bt) RobbieFitzpatrick 3 53
(Charles Smith) *s.i.s: sn pushed along in rr: rdn over 1f out: r.o: nt rch ldrs* **20/1**
3423 **5** ½ **Volcanic Dust (IRE)**[30] 7292 5-9-6 **53**........(t) RichardKingscote 1 51
(Milton Bradley) *chsd ldrs: rdn over 1f out: styd on same pce ins fnl f* **7/1**[3]
0005 **6** 1 ¼ **Cashel's Missile (IRE)**[42] 6994 3-8-13 **46**........(p) LukeMorris 9 40
(John Spearing) *hld up in tch: rdn over 1f out: styd on same pce fnl f* **25/1**
4210 **7** ½ **Borough Boy (IRE)**[9] 7772 3-9-7 **54**........(v) DaleSwift 8 46
(Derek Shaw) *pushed along in rr early: rdn over 1f out: nt trble ldrs* **9/2**[2]
0-00 **8** 1 ¾ **Ballinargh Girl (IRE)**[182] 2409 5-9-2 **52**........ SladeO'Hara(3) 5 37
(Danielle McCormick) *hld up: hdwy over 1f out: sn rdn: no ex ins fnl f* **25/1**
0002 **9** 10 **Tongalooma**[17] 7599 7-9-4 **51**........(p) GrahamLee 11
(James Moffatt) *sn pushed along and prom: rdn and wknd over 1f out* **8/1**
0000 **10** 2 ½ **La Sylphe**[11] 7730 3-8-12 **52**........ AdamMcLean(7) 10
(Derek Shaw) *chsd ldrs: rdn 1/2-way: wknd over 1f out* **33/1**

1m 2.96s (0.66) **Going Correction** +0.15s/f (Slow) **10** Ran SP% **116.4**
Speed ratings (Par 101): **100,99,98,95,95 93,92,89,73,69**
toteswingers 1&2 £2.30, 1&3 £5.80, 2&3 £10.40 CSF £10.16 CT £85.30 TOTE £2.90: £1.10, £2.60, £2.80; EX 15.40 Trifecta £147.00 Pool: £1931.97 - 9.85 winning units..
Owner J P Allen **Bred** Christoph Amerian **Trained** Stoodleigh, Devon

FOCUS
This was won in the first furlong. The well backed winner showed similar form to his penultimate C&D run.

7904 BOOKMAKERS.CO.UK H'CAP (DIV I) 5f 216y(P)
6:00 (6:02) (Class 6) (0-55,55) 3-Y-O+ **£1,940** (£577; £288; £144) **Stalls** Low

Form RPR
0543 **1** **Red Shadow**[7] 7808 4-9-2 **50**........(p) DaleSwift 8 58
(Alan Brown) *led 5f out: rdn over 1f out: all out* **8/1**
0054 **2** nse **Grace Hull**[73] 6075 3-9-4 **55**........ BillyCray(3) 6 63
(Garry Moss) *chsd ldrs: rdn over 1f out: hung rt ins fnl f: r.o* **14/1**
6060 **3** nse **Medam**[15] 7643 4-8-9 **48**........ ShirleyTeasdale(5) 2 56
(Shaun Harris) *s.i.s: hld up: hdwy u.p over 1f out: r.o wl* **6/1**[3]
-060 **4** 1 ½ **Angel Grigio**[56] 6604 3-8-7 **46**........ DavidBergin(5) 11 49
(David O'Meara) *mid-div: hdwy over 1f out: rdn and hung lft ins fnl f: r.o: nt rch ldrs* **20/1**
6302 **5** ¾ **Amelia Jay**[21] 7508 3-9-4 **52**........ GrahamLee 3 53
(Danielle McCormick) *led 1f: chsd ldrs: rdn over 1f out: styd on same pce ins fnl f* **5/1**[2]
1404 **6** ¾ **Boy The Bell**[38] 7101 6-9-0 **55**........(be) LauraBarry(7) 12 53
(Ollie Pears) *hld up: rdn over 1f out: r.o: nt trble ldrs* **4/1**[1]
5600 **7** hd **Kasbhom**[21] 7508 3-9-5 **53**........ WilliamCarson 1 51
(Anthony Carson) *hld up: hdwy and nt clr run 1f out: sn rdn and edgd lft: r.o: nt trble ldrs* **12/1**
3000 **8** nk **Actonetaketwo**[15] 7639 3-9-1 **49**........(p) RichardKingscote 5 46
(Ron Hodges) *prom: rdn over 1f out: styd on same pce fnl f* **25/1**
5600 **9** 2 ¼ **Flow Chart (IRE)**[39] 7079 6-8-10 **47**........ SladeO'Hara(3) 7 36
(Peter Grayson) *sn pushed along in rr: nvr on terms* **20/1**
0564 **10** nk **Wotalad**[15] 7644 3-8-13 **52**........(v[1]) GeorgeChaloner(5) 13 40
(Richard Whitaker) *chsd ldr 5f out: rdn over 2f out: wknd fnl f* **6/1**[3]
3-30 **11** 1 ½ **Marabout (IRE)**[41] 7030 3-9-7 **55**........ DuranFentiman 10 39
(Mel Brittain) *chsd ldrs: rdn over 2f out: wknd fnl f* **7/1**
0350 **12** nse **Celestial Dawn**[151] 3393 4-9-7 **55**........ LukeMorris 9 38
(John Weymes) *s.s: outpcd* **16/1**

1m 16.01s (1.01) **Going Correction** +0.15s/f (Slow) **12** Ran SP% **122.5**
Speed ratings (Par 101): **99,98,98,96,95 94,94,94,91,90 88,88**
toteswingers 1&2 £22.10, 1&3 £18.80, 2&3 £70.50 CSF £114.82 CT £740.19 TOTE £10.80: £2.70, £5.10, £3.80; EX 122.80 Trifecta £1189.70 Part won. Pool: £1586.32 - 0.25 winning units..
Owner S Pedersen **Bred** Mrs P A & M J Reditt **Trained** Yedingham, N Yorks

FOCUS
Again, getting the early lead proved all important. The winner is rated to her best form since last autumn.

7905 BOOKMAKERS.CO.UK H'CAP (DIV II) 5f 216y(P)
6:30 (6:31) (Class 6) (0-55,55) 3-Y-O+ **£1,940** (£577; £288; £144) **Stalls** Low

Form RPR
0-25 **1** **Ad Vitam (IRE)**[45] 6919 5-9-4 **52**........(bt) DuranFentiman 3 64
(Mel Brittain) *chsd ldrs: rdn over 2f out: led ins fnl f: r.o u.p to ld ins fnl f: sn clr* **6/1**[2]
0-00 **2** 2 ¾ **Slewtoo**[162] 3026 4-9-0 **48**........ GrahamLee 7 51
(James Given) *hld up: rdn and r.o ins fnl f: wnt 2nd nr fin: no ch w wnr* **14/1**
00 **3** nk **Legal Eagle (IRE)**[223] 1396 8-8-12 **49**........(p) MarkCoumbe(3) 4 51
(Noel Williams) *prom: rdn over 2f out: r.o* **20/1**
5406 **4** hd **Coastal Passage**[10] 7752 5-9-3 **51**........(bt) RobbieFitzpatrick 1 53
(Charles Smith) *sn pushed along into mid-div: hdwy u.p over 1f out: r.o* **25/1**
5466 **5** hd **Hamis Al Bin (IRE)**[29] 7323 4-9-6 **54**........(t) RichardKingscote 10 55
(Milton Bradley) *hld up: hdwy: nt clr run and swtchd lft ins fnl f: r.o: nt rch ldrs* **7/2**[1]
0530 **6** shd **Myjestic Melody (IRE)**[32] 7236 5-8-12 **46**........ BenCurtis 2 47
(Brian Ellison) *chsd ldr tl led over 3f out: rdn over 1f out: hdd and unable qck ins fnl f* **12/1**
3605 **7** ½ **Methaaly (IRE)**[21] 7512 10-9-0 **55**........(be) LewisStones(7) 13 54
(Michael Mullineaux) *hld up: racd on outer: hdwy over 1f out: nt rch ldrs* **10/1**
5-04 **8** ¾ **Interchoice Star**[22] 7485 8-9-0 **48**........(p) LukeMorris 8 45
(Ray Peacock) *chsd ldrs: rdn over 1f out: no ex ins fnl f* **7/1**[3]
6225 **9** nk **Doctor Hilary**[137] 3897 11-9-0 **48**........(v) FergusSweeney 5 44
(Mark Hoad) *hld up: hdwy over 1f out: styd on same pce ins fnl f* **10/1**
4666 **10** 2 ¼ **Vhujon (IRE)**[295] 349 8-8-9 **46** oh1........ SladeO'Hara(3) 9 34
(Peter Grayson) *hld up: rdn over 1f out: nvr on terms* **33/1**
5043 **11** 1 ½ **Coire Gabhail**[24] 7443 3-9-7 **55**........(p) SeanLevey 12 39
(Hughie Morrison) *led: hdd over 3f out: rdn over 2f out: wknd ins fnl f* **6/1**[2]
00 **12** 1 **Kai**[55] 6634 4-9-5 **53**........(b) CathyGannon 6 33
(Alan McCabe) *prom: hmpd and lost pl sn after s: rdn over 2f out: n.d after* **10/1**

1m 15.87s (0.87) **Going Correction** +0.15s/f (Slow) **12** Ran SP% **116.5**
Speed ratings (Par 101): **100,96,95,95,95 95,94,93,93,90 88,86**
CSF £83.03 CT £1575.21 TOTE £6.70: £1.80, £4.80, £8.00; EX 94.00 Trifecta £1091.80 Part won. Pool: £1455.77 - 0.09 winning units..
Owner Christian Bennett **Bred** Michelle Morgan **Trained** Warthill, N Yorks
■ Stewards' Enquiry : Luke Morris one-day ban: failed to ride to draw (Dec 4)
Sean Levey two-day ban: careless riding (Dec 2-3)

FOCUS
There was plenty of early pace on, the leaders tired badly in the straight and the time was 0.14sec quicker than the first division. The winner is rated back to his best.

7906 CORAL APP DOWNLOAD FROM THE APP STORE H'CAP 1m 1f 103y(P)
7:00 (7:00) (Class 3) (0-95,93) 3-Y-O **£7,246** (£2,168; £1,084; £542; £270) **Stalls Low**

Form RPR
2066 **1** **Come On Blue Chip (IRE)**[15] 7641 4-9-0 **86**................(p) SeanLevey 2 96
(Paul D'Arcy) *a.p: chsd ldr over 2f out: rdn to ld over 1f out: styd on u.p* **5/1**[2]
1160 **2** 1 1/4 **Zain Eagle**[21] 7497 3-9-4 **93**.................................... BenCurtis 5 101
(Gerard Butler) *hld up: hdwy over 2f out: rdn and hung lft fr over 1f out: chsd wnr fnl f: styd on* **5/4**[1]
1550 **3** 1 1/2 **Spirit Of The Law (IRE)**[49] 6801 4-8-9 **86**.............. GeorgeChaloner(5) 4 90
(Richard Fahey) *prom: edgd lft over 3f out: shkn up over 2f out: swtchd rt over 1f out: r.o* **20/1**
0150 **4** 2 3/4 **Marcret (ITY)**[48] 6838 6-9-7 **93**................................ DanielTudhope 3 91
(David O'Meara) *led: rdn and hdd over 1f out: no ex ins fnl f* **5/1**[2]
0450 **5** 4 **The Lock Master (IRE)**[87] 5613 6-8-13 **85**.................. AndrewMullen 6 75
(Michael Appleby) *chsd ldrs: rdn over 2f out: wknd over 1f out* **33/1**
0031 **6** 1 1/2 **Stevie Thunder**[9] 7765 8-8-7 **79** 6ex.....................(p) RichardKingscote 7 66
(Ian Williams) *chsd ldr tl rdn over 2f out: wknd over 1f out* **5/1**[2]
0004 **7** 4 1/2 **Ardmay (IRE)**[25] 7425 4-8-13 **85**..................................(p) GrahamLee 8 62
(Kevin Ryan) *hld up: hdwy over 4f out: rdn over 2f out: sn wknd* **10/1**[3]
3625 **8** 23 **Next Edition (IRE)**[40] 6499 5-8-11 **83**............................... LukeMorris 1 12
(Philip Kirby) *sn pushed along in rr: hmpd over 7f out: drvn along over 4f out: hmpd over 3f out: eased* **16/1**

2m 0.45s (-1.25) **Going Correction** +0.15s/f (Slow)
WFA 3 from 4yo+ 3lb **8** Ran SP% **117.1**
Speed ratings (Par 107): **111,109,108,106,102 101,97,76**
toteswingers 1&2 £3.40, 1&3 £20.70, 2&3 £7.60 CSF £11.97 CT £116.25 TOTE £7.70: £1.70, £2.20, £4.50; EX 14.60 Trifecta £237.70 Pool: £1709.93 - 5.39 winning units..
Owner Blue Chip Feed Ltd **Bred** Gerry Flannery Developments **Trained** Newmarket, Suffolk
FOCUS
A decent handicap, but the early pace wasn't hectic and the form is not the strongest for the grade. The winner's best run since this race last year.

7907 CORAL MOBILE "JUST THREE CLICKS TO BET" CLASSIFIED STKS 1m 1f 103y(P)
7:30 (7:31) (Class 6) 3-Y-O+ **£1,940** (£577; £288; £144) **Stalls Low**

Form RPR
2003 **1** **Minstrel Lad**[15] 7639 5-9-1 54.................................... GrahamLee 7 62
(Lydia Pearce) *a.p: chsd ldr over 1f out: shkn up to ld wl ins fnl f: r.o* **4/1**[2]
6024 **2** 1 3/4 **Attain**[29] 7321 4-8-10 51...................................(p) ShelleyBirkett(5) 9 58
(Julia Feilden) *trckd ldr tl led over 2f out: rdn over 1f out: hdd and unable qck wl ins fnl f* **11/2**[3]
3 2 1/2 **Koos (GER)**[84] 5-9-1 48...................................... LukeMorris 8 53
(Marco Botti) *chsd ldrs: pushed along over 3f out: n.m.r over 1f out: styd on same pce fnl f* **4/1**[2]
0501 **4** 1/2 **Quadriga (IRE)**[7] 7806 3-8-13 53........................ GeorgeChaloner(5) 2 59
(Robert Eddery) *hld up: hdwy over 2f out: rdn over 1f out: styd on same pce fnl f* **7/2**[1]
3445 **5** 5 **Well Owd Mon**[38] 7104 3-8-7 54.............................. JackDuern(5) 3 42
(Andrew Hollinshead) *hld up: pushed along 3f out: styd on fr over 1f out: nvr nrr* **8/1**
0034 **6** 3 1/2 **Lincolnrose (IRE)**[15] 7637 3-8-12 52......................(p) AndrewMullen 10 35
(Michael Appleby) *led: rdn and hdd over 2f out: wknd over 1f out* **16/1**
4020 **7** 4 **Platinum Proof (USA)**[9] 7770 3-8-7 48....................(bt) DavidBergin(5) 6 26
(David O'Meara) *chsd ldrs: rdn over 2f out: wknd wl over 1f out* **10/1**
0650 **8** 3 1/4 **Planchette**[58] 6518 3-8-12 40.................................. CathyGannon 5 20
(Jane Chapple-Hyam) *prom: drvn along over 4f out: wknd over 2f out* **50/1**
3V01 **9** 3 **Rock Diamond (IRE)**[123] 4345 3-8-12 50.................. RichardKingscote 1 13
(Brendan Powell) *a in rr: pushed along 3f out: sn wknd* **14/1**
400 **10** 24 **Operettist**[15] 7643 4-8-10 44................................. GeorgeDowning(5) 4
(Tony Carroll) *s.i.s: sn pushed along in rr: wknd over 3f out* **66/1**

2m 2.06s (0.36) **Going Correction** +0.15s/f (Slow)
WFA 3 from 4yo+ 3lb **10** Ran SP% **113.8**
Speed ratings (Par 101): **104,102,100,99,95 92,88,85,83,61**
toteswingers 1&2 £4.50, 1&3 £6.40, 2&3 £4.90 CSF £25.64 TOTE £4.20: £1.20, £2.10, £2.20; EX 26.40 Trifecta £109.40 Pool: £1831.58 - 12.55 winning units..
Owner S & M Supplies (Aylsham) Ltd **Bred** Theresa Fitsall **Trained** Newmarket, Suffolk
FOCUS
There was a reasonable gallop on here and the form is sound, if limited.
T/Plt: £224.50 to a £1 stake. Pool: £81067.50 - 263.55 winning tickets T/Qpdt: £46.50 to a £1 stake. Pool: £13063.01 - 207.50 winning tickets CR

7908 - 7921a (Foreign Racing) - See Raceform Interactive

7892 LINGFIELD (L-H)
Saturday, November 16

OFFICIAL GOING: Standard
Wind: virtually nil Weather: dry and bright

7922 CORAL APP DOWNLOAD FROM THE APP STORE H'CAP (DIV I) 1m 2f (P)
11:50 (11:50) (Class 6) (0-65,65) 3-Y-O+ **£2,045** (£603; £302) **Stalls Low**

Form RPR
-020 **1** **Brave Decision**[188] 625 6-8-10 **51** oh3............................ LukeMorris 2 57
(Suzy Smith) *in tch in midfield: lft in ld bnd after 1f: hdd 8f out and chsd ldr after: rdn to ld over 2f out: kpt on u.p fnl f* **33/1**
5152 **2** 1 1/2 **Sutton Sid**[23] 7321 3-8-13 **58**..(p) GrahamLee 5 61
(Chris Gordon) *in tch in midfield: lft chsng ldrs bnd after 1f: 3rd and drvn wl over 1f out: chsd wnr jst ins fnl f: kpt on but a hld* **7/1**[3]
6013 **3** 1 **Petersboden**[60] 6491 4-8-10 **51** oh2.............................. FergusSweeney 9 52
(Michael Blanshard) *in tch in midfield: hdwy to chse ldr jst over 2f out: drvn and kpt on same pce fr over 1f out: lost 3rd jst ins fnl f* **14/1**
0065 **4** 1 1/4 **Paddy's Saltantes (IRE)**[12] 7736 3-9-5 **64**...................(b) LiamJones 10 63
(J S Moore) *dwlt and rdn along early: in tch in midfield: drvn and effrt to chse ldrs jst over 2f out: kpt on ins fnl f but no threat to ldrs* **7/2**[2]
3-00 **5** 3 **Queen Of Skies (IRE)**[32] 7278 4-9-3 **58**.................... AndrewMullen 11 51
(Michael Appleby) *stdd and dropped in bhd after s: hld up in tch in rr: rdn and effrt over 1f out: no imp and one pce fnl f* **20/1**
0631 **6** 1 1/4 **Buster Brown (IRE)**[22] 7514 4-9-10 **65**........................ GeorgeBaker 8 55
(Gary Moore) *hld up in tch in last trio: clsd and looked to be travelling over 2f out: rdn and fnd nil over 1f out: wknd ins fnl f* **10/11**[1]
-000 **7** 4 **Hartlebury**[35] 7201 3-8-7 **52**..................................... SilvestreDeSousa 3 34
(James Bethell) *t.k.h: chsd ldr tl carried v wd bnd after 1f: lost pl and hld up in last pair after: effrt u.p on inner over 1f out: wknd fnl f* **14/1**
0005 **8** hd **Kindia (IRE)**[24] 7458 5-8-5 **51**.......................................(p) RyanTate(5) 6 33
(Michael Attwater) *t.k.h: chsd ldrs tl carried v wd bnd after 1f out: stuck wd and hld up in midfield after: rdn and no rspnse over 2f out: wknd over 1f out* **14/1**
0460 **9** 6 **Beep**[72] 6146 3-9-1 **65**...(e[1]) ShelleyBirkett(5) 1 35
(Lydia Richards) *sn led: hung bdly rt to paddock exit and hdd after 1f: rcvrd and dashed into ld 8f out: rdn and hdd over 2f out: wknd 2f out: fdd fnl f* **33/1**

2m 5.17s (-1.43) **Going Correction** -0.15s/f (Stan)
WFA 3 from 4yo+ 4lb **9** Ran SP% **117.7**
Speed ratings (Par 101): **99,97,97,96,93 92,89,89,84**
toteswingers 1&2 £9.40, 1&3 £14.20, 2&3 £4.30 CSF £247.74 CT £3386.77 TOTE £23.20: £4.30, £1.50, £2.80; EX 185.40 Trifecta £621.80 Pool: £1865.91 - 2.25 winning units..
Owner R Knight **Bred** K A Dasmal **Trained** Lewes, E Sussex
FOCUS
A moderate handicap to start the card and drama on the first bend where the leader Beep, in a first-time eyeshield, tried to run out and badly hampered both Kindia and Hartlebury in the process. It may be best to forgive the latter pair their respective efforts. The winner and third were out of the handicap and the form is rated a bit cautiously.

7923 CORAL APP DOWNLOAD FROM THE APP STORE H'CAP (DIV II) 1m 2f (P)
12:20 (12:21) (Class 6) (0-65,61) 3-Y-O+ **£2,045** (£603; £302) **Stalls Low**

Form RPR
5515 **1** **Lady Lunchalot (USA)**[16] 7637 3-9-3 **58**......................(p) LiamJones 9 69
(Laura Mongan) *in tch in midfield: hdwy to chse ldrs 5f out: upsides ldr 2f out: wd but rdn to ld bnd wl over 1f out: r.o wl: rdn out* **8/1**
0000 **2** 1 1/2 **Full Speed (GER)**[130] 4150 8-9-3 **61**.......................... EvaMoscrop(7) 3 69
(Philip Kirby) *hld up in tch in last quartet: rdn and gd hdwy on inner to chse wnr over 1f out: r.o but no imp on wnr fnl f* **20/1**
440 **3** 3 1/2 **Short Shrift (IRE)**[161] 3116 3-9-6 **61**............................ GeorgeBaker 4 62
(James Toller) *stdd after s: t.k.h: hld up in tch in midfield: rdn and effrt wl over 1f out: hdwy to chse clr ldng pair jst ins fnl f: no imp* **5/1**[3]
3000 **4** shd **Offbeat Safaris (IRE)**[71] 6153 5-9-3 **54**........................(p) LukeMorris 7 55
(Ronald Harris) *t.k.h: hld up in tch in midfield: rdn and hdwy over 1f out: battling for 3rd but no threat to ldng pair fnl f* **16/1**
0352 **5** 1 3/4 **Ground Ginger**[42] 7034 3-8-6 **47** oh1........................ SilvestreDeSousa 8 44
(James Bethell) *in tch in midfield: lost bnd and rdn bnd wl over 1f out: no threat to ldrs and kpt on same pce after* **3/1**[1]
1666 **6** nse **Entrance**[83] 5803 5-8-6 **48**.. ShelleyBirkett(5) 10 45
(Julia Feilden) *s.i.s and niggled along early: in tch in rr: hdwy over 1f out: kpt on fnl f: nvr trbld ldrs* **8/1**
3463 **7** 1 1/2 **Malih**[11] 7741 4-9-9 **60**.. FergusSweeney 11 54
(Jamie Osborne) *chsd ldrs: wnt 2nd 8f out tl led over 2f out: rdn and hdd wl over 1f out: 3rd and outpcd over 1f out: lost 3rd and wknd ins fnl f* **7/2**[2]
5200 **8** 1/2 **Final Delivery**[25] 7437 4-9-8 **59**...............................(b) WilliamCarson 1 52
(Jim Boyle) *hld up in tch: hmpd bnd over 8f out: rdn and no hdwy 2f out: nvr trbld ldrs* **12/1**
0000 **9** 1/2 **Byrd In Hand (IRE)**[75] 6038 6-8-10 **47** oh1....................... GrahamLee 2 39
(John Bridger) *t.k.h: hld up in tch: lost pl and rdn ent fnl 2f: wknd over 1f out* **33/1**
-005 **10** 1 1/4 **Roaring Rocks (FR)**[31] 7299 3-8-11 **52**.......................... AndreaAtzeni 6 42
(Heather Main) *led tl rdn and hdd over 2f out: awkward hd carriage u.p: wknd over 1f out* **10/1**
3400 **11** nk **Lady Barastar (IRE)**[39] 7091 5-8-12 **49**..........................(b) JimCrowley 5 38
(Amanda Perrett) *sn pushed along in last pair: in tch: rdn and no hdwy 2f out: sn wknd* **12/1**

2m 5.05s (-1.55) **Going Correction** -0.15s/f (Stan)
WFA 3 from 4yo+ 4lb **11** Ran SP% **124.2**
Speed ratings (Par 101): **100,98,96,95,94 94,93,92,92,91 91**
toteswingers 1&2 £19.10, 1&3 £5.20, 2&3 £28.40 CSF £163.88 CT £896.84 TOTE £9.30: £2.30, £6.00, £2.00; EX 281.00 Trifecta £1214.40 Part won. Pool: £1,619.24 - 0.46 winning units..
Owner Charlie's Starrs **Bred** Fred W Hertrich III **Trained** Epsom, Surrey
FOCUS
The winning time was 0.12sec faster than the first division but the form looks shaky again.

7924 LADBROKES CLAIMING STKS 1m (P)
12:50 (12:50) (Class 6) 3-Y-O **£2,045** (£603; £302) **Stalls High**

Form RPR
515 **1** **Tabaayun (IRE)**[26] 7425 3-9-5 75..............................(v) DanielTudhope 8 82
(David O'Meara) *led tl over 6f out: chsd ldr tl led and qcknd clr 2f out: in command fnl f: r.o wl: comf* **5/2**[1]
2200 **2** 3 1/2 **Cash Is King**[133] 4076 3-8-12 70...................................(b[1]) MartinLane 2 67
(Nick Littmoden) *wl in tch in midfield on inner: rdn and effrt to chse wnr over 1f out: no ex 1f out: one pce after* **6/1**
3411 **3** 3/4 **Poitin**[30] 7325 3-8-13 70.. LukeMorris 3 66
(Harry Dunlop) *niggled along in last trio: hdwy u.p ent fnl f: chsd ldng pair ins fnl f: kpt on* **7/2**[3]
0040 **4** 2 **Foie Gras**[16] 7643 3-8-2 45.. ShelleyBirkett(5) 1 56
(Chris Dwyer) *in tch in last pair: hdwy on inner and carried lft over 1f out: kpt on fnl f: no threat to wnr* **50/1**
5335 **5** nse **Taxiformissbyron**[23] 7489 3-8-8 65..............................(p) JoeFanning 7 57
(Michael Herrington) *chsd ldrs: rdn and unable qck 2f out: wknd u.p over 1f out* **6/1**
0415 **6** 3 1/4 **Admirals Walk (IRE)**[22] 7511 3-8-4 60....................(tp) JoshBaudains(5) 5 50
(Sylvester Kirk) *t.k.h: hld up wl in tch in midfield: rdn and unable qck whn edgd lft over 1f out: wknd fnl f* **16/1**
0502 **7** 2 **Not Rigg (USA)**[21] 7544 3-8-11 68....................................(t) ShaneKelly 6 47
(Gary Harrison) *midfield tl stdd after 1f: hld up in tch towards rr after: rdn and no hdwy wl over 1f out: wknd over 1f out* **3/1**[2]
0050 **8** 3 **Whitford (IRE)**[16] 7644 3-8-3 45 ow1.......................... NathanAlison(5) 9 38
(Chris Dwyer) *s.i.s: rcvrd and hdwy to ld over 6f out: rdn and hdd 2f out: wknd over 1f out: bhd fnl f* **100/1**

1m 36.65s (-1.55) **Going Correction** -0.15s/f (Stan) **8** Ran SP% **113.2**
Speed ratings (Par 98): **101,97,96,94,94 91,89,86**
toteswingers 1&2 £3.20, 1&3 £2.10, 2&3 £4.20 CSF £17.74 TOTE £2.70: £1.10, £2.20, £2.20; EX 19.00 Trifecta £98.80 Pool: £2649.35 - 20.09 winning units..
Owner Middleham Park Racing LVII & Partner **Bred** Ecurie Des Monceaux **Trained** Nawton, N Yorks
FOCUS
A moderate claimer, the form limited by the fourth.

7925 32RED/BRITISH STALLION STUDS EBF NOVICE STKS 1m (P)
1:25 (1:26) (Class 5) 2-Y-O **£2,911** (£866; £432; £216) **Stalls High**

Form RPR
225 **1** **Thewandaofu (IRE)**[35] 7194 2-8-11 90........................ FergusSweeney 4 84+
(Jamie Osborne) *mde all: rdn and qcknd 2f out: styd on wl fnl f: rdn out* **6/4**[1]

The Form Book Flat, Raceform Ltd, Compton, RG20 6NL.

2 **2** *2* **Epic Voyage (USA)**[94] 5405 2-9-0 0 RobertHavlin 2 83+
(John Gosden) *hld up in 3rd: chsd wnr ent fnl 2f: rdn and hung bdly lft over 1f out: continued to hang and no imp fnl f* **6/4**[1]

0564 **3** *3 1/2* **Steventon Star**[65] 6328 2-9-10 94 (b) SilvestreDeSousa 1 84
(Alan Bailey) *hld up in tch in last: rdn wl over 2f out: no imp over 1f out: wnt 3rd 1f out: nvr trbld ldrs* **4/1**[2]

001 **4** *1 3/4* **Applejack Lad**[9] 7780 2-9-2 75 (t) GrahamLee 3 72
(John Ryan) *chsd ldng pair: rdn over 2f out: outpcd and btn over 1f out: dropped to last and wknd 1f out* **16/1**[3]

1m 36.93s (-1.27) **Going Correction** -0.15s/f (Stan) **4** Ran SP% **105.9**
Speed ratings (Par 96): **100,98,94,92**
CSF £3.80 TOTE £2.40; EX 4.80 Trifecta £5.00 Pool: £2394.37 - 354.74 winning units..
Owner Fromthestables.Com & Partner **Bred** Mrs Eleanor Commins **Trained** Upper Lambourn, Berks

FOCUS
An interesting little novice event despite the small field, but the winner had it very much her own way in a falsely run race. Not form to take too literally and the winner is rated 4lb off her Rockfel form.

7926 DOWNLOAD THE LADBROKES APP H'CAP 1m (P)
2:00 (2:01) (Class 2) (0-105,97) 3-Y-0+ **£12,291** (£3,657; £1,827; £913) **Stalls** High

Form RPR

-100 **1** **Anaconda (FR)**[21] 7540 4-9-8 **95** RichardKingscote 10 105
(Tom Dascombe) *sn led and mde rest: rdn and qcknd over 1f out: a holding rivals fnl f and r.o wl: rdn out* **8/1**

60-5 **2** *1 1/4* **Marshgate Lane (USA)**[16] 7641 4-9-4 **91** JoeFanning 9 98
(Mark Johnston) *stuck wd: in tch in midfield: rdn and effrt ent fnl 2f: r.o u.p to go 2nd towards fin* **8/1**

0000 **3** *1/2* **Loyalty**[16] 7648 6-8-7 **87** (v) AdamMcLean(7) 1 93
(Derek Shaw) *chsd ldr tl over 6f out: chsd ldng pair after: rdn and effrt to chse wnr again wl over 1f out: styd on same pce fnl f: lost 2nd towards fin* **33/1**

1000 **4** *nse* **Clockmaker (IRE)**[21] 7540 7-9-7 **94** JimCrowley 7 100
(Conor Dore) *t.k.h: hld up wl in tch in midfield: rdn and effrt over 1f out: r.o wl u.p ins fnl f: no threat to wnr* **50/1**

3052 **5** *nk* **Solar Deity (IRE)**[21] 7540 4-9-9 **96** MartinHarley 6 101+
(Marco Botti) *hld up wl in tch in midfield: nt clr run and forced to switch rt ent fnl f: r.o wl ins fnl f: no threat to wnr* **5/2**[1]

/5-0 **5** *dht* **Mighty Ambition (USA)**[16] 7641 4-9-3 **90** SilvestreDeSousa 2 95+
(Charlie Appleby) *dwlt: sn rcvrd and wl in tch in midfield: gng for run towards inner over 1f out: travelling wl but nt clr run 1f out: fnlly swtchd rt wl ins fnl f: unable to chal* **6/1**[3]

3100 **7** *1/2* **Mia's Boy**[16] 7648 9-9-3 **93** RobertTart(3) 12 97
(Chris Dwyer) *stdd s: hld up wl in tch in rr: rdn and effrt on outer bnd 2f out: r.o wl ins fnl f: nt rch ldrs* **25/1**

1015 **8** *3/4* **Lowther**[21] 7542 8-9-3 **90** (v) GrahamLee 3 92
(Lee Carter) *wl in tch in midfield: rdn and effrt 2f out: unable qck over 1f out: styd on same pce fnl f* **25/1**

2030 **9** *3/4* **Tigers Tale (IRE)**[21] 7536 4-9-0 **87** (v) AndreaAtzeni 4 88
(Roger Teal) *bustled along leaving stalls: chsd wnr over 6f out tl wl over 1f out: unable qck over 1f out: wknd ins fnl f* **14/1**

1-00 **10** *shd* **Stasio (USA)**[252] 953 3-9-0 **89** MartinLane 5 88+
(David Simcock) *hld up in tch in rr: cl enough but nvr anywhere to go fr over 1f out: nvr able to chal* **25/1**

5-00 **11** *shd* **Bronze Angel (IRE)**[35] 7196 4-9-10 **97** MartinDwyer 8 97+
(Marcus Tregoning) *s.i.s: in tch and niggled along in last pair: hdwy on inner over 1f out: nvr enough room and no imp ins fnl f: nvr able to chal* **9/2**[2]

1105 **12** *3/4* **Roserrow**[98] 5255 4-9-2 **94** OisinMurphy(5) 11 92
(Andrew Balding) *chsd ldrs: rdn and unable qck over 1f out: wknd ins fnl f* **7/1**

1m 35.11s (-3.09) **Going Correction** -0.15s/f (Stan)
WFA 3 from 4yo+ 2lb **12** Ran SP% **118.9**
Speed ratings (Par 109): **109,107,107,107,106 106,106,105,104,104 104,103**
toteswingers 1&2 £12.10, 1&3 £74.40, 2&3 £61.80 CSF £66.37 CT £2042.34 TOTE £8.90: £2.40, £3.00, £8.30; EX 149.70 Trifecta £2130.80 Part won. Pool: £2,841.07 - 0.78 winning units..
Owner The MHS 8X8 Partnership **Bred** Haras Du Quesnay **Trained** Malpas, Cheshire
■ Stewards' Enquiry : Richard Kingscote two-day ban: careless riding (Nov 30,Dec 2)

FOCUS
A red-hot handicap, but in such a tight contest and with room to manoeuvre at such a premium, the best place to be is often out in front. Another personal best from the winner.

7927 CORAL.CO.UK CHURCHILL STKS (LISTED RACE) 1m 2f (P)
2:35 (2:39) (Class 1) 3-Y-0+
£20,982 (£7,955; £3,981; £1,983; £995; £499) **Stalls** Low

Form RPR

3461 **1** **Prince Alzain (USA)**[9] 7793 4-9-2 110 (p) OisinMurphy 5 108
(Gerard Butler) *hld up wl in tch in midfield: rdn and hdwy to press ldrs ent fnl f: led ins fnl f: edgd rt but sn qcknd clr: comf* **5/2**[1]

331 **2** *2 1/4* **Bancnuanaheireann (IRE)**[50] 6801 6-9-2 97 AndrewMullen 10 103
(Michael Appleby) *stuck wd thrght: in tch towards rr: hdwy 3f out: drvn 2f out: kpt on gamely fr over 1f out: chsd wnr fnl 75yds: no imp* **16/1**

600/ **3** *1/2* **Uramazin (IRE)**[14] 7498 7-9-2 99 [1] JimCrowley 7 102
(Philip Hide) *hld up in tch in rr: rdn wl over 1f out: stl plenty to do and swtchd rt 1f out: r.o strly ins fnl f: no threat to wnr* **66/1**

-512 **4** *1/2* **Tales Of Grimm (USA)**[35] 7196 4-9-2 108 PaulHanagan 6 101
(Richard Fahey) *hld up in tch in last pair: rdn 2f out: hdwy u.p 1f out: styd on same pce fnl 100yds* **3/1**[2]

0630 **5** *1/2* **Dick Doughtywylie**[52] 6742 5-9-2 100 RobertHavlin 3 100
(John Gosden) *restless in stalls: awkward s: wl in tch in midfield: rdn to press ldrs 2f out: no ex 1f out: styd on same pce ins fnl f* **12/1**

6204 **6** *1* **Tinshu (IRE)**[40] 7072 7-8-11 91 (p) GrahamLee 2 95+
(Derek Haydn Jones) *chsd ldrs: effrt on inner and pressing ldr whn nt clr run and hmpd 1f out: sme hdwy jst ins fnl f: no imp fnl 100yds: wknd towards fin* **20/1**

4651 **7** *nk* **Highland Knight (IRE)**[35] 7196 6-9-6 109 (t) DavidProbert 4 101
(Andrew Balding) *led: rdn ent fnl 2f: drvn and hdd ins fnl f: no ex and wknd fnl 75yds* **3/1**[2]

1005 **8** *1 3/4* **Sugar Boy (IRE)**[21] 7535 3-9-2 108 (b) MartinHarley 8 98
(Marco Botti) *chsd ldr tl over 1f out: sn btn: wknd ins fnl f* **8/1**[3]

66 **9** *7* **Charles Camoin (IRE)**[35] 7206 5-9-2 91 CathyGannon 9 80
(Sylvester Kirk) *wl in tch in midfield: rdn and struggling over 2f out: losing pl whn sltly hmpd wl over 1f out: bhd fnl f* **14/1**

-026 **10** *7* **Tosca (GER)**[140] 3835 3-8-7 82 [1] MartinLane 1 61
(Mrs Ilka Gansera-Leveque) *in tch in midfield: rdn and lost pl over 2f out: bhd over 1f out* **66/1**

2m 2.33s (-4.27) **Going Correction** -0.15s/f (Stan)
WFA 3 from 4yo+ 4lb **10** Ran SP% **117.7**
Speed ratings (Par 111): **111,109,108,108,108 107,106,105,99,94**
toteswingers 1&2 £7.60, 1&3 £37.90, 2&3 £51.40 CSF £44.58 TOTE £3.60: £1.40, £3.50, £12.10; EX 47.80 Trifecta £985.40 Pool: £2876.91 - 2.18 winning units..
Owner Asaad Al Banwan **Bred** Dermot Cantillon & Patrick Hayes **Trained** Newmarket, Suffolk
■ Stewards' Enquiry : David Probert three-day ban: careless riding (Nov 30,Dec2-3)

FOCUS
A decent Listed race in its own right, the Churchill Stakes is now a "Win & You're In" qualifier for the All-Weather Championships Middle Distance Final next April. The 3yo generation had taken four of the last five runnings of this race, but the classic generation were thinly represented this year and this was one for the older brigade. The pace was ordinary, as was the time for the grade. The winner went some way to confirming his latest Wolverhampton form.

7928 BEST ODDS AT BOOKMAKERS.CO.UK GOLDEN ROSE STKS (LISTED RACE) 6f (P)
3:10 (3:13) (Class 1) 3-Y-0+
£20,982 (£7,955; £3,981; £1,983; £995; £499) **Stalls** Low

Form RPR

4060 **1** **Valbchek (IRE)**[21] 7527 4-9-2 99 (b) ShaneKelly 1 108
(Jeremy Noseda) *hld up in midfield: swtchd lft and effrt over 1f out: rdn and qcknd to ld ins fnl f: drvn and hld on towards fin* **14/1**

010 **2** *nk* **Take Cover**[21] 7527 6-9-2 98 OisinMurphy 2 107
(David C Griffiths) *hdwy to press ldr 5f out: sn wnt clr: led over 2f out: pressed whn edgd rt u.p 1f out: hdd ins fnl f: rallied gamely u.p towards fin: hld cl home* **7/1**[3]

4110 **3** *1 1/4* **Lancelot Du Lac (ITY)**[22] 7495 3-9-2 98 JimCrowley 10 103+
(Dean Ivory) *hld up in last pair: clsd 2f out: swtchd rt and effrt jst over 1f out: r.o strly ins fnl f: nt rch ldrs* **10/1**

4002 **4** *3/4* **Hawkeyethenoo (IRE)**[21] 7527 7-9-2 104 GrahamLee 8 101
(Jim Goldie) *hld up in last pair: clsd 2f out: rdn and hdwy 1f out: r.o strly ins fnl f: nt rch ldrs* **4/1**[1]

00 **5** *1 1/4* **Tiddliwinks**[53] 6719 7-9-2 102 DanielTudhope 3 97
(Kevin Ryan) *chsd ldr for 1f: chsd clr ldng pair after: clsd 2f out: rdn to press wnr ent fnl f: carried rt and sltly hmpd jst ins fnl f: wknd fnl 75yds* **20/1**

1500 **6** *nk* **Hitchens (IRE)**[42] 7013 8-9-6 108 GrahamGibbons 9 100
(David Barron) *hld up in midfield: clsd 2f out: rdn and effrt over 1f out: styd on ins fnl f: nt rch ldrs* **7/1**[3]

-010 **7** *1/2* **Hoodna (IRE)**[43] 6990 3-8-11 97 SilvestreDeSousa 7 89
(Saeed bin Suroor) *stdd s: t.k.h: sn prom in chsng gp: clsd 2f out: rdn whn nt clr run and swtchd lft jst over 1f out: sn drvn: wknd ins fnl f* **6/1**[2]

0000 **8** *nse* **Fratellino**[56] 6647 6-9-2 97 (tp) MartinHarley 6 94
(Alan McCabe) *racd in last quartet: rdn and effrt on inner over 1f out: no imp 1f out: wknd ins fnl f* **33/1**

0605 **9** *2 1/4* **Tangerine Trees**[21] 7527 8-9-2 101 (v) PaulHanagan 5 87
(Bryan Smart) *prom in main gp: clsd 2f out: drvn and edgd lft over 1f out: wknd ins fnl f* **14/1**

1000 **10** *3 1/4* **Zanetto**[83] 5804 3-9-4 105 DavidProbert 11 78
(Andrew Balding) *hld up in last trio: clsd 2f out: rdn and no hdwy wl over 1f out: sn wknd* **14/1**

1030 **11** *2 1/2* **Ballista (IRE)**[77] 5984 5-9-2 108 RichardKingscote 4 68
(Tom Dascombe) *led: wnt clr w rival over 4f out: hdd over 2f out: rdn and lost 2nd over 1f out: fdd fnl f* **4/1**[1]

1m 9.42s (-2.48) **Going Correction** -0.15s/f (Stan) course record **11** Ran SP% **116.1**
Speed ratings (Par 111): **110,109,107,106,105 104,104,104,101,96 93**
toteswingers 1&2 £24.60, 1&3 £24.80, 2&3 £14.20 CSF £107.34 TOTE £19.80: £5.00, £2.70, £3.00; EX 139.50 Trifecta £1544.00 Pool: £3445.58 - 1.67 winning units..
Owner Richard Keen & Paul Smith **Bred** Kildaragh Stud **Trained** Newmarket, Suffolk

FOCUS
A decent Listed sprint and also a "Win & You're In" qualifier for the All-Weather Championships Sprint Final next April. The line-up contained two previous winners of the race. They went a searing pace thanks to a contested lead and, on a day when pace was holding up, it was little surprise that they lowered the track record. The form is rated around the principals with a few doubts over the field.

7929 COMPARE BOOKMAKERS AT BOOKMAKERS.CO.UK MEDIAN AUCTION MAIDEN STKS 6f (P)
3:45 (3:46) (Class 6) 3-5-Y-0 **£2,045** (£603; £302) **Stalls** Low

Form RPR

-505 **1** **Kerfuffle (IRE)**[28] 7380 4-8-9 44 (b) JackDuern(5) 3 53
(Simon Dow) *chsd ldrs: rdn and effrt over 1f out: chsd ldr jst over 1f out: kpt on u.p to ld cl home* **5/2**[1]

2 *nk* **Twilight Angel**[433] 5-9-0 0 RobertHavlin 4 52
(Pat Eddery) *chsd ldr: rdn to ld wl over 1f out: edgd rt u.p ins fnl f: hdd and no ex cl home* **5/2**[1]

-060 **3** *6* **Fleeting Indian (IRE)**[193] 2125 4-8-12 45 (p) DanielCremin(7) 1 36
(Linda Jewell) *chsd ldrs: 4th and rdn over 1f out: btn 1f out: wknd ins fnl f* **16/1**

0535 **4** *1/2* **Daneglow (IRE)**[35] 7203 3-8-9 45 GeorgeDowning(5) 5 31
(Mike Murphy) *led tl rdn and hdd wl over 1f out: 3rd and btn 1f out: wknd ins fnl f* **4/1**[2]

5044 **5** *1 3/4* **Mid Yorkshire Golf**[28] 7380 4-8-11 44 SladeO'Hara(3) 2 26
(Peter Grayson) *sn outpcd in rr: lost tch 3f out: no ch but kpt on ins fnl f* **5/1**[3]

5650 **6** *nse* **Kaahen (USA)**[24] 7459 3-9-2 43 (b) RobertTart(3) 6 30
(Pat Eddery) *sn outpcd in last pair: lost tch 3f out: no ch but kpt on ins fnl f* **5/1**[3]

1m 11.86s (-0.04) **Going Correction** -0.15s/f (Stan) **6** Ran SP% **116.4**
Speed ratings (Par 101): **94,93,85,84,82 82**
toteswingers 1&2 £2.40, 1&3 £3.30, 2&3 £5.60 CSF £9.36 TOTE £3.00: £1.50, £1.80; EX 9.30 Trifecta £77.20 Pool: £2632.35 - 25.54 winning units..
Owner J Taylor & W J Taylor **Bred** Oghill House Stud **Trained** Epsom, Surrey

FOCUS
An extremely tame end to a classy card with five of the six-strong field possessing official marks between 43 and 45. The time wasn't bad and the form could be rated a little higher.

T/Plt: £1156.10. Pool: £65,284.86 - 41.22 winning units. T/Qpdt: £66.60. Pool: £6322.50 - 70.24 winning units. SP

7900 WOLVERHAMPTON (A.W) (L-H)

Saturday, November 16

OFFICIAL GOING: Standard

Wind: Almost Nil Weather: Overcast

7930 DOWNLOAD THE LADBROKES APP H'CAP (DIV I) 1m 141y(P)

5:50 (5:50) (Class 6) (0-60,62) 3-Y-0+ £1,940 (£577; £288; £144) Stalls Low

Form RPR

6 1 **Pim Street (USA)**[50] 6814 3-8-12 **57** JulieBurke(3) 9 68
(David O'Meara) *chsd ldrs: pushed along over 2f out: led over 1f out: rdn out* **16/1**

6300 2 ½ **Litmus (USA)**[58] 6553 4-8-9 **48** (b) LukeMorris 10 58
(Simon Dow) *hld up: drvn along and hdwy over 2f out: hung lft ins fnl f: r.o u.p* **28/1**

3300 3 1 ½ **Tornado Battle**[50] 6804 3-8-1 **48** RyanTate(5) 6 55
(Phil McEntee) *chsd ldrs: rdn over 1f out: styd on same pce ins fnl f* **20/1**

0033 4 ¾ **Outlaw Torn (IRE)**[12] 7733 4-9-7 **60** (e) RobbieFitzpatrick 1 65
(Richard Guest) *led: clr 5f out tl over 2f out: rdn and hdd over 1f out: no ex wl ins fnl f* **11/4**[2]

04 5 ½ **Mojo Bear**[11] 7740 3-8-11 **58** JoshBaudains(5) 5 62
(Sylvester Kirk) *hld up: pushed along over 3f out: hdwy u.p over 1f out: nt rch ldrs* **12/1**

5430 6 ½ **Tukitinyasok (IRE)**[29] 7344 6-8-7 **46** oh1 [1] JamesSullivan 2 49
(Clive Mulhall) *chsd ldr: rdn over 3f out: lost 2nd over 2f out: styd on same pce fnl f* **25/1**

0361 7 ¾ **Delightful Sleep**[12] 7733 5-9-2 **62** EoinWalsh(7) 4 63
(David Evans) *hld up: nt clr run over 3f out: hdwy over 1f out: rdn and nt clr run ins fnl f: one pce* **2/1**[1]

400 8 shd **Brown Pete (IRE)**[22] 7515 5-9-4 **57** WilliamCarson 7 58
(Violet M Jordan) *sn pushed along in rr: r.o ins fnl f: nvr nrr* **7/1**[3]

0505 9 12 **Mr Chocolate Drop (IRE)**[240] 1100 9-8-11 **53** (t) RossAtkinson(3) 11 26
(Mandy Rowland) *hld up: effrt over 2f out: sn wknd* **25/1**

0-00 10 3 ¾ **Hooligan Sean**[8] 7808 6-8-9 **48** MartinDwyer 8 12
(Mark Usher) *hld up: hdwy u.p over 2f out: sn wknd* **40/1**

0433 P **La Rosiere (USA)**[24] 7458 4-9-3 **56** (p) FergusSweeney 3
(Pat Murphy) *chsd ldrs tl lost action and eased over 3f out: p.u fnl f: lame* **8/1**

1m 50.63s (0.13) **Going Correction** +0.05s/f (Slow)
WFA 3 from 4yo+ 3lb 11 Ran SP% **115.5**
Speed ratings (Par 101): **101,100,99,98,98 97,97,96,86,82**
toteswingers 1&2 £16.60, 1&3 £68.10, 2&3 £32.90 CSF £395.24 CT £8636.62 TOTE £23.60: £5.10, £3.10, £4.80; EX 365.00 Trifecta £1080.00 Pool: £2471.88 - 1.71 winning units..
Owner Dundalk Racing Club **Bred** Mr & Mrs D Probert, R Cowley & Darley **Trained** Nawton, N Yorks

FOCUS
Just a modest contest, but the winner is one to keep on side. It was run at a good pace and in a quicker time than division II. A slightly positive view has been taken of the form.

7931 DOWNLOAD THE LADBROKES APP H'CAP (DIV II) 1m 141y(P)

6:20 (6:20) (Class 6) (0-60,60) 3-Y-0+ £1,940 (£577; £288; £144) Stalls Low

Form RPR

0054 1 **Dansili Dutch (IRE)**[29] 7350 4-9-0 **53** DavidNolan 4 63
(David O'Meara) *mid-div: outpcd over 3f out: rallied over 2f out: nt clr run and swtchd rt over 1f out: rdn to ld ins fnl f: r.o* **11/1**

6215 2 1 ½ **Cantor**[22] 7514 5-9-7 **60** PatrickDonaghy 5 67
(Giles Bravery) *sn pushed along and prom: chsd ldr over 3f out: rdn to ld over 1f out: hdd and unable qck ins fnl f* **13/8**[1]

0300 3 1 ¼ **Aureolin Gulf**[80] 5903 4-8-7 **46** oh1 LiamJones 7 50
(Andrew Hollinshead) *hld up: hdwy over 2f out: rdn over 1f out: r.o* **28/1**

0626 4 ½ **Bond Artist (IRE)**[35] 7201 4-8-8 **50** WilliamTwiston-Davies(3) 10 53
(Geoffrey Oldroyd) *s.s: hld up: hdwy over 1f out: hung lft ins fnl f: styd on same pce* **5/1**[3]

3140 5 1 ¾ **Minimee**[16] 7639 3-9-2 **58** (v) PaddyAspell 2 57
(Phil McEntee) *chsd ldrs: rdn over 2f out: styd on same pce fnl f* **14/1**

006 6 hd **Bertie Blu Boy**[75] 6042 5-8-7 **46** (b) JamesSullivan 8 44
(Lisa Williamson) *plld hrd: w ldr tl led over 3f out: rdn and hdd over 1f out: no ex ins fnl f* **20/1**

6355 7 2 **Buaiteoir (FR)**[40] 7082 7-8-11 **55** RyanTate(5) 6 49
(Nikki Evans) *hld up: shkn up over 1f out: nvr trbld ldrs* **17/2**

4004 8 2 ½ **Direct Trade**[40] 7083 3-7-13 **46** oh1 (e) DanielMuscutt(5) 9 34
(Mark Usher) *hld up: t.k.h: hdwy on outer wl over 2f out: rdn and wknd over 1f out* **40/1**

300 9 17 **Claude Monet (BRZ)**[44] 6976 4-9-5 **58** LukeMorris 11 7
(Simon Dow) *s.i.s: hdwy over 7f out: rdn over 3f out: wknd over 2f out* **9/2**[2]

6060 10 ¾ **Ellaal**[11] 7754 4-9-4 **57** DaleSwift 1 4
(Ruth Carr) *led: rdn and hdd over 3f out: wknd over 2f out* **18/1**

1m 51.25s (0.75) **Going Correction** +0.05s/f (Slow)
WFA 3 from 4yo+ 3lb 10 Ran SP% **114.4**
Speed ratings (Par 101): **98,96,95,95,93 93,91,89,74,73**
toteswingers 1&2 £5.00, 1&3 £59.20, 2&3 £10.70 CSF £28.12 CT £502.35 TOTE £13.90: £4.20, £1.10, £5.70; EX 36.30 Trifecta £1822.10 Part won. Pool: £2,429.54 - 0.34 winning units..
Owner Direct Racing Partnership **Bred** Castlefarm Stud **Trained** Nawton, N Yorks
■ Stewards' Enquiry : Patrick Donaghy two-day ban: used whip above permitted level (Nov 30,Dec 2)

FOCUS
The second division of this 0-60 handicap once again highlighted the skills of David O'Meara. The pace collapsed and it was the slower division. The form makes sense.

7932 LADBROKES MOBILE MAIDEN STKS 1m 141y(P)

6:50 (6:50) (Class 5) 3-Y-0+ £2,587 (£770; £384; £192) Stalls Low

Form RPR

1 **Doldrums (USA)** 3-9-0 0 JoeFanning 3 78
(Mark Johnston) *led: hdd over 6f out: chsd ldr tl shkn up to ld wl over 1f out: rdn ins fnl f: r.o* **7/1**[3]

2 1 ¼ **Like A Diamond (IRE)**[55] 6677 3-9-5 78 GrahamLee 5 80
(Evan Williams) *s.i.s: sn chsng ldrs: hmpd over 6f out: rdn over 1f out: styd on to go 2nd wl ins fnl f: nt rch wnr* **3/1**[2]

2 3 2 ¼ **Bouclier (IRE)**[9] 7781 3-9-5 0 AndreaAtzeni 7 75
(Luca Cumani) *t.k.h: w ldr tl led over 6f out: rdn and hdd wl over 1f out: no ex wl ins fnl f* **1/2**[1]

4 6 **Charlotte Rhodes** 3-9-0 0 MartinHarley 9 56
(Marco Botti) *hld up: hdwy 2f out: nt trble ldrs* **16/1**

6 5 8 **Global Leader (IRE)**[8] 7802 3-9-5 0 (b[1]) FrederikTylicki 8 43
(Paul D'Arcy) *trckd ldrs: rdn over 3f out: wknd over 2f out* **40/1**

06 6 7 **Thomas Blossom (IRE)**[31] 7311 3-9-5 0 AdamBeschizza 4 27
(Nigel Tinkler) *sn pushed along in rr: hdwy over 5f out: rdn and wknd wl over 2f out* **66/1**

0 7 60 **Moves Like Jagger (IRE)**[231] 1236 3-9-5 0 PaddyAspell 2
(Phil McEntee) *hld up: a in rr: bhd fnl 4f* **50/1**

1m 50.15s (-0.35) **Going Correction** +0.05s/f (Slow) 7 Ran SP% **115.9**
Speed ratings (Par 103): **103,101,99,94,87 81,27**
toteswingers 1&2 £2.00, 1&3 £1.10, 2&3 £1.10 CSF £28.77 TOTE £7.80: £2.70, £2.40; EX 26.30 Trifecta £39.90 Pool: £2786.26 - 52.35 winning units..
Owner Sheikh Hamdan Bin Mohammed Al Maktoum **Bred** Lothenbach Stables Inc **Trained** Middleham Moor, N Yorks

FOCUS
Fair form from the leading trio, who pulled well clear. The race is rated around the runner-up.

7933 32RED NURSERY H'CAP 5f 216y(P)

7:20 (7:20) (Class 2) 2-Y-0 £8,821 (£2,640; £1,320; £660; £329) Stalls Low

Form RPR

2123 1 **Pound Piece (IRE)**[25] 7567 2-8-4 **78** LiamJones 6 83
(J S Moore) *hld up: hdwy and n.m.r 1/2-way: led over 1f out: rdn and edgd rt ins fnl f: r.o* **5/1**

120 2 1 **Invincible Strike (IRE)**[21] 7534 2-9-7 **95** LukeMorris 5 97
(James Tate) *a.p: chsd ldr over 2f out: rdn over 1f out: r.o* **5/2**[2]

2601 3 2 **Quickaswecan**[30] 7317 2-8-9 **83** JoeFanning 3 79
(Mark Johnston) *led: rdn and hdd over 1f out: styd on same pce ins fnl f* **13/8**[1]

0051 4 4 **Touch The Clouds**[10] 7771 2-8-1 **80** (p) ShaneGray(5) 4 64
(Kevin Ryan) *chsd ldrs: rdn over 2f out: wknd over 1f out* **12/1**

152 5 2 **Captain Midnight (IRE)**[21] 7545 2-8-12 **86** GrahamLee 2 64
(David Brown) *w ldr over 2f: hmpd 1/2-way: sn rdn: wknd over 1f out* **7/2**[3]

1m 14.72s (-0.28) **Going Correction** +0.05s/f (Slow) 5 Ran SP% **113.2**
Speed ratings (Par 102): **103,101,99,93,91**
CSF £18.22 TOTE £5.00: £3.20, £1.60; EX 10.60 Trifecta £102.40 Pool: £2177.80 - 15.94 winning units..
Owner G B Watts & J S Moore **Bred** Grangemore Stud **Trained** Upper Lambourn, Berks

FOCUS
A pretty useful nursery. Despite the small field it seemed truly run. The winner is rated to the revised level of his French form.

7934 32RED.COM EBF STALLIONS MAIDEN FILLIES' STKS 7f 32y(P)

7:50 (7:54) (Class 5) 2-Y-0 £2,911 (£866; £432; £108; £108) Stalls High

Form RPR

1 **Euro Charline** 2-9-0 0 PaoloSirigu 10 76+
(Marco Botti) *trckd ldr tl led and hung lft over 1f out: pushed out* **20/1**

4 2 3 **Alpine Storm (IRE)**[39] 7103 2-9-0 0 MartinLane 1 69
(Charlie Appleby) *led: t.k.h: rdn and hdd over 1f out: styd on same pce ins fnl f* **4/1**[2]

4 3 4 **Nice Life (IRE)**[16] 7645 2-9-0 0 SilvestreDeSousa 3 59
(Saeed bin Suroor) *chsd ldrs: rdn and hung lft over 1f out: no ex ins fnl f* **8/13**[1]

4 2 **Real Jazz (IRE)** 2-9-0 0 LukeMorris 6 54+
(Sir Mark Prescott Bt) *mid-div: hdwy u.p over 2f out: nt trble ldrs* **28/1**

00 4 dht **Pearlofthequarter**[25] 7449 2-9-0 0 MartinHarley 7 54
(Marco Botti) *chsd ldrs: rdn over 2f out: no ex fnl f* **8/1**[3]

00 6 hd **Twenty Roses (IRE)**[42] 7023 2-9-0 0 GrahamLee 11 54+
(Ed Walker) *hld up: hdwy over 2f out: sn rdn: nt trble ldrs* **40/1**

7 7 **Heavens Eyes (IRE)** 2-9-0 0 FergusSweeney 4 37+
(Pat Murphy) *s.i.s: a in rr: wknd over 2f out* **50/1**

8 1 ¼ **Belle Peinture (FR)** 2-9-0 0 DavidNolan 9 34+
(Richard Fahey) *s.i.s: sn pushed along and a in rr: wknd over 2f out* **33/1**

00 9 10 **Connexion Francais**[59] 6523 2-9-0 0 JamesSullivan 8 9
(Tim Etherington) *prom: t.k.h: rdn and wknd over 2f out* **100/1**

10 1 ¾ **Baytown Tigress** 2-9-0 0 PaddyAspell 2 5
(Phil McEntee) *s.i.s: a in rr: wknd over 2f out* **50/1**

1m 29.96s (0.36) **Going Correction** +0.05s/f (Slow) 10 Ran SP% **111.5**
Speed ratings (Par 93): **99,95,91,88,88 88,80,79,67,65**
toteswingers 1&2 £8.90, 2&3 £1.10, 1&3 £5.00 CSF £79.66 TOTE £18.90: £5.30, £1.30, £1.10; EX 118.50 Trifecta £287.30 Pool: £2905.98 - 7.58 winning units..
Owner Scuderia Blueberry **Bred** Brian Liversage **Trained** Newmarket, Suffolk

FOCUS
Doubtful there was much depth to this maiden, and it was steadily run, but plenty to like about the winner's performance. The form is rated around the second and third.

7935 32RED ON THE APP STORE NURSERY H'CAP 1m 141y(P)

8:20 (8:21) (Class 5) (0-70,70) 2-Y-0 £2,587 (£770; £384; £192) Stalls Low

Form RPR

4455 1 **Boogangoo (IRE)**[9] 7782 2-9-7 **70** SilvestreDeSousa 6 74
(Keith Dalgleish) *hld up: hdwy and nt clr run over 2f out: rdn to ld and hung lft ins fnl f: r.o* **9/2**

5430 2 1 ¼ **Avocadeau (IRE)**[39] 7088 2-9-5 **68** MartinDwyer 8 60
(William Muir) *trckd ldr tl led 2f out: sn rdn: edgd lft and hdd ins fnl f: styd on same pce* **16/1**

611 3 1 ¼ **Jazzy Lady (IRE)**[3] 7855 2-8-5 **61** 6ex EoinWalsh(7) 5 62+
(David Evans) *a.p: nt clr run fr over 1f out: nvr able to chal* **9/4**[1]

6500 4 ½ **Loving Your Work**[65] 6322 2-9-2 **65** [1] LukeMorris 1 63
(George Baker) *s.i.s: hld up: pushed along over 3f out: hdwy u.p over 2f out: rdn and ev ch over 1f out: hung lft and no ex ins fnl f* **20/1**

052P 5 3 **Maxie T**[42] 7017 2-9-6 **69** JoeFanning 3 60
(Mark Johnston) *led: rdn and hdd 2f out: wknd ins fnl f* **7/2**[3]

5230 6 ½ **Rockie Road (IRE)**[42] 7032 2-8-6 **55** RaulDaSilva 4 45
(Paul Green) *hld up: rdn over 1f out: nvr on terms* **20/1**

265 7 1 ¼ **Goleador (USA)**[54] 6689 2-9-3 **66** MartinHarley 9 54
(Marco Botti) *chsd ldrs: rdn over 2f out: wknd fnl f* **5/2**[2]

3640 8 21 **Evie Jay (IRE)**[84] 5773 2-9-3 **66** WilliamCarson 2 10
(Paul Green) *chsd ldrs: rdn over 3f out: wknd over 2f out* **33/1**

1m 52.44s (1.94) **Going Correction** +0.05s/f (Slow) 8 Ran SP% **118.1**
Speed ratings (Par 96): **93,91,90,90,87 87,86,67**
toteswingers 1&2 £7.80, 1&3 £2.60, 2&3 £7.70 CSF £68.69 CT £204.57 TOTE £5.20: £1.70, £4.80, £2.10; EX 62.50 Trifecta £177.00 Pool: £3018.36 - 12.78 winning units..
Owner Middleham Park Racing II **Bred** Marie & Mossy Fahy **Trained** Carluke, S Lanarks

FOCUS
A modest nursery. The gallop didn't look overly strong. The winner was entitled to win off this mark on her best form.

7936 32RED CASINO EBF STALLIONS MAIDEN STKS 1m 1f 103y(P)
8:50 (8:51) (Class 5) 2-Y-O £2,911 (£866; £432; £216) Stalls Low

Form RPR
52 **1** **Personal Opinion**[29] 7332 2-9-5 0 SilvestreDeSousa 7 76
(Charlie Appleby) *a.p: pushed along over 2f out: led over 1f out: rdn out* **10/11**[1]
6 **2** *2 ¼* **Conquerant**[29] 7339 2-9-5 0 MartinLane 3 72
(Charlie Appleby) *chsd ldrs: rdn over 1f out: styd on to go 2nd wl ins fnl f* **14/1**
3 **3** *1* **Al Busayyir (IRE)**[22] 7513 2-9-5 0 MartinHarley 2 70
(Marco Botti) *led: rdn and hdd over 1f out: no ex ins fnl f* **9/4**[2]
53 **4** *¾* **Loch Ma Naire (IRE)**[14] 7693 2-9-0 0 AndreaAtzeni 6 63
(Ed Dunlop) *prom: rdn over 2f out: hung lft ins fnl f: styd on same pce* **6/1**[3]
50 **5** *6* **Piton**[22] 7494 2-9-5 0 GrahamLee 5 57
(Mark Johnston) *s.i.s: hld up: pushed along and wknd over 2f out* **40/1**
60 **6** *2 ¾* **Late Shipment**[9] 7779 2-9-5 0 JoeFanning 1 52
(Mark Johnston) *hld up: rdn and wknd over 2f out* **20/1**
60 **7** *3 ½* **Flying Author (IRE)**[65] 6322 2-9-5 49 PaddyAspell 4 45
(Phil McEntee) *chsd ldr tl rdn over 2f out: wknd over 1f out* **100/1**

2m 2.86s (1.16) **Going Correction** +0.05s/f (Slow) **7** Ran SP% **112.3**
Speed ratings (Par 96): **96,94,93,92,87 84,81**
toteswingers 1&2 £3.60, 1&3 £1.10, 2&3 £6.50 CSF £14.90 TOTE £1.90: £1.10, £4.70; EX 12.10 Trifecta £36.90 Pool: £3421.32 - 69.40 winning units..
Owner Godolphin **Bred** Whitley Stud **Trained** Newmarket, Suffolk
FOCUS
Just an ordinary maiden. The winner is rated just to his mark in success.

7937 COMPARE BOOKMAKERS AT BOOKMAKERS.CO.UK H'CAP 5f 20y(P)
9:20 (9:20) (Class 5) (0-70,68) 3-Y-O+ £2,587 (£770; £384; £192) Stalls Low

Form RPR
0044 **1** **Passionada**[31] 7315 4-9-2 **63** GrahamLee 9 73
(Ed McMahon) *hld up: hdwy and edgd lft over 1f out: r.o to ld nr fin* **4/1**[1]
1606 **2** *½* **Different**[105] 4976 3-9-5 **66** JoeFanning 5 74
(Bryan Smart) *a.p: pushed along 1/2-way: rdn and ev ch wl ins fnl f: r.o* **7/1**[3]
405 **3** *shd* **Solemn**[26] 7432 8-9-7 **68** (v[1]) RichardKingscote 6 76
(Milton Bradley) *chsd ldrs: rdn over 1f out: r.o* **6/1**[2]
4003 **4** *nk* **Quality Art (USA)**[10] 7772 5-8-11 **61** BillyCray(3) 3 68
(Richard Guest) *led: rdn and edgd rt fr over 1f out: hdd nr fin* **14/1**
5310 **5** *1 ¼* **Never A Quarrel (IRE)**[52] 6745 3-9-6 **67** FergusSweeney 7 69
(Jeremy Gask) *chsd ldr: rdn over 1f out: no ex towards fin* **6/1**[2]
651 **5** *dht* **Dark Lane**[12] 7729 7-9-6 **67** SilvestreDeSousa 1 69
(David Evans) *prom: pushed along 1/2-way: rdn over 1f out: styd on* **4/1**[1]
0306 **7** *¾* **Captain Scooby**[18] 7594 7-9-5 **66** (e) RobbieFitzpatrick 10 65
(Richard Guest) *sn pushed along in rr: hdwy u.p over 1f out: styd on same pce ins fnl f* **14/1**
5301 **8** *nk* **Megaleka**[10] 7772 3-8-8 **60** TimClark(5) 12 58
(Alan Bailey) *s.i.s: hld up: hdwy over 1f out: styd on same pce ins fnl f* **11/1**
0000 **9** *2 ¼* **Prince Of Burma (IRE)**[18] 7601 5-8-11 **65** (b) EoinWalsh(7) 4 55
(David Evans) *s.i.s: a in rr* **16/1**
6360 **10** *2 ¾* **Mr Mo Jo**[42] 7029 5-9-6 **67** (b) DuranFentiman 8 47
(Lawrence Mullaney) *chsd ldrs to 1/2-way* **20/1**
0550 **11** *2 ¾* **Falasteen (IRE)**[166] 2918 6-9-5 **66** ChrisCatlin 11 36
(Milton Bradley) *a in rr: wknd 2f out* **22/1**

1m 2.38s (0.08) **Going Correction** +0.05s/f (Slow) **11** Ran SP% **117.7**
Speed ratings (Par 103): **101,100,100,99,97 97,96,95,92,87 83**
toteswingers 1&2 £6.40, 1&3 £5.30, 2&3 £12.30 CSF £31.86 CT £168.17 TOTE £5.00: £1.40, £3.30, £2.80; EX 46.00 Trifecta £444.10 Pool: £3219.63 - 5.43 winning units..
Owner Mia Racing **Bred** Mia Racing **Trained** Lichfield, Staffs
FOCUS
A run-of-the-mill sprint which was run at a good pace. Sound form.
T/Plt: £975.00. Pool: £121,173.53 - 90.72 winning units. T/Qpdt: £12.80. Pool: £13,802.52 - 795.59 winning units. CR

7392 CAULFIELD (R-H)
Saturday, November 16

OFFICIAL GOING: Turf: good

7938a SPORTINGBET SANDOWN CUP (LISTED QUALITY H'CAP) (3YO+) (TURF) 2m
1:50 (12:00) 3-Y-0+
£58,012 (£17,307; £8,653; £4,326; £2,403; £1,923)

RPR
1 **Caravan Rolls On**[11] 7760 5-8-9 **0** CraigAWilliams 1 104
(Peter Chapple-Hyam) *prom on inner early: midfield in tch fr bef 1/2-way: swtchd off rail and smooth hdwy to chal over 2f out: sn up and led over 1f out: styd on strly ins fnl f and sn clr: pushed out: easily* **5/4**[1]
2 *1 ¾* **Like A Carousel (AUS)**[11] 7760 4-8-9 **0** (b) CraigNewitt 9 106
(Ken Keys, Australia) **11/1**
3 *1* **Crafty Cruiser (AUS)**[11] 7760 6-8-9 **0** BenMelham 2 101
(Bryce Stanaway, Australia) **15/1**
4 *1 ¾* **Brayroan (NZ)**[11] 7760 7-8-9 **0** (b) GlenBoss 8 99
(Anthony Cummings, Australia) **20/1**
5 *hd* **Moudre (AUS)**[7] 7827 8-9-2 **0** (b) MichellePayne 3 106
(Ciaron Maher, Australia) **10/1**
6 *5* **Altonio (NZ)**[31] 7417 7-8-9 **0** (b) JamesWinks 5 93
(Pat Carey, Australia) **15/1**
7 *½* **Mujadale (AUS)**[11] 7760 6-8-9 **0** StephenBaster 10 93
(Paul A Jones, Australia) **18/5**[2]
8 *shd* **Planet Purple (AUS)**[11] 7760 7-8-9 **0** KerrinMcEvoy 7 93
(Kerry Parker, Australia) **17/2**[3]
9 *9* **Star Of Tralee (NZ)**[595] 5-8-9 **0** ChadSchofield 6 83
(David Hayes, Australia) **90/1**
10 *1* **Rowland (AUS)**[11] 7760 8-8-9 **0** DwayneDunn 4 82
(Robbie Laing, Australia) **40/1**

3m 23.82s (203.82) **10** Ran SP% **114.9**
PARI-MUTUEL (NSW TAB - all including 1 aud stake): WIN 2.20; PLACE 1.40, 2.90, 3.50; DF 11.60; SF 15.00.
Owner Qatar Racing Limited **Bred** Miss K Rausing **Trained** Newmarket, Suffolk

7116 MAISONS-LAFFITTE (R-H)
Saturday, November 16

OFFICIAL GOING: Turf: heavy
A rescheduled meeting after the fixture on November 5th was abandoned due to a strike by racecourse workers.

7939a CRITERIUM DE MAISONS-LAFFITTE (GROUP 2) (2YO) (TURF) 6f (S)
12:05 (12:00) 2-Y-0 **£88,048** (£33,983; £16,219; £10,813; £5,406)

RPR
1 **Kiram (FR)**[36] 7184 2-9-0 0 ChristopheSoumillon 12 112
(J-C Rouget, France) *hld up towards rr: prog on outside 1 1/2f out: rdn and r.o to ld fnl 150yds: drvn out: in control last 50yds* **17/10**[1]
2 *1 ¼* **This Time (FR)**[67] 6293 2-8-10 0 FabriceVeron 9 104
(H-A Pantall, France) *midfield on outer: hdwy to chse ldrs under 2f out: hrd rdn and ev ch 1f out: r.o fnl f: nt pce of wnr* **63/10**[3]
3 *shd* **Passing Burg (FR)**[25] 7567 2-8-10 0 ThierryThulliez 2 104
(L A Urbano-Grajales, France) *midfield: rdn to chse ldr 1 1/2f out: r.o u.p fnl f: nt pce of wnr* **30/1**
4 *1 ¼* **Another Party (FR)**[36] 7184 2-9-0 0 (b[1]) AntoineHamelin 5 104
(Matthieu Palussiere, France) *led: 2 l clr and shkn up over 1 1/2f out: hrd rdn and hdd 1f out: one pce fnl f* **16/1**
5 *hd* **High Duty**[36] 7184 2-9-0 0 AStarke 3 104
(P Schiergen, Germany) *chsd ldng pair: rdn and outpcd over 1f out: kpt on at same pce fnl f* **10/1**
6 *snk* **Hidden Oasis (IRE)**[27] 7403 2-9-0 0 (p) FMBerry 6 103
(David Wachman, Ire) *chsd ldng pair: rdn to ld 1f out: hdd 150yds out: no ex* **43/10**[2]
7 *1 ½* **No Leaf Clover (IRE)**[35] 7207 2-9-0 0 RobertWinston 8 99
(Ollie Pears) *towards rr: rdn and short-lived effrt over 1 1/2f out: one pce fnl f* **15/1**
8 *2* **Ragazzo (FR)**[29] 2-9-0 0 (b[1]) OlivierPeslier 10 93
(Mario Hofer, Germany) *towards rr: rdn and outpcd 2f out: nvr in contention* **11/1**
9 *snk* **Oeil De Tigre (FR)**[20] 7565 2-9-0 0 ThierryJarnet 4 92
(H-A Pantall, France) *trckd ldr: rdn and nt qckn 1 1/2f out: wknd u.p fnl f* **10/1**
10 *nk* **Mister Worldwide (FR)**[43] 2-9-0 0 NicolasPerret 11 91
(Y Gourraud, France) *towards rr: rdn and no imp fnl 2f: nvr trbld ldrs* **67/1**
11 *3 ½* **Master Of Gold (FR)**[27] 2-9-0 0 JeromeClaudic 1 81
(E J O'Neill, France) *dwlt: racd in fnl 3rd: rdn and btn ins fnl 2f: nvr figured* **53/1**
12 *4 ½* **Louarn (IRE)**[25] 2-8-10 0 ThomasHenderson 7 63
(J Heloury, France) *midfield: rdn and outpcd over 2f out: wknd and eased fnl f* **85/1**

1m 16.3s (2.90) **12** Ran SP% **116.0**
WIN (incl. 1 euro stake): 2.70. PLACES: 1.50, 2.20, 4.60. DF: 10.00. SF: 12.40.
Owner H H Aga Khan **Bred** H H The Aga Khan's Studs S C **Trained** Pau, France
FOCUS
The form is rated towards the lower end of the race averages.

7940a PRIX MIESQUE (GROUP 3) (2YO FILLIES) (TURF) 7f (S)
1:10 (12:00) 2-Y-0 **£32,520** (£13,008; £9,756; £6,504; £3,252)

RPR
1 **Lacarolina (FR)**[67] 6292 2-8-11 0 ChristopheSoumillon 4 100
(J-C Rouget, France) *dwlt sltly but qckly rcvrd and sn led: rdn and jnd ent fnl f: sustained battle w eventual runner-up: r.o and jst prevailed* **4/5**[1]
2 *shd* **Xcellence (FR)**[35] 2-8-11 0 MaximeGuyon 8 100
(F Doumen, France) *hld up in tch towards rr: rdn and hdwy over 1f out: jnd wnr ent fnl f and sustained battle: r.o but jst denied* **9/1**
3 *1 ½* **Artwork Genie (IRE)**[60] 2-8-11 0 Pierre-CharlesBoudot 6 96
(J-P Carvalho, France) *dwlt sltly and hld up in tch towards rr: rdn over 1f out: r.o and wnt 3rd ins fnl f: nt pce of front pair* **5/1**[3]
4 *1* **Champ D'Honneur**[35] 2-8-11 0 CristianDemuro 1 93
(J-P Gallorini, France) *racd alone against nr side' rail early: sn jnd remainder of field and trckd ldr: rdn and effrt to chal over 1f out: kpt on same pce and dropped to 4th ins fnl f* **21/1**
5 *2* **Sweltering (FR)**[35] 2-8-11 0 MathieuAndrouin 3 88
(P Monfort, France) *trckd ldr: rdn over 1f out: sn outpcd: kpt on for wl hld 5th* **24/1**
6 *3* **Momo No Sekku (FR)**[35] 2-8-11 0 OlivierPeslier 7 80
(S Kobayashi, France) *dwlt slt and hld up in last: rdn over 1f out: no imp and sn btn: nvr a factor* **16/1**
7 *2 ½* **Petits Potins (IRE)**[40] 7084 2-8-11 0 StephanePasquier 5 74
(Rod Collet, France) *midfield in tch: rdn 2f out: lost pl and btn ent fnl f: sn eased* **43/10**[2]
8 *3 ½* **Ultradargent (FR)**[21] 7589 2-8-11 0 FabriceVeron 2 65
(H-A Pantall, France) *t.k.h: trckd ldr: rdn over 2f out: sn lost pl and btn: dropped to last and eased ins fnl f* **23/1**

1m 31.9s (3.90) **8** Ran SP% **119.7**
WIN (incl. 1 euro stake): 1.80. PLACES: 1.20, 1.70, 1.60. DF: 10.50. SF: 11.30.
Owner O Carli & G Augustin-Normand **Bred** J-M Lapoujade **Trained** Pau, France

7941a PRIX DE SEINE-ET-OISE (GROUP 3) (3YO+) (TURF) 6f (S)
1:40 (12:00) 3-Y-0+ **£32,520** (£13,008; £9,756; £6,504; £3,252)

RPR
1 **Kolonel (GER)**[44] 4-8-11 0 OlivierPeslier 1 109+
(Mario Hofer, Germany) *chsd ldr: pushed along to chal over 1f out: rdn to ld ent fnl f: r.o strly and asserted: readily* **147/10**
2 *1 ¼* **Wedge Trust (IRE)**[40] 7085 3-8-8 0 IoritzMendizabal 2 102
(J-C Rouget, France) *dwlt sltly and hld up towards rr: rdn 2f out: r.o and wnt 2nd ins fnl f: fin wl but nt pce of wnr* **11/2**[3]
3 *2* **Myasun (FR)**[41] 7054 6-9-0 0 MaximeGuyon 7 102
(C Baillet, France) *midfield: rdn and effrt to chal over 1f out: nt pce of front pair ins fnl f: kpt on* **23/10**[1]

4 ½ **Abu Sidra (FR)**[83] 5806 4-9-0 0 .... ChristopheSoumillon 3 100
(J-F Bernard, France) *midfield: rdn 2f out: kpt on same pce fr over 1f out* **16/1**

5 2 **Dibajj (FR)**[41] 7054 3-8-10 0 .... AntoineHamelin 5 90
(A De Royer-Dupre, France) *dwlt and racd in rr: rdn 2f out: kpt on and tk wl hld 5th towards fin: nvr nrr* **7/1**

6 1 ¼ **Giant Sandman (IRE)**[62] 6-9-2 0 ....(p) LennartHammer-Hansen 9 92
(Rune Haugen, Norway) *led: 2 l clr 1/2-way: rdn and strly pressed over 1f out: hdd ent fnl f: no ex and btn: fdd* **78/10**

7 2 **Sorry Woman (FR)**[17] 3-8-8 0 .... FabriceVeron 4 77
(H-A Pantall, France) *chsd ldr: rdn over 2f out: kpt on tl no ex and fdd ins fnl f: eased towards fin* **17/1**

8 nse **Amarillo (IRE)**[35] 7190 4-9-0 0 .... AStarke 6 83
(P Schiergen, Germany) *hld up in midfield: rdn 2f out: outpcd and btn ins fnl f: fdd and dropped to last: eased towards fin* **14/5**[2]

U **Chopouest (FR)**[4] 6-8-11 0 .... FredericSpanu 8
(T Castanheira, France) *in rr: pushed along whn broke down 2f out and uns rdr: fatally injured* **37/1**

1m 15.1s (1.70) **9** Ran SP% **116.3**
WIN (incl. 1 euro stake): 15.70.PLACES: 3.60, 1.90, 1.40. DF: 35.30. SF: 70.00.
Owner Stall Helena **Bred** Rolf Brunner **Trained** Germany

7942 - 7943a (Foreign Racing) - See Raceform Interactive

7930

WOLVERHAMPTON (A.W) (L-H)
Monday, November 18

OFFICIAL GOING: Standard
Wind: Light across Weather: Overcast

7944 32RED CASINO NURSERY H'CAP — 1m 1f 103y(P)
2:00 (2:00) (Class 6) (0-65,68) 2-Y-O — **£1,940** (£577; £288; £144) **Stalls** Low

Form RPR

4131 1 **Earthflight**[6] 7846 2-9-3 **68** 6ex .... LouisSteward(7) 7 85+
(Philip McBride) *trckd ldr tl led over 4f out: qcknd clr 2f out: rdn and edgd lft over 1f out: easily* **5/4**[1]

0003 2 9 **Star Anise (FR)**[17] 7664 2-9-5 **63** .... LukeMorris 4 63
(Harry Dunlop) *dwlt: hld up: pushed along and hdwy over 2f out: rdn to go 2nd and edgd lft over 1f out: no ch w wnr* **12/1**

113 3 1 ¾ **Jazzy Lady (IRE)**[2] 7935 2-9-3 **61** 6ex .... StevieDonohoe 6 58
(David Evans) *hld up: pushed along over 3f out: hdwy over 2f out: styd on same pce fnl f* **5/2**[2]

5004 4 1 ½ **Loving Your Work**[2] 7935 2-9-7 **65** .... RobertHavlin 1 59
(George Baker) *chsd ldrs: rdn over 3f out: no ex fr over 1f out* **8/1**[3]

0000 5 ¾ **Hasta La Vista**[13] 7755 2-8-6 **50** .... JoeFanning 8 42
(Mark Johnston) *trckd ldrs: wnt 2nd over 3f out: rdn over 2f out: wknd fnl f* **16/1**

2552 6 shd **Nice Arty (IRE)**[19] 7630 2-9-3 **61** .... RichardKingscote 5 53
(Jamie Osborne) *s.i.s: hdwy over 4f out: rdn over 2f out: wknd over 1f out* **10/1**

0020 7 7 **Suni Dancer**[44] 7032 2-8-5 **49** .... RaulDaSilva 2 28
(Paul Green) *prom: racd keenly: rdn and n.m.r over 3f out: wknd over 2f out* **25/1**

000 8 ½ **Mestizo**[38] 7175 2-8-4 **51** .... NeilFarley(3) 3 29
(Declan Carroll) *led: hdd over 4f out: rdn and wknd over 2f out* **16/1**

2m 2.01s (0.31) **Going Correction** +0.125s/f (Slow) **8** Ran SP% **116.5**
Speed ratings (Par 94): **103,95,93,92,91 91,85,84**
toteswingers 1&2 £2.80, 1&3 £1.60, 2&3 £4.70 CSF £18.85 CT £34.99 TOTE £2.30: £1.10, £1.90, £1.20; EX 10.30 Trifecta £34.00 Pool: £1946.56 - 34.00 winning units..
Owner Four Winds Racing Partnership **Bred** Wood Farm Stud (Waresley) **Trained** Newmarket, Suffolk

FOCUS
A low-grade nursery, but an improving winner who routed these. Things will be a lot tougher off her new mark.

7945 32RED ON THE APP STORE CLAIMING STKS — 1m 141y(P)
2:30 (2:30) (Class 6) 2-Y-O — **£1,940** (£577; £288; £144) **Stalls** Low

Form RPR

0443 1 **Slinky McVelvet**[19] 7630 2-8-3 53 ow1 .... BillyCray(3) 6 58
(Garry Moss) *racd keenly: trckd ldr tl led wl over 1f out: rdn out* **9/2**[3]

0424 2 ½ **Heska (IRE)**[32] 7326 2-9-0 67 ....(v[1]) MartinHarley 1 65
(Mick Channon) *trckd ldrs: rdn to chse wnr fnl f: r.o* **10/11**[1]

310 3 4 **Howz The Family (IRE)**[35] 7252 2-9-0 70 ....(v[1]) RichardKingscote 3 57
(Tom Dascombe) *led: qcknd over 3f out: rdn over 2f out: hdd wl over 1f out: no ex fnl f* **2/1**[2]

6405 4 18 **Hija**[24] 7509 2-8-2 51 ....(b) RyanWhile(7) 2 14
(Bill Turner) *pushed along in rr early: in tch tl rdn and wknd over 2f out* **33/1**

1m 53.54s (3.04) **Going Correction** +0.125s/f (Slow) **4** Ran SP% **106.8**
Speed ratings (Par 94): **91,90,87,71**
CSF £9.04 TOTE £6.60; EX 9.20 Trifecta £10.80 Pool: £2024.15 - 139.87 winning units..
Owner Ron Hull **Bred** Jason Paxton **Trained** Tickhill, S Yorks

FOCUS
A pretty dire race and not form to dwell on.

7946 32RED.COM MAIDEN FILLIES' STKS — 7f 32y(P)
3:00 (3:00) (Class 5) 3-Y-O+ — **£2,587** (£770; £384; £192) **Stalls** High

Form RPR

33 1 **Enfijaar (IRE)**[19] 7624 3-8-13 0 ....(p) PaulHanagan 1 64+
(William Haggas) *mde all: racd keenly: rdn over 1f out: edgd lft ins fnl f: r.o* **6/4**[2]

2 3 ¼ **Winterwell (USA)**[172] 3-8-13 81 .... DanielTudhope 6 55
(David O'Meara) *sn prom: pushed along to chse wnr 2f out: rdn over 1f out: styd on same pce ins fnl f* **4/6**[1]

0-00 3 1 ¼ **Seraphima**[14] 7733 3-8-13 57 .... LiamJones 5 52
(James Unett) *trckd ldrs: rdn over 1f out: no ex ins fnl f* **50/1**

4663 4 3 ½ **Stoneacre Hull (IRE)**[14] 7730 4-8-11 50 .... SladeO'Hara(3) 4 44
(Peter Grayson) *hld up: effrt over 1f out: n.d* **33/1**[3]

0000 5 nk **Queen's Princess**[11] 7791 5-8-9 42 ....(p) AdamCarter(5) 3 43
(John Wainwright) *chsd wnr tl pushed along over 2f out: rdn and wknd over 1f out* **50/1**

1m 30.63s (1.03) **Going Correction** +0.125s/f (Slow)
WFA 3 from 4yo+ 1lb **5** Ran SP% **106.9**
Speed ratings (Par 100): **99,95,93,89,89**
CSF £2.64 TOTE £2.80: £1.20, £1.10; EX 2.30 Trifecta £8.80 Pool: £2406.98 - 202.99 winning units..
Owner Hamdan Al Maktoum **Bred** Shadwell Estate Company Limited **Trained** Newmarket, Suffolk

FOCUS
A really weak maiden run in a slow time, and shaky form. The winner did not need to find much on previous efforts.

7947 32RED H'CAP — 2m 119y(P)
3:30 (3:30) (Class 5) (0-75,75) 3-Y-O+ — **£2,587** (£770; £384; £192) **Stalls** Low

Form RPR

3222 1 **Flemish School**[3] 7894 3-9-2 **75** ....(p) WilliamTwiston-Davies(3) 8 84
(Gerard Butler) *s.i.s: hld up: hdwy over 2f out: rdn to ld ins fnl f: edgd rt: styd on* **7/2**[1]

0521 2 ¾ **Aiyana**[33] 7305 3-8-9 **65** .... RobertHavlin 3 73
(Hughie Morrison) *chsd ldrs: led over 2f out: rdn and edgd rt fr over 1f out: hdd ins fnl f: kpt on* **7/1**

620 3 1 ½ **Caterina De Medici (FR)**[24] 7504 4-9-11 **72** .... TomMcLaughlin 2 78
(Ed Walker) *led 1f: chsd ldrs: rdn over 2f out: styd on same pce ins fnl f* **12/1**

0122 4 1 ½ **Alpine Mysteries (IRE)**[24] 7510 3-9-3 **73** .... LukeMorris 6 78
(Harry Dunlop) *hld up: hdwy over 4f out: rdn over 2f out: nt clr run ins fnl f: styd on same pce* **5/1**[2]

41 5 2 ¼ **Eshtyaaq**[64] 6424 6-9-11 **72** .... MartinHarley 9 74
(David Evans) *led after 1f: rdn and hdd over 2f out: no ex ins fnl f* **7/2**[1]

250 6 3 ½ **Ampleforth**[36] 7217 5-9-8 **69** ....(b) FrederikTylicki 5 67
(Ian Williams) *prom: chsd ldr 14f out: rdn over 2f out: wknd ins fnl f* **7/1**

2105 7 10 **My History (IRE)**[19] 7627 3-9-5 **75** .... JoeFanning 1 61
(Mark Johnston) *prom: lost pl over 4f out: wknd over 1f out* **11/2**[3]

2560 8 31 **Hawk Mountain (UAE)**[37] 7210 8-9-6 **74** .... JoeDoyle(7) 4 22
(John Quinn) *hld up: hdwy 5f out: pushed along and wknd over 3f out* **10/1**

3m 43.32s (1.52) **Going Correction** +0.125s/f (Slow)
WFA 3 from 4yo+ 9lb **8** Ran SP% **118.3**
Speed ratings (Par 103): **101,100,99,99,98 96,91,77**
toteswingers 1&2 £4.60, 1&3 £10.40, 2&3 £15.60 CSF £29.61 CT £268.22 TOTE £5.30: £1.80, £2.50, £3.20; EX 47.10 Trifecta £801.00 Pool: £2707.03 - 2.53 winning units..
Owner Mrs Barbara M Keller **Bred** Horizon Bloodstock Limited **Trained** Newmarket, Suffolk

FOCUS
They went a steady pace. The winner and second found a bit, with the next three close to their marks.

7948 DOWNLOAD THE LADBROKES APP CLASSIFIED (S) STKS — 7f 32y(P)
4:00 (4:01) (Class 6) 3-Y-O+ — **£1,940** (£577; £288; £144) **Stalls** High

Form RPR

4604 1 **Illustrious Prince (IRE)**[4] 7885 6-9-4 73 .... NeilFarley(3) 7 80
(Declan Carroll) *chsd ldrs: led over 4f out: clr 3f out: rdn and hung lft over 1f out: styd on* **5/2**[3]

3160 2 2 ¾ **Pravda Street**[20] 7611 8-9-4 69 .... RobertTart(3) 5 73
(Brian Ellison) *sn pushed along in rr: hdwy over 1f out: wnt 2nd ins fnl f: r.o: no ch w wnr* **2/1**[1]

4206 3 4 **All Or Nothin (IRE)**[32] 7318 4-9-7 72 .... JoeFanning 1 62
(Paddy Butler) *prom: rdn over 2f out: styd on same pce fr over 1f out* **16/1**

0063 4 ¾ **Creek Falcon (IRE)**[51] 6843 4-9-7 69 ....(b[1]) DanielTudhope 6 60
(David O'Meara) *w ldr tl over 4f out: wnt 2nd over 2f out: rdn over 1f out: no ex fnl f* **9/4**[2]

5000 5 7 **Bachelor Knight (IRE)**[110] 4893 5-8-8 38 ....(e[1]) JordanVaughan(7) 4 35
(Suzzanne France) *hld up: rdn over 2f out: nvr on terms* **100/1**

0605 6 19 **Alpha Tauri (USA)**[11] 7792 7-9-7 70 ....(t) RobbieFitzpatrick 3
(Charles Smith) *led: hdd over 4f out: rdn over 2f out: wknd over 1f out* **8/1**

1m 29.83s (0.23) **Going Correction** +0.125s/f (Slow) **6** Ran SP% **110.7**
Speed ratings (Par 101): **103,99,95,94,86 64**
toteswingers 1&2 £1.20, 1&3 £5.60, 2&3 £3.10 CSF £7.68 TOTE £3.30: £1.70, £1.30; EX 9.80 Trifecta £70.70 Pool: £3102.63 - 32.86 winning units..There was no bid for the winner.
Owner Ray Flegg **Bred** Rathbarry Stud **Trained** Sledmere, E Yorks

FOCUS
Uncompetitive stuff, the form rated around the runner-up.

7949 LADBROKES MOBILE H'CAP — 7f 32y(P)
4:30 (4:31) (Class 4) (0-85,84) 3-Y-O+ — **£4,690** (£1,395; £697; £348) **Stalls** High

Form RPR

0500 1 **Al's Memory (IRE)**[18] 7648 4-9-3 **80** .... MartinHarley 4 89
(David Evans) *chsd ldrs: rdn over 1f out: r.o to ld wl ins fnl f* **8/1**

1213 2 nk **Living The Life (IRE)**[20] 7603 3-9-0 **78** ....(b) RichardKingscote 7 85
(Jamie Osborne) *sn led: rdn over 1f out: hdd wl ins fnl f* **9/2**[2]

5351 3 ½ **Ruwaiyan (USA)**[20] 7603 4-9-6 **83** ....(p) LukeMorris 8 90
(James Tate) *s.i.s: hld up: hdwy over 2f out: rdn over 1f out: r.o* **5/4**[1]

556 4 hd **Piddie's Power**[42] 7080 6-8-13 **79** .... RobertTart(3) 6 85
(Kevin Frost) *a.p: racd keenly: rdn over 1f out: r.o* **20/1**

0031 5 1 ¾ **Fortinbrass (IRE)**[11] 7792 3-9-1 **79** .... DanielTudhope 3 79
(David O'Meara) *chsd ldrs: rdn over 2f out: styd on* **7/1**[3]

0060 6 2 ¼ **Fieldgunner Kirkup (GER)**[62] 6496 5-9-4 **81** .... GrahamGibbons 2 76
(David Barron) *mid-div: hmpd and lost pl over 5f out: n.d after* **10/1**

000 7 nk **Docofthebay (IRE)**[18] 7648 9-9-7 **84** ....(v[1]) TomEaves 1 78
(Scott Dixon) *s.i.s: hld up: hdwy over 2f out: sn rdn: styd on same apce fr over 1f out* **20/1**

0000 8 15 **Oil Strike**[12] 7776 6-9-3 **80** .... JamesSullivan 9 34
(Michael Easterby) *chsd ldrs: rdn over 2f out: sn wknd* **66/1**

0025 9 13 **Personal Touch**[16] 7699 4-9-3 **80** .... PaulHanagan 5
(Richard Fahey) *plld hrd and prom: hung lft thrght: lost pl 1/2-way: eased* **7/1**[3]

1m 29.12s (-0.48) **Going Correction** +0.125s/f (Slow)
WFA 3 from 4yo+ 1lb **9** Ran SP% **118.8**
Speed ratings (Par 105): **107,106,106,105,103 101,100,83,68**
toteswingers 1&2 £8.10, 1&3 £3.80, 2&3 £1.90 CSF £44.18 CT £76.41 TOTE £12.80: £2.20, £1.80, £1.20; EX 60.00 Trifecta £216.40 Pool: £5153.80 - 17.85 winning units..
Owner Will Dawson **Bred** Brian Miller **Trained** Pandy, Monmouths

FOCUS
Quite a good handicap for the grade and the form is rated slightly positively.

7950 CORAL MOBILE "JUST THREE CLICKS TO BET" H'CAP — 1m 4f 50y(P)
5:00 (5:00) (Class 5) (0-75,75) 3-Y-O+ — **£2,587** (£770; £384; £192) **Stalls** Low

Form RPR

1 **Knockgraffon Lad (USA)**[32] 1762 6-9-6 **74**(tp)
WilliamTwiston-Davies(3) 6 82
(Brendan Powell) *hld up: hdwy over 1f out: shkn up to ld ins fnl f r.o wl* **12/1**

4334 2 ¾ **Incendo**[13] 7758 7-9-10 **75** .... StevieDonohoe 10 81
(Ian Williams) *s.i.s: hld up: hdwy and n.m.r over 1f out: sn rdn and ev ch: kpt on* **12/1**

6034 **3** 1 ½ **Mick Duggan**[45] 5954 3-8-10 **67** LukeMorris 5 71
(Simon Hodgson) *hld up in tch: rdn and swtchd lft over 1f out: ev ch 1f out: styd on same pce* **7/1**[3]
2000 **4** ¾ **Singzak**[24] 7498 5-9-7 **72** JamesSullivan 9 75
(Michael Easterby) *trckd ldr tl led over 4f out: rdn over 1f out: hdd and unable qck ins fnl f* **9/2**[2]
504 **5** ¾ **Sir Boss (IRE)**[41] 7115 8-9-7 **75** SladeO'Hara(3) 7 77
(Michael Mullineaux) *mid-div: hdwy over 5f out: rdn over 1f out: ev ch ins fnl f: styd on same pce* **10/1**
6 1 ½ **Rebel Force (IRE)**[59] 6615 3-8-13 **70** JoeFanning 3 69
(Mark Johnston) *hld up: hdwy over 2f out: rdn and edgd lft over 1f out: styd on same pce* **8/1**
6526 **7** 3 ½ **Yul Finegold (IRE)**[116] 4672 3-9-2 **73** AndreaAtzeni 2 67
(George Baker) *trckd ldrs: rdn over 2f out: wknd ins fnl f* **7/4**[1]
3600 **8** 1 ½ **Sommersturm (GER)**[115] 4714 9-8-10 **61** oh3 (t) RichardKingscote 1 52
(David Evans) *mid-div: shkn up over 1f out: sn wknd* **25/1**
0625 **9** *hd* **Waving**[23] 6044 4-8-12 **70** AidenBlakemore(7) 4 61
(Tony Carroll) *prom: chsd ldr 4f out tl rdn over 2f out: wknd fnl f* **25/1**
0605 **10** *84* **Venutius**[28] 7424 6-9-7 **72** RussKennemore 8
(Philip Kirby) *sn led: hdd over 4f out: rdn and wknd over 3f out* **16/1**

2m 41.9s (0.80) **Going Correction** +0.125s/f (Slow)
WFA 3 from 4yo+ 6lb **10** Ran SP% **116.2**
Speed ratings (Par 103): **102,101,100,100,99 98,96,95,95,39**
toteswingers 1&2 £12.40, 1&3 £12.00, 2&3 £9.20 CSF £146.11 CT £1082.03 TOTE £9.60: £2.00, £4.40, £2.60; EX 121.90 Trifecta £514.60 Pool: £4721.26 - 6.87 winning units..
Owner Nigel M Davies **Bred** M A Paulson & Diamond A Racing Corp **Trained** Upper Lambourn, Berks

FOCUS
Just a modest handicap. A personal best from the winner, the third and fourth helping with the standard.
T/Jkpt: £7,691.10 to a £1 stake. Pool: £415322.78 - 38.34 winning tickets T/Plt: £41.90 to a £1 stake. Pool: £95998.47 - 1668.56 winning tickets T/Qpdt: £3.70 to a £1 stake. Pool: £8535.44 - 1685.80 winning tickets CR

7881 SOUTHWELL (L-H)
Tuesday, November 19

OFFICIAL GOING: Standard
Wind: Fresh behind Weather: Fine

7951 CORAL.CO.UK BEST ODDS GUARANTEED ON RACING H'CAP 1m 4f (F)
12:10 (12:10) (Class 6) (0-55,55) 3-Y-O+ **£1,940** (£577; £288; £144) **Stalls** Low

Form RPR
0000 **1** **Hussar Ballad (USA)**[60] 6598 4-9-2 **50** PJMcDonald 7 61+
(Mel Brittain) *a.p: shkn up to ld over 1f out: rdn out* **12/1**
404 **2** 4 **Princeofthedesert**[42] 7099 7-9-4 **52** GrahamLee 10 56
(Garry Woodward) *led: hdd over 10f out: chsd ldr tl led again over 6f out: rdn and hdd over 2f out: ev ch over 1f out: styd on same pce fnl f* **6/1**[3]
0255 **3** ¾ **Miss Ella Jade**[43] 7081 4-8-10 **49** GeorgeChaloner(5) 11 52
(Richard Whitaker) *chsd ldrs: rdn over 2f out: ev ch over 1f out: styd on same pce fnl f* **9/1**
364- **4** *nk* **Mister Frosty (IRE)**[574] 1580 7-8-13 **54** EoinWalsh(7) 6 56
(Christine Dunnett) *s.i.s: hld up: hdwy 1/2-way: rdn and ev ch over 1f out: styd on same pce fnl f* **25/1**
022 **5** 1 ¼ **Goodlukin Lucy**[15] 7735 6-9-4 **52** TomEaves 13 53
(Keith Dalgleish) *a.p: chsd ldr 1/2-way: led over 2f out: rdn and hdd over 1f out* **13/2**
0660 **6** 5 **This Is Me**[141] 3909 5-9-7 **55** AndrewMullen 1 48
(Don Cantillon) *prom: pushed along and lost pl over 10f out: styd on u.p fr over 1f out: nvr trbld ldrs* **3/1**[1]
5353 **7** 2 **Goldie Horn**[54] 6783 5-8-11 **48** (t) WilliamTwiston-Davies(3) 4 38
(Nigel Twiston-Davies) *hld up: hdwy over 4f out: rdn over 2f out: wknd over 1f out* **14/1**
3300 **8** *nk* **Layla's Boy**[209] 1763 6-9-6 **54** (bt) LukeMorris 14 44
(Simon West) *hld up: hdwy over 3f out: rdn and wknd over 1f out* **18/1**
0063 **9** 8 **Lord Golan**[28] 7440 5-9-4 **52** (b) WilliamCarson 3 30
(Violet M Jordan) *prom: lost pl 1/2-way: n.d after* **14/1**
-004 **10** 4 ½ **Overrule (USA)**[54] 6783 9-9-5 **53** (b[1]) FrederikTylicki 5 24
(Chris Bealby) *chsd ldrs: lost pl 1/2-way: wknd over 4f out* **12/1**
0024 **11** ¾ **Like Clockwork**[31] 7376 4-9-4 **52** LiamJones 12 22
(Mark H Tompkins) *mid-div: sn pushed along: hdwy over 5f out: rdn and wknd over 3f out* **5/1**[2]
0000 **12** ¾ **Flying Applause**[20] 7636 8-8-11 **48** (b) MarkCoumbe(3) 9 17
(Roy Bowring) *w ldr: led over 10f out: hdd over 6f out: wknd 4f out* **25/1**
0005 **13** *66* **Follow The Flag (IRE)**[14] 7758 9-8-11 **52** (v) NatalieHambling-Yates(7) 8
(Alan McCabe) *sn outpcd and bhd* **66/1**

2m 40.6s (-0.40) **Going Correction** 0.0s/f (Stan) **13** Ran SP% **122.5**
Speed ratings (Par 101): **101,98,97,97,96 93,92,91,86,83 83,82,38**
toteswingers 1&2 £19.10, 2&3 £14.00, 1&3 £30.30 CSF £83.18 CT £697.56 TOTE £22.10: £6.70, £2.70, £4.90; EX 115.30 Trifecta £1626.60 Part won. Pool: £2168.87 - 0.72 winning units..
Owner Mel Brittain **Bred** Darley **Trained** Warthill, N Yorks

FOCUS
This competitive, if very ordinary handicap was run at a even tempo throughout. The form looks pretty solid rated around the second.

7952 DOWNLOAD THE LADBROKES APP H'CAP 1m (F)
12:40 (12:41) (Class 5) (0-70,70) 3-Y-O+ **£2,911** (£866; £432; £216) **Stalls** Low

Form RPR
3620 **1** **Chrissycross (IRE)**[28] 7446 4-9-7 **70** (v) RobertWinston 1 80+
(Roger Teal) *a.p: pushed along over 3f out: rdn to ld ins fnl f: styd on* **9/1**
2205 **2** *nk* **Emperatriz**[14] 7754 3-8-12 **63** RobertHavlin 10 71
(John Holt) *led over 3f: led again over 2f out: rdn over 1f out: hdd ins fnl f: styd on* **12/1**
3144 **3** 1 ½ **Uncle Brit**[13] 7778 7-8-13 **62** PJMcDonald 14 68
(Malcolm Jefferson) *prom: outpcd over 4f out: hdwy over 1f out: r.o* **8/1**[3]
0022 **4** 1 ¼ **Maakirr (IRE)**[25] 7512 4-8-11 **63** (t) MarkCoumbe(3) 11 66
(Roy Bowring) *chsd ldr: led over 4f out: hdd over 2f out: sn rdn: styd on same pce fnl f* **4/1**[2]
4331 **5** 1 ½ **Peter's Friend**[47] 6963 4-9-3 **66** TomEaves 7 66
(Michael Herrington) *chsd ldrs: rdn over 2f out: no ins ex fnl f* **11/4**[1]
4443 **6** 3 **Syncopate**[20] 7629 4-9-4 **70** RossAtkinson(3) 4 63
(Pam Sly) *hld up: drvn along 1/2-way: styd on u.p fr over 1f out: nvr trbld ldrs* **9/1**

5125 **7** *shd* **Icy Blue**[25] 7515 5-8-5 **59** (p) GeorgeChaloner(5) 12 51
(Richard Whitaker) *chsd ldrs: rdn over 2f out: wknd over 1f out* **12/1**
30/0 **8** 2 ¼ **Auden (USA)**[8] 7836 5-9-2 **65** FrederikTylicki 3 52
(J R Jenkins) *sn pushed along in rr: styd on appr fnl f: nvr on terms* **18/1**
-150 **9** 1 ¼ **Returntobrecongill**[45] 7028 3-9-5 **70** GrahamLee 2 53
(James Given) *s.i.s: hdwy over 6f out: rdn and wknd 3f out* **16/1**
-550 **10** *10* **Witch Way Went**[41] 7132 3-8-13 **64** (b[1]) PaulPickard 6 24
(Brian Ellison) *sn pushed along and a in rr* **25/1**
1160 **11** *8* **Tenbridge**[41] 7130 4-8-8 **60** (v) RosieJessop(3) 13
(Derek Haydn Jones) *s.i.s: hdwy over 6f out: rdn over 3f out: wknd wl over 1f out* **50/1**
000 **12** *44* **Nelson's Bay**[55] 6758 4-9-2 **65** JimmyQuinn 5
(Wilf Storey) *sn pushed along in rr: bhd fr 1/2-way* **80/1**

1m 43.31s (-0.39) **Going Correction** 0.0s/f (Stan)
WFA 3 from 4yo+ 2lb **12** Ran SP% **111.3**
Speed ratings (Par 103): **101,100,99,97,96 93,93,91,89,79 71,27**
CSF £98.86 CT £787.49 TOTE £7.80: £2.40, £4.00, £2.70; EX 145.60 Trifecta £1008.70 Part won. Pool: £1345.03 - 0.32 winning units..
Owner John Morton **Bred** David Watson & Shane Horan **Trained** Ashtead, Surrey
■ Uncle Dermot was withdrawn on vet's advice (10-1, deduct 5p in the £ under R4).

FOCUS
This was run at a searching pace from the outset and it required a strong-staying performance. Straightforward form rated around the front three.

7953 LADBROKES H'CAP 7f (F)
1:10 (1:10) (Class 5) (0-70,70) 3-Y-O+ **£2,587** (£770; £384; £192) **Stalls** Low

Form RPR
512 **1** **Big Storm Coming**[64] 6478 3-8-12 **62** BenCurtis 11 75+
(Brian Ellison) *mid-div: hdwy over 3f out: rdn and hung lft fr over 2f out: led ins fnl f: r.o* **5/1**[3]
2335 **2** 2 **Two No Bids (IRE)**[28] 7454 3-9-3 **67** (be) PaddyAspell 4 73
(Phil McEntee) *sn trcking ldrs: led over 3f out: clr over 2f out: rdn and hdd ins fnl f: styd on same pce* **12/1**
0401 **3** 4 ½ **Hellbender (IRE)**[14] 7754 7-9-6 **69** (t) JimmyQuinn 8 64
(Shaun Harris) *in rr: pushed along over 4f out: hdwy u.p over 2f out: styd on same pce fnl f* **7/2**[2]
0413 **4** 1 ½ **Schottische**[12] 7784 3-8-6 **59** (v) RosieJessop(3) 7 49
(Derek Haydn Jones) *prom: hmpd and lost pl 5f out: styd on appr fnl f* **16/1**
0402 **5** ½ **Delores Rocket**[35] 7281 3-8-12 **67** (b) ShaneGray(5) 10 55+
(Kevin Ryan) *s.i.s: sn pushed along in rr: rdn over 2f out: styd on appr fnl f: nvr nrr* **13/2**
4055 **6** 3 ¼ **Jebel Tara**[64] 6468 8-9-5 **68** (bt) PaulPickard 2 49
(Alan Brown) *chsd ldrs: rdn over 2f out: wknd over 1f out* **12/1**
-000 **7** 3 ½ **Starbotton**[114] 4807 3-8-1 **56** oh3 ShirleyTeasdale(5) 6 26
(James Bethell) *sn pushed along in rr: nvr nrr* **100/1**
0200 **8** 2 ½ **Dancing Maite**[5] 7885 8-9-4 **70** (b) MarkCoumbe(3) 9 34
(Roy Bowring) *s.i.s: sn trcking ldrs: led over 4f out: hdd over 3f out: sn rdn: wknd wl over 1f out* **16/1**
620 **9** 8 **Glenridding**[18] 7669 9-8-13 **62** (p) DaleSwift 3
(James Given) *sn drvn along w ldrs: lost pl over 4f out: sn wknd* **18/1**
163 **10** *10* **Fairy Wing (IRE)**[71] 6259 6-9-5 **68** (b) WilliamCarson 1
(Violet M Jordan) *sn led: hdd over 4f out: rdn over 3f out: sn wknd* **22/1**
0460 **11** *61* **Only Ten Per Cent (IRE)**[35] 7263 5-9-4 **67** FrederikTylicki 5
(J R Jenkins) *chsd ldrs: n.m.r and hmpd 5f out: rdn over 3f out: sn wknd: virtually p.u appr fnl f* **3/1**[1]

1m 28.98s (-1.32) **Going Correction** 0.0s/f (Stan)
WFA 3 from 5yo+ 1lb **11** Ran SP% **115.0**
Speed ratings (Par 103): **107,104,99,97,97 93,89,86,77,66**
toteswingers 1&2 £7.90, 2&3 £9.30, 1&3 £3.40 CSF £62.15 CT £240.56 TOTE £6.40: £2.40, £4.00, £1.20; EX 48.80 Trifecta £274.60 Pool: £1922.47 - 5.24 winning units..
Owner Fishlake Commercial Motors Ltd **Bred** Bearstone Stud **Trained** Norton, N Yorks

FOCUS
A fair race for the grade and the winner has more to offer again.

7954 32RED CASINO (S) STKS 7f (F)
1:40 (1:40) (Class 6) 2-Y-O **£2,045** (£603; £302) **Stalls** Low

Form RPR
2000 **1** **Black Vale (IRE)**[6] 7855 2-8-12 **59** (bt) PaddyAspell 8 64
(Phil McEntee) *sn pushed along to chse ldrs: led over 5f out: clr 4f out: rdn over 1f out: styd on* **6/1**[3]
4400 **2** 2 ¼ **Camatini (IRE)**[32] 7340 2-8-2 **56** (p) ConnorBeasley(5) 4 53
(Michael Dods) *sn led: hdd over 5f out: chsd wnr: rdn over 3f out: hung lft over 1f out: no ex wl ins fnl f* **10/1**
0640 **3** 3 ¾ **Severnwind (IRE)**[6] 7855 2-8-12 **54** (b) LukeMorris 3 48
(Ronald Harris) *s.i.s: sn drvn along and outpcd: r.o ins fnl f: nt rch ldrs* **10/1**
000 **4** ¾ **Hello Sweetness**[29] 7419 2-8-7 **45** BenCurtis 6 41
(Jason Ward) *sn pushed along in rr: hdwy u.p and hung lft fr over 2f out: styd on same pce appr fnl f* **66/1**
50 **5** *nse* **Little Tinka**[47] 6974 2-8-7 **0** LiamJones 7 41
(Mark H Tompkins) *chsd ldrs: pushed along over 4f out: styd on same pce fnl 2f* **5/2**[2]
4416 **6** *shd* **May Whi (IRE)**[21] 7604 2-8-12 **65** RobertWinston 2 45
(John Quinn) *chsd ldrs: rdn over 3f out: styd on same pce fnl 2f* **6/4**[1]
066 **7** 9 **Mishnah**[12] 7790 2-8-7 **57** RobertHavlin 1 16
(John Holt) *prom: lost pl over 5f out: rdn 1/2-way: wknd wl over 1f out: eased ins fnl f* **16/1**

1m 32.1s (1.80) **Going Correction** 0.0s/f (Stan) **7** Ran SP% **108.4**
Speed ratings (Par 94): **89,86,82,81,81 81,70**
toteswingers 1&2 £5.10, 2&3 £5.40, 1&3 £6.50 CSF £55.27 TOTE £4.90: £1.70, £3.10; EX 57.60 Trifecta £380.90 Pool: £2718.18 - 5.35 winning units..There was no bid for the winner.
Owner Mrs Rebecca McEntee **Bred** Michael Downey & Roalso Ltd **Trained** Newmarket, Suffolk

FOCUS
A weak race, even by selling standards, but it has to rate a personal best from the winner.

7955 32RED BRITISH STALLION STUDS EBF MAIDEN STKS 1m (F)
2:10 (2:11) (Class 5) 2-Y-O **£2,911** (£866; £432; £216) **Stalls** Low

Form RPR
55 **1** **Framed Masterpiece**[18] 7655 2-9-5 **0** (p) LukeMorris 3 70
(Paul Fitzsimons) *chsd ldr tl led over 4f out: pushed along and edgd rt over 3f out: rdn clr over 2f out: jst hld on* **11/2**[2]
2 ¾ **Lesha (IRE)** 2-9-5 **0** [1] DavidNolan 6 68+
(Kevin Ryan) *s.s: outpcd: hdwy over 1f out: r.o to go 2nd wl ins fnl f: nt quite rch wnr* **14/1**

0 **3** 2 1/4 **Lyngnale**88 5727 2-9-0 0........................ LiamJones 5 58
(Jo Hughes) *chsd ldrs: sn pushed along: rdn over 3f out: wnt 2nd wl over 1f out: no ex fnl f* **7/1**3

4 6 **New Colours** 2-9-5 0........................1 MartinDwyer 1 49+
(Marcus Tregoning) *s.s: outpcd: styd on appr fnl f: nvr nrr* **12/1**

52 **5** 4 **Stout Cortez**13 7773 2-9-5 0........................ JoeFanning 9 40
(Mark Johnston) *led: hdd over 3f out: chsd wnr: rdn 3f out: sn hung lft: wknd over 1f out* **8/11**1

0 **6** 2 3/4 **Master Dan**13 7774 2-9-5 0........................ DaleSwift 8 34
(James Given) *sn pushed along and prom: rdn over 4f out: wknd over 2f out* **50/1**

5604 **7** shd **Ice Mayden**14 7755 2-8-11 58........................ WilliamTwiston-Davies(3) 7 29
(Bryan Smart) *chsd ldrs: drvn along over 4f out: wknd over 2f out* **8/1**

0 **8** 13 **Worcharlie'Slass**48 6938 2-9-0 0........................ TomEaves 2
(Michael Herrington) *hld up: rdn and wknd 1/2-way* **50/1**

9 41 **Antioch (IRE)** 2-9-2 0........................ RossAtkinson(3) 4
(Pam Sly) *s.s: rn green and sn outpcd: hit rail over 6f out* **28/1**

1m 44.5s (0.80) **Going Correction** 0.0s/f (Stan) **9** Ran SP% **118.6**
Speed ratings (Par 96): **96,95,93,87,83 80,80,67,26**
toteswingers 1&2 £8.90, 2&3 £16.00, 1&3 £5.90 CSF £78.08 TOTE £8.90: £2.10, £3.00, £1.90; EX 106.50 Trifecta £642.10 Pool: £3366.69 - 3.93 winning units..
Owner Saxon Gate Bloodstock (Helene Moller) **Bred** Mrs Hugh Maitland-Jones **Trained** Upper Lambourn, Berks

FOCUS
It's hard to believe this was anything other than an ordinary maiden, and the favourite was below par. The winner is rated a slight improver.

7956 32RED.COM NURSERY H'CAP 6f (F)
2:40 (2:40) (Class 6) (0-60,57) 2-Y-O **£1,940** (£577; £288; £144) **Stalls** Low

Form RPR
0353 **1** **Dandys Perier (IRE)**14 7755 2-9-0 **50**........................ LiamJones 10 55
(Ronald Harris) *sn pushed along towards rr: hdwy over 3f out: rdn and edgd lft fr over 1f out: styd on u.p to nr fin* **9/4**1

000 **2** hd **Razin' Hell**40 7155 2-8-4 **45**........................(p) GeorgeChaloner(5) 1 50+
(Alan McCabe) *chsd ldrs: led over 3f out: rdn and edgd rt over 1f out: hdd nr fin* **10/1**

0003 **3** 4 1/2 **Biscuiteer**14 7756 2-9-0 **50**........................(p) TomEaves 6 41
(Scott Dixon) *w ldrs: rdn over 2f out: no ex ins fnl f* **8/1**

6604 **4** 2 **Modify**14 7756 2-9-4 **57**........................(p) WilliamTwiston-Davies(3) 11 44+
(Bryan Smart) *s.i.s: outpcd: r.o ins fnl f: nrst fin* **6/1**3

000 **5** 3 3/4 **Kopenhagen (IRE)**40 7155 2-9-4 **57**........................ RobertTart(3) 2 31
(Ed de Giles) *chsd ldrs: rdn 1/2-way: wknd over 1f out* **5/1**2

0004 **6** 1 **Clear Focus (IRE)**18 7665 2-8-9 **45**........................ MartinDwyer 5 16
(Brendan Powell) *prom: rdn over 2f out: wknd over 1f out* **7/1**

0000 **7** 2 **Cheeky Peta'S**11 7804 2-9-0 **50**........................ JamesSullivan 3 15
(James Given) *led: hdd over 3f out: sn rdn: wknd over 1f out* **25/1**

0600 **8** 2 1/2 **Blunos (IRE)**12 7788 2-9-0 **50**........................ RobertHavlin 7 7
(Rod Millman) *prom: lost pl over 4f out: bhd fr 1/2-way* **16/1**

1000 **9** 2 1/4 **White Flag**14 7755 2-9-4 **54**........................(b) DuranFentiman 8 5
(Tim Easterby) *sn pushed along and prom: rdn over 3f out: wknd over 2f out* **20/1**

0646 **10** 1 3/4 **Baileys Celebrate**12 7789 2-8-9 **45**........................ JoeFanning 9
(Mark Johnston) *s.i.s: sn pushed along in rr: bhd fr 1/2-way* **18/1**

1m 17.49s (0.99) **Going Correction** 0.0s/f (Stan) **10** Ran SP% **114.2**
Speed ratings (Par 94): **93,92,86,84,79 77,75,71,68,66**
toteswingers 1&2 £5.70, 2&3 £17.70, 1&3 £4.20 CSF £25.42 CT £156.16 TOTE £2.60: £1.10, £3.00, £2.20; EX 39.40 Trifecta £426.30 Pool: £2619.81 - 4.60 winning units..
Owner Farley, Mares & Ridge House Stables **Bred** John Doyle **Trained** Earlswood, Monmouths
■ Stewards' Enquiry : Liam Jones two-day ban: used whip above permitted level (Dec 3-4)

FOCUS
They went a frantic pace in this low-grade nursery and stamina very much won the day. The first pair were clear but it did look a poor race.

7957 COMPARE BOOKMAKERS AT BOOKMAKERS.CO.UK H'CAP (DIV I) 6f (F)
3:10 (3:12) (Class 6) (0-65,65) 3-Y-O+ **£1,940** (£577; £288; £144) **Stalls** Low

Form RPR
6600 **1** **Caramelita**28 7455 6-9-1 **59**........................(v) FrederikTylicki 12 70
(J R Jenkins) *w ldrs: led over 3f out: rdn over 1f out: styd on* **6/1**3

3345 **2** 2 **Amenable (IRE)**20 7634 6-9-5 **63**........................(p) BenCurtis 6 68
(Violet M Jordan) *prom: outpcd 4f out: hdwy over 1f out: r.o to go 2nd nr fin: nt rch wnr* **6/1**3

0400 **3** nk **Prince Of Passion (CAN)**15 7728 5-9-3 **61**........................ JoeFanning 3 65
(Derek Shaw) *weith ldrs: rdn over 2f out: styd on same pce ins fnl f: lost 2nd nr fin* **20/1**

0344 **4** nk **Fathom Five (IRE)**13 7772 9-8-10 **57**........................ BillyCray(3) 5 60
(Shaun Harris) *chsd ldrs: rdn over 2f out: styd on* **16/1**

-005 **5** 1 **Beachwood Bay**29 7427 5-9-2 **60**........................ RobertHavlin 2 60+
(Jo Hughes) *sn pushed along in rr: nt clr run over 1f out: r.o ins fnl f: nvr nrr* **11/2**2

2560 **6** 1/2 **Belle Bayardo (IRE)**11 7801 5-9-5 **63**........................ LiamJones 1 62
(Ronald Harris) *sn pushed along in rr: hdwy u.p over 1f out: nt trble ldrs* **16/1**

3022 **7** shd **Madame Kintyre**43 7068 5-8-7 **51**........................ MartinDwyer 14 49
(Rod Millman) *s.i.s: hdwy over 4f out: rdn 1/2-way: styd on same pce fnl f* **16/1**

0020 **8** 1 1/4 **Monnoyer**34 7315 4-9-5 **63**........................(p) TomEaves 9 58
(Scott Dixon) *s.i.s: in rr and rdn 1/2-way: nvr on terms* **11/2**2

6320 **9** hd **Ishiamiracle**28 7455 4-8-0 **51** oh6........................(p) DonnaCaldwell(7) 11 45
(Phil McEntee) *hmpd sn after s: rdn over 2f out: n.d* **16/1**

4000 **10** nse **Bapak Pesta (IRE)**15 7729 3-8-6 **55**........................(b) ShaneGray(5) 4 49
(Kevin Ryan) *sn pushed along in rr: hdwy u.p over 2f out: no ex fnl f* **16/1**

0300 **11** 4 1/2 **Divertimenti (IRE)**32 7347 9-8-10 **57**........................(b) MarkCoumbe(3) 13 37
(Roy Bowring) *led: hdd over 3f out: rdn and wknd over 1f out* **33/1**

4053 **12** 1/2 **Bond Club**32 7343 3-9-4 **65**........................(p) WilliamTwiston-Davies(3) 7 44
(Geoffrey Oldroyd) *sn pushed along and a in rr* **7/2**1

1m 16.89s (0.39) **Going Correction** 0.0s/f (Stan) **12** Ran SP% **118.7**
Speed ratings (Par 101): **97,94,93,93,92 91,91,89,89,89 83,82**
toteswingers 1&2 £5.70, 2&3 £21.10, 1&3 £22.40 CSF £41.96 CT £696.61 TOTE £6.50: £2.30, £2.40, £5.30; EX 47.20 Trifecta £1025.20 Pool: £2110.00 - 1.54 winning units..
Owner La Senoritas **Bred** R B Hill **Trained** Royston, Herts

FOCUS
A strongly run affair and straightforward form.

7958 COMPARE BOOKMAKERS AT BOOKMAKERS.CO.UK H'CAP (DIV II) 6f (F)
3:40 (3:44) (Class 6) (0-65,65) 3-Y-O+ **£1,940** (£577; £288; £144) **Stalls** Low

Form RPR
5463 **1** **Hannahs Turn**18 7663 3-9-2 **65**........................ ShelleyBirkett(5) 13 82+
(Chris Dwyer) *s.i.s: sn rcvrd to ld: clr fr over 2f out: easily* **10/3**1

4665 **2** 7 **Spitfire**81 5965 8-9-5 **63**........................(t) JoeFanning 7 59
(J R Jenkins) *sn outpcd: hdwy over 1f out: r.o to go 2nd nr fin: no ch w wnr* **7/1**

3500 **3** nk **Putin (IRE)**35 7262 5-9-0 **58**........................(bt) PaddyAspell 9 53
(Phil McEntee) *chsd ldrs: rdn over 2f out: styd on same pce fr over 1f out* **8/1**

3210 **4** 2 1/2 **Lees Anthem**32 7344 6-8-12 **56**........................ PJMcDonald 10 44
(Mel Brittain) *prom: rdn over 2f out: styd on same pce* **12/1**

6066 **5** 2 **Orwellian**32 7344 4-8-7 **54**........................(e) MarkCoumbe(3) 2 36+
(Bryan Smart) *s.i.s: outpcd: r.o ins fnl f: nvr nrr* **20/1**

0053 **6** hd **Pearl Noir**5 7886 3-8-7 **51** oh1........................ JamesSullivan 6 32
(Scott Dixon) *chsd ldrs: rdn and edgd along over 4f out: wknd over 1f out* **14/1**

6603 **7** 3 3/4 **Fortrose Academy (IRE)**29 7427 4-9-7 **65**........................ DavidProbert 5 35
(Andrew Balding) *mid-div: rdn 1/2-way: wknd over 1f out* **9/2**2

3010 **8** 1 **Megaleka**3 7937 3-8-13 **60**........................ RobertTart(3) 4 27
(Alan Bailey) *prom: rdn over 2f out: wknd over 1f out* **12/1**

3400 **9** 3 1/4 **Night Trade (IRE)**6 7862 6-9-2 **60**........................(p) LiamJones 3 17
(Ronald Harris) *sn outpcd* **33/1**

1601 **10** 1 1/2 **All Right Now**28 7454 6-9-5 **63**........................(p) ChrisCatlin 11 16
(Tony Newcombe) *sn outpcd* **6/1**3

50 **11** 8 **Ioannou**60 6610 4-8-13 **57**........................ BenCurtis 1
(Ian Williams) *chsd ldrs: drvn along over 3f out: wknd 2f out* **10/1**

60-0 **U** **Fair Bunny**60 6603 6-8-8 **52** oh4 ow1........................(b) RobertHavlin 12
(Alan Brown) *uns rdr leaving stalls* **50/1**

1m 15.01s (-1.49) **Going Correction** 0.0s/f (Stan) **12** Ran SP% **120.0**
Speed ratings (Par 101): **109,99,99,95,93 93,88,86,82,80 69,**
toteswingers 1&2 £6.00, 2&3 £8.00, 1&3 £8.20 CSF £26.47 CT £179.77 TOTE £6.10: £1.70, £3.50, £2.90; EX 24.70 Trifecta £241.60 Pool: £3090.19 - 9.58 winning units..
Owner Mrs K W Sneath **Bred** Wayland Stud **Trained** Newmarket, Suffolk

FOCUS
This looked marginally stronger than the first division but it produced the easiest winner of the day. However she will be hit by the handicapper for this.
T/Jkpt: Not won. T/Plt: £10,256.50 to a £1 stake. Pool of £63787.44 - 4.54 winning tickets.
T/Qpdt: £63.80 to a £1 stake. Pool of £7546.30 - 87.50 winning tickets. CR

7944 WOLVERHAMPTON (A.W) (L-H)
Tuesday, November 19

OFFICIAL GOING: Standard
Wind: Virtually nil Weather: Fine

7959 BEST ODDS AT BOOKMAKERS.CO.UK H'CAP 5f 216y(P)
4:00 (4:01) (Class 4) (0-85,86) 3-Y-O+ **£5,175** (£1,540; £769; £384) **Stalls** Low

Form RPR
0011 **1** **Fat Gary**21 7593 3-9-7 **82**........................(p) RichardKingscote 7 93
(Tom Dascombe) *trckd ldr: rdn to ld over 1f out: sn strly pressed: kpt on wl: asserted nr fin* **6/4**1

2122 **2** 3/4 **Burren View Lady (IRE)**15 7731 3-9-4 **79**........................(e) DavidAllan 6 88
(Tim Easterby) *led narrowly: hdd 4f out: trckd ldr: rdn to chal strly over 1f out: kpt on: hld nr fin* **7/4**2

5035 **3** 3 **Angelito**15 7731 4-9-3 **78**........................ SeanLevey 5 78
(Ed McMahon) *s.i.s: sn in tch: rdn to chse ldr on outer 2f out: one pce in 3rd fnl f* **7/1**3

4000 **4** 1 **Desert Strike**15 7731 7-8-11 **75**........................(p) RyanPowell(3) 8 72
(Conor Dore) *in tch: hdwy on outside to ld 4f out: rdn whn hdd over 1f out: no ex* **33/1**

1464 **5** 1/2 **Wild Sauce**13 7777 4-9-0 **75**........................(bt) GrahamLee 4 70
(Bryan Smart) *hld up in tch: rdn over 2f out: one pce and nvr threatened ldrs* **8/1**

2061 **6** 2 1/2 **Decision By One**15 7730 4-9-3 **78**........................(t) StephenCraine 3 66
(David Evans) *racd keenly: hld up in tch: rdn 2f out: sn btn* **16/1**

630 **7** 1 1/2 **Perfect Blossom**29 7420 6-8-11 **75**........................(t) SladeO'Hara(3) 2 58
(Alan Berry) *dwlt: hld up: nvr threatened* **33/1**

1m 14.36s (-0.64) **Going Correction** +0.05s/f (Slow) **7** Ran SP% **111.7**
Speed ratings (Par 105): **106,105,101,99,99 95,93**
toteswingers 1&2 £1.10, 2&3 £3.30, 1&3 £2.40 CSF £4.12 CT £11.10 TOTE £2.10: £1.20, £1.10; EX 4.60 Trifecta £13.90 Pool: £2660.70 - 142.96 winning units..
Owner Manor House Racing Club **Bred** J M Beever **Trained** Malpas, Cheshire

FOCUS
The early pace wasn't great for 6f, but the result looks right, with the two in-form market leaders contesting the finish. They are both thriving at the moment.

7960 32RED MAIDEN AUCTION STKS 5f 216y(P)
4:30 (4:31) (Class 5) 2-Y-O **£2,587** (£770; £384; £192) **Stalls** Low

Form RPR
3050 **1** **Jacquotte Delahaye**10 7817 2-8-8 69........................(b) DavidAllan 5 72
(Bryan Smart) *trckd ldr: led wl over 1f out: sn rdn clr: edgd lft ins fnl f: easily* **5/1**3

0 **2** 6 **Brigliadoro (IRE)**18 7655 2-9-1 0........................ WilliamCarson 2 61
(Philip McBride) *slowly away: hld up: hdwy to chse ldng pair over 2f out: rdn 2f out: one pce: wnt 2nd jst ins fnl f: no threat wnr* **4/7**1

3 5 **Mon Petit Secret** 2-8-8 0........................ BarryMcHugh 1 39
(Kevin Ryan) *hld up in tch: rdn over 2f out: sn btn: wnt poor 3rd fnl 50yds* **25/1**

33 **4** 3/4 **Definite Secret**21 7602 2-8-11 0........................ LukeMorris 6 40
(James Tate) *led: rdn whn hdd wl over 1f out: hung lft appr fnl f: sn lost 2nd and wknd* **9/2**2

4 **5** 1/2 **Jayeff Herring (IRE)**46 6999 2-9-3 0........................ StevieDonohoe 3 44
(Michael Bell) *hld up in tch: rdn over 2f out: sn wknd* **12/1**

1m 14.82s (-0.18) **Going Correction** +0.05s/f (Slow) **5** Ran SP% **110.0**
Speed ratings (Par 96): **103,95,88,87,86**
CSF £8.43 TOTE £5.40: £1.70, £1.20; EX 11.10 Trifecta £68.80 Pool: £3478.40 - 37.88 winning units..
Owner Just For Girls Partnership **Bred** A S Denniff **Trained** Hambleton, N Yorks

The Form Book Flat, Raceform Ltd, Compton, RG20 6NL.

FOCUS
The pace was decent and the winner put in a likeable performance, but there was no depth to this modest maiden. The winner bounced back to her early-season form.

7961 CORAL APP DOWNLOAD FROM THE CORAL STORE H'CAP 1m 1f 103y(P)
5:00 (5:00) (Class 5) (0-75,73) 3-Y-0+ £2,587 (£770; £384; £192) Stalls Low

Form RPR
3436 1 **Lean On Pete (IRE)**[11] 7805 4-9-2 73 JacobButterfield(5) 6 82
(Ollie Pears) *hld up: smooth hdwy on outside over 2f out: pushed along to chse ldr jst ins fnl f: qckng to ld 50yds out* **4/1[3]**
6330 2 1 1/2 **Brockfield**[29] 7425 7-9-1 67 DavidAllan 8 73
(Mel Brittain) *trckd ldr: led over 3f out: rdn over 2f out: kpt on same pce: hdd 50yds out* **12/1**
0352 3 nk **Eurystheus (IRE)**[20] 7632 4-9-6 72 AndrewMullen 3 77
(Michael Appleby) *s.i.s: hld up: rdn and hdwy 2f out: chsd ldr jst ins fnl f: one pce fnl 100yds* **5/2[2]**
1-51 4 2 3/4 **Fresa**[24] 7546 4-9-7 73 LukeMorris 2 73
(Sir Mark Prescott Bt) *trckd ldng pair: rdn over 2f out: wknd ins fnl f* **6/4[1]**
5054 5 1 1/2 **Egotist (IRE)**[24] 7544 5-9-4 70 (t) RichardKingscote 5 67
(Milton Bradley) *trckd ldng pair: rdn to chse ldr over 2f out: wknd fnl f* **25/1**
0533 6 11 **Everlasting Light**[28] 7439 3-8-11 66 DuranFentiman 7 42
(Tim Walford) *midfield: rdn over 2f out: sn wknd* **25/1**
1241 7 2 **Ana Shababiya (IRE)**[18] 7667 3-8-13 68 MartinLane 1 41
(Ismail Mohammed) *led: racd keenly: hdd over 3f out: wknd* **7/1**
0000 8 2 1/2 **Standpoint**[19] 7651 7-9-3 72 RyanPowell(3) 4 40
(Conor Dore) *midfield: rdn 3f out: sn wknd* **66/1**

2m 1.34s (-0.36) **Going Correction** +0.05s/f (Slow)
WFA 3 from 4yo+ 3lb **8 Ran SP% 117.9**
Speed ratings (Par 103): **103,101,101,98,97 87,86,83**
toteswingers 1&2 £11.40, 2&3 £5.80, 1&3 £3.20 CSF £49.43 CT £144.50 TOTE £5.50: £1.70, £3.30, £1.10; EX 61.60 Trifecta £325.30 Pool: £3968.96 - 9.14 winning units..
Owner K C West **Bred** Mrs T Mahon **Trained** Norton, N Yorks

FOCUS
The pace was solid, with two of the first three making ground from the rear. Straightforward form.

7962 CORAL MOBILE "JUST THREE CLICKS TO BET" H'CAP (DIV I) 1m 1f 103y(P)
5:30 (5:30) (Class 6) (0-52,52) 3-Y-0+ £1,940 (£577; £288; £144) Stalls Low

Form RPR
6000 1 **Shirazz**[116] 4714 4-9-1 46 GeorgeBaker 7 56+
(Seamus Durack) *hld up: pushed along over 3f out: r.o strly on wd outside fr over 1f out: led 110yds out: sn clr: comf* **7/1[3]**
6403 2 2 1/4 **Appyjack**[19] 7644 5-9-1 46 (t) LukeMorris 8 50
(Tony Carroll) *midfield: rdn over 2f out: hdwy to chse ldrs over 1f out: kpt on to go 2nd 100yds out: no ch w wnr* **7/2[1]**
4604 3 1/2 **Shamiana**[11] 7806 3-9-4 52 RichardKingscote 10 55
(Daniel Kubler) *midfield: rdn over 2f out: styd on: wnt 3rd 50yds out* **14/1**
0000 4 1 1/2 **Silver Fawn (IRE)**[18] 7666 3-8-12 46 oh1 (be) JimmyQuinn 5 46
(John Weymes) *racd keenly in tch: hdwy over 2f out: rdn to ld ent fnl f: hdd 110yds out: wknd and lost 2 more pls* **20/1**
0344 5 1 **Greyemkay**[15] 7733 5-9-0 50 JacobButterfield(5) 12 48
(Richard Price) *in tch: rdn over 2f out: one pce* **7/2[1]**
-066 6 1/2 **Mill I Am (USA)**[13] 7770 3-9-3 51 SeanLevey 2 48
(Stuart Williams) *led: rdn over 2f out: hdd ent fnl f: wknd* **14/1**
0226 7 2 3/4 **My Claire**[18] 7666 3-9-2 50 AdamBeschizza 6 42
(Nigel Tinkler) *midfield: rdn over 2f out: briefly n.m.r 2f out: no imp* **9/2[2]**
0-00 8 2 1/4 **Oriental Cavalier**[103] 5204 7-9-7 52 (v) MartinLane 4 40
(Mark Buckley) *in tch: rdn over 3f out: wknd 2f out* **16/1**
6000 9 nk **Zainda (IRE)**[25] 7498 3-9-4 52 BarryMcHugh 11 39
(John Wainwright) *trckd ldr: rdn over 2f out: wknd over 1f out* **14/1**
06-0 10 7 **Gifted Heir (IRE)**[96] 5429 9-9-1 46 oh1 WilliamCarson 13 20
(Ray Peacock) *hld up: nvr threatened* **100/1**
3000 10 dht **Meglio Ancora**[14] 7753 6-9-3 48 (t) GrahamLee 1 22
(Richard Ford) *trckd ldr: rdn 3f out: wknd 2f out* **12/1**
0000 12 hd **Addikt (IRE)**[43] 7081 8-9-7 52 JohnFahy 9 25
(John Spearing) *slowly away: hld up in rr: a bhd* **33/1**
050/ 13 18 **Shakedown**[1264] 2714 8-9-1 46 StevieDonohoe 3
(Kevin Frost) *hld up: a bhd: t.o* **66/1**

2m 2.79s (1.09) **Going Correction** +0.05s/f (Slow)
WFA 3 from 4yo+ 3lb **13 Ran SP% 118.9**
Speed ratings (Par 101): **97,95,94,93,92 91,89,87,87,80 80,80,64**
toteswingers 1&2 £4.50, 2&3 £7.40, 1&3 £16.40 CSF £30.71 CT £341.64 TOTE £9.50: £2.60, £1.30, £4.80; EX 35.20 Trifecta £374.90 Pool: £2791.91 - 5.58 winning units..
Owner Mrs Sally Doyle **Bred** Mrs Sally Doyle **Trained** Baydon, Wilts

FOCUS
A pretty weak race. A brisk pace set this up for the strong finishers, including the winner, who has the scope to do better.

7963 CORAL MOBILE "JUST THREE CLICKS TO BET" H'CAP (DIV II) 1m 1f 103y(P)
6:00 (6:00) (Class 6) (0-52,52) 3-Y-0+ £1,940 (£577; £288; £144) Stalls Low

Form RPR
212 1 **Poppy Bond**[18] 7667 3-9-4 52 GrahamGibbons 12 62
(Alan Bailey) *led after 1f: mde rest: strly pressed over 2f out: kpt on wl to assert fnl 110yds* **7/4[1]**
0004 2 1 1/2 **Galilee Chapel (IRE)**[14] 7752 4-9-3 48 (b[1]) BarryMcHugh 8 55
(Alistair Whillans) *racd keenly: trckd ldrs: rdn to press wnr over 2f out: one pce and hld fnl 110yds* **20/1**
5432 3 2 1/4 **Bladewood Girl**[14] 7752 5-9-7 52 FrederikTylicki 7 55
(J R Jenkins) *trckd ldrs: rdn over 2f out: one pce in 3rd fr over 1f out* **9/2[2]**
6006 4 shd **Daniel Thomas (IRE)**[98] 5377 11-9-3 48 (tp) WilliamCarson 10 51
(Violet M Jordan) *slowly away: hld up: rdn over 2f out: kpt on fnl f: nrst fin* **16/1**
1522 5 nk **Kyle Of Bute**[15] 7733 7-9-1 51 JoshBaudains(5) 5 53+
(Richard Ford) *hld up in midfield: sme hdwy 2f out: sn rdn: kpt on* **6/1[3]**
3600 6 hd **Elizabeth Coffee (IRE)**[14] 7753 5-9-5 50 (b) JimmyQuinn 9 52
(John Weymes) *in tch: rdn over 2f out: one pce* **25/1**
0005 7 2 1/4 **Just Five (IRE)**[14] 7752 7-8-10 46 (v) JoeyHaynes(5) 3 45
(John Weymes) *hld up: bmpd over 1f out: sme late hdwy: nvr threatened* **25/1**
0643 8 1/2 **Count Ceprano (IRE)**[38] 7201 9-9-2 47 GrahamLee 1 44
(Lydia Pearce) *midfield: rdn over 2f out: wknd over 1f out* **8/1**
0006 9 1 1/2 **Zed Candy Girl**[11] 7806 3-8-12 46 oh1 StephenCraine 4 40
(John Stimpson) *hld up: hmpd over 1f out: nvr threatened* **33/1**
2030 10 4 **Madame Blavatsky (FR)**[31] 7372 5-8-8 46 (v) EvaMoscrop(7) 11 32
(Simon West) *midfield on outside: briefly chsd ldr 3f out: wknd over 1f out* **33/1**
0202 11 9 **Ocean Power (IRE)**[13] 7770 3-9-1 49 LukeMorris 13 18
(Richard Phillips) *trckd ldr: rdn over 2f out: wknd over 1f out: eased* **8/1**
0000 12 6 **Smirfy's Silver**[25] 7514 9-9-1 46 oh1 StevieDonohoe 2 4
(Michael Mullineaux) *led for 1f: trckd ldrs: wknd 3f out* **50/1**

2m 2.49s (0.79) **Going Correction** +0.05s/f (Slow)
WFA 3 from 4yo+ 3lb **12 Ran SP% 117.2**
Speed ratings (Par 101): **98,96,94,94,94 94,92,91,90,86 78,73**
toteswingers 1&2 £14.80, 2&3 £15.30, 1&3 £2.00 CSF £46.34 CT £142.18 TOTE £2.40: £1.10, £6.90, £2.30; EX 38.20 Trifecta £224.70 Pool: £2501.18 - 8.34 winning units..
Owner North Cheshire Trading & Storage Ltd **Bred** North Cheshire Trading And Storage Ltd **Trained** Newmarket, Suffolk

FOCUS
After a dash to the first bend, the tempo softened to a medium one in mid-race. The winner is thriving at the moment.

7964 LADBROKES H'CAP (DIV I) 7f 32y(P)
6:30 (6:32) (Class 4) (0-77,77) 3-Y-0+ £5,175 (£1,540; £769; £384) Stalls High

Form RPR
2205 1 **Fantasy Gladiator**[14] 7742 7-9-3 73 LukeMorris 5 85
(John Quinn) *hld up in midfield: hdwy to trck ldrs gng wl over 2f out: rdn to ld over 1f out: kpt on wl* **9/2[2]**
-045 2 2 1/4 **Jubilee Brig**[62] 6525 3-9-5 76 (v) GeorgeBaker 10 81
(Gary Moore) *dwlt: hld up: smooth hdwy 2f out: sn rdn to chse ldrs: wnt 2nd ins fnl f: kpt on but nvr rching wnr* **4/1[1]**
0044 3 3 1/2 **Dream Scenario**[92] 5581 3-8-10 67 (v[1]) DavidAllan 9 64
(Mel Brittain) *prom on outside: rdn to ld 2f out: hdd over 1f out: lost 2nd ins fnl f: wknd* **20/1**
0025 4 1 3/4 **Emiratesdotcom**[11] 7801 7-8-13 69 (tp) RichardKingscote 1 63
(Milton Bradley) *trckd ldrs: rdn over 2f out: sn outpcd by ldrs and no threat after* **12/1**
1040 5 shd **Celtic Sixpence (IRE)**[10] 7824 5-8-10 71 (p) ShelleyBirkett(5) 6 64
(Nick Kent) *w ldr: rdn over 2f out: wknd over 1f out* **12/1**
0411 6 1/2 **One Way Or Another (AUS)**[11] 7808 10-8-5 68 (t) EoinWalsh(7) 8 60
(David Evans) *midfield towards outer: rdn over 2f out: sn no imp* **5/1[3]**
1542 7 3/4 **Red Art (IRE)**[35] 7269 4-9-7 77 ChrisCatlin 2 67
(Tony Newcombe) *led narrowly: rdn whn hdd 2f out: sn wknd* **5/1[3]**
64-2 8 shd **Crossley**[166] 3030 4-8-7 63 oh1 RaulDaSilva 7 53
(Geoffrey Oldroyd) *chsd ldrs: sn pushed along: wknd over 1f out* **12/1**
0201 9 1/2 **Just The Tonic**[21] 7594 6-9-2 77 NathanAlison(5) 4 66
(Marjorie Fife) *hld up: rdn over 3f out: a towards rr* **16/1**
4020 10 1 **Pashan Garh**[10] 7824 4-8-11 70 RobertTart(3) 3 56
(Pat Eddery) *midfield on inner: rdn over 2f out: wknd over 1f out* **8/1**

1m 29.01s (-0.59) **Going Correction** +0.05s/f (Slow)
WFA 3 from 4yo+ 1lb **10 Ran SP% 116.3**
Speed ratings (Par 105): **105,102,98,96,96 95,94,94,94,93**
toteswingers 1&2 £4.90, 2&3 £18.90, 1&3 £22.10 CSF £22.82 CT £334.63 TOTE £4.40: £1.70, £1.80, £7.20; EX 25.80 Trifecta £435.20 Pool: £2576.40 - 4.43 winning units..
Owner The Fantasy Fellowship **Bred** R S A Urquhart **Trained** Settrington, N Yorks

FOCUS
Despite half the field being rated in the 70s, this was a routine Polytrack event, and the fact that the exposed winner won so easily suggests that most of those behind him will have to improve. The winner's best effort for quite a while.

7965 LADBROKES H'CAP (DIV II) 7f 32y(P)
7:00 (7:01) (Class 4) (0-77,77) 3-Y-0+ £5,175 (£1,540; £769; £384) Stalls High

Form RPR
2115 1 **Jay Bee Blue**[4] 7896 4-9-2 77 (bt) OisinMurphy(5) 7 86
(Sean Curran) *hld up in midfield: hdwy 3f out: in tch and gng wl 2f out: rdn over 1f out: kpt on to ld 75yds out* **9/4[1]**
1030 2 1/2 **George Fenton**[4] 7896 4-9-0 73 (e) RyanPowell(3) 9 81
(Conor Dore) *trckd ldr: rdn to ld narrowly over 1f out: kpt on: hdd 75yds out* **20/1**
0021 3 3/4 **Bogsnog (IRE)**[26] 7486 3-9-0 76 JacobButterfield(5) 4 81
(Kristin Stubbs) *t.k.h early: trckd ldr: rdn to chal over 1f out: one pce ins fnl f* **4/1[2]**
0310 4 hd **Black Dave (IRE)**[14] 7743 3-8-10 67 StevieDonohoe 2 72
(David Evans) *hld up: rdn over 2f out: kpt on fnl f: nrst fin* **16/1**
0555 5 hd **Smalljohn**[26] 7486 7-8-13 69 (v) GrahamLee 8 74
(Bryan Smart) *led narrowly: rdn whn hdd over 1f out: no ex ins fnl f* **7/1**
0030 6 1/2 **One Scoop Or Two**[66] 6384 7-9-2 72 (v) GrahamGibbons 10 76
(Andrew Hollinshead) *prom towards outer: rdn over 2f out: stl ev ch jst ins fnl f: no ex* **8/1**
5000 7 10 **Steel Stockholder**[10] 7824 7-9-0 70 DavidAllan 5 49
(Mel Brittain) *hld up: rdn over 2f out: a towards rr* **8/1**
0202 8 7 **Relight My Fire**[26] 7487 3-9-4 75 (e) DuranFentiman 1 36
(Tim Easterby) *midfield: rdn over 2f out: sn wknd* **6/1[3]**
5620 9 7 **Celestial Bay**[62] 6527 4-9-0 70 LukeMorris 3 15
(Sylvester Kirk) *midfield: rdn 3f out: sn wknd: eased* **33/1**

1m 29.33s (-0.27) **Going Correction** +0.05s/f (Slow)
WFA 3 from 4yo+ 1lb **9 Ran SP% 113.4**
Speed ratings (Par 105): **103,102,101,101,101 100,89,81,73**
toteswingers 1&2 £6.10, 2&3 £13.40, 1&3 £2.40 CSF £50.56 CT £172.20 TOTE £2.30: £1.10, £3.70, £2.10; EX 45.80 Trifecta £137.00 Pool: £3039.55 - 16.63 winning units..
Owner Scuderia Vita Bella **Bred** L A C Ashby Newhall Estate Farm **Trained** Hatford, Oxon

FOCUS
The first three all came into this race in good shape, but the next three home showed signs of coming back to their best and are also worth keeping an eye on. Straightforward form.

7966 DOWNLOAD THE LADBROKES APP H'CAP 7f 32y(P)
7:30 (7:33) (Class 6) (0-60,60) 3-Y-O £1,940 (£577; £288; £144) Stalls High

Form RPR
3033 1 **Be Royale**[11] 7806 3-8-9 48 AndrewMullen 3 64
(Michael Appleby) *trckd ldr: rdn to ld over 1f out: kpt on wl* **4/1[2]**
5231 2 1 3/4 **Sakash**[97] 5407 3-9-4 57 FrederikTylicki 7 69
(J R Jenkins) *hld up: hdwy over 2f out: rdn to chse wnr appr fnl f: kpt on but a hld* **5/1[3]**
5010 3 3 **Kindlelight Storm (USA)**[27] 7458 3-9-3 56 RobertHavlin 10 60
(Nick Littmoden) *in tch: rdn and outpcd over 2f out: kpt on fnl f: no threat to ldng pair* **3/1[1]**
0351 4 nk **Sweet Vintage (IRE)**[19] 7644 3-9-2 55 LukeMorris 12 59
(Mark Brisbourne) *trckd ldrs: rdn and outpcd over 2f out: kpt on fnl f* **10/1**
002 5 2 1/4 **Triple Aitch (USA)**[11] 7808 3-8-12 58 JordanVaughan(7) 5 56
(Giles Bravery) *midfield: rdn and hdwy to chse ldrs 2f out: wknd ins fnl f* **7/1**
6664 6 1 3/4 **Elle Rebelle**[19] 7643 3-8-9 48 (p) MartinDwyer 1 42
(Mark Brisbourne) *led: rdn whn hdd over 1f out: wknd fnl f* **14/1**

2002 **7** ½ **Just A Pound (IRE)**[25] 7511 3-8-12 **58** HarryBurns(7) 8 51
(Jo Hughes) *hld up in midfield: rdn over 2f out: sn btn* **6/1**
615 **8** *shd* **Mysterious Wonder**[40] 7149 3-8-11 **57** (b) EvaMoscrop(7) 11 49
(Philip Kirby) *racd keenly: sn prom on outside: upsides over 1f out: wknd fnl f* **12/1**
054 **9** *shd* **Partner's Gold (IRE)**[57] 6682 3-8-9 **48** (b1) GrahamGibbons 9 40
(Alan Berry) *hld up in midfield: rdn over 2f out: nvr threatened* **20/1**
0003 **10** *nse* **Lucy Minaj**[25] 7512 3-8-8 **47** (p) DavidAllan 6 39
(Bryan Smart) *hld up: nvr threatened* **20/1**
000 **P** **Serendippidy**[167] 2979 3-9-2 **55** LiamJones 4
(James Unett) *midfield: lost pl qckly 1/2-way: sn t.o: p.u 2f out* **50/1**

1m 29.41s (-0.19) **Going Correction** +0.05s/f (Slow) 11 Ran SP% **123.4**
Speed ratings (Par 98): **103,101,97,97,94 92,92,91,91,91**
toteswingers 1&2 £4.70, 2&3 £4.00, 1&3 £3.50 CSF £25.16 CT £71.84 TOTE £6.60: £2.10, £2.60, £1.70; EX 55.30 Trifecta £172.90 Pool: £3256.15 - 14.11winning units..
Owner Wayne Brackstone, Steve Whitear **Bred** W Brackstone & S J Whitear **Trained** Danethorpe, Notts

FOCUS
This looked a modest race on paper, but the first three don't have many miles on the clock so it's likely to be a bit better than that. The form is rated on the positive side.
T/Plt: £39.00 to a £1 stake. Pool of £87818.47 - 1641.25 winning tickets. T/Qpdt: £15.30 to a £1 stake. Pool of £10956.72 - 527.58 winning tickets. AS

7736 CHANTILLY (R-H)
Tuesday, November 19

OFFICIAL GOING: Polytrack: standard; turf: heavy

7967a PRIX ISONOMY (LISTED RACE) (2YO) (ROUND COURSE) (TURF) 1m
12:15 (12:16) 2-Y-0 **£22,357** (£8,943; £6,707; £4,471; £2,235)

RPR
1 **Under The Radar (FR)**[24] 7589 2-8-11 0 CristianDemuro 7 98
(F Doumen, France) **135/10**
2 *shd* **Divina Comedia (FR)**[39] 2-8-8 0 ThierryThulliez 2 95
(N Clement, France) **9/5**1
3 *snk* **Aventador (FR)**[23] 2-8-11 0 ThierryJarnet 1 97
(T Castanheira, France) **11/2**2
4 1½ **Allez Henri (IRE)**[38] 2-8-11 0 ChristopheSoumillon 8 94
(M Delzangles, France) **12/1**
5 2 **Spoken To Me (IRE)**[18] 2-8-8 0 MaximeGuyon 10 87
(Mme Pia Brandt, France) **8/1**
6 *snk* **Bocaiuva (IRE)**[26] 2-8-8 0 IoritzMendizabal 3 86
(F Chappet, France) **29/1**
7 1½ **Itoobeboss (IRE)**[141] 2-8-11 0 StephanePasquier 4 86
(Rod Collet, France) **6/1**3
8 ¾ **Delicate Delight (IRE)**[51] 2-8-8 0 FabriceVeron 5 81
(P Schiergen, Germany) **14/1**
9 ½ **Farquhar (IRE)**[20] 7631 2-8-11 0 ShaneKelly 9 83
(Peter Chapple-Hyam) *t.k.h: hld up towards rr on outer: rdn 2f out: outpcd in rr ent fnl f: no imp* **13/1**
10 ½ **Cockney Bob**[24] 7589 2-8-11 0 (p) MatthiasLauron 6 82
(D Windrif, France) **11/1**

1m 45.28s (7.28) 10 Ran SP% **116.6**
WIN (incl. 1 euro stake): 14.50. PLACES: 2.70, 1.40, 1.80. DF: 20.90. SF: 39.10.
Owner Haras D'Ecouves **Bred** Uplifting Bloodstock Ltd **Trained** Bouce, France

7968a PRIX TANTIEME (LISTED RACE) (3YO+) (ROUND COURSE) (TURF) 1m
12:50 (1:00) 3-Y-0+ **£21,138** (£8,455; £6,341; £4,227; £2,113)

RPR
1 **Combat Zone (IRE)**[44] 7053 7-9-4 0 (p) NRichter 9 111
(Mario Hofer, Germany) **21/1**
2 1¾ **Boomshackerlacker (IRE)**[17] 7698 3-8-11 0 (p) JimCrowley 3 101
(George Baker) *midfield in tch: rdn and hdwy 2f out: hung rt u.p and wnt 2nd over 1f out: kpt on wl wout matching wnr ins fnl f* **16/1**
3 2 **Samana Cay (USA)**[17] 4-8-10 0 Pierre-CharlesBoudot 6 94
(A Fabre, France) **83/10**
4 *nk* **Maningrey (GER)**[30] 4-9-0 0 MarcLerner 2 98
(W Hickst, Germany) **15/2**
5 1½ **Gris De Reve (FR)**[18] 7685 4-9-0 0 IoritzMendizabal 12 94
(A Lyon, France) **7/1**3
6 *hd* **Hippolyte (FR)**[20] 4-9-0 0 ThierryJarnet 10 94
(T Clout, France) **58/10**1
7 ¾ **Ideal (GER)**[152] 3485 3-9-2 0 LennartHammer-Hansen 1 95
(Ferdinand J Leve, Germany) **36/1**
8 *nk* **Cielo Canarias (IRE)**[37] 5-9-4 0 (p) J-LMartinez 15 95
(E Leon Penate, Spain) **78/10**
9 1¼ **Paraggi**[28] 4-9-0 0 MaximeGuyon 4 88
(Mme Pia Brandt, France) **12/1**
10 ½ **Baie D'Honneur (FR)**[15] 3-8-13 0 Jean-BaptisteHamel 11 87
(D De Watrigant, France) **12/1**
11 ¾ **Daring Storm (GER)** 3-8-11 0 AnthonyCrastus 8 84
(J Hirschberger, Germany) **21/1**
12 1¾ **Celebrissime (IRE)**[141] 3913 8-9-4 0 FlavienPrat 7 86
(F Head, France) **9/1**
13 6 **Menardais (FR)**[39] 7186 4-9-4 0 StephanePasquier 16 72
(P Bary, France) **68/10**2

1m 42.17s (4.17) 13 Ran SP% **117.0**
WFA 3 from 4yo+ 2lb
WIN (incl. 1 euro stake): 22.00. PLACES: 6.80, 5.40, 3.50. DF: 101.80. SF: 83.70.
Owner Guido-Werner-Hermann-Schmitt **Bred** Twelve Oaks Stud **Trained** Germany
■ Hermival was withdrawn after getting loose before the start.

7873 KEMPTON (A.W) (R-H)
Wednesday, November 20

OFFICIAL GOING: Standard
Wind: Virtually nil Weather: Getting dark

7969 BOOK NOW FOR BOXING DAY MEDIAN AUCTION MAIDEN STKS 5f (P)
4:00 (4:00) (Class 6) 3-5-Y-0 **£1,940** (£577; £288; £144) **Stalls** Low

Form RPR
423 **1** **Poyle Vinnie**[12] 7802 3-9-2 65 RyanPowell(3) 6 70
(George Margarson) *trckd ldr 1/2-way: led wl over 1f out: pushed out* **10/11**1
0-04 **2** 1 **Dawn Catcher**[79] 6040 3-9-0 63 MartinHarley 2 61
(Geoffrey Deacon) *chsd ldrs: styd on to take 2nd jst ins fnl f: kpt on but a readily hld* **5/2**2
02 **3** 3 **Twist And Twirl**[300] 356 3-9-0 0 DaleSwift 5 51
(Derek Shaw) *in rr: drvn along 1/2-way: hdwy over 1f out: styd on to take 2nd in clsng stages but no ch w ldng duo* **8/1**3
5354 **4** *nk* **Daneglow (IRE)**[4] 7929 3-9-0 45 LukeMorris 4 50
(Mike Murphy) *t.k.h and sn led: hdd wl over 1f out: wknd ins fnl f and lost 3rd in clsng stages* **12/1**
0630 **5** 6 **Lily The Dragon (IRE)**[48] 6965 3-8-11 37 RobertTart(3) 3 28
(Mick Quinn) *outpcd* **33/1**
0420 **6** 3½ **College Doll**[29] 7454 4-9-0 47 (t) TomMcLaughlin 7 15
(Christine Dunnett) *racd on outer: in tch tl wknd ins fnl 2f* **14/1**

59.38s (-1.12) **Going Correction** -0.075s/f (Stan) 6 Ran SP% **109.4**
Speed ratings (Par 101): **105,103,98,98,88 82**
toteswingers 1&2 £1.20, 2&3 £2.20, 1&3 £1.60 CSF £3.10 TOTE £2.50: £1.20, £1.50; EX 4.10 Trifecta £8.30 Pool: £3472.47 - 312.15 winning units..
Owner Cecil And Miss Alison Wiggins **Bred** Cecil And Miss Alison Wiggins **Trained** Newmarket, Suffolk

FOCUS
A weak sprint maiden in which they went a decent gallop. The form makes sense.

7970 £500 FREE BETS AT BETDAQ H'CAP 1m 2f (P)
4:30 (4:30) (Class 5) (0-75,75) 3-Y-0+ **£2,587** (£770; £384; £192) **Stalls** Low

Form RPR
6052 **1** **Maria's Choice (IRE)**[13] 7785 4-9-8 **74** (p) MartinHarley 13 82
(Alan McCabe) *chsd ldr: led ins fnl 2f: hrd drvn fnl f: jst hld on* **8/1**
-130 **2** *shd* **Little Buxted (USA)**[9] 7840 3-9-5 **75** GrahamLee 4 83
(Robert Mills) *chsd ldrs: rdn and one pce 2f out: str run ins fnl f to chse wnr fnl 120yds: fin wl: nt quite get up* **6/1**2
6-06 **3** 1½ **Archie Rice (USA)**[119] 4638 7-9-2 **71** RobertTart(3) 8 76
(Tom Keddy) *in rr: hdwy on outer over 1f out: styd wl fnl f to take 3rd in clsng stages: nt rch ldng duo* **33/1**
-446 **4** ¾ **Odin (IRE)**[53] 3785 5-9-2 **75** JoeDoyle(7) 1 79
(Don Cantillon) *in rr: hdwy and n.m.r over 1f out: kpt on ins fnl f: nt rch ldrs* **14/1**
506 **5** ½ **Xinbama (IRE)**[20] 7651 4-9-3 **74** (t) ShelleyBirkett(5) 10 77
(J W Hills) *chsd ldrs: rdn 2f out: edgd rt over 1f out: styd on same pce* **8/1**
4102 **6** ½ **Oratorio's Joy (IRE)**[25] 7546 3-9-3 **73** FergusSweeney 9 75
(Jamie Osborne) *in tch: drvn to chse ldrs on outer over 2f out: styd on same pce fnl f* **13/2**3
3416 **7** ½ **Precision Five**[29] 7447 4-9-4 **70** (p) JimCrowley 11 71+
(Jeremy Gask) *towards rr: hdwy whn nt clr run over 1f out and ins fnl f: kpt on cl home: nt rcvr* **12/1**
50-6 **8** *hd* **Planetoid (IRE)**[15] 7739 5-9-9 **75** AmirQuinn 12 75
(Jim Best) *in rr: pushed along over 1f out and styd on fnl f: nt rch ldrs* **33/1**
4445 **9** ½ **Gabrial's Wawa**[19] 7661 3-9-4 **74** RobertHavlin 14 73
(Roger Ingram) *sn led: hdd ins fnl 2f: wknd fnl f* **14/1**
2050 **10** ¾ **Poetic Lord**[28] 7462 4-9-4 **70** LukeMorris 3 68
(Sylvester Kirk) *chsd ldrs: rdn 3f out: losing pl 2f out: hld whn n.m.r on inner over 1f out* **25/1**
1433 **11** *nk* **Perfect Cracker**[132] 4194 5-9-0 **71** RyanTate(5) 7 68+
(Clive Cox) *chsd ldrs: styng on same pce whn n.m.r on rails and eased ins fnl f* **7/1**
000 **12** *nk* **Reflect (IRE)**[49] 6936 5-9-9 **75** (vt) DaleSwift 2 71
(Derek Shaw) *outpcd* **25/1**
0420 **13** 1¼ **Emulating (IRE)**[81] 6003 3-9-2 **72** ShaneKelly 5 66
(James Fanshawe) *in rr: racd on outer and rdn over 2f out: hdwy sn after: wknd over 1f out* **9/2**1
4445 **14** 8 **Lady Bayside**[13] 7785 5-9-4 **70** TomMcLaughlin 6 48
(Malcolm Saunders) *chsd ldrs: rdn 3f out: sn btn* **20/1**

2m 6.44s (-1.56) **Going Correction** -0.075s/f (Stan) 14 Ran SP% **119.9**
WFA 3 from 4yo+ 4lb
Speed ratings (Par 103): **103,102,101,101,100 100,99,99,99,98 98,98,97,90**
toteswingers 1&2 £11.10, 2&3 £35.90, 1&3 £40.60 CSF £51.42 CT £1507.37 TOTE £8.70: £3.40, £2.80, £6.30; EX 68.70 Trifecta £2320.50 Part won. Pool: £3094.11 - 0.35 winning units..
Owner Craig and Maureen Buckingham **Bred** A Christodoulou **Trained** Averham Park, Notts

FOCUS
A fair handicap. The winner was close to this year's best.

7971 BRITISH STALLION STUDS EBF MAIDEN STKS (DIV I) 7f (P)
5:00 (5:03) (Class 5) 2-Y-0 **£2,911** (£866; £324; £324) **Stalls** Low

Form RPR
0 **1** **Secret Archive (USA)**[14] 7766 2-9-5 0 JimCrowley 7 72+
(Ralph Beckett) *mde all: rdn over 1f out: hld on wl in clsng stages* **6/1**3
2 *nk* **Quiet Warrior (IRE)** 2-9-5 0 MartinHarley 2 72+
(Marco Botti) *in tch hdwy 2f out: chsd wnr fnl f: fin strly: jst failed* **7/1**
0 **3** 1¾ **Hanno (USA)**[89] 5718 2-9-5 0 AndreaAtzeni 1 67
(Ed Dunlop) *chsd ldrs: rdn and styd on same pce fr over 1f out: jnd for 3rd last stride* **3/1**2
5 **3** *dht* **D'Avignon (USA)**[28] 7461 2-9-5 0 RobertHavlin 6 67
(John Gosden) *chsd ldrs: rdn and one pce 2f out: rallied fnl f and kpt on to share 3rd last stride* **5/4**1
5 1¼ **Shushu Sugartown (IRE)** 2-9-0 0 JamieSpencer 4 59
(Ian Williams) *chsd ldr: drvn and green over 1f out: wknd ins fnl f* **8/1**
6 ¾ **Castorienta** 2-9-0 0 LukeMorris 9 57+
(George Baker) *s.i.s: in rr: drvn over 2f out: kapet on fnl f: no imp on ldrs* **33/1**

The Form Book Flat, Raceform Ltd, Compton, RG20 6NL.

00 **7** 1 1/4 **Comanchero (IRE)**[14] 7766 2-9-5 0 DavidProbert 5 59
(Andrew Balding) *mid-div: rdn and sme hdwy 2f out: styd on same pce fr over 1f out* **50/1**
8 3 3/4 **Kirkman (IRE)** 2-9-5 0 TedDurcan 8 49
(James Bethell) *s.i.s: in rr: drvn and mod prog over 2f out: nvr any ch* **20/1**
9 1/2 **Stilla Afton** 2-9-0 0 MartinDwyer 3 43
(Marcus Tregoning) *s.i.s: outpcd* **25/1**

1m 27.41s (1.41) **Going Correction** -0.075s/f (Stan) **9** Ran SP% **120.9**
Speed ratings (Par 96): **88,87,85,85,84 83,81,77,77**WIN: Secret Archive: £8.30 Places: £2.10, £2.20. Hanno: £0.60 D'Avignon: £0.50 Secret Archive, £2.20 Quiet Warrior; Exacta: £74.00; CSF: £46.98; Trifecta: SA/QW/DA: £68.50, SA/Q £115.60; toteswinger:DA&QW £0.90, DA&SA, H&QW £1.50, H&SA £3.00, QW&SA £6.7027 CSF £Owner CT £Thurloe Thoroughbreds XXXII TOTE £Bred: £Hickory Tree Farm, £Trained, £Kimpton, Hants.

FOCUS
A modest juvenile maiden in terms of previous form, but a few decent types may well emerge from this contest.

7972 BRITISH STALLION STUDS EBF MAIDEN STKS (DIV II) 7f (P)
5:30 (5:33) (Class 5) 2-Y-O **£2,911** (£866; £432; £216) **Stalls** Low

Form RPR
0 **1** **Naadirr (IRE)**[28] 7467 2-9-5 0 MartinHarley 3 75+
(Marco Botti) *mde all: pushed clr over 1f out: unchal* **2/1**[1]
0 **2** 2 1/2 **Mr Greenspan (USA)**[19] 7654 2-9-5 0 GeorgeBaker 6 68+
(Richard Hannon) *s.i.s: in rr: hdwy over 1f out: styd on wl to take 2nd fnl 110yds: no ch w wnr* **16/1**
0 **3** 2 **Truancy (IRE)**[75] 6174 2-9-5 0 RobertWinston 9 63
(K R Burke) *chsd ldrs: wnt 2nd appr fnl f but nvr any ch w wnr: outpcd into 3rd fnl 110yds* **7/1**[3]
4 1/2 **Examiner (IRE)** 2-9-5 0 JoeFanning 7 62+
(William Haggas) *in rr: pushed along 2f out: styd on fnl f: kpt on in clsng stages* **8/1**
5 1/2 **Gone With The Wind (GER)** 2-9-5 0 GrahamLee 4 60+
(Jeremy Noseda) *chsd ldrs: drvn over 2f out: outpcd fnl f* **5/1**[2]
0 **6** 1 1/4 **Westminster (IRE)**[20] 7647 2-9-5 0 RobertHavlin 10 57
(John Gosden) *chsd ldrs: rdn 2f out: wknd appr fnl f* **7/1**[3]
00 **7** shd **Dalarosso**[28] 7469 2-9-5 0 AndreaAtzeni 2 57
(Ed Dunlop) *in rr: sme hdwy 2f out: wknd appr fnl f* **20/1**
8 6 **Moneypennie** 2-9-0 0 MartinDwyer 1 35+
(Marcus Tregoning) *slowly away: a in rr* **50/1**
224 **9** 1/2 **Travis Bickle (IRE)**[56] 6739 2-9-5 69 SeanLevey 5 39
(Sylvester Kirk) *in tch: rdn over 2f out: wknd wl over 1f out* **5/1**[2]
00 **10** 1 **Bonnie Fairy**[70] 6298 2-9-0 0 BenCurtis 8 31
(Michael Appleby) *in rr: sme hdwy over 2f out: sn wknd* **50/1**

1m 26.43s (0.43) **Going Correction** -0.075s/f (Stan) **10** Ran SP% **117.3**
Speed ratings (Par 96): **94,91,88,88,87 86,86,79,78,77**
toteswingers 1&2 £8.00, 2&3 £24.50, 1&3 £4.50 CSF £38.66 TOTE £2.60: £1.30, £5.00, £2.40; EX 36.70 Trifecta £282.00 Pool: £3888.65 - 10.33 winning units..
Owner Sheikh Mohammed Bin Khalifa Al Maktoum **Bred** Castlemartin Sky & Skymarc Farm **Trained** Newmarket, Suffolk

FOCUS
The second division of the juvenile maiden produced a taking winner.

7973 JUMP RACING HERE ON MONDAY 25.11.13 NURSERY H'CAP 7f (P)
6:00 (6:00) (Class 6) (0-65,65) 2-Y-O **£1,940** (£577; £288; £144) **Stalls** Low

Form RPR
0105 **1** **Fiftyshadesfreed (IRE)**[6] 7878 2-9-6 **64** JimCrowley 1 68
(George Baker) *chsd ldrs: drvn over 2f out: styd on u.p to ld fnl 75yds* **11/4**[2]
0605 **2** 1 **Drinkuptrig (IRE)**[61] 6605 2-9-3 **61** AdamBeschizza 6 62
(Stuart Williams) *s.i.s: sn rcvrd and led 4f out: pushed along over 2f out: kpt on tl hdd and outpcd fnl 75yds* **9/4**[1]
646 **3** nk **Mersad (IRE)**[20] 7646 2-9-7 **65** LukeMorris 8 65
(James Tate) *in rr: drvn 2f out: hdwy over 1f out: kpt on fnl f to cl on 2nd but no imp on wnr* **4/1**[3]
0000 **4** 2 1/4 **Charleys Angel**[6] 7878 2-7-13 **46** JemmaMarshall(3) 2 40
(Pat Phelan) *t.k.h: chsd ldrs: rdn over 2f out: wknd ins fnl f* **25/1**
4050 **5** 1 **Royal Bushida**[6] 7878 2-8-7 **51** RaulDaSilva 7 43
(Derek Shaw) *stdd s: swtchd rt and t.k.h: hdwy to dispute 2nd 2f out: sn rdn: wknd ins fnl f* **14/1**
4665 **6** 6 **Elite Freedom (IRE)**[21] 7623 2-9-0 **58** JoeFanning 4 34
(Jo Hughes) *sn led: hdd 4f out: wknd over 1f out* **7/1**
550 **7** 1 1/4 **Solent Lad (USA)**[50] 6923 2-8-11 **55** (p) AndreaAtzeni 3 27
(Robert Eddery) *outpcd most of way* **12/1**
0663 **8** 6 **Trinity Lorraine (IRE)**[13] 7788 2-8-1 **45** (p) NickyMackay 5
(Alan Bailey) *chsd ldrs on outside: wknd ins fnl 3f* **14/1**

1m 26.41s (0.41) **Going Correction** -0.075s/f (Stan) **8** Ran SP% **114.8**
Speed ratings (Par 94): **94,92,92,89,88 81,80,73**
toteswingers 1&2 £1.80, 2&3 £1.60, 1&3 £2.00 CSF £9.42 CT £23.50 TOTE £3.10: £1.10, £1.10, £2.10; EX 12.00 Trifecta £24.70 Pool: £2662.81 - 80.79 winning units..
Owner Team Fifty **Bred** Bernard Cloney **Trained** Manton, Wilts

FOCUS
A modest nursery.

7974 WINNERS ARE WELCOME AT BETDAQ E B F STALLIONS HYDE STKS (LISTED RACE) 1m (P)
6:30 (6:31) (Class 1) 3-Y-O+
£22,684 (£8,600; £4,304; £2,144; £1,076; £540) **Stalls** Low

Form RPR
1505 **1** **Sirius Prospect (USA)**[32] 7364 5-9-4 105 RobertWinston 3 103
(Dean Ivory) *chsd ldrs: led over 1f out: hrd pressed fnl 110yds: hld on wl cl home* **8/1**[3]
0022 **2** hd **Bertiewhittle**[46] 7014 5-9-2 102 GrahamGibbons 4 101
(David Barron) *in rr: hdwy ins fnl 2f: styd on wl fnl f to press wnr in clsng stages: a jst hld* **8/1**[3]
5422 **3** shd **Galician**[20] 7649 4-8-11 99 JoeFanning 11 95
(Mark Johnston) *sn led tl hdd wl over 4f out: styd chsng ldrs: styd on wl to press wnr in clsng stages but a jst hld* **14/1**
0254 **4** 2 1/4 **Enrol**[20] 7649 4-8-11 100 (p) ShaneKelly 6 90
(Sir Michael Stoute) *in tch: hdwy and nt clr run appr fnl f: styd on again in clsng stages: nt trble ldng trio* **14/1**
1411 **5** 1 **Graphic (IRE)**[14] 7775 4-9-2 110 (p) JamieSpencer 10 93
(William Haggas) *chsd ldrs: drvn and styd on same pce fnl 2f* **5/4**[1]
0313 **6** hd **Big Whiskey (IRE)**[15] 7742 3-9-0 80 JenniferFerguson 9 91?
(Edward Creighton) *chsd ldrs: led wl over 4f out: hdd over 1f out: wknd ins fnl f* **66/1**
1-03 **7** 1 1/4 **Tullius (IRE)**[18] 7698 5-9-2 109 DavidProbert 1 90
(Andrew Balding) *in rr: hdwy and drvn over 2f out: chsd ldrs over 1f out: wknd ins fnl f* **5/2**[2]
3144 **8** 3 1/4 **Emerald Wilderness (IRE)**[270] 777 9-9-2 0 FrederikTylicki 2 82
(Mark Rimmer) *in tch: hdwy to chse ldrs 2f out: wknd ins fnl f* **33/1**
2433 **9** 1 1/4 **It's My Time**[25] 7546 4-8-11 67 TonyHamilton 5 74?
(Richard Fahey) *s.i.s: towards rr most of way* **33/1**
6-00 **10** 4 1/2 **Malilla (IRE)**[11] 7821 3-8-9 88 JohnFahy 7 63
(Clive Cox) *chsd ldrs: wknd over 2f out* **50/1**

1m 37.45s (-2.35) **Going Correction** -0.075s/f (Stan)
WFA 3 from 4yo+ 2lb **10** Ran SP% **117.9**
Speed ratings (Par 111): **108,107,107,105,104 104,103,99,98,94**
toteswingers 1&2 £12.40, 2&3 £14.70, 1&3 £10.20 CSF £68.95 TOTE £9.50: £2.60, £3.20, £3.00; EX 70.20 Trifecta £684.30 Pool: £4187.39 - 4.58 winning units..
Owner Miss N Yarrow **Bred** Brookdale And Dr Ted Folkerth **Trained** Radlett, Herts
■ Stewards' Enquiry : Frederik Tylicki two-day ban: careless riding (Dec 4-5)

FOCUS
A good quality Listed contest. However there are doubts over the bare form with the sixth and ninth not beaten too far. The principals are rated bit off their bests in the circumstances.

7975 BETDAQ - THE SPORTS BETTING EXCHANGE H'CAP 2m (P)
7:00 (7:00) (Class 2) (0-105,91) 3-Y-O+
£11,827 (£3,541; £1,770; £885; £442; £222) **Stalls** Low

Form RPR
4364 **1** **Arch Villain (IRE)**[47] 6992 4-9-13 **90** (b) JimCrowley 4 101
(Amanda Perrett) *chsd ldrs: wnt 2nd ins fnl 3f: led u.p 1f out: styd on wl in clsng stages* **7/4**[1]
3420 **2** 3/4 **Theology**[10] 7660 6-9-9 **86** FrederikTylicki 9 96
(Steve Gollings) *trckd ldr: led over 3f out: drvn and styd on fr 2f out: hdd 1f out: kpt on but a jst hld by wnr* **14/1**
6021 **3** 7 **Perennial**[48] 6984 4-9-6 **83** GrahamLee 6 85
(Philip Kirby) *in tch: hdwy 3f out: styd on u.p fnl 2f: no imp on ldng duo* **4/1**[2]
-013 **4** nk **Shelford (IRE)**[19] 7660 4-9-9 **86** BenCurtis 2 87
(Michael Appleby) *chsd ldrs: hdwy to cl on ldrs over 3f out: outpcd fnl 2f* **9/1**
0 **5** nk **Cullentry Royal**[38] 7230 5-10-0 **91** (p) GaryCarroll 5 92
(J F Levins, Ire) *in rr: rdn on outer over 3f out: styd on u.p ins fnl f: nvr any ch* **8/1**
0310 **6** 3/4 **Be Perfect (USA)**[17] 7723 4-9-9 **86** TomEaves 1 86
(David Nicholls) *in rr but in tch: hdwy 3f out: chsd ldrs over 2f out: wknd over 1f out* **6/1**[3]
4400 **7** nk **Nave (USA)**[14] 7765 6-9-2 **79** MartinLane 3 79
(David Simcock) *in rr: rdn 3f out: mod prog fnl f* **20/1**
0001 **8** 73 **Masterful Act (USA)**[15] 7757 6-9-13 **90** JoeFanning 8
(Alan McCabe) *led: hdd over 3f out: wknd qckly: t.o* **8/1**

3m 24.44s (-5.66) **Going Correction** -0.075s/f (Stan) **8** Ran SP% **114.3**
Speed ratings (Par 109): **111,110,107,106,106 106,106,69**
toteswingers 1&2 £7.60, 2&3 £24.80, 1&3 £2.00 CSF £28.82 CT £87.67 TOTE £2.20: £1.20, £3.90, £1.80; EX 28.30 Trifecta £137.90 Pool: £2746.70 - 14.93 winning units..
Owner Mr & Mrs F Cotton, Mr & Mrs P Conway **Bred** Summerhill Bloodstock **Trained** Pulborough, W Sussex

FOCUS
A decent staying handicap in which they went a particularly solid gallop. The first pair were clear and the winner posted a personal best.

7976 BETDAQ 1ST UK RACE COMMISSION FREE H'CAP 1m 4f (P)
7:30 (7:30) (Class 4) (0-85,85) 3-Y-O+ **£4,690** (£1,395; £697; £348) **Stalls** Centre

Form RPR
2053 **1** **Presburg (IRE)**[15] 7739 4-8-12 **78** OisinMurphy(5) 6 89
(Joseph Tuite) *in tch: drvn and hdwy fr 2f out: styd on to ld fnl 150yds: styd on wl* **5/1**[2]
2310 **2** 1 3/4 **Grendisar (IRE)**[25] 7542 3-9-2 **83** (p) MartinHarley 4 91
(Marco Botti) *in rr gd hdwy fr 2f out: led wl over 1f out: hdd fnl 150yds: styd on same pce* **7/1**
3/0- **3** nk **Clerk's Choice (IRE)**[217] 3610 7-9-0 **75** SteveDrowne 12 83
(William Jarvis) *hld up in rr: shkn up 2f out: styd on wl fnl f to take 3rd in clsng stages* **20/1**
6254 **4** 1/2 **Burnham**[14] 7765 4-9-4 **79** (p) RobertHavlin 3 86
(Hughie Morrison) *chsd ldrs: led ins fnl 2f: hdd wl over 1f out: one pce fnl f* **14/1**
0365 **5** 3/4 **Icebuster**[54] 6801 5-9-10 **85** DavidProbert 9 91
(Rod Millman) *in rr: hdwy over 1f out: styd on in clsng stages* **6/1**[3]
3230 **6** 3/4 **Silver Dixie (USA)**[54] 6801 3-9-1 **82** JimCrowley 8 87
(Peter Hedger) *chsd ldrs: ev ch wl over 1f out: wknd ins fnl f* **7/1**
3125 **7** 2 1/4 **Nimiety**[74] 6200 4-9-4 **79** JoeFanning 1 80
(Mark Johnston) *chsd ldrs: ev ch ins fnl 2f: wknd fnl f* **16/1**
5450 **8** 5 **John Biscuit (IRE)**[14] 7765 5-9-5 **80** JamieSpencer 5 73
(Andrew Balding) *chsd ldrs: rdn on outer 3f out: sn btn* **16/1**
2202 **9** 1 **Scottish Star**[15] 7739 5-9-0 **80** RyanTate(5) 7 71
(James Eustace) *in rr: sme hdwy on outside 3f out: sn wknd* **7/1**
6000 **10** 1/2 **Nanton (USA)**[39] 7193 11-9-6 **81** GrahamLee 13 72
(Jim Goldie) *towards rr most of way* **33/1**
4163 **11** 1 **Deserted**[14] 7765 3-8-11 **78** AndreaAtzeni 2 67
(Luca Cumani) *led: hdd & wknd ins fnl 2f* **3/1**[1]
0430 **12** 1 3/4 **King Olav (UAE)**[56] 6750 8-8-12 **73** LukeMorris 10 59
(Tony Carroll) *chsd ldr: rdn over 3f out: wknd 2f out* **33/1**
0113 **13** 33 **One Pursuit (IRE)**[15] 7757 5-9-2 **77** GeorgeBaker 11 10
(Brendan Powell) *chsd ldrs 7f* **14/1**

2m 31.06s (-3.44) **Going Correction** -0.075s/f (Stan)
WFA 3 from 4yo+ 6lb **13** Ran SP% **129.2**
Speed ratings (Par 105): **108,106,106,106,105 105,103,100,99,99 98,97,75**
toteswingers 1&2 £11.40, 2&3 £61.70, 1&3 £36.80 CSF £42.77 CT £670.73 TOTE £6.70: £2.90, £1.90, £9.10; EX 53.70 Trifecta £1929.90 Part won. Pool: £2573.20 - 0.56 winning units..
Owner www.isehove.com **Bred** Limestone And Tara Studs **Trained** Great Shefford, Berks

FOCUS
A decent middle-distance handicap, and once again there was no hanging about. Sound form which could be rated slightly better.
T/Plt: £125.10 to a £1 stake. Pool of £78917.96 - 460.50 winning tickets. T/Qpdt: £22.50 to a £1 stake. Pool of £8893.25 - 292.30 winning tickets. ST

7922 LINGFIELD (L-H)

Wednesday, November 20

OFFICIAL GOING: Standard

Wind: light breeze across Weather: heavy showers

7977 32RED CASINO CLAIMING STKS 7f (P)

12:00 (12:02) (Class 6) 2-Y-O £2,045 (£603; £302) Stalls Low

Form RPR

004 1 **One Penny Piece**[83] 5926 2-7-11 72 (t) DannyBrock(5) 1 67
(Philip McBride) *disputing ld: clr ldr and sn 3 l clr 2f out: kpt on: rdn out* 7/4[2]

0365 2 1¼ **Sheacheval (IRE)**[33] 7352 2-8-1 62 ow1 (p) MartinLane 2 62
(J S Moore) *trckd ldrs: rdn over 2f out: hdwy ent fnl f: sn chsng wnr: drifted lft: kpt on* 9/2[3]

05 3 2½ **Rose Buck**[13] 7790 2-8-1 0 ow1 RaulDaSilva 5 55
(Paul Cole) *trckd ldrs: rdn 2f out: kpt on same pce* 14/1

3204 4 1¼ **Intense Feeling (IRE)**[8] 7846 2-8-3 74 LukeMorris 3 54
(David Evans) *disp ld tl rdn 2f out: sn hld by wnr: hung lft: wknd ent fnl f* 5/4[1]

0310 5 5 **El Duque**[161] 3189 2-8-2 58 ow1 (v[1]) RyanWhile(7) 4 46
(Bill Turner) *awkward leaving stalls: racd keenly for over 2f: trckd ldrs: rdn over 2f out: wknd over 1f out* 33/1

1m 25.62s (0.82) **Going Correction** -0.10s/f (Stan) 5 Ran SP% 108.6

Speed ratings (Par 94): **91,89,86,85,79**

CSF £9.51 TOTE £2.20: £1.10, £2.50; EX 12.40 Trifecta £32.20 Pool: £1272.95 - 29.56 winning units..

Owner P J McBride **Bred** Mrs Sarah Hamilton **Trained** Newmarket, Suffolk

FOCUS

Four fillies against one gelding in this moderate claimer following the withdrawal of Caroline's Beach at the start. Three of the five remaining runners carried 1lb overweight. They went a steady temp and the winner probably didn't need to match her balance of form.

7978 32RED/BRITISH STALLION STUDS E B F MAIDEN STKS 6f (P)

12:30 (12:31) (Class 5) 2-Y-O £3,067 (£905; £453) Stalls Low

Form RPR

4555 1 **Drive On (IRE)**[56] 6749 2-9-5 52 (p) JohnFahy 10 71
(Eve Johnson Houghton) *hld up in last trio: gd hdwy on inner wl over 1f out: swtchd rt jst ins fnl f: led fnl 120yds: r.o strly* 20/1

06 2 1¼ **Suitsus**[20] 7647 2-9-5 0 SteveDrowne 1 67
(Peter Makin) *mid-div: rdn and hdwy over 1f out: ev ch briefly 120yds: kpt on but nt gng pce of wnr* 66/1

65 3 ½ **Penny Sixpence (FR)**[29] 7435 2-9-0 0 (b[1]) RobertHavlin 8 61
(John Gosden) *mid-div: rdn over 1f out: sn hung rt: fin up on stands' side rails but styd on wl fnl f* 6/1

0 4 1 **Bretherton**[93] 5577 2-9-5 0 TonyHamilton 7 63+
(Richard Fahey) *s.i.s: sn pushed along towards rr of midfield: making hdwy whn hmpd over 1f out: running on whn hmpd again ins fnl f: kpt on to snatch 4th fnl stride* 7/2[1]

06 5 hd **Thataboy (IRE)**[124] 4477 2-9-5 0 RichardKingscote 6 62
(Tom Dascombe) *disp ld: rdn into def advantage jst over 1f out: kpt on but no ex whn hdd fnl 120yds: lost 4th fnl stride* 5/1[3]

3432 6 hd **Flicksta (USA)**[31] 7393 2-9-5 69 LukeMorris 12 62
(Ronald Harris) *mid-div: rdn whn nt clr run over 1f out tl ent fnl f: kpt on* 7/1

54 7 3¼ **Dutchartcollector**[7] 7860 2-9-5 0 GeorgeBaker 11 52
(Gary Moore) *s.i.s: bhd: sme late prog: nvr a danger* 10/1

0 8 nse **Locky Taylor (IRE)**[33] 7341 2-9-5 0 JamieSpencer 5 52
(Kevin Ryan) *disp ld rdn 2f out: hdd jst over 1f out: hld whn hanging bdly rt fnl 120yds* 9/2[2]

04 9 ½ **He's My Boy (IRE)**[20] 7638 2-9-5 0 FrederikTylicki 2 50
(James Fanshawe) *trckd ldrs: rdn 2f out: wknd fnl f* 9/2[2]

50 10 nse **Amontillado (IRE)**[165] 3107 2-9-0 0 KieranO'Neill 3 45
(Richard Hannon) *a struggling towards rr* 33/1

00 11 1¼ **Febrayer Star (IRE)**[13] 7790 2-9-5 0 JimCrowley 4 46
(Robert Cowell) *wnt to s early: trckd ldrs: rdn over 2f out: one pce whn hmpd ins fnl f* 100/1

000 12 1¼ **Warm Order**[31] 7393 2-9-0 55 DavidProbert 9 38
(Tony Carroll) *trckd ldrs: rdn 2f out: wknd jst ins fnl f* 100/1

1m 11.32s (-0.58) **Going Correction** -0.10s/f (Stan) 12 Ran SP% 122.3

Speed ratings (Par 96): **99,97,96,95,95 94,90,90,89,89 88,86**

toteswingers 1&2 £41.60, 2&3 £32.30, 1&3 £13.20 CSF £923.61 TOTE £33.90: £8.90, £18.80, £2.60; EX 540.20 Trifecta £1503.10 Part won. Pool: £2004.20 - 0.48 winning units..

Owner Miss E Johnson Houghton **Bred** Nicola And Eleanor Kent **Trained** Blewbury, Oxon

FOCUS

An ordinary maiden. The leaders may have gone off too quick and this was a race in which those held up were favoured. A compressed finish and the form is rated cautiously.

7979 32RED.COM NURSERY H'CAP 1m (P)

1:00 (1:00) (Class 5) (0-75,75) 2-Y-O £2,726 (£805; £402) Stalls High

Form RPR

5543 1 **Castle Combe (IRE)**[13] 7779 2-9-4 72 (v) MartinDwyer 3 78
(Marcus Tregoning) *little slowly away: racd keenly trcking ldrs: wnt 2nd after 2f: rdn to chal 2f out: led narrowly ent fnl f: strly pressed but holding on wl fnl 50yds: all out* 9/2[2]

01 2 nk **Elysian Prince**[78] 6079 2-9-7 75 JimCrowley 4 80+
(Paul Cole) *led: lost footing briefly over 2f out: sn rdn and strly pressed: narrowly hdd ent fnl f: kpt on w ev ch: hld fnl 50yds* 7/4[1]

6215 3 1 **Art Wave (IRE)**[49] 6935 2-9-7 75 MartinHarley 1 78
(Marco Botti) *w ldr for 2f: trckd ldng pair: rdn 2f out: kpt on ins fnl f but nt quite gng pce to get on terms* 7/4[1]

4064 4 2 **Dry Your Eyes (IRE)**[51] 6904 2-8-10 64 JoeFanning 2 62
(Mark Johnston) *trckd ldrs: rdn 2f out: sn one pce* 12/1

5340 5 2½ **Habdab**[35] 7309 2-9-1 69 SeanLevey 6 62
(Richard Hannon) *stdd s: in last pair but cl up: rdn 2f out: nvr gng pce to get involved* 20/1

603 6 ½ **Bognor (USA)**[29] 7441 2-9-1 69 LukeMorris 5 61
(Jo Hughes) *in last pair but cl up: rdn 2f out: nvr gng pce to get involved* 10/1[3]

1m 38.07s (-0.13) **Going Correction** -0.10s/f (Stan) 6 Ran SP% 112.5

Speed ratings (Par 96): **96,95,94,92,90 89**

toteswingers 1&2 £1.60, 2&3 £1.70, 1&3 £1.80 CSF £12.90 TOTE £6.40: £2.90, £1.10; EX 16.40 Trifecta £30.90 Pool: £1533.37 - 37.19 winning units..

Owner Gaskell, Wallis & Partners **Bred** Old Long Hill Ballinteskin Stud Ltd **Trained** Whitsbury, Hants

FOCUS

The gallop was modest in this ordinary nursery and those that raced up with the pace were favoured this time. The form makes sense but the runner-up was arguably unlucky.

7980 LADBROKES H'CAP (DIV I) 1m (P)

1:30 (1:30) (Class 6) (0-55,55) 3-Y-0+ £2,045 (£603; £302) Stalls High

Form RPR

0654 1 **Skidby Mill (IRE)**[28] 7465 3-9-2 52 JimCrowley 4 60
(Laura Mongan) *hld up: gd hdwy on inner fr 2f out: rdn over 1f out: led ins fnl f: kpt on wl* 8/1

4 2 ½ **Better Value (IRE)**[32] 7386 3-9-1 51 (p) BenCurtis 11 58
(Noel Quinlan) *led: rdn 2f out: hdd ins fnl f: kpt on gamely but no ex* 20/1

5014 3 ¾ **Quadriga (IRE)**[5] 7907 3-9-3 53 AndreaAtzeni 5 58
(Robert Eddery) *mid-div: smooth hdwy on inner fr over 3f out: effrt in 2nd over 1f out: sn sltly outpcd: styd on again fnl 120yds* 2/1[1]

5006 4 ½ **Purley Queen (IRE)**[12] 7807 4-9-5 53 MartinHarley 2 58
(Sylvester Kirk) *hld up: pushed along and hdwy 2f out: sn rdn to chse ldrs: kpt on same pce fnl f* 14/1

5022 5 2½ **Legal Legacy**[20] 7639 7-9-2 55 DannyBrock(5) 8 54
(Lee Carter) *mid-div: pushed along 2f out: rdn over 1f out: kpt on fnl f but nt gng pce to get on terms* 3/1[2]

0606 6 1½ **Birdie King**[34] 7322 3-9-4 54 [1] GeorgeBaker 1 49
(Gary Moore) *sn trcking ldr: rdn over 2f out: sn one pce* 10/1

0065 7 ½ **Strategic Action (IRE)**[13] 7784 4-9-6 54 (p) RobertHavlin 3 49
(Linda Jewell) *mid-div: outpcd wl over 1f out: kpt on but n.d fnl f* 6/1[3]

1000 8 3¼ **Thewinningmachine**[43] 7091 4-9-4 52 LiamJones 10 39
(Jo Hughes) *trckd ldrs: rdn over 2f out: wknd over 1f out* 25/1

4060 9 10 **South Kenter (USA)**[35] 7292 4-9-0 48 (p) JamieSpencer 7 12
(Heather Main) *stdd s: a towards rr: eased ins fnl f* 16/1

4400 R **Sakhee's Alround**[6] 7885 3-9-0 50 (b[1]) AdamBeschizza 6
(K F Clutterbuck) *wnt to s early: ref to r: tk no part* 20/1

1m 37.49s (-0.71) **Going Correction** -0.10s/f (Stan)

WFA 3 from 4yo+ 2lb 10 Ran SP% 118.7

Speed ratings (Par 101): **99,98,97,97,94 93,92,89,79,**

toteswingers 1&2 £17.10, 2&3 £13.10, 1&3 £3.50 CSF £158.11 CT £456.46 TOTE £9.40: £3.20, £6.80, £2.00; EX 158.10 Trifecta £385.40 Pool: £837.29 - 1.62 winning units..

Owner Ronnie Coates **Bred** Michael O'Mahony **Trained** Epsom, Surrey

FOCUS

A moderate handicap run a bit quicker than division II. The winner is rated up slightly on her 3yo form.

7981 LADBROKES H'CAP (DIV II) 1m (P)

2:00 (2:01) (Class 6) (0-55,55) 3-Y-0+ £2,045 (£603; £302) Stalls High

Form RPR

4022 1 **Squirrel Wood (IRE)**[20] 7644 5-9-5 53 JimCrowley 8 63
(George Baker) *trckd ldrs: rdn to ld ent fnl f: kpt on wl: rdn out* 7/2[1]

3200 2 ½ **Fonterutoli (IRE)**[21] 7622 6-9-4 52 (e) RobertHavlin 4 61
(Roger Ingram) *mid-div: rdn and hdwy over 1f out: kpt on to press wnr ins fnl f: a being jst hld* 8/1

1503 3 3 **Gypsy Rider**[20] 7643 4-9-0 55 NedCurtis(7) 3 57
(Roger Curtis) *mid-div: hdwy whn nt clr run and swtchd rt ent fnl f: r.o to snatch 3rd fnl stride* 16/1

3002 4 hd **Litmus (USA)**[4] 7930 4-9-0 48 (b) LukeMorris 2 49
(Simon Dow) *led: rdn and hdd ent fnl f: kpt on but no ex* 5/1[3]

34-0 5 ½ **Cativo Cavallino**[20] 7639 10-8-13 50 NataliaGemelova(3) 5 50
(John E Long) *mid-div rdn wl over 1f out: no imp tl r.o ins fnl f* 16/1

5300 6 1¼ **Birdie Queen**[51] 6902 3-9-5 55 [1] GeorgeBaker 1 51
(Gary Moore) *racd keenly trcking ldrs: rdn and ch ent fnl f: wknd fnl 140yds* 12/1

3066 7 nk **Uncle Fred**[13] 7784 8-9-2 55 DanielMuscutt(5) 9 52
(Patrick Chamings) *hld up bhd: sme late prog: nvr trble ldrs* 10/1

1640 8 ½ **Cuthbert (IRE)**[103] 5232 6-9-1 49 (b) JimmyQuinn 6 45
(Michael Attwater) *hld up towards rr: styd on fnl f: nvr trbld ldrs* 25/1

5004 9 nk **Arte Del Calcio**[14] 6491 4-9-0 48 DavidProbert 7 43
(Tony Carroll) *s.i.s: towards rr: styd on fnl f: nvr a threat* 33/1

0604 10 3¼ **Norphin**[34] 7322 3-9-4 54 (p) MartinHarley 10 40
(Denis Coakley) *w ldr: rdn over 2f out: wknd over 1f out* 10/1

6346 11 1¼ **Hamble**[29] 7455 4-9-1 54 (t) ShelleyBirkett(5) 12 39
(Julia Feilden) *s.i.s fr wd draw: towards rr: c wd u.p ent st: wknd fnl f* 9/2[2]

0-60 12 2½ **First Glance**[95] 5515 4-9-0 48 (p) BenCurtis 11 27
(Michael Appleby) *racd keenly: trckd ldrs tl wknd 2f out* 20/1

1m 37.77s (-0.43) **Going Correction** -0.10s/f (Stan)

WFA 3 from 4yo+ 2lb 12 Ran SP% 117.4

Speed ratings (Par 101): **98,97,94,94,93 92,92,91,91,88 86,84**

toteswingers 1&2 £5.80, 2&3 £26.40, 1&3 £7.30 CSF £30.42 CT £404.20 TOTE £4.10: £2.00, £3.20, £3.20; EX 32.10 Trifecta £482.40 Pool: £1751.74 - 2.72 winning units..

Owner Mrs Richard Hambro **Bred** Cotswold Stud **Trained** Manton, Wilts

FOCUS

The winning time was 0.28sec slower than the first division. A small best from the winner, whose penultimate run has been frnaked.

7982 COMPARE BOOKMAKERS AT BOOKMAKERS.CO.UK H'CAP 6f (P)

2:30 (2:32) (Class 3) (0-95,95) 3-Y-0+ £7,439 (£2,213; £1,106; £553) Stalls Low

Form RPR

6205 1 **Addictive Dream (IRE)**[12] 7803 6-9-6 94 TonyHamilton 8 103
(David Nicholls) *travelled wl w ldr: pushed along upsides over 1f out: led fnl 120yds: a holding on: rdn out* 20/1

1032 2 ¾ **If So**[20] 7642 4-9-3 91 FrederikTylicki 4 98
(James Fanshawe) *trckd ldrs: rdn over 2f out: no imp tl r.o ins fnl f: wnt 2nd towards fin* 11/4[1]

2046 3 hd **Naabegha**[12] 7803 6-9-0 88 AndreaAtzeni 7 94
(Ed de Giles) *towards rr of midfield: rdn over 1f out: r.o strly ins fnl f: wnt 3rd towards fin: nt quite rching wnr but nrly snatched 2nd* 8/1

0460 4 nk **Diamond Charlie (IRE)**[20] 7642 5-8-13 87 GrahamLee 2 92
(Simon Dow) *racd keenly: mid-div: rdn 2f out: wnt 4th over 1f out: lft 3rd briefly fnl 120yds: kpt on but no ex* 33/1

132 5 1¼ **Peace Seeker**[12] 7803 5-9-0 88 WilliamCarson 5 89
(Anthony Carson) *led: rdn and strly pressed fr over 1f out: hdd fnl 120yds: no ex and lost 3 pls nring fin* 12/1

0500 6 1 **Rivellino**[58] 6692 3-9-0 88 MartinHarley 10 86
(K R Burke) *mid-div: rdn over 2f out: kpt on same pce fnl f* 12/1

0054 7 1½ **Stonefield Flyer**[12] 7803 4-9-0 88 TomEaves 9 81
(Keith Dalgleish) *trckd ldrs: rdn over 2f out: sn one pce* 20/1

4220 8 1 **Trader Jack**[60] 6638 4-9-4 92 (b[1]) JimCrowley 1 82
(David Flood) *s.i.s: a towards rr* 8/1

500- 9 1 3/4 **Alben Star (IRE)**424 6468 5-9-6 **94**................................ JamieSpencer 6 78
(Richard Fahey) *a towards rr* **14/1**
1-20 10 1 1/2 **Blessington (IRE)**26 7507 3-9-0 **88**................................ RobertHavlin 12 67
(John Gosden) *steadily away fr wd draw: towards rr: rdn over 2f out: nvr any imp* **7/2**2
0044 11 1/2 **Fair Value (IRE)**78 6078 5-8-8 **87**................................ JackDuern(5) 11 65
(Simon Dow) *mid-div tl dropped in rr after 2f: nt a danger after* **33/1**
0005 12 33 **Prodigality**26 7495 5-9-7 **95**................................ LukeMorris 3 101
(Ronald Harris) *trckd ldrs: rdn in cl 3rd over 1f out: keeping on between ldrs whn lost action fnl 120yds: dismntd* **9/2**3

1m 9.73s (-2.17) **Going Correction** -0.10s/f (Stan) **12** Ran SP% **126.8**
Speed ratings (Par 107): **110,109,108,108,106 105,103,102,99,97 97,53**
toteswingers 1&2 £11.80, 2&3 £9.50, 1&3 £21.90 CSF £76.88 CT £507.45 TOTE £24.40: £6.40, £1.50, £2.50; EX 96.10 Trifecta £914.80 Pool: £3157.94 - 2.58 winning units..
Owner Brian Morton & Pinnacle Dream Partnership **Bred** Eugene Matthews **Trained** Sessay, N Yorks

FOCUS
A decent sprint handicap. The winner is rated to his best form in the past year.

7983 CORAL APP DOWNLOAD FROM THE APP STORE MAIDEN STKS 1m 2f (P)
3:00 (3:03) (Class 5) 3-Y-0+ **£2,726** (£805; £402) **Stalls** Low

Form RPR
203 1 **Swehan (IRE)**13 7781 3-9-5 **67**................................ JamieSpencer 5 75
(Kevin Ryan) *trckd ldrs: rdn to chal over 1f out: led jst ins fnl f: styd on wl* **6/4**1
222 2 1 1/4 **Wilhana (IRE)**13 7791 3-8-11 **69**................................ RossAtkinson(3) 7 67
(Pam Sly) *hld up 5th: rdn into 4th over 2f out: little imp tl styd on fnl f: wnt 2nd fnl stride* **3/1**2
6 3 hd **Frost Fire (USA)**44 7067 3-9-0 **0**................................ JoeFanning 8 67
(Mark Johnston) *pressed ldr: led over 3f out: rdn 2f out: sn pressed: hdd jst ins fnl f: no ex fnl 100yds: lost 2nd fnl stride* **7/2**3
0- 4 5 **Tumbledown (USA)**424 6489 3-9-0 **0**................................ JimCrowley 3 57
(Ed Walker) *trckd ldrs: rdn over 2f out: nt pce to chal: fdd ins fnl f* **9/2**
3050 5 7 **Kaylee**26 7508 4-9-1 **46**................................ WilliamTwiston-Davies(3) 4 43
(Brett Johnson) *slowly away: in last: tk clsr order 4f out: rdn over 2f out: sn btn* **66/1**
0 6 23 **Spessartine (IRE)**35 7311 3-9-5 **0**................................ AndreaAtzeni 1
(Robert Eddery) *led tl rdn over 3f out: wknd rapidly: t.o* **14/1**

2m 4.77s (-1.83) **Going Correction** -0.10s/f (Stan)
WFA 3 from 4yo 4lb **6** Ran SP% **113.6**
Speed ratings (Par 103): **103,102,101,97,92 73**
toteswingers 1&2 £1.40, 2&3 £2.50, 1&3 £1.30 CSF £6.44 TOTE £2.70: £1.10, £2.20; EX 5.60 Trifecta £15.60 Pool: £2992.04 - 143.56 winning units..
Owner Mubarak Al Naemi **Bred** Camogue Stud Ltd **Trained** Hambleton, N Yorks

FOCUS
A weak maiden. This could underrate the winner but the form isn't too convincing.

7984 CORAL MOBILE "JUST THREE CLICKS TO BET" AMATEUR RIDERS' H'CAP 1m 4f (P)
3:30 (3:30) (Class 6) (0-65,63) 3-Y-0+ **£1,975** (£607; £303) **Stalls** Low

Form RPR
5600 1 **Linkable**16 7735 4-10-9 **63**................................(tp) MissJenniferPowell(5) 12 69+
(Brendan Powell) *mid-div: hdwy over 3f out: rdn to ld over 1f out: jst hld on to a fast diminishing advantage* **8/1**
0053 2 hd **Royal Marskell**14 7778 4-11-0 **63**................................ MrPCollington 8 69
(K F Clutterbuck) *mid-div: hdwy over 3f out: rdn into 4th over 1f out: styd on strly ins fnl f: jst failed* **7/1**3
3156 3 1/2 **Cabuchon (GER)**14 7767 6-10-2 **56**................................(t) MissHDoyle(5) 6 61
(David Evans) *mid-div: hdwy 2f out: sn rdn: styd on strly ins fnl f: wnt 3rd fnl stride* **5/1**1
4500 4 hd **Epsom Salts**14 7767 8-9-13 **55**................................(p) MissLDempster(7) 1 60
(Pat Phelan) *s.i.s: towards rr: hdwy 5f out to trck ldrs 4f out: led over 3f out: rdn and hdd over 1f out: no ex and lost 2 pls fnl strides* **14/1**
365 5 1/2 **Opus (IRE)**16 7735 4-9-8 **50** oh2 ow1................................ MrSamDavis(7) 14 54+
(Lucy Wadham) *mid-div tl dropped in rr over 2f out: c wd st: swtchd lft fr over 1f out: fin v strly on far side rails: wnt 5th fnl strides* **20/1**
4056 6 1 **Super Duplex**7 7858 6-10-2 **58**................................(t) MissLWilliams(7) 16 60
(Roger Teal) *hld up towards rr: stdy prog on outer fr over 7f out: rdn and ev ch 2f out: fdd ins fnl f* **8/1**
0332 7 3/4 **Estibdaad (IRE)**20 7637 3-10-0 **60**................................(t) MissMBryant(5) 7 61
(Paddy Butler) *in tch whn squeezed up on bnd over 7f out: styd on same pce fr over 1f out* **8/1**
5060 8 shd **Merrjanah**132 4204 5-9-7 **49** oh3................................ MrAFrench(7) 9 50
(John Wainwright) *lost pl whn squeezed up after 2f: mid-div whn hmpd again over 7f out: towards rr and struggling over 2f out: styd on wl fr over 1f out but no ch* **33/1**
2000 9 1 **Gladstone (IRE)**127 4380 5-10-2 **51**................................ MissRachelKing 10 50
(Polly Gundry) *trckd ldrs tl lost pl over 5f out: stl in tch: rdn 2f out: styd on same pce* **8/1**
1213 10 3 1/4 **Baan (USA)**98 5409 10-10-5 **61**................................ MrDeanSmith(7) 3 55
(James Eustace) *stmbld leaving stalls but stl broke wl: restrained to rr: rdn 2f out: nvr threatened* **16/1**
-050 11 2 3/4 **Stadium Of Light (IRE)**9 7498 6-9-11 **49** oh4.......... MissAliceMills(3) 5 39
(Shaun Harris) *a towards rr* **20/1**
5160 12 2 1/4 **Josie's Dream (IRE)**50 4204 5-9-13 **53**.............. MrJamesHughes(5) 15 39
(Jo Hughes) *chsd ldrs tl over 2f out: sn wknd* **25/1**
056/ 13 2 3/4 **Cunning Plan (IRE)**136 7156 6-9-7 **49** oh4........... MissKARandall(7) 11 31
(Raymond York) *prom: led after 3f tl over 3f out: sn wknd* **66/1**
244/ 14 1/2 **What's Up Doc (IRE)**193 881 12-9-12 **54**................................ MrPPilley(7) 13 35
(Lawney Hill) *racd keenly: led for 3f: trckd ldrs tl wknd 2f out* **20/1**
1006 15 1 **Teide Peak (IRE)**90 5672 4-10-8 **62**................................ MrsRWilson(5) 2 41
(Paul D'Arcy) *steadily away: racd keenly towards rr: hdwy after 3f to sit promly 7f out: wknd over 2f out* **6/1**2
00-0 16 32 **Razzle Dazzle 'Em**27 4927 4-9-7 **49** oh4............(t) MissMeganHarris(7) 4
(Shaun Harris) *s.i.s: a bhd: t.o fnl 2f* **66/1**

2m 33.22s (0.22) **Going Correction** -0.10s/f (Stan)
WFA 3 from 4yo+ 6lb **16** Ran SP% **124.5**
Speed ratings (Par 101): **95,94,94,94,94 93,92,92,92,90 88,86,84,84,83 62**
toteswingers 1&2 £17.80, 2&3 £11.50, 1&3 £14.30 CSF £59.20 CT £317.13 TOTE £13.40: £3.30, £2.90, £1.50, £2.90; EX 113.50 Trifecta £1332.80 Pool: £2020.10 - 1.13 winning units..
Owner Jonathan H Ross **Bred** Juddmonte Farms Ltd **Trained** Upper Lambourn, Berks
■ Stewards' Enquiry : Miss Rachel King three-day ban: careless riding (Dec 4,16,tbn)

FOCUS
A moderate amateur riders' event to close the card and they rather finished in a heap. The form is ordinary at best.
T/Plt: £165.90 to a £1 stake. Pool of £51454.63, 226.40 winning tickets. T/Qpdt: £9.90 to a £1 stake. Pool of £4457.36, 331.58 winning tickets. TM

7969 KEMPTON (A.W) (R-H)
Thursday, November 21

OFFICIAL GOING: Standard
Wind: Moderate, half against Weather: Clear

7985 BETVICTOR.COM LIVE - CASINO CLAIMING STKS 6f (P)
4:10 (4:10) (Class 6) 3-Y-0+ **£1,940** (£577; £288; £144) **Stalls** Low

Form RPR
0205 1 **Kuanyao (IRE)**23 7593 7-9-1 **67**................................(v) JoeFanning 6 77
(David Nicholls) *mde all: rdn and hld on wl fnl 2f* **7/1**
/002 2 2 3/4 **Alis Aquilae (IRE)**37 7263 7-9-1 **61**................................ AdamBeschizza 8 69
(Tim Etherington) *a.p: rdn to chse wnr ins fnl f: no imp* **14/1**
0526 3 3/4 **Electric Qatar**23 7601 4-9-7 **78**................................ RichardKingscote 2 73
(Tom Dascombe) *chsd wnr tl no ex ins fnl f* **3/1**1
0050 4 1 **Divine Call**48 6995 6-8-9 **68**................................ DavidProbert 1 58
(Milton Bradley) *mid-div: rdn to chse ldrs over 1f out: styd on same pce* **7/1**
2400 5 3/4 **Red Explorer (USA)**82 5987 3-9-3 **82**................................ FergusSweeney 10 63
(Jamie Osborne) *bhd: pushed along 2f out: r.o fnl f: gng on at fin* **4/1**2
0300 6 1 1/4 **Torres Del Paine**51 6929 6-8-8 **60**.............. WilliamTwiston-Davies(3) 11 54
(Brett Johnson) *bhd tl styd on fnl f* **25/1**
0510 7 1 1/4 **R Woody**36 7314 6-9-1 **70**................................(e) MartinLane 4 54
(Robert Cowell) *chsd ldrs tl wknd over 1f out* **5/1**3
0300 8 1/2 **Steelcut**40 7197 9-8-11 **59**................................(p) MartinDwyer 9 48
(Mark Buckley) *stdd s: towards rr: rdn 2f out: nvr able to chal* **33/1**
4343 9 1/2 **Johnny Splash (IRE)**58 6732 4-8-2 **58**................(v) NathanAlison(5) 3 43
(Roger Teal) *mid-div tl lost pl over 2f out* **20/1**
0500 10 2 **Interakt**21 7652 6-8-6 **58**................................ JohnFahy 7 36
(Joseph Tuite) *s.s: outpcd: a wl bhd* **50/1**
0032 11 3 **Rothesay Chancer**17 7730 5-8-9 **73**................................ GrahamLee 5 30
(Jim Goldie) *in tch tl wknd over 2f out* **6/1**

1m 11.72s (-1.38) **Going Correction** -0.125s/f (Stan) **11** Ran SP% **121.1**
Speed ratings (Par 101): **104,100,99,98,97 95,93,93,92,89 85**
toteswingers 1&2 £14.20, 1&3 £5.90, 2&3 £11.30 CSF £97.91 TOTE £10.50: £3.10, £4.70, £1.10; EX 94.90 Trifecta £228.30 Pool: £3033.44 - 9.96 winning units..
Owner Matt & Lauren Morgan **Bred** Newlands House Stud **Trained** Sessay, N Yorks

FOCUS
This claimer saw a fair winning time.

7986 PHAR PARTNERSHIP NURSERY H'CAP 6f (P)
4:40 (4:42) (Class 6) (0-65,65) 2-Y-0 **£1,940** (£577; £288; £144) **Stalls** Low

Form RPR
6105 1 **Porteous**74 6233 2-9-2 **63**................................ WilliamTwiston-Davies(3) 11 70+
(Mick Channon) *prom: led over 1f out: rdn out* **6/1**3
0032 2 1 **Bazooka (IRE)**14 7788 2-9-2 **63**................................ RobertTart(3) 3 67
(Ed de Giles) *mid-div on rail: swtchd lft and rdn 2f out: r.o fnl f: jst snatched 2nd* **5/2**1
000 3 nk **Coiste Bodhar (IRE)**51 6923 2-9-4 **62**................................ TedDurcan 8 65
(Joseph Tuite) *towards rr: hrd rdn and r.o fnl 2f: clsng at fin* **8/1**
3421 4 nk **Debt Settler (IRE)**6 7900 2-9-7 **65** 6ex................................ JimmyQuinn 6 67
(Luke Dace) *in tch: rdn to chse wnr over 1f out: unable qck ins fnl f: lost 2nd nr fin* **3/1**2
0063 5 3 **Saffire Song**53 6872 2-9-2 **60**................................ RobertWinston 7 53
(Alan Bailey) *led tl over 1f out: wknd fnl f* **10/1**
5005 6 1 **Vodka Chaser (IRE)**47 7036 2-9-2 **60**................................ LiamJones 1 50
(J S Moore) *prom tl hrd rdn and wknd over 1f out* **25/1**
630 7 nk **Birikyno**57 6746 2-9-7 **65**................................ LiamKeniry 12 54
(Mark Usher) *bhd: rdn 2f out: styd on fnl f* **33/1**
5533 8 1 **Caesars Gift (IRE)**15 7771 2-8-13 **64**................................(v1) AdamMcLean(7) 10 50
(Derek Shaw) *plld hrd: wnt prom after 2f: rn wd on bnd 3f out: wknd over 1f out* **6/1**3
3205 9 11 **Zafraaj**32 7394 2-9-6 **64**................................(p) GeorgeBaker 4 17
(Ronald Harris) *s.i.s: a in rr: n.d fnl 2f* **20/1**
034 10 4 1/2 **Sweet Angelica**31 7419 2-9-7 **65**................................ GrahamLee 9 5
(James Given) *chsd ldrs: rdn along after 2f: wknd 2f out* **14/1**

1m 13.17s (0.07) **Going Correction** -0.125s/f (Stan) **10** Ran SP% **120.6**
Speed ratings (Par 94): **94,92,92,91,87 86,86,84,70,64**
toteswingers 1&2 £3.60, 1&3 £9.90, 2&3 £7.70 CSF £21.67 CT £127.74 TOTE £6.90: £2.50, £1.40, £2.50; EX 21.80 Trifecta £441.70 Pool: £3751.72 - 6.36 winning units..
Owner Imperial **Bred** Imperial & Mike Channon Bloodstock Ltd **Trained** West Ilsley, Berks

FOCUS
A moderate nursery. It was a fairly run contest and the form looks fair.

7987 LORICA EMPLOYEE BENEFITS MEDIAN AUCTION MAIDEN STKS 1m (P)
5:10 (5:10) (Class 6) 3-5-Y-0 **£1,940** (£577; £288; £144) **Stalls** Low

Form RPR
3424 1 **Pretty Bubbles**29 7458 4-9-2 **57**................................ FrederikTylicki 6 67
(J R Jenkins) *chsd ldr: led 2f out: rdn clr* **3/1**2
0635 2 2 1/2 **No Win No Fee**23 7605 3-9-5 **58**................................(p) BenCurtis 3 65
(Michael Appleby) *led tl 2f out: sn outpcd by wnr* **11/4**1
035 3 3 1/2 **Trulee Scrumptious**29 7470 4-9-2 **55**................................(be) JimmyQuinn 1 53
(Peter Charalambous) *rdn s: sn chsng ldrs on rail: drvn along and one pce fnl 2f* **6/1**3
3040 4 1/2 **Clary (IRE)**61 6655 3-9-0 **59**................................ RobertWinston 2 51
(James Unett) *bhd: hdwy on inner 4f out: one pce fnl 2f* **8/1**
22 5 2 **Memphis Magic (GER)**28 7490 3-9-5................................(t) GeorgeBaker 10 51
(Ed Walker) *wd: t.k.h: in tch: rdn and no imp fnl 2f* **11/4**1
0- 6 2 1/4 **Little Red Nell (IRE)**532 2864 4-9-2................................ RobertHavlin 5 42
(Martin Bosley) *s.i.s: sme hdwy 3f out: rdn and btn 2f out* **50/1**
052 7 2 1/2 **Clear Loch**7 7873 3-9-5 **60**................................ NickyMackay 8 41
(John Spearing) *chsd ldrs tl wknd 2f out* **14/1**
4-00 8 1/2 **Believe In Me**23 7610 3-8-9 **43**...............: sn struggling ShelleyBirkett(5) 4 34
(Julia Feilden) *twrds rr: rdn 4f out* **50/1**
30 9 2 **Boom**16 7738 3-9-0................................ GrahamLee 7 30
(Olivia Maylam) *t.k.h: dropped to rr 5f out: struggling fnl 3f* **25/1**

1m 38.4s (-1.40) **Going Correction** -0.125s/f (Stan)
WFA 3 from 4yo 2lb **9** Ran SP% **118.2**
Speed ratings (Par 101): **102,99,96,95,93 91,88,88,86**
toteswingers 1&2 £2.40, 1&3 £4.20, 2&3 £3.50 CSF £11.89 TOTE £3.50: £1.50, £1.20, £2.70; EX 16.80 Trifecta £102.20 Pool: £3841.11 - 28.16 winning units..
Owner Mark Goldstein & Mark Callow **Bred** Southill Stud **Trained** Royston, Herts

FOCUS
A weak maiden.

7988 ARBUTHNOT LATHAM 180 YEARS H'CAP (DIV I) 1m (P)
5:40 (5:41) (Class 4) (0-85,85) 3-Y-O+ **£4,690** (£1,395; £697; £348) **Stalls** Low

Form RPR
0300 **1** **Maverik**[21] 7641 5-9-7 **85** JimCrowley 6 95
(William Knight) *mde all: rdn and hld on wl fnl 2f* **7/2**[2]
6000 **2** 3/4 **Chapter And Verse (IRE)**[21] 7641 7-9-5 **83** FrederikTylicki 7 91
(Mike Murphy) *prom: chsd wnr 5f out: kpt on wl fnl f: a jst hld* **14/1**
0003 **3** 1 3/4 **Escape To Glory (USA)**[63] 6549 5-8-12 **76** GrahamLee 2 80
(Michael Dods) *chsd ldrs: rdn and kpt on fnl 2f* **12/1**
3004 **4** shd **Shamir**[42] 7157 6-9-7 **85** FergusSweeney 10 89
(Jo Crowley) *chsd ldrs: rdn over 2f out: kpt on fnl f: fin lame* **16/1**
1250 **5** 3/4 **Naaz (IRE)**[27] 7499 3-9-2 **82** GeorgeBaker 12 83
(Ed Dunlop) *bhd tl r.o u.p fr over 1f out* **12/1**
6401 **6** 3/4 **Well Painted (IRE)**[45] 7071 4-9-1 **84** (tp) NathanAlison(5) 9 85
(William Haggas) *s.i.s: sn in midfield: rdn and lost pl over 2f out: styd on same pce fnl f* **5/2**[1]
5241 **7** 1/2 **Soaring Spirits (IRE)**[26] 7531 3-9-1 **81** (b) RobertWinston 1 79
(Dean Ivory) *t.k.h: chsd wnr 3f: prom tl wknd over 1f out* **8/1**
0320 **8** nk **Noble Citizen (USA)**[21] 7648 8-8-11 **82** (b) LewisWalsh(7) 8 81
(David Simcock) *bhd: sme hdwy over 1f out: n.d* **8/1**
2150 **9** shd **Gracious George (IRE)**[61] 6642 3-8-10 **76** (b) TedDurcan 4 74
(Jimmy Fox) *dwlt: twrds rr: mod effrt 2f out: nvr able to chal* **6/1**[3]
1404 **10** 1/2 **Swift Cedar (IRE)**[70] 6337 3-8-11 **80** RobertTart(3) 3 76
(Alan Jarvis) *s.s: sn in tch on rail: rdn and wknd 2f out* **14/1**
0000 **11** 1 3/4 **Top Offer**[38] 7254 4-8-13 **77** ShaneKelly 5 70
(Peter Crate) *in tch tl rdn and btn 2f out* **25/1**

1m 38.42s (-1.38) **Going Correction** -0.125s/f (Stan)
WFA 3 from 4yo+ 2lb 11 Ran SP% **125.7**
Speed ratings (Par 105): **101,100,98,98,97 96,96,96,96,95 93**
toteswingers 1&2 £11.20, 1&3 £11.70, 2&3 £35.40 CSF £56.18 CT £563.71 TOTE £5.00: £2.30, £6.20, £3.90; EX 74.40 Trifecta £1095.80 Pool: £2528.71 - 1.73 winning units..
Owner A Brooks **Bred** J G Davis & Star Pointe Ltd **Trained** Patching, W Sussex

FOCUS
A competitive handicap.

7989 ARBUTHNOT LATHAM 180 YEARS H'CAP (DIV II) 1m (P)
6:10 (6:10) (Class 4) (0-85,85) 3-Y-O+ **£4,690** (£1,395; £697; £348) **Stalls** Low

Form RPR
-202 **1** **Dixie's Dream (IRE)**[51] 6925 4-9-3 **81** JoeFanning 2 92
(William Jarvis) *prom: drvn to ld ins fnl f: styd on* **6/1**[2]
021 **2** 1 1/2 **Tasrih (USA)**[14] 7781 4-9-1 **79** MartinHarley 7 87
(Alan McCabe) *led after 2f: kicked on and gng wl 3f out: hdd and unable qck ins fnl f* **3/1**[1]
0304 **3** 4 1/2 **Red Dragon (IRE)**[27] 7505 3-8-10 **76** FergusSweeney 3 73
(Michael Blanshard) *towards rr: rdn and hdwy over 1f out: r.o* **33/1**
0120 **4** shd **Legendary**[145] 3812 4-9-7 **85** [1] JimmyQuinn 9 82
(Ed Vaughan) *mid-div: effrt 2f out: styd on same pce* **6/1**[2]
2364 **5** 1 1/4 **Ree's Rascal (IRE)**[51] 6925 5-9-2 **85** NathanAlison(5) 8 80
(Jim Boyle) *rdn along early: bhd tl styd on wl in centre fnl 2f* **6/1**[2]
0050 **6** nse **Hill Of Dreams (IRE)**[38] 7256 4-9-0 **78** (p) RobertWinston 4 72
(Dean Ivory) *towards rr: effrt 2f out: styd on same pce appr fnl f* **25/1**
2514 **7** 1 1/4 **Greyfriarschorista**[20] 7661 6-9-4 **82** GeorgeBaker 10 74
(Tom Keddy) *prom: rdn 2f out: sn wknd* **12/1**[3]
00-3 **8** 1/2 **Indian Jack (IRE)**[21] 7648 5-9-6 **84** TomMcLaughlin 5 74
(Ed Walker) *mid-div: outpcd 2f out: sn btn* **3/1**[1]
6606 **9** 1 **Thistleandtworoses (USA)**[30] 7438 3-8-8 **74** ow1 GrahamGibbons 11 61
(David O'Meara) *s.i.s: plld hrd in rr: shkn up over 1f out: nvr trbld ldrs* **12/1**[3]
0055 **10** 3/4 **Mister Musicmaster**[15] 7769 4-9-0 **78** WilliamCarson 6 64
(Ron Hodges) *led 2f: prom tl wknd 2f out* **14/1**
10-0 **11** 9 **Munsarim (IRE)**[30] 7438 6-8-8 **77** DannyBrock(5) 1 43
(Lee Carter) *in tch on rail tl wknd over 2f out* **33/1**

1m 37.22s (-2.58) **Going Correction** -0.125s/f (Stan)
WFA 3 from 4yo+ 2lb 11 Ran SP% **124.6**
Speed ratings (Par 105): **107,105,101,100,99 99,98,97,96,96 87**
toteswingers 1&2 £2.80, 1&3 £16.80, 2&3 £22.20 CSF £25.48 CT £579.83 TOTE £8.50: £2.90, £1.40, £7.20; EX 20.40 Trifecta £1152.10 Pool: £2783.27 - 1.81 winning units..
Owner William Jarvis **Bred** Miss Joan Murphy **Trained** Newmarket, Suffolk

FOCUS
The second division of the 1m handicap was yet another race where racing handily proved a must due to the uneven pace.

7990 PCA CUP H'CAP (LONDON MIDDLE DISTANCE SERIES QUALIFIER) 1m 3f (P)
6:40 (6:40) (Class 3) (0-95,95) 3-Y-O+
£7,158 (£1,607; £1,607; £535; £267; £134) **Stalls** Low

Form RPR
6100 **1** **Shavansky**[55] 6801 9-8-10 **86** ShelleyBirkett(5) 2 94
(Rod Millman) *mid-div: gd hdwy to ld 1f out: hld on wl* **25/1**
0150 **2** 1/2 **Lowther**[5] 7926 8-9-0 **90** (v) OisinMurphy(5) 10 97
(Lee Carter) *mid-div: gd hdwy over 1f out: r.o wl: jst hld* **8/1**
2 dht **Litigant**[865] 5-9-3 **88** GeorgeBaker 6 95
(Seamus Durack) *s.i.s: bhd: rapid hdwy fnl f: fin wl* **16/1**
1064 **4** 3/4 **Super Say (IRE)**[14] 7793 7-8-10 **81** (t) BenCurtis 8 87
(Michael Appleby) *prom: led briefly wl over 1f out: kpt on u.p* **25/1**
2003 **5** nk **Spifer (IRE)**[56] 6772 5-9-8 **93** MartinHarley 11 99
(Marco Botti) *bhd: rdn and hdwy 2f out: kpt on fnl f* **7/1**[3]
2002 **6** 1 **Rio's Rosanna (IRE)**[12] 7823 6-8-11 **87** GeorgeChaloner(5) 4 91
(Richard Whitaker) *chsd ldrs: outpcd 2f out: styd on nr fin* **10/1**
6262 **7** 1/2 **Castilo Del Diablo (IRE)**[76] 6172 4-9-7 **92** (b) JimCrowley 14 95
(David Simcock) *dwlt: sn cl up on outer fr wdst stall: jnd ldr 5f out tl 2f out: no ex over 1f out* **11/8**[1]
63-0 **8** 2 **Franco Is My Name**[15] 7765 7-8-11 **82** (p) KierenFox 5 82
(Peter Hedger) *towards rr: hdwy 2f out: no ex ins fnl f* **33/1**
13 **9** 1 **Open Eagle (IRE)**[12] 7823 4-9-10 **95** DanielTudhope 7 93
(David O'Meara) *led after 1f tl wl over 1f out: sn wknd* **7/1**[3]
5-51 **10** nk **Layl (USA)**[14] 7794 3-8-10 **86** JoeFanning 3 84
(Mark Johnston) *led 1f: prom: led again briefly over 1f out: wknd fnl f* **6/1**[2]
4133 **11** hd **Lexington Bay (IRE)**[208] 1841 5-8-10 **81** oh1 TonyHamilton 9 79
(Richard Fahey) *mid-div tl outpcd 3f out* **25/1**
0000 **12** 3/4 **Nanton (USA)**[1] 7976 11-8-10 **81** GrahamLee 1 77
(Jim Goldie) *chsd ldrs on rail tl wknd 2f out* **33/1**

2m 19.57s (-2.33) **Going Correction** -0.125s/f (Stan)
WFA 3 from 4yo+ 5lb 12 Ran SP% **124.9**
CSF £Owner CT £The Links Partnership TOTE £Bred: £George Strawbridge, £Trained, £Kentisbeare, Devon.

FOCUS
A decent handicap and they went something of an uneven pace, resulting in a tight finish.

7991 CME GROUP CHALLLENGE H'CAP 7f (P)
7:10 (7:14) (Class 2) (0-105,99) 3-Y-O+
£11,827 (£3,541; £1,770; £885; £442; £222) **Stalls** Low

Form RPR
0003 **1** **Loyalty**[5] 7926 6-8-5 **87** (v) AdamMcLean(7) 1 96
(Derek Shaw) *trckd ldrs on rail: led 2f out: hrd rdn fnl f: jst hld on* **14/1**
0004 **2** nk **Clockmaker (IRE)**[5] 7926 7-9-5 **94** JimCrowley 3 102
(Conor Dore) *led tl 2f out: rallied fnl f: clsng again at fin* **8/1**
0503 **3** nk **George Guru**[21] 7641 6-9-3 **92** RobertHavlin 2 99
(Michael Attwater) *mid-div: rdn and hdwy 2f out: r.o* **7/1**
0101 **4** 1 **Common Touch (IRE)**[15] 7769 5-9-6 **95** RobertWinston 8 100
(Willie Musson) *towards rr: rdn and hdwy 2f out: n.m.r over 1f out: kpt on* **9/2**[3]
0455 **5** hd **Tarooq (USA)**[26] 7540 7-9-10 **99** GrahamGibbons 7 103
(David Barron) *chsd ldr tl 2f out: kpt on u.p* **4/1**[2]
2160 **6** 2 1/2 **Sir Reginald**[33] 7368 5-9-3 **92** TonyHamilton 9 90
(Richard Fahey) *towards rr: rdn over 2f out: styd on fnl f* **16/1**
115 **7** 3/4 **Brownsea Brink**[48] 6993 3-9-1 **91** SeanLevey 10 86
(Richard Hannon) *chsd ldrs on outer tl outpcd fnl 2f* **7/2**[1]
10 **8** 1 1/4 **Atlantis Crossing (IRE)**[21] 7641 4-9-0 **89** GrahamLee 4 82
(Jim Boyle) *missed break and lost 10 l: bhd: sme hdwy 2f out: nvr rcvrd* **10/1**
4120 **9** 3/4 **Favourite Treat (USA)**[12] 7820 3-9-2 **92** JoeFanning 5 82
(Mark Johnston) *mid-div: rdn 3f out: sn outpcd* **10/1**
3500 **10** 3/4 **Birdman (IRE)**[27] 7495 3-9-4 **94** MartinLane 6 82
(David Simcock) *prom tl wknd over 2f out* **33/1**

1m 23.43s (-2.57) **Going Correction** -0.125s/f (Stan)
WFA 3 from 4yo+ 1lb 10 Ran SP% **117.7**
Speed ratings (Par 109): **109,108,108,107,106 104,103,101,100,100**
toteswingers 1&2 £15.70, 1&3 £9.40, 2&3 £11.70 CSF £122.25 CT £631.17 TOTE £16.40: £3.90, £2.80, £2.90; EX 94.80 Trifecta £938.60 Pool: £3662.44 - 2.92 winning units..
Owner Brian Johnson (Northamptonshire) **Bred** Ecoutila Partnership **Trained** Sproxton, Leics

FOCUS
There was a solid pace on in this good-quality handicap.

7992 JLT H'CAP 7f (P)
7:40 (7:40) (Class 3) (0-90,88) 3-Y-O+
£7,158 (£2,143; £1,071; £535; £267; £134) **Stalls** Low

Form RPR
0000 **1** **Upavon**[38] 7254 3-9-3 **85** LiamKeniry 8 93
(David Elsworth) *towards rr: hdwy over 1f out: r.o to ld ins fnl f: drvn out* **33/1**
060 **2** 1/2 **Frontier Fighter**[12] 7820 5-9-6 **87** DanielTudhope 2 95
(David O'Meara) *led: hrd rdn over 1f out: hdd ins fnl f: kpt on* **7/2**[1]
2065 **3** nk **Corporal Maddox**[29] 7464 6-9-4 **85** (p) GeorgeBaker 12 92
(Ronald Harris) *bhd: nt best of runs fr over 1f out: gd hdwy fnl f: fin wl* **7/1**
3041 **4** 1 1/4 **Apollo D'Negro (IRE)**[16] 7742 5-8-7 **79** (v) RyanTate(5) 1 83
(Clive Cox) *prom on rail: rdn 2f out: one pce ins fnl f* **7/2**[1]
020 **5** nse **Tidentime (USA)**[70] 6337 4-8-13 **80** MartinHarley 10 84
(Mick Channon) *chsd ldrs: rdn over 2f out: styd on* **16/1**
1026 **6** 1/2 **Ocean Legend (IRE)**[15] 7769 8-8-10 **80** RobertTart(3) 9 83
(Tony Carroll) *mid-div on outer: rdn over 2f out: styd on same pce* **16/1**
0010 **7** hd **Apostle (IRE)**[15] 7769 4-9-5 **86** JimCrowley 7 88
(David Simcock) *chsd ldr tl no ex over 1f out* **6/1**[3]
0310 **8** 3/4 **Mr David (USA)**[29] 7464 6-9-4 **85** (b) DavidProbert 3 85
(Jamie Osborne) *chsd ldrs tl outpcd fnl f* **12/1**
3122 **9** 1/2 **Bowstar**[16] 7742 4-8-7 **74** (v[1]) RobertHavlin 5 73
(Michael Attwater) *s.s: bhd: sme hdwy over 1f out: nt rch ldrs and hld whn hmpd ins fnl f* **11/2**[2]
2110 **10** 7 **Showboating (IRE)**[12] 7820 5-9-7 **88** (tp) SeanLevey 6 69
(Alan McCabe) *s.s: a bhd* **16/1**
160 **11** 1/2 **Good Authority (IRE)**[113] 4879 6-9-1 **82** TedDurcan 4 61
(Karen George) *wnt lft s: mid-div on rail tl wknd 2f out* **15/2**

1m 23.99s (-2.01) **Going Correction** -0.125s/f (Stan)
WFA 3 from 4yo+ 1lb 11 Ran SP% **126.7**
Speed ratings (Par 107): **106,105,105,103,103 103,102,101,101,93 92**
toteswingers 1&2 £50.70, 1&3 £51.60, 2&3 £7.80 CSF £156.88 CT £969.23 TOTE £18.90: £5.90, £1.50, £3.50; EX 383.20 Trifecta £2215.20 Part won. Pool: £2953.70 - 0.23 winning units..
Owner McPabb Racing **Bred** Major-Gen Guy Watkins **Trained** Newmarket, Suffolk
■ Stewards' Enquiry : George Baker caution: careless riding.

FOCUS
Another competitive handicap to end proceedings.
T/Jkpt: Not won. T/Plt: £606.40. Pool: £97,731.55 - 117.65 winning units. T/Qpdt: £150.10. pool: £13,957.10 - 68.80 winning units. LM

6421 FONTAINEBLEAU
Thursday, November 21

OFFICIAL GOING: Turf: very soft

7993a PRIX CERES (LISTED RACE) (3YO FILLIES) (TURF) 7f
1:20 (12:00) 3-Y-O **£22,357** (£8,943; £6,707; £4,471; £2,235)

RPR
1 **Queen's Daughter (FR)**[36] 3-8-11 0 ThierryThulliez 2 101+
(N Clement, France) **165/10**
2 1 3/4 **Golbahar (IRE)**[16] 3-8-11 0 ThierryJarnet 4 96+
(X Thomas-Demeaulte, France) **14/1**
3 2 **Gyrella (IRE)**[28] 3-8-11 0 Pierre-CharlesBoudot 1 90
(A De Royer-Dupre, France) **33/1**

The Form Book Flat, Raceform Ltd, Compton, RG20 6NL.

4 1 1/4 **Liberating**[39] 7227 3-8-11 0....................................(p) KevinManning 6 87+
(Mrs John Harrington, Ire) *hld up towards rr: pushed along over 3f out: rdn and hdwy fr 2f out: kpt on and wnt 4th ins fnl f: nt pce to chal* **17/1**

5 2 **Roxanne (FR)**[24] 3-8-13 0 ow2........................ ChristopheSoumillon 5 84+
(Mme Pia Brandt, France) **4/1**[3]

6 1 **Holly Filly (IRE)**[16] 3-8-11 0.............................. NicolasPerret 3 79+
(D Guillemin, France) **60/1**

7 shd **Charming Touch (USA)**[22] 3-8-11 0.......................... FlavienPrat 13 79+
(F Head, France) **11/1**

8 2 1/2 **Hail Shower (IRE)**[59] 6706 3-8-11 0.............................. LukeMorris 7 72+
(James Evans) *prom: pushed along over 3f out: rdn and effrt to chal over 2f out: sn outpcd: steadily fdd* **36/1**

9 2 1/2 **Asteria (FR)**[24] 3-8-11 0.................................... StephanePasquier 9 65+
(J E Pease, France) **12/1**

10 2 **Vaunoise (IRE)**[50] 3-8-11 0.................................... GregoryBenoist 12 60+
(J-C Rouget, France) **23/10**[1]

11 2 1/2 **Discernable**[22] 3-8-11 0.. FabriceVeron 10 53+
(H-A Pantall, France) **27/1**

12 3 **Key To Peace (IRE)**[36] 7316 3-8-11 0........................ MaximeGuyon 11 45+
(A Fabre, France) *a towards rr: pushed along 1/2-way: rdn over 2f out: awkward u.p and sn no imp: eased whn btn and dropped to last* **7/2**[2]

1m 30.9s (90.90) **12** Ran SP% **117.3**

Owner Pierre-Paul Richou **Bred** P-P Richou **Trained** Chantilly, France

FOCUS
The first three were always to the fore and it proved hard to make ground. The third sets the standard.

7994a PRIX ZEDDAAN (LISTED RACE) (2YO) (TURF) 6f
1:50 (12:00) 2-Y-O **£22,357** (£8,943; £6,707; £4,471; £2,235)

RPR

1 **Zygmunt (FR)**[25] 7565 2-8-11 0.................................... AlexisBadel 1 96
(Mme M Bollack-Badel, France) **163/10**

2 1/2 **Rangali**[45] 7084 2-8-11 0.. MaximeGuyon 4 94
(H-A Pantall, France) **73/10**

3 nk **Silver Treasure (FR)**[21] 7653 2-8-11 0..................... IoritzMendizabal 2 93
(Amy Weaver) **63/10**[3]

4 3/4 **Little Big Shot (IRE)**[74] 6249 2-8-11 0........................ RonanThomas 6 91
(F-H Graffard, France) **7/2**[2]

5 snk **Atlantic City (FR)**[30] 7568 2-8-8 0.............................. ThierryJarnet 3 87
(H-A Pantall, France) **14/1**

6 5 **Marie D'o (FR)**[56] 6785 2-8-8 0.................................... NicolasPerret 7 72
(K Borgel, France) **18/1**

7 2 1/2 **Watouka (FR)**[92] 2-8-8 0..................................(p) Francois-XavierBertras 9 65
(F Rohaut, France) **13/2**

8 10 **Korba (FR)**[7] 2-8-8 0.. StephanePasquier 8 35
(Y Gourraud, France) **22/1**

9 7 **Easy Risk (FR)**[30] 7567 2-8-8 0.................................... AntoineHamelin 5 14
(F Chappet, France) **33/1**

10 5 **Queen Of Norway (IRE)**[25] 7559 2-8-8 0................. GregoryBenoist 11
(John Joseph Murphy, Ire) *dwlt sltly and pushed along to rcvr: midfield in tch and niggled along thrght: rdn over 2f out: kpt on wl u.p and wnt 3rd towards fin* **42/1**

11 4 **Son Cesio (FR)**[41] 7185 2-8-11 0.................................... FabriceVeron 10
(H-A Pantall, France) **5/2**[1]

1m 13.1s (73.10) **11** Ran SP% **117.2**
WIN (incl. 1 euro stake): 17.30. PLACES: 4.50, 2.70, 2.50. DF: 44.30. SF: 107.70.

Owner Mme Myriam Bollack-Badel **Bred** Mme M Bollack-Badel & Earl Haras De Pierrepont **Trained** Lamorlaye, France

7995a PRIX CONTESSINA (LISTED RACE) (3YO+) (TURF) 6f
2:20 (12:00) 3-Y-O+ **£21,138** (£8,455; £6,341; £4,227; £2,113)

RPR

1 **Eton Rifles (IRE)**[12] 7821 8-8-11 0.................................... AndreaAtzeni 1 105
(Stuart Williams) *travelled strly: disp ld: rdn to ld over 1f out: r.o: pushed out firmly and a doing enough* **16/5**[1]

2 nk **Aksil (FR)**[22] 3-8-8 0.. StephanePasquier 12 101+
(M Boutin, France) **15/2**

3 1 1/4 **Amberley (FR)**[44] 4-8-11 0.. FredericSpanu 2 100+
(E Moullec, France) **19/1**

4 shd **Athenian (IRE)**[17] 7731 4-8-8 0..................................(p) LukeMorris 8 97
(Sir Mark Prescott Bt) *pushed along to chse ldrs: rdn 3f out: kpt on wl but nt quite pce to chal and dropped to 4th fnl strides* **15/1**

5 1 1/4 **Zayade (FR)**[29] 4-8-8 0.. ThierryJarnet 10 93
(J Boisnard, France) **12/1**

6 1 1/2 **Ghor (FR)**[5] 5-8-11 0..(b) ValentinGambart 4 91
(M Boutin, France) **15/1**

7 4 **Caesaria (IRE)**[37] 7286 3-8-11 0..............................(b) KevinManning 3 78
(Y Gourraud, France) **49/1**

8 1/2 **Murcielago (GER)**[21] 6-8-11 0..................................(p) MaximeGuyon 15 77
(M Keller, Germany) **13/2**[3]

9 1/2 **Tariq Too**[12] 7820 6-8-11 0.. IoritzMendizabal 6 75
(Amy Weaver) *dwlt and sn pushed along in rr: rdn and sme hdwy on outer 2f out: kpt on but no imp on ldrs: eased towards fin: n.d* **11/1**

10 hd **Bilge Kagan (IRE)**[32] 7408 3-8-11 0........................ GregoryBenoist 13 75
(X Thomas-Demeaulte, France) **28/1**

11 3/4 **Veremeroad (FR)**[21] 3-8-11 0.................................... FabienLefebvre 5 72
(G Martin, Austria) **73/1**

12 6 **Lykea (IRE)**[45] 7085 3-8-8 0...................................... JeromeClaudic 14 50
(C Laffon-Parias, France) **14/1**

13 2 1/2 **Lucrece**[81] 4-8-8 0.. Francois-XavierBertras 7 42
(F Rohaut, France) **21/1**

14 nk **Navajo Nights**[25] 3-8-13 0 ow2........................ ChristopheSoumillon 11 46
(E Leon Penate, Spain) **58/10**[2]

15 dist **Nini Ok (IRE)**[25] 7560 4-8-8 0..................................(b) FabriceVeron 9
(John Joseph Murphy, Ire) *sn towards rr: last 1/2-way: btn and eased 2f out: t.o* **48/1**

1m 12.3s (72.30) **15** Ran SP% **117.2**

Owner The Eton Riflemen **Bred** Grangecon Stud **Trained** Newmarket, Suffolk

FOCUS
The second, third and sixth help with the standard.

7996 - 8001a (Foreign Racing) - See Raceform Interactive

[7959] WOLVERHAMPTON (A.W) (L-H)
Friday, November 22

OFFICIAL GOING: Standard
Wind: Light half-against Weather: Fine

8002 COMPARE THE BOOKMAKERS AT BOOKMAKERS.CO.UK APPRENTICE H'CAP 5f 216y(P)
4:10 (4:10) (Class 6) (0-60,60) 3-Y-0+ **£1,940** (£577; £288; £144) **Stalls** Low

Form RPR

2600 1 **Penbryn (USA)**[14] 7807 6-9-2 **55**.................................... JordanVaughan 5 65
(Nick Littmoden) *s.i.s: hld up: hdwy over 1f out: shkn up and r.o to ld nr fin* **6/1**

0600 2 1 **Marmot Bay (IRE)**[62] 6651 3-8-7 **46**.................................... EvaMoscrop 8 53
(Philip Kirby) *plld hrd and sn prom: rdn over 1f out: r.o* **6/1**

2310 3 1/2 **Prigsnov Dancer (IRE)**[14] 7808 8-9-2 **58**..................(p) DavidParkes(3) 4 63
(Deborah Sanderson) *trckd ldrs: rdn to ld wl ins fnl f: edgd lft: hdd nr fin* **10/1**

3463 4 1 1/4 **Amis Reunis**[24] 7598 4-8-10 **54**..............................(p) JordanHibberd(5) 2 55
(Alan Berry) *mid-div: hdwy over 1f out: r.o* **5/1**[3]

4450 5 1 1/4 **Above The Stars**[10] 7848 5-9-7 **60**..................................(p) JoeDoyle 10 57
(Conor Dore) *led 5f out: rdn over 1f out: hdd and no ex wl ins fnl f* **12/1**

6050 6 nk **Methaaly (IRE)**[7] 7905 10-8-9 **55**..............................(be) LewisStones(7) 1 51
(Michael Mullineaux) *hood removed late and s.s: bhd: swtchd lft and r.o ins fnl f: nt rch ldrs* **4/1**[2]

3000 7 3/4 **Divertimenti (IRE)**[3] 7957 9-8-11 **57**..............................(b) JoshQuinn(7) 9 51
(Roy Bowring) *s.i.s: hdwy over 4f out: pushed along 1/2-way: styd on same pce appr fnl f* **16/1**

00/0 8 4 1/2 **Wyatt Earp (IRE)**[58] 6760 12-9-6 **59**..............................(p) AdamMcLean 11 38
(Richard Guest) *racd keenly: trckd ldrs: rdn over 1f out: wknd fnl f* **20/1**

5306 9 1 1/4 **Lord Buffhead**[49] 6994 4-8-8 **54**..............................(e) MelissaThompson(7) 3 29
(Richard Guest) *s.i.s: hld up: rdn over 1f out: nvr on terms* **20/1**

003- 10 1 **Sujet Bellagio**[9] 7866 4-8-7 **46** oh1..............................(t) RobJFitzpatrick 7 18
(Damian Joseph English, Ire) *led 1f: chsd ldrs: rdn over 2f out: wknd over 1f out* **3/1**[1]

1m 16.33s (1.33) **Going Correction** +0.175s/f (Slow) **10** Ran SP% **122.4**
Speed ratings (Par 101): **98,96,96,94,92 92,91,85,83,82**
toteswingers 1&2 £11.30, 1&3 £9.90, 2&3 £16.60 CSF £44.17 CT £358.06 TOTE £5.80: £2.10, £2.70, £3.10; EX 49.30 Trifecta £789.50 Pool: £3520.66 - 3.34 winning units..

Owner Mrs K Graham, N Littmoden, A Highfield **Bred** Kilboy Estate Inc **Trained** Newmarket, Suffolk

FOCUS
A moderate handicap and they looked to go a fair pace.

8003 BEST ODDS AT BOOKMAKERS.CO.UK MAIDEN STKS 5f 216y(P)
4:40 (4:40) (Class 5) 3-4-Y-0 **£2,587** (£770; £384; £192) **Stalls** Low

Form RPR

32 1 **Discussiontofollow (IRE)**[86] 5884 3-9-5 0........................ ShaneKelly 2 78+
(Mike Murphy) *s.i.s: sn trcking ldrs: wnt 2nd 1/2-way: led on bit over 1f out: swtchd rt ins fnl f: sn clr: easily* **1/1**[1]

0445 2 5 **Mid Yorkshire Golf**[6] 7929 4-8-11 44........................ SladeO'Hara(3) 1 51
(Peter Grayson) *hld up: shkn up over 1f out: r.o ins fnl f: wnt 2nd post: no ch w wnr* **50/1**

42 3 shd **Random Success (IRE)**[14] 7802 3-9-0 0........................ MartinLane 5 51
(Roger Charlton) *trckd ldrs: led 4f out: rdn: edgd lft and hdd over 1f out: wknd ins fnl f: lost 2nd post* **11/10**[2]

5600 4 5 **Princess Bounty**[46] 7079 3-9-0 46.................................... PaddyAspell 7 35
(Phil McEntee) *hld up: hdwy over 2f out: sn rdn: wknd over 1f out* **66/1**

0300 5 1 1/2 **Shelling Peas**[8] 7886 4-8-7 48..............................(v) AdamMcLean(7) 3 30
(Derek Shaw) *led 2f: chsd ldrs: pushed along over 2f out: wknd over 1f out* **50/1**

6 6 **Jenny Twigg** 3-9-0 0.. JoeFanning 6 11
(Chris Fairhurst) *chsd ldr tl hung rt 1/2-way: sn pushed along: wknd over 1f out* **16/1**[3]

1m 16.12s (1.12) **Going Correction** +0.175s/f (Slow) **6** Ran SP% **108.9**
Speed ratings (Par 103): **99,92,92,85,83 75**
toteswingers 1&2 £2.20, 1&3 £1.10, 2&3 £3.00 CSF £39.54 TOTE £1.90: £1.10, £6.00; EX 16.50 Trifecta £34.00 Pool: £4529.13 - 99.70 winning units..

Owner D Spratt **Bred** Jerry O'Sullivan **Trained** Westoning, Beds

FOCUS
A weak race.

8004 32RED H'CAP 1m 5f 194y(P)
5:10 (5:10) (Class 5) (0-75,75) 3-Y-0+ **£2,587** (£770; £384; £192) **Stalls** Low

Form RPR

5160 1 **Scottish Boogie (IRE)**[36] 4167 6-10-0 **75**..................(t) GeorgeBaker 2 86
(Seamus Durack) *hld up: hdwy over 1f out: styd on to ld wl ins fnl f: comf* **20/1**

2446 2 1 1/4 **Montjess (IRE)**[62] 6629 3-9-1 **70**..................(v) RichardKingscote 4 79
(Tom Dascombe) *chsd ldr tl led 3f out: clr 1f out: rdn and hdd wl ins fnl f* **13/2**[3]

0002 3 6 **Evermore (IRE)**[10] 7847 3-8-2 **57**.................................... JoeFanning 8 58
(Mark Johnston) *prom: chsd ldr wl over 2f out: rdn and edgd lft over 1f out: wknd ins fnl f* **11/4**[1]

1004 4 4 **Rapid Heat Lad (IRE)**[128] 4406 4-9-12 **73**..........(tp) GrahamGibbons 10 68
(Andrew Hollinshead) *hld up: pushed along over 3f out: styd on fnl f: nvr nrr* **14/1**

1-00 5 3/4 **Peachez**[17] 7739 5-9-7 **73**..(p) AmyScott(5) 7 67
(Seamus Durack) *s.i.s: hld up: pushed along over 3f out: styd on ins fnl f: nvr on terms* **10/1**

0363 6 shd **Spiekeroog**[49] 6632 7-9-2 **63**..................................(v) DanielTudhope 3 57
(David O'Meara) *hld up in tch: rdn over 2f out: wknd fnl f* **14/1**

5563 7 3/4 **Gosforth Park**[38] 7278 7-9-3 **64**.................................... JimmyQuinn 6 57
(Mel Brittain) *prom: rdn over 2f out: wknd over 1f out* **10/1**

03 8 1/2 **Meetings Man (IRE)**[28] 7510 6-9-13 **74**..................(p) GrahamLee 1 66
(Ali Brewer) *trckd ldrs: rdn over 2f out: wknd over 1f out* **4/1**[2]

2440 9 1 1/2 **The Blue Dog (IRE)**[161] 3301 6-9-8 **72**........................ RobertTart(3) 5 62
(Phil McEntee) *hld up: rdn over 2f out: wknd over 1f out* **16/1**

1553 10 8 **Fly Solo**[14] 7805 4-9-13 **74**.................................... BenCurtis 9 53
(Alan Swinbank) *led: rdn and hdd 3f out: wknd wl over 1f out* **4/1**[2]

3m 4.74s (-1.26) **Going Correction** +0.175s/f (Slow)
WFA 3 from 4yo+ 8lb **10** Ran SP% **122.2**
Speed ratings (Par 103): **110,109,105,103,103 103,102,102,101,96**
toteswingers 1&2 £26.50, 1&3 £11.60, 2&3 £4.80 CSF £151.14 CT £482.62 TOTE £19.20: £5.60, £2.20, £2.10; EX 188.50 Trifecta £964.80 Pool: £3704.98 - 2.87 winning units..

Owner A A Byrne **Bred** Littleton Stud **Trained** Baydon, Wilts

■ Stewards' Enquiry : Ben Curtis one-day ban: failed to ride to draw (Dec 6)

FOCUS
An ordinary staying handicap.

8005 32RED.COM MAIDEN AUCTION STKS 7f 32y(P)
5:40 (5:41) (Class 6) 2-Y-O **£1,940** (£577; £288; £144) **Stalls** High

Form RPR

0 **1** **First Experience**[50] 6974 2-8-8 0 ChrisCatlin 3 65
(Rae Guest) *hld up: hdwy 2f out: shkn up to ld over 1f out: r.o wl: readily* **12/1**

5 **2** 1 ¾ **Bon Port**[39] 7251 2-8-8 0 AndreaAtzeni 6 60
(Hughie Morrison) *s.i.s: sn prom: rdn and ev ch over 1f out: edgd lft: styd on same pce ins fnl f* **11/2**[3]

3 nk **Spirit Or Soul (FR)** 2-8-11 0 MartinHarley 5 63
(Marco Botti) *a.p: trckd ldr 6f out: rdn and ev ch over 1f out: styd on same pce ins fnl f* **1/1**[1]

2262 **4** 1 **Supa U**[8] 7883 2-8-6 65 (e) JamesSullivan 1 55
(Tim Easterby) *led: rdn and hdd over 1f out: no ex ins fnl f* **7/2**[2]

06 **5** ½ **Gee Sharp**[18] 7732 2-8-11 0 BarryMcHugh 4 59
(Julie Camacho) *chsd ldr 1f: remained handy: rdn and edgd lft over 1f out: styd on same pce* **25/1**

5 **6** 3 ¾ **Singing Star (IRE)**[13] 7817 2-8-6 0 JimmyQuinn 2 45+
(Mel Brittain) *s.i.s and hmpd s: hld up: plld hrd: shkn up over 1f out: nvr trbld ldrs* **10/1**

05 **7** 8 **Day Star Lad**[136] 4154 2-8-11 0 DaleSwift 7 30
(Derek Shaw) *hld up: plld hrd: pushed along over 2f out: sn wknd* **50/1**

1m 32.36s (2.76) **Going Correction** +0.175s/f (Slow) **7 Ran SP% 110.2**
Speed ratings (Par 94): **91,89,88,87,86 82,73**
toteswingers 1&2 £7.10, 1&3 £4.90, 2&3 £2.40 CSF £69.77 TOTE £14.00: £4.30, £3.30; EX 93.20 Trifecta £225.40 Pool: £3187.08 - 10.60 winning units..
Owner Fitorfat Racing & Guy Carstairs **Bred** Northmore Stud **Trained** Newmarket, Suffolk

FOCUS
The bare form is probably just modest, but the race should produce winners.

8006 CORAL APP DOWNLOAD FROM THE APP STORE H'CAP 1m 1f 103y(P)
6:10 (6:10) (Class 6) (0-60,63) 3-Y-O+ **£1,940** (£577; £288; £144) **Stalls** Low

Form RPR

0263 **1** **Dubai Celebration**[28] 7514 5-9-2 55 BarryMcHugh 10 65
(Julie Camacho) *hld up: hdwy over 3f out: led over 2f out: rdn clr fnl f: eased nr fin* **6/1**

0520 **2** 1 ¾ **Marina Ballerina**[34] 7379 5-8-7 46 JimmyQuinn 13 52
(Roy Bowring) *hld up: pushed along over 3f out: hdwy and hung lft fr over 1f out: r.o: nt trble wnr* **66/1**

3006 **3** 1 ¼ **Joshua The First**[18] 7733 4-9-6 59 GrahamLee 11 63
(Ian Semple) *sn pushed along towards rr: hdwy over 2f out: rdn to chse wnr over 1f out: hung lft ins fnl f: styd on same pce* **16/1**

0242 **4** 1 **Attain**[7] 7907 4-8-7 51 (p) ShelleyBirkett(5) 9 53
(Julia Feilden) *hld up: hdwy over 3f out: nt clr run over 1f out: styd on* **11/2**[3]

5030 **5** ¾ **Geeaitch**[28] 7515 4-9-2 55 WilliamCarson 8 55
(Peter Hiatt) *prom: drvn along over 2f out: hung lft and styd on same pce fnl f* **20/1**

0431 **6** hd **Bitaphon (IRE)**[8] 7886 4-9-0 53 (t) LukeMorris 6 53
(Michael Appleby) *prom: rdn over 1f out: no ex ins fnl f* **5/1**[2]

3106 **7** 2 **Jordaura**[28] 7498 7-9-4 60 SladeO'Hara(3) 12 55
(Alan Berry) *s.i.s: hld up: shkn up over 1f out: nvr nrr* **14/1**

0000 **8** ¾ **King Of Windsor (IRE)**[175] 2845 6-9-2 55 (bt) GrahamGibbons 7 49
(John Wainwright) *s.i.s: hld up: rdn over 2f out: nvr nrr* **7/1**

0334 **9** 3 ½ **Outlaw Torn (IRE)**[6] 7930 4-9-7 60 (e) RobbieFitzpatrick 4 46
(Richard Guest) *led: rdn and hdd over 2f out: wknd fnl f* **8/1**

00-0 **10** 2 ¼ **Northgate Lodge (USA)**[86] 5897 8-8-7 46 oh1 JoeFanning 3 28
(Mel Brittain) *hld up: rdn over 2f out: nvr on terms* **66/1**

4210 **11** 4 **Solarmaite**[45] 7106 4-9-4 60 (b) MarkCoumbe(3) 5 33
(Roy Bowring) *prom: plld hrd: trckd ldr 6f out: rdn and ev ch over 2f out: wknd over 1f out* **20/1**

61 **12** 1 ¾ **Pim Street (USA)**[6] 7930 3-9-7 63 6ex DanielTudhope 2 33
(David O'Meara) *s.i.s: sn prom: rdn and wknd over 1f out* **9/2**[1]

503 **13** 2 ¾ **Hail Bold Chief (USA)**[59] 6723 6-9-2 55 BenCurtis 1 19
(Alan Swinbank) *chsd ldr over 2f: remained handy: rdn over 4f out: wknd over 3f out* **16/1**

2m 2.07s (0.37) **Going Correction** +0.175s/f (Slow)
WFA 3 from 4yo+ 3lb **13 Ran SP% 119.1**
Speed ratings (Par 101): **105,103,102,101,100 100,98,98,95,93 89,87,85**
toteswingers 1&2 £24.30, 1&3 £15.90, 2&3 £65.90 CSF £371.33 CT £5892.96 TOTE £5.80: £1.80, £9.30, £3.50; EX 307.70 Trifecta £1896.90 Part won. Pool: £2529.21 - 0.22 winning units..
Owner L Bolingbroke, N Gravett & J Camacho **Bred** Wheelers Land Stud **Trained** Norton, N Yorks

FOCUS
Just a moderate handicap.

8007 CORAL MOBILE "JUST THREE CLICKS TO BET" H'CAP 1m 1f 103y(P)
6:40 (6:41) (Class 4) (0-85,85) 3-Y-O+ **£4,690** (£1,395; £697; £348) **Stalls** Low

Form RPR

4662 **1** **Off The Pulse**[29] 7491 3-8-12 79 GrahamGibbons 8 89
(John Mackie) *trckd ldr tl led 3f out: shkn up over 1f out: drvn out* **3/1**[2]

0L45 **2** 1 **Halfsin (IRE)**[111] 5008 5-9-6 84 (t) MartinHarley 4 92
(Marco Botti) *trckd ldrs: rdn to chse wnr over 1f out: r.o* **5/1**

6063 **3** ¾ **Woody Bay**[31] 7438 3-8-9 76 GrahamLee 7 82
(James Given) *hld up: hdwy over 2f out: rdn over 1f out: r.o* **9/2**[3]

4101 **4** shd **Soul Intent (IRE)**[29] 7491 3-8-10 77 MartinLane 3 83+
(J W Hills) *hld up: rdn over 1f out: r.o ins fnl f: nt rch ldrs* **2/1**[1]

0001 **5** nk **Creme Anglaise**[21] 7656 5-8-13 80 WilliamTwiston-Davies(3) 6 85
(Michael Bell) *hdwy over 7f out: chsd wnr over 2f out tl rdn over 1f out: styd on* **7/1**

4505 **6** 7 **The Lock Master (IRE)**[7] 7906 6-9-2 85 ShirleyTeasdale(5) 1 76
(Michael Appleby) *led: pushed along and hdd 3f out: rdn over 1f out: wknd ins fnl f* **25/1**

1010 **7** 3 ½ **Sofias Number One (USA)**[94] 5615 5-8-13 80 (b) MarkCoumbe(3) 2 63
(Roy Bowring) *prom: lost pl over 7f out: rdn over 2f out: sn wknd* **20/1**

2m 2.59s (0.89) **Going Correction** +0.175s/f (Slow)
WFA 3 from 5yo+ 3lb **7 Ran SP% 114.3**
Speed ratings (Par 105): **103,102,101,101,101 94,91**
toteswingers 1&2 £2.40, 1&3 £2.90, 2&3 £5.00 CSF £18.30 CT £65.52 TOTE £3.50: £2.50, £3.30; EX 22.10 Trifecta £87.20 Pool: £2042.18 - 17.56 winning units..
Owner G B Maher **Bred** Mrs V E Hughes **Trained** Church Broughton , Derbys

FOCUS
This was run in a slower time than the preceding Class 6 handicap.

8008 DOWNLOAD THE LADBROKES APP H'CAP 1m 141y(P)
7:10 (7:10) (Class 5) (0-75,74) 3-Y-O+ **£2,587** (£770; £384; £192) **Stalls** Low

Form RPR

2360 **1** **No Dominion (IRE)**[23] 7632 4-9-7 74 GrahamLee 7 83
(James Given) *sn pushed along in rr: shkn up over 1f out: r.o u.p to ld wl ins fnl f* **11/4**[2]

0-13 **2** 1 ¼ **Miguel Grau (USA)**[31] 7446 3-9-0 70 (b) AndreaAtzeni 1 76
(Roger Varian) *w ldr tl led over 6f out: rdn over 1f out: hdd and unable qck wl ins fnl f* **9/4**[1]

0400 **3** 1 ¼ **Kung Hei Fat Choy (USA)**[13] 7824 4-9-2 74 (b) GeorgeChaloner(5) 3 78
(James Given) *a.p: rdn over 1f out: styd on same pce ins fnl f* **16/1**

0406 **4** ½ **Mister Marcasite**[23] 7632 3-8-11 67 (v[1]) JimmyQuinn 4 70
(Mel Brittain) *hld up: hdwy and n.m.r over 1f out: rdn and hung lft ins fnl f: styd on same pce* **20/1**

5003 **5** 1 ¼ **Al Raqeeb (IRE)**[15] 7785 3-9-4 74 MartinHarley 8 74
(Gary Harrison) *hld up: nt clr run over 1f out: sn rdn: styd on same pce ins fnl f* **11/2**[3]

0325 **6** ½ **Fame Again**[21] 7669 5-9-3 70 (e[1]) GrahamGibbons 2 69
(Michael Easterby) *s.i.s: sn rcvrd to ld: hdd over 6f out: chsd ldr: rdn over 2f out: no ex ins fnl f* **7/1**

0000 **7** 1 ¼ **Angel Cake (IRE)**[8] 7876 4-8-10 63 LukeMorris 5 59
(Michael Appleby) *chsd ldrs: rdn 3f out: wknd ins fnl f* **8/1**

2535 **8** nk **Caramack**[16] 4442 3-9-3 73 SteveDrowne 6 69
(Richard Lee) *hld up: pushed along 3f out: rdn over 1f out: styd on same pce* **25/1**

1m 50.41s (-0.09) **Going Correction** +0.175s/f (Slow)
WFA 3 from 4yo+ 3lb **8 Ran SP% 110.9**
Speed ratings (Par 103): **107,105,104,104,103 102,101,101**
toteswingers 1&2 £2.50, 1&3 £5.80, 2&3 £8.50 CSF £8.74 CT £74.10 TOTE £4.20: £1.60, £1.10, £3.80; EX 10.80 Trifecta £97.50 Pool: £2497.59 - 19.20 winning units..
Owner J Barson **Bred** N Cable & M Smith **Trained** Willoughton, Lincs

FOCUS
A modest handicap.
T/Plt: £424.40 to a £1 stake. Pool: £87003.38 - 149.65 winning tickets T/Qpdt: £132.90 to a £1 stake. Pool: £15139.17 - 84.26 winning tickets CR

8009 - 8011a (Foreign Racing) - See Raceform Interactive

7908 DUNDALK (A.W) (L-H)
Friday, November 22

OFFICIAL GOING: Standard

8012a DUNDALK STADIUM ON FACEBOOK RATED RACE 7f (P)
7:50 (7:51) 3-Y-O+ **£4,487** (£1,040; £455; £260)

RPR

1 **Doc Holliday (IRE)**[49] 7002 3-8-12 70 (t) RPDowney(7) 2 77
(Edward Lynam, Ire) *disp early: narrow advantage bef 1/2-way: rdn fr under 2f out and hdd ent fnl f: kpt on wl u.p far side to regain advantage fnl 50yds* **2/1**[1]

2 ¾ **Fleet Captain**[79] 6120 5-9-6 62 ShaneFoley 7 76
(Jane M Foley, Ire) *hld up towards rr: hdwy in 9th and swtchd rt to outer over 2f out: sn qcknd to ld ent fnl f where edgd lft: hdd u.p fnl 50yds: no ex* **16/1**

3 1 ½ **Ningaloo Reef (IRE)**[7] 7911 5-9-8 72 ConorHoban 13 74
(Garvan Donnelly, Ire) *hld up in tch: 7th 1/2-way: pushed along into st and clsd u.p to chse ldrs in 5th 1f out: wnt 3rd nr fin: nt trble principals* **5/1**[3]

4 ½ **Cool Athlete (IRE)**[75] 6244 7-9-6 69 (p) FergalLynch 3 71
(David Marnane, Ire) *trckd ldrs: cl 4th 1/2-way: swtchd lft to inner fr 2f out and rdn into 3rd briefly ins fnl f: kpt on same pce* **7/1**

5 1 ¼ **Lake George (IRE)**[49] 7002 5-8-13 66 DylanRobinson(7) 9 67
(James M Barrett, Ire) *disp early: cl 2nd bef 1/2-way: rdn 1 1/2f out and edgd rt u.p: sn no ex in 3rd: one pce towards fin* **10/1**

6 1 ¼ **Regal Power**[68] 6439 4-8-13 73 SimonTorrens(10) 1 67
(J P Murtagh, Ire) *hld up: 8th 1/2-way: tk clsr order 2f out: sn rdn and no imp on ldrs in 6th ins fnl f: kpt on same pce* **7/1**

7 2 **Penny Serenade (IRE)**[99] 5450 3-9-5 69 (t) NGMcCullagh 4 57
(Edward Lynam, Ire) *prom: settled bhd ldrs: t.k.h: cl 5th 1/2-way: hdwy fr 2f out: hmpd over 1f out: no imp after: wknd towards fin* **16/1**

8 1 ¾ **Imperator Augustus (IRE)**[60] 6702 5-8-13 70 JackGarritty(7) 11 54
(Patrick Holmes) *chsd ldrs: cl 6th 1/2-way: rdn and sn no ex fr 2f out: wknd* **14/1**

9 3 ¼ **Burnwynd Boy**[102] 5331 8-9-6 EmmetMcNamara 8 45
(Lee Smyth, Ire) *s.i.s and racd in rr: pushed along into st where sltly hmpd: no imp after: kpt on one pce fnl f* **33/1**

10 2 **Dusty In Memphis (USA)**[9] 7868 3-9-9 74 (v[1]) WJLee 10 43
(David Wachman, Ire) *trckd ldrs on outer: t.k.h: cl 3rd 1/2-way: rdn and wknd fr 2f out: lame* **9/2**[2]

1m 25.58s (85.58)
WFA 3 from 4yo+ 1lb **10 Ran SP% 123.6**
CSF £41.90 TOTE £3.00: £1.20, £2.30, £2.60; DF 43.80 Trifecta £194.60.
Owner Ms Aileen Lynam **Bred** J Costello & Lawman Syndicate **Trained** Dunshaughlin, Co Meath

FOCUS
A winner here the previous month, Doc Holliday saw it out best to win this.

8013 - 8015a (Foreign Racing) - See Raceform Interactive

7977 LINGFIELD (L-H)
Saturday, November 23

OFFICIAL GOING: Standard
Wind: Moderate, against Weather: Fine

8016 32RED ON THE APP STORE (S) STKS 1m (P)
11:50 (11:51) (Class 6) 2-Y-O **£2,045** (£603; £302) **Stalls** High

Form RPR

3652 **1** **Sheacheval (IRE)**[3] 7977 2-8-6 62 (p) LiamJones 1 54
(J S Moore) *chsd ldr: rdn to ld 2f out and wd bnd sn after: drvn fnl f: wknd nr fin: jst hld on* **9/4**[2]

0000 **2** nk **Penara**[18] 7755 2-8-6 54 AndreaAtzeni 8 53
(Philip Hide) *hld up in tch: rdn 3f out: outpcd over 2f out: hrd drvn over 1f out: styd on fnl f: tk 2nd and clsng at fin* **14/1**

4242 **3** *hd* **Heska (IRE)**[5] 7945 2-8-11 67........(v) MartinHarley 3 58
(Mick Channon) *pushed along early: sn in 6th: outpcd by ldng pair over 2f out: hrd rdn over 1f out: styd on fnl f: clsng at fin* **1/1**[1]

006 **4** *½* **Sexy Secret**[71] 6365 2-8-11 45........(b) RobertHavlin 2 57
(Noel Quinlan) *led at gd pce: drvn and hdd 2f out: chsd wnr after: wknd ins fnl f: lost 2 pls nr fin* **8/1**[3]

4500 **5** *10* **Aweebitowinker**[9] 7878 2-8-6 50........(p) JoeyHaynes(5) 5 34
(J S Moore) *chsd ldrs: outpcd over 2f out: wknd qckly over 1f out* **20/1**

330 **6** *3 ¼* **Hannah Louise (IRE)**[87] 5891 2-8-6 45........(t) LukeMorris 7 21
(Olivia Maylam) *dwlt: a in rr: struggling sn after 1/2-way: bhd fnl 2f* **20/1**

000 **7** *¾* **One Picture**[23] 7647 2-8-4 45........ CameronHardie(7) 4 25
(Richard Hannon) *a in last pair: rdn 5f out: bhd fnl 3f* **25/1**

00 **8** *½* **Princess Tilly**[9] 7882 2-8-3 0........ RyanPowell(3) 6 18
(Bill Turner) *disp 2nd to 3f out: hanging rt and wknd qckly over 2f out* **66/1**

1m 38.04s (-0.16) **Going Correction** -0.15s/f (Stan) **8** Ran SP% **113.4**
Speed ratings (Par 94): **94,93,93,93,83 79,79,78**
toteswingers 1&2 £5.30, 2&3 £4.40, 1&3 £1.50 CSF £28.94 TOTE £2.90: £1.30, £2.70, £1.10; EX 36.50 Trifecta £54.60 Pool: £2386.78 - 32.78 winning units..There was no bid for the winner.
Owner Eventmasters Racing **Bred** Michael Begley **Trained** Upper Lambourn, Berks

FOCUS
A moderate juvenile seller and not form to rely on.

8017 £32 FREE AT 32RED.COM/E.B.F. STALLIONS MAIDEN STKS 5f (P)
12:20 (12:20) (Class 5) 2-Y-O £3,067 (£905; £453) Stalls High

Form RPR

262 **1** **Flashy Queen (IRE)**[34] 7394 2-8-9 67........ GeorgeChaloner(5) 5 59
(Joseph Tuite) *pressed ldng pair: hanging rt and wd bnd 2f out: drvn and clsd fnl f to ld last strides* **7/4**[1]

0050 **2** *½* **Grande Mago (IRE)**[16] 7789 2-9-5 58........(v¹) MartinLane 1 62
(Robert Cowell) *led: rdn on inner 2f out: kpt on fr over 1f out: hdd last strides* **16/1**

00 **3** *¾* **Alumina (IRE)**[23] 7638 2-9-0 0........ DavidProbert 8 55
(Andrew Balding) *towards rr: rdn wl over 1f out: hanging lft but styd on fnl f to take 3rd post* **9/2**[3]

0035 **4** *nse* **Back On Baileys**[22] 7665 2-9-0 54........ LukeMorris 4 54
(Chris Dwyer) *pressed ldr: drvn 2f out: hld and lost 2nd ins fnl f: one pce and lost 3rd post* **8/1**

300 **5** *1 ¾* **Previous Acclaim (IRE)**[10] 7852 2-9-0 63........ SeanLevey 3 50
(Richard Hannon) *dwlt sltly: in tch in rr: rdn over 1f out: one pce and no imp* **7/2**[2]

4 **6** *hd* **Random**[28] 7541 2-9-0 0........ ShaneKelly 6 47
(John Stimpson) *hld up in rr: reminder over 1f out: no prog fnl f: nvr involved* **9/2**[3]

300 **7** *5* **Paradise Child**[22] 7665 2-9-0 45........[1] GrahamLee 2 29
(Bill Turner) *dwlt sltly: chsd ldrs: rdn over 1f out: fdd fnl f* **50/1**

8 *22* **Little Herbert** 2-9-5 0........ LiamJones 7
(Michael Attwater) *slowly away: sn t.o* **33/1**

59.27s (0.47) **Going Correction** -0.15s/f (Stan) **8** Ran SP% **116.8**
Speed ratings (Par 96): **90,89,88,87,85 84,76,41**
toteswingers 1&2 £7.30, 2&3 £17.90, 1&3 £2.70 CSF £34.26 TOTE £2.40: £1.10, £5.00, £2.20; EX 44.00 Trifecta £151.10 Pool: £2326.32 - 11.54 winning units..
Owner B Woodward,P & A Burton & B & A Lampard **Bred** Stourbank Stud **Trained** Great Shefford, Berks

FOCUS
A modest juvenile sprint maiden.

8018 32RED CONDITIONS STKS 7f (P)
12:55 (12:55) (Class 2) 2-Y-O £9,056 (£2,695; £1,346; £673) Stalls Low

Form RPR

612 **1** **Complicit (IRE)**[52] 6958 2-9-3 0........ GrahamLee 6 92+
(Paul Cole) *chsd ldr: reminders over 1f out: cajoled along fnl f and r.o to ld last 75yds* **9/2**[3]

31 **2** *1* **Sir Robert Cheval**[10] 7860 2-9-3 0........ MartinHarley 1 89+
(Marco Botti) *led: kicked for home over 1f out: r.o fnl f but hdd and outpcd last 75yds* **1/1**[1]

44 **3** *4 ½* **Ifrika**[57] 6799 2-8-9 0........ LukeMorris 2 69
(Clive Brittain) *chsd ldrs in 4th: rdn 4f out: hung rt bnd 2f out and no ch after: kpt on to take 3rd last strides* **16/1**

2 **4** *nk* **Yagheer (IRE)**[29] 7494 2-9-0 0........[1] AndreaAtzeni 3 73
(Roger Varian) *chsd ldng pair: rdn over 2f out: no imp over 1f out: wknd fnl f and lost 3rd last strides* **9/4**[2]

0500 **5** *12* **Sandsman's Girl (IRE)**[12] 7837 2-8-9 70........(b¹) DaleSwift 4 36
(James Given) *t.k.h early: hld up in last: wknd over 2f out: t.o* **100/1**

1m 22.67s (-2.13) **Going Correction** -0.15s/f (Stan) 2y crse rec **5** Ran SP% **105.8**
Speed ratings (Par 102): **106,104,99,99,85**
CSF £8.78 TOTE £5.60: £2.40, £1.10; EX 9.40 Trifecta £31.10 Pool: £2260.56 - 54.38 winning units..
Owner T A Rahman **Bred** Barouche Stud Ireland Ltd **Trained** Whatcombe, Oxon

FOCUS
A decent little juvenile conditions event and a "Win & You're In" Qualifier for the All-Weather Championships 3-Y-O Final over this C&D next April. The pace was solid - they took over a second off the 2yo course record - and the first two horses dominated the contest from the off.

8019 LADBROKES H'CAP 7f (P)
1:25 (1:27) (Class 6) (0-65,65) 3-Y-O+ £2,045 (£603; £302)

Form RPR

0000 **1** **Prince Of Burma (IRE)**[7] 7937 5-9-4 62........(v¹) DavidProbert 7 71
(David Evans) *hld up in rr: taken out wd and prog over 1f out: r.o wl to ld last 75yds* **5/2**[1]

0360 **2** *1* **Shifting Star (IRE)**[18] 7740 8-9-3 61........ SeanLevey 14 67
(John Bridger) *t.k.h: sn trckd ldr: chal 2f out: led ins fnl f: hdd and outpcd last 75yds* **20/1**

3500 **3** *½* **Magical Rose (IRE)**[60] 6734 3-9-6 65........(p) FrederikTylicki 8 69
(Paul D'Arcy) *slowly away: hld up in rr: prog over 1f out: tried to chal fnl f: outpcd last 75yds: styd on* **16/1**

0400 **4** *nk* **Perfect Haven**[65] 6556 3-9-6 65........ LukeMorris 10 68
(Clive Cox) *t.k.h: prom: rdn and nt qckn over 1f out: styd on same pce fnl f* **20/1**

5100 **5** *1 ¼* **Athletic**[9] 7880 4-9-6 64........(v) MartinLane 5 65+
(Andrew Reid) *hld up in last pair: tried to thread way through fr over 1f out: hd high and styd on same pce: nvr able to threaten* **20/1**

6206 **6** *hd* **West Leake (IRE)**[136] 4163 7-9-4 62........ LiamKeniry 9 62
(Paul Burgoyne) *prom: rdn 2f out: nt qckn over 1f out: one pce fnl f* **25/1**

3304 **7** *nk* **Golden Desert (IRE)**[9] 7880 9-9-7 65........ GrahamLee 2 64
(Simon Dow) *slowly away: hld up in last: coaxed along over 1f out: kpt on but nvr threatened* **6/1**[3]

606 **8** *hd* **Ovatory**[16] 7781 3-9-4 63........ AndreaAtzeni 12 61
(Amanda Perrett) *led: kicked on 2f out: hdd & wknd ins fnl f* **6/1**[3]

2106 **9** *1 ½* **Saskia's Dream**[18] 7743 5-9-5 63........(v) RobertHavlin 1 58
(Jane Chapple-Hyam) *wl in tch on inner: cl up and rdn over 1f out: nowhere to go sn after: eased fnl f* **25/1**

6056 **10** *2* **Rondeau (GR)**[23] 7652 8-8-13 62........ DanielMuscutt(5) 6 51
(Patrick Chamings) *slowly away: hld up in rr: tried to make prog and wd bnd 2f out: wknd fnl f* **12/1**

1-30 **11** *6* **Winter Song (IRE)**[122] 4636 3-9-5 64........ SteveDrowne 13 36
(Charles Hills) *facing sideways as tape wnt up: rcvrd to be prom on outer: wknd over 2f out* **33/1**

45 **12** *8* **Bint Alzain (IRE)**[169] 3051 4-8-13 60........ JemmaMarshall(3) 11 12
(Pat Phelan) *slowly away: effrt fr rr and wdst of all fr 3f out: lost grnd bnd 2f out: wknd* **25/1**

2155 **U** **Victorian Number (FR)**[53] 6928 5-9-7 65........ GeorgeBaker 3
(Geoffrey Deacon) *reluctant to line up: led in and uns rdr s* **7/2**[2]

1m 23.56s (-1.24) **Going Correction** -0.15s/f (Stan)
WFA 3 from 4yo+ 1lb **13** Ran SP% **121.7**
Speed ratings (Par 101): **101,99,99,98,97 97,96,96,95,92 85,76,**
toteswingers 1&2 £21.60, 2&3 £94.40, 1&3 £12.90 CSF £60.72 CT £716.03 TOTE £4.10: £1.90, £5.20, £4.50; EX 69.20 Trifecta £1047.00 Pool: £2206.86 - 1.58 winning units..
Owner E R Griffiths **Bred** P Burns **Trained** Pandy, Monmouths

FOCUS
Following an act of vandalism overnight, there was only one set of stalls available and, as this 13-runner field would have required two, it became a flip start which is never ideal in a Flat race. After the runners had burst through the tape once, on the second attempt the fancied Victorian Number was in the process of being led up behind the other runners when he suddenly stopped and sent George Baker over his head. Although they did their best to line up according to their draws, it was nowhere near a level start and this is not form to rely on.

8020 32RED.COM/BRITISH STALLION STUDS EBF FILLIES' H'CAP 1m (P)
2:00 (2:00) (Class 4) (0-85,85) 3-Y-O+ £6,630 (£1,973; £986; £493) Stalls High

Form RPR

400 **1** **Strictly Silca**[40] 7255 3-8-8 77 ow1........(v) WilliamTwiston-Davies(3) 3 85
(Mick Channon) *hld up in last pair: prog and squeezed through over 1f out: shkn up to ld last 150yds: pushed out* **14/1**

1231 **2** *½* **Araqella (IRE)**[9] 7876 3-8-9 75........ LiamJones 7 82
(William Haggas) *chsd ldr: rdn to chal 2f out: nt qckn 1f out: chsd wnr ins fnl f: styd on but a hld* **9/4**[1]

2143 **3** *1 ½* **Al Freej (IRE)**[25] 7608 4-8-12 76........ DaleSwift 9 81
(Brian Ellison) *led at gd pce: hrd pressed and sltly wd bnd 2f out: hdd and one pce last 150yds* **5/1**[3]

6300 **4** *½* **Queen Aggie (IRE)**[25] 7603 3-8-7 73........[1] MartinLane 4 75
(David Evans) *stdd s: hld up in last: urged along wl over 1f out: styd on fnl f to take 4th nr fin* **25/1**

3620 **5** *½* **Wakeup Little Suzy (IRE)**[9] 7876 3-8-9 75........(t) MartinHarley 5 76
(Marco Botti) *prom: drvn 2f out: tried to chal 1f out: wknd last 100yds* **10/1**

1200 **6** *1* **Young Dottie**[16] 7785 7-8-6 73........ JemmaMarshall(3) 1 73
(Pat Phelan) *hld up in rr: rdn on inner over 2f out: sme prog over 1f out: fdd fnl f* **33/1**

5422 **7** *nse* **Oasis Spirit**[12] 7841 3-8-6 72........(v) DavidProbert 2 71
(Andrew Balding) *hld up in midfield: gng strly 2f out: rdn over 1f out: hanging and fnd nil* **7/1**

4606 **8** *¾* **Movementneverlies**[63] 6642 3-8-5 71 oh3........ AndreaAtzeni 6 68
(Charles Hills) *prom: wl there jst over 2f out: hanging and wd bnd sn after: lost pl and nvr threatened after* **8/1**

60 **9** *6* **Lillebonne (FR)**[14] 7822 3-9-5 85........ DanielTudhope 8 68
(David O'Meara) *racd wd: in tch: wknd whn wd bnd 2f out* **7/2**[2]

1m 35.64s (-2.56) **Going Correction** -0.15s/f (Stan)
WFA 3 from 4yo+ 2lb **9** Ran SP% **115.8**
Speed ratings (Par 102): **106,105,104,103,103 102,101,101,95**
toteswingers 1&2 £14.60, 2&3 £2.40, 1&3 £13.10 CSF £45.92 CT £187.41 TOTE £18.70: £4.90, £1.10, £1.80; EX 80.60 Trifecta £597.80 Pool: £1656.88 - 2.07 winning units..
Owner Aldridge Racing Partnership **Bred** Aldridge Racing Partnership **Trained** West Ilsley, Berks

FOCUS
A decent fillies' handicap.

8021 BOOKMAKERS.CO.UK H'CAP 5f (P)
2:35 (2:38) (Class 4) (0-85,84) 3-Y-O+ £4,690 (£1,395; £697; £348) Stalls High

Form RPR

4203 **1** **Picansort**[56] 6850 6-9-7 84........(v) ShaneKelly 8 91
(Peter Crate) *hld up in last trio: shkn up and prog jst over 1f out: r.o wl fnl f to ld last strides* **14/1**

3102 **2** *hd* **Triple Dream**[46] 7112 8-9-3 80........(tp) DavidProbert 1 86
(Milton Bradley) *led 1f: chsd ldr after: rdn 2f out: rallied fnl f: upsides last strides: jst pipped* **7/1**

0350 **3** *nk* **Powerful Wind (IRE)**[93] 5669 4-8-10 73........ LukeMorris 9 78
(Ronald Harris) *forced to r wd early but led after 1f: drvn 2 l clr over 1f out: collared last strides* **33/1**

553 **4** *½* **Exotic Isle**[56] 6854 3-9-4 81........ AndreaAtzeni 3 84
(Ralph Beckett) *chsd ldrs: hrd rdn on inner over 1f out: styd on same pce: nvr quite able to chal* **4/1**[2]

0043 **5** *nk* **Senator Bong**[8] 7897 3-8-9 72........ LiamKeniry 2 74
(David Elsworth) *disp 2nd pl much of way: nt qckn 1f out: lost pls nr fin* **5/1**[3]

3056 **6** *nk* **Sandfrankskipsgo**[56] 6854 4-9-2 79........ SteveDrowne 10 80
(Peter Crate) *awkward s: wl in rr: effrt on wd outside over 1f out: kpt on fnl f: n.d* **16/1**

0051 **7** *shd* **Sir Pedro**[73] 6309 4-9-3 80........ GrahamLee 4 81+
(Robert Cowell) *hld up in tch: gng wl enough whn trapped bhd rivals fnl f: nt rcvr* **7/2**[1]

0003 **8** *1* **Cheworee**[33] 7420 4-9-7 84........ StephenCraine 5 81
(Tom Dascombe) *a in rr: rdn and no prog over 1f out* **8/1**

6215 **9** *nk* **Rocket Rob (IRE)**[72] 6331 7-9-4 81........ JamieMackay 6 77
(Willie Musson) *c out of the stalls v slowly: detached in last: one reminder fnl f: styd on quite takingly nr fin: nvr remotely involved* **10/1**

0064 **10** *2 ¾* **Royal Bajan (USA)**[9] 7887 5-9-1 78........(p) FrederikTylicki 7 64
(James Given) *chsd ldrs on outer: wknd wl over 1f out* **7/1**

58.41s (-0.39) **Going Correction** -0.15s/f (Stan) **10** Ran SP% **119.6**
Speed ratings (Par 105): **97,96,96,95,94 94,94,92,92,87**
toteswingers 1&2 £9.90, 2&3 £26.80, 1&3 £31.70 CSF £111.23 CT £3249.99 TOTE £11.50: £3.60, £2.70, £8.40; EX 60.80 Trifecta £2268.80 Part won. Pool: £3025.15 - 0.98 winning units..
Owner Peter Crate **Bred** Miss Brooke Sanders **Trained** Newdigate, Surrey

FOCUS
Fast and furious stuff in this good sprint handicap, yet the principals finished in a heap.

8022 BEST ODDS AT BOOKMAKERS.CO.UK H'CAP (DIV I) 6f (P)
3:10 (3:11) (Class 6) (0-60,62) 3-Y-0+ **£2,045** (£603; £302) **Stalls** Low

Form RPR
5312 **1** **Gregori (IRE)**[10] 7862 3-9-9 **62**.....(t) SeanLevey 5 79
(Brian Meehan) *mde all: clr over 2f out: rdn whn stmbld sltly over 1f out: unchal* **11/10**[1]
6125 **2** *4* **Metropolitan Chief**[23] 7644 9-9-1 **54**.....(p) TomMcLaughlin 7 58
(Paul Burgoyne) *chsd ldrs: rdn 2f out: kpt on to take 2nd jst ins fnl f: no ch w wnr* **25/1**
3300 **3** *1* **Chevise (IRE)**[23] 7652 5-9-7 **60**.....(p) AndreaAtzeni 2 61
(Steve Woodman) *sn in rr: outpcd fr 1/2-way: shkn up and styd on wl fnl f to take 3rd last strides* **10/1**
2533 **4** *½* **Homeboy (IRE)**[10] 7862 5-9-5 **58**..... MartinDwyer 6 57
(Marcus Tregoning) *chsd wnr: rdn and no imp 2f out: lost 2nd and one pce 1f out* **4/1**[2]
4531 **5** *¾* **Sarah Berry**[38] 7292 4-9-6 **59**.....(v) LukeMorris 1 56
(Chris Dwyer) *chsd ldng pair: rdn 2f out: wnt 2nd briefly 1f out: fdd fnl f* **10/1**
4262 **6** *hd* **Hinton Admiral**[23] 7643 9-9-4 **57**..... RobertHavlin 10 53
(Pat Eddery) *chsd ldrs on outer: no prog 2f out: plugged on ins fnl f* **8/1**[3]
4460 **7** *1* **Ryan Style (IRE)**[39] 7262 7-9-6 **59**.....(tp) GrahamLee 4 52
(Lisa Williamson) *towards rr: rdn fr 1/2-way: plugged on but nvr a factor* **14/1**
5465 **8** *1* **Baby Dottie**[23] 7652 6-9-1 **57**.....(tp) JemmaMarshall(3) 9 47
(Pat Phelan) *nvr beyond midfield: no prog 2f out: wl btn after* **12/1**
0400 **9** *6* **My Sweet Lord**[46] 7086 3-9-5 **58**..... LiamKeniry 8 28
(Mark Usher) *rel to r and lost many l: a bhd: t.o* **20/1**
000- **10** *¾* **Underwhelm**[367] 7813 3-8-13 **52**..... MartinLane 11 20
(Andrew Reid) *a in rr: struggling bef 1/2-way: t.o* **50/1**

1m 10.78s (-1.12) **Going Correction** -0.15s/f (Stan) **10** Ran SP% **121.8**
Speed ratings (Par 101): **101,95,94,93,92 92,91,89,81,80**
toteswingers 1&2 £8.10, 2&3 £27.10, 1&3 £4.00 CSF £41.34 CT £211.19 TOTE £2.10: £1.40, £4.50, £2.30; EX 56.10 Trifecta £346.90 Pool: £2391.54 - 5.17 winning units..
Owner Stephen Tucker **Bred** Mrs James Wigan **Trained** Manton, Wilts
FOCUS
A moderate handicap and few got into it.

8023 BEST ODDS AT BOOKMAKERS.CO.UK H'CAP (DIV II) 6f (P)
3:45 (3:47) (Class 6) (0-60,60) 3-Y-0+ **£2,045** (£603; £302)

Form RPR
1300 **1** **Clock Opera (IRE)**[32] 7454 3-8-13 **59**..... LouisSteward(7) 11 67
(William Stone) *hmpd and dropped to last trio after 1f: prog over 1f out: squeezed between rivals ins fnl f and r.o to ld last stride* **16/1**
5154 **2** *shd* **Pharoh Jake**[46] 7086 5-9-2 **55**..... KieranO'Neill 6 63
(John Bridger) *pressed ldr: rdn to ld 2f out: kpt on wl whn pressed ins fnl f: hdd last stride* **12/1**
3630 **3** *nk* **Proper Charlie**[53] 6928 5-9-5 **58**.....(v) AmirQuinn 1 65
(Lee Carter) *chsd ldng pair: rdn over 1f out: clsd to chal ins fnl f: nt qckn nr fin* **8/1**[3]
5003 **4** *½* **Putin (IRE)**[4] 7958 5-9-5 **58**.....(bt) PaddyAspell 4 63
(Phil McEntee) *led at gd pce: hdd 2f out: kpt on tl no ex last 50yds* **4/1**[1]
4156 **5** *¾* **Admirals Walk (IRE)**[7] 7924 3-9-5 **58**.....(p) LiamKeniry 7 61
(Sylvester Kirk) *chsd ldrs: rdn over 2f out: keeping on at same pce and wl hld whn nt clr run nr fin* **14/1**
550 **6** *1* **Diamond Vine (IRE)**[25] 7599 5-9-0 **53**.....(b) LukeMorris 12 53
(Ronald Harris) *towards rr and nt gng wl: taken wdst of all over 2f out: kpt on fnl f: n.d* **12/1**
2416 **7** *½* **New Rich**[12] 7841 3-9-7 **60**.....(p) JohnFahy 3 58
(Eve Johnson Houghton) *wl in rr: carried hd to one side whn asked for effrt fr 2f out: kpt on fnl f* **5/1**[2]
00 **8** *2* **Kai**[8] 7905 4-8-12 **51**.....(b) DavidProbert 9 43
(Alan McCabe) *chsd ldrs towards outer: rdn over 2f out: nt qckn over 1f out: fdd* **25/1**
0340 **9** *nse* **Catflap (IRE)**[16] 7783 4-9-6 **59**.....(p) GrahamLee 5 51
(Derek Haydn Jones) *covered up in midfield: nudged along and no prog over 1f out: lost pl fnl f* **16/1**
5133 **10** *2¼* **Dixie Gwalia**[244] 1155 5-9-4 **57**.....(v) RobertHavlin 8 41
(Michael Attwater) *a towards rr: struggling 2f out: no ch whn nt clr run jst ins fnl f* **12/1**
0004 **11** *½* **The Wee Chief (IRE)**[10] 7862 7-9-4 **57**.....(b) SeanLevey 2 40
(Jimmy Fox) *nvr bttr than midfield: no prog over 1f out: wknd fnl f* **4/1**[1]
01U4 **12** *1¼* **Bestfootforward**[37] 7319 4-8-12 **56**..... ShelleyBirkett(5) 10 35
(Julia Feilden) *mostly in last: lost tch over 2f out* **12/1**

1m 9.9s (-2.00) **Going Correction** -0.15s/f (Stan) **12** Ran SP% **120.8**
Speed ratings (Par 101): **107,106,106,105,104 103,102,100,100,97 96,94**
toteswingers 1&2 £31.10, 2&3 £15.20, 1&3 £21.20 CSF £198.76 CT £1684.90 TOTE £18.50: £4.70, £3.50, £2.40; EX 258.10 Trifecta £1402.30 Part won. Pool: £1869.74 - 0.65 winning units..
Owner Caroline Scott & Shane Fairweather **Bred** Ms H W Topping **Trained** West Wickham, Cambs
FOCUS
Another flip start and it took them a couple of attempts before they were allowed to go. For information purposes this division was 0.88 seconds quicker than the first, but the different start should be borne in mind when comparing times between the two legs.
T/Plt: £41.90 to a £1 stake. Pool of £61060.46 - 1061.34 winning tickets. T/Qpdt: £29.10 to a £1 stake. Pool of £4836.55 - 122.95 winning tickets. JN

8002 WOLVERHAMPTON (A.W) (L-H)
Saturday, November 23

OFFICIAL GOING: Standard
Wind: Light across Weather: Fine

8024 32RED.COM NURSERY H'CAP 5f 216y(P)
5:50 (5:50) (Class 5) (0-75,73) 2-Y-0 **£2,587** (£770; £384; £192) **Stalls** Low

Form RPR
1051 **1** **Porteous**[2] 7986 2-9-3 **69** 6ex..... JoeFanning 2 78
(Mick Channon) *a.p: chsd ldr 1/2-way: shkn up to ld wl ins fnl f: rdn out* **9/4**[1]
1100 **2** *2* **Captain Secret**[8] 7892 2-9-7 **73**..... MartinHarley 1 76
(Marco Botti) *led: rdn and hdd wl ins fnl f: styd on same pce* **9/2**[3]
2512 **3** *3¼* **Kodafine (IRE)**[8] 7900 2-8-11 **70**..... EoinWalsh(7) 6 63
(David Evans) *prom: lost pl 5f out: pushed along and hdwy over 1f out: nt trble ldrs* **7/2**[2]
0030 **4** *4½* **Captain Gee**[46] 7095 2-8-3 **62**..... JoeDoyle(7) 3 42
(John Quinn) *s.i.s: sn prom: rdn over 2f out: wknd over 1f out* **9/2**[3]
3040 **5** *½* **Outback Lover (IRE)**[17] 7771 2-8-10 **62**.....(b) LiamJones 5 40
(J S Moore) *chsd ldr to 1/2-way: sn pushed along: wknd over 1f out* **16/1**
0205 **6** *13* **Concrete Mac**[9] 7879 2-9-0 **73**.....(p) CharlieBennett(7) 4 12
(Hughie Morrison) *sn outpcd* **6/1**

1m 15.07s (0.07) **Going Correction** +0.075s/f (Slow) **6** Ran SP% **109.5**
Speed ratings (Par 96): **102,99,95,89,88 71**
toteswingers 1&2 £1.20, 1&3 £1.50, 2&3 £2.90 CSF £11.95 TOTE £2.50: £1.30, £2.10; EX 9.60 Trifecta £21.70 Pool: £2419.08 - 83.32 winning units..
Owner Imperial **Bred** Imperial & Mike Channon Bloodstock Ltd **Trained** West Ilsley, Berks
FOCUS
Only two mattered from the turn in.

8025 32RED CASINO (S) STKS 5f 216y(P)
6:20 (6:20) (Class 6) 2-Y-0 **£1,940** (£577; £288; £144) **Stalls** Low

Form RPR
2354 **1** **Little Big Man**[8] 7893 2-8-7 57.....(b) JoshBaudains(5) 2 67
(Sylvester Kirk) *chsd ldrs: rdn to ld over 1f out: r.o wl: comf* **5/2**[2]
0056 **2** *4* **Vodka Chaser (IRE)**[2] 7986 2-8-7 60..... LiamJones 1 48
(J S Moore) *chsd ldrs: outpcd over 3f out: rallied over 1f out: styd on to go 2nd wl ins fnl f: no ch w wnr* **7/2**[3]
3105 **3** *1½* **El Duque**[3] 7977 2-8-10 58.....(p) RyanWhile(7) 6 54
(Bill Turner) *disp ld tl wnt on wl over 1f out: rdn and hdd over 1f out: no ex ins fnl f* **14/1**
1056 **4** *4½* **Bird Of Light (IRE)**[9] 7882 2-8-12 67..... MartinHarley 3 35
(Jamie Osborne) *disp ld tl pushed along wl over 2f out: wknd fnl f* **7/2**[3]
0 **5** *8* **Vision Of Rome**[10] 7852 2-8-7 0..... JoeFanning 5
(Mick Channon) *hld up: hdwy 1/2-way: rdn over 2f out: wknd wl over 1f out* **9/4**[1]

1m 16.3s (1.30) **Going Correction** +0.075s/f (Slow) **5** Ran SP% **110.5**
Speed ratings (Par 94): **94,88,86,80,70**
CSF £11.48 TOTE £3.40: £2.00, £3.60; EX 11.90 Trifecta £36.80 Pool: £2242.50 - 45.65 winning units..There was no bid for the winner.
Owner N Simpson & S Kirk **Bred** Paul Merritt **Trained** Upper Lambourn, Berks
FOCUS
An ordinary race, but a smooth success from the winner.

8026 32RED E B F STALLIONS MAIDEN STKS 1m 141y(P)
6:50 (6:50) (Class 5) 2-Y-0 **£2,911** (£866; £432; £216) **Stalls** Low

Form RPR
00 **1** **Rite To Reign**[10] 7854 2-9-0 0..... DannyBrock(5) 4 73
(Philip McBride) *chsd ldrs: rdn to ld over 1f out: hung rt wl ins fnl f: jst hld on* **50/1**
0 **2** *shd* **Dragoon Guard (IRE)**[38] 7308 2-9-5 0..... MartinHarley 9 73+
(Marco Botti) *hld up: hdwy over 1f out: rdn and r.o wl ins fnl f: nt quite get there* **3/1**[2]
3 *1¾* **Fine Vintage (FR)** 2-9-5 0..... JoeFanning 3 70+
(Mark Johnston) *chsd ldrs: shkn up and ev ch 1f out: rdn and styng on whn hmpd and nt rcvr wl ins fnl f* **7/2**[3]
02 **4** *2½* **Alexanor (IRE)**[8] 7902 2-9-5 0.....(t) LukeMorris 1 64
(Marco Botti) *led: rdn and hdd over 1f out: no ex ins fnl f* **13/8**[1]
2 **5** *2¼* **Choice Of Destiny**[22] 7664 2-9-0 0..... WilliamCarson 2 54
(Philip McBride) *chsd ldr: rdn over 2f out: wknd ins fnl f* **9/2**
6 *3¼* **Market Storm (FR)** 2-9-2 0..... SladeO'Hara(3) 5 52
(Michael Mullineaux) *s.i.s: hld up: rdn over 2f out: n.d* **25/1**
0 **7** *nk* **Aptitude**[8] 7902 2-9-0 0..... AdamBeschizza 6 47
(Tobias B P Coles) *prom: rdn over 2f out: wknd over 1f out* **50/1**
8 *½* **Mahon Falls**[62] 6671 2-8-7 0..... EoinWalsh(7) 7 46
(David Evans) *s.i.s: hld up: rdn over 3f out: a in rr* **16/1**
00 **9** *8* **Secret Keeper**[9] 7874 2-9-0 0..... DanielTudhope 8 29
(Sir Mark Prescott Bt) *hld up: rdn and wknd over 2f out* **50/1**

1m 52.02s (1.52) **Going Correction** +0.075s/f (Slow) **9** Ran SP% **119.1**
Speed ratings (Par 96): **96,95,94,92,90 87,86,86,79**
toteswingers 1&2 £49.20, 1&3 £51.30, 2&3 £2.30 CSF £199.25 TOTE £30.40: £6.60, £1.50, £1.40; EX 249.90 Trifecta £925.40 Pool: £2534.33 - 3.05 winning units..
Owner Maelor Racing **Bred** Oscar Stud **Trained** Newmarket, Suffolk
■ Stewards' Enquiry : Danny Brock four-day ban: careless riding (Dec 7,9-11)
FOCUS
There was a turn-up in this maiden.

8027 32RED ON THE APP STORE H'CAP 2m 119y(P)
7:20 (7:20) (Class 6) (0-60,58) 3-Y-0+ **£1,940** (£577; £288; £144) **Stalls** Low

Form RPR
0064 **1** **Jawaab (IRE)**[22] 7668 9-9-3 **49**.....(e) JoeFanning 9 61
(Philip Kirby) *broke wl: hmpd and lost pl sn after s: hld up: hdwy over 4f out: shkn up to ld over 1f out: rdn out* **7/2**[1]
5/26 **2** *1¾* **Sergeant Pink (IRE)**[22] 5048 7-9-2 **53**.....(p) EmmaSayer(5) 13 63
(Dianne Sayer) *hld up: hdwy over 2f out: rdn over 1f out: styd on same pce ins fnl f* **16/1**
0631 **3** *½* **Lacey**[8] 7899 4-9-2 **53**.....(e) JackDuern(5) 10 62
(Andrew Hollinshead) *chsd ldr over 5f: remained handy: pushed along over 3f out: rdn over 1f out: styd on same pce ins fnl f* **9/2**[3]
P031 **4** *5* **Ice Apple**[25] 7612 5-9-2 **48**..... JimmyQuinn 4 51
(John E Long) *prom: rdn over 3f out: no ex fnl f* **4/1**[2]
260- **5** *2½* **Tokyo Brown (USA)**[381] 7629 4-9-7 **53**..... LukeMorris 1 53
(Heather Main) *prom: chsd ldr 11f out tl led 3f out: rdn and hdd over 1f out: wknd ins fnl f* **8/1**
0420 **6** *5* **Grandiloquent**[17] 7767 4-9-12 **58**.....(p) DanielTudhope 6 52
(Kevin Ryan) *led: rdn and hdd 3f out: wknd and eased fnl f* **9/2**[3]
56/0 **7** *11* **Compassion**[28] 7539 5-9-4 **57**..... JaneElliott(7) 3 38
(Emma Lavelle) *sn pushed along in rr: effrt over 3f out: wknd over 2f out* **25/1**
6-00 **8** *¾* **Primacy (IRE)**[152] 3618 4-9-6 **52**..... LiamKeniry 8 32
(Neil Mulholland) *prom: rdn over 3f out: wknd 2f out* **22/1**
1-04 **9** *15* **Dew Reward (IRE)**[225] 1513 5-9-4 **57**..... RyanWhile(7) 2 19
(Bill Turner) *mid-div: hmpd and lost pl over 14f out: bhd fnl 7f* **28/1**
-030 **10** *2* **Azerodegree (IRE)**[192] 1572 4-9-11 **57**..... GrahamLee 12 17
(Iain Jardine) *hld up: rdn over 4f out: sn wknd* **12/1**

The Form Book Flat, Raceform Ltd, Compton, RG20 6NL.

000/ 11 *14* **Until The Man (IRE)**[27] 4322 6-8-9 **48**....................(v) LouisSteward(7) 11
(Natalie Lloyd-Beavis) *chsd ldrs tl rdn and wknd over 4f out* **40/1**
3m 44.19s (2.39) **Going Correction** +0.075s/f (Slow) 11 Ran SP% **117.4**
Speed ratings (Par 101): **97,96,95,93,92 90,84,84,77,76 69**
toteswingers 1&2 £8.50, 1&3 £3.40, 2&3 £9.60 CSF £57.57 CT £259.15 TOTE £5.40: £1.80, £2.40, £1.70; EX 85.30 Trifecta £385.30 Pool: £2463.64 - 4.79 winning units..
Owner L & D Racing **Bred** Hascombe And Valiant Studs **Trained** Middleham, N Yorks
■ Stewards' Enquiry : Louis Steward one-day ban: careless riding (Dec 7)

FOCUS
A moderate staying handicap.

8028 LADBROKES CLAIMING STKS 1m 141y(P)
7:50 (7:50) (Class 6) 3-Y-O+ **£1,940** (£577; £288; £144) **Stalls** Low

Form RPR
6253 1 **Honey Of A Kitten (USA)**[36] 7350 5-8-4 67..................(b) EoinWalsh(7) 4 77
(David Evans) *plld hrd: trckd ldr: led over 5f out: clr fnl 2f* **9/1**
5151 2 *5* **Tabaayun (IRE)**[7] 7924 3-9-3 82..................................(v) DanielTudhope 7 76
(David O'Meara) *chsd ldrs: rdn over 2f out: styd on same pce* **11/10**[1]
0-00 3 *3* **Complexity**[19] 3945 3-8-10 73... LiamKeniry 3 62
(Seamus Mullins) *hld up: plld hrd: hdwy over 5f out: chsd ldr over 4f out: hung lft fr over 2f out: sn rdn: no ex fr over 1f out* **33/1**
04 4 *15* **Cumberworth**[9] 7884 3-8-0 0.................................... DanielleMooney(7) 1 28
(Michael Easterby) *led 1f: chsd ldrs: lost pl over 5f out: rdn and wknd over 3f out* **66/1**
2000 5 *1 ½* **Sam Nombulist**[14] 7820 5-8-13 78...................................(v) GrahamLee 2 28
(Ian Semple) *w ldr tl led over 7f out: hdd over 5f out: rdn and wknd over 3f out* **4/1**[3]
011 6 *54* **Alakhan (IRE)**[28] 7544 7-8-12 77................(p) WilliamTwiston-Davies(3) 5
(Ian Williams) *s.s: hld up: hdwy over 3f out: nt clr run fr over 2f out tl lost action over 1f out: virtually p.u sn after* **5/2**[2]
1m 50.61s (0.11) **Going Correction** +0.075s/f (Slow)
WFA 3 from 5yo+ 3lb 6 Ran SP% **110.6**
Speed ratings (Par 101): **102,97,94,81,80 32**
toteswingers 1&2 £3.30, 1&3 £9.30, 2&3 £9.10 CSF £19.01 TOTE £6.50: £3.70, £1.60; EX 27.00 Trifecta £129.90 Pool: £3008.19 - 17.35 winning units..There were no claims.
Owner Mrs E Evans **Bred** Kenneth L Ramsey And Sarah K Ramsey **Trained** Pandy, Monmouths

FOCUS
With a couple of the fancied runners failing to run to their best for one reason or another, this is probably questionable form.

8029 BOOKMAKERS.CO.UK H'CAP (DIV I) 5f 216y(P)
8:20 (8:22) (Class 5) (0-70,70) 3-Y-O+ **£2,911** (£866; £432; £216) **Stalls** Low

Form RPR
0104 1 **Iceblast**[15] 7801 5-8-12 **61**..(v) JamesSullivan 9 71
(Michael Easterby) *sn outpcd: hdwy over 1f out: rdn to ld and hung lft ins fnl f: r.o* **7/1**
4440 2 *2* **Indian Affair**[33] 7432 3-9-3 **66**.. DavidProbert 1 70
(Milton Bradley) *led: hung rt fr over 2f out: rdn over 1f out: hdd and unable qck ins fnl f* **13/2**[3]
3000 3 *½* **Sewn Up**[9] 7888 3-9-4 **67**..(e) ShaneKelly 8 70
(Andrew Hollinshead) *hld up: hdwy 1/2-way: nt clr run over 1f out: rdn and carried rt ins fnl f: nt run on* **13/2**[3]
3060 4 *3 ½* **Captain Scooby**[7] 7937 7-8-12 **64**....................................(e) BillyCray(3) 3 56
(Richard Guest) *sn outpcd: hdwy over 1f out: wknd wl ins fnl f* **14/1**
6003 5 *1 ¾* **Invigilator**[19] 7729 5-9-2 **65**..(t) RaulDaSilva 5 52
(Derek Shaw) *prom: rdn over 1f out: ev ch ins fnl f: sn wknd* **3/1**[1]
1360 6 *2 ¾* **Funding Deficit (IRE)**[25] 7603 3-9-4 **67**.................................[1] GrahamGibbons 2 46
(David Barron) *chsd ldr: rdn over 2f out: wknd over 1f out* **9/2**[2]
0201 7 *¾* **Speightowns Kid (USA)**[11] 7848 5-9-2 **65**.................(b) RobertHavlin 4 41
(Alan Berry) *chsd ldrs: rdn over 1f out: wknd ins fnl f* **3/1**[1]
2420 8 *1* **Wooden King (IRE)**[16] 7783 8-9-7 **70**......................(p) TomMcLaughlin 6 43
(Malcolm Saunders) *chsd ldrs: rdn over 2f out: wknd ins fnl f* **16/1**
1m 15.48s (0.48) **Going Correction** +0.075s/f (Slow) 8 Ran SP% **119.9**
Speed ratings (Par 103): **99,96,95,91,88 85,84,82**
toteswingers 1&2 £4.20, 1&3 £14.30, 2&3 £8.60 CSF £54.05 CT £319.23 TOTE £8.70: £2.30, £2.30, £2.50; EX 61.40 Trifecta £263.80 Pool: £3292.05 - 9.35 winning units..
Owner B Padgett **Bred** A C M Spalding **Trained** Sheriff Hutton, N Yorks
■ Stewards' Enquiry : David Probert caution: careless riding.

FOCUS
They went very fast in front and the race was set up for a closer.

8030 BOOKMAKERS.CO.UK H'CAP (DIV II) 5f 216y(P)
8:50 (8:51) (Class 5) (0-70,68) 3-Y-O+ **£2,911** (£866; £432; £216) **Stalls** Low

Form RPR
0050 1 **Monsieur Royale**[15] 7801 3-9-1 **65**............(b) WilliamTwiston-Davies(3) 4 73
(Geoffrey Oldroyd) *chsd ldr over 3f out: rdn to ld ins fnl f: styd on* **9/2**[3]
0060 2 *nk* **Colourbearer (IRE)**[15] 7801 6-9-6 **67**.............................(t) DavidProbert 5 74
(Milton Bradley) *trckd ldrs: wnt 2nd over 2f out: rdn and ev ch ins fnl f: styd on* **10/1**
1022 3 *1 ¼* **Trending (IRE)**[15] 7801 4-8-12 **66**..............................(bt) DavidParkes(7) 8 69
(Jeremy Gask) *plld hrd and prom: rdn over 1f out: edgd lft ins fnl f: styd on* **6/4**[1]
1405 4 *hd* **Bilash**[70] 6382 6-9-1 **67**... JackDuern(5) 3 70
(Andrew Hollinshead) *prom: rdn over 1f out: kpt on* **7/1**
0023 5 *nk* **Rise To Glory (IRE)**[11] 7848 5-9-4 **65**................................. DuranFentiman 7 67
(Shaun Harris) *led: rdn over 1f out: hdd ins fnl f: styd on same pce* **7/2**[2]
0400 6 *2* **Run It Twice (IRE)**[18] 7754 3-9-3 **64**...........................(b) MartinHarley 1 60
(David Evans) *hld up: rdn over 2f out: nvr trbld ldrs* **7/1**
1456 7 *16* **Sam Spade (IRE)**[162] 3289 3-9-0 **68**.............................. AdamMcLean(7) 9 16
(Derek Shaw) *hld up: rdn 1/2-way: wknd over 2f out* **20/1**
1m 15.62s (0.62) **Going Correction** +0.075s/f (Slow) 7 Ran SP% **119.3**
Speed ratings (Par 103): **98,97,95,95,95 92,71**
toteswingers 1&2 £5.10, 1&3 £2.40, 2&3 £4.30 CSF £49.52 CT £98.85 TOTE £7.40: £4.20, £3.90; EX 58.10 Trifecta £98.80 Pool: £3976.31 - 22.58 winning units..
Owner Casino Royale Racing **Bred** Bond Thoroughbred Corporation **Trained** Brawby, N Yorks

FOCUS
They went a more sensible gallop here, but the winning time wasn't far off the first division (0.14sec slower).

8031 CORAL APP DOWNLOAD FROM THE APP STORE H'CAP 1m 4f 50y(P)
9:20 (9:20) (Class 6) (0-60,61) 3-Y-O+ **£1,940** (£577; £288; £144) **Stalls** Low

Form RPR
0512 1 **Tracks Of My Tears**[28] 7543 3-8-7 **52**.......................... RyanPowell(3) 12 62+
(Giles Bravery) *hld up: hdwy over 5f out: chsd ldr over 1f out: rdn to ld ins fnl f: styd on* **3/1**[1]
6322 2 *hd* **Men Don't Cry (IRE)**[10] 7857 4-9-7 **60**......................... MarkCoumbe(3) 3 70
(Ed de Giles) *hld up: hdwy over 4f out: led over 2f out: rdn and hdd ins fnl f: styd on gamely* **11/2**[3]
6004 3 *16* **Rancho Montoya (IRE)**[33] 7422 3-9-3 **59**.....................(v) DavidProbert 2 45
(Andrew Balding) *prom: chsd ldr over 3f out: rdn and ev ch over 2f out: wknd over 1f out* **15/2**
4455 4 *¾* **Well Owd Mon**[8] 7907 3-8-4 **51**...................................(e[1]) JackDuern(5) 9 36
(Andrew Hollinshead) *hld up: hdwy over 3f out: rdn and wknd over 2f out* **16/1**
0400 5 *1 ¾* **Azabitmour (FR)**[25] 7610 3-8-11 **53**..............................(b[1]) LukeMorris 11 35
(John Best) *s.s: hld up: sme hdwy over 2f out: n.d* **16/1**
0313 6 *2* **Captain Caroline**[12] 7839 3-9-5 **61**.................................... ShaneKelly 10 40
(Mike Murphy) *prom: chsd ldr 9f out tl led over 5f out: rdn and hdd over 2f out: wknd over 1f out* **4/1**[2]
0552 7 *3 ¾* **High On A Hill (IRE)**[22] 7668 6-9-9 **59**.........................(b[1]) GrahamLee 6 32
(Iain Jardine) *hld up: hdwy over 3f out: rdn and wknd 2f out* **7/1**
4000 8 *1 ¼* **Call Of Duty (IRE)**[28] 6296 8-8-13 **54**..........................(p) EmmaSayer(5) 1 25
(Dianne Sayer) *hld up: rdn over 3f out: a in rr* **25/1**
-000 9 *24* **Red Willow**[31] 7458 7-8-11 **47**... JimmyQuinn 8
(John E Long) *prom tl rdn and wknd over 3f out* **40/1**
5040 10 *11* **Lalinde**[15] 7806 3-8-4 **46**.. KieranO'Neill 4
(Daniel Kubler) *hld up: rdn over 4f out: sn wknd* **40/1**
0005 11 *7* **Capetown Kid**[10] 7857 3-9-1 **57**.. LiamKeniry 5
(Sylvester Kirk) *hld up in tch: nt clr run and lost pl 4f out: sn wknd* **20/1**
6000 12 *99* **Jeer (IRE)**[89] 5833 9-9-0 **50**.......................................(b) GrahamGibbons 7
(Michael Easterby) *chsd ldr 3f: remained handy tl rdn and wknd 3f out: eased* **15/2**
2m 39.98s (-1.12) **Going Correction** +0.075s/f (Slow)
WFA 3 from 4yo+ 6lb 12 Ran SP% **121.7**
Speed ratings (Par 101): **106,105,95,94,93 92,89,88,72,65 60,**
toteswingers 1&2 £3.80, 1&3 £10.20, 2&3 £8.50 CSF £19.18 CT £115.45 TOTE £5.70: £1.10, £2.50, £2.40; EX 20.30 Trifecta £140.60 Pool: £3711.56 - 19.78 winning units..
Owner D B Clark **Bred** The Policy Setters **Trained** Newmarket, Suffolk

FOCUS
The first two came well clear.
T/Plt: £322.60. Pool: £109,834.76 - 248.47 winning units. T/Qpdt: £48.30. Pool: £11,492.32 - 175.79 winning units. CR

8032 - (Foreign Racing) - See Raceform Interactive

2700 TOKYO (L-H)
Sunday, November 24

OFFICIAL GOING: Turf: firm

8033a JAPAN CUP (GRADE 1) (3YO+) (TURF) 1m 4f
6:55 (12:00) 3-Y-O£1,800,624 (£717,184; £450,830; £269,618; £177,380)

RPR
1 **Gentildonna (JPN)**[28] 4-8-9 0.. RyanMoore 7 112
(Sei Ishizaka, Japan) *a.p: rdn to chal over 2f out: led over 1f out: styd on: strly pressed fnl strides: jst hld on* **11/10**[1]
2 *nse* **Denim And Ruby (JPN)**[14] 3-8-5 0.......................... SuguruHamanaka 9 114
(Katsuhiko Sumii, Japan) *hld up towards rr: rdn 3f out: short of room briefly 2f out: styd on strly and wnt 2nd cl home: pressed wnr fnl strides: jst failed* **29/1**
3 *nk* **Tosen Jordan (JPN)**[28] 7-9-0 0.. WilliamBuick 5 116
(Yasutoshi Ikee, Japan) *pushed along to go forward and trckd ldr: rdn to chal over 2f out: styd on wl but nt quite pce of wnr and dropped to 3rd cl home* **99/1**
4 *¾* **Admire Rakti (JPN)**[21] 5-9-0 0..................................... CraigAWilliams 6 115
(Tomoyuki Umeda, Japan) *midfield on inner: rdn over 2f out: styd on wl and wnt 4th cl home: nvr nrr* **201/10**
5 *nk* **Dunaden (FR)**[19] 7761 7-9-0 0..................................... JamieSpencer 10 115
(M Delzangles, France) *hld up in midfield on outer: rdn over 2f out: styd on steadily down wd outside and wnt 5th cl home: nvr nrr* **116/1**
6 *nk* **Lelouch (JPN)**[21] 5-9-0 0.. YuichiFukunaga 11 114
(Kazuo Fujisawa, Japan) *prom on outer: rdn over 2f out: kpt on same pce and nvr quite able to chal: dropped to 6th cl home* **247/10**
7 *nse* **Verxina (JPN)**[14] 4-8-9 0.. Yasunarilwata 1 109
(Yasuo Tomomichi, Japan) *broke wl and trckd ldr on inner: rdn over 2f out: kpt on same pce and nvr able to chal* **48/1**
8 *nk* **Uncoiled (FR)**[28] 4-9-0 0.. HirokiGoto 3 113
(Yoshito Yahagi, Japan) *midfield in tch: rdn over 2f out: kpt on same pce and nvr able to chal* **203/10**
9 *½* **Nakayama Knight (JPN)**[28] 5-9-0 0......................... YoshitomiShibata 2 113
(Yoshitaka Ninomiya, Japan) *midfield in tch on inner: rdn over 2f out: kpt on but nt pce to chal* **53/1**
10 *½* **Eishin Flash (JPN)**[28] 6-9-0 0.. MircoDemuro 4 112
(Hideaki Fujiwara, Japan) *led: pressed fr over 2f out: rdn and hdd over 1f out: sn no ex: fdd* **39/10**[3]
11 *nse* **Hit The Target (JPN)**[28] 5-9-0 0... YutakaTake 16 112
(Keiji Kato, Japan) *midfield on outer: rapid hdwy and prom 3f out: rdn to chal and ev ch 2f out: kpt on tl no ex and fdd ins fnl f* **34/1**
12 *nk* **Hokko Brave (JPN)**[21] 5-9-0 0.. KoseiMiura 12 111
(Yasutoshi Matsunaga, Japan) *midfield: rdn over 2f out: kpt on but sn no imp* **185/1**
13 *nse* **Simenon (IRE)**[19] 7761 6-9-0 0.. RichardHughes 14 111
(W P Mullins, Ire) *hld up in midfield on inner: swtchd rt and rdn over 2f out: sn outpcd: plugged on but n.d* **163/1**
14 *1 ¼* **Smart Gear (JPN)**[14] 8-9-0 0... KeitaTosaki 15 109
(Masaru Sayama, Japan) *hld up in rr: rdn over 2f out: sn outpcd: nvr a factor* **400/1**
15 *3 ½* **Gold Ship (JPN)**[49] 4-9-0 0... HiroyukiUchida 13 104
(Naosuke Sugai, Japan) *hld up in rr: last 1/2-way: rdn and sme hdwy on outer 3f out: no imp and btn in st: nvr a factor* **12/5**[2]
16 *3* **Fire (JPN)**[22] 5-9-0 0... NorihiroYokoyama 8 99
(Masaru Honda, Japan) *hld up and a in rr: rdn over 2f out: no imp and btn: eased: nvr a factor* **156/1**
17 *nk* **Joshua Tree (IRE)**[28] 7563 6-9-0 0.................................. JohnnyMurtagh 17 98
(Ed Dunlop) *midfield in tch on outer: rdn over 2f out: lost pl and dropped to rr over 1f out: eased whn btn* **111/1**
2m 26.1s (0.60)
WFA 3 from 4yo+ 6lb 17 Ran SP% **125.6**
PARI-MUTUEL (all including 100 jpy stake): WIN 210; SHOW 120, 510, 1220; DF 2500; SF 3330.
Owner Sunday Racing Co Ltd **Bred** Northern Racing **Trained** Japan

FOCUS
This year's Japan Cup didn't look to have a great deal of depth to it and there were two clear market leaders. It proved a tactical affair too, with only a modest early pace set, and there was a bunched finish.

8024 WOLVERHAMPTON (A.W) (L-H)
Monday, November 25

OFFICIAL GOING: Standard
Wind: virtually nil Weather: dry and bright

8034 COMPARE BOOKMAKERS AT BOOKMAKERS.CO.UK H'CAP (DIV I) 5f 20y(P)
1:55 (1:55) (Class 6) (0-60,60) 3-Y-O+ £1,940 (£577; £288; £144) Stalls Low

Form RPR
4060 1 **Danzoe (IRE)**[19] 7772 6-9-0 **60**..[1] EoinWalsh(7) 4 69
(Christine Dunnett) *mde all: pushed along and wnt clr over 1f out: kpt on wl ins fnl f* **9/2**[2]
4505 2 1 ½ **Above The Stars**[3] 8002 5-9-2 **58**..................(p) RyanPowell(3) 8 62
(Conor Dore) *chsd ldng trio: rdn and effrt to chse wnr wl over 1f out: no imp fnl 100yds* **6/1**[3]
40 3 2 ¼ **Enter The Red (IRE)**[37] 7386 4-8-13 **55**..................(bt) LeighRoche(3) 5 51
(Aidan Anthony Howard, Ire) *sn bustled along in midfield: effrt u.p on inner over 1f out: 3rd and kpt on same pce ins fnl f* **3/1**[1]
0006 4 1 ½ **Your Gifted (IRE)**[13] 7848 6-9-1 **57**.................... MarkCoumbe(3) 1 48
(Lisa Williamson) *stdd after s: hld up in last pair: rdn and hdwy on outer over 1f out: kpt on fnl f* **8/1**
1000 5 *shd* **Speedyfix**[13] 7848 6-9-2 **60**..................................(t) DanielMuscutt(5) 9 50
(Christine Dunnett) *in tch in midfield on outer: effrt u.p over 1f out: styd on same pce ins fnl f* **12/1**
6000 6 *hd* **Flow Chart (IRE)**[10] 7904 6-8-7 **49** oh1 ow3................ SladeO'Hara(3) 2 38
(Peter Grayson) *sn niggled along in last pair: clsng whn nt clr run and swtchd rt jst ins fnl f: styd on* **16/1**
5550 7 2 ¾ **Charming (IRE)**[62] 6732 4-9-5 **58**..............................(p) SteveDrowne 3 38
(Olivia Maylam) *chsd wnr tl wl over 1f out: sn drvn and no ex: wknd ins fnl f* **12/1**
624 8 *shd* **Jiminy**[20] 7759 3-9-4 **57**..(b) LukeMorris 7 36
(Scott Dixon) *in tch in midfield: n.m.r 2f out: rdn and no hdwy over 1f out: wknd fnl f* **3/1**[1]
0630 9 3 ¾ **Wicked Wilma (IRE)**[54] 6945 9-8-8 **47** oh1 ow1............(p) TomEaves 6 13
(Alan Berry) *chsd ldrs tl wl over 1f out: sn drvn and lost pl: wknd 1f out* **20/1**

1m 3.08s (0.78) **Going Correction** +0.20s/f (Slow) **9** Ran SP% **119.6**
Speed ratings (Par 101): **101,98,95,92,92 92,87,87,81**
toteswingers 1&2 £6.50, 1&3 £4.80, 2&3 £3.20 CSF £32.92 CT £95.74 TOTE £5.40: £2.30, £3.30, £1.10; EX 42.50 Trifecta £326.90 Pool: £1596.07 - 3.66 winning units..
Owner One For All **Bred** Miss Anne Ormsby **Trained** Hingham, Norfolk

FOCUS
A moderate sprint handicap and few with solid recent form. It's hard to rate the form any higher.

8035 COMPARE BOOKMAKERS AT BOOKMAKERS.CO.UK H'CAP (DIV II) 5f 20y(P)
2:30 (2:30) (Class 6) (0-60,60) 3-Y-O+ £1,940 (£577; £288; £144) Stalls Low

Form RPR
1040 1 **Give Us A Belle (IRE)**[12] 7850 4-8-7 **46**................(vt) AdamBeschizza 8 58
(Christine Dunnett) *chsd ldrs tl pushed into ld wl over 1f out: clr and in command whn edgd rt ins fnl f: r.o wl* **8/1**
3000 2 2 ¾ **Steelcut**[4] 7985 9-9-6 **59**..(v) MartinDwyer 2 61
(Mark Buckley) *s.i.s: sn rcvrd and in tch in midfield: effrt and drvn over 1f out: chsd wnr ins fnl f: edgd lft and no imp after* **5/1**
0600 3 ¾ **I'll Be Good**[110] 5138 4-9-4 **57**.. RobertHavlin 9 56
(Alan Berry) *chsd ldrs on outer: effrt u.p to chse clr wnr over 1f out: no imp and lost 2nd ins fnl f* **7/2**[2]
5010 4 1 ¾ **Compton Prince**[12] 7862 4-9-7 **60**..............................(b) LukeMorris 7 53
(Milton Bradley) *dwlt: sn rcvrd and wl in tch in midfield: unable qck u.p over 1f out: plugged on same pce fnl f* **9/2**[3]
3444 5 1 **Fathom Five (IRE)**[6] 7957 9-9-4 **57**.................................... JimmyQuinn 4 47
(Shaun Harris) *pressed ldr on inner: rdn and ev ch 2f out: no ex and btn ent fnl f: wknd fnl 100yds* **5/2**[1]
/00- 6 7 **Lucky Mellor**[503] 3949 6-8-5 **51**.. PaulBooth(7) 5 15
(Barry Murtagh) *led tl wl over 1f out: sn drvn and btn: wknd ent fnl f: fdd fnl f* **33/1**
-000 7 ½ **Johnson's Cat (IRE)**[286] 618 4-8-7 **46** oh1.......................... JohnFahy 6 9
(Mandy Rowland) *stdd s: wl off the pce in last pair: rdn and no hdwy 1/2-way: n.d* **50/1**
000 8 1 ¼ **Evens And Odds (IRE)**[21] 7728 9-9-2 **58**..................(p) SladeO'Hara(3) 1 16
(Peter Grayson) *sn wl in outpcd in detached last: nvr on terms* **20/1**
060 9 5 **Pavers Star**[21] 7728 4-9-2 **55**..............................(p[1]) DuranFentiman 3
(Noel Wilson) *reminder after s: wl in tch in midfield: drvn and dropped out ent fnl 2f: wl bhd fnl f* **12/1**

1m 2.66s (0.36) **Going Correction** +0.20s/f (Slow) **9** Ran SP% **114.1**
Speed ratings (Par 101): **105,100,99,96,95 83,83,81,73**
toteswingers 1&2 £6.90, 1&3 £6.80, 2&3 £5.60 CSF £46.12 CT £166.74 TOTE £9.60: £3.30, £1.60, £1.40; EX 50.40 Trifecta £339.20 Pool: £2858.56 - 6.32 winning units..
Owner F Butler & Mrs C Dunnett **Bred** Audrey Frances Stynes **Trained** Hingham, Norfolk

FOCUS
A bit faster than the first division, and the winner rates a length personal best.

8036 CORAL APP DOWNLOAD FROM THE APP STORE MAIDEN STKS 1m 1f 103y(P)
3:00 (3:00) (Class 5) 3-Y-O+ £2,587 (£770; £384; £192) Stalls Low

Form RPR
5523 1 **Nickels And Dimes (IRE)**[42] 7257 3-9-0 **74**.................... TonyHamilton 8 70
(Richard Fahey) *dwlt: sn niggled along in last trio: rdn and hdwy 3f out: drvn to chal over 1f out: led ins fnl f: edgd rt: drvn out* **11/10**[1]
6 2 *nk* **Strandfield Bay (IRE)**[11] 7885 7-9-3 **0**.................................. PaulQuinn 2 69
(Sharon Watt) *dwlt and short of room sn after s: hld up in tch in last trio: swtchd rt and hdwy 4f out: drvn and chsd ldrs 2f out: plugged on to ld 1f out: hdd ins fnl f: kpt on same pce after* **16/1**
04 3 6 **Perivale (USA)**[40] 7311 3-9-0 **0**.. JoeFanning 6 56
(Mark Johnston) *led: rdn and edgd rt wl over 1f out: hdd 1f out: wknd ins fnl f* **8/1**
2 4 3 ¼ **Crow Down (IRE)**[71] 6431 4-9-8 **0**.................................. RobertWinston 7 55
(Charles Hills) *dwlt and pushed along early: hdwy to chse ldrs after 2f: rdn and struggling over 3f out: wknd u.p 2f out* **4/1**[2]
2546 5 ¾ **Fatima's Gift**[30] 7546 3-9-0 **67**.. AndreaAtzeni 5 48
(Stuart Williams) *chsd ldr tl over 1f out: sn drvn and btn: wknd fnl f* **6/1**[3]
5 6 3 ¼ **Sonny Jim**[21] 7734 5-9-8 **0**..(v[1]) StephenCraine 4 46
(John Mackie) *t.k.h and chsd ldrs early: stdd bk towards rr after 2f: drvn and struggling 4f out: sn lost tch* **66/1**
0-4 7 4 ½ **Arch Ebony (USA)**[174] 2960 3-9-5 **0**.................................... DavidNolan 1 37
(David O'Meara) *chsd ldrs: pushed along 6f out: drvn and btn 2f out: wknd qckly over 1f out* **16/1**
0/ 8 3 **Paradise Sea (USA)**[760] 7118 4-9-3 **0**................................ GrahamLee 3 25
(Jo Hughes) *wnt lft s: in tch in last trio: swtchd to outer and hdwy 6f out: rdn and dropped out qckly over 3f out: bhd after* **7/1**

2m 3.87s (2.17) **Going Correction** +0.20s/f (Slow)
WFA 3 from 4yo+ 3lb **8** Ran SP% **118.8**
Speed ratings (Par 103): **98,97,92,89,88 85,81,79**
toteswingers 1&2 £8.50, 1&3 £2.80, 2&3 £34.30 CSF £23.53 TOTE £1.80: £1.10, £7.20, £2.20; EX 43.70 Trifecta £388.80 Pool: £2850.86 - 5.49 winning units..
Owner R A Fahey **Bred** James Waldron **Trained** Musley Bank, N Yorks
■ Stewards' Enquiry : Paul Quinn three-day ban: use of whip (9-11 Dec)
Tony Hamilton caution: careless riding

FOCUS
A weak maiden rated around the runner-up.

8037 LADBROKES H'CAP 7f 32y(P)
3:30 (3:31) (Class 5) (0-70,70) 3-Y-O+ £2,587 (£770; £384; £192) Stalls High

Form RPR
5032 1 **Kimbali (IRE)**[40] 7303 4-9-2 **65**.. GeorgeBaker 7 76
(David Evans) *v.s.a: in tch in rr: hdwy on outer over 2f out: rdn wl over 1f out: chal and carried rt ins fnl f: led fnl 50yds: r.o wl* **7/2**[1]
1 2 ½ **Barbados Bob (USA)**[11] 7884 3-8-12 **67**................ GeorgeChaloner(5) 1 76
(Michael Wigham) *t.k.h: hld up in tch in last trio: hdwy over 2f out: rdn to chal over 1f out: led and wnt rt 1f out: sn hrd pressed: hdd and no ex fnl 50yds* **5/1**[2]
4013 3 2 ¼ **Hellbender (IRE)**[6] 7953 7-9-6 **69**.................................(t) JimmyQuinn 2 73
(Shaun Harris) *hld up in tch in last trio: nt clr run ent fnl 2f: swtchd rt wl over 1f out: switching bk lft and hdwy over 1f out: r.o wl to go 3rd wl ins fnl f* **10/1**
5321 4 1 ¼ **Orpsie Boy (IRE)**[17] 7807 10-9-0 **63**.................................. LukeMorris 10 63
(Ruth Carr) *t.k.h: chsd ldrs on outer: rdn and unable qck over 1f out: outpcd fnl f* **7/1**[3]
-530 5 *hd* **Nelina**[34] 7455 3-8-10 **60**.. GrahamLee 8 59
(Robert Cowell) *chsd ldr after 1f out: rdn and sltly hmpd wl over 1f out: no ex and outpcd fnl f* **14/1**
0000 6 1 ¼ **Lastkingofscotland (IRE)**[12] 7858 7-8-7 **59**..............(b) RyanPowell(3) 9 55
(Conor Dore) *led: rdn wl over 1f out: hdd and no ex 1f out: wknd ins fnl f* **8/1**
60P0 7 2 ½ **Living Leader**[18] 7785 4-9-7 **70**..(p) MartinLane 3 60
(Nick Littmoden) *in tch in midfield: rdn and lost pl over 2f out: one pce and wl hld fr over 1f out* **5/1**[2]
0066 8 1 ½ **David's Secret**[103] 5393 3-8-12 **62**..................................(p) TomEaves 6 46
(Roy Brotherton) *t.k.h: hld up wl in tch in midfield: rdn and no rspnse over 2f out: wknd wl over 1f out* **66/1**
3032 9 2 ½ **Lucky Lodge**[41] 7282 3-9-1 **65**.. DavidAllan 4 43
(Mel Brittain) *in tch in midfield: lost pl and towards rr whn rdn over 1f out: wl hld and nt clr run ent fnl f* **14/1**
-000 10 1 ½ **Rugosa**[10] 7898 4-9-7 **70**.. RobertWinston 5 45
(Charles Hills) *chsd ldrs: rdn and unable qck over 2f out: wknd over 1f out: bhd and eased wl ins fnl f* **8/1**

1m 31.38s (1.78) **Going Correction** +0.20s/f (Slow)
WFA 3 from 4yo+ 1lb **10** Ran SP% **114.2**
Speed ratings (Par 103): **97,96,93,92,92 90,87,86,83,81**
toteswingers 1&2 £4.80, 1&3 £5.20, 2&3 £9.30 CSF £20.10 CT £160.77 TOTE £4.00: £1.30, £1.80, £3.60; EX 26.80 Trifecta £160.80 Pool: £3390.79 - 15.81 winning units..
Owner J A Wilcox **Bred** P Kelly **Trained** Pandy, Monmouths

FOCUS
This was competitive and might prove fair form for the grade. The first three finishers just about filled the last three positions at halfway.

8038 DOWNLOAD THE LADBROKES APP H'CAP 1m 141y(P)
4:00 (4:00) (Class 6) (0-65,65) 3-Y-O+ £1,940 (£577; £288; £144) Stalls Low

Form RPR
0541 1 **Dansili Dutch (IRE)**[9] 7931 4-8-12 **56**.......................... GrahamGibbons 2 65
(David O'Meara) *chsd ldrs: swtchd rt and effrt to ld wl over 1f out: edgd rt 1f out: kpt on wl: rdn out* **5/1**[3]
2314 2 1 **Candy Kitten**[24] 7669 3-9-4 **65**..(p) LukeMorris 6 72
(Alastair Lidderdale) *in tch in midfield: rdn 3f out: hdwy u.p over 1f out: chsd wnr and swtchd lft ins fnl f: kpt on* **9/2**[2]
3610 3 ¾ **Delightful Sleep**[9] 7930 5-9-4 **62**...................................... GeorgeBaker 1 67
(David Evans) *hld up in tch in midfield: n.m.r jst over 2f out: swtchd rt and effrt wl over 1f out: chsd wnr 1f out tl ins fnl f: swtchd lft and one pce fnl 75yds* **4/1**[1]
3240 4 *hd* **Khajaaly (IRE)**[11] 7880 6-9-6 **64**..................................(tp) JimmyQuinn 8 69
(Michael Appleby) *stdd s: hld up in tch in rr: rdn and hdwy jst over 1f out: kpt on wl u.p ins fnl f* **6/1**
2543 5 3 **Baile Atha Cliath (IRE)**[9] 7753 4-8-4 **51**..................(b[1]) NeilFarley(3) 5 49
(Declan Carroll) *t.k.h: chsd ldrs: wnt 2nd 5f out tl led over 2f out: rdn and hdd wl over 1f out: lost 2nd ent fnl f: wknd* **7/1**
6050 6 ½ **Exceedexpectations (IRE)**[11] 7880 4-9-4 **62**........................ GrahamLee 4 59
(Conor Dore) *led tl over 7f out: chsd ldr tl 5f out: rdn and unable qck wl over 1f out: wknd 1f out* **4/1**[1]
4466 7 1 **Flipping**[55] 6919 6-8-7 **51** oh1.. BarryMcHugh 3 45
(Nicky Richards) *in tch in last trio: rdn and effrt on outer over 2f out: no imp over 1f out: wknd ins fnl f* **16/1**
0056 8 8 **Boom To Bust (IRE)**[14] 7836 5-9-6 **64**..........................(b) RobertHavlin 7 40
(Barry Brennan) *dwlt: sn rdn along and hdwy to ld over 7f out: hdd over 2f out: drvn and wknd 2f out: bhd and eased wl ins fnl f* **12/1**

1m 51.57s (1.07) **Going Correction** +0.20s/f (Slow)
WFA 3 from 4yo+ 3lb **8** Ran SP% **115.2**
Speed ratings (Par 101): **103,102,101,101,98 98,97,90**
toteswingers 1&2 £3.60, 1&3 £3.30, 2&3 £4.40 CSF £27.95 CT £99.20 TOTE £4.60: £2.80, £1.40, £1.80; EX 23.60 Trifecta £108.20 Pool: £3155.91 - 21.85 winning units..
Owner Direct Racing Partnership **Bred** Castlefarm Stud **Trained** Nawton, N Yorks

The Form Book Flat, Raceform Ltd, Compton, RG20 6NL.

FOCUS
Just a moderate handicap but a winner who's back on the up and has scope do better again.

8039 32RED.COM NURSERY H'CAP 7f 32y(P)
4:30 (4:32) (Class 6) (0-60,60) 2-Y-O £1,940 (£577; £288; £144) Stalls High

Form RPR
3025 1 **Tyrsal (IRE)**[12] 7855 2-9-3 56 AndreaAtzeni 9 63
(Robert Eddery) *chsd ldr tl led 6f out: mde rest: rdn wl over 1f out: wnt lft u.p ins fnl f: stened and hld on wl fnl 50yds* 3/1[1]
000 2 *shd* **Spreadable (IRE)**[101] 5488 2-8-8 47 (b[1]) MartinLane 1 54+
(Nick Littmoden) *hld up in tch: clsd and travelling wl over 2f out: rdn and effrt over 1f out: edgd lft 1f out: str chal ins fnl f: kpt on but hld fnl 50yds* 7/2[2]
2031 3 3 1/2 **Starlight Princess (IRE)**[11] 7878 2-9-5 58 (b) JohnFahy 2 56
(J S Moore) *stdd s: hld up in rr: clsd 3f out: effrt u.p on inner over 1f out: wnt 3rd ins fnl f: no imp* 5/1[3]
0043 4 1 1/2 **My My My Diliza**[11] 7878 2-9-2 55 (b) LiamJones 6 49
(J S Moore) *dwlt and rdn along early: hdwy to chse ldrs over 5f out: rdn and chsd wnr wl over 1f out: no ex and btn 1f out: wknd and lost 2 pls ins fnl f* 8/1
2330 5 6 **Larsen Bay (IRE)**[40] 7309 2-9-6 59 (p) StephenCraine 7 39
(Tom Dascombe) *t.k.h: hld up in tch in midfield: short of room and hmpd 6f out: hdwy on outer to chse ldr 5f out tl 2f out: wknd over 1f out* 7/1
065 6 2 1/2 **Jana**[51] 7032 2-8-8 47 (p) LukeMorris 8 21
(Sylvester Kirk) *chsd ldrs: rdn and struggling over 2f out: wknd over 1f out* 10/1
006 7 14 **Booloo (IRE)**[12] 7859 2-8-13 52 (p) GrahamLee 5
(Garry Moss) *led tl 6f out: chsd ldr tl 5f out: chsd ldrs tl shuffled bk over 2f out: wknd qckly over 1f out: wl bhd fnl f* 10/1
1004 8 13 **Sakuramachi**[86] 5976 2-9-2 60 PhilipPrince(5) 3
(Nikki Evans) *s.i.s: rdn along thrght and a in rr: lost tch over 2f out: t.o and eased wl ins fnl f* 50/1

1m 31.88s (2.28) **Going Correction** +0.20s/f (Slow) 8 Ran SP% **107.6**
Speed ratings (Par 94): **94,93,89,88,81 78,62,47**
toteswingers 1&2 £2.40, 1&3 £2.50, 2&3 £4.00 CSF £11.95 CT £41.67 TOTE £3.80: £1.30, £1.60, £1.30; EX 15.70 Trifecta £75.60 Pool: £3883.03 - 38.48 winning units..
Owner Phillips, Fullerton & Riesebieter **Bred** Daniel Furini **Trained** Newmarket, Suffolk
■ Jaeger Connoisseur (10-1) was withdrawn on vet's advice. Deduct 5p in the £ under R4.
■ Stewards' Enquiry : Andrea Atzeni one-day ban: careless riding (9 December)

FOCUS
A very moderate nursery with a real lack of depth. A minor step up from the winner.

8040 32RED CASINO NURSERY H'CAP 1m 141y(P)
5:00 (5:00) (Class 6) (0-60,60) 2-Y-O £1,940 (£577; £288; £144) Stalls Low

Form RPR
0221 1 **Rural Affair**[26] 7630 2-9-3 56 LukeMorris 5 67
(Michael Appleby) *t.k.h: chsd ldr tl led 6f out: mde rest: gng best over 2f out: rdn and asserted over 1f out: r.o wl* 7/2[2]
650 2 2 3/4 **Columbian Roulette (IRE)**[16] 7818 2-8-8 47 MartinDwyer 4 52
(Charles Hills) *t.k.h: chsd ldrs: swtchd rt after 1f: hdwy to chse wnr 6f out: rdn over 2f out: outpcd and btn over 1f out: kpt on* 5/4[1]
023 3 2 3/4 **Chanceuse**[13] 7846 2-8-10 54 DanielMuscutt(5) 6 53
(Gay Kelleway) *t.k.h: hld up in tch: pushed rt after 1f: hdwy to trck ldrs 3f out: rdn and no imp 2f out: kpt on same pce after* 11/2
4431 4 5 **Slinky McVelvet**[7] 7945 2-9-3 59 6ex BillyCray(3) 3 48
(Garry Moss) *s.i.s: in tch in rr: rdn and effrt 3f out: sn struggling: 4th and wl hld over 1f out* 5/1[3]
0044 5 5 **Miss Lawlass (IRE)**[11] 7883 2-8-7 46 JamesSullivan 2 24
(James Given) *led tl 6f out: chsd ldrs: rdn 4f out: lost pl and btn over 2f out: wknd 2f out* 33/1
635 6 10 **Wilberfoss (IRE)**[11] 7883 2-9-7 60 DavidAllan 1 17
(Mel Brittain) *dropped to rr 6f out: rdn over 5f out: lost tch over 2f out: wl bhd and eased ins fnl f* 10/1

1m 53.39s (2.89) **Going Correction** +0.20s/f (Slow) 6 Ran SP% **110.8**
Speed ratings (Par 94): **95,92,90,85,81 72**
toteswingers 1&2 £1.60, 1&3 £1.30, 2&3 £1.70 CSF £8.07 TOTE £3.20: £1.60, £1.50; EX 10.70 Trifecta £33.40 Pool: £3944.56 - 88.54 winning units..
Owner Dallas Racing & T R Pearson **Bred** Stowell Hill Ltd **Trained** Danethorpe, Notts

FOCUS
Once taking command down the back straight, Luke Morris set what looked a muddling gallop aboard the winner. The form has been given a bit of a chance.

8041 32RED H'CAP 2m 119y(P)
5:30 (5:30) (Class 4) (0-85,83) 3-Y-O+ £4,690 (£1,395; £697; £348) Stalls Low

Form RPR
140 1 **Layline (IRE)**[34] 7453 6-9-2 76 DanielMuscutt(5) 1 85
(Gay Kelleway) *hld up in tch in last pair: rdn and effrt to chse ldng pair 2f out: styd on and str chal ins fnl f: led towards fin* 16/1
4462 2 *hd* **Montjess (IRE)**[3] 8004 3-8-6 70 (v) KieranO'Neill 2 79
(Tom Dascombe) *led for 2f: chsd ldr tl rdn to ld again 2f out: wandered lft u.p 1f out: hrd pressed ins fnl f: hdd towards fin* 3/1[2]
3605 3 3 1/2 **Noble Alan (GER)**[17] 7805 10-10-0 83 GrahamLee 4 88
(Nicky Richards) *t.k.h: chsd ldr tl led after 2f: hdd and rdn 2f out: keeping on same pce whn swtchd rt 1f out: one pce after* 7/4[1]
1402 4 5 **All The Winds (GER)**[17] 7805 8-9-8 80 (t) WilliamTwiston-Davies(3) 6 79
(Shaun Lycett) *s.i.s: in tch in last pair: rdn and unable qck ent fnl 2f: one pce and hld fnl 2f* 11/2
2246 5 1 3/4 **Murcar**[18] 2587 8-9-5 79 (b) PhilipPrince(5) 3 76
(Liam Corcoran) *chsd ldrs: rdn and unable qck ent fnl 2f: styd on same pce and hld fnl 2f* 6/1
251 6 44 **Toughness Danon**[8] 7597 7-9-1 70 TonyHamilton 5 14
(Ian Williams) *chsd ldrs: rdn and lost pl over 4f out: lost tch 3f out: t.o and eased ins fnl f* 9/2[3]

3m 42.74s (0.94) **Going Correction** +0.20s/f (Slow)
WFA 3 from 6yo+ 9lb 6 Ran SP% **115.1**
Speed ratings (Par 105): **105,104,103,100,100 79**
toteswingers 1&2 £11.10, 1&3 £9.00, 2&3 £1.10 CSF £65.01 TOTE £13.90: £6.80, £2.00; EX 42.30 Trifecta £277.30 Pool: £4007.70 - 10.83 winning units..
Owner M Bartram, R Smith & N Scandrett **Bred** Mrs M E Slade **Trained** Exning, Suffolk

FOCUS
An ordinary race for the grade and the front two finished clear. The winner was on a fair mark on his best form of the past year.
T/Plt: £28.80 to a £1 stake. Pool: £93911.94 - 2379.71 winning tickets T/Qpdt: £3.10 to a £1 stake. Pool: £9290.68 - 2187.70 winning tickets SP

7951 SOUTHWELL (L-H)
Tuesday, November 26

OFFICIAL GOING: Standard
Wind: Virtually nil Weather: Fine and dry

8042 LADBROKES AMATEUR RIDERS' H'CAP 1m (F)
12:10 (12:11) (Class 6) (0-60,60) 3-Y-O+ £1,871 (£580; £290; £145) Stalls Low

Form RPR
1500 1 **Mcconnell (USA)**[40] 7321 8-10-8 58 (b) MissHDoyle(5) 14 67
(Violet M Jordan) *trckd ldrs: smooth hdwy 3f out: chal over 1f out: rdn to ld appr fnl f: kpt on wl towards fin* 12/1
0034 2 3/4 **Putin (IRE)**[3] 8023 5-10-6 58 (tp) MissMBishop-Peck(7) 9 65
(Phil McEntee) *in tch: hdwy to trck ldrs over 3f out: rdn over 1f out: styd on to chal ins fnl f: kpt on same pce towards fin* 6/1[2]
2560 3 1 1/2 **Nezami (IRE)**[22] 7733 8-10-10 55 (b) MissSBrotherton 3 59
(Patrick Clinton) *prom: hdwy and slt ld wl over 3f out: rdn along 2f out: drvn and hdd appr fnl f: kpt on same pce* 15/2
2100 4 1 3/4 **Ivy Port**[27] 7636 3-10-9 56 MrRossBirkett 2 55
(Michael Appleby) *cl up: led after 2f: hdd and cl up over 3f out: rdn 2f out and ev ch tl drvn and wknd ent fnl f* 9/2[1]
0061 5 *nk* **On The Cusp (IRE)**[21] 7752 6-10-4 56 (b) MissEllaSmith(7) 6 55+
(Violet M Jordan) *dwlt and towards rr: hdwy over 3f out: rdn to chse ldrs wl over 1f out: no imp fnl f* 8/1
3616 6 *shd* **Hail Promenader (IRE)**[26] 7639 7-10-7 59 (p) MissMNicholls(7) 13 58
(Anthony Carson) *in tch: hdwy to chse ldrs over 3f out: rdn along 2f out: one pce appr fnl f* 7/1[3]
4046 7 6 **Boy The Bell**[11] 7904 6-10-5 55 (be) MissHDukes(5) 7 40+
(Ollie Pears) *s.i.s and bhd: hdwy 1/2-way: in tch and rdn whn swtchd rt wl over 1f out: sn drvn and edgd rt to stands' rail and no imp* 14/1
6125 8 *hd* **Elusive Warrior (USA)**[12] 7886 10-10-2 52 (p) MrBenFfrenchDavis(5) 8 36
(Alan McCabe) *dwlt: sn in midfield: effrt over 2f out: sn rdn and n.d* 16/1
2300 9 1 **Knight Charm**[35] 7437 3-10-4 58 MissAnne-SophieCrombez(7) 10 39
(Gay Kelleway) *nvr bttr than midfield* 25/1
1405 10 1 1/2 **Minimee**[10] 7931 3-10-3 57 (be[1]) MrJAMcEntee(7) 5 35
(Phil McEntee) *dwlt: a towards rr* 14/1
4 11 2 **Masked Dance (IRE)**[12] 7886 6-10-6 56 (p) MrKLocking(5) 12 30
(Scott Dixon) *prom: rdn along to chse ldng pair 3f out: drvn and wknd fnl 2f* 16/1
0002 12 22 **Viking Warrior (IRE)**[47] 7153 6-10-5 57 MissMeganHarris(7) 1
(Shaun Harris) *led 2f: cl up: rdn along wl over 3f out and sn wknd* 33/1
3320 13 3/4 **Estibdaad (IRE)**[6] 7984 3-10-8 60 (t) MissMBryant(5) 4
(Paddy Butler) *a towards rr* 11/1
0600 14 2 1/2 **Hazza The Jazza**[12] 7886 3-10-4 58 (e) MrRAsquith(7) 11
(Richard Guest) *dwlt and a in rr* 40/1

1m 44.38s (0.68) **Going Correction** +0.025s/f (Slow)
WFA 3 from 5yo+ 2lb 14 Ran SP% **118.2**
Speed ratings (Par 101): **97,96,94,93,92 92,86,86,85,83 81,59,59,56**
toteswingers 1&2 £19.90, 1&3 £24.40, 2&3 £14.60 CSF £79.49 CT £602.89 TOTE £11.00: £5.20, £2.10, £3.10; EX 95.50 Trifecta £430.30 Pool: £1867.35 - 3.25 winning units..
Owner Rakebackmypoker.com **Bred** Hall Et Al Farm **Trained** Moreton Morrell, Warwicks
■ Stewards' Enquiry : Mr K Locking two-day ban: careless riding (tba)

FOCUS
A moderate amateur riders' handicap. A straightforward level with the winner in his best form since 2012.

8043 DOWNLOAD THE LADBROKES APP MEDIAN AUCTION MAIDEN STKS 1m (F)
12:40 (12:40) (Class 5) 3-Y-O £2,587 (£770; £384; £192) Stalls Low

Form RPR
42 1 **Better Value (IRE)**[6] 7980 3-9-5 51 (p) BenCurtis 6 65
(Noel Quinlan) *mde all: wd st: rdn along 2f out and sn clr: edgd rt ins fnl f: kpt on* 9/4[1]
0536 2 5 **Pearl Noir**[7] 7958 3-9-5 51 LukeMorris 1 54
(Scott Dixon) *prom: pushed along and sltly outpcd 1/2-way: rdn and hdwy to chse wnr 2f out: drvn along wl over 1f out: sn one pce* 8/1[3]
3 3/4 **Stun Gun** 3-9-5 0 DaleSwift 2 52
(Derek Shaw) *dwlt and sn pushed along in rr: hdwy and in tch after 3f: rdn along on inner to chse ldng pair 2f out: sn drvn and kpt on one pce* 12/1
3 4 9 **Sugar Town**[12] 7884 3-9-0 0 TomEaves 5 26
(Peter Niven) *trckd ldrs: hdwy 1/2-way: chsd ldng pair 3f out: sn rdn and one pce fnl 2f* 9/2[2]
5 2 1/4 **Lateral Thinking (IRE)**[123] 4736 3-9-5 0 GeorgeBaker 7 26
(James Evans) *hld up: hdwy and in tch over 3f out: wd st and rdn wl over 2f out: sn wknd* 9/4[1]
3003 6 2 1/4 **Tornado Battle**[10] 7930 3-9-5 49 PaddyAspell 4 21
(Phil McEntee) *prom: sn chsng wnr: rdn along 3f out: sn drvn and wknd 2f out* 8/1[3]

1m 44.53s (0.83) **Going Correction** +0.025s/f (Slow) 6 Ran SP% **109.6**
Speed ratings (Par 102): **96,91,90,81,79 76**
toteswingers 1&2 £3.60, 1&3 £3.00, 2&3 £14.00 CSF £19.78 TOTE £4.80: £1.30, £3.50; EX 24.10 Trifecta £102.50 Pool: £1235.69 - 9.03 winning units..
Owner Miss M A Quinlan **Bred** J L Hassett **Trained** Newmarket, Suffolk

FOCUS
With the first two home having previously raced 31 times without success between them, this was a poor maiden. Improvement from the winner.

8044 32RED NOVICE STKS 7f (F)
1:10 (1:10) (Class 5) 2-Y-O £3,234 (£962; £481; £240) Stalls Low

Form RPR
22 1 **Resolute**[17] 7817 2-9-0 0 JoeFanning 1 88+
(William Haggas) *trckd ldng pair: hdwy and cl up 1/2-way: led 2f out: pushed clr over 1f out: unchal* 4/11[1]
0002 2 14 **Razin' Hell**[7] 7956 2-9-0 42 (p) LukeMorris 5 50
(Alan McCabe) *cl up: led over 4f out: rdn and jnd 3f out: hdd 2f out: sn drvn and kpt on: no ch w wnr* 10/1[3]
3 1 3/4 **La Paiva (FR)** 2-8-9 0 PJMcDonald 6 40
(Scott Dixon) *s.i.s: hdwy to chse ldrs over 4f out: rdn along and wd st: kpt on u.p fnl 2f* 20/1
3 4 3/4 **Rocked The Boat**[11] 7901 2-9-0 0 AdamBeschizza 2 44
(Tobias B P Coles) *dwlt and sn rdn along in rr: sme hdwy u.p wl over 2f out: nvr a factor* 5/1[2]

35 **5** *5* **Armelle (FR)**[17] 7818 2-8-9 0 TomEaves 4 26
(Scott Dixon) *slt ld tl hdd over 4f out: rdn along over 3f out: sn outpcd* **20/1**

50 **6** *19* **The Bunny Catcher**[206] 2025 2-8-9 0 PaulQuinn 3
(Sharon Watt) *dwlt: sn rdn along and a in rr: bhd fnl 3f* **100/1**

1m 29.6s (-0.70) **Going Correction** +0.025s/f (Slow) **6** Ran SP% **109.6**
Speed ratings (Par 96): **105,89,87,86,80 58**
toteswingers 1&2 £1.80, 1&3 £2.20, 2&3 £5.20 CSF £4.41 TOTE £1.20: £1.10, £2.70; EX 5.10 Trifecta £31.40 Pool: £2796.54 - 66.60 winning units..
Owner Cheveley Park Stud **Bred** Cheveley Park Stud Ltd **Trained** Newmarket, Suffolk

FOCUS
Despite this novice event being open to previous winners, it ended up attracting five maidens and a newcomer and it proved as one-sided as the betting would have suggested. A step up from the winner on his pre-race form.

8045 32RED.COM CLAIMING STKS 7f (F)
1:40 (1:41) (Class 6) 2-Y-O **£2,045** (£603; £302) **Stalls** Low

Form RPR

2104 **1** **Stoney Quine (IRE)**[12] 7882 2-8-10 64 TomEaves 3 65
(Keith Dalgleish) *led 2f: pushed along and sltly outpcd over 2f out: sn rdn: swtchd rt and drvn over 1f out: flashed tail but styd on wl fnl f to ld last 50yds* **9/4**[1]

0001 **2** *1* **Black Vale (IRE)**[7] 7954 2-8-12 55 (bt) PaddyAspell 4 64
(Phil McEntee) *cl up: led after 2f: rdn 2f out: drvn over 1f out: wandered and wknd ins fnl f: hdd last 50yds* **5/2**[2]

0064 **3** *4 1/2* **Sexy Secret**[3] 8016 2-8-11 45 (b) RobertHavlin 2 52
(Noel Quinlan) *sn trcking ldng pair: hdwy to chse ldr 3f out: rdn 2f out: drvn and one pce ent fnl f* **9/4**[1]

5000 **4** *20* **Mystic Angellina**[111] 5151 2-8-0 41 (t[1]) PaulQuinn 1
(Mrs Ilka Gansera-Leveque) *in tch on inner: rdn along whn hmpd over 3f out: sn wknd* **25/1**

6403 **5** *26* **Severnwind (IRE)**[7] 7954 2-8-13 52 LukeMorris 6
(Ronald Harris) *sn rdn along in rr: sme hdwy 1/2-way: edgd lft over 3f out: sn wknd and eased fnl 2f* **5/1**[3]

1m 32.31s (2.01) **Going Correction** +0.025s/f (Slow) **5** Ran SP% **110.6**
Speed ratings (Par 94): **89,87,82,59,30**
CSF £8.26 TOTE £2.30: £1.60, £1.80; EX 5.70 Trifecta £15.30 Pool: £3016.83 - 147.74 winning units..
Owner Middleham Park racing XXII **Bred** T Monaghan **Trained** Carluke, S Lanarks

FOCUS
A moderate claimer with a tail-swisher getting the better of a reluctant leader and the gamble appearing to go wrong. The front two are rated to their marks.

8046 CORAL APP DOWNLOAD FROM THE APP STORE MAIDEN STKS 1m 4f (F)
2:10 (2:10) (Class 5) 3-Y-O+ **£2,726** (£805; £402) **Stalls** Low

Form RPR

6203 **1** **Caterina De Medici (FR)**[8] 7947 4-9-6 72 TomMcLaughlin 10 74
(Ed Walker) *cl up: led 7f out: rdn wl over 1f out: kpt on wl and clr fnl f* **15/8**[1]

32 **2** *7* **Gwael (USA)**[152] 3711 3-9-0 0 LukeMorris 6 67
(James Tate) *stmbld s: sn trcking ldrs: hdwy to chse wnr 4f out: rdn 2f out: drvn appr fnl f and sn no imp* **3/1**[3]

3 *3/4* **Dan Emmett (USA)** 3-9-5 0 LiamKeniry 8 67+
(John Quinn) *green and s.i.s: sn pushed along and hdwy to trck ldrs after 2f: effrt 4f out: rdn along 3f out: kpt on same pce fnl 2f* **9/4**[2]

4 *18* **Hope For Glory**[30] 4-9-11 0 FrederikTylicki 5 40
(Jason Ward) *hld up: hdwy to chse ldrs 5f out: rdn along 3f out: sn outpcd* **14/1**

3540 **5** *2* **Samoset**[66] 6629 3-9-5 55 BenCurtis 1 37
(Alan Swinbank) *hld up in tch: hdwy to chse ldrs 4f out: rdn along over 3f out: sn drvn and outpcd* **8/1**

6 **6** *3/4* **Cedar Glory**[42] 7279 4-9-6 0 PaddyAspell 2 31
(Tim Walford) *a towards rr* **50/1**

60 **7** *1 1/2* **Felice (IRE)**[19] 7791 3-9-0 0 TomEaves 4 29
(Scott Dixon) *hld up: a towards rr* **33/1**

0000 **8** *24* **Penderyn**[36] 7422 6-9-3 34 (p) BillyCray(3) 9
(Charles Smith) *chsd ldrs: hdwy and cl up 1/2-way: rdn along over 4f out and sn wknd* **100/1**

00 **9** *88* **Baby Mac**[87] 5989 5-9-6 0 (b[1]) AdamCarter(5) 3
(Neville Bycroft) *led: rdn along and hdd 7f out: sn wknd: t.o fnl 3f* **100/1**

2m 40.67s (-0.33) **Going Correction** +0.025s/f (Slow)
WFA 3 from 4yo+ 6lb **9** Ran SP% **115.2**
Speed ratings (Par 103): **102,97,96,84,83 83,82,66,7**
toteswingers 1&2 £2.00, 1&3 £1.80, 2&3 £2.00 CSF £7.76 TOTE £3.10: £1.50, £1.10, £1.40; EX 8.90 Trifecta £20.80 Pool: £3481.24 - 125.07 winning units..
Owner S Stuckey **Bred** Az Ag Il Tiglio Di Amelia Prevedello **Trained** Newmarket, Suffolk

FOCUS
An uncompetitive maiden and the first three pulled miles clear of the rest. The winner did not quite need to produce her best.

8047 CORAL MOBILE "JUST THREE CLICKS TO BET" H'CAP 1m 4f (F)
2:40 (2:40) (Class 5) (0-75,75) 3-Y-O+ **£2,587** (£770; £384; £192) **Stalls** Low

Form RPR

1001 **1** **Honoured (IRE)**[21] 7758 6-9-1 66 (t) TomQueally 11 81
(Michael Appleby) *prom: cl up after 4f: led 4f out: rdn clr over 1f out: styd on strly* **9/2**[2]

2221 **2** *7* **Golden Jubilee (USA)**[13] 7857 4-9-1 69 (v) WilliamTwiston-Davies(3) 3 74
(Nigel Twiston-Davies) *led 2f: cl up: effrt to chse wnr 3f out: rdn 2f out: drvn and one pce appr fnl f* **9/4**[1]

5140 **3** *3/4* **Mediterranean Sea (IRE)**[44] 7217 7-9-8 73 FrederikTylicki 8 76
(J R Jenkins) *hld up towards rr: hdwy over 4f out: chsd ldrs 3f out and sn rdn: drvn wl over 1f out: kpt on fnl f* **14/1**

3300 **4** *1 3/4* **Gabrial The Thug (FR)**[19] 7786 3-8-5 62 ow1 (t) BarryMcHugh 4 63
(Richard Fahey) *bhd: hdwy 4f out: sn rdn and styd on to chse ldng pair whn edgd lft wl over 1f out and sn one pce* **20/1**

4000 **5** *2 3/4* **Northside Prince (IRE)**[91] 5868 7-9-10 75 BenCurtis 6 72
(Alan Swinbank) *trckd ldrs: hdwy 4f out: rdn along 3f out: drvn 2f out and sn one pce* **8/1**

0/24 **6** *7* **Poncho**[38] 7379 4-8-10 61 oh14 (p) ChrisCatlin 2 47
(Mark Rimell) *hld up towards rr: hdwy on inner 4f out: rdn to chse ldrs 3f out: sn drvn and wknd* **50/1**

2305 **7** *3/4* **Bavarian Nordic (USA)**[12] 7881 8-8-6 62 oh5 ow1 (v) GeorgeChaloner(5) 5 47
(Richard Whitaker) *chsd ldrs: rdn along 4f out: grad wknd* **16/1**

002 **8** *2 1/4* **Top Diktat**[39] 7346 5-9-3 68 GeorgeBaker 9 50
(Gary Moore) *hld up in tch: effrt to chse ldrs 4f out: rdn along over 3f out and sn wknd* **6/1**[3]

3-33 **9** *6* **Dontpaytheferryman (USA)**[44] 2509 8-9-0 65 (b) WilliamCarson 7 38
(Peter Hiatt) *prom: led after 2f: rdn along and hdd 4f out: drvn over 3f out and sn wknd* **20/1**

5250 **10** *29* **Ever Fortune (USA)**[42] 7275 4-9-8 73 TomEaves 10
(Brian Ellison) *hld up towards rr: hdwy on outer to chse ldrs 1/2-way: rdn along 4f out and sn wknd* **6/1**[3]

0-40 **11** *7* **Three White Socks (IRE)**[197] 2313 6-8-12 63 PaulPickard 1
(Brian Ellison) *sn rdn along in rr: a bhd* **28/1**

2m 38.26s (-2.74) **Going Correction** +0.025s/f (Slow)
WFA 3 from 4yo+ 6lb **11** Ran SP% **116.1**
Speed ratings (Par 103): **110,105,104,103,101 97,96,95,91,71 67**
toteswingers 1&2 £3.30, 1&3 £12.10, 2&3 £8.90 CSF £14.05 CT £130.75 TOTE £4.70: £1.50, £1.20, £4.40; EX 16.90 Trifecta £69.50 Pool: £2976.37 - 32.08 winning units..
Owner Dallas Racing **Bred** Kilfrush Stud **Trained** Danethorpe, Notts

FOCUS
An ordinary handicap in which the winning time was 2.41sec faster than the preceding maiden. A clear personal best from the winner.

8048 BEST ODDS AT BOOKMAKERS.CO.UK H'CAP (DIV I) 6f (F)
3:10 (3:10) (Class 6) (0-65,65) 3-Y-O+ **£1,940** (£577; £288; £144) **Stalls** Low

Form RPR

4445 **1** **Fathom Five (IRE)**[1] 8035 9-9-0 57 PaddyAspell 9 67
(Shaun Harris) *qckly away: mde all: rdn clr over 1f out: drvn and edgd rt ins fnl f: hld on gamely* **18/1**

0542 **2** *1 1/4* **Grace Hull**[11] 7904 3-8-10 56 BillyCray(3) 5 62
(Garry Moss) *n.m.r s and sn swtchd rt towards outer: in rr and hdwy 1/2-way: wd st: rdn wl over 1f out: styd on strly fnl f* **13/2**

0200 **3** *1/2* **Monnoyer**[7] 7957 4-9-6 63 (p) PJMcDonald 10 68
(Scott Dixon) *chsd wnr: rdn along 2f out: drvn jst over 1f out: kpt on same pce ins fnl f* **5/1**[2]

6001 **4** *2* **Caramelita**[7] 7957 6-9-8 65 6ex (v) FrederikTylicki 7 64
(J R Jenkins) *trckd ldrs: hdwy 1/2-way: rdn wl over 1f out: drvn and one pce appr fnl f* **7/2**[1]

3452 **5** *1 1/2* **Amenable (IRE)**[7] 7957 6-9-6 63 (p) WilliamCarson 2 57
(Violet M Jordan) *towards rr: hdwy over 2f out: sn rdn and no imp appr fnl f* **7/2**[1]

0604 **6** *4 1/2* **Captain Scooby**[3] 8029 7-9-7 64 (e) JoeFanning 4 45
(Richard Guest) *midfield: effrt over 2f out: sn rdn and no imp* **6/1**[3]

5306 **7** *2* **Somethingboutmary**[73] 6397 3-9-3 60 [1] DaleSwift 1 35
(Neville Bycroft) *in tch on inner: effrt and sme hdwy over 2f out: sn rdn and btn* **20/1**

120 **8** *1/2* **Shamrocked (IRE)**[22] 7729 4-9-4 61 TomEaves 8 34
(Ollie Pears) *dwlt and sn rdn along to chse ldrs: drvn over 2f out and sn btn* **16/1**

3200 **9** *1 1/4* **Ishiamiracle**[7] 7957 4-8-0 50 oh5 (p) DonnaCaldwell(7) 3 20
(Phil McEntee) *in tch: rdn along 1/2-way: sn wknd* **25/1**

0300 **10** *1* **Legal Bond**[54] 6980 4-8-11 57 (p) JulieBurke(3) 6 24
(David O'Meara) *chsd ldrs: rdn wl over 2f out: drvn and wknd wl over 1f out* **16/1**

1m 16.48s (-0.02) **Going Correction** +0.025s/f (Slow) **10** Ran SP% **114.4**
Speed ratings (Par 101): **101,99,98,96,94 88,85,84,83,81**
toteswingers 1&2 £20.90, 1&3 £29.00, 2&3 £9.90 CSF £128.00 CT £696.09 TOTE £16.90: £2.80, £2.70, £2.30; EX 94.00 Trifecta £1327.00 Pool: £2033.61 - 1.14 winning units..
Owner Nottinghamshire Racing **Bred** Eamonn Connolly **Trained** Carburton, Notts

■ Stewards' Enquiry : Billy Cray two-day ban: use of whip (10-11 Dec)

FOCUS
A moderate sprint handicap. Four of the first five home all ran in the same race over C&D seven days earlier. A step up on his recent form from the winner.

8049 BEST ODDS AT BOOKMAKERS.CO.UK H'CAP (DIV II) 6f (F)
3:40 (3:41) (Class 6) (0-65,65) 3-Y-O+ **£1,940** (£577; £288; £144) **Stalls** Low

Form RPR

6652 **1** **Spitfire**[7] 7958 8-9-5 63 (t) JoeFanning 6 73
(J R Jenkins) *trckd ldrs: hdwy 2f out: rdn to ld over 1f out: clr fnl f* **4/1**[2]

3520 **2** *5* **Thorpe Bay**[13] 7862 4-9-2 60 TomQueally 2 55
(Michael Appleby) *dwlt: in tch on inner: pushed along 1/2-way: swtchd rt to outer and hdwy over 2f out: rdn wl over 1f out: chsd wnr ins fnl f: sn no imp* **9/2**[3]

4003 **3** *2 3/4* **Prince Of Passion (CAN)**[7] 7957 5-9-3 61 GeorgeBaker 7 48
(Derek Shaw) *led: hdd and pushed along 1/2-way: rdn and sltly outpcd 2f out: kpt on u.p fnl f* **9/2**[3]

123 **4** *shd* **Insolenceofoffice (IRE)**[147] 3934 5-8-11 60 (p) JoshBaudains(5) 9 46
(Richard Ford) *cl up: chal over 2f out: sn rdn and ev ch tl drvn and wknd over 1f out* **10/3**[1]

0010 **5** *1 1/4* **Monzino (USA)**[54] 6963 5-8-13 64 PaulBooth(7) 3 47
(Michael Chapman) *s.i.s and bhd tl styd on wl appr fnl f: nrst fin* **25/1**

4136 **6** *1 1/4* **Bunce (IRE)**[19] 7792 5-9-4 65 (b) JulieBurke(3) 8 44
(David O'Meara) *cl up: led 1/2-way: rdn 2f out: hdd over 1f out: sn wknd* **6/1**

2104 **7** *shd* **Lees Anthem**[7] 7958 6-8-12 56 PJMcDonald 5 35
(Mel Brittain) *chsd ldrs on inner: rdn along wl over 2f out: sn wknd* **11/1**

0020 **8** *6* **Upper Lambourn (IRE)**[12] 7886 5-8-10 54 (t) ChrisCatlin 4 15
(Christopher Kellett) *sn outpcd and rdn along: a in rr* **16/1**

1m 15.91s (-0.59) **Going Correction** +0.025s/f (Slow) **8** Ran SP% **111.8**
Speed ratings (Par 101): **104,97,93,93,91 90,90,82**
toteswingers 1&2 £4.30, 1&3 £4.40, 2&3 £2.70 CSF £21.27 CT £81.93 TOTE £4.20: £1.80, £1.70, £1.70; EX 22.80 Trifecta £74.60 Pool: £3621.01 - 36.37 winning units..
Owner Mrs Wendy Jenkins **Bred** R B Hill **Trained** Royston, Herts

FOCUS
The winning time was 0.57sec quicker than the first division. The winner bounced back to last year's figure at this time of year.

T/Plt: £24.60. Pool: £51,624.69 - 1527.53 winning units. T/Qpdt: £1.60. Pool:4707.80 - 2084.06 winning units. JR

The Form Book Flat, Raceform Ltd, Compton, RG20 6NL.

[8034]WOLVERHAMPTON (A.W) (L-H)

Tuesday, November 26

OFFICIAL GOING: Standard

Wind: Light half-behind Weather: Overcast

8050 COMPARE BOOKMAKERS AT BOOKMAKERS.CO.UK H'CAP (DIV I) 5f 20y(P)

3:50 (3:52) (Class 6) (0-52,52) 3-Y-O+ **£1,940** (£577; £288; £144) **Stalls** Low

Form RPR

206- **1** **College Doll**[6] 7969 4-8-9 **47**....(t) EoinWalsh(7) 3 57
(Christine Dunnett) *mde all: edgd lft over 3f out: shkn up over 1f out: rdn out* **7/2**[2]

033- **2** *3* **Major Muscari (IRE)**[11] 7903 5-9-4 **49**.... JimmyQuinn 7 49
(Shaun Harris) *s.i.s: hdwy 1/2-way: rdn to go 2nd wl ins fnl f: edgd lft: nt rch wnr* **3/1**[1]

/00- **3** *¾* **Befortyfour**[20] 7772 8-9-7 **52**....(bt) RobertWinston 6 49
(Charles Smith) *a.p: chsd wnr 1/2-way: rdn and edgd lft over 1f out: styd on same pce ins fnl f* **4/1**[3]

00- **4** *½* **Ferocious Fran (IRE)**[169] 3154 5-9-1 **46** oh1.... ShaneKelly 5 41
(Emmet Michael Butterly, Ire) *hld up: pushed along 1/2-way: hdwy u.p over 1f out: nvr trbld ldrs* **10/1**

056- **5** *1 ¾* **Cashel's Missile (IRE)**[11] 7903 3-9-1 **46** oh1....(p) LiamJones 11 35
(John Spearing) *prom: pushed along 1/2-way: styd on same pce appr fnl f* **10/1**

065- **6** *1* **Ishetoo**[87] 5982 9-9-1 **46** oh1.... StephenCraine 9 31
(Peter Grayson) *chsd ldrs: rdn and hung rt 1/2-way: wknd fnl f* **33/1**

30- **7** *¾* **Bond Blade**[236] 1355 5-8-10 **46** oh1.... JacobButterfield(5) 8 28
(Suzzanne France) *sn pushed along in rr: rdn over 1f out: n.d* **33/1**

250- **8** *1 ¼* **Lexi's Beauty (IRE)**[170] 3134 3-9-1 **46**.... GrahamGibbons 1 24
(Brian Baugh) *chsd ldr: hmpd over 3f out: rdn 1/2-way: wknd ins fnl f* **6/1**

606- **9** *1 ¼* **Chateau Lola**[13] 7850 4-8-10 **48**....(v) AdamMcLean(7) 2 21
(Derek Shaw) *s.i.s: hld up: rdn over 1f out: a in rr* **8/1**

1m 3.07s (0.77) **Going Correction** +0.15s/f (Slow) **9** Ran SP% **116.7**
Speed ratings (Par 101): **99,94,93,92,89 87,86,84,82**
toteswingers 1&2 £2.70, 1&3 £3.60, 2&3 £3.30 CSF £14.63 CT £42.35 TOTE £5.00: £1.60, £1.40, £1.40; EX 15.10 Trifecta £113.90 Pool: £3484.62 - 22.92 winning units..
Owner P D West, A S Machin & C A Dunnett **Bred** Christine Dunnett & Brian Green **Trained** Hingham, Norfolk

FOCUS
A desperately weak handicap where the order changed little. Not form to be with.

8051 COMPARE BOOKMAKERS AT BOOKMAKERS.CO.UK H'CAP (DIV II) 5f 20y(P)

4:20 (4:21) (Class 6) (0-52,52) 3-Y-O+ **£1,940** (£577; £288; £144) **Stalls** Low

Form RPR

01- **1** **Iffranesia (FR)**[13] 7850 3-9-7 **52**....(p) MartinLane 3 70+
(Robert Cowell) *hld up: hdwy 2f out: hrd rdn over 1f out: r.o to ld wl ins fnl f* **7/2**[2]

401- **2** *½* **Give Us A Belle (IRE)**[1] 8035 4-9-0 **46**....(vt) EoinWalsh(7) 6 68
(Christine Dunnett) *chsd ldr: pushed along 1/2-way: rdn to ld over 1f out: hdd wl ins fnl f: styd on* **5/4**[1]

660- **3** *3 ¾* **Vhujon (IRE)**[11] 7905 8-8-12 **46** oh1.... SladeO'Hara(3) 2 49
(Peter Grayson) *chsd ldrs: pushed along 1/2-way: rdn over 1f out: styd on same pce fnl f* **20/1**

306- **4** *2* **Myjestic Melody (IRE)**[11] 7905 5-8-12 **46** oh1....(p) RobertTart(3) 1 42
(Brian Ellison) *led: rdn and hdd over 1f out: wknd ins fnl f* **7/2**[2]

000- **5** *2 ¾* **La Sylphe**[11] 7903 3-8-9 **47**.... AdamMcLean(7) 4 33
(Derek Shaw) *dwlt: hld up: hdwy over 1f out: sn rdn: wknd fnl f* **25/1**

300- **6** *3* **Chelsea Grey (IRE)**[40] 7323 3-8-10 **46** oh1....(b) PhilipPrince(5) 9 21
(Ronald Harris) *sn pushed along and prom: lost pl 4f out: sn bhd* **20/1**

350- **7** *½* **Rightcar**[55] 6930 6-9-3 **48**.... StephenCraine 5 21
(Peter Grayson) *sn pushed along in rr: rdn 1/2-way: n.d* **7/1**[3]

000- **8** *5* **Johnson's Cat (IRE)**[1] 8035 4-9-1 **46** oh1.... JimmyQuinn 7
(Mandy Rowland) *chsd ldrs: rdn 1/2-way: wknd wl over 1f out* **33/1**

1m 2.92s (0.62) **Going Correction** +0.15s/f (Slow) **8** Ran SP% **117.7**
Speed ratings (Par 101): **101,100,94,91,86 81,81,73**
toteswingers 1&2 £1.90, 1&3 £10.20, 2&3 £7.90 CSF £8.16 CT £75.07 TOTE £3.40: £1.50, £1.10, £5.40; EX 10.30 Trifecta £205.60 Pool: £4517.54 - 16.47 winning units..
Owner Cyril Humphris **Bred** Cyril Humphris **Trained** Six Mile Bottom, Cambs

FOCUS
This was significantly stronger the first division and the finish was fought out by the two recent winners in the line-up. The form is possibly worth slightly more.

8052 32RED FILLIES' H'CAP 5f 216y(P)

4:50 (4:52) (Class 5) (0-70,71) 3-Y-O+ **£3,234** (£962; £481; £240) **Stalls** Low

Form RPR

443- **1** **Dream Scenario**[7] 7964 3-9-4 **67**....(v) DavidAllan 3 76+
(Mel Brittain) *s.i.s: outpcd: rdn over 1f out: str run to ld wl ins fnl f: sn clr* **6/1**[2]

440- **2** *2 ¼* **Song Of Parkes**[14] 7845 6-9-1 **67**.... SladeO'Hara(3) 1 69
(Peter Grayson) *chsd ldrs: rdn over 1f out: ev ch wl ins fnl f: styd on same pce* **33/1**

310- **3** *nk* **Barbs Princess**[27] 7634 3-9-7 **70**.... RobertWinston 6 71
(Charles Hills) *w ldr: rdn over 2f out: led wl over 1f out: hdd and unable qck wl ins fnl f* **7/1**[3]

631- **4** *1 ¼* **Hannahs Turn**[7] 7958 3-9-3 **71** 6ex.... ShelleyBirkett(5) 9 69
(Chris Dwyer) *led: rdn and hdd over 1f out: no ex wl ins fnl f* **5/2**[1]

060- **5** *1 ½* **Saskia's Dream**[3] 8019 5-9-0 **63**....(v) LukeMorris 8 56
(Jane Chapple-Hyam) *mid-div: pushed along 1/2-way: r.o ins fnl f: nt trble ldrs* **6/1**[2]

012- **6** *½* **Tiger's Home**[14] 7845 3-8-8 **57**.... AdamBeschizza 11 49
(Julia Feilden) *sn pushed along towards rr: rdn and r.o ins fnl f: nvr nrr* **16/1**

346- **7** *½* **Ray Of Joy**[25] 7663 7-9-4 **67**.... LiamJones 5 57
(J R Jenkins) *sn pushed along in rr: r.o ins fnl f: nrst fin* **14/1**

412- **8** *2 ¾* **Beacon Tarn**[11] 7903 3-8-13 **62**.... GrahamGibbons 7 44
(Eric Alston) *prom: rdn over 2f out: wknd ins fnl f* **8/1**

004- **9** *1 ¾* **Economic Crisis (IRE)**[14] 7845 4-9-2 **65**.... RobertHavlin 10 42
(Alan Berry) *prom: rdn 1/2-way: wknd fnl f* **16/1**

10 *5* **Mandarin Bar**[155] 3-8-10 **64**.... DavidBergin(5) 4 26
(David O'Meara) *mid-div: rdn and lost pl 1/2-way: wknd over 2f out* **14/1**

104- **11** *3 ¾* **Batchworth Lady**[21] 7743 3-9-2 **65**.... JimmyQuinn 2 15
(Dean Ivory) *mid-div: hdwy 2f out: sn rdn: wknd fnl f: eased* **12/1**

1m 15.33s (0.33) **Going Correction** +0.15s/f (Slow) **11** Ran SP% **116.5**
Speed ratings (Par 100): **103,100,99,97,95 95,94,90,88,81 76**
toteswingers 1&2 £42.80, 1&3 £8.70, 2&3 £53.70 CSF £180.23 CT £1438.92 TOTE £5.60: £2.00, £7.00, £2.90; EX 178.80 Trifecta £3168.20 Part won. Pool: £4224.34 - 0.37 winning units..
Owner Northgate Black **Bred** R J Cornelius **Trained** Warthill, N Yorks

FOCUS
There's no doubt that Hannahs Turn brought the best recent form into this but she's clearly not as good on Polytrack and was again found wanting.

8053 LADBROKES H'CAP 7f 32y(P)

5:20 (5:23) (Class 4) (0-85,84) 3-Y-O+ **£5,175** (£1,540; £769; £384) **Stalls** High

Form RPR

356- **1** **Capo Rosso (IRE)**[26] 7648 3-9-5 **83**....(v) StephenCraine 1 93
(Tom Dascombe) *w ldr tl led 1/2-way: rdn over 1f out: r.o gamely* **7/1**

110- **2** *nk* **Iptisam**[43] 7241 4-9-7 **84**.... LukeMorris 2 94
(James Tate) *hmpd s: sn trcking ldrs: wnt 2nd over 2f out: rdn and ev ch fr over 1f out: r.o* **11/4**[1]

051- **3** *2* **Fantasy Gladiator**[7] 7964 7-9-2 **79** 6ex.... AndreaAtzeni 7 84
(John Quinn) *sn pushed along in rr: hdwy over 2f out: rdn over 1f out: styd on u.p* **9/2**[3]

132- **4** *2 ¼* **Living The Life (IRE)**[8] 7949 3-9-0 **78**....(b) DavidProbert 5 77
(Jamie Osborne) *chsd ldrs: rdn over 1f out: edgd lft and no ex ins fnl f* **3/1**[2]

606- **5** *4 ½* **Fieldgunner Kirkup (GER)**[8] 7949 5-9-4 **81**.... GrahamGibbons 4 70
(David Barron) *hld up: rdn over 2f out: nvr nrr* **8/1**

0/0- **6** *nk* **Suehail**[20] 7769 4-9-1 **78**.... SeanLevey 8 66
(Robert Cowell) *hld up: rdn over 1f out: nt trble ldrs* **33/1**

564- **7** *3 ½* **Piddie's Power**[8] 7949 6-8-13 **79**.... RobertTart(3) 6 59
(Kevin Frost) *chsd ldrs: pushed along whn hmpd over 2f out: wknd over 1f out* **16/1**

213- **8** *7* **Bogsnog (IRE)**[7] 7965 3-8-7 **76**.... JacobButterfield(5) 3 37
(Kristin Stubbs) *led to 1/2-way: sn rdn: wknd over 1f out* **8/1**

1m 28.87s (-0.73) **Going Correction** +0.15s/f (Slow)
WFA 3 from 4yo+ 1lb **8** Ran SP% **113.4**
Speed ratings (Par 105): **110,109,107,104,99 99,95,87**
toteswingers 1&2 £3.10, 1&3 £6.30, 2&3 £2.40 CSF £26.15 CT £96.96 TOTE £7.80: £2.50, £1.30, £1.70; EX 28.20 Trifecta £182.70 Pool: £4343.31 - 17.82 winning units..
Owner Deva Racing Red Clubs Partnership **Bred** Michael Wiley **Trained** Malpas, Cheshire

FOCUS
There was no shortage of pace on in this competitive handicap. The winner is rated back to his best.

8054 DOWNLOAD THE LADBROKES APP MAIDEN STKS 1m 141y(P)

5:50 (5:50) (Class 5) 3-Y-O+ **£2,587** (£770; £384; £192) **Stalls** Low

Form RPR

0/6- **1** **Jaladee**[21] 7738 3-9-5 0.... AndreaAtzeni 1 69+
(Roger Varian) *s.i.s: sn pushed along and given reminder: then plld hrd in rr: hdwy over 1f out: rdn and r.o to ld nr fin* **8/11**[1]

63- **2** *nse* **Frost Fire (USA)**[6] 7983 3-9-0 0.... AdrianNicholls 3 64
(Mark Johnston) *led: rdn over 1f out: edgd rt ins fnl f: hdd nr fin* **2/1**[2]

403- **3** *3* **Short Shrift (IRE)**[10] 7923 3-8-11 61.... RobertTart(3) 8 58
(James Toller) *chsd ldr: shkn up over 2f out: rdn over 1f out: lost 2nd and no ex wl ins fnl f* **6/1**[3]

604- **4** *7* **Medecis Mountain**[19] 7787 4-9-8 43....(p) PaddyAspell 7 48
(John Wainwright) *prom: rdn over 2f out: wknd over 1f out* **66/1**

0/0- **5** *15* **Dinkie**[77] 6289 3-9-0 45.... BarryMcHugh 6 12
(Geoffrey Oldroyd) *hld up: pushed along over 3f out: wknd over 2f out* **33/1**

046/ **6** *½* **Louis Vee (IRE)**[530] 3076 5-9-8 46.... LukeMorris 5 15
(Roy Brotherton) *plld hrd and prom: rdn and wknd over 2f out* **66/1**

1m 51.5s (1.00) **Going Correction** +0.15s/f (Slow)
WFA 3 from 4yo+ 3lb **6** Ran SP% **111.4**
Speed ratings (Par 103): **101,100,98,92,78 78**
toteswingers 1&2 £1.10, 1&3 £1.30, 2&3 £1.20 CSF £2.36 TOTE £2.00: £1.10, £1.20; EX 2.80 Trifecta £6.70 Pool: £3646.44 - 407.16 winning units..
Owner Sheikh Ahmed Al Maktoum **Bred** Darley **Trained** Newmarket, Suffolk

FOCUS
The market spoken heavily in the favour of the winner. The third and fourth set a solid, modest leve.

8055 LADBROKES MOBILE H'CAP (DIV I) 1m 141y(P)

6:20 (6:20) (Class 6) (0-52,52) 3-Y-O+ **£1,940** (£577; £288; £144) **Stalls** Low

Form RPR

042- **1** **Galilee Chapel (IRE)**[7] 7963 4-9-3 **48**....(b) BarryMcHugh 7 54
(Alistair Whillans) *s.s: in rr: pushed along over 3f out: rdn over 2f out: str run u.p to ld nr fin* **4/1**[2]

300- **2** *nk* **Do More Business (IRE)**[42] 7265 6-8-13 **49**....(bt) PhilipPrince(5) 11 54
(Liam Corcoran) *hld up: hdwy over 1f out: rdn to ld wl ins fnl f: edgd lft and hdd nr fin* **14/1**

306- **3** *nk* **Holli Deya**[21] 7753 3-8-9 **46** oh1....(v[1]) RobertTart(3) 2 51
(Andi Brown) *a.p: rdn over 1f out: ev ch ins fnl f: r.o* **12/1**

666- **4** *½* **Mill I Am (USA)**[7] 7962 3-9-3 **51**.... AndreaAtzeni 9 55
(Stuart Williams) *a.p: chsd ldr over 2f out: led over 1f out: sn rdn: hdd wl ins fnl f: hmpd nr fin* **7/2**[1]

003- **5** *½* **Aureolin Gulf**[10] 7931 4-9-1 **46** oh1.... LiamJones 3 49
(Andrew Hollinshead) *hld up: hdwy over 2f out: rdn over 1f out: r.o* **8/1**

066- **6** *1 ¾* **Bertie Blu Boy**[10] 7931 5-9-1 **46** oh1....(b) JamesSullivan 8 45
(Lisa Williamson) *led: rdn and hdd over 1f out: styd on same pce ins fnl f* **8/1**

050- **7** *¾* **Mr Chocolate Drop (IRE)**[10] 7930 9-9-5 **50**....(t) JimmyQuinn 6 47
(Mandy Rowland) *hld up: hdwy over 1f out: sn rdn: no ex ins fnl f* **16/1**

000- **8** *¾* **Benandonner (USA)**[13] 7858 10-9-7 **52**.... ShaneKelly 4 48
(Mike Murphy) *hld up: hdwy over 2f out: rdn over 1f out: styd on same pce* **9/2**[3]

456- **9** *1 ¾* **Justcallmehandsome**[50] 7083 11-8-10 **46** oh1....(p) JoshBaudains(5) 5 38
(Dominic Ffrench Davis) *s.i.s: hld up: n.d* **33/1**

600- **10** *4* **Poetic Belle**[12] 7886 3-8-13 **52**....(t) ShirleyTeasdale(5) 10 36
(Shaun Harris) *chsd ldr tl rdn over 2f out: wknd fnl f* **20/1**

600- 11 2 3/4 **Ellaal**[10] 7931 4-9-7 **52** DaleSwift 1 30
(Ruth Carr) *prom: rdn over 3f out: wknd over 1f out* **20/1**

1m 51.74s (1.24) **Going Correction** +0.15s/f (Slow)
WFA 3 from 4yo+ 3lb **11 Ran SP% 115.3**
Speed ratings (Par 101): **100,99,99,99,98 97,96,95,94,90 88**
toteswingers 1&2 £11.70, 1&3 £14.10, 2&3 £21.00 CSF £55.63 CT £628.57 TOTE £5.10: £1.70, £3.70, £3.80; EX 22.70 Trifecta £791.80 Pool: £2893.41 - 2.74 winning units..
Owner The Blues Gang **Bred** Tally-Ho Stud **Trained** Newmill-On-Slitrig, Borders

FOCUS
As weak a handicap as you'll get and routine, low-grade form.

8056 LADBROKES MOBILE H'CAP (DIV II) 1m 141y(P)
6:50 (6:51) (Class 6) (0-52,54) 3-Y-O+ **£1,940** (£577; £288; £144) **Stalls** Low

Form RPR
331- 1 **Be Royale**[7] 7966 3-9-6 **54** 6ex RobertWinston 6 67+
(Michael Appleby) *chsd ldrs: led over 1f out: shkn up ins fnl f: comf* **5/4**[1]
264- 2 2 1/4 **Bond Artist (IRE)**[10] 7931 4-9-2 **50** WilliamTwiston-Davies(3) 7 56+
(Geoffrey Oldroyd) *hld up: hdwy over 2f out: shkn up over 1f out: chsd wnr fnl f: no imp* **6/1**[2]
60- 3 6 **Hypnotism**[189] 2547 3-8-12 **46** LukeMorris 4 39
(Ronald Harris) *chsd ldrs: pushed along over 3f out: rdn over 2f out: styng on same pce whn hung lft ins fnl f* **7/1**[3]
000- 4 2 1/4 **Storey Hill (USA)**[42] 7266 8-9-1 **46** oh1 RobbieFitzpatrick 8 35
(Richard Guest) *hld up: hdwy u.p over 1f out: no ex ins fnl f* **50/1**
600- 5 1 1/2 **Bix (IRE)**[33] 7485 3-9-0 **48** (b) RobertHavlin 9 34
(Alan Berry) *hld up: rdn over 2f out: nvr nrr* **50/1**
605- 6 1/2 **Stoneacre Oskar**[26] 7639 4-9-0 **48** SladeO'Hara(3) 3 32
(Peter Grayson) *hld up: rdn over 1f out: nvr trbld ldrs* **20/1**
323- 7 3/4 **Bladewood Girl**[7] 7963 5-9-7 **52** FrederikTylicki 2 35
(J R Jenkins) *led: rdn and hdd over 1f out: wknd ins fnl f* **6/1**[2]
043- 8 1/2 **Shamiana**[7] 7962 3-9-4 **52** SteveDrowne 5 34
(Daniel Kubler) *chsd ldr tl rdn over 1f out: wknd fnl f* **16/1**
430- 9 1 1/4 **Stamp Duty (IRE)**[54] 6985 5-8-11 **47** (p) JacobButterfield(5) 11 26
(Suzzanne France) *hld up: pushed along over 2f out: nvr on terms* **10/1**
6/0- 10 6 **Huzzah (IRE)**[313] 240 8-9-4 **49** [1] IPoullis 10 16
(Jedd O'Keeffe) *prom: rdn over 2f out: sn wknd* **16/1**
000- 11 6 **World Freight Girl**[42] 7265 3-8-12 **46** oh1 (p) JimmyQuinn 1
(Dean Ivory) *prom: rdn over 3f out: wknd over 2f out* **33/1**

1m 51.47s (0.97) **Going Correction** +0.15s/f (Slow)
WFA 3 from 4yo+ 3lb **11 Ran SP% 118.0**
Speed ratings (Par 101): **101,99,93,91,90 89,89,88,87,82 77**
toteswingers 1&2 £3.00, 1&3 £4.40, 2&3 £6.50 CSF £8.50 CT £38.39 TOTE £2.50: £1.10, £2.90, £3.00; EX 8.20 Trifecta £65.40 Pool: £3239.91 - 37.12 winning units..
Owner Wayne Brackstone, Steve Whitear **Bred** W Brackstone & S J Whitear **Trained** Danethorpe, Notts

FOCUS
An emphatic success for the favourite.

8057 CORAL APP DOWNLOAD FROM THE APP STORE H'CAP 1m 1f 103y(P)
7:20 (7:20) (Class 4) (0-80,79) 3-Y-O+ **£4,690** (£1,395; £697; £348) **Stalls** Low

Form RPR
1/1- 1 **Epic Battle (IRE)**[19] 7786 3-9-4 **77** LiamJones 6 87+
(William Haggas) *a.p: pushed along over 3f out: rdn over 1f out: sn swvd lft: edgd rt ins fnl f: sn led and hung lft: r.o* **6/4**[1]
244- 2 1 1/2 **Ishikawa (IRE)**[14] 7849 5-9-0 **77** RobJFitzpatrick(7) 1 83
(K R Burke) *chsd ldrs: led over 1f out: rdn and hdd ins fnl f: styd on same pce* **5/1**[3]
152- 3 1 **Tatting**[28] 7605 4-9-0 **70** LukeMorris 7 74
(Chris Dwyer) *hld up: rdn over 1f out: edgd lft and r.o ins fnl f: nt rch ldrs* **7/1**
342- 4 1/2 **Incendo**[8] 7950 7-9-5 **75** StevieDonohoe 4 78
(Ian Williams) *hld up: hdwy over 1f out: r.o* **16/1**
102- 5 1 3/4 **Berlusca (IRE)**[14] 7849 4-9-7 **77** GrahamGibbons 2 77
(David O'Meara) *led: rdn and hdd over 1f out: no ex ins fnl f* **6/1**
361- 6 1 3/4 **Lean On Pete (IRE)**[7] 7961 4-9-4 **79** 6ex JacobButterfield(5) 3 76
(Ollie Pears) *hld up: shkn up over 1f out: nt trble ldrs* **7/2**[2]
241/ 7 1 1/2 **Laudate Dominum (IRE)**[451] 5818 3-9-4 **77** TonyHamilton 5 71
(Richard Fahey) *trckd ldr: plld hrd: rdn over 2f out: wknd fnl f* **14/1**

2m 2.49s (0.79) **Going Correction** +0.15s/f (Slow)
WFA 3 from 4yo+ 3lb **7 Ran SP% 118.2**
Speed ratings (Par 105): **102,100,99,99,97 96,94**
toteswingers 1&2 £2.10, 1&3 £4.20, 2&3 £4.10 CSF £10.05 TOTE £2.40: £1.50, £2.50; EX 14.30 Trifecta £45.50 Pool: £3936.32 - 64.78 winning units..
Owner Saleh Al Homaizi & Imad Al Sagar **Bred** Castlemartin Sky & Skymarc Farm **Trained** Newmarket, Suffolk

FOCUS
A fair race for the grade with a progressive winner. The first two have more to offer.
T/Jkpt: £9417.80. Pool: £99,484.68 - 7.50 winning units. T/Plt: £68.70. Pool: £103,254.47 - 1095.83 winning units. T/Qpdt: £34.50. Pool: £10,050.15 - 215.17 winning units. CR

7985 KEMPTON (A.W) (R-H)
Wednesday, November 27

OFFICIAL GOING: Standard
Wind: Almost nil Weather: Overcast

8058 BETDAQ - THE SPORTS BETTING EXCHANGE MAIDEN AUCTION STKS 5f (P)
4:00 (4:00) (Class 5) 2-Y-O **£2,587** (£770; £384; £192) **Stalls** Low

Form RPR
1 **National Service (USA)** 2-8-12 0 SeanLevey 4 72+
(Stuart Williams) *s.s: chsd ldrs: wnt 2nd over 1f out and readily clsd on ldr: rdn to ld last 150yds: sn clr* **7/4**[1]
003- 2 2 1/4 **Coiste Bodhar (IRE)**[6] 7986 2-8-6 62 GeorgeChaloner(5) 1 63
(Joseph Tuite) *chsd clr ldr: pushed along 1/2-way: tried to cl over 1f out but wnr swept past: kpt on to take 2nd nr fin* **11/4**[2]
643- 3 nk **Anfield**[26] 7665 2-8-5 51 WilliamCarson 2 56
(Mick Quinn) *led and sn clr: 4 l up 1/2-way: rdn over 1f out: tired and hdd last 150yds: lost 2nd nr fin* **5/1**[3]
060- 4 6 **Seven Lucky Seven**[45] 7218 2-8-11 55 (b[1]) JimmyQuinn 7 40
(Gary Harrison) *s.i.s: outpcd and rousted along: hanging whn rdn over 1f out: tk modest 4th ins fnl f* **6/1**
5 3 1/2 **My Girl Rio (IRE)** 2-8-8 0 PaulQuinn 6 25
(Geoffrey Harker) *chsd ldrs: no imp over 2f out: wknd wl over 1f out* **25/1**
6 22 **Little Miss Becky** 2-8-2 0 RyanPowell(3) 5
(Giles Bravery) *s.v.s: a wl t.o* **20/1**

59.95s (-0.55) **Going Correction** +0.025s/f (Slow) **6 Ran SP% 102.6**
Speed ratings (Par 96): **105,101,100,91,85 50**
toteswingers 1&2 £1.10, 1&3 £1.60, 2&3 £1.70 CSF £5.53 TOTE £3.50: £1.30, £1.40; EX 6.70 Trifecta £14.30 Pool: £2256.51 - 118.07 winning units..
Owner T W Morley **Bred** Three Chimneys Farm Llc **Trained** Newmarket, Suffolk

FOCUS
An ordinary maiden. The third, who set a strong pace, limits the form.

8059 WINNERS ARE WELCOME AT BETDAQ H'CAP (DIV I) 1m 2f (P)
4:30 (4:30) (Class 5) (0-70,70) 3-Y-O+ **£2,587** (£770; £384; £192) **Stalls** Low

Form RPR
000- 1 **Ssafa**[28] 7629 5-9-5 **68** (p) SteveDrowne 4 76
(Alastair Lidderdale) *trckd ldrs: rdn and prog fr 2f out: led jst ins fnl f: styd on wl* **33/1**
421- 2 1 1/2 **Bobs Her Uncle**[28] 7622 4-9-4 **67** TedDurcan 1 72
(James Bethell) *chsd ldr 3f: styd prom: rdn and nt qckn over 1f out: kpt on to take 2nd last strides* **9/4**[1]
000- 3 hd **Darnathean**[13] 7880 4-8-13 **62** (e[1]) FrederikTylicki 6 67
(Paul D'Arcy) *led: tried to kick on over 2f out: hdd and one pce jst ins fnl f: lost 2nd last strides* **14/1**
060- 4 1/2 **Woolston Ferry (IRE)**[16] 7836 7-9-5 **68** FergusSweeney 2 72
(Henry Candy) *dwlt: sn in midfield on inner: nt clr run jst over 1f out: styd on same pce fnl f* **8/1**
103- 5 1/2 **Whinging Willie (IRE)**[49] 7132 4-8-12 **68** (p) HectorCrouch(7) 10 71+
(Gary Moore) *hld up towards rr on inner: nt clr run over 1f out to ins fnl f: kpt on but no ch* **8/1**
600- 6 nse **Tartan Gigha (IRE)**[19] 7805 8-9-7 **70** (b) GrahamLee 8 73+
(Geoffrey Harker) *hld up in last: coaxed into 7th 1f out: rdn and kpt on one pce fnl f* **20/1**
560- 7 2 1/4 **Shalambar (IRE)**[140] 4166 7-9-3 **66** DavidProbert 3 64
(Tony Carroll) *settled in rr: shkn up and no prog 2f out: wl hld fnl f* **20/1**
000- 8 nk **Fearless Lad (IRE)**[36] 7446 3-8-11 **64** (t) LukeMorris 7 61
(John Best) *t.k.h: trckd ldr after 3f: rdn wl over 2f out: wknd over 1f out* **25/1**
160- 9 3/4 **Mountain Range (IRE)**[29] 7611 5-9-5 **68** RobertWinston 5 64
(Willie Musson) *towards rr on outer: nudged along and dropped to last trio 2f out: no ch whn shkn up ins fnl f* **5/2**[2]
500- 10 17 **Unmoothaj**[27] 7651 3-9-3 **70** (v[1]) LiamKeniry 9 32
(Pam Sly) *chsd ldrs on outer: rdn 3f out: wknd rapidly 2f out: t.o* **6/1**[3]

2m 7.87s (-0.13) **Going Correction** +0.025s/f (Slow)
WFA 3 from 4yo+ 4lb **10 Ran SP% 118.8**
Speed ratings (Par 103): **101,99,99,99,98 98,97,96,96,82**
toteswingers 1&2 £12.60, 1&3 £29.40, 2&3 £9.40 CSF £104.89 CT £1152.65 TOTE £20.80: £5.30, £1.30, £6.20; EX 111.80 Trifecta £472.00 Pool: £4502.46 - 7.15 winning units..
Owner Andy Weller **Bred** Newsells Park Stud **Trained** Lambourn, Berks

FOCUS
A modest handicap and a muddling affair. They went no pace and it turned into a sprint from the turn in. The winner sets the standard.

8060 WINNERS ARE WELCOME AT BETDAQ H'CAP (DIV II) 1m 2f (P)
5:00 (5:00) (Class 5) (0-70,70) 3-Y-O+ **£2,587** (£770; £384; £192) **Stalls** Low

Form RPR
244- 1 **Thankyou Very Much**[20] 7786 3-8-9 **62** TedDurcan 10 71
(James Bethell) *mostly trckd ldr to 1/2-way: styd prom: rdn to chse ldr 1f out: r.o to ld nr fin* **8/1**
215- 2 1/2 **Storm (IRE)**[33] 7504 3-9-3 **70** JimCrowley 4 78
(Charles Hills) *trckd ldrs: swtchd to inner and prog to ld jst over 1f out: styd on but hdd nr fin* **13/8**[1]
400- 3 nk **Spring Tonic**[16] 7840 4-9-0 **68** JackDuern(5) 2 76
(Simon Dow) *hld up in last trio: lots to do after pce lifted 2f out: gd prog on outer fnl f: tk 3rd nr fin and clsd on ldng pair* **6/1**[3]
556- 4 nk **Enriching (USA)**[28] 7629 5-9-2 **68** RyanPowell(3) 5 75
(Gary Harrison) *trckd ldrs: rdn and nt qckn over 1f out: styd on to chse ldng pair ins fnl f: clsd grad but lost 3rd nr fin* **16/1**
020- 5 2 1/4 **Shirataki (IRE)**[14] 7865 5-9-4 **67** ChrisCatlin 1 71
(Peter Hiatt) *t.k.h: hld up in midfield: tried to make prog on inner but chopped off over 1f out: nt rcvr: kpt on* **16/1**
600- 6 1/2 **Martinas Delight (USA)**[35] 7462 3-9-0 **70** RobertTart(3) 3 72
(Alan Jarvis) *hld up in last trio: lot to do whn pce lifted 2f out and also v wd bnd: styd on fnl f: no ch* **25/1**
420- 7 3/4 **Mr Lando**[13] 7881 4-9-2 **65** JimmyQuinn 8 65
(Tony Carroll) *t.k.h: hld up in midfield tl swift prog to trck ldr 1/2-way: rdn to chal 2f out: upsides over 1f out: wknd fnl f* **10/3**[2]
415- 8 1/2 **Arashi**[140] 4166 7-8-13 **69** (v) AdamMcLean(7) 7 68
(Derek Shaw) *s.s: hld up in last: no ch after pce qckned 2f out: kpt on* **25/1**
510- 9 1 1/2 **April Ciel**[58] 6898 4-9-5 **68** (p) LukeMorris 6 64
(Ronald Harris) *led at mod pce: drvn and hdd jst over 1f out: wknd* **20/1**
215- 10 5 **Time Square (FR)**[150] 3865 6-8-8 **62** JoeyHaynes(5) 9 48
(Tony Carroll) *t.k.h: trckd ldrs on outer: wknd 2f out* **16/1**

2m 8.49s (0.49) **Going Correction** +0.025s/f (Slow)
WFA 3 from 4yo+ 4lb **10 Ran SP% 116.7**
Speed ratings (Par 103): **99,98,98,98,96 95,95,94,93,89**
toteswingers 1&2 £3.00, 1&3 £9.20, 2&3 £3.00 CSF £20.84 CT £84.05 TOTE £8.80: £2.30, £1.10, £2.20; EX 25.40 Trifecta £164.20 Pool: £3798.42 - 17.34 winning units..
Owner Robert Gibbons **Bred** Robert Gibbons **Trained** Middleham Moor, N Yorks

FOCUS
The second, and slower, division of the modest 1m2f handicap. The winner built on her first try at 1m2f.

8061 BRITISH STALLION STUDS EBF MAIDEN STKS 6f (P)
5:30 (5:32) (Class 5) 2-Y-O **£2,911** (£866; £432; £216) **Stalls** Low

Form RPR
1 **Glorious Empire (IRE)** 2-9-5 0 GeorgeBaker 7 81+
(Ed Walker) *hld up in tch: smooth prog over 2f out to trck ldr over 1f out: pushed into ld last 150yds: v readily* **11/4**[1]
220- 2 1 1/2 **Nova Champ (IRE)**[18] 7817 2-9-5 72 SteveDrowne 5 73
(Stuart Williams) *led: fended off chalrs wl enough 2f out: clr of rest but no ch w wnr once hdd last 150yds* **7/2**[2]
006- 3 4 **Green Music**[13] 7878 2-9-0 58 LukeMorris 8 56
(James Eustace) *t.k.h: chsd ldr: nt qckn 2f out: lost 2nd and outpcd fr over 1f out* **16/1**
05- 4 1/2 **Tahchee**[26] 7664 2-9-5 0 FrederikTylicki 9 60
(James Fanshawe) *chsd ldrs: rdn and outpcd fr wl over 1f out* **12/1**

The Form Book Flat, Raceform Ltd, Compton, RG20 6NL.

00- 5 hd **Like A Prayer**49 7120 2-9-5 0 JimCrowley 6 59+
(Ralph Beckett) *stdd s: hld up in last pair: pushed along on outer over 2f out: reminder over 1f out: kpt on steadily: nt disgracd* 8/1
- 6 3/4 **Spring Fling** 2-9-0 0 FergusSweeney 3 52+
(Henry Candy) *settled in last trio: pushed along 2f out: sme prog jst over 1f out: one pce last 100yds* 6/1
00- 7 shd **Illegal Action (USA)**84 6110 2-9-5 0 (t) AndreaAtzeni 4 56
(Olly Stevens) *settled in midfield: shuffled along fr over 2f out: kpt on same pce after: nt disgracd* 16/1
54- 8 2 3/4 **Frangipanni (IRE)**14 7852 2-9-0 0 MartinLane 2 43
(Roger Charlton) *chsd ldng pair: rdn over 2f out: sn lost pl and struggling* 4/1[3]
00- 9 1 3/4 **Ignight**68 6590 2-9-5 0 DavidProbert 1 43
(Mark Usher) *nvr bttr than midfield: rdn over 2f out: wknd jst over 1f out* 50/1
10 7 **Fruit Pastille** 2-9-0 0 NickyMackay 11 17
(Hughie Morrison) *dwlt: rn green and a in last pair: bhd fnl 2f* 33/1
11 3/4 **Beastfromtheeast** 2-9-5 0 TomMcLaughlin 10 20
(Ed Walker) *rn green and racd wd towards rr: wknd 2f out* 33/1

1m 13.57s (0.47) **Going Correction** +0.025s/f (Slow) 11 Ran SP% **121.6**
Speed ratings (Par 96): **97,95,89,89,88 87,87,83,81,72 71**
toteswingers 1&2 £2.60, 1&3 £10.90, 2&3 £11.40 CSF £12.58 TOTE £3.70: £1.30, £2.00, £5.00; EX 17.20 Trifecta £131.70 Pool: £4173.06 - 23.76 winning units..
Owner Ms Judy Yap & Ms Salina Yang **Bred** Patrick Grogan **Trained** Newmarket, Suffolk
FOCUS
An ordinary juvenile maiden. The second and third set the opening level.

8062 £500 FREE BETS AT BETDAQ WILD FLOWER STKS (LISTED RACE) 1m 4f (P)
6:00 (6:00) (Class 1) 3-Y-O+
£22,684 (£8,600; £4,304; £2,144; £1,076; £540) **Stalls** Centre

Form RPR
353- 1 **Aussie Reigns (IRE)**21 7768 3-9-0 95 (v) AndreaAtzeni 7 102
(William Knight) *hld up in 6th and off the pce: clsd over 2f out: prog and rdn to ld 1f out: styd on wl* 8/1
305- 2 1 **Dick Doughtywylie**11 7927 5-9-6 98 RobertHavlin 6 100
(John Gosden) *hld up in 4th: clsd over 2f out: rdn to try to chal over 1f out but nt qckn: styd on to take 2nd last 75yds* 5/1[3]
504- 3 3/4 **Banoffee (IRE)**27 7650 3-8-11 103 JimCrowley 4 96
(Hughie Morrison) *t.k.h early: trckd ldng pair: wnt 2nd jst over 3f out and led jst over 2f out: sn drvn: hdd and one pce 1f out* 11/4[2]
132- 4 1/2 **Modernstone**12 7895 3-8-9 82 ShaneKelly 5 93
(William Knight) *hld up in 5th: clsd over 2f out: drvn and nt qckn on outer over 1f out: one pce after* 20/1
562- 5 1 1/2 **Livia's Dream (IRE)**27 7650 4-9-1 92 TomMcLaughlin 2 91
(Ed Walker) *chsd ldr to over 3f out: lost pl 2f out: one pce u.p after* 10/1
0/0- 6 shd **Jeanie Johnston (IRE)**55 6-9-1 82 MartinHarley 1 91?
(P Harley, Germany) *hld up in last and off the pce: clsd up over 2f out: prog to press ldrs wl over 1f out: effrt petered out fnl f* 14/1
563- 7 3 3/4 **Fattsota**25 7697 5-9-6 105 GrahamLee 3 90
(David O'Meara) *sn led and stretched field after 3f: rdn and hdd jst over 2f out: sn lost pl and btn* 7/4[1]

2m 32.79s (-1.71) **Going Correction** +0.025s/f (Slow)
WFA 3 from 4yo+ 6lb 7 Ran SP% **111.3**
Speed ratings (Par 111): **106,105,104,104,103 103,100**
toteswingers 1&2 £5.00, 1&3 £8.70, 2&3 £2.40 CSF £44.54 TOTE £12.50: £4.70, £3.10; EX 51.90 Trifecta £388.70 Pool: £3541.63 - 6.83 winning units..
Owner The Old Brokers **Bred** S Connolly **Trained** Patching, W Sussex
FOCUS
A weak Listed race.

8063 KEMPTON.CO.UK MEDIAN AUCTION MAIDEN STKS 7f (P)
6:30 (6:30) (Class 6) 3-5-Y-O **£1,940** (£577; £288; £144) **Stalls** Low

Form RPR
646- 1 **Wandsworth (IRE)**44 7253 3-9-5 67 AndreaAtzeni 9 81
(Roger Varian) *trckd ldr: led wl over 1f out: drvn and drew rt away* 5/2[2]
/54- 2 7 **Tarquin (IRE)**28 7624 4-9-1 65 JacobButterfield(5) 5 63
(Kristin Stubbs) *led: rdn and hdd wl over 1f out: no ch w wnr after: jst hld on for 2nd* 5/1[3]
3 hd **Great Conquest (USA)** 3-9-5 0 FergusSweeney 3 61
(Jamie Osborne) *trckd ldrs: rdn wl over 1f out: no ch w wnr but kpt on and nrly snatched 2nd* 8/1
255- 4 1/2 **Aomen Rock**28 7629 3-9-5 68 JimCrowley 4 60
(James Fanshawe) *trckd ldrs: shkn up jst over 2f out: nt qckn and sn no ch w wnr: kpt on* 11/10[1]
65- 5 3 1/4 **Global Leader (IRE)**11 7932 3-9-5 0 (b) FrederikTylicki 6 51
(Paul D'Arcy) *trckd ldrs: rdn wl over 1f out: steadily wknd* 33/1
000- 6 nse **Bahama Bay**50 7108 3-9-0 20 AdamBeschizza 7 46
(Stuart Williams) *hld up in rr: rdn 2f out: no great prog* 100/1
7 1 1/4 **Limon Squeezy** 4-9-1 0 ShaneKelly 1 44
(Mike Murphy) *s.s: mostly in last: shkn up over 2f out: nvr a factor* 25/1
0- 8 6 **Byron Again**83 6134 3-9-5 0 FrankieMcDonald 2 32
(Sean Curran) *in tch: rdn 1/2-way: struggling in rr over 2f out: wknd* 66/1
30- 9 3/4 **Natalia**22 7741 4-8-10 57 JackDuern(5) 8 26
(Andrew Hollinshead) *a in rr: rdn and wknd over 1f out* 25/1

1m 26.18s (0.18) **Going Correction** +0.025s/f (Slow)
WFA 3 from 4yo 1lb 9 Ran SP% **117.1**
Speed ratings (Par 101): **99,91,90,90,86 86,85,78,77**
toteswingers 1&2 £2.90, 1&3 £3.30, 2&3 £5.00 CSF £14.85 TOTE £3.90: £1.30, £2.00, £1.30; EX 14.20 Trifecta £86.70 Pool: £2981.02 - 25.77 winning units..
Owner H R H Sultan Ahmad Shah **Bred** Francois Drion & Ptns **Trained** Newmarket, Suffolk
FOCUS
A moderate maiden run in a slow time. The winner rates a clear personal best.

8064 BETDAQ 1ST UK RACE COMMISSION FREE H'CAP 6f (P)
7:00 (7:00) (Class 2) (0-100,100) 3-Y-O+
£11,827 (£3,541; £1,770; £885; £442; £222) **Stalls** Low

Form RPR
103- 1 **Lancelot Du Lac (ITY)**11 7928 3-9-5 **98** JimCrowley 3 109+
(Dean Ivory) *hld up in last trio: prog over 2f out: sustained effrt to ld jst over 1f out: hung lft but styd on wl* 5/4[1]
044- 2 3/4 **Picture Dealer**67 6621 4-8-11 **90** GrahamLee 9 99
(Lydia Pearce) *hld up in last trio: prog wl over 1f out: rdn to take 2nd last 100yds: r.o but unable to chal* 8/1
325- 3 1 1/4 **Peace Seeker**7 7982 5-8-9 **88** WilliamCarson 4 93
(Anthony Carson) *chsd ldng trio: rdn to chal wl over 1f out: kpt on same pce fnl f* 12/1
614- 4 nk **Athenian (IRE)**6 7995 4-8-9 **88** (p) LukeMorris 6 92
(Sir Mark Prescott Bt) *pressed ldr: rdn to ld wl over 1f out to jst over 1f out: one pce after* 4/1[2]
402- 5 1/2 **Love Island**14 7851 4-8-8 **92** GeorgeChaloner(5) 2 94
(Richard Whitaker) *trckd ldng pair: chal on inner fr 2f out to over 1f out: one pce fnl f* 12/1
530/ 6 3 3/4 **Hurry Up George**370 7826 4-8-6 **92** JaneElliott(7) 8 82
(Ralph Beckett) *wl in rr: pushed along on outer and no prog over 2f out: passed a few wkng rivals fnl f* 25/1
05- 7 1 **Tiddliwinks**11 7928 7-9-7 **100** TomQueally 1 87
(Kevin Ryan) *trckd ldrs: rdn and nt qckn 2f out: wknd fnl f* 6/1[3]
000- 8 shd **Fratellino**11 7928 6-9-2 **95** (t) MartinHarley 5 82
(Alan McCabe) *a struggling to go the pce: wknd fr 2f out* 25/1
300- 9 nk **La Fortunata**53 7021 6-9-0 **93** AndreaAtzeni 7 79
(Mike Murphy) *led at gd pce: hdd wl over 1f out: wknd* 25/1

1m 11.28s (-1.82) **Going Correction** +0.025s/f (Slow) 9 Ran SP% **116.8**
Speed ratings (Par 109): **113,112,110,109,109 104,102,102,102**
toteswingers 1&2 £3.60, 1&3 £5.50, 2&3 £6.80 CSF £11.98 CT £80.45 TOTE £2.50: £1.10, £3.00, £3.20; EX 14.30 Trifecta £89.20 Pool: £2682.74 - 22.54 winning units..
Owner M J Yarrow **Bred** Elektra Di Fausto Martellozzo & C Sas **Trained** Radlett, Herts
FOCUS
A decent sprint handicap run at a good pace. A smart effort from the winner.

8065 KEMPTON.CO.UK ALL WEATHER "HANDS AND HEELS" APPRENTICE SERIES H'CAP (RACING EXCELLENCE) 1m (P)
7:30 (7:31) (Class 7) (0-50,60) 3-Y-O+ **£1,617** (£481; £240; £120) **Stalls** Low

Form RPR
303- 1 **Boris The Bold**301 441 4-9-3 **46** GeorgeBuckell 12 58
(Martin Smith) *led after 2f: mde rest: hrd pressed fnl 2f: kpt on fnl f: hld on* 14/1
013- 2 1/2 **Olivers Mount**26 7667 3-9-2 **50** (t) CameronHardie(3) 5 60
(Ed Vaughan) *t.k.h early: prom: pressed wnr fr 1/2-way: chal 2f out: nt qckn and jst hld fnl f* 5/2[1]
000- 3 2 3/4 **Meglio Ancora**8 7962 6-9-5 **48** (tp) JoeDoyle 7 53
(Richard Ford) *wl in tch: pushed along to chse ldng trio over 2f out: kpt on same pce to take 3rd ins fnl f* 20/1
420- 4 2 3/4 **Katmai River (IRE)**61 6803 6-9-1 **47** CharlotteJenner(3) 11 45
(Mark Usher) *hld up wl in rr: prog 2f out: pushed along and kpt on fnl f to take 4th nr fin* 8/1
000- 5 1 **Kept**70 6518 4-9-0 **46** JonathanWilletts(3) 8 42
(Ronald Harris) *prom on outer: chsd ldng pair over 3f out: wd bnd sn after: no imp 2f out: fdd fnl f* 5/1[3]
006- 6 2 1/2 **Sun And Stars**174 3011 5-8-13 **45** DavidParkes(3) 14 35
(Brendan Powell) *reluctant to enter stalls: slowly away: wl in rr: pushed along and kpt on fnl 2f: no ch* 11/1
406- 7 3 1/2 **Silver Marizah (IRE)**23 6457 4-8-11 **45** RhiainIngram(5) 4 27
(Roger Ingram) *led 2f: urged along over 3f out and lost pl: n.d fnl 2f* 20/1
/00- 8 shd **Ellies Image**160 3511 6-9-2 **45** JordanVaughan 9 27
(Richard Ford) *towards rr: sme prog into midfield over 2f out: sn outpcd: wknd over 1f out* 33/1
032- 9 3/4 **Appyjack**8 7962 5-9-0 **46** (t) AidenBlakemore(3) 6 26
(Tony Carroll) *s.i.s: struggling in last bef 1/2-way: nvr a factor* 7/2[2]
005- 10 1 1/4 **Pastoral Dancer**13 7873 4-9-3 **46** LouisSteward 10 23
(Richard Rowe) *wl in tch: gng bttr than many 3f out: urged along over 2f out: sn btn* 16/1
003- 11 shd **Action Front (USA)**22 7752 5-9-5 **48** (v) AdamMcLean 3 25
(Derek Shaw) *in tch: urged along over 3f out: no prog and struggling in rr fnl 2f* 10/1

1m 40.87s (1.07) **Going Correction** +0.025s/f (Slow)
WFA 3 from 4yo+ 2lb 11 Ran SP% **121.0**
Speed ratings (Par 97): **95,94,91,89,88 85,82,81,81,79 79**
toteswingers 1&2 £4.90, 1&3 £51.50, 2&3 £17.50 CSF £49.36 CT £747.02 TOTE £13.00: £3.10, £1.20, £6.00; EX 60.00 Trifecta £409.90 Pool: £2179.06 - 3.98 winning units..
Owner Wee 3 Women **Bred** John Best **Trained** Newmarket, Suffolk
■ The first training success for Martin Smith.
FOCUS
A weak handicap and a muddling first half of the race, but the first two finished clear.
T/Jkpt: Not won. T/Plt: £174.20. Pool: £79,121.71 - 331.49 winning units. T/Qpdt: £39.00. Pool: £8108.68 - 153.54 winning units. JN

8016 LINGFIELD (L-H)
Wednesday, November 27

OFFICIAL GOING: Standard
Wind: virtually nil Weather: dull, dry

8066 32RED/BRITISH STALLION STUDS EBF MAIDEN STKS (DIV I) 1m (P)
12:00 (12:03) (Class 5) 2-Y-O **£3,067** (£905; £453) **Stalls** High

Form RPR
0- 1 **Hooded (USA)**16 7834 2-9-5 0 MartinLane 2 77+
(Roger Charlton) *mde all: rdn and qcknd wl over 1f out: in command and styd on wl ins fnl f: rdn out* 4/1[2]
2- 2 2 1/4 **Billy Blue (IRE)**20 7779 2-9-5 0 RobertHavlin 7 72
(John Gosden) *chsd ldrs: effrt to chse wnr wl over 1f out: awkward hd carriage and hung lft in bhd wnr 1f out: no imp fnl f: eased cl home* 4/5[1]
3 1/2 **Tacticus (USA)** 2-9-5 0 AndreaAtzeni 10 71+
(Lady Cecil) *dwlt: rcvrd to chse wnr after 1f tl wl over 1f out: 3rd and sltly outpcd over 1f out: rallied and styd on again fnl 100yds: no threat to wnr* 6/1[3]
4 1/2 **Shining Glitter (IRE)** 2-9-0 0 FrederikTylicki 1 65+
(James Fanshawe) *chsd ldrs: rdn and sltly outpcd 2f out: rallied and styd on again ins fnl f: no threat to wnr* 20/1
5 2 **Poker Gold (FR)** 2-9-5 0 (t) LiamKeniry 5 65+
(Heather Main) *s.i.s: t.k.h: hld up wl in tch in last trio: rdn and hdwy 1f out: kpt on fnl f: nvr trbld ldrs* 50/1
6 nse **Artful Rogue (IRE)** 2-9-5 0 JimCrowley 4 65+
(Amanda Perrett) *wl in tch in midfield: pushed along and rn green bnd 2f out: kpt on same pce fr over 1f out: swtchd rt nr fin* 16/1
7 1/2 **Clear Spell (IRE)** 2-9-5 0 LukeMorris 9 64+
(Ed Walker) *dwlt: rn green in last pair: rdn 3f out: edging lft over 1f out: hdwy jst ins fnl f: styd on fnl 100yds: pushed rt and hmpd nr fin* 20/1

8 nk **Light Of Asia (IRE)** 2-9-5 0 .... GrahamLee 6 63+
(Ed Dunlop) *s.i.s: hld up wl in tch in rr: rdn and hdwy 1f out: styd on fnl f: nvr trbld ldrs* **12/1**

60- 9 3 ½ **Wintour Leap**[21] 7764 2-9-0 0 .... SteveDrowne 8 50
(Roger Charlton) *t.k.h: wl in tch in midfield: rdn and lost pl over 1f out: sn wknd* **33/1**

0- 10 2 **Gobertier**[14] 7852 2-9-5 0 .... SeanLevey 3 50
(Richard Hannon Snr) *t.k.h: chsd wnr for 1f: styd prom tl lost pl over 2f out: bhd 1f out* **50/1**

1m 37.94s (-0.26) **Going Correction** -0.125s/f (Stan) **10** Ran SP% **119.8**
Speed ratings (Par 96): **96,93,93,92,90 90,90,89,86,84**
toteswingers: 1&2 £1.70, 1&3 £3.50, 2&3 £2.10. CSF £7.37 TOTE £4.50: £1.30, £1.10, £2.20; EX 9.40 Trifecta £45.10 Pool: £3072.39 - 51.02 winning units..

Owner K Abdullah **Bred** Juddmonte Farms Inc **Trained** Beckhampton, Wilts

FOCUS
A fair first division of a juvenile maiden in which they went an even gallop. The field was compressed and the time was ordinary.

8067 32RED/BRITISH STALLION STUDS EBF MAIDEN STKS (DIV II) 1m (P)
12:30 (12:33) (Class 5) 2-Y-O £3,067 (£905; £453) Stalls High

Form RPR

00- 1 **Chinotto (IRE)**[16] 7834 2-9-5 0 .... DavidProbert 6 78+
(Andrew Balding) *racd off the pce in midfield: rdn over 2f out: hdwy on outer over 1f out: styd on to ld fnl 100yds: kpt on wl* **33/1**

2 1 **Fair Share** 2-9-5 0 .... AndreaAtzeni 5 76+
(Lady Cecil) *s.i.s: rdn along in rr early: clsd 5f out: hdwy on inner whn nt clr run ent fnl f: str run ins fnl f: wnt 2nd last strides* **10/1**

00- 3 nk **Sharp Lookout**[21] 7766 2-9-5 0 .... GeorgeBaker 1 75
(Roger Charlton) *racd off the pce in last quartet: rdn over 2f out: str run and swtchd lft 1f out: chsd wnr wl ins fnl f: kpt on but lost 2nd last strides* **20/1**

22- 4 hd **Epic Voyage (USA)**[11] 7925 2-9-5 0 ....(b[1]) RobertHavlin 8 75
(John Gosden) *dwlt: styd wd and niggled along early: hdwy to ld 6f out and moved to inner: rdn wl over 1f out: racd awkwardly u.p and hdd fnl 100yds: btn but kpt on again cl home* **6/4[1]**

43- 5 shd **Canova (IRE)**[16] 7834 2-9-5 0 ....(t) MartinLane 9 74
(Roger Charlton) *chsd ldrs: rdn to chse ldr 2f out: edgd rt u.p over 1f out: styd on to ld ins fnl f: sn hdd and no ex* **5/1[3]**

6- 6 1 **Sea Here**[42] 7308 2-9-5 0 .... JimCrowley 10 72
(Ralph Beckett) *racd in midfield: effrt and chsd ldrs 2f out: hmpd and swtchd lft over 1f out: pressing ldrs ins fnl f: no ex fnl 100yds* **7/2[2]**

50- 7 ½ **Galaxy (IRE)**[70] 6513 2-9-5 0 .... MartinHarley 7 71
(Alan McCabe) *racd off the pce in last quartet: clsd and rdn over 1f out: swtchd rt 1f out: kpt on same pce ins fnl f* **66/1**

6- 8 6 **Excel Best**[12] 7901 2-9-5 0 .... LukeMorris 3 57
(James Tate) *chsd ldrs: drvn and edgd lft over 1f out: btn whn n.m.r 1f out: wknd ins fnl f* **25/1**

3- 9 1 ¼ **Jalingo (IRE)**[14] 7860 2-9-5 0 .... JoeFanning 4 54
(Mark Johnston) *led for 2f: chsd ldr tl 2f out: sn drvn: keeping on same pce and looked btn whn hmpd 1f out: wknd* **8/1**

10 3 ¼ **Sealed With A Kiss** 2-9-0 0 ....[1] FrederikTylicki 2 42
(James Fanshawe) *s.i.s: rn green and rdn along in last thrght: n.d* **25/1**

1m 36.52s (-1.68) **Going Correction** -0.125s/f (Stan) **10** Ran SP% **116.0**
Speed ratings (Par 96): **103,102,101,101,101 100,99,93,92,89**
toteswingers: 1&2 £28.00, 1&3 £62.30, 2&3 £26.30. CSF £309.39 TOTE £30.30: £6.90, £3.40, £5.20; EX 546.30 Trifecta £2541.30 Part won. Pool: £3388.46 - 0.34 winning units..

Owner Mick and Janice Mariscotti **Bred** Paget Bloodstock **Trained** Kingsclere, Hants

FOCUS
The second division of the juvenile maiden looked the stronger in terms of prior form, and they went an unsustainable gallop. The likes of the seventh will prove key to the level.

8068 LADBROKES CLAIMING STKS 7f (P)
1:00 (1:00) (Class 6) 3-Y-O+ £2,045 (£603; £302) Stalls Low

Form RPR

161- 1 **Four Winds**[18] 7824 7-8-12 81 ....(v) RossAtkinson(3) 7 77
(Tom Dascombe) *taken down early: t.k.h: hld up in tch in midfield: hdwy to chse ldrs and hung lft 1f out: stened and r.o wl fnl 100yds to ld last strides* **4/5[1]**

140- 2 hd **Capaill Liath (IRE)**[13] 7885 5-9-3 84 ....(p) TomQueally 3 78
(Kevin Ryan) *chsd ldrs: effrt u.p 2f out: styd on u.p to ld wl ins fnl f: hdd last strides* **5/1[3]**

565- 3 ½ **The Mongoose**[42] 7303 5-8-11 66 ....(t) MartinHarley 5 71
(David Evans) *chsd ldr tl led over 2f out: rdn and qcknd wl over 1f out: hdd and no ex wl ins fnl f* **16/1**

/00- 4 nk **Munsarim (IRE)**[6] 7989 6-8-13 77 ....(b) JoeDoyle(7) 6 79
(Lee Carter) *t.k.h: chsd ldrs: rdn and effrt 2f out: chsd ldr over 1f out: styd on and pressing ldr ins fnl f: one pce towards fin* **16/1**

145- 5 2 **Greensward**[36] 7436 7-9-0 74 ....(b) LiamKeniry 10 68
(Conor Dore) *stdd s: hld up in last trio: hdwy on outer over 1f out: kpt on fnl f: nvr trbld ldrs* **12/1**

426- 6 4 **Polar Kite (IRE)**[103] 5474 5-9-6 80 .... FrankieMcDonald 1 63
(Paul Morgan) *dwlt: hld up in last trio: pushed along and effrt on inner over 1f out: kpt on same pce fnl f: nvr trbld ldrs* **12/1**

102- 7 ¾ **Assembly**[38] 6310 3-8-9 70 ....(b) JemmaMarshall(3) 11 53
(Pat Phelan) *led tl over 2f out: wknd u.p over 1f out* **33/1**

005- 8 1 **Red Explorer (USA)**[6] 7985 3-8-12 82 .... FergusSweeney 4 50
(Jamie Osborne) *chsd ldrs: rdn and lost pl jst over 2f out: wknd over 1f out* **9/2[2]**

0/0- 9 ¾ **Bryant Park (USA)**[259] 990 4-8-10 0 .... EoinWalsh(7) 2 53
(Christine Dunnett) *t.k.h: hld up in last trio: pushed along over 1f out: nvr much room fr 1f out: nvr trbld ldrs* **50/1**

0- 10 24 **Miss Glorioso**[278] 752 4-8-5 0 .... JoeFanning 8
(Alexandra Dunn) *t.k.h: hld up in midfield: lost pl and rdn 3f out: sn lost tch* **66/1**

1m 23.91s (-0.89) **Going Correction** -0.125s/f (Stan)
WFA 3 from 4yo+ 1lb **10** Ran SP% **123.9**
Speed ratings (Par 101): **100,99,99,98,96 92,91,90,89,61**
toteswingers: 1&2 £1.90, 1&3 £7.00, 2&3 £17.30. CSF £5.63 TOTE £2.10: £1.10, £2.10, £3.30; EX 7.40 Trifecta £76.10 Pool: £1718.16 - 16.92 winning units..Four Winds was claimed by Claes Bjorling for £10,000. Capaill Liath was the subject of a friendly claim.

Owner T Dascombe **Bred** The Queen **Trained** Malpas, Cheshire

FOCUS
A decent claimer in which they went a good gallop. The third is the key to the form.

8069 COMPARE BOOKMAKERS AT BOOKMAKERS.CO.UK H'CAP 6f (P)
1:30 (1:31) (Class 5) (0-75,74) 3-Y-O+ £2,726 (£805; £402) Stalls Low

Form RPR

034- 1 **Jungle Bay**[12] 7896 6-9-7 74 ....(b) TedDurcan 3 83
(Jane Chapple-Hyam) *in tch in midfield: rdn and effrt to chse ldrs over 1f out: qcknd to ld ins fnl f: r.o wl* **5/1[2]**

006- 2 ¾ **Seek The Fair Land**[12] 7896 7-9-4 71 ....(b) AmirQuinn 5 78
(Lee Carter) *short of room sn after s: hld up towards rr: hdwy to chse ldrs whn nt clr run jst ins fnl f: swtchd rt ins fnl f: pushed along and hdwy to chse wnr wl ins fnl f: r.o* **7/1**

156- 3 nk **Smokethatthunders (IRE)**[71] 6506 3-9-5 72 .... LukeMorris 11 78
(James Toller) *taken down early: racd in last pair: rdn and effrt 2f out: hdwy on outer ins fnl f: r.o strly to go 3rd cl home* **5/1[2]**

515- 4 ½ **Dark Lane**[11] 7937 7-9-0 67 .... DavidProbert 7 71
(David Evans) *hld up in tch in midfield: nt clr run 2f out: hdwy ins fnl f: r.o wl fnl 100yds* **12/1**

560- 5 ½ **Captain Kendall (IRE)**[12] 7897 4-9-4 71 .... JimCrowley 4 73
(Harry Chisman) *chsd ldr: rdn and ev ch 2f out: led jst ins fnl f: sn hdd and no ex: wknd towards fin* **20/1**

065- 6 ¾ **Bapak Sayang (USA)**[13] 7888 3-9-7 74 .... TomQueally 1 74
(Kevin Ryan) *led: rdn wl over 1f out: hdd jst ins fnl f: no ex: wknd towards fin* **9/2[1]**

300- 7 ¾ **Intomist (IRE)**[36] 7436 4-9-6 73 ....(p) WilliamCarson 10 71
(Jim Boyle) *sn in rr: rdn and hdwy on inner over 1f out: kpt on fnl f: nvr trbld ldrs* **14/1**

046- 8 ½ **Rowe Park**[12] 7897 10-9-7 74 ....(p) LiamKeniry 2 70
(Linda Jewell) *chsd ldrs: drvn and effrt over 1f out: no ex and btn ins fnl f: eased wl ins fnl f* **14/1**

025- 9 nk **Valmina**[20] 7783 6-9-7 74 ....(t) GeorgeBaker 9 69
(Tony Carroll) *in tch towards rr but stuck wd: effrt 2f out: no imp u.p fr over 1f out* **6/1[3]**

324- 10 2 **Italian Tom (IRE)**[29] 7593 6-9-6 73 .... LiamJones 8 62
(Ronald Harris) *wl in tch in midfield: lost pl u.p wl over 1f out: wknd fnl f* **7/1**

001- 11 7 **Billy Red**[20] 7783 9-9-5 72 ....(b) JoeFanning 6 38
(J R Jenkins) *chsd ldng pair tl over 1f out: sn btn and wknd fnl f* **10/1**

1m 10.57s (-1.33) **Going Correction** -0.125s/f (Stan) **11** Ran SP% **125.7**
Speed ratings (Par 103): **103,102,101,100,100 99,98,97,97,94 85**
toteswingers: 1&2 £7.60, 1&3 £13.00, 2&3 £9.50. CSF £43.06 CT £194.52 TOTE £6.30: £2.30, £4.00, £2.10; EX 43.40 Trifecta £404.30 Pool: £1785.01 - 3.31 winning units..

Owner S Brewster & Essex Racing Club **Bred** Stowell Hill Ltd & Major & Mrs R B Kennard **Trained** Dalham, Suffolk

FOCUS
A fair sprint handicap in which they went a proper gallop. The form looks sound.

8070 BEST ODDS AT BOOKMAKERS.CO.UK MAIDEN STKS 6f (P)
2:00 (2:01) (Class 5) 3-Y-O £2,726 (£805; £402) Stalls Low

Form RPR

66- 1 **Assertive Agent**[58] 6902 3-9-0 57 .... LukeMorris 4 58
(Tony Carroll) *in tch in midfield: rdn and chsd ldrs over 1f out: r.o u.str.p fnl f to ld on post* **6/1[2]**

006- 2 nse **Birdie Queen**[7] 7981 3-9-0 55 .... FergusSweeney 1 58
(Gary Moore) *t.k.h: chsd ldrs: wnt 2nd 4f out tl led 2f out: rdn over 1f out: kpt on u.p fnl f: hdd on post* **12/1[3]**

- 3 1 **Ex Ex** 3-9-5 0 .... MartinLane 3 60
(Nick Littmoden) *s.i.s: rdn along in last pair early: clsd: in tch and travelling bttr 4f out: rdn and outpcd 2f out: rallied and styd on wl ins fnl f* **5/4[1]**

3/4- 4 ½ **Ostralegus**[35] 7459 3-9-5 0 .... JoeFanning 5 58
(John Gallagher) *led tl over 4f out: trckd ldng pair after: rdn and effrt on inner over 1f out: kpt on same pce ins fnl f* **5/4[1]**

0- 5 5 **Mrs Gorsky**[51] 7067 3-9-0 0 .... StevieDonohoe 2 37
(Patrick Holmes) *s.i.s: rdn along in last pair early: clsd: in tch and travelling bttr 4f out: rdn and effrt 2f out: wknd 1f out* **50/1**

05- 6 4 ½ **Harpers Ruby**[13] 7884 3-8-9 0 .... ShirleyTeasdale(5) 6 23
(Simon Griffiths) *pressed ldr tl led over 4f out: rdn and hdd 2f out: wknd over 1f out: fdd ins fnl f* **50/1**

1m 12.01s (0.11) **Going Correction** -0.125s/f (Stan) **6** Ran SP% **114.8**
Speed ratings (Par 102): **94,93,92,91,85 79**
toteswingers 1&2 £3.00, 1&3 £2.40, 2&3 £2.80 CSF £68.96 TOTE £6.00: £4.00, £6.90; EX 37.80 Trifecta £66.50 Pool: £2501.06 - 28.17 winning units..

Owner Wedgewood Estates **Bred** Miss Liza Judd **Trained** Cropthorne, Worcs

■ Stewards' Enquiry : Fergus Sweeney four-day ban: used whip in incorrect place (Dec 11-14)

FOCUS
A weak 3yo sprint maiden run in a slow time. The form is rated around the first and second's recent runs.

8071 CORAL APP DOWNLOAD FROM THE APP STORE H'CAP 1m 2f (P)
2:35 (2:36) (Class 2) (0-100,98) 3-Y-O+ £12,291 (£3,657; £1,827; £913) Stalls Low

Form RPR

503- 1 **Spirit Of The Law (IRE)**[12] 7906 4-8-6 85 .... GeorgeChaloner(5) 4 93
(Richard Fahey) *t.k.h: chsd ldr: rdn and ev ch 2f out: kpt on wl u.p: led wl ins fnl f: hld on wl: all out* **14/1**

502- 2 nse **Lowther**[6] 7990 8-9-1 89 ....(v) TomEaves 10 97
(Lee Carter) *hld up wl in tch: rdn and effrt over 1f out: str chal ins fnl f: r.o wl u.p: jst hld* **16/1**

/52- 3 1 ¼ **Marshgate Lane (USA)**[11] 7926 4-9-4 92 .... JoeFanning 1 97
(Mark Johnston) *sn led: rdn wl over 1f out: hrd pressed 1f out: kpt on tl hdd wl ins fnl f: wknd cl home* **3/1[1]**

640- 4 hd **True To Form (IRE)**[27] 7641 6-9-5 93 ....(p) MartinHarley 2 98+
(Alan McCabe) *stdd s: hld up in tch in rr: rdn and hdwy on inner over 1f out: r.o wl u.p fnl f: nt rch ldrs* **10/1**

046- 5 ½ **Tinshu (IRE)**[11] 7927 7-9-3 91 ....(p) GrahamLee 6 95
(Derek Haydn Jones) *broke wl: stdd bk into midfield after 1f: shuffled bk and swtchd rt over 1f out: hdwy 1f out: r.o ins fnl f: nt rch ldrs* **6/1[2]**

2/0- 6 ½ **Rhamnus**[18] 7820 3-8-7 85 .... AndreaAtzeni 8 88
(Richard Hannon Snr) *s.i.s: in tch in last trio: rdn and effrt over 2f out: styd on u.p fnl f: nvr trbld ldrs* **6/1[2]**

216- 7 1 **Persepolis (IRE)**[93] 5824 3-8-10 88 .... JimCrowley 3 89
(Brett Johnson) *chsd ldrs: drvn and effrt over 1f out: unable qck 1f out: wknd ins fnl f* **10/1**

The Form Book Flat, Raceform Ltd, Compton, RG20 6NL.

002- 8 1¼ **Proud Chieftain**[25] 7697 5-9-10 **98**..............(p) RobertHavlin 9 97
(Clifford Lines) *t.k.h early: chsd ldrs and stuck wd tl stdd and dropped in towards rr over 8f out: rdn over 2f out: kpt on same pce fr over 1f out* **7/1**[3]
000- 9 nk **Mia's Boy**[11] 7926 9-9-2 **93**.............. RobertTart(3) 5 91
(Chris Dwyer) *wl in tch in midfield: rdn and unable qck over 1f out: kpt on same pce fnl f* **14/1**
604- 10 1¼ **Viewpoint (IRE)**[56] 6957 4-9-5 **93**.............. SeanLevey 7 88
(Richard Hannon Snr) *chsd ldrs: rdn and unable qck over 1f out: wknd ins fnl f* **6/1**[2]
2m 2.58s (-4.02) **Going Correction** -0.125s/f (Stan)
WFA 3 from 4yo+ 4lb **10** Ran SP% **117.8**
Speed ratings (Par 109): **111,110,109,109,109 109,108,107,106,105**
toteswingers 1&2 £18.00, 1&3 £7.50, 2&3 £6.30 CSF £217.90 CT £856.75 TOTE £16.40: £5.10, £3.50, £1.10; EX 166.00 Trifecta £603.00 Pool: £3142.30 - 3.90 winning units..
Owner The Matthewman One Partnership **Bred** Georgestown Stud **Trained** Musley Bank, N Yorks
■ Stewards' Enquiry : Tom Eaves two-day ban: used whip above permitted level (Dec 11-12)
FOCUS
A good-quality handicap in which there was no hanging about. A compressed finish and the form is rated around the first two.

8072 CORAL MOBILE "JUST THREE CLICKS TO BET" H'CAP 1m 2f (P)
3:10 (3:10) (Class 6) (0-65,65) 3-Y-0+ **£2,045** (£603; £302) **Stalls** Low

Form RPR
151- 1 **Lady Lunchalot (USA)**[11] 7923 3-9-6 **65**..............(p) LiamJones 12 74
(Laura Mongan) *chsd ldr for 2f: styd chsng ldrs tl rdn to chal ent fnl f: led fnl 150yds: r.o wl: rdn out* **8/1**
456- 2 1 **Persian Patriot**[20] 7786 3-9-2 **61**.............. RobertHavlin 7 68
(William Jarvis) *t.k.h: hld up in tch in midfield: rdn and effrt bnd 2f out: hdwy 1f out: kpt on wl ins fnl f: wnt 2nd cl home* **9/2**[2]
654- 3 shd **Paddy's Saltantes (IRE)**[11] 7922 3-9-4 **63**..............(b) AndreaAtzeni 9 70
(J S Moore) *led: rdn wl over 1f out: hdd fnl 150yds: kpt on same pce after: lost 2nd cl home* **7/2**[1]
334- 4 1¼ **Santadelacruze**[14] 7858 4-9-1 **63**..............(b) NedCurtis(7) 3 67
(Gary Moore) *hld up in tch in midfield: rdn and hdwy on inner over 1f out: kpt on same pce fnl 100yds* **6/1**[3]
000- 5 nse **Special Mix**[81] 6217 5-9-10 **65**.............. MartinLane 11 69
(Martin Smith) *dwlt: hdwy on outer to chse ldr 8f out tl jst over 1f out: no ex and outpcd ins fnl f* **50/1**
055- 6 ¾ **The Wonga Coup (IRE)**[22] 7740 6-9-1 **56**.............. FergusSweeney 4 59
(Pat Phelan) *wl in tch in midfield: rdn and effrt over 1f out: kpt on but no real imp fnl f* **8/1**
360- 7 1 **Ogaritmo**[16] 7836 4-9-8 **63**..............(tp) GeorgeBaker 8 64
(Seamus Durack) *hld up in tch in last quartet: rdn and hdwy over 1f out: kpt on fnl f: nvr trbld ldrs* **16/1**
604- 8 ¾ **Harwoods Star (IRE)**[44] 7249 3-9-5 **64**..............(p) JimCrowley 1 63
(Amanda Perrett) *t.k.h: chsd ldrs: rdn and unable qck wl over 1f out: wknd ins fnl f* **7/2**[1]
550- 9 ½ **Scamperdale**[28] 7622 11-9-6 **61**..............(p) KierenFox 2 59
(Brian Baugh) *hld up in tch in last pair: rdn and effrt on inner over 1f out: kpt on but nvr trbld ldrs* **25/1**
225- 10 2½ **Legal Legacy**[7] 7980 7-9-0 **55**.............. TomEaves 13 48
(Lee Carter) *hld up in tch towards rr: rdn and no hdwy wl over 1f out: nvr trbld ldrs* **12/1**
345- 11 10 **Edgware Road**[120] 3954 5-9-5 **63**.............. RossAtkinson(3) 5 36
(Paul Morgan) *stdd s: a in rr and nvr travelling: drvn 4f out: lost tch over 2f out* **33/1**
2m 4.33s (-2.27) **Going Correction** -0.125s/f (Stan)
WFA 3 from 4yo+ 4lb **11** Ran SP% **121.5**
Speed ratings (Par 101): **104,103,103,102,102 101,100,100,99,97 89**
toteswingers 1&2 £7.40, 1&3 £5.70, 2&3 £5.20 CSF £44.80 CT £153.48 TOTE £4.40: £2.40, £2.80, £1.20; EX 53.30 Trifecta £192.10 Pool: £2912.60 - 11.36 winning units..
Owner Charlie's Starrs **Bred** Fred W Hertrich III **Trained** Epsom, Surrey
FOCUS
A modest handicap in which it paid to be prominent off an ordinary gallop. The winner more than confirmed her C&D latest with another personal best.

8073 DOWNLOAD THE LADBROKES APP APPRENTICE H'CAP 7f (P)
3:40 (3:42) (Class 6) (0-58,58) 3-Y-0+ **£2,045** (£603; £302) **Stalls** Low

Form RPR
056- 1 **Perfect Pastime**[14] 7862 5-9-1 **57**..............(b1) DanielCremin(5) 6 64
(Jim Boyle) *t.k.h: hld up in tch in midfield: swtchd rt and hdwy over 1f out: rdn and r.o wl to ld towards fin* **5/1**[1]
600- 2 hd **Larghetto (USA)**[23] 7733 5-9-4 **58**.............. PhilipPrince(3) 11 64
(John Stimpson) *hld up in tch towards rr: rdn and effrt over 1f out: str chal wl ins fnl f: jst hld* **12/1**
033- 3 nk **Gypsy Rider**[7] 7981 4-8-13 **55**.............. NedCurtis(5) 1 61
(Roger Curtis) *in tch in midfield: rdn and effrt over 1f out: str run to ld fnl 100yds: hdd and no ex towards fin* **6/1**[2]
405- 4 nk **Wishformore (IRE)**[27] 7643 6-9-0 **51**..............(p) RossAtkinson 10 56
(Zoe Davison) *w ldr: rdn and sltly outpcd over 1f out: rallied and ev ch ins fnl f: unable qck cl home* **25/1**
025- 5 ½ **Triple Aitch (USA)**[8] 7966 3-9-1 **58**.............. JordanVaughan(5) 5 60
(Giles Bravery) *chsd ldrs: rdn and effrt wl over 1f out: ev ch 1f out tl no ex and btn wl ins fnl f* **6/1**[2]
040- 6 ½ **My Learned Friend (IRE)**[50] 7109 9-8-12 **56**..............(v) RobHornby(7) 12 58
(Andrew Balding) *dwlt and swtchd lft sn after s: in tch in last trio: effrt on outer wl over 1f out: r.o wl ins fnl f: nt rch ldrs* **16/1**
064- 7 nk **Purley Queen (IRE)**[7] 7980 4-8-11 **53**.............. JoshBaudains(5) 7 54
(Sylvester Kirk) *in tch in midfield: rdn and effrt over 1f out: kpt on ins fnl f but nvr quite pce to chal* **8/1**[3]
U40- 8 shd **Bestfootforward**[4] 8023 4-9-2 **56**.............. ShelleyBirkett(3) 8 57
(Julia Feilden) *in tch in midfield tl shuffled bk towards rr 2f out: rdn and effrt over 1f out: kpt on same pce: nvr trbld ldrs* **16/1**
000- 9 ½ **Moortahan**[19] 7807 3-8-12 **57**..............[1] CameronHardie(7) 4 56
(Richard Hannon Snr) *chsd ldrs: rdn over 3f out: stl chsng ldrs but one pce whn pushed rt over 1f out: wknd ins fnl f* **16/1**
303- 10 hd **Proper Charlie**[4] 8023 5-9-0 **58**..............(v) PaigeBolton(7) 13 57
(Lee Carter) *t.k.h: led: pushed along and clr over 1f out: hdd ins fnl f: no ex and wknd towards fin* **5/1**[1]
650- 11 nk **Strategic Action (IRE)**[7] 7980 4-8-12 **54**..............(p) EoinWalsh(5) 3 52
(Linda Jewell) *in tch towards rr: nt clr run on bnd 2f out: swtchd rt and hdwy over 1f out: kpt on wl fnl f: nvr trbld ldrs* **10/1**
004- 12 ¾ **Offbeat Safaris (IRE)**[11] 7923 5-8-12 **54**..............(p) DanielMuscutt(5) 14 50
(Ronald Harris) *s.i.s: in tch in rr: rdn and effrt 2f out: kpt on wl fnl f: nvr trbld ldrs* **10/1**

554- 13 3¾ **Princess Sheila (IRE)**[29] 7600 3-8-5 **50**.............. DavidParkes(7) 9 35
(J S Moore) *short of room and dropped to rr sn after s: hung rt and v wd bnd 4f out: stl in tch under hung rt and v wd again bnd 2f out: no ch after* **20/1**
000- 14 6 **Courtland Avenue (IRE)**[27] 7644 4-8-10 **50**..............(b1) JackGarritty(3) 2 20
(Jonathan Portman) *chsd ldrs: hmpd 5f out: rdn and no ex over 1f out: wknd fnl f* **66/1**
1m 24.65s (-0.15) **Going Correction** -0.125s/f (Stan)
WFA 3 from 4yo+ 1lb **14** Ran SP% **126.6**
Speed ratings (Par 101): **95,94,94,94,93 92,92,92,91,91 91,90,86,79**
toteswingers 1&2 £17.70, 1&3 £5.50, 2&3 £9.60 CSF £68.20 CT £391.81 TOTE £5.50: £2.20, £5.80, £1.90; EX 101.50 Trifecta £364.40 Pool: £3840.65 - 7.90 winning units..
Owner Country Friends **Bred** R G & T E Levin **Trained** Epsom, Surrey
FOCUS
A moderate handicap for apprentice riders, with a bunch finish. The form makes some sense.
T/Plt: £2077.00 Pool: £61,031.64 - 21.45 winning units. T/Qpdt: £40.60. Pool: 6973.50 - 126.98 winning units. SP

8058 KEMPTON (A.W) (R-H)
Thursday, November 28

OFFICIAL GOING: Standard
Wind: virtually nil Weather: dry

8082 MIX BUSINESS AND PLEASURE AT KEMPTON APPRENTICE H'CAP 6f (P)
4:05 (4:06) (Class 7) (0-50,50) 3-Y-0+ **£1,617** (£481; £240; £120) **Stalls** Low

Form RPR
040- 1 **Spellmaker**[28] 7644 4-9-4 **49**.............. EoinWalsh 3 60
(Tony Newcombe) *stdd s: hld up in tch in rr: swtchd rt and gd hdwy over 1f out: led ent fnl f: r.o wl* **7/2**[1]
662- 2 1¼ **Errigal Lad**[51] 7101 8-9-5 **50**.............. TimClark 12 57
(Garry Woodward) *stdd and dropped in bhd after s: rdn and gd hdwy on inner over 1f out: r.o wl to chse wnr wl ins fnl f: no threat to wnr* **16/1**
040- 3 ¾ **Rosa Lockwood**[21] 7792 4-9-3 **48**.............. PatMillman 1 53+
(Ed McMahon) *mde most: rdn 2f out: hdd ent fnl f: styd on same pce after: lost 2nd wl ins fnl f* **16/1**
600- 4 3½ **Daneside (IRE)**[15] 7850 6-9-2 **50**.............. JordanVaughan(3) 7 43
(P J O'Gorman) *hld up towards rr: rdn and hdwy over 1f out: styd on fnl f: no threat to ldrs* **8/1**
505- 5 2 **Imjin River (IRE)**[15] 7850 6-9-4 **49**..............(t) LouisSteward 4 36
(William Stone) *taken down early: chsd ldrs: wnt 2nd briefly but unable qck wl over 1f out: 3rd and btn 1f out: wknd* **8/1**
5/4- 6 2 **Play The Blues (IRE)**[323] 117 6-9-3 **48**..............(t) JoshBaudains 6 29
(Dominic Ffrench Davis) *in tch in midfield: pushed along and effrt wl over 1f out: sn outpcd and btn: plugged on same pce fnl f* **8/1**
000- 7 2¼ **Actonetaketwo**[13] 7904 3-9-2 **47**..............(p) DanielMuscutt 5 20
(Ron Hodges) *chsd ldrs: rdn and unable qck over 2f out: wknd u.p over 1f out* **20/1**
/00- 8 2½ **Jemimaville (IRE)**[57] 6930 6-8-13 **47**..............(v) DanielCremin(3) 11 12
(Giles Bravery) *hld up towards rr: rdn and no real imp 2f out: wl hld but plugged on fnl f* **33/1**
052- 9 ¾ **Exkaliber**[15] 7850 4-9-0 **50**..............(bt) DavidParkes(5) 8 13
(Jeremy Gask) *pressed ldr tl ent fnl 2f: sn rdn and btn: wknd over 1f out: fdd fnl f* **4/1**[2]
603- 10 shd **Demoiselle Bond**[15] 7850 5-9-4 **49**.............. NedCurtis 9 12
(Lydia Richards) *taken down early: chsd ldrs tl lost pl jst over 2f out: wknd wl over 1f out* **10/1**
634- 11 2½ **Charlemagne Diva**[15] 7850 3-8-12 **48**..............(t) AlfieWarwick(5) 10
(Richard Guest) *in tch in midfield: lost pl and rdn over 2f out: sn wknd* **7/1**[3]
00- 12 2 **Ziefhd**[51] 7086 4-9-5 **50**..............(p) RyanWhile 2
(Tim McCarthy) *in tch in midfield: rdn and lost pl over 2f out: wknd 2f out* **16/1**
1m 12.9s (-0.20) **Going Correction** 0.0s/f (Stan) **12** Ran SP% **122.5**
Speed ratings (Par 97): **101,99,98,93,91 88,85,82,81,80 77,74**
toteswingers 1&2 £15.90, 2&3 £32.60, 1&3 £11.40 CSF £63.71 CT £828.95 TOTE £4.00: £1.10, £3.30, £4.40; EX 63.80 Trifecta £830.40 Pool: £3268.41 - 2.95 winning units..
Owner Joli Racing **Bred** Dxb Bloodstock Ltd **Trained** Yarnscombe, Devon
FOCUS
A very moderate handicap in which the decent gallop favoured those held up . The winner raced edged towards the centre late on. The winner had had fewer chances than most.

8083 £25 FREE BET AT BETVICTOR.COM MAIDEN FILLIES' STKS (DIV I) 7f (P)
4:35 (4:35) (Class 5) 2-Y-O **£2,587** (£770; £384; £192) **Stalls** Low

Form RPR
1 **Forever Cinderella** 2-9-0 0.............. KieranO'Neill 4 74+
(Jimmy Fox) *stdd s: hld up in tch in rr: effrt in centre and str run over 1f out: led fnl 100yds: r.o wl* **7/1**
2 ¾ **Perfect Persuasion** 2-9-0 0.............. JimCrowley 5 72
(William Haggas) *in tch in midfield: rdn and effrt 2f out: hdwy u.p over 1f out: ev ch ins fnl f: kpt on but outpcd by wnr fnl 75yds* **4/1**[2]
36- 3 1½ **Perfect Pursuit**[43] 7294 2-9-0 0.............. MartinHarley 8 68
(Clive Cox) *t.k.h: chsd ldrs: wnt 2nd after 2f tl rdn to ld wl over 1f out: drvn and hdd fnl 100yds: wknd towards fin* **12/1**
0- 4 1¼ **Blue Oyster**[14] 7875 2-9-0 0.............. WilliamCarson 7 65
(Philip McBride) *in tch in last pair: rdn ent fnl 2f: hdwy jst over 1f out: styd on wl ins fnl f: nvr trbld ldrs* **16/1**
62- 5 hd **A Legacy Of Love (IRE)**[43] 7295 2-9-0 0.............. AndreaAtzeni 3 64
(Amanda Perrett) *t.k.h: chsd ldrs: rdn and chsd wnr over 1f out tl jst ins fnl f: wknd fnl 100yds* **11/10**[1]
6 2 **Arabian Music (IRE)** 2-9-0 0.............. MartinLane 1 59
(David Simcock) *in tch towards rr: rdn over 3f out: outpcd over 1f out: wknd fnl f* **25/1**
0- 7 3¾ **Her Honour (IRE)**[28] 7645 2-9-0 0.............. RobertHavlin 11 48
(John Gosden) *awkward leaving stalls: in tch in midfield: hdwy to chse ldrs over 4f out: rdn and struggling over 1f out: wknd 1f out* **10/1**
03- 8 9 **Rush**[15] 7852 2-9-0 0.............. GrahamLee 2 24
(Paul Cole) *led for over 1f: chsd ldrs after: swtchd rt and effrt 2f out: sn btn: wknd over 1f out* **6/1**[3]

06- **9** 3 ¾ **Wedgewood Estates**[15] 7852 2-9-0 0 .... DavidProbert 6 14
(Tony Carroll) *t.k.h: chsd ldr tl led over 5f out: hdd wl over 1f out: sn btn and fdd: bhd and eased ins fnl f* **50/1**

1m 26.5s (0.50) **Going Correction** 0.0s/f (Stan) **9** Ran SP% **122.9**
Speed ratings (Par 93): **97,96,94,93,92 90,86,75,71**
toteswingers 1&2 £6.60, 2&3 £6.70, 1&3 £11.20 CSF £37.55 TOTE £8.40: £1.90, £1.70, £3.20; EX 34.30 Trifecta £451.30 Pool: £3748.21 - 6.22 winning units..
Owner Mrs Sarah-Jane Fox **Bred** Fittocks Stud **Trained** Collingbourne Ducis, Wilts

FOCUS
Division one of an ordinary maiden. The gallop was on the steady side to the straight and the winner came down the centre. Nice efforts from the first two but the bare form is just fair.

8084 £25 FREE BET AT BETVICTOR.COM MAIDEN FILLIES' STKS (DIV II) 7f (P)
5:05 (5:06) (Class 5) 2-Y-O **£2,587** (£770; £384; £192) **Stalls** Low

Form RPR

1 **Alzanti (USA)** 2-9-0 0 .... AndreaAtzeni 11 77+
(Amanda Perrett) *in tch in midfield: pushed along 3f out: swtchd rt and hdwy 2f out: str run to ld ins fnl f: r.o wl: readily* **7/1**[3]

4- **2** 1 ¾ **Venus Grace**[22] 7766 2-9-0 0 .... JimCrowley 3 73
(Ralph Beckett) *chsd ldng trio: effrt u.p to press ldrs over 1f out: kpt on same pce ins fnl f: wnt 2nd nr fin* **11/10**[1]

622- **3** *hd* **Minnaloushe (IRE)**[16] 7844 2-9-0 74 .... RobertHavlin 4 72
(John Gosden) *chsd ldrs tl wnt 2nd 1/2-way: rdn to ld wl over 1f out: hdd ins fnl f: styd on same pce after: lost 2nd nr fin* **5/2**[2]

500- **4** 4 ½ **Amontillado (IRE)**[8] 7978 2-9-0 0 .... SeanLevey 2 60
(Richard Hannon Snr) *led tl 1/2-way: rdn 3f out: drvn ent fnl 2f: outpcd over 1f out: wknd fnl f* **33/1**

- **5** *nk* **Walk With An Angel** 2-9-0 0 ....(t) WilliamCarson 8 59
(Philip McBride) *t.k.h: chsd ldrs tl wnt 2nd over 5f out: led 1/2-way: rdn and hdd wl over 1f out: wknd fnl f* **8/1**

30- **6** ¾ **Pieman's Girl**[95] 5797 2-9-0 0 .... MartinHarley 5 57
(Anthony Carson) *hld up in tch towards rr: rdn and switching lft over 1f out: no imp fnl f* **16/1**

7 4 **Sweetness Lady** 2-9-0 0 .... SteveDrowne 10 46
(Olly Stevens) *s.i.s: hdwy into midfield 5f out: rdn and struggling over 2f out: wknd over 1f out* **25/1**

8 4 ½ **Close Companion** 2-9-0 0 ....(t) MartinDwyer 7 34
(Hugo Palmer) *s.i.s: in tch in last trio: rdn wl over 2f out: sn struggling: wknd wl over 1f out* **25/1**

9 10 **I'm Lucy (IRE)** 2-9-0 0 .... LiamKeniry 1 7
(Linda Jewell) *a in rr: rdn 1/2-way: lost tch 2f out* **50/1**

1m 27.42s (1.42) **Going Correction** 0.0s/f (Stan) **9** Ran SP% **118.3**
Speed ratings (Par 93): **91,89,88,83,83 82,77,72,61**
toteswingers 1&2 £2.50, 2&3 £1.50, 1&3 £3.10 CSF £15.12 TOTE £7.70: £2.30, £1.40, £1.10; EX 19.00 Trifecta £46.10 Pool: £3825.72 - 62.19 winning units..
Owner K Abdullah **Bred** Juddmonte Farms Inc **Trained** Pulborough, W Sussex

FOCUS
This looked the stronger of the divisions, though the pace was again on the steady side. The winner ended up against the inside rail and was quite impressive. The fourth offers some perspective on the form.

8085 DOWNLOAD THE BETVICTOR APP MAIDEN AUCTION STKS 1m (P)
5:35 (5:36) (Class 6) 2-Y-O **£1,940** (£577; £288; £144) **Stalls** Low

Form RPR

4- **1** **Tucson Arizona**[50] 7128 2-8-11 0 .... WilliamCarson 3 70+
(Anthony Carson) *stdd after s: hld up in tch towards rr: hdwy into midfield 1/2-way: rdn and hdwy to ld over 1f out: in command and r.o wl fnl f: rdn out* **9/4**[1]

25- **2** 2 ¼ **Mr Wickfield**[21] 7779 2-8-13 0 .... SteveDrowne 12 67
(John Best) *chsd ldr after 1f: rdn and ev ch 2f out: chsd wnr ins fnl f: kpt on same pce and no imp* **8/1**

04- **3** ¾ **Percybelle**[21] 7780 2-8-7 0 .... ShaneKelly 9 59
(William Knight) *chsd ldr tl led after 1f: rdn and hdd over 1f out: outpcd and lost 2nd ins fnl f: kpt on same pce fnl 100yds* **9/2**[2]

6- **4** *shd* **L Ge R**[72] 6500 2-8-4 0 .... JimmyQuinn 4 56
(Peter Charalambous) *t.k.h: hld up in tch in rr: hmpd after 2f: swtchd lft 2f out: rdn and hdwy over 1f out: kpt on fnl f but no threat to wnr* **8/1**

0- **5** 1 ¼ **Ede's The Business**[21] 7779 2-7-12 0 .... SophieRalston(7) 1 54
(Pat Phelan) *dwlt and bustled along early: in tch in last trio: rdn and effrt whn swtchd lft over 1f out: styd on same pce fnl f* **50/1**

06- **6** ½ **Tipsy Star**[15] 7853 2-8-8 0 .... RobertHavlin 5 56
(Daniel Kubler) *led for 1f: stdd and wl in tch in midfield after: rdn and effrt to chse ldrs over 1f out: keeping on whn nt clr run and hmpd 1f out: nt rcvr and one pce after* **16/1**

60- **7** 1 ¾ **Charlies Mate**[21] 7779 2-8-10 0 .... MartinDwyer 7 54
(John Best) *t.k.h: in tch in midfield: rdn and no hdwy over 2f out: outpcd and btn over 1f out: wknd fnl f* **50/1**

53- **8** 1 **Lady Knight (IRE)**[21] 7780 2-8-6 0 ....(p) LiamJones 2 48
(J S Moore) *hld up in tch towards rr: hmpd after 2f: rdn over 3f out: drvn and struggling over 2f out: plugged on but n.d after* **5/1**[3]

60- **9** 5 **D'Arcy Indiana**[22] 7773 2-8-11 0 .... JimCrowley 10 41
(Amy Weaver) *chsd ldrs after 2f: rdn and struggling ent fnl 2f: wknd over 1f out* **16/1**

4- **P** **Spanish Artist**[29] 7631 2-9-0 0 .... LukeMorris 6
(Harry Dunlop) *chsd ldrs tl lost action and p.u after 2f: dismntd* **9/2**[2]

1m 41.74s (1.94) **Going Correction** 0.0s/f (Stan) **10** Ran SP% **121.7**
Speed ratings (Par 94): **90,87,87,86,85 85,83,82,77,**
toteswingers 1&2 £5.00, 2&3 £8.20, 1&3 £2.80 CSF £22.66 TOTE £3.50: £1.30, £2.80, £1.40; EX 25.10 Trifecta £107.20 Pool: £3443.03 - 24.06 winning units..
Owner Christopher Wright & Minster Stud **Bred** Minster Stud & Stratford Place Stud **Trained** Newmarket, Suffolk

FOCUS
The late defections of Racing's Dream and Isabella Beeton and the early pulling up of Spanish Artist, who was badly struck into, meant this race didn't take much winning. The gallop soon steadied and the winner drifted towards the far rail late on. Ther bare form looks modest.

8086 BOOK CHRISTMAS FESTIVAL TICKETS NOW CLAIMING STKS 1m (P)
6:05 (6:06) (Class 6) 2-Y-O **£1,940** (£577; £288; £144) **Stalls** Low

Form RPR

041- **1** **One Penny Piece**[8] 7977 2-8-4 72 ....(t) WilliamCarson 2 64
(Philip McBride) *mde all: rdn and fnd ex over 1f out: edgd lft but drew clr ins fnl f: rdn out* **4/6**[1]

616- **2** 3 **Sydney James (IRE)**[41] 7352 2-8-4 62 .... JackDuern(5) 3 60
(Lee Carter) *stdd s: hld up in tch in last: rdn and effrt over 1f out: chsd clr wnr and swtchd rt ins fnl f: no imp* **4/1**[2]

053- **3** ½ **Rose Buck**[8] 7977 2-8-0 0 .... RaulDaSilva 4 50
(Paul Cole) *chsd ldng pair: rdn to chse wnr wl over 1f out: outpcd and lost 2nd ins fnl f: kpt on same pce after* **5/1**[3]

200- **4** 1 ½ **Acquaint (IRE)**[14] 7878 2-8-11 64 .... SeanLevey 1 57
(Richard Hannon Snr) *chsd wnr tl drvn and no rspnse wl over 1f out: 4th and one pce fnl f* **7/1**

1m 43.91s (4.11) **Going Correction** 0.0s/f (Stan) **4** Ran SP% **109.2**
Speed ratings (Par 94): **79,76,75,74**
CSF £3.69 TOTE £1.70; EX 3.90 Trifecta £7.00 Pool: £1966.99 - 209.95 winning units..One Penny Piece was claimed by A Weaver for £8000.
Owner P J McBride **Bred** Mrs Sarah Hamilton **Trained** Newmarket, Suffolk

FOCUS
Not a competitive claimer. The pace was steady to the intersection and the winner raced in the centre. The form could be rated a few pounds higher.

8087 £175 CASH BONUS AT VICTOR'S LIVE CASINO H'CAP 1m (P)
6:35 (6:36) (Class 6) (0-65,65) 3-Y-O+ **£1,940** (£577; £288; £144) **Stalls** Low

Form RPR

030- **1** **Stormbound (IRE)**[127] 4623 4-9-7 **65** .... MartinLane 5 74
(Paul Cole) *hld up in tch towards rr: swtchd lft and hdwy over 1f out: str run u.p fnl f to ld cl home* **13/2**[3]

005- **2** *hd* **Byroness**[17] 7841 3-9-5 **65** .... AndreaAtzeni 7 73
(Heather Main) *in tch in midfield: rdn and hdwy wl over 1f out: chsd ldr ins fnl f: ev ch fnl 50yds: jst hld* **10/1**

400- **3** *nk* **Self Employed**[44] 7283 6-9-5 **63** .... GrahamLee 1 71
(Garry Woodward) *travelled wl: trckd ldrs tl led and stl gng wl 2f out: rdn and qcknd clr over 1f out: drvn fnl 100yds: hdd and lost 2 pls cl home* **10/1**

322- **4** 1 ¼ **Tee It Up Tommo (IRE)**[15] 7858 4-9-5 **63** .... JimCrowley 13 68+
(Michael Wigham) *stdd after s: hld up in rr: swtchd lft and hdwy over 1f out: chsd ldrs ins fnl f: kpt on* **5/2**[1]

062- **5** ¾ **Welsh Sunrise**[14] 7876 3-9-5 **65** ....(v) LukeMorris 6 68
(Ed Walker) *t.k.h: hld up in tch in midfield: rdn and effrt 2f out: kpt on same pce ins fnl f* **7/2**[2]

300- **6** 1 ¼ **Raamz (IRE)**[37] 7453 6-9-2 **60** .... JimmyQuinn 10 61
(Kevin Morgan) *s.i.s: pushed in tch in last trio: hdwy u.p on inner over 1f out: kpt on fnl f: nvr trbld ldrs* **33/1**

233- **7** *shd* **Celestial Ray**[164] 3401 4-9-7 **65** .... RobertHavlin 4 66
(Linda Jewell) *s.i.s: rcvrd and in midfield after 2f: effrt u.p to chse ldrs over 1f out: wknd ins fnl f* **12/1**

040- **8** 2 ¼ **Annes Rocket (IRE)**[15] 7858 8-8-9 **60** ....(p) CameronHardie(7) 11 55
(Jimmy Fox) *in tch towards rr: hdwy and pushed along over 3f out: rdn and kpt on same pce fr over 1f out* **33/1**

530- **9** ½ **Lutine Charlie (IRE)**[15] 7858 6-8-12 **59** ....(p) RobertTart(3) 12 53
(Pat Eddery) *t.k.h: w ldr tl rdn and unable qck over 1f out: wknd ins fnl f* **20/1**

331- **10** 2 ½ **My Gigi**[14] 7873 3-9-3 **63** ....(p) GeorgeBaker 8 51
(Gary Moore) *t.k.h: chsd ldrs: rdn and ev ch 2f out: outpcd over 1f out: wknd ins fnl f* **8/1**

640- **11** 1 **Dear Maurice**[15] 7858 9-8-13 **64** ....(t) AlfieWarwick(7) 9 50
(Tobias B P Coles) *wl in tch in midfield on outer: rdn and lost pl ent fnl 2f: wknd over 1f out* **33/1**

520- **12** 6 **Wordismybond**[28] 7652 4-9-7 **65** .... SteveDrowne 2 37
(Peter Makin) *led tl rdn and hdd 2f out: sn btn and wknd over 1f out: fdd fnl f* **20/1**

550- **13** 12 **La Belle Epoque (USA)**[27] 7663 3-8-11 **62** ....(p) JoeyHaynes(5) 3
(Gerard Butler) *in tch in midfield tl lost pl and bhd over 2f out: lost tch over 1f out: wl bhd fnl f* **25/1**

1m 38.94s (-0.86) **Going Correction** 0.0s/f (Stan)
WFA 3 from 4yo+ 2lb **13** Ran SP% **123.3**
Speed ratings (Par 101): **104,103,103,102,101 100,100,97,97,94 93,87,75**
toteswingers 1&2 £14.20, 2&3 £11.50, 1&3 £13.00 CSF £65.20 CT £671.73 TOTE £9.80: £2.70, £3.60, £3.90; EX 80.70 Trifecta £1174.20 Pool: £3641.04 - 2.32 winning units..
Owner P F I Cole Ltd **Bred** A Footstep Away Syndicate **Trained** Whatcombe, Oxon

FOCUS
A modest handicap run at an ordinary gallop. The winner came down the centre and is rated pretty much to his best.

8088 BETVICTOR'S NEW LIVE CASINO H'CAP 6f (P)
7:05 (7:06) (Class 4) (0-85,82) 3-Y-O+ **£4,690** (£1,395; £697; £348) **Stalls** Low

Form RPR

211- **1** **Interception (IRE)**[16] 7845 3-9-4 **80** .... TedDurcan 9 92+
(David Lanigan) *hld up in tch towards rr: effrt u.p over 1f out: hrd drvn and str run ins fnl f to ld last strides* **7/4**[1]

504- **2** *hd* **Foxtrot Jubilee (IRE)**[29] 7633 3-8-13 **82** .... PatrickO'Donnell(7) 4 90
(Ralph Beckett) *chsd ldrs: pushed along and led 2f out: forged ahd wl ins fnl f: hdd last strides* **16/1**

014- **3** ½ **Slip Sliding Away (IRE)**[64] 6744 6-9-4 **80** .... LiamKeniry 2 87
(Peter Hedger) *wl in tch in midfield: rdn and effrt to chal over 1f out: ev ch thrght fnl f: no ex fnl 50yds* **16/1**

353- **4** 1 **Kinglami**[15] 7856 4-9-4 **80** ....(tp) SteveDrowne 5 84
(Brian Gubby) *t.k.h: chsd ldr: rdn and ev ch 2f out tl ins fnl f: wknd towards fin* **7/2**[2]

060- **5** *shd* **Enderby Spirit (GR)**[45] 7241 7-9-3 **79** ....(t) GrahamLee 1 82
(Bryan Smart) *hld up in tch in midfield: rdn and effrt on inner over 1f out: kpt on ins fnl f: nt rch ldrs* **12/1**

136- **6** ½ **Dominium (USA)**[23] 7742 6-8-13 **78** ....(b) RobertTart(3) 3 80
(Jeremy Gask) *in tch in midfield: effrt u.p and swtchd rt wl over 1f out: hdd u.p 1f out: no imp fnl 75yds* **9/2**[3]

400- **7** ¾ **Palace Moon**[22] 7769 8-9-4 **80** ....(t) AndreaAtzeni 7 81+
(William Knight) *stdd s: hld up in tch in last trio: rdn and hdwy over 1f out: hmpd and swtchd rt 1f out: kpt on ins fnl f: nvr trbld ldrs* **8/1**

515- **8** *shd* **Commanche**[22] 7776 4-9-4 **80** .... LukeMorris 10 79
(Chris Dwyer) *t.k.h: chsd ldrs: drvn and ev ch wl over 1f out tl ent fnl f: outpcd fnl 150yds* **16/1**

214- **9** 1 ¾ **Generalyse**[14] 7888 4-9-3 **79** ....(b) JimCrowley 12 72
(Ben De Haan) *stdd s: hld up in tch in last trio: rdn and effrt over 1f out: kpt on but nvr trbld ldrs* **8/1**

000- **10** *nk* **Dorback**[61] 6850 6-9-2 **78** .... MartinHarley 6 70
(Tony Newcombe) *t.k.h: hld up in tch in midfield: rdn and unable qck ent fnl 2f: outpcd and btn over 1f out: kpt on same pce after* **33/1**

362- **11** *hd* **Tagula Night (IRE)**[45] 7255 7-9-2 **78** ....(bt) FergusSweeney 11 70
(Dean Ivory) *stdd s: t.k.h: hld up in tch in last trio: rdn and effrt over 1f out: no hdwy: nvr trbld ldrs* **16/1**

The Form Book Flat, Raceform Ltd, Compton, RG20 6NL.

350- **12** ½ **Diamond Belle**[23] 7742 4-9-2 **78** .... MartinLane 8 68
(Noel Quinlan) *led: rdn and hdd 2f out: lost pl qckly ent fnl f: wknd* **25/1**

1m 12.68s (-0.42) **Going Correction** 0.0s/f (Stan) **12** Ran SP% **137.0**
Speed ratings (Par 105): **102,101,101,99,99 98,97,97,95,95 94,94**
toteswingers 1&2 £7.30, 2&3 £17.30, 1&3 £5.90 CSF £42.20 CT £407.32 TOTE £5.00: £1.60, £4.60, £5.20; EX 44.70 Trifecta £607.70 Pool: £3525.82 - 4.35 winning units..
Owner B E Nielsen **Bred** Corduff Bloodstock Ltd & David Egan **Trained** Upper Lambourn, Berks

FOCUS
A useful handicap in which the majority were exposed performers. The gallop was reasonable and the winner came down the centre. The form is rated around the next three home.

8089 BACK OF THE NET AT BETVICTOR H'CAP — 2m (P)
7:35 (7:35) (Class 5) (0-75,75) 3-Y-O+ **£2,587** (£770; £384; £192) **Stalls** Low

Form RPR

062- **1** **Norfolk Sky**[24] 6736 4-9-6 **67** .... FergusSweeney 8 79
(Laura Mongan) *hld up in tch towards rr: stdy hdwy fr 1/2-way: chsd ldr 2f out: rdn to ld 1f out: r.o strly* **6/1**

15- **2** 3¼ **Eshtyaaq**[10] 7947 6-9-11 **72** .... MartinHarley 2 80
(David Evans) *led: rdn wl over 1f out: drvn and hdd 1f out: outpcd by wnr fnl f but kpt on for clr 2nd* **4/1**[1]

464- **3** 2¾ **Odin (IRE)**[8] 7970 5-10-0 **75** .... GeorgeBaker 1 80
(Don Cantillon) *hld up in tch in rr: hdwy over 2f out: 3rd and drvn over 1f out: kpt on same pce fnl f* **15/2**

004- **4** 1¼ **Bow To No One (IRE)**[83] 6173 7-9-5 **69** .... RobertTart(3) 6 72
(Alan Jarvis) *stdd s: hld up in tch in rr: rdn and effrt 2f out: kpt on u.p ins fnl f: nvr trbld ldrs* **8/1**

511- **5** ¾ **Bramshill Lass**[15] 7863 4-9-10 **71** .... JimCrowley 7 73
(Amanda Perrett) *hld up in tch in last quartet: rdn and effrt 2f out: wnt 4th but no imp 1f out: one pce after: swtchd lft wl ins fnl f* **9/2**[2]

625- **6** nk **Where's Susie**[15] 7863 8-9-8 **69** .... RobertHavlin 3 71
(Michael Madgwick) *in tch in midfield: lost pl 4f out and bhd whn rdn over 2f out: swtchd rt and sme hdwy u.p over 1f out: kpt on same pce ins fnl f* **20/1**

251- **7** 1½ **Lady Of Yue**[52] 7066 3-8-7 **63** .... JimmyQuinn 10 63
(Eugene Stanford) *in tch in midfield: rdn over 3f out: drvn and outpcd 2f out: wl hld and plugged on same pce fr over 1f out* **5/1**[3]

653- **8** 1¼ **Happy Families**[43] 7305 3-8-9 **65** .... AndreaAtzeni 13 64
(Heather Main) *chsd ldr tl unable qck u.p 2f out: outpcd and btn over 1f out: wknd fnl f* **12/1**

/30- **9** 18 **Yes Chef**[15] 7863 6-8-11 **58** .... LiamKeniry 11 35
(Chris Gordon) *t.k.h: chsd ldrs: rdn and no rspnse over 2f out: wknd qckly wl over 1f out* **20/1**

313- **10** 15 **Barachiel**[141] 4166 5-9-3 **64** .... SeanLevey 9 23
(Luke Dace) *chsd ldrs: lost pl and rdn 4f out: bhd and lost tch 2f out: t.o* **8/1**

3m 26.9s (-3.20) **Going Correction** 0.0s/f (Stan)
WFA 3 from 4yo+ 9lb **10** Ran SP% **120.3**
Speed ratings (Par 103): **108,106,105,104,104 103,103,102,93,85**
toteswingers 1&2 £7.70, 2&3 £6.20, 1&3 £11.50 CSF £31.31 CT £183.27 TOTE £7.70: £2.70, £1.60, £3.20; EX 46.50 Trifecta £567.50 Pool: £3029.47 - 4.00 winning units..
Owner Condover Racing **Bred** Farmers Hill Stud **Trained** Epsom, Surrey

FOCUS
Mainly exposed sorts in a fair handicap. The gallop was no more than fair and the winner raced towards the far rail. She is rated back to last winter's form.
T/Jkpt: Not won. T/Plt: £375.90 to a £1 stake. Pool of £81105.31 - 157.48 winning tickets.
T/Qpdt: £28.10 to a £1 stake. Pool of £10883.36 - 286.40 winning tickets. SP

8050 WOLVERHAMPTON (A.W) (L-H)
Friday, November 29

OFFICIAL GOING: Standard
Wind: Fresh across Weather: Overcast

8090 32RED.COM NURSERY H'CAP — 5f 20y(P)
3:55 (3:55) (Class 6) (0-65,65) 2-Y-O **£1,940** (£577; £288; £144) **Stalls** Low

Form RPR

214- **1** **Debt Settler (IRE)**[8] 7986 2-9-0 **65** .... JoshQuinn(7) 1 72+
(Luke Dace) *hld up: hdwy and nt clr run over 1f out: shkn up to ld wl ins fnl f: r.o* **9/4**[1]

513- **2** 1¼ **Skinny Love**[14] 7900 2-9-5 **63** ....(p) GrahamLee 5 64
(Robert Cowell) *a.p: rdn to ld ins fnl f: sn hdd: styd on same pce* **9/2**[3]

000- **3** 1 **Gauchita**[16] 7852 2-8-10 **54** .... LukeMorris 7 51
(Michael Bell) *mid-div: sn pushed along: hdwy 1/2-way: rdn over 1f out: hmpd ins fnl f: styd on same pce* **8/1**

400- **4** 1¼ **Argent Touch**[52] 7095 2-8-1 **45** .... AndrewMullen 9 37+
(Derek Shaw) *s.i.s: in rr tl r.o ins fnl f: nvr nrr* **20/1**

042- **5** nk **Where The Boys Are (IRE)**[28] 7665 2-9-2 **60** .... GrahamGibbons 8 51
(Ed McMahon) *disp ld to 1/2-way: rdn over 1f out: no ex ins fnl f* **3/1**[2]

000- **6** ½ **Cheeky Peta'S**[10] 7956 2-8-6 **50** ....(v[1]) MartinDwyer 3 40
(James Given) *disp ld tl led 1/2-way: rdn over 1f out: hdd and no ex ins fnl f* **20/1**

040- **7** 1¼ **Aussie Sky (IRE)**[34] 7541 2-7-8 **45** .... JoeDoyle(7) 6 30
(John Stimpson) *hmpd s: hld up: rdn and hung rt over 1f out: nvr on terms* **33/1**

635- **8** 1¾ **Saffire Song**[8] 7986 2-9-2 **60** ....(v[1]) RobertWinston 4 39
(Alan Bailey) *chsd ldrs: rdn over 1f out: wknd fnl f* **9/2**[3]

600- **9** 8 **Reale Silenzio**[48] 7198 2-8-2 **46** ow1 ....(b) DuranFentiman 2
(John Weymes) *prom: pushed along 1/2-way: rdn and wknd over 1f out* **66/1**

1m 3.28s (0.98) **Going Correction** +0.10s/f (Slow) **9** Ran SP% **117.2**
Speed ratings (Par 94): **96,94,92,90,89 89,87,84,71**
toteswingers 1&2 £3.10, 1&3 £4.10, 2&3 £5.00 CSF £12.37 CT £69.47 TOTE £3.40: £1.90, £2.10, £2.90; EX 11.10 Trifecta £63.50 Pool: £2619.28 - 30.89 winning units..
Owner Mark Benton **Bred** Patrick Monahan **Trained** Five Oaks, W Sussex
■ The first winner for Josh Quinn, the son of jockey Jimmy Quinn.

FOCUS
They went a decent pace in this nursery and the favourite scored in good style under a hold-up ride.

8091 32RED CASINO MEDIAN AUCTION MAIDEN STKS — 5f 216y(P)
4:25 (4:26) (Class 6) 2-Y-O **£1,940** (£577; £288; £144) **Stalls** Low

Form RPR

22- **1** **Angel Flores (IRE)**[31] 7592 2-9-0 0 .... TonyHamilton 1 70
(Richard Fahey) *a.p: chsd ldr who was clr 2f out: r.o u.p to ld nr fin* **11/10**[1]

334- **2** ½ **Oriental Relation (IRE)**[16] 7853 2-9-5 72 ....(b[1]) GrahamLee 7 73
(James Given) *led: clr over 4f out: rdn and wknd ins fnl f: hdd nr fin* **7/4**[2]

236- **3** 5 **Le Laitier (FR)**[18] 7837 2-9-5 66 .... TomEaves 3 57
(Scott Dixon) *chsd ldr: pushed along over 3f out: lost 2nd 2f out: styd on same pce fr over 1f out* **16/1**

5- **4** 7 **Techtycoon**[15] 7882 2-8-12 0 .... DanielleMooney(7) 6 35
(Michael Easterby) *chsd ldrs: rdn over 1f out: wkng whn hung rt fnl f* **40/1**

4- **5** 3¾ **Real Jazz (IRE)**[13] 7934 2-9-0 0 .... LukeMorris 2 18
(Sir Mark Prescott Bt) *sn pushed along in rr: bhd fr 1/2-way* **10/1**[3]

6 ¾ **O'Raghallaigh (IRE)** 2-8-9 0 .... SamanthaBell(5) 4 16
(Richard Fahey) *s.i.s: outpcd* **20/1**

56- **7** 1½ **Vale Mentor (IRE)**[20] 7817 2-9-5 0 .... DuranFentiman 5 16
(Tim Easterby) *hld up: rdn and wknd over 2f out* **25/1**

1m 15.69s (0.69) **Going Correction** +0.10s/f (Slow) **7** Ran SP% **110.0**
Speed ratings (Par 94): **99,98,91,82,77 76,74**
toteswingers 1&2 £1.10, 1&3 £3.30, 2&3 £3.50 CSF £2.85 TOTE £1.90: £1.60, £1.10; EX 4.10 Trifecta £15.50 Pool: £5937.07 - 287.17 winning units..
Owner R A Fahey **Bred** Pier House Stud **Trained** Musley Bank, N Yorks

FOCUS
The two market leaders pulled clear in this maiden, which was run at a fast pace.

8092 32RED MAIDEN STKS — 1m 5f 194y(P)
4:55 (4:56) (Class 5) 3-Y-O+ **£2,587** (£770; £384; £192) **Stalls** Low

Form RPR

052- **1** **Coconell**[18] 7838 3-9-0 63 .... GrahamLee 8 75
(Jeremy Noseda) *a.p: chsd ldr over 3f out: led over 2f out: drvn out* **2/1**[2]

35- **2** 2¾ **Fair Loch**[170] 3209 5-9-13 0 .... MartinHarley 5 76
(K R Burke) *trckd ldrs: wnt 2nd over 1f out: sn rdn and ev ch: nt run on* **5/4**[1]

3- **3** 12 **Resourceful Miss**[18] 7838 4-9-8 0 .... MartinDwyer 7 54
(Paul Webber) *hld up in tch: rdn over 2f out: wknd over 1f out* **10/1**

005- **4** 1½ **Sir Tyto (IRE)**[24] 7738 5-9-13 0 .... SteveDrowne 6 57
(Peter Makin) *led 2f: chsd ldr tl led again 4f out: rdn and hdd over 2f out: wknd over 1f out* **8/1**[3]

5 7 **Miss Tilly Oscar (IRE)**[15] 7-9-8 0 .... AdamKirby 3 42
(David Evans) *s.i.s: pushed along 9f out: a in rr* **10/1**

5/6- **6** 4 **Word Of Warning**[43] 5295 9-9-13 47 ....(e[1]) JimmyQuinn 2 42
(Philip Kirby) *hld up: rdn over 4f out: wknd 3f out* **20/1**

0- **7** 14 **Amberjam (IRE)**[14] 7894 3-9-5 0 .... MartinLane 1 22
(Martin Smith) *s.i.s: a in rr* **66/1**

8 38 **Roxy Beat**[211] 5-9-8 0 .... LukeMorris 4
(David Evans) *chsd ldr tl led 12f out: pushed along and hdd 4f out: sn wknd* **20/1**

3m 7.47s (1.47) **Going Correction** +0.10s/f (Slow)
WFA 3 from 4yo+ 8lb **8** Ran SP% **118.1**
Speed ratings (Par 103): **99,97,90,89,85 83,75,53**
toteswingers 1&2 £1.20, 1&3 £3.70, 2&3 £3.30 CSF £4.93 TOTE £3.10: £1.20, £1.10, £2.00; EX 6.60 Trifecta £25.30 Pool: £4422.83 - 131.02 winning units..
Owner Vimal Khosla **Bred** Vimal & Gillian Khosla & Templeton Stud **Trained** Newmarket, Suffolk

FOCUS
The two leading form contenders pulled a long way clear in this modest maiden.

8093 CORAL APP FROM THE APP STORE (S) STKS — 1m 1f 103y(P)
5:25 (5:25) (Class 6) 3-Y-O+ **£1,940** (£577; £288; £144) **Stalls** Low

Form RPR

206- **1** **Officer In Command (USA)**[34] 7544 7-9-7 69 ....(p) LiamKeniry 4 76
(John Butler) *hld up: hdwy over 3f out: chsd ldr over 2f out: styd on u.p to ld wl ins fnl f* **6/1**[3]

531- **2** 1 **Honey Of A Kitten (USA)**[6] 8028 5-9-0 67 ....(b) EoinWalsh(7) 5 74
(David Evans) *led: rdn over 1f out: hdd wl ins fnl f* **1/2**[1]

000- **3** 11 **West End Lad**[15] 7881 10-9-7 65 ....(v[1]) JimmyQuinn 2 51
(Roy Bowring) *chsd ldrs: drvn along over 3f out: wknd 2f out* **14/1**

251- **4** 3¼ **Banreenahreenkah (IRE)**[11] 7104 3-8-13 63 .... TomQueally 6 39
(Jennie Candlish) *plld hrd: trckd ldr tl rdn over 2f out: wknd over 1f out* **4/1**[2]

2m 2.96s (1.26) **Going Correction** +0.10s/f (Slow)
WFA 3 from 5yo+ 3lb **4** Ran SP% **107.6**
Speed ratings (Par 101): **98,97,87,84**
CSF £9.76 TOTE £7.30; EX 11.80 Trifecta £30.00 Pool: £2093.87 - 52.33 winning units..There was no bid for the winner
Owner J Butler **Bred** Blooming Hills Inc **Trained** Newmarket, Suffolk

FOCUS
The odds-on favourite was turned over in this small-field seller.

8094 LADBROKES H'CAP — 1m 141y(P)
5:55 (5:57) (Class 3) (0-95,91) 3-Y-O- **£7,246** (£2,168; £1,084; £542; £270) **Stalls** Low

Form RPR

/02- **1** **Star Links (USA)**[70] 6617 7-8-7 **77** ....(b) LukeMorris 2 89
(S Donohoe, Ire) *a.p: shkn up to ld over 1f out: drvn clr ins fnl f* **8/1**

400- **2** 6 **Verse Of Love**[29] 7641 4-9-3 **87** .... AdamKirby 1 85
(David Evans) *chsd ldrs: lost pl 7f out: pushed along 1/2-way: hdwy u.p over 1f out: r.o to go 2nd post: no ch w wnr* **6/1**[3]

421- **3** hd **Silverware (USA)**[17] 7849 5-8-13 **83** .... TomEaves 6 81
(Kristin Stubbs) *sn led: rdn over 2f out: hdd over 1f out: no ex ins fnl f* **6/1**[3]

/11- **4** 6 **That's Plenty (IRE)**[21] 7816 4-9-0 **84** .... LiamKeniry 3 68
(John Patrick Shanahan, Ire) *prom: chsd ldr over 6f out: rdn over 2f out: wknd fnl f* **6/4**[1]

000- **5** 3¼ **Docofthebay (IRE)**[11] 7949 9-9-0 **84** ....(b) TomQueally 5 60
(Scott Dixon) *s.s: outpcd: tk clsr order over 3f out: rdn and wknd over 2f out* **16/1**

504- **6** 3½ **Marcret (ITY)**[14] 7906 6-9-7 **91** .... GrahamGibbons 4 59
(David O'Meara) *plld hrd: trckd ldr tl over 6f out: remained handy: rdn over 2f out: wknd over 1f out* **5/2**[2]

1m 49.28s (-1.22) **Going Correction** +0.10s/f (Slow) **6** Ran SP% **114.1**
Speed ratings (Par 107): **109,103,103,98,95 92**
toteswingers 1&2 £9.80, 1&3 £3.70, 2&3 £2.50 CSF £54.00 TOTE £10.30: £4.90, £2.00; EX 45.30 Trifecta £154.40 Pool: £2198.10 - 10.67 winning units..
Owner Gerry Dolan & Mrs Marie E Dolan **Bred** Shell Bloodstock **Trained** Cootehill Road, Co Cavan

FOCUS
They went a stop-start gallop in this decent handicap. The two market leaders were disappointing but the winner powered clear.

8095 DOWNLOAD THE LADBROKES APP H'CAP 7f 32y(P)
6:25 (6:25) (Class 5) (0-75,75) 3-Y-O+ **£2,587** (£770; £384; £192) **Stalls** High

Form RPR
361- **1** **Eastern Dragon (IRE)**[100] 5644 3-8-8 **68** .... JackDuern(5) 9 78
(Michael Scudamore) *hld up: hdwy over 1f out: sn rdn: r.o to ld nr fin* **16/1**
352- **2** 3/4 **Two No Bids (IRE)**[10] 7953 3-8-12 **67** .... (be) PaddyAspell 11 75
(Phil McEntee) *s.i.s: hld up: hdwy on outer 2f out: nt clr run over 1f out: sn rdn: r.o wl* **8/1**[3]
302- **3** shd **George Fenton**[10] 7965 4-9-1 **72** .... (e) RyanPowell(3) 12 81
(Conor Dore) *chsd ldrs: pushed along over 2f out: rdn to ld ins fnl f: hung lft and hdd nr fin* **10/1**
0- **4** nk **Marciano (IRE)**[104] 5541 3-9-6 **75** .... (p) RobertHavlin 8 82
(Alan Brown) *hld up: hdwy 2f out: rdn over 1f out: r.o* **25/1**
555- **5** 1 1/4 **Smalljohn**[10] 7965 7-9-1 **69** .... (v) GrahamLee 6 74
(Bryan Smart) *chsd ldrs: rdn over 2f out: led over 1f out: hdd and unable qck ins fnl f* **6/1**[2]
003- **6** 2 1/2 **Chiswick Bey (IRE)**[14] 7898 5-8-9 **68** .... (p) SamanthaBell(5) 5 66
(Richard Fahey) *hld up: rdn over 1f out: r.o ins fnl f: nvr nrr* **8/1**[3]
653- **7** 1 1/2 **Dodina (IRE)**[36] 7487 3-9-1 **70** .... TomEaves 1 63
(Brian Ellison) *mid-div: hdwy 1/2-way: rdn over 1f out: no ex fnl f* **5/2**[1]
000- **8** 2 1/2 **Blazeofenchantment (USA)**[143] 4140 3-8-10 **68** .... BillyCray(3) 3 54
(Richard Guest) *hld up: nt clr run over 2f out: shkn up over 1f out: nvr nr to chal* **50/1**
312- **9** 1 1/4 **Ace Master**[30] 7633 5-9-4 **75** .... (b) MarkCoumbe(3) 2 59
(Roy Bowring) *led: rdn and hdd over 1f out: wknd ins fnl f* **8/1**[3]
000- **10** 2 **Ferdy (IRE)**[51] 7130 4-8-11 **65** .... LukeMorris 10 43
(Paul Green) *hld up: rdn over 1f out: n.d* **33/1**
104- **11** 2 1/4 **Piceno (IRE)**[14] 7898 5-8-13 **72** .... (p) TimClark(5) 7 44
(Scott Dixon) *chsd ldr: rdn over 3f out: wknd over 1f out* **10/1**
050- **12** nk **Strong Man**[20] 7824 5-9-3 **71** .... (b) GrahamGibbons 4 42
(Michael Easterby) *prom: pushed along over 3f out: wknd over 1f out* **6/1**[2]

1m 29.96s (0.36) **Going Correction** +0.10s/f (Slow)
WFA 3 from 4yo+ 1lb **12** Ran SP% **123.3**
Speed ratings (Par 103): **101,100,100,99,98 95,93,90,89,87 84,84**
toteswingers 1&2 £17.30, 1&3 £12.80, 2&3 £9.90 CSF £141.93 CT £934.99 TOTE £15.80: £4.50, £3.70, £1.90; EX 198.40 Trifecta £1396.50 Part won. Pool: £1862.06 - 0.63 winning units..
Owner JCG Chua & CK Ong **Bred** James Mahon **Trained** Bromsash, H'fords
FOCUS
They went a strong pace in this competitive handicap and the winner came from some way back.

8096 COMPARE BOOKMAKERS AT BOOKMAKERS.CO.UK H'CAP 5f 20y(P)
6:55 (6:55) (Class 5) (0-75,75) 3-Y-O+ **£2,587** (£770; £384; £192) **Stalls** Low

Form RPR
610- **1** **Pull The Pin (IRE)**[23] 7772 4-8-10 **64** .... (b) WilliamCarson 5 73
(Violet M Jordan) *mde all: rdn over 1f out: hung rt ins fnl f: r.o* **12/1**
053- **2** hd **Solemn**[13] 7937 8-9-0 **68** .... (v) AdamKirby 1 76
(Milton Bradley) *chsd wnr: pushed along 1/2-way: rdn and hung rt and ev ch ins fnl f: r.o* **5/1**[2]
645- **3** hd **Wild Sauce**[10] 7959 4-9-7 **75** .... (bt) GrahamLee 12 83
(Bryan Smart) *a.p: rdn and hung rt over 1f out: ev ch ins fnl f: r.o* **8/1**
010- **4** 2 1/4 **Speightowns Kid (USA)**[6] 8029 5-8-11 **65** .... (b) RobertHavlin 8 64+
(Alan Berry) *hld up: hmpd 4f out: hdwy over 1f out: sn rdn: r.o: nt rch ldrs* **8/1**
100- **5** nk **R Woody**[8] 7985 6-9-2 **70** .... (e) MartinLane 10 68
(Robert Cowell) *chsd ldrs: rdn and ev ch over 1f out: styd on same pce ins fnl f* **8/1**
400- **6** 1 **Mount Hollow**[24] 7742 8-9-1 **74** .... (e) JackDuern(5) 3 69+
(Andrew Hollinshead) *hmpd s: hld up: rdn and r.o ins fnl f: nt trble ldrs* **8/1**
006- **7** 1/2 **Cadeaux Pearl**[15] 7887 5-9-0 **68** .... (b) LukeMorris 6 61
(Scott Dixon) *prom: racd keenly: rdn over 1f out: no ex ins fnl f* **4/1**[1]
014- **8** 3 1/4 **Layla's Oasis**[39] 7432 3-8-13 **72** .... GeorgeChaloner(5) 11 53
(Richard Fahey) *hld up: hmpd 4f out: rdn 1/2-way: hung lft over 1f out: nt trble ldrs* **7/1**[3]
/5- **9** nk **Welliesinthewater (IRE)**[255] 1075 3-9-5 **73** .... TomEaves 4 53
(Derek Shaw) *mid-div: drvn along and lost pl 1/2-way: n.d after* **25/1**
340- **10** nk **Miako (USA)**[158] 3638 3-8-13 **67** .... AndrewMullen 2 46
(Michael Appleby) *chsd ldrs: pushed along over 3f out: rdn over 1f out: wknd ins fnl f* **33/1**
300- **11** 1 **Flirtinaskirt**[30] 7634 3-9-2 **70** .... GrahamGibbons 7 46
(Ed McMahon) *hld up: rdn over 1f out: n.d* **12/1**
500- **12** 1 1/4 **Midnight Dream (FR)**[31] 7601 3-9-2 **75** .... JacobButterfield(5) 13 46
(Kristin Stubbs) *hld up: swtchd lft 4f out: hdwy 1/2-way: rdn over 1f out: wknd fnl f* **16/1**

1m 2.53s (0.23) **Going Correction** +0.10s/f (Slow) **12** Ran SP% **121.7**
Speed ratings (Par 103): **102,101,101,97,97 95,94,89,89,88 87,85**
toteswingers 1&2 £9.60, 1&3 £11.90, 2&3 £3.90 CSF £72.91 CT £532.24 TOTE £9.30: £3.50, £2.30, £3.00; EX 73.50 Trifecta £136.50 Pool: £1788.33 - 9.82 winning units..
Owner Rakebackmypoker.com **Bred** T J Ryan **Trained** Moreton Morrell, Warwicks
FOCUS
The pace looked solid in this handicap but not many got involved and the first three were always prominent.
T/Plt: £281.70 to a £1 stake. Pool: £102771.31 - 266.27 winning tickets T/Qpdt: £96.50 to a £1 stake. Pool: £8620.16 - 66.10 winning tickets CR

8097 - 8111a (Foreign Racing) - See Raceform Interactive

8090 WOLVERHAMPTON (A.W) (L-H)
Saturday, November 30

OFFICIAL GOING: Standard
Wind: Almost nil Weather: Overcast

8112 COMPARE BOOKMAKERS AT BOOKMAKERS.CO.UK MAIDEN STKS 5f 20y(P)
5:50 (5:50) (Class 5) 3-Y-O+ **£2,587** (£770; £384; £192) **Stalls** Low

Form RPR
503- **1** **Robyn**[25] 7759 3-9-0 48 .... LukeMorris 2 53
(Scott Dixon) *mde all: racd keenly: set stdy pce tl qcknd 2f out: drvn out* **7/2**[2]
325- **2** 1 **Busy Bimbo (IRE)**[32] 7600 4-8-11 45 .... MarkCoumbe(3) 3 49
(Alan Berry) *chsd wnr: rdn over 1f out: r.o* **8/1**
544- **3** nk **Daneglow (IRE)**[10] 7969 3-9-0 45 .... (e[1]) FrederikTylicki 5 48
(Mike Murphy) *hld up in tch: rdn over 1f out: r.o* **9/2**[3]
00- **4** 3/4 **My Time**[147] 4074 4-8-12 52 .... LewisStones(7) 1 51
(Michael Mullineaux) *hld up: r.o ins fnl f: nt trble ldrs* **6/1**
023- **5** 3/4 **Twist And Twirl**[10] 7969 3-9-0 52 .... DaleSwift 4 43
(Derek Shaw) *sn pushed along to chse ldrs: rdn over 1f out: styd on same pce ins fnl f* **11/8**[1]

1m 5.09s (2.79) **Going Correction** +0.275s/f (Slow) **5** Ran SP% **107.9**
Speed ratings (Par 103): **88,86,85,84,83**
CSF £26.86 TOTE £4.50: £1.90, £2.90; EX 26.00 Trifecta £58.90 Pool: £2,405.57 - 30.62 winning units..
Owner P J Dixon & Partners **Bred** Mrs Yvette Dixon **Trained** Babworth, Notts
FOCUS
A poor maiden with all five runners having very lowly official ratings.

8113 32RED MAIDEN STKS 5f 20y(P)
6:20 (6:20) (Class 5) 2-Y-O **£2,587** (£770; £384; £192) **Stalls** Low

Form RPR
033- **1** **Biscuiteer**[11] 7956 2-9-0 49 .... (p) LukeMorris 4 62
(Scott Dixon) *chsd ldr tl shkn up to ld over 1f out: drvn out* **18/1**
2 nk **Ealain Aibrean (IRE)**[64] 6811 2-9-0 0 .... AdamKirby 5 62+
(David Evans) *a.p: racd keenly: rdn ins fnl f: r.o* **7/2**[2]
330- **3** 3/4 **Caesars Gift (IRE)**[9] 7986 2-9-5 63 .... (v) DaleSwift 2 63
(Derek Shaw) *trckd ldrs: racd keenly: pushed along 1/2-way: rdn and ev ch ins fnl f: unable qck towards fin* **8/1**
502- **4** 2 **Grande Mago (IRE)**[7] 8017 2-9-5 67 .... (v) MartinLane 3 56
(Robert Cowell) *led: rdn and hdd over 1f out: styd on same pce ins fnl f* **7/1**[3]
25- **5** 2 1/2 **Conflicting**[17] 7852 2-9-5 0 .... SeanLevey 6 47
(Richard Hannon Snr) *s.i.s: hdwy over 3f out: rdn over 1f out: wknd ins fnl f* **5/6**[1]
6- **6** 1/2 **Kinkohyo**[25] 7756 2-8-11 0 .... MarkCoumbe(3) 1 40
(Bryan Smart) *s.i.s: outpcd* **25/1**

1m 3.8s (1.50) **Going Correction** +0.275s/f (Slow) **6** Ran SP% **109.5**
Speed ratings (Par 96): **99,98,97,94,90 89**
toteswingers 1&2 £1.70, 1&3 £8.50, 2&3 £3.00 CSF £74.99 TOTE £9.00: £2.60, £1.70; EX 28.70 Trifecta £130.70 Pool: £3,147.50 - 18.05 winning units..
Owner P J Dixon & Partners **Bred** Mrs Fiona Denniff **Trained** Babworth, Notts
FOCUS
On the face of it another poor maiden.

8114 32RED.COM MAIDEN STKS 7f 32y(P)
6:50 (6:50) (Class 5) 2-Y-O **£2,587** (£770; £384; £192) **Stalls** Low

Form RPR
6- **1** **Bint Malyana (IRE)**[42] 7371 2-9-0 0 .... LukeMorris 6 70
(James Tate) *a.p: pushed along over 2f out: rdn to ld 1f out: edgd lft: r.o u.p* **8/1**[3]
04- **2** nk **Bretherton**[10] 7978 2-9-5 0 .... TonyHamilton 4 74
(Richard Fahey) *chsd ldrs: wnt 2nd 3f out: led over 1f out: sn rdn: hung lft and hdd: ev ch ins fnl f: r.o* **7/4**[2]
0- **3** 7 **Mahon Falls**[7] 8026 2-9-0 0 .... AdamKirby 3 52
(David Evans) *led at stdy pce tl qcknd over 2f out: rdn and hdd over 1f out: wknd ins fnl f* **14/1**
4- **4** 4 **Prestige Roses (IRE)**[39] 7450 2-9-0 0 .... MartinHarley 1 42
(Marco Botti) *hld up: hdwy over 2f out: sn rdn: wknd over 1f out* **1/1**[1]
00- **5** 1 **Aptitude**[7] 8026 2-9-0 0 .... AdamBeschizza 2 40+
(Tobias B P Coles) *hld up: pushed along 1/2-way: wknd over 2f out* **25/1**
00- **6** 4 **Sarlat**[166] 3391 2-9-0 0 .... GrahamGibbons 5 30
(Mark Brisbourne) *chsd ldr tl pushed along 3f out: wknd 2f out* **66/1**

1m 31.43s (1.83) **Going Correction** +0.275s/f (Slow) **6** Ran SP% **109.5**
Speed ratings (Par 96): **100,99,91,87,85 81**
toteswingers 1&2 £2.80, 1&3 £6.10, 2&3 £2.70 CSF £21.41 TOTE £7.70: £3.10, £1.50; EX 18.50 Trifecta £88.30 Pool: £3,624.48 - 30.75 winning units..
Owner Saif Ali **Bred** Eyrefield Lodge Stud **Trained** Newmarket, Suffolk
FOCUS
This probably didn't take a great deal of winning but the front two pulled clear and both deserve credit.

8115 CORAL APP DOWNLOAD FROM THE APP STORE H'CAP 1m 4f 50y(P)
7:20 (7:20) (Class 5) (0-70,70) 3-Y-O+ **£2,587** (£770; £384; £192) **Stalls** Low

Form RPR
200- **1** **St Ignatius**[18] 7239 6-9-10 **70** .... (v) RobertWinston 3 80
(Alan Bailey) *chsd ldr tl led over 4f out: shkn up over 1f out: rdn out* **5/1**
343- **2** 3/4 **Mick Duggan**[12] 7950 3-9-1 **67** .... LukeMorris 4 76
(Simon Hodgson) *a.p: chsd wnr over 3f out: rdn and ev ch over 1f out: styd on u.p* **11/4**[1]
130- **3** 4 **Yasir (USA)**[17] 7863 5-9-5 **65** .... (p) LiamKeniry 5 67
(Conor Dore) *s.i.s: hld up: hdwy over 2f out: rdn over 1f out: edgd rt and styd on same pce fnl f* **4/1**[3]
000- **4** 1 1/4 **Sommersturm (GER)**[12] 7950 9-8-6 **57** .... (t) EoinWalsh(5) 7 57
(David Evans) *hld up: pushed along over 3f out: styd on to go 4th ins fnl f: nt trble ldrs* **16/1**
332- **5** 1 **Lookbeforeyouleap**[16] 7881 3-9-4 **70** .... DavidNolan 2 69
(David O'Meara) *chsd ldrs: rdn over 2f out: wknd ins fnl f* **3/1**[2]
450- **6** 3 1/4 **Easydoesit (IRE)**[16] 7881 5-9-5 **65** .... JimmyQuinn 6 59
(Tony Carroll) *hld up: hdwy over 3f out: rdn over 2f out: wknd over 1f out* **7/1**
250- **7** 8 **Waving**[12] 7950 4-9-2 **65** .... MarkCoumbe(3) 1 46
(Tony Carroll) *led over 7f: rdn and wknd over 2f out* **25/1**

2m 42.61s (1.51) **Going Correction** +0.275s/f (Slow)
WFA 3 from 4yo+ 6lb **7** Ran SP% **110.6**
Speed ratings (Par 103): **105,104,101,101,100 98,92**
toteswingers 1&2 £4.60, 1&3 £4.20, 2&3 £2.20 CSF £17.83 TOTE £4.20: £2.70, £2.30; EX 18.10 Trifecta £139.90 Pool: £3,309.56 - 17.74 winning units..
Owner Allan McNamee & Alan Bailey **Bred** Simon And Helen Plumbly **Trained** Newmarket, Suffolk
FOCUS
Run-of-the-mill handicap form and the pace looked even enough.

8116 CORAL MOBILE "JUST THREE CLICKS TO BET" H'CAP 1m 1f 103y(P)
7:50 (7:52) (Class 6) (0-55,61) 3-Y-O+ **£1,940** (£577; £288; £144) **Stalls** Low

Form RPR
000- **1** **Mosman**[23] 7784 3-9-4 **55** .... (tp) FergusSweeney 11 64
(Dean Ivory) *a.p: chsd ldr over 3f out: led over 2f out: rdn over 1f out: styd on gamely* **8/1**[3]
631- **2** hd **Dubai Celebration**[8] 8006 5-9-8 **61** .... JacobButterfield(5) 8 70
(Julie Camacho) *chsd ldrs: rdn and ev ch fr over 1f out: styd on* **6/4**[1]

The Form Book Flat, Raceform Ltd, Compton, RG20 6NL.

202- **3** 1 1/2 **Marina Ballerina**[8] 8006 5-8-13 **47**.................................... JimmyQuinn 7 53
(Roy Bowring) *pushed along in rr early: hdwy over 2f out: rdn over 1f out: edgd lft ins fnl f: styd on* **11/1**

306- **4** 1 3/4 **Tukitinyasok (IRE)**[14] 7930 6-8-7 **46** oh1............. GeorgeChaloner(5) 13 48
(Clive Mulhall) *w ldr tl led over 3f out: rdn and hdd over 2f out: nt clr run and swtchd rt ins fnl f: styd on same pce* **16/1**

121- **5** 3/4 **Poppy Bond**[11] 7963 3-9-7 **58**.................................... GrahamGibbons 10 59
(Alan Bailey) *a.p: rdn over 2f out: styd on same pce fnl f* **3/1**[2]

600- **6** 1/2 **First Glance**[10] 7981 4-8-12 **46** oh1................................ AndrewMullen 2 46
(Michael Appleby) *prom: hmpd and lost pl sn after s: hld up: hdwy over 3f out: rdn over 2f out: styd on same pce fnl f* **33/1**

605- **7** 3 1/2 **Uncle Bernie (IRE)**[29] 7666 3-8-13 **50**..........................(p) ShaneKelly 12 42
(Andrew Hollinshead) *s.i.s: hld up: hdwy over 2f out: rdn and swtchd rt over 1f out: no ex fnl f* **14/1**

001- **8** 5 **Kheskianto (IRE)**[67] 6723 7-8-5 **46**.................................. PaulBooth(7) 9 28
(Michael Chapman) *s.i.s: sn pushed along in rr: nvr nrr* **40/1**

000- **9** 11 **Flying Applause**[11] 7951 8-8-12 **46** oh1.....................(v) RobertWinston 5 5
(Roy Bowring) *sn edgd lft and led: rdn and hdd over 3f out: wknd over 2f out* **20/1**

0/0- **10** 3 3/4 **Legal Pursuit**[233] 1497 4-8-12 **46** oh1............................ StevieDonohoe 4
(Edward Bevan) *s.i.s: hld up: plld hrd: a in rr* **66/1**

/00- **11** 6 **Gifted Heir (IRE)**[11] 7962 9-8-7 **46** oh1......................... JoeyHaynes(5) 1
(Ray Peacock) *mid-div: drvn along over 3f out: wknd over 2f out* **100/1**

006- **12** 35 **Elizabeth Coffee (IRE)**[11] 7963 5-9-1 **49**.......................(b) LukeMorris 6
(John Weymes) *chsd ldrs: drvn along over 4f out: wknd 3f out* **8/1**[3]

2m 4.06s (2.36) **Going Correction** +0.275s/f (Slow)
WFA 3 from 4yo+ 3lb 12 Ran SP% **120.7**
Speed ratings (Par 101): **100,99,98,96,96 95,92,88,78,75 69,38**
toteswingers 1&2 £4.70, 1&3 £21.20, 2&3 £4.00 CSF £20.09 CT £141.30 TOTE £9.40: £2.50, £1.40, £2.70; EX 19.80 Trifecta £446.40 Pool: £3,905.72 - 6.56 winning units..
Owner Mrs Elaine White William Harris P Blows **Bred** P A Blows **Trained** Radlett, Herts
■ Stewards' Enquiry : Robert Winston three-day ban: careless riding

FOCUS
Only a few of these came into this in any kind of form and the overall time was over seven seconds slower than RP standard. It produced a cracking finish.

8117 LADBROKES H'CAP 1m 141y(P)
8:20 (8:21) (Class 2) 3-Y-0+
£28,012 (£8,388; £4,194; £2,097; £1,048; £526) **Stalls** Low

Form RPR

525- **1** **Solar Deity (IRE)**[14] 7926 4-9-7 **96**.................................... MartinHarley 6 109
(Marco Botti) *a.p: pushed along over 2f out: n.m.r over 1f out: rdn to ld ins fnl f: r.o wl u.p* **10/3**[2]

223- **2** 3 1/2 **Galician**[10] 7974 4-9-10 **99**.. AdamKirby 7 104
(Mark Johnston) *chsd ldrs: rdn over 3f out: styd on same pce u.p ins fnl f: wnt 2nd nr fin* **6/1**[3]

001- **3** 3/4 **Haaf A Sixpence**[28] 7696 4-9-6 **95**...................................... JimCrowley 3 98
(Ralph Beckett) *led to 1/2-way: led again over 2f out: rdn over 1f out: hdd and unable qck ins fnl f: lost 2nd nr fin* **11/4**[1]

643- **4** nk **Laffan (IRE)**[21] 7820 4-9-3 **92**....................................(e) DuranFentiman 11 95
(Tim Easterby) *hld up: rdn over 1f out: r.o ins fnl f: nt rch ldrs* **25/1**

442- **5** 3/4 **Ishikawa (IRE)**[4] 8057 5-7-11 **77**.................................... JoeyHaynes(5) 1 78
(K R Burke) *chsd ldrs: rdn over 1f out: styd on same pce fnl f* **12/1**

002- **6** 1/2 **Verse Of Love**[1] 8094 4-8-12 **87**.................................... GrahamGibbons 9 87
(David Evans) *prom: chsd ldr over 6f out tl led 1/2-way: hdd over 2f out: sn rdn: no ex ins fnl f* **18/1**

345- **7** nk **Alfred Hutchinson**[23] 7793 5-9-0 **89**................................. SeanLevey 12 88
(Geoffrey Oldroyd) *hld up: r.o ins fnl f: nvr nrr* **12/1**

513- **8** 1/2 **Ruwaiyan (USA)**[12] 7949 4-8-8 **83**...............................(p) LukeMorris 8 81
(James Tate) *hld up: hdwy over 2f out: sn rdn: no ex fnl f* **7/1**

040- **9** nk **Tellovoi (IRE)**[21] 7820 5-8-9 **84**..................................(v) StevieDonohoe 5 81
(Ian Williams) *hld up in tch: rdn over 2f out: no ex fnl f* **33/1**

002- **10** 2 1/4 **Chapter And Verse (IRE)**[9] 7988 7-8-10 **85**.............. FrederikTylicki 10 77
(Mike Murphy) *s.i.s: hld up: rdn over 1f out: n.d* **25/1**

200- **11** 15 **Favourite Treat (USA)**[9] 7991 3-8-13 **91**...................... AdrianNicholls 4 48
(Mark Johnston) *hld up: rdn and wknd over 2f out* **12/1**

200- **12** 7 **Trader Jack**[10] 7982 4-9-3 **92**......................................(b) TonyHamilton 2 33
(David Flood) *plld hrd and prom: rdn over 2f out: sn wknd* **20/1**

1m 49.75s (-0.75) **Going Correction** +0.275s/f (Slow)
WFA 3 from 4yo+ 3lb 12 Ran SP% **120.3**
Speed ratings (Par 109): **114,110,110,109,109 108,108,108,107,105 92,86**
toteswingers 1&2 £5.20, 1&3 £3.40, 2&3 £2.40 CSF £22.89 CT £63.35 TOTE £4.70: £1.70, £1.90, £1.80; EX 32.80 Trifecta £23.50 Pool: £3,147.58 - 100.18 winning units..
Owner G Manfredini & A Tinkler **Bred** Castlemartin Stud And Skymarc Farm **Trained** Newmarket, Suffolk

FOCUS
Easily the best race on the card and a good-quality handicap.

8118 DOWNLOAD THE LADBROKES APP H'CAP (DIV I) 7f 32y(P)
8:50 (8:51) (Class 6) (0-55,55) 3-Y-0+ **£1,940** (£577; £288; £144) **Stalls** High

Form RPR

500- **1** **Rafaaf (IRE)**[263] 968 5-9-7 **55**.................................... GrahamGibbons 10 66
(Richard Phillips) *trckd ldrs: racd keenly: rdn to ld over 1f out: drvn clr* **3/1**[1]

064- **2** 3 **Coastal Passage**[15] 7905 5-9-1 **49**................................(tp) AdamKirby 2 52
(Charles Smith) *trckd ldrs: rdn over 2f out: styd on to go 2nd post: no ch w wnr* **7/2**[2]

500- **3** nk **Celestial Dawn**[15] 7904 4-9-5 **53**.................................(b[1]) LukeMorris 7 55
(John Weymes) *racd keenly: hdwy over 5f out: rdn over 1f out: styd on* **22/1**

040- **4** nse **Interchoice Star**[15] 7905 8-8-7 **46**..........................(p) JoeyHaynes(5) 11 48
(Ray Peacock) *chsd ldr tl led over 5f out: rdn and hdd over 1f out: no ex ins fnl f* **20/1**

006- **5** 1 1/4 **Mataajir (USA)**[16] 7886 5-9-4 **52**................................(v) DaleSwift 4 51
(Derek Shaw) *hld up: pushed along 1/2-way: r.o ins fnl f: nvr nrr* **10/1**

060- **6** 2 1/4 **Pendle Lady (IRE)**[145] 4109 4-9-4 **52**........................(e[1]) ShaneKelly 6 45
(Mark Brisbourne) *hld up: rdn over 2f out: r.o ins fnl f: nrst fin* **33/1**

600- **7** 1/2 **Blue Noodles**[54] 7079 7-9-2 **50**.................................(v) PaddyAspell 3 41
(John Wainwright) *mid-div: rdn over 2f out: styd on same pce fr over 1f out* **22/1**

140- **8** 1/2 **Kielty's Folly**[30] 7639 9-9-4 **52**.................................... JimCrowley 5 42
(Brian Baugh) *led: hdd over 5f out: chsd ldr tl rdn over 1f out: wknd fnl f* **4/1**[3]

003- **9** 3 1/4 **Legal Eagle (IRE)**[15] 7905 8-8-11 **48**........................(p) MarkCoumbe(3) 8 29
(Noel Williams) *hld up: rdn over 2f out: a in rr* **12/1**

025- **10** 1/2 **Amelia Jay**[15] 7904 3-9-0 **52**.. SladeO'Hara(3) 9 31
(Danielle McCormick) *prom: stmbld and lost pl after 1f: n.d after* **14/1**

00- **11** 2 **Kai**[7] 8023 4-8-7 **49**...(b) AaronJones(7) 12 23
(Alan McCabe) *sn pushed along and a in rr* **20/1**

400- **12** 1/2 **Vitznau (IRE)**[16] 7886 9-9-5 **53**.................................... AdamBeschizza 1 26
(K F Clutterbuck) *hld up: sme hdwy over 2f out: sn rdn and wknd* **25/1**

1m 32.12s (2.52) **Going Correction** +0.275s/f (Slow)
WFA 3 from 4yo+ 1lb 12 Ran SP% **115.7**
Speed ratings (Par 101): **96,92,92,92,90 88,87,87,83,82 80,79**
toteswingers 1&2 £2.40, 1&3 £17.40, 2&3 £8.90 CSF £11.25 CT £194.49 TOTE £5.10: £1.90, £1.40, £4.70; EX 19.90 Trifecta £293.70 Pool: £2,644.91 - 6.75 winning units..
Owner J A Gent **Bred** Oscar Stud **Trained** Adlestrop, Gloucs

FOCUS
A weak handicap in which very few brought solid recent form to the table.

8119 DOWNLOAD THE LADBROKES APP H'CAP (DIV II) 7f 32y(P)
9:20 (9:21) (Class 6) (0-55,55) 3-Y-0+ **£1,940** (£577; £288; £144) **Stalls** High

Form RPR

004- **1** **Munaawib**[15] 7903 5-9-3 **51**...(t) AdamKirby 9 61+
(David C Griffiths) *hld up: hdwy over 1f out: r.o u.p to ld wl ins fnl f* **2/1**[1]

/40- **2** 1/2 **Kalithea**[74] 6497 3-9-3 **52**...(e) LukeMorris 7 60
(Julie Camacho) *s.i.s: hld up: hdwy over 1f out: rdn and edgd lft ins fnl f: r.o* **4/1**[2]

603- **3** 1/2 **Medam**[15] 7904 4-8-10 **49**.................................... ShirleyTeasdale(5) 10 56+
(Shaun Harris) *hld up: hdwy over 2f out: led over 1f out: rdn and hdd wl ins fnl f* **9/1**

646- **4** 1 **Elle Rebelle**[11] 7966 3-8-13 **48**.. ShaneKelly 6 52
(Mark Brisbourne) *a.p: rdn over 2f out: r.o* **7/1**[3]

640- **5** 1/2 **Purley Queen (IRE)**[3] 8073 4-9-4 **52**................................. LiamKeniry 3 55
(Sylvester Kirk) *chsd ldrs: nt clr run fr over 2f out tl over 1f out: sn rdn: r.o* **7/1**[3]

066- **6** 1 3/4 **Knockamany Bends (IRE)**[25] 7759 3-9-5 **54**............... PaddyAspell 12 52
(John Wainwright) *led 6f out: rdn and hdd over 1f out: no ex ins fnl f* **33/1**

040/ **7** 3 **Reinvigorate (IRE)**[456] 5807 3-9-6 **55**......................... MartinHarley 5 44
(Emmet Michael Butterly, Ire) *sn chsng ldr: rdn over 2f out: wknd ins fnl f* **12/1**

000- **8** 3/4 **Ballinargh Girl (IRE)**[15] 7903 5-8-12 **49**..................... SladeO'Hara(3) 4 37
(Danielle McCormick) *chsd ldrs: rdn over 2f out: wknd fnl f* **50/1**

431- **9** hd **Red Shadow**[15] 7904 4-9-4 **52**..(p) DaleSwift 2 40
(Alan Brown) *led 1f: chsd ldrs: rdn over 2f out: wknd fnl f* **10/1**

400- **10** 1 1/2 **Scommettitrice (IRE)**[61] 6901 5-9-4 **52**....................... KieranO'Neill 8 36
(Nigel Twiston-Davies) *hld up: hung lft over 1f out: n.d* **25/1**

505- **11** 2 **Mon Chic**[43] 7354 3-8-11 **46** oh1...................................... JimmyQuinn 1 23
(Geoffrey Oldroyd) *s.i.s: in rr whn hmpd wl over 3f out: nvr on terms* **16/1**

1m 31.79s (2.19) **Going Correction** +0.275s/f (Slow)
WFA 3 from 4yo+ 1lb 11 Ran SP% **119.7**
Speed ratings (Par 101): **98,97,96,95,95 93,89,88,88,86 84**
toteswingers 1&2 £2.60, 1&3 £3.00, 2&3 £15.20 CSF £9.59 CT £60.02 TOTE £3.90: £1.60, £1.70, £2.60; EX 17.50 Trifecta £167.40 Pool: £2,638.08 - 11.81 winning units..
Owner Willie McKay **Bred** Shadwell Estate Company Limited **Trained** Bawtry, S Yorks

FOCUS
Low-grade handicap form.
T/Plt: £120.70 to a £1 stake. Pool: £108,725.87 - 657.23 winning units T/Qpdt: £8.90 to a £1 stake. Pool: £9,637.56 - 796.30 winning units CR

4335 HOLLYWOOD PARK (L-H)
Sunday, December 1

OFFICIAL GOING: Turf: firm

8120a HOLLYWOOD DERBY (GRADE 1) (3YO) (TURF) 1m 2f
11:04 (12:00) 3-Y-0
£92,024 (£30,674; £18,404; £9,202; £3,067; £153)

RPR

1 **Seek Again (USA)**[50] 7205 3-8-10 0.................................... CNakatani 4 113
(John Gosden) **26/5**

2 1 1/2 **Admiral Kitten (USA)**[57] 7039 3-8-10 0.........................(b) JRLeparoux 5 110+
(Michael J Maker, U.S.A) **3/1**[1]

3 3/4 **Amen Kitten (USA)**[50] 3-8-10 0.................................... JJCastellano 7 109+
(Wesley A Ward, U.S.A) **40/1**

4 1/2 **Gervinho (USA)**[30] 3-8-10 0.................................... RBejarano 2 108
(Carla Gaines, U.S.A) **26/5**

5 nse **Rookie Sensation (USA)**[30] 3-8-10 0.............................(b) VEspinoza 8 107
(John Shirreffs, U.S.A) **16/5**[2]

6 1 1/4 **Jack Milton (USA)**[57] 7039 3-8-10 0.................................... JRosario 3 105
(Todd Pletcher, U.S.A) **39/10**[3]

7 2 1/2 **Infinite Magic (USA)**[56] 3-8-10 0.................................... JTalamo 1 100
(Richard C Mettee, U.S.A) **116/10**

7 dht **Dry Summer (USA)**[30] 3-8-10 0.................................(b) MESmith 6 100
(Jeff Mullins, U.S.A) **201/10**

9 1/2 **Irish Surf (USA)**[30] 3-8-10 0.................................(b) JValdiviaJr 9 99
(Dan L Hendricks, U.S.A) **33/1**

2m 0.6s (120.60) 9 Ran SP% **119.5**
PARI-MUTUEL (all including 2 usd stake): WIN 12.40; PLACE (1-2) 7.40, 4.00; SHOW (1-2-3) 5.80, 3.40, 12.80; DF 30.00; SF 53.60.
Owner Juddmonte Farms Inc **Bred** Juddmonte Farms Inc **Trained** Newmarket, Suffolk
■ The final Hollywood Derby as the track is to close.

8082 KEMPTON (A.W) (R-H)
Monday, December 2

OFFICIAL GOING: Standard
Wind: virtually nil Weather: overcast

8121 COME JUMP RACING ON BOXING DAY H'CAP 1m 2f (P)
2:20 (2:21) (Class 6) (0-60,60) 3-Y-0+ **£1,940** (£577; £288; £144) **Stalls** Low

Form RPR

201- **1** **Brave Decision**[16] 7922 6-9-3 **56**.................................... MartinHarley 8 65
(Suzy Smith) *travelled: hld up wl in tch in midfield: rdn and effrt over 1f out: chal ins fnl f: led fnl 75yds: r.o wl* **14/1**

040- 2 nk **Derfenna Art (IRE)**[25] 7784 4-9-4 **57**............................(t) GeorgeBaker 5 65
(Seamus Durack) *sn led: rdn and edgd rt over 1f out: str pressed and edgd lft u.p ins fnl f: hdd fnl 75yds: kpt on wl but a jst hld* **9/2**[2]

031- 3 2 **Minstrel Lad**[17] 7907 5-9-3 **56**.. JimCrowley 3 62
(Lydia Pearce) *travelled wl: hld up in tch in midfield: effrt to chse wnr whn nt clr run and swtchd lft jst over 1f out: hdwy and pressing ldrs whn squeezed for room and hmpd ins fnl f: nt rcvr and one pce after* **3/1**[1]

600- 4 1 1/4 **Warden Bond**[19] 7857 5-9-2 **60**...........................(p) ShelleyBirkett(5) 7 62
(William Stone) *in tch in midfield: hdwy u.p over 1f out: kpt on ins fnl f: nvr quite pce to chal* **10/1**

000- 5 1 **Interakt**[11] 7985 6-9-2 **55**.. JohnFahy 9 55
(Joseph Tuite) *stdd s: hld up in rr: hdwy over 1f out: swtchd lft 1f out: r.o wl fnl f: nt rch ldrs* **50/1**

005- 6 nk **Queen Of Skies (IRE)**[16] 7922 4-9-3 **56**...................... AndrewMullen 1 55
(Michael Appleby) *led early: sn settled to chse ldrs: rdn and chsd wnr wl over 1f out tl ent fnl f: wknd fnl 100yds* **8/1**[3]

054- 7 nk **Fair Comment**[56] 7071 3-9-1 **57**.............................. FergusSweeney 11 55
(Michael Blanshard) *in tch in midfield: rdn and effrt wl over 1f out: styd on wl u.p ins fnl f: neer trbld ldrs* **33/1**

041- 8 3/4 **Entrapping**[34] 7610 3-9-1 **57**... JimmyQuinn 6 54
(John E Long) *hld up in tch in midfield: rdn and hdwy on inner over 1f out: no imp ins fnl f* **12/1**

30- 9 1 **Gung Ho (FR)**[44] 7375 4-9-6 **59**.. LiamKeniry 4 54
(Tony Newcombe) *s.i.s: in rr: rdn over 2f out: styd on ins fnl f: nvr trbld ldrs* **16/1**

450- 10 2 **Bint Alzain (IRE)**[9] 8019 4-9-1 **57**........................... JemmaMarshall(3) 2 48
(Pat Phelan) *stdd s: hld up in rr: rdn wl over 1f out: kpt on fnl f: nvr trbld ldrs* **50/1**

522- 11 6 **Sutton Sid**[16] 7922 3-9-4 **60**..(p) AdamKirby 12 39
(Chris Gordon) *chsd ldrs: drvn 3f out: struggling u.p 2f out: sn wknd* **8/1**[3]

650- 12 1 **Beggers Belief**[208] 2159 5-8-10 **52**......................(v[1]) RossAtkinson(3) 14 29
(Zoe Davison) *dwlt: rcvrd to chse ldr after 2f out tl wl over 1f out: sn wknd* **33/1**

535- 13 3/4 **Having A Ball**[61] 6952 9-9-4 **57**...................................... ChrisCatlin 10 32
(Geoffrey Deacon) *a towards rr: n.d* **8/1**[3]

/62- 14 4 1/2 **Red Catkin**[34] 7610 3-9-1 **60**....................................... RyanPowell(3) 13 26
(George Margarson) *dwlt: sn rcvrd and in tch in midfield: rdn and struggling after 2f out: wknd over 1f out: bhd fnl f* **8/1**[3]

2m 6.36s (-1.64) **Going Correction** -0.075s/f (Stan)
WFA 3 from 4yo+ 3lb **14** Ran SP% **126.8**
Speed ratings (Par 101): **103,102,101,100,99 99,98,98,97,95 91,90,89,86**
toteswingers 1&2 £9.90, 1&3 £6.70, 2&3 £4.10 CSF £78.55 CT £249.94 TOTE £12.40: £3.70, £1.90, £1.60; EX 52.10 Trifecta £272.00 Pool: £3094.98 - 8.53 winning units..
Owner R Knight **Bred** K A Dasmal **Trained** Lewes, E Sussex
■ Stewards' Enquiry : George Baker two-day ban: careless riding (16-17 Dec)

FOCUS
This moderate handicap was run at a sound pace. The form looks sound for the grade, the winner backing up his Lingfield latest.

8122 BETVICTOR NON-RUNNER FREE BET CHELTENHAM 2014 CLAIMING STKS 7f (P)

2:50 (2:50) (Class 5) 3-Y-O+ **£2,587** (£770; £384; £192) **Stalls** Low

Form RPR

402- 1 **Capaill Liath (IRE)**[5] 8068 5-9-4 **84**............................(p) JamieSpencer 1 88
(Kevin Ryan) *t.k.h: hld up in midfield: swtchd lft and hdwy over 1f out: rdn to chal and edgd rt 1f out: led fnl 150yds: styd on and asserted wl ins fnl f* **11/4**[1]

266- 2 1 1/4 **Ocean Legend (IRE)**[11] 7992 8-8-8 **79**........................ JoeDoyle(7) 4 82
(Tony Carroll) *chsd ldng trio: clsd and upsides ldrs on bit wl over 1f out: pushed into ld over 1f out: carried rt and hdd fnl 150yds: unable qck and outpcd towards fin* **6/1**[2]

100- 3 2 **Mr David (USA)**[11] 7992 6-9-1 **84**..................................(b) JimCrowley 7 77
(Jamie Osborne) *racd off the pce in last trio: rdn and gd hdwy on inner over 2f out: chsd ldrs and styd on same pce ins fnl f* **11/4**[1]

304- 4 3/4 **Comrade Bond**[41] 7452 5-9-3 **72**...................................... LiamJones 8 77
(Mark H Tompkins) *pressed ldr: rdn to ld ent fnl 2f: hdd and unable qck over 1f out: one pce fnl f* **14/1**

365- 5 nk **Balducci**[108] 5474 6-9-1 **90**... DavidNolan 2 74
(David O'Meara) *chsd ldrs: rdn over 2f out: drvn and sltly outpcd over 1f out: kpt on again ins fnl f: no threat to ldrs* **11/4**[1]

040- 6 12 **Rapid Water**[27] 7741 7-8-7 **43**.......................................(b) MartinLane 5 35
(Pat Eddery) *racd off the pce in last trio: rdn and no hdwy over 2f out: wknd over 1f out* **100/1**

000- 7 6 **Daisie Cutter**[38] 7511 3-7-8 **43**....................................... EilishMcCall(7) 3 13
(Graeme McPherson) *dwlt and hmpd s: swtchd rt and hmpd after 1f: swtchd lft and sn rdn: lost tch 2f out* **100/1**

616- 8 1 **Decision By One**[13] 7959 4-9-4 **75**................................. AdamKirby 6 27
(David Evans) *led tl drvn and hdd ent fnl 2f: wknd qckly over 1f out: bhd and eased wl ins fnl f* **10/1**[3]

1m 24.55s (-1.45) **Going Correction** -0.075s/f (Stan) **8** Ran SP% **112.0**
Speed ratings (Par 103): **105,103,101,100,100 86,79,78**
toteswingers 1&2 £4.10, 1&3 £2.30, 2&3 £3.90 CSF £19.51 TOTE £3.60: £1.50, £2.30, £1.10; EX 14.10 Trifecta £41.20 Pool: £3856.09 - 70.14 winning units..
Owner T A Rahman **Bred** Stanley Estate & Stud Co & Mount Coote Stud **Trained** Hambleton, N Yorks
■ Stewards' Enquiry : Jim Crowley two-day ban: careless riding

FOCUS
A fair claimer, run at a sound gallop. The winner's task was eased by below-par runs from the other co-favourites.

8123 CHELTENHAM 2014 NRRB AT BETVICTOR.COM MAIDEN STKS (DIV I) 1m (P)

3:20 (3:21) (Class 5) 2-Y-O **£2,587** (£770; £384; £192) **Stalls** Low

Form RPR

1 **Cloudscape (IRE)** 2-9-5 0.. NickyMackay 7 74+
(John Gosden) *stdd s: hld up in last pair: rdn and effrt 2f out: str run to ld 1f out: r.o strly and drew clr fnl 100yds* **14/1**

2 3 **Sufranel (IRE)** 2-9-5 0... MartinHarley 6 67+
(Marco Botti) *chsd ldr tl led ent fnl 2f: sn rdn hdd 1f out: outpcd by wnr fnl 100yds but kpt on for clr 2nd* **11/4**[2]

3 2 **Purple Spectrum** 2-9-5 0.. LiamJones 3 63+
(William Haggas) *dwlt: sn rcvrd to r in midfield: rdn ent fnl 2f: wnt 4th 1f out: kpt on fnl f* **6/1**[3]

3- 4 nk **Twin Point**[26] 7766 2-9-5 0.. RobertHavlin 9 62
(John Gosden) *t.k.h: hld up wl in tch: rdn to press ldr 2f out tl jst over 1f out: sn outpcd: wknd ins fnl f* **2/1**[1]

0- 5 hd **Curbyourenthusiasm (IRE)**[21] 7835 2-9-5 0.................... MartinLane 5 63+
(David Simcock) *dwlt and pushed along early: hmpd after 2f: racd in last quartet: rdn and hdwy on inner 2f out: no imp ent fnl f: one pce after* **20/1**

5- 6 1 1/4 **Ayers Rock (IRE)**[19] 7860 2-9-5 0................................. ShaneKelly 10 59
(Marcus Tregoning) *hld up towards rr: rdn and effrt over 2f out: sme hdwy u.p over 1f out: drvn and styd on ins fnl f: nvr trbld ldrs* **20/1**

2- 7 nk **Lesha (IRE)**[13] 7955 2-9-5 0.. JamieSpencer 12 58
(Kevin Ryan) *hld up in last quartet: swtchd lft and rdn ent fnl 2f: no imp u.p tl drvn and kpt on ins fnl f: nvr trbld ldrs* **8/1**

05- 8 nse **Lucky Jim**[19] 7854 2-9-5 0... GeorgeBaker 8 58
(Chris Wall) *chsd ldrs: rdn and effrt ent fnl 2f: outpcd and btn over 1f out: wknd fnl f* **25/1**

5- 9 1 **Tower Power**[19] 7859 2-9-5 0.. AdamKirby 2 56
(Ismail Mohammed) *in tch in midfield: rdn and effrt between horses to chse ldrs 2f out: sn drvn and outpcd: wknd fnl f* **14/1**

0- 10 2 1/4 **Moneypennie**[12] 7972 2-9-0 0.. MartinDwyer 13 45
(Marcus Tregoning) *v s.i.s: in rr: rdn over 2f out: kpt on ins fnl f: n.d* **66/1**

0- 11 2 1/4 **Astrovirtue**[34] 7607 2-9-5 0.. BenCurtis 4 45
(Mark H Tompkins) *chsd ldrs: rdn and unable qck ent fnl 2f: btn over 1f out: wknd fnl f* **100/1**

0- 12 9 **Wiggins (IRE)**[21] 7835 2-9-5 0.. JimCrowley 11 25
(Ralph Beckett) *in tch in midfield on outer: rdn and struggling over 2f out: sn wknd: bhd fnl f* **20/1**

06- 13 1/2 **The Cat**[31] 7662 2-9-0 0.. KieranO'Neill 1 18
(Nigel Twiston-Davies) *led: rdn and hdd ent fnl 2f: sn struggling and lost pl: bhd fnl f* **66/1**

1m 39.66s (-0.14) **Going Correction** -0.075s/f (Stan) **13** Ran SP% **120.8**
Speed ratings (Par 96): **97,94,92,91,91 90,89,89,88,86 84,75,74**
toteswingers 1&2 £11.50, 1&3 £15.90, 2&3 £5.50 CSF £49.73 TOTE £17.30: £4.10, £1.50, £3.10; EX 88.80 Trifecta £451.80 Pool: £3318.94 - 5.50 winning units..
Owner Lady Rothschild **Bred** Carwell Equities Ltd **Trained** Newmarket, Suffolk

FOCUS
A host of big stables in opposition for this 2yo maiden, which was run at a sound pace. The first three home were the only debutants. The winner impressed but the bare form is modest.

8124 CHELTENHAM 2014 NRRB AT BETVICTOR.COM MAIDEN STKS (DIV II) 1m (P)

3:50 (3:53) (Class 5) 2-Y-O **£2,587** (£770; £384; £192) **Stalls** Low

Form RPR

1 **Western Hymn** 2-9-5 0... RobertHavlin 8 87+
(John Gosden) *hld up in last quartet: stl plenty to do and rdn wl over 1f out: str run to ld ins fnl f: r.o strly and sn drew clr* **6/1**[3]

2 2 3/4 **Be My Gal** 2-9-0 0... FrederikTylicki 1 74+
(Roger Charlton) *chsd ldrs: rdn to chse ldr over 2f out: drvn to ld over 1f out: hdd ins fnl f: sn outpcd by wnr but kpt on for clr 2nd* **10/1**

002- 3 2 1/2 **Roskilly (IRE)**[40] 7460 2-9-5 **79**..................................... LiamKeniry 11 73
(Andrew Balding) *sn led: rdn ent fnl 2f: edgd lft u.p and hdd over 1f out: 3rd and outpcd fnl f* **5/1**[1]

4 1 3/4 **Damascene** 2-9-5 0.. MartinHarley 13 69+
(Marco Botti) *chsd ldr for 3f: styd chsng ldrs: rdn and effrt wl over 1f out: 4th and outpcd fnl f* **8/1**

0- 5 1 **Mairise**[21] 7835 2-9-5 0.. ShaneKelly 5 67+
(Sir Michael Stoute) *in tch in midfield: rdn and effrt 2f out: sme hdwy and swtchd rt ent fnl f: no imp after* **7/1**

0- 6 3/4 **Purple Lane (IRE)**[40] 7469 2-9-5 0.................................. MartinLane 9 65
(David Simcock) *wl in tch in midfield but stuck wd: effrt u.p jst over 2f out: outpcd and btn over 1f out: wknd ins fnl f* **7/1**

06- 7 1/2 **Cape Summit**[21] 7835 2-9-5 0.. AdamKirby 7 68+
(Ed Dunlop) *hld up towards rr: rdn and effrt over 1f out: switcing rt and nt clr run ent fnl f: kpt on: nvr trbld ldrs* **14/1**

4- 8 1/2 **New Colours**[13] 7955 2-9-5 0.. MartinDwyer 3 63
(Marcus Tregoning) *dwlt: rdn along in rr: kpt on fnl f: nvr trbld ldrs* **33/1**

9 1 1/4 **Confiture** 2-9-0 0.. FergusSweeney 10 55
(Michael Blanshard) *t.k.h: hld up wl in tch: hdwy to chse ldr 5f out tl jst over 2f out: sn struggling u.p: wknd over 1f out* **100/1**

4- 10 1/2 **Warbrook (IRE)**[31] 7655 2-9-5 0..................................... NickyMackay 12 59
(John Gosden) *t.k.h: chsd ldrs: rdn and unable qck whn sltly hmpd 2f out: outpcd and btn whn n.m.r 1f out* **11/2**[2]

11 1/2 **Bishan Bedi (IRE)** 2-9-5 0.. SteveDrowne 2 57
(William Jarvis) *dwlt: sn rcvrd and in tch in midfield: rdn and effrt on inner ent fnl 2f: outpcd and btn over 1f out: wknd fnl f* **33/1**

0- 12 3/4 **Stilla Afton**[12] 7971 2-9-0 0.. JimCrowley 6 51
(Marcus Tregoning) *a towards rr: rdn and no hdwy 2f: n.d* **20/1**

13 1/2 **Hoist The Colours (IRE)** 2-9-5 0...................................... GeorgeBaker 4 55
(David Lanigan) *s.i.s: a in rr: shkn up and no hdwy 2f out: n.d* **11/2**[2]

1m 40.92s (1.12) **Going Correction** -0.075s/f (Stan) **13** Ran SP% **121.5**
Speed ratings (Par 96): **91,88,85,84,83 82,81,81,80,79 79,78,77**
CSF £64.99 TOTE £7.40: £2.70, £5.10, £2.40; EX 91.60 Trifecta £731.60 Pool: £3917.79 - 4.01 winning units..
Owner RJH Geffen and Rachel Hood **Bred** Newsells Park Stud **Trained** Newmarket, Suffolk

FOCUS
The pace was steady for this maiden which did not look as strong as the first division. The bare form is limited but the winner was impressive.

8125 BOOK CHRISTMAS FESTIVAL TICKETS NOW H'CAP 1m (P)

4:20 (4:21) (Class 6) (0-60,60) 3-Y-O+ **£1,940** (£577; £288; £144) **Stalls** Low

Form RPR

241- 1 **Pretty Bubbles**[11] 7987 4-9-4 **57**.................................. FrederikTylicki 2 73
(J R Jenkins) *trckd ldrs and a travelling wl: wnt 2nd over 2f out: rdn to ld and qcknd clr over 1f out: clr and r.o wl fnl f: readily* **4/1**[2]

311- 2 3 1/2 **Princess Spirit**[47] 7299 4-8-12 **58**..................(p) JenniferFerguson(7) 9 66
(Edward Creighton) *hld up towards rr: rdn and hdwy wl over 1f out: chsd clr wnr ins fnl f: r.o for clr 2nd: no ch w wnr* **10/1**

632- 3 2 1/2 **Warbond**[61] 6932 5-9-6 **59**.......................................(p) GeorgeBaker 10 61
(Michael Madgwick) *stdd s: hld up in last pair: rdn and gd hdwy on inner 2f out: chsd clr wnr ent fnl f: no imp and lost 2nd fnl 150yds* **8/1**

0/2- 4 1 1/4 **Pearl Ransom (IRE)**[27] 7741 3-9-6 **60**........................ RobertWinston 4 59
(Lady Herries) *led: rdn ent fnl 2f: hdd over 1f out: immediately outpcd and btn: wknd fnl f* **8/1**

541- 5 1 3/4 **Skidby Mill (IRE)**[12] 7980 3-9-2 **56**................................. JimCrowley 11 51
(Laura Mongan) *s.i.s: bhd: camce wd and effrt over 2f out: wnt lft and racing against stands' rail fnl f: styd on: nvr trbld ldrs* **10/1**

200- 6 1/2 **Tartan Trip**[99] 5793 6-9-7 **60**...................................(t) AndrewMullen 13 54
(Michael Appleby) *in tch in midfield but stuck wd: rdn and effrt ent fnl 2f: outpcd and wl btn over 1f out* **6/1**[3]

430- 7 nk **Pastoral Jet**[238] 1426 5-9-3 **59**.. RyanPowell(3) 3 53
(Richard Rowe) *in tch in midfield: effrt u.p 2f out: sn outpcd and btn: plugged on fnl f* **20/1**

300- 8 ¾ **Lutine Charlie (IRE)**[4] 8087 6-9-6 **59**.................................. MartinLane 7 51
(Pat Eddery) *t.k.h: hld up wl in tch in midfield: rdn over 2f out: sn outpcd: plugged on but wl hld fr over 1f out* **16/1**

150- 9 nk **Tammuz (IRE)**[18] 7876 3-9-1 **60**............................... GeorgeDowning(5) 5 51
(Tony Carroll) *stdd after s: hld up in last trio: effrt but stls lost to do over 1f out: nt clr run 1f out: kpt on: nvr trbld ldrs* **25/1**

660- 10 ½ **Safwaan**[44] 7378 6-9-4 **57**.. LiamJones 6 47
(Michael Squance) *hld up in tch in midfield: rdn and no hdwy 2f out: n.d fr over 1f out* **33/1**

006- 11 1½ **Night's Watch**[33] 7622 3-9-3 **57**.................................... RobertHavlin 12 43
(William Jarvis) *in tch in midfield: rdn over 2f out: lost pl and towards rr whn hmpd 2f out: n.d after* **7/2**[1]

305- 12 ½ **Nelina**[7] 8037 3-9-6 **60**..(p) ShaneKelly 8 45
(Robert Cowell) *in tch in midfield: rdn and no hdwy ent fnl 2f: wknd over 1f out* **16/1**

450- 13 1 **Standing Strong (IRE)**[40] 5099 5-9-3 **59**...............(p) RossAtkinson(3) 1 42
(Zoe Davison) *in tch in midfield: rdn and effrt 2f out: no hdwy and wknd over 1f out* **66/1**

010- 14 3¾ **All Right Now**[13] 7958 6-9-7 **60**.................................... MartinHarley 14 34
(Tony Newcombe) *chsd ldr tl wl over 2f out: sn lost pl: bhd fnl f* **50/1**

1m 39.0s (-0.80) **Going Correction** -0.075s/f (Stan)
WFA 3 from 4yo+ 1lb **14** Ran SP% **123.7**
Speed ratings (Par 101): **101,97,95,93,92 91,91,90,90,89 88,87,86,82**
toteswingers 1&2 £3.30, 1&3 £5.80, 2&3 £5.80 CSF £42.90 CT £324.00 TOTE £3.80: £1.90, £2.10, £2.40; EX 17.10 Trifecta £74.30 Pool: £4249.52 - 42.86 winning units..
Owner Mark Goldstein & Mark Callow **Bred** Southill Stud **Trained** Royston, Herts

FOCUS
This open handicap was run at an honest pace. The third is a fair guide.

8126 BACK OF THE NET AT BETVICTOR.COM NURSERY H'CAP 7f (P)
4:50 (4:50) (Class 5) (0-75,71) 2-Y-O **£2,587** (£770; £384; £192) **Stalls** Low

Form RPR

551- 1 **Drive On (IRE)**[12] 7978 2-9-5 **69**..(p) JohnFahy 1 74
(Eve Johnson Houghton) *t.k.h: hld up in tch in last pair: rdn and effrt to chal over 1f out: led ins fnl f: r.o wl u.p* **3/1**[3]

410- 2 ½ **Go For Broke**[21] 7837 2-9-3 **67**.. KieranO'Neill 6 71
(Richard Hannon Snr) *wnt lft s: sn led: rdn ent fnl 2f: hrd pressed over 1f out: hdd ins fnl f: r.o but a jst hld* **5/1**

410- 3 1½ **Hipz (IRE)**[25] 7782 2-9-7 **71**.. JimCrowley 3 71
(George Baker) *chsd ldr: rdn and effrt ent fnl 2f: pressing ldr over 1f out: styd on same pce and outpcd fnl 100yds* **11/4**[2]

320- 4 1¾ **Bonjour Steve**[25] 7782 2-9-2 **66**... LiamKeniry 2 62
(J S Moore) *chsd ldng pair: rdn and effrt 2f out: unable qck ent fnl f: wknd fnl 100yds* **8/1**

006- 5 5 **Exceed And Exceed**[112] 5344 2-9-0 **64**............................ MartinHarley 5 47
(George Margarson) *t.k.h: hld up in tch in last pair: rdn and fnd little wl over 1f out: wknd fnl f* **5/2**[1]

1m 26.79s (0.79) **Going Correction** -0.075s/f (Stan) **5** Ran SP% **108.0**
Speed ratings (Par 96): **92,91,89,87,82**
CSF £16.72 TOTE £3.10: £1.60, £3.10; EX 11.70 Trifecta £24.10 Pool: £3320.68 - 102.99 winning units..
Owner Miss E Johnson Houghton **Bred** Nicola And Eleanor Kent **Trained** Blewbury, Oxon

FOCUS
They went a sound gallop for this handicap with the winner coming from the rear. He proved his maiden win was no fluke, with the third fitting in.

8127 DOWNLOAD THE BETVICTOR APP NOW H'CAP 7f (P)
5:20 (5:20) (Class 4) (0-85,85) 3-Y-O+ **£4,690** (£1,395; £697; £348) **Stalls** Low

Form RPR

212- 1 **Tasrih (USA)**[11] 7989 4-9-3 **81**.. MartinHarley 12 90+
(Alan McCabe) *mde all: rdn over 1f out: hld on wl u.p ins fnl f: all out* **7/2**[1]

653- 2 nk **Corporal Maddox**[11] 7992 6-9-7 **85**................................(p) GeorgeBaker 2 93
(Ronald Harris) *hld up wl in tch: clsd on inner 2f out: rdn to chse inner 1f out: ev ch ins fnl f: r.o but hld towards fin* **7/1**[3]

220- 3 ½ **Secret Beau**[27] 7742 3-9-2 **80**..(vt) AdamKirby 1 87
(David Evans) *chsd ldrs: rdn and effrt over 1f out: kpt on u.p ins fnl f* **7/1**[3]

042- 4 hd **Light From Mars**[25] 7792 8-8-13 **77**...............................(p) LiamJones 4 83
(Ronald Harris) *chsd ldrs: wnt 2nd over 2f out tl 1f out: kpt on again u.p fnl 100yds* **14/1**

600- 5 hd **Nassau Storm**[40] 7464 4-9-5 **83**......................................(t) JimCrowley 10 89+
(William Knight) *hld up off the pce in last trio: rdn and hdwy jst over 1f out: r.o strly ins fnl f: nt rch ldrs* **5/1**[2]

452- 6 1¼ **Jubilee Brig**[13] 7964 3-8-13 **77**..................................(v) FergusSweeney 8 80
(Gary Moore) *hld up in tch in midfield: nt clr run on inner and shuffled bk over 2f out: rallied and hdwy over 1f out: kpt on u.p: nt rch ldrs* **12/1**

600- 7 nk **My Kingdom (IRE)**[30] 7699 7-8-11 **75**........................(t) AdamBeschizza 9 77
(Stuart Williams) *hld up off the pce in last trio: rdn and hdwy jst over 1f out: styd on wl ins fnl f: nt rch ldrs* **25/1**

353- 8 nse **Panther Patrol (IRE)**[48] 7264 3-8-11 **75**..........................(p) JohnFahy 7 77
(Eve Johnson Houghton) *t.k.h: hld up in tch in midfield: rdn and no hdwy wl over 1f out: swtchd lft 1f out: styd on on fnl f: nt rch ldrs* **20/1**

220- 9 2½ **Bowstar**[11] 7992 4-8-10 **74**.......................................(p) RobertHavlin 3 69
(Michael Attwater) *chsd ldr tl over 2f out: sn rdn and struggling: wknd fnl f* **14/1**

600- 10 hd **Good Authority (IRE)**[11] 7992 6-8-8 **79**......................... RyanWhile(7) 13 73
(Karen George) *stdd and dropped in bhd after s: detached in last tl clsd 2f out: kpt on fnl f: nvr trbld ldrs* **33/1**

133- 11 hd **Liberty Jack (IRE)**[90] 6072 3-8-13 **77**........................... StephenCraine 6 71
(Jim Boyle) *in tch in midfield: rdn and unable qck 2f out: wknd u.p jst over 1f out* **16/1**

420- 12 2½ **Red Art (IRE)**[13] 7964 4-8-11 **75**.. ChrisCatlin 11 62
(Tony Newcombe) *sn pushed along in midfield on outer: rdn 1/2-way: wknd over 1f out* **25/1**

126- 13 3¾ **Perfect Mission**[47] 7306 5-8-4 **73**..........................(v) DanielMuscutt(5) 5 50
(Andrew Balding) *chsd ldrs: rdn and struggling ent fnl 2f: sn wknd* **25/1**

554- 14 nk **George Rooke (IRE)**[37] 7531 3-9-1 **79**......................... JamieSpencer 14 55
(Kevin Ryan) *in tch in midfield: rdn and unable qck over 2f out: sn struggling: wknd over 1f out* **9/1**

1m 24.42s (-1.58) **Going Correction** -0.075s/f (Stan) **14** Ran SP% **120.0**
Speed ratings (Par 105): **106,105,105,104,104 103,102,102,99,99 99,96,92,92**
toteswingers 1&2 £5.00, 1&3 £6.20, 2&3 £11.10 CSF £25.02 CT £170.49 TOTE £4.30: £1.40, £2.60, £2.90; EX 21.40 Trifecta £77.50 Pool: £3503.45 - 33.88 winning units..
Owner Craig and Maureen Buckingham **Bred** G Bolton, D Dipietro & R W Honour **Trained** Averham Park, Notts

FOCUS
A competitive handicap run at a solid pace. The front five finished in a bunch. The second and third set the level.

8128 BETVICTOR NON-RUNNER FREE BET AT CHELTENHAM '14 H'CAP 6f (P)
5:50 (5:51) (Class 5) (0-70,69) 3-Y-O+ **£2,587** (£770; £384; £192) **Stalls** Low

Form RPR

003- 1 **Bapak Bangsawan**[25] 7783 3-9-6 **68**................................ JamieSpencer 6 77
(Kevin Ryan) *mde all: styd on strly u.p fnl f: drvn out* **11/2**[2]

000- 2 1 **Burnhope**[17] 7897 4-8-13 **68**.....................................(p) MatthewHopkins(7) 2 74
(Scott Dixon) *rdn along early: sn wl in tch: effrt and rdn over 1f out: kpt on u.p ins fnl f: wnt 2nd last strides* **10/1**

460- 3 shd **Ray Of Joy**[6] 8052 7-9-5 **67**..(v[1]) FrederikTylicki 7 73
(J R Jenkins) *in tch in midfield on outer: rdn and hdwy 2f out: chsd ldrs fnl f: r.o to snatch 3rd last strides* **9/1**

000- 4 hd **Bajan Bear**[17] 7896 5-9-7 **69**.. MartinHarley 12 74
(Michael Blanshard) *stdd s: hld up in rr: clsd and swtchd rt 2f out: gd hdwy over 1f out: chsd ldrs ins fnl f: wnt 2nd wl ins fnl f: kpt on but lost 2 pls cl home* **12/1**

354- 5 nk **Rigolleto (IRE)**[17] 7897 5-9-6 **68**...................................... GeorgeBaker 5 72
(Anabel K Murphy) *chsd wnr: drvn over 1f out: kpt on same pce ins fnl f: lost 3 pls wl ins fnl f* **7/1**

420- 6 1 **Lujeanie**[17] 7897 7-9-7 **69**..(v[1]) ShaneKelly 3 70
(Peter Crate) *hld up towards rr: clsd 2f out: rdn and hdwy ent fnl f: r.o to chse ldrs ins fnl f: clsng whn nt clr run and swtchd lft cl home* **6/1**[3]

602- 7 2 **Colourbearer (IRE)**[9] 8030 6-9-7 **69**................................(t) AdamKirby 11 63
(Milton Bradley) *stdd s: hld up in last pair: clsd and carried rt 2f out: kpt on ins fnl f: nvr trbld ldrs* **16/1**

656- 8 nk **Drawnfromthepast (IRE)**[103] 5645 8-9-0 **69**................. JackGarritty(7) 8 63
(Luke Dace) *chsd ldrs: rdn ent fnl f: outpcd and btn 1f out: one pce after* **25/1**

006- 9 1¼ **Climaxfortackle (IRE)**[26] 7777 5-9-6 **68**............................ LiamJones 1 58
(Derek Shaw) *t.k.h: hld up in tch on inner: hmpd on bnd over 4f out: effrt wl over 1f out: no imp: n.d and one pce fnl f* **33/1**

030- 10 2½ **Fortrose Academy (IRE)**[13] 7958 4-9-2 **64**........................ LiamKeniry 4 46
(Andrew Balding) *in tch in midfield: rdn and unable qck over 2f out: wknd u.p over 1f out* **4/1**[1]

402- 11 ½ **Indian Affair**[9] 8029 3-9-4 **66**.. MartinLane 10 46
(Milton Bradley) *chsd ldrs: drvn and lost pl over 2f out: wknd over 1f out* **11/2**[2]

622- 12 2¼ **Starlight Angel (IRE)**[53] 7150 3-9-5 **67**....................... RobertWinston 9 40
(Ronald Harris) *towards rr and stuck wd: rdn and no hdwy over 2f out: wknd over 1f out* **12/1**

1m 12.07s (-1.03) **Going Correction** -0.075s/f (Stan) **12** Ran SP% **124.7**
Speed ratings (Par 103): **103,101,101,101,100 99,96,96,94,91 90,87**
toteswingers 1&2 £15.40, 1&3 £6.90, 2&3 £15.70 CSF £63.04 CT £509.12 TOTE £5.70: £2.30, £4.70, £3.40; EX 76.30 Trifecta £1227.20 Pool: £4020.69 - 2.45 winning units..
Owner H R H Sultan Ahmad Shah **Bred** Hrh Sultan Ahmad Shah **Trained** Hambleton, N Yorks
■ Stewards' Enquiry : Adam Kirby £140 fine: entered the parade ring after the signal to mount had been given
Liam Keniry £140 fine: entered the parade ring after the signal to mount had been given
Martin Lane £140 fine: entered the parade ring after the signal to mount had been given
Jamie Spencer £140 fine: entered the parade ring after the signal to mount had been given

FOCUS
The pace was strong for this wide-open contest. A personal best of about a length from the winner, with the next three setting an ordinary standard.
T/Jkpt: Not won. T/Plt: £44.80 to a £1 stake. Pool: £67463.99 - 1097.64 winning tickets T/Qpdt: £18.50 to a £1 stake. Pool: £7217.76 - 288.40 winning tickets SP

8112 WOLVERHAMPTON (A.W) (L-H)
Monday, December 2

OFFICIAL GOING: Standard
Wind: Light behind Weather: Overcast

8129 32RED CASINO H'CAP (FOR AMATEUR RIDERS) 1m 5f 194y(P)
12:55 (12:55) (Class 6) (0-65,65) 3-Y-O+ **£1,871** (£580; £290; £145) **Stalls** Low

Form RPR

/00- 1 **Royal Trooper (IRE)**[33] 7628 7-10-3 **57**......... MissBeckyBrisbourne(3) 2 65
(Mark Brisbourne) *hld up: hdwy over 3f out: chsd ldr over 2f out: led wl over 1f out: rdn out* **14/1**[3]

200- 2 1½ **Rock Of Ages**[34] 7612 4-10-1 **55**.......................(b) MrMichaelJMurphy(3) 1 61
(Michael Murphy) *s.i.s: hld up: hdwy over 2f out: rdn and hung lft fr over 1f out: styd on: nt rch wnr* **16/1**

023- 3 1¾ **Evermore (IRE)**[10] 8004 3-9-11 **60**........................... MrAlexFerguson(5) 5 64
(Mark Johnston) *s.i.s: hld up: hdwy 1/2-way: rdn over 1f out: styd on* **9/2**[2]

002- 4 1¾ **Full Speed (GER)**[16] 7923 8-10-9 **65**................................ MrPDennis(5) 10 66
(Philip Kirby) *chsd ldrs: rdn over 1f out: styd on same pce fnl f* **3/1**[1]

303- 5 3½ **Yasir (USA)**[2] 8115 5-11-0 **65**..(p) MissEJJones 9 61
(Conor Dore) *s.i.s: racd keenly and sn prom: led over 3f out: rdn and hdd wl over 1f out: wknd ins fnl f* **9/2**[2]

563- 6 1¼ **Cabuchon (GER)**[12] 7984 6-10-1 **57**...........................(t) MissHDoyle(5) 12 51
(David Evans) *mid-div: hdwy over 5f out: rdn and swtchd lft over 1f out: wknd fnl f* **9/2**[2]

/03- 7 4 **Herbalist**[28] 6971 3-10-5 **63**.. MrFMitchell 4 52
(Ben Pauling) *mid-div: pushed along over 6f out: lost pl over 4f out: n.d after* **14/1**[3]

440- 8 2 **Walter De La Mare (IRE)**[26] 7767 6-9-7 **47**......[1] MissJoannaMason(3) 8 33
(Anabel K Murphy) *hld up: pushed along over 2f out: a in rr* **25/1**

000- 9 2½ **King Of Windsor (IRE)**[10] 8006 6-9-10 **54** ow2............(p) MrKWood(7) 3 37
(John Wainwright) *s.i.s: hld up: a in rr* **20/1**

000- 10 4 **Natural High (IRE)**[19] 7863 8-10-6 **64**...............(bt) MissBHampson(7) 13 41
(Sean Curran) *disp ld tl over 3f out: rdn and wknd over 1f out* **14/1**[3]

4/0- 11 2 **What's Up Doc (IRE)**[12] 7984 12-9-4 **48**............................ MrPPilley(7) 7 22
(Lawney Hill) *disp ld tl pushed along over 3f out: wknd over 2f out* **50/1**

/00- 12 3¾ **Compassion**[9] 8027 5-9-10 **54**...(b[1]) MsPFeld(7) 6 23
(Emma Lavelle) *chsd ldrs tl rdn and wknd over 2f out* **40/1**

3m 9.46s (3.46) **Going Correction** +0.20s/f (Slow)
WFA 3 from 4yo+ 7lb **12** Ran SP% **118.4**
Speed ratings (Par 101): **98,97,96,95,93 92,90,89,87,85 84,82**
toteswingers 1&2 £30.80, 1&3 £9.00, 2&3 £11.80 CSF £208.98 CT £1177.21 TOTE £9.90: £2.60, £4.90, £1.70; EX 103.20 Trifecta £940.30 Pool: £2909.93 - 2.32 winning units..
Owner Mark Brisbourne **Bred** Western Bloodstock **Trained** Great Ness, Shropshire

FOCUS
Moderate stuff. The winner was down a long way in the weights and the next two are rated pretty much to form.

8130 32RED H'CAP — 2m 119y(P)
1:25 (1:25) (Class 5) (0-75,75) 3-Y-0+ — **£3,234** (£962; £481; £240) **Stalls** Low

Form — RPR
311- **1** **Mr Burbidge**[26] 7767 5-9-9 **70**.........................(b) LukeMorris 4 82
(Neil Mulholland) *chsd ldr: rdn over 3f out: hung lft fr over 1f out: styd on u.p to ld ins fnl f* **6/4**[1]
005- **2** 1 ¼ **Scribe (IRE)**[7] 7757 5-9-4 **65**.........................(bt) GrahamGibbons 3 75
(David Evans) *led: pushed along over 2f out: rdn: hdd and bmpd ins fnl f: eased nr fin* **10/1**
/15- **3** 18 **Secret Edge**[31] 7660 5-9-10 **71**......................... TedDurcan 6 64
(Alan King) *dwlt: sn given reminders to get in tch: rn in snatches: drvn along over 3f out: wknd over 2f out: eased fnl f* **2/1**[2]
541- **4** 4 ½ **Embsay Crag**[20] 7280 7-10-0 **75**......................... GrahamLee 1 58
(Philip Kirby) *prom: rdn over 5f out: wknd 4f out* **5/1**[3]
150- **5** 1 ¾ **Arashi**[5] 8060 7-9-8 **69**.........................(v) DaleSwift 5 50
(Derek Shaw) *hld up: rdn over 3f out: sn wknd* **12/1**
050- **6** 5 **Song Of The Siren**[18] 7881 5-8-10 **62**......................... DavidBergin(5) 2 37
(David O'Meara) *chsd ldrs: rdn over 4f out: wknd over 3f out* **25/1**
3m 45.07s (3.27) **Going Correction** +0.20s/f (Slow) 6 Ran SP% **110.6**
Speed ratings (Par 103): **100,99,90,88,88 85**
toteswingers 1&2 £3.40, 1&3 £1.40, 2&3 £3.50 CSF £16.49 TOTE £2.10: £1.10, £6.00; EX 17.20 Trifecta £48.10 Pool: £3405.64 - 53.08 winning units..
Owner Dajam Ltd **Bred** M Burbidge **Trained** Limpley Stoke, Wilts
FOCUS
An uncompetitive staying handicap in which the front two pulled well clear. A race that rather fell apart, rated around the runner-up to his spring form.

8131 32REDPOKER.COM CLAIMING STKS — 1m 1f 103y(P)
1:55 (1:56) (Class 6) 2-Y-0 — **£1,940** (£577; £288; £144) **Stalls** Low

Form — RPR
526- **1** **Nice Arty (IRE)**[14] 7944 2-8-5 60.........................(p) WilliamCarson 8 61
(Jamie Osborne) *mde all: set stdy pce tl qcknd over 3f out: rdn clr fr over 1f out: hung rt ins fnl f: eased nr fin* **7/2**[2]
430- **2** 5 **The Wallace Line (IRE)**[19] 7855 2-8-2 56......................... DanielCremin(7) 1 55
(Mick Channon) *hld up: rdn over 2f out: r.o to go 2nd nr fin: no ch w wnr* **7/2**[2]
603- **3** ½ **Kantara Castle (IRE)**[19] 7853 2-9-5 67......................... TedDurcan 6 64
(Richard Hannon Snr) *prom: chsd ldr over 7f out tl rdn over 2f out: styng on same pce whn wnt 2nd again and hung lft 1f out: lost 2nd nr fin* **2/1**[1]
003- **4** 1 ½ **Maupiti Express (FR)**[164] 3541 2-8-10 58......................... DavidBergin(5) 2 57
(David O'Meara) *prom: rdn over 3f out: styd on same pce fr over 1f out* **16/1**
54- **5** 1 ¼ **Techtycoon**[3] 8091 2-8-9 0......................... GrahamGibbons 7 48
(Michael Easterby) *racd keenly: trckd wnr tl over 7f out: remained handy: rdn to go 2nd again over 2f out wknd fnl f* **8/1**
002- **6** 2 ¾ **Penara**[9] 8016 2-8-2 60......................... LukeMorris 5 36
(Philip Hide) *prom: rdn over 3f out: wknd 2f out* **6/1**[3]
00- **7** 3 **Worcharlie'Slass**[13] 7955 2-8-2 0......................... DuranFentiman 4 30
(Michael Herrington) *hld up: rdn over 3f out: wknd over 2f out* **66/1**
000- **8** 1 ½ **Kitty Brown (IRE)**[27] 7755 2-7-9 43......................... JoeyHaynes(5) 3 26
(David Evans) *sn pushed along in rr: rdn over 3f out: sn wknd* **50/1**
2m 4.85s (3.15) **Going Correction** +0.20s/f (Slow) 8 Ran SP% **112.5**
Speed ratings (Par 94): **94,89,89,87,86 84,81,80**
toteswingers 1&2 £2.40, 1&3 £1.80, 2&3 £2.00 CSF £15.63 TOTE £4.50: £1.50, £1.40, £1.20; EX 15.40 Trifecta £42.70 Pool: £4042.18 - 70.89 winning units..
Owner B T McDonald **Bred** Patrick Gleeson **Trained** Upper Lambourn, Berks
FOCUS
A moderate claimer and straightforward form. The second and fourth help set the level.

8132 32RED ON THE APP STORE NURSERY H'CAP — 1m 141y(P)
2:30 (2:30) (Class 6) (0-65,64) 2-Y-0 — **£1,940** (£577; £288; £144) **Stalls** Low

Form — RPR
133- **1** **Jazzy Lady (IRE)**[14] 7944 2-9-5 **62**......................... GrahamGibbons 6 66
(David Evans) *hld up: hdwy over 1f out: rdn to ld ins fnl f: edgd lft: r.o* **7/1**
211- **2** hd **Rural Affair**[7] 8040 2-9-5 **62** 6ex......................... LukeMorris 4 66
(Michael Appleby) *led: rdn over 1f out: hdd ins fnl f: r.o* **2/1**[2]
032- **3** ½ **Star Anise (FR)**[14] 7944 2-9-5 **62**......................... GrahamLee 5 65
(Harry Dunlop) *trckd ldr: rdn and ev ch fr over 1f out: n.m.r ins fnl f: unable qck nr fin* **6/1**[3]
045- **4** 6 **Tortoise**[28] 7732 2-7-11 **45**......................... JoeyHaynes(5) 3 35
(Richard Guest) *chsd ldrs: rdn over 1f out: hung lft and wknd fnl f* **25/1**
004- **5** 8 **Ragged Robbin (FR)**[19] 7859 2-9-7 **64**......................... TedDurcan 2 37
(David Lanigan) *trckd ldrs: rdn over 2f out: wknd over 1f out: eased* **5/4**[1]
1m 53.76s (3.26) **Going Correction** +0.20s/f (Slow) 5 Ran SP% **108.4**
Speed ratings (Par 94): **93,92,92,87,79**
CSF £20.69 TOTE £7.10: £2.80, £1.50; EX 16.00 Trifecta £30.90 Pool: £3248.41 - 78.59 winning units..
Owner Will Dawson **Bred** Limestone And Tara Studs **Trained** Pandy, Monmouths
FOCUS
A modest nursery. The winner was entitled to win on these terms.

8133 £32 FREE AT 32RED.COM NURSERY H'CAP — 7f 32y(P)
3:00 (3:02) (Class 6) (0-60,62) 2-Y-0 — **£1,940** (£577; £288; £144) **Stalls** High

Form — RPR
630- **1** **Trinity Lorraine (IRE)**[12] 7973 2-8-1 **45**.........................(v[1]) TimClark(5) 5 53
(Alan Bailey) *a.p: chsd ldr 4f out: sn pushed along: rdn over 2f out: led ins fnl f: styd on wl* **20/1**
251- **2** 3 **Tyrsal (IRE)**[7] 8039 2-9-2 **62** 6ex......................... LouisSteward(7) 4 63
(Robert Eddery) *chsd ldr 3f: pushed along over 2f out: rdn and hung lft over 1f out: styd on to go 2nd nr fin* **7/2**[2]
002- **3** ½ **Spreadable (IRE)**[7] 8039 2-8-1 **47**.........................(b) JordanVaughan(7) 2 46
(Nick Littmoden) *led: hung lft over 1f out: hdd and no ex ins fnl f* **10/11**[1]
006- **4** nk **Twenty Roses (IRE)**[16] 7934 2-9-7 **60**......................... GrahamLee 7 59
(Ed Walker) *hld up: hdwy over 2f out: sn rdn: r.o: nt rch ldrs* **7/1**[3]
500- **5** 1 **Solent Lad (USA)**[12] 7973 2-8-6 **50**.........................(p) GeorgeChaloner(5) 3 46
(Robert Eddery) *s.i.s: sn prom: rdn over 2f out: r.o* **12/1**
505- **6** 7 **Royal Bushida**[12] 7973 2-8-11 **50** ow2......................... DaleSwift 1 29
(Derek Shaw) *sn pushed along in rr: nvr on terms* **16/1**
000- **7** 18 **Lord Lexington**[63] 6896 2-9-1 **54**.........................(v[1]) TedDurcan 6
(Richard Hannon Snr) *s.i.s: sn pushed along in rr: rdn 1/2-way: wknd over 2f out* **7/1**[3]
243- **8** 10 **Countess Lupus (IRE)**[75] 6511 2-8-4 **46** ow1.........(v) MarkCoumbe(3) 8
(Lisa Williamson) *outpcd* **50/1**
1m 31.89s (2.29) **Going Correction** +0.20s/f (Slow) 8 Ran SP% **119.9**
Speed ratings (Par 94): **94,90,90,89,88 80,59,48**
toteswingers 1&2 £9.50, 1&3 £5.30, 2&3 £1.70 CSF £93.14 CT £134.22 TOTE £20.80: £3.60, £1.10, £1.20; EX 11.50 Trifecta £265.30 Pool: £4698.27 - 13.27 winning units..
Owner Dr S P Hargreaves **Bred** B Kennedy **Trained** Newmarket, Suffolk
FOCUS
Few were ever involved in this moderate nursery. The form is rated around the runner-up.

8134 32RED.COM FILLIES' H'CAP — 7f 32y(P)
3:30 (3:30) (Class 5) (0-75,75) 3-Y-0+ — **£3,234** (£962; £481; £240) **Stalls** High

Form — RPR
023- **1** **Maggie Pink**[19] 7861 4-9-1 **69**......................... LukeMorris 7 79
(Michael Appleby) *chsd ldr tl led 2f out: sn rdn: r.o* **5/2**[1]
252- **2** 2 ¼ **Miss Avonbridge (IRE)**[112] 5353 3-9-7 **75**......................... RichardKingscote 4 79
(Tom Dascombe) *a.p: rdn over 2f out: chsd wnr over 1f out: styd on same pce ins fnl f* **3/1**[2]
025- **3** 1 ¼ **Delores Rocket**[13] 7953 3-8-8 **67**.........................(b) ShaneGray(5) 8 68
(Kevin Ryan) *chsd ldrs: rdn and hung rt over 2f out: styd on same pce fnl f* **25/1**
431- **4** 1 ¼ **Dream Scenario**[6] 8052 3-9-4 **72** 6ex.........................(v) DuranFentiman 3 69
(Mel Brittain) *hld up: hdwy and nt clr run over 1f out: sn rdn: styd on same pce fnl f* **8/1**
/41- **5** nse **Sugarformyhoney (IRE)**[21] 7836 4-9-3 **74**......................... RobertTart(3) 6 71
(Brendan Powell) *hld up: pushed along over 2f out: hdwy sn after: rdn over 1f out: no ex ins fnl f* **11/2**[3]
130- **6** 1 ½ **Imaginary World (IRE)**[61] 6941 5-8-10 **69**.........(p) GeorgeChaloner(5) 1 62
(John Balding) *prom: rdn over 2f out: wknd ins fnl f* **14/1**
/26- **7** 13 **Last Minute Lisa (IRE)**[73] 6613 3-8-10 **64**......................... WilliamCarson 5 22
(S Donohoe, Ire) *led: rdn and hdd 2f out: wknd over 1f out* **8/1**
531- **8** 1 **Fab Lolly (IRE)**[21] 7841 3-8-11 **65**......................... TedDurcan 2 20
(James Bethell) *hld up: rdn and wknd over 1f out: eased* **7/1**
1m 30.23s (0.63) **Going Correction** +0.20s/f (Slow) 8 Ran SP% **114.2**
Speed ratings (Par 100): **104,101,100,98,98 96,81,80**
toteswingers 1&2 £2.60, 1&3 £10.50, 2&3 £9.20 CSF £10.07 CT £146.13 TOTE £3.30: £1.10, £1.30, £5.50; EX 11.20 Trifecta £159.00 Pool: £3682.45 - 17.36 winning units..
Owner A W Bult **Bred** Harcourt Stud **Trained** Danethorpe, Notts
FOCUS
Not a bad fillies' handicap. The winner has a progressive Polytrack record.

8135 COMPARE BOOKMAKERS AT BOOKMAKERS.CO.UK H'CAP — 5f 20y(P)
4:05 (4:05) (Class 6) (0-65,65) 3-Y-0+ — **£1,940** (£577; £288; £144) **Stalls** Low

Form — RPR
605- **1** **Shawkantango**[26] 7772 6-9-5 **63**.........................(v) DaleSwift 8 74
(Derek Shaw) *hld up: pushed along 1/2-way: hdwy over 1f out: r.o u.p to ld wl ins fnl f* **7/1**
003- **2** 1 ¾ **I'll Be Good**[7] 8035 4-8-10 **57**......................... MarkCoumbe(3) 9 62
(Alan Berry) *led: rdn over 1f out: hdd wl ins fnl f* **6/1**[3]
000- **3** 1 ¼ **Roy's Legacy**[77] 6475 4-8-13 **62**......................... ShirleyTeasdale(5) 12 62
(Shaun Harris) *chsd ldrs: rdn over 1f out: styd on same pce ins fnl f* **20/1**
634- **4** nk **Hot Sugar (USA)**[28] 7728 4-9-4 **62**.........................(p) WilliamCarson 6 61+
(Michael Appleby) *hmpd s: hld up: rdn and r.o ins fnl f: nt rch ldrs* **4/1**[2]
100- **5** ¾ **Megaleka**[13] 7958 3-8-13 **57**......................... GrahamGibbons 13 53
(Alan Bailey) *prom: chsd ldr over 3f out: rdn and hung lft fr over 1f out: styd on same pce ins fnl f* **16/1**
034- **6** 1 **Quality Art (USA)**[16] 7937 5-9-0 **61**......................... BillyCray(3) 5 54
(Richard Guest) *hmpd s: hld up: r.o ins fnl f: nvr nrr* **8/1**
441- **7** hd **Passionada**[16] 7937 4-9-7 **65**......................... GrahamLee 11 57
(Ed McMahon) *w ldr tl over 3f out: rdn over 1f out: no ex ins fnl f* **5/2**[1]
033- **8** ½ **Prince Of Passion (CAN)**[6] 8049 5-9-0 **61**.........(p) RobertTart(3) 3 51
(Derek Shaw) *hmpd s: sn pushed along and prom: rdn over 1f out: no ex fnl f* **12/1**
052- **9** 1 **Above The Stars**[7] 8034 5-9-0 **58**.........................(p) TomEaves 4 45
(Conor Dore) *hmpd s: hld up: nt clr run 1/2-way and ins fnl f: nvr able to chal* **16/1**
005- **10** ½ **Speedyfix**[7] 8034 6-8-11 **60**.........................(t) EoinWalsh(5) 7 45
(Christine Dunnett) *mid-div: rdn and wknd over 1f out* **14/1**
315- **11** 4 ½ **Sarah Berry**[9] 8022 4-9-1 **59**.........................(v) LukeMorris 1 28
(Chris Dwyer) *wnt rt s: sn chsng ldrs: pushed along 1/2-way: rdn and wknd over 1f out* **16/1**
1m 3.04s (0.74) **Going Correction** +0.20s/f (Slow) 11 Ran SP% **123.2**
Speed ratings (Par 101): **102,99,97,96,95 93,93,92,91,90 83**
toteswingers 1&2 £9.20, 1&3 £22.10, 2&3 £32.80 CSF £51.19 CT £823.91 TOTE £12.70: £3.70, £3.00, £7.30; EX 65.40 Trifecta £2409.70 Part won. Pool: £3212.94 - 0.93 winning units..
Owner Shawthing Racing Partnership **Bred** Derek Shaw **Trained** Sproxton, Leics
FOCUS
A moderate but competitive sprint handicap. The race is rated around the back-to-form winner.
T/Plt: £21.60 to a £1 stake. Pool: £73938.07 - 2491.50 winning tickets T/Qpdt: £2.90 to a £1 stake. Pool: £8111.30 - 2015.15 winning tickets CR

8129 WOLVERHAMPTON (A.W) (L-H)
Tuesday, December 3

OFFICIAL GOING: Standard
Wind: Light behind Weather: Overcast

8136 CORAL APP DOWNLOAD FROM THE APP STORE AW "HANDS AND HEELS" APPRENTICE SERIES H'CAP — 1m 1f 103y(P)
2:10 (2:10) (Class 5) (0-75,73) 3-Y-0+ — **£2,911** (£866; £432; £216) **Stalls** Low

Form — RPR
026- **1** **Oratorio's Joy (IRE)**[13] 7970 3-9-1 **72**......................... RobHornby(3) 3 81
(Jamie Osborne) *a.p: chsd ldr over 1f out: shkn up to ld ins fnl f: edgd lft: r.o* **7/2**[3]
231- **2** 1 ¼ **Silly Billy (IRE)**[19] 7885 5-8-13 **65**.........................(p) JordanVaughan 5 72
(Brian Ellison) *trckd ldr tl led on bit 2f out: pushed along and hdd ins fnl f: styd on same pce* **2/1**[1]
514- **3** 4 ½ **Fresa**[14] 7961 4-9-7 **73**.........................(p) LouisSteward 4 71
(Sir Mark Prescott Bt) *chsd ldrs: pushed along over 3f out: edgd lft over 1f out: no ex ins fnl f* **5/2**[2]
504- **4** 7 **Ocean Applause**[22] 7841 3-9-1 **72**.........................(t) JordonMcMurray(3) 7 57
(John Ryan) *hld up: hdwy 1/2-way: pushed along over 2f out: hung lft and wknd over 1f out* **6/1**
060- **5** 2 **Jordaura**[11] 8006 7-8-2 **59** oh2......................... NicolaGrundy(5) 2 40
(Alan Berry) *dwlt: outpcd: nvr nrr* **20/1**

300- **6** ½ **Miami Gator (IRE)**[207] 2219 6-8-7 **62**...(v) BTTreanor(3) 1 42
(K R Burke) *led: pushed along and hdd 2f out: wknd over 1f out* **20/1**

000- **7** 7 **Standpoint**[14] 7961 7-9-0 **69**... JackGarritty(3) 6 36
(Conor Dore) *hld up: pushed along and wknd over 2f out* **33/1**

2m 3.11s (1.41) **Going Correction** +0.275s/f (Slow)
WFA 3 from 4yo+ 2lb **7** Ran SP% **110.9**
Speed ratings (Par 103): **104,102,98,92,90 90,84**
toteswingers 1&2 £1.90, 1&3 £1.90, 2&3 £1.50 CSF £10.18 TOTE £4.90: £2.80, £1.40; EX 11.40 Trifecta £26.50 Pool: £3959.33 - 111.88 winning units..
Owner Dominic Christian **Bred** R Mahon & J Reilly **Trained** Upper Lambourn, Berks

FOCUS
A modest "hands and heels" apprentice handicap, run at a fair pace. The winner has an obvious chance of a repeat win.

8137 32RED CASINO (S) STKS 7f 32y(P)
2:40 (2:40) (Class 6) 2-Y-O **£1,940** (£577; £288; £144) **Stalls** High

Form RPR

103- **1** **Howz The Family (IRE)**[15] 7945 2-9-3 66...(v) RichardKingscote 5 67+
(Tom Dascombe) *prom: lost pl over 4f out: pushed along and hdwy over 1f out: rdn to ld ins fnl f: sn clr* **9/4**[1]

36- **2** 3½ **Jaeger Connoisseur (IRE)**[26] 7788 2-8-7 52... MartinLane 7 48
(K R Burke) *hld up: hdwy over 2f out: sn chsng ldr: rdn over 1f out: styd on same pce ins fnl f* **5/1**[3]

012- **3** 2½ **Black Vale (IRE)**[7] 8045 2-9-3 60...(bt) PaddyAspell 6 52
(Phil McEntee) *s.i.s: hdwy over 5f out: led over 4f out: clr 3f out: rdn over 1f out: hdd and no ex ins fnl f* **6/1**

562- **4** 1¾ **Vodka Chaser (IRE)**[10] 8025 2-8-7 55... LukeMorris 8 38
(J S Moore) *chsd ldrs: rdn over 2f out: wknd ins fnl f* **7/1**

166- **5** 1¾ **May Whi (IRE)**[14] 7954 2-8-12 62...(b[1]) RobertWinston 3 39
(John Quinn) *chsd ldr tl over 4f out: wnt 2nd again 1/2-way: rdn over 1f out: wknd fnl f* **7/2**[2]

002- **6** 6 **Camatini (IRE)**[14] 7954 2-8-2 53...(p) ConnorBeasley(5) 4 19
(Michael Dods) *led: hdd over 4f out: rdn over 2f out: wkng whn hung lft over 1f out* **8/1**

05- **7** 1½ **Vision Of Rome**[10] 8025 2-8-0 0... DanielCremin(7) 2 15
(Mick Channon) *wnt lft s: hld up: pushed along 1/2-way: sn wknd* **25/1**

1m 31.96s (2.36) **Going Correction** +0.275s/f (Slow) **7** Ran SP% **111.4**
Speed ratings (Par 94): **97,93,90,88,86 79,77**
toteswingers 1&2 £3.00, 1&3 £2.00, 2&3 £5.90 CSF £13.03 TOTE £3.70: £1.70, £2.30; EX 14.00 Trifecta £93.60 Pool: £4236.52 - 33.93 winning units..There was no bid for the winner
Owner Ham N Eggers **Bred** S F Bloodstock LLC **Trained** Malpas, Cheshire

FOCUS
A moderate seller run at a strong pace. This suited the winner, who can rate back at around 70 in similar circumstances.

8138 32RED.COM MEDIAN AUCTION MAIDEN STKS 7f 32y(P)
3:10 (3:12) (Class 6) 2-Y-O **£1,940** (£577; £288; £144) **Stalls** High

Form RPR

03- **1** **Truancy (IRE)**[13] 7972 2-9-5 0... RobertWinston 5 71+
(K R Burke) *plld hrd and a.p: trckd ldr over 2f out: shkn up to ld ins fnl f: rdn out* **7/2**[3]

322- **2** *nk* **Bazooka (IRE)**[12] 7986 2-9-2 64... RobertTart(3) 9 70
(Ed de Giles) *mid-div: pushed along over 2f out: hdwy u.p over 1f out: r.o* **11/4**[2]

02- **3** 2¼ **Three Pips**[26] 7790 2-9-5 0... GrahamGibbons 2 66
(Ed McMahon) *chsd ldr tl led over 5f out: rdn and hdd ins fnl f: no ex towards fin* **5/2**[1]

45- **4** 3½ **Jayeff Herring (IRE)**[14] 7960 2-9-5 0... TomQueally 4 57+
(Michael Bell) *hld up: pushed along over 2f out: r.o u.p ins fnl f: nrst fin* **20/1**

0- **5** 2½ **Keep To The Beat**[125] 4880 2-8-9 0... ShaneGray(5) 7 46
(Kevin Ryan) *trckd ldrs: rdn over 1f out: wknd ins fnl f* **12/1**

6 1¼ **Honiton Lace** 2-9-0 0... MartinLane 6 42
(J W Hills) *s.i.s: sn pushed along in rr: n.d* **66/1**

34- **7** 4 **Nissaki Kasta**[50] 7244 2-9-0 0... MartinHarley 3 41+
(Hughie Morrison) *prom: hmpd and lost pl over 5f out: rdn and wknd over 1f out* **6/1**

40- **8** 1¾ **Classic Princess**[31] 7693 2-8-9 0... DanielMuscutt(5) 1 28
(Gay Kelleway) *led: hdd over 5f out: rdn over 2f out: wknd over 1f out* **25/1**

0- **9** 2¾ **Baytown Tigress**[17] 7934 2-9-0 0... PaddyAspell 10 21
(Phil McEntee) *sn pushed along in rr: hdwy over 5f out: rdn and wknd over 2f out* **100/1**

1m 31.81s (2.21) **Going Correction** +0.275s/f (Slow) **9** Ran SP% **110.5**
Speed ratings (Par 94): **98,97,95,91,88 86,82,80,77**
toteswingers 1&2 £2.50, 2&3 £2.00, 1&3 £2.90 CSF £12.45 TOTE £7.10: £2.40, £1.40, £1.10; EX 13.60 Trifecta £29.10 Pool: £5055.01 - 129.86 winning units..
Owner Market Avenue Racing Club Ltd **Bred** Keogh Family **Trained** Middleham Moor, N Yorks
■ Stewards' Enquiry : Graham Gibbons two-day ban: careless riding (Dec 17-18)

FOCUS
A modest maiden and something of a messy race. The winner built on his Kempton win.

8139 32RED H'CAP 1m 5f 194y(P)
3:40 (3:41) (Class 5) (0-75,75) 3-Y-O+ **£2,911** (£866; £432; £216) **Stalls** Low

Form RPR

042- **1** **Admirable Duque (IRE)**[8] 7220 7-9-2 **70**...(be) JoshBaudains(5) 3 78
(Dominic Ffrench Davis) *hld up: hdwy over 3f out: rdn over 1f out: styd on to ld wl ins fnl f* **12/1**

004- **2** ½ **Singzak**[15] 7950 5-9-8 **71**... GrahamGibbons 6 78
(Michael Easterby) *led at stdy pce tl qcknd over 2f out: rdn and hdd over 1f out: ev ch wl ins fnl f: styd on* **11/4**[1]

302- **3** 1¼ **Royal Alcor (IRE)**[28] 7758 6-9-7 **75**...(t) ShelleyBirkett(5) 2 80
(Gay Kelleway) *trckd ldrs: t.k.h: led over 1f out: sn rdn: hdd and unable qck wl ins fnl f* **3/1**[2]

023- **4** 3 **Gioia Di Vita**[35] 7596 3-9-4 **74**... TomEaves 7 75
(David Thompson) *prom: rdn and ev ch 2f out: no ex fnl f* **5/1**

005- **5** 2¾ **Peachez**[11] 8004 5-9-2 **70**...(p) AmyScott(5) 1 67
(Seamus Durack) *s.s: hld up and bhd: hdwy over 4f out: outpcd 3f out: n.d after* **8/1**

224- **6** ¾ **Alpine Mysteries (IRE)**[15] 7947 3-9-3 **73**... LukeMorris 5 69
(Harry Dunlop) *trckd ldr: pushed along and hmpd over 3f out: rdn over 2f out: sn outpcd* **4/1**[3]

430- **7** ½ **Tight Knit (USA)**[225] 1725 3-9-2 **72**... MartinHarley 4 67
(John Weymes) *s.i.s: hld up: rdn over 1f out: nvr trbld ldrs* **20/1**

3m 9.46s (3.46) **Going Correction** +0.275s/f (Slow)
WFA 3 from 5yo+ 7lb **7** Ran SP% **111.9**
Speed ratings (Par 103): **101,100,100,98,96 96,96**
toteswingers 1&2 £5.90, 1&3 £6.30, 2&3 £2.60 CSF £43.14 TOTE £18.50: £8.00, £2.80; EX 72.30 Trifecta £263.00 Pool: £4538.91 - 12.93 winning units..
Owner Mrs J E Taylor **Bred** Airlie Stud And R N Clay **Trained** Lambourn, Berks

FOCUS
An ordinary staying handicap and they didn't go much of a pace, resulting in a close finish. Straightforward form.

8140 LADBROKES MAIDEN STKS 7f 32y(P)
4:10 (4:12) (Class 5) 3-Y-O+ **£2,587** (£770; £384; £192) **Stalls** High

Form RPR

1 **Conversational (IRE)**[104] 5658 3-9-0 72... MartinHarley 1 72
(Mick Channon) *led 1f: remained handy: led on bit over 1f out: clr ins fnl f: easily* **11/10**[1]

304- **2** 4½ **Nifty Kier**[26] 7784 4-9-5 59... JohnFahy 3 62
(Martin Bosley) *hld up: hdwy over 2f out: rdn over 1f out: styd on to go 2nd nr fin: no ch w wnr* **8/1**[3]

002- **3** ¾ **Cash Is King**[17] 7924 3-9-5 69...(b) MartinLane 8 60
(Nick Littmoden) *led 6f out: rdn and hdd over 1f out: no ex ins fnl f* **5/4**[2]

452- **4** 1½ **Mid Yorkshire Golf**[11] 8003 4-8-11 46... SladeO'Hara(3) 4 51
(Peter Grayson) *hld up: rdn over 1f out: n.d* **25/1**

005- **5** 5 **Queen's Princess**[15] 7946 5-8-9 42...(p) AdamCarter(5) 5 39
(John Wainwright) *chsd ldr: rdn 1/2-way: wknd fnl f* **100/1**

00- **6** 6 **Moves Like Jagger (IRE)**[17] 7932 3-9-5 0... PaddyAspell 6 30
(Phil McEntee) *prom: rdn over 2f out: hung lft and wknd over 1f out* **50/1**

0/6- **7** 17 **Little Red Nell (IRE)**[12] 7987 4-9-0 0... RobertHavlin 2
(Martin Bosley) *prom: pushed along 1/2-way: wknd over 2f out: eased* **25/1**

1m 31.68s (2.08) **Going Correction** +0.275s/f (Slow) **7** Ran SP% **113.8**
Speed ratings (Par 103): **99,93,93,91,85 78,59**
toteswingers 1&2 £1.80, 1&3 £1.10, 2&3 £1.90 CSF £10.12 TOTE £1.90: £1.40, £2.60; EX 9.70 Trifecta £14.70 Pool: £7639.90 - 388.21 winning units..
Owner Mrs T Burns **Bred** South House Stud **Trained** West Ilsley, Berks

FOCUS
A very one-sided maiden, with the third below par.

8141 LADBROKES MOBILE MEDIAN AUCTION MAIDEN STKS 1m 141y(P)
4:40 (4:41) (Class 6) 3-5-Y-O **£1,940** (£577; £288; £144) **Stalls** Low

Form RPR

240- **1** **Heezararity**[81] 6358 5-9-7 66... GeorgeBaker 1 71+
(Jonathan Geake) *mde all: pushed clr over 1f out: comf* **6/4**[1]

05- **2** 5 **Eco Warrior**[115] 5281 3-9-5 0... MartinLane 5 61
(J W Hills) *s.i.s: hdwy over 5f out: rdn over 2f out: styd on same pce fr over 1f out: wnt 2nd wl ins fnl f* **4/1**[3]

/20- **3** 1¼ **Crossley**[14] 7964 4-9-7 60... BarryMcHugh 2 58
(Geoffrey Oldroyd) *chsd wnr: rdn over 2f out: no ex fr over 1f out* **7/2**[2]

4 9 **Another Journey**[168] 4-9-4 0... MarkCoumbe(3) 3 39
(Lisa Williamson) *s.i.s: hdwy over 4f out: rdn over 3f out: wknd over 2f out* **20/1**

5 1¾ **Echologic** 3-9-5 0... GrahamGibbons 4 35
(Brian Baugh) *chsd ldrs: rdn over 2f out: wknd over 1f out* **5/1**

0/0- **6** 9 **Cottam Stella**[46] 7345 5-8-11 42... AdamCarter(5) 6 11
(John Wainwright) *prom 4f* **33/1**

1m 53.69s (3.19) **Going Correction** +0.275s/f (Slow)
WFA 3 from 4yo+ 2lb **6** Ran SP% **106.6**
Speed ratings (Par 101): **96,91,90,82,80 72**
toteswingers 1&2 £1.80, 1&3 £1.40, 2&3 £1.20 CSF £6.87 TOTE £2.30: £1.30, £2.00; EX 4.40 Trifecta £11.20 Pool: £5853.09 - 391.00 winning units..
Owner Miss E J Tanner **Bred** D J Weston **Trained** Marlborough, Wilts

FOCUS
This was a particularly poor maiden. A straightforward victory for the winner, with the runner-up perhaps key.

8142 DOWNLOAD THE LADBROKES APP H'CAP 1m 141y(P)
5:10 (5:10) (Class 6) (0-55,55) 3-Y-O+ **£1,940** (£577; £288; £144) **Stalls** Low

Form RPR

024- **1** **Litmus (USA)**[13] 7981 4-9-3 **51**...(b) LukeMorris 7 60
(Simon Dow) *hld up in tch: trckd ldr over 3f out: led over 2f out: rdn and hung lft fnl f: styd on* **16/1**

143- **2** ¾ **Quadriga (IRE)**[13] 7980 3-9-3 **53**... JimmyQuinn 11 60
(Robert Eddery) *sn prom: edgd lft over 7f out: chsd wnr over 2f out: styd on u.p* **9/2**[3]

302- **3** 1 **Reggie Bond**[25] 7806 3-9-3 **53**...(p) RobertWinston 4 58
(Geoffrey Oldroyd) *mid-div: hmpd over 7f out: hdwy over 2f out: sn rdn: hung lft and styd on u.p to go 3rd wl ins fnl f: nt rch ldrs* **9/4**[1]

00- **4** 1 **Six Silver Lane**[181] 2982 5-9-5 **53**...(v) GeorgeBaker 6 56+
(Derek Shaw) *trckd ldrs: rdn over 1f out: styd on same pce ins fnl f* **11/4**[2]

000- **5** 4½ **Ellaal**[7] 8055 4-9-4 **52**... DaleSwift 9 46
(Ruth Carr) *prom: lost pl after 1f: rdn over 2f out: r.o ins fnl f: nt trble ldrs* **50/1**

0/0- **6** ¾ **Vegas Belle**[52] 7204 3-8-12 **48**... BarryMcHugh 2 40
(Geoffrey Oldroyd) *hld up: nt clr run over 2f out: styd on fr over 1f out: n.d* **66/1**

000- **7** *shd* **Starbotton**[14] 7953 3-8-8 **49**... ShirleyTeasdale(5) 3 44
(James Bethell) *led 1f: chsd ldrs: hmpd and lost pl wl over 1f out: n.d after* **50/1**

004- **8** ¾ **Silver Fawn (IRE)**[14] 7962 3-8-10 **46** oh1...(e[1]) MartinHarley 8 36
(John Weymes) *hld up: nvr on terms* **16/1**

303- **9** 2½ **Lambert Pen (USA)**[55] 7124 3-8-11 **54**... DanielCremin(7) 1 39
(Mick Channon) *prom: lost pl 4f out: rdn over 2f out: sn wknd* **12/1**

6/6- **10** 6 **Louis Vee (IRE)**[7] 8054 5-8-12 **46**... TomEaves 5 19
(Roy Brotherton) *s.i.s: hdwy 1/2-way: rdn and wknd over 2f out* **100/1**

604- **11** 7 **Angel Grigio**[18] 7904 3-8-10 **46** oh1... GrahamGibbons 13 4+
(David O'Meara) *plld hrd: led after 1f: rdn and hdd over 2f out: edgd lft: wknd over 1f out* **16/1**

050- **12** 14 **Follow The Flag (IRE)**[14] 7951 9-9-0 **48**...(v) TomQueally 10
(Alan McCabe) *sn outpcd* **25/1**

1m 52.2s (1.70) **Going Correction** +0.275s/f (Slow)
WFA 3 from 4yo+ 2lb **12** Ran SP% **111.2**
Speed ratings (Par 101): **103,102,101,100,96 95,95,95,92,87 81,68**
CSF £79.52 CT £223.90 TOTE £10.10: £2.80, £1.60, £1.20; EX 28.80 Trifecta £68.90 Pool: £5801.34 - 63.06 winning units..
Owner T G Parker **Bred** Millsec Ltd **Trained** Epsom, Surrey

FOCUS
A fair handicap for the grade, but despite the size of the field not many got into this. The winner improved a little on recent course form.
T/Plt: £20.20. Pool: £61,913.65 - 2235.13 winning units. T/Qpdt: £7.60. Pool: £8446.16 - 818.47 winning units. CR

7570 DEAUVILLE (R-H)
Tuesday, December 3

OFFICIAL GOING: Fibresand: standard

8143a PRIX SOLEIL (CONDITIONS) (2YO COLTS & GELDINGS) (ROUND COURSE) (FIBRESAND) 7f 110y
11:00 (12:00) 2-Y-O £13,821 (£5,528; £4,146; £2,764; £1,382)

RPR
1 **Complicit (IRE)**[10] 8018 2-9-0 0 GrahamLee 3 95
(Paul Cole) *trcking ldr 1/2-way: ldng whn c into view over 1f out: pushed out ins fnl f: comf* **13/5**[2]
2 ¾ **Zvarov (IRE)**[33] 2-9-0 0 IoritzMendizabal 4 93
(J-C Rouget, France) **4/5**[1]
3 2 **Darselect**[14] 2-9-0 0 GregoryBenoist 2 89
(Mme Pia Brandt, France) **78/10**
4 1 **Footclass (IRE)** 2-8-7 0 ThomasMessina 6 79
(X Nakkachdji, France) **25/1**
5 1½ **Arpegio (FR)**[90] 2-8-10 0 TheoBachelot 7 79
(S Wattel, France) **27/1**
6 1¼ **Mister Worldwide (FR)**[17] 7939 2-9-0 0 StephanePasquier 5 80
(Y Gourraud, France) **15/2**[3]
7 2½ **Teardrops (FR)** 2-9-0 0 AnthonyCrastus 8 74
(R Chotard, France) **32/1**
8 5 **Seven Des Aigles (FR)** 2-8-7 0 AntoineCoutier 1 55
(F Chappet, France) **62/1**
1m 31.94s (91.94) 8 Ran SP% **118.5**
WIN (incl. 1 euro stake): 3.60. PLACES: 1.10, 1.10, 1.10. DF: 2.10. SF: 4.60.
Owner T A Rahman **Bred** Barouche Stud Ireland Ltd **Trained** Whatcombe, Oxon

8144 - (Foreign Racing) - See Raceform Interactive

8121 KEMPTON (A.W) (R-H)
Wednesday, December 4

OFFICIAL GOING: Standard
Wind: Almost nil Weather: Clear

8145 £500 FREE BETS AT BETDAQ EBF MAIDEN FILLIES' STKS 6f (P)
3:50 (3:51) (Class 5) 2-Y-O £2,911 (£866; £432; £216) Stalls Low

Form RPR
03- 1 **Lady Crossmar (IRE)**[28] 7763 2-9-0 0 SeanLevey 10 73
(Richard Hannon Snr) *trckd ldr after 1f: led jst over 2f out: drvn over 1f out: styd on wl* **4/1**[3]
2 1¾ **Garraun (IRE)** 2-9-0 0 GrahamLee 7 68+
(Jeremy Noseda) *restless stalls: trckd ldrs in 4th: shkn up over 1f out: prog to take 2nd last 100yds: styd on but no imp on wnr* **9/4**[1]
3 2 **Rosie Prospects** 2-9-0 0 RobertHavlin 3 62
(Roger Ingram) *chsd ldr 1f: styd cl up in 3rd: rdn and tried to chal 2f out: one pce over 1f out* **33/1**
5- 4 ½ **Shushu Sugartown (IRE)**[14] 7971 2-9-0 0 TomQueally 6 60
(Ian Williams) *s.i.s: t.k.h in 5th: prog to chal 2f out: nt qckn and hld 1f out: wknd ins fnl f* **5/2**[2]
0- 5 ½ **Sweet Cherry (IRE)**[40] 7501 2-9-0 0 FergusSweeney 8 59
(Pat Murphy) *hld up in 6th: shkn up over 1f out: kpt on steadily wout threatening* **25/1**
0- 6 5 **Whispering Star (USA)**[114] 5352 2-9-0 0 MartinLane 2 44
(David Simcock) *a in last pair: struggling 2f out* **4/1**[3]
- 7 6 **Mirror (IRE)** 2-9-0 0 MartinHarley 5 26
(Ed Dunlop) *led to jst over 2f out: wknd rapidly* **7/1**
1m 14.27s (1.17) **Going Correction** -0.025s/f (Stan) 7 Ran SP% **118.6**
Speed ratings (Par 93): **91,88,86,85,84 78,70**
toteswingers 1&2 £2.50, 1&3 £9.20, 2&3 £5.70 CSF £14.23 TOTE £4.20: £2.70, £1.60; EX 11.70 Trifecta £149.90 Pool: £4230.59 - 21.16 winning units..
Owner Middleham Park Racing Vi **Bred** Scuderia San Pancrazio **Trained** East Everleigh, Wilts

FOCUS
Not much strength in depth to the opening fillies' maiden. The winner was firmly on top.

8146 BETDAQ - THE SPORTS BETTING EXCHANGE MAIDEN STKS 6f (P)
4:20 (4:20) (Class 5) 3-Y-O+ £2,587 (£770; £384; £192) Stalls Low

Form RPR
/25- 1 **Dutiful Son (IRE)**[47] 7345 3-9-5 65 GrahamLee 3 74+
(Jeremy Noseda) *dwlt sltly: hld up in last trio: swtchd lft and prog over 1f out: chsd ldr jst ins fnl f: one reminder and clsd to ld last 100yds: pushed out: readily* **11/10**[1]
3- 2 1 **Ex Ex**[7] 8070 3-9-5 0 MartinLane 5 71
(Nick Littmoden) *trckd ldrs gng easily: prog to ld wl over 1f out: drvn sn after: styd on but hdd and outpcd last 100yds* **7/4**[2]
/44- 3 3 **Ostralegus**[7] 8070 3-9-5 0 TomQueally 4 61
(John Gallagher) *chsd ldng pair: clsd to chal and upsides 2f out: chsd ldr tl jst ins fnl f: outpcd* **6/1**[3]
040- 4 5 **Monty Fay (IRE)**[30] 7729 4-9-5 46 LiamKeniry 6 45
(Derek Haydn Jones) *walked to post early: w ldr and clr of rest: lost 2nd wl over 1f out: wknd qckly fnl f* **25/1**
400- 5 nk **Christopher Chua (IRE)**[21] 7850 4-9-0 45 (v) JackDuern(5) 7 44
(Michael Scudamore) *s.s: mostly in last pair: rdn and tried to make prog over 2f out: no hdwy 1f out: wknd* **33/1**
062- 6 ½ **Minty Jones**[106] 5614 4-9-0 43 (v) JoeyHaynes(5) 1 43
(Michael Mullineaux) *racd freely: led to wl over 1f out: wknd qckly fnl f* **16/1**
6- 7 2½ **Vermuyden**[35] 7625 4-9-2 0 (t) RossAtkinson(3) 2 35
(Pam Sly) *in tch: reminders over 2f out: wknd over 1f out* **12/1**
650- 8 1¼ **Elounta**[106] 5602 3-9-0 44 [1] LukeMorris 9 26
(John Best) *a in rr: struggling over 2f out* **33/1**
1m 12.41s (-0.69) **Going Correction** -0.025s/f (Stan) 8 Ran SP% **121.6**
Speed ratings (Par 103): **103,101,97,91,90 89,86,84**
toteswingers 1&2 £1.10, 1&3 £1.90, 2&3 £2.60 CSF £3.43 TOTE £2.00: £1.10, £1.40, £1.90; EX 4.20 Trifecta £12.70 Pool: £5625.59 - 330.14 winning units..
Owner Nigel O'Sullivan **Bred** Lodge Park Stud **Trained** Newmarket, Suffolk

FOCUS
Once again, there was little depth to this maiden. There was a decent pace and the front two were entitled to pull clear. It was almost two seconds quicker than the opener. The third helps set the level.

8147 WINNERS ARE WELCOME AT BETDAQ NURSERY H'CAP 1m (P)
4:50 (4:51) (Class 5) (0-75,75) 2-Y-O £2,587 (£770; £384; £192) Stalls Low

Form RPR
110- 1 **Hedge End (IRE)**[27] 7782 2-9-6 74 SeanLevey 7 79
(Richard Hannon Snr) *hld up in last: gd prog fr 2f out to ld 1f out: drvn and styd on wl* **8/1**
030- 2 1¾ **Irish Tears**[49] 7302 2-9-3 71 (t) RobertHavlin 8 72
(John Gosden) *sn restrained into last pair: sme prog 2f out: nt qckn over 1f out: styd on fnl f to take 2nd last stride* **9/1**
051- 3 hd **Fiftyshadesfreed (IRE)**[14] 7973 2-9-0 68 JimCrowley 5 69
(George Baker) *w.w in 5th: prog to trck ldr wl over 1f out: clsd and upsides whn wnr wnt past 1f out: styd on same pce after: lost 2nd last stride* **4/1**[2]
431- 4 3¼ **Castle Combe (IRE)**[14] 7979 2-9-7 75 (v) MartinDwyer 1 68+
(Marcus Tregoning) *chsd clr ldr: rdn over 2f out: lost 2nd wl over 1f out: steadily fdd fnl f* **3/1**[1]
463- 5 ¾ **Mersad (IRE)**[14] 7973 2-8-12 66 LukeMorris 3 57+
(James Tate) *trckd ldng pair: rdn 2f out: tried to cl u.p but no hdwy over 1f out: fdd fnl f* **3/1**[1]
536- 6 1¾ **Captain Swift (IRE)**[27] 7782 2-9-4 72 MartinLane 4 59
(Brian Meehan) *hld up in 6th: pushed along and no prog over 2f out: wl btn whn shkn up over 1f out* **11/2**[3]
135- 7 3½ **Aspirant**[62] 6972 2-8-13 67 WilliamCarson 6 46
(Bill Turner) *led: set reasonable pce but 6 l clr 1/2-way: wandered u.p fr 2f out: hdd & wknd 1f out* **25/1**
404- 8 8 **Shore Patrol (IRE)**[19] 7901 2-8-13 67 TonyHamilton 2 28
(Richard Fahey) *in tch: u.p wl over 2f out: sn wknd and bhd* **25/1**
1m 39.48s (-0.32) **Going Correction** -0.025s/f (Stan) 8 Ran SP% **114.2**
Speed ratings (Par 96): **100,98,98,94,94 92,88,80**
toteswingers 1&2 £9.80, 1&3 £3.20, 2&3 £6.70 CSF £76.06 CT £328.57 TOTE £8.60: £2.20, £3.40, £1.30; EX 50.10 Trifecta £481.40 Pool: £4207.45 - 6.55 winning units..
Owner Grimes, Ivory, Bull, Hannon **Bred** Airlie Stud **Trained** East Everleigh, Wilts

FOCUS
9lb covered the field and a case could have made for most of these in what looked a fair race. An unsatisfactory result though with those who chased the strong pace set by Aspirant fading right out of it and the first three home all held up. The winner did it well off a very fair mark.

8148 BOOK NOW FOR BOXING DAY H'CAP (DIV I) 1m 4f (P)
5:20 (5:20) (Class 6) (0-55,55) 3-Y-O+ £1,940 (£577; £288; £144) Stalls Centre

Form RPR
334- 1 **Jamaica Grande**[21] 7857 5-9-7 55 GrahamLee 9 64
(Dave Morris) *t.k.h: hld up in last: prog over 3f out: rdn to chse ldr 1f out: styd on wl to ld last strides* **4/1**[2]
434- 2 nk **Princess Willow**[35] 7628 5-9-6 54 JimmyQuinn 5 63
(John E Long) *t.k.h early: trckd ldng trio: drvn to ld wl over 1f out: kpt on fnl f: hdd last strides* **8/1**
305- 3 2¾ **Geeaitch**[12] 8006 4-9-5 53 WilliamCarson 1 57
(Peter Hiatt) *led: 4 l clr 4f out: edgd lft and hdd wl over 1f out: one pce* **12/1**
556- 4 1 **Ice Tres**[157] 3854 4-9-2 50 DavidProbert 8 53
(Rod Millman) *chsd ldr: clsd to chal and upsides 2f out: one pce u.p after* **25/1**
445- 5 ½ **Greyemkay**[15] 7962 5-8-8 49 DanielCremin(7) 4 51
(Richard Price) *in tch in midfield: rdn 3f out: plugged on same pce fr over 2f out: n.d* **20/1**
3- 6 1¾ **Koos (GER)**[19] 7907 5-9-0 48 MartinHarley 12 47
(Marco Botti) *hld up in midfield: prog over 3f out to trck ldrs: rdn over 2f out: no imp over 1f out* **7/2**[1]
600- 7 ½ **The Yank**[16] 6137 4-9-2 50 LiamKeniry 7 48
(Tony Carroll) *dwlt: hld up in rr: prog over 3f out: nt clr run on inner over 2f out: no imp over 1f out: kpt on* **33/1**
600- 8 2¾ **Merrjanah**[14] 7984 5-8-13 47 PaddyAspell 6 41
(John Wainwright) *wl in rr: rdn over 3f out: lft bhd over 2f out and nt looking too keen: plugged on: lame* **25/1**
353- 9 13 **Trulee Scrumptious**[13] 7987 4-9-4 52 (be) RobertWinston 11 25
(Peter Charalambous) *racd wd in midfield: rdn 4f out: struggling over 2f out: eased and t.o* **20/1**
026- 10 4½ **El Libertador (USA)**[19] 7899 7-9-1 54 (b) JoeyHaynes(5) 3 20
(Eric Wheeler) *chsd ldng pair: u.p 3f out: wknd rapidly wl over 1f out: t.o* **16/1**
156- 11 ¾ **Instinctual**[48] 5178 3-8-8 50 ow1 (p) RobertTart(3) 10 15
(Brendan Powell) *a in rr: u.p on outer over 4f out: no prog: t.o* **8/1**
040- 12 5 **Jackaddock**[22] 7847 3-9-2 55 TedDurcan 14 12
(James Bethell) *dwlt: prog to trck ldrs after 2f and racd on outer: rdn 4f out: wknd over 2f out: eased and t.o* **6/1**[3]
/00- 13 44 **Granule**[41] 7490 3-8-13 52 ShaneKelly 2
(Peter Chapple-Hyam) *dwlt: sn in midfield: lost pl rapidly 4f out and sn last: wl t.o and eased* **16/1**
005- R **Azabitmour (FR)**[11] 8031 3-8-12 51 (b) LukeMorris 13
(John Best) *ref to r: tk no part* **14/1**
2m 33.42s (-1.08) **Going Correction** -0.025s/f (Stan)
WFA 3 from 4yo+ 5lb 14 Ran SP% **125.0**
Speed ratings (Par 101): **102,101,99,99,98 97,97,95,86,83 83,80,50,**
toteswingers 1&2 £6.00, 1&3 £10.50, 2&3 £16.00 CSF £34.69 CT £368.53 TOTE £3.30: £1.80, £2.00, £6.10; EX 17.80 Trifecta £329.30 Pool: £3041.69 - 6.92 winning units..
Owner Stuart Wood **Bred** Mrs J A Gawthorpe **Trained** Baxter's Green, Suffolk

FOCUS
A bit faster than division II, and sound form.

8149 BOOK NOW FOR BOXING DAY H'CAP (DIV II) 1m 4f (P)
5:50 (5:54) (Class 6) (0-55,54) 3-Y-O+ £1,940 (£577; £288; £144) Stalls Centre

Form RPR
606- 1 **This Is Me**[15] 7951 5-9-5 52 GrahamLee 11 63
(Don Cantillon) *hld up in midfield: prog to trck ldrs over 2f out: chsd ldr over 1f out: rdn to ld last 150yds: sn clr* **4/1**[2]
000- 2 2¼ **Bennelong**[48] 7321 7-9-3 50 (b) AmirQuinn 9 57
(Lee Carter) *sn trckd ldng pair: led over 2f out gng strly: rdn over 1f out: hdd and outpcd last 150yds* **10/1**
546- 3 1¼ **Celtic Charlie (FR)**[2] 1348 8-9-5 52 (t) FergusSweeney 6 57
(Pat Phelan) *hld up in last quartet: prog over 2f out gng wl: rdn over 1f out: styd on to take 3rd fnl f but ldng pair long gone* **14/1**

040- **4** 1 **Polydamos**[63] 6933 4-9-1 **48** AdamKirby 5 51
(Tony Carroll) *hld up in midfield: prog on inner over 2f out: disp 2nd briefly wl over 1f out: one pce after* **8/1**[3]
605- **5** ½ **Xclusive**[29] 7753 3-8-10 **48** LukeMorris 3 51
(Ronald Harris) *in tch in midfield: reminder 4f out: prog and cl up over 2f out: drvn to chse ldr 2f out to over 1f out: one pce* **16/1**
000- **6** ½ **Primacy (IRE)**[11] 8027 4-9-3 **50** LiamKeniry 8 52
(Neil Mulholland) *v reluctant to enter stalls: hld up in last pair: sme prog 2f out: rdn over 1f out: styd on fnl f: no ch* **50/1**
001- **7** hd **Shirazz**[15] 7962 4-9-6 **53** GeorgeBaker 14 54
(Seamus Durack) *hld up in rr: gng wl enough whn nt clr run jst over 2f out: pushed along and styd on fr over 1f out: no ch* **3/1**[1]
246- **8** ¾ **Poncho**[8] 8047 4-9-0 **47** (b[1]) ChrisCatlin 2 47
(Mark Rimell) *trckd ldr: rdn over 2f out: steadily fdd fr over 1f out* **14/1**
050- **9** 3 ¼ **Kindia (IRE)**[18] 7922 5-9-3 **50** (p) RobertHavlin 13 45
(Michael Attwater) *hld up in last pair: swtchd to outer and tried to make prog 2f out: no ch of being involved and passed only a few stragglers* **25/1**
000- **10** 1 ¼ **Hartlebury**[18] 7922 3-8-13 **51** TedDurcan 4 44
(James Bethell) *cl up bhd ldrs: nt qckn and lost pl jst over 2f out: sn btn* **25/1**
046- **11** hd **Day In Day Out**[29] 7741 3-9-0 **52** (p) JimCrowley 12 45
(Seamus Mullins) *trckd ldrs on outer: rdn 2f out: wknd over 1f out* **10/1**
4/4- **12** 3 ¼ **Mister Frosty (IRE)**[15] 7951 7-9-2 **54** EoinWalsh(5) 7 42
(Christine Dunnett) *racd wd towards rr: rdn and no rspnse over 2f out: wl btn after* **8/1**[3]
004- **13** 10 **Rhinestone Rebel (IRE)**[30] 7734 7-9-7 **54** WilliamCarson 1 26
(Peter Hiatt) *led at mod pce: hdd over 2f out: wknd rapidly: t.o* **20/1**
066- **14** 5 **Birdie King**[14] 7980 3-8-12 **50** TomQueally 10 14
(Gary Moore) *s.i.s: sn rcvrd and prom on outer: wknd over 2f out: t.o* **14/1**

2m 34.21s (-0.29) **Going Correction** -0.025s/f (Stan)
WFA 3 from 4yo+ 5lb **14** Ran SP% **125.7**
Speed ratings (Par 101): **99,97,96,96,95 95,95,94,92,91 91,89,82,79**
toteswingers 1&2 £11.30, 1&3 £12.40, 2&3 £32.00 CSF £44.13 CT £531.91 TOTE £6.60: £2.40, £5.30, £4.40; EX 70.30 Trifecta £2382.20 Pool: £3199.95 - 1.00 winning units..
Owner Don Cantillon **Bred** Peter E Clinton **Trained** Newmarket, Suffolk

FOCUS
More moderate fare in the uncompetitive second division, but arguably the more interesting division. The winner is the type to do better.

8150 BETDAQ 1ST UK RACE COMMISSION FREE H'CAP (LONDON MIDDLE DISTANCE SERIES QUALIFIER) 1m 3f (P)
6:20 (6:21) (Class 3) (0-95,95) 3-Y-O+
£7,158 (£2,143; £1,071; £535; £267; £134) **Stalls** Low

Form RPR
452- **1** **Halfsin (IRE)**[12] 8007 5-8-13 **84** (t) MartinHarley 3 94
(Marco Botti) *won battle for ld then set ordinary pce after 3f: mde all: wound up fr over 3f out: urged along and asserted over 1f out: rdn out* **10/1**
316- **2** 2 ½ **Stevie Thunder**[19] 7906 8-8-10 **81** (p) GrahamLee 1 87
(Ian Williams) *tried to ld but forced to trck wnr then t.k.h: rdn over 2f out: nt qckn over 1f out: kpt on* **16/1**
655- **3** 1 ½ **Icebuster**[14] 7976 5-8-8 **84** ShelleyBirkett(5) 2 87
(Rod Millman) *t.k.h: hld up in 5th: rapid prog on outer 4f out to press ldng pair over 3f out: nt qckn and lost pl 2f out: kpt on fnl f* **7/1**
531- **4** ¾ **Presburg (IRE)**[14] 7976 4-8-6 **82** GeorgeChaloner(5) 6 83
(Joseph Tuite) *hld up in last pair: shkn up whn dash for home sed over 2f out: kpt on but no ch of being involved* **7/2**[3]
215- **5** 2 ¼ **Nautilus**[49] 7304 3-9-6 **95** RobertHavlin 4 92
(John Gosden) *t.k.h: trckd ldrs: dropped to rr over 3f out: outpcd over 2f out: no imp on ldrs after* **9/4**[1]
1/0- **6** 1 **Miss Blakeney**[184] 2939 4-8-10 **81** oh1 (v) MartinDwyer 7 77
(Marcus Tregoning) *t.k.h: trckd ldrs: rdn to dispute 2nd 2f out: nt qckn over 1f out: wknd qckly fnl f* **25/1**
/01- **7** 4 ½ **Omar Khayyam**[66] 6869 4-9-0 **85** (t) DavidProbert 5 73
(Andrew Balding) *hld up in last pair: shkn up over 2f out: pce lifted and no ch after* **3/1**[2]

2m 20.58s (-1.32) **Going Correction** -0.025s/f (Stan)
WFA 3 from 4yo+ 4lb **7** Ran SP% **109.3**
Speed ratings (Par 107): **103,101,100,99,97 97,93**
toteswingers 1&2 £8.90, 1&3 £10.80, 2&3 £12.70 CSF £132.25 TOTE £13.30: £7.00, £3.80; EX 88.30 Trifecta £375.60 Pool: £3158.08 - 6.30 winning units..
Owner Dr Marwan Koukash **Bred** Glending Bloodstock **Trained** Newmarket, Suffolk

FOCUS
Easily the best race on the card and the final qualifier for the London Middle Distance Final worth £70,000 to be run next week. An uneven gallop and those prominent were favoured. Muddling form.

8151 MIX BUSINESS WITH PLEASURE AT KEMPTON H'CAP 7f (P)
6:50 (6:50) (Class 6) (0-60,60) 3-Y-O+ **£1,940** (£577; £288; £144) **Stalls** Low

Form RPR
500- **1** **Ivor's Princess**[23] 7836 4-9-6 **59** (b) SeanLevey 3 68
(Rod Millman) *rousted and reminders early: towards rr: prog on inner fr 2f out: drvn and r.o wl fnl f to ld last 75yds* **20/1**
013- **2** ¾ **One Last Dream**[21] 7858 4-9-4 **57** (b) DavidProbert 12 64
(Ron Hodges) *led: styd on wl whn pressed fr 2f out: hdd and outpcd last 75yds* **8/1**
112- **3** nk **Princess Spirit**[2] 8125 4-8-12 **58** (p) JenniferFerguson(7) 6 64+
(Edward Creighton) *hld up in last trio: rdn and prog over 1f out: styd on to take 3rd last 75yds: unable to chal* **3/1**[2]
561- **4** ¾ **Perfect Pastime**[7] 8073 5-8-11 **57** (b) DanielCremin(7) 14 61
(Jim Boyle) *t.k.h: trckd ldr: rdn to chal over 1f out: urged along and fdd last 100yds* **7/1**[3]
054- **5** 1 **Wishformore (IRE)**[7] 8073 6-8-9 **51** (p) RossAtkinson(3) 1 52
(Zoe Davison) *t.k.h: trckd ldng pair: rdn over 2f out: nt qckn over 1f out: one pce after* **25/1**
401- **6** ½ **Multitask**[42] 7465 3-9-6 **59** GeorgeBaker 11 59+
(Michael Madgwick) *stdd s: plld hrd: hld up in last trio: taken wd and pushed along over 2f out: no prog tl shkn up and styd on fnl f: no ch* **15/8**[1]
626- **7** ½ **Hinton Admiral**[11] 8022 9-9-4 **57** LukeMorris 5 56
(Pat Eddery) *wl in tch: rdn to chse ldrs 2f out: nt qckn over 1f out: one pce and no imp after* **20/1**
066- **8** ½ **West Leake (IRE)**[11] 8019 7-9-7 **60** LiamKeniry 9 57
(Paul Burgoyne) *nvr bttr than midfield: shkn up wl over 1f out: one pce and no threat to ldrs* **16/1**
230- **9** ½ **Hot Mustard**[27] 7784 3-9-4 **57** TomQueally 7 53
(Michael Bell) *hld up towards rr: pushed along and no prog 2f out: nvr on terms after* **10/1**
600- **10** shd **Ryan Style (IRE)**[11] 8022 7-9-2 **55** (tp) GrahamLee 4 51
(Lisa Williamson) *rrd bdly s and nrly uns rdr: racd in last: rdn 2f out: kpt on but n.d* **33/1**
000- **11** ¾ **My Sweet Lord**[11] 8022 3-9-2 **55** RichardKingscote 10 49
(Mark Usher) *trckd ldrs: rdn 2f out: no imp on ldrs over 1f out: fdd fnl f* **33/1**
200- **12** 19 **Dee Aitch Dove**[80] 6436 3-9-2 **55** (t) JimCrowley 2
(George Baker) *trckd ldrs tl wknd rapidly over 1f out: t.o* **33/1**

1m 25.97s (-0.03) **Going Correction** -0.025s/f (Stan) **12** Ran SP% **120.6**
Speed ratings (Par 101): **99,98,97,96,95 95,94,94,93,93 92,70**
toteswingers 1&2 £67.00, 1&3 £17.30, 2&3 £5.20 CSF £162.10 CT £631.68 TOTE £29.40: £4.30, £2.80, £1.40; EX 351.80 Trifecta £1616.80 Part won. Pool: £2155.85 - 0.76 winning units..
Owner P G Gibbins & Ivor Perry **Bred** The Three Point Partnership **Trained** Kentisbeare, Devon

FOCUS
A bit of a turn up with an out-of-form filly beating some in-form horses in this modest race. The winner is rated to his best form in the past year.

8152 KEMPTON.CO.UK H'CAP 6f (P)
7:20 (7:21) (Class 6) (0-60,62) 3-Y-O+ **£1,940** (£577; £288; £144) **Stalls** Low

Form RPR
160- **1** **New Rich**[11] 8023 3-9-5 **59** (p) JohnFahy 2 70
(Eve Johnson Houghton) *w.w in rr: prog on inner 2f out: drvn over 1f out: edgd lft but clsd to ld last 150yds: styd on* **7/1**
402- **2** ½ **Ivestar (IRE)**[30] 7729 8-9-2 **56** (v) GrahamGibbons 1 65
(Michael Easterby) *in tch in midfield: prog on inner over 2f out: drvn to ld wl over 1f out: hdd last 150yds: kpt on but hld* **7/2**[2]
006- **3** 1 ¼ **Lastkingofscotland (IRE)**[9] 8037 7-9-2 **59** (b) RyanPowell(3) 8 64+
(Conor Dore) *bdly squeezed out s: off the pce in last pair: rdn over 2f out: r.o fr over 1f out: tk 3rd nr fin* **14/1**
006- **4** 1 ¼ **Torres Del Paine**[13] 7985 6-9-3 **57** AdamKirby 10 58
(Brett Johnson) *wnt rt s: off the pce in last pair: shkn up 2f out: swtchd lft over 1f out: prog fnl f: one pce last 100yds* **11/2**[3]
340- **5** ½ **Alfresco**[104] 5677 9-9-2 **56** (v) GeorgeBaker 11 55
(Martin Bosley) *led at str pce: hdd and nt qckn wl over 1f out: one pce after* **25/1**
451- **6** ½ **Fathom Five (IRE)**[8] 8048 9-9-8 **62** 6ex PaddyAspell 3 60
(Shaun Harris) *trckd ldng trio: clsd to chal and upsides 2f out: nt qckn over 1f out: grad fdd* **16/1**
542- **7** 1 ¾ **Pharoh Jake**[11] 8023 5-9-3 **57** KieranO'Neill 12 49
(John Bridger) *chsd ldr to 2f out: steadily fdd* **12/1**
000- **8** ¾ **Night Trade (IRE)**[15] 7958 6-9-3 **57** (b[1]) LukeMorris 4 47
(Ronald Harris) *chsd ldng pair: drvn and cl up 2f out: sn nt qckn and btn: wknd fnl f* **20/1**
055- **9** 5 **Reginald Claude**[83] 6343 5-8-13 **58** DanielMuscutt(5) 5 32
(Mark Usher) *in tch: shkn up and no prog over 2f out: sn lost pl and btn* **14/1**
060- **10** 3 ¾ **Ovatory**[11] 8019 3-9-6 **60** (b[1]) JimCrowley 7 22
(Amanda Perrett) *wnt lft s: a wl in rr: rdn and no prog 2f out: wl btn after* **6/4**[1]

1m 12.07s (-1.03) **Going Correction** -0.025s/f (Stan) **10** Ran SP% **125.6**
Speed ratings (Par 101): **105,104,102,101,100 99,97,96,89,84**
toteswingers 1&2 £4.80, 1&3 £17.60, 2&3 £10.40 CSF £34.38 CT £360.95 TOTE £8.40: £2.50, £2.50, £2.80; EX 38.90 Trifecta £868.40 Pool: £2949.55 - 2.54 winning units..
Owner Eden Racing Club **Bred** Whitsbury Manor Stud And Mrs M E Slade **Trained** Blewbury, Oxon

FOCUS
Another modest race to close proceedings and the constant stream of money for Ovatory proved misplaced as he finished last. They went a decent clip courtesy of Alfresco and as a result it was faster than the two earlier maidens over the same distance. The runner-up is a fair guide to the form.

T/Jkpt: Part won. £17750.00 to a £1 stake. Pool: £25000.00 - 0.50 winning tickets. T/Plt: £313.10 to a £1 stake. Pool: £80223.61 - 187.02 winning tickets T/Qpdt: £194.10 to a £1 stake. Pool: £7818.92 - 29.80 winning tickets JN

8066 LINGFIELD (L-H)
Wednesday, December 4

OFFICIAL GOING: Standard
Wind: light, across Weather: dry

8153 32RED NURSERY H'CAP 1m (P)
12:00 (12:00) (Class 3) (0-95,93) 2-Y-O **£6,469** (£1,925; £962; £481) **Stalls** High

Form RPR
231- **1** **Pearl Spectre (USA)**[56] 7119 2-8-7 **79** JamieSpencer 6 80
(Andrew Balding) *mde virtually all: hung rt 3f out and again bnd 2f out: rdn: stl edging rt and racing lazily over 1f out: edgd bk lft u.p ins fnl f: a jst holding rival* **4/6**[1]
324- **2** shd **Our Gabrial (IRE)**[19] 7902 2-8-1 **73** JimmyQuinn 1 74
(Richard Fahey) *chsd wnr tl 3f out: rdn and chal ent fnl f: ev ch fnl f: a jst being hld cl home* **5/1**[3]
462- **3** 1 ½ **Capers Royal Star (FR)**[19] 7901 2-8-0 **72** oh3 LukeMorris 2 69
(Alastair Lidderdale) *stdd s: t.k.h: hld up in tch in last: effrt u.p over 1f out: pressing ldrs and styng on whn gap clsd and squeezed for room ins fnl f: one pce after* **16/1**
112- **4** nk **Spiritual Flame**[34] 7640 2-8-5 **77** LiamJones 4 74
(William Haggas) *niggled along thrght: wnt 2nd 3f out: carried rt fr 2f out tl swtchd rt 1f out: kpt on same pce ins fnl f* **3/1**[2]

1m 37.17s (-1.03) **Going Correction** -0.075s/f (Stan) **4** Ran SP% **107.5**
Speed ratings (Par 100): **102,101,100,100**
CSF £4.32 TOTE £1.70; EX 3.90 Trifecta £22.10 Pool: £1456.42 - 49.35 winning units..
Owner Pearl Bloodstock Ltd **Bred** Estate Of Edward P Evans **Trained** Kingsclere, Hants
■ Stewards' Enquiry : Jamie Spencer caution: careless riding.

FOCUS
Just the four runners went to post, and the highest-rated horse remaining after two were taken out was 16lb below the ceiling. The winner built a little on his Kempton form.

8154 LADBROKES MAIDEN STKS 1m (P)
12:30 (12:30) (Class 5) 3-Y-O+ £2,726 (£805; £402) Stalls High

Form RPR
1 **Grasped** 3-9-0 0 TomQueally 6 78+
(Lady Cecil) *s.i.s: rn green in rr: rdn along briefly 4f out: sme hdwy on outer 3f out: outpcd bnd 2f out: hdwy to chse clr ldng pair ins fnl f: str run and clsd rapidly to ld cl home* 5/2[1]

3/ 2 *hd* **Secular Society**[487] 4792 3-9-5 0 SeanLevey 3 77
(Brian Meehan) *chsd ldrs: rdn to press ldr and wnt clr 2f out: led 1f out: forged clr u.p ins fnl f: hdd cl home* 9/2

232- 3 *2 1/2* **Lady Guinevere**[49] 7311 3-9-0 64 DavidProbert 8 66
(Stuart Williams) *chsd ldr tl rdn to ld ent fnl 2f: sn clr w rival: hdd 1f out: no ex u.p fnl 100yds and wknd towards fin* 7/2[3]

4 *1 1/2* **Aldeburgh**[5] 4-9-6 0 GeorgeBaker 4 68
(Jim Old) *hld up in tch towards rr: rdn and effrt ent fnl 2f: kpt on u.p fnl f: no threat to ldrs* 33/1

0/4- 5 *shd* **Tumbledown (USA)**[14] 7983 3-9-0 0 LukeMorris 7 63
(Ed Walker) *in tch in midfield: rdn and chsd ldng pair ent fnl 2f: sn drvn and outpcd: plugged on same pce and lost 2 pls ins fnl f* 12/1

/06- 6 *5* **Revise (IRE)**[156] 3908 3-9-5 75 JamieSpencer 5 56
(David Elsworth) *stdd s: hld up in last pair: rdn and sme hdwy 2f out: 6th and no imp over 1f out: wknd ins fnl f* 3/1[2]

0/ 7 *2* **Tequila Sunrise**[510] 4011 3-9-0 0 MartinLane 2 46
(J W Hills) *chsd ldrs: rdn and lost pl ent fnl 2f: wknd and wl btn over 1f out* 12/1

06- 8 *9* **Spessartine (IRE)**[14] 7983 3-9-5 0 JimmyQuinn 9 31
(Robert Eddery) *stdd s: t.k.h: hld up in tch towards rr: rdn and dropped to last 3f out: sn toiling and bhd over 1f out* 66/1

00- 9 *3 1/4* **Echoes Of War**[169] 3435 4-9-6 0 RobertHavlin 1 23
(Michael Attwater) *led tl rdn and hdd ent fnl 2f: sn lost pl: bhd 1f out* 200/1

1m 36.58s (-1.62) **Going Correction** -0.075s/f (Stan)
WFA 3 from 4yo 1lb 9 Ran SP% **114.3**
Speed ratings (Par 103): **105,104,102,100,100 95,93,84,81**
toteswingers 1&2 £3.40, 1&3 £3.00, 2&3 £2.20 CSF £13.95 TOTE £4.80: £1.70, £1.10, £1.40; EX 15.30 Trifecta £37.40 Pool: £2125.78 - 42.57 winning units..
Owner K Abdullah **Bred** Juddmonte Farms Ltd **Trained** Newmarket, Suffolk

FOCUS
A decent maiden for older horses, rated around the second and third. Form to follow.

8155 COMPARE BOOKMAKERS AT BOOKMAKERS.CO.UK H'CAP 5f (P)
1:00 (1:00) (Class 2) (0-105,100) 3-Y-£01,971 (£3,583; £1,791; £896; £446) Stalls High

Form RPR
011- 1 **Forest Edge (IRE)**[26] 7803 4-9-6 99 (b) AdamKirby 4 108+
(David Evans) *bustled along leaving stalls: midfield tl short of room and dropped to rr after 1f: switching rt looking for a run fr over 1f out: in the clr fnl 100yds and qcknd smartly to ld wl ins fnl f: comf* 3/1[1]

051- 2 *1* **Addictive Dream (IRE)**[14] 7982 6-9-5 98 TonyHamilton 9 103
(David Nicholls) *t.k.h: w ldr: stl travelling strly and led 1f out: rdn ins fnl f: forged ahd fnl 100yds: sn hdd and outpcd by wnr* 4/1[2]

050- 3 *3/4* **Tangerine Trees**[18] 7928 8-9-7 100 (v) GrahamLee 5 103
(Bryan Smart) *led: rdn over 1f out: hdd 1f out: no ex and outpcd fnl 100yds* 5/1[3]

005- 4 *hd* **Ubetterbegood (ARG)**[21] 7851 5-8-13 92 SeanLevey 10 94
(Robert Cowell) *in tch towards rr: hdwy into midfield and rdn ent fnl 2f: kpt on same pce u.p ins fnl f* 12/1

0/0- 5 *nk* **Alben Star (IRE)**[14] 7982 5-8-8 92 GeorgeChaloner(5) 8 93+
(Richard Fahey) *taken down early: stdd s: hld up in tch in rr: swtchd rt over 1f out: clsng but stuck bhd horses 1f out: swtchd rt and r.o towards fin: nvr trbld ldrs* 12/1

031- 6 *1/2* **Picansort**[11] 8021 6-8-8 87 (v) ShaneKelly 7 89+
(Peter Crate) *hld up in tch in last pair: clsd whn bmpd and hmpd 1f out: styd on wl ins fnl f: nvr able to chal* 14/1

020- 7 *1/2* **Ajjaadd (USA)**[81] 6391 7-9-0 98 EoinWalsh(5) 1 95
(Ted Powell) *s.i.s: sn rcvrd and in midfield after 1f: rdn and effrt to chse ldrs on inner over 1f out: no ex and wknd fnl 75yds* 6/1

100- 8 *1/2* **Even Stevens**[21] 7851 5-8-11 90 (p) TomEaves 6 86
(Scott Dixon) *chsd ldrs: rdn and effrt over 1f out: keeping on same pce whn sltly hmpd jst ins fnl f: wknd towards fin* 20/1

620- 9 *2 1/4* **Jiroft (ITY)**[67] 6830 6-9-1 97 (p) RobertTart(3) 2 84
(Robert Cowell) *w ldrs tl drvn and unable qck over 1f out: wknd ins fnl f* 20/1

004- 10 *1 1/4* **Prohibit**[21] 7851 8-8-13 92 (p) JimCrowley 3 75
(Robert Cowell) *in tch in midfield: rdn and lost pl over 1f out: towards rr whn hmpd ent fnl f: sn wknd* 10/1

57.66s (-1.14) **Going Correction** -0.075s/f (Stan) 10 Ran SP% **116.6**
Speed ratings (Par 109): **106,104,103,102,102 101,100,100,96,94**
toteswingers 1&2 £2.80, 1&3 £4.40, 2&3 £4.40 CSF £14.71 CT £56.97 TOTE £3.50: £2.10, £2.20, £2.00; EX 13.60 Trifecta £58.00 Pool: £1843.31 - 23.79 winning units..
Owner P & K Swinnerton **Bred** Alberto Panetta **Trained** Pandy, Monmouths
■ Stewards' Enquiry : Adam Kirby one-day ban: careless riding (Dec 18)

FOCUS
With £19,000 up for grabs it was no wonder that this was ultra-competitive, but the form is still a little disappointing for the grade. Another personal best from the winner.

8156 CORAL APP DOWNLOAD FROM THE APP STORE CONDITIONS STKS 1m 2f (P)
1:30 (1:30) (Class 2) 3-Y-O+ £11,827 (£3,541; £1,770; £885; £442) Stalls Low

Form RPR
523- 1 **Marshgate Lane (USA)**[7] 8071 4-9-4 92 AdamKirby 4 102
(Mark Johnston) *mde all: qcknd gallop and wnt clr over 2f out: 3 l clr and rdn over 1f out: drvn ins fnl f: a jst lasting home* 5/2[2]

0/3- 2 *hd* **Uramazin (IRE)**[18] 7927 7-9-4 99 JimCrowley 2 102
(Philip Hide) *chsd wnr 8f out: rdn over 2f out: swtchd out rt and 3 l down over 1f out: styd on wl u.p fnl f: nvr quite getting to wnr* 5/1[3]

000- 3 *2 1/2* **Mia's Boy**[7] 8071 9-9-4 93 GeorgeBaker 1 97
(Chris Dwyer) *stdd after s: hld up in last pair: rdn and effrt 2f out: wnt 3rd but stl plenty to do over 1f out: kpt on but nvr a threat* 20/1

312- 4 *nk* **Bancnuanaheireann (IRE)**[18] 7927 6-9-4 100 TomQueally 3 96
(Michael Appleby) *stdd s: hld up in tch in last pair: rdn and effrt jst over 2f out: 4th and no imp over 1f out: kpt on fnl f: no threat to ldrs* 10/11[1]

5 *4* **Freewheel (IRE)**[217] 1939 3-9-1 0 TonyHamilton 5 88
(David Nicholls) *chsd wnr for 2f: rdn and unable qck over 2f out: dropped to last and wknd over 1f out* 20/1

2m 6.39s (-0.21) **Going Correction** -0.075s/f (Stan)
WFA 3 from 4yo+ 3lb 5 Ran SP% **107.1**
Speed ratings (Par 109): **97,96,94,94,91**
CSF £13.85 TOTE £2.50: £1.20, £2.00; EX 10.60 Trifecta £65.50 Pool: £2180.29 - 24.93 winning units..
Owner Sheikh Hamdan Bin Mohammed Al Maktoum **Bred** Edmund A Gann **Trained** Middleham Moor, N Yorks

FOCUS
Predictably tactical stuff in this 1m2f conditions contest, which provided Mark Johnston with a welcome winner. Smart form, rated around the runner-up.

8157 DOWNLOAD THE LADBROKES APP H'CAP (DIV I) 7f (P)
2:00 (2:00) (Class 5) (0-70,70) 3-Y-O+ £2,726 (£805; £402) Stalls Low

Form RPR
001- 1 **Shaunas Spirit (IRE)**[29] 7740 5-9-6 69 (p) AdamKirby 9 79+
(Dean Ivory) *hld up in tch in midfield: swtchd out rt and effrt over 1f out: hdwy u.p to ld ins fnl f: r.o wl: rdn out* 6/1[3]

005- 2 *1* **Athletic**[11] 8019 4-9-0 63 (v) JimCrowley 7 70
(Andrew Reid) *t.k.h: hld up in tch in midfield: swtchd out rt and hdwy to chal 1f out: ev ch ins fnl f: kpt on same pce fnl 100yds* 6/1[3]

653- 3 *hd* **The Mongoose**[7] 8068 5-9-3 66 (t) MartinHarley 8 72
(David Evans) *chsd ldrs: rdn and ev ch over 1f out: led jst ins fnl f: hdd and styd on same pce ins fnl f* 9/2[2]

300- 4 *2* **Kakapuka**[19] 7898 6-9-7 70 GeorgeBaker 5 71
(Anabel K Murphy) *broke fast: led: rdn over 1f out: hdd jst ins fnl f: wknd fnl 75yds* 12/1

006- 5 *shd* **Nubar Boy**[162] 3661 6-8-11 60 (v) StevieDonohoe 2 61
(Ian Williams) *hld up in midfield: switching out rt and hdwy over 1f out: kpt on u.p ins fnl f* 14/1

406- 6 *nk* **My Learned Friend (IRE)**[7] 8073 9-8-0 56 (v) RobHornby(7) 1 56
(Andrew Balding) *racd off the pce in last quartet: effrt on outer bnd 2f out: kpt on ins fnl f: nt rch ldrs* 16/1

12- 7 *shd* **Barbados Bob (USA)**[9] 8037 3-9-4 67 SeanLevey 11 67
(Michael Wigham) *stdd s: hld up off the pce in rr: hdwy on inner over 1f out: swtchd rt jst over 1f out: kpt on same pce fnl 100yds* 7/2[1]

200- 8 *1/2* **Lieutenant Dan (IRE)**[198] 2515 6-9-5 68 (v) TomQueally 10 66
(Michael Appleby) *s.i.s: bhd: rdn 4f out: c wd and sme hdwy over 1f out: kpt on wl ins fnl f: nvr trbld ldrs* 20/1

251/ 9 *3/4* **Dozy Joe**[354] 8133 5-9-0 70 NoraLooby(7) 4 66
(Joseph Tuite) *in tch in midfield: rdn and effrt on inner over 1f out: no imp: wknd ins fnl f* 20/1

240- 10 *1* **Another Try (IRE)**[19] 7896 8-9-5 68 LukeMorris 12 62
(Alan Jarvis) *stdd after s: hld up towards rr: rdn and hdwy 2f out: no imp over 1f out: wknd ins fnl f* 10/1

0/0- 11 *9* **Specialty (IRE)**[21] 7861 3-9-2 65 LiamKeniry 13 34
(Pam Sly) *chsd ldrs: rdn 4f out: losing pl ent fnl 2f: bhd and eased wl ins fnl f* 33/1

630- 12 *13* **Scottish Lake**[49] 7306 5-9-4 70 (b) RobertTart(3) 6 4
(Olivia Maylam) *w ldr tl wl over 1f out: sn btn and wknd: wl bhd and eased ins fnl f: b.b.v* 8/1

1m 23.7s (-1.10) **Going Correction** -0.075s/f (Stan) 12 Ran SP% **121.9**
Speed ratings (Par 103): **103,101,101,99,99 98,98,98,97,96 85,71**
toteswingers 1&2 £7.60, 1&3 £5.70, 2&3 £4.00 CSF £42.05 CT £182.02 TOTE £9.10: £2.50, £2.10, £1.80; EX 64.30 Trifecta £301.40 Pool: £3013.98 - 7.49 winning units..
Owner Cynthia Smith & Dean Ivory **Bred** Miss Breda Wright **Trained** Radlett, Herts

FOCUS
The first division of the 7f handicap. The pace was good and the form looks solid.

8158 DOWNLOAD THE LADBROKES APP H'CAP (DIV II) 7f (P)
2:30 (2:30) (Class 5) (0-70,70) 3-Y-O+ £2,726 (£805; £402) Stalls Low

Form RPR
051- 1 **Kuanyao (IRE)**[13] 7985 7-9-5 68 (v) TonyHamilton 11 77+
(David Nicholls) *led tl 5f out: chsd ldr after tl led ent fnl f: sn rdn and qcknd clr: r.o wl comf* 4/1[2]

600- 2 *1 1/4* **Club House (IRE)**[19] 7898 3-8-13 62 TomQueally 1 68
(Robert Mills) *s.i.s: in tch in last quartet: hdwy on inner over 1f out: chsd wnr ins fnl f: r.o but no threat* 16/1

104- 3 *1/2* **Black Dave (IRE)**[15] 7965 3-9-4 67 AdamKirby 12 71
(David Evans) *stdd s: hld up in rr: hdwy ent fnl f: rdn and r.o wl fnl 150yds: wnt 3rd towards fin: nvr trbld ldrs* 9/2[3]

000- 4 *3/4* **Repetition**[62] 6969 3-9-1 69 JacobButterfield(5) 2 71
(Kristin Stubbs) *in tch in midfield: rdn and effrt over 2f out: kpt on u.p ins fnl f: no threat to wnr* 33/1

55U- 5 *nk* **Victorian Number (FR)**[11] 8019 5-9-2 65 MartinHarley 6 66
(Geoffrey Deacon) *chsd wnr for over 1f: styd chsng ldrs: rdn and effrt wl over 1f out: chsd clr wnr ins fnl f: kpt on same pce: lost 3 pls wl ins fnl f* 16/1

050- 6 *1 1/2* **Eager To Bow (IRE)**[20] 7880 7-9-6 69 LiamKeniry 4 66
(Patrick Chamings) *hld up in tch in last quartet: effrt and clsd ent fnl f: rdn and styd on fnl 150yds: nvr trbld ldrs* 16/1

640- 7 *1/2* **Midnight Feast**[35] 7629 5-9-4 67 (v) AmirQuinn 7 63
(Lee Carter) *in tch in midfield: hdwy to chse ldrs over 2f out: rdn and unable qck over 1f out: wknd ins fnl f* 20/1

133- 8 *hd* **First Class**[20] 7880 5-9-1 64 DavidProbert 9 60
(Rae Guest) *in tch in midfield: rdn and unable qck over 2f out: rdn and outpcd 2f out: wknd 1f out* 6/1

212- 9 *nse* **Daring Dragon**[20] 7880 3-9-7 70 (b) GeorgeBaker 8 65
(Ed Walker) *stdd s: t.k.h: hdwy to ld 5f out: rdn and hdd jst over 1f out: lost 2nd ins fnl f: wknd fnl 75yds* 3/1[1]

000- 10 *3/4* **Russian Ice**[20] 7876 5-9-7 70 (b) JimCrowley 3 63
(Dean Ivory) *in tch in midfield: rdn and lost pl ent fnl 2f: wknd u.p over 1f out* 12/1

040- 11 *1/2* **Golden Desert (IRE)**[11] 8019 9-9-2 65 GrahamLee 10 57
(Simon Dow) *s.i.s: bhd: rdn over 1f out: swtchd lft jst ins fnl f: kpt on but nvr trbld ldrs* 16/1

400- 12 *3 1/4* **Princess Patsky (USA)**[74] 6655 3-8-4 60 (v) LouisSteward(7) 5 43
(Michael Bell) *in tch towards rr: hdwy into midfield and rdn over 2f out: wknd over 1f out* 33/1

1m 23.47s (-1.33) **Going Correction** -0.075s/f (Stan) 12 Ran SP% **119.3**
Speed ratings (Par 103): **104,102,102,101,100 99,98,98,98,97 96,93**
toteswingers 1&2 £16.20, 1&3 £4.80, 2&3 £17.60 CSF £65.37 CT £304.75 TOTE £7.50: £2.30, £8.90, £2.80; EX 93.80 Trifecta £2066.80 Part won. Pool: £2755.83 - 0.85 winning units..
Owner Matt & Lauren Morgan **Bred** Newlands House Stud **Trained** Sessay, N Yorks

FOCUS
The second division of the 7f handicap had more depth and was faster than the first, but it was taken apart by a rejuvenated performer. He's probably better than the bare form.

8159 CORAL MOBILE "JUST THREE CLICKS TO BET" H'CAP 1m 4f (P)
3:00 (3:00) (Class 4) (0-80,82) 3-Y-O+ £4,690 (£1,395; £697; £348) Stalls Low

Form RPR
152- 1 **Mallory Heights (IRE)**[23] 7840 3-9-3 76 AdamKirby 7 84+
(Luca Cumani) *in tch in midfield: swtchd rt 3f out: rdn and qcknd to ld over 2f out: clr 2f out: in command whn edgd lft ins fnl f: kpt on: pushed out* 5/4[1]
1- 2 ¾ **Knockgraffon Lad (USA)**[16] 7950 6-9-7 78 (tp) RobertTart(3) 5 85+
(Brendan Powell) *stdd s: t.k.h: hld up in rr: hdwy ent fnl 2f: r.o wl u.p fnl f: wnt 2nd fnl 75yds: r.o wl but nvr gng to rch wnr* 5/1[2]
502- 3 1 **Echo Brava**[23] 7839 3-8-7 66 JimmyQuinn 10 71
(Luke Dace) *t.k.h: chsd ldrs: rdn and effrt over 2f out: chsd wnr ent fnl f: kpt on but lost 2nd fnl 75yds* 10/1
045- 4 1 **Sir Boss (IRE)**[16] 7950 8-9-5 73 TomEaves 9 77
(Michael Mullineaux) *hld up in tch in last quartet: clsd and n.m.r over 2f out: rdn and hdwy to chse ldrs over 1f out: kpt on same pce ins fnl f: fin lame* 20/1
00- 5 1 ½ **Magnolia Ridge (IRE)**[47] 7361 3-8-13 77 JacobButterfield(5) 2 78
(Kristin Stubbs) *t.k.h: hld up in tch in midfield: nt clr run and shuffled bk over 2f out: rdn and rallied on outer over 1f out: kpt on wl fnl f* 14/1
604- 6 1 ¾ **King's Request (IRE)**[23] 7839 3-8-8 67 LiamJones 8 65
(Laura Mongan) *chsd ldr tl over 2f out: sn rdn and unable qck: btn over 1f out: wknd ins fnl f* 12/1
040- 7 nk **Laser Blazer**[23] 7840 5-9-6 74 (p1) JimCrowley 12 72
(Jeremy Gask) *v.s.a: sn swtchd lft and in tch in rr: rdn and effrt wl over 1f out: kpt on fnl f: nvr trbld ldrs* 16/1
050- 8 1 **My History (IRE)**[16] 7947 3-9-0 73 AdrianNicholls 6 69
(Mark Johnston) *led tl hdd and outpcd by wnr over 2f out: sn rdn: lost 2nd ent fnl f: wknd ins fnl f* 14/1
000- 9 ½ **Reflect (IRE)**[14] 7970 5-9-6 74 (vt) DaleSwift 1 70
(Derek Shaw) *hld up in tch in last quartet: rdn and effrt on inner 2f out: no imp over 1f out: wknd fnl f* 33/1
406- 10 nse **Thecornishcowboy**[43] 7453 4-9-8 76 (t) RobertWinston 4 71
(John Ryan) *chsd ldrs: nt clr run and shuffled bk over 2f out: lost any ch and nvr much room tl ins fnl f: no prog* 8/1[3]
400- 11 2 **The Blue Dog (IRE)**[12] 8004 6-9-1 69 PaddyAspell 3 61
(Phil McEntee) *chsd ldrs: rdn and unable qck ent fnl 2f: outpcd and btn over 1f out: wknd fnl f* 33/1

2m 32.01s (-0.99) **Going Correction** -0.075s/f (Stan)
WFA 3 from 4yo+ 5lb 11 Ran SP% 118.9
Speed ratings (Par 105): **100,99,98,98,97 96,95,95,94,94 93**
toteswingers 1&2 £3.00, 1&3 £3.70, 2&3 £5.20 CSF £7.12 CT £43.29 TOTE £2.10: £1.20, £2.40, £3.00; EX 8.40 Trifecta £42.20 Pool: £3032.89 - 53.87 winning units..
Owner Merry Fox Stud Limited **Bred** Merry Fox Stud Limited **Trained** Newmarket, Suffolk

FOCUS
Adam Kirby illustrated why he is the best jockey riding regularly on the AW, completing a four-timer with a masterclass in this 1m4f handicap. The winner only had to match his Kempton latest.

8160 32RED.COM AMATEUR RIDERS' H'CAP 2m (P)
3:30 (3:33) (Class 6) (0-60,60) 3-Y-O+ £1,975 (£607; £303) Stalls Low

Form RPR
004- 1 **Epsom Salts**[14] 7984 8-10-3 56 (p) MissLDempster(7) 3 68
(Pat Phelan) *hld up in midfield: clsd on ldrs 1/2-way: swtchd rt and hdwy over 3f out: pressed ldr and wnt clr 2f out: led ins fnl f: r.o wl* 7/1[3]
004- 2 3 ¼ **Sommersturm (GER)**[4] 8115 9-10-6 57 (t) MissHDoyle(5) 7 65
(David Evans) *hld up in rr early: hdwy and clsd on ldrs 1/2-way: chsd ldr 7f out tl led wl over 2f out: rdn and drew clr w wnr 2f out: hdd and no ex ins fnl f* 7/1[3]
005- 3 5 **Keep Kicking (IRE)**[19] 7899 6-10-6 57 MrGeorgeCrate(5) 4 59
(Simon Dow) *awkward leaving stalls: bhd: clsd on ldrs 1/2-way: rdn and hdwy over 3f out: 5th and no imp over 1f out: plugged on u.p to go 3rd towards fin* 16/1
065- 4 ½ **Dr Finley (IRE)**[28] 7767 6-10-11 57 (v) MrSWalker 14 59
(Lydia Pearce) *chsd ldrs: clsd 1/2-way: rdn over 4f out: 3rd and btn over 1f out: plugged on: lost 3rd towards fin* 7/1[3]
000- 5 5 **Ctappers**[18] 7159 4-9-11 50 (v) MrPPilley(7) 12 46
(Mick Channon) *in rr: clsd on ldrs 1/2-way: rdn and effrt 1/2-way: n.d but plugging on whn swtchd lft ins fnl f: n.d* 14/1
130- 6 1 ¾ **Baan (USA)**[14] 7984 10-10-6 59 MrDeanSmith(7) 8 52
(James Eustace) *towards rr: clsd on ldrs 1/2-way: pushed along and sme hdwy on inner over 2f out: no real imp fnl 2f: nvr trbld ldrs* 16/1
664- 7 nk **Entitlement**[28] 7767 4-10-8 59 MissKMargarson(5) 13 52
(James Fanshawe) *t.k.h: hld up in midfield: hdwy to chse ldrs 10f out: clsd to ld over 7f out tl rdn and hdd wl over 2f out: wknd and wl btn whn hung rt 1f out* 8/1
304- 8 shd **Galiotto (IRE)**[19] 7899 7-10-2 55 (v) MrGGorman(7) 6 48
(Gary Moore) *racd in midfield: clsd on ldrs 1/2-way: lost pl and reminder 6f out: rdn and no prog over 3f out: sn outpcd and no ch fnl 2f* 6/1[2]
040- 9 6 **Dew Reward (IRE)**[11] 8027 5-10-9 55 MissSBrotherton 10 41
(Bill Turner) *midfield: clsd on ldrs 1/2-way: rdn over 5f out: wknd wl over 2f out* 16/1
000/ 10 7 **Daldini**[581] 5764 11-10-4 55 MrKLocking(5) 11 32
(Scott Dixon) *w ldr and sn clr: c bk to field but led 8f out: sn hdd and dropped out: bhd fnl 3f* 20/1
200- 11 13 **Estibdaad (IRE)**[8] 8042 3-10-0 59 (t) MissMBryant(5) 1 21
(Paddy Butler) *racd in midfield: clsd on ldrs 1/2-way: rdn and struggling over 3f out: bhd over 1f out: t.o* 25/1
606- 12 ½ **Bethan**[22] 7847 4-10-13 59 MrRossBirkett 9 20
(Julia Feilden) *chsd ldrs: clsd 1/2-way: rdn over 4f out: wknd over 2f out: wl bhd and eased ins fnl f: t.o* 5/1[1]
22P/ 13 11 **Grandad Mac**[8] 5280 5-10-9 60 MrAlexFerguson(5) 2 8
(Alan Coogan) *led and sn clr w rival: c bk to field and hdd 8f out: sn dropped out: t.o over 2f out* 16/1

3m 22.86s (-2.84) **Going Correction** -0.075s/f (Stan)
WFA 3 from 4yo+ 8lb 13 Ran SP% 118.4
Speed ratings (Par 101): **104,102,99,99,97 96,96,96,93,89 83,82,77**
toteswingers 1&2 £9.10, 1&3 £14.60, 2&3 £26.50 CSF £54.84 CT £765.01 TOTE £5.40: £2.40, £2.60, £7.10; EX 62.60 Trifecta £1296.50 Pool: £3921.79 - 2.26 winning units..
Owner The Epsom Racegoers **Bred** Heatherwold Stud **Trained** Epsom, Surrey
■ A first winner on only her second ride for Laura Dempster.

FOCUS
A handicap for amateur riders, run at an unsustainable gallop from the outset courtesy of Daldini and Grandad Mac. The winner built on his latest form.
T/Plt: £43.10 to a £1 stake. Pool: £58490.71 - 988.85 winning tickets T/Qpdt: £13.00 to a £1 stake. Pool: £5676.41 - 322.74 winning tickets SP

8136 WOLVERHAMPTON (A.W) (L-H)
Thursday, December 5

OFFICIAL GOING: Standard
Wind: Strong and gusty; across Weather: Dry, windy

8162 LADBROKES APPRENTICE H'CAP 1m 141y(P)
3:50 (3:50) (Class 5) (0-70,70) 3-Y-O+ £2,587 (£770; £384; £192) Stalls Low

Form RPR
422- 1 **Keene**[72] 6737 3-8-9 63 [1] LouisSteward(5) 1 71
(Philip McBride) *chsd ldr for 2f: styd chsng ldrs: swtchd rt and chal between horses ins fnl f: kpt on wl to ld cl home* 3/1[1]
250- 2 nk **Icy Blue**[16] 7952 5-8-8 58 (p) GeorgeChaloner(3) 2 65
(Richard Whitaker) *awkward leaving stalls: sn rcvrd to chse ldrs: wnt 2nd 6f out tl rdn to ld wl over 1f out: wandered u.p 1f out: kpt on tl hdd and no ex cl home* 8/1
330- 3 ½ **It's My Time**[15] 7974 4-9-1 67 SamanthaBell(5) 5 73
(Richard Fahey) *taken down early: hld up in tch in last pair: rdn and effrt on outer jst over 2f out: ev ch ins fnl f: unable qck cl home* 7/2[2]
150- 4 1 **Mysterious Wonder**[16] 7966 3-8-2 56 (e1) EvaMoscrop(5) 3 60
(Philip Kirby) *t.k.h: hld up in midfield: rdn and pressed ldrs over 1f out: ev ch ins fnl f: no ex and outpcd fnl 75yds* 25/1
315- 5 5 **Mcmonagle (USA)**[113] 5383 5-9-9 70 (tp) RobertTart 8 62
(Alan Brown) *led tl rdn and hdd wl over 1f out: no ex ent fnl f: sn wknd* 10/1
001- 6 1 ½ **Prince Of Burma (IRE)**[12] 8019 5-8-13 65 (bt) EoinWalsh(5) 6 54
(David Evans) *s.i.s: in tch in rr: rdn and effrt 3f out: no imp over 1f out: sn wknd* 9/2[3]
204- 7 ½ **Unex Michelangelo (IRE)**[57] 7132 4-9-1 69 (v1) DanielleMooney(7) 4 57
(Michael Easterby) *in tch in midfield: rdn and no hdwy 3f out: wknd over 1f out* 7/2[2]

1m 52.92s (2.42) **Going Correction** +0.275s/f (Slow)
WFA 3 from 4yo+ 2lb 7 Ran SP% 111.7
Speed ratings (Par 103): **100,99,99,98,93 92,92**
toteswingers 1&2 £4.70, 1&3 £2.60, 2&3 £3.40 CSF £25.85 CT £84.32 TOTE £3.80: £2.70, £3.10; EX 29.50 Trifecta £106.60 Pool: £1950.73 - 13.71 winning units..
Owner Four Winds Racing Partnership **Bred** Wood Farm Stud (Waresley) **Trained** Newmarket, Suffolk

FOCUS
Punters had found it difficult to separate these and it duly served up a thrilling finish. Muddling form, rated around the second and third.

8163 DOWNLOAD THE LADBROKES APP H'CAP 7f 32y(P)
4:20 (4:21) (Class 6) (0-65,65) 3-Y-O+ £1,940 (£577; £288; £144) Stalls High

Form RPR
006- 1 **Run It Twice (IRE)**[12] 8030 3-9-4 62 (b) MartinHarley 2 72+
(David Evans) *hld up in tch in midfield: travelling wl but stuck bhd rivals 1f out: swtchd lft and effrt 1f out: drvn to ld ins fnl f: pricked ears in front: rdn out* 5/2[1]
416- 2 ½ **Harvest Mist (IRE)**[27] 7808 5-8-11 58 RobertTart(3) 4 65
(Shaun Lycett) *in tch in midfield: rdn and chsd ldrs over 1f out: pressed ldrs ins fnl f: kpt on to go 2nd cl home* 8/1
506- 3 nk **Exceedexpectations (IRE)**[10] 8038 4-9-4 62 LiamKeniry 1 68
(Conor Dore) *led early: sn settled in 4th: rdn and effrt on inner over 1f out: drvn to ld jst ins fnl f: hdd and lost 2 pls fnl 50yds* 8/1
214- 4 1 ½ **Orpsie Boy (IRE)**[10] 8037 10-9-5 63 LukeMorris 8 65
(Ruth Carr) *in tch in last trio: rdn and effrt to chse ldrs over 1f out: kpt on same pce u.p fnl f* 5/1[2]
200- 5 nk **Glenridding**[16] 7953 9-8-12 61 (p) EoinWalsh(5) 5 62
(James Given) *sn led: hdd after 1f and chsd ldr after: rdn to ld again 2f out: hdd jst ins fnl f: no ex and wknd towards fin* 20/1
403- 6 ¾ **Piccolo Express**[27] 7807 7-9-0 58 ShaneKelly 3 57
(Brian Baugh) *in tch in last pair: rdn and effrt on inner over 1f out: styd on same pce ins fnl f* 5/1[2]
504- 7 2 **Divine Call**[14] 7985 6-9-7 65 RichardKingscote 9 59
(Milton Bradley) *chsd ldrs after 1f: rdn and chsd ldr 2f out tl jst ins fnl f: sn wknd* 7/1[3]
000- 8 2 ½ **Basle**[27] 7807 6-9-1 59 (t) TomEaves 7 46
(Roy Brotherton) *stdd after s: hld up in last pair: shkn up 4f out: rdn and no hdwy 1f out: nvr trbld ldrs* 66/1
100- 9 2 ½ **Solarmaite**[13] 8006 4-8-12 59 (b) MarkCoumbe(3) 6 39
(Roy Bowring) *t.k.h: chsd ldrs tl led after 1f: sn clr tl rdn and hdd 2f out: sn struggling: fdd fnl f* 8/1

1m 32.26s (2.66) **Going Correction** +0.275s/f (Slow) 9 Ran SP% 114.0
Speed ratings (Par 101): **95,94,94,92,92 91,88,86,83**
toteswingers 1&2 £8.00, 1&3 £7.80, 2&3 £14.10 CSF £23.00 CT £138.43 TOTE £4.00: £1.40, £2.00, £3.60; EX 33.50 Trifecta £315.90 Pool: £3858.48 - 9.15 winning units..
Owner Shropshire Wolves 4 **Bred** Yeomanstown Stud **Trained** Pandy, Monmouths

FOCUS
The market can often prove the best guide in races at this modest level and that certainly proved the case on this occasion. The winner was on a good mark on his form in the spring.

8164 32RED NURSERY H'CAP 1m 1f 103y(P)
4:50 (4:50) (Class 5) (0-75,74) 2-Y-O £2,587 (£770; £384; £192) Stalls Low

Form RPR
041- 1 **Groovejet**[22] 7854 2-9-4 71 MartinHarley 4 76
(Peter Chapple-Hyam) *in tch in midfield: rdn and effrt to chse ldr wl over 1f out: led ins fnl f: styd on wl: rdn out* 7/2[2]
331- 2 ¾ **Jazzy Lady (IRE)**[3] 8132 2-9-1 68 6ex GrahamGibbons 2 72
(David Evans) *stdd s: hld up in last pair: rdn and gd hdwy 1f out: ev ch ins fnl f: no ex and one pce towards fin* 8/1
302- 3 2 ¼ **Avocadeau (IRE)**[19] 7935 2-9-2 69 MartinDwyer 6 68
(William Muir) *dwlt: t.k.h: sn rcvrd and led 7f out: rdn over 1f out: hdd jst ins fnl f: no ex and outpcd fnl 75yds* 8/1
436- 4 ½ **Wealth (IRE)**[29] 7766 2-9-1 68 TonyHamilton 5 66
(Richard Fahey) *hld up in tch in last pair: swtchd rt and effrt u.p over 1f out: kpt on same pce ins fnl f* 5/2[1]

502- **5** 1 1/4 **Branston De Soto**[36] 7631 2-9-0 **67** LiamJones 1 63
(Mark Johnston) *led tl 7f out: chsd ldr tl struggling u.p and lost 2nd 2f out: wknd ins fnl f* **7/2**[2]

551- **6** 3 **Boogangoo (IRE)**[19] 7935 2-9-7 **74** TomEaves 3 64
(Keith Dalgleish) *broke wl: stdd and hld up in tch in midfield: rdn and effrt over 1f out: no imp ins fnl f: btn and eased towards fin* **6/1**[3]

2m 7.07s (5.37) **Going Correction** +0.275s/f (Slow) **6** Ran SP% **109.5**
Speed ratings (Par 96): **87,86,84,83,82 80**
toteswingers 1&2 £2.50, 1&3 £4.40, 2&3 £9.00 CSF £28.36 TOTE £3.90: £2.00, £1.90; EX 14.30 Trifecta £103.00 Pool: £3742.43 - 27.24 winning units..
Owner Phil Cunningham **Bred** P M Cunningham **Trained** Newmarket, Suffolk

FOCUS
A fair race for the grade with three last-time-out winners involved, but a steady tempo and the form is far from solid.

8165 32RED.COM MAIDEN STKS 5f 216y(P)
5:20 (5:21) (Class 5) 2-Y-0 **£2,587** (£770; £384; £192) **Stalls** Low

Form RPR

202- **1** **Nova Champ (IRE)**[8] 8061 2-9-5 72 SeanLevey 1 70+
(Stuart Williams) *tok t.k.h: mde all: rdn and clr 2f out: in command and r.o wl fnl f: comf* **8/11**[1]

2 3 1/2 **Golden Steps (FR)** 2-9-5 0 MartinHarley 3 60+
(Marco Botti) *s.i.s: racd in last pair: clsd 4f out: rdn and effrt on inner over 1f out: chsd clr wnr 1f out: kpt on but no imp* **3/1**[2]

0- **3** 3/4 **Female Strategy (IRE)**[40] 7533 2-9-0 0 ChrisCatlin 6 52
(Peter Chapple-Hyam) *in tch in midfield: rdn and effrt wl over 1f out: 3rd and plugged on same pce fnl f* **8/1**[3]

4 4 1/2 **Libra Romana (IRE)** 2-9-0 0 LukeMorris 5 39
(Sir Mark Prescott Bt) *chsd ldrs: rdn to chse wnr 2f out: no imp and lost 2nd 1f out: wknd fnl f* **50/1**

5- **5** 3 3/4 **Chatsworth Express**[20] 7901 2-9-0 0 GeorgeChaloner[(5)] 2 33
(Richard Whitaker) *chsd wnr tl 2f out: sn struggling u.p: fdd fnl f* **12/1**

0- **6** 6 **Belle Peinture (FR)**[19] 7934 2-8-9 0 SamanthaBell[(5)] 7 10
(Richard Fahey) *in tch in midfield: rdn and struggling over 2f out: sn wknd* **20/1**

60- **7** 3 1/2 **Frankthetank (IRE)**[28] 7790 2-9-5 0 TomEaves 4 4
(Keith Dalgleish) *s.i.s: a bhd: lost tch 1/2-way* **33/1**

1m 16.78s (1.78) **Going Correction** +0.275s/f (Slow) **7** Ran SP% **111.4**
Speed ratings (Par 96): **99,94,93,87,82 74,69**
toteswingers 1&2 £1.10, 1&3 £2.50, 2&3 £4.00 CSF £2.82 TOTE £1.50: £1.30, £1.60; EX 4.00 Trifecta £15.80 Pool: £4114.13 - 195.16 winning units..
Owner Qatar Racing Limited **Bred** Hyde Park Stud & Paddy Conney **Trained** Newmarket, Suffolk

FOCUS
A modest maiden. The winner had plenty of form in the book that entitled him to win a race like this.

8166 32RED CASINO NURSERY H'CAP 5f 216y(P)
5:50 (5:50) (Class 6) (0-65,65) 2-Y-0 **£1,940** (£577; £288; £144) **Stalls** Low

Form RPR

020- **1** **Honey Meadow**[21] 7878 2-9-7 **65** MartinHarley 9 69+
(Robert Eddery) *broke wl and led early: stdd bk and hld up towards rr after 1f: rdn and hdwy on outer over 1f out: r.o wl u.p to ld wl ins fnl f* **7/1**[3]

065- **2** 3/4 **Thataboy (IRE)**[15] 7978 2-9-4 **62** RichardKingscote 4 64
(Tom Dascombe) *sn led: hdd 4f out but styd w ldr: rdn to ld over 1f out: drvn ins fnl f: hdd and unable qck wl ins fnl f* **7/4**[1]

541- **3** nse **Little Big Man**[12] 8025 2-9-2 **65** (b) JoshBaudains[(5)] 10 67
(Sylvester Kirk) *hld up in tch in rr: swtchd rt 4f out: effrt u.p 2f out: ev ch ent fnl f: edging lft and bmpd rival ins fnl f: kpt on same pce cl home* **6/1**[2]

531- **4** 1 **Dandys Perier (IRE)**[16] 7956 2-8-12 **56** LiamJones 8 55
(Ronald Harris) *broke wl: chsd ldrs tl shuffled bk towards rr 4f out: rdn 2f out: kpt on u.p ins fnl f* **6/1**[2]

123- **5** 3/4 **Black Vale (IRE)**[2] 8137 2-9-2 **60** (bt) PaddyAspell 2 56
(Phil McEntee) *w ldr tl led 4f out: rdn 2f out: hdd 1f out: wknd fnl 75yds* **8/1**

666- **6** 3 **Dont Have It Then**[114] 5371 2-9-4 **62** RobertWinston 5 49
(Willie Musson) *hld up in tch in rr: rdn 1/2-way: outpcd and btn over 1f out* **12/1**

053- **7** 1 1/4 **El Duque**[12] 8025 2-8-4 **55** (p) RyanWhile[(7)] 6 39
(Bill Turner) *chsd ldrs: rdn and effrt jst over 2f out: shifted rt and btn 1f out: sn wknd* **25/1**

056- **U** **Shamardyh (IRE)**[94] 6035 2-9-1 **59** GrahamGibbons 7 60+
(David Evans) *t.k.h: hld up wl in tch in midfield: trcking ldrs and stl travelling strly whn clipped heels and uns rdr 1f out* **8/1**

1m 17.08s (2.08) **Going Correction** +0.275s/f (Slow) **8** Ran SP% **111.2**
Speed ratings (Par 94): **97,96,95,94,93 89,87,**
toteswingers 1&2 £2.30, 1&3 £6.90, 2&3 £2.40 CSF £18.57 CT £75.35 TOTE £5.70: £2.40, £1.20, £1.80; EX 21.70 Trifecta £70.50 Pool: £3576.13 - 38.00 winning units..
Owner G & L Knight, J Mitchell & N Donaldson **Bred** R J Budge **Trained** Newmarket, Suffolk

FOCUS
A modest nursery run at a good pace. Fairly straightforward form.

8167 COMPARE BOOKMAKERS AT BOOKMAKERS.CO.UK H'CAP 5f 20y(P)
6:20 (6:21) (Class 4) (0-85,82) 3-Y-0+ **£4,690** (£1,395; £697; £348) **Stalls** Low

Form RPR

640- **1** **Royal Bajan (USA)**[12] 8021 5-9-2 **77** (v[1]) TomQueally 2 89+
(James Given) *taken down early: mde all: rdn and wnt clr ent fnl f: r.o strly: eased towards fin* **8/1**

060- **2** 2 1/4 **Threes Grand**[29] 7777 3-9-5 **80** TomEaves 5 82
(Scott Dixon) *hld up in tch towards rr: effrt u.p on inner over 1f out: kpt on ins fnl f to go 2nd towards fin: no ch w wnr* **14/1**

510- **3** hd **Sir Pedro**[12] 8021 4-9-5 **80** GrahamLee 7 81
(Robert Cowell) *hld up in tch in rr: effrt u.p over 1f out: r.o fnl 100yds: wnt 3rd towards fin: no ch w wnr* **7/4**[1]

022- **4** 1/2 **Triple Dream**[12] 8021 8-9-7 **82** (tp) DavidProbert 9 81
(Milton Bradley) *in tch in midfield: effrt u.p on outer over 1f out: kpt on ins fnl f: wnt 4th nr fin: no ch w wnr* **7/2**[2]

004- **5** nk **Desert Strike**[16] 7959 7-8-12 **73** (p) LiamKeniry 3 71
(Conor Dore) *taken down early: chsd ldrs: rdn and effrt wl over 1f out: chsd clr wnr jst ins fnl f: no imp: lost 2 pls towards fin* **16/1**

000- **6** 3/4 **Oil Strike**[17] 7949 6-9-0 **75** GrahamGibbons 6 71
(Michael Easterby) *chsd ldrs: rdn and chsd wnr wl over 1f out: outpcd and btn ent fnl f: wknd fnl 100yds* **7/1**

003- **7** 1 1/2 **Moorhouse Lad**[21] 7887 10-9-2 **80** BillyCray[(3)] 1 70
(Garry Moss) *taken down early: chsd wnr tl wl over 1f out: sn struggling: wknd fnl f* **6/1**[3]

1m 2.57s (0.27) **Going Correction** +0.275s/f (Slow) **7** Ran SP% **109.0**
Speed ratings (Par 105): **108,104,104,103,102 101,99**
toteswingers 1&2 £11.30, 1&3 £4.70, 2&3 £5.60 CSF £96.07 CT £257.26 TOTE £7.80: £3.10, £7.40; EX 73.40 Trifecta £472.50 Pool: £3680.91 - 5.84 winning units..
Owner The Cool Silk Partnership **Bred** West Wind Farm **Trained** Willoughton, Lincs

FOCUS
A fair sprint handicap and the winner is rated back to his best.

8168 BEST ODDS AT BOOKMAKERS.CO.UK H'CAP (DIV I) 5f 20y(P)
6:50 (6:50) (Class 6) (0-55,55) 3-Y-0+ **£1,940** (£577; £288; £144) **Stalls** Low

Form RPR

012- **1** **Give Us A Belle (IRE)**[9] 8051 4-9-4 **52** 6ex (vt) AdamBeschizza 4 69
(Christine Dunnett) *mde all: rdn clr over 1f out: edgd rt but styd on wl fnl f: comf* **6/4**[1]

550- **2** 2 **Sir Geoffrey (IRE)**[76] 6603 7-9-6 **54** (p) LukeMorris 3 63
(Scott Dixon) *chsd ldrs: wnt 2nd 3f out: rdn and styd on same pce fnl 2f* **7/1**[2]

100- **3** 2 1/4 **Borough Boy (IRE)**[20] 7903 3-9-5 **53** (v) TomEaves 10 54
(Derek Shaw) *t.k.h: hld up wl in tch in midfield: rdn and effrt in 3rd 2f out: one pce and no imp after* **8/1**[3]

006- **4** 2 3/4 **Flow Chart (IRE)**[10] 8034 6-8-9 **46** oh1 SladeO'Hara[(3)] 8 37
(Peter Grayson) *s.i.s: wl off the pce in rr: rdn and hdwy 1f out: styd on ins fnl f: nvr trbld ldrs* **20/1**

004- **5** 1 3/4 **Ferocious Fran (IRE)**[9] 8050 5-8-12 **46** oh1 MartinHarley 7 31
(Emmet Michael Butterly, Ire) *taken down early: dwlt and bustled along early: a midfield: rdn and no imp over 1f out: nvr trbld ldrs* **14/1**

060- **6** 1/2 **Lucky Mark (IRE)**[22] 7862 4-9-4 **55** (p) BillyCray[(3)] 1 38
(Garry Moss) *taken down early: chsd wnr tl hmpd and lost pl 3f out: rdn and struggling over 2f out: sn wknd* **12/1**

500- **7** 1/2 **Rightcar**[9] 8051 6-9-0 **48** StephenCraine 2 29
(Peter Grayson) *racd off the pce in last trio: rdn and effrt over 1f out: plugged on fnl f: n.d* **20/1**

/00- **8** 1 **Wyatt Earp (IRE)**[13] 8002 12-9-7 **55** (p) RobbieFitzpatrick 12 33
(Richard Guest) *racd off the pce in last trio: rdn over 1f out: no hdwy: n.d* **50/1**

565- **9** 4 **Cashel's Missile (IRE)**[9] 8050 3-8-12 **46** oh1 (p) LiamJones 5 9
(John Spearing) *taken down early: chsd ldrs: rdn and struggling over 2f out: wknd 2f out: fdd fnl f* **25/1**

1m 3.11s (0.81) **Going Correction** +0.275s/f (Slow) **9** Ran SP% **93.3**
Speed ratings (Par 101): **104,100,97,92,90 89,88,86,80**
toteswingers 1&2 £2.50, 1&3 £1.40, 2&3 £5.00 CSF £6.69 CT £27.94 TOTE £2.10: £1.10, £2.00, £2.60; EX 9.30 Trifecta £27.70 Pool: £1886.95 - 51.06 winning units..
Owner F Butler & Mrs C Dunnett **Bred** Audrey Frances Stynes **Trained** Hingham, Norfolk
■ Marmot Bay was withdrawn (4-1, unruly in stalls). Deduct 20p in the £ under R4.

FOCUS
A furiously run handicap. The winner comfirmed recent improvement, making all in a good time for the grade.

8169 BEST ODDS AT BOOKMAKERS.CO.UK H'CAP (DIV II) 5f 20y(P)
7:20 (7:20) (Class 6) (0-55,55) 3-Y-0+ **£1,940** (£577; £288; £144) **Stalls** Low

Form RPR

/05- **1** **The Dancing Lord**[273] 916 4-9-0 **55** RyanWhile[(7)] 6 70
(Bill Turner) *chsd ldr tl led wl over 1f out: rdn clr ent fnl f: in n.d after: rdn out* **10/1**

000- **2** 4 **Divertimenti (IRE)**[13] 8002 9-9-3 **54** (b) MarkCoumbe[(3)] 8 55
(Roy Bowring) *chsd ldrs: 3rd and effrt 2f out: outpcd and btn 1f out: chsd clr wnr fnl 100yds: no imp* **6/1**

060- **3** 3/4 **Chateau Lola**[9] 8050 4-9-0 **48** (v) TomEaves 2 46
(Derek Shaw) *t.k.h: chsd ldrs: rdn and outpcd over 1f out: no ch w wnr but plugged on fnl f to go 3rd towards fin* **20/1**

603- **4** nk **Vhujon (IRE)**[9] 8051 8-8-9 **46** oh1 SladeO'Hara[(3)] 11 43
(Peter Grayson) *stdd s: wl off the pce in rr: rdn and styd on ins fnl f: nvr trbld ldrs* **10/1**

0/0- **5** 1 **Reinvigorate (IRE)**[5] 8119 3-9-7 **55** MartinHarley 4 48
(Emmet Michael Butterly, Ire) *led tl rdn and hdd wl over 1f out: outpcd and btn 1f out: wknd ins fnl f* **3/1**[1]

003- **6** hd **Befortyfour**[9] 8050 8-9-4 **52** RobertWinston 7 45
(Charles Smith) *sn pushed along in midfield: rdn and racd awkwardly 2f out: hung lft and no imp over 1f out: plugged on fnl f* **4/1**[2]

060- **7** 5 **Lord Buffhead**[13] 8002 4-9-1 **52** (e) BillyCray[(3)] 5 27
(Richard Guest) *taken down early: racd off the pce in last trio: rdn and wd bnd 2f out: no prog: n.d* **11/2**[3]

060/ **8** 1/2 **King's Ciel**[504] 4237 4-9-0 **48** RichardKingscote 9 21
(Sean Curran) *sn pushed along in midfield: struggling u.p 1/2-way: bhd fnl f* **4/1**[2]

656- **9** hd **Ishetoo**[9] 8050 9-8-12 **46** oh1 StephenCraine 1 18
(Peter Grayson) *racd off the pce in last trio: n.d* **33/1**

1m 3.44s (1.14) **Going Correction** +0.275s/f (Slow) **9** Ran SP% **120.6**
Speed ratings (Par 101): **101,94,93,92,91 91,83,82,81**
toteswingers 1&2 £12.60, 1&3 £12.80, 2&3 £29.90 CSF £71.70 CT £1205.61 TOTE £10.20: £2.70, £2.70, £4.40; EX 71.00 Trifecta £344.80 Pool: £2904.46 - 6.31 winning units..
Owner Mrs M S Teversham **Bred** Mrs Monica Teversham **Trained** Sigwells, Somerset

FOCUS
This looked significantly weaker than the first division, but it's hard to fault the performance of the winner, who rates back to his standout 3yo figure.
T/Plt: £338.20. Pool: £85,701.36 - 184.97 winning units. T/Qpdt: £47.20. Pool: £12,529.53 - 196.04 winning units. SP

8153 LINGFIELD (L-H)
Friday, December 6

OFFICIAL GOING: Standard
Wind: Light; across Weather: Dry

8175 32RED/BRITISH STALLION STUDS EBF MAIDEN FILLIES' STKS (DIV I) 1m (P)
11:45 (11:46) (Class 5) 2-Y-0 **£3,067** (£905; £453) **Stalls** High

Form RPR

62- **1** **Gay Marriage (IRE)**[30] 7763 2-9-0 0 RobertHavlin 6 73+
(John Gosden) *dwlt: rcvrd to ld after 1f: mde rest: rdn wl over 1f out: kpt on strly: rdn out* **11/4**[2]

40- **2** *1 ½* **Merry Me (IRE)**[128] 4877 2-9-0 0 DavidProbert 8 70+
(Andrew Balding) *dwlt: hld up in tch in midfield: nt clr run over 2f out: swtchd rt bnd 2f out: hdwy: rn green and hung lft 1f out: r.o wl to go 2nd last strides* **7/1**

3 *hd* **Passing By** 2-9-0 0 SeanLevey 5 69+
(Richard Hannon Snr) *t.k.h: chsd ldrs: rdn to press ldrs whn rn green and wd bnd 2f out: rallied ent fnl f: chsd wnr fnl 75yds: no imp: lost 2nd last strides* **6/1**[3]

5- **4** *hd* **Sotise (IRE)**[22] 7874 2-9-0 0 MartinHarley 7 69
(Marco Botti) *chsd wnr 5f out: rdn and unable qckn wl over 1f out: kpt on same pce u.p fnl f* **6/4**[1]

0- **5** *1* **Al Shoogh**[45] 7449 2-9-0 0 MartinLane 3 66
(David Simcock) *led for 1f: chsd ldrs after: effrt u.p on inner over 1f out: no ex and outpcd fnl 100yds* **8/1**

6 *7* **Alphabetique** 2-9-0 0 RobertWinston 1 50
(Peter Chapple-Hyam) *dwlt: in tch in last trio: hdwy on outer over 2f out: no imp and outpcd 2f out: wknd fnl f* **20/1**

7 *1 ½* **Procks Girl** 2-9-0 0 AdamKirby 4 47
(Clive Cox) *rn green: in tch in midfield: rdn and struggling ent fnl 2f: sn outpcd: wknd fnl f* **12/1**

- **8** *7* **Sweet Charlie** 2-9-0 0 ShaneKelly 2 31
(Mike Murphy) *rn green and pushed along in last trio: rdn 4f out: lost tch over 2f out* **66/1**

9 *4 ½* **Hallaga** 2-9-0 0 JimCrowley 9 20
(William Jarvis) *v.s.a: rcvrd and in tch in last after 1f: rdn and lost tch 3f out* **33/1**

1m 37.74s (-0.46) **Going Correction** -0.10s/f (Stan) **9** Ran SP% **121.5**
Speed ratings (Par 93): **98,96,96,96,95 88,86,79,75**
toteswingers 1&2 £2.80, 1&3 £1.80, 2&3 £9.30 CSF £23.35 TOTE £4.20: £1.20, £2.20, £2.20; EX 17.00 Trifecta £93.90 Pool: £1,559.06 - 12.44 winning units.
Owner Martin Hughes & Michael Kerr-Dineen **Bred** Lodge Park Stud **Trained** Newmarket, Suffolk

FOCUS
No overnight frost, but low temperatures and bright with little wind. The first division of this juvenile fillies' maiden was run at a modest early pace and the form doesn't look anything out of the ordinary. They finished in a heap but the form is rated as straightforward.

8176 32RED/BRITISH STALLION STUDS EBF MAIDEN FILLIES' STKS (DIV II) 1m (P)
12:15 (12:17) (Class 5) 2-Y-O **£3,067** (£905; £453) **Stalls** High

Form RPR

2- **1** **Water Hole (IRE)**[22] 7875 2-9-0 0 RobertHavlin 3 81+
(John Gosden) *chsd ldrs: hdwy to go 2nd after 2f: led and travelling strly 2f out: rdn and clr over 1f out: kpt on u.p: rdn out* **8/15**[1]

330- **2** *2 ¾* **Tears Of The Sun**[76] 6644 2-9-0 74 ChrisCatlin 1 75
(Roger Varian) *chsd ldrs: rdn and effrt 2f out: chsd clr wnr over 1f out: kpt on but no imp* **7/1**[3]

45- **3** *½* **This Is The Day**[36] 7645 2-9-0 0 ShaneKelly 2 74
(William Haggas) *chsd ldrs: rdn over 2f out: 3rd and kpt on same pce u.p fr over 1f out: no threat to wnr* **9/2**[2]

4 *2 ¾* **Charmy Dukesse (IRE)** 2-9-0 0 MartinHarley 9 67+
(Marco Botti) *hld up in tch in last trio: rdn and hdwy wl over 1f out: 4th and no imp fr over 1f out* **16/1**

5 *5* **Cosquillas (IRE)** 2-9-0 0 LiamJones 7 56
(Mark Johnston) *rn green in last trio: reminder after 2f: rdn and effrt on outer 3f out: struggling ent fnl 2f: sn wknd* **25/1**

6 *3 ¾* **Lara Lipton (IRE)** 2-9-0 0 TedDurcan 5 47
(Jane Chapple-Hyam) *s.i.s: rn green: in tch in rr: rdn and struggling over 2f out: wknd wl over 1f out* **50/1**

5- **7** *hd* **Aristocratic Duty**[30] 7763 2-9-0 0 LiamKeniry 4 47
(Sylvester Kirk) *led: hdd and rdn 2f out: sn outpcd and btn: wknd fnl f* **14/1**

1m 37.16s (-1.04) **Going Correction** -0.10s/f (Stan) **7** Ran SP% **114.3**
Speed ratings (Par 93): **101,98,97,95,90 86,86**
toteswingers 1&2 £1.40, 1&3 £1.20, 2&3 £1.60 CSF £5.05 TOTE £1.40: £1.10, £3.20; EX 4.60 Trifecta £10.00 Pool: £3,120.85 - 232.68 winning units.
Owner W S Farish **Bred** Barronstown Stud **Trained** Newmarket, Suffolk

FOCUS
The pace was ordinary for the second division of the fillies' maiden, which looked a weaker event than the first. The winner got this done with the minimum of fuss.

8177 BEST ODDS AT BOOKMAKERS.CO.UK CLAIMING STKS 5f (P)
12:45 (12:45) (Class 6) 3-Y-O+ **£2,045** (£603; £302) **Stalls** Low

Form RPR

250- **1** **Hamoody (USA)**[77] 6583 9-8-12 82 MartinDwyer 1 89
(David Nicholls) *taken down early: pressed ldr tl led on inner 1/2-way: pushed along and qcknd clr over 1f out: r.o wl: comf* **3/1**[3]

006- **2** *2 ½* **Pabusar**[36] 7642 5-9-6 87 AdamKirby 2 88
(Jamie Osborne) *led tl 1/2-way: rdn 2f out: drvn and outpcd by wnr over 1f out: one pce after* **11/10**[1]

263- **3** *2* **Electric Qatar**[15] 7985 4-8-8 75 RichardKingscote 7 69
(Tom Dascombe) *pressed ldr tl 3rd and outpcd bnd 2f out: wl hld and plugged on same pce after* **9/4**[2]

400- **4** *3* **Girl At The Sands (IRE)**[25] 7841 3-8-3 62 JimmyQuinn 5 53
(Edward Creighton) *pushed along in rr: effrt u.p to go modest 4th over 1f out: no imp* **33/1**

460- **5** *2 ½* **Royal Award**[51] 7315 4-8-0 62 (b[1]) JamieMackay 4 41
(Jonathan Portman) *chsd ldng trio and rdn along early: hdwy on outer to chse ldrs 1/2-way: outpcd and wd bnd 2f out: sn wknd* **25/1**

58.22s (-0.58) **Going Correction** -0.10s/f (Stan) **5** Ran SP% **110.2**
Speed ratings (Par 101): **100,96,92,88,84**
CSF £6.77 TOTE £4.50: £2.40, £1.10; EX 6.20 Trifecta £11.00 Pool: £3,036.77 - 206.96 winning units.
Owner Hart Inn I **Bred** Ragged Mountain Farm **Trained** Sessay, N Yorks

FOCUS
A fair sprint claimer. The winner is more solid than most for the grade.

8178 LADBROKES H'CAP 1m (P)
1:20 (1:20) (Class 5) (0-75,75) 3-Y-O+ **£2,726** (£805; £402) **Stalls** High

Form RPR

461- **1** **Wandsworth (IRE)**[9] 8063 3-9-1 73 6ex RossAtkinson(3) 5 85+
(Roger Varian) *chsd ldrs tl led over 6f out: mde rest: rdn and qcknd bnd 2f out: clr ins fnl f: r.o wl* **3/1**[1]

540- **2** *1 ¼* **Just One Kiss**[78] 6566 3-9-6 75 JimCrowley 1 83
(Lady Cecil) *t.k.h: chsd ldrs: rdn to chse wnr 2f out: drvn and kpt on same pce fr over 1f out* **7/1**[3]

535- **3** *nk* **Flamborough Breeze**[22] 7876 4-9-6 74 (t) TedDurcan 9 81
(Ed Vaughan) *stdd s: hld up in last trio: hdwy into midfield 3f out: racd awkwardly u.p bnd 2f out: chsd ldrs and kpt on ins fnl f: no threat to wnr* **12/1**

012- **4** *1 ¾* **Duke Of Grazeon (IRE)**[42] 7505 3-9-0 69 MartinLane 2 72
(Mrs Ilka Gansera-Leveque) *t.k.h: chsd ldrs: effrt u.p ent fnl 2f: kpt on same pce ins fnl f* **16/1**

455- **5** *½* **Greensward**[9] 8068 7-9-6 74 (b) HayleyTurner 6 76
(Conor Dore) *stdd s: hld up in tch in last trio: hdwy u.p over 1f out: kpt on ins fnl f: no threat to wnr* **25/1**

024- **6** *shd* **Duke Of Destiny (IRE)**[29] 7785 4-9-7 75 (p) GeorgeBaker 7 77
(Ed Walker) *in tch in midfield: effrt ent fnl 2f: styd on same pce u.p fr over 1f out* **3/1**[1]

041- **7** *1 ¾* **Broughtons Charm (IRE)**[23] 7861 3-9-5 74 RobertWinston 11 72
(Willie Musson) *hld up in tch in last trio: pushed along and hdwy jst over 1f out: stl pushed along and kpt on same pce ins fnl f* **6/1**[2]

450- **8** *nk* **Gabrial's Wawa**[16] 7970 3-9-4 73 RobertHavlin 3 70
(Roger Ingram) *t.k.h: led tl over 6f out: rdn and lost 2nd 2f out: sn drvn and outpcd jst over 1f out: wknd ins fnl f* **16/1**

003- **9** *¾* **Kung Hei Fat Choy (USA)**[14] 8008 4-9-4 72 (b) FrederikTylicki 4 67
(James Given) *in tch in midfield: rdn over 2f out: outpcd u.p and btn over 1f out: wknd ins fnl f* **8/1**

506- **10** *shd* **Hill Of Dreams (IRE)**[15] 7989 4-9-7 75 (b) FergusSweeney 10 70
(Dean Ivory) *dwlt: sn in tch in midfield: rdn and edgd rt over 1f out: no imp and continued to hang rt ins fnl f* **25/1**

000- **11** *hd* **Top Offer**[15] 7988 4-9-4 72 ShaneKelly 12 66
(Peter Crate) *stdd s: hld up in tch in last pair: swtchd rt over 2f out: no hdwy over 1f out: n.d* **25/1**

000- **12** *7* **Rezwaan**[29] 7785 6-8-12 73 (b) NedCurtis(7) 8 51
(Murty McGrath) *stdd s: in tch towards rr: sme hdwy on outer 3f out: rdn and struggling ent fnl 2f: wknd over 1f out* **50/1**

1m 36.8s (-1.40) **Going Correction** -0.10s/f (Stan)
WFA 3 from 4yo+ 1lb **12** Ran SP% **120.9**
Speed ratings (Par 103): **103,101,101,99,99 99,97,97,96,96 96,89**
toteswingers 1&2 £6.30, 1&3 £9.10, 2&3 £13.90 CSF £23.94 CT £230.99 TOTE £4.10: £1.50, £2.90, £3.30; EX 23.70 Trifecta £308.00 Pool: £2,004.10 - 4.87 winning units.
Owner H R H Sultan Ahmad Shah **Bred** Francois Drion & Ptns **Trained** Newmarket, Suffolk

FOCUS
A slow early pace for this modest handicap. The winner more than confirmed his Kempton win.

8179 CORAL.CO.UK BEST ODDS GUARANTEED ON RACING H'CAP 1m 2f (P)
1:55 (1:57) (Class 5) (0-75,75) 3-Y-O+ **£2,726** (£805; £402) **Stalls** Low

Form RPR

436- **1** **Syncopate**[17] 7952 4-8-12 69 RossAtkinson(3) 3 78
(Pam Sly) *hld up in tch in midfield: swtchd rt and effrt ent fnl f: rdn and hands and heels and qcknd to ld wl ins fnl f: r.o wl: pushed out* **7/1**[2]

330- **2** *¾* **Perfect Cracker**[16] 7970 5-9-3 71 AdamKirby 7 79
(Clive Cox) *hld up in tch in last trio: nt clr run ent fnl 2f tl swtchd rt jst ins fnl f: r.o wl to go 2nd cl home* **7/2**[1]

440- **3** *nk* **Kelpie Blitz (IRE)**[25] 7840 4-9-3 71 (t) MartinHarley 6 78
(Seamus Durack) *stdd s: hld up in tch towards rr: clsd and nt clr run 2f out: swtchd lft and qcknd u.p over 1f out: ev ch ins fnl f: one pce fnl 75yds* **8/1**[3]

201- **4** *1 ¾* **Gaelic Silver (FR)**[23] 7865 7-9-4 72 GeorgeBaker 2 75
(Gary Moore) *hld up in tch in midfield: swtchd and chal whn bmpd ent fnl f: led jst ins fnl f: hdd and no ex fnl 100yds: wknd towards fin* **7/2**[1]

063- **5** *nk* **Archie Rice (USA)**[16] 7970 7-9-0 71 RobertTart(3) 1 74
(Tom Keddy) *chsd ldrs: rdn ent fnl 2f: stl pressing ldrs whn squeezed for room and hmpd 1f out: kpt on same pce ins fnl f* **10/1**

163- **6** *2 ¼* **Absent Amy (IRE)**[22] 7876 4-9-6 74 RobertHavlin 14 72
(Amy Weaver) *chsd ldrs: drvn and unable qck over 1f out: wknd ins fnl f* **10/1**

003- **7** *½* **Zaeem**[23] 7865 4-9-2 70 RobertWinston 9 67
(Dean Ivory) *chsd ldr tl rdn to ld wl over 1f out: bmpd ent fnl f: hdd jst ins fnl f: wknd fnl 100yds* **8/1**[3]

200- **8** *1 ½* **Apache Glory (USA)**[65] 6936 5-9-7 75 (p) StephenCraine 11 69
(John Stimpson) *hld up in tch in last quartet: pushed along and hdwy on outer 3f out: wd and lost pl bnd 2f out: trying to rally and edgd lft 1f out: kpt on same pce after* **50/1**

160- **9** *nk* **Precision Five**[16] 7970 4-9-2 70 (p) FergusSweeney 4 64
(Jeremy Gask) *in tch in midfield on outer: pushed along and no hdwy over 2f out: lost pl wl over 1f out: plugged on but n.d after* **20/1**

163- **10** *2 ¼* **Saharia (IRE)**[186] 2912 6-9-7 75 (p) ShaneKelly 8 64
(Jo Hughes) *stdd and dropped in bhd after s: hld up in rr: rdn and sme hdwy on inner over 1f out: no imp f1f out: wknd ins fnl f* **33/1**

065- **11** *shd* **Xinbama (IRE)**[16] 7970 4-9-0 73 (t) ShelleyBirkett(5) 10 62
(J W Hills) *s.i.s: hdwy on outer and in midfield after 2f: rdn and struggling ent fnl 2f: btn over 1f out: wknd fnl f* **12/1**

004- **12** *1* **Munsarim (IRE)**[9] 8068 6-9-5 73 (b) AmirQuinn 5 60
(Lee Carter) *t.k.h: led tl 2f out: sn rdn and stl pressing ldrs whn edgd rt jst over 1f out: sn btn: fdd ins fnl f* **12/1**

2m 4.12s (-2.48) **Going Correction** -0.10s/f (Stan)
WFA 3 from 4yo+ 3lb **12** Ran SP% **122.4**
Speed ratings (Par 103): **105,104,104,102,102 100,100,99,98,97 97,96**
toteswingers 1&2 £6.40, 1&3 £14.90, 2&3 £5.90 CSF £32.20 CT £208.22 TOTE £8.10: £2.70, £1.70, £3.60; EX 37.70 Trifecta £564.60 Pool: £2,949.40 - 3.91 winning units.
Owner Pam's People **Bred** Meon Valley Stud **Trained** Thorney, Cambs

FOCUS
A messy affair with a couple of hard-luck stories thanks to a pedestrian early pace and space being at a premium in the closing stages. Ordinary form.

8180 DOWNLOAD THE LADBROKES APP MAIDEN STKS 7f (P)
2:30 (2:30) (Class 5) 3-Y-O+ **£2,726** (£805; £402) **Stalls** Low

Form RPR

23- **1** **Bouclier (IRE)**[20] 7932 3-9-5 0 AdamKirby 6 88+
(Luca Cumani) *mde all: nudged along and readily wnt clr 2f out: in n.d after: easily* **2/7**[1]

2 *8* **Marble Statuette (USA)** 3-9-0 0 HayleyTurner 3 61
(Richard Fahey) *chsd ldrs: wnt 2nd 5f out: rdn over 2f out: sn brushed aside by wnr and wl btn: kpt on for clr 2nd* **5/1**[2]

402- **3** *5* **Maillot Jaune (IRE)**[66] 6919 3-8-7 50 JackGarritty(7) 1 48
(Patrick Holmes) *hld up in tch in last pair: outpcd by wnr ent fnl 2f: plugged on u.p to go modest 3rd ins fnl f: no imp* **16/1**

505- **4** *hd* **Kaylee**[16] 7983 4-9-0 46 ChrisCatlin 5 47
(Brett Johnson) *stdd s: hld up in rr: rdn over 2f out: outpcd by wnr and wd bnd 2f out: plugged on and battling for modest 3rd ins fnl f: kpt on* **33/1**

600- **5** *2 ¾* **Slip Of A Girl (IRE)**[91] 6178 3-9-0 51 StevieDonohoe 2 40
(Patrick Holmes) *pushed along early: chsd wnr tl 5f out: rdn over 2f out: sn outpcd and btn: wknd fnl f* **50/1**

5- **6** *1 ½* **Aeolian Blue**[29] 7781 3-9-0 0 ShaneKelly 4 36
(William Knight) *in tch in midfield: rdn and struggling over 2f out: outpcd and btn 2f out: wknd over 1f out* **8/1**[3]

1m 23.82s (-0.98) **Going Correction** -0.10s/f (Stan) **6** Ran SP% **116.3**
Speed ratings (Par 103): **101,91,86,85,82 81**
toteswingers 1&2 £1.10, 1&3 £2.70, 2&3 £3.10 CSF £2.49 TOTE £1.20: £1.10, £2.20; EX 2.90 Trifecta £10.60 Pool: £3,372.72 - 237.89 winning units.
Owner Wildenstein Stables Limited **Bred** Dayton Investments Ltd **Trained** Newmarket, Suffolk

FOCUS
A weak event but the winner recorded a good time. The bare form is limited.

8181 BOOKMAKERS.CO.UK H'CAP 6f (P)
3:05 (3:05) (Class 4) (0-85,85) 3-Y-0+ **£4,690** (£1,395; £697; £348) **Stalls** Low

Form RPR

021- **1** **Novellen Lad (IRE)**[21] 7897 8-9-2 **80** RobertWinston 3 90
(Willie Musson) *wl in tch in midfield: clsd and swtchd rt over 1f out: rdn to chal ins fnl f: led wl ins fnl f: a jst last home: rdn out* **7/2**[1]

545- **2** *hd* **Agerzam**[59] 7112 3-9-5 **83** AdamKirby 10 92+
(Roger Varian) *in tch in midfield: swtchd rt and effrt ent fnl f: str run to press wnr wl ins fnl f: clsng cl home but nvr quite getting to wnr* **4/1**[2]

122- **3** *1 ¼* **Glastonberry**[21] 7897 5-8-12 **76** HayleyTurner 5 81
(Geoffrey Deacon) *led: rdn wl over 1f out: hrd pressed but battled on gamely u.p tl hdd and no ex wl ins fnl f* **12/1**

200- **4** *hd* **Blessington (IRE)**[16] 7982 3-9-7 **85** RobertHavlin 2 90
(John Gosden) *chsd ldrs: effrt u.p and str chal ent fnl f: unable qck and one pce fnl 100yds* **9/2**[3]

250- **5** *½* **Kakatosi**[44] 7464 6-9-5 **83** ShaneKelly 4 86+
(Mike Murphy) *s.i.s: hld up in tch in rr: hdwy jst over 1f out: swtchd rt jst ins fnl f: r.o wl fnl 75yds: nt rch ldrs* **12/1**

054- **6** *½* **The Tichborne (IRE)**[42] 7507 5-8-13 **77** (p) MartinHarley 7 79
(Roger Teal) *in tch in midfield: effrt u.p over 1f out: styd on same pce ins fnl f* **6/1**

060- **7** *nk* **Tax Free (IRE)**[23] 7851 11-9-7 **85** MartinDwyer 9 86
(David Nicholls) *chsd ldr: rdn and ev ch 2f out: struggling to qckn whn pushed rt over 1f out: sltly outpcd 1f out: wknd fnl 100yds* **33/1**

151- **8** *½* **Jay Bee Blue**[17] 7965 4-9-2 **80** (bt) TomQueally 11 79
(Sean Curran) *stdd s: hld up in tch towards rr: effrt over 1f out: clsng whn pushed rt jst ins fnl f: kpt on same pce after* **10/1**

150- **9** *shd* **Commanche**[8] 8088 4-8-11 **80** ShelleyBirkett(5) 8 79
(Chris Dwyer) *t.k.h: wl in tch in midfield: rdn and effrt over 1f out: keeping on but looking hld whn pushed rt jst ins fnl f: one pce and no prog after* **20/1**

366- **10** *2 ¼* **Dominium (USA)**[8] 8088 6-8-7 **78** (b) DavidParkes(7) 1 69
(Jeremy Gask) *s.i.s: in tch in rr: rdn and effrt jst over 1f out: kpt on but no threat to ldrs: swtchd rt ins fnl f* **20/1**

460- **11** *nk* **Aye Aye Skipper (IRE)**[31] 7742 3-8-13 **77** JimCrowley 12 67
(Dean Ivory) *chsd ldrs on outer: rdn and struggling bnd 2f out: sn lost pl: wknd ent fnl f* **20/1**

150- **12** *nk* **Rocket Rob (IRE)**[13] 8021 7-9-2 **80** JamieMackay 6 70
(Willie Musson) *stdd s: hld up in rr on outer: pushed along wl over 1f out: no imp and hld whn pushed rt ins fnl f: eased towards fin* **20/1**

1m 10.79s (-1.11) **Going Correction** -0.10s/f (Stan) **12** Ran SP% **121.2**
Speed ratings (Par 105): **103,102,101,100,100 99,99,98,98,95 94,94**
toteswingers 1&2 £5.00, 1&3 £4.60, 2&3 £9.80 CSF £16.05 CT £157.36 TOTE £3.40: £2.10, £1.10, £2.50; EX 20.20 Trifecta £94.00 Pool: £3,597.82 - 28.69 winning units.
Owner Johnson & Broughton **Bred** Mrs Chris Harrington **Trained** Newmarket, Suffolk
■ Stewards' Enquiry : Shane Kelly one-day ban: careless riding (Dec 20)

FOCUS
A competitive handicap for the grade and the form looks solid. The winner built on his latest C&D defeat of the third.

8182 CORAL APP DOWNLOAD FROM THE APP STORE H'CAP 1m 4f (P)
3:35 (3:35) (Class 6) (0-65,64) 3-Y-0+ **£2,045** (£603; £302) **Stalls** Low

Form RPR

000- **1** **Dellbuoy**[37] 7629 4-9-8 **62** FergusSweeney 1 69
(Pat Phelan) *stdd s: hld up in rr: clsd wl over 1f out: rdn and hdwy 1f out: str run to ld fnl 75yds: pricked ears in front: r.o: comf* **7/1**[3]

350- **2** *¾* **Modem**[29] 7781 3-9-5 **64** (b[1]) MartinDwyer 6 70
(Rod Millman) *in tch in midfield: reminders 6f out: hdwy to join ldr and qcknd clr over 2f out: forged ahd ins fnl f: hdd: hung rt and no ex fnl 50yds* **7/4**[1]

445- **3** *½* **Perfect Delight**[38] 7611 4-9-3 **64** (p) JaneElliott(7) 7 69
(Ralph Beckett) *in tch in midfield: effrt over 1f out: swtchd rt and hdwy 1f out: kpt on wl ins fnl f* **9/2**[2]

345- **4** *¾* **India's Song**[62] 7038 3-9-1 **60** MartinLane 8 64
(David Simcock) *hld up in tch towards rr: rdn over 1f out: styd on u.p ins fnl f: sltly hmpd and swtchd rt nr fin* **9/2**[2]

300- **5** *1 ¼* **Yes Chef**[8] 8089 6-9-4 **58** (p) LiamJones 2 60
(Chris Gordon) *led: jnd and wnt clr w rival over 2f out: drvn 2f out: hdd jst ins fnl f: no ex and wknd towards fin* **10/1**

440- **6** *½* **Maison Brillet (IRE)**[174] 3328 6-9-8 **62** (p) RobertHavlin 3 63
(Clive Drew) *chsd ldrs: rdn and slty outpcd over 2f out: rallied u.p on inner and pressed ldrs 1f out: no ex and wknd wl ins fnl f* **14/1**

640- **7** *2* **London Skolar**[249] 1296 3-8-13 **58** MartinHarley 5 56
(James Eustace) *chsd ldr tl 3f out: sn rdn and sltly outpcd by ldng pair: tried to rally u.p over 1f out: wknd fnl 100yds* **14/1**

05R- **R** **Azabitmour (FR)**[2] 8148 3-8-6 **51** (b) JohnFahy 4
(John Best) *ref to r: tk no part* **12/1**

2m 32.48s (-0.52) **Going Correction** -0.10s/f (Stan)
WFA 3 from 4yo+ 5lb **8** Ran SP% **115.3**
Speed ratings (Par 101): **97,96,96,95,94 94,93,**
toteswingers 1&2 £4.50, 1&3 £3.10, 2&3 £2.70 CSF £19.89 CT £62.17 TOTE £11.10: £3.00, £1.50, £1.10; EX 25.60 Trifecta £150.00 Pool: £3,990.25 - 19.93 winning units.
Owner Timesquare Ltd **Bred** Ermyn Lodge Stud Limited **Trained** Epsom, Surrey

FOCUS
Moderate form but the pace wasn't bad.
T/Plt: £22.80 to a £1 stake. Pool: £46,048.73 - 1,474.24 winning units T/Qpdt: £8.60 to a £1 stake. Pool: £4,656.65 - 400.30 winning units SP

[8162] WOLVERHAMPTON (A.W) (L-H)
Friday, December 6

OFFICIAL GOING: Standard
Wind: Light behind Weather: Overcast

8183 CORAL APP DOWNLOAD FROM THE APP STORE APPRENTICE H'CAP 1m 1f 103y(P)
4:00 (4:00) (Class 6) (0-65,65) 3-Y-0+ **£1,940** (£577; £288; £144) **Stalls** Low

Form RPR

463- **1** **Mrs Micawber**[23] 7857 3-9-4 **62** LouisSteward 6 78
(Michael Bell) *mde all: pushed clr over 1f out: rdn out* **7/4**[1]

411- **2** *4 ½* **Dansili Dutch (IRE)**[11] 8038 4-8-13 **62** 6ex JoshDoyle(7) 5 69
(David O'Meara) *chsd ldrs: pushed along over 2f out: rdn over 1f out: edgd lft and wnt 2nd ins fnl f: styd on same pce* **5/1**[3]

103- **3** *3* **Delightful Sleep**[11] 8038 5-9-6 **62** EoinWalsh 1 63
(David Evans) *prom: chsd wnr over 3f out: rdn over 1f out: no ex ins fnl f* **11/4**[2]

105- **4** *1 ¼* **Monzino (USA)**[10] 8049 5-9-3 **64** PaulBooth(5) 4 62
(Michael Chapman) *s.s: in rr and pushed along over 5f out: rdn over 2f out: sn outpcd* **8/1**

060- **5** *2 ¼* **Elizabeth Coffee (IRE)**[6] 8116 5-8-6 **51** oh2 [1] JordanVaughan(3) 2 44
(John Weymes) *hld up: rdn and wknd over 2f out* **25/1**

500- **6** *14* **Mespone (FR)**[23] 7865 4-9-9 **65** TimClark 3 29
(Alan Bailey) *w wnr tl pushed along over 4f out: rdn and wknd over 2f out* **5/1**[3]

2m 2.77s (1.07) **Going Correction** +0.275s/f (Slow)
WFA 3 from 4yo+ 2lb **6** Ran SP% **111.3**
Speed ratings (Par 101): **106,102,99,98,96 83**
toteswingers 1&2 £1.60, 1&3 £1.30, 2&3 £2.50 CSF £10.73 TOTE £1.70: £1.10, £2.00; EX 11.00 Trifecta £16.80 Pool: £4264.41 - 189.63 winning units.
Owner W J Gredley **Bred** Stetchworth & Middle Park Studs **Trained** Newmarket, Suffolk

FOCUS
This handicap, confined to apprentice riders, was run at an honest pace. The winner stepped up and the second is getting close to his old best.

8184 CORAL MOBILE "JUST THREE CLICKS TO BET" H'CAP 1m 4f 50y(P)
4:30 (4:30) (Class 5) (0-70,68) 3-Y-0 **£2,587** (£770; £384; £192) **Stalls** Low

Form RPR

6- **1** **Rebel Force (IRE)**[18] 7950 3-9-7 **68** GrahamLee 5 77
(Mark Johnston) *a.p: chsd ldr over 5f out: rdn to ld 1f out: styd on* **3/1**[2]

510- **2** *nk* **Pixie Cut (IRE)**[44] 7573 3-9-7 **68** BarryMcHugh 3 76
(Alistair Whillans) *chsd ldrs: lost pl over 7f out: nt clr run 3f out: hdwy over 1f out: rdn and ev ch ins fnl f: styd on* **7/2**[3]

435- **3** *4 ½* **Akdam (IRE)**[20] 4222 3-9-7 **68** (p) LukeMorris 4 68
(Tony Carroll) *rn in snatches: in tch: rdn over 2f out: no ex ins fnl f* **9/4**[1]

215- **4** *½* **Poppy Bond**[6] 8116 3-8-11 **58** GrahamGibbons 6 58
(Alan Bailey) *hld up: plld hrd: hdwy to ld over 7f out: pushed along over 2f out: rdn and hdd 1f out: wknd ins fnl f* **3/1**[2]

5 *1* **Slipper Satin (IRE)**[17] 7390 3-9-7 **68** BenCurtis 2 66
(Noel Quinlan) *led: hdd over 7f out: chsd ldrs: rdn over 2f out: wknd over 1f out* **10/1**

2m 45.97s (4.87) **Going Correction** +0.275s/f (Slow) **5** Ran SP% **112.1**
Speed ratings (Par 102): **94,93,90,90,89**
CSF £13.85 TOTE £3.90: £1.70, £2.50; EX 15.00 Trifecta £36.80 Pool: £3799.99 - 76.63 winning units.
Owner Lady O'Reilly **Bred** Castlemartin Sky & Skymarc Farm **Trained** Middleham Moor, N Yorks

FOCUS
Plenty of pace on for this handicap with the front two pulling clear. The bare form is ordinary.

8185 CORAL.CO.UK BEST ODDS GUARANTEED ON RACING MAIDEN STKS 1m 1f 103y(P)
5:00 (5:00) (Class 5) 3-4-Y-0 **£2,587** (£770; £384; £192) **Stalls** Low

Form RPR

622- **1** **Hanalei Bay (IRE)**[35] 7669 3-9-5 63 TomEaves 4 71
(Keith Dalgleish) *mde all: rdn over 1f out: hung rt ins fnl f: styd on u.p* **7/4**[2]

632- **2** *1* **Frost Fire (USA)**[10] 8054 3-9-0 0 GrahamLee 5 64
(Mark Johnston) *sn trcking ldr: rdn over 2f out: styd on same pce ins fnl f* **8/11**[1]

3 *12* **Acton Gold** 4-9-2 0 GrahamGibbons 3 39
(Brian Baugh) *dwlt: sn pushed along and in tch: rdn 3f out: wknd 2f out* **33/1**

520- **4** *53* **Caerwyn**[31] 7740 3-9-5 64 LukeMorris 1
(Tony Carroll) *chsd ldrs: pushed along over 3f out: rdn and wknd over 2f out* **10/1**[3]

2m 4.05s (2.35) **Going Correction** +0.275s/f (Slow)
WFA 3 from 4yo 2lb **4** Ran SP% **106.3**
Speed ratings (Par 103): **100,99,88,41**
CSF £3.29 TOTE £2.50; EX 4.70 Trifecta £12.70 Pool: £2495.08 - 146.71 winning units.
Owner Mrs Francesca Mitchell **Bred** Holborn Trust Co **Trained** Carluke, S Lanarks

FOCUS
This weak maiden looked a match on the book and the market leaders were in command turning for home.

8186 CORAL.CO.UK H'CAP 1m 1f 103y(P)
5:30 (5:30) (Class 6) (0-60,59) 3-Y-0 **£1,940** (£577; £288; £144) **Stalls** Low

Form RPR

200- **1** **Berkeley Street (USA)**[48] 7376 3-9-4 **55** (p) GrahamLee 6 65+
(Jane Chapple-Hyam) *sn trcking ldr: swtchd lft after 1f: racd keenly: led over 3f out: clr over 2f out: rdn and hdd 1f out: rallied to ld post* **9/4**[2]

045- **2** *shd* **Mojo Bear**[20] 7930 3-9-1 **57** JoshBaudains(5) 5 65
(Sylvester Kirk) *wnt lft s: prom: hdwy and lost pl after 1f: hld up: pushed along over 3f out: hdwy u.p to chse wnr and edgd lft over 2f out: led 1f out: hdd post* **9/2**[3]

000- **3** *10* **Lucy Bee**[57] 7150 3-9-7 **58** AndrewMullen 4 45
(Michael Appleby) *hmpd s: chsd ldrs: rdn over 3f out: hmpd and wknd 2f out* **12/1**

03- **4** *6* **Hypnotism**[10] 8056 3-8-9 **46** LukeMorris 2 20
(Ronald Harris) *half-rrd and hmpd s: hld up: rdn over 3f out: nt clr run sn after: wknd over 2f out* **6/1**

040- **5** *28* **Silver Fawn (IRE)**[3] 8142 3-8-8 **45** (be) JimmyQuinn 1
(John Weymes) *hmpd s: chsd ldrs: rdn over 3f out: wknd over 2f out* **14/1**

421- **P** **Better Value (IRE)**[10] 8043 3-9-8 **59** 6ex........................(p) BenCurtis 3
(Noel Quinlan) *hmpd s: led: rdn and hdd over 3f out: sn eased: p.u and dismntd 2f out* **2/1**[1]
2m 4.88s (3.18) **Going Correction** +0.275s/f (Slow) **6** Ran SP% **110.9**
Speed ratings (Par 98): **96,95,87,81,56**
toteswingers 1&2 £1.90, 1&3 £3.60, 2&3 £6.00 CSF £12.37 TOTE £2.80: £1.30, £2.20; EX 10.80 Trifecta £60.00 Pool: £1765.33 - 22.04 winning units.
Owner Invictus **Bred** Darley **Trained** Dalham, Suffolk
■ Stewards' Enquiry : Josh Baudains caution: careless riding.
FOCUS
A modest contest run at a sound pace with the front two fighting out an exciting finish. The form is rated around the runner-up.

8187 LADBROKES CLASSIFIED CLAIMING STKS 1m 141y(P)
6:00 (6:00) (Class 5) 3-Y-0+ **£2,587** (£770; £384; £192) **Stalls** Low

Form RPR
602- **1** **Pravda Street**[18] 7948 8-8-4 69........................ BenCurtis 5 65
(Brian Ellison) *hld up: rdn over 2f out: hdwy and edgd lft over 1f out: led ins fnl f: r.o* **7/4**[1]
152- **2** ½ **Cantor**[20] 7931 5-8-3 60........................(v[1]) RyanPowell(3) 7 66
(Giles Bravery) *prom: pushed along over 3f out: nt clr run and lost pl over 2f out: swtchd rt 1f out: rdn and r.o wl* **9/2**[2]
340- **3** 2¼ **Prime Exhibit**[27] 7824 8-8-8 68........................(t) LukeMorris 4 63
(John Stimpson) *s.i.s: hld up: rdn over 1f out: styd on ins fnl f* **7/1**
003- **4** 1¼ **Complexity**[13] 8028 3-8-3 69........................ JoeyHaynes(5) 2 62
(Seamus Mullins) *led: plld hrd: shkn up over 2f out: rdn and hdd ins fnl f: no ex* **16/1**
020- **5** ½ **Not Rigg (USA)**[20] 7924 3-8-5 67........................(t) JordanVaughan(7) 8 65
(Gary Harrison) *a.p: trckd ldr 7f out: rdn over 1f out: no ex ins fnl f* **10/1**
355- **6** ¾ **Taxiformissbyron**[20] 7924 3-8-6 63........................ BarryMcHugh 6 57
(Michael Herrington) *chsd ldrs: rdn over 2f out: no ex ins fnl f* **14/1**
116- **7** ¾ **One Way Or Another (AUS)**[17] 7964 10-8-1 68..........(t) EoinWalsh(5) 1 53
(David Evans) *hld up: nt clr run over 2f out: shkn up over 1f out: nvr on terms* **6/1**[3]
556- **8** 3½ **Jebel Tara**[17] 7953 8-8-10 66........................(bt) DaleSwift 3 49
(Alan Brown) *mid-div: hdwy over 5f out: rdn and hung lft fr over 2f out: wknd ins fnl f* **16/1**
1m 51.76s (1.26) **Going Correction** +0.275s/f (Slow)
WFA 3 from 5yo+ 2lb **8** Ran SP% **108.9**
Speed ratings (Par 103): **105,104,102,101,101 100,99,96**
toteswingers 1&2 £1.90, 1&3 £3.50, 2&3 £5.30 CSF £8.40 TOTE £2.60: £1.20, £1.10, £1.70; EX 8.10 Trifecta £39.30 Pool: £1882.55 - 35.85 winning units.
Owner Koo's Racing Club **Bred** R A Instone **Trained** Norton, N Yorks
FOCUS
A tight claimer run at a fair pace. The winner was best in and the runner-up sets the standard.

8188 32RED MEDIAN AUCTION MAIDEN STKS 5f 20y(P)
6:30 (6:31) (Class 6) 2-Y-0 **£1,940** (£577; £288; £144) **Stalls** Low

Form RPR
66- **1** **Kinkohyo**[6] 8113 2-9-0 0........................ LukeMorris 7 58
(Bryan Smart) *sn pushed along and prom: rdn to ld over 1f out: styd on u.p* **12/1**
032- **2** shd **Coiste Bodhar (IRE)**[9] 8058 2-9-5 62........................ LiamKeniry 6 63
(Joseph Tuite) *a.p: chsd ldr over 3f out: rdn and ev ch ins fnl f: r.o* **5/4**[1]
340- **3** 1¼ **Sweet Angelica**[15] 7986 2-9-0 62........................(p) GrahamLee 4 54
(James Given) *pushed along to chse ldr tl over 3f out: remained handy: rdn over 1f out: r.o* **8/1**
050- **4** ½ **Day Star Lad**[14] 8005 2-9-5 50........................ DaleSwift 5 57+
(Derek Shaw) *sn pushed along in rr: rdn and r.o ins fnl f: nt rch ldrs* **20/1**
304- **5** 2 **Captain Gee**[13] 8024 2-9-5 59........................(b[1]) TomEaves 1 50
(John Quinn) *led: rdn: hung rt and hdd over 1f out: no ex whn hung lft ins fnl f* **7/2**[2]
6 shd **River Dreamer (IRE)** 2-9-0 0........................ AdamBeschizza 2 44
(Robert Stephens) *sn outpcd: r.o ins fnl f: nvr nrr* **16/1**
604- **7** 4½ **Seven Lucky Seven**[9] 8058 2-9-5 55........................(b) JimmyQuinn 8 33
(Gary Harrison) *wnt rt s: sn given reminders and wnt prom racing keenly: rdn over 1f out: wknd fnl f* **5/1**[3]
8 11 **The Brockster** 2-8-12 0........................ VictorSantos(7) 3
(Richard Ford) *s.s: outpcd* **66/1**
1m 4.78s (2.48) **Going Correction** +0.275s/f (Slow) **8** Ran SP% **114.3**
Speed ratings (Par 94): **91,90,88,88,84 84,77,59**
toteswingers 1&2 £4.90, 1&3 £5.10, 2&3 £4.40 CSF £27.53 TOTE £16.60: £2.80, £1.40, £2.30; EX 29.40 Trifecta £178.20 Pool: £2012.13 - 8.46 winning units.
Owner Crossfields Racing **Bred** Crossfields Bloodstock Ltd **Trained** Hambleton, N Yorks
■ Stewards' Enquiry : Tom Eaves caution: careless riding
FOCUS
The gallop was honest for this very weak maiden. The second helps with the level.

8189 COMPARE BOOKMAKERS AT BOOKMAKERS.CO.UK H'CAP 5f 216y(P)
7:00 (7:00) (Class 3) (0-95,92) 3-Y-0- **£7,246** (£2,168; £1,084; £542; £270) **Stalls** Low

Form RPR
110- **1** **Equitania**[28] 7803 3-8-10 **86**........................ TimClark(5) 5 95
(Alan Bailey) *broke wl: mde all: rdn clr over 1f out: styd on* **16/1**
604- **2** 1½ **Diamond Charlie (IRE)**[16] 7982 5-9-2 **87**........................ GrahamLee 8 91
(Simon Dow) *hld up: rdn: hung lft and r.o ins fnl f: wnt 2nd post: nt rch wnr* **8/1**
111- **3** shd **Fat Gary**[17] 7959 3-9-0 **85**........................ RichardKingscote 6 89
(Tom Dascombe) *a.p: rdn to chse wnr over 1f out: hung lft ins fnl f: r.o: lost 2nd post* **6/4**[1]
253- **4** 2¼ **Peace Seeker**[9] 8064 5-9-2 **87**........................ WilliamCarson 7 84
(Anthony Carson) *hld up in tch: rdn over 1f out: styd on same pce ins fnl f* **7/4**[2]
013- **5** shd **Arctic Feeling (IRE)**[28] 7803 5-8-10 **86**........................ SamanthaBell(5) 2 82
(Richard Fahey) *chsd ldrs: rdn over 1f out: styd on same pce fnl f* **5/1**[3]
045- **6** 2½ **My Son Max**[148] 4217 5-9-2 **87**........................ DaleSwift 3 75
(Michael Blake) *s.s: outpcd* **16/1**
000- **7** 2 **Aubrietia**[28] 7803 4-9-6 **91**........................(b) GrahamGibbons 1 73
(Alan McCabe) *trckd wnr tl rdn over 1f out: wknd fnl f* **25/1**
1m 14.64s (-0.36) **Going Correction** +0.275s/f (Slow) **7** Ran SP% **119.8**
Speed ratings (Par 107): **113,111,110,107,107 104,101**
CSF £139.83 CT £311.79 TOTE £14.10: £4.00, £5.30; EX 166.40 Trifecta £789.30 Pool: £1675.12 - 1.59 winning units.
Owner John Stocker **Bred** Longdon Stud **Trained** Newmarket, Suffolk
FOCUS
They went a decent gallop for this competitive contest. A personal best from the winner but not a race to take too literally.

T/Plt: £46.70 to a £1 stake. Pool: £76131.17 - 1189.28 winning tickets T/Qpdt: £9.60 to a £1 stake. Pool: £9367.39 - 715.85 winning tickets CR

8190 - 8197a (Foreign Racing) - See Raceform Interactive

8183 WOLVERHAMPTON (A.W) (L-H)
Saturday, December 7

OFFICIAL GOING: Standard
Wind: Light behind Weather: Cloudy

8198 LADBROKES H'CAP 7f 32y(P)
6:20 (6:20) (Class 5) (0-75,74) 3-Y-0+ **£2,587** (£770; £384; £192) **Stalls** High

Form RPR
023- **1** **George Fenton**[8] 8095 4-9-7 **74**........................(b[1]) HayleyTurner 3 82
(Conor Dore) *trckd ldr: racd keenly: pushed along over 2f out: rdn over 1f out: led and edgd lft ins fnl f: sn hdd: rallied to ld nr fin* **11/8**[1]
500- **2** shd **Strong Man**[8] 8095 5-9-1 **68**........................(b) GrahamGibbons 2 76
(Michael Easterby) *led: rdn and edgd lft over 1f out: hdd and n.m.r ins fnl f: r.o* **13/2**
133- **3** shd **Hellbender (IRE)**[12] 8037 7-9-2 **69**........................(t) JimmyQuinn 4 76
(Shaun Harris) *prom: pushed along 1/2-way: rdn and outpcd over 2f out: hdwy over 1f out: drvn to ld wl ins fnl f: edgd lft: hdd nr fin* **11/2**
001- **4** 5 **Hierarch (IRE)**[87] 6316 6-8-6 **66**........................ GeorgeBuckell(7) 5 60
(David Simcock) *prom: pushed along over 1f out: styd on same pce* **5/1**[3]
545- **5** nk **Egotist (IRE)**[18] 7961 5-9-1 **68**........................(t) RichardKingscote 1 61
(Milton Bradley) *chsd ldrs: rdn over 1f out: no ex fnl f* **4/1**[2]
1m 30.34s (0.74) **Going Correction** +0.225s/f (Slow) **5** Ran SP% **107.5**
Speed ratings (Par 103): **104,103,103,98,97**
toteswinger 1-2 £6.40 CSF £10.02 TOTE £1.90: £1.10, £2.50; EX 10.60 Trifecta £28.50 Pool: £3,050.97 - 80.03 winning tickets..
Owner Mrs Louise Marsh **Bred** R P Williams **Trained** Hubbert's Bridge, Lincs
■ Stewards' Enquiry : Jimmy Quinn two-day ban: excessive use of the whip (Dec 21,26)
FOCUS
A cracking finish to this open little handicap. Sound form.

8199 DOWNLOAD THE LADBROKES APP H'CAP 1m 141y(P)
6:50 (6:50) (Class 6) (0-60,63) 3-Y-0+ **£1,940** (£577; £288; £144) **Stalls** Low

Form RPR
166- **1** **Hail Promenader (IRE)**[11] 8042 7-9-5 **58**..................(tp) WilliamCarson 8 65
(Anthony Carson) *led 1f: chsd ldr: pushed along and n.m.r over 2f out: rdn and edgd lft over 1f out: styd on u.p to ld wl ins fnl f: jst hld on* **3/1**[2]
000- **2** nk **General Tufto**[178] 3195 8-8-7 **46** oh1........................(b) MartinLane 7 52
(Charles Smith) *hld up: pushed along and hdwy over 3f out: rdn over 1f out: r.o* **33/1**
311- **3** 2½ **Be Royale**[11] 8056 3-9-8 **63**........................ AndrewMullen 1 64
(Michael Appleby) *s.i.s: sn prom and racd keenly: led over 2f out: rdn and hung lft over 1f out: hdd and no ex wl ins fnl f* **11/10**[1]
002- **4** nk **Do More Business (IRE)**[11] 8055 6-8-7 **51**..............(bt) PhilipPrince(5) 2 51
(Liam Corcoran) *prom: pushed along and lost pl over 3f out: r.o ins fnl f* **12/1**
421- **5** 4½ **Galilee Chapel (IRE)**[11] 8055 4-8-12 **51**........................(b) BarryMcHugh 3 41
(Alistair Whillans) *led over 7f out: rdn and hdd over 2f out: wknd ins fnl f* **10/3**[3]
1m 52.89s (2.39) **Going Correction** +0.225s/f (Slow)
WFA 3 from 4yo+ 2lb **5** Ran SP% **106.3**
Speed ratings (Par 101): **98,97,95,95,91**
toteswinger 1-2 £37.90 CSF £54.57 TOTE £3.60: £1.70, £3.80; EX 88.90 Trifecta £173.90 Pool: £3,438.79 - 14.82 winning tickets..
Owner Richard Prince **Bred** Rathbarry Stud **Trained** Newmarket, Suffolk
FOCUS
Modest and shaky form, with the second 8lb wrong.

8200 CORAL APP DOWNLOAD FROM THE APP STORE MAIDEN STKS 1m 4f 50y(P)
7:20 (7:21) (Class 5) 3-Y-0+ **£2,587** (£770; £384; £192) **Stalls** Low

Form RPR
- **1** **Summer School (IRE)** 3-9-0 0........................ JoeFanning 6 86+
(Mark Johnston) *trckd ldr tl led 3f out: pushed clr 2f out: easily* **5/6**[1]
62- **2** 10 **Strandfield Bay (IRE)**[12] 8036 7-9-5 0........................ PaddyAspell 4 63
(Sharon Watt) *hld up: hdwy 5f out: rdn over 3f out: wnt 2nd 1f out: no ch w wnr* **7/1**[3]
322- **3** 8 **Gwael (USA)**[11] 8046 3-9-0 70........................(p) LukeMorris 2 50
(James Tate) *led: rdn and hdd 3f out: sn outpcd: wknd and lost 2nd 1f out: eased* **5/2**[2]
4 6 **I Am Who I Am** 3-9-0 0........................ TomEaves 3 41
(Iain Jardine) *s.i.s: hld up: bhd fnl 7f* **50/1**
56- **5** ½ **Sonny Jim**[12] 8036 5-9-10 0........................(vt) StephenCraine 7 45
(John Mackie) *prom: rdn over 6f out: wknd 4f out* **66/1**
036- **6** nk **The Bay Tigress**[36] 7667 3-9-0 45........................ RichardKingscote 5 39
(Lisa Williamson) *prom: pushed along 7f out: wknd 4f out* **14/1**
7 62 **Silent Sam** 5-9-10 0........................ AndrewMullen 1
(Michael Appleby) *trckd ldrs: racd keenly: rdn over 5f out: wknd 4f out* **25/1**
2m 43.56s (2.46) **Going Correction** +0.225s/f (Slow)
WFA 3 from 5yo+ 5lb **7** Ran SP% **109.6**
Speed ratings (Par 103): **100,93,88,84,83 83,42**
toteswingers 1&2 £1.10, 2&3 £1.70, 1&3 £1.10 CSF £6.73 TOTE £2.10: £1.10, £3.20; EX 7.20 Trifecta £16.60 Pool: £4,608.97 - 207.64 winning tickets..
Owner Sheikh Hamdan Bin Mohammed Al Maktoum **Bred** Darley **Trained** Middleham Moor, N Yorks
FOCUS
A weak and uncompetitive maiden, but an impressive start from the winner.

8201 32RED CASINO EBF STALLIONS MAIDEN STKS 7f 32y(P)
7:50 (7:52) (Class 5) 2-Y-0 **£2,911** (£866; £432; £216) **Stalls** High

Form RPR
430- **1** **Joohaina (IRE)**[23] 7875 2-9-0 75........................(b[1]) LukeMorris 8 72
(Marco Botti) *led 6f out: pushed clr 2f out: rdn over 1f out: styd on u.p* **7/2**[3]
2 ¾ **Outlawed** 2-9-5 0........................ GeorgeBaker 4 77+
(Ed Walker) *hld up in tch: shkn up to go 2nd and edgd lft fr over 1f out: r.o wl: nt rch wnr* **11/4**[1]
3 10 **Deano's Devil (IRE)** 2-8-9 0........................ GeorgeChaloner(5) 5 46
(Richard Fahey) *s.i.s: rcvrd to chse wnr over 5f out tl rdn over 2f out: wknd fnl f* **22/1**

25- 4 1/2 **Choice Of Destiny**[14] 8026 2-9-0 0 WilliamCarson 6 44
(Philip McBride) *led 1f: chsd ldrs: rdn to chse wnr over 2f out tl over 1f out: wknd fnl f* 13/2

- 5 2 3/4 **God's Speed (IRE)** 2-9-5 0 ChrisCatlin 3 43+
(Rae Guest) *broke wl enough: sn pushed along and lost pl: n.d after* 3/1[2]

6 1 1/4 **Best Tamayuz** 2-9-5 0 JoeFanning 7 40
(William Haggas) *hld up: plld hrd: hdwy over 5f out: rdn over 2f out: wknd wl over 1f out* 7/1

34- 7 1 3/4 **Rocked The Boat**[11] 8044 2-8-12 0 AlfieWarwick(7) 2 35+
(Tobias B P Coles) *hmpd sn after s: a in rr* 14/1

1m 31.68s (2.08) **Going Correction** +0.225s/f (Slow) 7 Ran SP% **110.7**
Speed ratings (Par 96): **97,96,84,84,81 79,77**
toteswingers 1&2 £1.90, 2&3 £12.00, 1&3 £7.40 CSF £12.65 TOTE £3.90: £2.10, £2.10; EX 11.90 Trifecta £181.40 Pool: £3,865.20 - 15.97 winning tickets..
Owner Sheikh Mohammed Bin Khalifa Al Maktoum **Bred** Kabansk Ltd & Rathbarry Stud **Trained** Newmarket, Suffolk
■ Stewards' Enquiry : William Carson two-day ban: careless riding (Dec 21,26)

FOCUS
No more than fair form from the first two, who finished clear. The early pace was steady.

8202 32RED H'CAP 1m 5f 194y(P)
8:20 (8:21) (Class 2) (0-105,93) 3-Y-£11,971 (£3,583; £1,791; £896; £446) Stalls Low

Form RPR
2- 1 **Litigant**[16] 7990 5-9-11 90 GeorgeBaker 5 101+
(Seamus Durack) *trckd ldr tl led on bit 2f out: rdn and hung lft fr over 1f out: r.o: eased nr fin* 9/4[1]

201- 2 3 1/2 **Gabrial's King (IRE)**[71] 6809 4-9-5 84 AdamKirby 1 90
(David Simcock) *trckd ldrs: rdn over 2f out: hung lft over 1f out: styng on same pce whn hung rt and wnt 2nd wl ins fnl f* 9/4[1]

030- 3 1/2 **Kiama Bay (IRE)**[28] 7823 7-9-3 87 GeorgeChaloner(5) 2 92
(Richard Fahey) *led: rdn and hdd 2f out: no ex ins fnl f* 5/1[2]

424- 4 7 **Incendo**[11] 8057 7-8-12 77 RichardKingscote 6 73
(Ian Williams) *hld up: hdwy over 2f out: rdn and hung lft over 1f out: wknd ins fnl f* 9/1

310- 5 hd **Swinging Hawk (GER)**[9] 7193 7-9-2 81 StevieDonohoe 3 76
(Ian Williams) *prom: rdn over 2f out: sn wknd* 17/2

6 12 **Kazlian (FR)**[273] 2521 5-10-0 93 BrendanPowell 4 71
(Johnny Farrelly) *hld up: rdn 3f out: wknd over 2f out* 7/1[3]

3m 4.36s (-1.64) **Going Correction** +0.225s/f (Slow) 6 Ran SP% **111.2**
Speed ratings (Par 109): **113,111,110,106,106 99**
toteswingers 1&2 £1.60, 2&3 £6.00, 1&3 £4.60 CSF £7.10 TOTE £2.90: £1.60, £1.30; EX 6.90 Trifecta £28.90 Pool: £2,901.28 - 75.14 winning tickets..
Owner A A Byrne **Bred** Darley **Trained** Baydon, Wilts

FOCUS
A good prize but the highest-rated of these was only 93, 12lb below the ceiling for the grade, so this wasn't as competitive as it could have been. The form is rated around the third.

8203 32RED.COM NURSERY H'CAP 5f 216y(P)
8:50 (8:50) (Class 2) 2-Y-0 £9,056 (£2,695; £1,346; £673) Stalls Low

Form RPR
643- 1 **Steventon Star**[21] 7925 2-9-7 93 (p) RobertWinston 5 97
(Alan Bailey) *s.i.s: hld up: hdwy over 1f out: rdn ins fnl f: r.o to ld nr fin* 8/1

511- 2 shd **Porteous**[14] 8024 2-8-2 74 MartinLane 1 78
(Mick Channon) *chsd ldrs: pushed along and nt clr run over 2f out: rdn to ld over 1f out: hdd nr fin* 5/2[1]

025- 3 nse **Wee Jean**[105] 5737 2-9-4 90 GeorgeBaker 8 94
(Mick Channon) *trckd ldrs: racd keenly: rdn and edgd rt over 1f out: r.o: fin 4th: plcd 3rd* 6/1[3]

062- 4 3/4 **Corncockle**[59] 7127 2-8-9 81 GrahamGibbons 9 82
(David O'Meara) *chsd ldrs: rdn and ev ch over 1f out: edgd rt wl ins fnl f: r.o: fin 3rd: plcd 4th* 12/1

231- 5 nse **Pound Piece (IRE)**[21] 7933 2-8-12 84 LiamJones 4 85
(J S Moore) *a.p: rdn to ld wl over 1f out: sn hdd: r.o* 4/1[2]

224- 6 1 3/4 **Scruffy Tramp (IRE)**[87] 6304 2-9-3 92 RobertTart(3) 3 88
(Alan Bailey) *sn pushed along in rr: hdwy over 1f out: styd on same pce ins fnl f* 10/1

1- 7 2 3/4 **Distant Past**[29] 7804 2-8-7 79 TomEaves 7 67+
(Kevin Ryan) *hld up: plld hrd: rdn over 1f out: hmpd sn after: no ex fnl f* 4/1[2]

303- 8 1 1/4 **Zalzilah**[42] 7545 2-9-4 90 (p) LukeMorris 2 74
(James Tate) *sn pushed along to ld: rdn over 2f out: hdd wl over 1f out: wknd ins fnl f* 17/2

103- 9 3 1/2 **Alfie Lunete (IRE)**[26] 7837 2-8-0 72 oh5 KieranO'Neill 6 45
(J S Moore) *trckd ldr: plld hrd: rdn over 2f out: wknd fnl f* 22/1

1m 15.34s (0.34) **Going Correction** +0.225s/f (Slow) 9 Ran SP% **125.6**
Speed ratings (Par 102): **106,105,104,104,104 102,98,97,92**
toteswingers 1&2 £9.00, 2&3 £8.50, 1&3 £12.70 CSF £31.00 CT £137.99 TOTE £9.00: £2.50, £1.60, £2.10; EX 55.60 Trifecta £382.60 Pool: £2,718.26 - 2.30 winning tickets..
Owner John Stocker **Bred** The National Stud **Trained** Newmarket, Suffolk

FOCUS
A cracking nursery for the time of year, and the form looks reliable.

8204 32RED ON THE APP STORE H'CAP 2m 119y(P)
9:20 (9:22) (Class 6) (0-65,65) 3-Y-0+ £1,940 (£577; £288; £144) Stalls Low

Form RPR
520- 1 **High On A Hill (IRE)**[14] 8031 6-9-8 59 (b) AdamKirby 7 68
(Iain Jardine) *hld up: hdwy 4f out: led 3f out: pushed clr 2f out: rdn: hung lft and rt ins fnl f: hld on* 7/2[2]

0/5- 2 1/2 **Tokyo Brown (USA)**[14] 8027 4-9-1 52 LukeMorris 1 60
(Heather Main) *hld up: hdwy over 2f out: rdn over 1f out: styd on wl* 5/1[3]

052- 3 5 **Scribe (IRE)**[5] 8130 5-10-0 65 (bt) GrahamGibbons 2 67
(David Evans) *chsd ldrs: nt clr run and lost pl over 2f out: rallied over 1f out: no imp ins fnl f* 5/4[1]

036- 4 4 **Epic Storm (IRE)**[32] 7758 5-9-10 64 (tp) RossAtkinson(3) 8 62
(Paul Morgan) *hld up: plld hrd: hdwy over 3f out: chsd wnr over 2f out: rdn over 1f out: wknd ins fnl f* 16/1

/50- 5 6 **Celebrian**[128] 2563 6-8-11 48 (t) ChrisCatlin 3 38
(Alex Hales) *chsd ldrs tl rdn and wknd over 2f out* 40/1

315- 6 1 1/2 **River Du Nord (FR)**[49] 7382 6-8-9 46 oh1 MartinLane 9 35
(Susan Gardner) *s.i.s: hdwy to trck ldr after 2f: led over 5f out: hdd 3f out: wknd wl over 1f out* 16/1

643- 7 18 **Waldsee (GER)**[263] 1080 8-8-9 46 oh1 (b) FrankieMcDonald 4 13
(Paul Morgan) *hld up: a in rr: wknd 3f out* 22/1

500- 8 16 **Underwritten**[39] 7597 4-9-9 60 (be) RobertWinston 5 8
(John Weymes) *prom: chsd ldr over 4f out tl over 3f out: rdn and wknd over 2f out* 14/1

220- 9 27 **Dubara Reef (IRE)**[25] 7847 6-9-1 52 (p) JoeFanning 6
(Paul Green) *sn led: pushed along over 7f out: hdd over 5f out: wknd over 3f out* 20/1

3m 48.36s (6.56) **Going Correction** +0.225s/f (Slow) 9 Ran SP% **113.3**
Speed ratings (Par 101): **93,92,90,88,85 85,76,69,56**
toteswingers 1&2 £2.80, 2&3 £2.00, 1&3 £1.60 CSF £20.32 CT £32.07 TOTE £3.50: £1.30, £1.60, £1.50; EX 16.60 Trifecta £46.10 Pool: £3,133.68 - 46.10 winning tickets..
Owner I J Jardine **Bred** Dominic Fagan **Trained** Bonchester Bridge, Borders

FOCUS
There didn't look to be much pace on early and the overall time was over 14secs slower than standard, so not form to take too literally. The winner's previous C&D run had been franked.
T/Plt: £126.70 to a £1 stake. Pool: £111,687.94 - 643.09 winning tickets. T/Qpdt: £6.30 to a £1 stake. Pool: £10,632.20 - 1236.07 winning tickets. CR

8205 - 8207a (Foreign Racing) - See Raceform Interactive

7564 SHA TIN (R-H)
Sunday, December 8

OFFICIAL GOING: Turf: good to firm

8208a LONGINES HONG KONG VASE (GROUP 1) (3YO+) (TURF) 1m 4f
6:00 (12:00) 3-Y-0+
£679,110 (£262,112; £119,142; £67,911; £39,316; £23,828)

RPR
1 **Dominant (IRE)**[21] 5-9-0 0 ZacPurton 12 119+
(J Moore, Hong Kong) *hld up in last pair: swtchd to outer and rdn 2f out: hdwy to ld over 1f out and qcknd clr: styd on: clsd down towards fin but in control* 33/1

2 3/4 **The Fugue**[36] 7712 4-8-10 0 WilliamBuick 3 115+
(John Gosden) *midfield: shuffled bk and towards rr 3f out: nt clr run and swtchd lft 2f out: sn rdn: styd on and wnt 2nd fnl strides: clsng on wnr but hld* 1/1[1]

3 shd **Dunaden (FR)**[14] 8033 7-9-0 0 JamieSpencer 11 118+
(M Delzangles, France) *stdd s: dropped in and hld up towards rr: last 3f out: rdn 2f out: swtchd rt to rail and hdwy over 1f out: styd on and wnt 2nd ins fnl f: chsd wnr and clsd but hld: dropped to 3rd fnl strides* 9/1

4 1 3/4 **Red Cadeaux**[33] 7761 7-9-0 0 GeraldMosse 10 115+
(Ed Dunlop) *hld up towards rr: hdwy into midfield on outer 1/2-way: rdn over 2f out: w ldrs and ev ch over 1f out: outpcd by wnr ins fnl f: styd on but dropped to 4th* 5/1[2]

5 1 1/2 **Simenon (IRE)**[14] 8033 6-9-0 0 RyanMoore 4 112+
(W P Mullins, Ire) *midfield in tch on inner: rdn over 2f out: w ldrs and ev ch over 1f out: styd on but outpcd and dropped to 5th ins fnl f* 16/1

6 2 3/4 **Ebiyza (IRE)**[42] 7566 3-8-5 0 Christophe-PatriceLemaire 6 104+
(A De Royer-Dupre, France) *hld up in midfield: rdn over 2f out: wnt 6th ent fnl f: styd on but nt pce of ldrs* 14/1

7 2 1/4 **Asuka Kurichan (JPN)**[35] 6-9-0 0 (t) YasunariIwata 9 104+
(Naosuke Sugai, Japan) *prom early: sn settled in midfield: rdn and hdwy over 2f out: outpcd and fdd over 1f out* 25/1

8 1/2 **Feuerblitz (GER)**[35] 7724 4-9-0 0 ThierryThulliez 8 104+
(M Figge, Germany) *hld up in rr: rdn over 2f out: outpcd and btn ins fnl f* 33/1

9 1 **Mount Athos (IRE)**[33] 7761 6-9-0 0 CraigAWilliams 5 102+
(Luca Cumani) *t.k.h: trckd ldr early and prom tl dropped to midfield 5f out: rdn 3f out: outpcd whn sltly hmpd over 1f out: no imp and sn btn* 11/2[3]

10 1 1/2 **Liberator (AUS)**[21] 6-9-0 0 (bt) BrettPrebble 7 100+
(D E Ferraris, Hong Kong) *sn trcking ldr: rdn to ld over 2f out: strly pressed and hdd over 1f out: no ex and wknd* 50/1

11 nk **Seismos (IRE)**[42] 7563 5-9-0 0 AndreaAtzeni 2 99+
(A Wohler, Germany) *dwlt sltly and pushed along early: midfield on inner: rdn over 2f out: in rr whn sltly hmpd over 1f out: sn btn* 25/1

12 4 1/2 **Nymphea (IRE)**[50] 7365 4-8-10 0 AStarke 1 88+
(P Schiergen, Germany) *led: rdn and hdd over 2f out: sn no ex and btn: wknd and dropped to last ins fnl f* 33/1

2m 27.29s (-0.91)
WFA 3 from 4yo+ 5lb 12 Ran SP% **123.1**
PARI-MUTUEL (all including 10 hkd stake): WIN 136.50; PLACE 29.50, 13.00, 23.50; DF 155.00.
Owner 10/11 John Moore Trainer Syndicate **Bred** Newhall Ltd **Trained** Hong Kong

FOCUS
A somewhat muddling edition of the Vase in which a few familiar names were seen off by a relatively unfancied local runner, but it would be wrong to conclude the winner completely fluked it. The sectionals show this was run at a slow-fast gallop (25.91, 24.22, 24.94, 25.05, 23.98, 23.19) and some found trouble, notably The Fugue. The winner rates back to his best.

8209a LONGINES HONG KONG SPRINT (GROUP 1) (3YO+) (TURF) 6f
6:40 (12:00) 3-Y-0+
£679,110 (£262,112; £119,142; £67,911; £39,316; £23,828)

RPR
1 **Lord Kanaloa (JPN)**[70] 6888 5-9-0 0 YasunariIwata 12 129
(Takayuki Yasuda, Japan) *midfield in tch: smooth hdwy 2f out: rdn to ld over 1f out: hung rt to rail but qcknd clr and sn in control: impressive* 11/8[1]

2 5 **Sole Power**[63] 7054 6-9-0 0 JohnnyMurtagh 9 113
(Edward Lynam, Ire) *restrained and hld up towards rr: rdn 2f out: r.o and wnt 2nd fnl strides: no ch w impressive wnr* 16/1

3 nk **Frederick Engels**[21] 4-9-0 0 ZacPurton 4 112
(J Moore, Hong Kong) *midfield: looking for room fr 2f out tl rdn over 1f out: r.o and wnt 2nd ins fnl 100yds: no ch w wnr and dropped to 3rd fnl strides* 8/1

4 1 **Cerise Cherry (SAF)**[21] 8-9-0 0 (bt) MatthewChadwick 3 109
(D Cruz, Hong Kong) *a.p on inner: rdn 2f out: kpt on same pce fr over 1f out* 18/1

5 shd **Sterling City (AUS)**[21] 5-9-0 0 TommyBerry 2 109
(J Moore, Hong Kong) *hld up towards rr on inner: rdn 2f out: nt clrest of runs in st but kpt on and wnt 5th post: nvr nrr* 7/1[3]

6 nk **Rich Tapestry (IRE)**[42] 5-9-0 0 (b) RyanMoore 6 108
(C W Chang, Hong Kong) *led: rdn and hdd over 1f out: readily outpcd by wnr but kpt on tl no ex towards fin: dropped to 6th post* 66/1

7 nk **Lucky Nine (IRE)**[29] 7825 6-9-0 0 BrettPrebble 5 107+
(C Fownes, Hong Kong) *rrd leaving stalls and dwlt: hld up towards rr: rdn over 1f out: kpt on and wnt 7th cl home: nvr able to chal* 11/2[2]

The Form Book Flat, Raceform Ltd, Compton, RG20 6NL.

8 shd **Time After Time (AUS)**[21] 6-9-0 0..............................(t) GeraldMosse 11 106
(W Y So, Hong Kong) *dwlt and hld up in last: swtchd lft and rdn over 1f out: kpt on and wnt 8th cl home: n.d* **50/1**

9 nk **Go Baby Go (AUS)**[68] 6-9-0 0.................................. TyeAngland 13 105
(C H Yip, Hong Kong) *trckd ldr: rdn to chal 2f out: readily outpcd by wnr 1f out: kpt on tl no ex and lost multiple pls towards fin* **50/1**

10 ½ **Slade Power (IRE)**[50] 7364 4-9-0 0............................ WayneLordan 10 104
(Edward Lynam, Ire) *dwlt sltly and pushed along to rcvr: midfield on outer: rdn over 2f out: kpt on same pce and n.d* **16/1**

11 ¾ **Charles The Great (IRE)**[21] 4-9-0 0..........................(t) DouglasWhyte 7 101
(J Moore, Hong Kong) *midfield in tch: gng wl enough but nt clr run at any stage in st: lost all ch and steadily shuffled bk towards rr* **10/1**

12 4 **Eagle Regiment (AUS)**[21] 6-9-0 0....................................... ODoleuze 8 89
(K L Man, Hong Kong) *midfield: rdn 2f out: sn no imp and btn* **16/1**

13 2 **Joy And Fun (NZ)**[253] 1265 10-9-0 0...............................(p) BrettDoyle 1 82
(D Cruz, Hong Kong) *midfield in tch on inner: rdn 2f out: lost pl ent fnl f: no ex: fdd and dropped to last: bdly hmpd by faller and almost uns rdr nr fin* **33/1**

F **Jwala**[63] 7054 4-8-10 0.. SteveDrowne 14
(Robert Cowell) *pushed along to go forward fr wdst draw and chsd ldr: rdn to chal 2f out: no ex and btn ent fnl f: wkng whn squeezed for room and fell towards fin: fatally injured* **25/1**

1m 8.25s (68.25) **14 Ran SP% 125.3**
PARI-MUTUEL (all including 10 hkd stake): WIN 18.00; PLACE 11.00, 161.00, 21.50; DF 702.00.
Owner Lord Horse Club **Bred** K I Farm **Trained** Japan

FOCUS
No depth to this year's Sprint and a few found trouble, but the Japanese-trained Lord Kanaloa was in a different league, producing a top-class performance. The runner-up is rated in line with his July Cup form.

8210a LONGINES HONG KONG MILE (GROUP 1) (3YO+) (TURF) 1m

7:50 (12:00) 3-Y-0+

£905,480 (£349,483; £158,856; £90,548; £52,422; £31,771)

RPR

1 **Glorious Days (AUS)**[189] 6-9-0 0...........................(b) DouglasWhyte 13 122
(J Size, Hong Kong) *stdd and hld up towards rr: rdn and hdwy on outer fr 2f out: r.o to ld wl ins fnl f and won gng away: readily* **14/1**

2 ¾ **Gold-Fun (IRE)**[21] 4-9-0 0.. ODoleuze 10 120
(R Gibson, Hong Kong) *broke wl and w ldr early: sn stdd and trckd ldr: rdn to chal and led over 1f out: r.o but clsd down and hdd wl ins fnl f: no ex* **7/2**[2]

3 ¾ **Packing Whiz (IRE)**[21] 5-9-0 0... BrettPrebble 9 119
(C Fownes, Hong Kong) *stdd and hld up towards rr on inner: rdn 2f out: r.o and wnt 3rd ins fnl f: nt pce of wnr* **16/1**

4 ½ **Gordon Lord Byron (IRE)**[50] 7366 5-9-0 0.................... WilliamBuick 4 117
(T Hogan, Ire) *midfield: rdn over 2f out: r.o and wnt 4th cl home: fin wl but nt pce to chal* **20/1**

5 ½ **Real Specialist (NZ)**[21] 6-9-0 0...................................(b[1]) TyeAngland 2 116
(J Size, Hong Kong) *midfield: rdn over 2f out: r.o but nt quite pce to chal and dropped to 5th cl home* **25/1**

6 1 **Moonlight Cloud**[63] 7059 5-8-10 0................................ ThierryJarnet 6 110
(F Head, France) *midfield on outer: shkn up 2f out and nt qckn: rdn over 1f out: kpt on wout threatening ins fnl f* **11/8**[1]

7 1 ¼ **Helene Spirit (IRE)**[21] 6-9-0 0.......................................(t) GeraldMosse 5 111
(C Fownes, Hong Kong) *sn trcking ldr on inner: rdn to ld over 2f out: hdd over 1f out: sn no ex: fdd* **16/1**

8 1 ¼ **Dan Excel (IRE)**[21] 5-9-0 0..(t) WCMarwing 7 108
(J Moore, Hong Kong) *prom on outer: rdn 2f out: no ex and btn ins fnl f: fdd* **25/1**

9 nk **Xtension (IRE)**[21] 6-9-0 0..(p) ZacPurton 12 108
(J Moore, Hong Kong) *stdd and hld up in last pair on inner: swtchd lft and rdn over 2f out: kpt on but no imp and nvr threatened* **40/1**

10 1 ¼ **Pure Champion (IRE)**[21] 6-9-0 0...........................(t) UmbertoRispoli 1 105
(A S Cruz, Hong Kong) *midfield in tch on inner: rdn and ev ch 2f out: outpcd whn slt bump ent fnl f: sn no imp: eased whn btn* **66/1**

11 ½ **Shamalgan (FR)**[35] 7724 6-9-0 0....................................... MaximeGuyon 14 103
(X Thomas-Demeaulte, France) *stdd and hld up in last pair on outer: rdn over 2f out: no imp in st: nvr a factor* **50/1**

12 3 ¼ **King Kreesa (USA)**[50] 4-9-0 0...(vt) MESmith 11 96
(Jeremiah C Englehart, U.S.A) *led: hdd over 2f out: rdn and sn no ex: wknd and bmpd rival ent fnl f: eased towards fin* **50/1**

13 1 ¼ **Linton (AUS)**[38] 7-9-0 0...(b) DamienOliver 3 93
(John D Sadler, Australia) *midfield on inner: rdn over 2f out: outpcd and btn over 1f out: fdd* **33/1**

14 4 ¾ **Sky Lantern (IRE)**[71] 6837 3-8-9 0.............................. RichardHughes 8 78
(Richard Hannon Snr) *midfield: rdn 2f out: dropped to rr and btn over 1f out: eased* **5/1**[3]

1m 33.6s (-1.10)
WFA 3 from 4yo+ 1lb **14 Ran SP% 122.7**
PARI-MUTUEL (all including 10 hkd stake): WIN 87.50; PLACE 30.50, 13.00, 25.00; DF 210.50.
Owner Tom Brown's Syndicate **Bred** Mr R Pietrykowski **Trained** Hong Kong

FOCUS
With Moonlight Cloud well below her best, this was an ordinary running the Mile - much the same standard as last year. They went a good, even pace (24.75, 22.95, 22.95, 22.95) and Glorious Days picked up from well back.

8211a LONGINES HONG KONG CUP (GROUP 1) (3YO+) (TURF) 1m 2f

8:30 (12:00) 3-Y-0+

£996,028 (£384,432; £174,741; £99,602; £57,664; £34,948)

RPR

1 **Akeed Mofeed**[21] 4-9-0 0... DouglasWhyte 1 118+
(R Gibson, Hong Kong) *midfield on inner: clsd over 2f out: swtchd lft off rail for clr run and rdn over 1f out: styd on and led towards fin: pushed out and won gng away: readily* **7/2**[2]

2 1 **Tokei Halo (JPN)**[42] 4-9-0 0... YutakaTake 5 116
(Hisashi Shimizu, Japan) *led and allowed to dictate modest pce: rdn over 1f out: styd on but hdd towards fin and no ex: jst hld on for 2nd* **14/1**

3 ½ **Cirrus Des Aigles (FR)**[50] 7367 7-9-0 0........... ChristopheSoumillon 10 115
(Mme C Barande-Barbe, France) *midfield: clsd over 2f out: rdn to chal and ev ch over 1f out: styd on but nt quite pce of front pair ins fnl f: jst hld on for 3rd* **5/1**[3]

4 nse **Military Attack (IRE)**[21] 5-9-0 0....................................... ZacPurton 9 115+
(J Moore, Hong Kong) *hld up in last pair on inner: swtchd off rail and rdn over 2f out: styd on and wnt 4th cl home: fin wl and almost snatched 3rd post but nvr able to chal* **9/4**[1]

5 nk **Side Glance**[36] 7702 6-9-0 0.. JamieSpencer 2 114+
(Andrew Balding) *hld up in midfield: rdn over 2f out: styd on wl but nt quite pce to chal* **20/1**

6 shd **Blazing Speed**[21] 4-9-0 0..(t) GeraldMosse 4 114+
(A S Cruz, Hong Kong) *dwlt sltly and hld up towards rr on inner: rdn 2f out: styd on wl but nt quite pce to chal* **16/1**

7 1 ¼ **Grandeur (IRE)**[74] 6742 4-9-0 0....................................... RyanMoore 7 111
(Jeremy Noseda) *midfield on inner: rdn 2f out: swtchd lft over 1f out: kpt on but nt pce to chal* **16/1**

8 ¾ **Neatico (GER)**[66] 6987 6-9-0 0... AStarke 11 110
(P Schiergen, Germany) *midfield: rdn over 2f out: kpt on same pce and nvr threatened* **33/1**

9 shd **Little Mike (USA)**[36] 7712 6-9-0 0.......................................(t) MESmith 6 110
(Dale Romans, U.S.A) *prom: rdn over 2f out: outpcd over 1f out: kpt on wout threatening ins fnl f* **16/1**

10 1 ¾ **Same World**[21] 5-9-0 0... TommyBerry 3 106
(J Moore, Hong Kong) *trckd ldr: rdn and effrt to chal over 2f out: outpcd over 1f out: steadily fdd and eased towards fin* **50/1**

11 1 ½ **Endowing (IRE)**[21] 4-9-0 0... TyeAngland 8 103
(J Size, Hong Kong) *hld up and a towards rr: rdn to try and improve on outer 2f out: sn no imp* **13/2**

12 nk **Rainbow Chic (IRE)**[21] 4-9-0 0.....................................(t) BrettPrebble 12 103
(C Fownes, Hong Kong) *dropped in fr wdst draw and hld up in last: rdn over 2f out: sn no imp* **50/1**

2m 1.96s (0.56) **12 Ran SP% 118.9**
PARI-MUTUEL (all including 10 hkd stake): WIN 29.50; PLACE 13.50, 40.50, 25.00; DF 269.50.
Owner Pan Sutong **Bred** Rabbah Bloodstock Limited **Trained** Hong Kong

FOCUS
The pace slowed at halfway before a sprint finish (25.74, 24.75, 25.27, 23.86, 22.34) and the Japanese-trained Tokei Halo very much had the run of the race in a clear lead. It paid to be handy.

8212 - (Foreign Racing) - See Raceform Interactive

8175 LINGFIELD (L-H)

Monday, December 9

OFFICIAL GOING: Standard
Wind: Light, half behind Weather: Fine, mild

8213 32RED MEDIAN AUCTION MAIDEN STKS (DIV I) 1m (P)

12:00 (12:01) (Class 6) 2-Y-O **£2,045** (£603; £302) **Stalls** High

Form RPR

5- 1 **Poker Gold (FR)**[12] 8066 2-9-5 0.....................................(t) LiamJones 6 68
(Heather Main) *pressed ldr: chal over 2f out: drvn to ld narrowly 1f out: kpt on wl* **8/1**[3]

6- 2 nk **Artful Rogue (IRE)**[12] 8066 2-9-5 0.............................. RobertHavlin 5 67
(Amanda Perrett) *led: jnd over 2f out: rdn and narrowly hdd 1f out: pressed wnr after: nt qckn nr fin* **12/1**

3 1 ¼ **Royal Warranty** 2-9-0 0.. LiamKeniry 2 59+
(Andrew Balding) *hld up in last trio: pushed along over 2f out: gd prog on outer fnl f: r.o to take 3rd last stride* **14/1**

00- 4 hd **Mary Le Bow**[48] 7450 2-9-0 0... FrederikTylicki 8 59
(Lucy Wadham) *hld up in rr: prog to trck ldng quartet over 2f out and shkn up: kpt on fnl f to take 3rd briefly nr fnish* **20/1**

04- 5 hd **Turnbury**[26] 7854 2-9-5 0...(t) TomQueally 7 64
(Robert Mills) *t.k.h early: trckd ldng pair: rdn wl over 1f out: nt qckn and hanging ins fnl f: lost pl nr fin* **16/1**

5- 6 nk **Racing's Dream**[45] 7494 2-9-5 0.. SeanLevey 3 63
(Brian Meehan) *trckd ldng pair: shkn up and nt qckn wl over 1f out: one pce after: lost pls nr fin* **2/1**[2]

7 2 ¾ **Harry's Summer (USA)** 2-8-12 0.......................... JordanVaughan[(7)] 1 57
(Nick Littmoden) *hld up in last trio: pushed along over 2f out: reminders and no prog over 1f out* **25/1**

3- 8 ½ **Special Miss**[25] 7874 2-9-0 0.. LukeMorris 4 50
(Marco Botti) *trckd ldrs: rdn bef 1/2-way and sn lost pl: struggling in rr fnl 3f* **11/10**[1]

9 15 **Hiorne Tower (FR)** 2-9-5 0... GeorgeBaker 9 21
(John Best) *s.i.s: a in last: t.o* **20/1**

1m 37.57s (-0.63) **Going Correction** -0.075s/f (Stan) **9 Ran SP% 125.7**
Speed ratings (Par 94): **100,99,98,98,98 97,95,94,79**
toteswingers 1&2 £11.30, 1&3 £18.80, 2&3 £20.10 CSF £102.35 TOTE £12.30: £2.60, £2.30, £3.60; EX 74.60 Trifecta £956.70 Pool: £3406.38 - 2.67 winning tickets..
Owner Mr & Mrs D R Guest **Bred** Guy Pariente **Trained** Kingston Lisle, Oxon

FOCUS
A modest maiden and they didn't appear to go too quick, with the front two filling those positions throughout. The winning time was half a second slower than the second division. The third looks sure to do better.

8214 32RED MEDIAN AUCTION MAIDEN STKS (DIV II) 1m (P)

12:30 (12:31) (Class 6) 2-Y-O **£2,045** (£603; £302) **Stalls** High

Form RPR

4- 1 **Examiner (IRE)**[19] 7972 2-9-5 0... LiamJones 10 77+
(William Haggas) *hld up in midfield: prog to trck ldng pair over 2f out: clsd on inner over 1f out: led jst ins fnl f: pushed clr: comf* **9/4**[1]

63- 2 2 ¼ **Sheila's Footsteps**[138] 4631 2-9-5 0................................. LukeMorris 4 72
(J S Moore) *trckd ldrs: prog to go 2nd over 2f out: drvn to ld wl over 1f out: hdd and outpcd jst ins fnl f* **5/1**[3]

6- 3 3 ½ **Armourer (IRE)**[53] 7320 2-9-5 0....................................... GeorgeBaker 8 64
(William Muir) *sn pressed ldr: led 5f out: drvn and hdd wl over 1f out: fdd fnl f* **20/1**

6- 4 ¾ **Old Town Boy**[24] 7902 2-9-5 0...................................... WilliamCarson 1 62
(Philip McBride) *wl in rr: rdn 1/2-way: nvr gng pce to make prog: styd on fr over 1f out* **6/1**

46- 5 hd **Spectator**[26] 7854 2-9-5 0.. LiamKeniry 6 62
(Andrew Balding) *trckd ldrs: wnt 2nd briefly 3f out: nt qckn and outpcd 2f out: one pce after* **9/2**[2]

05- 6 2 ¾ **Mairise**[7] 8124 2-9-5 0.. ShaneKelly 7 55
(Sir Michael Stoute) *chsd ldrs on outer: lost pl 1/2-way: wl in rr: after: plugged on* **9/2**[2]

60- 7 nk **Artistic Flame**[28] 7834 2-9-5 0.....................................(b) RobertHavlin 2 55
(Amanda Perrett) *v s.i.s: detached in last: rdn over 2f out: no great prog* **33/1**

8 ½ **My Red Devil (IRE)** 2-9-0 0... BarryMcHugh 5 48+
(Richard Fahey) *t.k.h: hld up in rr and rn green: prog on inner over 2f out: rchd 4th over 1f out: wknd sn after* **16/1**

0- 9 14 **Close Companion**[11] 8084 2-9-0 0...............................(bt[1]) MartinDwyer 9 16
(Hugo Palmer) *prom on outer: rdn over 3f out: sn wknd rapidly: t.o* **50/1**

004- **10** 9 **Mystic Angellina**[13] 8045 2-9-0 35..........(t) MartinLane 3
(Mrs Ilka Gansera-Leveque) *led to 5f out: sn u.p: wknd rapidly over 2f out: t.o* **100/1**

1m 37.0s (-1.20) **Going Correction** -0.075s/f (Stan) **10** Ran SP% **114.6**
Speed ratings (Par 94): **103,100,97,96,96 93,93,92,78,69**
toteswingers 1&2 £2.80, 1&3 £10.80, 2&3 £16.10 CSF £12.95 TOTE £3.70: £1.70, £1.10, £5.60; EX 13.80 Trifecta £109.20 Pool: £4673.40 - 32.07 winning tickets..
Owner Ian and Christine Beard **Bred** River Downs Stud **Trained** Newmarket, Suffolk

FOCUS
A modest maiden, but they went a solid enough pace and the winner came away in good style to win in a time half a second quicker than the first division.

8215 32RED.COM (S) STKS 6f (P)
1:00 (1:00) (Class 6) 2-Y-O **£2,045** (£603; £302) **Stalls** Low

Form RPR

350- **1** **Aspirant**[5] 8147 2-8-9 67..........RyanWhile(7) 7 68
(Bill Turner) *mde virtually all: shkn up and drew clr wl over 1f out: pushed out: unchal* **5/2[2]**

6- **2** 1 3/4 **Ain't No Surprise (IRE)**[141] 4564 2-8-7 0 ow1..........JohnFahy 2 57+
(Jamie Osborne) *hld up: stl last 2f out: prog on inner over 1f out: r.o to take 2nd last 100yds and cl on wnr: no ch to chal* **4/1[3]**

123- **3** 1 **Kodafine (IRE)**[16] 8024 2-8-11 70..........TomQueally 4 55
(David Evans) *hld up in tch: prog whn wd bnd 2f out: rdn to chse wnr over 1f out: no imp: lost 2nd last 100yds* **7/4[1]**

400- **4** 1 1/2 **Royal River**[48] 7568 2-8-11 59..........LiamKeniry 1 50
(J S Moore) *trckd ldng pair: trying to cl whn nt clr run briefly 2f out and lost pl: kpt on again ins fnl f* **5/1**

235- **5** 1 1/4 **Black Vale (IRE)**[4] 8166 2-8-9 64..........(bt) DonnaCaldwell(7) 5 52
(Phil McEntee) *t.k.h: prog to join wnr after 1f to 2f out: wknd and lost 2nd over 1f out* **14/1**

505- **6** 1 1/4 **Little Tinka**[20] 7954 2-8-6 54..........(b[1]) LiamJones 3 38
(Mark H Tompkins) *a in rr: pushed along bef 1/2-way: nvr on terms* **25/1**

440- **7** 2 3/4 **Maximilianthefirst**[115] 5494 2-8-11 44..........FrederikTylicki 6 35
(Mark Rimmer) *a in rr: pushed along bef 1/2-way: no prog* **100/1**

1m 11.69s (-0.21) **Going Correction** -0.075s/f (Stan) **7** Ran SP% **113.1**
Speed ratings (Par 94): **98,95,94,92,90 89,85**
toteswingers 1&2 £2.10, 1&3 £1.60, 2&3 £2.00 CSF £12.66 TOTE £4.30: £2.00, £1.80; EX 11.90 Trifecta £31.00 Pool: £4233.23 - 102.10 winning tickets..There was no bid for the winner
Owner The Huxley Partnership **Bred** Juddmonte Farms Ltd **Trained** Sigwells, Somerset

FOCUS
They didn't go particularly quick during the early stages of this seller. The form could have been rated 4lb higher.

8216 COMPARE BOOKMAKERS AT BOOKMAKERS.CO.UK H'CAP 5f (P)
1:30 (1:30) (Class 5) (0-70,70) 3-Y-O+ **£2,726** (£805; £402) **Stalls** High

Form RPR

121- **1** **Gregori (IRE)**[16] 8022 3-9-7 70..........(t) SeanLevey 5 81+
(Brian Meehan) *mde virtually all: pushed along and asserted wl over 1f out: rdn out* **10/11[1]**

500- **2** 1 1/2 **Falasteen (IRE)**[23] 7937 6-9-1 64..........LiamJones 6 70
(Milton Bradley) *broke wl: w wnr to 1/2-way: nt qckn 2f out: kpt on fnl f* **33/1**

104- **3** 1 3/4 **Novabridge**[35] 7730 5-9-4 67..........(b) LiamKeniry 2 67
(Neil Mulholland) *chsd ldng pair: rdn 2f out: outpcd but kpt on fnl f* **20/1**

136- **4** nk **Excellent Aim**[97] 6077 6-8-10 66..........JordanVaughan(7) 3 65+
(George Margarson) *trckd ldrs: pushed along 2f out: hanging sltly and nt qckn over 1f out: reminder and styd on to press for 3rd nr fin* **8/1[3]**

140- **5** 3/4 **Layla's Oasis**[10] 8096 3-9-7 70..........BarryMcHugh 1 66
(Richard Fahey) *chsd ldng pair on inner: rdn 2f out: sn outpcd: fdd ins fnl f* **16/1**

223- **6** 3/4 **Trending (IRE)**[16] 8030 4-9-3 66..........(bt) LukeMorris 4 59
(Jeremy Gask) *mostly in last trio: rdn over 2f out: no prog over 1f out: plugged on* **6/1[2]**

105- **7** hd **Never A Quarrel (IRE)**[23] 7937 3-8-10 66..........DavidParkes(7) 9 59
(Jeremy Gask) *hld up in last trio: effrt on wd outside 2f out: lost grnd and nvr on terms after* **16/1**

406- **8** 3/4 **Ada Lovelace**[32] 7783 3-9-2 65..........JimmyQuinn 7 55
(Dean Ivory) *dwlt: rcvrd to chse ldrs on outer: outpcd 2f out: pushed along over 1f out: fdd ins fnl f* **12/1**

154- **9** nk **Dark Lane**[12] 8069 7-9-3 66..........TomQueally 8 55
(David Evans) *a in rr: wd bnd 2f out: no ch after* **8/1[3]**

58.04s (-0.76) **Going Correction** -0.075s/f (Stan) **9** Ran SP% **116.1**
Speed ratings (Par 103): **103,100,97,97,96 94,94,93,92**
toteswingers 1&2 £11.90, 1&3 £8.10, 2&3 £75.70 CSF £39.58 CT £394.80 TOTE £1.90: £1.20, £5.60, £3.50; EX 32.60 Trifecta £876.70 Pool: £4849.68 - 4.14 winning tickets..
Owner Stephen Tucker **Bred** Mrs James Wigan **Trained** Manton, Wilts

FOCUS
It proved hard to make up ground in this modest sprint handicap but the progressive winner did it well. There was no depth to the race.

8217 LADBROKES CLAIMING STKS 7f (P)
2:00 (2:00) (Class 6) 3-Y-O+ **£2,045** (£603; £302) **Stalls** Low

Form RPR

463- **1** **Naabegha**[19] 7982 6-9-5 89..........TomQueally 1 88
(Ed de Giles) *plld hrd: hld up in 3rd: pressed ldr on inner over 1f out: led ins fnl f: jst hld on* **11/10[1]**

100- **2** nse **Apostle (IRE)**[18] 7992 4-9-5 85..........ChrisCatlin 3 88
(David Simcock) *led: set mod pce to 3f out: sltly wd bnd 2f out: drvn and hrd pressed over 1f out: hdd ins fnl f: rallied nr fin: jst failed* **5/2[2]**

003- **3** nse **Mr David (USA)**[7] 8122 6-9-1 84..........(b) LukeMorris 6 84
(Jamie Osborne) *t.k.h: hld up in 4th: drvn on outer over 1f out: clsng whn jockey dropped whip ins fnl f: r.o: jst failed* **3/1[3]**

266- **4** 2 1/2 **Polar Kite (IRE)**[12] 8068 5-9-2 78..........FrankieMcDonald 4 78
(Paul Morgan) *s.s: t.k.h in last: shkn up over 1f out: styd on but no ch of threatening ldrs* **16/1**

235- **5** 1 **Rise To Glory (IRE)**[16] 8030 5-8-10 64..........JimmyQuinn 5 69?
(Shaun Harris) *t.k.h: pressed ldr: rdn over 2f out: lost 2nd and wknd over 1f out* **25/1**

1m 24.49s (-0.31) **Going Correction** -0.075s/f (Stan) **5** Ran SP% **110.9**
Speed ratings (Par 101): **98,97,97,95,93**
CSF £4.18 TOTE £1.70: £1.10, £2.30; EX 4.10 Trifecta £7.30 Pool: £3282.19 - 334.77 winning tickets..Naabegha was claimed by Mr A. J. McCabe for £15,000.
Owner Tight Lines Partnership **Bred** Shadwell Estate Company Limited **Trained** Ledbury, H'fords

FOCUS
A couple of useful types contested this claimer and the front three finished in a line following a steady early pace.

8218 CORAL APP DOWNLOAD FROM THE APP STORE H'CAP 1m 2f (P)
2:30 (2:30) (Class 3) (0-95,90) 3-Y-O+ **£7,439** (£2,213; £1,106; £553) **Stalls** Low

Form RPR

342- **1** **Karam Albaari (IRE)**[33] 7765 5-9-1 84..........FrederikTylicki 2 91
(J R Jenkins) *trckd ldr: rdn to ld over 2f out: drvn 2 l clr 1f out: hld on to dwindling ld nr fin* **7/1**

423- **2** nk **Swing Alone (IRE)**[140] 4601 4-9-7 90..........LukeMorris 4 96
(Gay Kelleway) *hld up in 4th: rdn over 2f out: styd on to take 2nd ins fnl f: clsd on wnr nr fin* **5/2[1]**

160- **3** hd **Persepolis (IRE)**[12] 8071 3-9-0 86..........TomQueally 5 92
(Brett Johnson) *hld up in last pair: rdn over 2f out: prog to dispute 2nd fnl f: styd on and clsd on wnr nr fin* **8/1**

014- **4** shd **Soul Intent (IRE)**[17] 8007 3-8-5 77..........HayleyTurner 3 82
(J W Hills) *hld up in 5th: rdn over 2f out: nt qckn over 1f out: styd on fnl f: clsng at fin* **7/2[2]**

505- **5** 1/2 **Naaz (IRE)**[18] 7988 3-8-9 81..........ChrisCatlin 7 85
(Ed Dunlop) *stdd s: hld up in last: rdn on outer over 2f out: styd on fnl f to press for a pl last 75yds: no ex nr fin* **14/1**

225- **6** 1 **Mystery Bet (IRE)**[24] 7895 3-8-5 77..........BarryMcHugh 6 79
(Richard Fahey) *trckd ldng pair on outer: rdn over 2f out: nt qckn and lost pl fnl f* **6/1**

/06- **7** 1 **Rhamnus**[12] 8071 3-8-12 84..........SeanLevey 1 84
(Richard Hannon Snr) *led: set mod pce to 1/2-way: rdn and hdd over 2f out: chsd wnr tl ins fnl f: wknd* **9/2[3]**

2m 5.33s (-1.27) **Going Correction** -0.075s/f (Stan)
WFA 3 from 4yo+ 3lb **7** Ran SP% **113.5**
Speed ratings (Par 107): **102,101,101,101,101 100,99**
toteswingers 1&2 £3.30, 1&3 £10.30, 2&3 £5.90 CSF £24.52 TOTE £8.80: £3.80, £1.50; EX 25.10 Trifecta £181.90 Pool: £3712.41 - 15.29 winning tickets..
Owner Mark Goldstein **Bred** Morecool Stud **Trained** Royston, Herts

FOCUS
A reasonable handicap, although the pace was only modest and they finished in a bit of a heap. It's hard to rate form anything other than ordinary.

8219 DOWNLOAD THE LADBROKES APP H'CAP 1m (P)
3:00 (3:01) (Class 4) (0-85,85) 3-Y-O+ **£4,690** (£1,395; £697; £348) **Stalls** High

Form RPR

041- **1** **Scottish Glen**[32] 7785 7-9-2 80..........GeorgeBaker 6 88
(Patrick Chamings) *trckd ldrs: rdn and prog on outer over 1f out to ld jst ins fnl f: styd on wl* **7/2[2]**

204- **2** 3/4 **Legendary**[18] 7989 4-9-5 83..........JimmyQuinn 9 89
(Ed Vaughan) *racd wd early: led after 2f: drvn over 1f out: hdd jst ins fnl f: styd on but a hld* **5/1[3]**

410- **3** nse **Soaring Spirits (IRE)**[18] 7988 3-9-1 80..........(b) LiamKeniry 8 86
(Dean Ivory) *t.k.h: pressed ldr after 3f: chal 2 out: lost 2nd and nt qckn 1f out: styd on* **16/1**

203- **4** 1/2 **Secret Beau**[7] 8127 3-9-1 80..........(vt) LukeMorris 3 85
(David Evans) *racd freely: led 2f: styd cl up: tried to chal on inner over 1f out: kpt on same pce fnl f* **11/4[1]**

124- **5** hd **High Time Too (IRE)**[96] 6115 3-8-12 77..........MartinDwyer 7 81
(Hugo Palmer) *hld up and sn towards rr: rdn 2f out: no prog tl styd on ins fnl f: nrst fin* **8/1**

110- **6** 1 1/2 **Lions Arch (IRE)**[212] 2259 3-9-6 85..........KieranO'Neill 5 86
(Richard Hannon Snr) *trckd ldrs: rdn and nt qckn wl over 1f out: no imp after* **10/1**

100- **7** 1 1/2 **Imperator Augustus (IRE)**[17] 8012 5-8-0 71 oh2..........JackGarritty(7) 10 68
(Patrick Holmes) *swtchd sharply lft fr wd draw sn after s: hld up in last pair: pushed along 2f out: no real prog on inner after* **33/1**

016- **8** 3/4 **Well Painted (IRE)**[18] 7988 4-8-11 82..........(t) StephanieJoannides(7) 4 78
(William Haggas) *awkward s: bmpd after 100yds and hld up in last: nudged along on inner fr over 2f out: nvr on terms* **5/1[3]**

031- **9** 1 1/2 **Mahadee (IRE)**[101] 5948 8-8-11 78..........(b) MarkCoumbe(3) 1 70
(Ed de Giles) *s.s: hld up towards rr: rdn and fnd nil 2f out: wknd over 1f out* **16/1**

1m 37.87s (-0.33) **Going Correction** -0.075s/f (Stan)
WFA 3 from 4yo+ 1lb **9** Ran SP% **117.1**
Speed ratings (Par 105): **98,97,97,96,96 95,93,92,91**
toteswingers 1&2 £4.40, 1&3 £13.30, 2&3 £14.10 CSF £21.80 CT £248.21 TOTE £5.80: £2.00, £1.70, £5.40; EX 25.30 Trifecta £261.80 Pool: £4570.50 - 13.09 winning tickets..
Owner The Foxford House Partnership **Bred** Mrs Ann Jenkins **Trained** Baughurst, Hants
■ Stewards' Enquiry : Jack Garritty two-day ban: careless riding (Dec 26-27)

FOCUS
A competitive handicap in which the principals all raced handily with the pace modest. Ordinary form, the second to sixth close to their marks at face value.

8220 BEST ODDS AT BOOKMAKERS.CO.UK H'CAP 6f (P)
3:30 (3:32) (Class 6) (0-65,69) 3-Y-O+ **£2,045** (£603; £302) **Stalls** Low

Form RPR

154- **1** **Welsh Moonlight**[86] 6397 3-9-3 62..........SeanLevey 6 70
(Stuart Williams) *wl plcd bhd ldrs: rdn over 1f out: prog to take 2nd jst ins fnl f: drvn to ld narrowly 100yds out: hld on* **12/1**

005- **2** hd **Street Power (USA)**[25] 7880 8-9-5 64..........LiamKeniry 5 72+
(Jeremy Gask) *hld up in 7th: rdn and prog whn nt clr run jst over 1f out: swtchd ins and r.o fnl f: tk 2nd last stride: jst failed* **3/1[1]**

001- **3** nse **Clock Opera (IRE)**[16] 8023 3-8-10 62..........LouisSteward(7) 2 69
(William Stone) *led: rdn over 1f out: hdd fnl 100yds: styd on but lost 2nd last stride* **7/2[2]**

063- **4** 1 3/4 **Uprise**[55] 7263 4-9-4 63..........BarryMcHugh 11 64+
(George Margarson) *hld up and last tl wl over 2f out: pushed along and sme prog over 1f out: reminder and r.o fnl f to take 4th nr fin: nvr involved* **8/1**

035- **5** shd **Invigilator**[16] 8029 5-9-5 64..........(t) GeorgeBaker 9 65+
(Derek Shaw) *hld up in last trio: rdn wl over 1f out: styd on wl fnl f: nrst fin* **8/1**

003- **6** 1/2 **Roy's Legacy**[7] 8135 4-8-12 62..........ShirleyTeasdale(5) 10 61
(Shaun Harris) *chsd ldr tl jst ins fnl f: wknd* **16/1**

300- **7** 1 1/4 **Catalinas Diamond (IRE)**[116] 5447 5-9-3 62..........(t) MartinDwyer 3 57
(Pat Murphy) *trckd ldrs in 6th: rdn and n.m.r briefly over 1f out: no prog fnl f* **20/1**

/32- **8** 3/4 **Ghost Train (IRE)**[142] 4520 4-9-0 62..........(p) MarkCoumbe(3) 7 55
(Tim McCarthy) *settled in 8th: nowhere to go on inner over 1f out and snatched up: kpt on same pce fnl f* **14/1**

The Form Book Flat, Raceform Ltd, Compton, RG20 6NL.

200- **9** ¾ **Celestial Bay**[20] 7965 4-9-6 **65** .... TomQueally 8 56
(Sylvester Kirk) *s.i.s and n.m.r: hld up in last pair: dropped to last wl over 2f out: detached and drvn over 1f out: styd on ins fnl f* **25/1**

020- **10** 1 ½ **Assembly**[12] 8068 3-9-6 **65** ....(b) JimmyQuinn 4 51
(Pat Phelan) *pressed ldrs: rdn 2f out: wknd qckly jst over 1f out* **7/1**[3]

051- **11** 1 ¼ **Shawkantango**[7] 8135 6-9-3 **69** 6ex........................(v) AdamMcLean[(7)] 1 51
(Derek Shaw) *prom on inner: rdn wl over 1f out: sn lost pl: wknd qckly fnl f* **12/1**

1m 11.69s (-0.21) **Going Correction** -0.075s/f (Stan) **11** Ran SP% **118.5**
Speed ratings (Par 101): **98,97,97,95,95 94,92,91,90,88 87**
CSF £48.33 CT £158.36 TOTE £13.50: £4.00, £1.60, £1.50; EX 74.00 Trifecta £333.60 Pool: £5086.51 - 11.43 winning tickets..
Owner Orchard Stud **Bred** Mrs F Midwood & P Sells **Trained** Newmarket, Suffolk

FOCUS
The front three finished in a line, but this is probably reasonable form for the grade, rated around the third.
T/Plt: £439.10 to a £1 stake. Pool: £53392.2 - 88.75 winning tickets T/Qpdt: £14.40 to a £1 stake. Pool: £7211.79 - 370.55 winning tickets JN

8198 WOLVERHAMPTON (A.W) (L-H)
Monday, December 9

OFFICIAL GOING: Standard
Wind: Fresh behind Weather: Fine

8221 32RED MEDIAN AUCTION MAIDEN STKS 1m 141y(P)
2:10 (2:11) (Class 6) 2-Y-O **£1,940** (£577; £288; £144) **Stalls** Low

Form RPR

02- **1** **Dragoon Guard (IRE)**[16] 8026 2-9-5 0........................ MartinHarley 1 73+
(Marco Botti) *hld up: hdwy over 2f out: rdn over 1f out: led ins fnl f: edgd lft: pushed out* **5/4**[2]

6- **2** 1 ¾ **Market Storm (FR)**[16] 8026 2-9-5 0........................(be[1]) TomEaves 6 69
(Michael Mullineaux) *s.i.s: hdwy over 5f out: led over 3f out: rdn and hdd over 1f out: styd on same pce ins fnl f* **16/1**[3]

62- **3** nse **Itsnowcato**[26] 7853 2-9-5 0........................ RichardKingscote 2 69
(Ed Walker) *a.p: chsd ldr over 2f out: led over 1f out: sn rdn: hdd and unable qck ins fnl f* **8/11**[1]

0- **4** 4 ½ **Bourbondi**[102] 5924 2-9-5 0........................ RobertWinston 3 59
(Michael Murphy) *sn outpcd: hung rt 6f out: hdwy over 2f out: rdn over 1f out: wknd ins fnl f* **66/1**

00- **5** 20 **Rose Boeuf (FR)**[24] 7902 2-8-11 0........................(v[1]) JulieBurke[(3)] 5 8
(David O'Meara) *sn led: hdd over 7f out: chsd ldr tl pushed along over 3f out: rdn and wknd over 2f out* **66/1**

00- **6** 9 **Baytown Tigress**[6] 8138 2-9-0 0........................ PaddyAspell 4
(Phil McEntee) *led over 7f out: pushed along and hdd 3f out: wknd over 2f out* **66/1**

1m 53.1s (2.60) **Going Correction** +0.175s/f (Slow) **6** Ran SP% **112.7**
Speed ratings (Par 94): **95,93,93,89,71 63**
toteswingers 1&2 £1.60, 1&3 £1.02, 2&3 £1.60 CSF £18.76 TOTE £2.20: £1.20, £4.10; EX 17.50 Trifecta £28.70 Pool: £5280.08 - 137.65 winning tickets..
Owner Khalifa Dasmal **Bred** Kildaragh Stud **Trained** Newmarket, Suffolk

FOCUS
This was a routine maiden, with the two market leaders setting a respectable standard for the course.

8222 32RED.COM NURSERY H'CAP 5f 216y(P)
2:40 (2:40) (Class 6) (0-65,65) 2-Y-O **£1,940** (£577; £288; £144) **Stalls** Low

Form RPR

043- **1** **Exceeding Power**[48] 7451 2-9-5 **63**........................ MartinHarley 3 69+
(Michael Bell) *trckd ldr tl led over 1f out: rdn and edgd lft ins fnl f: r.o* **2/1**[1]

402- **2** 1 ½ **Dancing Sal (IRE)**[32] 7789 2-9-6 **64**........................ GrahamGibbons 2 66
(David Evans) *sn led: rdn and hdd over 1f out: styd on same pce ins fnl f* **4/1**[2]

322- **3** 3 ¼ **Coiste Bodhar (IRE)**[3] 8188 2-9-4 **62**........................ GrahamLee 4 54
(Joseph Tuite) *hld up in tch: racd keenly: rdn over 1f out: styd on same pce fnl f* **2/1**[1]

303- **4** 1 ¾ **Caesars Gift (IRE)**[9] 8113 2-9-7 **65**........................(v) DaleSwift 6 52
(Derek Shaw) *hld up: plld hrd: rdn over 1f out: styd on same pce* **7/1**[3]

510- **5** 1 ¼ **Just Rubie**[25] 7878 2-9-5 **63**........................ FergusSweeney 1 46
(Michael Blanshard) *s.i.s: sn prom: rdn over 1f out: wknd fnl f* **12/1**

062- **6** 5 **Astral Rose**[31] 7804 2-9-2 **60**........................(b) RichardKingscote 5 28
(Jonathan Portman) *hld up: rdn over 2f out: wknd over 1f out* **25/1**

1m 16.93s (1.93) **Going Correction** +0.175s/f (Slow) **6** Ran SP% **110.7**
Speed ratings (Par 94): **94,92,87,85,83 77**
toteswingers 1&2 £1.90, 1&3 £1.30, 2&3 £1.70 CSF £10.07 TOTE £2.80: £1.30, £2.00; EX 10.30 Trifecta £20.10 Pool: £3373.22 - 125.74 winning tickets..
Owner Dr Ali Ridha **Bred** Rabbah Bloodstock Limited **Trained** Newmarket, Suffolk

FOCUS
Some exposed types contested this nursery, but the more lightly raced winner is going the right way. Fair form for the grade.

8223 32RED CASINO H'CAP 1m 5f 194y(P)
3:10 (3:10) (Class 6) (0-65,65) 3-Y-O+ **£1,940** (£577; £288; £144) **Stalls** Low

Form RPR

313- **1** **Lacey**[16] 8027 4-9-0 **56**........................ JackDuern[(5)] 6 66+
(Andrew Hollinshead) *hld up: hdwy over 5f out: chsd ldr over 3f out: led and hung lft over 2f out: rdn clr 1f out: eased ins fnl f* **11/4**[1]

600- **2** 5 **Fire In Babylon (IRE)**[110] 5633 5-8-9 **46** oh1..........(b) AdamBeschizza 5 48
(Noel Quinlan) *led after 1f: rdn and hdd over 2f out: no ex fnl f* **25/1**

043- **3** 4 ½ **Rancho Montoya (IRE)**[16] 8031 3-8-13 **57**..................(v) DavidProbert 7 53
(Andrew Balding) *prom: rdn over 3f out: wknd 2f out* **7/2**[2]

506- **4** 1 ¾ **Song Of The Siren**[7] 8130 5-9-11 **62**........................(p) GrahamLee 2 55
(David O'Meara) *led 1f: chsd ldr tl rdn over 3f out: wknd over 2f out* **16/1**

404- **5** 12 **Authentication**[49] 7423 4-9-5 **56**........................ DuranFentiman 4 32
(Mel Brittain) *chsd ldrs: rdn over 3f out: wknd over 2f out* **5/1**[3]

1/3- **6** 34 **Vexillum (IRE)**[18] 7273 4-10-0 **65**........................(t) MartinHarley 1
(Simon Hodgson) *hld up: rdn and wknd over 5f out* **6/1**

004- **7** 62 **Gabrial The Thug (FR)**[13] 8047 3-9-2 **60**........................(t) TomEaves 3
(Richard Fahey) *hld up in tch: rdn and wknd 5f out* **7/2**[2]

3m 7.47s (1.47) **Going Correction** +0.175s/f (Slow)
WFA 3 from 4yo+ 7lb **7** Ran SP% **111.8**
Speed ratings (Par 101): **102,99,96,95,88 69,33**
toteswingers 1&2 £10.60, 1&3 £2.50, 2&3 £20.40 CSF £63.30 TOTE £3.50: £1.60, £8.00; EX 90.00 Trifecta £589.80 Pool: £3220.82 - 4.09 winning tickets..
Owner N S Sweeney **Bred** Millsec Limited **Trained** Upper Longdon, Staffs

FOCUS
This was uncompetitive, with most of the field either out of form or never having shown much in the first place. Weak form.

8224 COMPARE BOOKMAKERS AT BOOKMAKERS.CO.UK H'CAP 5f 216y(P)
3:40 (3:41) (Class 5) (0-75,75) 3-Y-O+ **£2,587** (£770; £384; £192) **Stalls** Low

Form RPR

321- **1** **Discussiontofollow (IRE)**[17] 8003 3-9-0 **68**........................ ShaneKelly 11 83+
(Mike Murphy) *hld up: hdwy 1/2-way: edgd lft fr over 1f out: shkn up to ld wl ins fnl f: comf* **11/4**[1]

003- **2** 1 **Lexi's Hero (IRE)**[31] 7801 5-8-9 **68**........................ SamanthaBell[(5)] 4 77
(Richard Fahey) *led: rdn over 1f out: hdd wl ins fnl f* **12/1**

203- **3** ¾ **Go Far**[179] 3253 3-8-13 **67**........................ RobertWinston 1 74
(Alan Bailey) *prom: pushed along 1/2-way: rdn over 1f out: kpt on* **10/1**

233- **4** 2 **Cape Of Hope (IRE)**[46] 7486 3-9-2 **75**........................ DavidBergin[(5)] 7 75
(David O'Meara) *w ldr tl rdn over 2f out: styd on same pce ins fnl f* **10/3**[2]

130- **5** ½ **Bogsnog (IRE)**[13] 8053 3-9-7 **75**........................ TomEaves 9 74
(Kristin Stubbs) *prom: effrt and hmpd over 1f out: styd on same pce ins fnl f* **10/1**

04- **6** hd **Marciano (IRE)**[10] 8095 3-9-7 **75**........................(v[1]) DaleSwift 12 73
(Alan Brown) *s.i.s: sn pushed along in rr: rdn over 1f out: edgd lft and r.o u.p ins fnl f: nvr nrr* **12/1**

112- **7** shd **Powerful Pierre**[24] 7896 6-8-11 **70**........................(b) JacobButterfield[(5)] 2 68
(Ollie Pears) *s.i.s: rdn over 2f out: r.o ins fnl f: nrst fin* **7/1**[3]

006- **8** 1 **Mount Hollow**[10] 8096 8-8-13 **72**........................(e) JackDuern[(5)] 8 66
(Andrew Hollinshead) *hld up: rdn over 1f out: running on whn n.m.r ins fnl f: nvr trbld ldrs* **10/1**

104- **9** 2 **Speightowns Kid (USA)**[10] 8096 5-8-11 **65**........................(b) RobertHavlin 3 53
(Alan Berry) *chsd ldrs: rdn over 2f out: wknd ins fnl f* **16/1**

350- **10** 2 **Cardinal**[24] 7896 8-9-2 **70**........................(p) GrahamLee 5 52
(Robert Cowell) *mid-div: lost pl over 4f out: n.d after* **25/1**

000- **11** 1 **Dorback**[11] 8088 6-9-7 **75**........................ MartinHarley 10 53
(Tony Newcombe) *mid-div: rdn over 2f out: wknd over 1f out* **20/1**

046- **12** 3 ½ **Captain Scooby**[13] 8048 7-8-5 **62**........................(e) BillyCray[(3)] 13 29
(Richard Guest) *sn outpcd* **50/1**

66- **13** 1 **Mambo Spirit (IRE)**[72] 6856 9-8-7 **64**........................ RossAtkinson[(3)] 6 28
(Tony Newcombe) *s.i.s: drvn along over 2f out: sn wknd* **50/1**

1m 15.36s (0.36) **Going Correction** +0.175s/f (Slow) **13** Ran SP% **123.3**
Speed ratings (Par 103): **104,102,101,99,98 98,97,96,93,91 89,85,83**
toteswingers 1&2 £10.60, 1&3 £7.10, 2&3 £15.30 CSF £37.25 CT £309.35 TOTE £5.30: £1.60, £5.40, £3.60; EX 55.40 Trifecta £487.00 Pool: £3694.73 - 5.68 winning tickets..
Owner D Spratt **Bred** Jerry O'Sullivan **Trained** Westoning, Beds
■ Stewards' Enquiry : Jacob Butterfield caution: careless riding.

FOCUS
This was a fair race of its type, with a number of the field in decent form. The form is rated slightly positively.

8225 CORAL APP DOWNLOAD FROM THE APP STORE H'CAP 1m 4f 50y(P)
4:10 (4:10) (Class 6) (0-60,60) 3-Y-O+ **£1,940** (£577; £288; £144) **Stalls** Low

Form RPR

564- **1** **Rainford Glory (IRE)**[196] 2709 3-9-0 **55**........................ MartinHarley 7 62
(David Simcock) *a.p: led 2f out: rdn over 1f out: all out* **7/1**

121- **2** shd **Tracks Of My Tears**[16] 8031 3-9-0 **58**........................ RyanPowell[(3)] 1 64
(Giles Bravery) *hld up: hdwy over 2f out: rdn over 1f out: ev ch wl ins fnl f: r.o* **1/1**[1]

225- **3** nk **Our Golden Girl**[44] 7543 3-8-11 **55**........................(b) RobertTart[(3)] 6 61
(Shaun Lycett) *hld up: hdwy on outer over 2f out: rdn and ev ch fr over 1f out: styd on* **9/2**[2]

054- **4** 13 **Sir Tyto (IRE)**[10] 8092 5-9-10 **60**........................(p) GrahamLee 5 45
(Peter Makin) *chsd ldr over 3f out: hdd 2f out: sn rdn: wknd fnl f* **12/1**

554- **5** 8 **Well Owd Mon**[16] 8031 3-8-8 **49**........................ DavidProbert 3 21
(Andrew Hollinshead) *chsd ldrs: pushed along over 5f out: rdn and wknd over 2f out* **6/1**[3]

010- **6** 12 **Rock Diamond (IRE)**[24] 7907 3-8-7 **48**................(p) RichardKingscote 2
(Brendan Powell) *led 9f: rdn and weakjened 2f out* **14/1**

040- **7** 39 **Jody Bear**[24] 7899 5-8-7 **46** oh1........................ MatthewLawson[(3)] 4
(Jonathan Portman) *hld up: rdn and wknd over 3f out* **33/1**

2m 43.53s (2.43) **Going Correction** +0.175s/f (Slow)
WFA 3 from 5yo 5lb **7** Ran SP% **112.3**
Speed ratings (Par 101): **98,97,97,89,83 75,49**
toteswingers 1&2 £2.80, 1&3 £5.00, 2&3 £1.30 CSF £13.95 CT £34.66 TOTE £8.40: £3.20, £1.10; EX 17.40 Trifecta £49.90 Pool: £6029.53 - 90.48 winning tickets..
Owner Dr Marwan Koukash **Bred** Her Diamond Necklace **Trained** Newmarket, Suffolk

FOCUS
This was a modest event, with the topweight having shown little in maidens. The first three were clear.

8226 CORAL MOBILE "JUST THREE CLICKS TO BET" H'CAP 1m 1f 103y(P)
4:40 (4:40) (Class 4) (0-80,78) 3-Y-O+ **£4,690** (£1,395; £697; £348) **Stalls** Low

Form RPR

351- **1** **Modernism**[39] 7651 4-9-7 **78**........................ MartinHarley 7 87
(David Simcock) *chsd ldr tl led 2f out: sn rdn: styd on u.p* **7/4**[1]

025- **2** nk **Berlusca (IRE)**[13] 8057 4-9-1 **77**........................ DavidBergin[(5)] 5 85
(David O'Meara) *trckd ldrs: shkn up and ev ch fr over 1f out: rdn ins fnl f: styd on* **7/1**

043- **3** 1 ¼ **Red Dragon (IRE)**[18] 7989 3-9-1 **74**........................ FergusSweeney 3 79
(Michael Blanshard) *plld hrd and prom: rdn over 1f out: styd on* **12/1**

616- **4** 1 ¾ **Lean On Pete (IRE)**[13] 8057 4-9-1 **77**........................ JacobButterfield[(5)] 6 79
(Ollie Pears) *hld up: rdn over 1f out: kpt on ins fnl f: nvr trbld ldrs* **6/1**[3]

1- **5** 4 **Doldrums (USA)**[23] 7932 3-9-3 **76**........................ JoeFanning 2 69
(Mark Johnston) *led: pushed along and hdd 2f out: wknd ins fnl f* **9/4**[2]

040- **6** 2 ½ **Munsarim (IRE)**[3] 8179 6-8-9 **73**........................(b) JoeDoyle[(7)] 4 61
(Lee Carter) *hld up in tch: plld hrd: rdn over 2f out: wkng whn hung rt fnl f* **16/1**

154- **7** 2 ¼ **Gabrial's Hope (FR)**[184] 3085 4-8-10 **67**........................(t) MartinLane 1 50
(David Simcock) *s.s: hld up: pushed along over 3f out: wknd over 2f out* **25/1**

2m 3.69s (1.99) **Going Correction** +0.175s/f (Slow)
WFA 3 from 4yo+ 2lb **7** Ran SP% **111.3**
Speed ratings (Par 105): **98,97,96,95,91 89,87**
toteswingers 1&2 £2.80, 1&3 £3.40, 2&3 £6.80 CSF £13.84 TOTE £2.90: £1.90, £3.50; EX 14.60 Trifecta £86.40 Pool: £6620.52 - 57.43 winning tickets..
Owner Dr Marwan Koukash **Bred** Darley **Trained** Newmarket, Suffolk

FOCUS
This is pretty solid AW form at this level, the winner getting close to his 3yo form.

8227 **LADBROKES H'CAP** **1m 141y(P)**
5:10 (5:10) (Class 5) (0-75,75) 3-Y-O+ **£2,587** (£770; £384; £192) **Stalls Low**

Form RPR
/06- 1 **Suehail**13 8053 4-9-7 **75** ShaneKelly 10 86
(Robert Cowell) *hld up: hdwy over 2f out: led over 1f out: drvn out* **20/1**
306- 2 1 3/4 **One Scoop Or Two**20 7965 7-9-3 **71** (v) GrahamGibbons 3 78
(Andrew Hollinshead) *a.p: rdn and ev ch over 1f out: sn hung lft: styd on same pce u.p ins fnl f* **6/1**2
/61- 3 3/4 **Jaladee**13 8054 3-9-3 **73** AndreaAtzeni 7 78
(Roger Varian) *s.i.s: hld up: hdwy over 3f out: rdn over 1f out: styd on same pce ins fnl f* **11/10**1
004- 4 1/2 **Ewell Place (IRE)**24 7898 4-9-0 **68** MartinHarley 8 72
(David Simcock) *hld up: hdwy over 1f out: sn rdn: styd on: nt rch ldrs* **6/1**2
004- 5 nse **Queen Aggie (IRE)**16 8020 3-9-2 **72** MartinLane 1 76
(David Evans) *hld up: racd keenly: pushed along and hdwy over 2f out: nt clr run over 1f out: r.o: nt rch ldrs* **10/1**3
155- 6 3/4 **Mcmonagle (USA)**4 8162 5-9-2 **70** (vt1) DaleSwift 6 72
(Alan Brown) *trckd ldr tl led over 3f out: rdn and hdd over 1f out: styd on same pce fnl f* **25/1**
260- 7 3 1/4 **Kyllachy Star**41 7608 7-9-0 **68** TomEaves 9 63
(Richard Fahey) *s.i.s: hld up: pushed along over 3f out: nvr on terms* **16/1**
350- 8 2 1/4 **Caramack**17 8008 3-9-0 **70** (p) RobertHavlin 4 60
(Richard Lee) *chsd ldr: rdn over 1f out: wknd fnl f* **33/1**
043- 9 41 **Perivale (USA)**14 8036 3-8-6 **62** JoeFanning 5
(Mark Johnston) *chsd ldrs: pushed along over 3f out: wknd 2f out: eased* **14/1**
064- 10 shd **Mister Marcasite**17 8008 3-8-8 **64** (v) DuranFentiman 2
(Mel Brittain) *led: rdn and hdd over 3f out: wknd over 2f out* **14/1**

1m 51.48s (0.98) **Going Correction** +0.175s/f (Slow)
WFA 3 from 4yo+ 2lb **10 Ran SP% 116.0**
Speed ratings (Par 103): **102,100,99,99,99 98,95,93,57,57**
toteswingers 1&2 £18.60, 1&3 £6.80, 2&3 £1.80 CSF £132.32 CT £252.24 TOTE £25.40: £6.30, £1.60, £1.30; EX 179.60 Trifecta £440.70 Pool: £5756.46 - 9.79 winning tickets..
Owner Malih Lahej Al Basti **Bred** Malih Al Basti **Trained** Six Mile Bottom, Cambs

FOCUS
Many of these are likely to win in their turn during the winter. The winner was on a good amrk on his Irish form.
T/Jkpt: £4,036.50 to a £1 stake. Pool: £68224.05 - 12.00 winning tickets T/Plt: £94.50 to a £1 stake. Pool: £80677.58 - 622.59 winning tickets T/Qpdt: £8.20 to a £1 stake. Pool: £9351.10 - 842.48 winning tickets CR

8042 SOUTHWELL (L-H)
Tuesday, December 10

OFFICIAL GOING: Standard
Wind: Virtually nil Weather: Fine and dry

8228 **32RED NURSERY H'CAP** **5f (F)**
12:00 (12:02) (Class 5) (0-75,71) 2-Y-O **£2,587** (£770; £384; £192) **Stalls High**

Form RPR
442- 1 **Pensax Lad (IRE)**29 7837 2-9-7 **71** RobertWinston 2 76+
(Ronald Harris) *trckd ldrs on outer: cl up 1/2-way: chal over 1f out: led appr fnl f: sn rdn and kpt on* **5/4**1
132- 2 1 1/4 **Skinny Love**11 8090 2-9-2 **66** (p) AdamBeschizza 5 64
(Robert Cowell) *cl up: led 1/2-way: rdn wl over 1f out: hdd appr fnl f: sn drvn and kpt on same pce* **11/2**3
610- 3 nk **Tautira (IRE)**29 7837 2-8-10 **67** LouisSteward(7) 4 64
(Michael Bell) *squeezed out and lost pl after 100yds: sn bhd: swtchd rt to stands' rail bef 1/2-way: hdwy 2f out: rdn and styng on to chse ldng pair whn hung lft ent fnl f: kpt on towards fin* **5/1**2
354- 4 4 **Back On Baileys**17 8017 2-8-7 **57** LukeMorris 8 40
(Chris Dwyer) *prom towards stands' rail: rdn along 2f out and sn edgd lft: wknd over 1f out* **12/1**
331- 5 1 1/2 **Biscuiteer**10 8113 2-8-6 **63** (p) MatthewHopkins(7) 3 40
(Scott Dixon) *chsd ldrs: rdn along and outpcd after 1 1/2f: sn in rr: plugged on u.p fr over 1f out* **6/1**
404- 6 1 **Sunningdale Rose (IRE)**28 7844 2-8-5 **60** (v) DanielMuscutt(5) 6 34
(Gay Kelleway) *cl up: rdn along over 2f out: drvn and wknd over 1f out* **20/1**
045- 7 4 1/2 **Anytimeatall (IRE)**25 7900 2-8-7 **62** TimClark(5) 7 19
(Alan Bailey) *t.k.h: slt ld: pushed along and hdd 1/2-way: sn rdn and wknd* **12/1**

1m 0.85s (1.15) **Going Correction** +0.125s/f (Slow) **7 Ran SP% 110.9**
Speed ratings (Par 96): **95,93,92,86,83 82,74**
toteswingers 1&2 £1.90, 2&3 £4.00, 1&3 £2.30 CSF £7.87 CT £23.54 TOTE £1.90: £1.20, £2.40; EX 8.10 Trifecta £32.20 Pool: £3049.90 - 70.92 winning units..
Owner S & A Mares **Bred** Seamus And James McMullan **Trained** Earlswood, Monmouths

FOCUS
A modest sprint nursery in which the sole colt proved too good for the six fillies. Four horses disputed the early lead.

8229 **32RED.COM H'CAP** **1m 6f (F)**
12:30 (12:32) (Class 6) (0-60,65) 3-Y-O+ **£1,940** (£577; £288; £144) **Stalls Low**

Form RPR
002- 1 **Rock Of Ages**8 8129 4-9-7 **55** (b) LiamJones 9 65
(Michael Murphy) *dwlt and reminders in rr s: rapid hdwy to ld after 3f: rdn along over 2f out: edgd rt wl over 1f out: drvn and kpt on wl fnl f* **7/2**2
304- 2 4 **Tobrata**53 7342 7-9-8 **56** DuranFentiman 6 61
(Mel Brittain) *led 3f: chsd wnr: rdn to chal over 2f out and ev ch whn n.m.r and sltly outpcd wl over 1f out: sn swtchd lft and drvn: styd on u.p fnl f* **15/2**
3 1/2 **Hazariban (IRE)**16 7041 4-9-10 **58** (e1) ShaneFoley 8 62
(Seamus Fahey, Ire) *trckd ldrs: hdwy 5f out: effrt on inner 3f out: rdn 2f out: drvn and one pce fnl f* **9/2**
344- 4 3/4 **Neighbourhood (USA)**35 7159 5-9-12 **60** (b) ChrisCatlin 10 63
(James Evans) *trckd ldrs on outer: hdwy and cl up 5f out: effrt over 2f out: sn rdn and ev ch tl drvn and one pce fnl f* **3/1**1
201- 5 1 3/4 **High On A Hill (IRE)**3 8204 6-10-3 **65** 6ex (b) AdamKirby 11 67
(Iain Jardine) *midfield: hdwy on outer 5f out: effrt to chse ldrs 3f out: rdn 2f out: drvn and no imp appr fnl f* **4/1**3
3U0- 6 8 **Miss Mohawk (IRE)**114 5560 4-8-12 **46** oh1 (p) DaleSwift 5 37
(Alan Brown) *prom: rdn along over 4f out: drvn 3f out and grad wknd* **66/1**
553- 7 6 **Miss Ella Jade**21 7951 4-9-1 **49** TonyHamilton 3 32
(Richard Whitaker) *chsd ldrs: rdn along over 4f out: sn wknd* **16/1**
400- 8 7 **Tamaletta (IRE)**25 7894 3-8-13 **54** JimmyQuinn 7 28
(Paul Burgoyne) *dwlt: a in rr* **25/1**
060- 9 12 **Anne's Valentino**52 7376 3-8-5 **46** oh1 AndrewMullen 2 4
(Malcolm Jefferson) *in tch on inner: rdn along 1/2-way: sn wknd* **40/1**
0- 10 2 3/4 **Diamond Pro (IRE)**6 5506 4-9-8 **56** (t) BenCurtis 4 10
(Christopher Kellett) *sn pushed along in rr: rdn along over 5f out and a bhd* **40/1**
/66- 11 14 **Ravens Nest**29 7839 3-8-13 **54** JohnFahy 1
(Ben Pauling) *prom on inner: pushed along 1/2-way: rdn 5f out: sn lost pl and bhd* **33/1**

3m 9.82s (1.52) **Going Correction** +0.075s/f (Slow)
WFA 3 from 4yo+ 7lb **11 Ran SP% 116.2**
Speed ratings (Par 101): **98,95,95,95,94 89,86,82,75,73 65**
toteswingers 1&2 £5.90, 2&3 £7.60, 1&3 £4.60 CSF £28.06 CT £120.34 TOTE £4.60: £2.10, £2.60, £2.00; EX 33.60 Trifecta £237.20 Pool: £3146.41 - 9.94 winning units..
Owner Bob W Smith **Bred** Cheveley Park Stud Ltd **Trained** Newmarket, Suffolk
■ Stewards' Enquiry : Shane Foley two-day ban: used whip above permitted level (Dec 26-27)

FOCUS
A moderate staying handicap and the pace wasn't that strong. Straightforward form.

8230 **BEST ODDS AT BOOKMAKERS.CO.UK CLASSIFIED CLAIMING STKS** **6f (F)**
1:00 (1:02) (Class 6) 3-Y-O+ **£2,045** (£603; £302) **Stalls Low**

Form RPR
056- 1 **Alpha Tauri (USA)**22 7948 7-8-0 67 (t) JackGarritty(7) 9 73
(Charles Smith) *trckd ldrs: hdwy 1/2-way: cl up over 2f out: led wl over 1f out: rdn ent fnl f: sn edgd rt and kpt on* **8/1**
521- 2 3/4 **Spitfire**14 8049 8-8-10 70 (t) JoeFanning 7 74
(J R Jenkins) *in tch: hdwy over 2f out: rdn along wl over 1f out: drvn and kpt on fnl f* **11/8**1
040- 3 nk **Angelo Poliziano**234 1694 7-7-11 67 ow1 (b) JosephineGordon(7) 3 67
(Jo Hughes) *towards rr: hdwy on outer over 2f out: rdn to chse ldrs over 1f out: styd on fnl f* **25/1**
003- 4 1 **Sewn Up**17 8029 3-8-12 67 (p1) LiamJones 8 72
(Andrew Hollinshead) *dwlt and towards rr: hdwy over 2f out: rdn wl over 1f out: styd on fnl f: nrst fin* **5/1**2
516- 5 1 **Fathom Five (IRE)**6 8152 9-8-2 61 JimmyQuinn 10 59
(Shaun Harris) *qckly away and led: rdn along over 2f out: hdd wl over 1f out and grad wknd* **13/2**3
30- 6 3/4 **Whisky Bravo**82 6568 4-8-5 65 DavidProbert 6 60
(David C Griffiths) *chsd ldr: hdwy on inner over 2f out: rdn and ev ch wl over 1f out: drvn and wknd fnl f* **9/1**
000- 7 1 1/4 **Dancing Maite**21 7953 8-8-4 66 ow2 MarkCoumbe(3) 5 58
(Roy Bowring) *dwlt: sn chsng ldrs: rdn along over 2f out and sn no hdwy* **25/1**
366- 8 2 **Bunce (IRE)**14 8049 5-7-11 63 ow2 (bt) JoshDoyle(7) 2 49
(David O'Meara) *chsd ldng pair: rdn along 1/2-way: sn wknd* **14/1**
060- 9 3 **Avonmore Star**26 7880 5-8-9 64 (e1) ShaneKelly 1 45
(Mike Murphy) *a towards rr* **14/1**
006- 10 12 **King Vahe (IRE)**115 5523 4-7-9 54 RhiainIngram(7) 4 2
(Olivia Maylam) *a towards rr: bhd fr 1/2-way* **66/1**

1m 16.81s (0.31) **Going Correction** +0.075s/f (Slow) **10 Ran SP% 115.7**
Speed ratings (Par 101): **100,99,98,97,95 94,93,90,86,70**
toteswingers 1&2 £4.00, 2&3 £8.70, 1&3 £34.50 CSF £18.92 TOTE £9.60: £2.70, £1.10, £4.80; EX 32.60 Trifecta £842.90 Pool: £3193.56 - 2.84 winning units..
Owner Willie McKay **Bred** Flaxman Holdings Ltd **Trained** Temple Bruer, Lincs

FOCUS
A moderate classified claimer but straightforward form.

8231 **LADBROKES H'CAP** **7f (F)**
1:30 (1:30) (Class 2) (0-105,99) 3-Y-O£11,971 (£3,583; £1,791; £896; £446) **Stalls Low**

Form RPR
500- 1 **Dubai Hills**53 7337 7-9-1 **93** GrahamLee 7 103
(Bryan Smart) *trckd ldrs: hdwy 3f out: cl up 2f out: rdn to take slt advantage ent fnl f: drvn out towards fin* **11/4**1
602- 2 nk **Frontier Fighter**19 7992 5-8-10 **88** GrahamGibbons 9 97
(David O'Meara) *prom: cl up 3f out: slt ld 2f out: sn rdn and hdd ent fnl f: drvn and kpt on wl: jst hld* **7/2**3
232- 3 5 **Galician**10 8117 4-9-7 **99** JoeFanning 6 95
(Mark Johnston) *in rr and swtchd rt to outer after 1f: hdwy and wd st: rdn over 2f out: styd on appr fnl f: nrst fin* **6/1**
102- 4 nse **Iptisam**14 8053 4-8-10 **88** LukeMorris 4 84
(James Tate) *t.k.h early: chsd ldrs: hdwy over 2f out: rdn to chse ldng pair whn hung lft over 1f out: sn drvn and wknd fnl f* **3/1**2
400- 5 1 **Tellovoi (IRE)**10 8117 5-7-13 **80** (v) RyanPowell(3) 5 73
(Ian Williams) *dwlt and in rr: hdwy over 2f out: rdn to chse ldrs over 1f out: no imp fnl f* **16/1**
042- 6 4 1/2 **Clockmaker (IRE)**19 7991 7-9-3 **95** HayleyTurner 3 77
(Conor Dore) *chsd ldrs: rdn along over 3f out: sn wknd* **12/1**
000- 7 1 **Aubrietia**4 8189 4-8-13 **91** (b) TomQueally 8 70
(Alan McCabe) *set str pce: rdn 3f out and sn jnd: hdd 2f out and sn wknd* **33/1**
434- 8 1/2 **Laffan (IRE)**10 8117 4-8-13 **91** (e) DuranFentiman 2 69
(Tim Easterby) *towards rr on inner: effrt 3f out: sn rdn and n.d* **8/1**
000- 9 1/2 **Fratellino**13 8064 6-9-0 **92** (tp) MartinHarley 1 69
(Alan McCabe) *prom on inner: rdn along wl over 2f out: sn wknd* **50/1**

1m 28.68s (-1.62) **Going Correction** +0.075s/f (Slow) **9 Ran SP% 117.8**
Speed ratings (Par 109): **112,111,105,105,104 99,98,97,97**
toteswingers 1&2 £4.40, 2&3 £4.80, 1&3 £3.80 CSF £12.95 CT £53.43 TOTE £4.00: £1.50, £1.60, £1.50; EX 18.50 Trifecta £71.60 Pool: £3798.32 - 39.75 winning units..
Owner Mrs F Denniff **Bred** A S Denniff **Trained** Hambleton, N Yorks

FOCUS
A cracking handicap and there was no hanging about. The first two have been rated to their marks.

8232 **BOOKMAKERS.CO.UK H'CAP** **5f (F)**
2:00 (2:02) (Class 3) (0-95,92) 3-Y-O+ **£7,439** (£2,213; £1,106; £553) **Stalls High**

Form RPR
640- 1 **Bedloe's Island (IRE)**142 4569 8-8-13 **84** MartinHarley 8 91
(Alan McCabe) *hld up: smooth hdwy to trck ldrs 2f out: effrt and nt clr run jst over 1f out: rdn and styd on strly last 100yds to lds nr line* **33/1**

The Form Book Flat, Raceform Ltd, Compton, RG20 6NL.

101- **2** *hd* **Equitania**[4] 8189 3-9-2 **92** 6ex.. TimClark(5) 13 99
(Alan Bailey) *cl up: led 2f out: rdn over 1f out: drvn and edgd rt ins fnl f: hdd and no ex nr line* **8/1**[3]

401- **3** *hd* **Royal Bajan (USA)**[5] 8167 5-8-12 **83** 6ex....................(v) TomQueally 12 89
(James Given) *racd wd towards stands' rail: chsd ldrs: hdwy wl over 1f out: rdn to chal ent fnl f and ev ch tl drvn and nt qckn nr fin* **10/1**

603- **4** *shd* **Silken Express (IRE)**[27] 7851 4-9-4 **89**.......................... MartinLane 1 95
(Robert Cowell) *prom: cl up 2f out: rdn to chal over 1f out and ev ch tl drvn and nt qckn wl ins fnl f* **5/1**[1]

352- **5** *shd* **Monsieur Jamie**[26] 7887 5-8-7 **78**.............................(v) JoeFanning 4 83
(J R Jenkins) *cl up: effrt 2f out and sn ev ch tl drvn ent fnl f and kpt on same pce last 100yds* **6/1**[2]

000- **6** *1 ¾* **Even Stevens**[6] 8155 5-9-5 **90**..............................(p) TomEaves 14 89
(Scott Dixon) *slt ld: rdn and hdd 2f out: cl up tl drvn and one pce ent fnl f* **6/1**[2]

230- **7** *1* **Sleepy Blue Ocean**[90] 6309 7-8-8 **79**..........................(p) LukeMorris 5 74
(John Balding) *chsd ldrs: rdn along wl over 1f out: grad wknd* **20/1**

000- **8** *1* **Doctor Parkes**[52] 7373 7-9-7 **92**.......................... AdamBeschizza 2 84
(Stuart Williams) *chsd ldrs: rdn along 2f out: grad wknd* **25/1**

236- **9** *2* **Clubland (IRE)**[73] 6822 4-8-9 **80**.............................. JimmyQuinn 3 65
(Roy Bowring) *dwlt and hmpd s: towards rr: gd hdwy to chse ldrs 2f out: sn rdn and grad wknd* **10/1**

004- **10** *¾* **Maglietta Fina (IRE)**[34] 7776 4-9-0 **85**...................... RobertHavlin 6 67
(Robert Cowell) *towards rr: hdwy to chse ldrs 1/2-way: rdn along over 2f out: sn wknd* **16/1**

602- **11** *3 ½* **Threes Grand**[5] 8167 3-8-2 **80**......................... MatthewHopkins(7) 7 49
(Scott Dixon) *a towards rr* **16/1**

103- **12** *1 ¼* **Cheveton**[34] 7776 9-9-2 **87**.. AdamKirby 10 52
(Richard Price) *a in rr* **10/1**

050- **13** *¾* **Khawatim**[154] 4138 5-9-4 **92**.................................... BillyCray(3) 11 54
(Richard Guest) *dwlt: a in rr* **33/1**

01- **14** *¾* **Sharaarah (IRE)**[26] 7888 3-8-11 **87**.......................(b) DavidBergin(5) 9 46
(David O'Meara) *a in rr* **6/1**[2]

59.3s (-0.40) **Going Correction** +0.125s/f (Slow) **14** Ran SP% **124.2**
Speed ratings (Par 107): **108,107,107,107,107 104,102,101,97,96 91,89,87,86**
toteswingers 1&2 £68.80, 2&3 £13.10, 1&3 £70.50 CSF £278.76 CT £2862.84 TOTE £35.40: £12.70, £2.80, £3.50; EX 603.40 Trifecta £2441.80 Part won. Pool: £3255.76 - 0.15 winning units..
Owner Matthew Timms **Bred** Dr Dean Harron **Trained** Averham Park, Notts

FOCUS
A competitive sprint handicap and a large horse blanket would have covered the front five at the line. Decent, straightforward form amongst the principals.

8233 LADBROKES WISHES PAULA WILSON HAPPY 50TH H'CAP 1m (F)
2:30 (2:31) (Class 6) (0-60,59) 3-Y-O+ **£1,940** (£577; £288; £144) **Stalls** Low

Form RPR

352- **1** **No Win No Fee**[19] 7987 3-9-4 **57**.........................(p) AndrewMullen 7 66
(Michael Appleby) *prom: led 3f out: hdd over 2f out and sn rdn: rallied u.p ent fnl f: styd on wl to ld last 100yds* **4/1**[2]

401- **2** *1 ½* **Frosty Friday**[35] 7753 5-9-0 **52**.....................(v) FrederikTylicki 9 58
(J R Jenkins) *trckd ldrs: hdwy 3f out and sn cl up: led over 2f out: rdn over 1f out: drvn and edgd rt ins fnl f: hdd and no ex last 100yds* **9/2**[3]

040- **3** *nk* **Xpres Maite**[26] 7881 10-9-1 **56**......................(v) MarkCoumbe(3) 8 61
(Roy Bowring) *dwlt and in rr: hdwy wl over 2f out: rdn to chse ldrs over 1f out: kpt on wl fnl f: nrst fin* **25/1**

065- **4** *1* **Mataajir (USA)**[10] 8118 5-8-13 **51**...........................(v) DaleSwift 11 54
(Derek Shaw) *racd wd: chsd ldrs: hdwy over 2f out: rdn wl over 1f out: drvn and kpt on same pce fnl f* **6/1**

002- **5** *2 ¾* **General Tufto**[3] 8199 8-8-7 **45**...........................(b) MartinLane 10 41
(Charles Smith) *dwlt and in rr: hdwy and wd st: rdn to chse ldrs wl over 1f out: sn no imp* **12/1**

0/2- **6** *9* **Fast On (IRE)**[26] 7886 4-8-12 **50**......................(be[1]) ShaneFoley 6 26
(Seamus Fahey, Ire) *a towards rr* **7/1**

001- **7** *2 ¼* **Hussar Ballad (USA)**[21] 7951 4-9-7 **59**...................... PJMcDonald 4 29
(Mel Brittain) *in tch: hdwy to chse ldrs 3f out: rdn over 2f out and sn wknd* **7/2**[1]

340- **8** *2 ¼* **Outlaw Torn (IRE)**[18] 8006 4-9-7 **59**..............(e) RobbieFitzpatrick 3 24
(Richard Guest) *a towards rr* **20/1**

/60- **9** *4 ½* **Andiamo Via**[85] 6464 6-9-6 **58**................................... GrahamLee 1 13
(Brian Ellison) *prom on inner: rdn along over 3f out and sn wknd* **10/1**

362- **10** *2* **Pearl Noir**[14] 8043 3-8-11 **50**.............................(b) LukeMorris 5
(Scott Dixon) *led: rdn along and hdd 3f out: sn wknd* **16/1**

/0U- **11** *17* **Fair Bunny**[21] 7958 6-8-9 **47**............................(b) JimmyQuinn 12
(Alan Brown) *dwlt: a in rr* **100/1**

/00- **12** *26* **Legal Pursuit**[10] 8116 4-8-4 **45**................................ RyanPowell(3) 2
(Edward Bevan) *dwlt and a in rr* **100/1**

1m 43.95s (0.25) **Going Correction** +0.075s/f (Slow)
WFA 3 from 4yo+ 1lb **12** Ran SP% **120.4**
Speed ratings (Par 101): **101,99,99,98,95 86,84,81,77,75 58,32**
toteswingers 1&2 £4.40, 2&3 £24.60, 1&3 £19.60 CSF £22.18 CT £404.38 TOTE £3.80: £1.60, £1.90, £7.00; EX 23.90 Trifecta £577.70 Pool: £3556.05 - 4.61 winning units..
Owner Stephen Almond **Bred** Bearstone Stud **Trained** Danethorpe, Notts

FOCUS
A moderate handicap and not many got into it. Routine, low-grade form.

8234 LADBROKES H'CAP (DIV I) 7f (F)
3:00 (3:03) (Class 6) (0-60,60) 3-Y-O+ **£1,940** (£577; £288; £144) **Stalls** Low

Form RPR

312- **1** **Sakash**[21] 7966 3-9-7 **60**.. FrederikTylicki 9 77+
(J R Jenkins) *prom: hdwy to ld over 3f out: rdn clr and hung bdly lft to inner wl over 1f out: drvn and kpt on fnl f* **9/4**[1]

004- **2** *2* **Ivy Port**[14] 8042 3-9-3 **56**...................................... AndrewMullen 10 68+
(Michael Appleby) *chsd ldrs on outer: wd st: hdwy over 2f out: rdn to chse wnr and hung bdly lft over 1f out: kpt on u.p fnl f* **9/4**[1]

600- **3** *8* **Vale Of Clara (IRE)**[26] 7886 5-8-11 **50**..................(be[1]) TomEaves 6 41
(Peter Niven) *in rr: hdwy wl over 2f out: rdn over 1f out: styd on fnl f: nrst fin* **20/1**

342- **4** *1 ½* **Putin (IRE)**[14] 8042 5-9-7 **60**.............................(tp) PaddyAspell 11 47
(Phil McEntee) *chsd ldrs: rdn along wl over 2f out: sn drvn and one pce* **9/2**[2]

000- **5** *1* **Red Star Lady (IRE)**[35] 7752 3-8-7 **46** oh1..................... JimmyQuinn 8 31
(Shaun Harris) *chsd ldrs: hdwy 3f out: rdn 2f out and sn no imp* **66/1**

665- **6** *1 ¼* **Orwellian**[21] 7958 4-8-13 **52**.................................(e) GrahamLee 4 33
(Bryan Smart) *dwlt and in rr tl sme late hdwy* **8/1**[3]

200- **7** *½* **Shamrocked (IRE)**[14] 8048 4-9-1 **59**..................... JacobButterfield(5) 7 39
(Ollie Pears) *slt ld: rdn along and hdd over 3f out: drvn wl over 2f out and sn wknd* **20/1**

060- **8** *2 ¼* **Somethingboutmary**[14] 8048 3-9-4 **57**............................ DaleSwift 3 31
(Neville Bycroft) *hld up a towards rr* **33/1**

200- **9** *5* **Upper Lambourn (IRE)**[14] 8049 5-8-8 **52**..............(t) JackDuern(5) 1 13
(Christopher Kellett) *chsd ldrs on inner: rdn along over 3f out: sn wknd* **33/1**

40- **10** *2* **Masked Dance (IRE)**[14] 8042 6-9-1 **54**.....................(p) LukeMorris 5
(Scott Dixon) *a towards rr* **14/1**

050- **11** *6* **Mousie**[109] 5709 4-8-2 **46** oh1...........................(p) ShirleyTeasdale(5) 2
(Alan McCabe) *cl up: rdn along 1/2-way: sn wknd* **50/1**

1m 30.28s (-0.02) **Going Correction** +0.075s/f (Slow) **11** Ran SP% **116.4**
Speed ratings (Par 101): **103,100,91,89,88 87,86,84,78,76 69**
toteswingers 1&2 £2.10, 2&3 £13.60, 1&3 £11.90 CSF £6.29 CT £76.85 TOTE £3.50: £1.50, £1.10, £4.70; EX 8.60 Trifecta £198.40 Pool: £4991.13 - 18.86 winning units..
Owner Mr & Mrs C Schwick **Bred** Mr & Mrs C Schwick **Trained** Royston, Herts
■ Stewards' Enquiry : Andrew Mullen two-day ban: used whip above permitted level (Dec 26-27)

FOCUS
A moderate handicap and there was a yawning gap between the two market leaders and the others. The winner is generally progressive.

8235 LADBROKES H'CAP (DIV II) 7f (F)
3:30 (3:30) (Class 6) (0-60,60) 3-Y-O+ **£1,940** (£577; £288; £144) **Stalls** Low

Form RPR

001- **1** **Izzy Boy (USA)**[46] 7508 3-9-2 **55**.................................. LiamJones 3 63
(Mark Johnston) *dwlt and in rr: hdwy 3f out: chsd ldrs on inner over 2f out: rdn to ld over 1f out: drvn ins fnl f: jst hld on* **7/2**[1]

640- **2** *nse* **Wotalad**[25] 7904 3-8-12 **51**...............................(p) TonyHamilton 4 59
(Richard Whitaker) *cl up: led after 2f: rdn along over 2f out and sn hdd: drvn over 1f out: rallied strly ins fnl f: jst failed* **25/1**

606- **3** *2 ¾* **Heidi's Delight (IRE)**[202] 2575 4-8-8 **47**....................... PJMcDonald 8 47
(Ann Duffield) *dwlt and in rr: hdwy on outer wl over 2f out: rdn over 1f out: styd on fnl f: nrst fin* **16/1**

422- **4** *nk* **Grace Hull**[14] 8048 3-9-4 **57**.................................... TomQueally 2 57
(Garry Moss) *led 2f: cl up tl led again 2f out: sn rdn and hdd wl over 1f out: wknd ent fnl f* **9/2**[2]

000- **5** *1 ¾* **Bapak Pesta (IRE)**[21] 7957 3-8-13 **52**......................... MartinHarley 1 47
(Kevin Ryan) *chsd ldrs on inner: rdn along and outpcd 1/2-way: kpt on u.p fnl 2f* **16/1**

250- **6** *hd* **Elusive Warrior (USA)**[14] 8042 10-8-6 **52**..........(p) AaronJones(7) 10 46
(Alan McCabe) *dwlt: hdwy on outer to chse ldrs after 2f: rdn wl over 2f out and sn one pce* **14/1**

330- **7** *3 ¼* **Prince Of Passion (CAN)**[8] 8135 5-9-7 **60**..............(p) JoeFanning 7 46
(Derek Shaw) *chsd ldrs: rdn over 2f out: sn wknd* **8/1**

654- **8** *½* **Guishan**[157] 4068 3-9-6 **59**..................................... AndrewMullen 5 43
(Michael Appleby) *cl up: rdn along wl over 2f out: grad wknd* **5/1**[3]

412- **9** *3 ¾* **Monte Cassino (IRE)**[32] 7807 8-9-5 **58**.....................(e) GrahamLee 9 32
(Bryan Smart) *in tch: rdn along over 3f out: sn wknd* **7/2**[1]

1m 31.19s (0.89) **Going Correction** +0.075s/f (Slow) **9** Ran SP% **112.7**
Speed ratings (Par 101): **97,96,93,93,91 91,87,86,82**
toteswingers 1&2 £19.30, 2&3 £23.60, 1&3 £14.90 CSF £89.39 CT £1227.73 TOTE £4.70: £1.80, £5.40, £4.70; EX 93.40 Trifecta £3410.70 Part won. Pool: £4547.65 - 0.99 winning units..
Owner Frank Bird **Bred** Pollock Farms & Darley **Trained** Middleham Moor, N Yorks

FOCUS
The winning time was 0.91sec slower than the first division. Modest form.
T/Jkpt: Not won. T/Plt: £79.10 to a £1 stake. Pool of £70796.46 - 653.25 winning tickets. T/Qpdt: £21.60 to a £1 stake. Pool of £6993.90 - 238.80 winning tickets. JR

8145 KEMPTON (A.W) (R-H)
Wednesday, December 11
8236 Meeting Abandoned - Fog.
Wind: Nil Weather: Meeting ABANDONED

8213 LINGFIELD (L-H)
Wednesday, December 11
OFFICIAL GOING: Standard (remainder of meeting abandoned after race 2 due to fog)
Wind: virtually nil Weather: foggy

8244 DOWNLOAD THE LADBROKES APP (S) STKS 7f (P)
12:30 (12:30) (Class 6) 3-Y-O+ **£2,045** (£603; £302) **Stalls** Low

Form RPR

051- **1** **The Dancing Lord**[6] 8169 4-8-11 55.............................. RyanWhile(7) 2 70
(Bill Turner) *in tch in midfield: swtchd rt and effrt to chse ldr over 1f out: led ins fnl f: r.o wl* **16/1**

533- **2** *½* **The Mongoose**[7] 8157 5-9-4 66..............................(t) AdamKirby 3 69
(David Evans) *chsd ldrs: rdn and chal 2f out: sn led and drvn: hdd ins fnl f: kpt on wl but hld towards fin* **5/4**[1]

660- **3** *2 ¾* **Abigails Angel**[30] 7836 6-8-7 67.............................. KieranO'Neill 9 50
(Brett Johnson) *stdd and dropped in bhd after s: hld up in rr: clsd on outer over 2f out: rdn and effrt to chse ldrs 1f out: no imp ins fnl f* **9/2**[2]

030- **4** *shd* **Copperwood**[49] 7462 8-9-4 67.................................... AmirQuinn 5 61
(Lee Carter) *hld up in last quartet: rdn and hdwy to chse ldrs 2f out: no ex and one pce ins fnl f* **6/1**[3]

060- **5** *2 ½* **Blue Deer (IRE)**[57] 7266 5-8-9 51......................(p) MarkCoumbe(3) 1 48
(Lee Carter) *hld up in last quartet: rdn and clsd 2f out: no imp 1f out: wknd ins fnl f* **33/1**

205- **6** *1 ½* **Fairy Mist (IRE)**[57] 7266 6-9-4 45.............................. SeanLevey 6 50
(John Bridger) *stdd s: hld up in last quartet: rdn and hdwy over 2f out: no imp over 1f out: wknd fnl f* **100/1**

060- **6** *dht* **Comadoir (IRE)**[63] 7124 7-8-12 52....................(p) RichardKingscote 8 44
(Jo Crowley) *in tch in midfield: rdn and effrt jst over 2f out: wknd ent fnl f* **25/1**

334- **8** *6* **Homeboy (IRE)**[18] 8022 5-9-4 57................................. MartinDwyer 4 34
(Marcus Tregoning) *taken down early: led tl wl over 1f out: sn rdn and struggling: fdd fnl f* **8/1**

063- **9** *nse* **All Or Nothin (IRE)**[23] 7948 4-9-4 70............................(t[1]) JoeFanning 7 34
(Paddy Butler) *chsd ldr tl ent fnl 2f: sn struggling: fdd fnl f* **10/1**
1m 23.42s (-1.38) **Going Correction** -0.25s/f (Stan) **9** Ran SP% **110.8**
Speed ratings (Par 101): **97,96,93,93,90 88,88,81,81**
toteswingers 1&2 £6.30, 2&3 £1.50, 1&3 £12.50 CSF £34.40 TOTE £16.10: £3.60, £1.10, £1.30; EX 29.60 Trifecta £191.10 Pool: £2856.72 - 11.20 winning units..The winner was bought by D Phelan for 3,800gns.
Owner Mrs M S Teversham **Bred** Mrs Monica Teversham **Trained** Sigwells, Somerset
FOCUS
Limited visibility for this seller but it appeared to be run at decent pace and required a solid staying performance.

8245 CORAL MOBILE "JUST THREE CLICKS TO BET" MEDIAN AUCTION MAIDEN STKS 1m 2f (P)
1:00 (1:08) (Class 6) 3-5-Y-O **£2,045** (£603; £302) **Stalls** Low

Form RPR
342- **1** **Vermont (IRE)**[28] 7864 3-9-5 82........................ AdamKirby 5 92+
(Luca Cumani) *s.i.s: hdwy to ld after 1f: sn clr and mde rest: wl clr 2f out: heavily eased ins fnl f* **1/6**[1]
4- **2** *16* **Charlotte Rhodes**[25] 7932 3-9-0 0........................ MartinHarley 4 54
(Marco Botti) *led for 1f: chsd clr wnr after: wl btn 2nd 2f out: kpt on same pce after* **8/1**[2]
3 *3 ½* **Tax Reform (IRE)**[105] 5905 3-9-5 77........................ RobertHavlin 2 52
(Mark Hoad) *chsd ldrs: 3rd and no ch w wnr 2f out: kpt on same pce after* **12/1**
4 *1* **Music Man (IRE)** 3-9-5 0........................ JimCrowley 7 50
(Jo Crowley) *s.i.s: chsd ldrs 5f out: 4th and wl btn 2f out: plugged on* **10/1**[3]
00- **5** *2* **Maygo's Joy**[99] 6062 3-9-5 0........................ JoeFanning 1 46
(Ralph Smith) *hld up in last pair: 5th and wl btn 2f out: plugged on* **100/1**
6 *24* **Ashcott Boy**[23] 5-9-8 0........................ LiamKeniry 3
(Neil Mulholland) *s.i.s: a in rr: lost tch 2f out: t.o fnl f* **50/1**
2m 2.92s (-3.68) **Going Correction** -0.25s/f (Stan)
WFA 3 from 5yo 3lb **6** Ran SP% **116.5**
Speed ratings (Par 101): **104,91,88,87,86 66**
toteswingers 1&2 £1.10, 2&3 £1.50, 1&3 £1.70 CSF £2.75 TOTE £1.20: £1.10, £2.20; EX 2.70 Trifecta £6.50 Pool: £3886.60 - 448.30 winning units..
Owner Wildenstein Stables Limited **Bred** Dayton Investments Ltd **Trained** Newmarket, Suffolk
FOCUS
A one-sided event run in poor visibility. Weak form, with the winner a class above.

8246 CORAL.CO.UK BEST ODDS GUARANTEED ON RACING H'CAP 1m 4f (P)
() (Class 5) (0-75,) 3-Y-0+ £

8247 LADBROKES H'CAP 7f (P)
() (Class 4) (0-85,) 3-Y-0+ £

8249 CORAL APP DOWNLOAD FROM THE APP STORE H'CAP 1m 2f (P)
() (Class 6) (0-65,) 3-Y-0+ £

8250 LADBROKES MOBILE ALL-WEATHER "HANDS AND HEELS" APPRENTICE SERIES H'CAP (EXCELLENCE INITIATIVE) 1m (P)
() (Class 6) (60-92,) 3-Y-0+ £

T/Jkpt: £37.20 to a £1 stake. Pool of £10000.00 - 190.50 winning units. T/Plt: £1.10 to a £1 stake. Pool of £69594.91 - 53306.84 winning units. SP

8145 KEMPTON (A.W) (R-H)
Thursday, December 12

OFFICIAL GOING: Standard
Wind: Almost nil Weather: Some cloud

8258 DON SILVEY 70TH BIRTHDAY H'CAP 7f (P)
3:50 (3:51) (Class 7) (0-50,50) 3-Y-0+ **£1,617** (£481; £240; £120) **Stalls** Low

Form RPR
404- **1** **Foie Gras**[26] 7924 3-8-13 **49**........................ ShelleyBirkett[(5)] 3 60
(Chris Dwyer) *hld up in midfield: hdwy 2f out: drvn to ld ins fnl f* **10/1**
033- **2** *nk* **Medam**[12] 8119 4-9-0 **50**........................ ShirleyTeasdale[(5)] 1 60
(Shaun Harris) *chsd ldrs: rdn to chal 1f out: kpt on* **6/1**[3]
000- **3** *1* **Blue Noodles**[12] 8118 7-9-3 **48**........................(v) LukeMorris 7 55+
(John Wainwright) *towards rr: hrd rdn and r.o fnl 2f: clsng at fin* **12/1**
064- **4** *1* **Misty Eyes**[34] 7807 4-9-4 **49**........................(v) JoeFanning 13 54
(Geoffrey Harker) *led: set modest pce: hdd and no ex ins fnl f* **10/1**
054- **5** *1 ½* **Ryedale Lass**[99] 6102 5-9-5 **50**........................ HayleyTurner 9 51
(Geoffrey Deacon) *chsd ldrs: rdn and styd on same pce fnl 2f* **5/1**[2]
004- **6** *1 ¾* **Daneside (IRE)**[14] 8082 6-9-4 **49**........................ GrahamGibbons 6 45
(P J O'Gorman) *chsd ldr: rdn over 2f out: wknd over 1f out* **7/2**[1]
25- **7** *¾* **Chester Deelyte (IRE)**[55] 7353 5-9-1 **49**........................(v) MarkCoumbe[(3)] 4 43
(Lisa Williamson) *prom tl wknd over 1f out* **12/1**
/00- **8** *1 ½* **Bryant Park (USA)**[15] 8068 4-9-5 **50**........................(t) AdamBeschizza 10 40
(Christine Dunnett) *dwlt: t.k.h in rr: rdn and sme hdwy over 1f out: nt rch ldrs* **8/1**
0/0- **9** *¾* **Underwhelm**[10] 8022 3-8-10 **48**........................ JordanVaughan[(7)] 8 36
(Andrew Reid) *towards rr: rdn 3f out: n.d* **66/1**
6/3- **10** *2 ¾* **Fen Flyer**[28] 7873 4-9-5 **50**........................ PaddyAspell 12 30
(John Berry) *nvr nr ldrs* **33/1**
000- **11** *2* **Prom Dress**[37] 7759 3-9-5 **50**........................ FrederikTylicki 2 25
(J R Jenkins) *mid-div tl wknd over 2f out* **16/1**
400- **12** *½* **Chandrayaan**[117] 5525 6-9-5 **50**........................(v) JimmyQuinn 11 24
(John E Long) *s.s: hdwy into midfield on outer after 2f: wknd 2f out* **20/1**
400- **13** *2 ½* **Cuthbert (IRE)**[22] 7981 6-9-3 **48**........................(b) RobertHavlin 5 15
(Michael Attwater) *a towards rr: bhd fnl 2f* **14/1**
1m 26.04s (0.04) **Going Correction** -0.025s/f (Stan) **13** Ran SP% **119.6**
Speed ratings (Par 97): **98,97,96,95,93 91,90,89,88,85 82,82,79**
toteswingers 1&2 £9.60, 2&3 £13.90, 1&3 £26.20 CSF £67.88 CT £766.05 TOTE £13.60: £3.60, £2.80, £2.60; EX 93.10 Trifecta £762.60 Pool: £2919.49 - 2.87 winning units..
Owner Mrs Shelley Dwyer **Bred** Sir Eric Parker **Trained** Newmarket, Suffolk
FOCUS
The pace was not very strong in this modest handicap and there was a tight finish. Straightforward, low-grade form.

8259 DINE IN THE PANORAMIC MAIDEN AUCTION STKS 7f (P)
4:20 (4:20) (Class 6) 2-Y-O **£1,940** (£577; £288; £144) **Stalls** Low

Form RPR
2- **1** **Isabella Beeton**[72] 6922 2-8-1........................ JemmaMarshall[(3)] 3 68+
(Pat Phelan) *trckd ldrs in 3rd: smooth hdwy to ld over 1f out: pushed clr: easily* **5/4**[1]
2 *2* **Indira** 2-8-4........................ MartinLane 4 60+
(John Berry) *hld up in 4th: rdn 4f out: outpcd 2f out: styd on fnl f: jst snatched 2nd* **16/1**
430- **3** *nse* **Island Kingdom (IRE)**[60] 7218 2-8-9 70........................ LiamJones 2 64
(J S Moore) *led: racd freely and restrained in front: hdd over 1f out: one pce: lost 2nd on line* **11/4**[2]
4 *½* **Lady Kathian (IRE)** 2-8-10........................ KieranO'Neill 1 64+
(Joseph Tuite) *s.s: bhd: rdn 3f out: sme hdwy over 1f out: one pce fnl f* **10/1**
64- **5** *1* **L Ge R**[14] 8085 2-8-4........................ LukeMorris 6 55
(Peter Charalambous) *trckd ldr: rdn over 2f out: sn outpcd* **3/1**[3]
1m 27.69s (1.69) **Going Correction** -0.025s/f (Stan) **5** Ran SP% **111.1**
Speed ratings (Par 94): **89,86,86,86,84**
CSF £20.57 TOTE £1.80: £1.10, £4.00; EX 23.00 Trifecta £44.70 Pool: £3227.16 - 54.08 winning units..
Owner Tony Smith **Bred** Ermyn Lodge Stud Limited **Trained** Epsom, Surrey
FOCUS
The leading form contender scored in good style in this weak maiden but the rest finished in a bunch. The winner is entitled to win at these weights.

8260 BETVICTOR NON-RUNNER FREE BET CHELTENHAM 2014 MEDIAN AUCTION MAIDEN STKS 1m 4f (P)
4:50 (4:50) (Class 6) 3-5-Y-O **£1,940** (£577; £288; £144) **Stalls** Centre

Form RPR
0- **1** **Phosphorescence (IRE)**[210] 2384 3-9-5........................ TomQueally 8 65+
(Lady Cecil) *sn led: dictated modest pce: hdd over 2f out: rallied and led again 1f out: rdn out* **11/10**[1]
533- **2** *1* **Kingston Eucalypt**[27] 7894 3-9-0 74........................ LiamKeniry 1 58+
(David Elsworth) *chsd ldrs: qcknd to ld over 2f out: hdd 1f out: one pce* **2/1**[2]
222- **3** *1 ¼* **Wilhana (IRE)**[22] 7983 3-9-0 69........................ AdamKirby 2 56+
(Pam Sly) *chsd wnr 2f: outpcd over 2f out: styd on again fnl f* **7/2**[3]
000- **4** *4 ½* **Rowlestone Lass**[37] 7738 3-9-0 40........................[1] ShaneKelly 7 48?
(Richard Price) *t.k.h in rr: wnt mod 4th 2f out: no imp* **100/1**
600- **5** *4* **Parsons Green**[57] 7305 4-9-5 40........................ LiamJones 5 42
(Michael Attwater) *hld up in 5th: rdn and btn over 2f out* **100/1**
6- **6** *5* **Share The Dosh**[63] 7158 5-9-5........................ FrederikTylicki 6 34
(J R Jenkins) *cl up: chsd wnr after 2f tl wknd over 2f out* **50/1**
4- **7** *hd* **Another Journey**[9] 8141 4-9-7........................ MarkCoumbe[(3)] 4 39
(Lisa Williamson) *stdd s: hld up in rr: rdn and lost tch over 2f out* **50/1**
5- **8** *5* **Lateral Thinking (IRE)**[16] 8043 3-9-5 68........................ ChrisCatlin 3 31
(James Evans) *hld up in 6th: rdn 3f out: sn wknd* **14/1**
2m 36.7s (2.20) **Going Correction** -0.025s/f (Stan)
WFA 3 from 4yo+ 5lb **8** Ran SP% **115.7**
Speed ratings (Par 101): **91,90,89,86,83 80,80,77**
toteswingers 1&2 £1.10, 2&3 £1.40, 1&3 £1.10 CSF £3.59 TOTE £2.70: £1.20, £1.10, £1.10; EX 3.80 Trifecta £6.70 Pool: £5197.87 - 581.28 winning units..
Owner Niarchos Family **Bred** Niarchos Family **Trained** Newmarket, Suffolk
FOCUS
The unexposed favourite showed a good attitude to win this maiden and the three market leaders pulled clear of the rest. Weak form, severely limited by the fourth anf fifth.

8261 CHELTENHAM 2014 NRFB AT BETVICTOR.COM NURSERY H'CAP 6f (P)
5:20 (5:20) (Class 4) (0-85,81) 2-Y-O **£3,752** (£1,116; £557; £278) **Stalls** Low

Form RPR
140- **1** **Harwoods Volante (IRE)**[82] 6640 2-9-1 **75**........................ RobertHavlin 3 83
(Amanda Perrett) *s.s: sn in midfield: hdwy to ld wl over 1f out: sn clr: rdn out* **9/2**
112- **2** *1 ½* **Porteous**[5] 8203 2-8-7 **74**........................ DanielCremin[(7)] 5 78
(Mick Channon) *hld up in 6th: hdwy to chse wnr over 1f out: kpt on: a hld* **3/1**[2]
363- **3** *2* **Le Laitier (FR)**[13] 8091 2-8-3 **63**........................ AndreaAtzeni 6 61
(Scott Dixon) *chsd ldrs: outpcd 2f out: styd on fnl f* **7/1**
210- **4** *¾* **Expect**[41] 7657 2-9-6 **80**........................ ShaneKelly 1 75
(Jeremy Noseda) *disp ld: led over 2f out tl wl over 1f out: edgd lft: one pce* **11/4**[1]
326- **5** *nk* **Sunset Shore**[43] 7626 2-9-7 **81**........................(p) LukeMorris 2 75
(Sir Mark Prescott Bt) *prom tl no ex over 1f out* **10/1**
130- **6** *nk* **Danfazi (IRE)**[145] 4528 2-8-9 **76**........................ GeorginaBaxter[(7)] 4 69
(Kristin Stubbs) *disp ld tl over 2f out: sn outpcd* **25/1**
600- **7** *½* **Basil Berry**[33] 7819 2-8-5 **68** ow1........................ RossAtkinson[(3)] 8 60
(Chris Dwyer) *towards rr: effrt on outer over 2f out: no imp* **25/1**
511- **8** *1* **Nova Princesse (GER)**[28] 7879 2-9-3 **77**........................(t) MartinHarley 7 66
(Marco Botti) *s.s: bhd: hdwy 2f out: wknd fnl f* **7/2**[3]
1m 11.95s (-1.15) **Going Correction** -0.025s/f (Stan) **8** Ran SP% **121.4**
Speed ratings (Par 98): **106,104,101,100,99 99,98,97**
toteswingers 1&2 £3.30, 2&3 £4.60, 1&3 £6.90 CSF £19.72 CT £94.07 TOTE £5.00: £1.80, £1.50, £2.40; EX 26.00 Trifecta £157.60 Pool: £36762.55 - 17.89 winning units..
Owner Harwoods Racing Club **Bred** Gerry And John Rowley **Trained** Pulborough, W Sussex
FOCUS
Two of the market leaders were a bit disappointing in this fair nursery but a big gamble was landed by an unexposed type. The form makes sense.

8262 BACK OF THE NET AT BETVICTOR.COM NURSERY H'CAP 1m (P)
5:50 (5:50) (Class 6) (0-60,60) 2-Y-O **£1,940** (£577; £288; £144) **Stalls** Low

Form RPR
540- **1** **Dutchartcollector**[22] 7978 2-9-7 **60**........................ GeorgeBaker 9 63+
(Gary Moore) *hld up towards rr: hdwy over 1f out: str run fnl f: led fnl strides* **2/1**[1]
313- **2** *hd* **Starlight Princess (IRE)**[17] 8039 2-9-5 **58**........................(b) JohnFahy 6 61+
(J S Moore) *bhd: gd hdwy over 1f out: drvn to ld fnl 50yds: jst ct* **8/1**
042- **3** *hd* **Plough Boy (IRE)**[28] 7878 2-9-2 **55**........................ RobertWinston 10 58
(Willie Musson) *bhd: gd hdwy fr over 1f out: fin wl* **9/2**[2]
000- **4** *nk* **Masterpaver**[44] 7607 2-9-2 **55**........................(v[1]) LiamKeniry 3 57
(Alan Bailey) *dwlt: sn in midfield: drvn along over 2f out: styd on wl fr over 1f out: nrest at fin* **5/1**[3]

The Form Book Flat, Raceform Ltd, Compton, RG20 6NL.

533- **5** *nk* **Rose Buck**[14] 8086 2-9-2 **58**.. MarkCoumbe(3) 4 59
(Lee Carter) *led after 1f: hld on wl tl hdd and one pce fnl 50yds* **25/1**

434- **6** *2 1/4* **My My My Diliza**[17] 8039 2-9-2 **55**................................(b) DavidProbert 2 51
(J S Moore) *chsd ldrs tl no ex fnl f* **12/1**

600- **7** *nse* **Artemis (IRE)**[88] 6423 2-9-2 **55**.. AndreaAtzeni 7 51
(Conrad Allen) *t.k.h: in tch: rdn to press ldr over 1f out: no ex ins fnl f* **25/1**

233- **8** *2 1/2* **Chanceuse**[17] 8040 2-8-10 **54**...................................... DanielMuscutt(5) 1 44
(Gay Kelleway) *led 1f: chsd ldr after tl outpcd fnl 2f* **16/1**

500- **9** *1 3/4* **Hostile Takeover (IRE)**[133] 4925 2-9-2 **55**........................ AdamKirby 8 41
(Jo Crowley) *nvr trbld ldrs* **16/1**

500- **10** *2 3/4* **Trigger Park (IRE)**[29] 7855 2-9-4 **57**................................. LukeMorris 5 37
(Ronald Harris) *prom tl wknd 2f out* **25/1**

336- **11** *2 1/4* **M'Lady Ermyn**[85] 6520 2-9-1 **57**............................ JemmaMarshall(3) 12 32
(Pat Phelan) *in tch tl wknd over 2f out* **12/1**

040- **12** *1/2* **Black Sceptre (IRE)**[106] 5891 2-9-5 **58**........................ JimmyQuinn 11 31
(Edward Creighton) *a towards rr: last and struggling 2f out* **50/1**

1m 41.32s (1.52) **Going Correction** -0.025s/f (Stan) **12** Ran SP% **119.9**
Speed ratings (Par 94): **91,90,90,90,90 87,87,85,83,80 78,77**
toteswingers 1&2 £3.80, 2&3 £3.50, 1&3 £2.50 CSF £17.98 CT £67.48 TOTE £3.40: £1.70, £2.10, £1.90; EX 18.20 Trifecta £58.40 Pool: £2701.31 - 34.66 winning units..
Owner R A Green **Bred** Cheveley Park Stud Ltd **Trained** Lower Beeding, W Sussex
■ Stewards' Enquiry : Liam Keniry two-day ban: used whip above permitted level (Dec 26-27)

FOCUS
There was an exciting five-way finish in this minor nursery and the well-backed favourite got up close home. It's hard to rate the bare form much higher.

8263 DOWNLOAD THE BETVICTOR APP NOW H'CAP 1m (P)
6:20 (6:24) (Class 2) (0-100,98) 3-Y-O+
£11,827 (£3,541; £1,770; £885; £442; £222) **Stalls** Low

Form RPR
140- **1** **String Theory (IRE)**[175] 3484 3-9-0 **92**.......................... MartinHarley 4 102
(Marco Botti) *led after 1f tl 5f out: led again wl over 1f out: drvn out* **5/1**[2]

001- **2** *1/2* **Captain Cat (IRE)**[42] 7641 4-9-4 **95**.......................... GeorgeBaker 3 104
(Roger Charlton) *led 1f: stdd bk into midfield: hdwy 2f out: drvn to chal ins fnl f: jst hld* **11/8**[1]

033- **3** *1* **George Guru**[21] 7991 6-9-1 **92**.. RobertHavlin 2 99
(Michael Attwater) *towards rr: rdn and r.o fnl 2f: nrest at fin* **8/1**

001- **4** *1 3/4* **Maverik**[21] 7988 5-8-12 **89**.. TomQueally 7 92
(William Knight) *anticipated s: prom: led after 3f tl wl over 1f out: one pce* **25/1**

050- **5** *1 1/4* **Roserrow**[26] 7926 4-9-1 **92**.. DavidProbert 1 92
(Andrew Balding) *sn towards rr: effrt over 2f out: styd on same pce* **10/1**

4/0- **6** *3/4* **Moonday Sun (USA)**[57] 4-9-3 **94**................................... AndreaAtzeni 5 92
(Amanda Perrett) *mid-div: lost pl over 3f out: n.d after* **20/1**

040- **7** *1 3/4* **Viewpoint (IRE)**[15] 8071 4-9-0 **91**................................... SeanLevey 9 85
(Richard Hannon Snr) *outpcd in rr: nvr rchd ldrs* **20/1**

021- **8** *4 1/2* **Dixie's Dream (IRE)**[21] 7989 4-8-9 **86**........................ JoeFanning 6 70
(William Jarvis) *hdwy to chse ldrs after 2f tl wknd 2f out* **6/1**[3]

440- **9** *16* **Emerald Wilderness (IRE)**[22] 7974 9-9-7 **98**............ FrederikTylicki 10 45
(Mark Rimmer) *mid-div on outer tl wknd over 2f out* **25/1**

000- **10** *1* **Stasio (USA)**[26] 7926 3-8-11 **89**.................................... JamieSpencer 8 33
(David Simcock) *chsd ldrs over 5f* **7/1**

1m 36.92s (-2.88) **Going Correction** -0.025s/f (Stan)
WFA 3 from 4yo+ 1lb **10** Ran SP% **123.0**
Speed ratings (Par 109): **113,112,111,109,108 107,106,101,85,84**
toteswingers 1&2 £2.50, 2&3 £3.50, 1&3 £6.40 CSF £12.33 CT £55.88 TOTE £5.30: £2.10, £1.20, £3.20; EX 18.90 Trifecta £109.30 Pool: £3465.60 - 23.77 winning units..
Owner Prince A A Faisal **Bred** Minch Bloodstock **Trained** Newmarket, Suffolk

FOCUS
The pace was fairly steady in this valuable handicap but the well-backed winner held off the favourite and the form looks solid. The least exposed pair were 1-2.

8264 BETVICTOR.COM NON-RUNNER FREE BET CHELTENHAM 2014 H'CAP 7f (P)
6:50 (6:50) (Class 3) (0-95,95) 3-Y-O+
£7,158 (£2,143; £1,071; £535; £267; £134) **Stalls** Low

Form RPR
026- **1** **Verse Of Love**[12] 8117 4-8-12 **86**.................................... MartinHarley 2 95
(David Evans) *mde all: hld on wl ins fnl f* **7/1**[3]

000- **2** *1/2* **Favourite Treat (USA)**[12] 8117 3-9-0 **88**..................... JoeFanning 1 96
(Mark Johnston) *prom: kpt on u.p to take 2nd ins fnl f: jst hld* **12/1**

560- **3** *hd* **Bravo Echo**[78] 6744 7-9-5 **93**.. RobertHavlin 4 100
(Michael Attwater) *chsd wnr: hrd rdn over 1f out: kpt on: lost 2nd ins fnl f* **10/1**

000- **4** *1/2* **Birdman (IRE)**[21] 7991 3-9-1 **89**...................................... MartinLane 5 95+
(David Simcock) *dwlt: bhd: hdwy over 1f out: styd on wl fnl f* **25/1**

031- **5** *1/2* **Loyalty**[21] 7991 6-8-9 **90**...(v) AdamMcLean(7) 8 94
(Derek Shaw) *towards rr: effrt and hrd rdn over 1f out: styd on same pce* **7/2**[2]

001- **6** *3/4* **Upavon**[21] 7992 3-8-13 **87**.. LiamKeniry 9 89
(David Elsworth) *in tch: rdn over 2f out: one pce* **3/1**[1]

426- **7** *hd* **Clockmaker (IRE)**[2] 8231 7-9-7 **95**................................. HayleyTurner 7 97
(Conor Dore) *plld hrd in midfield: effrt over 2f out: kpt on fnl f* **3/1**[1]

300- **8** *nk* **Kyllachy Rise**[33] 7820 3-9-4 **92**....................................... SeanLevey 3 93
(Richard Hannon Snr) *chsd ldrs: rdn 2f out: no ex fnl f* **7/1**[3]

143- **9** *nk* **Slip Sliding Away (IRE)**[14] 8088 6-8-7 **81**...................... JohnFahy 6 81
(Peter Hedger) *stdd s: bhd: gd hdwy on inner 2f out: wknd fnl f* **10/1**

1m 24.63s (-1.37) **Going Correction** -0.025s/f (Stan) **9** Ran SP% **126.9**
Speed ratings (Par 107): **106,105,105,104,104 103,102,102,102**
toteswingers 1&2 £21.10, 2&3 £19.70, 1&3 £15.80 CSF £85.12 CT £863.64 TOTE £8.00: £1.70, £3.50, £2.70; EX 119.30 Trifecta £771.00 Pool: £2298.67 - 2.23 winning units..
Owner Wayne Clifford **Bred** Mrs S Clifford **Trained** Pandy, Monmouths

FOCUS
They finished in a bunch in this decent handicap and visibility was poor due to fog. The winner is rated back to his best.
T/Jkpt: Not won. T/Plt: £17.20 to a £1 stake. Pool of £83475.97 - 3525.67 winning tickets. T/Qpdt: £3.90 to a £1 stake. Pool of £7900.18 - 1482.65 winning tickets. LM

8228 SOUTHWELL (L-H)
Friday, December 13

OFFICIAL GOING: Standard
Wind: Moderate across Weather: Cloudy

8265 32RED CASINO CLAIMING STKS 1m (F)
11:50 (11:50) (Class 6) 2-Y-O **£1,940** (£577; £288; £144) **Stalls** Low

Form RPR
314- **1** **Slinky McVelvet**[18] 8040 2-8-5 **58**.............................. AndrewMullen 6 75
(Garry Moss) *prom: led after 2f: pushed clr over 2f out: styd on strly: unchal* **3/1**[3]

034- **2** *18* **Maupiti Express (FR)**[11] 8131 2-8-8 **58**...................(v[1]) DavidBergin(5) 3 43
(David O'Meara) *trckd ldrs: hdwy over 3f out: sn chsng wnr: rdn along wl over 2f out and sn one pce* **9/2**

000- **3** *4 1/2* **Worcharlie'Slass**[11] 8131 2-8-4 **0**.................................. DuranFentiman 5 24
(Michael Herrington) *green and sn rdn along in rr: bhd 1/2-way: hdwy over 2f out: plugged on u.p to take poor 3rd ins fnl f* **33/1**

643- **4** *1 1/4* **Sexy Secret**[17] 8045 2-8-8 **63**.....................................(b) RobertHavlin 2 25
(Noel Quinlan) *trckd ldrs: effrt 3f out and sn rdn along: wknd over 2f out* **9/4**[2]

364- **5** *11* **Paddy's Bay**[63] 7168 2-8-11 **53**.....................................(p) MartinHarley 1 4
(Kevin Ryan) *qckly away: led 2f: cl up: rdn along 1/2-way: sn lost pl and bhd fnl 2f* **2/1**[1]

60- **6** *2* **L'Es Fremantle (FR)**[29] 7883 2-8-1 **0**............................ PaulBooth(7) 4
(Michael Chapman) *sn rdn along in rr: outpcd and bhd fr over 3f out* **100/1**

1m 45.1s (1.40) **Going Correction** +0.025s/f (Slow) **6** Ran SP% **111.2**
Speed ratings (Par 94): **94,76,71,70,59 57**
toteswingers 1&2 £1.90, 1&3 £14.40, 2&3 £22.60 CSF £16.31 TOTE £4.50: £1.30, £2.90; EX 14.30 Trifecta £97.20 Pool: £1093.33 - 8.43 winning units..
Owner Ron Hull **Bred** Jason Paxton **Trained** Tickhill, S Yorks

FOCUS
A moderate race, even by claiming standards. Improved form from the winner however viewed, but clearly little substance in behind.

8266 32RED.COM EBF MAIDEN STKS 7f (F)
12:20 (12:21) (Class 5) 2-Y-O **£3,067** (£905; £453) **Stalls** Low

Form RPR
06- **1** **Westminster (IRE)**[23] 7972 2-9-5 **0**................................. RobertHavlin 1 80+
(John Gosden) *cl up on inner: slt ld 4f out: rdn wl over 1f out: drvn clr ent fnl f: kpt on* **3/1**[2]

034- **2** *3 3/4* **Queenie's Home**[36] 7782 2-9-0 **73**................................... GrahamLee 5 65
(James Given) *cl up: effrt to dispute ld over 2f out: rdn wl over 1f out and ev ch tl drvn and one pce ent fnl f* **11/4**[1]

6- **3** *4* **Outback Warrior (IRE)**[119] 5482 2-9-5 **0**........................ MartinHarley 6 59+
(Kevin Ryan) *towards rr: hdwy 1/2-way: rdn to chse ldng pair over 2f out: sn no imp* **3/1**[2]

4 *12* **Ventura Reef (IRE)** 2-9-5 **0**.. TonyHamilton 8 27
(Richard Fahey) *dwlt: green and sn pushed along towards rr: sme hdwy 1/2-way: sn shkn up and n.d* **5/1**[3]

- **5** *3/4* **Rio Ranger (IRE)** 2-9-0 **0**.. JoeFanning 9 20+
(Bryan Smart) *s.i.s and in rr: hdwy over 2f out: swtchd lft and kpt on fnl f* **7/1**

06- **6** *4* **Belle Peinture (FR)**[8] 8165 2-8-9 **0**............................ SamanthaBell(5) 7 9
(Richard Fahey) *dwlt: a in rr* **25/1**

3- **7** *1 1/2* **La Paiva (FR)**[17] 8044 2-9-0 **0**.. TomEaves 2 5
(Scott Dixon) *led 2f: cl up: rdn along wl over 2f out: sn wknd* **14/1**

6- **8** *1* **Alba Verde**[31] 7844 2-9-0 **0**... LukeMorris 4 2
(Sir Mark Prescott Bt) *in tch: pushed along after 2f: rdn along 1/2-way: sn outpcd* **50/1**

0- **9** *6* **Skinny Latte**[56] 7348 2-9-5 **0**... PJMcDonald 3
(Micky Hammond) *a towards rr* **100/1**

1m 30.18s (-0.12) **Going Correction** +0.025s/f (Slow) **9** Ran SP% **119.3**
Speed ratings (Par 96): **101,96,92,78,77 73,71,70,63**
toteswingers 1&2 £2.40, 1&3 £2.20, 2&3 £3.00 CSF £12.08 TOTE £5.10: £1.10, £1.80, £1.50; EX 9.90 Trifecta £36.70 Pool: £1180.55 - 24.10 winning units..
Owner Highclere Thoroughbred Racing - Norfolk **Bred** Lismacue Mare Syndicate **Trained** Newmarket, Suffolk

FOCUS
A weak maiden and hard to get overly excited about the performance of the winner, but the time was decent. The form is rated around the second.

8267 32RED NURSERY H'CAP 7f (F)
12:55 (12:55) (Class 5) (0-75,73) 2-Y-O **£2,911** (£866; £432) **Stalls** Low

Form RPR
355- **1** **Black Vale (IRE)**[4] 8215 2-8-12 **64**..............................(bt) PaddyAspell 3 69
(Phil McEntee) *sn cl up: chal wl over 2f out: carried sltly rt and rdn wl over 1f out: sn led and rdr lost whip over 1f out: clr whn edgd lft ins fnl f: kpt on* **8/1**[3]

022- **2** *3* **Madame Mirasol (IRE)**[28] 7892 2-9-7 **73**......................... MartinHarley 1 70
(Kevin Ryan) *sn led: rdn and edgd rt wl over 1f out: sn hdd and drvn: kpt on same pce fnl f* **1/1**[1]

242- **3** *nse* **Our Gabrial (IRE)**[9] 8153 2-9-7 **73**................................. TomEaves 2 70
(Richard Fahey) *broke wl: stdd and trckd ldng pair: pushed along after 2f: rdn along and outpcd 1/2-way: drvn on inner 2f out: swtchd rt ent fnl f: kpt on u.p towards fin* **11/10**[2]

1m 31.41s (1.11) **Going Correction** +0.025s/f (Slow) **3** Ran SP% **108.7**
Speed ratings (Par 96): **94,90,90**
toteswingers 1&2 £2.40, 1&3 £2.20, 2&3 £3.00 CSF £16.01 TOTE £3.70; EX 7.60 Trifecta £18.10 Pool: £1898.31 - 78.37 winning units..
Owner Mrs Rebecca McEntee **Bred** Michael Downey & Roalso Ltd **Trained** Newmarket, Suffolk

FOCUS
A disappointing turnout for this and it saw something of an upset. Obvious doubts as to how literally this form can be taken.

8268 32RED ON THE APP STORE H'CAP 2m (F)
1:30 (1:30) (Class 6) (0-60,60) 3-Y-O+ **£1,940** (£577; £288; £144) **Stalls** Low

Form RPR
000/ **1** **The Young Master**[19] 1608 4-8-12 **46** oh1.......................(p) LiamKeniry 5 59
(Neil Mulholland) *a.p: chsd ldr fr 1/2-way: rdn along 3f out: 6 l down and drvn wl over 1f out: styd on u.p fnl f to ld nr fin* **8/1**[3]

444- **2** *nk* **Neighbourhood (USA)**[3] 8229 5-9-7 **60**....................(b) JoeyHaynes(5) 9 73
(James Evans) *hld up in rr: smooth hdwy 6f out: led 4f out: pushed 6 l clr over 2f out: stl clr ent fnl f: sn shkn up and edgd lft: wknd last 100yds: hdd nr fin* **10/11**[1]

314- **3** *13* **Ice Apple**[20] 8027 5-9-0 **48**.. JimmyQuinn 7 45
(John E Long) *hld up towards rr: hdwy over 5f out: rdn along to chse ldrs wl over 3f out: drvn and one pce fr over 2f out* **7/1**[2]

360/ **4** *nk* **Aureate**[258] 2391 9-8-10 **51**..................................(p) DanielCremin(7) 2 48
(Brian Forsey) *trckd ldrs on inner: hdwy 7f out: rdn along over 3f out: drvn over 2f out and plugged on same pce* **20/1**

005- **5** *18* **Generous George (IRE)**[59] 7279 4-9-4 **52**.................. PJMcDonald 10 27
(Mel Brittain) *chsd ldrs: rdn along over 5f out: drvn and outpcd fr 4f out* **10/1**

0/0- **6** *41* **Daldini**[9] 8160 11-9-7 **55**.. LukeMorris 3
(Scott Dixon) *rn in snatches: chsd ldrs and reminders after 3f: rdn along after 6f: drvn and outpcd fr 4f out* **12/1**

605- **7** *21* **Russian Link**[32] 7838 3-8-13 **55**... MartinLane 6
(John Berry) *led 3f: chsd ldr: rdn along after 7f: sn lost pl and bhd fnl 6f* **16/1**

330- **8** *17* **Generous Dream**[45] 7597 5-9-10 **58**.......................... DuranFentiman 8
(Mel Brittain) *in tch: rdn along over 6f out: sn wknd and bhd fnl 3f* **8/1**[3]

000- **9** *99* **Sings Poet**[37] 7770 3-8-4 **46** oh1...............................(p) WilliamCarson 1
(Peter Hiatt) *swtchd rt to wd outside sn after s: chsd ldrs tl led after 3f: rdn along 5f out: hdd 4f out and wknd qckly: t.o and virtually p.u fnl 2f* **33/1**

3m 45.92s (0.42) **Going Correction** +0.025s/f (Slow)
WFA 3 from 4yo+ 8lb **9** Ran SP% **117.5**
Speed ratings (Par 101): **99,98,92,92,83 62,52,43,**
toteswingers 1&2 £5.10, 1&3 £11.00, 2&3 £2.90 CSF £15.94 CT £57.18 TOTE £8.90: £2.80, £1.40, £1.30; EX 28.10 Trifecta £113.50 Pool: £980.84 - 6.47 winning units..
Owner Dajam Ltd **Bred** Brendan Boyle **Trained** Limpley Stoke, Wilts

FOCUS
A poor staying handicap and painful viewing for favourite backers. The time was slow and the level of the form is hard to gauge. The winner's first real Flat form.

8269 LADBROKES H'CAP 1m (F)
2:00 (2:03) (Class 4) (0-80,80) 3-Y-0+ **£4,690** (£1,395; £697; £348) **Stalls** Low

Form RPR

523- **1** **Tatting**[17] 8057 4-8-11 **70**.. HayleyTurner 9 82
(Chris Dwyer) *hld up towards rr: hdwy 3f out: trckd ldrs 2f out: swtchd lft and rdn to chse ldng pair ent fnl f: kpt on wl to ld last 75yds* **10/1**

030- **2** *¾* **Kung Hei Fat Choy (USA)**[7] 8178 4-8-13 **72**...............(b) GrahamLee 7 82
(James Given) *a.p: cl up 1/2-way: led 3f out: jnd and rdn 2f out: drvn ins fnl f: hdd and no ex last 75yds* **5/1**[1]

201- **3** *shd* **Chrissycross (IRE)**[24] 7952 4-9-0 **73**.....................(v) RobertWinston 12 83
(Roger Teal) *dwlt and in rr: sn swtchd wd: hdwy 1/2-way: wd st and effrt to chal 2f out: sn rdn and ev ch tl drvn ins fnl f and kpt on same pce* **5/1**[1]

100- **4** *3 ½* **Sofias Number One (USA)**[21] 8007 5-9-2 **78**........(b) MarkCoumbe(3) 4 80
(Roy Bowring) *dwlt and in rr: wd st: rdn and hdwy 2f out: kpt on u.p fnl f: nrst fin* **8/1**[3]

556- **5** *½* **My Single Malt (IRE)**[94] 6291 5-8-12 **71**..................... BarryMcHugh 13 72
(Julie Camacho) *hld up: hdwy over 3f out: chsd ldrs over 2f out: rdn wl over 1f out and one pce* **20/1**

056- **6** *1* **The Lock Master (IRE)**[21] 8007 6-9-7 **80**................. AndrewMullen 3 79
(Michael Appleby) *chsd ldrs: rdn along wl over 2f out: drvn wl over 1f out and sn one pce* **10/1**

005- **7** *1 ½* **Docofthebay (IRE)**[14] 8094 9-9-5 **78**.........................(b) PJMcDonald 11 73
(Scott Dixon) *towards rr: hdwy over 3f out: rdn and in tch 2f out: sn no imp* **6/1**[2]

521- **8** *1* **Maria's Choice (IRE)**[23] 7970 4-9-3 **76**.........................(p) MartinHarley 5 69
(Alan McCabe) *hld up in tch: hdwy on inner over 3f out: rdn to chse ldrs 2f out: drvn and wknd appr fnl f* **5/1**[1]

026- **9** *3 ¼* **Caldercruix (USA)**[29] 7888 6-8-12 **78**....................(v) DanielCremin(7) 14 63
(James Evans) *prom: rdn along 3f out: sn wknd* **14/1**

040- **10** *hd* **Piceno (IRE)**[14] 8095 5-8-7 **71**.......................................(p) TimClark(5) 2 56
(Scott Dixon) *led: rdn along and hdd 3f out: sn wknd* **25/1**

003- **11** *12* **Bay Knight (IRE)**[29] 7885 7-9-5 **78**..................................... AdamKirby 10 35
(Sean Curran) *prom: rdn along bef 1/2-way: sn lost pl and bhd fr over 2f out* **12/1**

000- **12** *3 ¾* **Sky Crossing**[50] 7486 4-8-11 **70**.. MartinLane 8 19
(Tom Tate) *sn rdn along and a in rr* **50/1**

033- **13** *nse* **Escape To Glory (USA)**[22] 7988 5-9-3 **76**............................ TomEaves 1 24
(Michael Dods) *cl up on inner: rdn along over 3f out: sn wknd* **18/1**

1m 42.4s (-1.30) **Going Correction** +0.025s/f (Slow)
WFA 3 from 4yo+ 1lb **13** Ran SP% **123.8**
Speed ratings (Par 105): **107,106,106,102,102 101,99,98,95,95 83,79,79**
toteswingers 1&2 £12.20, 1&3 £9.30, 2&3 £6.10 CSF £60.39 CT £290.21 TOTE £11.90: £4.00, £2.10, £1.60; EX 86.90 Trifecta £308.00 Pool: £3453.05 - 8.40 winning units..
Owner Mrs K W Sneath **Bred** Darley **Trained** Newmarket, Suffolk

FOCUS
A devilishly competitive feature.

8270 CORAL "JUST THREE CLICKS TO BET" H'CAP 1m 4f (F)
2:30 (2:31) (Class 6) (0-65,65) 3-Y-0+ **£1,940** (£577; £288; £144) **Stalls** Low

Form RPR

035- **1** **Yasir (USA)**[11] 8129 5-9-9 **64**.......................................(p) HayleyTurner 8 74
(Conor Dore) *bhd: stdy hdwy on outer 1/2-way: trckd ldrs over 3f out: wd st and hdwy to ld 2f out: jnd and rdn over 1f out: drvn ins fnl f: kpt on wl towards fin* **11/4**[1]

054- **2** *nk* **Monzino (USA)**[7] 8183 5-9-2 **64**.................................(b) PaulBooth(7) 5 73
(Michael Chapman) *dwlt and in rr: hdwy 1/2-way: in tch whn n.m.r bnd 4f out: wd st and rdn to chse wnr 2f out: edgd lft and chal over 1f out: ev ch ins fnl f tl no ex towards fin* **20/1**

655- **3** *6* **Flash Crash**[52] 7446 4-9-8 **63**.................................(tp) WilliamCarson 7 62
(Anthony Carson) *midfield: hdwy 4f out: rdn along wl over 2f out: swtchd rt to outer and drvn over 1f out: kpt on fnl f* **12/1**

224- **4** *nk* **Maakirr (IRE)**[24] 7952 4-9-5 **63**..............................(t) MarkCoumbe(3) 4 62
(Roy Bowring) *trckd ldrs: hdwy 4f out: rdn along 3f out: drvn and one pce fr over 1f out* **9/2**[2]

142- **5** *2 ¾* **Vittachi**[14] 7376 6-9-6 **61**..(p) AdamKirby 6 56
(Alistair Whillans) *in rr: hdwy on outer 5f out: chsd ldrs 3f out: rdn 2f out and sn one pce* **8/1**[3]

/40- **6** *1 ¾* **Mister Frosty (IRE)**[9] 8149 7-8-8 **54**............................. EoinWalsh(5) 13 46
(Christine Dunnett) *hld up: stdy hdwy 1/2-way: led 4f out: rdn along and hdd over 2f out: sn drvn and grad wknd* **14/1**

610- **7** *11* **Corn Maiden**[44] 7628 4-9-0 **55**.. PaddyAspell 11 29
(Lydia Pearce) *hld up: hdwy 5f out: in tch over 3f out: sn rdn and n.d* **8/1**[3]

405- **8** *4 ½* **Samoset**[17] 8046 3-8-9 **55**.. BenCurtis 3 22
(Alan Swinbank) *nvr bttr than midfield* **20/1**

056- **9** *3 ½* **Queen Of Skies (IRE)**[11] 8121 4-9-1 **56**.................... AndrewMullen 12 17
(Michael Appleby) *prom: cl up 1/2-way: rdn along over 3f out and sn wknd* **12/1**

050- **10** *9* **Bavarian Nordic (USA)**[17] 8047 8-9-1 **56**.................(v) RobertWinston 2 3
(Richard Whitaker) *chsd ldrs: rdn along 3f out: wknd over 2f out* **10/1**

000- **11** *14* **Kingaroo (IRE)**[50] 2860 7-8-5 **51** oh2................................ TimClark(5) 14
(Garry Woodward) *cl up: led 1/2-way: rdn along and hdd 4f out: sn wknd* **33/1**

360- **12** *13* **Goldmadchen (GER)**[207] 2511 5-9-4 **59**........................... GrahamLee 10
(James Given) *prom: rdn along 1/2-way: sn wknd* **16/1**

/0- **13** *9* **Indian Scout**[31] 7847 5-9-1 **56**......................................(p) MartinHarley 1
(Anabel K Murphy) *towards rr: bhd fr 1/2-way* **20/1**

100- **14** *2 ¼* **April Ciel**[16] 8060 4-9-10 **65**..(p) LiamJones 9
(Ronald Harris) *set str pce: pushed along and hdd 1/2-way: sn lost pl and bhd* **20/1**

2m 41.38s (0.38) **Going Correction** +0.025s/f (Slow)
WFA 3 from 4yo+ 5lb **14** Ran SP% **126.1**
Speed ratings (Par 101): **99,98,94,94,92 91,84,81,78,72 63,54,48,47**
toteswingers 1&2 £21.60, 1&3 £9.80, 2&3 £37.80 CSF £69.90 CT £604.42 TOTE £3.80: £1.10, £10.90, £3.90; EX 112.40 Trifecta £1185.50 Pool: £2741.50 - 1.73 winning units..
Owner Mrs Louise Marsh **Bred** Shadwell Farm LLC **Trained** Hubbert's Bridge, Lincs

FOCUS
They went a suicidal early pace and it that played right into the hands of the principals, who had raced second-last and last respectively in the early stages. The winner rates close to this year's best.

8271 COMPARE BOOKMAKERS AT BOOKMAKERS.CO.UK APPRENTICE H'CAP (DIV I) 5f (F)
3:05 (3:07) (Class 6) (0-60,60) 3-Y-0+ **£1,940** (£577; £288; £144) **Stalls** High

Form RPR

502- **1** **Sir Geoffrey (IRE)**[8] 8168 7-8-10 **54**..................(p) MatthewHopkins(5) 6 65
(Scott Dixon) *prom: led wl over 1f out: sn rdn and kpt on strly fnl f* **5/1**[1]

332- **2** *2 ¼* **Major Muscari (IRE)**[17] 8050 5-8-3 **49**..................(p) AlexHopkinson(7) 3 52
(Shaun Harris) *prom: chsd ldr 1/2-way: rdn wl over 1f out and ev ch tl drvn and one pce ins fnl f* **12/1**

234- **3** *1 ¼* **Insolenceofoffice (IRE)**[17] 8049 5-9-3 **59**.............(p) JoshBaudains(3) 5 57
(Richard Ford) *dwlt and in rr: rdn along and hdwy 1/2-way: styd on to chse ldng pair appr fnl f: sn drvn and no imp* **5/1**[1]

002- **4** *1* **Divertimenti (IRE)**[8] 8169 9-8-12 **54**.......................(b) LouisSteward(3) 11 49
(Roy Bowring) *chsd ldrs: rdn along and sltly outpcd wl over 1f out: kpt on u.p fnl f* **14/1**

050- **5** *¾* **Speedyfix**[11] 8135 6-9-2 **58**..(t) EoinWalsh(3) 7 50
(Christine Dunnett) *towards rr: hdwy 1/2-way: rdn wl over 1f out: kpt on same pce fnl f* **25/1**

346- **6** *1* **Quality Art (USA)**[11] 8135 5-9-0 **60**.......................... MelissaThompson(7) 1 49
(Richard Guest) *sn led: edgd rt fr 1/2-way: hdd wl over 1f out and grad wknd* **7/1**[2]

031- **7** *1* **Robyn**[13] 8112 3-8-6 **48**.. TimClark(3) 9 33
(Scott Dixon) *prom: rdn along over 2f out: grad wknd* **14/1**

064- **8** *nk* **Your Gifted (IRE)**[18] 8034 6-9-2 **55**.............................. ShirleyTeasdale 8 39
(Lisa Williamson) *towards rr: hdwy 1/2-way: swtchd lft and rdn 2f out: sn no imp* **8/1**[3]

515- **9** *hd* **Auntie Mildred (IRE)**[197] 2795 3-8-7 **53**......................... JoshDoyle(7) 12 36
(David O'Meara) *chsd ldrs: rdn along over 2f out: sn btn* **12/1**

520- **10** *1* **Exkaliber**[15] 8082 4-8-5 **49**..(bt) DavidParkes(5) 13 29
(Jeremy Gask) *in tch: rdn along 2f out: sn wknd* **8/1**[3]

315- **11** *nse* **Max The Machine**[31] 7848 3-9-1 **59**............................. AdamMcLean(5) 10 38
(Derek Shaw) *a in rr* **5/1**[1]

020- **12** *hd* **Cheyenne Red (IRE)**[60] 7236 7-8-4 **48**......................... PaulMcGiff(5) 2 27
(Michael Herrington) *dwlt: a towards rr* **25/1**

300- **13** *1 ¼* **Bond Blade**[17] 8050 5-8-7 **46** oh1..................................... JacobButterfield 4 20
(Suzzanne France) *a towards rr* **33/1**

1m 0.61s (0.91) **Going Correction** +0.25s/f (Slow) **13** Ran SP% **124.1**
Speed ratings (Par 101): **102,98,96,94,93 92,90,89,89,88 87,87,85**
toteswingers 1&2 £12.60, 1&3 £5.20, 2&3 £8.90 CSF £68.16 CT £325.16 TOTE £5.70: £2.20, £4.10, £1.30; EX 59.40 Trifecta £294.30 Pool: £2697.33 - 6.87 winning units..
Owner General Sir Geoffrey Howlett **Bred** P Rabbitte **Trained** Babworth, Notts

FOCUS
There was no hanging around in this low-grade sprint handicap. The form is rated around the runner-up.

8272 COMPARE BOOKMAKERS AT BOOKMAKERS.CO.UK APPRENTICE H'CAP (DIV II) 5f (F)
3:35 (3:36) (Class 6) (0-60,60) 3-Y-0+ **£1,940** (£577; £288; £144) **Stalls** High

Form RPR

202- **1** **Thorpe Bay**[17] 8049 4-9-2 **60**.. GeorgeBuckell(5) 6 71
(Michael Appleby) *prom: led 2f out: rdn clr ent fnl f: kpt on* **11/4**[1]

606- **2** *2 ½* **Lucky Mark (IRE)**[8] 8168 4-8-13 **55**............................ SamanthaBell(3) 9 57
(Garry Moss) *towards rr: hdwy wl over 1f out: swtchd rt and rdn over 1f out: styd on to chse wnr ins fnl f: sn no imp* **14/1**

240- **3** *2* **Jiminy**[18] 8034 3-8-11 **55**...............................(b) MatthewHopkins(5) 8 50
(Scott Dixon) *prom: effrt and cl up 2f out: sn rdn and kpt on same pce fnl f* **8/1**

251- **4** *nk* **Beach Rhythm (USA)**[28] 7903 6-9-0 **58**.................(v) JackGilligan(5) 12 52
(Jim Allen) *slt ld: rdn along and hdd 2f out: wknd ent fnl f* **3/1**[2]

603- **5** *½* **Chateau Lola**[8] 8169 4-8-2 **46**....................................(v) AdamMcLean(5) 1 38
(Derek Shaw) *in tch: hdwy on outer to chse ldrs over 2f out: sn rdn and one pce appr fnl f* **12/1**

142- **6** *1* **Coalburn**[45] 7598 5-8-7 **53**..(v) JackOsborn(7) 5 41
(Gary Harrison) *prom: rdn along 2f out: grad wknd* **8/1**

150- **7** *2 ¾* **Sarah Berry**[11] 8135 4-9-6 **59**....................................(v) ShelleyBirkett 3 37
(Chris Dwyer) *dwlt and in rr: hdwy on wd outside 2f out: sn rdn and n.d* **12/1**

0/6- **8** *shd* **Lucky Mellor**[18] 8035 6-8-5 **49**.......................................(t) PaulBooth(5) 2 27
(Barry Murtagh) *chsd ldrs: rdn along over 2f out: sn wknd* **33/1**

540- **9** *1 ½* **Ichimoku**[84] 6604 3-9-1 **54**......................................(t) JacobButterfield 7 27
(Bryan Smart) *sn rdn along and a in rr* **6/1**[3]

0/0- **10** *4* **King's Ciel**[8] 8169 4-8-9 **48**..(p) JoeyHaynes 11 6
(Sean Curran) *a in rr* **25/1**

The Form Book Flat, Raceform Ltd, Compton, RG20 6NL.

010- 11 6 **Sophie's Beau (USA)**[66] [7101] 6-8-4 **48**....................(b) JackGarritty(5) 10
(Michael Chapman) *t.k.h early: a in rr* **16/1**

1m 0.9s (1.20) **Going Correction** +0.25s/f (Slow) **11** Ran SP% **122.9**
Speed ratings (Par 101): **100,96,92,92,91 89,85,85,82,76 66**
toteswingers 1&2 £11.10, 1&3 £5.70, 2&3 £18.60 CSF £45.07 CT £288.56 TOTE £4.00: £1.60, £5.10, £2.40; EX 52.10 Trifecta £595.70 Pool: £2580.17 - 3.24 winning units..
Owner Dallas Racing **Bred** Clive Dennett **Trained** Danethorpe, Notts

FOCUS
A weakish race and slower than division I. The winner looks better than ever.
T/Plt: £275.20 to a £1 stake. Pool: £42266.43 - 112.11 winning tickets T/Qpdt: £183.50 to a £1 stake. Pool: £3900.12 - 15.72 winning tickets JR

8221 WOLVERHAMPTON (A.W) (L-H)

Friday, December 13

OFFICIAL GOING: Standard
Wind: Fresh behind Weather: Overcast

8273 32RED NURSERY H'CAP 5f 20y(P)
3:55 (3:57) (Class 6) (0-65,63) 2-Y-O **£1,940** (£577; £288; £144) **Stalls Low**

Form RPR
063- 1 **Green Music**[16] [8061] 2-9-0 **56**..(b1) LukeMorris 4 62
(James Eustace) *chsd ldr: pushed along 1/2-way: rdn to ld ins fnl f: edgd rt: r.o* **4/1**[2]

004- 2 3 **Argent Touch**[14] [8090] 2-8-3 **45**.............................. JoeFanning 2 40
(Derek Shaw) *hld up: hdwy 1/2-way: styd on same pce ins fnl f* **9/2**[3]

005- 3 ½ **Sandsman's Girl (IRE)**[20] [8018] 2-9-7 **63**......................(b) TomQueally 6 56
(James Given) *hmpd s: sn outpcd: rdn over 1f out: r.o ins fnl f: nrst fin* **8/1**

433- 4 ½ **Anfield**[16] [8058] 2-8-11 **56**.. RobertTart(3) 5 47
(Mick Quinn) *edgd rt s: sn led: shkn up whn rdr dropped whip 2f out: hdd and no ex ins fnl f* **7/2**[1]

430- 5 2 ¼ **Clapperboard**[44] [7623] 2-9-5 **61**.............................. RichardKingscote 3 44
(Paul Fitzsimons) *prom: rdn and nt clr run wl over 1f out: styd on same pce* **8/1**

000- 6 1 ¾ **Febrayer Star (IRE)**[23] [7978] 2-8-9 **51**..........................(v1) ShaneKelly 8 28
(Robert Cowell) *chsd ldrs: rdn 1/2-way: wknd over 1f out* **8/1**

006- 7 nk **Cheeky Peta'S**[14] [8090] 2-8-3 **45**..............................(v) MartinDwyer 7 21
(James Given) *chsd ldrs: pushed along 1/2-way: rdn over 1f out: sn wknd* **10/1**

245- 8 12 **Hot Amber (USA)**[56] [7348] 2-8-12 **54**.......................(v1) AdamBeschizza 1
(Robert Cowell) *sn outpcd* **7/1**

1m 3.77s (1.47) **Going Correction** +0.25s/f (Slow) **8** Ran SP% **115.3**
Speed ratings (Par 94): **98,93,92,91,88 85,84,65**
toteswingers 1&2 £3.40, 1&3 £5.40, 2&3 £5.60 CSF £22.57 CT £138.17 TOTE £4.30: £1.80, £1.60, £2.20; EX 22.00 Trifecta £151.30 Pool: £3346.29 - 16.58 winning units..
Owner J C Smith **Bred** Littleton Stud **Trained** Newmarket, Suffolk

FOCUS
Not much to dwell on in a moderate nursery with little depth. The gallop was sound and the winner edged away from the inside rail in the closing stages.

8274 32RED.COM NURSERY H'CAP 1m 1f 103y(P)
4:25 (4:25) (Class 6) (0-60,66) 2-Y-O **£1,940** (£577; £288; £144) **Stalls Low**

Form RPR
000- 1 **Big Kenny**[74] [6897] 2-8-6 **45**.. LukeMorris 1 58
(David Evans) *hld up: hdwy u.p over 2f out: led over 1f out: rdn clr ins fnl f* **8/1**

006- 2 9 **Sarlat**[13] [8114] 2-8-6 **45**.. MartinDwyer 4 41
(Mark Brisbourne) *hld up: hdwy over 1f out: sn rdn: styd on same pce: wnt 2nd wl ins fnl f* **33/1**

301- 3 1 ¼ **Trinity Lorraine (IRE)**[11] [8133] 2-8-9 **51** 6ex.................(v) RobertTart(3) 6 45
(Alan Bailey) *chsd ldrs: rdn over 2f out: wknd ins fnl f* **3/1**[2]

600- 4 hd **Flying Author (IRE)**[27] [7936] 2-8-10 **49**..............(v1) RichardKingscote 3 42
(Phil McEntee) *sn pushed along and prom: chsd ldr over 7f out tl led over 2f out: rdn and hdd over 1f out: wknd ins fnl f* **20/1**

005- 5 1 ½ **Hasta La Vista**[25] [7944] 2-8-6 **45**.. JoeFanning 2 35
(Mark Johnston) *chsd ldrs: pushed along over 3f out: rdn over 1f out: wknd fnl f* **6/1**[3]

000- 6 19 **Touche De Rouge (IRE)**[30] [7855] 2-8-11 **50**..................... TomQueally 5
(Peter Makin) *hld up: hdwy 3f out: rdn and wknd wl over 1f out* **12/1**

261- 7 42 **Nice Arty (IRE)**[11] [8131] 2-9-13 **66** 6ex...........................(p) GeorgeBaker 7
(Jamie Osborne) *led: rdn: hung rt and hdd over 2f out: wknd wl over 1f out: eased* **1/1**[1]

2m 4.42s (2.72) **Going Correction** +0.25s/f (Slow) **7** Ran SP% **115.8**
Speed ratings (Par 94): **97,89,87,87,86 69,32**
toteswingers 1&2 £10.60, 1&3 £3.40, 2&3 £4.20 CSF £199.18 TOTE £7.90: £2.20, £7.80; EX 253.80 Trifecta £768.30 Pool: £4934.84 - 4.81 winning units..
Owner P D Evans **Bred** O J Williams **Trained** Pandy, Monmouths

FOCUS
Both market leaders underperformed to varying degrees but this race saw a much-improved effort from the easy winner. The gallop was modest and the winner came down the centre. The form could be rated up to 8lb higher.

8275 CORAL MOBILE "JUST THREE CLICKS TO BET" H'CAP 1m 1f 103y(P)
4:55 (4:55) (Class 6) (0-60,60) 3-Y-O+ **£1,940** (£577; £288; £144) **Stalls Low**

Form RPR
064- 1 **Tukitinyasok (IRE)**[13] [8116] 6-8-7 **46** oh1........................ BarryMcHugh 6 57
(Clive Mulhall) *chsd ldr tl led over 2f out: sn pushed clr: styd on wl* **25/1**

001- 2 2 ¾ **Mosman**[13] [8116] 3-9-5 **60**..(tp) TomQueally 4 65
(Dean Ivory) *hld up: racd keenly: nt clr run over 2f out: hdwy over 1f out: rdn and r.o to go 2nd nr fin: nt rch wnr* **9/2**[3]

005- 3 nk **Secret Song**[178] [3435] 3-9-1 **56**.. LukeMorris 5 61
(Sir Mark Prescott Bt) *hld up: pushed along over 6f out: hdwy over 2f out: rdn to chse wnr over 1f out: hung lft ins fnl f: styd on same pce* **9/4**[2]

452- 4 3 ¼ **Mojo Bear**[7] [8186] 3-9-2 **57**.. LiamKeniry 3 55
(Sylvester Kirk) *prom: pushed along over 3f out: outpcd over 2f out: hung lft and styd on ins fnl f* **10/1**

402- 5 nk **Derfenna Art (IRE)**[11] [8121] 4-9-4 **57**...........................(t) GeorgeBaker 8 54
(Seamus Durack) *chsd ldrs: rdn over 2f out: no ex fnl f* **7/4**[1]

225- 6 3 ¼ **Kyle Of Bute**[24] [7963] 7-8-9 **51**.. SladeO'Hara(3) 1 41
(Richard Ford) *chsd ldrs: rdn over 2f out: wknd fnl f* **16/1**

660- 7 12 **David's Secret**[18] [8037] 3-9-4 **59**... TomEaves 7 24
(Roy Brotherton) *a in rr: rdn and wknd over 2f out* **50/1**

004- 8 3 **Six Silver Lane**[10] [8142] 5-9-0 **53**......................................(v) DaleSwift 2 12
(Derek Shaw) *led: rdn and hdd over 2f out: sn wknd* **12/1**

2m 3.85s (2.15) **Going Correction** +0.25s/f (Slow)
WFA 3 from 4yo+ 2lb **8** Ran SP% **113.8**
Speed ratings (Par 101): **100,97,97,94,94 91,80,77**
toteswingers 1&2 £13.80, 1&3 £11.30, 2&3 £2.60 CSF £132.15 CT £361.71 TOTE £15.80: £4.00, £2.00, £1.40; EX 110.10 Trifecta £613.50 Pool: £4104.59 - 5.01 winning units..
Owner Carl Chapman & Mrs C M Mulhall **Bred** Newlands House Stud **Trained** Scarcroft, W Yorks

FOCUS
Mainly exposed sorts in a moderate handicap. The gallop was no more than fair and the winner came down the centre. He's rated to this year's turf form.

8276 CORAL APP DOWNLOAD FROM THE APP STORE H'CAP 1m 4f 50y(P)
5:25 (5:25) (Class 4) (0-85,83) 3-Y-O+ **£4,690** (£1,395; £697; £348) **Stalls Low**

Form RPR
421- 1 **Magika**[60] [7258] 3-8-10 **74**..(t) MartinHarley 1 84+
(Marco Botti) *chsd ldr over 6f: wnt 2nd again over 3f out: led over 2f out: rdn and edgd lft ins fnl f: r.o: comf* **6/4**[1]

5/0- 2 1 ½ **Back Burner (IRE)**[61] [7228] 5-9-6 **82**................................. SHJames(3) 2 90
(David O'Meara) *trckd ldrs: racd keenly: chsd wnr 2f out: sn rdn: r.o* **10/1**

330- 3 5 **Lexington Bay (IRE)**[22] [7990] 5-9-6 **79**.......................... TonyHamilton 3 79
(Richard Fahey) *set stdy pce tl hdd over 4f out: sn pushed along: outpcd over 2f out: styd on ins fnl f* **8/1**

12- 4 3 ¾ **Knockgraffon Lad (USA)**[9] [8159] 6-9-5 **78**.....................(tp) LiamKeniry 4 72
(Brendan Powell) *s.i.s: hld up: plld hrd: hdwy 3f out: rdn over 1f out: wknd fnl f* **3/1**[2]

024- 5 1 ¾ **All The Winds (GER)**[18] [8041] 8-9-3 **79**...........................(t) RobertTart(3) 7 70
(Shaun Lycett) *plld hrd and prom: trckd ldr over 5f out: led over 4f out: hdd over 2f out: sn rdn: wknd fnl f* **4/1**[3]

250- 6 2 ½ **Next Edition (IRE)**[28] [7906] 5-9-1 **81**.............................. EvaMoscrop(7) 5 68
(Philip Kirby) *hld up: pushed along over 2f out: wknd over 1f out* **20/1**

640- 7 11 **Mica Mika (IRE)**[153] [4313] 5-9-3 **83**................................. JoshQuinn(7) 6 52
(Richard Fahey) *hld up: pushed along on outer 3f out: wknd 2f out* **8/1**

2m 44.78s (3.68) **Going Correction** +0.25s/f (Slow)
WFA 3 from 5yo+ 5lb **7** Ran SP% **121.1**
Speed ratings (Par 105): **97,96,92,90,89 87,80**
toteswingers 1&2 £2.90, 1&3 £2.30, 2&3 £8.60 CSF £19.76 TOTE £2.10: £1.10, £6.20; EX 14.70 Trifecta £75.70 Pool: £2771.16 - 27.42 winning units..
Owner Marco & Sara Moretti & Partner **Bred** Immobiliare Casa Paola SRL **Trained** Newmarket, Suffolk

FOCUS
A useful handicap in which a steady pace only increased turning for home and this bare form doesn't look reliable. The first two pulled clear and the winner edged towards the far rail in the straight. She is improving.

8277 COMPARE BOOKMAKERS AT BOOKMAKERS.CO.UK MEDIAN AUCTION MAIDEN STKS 5f 20y(P)
5:55 (5:55) (Class 6) 3-5-Y-O **£1,940** (£577; £288; £144) **Stalls Low**

Form RPR
443- 1 **Daneglow (IRE)**[13] [8112] 3-9-0 45.......................................(e) LukeMorris 5 56
(Mike Murphy) *prom: pushed along 1/2-way: rdn over 1f out: r.o u.p to ld wl ins fnl f* **7/2**[2]

524- 2 ¾ **Mid Yorkshire Golf**[10] [8140] 4-8-11 46.......................... SladeO'Hara(3) 7 53
(Peter Grayson) *sn outpcd: rdn over 1f out: r.o ins fnl f* **11/2**

303/ 3 1 ½ **Moss Quito (IRE)**[510] [4343] 3-9-2 60.................................. JulieBurke(3) 2 53
(David O'Meara) *sn led: edgd lft over 3f out: shkn up over 1f out: rdn: hung: lft and hdd wl ins fnl f* **3/1**[1]

252- 4 1 **Busy Bimbo (IRE)**[13] [8112] 4-8-11 45.......................... MarkCoumbe(3) 4 44
(Alan Berry) *chsd ldrs: rdn and rdr dropped reins over 1f out: ev ch ins fnl f: no ex towards fin* **4/1**[3]

500- 5 3 **Lexi's Beauty (IRE)**[17] [8050] 3-9-0 45................................. TomEaves 1 34
(Brian Baugh) *w ldr tl n.m.r over 3f out: rdn over 1f out: wknd ins fnl f* **16/1**

235- 6 2 ½ **Twist And Twirl**[13] [8112] 3-9-0 50.. DaleSwift 6 25
(Derek Shaw) *sn pushed along and prom: chsd ldr over 3f out: rdn over 1f out: wknd fnl f* **7/2**[2]

1m 3.72s (1.42) **Going Correction** +0.25s/f (Slow) **6** Ran SP% **110.7**
Speed ratings (Par 101): **98,96,94,92,88 84**
toteswingers 1&2 £5.60, 1&3 £2.60, 2&3 £6.20 CSF £21.76 TOTE £3.40: £1.20, £3.10; EX 22.50 Trifecta £184.30 Pool: £1957.04 - 7.96 winning units..
Owner Mrs J E A Thompson **Bred** David Brickley **Trained** Westoning, Beds

FOCUS
A low-grade maiden in which the gallop was reasonable. The winner came down the centre and the form has been given a minor chance.

8278 DOWNLOAD THE LADBROKES APP H'CAP 7f 32y(P)
6:25 (6:27) (Class 6) (0-60,60) 3-Y-O+ **£1,940** (£577; £288; £144) **Stalls High**

Form RPR
006- 1 **Tartan Trip**[11] [8125] 6-9-7 **60**...(v) AndrewMullen 6 77
(Michael Appleby) *s.i.s: sn pushed along in rr: hdwy to ld over 1f out: sn rdn: hung lft and styd on wl* **7/2**[2]

514- 2 5 **Sweet Vintage (IRE)**[24] [7966] 3-9-2 **55**............................... LukeMorris 1 58
(Mark Brisbourne) *chsd ldrs: rdn over 3f out: styd on same pce fnl f* **12/1**

063- 3 ½ **Lastkingofscotland (IRE)**[9] [8152] 7-9-4 **57**................(b) HayleyTurner 5 59
(Conor Dore) *hld up: hdwy over 2f out: rdn over 1f out: styd on same pce fnl f* **2/1**[1]

162- 4 2 ¾ **Harvest Mist (IRE)**[8] [8163] 5-9-2 **58**.................................. RobertTart(3) 3 52
(Shaun Lycett) *prom: chsd ldr over 5f out: rdn and ev ch over 1f out: wknd ins fnl f* **8/1**

251- 5 shd **Ad Vitam (IRE)**[28] [7905] 5-9-5 **58**..................................(vt) DuranFentiman 8 52
(Mel Brittain) *hld up: rdn over 2f out: kpt on ins fnl f: nvr nrr* **8/1**

063- 6 ¾ **Exceedexpectations (IRE)**[8] [8163] 4-9-4 **60**................ RyanPowell(3) 4 52
(Conor Dore) *chsd ldrs: led wl over 1f out: sn rdn and hdd: wknd ins fnl f* **5/1**[3]

036- 7 1 **Piccolo Express**[8] [8163] 7-9-5 **58**.. TomQueally 10 47
(Brian Baugh) *prom: lost pl 4f out: rdn over 1f out: hung lft and wknd ins fnl f* **12/1**

000- 8 ½ **Basle**[8] [8163] 6-9-6 **59**..(t) TomEaves 2 47
(Roy Brotherton) *mid-div: hdwy and nt clr run over 2f out: rdn over 1f out: wknd ins fnl f* **33/1**

103- 9 1 ¼ **Prigsnov Dancer (IRE)**[21] [8002] 8-9-0 **58**....................(p) JackDuern(5) 11 43
(Deborah Sanderson) *sn led: rdn and hdd wl over 1f out: wknd fnl f* **14/1**

003- 10 21 **Seraphima**[25] [7946] 3-9-4 **57**.. LiamJones 9
(James Unett) *s.i.s: hdwy over 5f out: wknd 3f out* **33/1**

1m 31.47s (1.87) **Going Correction** +0.25s/f (Slow) **10** Ran SP% **122.4**
Speed ratings (Par 101): **99,93,92,89,89 88,87,86,85,61**
toteswingers 1&2 £18.50, 1&3 £3.50, 2&3 £10.10 CSF £47.74 CT £110.40 TOTE £5.50: £2.10, £3.20, £2.00; EX 48.80 Trifecta £236.30 Pool: £2219.81 - 7.04 winning units..

Owner M Andrews **Bred** Kingsclere Stud **Trained** Danethorpe, Notts
FOCUS
A moderate handicap run at a fair gallop. The winner came down the centre in the straight and the form is potentially fair for the grade.

8279 LADBROKES H'CAP — 1m 141y(P)
6:55 (6:55) (Class 7) (0-50,50) 3-Y-O+ — **£1,940** (£577; £288; £144) **Stalls** Low

Form — RPR

003- **1** **Meglio Ancora**[16] 8065 6-8-12 **47**....(tp) JoshBaudains(5) 11 — 56
(Richard Ford) *a.p: chsd ldr over 1f out: styd on to ld wl ins fnl f* **8/1**

000- **2** *shd* **Classy Trick (USA)**[209] 2464 3-9-4 **50**....(p) MartinHarley 5 — 59
(Patrick Morris) *sn led: hdd over 6f out: chsd ldr tl led again over 3f out: rdn clr 2f out: hdd wl ins fnl f* **14/1**

005- **3** *nse* **Ellaal**[10] 8142 4-9-5 **49**.... DaleSwift 13 — 58
(Ruth Carr) *mid-div: hdwy over 3f out: rdn over 2f out: hung lft ins fnl f: r.o* **11/2**[3]

/06- **4** *4 ½* **Vegas Belle**[10] 8142 3-9-2 **48**.... BarryMcHugh 9 — 47
(Geoffrey Oldroyd) *hld up: hdwy u.p over 1f out: edgd lft ins fnl f: nt trble ldrs* **20/1**

050- **5** *¾* **Tony Hollis**[98] 6180 5-9-4 **48**....(t) AndrewMullen 7 — 45
(Michael Appleby) *prom: rdn to chse ldr over 2f out tl over 1f out: no ex fnl f* **8/1**

204- **6** *1 ¼* **Katmai River (IRE)**[16] 8065 6-8-9 **46**....(v) CharlotteJenner(7) 1 — 40
(Mark Usher) *hld up: pushed along 1/2-way: styd on ins fnl f: nvr nrr* **10/1**

320- **7** *½* **Appyjack**[16] 8065 5-9-2 **46**....(t) LukeMorris 4 — 39
(Tony Carroll) *mid-div: drvn along over 3f out: nvr trbld ldrs* **4/1**[2]

056- **8** *shd* **Stoneacre Oskar**[17] 8056 4-8-13 **46**.... SladeO'Hara(3) 10 — 39
(Peter Grayson) *hld up: styd on ins fnl f: nvr nrr* **16/1**

606- **9** *15* **Pendle Lady (IRE)**[13] 8118 4-9-6 **50**....(e) LiamJones 3 — 8
(Mark Brisbourne) *mid-div: rdn 1/2-way: wknd over 2f out* **25/1**

036- **10** *¾* **Tornado Battle**[17] 8043 3-9-2 **48**.... PaddyAspell 2 — 4
(Phil McEntee) *w ldr tl led over 6f out: hdd over 3f out: sn rdn: wknd 2f out* **10/1**

006/ **11** *1 ¼* **Zavier (FR)**[447] 6480 4-9-6 **50**.... GeorgeBaker 8 — 4
(Gary Brown) *hld up: pushed along 3f out: wknd over 2f out* **7/2**[1]

1m 53.0s (2.50) **Going Correction** +0.25s/f (Slow)
WFA 3 from 4yo+ 2lb — **11** Ran SP% **119.2**
Speed ratings (Par 97): **98,97,97,93,93 92,91,91,78,77 76**
toteswingers: 1&2 £21.40, 1&3 £13.50, 2&3 £6.80 CSF £115.75 CT £687.67 TOTE £8.80: £2.30, £3.50, £4.20; EX 75.90 Trifecta £960.20 Part won. Pool: £1280.33 - 0.88 winning units..
Owner Sports 360 **Bred** Mrs R Pease **Trained** Garstang, Lancs
■ Stewards' Enquiry : Martin Harley two-day ban: used whip above permitted level (Dec 27-28)
FOCUS
A low-grade handicap run at an ordinary gallop. The first three (clear of rest) finished in a line and winner raced against the far rail. The form makes sense.
T/Plt: £2,019.80 to a £1 stake. Pool: £74403.11 - 26.89 winning tickets T/Qpdt: £26.20 to a £1 stake. Pool: £12286.85 - 345.90 winning tickets CR

8280 - 8292a (Foreign Racing) - See Raceform Interactive

8265 SOUTHWELL (L-H)
Saturday, December 14

OFFICIAL GOING: Standard
Wind: Moderate across Weather: Light cloud and dry

8293 LADBROKES H'CAP — 7f (F)
12:05 (12:06) (Class 6) (0-55,55) 3-Y-O+ — **£1,940** (£577; £288; £144) **Stalls** Low

Form — RPR

302- **1** **George Benjamin**[30] 7885 6-9-3 **51**....(t) AndrewMullen 5 — 64
(Michael Appleby) *dwlt and bhd: swtchd rt to outer and hdwy 1/2-way: wd st: rdn to chal and edgd lft over 1f out: led ent fnl f: drvn out* **5/4**[1]

041- **2** *1* **Munaawib**[14] 8119 5-9-7 **55**....(t) AdamKirby 13 — 65
(David C Griffiths) *trckd ldrs: hdwy 3f out: led 2f out: rdn over 1f out: edgd lft and hdd ent fnl f: kpt on same pce* **7/2**[2]

004- **3** *1* **Storey Hill (USA)**[18] 8056 8-8-12 **46** oh1.... RobbieFitzpatrick 4 — 53
(Richard Guest) *in tch: hdwy over 2f out: sn rdn and kpt on fnl f: nrst fin* **9/1**[3]

540- **4** *nk* **Rutterkin (USA)**[89] 6471 5-8-5 **46**.... VictorSantos(7) 11 — 53
(James Moffatt) *dwlt and in rr: swtchd lft to inner after 1f: hdwy 3f out: cl up wl over 1f out: sn rdn and ev ch tl drvn and one pce fnl f* **16/1**

000- **5** *5* **Mucky Molly**[39] 7753 5-9-2 **50**....(vt) TomEaves 12 — 44
(Alison Hutchinson) *cl up: led after 2f: rdn along and hdd 2f out: grad wknd* **16/1**

040- **6** *3* **Angel Grigio**[11] 8142 3-8-9 **46** oh1.... SHJames(3) 14 — 32
(David O'Meara) *cl up: rdn along wl over 2f out: grad wknd* **25/1**

000- **7** *1 ½* **Ishiamiracle**[18] 8048 4-8-12 **46** oh1....(p) PaddyAspell 9 — 28
(Phil McEntee) *midfield: effrt and sme hdwy over 2f out: sn rdn and n.d* **25/1**

050- **8** *3 ¾* **Mon Chic**[14] 8119 3-8-12 **46** oh1.... BarryMcHugh 6 — 18
(Geoffrey Oldroyd) *a towards rr* **50/1**

600- **9** *2 ¾* **Seamster**[39] 7752 6-9-2 **50**....(vt) GrahamLee 3 — 15
(Richard Ford) *led 2f: cl up: rdn along wl over 2f out and sn wknd* **10/1**

004- **10** *1* **Frosted Off**[39] 7753 3-8-12 **46** oh1.... NickyMackay 2 — 8
(John Spearing) *a towards rr* **16/1**

346- **11** *¾* **Lincolnrose (IRE)**[29] 7907 3-9-2 **50**....(p) LukeMorris 1 — 10
(Michael Appleby) *chsd ldrs on inner: rdn along over 3f out: sn wknd* **16/1**

500- **12** *shd* **Strategic Action (IRE)**[17] 8073 4-9-4 **52**....(p) RobertHavlin 8 — 12
(Linda Jewell) *chsd ldrs: rdn along wl over 2f out: sn wknd* **16/1**

1m 31.36s (1.06) **Going Correction** +0.20s/f (Slow) — **12** Ran SP% **124.8**
Speed ratings (Par 101): **101,99,98,98,92 89,87,83,80,78 78,77**
toteswingers: 1&2 £1.60, 1&3 £4.00, 2&3 £6.20. CSF £5.43 CT £30.84 TOTE £2.40: £1.40, £1.50, £3.50; EX 7.10 Trifecta £56.40 Pool: £1744.27 - 23.16 winning units..
Owner Mick Appleby Racing **Bred** Mascalls Stud **Trained** Danethorpe, Notts
FOCUS
A low-grade handicap, but it might be all right for the class as the winner used to be better than this, the runner-up is a previous winner here and the third is bred for the surface.

8294 DOWNLOAD THE LADBROKES APP (S) STKS — 1m (F)
12:35 (12:37) (Class 6) 3-Y-O+ — **£2,045** (£603; £302) **Stalls** Low

Form — RPR

021- **1** **Pravda Street**[8] 8187 8-9-8 **69**.... DaleSwift 5 — 79
(Brian Ellison) *s.i.s and sn pushed along in rr: hdwy and in tch 1/2-way: trckd ldrs 3f out: led on bit 2f out: sn pushed clr: readily* **9/2**[3]

006- **2** *9* **Miami Gator (IRE)**[11] 8136 6-8-9 **58**....(v) BTTreanor(7) 8 — 52
(K R Burke) *cl up: slt ld over 3f out: sn rdn and hdd 2f out: drvn and kpt on one pce* **14/1**

560- **3** *1 ¼* **Staff Sergeant**[46] 7605 6-9-8 **67**.... AndrewMullen 7 — 55
(Michael Appleby) *slt ld: rdn along and hdd over 3f out: drvn and one pce fr over 2f out* **11/10**[1]

0/2- **4** *6* **Roger Thorpe**[106] 5962 4-8-11 **0**.... JackDuern(5) 9 — 36
(Deborah Sanderson) *s.i.s and in rr: hdwy to chse ldrs 1/2-way: rdn along over 3f out: sn one pce* **16/1**

/00- **5** *2 ¼* **Pelican Rock (IRE)**[220] 2168 4-8-9 **42**.... RobJFitzpatrick(7) 2 — 30
(David Thompson) *outpcd and bhd fr 1/2-way* **50/1**

561- **6** *1* **Alpha Tauri (USA)**[4] 8230 7-9-8 **67**....(t) AdamKirby 4 — 34
(Charles Smith) *trckd ldng pair: hdwy 3f out: rdn along over 2f out: sn wknd* **5/2**[2]

000- **7** *20* **Red Joker (IRE)**[160] 4100 3-9-1 **70**.... BenCurtis 3
(Alan Swinbank) *sn outpcd and bhd fr 1/2-way* **20/1**

1m 45.59s (1.89) **Going Correction** +0.20s/f (Slow)
WFA 3 from 4yo+ 1lb — **7** Ran SP% **113.6**
Speed ratings (Par 101): **98,89,87,81,79 78,58**
toteswingers: 1&2 £10.00, 1&3 £1.70, 2&3 £3.80. CSF £60.42 TOTE £5.40: £2.60, £7.60; EX 76.50 Trifecta £161.90 Pool: £3759.23 - 17.41 winning units..Winner sold to Mr K Edwardson for 6,400gns. Alpha Tauri was claimed by R C Guest for £6,000.
Owner Koo's Racing Club **Bred** R A Instone **Trained** Norton, N Yorks
FOCUS
A strong pace for this seller. The winner has been rated as stepping up on this year's form.

8295 LADBROKES MOBILE H'CAP — 1m (F)
1:10 (1:10) (Class 6) (0-65,67) 3-Y-O+ — **£1,940** (£577; £288; £144) **Stalls** Low

Form — RPR

204- **1** **Mishrif (USA)**[31] 7858 7-9-7 **65**....(v) FrederikTylicki 13 — 77
(J R Jenkins) *trckd ldrs: hdwy wl over 2f out: led wl over 1f out: rdn clr ent fnl f: styd on* **10/1**

316- **2** *5* **Bitaphon (IRE)**[22] 8006 4-9-0 **58**....(t) AndrewMullen 12 — 59
(Michael Appleby) *prom on outer: clsd up 1/2-way: led wl over 2f out: rdn and hdd wl over 1f out: swtchd rt and drvn appr fnl f: one pce* **7/1**

443- **3** *2 ¾* **Uncle Brit**[25] 7952 7-9-4 **62**.... PJMcDonald 2 — 56
(Malcolm Jefferson) *midfield: hdwy whn nt clr run and sltly hmpd over 3f out: swtchd rt to outer wl over 1f out: kpt on fnl f: nrst fin* **6/1**[3]

330- **4** *2 ¼* **Celestial Ray**[16] 8087 4-9-5 **63**.... LukeMorris 1 — 52
(Linda Jewell) *trckd ldrs: hdwy over 2f out: rdn to chse ldng pair over 1f out: sn drvn and one pce* **7/1**

121- **5** *3 ¼* **Camerooney**[61] 7238 10-9-2 **65**....(p) NathanAlison(5) 7 — 47
(Marjorie Fife) *slt ld: hdd wl over 3f out: rdn along over 2f out: sn drvn and wknd* **6/1**[3]

134- **6** *nk* **Schottische**[25] 7953 3-8-11 **59**....(v) RosieJessop(3) 11 — 40
(Derek Haydn Jones) *cl up: led wl over 3f out: rdn along and hdd wl over 2f out: grad wknd* **20/1**

P/0- **7** *nk* **Grandad Mac**[10] 8160 5-8-11 **55**.... LiamKeniry 6 — 35
(Alan Coogan) *bhd tl sme late hdwy* **50/1**

061- **8** *½* **Run It Twice (IRE)**[9] 8163 3-9-7 **66**....(b) MartinHarley 10 — 45
(David Evans) *towards rr: effrt and sme hdwy wl over 2f out: sn rdn and n.d* **5/1**[2]

400- **9** *nk* **Dear Maurice**[16] 8087 9-8-11 **62**....(t) AlfieWarwick(7) 9 — 40
(Tobias B P Coles) *a in rr* **50/1**

312- **10** *1 ¼* **Silly Billy (IRE)**[11] 8136 5-9-9 **67**....(p) PaulPickard 5 — 42
(Brian Ellison) *hld up: effrt on inner whn n.m.r and hmpd over 3f out: bhd after* **4/1**[1]

424- **11** *3* **Putin (IRE)**[4] 8234 5-8-9 **60**....(tp) DonnaCaldwell(7) 4 — 29
(Phil McEntee) *prom: rdn along wl over 3f out: sn hung lft and wknd* **16/1**

112- **12** *1* **Dansili Dutch (IRE)**[8] 8183 4-9-1 **62**.... SHJames(3) 8 — 28
(David O'Meara) *trckd ldrs: rdn along over 3f out: sn wknd* **10/1**

0- **13** *15* **Mandarin Bar**[18] 8052 3-9-0 **62**.... JulieBurke(3) 3
(David O'Meara) *a towards rr* **50/1**

1m 43.57s (-0.13) **Going Correction** +0.20s/f (Slow)
WFA 3 from 4yo+ 1lb — **13** Ran SP% **124.9**
Speed ratings (Par 101): **108,103,100,98,94 94,94,93,93,92 89,88,73**
toteswingers: 1&2 £13.60, 1&3 £8.80, 2&3 £6.20. CSF £80.12 CT £480.94 TOTE £13.90: £4.00, £2.70, £2.00; EX 122.50 Trifecta £690.80 Pool: £3581.41 - 3.88 winning units..
Owner Mrs Wendy Jenkins **Bred** Mr & Mrs Theodore Kuster Et Al **Trained** Royston, Herts
■ Stewards' Enquiry : Donna Caldwell three-day ban: careless riding (Dec 28-30)
FOCUS
Another strong pace for this competitive-looking 51-65 handicap. It's a long time since the winner was rated this high (early 2012), but this was only his second try here and the level looks okay with the likes of the runner-up down to the fifth all proven here.

8296 32RED.COM NURSERY H'CAP — 1m (F)
1:45 (1:47) (Class 6) (0-65,64) 2-Y-O — **£1,940** (£577; £288; £144) **Stalls** Low

Form — RPR

000- **1** **Bonnie Fairy**[24] 7972 2-8-2 **45**.... AndrewMullen 6 — 51+
(Michael Appleby) *trckd ldng pair: hdwy on outer and cl up 3f out: chal 2f out and sn rdn: led ent fnl f: drvn and kpt on wl towards fin* **5/1**[3]

530- **2** *1* **Lady Knight (IRE)**[16] 8085 2-9-6 **63**.... LiamJones 4 — 67
(J S Moore) *trckd ldr: cl up over 3f out: rdn along over 2f out: led wl over 1f out: edgd lft and hdd ent fnl f: drvn and no ex last 100yds* **4/1**[2]

041- **3** *4* **Stoney Quine (IRE)**[18] 8045 2-9-7 **64**.... TomEaves 3 — 59
(Keith Dalgleish) *set stdy pce: qcknd over 3f out: rdn along over 2f out: hdd wl over 1f out: sn one pce* **7/4**[1]

132- **4** *7* **Starlight Princess (IRE)**[2] 8262 2-9-1 **58**....(b) JohnFahy 1 — 37
(J S Moore) *hld up in tch: hdwy 3f out and sn chsng ldrs: rdn over 2f out and sn btn* **7/4**[1]

1m 47.33s (3.63) **Going Correction** +0.20s/f (Slow) — **4** Ran SP% **109.4**
Speed ratings (Par 94): **89,88,84,77**
CSF £22.44 TOTE £7.00; EX 21.20 Trifecta £64.80 Pool: £2502.06 - 20.91 winning units..
Owner Mrs Lucille Bone **Bred** Triple H Stud Ltd **Trained** Danethorpe, Notts
FOCUS
Just an ordinary pace for an intriguing nursery despite the fact there were only four runners. The fourth failed to give her running so the form looks dubious.

8297 32RED MAIDEN STKS — 1m (F)
2:20 (2:20) (Class 5) 2-Y-O — **£2,911** (£866; £432; £216) **Stalls** Low

Form — RPR

20- **1** **Lesha (IRE)**[12] 8123 2-9-5 **0**.... DavidNolan 3 — 70
(Kevin Ryan) *hld up: hdwy to trck ldrs over 3f out: chsd ldng pair whn swtchd rt over 1f out: rdn to ld appr fnl f: styd on* **7/4**[2]

06- **2** *2 ¼* **Master Dan**[25] 7955 2-9-5 **0**.... GrahamLee 5 — 65
(James Given) *cl up: effrt wl over 2f out: sn rdn and ev ch tl drvn appr fnl f and kpt on same pce* **12/1**

The Form Book Flat, Raceform Ltd, Compton, RG20 6NL.

60- **3** *hd* **Excel Best**[17] 8067 2-9-5 0....................(p) LukeMorris 1 64
(James Tate) *cl up on inner: led wl over 2f out: rdn: hung lft and put hd in air over 1f out: sn hdd and drvn: one pce* **6/1**[3]

452- **4** *14* **Alfaayza (IRE)**[53] 7435 2-9-0 73.................... MartinHarley 4 27
(K R Burke) *led: rdn along and hdd wl over 2f out: sn wknd* **11/10**[1]

5 *20* **Sweet Summer** 2-9-0 0.................... RobertHavlin 6
(John Holt) *chsd ldrs on outer: pushed along 1/2-way: sn outpcd and bhd* **20/1**

1m 46.58s (2.88) **Going Correction** +0.20s/f (Slow) 5 Ran SP% **110.7**
Speed ratings (Par 96): **93,90,90,76,56**
CSF £20.16 TOTE £2.40: £1.40, £4.60; EX 24.40 Trifecta £63.60 Pool: £2917.23 - 34.35 winning units..
Owner Mubarak Al Naemi **Bred** Michael Conlon **Trained** Hambleton, N Yorks

FOCUS
An uncompetitive maiden. The winner has been rated to his debut form here.

8298 CORAL APP DOWNLOAD FROM THE APP STORE MAIDEN STKS 1m 4f (F)
2:55 (2:55) (Class 5) 3-4-Y-O **£2,911** (£866; £432; £216) **Stalls** Low

Form RPR

24- **1** **Crow Down (IRE)**[19] 8036 4-9-10 0....................(b[1]) LukeMorris 1 76
(Charles Hills) *trckd ldrs on inner: hdwy over 4f out: led 3f out: rdn clr over 2f out: readily* **8/1**

3- **2** *8* **Dan Emmett (USA)**[18] 8046 3-9-5 0.................... LiamKeniry 3 66
(John Quinn) *sn rdn along in rr: hdwy 5f out: drvn to chse ldrs 3f out: plugged on same pce u.p fnl 2f: no ch w wnr* **6/4**[1]

000- **3** *6* **Zainda (IRE)**[25] 7962 3-9-0 49.................... PaddyAspell 4 49
(John Wainwright) *prom: rdn along 4f out: drvn wl over 2f out and plugged on same pce* **33/1**

/60- **4** *1 ½* **Newsreader (USA)**[39] 7738 3-9-5 70.................... JoeFanning 5 52
(Mark Johnston) *prom: led over 4f out: rdn along and hdd 3f out: drvn 2f out and sn wknd* **9/4**[2]

00- **5** *22* **Amberjam (IRE)**[15] 8092 3-9-5 0.................... MartinLane 8 16
(Martin Smith) *in rr: racd wd and rdn along bef 1/2-way: sn bhd* **50/1**

0/0- **6** *1 ½* **Paradise Sea (USA)**[19] 8036 4-9-5 0....................(p) AdamKirby 6 9
(Jo Hughes) *led: rdn along and hdd over 4f out: sn wknd* **8/1**

66- **7** *2 ¾* **Cedar Glory**[18] 8046 4-9-5 0.................... DuranFentiman 2 5
(Tim Walford) *chsd ldrs: lost pl after 4f: bhd fr 1/2-way* **50/1**

004/ **8** *3 ½* **Sanctioned**[491] 5048 4-9-10 77.................... GrahamLee 7 4
(Robert Stephens) *in tch: rdn along over 4f out: sn outpcd and bhd* **9/2**[3]

2m 43.17s (2.17) **Going Correction** +0.20s/f (Slow)
WFA 3 from 4yo 5lb 8 Ran SP% **118.0**
Speed ratings (Par 103): **100,94,90,89,75 74,72,69**
toteswingers 1&2 £4.20, 1&3 £8.60, 2&3 £9.10 CSF £21.12 TOTE £7.20: £2.30, £1.20, £4.60; EX 19.60 Trifecta £168.20 Pool: £3532.11 - 15.74 winning units..
Owner B W Hills **Bred** Conor Cashman & Tim Magner **Trained** Lambourn, Berks

FOCUS
A modest maiden with most of the field labouring badly with four furlongs to go, eventually finishing well strung out, and the form should be treated with caution. Weak form with the favourite not travelling and the fourth dropping out tamely again.

8299 CORAL MOBILE "JUST THREE CLICKS TO BET" H'CAP 1m 3f (F)
3:30 (3:31) (Class 5) (0-75,73) 3-Y-O+ **£2,587** (£770; £384; £192) **Stalls** Low

Form RPR

400- **1** **Dame Nellie Melba**[39] 7739 3-9-3 **70**.................... JoeFanning 4 84
(Mark Johnston) *trckd ldrs: hdwy 3f out: swtchd rt and rdn to chal 2f out: sn led: drvn and edgd lft ins fnl f: hld on gamely* **12/1**

500- **2** *nk* **Returntobrecongill**[25] 7952 3-9-1 **68**.................... GrahamLee 3 81
(James Given) *led 3f: cl up tl led again 4f out: rdn and jnd 2f out: sn hdd and drvn: ev ch whn sltly hmpd ins fnl f: no ex towards fin* **10/1**

450/ **3** *7* **Gogeo (IRE)**[750] 6151 6-9-10 **73**.................... BenCurtis 2 74
(Alan Swinbank) *chsd ldrs: hdwy 4f out: rdn to chse ldng pair 2f out: sn drvn and no imp fnl f* **8/1**

061- **4** *nk* **Dynastic**[30] 7881 4-8-10 **66**.................... LauraBarry[(7)] 5 67
(Tony Coyle) *in tch: effrt over 4f out: rdn along over 3f out: plugged on one pce fnl 2f* **5/2**[2]

000- **5** *7* **Triple Eight (IRE)**[50] 7498 5-9-2 **72**....................(e[1]) EvaMoscrop[(7)] 8 61
(Philip Kirby) *hld up towards rr: rdn along and sme hdwy 3f out: n.d* **12/1**

302- **6** *8* **Brockfield**[25] 7961 7-9-4 **67**.................... PJMcDonald 7 42
(Mel Brittain) *cl up: slt ld after 3f: rdn along and hdd 4f out: cl up tl drvn wl over 2f out and sn wknd* **9/4**[1]

403- **7** *17* **Mediterranean Sea (IRE)**[18] 8047 7-9-10 **73**.................... FrederikTylicki 1 19
(J R Jenkins) *towards rr: effrt and sme hdwy over 5f out: rdn along 4f out and sn btn* **5/1**[3]

336- **8** *2 ¾* **Everlasting Light**[25] 7961 3-8-12 **65**.................... DuranFentiman 6 7
(Tim Walford) *a towards rr: bhd fnl 3f* **25/1**

2m 27.72s (-0.28) **Going Correction** +0.20s/f (Slow)
WFA 3 from 4yo+ 4lb 8 Ran SP% **115.4**
Speed ratings (Par 103): **109,108,103,103,98 92,80,78**
toteswingers 1&2 £10.70, 1&3 £6.30, 2&3 £9.80 CSF £123.95 CT £1022.01 TOTE £9.90: £2.70, £3.30, £2.60; EX 79.70 Trifecta £1269.00 Pool: £3107.52 - 1.83 winning units..
Owner Miss K Rausing **Bred** Miss K Rausing **Trained** Middleham Moor, N Yorks

FOCUS
A trappy 61-75 middle-distance handicap with plenty given chances if putting their best foot forward. However, the way the race panned out off an even pace, few got involved. The runner-up has been rated in line with a better view of his turf form.
T/Plt: £456.00. Pool: £52,812.60 - 84.53 winning units. T/Qpdt: £65.20. Pool: £4556.50 - 51.70 winning units. JR

8273 WOLVERHAMPTON (A.W) (L-H)
Saturday, December 14

OFFICIAL GOING: Standard
Wind: Strong behind Weather: Overcast

8300 32RED MAIDEN STKS 5f 20y(P)
6:20 (6:20) (Class 5) 2-Y-O **£2,587** (£770; £384; £192) **Stalls** Low

Form RPR

342- **1** **Oriental Relation (IRE)**[15] 8091 2-9-5 73....................(b) GrahamLee 3 80
(James Given) *mde all: shkn up over 1f out: clr fnl f: easily* **13/8**[2]

0- **2** *5* **Royal Birth**[97] 6234 2-9-5 0.................... JamieSpencer 1 62
(Stuart Williams) *trckd wnr: t.k.h: rdn over 1f out: styd on same pce fnl f* **5/4**[1]

2- **3** *8* **Ealain Aibrean (IRE)**[14] 8113 2-9-0 0....................(v) AdamKirby 5 28
(David Evans) *chsd ldrs: rdn 1/2-way: wknd over 1f out* **5/1**[3]

4- **4** *3* **Libra Romana (IRE)**[9] 8165 2-9-0 0.................... LukeMorris 4 17
(Sir Mark Prescott Bt) *hld up: shkn up over 1f out: sn wknd* **28/1**

200- **5** *6* **Annie's Rose**[72] 6967 2-9-0 53.................... JoeFanning 2
(Bryan Smart) *chsd ldrs: pushed along over 3f out: wknd 1/2-way* **33/1**

1m 2.3s **Going Correction** +0.30s/f (Slow) 5 Ran SP% **105.6**
Speed ratings (Par 96): **112,104,91,86,76**
CSF £3.62 TOTE £2.90: £1.40, £1.70; EX 4.80 Trifecta £8.50 Pool: £2642.20 - 232.02 winning units..
Owner The Cool Silk Partnership **Bred** Brendan Laffan & Michael McCormick **Trained** Willoughton, Lincs

FOCUS
Probably just ordinary maiden form. The winner has been rated back to his best.

8301 CORAL MOBILE H'CAP 1m 1f 103y(P)
6:50 (6:50) (Class 2) 3-Y-O+
£28,012 (£8,388; £4,194; £2,097; £1,048; £526) **Stalls** Low

Form RPR

231- **1** **Marshgate Lane (USA)**[10] 8156 4-9-4 **99**.................... AdamKirby 6 109
(Mark Johnston) *led over 8f out: rdn clr 2f out: all out* **10/1**

251- **2** *hd* **Solar Deity (IRE)**[14] 8117 4-9-8 **103**.................... MartinHarley 5 115+
(Marco Botti) *prom: lost pl over 3f out: hdwy and nt clr run over 1f out: rdn and r.o wl ins fnl f: nt quite get up* **15/8**[1]

106- **3** *1 ½* **Teolagi (IRE)**[40] 7736 3-7-9 **81** oh8.................... JoeyHaynes[(5)] 10 90
(J S Moore) *hld up: pushed along and hdwy over 1f out: rdn and hung lft ins fnl f: styd on* **40/1**

/11- **4** *1 ¾* **Epic Battle (IRE)**[18] 8057 3-8-1 **84**....................(p) LiamJones 13 87
(William Haggas) *t.k.h and sn prom: pushed along over 2f out: rdn over 1f out: styd on same pce ins fnl f* **9/2**[2]

021- **5** *1 ¾* **Star Links (USA)**[15] 8094 7-8-3 **84**....................(b) LukeMorris 2 83
(S Donohoe, Ire) *hld up: hdwy over 3f out: rdn over 2f out: hmpd over 1f out: styd on ins fnl f* **14/1**

060- **6** *hd* **Dance And Dance (IRE)**[42] 7696 7-8-11 **92**.................... AndreaAtzeni 7 91
(Ed Vaughan) *hld up: plld hrd: hdwy over 3f out: rdn over 1f out: hung lft and no ex ins fnl f* **6/1**[3]

002- **7** *4 ½* **Favourite Treat (USA)**[2] 8264 3-8-5 **88**.................... JoeFanning 4 77
(Mark Johnston) *led 1f: chsd ldrs: rdn over 2f out: wknd fnl f* **16/1**

031- **8** *hd* **Spirit Of The Law (IRE)**[17] 8071 4-8-3 **89**.................... SamanthaBell[(5)] 11 78
(Richard Fahey) *hmpd s: hld up: pushed along over 2f out: nvr nrr* **22/1**

62/ **9** *¾* **High Net Worth**[29] 7914 4-8-0 **79** oh2....................(p) JimmyQuinn 8 68
(Gordon Elliott, Ire) *s.i.s and hmpd s: hmpd again over 7f out: hdwy over 5f out: rdn and hung lft over 1f out: sn wknd* **25/1**

511- **10** *3* **Modernism**[5] 8226 4-8-3 **84** 6ex.................... ChrisCatlin 12 65
(David Simcock) *hmpd s: hdwy to chse ldr over 7f out: rdn over 2f out: hmpd and wknd over 1f out* **12/1**

404- **11** *2 ½* **Sweet Lightning**[57] 7361 8-9-10 **105**.................... DavidNolan 3 81
(David O'Meara) *s.i.s: hld up: pushed along and wknd over 2f out* **22/1**

022- **12** *28* **Lowther**[17] 8071 8-8-11 **92**....................(v) TomEaves 1 9
(Lee Carter) *prom: rdn over 3f out: wknd over 2f out* **16/1**

2m 1.27s (-0.43) **Going Correction** +0.30s/f (Slow)
WFA 3 from 4yo+ 2lb 12 Ran SP% **117.4**
Speed ratings (Par 109): **113,112,111,109,108 108,104,104,103,100 98,73**
toteswingers 1&2 £5.30, 1&3 £72.20, 2&3 £38.50 CSF £27.44 CT £747.39 TOTE £10.90: £3.70, £1.10, £9.70; EX 40.90 Trifecta £2494.80 Part won. Pool: £3326.50 - 0.98 winning units..
Owner Sheikh Hamdan Bin Mohammed Al Maktoum **Bred** Edmund A Gann **Trained** Middleham Moor, N Yorks

■ Stewards' Enquiry : Martin Harley two-day ban: used whip above permitted level (Dec 29-30)

FOCUS
A valuable prize and Adam Kirby was allowed too much leeway up front and he pinched this aboard Marshgate Lane. The runner-up looked the moral winner, while the third puts a question mark over the true value of the form.

8302 CORAL APP DOWNLOAD FROM THE APP STORE H'CAP 1m 4f 50y(P)
7:20 (7:20) (Class 6) (0-60,59) 3-Y-O+ **£1,940** (£577; £288; £144) **Stalls** Low

Form RPR

641- **1** **Funky Munky**[10] 7375 8-8-11 **46**....................(p) PJMcDonald 3 54
(Alistair Whillans) *a.p: chsd ldr 5f out: led over 3f out: rdn over 2f out: all out* **16/1**

010- **2** *hd* **Shirazz**[10] 8149 4-9-3 **52**....................(t) GeorgeBaker 7 60+
(Seamus Durack) *hld up: hdwy 1/2-way: chsd wnr over 2f out: sn rdn: styd on u.p* **5/2**[1]

000- **3** *1* **Layla's Boy**[25] 7951 6-9-1 **50**....................(bt) AdamKirby 4 56
(Simon West) *chsd ldrs: rdn over 1f out: edgd lft ins fnl f: styd on u.p* **13/2**

253- **4** *3 ½* **Our Golden Girl**[5] 8225 3-8-12 **55**....................(b) RobertTart[(3)] 2 55
(Shaun Lycett) *hld up: pushed along 1/2-way: hdwy over 3f out: rdn over 2f out: styd on same pce fnl f* **11/4**[2]

002- **5** *9* **Bennelong**[10] 8149 7-9-4 **53**....................(b) LukeMorris 9 39
(Lee Carter) *s.s: hld up: hdwy over 3f out: rdn over 2f out: wknd over 1f out* **7/2**[3]

400- **6** *2 ¼* **Walter De La Mare (IRE)**[12] 8129 6-8-11 **46**.................... MartinHarley 1 28
(Anabel K Murphy) *hld up: a in rr: wknd over 2f out* **16/1**

500- **7** *8* **Waving**[14] 8115 4-9-7 **59**....................(t) MarkCoumbe[(3)] 6 29
(Tony Carroll) *led: hdd over 9f out: chsd ldr tl 5f out: rdn and wknd 3f out* **14/1**

000- **8** *3 ¾* **Sweet Louise (IRE)**[26] 6964 3-8-0 **45**....................(t) JoeyHaynes[(5)] 8 9
(Barry Brennan) *w ldr tl led over 9f out: hdd over 3f out: sn rdn and wknd* **40/1**

000/ **9** *4* **Nelson's Muse**[351] 8262 3-8-5 **45**.................... MartinLane 5 2
(Tobias B P Coles) *sn pushed along in rr: sme hdwy u.p over 5f out: wknd 3f out* **33/1**

2m 43.77s (2.67) **Going Correction** +0.30s/f (Slow)
WFA 3 from 4yo+ 5lb 9 Ran SP% **114.6**
Speed ratings (Par 101): **103,102,102,99,93 92,87,84,81**
toteswingers 1&2 £8.10, 1&3 £6.50, 2&3 £3.60 CSF £55.71 CT £295.78 TOTE £9.60: £2.70, £1.40, £2.30; EX 41.30 Trifecta £280.20 Pool: £2995.08 - 8.01 winning units..
Owner The Twelve Munkys **Bred** Mrs S Corbett **Trained** Newmill-On-Slitrig, Borders

FOCUS
A weak handicap in which it paid to be prominent when the pace lifted three out. The form is a bit muddling.

8303 LADBROKES MAIDEN STKS 7f 32y(P)
7:50 (7:50) (Class 5) 3-Y-O+ **£2,587** (£770; £384; £192) **Stalls** High

Form RPR

5- **1** **Love Excel**[236] 1713 3-9-5 0.................... JamieSpencer 2 84+
(Charles Hills) *trckd ldr tl led 2f out: sn edgd lft: shkn up and r.o wl fnl f: easily* **1/1**[1]

32- **2** 4 **Ex Ex**[10] 8146 3-9-5 0 .... MartinLane 5 73
(Nick Littmoden) *chsd ldrs: rdn over 2f out: styd on same pce ins fnl f* **5/2**[2]
3 3/4 **Coillte Cailin (IRE)** 3-9-0 0 .... ShaneKelly 6 66
(Daniel Mark Loughnane) *dwlt: hld up: hdwy over 2f out: shkn up over 1f out: edgd rt ins fnl f: styd on to go 3rd nr fin: nt trble ldrs* **16/1**
3/ **4** 3/4 **Slope**[79] 3-9-0 0 .... GrahamGibbons 3 64
(David O'Meara) *led: clr 5f out: pushed along and hdd 2f out: sn rdn: no ex fnl f* **7/2**[3]
00- **5** 21 **Lady Faye**[51] 7488 4-8-9 0 .... JackDuern(5) 1 7
(Andrew Hollinshead) *hld up: t.k.h: rdn and wknd over 2f out* **40/1**

1m 31.97s (2.37) **Going Correction** +0.30s/f (Slow) **5 Ran SP% 109.1**
Speed ratings (Par 103): **98,93,92,91,67**
CSF £3.68 TOTE £2.00: £1.50, £1.30; EX 3.90 Trifecta £21.40 Pool: £3798.52 - 132.68 winning units..
Owner Robert Ng **Bred** G S Bishop **Trained** Lambourn, Berks

FOCUS
This looked a three-cornered affair on paper but it proved very one-sided. Muddling form.

8304 DOWNLOAD THE LADBROKES APP H'CAP 7f 32y(P)
8:20 (8:21) (Class 5) (0-75,75) 3-Y-O+ **£2,587** (£770; £384; £192) **Stalls High**

Form RPR
522- **1** **Two No Bids (IRE)**[15] 8095 3-9-0 **68** ....(be) PaddyAspell 8 81
(Phil McEntee) *hld up: hdwy 1/2-way: led over 1f out: rdn out* **8/1**
120- **2** 2 1/2 **Barbados Bob (USA)**[10] 8157 3-9-2 **70** .... AndreaAtzeni 2 76
(Michael Wigham) *hld up: hdwy over 2f out: rdn over 1f out: styd on same pce ins fnl f* **7/1**
000- **3** 1 3/4 **My Kingdom (IRE)**[12] 8127 7-9-6 **74** ....(t[1]) AdamBeschizza 6 75
(Stuart Williams) *s.i.s: hld up: hdwy 3f out: rdn over 1f out: styd on same pce fnl f* **9/2**[2]
062- **4** 3/4 **Seek The Fair Land**[17] 8069 7-9-4 **72** ....(b) LukeMorris 5 72
(Lee Carter) *chsd ldrs: led over 2f out: rdn and hdd over 1f out: no ex ins fnl f* **7/2**[1]
500- **5** 2 1/2 **Valdaw**[39] 7742 5-9-0 **68** .... ShaneKelly 7 61
(Mike Murphy) *prom: lost pl 1/2-way: n.d after* **25/1**
231- **6** 3/4 **George Fenton**[7] 8198 4-9-7 **75** ....(b) HayleyTurner 4 66
(Conor Dore) *hld up: pushed along over 2f out: nvr on terms* **5/1**[3]
101- **7** nse **Menelik (IRE)**[143] 4637 4-9-1 **69** .... GeorgeBaker 3 60
(Tom Dascombe) *hld up: pushed along 1/2-way: nt clr run over 2f out: n.d* **5/1**[3]
555- **8** 2 1/2 **Smalljohn**[15] 8095 7-9-0 **68** ....(v) GrahamLee 1 52
(Bryan Smart) *led 1f: led again 4f out: rdn and hdd over 2f out: wknd fnl f* **8/1**
160- **9** 27 **Decision By One**[12] 8122 4-9-5 **73** .... AdamKirby 9
(David Evans) *w ldr tl led 6f out: hdd 4f out: rdn 1/2-way: wknd over 2f out* **20/1**

1m 31.48s (1.88) **Going Correction** +0.30s/f (Slow) **9 Ran SP% 117.1**
Speed ratings (Par 103): **101,98,96,95,92 91,91,88,57**
toteswingers 1&2 £7.60, 1&3 £9.60, 2&3 £7.50 CSF £63.56 CT £288.14 TOTE £9.10: £2.30, £3.10, £2.00; EX 83.60 Trifecta £1790.30 Pool: £3214.46 - 1.34 winning units..
Owner Eventmaker Racehorses **Bred** Marston & Dean Fleming Thoroughbreds **Trained** Newmarket, Suffolk

FOCUS
Quite a competitive little handicap but the early pace looked quite strong and that enabled the hold-up horses to work their way into contention by the home turn. The time was modest, suggesting the pace was a bit overdone.

8305 COMPARE BOOKMAKERS AT BOOKMAKERS.CO.UK H'CAP 5f 216y(P)
8:50 (8:50) (Class 3) (0-90,87) 3-Y-O+ **£7,439** (£2,213; £1,106; £553) **Stalls Low**

Form RPR
006- **1** **Rivellino**[24] 7982 3-9-7 **87** .... MartinHarley 7 98
(K R Burke) *trckd ldr tl led over 1f out: edgd lft and rdn clr ins fnl f* **5/2**[2]
510- **2** 3 1/4 **Jay Bee Blue**[8] 8181 4-9-0 **80** ....(bt) JohnFahy 8 81
(Sean Curran) *hld up: hdwy 2f out: sn rdn: styd on to go 2nd wl ins fnl f: no ch w wnr* **17/2**
001- **3** nk **Al's Memory (IRE)**[26] 7949 4-9-2 **82** .... AdamKirby 6 82
(David Evans) *led: rdn and hdd over 1f out: no ex ins fnl f* **2/1**[1]
500- **4** 1 1/2 **Commanche**[8] 8181 4-8-12 **78** .... LukeMorris 4 73
(Chris Dwyer) *prom: rdn over 2f out: styd on same pce fnl f* **14/1**
030- **5** 1 **Cheworee**[21] 8021 4-9-3 **83** .... JamieSpencer 3 75
(Tom Dascombe) *hld up: rdn and r.o ins fnl f: nvr on terms* **10/1**
135- **6** shd **Arctic Feeling (IRE)**[8] 8189 5-9-0 **85** .... SamanthaBell(5) 1 76
(Richard Fahey) *hld up: hdwy 2f out: rdn over 1f out: wknd ins fnl f* **8/1**[3]
055- **7** 1 **Master Bond**[30] 7887 4-8-10 **76** ....(v[1]) GrahamGibbons 5 64
(David O'Meara) *trckd ldrs: plld hrd: rdn over 1f out: wknd fnl f* **10/1**
010- **8** 6 **Sharaarah (IRE)**[4] 8232 3-9-2 **87** ....(b) DavidBergin(5) 2 56
(David O'Meara) *dwlt: hld up: a in rr: wknd over 1f out* **18/1**

1m 15.92s (0.92) **Going Correction** +0.30s/f (Slow) **8 Ran SP% 113.7**
Speed ratings (Par 107): **105,100,100,98,96 96,95,87**
toteswingers 1&2 £5.40, 1&3 £1.60, 2&3 £6.10 CSF £23.69 CT £48.98 TOTE £4.00: £1.50, £2.60, £1.30; EX 22.90 Trifecta £58.70 Pool: £3233.81 - 41.25 winning units..
Owner Mrs Melba Bryce **Bred** Castlemartin Sky & Skymarc Farm **Trained** Middleham Moor, N Yorks

FOCUS
The gallop looked even enough thanks to Al's Memory. No great depth to the race and the winner has been rated in line with his better form.

8306 BEST ODDS AT BOOKMAKERS.CO.UK H'CAP 5f 216y(P)
9:20 (9:20) (Class 6) (0-65,65) 3-Y-O+ **£1,940** (£577; £288; £144) **Stalls Low**

Form RPR
256- **1** **New Decade**[38] 7772 4-9-6 **64** .... AdamKirby 7 72
(Milton Bradley) *hld up: t.k.h: hdwy over 2f out: hung lft fr over 1f out: r.o u.p to ld post* **5/1**[1]
000- **2** nse **My Sweet Lord**[10] 8151 3-8-8 **52** .... DavidProbert 1 60
(Mark Usher) *sn pushed along and prom: rdn over 2f out: styd on to ld wl ins fnl f: hdd post* **22/1**
560- **3** nk **Parisian Pyramid (IRE)**[158] 4149 7-9-4 **62** .... JamieSpencer 10 69
(Richard Fahey) *trckd ldrs: shkn up over 1f out: rdn and hung lft ins fnl f: r.o* **8/1**[3]
355- **4** 1/2 **Invigilator**[5] 8220 5-9-6 **64** ....(t) GeorgeBaker 2 70+
(Derek Shaw) *hld up: hdwy and hmpd 1f out: r.o wl: nt rch ldrs* **11/2**[2]
024- **5** nk **Consistant**[164] 3949 5-8-13 **57** .... GrahamGibbons 11 61
(Brian Baugh) *a.p: chsd ldr over 3f out: rdn to ld over 1f out: hdd and unable qck wl ins fnl f* **12/1**
040- **6** 1/2 **Divine Call**[9] 8163 6-9-4 **62** .... LiamJones 9 65
(Milton Bradley) *hld up: hdwy and nt clr run ins fnl f: r.o: nt rch ldrs* **18/1**
520- **7** nk **Above The Stars**[12] 8135 5-9-0 **58** ....(p) HayleyTurner 13 60+
(Conor Dore) *hld up: hmpd ins fnl f: r.o: nt trble ldrs* **22/1**
155- **8** 1 1/4 **Gaelic Wizard (IRE)**[57] 7347 5-8-13 **62** ....(p) JoshBaudains(5) 8 60
(Dominic Ffrench Davis) *sn led: rdn and hdd over 1f out: styng on same pce whn nt clr run wl ins fnl f* **8/1**[3]
002- **9** hd **Steelcut**[19] 8035 9-9-1 **59** ....(v) MartinDwyer 4 56
(Mark Buckley) *plld hrd and prom: rdn over 2f out: no ex ins fnl f* **11/1**
001- **10** nk **Penbryn (USA)**[22] 8002 6-8-9 **60** .... JordanVaughan(7) 6 56
(Nick Littmoden) *hld up: r.o ins fnl f: nvr nrr* **8/1**[3]
60/ **11** nse **Back In The Frame**[52] 3-9-2 **65** .... DavidBergin(5) 12 61
(David O'Meara) *hld up: pushed along over 2f out: nvr on terms* **33/1**
030- **12** 1 1/4 **Proper Charlie**[17] 8073 5-9-1 **59** ....(v) LukeMorris 3 51
(Lee Carter) *chsd ldrs: rdn over 1f out: no ex ins fnl f* **5/1**[1]
000- **13** 1/2 **Bussa**[43] 7669 5-8-11 **62** .... GearoidBrouder(7) 5 52
(David Evans) *hld up: pushed along over 1f out: n.d* **16/1**

1m 17.0s (2.00) **Going Correction** +0.30s/f (Slow) **13 Ran SP% 120.9**
Speed ratings (Par 101): **98,97,97,96,96 95,95,93,93,93 93,91,90**
toteswingers 1&2 £43.80, 1&3 £9.50, 2&3 £75.90 CSF £119.79 CT £911.66 TOTE £6.20: £2.30, £4.00, £4.30; EX 156.60 Trifecta £2071.90 Part won. Pool: £2762.58 - 0.53 winning units..
Owner J M Bradley **Bred** Cheveley Park Stud Ltd **Trained** Sedbury, Gloucs

FOCUS
A bunch finish to this wide open low-grade handicap. The winner has been rated close to the level of his C&D win in April.
T/Plt: £42.70. Pool: £122,406.65 - 2091.04 winning units. T/Qpdt: £24.40. Pool: £9152.77 - 277.08 winning units. CR

8307 - (Foreign Racing) - See Raceform Interactive

8300

WOLVERHAMPTON (A.W) (L-H)
Monday, December 16

OFFICIAL GOING: Standard
Wind: Light half-behind Weather: Overcast

8308 CORAL MOBILE "JUST THREE CLICKS TO BET" AMATEUR RIDERS' H'CAP 1m 1f 103y(P)
1:55 (1:55) (Class 5) (0-75,74) 3-Y-O+ **£2,495** (£774; £386; £193) **Stalls Low**

Form RPR
33/- **1** **Fujin Dancer (FR)**[227] 6303 8-11-0 **74** .... MissHBethell 13 86
(Brian Ellison) *hld up: hdwy over 2f out: shkn up to ld ins fnl f: r.o wl* **10/1**
312- **2** 3 1/2 **Honey Of A Kitten (USA)**[17] 8093 5-10-5 **70** ....(b) MissHDoyle(5) 2 75
(David Evans) *led: racd keenly: clr over 6f out: rdn over 1f out: hdd and no ex ins fnl f* **6/1**[3]
040- **3** nk **Unex Michelangelo (IRE)**[11] 8162 4-10-6 **66** .... MissSBrotherton 11 70
(Michael Easterby) *sn pushed along and prom: chsd ldr 2f out: rdn and edgd lft over 1f out: styd on same pce ins fnl f* **9/4**[1]
602- **4** 2 3/4 **Aldwick Bay (IRE)**[56] 7431 5-10-3 **70** .... MissCAGreenway(7) 3 68+
(Tom Dascombe) *hld up: rdn over 2f out: r.o ins fnl f: nvr nrr* **17/2**
060- **5** 1 **Teide Peak (IRE)**[26] 7984 4-9-9 **60** .... MrsRWilson(5) 8 56
(Paul D'Arcy) *s.i.s: hld up: hdwy over 2f out: nt trble ldrs* **14/1**
040- **6** 1/2 **Capitol Gain (IRE)**[108] 5947 4-9-13 **64** ....[1] MrORJSangster(5) 1 59
(George Baker) *s.i.s: sn prom: rdn over 2f out: styd on same pce* **14/1**
014- **7** 6 **Gaelic Silver (FR)**[10] 8179 7-10-9 **72** .... MissHayleyMoore(3) 6 54
(Gary Moore) *chsd ldrs: wnt 2nd over 3f out tl rdn 2f out: wknd fnl f* **3/1**[2]
020- **8** 1 1/4 **Just A Pound (IRE)**[27] 7966 3-9-7 **60** oh3 .... MrJamesHughes(5) 7 40
(Jo Hughes) *prom: rdn over 3f out: wknd 2f out* **25/1**
540/ **9** 1 **Ibiza Sunset (IRE)**[8] 4042 5-9-11 **62** .... MissJenniferPowell(5) 12 40
(Brendan Powell) *s.i.s: pushed along over 3f out: a in rr* **33/1**
402- **10** 1 1/4 **Flag Of Glory**[130] 5171 6-10-3 **68** .... MissMEdden(5) 4 43
(Peter Hiatt) *chsd ldr tl pushed along over 3f out: wknd wl over 1f out* **16/1**
505- **11** 15 **Arashi**[14] 8130 7-9-13 **66** ....(p) MrJMorris(7) 9 10
(Derek Shaw) *hld up: a in rr: bhd fnl 5f* **50/1**
140/ **12** 6 **Costa Del Fortune (IRE)**[794] 6829 4-10-5 **72** .... MissBHampson(7) 10
(Paul Morgan) *hld up: rdn over 3f out: sn wknd* **33/1**

2m 2.28s (0.58) **Going Correction** +0.075s/f (Slow)
WFA 3 from 4yo+ 2lb **12 Ran SP% 120.6**
Speed ratings (Par 103): **100,96,96,94,93 92,87,86,85,84 71,65**
toteswingers 1&2 £4.70, 1&3 £7.00, 2&3 £4.00 CSF £68.06 CT £186.41 TOTE £13.00: £4.30, £1.70, £1.10; EX 46.10 Trifecta £128.10 Pool: £2670.06 - 15.62 winning units..
Owner W A Bethell **Bred** Loughtown Stud Ltd **Trained** Norton, N Yorks

FOCUS
A modest race. The winner seems as good as ever and the second was close to form.

8309 CORAL APP DOWNLOAD FROM THE APP STORE (S) STKS 1m 4f 50y(P)
2:30 (2:30) (Class 6) 3-Y-O+ **£1,940** (£577; £288; £144) **Stalls Low**

Form RPR
311- **1** **Matraash (USA)**[149] 4522 7-9-8 75 ....(be) ShaneKelly 5 83+
(Daniel Mark Loughnane) *hld up: hdwy over 2f out: sn trcking ldr: led on bit ins fnl f: shkn up: jst hld on* **5/2**[1]
0/0- **2** nse **A Little Bit Dusty**[4] 7544 5-9-4 77 ....(p) HayleyTurner 4 78
(Conor Dore) *a.p: chsd ldr 3f out: led over 2f out: rdn over 1f out: hdd ins fnl f: styd on u.p* **3/1**[2]
045/ **3** 13 **Ballyheigue (IRE)**[432] 6976 4-9-4 70 ....(b) GeorgeBaker 1 57
(Gary Moore) *chsd ldr over 4f: remained handy: rdn over 2f out: wknd over 1f out* **5/2**[1]
364- **4** 2 1/4 **Epic Storm (IRE)**[9] 8204 5-9-4 63 ....(tp) AdamKirby 7 54
(Paul Morgan) *hld up: hdwy to chse ldr over 7f out: led over 3f out: rdn and hdd over 2f out: wknd over 1f out* **9/2**[3]
064- **5** 3 1/4 **Song Of The Siren**[7] 8223 5-8-10 59 ....(p) SHJames(3) 6 43
(David O'Meara) *led over 8f: rdn and wknd over 2f out* **10/1**
000- **6** 28 **Alsaqi (IRE)**[195] 2952 3-8-13 52 ....(b) FrankieMcDonald 3 4
(John Butler) *prom: rdn over 4f out: wknd over 3f out* **100/1**

2m 41.49s (0.39) **Going Correction** +0.075s/f (Slow)
WFA 3 from 4yo+ 5lb **6 Ran SP% 110.4**
Speed ratings (Par 101): **101,100,92,90,88 69**
toteswingers 1&2 £2.00, 1&3 £1.80, 2&3 £2.10 CSF £9.95 TOTE £3.20: £1.70, £1.40; EX 7.70 Trifecta £10.30 Pool: £3098.24 - 224.42 winning units..There was no bid for the winner. Epic Storm was claimed by M Keighley for £6000.
Owner Over The Moon Racing **Bred** Shadwell Farm LLC **Trained** Baldwin's Gate, Staffs

FOCUS
An ordinary seller. The first pair were clear but there is some doubt over the current form of these.

8310 32RED H'CAP 1m 5f 194y(P)
3:05 (3:05) (Class 5) (0-75,74) 3-Y-O+ £2,587 (£770; £384; £192) Stalls Low

Form RPR
643- 1 **Odin (IRE)**[18] 8089 5-9-11 74 GeorgeBaker 4 84
(Don Cantillon) *a.p: trckd ldr 3f out: shkn up to ld 1f out: styd on* 9/4[2]
523- 2 ½ **Scribe (IRE)**[9] 8204 5-9-5 68 (bt) AdamKirby 5 77
(David Evans) *led: rdn over 2f out: hdd 1f out: styd on* 4/1[3]
502- 3 6 **Alborz (IRE)**[25] 7278 4-9-6 69 LeeTopliss 1 70
(Tim Vaughan) *trckd ldr tl pushed along 3f out: rdn over 2f out: no ex fnl f* 16/1
622- 4 1 **Montjess (IRE)**[21] 8041 3-9-3 73 (v) RichardKingscote 3 73
(Tom Dascombe) *prom: pushed along over 3f out: nt clr run over 1f out: styd on same pce* 6/4[1]
001- 5 16 **Artistical (IRE)**[32] 7877 3-9-2 72 TomEaves 2 49
(Lee Carter) *hld up: hdwy over 2f out: sn rdn: wknd over 1f out* 11/2
3m 5.79s (-0.21) **Going Correction** +0.075s/f (Slow)
WFA 3 from 4yo+ 7lb 5 Ran SP% 112.0
Speed ratings (Par 103): **103,102,99,98,89**
CSF £11.62 TOTE £3.80: £1.50, £1.90; EX 10.90 Trifecta £73.10 Pool: £2841.59 - 29.11 winning units..
Owner Mrs Catherine Reed **Bred** Littleton Stud **Trained** Newmarket, Suffolk

FOCUS
A modest staying event. The winner is rated back to his best.

8311 32RED CASINO CLAIMING STKS 1m 141y(P)
3:40 (3:41) (Class 6) 2-Y-O £1,940 (£577; £288; £144) Stalls Low

Form RPR
033- 1 **Kantara Castle (IRE)**[14] 8131 2-9-6 67 SeanLevey 2 70
(Richard Hannon Snr) *mde virtually all: set stdy pce tl qcknd 3f out: rdn over 1f out: styd on u.p* 4/1[3]
312- 2 ½ **Jazzy Lady (IRE)**[11] 8164 2-9-5 70 AdamKirby 4 68
(David Evans) *trckd ldrs: rdn over 1f out: r.o* 5/4[1]
031- 3 1 **Howz The Family (IRE)**[13] 8137 2-9-0 70 (v) RichardKingscote 1 61
(Tom Dascombe) *trckd wnr: rdn and hung lft fr over 1f out: nt run on* 6/4[2]
162- 4 34 **Sydney James (IRE)**[18] 8086 2-9-6 68 TomEaves 3
(Lee Carter) *s.i.s: hdwy over 6f out: rdn and wknd over 2f out* 20/1
1m 54.33s (3.83) **Going Correction** +0.075s/f (Slow) 4 Ran SP% 109.2
Speed ratings (Par 94): **85,84,83,53**
CSF £9.56 TOTE £5.00; EX 10.20 Trifecta £19.30 Pool: £2980.33 - 115.35 winning units..Howz The Family was claimed by John Spearing for £7,000.
Owner Middleham Park Racing Xxv **Bred** Tally-Ho Stud **Trained** East Everleigh, Wilts

FOCUS
Only three mattered in this claimer. The winner very much had the run of the race, but is credited with fractional improvement.

8312 32RED.COM MEDIAN AUCTION MAIDEN STKS 1m 1f 103y(P)
4:10 (4:10) (Class 6) 2-Y-O £1,940 (£577; £288; £144) Stalls Low

Form RPR
442- 1 **Power Up**[69] 7110 2-9-0 68 JoeFanning 4 73
(Mark Johnston) *chsd ldr tl led over 2f out: shkn up and hung rt over 1f out: rdn and edgd lft ins fnl f: styd on* 7/4[2]
2 1½ **L'Avenue (IRE)** 2-9-0 0 LukeMorris 3 70
(James Tate) *s.i.s: rn green in rr: hdwy u.p to chse wnr 2f out: styd on* 9/2[3]
3 14 **Nixyba** 2-9-0 0 LeeTopliss 2 44
(Tim Vaughan) *chsd ldrs: rdn over 3f out: wknd wl over 1f out* 33/1
63- 4 ½ **Armourer (IRE)**[7] 8214 2-9-5 0 MartinDwyer 1 48
(William Muir) *sn led: rdn and hdd over 2f out: wknd fnl f* 5/4[1]
5 5 **Haleo** 2-9-5 0 GeorgeBaker 5 38
(William Muir) *prom: rdn over 3f out: wknd over 2f out* 16/1
- 6 16 **Grey Odyssey** 2-9-5 0 AdamKirby 6 8
(Dean Ivory) *s.s: outpcd* 9/1
2m 2.41s (0.71) **Going Correction** +0.075s/f (Slow) 6 Ran SP% 117.8
Speed ratings (Par 94): **99,97,85,84,80 66**
toteswingers 1&2 £1.80, 1&3 £7.00, 2&3 £9.90 CSF £10.82 TOTE £2.80: £1.40, £3.00; EX 6.70 Trifecta £86.00 Pool: £4387.62 - 38.24 winning units..
Owner Mrs Christine E Budden **Bred** Mrs C E Budden & Partners **Trained** Middleham Moor, N Yorks

FOCUS
Only two of these had previous experience and one of them, Armourer, disappointed so it's hard to know exactly what to make of the form, but for now at least it's probably worth being positive about the front two, who finished well clear. A slight step up from the winner.

8313 LADBROKES MAIDEN STKS 1m 141y(P)
4:40 (4:42) (Class 5) 3-Y-O+ £2,587 (£770; £384; £192) Stalls Low

Form RPR
1 **Fleckerl (IRE)** 3-9-5 0 MartinDwyer 8 78+
(William Muir) *dwlt: hld up: hdwy 2f out: shkn up to ld ins fnl f: r.o wl: readily* 16/1
554- 2 1½ **Aomen Rock**[19] 8063 3-9-5 67 HayleyTurner 5 72
(James Fanshawe) *trckd ldrs: led over 1f out: rdn and hdd ins fnl f: styd on same pce* 5/2[2]
203- 3 5 **Severiano (USA)**[153] 4381 3-9-5 68 [1] AndreaAtzeni 1 61+
(Roger Varian) *trckd ldrs: racd keenly: nt clr run over 2f out: shkn up over 1f out: no ex fnl f* 5/4[1]
3- 4 4 **Great Conquest (USA)**[19] 8063 3-9-5 0 FergusSweeney 4 51
(Jamie Osborne) *hld up: plld hrd: hdwy 2f out: sn rdn: wknd fnl f* 3/1[3]
5 2¼ **Glee Club**[31] 3-9-0 0 TomEaves 7 41
(Noel Quinlan) *chsd ldr tl led over 2f out: rdn and hdd over 1f out: wknd ins fnl f* 20/1
5- 6 23 **Echologic**[13] 8141 3-9-5 0 GrahamGibbons 6
(Brian Baugh) *led: rdn and hdd over 2f out: wknd over 1f out* 50/1
0- 7 4½ **Silent Sam**[9] 8200 5-9-7 0 AndrewMullen 2
(Michael Appleby) *s.i.s: hld up: plld hrd: nt clr run 6f out: rdn over 2f out: sn wknd* 50/1
1m 50.76s (0.26) **Going Correction** +0.075s/f (Slow)
WFA 3 from 5yo 2lb 7 Ran SP% 112.6
Speed ratings (Par 103): **101,99,95,91,89 69,65**
toteswingers 1&2 £6.40, 1&3 £5.10, 2&3 £1.10 CSF £54.17 TOTE £17.50: £8.30, £1.50; EX 72.10 Trifecta £238.50 Pool: £6879.55 - 21.63 winning units..
Owner F Hope **Bred** Yeguada De Milagro Sa **Trained** Lambourn, Berks

FOCUS
Just an ordinary maiden, but a nice performance on debut from Fleckerl. Muddling form, rated around the runner-up.

8314 DOWNLOAD THE LADBROKES APP H'CAP 1m 141y(P)
5:10 (5:12) (Class 5) (0-75,72) 3-Y-O+ £2,587 (£770; £384; £192) Stalls Low

Form RPR
523- 1 **Eurystheus (IRE)**[27] 7961 4-9-7 72 AndrewMullen 3 85
(Michael Appleby) *s.i.s: hld up: hdwy and nt clr run over 2f out: led over 1f out: rdn and edgd rt ins fnl f: r.o* 2/1[1]
234- 2 1½ **Aqua Ardens (GER)**[84] 6701 5-9-6 71 (t) GeorgeBaker 7 81
(George Baker) *chsd ldrs: rdn over 1f out: chsd wnr and hung lft ins fnl f: no imp* 7/2[2]
256- 3 2¾ **Fame Again**[24] 8008 5-9-3 68 GrahamGibbons 1 72
(Michael Easterby) *led: rdn and hdd over 1f out: styd on same pce fnl f* 7/1
062- 4 shd **One Scoop Or Two**[7] 8227 7-9-6 71 (v) ShaneKelly 9 74
(Andrew Hollinshead) *hld up: pushed along 3f out: rdn over 1f out: hung lft and r.o ins fnl f: nt trble ldrs* 9/2[3]
460- 5 nse **Waverunner**[39] 7785 3-9-3 70 JoeFanning 2 73
(Mark Johnston) *chsd ldrs: rdn over 1f out: no ex ins fnl f* 14/1
160- 6 ¾ **One Way Or Another (AUS)**[10] 8187 10-8-9 65 (t) EoinWalsh[(5)] 4 67
(David Evans) *hld up: hdwy 2f out: rdn over 1f out: no ex ins fnl f* 25/1
060- 7 12 **Hill Of Dreams (IRE)**[10] 8178 4-9-7 72 (b) FergusSweeney 5 46
(Dean Ivory) *prom: rdn over 3f out: wknd fnl f* 25/1
401- 8 3¾ **Heezararity**[13] 8141 5-9-4 69 AdamKirby 10 34
(Jonathan Geake) *chsd ldr tl rdn over 2f out: wknd over 1f out* 7/1
450- 9 7 **Edgware Road**[19] 8072 5-8-6 60 RossAtkinson[(3)] 6 9
(Paul Morgan) *hld up: rdn 1/2-way: wknd over 3f out* 66/1
1m 49.82s (-0.68) **Going Correction** +0.075s/f (Slow)
WFA 3 from 4yo+ 2lb 9 Ran SP% 114.6
Speed ratings (Par 103): **106,104,102,102,102 101,90,87,81**
toteswingers 1&2 £2.20, 1&3 £3.90, 2&3 £5.00 CSF £8.69 CT £39.53 TOTE £2.90: £1.20, £1.30, £2.00; EX 10.70 Trifecta £68.70 Pool: £6792.13 - 74.14 winning units..
Owner Midest Partnership **Bred** Calley House Uk **Trained** Danethorpe, Notts

FOCUS
A modest handicap run at a fair pace. Decent form for the level.
T/Plt: £159.90 to a £1 stake. Pool: £75505.71 - 344.66 winning tickets T/Qpdt: £36.40 to a £1 stake. Pool: £6014.66 - 122.20 winning tickets CR

8293 SOUTHWELL (L-H)
Tuesday, December 17

OFFICIAL GOING: Standard
Wind: Light across Weather: Fine & dry

8315 LADBROKES H'CAP 7f (F)
12:30 (12:30) (Class 6) (0-65,65) 3-Y-O+ £1,940 (£577; £288; £144) Stalls Low

Form RPR
514- 1 **Arabian Flight**[60] 7354 4-9-2 60 AndrewMullen 6 71
(Michael Appleby) *mde most: jnd and rdn 2f out: slt ld whn drvn and edgd rt ins fnl f: kpt on wl towards fin* 6/4[1]
055- 2 1 **Beachwood Bay**[28] 7957 5-9-1 59 RobertHavlin 4 67
(Jo Hughes) *trckd ldrs: smooth hdwy 3f out: chal 2f out: rdn over 1f out and ev ch tl drvn and one pce wl ins fnl f* 2/1[2]
100- 3 9 **All Right Now**[15] 8125 6-8-11 55 (t) MartinHarley 2 39
(Tony Newcombe) *prom on inner: pushed along 3f out: rdn over 2f out: styd on same pce* 8/1
656- 4 1 **Orwellian**[7] 8234 4-8-8 52 JoeFanning 5 33
(Bryan Smart) *trckd ldrs: hdwy on outer and cl up 1/2-way: rdn along 2f out: sn one pce* 6/1[3]
406- 5 1¾ **Rapid Water**[15] 8122 7-8-7 51 oh6 (b) MartinLane 3 28
(Pat Eddery) *dwlt: sn swtchd rt to outer and reminders: hdwy to trck ldrs after 2f: rdn along wl over 2f out: sn btn* 33/1
005- 6 nk **Art Dzeko**[101] 6219 4-9-4 62 TomEaves 7 38
(Brian Baugh) *cl up: rdn along 3f out: wknd 2f out* 12/1
306- 7 34 **Whisky Bravo**[7] 8230 4-9-7 65 (v[1]) LukeMorris 1
(David C Griffiths) *sn rdn along and outpcd in rr: bhd fr 1/2-way* 14/1
1m 29.45s (-0.85) **Going Correction** +0.075s/f (Slow) 7 Ran SP% 116.0
Speed ratings (Par 101): **107,105,95,94,92 92,53**
toteswingers 1&2 £1.20, 1&3 £2.40, 2&3 £4.00 CSF £4.86 TOTE £2.20: £1.10, £2.20; EX 6.20 Trifecta £19.90 Pool: £3791.09 - 142.16 winning units..
Owner Dallas Racing **Bred** Mr & Mrs A E Pakenham **Trained** Danethorpe, Notts

FOCUS
A modest handicap but featuring several with decent course records. The market leaders had it between them from halfway up the straight. The winner is rated back to his best level.

8316 32RED FILLIES' H'CAP 1m (F)
1:00 (1:00) (Class 5) (0-75,73) 3-Y-O+ £2,911 (£866; £432; £216) Stalls Low

Form RPR
322- 1 **Frost Fire (USA)**[11] 8185 3-8-12 65 JoeFanning 5 77+
(Mark Johnston) *mde all: rdn wl over 1f out: kpt on strly u.p fnl f* 11/4[2]
042- 2 1¾ **Ivy Port**[7] 8234 3-8-6 59 oh3 AndrewMullen 6 67
(Michael Appleby) *pushed along s and sn trcking ldrs: hdwy on outer 3f out: chal 2f out and sn rdn: ev ch tl drvn ent fnl f and kpt on same pce* 7/4[1]
636- 3 1¼ **Absent Amy (IRE)**[11] 8179 4-9-7 73 HayleyTurner 4 79
(Amy Weaver) *hld up: sn pushed along in rr: wd st: rdn and hdwy 2f out: styd on fnl f: nrst fin* 8/1
052- 4 1¾ **Emperatriz**[28] 7952 3-8-12 65 RobertHavlin 1 66
(John Holt) *trckd ldrs on inner: effrt 3f out: rdn along 2f out: drvn and one pce appr fnl f* 6/1[3]
306- 5 hd **Imaginary World (IRE)**[15] 8134 5-9-1 67 (p) MartinHarley 7 69
(John Balding) *hld up in tch: hdwy 3f out: chsd ldrs over 2f out: sn rdn and no imp* 8/1
452- 6 2¼ **Dance For Georgie**[87] 6634 4-9-1 67 PatrickDonaghy 8 63
(Ben Haslam) *cl up: rdn along wl over 2f out: drvn wl over 1f out: grad wknd* 16/1
001- 7 12 **Ivor's Princess**[13] 8151 4-8-11 63 (p) GrahamLee 3 32
(Rod Millman) *sn rdn along in rr: bhd fnl 3f* 25/1

0- 8 4 1/2 **Hail Shower (IRE)**[26] 7993 3-9-4 71 .... LukeMorris 2 29
(James Evans) *trckd ldrs: rdn along over 3f out: sn wknd* **20/1**
1m 44.11s (0.41) **Going Correction** +0.075s/f (Slow)
WFA 3 from 4yo+ 1lb 8 Ran SP% **114.0**
Speed ratings (Par 100): **100,98,97,95,95 92,80,76**
toteswingers 1&2 £1.40, 1&3 £3.40, 2&3 £4.40 CSF £7.90 CT £31.80 TOTE £3.60: £1.20, £1.30, £2.20; EX 8.80 Trifecta £31.90 Pool: £2867.54 - 67.37 winning units..
Owner Sheikh Hamdan Bin Mohammed Al Maktoum **Bred** Woodford Thoroughbreds LLC **Trained** Middleham Moor, N Yorks

FOCUS
Lack of previous course experience proved no barrier for the winner. Improved form from her, with the race rated slightly positively.

8317 32RED.COM NURSERY H'CAP 6f (F)
1:30 (1:31) (Class 6) (0-60,60) 2-Y-O **£1,940** (£577; £288; £144) **Stalls** Low

Form RPR
022- 1 **Razin' Hell**[21] 8044 2-8-11 **50** .... (v[1]) MartinHarley 3 56
(Alan McCabe) *mde all: rdn clr wl over 1f out: drvn ins fnl f: jst hld on* **7/4**[1]
435- 2 *shd* **Hot Stock (FR)**[111] 5898 2-9-5 **58** .... JoeFanning 9 64
(Jo Hughes) *trckd wnr: effrt 2f out: sn rdn and edgd lft: drvn and stay wl fnl f: jst failed* **4/1**[3]
334- 3 5 **Definite Secret**[28] 7960 2-9-7 **60** .... LukeMorris 7 51
(James Tate) *chsd ldrs: rdn along over 2f out: n.m.r and drvn appr fnl f: kpt on towards fin* **7/1**
504- 4 *hd* **Day Star Lad**[11] 8188 2-9-5 **58** .... DaleSwift 8 48
(Derek Shaw) *towards rr: hdwy on outer and wd st: rdn to chse ldrs 2f out: drvn and one pce fnl f* **10/1**
056- 5 *nk* **Royal Bushida**[15] 8133 2-7-13 **45** .... AdamMcLean(7) 5 34
(Derek Shaw) *hld up: hdwy on inner 1/2-way: chsd ldrs 2f out: sn rdn and one pce* **16/1**
314- 6 3 1/4 **Dandys Perier (IRE)**[12] 8166 2-9-3 **56** .... LiamJones 1 35
(Ronald Harris) *a towards rr* **7/2**[2]
000- 7 *nk* **Mavree (IRE)**[60] 7340 2-8-6 **45** .... (b) DuranFentiman 6 24
(Tim Easterby) *sn outpcd and a in rr* **50/1**
000- 8 3/4 **Genax (IRE)**[102] 6174 2-9-3 **56** .... RobbieFitzpatrick 4 32
(Richard Guest) *dwlt: sn chsng ldrs: rdn along 1/2-way: wknd over 2f out* **25/1**
403- 9 3 1/2 **Sweet Angelica**[11] 8188 2-9-5 **58** .... (p) GrahamLee 2 24
(James Given) *stmbld s: prom and sn rdn along: lost pl bef 1/2-way and sn in rr* **14/1**
1m 17.66s (1.16) **Going Correction** +0.075s/f (Slow) 9 Ran SP% **118.5**
Speed ratings (Par 94): **95,94,88,87,87 83,82,81,77**
toteswingers 1&2 £1.90, 1&3 £3.40, 2&3 £4.30 CSF £9.13 CT £40.09 TOTE £2.60: £1.30, £2.00, £1.20; EX 12.90 Trifecta £57.60 Pool: £2557.41 - 33.28 winning units..
Owner Timms, Timms, McCabe & Warke **Bred** Alan J McCabe **Trained** Averham Park, Notts

FOCUS
A moderate sprint nursery in which the first two dominated throughout. The winner is going the right way from a very low base.

8318 CORAL APP DOWNLOAD FROM THE APP STORE CLAIMING STKS 1m 3f (F)
2:00 (2:00) (Class 6) 3-Y-O+ **£1,940** (£577; £288; £144) **Stalls** Low

Form RPR
230- 1 **La Estrella (USA)**[182] 3423 10-9-7 87 .... GrahamLee 4 90
(Don Cantillon) *cl up: led 1/2-way: pushed clr 2f out: unchal* **8/11**[1]
/00- 2 23 **Cottesmore (USA)**[41] 7778 4-8-6 65 ow2 .... (vt[1]) JoshBaudains(5) 2 43
(Richard Ford) *trckd ldrs: hdwy 4f out: chsd wnr 3f out and sn rdn: drvn and one pce fnl 2f* **8/1**[3]
060- 3 3/4 **Silver Marizah (IRE)**[20] 8065 4-7-11 43 .... (e[1]) RhiainIngram(7) 1 35
(Roger Ingram) *slt ld to 1/2-way: rdn along 4f out: plugged on u.p fnl 2f* **50/1**
512- 4 30 **Tabaayun (IRE)**[24] 8028 3-9-4 80 .... (v) SHJames(3) 5 8
(David O'Meara) *cl up on outer: pushed along 1/2-way: rdn 4f out: drvn 3f out: sn btn and bhd whn eased fnl 2f* **7/4**[2]
2m 27.28s (-0.72) **Going Correction** +0.075s/f (Slow)
WFA 3 from 4yo+ 4lb 4 Ran SP% **107.3**
Speed ratings (Par 101): **105,88,87,65**
CSF £6.79 TOTE £1.70; EX 3.50 Trifecta £28.00 Pool: £2039.87 - 54.44 winning units..
Owner Don Cantillon **Bred** Five Horses Ltd And Theatrical Syndicate **Trained** Newmarket, Suffolk

FOCUS
This claimer concerned only two judged on the ratings. The winner looked as good as ever.

8319 BEST ODDS AT BOOKMAKERS.CO.UK H'CAP 5f (F)
2:30 (2:32) (Class 5) (0-75,75) 3-Y-O+ **£2,911** (£866; £432; £216) **Stalls** High

Form RPR
503- 1 **Powerful Wind (IRE)**[24] 8021 4-9-6 **74** .... LukeMorris 1 86
(Ronald Harris) *cl up: led after 1 1/2f: clr 2f out: rdn and kpt on strly fnl f* **16/1**
060- 2 2 3/4 **Cadeaux Pearl**[18] 8096 5-8-4 **65** .... (v[1]) MatthewHopkins(7) 9 67
(Scott Dixon) *prom: rdn along and sltly outpcd 2f out: styd on u.p fnl f: no ch w wnr* **8/1**[3]
314- 3 1 1/4 **Hannahs Turn**[21] 8052 3-9-7 **75** .... HayleyTurner 3 73
(Chris Dwyer) *hld up: hdwy 1/2-way: rdn to chse wnr over 1f out: sn drvn and one pce* **5/4**[1]
102- 4 1 3/4 **Rambo Will**[33] 7888 5-8-12 **71** .... ShelleyBirkett(5) 5 62
(J R Jenkins) *n.m.r s and sn swtchd lft to far side: hdwy 2f out: sn rdn and kpt on fnl f* **9/2**[2]
034- 5 3/4 **Sewn Up**[7] 8230 3-8-13 **67** .... (p) LiamJones 6 56
(Andrew Hollinshead) *sn outpcd and bhd: hdwy wl over 1f out: rdn and kpt on fnl f: nrst fin* **10/1**
200- 6 *nk* **Majestic Manannan (IRE)**[49] 7593 4-9-5 **73** .... AdrianNicholls 10 61
(David Nicholls) *chsd ldrs: rdn along 2f out: grad wknd* **16/1**
062- 7 3 1/2 **Different**[31] 7937 3-8-12 **66** .... JoeFanning 2 41
(Bryan Smart) *dwlt: sn chsng ldrs: rdn along 2f out and grad wknd* **8/1**[3]
000- 8 1/2 **Flirtinaskirt**[18] 8096 3-8-13 **67** .... MartinHarley 8 40
(Ed McMahon) *a towards rr* **16/1**
400- 9 *hd* **Flash City (ITY)**[33] 7888 5-9-7 **75** .... (vt) GrahamLee 11 47
(Bryan Smart) *a towards rr* **25/1**
330- 10 10 **Come On Dave (IRE)**[94] 6388 4-9-7 **75** .... AndrewMullen 12 11
(David Nicholls) *led 1 1/2f: chsd wnr: rdn 2f out and sn wknd* **10/1**
59.95s (0.25) **Going Correction** +0.125s/f (Slow) 10 Ran SP% **124.5**
Speed ratings (Par 103): **103,98,96,93,92 92,86,85,85,69**
toteswingers 1&2 £27.80, 1&3 £6.90, 2&3 £4.90 CSF £146.92 CT £288.55 TOTE £20.80: £3.70, £3.20, £1.30; EX 202.30 Trifecta £2467.30 Part won. Pool: £3289.75 - 0.81 winning units..
Owner Anthony Cooke **Bred** Miss Ciara Doyle **Trained** Earlswood, Monmouths

FOCUS
A competitive sprint handicap on paper, but turned into a procession by the winner who could be made for sprinting here.

8320 COMPARE BOOKMAKERS AT BOOKMAKERS.CO.UK MEDIAN AUCTION MAIDEN STKS 6f (F)
3:00 (3:01) (Class 6) 3-5-Y-O **£1,940** (£577; £288; £144) **Stalls** Low

Form RPR
620- 1 **Pearl Noir**[7] 8233 3-8-12 50 .... (b) MatthewHopkins(7) 8 60
(Scott Dixon) *dwlt: sn led and clr: rdn wl over 1f out: drvn ins fnl f: jst hld on* **3/1**[2]
006- 2 *nk* **Ishisoba**[53] 7508 3-9-0 47 .... LukeMorris 3 54
(Ronald Harris) *prom: hdwy to chse wnr 1/2-way: rdn wl over 1f out: drvn and styd on wl fnl f: jst hld* **5/1**
666- 3 2 1/2 **Knockamany Bends (IRE)**[17] 8119 3-9-5 52 .... PaddyAspell 4 52
(John Wainwright) *chsd ldrs: hdwy over 2f out: rdn wl over 1f out: kpt on same pce fnl f* **9/2**[3]
524- 4 3/4 **Busy Bimbo (IRE)**[4] 8277 4-8-11 45 .... (b) MarkCoumbe(3) 6 44
(Alan Berry) *in rr: wd st: hdwy 2f out: sn rdn and kpt on appr fnl f: nrst fin* **12/1**
050- 5 4 **Chessfield Park**[42] 7759 3-9-5 46 .... (p) GrahamLee 7 37
(Bryan Smart) *chsd wnr: rdn along 1/2-way: sn one pce* **7/1**
000- 6 1 1/2 **Jillywinks**[63] 7263 3-9-0 58 .... FrederikTylicki 2 28
(Scott Dixon) *in tch: rdn along bef 1/2-way: n.d* **2/1**[1]
055- 7 6 **Queen's Princess**[14] 8140 5-8-9 42 .... (v[1]) AdamCarter(5) 1 10
(John Wainwright) *sn outpcd and a bhd* **50/1**
1m 17.97s (1.47) **Going Correction** +0.075s/f (Slow) 7 Ran SP% **115.3**
Speed ratings (Par 101): **93,92,89,88,82 80,72**
toteswingers 1&2 £3.10, 1&3 £3.10, 2&3 £4.30 CSF £18.67 TOTE £3.90: £2.50, £3.80; EX 21.60 Trifecta £96.70 Pool: £4266.70 - 33.09 winning units..
Owner P J Dixon & Partners **Bred** Mrs Yvette Dixon **Trained** Babworth, Notts

FOCUS
A poor sprint maiden for older horses and run 0.31secs slower than the earlier nursery. Not a race to be taking positives from.

8321 BOOKMAKERS.CO.UK H'CAP 6f (F)
3:30 (3:32) (Class 5) (0-75,74) 3-Y-O+ **£2,587** (£770; £384; £192) **Stalls** Low

Form RPR
000- 1 **Mappin Time (IRE)**[43] 7731 5-9-0 **72** .... (be) AdamCarter(5) 6 83
(Tim Easterby) *hld up: hdwy to trck ldrs wl over 2f out: swtchd rt and rdn to ld over 1f out: drvn out* **5/1**[2]
032- 2 3/4 **Lexi's Hero (IRE)**[8] 8224 5-8-10 **68** .... SamanthaBell(5) 12 77
(Richard Fahey) *prom: hdwy and cl up 1/2-way: led 2f out: sn rdn and hdd over 1f out: kpt on same pce fnl f* **11/4**[1]
120- 3 1/2 **Ace Master**[18] 8095 5-9-4 **74** .... (b) MarkCoumbe(3) 3 81
(Roy Bowring) *led 1f: cl up: rdn 2f out and ev ch tl drvn and no ex ins fnl f* **10/1**
002- 4 1 **Burnhope**[15] 8128 4-8-8 **68** .... (p) MatthewHopkins(7) 2 72
(Scott Dixon) *trckd ldrs on inner: swtchd rt and effrt whn n.m.r over 2f out: sn swtchd lft and rdn: ev ch over 1f out: drvn and one pce fnl f* **5/1**[2]
200- 5 5 **Red Art (IRE)**[15] 8127 4-9-5 **72** .... ChrisCatlin 10 61
(Tony Newcombe) *s.i.s and bhd: hdwy wl over 2f out: rdn over 1f out: kpt on fnl f: nrst fin* **10/1**
060- 6 1 1/4 **Mount Hollow**[8] 8224 8-9-0 **72** .... (p[1]) JackDuern(5) 11 58
(Andrew Hollinshead) *dwlt and bhd: wd st: sme late hdwy* **7/1**[3]
200- 7 3/4 **Dreaming Of Rubies**[108] 5985 4-9-3 **70** .... (vt[1]) GrahamLee 5 53
(Ben Haslam) *cl up: led after 1f: rdn along and hdd 2f out: sn drvn and wknd* **25/1**
660- 8 *nk* **Point North (IRE)**[33] 7888 6-9-5 **72** .... (b) LukeMorris 9 54
(John Balding) *chsd ldrs: rdn along wl over 2f out: grad wknd* **8/1**
603- 9 1/2 **Ray Of Joy**[15] 8128 7-9-0 **67** .... (v) FrederikTylicki 8 48
(J R Jenkins) *chsd ldrs: rdn along 1/2-way: sn wknd* **10/1**
240- 10 3/4 **Italian Tom (IRE)**[20] 8069 6-9-3 **70** .... LiamJones 1 49
(Ronald Harris) *sn outpcd and rdn along: a bhd* **12/1**
006- 11 1 1/2 **Oil Strike**[12] 8167 6-8-13 **73** .... DanielleMooney(7) 4 47
(Michael Easterby) *trckd ldrs: rdn over 2f out and sn wknd* **25/1**
1m 16.7s (0.20) **Going Correction** +0.075s/f (Slow) 11 Ran SP% **126.3**
Speed ratings (Par 103): **101,100,99,98,91 89,88,88,87,86 84**
toteswingers 1&2 £3.50, 1&3 £11.30, 2&3 £8.30 CSF £20.68 CT £140.09 TOTE £7.30: £2.50, £1.70, £2.60; EX 28.30 Trifecta £203.60 Pool: £2244.81 - 8.26 winning units..
Owner P Baillie **Bred** J Jamgotchian **Trained** Great Habton, N Yorks
■ Stewards' Enquiry : Adam Carter two-day ban; used whip above permitted level (31st Dec 2013, 1st Jan 2014)

FOCUS
This competitive handicap was unsurprisingly run nearly a second faster than the quickest of the two earlier races over the trip. The winner was fully entitled to win off this mark.
T/Plt: £18.40. Pool: £63,714.21 - 153.29 winning units. T/Qpdt: £11.00. Pool: £5246.14 - 350.30 winning units. JR

8258 KEMPTON (A.W) (R-H)
Wednesday, December 18

OFFICIAL GOING: Standard
Wind: Strong, half behind Weather: Overcast, raining final 2 races

8322 BETDAQ - THE SPORTS BETTING EXCHANGE NURSERY H'CAP 5f (P)
3:50 (3:50) (Class 5) (0-75,73) 2-Y-O **£2,587** (£770; £384; £192) **Stalls** Low

Form RPR
441- 1 **Pushkin Museum (IRE)**[33] 7893 2-9-6 **72** .... GeorgeBaker 5 81+
(Gary Moore) *mde all: shkn up and drew 3 l clr over 1f out: in n.d after: eased last 50yds* **6/4**[1]
446- 2 1 3/4 **Royal Brave (IRE)**[33] 7893 2-8-10 **62** .... AndreaAtzeni 1 62
(William Muir) *in tch on inner: prog 2f out: rdn and nt qckn over 1f out: wnt 2nd jst ins fnl f: no ch w wnr* **7/1**[3]
233- 3 *nk* **Kodafine (IRE)**[9] 8215 2-9-4 **70** .... AdamKirby 3 69
(David Evans) *in tch: prog 2f out: rdn and kpt on to take 3rd ins fnl f: no threat to wnr* **7/1**[3]
235- 4 *nse* **Douneedahand**[109] 5976 2-8-13 **65** .... LiamKeniry 6 63
(Seamus Mullins) *s.i.s: in last pair tl rdn and prog 2f out: styd on to press for a pl ins fnl f* **25/1**
631- 5 2 **Green Music**[5] 8273 2-8-10 **62** 6ex .... (b) LukeMorris 2 53
(James Eustace) *chsd wnr: rdn 2f out: fnd little over 1f out: lost 2nd jst ins fnl f and wknd* **7/2**[2]

The Form Book Flat, Raceform Ltd, Compton, RG20 6NL.

141- 6 1 3/4 **Debt Settler (IRE)**19 8090 2-9-0 **73** JoshQuinn(7) 7 58
(Luke Dace) *awkward s: racd wd: in tch in rr: pushed along and no prog fr 2f out* **9/1**
544- 7 3 1/4 **Back On Baileys**8 8228 2-8-5 **57** HayleyTurner 4 30
(Chris Dwyer) *racd wd: chsd ldng pair to over 2f out: wknd* **20/1**
200- 8 1 **Wiki Tiki**165 4073 2-8-11 **63** DavidProbert 8 33
(Stuart Williams) *s.s: a last: pushed along and no prog 2f out* **12/1**
59.75s (-0.75) **Going Correction** -0.05s/f (Stan) **8** Ran SP% **113.5**
Speed ratings (Par 96): **104,101,100,100,97 94,89,87**
Tote Swingers: 1&2 £2.40, 1&3 £8.20, 2&3 £4.10 CSF £12.48 CT £56.31 TOTE £2.40: £1.20, £3.80, £2.00; EX 17.40 Trifecta £126.70 Pool: £3,913.24 - 23.16 winning units..
Owner R A Green **Bred** Miss Nicola Cullen **Trained** Lower Beeding, W Sussex
FOCUS
A couple of unexposed sorts in a fair nursery. The gallop was an ordinary one and the winner raced towards the inside rail in the straight. The second and third underpin the form.

8323 £500 FREE BETS AT BETDAQ H'CAP 1m 2f (P)
4:20 (4:20) (Class 5) (0-70,70) 3-Y-O+ **£2,587** (£770; £384; £192) **Stalls** Low

Form RPR
132- 1 **Miguel Grau (USA)**26 8008 3-9-4 **70** (b) AndreaAtzeni 12 82+
(Roger Varian) *wl in tch: prog to take 3rd over 2f out: sn rdn: clsd to ld over 1f out: styd on wl* **9/4** 1
511- 2 1 3/4 **Lady Lunchalot (USA)**21 8072 3-9-3 **69** (p) LiamJones 6 75
(Laura Mongan) *prom: chsd ldr 4f out: drvn over 2f out: trying to cl whn wnr wnt by over 1f out: kpt on to take 2nd again post* **9/1**
462- 3 nse **Understory (USA)**35 7865 6-9-6 **69** HayleyTurner 10 75
(Tim McCarthy) *trckd ldr after 2f: led over 5f out: drvn over 1f out: sn hdd and nt qckn: lost 2nd post* **9/1**
564- 4 3/4 **Enriching (USA)**21 8060 5-9-5 **68** JimmyQuinn 5 73
(Gary Harrison) *in tch in midfield: rdn over 2f out: wnt 4th over 1f out: no imp on ldrs after* **12/1**
003- 5 1/2 **Spring Tonic**21 8060 4-9-1 **69** JackDuern(5) 7 73+
(Simon Dow) *hld up in 8th: shkn up 2f out: sme prog over 1f out: kpt on but nvr cl enough to chal* **7/2** 2
600- 6 1 1/4 **Storm Runner (IRE)**41 7785 5-9-4 **70** RyanPowell(3) 11 71
(George Margarson) *hld up in midfield: shkn up 2f out: prog over 1f out: fdd ins fnl f* **33/1**
201- 7 1/2 **Bloodsweatandtears**35 7858 5-9-3 **66** TomQueally 9 66
(William Knight) *t.k.h: hld up in last trio: rdn on outer over 2f out: plugged on: nvr on terms* **14/1**
300- 8 1/2 **King Olav (UAE)**28 7976 8-9-7 **70** LukeMorris 4 69
(Tony Carroll) *led 1f: steadily lost pl fr 4f out: in last pair over 1f out: shuffled along and threatened to stay on again fnl f* **10/1**
000- 9 nk **Imperator Augustus (IRE)**9 8219 5-8-13 **69** JackGarritty(7) 8 67
(Patrick Holmes) *stdd s: hld up in last pair: shkn up and sme prog on inner 2f out: no prog 1f out: fdd* **20/1**
045- 10 shd **Whitby Jet (IRE)**35 7865 5-9-3 **66** WilliamCarson 14 64
(Ed Vaughan) *a in last trio: rdn and no prog over 2f out* **8/1** 3
600- 11 4 **Shalambar (IRE)**21 8059 7-9-2 **65** AdamKirby 2 55
(Tony Carroll) *pushed up to ld after 1f: hdd over 5f out: wknd fr over 3f out* **16/1**
2m 5.89s (-2.11) **Going Correction** -0.05s/f (Stan)
WFA 3 from 4yo+ 3lb **11** Ran SP% **121.1**
Speed ratings (Par 103): **106,104,104,103,103 102,102,101,101,101 98**
Tote Swingers: 1&2 £3.70, 1&3 £5.40, 2&3 £10.20 CSF £24.37 CT £160.76 TOTE £3.20: £1.50, £2.10, £2.50; EX 19.20 Trifecta £60.70 Pool: £3,719.84 - 45.90 winning units..
Owner J Barton & C Pizarro **Bred** Sea Horse Breeders **Trained** Newmarket, Suffolk
FOCUS
A modest handicap in which an ordinary gallop suited the prominent-racers. The winner edged towards the far side in the straight. The winner is rated a bit better than the bare form.

8324 WINNERS ARE WELCOME AT BETDAQ H'CAP 5f (P)
4:50 (4:50) (Class 4) (0-85,85) 3-Y-O+ **£4,690** (£1,395; £697; £348) **Stalls** Low

Form RPR
600- 1 **Tax Free (IRE)**12 8181 11-9-5 **83** MartinDwyer 6 92
(David Nicholls) *disp ld: rdn to take narrow ld over 1f out: hrd pressed ins fnl f: styd on gamely* **8/1**
143- 2 3/4 **Nafa (IRE)**141 4866 5-9-5 **83** ShaneKelly 1 89
(Daniel Mark Loughnane) *wl in tch: prog on inner 2f out: angled out 1f out and sn pressed wnr: styd on but hld last 75yds* **12/1**
456- 3 1 1/4 **My Son Max**12 8189 5-9-7 **85** MartinLane 3 87
(Michael Blake) *s.i.s: hld up in last trio: pushed along and prog over 1f out: stl pushed along and styd on to take 3rd last 100yds: unable to chal* **8/1**
062- 4 1 3/4 **Pabusar**12 8177 5-9-7 **85** (p) AdamKirby 2 80
(Jamie Osborne) *chsd ldng pair: rdn wl over 1f out: one pce and no imp* **7/2** 1
000- 5 1 3/4 **Island Legend (IRE)**257 1370 7-8-13 **77** (p) RichardKingscote 5 66
(Milton Bradley) *disp ld to over 1f out: wknd fnl f* **20/1**
103- 6 1 1/2 **Sir Pedro**13 8167 4-9-2 **80** SeanLevey 4 64
(Robert Cowell) *t.k.h bhd ldng pair: rdn and fnd nil wl over 1f out: sn lost pl and btn* **4/1** 2
000- 7 hd **Profile Star (IRE)**89 6583 4-9-5 **83** GrahamGibbons 7 66
(David Barron) *mostly in last trio: shkn up and no prog over 1f out* **5/1** 3
013- 8 1 **Royal Bajan (USA)**8 8232 5-9-5 **83** (v) TomQueally 9 62
(James Given) *racd wd: chsd ldrs: rdn 2f out: wknd over 1f out* **4/1** 2
234- 9 1/2 **Sulis Minerva (IRE)**155 4368 6-8-10 **81** DavidParkes(7) 8 58
(Jeremy Gask) *a in last trio: pushed along in last whn nt clr run 1f out* **20/1**
59.52s (-0.98) **Going Correction** -0.05s/f (Stan) **9** Ran SP% **118.3**
Speed ratings (Par 105): **105,103,101,99,96 93,93,91,91**
Tote Swingers: 1&2 £25.50, 1&3 £12.20, 2&3 £9.40 CSF £100.69 CT £794.08 TOTE £16.20: £4.00, £2.00, £2.40; EX 138.00 Trifecta £241.20 Pool: £3,988.94 - 12.39 winning units..
Owner D Nicholls & Mrs J Love **Bred** Denis And Mrs Teresa Bergin **Trained** Sessay, N Yorks
FOCUS
Exposed performers in a useful handicap and several market leaders underperformed. The gallop was reasonable and the winner raced centre-to-far side in the straight. The time was onlu slightly slower than the nursery and the form isn't rated too positively.

8325 BETDAQ 1ST UK RACE COMMISSION FREE (S) STKS 7f (P)
5:20 (5:20) (Class 6) 2-Y-O **£1,940** (£577; £288; £144) **Stalls** Low

Form RPR
501- 1 **Aspirant**9 8215 2-8-9 67 RyanWhile(7) 5 73
(Bill Turner) *racd freely: mde all: clr 3f out: hld together tl rdn jst over 1f out: wandered but kpt on wl* **9/4** 1
62- 2 2 1/4 **Ain't No Surprise (IRE)**9 8215 2-8-6 0 WilliamCarson 2 57+
(Jamie Osborne) *t.k.h: hld up: prog to chse clr wnr 2f out: limited rspnse to press over 1f out: grad clsd fnl f: no threat* **9/4** 1
044- 3 7 **Intense Feeling (IRE)**28 7977 2-8-11 70 MartinHarley 8 43
(David Evans) *chsd wnr: lft bhd u.p fr 3f out: wknd 2f out* **11/4** 2
105- 4 2 1/2 **Just Rubie**9 8222 2-8-11 63 FergusSweeney 1 36
(Michael Blanshard) *trckd ldng pair: rdn to dispute 2nd briefly 2f out: sn wknd* **14/1**
030- 5 2 1/4 **Nick The Odds (IRE)**57 7451 2-8-4 67 HarryBurns(7) 3 30
(Jo Hughes) *plld hrd: hld up: rdn and wknd over 2f out* **13/2** 3
000- 6 1 **Polar Express**34 7878 2-8-8 54 (b1) MatthewLawson(3) 4 28
(Jonathan Portman) *t.k.h: hld up: last and struggling sn after 1/2-way* **20/1**
1m 26.78s (0.78) **Going Correction** -0.05s/f (Stan) **6** Ran SP% **113.0**
Speed ratings (Par 94): **93,90,82,79,77 75**
Tote Swingers: 1&2 £1.70, 1&3 £1.70, 2&3 £1.30 CSF £7.70 TOTE £3.20: £1.50, £2.20; EX 10.00 Trifecta £14.00 Pool: £4,591.89 - 244.84 winning units..The winner was bought in for 10,800gns.
Owner The Huxley Partnership **Bred** Juddmonte Farms Ltd **Trained** Sigwells, Somerset
FOCUS
A decent seller in which the gallop was steady to the home turn. The winner came down the centre and the first two pulled clear. The winner confirmed recent form with the runner-up.

8326 DINE IN THE PANORAMIC MEDIAN AUCTION MAIDEN STKS 6f (P)
5:50 (5:55) (Class 6) 2-Y-O **£1,940** (£433; £433; £144) **Stalls** Low

Form RPR
2- 1 **Quiet Warrior (IRE)**28 7971 2-9-5 0 MartinHarley 6 80+
(Marco Botti) *t.k.h: trckd ldrs: clsd smoothly to ld over 1f out: pushed out: comf* **4/5** 1
00- 2 4 1/2 **Gobertier**21 8066 2-9-5 0 KieranO'Neill 7 63
(Richard Hannon Snr) *chsd ldr: rdn and lost 2nd over 2f out: kpt on again u.p fr over 1f out: no ch w wnr* **50/1**
3- 2 dht **Rosie Prospects**14 8145 2-9-0 0 RobertHavlin 4 58
(Roger Ingram) *led: drvn and hdd over 1f out: no ch w wnr after: jnd for 2nd pl post* **20/1**
0- 4 hd **Sweetness Lady**20 8084 2-9-0 0 AndreaAtzeni 5 57+
(Olly Stevens) *t.k.h: hld up in 6th: pushed along over 2f out: styd on fr over 1f out: pressed for a pl nr fin* **25/1**
363- 5 1 1/4 **Perfect Pursuit**20 8083 2-9-0 75 AdamKirby 12 53
(Clive Cox) *prom: rdn to chse ldr over 2f out to wl over 1f out: one pce after: fdd nr fin* **5/1** 3
243- 6 1/2 **Costa Filey**118 5665 2-9-5 70 1 GeorgeBaker 10 57+
(Ed Vaughan) *stdd s: hld up in last pair: wl bhd whn swtchd fr inner to outer 2f out: shkn up and styd on wl fnl f: nvr involved* **12/1**
7 nk **Mercury Magic** 2-9-5 0 JimCrowley 11 56+
(Ralph Beckett) *v difficult to load into stalls: trckd ldrs: shkn up and outpcd over 2f out: styd on fnl f* **9/2** 2
8 3/4 **Perrydot (IRE)** 2-9-0 0 FergusSweeney 1 49
(Jo Crowley) *v difficult to load into stalls: wnt lft s: in tch: shkn up and outpcd over 2f out: styd on fnl f* **16/1**
0- 9 2 **Fruit Pastille**21 8061 2-9-0 0 NickyMackay 3 43
(Hughie Morrison) *sltly impeded s: hld up in rr: pushed along and sme prog 2f out: no hdwy over 1f out* **50/1**
0- 10 1 1/2 **Risk 'N' Reward (IRE)**137 5000 2-9-0 0 DavidKenny(5) 8 43
(Amy Weaver) *a towards rr: rdn and struggling 3f out* **33/1**
6- 11 12 **Little Miss Becky**21 8058 2-9-0 0 PatrickDonaghy 9 2
(Giles Bravery) *s.s: a in last pair: t.o* **66/1**
12 1/2 **Minnie Miracle** 2-9-0 0 LiamKeniry 2
(Mark Usher) *sltly impeded s: a in rr: wknd over 2f out: t.o* **50/1**
1m 13.57s (0.47) **Going Correction** -0.05s/f (Stan) **12** Ran SP% **122.9**
Speed ratings (Par 94): **94,88,88,87,86 85,85,84,81,79 63,62**
WIN: 1.80 Quiet Warrior; PL: 11.10 Gobertier, 4.10 Rosie Prospects, 1.10 Quiet Warrior; EX: 22.70, 8.90; CSF: 38.37, 13.08; TC: ; TF: 405.70, 319.50;.
Owner Global First Racing **Bred** John R Jeffers **Trained** Newmarket, Suffolk
FOCUS
Little strength in depth but a fair effort from the ready winner, who came down the centre in the straight. The gallop was no more than fair. The winner was value for extra but the form was compressed in behind.

8327 BETDAQ - THE SPORTS BETTING EXCHANGE H'CAP (LONDON MIDDLE DISTANCE SERIES FINAL) 1m 3f (P)
6:20 (6:23) (Class 2) 3-Y-O+
£37,350 (£11,184; £5,592; £2,796; £1,398; £702) **Stalls** Low

Form RPR
141- 1 **I'm Fraam Govan**70 7121 5-9-3 **87** (t) JimCrowley 6 99+
(George Baker) *settled disputing 7th: looking for room 2f out: swtchd to outer and prog over 1f out: drvn and r.o to ld last 100yds* **9/2** 1
620- 2 1 **Castilo Del Diablo (IRE)**27 7990 4-9-8 **92** (b) AdamKirby 14 101
(David Simcock) *hld up in last pair: gd prog on outer jst over 2f out: drvn to chal ins fnl f: nt qckn but styd on to take 2nd last strides* **5/1** 2
553- 3 nk **Icebuster**14 8150 5-8-13 **83** DavidProbert 10 92
(Rod Millman) *trckd ldng quartet: pushed along and clsd to ld wl over 1f out: drvn fnl f: hdd and one pce last 100yds* **12/1** 3
314- 4 2 1/4 **Presburg (IRE)**14 8150 4-8-8 **81** ConorHoban(3) 9 87+
(Joseph Tuite) *hld up disputing 9th: rdn over 2f out: bdly hmpd wl over 1f out: styd on fnl f on outer: nrst fin* **16/1**
3/1- 5 3/4 **Troopingthecolour**77 6936 7-9-6 **90** (t) RobertWinston 4 93+
(Steve Gollings) *hld up disputing 9th: rdn over 2f out: trying to make prog whn nt clr run over 1f out: swtchd to outer and kpt on fnl f* **5/1** 2
201- 6 1 1/2 **Jazz Master**49 7627 3-8-12 **86** (b) AndreaAtzeni 5 87
(Luca Cumani) *hld up disputing 7th: tried to make prog on inner fr 2f out: no hdwy fnl f* **9/2** 1
510- 7 1 1/4 **Layl (USA)**27 7990 3-8-12 **86** JoeFanning 7 84
(Mark Johnston) *trckd ldng pair: led briefly 2f out: wknd qckly fnl f* **16/1**
001- 8 hd **Shavansky**27 7990 9-9-0 **89** ShelleyBirkett(5) 1 87
(Rod Millman) *t.k.h: hld up disputing 5th: rdn towards inner 2f out and wl in tch: fdd over 1f out* **16/1**
231- 9 7 **Zamoyski**38 4167 3-8-12 **86** SeanLevey 2 71
(Steve Gollings) *trckd ldng pair: rdn over 2f out: wknd towards inner over 1f out* **20/1**
521- 10 1 1/2 **Halfsin (IRE)**14 8150 5-9-5 **89** (t) MartinHarley 12 72
(Marco Botti) *tried to ld but pressed then hdd after 2f: drvn over 1f out: wknd over 1f out: eased* **12/1** 3
130- 11 7 **Open Eagle (IRE)**27 7990 4-9-10 **94** GrahamGibbons 3 64
(David O'Meara) *won battle for ld after 2f: hdd & wknd 2f out: eased fnl f: t.o* **20/1**

035- 12 *shd* **Spifer (IRE)**[27] 7990 5-9-9 **93**....(p) LukeMorris 13 63
(Marco Botti) *hld up in last pair: shuffled along towards inner 2f out: no prog and sn wknd: eased and t.o* **14/1**

2m 18.34s (-3.56) **Going Correction** -0.05s/f (Stan)
WFA 3 from 4yo+ 4lb **12 Ran SP% 118.9**
Speed ratings (Par 109): **110,109,109,107,106 105,104,104,99,98 93,93**
CSF £26.56 CT £250.35 TOTE £5.00: £2.10, £2.30, £4.00; EX 32.40 Trifecta £457.50 Pool: £3,670.91 - 6.01 winning units..
Owner Sir Alex Ferguson **Bred** M Kehoe **Trained** Manton, Wilts
■ This race was rescheduled having been part of the abandoned card a week earlier.

FOCUS
A very useful and competitive handicap featuring several last-time-out winners. A fair gallop soon steadied and the winner came down the centre. The form is solid with the third a reliable guide.

8328 BOOK CHRISTMAS FESTIVAL TICKETS NOW MAIDEN AUCTION STKS 1m (P)
6:50 (6:52) (Class 6) 2-Y-O **£1,940** (£577; £288; £144) **Stalls** Low

Form RPR
40- 1 **New Colours**[16] 8124 2-8-13 0.... MartinDwyer 7 70
(Marcus Tregoning) *mde all: jinked lft and rdn 2f out: jnd fnl f: hld on wl nr fin* **10/1**
3- 2 *hd* **Spirit Or Soul (FR)**[26] 8005 2-8-10 0.... MartinHarley 1 67
(Marco Botti) *trckd ldrs: shkn up over 2f out: rdn to take 2nd wl over 1f out: jnd wnr fnl f: nt qckn nr fin* **5/4**[1]
0- 3 *nk* **Confiture**[16] 8124 2-8-7 0.... DavidProbert 10 63
(Michael Blanshard) *hld up wl in rr: prog fr 2f out: wnt 3rd fnl f: styd on and clsd on ldng pair fin: jst hld* **25/1**
4 *1* **Marphilly (IRE)** 2-8-5 0.... LukeMorris 5 59
(John Best) *slowly away: wl in rr: prog towards inner 2f out: rdn and styd on same pce fnl f: nvr quite able to chal* **10/1**
05- 5 *nk* **Ede's The Business**[20] 8085 2-8-5 0.... LiamJones 2 58
(Pat Phelan) *prom: rdn to dispute 2nd wl over 1f out: one pce after* **16/1**
6 *nk* **Sea Spear** 2-8-11 0.... GrahamGibbons 3 63+
(David Barron) *slowly away: wl in rr: rdn over 2f out: prog wl over 1f out: styd on wl fnl f: nrst fin* **7/1**[3]
0- 7 *½* **Hallaga**[12] 8175 2-8-5 0.... JimmyQuinn 6 56
(William Jarvis) *awkward s: towards rr: rdn and prog towards inner fr 2f out: kpt on one pce fnl f* **66/1**
00- 8 *¾* **Moneypennie**[16] 8123 2-8-7 0.... HayleyTurner 12 56
(Marcus Tregoning) *t.k.h: trckd wnr: pushed along over 2f out: lost 2nd and shkn up wl over 1f out: grad fdd* **25/1**
6- 9 *1 ¾* **Swale Star**[203] 2774 2-8-0 0.... JoeyHaynes(5) 4 50
(Seamus Mullins) *prom: drvn over 2f out: fdd over 1f out* **50/1**
252- 10 *3* **Mr Wickfield**[20] 8085 2-8-13 71.... FrederikTylicki 9 51
(John Best) *nt that wl away but sn prom on outer: rdn over 2f out: wknd wl over 1f out* **9/2**[2]
11 *nk* **Footsieonehundred (IRE)** 2-8-5 0.... AdamBeschizza 14 43
(Patrick Gilligan) *a towards rr: rdn over 2f out: no prog* **33/1**
12 *7* **French Accent** 2-8-10 0.... FergusSweeney 11 32+
(John Best) *s.v.s: mostly in last pair and nvr on terms* **33/1**
- 13 *1 ¾* **Zealand (IRE)** 2-8-13 0.... JohnFahy 13 31
(John Best) *sn restrained into last pair: wl bhd 3f out: nvr a factor* **25/1**
000- 14 *1* **Artemis (IRE)**[6] 8262 2-8-5 55.... AndreaAtzeni 8 20
(Conrad Allen) *trckd ldrs on outer: gng bttr than most over 2f out: sn rdn and wknd qckly* **14/1**

1m 42.01s (2.21) **Going Correction** -0.05s/f (Stan) **14 Ran SP% 126.7**
Speed ratings (Par 94): **86,85,85,84,84 83,83,82,80,77 77,70,68,67**
CSF £22.68 TOTE £11.70: £2.70, £1.10, £10.50; EX 33.60 Trifecta £925.60 Pool: £3,151.38 - 2.55 winning units..
Owner J A Tabet **Bred** Mr & Mrs G Middlebrook **Trained** Whitsbury, Hants

FOCUS
A modest maiden and one in which the gallop was on the steady side, resulting in a slow time. The winner came down the centre.

8329 KEMPTON.CO.UK ALL WEATHER "HANDS AND HEELS" APPRENTICE SERIES H'CAP (RACING EXCELLENCE) 1m (P)
7:20 (7:20) (Class 6) (0-60,60) 4-Y-O+ **£1,940** (£577; £288; £144) **Stalls** Low

Form RPR
002- 1 **Larghetto (USA)**[21] 8073 5-9-3 **59**.... CharlieElliott(3) 8 67
(Daniel Mark Loughnane) *hld up in last trio: prog over 3f out to press ldr wl over 1f out: led jst ins fnl f: hld on* **6/1**[3]
424- 2 *½* **Attain**[26] 8006 4-9-0 **53**....(p) AdamMcLean 3 60
(Julia Feilden) *trckd ldng pair: n.m.r on inner over 2f out: nt qckn over 1f out: styd on to take 2nd nr fin* **7/1**
046- 3 *½* **Katmai River (IRE)**[5] 8279 6-8-4 **46**.... CharlotteJenner(3) 6 52
(Mark Usher) *disp ld: def advantage jst over 2f out: hdd jst ins fnl f: no ex and lost 2nd nr fin* **10/1**
221- 4 *1 ½* **Squirrel Wood (IRE)**[28] 7981 5-9-4 **57**.... LouisSteward 4 59
(George Baker) *pushed along in last and struggling 1/2-way: effrt on wd outside over 2f out: kpt on but nvr able to chal* **3/1**[1]
042- 5 *1 ¼* **Nifty Kier**[15] 8140 4-9-6 **59**.... RobJFitzpatrick 5 58
(Martin Bosley) *trckd ldrs: effrt and cl enough wl over 1f out: kpt on same pce after* **7/1**
630- 6 *10* **Malih**[32] 7923 4-9-3 **59**.... RobHornby(3) 1 35
(Jamie Osborne) *disp ld to jst over 2f out: wknd qckly* **5/1**[2]
060- 7 *½* **Ermyntrude**[133] 5123 6-8-9 **51**....(v) SophieRalston(3) 2 26
(Pat Phelan) *lost pl on inner 5f out and in rr after: no prog 2f out: wl btn over 1f out* **10/1**
000- 8 *½* **Hooligan Sean**[32] 7930 6-8-7 **46** oh1....(v[1]) DanielCremin 7 20
(Mark Usher) *trckd ldrs: pushed along over 3f out: wknd 2f out* **33/1**
205- 9 *nk* **Voice From Above (IRE)**[14] 6700 4-9-4 **60**....(v[1]) JackGarritty(3) 10 33
(Patrick Holmes) *racd wd: in tch: wknd over 2f out* **20/1**
000- 10 *4* **Lutine Charlie (IRE)**[16] 8125 6-9-4 **57**.... MatthewHopkins 11 21
(Pat Eddery) *prom on outer tl wknd qckly over 2f out* **12/1**
00- 11 *1 ½* **Ioannou**[29] 7958 4-9-2 **55**.... JordanVaughan 9 16
(Ian Williams) *in tch tl wknd over 2f out* **6/1**[3]

1m 40.54s (0.74) **Going Correction** -0.05s/f (Stan) **11 Ran SP% 128.8**
Speed ratings (Par 101): **94,93,93,91,90 80,79,79,78,74 73**
Tote Swingers: 1&2 £4.10, 1&3 £3.90, 2&3 £3.40 CSF £52.63 CT £438.52 TOTE £5.00: £1.50, £3.00, £4.30; EX 73.50 Trifecta £516.20 Pool: £2,869.94 - 4.16 winning units..
Owner Mrs C Loughnane **Bred** Barr Inman & Giant's Causeway Syndicate **Trained** Baldwin's Gate, Staffs
■ Stewards' Enquiry : Sophie Ralston seven-day ban: used whip contrary to race conditions (Jan 12,14,15,22,24,30,31)
Charlie Elliott seven-day ban: used whip contrary to race conditions (Jan 5-6,8-10,12,14)

FOCUS
A moderate handicap run at a reasonable gallop. The winner came down the centre and the form is ordinary for the grade.
T/Plt: £48.60 to a £1 stake. Pool: £77,972.62 - 1,171.01 winning tickets. T/Qpdt: £28.60 to a £1 stake. Pool: £9,269.09 - 239.15 winning tickets. JN

8244 LINGFIELD (L-H)
Wednesday, December 18
OFFICIAL GOING: Standard

8330 BEST ODDS AT BOOKMAKERS.CO.UK H'CAP 6f (P)
12:00 (12:00) (Class 6) (0-65,65) 3-Y-O+ **£2,045** (£603; £302) **Stalls** Low

Form RPR
231- 1 **Welease Bwian (IRE)**[85] 6732 4-9-5 **63**.... AdamBeschizza 3 71
(Stuart Williams) *hld up in tch towards rr: swtchd rt and effrt over 1f out: str run under hands and heels riding ins fnl f to ld cl home* **7/1**[3]
443- 2 *shd* **Joyous**[72] 7073 3-9-2 **60**.... RobertWinston 12 68+
(Dean Ivory) *stdd s: hld up in last trio: swtchd lft and gd hdwy ent fnl f: swtchd rt and str chal wl ins fnl f: r.o* **4/1**[1]
605- 3 *nk* **Saskia's Dream**[22] 8052 5-9-3 **61**....(v) GrahamLee 4 68
(Jane Chapple-Hyam) *wl in tch in midfield: swtchd lft and effrt over 1f out: hdwy u.p to ld ins fnl f: r.o but lost 2 pls cl home* **14/1**
055- 4 *2 ½* **Perfect Venture**[33] 7897 3-9-7 **65**.... AdamKirby 2 64
(Clive Cox) *led tl 4f out: chsd ldr tl drvn and hdwy to chal ent fnl f: no ex and outpcd fnl 75yds* **5/1**[2]
106- 5 *½* **Two In The Pink (IRE)**[155] 4385 3-9-5 **63**.... JoeFanning 7 60
(Ralph Smith) *hld up in last quartet: swtchd rt over 1f out: r.o wl ins fnl f: nvr trbld ldrs* **16/1**
002- 6 *shd* **Falasteen (IRE)**[9] 8216 6-9-6 **64**.... LiamJones 8 61
(Milton Bradley) *chsd ldr tl led 4f out: drvn over 1f out: hdd ins fnl f: no ex and outpcd fnl 75yds* **7/1**[3]
606- 7 *hd* **Belle Bayardo (IRE)**[29] 7957 5-9-3 **61**.... LukeMorris 5 57
(Ronald Harris) *in tch in midfield: outpcd and rdn wl over 1f out: rallied and kpt on ins fnl f* **8/1**
310- 8 *½* **My Gigi**[20] 8087 3-9-4 **62**....(p) GeorgeBaker 10 57
(Gary Moore) *stdd s: hld up in last trio: swtchd rt and effrt over 1f out: kpt on ins fnl f: nvr trbld ldrs* **8/1**
300- 9 *2 ½* **Fortrose Academy (IRE)**[16] 8128 4-9-4 **62**....(v[1]) DavidProbert 11 49
(Andrew Balding) *chsd ldrs: drvn and unable qck over 1f out: wknd ins fnl f* **8/1**
320- 10 *1 ¼* **Ghost Train (IRE)**[9] 8220 4-8-13 **60**....(p) MarkCoumbe(3) 6 43
(Tim McCarthy) *hld up in last trio: wd and effrt bnd 2f out: no hdwy: n.d* **20/1**
145- 11 *hd* **Mrs Warren**[64] 7269 3-9-4 **62**....(p) JimCrowley 1 44
(George Baker) *wl in tch in midfield: rdn and unable qck over 1f out: wknd fnl f* **16/1**

1m 10.96s (-0.94) **Going Correction** -0.15s/f (Stan) **11 Ran SP% 118.2**
Speed ratings (Par 101): **100,99,99,96,95 95,95,94,91,89 89**
Tote Swingers: 1&2 £4.60, 1&3 £22.50, 2&3 £21.90 CSF £35.30 CT £394.14 TOTE £6.60: £2.50, £1.90, £5.80; EX 44.40 Trifecta £839.80 Pool: £2,230.26 - 1.99 winning units..
Owner W E Enticknap **Bred** Nils Koop **Trained** Newmarket, Suffolk

FOCUS
A moderate sprint handicap run at a good pace. The winner is rated close to his old best.

8331 32RED CASINO H'CAP 2m (P)
12:30 (12:32) (Class 5) (0-70,70) 3-Y-O+ **£2,726** (£805; £402) **Stalls** Low

Form RPR
03/- 1 **Outrageous Request**[17] 1880 7-9-7 **70**.... LouisSteward(7) 5 77
(William Stone) *t.k.h: led for over 1f: stdd and hld up wl in tch in midfield: effrt u.p to ld 1f out: hld on gamely cl home: all out* **12/1**
044- 2 *nse* **Bow To No One (IRE)**[20] 8089 7-9-9 **68**.... RobertTart(3) 2 75
(Alan Jarvis) *hld up in midfield: hdwy u.p over 1f out: str chal fnl 100yds: r.o: jst hld* **10/1**
053- 3 *½* **Keep Kicking (IRE)**[14] 8160 6-9-0 **56**.... LukeMorris 11 62+
(Simon Dow) *hld up in midfield: rdn over 3f out: wd and no imp bnd 2f out: styd on strly u.p ins fnl f: nt quite rch ldrs* **25/1**
055- 4 *1 ½* **Peachez**[15] 8139 5-9-11 **67**....(p) GeorgeBaker 9 72
(Seamus Durack) *stdd s: hld up towards rr: rdn and hdwy 2f out: swtchd rt over 1f out: hdwy u.p 1f out: styd on same pce fnl 100yds* **12/1**
041- 5 *1 ½* **Epsom Salts**[14] 8160 8-9-6 **62**....(p) FergusSweeney 1 65
(Pat Phelan) *hld up in tch in midfield: rdn and effrt 2f out: hdwy and n.m.r over 1f out: kpt on same pce ins fnl f* **6/1**[2]
610- 6 *nse* **Honest Strike (USA)**[210] 2570 6-9-6 **62**....(b) ShaneKelly 4 65+
(Daniel Mark Loughnane) *stdd s: hld up in last trio: rdn and hdwy on inner over 1f out: swtchd rt ins fnl f: no imp fnl 100yds* **20/1**
046- 7 *hd* **King's Request (IRE)**[14] 8159 3-9-1 **65**.... LiamJones 7 68
(Laura Mongan) *chsd ldrs: rdn and unable qck over 1f out: keeping on same pce whn jostling match w rival and hmpd ins fnl f* **16/1**
131- 8 *½* **Lacey**[9] 8223 4-9-1 **62** 6ex.... JackDuern(5) 3 64
(Andrew Hollinshead) *hld up in tch in midfield: hdwy 1/2-way: rdn and widish bnd 2f out: kpt on same pce and no imp fnl f* **5/1**[1]
/52- 9 *½* **Tokyo Brown (USA)**[11] 8204 4-9-0 **56**.... AndreaAtzeni 12 57
(Heather Main) *t.k.h: led over 14f out: rdn over 2f out: hdd and unable qck 1f out: keeping on same pce and hld whn short of room and hmpd ins fnl f* **10/1**
63- 10 *2* **Swift Blade (IRE)**[35] 7863 5-9-12 **68**.... RobertWinston 14 67
(Lady Herries) *t.k.h: hld up in tch in midfield: hdwy to chse ldr 10f out: rdn and ev ch over 2f out tl 1f out: wknd fnl 100yds* **8/1**[3]
042- 11 *1 ¼* **Sommersturm (GER)**[14] 8160 9-9-3 **59**.... AdamKirby 13 56
(David Evans) *stdd s: t.k.h: hld up in last trio: rdn and effrt wl over 1f out: kpt on: nvr trbld ldrs* **5/1**[1]
640- 12 *½* **Entitlement**[14] 8160 4-9-1 **57**.... HayleyTurner 10 54
(James Fanshawe) *stdd s: hld up in rr: nt clr run jst over 2f out: rdn and styd on same pce fr over 1f out: n.d* **20/1**
002- 13 *8* **Hazzaat (IRE)**[33] 7899 3-8-12 **62**.... JimmyQuinn 6 49
(Gary Harrison) *in tch in midfield: hdwy to chse ldrs 6f out: rdn and struggling over 2f out: wknd over 1f out* **12/1**

130- **14** *24* **Barachiel**[20] 8089 5-9-6 **62**........................ JimCrowley 8 20
(Luke Dace) *t.k.h: chsd ldr tl 10f out: lost pl and bhd over 2f out: eased wl over 1f out: t.o* **20/1**

3m 25.16s (-0.54) **Going Correction** -0.15s/f (Stan)
WFA 3 from 4yo+ 8lb **14** Ran SP% **124.0**
Speed ratings (Par 103): **95,94,94,93,93 93,93,92,92,91 90,90,86,74**
CSF £123.32 CT £2969.09 TOTE £12.40: £3.90, £4.70, £5.40; EX 140.70 Trifecta £1696.80 Part won. Pool: £2,262.51 - 0.18 winning units..
Owner Miss Caroline Scott **Bred** Patrick Eddery Ltd **Trained** West Wickham, Cambs
■ Stewards' Enquiry : Louis Steward one-day ban: failed to ride to draw (Jan 1)
Shane Kelly caution: careless riding.
Liam Jones caution: careless riding.

FOCUS
They went no pace early in this modest event, which probably didn't help the guaranteed stayers. A congested finish makes the bare form very ordinary.

8332 32RED.COM/BRITISH STALLION STUDS EBF MAIDEN FILLIES' STKS 7f (P)
1:00 (1:02) (Class 5) 2-Y-O **£3,067** (£905; £453) **Stalls** Low

Form RPR

1 **Betimes** 2-9-0 0........................ RobertHavlin 6 86+
(John Gosden) *wl in tch in midfield and a travelling wl: hdwy to ld wl over 1f out: shkn up and qcknd clr over 1f out: eased wl ins fnl f: impressive* **3/1**[2]

2 *4* **Outbacker (IRE)** 2-9-0 0........................ JoeFanning 14 71+
(Mark Johnston) *chsd ldrs: rdn and effrt wl over 1f out: kpt on to go 2nd fnl 100yds: no ch w wnr* **25/1**

3- **3** *1* **Passing By**[12] 8175 2-9-0 0........................ SeanLevey 2 69
(Richard Hannon Snr) *chsd ldrs: rdn and chsd wnr wl over 1f out: sn brushed aside by wnr and styd on same pce fnl f: lost 2nd fnl 100yds* **6/4**[1]

55- **4** *1 3/4* **Serena Grae**[86] 6690 2-9-0 0........................[1] MartinDwyer 5 64
(Marcus Tregoning) *hld up in midfield: rdn over 2f out: hdwy u.p over 1f out: styd on wl ins fnl f: no ch w wnr* **12/1**

443- **5** *1/2* **Ifrika**[25] 8018 2-9-0 71........................ LukeMorris 12 62
(Clive Brittain) *chsd ldrs on outer: rdn and hung rt bnd 2f out: no ch w wnr and kpt on same pce after* **6/1**[3]

6 *hd* **Joyful Friend** 2-9-0 0........................ NickyMackay 3 62
(John Gosden) *hld up in midfield: effrt on inner wl over 1f out: no ch w wnr kpt on same pce fnl f* **20/1**

7 *2 1/2* **Platinum Pearl** 2-9-0 0........................ AndreaAtzeni 11 55
(Peter Chapple-Hyam) *in tch in midfield on outer: effrt and pushed wdr bnd 2f out: n.d after: kpt on* **16/1**

6- **8** *1 3/4* **Arabian Music (IRE)**[20] 8083 2-9-0 0........................ MartinLane 4 50
(David Simcock) *in tch in midfield: rdn and outpcd ent fnl 2f: wknd over 1f out* **33/1**

9 *1/2* **Secret Pursuit (IRE)** 2-9-0 0........................ HayleyTurner 9 49
(Marcus Tregoning) *chsd ldr tl ent fnl 2f: sn lost pl and btn: wknd over 1f out* **20/1**

10 *nse* **Madame Mime Artist** 2-9-0 0........................ FergusSweeney 10 49
(Alastair Lidderdale) *s.i.s: hld up in last trio: rdn over 2f out: no prog wl over 1f out: n.d* **66/1**

0- **11** *1/2* **Borough Belle**[39] 7817 2-8-9 0........................ AmyScott(5) 7 48
(Henry Candy) *s.i.s: a towards rr: rdn over 2f out: no hdwy: n.d* **14/1**

00- **12** *2* **Bed Bed**[48] 7645 2-9-0 0........................ TomQueally 13 42
(Michael Bell) *s.i.s: a in rr: n.d* **100/1**

13 *3/4* **Up Hill Battle'S** 2-9-0 0........................ StephenCraine 8 40
(Daniel Mark Loughnane) *s.i.s: a in rr: n.d* **100/1**

026- **14** *nk* **Penara**[16] 8131 2-9-0 59........................(b[1]) TomEaves 1 39
(Philip Hide) *led tl 2f out: sn dropped: fdd over 1f out* **50/1**

1m 23.3s (-1.50) **Going Correction** -0.15s/f (Stan) **14** Ran SP% **121.3**
Speed ratings (Par 93): **102,97,96,94,93 93,90,88,88,88 87,85,84,83**
CSF £84.66 TOTE £6.10: £2.10, £4.40, £1.10; EX 118.00 Trifecta £276.40 Pool: £5,219.11 - 14.15 winning units..
Owner HRH Princess Haya Of Jordan **Bred** Whitsbury Manor Stud And Mrs M E Slade **Trained** Newmarket, Suffolk

FOCUS
Quite a strong maiden for the time of year and the winner was impressive and value for extra.

8333 32RED/EBF STALLIONS MAIDEN STKS (C&G) 7f (P)
1:30 (1:31) (Class 5) 2-Y-O **£3,067** (£905; £453) **Stalls** Low

Form RPR

1 **The Third Man** 2-9-0 0........................ RobertHavlin 11 75+
(John Gosden) *chsd ldrs: rdn to chse ldr over 1f out: r.o strly under hands and heels riding to ld wl ins fnl f: gng away at fin* **5/4**[1]

0- **2** *3/4* **Clear Spell (IRE)**[21] 8066 2-9-0 0........................ LukeMorris 1 71
(Ed Walker) *chsd ldr tl rdn and qcknd to ld 2f out: clr over 1f out: r.o u.p tl hdd and outpcd wl ins fnl f* **8/1**[3]

3 *4 1/2* **Bowie Boy (IRE)** 2-9-0 0........................ JimCrowley 7 59+
(Ralph Beckett) *hld up in midfield: swtchd lft and effrt wl over 1f out: styd on to go 3rd fnl 100yds: no ch w ldng pair* **10/1**

4 *1* **Here For Good (IRE)** 2-9-0 0........................ SeanLevey 3 56
(Richard Hannon Snr) *wl in tch in midfield: rdn and effrt ent fnl 2f: outpcd and no ch w ldng pair over 1f out: kpt on* **8/1**[3]

0- **5** *hd* **What A Dandy (IRE)**[205] 2723 2-9-0 0........................ StephenCraine 12 56+
(Jim Boyle) *t.k.h: stuck wd and chsd ldrs for 1f: stdd into midfield after: rdn and outpcd 2f out: n.d and one pce fnl f* **100/1**

00- **6** *1* **Mighty Force (IRE)**[63] 7308 2-8-7 0........................ JordanVaughan(7) 2 53
(Nick Littmoden) *led and set stdy gallop tl hdd 2f out: sn rdn and outpcd: wknd and lost 3rd fnl 100yds: fdd towards fin* **50/1**

7 *1 1/4* **Guaracha** 2-9-0 0........................ FrederikTylicki 9 50
(Clive Brittain) *in tch in midfield: rdn and outpcd ent fnl 2f: n.d and one pce fr over 1f out* **33/1**

8 *1 3/4* **Notebook** 2-9-0 0........................ LiamJones 8 45
(William Haggas) *hld up in last: trio: effrt but no hdwy on inner wl over 1f out: kpt on but n.d* **5/1**[2]

9 *hd* **Emperor Ferdinand (IRE)** 2-9-0 0........................ HayleyTurner 10 44
(Marcus Tregoning) *stdd s: hld up in last trio: rdn ent fnl f: kpt on same pce: n.d* **25/1**

10 *nk* **Shannon Haven (IRE)** 2-9-0 0........................ ShaneKelly 4 43
(Daniel Mark Loughnane) *hld up in midfield: swtchd rt and effrt 2f out: sn outpcd and wl btn over 1f out* **33/1**

11 *4* **Timeless War (USA)** 2-9-0 0........................ GrahamLee 5 33
(William Haggas) *chsd ldng trio: rdn over 2f out: sn struggling: wknd over 1f out* **8/1**[3]

12 *2* **Izbushka (IRE)** 2-9-0 0........................ StevieDonohoe 6 27
(Ian Williams) *sn outpcd in rr and rdn: n.d* **33/1**

1m 26.4s (1.60) **Going Correction** -0.15s/f (Stan) **12** Ran SP% **119.2**
Speed ratings (Par 96): **84,83,78,76,76 75,74,72,71,71 66,64**
CSF £11.21 TOTE £2.00: £1.40, £1.60, £3.00; EX 10.70 Trifecta £94.40 Pool: £4,743.72 - 37.67 winning units..
Owner Lady Rothschild **Bred** Kincorth Investments Inc **Trained** Newmarket, Suffolk

FOCUS
They didn't go a great pace here and the winning time was more than three seconds slower than the preceding fillies' event. The winner in particular should prove a lot better than this.

8334 COMPARE BOOKMAKERS AT BOOKMAKERS.CO.UK H'CAP 6f (P)
2:00 (2:02) (Class 2) 3-Y-O+ **£28,012** (£8,388; £4,194; £2,097; £1,048; £526) **Stalls** Low

Form RPR

555- **1** **Tarooq (USA)**[27] 7991 7-9-2 **99**........................ GrahamGibbons 4 110
(David Barron) *hld up towards rr: gd hdwy on inner over 1f out: rdn and qcknd to ld jst ins fnl f: r.o strly* **7/1**

024- **2** *1 1/2* **Hawkeyethenoo (IRE)**[32] 7928 7-9-5 **102**........................ GrahamLee 6 108
(Jim Goldie) *dwlt: sn bustled along towards rr: hdwy u.p over 1f out: r.o wl to go 2nd nr fin: no threat to wnr* **5/1**[3]

031- **3** *nk* **Lancelot Du Lac (ITY)**[21] 8064 3-9-6 **103**........................ JimCrowley 3 108
(Dean Ivory) *hld up in tch in midfield: rdn and effrt over 1f out: pressed wnr and drvn ins fnl f: no ex and wknd fnl 75yds: lost 2nd nr fin* **5/2**[1]

/05- **4** *1/2* **Alben Star (IRE)**[14] 8155 5-8-9 **92**........................ TonyHamilton 8 96
(Richard Fahey) *taken down early: hld up in tch in midfield: rdn and effrt wl over 1f out: styd on wl u.p fnl f: no threat to wnr* **10/1**

344- **5** *3/4* **Hoof It**[39] 7821 6-9-10 **107**........................ MartinHarley 1 108
(Michael Easterby) *chsd ldrs: swtchd rt and effrt over 1f out: drvn and unable qck 1f out: no ex and one pce ins fnl f* **4/1**[2]

111- **6** *nk* **Forest Edge (IRE)**[14] 8155 4-9-8 **105**........................(b) AdamKirby 5 105
(David Evans) *rrd as stalls opened and s.i.s: in rr: swtchd lft and hdwy 1f out: styd on same pce fnl 100yds* **7/1**

300- **7** *3 1/2* **Ballista (IRE)**[32] 7928 5-9-9 **106**........................ RichardKingscote 11 95
(Tom Dascombe) *hld up in tch in last quartet: shkn up 1f out: rdn and kpt on same pce ins fnl f: nvr trbld ldrs* **50/1**

012- **8** *1/2* **Equitania**[8] 8232 3-8-2 **90**........................ TimClark(5) 10 77
(Alan Bailey) *w ldr: ev ch and rdn 2f out: unable qckn over 1f out: wknd fnl f* **20/1**

512- **9** *hd* **Addictive Dream (IRE)**[14] 8155 6-9-3 **100**........................ JoeFanning 7 87
(David Nicholls) *led: rdn wl over 1f out: drvn and hdd jst ins fnl f: wknd fnl 150yds* **14/1**

200- **10** *3/4* **Ajjaadd (USA)**[14] 8155 7-8-9 **97**........................ EoinWalsh(5) 12 81
(Ted Powell) *stdd s: hld up in rr: effrt on outer bnd 2f out: no hdwy: n.d* **33/1**

051- **11** *4* **Shafaani**[72] 7080 3-8-9 **92**........................(bt) FrederikTylicki 2 64
(Clive Brittain) *chsd ldrs: rdn and effrt to press ldrs over 2f out: drvn and lost pl over 1f out: sn wknd* **25/1**

054- **12** *14* **Ubetterbegood (ARG)**[14] 8155 5-8-9 **92**........................ SeanLevey 9 19
(Robert Cowell) *in tch in midfield on outer: hung rt and lost pl bnd 2f out: sn lost tch and eased ins fnl f: t.o* **33/1**

1m 8.75s (-3.15) **Going Correction** -0.15s/f (Stan) course record **12** Ran SP% **122.4**
Speed ratings (Par 109): **115,113,112,111,110 110,105,105,104,103 98,79**
CSF £40.99 CT £114.87 TOTE £9.10: £2.90, £2.20, £1.10; EX 48.70 Trifecta £101.90 Pool: £5,071.33 - 37.30 winning units..
Owner EPL Investments **Bred** Kirsten Rausing **Trained** Maunby, N Yorks

FOCUS
This valuable sprint handicap was rescheduled to this meeting after fog had caused racing to be abandoned after just two contests here seven days earlier. With so many who normally like to force it in opposition, a strong pace was a certainty and they knocked 0.67sec off the course record. Those who raced up with, or close to, the sizzling early tempo, most notably Addictive Dream, Equitania and Shafaani, understandably paid for it later on. Strong form, the winner stepping up on last winter's progress.

8335 CORAL APP DOWNLOAD FROM THE APP STORE CLASSIFIED (S) STKS 1m 2f (P)
2:35 (2:35) (Class 6) 3-Y-O+ **£2,045** (£603; £302) **Stalls** Low

Form RPR

304- **1** **Copperwood**[7] 8244 8-9-9 67........................ AmirQuinn 4 67
(Lee Carter) *t.k.h: hld up in tch towards rr: swtchd rt and effrt over 1f out: r.o wl to ld towards fin* **16/1**

122- **2** *1/2* **Honey Of A Kitten (USA)**[2] 8308 5-9-9 70........................(v) AdamKirby 10 66
(David Evans) *chsd ldr tl rdn to ld over 2f out: hrd drvn and kpt on fr over 1f out: hdd and no ex towards fin* **6/4**[1]

030- **3** *3/4* **Herbalist**[16] 8129 3-9-0 60........................(b) JohnFahy 6 59
(Ben Pauling) *led for 2f: styd chsng ldrs: rdn 2f out: pressing ldrs fnl 100yds: styd on same pce after* **33/1**

006- **4** *shd* **Tartan Gigha (IRE)**[21] 8059 8-9-3 70........................(b) GrahamLee 2 58
(Geoffrey Harker) *in tch in midfield: rdn and effrt to chse ldr jst over 2f out: unable qck and one pce ins fnl f* **4/1**[2]

530- **5** *1/2* **Conducting**[61] 7346 5-9-4 68........................ ShelleyBirkett(5) 1 63
(Gay Kelleway) *in tch in midfield: rdn and effrt 2f out: chsng ldrs and nt clr run ins fnl f: kpt on* **8/1**

603- **6** *1/2* **Abigails Angel**[7] 8244 6-9-3 67........................ TomQueally 9 56
(Brett Johnson) *s.i.s and rdn along: effrt u.p and wd bnd 2f out: kpt on u.p fnl f* **6/1**[3]

/60- **7** *1* **Zenarinda**[57] 7453 6-9-3 68........................ JoeFanning 5 54
(Mark H Tompkins) *in tch in midfield on outer: rdn and effrt over 2f out: outpcd and btn over 1f out: styd on same pce fnl f* **10/1**

005- **8** *1 1/4* **Dolly Colman (IRE)**[129] 5311 5-9-0 44........................(p) RossAtkinson(3) 3 52
(Zoe Davison) *chsd ldrs: rdn and effrt ent fnl 2f: outpcd and btn over 1f out: wknd fnl f* **66/1**

540- **9** *1 1/2* **Gabrial's Hope (FR)**[9] 8226 4-9-9 67........................(t) MartinHarley 7 55
(David Simcock) *s.i.s: rdn and rcvrd to ld after 2f: rdn and hdd over 2f out: sn struggling: wknd over 1f out* **10/1**

0/0- **10** *79* **Tuxedo**[35] 7857 8-9-3 55........................(b) ChrisCatlin 11
(Peter Hiatt) *stuck wd first bnd: dropped to last pair and niggled along 8f out: lost tch 4f out: t.o and eased fnl 2f* **25/1**

2m 4.82s (-1.78) **Going Correction** -0.15s/f (Stan)
WFA 3 from 4yo+ 3lb **10** Ran SP% **117.7**
Speed ratings (Par 101): **101,100,100,99,99 99,98,97,96,32**
Tote Swingers: 1&2 £6.40, 1&3 £49.10, 2&3 £16.90 CSF £40.44 TOTE £26.00: £5.00, £1.20, £7.80; EX 62.10 Trifecta £2602.30 Part won. Pool: £3,469.79 - 0.73 winning units..No bid for the winner.
Owner Miss Victoria Baalham **Bred** Hertford Offset Press **Trained** Epsom, Surrey

FOCUS
They didn't go much of a pace in this moderate seller and the front six finished in a heap. Muddling form, limited by the sixth and the eighth.

8336 CORAL MOBILE "JUST THREE CLICKS TO BET" H'CAP 1m 2f (P)
3:10 (3:11) (Class 4) (0-85,82) 3-Y-O+ **£4,690** (£1,395; £697; £348) **Stalls** Low

Form RPR
503- **1** **Rakaan (IRE)**[184] 3416 6-9-5 **80** .... FergusSweeney 9 88
(Jamie Osborne) *s.i.s: hld up in rr: rdn and hdwy ent fnl f: str run to ld cl home* **16/1**
306- **2** *nk* **Silver Dixie (USA)**[28] 7976 3-9-2 **80** .... GrahamLee 11 87
(Peter Hedger) *t.k.h: chsd ldr for 2f: wnt 2nd again 4f out: drvn to ld 1f out: kpt on wl tl hdd and no ex cl home* **5/1**[3]
425- **3** *nk* **Ishikawa (IRE)**[18] 8117 5-9-4 **79** .... MartinHarley 7 84
(K R Burke) *hld up in tch in midfield: rdn and effrt to chse ldrs wl over 1f out: styd on same pce ins fnl f: fin 4th: plcd 3rd* **3/1**[1]
261- **4** *nk* **Oratorio's Joy (IRE)**[15] 8136 3-8-6 **77** .... RobHornby(7) 8 82
(Jamie Osborne) *in tch in midfield: rdn and effrt to chse ldrs 1f out: kpt on same pce ins fnl f: fin 5th: plcd 4th* **8/1**
020- **5** *½* **Scottish Star**[28] 7976 5-8-11 **79** .... LouisSteward(7) 5 83
(James Eustace) *in tch in last trio: rdn and effrt over 1f out: kpt on u.p ins fnl f: nt rch ldrs: fin 6th: plcd 5th* **9/2**[2]
250- **6** *nse* **Nimiety**[28] 7976 4-9-2 **77** .... JoeFanning 2 81
(Mark Johnston) *chsd ldrs: wnt 2nd 8f out tl led 7f out: rdn ent fnl 2f: hdd 1f out and sn edgd rt u.p: outpcd fnl 100yds: fin 7th: plcd 6th* **7/1**
/06- **7** *1* **Miss Blakeney**[14] 8150 4-9-3 **78** ....(v) MartinDwyer 3 80
(Marcus Tregoning) *in tch in midfield: shuffled bk to rr but stl in tch 3f out: rdn and hdwy on inner over 1f out: no ex ins fnl f: wknd towards fin: fin 8th: plcd 7th* **16/1**
006- **8** *4 ½* **Timothy T**[33] 7898 5-8-7 **68** oh1 .... TomEaves 1 61
(Philip Hide) *rdn along leaving stalls: sn led: hdd 8f out: chsd ldr tl 4f out: rdn and unable qck over 1f out: wknd ins fnl f: fin 9th: plcd 8th* **25/1**
361- **D** *1 ¼* **Syncopate**[12] 8179 4-8-9 **73** .... RossAtkinson(3) 6 78
(Pam Sly) *short of room so s: racd in last trio: rdn and effrt 2f out: styd on u.p ins fnl f: nt rch ldrs: fin 3rd: disqualified: rdr failed to weigh-in* **5/1**[3]

2m 4.59s (-2.01) **Going Correction** -0.15s/f (Stan)
WFA 3 from 4yo+ 3lb 9 Ran SP% **115.7**
Speed ratings (Par 105): **102,101,100,100,99 99,99,95,100**
CSF £94.15 CT £311.48 TOTE £15.50: £5.30, £2.40; EX 145.30 Trifecta £582.00 Pool: £3,478.85 - 4.48 winning units..
Owner Leslie Marshall **Bred** L Mulryan & M Fahy **Trained** Upper Lambourn, Berks
■ Stewards' Enquiry : Ross Atkinson seven-day ban: failed to weigh in (Jan 1-7)

FOCUS
A good handicap, but the pace was ordinary and is developed into a bit of a sprint. The time was only 0.23sec quicker than the seller. A bunch finish, but the form is taken at something like face value.

8337 CORAL.CO.UK BEST ODDS GUARANTEED ON RACING APPRENTICE H'CAP 1m 4f (P)
3:40 (3:41) (Class 5) (0-70,70) 3-Y-O+ **£2,726** (£805; £402) **Stalls** Low

Form RPR
023- **1** **Echo Brava**[14] 8159 3-9-3 **66** .... RossAtkinson 8 74
(Luke Dace) *hld up towards rr: hdwy to chse ldrs ent fnl 2f: rdn and chal ins fnl f: led fnl 50yds: r.o wl* **7/1**
005- **2** *1 ¼* **Special Mix**[21] 8072 5-9-0 **65** .... BradleyBosley(7) 3 71
(Martin Smith) *short of room leaving stalls: in tch in midfield: chsd ldrs 5f out: rdn to chse ldr over 2f out: ev ch fnl 100yds: kpt on same pce fnl 50yds* **25/1**
221- **3** *nk* **Keene**[13] 8162 3-8-12 **66** .... LouisSteward(5) 4 72
(Philip McBride) *chsd ldr tl led 3f out: drvn over 1f out: hdd fnl 50yds: no ex* **3/1**[1]
532- **4** *6* **Royal Marskell**[28] 7984 4-9-2 **65** .... TimClark(5) 1 61
(K F Clutterbuck) *t.k.h: led tl hdd and rdn 3f out: outpcd and btn over 1f out: wknd ins fnl f* **8/1**
463- **5** *¾* **Celtic Charlie (FR)**[14] 8149 8-8-5 **56** oh3 ....(t) SophieRalston(7) 6 51
(Pat Phelan) *hld up in detached last: rdn and effrt wl over 1f out: kpt on ins fnl f: nvr trbld ldrs* **12/1**
024- **6** *2 ¼* **Mcbirney (USA)**[35] 7865 6-9-7 **68** .... ShelleyBirkett(3) 7 59
(Paul D'Arcy) *hld up in tch towards rr: clsd and n.m.r ent fnl 2f: rdn and no hdwy over 1f out: wknd fnl f* **9/2**[3]
432- **7** *½* **Mick Duggan**[18] 8115 3-9-7 **70** ....(p) RobertTart 2 60
(Simon Hodgson) *chsd ldrs tl lost pl 4f out: rdn and wknd ent fnl 2f* **7/2**[2]
636- **8** *2 ½* **Cabuchon (GER)**[16] 8129 6-8-7 **56** .... EoinWalsh(5) 5 42
(David Evans) *chsd ldrs: rdn and struggling ent fnl 2f: wknd qckly over 1f out* **7/1**

2m 29.77s (-3.23) **Going Correction** -0.15s/f (Stan)
WFA 3 from 4yo+ 5lb 8 Ran SP% **113.1**
Speed ratings (Par 103): **104,103,102,98,98 96,96,94**
CSF £149.70 CT £631.58 TOTE £8.20: £3.10, £7.00, £1.40; EX 153.60 Trifecta £759.50 Pool: £5,034.16 - 4.97 winning units..
Owner Mark Benton **Bred** Adweb Ltd **Trained** Five Oaks, W Sussex
■ Stewards' Enquiry : Sophie Ralston ten-day ban: failed to take all reasonable and permissable measures to obtain best possible placing (Jan 1-10)

FOCUS
They only went an ordinary pace in this modest apprentice handicap. The winner had one turf run that could be rated a bit better.
T/Jkpt: Not won. T/Plt: £115.10 to a £1 stake. Pool: £66,314.17 - 420.51 winning tickets. T/Qpdt: £3.90 to a £1 stake. Pool: £7,390.35 - 1,396.43 winning tickets. SP

8322 KEMPTON (A.W) (R-H)
Thursday, December 19

OFFICIAL GOING: Standard
Wind: Moderate across Weather: wet

8338 COME RACING ON BOXING DAY H'CAP 6f (P)
4:00 (4:00) (Class 7) (0-50,55) 3-Y-O+ **£1,617** (£481; £240; £120) **Stalls** Low

Form RPR
041- **1** **Foie Gras**[7] 8258 3-9-3 **55** 6ex .... ShelleyBirkett(5) 3 66
(Chris Dwyer) *in tch: hdwy over 2f out: led wl over 1f out: hrd pressed fnl f: hld on wl in clsng stages* **7/4**[1]
322- **2** *hd* **Major Muscari (IRE)**[6] 8271 5-9-2 **49** ....(p) JimmyQuinn 12 59
(Shaun Harris) *s.i.s: in rr: hdwy 2f out: chsd wnr 1f out: str chal in clsng stages but a jst hld* **8/1**
242- **3** *4* **Mid Yorkshire Golf**[6] 8277 4-8-13 **49** .... SladeO'Hara(3) 5 46
(Peter Grayson) *in rr: drvn and hdwy appr fnl f: styd on to take 3rd last stride but no ch w ldng duo* **7/1**[3]
500- **4** *nse* **Sherjawy (IRE)**[187] 3325 9-9-0 **50** .... RossAtkinson(3) 2 47
(Zoe Davison) *chsd ldrs: styd on for one pce 3rd ins fnl f: dropped to 4th last strides* **20/1**
560- **5** *2* **Sally Bruce**[63] 7323 3-8-10 **50** ....(b[1]) JenniferFerguson(7) 4 41
(Edward Creighton) *chsd ldrs: rdn over 2f out: wknd fnl f* **11/1**
000- **5** *dht* **Kasbhom**[34] 7904 3-9-3 **50** ....(t) WilliamCarson 7 41
(Anthony Carson) *stdd s: in rr: styd on fnl f: nt rch ldrs* **3/1**[2]
000- **7** *1 ¼* **Wyatt Earp (IRE)**[14] 8168 12-9-3 **50** ....(p) MartinHarley 10 37
(Richard Guest) *sn led: hdd wl over 1f out: sn btn* **20/1**
34- **8** *1* **Stoneacre Hull (IRE)**[31] 7946 4-9-3 **50** .... StephenCraine 6 33
(Peter Grayson) *outpcd* **20/1**
220- **9** *5* **Madame Kintyre**[30] 7957 5-8-10 **50** .... PatMillman(7) 11 17
(Rod Millman) *chsd ldrs over 3f* **10/1**

1m 12.43s (-0.67) **Going Correction** +0.025s/f (Slow) 9 Ran SP% **116.7**
Speed ratings (Par 97): **105,104,99,99,96 96,95,93,87**
toteswingers 1&2 £3.60, 2&3 £3.00, 1&3 £3.60 CSF £16.22 CT £77.50 TOTE £3.00: £1.10, £2.10, £2.10; EX 15.80 Trifecta £54.90 Pool: £1732.09 - 23.63 winning units..
Owner Mrs Shelley Dwyer **Bred** Sir Eric Parker **Trained** Newmarket, Suffolk

FOCUS
A weak but competitive handicap, and unconvincing form. The front two pulled clear and it would be taking a leap of faith to think the remainder of the field are capable of winning any time soon.

8339 CONSTANTINE, ENA FETTEL & LINDA EMERY MEMORIAL CLAIMING STKS 1m (P)
4:30 (4:30) (Class 6) 3-Y-O **£1,940** (£577; £288; £144) **Stalls** Low

Form RPR
205- **1** **Wakeup Little Suzy (IRE)**[26] 8020 3-8-8 74 ....(t) MartinHarley 3 72+
(Marco Botti) *broke wl: stdd in tch: hdwy to ld appr fnl f: hrd drvn sn after: styd on wl in clsng stages* **7/4**[1]
340- **2** *nk* **Gabrial The Boss (USA)**[54] 7544 3-8-8 70 ....(t) RichardKingscote 2 71
(David Simcock) *hld up in rr: hdwy and rdn fr 2f out to chal 1f out: styd on wl fnl f but nt gng pce of wnr in clsng stages* **8/1**
044- **3** *¾* **Ocean Applause**[16] 8136 3-9-1 70 ....(t) AdamKirby 8 76
(John Ryan) *chsd ldr: chal fr ins fnl 2f tl appr fnl f: styd on same pce fnl 120yds* **7/2**[2]
040- **4** *nk* **Swift Cedar (IRE)**[28] 7988 3-8-12 78 .... RobertTart(3) 5 76
(Alan Jarvis) *hld up in rr: hdwy over 1f out: styd on wl in clsng stages: nt rch ldrs* **4/1**[3]
212- **5** *½* **Exclusive Waters (IRE)**[60] 6612 3-9-1 70 ....(b[1]) FergusSweeney 1 74
(Gary Moore) *chsd ldrs: rdn and slt ld ins fnl 2f: hdd over 1f out: styd on same pce* **9/2**
205- **6** *5* **Not Rigg (USA)**[13] 8187 3-8-10 65 ....(t) JimmyQuinn 4 58
(Gary Harrison) *sn led: narrowly hdd ins fnl 2f: wknd fnl f* **14/1**
560- **7** *12* **East Texas Red (IRE)**[51] 7610 3-8-4 41 .... ShelleyBirkett(5) 7 29
(Mick Quinn) *in rr: sme hdwy 3f out: sn wknd* **100/1**
606- **8** *nse* **Gold Weight**[58] 7443 3-8-4 46 ....(v[1]) PhilipPrince(5) 6 29
(Michael Madgwick) *t.k.h: chsd ldrs over 5f* **100/1**

1m 40.3s (0.50) **Going Correction** +0.025s/f (Slow) 8 Ran SP% **116.5**
Speed ratings (Par 98): **98,97,96,96,96 91,79,79**
toteswingers 1&2 £4.60, 2&3 £5.50, 1&3 £2.00 CSF £17.66 TOTE £2.20: £1.10, £3.70, £1.90; EX 17.50 Trifecta £60.10 Pool: £5376.54 - 67.01 winning units..Swift Cedar was claimed by J. R. Gask for £12000.
Owner Philip Newton **Bred** Philip Newton **Trained** Newmarket, Suffolk

FOCUS
There was a blanket finish to what on paper looked a tight-knit claimer. Muddling form, limited by the third.

8340 KEMPTON.CO.UK MAIDEN STKS 1m (P)
5:00 (5:01) (Class 5) 2-Y-O **£2,587** (£770; £384; £192) **Stalls** Low

Form RPR
22- **1** **Billy Blue (IRE)**[22] 8066 2-9-5 0 .... RobertHavlin 1 75
(John Gosden) *chsd ldr 4f and again 2f out: sn drvn and hd to one side: led 1f out: kpt on and a doing enough fnl 50yds* **5/2**[1]
4- **2** *½* **Damascene**[17] 8124 2-9-5 0 .... MartinHarley 5 74
(Marco Botti) *chsd ldrs: wnt 2nd 4f out: rdn and cl 3rd 2f out: styd on u.p fnl f to press wnr but a jst hld fnl 50yds* **7/2**[2]
3 *nk* **Anglo Irish** 2-9-5 0 .... NickyMackay 6 73+
(John Gosden) *chsd ldrs: drvn 2f out: styd on wl fnl f but nvr quite gng pce of ldng duo in clsng stages* **12/1**
33- **4** *½* **Al Busayyir (IRE)**[33] 7936 2-9-5 0 .... LukeMorris 3 72
(Marco Botti) *led: rdn over 2f out: hdd 1f out: styd on fnl f: outpcd fnl 100yds* **4/1**[3]
5 *3 ½* **Raging Bob (IRE)** 2-9-5 0 .... RichardKingscote 8 64+
(Ralph Beckett) *s.i.s: sn mid-div: hdwy over 1f out: kpt on fnl f: nt trble ldrs* **8/1**
6 *1 ½* **Galuppi** 2-9-5 0 .... AdamKirby 10 61+
(Luca Cumani) *towards rr: [pushed along over 2f out: styd on fnl f: gng on in clsng stages* **10/1**
7 *nk* **Witch From Rome** 2-8-12 0 .... PatrickO'Donnell(7) 7 60
(Ralph Beckett) *chsd ldrs: outpcd fnl f* **40/1**
0- **8** *hd* **Next Stop**[43] 7764 2-8-11 0 .... MarkCoumbe(3) 4 54
(Lee Carter) *broke wl: stdd in mid-div: kpt on fr over 1f out: nvr a threat* **50/1**
9 *½* **Rosarina** 2-9-0 0 .... FergusSweeney 9 53
(Jo Crowley) *s.i.s: in rr: styd on fr over 1f out* **50/1**
0- **10** *¾* **Fractal**[38] 7835 2-9-5 0 .... MartinLane 11 56
(David Simcock) *s.i.s: styd on fr over 1f out* **25/1**
0- **11** *1 ¾* **Attenzione (IRE)**[62] 7335 2-9-5 0 ....(t) PaoloSirigu 12 52
(Marco Botti) *chsd ldrs: rdn 3f out: wknd 2f out* **20/1**
0- **12** *nse* **Hoist The Colours (IRE)**[17] 8124 2-9-5 0 .... TomQueally 2 52
(David Lanigan) *s.i.s: in rr: mod late prog* **16/1**
0- **13** *¾* **Kirkman (IRE)**[29] 7971 2-9-5 0 .... JimmyQuinn 13 51
(James Bethell) *a in rr* **66/1**
00- **14** *8* **Desert Island Dusk**[36] 7859 2-9-5 0 .... KieranO'Neill 14 32
(John Bridger) *sn bhd* **100/1**

1m 40.42s (0.62) **Going Correction** +0.025s/f (Slow) 14 Ran SP% **122.0**
Speed ratings (Par 96): **97,96,96,95,92 90,90,90,89,88 87,87,86,78**
CSF £10.45 TOTE £3.60: £1.80, £1.50, £4.90; EX 12.20 Trifecta £69.50 Pool: £3810.82 - 41.06 winning units..
Owner R Van Gelder **Bred** Kabansk Ltd & Rathbarry Stud **Trained** Newmarket, Suffolk

The Form Book Flat, Raceform Ltd, Compton, RG20 6NL.

FOCUS
A couple brought fair form into this maiden. The winner found a little on his Lingfield efforts.

8341 BETVICTOR NON-RUNNER FREE BET CHELTENHAM 2014 H'CAP 1m (P)
5:30 (5:30) (Class 6) (0-55,55) 3-Y-O+ **£1,940** (£577; £288; £144) **Stalls** Low

Form RPR
040- **1** **Spirit Of Gondree (IRE)**[145] 4755 5-9-3 **55**....................(b) AdamKirby 7 65
(Milton Bradley) *stdd s: hld up in rr: gng wl whn nt much daylight fr 2f out: drvn and qcknd over 1f out: str run fnl f to ld fnl 25yds: readily* **7/1**[3]
042- **2** 1 **Up Tipp**[44] 7740 3-9-2 **55**.. AndreaAtzeni 2 62+
(Mike Murphy) *chsd ldrs: led ins fnl 2f: hdd over 1f out: rallied ins fnl f to take 2nd last strides but no ch w wnr* **15/8**[1]
600- **3** shd **Safwaan**[17] 8125 6-9-3 **55**.. MartinHarley 11 62
(Michael Squance) *s.i.s: in rr: hdwy on ins over 2f out: led over 1f out: hdd and nt pce of wnr fnl 25yds: dropped to 3rd last stride* **20/1**
300- **4** 1/2 **Cabal**[82] 6851 6-9-3 **55**..(b) SeanLevey 5 61
(Andrew Crook) *s.i.s: in rr: hdwy over 2f out: styd on u.p fnl f: kpt on in clsng stages* **25/1**
241- **5** 2 1/2 **Litmus (USA)**[16] 8142 4-9-2 **54**......................................(b) LukeMorris 13 55
(Simon Dow) *chsd ldrs: rdn over 2f out: styd on fnl f* **10/1**
333- **6** 2 1/4 **Gypsy Rider**[22] 8073 4-8-10 **55**.. NedCurtis(7) 3 50+
(Roger Curtis) *mid-div: pushed along 2f out: kpt on in clsng stages: nvr a threat* **12/1**
103- **7** 1 3/4 **Kindlelight Storm (USA)**[30] 7966 3-9-2 **55**.................... RobertHavlin 6 45
(Nick Littmoden) *in rr: pushed along over 2f out: styd on ins fnl f* **7/2**[2]
000- **8** 1/2 **Striker Torres (IRE)**[181] 3543 7-9-3 **55**.....................(v) StephenCraine 1 45
(Daniel Mark Loughnane) *chsd ldrs: rdn 2f out: wknd appr fnl f* **16/1**
000- **9** nk **Moortahan**[22] 8073 3-9-2 **55**.. KieranO'Neill 9 44
(Richard Hannon Snr) *led: hdd over 4f out: led ins fnl 3f: hdd ins fnl 2f: wknd over 1f out* **20/1**
400- **10** 3/4 **Bestfootforward**[22] 8073 4-8-11 **54**........................... ShelleyBirkett(5) 14 42
(Julia Feilden) *led over 4f out: hdd ins fnl 3f: wknd ins fnl 2f* **25/1**
020- **11** hd **Viking Warrior (IRE)**[23] 8042 6-9-3 **55**.......................... JimmyQuinn 4 42
(Shaun Harris) *chsd ldrs: wknd ins fnl 2f* **33/1**
500- **12** 27 **Bint Alzain (IRE)**[17] 8121 4-9-3 **55**............................ FergusSweeney 12
(Pat Phelan) *t.k.h: chsd ldrs tl wknd wl over 2f out* **20/1**
050- **P** **Substantivo (IRE)**[96] 6400 3-8-13 **55**.............................. RobertTart(3) 8
(Alan Jarvis) *stmbld after 2f: wknd and p.u bnd 3f out* **16/1**

1m 39.1s (-0.70) **Going Correction** +0.025s/f (Slow)
WFA 3 from 4yo+ 1lb 13 Ran SP% **123.0**
Speed ratings (Par 101): **104,103,102,102,99 97,95,95,95,94 94,67,**
toteswingers 1&2 £3.70, 2&3 £10.20, 1&3 £17.80 CSF £18.88 CT £276.04 TOTE £10.80: £3.10, £1.10, £7.80; EX 26.90 Trifecta £690.20 Pool: £2822.37 - 3.06 winning units..
Owner Paul & Ann de Weck & Partner **Bred** Windflower Overseas Holdings Inc **Trained** Sedbury, Gloucs
■ Stewards' Enquiry : Andrea Atzeni caution: careless riding.
FOCUS
A competitive albeit low-grade handicap. Routine form, with the first two from the rear.

8342 CHELTENHAM 2014 NRFB AT BETVICTOR.COM MEDIAN AUCTION MAIDEN STKS 7f (P)
6:00 (6:01) (Class 5) 2-Y-O **£2,587** (£770; £384; £192) **Stalls** Low

Form RPR
4- **1** **Reimpose (USA)**[176] 3673 2-9-0 0.. AdamKirby 1 70
(Pat Eddery) *mde all: rdn over 2f out: styd on strly thrght fnl f* **12/1**
000- **2** 1 3/4 **Stan Nineteen (IRE)**[34] 7893 2-9-5 0.............................. RobertHavlin 5 70
(George Baker) *sn chsng wnr: one pce u.p into 3rd over 1f out: styd on u.p fnl f to retake 2nd last strides but no ch w wnr* **8/1**[3]
3 nk **Normanna (IRE)** 2-9-0 0... MartinHarley 3 64+
(Marco Botti) *chsd ldrs: rdn to chse wnr over 1f out: no imp fnl f: dropped to 3rd last strides* **2/1**[1]
4 1 3/4 **Why Not Now** 2-9-0 0.. MartinLane 8 59+
(Roger Charlton) *in rr: hdwy over 2f out: styd on fnl f* **16/1**
32- **5** shd **Cincuenta Pasos (IRE)**[36] 7852 2-9-5 0............................ LiamKeniry 13 64
(Joseph Tuite) *in rr: swtchd lft wl over 1f: styd on wl fnl f: kpt on in clsng stages* **9/2**[2]
6 shd **Speechday (IRE)** 2-9-0 0... AndreaAtzeni 6 59
(Marco Botti) *in rr: hdwy over 2f out: styd on same pce fnl f* **16/1**
000- **7** 1/2 **Henry Grace (IRE)**[43] 7766 2-9-5 0................................ KieranO'Neill 2 63
(Jimmy Fox) *chsd ldrs: pushed along over 2f out: kpt on same pce fr over 1f out* **100/1**
0- **8** 1 1/2 **Stapleford Lad**[48] 7655 2-9-5 0.. KierenFox 12 59
(Stuart Williams) *t.k.h towards rr: racd on outside: styd on fnl f* **33/1**
9 3 1/2 **Pactolus (IRE)** 2-9-5 0.. AdamBeschizza 7 49
(Stuart Williams) *t.k.h: hld up towards rr: n.m.r and shkn up over 2f out: pushed along and no further prog* **2/1**[1]
60- **10** 1 1/4 **Alba Verde**[6] 8266 2-9-0 0.. LukeMorris 4 41
(Sir Mark Prescott Bt) *in rr: rdn over 2f out: one pce* **66/1**
- **11** hd **Dansante** 2-9-0 0.. SeanLevey 14 40
(Richard Hannon Snr) *stdd s and swtchd rt: rdn and n.m.r over 2f out: no ch after* **8/1**[3]
12 1 1/4 **Appellez Baileys (FR)** 2-9-5 0.. HayleyTurner 9 42
(Chris Dwyer) *chsd ldrs tl wknd fr 2f out* **40/1**
0- **13** 2 **Beastfromtheeast**[22] 8061 2-9-5 0.................................. GeorgeBaker 10 36
(Ed Walker) *hdwy to chse ldrs 4f out: wknd over 2f out* **50/1**

1m 28.95s (2.95) **Going Correction** +0.025s/f (Slow) 13 Ran SP% **136.4**
Speed ratings (Par 96): **84,82,81,79,79 79,78,77,73,71 71,70,67**
CSF £117.43 TOTE £15.30: £3.70, £2.90, £1.20; EX 165.50 Trifecta £2161.10 Pool: £3570.49 - 1.23 winning units..
Owner K Abdullah **Bred** Juddmonte Farms Inc **Trained** Nether Winchendon, Bucks
FOCUS
A median auction maiden for 2yos that lacked strength in depth. The field finished very compressed off a slow pace set by the winner.

8343 BACK OF THE NET AT BETVICTOR.COM FILLIES' H'CAP 1m 4f (P)
6:30 (6:30) (Class 5) (0-75,73) 3-Y-O+ **£2,587** (£770; £384; £192) **Stalls** Low

Form RPR
601- **1** **Asia Minor (IRE)**[50] 7628 4-9-4 **67**....................................(t) MartinLane 8 77+
(Dr Jon Scargill) *stdd s: hld up in rr: hdwy on outside fr 2f out: str run u.p to take slt ld fnl 120yds: kpt on wl* **3/1**[2]
562- **2** 1/2 **Persian Patriot**[22] 8072 3-8-9 **63**...................................... RobertHavlin 4 72
(William Jarvis) *chsd ldrs: led and edgd lft u.p fr over 1f out: hdd and one pce fnl 120yds* **5/1**[3]
256- **3** 3 1/4 **Where's Susie**[21] 8089 8-9-4 **67**.. GeorgeBaker 3 71
(Michael Madgwick) *led: rdn over 2f out: hdd over 1f out and sn pushed lft: wl hld whn eased last strides* **7/1**
006- **4** nk **Martinas Delight (USA)**[22] 8060 3-8-12 **69**..................... RobertTart(3) 2 72
(Alan Jarvis) *hld up in rr: hdwy 2f out: styd on to cl on 3rd in clsng stages but no ch w ldng duo* **12/1**
513- **5** 1 1/4 **Atalanta Bay (IRE)**[34] 7899 3-8-12 **66**............................ HayleyTurner 1 67
(Marcus Tregoning) *t.k.h: chsd ldrs: rdn and one pce whn n.m.r over 1f out: wknd ins fnl f* **5/2**[1]
130- **6** 3 3/4 **Dazzling Valentine**[119] 5672 5-9-0 **68**....................... NatashaEaton(5) 9 63
(Alan Bailey) *in rr: pushed along and no prog fr over 2f out* **25/1**
000- **7** 1/2 **The Blue Dog (IRE)**[15] 8159 6-9-2 **65**.......................... WilliamCarson 7 60
(Phil McEntee) *chsd ldr: rdn over 2f out: sn btn* **25/1**
521- **8** 16 **Coconell**[20] 8092 3-9-5 **73**.. ShaneKelly 5 42
(Jeremy Noseda) *in rr: hdwy to chse ldr 6f out: shkn up 4f out: wknd ins fnl 3f* **6/1**

2m 32.76s (-1.74) **Going Correction** +0.025s/f (Slow)
WFA 3 from 4yo+ 5lb 8 Ran SP% **112.4**
Speed ratings (Par 100): **106,105,103,103,102 99,99,88**
toteswingers 1&2 £6.20, 2&3 £8.10, 1&3 £4.60 CSF £17.75 CT £93.63 TOTE £3.60: £1.40, £2.20, £2.60; EX 20.90 Trifecta £159.80 Pool: £3008.32 - 14.11 winning units..
Owner Strawberry Fields Stud **Bred** Darley **Trained** Newmarket, Suffolk
FOCUS
Plenty came into this fillies' handicap at the top of their game and the pace was solid. The first two are on the up.

8344 DOWNLOAD THE BETVICTOR APP NOW CONDITIONS STKS 7f (P)
7:00 (7:00) (Class 2) 3-Y-O+
£11,827 (£3,541; £1,770; £885; £442; £222) **Stalls** Low

Form RPR
616- **1** **Mont Ras (IRE)**[82] 6834 6-9-4 103.. DavidNolan 5 104
(David O'Meara) *led 1f: chsng ldrs whn n.m.r: rdn and lost position over 4f out: rdn over 3f out: styd on u.p fr 2f out to ld fnl 100yds: hld on wl* **9/2**[2]
331- **2** 1/2 **Grey Mirage**[36] 7856 4-9-4 96.. MartinHarley 8 103
(Marco Botti) *chsd ldr after 2f: led over 2f out and sn rdn: hdd fnl 100yds: kpt on same pce* **4/6**[1]
261- **3** 3 **Verse Of Love**[7] 8264 4-9-4 86.. AdamKirby 4 95
(David Evans) *drvn to ld after 1f: rdn and hdd over 2f out: wknd fnl 120yds* **12/1**
603- **4** 1 1/4 **Bravo Echo**[7] 8264 7-9-4 93.. RobertHavlin 7 92
(Michael Attwater) *chsd ldrs: rdn over 2f out: styd on same pce* **14/1**
605- **5** shd **Captain Kendall (IRE)**[22] 8069 4-9-4 70............................ LukeMorris 9 91?
(Harry Chisman) *in rr: drvn and hdwy ins fnl 2f: styd on same pce appr fnl f* **100/1**
532- **6** 6 **Corporal Maddox**[17] 8127 6-9-4 86..........................(be[1]) GeorgeBaker 3 75
(Ronald Harris) *in rr: hdwy on ins over 2f out: sn hung bdly rt on to rail and no ch after* **8/1**[3]
050- **7** 1/2 **Tiddliwinks**[22] 8064 7-9-4 97.. TomQueally 1 74
(Kevin Ryan) *chsd ldrs: rdn over 2f out: wknd u.p over 1f out* **10/1**
360- **8** 2 **Capone (IRE)**[285] 944 8-9-4 97.. ShaneKelly 2 68
(Michael Attwater) *s.i.s: a towards rr* **25/1**

1m 25.19s (-0.81) **Going Correction** +0.025s/f (Slow) 8 Ran SP% **117.6**
Speed ratings (Par 109): **105,104,101,99,99 92,92,89**
toteswingers 1&2 £1.20, 2&3 £3.60, 1&3 £9.10 CSF £8.08 TOTE £7.00: £1.70, £1.02, £2.90; EX 11.20 Trifecta £59.30 Pool: £3707.82 - 46.83 winning units..
Owner Colne Valley Racing **Bred** Patrick M Ryan **Trained** Nawton, N Yorks
FOCUS
A mixture of abilities were on offer in this conditions event. The time was ordinary and the fifth close enough, but the form is rated at face value.

8345 BETVICTOR.COM NON-RUNNER FREE BET CHELTENHAM 2014 H'CAP 7f (P)
7:30 (7:30) (Class 5) (0-75,75) 3-Y-O **£2,587** (£770; £384; £192) **Stalls** Low

Form RPR
30- **1** **Firmdecisions (IRE)**[140] 4922 3-9-7 **75**............................ AdamKirby 11 89
(Brett Johnson) *mde virtually all: styd on wl u.p fr over 1f out: kpt on strly* **8/1**[3]
124- **2** 2 1/2 **Duke Of Grazeon (IRE)**[13] 8178 3-9-0 **68**.................... FrederikTylicki 9 75
(Mrs Ilka Gansera-Leveque) *sn chsng wnr: rdn over 2f out: outpcd fnl f but hld on wl for 2nd* **10/1**
033- **3** 1 1/4 **Go Far**[10] 8224 3-8-8 **67**.. TimClark(5) 7 71
(Alan Bailey) *chsd ldrs: rdn over 2f out: styd on same pce fr over 1f out* **8/1**[3]
1- **4** hd **Triple Chocolate**[50] 7624 3-9-6 **74**................................... JimmyQuinn 12 77
(Roger Ingram) *s.i.s: sn rcvrd to chse ldrs: rdn over 2f out: one pce fr over 1f out* **8/1**[3]
004- **5** 1 1/2 **Repetition**[15] 8158 3-8-9 **68**.. JacobButterfield(5) 5 67+
(Kristin Stubbs) *in rr: hdwy fr 2f out: kpt on fnl f* **25/1**
500- **6** 1 **Gracious George (IRE)**[28] 7988 3-9-7 **75**....................(b) KieranO'Neill 3 72
(Jimmy Fox) *in rr: hdwy over 1f out: kpt on in clsng stages* **7/1**[2]
/10- **7** 1/2 **Emperor Julius (IRE)**[246] 1612 3-9-7 **75**.................... FergusSweeney 4 70
(Jo Crowley) *chsd ldrs: rdn over 2f out: wknd fnl f* **25/1**
410- **8** shd **Broughtons Charm (IRE)**[13] 8178 3-9-6 **74**.................... TomQueally 6 69
(Willie Musson) *in tch: hdwy 2f out: edgd rt u.p over 1f out: sn btn* **10/1**
504- **9** nk **Lucky Di**[36] 7861 3-9-4 **72**.. GeorgeBaker 13 66
(Peter Hedger) *in rr: hdwy over 1f out: styd on cl home* **6/1**[1]
052- **10** 3/4 **Byroness**[21] 8087 3-8-13 **67**.. AndreaAtzeni 1 59
(Heather Main) *towards rr: hdwy on ins 2f out: sn nt much room on rail: no ch after* **7/1**[2]
035- **11** 3/4 **Al Raqeeb (IRE)**[27] 8008 3-9-5 **73**...................................... LukeMorris 10 63
(Gary Harrison) *in tch: wknd 2f out* **8/1**[3]
611- **12** nk **Eastern Dragon (IRE)**[20] 8095 3-8-12 **71**.................... JackDuern(5) 8 60
(Michael Scudamore) *in rr: rdn and no prog wl over 2f out* **8/1**[3]
600- **13** 1 1/4 **Aye Aye Skipper (IRE)**[13] 8181 3-9-0 **75**...................... PaulBooth(7) 14 61
(Dean Ivory) *s.i.s: a in rr* **40/1**
125- **14** 6 **Bapak Muda (USA)**[94] 6475 3-9-1 **74**............................ ShaneGray(5) 2 44
(Kevin Ryan) *chsd ldrs: wknd over 2f out* **16/1**

1m 26.13s (0.13) **Going Correction** +0.025s/f (Slow) 14 Ran SP% **129.0**
Speed ratings (Par 102): **100,97,95,95,93 92,92,91,91,90 89,89,88,81**
toteswingers 1&2 £28.50, 2&3 £18.50, 1&3 £19.80 CSF £90.51 CT £684.50 TOTE £8.60: £2.50, £4.60, £2.80; EX 166.50 Trifecta £2196.10 Part won. Pool: £2928.25 - 0.46 winning units..
Owner White Bear Racing **Bred** Thomas O'Meara **Trained** Epsom, Surrey
■ Stewards' Enquiry : Tom Queally caution: careless riding.
FOCUS
The market told that the closing 7f handicap for 3yos was an open and competitive affair. Adam Kirby was able to dictate a modest tempo on the winner and those who raced off the pace had no chance. The form has been rated slightly positively, though.
T/Jkpt: Not won. T/Plt: £15.20 to a £1 stake. Pool of £86329.39 - 4132.27 winning tickets. T/Qpdt: £9.30 to a £1 stake. Pool of £9875.05 - 783.0 winning tickets. ST

[8315] SOUTHWELL (L-H)

Thursday, December 19

OFFICIAL GOING: Standard

Wind: Fresh across Weather: Fine and dry

8346 32RED BRITISH STALLION STUDS EBF MAIDEN STKS 7f (F)

12:00 (12:00) (Class 5) 2-Y-O **£2,911** (£866; £432; £216) **Stalls** Low

Form RPR

5- **1** **Grandest**[145] 4764 2-9-5 0....................(p) RobertHavlin 9 82+
(John Gosden) *trckd ldrs: cl up 1/2-way: led wl over 2f out: rdn clr appr fnl f: styd on* **4/9**[1]

30- **2** 3¾ **Jalingo (IRE)**[22] 8067 2-9-5 0.................... JoeFanning 8 74
(Mark Johnston) *cl up: effrt to dispute ld 3f out: sn rdn and ev ch tl one pce appr fnl f* **7/2**[2]

3 11 **Playtothewhistle** 2-9-5 0.................... GrahamLee 2 42
(Bryan Smart) *towards rr: hdwy 3f out: rdn 2f out: styd on fnl f* **20/1**

45- **4** 1¼ **Real Jazz (IRE)**[20] 8091 2-9-0 0.................... LukeMorris 10 34
(Sir Mark Prescott Bt) *dwlt: sn trcking ldrs: hdwy to chse ldng pair over 2f out: sn rdn and one pce* **14/1**

065- **5** 5 **Gee Sharp**[27] 8005 2-9-5 0.................... BarryMcHugh 1 25
(Julie Camacho) *towards rr: effrt 3f out: sn rdn and sme late hdwy* **25/1**

6 6 **This Charming Man (IRE)** 2-9-5 0.................... TomEaves 3
(Keith Dalgleish) *led: rdn along over 3f out: sn hdd & wknd* **14/1**

7 4 **St Paul'S (IRE)** 2-9-5 0.................... BenCurtis 5
(David C Griffiths) *dwlt: a in rr* **33/1**

00- **8** 2¾ **Skinny Latte**[6] 8266 2-9-5 0.................... PJMcDonald 7
(Micky Hammond) *chsd ldrs to 1/2-way: sn wknd* **100/1**

6- **9** nse **O'Raghallaigh (IRE)**[20] 8091 2-8-7 0.................... JoshQuinn(7) 6
(Richard Fahey) *a towards rr* **50/1**

10 1¼ **Disco Dale (IRE)** 2-9-5 0.................... TonyHamilton 11
(Richard Fahey) *dwlt: sn chsng ldrs on outer: rdn along and wd st: sn wknd: edgd lft and bhd fr wl over 1f out* **10/1**[3]

1m 29.56s (-0.74) **Going Correction** +0.05s/f (Slow) **10 Ran SP% 128.4**
Speed ratings (Par 96): **106,101,89,87,82 75,70,67,67,65**
toteswingers 1&2 £1.20, 2&3 £8.40, 1&3 £4.90 CSF £2.56 TOTE £1.30: £1.10, £1.70, £4.70; EX 3.40 Trifecta £40.80 Pool: £4905.44 - 90.14 winning units..
Owner Lady Rothschild **Bred** Kincorth Investments Inc **Trained** Newmarket, Suffolk

FOCUS
There was little strength in depth in this maiden but the hot favourite beat his main market rival with something in hand and the pair pulled a long way clear. The second has been rated as improving.

8347 32RED CASINO (S) STKS 1m (F)

12:30 (12:30) (Class 6) 2-Y-O **£2,045** (£603; £302) **Stalls** Low

Form RPR

413- **1** **Stoney Quine (IRE)**[5] 8296 2-8-11 64.................... TomEaves 2 61
(Keith Dalgleish) *trckd ldrs: hdwy to ld 2f out: rdn over 1f out: styd on fnl f* **1/1**[1]

434- **2** 4 **Sexy Secret**[6] 8265 2-8-11 63....................(p) PaddyAspell 4 52
(Noel Quinlan) *cl up: rdn along 2f out and ev ch tl drvn and one pce appr fnl f* **4/1**[3]

026- **3** 5 **Camatini (IRE)**[16] 8137 2-8-6 51....................(p) BarryMcHugh 1 36
(Michael Dods) *led 2f: pushed along on inner and sltly outpcd 1/2-way: rdn and hdwy wl over 2f out: ev ch on inner over 1f out: sn btn* **8/1**

342- **4** 4 **Maupiti Express (FR)**[6] 8265 2-8-8 60....................(b[1]) SHJames(3) 3 31
(David O'Meara) *cl up: led after 2f: rdn along 3f out: hdd 2f out and sn wknd* **9/4**[2]

1m 46.51s (2.81) **Going Correction** +0.05s/f (Slow) **4 Ran SP% 111.9**
Speed ratings (Par 94): **87,83,78,74**
CSF £5.55 TOTE £2.00; EX 3.90 Trifecta £14.40 Pool: £2067.40 - 107.20 winning units..There was no bid for winner.
Owner Middleham Park racing XXII **Bred** T Monaghan **Trained** Carluke, S Lanarks

FOCUS
The favourite had to work hard but showed a good attitude to forge clear in this seller. The form looks par for the grade.

8348 32RED.COM MAIDEN FILLIES' STKS 1m (F)

1:00 (1:01) (Class 5) 3-Y-O+ **£2,587** (£770; £384; £192) **Stalls** Low

Form RPR

1 **Curious Mind** 3-9-0 0.................... LukeMorris 5 76+
(Sir Mark Prescott Bt) *chsd ldrs on outer: pushed along over 3f out: rdn and green over 2f out: sn led: kpt on wl u.p fnl f* **9/2**[3]

2- **2** 1½ **Marble Statuette (USA)**[13] 8180 3-9-0 0.................... TonyHamilton 6 73
(Richard Fahey) *trckd ldrs: hdwy on inner 3f out: cl up over 2f out: rdn and ev ch whn edgd lft over 1f out: drvn and edgd lft ins fnl f: kpt on* **7/4**[1]

430- **3** 9 **Shamiana**[23] 8056 3-9-0 51....................(b[1]) RichardKingscote 7 52
(Daniel Kubler) *cl up: led briefly over 2f out: sn rdn and hdd: one pce* **12/1**

4 5 **Missy Wells** 3-9-0 0.................... GrahamGibbons 2 40
(Tim Walford) *sn swtchd wd and rdn along in rr: swtchd to inner and hdwy 3f out: sn rdn and kpt on: nrst fin* **33/1**

34- **5** 2 **Sugar Town**[23] 8043 3-9-0 0.................... GrahamLee 4 36
(Peter Niven) *in tch: rdn along 3f out: sn wknd* **8/1**

506- **6** 6 **Una Bella Cosa**[113] 5902 3-9-0 45....................(v) BenCurtis 3 22
(Alan McCabe) *cl up: rdn along bef 1/2-way and sn outpcd* **14/1**

2- **7** 12 **Winterwell (USA)**[31] 7946 3-9-0 77....................(b[1]) TomEaves 1
(David O'Meara) *sn led: rdn along and hdd over 2f out: sn wknd* **5/2**[2]

8 28 **Missfire** 3-9-0 0.................... DuranFentiman 8
(Brian Baugh) *s.i.s and a wl bhd* **40/1**

1m 44.05s (0.35) **Going Correction** +0.05s/f (Slow) **8 Ran SP% 114.0**
Speed ratings (Par 100): **100,98,89,84,82 76,64,36**
CSF £12.70 TOTE £3.60: £1.70, £1.10, £2.70; EX 18.60 Trifecta £157.10 Pool: £3128.63 - 14.92 winning units..
Owner Denford Stud **Bred** Denford Stud Ltd **Trained** Newmarket, Suffolk

FOCUS
A well-backed newcomer beat the favourite in this weak fillies' maiden and the pair finished clear. The third anchors the form.

8349 32RED ON THE APP STORE H'CAP 1m 6f (F)

1:30 (1:30) (Class 6) (0-65,69) 3-Y-O+ **£1,940** (£577; £288; £144) **Stalls** Low

Form RPR

225- **1** **Goodlukin Lucy**[30] 7951 6-9-2 51.................... TomEaves 1 59
(Keith Dalgleish) *cl up: led after 2f: rdn along over 2f out: drvn over 1f out: edgd rt ins fnl f: kpt on gamely towards fin* **12/1**

042- **2** 1 **Tobrata**[9] 8229 7-9-7 56.................... DuranFentiman 4 63
(Mel Brittain) *led 2f: trckd wnr: effrt 3f out: rdn along and sltly outpcd 2f out: drvn and styd on to chse wnr whn swtchd lft ins fnl f: sn drvn and no imp towards fin* **3/1**[3]

351- **3** nk **Yasir (USA)**[6] 8270 5-10-6 69 6ex....................(p) HayleyTurner 7 76
(Conor Dore) *hld up in rr: hdwy on wd outside 1/2-way: trckd ldrs 4f out: effrt 3f out: rdn 2f out and sn ev ch tl drvn and one pce ins fnl f* **6/4**[1]

505- **4** nk **Celebrian**[12] 8204 6-8-11 46....................(t) ChrisCatlin 5 52
(Alex Hales) *chsd ldng pair: pushed along over 4f out: rdn and sltly outpcd wl 1f out: rallied u.p ins fnl f: kpt on* **25/1**

434- **5** 2 **Omega Omega**[38] 7838 4-8-11 46....................(b) AdamBeschizza 6 49
(Julia Feilden) *trckd ldrs: hdwy 4f out: chsd wnr wl over 1f out: sn rdn: drvn and wknd fnl f* **20/1**

061- **6** 10 **This Is Me**[15] 8149 5-9-11 60.................... GrahamLee 3 49
(Don Cantillon) *trckd ldrs on inner: pushed along over 4f out: rdn over 3f out and sn wknd* **11/4**[2]

330- **7** 20 **Dontpaytheferryman (USA)**[23] 8047 8-9-11 60............(b) LukeMorris 8 21
(Peter Hiatt) *chsd ldrs: rdn along over 4f out: sn lost pl and bhd* **14/1**

3m 9.06s (0.76) **Going Correction** +0.05s/f (Slow) **7 Ran SP% 114.6**
Speed ratings (Par 101): **99,98,98,98,96 91,79**
toteswingers 1&2 £3.70, 2&3 £1.80, 1&3 £4.20 CSF £48.13 CT £86.67 TOTE £15.70: £5.10, £2.10; EX 30.60 Trifecta £99.30 Pool: £3968.57 - 29.94 winning units..
Owner Evergreen Racing **Bred** Moretail Ventures **Trained** Carluke, S Lanarks

FOCUS
There was not much separating the first five in this handicap but the winner put in a gutsy front-running display. The bare form is ordinary at best.

8350 LADBROKES H'CAP 7f (F)

2:00 (2:04) (Class 4) (0-85,81) 3-Y-O+ **£4,690** (£1,395; £697; £348) **Stalls** Low

Form RPR

221- **1** **Two No Bids (IRE)**[5] 8304 3-9-0 74 6ex....................(be) PaddyAspell 6 84
(Phil McEntee) *hld up towards rr: wd st: hdwy over 2f out: sn chsng ldrs: rdn to challaenge and edgd lft ent fnl f: led last 100yds: styd on* **9/2**[2]

400- **2** 1¼ **Piceno (IRE)**[6] 8269 5-8-4 71....................(b) MatthewHopkins(7) 8 78
(Scott Dixon) *cl up: effrt over 2f out: rdn to ld wl over 1f out: drvn ins fnl f: hdd and no ex last 100yds* **16/1**

120- **3** 1½ **Silly Billy (IRE)**[5] 8295 5-8-7 67....................(p) BenCurtis 12 70
(Brian Ellison) *in tch: effrt on outer whn n.m.r wl over 1f out: styd on u.p fnl f: nrst fin* **6/1**[3]

341- **4** 1 **The Great Gabrial**[34] 7898 4-9-5 79....................(v) AndrewMullen 1 80
(Alan McCabe) *cl up on inner: slt ld 1/2-way: rdn over 2f out: drvn and hdd wl over 1f out: kpt on same pce* **12/1**

140- **5** ½ **Greyfriarschorista**[28] 7989 6-9-7 81.................... GrahamLee 11 80
(Tom Keddy) *chsd ldrs: rdn 2f out: drvn and one pce fnl f* **4/1**[1]

424- **6** 3½ **Light From Mars**[17] 8127 8-9-3 77....................(p) LiamJones 4 67
(Ronald Harris) *trckd ldrs whn n.m.r and sltly hmpd 1/2-way: rdn along over 2f out: sn no imp* **14/1**

030- **7** nk **Conry (IRE)**[40] 7820 7-8-8 68.................... StevieDonohoe 7 57
(Ian Williams) *dwlt and bhd tl styd on fnl 2f* **7/1**

640- **8** hd **Johnny Cavagin**[45] 7731 4-9-1 75....................(t) BarryMcHugh 10 64
(Richard Guest) *in tch: rdn along 3f out: n.d* **16/1**

050- **9** 1½ **Docofthebay (IRE)**[6] 8269 9-9-4 78....................(b) PJMcDonald 2 63
(Scott Dixon) *dwlt: a towards rr* **12/1**

005- **10** 8 **Sam Nombulist**[26] 8028 5-9-1 75....................(b[1]) TomEaves 5 39
(Ian Semple) *slt ld: rdn along and hdd 1/2-way: sn wknd* **25/1**

034- **11** 22 **Secret Beau**[10] 8219 3-9-6 80.................... GrahamGibbons 9
(David Evans) *towards rr: rdn along 1/2-way: sn outpcd* **9/2**[2]

1m 29.25s (-1.05) **Going Correction** +0.05s/f (Slow) **11 Ran SP% 120.8**
Speed ratings (Par 105): **108,106,104,103,103 99,98,98,96,87 62**
CSF £76.43 CT £452.24 TOTE £6.30: £2.30, £6.40, £2.40; EX 102.60 Trifecta £756.60 Pool: £5438.78 - 5.39 winning units..
Owner Eventmaker Racehorses **Bred** Marston & Dean Fleming Thoroughbreds **Trained** Newmarket, Suffolk

FOCUS
A decent handicap. It was run at a fair pace and the winner scored with a bit more in hand than the winning margin. He posted another personal best.

8351 COMPARE BOOKMAKERS AT BOOKMAKERS.CO.UK H'CAP (DIV I) 5f (F)

2:30 (2:31) (Class 6) (0-65,65) 3-Y-O+ **£1,940** (£577; £288; £144) **Stalls** High

Form RPR

466- **1** **Quality Art (USA)**[6] 8271 5-9-2 60.................... RobbieFitzpatrick 6 71+
(Richard Guest) *trckd ldrs: nt clr run and swtchd rt over 1f out: sn rdn and styd on strly fnl f to ld nr line* **8/1**

150- **2** shd **Max The Machine**[6] 8271 3-9-1 59....................(v) DaleSwift 1 67
(Derek Shaw) *hld up: hdwy on outer 2f out: rdn to ld ins fnl f: sn drvn: hdd nr liine* **12/1**

620- **3** 1 **Master Of Disguise**[199] 2918 7-9-7 65.................... GrahamGibbons 2 69
(Brian Baugh) *cl up: rdn to ld wl over 1f out: drvn and hdd ins fnl f: one pce towards fin* **20/1**

330- **4** 1½ **Confidential Creek**[37] 7848 3-8-13 62....................(p) JacobButterfield(5) 11 61
(Ollie Pears) *slt ld: rdn along 2f out: hdd wl over 1f out: drvn and one pce fnl f* **14/1**

505- **5** 1 **Speedyfix**[6] 8271 6-8-8 57....................(t) EoinWalsh(5) 8 52
(Christine Dunnett) *sltly hmpd s and in rr: hdwy over 2f out: rdn to chse ldrs over 1f out: no imp fnl f* **20/1**

602- **6** ½ **Cadeaux Pearl**[2] 8319 5-9-0 65....................(b) MatthewHopkins(7) 5 59
(Scott Dixon) *in rr and pushed along 1/2-way: rdn wl over 1f out: kpt on u.p fnl f* **5/4**[1]

403- **7** hd **Jiminy**[6] 8272 3-8-11 55....................(b) PJMcDonald 7 48
(Scott Dixon) *cl up: rdn along 2f out: drvn and wknd over 1f out* **7/1**[3]

400- **8** 2¼ **Miako (USA)**[20] 8096 3-9-6 64.................... AndrewMullen 9 49
(Michael Appleby) *cl up: rdn along over 2f out: sn drvn and btn* **4/1**[2]

046- **9** 2 **Daneside (IRE)**[7] 8258 6-8-5 52 oh2 ow1............ MatthewLawson(3) 10 30
(P J O'Gorman) *dwlt: swtchd rt to stands' rail after s: a in rr* **33/1**

400- **10** 1¼ **Ichimoku**[6] 8272 3-8-10 54....................(t) JoeFanning 4 27
(Bryan Smart) *towards rr: swtchd lft to outer after 1f: rdn along over 2f out: n.d* **14/1**

056- **11** 2½ **Lothian Countess**[159] 4292 3-8-7 51 oh1.................... BarryMcHugh 3 15
(Ian Semple) *chsd ldrs: rdn along 1/2-way: sn wknd* **33/1**

1m 0.48s (0.78) **Going Correction** +0.15s/f (Slow) **11 Ran SP% 124.5**
Speed ratings (Par 101): **99,98,97,94,93 92,92,88,85,83 79**
CSF £99.77 CT £1914.67 TOTE £17.10: £3.80, £5.30, £3.80; EX 90.50 Trifecta £2254.50 Pool: £3602.25 - 1.19 winning units..
Owner Mrs Alison Guest **Bred** Farfellow Farms & Darley Stud Management **Trained** Wetherby, W Yorks

The Form Book Flat, Raceform Ltd, Compton, RG20 6NL.

FOCUS
The clear favourite was disappointing in the sprint handicap but the winner finished well to snatch the prize. He rates a bit better than the bare form.

8352 COMPARE BOOKMAKERS AT BOOKMAKERS.CO.UK H'CAP (DIV II) 5f (F)
3:00 (3:00) (Class 6) (0-65,65) 3-Y-O+ **£1,940** (£577; £288; £144) **Stalls** High

Form RPR
120- 1 **Beacon Tarn**[23] 8052 3-9-1 **62**............ NeilFarley(3) 3 78
(Eric Alston) *mde all: rdn clr over 1f out: readily* **5/1**[1]
2 4 1/2 **Commandable (AUS)**[522] 9-8-11 **55**............ TomEaves 4 55
(Ian Semple) *cl up: rdn 2f out: drvn over 1f out: kpt on u.p fnl f: no ch w wnr* **20/1**
165- 3 1 1/4 **Fathom Five (IRE)**[9] 8230 9-9-3 **61**............ PaddyAspell 9 56
(Shaun Harris) *chsd ldng pair: rdn along wl over 1f out: drvn: edgd lft a and one pce appr fnl f* **5/1**[3]
310- 4 3/4 **Robyn**[6] 8271 3-8-1 **52** oh3 ow1............ MatthewHopkins(7) 7 45
(Scott Dixon) *towards rr: rdn along 1/2-way: kpt on fnl f: n.d* **10/1**
005- 5 1 1/2 **Megaleka**[17] 8135 3-8-13 **57**............ RobertWinston 8 44
(Alan Bailey) *chsd ldrs: swtchd lft and rdn wl over 1f out: sn one pce* **7/1**
601- 6 3/4 **Danzoe (IRE)**[24] 8034 6-9-2 **65**............ EoinWalsh(5) 10 50
(Christine Dunnett) *dwlt and reminders sn after s: a in rr* **4/1**[2]
220- 7 1/2 **Starlight Angel (IRE)**[17] 8128 3-9-2 **65**............ JackDuern(5) 5 48
(Ronald Harris) *chsd ldrs: rdn along over 2f out: sn wknd* **5/1**[3]
130- 8 19 **La Luz Del Sol**[205] 2756 3-8-8 **59**............ JoshQuinn(7) 6
(Richard Fahey) *v.s.i.s: a bhd: eased fnl 2f* **14/1**

1m 0.16s (0.46) **Going Correction** +0.15s/f (Slow) **8** Ran SP% **114.9**
Speed ratings (Par 101): **102,94,92,91,89 88,87,56**
toteswingers 1&2 £6.10, 2&3 £11.70, 1&3 £4.00 CSF £55.16 CT £236.13 TOTE £3.40: £1.10, £5.40, £2.50; EX 31.10 Trifecta £174.60 Pool: £4164.94 - 17.88 winning units..
Owner Mr & Mrs G Middlebrook **Bred** Mr & Mrs G Middlebrook **Trained** Longton, Lancs

FOCUS
There was an emphatic winner in this second division of a sprint handicap. It was the faster time and the form is rated around that and the winner's C&D maiden win.

8353 CORAL MOBILE JUST THREE CLICKS TO BET H'CAP 1m 4f (F)
3:30 (3:30) (Class 4) (0-85,82) 3-Y-O+ **£4,690** (£1,395; £697; £348) **Stalls** Low

Form RPR
001- 1 **St Ignatius**[19] 8115 6-9-3 **75**............(v) RobertWinston 7 85
(Alan Bailey) *towards rr and pushed along after 3f: swtchd rt to outer and hdwy 5f out: rdn along to chse ldrs over 2f out: drvn over 1f out: styd on wl fnl f to ld nr fin* **7/1**
011- 2 nk **Honoured (IRE)**[23] 8047 6-9-3 **75**............(t) AndrewMullen 5 84
(Michael Appleby) *prom: led wl over 2f out: rdn clr and edgd lft over 1f out: drvn and edgd rt ins fnl f: hdd and no ex nr fin* **7/4**[1]
01- 3 3 1/4 **Layline (IRE)**[16] 8041 6-9-3 **80**............ DanielMuscutt(5) 2 84
(Gay Kelleway) *trckd ldrs on inner: cl up after 3f: led over 4f out: rdn along and hdd wl over 2f out: drvn and kpt on same pce fnl f* **20/1**
/02- 4 3/4 **Back Burner (IRE)**[6] 8276 5-9-7 **82**............ SHJames(3) 6 85
(David O'Meara) *hld up: hdwy on inner to trck ldrs 1/2-way: rdn wl over 2f out: drvn appr fnl f and kpt on same pce* **5/1**
212- 5 1/2 **Sherman McCoy**[50] 7635 7-9-5 **77**............ DaleSwift 4 79
(Brian Ellison) *trckd ldrs: pushed along over 4f out: rdn along over 3f out: drvn and one pce fnl 2f* **9/2**[3]
005- 6 12 **Northside Prince (IRE)**[23] 8047 7-9-1 **73**............ BenCurtis 1 56
(Alan Swinbank) *hld up: a in rr* **12/1**
500- 7 4 1/2 **My History (IRE)**[15] 8159 3-8-8 **71**............ JoeFanning 3 47
(Mark Johnston) *led: pushed along 1/2-way: hdd over 4f out and sn wknd* **4/1**[2]

2m 39.6s (-1.40) **Going Correction** +0.05s/f (Slow)
WFA 3 from 5yo+ 5lb **7** Ran SP% **116.2**
Speed ratings (Par 105): **106,105,103,103,102 94,91**
toteswingers 1&2 £3.40, 2&3 £3.60, 1&3 £7.90 CSF £20.35 TOTE £7.30: £2.70, £1.10; EX 20.10 Trifecta £103.70 Pool: £2887.09 - 20.86 winning units..
Owner Allan McNamee & Alan Bailey **Bred** Simon And Helen Plumbly **Trained** Newmarket, Suffolk

FOCUS
They went a steady pace in this fair handicap but the first two pulled clear and the form looks solid. A personal best from the winner.
T/Plt: £295.60 to s £1 stake. Pool of £49052.65 - 121.10 winning tickets. T/Qpdt: £142.20 to a £1 stake. Pool of £5075.30 - 26.40 winning tickets. JR

8307 DEAUVILLE (R-H)
Thursday, December 19
OFFICIAL GOING: Fibresand: standard

8354a PRIX HABITAT (CONDITIONS) (2YO) (FIBRESAND) 7f 110y
11:00 (12:00) 2-Y-O **£11,788** (£4,715; £3,536; £2,357; £1,178)

RPR
1 **Nabbaash** 2-9-0 0............ FranckBlondel 1 81
(J-C Rouget, France) **9/10**[1]
2 3/4 **Naloudia (IRE)**[56] 2-8-10 0............ FabriceVeron 7 75
(H-A Pantall, France) **137/10**
3 3/4 **Berrahri (IRE)**[35] 7889 2-8-11 0 ow1............ Pierre-CharlesBoudot 8 74
(John Best) *sn led: shkn up and qcknd 2f out: rallied u.p whn pressed fr 1 1/2f out: hdd ent fnl f: kpt on at same pce* **156/10**
4 nk **Zlatan Dream (FR)**[16] 2-9-0 0............ RonanThomas 4 76
(P Van De Poele, France) **49/10**[2]
5 3 1/2 **Elliot Carver (FR)**[15] 2-9-0 0............ TheoBachelot 9 68
(M Munch, Germany) **68/10**[3]
6 shd **Anzi Star (FR)** 2-8-10 0............ FlavienPrat 3 64
(D Guillemin, France) **156/10**
7 1 1/4 **Sixtine's Lucky**[35] 2-8-7 0............ AntoineHamelin 2 58
(N Bertran De Balanda, France) **103/10**
8 1 1/2 **Teardrops (FR)**[16] 8143 2-9-4 0............ AnthonyCrastus 5 65
(R Chotard, France) **41/1**
9 nk **Collani (IRE)**[30] 2-9-0 0............(b) StephanePasquier 6 61
(M Nigge, France) **25/1**

1m 31.06s (91.06) **9** Ran SP% **116.3**
WIN (incl. 1 euro stake): 1.90. PLACES: 1.20, 2.60, 3.00. DF: 13.30. SF: 18.00.
Owner Hamdan Al Maktoum **Bred** Card Bloodstock **Trained** Pau, France

8346 SOUTHWELL (L-H)
Friday, December 20
OFFICIAL GOING: Standard
Wind: Moderate across Weather: Fine and dry

8360 LADBROKES H'CAP 1m (F)
12:10 (12:10) (Class 6) (0-65,71) 3-Y-O+ **£2,264** (£673; £336; £168) **Stalls** Low

Form RPR
524- 1 **Emperatriz**[3] 8316 3-9-6 **65**............ RobertHavlin 9 76
(John Holt) *hld up in tch: hdwy over 3f out: chal wl over 1f out: rdn to ld jst ins fnl f: kpt on* **5/1**[2]
460- 2 2 1/2 **Amtired**[36] 7881 7-9-1 **59**............(p) MartinHarley 8 65
(Marjorie Fife) *trckd ldrs: smooth hdwy 3f out: cl up over 2f out: rdn to take slt ld wl over 1f out: drvn and hdd jst ins fnl f: kpt on same pce* **12/1**
000- 3 1 1/4 **Mitchell**[16] 7881 3-8-6 **58**............ RobJFitzpatrick(7) 4 60
(David Thompson) *led: rdn along 3f out: hdd wl over 1f out and sn drvn: cl up tl kpt on same pce fnl f* **50/1**
041- 4 3 **Mishrif (USA)**[6] 8295 7-9-13 **71** 6ex............(v) FrederikTylicki 7 67
(J R Jenkins) *towards rr and pushed along 1/2-way: swtchd rt towards outer st: hdwy 2f out: rdn to chse ldrs over 1f out: edgd lft and no imp fnl f* **7/4**[1]
21P- 5 3 1/2 **Better Value (IRE)**[14] 8186 3-9-1 **60**............(p) AdamBeschizza 10 47
(Noel Quinlan) *prom: effrt on inner 3f out and sn cl up: rdn 2f out and grad wknd appr fnl f* **12/1**
003- 6 3/4 **West End Lad**[21] 8093 10-9-5 **63**............(p) LiamJones 5 50
(Roy Bowring) *sn pushed along in rr: swtchd rt to outer after 2f: wd st: rdn and hdwy 2f out: nt rch ldrs* **33/1**
060- 7 1 1/2 **Chief Executive (IRE)**[93] 6521 3-9-4 **63**............ JoeFanning 11 45
(Jo Hughes) *dwlt: sn trcking ldrs: effrt 3f out: rdn along over 2f out and grad wknd* **8/1**[3]
522- 8 2 1/2 **Cantor**[14] 8187 5-9-4 **62**............(b) AdamKirby 14 40
(Paul Morgan) *chsd ldrs on wd outside: hdwy and cl up 1/2-way: effrt and ev ch 3f out: sn rdn and wknd fnl 2f* **8/1**[3]
600- 9 1 1/2 **Master Of Song**[56] 7515 6-9-1 **62**............(p) MarkCoumbe(3) 13 36
(Roy Bowring) *v s.i.s and bhd: wd st: sn rdn and sme late hdwy* **20/1**
636- 10 3 1/4 **Exceedexpectations (IRE)**[7] 8278 4-9-4 **62**............ HayleyTurner 2 29
(Conor Dore) *in tch: n.m.r on inner 3f out: sn rdn along and wknd* **20/1**
321- 11 6 **Uncle Dermot (IRE)**[52] 7608 5-9-4 **62**............ TomQueally 3 15
(Brendan Powell) *chsd ldrs: rdn along wl over 3f out: drvn and wknd wl over 2f out* **8/1**[3]
455- 12 4 1/2 **Egotist (IRE)**[13] 8198 5-9-7 **65**............(t) RobertWinston 6 7
(Milton Bradley) *in rr: swtchd rt towards outer and sme hdwy 3f out: rdn over 2f out and n.d* **16/1**
004- 13 8 **Rockgoat (IRE)**[190] 3252 4-8-7 **51** oh5............(e[1]) AndreaAtzeni 1
(Daniel Mark Loughnane) *chsd ldrs on inner: rdn along over 3f out: sn wknd* **33/1**

1m 42.29s (-1.41) **Going Correction** -0.05s/f (Stan)
WFA 3 from 4yo+ 1lb **13** Ran SP% **125.0**
Speed ratings (Par 101): **105,102,101,98,94 94,92,90,88,85 79,74,66**
toteswingers 1&2 £16.70, 1&3 £96.70, 2&3 £173.20 CSF £62.50 CT £2738.24 TOTE £8.10: £2.20, £3.60, £16.70; EX 81.90 Trifecta £3761.10 Part won..
Owner Eric Boumans **Bred** D R Botterill **Trained** Peckleton, Leics

FOCUS
Modest form.

8361 LADBROKES CLASSIFIED STKS 7f (F)
12:40 (12:40) (Class 6) 3-Y-O+ **£1,940** (£577; £288; £144) **Stalls** Low

Form RPR
005- 1 **Kept**[23] 8065 4-9-0 45............[1] LiamJones 3 54
(Ronald Harris) *dwlt and sn swtchd to wd outside: hdwy 1/2-way and sn cl up: rdn to chal 2f out: led and edgd lft appr fnl f: kpt on wl towards fin* **5/1**
005- 2 1/2 **Bapak Pesta (IRE)**[10] 8235 3-9-0 52............(p) JamieSpencer 6 53
(Kevin Ryan) *led: pushed along and swtchd rt over 2f out: rdn over 1f out: hdd appr fnl f: sn hrd drvn and edgd lft u.p: no ex last 100yds* **9/2**[3]
432- 3 1 **Quadriga (IRE)**[17] 8142 3-9-0 55............ AndreaAtzeni 5 50
(Robert Eddery) *trckd ldr on inner: pushed along over 2f out: rdn wl over 1f out: sn drvn and kpt on same pce* **5/4**[1]
4 nk **Mont Ventoux (FR)**[39] 3-9-0 53............ FrederikTylicki 1 49
(Philip Mitchell) *dwlt: sn rdn along in rr and detached after 1f: bhd 1/2-way: hdwy 2f out: styd on strly u.p fnl f: nrst fin* **20/1**
504- 5 nk **Mysterious Wonder**[15] 8162 3-8-7 55............(e) EvaMoscrop(7) 2 49
(Philip Kirby) *trckd ldrs: effrt 3f out: rdn along 2f out: kpt on fnl f: nrst fin* **4/1**[2]
000- 6 8 **Poetic Belle**[24] 8055 3-8-9 49............(t) ShirleyTeasdale(5) 4 28
(Shaun Harris) *chsd ldrs: rdn along 3f out: sn wknd* **25/1**
030- 7 7 **Lucy Minaj**[31] 7966 3-9-0 44............(p) JoeFanning 7 10
(Bryan Smart) *trckd ldng pair: rdn along over 3f out: sn wknd* **10/1**

1m 31.24s (0.94) **Going Correction** -0.05s/f (Stan) **7** Ran SP% **117.0**
Speed ratings (Par 101): **92,91,90,89,89 80,72**
toteswingers 1&2 £4.00, 1&3 £2.40, 2&3 £2.30 CSF £28.58 TOTE £7.60: £2.50, £2.90; EX 33.90 Trifecta £86.60 Pool: £4330.87 - 37.49 winning units..
Owner Robert & Nina Bailey **Bred** Coleman Bloodstock & Cheveley Park Stud **Trained** Earlswood, Monmouths

FOCUS
A 0-55 classified event for horses who hadn't won more than one race, and there was a slow-motion finish.

8362 32RED FILLIES' MAIDEN STKS 1m (F)
1:10 (1:12) (Class 5) 2-Y-O **£2,587** (£770; £384; £192) **Stalls** Low

Form RPR
302- 1 **Tears Of The Sun**[14] 8176 2-9-0 74............ JamieSpencer 5 67+
(Roger Varian) *swtchd to outer sn after s and hld up in tch: hdwy 3f out: led 2f out: sn edgd lft and rdn: drvn and hung rt over 1f out: edgd lft and kpt on fnl f* **4/6**[1]
2 1 1/4 **Wildcat Lass (USA)** 2-8-11 0............ SHJames(3) 2 64+
(David O'Meara) *trckd ldrs: hdwy 3f out: effrt to chse wnr whn swtchd lft over 1f out: rdn and ev ch whn rn green and hung lft ins fnl f: no ex* **9/2**[3]
020- 3 3 **Volodina (IRE)**[115] 5865 2-9-0 53............(v) BenCurtis 3 57
(Alan McCabe) *led: rdn along 3f out: hdd 2f out: drvn over 1f out: n.m.r and kpt on same pce fnl f* **33/1**

4 1 1/4 **Windshield** 2-9-0 0 LiamJones 1 54+
(Sir Mark Prescott Bt) *trckd ldrs on inner: effrt 2f out: sn rdn and green: n.m.r and kpt on same pce fnl f* **14/1**
60- 5 3 **Vera Lou (IRE)**48 7692 2-9-0 0 JoeFanning 7 47
(Pat Eddery) *chsd ldr: rdn along wl over 2f out: grad wknd* **20/1**
05- 6 1/2 **Keep To The Beat**17 8138 2-8-9 0 ShaneGray(5) 4 46
(Kevin Ryan) *t.k.h early: hld up: sme hdwy wl over 2f out: sn rdn and btn* **25/1**
44- 7 10 **Prestige Roses (IRE)**20 8114 2-9-0 0 MartinHarley 8 23
(Marco Botti) *chsd ldrs on outer: rdn along 3f out: sn wknd* **4/1**2
1m 44.63s (0.93) **Going Correction** -0.05s/f (Stan) 7 Ran SP% **116.4**
Speed ratings (Par 93): **93,91,88,87,84 84,74**
toteswingers 1&2 £2.40, 1&3 £4.30, 2&3 £12.50 CSF £4.14 TOTE £1.70: £1.70, £2.40; EX 5.70 Trifecta £66.90 Pool: £4713.47 - 52.82 winning units..
Owner Qatar Racing Limited **Bred** Dr Bridget Drew & John Burke **Trained** Newmarket, Suffolk

FOCUS
A weak maiden. The winner didn't look the most straightforward and has been rated a bit below form in success.

8363 32RED CASINO NURSERY H'CAP 7f (F)
1:40 (1:40) (Class 6) (0-60,58) 2-Y-O **£2,264** (£673; £336; £168) **Stalls** Low

Form RPR
001- 1 **Big Kenny**7 8274 2-8-9 51 6ex EoinWalsh(5) 8 64+
(David Evans) *trckd ldrs on outer: cl up after 3f: led wl over 2f out: rdn clr over 1f out: readily* **9/4**2
004- 2 5 **Masterpaver**8 8262 2-9-4 55 (v) RobertWinston 1 53+
(Alan Bailey) *sn rdn along towards rr: hdwy on inner 3f out: drvn over 1f out: edgd rt and styd on fnl f: tk 2nd towards fin* **9/2**3
005- 3 nk **Solent Lad (USA)**18 8133 2-8-6 48 (p) DanielMuscutt(5) 2 45
(Robert Eddery) *cl up on inner: pushed along 1/2-way: rdn over 2f out: kpt on one pce u.p fnl f* **10/1**
352- 4 3 **Hot Stock (FR)**3 8317 2-9-7 58 JoeFanning 7 47
(Jo Hughes) *sn led: jnd and rdn over 3f out: hdd wl over 1f out: swtchd rt over 1f out and sn wknd* **6/4**1
330- 5 2 **Chanceuse**8 8262 2-8-10 54 (b1) JoeDoyle(7) 5 38
(Gay Kelleway) *in rr: rdn along 1/2-way: n.d* **8/1**
454- 6 6 **Tortoise**18 8132 2-8-3 45 TimClark(5) 6 14
(Richard Guest) *chsd ldrs: rdn along 3f out: sn wknd* **25/1**
400- 7 14 **Maximilianthefirst**11 8215 2-8-8 45 AdrianNicholls 4
(Mark Rimmer) *t.k.h: trckd ldrs: rdn along wl over 2f out: sn wknd* **33/1**
1m 31.06s (0.76) **Going Correction** -0.05s/f (Stan) 7 Ran SP% **115.9**
Speed ratings (Par 94): **93,87,86,83,81 74,58**
CSF £13.28 CT £83.44 TOTE £4.60: £2.60, £1.90; EX 13.90 Trifecta £84.50 Pool: £5267.10 - 25.47 winning units..
Owner P D Evans **Bred** O J Williams **Trained** Pandy, Monmouths

FOCUS
This nursery fell apart and the well-handicapped winner had a straightforward task. The winner was more than confirming his previous step up, while the runner-up faced kickback from an early stage and can do a little better here in future.

8364 32RED.COM NURSERY H'CAP 6f (F)
2:10 (2:13) (Class 5) (0-75,77) 2-Y-O **£2,587** (£770; £384; £192) **Stalls** Low

Form RPR
002- 1 **Captain Secret**27 8024 2-9-7 75 AdamKirby 7 83
(Marco Botti) *mde all: rdn clr over 1f out and sn edgd lft: kpt on fnl f* **9/4**2
413- 2 3 1/2 **Little Big Man**15 8166 2-8-12 66 (b) LiamKeniry 6 63
(Sylvester Kirk) *chsd wnr: rdn 2f out: drvn and edgd lft over 1f out: no imp fnl f* **8/1**
355- 3 1 **Armelle (FR)**24 8044 2-7-9 56 (p) JoeDoyle(7) 8 50
(Scott Dixon) *towards rr: wd st: sn rdn and hdwy 2f out: styd on wl appr fnl f: nrst fin* **7/1**3
421- 4 6 **Pensax Lad (IRE)**10 8228 2-9-9 77 6ex RobertWinston 2 53
(Ronald Harris) *trckd ldrs: pushed along and sltly outpcd 1/2-way: rdn and hung lft 2f out: sn drvn and no imp* **6/4**1
160- 5 4 **Casper Lee (IRE)**63 7340 2-8-8 62 RobertHavlin 4 26
(Alan Berry) *in tch: rdn along 1/2-way: sn outpcd* **20/1**
551- 6 nk **Black Vale (IRE)**7 8267 2-8-13 67 6ex (bt) PaddyAspell 1 30
(Phil McEntee) *chsd ldng pair: rdn along over 2f out: grad wknd* **8/1**
300- 7 3 3/4 **Birikyno**29 7986 2-8-2 61 JoeyHaynes(5) 3 13+
(Mark Usher) *stmbld bdly s and a bhd* **16/1**
1m 16.74s (0.24) **Going Correction** -0.05s/f (Stan) 7 Ran SP% **116.1**
Speed ratings (Par 96): **96,91,90,82,76 76,71**
CSF £21.09 CT £109.94 TOTE £3.00: £1.20, £4.80; EX 21.30 Trifecta £155.00 Pool: £3385.36 - 24.26 winning units..
Owner Scuderia Blueberry **Bred** R G Percival **Trained** Newmarket, Suffolk

FOCUS
Few got into this ordinary nursery. The winner was well positioned throughout.

8365 COMPARE BOOKMAKERS AT BOOKMAKERS.CO.UK CLAIMING STKS 6f (F)
2:45 (2:45) (Class 6) 3-Y-O+ **£1,940** (£577; £288; £144) **Stalls** Low

Form RPR
315- 1 **Fortinbrass (IRE)**32 7949 3-8-11 78 SHJames(3) 1 83
(David O'Meara) *trckd ldng pair: hdwy on inner to chse ldr over 2f out: rdn wl over 1f out: drvn ins fnl f: styd on wl to ld last 75yds* **7/4**1
403- 2 3/4 **Angelo Poliziano**10 8230 7-8-1 67 (b) JosephineGordon(7) 2 75
(Jo Hughes) *trckd ldrs: smooth hdwy over 2f out: led over 1f out: rdn ins fnl f: hdd and no ex last 75yds* **12/1**
300- 3 4 **New Leyf (IRE)**52 7595 7-8-0 79 RobJFitzpatrick(7) 5 61
(David Thompson) *trckd ldr: pushed along and sltly outpcd over 2f out: kpt on same pce u.p fnl f* **8/1**
220- 4 2 **Greenhead High**217 2409 5-8-10 75 (v) AdrianNicholls 4 58
(David Nicholls) *led: rdn along over 2f out: hdd over 1f out: sn edgd lft and wknd* **2/1**2
106- 5 shd **Gabrial's Gift (IRE)**66 7264 4-8-7 77 MatthewHopkins(7) 3 61
(Scott Dixon) *chsd ldrs on outer: rdn along 2f out: sn one pce* **3/1**3
1m 16.63s (0.13) **Going Correction** -0.05s/f (Stan) 5 Ran SP% **113.5**
Speed ratings (Par 101): **97,96,90,88,87**
CSF £21.36 TOTE £2.40: £1.20, £3.10; EX 13.80 Trifecta £104.60 Pool: £4616.94 - 190.78 winning units..Fortinbrass was bought by Mr John Balding for £12,000. New Leyf was claimed by Mr J. R. Gask for £5,000
Owner Middleham Park Racing XVIII & Partner **Bred** Tom Wallace **Trained** Nawton, N Yorks

FOCUS
A fair claimer.

8366 CORAL APP DOWNLOAD FROM THE APP STORE H'CAP 1m 3f (F)
3:20 (3:20) (Class 5) (0-70,70) 3-Y-O **£2,587** (£770; £384; £192) **Stalls** Low

Form RPR
002- 1 **Returntobrecongill**6 8299 3-9-5 68 GrahamLee 3 87+
(James Given) *mde all: pushed clr over 2f out: styd on strly: unchal* **4/7**1
300- 2 19 **Tight Knit (USA)**17 8139 3-9-2 70 (b) JoeyHaynes(5) 4 57
(John Weymes) *trckd ldng pair on outer: hdwy 4f out: rdn along 3f out: chsd wnr 2f out: sn drvn and one pce* **12/1**3
605- 3 4 **Waverunner**4 8314 3-9-7 70 (b1) JoeFanning 2 50
(Mark Johnston) *t.k.h: trckd ldrs: hdwy to chse wnr over 4f out: rdn along 3f out: drvn 2f out and sn outpcd* **11/4**2
5- 4 9 **Slipper Satin (IRE)**14 8184 3-9-2 65 (b1) AdamKirby 5 30
(Noel Quinlan) *chsd ldrs on outer: rdn along 5f out: sn outpcd and bhd fnl 3f* **16/1**
644- 5 23 **Helmsley Flyer (IRE)**207 2716 3-8-4 56 oh1 JulieBurke(3) 1
(David O'Meara) *chsd wnr on inner: rdn along 1/2-way: sn lost pl and bhd fnl 3f* **14/1**
2m 24.74s (-3.26) **Going Correction** -0.05s/f (Stan) 5 Ran SP% **110.6**
Speed ratings (Par 102): **109,95,92,85,69**
CSF £8.72 TOTE £1.40: £1.20, £5.10; EX 26.60 Trifecta £18.10 Pool: £4616.94 - 190.78 winning units..
Owner The Cool Silk Partnership **Bred** Miss S E Hall **Trained** Willoughton, Lincs

FOCUS
An uncompetitive handicap.
T/Plt: £411.50 to a £1 stake. Pool: £53825.40 - 95.48 winning tickets T/Qpdt: £14.20 to a £1 stake. Pool: £4679.15 - 242.85 winning tickets JR

8308 WOLVERHAMPTON (A.W) (L-H)
Friday, December 20

OFFICIAL GOING: Standard
Wind: Fresh behind Weather: Overcast

8367 32RED.COM MAIDEN AUCTION STKS 7f 32y(P)
3:50 (3:50) (Class 6) 2-Y-O **£1,940** (£577; £288; £144) **Stalls** High

Form RPR
52- 1 **Bon Port**28 8005 2-8-10 0 AndreaAtzeni 5 64
(Hughie Morrison) *trckd ldr tl led over 2f out: rdn clr over 1f out: styd on* **3/1**2
6- 2 3 1/4 **Final Countdown**49 7655 2-9-0 0 WilliamCarson 4 60
(Anthony Carson) *hld up: pushed along over 2f out: hdwy over 1f out: rdn to go 2nd and hung lft ins fnl f: nt trble wnr* **7/2**3
3 3 1/4 **Captain Mo** 2-9-0 0 MartinHarley 2 51
(Marco Botti) *chsd ldrs: pushed along to go 2nd 2f out: sn rdn: no ex fnl f* **1/1**1
40- 4 5 **Tara's Treasure (IRE)**37 7853 2-8-12 0 TomQueally 3 36
(Gary Moore) *led: pushed along and hdd over 2f out: wknd over 1f out* **7/1**
1m 31.51s (1.91) **Going Correction** +0.175s/f (Slow) 4 Ran SP% **109.7**
Speed ratings (Par 94): **96,92,88,82**
CSF £12.96 TOTE £2.10; EX 9.00 Trifecta £18.60 Pool: £21410.36 - 96.83 winning units..
Owner A C Pickford & Partners **Bred** Llety Stud **Trained** East Ilsley, Berks

FOCUS
An uncompetitive maiden and one run at an ordinary gallop to the home turn. The winner raced against the inside rail in the straight.

8368 32RED MAIDEN STKS 5f 216y(P)
4:20 (4:20) (Class 5) 2-Y-O **£2,587** (£770; £384; £192) **Stalls** Low

Form RPR
342- 1 **Queenie's Home**7 8266 2-9-0 73 TomQueally 2 71
(James Given) *trckd ldrs: rdn over 1f out: styd on u.p to ld wl ins fnl f: edgd rt towards fin* **5/2**2
2 1/2 **Chunghua (USA)** 2-9-5 0 GeorgeBaker 3 75+
(Ed Walker) *a.p: led over 1f out: shkn up: edgd lft and hdd wl ins fnl f* **8/1**3
3 6 **Have A Great Day (IRE)**14 8190 2-9-5 0 (t) MartinHarley 5 57
(A Oliver, Ire) *chsd ldr: rdn and ev ch over 1f out: wknd ins fnl f* **4/5**1
44- 4 2 **Libra Romana (IRE)**6 8300 2-9-0 0 LukeMorris 4 46+
(Sir Mark Prescott Bt) *hld up: hdwy over 1f out: wknd fnl f* **20/1**
5 nk **Cocoa's Princess** 2-9-0 0 TonyHamilton 7 45
(Richard Fahey) *s.i.s: hld up: pushed along and hung lft over 1f out: n.d* **16/1**
03- 6 1 3/4 **Mahon Falls**20 8114 2-8-9 0 EoinWalsh(5) 8 39
(David Evans) *sn led: rdn and hdd over 1f out: wknd fnl f* **25/1**
05- 7 2 1/4 **Motamayezah**45 7756 2-9-0 0 (b1) LiamJones 1 33
(Ismail Mohammed) *s.i.s: hdwy over 4f out: rdn and wknd over `1f out* **28/1**
1m 16.5s (1.50) **Going Correction** +0.175s/f (Slow) 7 Ran SP% **113.2**
Speed ratings (Par 96): **97,96,88,85,85 82,79**
CSF £21.26 TOTE £4.20: £1.90, £3.60; EX 28.80 Trifecta £43.70 Pool: £4787.84 - 82.00 winning units..
Owner The Cool Silk Partnership **Bred** Newsells Park Stud **Trained** Willoughton, Lincs

FOCUS
Not much strength in depth but fair form from the first two, who pulled clear in the straight. The gallop was reasonable and the winner came down the centre. The winner limits the form.

8369 BEST ODDS AT BOOKMAKERS.CO.UK H'CAP 5f 216y(P)
4:50 (4:50) (Class 2) (0-105,92) 3-Y-O£11,971 (£3,583; £1,791; £896; £446) **Stalls** Low

Form RPR
121- 1 **Trinityelitedotcom (IRE)**78 6977 3-9-0 85 RichardKingscote 1 96
(Tom Dascombe) *mde all: rdn over 1f out: edgd rt wl ins fnl f: jst hld on* **5/1**3
024- 2 nse **Iptisam**10 8231 4-9-3 88 (p) LukeMorris 3 99
(James Tate) *chsd wnr: pushed along over 2f out: rdn over 1f out: r.o u.p: carried rt towards fin* **5/1**3
054- 3 1 **Alben Star (IRE)**2 8334 5-9-7 92 TonyHamilton 7 100
(Richard Fahey) *hld up in tch: rdn over 1f out: r.o* **15/8**1
534- 4 3 3/4 **Peace Seeker**14 8189 5-9-2 87 WilliamCarson 6 83
(Anthony Carson) *hld up: hdwy over 1f out: sn rdn: nt trble ldrs* **10/1**
013- 5 1/2 **Al's Memory (IRE)**6 8305 4-8-11 82 MartinHarley 5 76
(David Evans) *prom: rdn over 2f out: styd on same pce fr over 1f out* **7/1**
356- 6 3/4 **Arctic Feeling (IRE)**6 8305 5-8-9 85 SamanthaBell(5) 4 77
(Richard Fahey) *hld up: nt clr run over 1f out: n.d* **25/1**

022- **7** *nse* **Frontier Fighter**[10] 8231 5-9-3 **88**.......... GrahamGibbons 2 79
(David O'Meara) *chsd ldrs: rdn over 2f out: no ex fnl f* **9/2**[2]

60- **8** *2 1/4* **Caspian Prince (IRE)**[50] 4-9-0 **88**..........[1] MarkCoumbe[(3)] 9 72
(Tony Carroll) *prom: plld hrd: rdn over 2f out: wknd fnl f* **33/1**

1m 14.76s (-0.24) **Going Correction** +0.175s/f (Slow) **8** Ran SP% **114.7**
Speed ratings (Par 109): **108,107,106,101,100 99,99,96**
toteswingers 1&2 £4.20, 1&3 £3.40, 2&3 £2.40 CSF £30.21 CT £63.03 TOTE £5.60: £1.80, £2.00, £1.10; EX 18.20 Trifecta £90.30 Pool: £3888.03 - 32.29 winning units..
Owner Manor House Racing Club **Bred** Natasha Newsome **Trained** Malpas, Cheshire
■ Stewards' Enquiry : Richard Kingscote caution; careless riding.

FOCUS
Mainly exposed performers but a useful handicap. An ordinary gallop suited those right up with the pace and the winner came down the centre in the straight. The first three pulled clear.

8370 COMPARE BOOKMAKERS AT BOOKMAKERS.CO.UK H'CAP 5f 20y(P)
5:20 (5:20) (Class 6) (0-55,55) 3-Y-O+ **£1,940** (£577; £288; £144) **Stalls** Low

Form RPR

04- **1** **My Time**[20] 8112 4-9-2 **50**.......... TomEaves 10 58
(Michael Mullineaux) *chsd ldrs: pushed along 1/2-way: r.o u.p to ld wl ins fnl f* **8/1**

640- **2** *1 1/4* **Your Gifted (IRE)**[7] 8271 6-9-4 **55**..........(v[1]) MarkCoumbe[(3)] 2 59
(Lisa Williamson) *dwlt: hdwy u.p over 1f out: r.o* **15/2**

506- **3** *hd* **Methaaly (IRE)**[28] 8002 10-8-12 **53**..........(be) LewisStones[(7)] 5 56
(Michael Mullineaux) *stmbld s: outpcd: swtchd lft and r.o wl ins fnl f: nrst fin* **9/1**

061- **4** *nk* **College Doll**[24] 8050 4-9-1 **54**..........(t) EoinWalsh[(5)] 4 56+
(Christine Dunnett) *chsd ldr tl led over 1f out: sn rdn: hdd and unable qck wl ins fnl f* **15/8**[1]

035- **5** *nk* **Chateau Lola**[7] 8272 4-8-5 **46**..........(v) AdamMcLean[(7)] 6 47
(Derek Shaw) *s.i.s: sn pushed along in rr: hdwy 2f out: rdn over 1f out: styd on* **14/1**

024- **6** *1 1/4* **Divertimenti (IRE)**[7] 8271 9-8-13 **54**..........(b) LouisSteward[(7)] 9 50
(Roy Bowring) *prom: drvn along and outpcd 1/2-way: styd on u.p ins fnl f* **5/1**[3]

360- **7** *1 1/4* **Balatina**[38] 7845 3-9-6 **54**.......... LukeMorris 11 46
(Chris Dwyer) *led: rdn and hdd over 1f out: no ex wl ins fnl f* **7/2**[2]

1m 4.05s (1.75) **Going Correction** +0.175s/f (Slow) **7** Ran SP% **113.2**
Speed ratings (Par 101): **93,91,90,90,89 87,85**
toteswingers 1&2 £4.40, 1&3 £9.00, 2&3 £4.90 CSF £63.23 CT £549.30 TOTE £11.80: £4.30, £3.40; EX 93.00 Trifecta £435.20 Pool: £2087.40 - 3.59 winning units..
Owner Mark Kilner **Bred** John Heywood & Michael Mullineaux **Trained** Alpraham, Cheshire
■ Stewards' Enquiry : Tom Eaves seven-day ban; used whip above permitted level (5th-9th Jan).

FOCUS
A moderate handicap and a depleted field. The gallop was strong and the winner came down the centre.

8371 LADBROKES H'CAP 1m 141y(P)
5:55 (5:55) (Class 7) (0-50,50) 3-Y-O+ **£1,940** (£577; £288; £144) **Stalls** Low

Form RPR

053- **1** **Ellaal**[7] 8279 4-9-6 **49**.......... DaleSwift 9 61
(Ruth Carr) *trckd ldrs: pushed along over 2f out: rdn to ld 1f out: sn hung lft: r.o wl: eased nr fin* **5/1**[2]

/ **2** *3* **Disco Dave (IRE)**[502] 4855 5-9-7 **50**.......... ShaneKelly 5 55
(Daniel Mark Loughnane) *hld up in tch: racd keenlu: rdn over 1f out: sn ev ch: edgd lft and styd on same pce ins fnl f* **8/1**

505- **3** *1/2* **Tony Hollis**[7] 8279 5-9-5 **48**..........(t) AndrewMullen 7 52
(Michael Appleby) *trckd ldr: chal over 2f out: sn rdn: styd on same pce ins fnl f* **10/1**

035- **4** *hd* **Aureolin Gulf**[24] 8055 4-8-11 **45**.......... JackDuern[(5)] 13 49
(Andrew Hollinshead) *hld up: pushed along and hdwy on outer over 2f out: rdn over 1f out: styd on* **14/1**

/00- **5** *3/4* **Huzzah (IRE)**[24] 8056 8-9-3 **46**..........(t) LukeMorris 1 48
(Michael Appleby) *hld up: pushed along over 2f out: hdwy over 1f out: nt trble ldrs* **16/1**

002- **6** *1* **Classy Trick (USA)**[7] 8279 3-9-5 **50**.......... MartinHarley 8 50
(Patrick Morris) *led: rdn and hdd 1f out: no ex ins fnl f* **11/2**[3]

024- **7** *hd* **Do More Business (IRE)**[13] 8199 6-9-2 **50**..........(bt) PhilipPrince[(5)] 2 49
(Liam Corcoran) *hld up: pushed along over 3f out: r.o ins fnl f: nvr nrr* **14/1**

664- **8** *3 1/4* **Mill I Am (USA)**[24] 8055 3-9-5 **50**.......... AndreaAtzeni 11 42
(Stuart Williams) *hld up: plld hrd: hdwy over 2f out: rdn over 1f out: wknd ins fnl f* **5/2**[1]

106- **9** *6* **Rock Diamond (IRE)**[11] 8225 3-9-3 **48**..........(p) GrahamLee 3 26
(Brendan Powell) *chsd ldrs: rdn over 3f out: wknd 2f out* **25/1**

0/5- **10** *nk* **Beauchamp Sunset**[212] 2566 3-9-5 **50**.......... RichardKingscote 10 27
(Paul Fitzsimons) *hld up: pushed along over 2f out: sn wknd* **25/1**

545- **11** *1* **Ryedale Lass**[8] 8258 5-9-7 **50**.......... HayleyTurner 6 25
(Geoffrey Deacon) *hld up: rdn over 3f out: a in rr* **8/1**

060- **12** *2 1/4* **Pendle Lady (IRE)**[7] 8279 4-9-7 **50**.......... LiamJones 12 20
(Mark Brisbourne) *sn pushed along and prom: rdn whn hmpd 3f out: wknd 2f out* **66/1**

560- **13** *1 1/2* **Stoneacre Oskar**[7] 8279 4-9-0 **46**.......... SladeO'Hara[(3)] 4 12
(Peter Grayson) *mid-div: lost pl 4f out: wknd over 2f out* **25/1**

1m 51.79s (1.29) **Going Correction** +0.175s/f (Slow)
WFA 3 from 4yo+ 2lb **13** Ran SP% **124.2**
Speed ratings (Par 97): **101,98,97,97,97 96,95,93,87,87 86,84,83**
toteswingers 1&2 £11.30, 1&3 £12.60, 2&3 £18.90 CSF £45.02 CT £398.55 TOTE £6.80: £2.30, £4.30, £4.50; EX 60.60 Trifecta £728.40 Pool: £1880.01 - 1.93 winning units..
Owner The Bottom Liners & Paul Saxton **Bred** W And R Barnett Ltd **Trained** Huby, N Yorks

FOCUS
A very moderate handicap in which the gallop was an ordinary one. The winner came down the centre in the straight.

8372 CORAL APP DOWNLOAD FROM THE APP STORE H'CAP 1m 1f 103y(P)
6:30 (6:30) (Class 6) (0-65,65) 3-Y-O **£1,940** (£577; £288; £144) **Stalls** Low

Form RPR

201- **1** **Luv U Whatever**[202] 2175 3-9-7 **65**.......... LiamJones 4 75+
(Jo Hughes) *hld up: racd keenly: hdwy 2f out: shkn up to ld and hung lft ins fnl f: rdn out* **5/1**[2]

556- **2** *2 3/4* **Taxiformissbyron**[14] 8187 3-9-2 **60**.......... TomEaves 3 64
(Michael Herrington) *a.p: rdn to ld over 1f out: hdd ins fnl f: styd on same pce* **16/1**

/40- **3** *2 3/4* **Arch Ebony (USA)**[25] 8036 3-9-4 **62**..........(v[1]) GrahamGibbons 7 60
(David O'Meara) *sn pushed along and prom: chsd ldr 6f out: rdn over 2f out: nt clr run and no ex ins fnl f* **10/1**

033- **4** *2 1/2* **Short Shrift (IRE)**[24] 8054 3-9-4 **62**.......... TonyHamilton 2 55
(Richard Fahey) *sn pushed along and prom: lost pl 6f out: nt clr run fr over 3f out tl hdwy over 1f out: sn rdn: wknd ins fnl f* **7/1**[3]

003- **5** *shd* **Lucy Bee**[14] 8186 3-8-13 **57**.......... AndrewMullen 8 50
(Michael Appleby) *led: rdn and hdd over 1f out: wknd ins fnl f* **9/1**

001- **6** *16* **Berkeley Street (USA)**[14] 8186 3-9-2 **60**..........(p) GrahamLee 5 19
(Jane Chapple-Hyam) *hld up: hdwy 6f out: rdn over 2f out: wknd over 1f out* **10/11**[1]

600- **7** *12* **Somethingboutmary**[10] 8234 3-8-13 **57**.......... DaleSwift 6
(Neville Bycroft) *chsd ldr over 2f: remained handy: rdn over 3f out: wknd 2f out* **40/1**

610- **8** *13* **Pim Street (USA)**[28] 8006 3-9-1 **62**.......... JulieBurke[(3)] 1
(David O'Meara) *hld up: a in rr: wknd over 2f out* **16/1**

2m 3.53s (1.83) **Going Correction** +0.175s/f (Slow) **8** Ran SP% **114.8**
Speed ratings (Par 98): **98,95,93,90,90 76,65,54**
toteswingers 1&2 £4.70, 1&3 £7.90, 2&3 £20.30 CSF £78.57 CT £768.37 TOTE £5.60: £2.20, £3.40, £3.40; EX 50.00 Trifecta £305.50 Pool: £2105.83 - 5.16 winning units..
Owner 21C Telecom.co.uk **Bred** Richard Hunt **Trained** Lambourn, Berks

FOCUS
A modest handicap run at an ordinary gallop. The winner edged from the centre towards the far rail in the closing stages.

8373 CORAL MOBILE "JUST THREE CLICKS TO BET" H'CAP 1m 4f 50y(P)
7:00 (7:00) (Class 6) (0-65,69) 3-Y-O+ **£1,940** (£577; £288; £144) **Stalls** Low

Form RPR

542- **1** **Monzino (USA)**[7] 8270 5-9-0 **62**..........(b) PaulBooth[(7)] 5 73
(Michael Chapman) *s.i.s: hld up: hdwy over 1f out: r.o to ld wl ins fnl f: sn clr* **11/4**[2]

564- **2** *5* **Ice Tres**[16] 8148 4-8-10 **51** oh2.......... AndreaAtzeni 6 54
(Rod Millman) *chsd ldr tl led over 2f out: rdn over 1f out: hdd and no ex wl ins fnl f* **5/1**[3]

033- **3** *1 1/2* **Star Of Namibia (IRE)**[36] 7877 3-9-5 **65**..........(be) TomEaves 2 66
(Michael Mullineaux) *chsd ldrs: rdn over 2f out: styd on same pce fnl f* **14/1**

053- **4** *5* **Geeaitch**[16] 8148 4-8-12 **53**..........(b[1]) WilliamCarson 1 46
(Peter Hiatt) *led: rdn and hdd over 2f out: hung lft and wknd fnl f* **5/2**[1]

534- **5** *1/2* **Our Golden Girl**[6] 8302 3-8-2 **55**..........(b) MatthewHopkins[(7)] 3 47
(Shaun Lycett) *hld up: pushed along over 4f out: hdwy u.p over 1f out: wknd fnl f* **5/1**[3]

100/ **6** *18* **Reality Show (IRE)**[492] 5224 6-9-4 **59**.......... JimmyQuinn 7 22
(Shaun Harris) *prom tl rdn and wknd over 2f out* **6/1**

00- **7** *1 1/4* **Diamond Pro (IRE)**[10] 8229 4-9-1 **56**..........(bt[1]) BenCurtis 8 17
(Christopher Kellett) *s.i.s: sn pushed along in rr: reminders over 8f out: rdn and wknd 3f out* **25/1**

0/0- **8** *24* **Good As New**[206] 2762 3-8-0 **51** oh2.......... TimClark[(5)] 4
(Denis Quinn) *chsd ldrs: rdn over 3f out: sn wknd* **50/1**

2m 42.94s (1.84) **Going Correction** +0.175s/f (Slow)
WFA 3 from 4yo+ 5lb **8** Ran SP% **115.3**
Speed ratings (Par 101): **100,96,95,92,92 80,79,63**
toteswingers 1&2 £2.80, 1&3 £3.70, 2&3 £7.80 CSF £17.17 CT £161.89 TOTE £2.90: £1.30, £1.90, £2.10; EX 18.80 Trifecta £176.10 Pool: £1998.78 - 8.51 winning units..
Owner Mrs M Chapman **Bred** Pillar Property Services Inc **Trained** Market Rasen, Lincs

FOCUS
A moderate handicap in which an ordinary gallop picked up leaving the back straight. The winner came down the centre.
T/Plt: £1,455.00 to a £1 stake. Pool: £72654.97 - 36.45 winning tickets T/Qpdt: £155.00 to a £1 stake. Pool: £12675.34 - 60.50 winning tickets CR

8374 - 8381a (Foreign Racing) - See Raceform Interactive

8330 LINGFIELD (L-H)
Saturday, December 21

OFFICIAL GOING: Standard
Wind: strong, behind Weather: rain, windy

8382 32RED NOVICE STKS 1m (P)
12:20 (12:20) (Class 5) 2-Y-O **£2,726** (£805; £402) **Stalls** High

Form RPR

5- **1** **Impulsive Moment (IRE)**[57] 7500 2-9-0 0.......... DavidProbert 6 76+
(Andrew Balding) *dwlt: rcvrd to chse ldr after 1f: rdn and effrt over 1f out: drvn to ld jst ins fnl f: r.o wl: rdn out* **5/4**[2]

41- **2** *1/2* **Examiner (IRE)**[12] 8214 2-9-2 78.......... LiamJones 5 77
(William Haggas) *hld up in tch: rdn and effrt on outer wl over 1f out: hdwy u.p to press wnr ins fnl f: r.o but a hld* **11/10**[1]

500- **3** *2* **Galaxy (IRE)**[24] 8067 2-9-0 72..........(v[1]) MartinHarley 7 70
(Alan McCabe) *stdd s: hld up in tch in rr: effrt and drvn over 1f out: edgd rt but styd on to go 3rd fnl 100yds: no imp after* **14/1**

01- **4** *1* **First Experience**[29] 8005 2-8-11 0.......... ChrisCatlin 2 64
(Rae Guest) *t.k.h: chsd ldr for 1f: styd chsng ldrs: drvn and effrt on inner over 1f out: outpcd fnl 100yds* **8/1**[3]

335- **5** *hd* **Rose Buck**[9] 8262 2-8-6 58.......... MarkCoumbe[(3)] 4 62
(Lee Carter) *led: rdn over 2f out: drvn and hdd jst ins fnl f: no ex and outpcd fnl 100yds* **50/1**

1m 38.42s (0.22) **Going Correction** -0.025s/f (Stan) **5** Ran SP% **111.8**
Speed ratings (Par 96): **97,96,94,93,93**
CSF £3.02 TOTE £2.00: £1.10, £1.60; EX 3.40 Trifecta £8.40 Pool: £2749.18 - 245.28 winning units..
Owner Weston Brook Farm Bromfield & Whitaker **Bred** Mrs Evie Stockwell **Trained** Kingsclere, Hants

FOCUS
A reasonable race for the class. The form fits, but the seemingly outclassed fifth does limit it.

8383 32RED.COM CLAIMING STKS 6f (P)
12:55 (12:55) (Class 6) 2-Y-O **£2,045** (£603; £302) **Stalls** Low

Form RPR

514- **1** **Touch The Clouds**[35] 7933 2-9-4 79.......... TomEaves 4 74
(Kevin Ryan) *mde all: rdn wl over 1f out: hrd pressed and drvn fnl f: hld on gamely: all out* **7/2**[2]

333- **2** *nse* **Kodafine (IRE)**[3] 8322 2-8-8 67 ow1.......... MartinHarley 1 64
(David Evans) *hld up in tch in last pair: rdn and hdwy over 1f out: nt clr run and swtchd rt ins fnl f: str run and chal wl ins fnl f: jst failed* **7/2**[2]

103- **3** *1/2* **Hipz (IRE)**[19] 8126 2-8-11 71.......... JimCrowley 3 65
(George Baker) *in tch in midfield: effrt u.p on inner over 1f out: ev ch ins fnl f: styd on same pce cl home* **3/1**[1]

245- **4** *nk* **Sebs Sensei (IRE)**[114] 5926 2-8-13 67................................ SeanLevey 6 66
(Richard Hannon Snr) *dwlt: hld up in last pair: effrt u.p on outer over 1f out: r.o wl ins fnl f: nt quite rch ldrs* **4/1**[3]

624- **5** *1 1/2* **Vodka Chaser (IRE)**[18] 8137 2-8-5 52..........................(b[1]) LiamJones 2 54
(J S Moore) *chsd ldrs: rdn and effrt to chal over 1f out: no ex and btn fnl 100yds: wknd towards fin* **25/1**

346- **6** *1 3/4* **My My My Diliza**[9] 8262 2-8-7 53.................................... DavidProbert 5 50
(J S Moore) *in tch in midfield: rdn and effrt ent fnl 2f: no imp 1f out: wknd ins fnl f* **20/1**

002- **7** *nse* **Gobertier**[3] 8326 2-9-2 0.. KieranO'Neill 7 59
(Richard Hannon Snr) *chsd ldr tl bnd wl over 1f out: styng on same pce u.p whn squeezed for room and hmpd ins fnl f: nt rcvr and hld after* **6/1**

005- **8** *2* **Previous Acclaim (IRE)**[28] 8017 2-8-2 59................. ShelleyBirkett(5) 8 43
(Julia Feilden) *hld up in tch in midfield: rdn and effrt over 1f out: no imp: wknd ins fnl f* **25/1**

1m 12.23s (0.33) **Going Correction** -0.025s/f (Stan) 8 Ran SP% **116.2**
Speed ratings (Par 94): **96,95,95,94,92 90,90,87**
toteswingers 1&2 £4.20, 1&3 £2.90, 2&3 £3.90 CSF £16.01 TOTE £4.10: £1.90, £1.50, £1.50; EX 14.40 Trifecta £25.10 Pool: £2820.02 - 84.17 winning units..
Owner Matt & Lauren Morgan 1 **Bred** Stuart McPhee Bloodstock Ltd **Trained** Hambleton, N Yorks
■ Stewards' Enquiry : Martin Harley two-day ban; careless riding (4th,5th Jan).

FOCUS
A modest claimer. The fifth is the key to the level.

8384 COMPARE BOOKMAKERS AT BOOKMAKERS.CO.UK H'CAP 5f (P)
1:25 (1:27) (Class 5) (0-70,70) 3-Y-O+ **£2,726** (£805; £402) **Stalls** High

Form RPR

040/ **1** **Expose**[443] 6824 5-9-0 **70**.................................... AliRawlinson(7) 9 78
(Michael Appleby) *stdd and awkward leaving stalls: t.k.h: hld up in rr: hdwy ent fnl 2f: waiting for gap jst over 1f out: rdn and str run ins fnl f to ld last stride* **12/1**

560- **2** *shd* **Drawnfromthepast (IRE)**[19] 8128 8-9-4 **67**..................... JimCrowley 2 75
(Luke Dace) *racd in midfield: clsd on ldrs over 1f out: drvn to ld ins fnl f: r.o u.p: hdd last stride* **5/1**

050- **3** *1/2* **Never A Quarrel (IRE)**[12] 8216 3-9-1 **64**..................... FergusSweeney 1 70
(Jeremy Gask) *taken down early: w ldr and clr tl over 2f out: ev ch u.p 1f out: no ex and one pce towards fin* **16/1**

231- **4** *1/2* **Poyle Vinnie**[31] 7969 3-9-1 **67**.................................... RyanPowell(3) 5 71
(George Margarson) *s.i.s: racd in last trio: clsd on ldrs over 2f out: effrt u.p on outer over 1f out: styd on wl ins fnl f* **7/2**[2]

206- **5** *3/4* **Lujeanie**[19] 8128 7-9-6 **69**..(b) ShaneKelly 4 70
(Peter Crate) *led and clr w rival tl over 2f out: rdn over 1f out: edgd rt and hdd ins fnl f: wknd towards fin: burst blood vessel* **8/1**

344- **6** *hd* **Hot Sugar (USA)**[19] 8135 4-8-13 **62**........................(p) AndrewMullen 3 63
(Michael Appleby) *racd in midfield: clsd on ldrs over 2f out: effrt u.p on inner over 1f out: kpt on ins fnl f* **9/2**[3]

361- **7** *1/2* **Haadeeth**[47] 7728 6-9-6 **69**..(t) AdamKirby 7 68
(David Evans) *chsd clr ldng pair: clsd on ldrs over 2f out: rdn and effrt over 1f out: styd on same pce ins fnl f* **3/1**[1]

501- **8** *shd* **Monsieur Royale**[28] 8030 3-9-5 **68**..............................(b) SeanLevey 6 66
(Geoffrey Oldroyd) *in tch in midfield: rdn and effrt over 1f out: styd on same pce fnl f* **8/1**

320- **9** *4 1/2* **Where's Reiley (USA)**[87] 6745 7-9-7 **70**.....................(v) LukeMorris 10 52
(Michael Attwater) *sn rdn along towards rr dropped to last and struggling 1/2-way: wknd over 1f out* **20/1**

58.03s (-0.77) **Going Correction** -0.025s/f (Stan) 9 Ran SP% **122.6**
Speed ratings (Par 103): **105,104,104,103,102 101,100,100,93**
toteswingers 1&2 £8.90, 1&3 £34.40, 2&3 £21.20 CSF £75.30 CT £997.00 TOTE £17.40: £4.60, £2.90, £5.70; EX 107.20 Trifecta £2427.30 Pool: £3346.89 - 1.03 winning units..
Owner The Giggle Factor Partnership **Bred** John And Susan Davis **Trained** Danethorpe, Notts
■ Stewards' Enquiry : Fergus Sweeney caution; careless riding.

FOCUS
A typically competitive sprint handicap.

8385 LADBROKES CONDITIONS STKS 1m (P)
2:00 (2:01) (Class 3) 3-Y-O+ **£7,439** (£2,213; £1,106; £553) **Stalls** High

Form RPR

450- **1** **Alfred Hutchinson**[21] 8117 5-8-9 87........................ RobertTart(3) 8 97
(Geoffrey Oldroyd) *chsd ldrs tl led over 3f out: rdn 2f out: kpt on wl u.p fnl f: drvn out* **5/2**[1]

400- **2** *1* **Emerald Wilderness (IRE)**[9] 8263 9-8-12 96............. FrederikTylicki 3 95
(Mark Rimmer) *in tch in midfield: hdwy to chse wnr 3f out: rdn over 2f out: kpt on u.p fnl f* **10/1**

060- **3** *2* **Rhamnus**[12] 8218 3-8-11 84.. SeanLevey 9 89
(Richard Hannon Snr) *dwlt: sn rcvrd and in tch in midfield: rdn and effrt over 2f out: wnt 3rd over 1f out: kpt on* **14/1**

003- **4** *nk* **Mia's Boy**[17] 8156 9-8-12 91... LukeMorris 5 89
(Chris Dwyer) *s.i.s: racd in last pair: rdn and effrt over 2f out: hdwy over 1f out: styd on wl ins fnl f: nt rch ldrs* **4/1**[2]

004- **5** *1/2* **Crius (IRE)**[170] 3984 4-8-12 86.............................. RichardKingscote 6 88
(Daniel Kubler) *hld up in last trio: nt clr run and hmpd ent fnl 2f: swtchd rt over 1f out: styd on wl ins fnl f: unable to chal* **12/1**

060- **6** *1 3/4* **Silverheels (IRE)**[63] 7368 4-8-12 83.................................... JimCrowley 1 84
(Paul Cole) *in tch in midfield: rdn over 1f out: fnd little and sn outpcd: plugged on same pce fnl f* **8/1**[3]

5- **7** *1/2* **Freewheel (IRE)**[17] 8156 3-9-0 0.................................... TonyHamilton 7 85
(David Nicholls) *hld up in last pair: rdn and effrt over 2f out: no imp: nvr trbld ldrs* **20/1**

121- **8** *9* **Tasrih (USA)**[19] 8127 4-9-3 83... MartinHarley 2 67
(Alan McCabe) *led tl 1/2-way: rdn and struggling over 2f out: btn over 1f out and sn fdd* **5/2**[1]

000- **9** *9* **Trader Jack**[21] 8117 4-8-7 87..................................(b) JoshBaudains(5) 4 42
(David Flood) *dwlt: sn rcvrd to chse ldr: led 4f out tl over 3f out: lost pl ent fnl 2f: bhd 1f out* **33/1**

1m 36.17s (-2.03) **Going Correction** -0.025s/f (Stan)
WFA 3 from 4yo+ 1lb 9 Ran SP% **119.4**
Speed ratings (Par 107): **109,108,106,105,105 103,102,93,84**
toteswingers 1&2 £4.60, 1&3 £7.70, 2&3 £26.40 CSF £30.68 TOTE £3.20: £2.00, £3.10, £3.20; EX 26.00 Trifecta £248.00 Pool: £5342.06 - 16.15 winning units..
Owner R C Bond **Bred** R C Bond **Trained** Brawby, N Yorks
■ Stewards' Enquiry : Jim Crowley £80.00 fine; entered wrong stall.

FOCUS
Form to tread carefully with.

8386 CORAL APP DOWNLOAD FROM THE APP STORE QUEBEC STKS (LISTED RACE) 1m 2f (P)
2:35 (2:35) (Class 1) 3-Y-O+
£20,982 (£7,955; £3,981; £1,983; £995; £499) **Stalls** Low

Form RPR

052- **1** **Dick Doughtywylie**[24] 8062 5-9-3 98............................(t) RobertHavlin 9 107
(John Gosden) *s.i.s: rcvrd to ld 8f out: mde rest: rdn 2f out: edging rt u.p but hld on gamely fnl f: drvn out* **5/1**[2]

232- **2** *1/2* **Gatewood**[45] 7768 5-9-3 106.. WilliamBuick 5 106
(John Gosden) *in tch towards rr: hdwy to chse wnr over 7f out: rdn and effrt 2f out: ev ch and carried rt ins fnl f: no ex and hld towards fin* **5/4**[1]

323- **3** *nk* **Galician**[11] 8231 4-8-12 99... JoeFanning 1 100
(Mark Johnston) *sn led: hdd 8f out and chsd ldrs after: effrt u.p ent fnl f: ev ch ins fnl f: unable qck fnl 75yds* **7/1**[3]

6/0- **4** *hd* **Energia Davos (BRZ)**[324] 462 5-9-3 102......................... MartinHarley 8 105
(Marco Botti) *hld up in tch towards rr: effrt and hdwy on outer over 1f out: styng on whn nt clr run and swtchd rt wl ins fnl f: nt quite rch ldrs* **16/1**

465- **5** *3/4* **Tinshu (IRE)**[24] 8071 7-8-12 91......................................(p) HayleyTurner 2 99
(Derek Haydn Jones) *broke wl: stdd bk and hld up in tch in rr: swtchd lft and hdwy on inner over 1f out: styd on same pce wl ins fnl f* **12/1**

020- **6** *1/2* **Proud Chieftain**[24] 8071 5-9-3 97......................................(v[1]) AdamKirby 3 103
(Clifford Lines) *t.k.h: hld up wl in tch in midfield: rdn and effrt 2f out: drvn and kpt on same pce ins fnl f* **12/1**

124- **7** *1 1/4* **Tales Of Grimm (USA)**[35] 7927 4-9-3 107.................. TonyHamilton 10 100
(Richard Fahey) *t.k.h early: hld up wl in tch in midfield: rdn and effrt ent fnl f: nt qckn over 1f out: wknd ins fnl f* **5/1**[2]

113- **8** *1 1/2* **Poitin**[35] 7924 3-8-9 69.. RichardKingscote 4 92?
(Harry Dunlop) *hld up in tch in midfield: rdn and effrt on inner over 1f out: no imp 1f out: wknd ins fnl f* **66/1**

404- **9** *3/4* **True To Form (IRE)**[24] 8071 6-9-3 94............................(p) LukeMorris 11 96
(Alan McCabe) *hld up in tch towards rr: rdn and effrt over 2f out: no imp over 1f out: wknd ins fnl f* **8/1**

2m 5.03s (-1.57) **Going Correction** -0.025s/f (Stan)
WFA 3 from 4yo+ 3lb 9 Ran SP% **124.1**
Speed ratings (Par 111): **105,104,104,104,103 103,102,101,100**
toteswingers 1&2 £2.30, 1&3 £6.60, 2&3 £3.10 CSF £12.59 TOTE £6.80: £1.70, £1.50, £2.00; EX 18.70 Trifecta £93.40 Pool: £4394.11 - 35.28 winning units..
Owner Ms Rachel D S Hood **Bred** Ms Rachel Hood **Trained** Newmarket, Suffolk

FOCUS
This Listed contest attracted a decent enough field, but they went steady and it paid to be handy.

8387 CORAL MOBILE "JUST THREE CLICKS TO BET" H'CAP 1m 4f (P)
3:10 (3:10) (Class 2) (0-100,94) 3-Y-O+ **£12,291** (£3,657; £1,827; £913) **Stalls** Low

Form RPR

324- **1** **Modernstone**[24] 8062 3-8-10 **85**................................ AndreaAtzeni 7 95
(William Knight) *stdd and dropped in bhd after s: hld up in rr: hdwy to chse ldrs 2f: rdn and effrt over 1f out: r.o to chal fnl 100yds: led last stride* **4/1**[2]

102- **2** *shd* **Grendisar (IRE)**[31] 7976 3-8-8 **83**..................................(p) MartinHarley 5 93
(Marco Botti) *hld up in tch in last trio: clsd and travelling wl 2f out: rdn and qcknd to ld jst ins fnl f: r.o u.p: hdd last stride* **11/4**[1]

206- **3** *2 3/4* **Mawaakef (IRE)**[46] 7757 5-8-13 **83**.................................. FrederikTylicki 1 88
(J R Jenkins) *chsd ldr for 2f: styd chsng ldrs: effrt u.p 2f out: ev ch 1f out: no ex and outpcd fnl 100yds* **10/1**

644- **4** *1 3/4* **Super Say (IRE)**[30] 7990 7-8-12 **82**..............................(t) AndrewMullen 3 85
(Michael Appleby) *taken down early: led: rdn 2f out: hdd and squeezed for room jst ins fnl f: wknd fnl 100yds* **5/1**[3]

155- **5** *3/4* **Nautilus**[17] 8150 3-9-5 **94**... WilliamBuick 6 95
(John Gosden) *dwlt and pushed along early: hdwy to chse ldr 10f out: rdn 2f out: unable qck and n.m.r ent fnl f: wknd fnl 150yds* **11/4**[1]

220- **6** *3/4* **Lowther**[7] 8301 8-9-8 **92**..(v) TomEaves 4 92
(Lee Carter) *in tch in midfield: rdn 3f out: chsd ldrs and drvn over 1f out: no ex 1f out and wknd ins fnl f* **8/1**

404- **7** *7* **Lady Rosamunde**[162] 4234 5-8-13 **83**...........................(v) MartinDwyer 2 72
(Marcus Tregoning) *in tch in last trio: rdn and dropped to last 3f out: sn struggling: wknd wl over 1f out* **16/1**

2m 29.82s (-3.18) **Going Correction** -0.025s/f (Stan)
WFA 3 from 5yo+ 5lb 7 Ran SP% **116.1**
Speed ratings (Par 109): **109,108,107,105,105 104,100**
toteswingers 1&2 £2.60, 1&3 £8.90, 2&3 £6.20 CSF £15.92 TOTE £5.60: £2.60, £1.80; EX 9.00 Trifecta £80.90 Pool: £4138.41 - 38.34 winning units..
Owner Biddestone Racing Club **Bred** Oscar Stud **Trained** Patching, W Sussex

FOCUS
Not a great turnout for this Class 2 handicap, but the front pair are going the right way.

8388 FREDERICK JAMES BOUCH MEMORIAL CORAL.CO.UK H'CAP 1m 4f (P)
3:40 (3:42) (Class 6) (0-65,65) 3-Y-O **£2,045** (£603; £302) **Stalls** Low

Form RPR

502- **1** **Modem**[15] 8182 3-9-7 **65**...(b) AndreaAtzeni 13 74
(Rod Millman) *t.k.h: chsd ldrs: wnt 2nd 10f out tl rdn to ld 2f: kpt on gamely u.p fnl f: jst hld on* **11/4**[2]

360- **2** *hd* **Tornado Battle**[8] 8279 3-8-3 **47**......................................(t) DavidProbert 4 55
(Phil McEntee) *hld up in midfield: swtchd lft and hdwy ent fnl f: gd hdwy to chal fnl 75yds: r.o wl: jst hld* **25/1**

641- **3** *1/2* **Rainford Glory (IRE)**[12] 8225 3-9-0 **58**.......................... MartinHarley 5 65
(David Simcock) *hld up in midfield: hdwy u.p to chse ldrs over 1f out: kpt on same pce fnl 100yds* **5/1**[3]

540- **4** *1 1/4* **Fair Comment**[19] 0121 3-8-11 **55**................................ FergusSweeney 6 60
(Michael Blanshard) *t.k.h: hld up wl in tch in midfield: hdwy to chse ldrs 3f out: rdn and effrt over 1f out: drvn and one pce fnl f* **14/1**

543- **5** *3 1/4* **Paddy's Saltantes (IRE)**[24] 8072 3-9-7 **65**........................(b) AdamKirby 12 65
(J S Moore) *chsd ldrs: rdn over 2f out: no ex u.p over 1f out: wknd ins fnl f* **2/1**[1]

00- **6** *nse* **Anjuna Beach (USA)**[38] 7857 3-9-3 **61**............................ GeorgeBaker 9 61
(Gary Moore) *stdd and dropped in bhd after s: hld up in rr: hdwy over 2f out: rdn and effrt over 1f out: no imp fnl f* **12/1**

020- **7** *1 1/2* **Ocean Power (IRE)**[32] 7963 3-7-11 **48**..............................[1] JoeDoyle(7) 1 46
(Richard Phillips) *in tch in midfield: effrt u.p on inner over 1f out: no imp 1f out: wknd ins fnl f* **20/1**

430- **8** *nk* **Perivale (USA)**[12] 8227 3-9-2 **60**... JoeFanning 2 57
(Mark Johnston) *led tl 10f out: chsd ldrs after: drvn and unable qck over 1f out: wknd ins fnl f* **10/1**

506- 9 1 ½ **Icanboogie**[264] 1289 3-8-2 **46** oh1 .... KieranO'Neill 10 41
(Anthony Middleton) *hld up towards rr: hdwy over 1f out: rdn and no imp over 1f out: wknd fnl f* **50/1**
620- 10 *hd* **Red Catkin**[19] 8121 3-8-12 **59** ....(b¹) RyanPowell(3) 11 53
(George Margarson) *t.k.h: hld up wl in tch in midfield: rdn and unable qck 2f out: wknd ent fnl f* **20/1**
240- 11 6 **Countess Lovelace**[222] 2325 3-9-7 **65** .... LukeMorris 3 50
(Pat Phelan) *t.k.h: chsd ldr tl 10f out: rdn and hdd 2f out: lost pl over 1f out: wknd fnl f* **14/1**
060- 12 21 **Feather Dancer**[101] 6312 3-8-2 **46** oh1 .... FrankieMcDonald 7
(Jamie Poulton) *a towards rr and pushed along at times: effrt on outer 3f out: sn btn: wknd 2f out* **66/1**

2m 34.16s (1.16) **Going Correction** -0.025s/f (Stan) 12 Ran SP% **123.6**
Speed ratings (Par 98): **95,94,94,93,91 91,90,90,89,89 85,71**
toteswingers 1&2 £9.90, 1&3 £3.30, 2&3 £18.00 CSF £80.88 CT £345.08 TOTE £3.70: £1.10, £7.30, £1.60; EX 48.60 Trifecta £450.20 Pool: £1611.89 - 2.68 winning units..
Owner D J Deer **Bred** D J And Mrs Deer **Trained** Kentisbeare, Devon

FOCUS
A race run in near darkness.
T/Plt: £98.30. Pool: £82,215.68 - 610.54 winning units. T/Qpdt: £85.80. Pool: £5091.55 - 43.90 winning units. SP

8382 LINGFIELD (L-H)
Sunday, December 22

OFFICIAL GOING: Standard
Wind: strong, half behind Weather: dry, breeezy

8389 32RED.COM MAIDEN STKS 1m (P)
1:30 (1:34) (Class 5) 2-Y-O £2,587 (£770; £384; £192) Stalls High

Form RPR
632- 1 **Sheila's Footsteps**[13] 8214 2-9-5 73 .... DavidProbert 4 72
(J S Moore) *chsd ldrs: rdn and effrt whn bmpd jst over 2f out: styd on wl u.p ins fnl f to ld cl home* **3/1²**
302- 2 *nk* **Irish Tears**[18] 8147 2-9-5 73 ....(t) RobertHavlin 6 71
(John Gosden) *t.k.h: led: rdn wl over 1f out: drvn 1f out: kpt on tl hdd and no ex cl home* **7/4¹**
0- 3 1 ¾ **Timeless War (USA)**[4] 8333 2-9-5 0 .... LiamJones 5 67
(William Haggas) *in tch in rr: pushed along 4f out: rdn over 2f out: swtchd lft 1f out: kpt on u.p: wnt 3rd cl home* **20/1**
56- 4 ½ **Ayers Rock (IRE)**[20] 8123 2-9-5 0 .... ShaneKelly 2 66
(Marcus Tregoning) *stdd s: t.k.h: hdwy to chse ldrs 5f out: wnt 2nd over 2f out: effrt u.p wl over 1f out: no ex ins fnl f: wknd towards fin* **8/1³**
0- 5 10 **Confucius Legend (IRE)**[66] 7320 2-9-5 0 .... StephenCraine 3 43
(Jim Boyle) *awkward leaving stalls and s.i.s: hdwy to join ldr after 2f: rdn 3f out: losing pl whn wandered u.p jst over 2f out: wknd over 1f out* **100/1**
3- 6 2 ¼ **Fine Vintage (FR)**[29] 8026 2-9-5 0 .... AdamKirby 1 38
(Mark Johnston) *t.k.h: hld up wl in tch: pushed along 4f and nvr looked happy after: rdn wl over 1f out: no hdwy and wknd 1f out* **7/4¹**

1m 38.77s (0.57) **Going Correction** -0.05s/f (Stan) 6 Ran SP% **114.6**
Speed ratings (Par 96): **95,94,92,92,82 80**
toteswingers 1&2 £1.50, 1&3 £9.40, 2&3 £6.90 CSF £8.98 TOTE £3.30: £1.10, £2.00; EX 6.30 Trifecta £104.90 Pool: £4075.74 - 29.12 winning units..
Owner Ray Styles & J S Moore **Bred** J S B Anderson **Trained** Upper Lambourn, Berks

FOCUS
Despite one joint-favourite disappointing, the form looks reliable with two 73-rated rivals fighting out the finish. Straightforward but limited form.

8390 DOWNLOAD THE LADBROKES APP H'CAP 1m (P)
2:00 (2:03) (Class 6) (0-52,52) 3-Y-O+ £1,940 (£577; £288; £144) Stalls High

Form RPR
040- 1 **Archelao (IRE)**[74] 7124 5-9-7 52 .... AmirQuinn 12 61
(Lee Carter) *hld up in midfield: smooth hdwy over 2f out: rdn and effrt over 1f out: led ins fnl f: rdn out* **7/2¹**
404- 2 ¾ **Polydamos**[18] 8149 4-9-2 47 .... AdamKirby 3 54
(Tony Carroll) *hld up in midfield: rdn 2f out: hdwy u.p over 1f out: chsd wnr wl ins fnl f: r.o wl* **4/1²**
000- 3 2 ¼ **Starbotton**[19] 8142 3-8-9 46 .... ShirleyTeasdale(5) 10 47
(James Bethell) *led: fnd ex u.p wl over 1f out: hdd ins fnl f: wknd towards fin* **20/1**
025- 4 *nse* **Bennelong**[8] 8302 7-9-4 52 ....(b) MarkCoumbe(3) 5 54
(Lee Carter) *hld up in last quartet: switching to outer and hdwy bnd 2f out: styd on wl u.p fnl f: nvr trbld ldrs* **8/1**
/05- 5 3 ¼ **Cativo Cavallino**[32] 7981 10-9-0 48 .... NataliaGemelova(3) 11 43
(John E Long) *bustled along early: chsd ldrs: rdn to chse ldr over 2f out: no ex and outpcd over 1f out: wknd ins fnl f* **7/1³**
031- 6 1 ½ **Meglio Ancora**[9] 8279 6-9-1 51 ....(tp) JoshBaudains(5) 4 42
(Richard Ford) *hld up in midfield: nt clr run over 2f out: effrt on inner over 1f out: no imp u.p 1f out: wknd ins fnl f* **7/1³**
000- 7 ½ **Byrd In Hand (IRE)**[36] 7923 6-8-8 46 oh1 ....(p) RyanWhile(7) 2 36
(John Bridger) *chsd ldrs: drvn and no ex wl over 1f out: wknd ent fnl f* **20/1**
605- 8 3 ½ **Blue Deer (IRE)**[11] 8244 5-9-6 51 ....(v) KierenFox 8 33
(Lee Carter) *hld up in last quartet: pushed along and effrt on outer over 3f out: struggling ent fnl 2f: sn wknd* **12/1**
000- 9 1 ¾ **Cuthbert (IRE)**[10] 8258 6-9-1 46 ....(v) RobertHavlin 1 24
(Michael Attwater) *hld up in last quartet: n.d* **12/1**
055- 10 3 ¼ **Meetha Achar**[244] 1711 3-9-2 48 .... StephenCraine 9 17
(Jim Boyle) *v.s.a: rcvrd and in tch in last quartet after 1f out: bhd and no hdwy whn nt clr run over 1f out: n.d* **8/1**
/40- 11 4 **Ottavino (IRE)**[99] 6400 4-9-2 47 .... LiamJones 7 8
(Jane Chapple-Hyam) *rdn along early: chsd ldr tl over 2f out: wknd qckly wl over 1f out: bhd fnl f* **20/1**

1m 37.35s (-0.85) **Going Correction** -0.05s/f (Stan)
WFA 3 from 4yo+ 1lb 11 Ran SP% **119.1**
Speed ratings (Par 101): **102,101,99,98,95 94,93,90,88,85 81**
toteswingers 1&2 £3.60, 1&3 £15.60, 2&3 £17.00 CSF £16.89 CT £235.79 TOTE £4.10: £1.80, £1.90, £8.80; EX 19.20 Trifecta £439.40 Pool: £4211.21 - 7.18 winning units..
Owner Miss Victoria Baalham **Bred** Mount Coote Stud And M H Dixon **Trained** Epsom, Surrey

FOCUS
A moderate handicap.

8391 LADBROKES H'CAP 7f (P)
2:30 (2:34) (Class 3) (0-90,90) 3-Y-O+
£7,158 (£2,143; £1,071; £535; £267; £134) Stalls Low

Form RPR
033- 1 **Mr David (USA)**[13] 8217 6-8-13 82 ....(b) DavidProbert 2 91
(Jamie Osborne) *chsd ldrs: rdn and effrt over 1f out: qcknd and str run to ld wl ins fnl f: sn in command and gng away at fin* **14/1**
315- 2 1 ½ **Loyalty**[10] 8264 6-9-0 90 ....(v) AdamMcLean(7) 3 95
(Derek Shaw) *hld up in tch in midfield: rdn and effrt over 1f out: hdwy whn nt clr run and swtchd rt ins fnl f: r.o wl to snatch 2nd on post: no threat to wnr* **8/1³**
341- 3 *nse* **Jungle Bay**[25] 8069 6-8-8 77 ....(b) MartinDwyer 5 82
(Jane Chapple-Hyam) *dwlt: swtchd lft and hdwy to chse ldrs after 1f and t.k.h: rdn and ev ch over 1f out: led ins fnl f: sn hdd and one pce after: lost 2nd on post* **14/1**
001- 4 ½ **Strictly Silca**[29] 8020 3-8-5 81 ....(v) DanielCremin(7) 6 84
(Mick Channon) *hld up in tch in midfield: rdn and effrt over 1f out: swtchd lft ins fnl f: kpt on wl u.p but no threat to wnr* **7/1²**
412- 5 ½ **Noble Deed**[134] 5260 3-9-7 90 .... LiamJones 10 92
(Michael Attwater) *led to s and mounted at s: t.k.h: chsd ldr: rdn 2f out: drvn and led 1f out: sn hdd and no ex: wknd fnl 75yds* **20/1**
213- 6 ¾ **Emkanaat**[37] 7896 5-8-3 79 .... LouisSteward(7) 1 79
(Amy Weaver) *led: rdn wl over 1f out: hdd and no ex 1f out: wknd fnl 75yds* **10/1**
005- 7 *shd* **Nassau Storm**[20] 8127 4-9-0 83 ....(t) JimCrowley 8 83
(William Knight) *hld up in last trio: hdwy on inner over 1f out: clsng whn nt clr run ins fnl f: nt rcvr: swtchd rt and kpt on towards fin* **7/4¹**
330- 8 ½ **Liberty Jack (IRE)**[20] 8127 3-8-7 76 .... WilliamCarson 7 74
(Jim Boyle) *s.i.s and swtchd lft after s: rdn and effrt over 1f out: kpt on ins fnl f: nvr trbld ldrs* **16/1**
021- 9 1 **Capaill Liath (IRE)**[20] 8122 5-9-0 83 ....(p) RobertWinston 9 79
(Kevin Ryan) *in tch in last trio: rdn and wd bnd 2f out: kpt on same pce and no imp after* **8/1³**

1m 23.41s (-1.39) **Going Correction** -0.05s/f (Stan) 9 Ran SP% **104.2**
Speed ratings (Par 107): **105,103,103,102,102 101,101,100,99**
toteswingers 1&2 £14.10, 1&3 £18.00, 2&3 £19.70 CSF £97.92 CT £1167.87 TOTE £12.70: £3.20, £2.60, £3.80; EX 121.10 Trifecta £1223.40 Pool: £4150.31 - 2.54 winning units..
Owner Steve Jakes & S J Piper Partnership **Bred** Mr & Mrs R David Randal **Trained** Upper Lambourn, Berks
■ Stewards' Enquiry : Martin Dwyer one-day ban; careless riding (5th Jan).
Daniel Cremin one-day ban; careless riding (5th Jan).

FOCUS
A competitive handicap that saw a bit of jostling late on and a bunched finish after a steady early pace.

8392 32RED H'CAP 2m (P)
3:00 (3:05) (Class 4) (0-85,86) 3-Y-O+ £4,851 (£1,443; £721; £360) Stalls Low

Form RPR
0/3- 1 **Clerk's Choice (IRE)**[32] 7976 7-9-4 75 .... JimCrowley 7 85
(William Jarvis) *hld up in midfield: rdn and hdwy on inner 2f out: chsd wnr and swtchd rt over 1f out: r.o wl u.p to ld fnl 50yds* **11/4²**
106- 2 *nk* **Be Perfect (USA)**[32] 7975 4-10-0 85 .... TonyHamilton 5 95
(David Nicholls) *led: rdn over 1f out: drvn ins fnl f: kpt on tl hdd and no ex fnl 50yds* **9/2³**
601- 3 4 ½ **Scottish Boogie (IRE)**[30] 8004 6-9-10 81 ....(t) GeorgeBaker 3 86
(Seamus Durack) *stdd s: hld up in last pair: rdn and hdwy on outer wl over 1f out: styd on ins fnl f to snatch 3rd on post: no threat to ldrs* **6/1**
621- 4 *nk* **Norfolk Sky**[24] 8089 4-9-2 73 .... FergusSweeney 4 77
(Laura Mongan) *chsd ldrs tl wnt 2nd wl over 3f out: rdn over 2f out: lost 2nd and unable qck over 1f out: wknd ins fnl f* **5/1**
000- 5 1 ¾ **Nave (USA)**[32] 7975 6-9-5 76 .... LiamKeniry 9 78
(David Simcock) *in tch in midfield: rdn and effrt ent fnl 2f: outpcd and btn over 1f out: wknd ins fnl f* **14/1**
341- 6 1 ¾ **Spiritoftomintoul**[116] 5895 4-10-0 85 .... AdamKirby 2 85
(Tony Carroll) *stdd s: hld up in last pair: rdn and hdwy on outer to chse ldrs over 2f out: no ex and btn over 1f out: wknd ins fnl f* **5/2¹**
0/0- 7 16 **Tuscan Gold**[224] 1670 6-9-4 75 .... LiamJones 8 56
(Laura Mongan) *t.k.h: chsd ldr tl wl over 3f out: sn rdn and lost pl: bhd over 1f out* **33/1**
100- 8 16 **Wildomar**[231] 2044 4-9-8 86 .... JoeDoyle(7) 1 48
(Tony Carroll) *in tch in midfield: rdn and lost pl over 3f out: lost tch over 2f out: t.o fnl f* **33/1**

3m 20.24s (-5.46) **Going Correction** -0.05s/f (Stan) 8 Ran SP% **116.9**
Speed ratings (Par 105): **111,110,108,108,107 106,98,90**
toteswingers 1&2 £3.30, 1&3 £3.80, 2&3 £4.60 CSF £16.06 CT £67.07 TOTE £3.60: £1.30, £2.10, £2.20; EX 16.00 Trifecta £86.30 Pool: £4680.42 - 40.63 winning units..
Owner M C Banks **Bred** N Coman **Trained** Newmarket, Suffolk

FOCUS
This was run at a steady pace giving those racing prominently an advantage.

8393 BEST ODDS AT BOOKMAKERS.CO.UK H'CAP 6f (P)
3:30 (3:32) (Class 6) (0-52,50) 3-Y-O+ £1,940 (£577; £288; £144) Stalls Low

Form RPR
005- 1 **Kasbhom**[3] 8338 3-9-7 50 ....(t) WilliamCarson 9 60
(Anthony Carson) *in tch in midfield on outer: hdwy to chse ldrs over 2f out: effrt u.p over 1f out: edgd lft u.p but r.o to ld wl ins fnl f: drvn out* **5/2¹**
005- 2 1 **Christopher Chua (IRE)**[18] 8146 4-8-11 45 ....(v) DavidKenny(5) 10 52
(Michael Scudamore) *hld up in tch towards rr: rdn and gd hdwy on inner over 1f out: led ins fnl f: hdd and one pce wl ins fnl f* **16/1**
400- 3 *shd* **Microlight**[66] 7323 5-9-2 45 ....(b) JimmyQuinn 5 51
(John E Long) *chsd ldr: rdn and effrt 2f out: ev ch 1f out: carried lft ins fnl f: unable qck and hung lft cl home* **20/1**
030- 4 ½ **Demoiselle Bond**[24] 8082 5-9-5 48 .... RobertHavlin 3 53
(Lydia Richards) *taken down early: led: rdn and edgd rt over 1f out: hdd ins fnl f: carried lft and one pce wl ins fnl f: bmpd and eased last strides* **8/1**
600- 5 ¾ **Surrey Dream (IRE)**[52] 7644 4-9-2 45 ....(v¹) MartinDwyer 2 47
(John Bridger) *chsd ldrs: rdn and ev ch 1f out: styd on same pce ins fnl f: hld whn hmpd last strides* **25/1**
404- 6 *hd* **Rutterkin (USA)**[8] 8293 5-8-10 46 .... VictorSantos(7) 8 48
(James Moffatt) *stdd: awkward leaving stalls and slowly away: bhd: hdwy over 1f out: running on whn n.m.r and squeezed between horses ins fnl f: nt clr run and swtchd rt towards fin: r.o: nt rch ldrs* **7/1³**

605- 7 3/4 **Sally Bruce**[3] 8338 3-9-0 50................................(b) JenniferFerguson(7) 12 49
(Edward Creighton) *hld up in tch towards rr: hdwy to chse ldrs and n.m.r ent fnl f: nvr much room and styd on same pce ins fnl f* **25/1**

/46- 8 nse **Play The Blues (IRE)**[24] 8082 6-8-13 47.................(t) JoshBaudains(5) 6 46
(Dominic Ffrench Davis) *in tch in midfield: bmpd bnd ent fnl 2f: rdn and effrt over 1f out: ev ch 1f out: no ex and btn wl ins fnl f: nt clr run and eased nr fin* **14/1**

055- 9 2 **Imjin River (IRE)**[24] 8082 6-8-12 48........................(t) LouisSteward(7) 11 41
(William Stone) *hld up in last pair: rdn and effrt over 1f out: no real imp fnl f: nvr trbld ldrs* **10/1**

054- 10 1 **Kaylee**[16] 8180 4-9-6 49.. AdamKirby 1 39
(Brett Johnson) *in tch in midfield: nt clr run and hmpd bnd ent fnl 2f: rdn and no hdwy over 1f out* **8/1**

/00- 11 6 **Chiltern Secret**[188] 3417 3-9-3 46................................. RobertWinston 4 16
(Dean Ivory) *chsd ldrs: edgd lft and bmpd rival bnd ent fnl 2f: lost pl wl over 1f out: sn wknd* **3/1**[2]

1m 11.81s (-0.09) **Going Correction** -0.05s/f (Stan) **11** Ran SP% **122.4**
Speed ratings (Par 101): **98,96,96,95,94 94,93,93,90,89 81**
toteswingers 1&2 £14.50, 1&3 £19.20, 2&3 £64.60 CSF £45.61 CT £670.92 TOTE £3.70: £1.90, £8.10, £7.10; EX 64.70 Trifecta £1608.80 Pool: £4129.93 - 1.92 winning units..
Owner Macattack, William Lea Screed & Form IT **Bred** Darley **Trained** Newmarket, Suffolk

FOCUS
A moderate affair producing a bunched finish. The winner and third delivered their challenges wide and veered towards the middle.
T/Plt: £48.90. Pool: £74,231.86 - 1106.21 winning units. T/Qpdt: £31.10. Pool: 7629.70 - 181.40 winning units. SP

8394 - (Foreign Racing) - See Raceform Interactive

8367 WOLVERHAMPTON (A.W) (L-H)

Thursday, December 26

OFFICIAL GOING: Standard
Wind: Light; behind Weather: Dry; chilly

8395 COMPARE BOOKMAKERS AT BOOKMAKERS.CO.UK CONDITIONS STKS 5f 216y(P)

1:40 (1:40) (Class 2) 3-Y-O+ **£11,827** (£3,541; £1,770; £885) **Stalls** Low

Form RPR

000- 1 **Ballista (IRE)**[8] 8334 5-9-4 106.................................... RichardKingscote 1 109
(Tom Dascombe) *trckd ldng pair: rdn and effrt on inner wl over 1f out: ev ch 1f out: led wl ins fnl f: r.o wl* **3/1**[2]

200- 2 nk **Masamah (IRE)**[82] 7010 7-9-4 103.................................... PaddyAspell 3 108
(Marco Botti) *t.k.h: chsd ldr: rdn and effrt wl over 1f out: ev ch over 1f out: led ins fnl f: hdd wl ins fnl f: kpt on but hld towards fin* **7/2**[3]

120- 3 2 1/4 **Addictive Dream (IRE)**[8] 8334 6-9-4 100................. TonyHamilton 2 101
(David Nicholls) *led and set stdy gallop: qcknd 2f out: hdd jst ins fnl f: stl ev ch whn edgd lft fnl 100yds: sn btn and wknd towards fin* **6/1**

116- 4 3 1/4 **Forest Edge (IRE)**[8] 8334 4-9-4 105........................(b) AdamKirby 4 90
(David Evans) *dwlt and sn niggled along in tch in rr: drvn 1/2-way: hdwy u.p on outer over 1f out: no ex and btn fnl 100yds: eased towards fin* **5/4**[1]

1m 15.81s (0.81) **Going Correction** +0.25s/f (Slow) **4** Ran SP% **106.0**
Speed ratings (Par 109): **104,103,100,96**
CSF £12.37 TOTE £4.30; EX 9.70 Trifecta £36.10 Pool: £661.41 - 13.72 winning units..
Owner Well Done Top Man Partnership **Bred** Sj Partnership **Trained** Malpas, Cheshire

FOCUS
A tight conditions sprint to commence the card with only 6lb splitting four rivals. The form makes sense on paper but it was a small field conditions race in which the favourite disappointed, so it's not bombproof.

8396 32RED.COM EBF STALLIONS MAIDEN STKS 5f 20y(P)

2:10 (2:10) (Class 5) 2-Y-O **£2,911** (£866; £432; £216) **Stalls** Low

Form RPR

02- 1 **Royal Birth**[12] 8300 2-9-5 0.. AdamKirby 3 84+
(Stuart Williams) *mde all: shkn up and qcknd clr 2f out: in n.d after: eased towards fin* **5/6**[1]

56U- 2 6 **Shamardyh (IRE)**[21] 8166 2-9-0 59................................. DavidProbert 4 55
(David Evans) *dwlt: sn rcvrd to chse ldng pair: wnt 2nd 3f out: rdn and outpcd by wnr 2f out: no ch w wnr but kpt on for clr 2nd* **6/1**[3]

306- 3 4 1/2 **Pieman's Girl**[28] 8084 2-9-0 65.................................. WilliamCarson 1 39
(Anthony Carson) *pushed along early: in tch in last pair: rdn and outpcd 2f out: no ch after: wnt modest 3rd ins fnl f* **14/1**

003- 4 3 1/4 **Broadway Ranger (IRE)**[47] 7818 2-9-5 72................. RobertWinston 2 32
(Charles Hills) *chsd wnr tl 3f: rdn 2f out: sn outpcd and hung lft: wknd fnl f* **5/2**[2]

0- 5 9 **Mirror (IRE)**[22] 8145 2-9-0 0....................................... RichardKingscote 6
(Ed Dunlop) *stdd s: t.k.h: hld up in tch in last pair: hung rt and rdn 2f out: sn btn and bhd* **16/1**

1m 2.59s (0.29) **Going Correction** +0.25s/f (Slow) **5** Ran SP% **110.0**
Speed ratings (Par 96): **107,97,90,85,70**
CSF £6.41 TOTE £1.70: £1.50, £1.90; EX 6.80 Trifecta £36.70 Pool: £1,525.24 - 31.09 winning units..
Owner Qatar Racing Limited **Bred** Old Mill Stud & S Williams & J Parry **Trained** Newmarket, Suffolk

FOCUS
On paper this didn't appear a one-horse race but with a couple of runners performing well below their official ratings it turned into one. The winner was given a good ride, but he thrashed his rivals and doubt this form flatters him.

8397 32RED NURSERY H'CAP 1m 141y(P)

2:40 (2:40) (Class 4) (0-85,83) 2-Y-O **£3,752** (£1,116; £557; £278) **Stalls** Low

Form RPR

214- 1 **Act Of Charity (IRE)**[62] 7492 2-9-7 83.......................... DavidProbert 2 87
(Gay Kelleway) *mde all: rdn and qcknd 2f out: styd on wl u.p fnl f: drvn out* **3/1**[2]

221- 2 1 1/2 **Resolute**[30] 8044 2-9-3 79.. LiamJones 3 79+
(William Haggas) *awkward leaving stalls: t.k.h: chsd ldr tl dropped to last but stl wl in tch over 6f out: rdn 2f out and outpcd over 1f out: rallied u.p ins fnl f: styd on to snatch 2nd last strides* **10/11**[1]

41- 3 hd **Tucson Arizona**[28] 8085 2-8-12 74.............................. WilliamCarson 4 74
(Anthony Carson) *hld up wl in tch: chsd wnr over 6f out: rdn and sltly outpcd in 3rd over 1f out: rallied and styd on u.p fnl 75yds* **4/1**[3]

122- 4 shd **Jazzy Lady (IRE)**[10] 8311 2-8-3 70................................ JoeyHaynes(5) 1 70
(David Evans) *niggled along but wl in tch: effrt on inner to chse wnr u.p over 1f out: no ex ins fnl f: plugged on same pce and lost 2 pls last strides* **7/1**

1m 52.78s (2.28) **Going Correction** +0.25s/f (Slow) **4** Ran SP% **109.9**
Speed ratings (Par 98): **99,97,97,97**
CSF £6.33 TOTE £4.00; EX 5.20 Trifecta £8.20 Pool: £1,342.83 - 121.52 winning units..
Owner Andy Wong **Bred** J Kenny **Trained** Exning, Suffolk

FOCUS
Just the four runners, but still an interesting nursery. There was a steady pace, dictated by the winner, and it's not form to rely on too heavily.

8398 CORAL APP DOWNLOAD FROM THE APP STORE H'CAP 1m 1f 103y(P)

3:15 (3:18) (Class 2) (0-105,95) 3-Y-O£11,971 (£3,583; £1,791; £896; £446) **Stalls** Low

Form RPR

401- 1 **String Theory (IRE)**[14] 8263 3-9-7 95.............................. AdamKirby 1 105+
(Marco Botti) *mde all: rdn 2f out: drvn clr and in command 1f out: eased towards fin* **11/10**[1]

063- 2 2 1/4 **Teolagi (IRE)**[12] 8301 3-8-6 85.................................. JoeyHaynes(5) 2 90
(J S Moore) *t.k.h: chsd ldng pair: rdn wl over 2f out: battling for 2nd but outpcd by wnr over 1f out: kpt on same pce and wnt 2nd wl ins fnl f* **5/1**

114- 3 1/2 **Epic Battle (IRE)**[12] 8301 3-8-10 84................................(p) LiamJones 5 88
(William Haggas) *chsd wnr: drvn 3f out: outpcd by wnr over 1f out: kpt on same pce after: lost 2nd wl ins fnl f* **7/2**[2]

232- 4 2 3/4 **Swing Alone (IRE)**[17] 8218 4-9-4 90.......................... DavidProbert 4 88
(Gay Kelleway) *in tch in last pair: rdn over 3f out: 4th and outpcd u.p 2f out: wl hld but plugged on ins fnl f* **9/2**[3]

350- 5 8 **Spifer (IRE)**[8] 8327 5-9-7 93..(p) PaddyAspell 3 75
(Marco Botti) *s.i.s: in tch in rr: rdn over 3f out: struggling over 2f out: wknd 2f out* **14/1**

2m 2.88s (1.18) **Going Correction** +0.25s/f (Slow)
WFA 3 from 4yo+ 2lb **5** Ran SP% **111.4**
Speed ratings (Par 109): **104,102,101,99,92**
CSF £7.15 TOTE £1.70: £1.30, £2.90; EX 8.40 Trifecta £17.80 Pool: £2,193.21 - 91.98 winning units..
Owner Prince A A Faisal **Bred** Minch Bloodstock **Trained** Newmarket, Suffolk

FOCUS
A Boxing Day treat for all-weather fans with five smart performers fighting it out. The winner built on his Kempton win and can rate higher again, while the third confirmed his latest effort in a good race.

8399 CORAL.CO.UK BEST ODDS GUARANTEED ON RACING H'CAP 1m 1f 103y(P)

3:45 (3:46) (Class 6) (0-60,60) 3-Y-O+ **£1,940** (£577; £288; £144) **Stalls** Low

Form RPR

240- 1 **Do More Business (IRE)**[6] 8371 6-8-6 50..............(vt) PhilipPrince(5) 10 59
(Liam Corcoran) *hld up in tch towards rr: rdn and hdwy on outer over 2f out: chal ins fnl f: led and edgd lft fnl 75yds: hld on wl towards fin: all out* **16/1**

025- 2 nk **General Tufto**[16] 8233 8-8-3 47....................................(b) JoeyHaynes(5) 8 55
(Charles Smith) *hld up in midfield: hdwy u.p over 1f out: str chal wl ins fnl f: r.o but hld towards fin* **25/1**

641- 3 2 **Tukitinyasok (IRE)**[13] 8275 6-9-0 53............................. BarryMcHugh 6 57
(Clive Mulhall) *chsd ldrs: wnt 2nd over 6f out: rdn and ev ch 2f out: edgd lft and led jst ins fnl f: hdd and no ex fnl 75yds* **15/2**

562- 4 1/2 **Taxiformissbyron**[6] 8372 3-9-5 60.................................... TomEaves 3 63
(Michael Herrington) *chsd ldrs: effrt u.p wl over 1f out: swtchd lft ins fnl f: styd on u.p fnl 75yds* **6/1**[3]

053- 5 3/4 **Secret Song**[13] 8275 3-9-2 57.. ChrisCatlin 5 59
(Sir Mark Prescott Bt) *sn led: rdn over 3f out: drvn wl over 1f out: hdd and no ex jst ins fnl f: wknd fnl 75yds* **9/4**[1]

300- 6 3/4 **Stamp Duty (IRE)**[30] 8056 5-8-7 46 oh1..................... WilliamCarson 12 46
(Suzzanne France) *hld up in last trio: hdwy on inner over 1f out: nt clr run and swtchd rt jst ins fnl f: r.o wl: nt rch ldrs* **33/1**

524- 7 1 3/4 **Mojo Bear**[13] 8275 3-9-3 58..(p) AdamKirby 7 54
(Sylvester Kirk) *chsd ldrs: rdn over 3f out: drvn and hdwy to chse ldrs over 1f out: no ex ins fnl f: wknd fnl 75yds* **5/1**[2]

500- 8 1 **Scamperdale**[29] 8072 11-9-2 58................................(p) RyanPowell(3) 11 52
(Brian Baugh) *hld up in tch towards rr: clsd and nt clr run over 2f out: rdn and hdwy over 1f out: keeping on same pce whn pushed lft and hmpd ins fnl f: wknd fnl 75yds* **12/1**

560- 9 1 **Justcallmehandsome**[30] 8055 11-8-0 46 oh1(be) JosephineGordon(7) 13 38
(Dominic Ffrench Davis) *chsd ldrs: rdn over 2f out: struggling u.p over 1f out: wknd ins fnl f* **33/1**

000- 10 3/4 **Rosie's Lady (IRE)**[57] 7636 4-9-6 59............................. RobertWinston 1 50
(Paul Green) *in tch in midfield: rdn and unable qck over 1f out: no hdwy 1f out: wknd ins fnl f* **16/1**

040- 11 3 1/4 **Six Silver Lane**[13] 8275 5-8-12 51................................. TonyHamilton 4 35
(Derek Shaw) *rdn along leaving stalls: chsd ldr tl over 6f out: styd chsng ldrs: rdn and losing pl 3f out: bhd fnl f* **20/1**

000- 12 3/4 **Ferryview Place**[70] 7321 4-9-3 56..........................(tp) StevieDonohoe 2 38
(Ian Williams) *in tch in midfield: rdn and no hdwy over 1f out: swtchd rt and wknd ins fnl f* **10/1**

300- 13 1 1/4 **Gung Ho (FR)**[24] 8121 4-9-1 57................................... RossAtkinson(3) 9 36
(Tony Newcombe) *a in rr: rdn over 3f out: wknd wl over 1f out: bhd fnl f* **14/1**

2m 4.18s (2.48) **Going Correction** +0.25s/f (Slow)
WFA 3 from 4yo+ 2lb **13** Ran SP% **123.2**
Speed ratings (Par 101): **98,97,95,95,94 94,92,91,90,90 87,86,85**
toteswingers 1&2 £28.00, 1&3 £20.60, 2&3 £56.70 CSF £378.30 CT £3231.73 TOTE £20.70: £5.70, £8.60, £2.30; EX 360.00 Trifecta £1939.00 Part won. Pool: £2,585.34 - 0.31 winning units..
Owner Richard Prince **Bred** Hardys Of Kilkeel Ltd **Trained** Lovington, Somerset

FOCUS
An open handicap. The runner-up confirmed the level he ran to when last here, and is at his best since early last year.

8400 CORAL MOBILE "JUST THREE CLICKS TO BET" H'CAP 1m 4f 50y(P)

4:15 (4:15) (Class 5) (0-75,80) 3-Y-O+ **£2,587** (£770; £384; £192) **Stalls** Low

Form RPR

431- 1 **Odin (IRE)**[10] 8310 5-10-1 80 6ex.................................... GeorgeBaker 8 89+
(Don Cantillon) *chsd ldr: clsd and gng best over 2f out: shkn up to ld over 1f out: in command and rdn hands and heels ins fnl f: comf* **9/4**[1]

042- 2 1/2 **Singzak**[23] 8139 5-9-8 73.. TomEaves 4 79
(Michael Easterby) *led: rdn over 2f out: hdd and drvn over 1f out: kpt on u.p ins fnl f* **9/4**[1]

005- 3 3/4 **Triple Eight (IRE)**12 8299 5-8-12 **70**..........................(p) EvaMoscrop(7) 6 75
(Philip Kirby) *t.k.h: hld up in last pair: rdn and hdwy on inner over 1f out: kpt on same pce ins fnl f* **16/1**
143- 4 3 3/4 **Fresa**23 8136 4-9-8 **73**.. ChrisCatlin 7 72
(Sir Mark Prescott Bt) *hld up in last pair: effrt on outer wl over 1f out: sn outpcd and no threat to ldrs: plugged on to go 4th and edgd lft ins fnl f* **6/1**3
005- 5 2 3/4 **Magnolia Ridge (IRE)**22 8159 3-9-0 **75**................ JacobButterfield(5) 5 70
(Kristin Stubbs) *chsd ldrs: rdn over 2f out: outpcd u.p and btn over 1f out: wknd fnl f* **6/1**3
060- 6 1 1/4 **Thecornishcowboy**22 8159 4-9-9 **74**..........................(t) RobertWinston 2 67
(John Ryan) *chsd ldrs: rdn wl over 2f out: outpcd and btn over 1f out: wknd fnl f* **9/2**2

2m 43.58s (2.48) **Going Correction** +0.25s/f (Slow)
WFA 3 from 4yo+ 5lb **6** Ran SP% **114.2**
Speed ratings (Par 103): **101,100,100,97,95 95**
toteswingers 1&2 £1.30, 1&3 £9.70, 2&3 £4.80 CSF £7.56 CT £60.46 TOTE £3.60: £1.90, £1.10; EX 7.90 Trifecta £79.20 Pool: £4,502.02 - 42.62 winning units..
Owner Mrs Catherine Reed **Bred** Littleton Stud **Trained** Newmarket, Suffolk

FOCUS
A few came into this handicap with questions to answer and it was the two in-form stayers who fought out the finish. The runner-up had an easy time of it in front and sets the standard.

8401 LADBROKES H'CAP 7f 32y(P)
4:45 (4:45) (Class 5) (0-75,79) 3-Y-0+ £2,587 (£770; £384; £192) Stalls High

Form RPR
120- 1 **Powerful Pierre**17 8224 6-8-11 **70**.......................(b) JacobButterfield(5) 3 80
(Ollie Pears) *dwlt: niggled along in tch towards rr of main gp: hdwy u.p on outer over 1f out: styd on wl to ld towards fin* **16/1**
500- 2 1/2 **Pearl Nation (USA)**215 2659 4-9-7 **75**.................... AdamKirby 12 83+
(Brian Baugh) *in tch in midfield: hdwy to chse ldrs over 2f out: rdn and ev ch 2f out: led ins fnl f: hdd and no ex towards fin* **6/1**
333- 3 1/2 **Hellbender (IRE)**19 8198 7-9-1 **69**................................(t) DavidProbert 6 76
(Shaun Harris) *in tch in midfield: hdwy to chse ldrs 2f out: swtchd lft 1f out: ev ch ins fnl f: no ex towards fin* **12/1**
211- 4 1/2 **Two No Bids (IRE)**7 8350 3-9-11 **79** 6ex.....................(bt) PaddyAspell 7 85
(Phil McEntee) *hld up in midfield: hdwy to chse ldrs 2f out: drvn over 1f out: kpt on same pce ins fnl f* **3/1**1
316- 5 2 1/2 **George Fenton**12 8304 4-9-7 **75**..................................(p) GeorgeBaker 9 74
(Conor Dore) *chsd ldrs: wnt 2nd over 2f out: rdn to ld 2f out: hdd ins fnl f: wknd fnl 75yds* **12/1**
522- 6 4 1/2 **Miss Avonbridge (IRE)**24 8134 3-9-7 **75**............ RichardKingscote 5 62
(Tom Dascombe) *chsd ldrs: rdn to chse ldr 3f out tl over 2f out: outpcd and btn 2f out: wknd ent fnl f* **7/2**2
002- 7 3/4 **Strong Man**19 8198 5-9-0 **68**..(b) TomEaves 8 53
(Michael Easterby) *led: rdn over 2f out: hdd 2f out: btn over 1f out and wknd fnl f* **9/1**
202- 8 1 **Barbados Bob (USA)**12 8304 3-9-2 **70**..................... WilliamCarson 10 52
(Michael Wigham) *hld up in tch in rr of main gp: rdn and no hdwy wl over 1f out: wknd over 1f out* **5/1**3
555- 9 1/2 **Greensward**20 8178 7-9-1 **72**......................................(b) RyanPowell(3) 1 53
(Conor Dore) *dwlt: sn detached in last and nvr travelling wl: n.d* **16/1**
000- 10 5 **Striking Echo**41 7898 3-8-6 **65**...................................(p) JoeyHaynes(5) 11 32
(Andrew Hollinshead) *in tch in rr of main gp: rdn and effrt over 3f out: struggling u.p over 2f out: wknd over 1f out* **40/1**
000- 11 27 **Rugosa**31 8037 4-8-13 **67**...(b1) RobertWinston 2
(Charles Hills) *chsd ldr tl 3f out: sn dropped out: t.o and eased ins fnl f* **20/1**

1m 29.8s (0.20) **Going Correction** +0.25s/f (Slow) **11** Ran SP% **122.5**
Speed ratings (Par 103): **108,107,106,106,103 98,97,96,95,90 59**
toteswingers 1&2 £27.20, 1&3 £24.40, 2&3 £23.70 CSF £113.65 CT £1245.93 TOTE £15.20: £4.10, £2.90, £4.70; EX 164.40 Trifecta £1082.90 Pool: £5,371.70 - 3.72 winning units..
Owner Terence Elsey **Bred** Hedsor Stud **Trained** Norton, N Yorks

FOCUS
Competitive stuff in the finale. The time was good and the form is solid, with the winner better than ever and the runner-up back to form off a break. The third helps set the standard and the in-form fourth has been rated pretty much to his latest Southwell figures.
T/Plt: £940.50 to a £1 stake. Pool: £44,490.45 - 34.53 winning units T/Qpdt: £115.60 to a £1 stake. Pool: £3,024.40 - 19.35 winning units SP

8360 SOUTHWELL (L-H)
Friday, December 27

OFFICIAL GOING: Standard
Wind: Fresh; across Weather: Cloudy with sunny periods

8404 32RED NURSERY H'CAP 5f (F)
12:25 (12:25) (Class 5) (0-75,78) 2-Y-0 £2,587 (£770; £384; £192) Stalls High

Form RPR
421- 1 **Oriental Relation (IRE)**13 8300 2-9-7 **75**........................(b) TomEaves 2 81
(James Given) *trckd ldng pair: hdwy on outer and cl up 2f out: effrt to ld over 1f out and sn edgd rt: rdn and styd on wl fnl f* **11/8**1
411- 2 2 **Pushkin Museum (IRE)**9 8322 2-9-10 **78** 6ex............... GeorgeBaker 1 77
(Gary Moore) *slt ld: rdn along 2f out: hdd and n.m.r over 1f out: sn swtchd lft and drvn: kpt on same pce* **13/8**2
221- 3 hd **Razin' Hell**10 8317 2-8-2 **56** 6ex.....................................(v) AndrewMullen 4 54
(Alan McCabe) *sn pushed along and cl up: rdn to chal 1/2-way and ev ch tl drvn: edgd rt and one pce appr fnl f* **10/3**3
315- 4 6 **Biscuiteer**17 8228 2-7-13 **60**..................................(p) MatthewHopkins(7) 5 36
(Scott Dixon) *fly-jmpd s: pushed along to chse ldrs and sn swtchd lft: rdn 1/2-way: sn one pce* **25/1**

59.64s (-0.06) **Going Correction** -0.025s/f (Stan) **4** Ran SP% **107.1**
Speed ratings (Par 96): **99,95,95,85**
CSF £3.87 TOTE £2.00; EX 3.10 Trifecta £2.70 Pool: £1,429.29 - 382.87 winning units..
Owner The Cool Silk Partnership **Bred** Brendan Laffan & Michael McCormick **Trained** Willoughton, Lincs

FOCUS
Only four runners, but probably fair enough form. The winner was confirming himself back to his best, while the runner-up has been rated just about to form.

8405 32RED.COM (S) STKS 5f (F)
12:55 (12:55) (Class 6) 2-Y-0 £1,940 (£577; £288; £144) Stalls High

Form RPR
141- 1 **Touch The Clouds**6 8383 2-9-3 **79**..................................... DavidNolan 2 63
(Kevin Ryan) *mde most: rdn along over 2f out: drvn and hdd ins fnl f: kpt on wl to ld again nr fin* **2/5**1
2 1/2 **Meebo (IRE)**65 7472 2-8-2 **0**... ShelleyBirkett(5) 5 51
(J R Jenkins) *chsd ldng pair: hdwy 2f out: rdn to chal over 1f out: slt ld ins fnl f: hdd and no ex towards fin* **7/1**3
000- 3 4 1/2 **Who Splashed Me**70 7348 2-8-0 **43**........................... AdamMcLean(7) 1 35
(J R Jenkins) *racd wd: prom: rdn along over 2f out and sn one pce* **66/1**
030- 4 10 **Sweet Angelica**10 8317 2-8-9 **57** ow2.............................(p) TomEaves 3 1
(James Given) *chsd ldrs: rdn along after 1f out: outpcd and bhd fr 1/2-way* **14/1**
5 5 **Sleet (IRE)** 2-8-12 **0**.. AndrewMullen 4
(Michael Appleby) *s.i.s and green: sn rdn: a outpcd and bhd* **9/2**2

1m 0.93s (1.23) **Going Correction** -0.025s/f (Stan) **5** Ran SP% **110.3**
Speed ratings (Par 94): **89,88,81,65,57**
CSF £3.90 TOTE £1.40: £1.10, £2.00; EX 3.50 Trifecta £28.20 Pool: £2,577.40 - 68.45 winning units..The winner sold to William Stone for 7,000gns.
Owner Matt & Lauren Morgan 1 **Bred** Stuart McPhee Bloodstock Ltd **Trained** Hambleton, N Yorks

FOCUS
Ordinary selling form. The third is the key to the level.

8406 COMPARE BOOKMAKERS AT BOOKMAKERS.CO.UK CLAIMING STKS 5f (F)
1:25 (1:25) (Class 6) 3-Y-0+ £1,940 (£577; £288; £144) Stalls High

Form RPR
510- 1 **Shawkantango**18 8220 6-8-8 **69**.................................(v) AdamMcLean(7) 3 77
(Derek Shaw) *dwlt and hmpd s: in rr and swtchd lft to outer after 1f: rdn along 2f out: styd on u.p nr far rail to ld ins fnl f: kpt on* **9/2**
003- 2 3/4 **Monnoyer**31 8048 4-8-4 **63**.......................................(b) MatthewHopkins(7) 1 70
(Scott Dixon) *led: rdn along wl over 1f out: drvn and edgd lft ent fnl f: sn hdd and kpt on same pce* **5/2**1
661- 3 3/4 **Quality Art (USA)**8 8351 5-8-11 **59**............................... RobertWinston 8 68
(Richard Guest) *swtchd lft sn after s and trckd ldrs: smooth prog and cl up over 2f out: shkn up to chal ent fnl f: sn rdn and one pce* **3/1**2
000- 4 2 1/2 **Solarmaite**22 8163 4-8-7 **57**.......................................(b) MarkCoumbe(3) 2 58
(Roy Bowring) *cl up: rdn along over 2f out: drvn over 1f out: sn edgd rt and one pce* **12/1**
000- 5 shd **Upper Lambourn (IRE)**17 8234 5-8-3 **49** ow3......(t) RobJFitzpatrick(7) 6 57
(Christopher Kellett) *chsd ldrs: rdn along wl over 1f out: edgd rt and grad wknd* **33/1**
104- 6 2 1/4 **Robyn**8 8352 3-8-2 **47**... NickyMackay 7 41
(Scott Dixon) *cl up: rdn along over 2f out: grad wknd* **25/1**
032- 7 1 1/4 **Angelo Poliziano**7 8365 7-8-5 **67**.......................(b) JosephineGordon(7) 5 47
(Jo Hughes) *wnt lft and sltly hmpd s: in rr and swtchd rt towards stands' rail after 2f: hdwy over 2f out: sn rdn and btn* **4/1**3
030- 8 1/2 **Jiminy**8 8351 3-8-13 **52**...(b) TomEaves 4 46
(Scott Dixon) *prom: rdn along over 2f out: sn wknd* **16/1**

59.54s (-0.16) **Going Correction** -0.025s/f (Stan) **8** Ran SP% **112.1**
Speed ratings (Par 101): **100,98,97,93,93 89,87,87**
toteswingers 1&2 £3.20, 1&3 £3.60, 2&3 £3.50 CSF £15.51 TOTE £8.10: £2.40, £1.10, £1.20; EX 20.50 Trifecta £91.60 Pool: £2,790.00 - 22.83 winning units..
Owner Shawthing Racing Partnership **Bred** Derek Shaw **Trained** Sproxton, Leics

FOCUS
A modest claimer in which the action unfolded towards the far side. The winner has been rated to his best and the runner-up to his best since his C&D win in April. The fourth and fifth help set the standard.

8407 BEST ODDS AT BOOKMAKERS.CO.UK MAIDEN STKS 6f (F)
1:55 (1:58) (Class 5) 3-Y-0+ £2,587 (£770; £384; £192) Stalls Low

Form RPR
333- 1 **Go Far**8 8345 3-9-5 **67**...(v1) RobertWinston 5 74
(Alan Bailey) *trckd ldr: hdwy to ld 1/2-way: rdn and hdd wl over 1f out: cl up: drvn and rallied ent fnl f: edgd rt and led last 100yds* **5/4**1
244- 2 1/2 **Maakirr (IRE)**14 8270 4-9-2 **62**..................................(tp) MarkCoumbe(3) 3 72
(Roy Bowring) *trckd ldrs: hdwy 1/2-way and sn cl up: rdn to ld wl over 1f out: drvn and edgd lft 1f out: hdd and no ex last 100yds* **7/4**2
663- 3 9 **Knockamany Bends (IRE)**10 8320 3-9-5 **52**................. PaddyAspell 7 44
(John Wainwright) *chsd ldrs: rdn along 2f out: sn one pce* **20/1**
00- 4 8 **The Troyster**221 2507 3-9-5 **0**....................................... PaulPickard 8 18
(Brian Ellison) *dwlt: green and bhd: hdwy over 2f out: sn rdn and plugged on: n.d* **22/1**
3/4- 5 1 1/2 **Slope**13 8303 3-9-0 **75**... TomEaves 1 8
(David O'Meara) *trckd ldrs: effrt 1/2-way: sn rdn and wknd over 2f out* **4/1**3
000- 6 6 **Mrs Medley**52 7759 7-8-10 **20** ow1.................................. AnnStokell(5) 4
(Ann Stokell) *t.k.h: led: rdn and hdd 1/2-way: sn wknd* **100/1**

1m 16.06s (-0.44) **Going Correction** -0.025s/f (Stan) **6** Ran SP% **110.9**
Speed ratings (Par 103): **101,100,88,77,75 67**
toteswingers 1&2 £1.10, 1&3 £2.40, 2&3 £3.10 CSF £3.57 TOTE £2.10: £1.20, £1.30; EX 4.30 Trifecta £18.60 Pool: £2,059.95 - 82.68 winning units..
Owner R West **Bred** Michael Turner **Trained** Newmarket, Suffolk

FOCUS
A moderate maiden. The first two have been rated pretty much to their marks.

8408 LADBROKES H'CAP 1m (F)
2:25 (2:26) (Class 4) (0-85,83) 3-Y-0+ £4,690 (£1,395; £697; £348) Stalls Low

Form RPR
405- 1 **Greyfriarschorista**8 8350 6-9-0 **81**........................... ShelleyBirkett(5) 9 93
(Tom Keddy) *hld up: gd hdwy on inner over 3f out: led 2f out: rdn and edgd rt jst over 1f out: kpt on* **6/1**
302- 2 1 1/2 **Kung Hei Fat Choy (USA)**14 8269 4-8-11 **73**................(b) TomEaves 6 81
(James Given) *prom: cl up 3f out: rdn and ev ch whn n.m.r and swtchd lft jst over 1f out: kpt on u.p fnl f* **3/1**1
013- 3 hd **Chrissycross (IRE)**14 8269 4-8-12 **74**....................(v) RobertWinston 4 82
(Roger Teal) *trckd ldrs: hdwy 3f out: cl up 2f out: sn rdn and ev ch tl drvn and kpt on same pce ins fnl f* **6/1**
566- 4 2 1/2 **The Lock Master (IRE)**14 8269 6-8-9 **78**............... AliRawlinson(7) 3 80
(Michael Appleby) *in rr and sn pushed along: wd st and hdwy over 2f out: sn rdn and kpt on: nrst fin* **8/1**

615- 5 *shd* **First Post (IRE)**[58] 7632 6-9-7 **83**.................................... FrederikTylicki 10 85
(Derek Haydn Jones) *in tch on outer: rdn along wl over 2f out: drvn and one pce fr wl over 1f out* **4/1**[2]

221- 6 *7* **Frost Fire (USA)**[10] 8316 3-8-8 **71** 6ex.................................... LiamJones 1 56
(Mark Johnston) *dwlt: sn led: hdd after 3f and cl up on inner tl led again 3f out: sn rdn and hdd 2f out: sn wknd* **5/1**[3]

1/0- 7 *3/4* **Laudate Dominum (IRE)**[31] 8057 3-8-12 **75**................ TonyHamilton 5 58
(Richard Fahey) *chsd ldrs: rdn along over 3f out and sn wknd* **25/1**

416- 8 *5* **Goal (IRE)**[22] 8102 5-8-6 **75**................................(t) JackGarritty(7) 2 48
(Charles Smith) *sn rdn along and a in rr: bhd fnl 3f* **28/1**

002- 9 *16* **Piceno (IRE)**[8] 8350 5-8-0 **69** oh1.........................(b) MatthewHopkins(7) 7 5
(Scott Dixon) *cl up: led after 3f: rdn along and hdd 3f out: sn wknd* **11/1**

1m 42.56s (-1.14) **Going Correction** -0.025s/f (Stan)
WFA 3 from 4yo+ 1lb **9** Ran SP% **117.0**
Speed ratings (Par 105): **104,102,102,99,99 92,91,86,70**
toteswingers 1&2 £4.90, 1&3 £6.60, 2&3 £3.80 CSF £24.70 CT £114.95 TOTE £7.30: £3.10, £1.50, £2.10; EX 35.60 Trifecta £77.20 Pool: £1,809.00 - 17.55 winning units..
Owner Hayley Keddy, Lynn Lambert, Val Beeson **Bred** Castlemartin Stud And Skymarc Farm **Trained** Newmarket, Suffolk

FOCUS
A good handicap. It's been rated through the runner-up and third to their latest C&D efforts.

8409 DOWNLOAD THE LADBROKES APP H'CAP 1m (F)
3:00 (3:03) (Class 6) (0-60,59) 3-Y-0+ **£1,940** (£577; £288; £144) **Stalls** Low

Form RPR

065- 1 **Dandarrell**[53] 7733 6-9-4 **56**...(p) FrederikTylicki 8 75
(Julie Camacho) *trckd ldrs: smooth hdwy 3f out: led wl over 1f out: sn pushed clr: readily* **5/2**[1]

000- 2 *9* **Flying Applause**[27] 8116 8-8-2 **45**....................................(bt) TimClark(5) 2 43
(Roy Bowring) *cl up: rdn along and outpcd over 3f out: styd nr inner rail and drvn 2f out: kpt on fnl f: no ch w wnr* **25/1**

011- 3 *2* **Izzy Boy (USA)**[17] 8235 3-9-6 **59**.. LiamJones 3 52
(Mark Johnston) *trckd ldrs: hdwy to ld over 3f out: rdn over 2f out: hdd wl over 1f out: sn drvn and one pce* **11/4**[2]

654- 4 *1* **Mataajir (USA)**[17] 8233 5-8-5 **50**...............................(v) AdamMcLean(7) 1 41
(Derek Shaw) *led: rdn along and hdd over 3f out: drvn and hung rt 2f out: sn wknd* **9/2**[3]

050- 5 *1 1/4* **Minimee**[31] 8042 3-9-2 **55**...(bt) PaddyAspell 7 43
(Phil McEntee) *dwlt and in rr tl styd on fnl 2f: nrst fin* **12/1**

052- 6 *2* **Bapak Pesta (IRE)**[7] 8361 3-8-11 **50**...............................(tp) TomEaves 6 33
(Kevin Ryan) *prom: cl up 3f out: sn rdn and wknd 2f out* **8/1**

403- 7 *2 3/4* **Xpres Maite**[17] 8233 10-9-2 **57**....................................(v) MarkCoumbe(3) 9 35
(Roy Bowring) *s.i.s: a bhd* **6/1**

500- 8 *6* **Mr Chocolate Drop (IRE)**[31] 8055 9-8-7 **48**............(t) RossAtkinson(3) 4 12
(Mandy Rowland) *a towards rr* **22/1**

1m 42.35s (-1.35) **Going Correction** -0.025s/f (Stan)
WFA 3 from 4yo+ 1lb **8** Ran SP% **114.7**
Speed ratings (Par 101): **105,96,94,93,91 89,87,81**
toteswingers 1&2 £13.80, 1&3 £2.30, 2&3 £11.00 CSF £62.94 CT £184.55 TOTE £4.10: £1.10, £7.50, £1.30; EX 96.70 Trifecta £742.20 Pool: £3,185.29 - 3.21 winning units..
Owner Jocelyn Waller **Bred** Peter Onslow **Trained** Norton, N Yorks
■ Stewards' Enquiry : Tim Clark four-day ban; used whip above permitted level (10th-13th Jan).

FOCUS
A low-grade handicap, but a runaway winner. The form is tricky to pin down given the winning margin, but the winner was always a bit better here than elsewhere.

8410 CORAL APP DOWNLOAD FROM THE APP STORE H'CAP 1m 3f (F)
3:35 (3:35) (Class 5) (0-70,65) 3-Y-0+ **£2,587** (£770; £384; £192) **Stalls** Low

Form RPR

603- 1 **Staff Sergeant**[13] 8294 6-9-2 **64**.. AliRawlinson(7) 5 74
(Michael Appleby) *trckd ldrs: smooth hdwy 4f out: led over 3f out: styd nr inner rail and pushed clr wl over 1f out: rdn ins fnl f: kpt on* **9/2**[3]

500- 2 *3/4* **Bavarian Nordic (USA)**[14] 8270 8-8-13 **54**..............(b[1]) TonyHamilton 4 63
(Richard Whitaker) *prom: trckd ldrs 1/2-way: rdn along and sltly outpcd wl over 1f out: sn drvn and kpt on wl u.p fnl f* **14/1**

016- 3 *6* **Berkeley Street (USA)**[7] 8372 3-9-0 **59**....................(v[1]) FrederikTylicki 7 58
(Jane Chapple-Hyam) *cl up: led after 1f: hdd over 3f out and sn rdn along: drvn and one pce fr wl over 1f out* **11/4**[1]

036- 4 *1 1/4* **West End Lad**[7] 8360 10-9-8 **63**.......................................(v) LiamJones 3 60
(Roy Bowring) *chsd ldrs: rdn along 4f out: drvn to chse ldng pair over 1f out: one pce* **16/1**

312- 5 *4* **Dubai Celebration**[27] 8116 5-9-10 **65**............................ BarryMcHugh 2 55
(Julie Camacho) *trckd ldrs: effrt 4f out: rdn along 3f out: drvn over 2f out and sn wknd* **7/2**[2]

600- 6 *3/4* **Goldmadchen (GER)**[14] 8270 5-9-1 **56**.............................. TomEaves 8 45
(James Given) *led 1f: prom tl rdn along and wknd over 3f out* **10/1**

341- 7 *6* **Jamaica Grande**[23] 8148 5-9-4 **59**................................ WilliamCarson 6 37
(Dave Morris) *hld up in tch: hdwy to chse ldrs 4f out: rdn along wl over 2f out and sn wknd* **7/2**[2]

/00- 8 *76* **Grandad Mac**[13] 8295 5-8-8 **52**...................................... RossAtkinson(3) 1
(Alan Coogan) *a in rr: t.o and virtually p.u over 2f out* **20/1**

2m 26.64s (-1.36) **Going Correction** -0.025s/f (Stan)
WFA 3 from 5yo+ 4lb **8** Ran SP% **115.7**
Speed ratings (Par 103): **103,102,98,97,94 93,89,34**
toteswingers 1&2 £6.90, 1&3 £3.70, 2&3 £7.50 CSF £64.23 CT £204.62 TOTE £5.30: £2.00, £3.40, £2.30; EX 43.10 Trifecta £303.20 Pool: £2,064.86 - 5.10 winning units..
Owner Mick Appleby Racing **Bred** Darley **Trained** Danethorpe, Notts

FOCUS
A modest handicap. The pace and time were okay, though, and the runner-up looks the key to the level.
T/Plt: £13.00 to a £1 stake. Pool: £49,629.86 - 2,775.65 winning units T/Qpdt: £4.90 to a £1 stake. Pool: £4,472.20 - 674.00 winning units JR

8395 WOLVERHAMPTON (A.W) (L-H)
Friday, December 27

OFFICIAL GOING: Standard
Wind: strong, behind Weather: dry, windy

8411 COMPARE BOOKMAKERS AT BOOKMAKERS.CO.UK H'CAP 5f 20y(P)
3:55 (3:55) (Class 6) (0-60,60) 3-Y-0+ **£1,940** (£577; £288; £144) **Stalls** Low

Form RPR

121- 1 **Give Us A Belle (IRE)**[22] 8168 4-9-4 **59**.................(vt) AdamBeschizza 5 72
(Christine Dunnett) *chsd ldrs and travelled wl: rdn and effrt on inner over 1f out: drvn to ld and edgd rt jst ins fnl f: clr fnl 100yds: hrd pressed cl home: jst lasted: all out* **11/4**[2]

011- 2 *shd* **Iffranesia (FR)**[31] 8051 3-9-4 **59**...(p) ShaneKelly 6 72+
(Robert Cowell) *stdd s: hld up in last quartet: rdn and hdwy on outer wl over 1f out: edgd lft u.p but chsd wnr ins fnl f: drvn and r.o strly fnl 100yds: jst failed* **5/2**[1]

020- 3 *3* **Steelcut**[13] 8306 9-9-4 **59**...(v) GeorgeBaker 12 61
(Mark Buckley) *stdd s: hld up in last quartet: hdwy and swtchd lft jst ins fnl f: styd on: no threat to ldng pair* **16/1**

460- 4 *hd* **Captain Scooby**[18] 8224 7-9-4 **59**.................................(e) AndrewMullen 2 60
(Richard Guest) *sn bustled along in last trio: hdwy and switching rt ins fnl f: r.o wl fnl 100yds: nvr trbld ldrs* **14/1**

036- 5 *1 1/4* **Roy's Legacy**[18] 8220 4-9-0 **60**................................ ShirleyTeasdale(5) 10 57
(Shaun Harris) *chsd ldrs: drvn and unable qck over 1f out: outpcd and btn 1f out: wknd fnl 100yds* **8/1**

514- 6 *hd* **Beach Rhythm (USA)**[14] 8272 6-8-9 **57**....................(b) JackGilligan(7) 1 53
(Jim Allen) *led: rdn wl over 1f out: drvn and hdd jst ins fnl f: no ex: wknd fnl 100yds* **5/1**[3]

030- 7 *shd* **Prigsnov Dancer (IRE)**[14] 8278 8-8-12 **58**...............(p) JackDuern(5) 9 54
(Deborah Sanderson) *in tch in midfield: rdn and unable qck over 1f out: sn outpcd and btn 1f out: plugged on same pce after* **20/1**

000- 8 *shd* **Bussa**[13] 8306 5-8-11 **59**... GearoidBrouder(7) 13 54
(David Evans) *racd off the pce in last quartet: rdn over 2f out: plugged on fnl f: nvr trbld ldrs* **16/1**

200- 9 *2* **Above The Stars**[13] 8306 5-9-3 **58**................................(p) HayleyTurner 4 46
(Conor Dore) *t.k.h: in tch in midfield on inner: rdn and btn over 1f out: no ch and eased fnl 100yds* **12/1**

060- 10 *2 1/4* **Spic 'n Span**[103] 6436 8-9-5 **60**...(b) DavidProbert 8 40
(Ronald Harris) *taken down early: chsd ldr tl over 1f out: sn btn and fdd fnl f* **20/1**

1m 2.88s (0.58) **Going Correction** +0.15s/f (Slow) **10** Ran SP% **118.7**
Speed ratings (Par 101): **101,100,96,95,93 93,93,93,89,86**
toteswingers 1&2 £1.80, 1&3 £6.90, 2&3 £10.60 CSF £10.28 CT £90.21 TOTE £3.90: £2.00, £1.10, £4.70; EX 8.00 Trifecta £93.40 Pool: £3930.95 - 31.53 winning units..
Owner F Butler & Mrs C Dunnett **Bred** Audrey Frances Stynes **Trained** Hingham, Norfolk
■ Stewards' Enquiry : George Baker one-day ban; careless riding (10th Jan).

FOCUS
A moderate handicap in which the gallop was sound and it's worth taking a positive view about the first two, who pulled clear in the centre late on. The first two are on the up and the third has been rated to his recent best.

8412 BEST ODDS AT BOOKMAKERS.CO.UK H'CAP (DIV I) 5f 216y(P)
4:25 (4:25) (Class 6) (0-55,55) 3-Y-0+ **£1,940** (£577; £288; £144) **Stalls** Low

Form RPR

000- 1 **Pick A Little**[53] 7729 5-9-4 **55**.. RobertTart(3) 8 64
(Michael Blake) *in tch in midfield: rdn and effrt wl over 1f out: hdwy to chal 1f out: led ins fnl f: r.o wl: rdn out* **5/2**[1]

003- 2 *nk* **Celestial Dawn**[27] 8118 4-9-5 **53**.................................(b) AdamKirby 10 61
(John Weymes) *stdd after s: hld up off the pce in last quartet: stdy hdwy 3f out: rdn to chal ins fnl f: hrd drvn fnl 100yds: nt qckn and hld cl home* **10/1**

310- 3 *2* **Red Shadow**[27] 8119 4-9-4 **52**..(p) DaleSwift 9 54
(Alan Brown) *chsd ldr: drvn to ld over 1f out: hdd ins fnl f: no ex and wknd towards fin* **10/1**

063- 4 *3/4* **Methaaly (IRE)**[7] 8370 10-8-12 **53**.............................(be) LewisStones(7) 3 52
(Michael Mullineaux) *stdd after s: hld up in rr and grad moving to outer: v wd bnd 2f out: rdn over 1f out: styd on wl ins fnl f: nt rch ldrs* **8/1**

506- 5 *nk* **Diamond Vine (IRE)**[34] 8023 5-8-13 **52**.....................(p) DarylByrne(5) 2 50
(Ronald Harris) *s.i.s: sn drvn along and detached in last: hdwy u.p over 1f out: styd on wl ins fnl f: nt rch ldrs* **7/1**

000- 6 *1/2* **Scommettitrice (IRE)**[27] 8119 5-9-1 **49**.....................(p) KieranO'Neill 4 46
(Nigel Twiston-Davies) *chsd ldrs: nt clr run wl over 1f out: rdn and unable qck ent fnl f: struggling and swtchd lft ins fnl f: wknd fnl 100yds* **25/1**

002- 7 *1/2* **My Sweet Lord**[13] 8306 3-9-6 **54**.. DavidProbert 1 49
(Mark Usher) *chsd ldrs on inner: hrd drvn over 1f out: no ex ins fnl f: wknd fnl 100yds* **11/4**[2]

002- 8 *3 3/4* **Slewtoo**[42] 7905 4-8-13 **47**.. HayleyTurner 6 30
(James Given) *in tch in midfield: rdn: no rspnse and lost pl over 1f out: btn whn swtchd rt ins fnl f: sn wknd* **9/2**[3]

060- 9 *1* **Avonlini**[70] 7354 7-8-7 **46**.. JoshBaudains(5) 5 26
(Richard Ford) *led tl drvn and hdd over 1f out: sn btn: fdd fnl f* **33/1**

406- 10 *2 1/4* **Angel Grigio**[13] 8293 3-8-12 **46** oh1..................................... AndrewMullen 11 19
(David O'Meara) *taken down early: in tch but stuck wd in midfield: rdn and lost pl 2f out: bhd over 1f out* **25/1**

1m 16.47s (1.47) **Going Correction** +0.15s/f (Slow) **10** Ran SP% **125.8**
Speed ratings (Par 101): **96,95,92,91,91 90,90,85,83,80**
toteswingers 1&2 £7.90, 1&3 £7.60, 2&3 £10.10 CSF £30.65 CT £201.85 TOTE £7.10: £2.50, £3.20, £4.00; EX 42.20 Trifecta £483.20 Pool: £5392.44 - 8.36 winning units..
Owner C Weare and A Pierce **Bred** D R Tucker **Trained** Trowbridge, Wilts

FOCUS
Division one of a moderate handicap. The gallop was sound and the winner raced in the centre. Not solid form, with the winner having shown little since his Kempton win in March, but he was well backed on this drop in grade.

8413 BEST ODDS AT BOOKMAKERS.CO.UK H'CAP (DIV II) 5f 216y(P)
4:55 (4:55) (Class 6) (0-55,54) 3-Y-0+ **£1,940** (£577; £288; £144) **Stalls** Low

Form RPR

222- 1 **Major Muscari (IRE)**[8] 8338 5-8-11 **49**.......................(p) AdamCarter(5) 11 61
(Shaun Harris) *travelled wl: hld up wl in tch: clsd to chse clr ldr 2f out: swtchd lft and rdn 1f out: r.o u.p to ld fnl 100yds: a doing enough after: rdn out* **5/2**[2]

665- **2** 1/2 **Hamis Al Bin (IRE)**[42] 7905 4-9-6 **53**................................(t) AdamKirby 9 63
(Milton Bradley) *stdd and dropped in bhd after s: hld up in last trio: hdwy over 2f out: rdn over 1f out: styd on wl u.p ins fnl f: wnt 2nd last strides* **2/1**[1]

404- **3** *hd* **Interchoice Star**[27] 8118 8-8-13 **46**..............................(p) DavidProbert 10 55
(Ray Peacock) *chsd ldr tl led over 3f out: rdn clr 2f out: drvn 1f out: hdd fnl 100yds: kpt on same pce after* **8/1**

634- **4** 2 3/4 **Amis Reunis**[35] 8002 4-9-7 **54**......................................(p) RobertHavlin 7 55
(Alan Berry) *in tch in midfield: effrt u.p to chse ldrs over 1f out: no ex ins fnl f: wknd towards fin* **7/1**

546- **5** 1/2 **Littlecote Lady**[234] 2125 4-9-7 **54**.................................... HayleyTurner 8 53
(Mark Usher) *hld up towards rr: clsd 2f out: rdn and hdwy over 1f out: kpt on same pce and no imp ins fnl f* **12/1**

062- **6** 2 1/4 **Lucky Mark (IRE)**[14] 8272 4-9-6 **53**................................ AndrewMullen 3 45
(Garry Moss) *taken down early: sn bustled along to ld: hdd and rdn over 1f out: wknd fnl f* **11/2**[3]

000- **7** 6 **Olynard (IRE)**[182] 3754 7-8-7 **45**..............................(be) JoeyHaynes(5) 4 18
(Michael Mullineaux) *s.i.s: a in rr* **25/1**

000- **8** *nse* **Jemimaville (IRE)**[29] 8082 6-8-12 **45**.......................... AdamBeschizza 1 17
(Giles Bravery) *s.i.s: sn rcvrd and in tch in midfield: rdn and lost pl 2f out: sn wknd* **33/1**

1m 15.97s (0.97) **Going Correction** +0.15s/f (Slow) 8 Ran SP% **115.4**
Speed ratings (Par 101): **99,98,98,94,93 90,82,82**
toteswingers 1&2 £1.80, 1&3 £6.90, 2&3 £8.00 CSF £8.01 CT £32.95 TOTE £3.30: £1.20, £1.10, £2.20; EX 9.70 Trifecta £63.60 Pool: £3592.38 - 42.33 winning units..
Owner J Morris **Bred** Simon Holt David Thorpe & R J Beggan **Trained** Carburton, Notts

FOCUS
Mainly exposed sorts in division two of this moderate event. The gallop was reasonable and the winner edged towards the far rail late on. Solid form which has been rated slightly positively.

8414 32RED.COM MAIDEN AUCTION STKS 5f 216y(P)
5:25 (5:25) (Class 6) 2-Y-O **£1,940** (£577; £288; £144) **Stalls** Low

Form RPR
023- **1** **Three Pips**[24] 8138 2-8-12 65... ChrisCatlin 3 72
(Ed McMahon) *chsd ldr tl led over 4f out: mde rest: rdn over 1f out: in command and edgd rt ins fnl f: kpt on: rdn out* **5/2**[2]

\- **2** 1 1/4 **Jaeger Train (IRE)** 2-9-3 0...................................... RichardKingscote 4 73+
(K R Burke) *chsd ldrs: chsd wnr over 2f out: rdn and effrt over 1f out: kpt on same pce and swtchd lft ins fnl f* **5/4**[1]

022- **3** 1 3/4 **Dancing Sal (IRE)**[18] 8222 2-8-7 65................................. DavidProbert 1 58
(David Evans) *broke fast: led tl over 4f out: chsd wnr tl over 2f out: rdn and unable qck over 1f out: edgd rt 1f out: wknd ins fnl f* **3/1**[3]

343- **4** 2 1/4 **The Doyle Machine (IRE)**[92] 6776 2-9-0 65...........(p) AdamBeschizza 2 58
(Noel Quinlan) *t.k.h: chsd ldrs: rdn and unable qck over 1f out: wknd ins fnl f* **10/1**

00- **5** 32 **Desert Flute**[163] 4414 2-9-0 0... AdamKirby 5
(Michael Blake) *s.i.s: racd wd and a detached in last: t.o 1/2-way: eased ins fnl f* **25/1**

1m 16.92s (1.92) **Going Correction** +0.15s/f (Slow) 5 Ran SP% **111.0**
Speed ratings (Par 94): **93,91,89,86,43**
CSF £6.11 TOTE £3.10: £1.10, £1.80; EX 7.00 Trifecta £12.50 Pool: £2476.67 - 148.46 winning units..
Owner Whittle, Kent & Lees-Jones **Bred** W T Whittle And Mickley Stud Ltd **Trained** Lichfield, Staffs

FOCUS
A modest maiden run at an ordinary gallop. The winner has been rated as stepping up on his previous efforts.

8415 32RED MAIDEN STKS 1m 141y(P)
5:55 (5:57) (Class 5) 2-Y-O **£2,587** (£770; £384; £192) **Stalls** Low

Form RPR
\- **1** **Dutch Rifle** 2-8-9 0.. HarryPoulton(5) 9 75+
(James Tate) *led to post: a travelling wl: led early: chsd ldr tl led on bit over 2f out: rdn hands and heels and readily qcknd clr over 1f out: r.o: easily* **3/1**[2]

0- **2** 2 1/4 **Captain Morley**[46] 7834 2-9-5 0....................................... HayleyTurner 7 76+
(David Simcock) *stdd s: hld up in tch in rr of main gp: clsd over 2f out: rdn and hdwy on inner over 1f out: drvn to chse wnr ins fnl f: kpt on but no imp* **7/2**[3]

4- **3** 2 1/4 **Charmy Dukesse (IRE)**[21] 8176 2-9-0 0.......................... AdamKirby 10 66
(Marco Botti) *t.k.h: chsd ldrs: effrt and rn green ent fnl 2f: hdwy to chse clr wnr 1f out tl ins fnl f: lost 2nd and edgd lft fnl 100yds* **5/2**[1]

62- **4** 1 1/2 **Market Storm (FR)**[18] 8221 2-9-5 0...............................(be) TomEaves 2 68
(Michael Mullineaux) *sn rdn along to ld: rdn and hdd over 2f out: drvn and btn 1f out: wknd ins fnl f* **10/1**

5 *nk* **Mbhali (IRE)** 2-9-2 0.. MichaelJMMurphy(3) 3 67
(Mark Johnston) *in tch in midfield: rdn 5f out: hdwy u.p to chse ldrs on inner 2f out: sn outpcd: plugged on same pce fnl f* **7/1**

4- **6** 1 1/2 **Here For Good (IRE)**[9] 8333 2-9-5 0............................. KieranO'Neill 12 64+
(Richard Hannon Snr) *hld up in tch in midfield on outer: rdn and wd bnd 2f out: sn outpcd and btn: wl hld and hung lft ins fnl f* **7/1**

7 8 **Fiftyshadesdarker (IRE)** 2-9-5 0.................................(t) JimmyQuinn 1 47
(George Baker) *chsd ldrs: edging rt bnd over 2f out: rdn and btn 2f out: sn wknd* **20/1**

0- **8** 29 **Miss Verdoyante**[184] 3689 2-9-0 0.................................... ChrisCatlin 6
(Sir Mark Prescott Bt) *s.i.s: rdn and detached in last pair: lost tch 3f out: t.o fnl 2f* **33/1**

9 3 1/2 **Imperial Ike** 2-9-2 0... MarkCoumbe(3) 4
(Lisa Williamson) *s.i.s: rdn and detached in last pair: lost tch 3f out: t.o fnl 2f* **100/1**

04- **10** 40 **Bourbondi**[18] 8221 2-9-5 0.. ShaneKelly 8
(Michael Murphy) *hld up in midfield: lost pl qckly over 3f out: t.o fnl 2f: virtually p.u ins fnl f* **20/1**

1m 51.65s (1.15) **Going Correction** +0.15s/f (Slow) 10 Ran SP% **123.3**
Speed ratings (Par 96): **100,98,96,94,94 93,85,60,57,21**
toteswingers 1&2 £5.70, 1&3 £2.90, 2&3 £4.20 CSF £14.37 TOTE £5.60: £1.70, £1.60, £1.80; EX 28.00 Trifecta £90.70 Pool: £3031.13 - 25.06 winning units..
Owner Saeed Manana **Bred** Mr And Mrs R Newman **Trained** Newmarket, Suffolk

FOCUS
A fair maiden in which the gallop soon steadied. The comfortable winner came down the centre in the straight. The third and fourth offer hope that this level is correct.

8416 CORAL APP DOWNLOAD FROM THE APP STORE H'CAP 1m 1f 103y(P)
6:25 (6:26) (Class 4) (0-85,83) 3-Y-O+ **£4,690** (£1,395; £697; £348) **Stalls** Low

Form RPR
252- **1** **Berlusca (IRE)**[18] 8226 4-8-13 **78**.................................... SHJames(3) 11 88
(David O'Meara) *wl in tch in midfield: hdwy to chse ldr over 1f out: rdn to ld ins fnl f: kpt on wl* **12/1**

133- **2** 3/4 **Excellent Puck (IRE)**[63] 7505 3-8-10 **77**......................... RobertTart(3) 12 85
(Shaun Lycett) *wl in tch in midfield: hdwy to chse ldrs over 2f out: rdn to ld 2f out: hdd ins fnl f: kpt on same pce after* **7/1**

231- **3** 1/2 **Eurystheus (IRE)**[11] 8314 4-9-2 **78** 6ex.......................... AndrewMullen 5 85+
(Michael Appleby) *dwlt and bustled along leaving stalls: in tch in midfield: n.m.r wl over 1f out: hdwy u.p to chse ldrs ins fnl f: styd on wl fnl 100yds: nt rch ldrs* **3/1**[1]

621- **4** 3 1/4 **Off The Pulse**[35] 8007 3-9-4 **82**... GeorgeBaker 9 83
(John Mackie) *in tch in midfield: clsd to chse ldrs on outer 2f out: no ex u.p 1f out: wknd ins fnl f* **9/2**[2]

213- **5** 2 **Silverware (USA)**[28] 8094 5-9-7 **83**.............................. TonyHamilton 6 79
(Kristin Stubbs) *led: rdn and hdd 2f out: no ex u.p ent fnl f: sn wknd* **16/1**

201- **6** *nk* **Investment Expert (IRE)**[81] 7075 3-9-1 **79**........................ DaleSwift 4 75
(Brian Ellison) *hld up in last trio: hdwy but stl plenty to do whn nt clr run and swtchd rt 1f out: hung lft and plugged on ins fnl f: nvr trbld ldrs* **6/1**

043- **7** 1/2 **Sound Advice**[50] 7793 4-9-6 **82**... TomEaves 2 77
(Keith Dalgleish) *chsd ldng pair tl 2f out: sn drvn and unable qck: wknd ins fnl f* **12/1**

631- **8** 1 3/4 **Mrs Micawber**[21] 8183 3-8-6 **70**..................................... HayleyTurner 10 61
(Michael Bell) *t.k.h: chsd ldr tl ent fnl 2f: struggling whn short of room over 1f out: sn wknd* **11/2**[3]

4/0- **9** 2 **Buzz Law (IRE)**[262] 1442 5-8-2 **69**.................................. JoeyHaynes(5) 7 56
(K R Burke) *hld up in last trio: rdn 3f out: no prog: nvr trbld ldrs* **33/1**

506- **10** 9 **Next Edition (IRE)**[14] 8276 5-8-7 **76**.............................. EvaMoscrop(7) 1 44
(Philip Kirby) *a bhd: rdn and struggling over 3f out: bhd fnl 2f* **33/1**

061- **11** 1/2 **Suehail**[18] 8227 4-9-4 **80**... ShaneKelly 8 47
(Robert Cowell) *t.k.h: hld up in tch in midfield: rdn and btn 2f out: sn bhd* **10/1**

2m 0.27s (-1.43) **Going Correction** +0.15s/f (Slow)
WFA 3 from 4yo+ 2lb 11 Ran SP% **121.6**
Speed ratings (Par 105): **112,111,110,108,106 105,105,103,102,94 93**
toteswingers 1&2 £5.70, 1&3 £2.90, 2&3 £4.20 CSF £96.76 CT £322.44 TOTE £12.80: £3.40, £2.70, £1.90; EX 76.50 Trifecta £1495.20 Part won. Pool: £1993.69 - 0.84 winning units..
Owner Peter R Ball **Bred** Value Bloodstock **Trained** Nawton, N Yorks

FOCUS
A useful handicap in which the gallop was reasonable. The winner raced towards the far rail in the straight and the first three pulled clear. The winner and runner-up have been rated as running personal bests, while the fourth is solid around here.

8417 CORAL MOBILE "JUST THREE CLICKS TO BET" H'CAP 1m 4f 50y(P)
6:55 (6:56) (Class 6) (0-60,60) 3-Y-O+ **£1,940** (£577; £288; £144) **Stalls** Low

Form RPR
616- **1** **This Is Me**[8] 8349 5-9-10 **60**... GeorgeBaker 4 69+
(Don Cantillon) *restless in stalls: hld up in rr: clsd and in tch 8f out: effrt to chal wl over 1f out: rdn to ld ins fnl f: styd on wl* **9/4**[2]

450- **2** 1 **Impeccability**[45] 7847 3-8-5 **46** oh1.................................. JimmyQuinn 8 53
(John Mackie) *midfield: clsd on ldrs 8f out: chsd ldr 6f out tl led 3f out: drvn wl over 1f out: hdd ins fnl f: one pce after* **16/1**

534- **3** *hd* **Geeaitch**[7] 8373 4-9-3 **53**.. WilliamCarson 3 60
(Peter Hiatt) *hld up off the pce in last quartet: clsd and in tch 8f out: chsd ldrs and rdn 2f out: unable qck over 1f out: kpt on u.p towards fin* **11/4**[3]

454- **4** 8 **India's Song**[21] 8182 3-9-5 **60**... AdamKirby 6 54
(David Simcock) *hld up off the pce in last quartet: clsd and in tch 8f out: chsd ldrs and rdn wl over 1f out: hung lft and btn 1f out: wknd* **6/4**[1]

000- **5** 2 3/4 **Willow Island (IRE)**[59] 7612 4-8-10 **46** oh1...................... DavidProbert 2 36
(David Evans) *chsd ldrs: wnt 2nd 9f out tl 6f out: nt clr run and shuffled bk ent fnl 2f: rdn and wknd over 1f out* **16/1**

000- **6** 3 1/2 **Waving**[13] 8302 4-9-2 **55**..(t) MarkCoumbe(3) 5 39
(Tony Carroll) *sn led: rdn and hdd 3f out: lost pl u.p ent fnl 2f: wknd over 1f out* **16/1**

060- **7** 7 **Icanboogie**[6] 8388 3-8-5 **46** oh1... KieranO'Neill 7 19
(Anthony Middleton) *v.s.a: t.k.h: hld up in rr: clsd and in tch 8f out: rdn 2f out: sn wknd* **33/1**

000- **8** 59 **Underwritten**[20] 8204 4-9-0 **55**.................................(b) JoeyHaynes(5) 1
(John Weymes) *chsd ldr tl 9f out: sn rdn and steadily lost pl: bhd 5f out: lost tch and t.o over 2f out* **12/1**

2m 42.81s (1.71) **Going Correction** +0.15s/f (Slow)
WFA 3 from 4yo+ 5lb 8 Ran SP% **125.7**
Speed ratings (Par 101): **100,99,99,93,92 89,85,45**
toteswingers 1&2 £6.90, 1&3 £1.80, 2&3 £7.30 CSF £41.75 CT £110.82 TOTE £3.40: £1.90, £5.60, £1.10; EX 47.20 Trifecta £184.80 Pool: £2631.20 - 10.67 winning units..
Owner Don Cantillon **Bred** Peter E Clinton **Trained** Newmarket, Suffolk

FOCUS
A moderate handicap in which the gallop was an ordinary one. The winner came down the centre and the first three pulled clear. The runner-up has been rated as running a small pb, with the third in line with his recent form.

8418 LADBROKES H'CAP 7f 32y(P)
7:25 (7:25) (Class 7) (0-50,56) 3-Y-O+ **£1,940** (£577; £288; £144) **Stalls** High

Form RPR
043- **1** **Storey Hill (USA)**[13] 8293 8-9-3 **46**............................... TonyHamilton 1 60
(Richard Guest) *taken down early: chsd ldrs: rdn and outpcd over 2f out: swtchd lft wl over 1f out: rallied u.p to chse ldr and swtchd rt 1f out: styd on to ld fnl 100yds: sn forged clr: drvn out* **9/2**[2]

000- **2** 2 1/4 **Seamster**[13] 8293 6-8-13 **47**..................................(bt[1]) JoshBaudains(5) 6 55
(Richard Ford) *w ldr tl led 3f out: rdn 2 l clr 2f out: drvn and tired jst ins fnl f: hdd fnl 100yds: wknd towards fin* **10/1**

053- **3** *hd* **Tony Hollis**[7] 8371 5-9-4 **47**...(t) AndrewMullen 4 54
(Michael Appleby) *led: hdd 3f out: drvn and outpcd ent fnl 2f: edgd rt wl over 1f out: plugged on same pce u.p fnl f* **9/4**[1]

024- **4** 2 1/4 **Windsor Secret**[56] 7667 3-9-3 **46**... TomEaves 10 48
(Keith Dalgleish) *hld up in rr of main gp: rdn and effrt over 2f out: edgd lft and plugged on ins fnl f: nvr trbld ldrs* **7/1**

403- **5** *shd* **Rosa Lockwood**[29] 8082 4-9-5 **48**....................................... AdamKirby 2 49
(Ed McMahon) *chsd ldrs: wnt 3rd over 3f out: drvn and unable qck 2f out: wknd ins fnl f* **11/2**[3]

030- **6** 3 1/2 **Legal Eagle (IRE)**[27] 8118 8-9-1 **47**..........................(p) MarkCoumbe(3) 7 39
(Noel Williams) *sn outpcd and in last trio: sme hdwy u.p over 1f out: no imp fnl f* **20/1**

006- **7** 7 **Bahama Bay**[30] 8063 3-9-2 **45**.................... AdamBeschizza 12 19
(Stuart Williams) *t.k.h: chsd ldrs: rdn 2f out: sn btn and wknd over 1f out: fdd fnl f* **8/1**

610- **8** 9 **Ficelle (IRE)**[50] 7792 4-9-1 **47**..........................(p) MatthewCosham(3) 3
(Nikki Evans) *pushed along leaving stalls: in tch in midfield: drvn and no hdwy 3f out: wknd 2f out: eased wl ins fnl f* **20/1**

505- **9** 2 3/4 **Loulou Vuitton**[123] 5818 3-9-2 **50**.................... JackDuern(5) 9
(Steph Hollinshead) *led rdrless to post: awkward leaving stalls and s.i.s: rdn along thrght and a bhd: eased ins fnl f* **14/1**

000- **10** 14 **Top Line Banker**[81] 7067 3-9-1 **47**..........................(be1) RobertTart(3) 5
(Michael Mullineaux) *dwlt: sn detached in last: t.o 4f out: eased fr wl over 1f out* **25/1**

1m 31.33s (1.73) **Going Correction** +0.15s/f (Slow) **10** Ran SP% **117.1**
Speed ratings (Par 97): **96,93,93,90,90 86,78,68,65,49**
toteswingers 1&2 £8.70, 1&3 £3.10, 2&3 £5.90 CSF £47.31 CT £129.81 TOTE £3.50: £1.20, £4.40, £1.10; EX 51.20 Trifecta £230.50 Pool: £2272.47 - 7.39 winning units..
Owner Mrs Alison Guest **Bred** Mr And Mrs Richard S Kaster **Trained** Wetherby, W Yorks

FOCUS
A very moderate handicap in which the gallop was no more than fair. The winner raced centre-to-far side in the straight. Little solid, as befits the grade, but the winner used to be a lot better and the runner-up may have improved for the blinkers.
T/Plt: £18.60. Pool: £103,883.05 - 4057.20 winning units. T/Qpdt: £5.30. Pool: £12,939.09 - 1779.99 winning units. SP

8419 - 8424a (Foreign Racing) - See Raceform Interactive

8389 LINGFIELD (L-H)
Saturday, December 28

OFFICIAL GOING: Standard
Wind: Moderate, behind Weather: Sunny

8425 32RED.COM / BRITISH STALLION STUDS EBF MAIDEN STKS 7f (P)
11:40 (11:41) (Class 5) 2-Y-O £3,067 (£905; £453) Stalls Low

Form RPR

302- **1** **Jalingo (IRE)**[9] 8346 2-9-5 72.................... AdamKirby 6 74
(Mark Johnston) *mde all: rdn and r.o wl fnl 2f: readily* **5/2**[1]

06- **2** 2 1/4 **Treasure Cay (IRE)**[51] 7779 2-9-5 0.................... MartinLane 5 68
(Paul Cole) *chsd ldrs: rdn over 2f out: r.o to take 2nd ins fnl f* **25/1**

6- **3** 1 3/4 **Castorienta**[38] 7971 2-9-0 0.................... JimCrowley 10 59
(George Baker) *chsd wnr: one pce fnl 2f: lost 2nd ins fnl f* **25/1**

40- **4** hd **Warbrook (IRE)**[26] 8124 2-9-5 0....................[1] RobertHavlin 2 63
(John Gosden) *dwlt: sn in midfield: rdn and styd on fnl 2f* **7/2**[2]

5 nk **Ganymede** 2-9-5 0.................... JohnFahy 11 62
(Eve Johnson Houghton) *stdd s: towards rr: hdwy on inner over 1f out: styd on fnl f* **5/1**

6 nk **War Of Art (IRE)** 2-9-5 0....................[1] RichardKingscote 8 62+
(Tom Dascombe) *chsd ldrs: rdn 3f out: sltly wd home turn: kpt on fnl f* **14/1**

7 3/4 **Spirit Of Winning** 2-9-0 0.................... NickyMackay 4 55+
(John Gosden) *mid-div: rdn 4f out: styd on same pce fnl 2f* **9/2**[3]

0- **8** 1 1/2 **Notebook**[10] 8333 2-9-5 0.................... LiamJones 1 56
(William Haggas) *chsd ldrs tl wknd 1f out* **12/1**

9 1/2 **Royal Encounter** 2-9-5 0.................... JimmyQuinn 9 54
(Ed Vaughan) *dwlt: hld up towards rr: shkn up over 1f out: nvr rchd ldrs* **25/1**

06- **10** 1/2 **Caroline's Beach (IRE)**[93] 6776 2-9-0 0.................... LiamKeniry 3 48
(J S Moore) *prom tl wknd 1f out* **100/1**

11 1 **Anjin (IRE)** 2-9-5 0.................... ChrisCatlin 14 50
(Sir Mark Prescott Bt) *stdd s: a towards rr* **33/1**

0- **12** nk **Emperor Ferdinand (IRE)**[10] 8333 2-9-5 0.................... HayleyTurner 7 50
(Marcus Tregoning) *a towards rr* **33/1**

0- **13** 3 **Izbushka (IRE)**[10] 8333 2-9-5 0.................... StevieDonohoe 13 42
(Ian Williams) *a bhd* **100/1**

1m 24.64s (-0.16) **Going Correction** -0.10s/f (Stan) **13** Ran SP% **119.4**
Speed ratings (Par 96): **96,93,91,91,90 90,89,87,87,86 85,85,81**
CSF £75.60 TOTE £3.20: £1.20, £11.40, £5.40; EX 80.80 Trifecta £1220.20 Pool: £2785.66 - 1.71 winning units..
Owner Sheikh Hamdan Bin Mohammed Al Maktoum **Bred** Gerrardstown House Stud **Trained** Middleham Moor, N Yorks

FOCUS
An ordinary maiden in which the first three were always on the pace, but the race should produce a few winners. The winner has been rated as replicating his improved recent run.

8426 32RED CASINO NURSERY H'CAP 7f (P)
12:10 (12:11) (Class 2) 2-Y-O £9,056 (£2,695; £1,346; £673) Stalls Low

Form RPR

511- **1** **Drive On (IRE)**[26] 8126 2-8-5 **74**..........................(p) JohnFahy 1 79
(Eve Johnson Houghton) *hld up: hdwy over 1f out: drvn to ld ins fnl f* **6/1**

014- **2** 1/2 **Applejack Lad**[42] 7925 2-8-6 **75**..........................(t) DavidProbert 8 79
(John Ryan) *prom: rdn 3f out: kpt on fnl f* **10/1**

254- **3** nk **Wee Jean**[21] 8203 2-9-7 **90**.................... GeorgeBaker 9 93
(Mick Channon) *prom: sltly outpcd over 1f out: r.o again nr fin* **7/2**[2]

612- **4** 1/2 **Lady Frances**[121] 5927 2-9-2 **85**.................... AdamKirby 3 87
(Mark Johnston) *led: rdn over 2f out: hdd ins fnl f: one pce* **9/2**[3]

031- **5** 3/4 **Truancy (IRE)**[25] 8138 2-7-10 **70**.................... JoeyHaynes(5) 7 70
(K R Burke) *mid-div: rdn 3f out: kpt on fnl f* **9/4**[1]

623- **6** nk **Capers Royal Star (FR)**[24] 8153 2-8-1 **70**.................... KieranO'Neill 6 69
(Alastair Lidderdale) *s.i.s: bhd: sme hdwy on inner over 1f out: one pce fnl f* **14/1**

002- **7** 1/2 **Stan Nineteen (IRE)**[9] 8342 2-8-0 **69**.................... JimmyQuinn 4 67
(George Baker) *chsd ldrs: hrd rdn over 1f out: no ex fnl f* **10/1**

324- **8** 1/2 **Starlight Princess (IRE)**[14] 8296 2-7-7 **69** oh10.(b) CameronHardie(7) 2 66
(J S Moore) *dwlt: towards rr: rdn 2f out: nvr able to chal* **50/1**

1m 24.21s (-0.59) **Going Correction** -0.10s/f (Stan) **8** Ran SP% **112.3**
Speed ratings (Par 102): **99,98,98,97,96 96,95,95**
CSF £60.78 CT £240.57 TOTE £7.60: £2.30, £2.00, £1.90; EX 96.30 Trifecta £349.60 Pool: £2296.19 - 4.92 winning units..
Owner J H Widdows **Bred** Nicola And Eleanor Kent **Trained** Blewbury, Oxon

FOCUS
A decent nursery for which the winning time was 0.43sec quicker than the opening maiden. The form looks okay rated around the first four.

8427 LADBROKES MAIDEN STKS 1m (P)
12:40 (12:41) (Class 5) 3-Y-O+ £2,726 (£805; £402) Stalls High

Form RPR

1 **Big Baz (IRE)** 3-9-5.................... MartinDwyer 1 77
(William Muir) *dwlt: bhd: gd hdwy on inner over 1f out: qcknd wl to ld ins fnl f: easily* **5/1**[2]

2 2 3/4 **Gambol (FR)** 3-9-5.................... GeorgeBaker 11 71
(J W Hills) *sn led: hrd rdn and hdd ins fnl f: one pce* **6/1**[3]

3/2- **3** 1/2 **Secular Society**[24] 8154 3-9-5.................... SeanLevey 3 70
(Brian Meehan) *chsd ldrs: effrt and nt clr run jst over 1f out: kpt on fnl f* **1/1**[1]

05- **4** 1 1/4 **Sweet Marwell (IRE)**[165] 4382 3-9-0.................... JohnFahy 6 62
(Jo Crowley) *in tch: effrt on inner over 1f out: one pce* **14/1**

3- **5** nse **Tax Reform (IRE)**[17] 8245 3-9-5 72..........................(p) RobertHavlin 10 67
(Mark Hoad) *prom tl no ex over 1f out* **20/1**

4- **6** 3/4 **Aldeburgh**[24] 8154 4-9-6.................... LiamKeniry 12 66
(Jim Old) *prom: hrd rdn and edgd lft over 1f out: no ex* **14/1**

60- **7** 3 3/4 **Cataria Girl (USA)**[109] 6289 4-9-1.................... HayleyTurner 2 53
(Marcus Tregoning) *mid-div: rdn and no hdwy fnl 2f* **50/1**

34- **8** nk **Great Conquest (USA)**[12] 8313 3-9-5.................... FergusSweeney 9 56
(Jamie Osborne) *in tch: outpcd over 2f out: sn btn* **14/1**

9 1 3/4 **Lapis Blue (IRE)**[129] 5658 3-9-1 67 ow1.................... AdamKirby 5 48
(David Evans) *towards rr: last and struggling 3f out: sme late hdwy* **16/1**

000- **10** 5 **Echoes Of War**[24] 8154 4-9-6 30.................... LiamJones 4 41
(Michael Attwater) *a in rr* **100/1**

005- **11** 1 **Maygo's Joy**[17] 8245 3-9-5 44.................... DavidProbert 7 38
(Ralph Smith) *a towards rr* **25/1**

12 1 **Joyful Risk (IRE)** 3-9-0.................... JimCrowley 8 31
(Martin Bosley) *a outpcd in rr* **66/1**

1m 36.65s (-1.55) **Going Correction** -0.10s/f (Stan)
WFA 3 from 4yo 1lb **12** Ran SP% **119.9**
Speed ratings (Par 103): **103,100,99,98,98 97,93,93,91,86 85,84**
CSF £34.07 TOTE £6.20: £2.10, £2.10, £1.10; EX 24.30 Trifecta £143.30 Pool: £1848.35 - 9.67 winning units..
Owner The Big Baz Partnership **Bred** Haras De La Perelle **Trained** Lambourn, Berks

FOCUS
Older-horse maidens at this time of year tend to be modest affairs, but this one produced a dramatic debut performance from the winner.

8428 LADBROKES H'CAP 1m (P)
1:10 (1:10) (Class 2) (0-105,99) 3-Y-£11,971 (£3,583; £1,791; £896; £446) Stalls High

Form RPR

233- **1** **Galician**[7] 8386 4-9-9 **98**.................... AdamKirby 2 106
(Mark Johnston) *chsd ldrs: led over 2f out and sn rdn 4 l clr: hld on wl fnl f* **2/1**[1]

152- **2** 1 3/4 **Loyalty**[6] 8391 6-8-8 **90**..........................(v) AdamMcLean(7) 3 94
(Derek Shaw) *in tch: trapped on rail whn wnr qcknd clr 2f out: effrt on inner and wnt 2nd over 1f out: kpt on: a hld* **9/2**[2]

001- **3** 1 3/4 **Dubai Hills**[18] 8231 7-9-10 **99**.................... JimCrowley 6 99
(Bryan Smart) *towards rr: rdn 3f out: styd on fnl f* **6/1**

613- **4** shd **Verse Of Love**[9] 8344 4-8-13 **88**.................... DavidProbert 5 88
(David Evans) *led 1f: chsd ldr after tl over 2f out: one pce* **8/1**

260- **5** 2 3/4 **Clockmaker (IRE)**[16] 8264 7-9-5 **94**.................... HayleyTurner 7 87
(Conor Dore) *led after 1f tl over 2f out: wknd over 1f out* **6/1**

1/0- **6** 7 **Deia Sunrise (IRE)**[18] 3559 4-9-8 **97**..........................(t) MartinDwyer 4 74
(Paul Webber) *bhd: rdn 3f out: nvr trbld ldrs* **25/1**

004- **U** **Birdman (IRE)**[16] 8264 3-8-13 **89**.................... MartinLane 1
(David Simcock) *wnt lft and uns rdr leaving stalls* **5/1**[3]

1m 35.32s (-2.88) **Going Correction** -0.10s/f (Stan)
WFA 3 from 4yo+ 1lb **7** Ran SP% **111.7**
Speed ratings (Par 109): **110,108,106,106,103 96,**
toteswingers 1&2 £2.00, 1&3 £2.30, 2&3 £3.30 CSF £10.56 TOTE £2.20: £1.10, £3.20; EX 10.80 Trifecta £27.10 Pool: £2478.57 - 68.42 winning units..
Owner Sheikh Hamdan Bin Mohammed Al Maktoum **Bred** Darley **Trained** Middleham Moor, N Yorks

FOCUS
A decent handicap, though weakened a little when Birdman unshipped his rider after exiting the stalls.

8429 32RED H'CAP 2m (P)
1:40 (1:41) (Class 2) (0-105,94) 3-Y-£11,971 (£3,583; £1,791; £896; £446) Stalls Low

Form RPR

202- **1** **Theology**[38] 7975 6-9-9 **89**.................... FrederikTylicki 8 99
(Steve Gollings) *trckd ldr: led 1/2-way: rdn and hld on wl fnl 2f* **8/1**

062- **2** 1 **Be Perfect (USA)**[6] 8392 4-9-5 **85**.................... TonyHamilton 1 94
(David Nicholls) *led tl 1/2-way: remained prom: rdn to regain 2nd over 1f out: kpt on* **9/2**[3]

012- **3** nk **Gabrial's King (IRE)**[21] 8202 4-9-5 **85**..........................(p) AdamKirby 4 94
(David Simcock) *hld up towards rr: hdwy whn rn wd home turn: edgd lft fnl f: styd on* **8/1**

641- **4** 1 1/4 **Arch Villain (IRE)**[38] 7975 4-10-0 **94**..........................(b) JimCrowley 6 101
(Amanda Perrett) *prom: rdn over 2f out: one pce appr fnl f* **2/1**[1]

533- **5** nse **Icebuster**[10] 8327 5-9-5 **85**.................... DavidProbert 5 92
(Rod Millman) *stdd s: hld up in rr: rdn over 2f out: styd on fnl f* **10/1**

/31- **6** 3 1/4 **Clerk's Choice (IRE)**[6] 8392 7-9-1 **81** 6ex.................... HayleyTurner 3 84
(William Jarvis) *chsd ldrs: rdn 3f out: btn 2f out* **11/4**[2]

105- **7** 1/2 **Swinging Hawk (GER)**[21] 8202 7-8-13 **79**.................... StevieDonohoe 2 82
(Ian Williams) *in tch: outpcd 2f out: sn btn* **25/1**

3m 19.9s (-5.80) **Going Correction** -0.10s/f (Stan) course record **7** Ran SP% **113.3**
Speed ratings (Par 109): **110,109,109,108,108 107,106**
CSF £42.61 CT £297.65 TOTE £7.70: £4.60, £3.20; EX 43.00 Trifecta £265.00 Pool: £2225.01 - 6.29 winning units..
Owner P J Martin **Bred** Giacinto Guglielmi **Trained** Scamblesby, Lincs

The Form Book Flat, Raceform Ltd, Compton, RG20 6NL.

FOCUS
A decent handicap but, as is often the case in staying races around here, the early pace was modest and it developed into something of a sprint. Despite that they managed to lower the course record, but these were much better horses than you normally get in 2m races around here.

8430 BOOKMAKERS.CO.UK H'CAP (DIV I) 6f (P)
2:10 (2:12) (Class 4) (0-85,85) 3-Y-O+ **£4,690** (£1,395; £697; £348) **Stalls** Low

Form RPR
31/ **1** **Absolutely So (IRE)**[402] 7813 3-8-13 **77**........ DavidProbert 2 87
(Andrew Balding) *bmpd early and towards rr: gd hdwy over 1f out: r.o to ld nr fin* **11/4**[1]
000- **2** *hd* **Palace Moon**[30] 8088 8-9-0 **78**........(t) JimCrowley 1 87
(William Knight) *chsd ldrs: led over 1f out: kpt on u.p fnl f: hdd nr fin* **5/1**
004- **3** *1 ¾* **Blessington (IRE)**[22] 8181 3-9-7 **85**........(t) RobertHavlin 6 88
(John Gosden) *hld up in 5th and gng wl: rdn over 1f out: r.o ins fnl f* **3/1**[2]
511- **4** *shd* **Kuanyao (IRE)**[24] 8158 7-8-9 **73**........(v) TonyHamilton 5 76
(David Nicholls) *led tl over 1f out: one pce* **9/2**[3]
000- **5** *hd* **Intomist (IRE)**[31] 8069 4-8-8 **72**........(p) WilliamCarson 4 74
(Jim Boyle) *sn lost pl and towards rr: rdn and hdwy fr over 1f out: nrest at fin* **33/1**
042- **6** *1 ½* **Foxtrot Jubilee (IRE)**[30] 8088 3-8-13 **84**........ PatrickO'Donnell(7) 7 82
(Ralph Beckett) *in tch on outer: rdn 2f out: styd on same pce* **12/1**
223- **7** *½* **Glastonberry**[22] 8181 5-8-12 **76**........ HayleyTurner 10 72
(Geoffrey Deacon) *chsd ldr tl over 1f out: sn wknd* **14/1**
530- **8** *nse* **Panther Patrol (IRE)**[26] 8127 3-8-10 **74**........(p) JohnFahy 3 70
(Eve Johnson Houghton) *bmpd early and sn last: sme hdwy on inner over 1f out: nvr able to chal* **10/1**
50- **9** *3* **Welliesinthewater (IRE)**[29] 8096 3-7-12 **69**........ AdamMcLean(7) 8 55
(Derek Shaw) *dwlt: a bhd* **66/1**
566- **10** *6* **Sandfrankskipsgo**[35] 8021 4-9-0 **78**........ ShaneKelly 11 45
(Peter Crate) *plld hrd on outer: prom tl wnt wd and wknd ent st* **25/1**

1m 10.5s (-1.40) **Going Correction** -0.10s/f (Stan) **10** Ran SP% **118.2**
Speed ratings (Par 105): **105,104,102,102,102 100,99,99,95,87**
CSF £16.93 CT £45.42 TOTE £3.90: £1.90, £2.30, £1.20; EX 23.90 Trifecta £71.90 Pool: £3998.16 - 41.70 winning units..
Owner Jackie & George Smith **Bred** L Mulryan **Trained** Kingsclere, Hants
FOCUS
A fair sprint handicap with the finish being fought out between a progressive colt and a gelding once rated as high as 110, so this may be form to treat positively.

8431 BOOKMAKERS.CO.UK H'CAP (DIV II) 6f (P)
2:45 (2:48) (Class 4) (0-85,85) 3-Y-O+ **£4,690** (£1,395; £697; £348) **Stalls** Low

Form RPR
452- **1** **Agerzam**[22] 8181 3-9-7 **85**........ AdamKirby 8 95
(Roger Varian) *in tch: effrt 2f out: led 1f out: sn in command: rdn out* **6/4**[1]
563- **2** *1* **Smokethatthunders (IRE)**[31] 8069 3-8-8 **72**........ RobertHavlin 12 79
(James Toller) *stdd s and swtchd lft: hld up in rr: gd hdwy over 1f out: r.o fnl f* **8/1**
004- **3** *nk* **Bajan Bear**[26] 8128 5-8-5 **69**........ DavidProbert 4 75
(Michael Blanshard) *towards rr: gd hdwy over 1f out: r.o fnl f* **12/1**
211- **4** *3 ¼* **Gregori (IRE)**[19] 8216 3-8-11 **75**........(t) SeanLevey 2 70
(Brian Meehan) *prom: led 2f out tl 1f out: wknd fnl f* **9/2**[2]
413- **5** *½* **Jungle Bay**[6] 8391 6-8-13 **77**........(b) MartinDwyer 9 71
(Jane Chapple-Hyam) *towards rr on outer: sme hdwy whn carried v wd home turn: styd on fnl f* **6/1**[3]
605- **6** *hd* **Enderby Spirit (GR)**[30] 8088 7-9-0 **78**........(t) FergusSweeney 10 71
(Bryan Smart) *chsd ldrs: carried wd home turn: sn btn* **14/1**
500- **7** *1 ¼* **Rocket Rob (IRE)**[22] 8181 7-9-0 **78**........ StevieDonohoe 3 67
(Willie Musson) *dwlt: bhd: rdn 2f out: modest late hdwy* **25/1**
310- **8** *½* **Amosite**[45] 7861 7-8-5 **74**........(v) JoeyHaynes(5) 1 62
(J R Jenkins) *in tch: effrt over 2f out: wknd over 1f out* **33/1**
045- **9** *¾* **Desert Strike**[23] 8167 7-8-8 **72**........(p) HayleyTurner 6 57
(Conor Dore) *mid-div tl outpcd and btn 2f out* **33/1**
640- **10** *3* **Piddie's Power**[32] 8053 6-8-11 **78**........ RobertTart(3) 11 54
(Kevin Frost) *mid-div: rdn over 2f out: sn outpcd and sltly wd into st* **25/1**
600- **11** *6* **Decision By One**[14] 8304 4-8-5 **72**........ RossAtkinson(3) 7 28
(David Evans) *prom tl carried wd and wknd ent st* **20/1**
101- **12** *5* **Pull The Pin (IRE)**[29] 8096 4-8-2 **66**........(b) WilliamCarson 5 6
(Ann Stokell) *led tl 2f out: rn wd and wknd ent st* **20/1**

1m 9.73s (-2.17) **Going Correction** -0.10s/f (Stan) **12** Ran SP% **117.8**
Speed ratings (Par 105): **110,108,108,103,103 103,101,100,99,95 87,81**
CSF £12.56 CT £110.96 TOTE £2.20: £1.10, £2.90, £4.50; EX 19.50 Trifecta £145.90 Pool: £3032.18 - 15.57 winning units..
Owner Saleh Al Homaizi & Imad Al Sagar **Bred** Saleh Al Homaizi & Imad Al Sagar **Trained** Newmarket, Suffolk
FOCUS
The winning time was 0.77sec quicker than the first division, but it was still a rather messy race with the leader Pull The Pin hanging badly right off the final bend, effectively taking out Jungle Bay, Enderby Spirit and Decision By One.

8432 DOWNLOAD THE LADBROKES APP H'CAP 7f (P)
3:20 (3:23) (Class 6) (0-65,65) 3-Y-O+ **£2,045** (£603; £302) **Stalls** Low

Form RPR
004- **1** **Perfect Haven**[35] 8019 3-9-3 **64**........ AdamKirby 12 73
(Clive Cox) *mde all: kicked on over 2f out: pushed along and edgd lft ins fnl f: hld on wl* **10/1**
625- **2** *1 ¼* **Welsh Sunrise**[30] 8087 3-9-4 **65**........ GeorgeBaker 7 71
(Ed Walker) *in tch: effrt over 2f out: wnt 2nd ins fnl f: hld whn hmpd nr fin* **7/2**[1]
5U5- **3** *hd* **Victorian Number (FR)**[24] 8158 5-9-3 **64**........ HayleyTurner 8 69
(Geoffrey Deacon) *chsd wnr: rdn over 2f out: one pce ent fnl f* **12/1**
003- **4** *¾* **Magical Rose (IRE)**[35] 8019 3-9-4 **65**........(p) LiamKeniry 9 69
(Paul D'Arcy) *mid-div: hdwy and edgd lft over 1f out: r.o fnl f* **16/1**
016- **5** *½* **Prince Of Burma (IRE)**[23] 8162 5-9-4 **65**........(v) DavidProbert 3 67
(David Evans) *hld up in rr: gd hdwy fnl f: fin wl* **6/1**[3]
021- **6** *nk* **Larghetto (USA)**[10] 8329 5-9-2 **63**........ ShaneKelly 6 64
(Daniel Mark Loughnane) *bhd: hdwy on inner over 1f out: one pce fnl f* **10/1**
300- **7** *1* **Bold Ring**[47] 7836 7-8-11 **65**........ JenniferFerguson(7) 11 64
(Edward Creighton) *towards rr tl styd on fr over 1f out* **25/1**
/30- **8** *½* **Al Aqabah (IRE)**[194] 3404 8-9-4 **65**........(b) MartinLane 2 63
(Brian Gubby) *chsd ldrs: rdn over 2f out: wknd over 1f out* **66/1**
002- **9** *½* **Club House (IRE)**[24] 8158 3-8-13 **63**........ RobertTart(3) 13 59
(Robert Mills) *dwlt: sme hdwy on outer over 3f out: sltly wd and outpcd home turn* **9/2**[2]
014- **10** *1 ¾* **Caramelita**[32] 8048 6-9-2 **63**........(v) FrederikTylicki 4 55
(J R Jenkins) *t.k.h: prom tl wknd over 1f out* **25/1**
554- **11** *3 ¾* **Invigilator**[14] 8306 5-9-3 **64**........(t) JimCrowley 14 46
(Derek Shaw) *t.k.h: a bhd on outer: n.d whn rn v wd home turn* **12/1**
262- **12** *hd* **Pucker Up**[59] 7625 3-9-3 **64**........ SeanLevey 10 45
(David Brown) *t.k.h: mid-div: outpcd and btn 2f out* **7/1**

1m 24.88s (0.08) **Going Correction** -0.10s/f (Stan) **12** Ran SP% **115.8**
Speed ratings (Par 101): **95,93,93,92,91 91,90,89,89,87 83,82**
CSF £43.11 CT £438.66 TOTE £9.50: £2.80, £1.80, £3.20; EX 42.50 Trifecta £752.80 Pool: £3244.92 - 3.23 winning units..
Owner John Drew and Dr Bridget Drew **Bred** Worksop Manor Stud **Trained** Lambourn, Berks
■ Stewards' Enquiry : Adam Kirby two-day ban; careless riding (11th, 12th Jan).
FOCUS
Only 2lb covered the entire field in this modest handicap and it paid to race handily.
T/Plt: £49.60 to a £1 stake. Pool: £67661.02 - 994.25 winning tickets T/Qpdt: £9.70 to a £1 stake. Pool: £6703.91 - 507.36 winning tickets LM

8404 SOUTHWELL (L-H)
Sunday, December 29

OFFICIAL GOING: Standard
Wind: Moderate across Weather: Fine, crisp and dry

8433 32RED H'CAP 2m (F)
12:20 (12:20) (Class 5) (0-75,75) 3-Y-O+ **£2,911** (£866; £432; £216) **Stalls** Low

Form RPR
111- **1** **Mr Burbidge**[27] 8130 5-10-0 **75**........(b) LiamKeniry 6 88
(Neil Mulholland) *trckd ldr: cl up 6f out: led over 3f out: pushed clr over 2f out: kpt on strly* **2/1**[1]
513- **2** *8* **Yasir (USA)**[10] 8349 5-9-8 **69**........(p) HayleyTurner 7 72
(Conor Dore) *hld up in tch: tk clsr order 6f out: pushed along 4f out: rdn to chse wnr wl over 2f out: drvn over 1f out and no imp* **11/4**[2]
030- **3** *3 ½* **Mediterranean Sea (IRE)**[15] 8299 7-9-10 **71**........ FrederikTylicki 3 70
(J R Jenkins) *trckd ldng pair: pushed along 4f out: rdn 3f out: kpt on same pce fnl 2f* **11/1**
421- **4** *1 ¾* **Monzino (USA)**[9] 8373 5-9-2 **70**........(b) PaulBooth(7) 5 67
(Michael Chapman) *dwlt and in rr: hdwy and in tch 1/2-way: rdn along and outpcd over 4f out: sme late hdwy* **10/1**[3]
232- **5** *15* **Scribe (IRE)**[13] 8310 5-9-8 **69**........(bt) AdamKirby 2 48
(David Evans) *led: rdn along over 4f out: hdd over 3f out and sn wknd* **2/1**[1]

3m 41.12s (-4.38) **Going Correction** -0.05s/f (Stan) **5** Ran SP% **110.8**
Speed ratings (Par 103): **108,104,102,101,93**
CSF £7.87 TOTE £2.20: £1.10, £2.10; EX 8.20 Trifecta £37.30 Pool: £2006.12 - 40.27 winning units..
Owner Dajam Ltd **Bred** M Burbidge **Trained** Limpley Stoke, Wilts
FOCUS
Not a bad little staying handicap for the grade.

8434 32RED.COM NURSERY H'CAP 1m (F)
12:50 (12:50) (Class 6) (0-65,65) 2-Y-O **£1,940** (£577; £288; £144) **Stalls** Low

Form RPR
603- **1** **Excel Best**[15] 8297 2-9-7 **65**........(b[1]) PaddyAspell 4 78
(James Tate) *mde all: pushed clr over 2f out: rdn over 1f out: styd on strly* **4/1**[2]
604- **2** *6* **Evacusafe Lady**[45] 7878 2-9-7 **65**........(tp) AdamKirby 8 64
(John Ryan) *trckd ldrs on wd outside: hdwy 3f out: chsd wnr over 2f out and sn rdn: drvn over 1f out and sn no imp* **5/1**[3]
011- **3** *nk* **Big Kenny**[9] 8363 2-8-11 **62**........ GearoidBrouder(7) 2 60
(David Evans) *chsd ldrs on inner: hdwy 3f out: swtchd rt and rdn to chse ldng pair wl over 1f out: drvn and hung lft ent fnl f: kpt on same pce* **2/1**[1]
553- **4** *6* **Armelle (FR)**[9] 8364 2-8-12 **56**........(p) TomEaves 6 41
(Scott Dixon) *chsd wnr: rdn along 3f out: drvn over 2f out and grad wknd* **8/1**
U10- **5** *1 ½* **Cascadia (IRE)**[74] 7309 2-8-10 **61**........ RobJFitzpatrick(7) 7 42
(K R Burke) *towards rr: rdn along wl over 3f out: sme late hdwy* **20/1**
065- **6** *nk* **Three Heart's**[74] 7310 2-9-2 **60**........ MartinDwyer 9 40
(Hugo Palmer) *dwlt and in rr whn swtchd to outer: in tch: rdn along wl over 3f out: sn outpcd* **5/1**[3]
055- **7** *3* **Hasta La Vista**[16] 8274 2-8-1 **45**........(b[1]) AndrewMullen 5 18
(Mark Johnston) *chsd ldrs: rdn along over 3f out: sn wknd* **10/1**
203- **8** *2 ½* **Volodina (IRE)**[9] 8362 2-8-9 **60**........(v) AaronJones(7) 1 28
(Alan McCabe) *chsd ldrs: rdn along 3f out: wknd over 2f out: hung bdly rt wl over 1f* **20/1**
003- **9** *½* **Worcharlie'Slass**[16] 8265 2-8-1 **45**........ JimmyQuinn 3 12
(Michael Herrington) *a in rr: bhd fnl 3f* **40/1**

1m 43.88s (0.18) **Going Correction** -0.05s/f (Stan) **9** Ran SP% **118.8**
Speed ratings (Par 94): **97,91,90,84,83 82,79,77,76**
toteswingers 1&2 £4.40, 1&3 £2.40, 2&3 £3.30 CSF £24.45 CT £52.04 TOTE £4.10: £1.10, £2.30, £1.10; EX 24.00 Trifecta £56.20 Pool: £3600.32 - 48.03 winning units..
Owner Sheikh Juma Dalmook Al Maktoum **Bred** Best Breeding **Trained** Newmarket, Suffolk
■ Stewards' Enquiry : Gearoid Brouder 15-day ban; used whip above permitted level (12th-27th Jan)
FOCUS
A weak handicap, run at a strong pace. The placed horses have been rated near their recent form.

8435 32RED CASINO MAIDEN AUCTION STKS 5f (F)
1:25 (1:25) (Class 6) 2-Y-O **£1,940** (£577; £288; £144) **Stalls** High

Form RPR
004- **1** **Under Approval**[164] 4443 2-9-4 0........ DavidNolan 5 65
(David O'Meara) *trckd ldrs: effrt over 1f out: sn rdn and kpt on u.p to ld last 50yds* **16/1**
556- **2** *hd* **Diamondsinthesky (IRE)**[51] 7804 2-8-1 59........ AdamMcLean(7) 7 54
(Derek Shaw) *racd nr stands' rail: led 1f: prom tl rdn to ld again ent fnl f: hdd and no ex last 50yds* **8/1**
334- **3** *½* **Anfield**[16] 8273 2-8-7 55........ WilliamCarson 3 51
(Mick Quinn) *cl up: led after 1f: rdn along over 1f out: hdd and drvn ent fnl f: kpt on same pce* **7/4**[2]
223- **4** *nk* **Coiste Bodhar (IRE)**[20] 8222 2-8-13 62........ RobertWinston 6 56
(Joseph Tuite) *chsd ldrs: rdn along and outpcd after 2f: drvn and hdwy on outer wl over 1f out: kpt on u.p fnl f* **6/4**[1]
060- **5** *2 ¼* **Cheeky Peta'S**[16] 8273 2-8-9 45........(v) TomEaves 4 44
(James Given) *cl up: rdn along 2f out: drvn and wknd ent fnl f* **20/1**

5- **6** *4 1/2* **Sleet (IRE)**[2] 8405 2-9-4 0 .... AndrewMullen 1 37
(Michael Appleby) *dwlt and wnt lft s: sn outpcd and rdn along: a bhd* **6/1**[3]

1m 0.98s (1.28) **Going Correction** +0.075s/f (Slow) **6** Ran SP% **112.4**
Speed ratings (Par 94): **92,91,90,90,86 79**
toteswingers 1&2 £9.50, 1&3 £6.30, 2&3 £3.30 CSF £127.61 TOTE £18.70: £10.00, £3.70; EX 111.60 Trifecta £653.00 Pool: £2545.31 - 2.92 winning units..
Owner Richard Collins **Bred** Mickley Stud **Trained** Nawton, N Yorks
■ Stewards' Enquiry : Adam McLean two-day ban; used whip above permitted level (12th-13th Jan).

FOCUS
A desperately weak maiden. The first notable form from the winner, ruining his 45 mark in the process, but he's in good hands and could improve from here.

8436 CORAL MOBILE JUST THREE CLICKS TO BET (S) H'CAP 1m 3f (F)
1:55 (1:55) (Class 6) (0-60,60) 3-Y-O+ **£1,940** (£577; £288; £144) **Stalls** Low

Form RPR

/00- **1** **Auden (USA)**[40] 7952 5-9-10 **60** ....(v) FrederikTylicki 4 72
(J R Jenkins) *trckd ldr: smooth hdwy over 3f out: cl up over 2f out: led wl over 1f out: rdn ent fnl f: drvn and jst hld on nr line* **11/4**[1]

615- **2** *shd* **On The Cusp (IRE)**[33] 8042 6-9-5 **55** ....(b) WilliamCarson 12 67
(Ann Stokell) *set str pce: pushed along over 3f out: rdn over 2f out: hdd wl over 1f out: drvn and rallied ins fnl f: jst failed* **7/2**[2]

530- **3** *11* **Miss Ella Jade**[19] 8229 4-8-12 **48** ....(p) TonyHamilton 6 41
(Richard Whitaker) *chsd ldng pair: rdn along over 3f out: drvn over 2f out and plugged on one pce* **8/1**[3]

066- **4** *1 1/4* **Una Bella Cosa**[10] 8348 3-8-6 **46** oh1 ....(p) AndrewMullen 9 37
(Alan McCabe) *chsd ldrs: rdn along wl over 3f out: drvn over 2f out: kpt on one pce* **20/1**

333- **5** *nse* **Naughtybychoice**[297] 910 3-8-6 **51** ....(v[1]) JacobButterfield(5) 3 42
(Ollie Pears) *chsd ldrs: rdn along wl over 3f out: drvn 2f out: plugged on same pce* **8/1**[3]

0/4- **6** *nk* **Aureate**[16] 8268 9-8-7 **50** ....(p) DanielCremin(7) 2 41
(Brian Forsey) *midfield: rdn along wl over 3f out: sme late hdwy* **12/1**

065- **7** *1* **Rapid Water**[12] 8315 7-8-10 **46** oh1 ....(p) LiamJones 11 35
(Pat Eddery) *towards rr: hdwy and in tch over 4f out: rdn along over 3f out: drvn over 2f out: no imp* **25/1**

060- **8** *2 1/4* **Inside Knowledge (USA)**[30] 6565 7-8-8 **49** ....(p) TimClark(5) 14 34
(Garry Woodward) *in rr tl sme hdwy fnl 3f: n.d* **20/1**

00/- **9** *8* **Botanist**[452] 6771 6-8-11 **47** .... PaddyAspell 10 18
(Shaun Harris) *a in rr* **16/1**

605- **10** *4* **Jordaura**[26] 8136 7-9-2 **55** .... SladeO'Hara(3) 8 20
(Alan Berry) *midfield: rdn along 1/2-way: nvr a factor* **10/1**

006- **11** *2* **Primacy (IRE)**[25] 8149 4-8-12 **48** .... LiamKeniry 5 9
(Neil Mulholland) *in tch: rdn along 4f out: sn wknd* **16/1**

400- **12** *nk* **Dew Reward (IRE)**[25] 8160 5-8-9 **52** ....(p) RyanWhile(7) 13 13
(Bill Turner) *a in rr* **25/1**

000- **13** *34* **Sir Dylan**[112] 2828 4-9-6 **56** .... RobertWinston 7
(Ronald Harris) *a towards rr: bhd fnl 3f* **10/1**

2m 27.85s (-0.15) **Going Correction** -0.05s/f (Stan)
WFA 3 from 4yo+ 4lb **13** Ran SP% **126.0**
Speed ratings (Par 101): **98,97,89,89,88 88,88,86,80,77 76,76,51**
toteswingers 1&2 £3.00, 1&3 £3.90, 2&3 £4.20 CSF £11.86 CT £71.17 TOTE £4.50: £2.10, £1.30, £3.50; EX 14.60 Trifecta £67.10 Pool: £2489.11 - 27.80 winning units..There was no bid for the winner.
Owner Ms Aurelija Juskaite **Bred** Darley **Trained** Royston, Herts
■ Stewards' Enquiry : William Carson one-day ban; careless riding (12th Jan).
Frederik Tylicki two-day ban; used whip above permitted level (12th-13th Jan).

FOCUS
This very weak handicap was run at a strong pace.

8437 DOWNLOAD THE LADBROKES APP MAIDEN STKS 7f (F)
2:30 (2:31) (Class 5) 3-Y-O+ **£2,911** (£866; £432; £216) **Stalls** Low

Form RPR

3- **1** **Stun Gun**[33] 8043 3-9-5 0 .... DaleSwift 6 66
(Derek Shaw) *trckd ldrs: hdwy and cl up wl over 2f out: sn rdn: led appr fnl f: drvn out* **4/1**[2]

033- **2** *1 1/2* **Severiano (USA)**[13] 8313 3-9-5 67 .... AdamKirby 4 63
(Roger Varian) *trckd ldrs: pushed along 1/2-way: effrt over 2f out: sn rdn and ch tl drvn and one pce fnl f* **10/11**[1]

062- **3** *hd* **Ishisoba**[12] 8320 3-9-0 49 .... LiamJones 3 57
(Ronald Harris) *led 3f: cl up: led again wl over 2f out: sn rdn: jnd and drvn wl over 1f out: hdd appr fnl f: kpt on same pce* **8/1**

0- **4** *9* **Limon Squeezy**[32] 8063 4-9-0 0 .... RobertWinston 9 34
(Mike Murphy) *dwlt and towards rr: hdwy on outer over 2f out: sn rdn and kpt on fnl f: nrst fin* **16/1**

05- **5** *1/2* **Mobley Chaos**[114] 6155 3-9-0 0 .... DarylByrne(5) 5 37
(Ronald Harris) *in rr: sme hdwy over 2f out: sn rdn and n.d* **100/1**

244- **6** *1 1/2* **Busy Bimbo (IRE)**[12] 8320 4-8-11 45 .... MarkCoumbe(3) 10 28
(Alan Berry) *in tch: hdwy on wd outside and cl up over 2f out: rdn and edgd lft wl over 1f out: sn wknd* **25/1**

0/0- **7** *1 3/4* **Back In The Frame**[15] 8306 3-8-11 62 ....(v[1]) SHJames(3) 11 24
(David O'Meara) *s.i.s: a towards rr* **6/1**[3]

006- **8** *1/2* **Jillywinks**[12] 8320 3-8-7 55 ....(p) MatthewHopkins(7) 1 23
(Scott Dixon) *prom on inner: led after 3f: rdn along 3f out: sn hdd & wknd over 2f out* **20/1**

00/ **9** *13* **Les Andelys**[1186] 6499 7-9-5 0 .... PaddyAspell 7
(Michael Murphy) *a towards rr* **100/1**

0- **10** *9* **Law Hill**[305] 814 4-9-5 0 ....(t) WilliamCarson 8
(Michael Murphy) *s.i.s: a in rr* **20/1**

00- **11** *29* **Missie Snaffles**[222] 2538 3-9-0 0 .... MartinDwyer 2
(Alan Swinbank) *chsd ldrs: rdn along bef 1/2-way: sn wknd* **25/1**

1m 30.14s (-0.16) **Going Correction** -0.05s/f (Stan) **11** Ran SP% **122.9**
Speed ratings (Par 103): **98,96,96,85,85 83,81,80,66,55 22**
CSF £7.83 TOTE £5.50: £1.60, £1.10, £2.70; EX 13.20 Trifecta £57.20 Pool: £3633.05 - 47.56 winning units..
Owner John R Saville **Bred** Rothmere Bloodstock **Trained** Sproxton, Leics

FOCUS
An ordinary maiden.

8438 BEST ODDS AT BOOKMAKERS.CO.UK CLASSIFIED STKS 6f (F)
3:00 (3:00) (Class 6) 3-Y-O+ **£1,940** (£577; £288; £144) **Stalls** Low

Form RPR

003- **1** **Borough Boy (IRE)**[24] 8168 3-9-0 52 ....(v) DaleSwift 8 62
(Derek Shaw) *in tch on outer: wd st: hdwy 2f out: rdn to chse ldr and edgd lft over 1f out: styd on wl fnl f to ld last 75yds* **5/2**[2]

201- **2** *1 1/4* **Pearl Noir**[12] 8320 3-8-7 55 ....(b) MatthewHopkins(7) 9 58
(Scott Dixon) *led: rdn clr over 2f out: drvn ins fnl f: hdd and no ex last 75yds* **7/4**[1]

005- **3** *7* **Red Star Lady (IRE)**[19] 8234 3-9-0 40 .... JimmyQuinn 5 36
(Shaun Harris) *trckd ldng pair: hdwy to chse ldr 1/2-way: rdn along 2f out: sn drvn and one pce* **16/1**

540- **4** *4 1/2* **Partner's Gold (IRE)**[40] 7966 3-9-0 46 ....(b) RobertHavlin 1 21
(Alan Berry) *in tch: rdn along and outpcd 1/2-way: kpt on u.p fnl 2f: n.d* **12/1**

405- **5** *1/2* **Island Express (IRE)**[115] 6145 6-8-10 51 ow1 ....(tp) AnnStokell(5) 10 21
(Ann Stokell) *dwlt and towards rr tl sme hdwy fnl 2f: nvr a factor* **16/1**

644- **6** *5* **Misty Eyes**[17] 8258 4-9-0 48 ....(v) AndrewMullen 3 4
(Geoffrey Harker) *chsd ldr: rdn along 1/2-way: drvn 2f out and sn wknd* **7/2**[3]

000- **7** *4* **Bond Blade**[16] 8271 5-9-0 40 .... TomEaves 6
(Suzzanne France) *dwlt: a in rr* **25/1**

006- **8** *4 1/2* **Chelsea Grey (IRE)**[33] 8051 3-9-0 43 ....(p) LiamJones 7
(Ronald Harris) *a in rr* **20/1**

1m 16.21s (-0.29) **Going Correction** -0.05s/f (Stan) **8** Ran SP% **115.2**
Speed ratings (Par 101): **99,97,88,82,81 74,69,63**
toteswingers 1&2 £1.60, 1&3 £9.40, 2&3 £6.10 CSF £7.34 TOTE £3.10: £1.30, £1.50, £4.20; EX 10.50 Trifecta £73.60 Pool: £1162.82 - 11.84 winning units..
Owner Brian Johnson (Northamptonshire) **Bred** E Kopica And M Rosenfeld **Trained** Sproxton, Leics

FOCUS
Another weak affair.

8439 COMPARE BOOKMAKERS AT BOOKMAKERS.CO.UK H'CAP 5f (F)
3:30 (3:31) (Class 5) (0-75,83) 3-Y-O+ **£2,587** (£770; £384; £192) **Stalls** High

Form RPR

021- **1** **Thorpe Bay**[16] 8272 4-8-11 **65** .... AndrewMullen 8 78
(Michael Appleby) *prom: effrt and cl up 2f out: sn rdn: drvn to ld ins fnl f: kpt on wl towards fin* **5/1**[3]

031- **2** *1 3/4* **Powerful Wind (IRE)**[12] 8319 4-9-10 **83** .... DarylByrne(5) 2 90
(Ronald Harris) *prom: led over 2f out: sn rdn: jnd and drvn over 1f out: hdd ins fnl f: kpt on same pce* **3/1**[1]

021- **3** *1/2* **Sir Geoffrey (IRE)**[16] 8271 7-8-0 **61** oh1 ....(p) MatthewHopkins(7) 10 66
(Scott Dixon) *towards rr: swtchd lft and hdwy 2f out: sn rdn: styd on fnl f: nrst fin* **12/1**

550- **4** *nk* **Master Bond**[15] 8305 4-9-3 **74** .... SHJames(3) 11 78
(David O'Meara) *towards rr: hdwy over 2f out: rdn wl over 1f out: kpt on fnl f: nrst fin* **6/1**

032- **5** *1 1/2* **I'll Be Good**[27] 8135 4-8-5 **62** oh3 ow1 .... MarkCoumbe(3) 12 61
(Alan Berry) *dwlt: sn in tch: hdwy to chse ldrs 1/2-way: rdn along wl over 1f out: one pce* **20/1**

032- **6** *hd* **Monnoyer**[2] 8406 4-8-9 **63** ....(be) PJMcDonald 9 61
(Scott Dixon) *dwlt: sn rdn along and bhd tl styd on fnl f: nrst fin* **8/1**

060- **7** *1/2* **Climaxfortackle (IRE)**[27] 8128 5-8-12 **66** .... LiamJones 4 62
(Derek Shaw) *dwlt: sn swtchd lft and rdn along in rr: hdwy over 1f out: kpt on fnl f: nrst fin* **20/1**

532- **8** *1/2* **Solemn**[30] 8096 8-9-2 **70** ow1 ....(v) AdamKirby 6 64
(Milton Bradley) *chsd ldrs: effrt 2f out: sn rdn and edgd lft: wknd appr fnl f* **6/1**

653- **9** *1/2* **Fathom Five (IRE)**[10] 8352 9-8-7 **61** oh1 .... JimmyQuinn 5 54
(Shaun Harris) *led: rdn along over 2f out: sn hdd & wknd wl over 1f out* **20/1**

656- **10** *4* **Bapak Sayang (USA)**[32] 8069 3-9-5 **73** ....[1] TomEaves 7 51
(Kevin Ryan) *prom: rdn along over 2f out: sn wknd* **9/2**[2]

630- **11** *nk* **Fairy Wing (IRE)**[40] 7953 6-8-12 **66** ....(b) WilliamCarson 1 43
(Ann Stokell) *in tch on wd outside: rdn along 1/2-way: sn wknd* **33/1**

59.33s (-0.37) **Going Correction** +0.075s/f (Slow) **11** Ran SP% **124.5**
Speed ratings (Par 103): **105,102,101,100,98 97,96,95,89 88**
CSF £20.53 CT £183.15 TOTE £5.90: £2.00, £1.90, £1.90; EX 29.10 Trifecta £123.20 Pool: £1525.58 - 9.28 winning units..
Owner Dallas Racing **Bred** Clive Dennett **Trained** Danethorpe, Notts

FOCUS
A modest sprint handicap and solid enough form for the class.
T/Plt: £62.40. Pool: £70,575.88 - 824.95 winning units. T/Qpdt: £35.40. Pool: £5575.65 - 116.50 wining units. JR

[8354] DEAUVILLE (R-H)
Sunday, December 29

OFFICIAL GOING: Fibresand: standard

8440a PRIX MISS SATAMIXA (LISTED RACE) (3YO+ FILLIES & MARES) (FIBRESAND) 7f 110y
12:15 (12:15) 3-Y-O+ **£21,138** (£8,455; £6,341; £4,227; £2,113)

RPR

1 **L'Amour De Ma Vie (USA)**[26] 8144 4-8-11 0 .... MaximeGuyon 1 106
(Mme Pia Brandt, France) **9/2**[3]

2 *1/2* **Vaunoise (IRE)**[38] 7993 3-8-11 0 .... MatthiasLauron 16 105+
(J-C Rouget, France) **183/10**

3 *1 3/4* **Bayargal (USA)**[25] 8161 3-9-2 0 .... Pierre-CharlesBoudot 5 105
(A Fabre, France) **57/10**

4 *nk* **Gaga A (URU)**[48] 7843 4-8-11 0 .... AlexisBadel 10 100
(D Smaga, France) **43/10**[2]

5 *3/4* **Mon Choix (FR)**[15] 8307 4-8-11 0 .... MorganDelalande 8 98
(Y Darberot, France) **28/1**

6 *1/2* **Sargasses (FR)**[6] 7-8-11 0 .... EddyHardouin 15 97
(Mlle V Dissaux, France) **213/10**

7 *1 1/4* **Harmonic Note**[58] 7673 3-8-11 0 .... TheoBachelot 7 93
(F-H Graffard, France) **188/10**

8 *1 1/2* **Zayade (FR)**[38] 7995 4-8-11 0 .... AdrienFouassier 14 90
(J Boisnard, France) **269/10**

9 *shd* **Ostourah (USA)**[15] 8307 3-8-11 0 .... AntoineHamelin 9 89
(A De Royer-Dupre, France) **40/1**

10 *hd* **Fancy Green (FR)**[25] 3-8-11 0 .... AurelienLemaitre 11 89
(E Legrix, France) **61/1**

11 *hd* **Rocaille (FR)**[25] 8161 3-8-11 0 ....(b) CristianDemuro 4 88
(Mme C Head-Maarek, France) **39/10**[1]

12 *1 1/2* **Carnoustie (FR)**[57] 7706 4-8-11 0 ....(b) JimmyMartin 6 85
(X Thomas-Demeaulte, France) **56/1**

13 *nk* **Roxanne (FR)**[38] 7993 3-8-11 0 .... FlavienPrat 12 84
(H-A Pantall, France) **27/1**
14 *nk* **Yojojo (IRE)**[67] 7470 4-8-11 0 .... MickaelForest 3 83
(Gay Kelleway) *settled towards rr: rdn and short-lived effrt ins fnl 2f: sn no further imp: nvr in contention* **176/10**
15 *3* **Seventh Sense (GER)**[25] 3-8-11 0 .... RonanThomas 2 76
(P Van De Poele, France) **132/10**
16 *dist* **Day For Night (IRE)**[67] 3-8-11 0 .... AntoineWerle 13
(H-A Pantall, France) **109/1**

1m 29.06s (89.06) **16** Ran SP% **116.8**
WIN (incl. 1 euro stake): 5.50. PLACES: 2.20, 5.60, 2.10. DF: 63.60. SF: 100.00.
Owner Md Bloodstock Limited **Bred** Palides Investments N.V. Inc **Trained** France

8441a PRIX DE MORICAND (CLAIMER) (3YO) (LADY RIDERS) (FIBRESAND) 7f 110y
1:50 (1:50) 3-Y-O £**6,910** (£2,764; £2,073; £1,382; £691)

RPR
1 **Jolly Old Chap (FR)**[11] 3-9-3 0 ....(p) MlleAngelaLeCorre(5) 14 88
(M Nigge, France) **29/10**[1]
2 *1 1/2* **Echo Of Silence (FR)**[63] 3-9-4 0 .... DelphineSantiago 13 80
(J-M Capitte, France) **33/10**[2]
3 *4* **One And Only (FR)**[103] 3-8-5 0 .... MlleAmelieFoulon(3) 2 60
(P Decouz, France) **26/1**
4 *shd* **Vesper (GER)**[16] 3-8-3 0 .... PamelaBoehm(5) 3 60
(M Munch, Germany) **61/10**[3]
5 *nk* **Knight Charm**[33] 8042 3-8-11 0 .... CarlaO'Halloran 5 62
(Gay Kelleway) *t.k.h: trckd ldng gp: rdn 1 1/2f out: kpt on ins fnl f: nt pce to chal* **50/1**
6 *snk* **Perrecalla (FR)**[16] 3-8-3 0 .... MllePaulineDominois(5) 9 59
(J Van Handenhove, France) **99/10**
7 *1 3/4* **Slice Of Life (FR)**[78] 3-8-7 0 .... LauraGrosso(6) 10 59
(Mme M Bollack-Badel, France) **94/10**
8 *snk* **Khefyn (IRE)**[80] 7150 3-9-1 0 .... CelineLaunay 8 61
(J Reynier, France) **102/10**
9 *1* **Dark Woman**[15] 3-8-6 0 .... MlleCassandraMillet(5) 7 54
(H-A Pantall, France) **269/10**
10 *1 1/2* **Whipper Snapper (FR)**[16] 3-8-6 0 ....(b) MlleMarie-AnneBernadet(5) 4 51
(E J O'Neill, France) **173/10**
11 *1 1/4* **Ryedale Valley**[15] 3-8-6 0 .... MlleJeanneCotta(5) 6 48
(Mlle M Henry, France) **148/1**
12 *1 1/2* **Storm Fall (FR)**[16] 3-8-11 0 .... PaulineProd'homme 15 44
(D Prod'Homme, France) **26/1**
13 *7* **Lionel (FR)** 3-8-11 0 ....(b[1]) SibylleVogt 12 26
(Carmen Bocskai, Switzerland) **64/1**
14 *1/2* **Our Three Graces (IRE)**[118] 6038 3-8-8 0 ..... MlleAnnaVanDenTroost 1 22
(Andre Hermans, Belgium) **71/1**
15 *12* **Sarrebourg (FR)** 3-8-6 0 .... MlleZoePfeil(5) 11
(J-P Gauvin, France) **26/1**

1m 29.48s (89.48) **15** Ran SP% **116.4**
WIN (incl. 1 euro stake): 3.90. PLACES: 1.90, 1.90, 5.20. DF: 6.80. SF: 16.10.
Owner Mme Christa Zass **Bred** Janus Bloodstock **Trained** France

8425 LINGFIELD (L-H)
Monday, December 30

OFFICIAL GOING: Standard
Wind: Behind; very strong but gradually moderating Weather: Raining first 3 races - becoming brighter

8442 32RED NURSERY H'CAP 6f (P)
12:00 (12:01) (Class 4) (0-85,83) 2-Y-O £**3,752** (£1,116; £557; £278) **Stalls** Low

Form RPR
652- **1** **Thataboy (IRE)**[25] 8166 2-8-1 **63** .... KieranO'Neill 2 71+
(Tom Dascombe) *w.w in midfield: prog jst over 2f out: clsd qckly to ld ins fnl f: pushed clr* **7/2**[2]
425- **2** *2* **Searchlight**[82] 7127 2-8-13 **75** .... TonyHamilton 3 77
(Kevin Ryan) *led but pressed: drvn over 1f out: hdd and one pce ins fnl f* **14/1**
332- **3** *2 1/4* **Kodafine (IRE)**[9] 8383 2-8-4 **69** .... RossAtkinson(3) 6 64
(David Evans) *sn pushed along in last pair and wl off the pce: prog 2f out: styd on to take 3rd ins fnl f: no ch* **12/1**
401- **4** *2 1/4* **Harwoods Volante (IRE)**[18] 8261 2-9-7 **83** ....[1] RobertHavlin 8 72
(Amanda Perrett) *pushed along in 7th after 2f: kpt on fr over 1f out: nvr a threat* **7/4**[1]
306- **5** *1 1/4* **Danfazi (IRE)**[18] 8261 2-8-12 **74** .... TomEaves 5 59
(Kristin Stubbs) *trckd ldng pair: swung quite wd bnd 2f out and lost pl: no prog after* **16/1**
623- **6** *1* **Corncockle**[23] 8203 2-9-2 **81** .... SHJames(3) 7 63
(David O'Meara) *chsd ldrs: wnt 3rd briefly wl over 1f out: sn drvn and wknd* **6/1**[3]
011- **7** *1/2* **Aspirant**[12] 8325 2-8-9 **78** .... RyanWhile(7) 1 58
(Bill Turner) *w ldr to wl over 1f out: styd on inner and wknd rapidly fnl f* **10/1**
462- **8** *nk* **Royal Brave (IRE)**[12] 8322 2-8-0 **62** .... JimmyQuinn 9 41
(William Muir) *a wl in rr: struggling over 2f out* **8/1**
031- **9** *1* **Lady Crossmar (IRE)**[26] 8145 2-9-0 **76** .... SeanLevey 4 52
(Richard Hannon Snr) *chsd ldrs: rdn and lost pl over 2f out: steadily wknd* **7/1**

1m 11.28s (-0.62) **Going Correction** -0.125s/f (Stan) **9** Ran SP% **125.8**
Speed ratings (Par 99): **99,96,93,90,88 87,86,86,84**
toteswingers 1&2 £14.90, 1&3 £12.40, 2&3 £25.90 CSF £56.19 CT £556.89 TOTE £4.50: £1.40, £3.50, £3.50; EX 55.90 Trifecta £1159.80 Pool: £1748.29 - 1.13 winning units..
Owner David Lowe & Laurence Bellman **Bred** Mrs Brid Cosgrove **Trained** Malpas, Cheshire

FOCUS
Several in-form runners in a useful nursery but the market leader disappointed and not many figured. The gallop was sound and the winner raced towards the inside rail the in the straight. The winner is progressing and is likely to rate a bit higher again.

8443 DOWNLOAD THE LADBROKES APP H'CAP 1m (P)
12:30 (12:31) (Class 6) (0-65,65) 3-Y-O £**2,045** (£603; £302) **Stalls** High

Form RPR
610- **1** **Run It Twice (IRE)**[16] 8295 3-9-7 **65** ....(b) AdamKirby 4 75
(David Evans) *wl plcd bhd ldrs: wnt 2nd over 2f out: led over 1f out: shkn up and r.o wl* **11/4**[1]
016- **2** *1 1/4* **Multitask**[26] 8151 3-9-1 **59** .... LiamKeniry 2 66
(Michael Madgwick) *t.k.h: hld up in rr: prog 2f out: edgd rt but r.o to take 2nd last 100yds: no imp on wnr* **5/1**[3]
020- **3** *1 1/4* **Club House (IRE)**[2] 8432 3-8-12 **63** .... GeorgeBuckell(7) 1 67
(Robert Mills) *hld up in midfield: prog 2f out: rdn to take 2nd briefly jst ins fnl f: one pce after* **9/2**[2]
000- **4** *1/2* **Fearless Lad (IRE)**[33] 8059 3-9-4 **62** ....(t) HayleyTurner 3 65
(John Best) *w ldr: led 1/2-way: hdd and one pce over 1f out* **8/1**
400- **5** *3 1/4* **Countess Lovelace**[9] 8388 3-9-2 **60** .... FergusSweeney 12 56
(Pat Phelan) *hld up in last pair: wdst of all bnd 2f out: shkn up briefly over 1f out: kpt on but nvr involved* **25/1**
600- **6** *hd* **Chief Executive (IRE)**[10] 8360 3-9-2 **60** .... ShaneKelly 5 55
(Jo Hughes) *t.k.h: trckd ldrs: lost pl fr 3f out: outpcd fr 2f out* **5/1**[3]
530- **7** *1 1/2* **Bond Club**[41] 7957 3-9-2 **63** ....(b[1]) RobertTart(3) 10 55
(Geoffrey Oldroyd) *t.k.h: pressed ldrs: rdn and quite wd bnd 2f out: steadily fdd* **12/1**
005- **8** *4* **Gentlemax (FR)**[93] 6824 3-9-7 **65** .... WilliamCarson 7 48
(Jim Boyle) *stdd s: hld up in last pair: nvr more than pushed along on inner fr over 2f out: nvr remotely involved* **20/1**
000- **9** *3* **Overrider**[108] 6362 3-9-3 **61** ....(t) RichardKingscote 11 37
(Alastair Lidderdale) *led to 1/2-way: wknd over 2f out* **12/1**
430- **10** *4* **Lady Who**[53] 7786 3-9-7 **65** .... MartinDwyer 8 31
(William Muir) *racd wd in midfield: lost pl and struggling fr 1/2-way: sn no ch* **7/1**

1m 38.67s (0.47) **Going Correction** -0.125s/f (Stan) **10** Ran SP% **125.8**
Speed ratings (Par 98): **92,90,89,89,85 85,84,80,77,73**
toteswingers 1&2 £3.80, 1&3 £2.70, 2&3 £4.90 CSF £18.04 CT £63.91 TOTE £3.50: £1.10, £2.10, £1.70; EX 24.10 Trifecta £45.60 Pool: £2604.92 - 42.81 winning units..
Owner Shropshire Wolves 4 **Bred** Yeomanstown Stud **Trained** Pandy, Monmouths

FOCUS
A modest handicap in which the gallop was an ordinary one. The winner came down the centre in the straight.

8444 CORAL MOBILE "JUST THREE CLICKS TO BET" MAIDEN STKS 1m 2f (P)
1:00 (1:01) (Class 5) 3-Y-O £**2,726** (£805; £402) **Stalls** Low

Form RPR
4- **1** **Music Man (IRE)**[19] 8245 3-9-5 0 .... JimCrowley 4 79
(Jo Crowley) *trckd ldng trio: pushed along 3f out: clsd on outer to ld jst over 1f out: rdn out* **4/1**[2]
2 *1* **Avidly**[89] 3-8-9 0 .... ShelleyBirkett(5) 8 72
(Julia Feilden) *hld up and last to 3f out: stl only 6th 2f out: shkn up and prog on outer jst over 1f out: r.o to take 2nd last 100yds: too much to do* **8/1**[3]
254- **3** *1 3/4* **Conserve (IRE)**[65] 7546 3-9-0 74 .... HayleyTurner 2 69
(Amy Weaver) *trckd ldng pair: rdn to chal and upsides over 1f out: edgd rt and nt qckn* **9/4**[1]
223- **4** *hd* **Wilhana (IRE)**[18] 8260 3-9-0 70 ....(b) AdamKirby 1 68
(Pam Sly) *roused to ld: rdn and tried to kick on 3f out: hdd and nt qckn jst over 1f out* **9/4**[1]
5 *2 3/4* **Alpine Mist** 3-9-0 0 .... FergusSweeney 6 63
(Pat Murphy) *hld up in last pair: in tch and gng wl enough over 2f out: shkn up and outpcd on inner over 1f out: nt disgracd* **25/1**
22- **6** *3 1/4* **Marble Statuette (USA)**[11] 8348 3-9-0 0 .... TonyHamilton 5 56
(Richard Fahey) *trckd ldr: rdn to chal over 1f out: wknd qckly sn after* **4/1**[2]
000/ **7** *39* **Veronica's Pursuit**[374] 8201 3-9-0 49 ....[1] LiamKeniry 3
(Peter Hedger) *in tch tl wknd rapidly jst over 3f out: t.o* **50/1**

2m 5.84s (-0.76) **Going Correction** -0.125s/f (Stan) **7** Ran SP% **118.5**
Speed ratings (Par 102): **98,97,95,95,93 90,59**
toteswingers 1&2 £5.00, 1&3 £2.10, 2&3 £3.80 CSF £36.83 TOTE £5.10: £2.10, £4.50; EX 48.20 Trifecta £97.00 Pool: £3530.87 - 27.29 winning units..
Owner Kilstone Limited **Bred** Swordlestown Stud **Trained** Whitcombe, Dorset

FOCUS
No more than a fair maiden. The gallop was an ordinary one and the winner came down the centre.

8445 LADBROKES H'CAP 1m (P)
1:30 (1:31) (Class 3) (0-95,92) 3-Y-O+ £**7,439** (£2,213; £1,106; £553) **Stalls** High

Form RPR
501- **1** **Alfred Hutchinson**[9] 8385 5-9-4 **92** .... RobertTart(3) 8 102
(Geoffrey Oldroyd) *trckd ldrs: clsd 2f out: rdn to ld jst over 1f out: sn in command: pushed out* **7/2**[2]
160- **2** *3/4* **Well Painted (IRE)**[21] 8219 4-8-6 **82** .... NathanAlison(5) 7 90
(William Haggas) *sltly awkward s: hld up in last pair: prog on inner wl over 1f out: wnt 2nd ins fnl f: styd on but nvr really able to threaten wnr* **12/1**
303- **3** *1 3/4* **Veeraya**[84] 7063 3-8-13 **85** ....(p) AdamBeschizza 4 88
(Julia Feilden) *in tch towards rr: rdn over 2f out: styd on fr over 1f out to take 3rd ins fnl f: nt pce to chal* **14/1**
014- **4** *nk* **Maverik**[18] 8263 5-9-3 **88** .... JimCrowley 6 92
(William Knight) *trckd ldr: rdn to chal on outer over 2f out: nt qckn wl over 1f out: one pce after* **6/1**[3]
031- **5** *3/4* **Rakaan (IRE)**[12] 8336 6-9-0 **85** .... FergusSweeney 3 87
(Jamie Osborne) *stdd s: hld up in last: stl there jst over 2f out: sme prog between rivals over 1f out: rdn and one pce ins fnl f: nvr involved* **12/1**
134- **6** *3/4* **Verse Of Love**[2] 8428 4-9-3 **88** .... AdamKirby 5 88
(David Evans) *led: urged along 3f out: hdd and fdd over 1f out* **8/1**
611- **7** *nk* **Wandsworth (IRE)**[24] 8178 3-8-3 **78** .... RossAtkinson(3) 2 76
(Roger Varian) *trckd ldng pair: rdn to chal over 2f out: led briefly over 1f out: wknd fnl f* **7/4**[1]
020- **8** *1 1/4* **Favourite Treat (USA)**[16] 8301 3-9-0 **89** .... MichaelJMMurphy(3) 9 85
(Mark Johnston) *t.k.h: trckd ldrs on outer: rdn and struggling 3f out: sn lost pl and btn* **10/1**

0/0- 9 nk **Snow King (USA)**[243] 1921 3-8-13 **90**.................................. EoinWalsh(5) 1 85
(Ted Powell) *chsd ldrs: pushed along over 3f out: rdn and no prog wl over 1f out: fdd* **33/1**

1m 35.6s (-2.60) **Going Correction** -0.125s/f (Stan)
WFA 3 from 4yo+ 1lb 9 Ran SP% **118.1**
Speed ratings (Par 107): **108,107,105,105,104 103,103,102,101**
toteswingers 1&2 £8.00, 1&3 £10.50, 2&3 £29.80 CSF £45.86 CT £533.14 TOTE £3.50: £1.20, £4.40, £5.80; EX 44.90 Trifecta £1176.00 Pool: £4546.66 - 2.89 winning units..
Owner R C Bond **Bred** R C Bond **Trained** Brawby, N Yorks

FOCUS
A very useful handicap but one that didn't take as much winning as seemed likely with the market leader underperforming. The gallop was an ordinary one and the winner came down the centre.

8446 LADBROKES MOBILE H'CAP 7f (P)
2:05 (2:07) (Class 6) (0-55,55) 3-Y-O+ **£2,045** (£603; £302) **Stalls** Low

Form RPR
650- 1 **Mick Dundee (IRE)**[52] 7808 3-9-4 **54**..............................(bt) AdamKirby 2 66
(John Ryan) *racd freely: mde all: kicked at least 3 l clr over 2f out: drvn over 1f out: kpt on: unchal* **9/4**[1]

062- 2 2 ¼ **Birdie Queen**[33] 8070 3-9-5 **55**.................................. GeorgeBaker 1 61
(Gary Moore) *chsd wnr: rdn and nt qckn wl over 2f out: kpt on after but nvr able to chal* **6/1**[2]

405- 3 1 ¼ **Alfresco**[26] 8152 9-9-4 **54**..(v) RobertHavlin 9 57
(Martin Bosley) *restless in stalls: dwlt: sn in 8th: prog over 2f out: rdn and styd on fr over 1f out to take 3rd nr fin* **14/1**

260- 4 nk **Hinton Admiral**[26] 8151 9-9-5 **55**.................................. RobertWinston 8 57
(Pat Eddery) *wl in tch: outpcd over 2f out: chsd ldng pair wl over 1f out: kpt on but lost 3rd nr fin* **8/1**

064- 5 3 **Torres Del Paine**[26] 8152 6-9-5 **55**.................................. DavidProbert 11 49
(Brett Johnson) *dwlt: hld up in last trio: no ch once wnr kicked on over 2f out: prog over 1f out: shkn up and kpt on fnl f: nvr involved* **7/1**[3]

332- 6 1 **Medam**[18] 8258 4-9-2 **52**.. DuranFentiman 13 43
(Shaun Harris) *chsd ldrs: outpcd over 2f out: no imp fr over 1f out* **8/1**

066- 7 ½ **My Learned Friend (IRE)**[26] 8157 9-8-12 **55**............(v) RobHornby(7) 4 45
(Andrew Balding) *chsd ldng pair tl steadily wknd fr wl over 1f out* **8/1**

000- 8 ½ **Basle**[17] 8278 6-9-5 **55**..(t) TomEaves 6 43
(Roy Brotherton) *towards rr: wl off the pce once wnr kicked on over 2f out: rdn and one pce fr over 1f out* **25/1**

000- 9 2 ½ **Compton Silver**[82] 7124 3-9-3 **53**..................................(p) ChrisCatlin 10 34
(Paul Fitzsimons) *trckd ldrs: rdn over 2f out: fnd nil and sn lost pl* **25/1**

/00- 10 7 **Grand Piano (IRE)**[215] 2773 6-8-12 **55**...............(v) JonathanWilletts(7) 7 18
(Andrew Balding) *hld up in last: in danger of being t.o over 2f out: nudged along and no prog after* **33/1**

000- 11 1 ½ **Moortahan**[11] 8341 3-9-3 **53**..(b1) SeanLevey 3 12
(Richard Hannon Snr) *chsd ldrs but nvr gng wl: wknd 2f out: eased fnl f* **8/1**

030- 12 1 ½ **Waterloo Dock**[193] 3499 8-9-1 **54**.................................. RobertTart(3) 14 8
(Mick Quinn) *nvr gng wl in last pair: wl bhd over 2f out* **33/1**

1m 23.84s (-0.96) **Going Correction** -0.125s/f (Stan) 12 Ran SP% **122.2**
Speed ratings (Par 101): **100,97,96,95,92 91,90,89,87,79 77,75**
toteswingers 1&2 £4.40, 1&3 £9.80, 2&3 £12.70 CSF £15.17 CT £159.16 TOTE £4.20: £1.60, £1.80, £5.70; EX 19.90 Trifecta £170.90 Pool: £3171.95 - 13.91 winning units..
Owner Power Bloodstock Ltd **Bred** Kildare Racing Syndicate **Trained** Newmarket, Suffolk

FOCUS
A moderate handicap in which a reasonable gallop picked up on the approach to the home turn. The winner came down the centre and very few figured in a race where the first four pulled clear.

8447 CORAL.CO.UK BEST ODDS GUARANTEED ON RACING H'CAP 1m 4f (P)
2:40 (2:40) (Class 5) (0-70,70) 3-Y-O+ **£2,726** (£805; £402) **Stalls** Low

Form RPR
630- 1 **Swift Blade (IRE)**[12] 8331 5-9-7 **67**.................................. RobertWinston 9 75
(Lady Herries) *stdd s: hld up in last trio and off the pce: prog fr over 3f out: rdn over 1f out: r.o to ld last 120yds: sn clr* **6/1**[2]

000- 2 1 ¼ **The Blue Dog (IRE)**[11] 8343 6-9-2 **62**.................................. WilliamCarson 7 68
(Phil McEntee) *t.k.h early: prom: pressed ldr 3f out: rdn to ld over 2f out and sn booted 2 l clr: hdd and outpcd last 120yds* **14/1**

P00- 3 hd **Living Leader**[35] 8037 4-9-7 **67**....................................(v) RobertHavlin 10 73
(Nick Littmoden) *trckd ldrs: effrt on inner over 2f out: rdn over 1f out: styd on same pce after* **10/1**

165- 4 ½ **Comedy House**[20] 6458 5-9-4 **64**..................................(v1) GeorgeBaker 11 69
(Michael Madgwick) *hld up in last pair and wl off the pce: prog on outer fr over 2f out: rdn over 1f out: styd on ins fnl f: nrst fin but no ch to threaten* **10/1**

460- 5 1 **King's Request (IRE)**[12] 8331 3-8-13 **64**.................................. LiamJones 2 67
(Laura Mongan) *trckd ldrs: rdn and cl up 2f out: one pce fr over 1f out* **7/1**[3]

001- 6 1 ½ **Dellbuoy**[24] 8182 4-9-7 **67**.. FergusSweeney 6 68
(Pat Phelan) *stdd s: hld up in last pair and wl off the pce: prog over 4f out: trckd ldrs wl over 1f out: pushed along and nt qckn after: one reminder ins fnl f* **7/4**[1]

656- 7 ¾ **If I Were A Boy (IRE)**[97] 5762 6-8-12 **63**............(b) JoshBaudains(5) 13 63
(Dominic Ffrench Davis) *hld up in 9th: prog 1/2-way: trckd ldrs 4f out: rdn over 2f out: fdd fnl f* **16/1**

000- 8 4 ½ **Thane Of Cawdor (IRE)**[61] 7628 4-8-10 **56** oh1.................. ShaneKelly 5 48
(Joseph Tuite) *hld up in 7th: prog to trck ldng pair 1/2-way: led 3f out to over 2f out: wknd qckly over 1f out* **14/1**

046/ 9 13 **Magicalmysterytour (IRE)**[543] 3794 10-8-12 **58**........ StevieDonohoe 3 30
(Willie Musson) *hld up towards rr: shkn up and wknd 3f out: t.o* **25/1**

005- 10 3 ¾ **Yes Chef**[24] 8182 6-8-10 **56** oh1..(v1) LiamKeniry 8 22
(Chris Gordon) *t.k.h: pressed ldr: led 5f out to 3f out: wknd rapidly: t.o* **10/1**

0/0- 11 8 **Ibiza Sunset (IRE)**[14] 8308 5-8-12 **58**........................(t) FrederikTylicki 12 11
(Brendan Powell) *chsd ldrs to 1/2-way: sn dropped to rr and btn: t.o* **25/1**

42/- 12 2 ¼ **Sugar Hiccup (IRE)**[39] 4731 5-9-10 **70**.................................. AmirQuinn 1 19
(Jim Best) *led at str pce to 5f out: wknd rapidly: t.o* **12/1**

2m 30.13s (-2.87) **Going Correction** -0.125s/f (Stan)
WFA 3 from 4yo+ 5lb 12 Ran SP% **125.0**
Speed ratings (Par 103): **104,103,103,102,102 101,100,97,88,86 81,79**
toteswingers 1&2 £14.40, 1&3 £14.80, 2&3 £52.20 CSF £92.19 CT £839.45 TOTE £6.70: £1.80, £4.40, £4.50; EX 75.90 Trifecta £887.30 Pool: £3844.97 - 3.24 winning units..
Owner Angmering Park **Bred** Messrs Mark Hanly & James Hanly **Trained** Patching, W Sussex

FOCUS
A modest handicap run at a reasonable gallop. The winner came down the centre.

8448 CORAL.CO.UK H'CAP (DIV I) 1m 2f (P)
3:15 (3:16) (Class 6) (0-55,58) 3-Y-O+ **£2,045** (£603; £302) **Stalls** Low

Form RPR
600- 1 **The Ginger Berry**[83] 7104 3-8-9 **49**.................................[1] RobertTart(3) 4 56
(Dr Jon Scargill) *prom: rdn over 2f out: wnt 2nd wl over 1f out: drvn into ld ins fnl f: edgd rt but kpt on wl* **16/1**

242- 2 ½ **Attain**[12] 8329 4-9-2 **55**..(p) ShelleyBirkett(5) 9 61
(Julia Feilden) *trckd ldng pair: led over 6f out: rdn 2f out: hdd ins fnl f: fought on wl but hld nr fin* **9/2**[2]

401- 3 nk **Archelao (IRE)**[8] 8390 5-9-10 **58** 6ex..................................(t) AmirQuinn 8 63
(Lee Carter) *trckd ldrs: gng strly over 2f out: brought to chal over 1f out: sltly intimidated fnl f and didn't find much* **4/1**[1]

133- 4 ½ **Petersboden**[44] 7922 4-9-3 **51**.................................. LiamKeniry 7 55
(Michael Blanshard) *hld up in midfield: prog 2f out: chsd ldrs over 1f out: kpt on u.p: nvr quite able to chal* **12/1**

/00- 5 2 ¼ **Lisahane Bog**[235] 1054 6-9-4 **52**..(v) AdamKirby 6 52
(Peter Hedger) *hld up in midfield: sme prog to chse ldrs 2f out: rdn and nt qckn over 1f out* **8/1**

323- 6 1 ¼ **Quadriga (IRE)**[10] 8361 3-9-4 **55**.................................. JimmyQuinn 3 52
(Robert Eddery) *trckd ldr 3f: wnt 2nd again 4f out to wl over 1f out: wknd* **5/1**[3]

556- 7 nk **The Wonga Coup (IRE)**[33] 8072 6-9-7 **55**.................. FergusSweeney 10 52
(Pat Phelan) *t.k.h early: hld up in rr: gng wl enough but only 9th over 2f out: shkn up over 1f out: one pce after* **8/1**

660- 8 4 ½ **Hawaiian Freeze**[69] 7440 4-8-12 **46** oh1.................................. ShaneKelly 1 34
(John Stimpson) *restrained into last pair: shkn up 2f out: no ch after: nvr in it* **50/1**

050- 9 ½ **Dolly Colman (IRE)**[12] 8335 5-8-9 **46** oh1...............(p) RossAtkinson(3) 5 33
(Zoe Davison) *restrained into last pair: stl there and rdn 2f out: nvr in it* **25/1**

060- 10 2 ½ **Rock Diamond (IRE)**[10] 8371 3-8-9 **46** oh1..............[1] StevieDonohoe 12 28
(Brendan Powell) *nvr bttr than midfield: rdn and struggling 3f out: sn btn* **25/1**

00- 11 2 ¼ **Brown Pete (IRE)**[44] 7930 5-9-7 **55**..........................(b) WilliamCarson 11 32
(Ann Stokell) *dwlt: rchd midfield after 4f: rdn over 3f out: wknd over 2f out* **5/1**[3]

550- 12 13 **Buaiteoir (FR)**[44] 7931 7-9-2 **53**.................................. MatthewCosham(3) 2
(Nikki Evans) *rdn to ld: hdd over 6f out: wknd qckly over 3f out: t.o* **20/1**

2m 4.74s (-1.86) **Going Correction** -0.125s/f (Stan)
WFA 3 from 4yo+ 3lb 12 Ran SP% **121.7**
Speed ratings (Par 101): **102,101,101,100,99 98,97,94,93,91 90,79**
toteswingers 1&2 £16.80, 1&3 £16.30, 2&3 £3.90 CSF £85.58 CT £356.46 TOTE £19.20: £5.20, £1.80, £1.40; EX 135.70 Trifecta £791.80 Pool: £4350.90 - 4.12 winning units..
Owner Strawberry Fields Stud & Stuart Howard **Bred** Strawberry Fields Stud **Trained** Newmarket, Suffolk

FOCUS
A moderate handicap in which the gallop was an ordinary one. The winner came down the centre.

8449 CORAL.CO.UK H'CAP (DIV II) 1m 2f (P)
3:45 (3:46) (Class 6) (0-55,55) 3-Y-O+ **£2,045** (£603; £302) **Stalls** Low

Form RPR
002- 1 **Fonterutoli (IRE)**[40] 7981 6-9-7 **55**..............................(e) RobertWinston 9 65
(Roger Ingram) *hld up in last: sweeping move on wd outside to go 2nd over 2f out: led over 1f out and cajoled along: rdn out nr fin* **4/1**[2]

000- 2 1 ½ **Salient**[74] 7321 9-9-1 **49**.. KierenFox 6 55
(Michael Attwater) *trckd ldrs: prog to ld wl over 2f out: sn rdn: hdd over 1f out: one pce* **20/1**

030- 3 ¾ **Kindlelight Storm (USA)**[11] 8341 3-9-3 **54**...............(b1) RobertHavlin 3 59
(Nick Littmoden) *hld up in midfield: wl in tch whn trapped bhd wkng rivals over 2f out: prog over 1f out: styd on to take 3rd last strides* **6/1**

440- 4 hd **Royal Etiquette (IRE)**[61] 7628 6-9-7 **55**..........................(vt) AdamKirby 4 59
(Lawney Hill) *hld up towards rr: prog to trck ldrs whn nt clr run over 2f out: hdwy to chse ldng pair 1f out: kpt on but lost 3rd last strides* **9/4**[1]

005- 5 3 ½ **Interakt**[28] 8121 6-9-5 **53**.. JimCrowley 11 50
(Joseph Tuite) *trckd ldrs: rdn to go 3rd 2f out but sn outpcd: wknd 1f out* **12/1**

0/6- 6 nk **Reality Show (IRE)**[10] 8373 6-9-7 **55**.................................. DuranFentiman 8 52
(Shaun Harris) *in tch: bustled along 4f out: outpcd over 2f out: one pce after* **16/1**

254- 7 4 **Bennelong**[8] 8390 7-9-1 **52**..(b) MarkCoumbe(3) 2 41+
(Lee Carter) *hld up in last pair: gng wl enough whn trapped on inner over 2f out: no ch after* **9/2**[3]

000- 8 1 ¾ **Red Willow**[37] 8031 7-8-12 **46**.. JimmyQuinn 1 31
(John E Long) *in tch: nt clr run over 2f out: n.d after* **25/1**

/06- 9 7 **Paradise Sea (USA)**[16] 8298 4-8-12 **46** oh1.................(tp) ShaneKelly 5 17
(Jo Hughes) *w ldr to wl over 2f out: wknd sn after: eased fnl f* **16/1**

100- 10 ¾ **Corn Maiden**[17] 8270 4-9-0 **53**.................................. ShelleyBirkett(5) 7 23
(Lydia Pearce) *prom: rdn over 4f out: wknd over 2f out* **12/1**

000- 11 2 **Byrd In Hand (IRE)**[8] 8390 6-8-12 **46** oh1.......................... SeanLevey 10 12
(John Bridger) *mde most to wl over 2f out: wknd qckly 2f out* **33/1**

2m 4.7s (-1.90) **Going Correction** -0.125s/f (Stan)
WFA 3 from 4yo+ 3lb 11 Ran SP% **121.9**
Speed ratings (Par 101): **102,100,100,100,97 97,93,92,86,86 84**
toteswingers 1&2 £19.80, 1&3 £5.90, 2&3 £24.80 CSF £86.49 CT £488.67 TOTE £3.40: £1.20, £3.80, £1.50; EX 104.20 Trifecta £442.10 Pool: £3863.95 - 6.55 winning units..
Owner Mrs Cathy Hallam & Martyn Cruse **Bred** Massimo Parri **Trained** Epsom, Surrey

FOCUS
Not many in form types in the second division of a moderate handicap. The gallop was on the steady side and the winner came down the centre in the straight.

T/Plt: £3774.70. Pool: £77,305.71 - 14.95 winning units. T/Qpdt: £782.90. Pool: £8887.47 - 8.4 winning units. JN

8442 LINGFIELD (L-H)

Tuesday, December 31

OFFICIAL GOING: Standard

Wind: strong, behind Weather: rain, breezy

8450 LADBROKES APPRENTICE (S) STKS 1m (P)

12:00 (12:00) (Class 6) 3-Y-0+ £2,045 (£603; £302) Stalls High

Form RPR

443- 1 **Ocean Applause**[12] 8339 3-9-3 70....(tp) JoeDoyle(3) 2 74
(John Ryan) *chsd ldrs: clsd to trck ldrs and nt clr run over 1f out: gap opened ins fnl f: rdn and qcknd to ld wl ins fnl f: r.o wl* 7/2[2]

403- 2 ½ **Prime Exhibit**[25] 8187 8-9-7 64....(t) LouisSteward 4 74
(Daniel Mark Loughnane) *in tch: hdwy to chse ldrs and rdn wl over 1f out: ev ch ent fnl f: drvn to ld ins fnl f: hdd wl ins fnl f: kpt on* 5/1

124- 3 2 **Hillbilly Boy (IRE)**[13] 918 3-9-6 70....(p) RyanWhile 6 68
(Bill Turner) *chsd ldr tl jnd ldr ent fnl 2f: rdn to ld over 1f out: hdd ins fnl f: no ex and wknd towards fin* 20/1

036- 4 1 **Abigails Angel**[13] 8335 6-8-5 62.... DavidParkes(5) 7 56
(Brett Johnson) *s.i.s: racd off the pce in last trio: rdn and hdwy over 2f out: kpt on u.p ins fnl f: nt rch ldrs* 6/1

041- 5 nse **Copperwood**[13] 8335 8-9-0 68.... PaigeBolton(7) 8 67
(Lee Carter) *stdd and dropped in bhd after s: hld up off the pce in last trio: pushed along and hdwy on inner over 1f out: swtchd rt ins fnl f: styd on wl: nt rch ldrs* 8/1

222- 6 1¾ **Honey Of A Kitten (USA)**[13] 8335 5-9-7 70....(v) EoinWalsh 5 63
(David Evans) *restless in stalls: led: jnd and rdn 2f out: hdd over 1f out: wknd ins fnl f* 11/4[1]

310- 7 6 **Mahadee (IRE)**[22] 8219 8-9-7 76....(b) MatthewHopkins 3 49
(Ed de Giles) *awkward leaving stalls and s.i.s: racd off the pce in last trio: rdn and no hdwy wl over 1f out* 9/2[3]

056- 8 2½ **Fairy Mist (IRE)**[20] 8244 6-9-7 45.... PatMillman 1 43
(John Bridger) *t.k.h: chsd ldrs: lost pl over 3f out: bhd and rdn wl over 1f out: sn wknd* 100/1

1m 37.89s (-0.31) **Going Correction** -0.10s/f (Stan)
WFA 3 from 5yo+ 1lb 8 Ran SP% **114.9**
Speed ratings (Par 101): **97,96,94,93,93 91,85,83**
toteswingers 1&2 £6.30, 1&3 £7.00, 2&3 £8.00 CSF £21.49 TOTE £6.60: £1.70, £1.90, £3.10; EX 29.30 Trifecta £338.00.The winner was bought in for 8,400gns.
Owner W McLuskey **Bred** R G Levin **Trained** Newmarket, Suffolk
■ Stewards' Enquiry : Matthew Hopkins five-day ban; used whip when out of contention (14th-18th Jan).
Joe Doyle one-day ban; careless riding (14th Jan).

FOCUS
Fair efforts from the leading pair in this seller.

8451 32RED.COM MEDIAN AUCTION MAIDEN STKS 7f (P)

12:30 (12:30) (Class 6) 2-Y-0 £2,045 (£603; £302) Stalls Low

Form RPR

2- 1 **Perfect Persuasion**[33] 8083 2-9-0 0.... JimCrowley 2 75+
(William Haggas) *chsd ldrs: chsd clr ldr 2f out: chal over 1f out: led 1f out and stormed clr: r.o wl: readily* 3/1[2]

2- 2 5 **Outbacker (IRE)**[13] 8332 2-9-0 0.... AdamKirby 3 61
(Mark Johnston) *led: rdn and wnt 2 l clr 2f out: hrd pressed over 1f out: hdd 1f out and sn btn: hung bdly rt ins fnl f* 8/11[1]

05- 3 hd **What A Dandy (IRE)**[13] 8333 2-9-5 0.... StephenCraine 10 65
(Jim Boyle) *hld up in midfield: swtchd lft and hdwy over 1f out: styd on wl ins fnl f: no ch w wnr* 66/1

04- 4 nk **Sweetness Lady**[13] 8326 2-9-0 0.... SeanLevey 6 60
(Olly Stevens) *in tch in midfield: effrt over 2f out: chsd clr ldng pair 1f out: kpt on ins fnl f: no ch w wnr* 16/1

60- 5 hd **Arabian Music (IRE)**[13] 8332 2-9-0 0.... LiamKeniry 9 59+
(David Simcock) *hld up in midfield: pushed along and effrt 2f out: hdwy 1f out: styd on wl ins fnl f: nvr trbld ldrs* 66/1

0- 6 2¾ **Harry's Summer (USA)**[22] 8213 2-8-12 0.... JordanVaughan(7) 4 57
(Nick Littmoden) *chsd ldrs: rdn ent fnl 2f: outpcd and btn over 1f out: wl hld but kpt on fnl f* 33/1

7 ¾ **Sand Stormer (IRE)** 2-9-5 0.... MartinDwyer 1 55+
(William Muir) *s.i.s: wl off the pce in last pair and pushed along: clsd over 2f out: styd on steadily ins fnl f: n.d* 10/1

4- 8 shd **Ventura Reef (IRE)**[18] 8266 2-9-5 0.... TonyHamilton 7 54
(Richard Fahey) *hld up in midfield: rdn and outpcd jst over 2f out: wl hld but plugged on fnl f* 25/1

4- 9 1 **Why Not Now**[12] 8342 2-9-0 0.... MartinLane 5 47
(Roger Charlton) *w ldr tl rdn and unable qck 2f out: 3rd and btn over 1f out: wknd ins fnl f* 8/1[3]

00- 10 1 **Risk 'N' Reward (IRE)**[13] 8326 2-9-0 0.... DavidKenny(5) 13 49
(Amy Weaver) *hld up off the pce towards rr: rdn and effrt 2f out: no imp: n.d* 100/1

6- 11 ½ **Honiton Lace**[28] 8138 2-9-0 0.... RichardKingscote 8 43
(J W Hills) *chsd ldrs: rdn over 2f out: struggling 2f out: lost pl and towards rr whn sltly hmpd jst over 1f out: wknd ins fnl f* 50/1

12 4 **Haaffa Sovereign** 2-9-5 0.... ShaneKelly 11 37
(George Margarson) *s.i.s and swtchd lft after s: a bhd* 66/1

13 8 **Marti's Boy** 2-9-5 0.... LiamJones 12 15
(J S Moore) *s.i.s: a in rr* 100/1

1m 24.54s (-0.26) **Going Correction** -0.10s/f (Stan) 13 Ran SP% **124.2**
Speed ratings (Par 94): **97,91,91,90,90 87,86,86,85,84 83,78,69**
toteswingers 1&2 £1.10, 1&3 £22.60, 2&3 £20.00 CSF £5.55 TOTE £4.10: £1.30, £1.10, £8.10; EX 6.50 Trifecta £203.20.
Owner Clipper Logistics **Bred** The National Stud **Trained** Newmarket, Suffolk

FOCUS
Possibly not the strongest maiden and, while the winner was impressive, the runner-up, who set a good pace, looks to have run below form.

8452 32RED NURSERY H'CAP 7f (P)

1:00 (1:01) (Class 5) (0-75,75) 2-Y-0 £2,726 (£805; £402) Stalls Low

Form RPR

635- 1 **Mersad (IRE)**[27] 8147 2-8-12 66....(p) JimCrowley 7 71+
(James Tate) *hld up in midfield: hdwy u.p over 1f out: chsd ldrs 1f out: str run to ld fnl 50yds: r.o wl u.p* 9/2[3]

454- 2 ½ **Sebs Sensei (IRE)**[10] 8383 2-9-2 70.... SeanLevey 8 74
(Richard Hannon Snr) *chsd ldrs: wnt 2nd over 3f out: drvn to ld over 1f out: r.o wl u.p tl hdd fnl 50yds: kpt on* 14/1

000- 3 2¼ **Basil Berry**[19] 8261 2-8-11 65.... HayleyTurner 11 63
(Chris Dwyer) *stdd s: t.k.h: hld up in tch in last trio: hdwy u.p over 1f out: styd on wl to go 3rd last strides* 14/1

142- 4 hd **Applejack Lad**[3] 8426 2-9-7 75....(t) AdamKirby 9 72
(John Ryan) *chsd ldr tl led over 5f out: rdn and hrd pressed 2f out: hdd over 1f out: edgd rt and wknd towards fin* 2/1[1]

000- 5 nk **Illegal Action (USA)**[34] 8061 2-8-3 57....(t) WilliamCarson 4 54
(Olly Stevens) *t.k.h: hld up wl in tch in midfield: rdn and effrt 2f out: styd on ins fnl f: pressing for 3rd whn squeezed for room and hmpd nr fin* 12/1

004- 6 1¼ **Amontillado (IRE)**[33] 8084 2-8-9 63.... KieranO'Neill 3 56
(Richard Hannon Snr) *led tl over 5f out: chsd ldr tl over 3f out: sn u.p: outpcd over 1f out: styd on same pce after* 25/1

360- 7 hd **M'Lady Ermyn**[19] 8262 2-8-0 54.... FrankieMcDonald 1 47
(Pat Phelan) *in tch in midfield: rdn and effrt ent fnl 2f: styd on same pce and no imp fr over 1f out* 50/1

510- 8 hd **Sweet Alibi (IRE)**[129] 5773 2-8-10 69.... JoeyHaynes(5) 2 61
(J S Moore) *in tch in midfield: nt clr run and shuffled bk towards rr over 2f out: swtchd rt and rallied 1f out: edgd rt but styd on fnl f: no threat to ldrs* 33/1

61- 9 ½ **Alderley**[74] 7348 2-8-9 70.... LouisSteward(7) 6 61
(Martyn Meade) *in tch in last trio: pushed along and struggling 3f out: swtchd to outer and effrt bnd wl over 1f out: kpt on but no threat to ldrs* 12/1

236- 10 1½ **Capers Royal Star (FR)**[3] 8426 2-9-2 70....(p) FergusSweeney 5 57
(Alastair Lidderdale) *s.i.s: in tch in rr: sme hdwy but no threat to ldrs 1f out: n.m.r and no hdwy ins fnl f* 10/1

022- 11 shd **Irish Tears**[9] 8389 2-9-5 73....(t) RobertHavlin 10 59
(John Gosden) *steadid s: t.k.h: chsd ldrs: rdn and unable qck over 2f out: wknd and bhd jst ins fnl f* 7/2[2]

1m 24.66s (-0.14) **Going Correction** -0.10s/f (Stan) 11 Ran SP% **120.3**
Speed ratings (Par 96): **96,95,92,92,92 90,90,90,89,88 88**
toteswingers 1&2 £12.10, 1&3 £14.50, 2&3 £29.00 CSF £66.11 CT £830.40 TOTE £5.50: £1.90, £2.90, £3.90; EX 63.70 Trifecta £1186.40.
Owner Sultan Ali **Bred** Lynn Lodge Stud **Trained** Newmarket, Suffolk

FOCUS
A fair nursery. The pace steadied after 2f or so and not really picking up again until approaching the straight. The winner, who had excuses last time, has been rated as running a small pb here.

8453 DOWNLOAD THE LADBROKES APP H'CAP (DIV I) 1m (P)

1:30 (1:31) (Class 5) (0-75,75) 3-Y-0+ £2,726 (£805; £402) Stalls High

Form RPR

546- 1 **The Tichborne (IRE)**[25] 8181 5-9-7 75....(v) RobertWinston 2 85
(Roger Teal) *stdd s: hld up in tch in last trio: hdwy and swtchd rt wl over 1f out: drvn to chal jst ins fnl f: led fnl 100yds: r.o wl u.p* 10/1

342- 2 ¾ **Aqua Ardens (GER)**[15] 8314 5-9-5 73.... GeorgeBaker 7 81
(George Baker) *wl in tch in midfield: effrt to chal over 1f out: led 1f out: hdd and one pce fnl 100yds* 4/1[2]

625- 3 1 **Wilfred Pickles (IRE)**[50] 7836 7-9-2 70....(p) AdamKirby 9 76
(Jo Crowley) *stdd s: hld up in tch in last trio: hdwy and nt clr run over 1f out: swtchd rt 1f out: r.o wl ins fnl f* 8/1

010- 4 ½ **Bloodsweatandtears**[13] 8323 5-8-12 66.... JimCrowley 6 71
(William Knight) *stdd s: hld up in tch in last trio: rdn and effrt on outer over 1f out: hdwy jst ins fnl f: styd on* 12/1

031- 5 2¾ **Swehan (IRE)**[41] 7983 3-9-6 75.... TomEaves 11 73
(Kevin Ryan) *w ldr: rdn and ev ch 2f out: drvn to ld and edgd rt ent fnl f: sn hdd: wknd fnl 100yds* 16/1

303- 6 1 **It's My Time**[26] 8162 4-9-0 68.... TonyHamilton 4 64
(Richard Fahey) *chsd ldrs: rdn and unable qck whn edgd out rt wl over 1f out: wknd fnl 150yds* 14/1

203- 7 2 **Sheikh The Reins (IRE)**[56] 7743 4-9-3 71....(v) HayleyTurner 8 63
(John Best) *tk keen hodl early: chsd ldrs tl stdd into midfield after 1f: rdn and no hdwy wl over 1f out: wknd ins fnl f* 25/1

323- 8 ¾ **Leitrim Pass (USA)**[146] 5146 3-9-6 75.... ShaneKelly 10 64
(William Haggas) *chsd ldrs on outer: rdn and effrt over 2f out: struggling 2f out and btn over 1f out: wknd fnl f* 2/1[1]

500- 9 2¾ **Gabrial's Wawa**[25] 8178 3-9-1 70.... RobertHavlin 3 53
(Roger Ingram) *led: rdn ent fnl 2f: hdd ent fnl f: sn btn and fdd fnl f* 20/1

010- 10 1¼ **Menelik (IRE)**[17] 8304 4-9-0 68....(p) RichardKingscote 5 49
(Tom Dascombe) *in tch in midfield: rdn and unable qck wl over 1f out: sn btn: fdd fnl f* 6/1[3]

360- 11 4½ **Mafi (IRE)**[190] 3642 5-8-10 64....(t) WilliamCarson 1 34
(Mark Hoad) *in tch in midfield: rdn and struggling 2f out: btn over 1f out: fdd fnl f* 33/1

1m 36.29s (-1.91) **Going Correction** -0.10s/f (Stan)
WFA 3 from 4yo+ 1lb 11 Ran SP% **119.6**
Speed ratings (Par 103): **105,104,103,102,100 99,97,96,93,92 87**
toteswingers 1&2 £8.70, 1&3 £16.40, 2&3 £7.40 CSF £49.57 CT £352.27 TOTE £12.40: £2.40, £2.30, £3.20; EX 63.40 Trifecta £353.40.
Owner Chris Simpson & Mick Waghorn **Bred** Ms Alyson Flower And Chris Simpson **Trained** Ashtead, Surrey

FOCUS
A fair handicap which was run at a sound pace.

8454 DOWNLOAD THE LADBROKES APP H'CAP (DIV II) 1m (P)

2:00 (2:00) (Class 5) (0-75,75) 3-Y-0+ £2,726 (£805; £402) Stalls High

Form RPR

1- 1 **Fleckerl (IRE)**[15] 8313 3-9-4 73.... MartinDwyer 4 83+
(William Muir) *t.k.h: hld up in tch towards rr: hdwy and edgd rt bnd 2f out: chsd ldrs u.p 1f out: drvn and chal ins fnl f: styd on to ld wl ins fnl f: kpt on* 7/2[1]

406- 2 nk **Munsarim (IRE)**[22] 8226 6-9-2 70....(b) AmirQuinn 11 80
(Lee Carter) *stdd and dropped in bhd after s: hld up in rr: hdwy on outer bnd wl over 1f out: str run u.p ins fnl f: wnt 2nd towards fin: nt quite rch wnr* 20/1

242- 3 ¾ **Duke Of Grazeon (IRE)**[12] 8345 3-9-0 69.... FrederikTylicki 9 77
(Mrs Ilka Gansera-Leveque) *in tch in midfield: rdn 3f out: hdwy u.p to join ldr jst over 2f out: sustained duel w rival tl led ins fnl f: hdd wl ins fnl f: no ex and outpcd towards fin* 9/2[2]

402- 4 ¾ **Just One Kiss**[25] 8178 3-9-6 75.... JimCrowley 3 81
(Lady Cecil) *in tch in midfield: hdwy to ld ent fnl 2f: drvn and sustained duel w rival fr over 1f out: hdd ins fnl f: no ex and wknd towards fin* 7/2[1]

550- 5 1¾ **Mister Musicmaster**[40] 7989 4-9-7 75.... WilliamCarson 2 78
(Ron Hodges) *chsd ldrs: rdn whn bdly hmpd and lost pl bnd ent fnl 2f: rallied and 5th 1f out: styd on but no threat to ldrs* 8/1[3]

300- **6** *4* **Titan Triumph**[160] 4637 9-8-9 **63**....(t) RobertHavlin 6 57
(Michael Attwater) *broke wl: sn stdd to chse ldr: 3rd and rdn 2f out: btn ent fnl f: fdd fnl 150yds* **33/1**
036- **7** *nk* **Chiswick Bey (IRE)**[32] 8095 5-8-13 **67**.... TonyHamilton 10 60
(Richard Fahey) *hld up in tch in rr: rdn and no hdwy wl over 1f out: wl hld fnl f* **16/1**
360- **8** *½* **Poor Duke (IRE)**[62] 7629 3-8-13 **68**.... FergusSweeney 5 59
(Jamie Osborne) *in tch towards rr: swtchd rt and hdwy u.p wl over 3f out: struggling 2f out: wknd over 1f out* **14/1**
045- **9** *1 ½* **Queen Aggie (IRE)**[22] 8227 3-9-2 **71**.... AdamKirby 1 58
(David Evans) *in tch in midfield: hmpd and lost pl bnd ent fnl 2f: nt rcvr and n.d after* **9/2**[2]
556- **10** *4 ½* **Mcmonagle (USA)**[22] 8227 5-9-0 **68**....(vt) DaleSwift 7 46
(Alan Brown) *sn led: drvn and hdd jst over 2f out: wknd over 1f out: fdd fnl f* **20/1**

1m 36.19s (-2.01) **Going Correction** -0.10s/f (Stan) **10** Ran SP% **116.9**
WFA 3 from 4yo+ 1lb
Speed ratings (Par 103): **106,105,104,104,102 98,98,97,96,91**
toteswingers 1&2 £14.90, 1&3 £3.30, 2&3 £19.90 CSF £78.36 CT £329.30 TOTE £4.30: £1.80, £4.60, £1.70; EX 99.40 Trifecta £899.10.
Owner F Hope **Bred** Yeguada De Milagro Sa **Trained** Lambourn, Berks
■ Stewards' Enquiry : Martin Dwyer two-day ban; careless riding (14th-15th Jan).

FOCUS
As in the first division, the pace looked sound enough and the form should hold up.

8455 LADBROKES H'CAP 7f (P)
2:30 (2:31) (Class 4) (0-85,84) 3-Y-O+ **£4,690** (£1,395; £697; £348) **Stalls** Low

Form RPR
320/ **1** **Oblitereight (IRE)**[452] 6830 4-9-6 **83**.... GeorgeBaker 12 90
(William Knight) *hld up in tch towards rr: rdn and gd hdwy towards inner over 1f out: led wl ins fnl f: kpt on u.p* **5/1**[2]
505- **2** *nk* **Kakatosi**[25] 8181 6-9-5 **82**.... ShaneKelly 8 88
(Mike Murphy) *hld up in tch in rr: stl last over 1f out: swtchd lft and gd hdwy ins fnl f: ev ch cl home: r.o* **7/1**[3]
106- **3** *nk* **Lions Arch (IRE)**[22] 8219 3-9-7 **84**.... SeanLevey 1 89
(Richard Hannon Snr) *dwlt and pushed along leaving stalls: rcvrd to chse ldrs 4f out: drvn and ev ch 1f out: kpt on but unable qck cl home* **8/1**
136- **4** *shd* **Emkanaat**[9] 8391 5-8-11 **79**....(b[1]) DavidKenny[(5)] 6 84
(Amy Weaver) *hld up in tch in midfield: nt clr run wl over 1f out: swtchd lft and hdwy 1f out: r.o wl ins fnl f* **12/1**
460- **5** *½* **Glanely (IRE)**[66] 7531 3-8-7 **77**.... LouisSteward[(7)] 3 81
(Martyn Meade) *in tch in midfield: gd hdwy on inner over 1f out: ev ch 1f out: no ex fnl 100yds* **16/1**
005- **6** *nk* **Intomist (IRE)**[3] 8430 4-8-9 **72**....(p) WilliamCarson 4 75
(Jim Boyle) *in tch in midfield: swtchd rt and effrt u.p over 1f out: kpt on same pce ins fnl f* **12/1**
620- **7** *nk* **Tagula Night (IRE)**[33] 8088 7-9-0 **77**....(tp) RobertWinston 2 79
(Dean Ivory) *led: rdn ent fnl 2f: hdd ins fnl f: no ex and kpt on same pce fnl 100yds* **33/1**
526- **8** *¾* **Jubilee Brig**[29] 8127 3-9-0 **77**....(v) FergusSweeney 5 77
(Gary Moore) *wl in tch in midfield: rdn and effrt over 1f out: styd on same pce ins fnl f* **10/1**
340- **9** *½* **Secret Beau**[12] 8350 3-9-3 **80**....(t) AdamKirby 9 79
(David Evans) *chsd ldrs: rdn and effrt 2f out: no ex u.p 1f out: wknd ins fnl f* **8/1**
050- **10** *½* **Nassau Storm**[9] 8391 4-9-6 **83**....(t) JimCrowley 7 80
(William Knight) *hld up in tch in last trio: rdn and effrt over 1f out: styd on same pce ins fnl f* **11/4**[1]
210- **11** *1 ¼* **Capaill Liath (IRE)**[9] 8391 5-9-6 **83**....(b) TomEaves 11 77
(Kevin Ryan) *t.k.h: chsd ldr tl jst over 1f out: wknd ins fnl f* **25/1**
004- **12** *2 ½* **Commanche**[17] 8305 4-8-12 **75**.... HayleyTurner 10 62
(Chris Dwyer) *t.k.h early: chsd ldrs: stdd into midfield 4f out: rdn and struggling 2f out: wknd 1f out* **25/1**

1m 23.56s (-1.24) **Going Correction** -0.10s/f (Stan) **12** Ran SP% **119.0**
Speed ratings (Par 105): **103,102,102,102,101 101,100,100,99,98 97,94**
CSF £39.28 CT £284.74 TOTE £5.40: £1.90, £2.20, £2.90; EX 38.50 Trifecta £282.70.
Owner The Oil Men Partnership **Bred** Lodge Park Stud **Trained** Patching, W Sussex
■ Stewards' Enquiry : Sean Levey two-day ban; used whip above permitted (14th-15th Jan).

FOCUS
A fairly useful contest. The gallop didn't look that strong initially, but that didn't convey any advantage on those racing handily, the leading pair both coming from the rear.

8456 COMPARE BOOKMAKERS AT BOOKMAKERS.CO.UK H'CAP 6f (P)
3:00 (3:01) (Class 6) (0-65,65) 3-Y-O+ **£2,045** (£603; £302) **Stalls** Low

Form RPR
554- **1** **Perfect Venture**[13] 8330 3-9-6 **64**.... AdamKirby 12 74
(Clive Cox) *taken down early: broke fast to ld and crossed to inner: rdn 2f out: edgd rt u.p and clr w rival over 1f out: hdd ins fnl f: edgd lft u.p but rallied gamely to ld again cl home* **8/1**
423- **2** *hd* **Random Success (IRE)**[39] 8003 3-9-0 **58**.... MartinLane 3 67
(Roger Charlton) *chsd ldrs: rdn to chse wnr wl over 1f out: ev ch and clr w wnr over 1f out: led ins fnl f: kpt on tl hdd and no ex cl home* **7/1**
600- **3** *1 ½* **Avonmore Star**[21] 8230 5-9-4 **62**....(e) ShaneKelly 5 67
(Mike Murphy) *in tch: effrt 2f out: chsd ldrs and swtchd lft ins fnl f: kpt on u.p fnl 100yds* **16/1**
052- **4** *½* **Street Power (USA)**[22] 8220 8-9-7 **65**.... LiamKeniry 9 68
(Jeremy Gask) *hld up in last trio: rdn and hdwy ent fnl f: styd on wl fnl 100yds: nt rch ldrs* **3/1**[1]
355- **5** *shd* **Rise To Glory (IRE)**[22] 8217 5-9-6 **64**.... DuranFentiman 2 67
(Shaun Harris) *chsd wnr tl wl over 1f out: kpt on same pce u.p fr over 1f out* **16/1**
614- **6** *½* **Perfect Pastime**[27] 8151 5-8-8 **59**....(b) DanielCremin[(7)] 4 61
(Jim Boyle) *in tch in midfield: rdn and unable qck wl over 1f out: edgd rt 1f out: kpt on same pce ins fnl f* **8/1**
010- **7** *¾* **Penbryn (USA)**[17] 8306 6-8-8 **59**.... JordanVaughan[(7)] 11 58
(Nick Littmoden) *hld up in tch on outer: rdn and effrt over 1f out: drvn and kpt on same pce ins fnl f* **25/1**
053- **8** *nse* **Saskia's Dream**[13] 8330 5-9-5 **63**....(v) FrederikTylicki 10 62
(Jane Chapple-Hyam) *in tch in midfield: rdn and outpcd wl over 1f out: kpt on again ins fnl f: no threat to ldrs* **14/1**
660- **9** *nse* **West Leake (IRE)**[27] 8151 7-9-0 **58**....(p) JimmyQuinn 8 57
(Paul Burgoyne) *stdd s: hld up in tch in rr: clsd ent fnl f: n.m.r and swtchd lft ins fnl f: sme hdwy but n.d: eased towards fin* **20/1**
020- **10** *½* **Indian Affair**[29] 8128 3-9-7 **65**.... RichardKingscote 6 63
(Milton Bradley) *chsd ldrs: rdn and unable qck ent fnl 2f: lost pl and btn ent fnl f: wknd fnl 100yds* **6/1**[3]
050- **11** *2* **Pastoral Dancer**[34] 8065 4-8-7 **51** oh6.... ChrisCatlin 1 43
(Richard Rowe) *hld up in tch in last trio: rdn and effrt on inner over 1f out: kpt on but no real imp* **100/1**
065- **12** *1* **Nubar Boy**[27] 8157 6-9-1 **59**....(v) StevieDonohoe 7 48
(Ian Williams) *hld up in tch towards rr: rdn and effrt over 1f out: no imp whn n.m.r ent fnl f: n.d* **5/1**[2]

1m 11.04s (-0.86) **Going Correction** -0.10s/f (Stan) **12** Ran SP% **118.7**
Speed ratings (Par 101): **101,100,98,98,97 97,96,96,96,95 92,91**
CSF £62.01 CT £897.56 TOTE £7.30: £2.30, £2.60, £4.50; EX 37.80 Trifecta £576.50.
Owner Mildmay Racing **Bred** Mildmay Bloodstock Ltd **Trained** Lambourn, Berks

FOCUS
A sprint that few ever got into, the pace not being strong for a race of this nature.

8457 BEST ODDS AT BOOKMAKERS.CO.UK H'CAP 5f (P)
3:30 (3:31) (Class 6) (0-65,65) 3-Y-O+ **£2,045** (£603; £302) **Stalls** High

Form RPR
420- **1** **Pharoh Jake**[27] 8152 5-8-13 **57**.... KieranO'Neill 1 63
(John Bridger) *chsd ldrs: drvn and effrt on inner over 1f out: ev ch ins fnl f: r.o u.p to ld fnl 50yds: drvn out* **8/1**
322- **2** *hd* **Mossgo (IRE)**[92] 6901 3-9-4 **62**....(t) GeorgeBaker 4 67
(John Best) *led: rdn over 1f out: drvn 1f out: hdd fnl 50yds: kpt on wl but hld after* **5/1**[2]
365- **3** *nse* **Roy's Legacy**[4] 8411 4-9-2 **60**....(t) DuranFentiman 3 65
(Shaun Harris) *chsd ldr: rdn 2f out: ev ch ins fnl f: kpt on wl towards fin* **6/1**[3]
550- **4** *1* **Imjin River (IRE)**[9] 8393 6-8-3 **54** oh3 ow3....(t) LouisSteward[(7)] 7 56
(William Stone) *in tch in rr of main gp: swtchd rt ent fnl 2f: hdwy 1f out: styd on wl ins fnl f: nt rch ldrs* **25/1**
043- **5** *¾* **Novabridge**[22] 8216 5-9-7 **65**....(b) AdamKirby 2 64+
(Neil Mulholland) *in tch towards rr: rdn and effrt 2f out: hdwy u.p jst ins fnl f: kpt on u.p but nvr able to chal* **9/4**[1]
016- **6** *nk* **Danzoe (IRE)**[12] 8352 6-9-7 **65**.... AdamBeschizza 9 63
(Christine Dunnett) *in tch in midfield: effrt u.p wl over 1f out: styd on same pce and no imp ins fnl f* **10/1**
503- **7** *nse* **Never A Quarrel (IRE)**[10] 8384 3-8-13 **64**.... DavidParkes[(7)] 6 62
(Jeremy Gask) *taken down early: chsd ldrs: rdn and unable qck wl over 1f out: btn and kpt on same pce ins fnl f* **5/1**[2]
616- **8** *2 ¼* **Imaginary Diva**[133] 5608 7-8-9 **60**.... JordanVaughan[(7)] 5 49
(George Margarson) *in tch in midfield: effrt and unable qck u.p over 1f out: wknd ins fnl f* **33/1**
026- **9** *2* **Falasteen (IRE)**[13] 8330 6-9-5 **63**.... LiamJones 8 45
(Milton Bradley) *rdr slow to remove hood: in tch on outer: rdn and hdwy over 2f out: no imp u.p 1f out: wknd ins fnl f* **7/1**
500- **10** *2 ¾* **Sarah Berry**[18] 8272 4-8-8 **57**....(v) ShelleyBirkett[(5)] 10 29
(Chris Dwyer) *s.i.s: a bhd* **25/1**

58.44s (-0.36) **Going Correction** -0.10s/f (Stan) **10** Ran SP% **121.7**
Speed ratings (Par 101): **98,97,97,96,94 94,94,90,87,83**
CSF £48.96 CT £222.08 TOTE £13.50: £3.30, £2.00, £2.10; EX 60.80 Trifecta £341.90.
Owner The Hair & Haberdasher Partnership **Bred** J J Bridger **Trained** Liphook, Hants

FOCUS
A run-of-the-mill sprint to conclude proceedings.
T/Jkpt: Part won. £33,376.40. Pool: £47,009.12 - 0.50 winning units. £23,504.56 carried forward to Cheltenham on Wednesday the 1st January. T/Plt: £171.80. Pool: £104,152.81 - 442.52 winning units. T/Qpdt: £51.80. Pool: 12,194.93 - 173.96 winning units. SP

INDEX TO FLAT RACING

Horses are shown in alphabetical order; the trainer's name follows the name of the horse. The figures to the right are current master ratings for all-weather and turf; the all-weather rating is preceded by the letter 'a'.Underneath the horse's name is its age, colour and sex in abbreviated format e.g. 6 b g indicates the horse is six-years-old, bay in colour, and a gelding.The descriptive details are followed by the race numbers of the races in which it has taken part in chronological order; a superscript figure indicates its finishing position in that race (brackets indicate it was the winner of the race).

Aalim *Saeed bin Suroor* a77 77
3 b g Nayef(USA) Anna Palariva (IRE) (Caerleon (USA))
6926^{5} ◆ 7422^{2} (7734)

Aaranyow (IRE) *Clifford Lines* a58 59
5 ch g Compton Place Cutpurse Moll (Green Desert (USA))
1516^{4} ◆ 1929^{2} 2638^{3} 3246^{2} 3738^{5} 4120^{6} 4496^{7} 4999^{7} 5798^{5} 5930^{2}

Aarhus (SPA) *M Delcher Sanchez* a74 99
3 ch c Dyhim Diamond(IRE) Ensis (SPA) (Zieten (USA))
1799a^{3}

Aaronkayzo (IRE) *Peter McCreery* a24 48
4 b g Great Exhibition(USA) Spoofy Chic (IRE) (Kalanisi (IRE))
7514^{9}

Aather (IRE) *David Arbuthnot* a56 73
8 b g Key Of Luck(USA) Alkaffeyeh (IRE) (Sadler's Wells (USA))
789^{11}

Aazif (IRE) *Donald McCain* a82 89
4 ch g Nayef(USA) Ayun (USA) (Swain (IRE))
3685^{13}

Abace (IRE) *D Allard* a66
3 b c Astronomer Royal(USA) Cours De La Reine (IRE) (Fasliyev (USA))
191a^{10}

Abanoas (USA) *Alan Coogan* a2 45
3 bb f Proud Citizen(USA) Alabaq (USA) (Riverman (USA))
1288^{4} 1640^{12} 1911^{6} 2362^{4} 2508^{12} 2737^{5} 3016^{6} 3219^{8} 7753^{12}

Abated *Roger Charlton* a79 81
3 b f Dansili Tantina (USA) (Distant View (USA))
1732^{4} (3576) 4603^{2} 6045^{2} 6524^{5}

Abatis (USA) *Charles Hills* 44
2 bb f Aptitude(USA) Rouwaki (USA) (Miswaki (USA))
5061^{7}

Abbakova (IRE) *David O'Meara* 92
2 ch f Dandy Man(IRE) Over Rating (Desert King (IRE))
2675a^{3} 5476^{6} 7011^{10}

Abbey Vale (IRE) *G M Lyons* a92 92
3 b g Moss Vale(IRE) Cloonkeary (In The Wings)
4465a^{14} 6025a^{13}

Abbey Village (IRE) *Richard Fahey* 52
2 ch g Aqlaam Balladonia (Primo Dominie)
5145^{7}

Abbotsfield (IRE) *Ben Haslam* a32 69
3 ch f Sakhee's Secret May Day Queen (IRE) (Danetime (IRE))
6178^{2} 6497^{6} 7791^{6}

Abbraccio *Fergal O'Brien* a75 70
5 b g Pivotal Embraced (Pursuit Of Love)
2739^{4} 3156^{4} 4153^{3} 4838^{4} 5070^{8}

Abdel (FR) *J-M Osorio* 107
5 b c Dyhim Diamond(IRE) Leonor De Guzman (SPA) (Glauco (SPA))
(5465a) 7142a^{6}

Abendwind (GER) *W Hickst* 103
2 b c Wiesenpfad(FR) Adela (GER) (Tannenkonig (IRE))
(5911a)

Abhaath (USA) *Ronald Harris* a73 74
4 b g Hard Spun(USA) Above Perfection (USA) (In Excess)
97^{3} 229^{3} 317^{2} 380^{3} 490^{4} 705^{5} 791^{5} 976^{9} 1039^{2} 1170^{3} 1179^{2} 1401^{5} (1886) 2565^{11} (2948)

Abigails Angel *Brett Johnson* a76 74
6 br m Olden Times Make Ready (Beveled (USA))
159^{2} 720^{5} 6337^{6} 7256^{6} 7836^{8} 8244^{3} 8335^{6} 8450^{4}

Abilene *F-H Graffard* a90 95
3 ch f Samum(GER) Altamira (Peintre Celebre (USA))
(1611) 1933^{3} 3834^{6} 7116a^{4}

Abi Scarlet (IRE) *Hughie Morrison* a69
4 b f Baltic King Petarga (Petong)
7151^{10} 3906^{6}

Abisko (IRE) *Brian Ellison* 61
2 ch f Tagula(IRE) Strawberry Sands (Lugana Beach)
2161^{3} 2426^{11} 4808^{9} 5380^{9} 6073^{12}

Able Dash *Ed Walker* a40 53
3 ch g Dutch Art Evasive Quality (FR) (Highest Honor (FR))
3250^{9} 3539^{5} 4151^{10}

Able Master (IRE) *David O'Meara* a62 101
7 b g Elusive City(USA) Foresta Verde (USA) (Green Forest (USA))
2310^{10} 3088^{2} 3825^{6} (4101) 4342^{2} 4758^{2} 5026^{11} 5681^{11}

Abou Ben (IRE) *A Oliver* a67 71
11 bb g Beneficial Sister Ruth (IRE) (Satco (FR))
7230a^{27}

About Turn *Saeed bin Suroor* a78
2 ch c Pivotal Doctor's Glory (USA) (Elmaamul (USA))
(4379) ◆

Above Standard (IRE) *Michael Easterby* a86 96
5 ch g Shamardal(USA) Prealpina (IRE) (Indian Ridge)
(2755) (3299) 4983^{4} 5651^{6} 6190^{6} 6845^{7} 7171^{4}

Above The Stars *Conor Dore* a71 70
5 b f Piccolo Swindling (Bahamian Bounty)
101^{3} 135^{2} 379^{3} 494^{10} 611^{3} 687^{6} 842^{5} (2074) (2364) (2530) 2789^{3} (2926) 3691^{6} 3904^{3} 4636^{8} 5165^{6} 5674^{11} 5973^{2} 6255^{4} 6463^{4} 7730^{5} 7848^{7} 8002^{5} 8034^{2} 8135^{9} 8306^{7} 8411^{9}

A Boy Named Suzi *Andrew Balding* a100 103
5 b g Medecis Classic Coral (USA) (Seattle Dancer (USA))
1382^{3} 2428^{4}

Abraham Monro *Ruth Carr* 59
3 gr g Kyllachy Pendulum (Pursuit Of Love)
2756^{7} 3592^{5} 4114^{2} (4544) 5184^{2} 5487^{4} 5878^{9} 6760^{6}

Abraq *Ed Dunlop* a70 69
3 b c Danehill Dancer(IRE) Nordhock (USA) (Luhuk (USA))
141^{5} 428^{6}

Abrasivo (ITY) *P Caravati* a61
4 ch c Munir Medullia (IRE) (Turtle Island (IRE))
498a^{9}

Absconder (IRE) *Mark Johnston* 19
2 br c Shamardal(USA) Desertion (IRE) (Danehill (USA))
4053^{13} 4289^{6} 4963^{8} 6494^{12} 7036^{10}

Absent Amy (IRE) *Amy Weaver* a80 80
4 b f Redback Twitcher's Delight (Polar Falcon (USA))
878^{4} ◆ (1013) (3496) 5153^{3} 5881^{2} (6730) 6952^{6} 7876^{3} 8179^{6} 8316^{3}

Absolute Bearing (IRE) *Tim Etherington* a38 54
4 b g Majestic Missile(IRE) Garnock Academy (USA) (Royal Academy (USA))
2634^{4} 3026^{6}

Absolute Diamond *John Quinn* 63
3 ch f Monsieur Bond(IRE) Tibesti (Machiavellian (USA))
2027^{5} 2503^{7} 2765^{7} (4158) 5089^{2} 5471^{13} 6074^{7}

Absolute Fun (IRE) *Tim Easterby* a27 57
4 b f Lawman(FR) Jallaissine (IRE) (College Chapel)
26^{7}

Absolutely Me (IRE) *Willie Musson* a55 45
4 ch f Barathea(IRE) Attymon Lill (IRE) (Marju (IRE))
1350^{6} 2642^{9} 3256^{4} (7379)

Absolutely Right (IRE) *George Margarson* a71 53
3 b f Teofilo(IRE) Dabawiyah (IRE) (Intikhab (USA))
6734^{5} 7447^{8} 7786^{8}

Absolutely So (IRE) *Andrew Balding* a87 81
3 b c Acclamation Week End (Selkirk (USA))
(8430) ◆

Abstraction (IRE) *Sarah Dawson* a79 108
3 b c Majestic Missile(IRE) Bronze Queen (IRE) (Invincible Spirit (IRE))
2374a^{4} 5772a^{5}

Abundantly *Hughie Morrison* a34 81
4 b f Sakhee(USA) Composing (IRE) (Noverre (USA))
1728^{3} 1973^{2} 3344^{4} 4029^{8} 5746^{8} 6377^{6} ◆ 6960^{2} 7396^{2}

Abushamah (IRE) *Kevin Prendergast* 78
2 b c Nayef(USA) Adaala (USA) (Sahm (USA))
7050a^{3}

Abu Sidra (FR) *J-F Bernard* a91 114
4 gr c Shirocco(GER) Mary Doun (FR) (Smadoun (FR))
961a^{3} (3851a) 5040a^{7} 5806a^{5} 7941a^{4}

Acapulco Bay *Dai Burchell* a51 56
9 b g Pursuit Of Love Lapu-Lapu (Prince Sabo)
(2350) 3953^{10}

Accession (IRE) *Clive Cox* a94 97
4 b g Acclamation Pivotal's Princess (IRE) (Pivotal)
1675^{6} ◆ 2013^{8} 2618^{8} ◆ 3411^{9} 4067^{5} 4879^{3} ◆ 6959^{5}

Acclio (IRE) *Clive Brittain* a69 65
2 b f Acclamation Hovering (IRE) (In The Wings)
6107^{2} 7296^{5} 7533^{3}

Ace Master *Roy Bowring* a81 73
5 ch g Ballet Master(USA) Ace Maite (Komaite (USA))
54^{3} 437^{2} (616) 1205^{2} (1334) (1521) 2236^{5} 2932^{7} 3196^{3} 3446^{4} 4009^{10} 5373^{2} 5841^{2} 6757^{5} 6969^{3} (7315) 7633^{2} 8095^{9} 8321^{3}

Ace Of Spies (IRE) *Mandy Rowland* a72 61
8 br g Machiavellian(USA) Nadia (Nashwan (USA))
77^{11} 323^{7} 523^{4} 537^{5} (1310) 1455^{4} 2168^{5} 2578^{7} 5198^{14}

Ace Of Valhalla *Olly Stevens* a45 87
4 b g Authorized(IRE) Trick Of Ace (USA) (Clever Trick (USA))
2671^{11} 6559^{9}

Acertainplace *David Elsworth*
2 ch f Compton Place Phoenix Rising (Dr Fong (USA))
7852^{12}

Achalas (IRE) *Heather Main* a80 81
5 b g Statue Of Liberty(USA) Princess Of Iona (IRE) (Fasliyev (USA))
1302^{7} 1586^{2} 2102^{5} 2598^{4} 2849^{6}

A Childs Dream (IRE) *Richard Hannon Snr* a67 64
2 b f Intense Focus(USA) Keriyka (IRE) (Indian Ridge)
2090^{5} (2771) 4232^{5} 5850^{4} 6695^{9}

Achnaha (IRE) *P D Deegan* 86
2 b f Haatef(USA) Sanna Bay (IRE) (Refuse To Bend (IRE))
7720a^{2}

Achtung *Jeremy Noseda* a47 60
3 b c Montjeu(IRE) Funsie (FR) (Saumarez)
3021^{12} 3957^{9} 4223^{9} 7434^{9}

Achtung (SPA) *J Lopez Sanchez* 95
5 ch g Sulamani(IRE) Aurea (GER) (Silvano (GER))
6252a^{5} 7060a^{9}

Aciano (IRE) *Brendan Powell* a73 76
5 b g Kheleyf(USA) Blue Crystal (IRE) (Lure (USA))
1696^{5} 2057^{7} 3429^{6} 5327a^{4}

Acquaint (IRE) *Richard Hannon Snr* a65 57
2 gr f Verglas(IRE) Azia (IRE) (Desert Story (IRE))
3471^{8} 4589^{8} 5603^{3} 6311^{2} 7309^{15} 7878^{11} 8086^{4}

Across The Cape *Michael Bell* 43
2 ch f Manduro(GER) Cape Marien (IRE) (Cape Cross (IRE))
7449^{7}

Across The Rhine (USA) *S Seemar* a86 99
7 ch g Cuvee(USA) Seductive Smile (USA) (Silver Hawk (USA))
745a^{8} 838a^{6}

Action Front (USA) *Derek Shaw* a55 71
5 bb g Aptitude(USA) Palisade (USA) (Gone West (USA))
1794^{8} 2435^{11} 2785^{7} 3534^{2} 4071^{5} 4504^{3} 5377^{7} 7383^{10} 7752^{3} 8065^{11}

Activate *Keith Dalgleish* a79 85
6 b g Motivator Princess Manila (CAN) (Manila (USA))
(84) 183^{3} 227^{3} 318^{6} 432^{2} 524^{2} 816^{2} (929) 1251^{2} 1390^{4} 2221^{2} (2509) 2973^{3} (3085) 3333^{7} 3726^{5} 4110^{5} 4559^{2} 4822^{5}

Act Of Charity (IRE) *Gay Kelleway* a87 83
2 b c Royal Applause Kay Es Jay (FR) (Xaar)
5698^{6} ◆ 6378^{2} (6773) 7492^{4} (8397)

Actonetaketwo *Ron Hodges* a56 4
3 b f Act One Temple Dancer (Magic Ring (IRE))
136^{6} 442^{5} 732^{2} 1055^{3} (1118) 1319^{3} 1367^{3} 2362^{10} 7322^{10} 7639^{13} 7904^{8} 8082^{7}

Acton Gold *Brian Baugh* a39
4 b f And Beyond(IRE) Antonia Bertolini (Bertolini (USA))
8185^{3}

Acton Jenson *Brian Baugh* a38
4 gr g Proclamation(IRE) Crystal Attraction (Mon Tresor)
800^{5}

Act Your Shoe Size *Keith Dalgleish* 87
4 b f Librettist(USA) Howards Heroine (IRE) (Danehill Dancer (IRE))
1990^{8} 2220^{6} 2704^{4} 2915^{2} 3349^{16} 3567^{3} (3712) 4101^{4} 4760^{4} 5880^{6} 6550^{8} 6683^{2} 6875^{9}

Adaeze (IRE) *Jonathan Portman* a53 54
5 b f Footstepsinthesand Ringmoor Down (Pivotal)
143^{2} 339^{5} 551^{11} 819^{10}

Ada Lovelace *Dean Ivory* a71 53
3 b f Byron Satin Braid (Diktat)
(374) ◆ 531^{4} 894^{5} 5060^{9} 6100^{4} 7262^{9} ◆ 7783^{6} 8216^{8}

Adam's Ale *Paul Midgley* 82
4 b g Ishiguru(USA) Aqua (Mister Baileys)
1392^{2} 1687^{5} (2757) 3444^{7} 3778^{6} (4510) 5108^{2} 5381^{8} 6309^{8} 6771^{6}

Addictive Dream (IRE) *David Nicholls* a103 103
6 ch g Kheleyf(USA) Nottambula (IRE) (Thatching)
150a^{15} 365a^{13} 4058^{6} 4493^{4} 5375^{4} 5991^{5} 6391^{6} ◆ 6719^{2} 7527^{18} 7803^{5} (7982) 8155^{2} 8334^{9} 8395^{3}

Addictive Nature (IRE) *Clive Cox* a58 54
3 b g Acclamation Movie Queen (Danehill (USA))
2448^{10} 3401^{6}

Addikt (IRE) *John Spearing* a63 62
8 b h Diktat Frond (Alzao (USA))
1303^{7} 2982^{9} 5002^{14} 6782^{8} 7081^{8} 7962^{12}

Address Unknown *Richard Fahey* a70 84
6 b g Oasis Dream Return (USA) (Sadler's Wells (USA))
(2149) 2668^{3} 3824^{15}

Adena (FR) *T Mercier* a72 56
6 b m North Light(IRE) Bog Wild (USA) (Once Wild (USA))
5464a^{5}

Adeste Fideles (USA) *A P O'Brien* 84
2 bb f Giant's Causeway(USA) Imagine (IRE) (Sadler's Wells (USA))
2944a^{5}

Adhwaa *J W Hills* 93
2 br f Oasis Dream Hammiya (IRE) (Darshaan)
3057^{11} 3833^{2} (4432) 5284^{4} 6185^{2} 7695^{2}

Adiator *Neville Bycroft* 67
5 b f Needwood Blade Retaliator (Rudimentary (USA))
2504^{2} 2765^{4} 3593^{2} 4007^{9} 4623^{4} 5876^{5} (7345)

Adili (IRE) *Brian Ellison* a74 56
4 ch g Dubai Destination(USA) Adirika (IRE) (Miswaki (USA))
2886^{10} 3301^{11} 5052^{7} 5966^{5} 6632^{8} 7099^{8} 7423^{5}

Adiynara (IRE) *Neil Mulholland* a76 81
5 b f Halling(USA) Adirika (IRE) (Miswaki (USA))
57^{5} 2750^{5}

Admirable Art (IRE) *Tony Carroll* a44 72
3 b g Excellent Art Demi Voix (Halling (USA))
2321^{12} 2746^{4} 3242^{3} 3621^{3} 4829^{7} 6042^{5} 6587^{6} 7109^{4} (7246) 7430^{3}

Admirable Duque (IRE) *Dominic Ffrench Davis* a81 75
7 b g Selkirk(USA) Stunning (USA) (Nureyev (USA))
208^{4} 642^{4} 905^{3} (948) ◆ (1117) 1182^{4} 1733^{4} 1949^{2} ◆ (3110) 3587^{8} 4643^{6} 5823^{7} 6809^{3} 6960^{8} 7166^{4} 7220^{2} (8139)

Admiral Kitten (USA) *Michael J Maker* 112
3 b c Kitten's Joy(USA) Reachinforthestars (USA) (Grand Slam (USA))
(5551a) 8120a^{2}

Admiralofthesea (USA) *Robert Eddery* a74 69
3 b g Henrythenavigator(USA) Duchess Royale (IRE) (Danehill (USA))
(1301) (1427) 1608^{2} 1832^{5} 3404^{5} 3782^{7} 4670^{4} 5273^{5} 6039^{7} 6560^{7} 6932^{5} 7109^{2}

Admirals Walk (IRE) *Sylvester Kirk* a64 63
3 b g Tagula(IRE) Very Racy (USA) (Sri Pekan (USA))
2935^{6} 3665^{7} 4503^{5} 4829^{4} 5217^{3} 5525^{2} 5890^{8} 6155^{4} 6698^{2} 7511^{5} 7924^{6} 8023^{5}

Admiralty *Ismail Mohammed* a91 66
4 b c Iffraaj Camp Riverside (USA) (Forest Camp (USA))
(740) (1430) 4181^{4} 6203^{8}

Admirer (IRE) *David Simcock* 44
3 b c Henrythenavigator(USA) Rags To Riches (USA) (A.P. Indy (USA))
5588^{9}

Admire Rakti (JPN) *Tomoyuki Umeda* 115
5 b c Heart's Cry(JPN) Admire Teresa (JPN) (Helissio (FR))
1868a^{4} 8033a^{4}

Adorable Choice (IRE) *Tom Dascombe* a72 68
5 bb f Choisir(AUS) Burnin' Memories (USA) (Lit De Justice (USA))
675^{6} 978^{5} 1610^{3} 2796^{4} 3910^{6} 4341^{5} 5332^{9}

Adore *Sir Michael Stoute* a68 67
2 b f Oasis Dream Fantasize (Groom Dancer (USA))
5394^{11} 6512^{2} 6949^{4} 7326^{3}

Adoya (GER) *Andreas Lowe* 105
3 b f Doyen(IRE) Akasha (GER) (Dashing Blade)
3146a^{4} 5044a^{3} (6010a)

Adriana (GER) *M Rulec* 109
5 b f Poliglote An Angel (GER) (Trempolino (USA))
6010a^{3} 7558a^{4} (7831a)

Adriano (FR) *M Delzangles* 60
3 b c Anabaa(USA) Ballymena Lassie (Giant's Causeway (USA))
7569a^{7}

Adroitly (AUS) *Saeed bin Suroor* a79 101
6 br g Octagonal(NZ) Easy Out (AUS) (Anabaa (USA))
462a^{5} 661a^{11} 833a^{9}

Ad Value (IRE) *Alan Kirtley* a48 67
5 b g Ad Valorem(USA) Sopran Marida (IRE) (Darshaan)
1251^{6} 2540^{9} 2720^{8} 2975^{3}

Advanced *Kevin Ryan* a88 97
10 b g Night Shift(USA) Wonderful World (GER) (Dashing Blade)
60^{6} 966^{5} 1646^{9}

Adventure Seeker (IRE) *Ed Vaughan* a76 73
2 gr c Dalakhani(IRE) Adventure (USA) (Unbridled's Song (USA))
3689^{6} 5188^{4} (6168) 6935^{4}

Advisor (FR) *Mark Gillard* 23
7 gr g Anabaa(USA) Armilina (FR) (Linamix (FR))
6960^{10}

Advisory *Mark Johnston* 67
3 ch g Street Cry(IRE) Abhisheka (IRE) (Sadler's Wells (USA))
4805^{5} 6062^{6} 6498^{6} 7220^{10}

Ad Vitam (IRE) *Mel Brittain* a64 58
5 ch g Ad Valorem(USA) Love Sonnet (Singspiel (IRE))
6760^{2} 6919^{5} (7905) 8278^{5}

Aegaeus *Ed Dunlop* a95 83
4 b g Monsun(GER) Ouija Board (Cape Cross (IRE))
1422^{2} 2478^{10} 3293^{4} 3791^{6} 5712^{9} (6108) 6802^{7} 7542^{4}

Aegean Destiny *John Mackie* a51 65
6 b m Beat Hollow Starlist (Observatory (USA))
755^{6} 973^{7} 6787^{8} 7099^{3} 7375^{4}

Aegean King *Michael Wigham* a57 55
7 b g Falbrav(IRE) Aegean Dream (IRE) (Royal Academy (USA))
110^{6} 334^{5} 510^{8}

Aeolian Blue *William Knight* a52
3 ch f Bahamian Bounty Blue Mistral (IRE) (Spinning World (USA))
7781^{5} 8180^{6}

Aeolus *Ed McMahon* 99
2 b c Araafa(IRE) Bright Moll (Mind Games)
4505^{5} (6383) (7170) 7525^{2}

Aerobic (GER) *M Schwinn* 28
4 b f Shirocco(GER) Aerope (Celestial Storm (USA))
5601a^{17}

Aerodynamic (IRE) *Michael Easterby* a81 84
6 b g Oratorio(IRE) Willowbridge (IRE) (Entrepreneur)
1115^{11} 1363^{5} 1686^{8} 2081^{6} 3628^{13} 4928^{9} (5426) 5713^{3} 5861^{3} 6236^{9} 7130^{10} 7275^{9}

Aeronwyn Bryn (IRE) *Michael Dods* a69 95
3 b f Dylan Thomas(IRE) Hecuba (Hector Protector (USA))
1697^{7} 2080^{5} (3629) (3772) 4581^{2} 4890^{2} 5496^{5} (6210) 6624^{9}

Aertex (IRE) *Richard Hannon Snr* a73 70
2 b f Exceed And Excel(AUS) Gingham (Barathea (IRE))
6739^{8} 7245^{4} (7435)

Aesop's Fables (USA) *Saeed bin Suroor* a83 118
4 b g Distorted Humor(USA) Abhisheka (IRE) (Sadler's Wells (USA))
466a^{4} 957a^{12} 1267a^{14} 4276^{7} 4811^{3} 5739^{8} 6530^{7}

Aetna *Michael Easterby* 92
3 b f Indesatchel(IRE) On The Brink (Mind Games)
(1114) 1683^{10} 2371^{8} (2888) 3584^{2} 6583^{3} ◆ 7373^{3}

Affaire Solitaire (IRE) *A Fabre* a88 93
3 b c Danehill Dancer(IRE) Arlesienne (IRE) (Alzao (USA))
1511a3

Aficionado *Ed Dunlop* a67 73
3 ch g Halling(USA) Prithee (Barathea (IRE))
18826 24429 (2769) ◆ 32439 35352

Afkar (IRE) *Clive Brittain* a82 78
5 b g Invincible Spirit(IRE) Indienne (IRE) (Indian Ridge)
6294 109211 17827 24254 31722 39934 62046 66487

Afonso De Sousa (USA) *A P O'Brien* a106 109
3 br c Henrythenavigator(USA) Mien (USA) (Nureyev (USA))
7005a3 7361a3

African Art (USA) *P Schaerer* a76 75
7 ch g Johannesburg(USA) Perovskia (USA) (Stravinsky (USA))
514a7 701a9

African Oil (FR) *Charles Hills* a82 92
3 b g Royal Applause Ahdaaf (USA) (Bahri (USA))
19586 ◆ 24396 (4366) 51345 67923 70632

African Story *Saeed bin Suroor* a121 120
6 ch g Pivotal Blixen (USA) (Gone West (USA))
(957a) 1269a5

African Waters (USA) *J-C Rouget* a73
3 b c Henrythenavigator(USA) Louve Des Reves (IRE) (Sadler's Wells (USA))
(604a)

Afro *Peter Hedger* a72 71
3 b f Araafa(IRE) Largo (IRE) (Selkirk (USA))
(2800) 51025 61583

Afsare *Luca Cumani* a91 121
6 b g Dubawi(IRE) Jumaireyah (Fairy King (USA))
34578 40272 (5446) (5739) ◆

After The Goldrush *Richard Hannon Snr* 72
2 b g Kyllachy Fine Lady (Selkirk (USA))
47732 ◆ 498716 58435 70887

After The Storm *John O'Shea* a57 66
4 b g Dylan Thomas(IRE) Inchiri (Sadler's Wells (USA))
74225

Agama (GER) *C Sprengel* 95
3 ch f Sholokhov(IRE) Ariana (GER) (Dashing Blade)
2910a11 4092a9

Agent Allison *Peter Chapple-Hyam* 103
3 b f Dutch Art Loquacity (Diktat)
16762 204711 352413 494910 65365 70204 782210

Agent Mimi (FR) *J-P Carvalho* a64 78
3 bb f Medecis Azucar (IRE) (Desert Prince (IRE))
7412a3

Agent Secret (IRE) *F Rohaut* a87 108
7 b h Pyrus(USA) Ron's Secret (Efisio)
7142a5

Agerzam *Roger Varian* a95 75
3 b g Holy Roman Emperor(IRE) Epiphany (Zafonic (USA))
202213 34743 51034 65755 68544 71125 81812 (8431)

Aglaophonos *Ian Williams* a78 79
3 ch g Dutch Art Lasting Image (Zilzal (USA))
17322 29343 39273 501611 (7065) 73074

A Good Year (IRE) *J W Hills* a54 41
3 b f Montjeu(IRE) Noble Pearl (GER) (Dashing Blade)
18768 323711 497810 55927 60446

Agosto (GER) *N Minner* 64
4 bb g Mamool(IRE) Almudena (GER) (Law Society (USA))
3647a2

Agresivo (USA) *S Ozolke* 86
4 b c Harlan's Holiday(USA) Maddalena (USA) (Good And Tough (USA))
6254a9

Agy (IRE) *J-C Rouget* a89
3 b c Dylan Thomas(IRE) Diamond Star (IRE) (Daylami (IRE))
5805a3

Ahern *David Barron* 104
3 ch g Dutch Art Petra Nova (First Trump)
192112 334810 382313 42556 478017 553812 630811

Ahfir (IRE) *S Wattel* a60
3 b f Ramonti(FR) Amaniy (USA) (Dayjur (USA))
126a9

Ahouva (FR) *F Chappet* a45 66
2 b f Falco(USA) Ask For Love (IRE) (Montjeu (IRE))
7568a12

Ahoy There (IRE) *Tom Tate* 68
2 ch g Captain Rio Festivite (IRE) (Fasliyev (USA))
29854 35002 43127 50834 55436 62756 (7309) 749210

Ahtoug *Charlie Appleby* a103 104
5 b h Byron Cherokee Rose (IRE) (Dancing Brave (USA))
290a6 42755 48004 (5257)

A Huge Dream (IRE) *F Rohaut* 99
4 b f Refuse To Bend(IRE) Great Joy (IRE) (Grand Lodge (USA))
4935a4 5806a8 6445a5 7085a2

Ahzeemah (IRE) *Saeed bin Suroor* a84 117
4 b g Dubawi(IRE) Swiss Roll (IRE) (Entrepreneur)
246a2 555a2 (870a) 1263a2 42132 49192 (5724) 6441a2 73639

Aiken *John Gosden* 116
5 b c Selkirk(USA) Las Flores (IRE) (Sadler's Wells (USA))
55316 6447a11 736312 782311

Ailsa Craig (IRE) *Edwin Tuer* a66 78
7 b m Chevalier(IRE) Sharplaw Destiny (IRE) (Petardia)
17753 25557 29564 35433 39474 45438 (5370) 58333 (6130) 66314 71007 749811

Ainmire *John Quinn* 59
2 b c Tobougg(IRE) Ames Souer (IRE) (Fayruz)
51404 58265 62717 70874

Aint Got A Scooby (IRE) *Clive Cox* a74 79
3 br c Red Clubs(IRE) La Bataille (USA) (Out Of Place (USA))
(1770) 23226 31735 45932 60034 63356 67342

Ain't No Surprise (IRE) *Jamie Osborne* a63 68
2 b f Kheleyf(USA) Harmonist (USA) (Hennessy (USA))
26756 82152 83252

Air Mail (IRE) *A Giorgi* 87
3 b f Choisir(AUS) Alexander Express (IRE) (Sri Pekan (USA))
2697a7 3616a8

Air Of Glory (IRE) *Charlie Appleby* a84
3 ch g Shamardal(USA) Balloura (USA) (Swain (IRE))
(2952) ◆ 34707 669411

Aiyana *Hughie Morrison* a73 71
3 ch f Indian Haven Coventina (IRE) (Daylami (IRE))
34696 39073 51007 57627 63635 70662 (7305) 79472

A J Cook (IRE) *Ron Barr* a68 64
3 b g Mujadil(USA) Undertone (IRE) (Noverre (USA))
12154 ◆ 20768 22182 27565 (3547) 41147 489211 66045 703010 75988

Ajeeb (USA) *Michael Scudamore* a85 49
5 b g Harlan's Holiday(USA) Fair Settlement (USA) (Easy Goer (USA))
322 1832 4965 5858 8823 10379 13276 184912 35797 39768 48317 56315 64737 70824 737810

Ajig *Eve Johnson Houghton* a73 70
2 ch f Bahamian Bounty Atwirl (Pivotal)
38963 45897 (5891) 640111 70885

Ajjaadd (USA) *Ted Powell* a101 104
7 b g Elusive Quality(USA) Millstream (USA) (Dayjur (USA))
(1765) 286511 427510 49862 63919 81557 833410

Ajman Bridge *Luca Cumani* a82 95
3 ch c Dubawi(IRE) Rice Mother (IRE) (Indian Ridge)
(6563) ◆ 70222 ◆ 74973

Ajmany (IRE) *Luca Cumani* a94 96
3 b g Kheleyf(USA) Passarelle (USA) (In The Wings)
22093 28576 (4502) 491710 67515

Ajraam (USA) *Charles Hills* 97
3 b g Daaher(CAN) Abby Road (IRE) (Danehill (USA))
(1635) (3028) 345521 55107 665013

Akarali (IRE) *Th Von Ballmoos* a53
4 ch g Halling(USA) Akaliya (IRE) (Daylami (IRE))
513a7

Akarana (IRE) *Willie Musson* a55
6 b g Danehill Dancer(IRE) Castle Quest (IRE) (Grand Lodge (USA))
8528 11202 25115 29915

Akasaka (IRE) *Edward Lynam* a102 94
6 b g King's Best(USA) Daganya (IRE) (Danehill Dancer (IRE))
3869a6

Akdam (IRE) *Tony Carroll* a68 71
3 br g Dubai Destination(USA) Akdara (IRE) (Sadler's Wells (USA))
(925) 18854 23123 42225 81843

Akeed Dubawi *William Haggas* a80 80
3 b c Dubawi(IRE) Anosti (Act One)
35855 41523 44952 (5867)

Akeed Mofeed *R Gibson* 118
4 b c Dubawi(IRE) Wonder Why (GER) (Tiger Hill (IRE))
1872a5 (8211a)

Akeed Wafi (IRE) *A Al Raihe* a75 101
4 b c Street Cry(IRE) Shy Lady (FR) (Kaldoun (FR))
149a12 241a14 462a12

Akemi (IRE) *X Thomas-Demeaulte* a88 102
3 b f Footstepsinthesand Hitra (USA) (Langfuhr (CAN))
4468a4 (6124a) 6890aP

Akira (IRE) *Patrick J Flynn* 94
3 b f Acclamation Saik (USA) (Riverman (USA))
3845a12 7051a6

Aksil (FR) *M Boutin* 105
3 b f Spirit One(FR) Nera Zilzal (IRE) (Zilzal (USA))
7995a2

Akua'da (GER) *A Wohler* 106
3 bb f Shamardal(USA) Akua'Ba (IRE) (Sadler's Wells (USA))
2065a7 (2910a) 3852a2 5940a11 6451a2 7053a7

Aladdins Cave *C A Murphy* a91 93
9 b g Rainbow Quest(USA) Flight Of Fancy (Sadler's Wells (USA))
3599a8

A Ladies Man (IRE) *Richard Hannon Snr* a74 71
3 b c Kyllachy Ego (Green Desert (USA))
14775 163614 (1903) 23932

Alakhan (IRE) *Ian Williams* a79 81
7 gr g Dalakhani(IRE) Alte Kunst (IRE) (Royal Academy (USA))
16739 56138 (6756) (7544) 80286

Al Amaan *Gary Moore* a68 72
8 b g Nayef(USA) Siobhan (Generous (IRE))
3386 12072 17158

Al Aqabah (IRE) *Brian Gubby* a75 70
8 ch m Redback Snow Eagle (IRE) (Polar Falcon (USA))
19543 340411 84328

Al Arish (IRE) *Lady Cecil* a77 77
3 b g Iffraaj Flash And Dazzle (IRE) (Bertolini (USA))
45903 52333 58924

Alaskan (IRE) *Richard Hannon Snr* 66
2 b c Kodiac Olympia Theatre (Galileo (IRE))
24119 49588 (Dead)

Alaskan Bullet (IRE) *Brian Ellison* a91 86
4 b g Kodiac Czars Princess (IRE) (Soviet Star (USA))
1969 3193 4576 16496 19642

Alaskan Night (IRE) *Kevin Ryan* a56 55
2 b g Kodiac Fingal Nights (IRE) (Night Shift (USA))
23144 45398 49639 69144 72006 75097

Alazan (IRE) *Philip Hobbs* a84 87
7 ch g Dubai Destination(USA) Marion Haste (IRE) (Ali-Royal (IRE))
527

Alazeyab (USA) *A Al Raihe* a88 107
7 b g El Prado(IRE) Itnab (Green Desert (USA))
465a13 575a4 660a12 838a9 955a10

Al Baahi (IRE) *Roger Varian* a46
3 b g Shamardal(USA) Lanzana (IRE) (Kalanisi (IRE))
192611

Albaasil (IRE) *Doug Watson* 115
5 b c Dansili Wrong Key (IRE) (Key Of Luck (USA))
466a5

Albamara *Sir Mark Prescott Bt* a92 102
4 bb f Galileo(IRE) Albanova (Alzao (USA))
24076 43098

Albaqaa *P J O'Gorman* a91 97
8 ch g Medicean Basbousate Nadia (Wolfhound (USA))
7236 ◆ 8818 11218 153813 228611 24502 (2659) 30605 35868 38112 42585 44152 48593 ◆ 49604 52855 (5613) 62785 657116 68019

Albasharah (USA) *Saeed bin Suroor* a90 114
4 b f Arch(USA) Desert Gold (USA) (Seeking The Gold (USA))
(2440) 35255 ◆ 40593 4732U

Alba Verde *Sir Mark Prescott Bt* a36
2 gr f Verglas(IRE) Algarade (Green Desert (USA))
78446 82668 834210

Al Baz *James Tate* a81 87
2 b c Sixties Icon Aileen's Gift (IRE) (Rainbow Quest (USA))
19304 27418 31482 (3588) 43005 (4833) 60645 (6628) 68445

Alben Star (IRE) *Richard Fahey* a100 101
5 b g Clodovil(IRE) Secret Circle (Magic Ring (IRE))
79829 81555 ◆ 83344 ◆ 83693

Albert Bridge *Ralph Beckett* a83 95
5 gr g Hernando(FR) Alvarita (Selkirk (USA))
15478 26547 65852 66265 719320

Alberto *Paul Fitzsimons* a47 15
3 b g Bertolini(USA) Al Awaalah (Mukaddamah (USA))
48398 53456 58459 707910 72669

Alberto Hawaii (GER) *Elfie Schnakenberg*
4 bb c Lord Of England(GER) Aloha Hawaii (GER) (Highland Chieftain)
702a3

Albert Tatlock (IRE) *John Butler* 73
4 b g Antonius Pius(USA) Double Precedent (Polish Precedent (USA))
306816 40723 56457

Albion *A Fabre* 110
4 b c With Approval(CAN) Alborada (Alzao (USA))
3165a7 4421a8

Albonny (IRE) *Alan Jarvis* a76 78
4 b g Aussie Rules(USA) Silk Law (IRE) (Barathea (IRE))
(1927) ◆ (2545) 40299 51855

Alborz (IRE) *Tim Vaughan* a78 77
4 b g Dubai Destination(USA) Mount Elbrus (Barathea (IRE))
3092 ◆ 6425 60719 72782 83103

Al Busayyir (IRE) *Marco Botti* a72
2 b c Amadeus Wolf Helen Wells (IRE) (Sadler's Wells (USA))
75133 79363 83404

Alcaeus *Sir Mark Prescott Bt* a82 100
3 b c Hernando(FR) Alvarita (Selkirk (USA))
(2508) (2799) (3055) (3257) (4770) 5326a13 (6876)

Alcando (IRE) *Denis Coakley* a81 87
3 ch g Alhaarth(IRE) Cantando (IRE) (Hamas (IRE))
162514 36346 43674 47976 55415

Alcohuaz (CHI) *Lennart Reuterskiold Jr* a106 86
8 b g Merchant Of Venice(USA) Giverny (CHI) (Hussonet (USA))
2145a2 5325a5

Aldborough (IRE) *Ralph Beckett* 75
3 b g Danehill Dancer(IRE) Kitty O'Shea (Sadler's Wells (USA))
16786 ◆

Aldeburgh *Jim Old* a68
4 b g Oasis Dream Orford Ness (Selkirk (USA))
81544 84276

Alderley *Martyn Meade* a66
2 b f Three Valleys(USA) Doctor's Note (Pursuit Of Love)
69316 (7348) 84529

Aldershot (FR) *Mlle L Payet-Burin* 9
7 ch m Lomitas Amazing Story (FR) (Cricket Ball (USA))
6058a6

Aldo Bere (FR) *C Boutin* a88 86
3 b c Hurricane Cat(USA) Relicia Bere (FR) (Until Sundown (USA))
286a3 2557a10

Aldreth *Michael Easterby* 56
2 b g Champs Elysees Rowan Flower (IRE) (Ashkalani (IRE))
49258 54828 658110 717510

Aldwick Bay (IRE) *Tom Dascombe* a87 90
5 b g Danehill Dancer(IRE) Josie Doocey (IRE) (Sadler's Wells (USA))
13024 17287 38389 41675 46385 48324 55356 707211 74312 83084 ◆

A Legacy Of Love (IRE) *Amanda Perrett* a74
2 b f Sea The Stars(IRE) Nashmiah (IRE) (Elusive City (USA))
66916 72952 80835

Alegra *Lady Cecil* a65 90
3 gr f Galileo(IRE) Altitude (Green Desert (USA))
43824 (4968) ◆ 59602 70725

Alejandro (IRE) *Richard Fahey* a64 96
4 b g Dark Angel(IRE) Carallia (IRE) (Common Grounds)
123215 154214 17877 23107 28822 309610 37574 (4340) 48792 (5238) 59927 63844 68269 72414

Aleksandar *Jim Goldie* a75 78
4 ch g Medicean Alexander Celebre (IRE) (Peintre Celebre (USA))
204011 27984 32842 39303 41592 478210 56405 64667 662613 721017

Al Emirati (IRE) *Marco Botti* a66 71
3 b c Tamayuz Corrine (IRE) (Spectrum (IRE))
14007 27279

Al Enbess (IRE) *David Simcock* a72 43
3 b g Kyllachy Taghreed (IRE) (Zamindar (USA))
(580) 7385 31737 38619

Alexandrakollontai (IRE) *Alistair Whillans* a55 76
3 b f Amadeus Wolf Story (Observatory (USA))
12757 17596 (2409) 48216 52634 57043 60523 66644 69169 (7149) 73444

Alexanor (IRE) *Marco Botti* a70 49
2 b c Pivotal Butterfly Cove (USA) (Storm Cat (USA))
76077 79022 80264

Alex My Boy (IRE) *Mark Johnston* 76
2 b c Dalakhani(IRE) Alexandrova (IRE) (Sadler's Wells (USA))
72742

Alex Vino (IRE) *Sir Michael Stoute* a79 76
2 b c High Chaparral(IRE) Rare Ransom (Oasis Dream)
57183 (6733)

Alezanna *James Toller* a62
4 ch f Halling(USA) Denica (IRE) (Night Shift (USA))
2004 8405 14016

Alfaayza (IRE) *K R Burke* a70 68
2 b f Dansili Ayun (USA) (Swain (IRE))
24195 53854 67895 74352 82974

Alfaisaliah (IRE) *J S Moore* a57
3 b f Red Clubs(IRE) Falcolnry (IRE) (Hawk Wing (USA))
2163 3369

Alfie Joe *Ron Hodges* a36 49
4 b g Bandmaster(USA) The Grey Bam Bam (Baryshnikov (AUS))
11618 18939 20578

Alfie Lunete (IRE) *J S Moore* a65 68
2 b f Footstepsinthesand La Lunete (Halling (USA))
45894 50903 55935 (6320) 669510 78373 82039

Alfraamsey *Sheena West* a78 75
5 b g Fraam Evanesce (Lujain (USA))
52313 ◆ 59334

Alfred Hutchinson *Geoffrey Oldroyd* a102 89
5 ch g Monsieur Bond(IRE) Chez Cherie (Wolfhound (USA))
(6) 6903 9457 202911 236511 61645 65385 69883 71724 77935 81177 (8385) (8445)

Alfred The Great *Richard Ford*
3 ch g Proclamation(IRE) Synergie (IRE) (Exit To Nowhere (USA))
393210 59628

Al Freej (IRE) *Brian Ellison* a82 78
4 b f Iffraaj Why Now (Dansili)
(159) 5892 13984 15402 16862 (5353) 67274 76083 80203

Alfresco *Martin Bosley* a57 62
9 b g Mtoto Maureena (IRE) (Grand Lodge (USA))
38413 43884 56778 81525 84463

Al Furat (USA) *Ron Barr* a40 71
5 b g El Prado(IRE) No Frills (IRE) (Darshaan)
17892 26297 32873 35047 407114 45634 49517 54662 62397 66327

Algar Lad *Jim Goldie* 81
3 ch g Kheleyf(USA) Winding (USA) (Irish River (FR))
(2317) 28884 35664 (5266) 658619 72406

Al Gharrafa *Rae Guest* a66 35
3 b f Dutch Art Smart Ass (IRE) (Shinko Forest (IRE))
2253 8174 10146 15245 296211 63979

Al Ghashamiya (IRE) *Marco Botti* 6
2 b f Amadeus Wolf Ryninch (IRE) (Dr Devious (IRE))
543510

Algorithmic (IRE) *Michael Bell* a56 58
3 b g Danehill Dancer(IRE) Tanami Desert (Lycius (USA))
142310 17139 250810 37936 53919

Al Guwair (IRE) *Lady Cecil* a69
3 b g Shirocco(GER) Katariya (IRE) (Barathea (IRE))
38214 52812 61165

Alhaarth Beauty (IRE) *Ismail Mohammed* a66 74
3 b f Alhaarth(IRE) Endis (IRE) (Distant Relative)
12152 17627 (2962) 36785 53005 636210 78455

Alhaban (IRE) *Ronald Harris* a80 76
7 gr g Verglas(IRE) Anne Tudor (IRE) (Anabaa (USA))
7473 7913 11044 (1170) 13535 14963 17886 19255

Alhebayeb (IRE) *Richard Hannon Snr* 109
3 gr c Dark Angel(IRE) Miss Indigo (Indian Ridge)
16215 26614 42163 5120a7

Alhellal (IRE) *M Phelan* a83 89
7 b g Kalanisi(IRE) Zafayana (IRE) (Mark Of Esteem (IRE))
3599a5 7230a25

Alice Rose (IRE) *Rae Guest* 73
4 ch f Manduro(GER) Bold Assumption (Observatory (USA))
(1914) 27117 36619 44969 51529

Alice's Dancer (IRE) *William Muir* a77 87
4 br f Clodovil(IRE) Islandagore (IRE) (Indian Ridge)
154211 18788 (2531) 31583 35326 40973 45254 54935

Alis Aquilae (IRE) *Tim Etherington* a69 54
7 b g Captain Rio Garnock Academy (USA) (Royal Academy (USA))
651611 675710 72632 79852

Alisios (GR) *Luca Cumani* 78
2 b c Ialysos(GR) Macanuda (IRE) (Slickly (FR))
5199^6 6277^2 7023^2 7471^7
Alito *W Hickst* 82
3 b c Big Shuffle(USA) Alanda (GER) (Lando (GER))
6713a^{15}
A Little Bit Dusty *Conor Dore* a84 83
5 ch g Needwood Blade Dusty Dazzler (IRE) (Titus Livius (FR))
7544^7 8309^2
Alive Alive Oh *T Stack* 102
3 b f Duke Of Marmalade(IRE) Higher Love (IRE) (Sadler's Wells (USA))
6416a^7
Alive And Kicking *Richard Fahey* a45 83
5 b g Compton Place Strawberry Dale (IRE) (Bering)
86^{10}
Aljamaaheer (IRE) *Roger Varian* 119
4 ch c Dubawi(IRE) Kelly Nicole (IRE) (Rainbow Quest (USA))
1835^2 2446^3 ◆ 3419^2 (4276) 5314a^8
Al Jamal *Saeed bin Suroor* a87 88
3 b f Authorized(IRE) Kydd Gloves (USA) (Dubai Millennium)
2054^6 (5589) 6115^3 6531^5
Al Jar (IRE) *S Sordi* 85
3 b f Iffraaj Hartal (Alhaarth (IRE))
1866a^9
Aljosan *Frank Sheridan* a52 48
4 b f Compton Place Little Caroline (IRE) (Great Commotion (USA))
240^6 381^9 408^8 565^{11} 1043^9 1395^{11} 1519^2 1929^8
Al Kazeem *Roger Charlton* 126
5 b c Dubawi(IRE) Kazeem (Darshaan)
(1846) (2688a) (3457) (4082) 5654^3 6226a^2 7058a^6
Alkcama (IRE) *John Weymes* 53
3 b g Camacho Alkifaf (USA) (Mtoto)
2501^{16}
Alketios (GR) *Luca Cumani* 67
2 b c Kavafi(IRE) Mazea (IRE) (Montjeu (IRE))
5472^6
Al Khan (IRE) *Violet M Jordan* a85 91
4 b g Elnadim(USA) Popolo (IRE) (Fasliyev (USA))
113^4 822^5 (878) 996^2 1096^2 1308^7 (1599) 2046^{13} 2214^4 2834^{11} 3096^3 3351^6 3980^2 (4235) 4560^3 4778^3 5019a^5 5738^9 6161^6 6331^{14}
Alkhataaf (USA) *Lydia Pearce* a8 83
6 b g Green Desert(USA) Elrafa Ah (USA) (Storm Cat (USA))
6310^{10} 6929^{11} 7454^{14}
Al Khawaneej Star (USA) *Michael Bell* a54 65
2 bb g Arch(USA) Frolic Away (USA) (Pentelicus (USA))
5244^9 5852^3 6688^6
Alkimos (IRE) *Saeed bin Suroor* a89 105
5 b g High Chaparral(IRE) Bali Breeze (IRE) (Common Grounds)
462a^{13} (Dead)
All Ablaze (IRE) *Damian Joseph English* a82 77
3 b f Antonius Pius(USA) Strawberry Sands (Lugana Beach)
2213^{10}
Allanit (GER) *Des Donovan* a66 72
9 b g Tiger Hill(IRE) Astilbe (GER) (Monsun (GER))
4411^8
All Annalena (IRE) *Lucy Wadham* a63 88
7 b m Dubai Destination(USA) Alla Prima (IRE) (In The Wings)
2440^5 2849^4 4166^6
All Black Rose *Ann Duffield*
3 b f Vita Rosa(JPN) All A Dream (Desert Story (IRE))
4356^{10}
All Cash (USA) *D Wayne Lukas* a96 85
2 ch c English Channel(USA) Andover The Money (USA) (Dynaformer (USA))
7688a^{13}
All Dynamite (FR) *Braem Horse Racing Sprl* a79 71
4 b c Kentucky Dynamite(USA) All Risk (BEL) (Pyramus (USA))
3647a^6
Allegation (FR) *David Lanigan* 55
2 b f Lawman(FR) Anja (IRE) (Indian Ridge)
5472^{11}
Allegra Clairmont *John Best* a40
4 b f Byron Villarosi (IRE) (Rossini (USA))
7154^6 7625^7
Allegra Tak (ITY) *H Rogers* a66 92
7 b m Invincible Spirit(IRE) No Tiktak (IRE) (Diktat)
4647a^{10} 7719a^{14}
Allergic Reaction (IRE) *William Knight* a54 55
2 b g Kyllachy Wood Chorus (Singspiel (IRE))
4987^{15} 5698^8 6485^7 6924^6
Allez Henri (IRE) *M Delzangles* 94
2 b c Footstepsinthesand Macotte (FR) (Nicolotte)
7967a^4
Allez Viv (FR) *P Van De Poele* a77 71
3 ch g Stormy River(FR) Autumn Forest (FR) (Exit To Nowhere (USA))
7569a^5
Allied Answer *Steve Gollings* 79
5 gr g Danehill Dancer(IRE) Hotelgenie Dot Com (Selkirk (USA))
7635^4
Allied Powers (IRE) *Michael Bell* a70 110
8 b g Invincible Spirit(IRE) Always Friendly (High Line)
1674^5 2184a^5 2407^5 6385^3
Allnecessaryforce (FR) *Richard Fahey* a84 87
3 gr g Verglas(IRE) Kosmic View (USA) (Distant View (USA))
1109^2 1470^2 2432^4 2879^8 4804^4 5223^P 5582^2 7369^{12}
All On Red (IRE) *George Baker* 83
3 b f Red Clubs(IRE) Champion Tipster (Pursuit Of Love)
2783^5 5541^9
All Or Nothin (IRE) *Paddy Butler* a62 92
4 b g Majestic Missile(IRE) Lady Peculiar (CAN) (Sunshine Forever (USA))
1232^{10} 1720^{11} 2214^{13} (2752) (3592) 4012^4 5301^2 5793^{12} 7318^6 7948^3 8244^9
All Right Now *Tony Newcombe* a60 59
6 b g Night Shift(USA) Cookie Cutter (IRE) (Fasliyev (USA))
2345^9 4155^{12} 5097^5 (5817) 6101^6 7092^8 (7454) 7958^{10} 8125^{14} 8315^3
All Set To Go (IRE) *A Oliver* 98
2 gr c Verglas(IRE) Firecrest (IRE) (Darshaan)
2943a^4 6884a^4 7548a^4
All Talk N No Do (IRE) *Seamus Durack* a74 76
2 b c Kodiac Woodren (USA) (Woodman (USA))
4640^9 5188^2 5698^4 6299^2 7129^{10} 7460^4 7640^6
All That Remains (IRE) *Brian Ellison* a59 53
8 b g King's Theatre(IRE) Morning Breeze (IRE) (Bigstone (IRE))
1445^{10}
All The Aces (IRE) *Nicky Henderson* a113 96
8 b g Spartacus(IRE) Lili Cup (FR) (Fabulous Dancer (USA))
2044^9 3297^5 4313^6 4782^3 5655^4 6591^7 7496^{11}
All The Winds (GER) *Shaun Lycett* a86 83
8 ch g Samum(GER) All Our Luck (GER) (Spectrum (IRE))
52^6 309^P 797^2 ◆ (1083) 1212^4 7115^{10} 7805^2 8041^4 8276^5
Alluring Star *Michael Easterby* a67 71
5 b f Gentleman's Deal(IRE) Alustar (Emarati (USA))
975^3 1214^3 1394^3 (1610) 1932^2 2162^8 3395^2 3686^4 4823^3 5139^2 5614^4 5830^4 6367^3 6761^8 7381^5 7663^5
All Yours (IRE) *William Knight* a35 67
2 gr f Verglas(IRE) Totally Yours (IRE) (Desert Sun)
4921^{15} 5394^{13} 6140^8 6807^7 7309^9
Ally Pally (FR) *G Botti* a71 46
3 ch c Green Tune(USA) Castilly (Inchinor)
1850a^{10}
Almada (FR) *K Borgel* 55
3 b f Loup Solitaire(USA) Change Partner (FR) (Turtle Island (IRE))
5692a^7
Almadaa *David Marnane* a96 74
6 b g Exceed And Excel(AUS) Masaader (USA) (Wild Again (USA))
679a^2 6883a^{10} 7521a^4
Almadan (IRE) *Ferdy Murphy* a33 77
5 b g Azamour(IRE) Alamouna (IRE) (Indian Ridge)
622^4
Almagest *David O'Meara* 93
5 br g Galileo(IRE) Arabesque (Zafonic (USA))
3607^3 4264^6 4626^3 4804^6 (5109) ◆ (5423) 6585^9 7064^3 7496^{13}
Almail (USA) *Jamie Osborne* a84 74
7 b g Swain(IRE) Khassah (Green Desert (USA))
6158^{10}
Almalekiah (IRE) *J S Moore* a75 82
3 gr f Clodovil(IRE) Majestic Night (IRE) (Mujadil (USA))
1515^2 2415^7 2983^3 3591^2 (3677)
Almalyk (FR) *A De Royer-Dupre* 103
4 gr g Oratorio(IRE) Alnamara (FR) (Linamix (FR))
6447a^7
Al Manaal *Saeed bin Suroor* a68 82
3 b f Echo Of Light Mall Queen (USA) (Sheikh Albadou)
(3149) 3828^3 4219^2 5125^7
Almanack *T Stack* a91 78
3 b c Haatef(USA) Openness (Grand Lodge (USA))
2213^9
Almargo (IRE) *Charlie Appleby* a67 68
2 b c Invincible Spirit(IRE) Alexander Youth (IRE) (Exceed And Excel (AUS))
6110^3 6931^5 7119^7
Almashooqa (USA) *Roger Varian* a66
2 bb f Dubawi(IRE) Almoutezah (USA) (Storm Cat (USA))
7764^5
Almaty Express *John Weymes* a65 55
11 b g Almaty(IRE) Express Girl (Sylvan Express)
559^5 736^8 1042^4 1356^2 (1395) 1731^8 3197^{11} 4148^{10} (4621) 4836^3 5674^{10} 6478^7 6651^3 6808^{10}
Almax *Michael Bell* 5
2 b c Rock Of Gibraltar(IRE) Inya Lake (Whittingham (IRE))
7817^{13}
Al Meezan *David Simcock* a68
3 ch g Nayef(USA) Festivale (IRE) (Invincible Spirit (IRE))
1069^7 1478^5 1653^7
Almerzem (USA) *Saeed bin Suroor* 56
2 bb c Medaglia d'Oro(USA) Tashawak (IRE) (Night Shift (USA))
5490^5
Almond Branches *Sharon Watt* 82
4 ch f Dutch Art Queens Jubilee (Cayman Kai (IRE))
2122^6 2410^{10} 3569^{13}
Almond Grace *Mme M Bollack-Badel* a50 66
2 b f Manduro(GER) King's Folly (FR) (King's Best (USA))
4651a^6 6059a^6
Almost Famous (IRE) *Jamie Osborne* a44 54
2 b c Acclamation Array Of Stars (IRE) (Barathea (IRE))
3853^7 4439^6 4906^6 5610^{10} 6979^6 7198^6 7665^6
Almost Gemini (IRE) *Don Cantillon* a72 70
4 gr g Dylan Thomas(IRE) Streetcar (IRE) (In The Wings)
(1080) (1744) (2980) 5933^7 6942^5 7280^4 7506^3
Almowj *George Jones* a34 41
10 b g Fasliyev(USA) Tiriana (Common Grounds)
4036^6
Almuhalab *Charles Hills* 59
2 bb c Dansili Ghanaati (USA) (Giant's Causeway (USA))
5718^{10}
Al Muheer (IRE) *Ruth Carr* a63 96
8 b g Diktat Dominion Rose (USA) (Spinning World (USA))
1723^9 2078^7 2463^5 ◆ 2665^3 ◆ (3096) 3368^7 3684^{15} 4055^5 4308^3 5014^{16} 5268^8 5613^6 5987^4 6384^5 6496^4 6756^2 6822^4 7031^5
Almuheet *Sir Michael Stoute* 85
2 b c Dansili Arwaah (IRE) (Dalakhani (IRE))
(5244) 6697^6
Al Mukhdam *Peter Chapple-Hyam* 90
3 b g Exceed And Excel(AUS) Sakhya (IRE) (Barathea (IRE))
(1683) ◆ 2259^2 3763^5 4236^7 5886^2 6951^3
Al Muthana (FR) *F-H Graffard* a94 102
2 bb c Pastoral Pursuits Annabelle Ja (FR) (Singspiel (IRE))
4816a^2 5573a^7 6293a^5 7056a^7 7570a^3
Alnawiyah *Charles Hills* 73
3 b f Dalakhani(IRE) Mokaraba (Unfuwain (USA))
3237^5 6997^6
Alnoomaas (IRE) *Luke Dace* a82 82
4 b g Oasis Dream Remarkable Story (Mark Of Esteem (IRE))
(11) 372^3 627^6 812^2 1346^3 2425^7 3018^2 3415^3 3733^8 4235^6 4983^{19} 5398^2 5636^4 6204^8 6403^9 6647^5 7165^4 7444^9
Aloha *Roger Varian* a67 80
3 b f With Approval(CAN) Almamia (Hernando (FR))
2762^2 3820^2 4352^3 (6405)
Aloha Iwanaga (GER) *R Dzubasz*
4 ch f Samum(GER) Anavera (GER) (Acatenango (GER))
7890a^{12}
Along Again (IRE) *Sir Michael Stoute* a79 98
2 b f Elusive City(USA) American Adventure (USA) (Miswaki (USA))
3863^2 (4408) 4742^3
Along Came Casey (IRE) *D K Weld* a100 111
5 b f Oratorio(IRE) Secretariat's Tap (USA) (Pleasant Tap (USA))
3964a^2 4696a^3 6023a^7
Aloof (IRE) *David Wachman* a97 107
4 b f Galileo(IRE) Airwave (Air Express (IRE))
1862a^3 2678a^5 3142a^4 3798a^2 4567a^4 6023a^2 6674a^4
Alo Pura *D Selvaratnam* a103 88
9 b m Anabaa(USA) Rubies From Burma (USA) (Forty Niner (USA))
244a^{12}
Alpe Doloise (FR) *J Phelippon* a68 72
9 b m Marchand De Sable(USA) Clarecastle (IRE) (Caerleon (USA))
5601a^9
Alpetetim *Stuart Kittow* a18 50
4 gr g Proclamation(IRE) Krismick (IRE) (Orpen (USA))
5813^4 6402^{14}
Alpha (USA) *Kiaran McLaughlin* a119
4 b c Bernardini(USA) Munnaya (USA) (Nijinsky (CAN))
556a^{12} 1262a^5 7689a^8
Alphabetique *Peter Chapple-Hyam* a50
2 b f Zamindar(USA) Almamia (Hernando (FR))
8175^6
Alphabet Rap (IRE) *David Barron* 87
2 b g Amadeus Wolf Pearls Of Wisdom (Kyllachy)
5380^3 (6234)
Alpha Delta Whisky *John Gallagher* a77 74
5 ch g Intikhab(USA) Chispa (Imperial Frontier (USA))
(1058) (1467) 1814^6 2550^8 3010^5 4197^6 4712^5 4860^{16} (5796) 6745^5 7634^{14}
Alpha Tauri (USA) *Charles Smith* a80 50
7 b g Aldebaran(USA) Seven Moons (JPN) (Sunday Silence (USA))
645^3 912^2 (965) 986^5 1276^7 2580^4 3024^3 3197^{12} 3660^6 7601^9 7792^5 7948^6 (8230) 8294^6
Alpine Flower (IRE) *Tim Easterby* 66
2 b f Intense Focus(USA) Wine House (IRE) (Sadler's Wells (USA))
3077^2 3280^3
Alpine Mist *Pat Murphy* a63
3 b f Elusive Quality(USA) Snowtime (IRE) (Galileo (IRE))
8444^5
Alpine Mysteries (IRE) *Harry Dunlop* a79 66
3 b f Elusive City(USA) Alpine Gold (IRE) (Montjeu (IRE))
1289^2 1879^3 (3432) 3675^2 4584^6 6109^8 (6996) 7166^2 7510^2 7947^4 8139^6
Alpine Retreat (USA) *Charlie Appleby* a84
2 ch c Distorted Humor(USA) Indy's Windy (USA) (A.P. Indy (USA))
5924^2 6733^6
Alpine Storm (IRE) *Charlie Appleby* a71 64
2 b f Raven's Pass(USA) Lurina (IRE) (Lure (USA))
7103^4 7934^2
Alpinist *J S Bolger* 81
3 b c New Approach(IRE) Alouette (Darshaan)
1558a^5
Alps *David Simcock* 34
2 b f Danehill Dancer(IRE) Mountain Chain (USA) (Royal Academy (USA))
7493^{11}
Alquimia (IRE) *Ed Dunlop* a52 65
2 gr f Medicean Cleide Da Silva (USA) (Monarchos (USA))
3536^6 5352^5 5740^2
Al Raqeeb (IRE) *Gary Harrison* a81 78
3 b g Lawman(FR) Caerlina (IRE) (Caerleon (USA))
(160) 533^3 920^3 5721^5 6642^{12} 7224^{15} 7785^3 8008^5 8345^{11}
Al Saham *Saeed bin Suroor* a94 97
4 b g Authorized(IRE) Local Spirit (USA) (Lion Cavern (USA))
2052^{12} (3208) 4028^4 4765^5 6927^4
Alsahil (USA) *Alan Swinbank* a91 80
7 ch g Diesis Tayibah (IRE) (Sadler's Wells (USA))
1463^{11} 2316^8 2798^6 3480^4 5086^7 5833^{13}
Alsaqi (IRE) *John Butler* a45
3 b g Singspiel(IRE) Oriental Dance (Fantastic Light (USA))
2496^7 2709^7 2952^9 8309^6
Al Senad *Peter Chapple-Hyam* 69
2 ch c Exceed And Excel(AUS) Waafiah (Anabaa (USA))
6569^3 ◆
Alshan Fajer *Roger Ingram* a68 69
3 ch g Lemon Drop Kid(USA) Illuminise (IRE) (Grand Lodge (USA))
396^6 580^8 824^4 1098^2 2156^3 2599^2 3653^3 3820^3 4352^2 7298^{12}
Al Shemali *A Al Raihe* a100 105
9 ch h Medicean Bathilde (IRE) (Generous (IRE))
152a^8 242a^4
Al Shoogh *David Simcock* a66 24
2 b f Nayef(USA) Bakhoor (IRE) (Royal Applause)
7449^{10} 8175^5
Al's Memory (IRE) *David Evans* a93 94
4 b g Red Clubs(IRE) Consensus (IRE) (Common Grounds)
(34) (80) (345) 400^5 629^5 751^2 (844) 947^3 (1160) 1385^3 1720^3 2310^{12} 2460^9 2868^8 3093^{15} 4067^3 (4285) 4472^4 ◆ 4780^{13} 5027^8 5696^{11} 5991^9 6822^5 7080^8 7648^{11} (7949) 8305^3 8369^5
Al Sulaimi (IRE) *Ronald Harris* a53
3 br c Jeremy(USA) Capital Gain (FR) (Bluebird (USA))
491^4 673^3
Alta Lilea (IRE) *Mark Johnston* 103
3 b f Galileo(IRE) In My Life (IRE) (Rainbow Quest (USA))
1623^4 (1761) 2261^4 2879^7 (3834) 3990^7 4286^2 4473^2 4920^3 5779a^3 5993^8 6329^3
Altano (GER) *A Wohler* 116
7 b g Galileo(IRE) Alanda (GER) (Lando (GER))
(2492a) 3483^5 4919^3 6248a^5 (7060a) 7566a^8
Alta Quota (IRE) *G Vizzini* 92
4 ch f Refuse To Bend(IRE) Red Zinger (USA) (Red Ransom (USA))
1563a^4
Altaria *Seamus Durack* a81 33
4 b f Rail Link Costa Rica (IRE) (Sadler's Wells (USA))
7504^{14} 7865^{11}
Alta Stima (IRE) *E Lellouche* 102
3 b f Raven's Pass(USA) En Public (FR) (Rainbow Quest (USA))
6484a^8 6962a^9
Alterite (FR) *Chad C Brown* 113
3 b f Literato(FR) Ana Luna (Dream Well (FR))
2299a^{10} 2693a^2 3385a^6 7708a^3
Al Thakhira *Marco Botti* 110
2 b f Dubawi(IRE) Dahama (Green Desert (USA))
(6500) ◆ (7194) 7690a^{14}
Altharoos (IRE) *Sir Michael Stoute* 97
3 br g Sakhee(USA) Thamara (USA) (Street Cry (IRE))
3020^4 ◆ (4007) 4733^2 5287^8 (6208) ◆ 6537^3
Al Thumama *Kevin Ryan* a49 72
3 b f Byron Tanwir (Unfuwain (USA))
2331^4 (2796) (3735) 4401^5 5483^6
Altnaharra *Jim Goldie* a37 55
4 b g Halling(USA) Gargoyle Girl (Be My Chief (USA))
1279^8 1993^{11} 2971^5 3199^9 4343^2 4951^9 5267^5 5862^8
Altonio (NZ) *Pat Carey* 93
7 b g Savabeel(AUS) Shafty Lady (NZ) (Last Tycoon)
7417a^{11} 7938a^6
Altruistic (IRE) *J P Murtagh* 104
2 ch c Galileo(IRE) Altesse Imperiale (IRE) (Rock Of Gibraltar (IRE))
6884a^3 7528^3
Al Udeid (IRE) *Kevin Ryan* a80 82
3 gr g Verglas(IRE) Gold Strike (IRE) (Rainbow Quest (USA))
1444^4 2190^{11} 3053^2 3582^3 4056^5 4905^2 5537^{11} (5820)
Alumina (IRE) *Andrew Balding* a55 35
2 b f Invincible Spirit(IRE) La Reine Mambo (USA) (High Yield (USA))
7245^8 7638^8 8017^3
Alumna (USA) *A Fabre* a82 109
3 b f Mr Greeley(USA) Alma Mater (Sadler's Wells (USA))
2693a^4 3877a^7 4792a^3
Alutiq (IRE) *Eve Johnson Houghton* a80 99
2 b f Kodiac Marasem (Cadeaux Genereux)
(1421) 2053^3 (2414) 3459^7 4528^5 5680^5 6142^4 6836^7
Al Waab (IRE) *Lady Cecil* 111
3 ch c Danehill Dancer(IRE) Aunt Julia (In The Wings)
1811^6 2812^4 4526^2 5760^2 7049a^9
Always Be Closing *John Quinn* 16
2 b c Sleeping Indian Hiraeth (Petong)
3724^{11} 4538^8
Always Fabulous *Mark Johnston* a44
3 b f Mount Nelson Really Polish (USA) (Polish Numbers (USA))
102^6 324^5 532^6
Always Gentle (IRE) *George Margarson* a14
3 ch f Redback Always Friendly (High Line)
1352^5 1611^8
Always Resolute *Alan Jarvis* a61 57
2 b c Refuse To Bend(IRE) Mad Annie (USA) (Anabaa (USA))
4483^9 6168^9 6635^{12}
Always The Gent *Matthieu Palussiere* 62
2 b c Elnadim(USA) Aunt Susan (Distant Relative)
5362a^5
Alwilda *Sir Mark Prescott Bt* a88 90
3 gr f Hernando(FR) Albanova (Alzao (USA))
3214^4 3908^2 (4899) 5109^3 6196^2 6540^3 7338^9 7650^8

Al Wuseil (FR) *Kevin Ryan* 17
2 ch c Sholokhov(IRE) Lady Kristinne (IRE) (Night Shift (USA))
6513[13]

Alys Love *William Muir* 78
2 b f New Approach(IRE) Porthcawl (Singspiel (IRE))
5740[4] ◆ 6140[2] 6973[2]

Al Zaman Thaman (FR) *Marco Botti* 10
2 b c Nayef(USA) Angie Eria (FR) (Galileo (IRE))
6938[10] 7332[10]

Alzammaar (USA) *Charles Hills* 41
2 b c Birdstone(USA) Alma Mater (Sadler's Wells (USA))
7469[12]

Alzanti (USA) *Amanda Perrett* a77
2 b f Arch(USA) Proud Fact (USA) (Known Fact (USA))
(8084) ◆

Alzavola *Sir Mark Prescott Bt* a58 72
3 gr f With Approval(CAN) Alizadora (Zilzal (USA))
(4657) 4939[3] 5605[5]

Al Zein *Richard Hannon Snr* a52 47
3 b c Notnowcato Luminda (IRE) (Danehill (USA))
1955[6] 2362[7] 2800[6] 3918[6]

Amadaffair *Tom Dascombe* a63 59
2 b f Amadeus Wolf Italian Affair (Fumo Di Londra (IRE))
5350[2] 5593[4] 6013[3] 6474[2] 6605[2] 7202[9] 7882[3]

Amadeus Denton (IRE) *Michael Dods* a63 74
4 b g Amadeus Wolf Wood Sorrel (IRE) (Woodman (USA))
2703[6] 3190[4] 3462[6] 4018[9] 4430[8] 4892[4]

Amadeus Wolfe Tone (IRE) *Jamie Osborne* a100 99
4 b g Amadeus Wolf Slieve (Selkirk (USA))
1542[15] 2046[14] 2444[13] 3367[11] 3973[4] 4440[2] 4677[5] 5437[8]

Amadiva (IRE) *Dean Ivory* a23
2 b f Amadeus Wolf Divine Quest (Kris)
7327[8] 7853[8]

Amahoro *Mick Channon* 77
2 b f Sixties Icon Evanesce (Lujain (USA))
6561[8] (6947) ◆

Amana (USA) *Mark Brisbourne* a68 68
9 b m Diesis Ma-Arif (IRE) (Alzao (USA))
219[9] 429[12] 520[6] 722[2] 789[2] 914[5] 1097[7]

Amanda Wolf (IRE) *James Given* a34 38
3 b f Amadeus Wolf Alexander Phantom (IRE) (Soviet Star (USA))
1114[6] 1329[5] 1687[10]

Amanee (AUS) *M F De Kock* a101 102
5 b m Pivotal Moon Is Up (USA) (Woodman (USA))
154a[13] 366a[DSQ] 836a[8]

Amantius *Johnny Farrelly* a77 50
4 b g Multiplex Ghana (GER) (Bigstone (IRE))
5979[2] (6479) 6558[3] 7379[2] (7735) 7847[4]

Amarillo (IRE) *P Schiergen* 115
4 b c Holy Roman Emperor(IRE) Alte Kunst (IRE) (Royal Academy (USA))
1564a[7] 2202a[4] (3101) 4093a[2] 5804a[4] 7190[2] 7941a[8]

Amaron *Andreas Lowe* 117
4 ch c Shamardal(USA) Amandalini (Bertolini (USA))
1456a[3] 2446[8] 6451a[4] 7047a[13] (7685a)

Amarysia (FR) *C Laffon-Parias* a90 81
3 ch f Medicean Light Quest (USA) (Quest For Fame)
4468a[10] 5361a[10] 6031a[8]

Amaseena (IRE) *Roger Varian* a70 76
2 gr f Shamardal(USA) Indian Belle (IRE) (Indian Ridge)
6690[4] 7102[2] ◆ 7695[8]

Amaze *Brian Ellison* 90
5 ch g Pivotal Dazzle (Gone West (USA))
1237[6] 1840[3] 2191[8] 2478[6] 5055[7] 7131[2] 7312[5]

Amazing Amoray (IRE) *David Barron* 93
5 b g Tagula(IRE) Amistad (GER) (Winged Love (IRE))
(2541) 2858[14]

Amazing Beauty (GER) *M Figge* a96 99
6 ch m Bahamian Bounty Amidala (GER) (Monsagem (USA))
(514a) 701a[5]

Amazing Blue Sky *Ruth Carr* a43 84
7 b g Barathea(IRE) Azure Lake (USA) (Lac Ouimet (USA))
970[4] 1239[12] 1775[9] 2435[9] 2785[4] 2886[9] 3195[3] 3543[4] (3727) 4099[7] 5142[4] 5840[7] 6470[9] 6598[9]

Amazing Maria (IRE) *Ed Dunlop* 106
2 gr f Mastercraftsman(IRE) Messias Da Silva (USA) (Tale Of The Cat (USA))
3664[7] 4484[3] ◆ (4921) (5737)

Amazonas (IRE) *Ed Dunlop* 102
3 b f Cape Cross(IRE) Francesca D'Gorgio (USA) (Proud Citizen (USA))
(5271) 7043a[8]

Amber Heights *Henry Candy* a70 67
5 b f Kyllachy Jumairah Sun (IRE) (Scenic)
(1472) 1957[4] 3042[7] 4034[5] 4487[8] 5104[4] 5447[4]

Amber Isle (USA) *Roger Charlton* 75
2 b f First Defence(USA) Family (USA) (Danzig (USA))
3664[4]

Amberjam (IRE) *Martin Smith* a22
3 b g Duke Of Marmalade(IRE) Makarova (IRE) (Sadler's Wells (USA))
7894[10] 8092[7] 8298[5]

Amberley (FR) *E Moullec* a74 100
4 b g Anabaa(USA) Desert Jewel (USA) (Caerleon (USA))
7995a[3]

Amberley Heights (IRE) *Richard Hannon Snr* 75
3 b f Elnadim(USA) Fawaayid (USA) (Vaguely Noble)
1620[12] 2449[9]

Amber Moon *Ann Stokell* a50 49
8 ch m Singspiel(IRE) Merewood (USA) (Woodman (USA))
845 1931[0] 517[8] 664[2] 805[4] 839[4] 1056[6] 1162[2] 1473[8]

Ambiance (IRE) *Mick Channon* 102
2 b c Camacho Thawrah (IRE) (Green Desert (USA))
2411[11] (2955) 3481[4] (4025) 4572a[6] 4855[3] 5319a[4] 6347[7]

Ambitious Boy *Andrew Hollinshead* a74 83
4 bl g Striking Ambition Cherished Love (IRE) (Tomba)
3733[3] 4884[9] (5273) 6476[6] 6977[2]

Ambitious Dragon (NZ) *A T Millard* 124
7 b g Pins(AUS) Golden Gamble (NZ) (Oregon (USA))
1872a[6]

Ambitious Icarus *Richard Guest* a65 88
4 b g Striking Ambition Nesting Box (Grand Lodge (USA))
885[11] 998[6] 1205[9] 1283[6] 1758[9] 2222[5] 2409[11] 2702[9] 2780[4] 3200[5] 3738[4] 4930[8] (5373) 5708[4] 5832[11] 6052[6] 6287[5] (6603) (6848) 6948[3] ◆ 7314[2] 7777[2]

Ambivalent (IRE) *Roger Varian* a69 111
4 b f Authorized(IRE) Darrery (Darshaan)
2397[2] 3100[3] (3870a) 4985[9] 6253a[2]

Ambleside *Mark Johnston* a68 85
3 b g Cape Cross(IRE) Zarara (USA) (Manila (USA))
799[4] 1009[2] ◆ 1274[2] (1609) 2153[5] 3048[3] 4116[2] 4480[2] 4950[4] (5223) (5549) 5764[11] 5888[2] ◆

Ambria's Fury (IRE) *Mick Channon* a54 61
2 b c Thousand Words Ambria (ITY) (Final Straw)
5244[11] 5472[12] 5950[5] 6152[3] 6474[8] 6749[9] 6983[10] 7630[6]

Ameli (FR) *J Heloury* 84
2 ch f Vatori(FR) Zhuhai (IRE) (Indian Lodge (IRE))
6786a[11] 7653a[9]

Amelia Hull *Karen George* a57 9
3 b f Byron Sweetypie (IRE) (Golan (IRE))
(103) 427[2] 547[3] 1428[6]

Amelia Jay *Danielle McCormick* a54 55
3 b f Avonbridge Rainbow Spectrum (FR) (Spectrum (IRE))
1764[9] 2405[7] 2581[2] 2998[5] (5265) 5336[9] 5788[6] 6682[3] 7079[8] 7508[2] 7904[5] 8118[10]

Amelie Beat (GER) *D Moser* 57
4 b f Electric Beat Adora (GER) (Danehill (USA))
7821[17]

Amen (IRE) *Gary Moore* a57 73
5 b g Galileo(IRE) Kitza (IRE) (Danehill (USA))
816[9] 1060[5] 1325[6]

Amenable (IRE) *Violet M Jordan* a71 80
6 b g Bertolini(USA) Graceful Air (IRE) (Danzero (AUS))
56[6] 232[7] 493[10] 687[10] 806[9] 1088[9] 2170[10] 2832[6] 2997[5] 3190[7] ◆ 3660[4] 4448[4] ◆ (4814) (5047) (5165) 5376[3] 5523[5] 5701[8] 6461[3] 6771[3] 6908[4] 7634[5] 7957[2] 8048[5]

Amen Kitten (USA) *Wesley A Ward* 109
3 b g Kitten's Joy(USA) Crumbs Of Comfort (USA) (Pulpit (USA))
5551a[6] 8120a[3]

American Devil (FR) *J Van Handenhove* 114
4 b c American Post Alcestes Selection (Selkirk (USA))
2897a[6] 3851a[5] 5040a[5] 5806a[10] 7059a[5]

American Kiss (SWE) *Robin Dickin* a39
4 b f American Post Power Kiss (SWE) (Richard Of York)
1070[9] 1371[5] 1611[10] 5429[13]

American Lover (FR) *John Wainwright* a54 48
6 b m American Post Lovarisk (FR) (Take Risks (FR))
41[3] ◆ 192[4] 375[7] 1017[5] 1221[9] 1603[10]

American Spin *Luke Dace* a72 14
9 ch g Groom Dancer(USA) Sea Vixen (Machiavellian (USA))
3560[14]

Amethyst Dawn (IRE) *Alan McCabe* a73 68
7 gr m Act One A L'Aube (IRE) (Selkirk (USA))
728[4] 790[2] 902[4] 1063[2] 1173[3] (1398) 1798[10] 2225[8] 2516[5] 2745[4] 3496[3] 4149[2] 4637[2] 5353[4] 5614[6] 6568[4] 7076[8]

Ametrine (IRE) *William Jarvis* 62
2 b f Fastnet Rock(AUS) Amethyst (IRE) (Sadler's Wells (USA))
7448[4] 7693[5]

Ametyst (DEN) *Bent Olsen*
2 b f Bosun's Watch Pearl Of York (DEN) (Richard Of York)
6452a[3]

Amigo Tonio (FR) *Robert Collet* a74 84
3 b c Falco(USA) Veliana (FR) (Vettori (IRE))
1756a[0]

Aminah *Robert Cowell* a67 67
3 b f Dubawi(IRE) Why Dubai (USA) (Kris S (USA))
2308[12] 2743[2] 3418[9] 5528[2] 6522[4] 6964[6]

Amir Pasha (UAE) *Micky Hammond* a42 58
8 br g Halling(USA) Clarinda (IRE) (Lomond (USA))
1763[12] 2120[3] (2720) 3089[7] 3589[4] 3944[2] 4403[9] 4563[5] 4622[6] 7099[5] 7375[5]

Amisfield Lad *Michael Smith* 21
4 b g Zafeen(FR) Flying Wind (Forzando)
3465[4]

Amis Reunis *Alan Berry* a66 66
4 b f Bahamian Bounty Spring Clean (FR) (Danehill (USA))
162[4] (346) 497[5] 1657[3] 1783[4] 2932[11] 4388[2] 4691[5] 5232[8] 6568[5] 6761[7] 6944[8] 7077[3] 7236[4] 7347[6] 7598[3] 8002[4] 8413[4]

Amnesia (IRE) *William Haggas* 83
2 b f Invincible Spirit(IRE) Applauded (IRE) (Royal Applause)
4215[8] 4912[3] (6034) 6644[9] 7016[7]

Amno Dancer (IRE) *Keith Dalgleish* a53 54
6 b g Namid Special Dancer (Shareef Dancer (USA))
2319[5] 2977[6] 3286[3] 3770[9]

Among Equals *Doug Watson* a74 91
4 b c Oasis Dream First (Highest Honor (FR))
412a[4] 503a[10]

Amontillado (IRE) *Richard Hannon Snr* a60 45
2 b f Pastoral Pursuits Almost Amber (USA) (Mt. Livermore (USA))
2744[5] 3107[12] 7978[10] 8084[4] 8452[6]

Amood (IRE) *Charles Hills* 74
2 ch c Elnadim(USA) Amanah (USA) (Mr Prospector (USA))
5539[3] ◆ 6184[6] 7308[9]

Amosite *J R Jenkins* a78 76
7 b m Central Park(IRE) Waterline Dancer (IRE) (Danehill Dancer (IRE))
271[2] 546[4] (778) 1013[5] 1503[P] (2092) (3111) 3988[7] 5205[4] 5798[3] (7663) 7861[10] 8431[8]

Amoya (GER) *Philip McBride* a50 87
6 b m Royal Dragon(USA) Arkona (GER) (Aspros (GER))
2422[8] 2761[7] 3095[4] 3785[2] 7131[13] 7546[5]

Ampleforth *Ian Williams* a67 76
5 ch g Pivotal Anna Amalia (IRE) (In The Wings)
4754[8] (5409) 5879[2] 6424[5] 7217[7] 7947[6]

Amralah (IRE) *Mick Channon* 96
3 b c Teofilo(IRE) Sharp Mode (USA) (Diesis)
5401[3] 6353[2] (6841) ◆ 7196[9]

Amtired *Marjorie Fife* a70 64
7 gr g Beauchamp King Rising Talisker (Primitive Rising (USA))
(888) 970[2] 989[2] 2961[4] 3301[6] 7881[11] 8360[2]

Amulet *Eve Johnson Houghton* a71 90
3 gr f Ishiguru(USA) Loveofmylife (Dr Fong (USA))
5152[8] (6153) 6735[2] (7130) (7505) 7632[4] 7822[6]

Amy Farah Fowler (IRE) *Ian Williams* a41 43
4 b f Oratorio(IRE) Fay (IRE) (Polish Precedent (USA))
4999[5] 6019[5] 6804[7] 6919[8]

Anaconda (FR) *Tom Dascombe* a105 69
4 b g Anabaa(USA) Porretta (IRE) (Indian Ridge)
(407) 7014[16] 7540[7] (7926)

Ana Emaratiya *A Al Raihe* a75 80
3 b f Sleeping Indian Vale Of Belvoir (IRE) (Mull Of Kintyre (USA))
243a[6] 553a[15]

Anaerobio (ARG) *M F De Kock* a81 108
6 b h Catcher In The Rye(IRE) Potra Anala (ARG) (Potrillon (ARG))
154a[3] 242a[5] ◆ 462a[6] 657a[2] (838a)

Anaita (GER) *P Harley* 81
4 b f Dubawi(IRE) Aliette (FR) (Lando (GER))
7233a[11]

Anan *Kevin Morgan* 40
7 br g Cape Cross(IRE) Hawafiz (Nashwan (USA))
2218[6]

Ana Shababiya (IRE) *Ismail Mohammed* a74 65
3 ch f Teofilo(IRE) Call Later (USA) (Gone West (USA))
5072[4] (5615) 6406[2] 7204[4] (7667) 7961[7]

Anatol Artist (GER) *J Hirschberger* 98
3 b c Doyen(IRE) Anna Spectra (IRE) (Spectrum (IRE))
1708a[6]

Anatolian *Mahmood Al Zarooni* 108
5 ch g Pivotal Poseidon's Bride (USA) (Seeking The Gold (USA))
(246a) (661a)

Anaxis (FR) *S Wattel* a98 103
6 ch g Muhtathir Monadis (USA) (Miswaki (USA))
(125a) 960a[3]

Anazone (IRE) *F Rossi* a99 106
3 gr f Anabaa(USA) Ozone Bere (FR) (Verglas (IRE))
(7316a)

An Cat Dubh (IRE) *Nicky Vaughan* a80 83
4 b g One Cool Cat(USA) Bella Estella (GER) (Sternkoenig (IRE))
1746[3] 2646[4] 3094[10] 3570[6] 4250[6]

An Chulainn (IRE) *Mark Johnston* a73 81
2 ch f Tamayuz Livius Lady (IRE) (Titus Livius (FR))
5105[4] 5421[4] 5773a[3] 6141[3] 6581[4] (7790)

Ancient Cross *Michael Easterby* a73 106
9 b g Machiavellian(USA) Magna Graecia (IRE) (Warning)
1232[16] 1607[5] (2396) 2669[12] 3558[16] 3776[2] 4275[13] 5651[13] 6391[7] (6621) 7208[7] 7495[20]

Ancient Greece *George Baker* a83 83
6 b g Pivotal Classicism (USA) (A.P. Indy (USA))
79[4] (513a) (609a) (702a) 1849[4] 2380a[3] 4879[4] 5310[6]

Ancient King (IRE) *S Botti* 100
3 b c Ramonti(FR) Queen Of Rap (IRE) (Alhaarth (IRE))
2490a[3]

Ancient Sands (IRE) *Ms Joanna Morgan* a82 98
5 b g Footstepsinthesand Antiguan Wells (IRE) (Sadler's Wells (USA))
7723a[7]

Anderiego (IRE) *David O'Meara* 101
5 b g Invincible Spirit(IRE) Anna Frid (GER) (Big Shuffle (USA))
1235[21] 2029[2] ◆ 2399[3] 3527[24] 4308[8] 5681[8] 6025a[12] 6396[7] 7172[13]

Anderton (IRE) *Richard Fahey* 75
3 b g Invincible Spirit(IRE) Alarme Belle (Warning)
1722[3] 2317[5]

Andhesontherun (IRE) *Roger Varian* a81 95
2 b c Captain Rio Harvest Joy (IRE) (Daggers Drawn (USA))
(2497) 2809[2] 3424[12] (4434) 4918[8]

Andiamo Via *Brian Ellison* a13 51
6 b g Mujahid(USA) Efizia (Efisio)
5711[6] 6464[8] 8233[9]

Andi'Amu (FR) *C Ferland* a70
3 b g Walk In The Park(IRE) Sainte Parfaite (FR) (Septieme Ciel (USA))
3129a[8]

Andolini (GER) *A Wohler* 104
4 bb c Kallisto(GER) Auenpracht (GER) (General Assembly (USA))
2822a[7] 3879a[7] 5778a[4]

Andreas (GER) *Markus Klug* 102
4 ch c Dr Fong(USA) Annouche (GER) (Unfuwain (USA))
6248a[7]

Andrina (IRE) *H J Groschel* 80
2 b f Tertullian(USA) Algoma (GER) (Monsun (GER))
5939a[7]

Android (IRE) *Clive Cox* 23
2 ch g Dandy Man(IRE) Noble View (USA) (Distant View (USA))
5757[5]

Anducas (FR) *G Henrot* a76 85
4 ch g Rock Of Gibraltar(IRE) Anna Mona (GER) (Monsun (GER))
5735a[13]

Andy Dandy (IRE) *Tom Dascombe* a73 60
2 b c Dandy Man(IRE) Chimay (IRE) (Kris Kin (USA))
2712[6] (5675) 6934[2]

Aneedh *Jedd O'Keeffe* a76 79
3 b g Lucky Story(USA) Seed Al Maha (USA) (Seeking The Gold (USA))
1891[2] (2507) 3062[5] 3995[5] 4672[3] (4940) 6051[2] 6601[2]

Anfield *Mick Quinn* a56 50
2 b f Captain Gerrard(IRE) Billie Holiday (Fairy King (USA))
1749[4] 1910[5] 2740[8] 3217[4] 4451[2] 5066[2] 5648[3] 6073[6] 6967[4] 7665[3] 8058[3] 8273[4] 8435[3]

Angela's Dream (IRE) *G M Lyons* a90 88
3 b f Chineur(FR) Church Mice (IRE) (Petardia)
3845a[9]

Angel Cake (IRE) *Michael Appleby* a72 52
4 b f Dark Angel(IRE) Royal Jelly (King's Best (USA))
4070[8] (4834) (5072) 5354[5] 6210[9] 6702[10] 7383[8] 7876[8] 8008[7]

Angelena Ballerina (IRE) *Sean Curran* a62 70
6 ch m Indian Haven Nom Francais (First Trump)
456[2] 522[6] 625[2] 852[3] (1070) 1298[6] 1730[2] 1987[2]

Angel Flores (IRE) *Richard Fahey* a72 69
2 b f Art Connoisseur(IRE) Emmas Princess (IRE) (Bahhare (USA))
7078[2] 7592[2] (8091)

Angel Gabrial (IRE) *Ian Williams* a77 96
4 b g Hurricane Run(IRE) Causeway Song (USA) (Giant's Causeway (USA))
1273[11] 1728[2] ◆ (2251) 3115[10] 4060[16] 4310[6]

Angel Grigio *David O'Meara* a49 36
3 gr f Dark Angel(IRE) Owdbetts (IRE) (High Estate)
5184[9] 5864[6] 6604[12] 7904[4] ◆ 8142[11] 8293[6] 8412[10]

Angelic Air *John Gosden* 77
2 b f Oasis Dream Innocent Air (Galileo (IRE))
7692[3] ◆

Angelic Upstart (IRE) *Andrew Balding* a87 83
5 b g Singspiel(IRE) Rada (IRE) (Danehill (USA))
6[5] 272[5] 4243[3] (4960) 5825[2] 6694[4] 7131[7]

Angelito *Ed McMahon* a78 86
4 ch g Primo Valentino(IRE) Supreme Angel (Beveled (USA))
2031[2] ◆ 2755[6] 4123[2] 4620[5] 5832[8] 6822[3] 7731[5] 7959[3]

Angelo Poliziano *Jo Hughes* a75 79
7 ch g Medicean Helen Sharp (Pivotal)
727[3] (1101) 1283[10] 1431[4] 1694[8] 8230[3] 8365[2] 8406[7]

Angelot Du Berlais (FR) *Dr Richard Newland* a67 86
4 b g Poliglote Afragha (IRE) (Darshaan)
6557[8]

Angel Rosa *Keith Dalgleish* 62
2 b f Multiplex Rosi Quest (Rainbow Quest (USA))
(2793) 4108[4] 5136[7] 5235[3] 5703[5] 6085[5] 6465[4] 6726[7]

Angels Calling *K R Burke* a57 64
3 b f Multiplex Angel Voices (IRE) (Tagula (IRE))
1011[4] 1476[5] 1906[2] 2512[8] 2916[4] 3216[6] 4410[8] 4722[2] (4916) 5644[6] 6698[3] 7148[5] 7512[10]

Angel Spirit (IRE) *Matthieu Palussiere* 87
2 b f Invincible Spirit(IRE) Fleche Brisee (USA) (Dynaformer (USA))
3752a[5]

Angel's Pursuit (IRE) *David Marnane* a92 91
6 ch g Pastoral Pursuits Midnight Angel (Machiavellian (USA))
2676a[15] 3846a[26]

Angels Will Fall (IRE) *Charles Hills* a93 106
4 b f Acclamation Coconut Squeak (Bahamian Bounty)
1637[7] 2019[15] 2368[16] 3102[4] 3420[17] 5651[11] (6391) ◆ 6639[6] 7021[5] 7227a[2] 7521a[3]

Angel Way (IRE) *Mike Murphy* a79 80
4 br f Trans Island Zilayah (USA) (Zilzal (USA))
2745[7] 3691[2] 4389[6] 5036[2] (5441) 5956[5] 6652[4]

Angilina *Kevin Ryan* a41 52
3 b f Teofilo(IRE) Finnmark (Halling (USA))
2175[4] 2716[15]

Anginola (IRE) *Laura Mongan* a56 64
4 b f Kodiac Lady Montekin (Montekin)
3056[4] 4355[2] 4411[5] (5123) 5854[8] 6458[9] 6737[10]

Angleterre (FR) *Richard Hannon Snr* 73
2 b f Pivotal Ailette (Second Set (IRE))
4921[4] 5716[5]

Anglo Irish *John Gosden* a75
2 b c Dansili Tebee (Selkirk (USA))
8340[3]

Anglophile *Charlie Appleby* a59 81
2 ch g Dubawi(IRE) Anna Palariva (IRE) (Caerleon (USA))
3689[7] 4662[2] (5122) (5951) ◆ 7471[4]

Angola (AUS) *Pat Carey* 85
5 b g Helenus(AUS) Nyasa (AUS) (Don't Say Halo (USA))
7417a[7] 7827a[12]

Angry Kitten (USA) *Gianluca Bietolini* a70 94
3 b c Kitten's Joy(USA) Spine Tingling (USA) (Devil His Due (USA))
7188a[18]

Angus Glens *David Dennis* 80
3 gr g Dalakhani(IRE) Clara Bow (IRE) (Sadler's Wells (USA))
4590[5] 5495[3] 6062[4] ◆ 6743[5] 7257[4]

Angus Mac Og (IRE) *Nigel Tinkler*
2 b g Elnadim(USA) Banba (IRE) (Docksider (USA))
3298[13] 5834[6] 6206[12] 6494[10]

Angus Og *K R Burke* a83 89
3 b g Pastoral Pursuits Winter Moon (Mujadil (USA))
1844[2] 2083[3] 2708[6] 3591[8] 4112[2] 5057[3] (5340) 6583[19] 7373[6]

Animal Kingdom (USA) *H Graham Motion* a124 123
5 ch c Leroidesanimaux(BRZ) Dalicia (GER) (Acatenango (GER))
(1269a) 3419[11]

Anipa *Ed Dunlop* a71 74
2 ch f Sea The Stars(IRE) Anna Amalia (IRE) (In The Wings)
4491[7] 5279[3] 5988[2] 6688[4]

Anjaal *Richard Hannon Snr* 110
2 ch c Bahamian Bounty Ballymore Celebre (IRE) (Peintre Celebre (USA))
2048[8] (3077) (4212) ◆ 7192[4]

Anjin (IRE) *Sir Mark Prescott Bt* a51
2 b c Danehill Dancer(IRE) Twyla Tharp (IRE) (Sadler's Wells (USA))
8425[11]

Anjuna Beach (USA) *Gary Moore* a70 61
3 b c Artie Schiller(USA) Hidden Temper (USA) (Miswaki (USA))
2727[11] 2935[10] 3528[8] 7446[10] 7857[7] 8388[6]

Annaley My Darling (IRE) *Mark Rimmer* a67
3 b f Shamardal(USA) Unreal (Dansili)
1051[3] 1216[3] 1906[5] 2135[8] 2873[3] 3134[11] 3639[4]

Annalova *Richard Fahey* a41 27
3 b f Araafa(IRE) Danalova (Groom Dancer (USA))
310[7] 507[6] 2341[9] 2716[13]

Annaluna (IRE) *David Evans* a57 62
4 b f Whipper(USA) Annaletta (Belmez (USA))
2922[4] (3884)

Anna's Arch (IRE) *Alan Swinbank* a79 72
6 b g Arch(USA) Lady Angharad (IRE) (Tenby)
(1454)

Anna's Pearl *Ralph Beckett* 110
3 ch c Pivotal Mi Anna (GER) (Lake Coniston (IRE))
1621[10] (3278) 3876a[10] 6191[8] 6624[10] 7247[5]

Anna's Vision (IRE) *Jeremy Noseda* a65
2 b f Invincible Spirit(IRE) House In Wood (FR) (Woodman (USA))
7294[4] ◆

Annawi *Henry Candy* 86
3 b f Dubawi(IRE) Anna Of Brunswick (Rainbow Quest (USA))
4500[3] 5038[4] 5942[3] (6531)

Annecdote *Jonathan Portman* 106
3 b f Lucky Story(USA) May Fox (Zilzal (USA))
2195[6] (2449) (3460) 4705[4] (4949) 6327[4]

Annelko *Michael Blake* a67 64
6 b g Sulamani(IRE) Creeking (Persian Bold)
53[2] 520[4]

Annes Rocket (IRE) *Jimmy Fox* a63 78
8 b h Fasliyev(USA) Aguilas Perla (IRE) (Indian Ridge)
2255[19] 3315[4] 3955[7] 4685[9] 5404[2] 6096[3] 6606[5] 6937[9] 7652[4] 7858[7] 8087[8]

Anne's Valentino *Malcolm Jefferson* a4 36
3 b f Primo Valentino(IRE) Annie's Gift (IRE) (Presenting)
5071[11] 5484[9] 6566[6] 7376[7] 8229[9]

Annia Galeria (IRE) *John Berry* a54 34
6 b m Antonius Pius(USA) Jay Gee (IRE) (Second Set (IRE))
2747[11] 3026[12]

Annie Besant *Michael Mullineaux* a49 49
3 ch f Sir Percy Caribana (Hernando (FR))
2345[6] 2770[7] 3509[8] 5512[5] 6154[11] 6361[11]

Annie Gogh *Tim Easterby* a61 66
3 b f Dutch Art Spunger (Fraam)
2241[2] 2756[6] 3082[8] 3281[7] 4114[5] 4544[6] 5916[2] 6180[9] 6655[5] 6843[4] 7354[3]

Annie's Fortune (IRE) *Alan Jarvis* 100
3 b f Montjeu(IRE) Semaphore (Zamindar (USA))
2429[7] 3460[25] 4078[8]

Annie's Rose *Bryan Smart* a52 55
2 b f Captain Gerrard(IRE) Annie Harvey (Fleetwood (IRE))
5638[4] 5900[2] 6627[8] 6967[8] 8300[5]

Annina (IRE) *Henry Candy* 86
3 b f Singspiel(IRE) Lysandra (IRE) (Danehill (USA))
6356[8] ◆ 6767[7] 7699[7]

Announcement *Karen Tutty* 73
2 ch f Proclamation(IRE) Anapola (GER) (Polish Precedent (USA))
(3624)

Annunciation *Richard Hannon Snr* a100 103
3 b c Proclamation(IRE) Rockburst (Xaar)
999a[7] (1112) 2039[7] 2621[6] 4058[4] (5260) 5844[4]

Anodin (IRE) *F Head* 109
3 b c Anabaa(USA) Born Gold (USA) (Blushing Groom (FR))
2298a[7] (3128a) 3876a[7] 6450a[3] 7059a[7]

Anomaly *Charlie Appleby* a39 99
4 ch g Pivotal Anna Palariva (IRE) (Caerleon (USA))
5283[8] 6163[5] 6927[7]

Another Citizen (IRE) *Tim Easterby* a81 82
5 b g Byron Royal Rival (IRE) (Marju (IRE))
1431[3] (1649) 1807[9] 2268[6] 3505[2] 4479[11] 5294[12]

Another Claret *Richard Fahey* a31 72
3 b g Avonbridge Sylvan (IRE) (Shinko Forest (IRE))
1450[5] 1829[11] 2556[3] 3025[9] 3730[10] 4544[9]

Another Cocktail *Hughie Morrison* a81 98
3 b g Dalakhani(IRE) Yummy Mummy (Montjeu (IRE))
(1478) 1767[2] 2262[4] 3486[5] 4279[5] 6186[13]

Another For Joe *Jim Goldie* 80
5 b g Lomitas Anna Kalinka (GER) (Lion Cavern (USA))
1831[8] 2220[7] 2976[2] 3204[6] 3464[4] 4101[3] 4746[11] 5332[4] 5918[6] 6548[4] 7152[12] 7498[10]

Another Journey *Lisa Williamson* a39
4 b g Rail Link Singasongosixpence (Singspiel (IRE))
8141[4] 8260[7]

Another Name (IRE) *Paul Cole* a55 38
3 b g Red Clubs(IRE) Pure Gold (Dilum (USA))
3898[4] 6113[4] 6366[8] 7465[5]

Another Party (FR) *Matthieu Palussiere* 106
2 ch c Pomellato(GER) Jummana (FR) (Cadeaux Genereux)
3875a[2] 4572a[7] 5082a[3] 6293a[2] 7056a[8] 7184a[3] 7939a[4]

Another Royal *Tim Easterby* 59
2 b f Byron Royal Punch (Royal Applause)
2751[8] 3826[3] 4539[6] 4965[6] 5703[3] 6285[3] 7096[3]

Another Squeeze *Peter Hiatt* a46 55
5 gr f Proclamation(IRE) Tight Squeeze (Petoski)
2534[10] 4241[4] 4711[4] 5126[3] 5434[3] ◆ 5934[6] 6097[5]

Another Try (IRE) *Alan Jarvis* a84 90
8 b g Spinning World(USA) Mad Annie (USA) (Anabaa (USA))
1922[10] 2664[10] 2868[12] 3980[5] 4440[4] 5219[5] ◆ 5928[9] 7106[2] ◆ 7444[4] 7896[8] 8157[10]

Another Wise Kid (IRE) *Paul Midgley* 93
5 b g Whipper(USA) Romancing (Dr Devious (IRE))
1232[6] 1807[6] 2007[3] 3299[8] 3682[5] (4507) 4800[16] 5108[10] 5519[11] 6699[9]

Anrheg *Dai Burchell* a43 35
5 b f Diktat Dim Ots (Alhijaz)
630[8] 915[7] 1521[11] 1664[11] 1974[6] 2360[9]

Ansaab *Kevin Prendergast* a89 100
5 b g Cape Cross(IRE) Dawn Raid (IRE) (Docksider (USA))
1168a[10]

An Saighdiur (IRE) *Andrew Slattery* a99 104
6 b g Acclamation Brief Sentiment (IRE) (Brief Truce (USA))
1255a[6] 3846a[17] 5019a[4] 6621[3] 7208[12] 7527[9]

Ansells Pride (IRE) *Bill Turner* a63 72
10 b g King Charlemagne(USA) Accounting (Sillery (USA))
4520[7] 5523[7]

Ansgar (IRE) *Sabrina J Harty* a99 109
5 b g Celtic Swing Jemmy's Girl (IRE) (Pennekamp (USA))
1034[8] 3142a[8] (3869a) 4869a[17] 5453a[2] 6025a[4] 6440a[2] 7190[7]

An Spailpin Fanach (USA) *Paul Midgley* a57 69
6 ch g Purge(USA) Wild Crazy Lady (USA) (Touch Gold (USA))
5840[14]

Anticipated (IRE) *Richard Hannon Snr* 106
2 b c Whipper(USA) Foreplay (IRE) (Lujain (USA))
(1580) ◆ (1917) ◆ 3424[3] 4572a[5] 4855[2] 5573a[9] 6637[6] 7026[7] 7534[11]

Antioch (IRE) *Pam Sly*
2 b g Papal Bull Sharadja (IRE) (Doyoun)
7955[9]

Antious (ARG) *David Marnane* 94
6 ch g Pure Prize(USA) Adira (USA) (Affirmed (USA))
2676a[13] 3848a[9]

Anton (IRE) *Mme Pia Brandt* a76
5 b g Antonius Pius(USA) Seasonal Pleasure (USA) (Graustark (USA))
127a[3]

Anton Chigurh *Tom Dascombe* a87 94
4 b g Oasis Dream Barathiki (Barathea (IRE))
1168a[20] 3825[9] 5546[8] 5838[10] 6989[5] 7337[5] 7536[4]

Anton Dolin (IRE) *Dr Richard Newland* a80 87
5 ch g Danehill Dancer(IRE) Ski For Gold (Shirley Heights)
6217[5]

Antonio Gramsci *David Barron* a56 86
3 b g Misu Bond(IRE) La Corujera (Case Law)
829[3] 964[5] (1988) 2408[2] (2987) 3320[5] 4117[6]

Antonius *Kristin Stubbs* a43 57
3 b g Antonius Pius(USA) Queen Of Poland (FR) (Polish Precedent (USA))
1772[11] 2274[14]

Anya *Ed Walker* a80 82
4 b f Monsieur Bond(IRE) Dyanita (Singspiel (IRE))
3215[3] 3864[5] 6359[4]

Anya's Angel *David Simcock* 37
2 b f Holy Roman Emperor(IRE) Someone's Angel (USA) (Runaway Groom (CAN))
2744[7] 3217[6] 3663[12]

Any Given Dream (IRE) *Lee Carter* a72
4 b g Bahri(USA) Anazara (USA) (Trempolino (USA))
1059[9]

Anytimeatall (IRE) *Alan Bailey* a58 63
2 b f Kodiac Under My Skin (IRE) (Mark Of Esteem (IRE))
2189[8] 3510[3] 4142[2] 5106[2] 5595[7] (6073) 6320[5] 6967[9] 7771[4] 7900[5] 8228[7]

Anzi Star (FR) *D Guillemin* a64
2 b f Anzillero(GER) L'Eclipse Francaise (FR) (Jeune Homme (USA))
8354a[6]

Aolida (FR) *F Chappet* a69 74
3 b f Anabaa(USA) Comete (FR) (Jeune Homme (USA))
126a[7]

Aomen Rock *James Fanshawe* a73 63
3 b g Rock Of Gibraltar(IRE) Siren Sound (Singspiel (IRE))
5845[6] 6555[2] 6950[5] 7629[5] 8063[4] 8313[2]

Aotearoa (USA) *Leonard Powell* a80 100
2 ch g Good Journey(USA) Madera Royal (USA) (Lil Tyler (USA))
7688a[7]

Aouasif (IRE) *E Lellouche* a78 80
3 ch c Shirocco(GER) Greta Road (FR) (Grape Tree Road)
7412a[2]

Apache (IRE) *Jane Chapple-Hyam* a94 93
5 b g Galileo(IRE) Charroux (IRE) (Darshaan)
1382[6] ◆ 2044[8] 3099[5] ◆ 3423[14]

Apache Glory (USA) *John Stimpson* a71 83
5 bb f Cherokee Run(USA) Jumeirah Glory (USA) (Deputy Minister (CAN))
147[3] 477[7] 709[5] 921[3] ◆ (1082) (1381) (1775) 2311[2] 3083[2] 3204[11] 6936[9] 8179[8]

Apache Rising *Bryan Smart* a80 68
3 ch g Sleeping Indian Distant Music (Darshaan)
(623) 826[3] (1206) ◆ (1330) 1577[5] 1991[7] 5870[3] 6301[10] 6602[3]

Apache Spirit *A Fabre* 90
2 b c Invincible Spirit(IRE) Agathe Rare (IRE) (Sadler's Wells (USA))
5313a[5]

Aphrodite's Dream *Derek Shaw* a12
3 b f Manduro(GER) Trick Of Ace (USA) (Clever Trick (USA))
2331[8]

Aphrodite Spirit (IRE) *Pat Eddery* a52 47
3 b f Key Of Luck(USA) Rosewater (GER) (Winged Love (IRE))
527[5] 804[2] 1326[4] 1897[8] 3432[2] 3820[4] 4352[6] 5178[4] 5934[5] 6103[4] 6491[9] 7104[P] (Dead)

Apisata (GER) *Mervyn Torrens* a52 53
4 b f Mamool(IRE) Api Sa (IRE) (Zinaad)
5021a[7]

Apollo D'Negro (IRE) *Clive Cox* a84 85
5 br g Fasliyev(USA) Special One (Aragon)
(2128) 2255[5] 2725[4] 3415[8] 3720[3] 4235[4] 4746[3] 4983[22] 7264[4] (7742) 7992[4]

Apollon D'Olivate (FR) *P Van De Poele* a82 88
3 b g Epalo(GER) Saintete (FR) (Saint Des Saints (FR))
2434a[0]

Apolskapart (IRE) *Michael Smith* a55 51
5 b g Red Ransom(USA) Polska (USA) (Danzig (USA))
3947[7]

Apostle (IRE) *David Simcock* a95 68
4 gr g Dark Angel(IRE) Rosy Dudley (IRE) (Grand Lodge (USA))
6384[10] 6826[11] (7436) 7769[7] 7992[7] 8217[2]

Apparently *Charlie Appleby* a80 78
3 b c New Approach(IRE) Illustrious Miss (USA) (Kingmambo (USA))
3923[2] ◆ 5064[5] 5484[6] 6313[2]

Appease *Richard Hannon Snr* a77 84
4 b g Oasis Dream Penchee (Grand Lodge (USA))
(6555) 6898[2]

Appellez Baileys (FR) *Chris Dwyer* a37
2 b c Halling(USA) Bitza Baileys (IRE) (Zamindar (USA))
8342[12]

Appleby (GER) *S Smrczek* a91 96
5 b c Mamool(IRE) Almudena (GER) (Law Society (USA))
125a[5]

Applejack Lad *John Ryan* a78 64
2 ch g Three Valleys(USA) Fittonia (FR) (Ashkalani (IRE))
1749[7] 7467[8] (7780) 7925[4] 8426[2] 8452[4]

Application *Bryan Smart* 44
2 ch g Major Cadeaux Choisette (Choisir (AUS))
5482[12] 6829[13]

Appointee (IRE) *Robert Cowell* a95 88
4 b f Exceed And Excel(AUS) Anna Wi'Yaak (JPN) (Dubai Millennium)
4217[11] 4677[4] 5308[8] 6135[12] 7445[10]

Approach The West (IRE) *James Tate* 73
2 b f New Approach(IRE) Damsel (Danzero (AUS))
6256[4] (6754)

Appyjack *Tony Carroll* a51 40
5 b g Royal Applause Petrikov (IRE) (In The Wings)
4350[9] 5171[8] 6097[6] 6399[4] 6851[8] 7644[3] 7962[2] 8065[9] 8279[7]

Apricot Sky *Henry Candy* a70 78
3 ch g Pastoral Pursuits Miss Apricot (Indian Ridge)
2051[5] (2499) 6744[5]

April Ciel *Ronald Harris* a64 73
4 b g Septieme Ciel(USA) By Definition (IRE) (Definite Article)
1586[9] (1948) 2348[2] 2826[4] 2923[2] 3273[5] 3917[7] 5479[6] 5855[7] 6325[5] (6491) 6898[14] 8060[9] 8270[14]

April Fool *Ronald Harris* a87 87
9 ch g Pivotal Palace Affair (Pursuit Of Love)
34[4] 221[4]

Apsis Dream (FR) *T Castanheira* a78 48
2 b c Apsis Vestale Bleue (Anabaa (USA))
2433a[7]

Aptitude *Tobias B P Coles* a48
2 ch f With Approval(CAN) Moi Aussi (USA) (Mt. Livermore (USA))
7902[9] 8026[7] 8114[5]

Aqlaam Vision *Clive Brittain* 95
2 b f Aqlaam Dream Vision (USA) (Distant View (USA))
2419[3] 2869[2] 4877[7] 5951[2] (6326) 6644[6] 7016[6] (7537)

Aqua Ardens (GER) *George Baker* a81 76
5 b g Nayef(USA) Arduinna (GER) (Winged Love (IRE))
493[3] 1366[7] 1681[13] (3015) (3926) 4426[2] 5124[3] 6701[4] 8314[2] 8453[2]

Aquarian Spirit *Richard Fahey* a81 78
6 b g Fantastic Light(USA) Notable Lady (IRE) (Victory Note (USA))
1292[6] 1788[9] 2278[13] 3395[5] 3727[6]

Aquatinta (GER) *Clive Cox* 104
3 b f Samum(GER) Arpista (GER) (Chief Singer)
1358a[7] 1869a[6] 4792a[5] 6000[8]

Aquilifer (IRE) *Mrs K Burke* a79 56
5 b g Holy Roman Emperor(IRE) Sassy Bird (USA) (Storm Bird (CAN))
370[6]

Aquilla (IRE) *David Simcock* 99
4 b f Teofilo(IRE) Dance Troupe (Rainbow Quest (USA))
5038[3] (6498) 7189a[3]

Aquilonius (IRE) *Stuart Williams* a94 88
4 b c Soviet Star(USA) Via Verbano (IRE) (Caerleon (USA))
6[2] 273[7] 495[8] (585) 865[3] 1037[3] 1159[2] 1382[4] 2251[9] 2867[8] 3607[6] 4075[2] (4407) 5302[2] (6066)

Araajmh (USA) *James Tate*
3 b f Street Cry(IRE) Rajeem (Diktat)
1291[10]

Arabda *Mark Johnston* 66
2 bb f Elnadim(USA) Ghizlaan (USA) (Seeking The Gold (USA))
(2612) 3522[19] 4134[4] 7147[7]

Arab Dawn *Hughie Morrison* a64 51
2 gr c Dalakhani(IRE) Victoire Celebre (USA) (Stravinsky (USA))
6355[10] 6953[11] 7460[7]

Arabela (IRE) *James Unett* a65 64
4 ch f Medicean Arameen (IRE) (Halling (USA))
(921) 2982[5]

Arabian Beauty (IRE) *Saeed bin Suroor* 73
2 b f Shamardal(USA) Express Way (ARG) (Ahmad (ARG))
7103[8] 7493[2]

Arabian Comet (IRE) *Charlie Appleby* a65 67
2 b f Dubawi(IRE) Aviacion (BRZ) (Know Heights (IRE))
5131[5] 6063[5] 6597[7]

Arabian Flight *Michael Appleby* a71 44
4 b f Exceed And Excel(AUS) Emirates First (IRE) (In The Wings)
98[2] 347[3] 435[2] 587[4] 705[3] 813[5] 1054[5] 1211[5] 4357[6] 4834[2] 5596[8] 5903[2] 6276[13] 6553[5] (7124) 7354[4] (8315)

Arabian Heights *Anthony Middleton* a37 57
5 gr g Araafa(IRE) Makhsusah (IRE) (Darshaan)
4683[7]

Arabian Music (IRE) *David Simcock* a59
2 b f Kheleyf(USA) Areyaam (USA) (Elusive Quality (USA))
8083[6] 8332[8] 8451[5] ◆

Arabian Star (IRE) *Alan McCabe* a61 97
5 b g Green Desert(USA) Kassiopeia (IRE) (Galileo (IRE))
4308[13] 5285[11] 5613[3] 6288[12] 6984[4] 7651[11]

Arabian Sunset (IRE) *Brendan Powell* 48
2 b f Dubawi(IRE) Summer Sunset (IRE) (Grand Lodge (USA))
5529[13] 6408[3] 6973[9] 7394[6]

Arable *Charles Hills* 71
2 ch c Three Valleys(USA) Cut Corn (King's Theatre (IRE))
5957[11] 6762[7]

Arabougg *Nikki Evans* a33
3 b g Tobougg(IRE) Arabellas Homer (Mark Of Esteem (IRE))
102[7] 479[5] 904[6]

Arab Spring (IRE) *Sir Michael Stoute* 95
3 b c Monsun(GER) Spring Symphony (IRE) (Darshaan)
2384[2]

Arachnophobia (IRE) *Martin Bosley* a63 51
7 b g Redback La Mata (IRE) (Danehill Dancer (IRE))
223[2] 665[4] 1426[7] 4623[8] 7124[5] 7643[6]

Aragorn Rouge *Keith Dalgleish* a80 75
5 b g Aragorn(IRE) Red Top (IRE) (Fasliyev (USA))
61[3] 192[2] 218[3] 546[5]

Aragosta *James Fanshawe* 72
3 ch f Pivotal Langoustine (AUS) (Danehill (USA))
2519[3] ◆

Araldo *Michael Moroney* 112
5 b c High Chaparral(IRE) Alanda (GER) (Lando (GER))
7700a[3]

Aramadyh *James Tate* a72 31
2 gr f Authorized(IRE) Swift Dispersal (Shareef Dancer (USA))
5968[8] 6365[4] (6999)

Aramist (IRE) *Alan Swinbank* 78
3 gr g Aussie Rules(USA) Mistic Sun (Dashing Blade)
1845[4] 2538[4] 2754[4] 6301[4] (6686) 7242[4]

Arango (GER) *S Smrczek* 102
3 b c Dai Jin Autriche (IRE) (Acatenango (GER))
6248a[3]

Aran Sky (IRE) *K R Burke* 70
2 b g Arakan(USA) Fayr Sky (IRE) (Fayruz)
6754[4] 7817[9]

Arantes *Mick Channon* a78 76
2 b c Sixties Icon Black Opal (Machiavellian (USA))
5698[7] 6355[2] 6773[3] 7162[2] 7513[2]

Araqella (IRE) *William Haggas* a82 73
3 b f Oasis Dream Bourbonella (Rainbow Quest (USA))
(5618) 6106[2] 6657[3] (7876) 8020[2]

Arashi *Derek Shaw* a74 72
7 b g Fantastic Light(USA) Arriving (Most Welcome)
592[5] 709[10] 883[5] (1060) (2087) 2545[4] 2980[4] (3473) 4166[5] 8060[8] 8130[5] 8308[11]

Arbaab *Sir Michael Stoute* 70
2 br c Dynaformer(USA) Kaseema (USA) (Storm Cat (USA))
6739[7] 7339[3]

Arbaah (USA) *Brian Meehan* a75 86
3 b f Invasor(ARG) Alshadiyah (USA) (Danzig (USA))
1671[5] ◆ (1955) 2390[2] 2846[2] (3783) 4681[6] 6649[8]

Arbeejay *Simon Hodgson* a37 36
4 b f Iceman Diliza (Dilum (USA))
33[6] 458[12]

Arbeel *Peter Chapple-Hyam* 80
3 b f Royal Applause Waafiah (Anabaa (USA))
2215[4] 2872[2] 3787[4] 4751[5] 5515[10]

Arbitrageur (IRE) *Donal Kinsella* a83 87
4 b g Elusive City(USA) Mother's Hope (IRE) (Idris (IRE))
3846a[21]

Arcadian Legend (USA) *Jeremy Noseda* a54 68
3 b f Van Nistelrooy(USA) Miss Zafonic (FR) (Zafonic (USA))
3787[3] (4176) 6315[13] 7163[6]

Archambo *Mark Johnston*
2 b c Shamardal(USA) Silversword (FR) (Highest Honor (FR))
7654[11]

Archbishop (USA) *Brian Meehan* 111
4 b c Arch(USA) Avaricity (USA) (Carson City (USA))
5725[6]

Arch Duchess (FR) *A De Royer-Dupre* 101
3 bl f Arch(USA) Jacira (FR) (Sillery (USA))
7316a[4]

Archduchess *Rae Guest* 22
2 b f Archipenko(USA) Eminencia (Sadler's Wells (USA))
7466[15]

Arch Ebony (USA) *David O'Meara* a60 64
3 bb g Arch(USA) Dot C C (USA) (Cozzene (USA))
2960[4] 8036[7] 8372[3]

Archelao (IRE) *Lee Carter* a63 28
5 br g Cape Cross(IRE) Brindisi (Dr Fong (USA))
94[9] 508[9] 1183[4] (1473) 5528[3] 5631[6] 6399[9] 6737[4] 7124[7] (8390) 8448[3]

Arch Event *Bernard Llewellyn* a44 65
8 ch m Umistim Arch Angel (IRE) (Archway (IRE))
2828[5] 2921[6] 3312[3] 3953[4] 4238[2] 4713[2] (5093) (5433) ◆

Archibald Thorburn (IRE) *Ed McMahon* a74 63
2 br g Duke Of Marmalade(IRE) Winged Harriet (IRE) (Hawk Wing (USA))
4513[3] 5826[4] 6340[2] (6807) 7463[6]

Archie Rice (USA) *Tom Keddy* a76 50
7 b g Arch(USA) Gold Bowl (USA) (Seeking The Gold (USA))
3889[11] 4638[6] 7970[3] ◆ 8179[5]

Archie Stevens *Amy Weaver* a86 69
3 b g Pastoral Pursuits Miss Wells (IRE) (Sadler's Wells (USA))
(4) 85[2] 2190[8] 2593[6] 3104[9] (3639) 4353[2]

Archive *Lady Cecil* 82
3 b f Dansili Modesta (IRE) (Sadler's Wells (USA))
2931[2] ◆ 3530[3] 5478[5]

Arch Villain (IRE) *Amanda Perrett* a101 96
4 b g Arch(USA) Barzah (IRE) (Darshaan)
(2385) (2654) 3824[8] 5288[4] 6066[3] 6646[6] 6992[4] (7975) 8429[4]

Arch Walker (IRE) *John Weymes* a48 67
6 ch g Choisir(AUS) Clunie (Inchinor)
2074[6] 2338[7] 3024[7] 4009[8] 4388[3] 4691[2] 4761[4] (4943) 5388[4] 5670[5] 6901[8]

Arc Light (IRE) *Tim Easterby* a42 81
5 b g Shamardal(USA) Banakill (FR) (Funambule (USA))
990[5] 1282[4] 1567[4] (2539) (2886) 3301[10] 3651[4] 4055[4] 4542[5] (4810) 5382[5] 6236[7] 6563[11] 7028[5] 7424[6]

Arctic (IRE) *Tracey Collins* 107
6 gr g Shamardal(USA) Shawanni (Shareef Dancer (USA))
2676a[6] 3846a[12] 7227a[6] 7719a[11]

Arctic Admiral (IRE) *Richard Hannon Snr* a81 78
3 gr c Verglas(IRE) Fag End (IRE) (Treasure Kay)
1323[2] 1769[6] (2229) 2420[2]

Arctic Feeling (IRE) *Richard Fahey* a89 92
5 ch g Camacho Polar Lady (Polar Falcon (USA))
1245[10] 1607[4] 2366[14] (2868) 3561[4] 4263[6] 4860[5] 4983[15] 5544[17] 6331[13] 6831[10] (7420) 7803[3] 8189[5] 8305[6] 8369[6]

Arctic Lynx (IRE) *Robert Cowell* a88 90
6 b g One Cool Cat(USA) Baldemara (FR) (Sanglamore (USA))
1984[4] 2388[8] 2724[3] 3220[5] 3586[7] (4165) 4690[2] 5062[7] 6189[F] 7080[9]

Arctic Moon (USA) *Charlie Appleby* 41
2 bb f Raven's Pass(USA) Golden Sphinx (USA) (Storm Cat (USA))
6112[8]

Ardaal *James Fanshawe* a46 51
3 ch c Singspiel(IRE) Moonmaiden (Selkirk (USA))
2157[10] 2754[7] 3402[8]

Ardingly (IRE) *Roger Varian* a77 76
3 b f Danehill Dancer(IRE) Asnieres (USA) (Spend A Buck (USA))
2850[4] (3469) 4066[5] 5169[4]

Ardlui (IRE) *Alan King* 102
5 b g Galileo(IRE) Epping (Charnwood Forest (IRE))
(1841) 3824[11] 4857[12]

Ardmay (IRE) *Kevin Ryan* a62 96
4 b g Strategic Prince Right After Moyne (IRE) (Imperial Ballet (IRE))
1688[11] (2477) 2958[10] 5838[12] 6625[11] 6792[10] 7425[4] 7906[7]

Area Fifty One *Richard Fahey* a87 108
5 b g Green Desert(USA) Secret History (USA) (Bahri (USA))
(1768) 2185[4] 2839[2] (3094) 4310[19] 5270[4] 5760[4] 6385[5] 6838[18] 7206[2]

Ares D'Emra (FR) *C Delcher-Sanchez* 107
3 b c Desert Style(IRE) Belga (GER) (Lomitas)
1419a[5] 2907a[12]

Are You Mine (IRE) *Ralph Beckett* a74 77
3 b f Nayef(USA) Celtic Slipper (IRE) (Anabaa (USA))
3469[3] 4633[5] 5030[3] 5548[3] 6062[3] (6684)

Argaki (IRE) *Keith Dalgleish* a63 84
3 ch g Strategic Prince Amathusia (Selkirk (USA))
950[5] 1965[3] 2342[7] 2971[7] 3202[2] 3465[2] (3711) (4098) 4293[2] 4446[2] 4994[9] (5642) 5918[4] 6551[7]

Argaum (IRE) *Richard Price* a21 76
6 ch g Medicean Poppy Carew (IRE) (Danehill (USA))
7734[6]

Argent Knight *William Jarvis* a65 94
3 gr g Sir Percy Tussah (Daylami (IRE))
(2233) 2602[2] 3206[2] 3982[4] (4417) (5288) 6066[9] 6992[3]

Argent Touch *Derek Shaw* a53 31
2 gr g Elnadim(USA) The Manx Touch (IRE) (Petardia)
3979[4] 4963[11] 7095[8] 8090[4] 8273[2]

Argot *Anthony Carson* 73
2 b c Three Valleys(USA) Tarot Card (Fasliyev (USA))
(7126)

Ariete Arrollador *G Arizkorreta Elosegui* a104 102
6 b h Kingsalsa(USA) Proud Douna (FR) (Kaldoun (FR))
149a[2] 465a[8] 557a[5] 744a[4] 3969a[2]

Aristocracy *Mick Channon* a64 73
2 b c Royal Applause Pure Speculation (Salse (USA))
3853[8] 4304[5] 4513[4] 5034[6] 5893[2] 6401[10] (6897) 7107[4]

Aristocratic Duty *Sylvester Kirk* a63
2 b f Zamindar(USA) Duty Paid (IRE) (Barathea (IRE))
7763[5] 8176[7]

Aristoteles (FR) *M Delzangles* 91
3 b c Peintre Celebre(USA) Khaliyna (IRE) (Danehill (USA))
4815a[2]

Arizona John (IRE) *John Mackie* a78 85
8 b g Rahy(USA) Preseli (IRE) (Caerleon (USA))
1212[3] ◆ 1463[3] 1774[2] 2277[3] (2552)

Arjawan *Clive Brittain* a58 42
3 b g Byron Al Hawa (USA) (Gulch (USA))
807[9] 2455[9] 2746[12] 3191[6]

Arkaim *Pam Sly* a73 31
5 b g Oasis Dream Habariya (IRE) (Perugino (USA))
3138[8]

Arkhip *M Delzangles* 90
3 b c Arch(USA) Slow Down (USA) (Seattle Slew (USA))
7046a[8]

Arlecchino (IRE) *Ed McMahon* a64 78
3 b g Hernando(FR) Trullitti (IRE) (Bahri (USA))
2271[4] 2827[3] 3502[6] (4509) 5189[3] 5847[8] 6258[5] 7491[5]

Arluno (FR) *J-Y Artu* a93 64
4 gr c Chichicastenango(FR) Ambrosianella` (FR) (Take Risks (FR))
4467a[14] 5042a[14]

Armada Bay (IRE) *Bryan Smart* a53 51
3 b g Tamayuz Yara (IRE) (Sri Pekan (USA))
102[3] 310[2] 459[2] 717[6] 1064[8] 1764[8] 1967[7] 6683[4]

Armelle (FR) *Scott Dixon* a54 48
2 b f Milk It Mick Park Ave Princess (IRE) (Titus Livius (FR))
7509[3] 7818[5] 8044[5] 8364[3] 8434[4]

Armourer (IRE) *William Muir* a64 43
2 b c Azamour(IRE) Engraving (Sadler's Wells (USA))
7320[6] 8214[3] 8312[4]

Arms (IRE) *J W Hills* a81 73
3 b c Excellent Art Enchanting Way (Linamix (FR))
1735[2] 2192[7] 6950[6] 7253[3] (7787)

Arnold Lane (IRE) *Mick Channon* a107 111
4 b h Footstepsinthesand Capriole (Noverre (USA))
154a[8] 465a[6] 834a[2] 1413a[5] (1691) (1944a) 6392[7] 6595[8] 7014[4] 7190[8] 7821[8]

Arod (IRE) *Peter Chapple-Hyam* a75
2 b c Teofilo(IRE) My Personal Space (USA) (Rahy (USA))
7835[3]

Arpegio (FR) *S Wattel* a79 55
2 b c King's Best(USA) Fongagain (IRE) (Dr Fong (USA))
8143a[5]

Arpinati *S Botti* 105
2 br c Lucky Story(USA) Lola Sapola (IRE) (Benny The Dip (USA))
(3880a) 7235a[3]

Arranger (IRE) *Richard Hannon Snr* 76
2 b f Bushranger(IRE) El Morocco (USA) (El Prado (IRE))
4877[10] (5949) ◆ 6326[5]

Arr' Kid (USA) *Keith Dalgleish* a52 77
3 b c Medaglia d'Oro(USA) Viaduct (USA) (Thunder Gulch (USA))
2538[2] ◆ 3201[3] 4139[3] 5264[3] 6601[4] 6917[2] 7369[2] 7510[7]

Arrowzone *Garry Moss* 72
2 b g Iffraaj Donna Giovanna (Mozart (IRE))
3536[7] 4505[9] 4925[6] 5482[2] 5941[8] 7097[3] 7309[3] 7529[9]

Arsaadi (IRE) *William Haggas* a87 105
4 b f Dubawi(IRE) Arsad (IRE) (Cape Cross (IRE))
777[7] 2253[9] 3458[3] 4525[2] 4811[4] 6231a[2] 6838[31]

Arsalan *F Rodriguez Puertas* 65
4 b c Halling(USA) Kali (Linamix (FR))
2380a[5]

Arsheef (USA) *J-C Rouget* a83 97
3 b f Hard Spun(USA) Atayeb (USA) (Rahy (USA))
1972a[4]

Ars Nova (GER) *W Figge* 100
3 b f Soldier Hollow Asuma (GER) (Surumu (GER))
2065a[4] (3146a) 4092a[3] 5044a[13] 6010a[7] 6987a[6]

Art Contemporain (USA) *P Bary* a87 107
3 rg c Smart Strike(CAN) Super Lina (FR) (Linamix (FR))
1737a[3] 2297a[4] 3645a[4]

Art Dzeko *Brian Baugh* a71 57
4 b g Acclamation Delitme (IRE) (Val Royal (FR))
1309[3] 1693[9] 2338[3] 2702[6] 3714[11] 4146[3] 5088[7] 5674[13] 6219[5] 8315[6]

Arte Del Calcio *Tony Carroll* a60 66
4 b g Manduro(GER) Movie Queen (Danehill (USA))
531[1] 508[10] 737[5] 4350[8] 6137[7] 6491[4] 7981[9]

Artemis (IRE) *Conrad Allen* a55 46
2 b f Marju(IRE) Silver Arrow (USA) (Shadeed (USA))
5609[6] 6107[8] 6423[10] 8262[7] 8328[14]

Artemis Agrotera (USA) *Michael Hushion* a108
2 b f Roman Ruler(USA) Indy Glory (USA) (A.P. Indy (USA))
7707a[5]

Artemisia (IRE) *P Schiergen* 93
3 ch f Peintre Celebre(USA) Antique Rose (GER) (Desert King (IRE))
2065a[6] 3146a[3] 6010a[10] 6962a[13]

Artemus Gordon (IRE) *Robert Collet* 72
2 b c Sinndar(IRE) Lexington Dream (FR) (Peintre Celebre (USA))
5875a[6]

Artemus Kitten (USA) *Michael J Maker* a94 101
5 ch f Kitten's Joy(USA) Chianti Red (USA) (Woodman (USA))
5552a[8]

Artful Dodger *Olivia Maylam* a34
6 b g Josr Algarhoud(IRE) Artistic Belle (IRE) (Orpen (USA))
515[9]

Artful Lady (IRE) *George Margarson* a61 68
4 br f Excellent Art Fear And Greed (IRE) (Brief Truce (USA))
277[2] 423[4] (471) 863[2] 1196[4] 1748[3] (2281) 3223[8] (5602) 6075[10] 7347[8]

Artful Prince *James Given* 85
3 ch g Dutch Art Royal Nashkova (Mujahid (USA))
2274[9] 2464[13] (4391) (5334) (5497) 5990[2] (6297) (6598) 6788[6] 7424[9]

Artful Rogue (IRE) *Amanda Perrett* a67
2 b g Excellent Art Szabo (IRE) (Anabaa (USA))
8066[6] 8213[2]

Art History (IRE) *David O'Meara* a90 86
5 gr g Dalakhani(IRE) What A Picture (FR) (Peintre Celebre (USA))
1677[7] 378[3] 3609[3] 4313[8] 4782[9] 5640[7]

Arthur's Melody *Bill Turner* 55
2 b g Oratorio(IRE) Poilane (Kris)
3255[5] 3541[2] 6896[6] 6983[11]

Arthurs Secret *John Quinn* a76 80
3 ch g Sakhee's Secret Angry Bark (USA) (Woodman (USA))
1109[3] 1604[7] 2432[10] 3502[7]

Arthur's Tale (USA) *Mahmood Al Zarooni* a102
5 b c Bernardini(USA) Owsley (USA) (Harlan (USA))
151a[5] 362a[6] 552a[2] 871a[8]

Arthur The King (IRE) *Y Durepaire* 83
3 ch c Medicean Applauded (IRE) (Royal Applause)
(2557a)

Artibai *M Delzangles* 101
3 b c Aussie Rules(USA) Tequila Brown (FR) (Kendor (FR))
3386a[9]

Artillery Train (IRE) *Tim Etherington* a50 52
4 b g Amadeus Wolf Another Valentine (FR) (Bering)
2636[9] 3030[11] 3946[14] 6084[8] 7380[7]

Artiste Celebre (FR) *W Menuet* 77
2 b f Excellent Art Golly Gree (USA) (Mr Greeley (USA))
(5323a)

Artiste Divine *A Fabre* 109
3 b f Peintre Celebre(USA) Aquarelliste (FR) (Danehill (USA))
2693a[4] 5315a[2]

Artistic Acclaim (IRE) *John Weymes* 31
2 b f Acclamation Ballet Dancer (IRE) (Refuse To Bend (IRE))
4073[12] 4617[3] 5467[7]

Artistical (IRE) *Lee Carter* a76 67
3 b c Excellent Art Royale Figurine (IRE) (Dominion Royale)
1243[4] 6486[3] 7067[8] 7505[7] (7877) 8310[5]

Artistic Charm *David Simcock* 84
2 b f Dutch Art Greenfly (Green Desert (USA))
3781[2] 5385[3] (6974)

Artistic Flame *Amanda Perrett* a56
2 b g Archipenko(USA) Umlilo (Mtoto)
7442[6] 7834[12] 8214[7]

Artistic Jewel (IRE) *Ed McMahon* a97 110
4 ch f Excellent Art Danish Gem (Danehill (USA))
(3102) (5561) 6414a[2]

Art Mistress (IRE) *Tim Easterby* 68
3 b f Excellent Art Hammrah (Danehill (USA))
2080[6] 2616[12]

Art Obsession (IRE) *David Barron* a76 71
2 b g Excellent Art Ghana (IRE) (Lahib (USA))
6581[2] ◆ 7237[4] (7602)

Art Of Dreams (FR) *B Grizzetti* 98
4 b c Dutch Art Giant Dream (Giant's Causeway (USA))
2491a[8] 7416a[3] 7706a[6]

Art Official (IRE) *Richard Hannon Snr* 88
2 b c Excellent Art Dama'A (IRE) (Green Desert (USA))
2401[2] 3374[4] 4218[2] (4676) (4988) 6328[14] 7336[4]

Art Of War (IRE) *Tom Dascombe* 89
2 b g Invincible Spirit(IRE) Chica Roca (USA) (Woodman (USA))
6184[2]

Artplace (IRE) *C Ferland* a75 92
3 b c Teofilo(IRE) Ginostra (Oasis Dream)
72a[7] 2334a[5]

Art Scholar (IRE) *Michael Appleby* a92 102
6 b g Pyrus(USA) Marigold (FR) (Marju (IRE))
246a[6] 362a[4] 555a[13] 871a[10] 1110[3] 3559[13] ◆ 4262[5] 4501[5] 4979[12]

Art Thief *Michael Appleby* a39 51
5 b g Catcher In The Rye(IRE) Eurolink Sundance (Night Shift (USA))
4355[5] 4835[11] 5123[4]

Art Wave (IRE) *Marco Botti* a78 74
2 ch c Art Connoisseur(IRE) Musical Review (UAE) (Jade Robbery (USA))
4386[3] 4926[6] 5279[2] (6340) 6935[5] 7979[3]

Artwork Genie (IRE) *J-P Carvalho* 96
2 b f Excellent Art Brief Escapade (IRE) (Brief Truce (USA))
7940a[3]

Arty Campbell (IRE) *David Simcock* a67 70
3 b g Dylan Thomas(IRE) Kincob (USA) (Kingmambo (USA))
5892[6] 6557[7] 7279[2]

Aryal *Mark Johnston* a74 82
3 b g Singspiel(IRE) Majoune (FR) (Take Risks (FR))
743 ◆ 479[2] 663[2] 774[2] (911) (1604) 1803[3]

Aryizad (IRE) *Alan Swinbank* 74
4 b f Hurricane Run(IRE) Daziyra (IRE) (Doyoun)
2279[13] 5058[3] 5707[2] 6051[5] (6599) 6846[6]

Asatir (USA) *Saeed bin Suroor* a94 101
4 b g Elusive Quality(USA) Valid Warning (USA) (Valid Appeal (USA))
2841[13] (3697) 4080[5] 4946[18] 6001[15] 6767[3] 7172[9]

Asbaab (USA) *Brian Meehan* 101
3 ch g Jazil(USA) Alsaabeqa (USA) (Sakhee (USA))
2442[7] 3059[4] (4719) 6144[2] ◆

Ascalon *Pat Eddery* a76 45
9 ch h Galileo(IRE) Leaping Flame (USA) (Trempolino (USA))
4166[4] 5231[8]

Ascendant *J R Jenkins* a87 70
7 ch g Medicean Ascendancy (Sadler's Wells (USA))
167[4] 830[4] (1182) 2052[8]

Ascha (FR) *Mme Pia Brandt* a59 76
3 b g Piccolo Polliwilline (IRE) (Mull Of Kintyre (USA))
331a[0]

Ascot Memory (IRE) *S Wattel* 93
2 b f Iffraaj Flash And Dazzle (IRE) (Bertolini (USA))
5363a[8] (6059a) 6786a[5] 7084a[3] 7571a[10]

Ascription (IRE) *Hugo Palmer* 113
4 b g Dansili Lady Elgar (IRE) (Sadler's Wells (USA))
1576[6] 2232[2] 2424[6] (4859) 5268[2] (6396) ◆ 7014[14]

As De Bigorre (IRE) *C Ferland* 84
3 b c Johannesburg(USA) Ardere (USA) (El Prado (IRE))
(1594a) 2335a[6]

As Des Flandres (FR) *Y Barberot* a102 100
3 b c King's Best(USA) Agnes For Ransom (USA) (Red Ransom (USA))
7705a[5]

Asgardella (IRE) *Richard Fahey* 92
3 b f Duke Of Marmalade(IRE) Peaceful Kingdom (USA) (King Of Kings (IRE))
1773[2] 2271[3] 2412[5] 3080[3] 6208[5] 6823[7] 7211[6] (7424)

Ashaadd (IRE) *Roger Varian* a84 101
3 b g Dansili Vital Statistics (Indian Ridge)
2655[5] ◆ (3020) ◆ 3339[6] (4062) ◆ 4744[16]

Ashamaly *James Tate* a90
3 br c Shamardal(USA) Tullynally (Dansili)
129[2] (325) (533) 1033[7] 1543[5] 2844[13] 3472[7]

Ash Cape *Brian Rothwell*
3 bg g Cape Town(IRE) Chili Pepper (Chilibang)
7884[6]

Ashcott Boy *Neil Mulholland*
5 ch g Lahib(USA) Last Ambition (IRE) (Cadeaux Genereux)
8245[6]

Ashdan *John Gosden* 109
3 b c Dansili Bonash (Rainbow Quest (USA))
4216[2] 4907[2]

Ashdeuzo (FR) *E Puente Simon* a75 79
7 b g Poliglote Khazana (FR) (Saumarez)
6680a[2]

Ashdown Lad *William Jarvis* a70 83
4 ch g Sir Percy Antibes (IRE) (Grand Lodge (USA))
2234[2] (2739) ◆ 3321[3] 3765[2] ◆

Ashkalara *Stuart Howe* a67 60
6 b m Footstepsinthesand Asheyana (IRE) (Soviet Star (USA))
520[7] 1059[4]

Ashkannd (FR) *A De Royer-Dupre* 84
2 b c Sinndar(IRE) Ashalanda (FR) (Linamix (FR))
5875a[5]

Ashkari (IRE) *Clive Cox* 66
2 ch c Dutch Art Frivolity (Pivotal)
7270[5]

Ashkiyr (FR) *J Moore* 113
4 b g Rock Of Gibraltar(IRE) Asharna (IRE) (Darshaan)
1872a[13]

Ashpan Sam *John Spearing* a78 102
4 b g Firebreak Sweet Patoopie (Indian Ridge)
1726[7] 2097[3] 2460[3] 3487[2] 3682[6] 4165[6] 5062[2] (5971) (6162) 6586[6] (7222)

Asia Minor (IRE) *Dr Jon Scargill* a77 54
4 ch f Pivotal Anka Britannia (USA) (Irish River (FR))
(418) ◆ 653[3] 816[3] 1654[6] 3437[7] (7628) (8343)

Asian Prince (IRE) *Alastair Lidderdale*
4 b g Strategic Prince Asian Alliance (IRE) (Soviet Star (USA))
6738[8]

Asian Rocket (FR) *C Boutin* 70
3 b c Indian Rocket Singapore City (FR) (Sagacity (FR))
2335a[0]

Asian Trader *William Haggas* a67 89
4 b g Acclamation Tiger Waltz (Pivotal)
(1896) ◆ (3018) 3371[2] 3786[3]

Askania Nova (IRE) *A De Royer-Dupre* 91
3 ch f New Approach(IRE) Bal De La Rose (IRE) (Cadeaux Genereux)
5461a[11] 6124a[7]

Askar Tau (FR) *Marcus Tregoning* a106 115
8 b g Montjeu(IRE) Autriche (IRE) (Acatenango (GER))
1920[9] 2810[9] 4919[10] 5724[7]

Askaud (IRE) *Scott Dixon* a81 95
5 b f Iffraaj Tarabaya (IRE) (Warning)
4951[1] 644[4] 810[2] 995[5] 1237[9] 1422[5] 1823[7] (3322) (4067) 4879[6] (5493) 6650[11] 7172[15] 7368[16]

Ask Dad *Michael Dods* 97
3 b c Intikhab(USA) Don't Tell Mum (IRE) (Dansili)
2374a[11] 2677a[10] 3846a[9] 5019a[13] 6792[14] 7176[13]
Asker (IRE) *Zoe Davison* 91
5 b g High Chaparral(IRE) Pay The Bank (High Top)
6992[13]
Ask The Guru *Michael Attwater* a88 89
3 b c Ishiguru(USA) Tharwa (IRE) (Last Tycoon)
1033[12] 1362[4] 1808[7] 2083[5] 5998[11] 6429[5] 6900[5] 7264[8] 7445[7] 7783[4]
A Southside Boy (GER) *Jim Goldie* 69
5 b g Samum(GER) Anthurium (GER) (Hector Protector (USA))
1572[7] (2798) 3199[6] (3709) 4822[2] 5920[3] 6552[8]
Aspenbreeze *Alan Bailey* a44
2 b c Champs Elysees Llanito (Rock Of Gibraltar (IRE))
3112[14] 4833[4] 5101[9] 5865[5] 6520[10] 7032[7]
Aspidistra (GER) *W Giedt* 84
3 b f Hernando(FR) Astilbe (GER) (Monsun (GER))
3604a[9]
Aspirant *Bill Turner* a73 66
2 b g Rail Link Affluent (Oasis Dream)
3155[6] 3836[5] 4477[4] (6104) 6376[3] 6972[5] 8147[7] (8215) (8325) 8442[7]
Assembly *Pat Phelan* a70 73
3 ch g Kyllachy Constitute (USA) (Gone West (USA))
1618[8] 2340[3] 2535[5] (5200) 5477[10] 6310[2] 8068[7] 8220[10]
Assertive Agent *Tony Carroll* a58 64
3 b f Assertive Agent Kensington (Mujahid (USA))
1660[3] ◆ 1896[4] 3016[5] 5177[6] 6902[6] (8070)
Assinie Fix (FR) *J-P Gallorini*
4 b f Smadoun(FR) Ifaty (FR) (Rose Laurel)
963a[0]
Assizes *Ruth Carr* a93 96
4 gr g Teofilo(IRE) Requesting (Rainbow Quest (USA))
926[7] 2185[7] 2478[9] 2881[3] 3113[6] 3349[6] 3804[3] 3976[6] 5355[8] 5918[9] 6717[4] 6759[4] 7238[6]
Assoluta (IRE) *Sylvester Kirk* a58 46
2 ch f Danehill Dancer(IRE) A P Easy (USA) (A.P. Indy (USA))
3107[11] 5131[7] 5790[12] 6311[7] 7032[2] 7168[7]
Astaire (IRE) *Kevin Ryan* 116
2 b c Intense Focus(USA) Runway Dancer (Dansili)
(2670) 4212[6] (4768) (5765) (7191)
A Star In My Eye (IRE) *Kevin Ryan* 87
3 b f Authorized(IRE) Vyatka (Lion Cavern (USA))
1636[10] 2231[3] (3201) 4878[6] 5496[7] (6514)
Asterales *Jo Hughes* a57 64
6 b m Royal Applause Shalimar (IRE) (Indian Ridge)
201[5] 406[10]
Asteria (FR) *J E Pease* a86 90
3 b f Orpen(USA) Latona (FR) (Kendor (FR))
2334a[6] 4274a[9] 7993a[9]
Asterism *Ian Williams* a80 56
5 b f Motivator Star Cluster (Observatory (USA))
433[4] 675[4]
Asteroidea *Pam Sly* 56
2 b f Sea The Stars(IRE) Speciosa (IRE) (Danehill Dancer (IRE))
6125[10] 6643[13]
Aster's Approval *Tim Vaughan* 20
3 b g With Approval(CAN) Aster (IRE) (Danehill (USA))
4404[8] 5064[11]
Astonishing (IRE) *Sir Michael Stoute* a94 110
3 b f Galileo(IRE) Amazing Krisken (USA) (Kris S (USA))
3239[3] (3957) 5795[2] 6649[2] (6764)
Astorgs Galaxy *Sir Michael Stoute* a72 72
3 b f Galileo(IRE) Astorg (USA) (Lear Fan (USA))
2803[3] 3606[2] 5233[4] 6313[4] 6978[9]
Astorya (TUR) *U Bilik* 105
4 b c Sri Pekan(USA) Melita (IRE) (Tagula (IRE))
6254a[4]
Astra (GER) *W Hickst* 66
4 b f Soldier Hollow Aarau (GER) (Platini (GER))
963a[0]
Astra Hall *Ralph Beckett* a49 87
4 ch f Halling(USA) Star Precision (Shavian)
(2349) 2923[4] (4914) 5795[8] 6490[2] 7504[2] 7822[11]
Astral Pursuits *Nigel Tinkler* 42
2 ch f Pastoral Pursuits Wish You Luck (Dubai Destination (USA))
2883[12] 3541[6] 4065[8] 4387[4] 4617[5] 5970[8] 6494[7]
Astral Rose *Jonathan Portman* a57 42
2 b f Pastoral Pursuits Rosapenna (IRE) (Spectrum (IRE))
1659[12] 2723[7] 3174[10] 6409[10] 6922[9] 7426[6] 7804[2] 8222[6]
Astrogold *Mark H Tompkins* 54
4 ch f Motivator Mega (IRE) (Petardia)
2136[3] 3790[5]
Astromagick *Mark H Tompkins* 81
5 b f Rainbow Quest(USA) Astrocharm (IRE) (Charnwood Forest (IRE))
2009[4] 2587[F]
Astrosapphire *Mark H Tompkins* a69 73
3 b f Manduro(GER) Astromancer (USA) (Silver Hawk (USA))
1934[6] 2386[4] 2967[3] 4882[8] 5203[4] 6335[5] 6952[7]
Astroscarlet *Mark H Tompkins* a66 52
4 ch f Carnival Dancer Astrolove (IRE) (Bigstone (IRE))
2567[7] 3168[5] 3792[3] 4179[5]
Astrovirtue *Mark H Tompkins* a49
2 b c Virtual Astrolove (IRE) (Bigstone (IRE))
7607[11] 8123[11]
Astrowolf *Mark H Tompkins* 64
2 b g Halling(USA) Optimistic (Reprimand)
4926[3] 5852[6] 6570[7] 7418[12]
Astrum *Rod Millman* a80 78
3 gr g Haafhd Vax Star (Petong)
(1289) 1685[3] (2095) 2742[4] 3232[2] 3893[2] 4634[2] 4899[2] 5953[5] 6202[7]
Asuka Kurichan (JPN) *Naosuke Sugai* 111
6 b h Sterling Rose(JPN) Laurel Waltz (JPN) (Dyna Letter (JPN))
8208a[7]
Asulaman (GER) *S Cerulis* a84 82
6 b g Sulamani(IRE) Andrelhina (Tirol)
127a[10]
Asyad (IRE) *Sir Michael Stoute* 80
2 b f New Approach(IRE) Elle Danzig (GER) (Roi Danzig (USA))
6141[4] (7450)
Asyl (IRE) *F Rohaut* a84 89
4 b f Peintre Celebre(USA) Coup D'Eclat (IRE) (Rainbow Quest (USA))
2969a[0]
Atacama Sunrise *John Butler* a53 70
7 b m Desert Sun Top Of The Morning (Keen)
456[6] 852[6] 900[5] 1093[13]
At A Clip *Ralph Beckett* a37 71
3 b f Green Desert(USA) First Bloom (USA) (Fusaichi Pegasus (USA))
1666[10] ◆ (2226) ◆ 2572[10]
Atalanta Bay (IRE) *Marcus Tregoning* a69 54
3 b f Strategic Prince Wood Sprite (Mister Baileys)
1487[5] (7770) 7899[3] 8343[5]
Ataraxis (FR) *Sir Henry Cecil* 74
3 b c Nayef(USA) Seven Magicians (USA) (Silver Hawk (USA))
2568[3]
Athaakeel (IRE) *Ronald Harris* a61 63
7 b m Almutawakel Asaafeer (USA) (Dayjur (USA))
42[9] (88) 355[3] 471[6] 551[5] (611) 754[2] 863[6] 916[4] 1195[7] 1397[7]
Athania (IRE) *S Arthur* a62 43
7 ch m Fath(USA) Xania (Mujtahid (USA))
1313a[5] 1739a[7] 7145a[5]
Atheera (IRE) *Mark Johnston* a67 67
2 ch f Shamardal(USA) Alshamatry (USA) (Seeking The Gold (USA))
2744[6] 3205[4] (3680) 4246[8] 5235[4] 5926[3] 6582[14] 7062[10]
Athenian (IRE) *Sir Mark Prescott Bt* a97 97
4 b f Acclamation Ziria (IRE) (Danehill Dancer (IRE))
2476[2] 2848[5] 6665[3] 7222[6] (7731) 7995a[4] 8064[4]
Athletic *Andrew Reid* a71 40
4 b g Doyen(IRE) Gentle Irony (Mazilier (USA))
312[6] 510[5] 631[2] 737[2] (794) 1100[2] 1193[2] 2134[9] 2565[2] 2773[6] 3434[5] 4637[5] (5398) 7262[8] 7880[9] 8019[5] 8157[2]
Athwaab *Simon Hodgson* a65 34
6 b m Cadeaux Genereux Ahdaaf (USA) (Bahri (USA))
728[8] 790[7] 1065[2] 1195[3] 1475[5] 1902[9] 2126[6] 3660[9] 4197[8]
Atilia *Harry Dunlop* a30 10
3 ch f Notnowcato Gib (IRE) (Rock Of Gibraltar (IRE))
2346[7] 3016[8]
Atlantic Affair (IRE) *Mark Johnston* 80
2 gr f Clodovil(IRE) Adultress (IRE) (Ela-Mana-Mou)
1605[4] 1839[4] 2204[4] 2497[2] 3092[6] (3648) 4108[3] 5136[3] 5773a[2] 6326[12] 7026[22]
Atlantic Beach *Milton Bradley* a75 82
8 ch g Kyllachy Amused (Prince Sabo)
135[4] 369[6] 537[7] 760[8]
Atlantic City (FR) *H-A Pantall* a85 87
2 b f Holy Roman Emperor(IRE) Bog Wild (USA) (Once Wild (USA))
2433a[3] 5363a[3] (7568a) 7994a[5]
Atlantic Isle (GER) *Sir Henry Cecil* a63 49
3 b f Tertullian(USA) All Time Great (Night Shift (USA))
1713[6] 2084[12] 2930[6]
Atlantis City (FR) *Richard Hannon Snr* a79 51
3 b g Elusive City(USA) Feld Marechale (FR) (Deputy Minister (CAN))
2560[2] 2786[5] 3294[11] 3858[8] 6003[11]
Atlantis Crossing (IRE) *Jim Boyle* a95 60
4 b g Elusive City(USA) Back At De Front (IRE) (Cape Cross (IRE))
25[2] (217) 443[3] 690[5] (1061) 7641[12] 7991[8]
Atmanna *Zoe Davison* a48 53
4 br f Manduro(GER) Samdaniya (Machiavellian (USA))
1882[12] 2963[4] 3437[6] 7298[11]
Atomic Bere (FR) *Mlle C Cardenne* a71 87
3 b g Hurricane Cat(USA) Arrondie (FR) (Inchinor)
(72a)
Atomic Waves *P Bary* a87 90
4 ch g Hernando(FR) Atlantic Blue (USA) (Nureyev (USA))
5042a[6]
Attain *Julia Feilden* a61 56
4 b g Dansili Achieve (Rainbow Quest (USA))
1893[5] 2845[4] 3513[6] 4144[10] 6518[2] 7321[4] 7907[2] 8006[4] 8329[2] 8448[2]
Attansky (IRE) *Tim Easterby* 62
3 b g Ivan Denisovich(IRE) Attanagh (IRE) (Darnay)
1393[6] 2769[5] 3194[2] 3653[5] 4587[3] 5010[5] 5295[4] 6552[5]
Attention Seaker *Tim Easterby* 73
3 b f Bollin Eric Pay Attention (Revoque (IRE))
2164[5] 2465[5] 2833[3] 3394[4] 3893[3] (4587) 5137[2]
Attenzione (IRE) *Marco Botti* a52 57
2 b c Shamardal(USA) Fig Tree Drive (USA) (Miswaki (USA))
7335[8] 8340[11]
Attraction Ticket *David Simcock* a75 65
4 b g Selkirk(USA) Trick (IRE) (Shirley Heights)
2418[5] (2777) 2982[8] (4904) 5587[5] 7000[8]
Attwaal (IRE) *Neil King* a73 83
4 b g Teofilo(IRE) Qasirah (IRE) (Machiavellian (USA))
403[5] 709[3] (866) (1586) (1884) 2385[7] 6504[6]
Aubrietia *Alan McCabe* a102 92
4 b f Dutch Art Petong's Pet (Petong)
(101) 196[2] (234) (526) (913) (966) 1287[3] 2145a[8] 2647[8] 6665[13] 7313[11] 7540[8] 7803[10] 8189[7] 8231[7]
Auction (IRE) *Ed Dunlop* a77 101
3 b f Mr Greeley(USA) Exhibit One (USA) (Silver Hawk (USA))
(1986) (2387) (2622) 3460[2] ◆ 4081[4] 4705[9]
Audacia (IRE) *Hugo Palmer* a68 85
3 b f Sixties Icon Indiannie Moon (Fraam)
(2804) 4468a[6] 6536[7] 7404a[10]
Auden (USA) *J R Jenkins* a72 67
5 b g Librettist(USA) Moyesii (USA) (Diesis)
7836[11] 7952[8] (8436)
Auditor (USA) *C Ferland* a99 102
3 ch c Kingmambo(USA) Queen Of Money (USA) (Corporate Report (USA))
7116a[8]
Augusta Ada *Ollie Pears* 81
2 b f Byron Preference (Efisio)
2075[3] 2401[5] 2751[2] 3605[2] (4616) 5005[9] 5787[5]
August Rush (SAF) *Seth Benzel* a108 112
7 ch g Var(USA) Bushgirl (ZIM) (Huntingdale (IRE))
955a[8]
Augustus John (IRE) *Roy Brotherton* a53 73
10 gr g Danehill(USA) Rizerie (FR) (Highest Honor (FR))
22[10]
Auld Alliance (IRE) *Sir Michael Stoute* a72 88
3 b f Montjeu(IRE) Highland Gift (IRE) (Generous (IRE))
1813[3] 2423[2] (3272) 4029[5] 4480[3]
Auntie Mildred (IRE) *David O'Meara* a36 58
3 b f Elnadim(USA) Nahrayn (USA) (Elusive Quality (USA))
706[9] 1447[9] ◆ 1760[5] (2336) 2795[5] 8271[9]
Aura Bora (USA) *Tim Easterby* a31 17
5 b g North Light(IRE) A Rose For Chris (USA) (Will's Way (USA))
849[9] 911[6] 1072[5] 2720[11]
Aureate *Brian Forsey* a48 30
9 ch g Jade Robbery(USA) Anne D'Autriche (IRE) (Rainbow Quest (USA))
8268[4] 8436[6]
Aurelia Cotta (IRE) *Charles Hills* a57 57
2 b f Holy Roman Emperor(IRE) Art Work (Zafonic (USA))
6789[7] 7200[3] 7763[13]
Au Renoir *Kevin Ryan*
3 ch f Peintre Celebre(USA) Goodbye (Efisio)
377[5]
Aurens (IRE) *Michael Attwater* a72 64
4 b g One Cool Cat(USA) Al Aqabah (IRE) (Redback)
4176[9] 4677[RR]
Aureolin Gulf *Andrew Hollinshead* a53 59
4 b g Proclamation(IRE) Vermilion Creek (Makbul)
435[12] 587[10] 4503[9] 5073[3] 5429[7] 5903[9] 7931[3] 8055[5] 8371[4]
Au Revoir (IRE) *A Fabre* 112
3 b c Singspiel(IRE) First (Highest Honor (FR))
4325a[5] 5041a[5] (5779a) 6250a[4]
Aurora Borealis (IRE) *Ed Dunlop* 62
2 b f Montjeu(IRE) Elaflaak (USA) (Gulch (USA))
7493[7]
Aussie Blue (IRE) *Charles Pogson* a75 65
9 b g Bahamian Bounty Luanshya (First Trump)
2932[14] 3246[4] 3630[12] 4504[8] 5373[8]
Aussie Lyrics (FR) *F Chappet* a77 84
3 gr c Aussie Rules(USA) Operam (Kris)
2584[6] 4384[5] 5960[3] 6743[2] 7412a[7] 7736a[12]
Aussie Reigns (IRE) *William Knight* a102 99
3 b g Aussie Rules(USA) Rohain (IRE) (Singspiel (IRE))
2193[6] (2727) 2935[11] (3537) 3780[2] 4295[6] 4917[2] 5792[2] 6332[8] 6868[3] 7022[5] 7768[3] (8062)
Aussie Sky (IRE) *John Stimpson* a33 33
2 b f Aussie Rules(USA) Skyscape (Zafonic (USA))
6160[7] 7317[4] 7541[7] 8090[7]
Australia *A P O'Brien* 113
2 ch c Galileo(IRE) Ouija Board (Cape Cross (IRE))
(6223a)
Australia Day (IRE) *Paul Webber* a93 93
10 gr g Key Of Luck(USA) Atalina (FR) (Linamix (FR))
1615[8] 2251[10] 4029[3] 5465a[5] 6252a[4]
Ausus (USA) *Daniel Peitz* a97 104
4 ch f Invasor(ARG) El Raabi (USA) (Fusaichi Pegasus (USA))
5552a[3]
Authentication *Mel Brittain* a66 70
4 b g Authorized(IRE) Valley Of Gold (FR) (Shirley Heights)
3480[6] 3627[10] 4969[6] 5185[8] 5831[4] 6177[4] 6565[10] 6942[4] 7280[9] 7423[4] 8223[5]
Authenticity *John Butler* 30
2 b c Authorized(IRE) Jubilee (Selkirk (USA))
7654[8]
Authenticity (USA) *Todd Pletcher* a111
6 b m Quiet American(USA) Court Of Appeal (USA) (Deputy Minister (CAN))
7691a[3]
Authoritarian *Richard Hannon Snr* a64 81
4 b f Authorized(IRE) Favourita (Diktat)
1583[11] 2531[4] 3158[5] 3416[6] 4718[7] 5181[6] 7429[4] 7741[5]
Authorized Too *William Haggas* a66 51
2 b c Authorized(IRE) Audaz (Oasis Dream)
7219[6] 7902[3]
Authorship (IRE) *Charlie Appleby* 87
3 b g Authorized(IRE) Desert Frolic (IRE) (Persian Bold)
4882[5] 5483[2]
Auto Mac *Neville Bycroft* a58 66
5 b g Auction House(USA) Charlottevalentina (IRE) (Perugino (USA))
2752[7] 4888[3] 5341[7] 6276[11] (6759) 7027[4]
Automated *Clive Brittain* 62
2 b c Authorized(IRE) Red Blooded Woman (USA) (Red Ransom (USA))
6581[6] ◆ 7694[3]
Automotive *Julia Feilden* a63 69
5 b g Beat Hollow Bina Ridge (Indian Ridge)
14[3] 510[4] 1294[7] 1498[5] 1909[6] 2875[2] (3244) 3882[4] 5032[6] (5793) 6130[3] 6794[8]
Autopilot *Anabel K Murphy* a55 70
2 b c Kyllachy Khyber Knight (IRE) (Night Shift (USA))
3836[4] ◆ 4351[6] 4827[4] 5850[6] (6279) 7088[6]
Autrisk (IRE) *Marco Botti* a63 54
3 b c Authorized(IRE) Maid To Order (IRE) (Zafonic (USA))
708[5] 994[4] 1425[3] 1685[7]
Autspread *Marco Botti* 83
3 b c Authorized(IRE) Ridotto (Salse (USA))
(1291) 2857[9]
Autumn Draw *Ralph Beckett* 35
3 b g Marju(IRE) Shallow Ground (IRE) (Common Grounds)
3858[10]
Autumn Lily (USA) *Charlie Appleby* 99
2 b f Street Cry(IRE) Arlette (IRE) (King Of Kings (IRE))
(3205) 3555[12] (4277) 5536[11] (6839)
Autumns Blush (IRE) *Jeremy Noseda* 77
2 b f Kheleyf(USA) Park Romance (IRE) (Dr Fong (USA))
1634[8] (2131) 5476[5]
Autumn Sunrise (IRE) *Richard Hannon Snr* 81
2 ch f Camacho Convenience (IRE) (Ela-Mana-Mou)
3664[2] 4484[2] 4877[4] (5307)
Autumn Tide (IRE) *John Quinn* 50
2 b f Jeremy(USA) September Tide (IRE) (Thatching)
3391[8] 3943[5] 4450[2] 5480[5] 5970[6]
Autumnus (IRE) *Ismail Mohammed* a50 48
4 b g Manduro(GER) Turning Light (GER) (Fantastic Light (USA))
381[8] 2764[14]
Autun (USA) *Lady Cecil* a95 85
3 b c Empire Maker(USA) Sense Of Joy (Dansili)
2416[3] 3470[2] 4167[2] 4980[4] 6115[2] (6559)
Available (IRE) *John Mackie* a68 85
4 b f Moss Vale(IRE) Divert (IRE) (Averti (IRE))
1398[5] 1650[5] (1802) 2255[18] (2711) 3322[9] 4671[8] 6072[5] 6274[7] 7163[2] 7381[3] 7845[3]
Availed Speaker (IRE) *Richard Fahey* a71 53
4 ch g Iffraaj Privileged Speech (USA) (General Assembly (USA))
146[5] 511[9] 718[5] 974[3] 1104[2] 1239[5] 1603[4] 1842[5] 2977[7] 3397[7]
Avante *J-M Osorio* 95
4 b c Shamardal(USA) Se Me Va (USA) (Bahri (USA))
5465a[3]
Avanzini (USA) *G Botti* a79
3 b c Mr Greeley(USA) Spira (IRE) (Sadler's Wells (USA))
72a[2]
Ava Schmetterling *Garry Moss* a29 13
3 b f Avonbridge Manila Selection (USA) (Manila (USA))
1044[6] 1202[5]
Ava Star (IRE) *David Wachman* a77 82
2 b f Amadeus Wolf Star Of The West (Galileo (IRE))
5773a[4]
Avatar Star (IRE) *Marco Botti* a79 70
3 b g Peintre Celebre(USA) Homegrown (IRE) (Mujadil (USA))
1293[6] 1958[8] 2737[2] 2949[3] 4383[6] (4881) (5393) 6476[2]
Avec Rose *Richard Fahey* a75 78
3 b f Tagula(IRE) Rose Siog (Bahamian Bounty)
1806[11] 3813[8] 4117[8]
Aventador (FR) *T Castanheira* 97
2 b c Zafeen(FR) Day Of Dream (IRE) (Rainbows For Life (CAN))
7160a[5] 7967a[3]
Aventure Love (FR) *M Gentile* 95
2 bb f Orpen(USA) Kshanti (USA) (Diesis)
1894a[2] 2433a[4] 5460a[2]
Avenue Gabriel *P D Deegan* 104
2 b f Champs Elysees Vas Y Carla (USA) (Gone West (USA))
4462a[3] ◆ 5318a[3] 6798[5]
Averroes (IRE) *Ernst Oertel* a107 114
6 ch h Galileo(IRE) Shapely (USA) (Alleged (USA))
1263a[9]
Avertis *Alastair Lidderdale* a78 75
8 b g Averti(IRE) Double Stake (USA) (Kokand (USA))
(138) 272[7] 689[3] 1181[2] 1878[10] 2573[5]
Avidly *Julia Feilden* a72 75
3 b f Beat Hollow Balmy (Zafonic (USA))
8444[2]
Aviso (GER) *David Evans* a71 57
9 b g Tertullian(USA) Akasma (GER) (Windwurf (GER))
73[5] 190[3] 314[7] 639[9] 747[5] 1700[4] 1949[5] 2570[6]
Avison (IRE) *Lawney Hill* a58 67
5 b g Diamond Green(FR) Actoris (USA) (Diesis)
417[12] 524[4]
Avocadeau (IRE) *William Muir* a69 67
2 b c Lawman(FR) Christmas Cracker (FR) (Alhaarth (IRE))
5819[5] 6139[4] 6656[3] 7088[8] 7935[2] 8164[3]
Avomcic (IRE) *M Maroni* 93
3 ch f Avonbridge Ulanova (IRE) (Noverre (USA))
1866a[13] 6890a[9]
Avon Breeze *Richard Whitaker* a71 89
4 b f Avonbridge African Breeze (Atraf)
(2479) 2755[2] (3682) 4217[3] 4954[4] 5544[3] 6273[5] 6665[5] 7420[11]
Avon Ferry *F Perez* 72
6 b m Avonbridge I'm Connected (USA) (Palmister (USA))
2380a[2]
Avonlini *Richard Ford* a54 54
7 b m Bertolini(USA) Avondale Girl (IRE) (Case Law)
6344[10] 6930[6] 7354[11] 8412[9]

Avonmore Star *Mike Murphy* a85 87
5 b g Avonbridge Pooka's Daughter (IRE) (Eagle Eyed (USA))
358[7] 650[4] 822[4] 6526[9] 6929[9] 7303[6] 7880[13] 8230[9] 8456[3]

Avon Pearl *Rune Haugen* a90 99
4 ch c Avonbridge Warden Rose (Compton Place)
5809a[8]

Avon River *Dean Ivory* a70 65
6 ch g Avonbridge Night Kiss (FR) (Night Shift (USA))
3721[5]

Avonrose *Derek Shaw* a81 78
6 b m Avonbridge Loveleaves (Polar Falcon (USA))
116[3] 234[2] 358[8] 4064[7]

Avon Supreme *Gay Kelleway* a61 57
5 ch f Avonbridge Fredora (Inchinor)
381[6] 441[7] 565[4] 725[2] 907[7]

Avonvalley *Peter Grayson* a72 65
6 b m Avonbridge Piper's Ash (USA) (Royal Academy (USA))
101[5] 582[7] 790[5] (971) 1351[4] 1957[5] 2410[11] 3569[7] 4385[10] 4636[4] 4837[5]

Await The Dawn (USA) *M F De Kock* a100 122
6 b h Giant's Causeway(USA) Valentine Band (USA) (Dixieland Band (USA))
556a[9] (741a) 956a[2] 1268a[5]

Awake My Soul (IRE) *David O'Meara* 101
4 ch g Teofilo(IRE) Field Of Hope (IRE) (Selkirk (USA))
(1777) (2240) ◆ 2431[3] (2976) 3832[3] 4310[4] 4979[8] 5269[14] 6772[6] 7312[3] 7823[8]

Award (IRE) *John Gosden* a66
2 b f Tamayuz Fantastic Account (Fantastic Light (USA))
7260[4]

Awattan *Ed Vaughan* a69
3 b f Singspiel(IRE) Mureefa (USA) (Bahri (USA))
580[3] ◆ 864[2] 972[2] 7033[6]

Aweebitowinker *J S Moore* a48 50
2 ch g Winker Watson French Connexion (IRE) (Chineur (FR))
1432[3] 1749[6] 3659[4] 3914[5] 7117[8] 7878[12] 8016[5]

Awesome Rock (IRE) *Roger Ingram* a56 44
4 ch g Rock Of Gibraltar(IRE) Dangerous Diva (IRE) (Royal Academy (USA))
94[8] 226[5] 5934[8] 7440[11]

Axiom *Ed Walker* a104 99
9 ch g Pivotal Exhibitor (USA) (Royal Academy (USA))
3060[6] 5533[3] 5738[13] 6204[5] 6792[6]

Ayaar (IRE) *Mick Channon* 102
3 bb c Rock Of Gibraltar(IRE) Teide Lady (Nashwan (USA))
1621[4] 2024[6] 2526a[6] 3484[10] 5287[5] 5510[3] 5992[8] 6650[7] (6840)

Aya's Gift *Ed Walker* a64 46
2 ch c Compton Place Ringarooma (Erhaab (USA))
3631[6] 4379[5] 5000[4] ◆

Ayasha *Bryan Smart* a67 73
3 b f Indesatchel(IRE) Nizhoni (USA) (Mineshaft (USA))
923[8] 1073[3] 1647[4] 2076[12] 2959[10] (3611) 3934[2] 4510[3] 5150[9]

Aye Aye Digby (IRE) *Patrick Chamings* a91 83
8 b g Captain Rio Jane Digby (IRE) (Magical Strike (USA))
(2196) 2657[3] 3415[5] 4210[6] 5219[10] (5701) 6525[7] 6744[7]

Aye Aye Skipper (IRE) *Dean Ivory* a77 82
3 b g Captain Marvelous(IRE) Queenfisher (Scottish Reel)
2984[9] 3782[8] (4962) 5477[4] 6461[6] 7742[11] 8181[11] 8345[13]

Ayers Rock (IRE) *Marcus Tregoning* a66
2 b g Bushranger(IRE) Red Fuschia (Polish Precedent (USA))
7860[5] 8123[6] 8389[4]

Aylin (FR) *N Clement* a90 93
3 ch f Gold Away(IRE) Street Lightning (FR) (Best Of The Bests (IRE))
5779a[6]

Ayr Missile *Kevin Ryan* 70
3 b f Cadeaux Genereux Venoge (IRE) (Green Desert (USA))
1447[6] 2010[9] 2318[5]

Ay Tay Tate (IRE) *Noel Wilson* a72 72
7 b g Catcher In The Rye(IRE) Vintage Belle (IRE) (Waajib)
4435[9] 5059[9] 5934[11] 6722[5] 6907[12]

Azabitmour (FR) *John Best* a68 66
3 b g Azamour(IRE) Brixa (FR) (Linamix (FR))
191a[4] 1511a[8] 1850a[9] 2403a[5] 3129a[15] 4509[4] 6788[8] 7610[8] 8031[5] 8148[RR] 8182[RR]

Azafata (SPA) *J Lopez Sanchez* 90
4 b f Motivator Anysheba (USA) (Alysheba (USA))
6252a[2]

Azagal (IRE) *Tim Easterby* 98
2 b f Azamour(IRE) Brave Madam (IRE) (Invincible Spirit (IRE))
1642[5] 2458[3] 2645[5] 3366[2] (4053) (4726) 5005[7] 5680[6] 6328[2] 6622[10] 7026[6] 7537[8]

Azelle *Brendan Powell* a28 68
3 b f Starcraft(NZ) Zola (NZ) (Volksraad)
1828[5] 2597[6] 3039[4] 3530[4] 4030[2] 4345[2] 5170[7] 5275[3] 6339[9]

Azenzar *Roger Varian* a72 77
3 b f Danehill Dancer(IRE) Dashing (IRE) (Sadler's Wells (USA))
(1364) ◆ 2449[10] 3292[3] 4385[3] 5181[4] 6535[2] 7821[14]

Azerodegree (IRE) *Iain Jardine* a66 60
4 b g Azamour(IRE) Fairy (USA) (Gulch (USA))
1084[8] 1251[3] 1572[9] 8027[10]

Aziyadee (FR) *U Suter* a43
3 b f Whipper(USA) Askeagh (IRE) (Daylami (IRE))
962a[0]

Azma (USA) *Conrad Allen* a72 83
3 b f Bernardini(USA) Dyna's Destiny (USA) (Dynaformer (USA))
188[4] 731[4] 1697[6] 2387[3] 3292[6] (3780) 4258[8] 4721[3] (5491) 6538[10]

Azrael *Alan McCabe* a88 88
5 b g Makbul Fontaine Lady (Millfontaine)
104[3] 370[3] 517[2] (1292) 1576[4] 1819[10] 2496[4] 2752[3] (2964) 3368[6] 4067[2] 4864[4] 5437[7] 5621[6] 6215[4]

Azrag (USA) *Gerard Butler* a90 88
5 rg g Mizzen Mast(USA) Call Account (USA) (Private Account (USA))
(5672) 5823[2] 6336[14] (7115) 7542[6]

Azrur (IRE) *Michael Bell* 92
3 b g Sir Percy Tiger Spice (Royal Applause)
2024[7] 2445[6] (3582) 5287[6] 6571[7]

Aztec Brave (FR) *E J O'Neill* 84
2 b c Pyrus(USA) Azteca (Spinning World (USA))
6293a[9]

Azubara (USA) *M Delzangles* 63
2 b c Speightstown(USA) Union City (USA) (Dixie Union (USA))
7185a[6]

Azucardel (FR) *T Lallie* a72 58
2 b c Della Francesca(USA) Azucar (IRE) (Desert Prince (IRE))
6961a[7]

Azzurra Du Caprio (IRE) *Ben Haslam* 85
5 ch f Captain Rio Dunbrody (FR) (Jeune Homme (USA))
1692[3] ◆ (2166) 2711[5] 3351[18] 6774[9]

Baan (USA) *James Eustace* a62 66
10 ch g Diesis Madaen (USA) (Nureyev (USA))
22[2] 430[5] 851[4] 1953[5] (3256) 4173[2] (4867) 5409[3] 7984[10] 8160[6]

Baarez (USA) *Roger Varian* 87
2 ch c Hard Spun(USA) Sortita (GER) (Monsun (GER))
6799[2] (7335)

Baars Causeway (IRE) *Alan Jarvis* a71 72
2 ch f Intense Focus(USA) Barbera (GER) (Night Shift (USA))
3663[3] ◆ 4484[5] 5891[2] 6821[9] 7062[2] 7441[4]

Baba O'Riley (IRE) *W Walton* a60 90
3 b c Whipper(USA) Speckled Hen (IRE) (Titus Livius (FR))
3708a[6]

Babaway (FR) *Mlle M Henry* a69
3 bb g Gold Away(IRE) Grande Aphrodite (USA) (Grand Slam (USA))
2335a[0]

Babel Ouest (FR) *J Van Handenhove* a88 75
5 b c Bachir(IRE) Belle De L'Ouest (FR) (Quai Voltaire (USA))
498a[7] 960a[6]

Babushka's Girl *Lisa Williamson* a13
4 b f Central Park(IRE) Shaymee's Girl (Wizard King)
2628[15] 4381[12] 4887[13] 5354[9] 6921[10]

Baby Bush (IRE) *Richard Hannon Snr* 79
2 b f Holy Roman Emperor(IRE) Mainstream Opinion (IRE) (Indian Ridge)
(3986) 5284[8] 6955[3]

Baby Dottie *Pat Phelan* a66 54
6 ch m Dr Fong(USA) Auntie Dot Com (Tagula (IRE))
156[2] (233) 323[2] 354[2] 493[6] 665[8] 3955[5] 4909[4] 6019[6] 7652[5] 8022[8]

Babyfact *Malcolm Saunders* 9
2 b f Piccolo Pennyspider (IRE) (Redback)
5584[10]

Baby Foot (IRE) *F Rossi* 104
2 b c Footstepsinthesand Baby Houseman (Oasis Dream)
5628a[2] 7056a[6]

Baby Judge (IRE) *Michael Chapman* a53 18
6 ch g Captain Rio Darling Clementine (Lion Cavern (USA))
3897[6]

Baby Mac *Neville Bycroft*
5 b g Presidium Nishara (Nishapour (FR))
5783[7] 5989[10] 8046[9]

Baby Queen (IRE) *Brian Baugh* a66 74
7 b m Royal Applause Kissing Time (Lugana Beach)
3042[2] 3569[12] 4074[7] 4712[2] 5227[10] 5669[7]

Baby Strange *Derek Shaw* a89 93
9 gr g Superior Premium The Manx Touch (IRE) (Petardia)
2214[9] 2460[10] 2868[4] (3823) 4983[8] 5537[3] 6331[6] 6831[5]

Baccarat (IRE) *Richard Fahey* a74 105
4 ch g Dutch Art Zut Alors (IRE) (Pivotal)
(1646) 3527[9] 4780[6] ◆ (5545) ◆ 6623[5] 7208[14]

Bacchelli *S Botti* 102
5 b c Mujahid(USA) Bugia (GER) (Kendor (FR))
7591a[5]

Bachelor Knight (IRE) *Suzzanne France* a41 59
5 b g Bachelor Duke(USA) Labetera (Lujain (USA))
42[8] 422[3] 551[7] 754[7] 909[11] 2752[5] 3029[7] 4005[10] 4893[10] 7948[5]

Bachotheque (IRE) *Tim Easterby* 85
3 b g Chineur(FR) Bacchanalia (IRE) (Blues Traveller (IRE))
2430[6] 3066[10] 3478[4] ◆ 4056[7] 5056[9] 6238[10]

Backbone (AUS) *Michael Kent* 101
5 b g Mossman(AUS) Fuss (AUS) (At Talaq (USA))
(7417a)

Back Burner (IRE) *David O'Meara* a93 95
5 br g Big Bad Bob(IRE) Marl (Lycius (USA))
3869a[13] 8276[2] 8353[4]

Back For Tea (IRE) *Phil McEntee* a48 28
5 b g Redback Jasmine Pearl (IRE) (King Of Kings (IRE))
114[6] 274[7] 322[3] 346[6] 449[5] 565[5] 667[5] 825[8] 1150[5] 1193[8] 1294[8] 1656[11] 2529[5]

Back In The Frame *David O'Meara* a61 64
3 b f Dutch Art Ile Deserte (Green Desert (USA))
8306[11] 8437[7]

Back Lane *Richard Fahey* 82
2 b c Invincible Spirit(IRE) Rivalry (Medicean)
3681[7] 4370[2] (4808) 5236[2] 6584[8] 7333[10]

Back On Baileys *Chris Dwyer* a55 15
2 b f Kyllachy Baileys Gleam (Compton Place)
1634[17] 6213[7] 6746[10] 7293[3] 7665[5] 8017[4] 8228[4] 8322[7]

Back On The Trail *Brian Ellison* a74 53
3 b g Singspiel(IRE) Boleyna (USA) (Officer (USA))
734[2] (1106) 1903[3] 2827[6] 5132[9] 6810[8]

Backstage Tour *A bin Huzaim* a68 68
3 ch c Manduro(GER) Welsh Diva (Selkirk (USA))
7683a[5]

Baddilini *Alan Bailey* a83 92
3 b g Bertolini(USA) Baddi Heights (FR) (Shirley Heights)
2188[6] 3342[14] 3840[11] 4217[7] 5009[11] 6506[2] 6575[2]

Badea *Martin Todhunter* a77 74
4 b g Cockney Rebel(IRE) Gibraltar Bay (IRE) (Cape Cross (IRE))
3043[4] 3652[2] 4016[6] 4809[7] 5059[6] 6632[10]

Badged *Lucy Normile* 71
4 b g High Chaparral(IRE) Meshhed (USA) (Gulch (USA))
1993[9]

Badger Or Bust (IRE) *Stephen Michael Cox* a51 55
8 b g Orpen(USA) Peace Dividend (IRE) (Alzao (USA))
5021a[13] (Dead)

Bad Medicine *Colin Teague*
3 b f Motivator Sagina (Shernazar)
6272[8] 6498[12]

Bad Mistone (FR) *E Nicoleau* a70 61
6 b g Bad As I Wanna Be(IRE) Miss Bahamas (FR) (Shining Steel)
127a[0]

Badr Al Badoor (IRE) *James Fanshawe* a94 88
3 b f Acclamation Dani Ridge (IRE) (Indian Ridge)
1620[11] 2708[8] (3691) (5103) ◆ 5700[6] 6692[4]

Bad Sir Brian (IRE) *M Ameye* 42
8 b g Bach(IRE) Ballyverane Pride (IRE) (Presenting)
3647a[9]

Bahaa (FR) *F Head* a73 72
3 b f Kentucky Dynamite(USA) La Bahamienne (IRE) (Fasliyev (USA))
1756a[0]

Bahama Bay *Stuart Williams* a46
3 b f Bahamian Bounty Green Bonnet (IRE) (Green Desert (USA))
3731[8] 4182[9] 7108[10] 8063[6] 8418[7]

Bahamamay *Richard Fahey* a47 68
3 ch g Bahamian Bounty May West (Act One)
1522[6] 3232[7] 3893[10] (4374) 4853[5] 5483[4] 5990[5] 6686[4]

Bahamian C *Richard Fahey* 78
2 b g Bahamian Bounty Amandian (IRE) (Indian Ridge)
3350[2] 4312[5] 5558[5] 6234[9] 7170[17]

Bahamian Heights *Clive Brittain* a93 97
2 b c Bahamian Bounty Tahirah (Green Desert (USA))
1619[5] 2591[6] 3291[3] (3991) 4212[7] 4918[10] (5656) 6201[4] 6584[7]

Bahamian Squall (USA) *David Fawkes* a118
4 bb c Gone West(USA) Midway Squall (USA) (Storm Bird (CAN))
7713a[6]

Bahrain Storm (IRE) *Noel Quinlan* a73 85
10 b g Bahhare(USA) Dance Up A Storm (USA) (Storm Bird (CAN))
654[7] 1927[5] 2197[7]

Bahri Sheen (IRE) *John Best* a65 40
5 b g Bahri(USA) Kama's Wheel (Magic Ring (IRE))
347[4]

Baiadera (GER) *R Dzubasz* a81 96
6 ch m Tertullian(USA) Belinga (GER) (Tannenkonig (IRE))
3970a[6]

Baie D'Honneur (FR) *D De Watrigant* 106
3 gr f Baroud D'Honneur(FR) Belle Lagune (Barathea (IRE))
2299a[11] 5461a[9] 7968a[10]

Baihas *Sir Michael Stoute* 90
3 b g Nayef(USA) Allegretto (IRE) (Galileo (IRE))
2055[2] ◆ (2967) 3526[9]

Bailadeira *Tim Etherington* a68 62
5 bb f Intikhab(USA) Sainte Gig (FR) (Saint Cyrien (FR))
(516) 760[5] 1355[4] 1596[5] 2542[7]

Baile Atha Cliath (IRE) *Declan Carroll* a55 34
4 b g Barathea(IRE) Danielli (IRE) (Danehill (USA))
1282[9] 2507[10] 6218[2] 6472[5] 6985[4] ◆ 7753[3] 8038[5]

Baileys Auteur (FR) *W Walton* a77
3 b c Librettist(USA) Perusha (USA) (Southern Halo (USA))
445a[2] 605a[2]

Baileys Celebrate *Mark Johnston* a28 39
2 b f Royal Applause Southern Psychic (USA) (Alwasmi (USA))
2419[7] 3766[7] 4539[11] 5634[8] 5898[6] 7094[4] 7789[6] 7956[10]

Baileys Forever *James Given* a43 69
2 ch f Mount Nelson Forever Fine (USA) (Sunshine Forever (USA))
3084[5] 4847[3] (5338) 7609[8] 7892[9]

Baileys Jubilee *Mark Johnston* a83 105
3 b f Bahamian Bounty Missisipi Star (IRE) (Mujahid (USA))
1622[10] 5984[14] 6235[11] 6505[4] 6685[5] 6989[11]

Baino Rock (FR) *J-C Rouget* 105
4 b f Rock Of Gibraltar(IRE) Baino Ridge (FR) (Highest Honor (FR))
5360a[8] 7843a[11]

Bain's Pass (IRE) *Kevin Ryan* a68 65
3 ch g Johannesburg(USA) Rose Bourbon (USA) (Woodman (USA))
849[4] (1064) 1372[2] 1609[5] 1743[2] 2079[3] 2924[5] (3194)

Bajan Bear *Michael Blanshard* a75 81
5 ch g Compton Place Bajan Rose (Dashing Blade)
2929[3] 3322[DSQ] 4303[2] ◆ (4884) 5062[3] 5489[8] 6648[5] 6977[9] 7742[12] 7896[7] 8128[4] 8431[3]

Bajan Beauty (IRE) *Charles Hills* 70
2 b f Footstepsinthesand Blue Crystal (IRE) (Lure (USA))
4347[7] 4921[6] 5983[3]

Bajan Rebel *Michael Easterby* a48 60
2 ch f Bahamian Bounty Silca Key (Inchinor)
2117[2] 4370[6] 5366[5] 6284[7] 6726[2] 7855[7]

Bajan Story *Michael Blanshard* a66 66
4 b g Lucky Story(USA) Bajan Rose (Dashing Blade)
840[4] 1303[2] 1617[10] 2228[2] 2574[7] 2932[8] 3434[12] 4126[9] 4996[7] 5596[3] 6400[8] 6737[7] 7124[8]

Bajan Tryst (USA) *Kevin Ryan* a101 105
7 bb g Speightstown(USA) Garden Secrets (USA) (Time For A Change (USA))
319[5] 3334[5] 3846a[23] 5544[16]

Baker Man (IRE) *Sylvester Kirk* a56 70
2 b g Dandy Man(IRE) Anne Bonney (Jade Robbery (USA))
3175[5] 6635[5] 6981[3] 7243[6]

Baker's Pursuit *Jim Goldie* a9 66
3 b f Pastoral Pursuits Little Caroline (IRE) (Great Commotion (USA))
3283[12] 5265[2] 5641[3] 5916[5] 6547[14] 6945[9] 7728[10]

Balad (IRE) *Saeed bin Suroor* 21
3 b c Exceed And Excel(AUS) Bright Morning (Dubai Millennium)
1618[10] (Dead)

Balady (IRE) *Dominic Ffrench Davis* a78 80
4 b f Zamindar(USA) Faydah (USA) (Bahri (USA))
1422[8] 1673[11] 2155[4] 2606[10] 2845[6] 3412[2] 4208[5] 4894[8] 5762[4] 6325[12]

Balashkova (FR) *J-C Rouget* 98
3 b f Montjeu(IRE) Ecume Du Jour (FR) (Hawk Wing (USA))
2970a[4]

Balatina *Chris Dwyer* a59 51
3 ch f Byron Primavera (Anshan)
1050[2] 1157[3] (1742) 2091[5] 2965[3] 3638[6] 7845[8] 8370[7]

Balaton *William Muir* a38 5
4 br f Singspiel(IRE) Traverse City (USA) (Halo (USA))
1953[8] 2828[12]

Balcibin (TUR) *Z Bektas* 95
5 b f Strike The Gold(USA) Candy Cove (Reprimand)
6231a[7]

Bal De France (FR) *S Kobayashi* 81
2 b c Della Francesca(USA) Baldoranic (FR) (Panoramic)
7828a[7]

Baldemar *Richard Fahey* a60 88
8 b g Namid Keen Melody (USA) (Sharpen Up)
1205[8] 1644[2] 2239[12] 3441[2] 4210[5] 4730[16] 5851[6]

Balder Succes (FR) *Alan King* a63 65
5 b g Goldneyev(USA) Frija Eria (FR) (Kadalko (FR))
6402[5] 6696[4]

Balducci *David O'Meara* a74 99
6 b g Dansili Miss Meltemi (IRE) (Miswaki Tern (USA))
3725[3] 4825[6] 5474[5] 8122[5]

Balinka *Mel Brittain* 70
3 b f Bahamian Bounty Eurolinka (IRE) (Tirol)
2076[9] 2544[9] 3946[11] 4727[4] 5141[3] 5422[10] 6604[3] 6944[6] 7772[15]

Balladry (USA) *Mahmood Al Zarooni* a102 77
5 gr c Unbridled's Song(USA) Storm Song (USA) (Summer Squall (USA))
870a[10]

Ballarina *Eric Alston* a61 66
7 b m Compton Place Miss Uluwatu (IRE) (Night Shift (USA))
3024[2] 5227[5] ◆ 5305[6]

Ballesteros *Richard Fahey* 108
4 ch g Tomba Flamenco Dancer (Mark Of Esteem (IRE))
2865[17] 3420[19] 6639[5] 7054a[9] 7527[8] 7821[11]

Ballinargh Girl (IRE) *Danielle McCormick* a61 69
5 b f Footstepsinthesand Rack And Ruin (IRE) (King's Best (USA))
2043[11] 2409[14] 7903[8] 8119[8]

Ballinderry Boy *Andrew Balding* a86 100
3 b g Kayf Tara Spring Dream (IRE) (Kalanisi (IRE))
1898[3] 2602[3] 5102[2] ◆ (6202) ◆ (6992) ◆ 7660[2]

Ballista (IRE) *Tom Dascombe* a113 113
5 b g Majestic Missile(IRE) Ancient Secret (Warrshan (USA))
365a[7] 660a[13] 868a[2] 954a[10] (2152) 2662[10] 5027[3] 5984[15] 7928[11] 8334[7] (8395)

Ball Lightning (FR) *E Libaud* a80 89
3 b c Sir Percy Tunguska (Silver Patriarch (IRE))
(3129a)

Ballybacka Queen (IRE) *P A Fahy* 97
2 b f Hurricane Run(IRE) Zankara (FR) (Linamix (FR))
6798[8]

Ballyheigue (IRE) *Gary Moore* a76 68
4 b g High Chaparral(IRE) Lypharden (IRE) (Lyphard's Special (USA))
8300[3]

Ballyorban (IRE) *K J Condon* 90
3 b g Cape Cross(IRE) Macheera (IRE) (Machiavellian (USA))
1555a[8] 7719a[15]

Ballyshonagh *Chris Wall* a68
3 b f Tiger Hill(IRE) Shamara (IRE) (Spectrum (IRE))
5925[7] 6312[7] 7864[5]

Balmont Mast (IRE) *Edward Lynam* a115 110
5 b g Balmont(USA) Corn Futures (Nomination)
150a[10] 365a[2] 660a[4] 955a[3] 1266a[2] 6414a[5] (7227a) 7364[11]

Balmoral Castle *Jonathan Portman* a61 73
4 b g Royal Applause Mimiteh (USA) (Maria's Mon (USA))
600[7] 993[2] 2089[2] 2395[3] (2845) (3106) 3244[8] 5479[3] 5793[9] 6794[3] 7430[5]

Balthazar (USA) *Dale Romans* 93
3 ch c Red Giant(USA) Dina Gold (USA) (Seeking The Gold (USA))
5551a[7]

Baltic Baroness (GER) *A Fabre* a74 108
3 b f Shamardal(USA) Born Wild (GER) (Sadler's Wells (USA))
1602a[2] (2381a) 3385a[10] 7048a[4]

Baltic Blade (IRE) *Gary Moore* a65 66
3 b g Baltic King Anita's Contessa (IRE) (Anita's Prince)
2016[4] 2447[7] ◆ 2872[8] *4169[9] 4755[5]* 5216[3]

Baltic Bomber (IRE) *John Quinn* 66
4 b g Baltic King Dieci Anno (IRE) (Classic Music (USA))
1283[9] 2343[4] 2835[4] 3090[10] 3190[8] 4009[12] 4292[5] 4761[9] 5486[6]

Baltic Brave (IRE) *Hughie Morrison* a69 60
2 b c Baltic King Negria (IRE) (Al Hareb (USA))
7125[4] 7426[4] *7790[3]*

Baltic Fire (IRE) *K R Burke* 58
2 b g Baltic King Teutonic (IRE) (Revoque (IRE))
1642[11] 1960[5] 2712[8] 4618[3] 5136[6] 5424[3] 6275[5]

Baltic Gin (IRE) *Malcolm Saunders* a52 63
3 b f Baltic King Deeday Bay (IRE) (Brave Act)
1978[3] 2394[12] 4240[4] 4881[4] 5431[5] 5817[8] 6902[9]

Baltic Knight (IRE) *Richard Hannon Snr* a83 113
3 b c Baltic King Night Of Joy (IRE) (King's Best (USA))
(1668) 2453[3] 2857[2] (3347) 4945[7]

Baltic Prince (IRE) *Paul Green* a63 68
3 b c Baltic King Brunswick (Warning)
923[10] 985[2] (1066) 1118[2] 1284[5] 1764[13] (2080) *2330[5]* (2916) 3232[8] 3683[3] 3758[4] 4056[3] (4288) 4806[3] 5273[12] 5676[7] 5886[5]

Baltic Spirit (IRE) *Keith Dalgleish* 63
2 b f Baltic King Beau Petite (Kyllachy)
3826[5] 5578[2] 5857[4] 6663[9] 6872[2]

Balti's Sister (IRE) *Martin Smith* a84 67
4 b f Tiger Hill(IRE) Itsibitsi (IRE) (Brief Truce (USA))
25[5] (358) 5437[9] 5758[7] *6341[6] 6608[6] 7861[2]*

Balty Boys (IRE) *Brian Ellison* 100
4 b g Cape Cross(IRE) Chatham Islands (USA) (Elusive Quality (USA))
1830[9] 2210[9] 3220[3] 3415[4] (3974) 4281[6] 4895[3] 5474[2] (5783) 6384[2] 6834[2] 7368[14]

Balu *J Hirschberger* 72
3 gr c With Approval(CAN) Hermanita (Hernando (FR))
1867a[8]

Banaadeer (IRE) *Richard Hannon Snr* 82
2 ch c Tamayuz Loose Julie (IRE) (Cape Cross (IRE))
3490[2] ◆ (3815) ◆ 4703[2] 5656[5]

Bana Wu *Andrew Balding* a85 106
4 ch f Shirocco(GER) My Way (IRE) (Marju (IRE))
2045[4] 2656[4] 3525[3] 5402[5] 6530[3] 7697[4]

Bancnuanaheireann (IRE) *Michael Appleby* a103 100
6 b g Chevalier(IRE) Alamanta (IRE) (Ali-Royal (IRE))
1235[15] 1840[6] (2193) 3339[9] 3697[6] 5007[3] 6427[3] (6801) *7927[2] 8156[4]*

Bandanaman (IRE) *Alan Swinbank* a16 68
7 b g Danehill Dancer(IRE) Band Of Angels (IRE) (Alzao (USA))
2720[10] 3771[4] 5048[7]

Bandolier *Richard Fahey* 66
2 b c Bahamian Bounty Todber (Cape Cross (IRE))
1680[4] 2005[4] 2955[8] 3767[4] 4990[2] (6047) 6493[7]

Bandstand *Bryan Smart* a85 74
7 b g Royal Applause Incise (Dr Fong (USA))
58[12] 526[5] 966[4] ◆ *1334[6]*

Bandy Bob *Iain Jardine* a46 39
4 b g Distant Music(USA) Angelic Girl (USA) (Swain (IRE))
1022[9] 1270[9] 1578[7]

Bang Tidy (IRE) *Brian Ellison* a63 67
4 b g Moss Vale(IRE) Bound To Glitter (USA) (Boundary (USA))
96[2] 1521[8] (1801) 2089[7] *2565[13]* 3444[9] *4155[4] 5072[3] 5594[8]*

Bank Of Burden (USA) *Niels Petersen* a104 104
6 ch g Hawk Wing(USA) Wewantitall (Pivotal)
462a[8] 661a[9] 873a[6] 3188a[3] 4095a[3] (5045a) 5809a[4] 6453a[2]

Bank On Me *Philip McBride* a90 85
4 ch g Medicean Red Garland (Selkirk (USA))
3368[3] 3812[3] 4765[4] 5124[2] ◆ 6236[10] *6694[7]* 6801[12] *7438[7]*

Bankroll *Jonjo O'Neill* a72 91
6 b g Pivotal Lady Bountiful (Spectrum (IRE))
1115[12] *1430[5] 2574[6]* 3901[5] 4593[10] *5135[13] 5677[9]* 6323[11] *7082[8]*

Banna Boirche (IRE) *M Halford* a103 101
7 b g Lucky Owners(NZ) Ziet D'Alsace (FR) (Zieten (USA))
241a[4] 463a[4] 557a[9] 836a[2] 3869a[9]

Bannock (IRE) *Charlie Appleby* a109 113
4 b g Bertolini(USA) Laoub (USA) (Red Ransom (USA))
838a[11] 4514[3] 5013[4]

Bannockburn Boy *Tim Easterby* 26
3 b g Motivator Senta's Dream (Danehill (USA))
1845[7] 2340[6] 2960[8]

Banoffee (IRE) *Hughie Morrison* a96 105
3 b f Hurricane Run(IRE) Nanabanana (IRE) (Anabaa (USA))
(1671) (2148) 2842[7] 4059[5] 4985[14] *7650[4] 8062[3]*

Banovallum *Sylvester Kirk* a68 81
3 b g Invincible Spirit(IRE) Sinduda (Anabaa (USA))
2285[6] 3020[5] ◆ 3582[9] 5401[8] *7264[5]*

Banreenahreenkah (IRE) *Jennie Candlish* a62 71
3 b f Steppe Dancer(IRE) Carmencita (Rock Of Gibraltar (IRE))
1904[4] 3241[4] *3641[4]* 4656[2] 5605[2] 6492[5] (7104) *8093[4]*

Bantam (IRE) *Ed Dunlop* a91 97
3 b f Teofilo(IRE) Firecrest (IRE) (Darshaan)
2442[5] ◆ 2804[2] 3239[2] *3908[4]* (4594) 5015[2] (5445) 5795[3] 7072[2] *7650[5]*

Banu (GER) *J-P Carvalho* a82 78
3 b f Lateral Barbea (GER) (Kallisto (GER))
7188a[3]

Bapak Bangsawan *Kevin Ryan* a77 72
3 b g Pastoral Pursuits Nsx (Roi Danzig (USA))
829[2] 915[2] (1051) 1524[2] 1791[6] 2076[3] 2614[3] 2888[3] 2959[7] *7444[11] 7783[3] (8128)*

Bapak Besar (CAN) *Kevin Ryan* a53 40
3 ch g Speightstown(USA) Valid Move (USA) (Valid Expectations (USA))
1965[6] *2330[9]*

Bapak Chinta (USA) *Kevin Ryan* 80
4 rg g Speightstown(USA) Suena Cay (USA) (Maria's Mon (USA))
1249[6] 2366[9] 3558[18] 4263[14] 6920[10] 7171[16]

Bapak Muda (USA) *Kevin Ryan* a72 80
3 ch c Distorted Humor(USA) Shiva (JPN) (Hector Protector (USA))
1461[2] 2167[6] *4144[2] (4378)* (5184) 5300[2] *6475[5] 8345[14]*

Bapak Pesta (IRE) *Kevin Ryan* a53 63
3 b g Haatef(USA) Penny Fan (Nomination)
1608[7] 4114[8] 5365[3] 5704[4] 6919[13] *7512[8] 7729[7] 7957[10] 8235[5] 8361[2] 8409[6]*

Bapak Sayang (USA) *Kevin Ryan* a77 82
3 b g Medaglia d'Oro(USA) Emily Ring (USA) (Fit To Fight (USA))
1645[8] 2022[5] ◆ 2452[8] 3097[2] 3591[5] 4734[12] 5057[6] *7888[5] 8069[6] 8439[10]*

Baraboy (IRE) *Barry Murtagh* a19 64
3 b g Barathea(IRE) Irina (IRE) (Polar Falcon (USA))
2274[6] 3394[8] 3772[6] 4826[4] 5142[3] 5334[7] 6600[8] (7153)

Barachiel *Luke Dace* a68 67
5 b g Pivotal Coveted (Sinndar (IRE))
118[3] 508[3] 896[3] 1158[4] 1325[3] (3688) 4166[3] 8089[10] 8331[14]

Barack (IRE) *W McCreery* a90 104
7 b g Pyrus(USA) Morna's Fan (FR) (Lear Fan (USA))
4465a[8]

Baradari (IRE) *J-C Rouget* 103
3 br g Manduro(GER) Behra (IRE) (Grand Lodge (USA))
1046a[3]

Baranain (SPA) *T Martins*
4 ch f Dyhim Diamond(IRE) Zaniah (SPA) (Sorcerous)
6252a[9]

Baratella (FR) *L Racco* 89
4 b f Orpen(USA) Brailovskaya (ITY) (Darshaan)
6890a[5]

Barathea Dancer (IRE) *Christine Dunnett* a51 81
5 b f Barathea(IRE) Showering (Danehill (USA))
3399[11] 3688[10]

Barbados Bob (USA) *Michael Wigham* a76 76
3 b g Speightstown(USA) Lemon Lady (USA) (Lemon Drop Kid (USA))
(7884) 8037[2] 8157[7] 8304[2] 8401[8]

Barbara Elizabeth *Tony Coyle* 39
2 b f Sir Percy Fair View (GER) (Dashing Blade)
2553[7] 3064[9] 5577[9] 6755[7]

Barbary (IRE) *James Fanshawe* a57 55
2 b g Rock Of Gibraltar(IRE) Silver Cache (USA) (Silver Hawk (USA))
3366[8] 3991[8] 5843[9] *7352[4]*

Barbecue Eddie (USA) *Doug Watson* a113 94
9 br g Stormy Atlantic(USA) The Green Owl (USA) (Carson City (USA))
(153a) 659a[3] 957a[13] 1262a[11]

Barbican *Alan Bailey* a114 108
5 b g Hurricane Run(IRE) The Faraway Tree (Suave Dancer (USA))
4796[4]

Barbsiz (IRE) *Mark H Tompkins* a57 42
3 ch f Elnadim(USA) Bianca Cappello (IRE) (Glenstal (USA))
904[5] 2762[8] 4071[13] 6971[7]

Barbs Princess *Charles Hills* a77 75
3 ch f Bahamian Bounty Halland Park Girl (IRE) (Primo Dominie)
1476[6] 1832[9] 2919[3] (3533) 7634[12] *8052[3]*

Barista (IRE) *Brian Forsey* a40 70
5 b g Titus Livius(FR) Cappuccino (IRE) (Mujadil (USA))
6932[9] (7109) 7430[4]

Barkston Ash *Eric Alston* 86
5 b g Kyllachy Ae Kae Ae (USA) (King Of Kings (IRE))
1113[6] 1646[3] 1838[6] 3200[2] 3714[5] 3980[7] 4560[5] 4812[4] 5292[9] 5705[6] (6287) 6548[9] 6822[10] (6908) 6977[14]

Barleycorn *Tim Easterby* 49
2 ch c Captain Gerrard(IRE) Barley Bree (IRE) (Danehill Dancer (IRE))
2075[8] 2475[5] 4156[6] 4538[5] 6511[10]

Barley Mow (IRE) *Richard Hannon Snr* 109
2 b c Zamindar(USA) Harvest Queen (IRE) (Spinning World (USA))
(5473) 6351[2] ◆ 7056a[5]

Barlovento (FR) *J Rossi* a80 72
7 gr g Tobougg(IRE) Tempete Tropicale (FR) (Kaldoun (FR))
960a[4]

Barnaby Brook (CAN) *Nick Littmoden* a73 37
3 b g North Light(IRE) Mascara (USA) (Milwaukee Brew (USA))
(895) 2050[8] 2641[5] 5960[7] *7786[10] 7877[4]*

Barnacle *Pat Eddery* a56 56
4 b g Compton Place Bombalarina (IRE) (Barathea (IRE))
1325[4] 1744[4] 2777[5] (2991) 4147[4]

Barnet Fair *Richard Guest* a100 103
5 br g Iceman Pavement Gates (Bishop Of Cashel)
947[8] 2207[11] 2669[6] 3334[3] ◆ 4275[15] 4472[8] (4800) 4986[12] 5651[5] 6391[17] 6830[5]

Barney McGrew (IRE) *Michael Dods* a78 85
10 b g Mark Of Esteem(IRE) Success Story (Sharrood (USA))
1787[8] 2441[4] 2914[11] 3351[10] 3811[5] 4198[3] (4577) 5481[4] 5974[13]

Barnmore *Peter Hedger* a71 29
5 b g Royal Applause Veronica Franco (Darshaan)
4169[12] (5098) 5387[10]

Baronia (SPA) *G Arizkorreta Elosegui* 95
6 b m Bahhare(USA) Lonia (GER) (Royal Academy (USA))
2969a[7]

Baron Run *K R Burke* a71 76
3 ch g Bertolini(USA) Bhima (Polar Falcon (USA))
1299[3] 1911[2] 2672[5] *3212[5]* 4814[8] 5184[5] (5919) (6664) 6977[8]

Barons Spy (IRE) *Richard Price* a84 93
12 b g Danzero(AUS) Princess Accord (USA) (D'Accord (USA))
1287[5] 1726[15] 2214[11] 2825[8] 3038[5] 3411[10] 4884[10] 5304[9]

Barracuda Boy (IRE) *Tom Dascombe* a99 99
3 b g Bahamian Bounty Madame Boulangere (Royal Applause)
1808[3] 3348[3] 3823[7] 4255[14] 5260[3] *6692[2]* 6830[9]

Barren Brook *Michael Easterby* 88
6 b g Beat Hollow Carinthia (IRE) (Tirol)
1576[8] 3349[5] 3683[15] 4264[2] 4810[4] 5546[12] 5860[7] 6236[5] 7028[3] 7211[12]

Barsam (FR) *P Bary* a71 71
3 ch c Tomorrows Cat(USA) Belga Wood (USA) (Woodman (USA))
1850a[8] 2434a[3]

Bar Shy *Tim Easterby* 53
2 b g Dutch Art Notable Lady (IRE) (Victory Note (USA))
2883[8] 4044[7] 4556[4] 6284[8]

Bartack (IRE) *Luca Cumani* a87 85
3 b g Acclamation Bentley's Bush (IRE) (Barathea (IRE))
1577[2] 2309[2] (3011) 3683[12] 4425[2] *(5134)* 6356[6] *6925[3]*

Bartley *Bryan Smart* a67 76
4 ch g Monsieur Bond(IRE) Annie Harvey (Fleetwood (IRE))
162[6] 435[11] 523[3]

Barton Bounty *Peter Niven* a65 61
6 b g Bahamian Bounty Tenebrae (IRE) (In The Wings)
1790[4] (2972) 3543[5] (4099) 4516[4] *6339[8]* 6722[4] *7169[8]*

Barwick *Mark H Tompkins* a68 87
5 b g Beat Hollow Tenpence (Bob Back (USA))
1751[6] 2659[6] 3019[3] 4957[9] 5947[3] 6360[3] 6538[4] 7608[10]

Baschar *M G Mintchev* 115
6 b h Starcraft(NZ) Belle Et Deluree (USA) (The Minstrel (CAN))
3879a[5] 4819a[6]

Bashama *Nikki Evans* a57 58
5 ch f Dubai Destination(USA) My Amalie (IRE) (Galileo (IRE))
476[5] 707[3] 901[3] 1070[6] 1353[6]

Bashart (USA) *Todd Pletcher* a102 102
2 b c War Front(USA) Busy Windsong (USA) (Clever Trick (USA))
7688a[6]

Bashiba (IRE) *Nigel Tinkler* 43
2 ch c Iffraaj Nightswimmer (IRE) (Noverre (USA))
4724[9] 5105[7] 6790[9] 7147[6]

Basil Berry *Chris Dwyer* a69 60
2 b g Tobougg(IRE) Dolly Coughdrop (IRE) (Titus Livius (FR))
2758[7] 3581[10] 4218[10] *5068[3] 5634[5]* ◆ *(6170) 6731[6] 7463[8]* 7819[10] *8261[7] 8452[3]*

Basingstoke (IRE) *Keith Dalgleish* a62 68
4 b g Elusive City(USA) Ryninch (IRE) (Dr Devious (IRE))
548[6] 1568[8]

Basle *Roy Brotherton* a67 61
6 b m Trade Fair Gibaltarik (IRE) (Jareer (USA))
(50) 346[4] 616[3] 1657[10] 1887[7] 2364[2] 2596[5] 3270[4] *(3644) 4385[11] 7163[8] 7807[9]* 8163[8] 8278[8] 8446[8]

Bassara (IRE) *Chris Wall* 89
4 b f Oasis Dream Sauvage (FR) (Sri Pekan (USA))
(2639) ◆ (3368) 4258[6] 4960[8] 6988[14]

Basseterre (IRE) *Charles Hills* a93 96
4 b c Cape Cross(IRE) Higher Love (IRE) (Sadler's Wells (USA))
2018[5] ◆ 2592[7] 3113[4] 3570[3] (4258)

Bassett Road (IRE) *Keith Dalgleish* a76 72
5 ch g Byron Topiary (IRE) (Selkirk (USA))
(194) 380[8] 603[5] 812[9] 1253[9] 1460[4] 1995[4] 2037[6] 2797[3] 3714[8] 4102[11] 4338[10] 7344[2] *7652[2] 7754[2]* 7801[6]

Bass Strait (NZ) *David Hayes* 102
4 b g Holy Roman Emperor(IRE) Crystalline (NZ) (Zabeel (NZ))
7700a[12]

Bastiani (IRE) *L Racco* 96
3 b c Shamardal(USA) Bessie Bennett (IRE) (Be My Guest (USA))
1865a[6] 7725a[8]

Bastion (USA) *Roger Varian* a65 79
3 b g Giant's Causeway(USA) Marital Spook (USA) (Silver Ghost (USA))
1722[2] 4011[5]

Batchelors Star (IRE) *Seamus Durack* a70 79
5 ch g Fath(USA) Batchelor's Button (FR) (Kenmare (FR))
1346[8] 2574[8] 2920[4] 3617[6] 5694[3] 6158[U]

Batchworth Firefly *Dean Ivory* a57 30
5 b f Piccolo Batchworth Belle (Interrex (CAN))
1781[10] 2126[5] 2345[12] 2789[4]

Batchworth Lady *Dean Ivory* a70 65
3 b f Pastoral Pursuits Batchworth Belle (Interrex (CAN))
114[2] 416[3] 561[4] (1050) 2091[2] (2347) 2829[5] *(6560)* 7106[11] *7743[4] 8052[11]*

Batgirl *Martin Smith* a65 74
6 ch m Mark Of Esteem(IRE) Serriera (FR) (Highest Honor (FR))
354[8] 4671[4] ◆ 4909[2] 5152[3] 5802[3] 6068[8] 6794[5] 6952[2]

Bathcounty (IRE) *Barry Brennan* a41
6 ch g Tobougg(IRE) Seasons Estates (Mark Of Esteem (IRE))
521[5]

Bathwick Street *David Evans* a73 80
4 ch g Compton Place Bahawir Pour (USA) (Green Dancer (USA))
948[4] 1445[6] (1899) (2284)

Bathyrhon (GER) *S Arslangirej* a78 75
3 b c Monsun(GER) Be My Lady (GER) (Be My Guest (USA))
5576a[7]

Battalion (IRE) *William Haggas* 102
3 b c Authorized(IRE) Zigarra (Halling (USA))
2151[5] 3491[2] 3989[4] (5058) (6503) ◆ 7705a[3]

Battante (FR) *J-V Toux* a75
3 b f Muhtathir Bahama Love (USA) (Hennessy (USA))
962a[5]

Battersea *Roger Varian* 75
2 b c Galileo(IRE) Gino's Spirits (Perugino (USA))
7019[9] 7332[3]

Battibecco (IRE) *Robert Cowell* 90
4 b g Le Vie Dei Colori Agata Laguna (IRE) (Elnadim (USA))
3897[3] 5155[5]

Battier (ITY) *L Polito* 72
3 b c Blu Air Force(IRE) Luisa Regina (ITY) (Central Park (IRE))
1865a[11]

Battle Command (USA) *Peter Chapple-Hyam* 57
2 bb c Stormy Atlantic(USA) Charmsil (USA) (Silver Charm (USA))
7467[10]

Battlefront (USA) *J-C Rouget* a89 84
2 b c War Front(USA) Baroness Richter (IRE) (Montjeu (IRE))
5628a[9] *7570a[7]*

Battle Of Marengo (IRE) *A P O'Brien* 118
3 b c Galileo(IRE) Anna Karenina (IRE) (Green Desert (USA))
(1558a) (2290a) 2866[4] 3523[2] 4325a[7]

Battleoftheboyne (IRE) *Michael Mulvany* a79 94
4 b c Majestic Missile(IRE) Khaytada (IRE) (Doyoun)
3846a[30] 5019a[12]

Bavarian Nordic (USA) *Richard Whitaker* a63 61
8 b g Barathea(IRE) Dubai Diamond (Octagonal (NZ))
2961[7] 3652[3] 4809[2] 5059[3] 6290[14] *7881[5] 8047[7] 8270[10] 8410[2]*

Bayan (IRE) *Gordon Elliott* a68 86
4 b g Danehill Dancer(IRE) Kindling (Dr Fong (USA))
3599a[6] 7723a[3]

Bayan Kasirga (IRE) *Richard Fahey* a66 89
3 b f Aussie Rules(USA) Gwyllion (USA) (Red Ransom (USA))
1772[2] 2420[7] 2915[4] 4049[3] 4401[2] (5343) 5920[U] (6470) 6631[7] (7100) ◆ (7239)

Bayargal (USA) *A Fabre* a105 99
3 b f Bernstein(USA) Bailonguera (ARG) (Southern Halo (USA))
4700a[7] *8440a[3]*

Baybshambles (IRE) *Tina Jackson* 60
9 b g Compton Admiral Payvashooz (Ballacashtal (CAN))
4621[8] 4892[8] 5889[9] 6180[7] 6760[9] 6944[11]

Bay Knight (IRE) *Sean Curran* a82 92
7 b g Johannesburg(USA) Sabeline (IRE) (Caerleon (USA))
(5063) 5759[4] 6988[15] 7224[12] *7885[3] 8269[11]*

Bay Laurel (IRE) *Mrs K Burke* a64 39
3 b f Baltic King Bayleaf (Efisio)
17[3] 195[7]

Bayleyf (IRE) *John Best* a96 96
4 b g Kheleyf(USA) Hi Katriona (IRE) (Second Empire (IRE))
1215[5] 1913[10] 3153[7] 4198[12] 4425[3] *6525[10] 7123[13] 7462[13]*

Baynunah (USA) *James Fanshawe* a66
2 br f Medaglia d'Oro(USA) Damaniyat Girl (USA) (Elusive Quality (USA))
7295[5] 7764[4]

Bay Street Belle *Philip Kirby*
2 ch f Bahamian Bounty Donna Anna (Be My Chief (USA))
6512[9]

Baytown Bertie *Lydia Richards* a38 7
4 b g Orientor Baytown Flyer (Whittingham (IRE))
748[7] 1057[10] 1178[8] 1473[7] 7093[10]

Baytown Kestrel *Brian Ellison* a81 73
2 b f Captain Gerrard(IRE) Litewska (IRE) (Mujadil (USA))
(2947) 3459[21] 3767[2] 4261[2] 4783[4] *(5351)* 5767[5] 6376[8] *(6731)*

Baytown Tigress *Phil McEntee* a21
2 b f Tiger Hill(IRE) House Maiden (IRE) (Rudimentary (USA))
7934[10] 8138[9] 8221[6]

Bay Willow (IRE) *S Seemar* a102 90
6 b g Singspiel(IRE) Tree House (USA) (Woodman (USA))
(362a) 555a[8] *833a[4]*

Baz (FR) *F-H Graffard* a78 82
3 b g Mount Nelson Zelah (IRE) (Alzao (USA))
2034a[2] 2403a[2] *3129a[7]*

Bazart *Bernard Llewellyn* a76 62
11 b g Highest Honor(FR) Summer Exhibition (Royal Academy (USA))
4915[7]

Bazooka (IRE) *Ed de Giles* a70 51
2 b c Camacho Janadam (IRE) (Mukaddamah (USA))
6477[9] 6746[7] 7394[3] *7788[2] 7986[2] 8138[2]*

Beach Bar (IRE) *William Knight* a77 66
2 b g Azamour(IRE) Toasted Special (USA) (Johannesburg (USA))
4987[10] 6277[5] *(7779)*

Beach Candy (IRE) *Phil McEntee* a64 78
4 ch f Footstepsinthesand Endure (IRE) (Green Desert (USA))
(111) (128) 369^{9} 398^{12}

Beach Club *David Brown* a88 94
3 b c Footstepsinthesand Dunya (Unfuwain (USA))
1477^{2} ◆ 2285^{8} 3234^{2} (4078)

Beach Of Falesa (IRE) *A P O'Brien* 100
4 b f Dylan Thomas(IRE) Leonia (IRE) (Sadler's Wells (USA))
1166a^{5} 3381a^{8} 5115a^{5}

Beach Rhythm (USA) *Jim Allen* a62 37
6 ch g Footstepsinthesand Queen's Music (USA) (Dixieland Band (USA))
2395^{9} *2998^{4}* 3700^{7} *4635^{6} 5230^{4} (5864)* 6436^{9} *6994^{2} 7508^{5} (7903) 8272^{4} 8411^{6}*

Beachwood Bay *Jo Hughes* a69 49
5 b g Tobougg(IRE) The Terrier (Foxhound (USA))
4884^{13} 5876^{8} 7427^{5} *7957^{5} 8315^{2}*

Beacon Lady *William Knight* a29 93
4 ch f Haafhd Oriental Lady (IRE) (King's Best (USA))
1949^{11} 2533^{13} 3151^{2} (3655) 3924^{2} 4429^{2} (4663) (5168) (5216) (5823) 6016^{4} 6646^{10} 7250^{8}

Beacon Lodge (IRE) *T Stack* 104
8 b g Clodovil(IRE) Royal House (FR) (Royal Academy (USA))
1691^{8} 2399^{13} 2477^{6} 3335^{5} 3564^{3} 3931^{3} 4062^{7} 4803^{4} 7388a^{3} 7719a^{13}

Beacon Tarn *Eric Alston* a78 52
3 b f Shamardal(USA) Baize (Efisio)
1349^{6} 1962^{9} 2317^{4} 3134^{4} 3626^{4} *(7759) 7903^{2} 8052^{8} (8352)*

Be A Flirt (IRE) *J E Hammond* a66 67
3 b f Refuse To Bend(IRE) Dark Hyacinth (IRE) (Darshaan)
7736a^{3}

Beakers N Num Nums (IRE) *William Jarvis* a52
2 b c Iffraaj Ivy League Star (IRE) (Sadler's Wells (USA))
7327^{7}

Beam Of Light *Jamie Osborne* a48 72
3 b f Bertolini(USA) Lighted Way (Kris)
5758^{8} *6316^{12} 7163^{9}*

Bear Behind (IRE) *Tom Dascombe* a96 107
4 b g Kodiac Gerobies Girl (USA) (Deposit Ticket (USA))
150a^{3} 464a^{3} 746a^{4} *1032^{6}* 2300a^{5} 2768^{5} 5257^{9} 6129^{3} 6830^{13}

Be A Rebel *John E Long*
3 b f Cockney Rebel(IRE) Star Apple (Barathea (IRE))
7781^{10} 7894^{11}

Bearing Kisses (IRE) *Shaun Harris* 37
2 gr f Clodovil(IRE) Masakira (IRE) (Royal Academy (USA))
1534^{5} 2147^{9} 5773a^{17}

Bear Power (GER) *C Sprengel* 69
2 b c Desert Prince(IRE) Bearall (IRE) (Al Hareb (USA))
7232a^{9}

Bearskin (IRE) *Ann Duffield* 62
2 br g Kodiac Dark Arts (USA) (Royal Anthem (USA))
6206^{9} 6769^{4} 7419^{5}

Beastfromtheeast *Ed Walker* a31
2 b g Oratorio(IRE) Bronze Star (Mark Of Esteem (IRE))
8061^{11} 8342^{13}

Beatabout The Bush (IRE) *Charles Hills* 56
2 bb g Bushranger(IRE) Queen Of Fibres (IRE) (Scenic)
4795^{8} 5584^{5} 6590^{10}

Beat Baby (IRE) *Niels Petersen* a99 103
6 ch g Johannesburg(USA) Najiya (Nashwan (USA))
464a^{8} 746a^{8} *(2145a) 5325a^{3}*

Beat Of The Drum (IRE) *Richard Hannon Snr* a70 71
3 b f Duke Of Marmalade(IRE) Square Pants (USA) (King Of Kings (IRE))
(1499) 2223^{4} 3842^{7}

Beatrice *H-A Pantall* a84 104
3 b f Dr Fong(USA) Brangane (IRE) (Anita's Prince)
(2065a) 2910a^{4} 4092a^{12} (6231a)

Beatrice Aurore (IRE) *Ed Dunlop* 109
5 b f Danehill Dancer(IRE) Mondschein (Rainbow Quest (USA))
2838^{9} 3456^{4} ◆ 4985^{13} 5809a^{2}

Beat Route *Michael Attwater* a79 71
6 ch g Beat Hollow Steppin Out (First Trump)
1193 809^{2} 1031^{5} (1158) 1615^{7} 2197^{3} 3587^{5} *3959^{10} 5231^{2}*

Beat The Bell *Jamie Osborne* a80 86
8 b g Beat All(USA) Bella Beguine (Komaite (USA))
92^{3}

Beat The Shower *Peter Niven* a46 71
7 b g Beat Hollow Crimson Shower (Dowsing (USA))
1390^{10} 1805^{11} 2242^{4} 2540^{6} 2990^{4} 3627^{2} 4989^{4} 5831^{0} 6290^{4} 6632^{5} 7099^{2}

Beat The Tide *Michael Dods* 80
3 b g Black Sam Bellamy(IRE) Sablonne (USA) (Silver Hawk (USA))
2624^{2} 4023^{6} (4822) 5549^{3} 6917^{5}

Beau Amadeus (IRE) *David Nicholls* a68 72
4 b g Amadeus Wolf Degree Of Honor (FR) (Highest Honor (FR))
976^{6} 4807^{5} 5832^{7} 6209^{2} 6728^{5} 7343^{5}

Beauchamp Astra *Hans Adielsson* a38
3 b f Observatory(USA) Ashford Castle (USA) (Bates Motel (USA))
4356^{9}

Beauchamp Sunset *Paul Fitzsimons* a47
3 b g Tiger Hill(IRE) Orange Sunset (IRE) (Roanoke (USA))
2566^{5} 8371^{10}

Beauchamp Xerxes *Hans Adielsson* a74 56
7 ch g Compton Admiral Compton Astoria (USA) (Lion Cavern (USA))
1310 478^{9} 840^{6} (1162) 1311^{6} 3054^{7} *3434^{4} (3642)* 3889^{7} *6105^{7}* 6802^{8}

Beaufort Twelve *William Jarvis* a63 97
4 b g Hurricane Run(IRE) Violette (Observatory (USA))
3113^{3} 3832^{8} 4301^{4} 5147^{3} 5259^{9} 6001^{13} *6936^{11}*

Beau Michael *Adrian McGuinness* a74 87
9 b g Medicean Tender Moment (IRE) (Caerleon (USA))
5021a^{17}

Beau Mistral (IRE) *Paul Green* a80 88
4 ch f Windsor Knot(IRE) Carpet Lover (IRE) (Fayruz)
966^{6} 1370^{9} 1649^{8} 2028^{11} *2513^{6}* 3236^{7} 3682^{9} 4479^{6} 4930^{7} 5227^{2} (5376) 5775a^{6} 6161^{3} 6515^{5} (6757) 7634^{11}

Beaumont Cooper *Anabel K Murphy* 67
4 b g Invincible Spirit(IRE) Atlantide (USA) (Southern Halo (USA))
2089^{12} 2710^{13}

Beaumont's Party (IRE) *Brian Ellison* a71 101
6 b g High Chaparral(IRE) Miss Champagne (FR) (Bering)
(1391) (1538) 2185^{3} 2407^{2} 3559^{10} 4060^{9} 4310^{9} 5283^{9} 6551^{2} 6801^{15} 7536^{2} 7775^{3}

Beau Nash (IRE) *Richard Hannon Snr* a88 86
2 b c Dandy Man(IRE) Dathuil (IRE) (Royal Academy (USA))
1360^{2} ◆ 1659^{2} (2391) 3424^{14} 4232^{7} 5745^{3} *6132^{2} 7122^{3}*

Beau Sakhee *Adrian McGuinness* a53 53
3 b g Sakhee's Secret Pure Speculation (Salse (USA))
5^{3} 38^{3} 55^{9}

Beau Select (IRE) *Robert Eddery* a68 67
3 b g Lucky Story(USA) Practicallyperfect (IRE) (King Charlemagne (USA))
632^{2} 1219^{4} 1424^{2} 2272^{3} 2324^{7} 3062^{11} 3722^{4} 4665^{5} 5491^{10}

Beau Slam (FR) *H-A Pantall* a70
3 b c Grand Slam(USA) Great Lady Slew (USA) (Seattle Slew (USA))
331a^{0}

Beautiful Day *Kevin Ryan* a89 69
5 b g Piccolo Evening (Mark Of Esteem (IRE))
(49) 400^{7}

Beautiful Forest *Saeed bin Suroor* 53
2 ch f Nayef(USA) Baya (USA) (Nureyev (USA))
6754^{7}

Beautiful Life *David Simcock* a50
3 b f Footstepsinthesand My Heart's Deelite (USA) (Afternoon Deelites (USA))
1213^{5}

Beautiful Story (IRE) *Mick Channon* a61 61
3 gr f Verglas(IRE) To The Skies (USA) (Sky Classic (CAN))
1499^{6} 1928^{5} 2324^{11} 3041^{7}

Beautiful Stranger (IRE) *Keith Dalgleish* a62 65
2 b c Iffraaj Monarchy (IRE) (Common Grounds)
4576^{3} 6581^{5} 7341^{4} *7788^{5}*

Beautiful View *Richard Hannon Snr* 86
3 ch f Dubawi(IRE) Flamenco Dancer (Mark Of Esteem (IRE))
3334^{8} 3784^{6} 4252^{9} 7272^{2} 7538^{7}

Beautifulwildthing *William Kinsey* 60
3 b f Mount Nelson Euro Empire (USA) (Bartok (IRE))
2742^{9}

Beauty Pageant (IRE) *David Brown* a82 81
6 ch m Bahamian Bounty My American Beauty (Wolfhound (USA))
58^{11} 196^{11} 518^{7} 778^{8} 878^{11} 1102^{8} 1324^{2} 1398^{6} 2132^{5} 5155^{3} 5796^{4} 6088^{5} 6753^{3} (6879) 6994^{3} 7236^{2}

Beauty Parlour *Sir Henry Cecil* 119
4 b f Deep Impact(JPN) Bastet (IRE) (Giant's Causeway (USA))
2694a^{6}

Becausewecan (USA) *Brian Ellison* a57 93
7 b g Giant's Causeway(USA) Belle Sultane (USA) (Seattle Slew (USA))
7230a^{26} 7597^{9} *7735^{3}*

Beckermet (IRE) *Ruth Carr* a78 93
11 b g Second Empire(IRE) Razida (IRE) (Last Tycoon)
1280^{3} 1459^{4} (1964) 2275^{4} 2664^{6} 3068^{12} 3501^{3} 3945^{10} 4338^{2} 4577^{4} 5049^{3} 5832^{3} 6052^{2} 6291^{5} 6905^{3} 7281^{5} (7344) 7595^{4} 7824^{13}

Beck's Bolero (IRE) *Mrs A Corson* a18 58
7 ch g Haafhd Prealpina (IRE) (Indian Ridge)
2302a^{2} 7145a^{6}

Becquanis (FR) *E Wianny* a80 38
4 bb g Panis(USA) Berangele (FR) (Medaaly)
963a^{6}

Becquarius (FR) *Y Fouin* a68 57
3 b c Medecis Berangele (FR) (Medaaly)
1495a^{8}

Bed Bed *Michael Bell* a42
2 b f Nayef(USA) Bedara (Barathea (IRE))
7450 ^{9} *7645^{12} 8332^{12}*

Bedetti *F Brogi* 103
5 b c Ekraar(USA) Buenos Aires (ITY) (Mukaddamah (USA))
2295a^{5} 2489a^{9}

Bedibyes *Richard Mitchell* a61 59
5 b f Sleeping Indian Aunt Sadie (Pursuit Of Love)
1298^{8}

Bedloe's Island (IRE) *Alan McCabe* a91 90
8 b g Statue Of Liberty(USA) Scenaria (IRE) (Scenic)
1807^{4} (2031) 2396^{8} 2505^{6} 3299^{4} 4047^{9} *(8232)*

Bedouin Invader (IRE) *Sir Michael Stoute* a87 73
3 b g Oasis Dream Hovering (IRE) (In The Wings)
1882^{2} *(2953)* 3862^{5}

Beedee *Richard Hannon Snr* a88 92
3 b c Beat Hollow Dawnus (IRE) (Night Shift (USA))
4415^{3} 4897^{8} 5401^{2} 6868^{10} 7205^{7} 7656^{4}

Bee Jay Kay *Brian Ellison* a63 78
3 ch f Sixties Icon Straight Sets (IRE) (Pivotal)
1666^{8} *1904^{5}* 2016^{3} 3039^{3} 3376^{5} 3528^{3} *3820^{6}* 4196^{2} (4474) 4950^{6} 5448^{4} (5791) 6869^{P}

Beep *Lydia Richards* a37 71
3 b f Beat Hollow Dialing Tone (USA) (Distant View (USA))
1828^{7} 2519^{4} 5588^{6} 6146^{7} *7922^{9}*

Be Excellent *Joseph Tuite* a23 28
3 b f Oratorio(IRE) Saphila (IRE) (Sadler's Wells (USA))
1035^{7} 2099^{7}

Before Bruce *Brendan Powell* a51 67
6 b g Danbird(AUS) Bisque (Inchinor)
12^{8} 418^{10}

Befortyfour *Charles Smith* a49 53
8 b g Kyllachy Ivania (First Trump)
7729^{8} 7772^{13} *8050^{3} 8169^{6}*

Beggers Belief *Zoe Davison* a60 62
5 ch g Bertolini(USA) Dropitlikeit's Hot (IRE) (Tagula (IRE))
94^{11} 722^{4} 983^{2} 1090^{6} 1715^{5} 2159^{8} 8121^{12}

Be Gifted *John E Long*
3 b f Sakhee(USA) Be Decisive (Diesis)
5277^{9} 5932^{8}

Beholder (USA) *Richard E Mandella* a123
3 b f Henny Hughes(USA) Leslie's Lady (USA) (Tricky Creek (USA))
(7691a)

Bejeweled (IRE) *Lady Cecil* a61 71
3 br f Rock Of Gibraltar(IRE) Gems Of Araby (Zafonic (USA))
4182^{2} ◆ *5133^{4} 6133^{4}* 6794^{6} *7434^{8}*

Belango (GER) *R Dzubasz* 102
7 ch g Tertullian(USA) Brighella (GER) (Lomitas)
6987a^{9} 7831a^{6}

Belayer (IRE) *Kevin Ryan* 77
2 b g Whipper(USA) Stella Del Mattino (USA) (Golden Gear (USA))
(4370) 4948^{18} 6194^{3} 7492^{8}

Beldale Memory (IRE) *Clive Cox* 91
2 b f Camacho Hartstown House (IRE) (Primo Dominie)
(1659) (2426) 3459^{14}

Belgian Bill *George Baker* a110 107
5 b c Exceed And Excel(AUS) Gay Romance (Singspiel (IRE))
149a^{10} 241a^{11} 1244^{2} 1675^{15} (3458) 4297^{14} 5808a^{2} 6451a^{6} 6838^{10}

Believe In Me *Julia Feilden* a39 34
3 b f Bertolini(USA) Zephrina (Zafonic (USA))
3013^{7} 7610^{9} *7987^{8}*

Belinsky (IRE) *Julie Camacho* a70 68
6 b g Compton Place Westwood (FR) (Anabaa (USA))
95^{3} 3811^{12} 4669^{9} 5487^{5} 6761^{12} *7743^{10} 7896^{9}*

Bella Bijou *Christopher Kellett* a14 21
3 br f Multiplex Madam Bijou (Atraf)
3641^{11}

Bella Cinderella *George Moore* a35
3 b f Tiger Hill(IRE) Design Perfection (USA) (Diesis)
148^{7} 706^{10} 972^{6}

Bella Michelle *Sylvester Kirk* 32
3 b f Sakhee's Secret Michelle Ma Belle (IRE) (Shareef Dancer (USA))
2099^{6} 2597^{13}

Bell'Arte (IRE) *Laura Mongan* a55 64
3 b f Zamindar(USA) Art Eyes (USA) (Halling (USA))
1393^{3} *2175^{6}* 2508^{6} *5528^{11}* 6257^{4} *7118^{6} 7331^{2}*

Bella's Charm *James Tate* 29
3 b f Hernando(FR) Odabella's Charm (Cadeaux Genereux)
3272^{9}

Bella Sheba (FR) *Mme L Poulain de la Fontaine* a69 69
4 b f Slickly(FR) Bahia Star (FR) (Mansonnien (FR))
7573a^{5}

Bella Varenna (IRE) *Marco Botti* 62
2 b f Lawman(FR) Sarawati (IRE) (Haafhd)
5282^{10} 6828^{7}

Belle Aumone (FR) *S Jesus* a63 57
5 b f Miesque's Son(USA) Salut Simone (FR) (Simon Du Desert (FR))
7573a^{13}

Belle Bayardo (IRE) *Ronald Harris* a74 74
5 b g Le Vie Dei Colori Heres The Plan (IRE) (Revoque (IRE))
11^{4} 86^{5} 535^{7} 583^{4} 688^{2} 775^{7} 971^{11} 2918^{2} 3529^{7} 3622^{2} 4034^{4} 4428^{4} 4712^{3} 5278^{5} 5389^{2} 5669^{5} 6096^{6} 7801^{10} 7957^{6} 8330^{7}

Belle De Crecy (IRE) *J P Murtagh* 112
4 b f Rock Of Gibraltar(IRE) Bloemfontain (IRE) (Cape Cross (IRE))
6225a^{4} (6416a) 7365^{2}

Belle Isle *Jeremy Noseda* a42
3 br f Pastoral Pursuits Bowness (Efisio)
549^{4} 979^{7}

Belle Noverre (IRE) *John Butler* a62 83
9 b m Noverre(USA) Belle Etoile (FR) (Lead On Time (USA))
435^{7} 1070^{8}

Belle Park *Karen George* a54 60
6 b m Hamairi(IRE) Cape Siren (Warning)
1730^{6} 3314^{9} 3954^{3} 5434^{2} 6492^{6} *7458^{10}*

Belle Peinture (FR) *Richard Fahey* a44
2 ch f Peintre Celebre(USA) Grosgrain (USA) (Diesis)
7934^{8} 8165^{6} 8266^{6}

Belliche *Marco Gasparini* 52
5 b f Halling(USA) Emanant (Emarati (USA))
1563a^{10}

Bellinda *Martin Bosley* a41
4 b f Aussie Rules(USA) Bonnie Belle (Imperial Ballet (IRE))
59^{8}

Bellitudo (IRE) *Marco Botti* a69 4
3 ch f Shamardal(USA) Night Life (IRE) (Night Shift (USA))
1892^{7} 2763^{7} *3216^{8}*

Belly To Belly (IRE) *S Botti* 90
4 b f Dubawi(IRE) Penfection (IRE) (Orpen (USA))
1563a^{8}

Belonging *A Fabre* 102
3 ch f Raven's Pass(USA) Desired (Rainbow Quest (USA))
3877a^{8} 5461a^{4} 6124a^{6}

Belrog *Ralph Beckett* a74 74
2 ch c New Approach(IRE) Millennium Dash (Nashwan (USA))
6953^{4} ◆ *7834^{4}*

Beltaine (IRE) *Brendan Powell*
4 b c Danehill Dancer(IRE) May Kiersey (IRE) (Sadler's Wells (USA))
2516^{10} 3011^{7}

Beltor *Michael Dods* 70
2 b g Authorized(IRE) Carahill (AUS) (Danehill (USA))
2955^{11} 3439^{4} 4107^{3} 5364^{3} 5827^{3} 6628^{6}

Be Lucky *Michael Easterby* a67 71
3 ch f Kyllachy Spritzeria (Bigstone (IRE))
1821^{3} ◆ *2169^{2}* (5989)

Be My Award (SWE) *Lennart Reuterskiold Jr* a91
3 b c Academy Award(IRE) Bea Apache (SWE) (Be My Chief (USA))
5326a^{3}

Be My Gal *Roger Charlton* a74
2 b f Galileo(IRE) Longing To Dance (Danehill Dancer (IRE))
8124^{2}

Be My Icon *Roger Charlton* a59 45
2 b f Sixties Icon Marathea (FR) (Marathon (USA))
6523^{10} 7245^{5}

Be My Rock *Rae Guest* a71 79
4 b f Rock Of Gibraltar(IRE) Supa Sal (King's Best (USA))
3434^{7} 4813^{2} 5758^{4} (6283) 6491^{7}

Benadalid (FR) *L Lallie* a92 85
6 b g Green Tune(USA) Agapimou (IRE) (Spectrum (IRE))
960a^{0}

Benandonner (USA) *Mike Murphy* a70 59
10 ch g Giant's Causeway(USA) Cape Verdi (IRE) (Caerleon (USA))
840^{3} 1054^{6} 1322^{2} 1496^{4} 1780^{9} 2057^{9} 2845^{13} 3406^{12} 3657^{2} 3924^{4} 4623^{12} 5171^{4} 6038^{10} 6457^{7} 7858^{8} 8055^{8}

Benash (IRE) *John G Carr* 82
9 br g Beneficial Ash Dame (IRE) (Strong Gale)
5021a^{3}

Ben Hall (IRE) *John Gosden* 98
2 b c Bushranger(IRE) Sassy Gal (IRE) (King's Best (USA))
2653^{4} (3045) ◆ 3424^{7} 4918^{6} 6328^{10} 7026^{17}

Benidorm *John Wainwright* a47 56
5 b g Bahamian Bounty Famcred (Inchinor)
2634^{6} 3593^{6} 4400^{9} *6806^{6} 7083^{10}*

Benjamin (FR) *L A Urbano-Grajales* a84 90
8 b g Highest Honor(FR) Mia's Baby (USA) (Rahy (USA))
498a^{5}

Benji's Empire (AUS) *S Burridge* 99
7 b g King Charlemagne(USA) Margareda (AUS) (Eagle Eyed (USA))
150a^{14} 467a^{14}

Bennelong *Lee Carter* a62 71
7 b g Bahamian Bounty Bundle Up (USA) (Miner's Mark (USA))
132^{8} 361^{8} 7090^{8} 7321^{12} *8149^{2} 8302^{5} 8390^{4} 8449^{7}*

Benodet (FR) *C Boutin* 86
2 b f Orpen(USA) Anchusa (IRE) (Nashwan (USA))
1894a^{5} (4599a)

Benoni *Henry Candy* a83 75
3 b g Bertolini(USA) Ladykirk (Slip Anchor)
1582^{6} 1832^{4} 2495^{4} (3289) 3782^{4} 4281^{3} 5437^{6} *6214^{2} 6642^{8} (7487)*

Benoordenhout (IRE) *Jonathan Portman* 38
2 br g Footstepsinthesand Tara Too (IRE) (Danetime (IRE))
4414^{15} 5442^{9} 6095^{4}

Benozzo Gozzoli *Simon Earle* a46 62
7 ch g Medicean Star Precision (Shavian)
343^{13}

Bens Boy (IRE) *Derek Shaw* 57
2 b c Holy Roman Emperor(IRE) Final Opinion (IRE) (King's Theatre (IRE))
2421^{4} 2670^{P} (Dead)

Bentley *Brian Baugh* a56 62
9 b g Piccolo April Lee (Superpower)
600^{2} 884^{2} 993^{6} 1311^{5}

Bentons Lad *George Moore* 53
2 br g Bollin Eric Spirit Of Ecstacy (Val Royal (FR))
2474^{7} 2985^{9} 4925^{7} 7418^{10}

Benvenue (IRE) *R Biondi* 96
4 ch c Iffraaj Guest Harbour (IRE) (Be My Guest (USA))
2489a^{4}

Benzanno (IRE) *Andrew Balding* a100 98
4 b g Refuse To Bend(IRE) Crossanza (IRE) (Cape Cross (IRE))
(1036) 1485^{5} 2018^{10} 2185^{5} 2841^{5} 4028^{5} 4923^{4} 5824^{2} 6638^{9} 6868^{2} 7206^{9}

Be On The Bell *Jamie Osborne* a72 54
3 b f Byron Bella Beguine (Komaite (USA))
4^{3}

Be Perfect (USA) *David Nicholls* a99 96
4 b g Street Cry(IRE) Binya (GER) (Royal Solo (IRE))
401^{7} 585^{10} 1843^{3} 2240^{4} 4979^{7} 5382^{6} 6211^{3} 6626^{11} 6846^{3} (7210) ◆ 7723a^{10} *7975^{6} 8392^{2} 8429^{2}*

Berberana (IRE) *Jeremy Gask* a68 73
5 b f Acclamation Barbera (GER) (Night Shift (USA))
360^{4}

Berbice (IRE) *Linda Perratt* a72 64
8 gr g Acclamation Pearl Bright (FR) (Kaldoun (FR))
1994^{8} 2319^{9} 3770^{6} 4109^{9} 4339^{5} 4615^{3} 4823^{5} 5239^{4} 5261^{4} 5331^{4}

Be Ready (IRE) *Saeed bin Suroor* 108
2 ch c New Approach(IRE) Call Later (USA) (Gone West (USA))
5530[2] ◆ (6351)

Bereka *James Tate* a64 60
2 b f Firebreak Alexander Ballet (Mind Games)
6110[4] 6477[4]

Berengar (IRE) *John Butler* a76 62
4 b g Holy Roman Emperor(IRE) Double Fantasy (GER) (Indian Ridge)
7163[10] 7622[11]

Bereni Ka (FR) *Y Gourraud* 101
2 b f Vadasin(IRE) Ile Aux Moines (IRE) (Bering)
7571a[4] 7828a[2]

Berkeley Street (USA) *Jane Chapple-Hyam* a65 61
3 b g Street Cry(IRE) Dream Ticket (USA) (Danzig (USA))
2930[7] 6407[2] 6787[11] 7376[10] (8186) 8372[6] 8410[3]

Berkeley Vale *Roger Teal* a38 65
2 b c Three Valleys(USA) Intriguing Glimpse (Piccolo)
5957[5] 6739[11] 7302[13]

Berkshire (IRE) *Paul Cole* 111
2 b c Mount Nelson Kinnaird (IRE) (Dr Devious (IRE))
2411[3] (3555) (6835)

Berlin Berlin *Markus Klug* 104
4 b f Dubai Destination(USA) Bombazine (IRE) (Generous (IRE))
3879a[DSQ] 6678a[5]

Berling (IRE) *Jessica Long* 106
6 gr g Montjeu(IRE) Danaskaya (IRE) (Danehill (USA))
3188a[2] 4095a[8] 5045a[2] (5809a) 6453a[6]

Berlusca (IRE) *David O'Meara* a88 79
4 b g Holy Roman Emperor(IRE) Shemanikha (FR) (Sendawar (IRE))
(61) ◆ (83) 593[2] 759[5] 832[7] 3506[7] 3945[8] 4482[4] 5070[4] 5369[9] 6306[8] (6877) 7211[9] 7849[2] 8057[5] 8226[2] (8416)

Bermondsey Bob (IRE) *John Spearing* a14 71
7 b g Trans Island Tread Softly (IRE) (Roi Danzig (USA))
2196[12] 2596[9] 3247[5] 3431[2] ◆

Bermuda Reef (IRE) *P Schiergen* 93
3 b c Oasis Dream Borgia (GER) (Acatenango (GER))
2696a[3] 4103a[16] 5576a[3] 6987a[7]

Bernardino *David Barron* 54
3 b g Bertolini(USA) Moon Royale (Royal Abjar (USA))
1759[11] 3025[11]

Bernie The Bolt (IRE) *Andrew Balding* a50 93
7 br g Milan Chaparral Lady (IRE) (Broken Hearted)
2451[12] 5288[12]

Bernie The Jet (USA) *Gary Contessa* 90
3 bb c Bernstein(USA) Amaretta (USA) (Woodman (USA))
3360a[11]

Bernisdale *John Flint* a68 73
5 ch f Bertolini(USA) Carradale (Pursuit Of Love)
429[6] 675[3] 929[3] (1068) 1176[4] 1586[4] 1974[5]

Bernix *Julie Camacho* a38 58
11 gr g Linamix(FR) Bernique (USA) (Affirmed (USA))
2332[7]

Bern Me Baby (USA) *Marco Botti* a89 93
3 bb f Bernstein(USA) Clever Maid (USA) (Confide (USA))
4493[2] 4767[9] 6282[4] 7642[7] 7851[6]

Be Royale *Michael Appleby* a67 45
3 b f Byron Sofia Royale (Royal Applause)
4813[3] 5091[9] 7465[3] 7806[3] (7966) (8056) 8199[3]

Beroye (FR) *Mme Pia Brandt* a81 76
3 ch f Indian Rocket La Teignouse (FR) (Green Tune (USA))
7736a[4]

Berrahri (IRE) *John Best* a74 73
2 b c Bahri(USA) Band Of Colour (IRE) (Spectrum (IRE))
5399[9] 6641[3] 7120[10] 7451[2] 7889a[4] 8354a[3]

Berrymead *Ann Stokell* a52 18
8 br m Killer Instinct Mill End Quest (King's Signet (USA))
1598[4] 6606[10] 6995[10]

Bertha Burnett (IRE) *Brian Rothwell* a11 58
2 gr f Verglas(IRE) Starsazi (Observatory (USA))
3064[7] 3648[5] 4977[10] 5865[7] 6284[3]

Bertie Baby *Ralph Smith* 13
2 br f Bertolini(USA) Los Organos (IRE) (Turtle Island (IRE))
7244[7]

Bertie Blu Boy *Lisa Williamson* a63 54
5 b g Central Park(IRE) Shaymee's Girl (Wizard King)
110[2] 435[9] 587[6] 3643[11] 4834[7] 5232[7] 6042[6] 7931[6] 8055[6]

Bertie Bob *Dai Burchell*
7 b g Bertolini(USA) Quartermark (IRE) (General Monash (USA))
1653[11]

Bertie Moon *Geoffrey Deacon* a70 62
3 b c Bertolini(USA) Fleeting Moon (Fleetwood (IRE))
1711[4] 2154[2] (3495) 5098[2] 5387[6] 6109[6] (6968) 7437[11]

Bertiewhittle *David Barron* a101 108
5 ch g Bahamian Bounty Minette (Bishop Of Cashel)
2254[2] 3527[10] 3825[2] 4297[18] 4744[19] 6352[2] 7014[2] 7974[2]

Bertinoro (IRE) *S Botti* 97
2 b c Aussie Rules(USA) Swirling (IRE) (Galileo (IRE))
7678a[2]

Bert The Alert *Laura Mongan* a77 53
5 b g Proclamation(IRE) Megalex (Karinga Bay)
403[2] 850[7] 1010[3] 4205[7] 4771[7] 6114[3] 7622[9] 7857[12]

Berwin (IRE) *Sylvester Kirk* a74 73
4 b f Lawman(FR) Topiary (IRE) (Selkirk (USA))
1974[3] 2413[4] 2606[12] 3106[14] 3635[10]

Be Seeing You *Roger Charlton* a69 74
2 ch g Medicean Oshiponga (Barathea (IRE))
6641[4] 7069[2] 7835[4]

Besito (IRE) *H-F Devin* a55 74
4 b f Kodiac Christmas Kiss (Taufan (USA))
7408a[4]

Besnardine (FR) *J Merienne* a65 55
2 bl f Early March Shark Bay (Anabaa (USA))
5213a[3]

Best Be Careful (IRE) *Mark Usher* a64 81
5 b f Exceed And Excel(AUS) Precautionary (Green Desert (USA))
2227[7] 3018[8] 3577[4] 3667[8] 3920[5] 4364[3] 4707[3] 5376[2] 5956[6] 6381[3] 6745[11]

Bestfootforward *Julia Feilden* a57 64
4 ch f Motivator Best Side (IRE) (King's Best (USA))
841[6] 1090[13] 1916[9] 2533[14] (6462) 7086[U] 7319[4] 8023[12] 8073[8] 8341[10]

Best Kept *Amanda Perrett* a78 56
2 ch c Sakhee's Secret Ashlinn (IRE) (Ashkalani (IRE))
6739[10] (7120)

Best Of Order (IRE) *E J O'Neill* a89 94
6 ch h Pivotal Groom Order (Groom Dancer (USA))
4297[8]

Best Regards (IRE) *P Harley* a77 103
3 bb f Tamayuz Neverletme Go (IRE) (Green Desert (USA))
3970a[3] 5804a[5]

Best Tamayuz *William Haggas* a43
2 ch c Tamayuz Pink Ivory (Sakhee (USA))
8201[6]

Best Tango (ITY) *Gianluca Bietolini* 103
3 b c Mujahid(USA) Nikita Tango (FR) (Sicyos (USA))
(1865a) 2490a[7]

Best Trip (IRE) *Brian Ellison* a89 93
6 b g Whipper(USA) Tereed Elhawa (Cadeaux Genereux)
1787[13] (2119) 3096[4] 3684[8] 4983[10] ◆ 5544[5] 6162[4] 6586[4] 7176[5] (7776)

Bethan *Julia Feilden* a62 61
4 b f Nayef(USA) Elizabethan Age (FR) (King's Best (USA))
6116[6] 6532[6] 7253[7] 7847[6] 8160[12]

Bethany Bay (IRE) *John Patrick Shanahan* a24 84
3 b f Dylan Thomas(IRE) Spinney (Unfuwain (USA))
2108a[7] (2650) 6327[7]

Bethel (USA) *Gennadi Dorochenko* a81 81
3 ch c Pulpit(USA) Cunning (USA) (Lord At War (ARG))
5551a[13]

Betimes *John Gosden* a86
2 ch f New Approach(IRE) See You Later (Emarati (USA))
(8332) ◆

Bet Noir (IRE) *Tony Carroll* a30 64
8 b m King's Best(USA) Ivowen (USA) (Theatrical (IRE))
132[10] 469[11] 755[10]

Better Life (AUS) *Hideyuki Takaoka* 109
5 ch m Smarty Jones(USA) Quiet Life (USA) (Sunday Silence (USA))
2494a[7]

Better Lucky (USA) *Thomas Albertrani* 113
4 b f Ghostzapper(USA) Sahara Gold (USA) (Seeking The Gold (USA))
(7043a)

Better Value (IRE) *Noel Quinlan* a65 54
3 b g Ad Valorem(USA) Varmint Lady (IRE) (Orpen (USA))
6944[4] 7980[2] (8043) 8186[P] 8360[5]

Bettolle (ITY) *Jessica Lari* 102
4 b f Blu Air Force(IRE) Happy Sue (IRE) (City On A Hill (USA))
(1563a) 2491a[4] 4527[4] 4947[14] 7830a[7]

Betty Boo (IRE) *Shaun Harris* a29 53
3 ch f Thousand Words Poker Dice (Primo Dominie)
1682[8] 1988[7] 2501[10] 3463[13] 3743[2] 4143[4] 4888[4] 5197[5] 5990[4] 6361[12] 7035[9] 7610[6]

Betty Lou (GER) *Markus Klug* 94
3 b f Dai Jin Bali's Dream (FR) (Big Shuffle (USA))
3604a[7] 4092a[11]

Betty The Thief (IRE) *Tom Dascombe* 60
2 b f Teofilo(IRE) Siphon Melody (USA) (Siphon (BRZ))
6828[8]

Between The Lines (IRE) *Anthony Middleton* a62 53
4 gr g Dalakhani(IRE) Stage Struck (IRE) (Sadler's Wells (USA))
1653[6] 1882[10] 2777[3] 2968[5] 4166[9] 4380[4] ◆ 4838[7] 5846[8]

Between Us *Sir Mark Prescott Bt* a66 92
4 b f Galileo(IRE) Confidante (USA) (Dayjur (USA))
2855[3] 3608[3] 4532[4] 5237[7]

Betzyoucan *Robert Stephens* a58 63
3 b f Royal Applause Mint Royale (IRE) (Cadeaux Genereux)
209[6] 402[3] 447[3] 6985[10] 7643[11]

Bewitchment *Sir Mark Prescott Bt* a70 67
2 b f Pivotal Hypnotize (Machiavellian (USA))
2774[2] 3426[2] 3640[3] 4589[3] 5194[3]

Beyeh (IRE) *Michael Appleby* a49 68
5 b f King's Best(USA) Cradle Rock (IRE) (Desert Sun)
1464[3] 1979[2] 2545[5]

Beyond (IRE) *David Pipe* a81 94
6 ch g Galileo(IRE) Run To Jane (IRE) (Doyoun)
(3856) 4873[17] 6424[11]

Beyond Conceit (IRE) *Andrew Balding* 98
4 b g Galileo(IRE) Baraka (IRE) (Danehill (USA))
1536[2] (1766) 2654[3] 3099[3] 4873[4] ◆

Beyond Smart (USA) *John Gosden* a71 72
2 b c Smart Strike(CAN) Beyond The Waves (USA) (Ocean Crest (USA))
6829[4] 7276[2] 7766[2]

Beyond Thankful (IRE) *J S Bolger* 102
3 b c Whipper(USA) Beyond Compare (IRE) (Galileo (IRE))
1558a[4] 2907a[14] 4869a[12]

B Fifty Two (IRE) *J W Hills* a101 101
4 br g Dark Angel(IRE) Petite Maxine (Sharpo)
2207[12] 2937[5] 3299[13] 5998[10] (6648) 6831[15]

Bheleyf (IRE) *Joseph Tuite* a72 72
3 b f Kheleyf(USA) Carraigoona (IRE) (Rock Of Gibraltar (IRE))
1616[5] 2098[11] 2572[8] 4244[9] 4369[8] 5128[11] 6157[7] 7031[7]

Bibactic (IRE) *J E Pease* a59 69
3 b c Montjeu(IRE) Alice Town (Darshaan)
5914a[3] 7736a[10]

Bible Belt (IRE) *Mrs John Harrington* 106
5 br f Big Bad Bob(IRE) Shine Silently (IRE) (Bering)
4567a[7]

Bidable *Bryn Palling* a56 51
9 b m Auction House(USA) Dubitable (Formidable (USA))
110[11]

Bien Determinee (FR) *X Betron* a66 63
3 ch f Chichi Creasy(FR) Bright Princess (FR) (Linamix (FR))
711a[5] 2034a[6]

Bienvenido (FR) *P Prunet-Foch* a39 28
8 b g Starborough Queen Mat (IRE) (Fairy King (USA))
6058a[5]

Bifocal *David Brown* 61
2 b g Footstepsinthesand Clear Vision (Observatory (USA))
6082[3]

Big Baz (IRE) *William Muir* a77
3 b g Pivotal Gracefully (IRE) (Orpen (USA))
(8427) ◆

Big Blue Kitten (USA) *Chad C Brown* a101 116
5 b c Kitten's Joy(USA) Spent Gold (USA) (Unaccounted For (USA))
7712a[8]

Big Boned (USA) *Ed Dunlop* a68
2 b f Street Sense(USA) Lizzy Cool (USA) (Saint Ballado (CAN))
6691[5] 7078[3] 7435[9]

Big Break *D K Weld* 107
3 br f Dansili Fame At Last (USA) (Quest For Fame)
2689a[4] 3524[7] 7051a[2] 7719a[2]

Big City Boy (IRE) *Phil McEntee* a52
5 b g Tamarisk(IRE) Cuddles (IRE) (Taufan (USA))
564[3] 602[4] 1017[8] 1161[6] 1297[9]

Big Easy (GER) *Philip Hobbs* 95
6 b g Ransom O'War(USA) Basilea Gold (GER) (Monsun (GER))
3423[8] 7193[21]

Bigger Picture (IRE) *John Butler* 74
3 ch f Raven's Pass(USA) Rababah (USA) (Woodman (USA))
7246[5] 7455[15]

Biggins Boy (IRE) *Alan Swinbank* a83
4 b g Motivator Optimal (IRE) (Green Desert (USA))
(215)

Big John Cannon (IRE) *David Barron* a25 59
3 b g High Chaparral(IRE) Bakiya (USA) (Trempolino (USA))
1648[8] 2279[10] 2480[3] 3194[9] 4143[5]

Big Johnny D (IRE) *David Barron* 103
4 ch g Alhaarth(IRE) Bakiya (USA) (Trempolino (USA))
1282[3] (1570) (5292) (6164) 7014[17]

Big Jones (FR) *Mlle M-L Mortier*
3 gr c Nombre Premier Cardamome (FR) (Cardoun (FR))
191a[0]

Big Kahuna *Jane Chapple-Hyam* a48 37
6 br g Trade Fair Pistoia (Alzao (USA))
157[6] 841[7] 1291[6] 2171[7]

Big Kenny *David Evans* a64 52
2 b g Multiplex Jezadil (IRE) (Mujadil (USA))
3267[6] 3640[10] 3948[7] 5893[8] 6897[8] (8274) ◆ (8363) 8434[3]

Big Moza *John Best* a59
3 b f Pastoral Pursuits Zaynah (IRE) (Kahyasi)
90[4]

Big Orange *Michael Bell* 72
2 b g Duke Of Marmalade(IRE) Miss Brown To You (IRE) (Fasliyev (USA))
7219[4] ◆ 7469[6]

Big Storm Coming *Brian Ellison* a75 27
3 b g Indesatchel(IRE) Amber Valley (Foxhound (USA))
202[5] 525[5] (6343) 6478[2] (7953)

Big Sylv (IRE) *James Unett* a70 49
4 gr f Clodovil(IRE) Casual Remark (IRE) (Trans Island)
61[2] (271) ◆ 778[2] 919[2] 1107[3] (1211) 1503[2]

Big Thing Coming *Patrick Gilligan* a11
5 b g Kyllachy Lady's Walk (IRE) (Charnwood Forest (IRE))
1187[5]

Big Thunder *Sir Mark Prescott Bt* a80 102
3 gr g Dalakhani(IRE) Charlotte O Fraise (IRE) (Beat Hollow)
2742[3] (3014) 3173[2] (4194) (4516) (4748) 5274[5] (6793)

Big Time (IRE) *John Joseph Murphy* 112
2 br c Kheleyf(USA) Beguine (USA) (Green Dancer (USA))
3847a[2] 5319a[2]

Big Time Billy (IRE) *Peter Bowen* a51 82
7 b m Definite Article Zaratu (IRE) (Key Of Luck (USA))
12[7] (2990) (3726) 4313[4] 5288[8]

Big Typhoon (IRE) *T G McCourt* a61 64
6 b g Fasliyev(USA) Dane's Lane (IRE) (Danehill (USA))
679a[5]

Big Wave (IRE) *Alison Hutchinson* a73 80
5 b f Choisir(AUS) Mystery Solved (USA) (Royal Academy (USA))
1802[3] 2338[5] 2781[10] 3223[2] (3489) 4064[4] 4690[3] 4982[4] (5154) 5498[2] 5798[7] 6209[5]

Big Whiskey (IRE) *Edward Creighton* a91 82
3 ch g Ad Valorem(USA) El Opera (IRE) (Sadler's Wells (USA))
5134[3] 5541[4] 6003[7] 6556[3] (6735) 7742[3] 7974[6]

Bijou Bijou (FR) *Laura Grizzetti* a79
3 b c Shirocco(GER) Andriana (IRE) (Second Empire (IRE))
461a[2]

Bijou Dan *George Moore* a49 63
12 ch g Bijou D'Inde Cal Norma's Lady (IRE) (Lyphard's Special (USA))
1721[10] 2120[6] 3089[10] 3944[6] 4969[10] 5885[6]

Bilash *Andrew Hollinshead* a70 73
6 gr g Choisir(AUS) Goldeva (Makbul)
(2825) 4479[4] 5537[14] 6382[5] 8030[4]

Bilge Kagan (IRE) *X Thomas-Demeaulte* a88 88
3 br c Whipper(USA) Privet (IRE) (Cape Cross (IRE))
(7408a) 7995a[10]

Bilidn *Ben De Haan* a71 94
5 b f Tiger Hill(IRE) Brightest Star (Unfuwain (USA))
6750[10]

Bilimbi (IRE) *William Haggas* 79
2 b g Duke Of Marmalade(IRE) Starship (IRE) (Galileo (IRE))
6184[10] 7270[4] (7606)

Billingsgate (IRE) *Charlie Appleby* a75
2 b c Exceed And Excel(AUS) Island Babe (USA) (Kingmambo (USA))
(7461)

Billion Dollar Kid *Jo Davis* a72 70
8 br g Averti(IRE) Fredora (Inchinor)
2057[12]

Bill Of Rights *Michael Bell* a49 53
3 b f Kyllachy Bijou A Moi (Rainbow Quest (USA))
1364[6] 1986[6] 2499[5] 3643[7]

Billowing (IRE) *John Gosden* a73
2 ch f Candy Ride(ARG) Cloudspin (USA) (Storm Cat (USA))
7296[2] 7764[3]

Billy Blue (IRE) *John Gosden* a75
2 b c High Chaparral(IRE) Silk Dress (IRE) (Gulch (USA))
7779[2] 8066[2] (8340)

Billy Budd (IRE) *S Bazzani* 98
5 b c Shamardal(USA) Baranja (USA) (St Jovite (USA))
3881a[8]

Billyford (IRE) *Liam Roche* a96 93
8 b g Lil's Boy(USA) Alamanta (IRE) (Ali-Royal (IRE))
4869a[18]

Billyrayvalentine (CAN) *George Baker* a63 79
4 b g Elusive Quality(USA) Sweet And Careless (USA) (Hennessy (USA))
4364[6] 5722[6] 6155[2] 6489[3] 7106[4]

Billy Red *J R Jenkins* a80 80
9 ch g Dr Fong(USA) Liberty Bound (Primo Dominie)
29[2] 232[4] (687) (1198) 1517[2] 1985[9] 3171[8] 3658[7] 6506[8] 7444[7] (7783) 8069[11]

Billy Redpath *Frederick Watson* 22
5 b g Distant Music(USA) Shardda (Barathea (IRE))
2507[11] 3398[9]

Bin End *Barry Brennan* a40 28
7 b g King's Best(USA) Overboard (IRE) (Rainbow Quest (USA))
1927[8]

Bin Manduro *James Tate* a67 57
3 b g Manduro(GER) Dust Dancer (Suave Dancer (USA))
333[3] 1069[5] 1923[5] 3674[5]

Bin Singspiel *James Tate* a96 85
3 br g Singspiel(IRE) Mexican Hawk (USA) (Silver Hawk (USA))
1296[2] 2878[6] 3491[3] (6942) ◆ 7210[6] (7542) ◆

Bint Alzain (IRE) *Pat Phelan* a78 56
4 b f Marju(IRE) Barconey (IRE) (Danehill Dancer (IRE))
1155[4] 1479[4] 3051[5] 8019[12] 8121[10] 8341[12]

Bint Malyana (IRE) *James Tate* a69 14
2 b f Bahamian Bounty Malyana (Mtoto)
7371[6] (8114)

Bint Youmzain (IRE) *M Ramadan* 56
3 b f Exceed And Excel(AUS) Chaussons (IRE) (Indian Ridge)
243a[10] 553a[16]

Biographer *David Lanigan* a91 112
4 b c Montjeu(IRE) Reflective (USA) (Seeking The Gold (USA))
2451[4] 4083[2] ◆ 5531[7] 6349[4] 7363[6]

Biography *Richard Hannon Snr* 81
2 ch g Assertive Dahshah (Mujtahid (USA))
1669[12] 2823[2] (3288) 3857[4] 4528[17]

Biotic *Rod Millman* 49
2 b g Aqlaam Bramaputra (IRE) (Choisir (AUS))
4883[4] 5584[7] 6589[7]

Bircham (IRE) *Ismail Mohammed* a74 83
3 ch c Dubawi(IRE) Royale Danehill (IRE) (Danehill (USA))
245a[14] 553a[12] 7683a[3]

Bird Dog *Phil McEntee* a56 43
7 ch g Compton Place Form At Last (Formidable (USA))
537[11] 618[10] 716[5] 968[10] 1294[12] 2516[9] 2643[6] 5085[13] 5864[13]

Bird Flown *A Fabre* 84
2 b f Oasis Dream Silver Star (Zafonic (USA))
(5419a)

Birdie King *Gary Moore* a59 60
3 b g Dutch Art Daughters World (Agnes World (USA))
3438[8] 5220[6] 5602[8] 7322[6] 7980[6] 8149[14]

Birdie Queen *Gary Moore* a61 52
3 b f Pastoral Pursuits Silver Miss (FR) (Numerous (USA))
2226[5] ◆ 3091[3] 4999[9] 6902[7] 7981[6] 8070[2] 8446[2]

Birdman (IRE) *David Simcock* a95 98
3 b g Danehill Dancer(IRE) Gilded Vanity (IRE) (Indian Ridge)
1621[6] 2008[3] 2843[5] 6990[14] 7495[18] 7991[10] 8264[4] 8428[U]

Bird Of Light (IRE) *Jamie Osborne* a36 69
2 b f Elnadim(USA) Lady Docker (IRE) (Docksider (USA))
(2067) 4528[18] 5175[5] 7882[6] 8025[4]

Birdy Boy (USA) *Mark Johnston* a69 63
3 ch g Elusive Quality(USA) Flip Flop (FR) (Zieten (USA))
527[6] (910) 1016[2] (1373) 1655[4] 2080[7] 2743[9] 3463[7] 4008[2] 4160[13] 4955[4] 5369[8] 5870[4] 6657[5] 6968[2] 7515[8]

Birikyno *Mark Usher* a54 55
2 b g Piccolo Alvarinho Lady (Royal Applause)
5866[6] 6354[3] 6746[8] 7986[7] 8364[7]

Birkacre (IRE) *Richard Fahey* 63
2 b f Dandy Man(IRE) Shenkara (IRE) (Night Shift (USA))
3942[3] 4259[5] 5421[6]

Birthday Sun (GER) *W Hickst* a76 52
5 b f Areion(GER) Boucheron (GER) (Turfkonig (GER))
(127a)

Biscuiteer *Scott Dixon* a61 24
2 ch f Byron Ginger Cookie (Bold Edge)
3366[10] 4073[9] 5609[8] 7756[3] 7956[3] (8113) 8228[5] 8404[4]

Bishan Bedi (IRE) *William Jarvis* a57
2 b c Intikhab(USA) Knockatotaun (Spectrum (IRE))
8124[11]

Bishop Of Ruscombe *Andrew Balding* 68
2 b c Mount Nelson Pain Perdu (IRE) (Waajib)
7631[3]

Bishop Roko *Roger Charlton* a102 100
4 b g Rock Of Gibraltar(IRE) Kirk (Selkirk (USA))
2775[4] 3960[3] (4796) 5766[13] 6394[5]

Bishop's Castle (USA) *Brian Ellison* a80 85
4 b g Distorted Humor(USA) Miss Caerleona (FR) (Caerleon (USA))
(950) 5521[2] 6236[3]

Bishop Wulstan (IRE) *Richard Hannon Snr* a49 52
2 b c Oratorio(IRE) Laurentine (USA) (Private Account (USA))
7320[5] 7647[8] 7835[14]

Bison Grass *Giles Bravery* a64 69
3 b g Halling(USA) Secret Blend (Pivotal)
6555[6] 7067[2] 7490[7]

Bispham Green *Richard Fahey* a72 86
3 b c Green Desert(USA) Royal Grace (Royal Applause)
(1150) 1482[6] 1690[2] 2213[2] 2430[9] 3299[5] 5769[5] 6699[11]

Bitaphon (IRE) *Michael Appleby* a67 70
4 br g Acclamation Pitrizzia (Lando (GER))
54[6] 162[2] 436[3] (603) 912[9] 965[2] 986[6] 1498[6] 1887[9] 6610[5] 6803[8] 7197[4] 7383[3] (7886) 8006[6] 8295[2]

Bite Of The Cherry *Michael Bell* a85 101
4 ro f Dalakhani(IRE) Bianca Nera (Salse (USA))
2012[4] 2668[2] 4083[6] 5035[9] 5683[9] 5993[2] 7650[12]

Bitusa (USA) *Alan Swinbank* 67
3 b g Roman Ruler(USA) Richen (USA) (Well Decorated (USA))
1392[3] 1575[4] 1965[8] 2464[2] 4806[8] 5016[8] 5642[3] 6049[8] 6907[7] 7027[8]

Bit Windy *Chris Dwyer* a51 17
4 b f Librettist(USA) Primavera (Anshan)
925[5] 1035[6] 1187[4] 1520[3] 3222[5] 3580[8]

Bix (IRE) *Alan Berry* a71 52
3 b g Holy Roman Emperor(IRE) Belle Rebelle (IRE) (In The Wings)
547[4] 827[4] 1275[8] 1761[3] 2237[6] 2794[7] 3931[4] 4514[4] (5916) 6180[11] 6685[6] 6843[7] 7485[10] 8056[5]

Biz The Nurse (IRE) *S Botti* 111
3 b c Oratorio(IRE) Biz Bar (Tobougg (IRE))
(2490a) (3147a) (6679a) 7414a[2]

Bizzy Nizzy (FR) *S Wattel* a57 76
3 b f Great Journey(JPN) Risky Nizzy (Cape Cross (IRE))
5913a[4]

Blackamoor Harry *Richard Ford* a34 47
4 b g Indesatchel(IRE) Libretta (Highest Honor (FR))
2168[8] 2536[15] 4826[2] 5092[3] 6323[9] 7752[8]

Black Annis Bower *Michael Easterby* 72
5 gr f Proclamation(IRE) Bow Bridge (Bertolini (USA))
1681[3] ◆ (2343) 2702[3] (3078) 4074[5] 4821[4] 4993[8] 5537[7] 6075[5]

Blackball (USA) *David Lanigan* a58 72
3 br g Speightstown(USA) Wild Decision (USA) (Wild Again (USA))
(2762) ◆ 3546[8] 4829[5]

Black Cadillac (IRE) *Andrew Balding* a80 50
5 bl g Kheleyf(USA) Desert Design (Desert King (IRE))
95[7] 372[8] 582[3] (688) 775[9] 4120[8] 4487[9] 5349[RR]

Black Caesar (IRE) *Richard Hannon Snr* 81
2 b c Bushranger(IRE) Evictress (IRE) (Sharp Victor (USA))
5957[9] (6589) 7221[3] 7819[4]

Black Dave (IRE) *David Evans* a72 69
3 b g Excellent Art Miss Latina (IRE) (Mozart (IRE))
(228) (357) 533[2] 674[3] 738[2] 920[5] 1099[6] 1832[10] 2308[9] 3050[3] (3221) 7743[7] 7965[4] 8158[3] ◆

Black Douglas *Jim Goldie* a42 63
4 b g Kyllachy Penmayne (Inchinor)
2222[6] 2757[8] 4102[9] 4582[4] 4891[4] (5487) 6180[10] 6604[2] 6761[3] 6916[7] 6945[2] 7149[7]

Blackdown Spirit *Paul D'Arcy* a79 87
3 b g Ishiguru(USA) Shielaligh (Aragon)
550[3]

Black Eyed Girl (IRE) *J S Moore* a55 52
3 br f Jeremy(USA) Holda (IRE) (Docksider (USA))
3915[3] 4410[9] 5173[3] 6321[4]

Black Geronimo *David Evans* a65 51
2 b c Sleeping Indian Voice (Zamindar (USA))
2823[5] 3640[4] 4351[8] 5634[12] 6311[11] 7198[2] 7623[7] (7882)

Blackie (NZ) *Jarrod McLean* 107
6 ch g Black Minnaloushe(USA) Diamond Babe (NZ) (Stravinsky (USA))
7826a[11]

Black Label *Harry Dunlop* a71 47
2 b g Medicean Black Belt Shopper (IRE) (Desert Prince (IRE))
5442[7] 6079[2] ◆ 6688[2]

Black Rider (IRE) *Julie Camacho* a57 74
3 b g Elnadim(USA) Barracade (IRE) (Barathea (IRE))
236[3] 404[4] 525[4] (2308) 2763[2] (3730) 4288[3] 4890[4] 6602[5] 7024[17]

Black Rodded *Hughie Morrison* 70
2 ch f Bahamian Bounty Palace Affair (Pursuit Of Love)
4484[12] 5529[9] 6644[13] 7317[2] (7393)

Black Sceptre (IRE) *Edward Creighton* a53 49
2 br c Diamond Green(FR) Salford Princess (IRE) (Titus Livius (FR))
4175[12] 5167[4] 5891[9] 8262[12]

Black Schnapps (IRE) *William Muir* a80 78
2 b c Manduro(GER) Ornellaia (IRE) (Mujadil (USA))
6953[2] (7301) 7662[5]

Black Shadow *Amanda Perrett* a73
2 b c New Approach(IRE) Shadow Dancing (Unfuwain (USA))
7302[6]

Black Snowflake (USA) *S Seemar* a79 79
6 b g Elusive Quality(USA) Black Escort (USA) (Southern Halo (USA))
412a[6]

Blacksou (FR) *P Adda* a68
3 b g Blackdoun(FR) Cadline (FR) (Cardoun (FR))
126a[0] 2335a[0]

Black Spirit (USA) *Clive Cox* a104 112
6 b g Black Minnaloushe(USA) L'Extra Honor (USA) (Hero's Honor (USA))
4027[8] 4526[4] 5270[8] 6332[4] 6638[10] 7206[11]

Blackstone Vegas *Derek Shaw* a63 72
7 ch g Nayef(USA) Waqood (USA) (Riverman (USA))
1794[7] 2087[6] 2563[5] 4035[4] 5560[7] ◆

Black Tie Dancer (IRE) *Gay Kelleway* a24 8
2 b g Mastercraftsman(IRE) Opera Star (IRE) (Sadler's Wells (USA))
5490[7] 6546[9] 7883[6]

Black Treacle (IRE) *Keith Dalgleish* a67 83
2 b g Kodiac Treacle Noir (IRE) (Raise A Grand (IRE))
3928[3] 4156[3] (4583) 5351[2] 5591[4] (5834) 6465[2] (6582)

Black Truffle (FR) *Mark Usher* a63 51
3 b c Kyllachy Some Diva (Dr Fong (USA))
122[3] 442[3] 732[3] 848[4] (1055) 1319[2] 1710[2] 1978[5] (2950) 3405[5] 4885[8] 5232[2] 5594[3] 6316[7] 6902[4]

Black Vale (IRE) *Phil McEntee* a69 16
2 b g Moss Vale(IRE) Limit (IRE) (Barathea (IRE))
4351[9] 5193[3] 5866[2] 6320[9] 6966[8] 7855[13] (7954) 8045[2] 8137[3] 8166[5] 8215[5] (8267) 8364[6]

Blades Boy *Richard Fahey* 49
2 ch g Winker Watson Blades Baby (Bertolini (USA))
1606[7] 2025[4] 2883[11] 3440[5]

Blades Lad *Peter Niven* a76 75
4 ch g Haafhd Blades Girl (Bertolini (USA))
914[3] (1076) 1391[3] 1936[7] 6346[11]

Bladewood Girl *J R Jenkins* a68 51
5 b f Needwood Blade Willmar (IRE) (Zafonic (USA))
536[5] 3635[11] 4169[5] 5135[8] 5961[5] 7124[4] 7351[3] 7752[2] 7963[3] 8056[7]

Blaine *Kevin Ryan* 108
3 ch g Avonbridge Lauren Louise (Tagula (IRE))
2334a[7] 3455[14] 4986[21] 5545[20]

Blanc De Chine (IRE) *Peter Makin* a86 95
4 gr f Dark Angel(IRE) Nullarbor (Green Desert (USA))
1652[6] (2227) 3135[3] (4123) 4800[8] 5519[7]

Blarney Stone (JPN) *Yasutoshi Ikee* 105
6 gr g Kurofune(USA) Fermoy (USA) (Irish River (FR))
6445a[6] 7059a[8]

Blazeofenchantment (USA) *Richard Guest* a68 51
3 b g Officer(USA) Willow Rush (USA) (Wild Rush (USA))
195[6] (845) 1400[6] 1832[11] 2272[8] 4140[7] 8095[8]

Blazers Rock (IRE) *Kevin Ryan* 71
2 b g Amadeus Wolf Nawaji (USA) (Trempolino (USA))
6125[5] 6716[3] 7276[6]

Blazing Chilli *Bill Turner*
2 b g Firebreak Janet Girl (Polar Falcon (USA))
1344[7]

Blazing Desert *William Kinsey* a76 69
9 b g Beat All(USA) Kingsfold Blaze (Mazilier (USA))
22[4] (430) 592[2] (1045) 1212[2] 1523[3] 1831[9] 2174[4] 2629[8] 3133[4] 3231[7] 4838[8]

Blazing Knight (IRE) *Ralph Beckett* a80 69
3 b g Red Clubs(IRE) Johar Jamal (IRE) (Chevalier (IRE))
(225) 550[6] ◆ 1892[10] 3050[6] 3212[7] 5278[6] 6135[9] (6777)

Blazing Speed *A S Cruz* 114
4 b g Dylan Thomas(IRE) Leukippids (IRE) (Sadler's Wells (USA))
8211a[6]

Blazon (FR) *P Van De Poele* a88 86
6 gr h Verglas(IRE) Hidden Silver (Anabaa (USA))
4467a[4]

Blessing Box *Chris Wall* a62 77
3 b f Bahamian Bounty Bible Box (IRE) (Bin Ajwaad (IRE))
2962[2] 3509[3] (4390) 5800[3] 6928[11]

Blessington (IRE) *John Gosden* a90 91
3 b c Kheleyf(USA) Madam Ninette (Mark Of Esteem (IRE))
6990[2] 7507[8] 7982[10] 8181[4] 8430[3]

Blewit (IRE) *William Kinsey* a35 48
5 b g Iffraaj Privileged Speech (USA) (General Assembly (USA))
3406[10] 4147[8]

Blhadawa (IRE) *James Tate* 77
2 b f Iffraaj Trois Heures Apres (Soviet Star (USA))
1634[2] 2869[4]

Blighty (IRE) *Lady Cecil* a84 89
3 ch g Beat Hollow Brisk Breeze (GER) (Monsun (GER))
3435[2] 4927[2] (5962) ◆ 6563[5] 7257[10]

Bling King *Geoffrey Harker* a89 88
4 b g Haafhd Bling Bling (IRE) (Indian Ridge)
1281[6] 1576[3] ◆ 2078[2] 2339[4] 2705[6] 5367[4] 6126[9] 6468[7] (6700) 6909[3] (7027)

Blithe Spirit *Eric Alston* a43 88
2 b f Byron Damalis (IRE) (Mukaddamah (USA))
1399[6] (1642) 2147[2] 2426[6] 3459[13] 4248[4] 5012[4] (5509) 6584[6] (6825)

Blizzard Blues (USA) *Aytach Sadik* a71 104
7 ch g Mr Greeley(USA) Blush Damask (USA) (Green Dancer (USA))
2[3] 166[4] 430[4] 563[6]

Blockade (IRE) *James Tate* a73 99
2 br f Kheleyf(USA) Barracade (IRE) (Barathea (IRE))
1634[9] 1924[3] (2327) 2767[5] 3439[2] 4006[2] 4528[14] (5468) (5994) 6622[8] 7194[2]

Blodwen Abbey *Michael Mullineaux* a61 60
4 b f Firebreak Miss Mirasol (Sheikh Albadou)
101[6] 431[7] 1397[8]

Bloodsweatandtears *William Knight* a72 79
5 b g Barathea(IRE) Celestial Princess (Observatory (USA))
89[5] 1056[2] 1303[9] 1779[7] 2787[4] (6459) 7092[2] 7318[8] 7858[2] 8323[7] 8453[4]

Blossom Lane *John Gosden* a61 50
2 ch f New Approach(IRE) Monturani (IRE) (Indian Ridge)
7103[10] 7449[6] 7874[9]

Blown It (USA) *Keith Dalgleish* a76 74
7 bb g More Than Ready(USA) Short Shadow (USA) (Out Of Place (USA))
56[5] 214[12]

Blu Axara (ITY) *F Chappet* a58 74
2 b f Blu Air Force(IRE) Silvaris (IRE) (Wixim (USA))
4599a[3] (5363a) 6293a[10] 6786a[8] 7184a[5]

Blue Anchor Bay (IRE) *Rod Millman* 46
2 b g Ad Valorem(USA) New Foundation (IRE) (College Chapel)
1580[6] 2067[4]

Blue Atlantic (USA) *Mark Johnston* 70
2 b c Stormy Atlantic(USA) Bluemamba (USA) (Kingmambo (USA))
3588[6] 4556[2] 4906[3] 6275[3]

Blue Bajan (IRE) *David O'Meara* a98 106
11 b g Montjeu(IRE) Gentle Thoughts (Darshaan)
3297[4] 3423[6] 3824[9] 4313[10] 5655[6] 6192[9]

Bluebell (IRE) *A P O'Brien* 88
2 b f Mastercraftsman(IRE) Sogno Verde (IRE) (Green Desert (USA))
3868a[5] 6021a[5]

Blue Bounty *Mark H Tompkins* a68 57
2 ch g Bahamian Bounty Laheen (IRE) (Bluebird (USA))
3493[2] 5025[4] 5364[9] 7451[7]

Blue Charm *Ian McInnes* a44 68
9 b g Averti(IRE) Exotic Forest (Dominion)
1455[8]

Blue Chocolate (IRE) *D Prod'Homme* a53 47
2 b f Halling(USA) Blue Fiji (IRE) (Dansili)
7185a[13] 7568a[14]

Blue Clumber *Shaun Harris* a29 82
3 b f Sleeping Indian Blue Nile (IRE) (Bluebird (USA))
1275[10] 1616[8] 1786[9] 3082[6] 3611[4] 4008[14] 5091[8] (5431) 5916[3] 6156[8] 6902[11] 7323[15] 7454[12]

Blue Corner (IRE) *Saeed bin Suroor* a7 101
4 b g Teofilo(IRE) Indian Belle (IRE) (Indian Ridge)
242a[7] 552a[11]

Blue Deer (IRE) *Lee Carter* a69 56
5 b g Bahamian Bounty Jaywick (UAE) (Jade Robbery (USA))
115[2] 689[5] 813[13] 978[10] 1194[9] 2948[4] 3433[9] 3661[7] 4423[8] 4904[2] 5234[12] 6105[6] 7266[7] 8244[5] 8390[8]

Blue Eyed (FR) *J-P Gallorini* a77 79
3 b f One Cool Cat(USA) Beriosova (FR) (Starborough)
(7187a)

Bluegrass Blues (IRE) *Paul Cole* a94 91
3 gr g Dark Angel(IRE) Dear Catch (IRE) (Bluebird (USA))
(1299) ◆ 1625[8] (1892) 2452[7] 3066[4] 3279[9] 4274a[4] (5004) 5886[3] 6204[2] 6403[3]

Blue Jack *Stuart Williams* a98 98
8 b g Cadeaux Genereux Fairy Flight (IRE) (Fairy King (USA))
358[5] ◆ (582) 880[2] 1160[4] 1814[13] 2097[2] ◆ 2388[6] 2868[6] 3415[2]

Blue Lotus (IRE) *Tim Easterby* 77
3 ch g Elnadim(USA) Saffa Garden (IRE) (King's Best (USA))
1444[9] 2371[12] 3591[6] 4117[7]

Blue Maisey *Edwin Tuer* a38 72
5 b f Monsieur Bond(IRE) Blue Nile (IRE) (Bluebird (USA))
914[4] 1442[2] 1932[6] 2278[4] 2539[6] 2915[5] (3546) 4007[7] 4375[2] 4967[6] 5974[3] 6301[7] 6941[2] 7283[3] 7344[7]

Blue Mood (IRE) *Charlie Appleby* a77 80
2 b f Invincible Spirit(IRE) Cabriole (Dansili)
(4191) 4653[3] 5228[3]

Blue Noodles *John Wainwright* a59 55
7 b g Reset(AUS) Gleam Of Light (IRE) (Danehill (USA))
88[4] 327[3] 423[3] 551[6] 649[3] 733[4] (1020) 1043[3] 1194[7] 1656[5] 1886[2] 2126[2] 3654[4] 4005[11] 4377[6] 4834[10] 7079[11] 8118[7] 8258[3]

Blue Oyster *Philip McBride* a65
2 b f Medicean Bluebelle (Generous (IRE))
7875[9] 8083[4]

Blue Panis (FR) *F Chappet* a84 96
6 b g Panis(USA) Rhapsody In Blue (FR) (Bering)
5735a[14]

Blue Pencil *Roger Curtis* a45 36
4 b g Ishiguru(USA) Gold And Blue (IRE) (Bluebird (USA))
703[11] (2304a) 2563[12]

Blue Planet (GER) *Christina Bucher* a81 88
4 ch c Paolini(GER) Blue Amour (IRE) (Bluebird (USA))
7890a[6]

Blues Buddy *H Edward Haynes* 39
6 b m Dubai Destination(USA) Swift Spring (FR) (Bluebird (USA))
3619[5] 4223[10]

Blue Shining (USA) *T Clout* a73 71
3 bb f Henrythenavigator(USA) Brilliance (FR) (Priolo (USA))
5119a[6]

Blue Shoes (IRE) *Tim Easterby* 75
4 b f Kodiac Alexander Capetown (IRE) (Fasliyev (USA))
1692[13] 2479[4] 3090[5] 3392[4] 4161[5] 4727[9] 5365[5] 5887[7] ◆

Blueskiesnrainbows (USA) *Jerry Hollendorfer* a112 69
4 ch c English Channel(USA) Cho Cho San (USA) (Deputy Minister (CAN))
7687a[2]

Blue Soave (FR) *F Chappet* a94 114
5 ch g Soave(GER) Rhapsody In Blue (FR) (Bering)
1945a[10] 2897a[12] 4093a[7] 4935a[9]

Blue Sonic *Jim Goldie* 9
3 gr f Proclamation(IRE) Big Mystery (IRE) (Grand Lodge (USA))
5919[6]

Blues Orchestra (FR) *J-V Toux* 58
2 b f Orpen(USA) Blanc Sur Blanc (IRE) (Hold That Tiger (USA))
6059a[9]

Blue Surf *Amanda Perrett* 104
4 ch g Excellent Art Wavy Up (IRE) (Brustolon)
2839[4] 3559[7] 4854[8] 5766[6] 6741[5]

Blue Talisman (IRE) *Tim Easterby* 56
2 ch g Alhaarth(IRE) Amaniy (USA) (Dayjur (USA))
2985[11] 5338[7] 5785[3] 6275[7] 6755[5] 6946[3]

Blue Top *Tim Walford* a56 65
4 b g Millkom Pompey Blue (Abou Zouz (USA))
2118[6] 2333[2] 2511[6] 2986[3] 3595[3] 4010[2] 4403[8] 4809[9] (5833) (6290) 7151[2]

Blue Twister *Andrew Balding* a48 61
3 ch g Pivotal Blue Siren (Bluebird (USA))
3109[4] 3509[7] 3956[7]

Blue Wave (IRE) *Mark Johnston* a83 90
3 b g Raven's Pass(USA) Million Waves (IRE) (Mull Of Kintyre (USA))
359[6] 474[3] (1470) (1719) 1834[3] 2216[5] 2660[2] 2879[5] 3486[18] 3982[8] 4301[8] 7635[7]

Blue Whip (IRE) *U Suter* a67 70
3 b f Whipper(USA) Brewing Storm (IRE) (King Charlemagne (USA))
962a[6]

Blunos (IRE) *Rod Millman* a28 55
2 b g Haatef(USA) Jemalina (USA) (Trempolino (USA))
3914[9] 4304[7] 5307[6] 6979[12] 7788[9] 7956[8]

Blurred Vision *William Jarvis* 88
2 b c Royal Applause Sparkling Eyes (Lujain (USA))
3017[6] ◆ 4858[7] ◆ 5199[2] 5656[3] 7207[4]

Blyde River (IRE) *F Doumen* 71
2 b c Shamardal(USA) Bunting (USA) (Private Account (USA))
5875a[4]

Boadicee *Rae Guest* 72
2 b f Aqlaam Fen Guest (Woodborough (USA))
(4883) 6572[5]

Boastful (IRE) *K R Burke* a81 104
5 gr f Clodovil(IRE) Vanity (IRE) (Thatching)
6327[8]

Boat Trip (USA) *Michael Pender* 105
4 b c Harlan's Holiday(USA) Turning Wheel (USA) (Seeking The Gold (USA))
7710a[12]

Boban (AUS) *Chris Waller* 115
4 br g Bernardini(USA) Kenbelle (AUS) (Kenmare (FR))
(7826a)

Bobbyow *K F Clutterbuck* a56 45
5 b g Bertolini(USA) Brooklyn's Sky (Septieme Ciel (USA))
111[9] 2425[12] 3247[12] 3922[9]

Bobbyscot (IRE) *Gary Moore* a77 79
6 b g Alhaarth(IRE) Sogno Verde (IRE) (Green Desert (USA))
2808[7] 4167[4] 4831[2] 6200[7] 6405[7]

Bobby's Kitten (USA) *Chad C Brown* 112
2 b c Kitten's Joy(USA) Celestial Woods (USA) (Forestry (USA))
7688a[3]

Bobby Two Shoes *Brett Johnson* a74 64
3 b g Byron Taminoula (IRE) (Tagula (IRE))
4592[6] 5280[8] 6412[9] 6928[10]

Bob Le Beau (IRE) *Mrs John Harrington* a90 101
6 br g Big Bad Bob(IRE) Shine Silently (IRE) (Bering)
246a[11] 555a[4] 661a[5] 833a[8]

Boblini *Mark Usher* a43 38
5 b f Bertolini(USA) Boojum (Mujtahid (USA))
1539[9] 2123[4]

Bob Masnicken *Scott Dixon* a24 61
2 b g Dandy Man(IRE) Twilight Belle (IRE) (Fasliyev (USA))
4602[4] 4963[10] 6477[11]

Boboli Gardens *Mrs Ilka Gansera-Leveque* a35
3 b g Medicean Park Crystal (IRE) (Danehill (USA))
6133[9] 7311[9]

Bobs Her Uncle *James Bethell* a73 69
4 b f Fair Mix(IRE) Shazana (Key Of Luck (USA))
1579[2] 2311[3] 2956[5] 3610[4] 4016[3] 4584[5] 6153[4] 6599[2] (7622) 8059[2]

Bocaiuva (IRE) *F Chappet* 86
2 ch f Teofilo(IRE) Breath Of Love (USA) (Mutakddim (USA))
7967a[6]

Bocamix (FR) *Andrew Crook* a69 69
7 gr g Linamix(FR) Bocanegra (FR) (Night Shift (USA))
539[4]

Boccalino (GER) *P Schaerer* a37 98
5 b c Iron Mask(USA) Bella Monica (GER) (Big Shuffle (USA))
700a[6]

Body And Soul (IRE) *Tim Easterby* 107
3 b f Captain Rio Goodwood March (Foxhound (USA))
2476[5] (3348) 4260[6]

Body Language (IRE) *Ian Williams* a82 99
5 b f Beat Hollow Banco Suivi (IRE) (Nashwan (USA))
2598[6] 3099[8] (4372) 6237[6] 6646[2] 6766[3]

Bogart *Kevin Ryan* 109
4 ch g Bahamian Bounty Lauren Louise (Tagula (IRE))
1483[3] 2019[17] 2368[8] 2669[15] 4780[U] (5651) 6391[14] 6623[19] 7208[15]

Bognor (USA) *Jo Hughes* a65 61
2 b g Hard Spun(USA) Ms Blue Blood (USA) (A.P. Indy (USA))
3717[6] 4414[12] 7441[3] 7979[6]

Bogsnog (IRE) *Kristin Stubbs* a81 75
3 b g Moss Vale(IRE) Lovers Kiss (Night Shift (USA))
(1791) 2408[6] 3104[7] 3591[9] 4734[9] 5141[6] 5611[2] 6072[9] 6664[8] 7164[2] (7486) 7965[3] 8053[8] 8224[5]

Bohemian Dance (IRE) *Sir Michael Stoute* 82
3 br f Dansili Islington (IRE) (Sadler's Wells (USA))
1671[8] ◆ 2206[10] 3237[3] 5064[3] (6046) 7504[13]

Bohemian Rhapsody (IRE) *Seamus Durack* a69 94
4 b g Galileo(IRE) Quiet Mouse (USA) (Quiet American (USA))
(4714) (4915) (5390) 5719[3] 7823[4]

Boissey (FR) *Mme Pia Brandt* a69
3 b f Authorized(IRE) Castillon (IRE) (Gone West (USA))
3129a[10]

Boite (IRE) *Peter Chapple-Hyam* 96
3 b c Authorized(IRE) Albiatra (USA) (Dixieland Band (USA))
1679[2] (1931) 2490a[8] 3526[3] 4211[8]

Bold Adventure *Willie Musson* a65 65
9 ch g Arkadian Hero(USA) Impatiente (USA) (Vaguely Noble)
12[2] (109) 351[2] 1040[4] (1348) 2980[5] 3688[4]

Bold And Free *David Thompson* a66 69
3 b g Bertolini(USA) Lady Broughton (IRE) (Grand Lodge (USA))
2935[13] 3418[7] 4122[2] 4374[3] 5099[8] 6357[3] (6717) 7881[6]

Bold Assertion *John Best* a68 68
3 ch c Assertive Fanciful Dancer (Groom Dancer (USA))
1057[7] 1300[7] 1741[2] 2233[3] 2784[5] 3257[5] 4352[7] 4753[4] 6787[7] 7331[10]

Bold Captain (IRE) *John Quinn* 73
2 ch g Captain Rio Indianaca (IRE) (Indian Danehill (IRE))
6513[2] 7175[6] 7339[2]

Bold Citizen (IRE) *Ed Dunlop* a64 58
3 b c New Approach(IRE) Claxon (Caerleon (USA))
5110[6] 5678[12] 6062[8] 7305[7] 7543[8]

Bold Cross (IRE) *Edward Bevan* a71 73
10 b g Cape Cross(IRE) Machikane Akaiito (IRE) (Persian Bold)
1699[9] 1948[4] 2413[6] 2710[10] 2826[5] 3312[2] 3662[8] (4365) 4714[4] 5312[6] 5671[2] (5980) 6898[13]

Bold Duke *Edward Bevan* a50 80
5 b g Sulamani(IRE) Dominant Duchess (Old Vic)
1366[6] 1585[4] 1889[5] 2418[4] 2785[3] (6492) (6794) 7211[18]

Bold Forest (USA) *Patrick J Quick* 81
4 ch g Forestry(USA) Delicatessa (USA) (Dare And Go (USA))
3361a[5]

Bold Jack Donahue (IRE) *Ralph Beckett* 50
2 bb g Bushranger(IRE) Mother's Hope (IRE) (Idris (IRE))
2741[10] 3374[10] 4773[6] 5276[5]

Bold Lass (IRE) *David Lanigan* a73 79
2 b f Sea The Stars(IRE) My Branch (Distant Relative)
(7102) ◆ 7463[4]

Bold Marc (IRE) *Mrs K Burke* a74 58
11 b g Bold Fact(USA) Zara's Birthday (IRE) (Waajib)
97[4] 540[4] 967[2] 1184[2] 1597[4] 2221[3] 2514[9]

Bold Max *Zoe Davison* a44 49
2 b g Assertive Jane's Payoff (IRE) (Danetime (IRE))
1880[6] 2282[6] 2562[10] 2978[5]

Bold Mistress (FR) *F Vermeulen* a67 76
3 b f Peintre Celebre(USA) Mysterious Guest (FR) (Barathea (IRE))
7187a[4]

Bold Prediction (IRE) *K R Burke* a82 86
3 b g Kodiac Alexander Eliott (IRE) (Night Shift (USA))
(992) 1444[7] 1892[3] 2626[5] 3582[5] 3828[2] 4508[3] (4581) 5287[4] 7063[4]

Bold Ring *Edward Creighton* a72 63
7 ch m Bold Edge Floppie Disk (Magic Ring (IRE))
1161[4] 1783[2] (1873) (2125) 2565[3] 2792[4] 4163[5] (4385) 4637[3] 4746[6] 6702[9] 7092[3] 7297[7] 7836[9] 8432[7]

Bold Runner *Sean Curran* 56
2 ch g Mount Nelson Music In Exile (USA) (Diesis)
5473[11] 6954[8] 7502[9]

Bold Sniper *Sir Michael Stoute* 105
3 b g New Approach(IRE) Daring Aim (Daylami (IRE))
1678[7] (2465) ◆ (2927) 3486[3] ◆ (4279) 4984[7] ◆

Bold Spirit *Richard Hannon Snr* 72
2 b g Invincible Spirit(IRE) Far Shores (USA) (Distant View (USA))
4231[6] 4827[2]

Bold Thady Quill (IRE) *K J Condon* a94 108
6 ch g Tale Of The Cat(USA) Jazzie (FR) (Zilzal (USA))
1168a[3] (1255a) 1413a[4] 1556a[2] 2288a[4] 3262a[4] 4549a[4] 6440a[8] 7051a[5] 7719a[8]

Boleyn *Olly Stevens* a63 67
3 b f Sir Percy Moody Margaret (Bahamian Bounty)
1319[6] 1697[8] 2963[5]

Bolivia (GER) *Lucy Wadham* a88 92
7 ch m Monsun(GER) Be My Lady (GER) (Be My Guest (USA))
2040[4] 4029[2]

Bollin Billy *Tim Easterby* 49
3 b g Lucky Story(USA) Bollin Jeannie (Royal Applause)
4374[4] 5142[7] 5240[7]

Bollin Bob *Tim Easterby* 60
4 b g Bollin Eric Bollin Roberta (Bob's Return (IRE))
3398[8] 4139[5] 4481[3] 5241[4]

Bollin Dolly *James Moffatt* 72
10 ch m Bien Bien(USA) Bollin Roberta (Bob's Return (IRE))
4888[8] 5087[6]

Bollin Fergus *Mrs J L Le Brocq* 57
9 br g Vettori(IRE) Bollin Harriet (Lochnager)
5329a[7] 7144a[8]

Bollin Freddie *Alan Lockwood* a53 6
9 ch g Golden Snake(USA) Bollin Roberta (Bob's Return (IRE))
5142[9]

Bollin Greta *Tim Easterby* a47 92
8 bb m Mtoto Bollin Zola (Alzao (USA))
1463[8] 1805[10] 2269[7] 2369[4] ◆ 2671[10] 3284[6] 3891[2] (4015) 4262[7] 4512[4]

Bollin Judith *Jim Best* a51 61
7 br m Bollin Eric Bollin Nellie (Rock Hopper)
5168[13]

Bollywood (IRE) *Alison Batchelor* a22 51
10 ch g Indian Rocket La Fille De Cirque (Cadeaux Genereux)
3580[12] 4380[13]

Bolt (FR) *P Vidotto* a66 66
5 b g Night Tango(GER) Roannaise (FR) (Octagonal (NZ))
6680a[4]

Bomar (IRE) *Wido Neuroth* a86 94
4 b c Sir Percy Rubileo (Galileo (IRE))
3188a[4] 4095a[9] 5045a[5] 6453a[7]

Bombardier *James Fanshawe* 68
3 ch g Manduro(GER) Lady Stardust (Spinning World (USA))
1882[9] 2321[7] 2938[5]

Bombardment (USA) *Charlie Appleby* a57
2 gr c War Front(USA) Niceling (USA) (Maria's Mon (USA))
6168[12]

Bomber Thorn *Tom Dascombe* 86
3 b g Manduro(GER) Treble Heights (IRE) (Unfuwain (USA))
2589[2] ◆ 3209[2] ◆ 4445[2]

Bon Accord (USA) *Antonio Sano* a98 103
2 ch c Showing Up(USA) Best Regards (USA) (Street Cry (IRE))
7688a[4]

Bonanza Creek (IRE) *Luca Cumani* 84
3 b f Anabaa(USA) Bright Moon (USA) (Alysheba (USA))
3237[4] 4500[2] ◆ (5478) 7020[U] 7822[15]

Bon A Savoir *Peter Chapple-Hyam*
2 ch g Layman(USA) Nice To Know (FR) (Machiavellian (USA))
7500[11]

Bonbon Bonnie *Phil McEntee* a40 22
5 b f Storming Home Form At Last (Formidable (USA))
202[4] 416[5] 438[3] 581[6]

Bond Artist (IRE) *Geoffrey Oldroyd* a56 64
4 b f Excellent Art Pitrizza (IRE) (Machiavellian (USA))
2503[6] 3644[9] 4834[6] 6986[2] ◆ 7201[6] 7931[4] 8056[2]

Bond Blade *Suzzanne France* a46 46
5 ch g Needwood Blade Bond Cat (IRE) (Raise A Grand (IRE))
423[11] 1077[3] 1355[9] 8050[7] 8271[13] 8438[7]

Bond Club *Geoffrey Oldroyd* a55 70
3 b g Misu Bond(IRE) Bond Platinum Club (Pivotal)
2756[4] 5150[7] 6664[5] 7343[3] 7957[12] 8443[7]

Bondesire *David O'Meara* 92
3 b f Misu Bond(IRE) Lawless Bridget (Alnasr Alwasheek)
1935[3] 2593[10] (2959) (3779) 4117[3] 4757[4] (5057) 6238[5] 7373[2]

Bond Holder (USA) *Doug O'Neill* a111
2 b c Mineshaft(USA) Cielo Girl (USA) (Conquistador Cielo (USA))
7711a[4]

Bondi (GER) *Frau J Mayer* 87
2 rg f It's Gino(GER) Bear Nora (GER) (Highest Honor (FR))
7409a[5]

Bondi Beach Boy *James Turner* 88
4 b g Misu Bond(IRE) Nice One (Almaty (IRE))
2217[4] (2611) (3024) (3654) 3933[3] (4009) 4728[3] (4852) (5381) (5579) 6273[3] 6586[16]

Bondi Mist (IRE) *Jonathan Geake* a56 68
4 gr f Aussie Rules(USA) Akoya (IRE) (Anabaa (USA))
753[8] 2360[8] 3412[6] (3953) 5434[11] 6899[9] 7305[8]

Bonfire *Andrew Balding* 116
4 b g Manduro(GER) Night Frolic (Night Shift (USA))
1639[3] 2186[7] 6592[3] 7142a[2]

Bon Grain (FR) *S Seemar* a85 66
8 br g Muhtathir Such Is Life (FR) (Akarad (FR))
871a[11]

Bonjour Steve *J S Moore* a62 68
2 b g Bahamian Bounty Anthea (Tobougg (IRE))
2359[3] 2917[2] 3175[4] 4121[4] 4519[7] 7327[3] 7568a[2] 7782[12] 8126[4]

Bonne Amie (FR) *Tom Dascombe* 62
3 b f Elusive City(USA) Sintra (IRE) (Kris)
2628[7] 3203[4]

Bonnie Charlie *David Nicholls* a76 84
7 ch g Intikhab(USA) Scottish Exile (IRE) (Ashkalani (IRE))
1248[8] 2007[13] 2460[13] (2664) 2988[5] 3351[4] 3714[4] 4730[13] 5294[6] 5705[4] 6205[3] 6583[5] 6908[12]

Bonnie Echo *Michael Dods* 56
6 b m Overbury(IRE) Sunday News'N'Echo (USA) (Trempolino (USA))
1777[4] 2279[7] 2405[5] 2798[9] 3728[14]

Bonnie Fairy *Michael Appleby* a50 29
2 b f Notnowcato Cheviot Heights (Intikhab (USA))
5140[7] 6298[10] 7972[10] (8296)

Bonnie Prince Blue *Ian McInnes* a68 65
10 ch g Tipsy Creek(USA) Heart So Blue (Dilum (USA))
98[8] 600[5] 884[3] 1311[3] 1455[6] 2171[5]

Bonnie Wee Lassie *Richard Hannon Snr* a40 41
2 b f Exceed And Excel(AUS) Scottish Exile (IRE) (Ashkalani (IRE))
1512[5] 1724[9] 3009[4] 3414[11]

Bon Port *Hughie Morrison* a64 36
2 b f Major Cadeaux Miss Poppy (Averti (IRE))
7251[5] 8005[2] (8367)

Bontoni (FR) *H-A Pantall* a82 82
3 ro c Silvano(GER) Brictop (USA) (Mizzen Mast (USA))
2335a[4]

Bon Voyage *Richard Hannon Snr* 95
2 b c Kyllachy Coming Home (Vettori (IRE))
5718[2] 6184[3] 6645[4] 7017[3] 7494[4]

Boogangoo (IRE) *Keith Dalgleish* a74 74
2 b f Acclamation Spice World (IRE) (Spinning World (USA))
3680[4] ◆ 4053[3] (4443) 5029[8] 5703[4] 6085[2] 6545[4] 6619[4] 7202[4] 7463[5] 7782[5] (7935) 8164[6]

Boogie Dancer *Jim Best* a29 34
9 b m Tobougg(IRE) Bolero (Rainbow Quest (USA))
3213[7]

Boogie De Bispo *Stuart Kittow* 52
3 b f Tobougg(IRE) Mellifluous (IRE) (Noverre (USA))
2362[9] 2924[4] 4035[7]

Boogy Man (ITY) *G Botti* a78 81
2 b c Orpen(USA) Little Lodge (IRE) (Grand Lodge (USA))
5362a[6] 6059a[11]

Bookmaker *Olly Stevens* 57
3 b g Byron Cankara (IRE) (Daggers Drawn (USA))
7073[5]

Book Review (USA) *Bob Baffert* a110
4 ch f Giant's Causeway(USA) Clever Babe (USA) (Distorted Humor (USA))
7709a[9]

Booktheband (IRE) *Clive Brittain* a60 48
3 ch g Dubawi(IRE) Songbook (Singspiel (IRE))
774[4] 1098[4] 1469[8] 2566[4] 2800[4] 4405[8]

Booloo (IRE) *Garry Moss* a36 43
2 b g Bushranger(IRE) Ink Pot (USA) (Green Dancer (USA))
6975[12] 7341[7] 7859[6] 8039[7]

Boom *Olivia Maylam* a43
3 b f Tiger Hill(IRE) Humility (Polar Falcon (USA))
7377[3] 7738[9] 7987[9]

Boom And Bloom (IRE) *W McCreery* a69 80
3 bb f Lawman(FR) Mamela (GER) (Protektor (GER))
2374a[4]

Boom And Bust (IRE) *Marcus Tregoning* a69 111
6 b g Footstepsinthesand Forest Call (Wolfhound (USA))
1639[4] 1919[5] 4856[3] 5446[2] 5794[2] 6427[2] 6797[5]

Boomerang Bob (IRE) *J W Hills* a73 107
4 b c Aussie Rules(USA) Cozzene's Pride (USA) (Cozzene (USA))
2257[3] (2936)

Boomshackerlacker (IRE) *George Baker* a43 108
3 gr g Dark Angel(IRE) Allegrina (IRE) (Barathea (IRE))
2526a[5] 2843[6] 4043a[6] 6530[2] 7116a[9] 7698[4] 7968a[2]

Boom The Groom (IRE) *David Marnane* 95
2 b c Kodiac Ecco Mi (IRE) (Priolo (USA))
5771a[3] 6021a[4]

Boom To Bust (IRE) *Barry Brennan* a84 84
5 br g Big Bad Bob(IRE) Forever Phoenix (Shareef Dancer (USA))
239[4] 563[7] 889[8] 2450[14] 3416[5] 3951[7] 7224[14] 7544[5] 7836[6] 8038[8]

Boonga Roogeta *Peter Charalambous* a78 99
4 b f Tobougg(IRE) Aberlady Bay (IRE) (Selkirk (USA))
(1663) (1825) (2018) 2045[6] 2656[5] 2839[7] 5255[10] 6838[29]

Boots And Spurs *K R Burke* a81 97
4 b g Oasis Dream Arctic Char (Polar Falcon (USA))
1233[2] 1583[9] (2265) (3411) 4062[11] 4744[13] 5019a[8] 5738[3] 6621[5] 7368[6]

Bop It *David O'Meara* a80 94
4 b g Misu Bond(IRE) Forever Bond (Danetime (IRE))
2441[11] 3200[8] 4730[4] ◆ 5183[3] ◆ 5294[3] (6161) ◆ 6586[22] 7171[9] 7495[17]

Bordah (USA) *Roger Varian* 40
3 b g Elusive Quality(USA) Alzerra (UAE) (Pivotal)
4813[4] 5110[9]

Border Bandit (USA) *Tracy Waggott* 70
5 b g Selkirk(USA) Coretta (IRE) (Caerleon (USA))
1572[6] 1790[5] 2886[4] 3397[4] (4119) 4557[7] 5239[2] 5637[2] 6301[2] (6721) 7283[8]

Border Legend *Roger Charlton* a89 94
4 ch g Selkirk(USA) Bonnie Doon (IRE) (Grand Lodge (USA))
1675[16] 2424[8] 6167[3] (7131) 7823[16]

Borderlescott *Robin Bastiman* a90 111
11 b g Compton Place Jeewan (Touching Wood (USA))
4311[6] 4947[11] 5545[7] 5984[3] 6305[5] 6719[4] 7208[17]

Border Revia (IRE) *Richard Fahey* 82
4 b g Celtic Swing Maraami (Selkirk (USA))
1290[6] 1569[4] 1827[8]

Boris Grigoriev (IRE) *Michael Easterby* a81 80
4 bb g Excellent Art Strategy (Machiavellian (USA))
5333[5] (6547)

Boris The Bold *Martin Smith* a58
4 b g Librettist(USA) Santiburi Girl (Casteddu)
220[3] 335[8] 441[3] (8065)

Born To Fly (IRE) *Gary Harrison* a52 62
2 b f Kodiac Cayambe (IRE) (Selkirk (USA))
4370[4] (5151) 5699[5] 6474[6]

Born To Perform *Alan Swinbank* 66
8 b g Theatrical(IRE) My Hansel (USA) (Hansel (USA))
165[7]

Born To Reign *Michael Bell* 21
2 b g Sir Percy Oat Cuisine (Mujahid (USA))
7654[10]

Born To Run *Hugo Palmer* a48
3 b f Ishiguru(USA) Maid For Running (Namaqualand (USA))
849[7] 1323[9] 1781[4] 2124[7]

Born To Run (GER) *R Dzubasz* 102
2 b c Shirocco(GER) Bravo Gorl (GER) (Tauchsport (GER))
(7232a)

Born To Shine (USA) *Alan Swinbank* 39
5 b g Suave(USA) Sentimental Keep (USA) (Behrens (USA))
2041[9]

Born To Surprise *Michael Bell* 101
4 b g Exceed And Excel(AUS) Dubai Surprise (IRE) (King's Best (USA))
2254[13] 2858[6] 3060[7] 5533[4] 6183[14] 6989[10]

Borough Belle *Henry Candy* a48 32
2 ch f Bertolini(USA) Sheesha (USA) (Shadeed (USA))
7817[7] 8332[11]

Borough Boy (IRE) *Derek Shaw* a65 57
3 b g Jeremy(USA) Ostrusa (AUT) (Rustan (HUN))
1742[12] 2347[5] 3134[5] 3323[2] 3540[4] 5067[6] 5305[4] 5890[10] 6651[8] 6930[3] 6994[4] 7203[2] (7380) 7772[9] 7903[7] 8168[3] (8438)

Bosham *William Jarvis* a72 73
3 b g Shamardal(USA) Awwal Malika (USA) (Kingmambo (USA))
2192[6] 2455[5] 2872[6] 3221[2] ◆ 3509[2] (3956) (4661) 5150[10] 6018[5]

Bossa Nova Baby (IRE) *Charles Hills* a64 69
3 b f High Chaparral(IRE) Attilia (GER) (Tiger Hill (IRE))
1636[12] 2423[3] 3364[6] 6313[6]

Bossy Jane *Zoe Davison* a20
3 b f Assertive Jane's Payoff (IRE) (Danetime (IRE))
6519[6] 7073[10]

Boston Alex (IRE) *Conor Dore* a57 55
2 br f Baltic King Petite Boulangere (IRE) (Namid)
3324[4] 4142[3] 5000[8] 6104[5] 6364[4] 6654[7] 7665[11]

Boston Blue *Tony Carroll* a64 78
6 b g Halling(USA) City Of Gold (IRE) (Sadler's Wells (USA))
39[7] 208[6] 418[12] 635[5] 1111[3] 1586[8] (2563) 2980[3] 3473[4] 7767[12]

Bostonian *Mark Johnston* 91
3 b g Dubawi(IRE) Bolshaya (Cadeaux Genereux)
4404[3] 4719[2] 5286[2]

Boston Rocker (IRE) *Edward Lynam* 102
3 b f Acclamation Rocking (Oasis Dream)
2374a[2] 3263a[2] 4647a[3] 7227a[4] 7719a[5]

Bosun Breese *David Barron* a61 98
8 b g Bahamian Bounty Nellie Melba (Hurricane Sky (AUS))
1607[9] 2031[9] 2461[2] 2669[11] 2880[3] 3334[12] 3561[8] 4217[8]

Botanist *Shaun Harris* a54 69
6 b g Selkirk(USA) Red Camellia (Polar Falcon (USA))
8436[9]

Botteen (IRE) *David O'Meara* a69 38
3 b g Invincible Spirit(IRE) Dundel (IRE) (Machiavellian (USA))
425[5] 636[3] (807) 2229[4] 4045[8] 6943[10] 7283[12]

Boucher Garcon (IRE) *Declan Carroll* a51 68
5 b g Spartacus(IRE) Valamander (IRE) (Val Royal (FR))
1283[2] 1465[10] 2410[8] 2479[6] 2832[13] 6469[9] 7101[10] 7599[8]

Bouclier (IRE) *Luca Cumani* a88
3 ch c Zamindar(USA) Bastet (IRE) (Giant's Causeway (USA))
7781[2] ◆ 7932[3] (8180)

Bougaloo *Alan McCabe* a67 52
3 b g Tobougg(IRE) Benjarong (Sharpo)
1330[2] 1772[9] 1967[5] 2576[7] 3657[13] 4143[9]

Bouggatti *Lady Herries* a71 78
5 b g Tobougg(IRE) Western Sal (Salse (USA))
2418[9]

Bouggler *Emma Lavelle* 60
8 b g Tobougg(IRE) Rush Hour (IRE) (Night Shift (USA))
5862[5]

Bound Copy (USA) *Mark Johnston* 59
3 b f Street Cry(IRE) In A Bound (AUS) (Ashkalani (IRE))
6684[3]

Bountiful Bess *Pam Sly* a61 62
3 ch f Bahamian Bounty Saida Lenasera (FR) (Fasliyev (USA))
1712[5] 2156[6]

Bountiful Catch *Pam Sly* a54 54
4 ch g Bahamian Bounty Saida Lenasera (FR) (Fasliyev (USA))
1617[12]

Bountiful Forest *Noel Wilson* 59
2 ch f Bahamian Bounty Through The Forest (USA) (Forestry (USA))
2740[6] 3189[2] 3826[6] 5226[4] (5578) 6082[4] 6467[3] 6872[6]

Bountiful Girl *Neville Bycroft* a67 78
4 b f Bahamian Bounty Cheeky Girl (College Chapel)
2673[11] 2845[8] 4771[3] 5032[7] 5427[8] 5793[6]

Bountiful Sin *George Margarson* a61 49
2 ch g Sinndar(IRE) Tropical Barth (IRE) (Peintre Celebre (USA))
7069[7] *7301[3] 7853[5]*

Bountybeamadam *George Baker* a72 75
3 b f Bahamian Bounty Madamoiselle Jones (Emperor Jones (USA))
1875[2] 2449[7] 3091[4] (6319) 7824[21]

Bounty Girl (IRE) *Tim Easterby* a62 68
2 b f Bushranger(IRE) Josphiel (IRE) (Okawango (USA))
2955[3] 3500[3] 4046[3] 4259[2] 4808[10] 6194[4] 6467[2] 6825[9] 7095[2] *7541[3]*

Bounty Hunter (IRE) *Tom Dascombe* 89
2 b g Bahamian Bounty Lindesberg (Doyoun)
1680[3] 2401[6] 2741[5] 3245[4] 4019[2] (4602) 5028[4] 5858[2] (6432) (7074)

Bounty Seeker (USA) *Mark Johnston* a79 78
4 b g A.P. Indy(USA) Plenty Of Light (USA) (Colony Light (USA))
2739[8] 3363[2] (3790) 4159[6]

Bourbon (IRE) *Mark Johnston* 75
3 b c Raven's Pass(USA) Traou Mad (IRE) (Barathea (IRE))
3539[4] 5110[7] ◆ 5786[9]

Bourbondi *Michael Murphy* a58
2 b c Sakhee(USA) Lake Diva (Docksider (USA))
5924[12] 8221[4] 8415[10]

Bourbon Prince *Michael Bell* 25
2 ch g Aqlaam Good Enough (FR) (Mukaddamah (USA))
7607[10] 7774[10]

Bousatet (FR) *Kevin Ryan* 79
3 b f Muhtathir Miss Mission (IRE) (Second Empire (IRE))
1828[8] (2503) 3396[3] 4955[2] 5581[2] (5975) (6602)

Bousfield *Declan Carroll* a73
2 b g Duke Of Marmalade(IRE) Exodia (Dr Fong (USA))
5675[5] (7883)

Bouyrin (IRE) *Michael Bell* a77
3 b f Invincible Spirit(IRE) Needles And Pins (IRE) (Fasliyev (USA))
197[2] 425[2] (821) 7663[2] ◆ *7861[9]*

Bow Creek (IRE) *Mark Johnston* 100
2 b c Shamardal(USA) Beneventa (Most Welcome)
3112[9] 5145[4] 5727[3] (5941) 6233[11] (6640) 7421[4]

Bowdler's Magic *David Thompson* a92 91
6 b g Hernando(FR) Slew The Moon (ARG) (Kitwood (USA))
1536[13] 1805[12] 2369[18] 6165[2] 6466[2] 7210[13]

Bowie Boy (IRE) *Ralph Beckett* a61
2 b c Intikhab(USA) Catatonic (Zafonic (USA))
8333[3] ◆

Bowlands Legacy *Richard Ford* a23 26
4 b f Grape Tree Road Bowlands Madam (Keen)
2169[9] 2634[7]

Bow Quarter *J S Moore* a26
2 b f Exceed And Excel(AUS) Jeritza (Rainbow Quest (USA))
7111[5] 7301[8]

Bowsers Bold *Marcus Tregoning* 68
2 b g Firebreak Cristal Clear (IRE) (Clodovil (IRE))
3374[9] 3836[8] 4121[3] 4988[11] 6285[8]

Bowstar *Michael Attwater* a80 65
4 b f Oasis Dream Bold Empress (USA) (Diesis)
(347) 652[2] 878[8] 6315[3] (6937) 7462[2] 7742[2] 7992[9] 8127[9]

Bow To No One (IRE) *Alan Jarvis* a79 79
7 b m Refuse To Bend(IRE) Deadly Buzz (IRE) (Darshaan)
823[6] 1615[6] 2205[4] 2587[10] 3726[11] *6173[4] 8089[4] 8331[2]*

Boxing Shadows *Bryan Smart* a75 71
3 b g Camacho Prima Ballerina (Pivotal)
85[6] 203[2] (710) 1791[5] 2076[2] 2544[10] 3320[3] 3591[4] 4136[8] *5673[7]* 5985[7] 6682[F] *7601[7]*

Boy In The Bar *David Barron* 65
2 ch g Dutch Art Lipsia (IRE) (Dubai Destination (USA))
6790[6]

Boy Ranger (IRE) *Ann Duffield* 36
2 b g Bushranger(IRE) Nonsense (IRE) (Soviet Star (USA))
4289[7] 4538[6] 5482[11] 6465[5]

Boy The Bell *Ollie Pears* a63 60
6 b g Choisir(AUS) Bella Beguine (Komaite (USA))
(24) 380[5] 523[6] 1020[3] 1397[5] 1757[7] 2273[12] *2578[5]* 2932[2] 3444[6] (4623) 4893[4] 5614[9] 7101[4] *7904[6]* ◆ 8042[7]

Boyzee *Linda Jewell* a63
5 b g Resplendent Glory(IRE) Busy (IRE) (In The Wings)
807[10] 1162[5] 1710[13]

Brabazon (IRE) *Emmet Michael Butterly* a65 70
10 b g In The Wings Azure Lake (USA) (Lac Ouimet (USA))
6404[5] 7863[10]

Bracelet (IRE) *A P O'Brien* 90
2 b f Montjeu(IRE) Cherry Hinton (Green Desert (USA))
2944a[8]

Bracing Breeze *D K Weld* a89 96
3 b f Dansili Nebraska Tornado (USA) (Storm Cat (USA))
3460[8]

Bradbury (IRE) *Donald McCain* a76 76
5 ch g Redback Simonaventura (IRE) (Dr Devious (IRE))
107[5] (378)

Brae Hill (IRE) *Richard Fahey* a74 104
7 b g Fath(USA) Auriga (Belmez (USA))
1235[3] 1675[19] 2399[5] 2841[7] 3346[10] 4297[19] (4895) 5992[2] 6624[2] 6834[7] 7172[19]

Braidley (IRE) *James Bethell* 90
2 b g Dylan Thomas(IRE) All Our Hope (USA) (Gulch (USA))
4505[3] ◆ (5083) 5829[2] (6303) ◆ 6619[6]

Brakina (FR) *J Helouiry* a54 75
3 b f Early March Capuccina (FR) (Lavirco (GER))
1756a[0]

Bramshill Lass *Amanda Perrett* a78 63
4 ch f Notnowcato Disco Ball (Fantastic Light (USA))
668[2] 866[3] 1062[2] 1348[4] 1899[5] 2197[5] 2570[2] 2921[2] ◆ *3328[5] (7159) (7863)* 8089[5]

Branderburgo (IRE) *M Grassi* 104
6 b h High Chaparral(IRE) Farhad (Red Ransom (USA))
2295a[9] 3881a[9]

Brandy Snapping *Mark Brisbourne* a52
4 ch f Needwood Blade Sunisa (IRE) (Daggers Drawn (USA))
226[6] 530[6] 704[2] 820[12]

Brandywell Boy (IRE) *Dominic Ffrench Davis* a61 56
10 b g Danetime(IRE) Alexander Eliott (IRE) (Night Shift (USA))
124[5] 233[0] 276[4] 649[7] 862[3] 3325[7] 3667[6] 3888[5] 4659[6] 4943[6] 5670[4] 5982[7] 6101[3] 6901[7]

Branston De Soto *Mark Johnston* a63 70
2 b g Hernando(FR) Julatten (IRE) (Alhaarth (IRE))
6939[5] 7209[13] 7631[2] *8164[5]*

Branston Jubilee *Geoffrey Harker* 30
3 ch f Assertive Branston Jewel (IRE) (Prince Sabo)
1447[7] 1961[7] 5614[14]

Brasingaman Eric *George Moore* a51 72
6 b g Bollin Eric Serene Pearl (IRE) (Night Shift (USA))
1279[7] 1572[4] 1993[2] 2313[2] 2720[2] 3065[6] 3726[2] 5109[4]

Brasingaman Espee *George Moore* 58
4 b c Silver Patriarch(IRE) Serene Pearl (IRE) (Night Shift (USA))
6788[10]

Brass Ring *John Gosden* 100
3 b g Rail Link Moraine (Rainbow Quest (USA))
1684[5] ◆ (1826) ◆ (2457) ◆

Brave Acclaim (IRE) *Tom Dascombe* 81
3 b c Acclamation Indienne (IRE) (Indian Ridge)
1678[16] 2628[3] (3047) 3571[7]

Brave Boy (IRE) *Saeed bin Suroor* a90 99
2 b g Invincible Spirit(IRE) Chan Tong (BRZ) (Hampstead (URU))
2543[3] ◆ (4497) (5372) *6201[6]* 7207[3] 7525[5]

Brave Decision *Suzy Smith* a65 53
6 gr g With Approval(CAN) Brave Vanessa (USA) (Private Account (USA))
158[8] 530[2] 625[11] (7922) (8121)

Braveheart Move (IRE) *Geoffrey Harker* a78 84
7 b g Cape Cross(IRE) Token Gesture (IRE) (Alzao (USA))
5055[6] 5559[4] 6211[11] 6499[6]

Brave Helios *Jonathan Portman* 60
3 b g High Chaparral(IRE) Renowned (IRE) (Darshaan)
1727[7] 2321[14] 3021[9] 4714[7] 5500[6]

Brave Imp *Kevin Ryan* a50 67
2 b g Sleeping Indian Impetuous (Inchinor)
2189[9] 6517[3] *6966[4]*

Brave Mariner *Bill Turner*
2 b c Pastoral Pursuits Rouge Dancer (Elusive City (USA))
6079[11]

Bravestar (IRE) *David Lanigan* a75 51
3 b g Lawman(FR) High Fidelity (GER) (Peintre Celebre (USA))
1926[7] 2953[5] 3417[9] *5356[8] 6398[11]*

Bravia *F Rohaut* a91 90
4 ch f Shamardal(USA) Albahaca (USA) (Green Dancer (USA))
3969a[5]

Bravo Bravo *Mark Gillard* a38 61
6 b g Sadler's Wells(USA) Top Table (Shirley Heights)
6558[11]

Bravodino (USA) *J E Pease* 111
3 bb c Dynaformer(USA) Angel In My Heart (FR) (Rainbow Quest (USA))
2035a[2] 2907a[7] 7142a[7]

Bravo Echo *Michael Attwater* a100 89
7 b g Oasis Dream Bold Empress (USA) (Diesis)
1061[2] 1385[4] 1542[3] 2013[6] 2207[10] 2618[3] 3274[2] *(3969a)* 4960[7] 5187[5] 6067[6] 6744[11] *8264[3]* 8344[4]

Bravo Youmzain (IRE) *A Al Raihe* a77 89
3 b c Invincible Spirit(IRE) Grizel (Lion Cavern (USA))
245a[8] 553a[10]

Brayroan (NZ) *Anthony Cummings* 99
7 b g Zabeel(NZ) Compulsion (AUS) (Danehill (USA))
7760a[11] 7938a[4]

Brazen *David Simcock* a93 97
3 b c Kyllachy Molly Brown (Rudimentary (USA))
2022[2] ◆ 2452[12] 3104[3] *(3474)* 4247[5] (5303)

Brazos (IRE) *Clive Brittain* 96
2 gr c Clodovil(IRE) Shambodia (IRE) (Petardia)
4031[2] 4312[2] (4858) 5652[5] 6351[4] 6765[4]

Breakable *Tim Easterby* 67
2 ch f Firebreak Magic Myth (IRE) (Revoque (IRE))
3943[6] 4616[4] ◆ 6627[3] 7062[5] 7418[5]

Breakheart (IRE) *Andrew Balding* a69 80
6 b g Sakhee(USA) Exorcet (FR) (Selkirk (USA))
(13) 89[4] 222[5] 415[4] 477[2] 2413[10] 2594[2] 3043[3] (3854) 3954[2] (4638) 5521[8] 6359[7] 6802[3]

Breaking The Bank *William Muir* a68 86
4 ch g Medicean Russian Dance (USA) (Nureyev (USA))
1836[4] 2234[6] (3156) 3854[2] 4126[6] (4831) (5587) 5824[7] 6596[7] (6956) 7431[6]

Break Rank (USA) *Ed de Giles* a92 91
4 b g Broken Vow(USA) Divert (USA) (Chester House (USA))
2191[5] 2728[9] *3434[3]* (3971) 4882[2] (5824) *6927[2]* 7536[8]

Brean Splash Susie *Bill Turner* a33
2 b f Tobougg(IRE) Straight As A Die (Pyramus (USA))
5229[5] 6131[7] 7036[7]

Breccbennach *Seamus Durack* a78 77
3 b g Oasis Dream Next (In The Wings)
2093[6] 2935[3] 3241[P] 3528[5] 5304[4] 5815[3] (6072) 6647[4] *7603[4]*

Breden (IRE) *John Gosden* a83 95
3 b g Shamardal(USA) Perfect Touch (USA) (Miswaki (USA))
(4382) (5287) ◆ 5958[4] 6356[5] (7022) ◆

Breezealong Riley *Zoe Davison*
4 b f Arkadian Hero(USA) Mountain Magic (Magic Ring (IRE))
7154[10]

Breezolini *Ollie Pears* a54 71
5 b m Bertolini(USA) African Breeze (Atraf)
1692[9] 2031[15] 2834[10] 3778[7] 4821[7] 4993[6] 7315[5] 7772[2]

Bremner *Kevin Ryan* 89
2 b c Manduro(GER) Maggie Lou (IRE) (Red Ransom (USA))
4731[3] (5262) (6545)

Brendan Brackan (IRE) *G M Lyons* a98 114
4 b g Big Bad Bob(IRE) Abeyr (Unfuwain (USA))
3844a[6] (4869a) 4946[13] (6440a) 7388a[2]

Bretherton *Richard Fahey* a73 25
2 ch c Exceed And Excel(AUS) Cliche (IRE) (Diktat)
5577[11] *7978[4] 8114[2]*

Breton Rock (IRE) *David Simcock* 108
3 b g Bahamian Bounty Anna's Rock (IRE) (Rock Of Gibraltar (IRE))
2188[2] ◆ 2655[7] (6308) ◆ 6990[3] (7368) 7775[2]

Brian Noble *Richard Fahey* 81
2 b c Royal Applause Little Greenbird (Ardkinglass)
(6127)

Brick Rising *Andrew Balding* a58 63
3 ch g Phoenix Reach(IRE) Comtesse Noire (CAN) (Woodman (USA))
1177[5] 1425[7] 1613[5] (1885) 2599[11] 4345[7]

Bridge Builder *Peter Hedger* 60
3 b g Avonbridge Amazing Dream (IRE) (Thatching)
2447[5] 2872[11] 3731[7]

Bridgehampton *Michael Bell* a82 81
4 b g Lando(GER) Gaze (Galileo (IRE))
4643[5] (5157) 5520[3] 6377[9] *7510[4]*

Bridge Of Avon *Mel Brittain* 26
2 b f Avonbridge Out Like Magic (Magic Ring (IRE))
1108[10] 3624[12] 5380[10] *5865[9]* 6914[5]

Bridge Orteip (IRE) *Filippo Sbariggia* 53
2 b c Amadeus Wolf Lovers Nest (Groom Dancer (USA))
7678a[7]

Bridge That Gap *Roger Ingram* a70 69
5 b c Avonbridge Figura (Rudimentary (USA))
94[6] (508) (789) 1381[2] 1836[3] 2413[5] *2982[7]*

Bridge To My Heart *Olivia Maylam*
3 b f Avonbridge Anatase (Danehill (USA))
5962[7] 6748[11] 7377[5]

Bridge Valley *Jason Ward* a53 53
6 ch g Avonbridge Go Between (Daggers Drawn (USA))
1280[4] 2276[8] 2795[7] 3026[10]

Bridle Belle *Richard Fahey* a73 93
5 b f Dansili River Belle (Lahib (USA))
2365[9] 2671[4] 3409[7] 3755[3] 4262[2]

Brigadoon *Philip Kirby* a82 87
6 b g Compton Place Briggsmaid (Elegant Air)
759[7] 889[7] 1081[5] 1442[11] 1819[7] 2278[6] 2435[4] ◆ *4150[3]* (4612) (4851) 5520[2]

Brigantin (USA) *Pat Carey* a65 114
6 ch h Cozzene(USA) Banyu Dewi (GER) (Poliglote)
7483a[7]

Brigh (IRE) *David Simcock* a77 90
3 ch f Galileo(IRE) La Vida Loca (IRE) (Caerleon (USA))
(774) 3437[3] (3925)

Bright Abbey *Dianne Sayer* a73 80
5 ch g Halling(USA) Bright Hope (IRE) (Danehill (USA))
6585[12]

Bright Applause *Tracy Waggott* a57 78
5 b g Royal Applause Sadaka (USA) (Kingmambo (USA))
(1763) (2165) 2706[3] 3480[3] 4543[6] 4851[4] 5059[4] 6211[8] 6631[6]

Bright Cecily (IRE) *Clive Cox* 75
2 b f Excellent Art Roman Love (IRE) (Perugino (USA))
4702[9] (5443)

Bright Glow *David Lanigan* a74 77
3 ch f Exceed And Excel(AUS) Lighthouse (Warning)
(2129) 2572[2] 2806[7] (4751) 5152[4]

Bright Society (IRE) *J S Moore* 12
2 b g Diamond Green(FR) Soul Society (IRE) (Inchinor)
3175[9] 3574[8] *4630[5]*

Bright Strike (USA) *John Gosden* a97 105
3 b c Smart Strike(CAN) Seebe (USA) (Danzig (USA))
(1199) (1714) 2298a[10]

Bright Thought (USA) *Jorge Gutierrez* 111
4 bb c Hat Trick(JPN) Smart Thought (USA) (Smart Strike (CAN))
7714a[10]

Brigliadoro (IRE) *Philip McBride* a61 46
2 ch c Excellent Art Milady's Pride (Machiavellian (USA))
7655[8] *7960[2]*

Brillantissimo (FR) *J-M Reillier* a65 59
8 ch g Gold Away(IRE) Brilliante (Sillery (USA))
6680a[3]

Brimstone Hill (IRE) *Anthony Carson* a86 82
4 b c Royal Applause Right As Rain (Rainbow Quest (USA))
420[3] 614[3] 1092[2] 1327[5] 2498[5]

Britain (IRE) *David C Griffiths* a62 27
2 b f Manduro(GER) Unreal (Dansili)
4073[8] 4177[4] *(5900) 6967[10]*

Broadcaster (IRE) *Ed McMahon* 77
2 b c Jeremy(USA) River Abouali (Bluebird (USA))
3233[7] 3724[2] 4337[2] 4802[3] 5710[2] 6493[4]

Broadway Duchess (IRE) *Richard Hannon Snr* 89
3 ch f New Approach(IRE) Annee Lumiere (IRE) (Giant's Causeway (USA))
2448[3] ◆ (3116) 3532[3] 5440[3] ◆ 6004[12] 6596[2]

Broadway Empire (USA) *Robertino Diodoro* a110
3 b g Empire Maker(USA) Broadway Hoofer (USA) (Belong To Me (USA))
7689a[9]

Broadway Musical (IRE) *Richard Hannon Snr* a59
2 b f Exceed And Excel(AUS) Broadway Hit (Sadler's Wells (USA))
7260[6] 7764[7]

Broadway Ranger (IRE) *Charles Hills* a53 64
2 b c Bushranger(IRE) Broadways Millie (IRE) (Imperial Ballet (IRE))
6931[7] 7638[9] 7818[3] *8396[4]*

Brockfield *Mel Brittain* a73 74
7 ch g Falbrav(IRE) Irish Light (USA) (Irish River (FR))
1237[10] 1391[5] 1775[6] 6758[3] 6943[3] ◆ 7425[9] *7961[2] 8299[6]*

Brockholes Flyer (IRE) *Brendan Powell* a49 43
2 b g Balmont(USA) Condilessa (IRE) (Key Of Luck (USA))
1344[5] 1512[4] 1659[14] *2562[9] 5066[13]* 5610[8] 6076[7] *6311[10]* 6322[6] 6726[6]

Brocklebank (IRE) *Simon Dow* a81 88
4 b g Diamond Green(FR) La Stellina (IRE) (Marju (IRE))
629[7] 792[7] 984[2] (1181) 1500[8] 2101[7] *3215[9] 3693[8]* (4237) 5124[8] 5621[2] (6337) 6871[10] 6988[8]

Brockwell *Tom Dascombe* 97
4 b g Singspiel(IRE) Noble Plum (IRE) (King's Best (USA))
1766[8] 2427[3] 3099[4] 3824[3] 4873[5] 5256[7] 6646[3] 7193[9] 7496[6]

Broctune Papa Gio *Keith Reveley* 76
6 b g Tobougg(IRE) Fairlie (Halling (USA))
3544[4] 3777[4] 4628[4] 5138[3] 6943[8] 7024[5] 7344[5] ◆

Brog Deas (IRE) *Patrick J Flynn* a93 96
4 b g Arakan(USA) Whitegate Way (Greensmith)
4465a[4] 4869a[2]

Broken Spirit (FR) *T Larriviere* 66
3 bl f Spirit One(FR) Broken Innate (IRE) (Broken Hearted)
711a[9]

Bronte *David Wachman* a83 94
3 b f Oasis Dream Interchange (IRE) (Montjeu (IRE))
5688a[6]

Bronze Angel (IRE) *Marcus Tregoning* a97 106
4 b g Dark Angel(IRE) Rihana (IRE) (Priolo (USA))
6838[23] 7196[8] *7926[11]* ◆

Bronze Beau *Kristin Stubbs* a59 88
6 ch g Compton Place Bella Cantata (Singspiel (IRE))
1649[11] 2122[4] 2410[3] (2736) 3069[2] 3236[6] 3855[10] 4579[5] 5381[7] (5985) 6309[10] 6848[8] 7314[7] *7731[10]*

Bronze Prince *Michael Attwater* a104 98
6 b g Oasis Dream Sweet Pea (Persian Bold)
1036[5] (1244) 2254[21] 2585[4] 4859[17] 5794[7] 6451a[12]

Brooke's Bounty *Richard Fahey* 75
3 ch g Bahamian Bounty Choysia (Pivotal)
1272[2] (1648) 2259[6] 2876[8] 3730[8]

Brooklyn Bowl (USA) *F Rohaut* a80 92
3 b g Henrythenavigator(USA) Turtle Bow (FR) (Turtle Island (IRE))
7188a[2]

Broon Troot (IRE) *Marcus Tregoning* a32
3 b g Jeremy(USA) Special Park (USA) (Trempolino (USA))
6748[10] 7781[8] 7873[6]

Brother Duke *Garry Moss* a53 36
3 b g Bachelor Duke(USA) Kathy's Rocket (USA) (Gold Legend (USA))
3650[5] *4356[5]* 4813[8]

Brother Tiger *David C Griffiths* a79 72
4 b g Singspiel(IRE) Three Secrets (IRE) (Danehill (USA))
(6289) 7281[8] *(7896)*

Broughton (GER) *Mark Johnston* 95
3 b g Teofilo(IRE) Boccassini (GER) (Artan (IRE))
(2989) 3502[2] (3756) ◆ 4063[2] 4279[6] (4917) 5258[6] 5792[6] 6868[6] 7206[12]

Broughton Place *Willie Musson* a54
5 b f Compton Place Classic Millennium (Midyan (USA))
343[9] 512[7]

Broughtons Bandit *Willie Musson* a64 44
6 b g Kyllachy Broughton Bounty (Bahamian Bounty)
361[2] 635[2] 928[4] 1062[6] 1953[2]

Broughtons Charm (IRE) *Willie Musson* a80 72
3 b f Invincible Spirit(IRE) Parisian Elegance (Zilzal (USA))
3956[4] 5280[2] ◆ 6977[13] *7663[4] (7861)* 8178[7] *8345[8]*

Broughtons Day *M Ramadan* a68 59
6 b g Mujahid(USA) Rainy Day Song (Persian Bold)
394a[6]

Broughtons Secret *Willie Musson* 82
2 b f Aqlaam Hidden Meaning (Cadeaux Genereux)
6644[12] 7016[8] 7493[3]

Brown Diamond (IRE) *Charles Hills* 78
2 b f Fastnet Rock(AUS) Adjalisa (IRE) (Darshaan)
6643[4]

Brown Eyed Honey *William Haggas* 75
2 b f Elusive City(USA) Tiger Mist (IRE) (Galileo (IRE))
3781[4] (4610)

Brown Panther *Tom Dascombe* a75 120
5 b c Shirocco(GER) Treble Heights (IRE) (Unfuwain (USA))
(3608) (4919) 6742[5] 7761a[8]

Brown Pete (IRE) *Ann Stokell* a73 65
5 bb g Aussie Rules(USA) Banba (IRE) (Docksider (USA))
83[7] 138[4] 450[3] 1220[7] 1297[2] 1366[3] 1884[7] 2220[3] 2413[2] 2640[3] 3022[8] 3218[6] 3977[5] ◆ 4441[3] 5124[12] 5304[5] 5605[3] 6037[4] 6258[2] 6459[4] 7091[10] 7515[9] 7930[8] 8448[11]

Brownsea Brink *Richard Hannon Snr* a86 97
3 b c Cadeaux Genereux Valiantly (Anabaa (USA))
(4957) (5958) (6650) 6993[5] 7991[7]

Brown Sugar (IRE) *Richard Hannon Snr* a110 108
2 b c Tamayuz Lady Livius (IRE) (Titus Livius (FR))
3112[2] ◆ (3695) ◆ 4212[10] (4855) 5573a[5] (6201) 7191[9]

Brownsville (USA) *Mark Johnston* 74
2 b g Bernstein(USA) Net Worth (USA) (Forty Niner (USA))
3461[4] 3717[2] 4026[7] 4477[5] 5400[5] 7592[3]

Brown Volcano (IRE) *John O'Shea* a60 61
4 b g Waky Nao Lavish Spirit (USA) (Southern Halo (USA))
54[5] 409[3] 437[3] 617[5] 2345[8] 3268[0] (4659) 4943[9] 5154[5] 6610[10]

Broxbourne (IRE) *Mark Johnston* a84 98
4 b f Refuse To Bend(IRE) Rafting (IRE) (Darshaan)
21[6] 198[4] (343) (562) (675) (809) 948[3] 1463[5] 1805[2] (4704) (4873) 5256[6] (5655) 6066[6] 6646[12] 7193[31]

Brujo De Olleros (BRZ) *Richard C Mettee* a111 84
5 ch h Wild Event(USA) Hit Oil (BRZ) (Roy (USA))
7689a[3]

Brundon *Ken Wingrove* a44 59
4 ch f Refuse To Bend(IRE) Anna Of Brunswick (Rainbow Quest (USA))
925[9]

Brunello *Philip Kirby* a68 68
5 b g Leporello(IRE) Lydia Maria (Dancing Brave (USA))
887[4] 1045[2] 1350[5] 1763[4] 2120[4] 2435[6] 2990[10] 3589[6] 3947[3] 4951[5] 5466[4] 5831[7] 6087[6] 6782[2] 7081[6]

Brunhilde *Tom Dascombe* 68
2 ch f Bahamian Bounty Glory Oatway (IRE) (Desert Prince (IRE))
2740[3] 3205[5] 3914[3]

Bruni Heinke (IRE) *Richard Fahey* 55
2 ch f Dutch Art Penchant (Kyllachy)
3760[11]

Brunston *Anthony Middleton* a91 35
7 gr g High Chaparral(IRE) Molly Mello (GER) (Big Shuffle (USA))
144[6] 592[3] 928[5] 1097[6]

Bryant Park (USA) *Christine Dunnett* a53
4 ch g Street Cry(IRE) Cala (FR) (Desert Prince (IRE))
990[7] 8068[9] 8258[8]

Brynford *Chris Dwyer* a67 50
3 b f Sir Percy Bull's Crown (USA) (Holy Bull (USA))
796[5] (1367) 1697[3] 2330[7] 2802[10] 3405[3] 3903[2] 5397[2] 5890[2] (6362) 6655[6]

Buaiteoir (FR) *Nikki Evans* a67 79
7 b g Mineshaft(USA) Witching Hour (FR) (Fairy King (USA))
974[2] 1890[5] 3399[6] 3910[3] 5073[5] 7082[5] 7931[7] 8448[12]

Bubblina *Alastair Lidderdale* a52
6 b m Pastoral Pursuits Streccia (Old Vic)
332[4] 1710[11]

Bubbly Bailey *Alan Bailey* a60 44
3 b g Byron Night Gypsy (Mind Games)
141[7] 195[5] 580[6] 1118[3] 1210[2] 1759[15] 1903[5]

Bubbly Ballerina *Alan Bailey* a82 83
4 ch f Footstepsinthesand Pain Perdu (IRE) (Waajib)
58[7] 196[7] 627[3] (1052) 1160[8] 1308[9] 1517[6] 3093[12] 3577[3] 3658[5]

Bubbly Bellini (IRE) *Adrian McGuinness* a65 97
6 b g Mull Of Kintyre(USA) Gwapa (IRE) (Imperial Frontier (USA))
2254[19] 3846a[8] 5019a[9] 6883a[13] 7368[25] 7719a[6]

Bubbly Braveheart (IRE) *Phil McEntee* a65 43
6 b g Cape Cross(IRE) Infinity (FR) (Bering)
200[5] 417[7] 625[5] 852[11] 921[11] 1146[3] 1162[7] 1297[7] 1502[10] 1752[8] 2509[6]

Buchanan *Henry Candy* a88 84
3 b c Dansili Because (IRE) (Sadler's Wells (USA))
(4632) 5146[2] 7250[6]

Buckie Boy (IRE) *Nicky Henderson* a69 75
7 b g Bahri(USA) Woodren (USA) (Woodman (USA))
351[8] 654[5] 1207[P]

Buckland (IRE) *Hans Adielsson* a103 106
5 b g Oratorio(IRE) Dollar Bird (IRE) (Kris)
133[4] 222[3] 705[6] (720) ◆ (882) (1037) (1242) ◆ 1547[2] 1920[4] 2149[12] 3559[16] 4796[9]

Buckland Beau *Hans Adielsson* a25
2 b g Rock Of Gibraltar(IRE) Heavenly Whisper (IRE) (Halling (USA))
3211[8]

Buckley Boy *K F Clutterbuck* a48 12
4 b g Araafa(IRE) Waseyla (IRE) (Sri Pekan (USA))
155[4]

Buckstay (IRE) *Peter Chapple-Hyam* a76 92
3 b g Lawman(FR) Stella Del Mattino (USA) (Golden Gear (USA))
1934[3] 2432[6] ◆ 2717[2] 4917[8] 5534[3] 6538[2] 7696[3]

Buckwheat *A Fabre* 111
3 b c Manduro(GER) Russian Snows (IRE) (Sadler's Wells (USA))
(3645a) 4573a[7] 5462a[6] 7049a[13]

Buds Bruvver *Brian Baugh* 21
4 ch g Reel Buddy(USA) Spectrum Queen (IRE) (Spectrum (IRE))
3047[8] 3919[9] 5073[U] 6155[6]

Bugsy's Babe *George Baker* a23 36
3 ch f Tobougg(IRE) Oak Tree Miss (USA) (Woodman (USA))
1367[7]

Bugsy's Boy *George Baker* a64 77
9 b g Double Trigger(IRE) Bugsy's Sister (Aragon)
1031[8]

Bull Bay *Jane Chapple-Hyam* a70 60
4 b g Bahamian Bounty Buffy Boo (Agnes World (USA))
898[9]

Bull Five *Nick Littmoden* a62
6 b g Intikhab(USA) Digamist Girl (IRE) (Digamist (USA))
3399[8]

Bull Market (IRE) *Alan Jones* a24 36
10 b g Danehill(USA) Paper Moon (IRE) (Lake Coniston (IRE))
6217[9]

Bullseye Babe *Mark Usher* a51 37
3 ch f Notnowcato Mary Sea (FR) (Selkirk (USA))
651[5] 1499[9] 2154[5] 2762[7] 3495[4] 5935[7] 6361[6] 7204[5]

Bunairgead (IRE) *J S Bolger* a73 102
3 b f New Approach(IRE) Montecito (USA) (Seeking The Gold (USA))
1557a[5] 2108a[2] 2689a[8] 4465a[9] 5115a[2] 6023a[4]

Bunce (IRE) *David O'Meara* a74 69
5 b g Good Reward(USA) Bold Desire (Cadeaux Genereux)
2441[7] 2707[5] 2752[2] 3068[2] 3392[5] 4119[7] 4966[6] 5239[3] 5713[8] 6181[8] 6606[4] (6905) 7282[3] 7792[6] 8049[6] 8230[8]

Bungle Inthejungle *Mick Channon* 108
3 b c Exceed And Excel(AUS) Licence To Thrill (Wolfhound (USA))
1620[4] 2019[14] 3420[10] 4079[4] 4947[12] 5726[14] 6305[11]

Bunker (IRE) *Richard Hannon Snr* 105
2 br c Hurricane Run(IRE) Endure (IRE) (Green Desert (USA))
(2591) ◆ 3555[2] ◆ (5313a)

Buonarroti (IRE) *A P O'Brien* 102
2 b c Galileo(IRE) Beauty Is Truth (IRE) (Pivotal)
(7050a) ◆ 7528[5]

Burano (IRE) *Brian Meehan* a103 107
4 ch h Dalakhani(IRE) Kalimanta (IRE) (Lake Coniston (IRE))
363a[2] 657a[10] 873a[3] 956a[7] 1241[2] 1643[2] 1846[4]

Bureau (IRE) *Mark Johnston* 79
2 ch f Halling(USA) Embassy (Cadeaux Genereux)
3290[2] ◆ 3555[14] (4386) 4988[10] (6085) 6839[8] 7129[9]

Burgoyne (USA) *Hughie Morrison* a73
3 b g Officer(USA) Married For Money (USA) (Not For Love (USA))
814[6] (1072) 1453[4] 2322[9] 3893[12]

Burj Alzain (IRE) *Fawzi Abdulla Nass* a103
5 b c Marju(IRE) Bahareeya (USA) (Riverman (USA))
463a[12] 869a[7]

Burke's Rock *Jeremy Noseda* a100 103
4 br f Cape Cross(IRE) Miss Lacey (IRE) (Diktat)
1544[4] (2015) 3458[8]

Burma Days (USA) *Sylvester Kirk* a38 52
3 b g Medaglia d'Oro(USA) Becky In Pink (USA) (Formal Gold (CAN))
2095[3] 2599[14] 2743[8] 3040[7]

Burmese Breeze *Chris Wall*
2 b g Shirocco(GER) Crimson Topaz (Hernando (FR))
7219[11]

Burnbrake *Richard Rowe* a45 17
8 b g Mujahid(USA) Duena (Grand Lodge (USA))
131[9] 418[8] 635[7] 1090[10] 2159[9] 5216[9] 5586[10]

Burnham *Hughie Morrison* a86 84
4 b g Nayef(USA) Salim Toto (Mtoto)
1586[5] 2739[2] (3617) 4280[3] 5513[6] 6108[2] 6646[5] 7765[4] 7976[4]

Burnhope *Scott Dixon* a82 76
4 b g Choisir(AUS) Isengard (USA) (Cobra King (USA))
(353) 526[2] 881[5] 1692[4] 2007[16] 3981[7] 4389[7] 6205[7] 6547[13] 7445[8] 7897[9] 8128[2] 8321[4]

Burning Blaze *Kevin Ryan* 96
3 b g Danroad(AUS) Demeter (USA) (Diesis)
2452[5] 3342[3] 4767[6] 4922[8]

Burning Dawn (USA) *David Brown* a81 77
3 b f Bernstein(USA) Winter Morning (USA) (Rahy (USA))
(2135) 3058[7] 4453[2] 5676[4] 6476[4] (6780)

Burning Thread (IRE) *Tim Etherington* a46 97
6 b g Captain Rio Desert Rose (Green Desert (USA))
2768[8] 3038[6] 4047[7] (4364) 4613[7] 5294[8] 5519[2] (5998) 6830[12] 7803[12]

Burns Night *Philip Kirby* a66 67
7 ch g Selkirk(USA) Night Frolic (Night Shift (USA))
6470[3] 7239[8]

Burnt Cream *Martin Bosley* a54 60
6 b m Exceed And Excel(AUS) Basbousate Nadia (Wolfhound (USA))
111[4] (529) 3425[6] 3994[4] 4427[3] 5221[6] 5408[2] (5982) 6901[4] 7292[6]

Burnt Fingers (IRE) *Rod Millman* 62
3 b f Kheleyf(USA) Play With Fire (FR) (Priolo (USA))
1364[3] 1660[7]

Burn The Boats (IRE) *G M Lyons* a73 94
4 br g Big Bad Bob(IRE) Forever Phoenix (Shareef Dancer (USA))
2444[4] (3846a) 4297[9] 7227a[8]

Burnt Sienna (IRE) *John Joseph Murphy* 75
3 ch f Papal Bull Lucky Achievement (USA) (St Jovite (USA))
6490[5]

Burnwynd Boy *Lee Smyth* a54 61
8 b g Tobougg(IRE) Cadeau Speciale (Cadeaux Genereux)
4339[3] ◆ 4615[2] 5331[5] 8012a[9]

Burren View Lady (IRE) *Tim Easterby* a90 62
3 br f Dansili Westerly Gale (USA) (Gone West (USA))
1392[7] 1722[4] 1962[2] 2916[10] (4840) 5139[4] (5674) 6655[2] (6982) 7381[2] 7731[2] 7959[2]

Bursledon (IRE) *Richard Hannon Snr* a72 75
3 b g Jeremy(USA) Desert Drama (IRE) (Green Desert (USA))
1300[3] 2416[4] 2846[3] 3636[4] 3990[4] 4417[7] 4961[7] 5694[5] 6153[2] 6734[4]

Burwaaz *Ed Dunlop* a104 100
4 b c Exceed And Excel(AUS) Nidhaal (IRE) (Observatory (USA))
1835[3] 2257[6] 3458[26] 4297[7] 4986[3] 5314a[11] 6391[19] 7366[12]

Bury Pacer (IRE) *Richard Hannon Snr* a74 67
2 b c Lawman(FR) Distant Drama (USA) (Distant View (USA))
7070[5] 7461[2]

Busatto (USA) *Mark Johnston* a73 82
3 bb c Bernardini(USA) Lyphard's Delta (USA) (Lyphard (USA))
6134[5] 6497[2] (6824)

Bush Beauty (IRE) *Clive Brittain* 70
2 b f Bushranger(IRE) Scottendale (Zilzal (USA))
2131[2] 5199[5]

Bushcraft (IRE) *Ed Walker* a82 91
2 b c Bushranger(IRE) Lady Lucia (IRE) (Royal Applause)
3288[3] (4142) (4639) 5509[2]

Bushel (USA) *Mark Johnston* 90
3 b g Street Cry(IRE) Melhor Ainda (USA) (Pulpit (USA))
3805[3] 4223[2] 4454[3] (5107) ◆ 5258[2]

Bushy Glade (IRE) *Julia Feilden* 48
2 b f Bushranger(IRE) Cladantom (IRE) (High Estate)
2382[11] 4861[5]

Bussa *David Evans* a76 71
5 b g Iceman Maid To Dance (Pyramus (USA))
(35) 139[2] 380[2] 426[2] (546) 650[2] 705[7] 981[3] 2736[8] 3622[9] 4120[5] 4608[7] 5349[P] 5841[3] 6317[5] 6606[7] 6928[8] 7669[9] 8306[13] 8411[8]

Buster Brown (IRE) *Gary Moore* a74 75
4 ch c Singspiel(IRE) Gold Dodger (USA) (Slew O'Gold (USA))
2417[7] 2886[7] 4889[4] 5179[5] 5833[8] 6730[7] 7132[6] 7378[3] (7514) 7922[6]

Bustling Darcey *Mark Gillard* 37
3 ch f Assertive Bint Baddi (FR) (Shareef Dancer (USA))
2597[11] 3176[10] 3915[4] 4607[8] 6486[7] 6956[4]

Bustopher (USA) *Mahmood Al Zarooni* 88
3 bb g Elusive Quality(USA) Catstar (USA) (Storm Cat (USA))
1635[2]

Busy Bimbo (IRE) *Alan Berry* a49 52
4 b f Red Clubs(IRE) Unfortunate (Komaite (USA))
326[10] 610[10] 2317[8] 2757[10] 3091[7] 3475[6] 4292[3] 4371[2] 4621[3] 4761[3] 4982[3] 5047[2] 5273[13] 5486[3] 5641[5] 5709[6] 6289[5] 6604[9] 6940[7] 7101[5] 7203[3] 7380[2] 7600[5] 8112[2] 8277[4] 8320[4] 8437[6]

Butterfly McQueen (USA) *Andrew Balding* 100
3 b f Curlin(USA) Distant Roar (CAN) (Storm Cat (USA))
2151[2] (2803) 3240[9] (4278) 4743[5] 6124a[2] 7205[8]

Button Down *Lady Cecil* a59
2 b f Oasis Dream Modesta (IRE) (Sadler's Wells (USA))
7763[7]

Button Moon (IRE) *Paul Fitzsimons* a74 84
5 ch f Compton Place Portelet (Night Shift (USA))
101[8]

Buxton *Roger Ingram* a64 79
9 b g Auction House(USA) Dam Certain (IRE) (Damister (USA))
80[8]

Buy And Sell (IRE) *David Brown* a69
2 b c Captain Rio Balance The Books (Elmaamul (USA))
4379[8] 6654[2] 6981[2] 7348[2]

Buy Art *Gary Moore* a71 72
3 b g Acclamation Kondakova (IRE) (Soviet Star (USA))
402[4] 710[7] (1157) 1180[5] 1661[6] 2098[3] 3050[2] 3533[5] (3732)

Buy Back Bob (IRE) *A J Martin* a88 88
6 b g Big Bad Bob(IRE) Abeyr (Unfuwain (USA))
3599a[4]

Buy Out Boy *Jo Hughes* a45 59
2 gr g Medicean Tiger's Gene (GER) (Perugino (USA))
5101[7] 6378[5] 6666[6]

Buzz Law (IRE) *K R Burke* a60 75
5 b g Fasliyev(USA) Buzz Two (IRE) (Case Law)
1442[12] 8416[9]

By A Wiska *Ann Duffield* a45 53
3 b g Kheleyf(USA) Tropical Breeze (IRE) (Kris)
237[6] 1747[6] 1842[9]

Bye Bye Birdie (IRE) *A P O'Brien* 105
2 b f Oasis Dream Sleek Slink (Selkirk (USA))
3459[12] (3868a) 4253[6]

Bygones For Coins (IRE) *Robert Johnson* a55 66
5 ch f Danroad(AUS) Reservation (IRE) (Common Grounds)
63[4] 99[7] 349[10] (3728) 4052[5] 4760[2] 5048[3] 5143[10]

By Jupiter *Michael Bell* a64 64
2 ch f Sea The Stars(IRE) Maid Of Killeen (IRE) (Darshaan)
6643[11] 7764[6]

Byrd In Hand (IRE) *John Bridger* a58 68
6 b g Fasliyev(USA) Military Tune (IRE) (Nashwan (USA))
441[4] 530[4] 630[4] 737[11] 1381[5] 2057[2] 2534[6] 2747[3] 2845[12] 4752[8] 4996[8] 6038[8] 7923[9] 8390[7] 8449[11]

By Rights *Tony Carroll* a54 62
2 b f Byron Legend House (FR) (Grand Lodge (USA))
5350[4] 5593[8] 6947[3] 7426[2]

Byron Again *Sean Curran* a32
3 b g Byron Kiss Me Again (IRE) (Cyrano De Bergerac)
6134[12] 8063[8]

Byroness *Heather Main* a73 64
3 b f Byron Parting Gift (Cadeaux Genereux)
371[4] 506[3] (632) ◆ (817) 1714[6] 2449[6] 2984[6] 3039[6] 6556[5] 6925[9] 7629[8] 7841[5] 8087[2] 8345[10]

Byron Gala *Marco Botti* a62 44
2 b g Byron Tenuta Di Gala (IRE) (Nashwan (USA))
5405[6] 6365[2] 7113[3] 7604[2]

Byron's Dream *Jedd O'Keeffe* a54 62
3 b g Byron Fresher (Fabulous Dancer (USA))
1772[2] 7109[9]

Byron's Gold *Ben De Haan* a64 54
2 ch f Byron Dance To The Blues (IRE) (Danehill Dancer (IRE))
7393[4] 7737[4]

By The Light (IRE) *Mark Johnston* a59 61
2 gr g Verglas(IRE) Margarita (IRE) (Marju (IRE))
2161[5] 2502[8] 3426[4] 5424[4] 5865[6] 6852[3] 7168[3]

Cabaan (IRE) *Brian Meehan* a55 60
2 b c Acclamation Abington Angel (Machiavellian (USA))
3374[8] 4483[8] 5025[8] 5634[11] 5865[2] 6131[3] 6311[8]

Cabal *Andrew Crook* a61 63
6 br m Kyllachy Secret Flame (Machiavellian (USA))
83[5] 1015[2] 2956[3] 3337[4] 3895[3] 4376[3] 4469[7] 5521[3] 6276[9] 6851[7] 8341[4]

Cable Bay (IRE) *Charles Hills* 115
2 b c Invincible Spirit(IRE) Rose De France (IRE) (Diktat)
2543[4] (2925) 4918[2] 5765[4] 6390[3] 6765[2] 7192[2]

Cabuchon (GER) *David Evans* a61 61
6 b g Fantastic Light(USA) Catella (GER) (Generous (IRE))
4605[3] 5093[9] 5934[3] (6044) 6325[11] 6782[3] (6895) 7305[5] 7767[6] 7984[3] 8129[6] 8337[8]

Cactus Valley (IRE) *Roger Charlton* a71 95
4 b g Lawman(FR) Beech Gardens (Sadler's Wells (USA))
1673[4] ◆ 2422[4] (3157)

Cadeaux Pearl *Scott Dixon* a69 82
5 b g Acclamation Anneliina (Cadeaux Genereux)
1248[2] 1581[5] 2014[8] 4860[9] 5108[11] 7112[7] 7887[6] 8096[7] 8319[2] 8351[6]

Cadeaux Power *Clive Brittain* 67
2 b f Major Cadeaux Right Answer (Lujain (USA))
7692[5]

Cadeaux Royale *Dominic Ffrench Davis* 37
5 b f Piccolo Sundial (Cadeaux Genereux)
3176[13] 5176[5] 5645[8] 6261[11]

Cadette D'Authie (FR) *O Regley* 33
3 b f Califet(FR) Vertige (USA) (Gulch (USA))
5692a[9]

Cadgers Brig *Barry Murtagh* a72 68
5 ch g Halling(USA) Burghmuir (IRE) (Cadeaux Genereux)
3768[5] 4355[10]

Cadmium *Harry Dunlop* a64
2 b f Major Cadeaux Miss Mirasol (Sheikh Albadou)
5443[10] 5891[5] 6923[5]

Cadmium Loch *Reg Hollinshead* a66 64
5 b g Needwood Blade Vermilion Creek (Makbul)
24[9] 423[10] 551[2] 670[4] 1020[8]

Caerwyn *Tony Carroll* a68 65
3 ch g Pastoral Pursuits Preference (Efisio)
5444[3] 5845[5] 7325[2] 7740[9] 8185[4]

Caesaria (IRE) *Y Gourraud* 87
3 br c Hannouma(IRE) Sweet Shop (Grand Lodge (USA))
7995a[7]

Caesars Gift (IRE) *Derek Shaw* a62 62
2 b g Holy Roman Emperor(IRE) Jazz Up (Cadeaux Genereux)
1792[5] 2082[5] 7200[5] 7623[3] 7771[3] 7986[8] 8113[3] 8222[4]

Cafe Society (FR) *David Simcock* a98 97
3 b g Motivator Mishina (FR) (Highest Honor (FR))
1834[2] 2457[3] (3698) ◆ 4279[2] ◆ 6186[5] 7304[2]

Cafetiere *Paul Cole* a76 75
2 b f Iffraaj Coffee Cream (Common Grounds)
1240[7] 1634[13] (2320) 4519[6] 7568a[4]

Cagoule *P Bary* 84
2 b c Oasis Dream Pretty Face (Rainbow Quest (USA))
7889a[3]

Cahal (IRE) *David Nicholls* 53
2 b g Bushranger(IRE) Cabopino (IRE) (Captain Rio)
6842[10] 7209[10] 7592[4]

Caim Hill (IRE) *Philip Fenton* 90
10 b g Deploy Glen's Gale (IRE) (Strong Gale)
7230a[23]

Cairanne *Tom Keddy* a57 64
5 b f High Chaparral(IRE) Celestial Choir (Celestial Storm (USA))
62[3] 201[7]

Cai Shen (IRE) *Richard Hannon Snr* a109 112
5 ch g Iffraaj Collada (IRE) (Desert Prince (IRE))
1034[3] 1241[5]

Caja (FR) *H-A Pantall* a81 88
2 ch f Touch Down(GER) Centinela (Caerleon (USA))
5555a[5] 7570a[5]

Cakal Carlos (TUR) *I Kapusiz* a99
3 b c Artie Schiller(USA) Divine Diva (USA) (Theatrical (IRE))
6232a[3]

Calabash Cove (USA) *E Charpy* a30 19
9 ch g Rahy(USA) I Need A Holiday (USA) (Nureyev (USA))
7679a[7]

Calaf *Brian Ellison* a77 89
5 b g Dubai Destination(USA) Tarandot (IRE) (Singspiel (IRE))
239[7] 329[3] 3094[4] 3685[8] 4854[15] 4923[11] 5559[2] 6211[6] 6801[23] (7596)

Calculated Risk *John Quinn* a61 78
4 ch g Motivator Glen Rosie (IRE) (Mujtahid (USA))
4995[6] (6552) 7239[6]

Calculating (IRE) *Mark Usher* a67 69
9 b g Machiavellian(USA) Zaheemah (USA) (El Prado (IRE))
624[5] 887[5] 1080[9] (1189) 1306[2] 1601[4] 1744[6] 2174[5]

Caldercruix (USA) *James Evans* a86 79
6 ch g Rahy(USA) Al Theraab (USA) (Roberto (USA))
11[5] 104[8] (912) 1148[3] 1203[6] 1599[5] 1849[8] 4237[7] (5899) 6203[11] 6609[5] 6792[8] 7224[11] 7603[2] 7888[6] 8269[9]

Caledonia *Jim Goldie* 72
6 b g Sulamani(IRE) Vanessa Bell (IRE) (Lahib (USA))
2462[4] 2971[3] 5484[11] 6166[3] 6668[5] 7210[4]

Caledonia Lady *Jo Hughes* 105
4 b f Firebreak Granuaile O'Malley (IRE) (Mark Of Esteem (IRE))
1662[3] 2019[12] 5726[10] 5984[12] 6639[11] 7010[9] 7821[5]

Caledonia Laird *Jo Hughes* 61
2 b c Firebreak Granuaile O'Malley (IRE) (Mark Of Esteem (IRE))
1659[9] 2411[10] 3883[5] 4703[7] 5371[7] 7451[13]

Caledonia Prince *Jo Hughes* a81 55
5 b g Needwood Blade Granuaile O'Malley (IRE) (Mark Of Esteem (IRE))
49[3] (540) (832) 889[3] 1203[3] 1752[3] 2580[7]

Caletta Bay *Mick Channon* 73
2 b f Rock Of Gibraltar(IRE) Cartimandua (Medicean)
2204[3] 2601[4] 3057[7] (Dead)

Calgacus (IRE) *John Patrick Shanahan* a71 89
4 ch g Galileo(IRE) Katdogawn (Bahhare (USA))
5759[5]

Califante *William Muir* a82 88
3 b f Kyllachy Call Mariah (USA) (Dixie Union (USA))
1676[8] 2429[5] 3460[17] 4252[6] 4766[9] 5202[3] 5896[4] 6524[7] 7256[8]

California English (IRE) *Marco Botti* a81 69
4 b g Oasis Dream Muwali (USA) (Kingmambo (USA))
49[2] 222[6] 593[5] 1081[2] 1354[3]

California Memory (USA) *A S Cruz* 121
7 gr g Highest Honor(FR) Kalpita (USA) (Spinning World (USA))
1872a[2]

Call Ahead *Sir Michael Stoute* a59 68
3 ch f Three Valleys(USA) Payphone (Anabaa (USA))
1640[4] 1891[5] 2872[4]

Calling *Brian Meehan* a32 71
3 b f Dalakhani(IRE) Almatinka (IRE) (Indian Ridge)
3237[12] 3860[3] 5064[4] 5694[8] 6810[6]

Callisto Moon *Jo Hughes* a29 83
9 b g Mujahid(USA) Nursling (IRE) (Kahyasi)
(2069) 6424[9]

Callmeakhab (IRE) *Charles Hills* a61 73
3 b f Intikhab(USA) Viola Royale (IRE) (Royal Academy (USA))
1640[5] ◆ (2215) 2622[4] 2951[7] 5096[3] 5975[4] 6306[12]

Call Me Bubbles (FR) *W P Mullins* a59 90
4 gr g Stormy River(FR) Tempete Tropicale (FR) (Kaldoun (FR))
7230a[3] 7723a[8]

Call Me Marilyn (USA) *Paul Cole* a23 27
3 ch f Henny Hughes(USA) Ball Gown (USA) (Silver Hawk (USA))
5176[8]

Call Of Duty (IRE) *Dianne Sayer* a25 67
8 br g Storming Home Blushing Barada (USA) (Blushing Groom (FR))
2316[7] 2629[6] 3043[6] 3397[3] 3466[5] 4052[3] 5052[4] 5466[8] 5882[7] 6296[8] 8031[8]

Calm Attitude (IRE) *Rae Guest* 67
3 ch f Dutch Art Turban Heights (IRE) (Golan (IRE))
1660[8] 2241[4] 2824[6] 3376[3] (4885) (5092) (6357)

Calon Lad (IRE) *George Baker* a69 65
3 ch g Redback Flames (Blushing Flame (USA))
3902[5] 4590[7] 5064[8] 6109[3] ◆ 6522[5] 7104[4] 7273[4]

Calrissian (GER) *Fredrik Reuterskiold* a100 101
9 ch g Efisio Centaine (Royal Academy (USA))
3970a[7] 7085a[5]

Calrissian (IRE) *Alan Jarvis* a61 77
2 ch c Lando(GER) Dallaah (Green Desert (USA))
3555[8] 4026[5] 4483[6] 5309[2] 7061[6] 7442[5]

Calvin Williams (FR) *E Lellouche* a101 101
3 gr c Carlotamix(FR) Quellaffaire (FR) (Charge D'Affaires)
(286a) 999a[4] 1357a[6]

Calypso Cay *Peter Salmon* a67 65
5 b g Tiger Hill(IRE) Tessa Reef (IRE) (Mark Of Esteem (IRE))
24[5]

Calypso Magic (IRE) *Olivia Maylam* a86 92
5 gr g Aussie Rules(USA) Calypso Dancer (FR) (Celtic Swing)
21[5] 94[5]

Calyxa *Ferdinand J Leve* 110
3 b f Pivotal Chantra (GER) (Lando (GER))
2065a[3] 2910a[2] 3852a[6] 5044a[7] 7053a[2]

Camacarin *G Collet* a51
5 ch f Domedriver(IRE) Thunder Queen (USA) (Thunder Gulch (USA))
498a[8]

Camache Queen (IRE) *Joseph Tuite* a83 82
5 b f Camacho Alinda (IRE) (Revoque (IRE))
1472[3] 2395[15] 2513[5] 5104[6] 5349[9] 5674[8] 6436[4] 6980[9] 7246[4] 7427[4] 7845[6]

Camachoice (IRE) *Marco Botti* a82 68
3 b g Camacho Nouvelle Reve (GER) (Acatenango (GER))
168[4] (414) (1099) 1683[7] 2776[6]

Camanche Grey (IRE) *Ben Haslam* a55 35
2 gr c Camacho Sense Of Greeting (IRE) (Key Of Luck (USA))
6517[11] 7804[4]

Camaretz (USA) *J-C Rouget* a86 102
3 ch g Mr Greeley(USA) Drums Of Freedom (USA) (Green Forest (USA))
782a[7] 1737a[6]

Camatini (IRE) *Michael Dods* a53 62
2 b f Camacho Trentini (IRE) (Singspiel (IRE))
3476[8] 4053[5] 4801[4] 6085[4] 6755[8] 7340[12] 7954[2] 8137[6] 8347[3]

Camborne *John Gosden* a92 116
5 b g Doyen(IRE) Dumnoni (Titus Livius (FR))
4857[2] 5741[4] (6348) (6636)

Cambridge *Charles Hills* 86
2 b f Rail Link Alumni (Selkirk (USA))
(6949) ◆

Cameley Dawn *Malcolm Saunders* 61
2 b f Alhaarth(IRE) Apply Dapply (Pursuit Of Love)
5473[10] 5812[5] 6334[4]

Camelopardalis *Tobias B P Coles* a54 57
4 b f Tobougg(IRE) Bonne Etoile (Diesis)
2971[8] 3907[7] 5093[3] 6558[9]

Camelot *A P O'Brien* 126
4 b c Montjeu(IRE) Tarfah (USA) (Kingmambo (USA))
(2105a) 2688a[2] 3457[4]

Cameo Tiara (IRE) *Richard Hannon Snr* a72 51
2 b f High Chaparral(IRE) Cuilaphuca (IRE) (Danetime (IRE))
7296[3] 7532[7]

Cameron Highland (IRE) *Roger Varian* 111
4 b c Galileo(IRE) Landmark (USA) (Arch (USA))
2652[4] 3830[4] (4907) (5761) ◆ 6385[6]

Camerooney *Marjorie Fife* a69 72
10 b g Sugarfoot Enkindle (Relkino)
5713[11] 6053[3] (6907) 7082[2] (7238) 8295[5]

Camilla De Rossi *Rae Guest* a39 25
3 b f Oratorio(IRE) Supa Sal (King's Best (USA))
1595[6] 2748[4]

Caminel (IRE) *Jeremy Gask* a44
2 b f Kyllachy Jalissa (Mister Baileys)
6477[7] 6931[8]

Camisole (IRE) *Charles Hills* 42
3 br f Teofilo(IRE) Sleeveless (USA) (Fusaichi Pegasus (USA))
5588[8] 6532[7]

Campanology *J P Murtagh* a95 101
4 b g Royal Applause Savannah Belle (Green Desert (USA))
1168a[15] 3527[15] 4869a[9] 6025a[3]

Canadian Run (IRE) *Robert Mills* a89 79
3 ch g Hurricane Run(IRE) Vale View (FR) (Anabaa (USA))
1767[7] 2604[6] 3633[9] 4442[2] 6359[5] (6734)

Canary Lad (IRE) *Alan Jarvis* 46
2 ch c Iffraaj Sweet Myrtle (USA) (Mutakddim (USA))
4121[8]

Canary Row (IRE) *P J Prendergast* 98
3 b c Holy Roman Emperor(IRE) Fresh Mint (IRE) (Sadler's Wells (USA))
1555a[5]

Canary Wharf (IRE) *Marco Botti* a81 64
4 b c Danehill Dancer(IRE) Wedding Morn (IRE) (Sadler's Wells (USA))
146[4] (439) 1238[7]

Candelita *Jo Hughes* a67 67
6 b m Trade Fair Gramada (IRE) (Cape Cross (IRE))
429[5] 714[3] 4403[3] (4655) 4938[3]

Candoluminescence *Roger Charlton* a78 76
3 br f Dansili Flash Of Gold (Darshaan)
3372[4] 4172[3] 5132[3] 6081[4] 6978[3] 7395[6] 7863[4]

Candy Apples (IRE) *P J Prendergast* a73 90
2 b f Footstepsinthesand Candy Ride (IRE) (Pivotal)
5771a[7]

Candycakes (IRE) *Michael Bell* a70 82
4 b f Cape Cross(IRE) Charita (IRE) (Lycius (USA))
1825[5] 2253[8] 2606[9]

Candy Critic (GER) *H-A Pantall* a60 65
3 b f Desert Prince(IRE) Chatcat (SWI) (Brief Truce (USA))
962a[8]

Candy Kitten *Alastair Lidderdale* a72 68
3 b f Assertive Birthday Venture (Soviet Star (USA))
1908[7] 3696[2] 4799[6] 6319[2] 6734[3] (7377) 7669[4] 8038[2]

Candyman Can (IRE) *Dominic Ffrench Davis* a66 76
3 b g Holy Roman Emperor(IRE) Palwina (FR) (Unfuwain (USA))
141[3] 5391[2] 5854[7] 6435[2] 6976[11] 7396[3]

Cane Cat (IRE) *Tony Carroll* a58 69
6 bb m One Cool Cat(USA) Seven Wonders (USA) (Rahy (USA))
919[7] 1068[4] 1298[9] 1893[2] 2714[4] 3138[2] 3314[5] 4350[6] 5002[12] 5803[2] 6851[6]

Canna (IRE) *Ali Brewer* a72 82
5 b g High Chaparral(IRE) Brave Madam (IRE) (Invincible Spirit (IRE))
3579[5]

Cannock Chase (USA) *Sir Michael Stoute* a72
2 b c Lemon Drop Kid(USA) Lynnwood Chase (USA) (Horse Chestnut (SAF))
7119[2]

Cannons Hall (IRE) *Paul Midgley* 13
4 b g Desert Millennium(IRE) Romanovna (IRE) (Mummy's Pet)
1962[11] 2503[9]

Canon Law (IRE) *Luca Cumani* a77 76
3 b g Holy Roman Emperor(IRE) Delisha (Salse (USA))
2306[8] 2931[4] (5845) 6203[13] 6735[3]

Canova (IRE) *Roger Charlton* a74 67
2 ch g Art Connoisseur(IRE) Rain Dancer (IRE) (Sadler's Wells (USA))
7500[4] 7834[3] 8067[5]

Cantara *Eric Alston*
3 b f Piccolo Damalis (IRE) (Mukaddamah (USA))
1962[15] 3932[9]

Can't Change It (IRE) *David Simcock* a66
2 gr g Verglas(IRE) All Tied Up (IRE) (Desert Prince (IRE))
7513[4]

Cantor *Paul Morgan* a67 69
5 b g Iceman Choir Mistress (Chief Singer)
6458[6] 6851[2] (7201) 7514[5] 7931[2] 8187[2] 8360[8]

Canwinn (IRE) *D Selvaratnam* a95 97
7 b g Refuse To Bend(IRE) Born To Glamour (Ajdal (USA))
149a[8] 367a[9] 744a[7]

Canyari (IRE) *Richard Fahey* 88
2 b c Dandy Man(IRE) Morna's Fan (FR) (Lear Fan (USA))
(2307) 4212[11]

Can You Conga *Kevin Ryan* a76 93
3 b g Piccolo Takes Two To Tango (Groom Dancer (USA))
729[2] 1392[4] (2006) 3066[7] 4797[2] (5538)

Capaill Liath (IRE) *Kevin Ryan* a90 97
5 gr g Iffraaj Bethesda (Distant Relative)
947[9] 1235[10] 1675[18] 3300[10] (3564) 4080[15] 4746[9] 4859[15] 5285[8] 6625[8] (7031) 7792[4] 7885[7] 8068[2] (8122) 8391[9] 8455[11]

Cape Alex *Clive Brittain* a68 56
4 b f Cape Cross(IRE) Alexander Three D (IRE) (Pennekamp (USA))
1217[2] (1350) 1654[4] (2159) 2739[6] 3168[2] 6565[11]

Cape Appeal *Richard Hannon Snr* a58 55
3 b f Cape Cross(IRE) Sheboygan (IRE) (Grand Lodge (USA))
2084[9] 2658[9] 3036[3] 6753[9] 7802[5]

Cape Arrow *Paul Cole* a60 60
2 b g Cape Cross(IRE) Aiming (Highest Honor (FR))
2653[7] 3238[9] 4026[9] 6924[5] 7428[3] 7640[7]

Cape Caster (IRE) *Ralph Beckett* a74
2 b g Cape Cross(IRE) Playboy Mansion (IRE) (Grand Lodge (USA))
6733[3]

Cape Castle (IRE) *Clive Brittain* 14
2 b f Cape Cross(IRE) Kaabari (USA) (Seeking The Gold (USA))
7693[10]

Cape Classic (IRE) *William Haggas* a71 106
5 b g Cape Cross(IRE) Politesse (USA) (Barathea (IRE))
1830[3] 2254[3]

Cape Crossing *Andrew Balding* a60 59
4 br f Cape Cross(IRE) Dame Hester (IRE) (Diktat)
108[2] 347[7] 4709[3] 5177[4] (5387) 6261[5] 6554[4] ◆ (6933)

Cape Explorer *Brian Ellison* a66 79
4 b g Cape Cross(IRE) Eve (Rainbow Quest (USA))
3729[9]

Cape Factor (IRE) *Rae Guest* a68 91
2 b f Oratorio(IRE) Crossanza (IRE) (Cape Cross (IRE))
(4175) (5634) 6076[4] (7451) (7657)

Cape Joy (IRE) *Sylvester Kirk* a60 73
4 b f Cape Cross(IRE) Perils Of Joy (IRE) (Rainbow Quest (USA))
1381[6] 1480[4] 1715[9] 1974[7] 2395[16] 3213[10]

Capelena *Clive Brittain* 40
2 b f Cape Cross(IRE) Roslea Lady (IRE) (Alhaarth (IRE))
5983[9]

Capellanus (IRE) *Brian Ellison* a82 81
7 b g Montjeu(IRE) Secret Dream (IRE) (Zafonic (USA))
563[10] 928[2] 1018[2] 1218[2] 2069[4] 2316[4] (3333) 3726[6]

Capella's Song (IRE) *Michael Bell* a76 75
3 b f Oratorio(IRE) Bright Bank (IRE) (Sadler's Wells (USA))
2099[3] (4356) 4898[4] 5491[4] 5758[3] 6335[3] 6780[7] (7489)

Capellini *Charles Egerton* a60 84
6 b g Cape Cross(IRE) Red Stella (FR) (Rainbow Quest (USA))
475[6] 646[7] 788[8]

Cape Of Approval (IRE) *T Stack* 110
4 b g Cape Cross(IRE) Wyola (USA) (Sadler's Wells (USA))
1255a[2] 1704a[7] 6414a[6] 7054a[15] 7364[13]

Cape Of Hope (IRE) *David O'Meara* a80 80
3 b c Cape Cross(IRE) Bright Hope (IRE) (Danehill (USA))
3253[2] (3759) (4428) 4661[2] 5406[3] 7486[3] 8224[4]

Cape Of Storms *Roy Brotherton* a71 24
10 b g Cape Cross(IRE) Lloc (Absalom)
88[9] 422[9]

Cape Parade (IRE) *Clive Cox* 16
2 b c Cape Cross(IRE) Blue Parade (IRE) (Singspiel (IRE))
7128[11]

Cape Peron *Henry Candy* 113
3 b g Beat Hollow Free Offer (Generous (IRE))
(1678) ◆ (2438) 3484[5] ◆ 4946[2] ◆ (7186a)

Caperina (IRE) *Ralph Beckett* 59
3 b f Cape Cross(IRE) Catherine Palace (Grand Lodge (USA))
2384[9] 3239[8]

Cape Rosa *James Moffatt* 45
3 b f Sir Percy Cashema (IRE) (Cape Cross (IRE))
4887[9] 5715[8] 6166[6] 6479[10]

Capers Royal Star (FR) *Alastair Lidderdale* a69 64
2 b c What A Caper(IRE) Arundhati (IRE) (Royal Academy (USA))
6934[4] 7467[6] 7901[2] 8153[3] 8426[6] 8452[10]

Cape Samba *Ismail Mohammed* a83 79
4 b g Cape Cross(IRE) Dancing Feather (Suave Dancer (USA))
5064[7] (5713) 6301[6] (6943) (7462)

Cape Schanck *Alan Coogan* a31 74
9 b g Observatory(USA) Sally Gardens (Alzao (USA))
3256[8]

Cape Summit *Ed Dunlop* a68 47
2 ch g Tamayuz Peace Summit (Cape Cross (IRE))
5957[12] 7835[6] 8124[7] ◆

Capetown Kid *Sylvester Kirk* a62 55
3 gr g Cape Town(IRE) Doris Souter (IRE) (Desert Story (IRE))
815[8] 4151[8] 4590[9] 6109[11] 7857[5] 8031[11]

Cape Wrath *Richard Hannon Snr* 80
2 rg c Verglas(IRE) Capades Dancer (USA) (Gate Dancer (USA))
(6590) ◆ 7468[3]

Cap Honor (FR) *D Turquet*
8 ch g Highest Honor(FR) Capades (USA) (Overskate (CAN))
6680a[8]

Capital Attraction (USA) *Ernst Oertel* a113 115
6 ch g Speightstown(USA) Cecilia's Crown (USA) (Chief's Crown (USA))
(241a) 659a[8] 957a[2] 1262a[10]

Capitol Gain (IRE) *George Baker* a59 77
4 b g Bahamian Bounty Emmas Princess (IRE) (Bahhare (USA))
1838[11] 2196[9] 2673[6] 3106[9] 3244[2] 4440[8] 5065[4] 5947[7] 8308[6]

Capitulate *Ed McMahon* 68
2 b c Avonbridge Succumb (Pursuit Of Love)
1659[3] 2497[6] 3045[4]

Capo Bastone (USA) *Todd Pletcher* a110 94
3 ch c Street Boss(USA) Fight To Love (USA) (Fit To Fight (USA))
7710a[13]

Caponata (USA) *D K Weld* 113
4 b f Selkirk(USA) Daring Diva (Dansili)
(1862a) ◆ 3844a[4] 4567a[3] 5317a[2] 6224a[10] 6674a[6]

Capone (IRE) *Michael Attwater* a106 91
8 b g Daggers Drawn(USA) Order Of The Day (USA) (Dayjur (USA))
480[3] 776[6] 944[8] 8344[8]

Capo Rosso (IRE) *Tom Dascombe* a93 92
3 b g Red Clubs(IRE) Satin Cape (IRE) (Cape Cross (IRE))
1625[10] (2285) 2666[2] 3484[24] 4062[5] 4812[7] 5510[9] 6608[3] 6874[5] 7648[6] (8053)

Cap O'Rushes *Charlie Appleby* a85 113
3 b c New Approach(IRE) Valley Of Gold (FR) (Shirley Heights)
1667[3] ◆ 3486[4] ◆ 3849a[4] (4874) 5653[6] 6393[11]

Capote Star (JPN) *Yoshito Yahagi* 116
4 b c Heart's Cry(JPN) Sabbiare (USA) (Capote (USA))
1868a[15]

Capponi (IRE) *Mahmood Al Zarooni* a120 110
6 ch g Medicean Nawaiet (USA) (Zilzal (USA))
1269a[12]

Cappuccino (SWI) *P Schaerer* a69 70
5 ch g Blue Canari(FR) Karapucha (IRE) (Kaldoun (FR))
609a[4] 702a[11]

Caprella *P D Deegan* a92 101
4 b f Kheleyf(USA) Angie And Liz (IRE) (Spectrum (IRE))
2108a[4]

Capriska *Willie Musson* a56 55
4 b f Bahri(USA) Guignol (IRE) (Anita's Prince)
1183[9] 1909[9] 2764[5] 3213[6] 3997[3] 4867[2] 5801[2] 7159[5] (7382)

Captain Baldwin *Jim Goldie* a39 55
4 b g Dubai Destination(USA) Tripti (IRE) (Sesaro (USA))
3285[4] 4824[3] 5143[7] (5261) 5921[7] 6921[8]

Captain Bellamy (USA) *Hughie Morrison* a84 15
5 ch g Bellamy Road(USA) Thesky'sthelimit (USA) (Northern Prospect (USA))
713[P]

Captain Bertie (IRE) *Jane Chapple-Hyam* 100
5 ch g Captain Rio Sadika (IRE) (Bahhare (USA))
1235[16] 1675[8] (2210) 3458[21] 4946[16] 5838[3] 6838[17] 7186a[7]

Captain Bob (IRE) *Charles Hills* 79
2 b g Dark Angel(IRE) Birthday Present (Cadeaux Genereux)
4121[5] 4483[3] 5399[2] 5843[2] 6328[15]

Captain Brown *James Moffatt* 21
5 b g Lomitas Nicola Bella (IRE) (Sadler's Wells (USA))
6668[6]

Captain Cardington (IRE) *John O'Shea* a66 72
4 b g Strategic Prince Alkaffeyeh (IRE) (Sadler's Wells (USA))
4238[6]

Captain Carey *Malcolm Saunders* a99 52
7 b g Fraam Brigadiers Bird (IRE) (Mujadil (USA))
1483[7] 2014[9] 5519[14]

Captain Caroline *Mike Murphy* a65 28
3 b f Multiplex Nut (IRE) (Fasliyev (USA))
4151[9] 5495[10] 6522[3] (7081) 7839[3] 8031[6]

Captain Cat (IRE) *Roger Charlton* a104 96
4 bb g Dylan Thomas(IRE) Mother Of Pearl (IRE) (Sadler's Wells (USA))
4859[16] 5749[7] (7641) 8263[2]

Captain Cavallo *Nicky Vaughan* a42 34
6 b g Pastoral Pursuits Nopalea (Warrshan (USA))
707[4] 909[8] 2074[13] 2575[13]

Captain Cleo (IRE) *David Peter Nagle* 34
2 b f Captain Rio Positano Princess (Tobougg (IRE))
4044[6]

Captain Cullen (IRE) *Gerard Keane* a76 85
4 b g Strategic Prince Missouri (Charnwood Forest (IRE))
4869a[13] 5019a[6]

Captain Devious *David Evans* 49
2 b c Captain Gerrard(IRE) Aspen Ridge (IRE) (Namid)
5428[4] 5843[10] 6981[6]

Captain Dunne (IRE) *Tim Easterby* a107 101
8 b g Captain Rio Queen Bodicea (IRE) (Revoque (IRE))
2150[2] 2865[7] 3334[16] 3776[9] 4507[8] 4954[11] 5519[13] 5991[6] 6848[12]

Captain Gee *John Quinn* a50 58
2 b c Captain Gerrard(IRE) Gagajulu (Al Hareb (USA))
4107[7] 4724[8] 6561[3] 7095[7] 8024[4] 8188[5]

Captain Joe *Michael Easterby* 70
2 ch g Captain Gerrard(IRE) Bond Shakira (Daggers Drawn (USA))
7173[6] 7370[2] 7592[6]

Captain Joy (IRE) *Tracey Collins* a105 109
4 gr g Dark Angel(IRE) Ardea Brave (IRE) (Chester House (USA))
1415a[5] 3142a[5] 3844a[3] 4869a[11] 7005a[4]

Captain Kendall (IRE) *Harry Chisman* a91 61
4 b g Clodovil(IRE) Queen's Lace (IRE) (King's Best (USA))
(115) ◆ 358[4] (535) 1694[5] 2516[6] 7897[10] 8069[5] 8344[5]

Captain Midnight (IRE) *David Brown* a86 82
2 b c Bushranger(IRE) Beverley Macca (Piccolo)
1605[3] 1989[3] 2955[9] 4107[2] 4808[3] 5145[2] 5380[4] (5787) 6065[5] 7545[2] 7933[5]

Captain Mo *Marco Botti* a51
2 b c Captain Gerrard(IRE) Plum Blossom (Beat All (USA))
8367[3]

Captain Morley *David Simcock* a76
2 b c Hernando(FR) Oval Office (Pursuit Of Love)
7834[10] ◆ 8415[2] ◆

Captain Myles (IRE) *Nicky Vaughan* a78 75
2 ch g Captain Rio Untimely (Inchinor)
5350[3] ◆ 5877[2]

Captain Oats (IRE) *Pam Ford* a54 59
10 b g Bahhare(USA) Adarika (Kings Lake (USA))
2714[7] 3406[9] 5432[4] 6153[9]

Captain Ramius (IRE) *Kevin Ryan* a89 114
7 b g Kheleyf(USA) Princess Mood (GER) (Muhtarram (USA))
154a[16] 467a[11] 1234[2] 1637[6] 5545[14]

Captain Rhyric *James Moffatt* 52
4 ch g Dylan Thomas(IRE) Nuts In May (USA) (A.P. Indy (USA))
3047[7] 3398[10] 3711[3] 4099[4] 5370[7] 6050[3]

Captain Royale (IRE) *Tracy Waggott* a46 75
8 ch g Captain Rio Paix Royale (Royal Academy (USA))
1961[4] 2276[5] 2409[2] 3283[10] 3446[3] 3630[10] 3654[11] 4619[4] (4761) 5139[13] 5365[4] (5889) (6088) 6547[7] 6771[5] 7030[6] 7281[4] 7594[2]

Captain Ryan *Peter Makin* a61 68
2 b g Captain Gerrard(IRE) Ryan's Quest (IRE) (Mukaddamah (USA))
2359[6] 2617[3] 3310[3] (3914) 4639[3] 5595[4] 6111[5] 7074[6]

Captain Scooby *Richard Guest* a70 82
7 b g Captain Rio Scooby Dooby Do (Atraf)
885[7] 998[4] (1283) 1370[10] 1649[5] 2268[5] 2410[7] 2834[8] 3462[3] 3933[4] 4728[4] 4814[5] 4884[7] 5901[4] 5971[7] 6287[2] 6547[5] 6977[4] 7029[9] 7262[3] 7432[8] 7594[6] 7937[7] 8029[4] 8048[6] 8224[12] 8411[4]

Captain's Dream (IRE) *Jedd O'Keeffe* 57
3 b g Kheleyf(USA) Somaggia (IRE) (Desert King (IRE))
1393[9]

Captain Secret *Marco Botti* a93 75
2 ch f Captain Gerrard(IRE) Obsessive Secret (IRE) (Grand Lodge (USA))
4154[3] ◆ (4668) (6132) 6839[12] 7892[8] 8024[2] (8364)

Captain Sharpe *Bernard Llewellyn* a63 69
5 ch g Tobougg(IRE) Helen Sharp (Pivotal)
1664[3] 1980[6] 3271[9] 4238[5]

Captain Starlight (IRE) *Jo Crowley* a77
3 b g Captain Marvelous(IRE) Jewell In The Sky (IRE) (Sinndar (IRE))
(14) 4383[11]

Captain Swift (IRE) *Brian Meehan* a74 57
2 br g Captain Rio Grannys Reluctance (IRE) (Anita's Prince)
6799[14] 7128[5] 7442[3] 7782[6] 8147[6]

Captain Whoosh (IRE) *Tom Dascombe* 71
2 gr g Dandy Man(IRE) Caerella (IRE) (Alzao (USA))
3045[3] (3883) 4434[4] 5842[4]

Caracal *Adrian McGuinness* a64 1
6 b g Dubai Destination(USA) Desert Lynx (IRE) (Green Desert (USA))
7[12] 41[9]

Cara Gina *William Haggas* 76
3 b f Bahamian Bounty Princess Georgina (Royal Applause)
1962[7] 2267[5] 2762[10] (3316) (3679) (3920) 4221[3] 5150[6]

Caramack *Richard Lee* a69 82
3 ch g Danehill Dancer(IRE) Oshiponga (Barathea (IRE))
1881[3] 2224[2] 2593[3] 3011[2] 3322[4] 3902[3] 4442[5] 8008[8] 8227[8]

Caramelita *J R Jenkins* a71 66
6 b m Deportivo Apple Of My Eye (Fraam)
159[6] 603[7] 1914[7] 5677[6] 6535[6] 6937[12] 7455[7] (7957) 8048[4] 8432[10]

Caramel Sundae *Robert Eddery* a47 58
3 b f Oratorio(IRE) Sundae Girl (USA) (Green Dancer (USA))
1071[7] 1487[9]

Caranbola *Mel Brittain* a65 88
7 br m Lucky Story(USA) Ladywell Blaise (IRE) (Turtle Island (IRE))
1607[7] 2476[9] 2664[11] 3351[14] 4047[6] 4588[7] 4730[9] 4852[9] 5011[2] 5294[2] 5381[11] 5498[5]

Cara's Delight (AUS) *Frederick Watson* 30
6 b m Fusaichi Pegasus(USA) Carahill (AUS) (Danehill (USA))
1962[16] 2504[6] 4582[7] 4991[9]

Cara's Request (AUS) *Michael Dods* a55 69
8 gr g Urgent Request(IRE) Carahill (AUS) (Danehill (USA))
(1994) 2280[4] 4956[4] (6464)

Caravan Rolls On *Peter Chapple-Hyam* a84 104
5 b c Hernando(FR) Grain Only (Machiavellian (USA))
2451[4] 3559[4] 4233[2] 5766[11] 7760a[3] (7938a)

Carazam (IRE) *Bernard Llewellyn* a76 80
6 b g Azamour(IRE) Carallia (IRE) (Common Grounds)
(906) 1538[9] (1849) 2339[7] 2498[6] 2981[6] 4028[10] 5302[5] 6435[10]

Carbas (ITY) *Bill Turner*
3 b c Acclamation Carya (IRE) (Sri Pekan (USA))
1367[7]

Card High (IRE) *Wilf Storey* 47
3 b g Red Clubs(IRE) Think (FR) (Marchand De Sable (USA))
2719[9] 3479[4] 4118[10]

Cardinal *Robert Cowell* a82 80
8 ch h Pivotal Fictitious (Machiavellian (USA))
27[3] (308) 481[2] 795[7] 1431[6] 1581[7] 2425[11] 5901[11] 6461[2] 7324[3] 7633[5] 7896[11] 8224[10]

Cardinal Palace (IRE) *John Joseph Murphy* a100 92
3 b g Papal Bull Heat (King's Best (USA))
5258[9] 7361a[6]

Cardinal Pioneer (TUR) *J W Hills* a32
3 ch c Galileo(IRE) Bartrobel (TUR) (Dilum (USA))
5678[9] 6402[13]

Cardinal Walter (IRE) *David Simcock* 98
4 bb g Cape Cross(IRE) Sheer Spirit (IRE) (Caerleon (USA))
1843[5]

Cardmaster (IRE) *Eve Johnson Houghton* 70
3 gr g Red Clubs(IRE) El Morocco (USA) (El Prado (IRE))
1612[12] 4515[7] 5201[2]

Cards *Kevin Ryan* a41
3 b f Tobougg(IRE) Card Games (First Trump)
1019[7]

Caridadi (IRE) *Charlie Appleby* 76
2 b g Invincible Spirit(IRE) Charity Belle (USA) (Empire Maker (USA))
6125[8] 6829[3] 7089[3] 7335[4]

Carina Palace *Jamie Osborne* a66
3 b f Dutch Art Ellcon (IRE) (Royal Applause)
1301[2] 1427[2] 1616[2] 1874[2]

Carinya (IRE) *Amy Weaver* a64 63
5 br f Iffraaj Ma N'leme Biche (USA) (Key To The Kingdom (USA))
2349[6] 5021a[8]

Carla Allegra *Jim Goldie* 32
4 ch f Byron Big Mystery (IRE) (Grand Lodge (USA))
1272[5] 1994[9] 3203[11] 4099[8]

Carla Bianca (IRE) *D K Weld* 102
2 gr f Dansili Majestic Silver (IRE) (Linamix (FR))
6024a[4] ◆

Carlarajah *Michael Bell* a65 68
3 ch g Sleeping Indian Carla (FR) (Cardoun (FR))
4637[10] 5541[8] 6154[7] 6752[8] 7454[7]

Carletti (IRE) *G Botti* a74
3 b g Zamindar(USA) Alsace (King's Best (USA))
270a[2] 460a[0]

Carlitoome (FR) *G Pannier*
3 b c Miesque's Son(USA) Inquisitive (Nashwan (USA))
191a[0]

Carlton Blue (IRE) *D Windrif* a94 82
3 gr c Aussie Rules(USA) Nurama (Daylami (IRE))
692a[2] 7736a[11]

Carlton Scroop (FR) *Paddy Butler* a66 57
10 ch g Priolo(USA) Elms Schooldays (Emarati (USA))
704[12]

Carmagnola (ITY) *F Camici* 92
2 b f Rattle And Hum(ITY) Special Milady (IRE) (Dolphin Street (FR))
7415a[8]

Carneades (IRE) *Ed Walker* a42 31
3 b g Exceed And Excel(AUS) Ivy League Star (IRE) (Sadler's Wells (USA))
1732[7] 2267[4] 2950[9] 3495[6] 3903[8]

Carnevale *Ralph Beckett* a69
2 ch f New Approach(IRE) Festivale (IRE) (Invincible Spirit (IRE))
7875[6]

Carnoustie (FR) *X Thomas-Demeaulte* a85 99
4 b f Acclamation Matin De Tempete (FR) (Cardoun (FR))
7706a[7] 8440a[12]

Caroline's Beach (IRE) *J S Moore* a48 43
2 ch f Footstepsinthesand Rohain (IRE) (Singspiel (IRE))
6423[8] 6776[6] 8425[10]

Caroun (IRE) *Patrick F Ryan* 68
5 b g Montjeu(IRE) Carlitta (USA) (Olympio (USA))
7760a[15]

Caroz (FR) *J-P Gauvin* a81
6 b g Sevres Rose(IRE) Calling Grace (FR) (General Assembly (USA))
5042a[4]

Carpentras *Dr Jon Scargill* a49 57
5 b f Val Royal(FR) Molly Brown (Rudimentary (USA))
62[5] 220[11]

Carragold *Mel Brittain* a54 82
7 b g Diktat Shadow Roll (IRE) (Mark Of Esteem (IRE))
1238[8] 1448[2] ◆ (1567) 2277[5] 2369[14] 2766[4] 3651[7] 4264[12] 4810[11]

Carrera *J W Hills* a64 55
3 b g Sixties Icon Aileen's Gift (IRE) (Rainbow Quest (USA))
1519[3] 2129[6] 2727[7] 3178[5] 3376[4] 5923[3] 6399[5] 6851[9] 7249[6]

Carrie's Magic *Alistair Whillans* a47 57
6 b m Kyllachy Carrie Pooter (Tragic Role (USA))
4471[6] ◆ 5331[3] 5708[3] 5876[9] 6687[6] 6918[7]

Carronade *Olivia Maylam* a37
3 b f Echo Of Light Romantic Retreat (Rainbow Quest (USA))
1499[10] 1741[5]

Carry On Sydney *Richard Hannon Snr* a87 92
3 ch g Notnowcato River Fantasy (USA) (Irish River (FR))
1099[2] 1250[2] 1847[2] 2050[5] 3486[13] 4084[7] 7312[8] 7431[3]

Carter *Ian Williams* a72 69
7 b g Reset(AUS) Cameo Role (GER) (Acatenango (GER))
73[3]

Carthage (IRE) *Richard Hannon Snr* 82
2 b c Mastercraftsman(IRE) Pitrizzia (Lando (GER))
6762[6] 7219[2] 7502[3]

Carthaginian (IRE) *Richard Fahey* a54 81
4 b g Azamour(IRE) Khayrat (IRE) (Polar Falcon (USA))
2041[4] (2885) 3607[4] 4810[10]

Casa Tua (FR) *David O'Meara* a54
3 b f Oasis Dream Cattiva Generosa (Cadeaux Genereux)
2034a[8] 6476 [10]

Cascadia (IRE) *K R Burke* a58 56
2 br f Mujadil(USA) Tucum (IRE) (Diktat)
(3440) 4134[5] 5235[6] 5467[U] (5963) 7309[13] 8434[5]

Cascading *Hughie Morrison* 69
2 b f Teofilo(IRE) Angel Falls (Kingmambo (USA))
6828[4] 7532[3]

Caserta *A Fabre* a91 100
4 b f Dansili Daring Miss (Sadler's Wells (USA))
3387a[5]

Cashel's Missile (IRE) *John Spearing* a51 44
3 b g Majestic Missile(IRE) Cashel Mead (Bishop Of Cashel)
4635[9] 5818[11] 6436[7] 6994[5] 7903[6] 8050[5] 8168[9]

Cash Injection *Karen George* a46 53
4 b g Halling(USA) Cape Siren (Warning)
1117[3] 1744[5]

Cash Is King *Nick Littmoden* a69 69
3 b g Bahamian Bounty Age Of Chivalry (IRE) (Invincible Spirit (IRE))
1293[2] 2272[2] 3294[7] 4076[7] 7924[2] 8140[3]

Cash Or Casualty (IRE) *Damian Joseph English* a84 91
5 b g Footstepsinthesand La Quinta (IRE) (Indian Ridge)
2214[3] 5019a[7] 5775a[10] 6025a[8] 6883a[21]

Cashpoint *Ian Williams* a89 90
8 b g Fantastic Light(USA) Cashew (Sharrood (USA))
1448[12] 2417[2] (3022) 4028[3] 4798[5] 6868[4] (6976) 7536[3] 7823[13]

Cash Rich *Jamie Osborne* a20
3 ch g Assertive Dahshah (Mujtahid (USA))
482[9]

Caspar Netscher *David Simcock* 119
4 b c Dutch Art Bella Cantata (Singspiel (IRE))
4856[2] 5532[4] 6392[4] 7025[2] 7366[10]

Casper Lee (IRE) *Alan Berry* a30 65
2 b g Kheleyf(USA) Shallop (Salse (USA))
3724[7] 4312[10] 4977[7] 5834[4] 5970[4] 6279[8] (6494) 6725[6] 7340[9] 8364[5]

Caspian Prince (IRE) *Tony Carroll* a72 98
4 ch g Dylan Thomas(IRE) Crystal Gaze (IRE) (Rainbow Quest (USA))
4935a[6] 6445a[7] 8369[8]

Casquito (IRE) *F Chappet* a78 93
5 b g Blue Canari(FR) Copacabana (IRE) (Entrepreneur)
(4467a)

Cassie Jem *David C Griffiths* a48
3 ch f Dubai Destination(USA) Generous Jem (Generous (IRE))
7791[5]

Cassini (FR) *Mme Pia Brandt* a83 74
3 b c Astronomer Royal(USA) Mulled Wine (FR) (Night Shift (USA))
7188a[11]

Castagna Girl *Denis Coakley* 64
2 ch f Major Cadeaux Ewenny (Warrshan (USA))
3663[6] 4708[4] 6095[2]

Castell Avon *Milton Bradley*
3 b f Avonbridge Castellina (USA) (Danzig Connection (USA))
1288[5] 1429[11] 1660[13]

Castilo Del Diablo (IRE) *David Simcock* a102 89
4 br g Teofilo(IRE) Hundred Year Flood (USA) (Giant's Causeway (USA))
2052[5] 3099[6] 3960[2] 5723[6] 6172[2] 7990[7] 8327[2]

Castle Combe (IRE) *Marcus Tregoning* a77 68
2 b c Dylan Thomas(IRE) Mundus Novus (USA) (Unbridled's Song (USA))
5790[5] 6593[5] 7089[4] 7779[3] (7979) 8147[4]

Castle Myth (USA) *Jim Best* a31 65
7 bb g Johannesburg(USA) Castlemania (CAN) (Bold Ruckus (USA))
73[9]

Castorienta *George Baker* a59
2 ch f Orientor The Lady Caster (City On A Hill (USA))
7971[6] 8425[3]

Casual Smile *Andrew Balding* 89
2 ch f Sea The Stars(IRE) Casual Look (USA) (Red Ransom (USA))
5282[2] ◆ 6185[3] 6643[2]

Catalinas Diamond (IRE) *Pat Murphy* a73 66
5 b f One Cool Cat(USA) Diamondiferous (USA) (Danzig (USA))
77[4] 372[6] (728) 1052[5] 1173[4] 1516[7] 1957[2] 2745[6] 3315[6] 3949[8] 4368[3] 4659[3] 5104[8] 5447[7] 8220[7]

Catalyze *Charles Smith* a70 83
5 b g Tumblebrutus(USA) Clarita Dear (CHI) (Hussonet (USA))
537[10]

Cataria Girl (USA) *Marcus Tregoning* a53 46
4 b f Discreet Cat(USA) Elaflaak (USA) (Gulch (USA))
5444[6] 6289[11] 8427[7]

Catawollow *Richard Guest* a23 52
6 b m Beat Hollow Catalonia (IRE) (Catrail (USA))
220[13] 330[10] 417[13] 2004[6]

Catcall (FR) *P Sogorb* 117
4 b g One Cool Cat(USA) Jurata (IRE) (Polish Precedent (USA))
(2300a) 2909a[2] 5040a[8] 6445a[3] 7054a[2]

Catchanova (IRE) *Eve Johnson Houghton* a62 68
6 b g Catcher In The Rye(IRE) Head For The Stars (IRE) (Head For Heights)
1925[11] 2514[6] 3399[4] 3687[4] 5234[3] 5615[5] 5793[5] 6146[5] 6737[11]

Catch The Cider *Hans Adielsson* a72
3 b g Medicean Zanna (FR) (Soviet Star (USA))
4381[6] 5133[8] 5892[11] 6937[6] 7836[10]

Categorical *Keith Reveley* a69 77
10 b g Diktat Zibet (Kris)
1805[7] 7342[7]

Caterina De Medici (FR) *Ed Walker* a78 53
4 b f Redoute's Choice(AUS) Night Dhu (Montjeu (IRE))
6312[6] 6997[2] 7504[11] 7947[3] (8046)

Catflap (IRE) *Derek Haydn Jones* a65 64
4 b f One Cool Cat(USA) Consignia (IRE) (Definite Article)
790[6] 1058[3] 1196[5] 1467[4] 3498[5] 3949[5] (4344) 4608[8] 6040[3] 6412[4] 7783[9] 8023[9]

Cathedral *Michael Wigham* a51 82
4 b g Invincible Spirit(IRE) Capades Dancer (USA) (Gate Dancer (USA))
511[11]

Cativo Cavallino *John E Long* a57 74
10 ch g Bertolini(USA) Sea Isle (Selkirk (USA))
7639[7] 7981[5] 8390[5]

Cat O'Mountain (USA) *Charlie Appleby* a108 96
3 bb g Street Cry(IRE) Thunder Kitten (USA) (Storm Cat (USA))
3061[4] 4301[3] 5749[5] (6172) (6751)

Cats Eyes *Robert Cowell* a49 81
4 b f Echo Of Light Desert Lynx (IRE) (Green Desert (USA))
2561[7] 3078[3] 3487[3] 4017[9]

Cauberg *Roger Varian* 30
3 b g Green Desert(USA) Thorntoun Piccolo (Groom Dancer (USA))
2224[8] 2556[6] 3176[9]

Caucus *John Gosden* 113
6 b g Cape Cross(IRE) Maid To Perfection (Sadler's Wells (USA))
1920[2] (4083) 4919[9] 5724[4] (6766) 7363[11]

Caunay *Neil Mulholland* a65 59
6 ch g Generous(IRE) Chantilly Lady (Rising)
12[12]

Causeway Foot (USA) *Jedd O'Keeffe* a56 65
3 ch g Giant's Causeway(USA) Flat Fleet Feet (USA) (Afleet (CAN))
1776[6] 3653[12] 6909[10]

Cavaleiro (IRE) *Marcus Tregoning* a101 104
4 ch g Sir Percy Khibraat (Alhaarth (IRE))
1484[4] 4857[11] 6144[4] 6766[7] 7542[9]

Cavalieri (IRE) *William Jarvis* a72 66
3 b g Oratorio(IRE) Always Attractive (IRE) (King's Best (USA))
877[2] 1891[4] 2306[9] 2957[4]

Cavalryman *Saeed bin Suroor* a114 117
7 b h Halling(USA) Silversword (FR) (Highest Honor (FR))
956a[3] (1263a) 2810[5] 4213[3] 4919[6]

Cave Man (NOR) *Are Hyldmo* a65
4 b c Academy Award(IRE) Romola (Wolfhound (USA))
5325a[9]

Caviar On Sunday (FR) *Mme A-M Poirier* a71
3 b g Sunday Break(JPN) Danseuse Classique (USA) (Green Dancer (USA))
191a[7]

Cawett Cove (IRE) *Jane Chapple-Hyam* a70 82
5 ch c Hawk Wing(USA) Memory Motel (DEN) (Always Fair (USA))
239[9] 1092[10] 1753[3] 2191[11] 3019[11] 3404[9]

Cay Dancer *Richard Hannon Snr* 72
2 gr f Danehill Dancer(IRE) White Cay (Dalakhani (IRE))
2601[6] 3986[3] 6318[3] 7533[7]

Cayman Cry (USA) *Brian Meehan* 50
2 ch f Street Cry(IRE) On A Cloud (USA) (Silver Hawk (USA))
4921[11]

Cayman Fox *Linda Perratt* a57 59
8 ch m Cayman Kai(IRE) Kalarram (Muhtarram (USA))
2043[10] 2632[3] 2795[10] 3933[8] 4102[13] 4448[11] 5641[6]

Cayuga *Brett Johnson* a86 87
4 b g Montjeu(IRE) Ithaca (USA) (Distant View (USA))
318[5] 1883[4] 2422[2] 2867[7] 3293[5] 4907[3] 5190[7] 6868[5] (7438) 7696[16]

Ceannline (IRE) *Venetia Williams* a80 67
7 b m Lil's Boy(USA) Scarpetta (USA) (Seattle Dancer (USA))
5847[6] 6490[6]

Cease (USA) *David Jacobson* a106 101
6 b g War Chant(USA) Limit (USA) (Cox's Ridge (USA))
7687a[9]

Cebuano *M Halford* a85 84
8 ch g Fraam Ideal Figure (Zafonic (USA))
7230a[12]

Cecily Parsley *Hughie Morrison* a61 49
7 b m Fantastic Light(USA) Salim Toto (Mtoto)
635[3] 1189[6]

Cedar Glory *Tim Walford* a31 48
4 b f Josr Algarhoud(IRE) Cedar Jeneva (Muhtarram (USA))
7279[6] 8046[6] 8298[7]

Ceekay's Girl *R Mike Smith* a50 47
3 ch f Medicean Duena (Grand Lodge (USA))
824[13] 1016[5] 1332[2] 1842[4] 2237[7] 2748[6] 4113[7] 4339[7] 4474[7]

Ceelo *Sylvester Kirk* a76 78
3 b g Green Desert(USA) Mindsharp (USA) (Gone West (USA))
1295[6] 1620[9] 2738[3] 3342[7] 3818[2] 4303[4] 4797[7] 6072[6] 6214[4] 6657[4] 7444[8]

Celebrian *Alex Hales* a52 19
6 b m Fasliyev(USA) Triplemoon (USA) (Trempolino (USA))
2333[5] 2563[8] 8204[5] 8349[4]

Celebrissime (IRE) *F Head* a89 113
8 ch g Peintre Celebre(USA) Ring Beaune (USA) (Bering)
1456a[4] 3913a[7] 7968a[12]

Celestial Bay *Sylvester Kirk* a56 77
4 b f Septieme Ciel(USA) Snowy Mantle (Siberian Express (USA))
2597[4] ◆ 2824[2] (3508) 3988[5] 4709[6] 6381[2] 6527[9] 7965[9] 8220[9]

Celestial Dawn *John Weymes* a61 69
4 b f Echo Of Light Celestial Welcome (Most Welcome)
1271[9] 1665[10] 2037[3] 2835[5] 3393[7] 7904[12] 8118[3] 8412[2]

Celestial Knight *James Fanshawe* a69
2 b g Compton Place Garter Star (Mark Of Esteem (IRE))
7328[3]

Celestial Prospect (AUS) *Martin Brassil* a50 71
7 b g Galileo(IRE) Space Ritual (IRE) (Top Ville)
7230a[17]

Celestial Ray *Linda Jewell* a72
4 ch g Pivotal Heavenly Ray (USA) (Rahy (USA))
2576[2] 3170[3] 3401[3] 8087[7] 8295[4]

Celtic Charlie (FR) *Pat Phelan* a61 43
8 ch g Until Sundown(USA) India Regalona (USA) (Dehere (USA))
343[4] 668[5] 788[4] 1348[6] 8149[3] 8337[5]

Celtic Filly (IRE) *E J O'Neill* 87
3 b f Footstepsinthesand Fiordiligi (Mozart (IRE))
(647a) 2047[13]

Celtic Ice (IRE) *Alan McCabe* a28 27
2 gr g Verglas(IRE) Dilinata (IRE) (Spinning World (USA))
3132[6] 5145[10] 5379[8] 5675[8]

Celtic Legacy *Michael Murphy* a55 36
6 ch m Where Or When(IRE) An Cailin Rua (Aragon)
1518[7] 1804[9] 2995[6] 3884[11]

Celtic Man (IRE) *David Marnane* a93 93
2 b c Lawman(FR) Celtic Silhouette (FR) (Celtic Swing)
5771a[9] 7026[11]

Celtic Rock *J C Fernandez* 106
4 ch c Rock Of Gibraltar(IRE) Luna Celtica (IRE) (Celtic Swing)
5465a[2] (7142a)

Celtic Sixpence (IRE) *Nick Kent* a75 79
5 b f Celtic Swing Penny Ha'Penny (Bishop Of Cashel)
27[8] 1540[3] 1802[6] 2425[6] 2780[2] 4970[4] 5564[4] (5974) 6496[11] 7486[4] 7824[11] 7964[5]

Celtic Step *Peter Niven* a66 59
9 br g Selkirk(USA) Inchiri (Sadler's Wells (USA))
2961[8] 3727[13] 5840[12]

Celticus (IRE) *S Botti* 96
3 b c Stroll(USA) Bois Joli (IRE) (Orpen (USA))
2490a[12]

Centralinteligence (USA) *Ronald W Ellis* a118
5 ch g Smarty Jones(USA) Shootforthestars (USA) (Seattle Slew (USA))
7689a[11]

Centrality *Mark Johnston* 63
2 b c Pivotal Calista (Caerleon (USA))
1946[7] 2358[5] 4497[4] 5068[10]

Centred (IRE) *Sir Michael Stoute* a71 95
3 gr f Dalakhani(IRE) Drama Class (IRE) (Caerleon (USA))
(1933) 2619[2] (3891) ◆ 7250[4] 7526[11]

Centre Haafhd *David Barron* 76
2 b g Haafhd Deira Dubai (Green Desert (USA))
3077[5] (3461) 4019[3]

Centurius *Marco Botti* 101
3 ch c New Approach(IRE) Questina (FR) (Rainbow Quest (USA))
(1684) 2023[2] 3485[12] 4452[3] 4979[6] 6163[3] 6834[5] 7205[3]

Century (IRE) *A P O'Brien* 86
2 b c Montjeu(IRE) Mixed Blessing (Lujain (USA))
7528[11]

Century Gold (USA) *Rafael A Fernandez* 40
7 b g Century City(IRE) Jump With Joy (USA) (Linkage (USA))
1001a[10]

Ceramick (FR) *F Doumen* a70 73
2 b f Slickly(FR) Hertzienne (FR) (Hernando (FR))
6786a[7]

Ceremonial Jade (UAE) *Marco Botti* a94 82
10 b g Jade Robbery(USA) Talah (Danehill (USA))
2028[9]

Cerise Cherry (SAF) *D Cruz* 114
8 ch g Goldkeeper(USA) Cherry Girl (ZIM) (Pochard (ARG))
8209a[4]

Certavi (IRE) *Brendan Powell* a85 81
4 b g Antonius Pius(USA) The Quiet Woman (IRE) (Barathea (IRE))
1711[7] 3410[5] (3954) 4350[2] (5312) 5706[4] 6336[3] 6869[2] (7840)

Certerach (IRE) *M Halford* a96 110
5 b g Halling(USA) Chartres (IRE) (Danehill (USA))
246a[5] 555a[3] 870a[2] 6441a[8] 7005a[5] 7723a[11]

Certificate *Roger Varian* 35
2 ch c Pivotal Graduation (Lomitas)
7654[7]

Certification (IRE) *Mark Johnston* a81 79
3 b g Authorized(IRE) Most Charming (FR) (Darshaan)
4633[4] 5058[2] 5892[2]

Certral *Mel Brittain* a81 86
5 b f Iffraaj Craigmill (Slip Anchor)
3349[13] 4201[5] 6288[15] 6756[4] 7027[3]

Cerys *Derek Haydn Jones* a38 33
3 ch f Three Valleys(USA) Tenebrae (IRE) (In The Wings)
134[7]

Cesta Punta (FR) *Mlle V Dissaux* a36 47
3 bb f Azamour(IRE) Kid Sister (IRE) (Danehill Dancer (IRE))
5119a[11]

Chabal'Ozor (FR) *Mlle C Cardenne* a90 92
4 b g Della Francesca(USA) Mysteryonthebounty (USA) (Mystery Storm (USA))
7060a[7]

Chain Of Events *Sarah Humphrey* a76 86
6 ch g Nayef(USA) Ermine (IRE) (Cadeaux Genereux)
1753[10]

Chain Reactor *Amy Weaver* a55
7 b g Hamas(IRE) Rose Tina (Tina's Pet)
157[4] 521[6] 712[7]

Chainsaw *Stuart Williams* a51 65
2 b c Pastoral Pursuits Roodeye (Inchinor)
3112[13] 5438[3] 6569[5] 6966[3]

Chalnetta (FR) *C Ferland* a87 110
3 gr f Oratorio(IRE) Aifa (Johann Quatz (FR))
3614a[2] 5297a[2] 7048a[2] 7843a[6]

Chamberlain *Alan McCabe* a49 67
2 b g Indesatchel(IRE) Citron (Reel Buddy (USA))
1606[3] 1930[7] 3648[4] 4053[11] 6206[3] 7902[8]

Chambles *Andrew Reid* a74 61
4 b f Shamardal(USA) Pants (Pivotal)
116[5] 271[4] (446) 778[4] 903[10] 1079[6] 3643[10]

Chamois (USA) *Christophe Clement* 110
3 ch c Smart Strike(CAN) Meridiana (GER) (Lomitas)
3360a[3]

Chamonix (IRE) *A P O'Brien* 112
4 b c Galileo(IRE) L'Ancresse (IRE) (Darshaan)
2864[5] 6441a[9]

Champagne Babe *Keith Dalgleish* a62 73
2 b f Captain Rio Oceanico Dot Com (IRE) (Hernando (FR))
(2025) 2426[7] 2767[9] 3332[6] 7545[7]

Champagne Rules *Sharon Watt* 51
2 gr g Aussie Rules(USA) Garabelle (IRE) (Galileo (IRE))
3588[4]

Champagne Sydney (IRE) *Richard Hannon Snr* a86
2 ch c Iffraaj Special Touch (IRE) (Spinning World (USA))
(6922) ◆

Champ D'Honneur *J-P Gallorini* 93
2 b f Champs Elysees Marla (GER) (Pentire)
7940a[4]

Championship (IRE) *Richard Hannon Snr* 89
2 ch c Exceed And Excel(AUS) Aljafliyah (Halling (USA))
(2411) 3422[14] 6765[6]

Chancealot *Neil Mulholland* a21
5 b g Reel Buddy(USA) Party Charmer (Charmer)
619[4]

Chance Of Romance (IRE) *Clive Cox* a30 57
2 b f Moss Vale(IRE) Evening Promise (Aragon)
2230[5] 2617[7] 3574[3] 5034[7] 5610[12] 6979[9]

Chancery (USA) *David O'Meara* a85 103
5 bb g Street Cry(IRE) Follow That Dream (Darshaan)
1826[3] 2030[3] 2402[15] (4020) (4264) ◆ 5269[10] (5723) 6800[4] 7174[11]

Chanceuse *Gay Kelleway* a53 43
2 b f Lucky Story(USA) Miss Madame (IRE) (Cape Cross (IRE))
3189[6] 4422[5] 4862[3] (5229) 6059a[16] 7755[2] 7846[3] 8040[3] 8262[8] 8363[5]

Chandelle Celeste *James Toller* a50 16
3 ch f Septieme Ciel(USA) First Candlelight (First Trump)
2950[10] 3699[11]

Chandlery (IRE) *Richard Hannon Snr* 95
4 b c Choisir(AUS) Masai Queen (IRE) (Mujadil (USA))
1535[6] 1919[8] 2585[9] 3558[21]

Chandrayaan *John E Long* a59 55
6 ch g Bertolini(USA) Muffled (USA) (Mizaaya)
(655) 806[8] (1093) 1497[5] 1981[4] 5232[11] 5525[7] 8258[12]

Change The Subject (USA) *Richard Guest* a84 78
5 rg g Maria's Mon(USA) Victory Lap (USA) (Touch Gold (USA))
239[5] 4475[5] 4850[6] 5264[6] 5713[10]

Chankillo *Mark H Tompkins* a61 64
4 ch g Observatory(USA) Seasonal Blossom (IRE) (Fairy King (USA))
1916[8] (2986) 4010[9] 4178[4]

Chant (IRE) *Ann Duffield* a68 77
3 b g Oratorio(IRE) Akarita (IRE) (Akarad (FR))
1776[4] 1965[4] 2769[3] (3394) (3809) 4447[7] 5582[3] 6514[2] 6775[3]

Chantrea (IRE) *Lady Cecil*
2 br f Dansili Celestial Lagoon (JPN) (Sunday Silence (USA))
3605[11]

Chapman (GER) *P Schiergen* a88 78
4 b c Big Shuffle(USA) Cominales (IRE) (Primo Dominie)
700a[7]

Chapter And Verse (IRE) *Mike Murphy* a96 80
7 gr g One Cool Cat(USA) Beautiful Hill (IRE) (Danehill (USA))
10[2] 60[2] 407[3] 945[3] 1545[4] 1922[7] 3368[4] 4957[6] 6199[12] 6701[10] 7641[14] 7988[2] 8117[10]

Chapter Five *Ian Williams* a58 73
6 b m Grape Tree Road Northern Shadows (Rock Hopper)
1060[4] 1664[4] 2545[3] 2922[5] (4035) 4775[2] (5666) (5977) 6377[2] 6424[2] 6960[6]

Chapter Nine (IRE) *Tony Carroll* a54 61
7 b g Expelled(USA) Abbey Ever After (Glenstal (USA))
1070[7] 1120[5] 1949[12]

Chapter Seven *Stuart Williams* a93 111
4 ch g Excellent Art My First Romance (Danehill (USA))
1235[6] 1675[3] 2864[4] 3525[7] 6001[12] 6638[2] 7196[3] 7697[5]

Characterise *Mick Channon* 51
2 ch g Winker Watson Artistic License (IRE) (Chevalier (IRE))
6635[9] 6975[13]

Chardonney Tcheque (FR) *T Satra* 95
5 bb c One Cool Cat(USA) Genevale (FR) (Unfuwain (USA))
3881a[6]

Charismas Birthday (IRE) *Philip M Byrne* a43 51
5 b f Choisir(AUS) Paradise Blue (IRE) (Bluebird (USA))
4369[5] 4520[4] 4608[6]

Charitable Act (FR) *Gary Moore* a79 83
4 b g Cadeaux Genereux Acatama (USA) (Efisio)
1849[2] 2193[8] 3019[14] 3974[9] 4685[2] 5398[6] 6259[2] 7130[13] (7318)

Charity Box *Chris Wall* a63 76
4 b f Haafhd Bible Box (IRE) (Bin Ajwaad (IRE))
2255[25] 2638[6]

Charity Line (IRE) *S Botti* 107
3 ch f Manduro(GER) Holy Moon (IRE) (Hernando (FR))
(2697a) (7558a)

Charlcot *James Bethell* a71
5 ch g Monsieur Bond(IRE) Miss Apricot (Indian Ridge)
(51)

Charlemagne Diva *Richard Guest* a56 67
3 b f Holy Roman Emperor(IRE) Opera Ridge (FR) (Indian Ridge)
910[6] 1284[4] 1458[6] 1651[3] 1742[5] 2133[2] 2542[8] (3025) 3762[6] 4064[6] (4727) 4982[10] 5583[6] 5704[6] 6478[3] 6808[7] 7106[6] 7265[3] 7850[4] 8082[11]

Charles Camoin (IRE) *Sylvester Kirk* a80 98
5 b g Peintre Celebre(USA) Birthday (IRE) (Singspiel (IRE))
(4798) 5768[8] 6741[6] 7206[6] 7927[9]

Charles Darwin (GER) *D Moser* 93
4 b c Tannenkonig(IRE) Conga (Robellino (USA))
3970a[9]

Charles De Mille *George Moore* 68
5 b g Tiger Hill(IRE) Apple Town (Warning)
6600[7]

Charles Molson *Henry Candy* a82 85
2 b g Monsieur Bond(IRE) Arculinge (Paris House)
5033[6] 6169[2] ◆ (7394) ◆ 7658[3]

Charles Parnell (IRE) *Simon Griffiths* a62 48
10 b g Elnadim(USA) Titania (Fairy King (USA))
1280[6] 1388[6]

Charles The Great (IRE) *J Moore* 115
4 b g Holy Roman Emperor(IRE) Jojeema (Barathea (IRE))
8209a[11]

Charles Tyrwhitt *George Baker* a26 65
4 b g Iffraaj Riverside Dancer (USA) (Stravinsky (USA))
1498[8]

Charleys Angel *Pat Phelan* a40
2 b f Myboycharlie(IRE) Muwasim (USA) (Meadowlake (USA))
4631[7] 6079[7] 7261[9] 7878[9] 7973[4]

Charlies Mate *John Best* a54
2 br c Myboycharlie(IRE) Retainage (USA) (Polish Numbers (USA))
7441[6] 7779[10] 8085[7]

Charlie's Wish (FR) *Conrad Allen* 28
2 b f Myboycharlie(IRE) Lindsey's Wish (USA) (Trippi (USA))
3510[6]

Charlie Wells (IRE) *Eve Johnson Houghton* 68
2 b g High Chaparral(IRE) Numbers Game (Rainbow Quest (USA))
3374[5] 5299[6] 5811[4] 6640[6]

Charlotte Rhodes *Marco Botti* a56
3 br f Halling(USA) Kunda (IRE) (Intikhab (USA))
7932[4] 8245[2]

Charlotte Rosina *Roger Teal* a95 96
4 b f Choisir(AUS) Intriguing Glimpse (Piccolo)
1726[6] (2088) 2848[3] 3973[3] 4534[4]

Charlotte's Day *Sir Mark Prescott Bt* 71
2 b f Dalakhani(IRE) Charlotte O Fraise (IRE) (Beat Hollow)
3753[4] ◆ 4723[4] 5330[2] 6378[3]

Charm Cry (USA) *Mark Johnston* a68
3 b f Street Cry(IRE) Nasheej (USA) (Swain (IRE))
212[P] 411[6]

Charmel's Delight *Geoffrey Oldroyd* a51 49
4 b f Monsieur Bond(IRE) Jane's Delight (IRE) (Namid)
148[5] 422[8]

Charming (IRE) *Olivia Maylam* a72 74
4 b f Invincible Spirit(IRE) Nofa's Magic (IRE) (Rainbow Quest (USA))
(124) 156[7] (448) 627[8] 719[4] 842[3] 1952[9] 2550[13] 2870[7] 3498[6] 3667[5] 3994[2] 4635[5] 5796[5] 5930[5] 6732[7] 8034[7]

Charming Kitten (USA) *Todd Pletcher* a109 105
3 bb c Kitten's Joy(USA) Iteration (USA) (Wild Again (USA))
2033a[9]

Charming Touch (USA) *F Head* a90 92
3 b f Elusive Quality(USA) Charmgoer (USA) (Nureyev (USA))
7993a[7]

Charm Spirit (IRE) *F Head* 112
2 b c Invincible Spirit(IRE) L'Enjoleuse (IRE) (Montjeu (IRE))
7056a[3]

Charmy Dukesse (IRE) *Marco Botti* a66
2 b f Duke Of Marmalade(IRE) Nashatara (USA) (Nashwan (USA))
8176[4] 8415[3]

Charpoy (USA) *Keith Dalgleish* a84 84
5 b g Street Cry(IRE) Honolua Bay (USA) (Storm Bird (CAN))
6943[13] 7238[7]

Charter (IRE) *Michael Wigham* a70 80
3 b g Elusive City(USA) Lucky Norwegian (IRE) (Almutawakel)
2169[3] 3159[2] ◆

Chasing Dreams *Kevin Ryan* a78 77
3 ch f Pastoral Pursuits Welanga (Dansili)
1682[3] 2166[4] 2430[12] 2994[2] 6664[3] 6982[3] 7282[9] (Dead)

Chasin' Rainbows *Sylvester Kirk* a61 57
5 b f Piccolo Tamara (Marju (IRE))
2710[6] 3169[9] 3662[6] 4605[2] 5127[4] 5934[4] 6137[4] 7201[5] 7321[3] 7458[6]

Chat (USA) *John Gosden* 82
3 bb f Dynaformer(USA) Verbal (USA) (Kingmambo (USA))
1918[5]

Chateau Lola *Derek Shaw* a56 28
4 b f Byron Glensara (Petoski)
81[6] 142[5] 529[7] 610[6] 670[9] (756) 862[5] 1077[4] 1186[5] 1355[6] 2326[8] 7850[6] 8050[9] 8169[3] 8272[5] 8370[5]

Chatez (IRE) *Alan King* 79
2 b g Dandy Man(IRE) Glory Days (GER) (Tiger Hill (IRE))
5843[3] 6975[3] (7502)

Chatsworth Express *Richard Whitaker* a54
2 b g Redoubtable(USA) Teo Torriate (IRE) (Daggers Drawn (USA))
7901[5] 8165[5]

Chattanooga Line *George Baker* a65
3 b f Rail Link Gay Romance (Singspiel (IRE))
5925[2] 6557[6] 7158[4]

Chaudhary (SWI) *U Suter* a76 75
3 b g Zamindar(USA) Chelsea (SWI) (Danehill Dancer (IRE))
6713a[16]

Chebika *Michael Bell*
3 b f Oasis Dream Dancing Abbie (USA) (Theatrical (IRE))
994[9]

Checkpoint *Tony Coyle* a76 81
4 ch g Zamindar(USA) Kalima (Kahyasi)
1898[5] 3468[5] 6105[2] 6748[2] (7118) 7369[13]

Cheektocheek (IRE) *Marco Botti* a74 70
3 b g Chineur(FR) Diamond Soles (IRE) (Danetime (IRE))
210[3] (Dead)

Cheeky Peta'S *James Given* a62 60
2 b f Compton Place Cheeky Girl (College Chapel)
2510[2] 2993[4] 3476[F] 4351[2] 5106[4] 5543[5] 6073[4] 6474[10] 6695[14] 7094[11] 7509[8] 7804[7] 7956[7] 8090[6] 8273[7] 8435[5]

Cheeky Wee Red *Alistair Whillans* a47 64
5 ch f Pastoral Pursuits Swynford Elegance (Charmer)
6919[11]

Cheers Big Ears (IRE) *Richard Price* a46 53
7 gr g Kheleyf(USA) Grey Galava (Generous (IRE))
1951[2] 3270[6] 3513[4] 4077[5] 5092[5] 5614[10] 5816[7] 6324[6] 6986[3] 7351[7]

Cheers Buddy (IRE) *Keith Dalgleish* a66 63
5 b g Acclamation Victorian Dancer (IRE) (Groom Dancer (USA))
5369[4] (5921) 6301[11]

Cheers For Thea (IRE) *Tim Easterby* a77 69
8 gr m Distant Music(USA) Popiplu (USA) (Cozzene (USA))
208[3] 429[8] 798[3] 1579[3] 2311[7] 2796[7] 4119[5]

Chef Chaudard (FR) *J-C Rouget* a72 55
3 ch c Turtle Bowl(IRE) Scottish Diva (Selkirk (USA))
2034a[5] 5914a[7]

Chellalla *Ian Williams* a42 64
4 b f Elnadim(USA) Cheloca (Selkirk (USA))
5518[9] 5742[10] 6126[12] 7594[4] 7861[7]

Chella Thriller (SPA) *Alastair Lidderdale* a68 58
4 b f Chevalier(IRE) Arundhati (IRE) (Royal Academy (USA))
(200) 1054[4] (1298) 1585[14] 2311[6]

Chelsea Grey (IRE) *Ronald Harris* a49 45
3 gr f Verglas(IRE) Kapera (FR) (Linamix (FR))
55[8] 310[5] (442) 848[5] 1066[5] 1742[8] 3679[8] 5128[5] 6157[3] 6902[12] 7323[12] 8051[6] 8438[8]

Chelwood Gate (IRE) *Roger Varian* a80 86
3 gb g Aussie Rules(USA) Jusoor (USA) (El Prado (IRE))
3342[10] 3803[6] 4922[16] 6925[6]

Chene Boppe (FR) *F-X De Chevigny* a77 77
3 ch c Turtle Bowl(IRE) Beggars Belief (IRE) (Common Grounds)
72a[8] 1756a[3] 2557a[6] 6713a[6]

Chennai Wind *Derek Shaw* a12 35
2 ch g Piccolo Madrasee (Beveled (USA))
6966[9] 7370[3] 7541[10]

Cherokee Princess (IRE) *Tim Pitt* 56
3 ch f Iffraaj Radiancy (IRE) (Mujtahid (USA))
3136[8] 4500[5] 4927[7]

Cherry Princess *Stuart Williams* a37 59
3 ch f Act One Francia (Legend Of France (USA))
979[6] 1640[14] 2519[11] 3403[6] 4679[4] 4961[10] (5702) 6202[10] 7395[7]

Cherry Tiger *James Toller* a63 56
3 b g Tiger Hill(IRE) Lolla's Spirit (IRE) (Montjeu (IRE))
1904[6] 3011[5] 4383[9] 5098[9] 6737[6] 7610[3]

Cherry Tree Hill (IRE) *Alan Swinbank* a53 59
5 b g Ivan Denisovich(IRE) Ring Pink (USA) (Bering)
1522[5] 2332[3] 2972[4] 3203[13]

Chesil Beach *Andrew Balding* 14
2 b f Phoenix Reach(IRE) Seaflower Reef (IRE) (Robellino (USA))
7310[7]

Ches Jicaro (IRE) *James Unett* a51
5 ch g Majestic Missile(IRE) Kelso Magic (USA) (Distant View (USA))
51^{3} 236^{6} 516^{10} 610^{4} 756^{4} 997^{2} 2326^{6}

Chessfield Park *Bryan Smart* a43 36
3 ch g Byron Annie Harvey (Fleetwood (IRE))
6176^{4} 6289^{10} 6965^{5} 7759^{7} 8320^{5}

Chess Valley *Rae Guest* 73
2 b f Shamardal(USA) Grecian Air (FR) (King's Best (USA))
(3717) 5371^{3} 6644^{10}

Chester Aristocrat *Eric Alston* a76 92
4 ch g Sakhee(USA) New Light (Generous (IRE))
1692^{2} 2028^{3} (2663) (2797) 3093^{4} 3823^{2} 4138^{6} 4285^{6} 4472^{12} 6052^{13} 6831^{9} 7314^{14}

Chester Deelyte (IRE) *Lisa Williamson* a55 47
5 b f Desert Style(IRE) Bakewell Tart (IRE) (Tagula (IRE))
163^{5} 327^{4} 551^{8} 917^{3} 1221^{5} 4371^{8} 4840^{3} 5230^{5} 5818^{3} 6101^{5} 7266^{2} 7353^{5} 8258^{7}

Chesterfield (IRE) *Charlie Appleby* 93
3 ch g Pivotal Antique (IRE) (Dubai Millennium)
3061^{3} (3990) 5258^{10} 6380^{4} 7223^{4}

Chester Row *James Toller* 61
3 ch c Compton Place Sophie's Girl (Bahamian Bounty)
1750^{2}

Chester'Slittlegem (IRE) *Jo Hughes* a64 57
4 b f Atraf Ceylon Round (FR) (Royal Applause)
162^{9} 1665^{12} 2074^{3} 2582^{11} 3042^{6} 3501^{6} 4660^{2} 4943^{2} 5670^{2} 5982^{2} 6017^{3} (6101) 6669^{4}

Chesturo (IRE) *Mick Channon* 77
2 ch f Manduro(GER) Joyfullness (USA) (Dixieland Band (USA))
2583^{4} (4723)

Chevalgris *Alan Swinbank* 82
3 gr g Verglas(IRE) Danzelline (Danzero (AUS))
2027^{4} (2405) 3067^{4}

Cheval Rouge (IRE) *H Rogers* a53 87
6 ch m Tagula(IRE) Izibi (FR) (Saint Cyrien (FR))
1168a^{2}

Cheveton *Richard Price* a52 88
9 ch g Most Welcome Attribute (Warning)
2366^{12} 3249^{10} 4690^{5} 6309^{15} 6586^{8} 6831^{7} (7314) 7420^{7} 7776^{3} 8232^{12}

Cheviot (USA) *Ian Semple* a70 109
7 b g Rahy(USA) Camlet (Green Desert (USA))
150a^{12} 244a^{7} 2396^{14} 3334^{11} 3776^{11} 4263^{7} 4800^{11} (5108) 5651^{8} 5984^{8} 6621^{10} 6830^{8} 7171^{5}

Chevise (IRE) *Steve Woodman* a68 64
5 b f Holy Roman Emperor(IRE) Lipica (IRE) (Night Shift (USA))
650^{11} 778^{5} (903) 1063^{10} 1173^{2} 1324^{5} 1957^{3} 2588^{2} 3529^{2} 4120^{10} 5697^{3} 6019^{3} 7086^{8} 7652^{8} 8022^{3}

Cheworee *Tom Dascombe* a81 87
4 b f Milk It Mick Jodrell Bank (IRE) (Observatory (USA))
(1581) 2396^{9} 2724^{11} 3114^{13} 7420^{3} 8021^{8} 8305^{5}

Cheyenne Red (IRE) *Michael Herrington* a38 53
7 br g Namid Red Leggings (Shareef Dancer (USA))
128^{6} 327^{10} 991^{7} 3024^{9} 5365^{2} 5876^{7} 6879^{2} 7236^{9} 8271^{12}

Chez Vrony *Dave Morris* a54 22
7 b g Lujain(USA) Polish Abbey (Polish Precedent (USA))
900^{10} 1311^{4} 2575^{3} 5614^{11} 6399^{8} 7265^{2} 7753^{8}

Chiara Wells (IRE) *A Floris* 95
4 gr f Refuse To Bend(IRE) Docklands Grace (USA) (Honour And Glory (USA))
1563a^{9} 2491a^{13} 7830a^{6}

Chiberta King *Andrew Balding* 111
7 b g King's Best(USA) Glam Rock (Nashwan (USA))
2443^{5} (3560) 4083^{3} 6349^{6} 7193^{4}

Chicago (IRE) *John Patrick Shanahan* 101
4 b g Montjeu(IRE) Lady Karr (Mark Of Esteem (IRE))
246a^{13} 555a^{5} 870a^{8} 3073a^{7}

Chicago Girl (IRE) *J P Murtagh* 104
2 b f Azamour(IRE) Angelic Sounds (IRE) (The Noble Player (USA))
6881a^{2}

Chicquita (IRE) *A De Royer-Dupre* 114
3 b f Montjeu(IRE) Prudenzia (IRE) (Dansili)
3385a^{2} (4550a)

Chief Barker (IRE) *Richard Hannon Snr* 101
2 b c Azamour(IRE) Millay (Polish Precedent (USA))
(5188) (5717) (6195) 7528^{6}

Chief Executive (IRE) *Jo Hughes* a62 75
3 gr g Dalakhani(IRE) Lucky (IRE) (Sadler's Wells (USA))
1679^{6} ◆ 2030^{5} 2846^{7} 5390^{6} 6521^{10} 8360^{7} 8443^{6}

Chief Monolulu *Pat Phelan*
3 b g Sleeping Indian Chispa (Imperial Frontier (USA))
3578

Chigun *Lady Cecil* a68 114
4 b f Oasis Dream Stormy Weather (Nashwan (USA))
2045^{2} (2678a) 3456^{6} 4817a^{9} 6224a^{7} 6837^{7}

Chika Dream (FR) *Y Barberot* a77 103
3 ch c Danehill Dancer(IRE) Smala Tica (FR) (Loup Solitaire (USA))
72a^{6} 5361a^{8}

Chik's Dream *Derek Haydn Jones* a52 48
6 ch g Dreams End Chik's Secret (Nalchik (USA))
99^{9} 852^{4} 1082^{2} 1797^{6} 3580^{7} 4604^{5}

Childa (IRE) *S Wattel* 109
3 gr f Duke Of Marmalade(IRE) Chill (FR) (Verglas (IRE))
1602a^{6} 2381a^{7} 6484a^{2} 7410a^{3} 7843a^{9}

Chilli Green *Julia Feilden* a93 92
6 b m Desert Sun Jade Pet (Petong)
1544^{12} 1835^{5} 2270^{6} 2531^{5} 3472^{11}

Chilly In Rio (IRE) *William Muir* a54 52
2 gr f Verglas(IRE) Brazilian Spirit (IRE) (Invincible Spirit (IRE))
1432^{7} 1724^{11} 2068^{5} 3414^{9} 4141^{5} 4910^{6} 5467^{2} 5963^{2} 6131^{5} 6779^{3} 6983^{7}

Chiltern Secret *Dean Ivory* a34 46
3 ch f Sakhee's Secret Regal Curtsy (Royal Applause)
2519^{10} 3417^{15} 8393^{11}

Chil The Kite *Hughie Morrison* 111
4 b g Notnowcato Copy-Cat (Lion Cavern (USA))
1810^{3} 2446^{4} 3419^{7} 5760^{3} 6254a^{2} 7186a^{4}

Chilworth Diva *Mick Channon*
3 b f Sixties Icon Cibenze (Owington)
3109^{7}

Chilworth Icon *Mick Channon* a85 103
3 b c Sixties Icon Tamara Moon (IRE) (Acclamation)
1621^{8} 2452^{3} 3348^{13} 3584^{5} 4255^{17} 4922^{11} 5260^{4} 5538^{6} 6308^{12} 6990^{15}

China Creek (IRE) *Mark Johnston* a57 82
3 b f Street Cry(IRE) Adonesque (IRE) (Sadler's Wells (USA))
4667^{2} ◆ 4978^{8} 5484^{5} 5867^{2} (6495)

China Excels *Sue Smith* 68
6 b g Exceed And Excel(AUS) China Beauty (Slip Anchor)
(3196) 3569^{11} 4047^{11} 4814^{4} 5365^{12} 6568^{8} 6945^{8}

China In My Hands *Mick Channon* a62 65
2 gr f Dark Angel(IRE) Cheap Thrills (Bertolini (USA))
5529^{7} 5740^{7} 5976^{2} 6333^{3} 6749^{6} 7202^{6}

Chinese Jade *Sir Mark Prescott Bt* a52 78
2 gr g Cape Cross(IRE) Chinese White (IRE) (Dalakhani (IRE))
3233^{8} 3905^{6} 4386^{2} (4662) (5242) 5952^{4}

Chinotto (IRE) *Andrew Balding* a77 33
2 b c Duke Of Marmalade(IRE) Muskoka Dawn (USA) (Miswaki (USA))
6762^{18} 7834^{11} (8067)

Chippy *John Holt* 20
5 b g Diktat French Mannequin (IRE) (Key Of Luck (USA))
4888^{9}

Chips All In (USA) *Jeff Mullins* a33 110
4 b c North Light(IRE) Maria's Mirage (USA) (Maria's Mon (USA))
7710a^{9}

Chiriqui (FR) *S Wattel* a65 76
3 b f Trempolino(USA) Chenoa (Red Ransom (USA))
1602a^{9}

Chiswick Bey (IRE) *Richard Fahey* a73 88
5 b g Elusive City(USA) Victoria Lodge (IRE) (Grand Lodge (USA))
844^{7} 1067^{8} 1363^{7} 1838^{12} 2450^{13} 3575^{2} 4482^{5} 5011^{8} 5378^{2} 6549^{5} (6727) 6943^{5} 7374^{11} 7699^{13} 7898^{3} 8095^{6} 8454^{7}

Chivers (IRE) *Tim Easterby* 51
2 b c Duke Of Marmalade(IRE) Thara (USA) (Hennessy (USA))
4556^{5} 5968^{6} 6299^{9}

Chjimes (IRE) *Conor Dore* a71 79
9 b g Fath(USA) Radiance (IRE) (Thatching)
233^{0} 322^{5} 449^{8} 862^{6}

Chloe's Dream (IRE) *Ann Duffield* a61 68
3 gr f Clodovil(IRE) Extravagance (IRE) (King's Best (USA))
1742^{3} 1961^{3} 2336^{3} 2795^{2} 3134^{2} 3594^{8} 4290^{3} 4448^{2} 5054^{6} (5788) 6669^{7}

Chloe's Image *Philip Kirby* 60
3 b f Lucky Story(USA) Iwunder (IRE) (King's Best (USA))
2794^{2} 3251^{6} 4049^{2} 4953^{7} (5856)

Chocala (IRE) *Alan King* a80 91
3 b g Rock Of Gibraltar(IRE) Arbella (Primo Dominie)
2432^{5} (2784) 5102^{3} (6389) 7250^{2}

Choc'A'Moca (IRE) *Paul Midgley* a29 71
6 b g Camacho Dear Catch (IRE) (Bluebird (USA))
1465^{2} 2611^{2} ◆ 3190^{2} 3630^{16} (4371) 4448^{10} 4891^{5} 5470^{11} 5889^{2} 6515^{10} 6757^{11}

Chock Dee (FR) *Y Barberot* a84 78
8 b g Cardoun(FR) Cometina (FR) (Arctic Tern (USA))
4467a^{7} 5601a^{5}

Chocolate Block (IRE) *Pat Phelan* a57 68
3 br f Singspiel(IRE) Pingus (Polish Precedent (USA))
(1879) 3497^{6} 4049^{4} (5065) 5535^{5} 7258^{9}

Chocolate Caviar (IRE) *Gary Moore* 68
3 ch f Tamayuz Jazz Up (Cadeaux Genereux)
2850^{7} 3417^{5}

Choice Of Destiny *Philip McBride* a62
2 ch f Haafhd Lumpini Park (Halling (USA))
7664^{2} 8026^{5} 8201^{4}

Choisan (IRE) *Tim Easterby* 82
4 b g Choisir(AUS) Attanagh (IRE) (Darnay)
2369^{17} 2706^{9} 3480^{2} 4313^{14} 4804^{2} (5059) 5706^{13} 6211^{12} 6626^{14} 6846^{10} 7498^{4} 7778^{2}

Choisirez (IRE) *John Panvert* 40
4 b f Choisir(AUS) Filimeala (IRE) (Pennekamp (USA))
2074^{14} 2392^{12} 2921^{8}

Chokidar (IRE) *Scott Dixon* a80 78
5 b g Sleeping Indian Lola Sapola (IRE) (Benny The Dip (USA))
358^{2} 844^{3} 1252^{9}

Chookie Avon *Keith Dalgleish* a83 79
6 ch g Avonbridge Lady Of Windsor (IRE) (Woods Of Windsor (USA))
217^{3} 644^{6} 822^{2} 3200^{4} 3592^{4} 3683^{6} ◆ 3945^{9} 4341^{4} 4577^{3} 5051^{4} 5138^{6}

Chookie Hamilton *Keith Dalgleish* a81 83
9 ch g Compton Place Lady Of Windsor (IRE) (Woods Of Windsor (USA))
7805^{P}

Chookie Royale *Keith Dalgleish* a104 93
5 ch g Monsieur Bond(IRE) Lady Of Windsor (IRE) (Woods Of Windsor (USA))
621^{3} (995) 1675^{13} 2240^{8} 2541^{5} 2882^{4} 3335^{3} ◆ 3590^{6} 3684^{2} 4055^{8} 4342^{7} 5051^{2} 6550^{12} 6625^{9} (7241) (7464) 7641^{2} 7769^{2} 7793^{2}

Chookie's Lass *Keith Dalgleish* a65 62
2 ch f Compton Place Lady Of Windsor (IRE) (Woods Of Windsor (USA))
4470^{4} ◆ 5083^{3} 5826^{8} 6914^{8} (7789)

Chooseday (IRE) *Kevin Ryan* 93
4 b g Choisir(AUS) Break Of Day (USA) (Favorite Trick (USA))
1232^{7} 2239^{4} 2460^{7} 3093^{2} 3299^{7} ◆ 3802^{7} 4983^{3} 5544^{4} 6621^{12} 6845^{10} (7452)

Chopin (GER) *A Wohler* 116
3 b c Santiago(GER) Caucasienne (FR) (Galileo (IRE))
(1708a) 2866^{7} 3485^{7}

Chopouest (FR) *T Castanheira* a100 107
6 b g Indian Rocket Free Track (FR) (Solid Illusion (USA))
961a^{6} 3851a^{6} 7941a^{U}

Choral Clan (IRE) *Philip Mitchell* a61 57
2 b c Oratorio(IRE) Campbellite (Desert Prince (IRE))
3174^{6} 3689^{10} 4414^{8} 5276^{2} 6749^{11} 7855^{2}

Choral Festival *John Bridger* a65 83
7 b m Pivotal Choirgirl (Unfuwain (USA))
1585^{5} 1884^{8} 2413^{3} 2729^{6} 2808^{2} 3244^{5} (3900) 5063^{3} 5190^{3} 5445^{6} 6358^{5} 7075^{10} 7267^{7} 7539^{7} 7865^{8}

Choral Prince (IRE) *Mike Murphy* a66 77
3 b g Oratorio(IRE) Princess Of Iona (IRE) (Fasliyev (USA))
1725^{11} 2935^{12} (3403) 3809^{4} (4392) 5157^{3} 6202^{6}

Choral Rhythm (IRE) *Tony Carroll* a24 48
3 b f Oratorio(IRE) Sierra (Dr Fong (USA))
2362^{6} 3041^{4} 3885^{3}

Chord Chart (IRE) *Charlie Appleby* a82 83
2 b c Acclamation Musical Bar (IRE) (Barathea (IRE))
3245^{5} (3640) 4232^{6} 4519^{2} 5927^{4} 6493^{5} 7300^{5}

Chorister Choir (IRE) *Tim Easterby* 60
3 b f Choisir(AUS) Cape Jasmine (IRE) (Danehill (USA))
5517^{10} 5989^{6} 7236^{10}

Chorister Girl *Richard Ford* a31 51
4 b f Acclamation Hazelhurst (IRE) (Night Shift (USA))
105^{9} 545^{6}

Chorlton Manor (IRE) *Nicky Vaughan* a78 70
2 b g Kheleyf(USA) Pearl Of The Sea (IRE) (Fusaichi Pegasus (USA))
4351^{4} 5558^{4} 6213^{2} (6477)

Chortle *Charlie Appleby* 65
2 b f Dubawi(IRE) Portmanteau (Barathea (IRE))
6281^{6} 6949^{5} 7449^{5}

Chosen Character (IRE) *Tom Dascombe* 101
5 b g Choisir(AUS) Out Of Thanks (IRE) (Sadler's Wells (USA))
1235^{18} 1688^{10} 2210^{2} 2649^{7} 3564^{8} 3984^{5} 5026^{2} 5268^{10} 5943^{3} 6826^{8} 7337^{3} 7820^{16}

Chosen Forever *Geoffrey Oldroyd* a86 52
8 b g Choisir(AUS) Forever Bond (Danetime (IRE))
146^{7} 238^{3} 433^{5} (801) 1107^{2} 1394^{6} 4504^{5}

Chosen One (IRE) *Ruth Carr* a29 71
8 ch g Choisir(AUS) Copious (IRE) (Generous (IRE))
1077^{9} 1388^{2} (1465) (1665) (2122) 2343^{7} 2832^{4} 3236^{9} 3769^{2} 4102^{10} 4479^{10} (5148) 5579^{10} 6471^{8} 6771^{11} 7029^{12}

Chriselliam (IRE) *Charles Hills* 114
2 b f Iffraaj Danielli (IRE) (Danehill (USA))
2625^{9} (4218) 5555a^{9} 6195^{2} (6798) (7690a)

Chrisnickdave (FR) *Michael Easterby* a39 51
3 b f Sleeping Indian Vagabond Chanteuse (Sanglamore (USA))
915^{5} 1114^{8} 1648^{4} 3203^{12}

Chrissycross (IRE) *Roger Teal* a83 58
4 b f Cape Cross(IRE) Penang (IRE) (Xaar)
159^{3} 451^{5} 1013^{2} 1176^{2} 2845^{7} 3330^{3} 3635^{4} 4523^{3} 5001^{6} 6963^{2} 7446^{7} (7952) 8269^{3} 8408^{3}

Christmas Light *Brian Ellison* a79 86
6 b m Zafeen(FR) Arabian Dancer (Dansili)
2551^{4} (3083) (3349) 3567^{4} 4264^{5} 4777^{6} 6236^{17} 6801^{6} 7211^{5}

Christmas Wish *Mick Channon* a60 66
2 b f Pastoral Pursuits Christmas Tart (IRE) (Danetime (IRE))
5282^{6} 5988^{7} 6409^{4} 6724^{5} 7327^{4}

Christopher Chua (IRE) *Michael Scudamore* a58 56
4 gr g Clodovil(IRE) Pearls Of Wisdom (Kyllachy)
139^{8} 471^{3} 862^{4} 1042^{5} 2096^{6} 6651^{11} 6930^{4} 7323^{7} 7850^{7} 8146^{5} 8393^{2}

Christopher Wren (USA) *Nick Gifford* a60 83
6 ch g D'Wildcat(USA) Ashley's Coy (USA) (Country Pine (USA))
6596^{11}

Chroussa (IRE) *J S Bolger* 94
2 b f Holy Roman Emperor(IRE) Violet Spring (IRE) (Exactly Sharp (USA))
4742^{10} 6881a^{7}

Chrysos (GER) *J-C Rouget* a67 64
3 b g Big Shuffle(USA) Centre Point (Pivotal)
270a^{5}

Chuckamental *Bryan Smart* a41 63
2 b g Captain Marvelous(IRE) Stoneacre Sarah (Cadeaux Genereux)
3766^{5} 4724^{4} 5350^{5} 6718^{5}

Chunghua (USA) *Ed Walker* a75
2 ch c Elusive Quality(USA) Mananiyya (IRE) (Ashkalani (IRE))
8368^{2} ◆

Chunky Diamond (IRE) *Ruth Carr* 88
4 b g Diamond Green(FR) Balance The Books (Elmaamul (USA))
1232^{18} 1644^{8} 2031^{19} 2441^{13} 2755^{11} 3505^{9} (4018) 4203^{5} 4235^{8} 4620^{6} 5108^{14} 5579^{5} 5985^{8} 6159^{10} 6515^{12} 6843^{6}

Churada (IRE) *J-M Lefebvre* a68 62
3 b f Green Tune(USA) Agiel (FR) (Bering)
2434a^{9} 5692a^{2} 7569a^{4}

Church Music (IRE) *Michael Scudamore* a94 85
4 b c Amadeus Wolf Cappella (IRE) (College Chapel)
1765^{9} 2207^{15} (2561) 2865^{13} 3249^{9} 3786^{6} 6189^{10} 7254^{2}

Churt *Christopher Kellett* a34 19
4 b g Namid Darayna (IRE) (Shernazar)
5845^{8} 6113^{5} 6555^{12} 7082^{10} 7273^{5}

Chutney (IRE) *Richard Hannon Snr* 75
2 b f Exceed And Excel(AUS) Crackle (Anshan)
3057^{9} (3694) 5005^{14} 6326^{13}

Cider Time (IRE) *David Evans*
2 ch f Captain Rio North Cider Rose (IRE) (Goldmark (USA))
6318^{11}

Ciel D'Automne (FR) *J-P Delaporte* a69
3 b c Vespone(IRE) Nuit D'Irlande (IRE) (Royal Academy (USA))
331a^{3} 1756a^{0}

Cielo Canarias (IRE) *E Leon Penate* 105
5 b g Exceed And Excel(AUS) Summer Dance (Sadler's Wells (USA))
7968a^{8}

Cihanim (TUR) *S Bektas* 98
4 b c Bin Ajwaad(IRE) Roxie Hart (IRE) (Danehill (USA))
6253a^{9}

Cincinnati Kit *Stuart Williams* a66 86
4 br f Cape Cross(IRE) Princess Georgina (Royal Applause)
529^{4} (670) (924) 2643^{7} (3317) (4017) ◆ (4536) 5027^{9}

Cincuenta Pasos (IRE) *Joseph Tuite* a76
2 ch c Footstepsinthesand Sweet Nicole (Okawango (USA))
7261^{3} 7852^{2} 8342^{5}

Cinderslipper (IRE) *Ann Duffield* a8 66
3 b f Jeremy(USA) Love City (IRE) (Spectrum (IRE))
1772^{3} 2506^{8} 3396^{10} 4143^{10} 7343^{8}

Cinematique (IRE) *Laura Mongan* a39
5 br g King's Theatre(IRE) Chantoue Royale (FR) (Cadoudal (FR))
227^{5}

Cinnamon Spice *Harry Dunlop* 52
2 bb g High Chaparral(IRE) Hot And Spicy (Grand Lodge (USA))
7500^{6}

Cinnilla *Ralph Beckett* 43
2 b f Authorized(IRE) Caesarea (GER) (Generous (IRE))
7532^{8}

Ciocco Sam (GER) *C Von Der Recke*
5 bb g Samum(GER) Cioccolata (GER) (Winged Love (IRE))
702a^{8}

Cio Cio San (IRE) *Bill Turner* a48 62
3 ch f Dalakhani(IRE) Unreachable Star (Halling (USA))
3216^{11} 3917^{8} 4521^{6} 4881^{6}

Circle Of Angels *Mark Johnston* a23 69
5 b f Royal Applause City Of Angels (Woodman (USA))
2511^{12} 3768^{2} 3971^{8} (4135)

Circuitous *Keith Dalgleish* a61 82
5 b g Fasliyev(USA) Seren Devious (Dr Devious (IRE))
2707^{2} 3393^{3} 3770^{3} (4051) 4338^{4} (5263) 6052^{4} 6548^{2} (6586)

Circumvent *Paul Cole* a109 88
6 ch g Tobougg(IRE) Seren Devious (Dr Devious (IRE))
2839^{6} 3864^{6} 6596^{6}

Circus Turn (USA) *Sir Michael Stoute* a83 94
3 b g Street Cry(IRE) Showlady (USA) (Theatrical (IRE))
1679^{12} 2548^{3} 2952^{2} (4084) 4537^{5} (5792) 5986^{3}

Cirrus Des Aigles (FR) *Mme C Barande-Barbe* a107 132
7 b g Even Top(IRE) Taille De Guepe (FR) (Septieme Ciel (USA))
3615a^{5} 4745^{4} 5298a^{2} 5807a^{5} (6618a) (7049a) 7367^{2} 8211a^{3}

Citizen Kaine (IRE) *Jo Hughes* 63
2 ch g Manduro(GER) Precious Citizen (USA) (Proud Citizen (USA))
3555^{19} 3833^{4} ◆ 4386^{4} 6619^{10}

City Chope (FR) *C Boutin* a66 72
3 b f Sagacity(FR) Grenoble (FR) (Marignan (USA))
647a^{6}

City Girl (IRE) *Ralph Beckett* a78 103
3 b f Elusive City(USA) Lochridge (Indian Ridge)
2415^{2} 3102^{7} (3784) 4260^{7} 5561^{6} 7821^{15}

City Ground (USA) *Michael Easterby* a70 70
6 bb g Orientate(USA) Magnet (USA) (Seeking The Gold (USA))
(2875) 3889^{8} (4376) 4951^{8} 6217^{3} 7498^{17}

City Image (IRE) *Richard Hannon Snr* 99
3 gr f Elusive City(USA) Photophore (IRE) (Clodovil (IRE))
1676^{6} 2429^{9}

City Line (IRE) *Karl Thornton* a42 46
6 b g Antonius Pius(USA) Indian Myth (USA) (Lear Fan (USA))
7379^{11}

City Of Culture (IRE) *W McCreery* a65 73
5 b f Elusive City(USA) Danestar (Danehill (USA))
3796a^{9}

City Of The Kings (IRE) *Tracy Waggott* a64 76
8 b g Cape Cross(IRE) Prima Volta (Primo Dominie)
1603^{7} 4888^{6}

Cityscape *Roger Charlton* 123
7 ch h Selkirk(USA) Tantina (USA) (Distant View (USA))
2446^{12}

City Style (USA) *Charlie Appleby* a107 119
7 ch g City Zip(USA) Brattothecore (CAN) (Katahaula County (CAN))
466a[2] 959a[3] 1267a[6] 5270[6] (5725)

City Zen (IRE) *Tony Coyle* 91
2 b f Baltic King Queen Cobra (IRE) (Indian Rocket)
4724[2] 5380[2] 5767[3] 6622[9] (7173)

C J Mon (USA) *Norris Davidson*
3 bb c Monarchos(USA) Charming Jenny (USA) (Home At Last (USA))
786a[11]

Claim (IRE) *Sir Michael Stoute* 77
3 b g Acclamation Raysiza (IRE) (Alzao (USA))
1912[5] 3279[6]

Claim The Roses (USA) *Ed Vaughan* a91 69
2 bb c Speightstown(USA) Reboot (USA) (Rubiano (USA))
(3905) 4717[6] (5927) 7122[2]

Claire Song (IRE) *S Botti* 90
3 b f Singspiel(IRE) Clara House (Shirley Heights)
2697a[6]

Clancy Avenue (USA) *T Stack* a80 98
3 br g Henrythenavigator(USA) Saintly Speech (USA) (Southern Halo (USA))
1620[2] 3103[8] 3846a[5]

Clapped *Ed Vaughan* a63 41
4 b g Royal Applause Susun Kelapa (USA) (St Jovite (USA))
418[7] 1100[9]

Clapperboard *Paul Fitzsimons* a61 31
2 b f Royal Applause Roseum (Lahib (USA))
5174[5] *6107[6] 6342[4] 7199[3] 7623[10] 8273[5]*

Clara Bel La (IRE) *John E Kiely* 82
7 b m Accordion(IRE) Home At Last (IRE) (Mandalus)
7230a[29]

Clarice *Sir Mark Prescott Bt* a49
2 b f Cape Cross(IRE) Phillipina (Medicean)
2577[5] 3211[5] 3493[4]

Clarion Call *Graeme McPherson* a67 69
5 b g Beat Hollow Fanfare (Deploy)
6130[2] 6336[7]

Clary (IRE) *James Unett* a65 66
3 b f Clodovil(IRE) Kibarague (Barathea (IRE))
849[5] 1019[3] 2215[2] *3216[3]* 3758[8] *4356[4] 6655[8] 7987[4]*

Classical Art (IRE) *Roger Varian* 74
2 ch c Excellent Art Ask Carol (IRE) (Foxhound (USA))
6975[9] 7320[2]

Classical Chloe *Tim Fitzgerald* 16
5 b f Sleeping Indian Mana Pools (IRE) (Brief Truce (USA))
6722[6]

Classical Diva *Declan Carroll* a4 71
2 b f Amadeus Wolf America Lontana (FR) (King's Theatre (IRE))
2715[2] (3280) 4261[6] 4965[7] 5648[5] *6170[7]* 6467[3] 7127[10] 7771[7]

Classic Art *Roger Teal* a21 64
3 ch g Excellent Art Sensibility (Halling (USA))
2017[11] 3861[10]

Classic Blade (IRE) *Doug Watson* a87 83
7 b h Daggers Drawn(USA) Queen Bodicea (IRE) (Revoque (IRE))
412a[8]

Classic Colori (IRE) *David O'Meara* a83 96
6 b g Le Vie Dei Colori Beryl (Bering)
23[3] (517) (1039) 1113[4] 1281[7] *(1368)* 1538[10] 1786[2] *1890[3]* 2659[2] (2881) 3346[9] 3812[6] 4895[2] 5355[6] 6801[24]

Classic Devotion (USA) *Charlie Appleby* a62
2 b c Street Cry(IRE) Serenading (USA) (A.P. Indy (USA))
7834[9]

Classic Mission *Jonathan Portman* 68
2 ch g Bahamian Bounty Triple Cee (IRE) (Cape Cross (IRE))
5344[10] 6333[5] 6739[5]

Classic Princess *Gay Kelleway* a63 11
2 b f Proclamation(IRE) Classic Lass (Dr Fong (USA))
6171[4] 7693[11] *8138[8]*

Classic Punch (IRE) *Tim Etherington* a78 93
10 b g Mozart(IRE) Rum Cay (USA) (Our Native (USA))
(2077) 2766[7] 3685[15] (4435) (5382) *6927[5]*

Classic Pursuit *Ronald Harris* 74
2 b c Pastoral Pursuits Snake's Head (Golden Snake (USA))
3948[5] 4347[2] (4827) 5371[5]

Classic Voice (IRE) *Roy Brotherton* a3 48
5 b g Oratorio(IRE) Pearly Brooks (Efisio)
2496[5] 3252[9] 3919[11] *4153[8]*

Classified Weapon (USA) *David Simcock* a66 66
2 b c Exchange Rate(USA) Perfect Paula (USA) (Songandaprayer (USA))
3493[3] 6064[4]

Classy Anne *Jim Goldie* 47
3 ch f Orientor Class Wan (Safawan)
5517[11] 5919[5] 6879[8] 6944[7] 7150[4]

Classy Lassy (IRE) *Brian Ellison* a44 81
2 b f Tagula(IRE) Classic Style (IRE) (Desert Style (IRE))
1642[8] 2025[2] 2426[3] 2883[6] *4154[4]* 5970[2] 6284[4]

Classy Trick (USA) *Patrick Morris* a59 31
3 b g Hat Trick(JPN) Classiest Gem (CAN) (Dehere (USA))
1314[4] 1685[11] *2124[8]* 2464[8] *8279[2] 8371[6]*

Claude Greenwood *Roger Curtis* a75 74
3 b g Lucky Story(USA) Greenmeadow (Sure Blade (USA))
628[8] 811[7] 1118[5] 1695[3] 1903[6] 2129[2] (2737) 3219[2] 3739[10] 4722[12]

Claude Monet (BRZ) *Simon Dow* a66 67
4 ch g Vettori(IRE) Femme Fatale (BRZ) (Clackson (BRZ))
2605[9] 3157[9] 4441[6] *5234[4]* 5631[3] *6398[8]* 6976[13] *7931[9]*

Claudia Octavia *Brian Ellison* a29 38
2 br f Holy Roman Emperor(IRE) Chalosse (Doyoun)
1449[5] 1642[7] 1930[10] 4990[3] *5865[4]*

Claudinho (FR) *C Ferland* a82 84
3 b c Lawman(FR) Full Snow Moon (USA) (Vindication (USA))
1972a[5]

Clayton *Kevin Ryan* a87 102
4 b g Peintre Celebre(USA) Blossom (Warning)
1768[2] 2365[6] 3346[13] (4765) 5283[3] 6551[4]

Clean Blow (USA) *David Brown* a54 76
3 bb f Street Boss(USA) Strike Hard (IRE) (Green Desert (USA))
1682[7] 2098[12] (3134) 3446[9]

Clear Focus (IRE) *Brendan Powell* a37 53
2 ch f Intense Focus(USA) Sofistication (IRE) (Dayjur (USA))
3896[8] 5529[8] *6213[10] 6979[7] 7665[4] 7956[6]*

Clearing *Jim Boyle* a67 54
3 br f Sleeping Indian Spring Clean (FR) (Danehill (USA))
1174[3] 1750[6] *3212[4] (3499)* 4283[4]

Clear Loch *John Spearing* a64 67
3 gr g Proclamation(IRE) Loch Shiel (IRE) (Selkirk (USA))
4[4] 3739[7] *7624[5] 7873[2] 7987[7]*

Clear Pearl (USA) *Ed Vaughan* a73 75
3 ch f Giant's Causeway(USA) Clear In The West (USA) (Gone West (USA))
1876[3] 2760[2] (4689) *5353[5]*

Clear Praise (USA) *Simon Dow* a88 83
6 b g Songandaprayer(USA) Pretty Clear (USA) (Mr Prospector (USA))
1643 723[7] 881[7] (1067) 1814[9] 2255[12] 2871[6] 3315[3] 3733[4] 4303[9] (5278) 5851[2] 6067[10] *7080[10]*

Clear Spell (IRE) *Ed Walker* a73
2 b g Tamayuz Beat The Rain (Beat Hollow)
8066[7] 8333[2] ◆

Clear Spring (IRE) *John Spearing* a69 100
5 b c Chineur(FR) Holly Springs (Efisio)
1838[10] 2255[22] 3010[3] (3315) (3973) 4389[2] 5009[4] ◆ (5544) 5696[3] 6078[2] 6621[11] 7495[14]

Clef D'Or (FR) *Y Durepaire* a68 79
3 b g Archange D'Or(IRE) Circus Key (IRE) (Key Of Luck (USA))
4575a[2] 5914a[5]

Clement (IRE) *John O'Shea* a77 80
3 b g Clodovil(IRE) Winnifred (Green Desert (USA))
1014[2] 1486[7] *(1928) (2951) 3438[5]* 4033[3] (4772) 6488[6]

Clement Rock (USA) *Mark Casse* 102
5 b c Strong Hope(USA) Ellesmere (USA) (Tabasco Cat (USA))
608a[3]

Clenor (IRE) *Doug O'Neill* 100
2 b f Oratorio(IRE) Chantarella (IRE) (Royal Academy (USA))
3868a[3] 7690a[8]

Cleofila (IRE) *J S Bolger* 86
4 b f Teofilo(IRE) Altarejos (IRE) (Vettori (IRE))
1862a[4]

Clerk's Choice (IRE) *William Jarvis* a85 25
7 b g Bachelor Duke(USA) Credit Crunch (IRE) (Caerleon (USA))
7976[3] (8392) 8429[6]

Clever Man *P Vovcenko* a75 70
5 b g Librettist(USA) Lindesberg (Doyoun)
5804a[11]

Clever Miss *Alan McCabe* a76 74
2 b f Mount Nelson Clever Millie (USA) (Cape Canaveral (USA))
2751[4] 3064[12] *3905[2] (4154)* 5284[7] 5829[5] 7088[4] *7463[10]*

Cliffords Reprieve *Eric Wheeler* a67 55
5 b g Kheleyf(USA) Bijan (IRE) (Mukaddamah (USA))
449[9]

Climaxfortackle (IRE) *Derek Shaw* a77 64
5 b f Refuse To Bend(IRE) Miss Asia Quest (Rainbow Quest (USA))
101[2] 214[2] 271[3] (431) (790) 1596[2] 1798[2] 2088[5] 6982[8] 7164[10] 7777[6] 8128[9] 8439[7]

Clockmaker (IRE) *Conor Dore* a102 102
7 b g Danetime(IRE) Lady Ingabelle (IRE) (Catrail (USA))
1571[6] 2214[6] 2649[2] 3088[5] (3335) 3754[2] *5894[7] (5992) 6199[11]* 6650[12] *7540[11] 7926[4] 7991[2] 8231[6] 8264[7]* 8428[5]

Clock On Tom *Michael Easterby* a59 67
3 b g Trade Fair Night Owl (Night Shift (USA))
1367[2] 1759[2] 1967[2] 2080[2] (2770) 3082[5] 4119[11] 4725[5] *6214[11]*

Clock Opera (IRE) *William Stone* a69 65
3 b f Excellent Art Moving Diamonds (Lomitas)
37[2] 416[2] 1447[2] 1911[4] *2772[5]* 3540[6] (5300) 6075[3] 6535[8] 7454[8] *(8023) 8220[3]*

Clodoaldo (IRE) *Brian Meehan* 58
2 b g Clodovil(IRE) Salonga (IRE) (Shinko Forest (IRE))
5033[11] 7019[11]

Clon Brulee (IRE) *David Barron* a36 105
4 ch g Modigliani(USA) Cloneden (IRE) (Definite Article)
(2478) (2718) ◆ 4310[5] 4854[12] (6332) 6620[3]

Clondinnery (IRE) *A Oliver* a82 73
5 b g Choisir(AUS) Grand Lili (Linamix (FR))
3869a[11]

Clorofilla (IRE) *Marco Gasparini* 97
3 b f Refuse To Bend(IRE) Crudelia (IRE) (Great Commotion (USA))
1563a[2] 1866a[3] 6890a[3] (7416a)

Close At Hand *John Gosden* 87
3 b f Exceed And Excel(AUS) Classic Remark (IRE) (Dr Fong (USA))
2658[2] 3136[3] (3860) 4878[7] (5960) 6536[6]

Close Companion *Hugo Palmer* a34
2 b f Azamour(IRE) Vittoria Vetra (Danehill Dancer (IRE))
8084[8] 8214[9]

Close Hatches (USA) *William Mott* a118
3 bb f First Defence(USA) Rising Tornado (USA) (Storm Cat (USA))
7691a[2]

Close Together (IRE) *Robert Mills* a64 46
3 b f Dylan Thomas(IRE) Maritana (USA) (Rahy (USA))
507[2] 634[4] 824[2] 1301[4] 1712[10] 2362[8]

Close To Heaven (GER) *A Trybuhl* a88 84
6 gr g Diktat Caronment (Environment Friend)
960a[0]

Cloud (IRE) *L Riccardi* 96
3 bb c Clodovil(IRE) Noble Indiana (ITY) (Indian Ridge)
2491a[9]

Cloudgazer (IRE) *Giles Bravery* a77 79
5 b g Dalakhani(IRE) City Zone (IRE) (Zafonic (USA))
4204[13]

Cloud Monkey (IRE) *Martin Todhunter* a76 88
3 bb g Marju(IRE) Sweet Clover (Rainbow Quest (USA))
7211[17]

Cloudscape (IRE) *John Gosden* a78
2 b c Dansili Set The Scene (IRE) (Sadler's Wells (USA))
(8123) ◆

Cloudwalker (USA) *Ed Vaughan* a70 77
3 bb f Tale Of The Cat(USA) Angel Flying (USA) (Saint Ballado (CAN))
2224[4] 3116[5] 3860[2]

Cloudy Spirit *Andrew Hollinshead* a69 84
8 gr m Silver Patriarch(IRE) Miss Lacroix (Picea)
2402[5] 3560[5] 4873[10]

Cloudy Start *Violet M Jordan* a67 77
7 b g Oasis Dream Set Fair (USA) (Alleged (USA))
6853[8] 7382[8]

Clover Nova *Jo Davis* a46
6 b m Exit To Nowhere(USA) Catriona (Bustino)
752[5]

Clowance Estate (IRE) *Roger Charlton* 101
4 b g Teofilo(IRE) Whirly Bird (Nashwan (USA))
(3293) 3838[3] 4857[6] 5746[3] 6192[2] 7193[14]

Club Electra (IRE) *Tobias B P Coles* a55
3 br f Red Clubs(IRE) Princess Electra (IRE) (Lake Coniston (IRE))
197[7] 509[2] 817[3] 923[6] 1066[6]

Club House (IRE) *Robert Mills* a76 74
3 b g Marju(IRE) Idesia (IRE) (Green Desert (USA))
(18) (188) 359[4] 444[3] 1011[3] 1099[4] 1477[8] 1770[9] 2209[12] 3178[10] 3665[2] 3927[4] 4504[2] *5280[6]* 5604[6] 7307[9] 7898[9] 8158[2] ◆ 8432[9] 8443[3]

Clubhouse Ride (USA) *Craig A Lewis* a111
5 ch c Candy Ride(ARG) Seeking Results (USA) (Seeking The Gold (USA))
4106a[4]

Clubland (IRE) *Roy Bowring* a85 81
4 b g Red Clubs(IRE) Racjilanemm (Kyllachy)
(454) (885) 1331[4] 1681[8] 2343[5] *2515[7]* (2781) 3441[3] 4007[12] (4669) 4884[2] *5901[2]* 6209[3] 6822[6] *8232[9]*

Club Wexford (IRE) *J S Bolger* 95
2 b c Lawman(FR) Masnada (IRE) (Erins Isle)
2675a[2] 2943a[3] ◆

Cluin Aine (IRE) *Kieran P Cotter* a66 42
4 br m Big Bad Bob(IRE) Gold Valley Hope (IRE) (Catrail (USA))
2616[11]

Clumber Place *James Given* a39 66
7 ch m Compton Place Inquirendo (USA) (Roberto (USA))
2884[11] 3445[11] 4198[10] 4967[4] 5263[3] 5331[11] 6633[5] 7153[11] 7455[2] *7808[5]*

Clumber Street *Ed McMahon* a75 71
2 ch c Compton Place Tinnarinka (Observatory (USA))
5665[2] *6213[9] 6746[2]*

Coach House (IRE) *A P O'Brien* 104
2 b c Oasis Dream Lesson In Humility (IRE) (Mujadil (USA))
(2675a) ◆ 3481[2] 3847a[3]

Coach Montana (IRE) *Jane Chapple-Hyam* a56 47
4 b g Proud Citizen(USA) Market Day (Tobougg (IRE))
2134[8] 3326[7] 3738[3] *5869[5]* 7323[16]

Coalburn *Gary Harrison* a41 56
5 ch g Captain Rio Pusey Street Girl (Gildoran)
5408[5] 6017[4] (6436) 7323[4] 7598[2] *8272[6]*

Coastal Passage *Charles Smith* a60 59
5 b g Ishiguru(USA) Elcon (IRE) (Royal Applause)
(105) 2401[0] 1239[13] 2170[7] 2926[3] ◆ 3029[6] *3644[5] 3910[4]* 4660[7] *7752[6] 7905[4] 8118[2]*

Coastal Storm *Hughie Morrison* a52 42
2 b f Manduro(GER) Ruff Shod (USA) (Storm Boot (USA))
7069[9] *7442[7] 7764[12]*

Coax *Patrick Holmes* a55 67
5 b g Red Ransom(USA) True Glory (IRE) (In The Wings)
6086[8] 6723[6] 6921[5]

Cockney Belle *Marco Botti* a69 63
2 br f Cockney Rebel(IRE) Fustaan (IRE) (Royal Applause)
2740[5] 3324[3] *4408[4] 5634[3]*

Cockney Bob *D Windrif* a81 90
2 b g Cockney Rebel(IRE) Wizby (Wizard King)
1360[4] 1749[2] 2011[2] 2358[3] *3436[2]* 3574[2] 4044[2] 4599a[2] (5214a) *(5848a)* 7967a[10]

Cockney Class (USA) *Dave Roberts* a96 90
6 rg g Speightstown(USA) Snappy Little Cat (USA) (Tactical Cat (USA))
2976[5]

Cockney Dancer *Charles Hills* a88 83
4 ch f Cockney Rebel(IRE) Roo (Rudimentary (USA))
60[7]

Cockney Sparrow *John Quinn* a72 92
4 b f Cockney Rebel(IRE) Compose (Anabaa (USA))
2369[6] 5712[2] (6626)

Cocktail Charlie *Tim Easterby* a76 79
5 b g Danbird(AUS) Royal Punch (Royal Applause)
2505[4] 2755[3] 3351[13] 4560[4] 5011[6] 5108[8] 5381[5] 5971[10] *6653[2]* 7030[3]

Cocktail Queen (IRE) *David Elsworth* a81 101
3 b f Motivator Premier Prize (Selkirk (USA))
1546[4] 2299a[17] 7535[3] 7822[2]

Cocoa's Princess *Richard Fahey* a45
2 b f Kyllachy Princess Cocoa (IRE) (Desert Sun)
8368[5]

Cocohatchee *Pat Phelan* a60 74
5 b g Avonbridge Chilly Cracker (Largesse)
2096[10] *2773[12] 3404[8] 4169[13]*

Coconell *Jeremy Noseda* a75
3 b f Rock Of Gibraltar(IRE) Marula (IRE) (Sadler's Wells (USA))
6557[9] 7488[5] 7838[2] (8092) 8343[8]

Coconut Kisses *Bill Turner* a57 67
3 ch f Bahamian Bounty Royal Mistress (Fasliyev (USA))
2873[4] 3494[3] 3904[5] 4353[3] 5054[2] 5644[9] 6436[3] 6902[15] *7292[7] 7730[6]*

Cocozza (USA) *K F Clutterbuck* a69 74
5 b g Elusive Quality(USA) Watership Crystal (IRE) (Sadler's Wells (USA))
2782[4] 3831[9] 5006[9] *5355[7] 6473[8] 6937[10] 7163[4]* 7455[3]

Codebreaker *Hughie Morrison* a68 68
3 ch g Sakhee's Secret Folly Lodge (Grand Lodge (USA))
1923[7] 3861[3] *6081[6] 6968[4]*

Code Of Conduct (USA) *Wayne Catalano* a89 103
5 b c Tapit(USA) Rumba Punch (USA) (Green Dancer (USA))
5550a[4]

Code Of Honor *Henry Candy* a89 112
3 b c Zafeen(FR) Verbal Intrigue (USA) (Dahar (USA))
1543[4] 2661[9] (4028) ◆ 4917[5] 5792[3] 6838[2]

Code Six (IRE) *Bryan Smart* a54 68
4 gr f Kodiac Grey Pursuit (IRE) (Pursuit Of Love)
101[4] 436[8] 1147[8] 1388[3] 2043[2] 2632[6] 3246[15] *4148[12]* 5486[8] *5864[7] 7077[7]*

Coillte Cailin (IRE) *Daniel Mark Loughnane* a66
3 b f Oratorio(IRE) Forest Walk (IRE) (Shinko Forest (IRE))
8303[3]

Coin Broker (IRE) *David O'Meara* 64
2 b f Montjeu(IRE) Cash Run (USA) (Seeking The Gold (USA))
5826[3] 6597[8]

Coincidently *Alan Bailey* a76 80
3 b f Acclamation Miss Chaussini (IRE) (Rossini (USA))
949[6] 1622[12] 3988[8] 4690[4] 6758[6] (6875)

Coire Gabhail *Hughie Morrison* a54 63
3 ch f Sakhee's Secret Glencal (Compton Place)
3109[5] 3837[6] 4200[5] *6560[8] 6965[4] 7443[3] 7905[11]*

Coiste Bodhar (IRE) *Joseph Tuite* a65 59
2 b g Camacho Nortolixa (FR) (Linamix (FR))
5399[11] 6590[7] *6923[10] 7986[3] 8058[2] 8188[2] 8222[3] 8435[4]*

Colamandis *H A McWilliams* a40 44
6 b m Lucky Story(USA) Merry Mary (Magic Ring (IRE))
88[8]

Colbyor *Richard Fahey* a74 77
4 ch g Orientor College Maid (IRE) (College Chapel)
(27) 453[5] 4338[7] 4992[5] (5973)

Colinca's Lad (IRE) *Peter Charalambous* a49 84
11 b g Lahib(USA) Real Flame (Cyrano De Bergerac)
2478[7] 2867[3] (3791) 4208[6] 6573[2] *7115[8]* 7611[6] *7857[6]*

Collaboration *Andrew Balding* 75
2 b g Halling(USA) Red Shareef (Marju (IRE))
3290[9] 4256[10] (7320)

Collani (IRE) *M Nigge* a66 74
2 b c Aussie Rules(USA) Les Planches (Tropular)
8354a[9]

College Doll *Christine Dunnett* a57 51
4 ch f Piccolo Southwarknewsflash (Danetime (IRE))
5499[7] 5930[4] *6651[2]* 7454[11] *7969[6] (8050) 8370[4]*

College Succes (FR) *Robert Collet* a69 77
2 b g Miesque's Son(USA) Sometimes Perhaps (FR) (Munir)
2558a[6] 5214a[10]

Colliding Worlds (IRE) *John Patrick Shanahan* a75 105
4 b f High Chaparral(IRE) Wee Mad Snout (IRE) (Soviet Star (USA))
153a[9] 743a[7]

Collingbourneducis (IRE) *Michael Dods* a62 72
3 b g Bahamian Bounty Quickstyx (Night Shift (USA))
(7269)

Collodi (GER) *Roger Curtis* a68 94
4 b g Konigstiger(GER) Codera (GER) (Zilzal (USA))
6562[9] 7075[11] (7430) 7608[6]

Collusiva (IRE) *G Botti* a86 95
3 b f Shamardal(USA) Strategic Tactics (IRE) (Bigstone (IRE))
1866a[4] 2697a[8] *7649[11]*

Colmar Kid (IRE) *Richard Hannon Snr* a80 81
3 b c Choisir(AUS) Roselyn (Efisio)
1770[10]

Colonel Joan (USA) *Eoin Harty* 107
2 b f Colonel John(USA) Live 'n Laugh (USA) (Dixieland Band (USA))
7690a[3]

Colonel Mak *David Barron* a86 111
6 br g Makbul Colonel's Daughter (Colonel Collins (USA))
1232[13] 1537[18] 1720[7] 2207[14] 2460[6] (4812) 5009[2] 6621[25] 6685[3]

Colonial Flag (USA) *Michael Matz* 105
4 bb f Pleasant Tap(USA) Silk N' Sapphire (USA) (Smart Strike (CAN))
6454a[2] 7562a[9]

Color Code (FR) *S Wattel* a67 68
2 ch c Desert Prince(IRE) Chatcat (SWI) (Brief Truce (USA))
5362a[4] 5848a[4] 7568a[5]

Colorful Notion (IRE) *Mme J Bidgood* a87 85
4 b f Danehill Dancer(IRE) Red Yellow Blue (USA) (Sky Classic (CAN))
3969a[9]

Color Shades *Clive Cox* a68 68
3 ch f Galileo(IRE) Red Yellow Blue (USA) (Sky Classic (CAN))
1803[4] 2127[5] 2602[7]

Colourbearer (IRE) *Milton Bradley* a79 61
6 ch g Pivotal Centifolia (FR) (Kendor (FR))
76[4] (214) 493[8] 760[6] 831[2] 898[4] (1102) 1430[4] 1665[4] 2781[11] 3247[8] 3949[12] 4837[10] 5817[6] 7801[8] 8030[2] 8128[7]

Colour Blue (IRE) *W McCreery* 88
2 b f Holy Roman Emperor(IRE) Catch The Blues (IRE) (Bluebird (USA))
3868a[4] 6881a[4]

Colour My World *Ed McMahon* a43 60
3 gr g With Approval(CAN) Nadeszhda (Nashwan (USA))
6166[5] 6781[4]

Colours Of Nature *Eric Alston* 57
3 b g Lucky Story(USA) Sweetly Sharp (IRE) (Daggers Drawn (USA))
4544[14] 5704[9] 5878[13]

Colour Vision (FR) *Saeed bin Suroor* a121 118
5 gr g Rainbow Quest(USA) Give Me Five (GER) (Monsun (GER))
2810[7] 3483[4] 4919[7] 5724[6] 6349[5]

Columbian Roulette (IRE) *Charles Hills* a58 42
2 b c Bushranger(IRE) Rainbow Lyrics (IRE) (Rainbow Quest (USA))
7501[6] 7654[5] 7818[10] 8040[2]

Comadoir (IRE) *Jo Crowley* a64 68
7 ch g Medecis Hymn Of The Dawn (USA) (Phone Trick (USA))
750[6] 1783[12] 3051[6] 7124[12] 8244[6]

Comanchero (IRE) *Andrew Balding* a60 3
2 b c Camacho Trempjane (Lujain (USA))
7251[9] 7766[12] 7971[7]

Combat Zone (IRE) *Mario Hofer* a88 111
7 b g Refuse To Bend(IRE) Zeiting (IRE) (Zieten (USA))
2202a[3] 3612a[8] 4333a[4] 5940a[7] 6451a[9] 7053a[3] (7968a)

Combustible (IRE) *John Stimpson* a78 81
3 b f Halling(USA) Jazz Baby (IRE) (Fasliyev (USA))
148[6] 964[4] 1150[2] (1202) 4145[2] (5096) 6642[13] 7297[4]

Comedy House *Michael Madgwick* a69 64
5 b g Auction House(USA) Kyle Akin (Vettori (IRE))
343[2] 668[4] 1466[6] 1899[6] 3985[2] (4754) 5231[6] 6458[5] 8447[4]

Come Here Yew (IRE) *Declan Carroll* 80
5 ch g Refuse To Bend(IRE) Red Zinger (USA) (Red Ransom (USA))
1390[5] 2402[3] 3065[4] 3726[7] 4782[8] (5048) 5560[3]

Come Hither *John Norton* a43 67
4 b f Pastoral Pursuits Stolen Glance (Mujahid (USA))
5840[13] 6518[16]

Come On Blue Chip (IRE) *Paul D'Arcy* a100 95
4 b g Holy Roman Emperor(IRE) Rapid Action (USA) (Quest For Fame)
945[10] 1501[7] (2101) 2728[2] 3157[2] 3832[5] 4280[2] 4979[2] 5723[8] 6927[6] 7641[6] (7906)

Come On Dave (IRE) *David Nicholls* a69 80
4 b g Red Clubs(IRE) Desert Sprite (IRE) (Tagula (IRE))
1253[2] 1649[10] 2031[7] 2459[11] 3331[8] 4588[4] 5148[3] 5579[3] 6388[9] 8319[10]

Come On Flo *Michael Mullineaux*
3 b f Avonbridge Nefeli (First Trump)
5301[6] 5942[11] 6806[8]

Come On Lila *Alex Hales* 30
2 b f Dutch Art Exchanging Glances (Diktat)
3986[14] 6589[10] 7078[8]

Come On Sunshine *Richard Fahey* 68
2 b c Authorized(IRE) Tagula Sunrise (IRE) (Tagula (IRE))
6330[9] 6829[15] 7332[4]

Cometography (IRE) *Lawrence Mullaney* a65 54
4 b g Teofilo(IRE) Halle Bop (Dubai Millennium)
3252[6] 6598[10]

Come To Heel (IRE) *David Wachman* 105
2 ch f Elnadim(USA) Give A Whistle (IRE) (Mujadil (USA))
(5771a) 6836[4]

Comfort And Joy (IRE) *Lee Carter* a19
3 b f Byron Dodona (Lahib (USA))
7781[9]

Comical *George Moore* a52 45
4 b g Dubai Destination(USA) Amusing Time (IRE) (Sadler's Wells (USA))
2886[11] 3199[7]

Comino (IRE) *Kevin Ryan* 81
2 b g Tagula(IRE) Malta (USA) (Gone West (USA))
(6206) 7026[12] 7529[7]

Commanche *Chris Dwyer* a79 86
4 ch g Sleeping Indian Happy Memories (IRE) (Thatching)
199[3] 1316[3] 1475[2] 1985[6] 2516[3] (2949) (3431) 4120[3] 4494[7] 4863[2] 5219[3] 5489[3] 6067[5] 6309[2] 6699[5] 7080[5] (7427) 7776[5] 8088[8] 8181[9] 8305[4] 8455[12]

Commanche Raider (IRE) *Michael Dods* a57 78
6 b g Tale Of The Cat(USA) Alsharq (IRE) (Machiavellian (USA))
1692[16] 2275[12] 2702[4] 3069[8] 3569[4] 4051[5] 4814[6] 5470[2] 5973[7] 6471[5] 6757[12] 7030[8] 7599[3]

Commandable (AUS) *Ian Semple* a55
9 b g Commands(AUS) Achievable (AUS) (Waajib)
8352[2]

Commander (USA) *Troy Taylor* a106
5 b g Broken Vow(USA) Pout (USA) (Deputy Minister (CAN))
7687a[8]

Commanding Force *John Bridger* a17 25
2 b g Authorized(IRE) Ghazal (USA) (Gone West (USA))
4631[14] 5443[11] 6460[10] 7087[6] 7442[11]

Commandingpresence (USA) *John Bridger* a65 75
7 bb m Thunder Gulch(USA) Sehra (USA) (Silver Hawk (USA))
(1929) 2530[6] 2588[4] 3181[7] 3498[4] 4385[9] (4999) 5104[7] 5447[6] 5701[7] 6255[3] 6412[6] 6929[6] 7432[11]

Commando Cat (FR) *P Nicot* a75
6 b g Munaafis(USA) Coopina (FR) (Dear Doctor (FR))
648a[8]

Commend *Sir Michael Stoute* a80 92
4 ch g Pivotal Reputable (Medicean)
2422[7] 3019[6] 3697[5] 4280[4] 4923[10]

Commerce *Dai Burchell* a43 70
6 b m Trade Fair Well Away (IRE) (Sadler's Wells (USA))
704[5] 974[7] 1350[8]

Commercial (IRE) *Jamie Osborne* a62 28
5 br g Kodiac Call Collect (IRE) (Houmayoun (FR))
(220) 630[2] 737[8]

Commissar *Ian Williams* a79 76
4 b g Soviet Star(USA) Sari (Faustus (USA))
2813[9] 3961[5] 5006[3] 5742[8] 6667[6] (7439) ◆ 7840[5]

Commissioned (IRE) *Mark Johnston* 104
3 b g Authorized(IRE) Zelda (IRE) (Caerleon (USA))
3902[2] (5469) (7242) ◆

Commitment *Neil Mulholland* 92
4 b g Motivator Courting (Pursuit Of Love)
1673[13]

Common Cents *Ronald Harris* a70 63
4 ch g Pivotal Small Change (IRE) (Danzig (USA))
(1078) 1351[12] 2780[8]

Common Courtesy *John Butler* a60
3 b f Motivator Crystal Swan (IRE) (Dalakhani (IRE))
1089[6] 4152[10] 5234[13]

Common Touch (IRE) *Willie Musson* a101 96
5 ch g Compton Place Flying Finish (FR) (Priolo (USA))
2585[7] 3060[13] 3538[6] 4258[7] 4744[7] 5285[9] 5533[13] (6988) 7368[19] (7769) 7991[4]

Communicator *Andrew Balding* a95 102
5 b g Motivator Goodie Twosues (Fraam)
2212[3] 3559[11] 4060[17] 5513[4] 7823[5]

Community (USA) *Jamie Osborne* a67 59
5 b f Proud Citizen(USA) Rimini Road (USA) (Dynaformer (USA))
205[5] 347[8]

Commute *D Smaga* 100
3 b f Rail Link Zorleni (Zafonic (USA))
5315a[5] 6031a[5] 7891a[11]

Company Secretary (USA) *Jo Hughes* 24
2 gr c Awesome Again(CAN) Maria Elena (USA) (El Prado (IRE))
5442[10] 6513[9]

Compassion *Emma Lavelle* a38 60
5 b f Tiger Hill(IRE) Windmill (Ezzoud (IRE))
7539[9] 8027[7] 8129[12]

Complexity *Seamus Mullins* a62 62
3 b g Multiplex Asinara (GER) (Big Shuffle (USA))
1714[9] 3945[13] 8028[3] 8187[4]

Complicator *Kevin Ryan* 59
3 br g Pastoral Pursuits Thara'A (IRE) (Desert Prince (IRE))
1114[7] 1566[5] 1764[3]

Complicit (IRE) *Paul Cole* a95 95
2 b c Captain Rio Molomo (Barathea (IRE))
3752a[6] (4539) 6958[2] (8018) (8143a)

Complimentor (IRE) *X Thomas-Demeaulte* a104 104
3 ch c Acclamation Lovely Blossom (FR) (Spinning World (USA))
999a[2] 3455[15]

Compton *Robert Cowell* a73 102
4 ch g Compton Place Look So (Efisio)
1672[6] 2366[7] 2868[7] 3249[8] 3825[5] 4744[29] 5838[14] 6526[6] 7123[11] 7313[7]

Compton Albion (IRE) *Jeremy Gask* a57 48
3 ch f Compton Place Yomalo (IRE) (Woodborough (USA))
197[5] 3246[14] 4607[3] 5067[2] 5890[6] 6651[4]

Compton Bird *Hans Adielsson* a67 69
4 b f Motivator Noble Peregrine (Lomond (USA))
903[13] 3399[9] 3687[3] 5429[3] (6137) 6398[9] 6558[6] 6802[4] 6933[2] (7091) 7321[5]

Compton Crofter *Hans Adielsson* a52 52
4 ch g Sleeping Indian Crofters Ceilidh (Scottish Reel)
226[8] 441[2] 631[6] 725[5]

Compton Heights *Jim Goldie* 68
4 ch g Compton Place Harrken Heights (IRE) (Belmez (USA))
1392[6] 1687[4] 2218[4] 2632[7] 3283[7] 4582[5] 4821[8] 5336[7] 6053[2] 6687[4] 6878[2] (6916) 7148[7]

Compton Prince *Milton Bradley* a73 69
4 ch g Compton Place Malelane (IRE) (Prince Sabo)
3051[9] 3268[3] 3499[4] 3949[14] 5220[5] 6324[9] (6901) 7862[10] 8035[4]

Compton Rainbow *Hans Adielsson* a89 60
4 b f Exceed And Excel(AUS) Rainbow Goddess (Rainbow Quest (USA))
(90) (421) 601[2] (980) 1544[5] 2085[8]

Compton Silver *Paul Fitzsimons* a62
3 ch g Haafhd Anna Oleanda (IRE) (Old Vic)
129[6] 977[6] (1210) 1349[5] 3495[5] 3621[6] 5935[11] 6610[9] 7124[11] 8446[9]

Comptonspirit *Brian Baugh* a29 78
9 ch m Compton Place Croeso Cynnes (Most Welcome)
1976[3] 2703[8] 3078[8] 3920[2] (4197) 4369[4] 5148[5] 6096[5]

Compton Target (IRE) *Milton Bradley* a61 55
4 b g Strategic Prince Tarakana (USA) (Shahrastani (USA))
42[2] 117[3] 349[8] 441[5] 537[6] 1657[8] 1951[13]

Comrade Bond *Mark H Tompkins* a77 82
5 ch g Monsieur Bond(IRE) Eurolink Cafe (Grand Lodge (USA))
1913[4] 2450[8] 2665[10] 3741[3] 4864[5] 6571[3] 7123[9] 7452[4] 8122[4]

Con Artist (IRE) *Saeed bin Suroor* a110 108
6 b g Invincible Spirit(IRE) Hoodwink (IRE) (Selkirk (USA))
241a[6] 463a[2] (742a) 871a[2]

Conas Ata Tu *Derek Shaw* a54
4 b f Medicean Sociable (Danehill (USA))
590[4] 706[5] 815[6] 1151[4] 1298[11] 1657[7]

Concave (CAN) *Doug O'Neill* a104
2 b f Colonel John(USA) Galadriel (CAN) (Ascot Knight (CAN))
7707a[9]

Concise *Ed Dunlop* a90 100
3 b f Lemon Drop Kid(USA) Cut Short (USA) (Diesis)
1546[3] 2049[8] 2412[4]

Concordat *S Seemar* a83 84
5 ch g Selkirk(USA) African Peace (USA) (Roberto (USA))
246a[12]

Concordia Notte (IRE) *Violet M Jordan* a50 56
4 b f Elusive City(USA) Laylati (IRE) (Green Desert (USA))
733[11] 1450[7]

Concrete Mac *Hughie Morrison* a64 71
2 b g Mastercraftsman(IRE) Merry Diva (Bahamian Bounty)
4347[10] 4708[2] 7218[11] 7879[5] 8024[6]

Conduct (IRE) *William Haggas* 111
6 gr g Selkirk(USA) Coventina (IRE) (Daylami (IRE))
5283[5] 6332[3] (7823)

Conducting *Gay Kelleway* a74 69
5 b g Oratorio(IRE) Aiming (Highest Honor (FR))
(73) (403) 639[3] 720[4] 1010[2] 1176[5] 2710[12] (3410) 3997[2] 4350[4] 5042a[12] (6114) 6473[5] 6759[3] 7346[13] 8335[5]

Confessional *Tim Easterby* a92 110
6 b g Dubawi(IRE) Golden Nun (Bishop Of Cashel)
150a[11] 244a[13] 1234[5] 1672[4] 2152[6] 2865[9] 3334[9] 3776[12] 5545[17] (6190) 6391[18] 6830[4] 7208[18] 7373[5] 7527[11]

Confidential Creek *Ollie Pears* a67 62
3 b g Sakhee's Secret Upstream (Prince Sabo)
1651[2] 1762[3] 2336[4] (2996) 3594[3] 4558[3] 7848[10] 8351[4]

Confirmed *Sean Curran* a60 70
4 b g Authorized(IRE) Vas Y Carla (USA) (Gone West (USA))
403[9] 600[9] 722[8] 907[8] 3657[14] 5098[8] 6033[8]

Confiture *Michael Blanshard* a63
2 b f Duke Of Marmalade(IRE) Sandtime (IRE) (Green Desert (USA))
8124[9] 8328[3]

Conflicting *Richard Hannon Snr* a62 76
2 b c Kyllachy Piper's Ash (USA) (Royal Academy (USA))
7125[2] 7852[5] 8113[5]

Confucius Legend (IRE) *Jim Boyle* a60 17
2 b g Oratorio(IRE) Midnight Partner (IRE) (Marju (IRE))
7320[8] 8389[5]

Confusing *David O'Meara* a57 77
3 b f Refuse To Bend(IRE) Ruse (Diktat)
2480[5] 2916[6] 3445[3] 3629[3] 5342[2] 5425[3] (6301)

Conjuror's Bluff *Frederick Watson* 51
5 b g Tiger Hill(IRE) Portmeirion (Polish Precedent (USA))
2163[8] 3203[7] 3395[4] 3546[5] 4577[6] 5783[6] 6083[4]

Con Leche *Scott Dixon* a59 11
3 br g Milk It Mick Capital Lass (Forzando)
438[2] 686[4] 828[5] 1458[11]

Connaught Water (IRE) *Jonathan Portman* 56
2 b c Aussie Rules(USA) Chingford (IRE) (Redback)
2359[8] 3174[5] 3631[5] 6111[9]

Connexion Francais *Tim Etherington* a24 40
2 b f Lucarno(USA) Sainte Gig (FR) (Saint Cyrien (FR))
5983[10] 6523[13] 7934[9]

Connishka *Alan Bailey* a50 46
4 gr f Verglas(IRE) Profit Alert (IRE) (Alzao (USA))
158[6]

Cono Zur (FR) *Ruth Carr* a74 81
6 b g Anabaa(USA) Alaskan Idol (USA) (Carson City (USA))
1354[5] 1569[7] 1827[9] 2278[2] 2406[3] 2659[11] 3027[3] 3506[2] 3895[10] 4373[2] (4482) (4609) 5332[8] 6126[11] 6562[8] 7152[13]

Conquerant *Charlie Appleby* a72 51
2 ch c Dubawi(IRE) The World (Dubai Destination (USA))
7339[6] 7936[2]

Conquestadim *Hughie Morrison* a71 66
3 b c Elnadim(USA) Conquestadora (Hernando (FR))
1727[4] 2157[4] 3435[3] 5762[11] 6202[8]

Conquest Titan (USA) *Mark Casse* a95
2 bb c Birdstone(USA) Miner's Secret (USA) (Mineshaft (USA))
7711a[13]

Conry (IRE) *Ian Williams* a79 80
7 ch g Captain Rio Altizaf (Zafonic (USA))
6384[9] 6648[6] 6871[9] 7699[3] 7820[11] 8350[7]

Conserve (IRE) *Amy Weaver* a76 76
3 b f Duke Of Marmalade(IRE) Minor Point (Selkirk (USA))
5071[2] 5678[2] 5942[5] 7546[4] 8444[3]

Consign *Jeremy Noseda* a77 100
3 b g Dutch Art Maid To Dance (Pyramus (USA))
1636[7] 2727[3] (3062) (4124) 4642[5] 5437[3] (5987) 6650[3] (6993) 7696[9]

Consistant *Brian Baugh* a61 71
5 b g Reel Buddy(USA) Compact Disc (IRE) (Royal Academy (USA))
705[11] 1525[7] 3068[11] 3392[2] 3949[4] 8306[5]

Constant Dream *James Given* a65 44
3 br f Kheleyf(USA) Pizzicato (Statoblest)
1742[6] 2512[2] 2996[6] 4892[9] 5265[6]

Constantine *Richard Hannon Snr* a81 74
2 b g Holy Roman Emperor(IRE) Whatami (Daylami (IRE))
2543[5] 3155[4] (3413) 5927[3] 6645[9] 7463[7] (7892)

Contesurmoi (FR) *A Bonin* a71 62
3 b g One Cool Cat(USA) Ymlaen (IRE) (Desert Prince (IRE))
2335a[0]

Continental Divide (IRE) *Jamie Osborne* a67 66
3 ch g Kheleyf(USA) Leenane (IRE) (Grand Lodge (USA))
350[3] 1178[2] (1522) 2325[5] 3735[6] 5789[8] 6657[9] 7325[6] 7666[3]

Continental Drift (USA) *Roger Charlton* a76
2 bb f Smart Strike(CAN) Intercontinental (Danehill (USA))
(7294) ◆

Continuum *Lady Cecil* 98
4 bb g Dansili Clepsydra (Sadler's Wells (USA))
1837[2] (2589) (3370) 4020[2] 5475[2] 6591[6] 7174[6]

Contradict *Mick Channon* a72 88
3 b f Raven's Pass(USA) Acts Of Grace (USA) (Bahri (USA))
2017[3] ◆ (2390) 2586[4] 3614a[9] 4541[5] 7822[16]

Contributer (IRE) *Ed Dunlop* a85 107
3 b c High Chaparral(IRE) Serisia (FR) (Exit To Nowhere (USA))
(1667) 2211[2] 2620[2] 3523[4]

Controversy *Saeed bin Suroor* a77 78
3 ch f Elusive Quality(USA) Forum Floozie (NZ) (Danasinga (AUS))
3136[6] (3469) 4015[4] 4678[5]

Conversational (IRE) *Mick Channon* a72 73
3 b f Thousand Words Alpine Flair (IRE) (Tirol)
(8140)

Conversing (USA) *Mark Johnston* a57 59
3 ch c Raven's Pass(USA) Mini Chat (USA) (Deputy Minister (CAN))
757[6] 910[2] 1098[3] 1314[3] 1425[4] 2124[2] 2341[2]

Cookie Crumbles (IRE) *Adrian McGuinness* a55 60
6 ch m Bahamian Bounty Diaspora (IRE) (Kris)
7148[6]

Cool And Clear (IRE) *Pat Eddery* a26 50
3 b g One Cool Cat(USA) Manon's Song (IRE) (Sadler's Wells (USA))
1289[7] 2950[14] 3859[10] 4378[8] 6043[4] 7035[8] 7104[8]

Cool Athlete (IRE) *David Marnane* a72 67
7 b g Bahri(USA) Perfect Fun (Marju (IRE))
8012a[4]

Cool Bahamian (IRE) *Eve Johnson Houghton* 92
2 b g Bahamian Bounty Keritana (FR) (One Cool Cat (USA))
(2260) 2863[5] (3890) 4486[4] 5028[3] 5952[2] 6351[5]

Cool Hand Jake *Ben De Haan* a71 58
7 b g Storming Home Monawara (IRE) (Namaqualand (USA))
5135[2] 6398[10] 7740[6]

Cool Hand Luke (IRE) *Ian Williams* a71 56
4 br g Le Vie Dei Colori Thelma Louise (IRE) (Desert Style (IRE))
2629[4]

Coolibah (IRE) *Charles O'Brien* 91
3 b f Peintre Celebre(USA) Honour Bright (IRE) (Danehill (USA))
1862a[6] 7404a[11]

Cool Kid *Ian Williams* a61 60
5 b g Iceman Clashfern (Smackover)
9[2]

Coolnagree (IRE) *W McCreery* 101
4 gr f Dark Angel(IRE) Win Cash (IRE) (Alhaarth (IRE))
3263a[9] 3964a[8]

Cool Sky *William Knight* a88 89
4 b g Millkom Intersky High (USA) (Royal Anthem (USA))
(144) 208[2] 1037[6] 1290[2] 1728[4] 2587[5] (3344)

Cool Strike (UAE) *Alex Hales* a4 96
7 b g Halling(USA) Velour (Mtoto)
5356[10]

Copano Jingu (JPN) *Toru Miya* 100
8 bb h Agnes Tachyon(JPN) Wedding Oak (JPN) (Tony Bin)
1868a[17]

Copper Canyon *Vanja Sandrup* a84 88
5 ch g Haafhd Deep Ravine (USA) (Gulch (USA))
2146a[4]

Copper Cavalier *Robert Cowell* a32
2 ch c Haafhd Elle Crystal (Mozart (IRE))
6776[8] 6981[5] 7327[9]

Copper Dock (IRE) *T G McCourt* a84 63
9 b g Docksider(USA) Sundown (Polish Precedent (USA))
679a[6]

Copper Falls *Brendan Powell* a56 64
4 b f Trade Fair Strat's Quest (Nicholas (USA))
1738a[5]

Copper Leyf *Jeremy Gask* a49 18
3 ch g Kheleyf(USA) Silver Quest (Rainbow Quest (USA))
356[6] ◆ 2347[6] 3247[14] 3888[11] 4410[4] 4836[12] 5230[6] 6343[8]

Copper Rag *J S Moore* a40 39
3 ch g Kirkwall Pajada (Bertolini (USA))
4423[5] 4996[U]

Copper To Gold *Robin Bastiman* a29 51
4 ch f Avonbridge Faithful Beauty (IRE) (Last Tycoon)
2006[P] 4050[4] 4892[3] 5331[9] 6323[4] 7454[6]

Copper Trade *Eve Johnson Houghton* a49 67
3 b g Trade Fair Madrigale (Averti (IRE))
4176[3] 4774[3] 5277[8] 6074[3] 6323[2] 7092[7]

Copperwood *Lee Carter* a80 84
8 ch g Bahamian Bounty Sophielu (Rudimentary (USA))
25[4] 79[5] 239[8] 415[9] 593[4] 644[5] 850[4] 889[6] 1081[3] 1203[2] 1334[3] 1514[9] 1827[11] 2163[2] 2315[4] (2807) 3081[10] (3193) 3570[5] 3683[4] 4007[2] (4207) 4859[13] 4923[13] 5014[15] 5613[5] 5987[8] 6538[8] 7306[3] 7462[12] 6801[22] 7024[12] 8244[4] (8335) 8450[5]
Coprah *Cathrine Erichsen* a6 100
5 b g Bertolini(USA) Oatcake (Selkirk (USA))
4936a[4] 5809a[3]
Copybook *Mark Johnston* a49 62
3 b f Singspiel(IRE) Billbill (USA) (Storm Cat (USA))
4157[3] 6166[2] 6847[6] 7510[6]
Coquet *Hughie Morrison* a79 110
4 b f Sir Percy One So Marvellous (Nashwan (USA))
2012[6] 4059[8] 5683[6] 6329[8]
Coralhasi (FR) *Mlle I Gallorini* 81
11 b g Kahyasi Coral Bird (FR) (Deep Roots (IRE))
7060a[10]
Coral Mist *Charles Hills* 98
2 ch f Bahamian Bounty Treasure Trove (USA) (The Minstrel (CAN))
4877[3] ◆ (6160) (6622)
Coral Sands (IRE) *Alan Swinbank* a49 69
5 bl g Footstepsinthesand Daziyra (IRE) (Doyoun) (2042) (2406) 2705[8] 5264[5]
Cordial *John Gosden* a72 65
2 b f Oasis Dream Mirabilis (USA) (Lear Fan (USA))
4491[8] 6140[11] 6691[3]
Cordite (IRE) *Michael Appleby* 94
2 ch c Footstepsinthesand Marion Haste (IRE) (Ali-Royal (IRE))
6234[8] 6517[2] (7271) 7534[4]
Core Element (IRE) *P J Prendergast* a84 94
6 b m Consolidator(USA) Millstream (USA) (Dayjur (USA))
3263a[12] 3845a[20]
Corncockle *David O'Meara* a82 81
2 b f Invincible Spirit(IRE) Alovera (IRE) (King's Best (USA))
2204[5] (2419) 2944a[6] 3459[22] 4019[10] 6376[6] 7127[2] 8203[4] 8442[6]
Corniche (FR) *David Elsworth* a64
3 b f Manduro(GER) Halska (Unfuwain (USA))
5119a[9]
Cornish Beau (IRE) *Dr Richard Newland* a70 65
6 ch g Pearl Of Love(IRE) Marimar (IRE) (Grand Lodge (USA))
(3168) 3579[2] 3721[2]
Cornish Path *Henry Candy* a72 77
2 b f Champs Elysees Quintrell (Royal Applause)
3175[6] (3958) 4717[2] 5536[5] 6326[3] 6839[6]
Corn Maiden *Lydia Pearce* a58 62
4 b f Refuse To Bend(IRE) Namat (IRE) (Daylami (IRE))
169[9] 539[2] (714) 888[4] (1916) 2642[7] 2968[4] 5803[4] 6216[6] (7090) 7628[8] 8270[7] 8449[10]
Cornrow *John Gosden* a94 61
3 ch c New Approach(IRE) Needlecraft (IRE) (Mark Of Esteem (IRE))
5495[6] (6133) (6694)
Corn Snow (USA) *Mark Johnston* a74 81
3 b c Raven's Pass(USA) Zofzig (USA) (Danzig (USA))
(1185) 1614[6] (1965) 2272[5] 2627[3] 2876[2] 3117[9] 7224[7] 7491[9]
Cornus *Alan McCabe* a66 71
11 ch g Inchinor Demerger (USA) (Distant View (USA))
77[6] 436[6]
Corporal Maddox *Ronald Harris* a93 90
6 b g Royal Applause Noble View (USA) (Distant View (USA))
60[5] 2265[4] 2618[11] 3019[9] 4243[5] 4494[6] 4730[3] ◆ 5219[8] (5775a) 6161[2] 6352[8] 6831[6] 7464[5] 7992[3] 8127[2] 8344[6]
Correggio *Micky Hammond* 80
3 ch g Bertolini(USA) Arian Da (Superlative)
1649[3] 2121[2] 2507[3] 2960[5] 3650[2] 4508[4] ◆ (5146) 5835[5] 6563[3]
Corres (IRE) *Paul Fitzsimons* a53 73
6 b g Peintre Celebre(USA) Kesh Kumay (IRE) (Danehill (USA))
2[5] 343[11] 724[12]
Correspondent *Brian Meehan* a89 106
3 ch c Exceed And Excel(AUS) Indian Love Bird (Efisio)
1677[4] 2021[11] 2453[6] (3803) 4284[4] 4922[13] (5510) 5992[11] 6595[6]
Corrib (IRE) *Bryn Palling* a59 60
10 b m Lahib(USA) Montana Miss (IRE) (Earl Of Barking (IRE))
98[7]
Cortogna (USA) *N Clement* a81 75
3 bb f Belong To Me(USA) Gingivere (USA) (Chester House (USA))
5119a[5]
Corton Lad *Keith Dalgleish* a78 82
3 b g Refuse To Bend(IRE) Kelucia (IRE) (Grand Lodge (USA))
2167[4] 2799[6] (3202) 4100[2] 4294[2] 4446[5] (4995) 5888[3] 6626[8] 7239[3] 7627[4] 7794[3]
Cosette (IRE) *Henry Candy* 63
2 b f Champs Elysees Luanas Pearl (IRE) (Bahri (USA))
4483[12] 6281[4] 6954[4]
Coside (USA) *E Leon Penate* 87
5 rg c Cozzene(USA) Fairy Heights (IRE) (Fairy King (USA))
6252a[6]
Cosimo de Medici *Hughie Morrison* a90 90
6 b g Medicean Wish (Danehill (USA))
1733[6] 2587[2] 3560[13] 3959[8] 4643[3] 5288[6] (5868) 6646[4] 7193[19] 7757[2]
Cosmic Chatter *David Barron* 102
3 b g Paris House Paradise Eve (Bahamian Bounty)
2400[3] ◆ 3348[12] 3584[3] 4247[4] 5769[7]
Cosmic Curious (GER) *Lady Cecil* 85
3 gr c Rock Of Gibraltar(IRE) Cosmic Fire (FR) (Dalakhani (IRE))
4223[4] 4978[2]
Cosmic Dream *Garry Moss* a27 31
3 b g Refuse To Bend(IRE) Cosmic Case (Casteddu)
1781[8] 2512[9]
Cosmic Halo *Richard Fahey* a74 85
4 ch f Halling(USA) Cosmic Case (Casteddu)
107[2] (2311) 2976[8] 4015[5] 4584[2] 4995[2] 5521[9] 5706[10] (6236) 6832[8] 7765[12]
Cosmic Moon *Richard Fahey* 66
5 b f Doyen(IRE) Cosmic Case (Casteddu)
1270[8] 1790[7] 2435[3] 2975[8]
Cosmic Sun *Richard Fahey* a80 80
7 b g Helissio(FR) Cosmic Case (Casteddu)
1273[12] 2369[13] (2706) 3345[9] 4110[4] 4804[7] 5706[3] 6239[3] 6876[2] 7121[3]
Cospirator (IRE) *S Botti* 73
2 b c Ivan Denisovich(IRE) Biz Bar (Tobougg (IRE))
7678a[6]
Cosquillas (IRE) *Mark Johnston* a54
2 b f Selkirk(USA) Crystany (IRE) (Green Desert (USA))
8176[5]
Cosseted *James Fanshawe* 80
3 b f Pivotal Fondled (Selkirk (USA))
2231[9] 2548[2] ◆ 4667[3] (5563) 6531[2] 7470[4]
Costa Del Fortune (IRE) *Paul Morgan* a3 79
4 ch f Heliostatic(IRE) Midris (IRE) (Namid)
8308[12]
Costa Filey *Ed Vaughan* a71 68
2 b g Pastoral Pursuits Cosmic Destiny (IRE) (Soviet Star (USA))
2250[5] 2771[2] 3288[4] 5665[3] 8326[6]
Cote Reveur *Michael Mullineaux* 30
3 b f Croco Rouge(IRE) Reveur (Rossini (USA))
6824[6] 7108[8]
Cottam Maybel *Mel Brittain* 33
4 b f Doyen(IRE) Northern Bird (Interrex (CAN))
4968[6]
Cottam Stella *John Wainwright* a11 26
5 br f Diktat Flower Breeze (USA) (Rahy (USA))
7345[10] 8141[6]
Cottesmore (USA) *Richard Ford* a83 40
4 b g Medaglia d'Oro(USA) Racing Heart (USA) (Fusaichi Pegasus (USA))
7396[9] 7778[12] 8318[2]
Cotton Club (IRE) *Rod Millman* 65
2 b g Amadeus Wolf Slow Jazz (USA) (Chief's Crown (USA))
3574[5] 3853[5]
Cotton King *Lady Herries* a84 74
6 b g Dubawi(IRE) Spinning The Yarn (Barathea (IRE))
1670[4] 2205[6] 2545[10]
Could Be (IRE) *David Simcock* a76 73
3 b c Sakhee(USA) Catch Us (FR) (Selkirk (USA))
895[7] 1089[2] 1478[4] 1898[2] 2641[3] 3402[3] (3907)
Couloir Extreme (IRE) *Gary Moore* a76 83
3 gr g Verglas(IRE) Chica Roca (USA) (Woodman (USA))
1770[3] 2017[4] 2786[2] (3418) (3636) 4950[12] 6136[6]
Coulsty (IRE) *Richard Hannon Snr* 98
2 b c Kodiac Hazium (IRE) (In The Wings)
(2712) ◆ 3481[11] 4768[2] 5313a[3] 5656[2] 6328[7]
Count Ceprano (IRE) *Lydia Pearce* a51 52
9 b g Desert Prince(IRE) Camerlata (Common Grounds)
110[7] 147[5] 709[8] 927[6] 1120[4] 7201[3] 7963[8]
Counterglow (IRE) *Mahmood Al Zarooni* a103 99
4 b g Echo Of Light Quintellina (Robellino (USA))
363a[3]
Countess Lovelace *Pat Phelan* a66
3 b f Byron Muwasim (USA) (Meadowlake (USA))
373[2] 815[4] 2325[8] 8388[11] 8443[5]
Countess Lupus (IRE) *Lisa Williamson* a42 44
2 b f Amadeus Wolf Papaha (FR) (Green Desert (USA))
1573[9] 1946[4] 2189[10] 3391[10] 4952[4] 5229[2] 5964[4] 6511[3] 8133[8]
Count Of Limonade (IRE) *A P O'Brien* a102 110
3 b c Duke Of Marmalade(IRE) Hoity Toity (Darshaan)
2687a[3] (3844a)
Country Blue (FR) *Mrs A Malzard* 23
4 bl c Country Reel(USA) Exica (FR) (Exit To Nowhere (USA))
1312a[7] 1739a[8] 5327a[7] 7143a[3]
Country Drive (USA) *Ed Dunlop* 71
2 ch f Shirocco(GER) Call Mariah (USA) (Dixie Union (USA))
5529[5] ◆
Countryman *Amy Weaver* a75 78
3 b g Pastoral Pursuits Baileys Silver (USA) (Marlin (USA))
1471[6] 2209[6] 2593[4] 3279[5] (4710) 4998[2] 7792[7]
Country Western *Charles Hills* a86 95
3 b c Oasis Dream Musical Horizon (USA) (Distant View (USA))
(1243) (1645) 2024[4] 2661[5] 3117[3] 3563[4] 4859[10] 6826[4]
Countrywide Flame *John Quinn* a63 97
5 b g Haafhd Third Party (Terimon)
2149[5]
Coup De Grace (IRE) *Pat Phelan* a68 63
4 b g Elusive City(USA) No Way (IRE) (Rainbows For Life (CAN))
(12)
Coup De Theatre (FR) *P Van De Poele* a97 107
4 ch c Gold Away(IRE) Storma (FR) (Starborough)
1945a[6] 2897a[11] 3851a[11]
Courageous (IRE) *Milton Bradley* a92 81
7 ch g Refuse To Bend(IRE) Bella Bella (IRE) (Sri Pekan (USA))
372[9] 583[10] 719[2] 924[9] 1058[6] 1286[8] 1902[8] 2096[11] 2364[7] 3270[7] 3660[8] 4423[7] 4660[5] 5166[7] 5221[5] 6157[5]
Courageous Rock (USA) *Ed Vaughan* a73 73
2 bb c Rock Hard Ten(USA) To The Brim (CAN) (Ascot Knight (CAN))
6330[5] 7442[4]
Courcy (FR) *J-C Rouget* a102 77
3 b c Mizzen Mast(USA) Insan Mala (IRE) (Bahhare (USA))
286a[2] 1562a[6]
Court Circle *Rune Haugen* 101
6 ch g Pivotal Noble Lady (Primo Dominie)
462a[11] 661a[13]
Courtesy Call (IRE) *Nicky Henderson* a88 93
4 br g Manduro(GER) Three Wrens (IRE) (Second Empire (IRE))
3560[11] 5288[7]
Courtezan *Jamie Osborne*
2 gr f Captain Gerrard(IRE) Ultimate Court (IRE) (Kendor (FR))
3414[12]
Courtland Avenue (IRE) *Jonathan Portman* a30 67
4 b g Kodiac Chingford (IRE) (Redback)
2364[9] 6436[10] 7109[10] 7644[13] 8073[14]
Court Life (IRE) *Ismail Mohammed* 72
3 ch c New Approach(IRE) Tudor Court (IRE) (Cape Cross (IRE))
4022[4]
Court Pastoral *Lady Cecil* 103
3 b f Mount Nelson Teggiano (IRE) (Mujtahid (USA))
(2938) (3976) (5015) 6294a[4] 6764[8]
Court Politics *A Fabre* a71 69
3 b c Sinndar(IRE) Russian Society (Darshaan)
1850a[4]
Cousin Khee *Hughie Morrison* a91 90
6 b g Sakhee(USA) Cugina (Distant Relative)
473[2] ◆ (637) 1884[4] (2369) 2654[6] 3685[3] 4301[7] 5895[2] 6192[7] ◆ 7193[29] 7823[17]
Cowslip *George Moore* a14 61
4 b f Tobougg(IRE) Forsythia (Most Welcome)
3089[11] 3947[6] 5137[3] (5862) 7280[6] 7423[2]
Cozy Tiger (USA) *Willie Musson* a70 48
8 gr g Hold That Tiger(USA) Cozelia (USA) (Cozzene (USA))
343[10] 983[4] 1175[6] 1502[8]
Crackentorp *Tim Easterby* a91 103
8 b g Generous(IRE) Raspberry Sauce (Niniski (USA))
1841[10] 2427[8] 3345[12] 3824[10] 4782[11] 5655[16] 6302[7]
Crackerjack (FR) *D Cruz* a112 105
4 gr g Kahyasi Mikalia (FR) (Kaldoun (FR))
1872a[14]
Cracker Mill *Michael Madgwick* a33
4 b g Act One Linda's Schoolgirl (IRE) (Grand Lodge (USA))
1468[9] 1898[6]
Cracking Choice (IRE) *Michael Dods* a64 67
3 ch g Choisir(AUS) Champagne Cracker (Up And At 'Em)
1566[2] 1791[2] 1988[4] 2317[6] 3198[6] 3779[3] 4544[7] 5265[4] 5485[3] 6176[5] 7077[4]
Cracking Lass (IRE) *Richard Fahey* 103
6 b m Whipper(USA) Lady From Limerick (IRE) (Rainbows For Life (CAN))
1110[4]
Crackos (FR) *F Belmont* 66
3 gr g Sunday Break(JPN) Jenauraisjamaiscru (FR) (Kendor (FR))
2434a[0]
Cradle Of Life (IRE) *Ed Dunlop* 61
2 ch f Notnowcato Pursuit Of Life (Pursuit Of Love)
6828[11] 7532[6]
Crafted (IRE) *Mark Johnston* a42
2 b g Shamardal(USA) Designed (Zamindar (USA))
7328[6] 7766[11]
Craftsman (IRE) *A P O'Brien* 104
2 b c Mastercraftsman(IRE) Weekend Fling (USA) (Forest Wildcat (USA))
(7548a)
Craftsmanship (FR) *Robert Eddery* a64 70
2 ch c Mastercraftsman(IRE) Jennie Jerome (IRE) (Pivotal)
3717[5] 4414[10] 5307[3] 5926[6] 7451[5]
Craftybird *Brett Johnson* a19 24
2 ch f Mastercraftsman(IRE) Tobaranama (IRE) (Sadler's Wells (USA))
5394[14] 6079[9] 6409[8] 6896[8]
Crafty Cruiser (AUS) *Bryce Stanaway* 102
6 ch g Good Journey(USA) Sly One (NZ) (O'Reilly (NZ))
7483a[4] 7760a[13] 7938a[3]
Crafty Exit *William Knight* 67
2 gr c Mastercraftsman(IRE) Demerger (USA) (Distant View (USA))
5718[7]
Crafty Spell *Mark Johnston* 37
2 b f Mastercraftsman(IRE) Isle Of Flame (Shirley Heights)
5983[11] 7061[9]
Crafty Wonder (IRE) *David Evans* a42 24
3 b g Refuse To Bend(IRE) Crafty Fancy (IRE) (Intikhab (USA))
103[10] 237[8]
Craggaknock *Tim Walford* 67
2 b g Authorized(IRE) Goodie Twosues (Fraam)
3810[2] 4925[10]
Crakehall Lad (IRE) *Alan Swinbank* 67
2 ch c Manduro(GER) My Uptown Girl (Dubai Destination (USA))
2793[5] 4044[4] 6175[2] 6628[5] ◆ 7129[7]
Cranach *Tom Keddy* a90 84
4 b g Rail Link Hachita (USA) (Gone West (USA))
(2754) 3692[3] ◆ 4720[P]
Crassula *Paul Fitzsimons* a77 89
5 b f Cacique(IRE) Neath (Rainbow Quest (USA))
2579[5]
Cravat *Ed de Giles* a75 78
4 b g Dubai Destination(USA) Crinolette (IRE) (Sadler's Wells (USA))
1514[6] 1780[5] 2710[3]
Crave *William Jarvis* 63
3 b f Sakhee's Secret Bolsena (USA) (Red Ransom (USA))
2231[8] 2637[2] 3149[2]
Crazee Diamond *Mick Channon* 32
2 b f Rock Of Gibraltar(IRE) Final Dynasty (Komaite (USA))
6789[11]
Crazy Brenda (IRE) *Sylvester Kirk* a19 7
2 b f Amadeus Wolf Glencoe Solas (IRE) (Night Shift (USA))
2805[7] 4154[12] 4880[11] 5350[8] 6131[8]
Crazy Dancer *Richard Guest* a8 21
2 b f Byron Ballet Princess (Muhtarram (USA))
2612[5] 5827[9] 7664[8]
Creative Spirit *David Brown* a15 59
2 ch f Pastoral Pursuits Creative Mind (IRE) (Danehill Dancer (IRE))
2458[8] 2701[5] 3318[8] 4141[6] 6340[7]
Crecora (IRE) *John Joseph Murphy* 55
2 ch c Papal Bull Prima Figlia (IRE) (Inchinor)
7050a[13]
Credit Swap *Michael Wigham* a84 97
8 b g Diktat Locharia (Wolfhound (USA))
6989[6] 7696[10]
Creek Falcon (IRE) *David O'Meara* a73 87
4 b g Elnadim(USA) Jewaar (USA) (Diesis)
217[4] 376[6] 540[8] (1800) 2255[13] (2929) ◆ 4014[7] 4628[9] 6473[6] 6843[3] 7948[4]
Creme Anglaise *Michael Bell* a85 85
5 b f Motivator Reading Habit (USA) (Half A Year (USA))
4878[10] 5283[7] 5795[9] 6433[7] (7656) 8007[5]
Cresta Rise *Alan Bailey* a11
2 br f Authorized(IRE) Cresta Gold (Halling (USA))
7902[10]
Crew Cut (IRE) *Jeremy Gask* a88 92
5 gb g Acclamation Carabine (USA) (Dehere (USA))
121[4] 408[8] (723) (880) 1245[7] 1838[2] 2207[3] 2868[14] 4235[5] (5537) 6621[13] 7368[18]
Cricklewood Green (USA) *Richard Hannon Snr* 85
2 ch g Bob And John(USA) B Berry Brandy (USA) (Event Of The Year (USA))
(3853) (5034)
Crimson Knight *Brian Meehan* 72
5 ch g Zafeen(FR) Kaylianni (Kalanisi (IRE))
2102[3]
Crimson Knot (IRE) *Alan Berry* 86
5 b f Red Ransom(USA) Green Minstrel (FR) (Green Tune (USA))
1253[7] 2476[8] 3331[9] 3561[3] 3769[7] 4613[8] 4821[3] 4954[5] 5266[4] 5579[8]
Crimson Monarch (USA) *Peter Hiatt* a54 51
9 b g Red Ransom(USA) Tolltally Light (USA) (Majestic Light (USA))
100[5] 406[3] 788[6] 846[2] (1022) 1175[5] 1217[7] 1520[10] 1794[3] 2159[6]
Crimson Queen *Roy Brotherton* a75 85
6 b m Red Ransom(USA) Rainbow Queen (Rainbow Quest (USA))
308[8] 481[4] 558[4] 795[6] (3667) 4017[4] 4487[7] 5956[7] (6096)
Crissolo (ITY) *B Grizzetti*
2 b c Red Rocks(IRE) Pesach (IRE) (Indian Danehill (IRE))
7235a[7]
Cristaliyev *David Evans* a65 59
5 b g Fasliyev(USA) Desert Cristal (IRE) (Desert King (IRE))
2345[10] 2918[7] 3246[10] 5097[10] 5818[10] 6038[7] 6901[6] 7323[3]
Cristoforo Colombo (USA) *A P O'Brien* a100 111
3 b c Henrythenavigator(USA) La Traviata (USA) (Johannesburg (USA))
2021[5] 6414a[8] 7227a[7] 7714a[7]
Criteria (IRE) *John Gosden* 75
2 b f Galileo(IRE) Aleagueoftheirown (IRE) (Danehill Dancer (IRE))
6063[4] ◆ 6643[5]
Crius (IRE) *Daniel Kubler* a88 100
4 b c Heliostatic(IRE) Fearless Flyer (IRE) (Brave Act)
1675[22] 2424[11] 2858[12] 3984[4] ◆ 8385[5] ◆
Croeso Mawr *John Spearing* 77
7 ch m Bertolini(USA) Croeso-I-Cymru (Welsh Captain)
2920[6] 3269[6] 6433[6] 7429[7]
Croftamie *Tracy Waggott* a71 58
4 b f Selkirk(USA) Embraced (Pursuit Of Love)
967[7] 1579[5] 1790[6] 2555[4] 3625[13] 5367[6] 5420[6] 5833[14]
Croi An Or (IRE) *T Stack* a97 102
4 b g Windsor Knot(IRE) Exponent (USA) (Exbourne (USA))
1168a[8] 3844a[8] 7388a[4]
Cromwell Rose (IRE) *John Weymes* a40 48
3 ch f Haafhd Bonny Rose (Zaha (CAN))
207[6] 442[7] 848[9] 1764[12]
Cropley (IRE) *Tony Carroll* a62 75
4 gr g Galileo(IRE) Niyla (IRE) (Darshaan)
5542[5]
Croquembouche (IRE) *Ed de Giles* a63 92
4 b g Acclamation Wedding Cake (IRE) (Groom Dancer (USA))
1422[7] 1796[8] 2551[5] 3157[4] (3676) 4366[3] 4908[2] (5348) (6428) 6772[2]
Crossley *Geoffrey Oldroyd* a58 67
4 ch g Monsieur Bond(IRE) Dispol Diamond (Sharpo)
3030[2] 7964[8] 8141[3]
Cross My Heart *William Haggas* a47 70
3 b f Sakhee's Secret Sacre Coeur (Compton Place)
2135[4] 6362[7] 6900[10]
Cross Pattee (IRE) *Ed Vaughan* a72 53
3 b f Oasis Dream Victoria Cross (IRE) (Mark Of Esteem (IRE))
3787[5]
Cross The Boss (IRE) *David O'Meara* a62 64
6 b g Cape Cross(IRE) Lady Salsa (IRE) (Gone West (USA))
1788[2] ◆ 2889[11] 3030[3] 4109[7] 4562[6] 4893[14]

Crowdmania *Mark Johnston* 81
2 ch g Shamardal(USA) Riotous Applause (Royal Applause)
2048[5] ◆ 3295[6] 4231[4] 4618[6] 5083[5] 6065[6] 6865[6]

Crow Down (IRE) *Charles Hills* a76 68
4 b g Oratorio(IRE) Louve Sereine (FR) (Sadler's Wells (USA))
6431[2] *8036[4] (8298)*

Crowley's Law *Tom Dascombe* 79
2 b f Dubawi(IRE) Logic (Slip Anchor)
4702[5] (6512)

Crown Choice *Paul Midgley* a86 89
8 b g King's Best(USA) Belle Allemande (CAN) (Royal Academy (USA))
913[6] 1113[8] 1442[9] 6905[6]

Crowning Star (IRE) *Gay Kelleway* a73 75
4 b g Royal Applause Dossier (Octagonal (NZ))
13[5] 138[7] 478[8] 638[5] 878[13]

Crown Pleasure (IRE) *Clive Brittain* a64 68
2 b f Royal Applause Tarbiyah (Singspiel (IRE))
4215[5] *5131[4]* 7695[12]

Crucis Abbey (IRE) *Mark Brisbourne* a56 54
5 b g Acclamation Golden Ribes (USA) (Charismatic (USA))
42[6] 220[4] 441[9] 900[2] (927) 1093[3] 1222[5] 1473[5] 1893[4] 2072[4] (3910) 4658[2] 5072[10] 5387[4] 5921[4] 6472[6] 6804[6] 6985[2] 7753[7]

Cruck Realta *Mick Channon* 97
3 b f Sixties Icon Wansdyke Lass (Josr Algarhoud (IRE))
1667[2] 1918[3] 2049[5] 2412[2] (3240) 3870a[9] 4473[4] 4917[7] 5986[5] 6832[2] 7022[6] 7497[5]

Cruiser *William Muir* a91 86
5 b g Oasis Dream Good Girl (IRE) (College Chapel)
1500[2] 1905[2] 2278[7] 2761[3] (3416) 3492[2] (3886) 4415[4] 5310[2] *6167[5] 6694[8]* 7075[9]

Cruise Tothelimit (IRE) *Ian Williams* a60 87
5 b g Le Vie Dei Colori Kiva (Indian Ridge)
1581[2] 1814[8] 2459[10] 3236[4] 3802[6] 4123[3] 4728[2] 4860[3] 5219[2] 5696[10] 6647[9] (6822) 7222[9]

Cruising Along *Ed McMahon* 41
3 ch g Byron Rosapenna (IRE) (Spectrum (IRE))
4011[7] 4774[7]

Cry For The Moon (USA) *J H Culloty* a70 87
7 b g Street Cry(IRE) Kafaf (USA) (Zilzal (USA))
3599a[10]

Cry Fury *Gary Moore* a88 96
5 b g Beat Hollow Cantanta (Top Ville)
1242[11] 3832[10] 5259[10]

Cry Joy (USA) *Charlie Appleby* a70
2 b c Street Cry(IRE) Blushing Ogygian (USA) (Ogygian (USA))
7460[5]

Cryptic Choice (IRE) *S Arthur* a70 74
4 b g Johannesburg(USA) Royal Fupeg (USA) (Fusaichi Pegasus (USA))
1312a[9]

Crystal Earth (IRE) *Peter Fahey* 82
6 b m Muhtarram(USA) Dochas (IRE) (King's Theatre (IRE))
7230a[13]

Crystal High *Mrs Ilka Gansera-Leveque* 51
5 b f High Chaparral(IRE) Park Crystal (IRE) (Danehill (USA))
3252[10] *4380[12]*

Crystalized (IRE) *Richard Hannon Snr* 57
2 ch f Rock Of Gibraltar(IRE) Magnificent Bell (IRE) (Octagonal (NZ))
5344[9] 5740[6] 6354[6]

Crystal Lake (IRE) *Ralph Beckett* a73
2 gr c Verglas(IRE) Entail (USA) (Riverman (USA))
6169[6] 7602[2]

Crystal Mist *Harry Dunlop* 66
3 bg f Dalakhani(IRE) Snow Crystal (IRE) (Kingmambo (USA))
1636[13] 2392[11] 3243[8] 4222[3] 4587[8]

Crystal Monarch (IRE) *Lady Cecil* a59 59
4 b g Dalakhani(IRE) Top Crystal (IRE) (Sadler's Wells (USA))
3953[9] *5526[3]* 6290[12]

Crystal Nymph (IRE) *Richard Hannon Snr* 69
2 ch f Rock Of Gibraltar(IRE) Flower Of Kent (USA) (Diesis)
5442[5] 5790[7] ◆ 7175[4] 7532[4]

Crystal Peaks *James Given* a69 60
3 b f Intikhab(USA) Crozon (Peintre Celebre (USA))
134[3] (534) 803[P]

Crystal Pearl *Mark H Tompkins* a73 39
2 b f Beat Hollow Missouri (Charnwood Forest (IRE))
7466[11] *(7874)*

Crystal Tiger *Alan Jarvis* a20 50
3 b f Tiger Hill(IRE) Moon Crystal (Fasliyev (USA))
4381[11] 5386[6] *6133[11]*

Ctappers *Mick Channon* a66 70
4 b g Imperial Dancer Stride Home (Absalom)
809[3] 1062[7] 1445[7] 1664[6] *1953[3] 2563[4]* 2921[4] 3271[8] 3884[12] *7159[9] 8160[5]*

Cubalibre (FR) *P Sogorb* 82
3 bb g Early March Shereda (IRE) (Indian Ridge)
(6713a)

Cubanita *Ralph Beckett* 109
4 ch f Selkirk(USA) Caribana (Hernando (FR))
2397[5] 3381a[3] 6385[2] (7535)

Cuckoo Rock (IRE) *Jonathan Portman* a54 67
6 b g Refuse To Bend(IRE) Ringmoor Down (Pivotal)
2350[5] 3406[3] 5032[8] 6325[15] (7220) 7433[4] 7778[5]

Cueca (FR) *Jonathan Portman* a47 56
2 b f Country Reel(USA) Costa Packet (IRE) (Hussonet (USA))
3107[9] *5131[11]* 6590[5] 7426[5]

Cufflink *Iain Jardine* a75 78
4 b f Rail Link Fred's Dream (Cadeaux Genereux)
984[11] 1237[11] 1442[16] 1763[13] 2219[6] (2764) 2972[7] 3728[12] 4109[12] 4559[4] 4826[5]

Cul Baire (IRE) *J S Bolger* a85 90
5 ch g King's Best(USA) Voronova (IRE) (Sadler's Wells (USA))
3560[8] ◆

Culdaff (IRE) *Charles Hills* 82
2 b c Aqlaam Nenuphar (IRE) (Night Shift (USA))
1880[2] 2194[5] 3374[2] (4061) 4717[4] 5400[4] 6619[8]

Cullentry Royal *J F Levins* a95 93
5 b g Royal Applause Fleur A Lay (USA) (Mr Greeley (USA))
7230a[24] 7975[5]

Culture Trip *Gary Moore* a50 40
3 b g Royal Applause Spanish Springs (IRE) (Xaar)
396[8] 580[9] 841[4] 3041[8] 3918[7] 5126[5] *6102[6]* 6260[8]

Cumberworth *Michael Easterby* a35 28
3 b g Ishiguru(USA) Sumitra (Tragic Role (USA))
7345[9] *7884[4] 8028[4]*

Cumbrian Craic *Tim Easterby* 76
3 b g Pastoral Pursuits Bollin Janet (Sheikh Albadou)
2987[7] 3566[7] 4048[8]

Cunning Plan (IRE) *Raymond York* a31 24
6 ch g Bachelor Duke(USA) Madamaa (IRE) (Alzao (USA))
7984[13]

Cupertino *Kevin Ryan* 77
3 b g Sakhee(USA) Arantxa (Sharpo)
1845[5] 2279[3] (4118) 5182[6] 5642[9]

Curbyourenthusiasm (IRE) *David Simcock* a67
2 gr g Mastercraftsman(IRE) Mohican Princess (Shirley Heights)
7835[10] 8123[5]

Curious Mind *Sir Mark Prescott Bt* a76
3 b f Dansili Intrigued (Darshaan)
(8348)

Curl (IRE) *Michael Dods* 69
3 b f Duke Of Marmalade(IRE) Fringe (In The Wings)
1486[5] 1965[5] 2506[4] 2916[9] 3488[2] (4030)

Curly Come Home *Chris Wall* a87 84
4 b f Notnowcato Cuyamaca (IRE) (Desert King (IRE))
1836[2] 2311[4] 3063[2] (3814) 4489[3] (5169) 6016[5] *6936[3]*

Curly Wee (IRE) *David Wachman* 89
3 b f Excellent Art Pietra Dura (Cadeaux Genereux)
3845a[7]

Currently Inlondon (IRE) *Mick Channon* 30
2 b f Compton Place Mrs Beeton (IRE) (Dansili)
3986[15] 4347[11] 4617[6]

Curro Perote (FR) *X Nakkachdji* a95 82
6 gr g Smadoun(FR) First Choice (FR) (Exit To Nowhere (USA))
4467a[10]

Cushion *John Gosden* 103
3 b f Galileo(IRE) Attraction (Efisio)
1813[5] 2389[2] (3239) 5035[3] ◆ 6484a[6] 7020[2] 7822[3]

Custom Cut (IRE) *George J Kent* a104 111
4 b g Notnowcato Polished Gem (IRE) (Danehill (USA))
1168a[16] (1413a) 2288a[2] 2840[6] 5453a[4] 5794[8]

Custom House (IRE) *John E Long* a62 67
5 b g Tale Of The Cat(USA) L'Acajou (CAN) (Gulch (USA))
794[3] 903[8] 1474[4] 1873[4] 2126[7]

Cut Across (IRE) *Nick Littmoden* a94 77
5 b g Cape Cross(IRE) Incise (Dr Fong (USA))
58[2]

Cuthbert (IRE) *Michael Attwater* a54 75
6 ch g Bertolini(USA) Tequise (IRE) (Victory Note (USA))
35[2] 346[2] 497[3] 725[9] 903[11] 1194[6] 1473[3] 1783[10] (1981) 3054[6] 3329[4] 5232[10] 7981[8] 8258[13] 8390[9]

Cut No Ice (IRE) *Paul Cole* a78 74
3 gr f Verglas(IRE) Limpopo (Green Desert (USA))
5541[6]

Cut The Cackle (IRE) *Violet M Jordan* a69 70
7 b m Danetime(IRE) Alexander Anapolis (IRE) (Spectrum (IRE))
77[9] 117[9] 323[3] 440[3] 565[10]

Cyclone *J P Murtagh* a60 88
3 b c Teofilo(IRE) Ascot Cyclone (USA) (Rahy (USA))
4465a[13]

Cyflymder (IRE) *David C Griffiths* a74 78
7 b g Mujadil(USA) Nashwan Star (IRE) (Nashwan (USA))
80[5] 217[8] 370[2] 749[2] 839[3] 2574[3] 2837[6] *3172[5]* 3534[10] 3895[6] 4245[6] 4615[4] 5427[9]

Cymeriad *Michael Easterby* a56 50
3 ch f Choisir(AUS) Danifah (IRE) (Perugino (USA))
3323[5] 3594[5] 4160[7] 4398[4] 4722[5] *5067[5]* 5644[5] *6344[5]* 6843[5]

Czech It Out (IRE) *Amanda Perrett* 84
3 b g Oratorio(IRE) Naval Affair (IRE) (Last Tycoon)
2016[5] (2448) 3020[3] ◆ 4922[15]

Daar Zayed (USA) *M Al Muhairi* a75
3 b f Kheleyf(USA) Lonely Ahead (USA) (Rahy (USA))
243a[7] 554a[8]

Dabbitse (GER) *C Zschache* 106
4 b c Soldier Hollow Djidda (GER) (Lando (GER))
(3970a)

Da Capo (IRE) *Mme Pia Brandt* a82 90
7 b g Peintre Celebre(USA) Specificity (USA) (Alleged (USA))
7566a[15]

Daddy Long Legs (USA) *M F De Kock* a115 111
4 ch h Scat Daddy(USA) Dreamy Maiden (USA) (Meadowlake (USA))
659a[13] 871a[4] 958a[13] 7698[5]

Daddy Warbucks (IRE) *David Nicholls* a73 81
4 b g Multiplex Skerries (IRE) (Dr Fong (USA))
3349[9] 3895[11] 4264[10] 5861[7] 6548[12]

Da Do Run Run *Brian Meehan* 80
3 b g Sixties Icon Fascinatin Rhythm (Fantastic Light (USA))
2099[2] (2568) 3526[14]

Dafeef *Doug Watson* a96 112
6 b g Medicean Almahab (USA) (Danzig (USA))
154a[10]

Dagda Mor (ITY) *S Botti* 64
6 b h Martino Alonso(IRE) Bagnolese (ITY) (Cape Cross (IRE))
2491a[14]

Daggers Bond (IRE) *Aidan Anthony Howard* 74
7 ch g Daggers Drawn(USA) Faithfulbond (IRE) (Elbio)
22[12]

Daghash *Clive Brittain* a82 83
4 b g Tiger Hill(IRE) Zibet (Kris)
1159[5] 1242[7] 1766[7] 3157[3] 6537[7]

Dai Bando (IRE) *P J Prendergast* 91
2 b c Montjeu(IRE) Ghurra (USA) (War Chant (USA))
4547a[6] 7050a[7]

Dairam (USA) *Charles Hills* a69 78
3 b c Jazil(USA) Tarteel (USA) (Bahri (USA))
1575[2] 2346[2] 2765[2] 3278[2] (3650) 4251[3]

Daisie Cutter *Graeme McPherson* a53 55
3 b f Tobougg(IRE) Bowled Out (GER) (Dansili)
31[6] 207[4] 848[6] 1116[3] 2133[7] 2762[11] 6902[13] *7511[8] 8122[7]*

Daisy Boy (IRE) *Stuart Williams* 58
2 b g Cape Cross(IRE) Muluk (IRE) (Rainbow Quest (USA))
4906[5] 6534[7] 7818[9]

Daisy Devine (USA) *Andrew McKeever* a111 113
5 b f Kafwain(USA) Devil's Dispute (USA) (Devil's Bag (USA))
7043a[3]

Dakatari (FR) *F Head* a81 95
3 gr f Dalakhani(IRE) Tiyi (FR) (Fairy King (USA))
6031a[4] 6962a[7]

Dakota Canyon (IRE) *Richard Fahey* a79 76
4 b g Rock Of Gibraltar(IRE) Dakota Sioux (IRE) (College Chapel)
82[5] 314[3] 614[5] (850) 995[7] 1538[16] 1932[4] 2406[4] 2753[4] 3349[17] 4294[6]

Daksha (FR) *W Hickst* 101
3 b f Authorized(IRE) Dareen (IRE) (Rahy (USA))
3146a[5] 4092a[8] 5315a[8] 6887a[5]

Dalaki (IRE) *Clive Brittain* 68
2 b g Dalakhani(IRE) Lunda (IRE) (Soviet Star (USA))
2741[12] 5025[7] 5309[4] 5852[2] 6763[8] 7492[5]

Dalaklear (IRE) *David Lanigan* 59
3 b g Dalakhani(IRE) Clear Vision (Observatory (USA))
1679[11] 2605[11]

Dalandra *Michael Dods* a58 58
3 b f Montjeu(IRE) Dalasyla (IRE) (Marju (IRE))
6049[5] 6518[4] 6918[9]

Dalarosso *Ed Dunlop* a61 65
2 b c Dalakhani(IRE) Jamboretta (IRE) (Danehill (USA))
6762[17] 7469[10] *7972[7]*

Dalaway (IRE) *Mick Channon* a60 61
3 gr f Dalakhani(IRE) In The Limelight (IRE) (Sadler's Wells (USA))
1364[4] *1697[4]* 2546[4] 3013[5] 3675[3] 4049[6] 4405[6]

Daldini *Scott Dixon* a32
11 b g Josr Algarhoud(IRE) Arianna Aldini (Habitat)
8160[10] 8268[6]

Dalgig *Jamie Osborne* a71 79
3 b g New Approach(IRE) Bright Halo (IRE) (Bigstone (IRE))
1423[5] 2151[4] 2833[2] *6738[6]*

Dalhousie Lassie *James Unett* a25 31
3 b f Indesatchel(IRE) Miss Mirasol (Sheikh Albadou)
1044[8] 1216[4]

Daliance (IRE) *Lucy Wadham* a88 83
4 ch g Dalakhani(IRE) Everlasting Love (Pursuit Of Love)
3960[9]

Dalilar (USA) *A De Royer-Dupre* 81
3 b c Dynaformer(USA) Daltaya (FR) (Anabaa (USA))
(5692a)

Dali's Lover (IRE) *Charles Hills* a66 76
3 b f Excellent Art Hendrina (IRE) (Daylami (IRE))
373[9] (473) 1609[3] (2153) 2602[8] 3313[2] 3806[2] 4417[8]

Dalkala (USA) *A De Royer-Dupre* 115
4 b f Giant's Causeway(USA) Daltaya (FR) (Anabaa (USA))
1420a[4] (2397) 3615a[9] 5574a[3] (7057a) 7365[4]

Dalliefour (IRE) *Michael Bell* 58
3 b f Cape Cross(IRE) Daliyana (IRE) (Cadeaux Genereux)
1671[15] 2093[8] 2547[6] 3013[3] 3918[2] 4391[4] 5633[4]

Dalmarella Dancer (IRE) *K R Burke* 52
2 b f Mastercraftsman(IRE) Ting A Greeley (Mr Greeley (USA))
6409[7] 6828[10]

Dalmatia (IRE) *Sir Michael Stoute* 61
2 gr f Cape Cross(IRE) Dalataya (IRE) (Sadler's Wells (USA))
4491[9]

Daloisi (FR) *C Scandella* a57
3 b f Marchand De Sable(USA) Aloisi (Kalanisi (IRE))
461a[9]

Dalwari (USA) *J-C Rouget* a82 110
3 b g More Than Ready(USA) Dalmiya (IRE) (Kalanisi (IRE))
(2355a) 2907a[9] 4573a[3]

Damaah (USA) *Mark Johnston* 66
2 b f Lemon Drop Kid(USA) Ekleel (IRE) (Danehill (USA))
4610[4] 5180[6] 5877[5] (6295) 6582[8]

Dama De La Noche (IRE) *Richard Hannon Snr* a61 66
3 b f Teofilo(IRE) Alessia (GER) (Warning)
1666[9] *1876[7]* 2658[6] 3014[2] 3977[8] 4715[3] 6098[4]

Damascene *Marco Botti* a74
2 b c Oasis Dream Acts Of Grace (USA) (Bahri (USA))
8124[4] 8340[2]

Dambuster (IRE) *Sir Michael Stoute* a68 83
3 b g Dalakhani(IRE) Threefold (USA) (Gulch (USA))
3021[6] 3417[7] *4381[5]* (5203) ◆

Dame Nellie Melba *Mark Johnston* a84 78
3 gr f Aussie Rules(USA) Scandalette (Niniski (USA))
4013[5] 4373[3] ◆ (4629) 5055[2] 5649[4] 7100[8] *7739[7] (8299)*

Damsah (USA) *D De Watrigant* a93 89
3 bb f Mr Greeley(USA) Modeeroch (IRE) (Mozart (IRE))
1495a[2] 4274a[5] 7085a[6]

Danadana (IRE) *Luca Cumani* a110 117
5 b c Dubawi(IRE) Zeeba (IRE) (Barathea (IRE))
(2186) 2811[5] 4213[6] 5725[2] *(6232a)*

Dana's Present *George Baker* a77 76
4 ch g Osorio(GER) Euro Empire (USA) (Bartok (IRE))
1780[7] ◆ 2780[10] 3575[7] (4241) 4517[2] *6089a[6]* (6306) *7306[10]*

Danat Al Atheer *William Haggas* 93
3 ch f Shamardal(USA) Height Of Vanity (IRE) (Erhaab (USA))
(1829) 2704[2] (3666) 3755[2] 4537[4] 5035[6] 5986[4]

Dancarina *Tim Easterby* 37
2 b f Multiplex Sambarina (IRE) (Victory Note (USA))
2715[10]

Dance *Rod Millman* 36
4 b f Erhaab(USA) Shi Shi (Alnasr Alwasheek)
2389[11] 2713[10] 3272[10]

Dancealot *Clive Brittain* a76 83
2 b f Lawman(FR) Dance Of Light (USA) (Sadler's Wells (USA))
2744[2] ◆ *3471[2]* 4491[4] 5005[3] (5536) 5952[3] 6501[5]

Dance And Dance (IRE) *Ed Vaughan* a95 109
7 b g Royal Applause Caldy Dancer (IRE) (Soviet Star (USA))
1244[6] 1675[24] 2018[11] 2399[8] 3725[6] 4297[4] ◆ 4946[10] 5533[2] 6025a[11] 6838[6] 7696[12] *8301[6]*

Dance Bid *Clive Brittain* a59 77
2 b f Authorized(IRE) Dancing Fire (USA) (Dayjur (USA))
3689[5] 5394[12] (5988) 6395[3] 6839[9]

Dance Card (USA) *Kiaran McLaughlin* a114
4 rg f Tapit(USA) Tempting Note (USA) (Editor's Note (USA))
7709a[3]

Dance Express (IRE) *Clive Cox* a83 79
4 b f Rail Link Swingsky (IRE) (Indian Ridge)
3842[3] 4237[10]

Dance For Georgie *Ben Haslam* a73 73
4 ch f Motivator Chetwynd (IRE) (Exit To Nowhere (USA))
1788[10] 3027[6] 3649[3] 5369[3] ◆ 5637[4] 6301[5] 6634[2] *8316[6]*

Dance In The Park (FR) *D Guillemin* 104
3 b f Walk In The Park(IRE) Danse D'Amour (Dansili)
2905a[3] 7843a[10]

Danceintothelight *Micky Hammond* a60 62
6 gr g Dansili Kali (Linamix (FR))
1464[7] 2120[7] 5048[2] 5885[2] 6632[2] 7098[4]

Dance King *David Lanigan* 87
3 ch g Danehill Dancer(IRE) One So Wonderful (Nashwan (USA))
2384[5] 2931[3] 3542[2] (6036) 7028[13]

Dance Moves *A Fabre* 111
5 b c Dansili Dance Routine (Sadler's Wells (USA))
2908a[5] 5575a[3] 6447a[9]

Dance Of Heroes *Jeremy Noseda* a71 62
2 b c Danehill Dancer(IRE) Helena Molony (IRE) (Sadler's Wells (USA))
7019[8] *7646[3]*

Dancer Destination *B Grizzetti* 100
3 b f Dubai Destination(USA) Mara Dancer (Shareef Dancer (USA))
(1866a) 2697a[2]

Dance To Bristol (USA) *Ollie Figgins III* a112
4 ch f Speightstown(USA) Dance To Dawn (USA) (Louis Quatorze (USA))
7709a[6]

Dance To Destiny *K F Clutterbuck* a41
5 ch f Carnival Dancer Java Dawn (IRE) (Fleetwood (IRE))
6554[9] 6986[6] 7351[10]

Dance With Dragons (IRE) *William Stone* a84 83
3 b g Namid Duck Over (Warning)
2022[8] 2495[2] 3582[6] 3782[2] 4492[4] 5541[3] 6072[8] (Dead)

Dance With Fate (USA) *Peter Eurton* a106
2 bb c Two Step Salsa(USA) Flirting With Fate (USA) (Saint Ballado (CAN))
7711a[8]

Dance With Me (IRE) *Jonathan Geake* a5 73
4 b g Danehill Dancer(IRE) Perpetual Time (Sadler's Wells (USA))
5954[10] *6855[9]*

Dancewiththedevil (SAF) *Roger Varian* 115
7 b m Modus Vivendi Emperor's Dance (SAF) (Caesour (USA))
3456[8]

Danchai *William Haggas* 104
4 gr g Authorized(IRE) Scarlet Empire (IRE) (Red Ransom (USA))
2018[2] 3339[2] ◆ 4080[6] (4310) 5269[13] 6001[7] 6838[24]

Dancheur (IRE) *K R Burke* a80 92
4 ch f Chineur(FR) Daneville (IRE) (Danetime (IRE))
1318[7] 2088[2] 2513[2] (3223) 3407[8] 4580[2] 5294[5] 5700[7] (6665) 6831[13]

Dancing Chief (IRE) *Alan Jarvis* a39 21
3 ch c Fracas(IRE) Dance Fontaine (IRE) (Danehill Dancer (IRE))
1469[5] 1613[8] 2566[7] 4122[6]

Dancing Cosmos (IRE) *John Patrick Shanahan* a73 60
3 b f Holy Roman Emperor(IRE) The Real Thing (IRE) (Traditionally (USA))
4448[5] 4471[5] *(6803) (7383)*

Dancing Ellie Mae *Derek Shaw* a32
4 b f Proclamation(IRE) Park Star (Gothenberg (IRE))
114^7 326^7

Dancing Freddy (IRE) *Violet M Jordan* a81 95
6 b g Chineur(FR) Majesty's Dancer (IRE) (Danehill Dancer (IRE))
29^3 187^9 398^6 ◆ *494^3*

Dancing House (USA) *Kiaran McLaughlin* a84 104
2 rg f Tapit(USA) Tout Charmant (USA) (Slewvescent (USA))
7690a^5

Dancing Juice *Alan Jarvis* a55 49
2 b c Major Cadeaux Mancunian Way (Green Desert (USA))
3408^6 3826^8 4282^6 *7117^9 7293^4*

Dancing Maite *Roy Bowring* a76 67
8 ch g Ballet Master(USA) Ace Maite (Komaite (USA))
86^7 2236^4 2780^6 (2932) 5515^9 6075^8 6568^{10} 6702^2 7109^{16} *7885^8 7953^8 8230^7*

Dancing Paddy (IRE) *Alan Swinbank* a49 39
5 b g Azamour(IRE) Moucha (FR) (Fabulous Dancer (USA))
1600^5 2991^6

Dancing Primo *Mark Brisbourne* a41 87
7 b m Primo Valentino(IRE) Tycoon's Last (Nalchik (USA))
1290^5 2004^5 3095^6 3345^{13} 4020^6 ◆ 4489^6 5222^6 6239^{10}

Dancing Sal (IRE) *David Evans* a66 64
2 b f Azamour(IRE) Miss Tango Hotel (Green Desert (USA))
1659^8 1946^6 2474^3 2645^4 3753^5 4246^3 *5068^7 5926^8* 6041^4 6821^8 *6979^2* 7096^4 *7352^7 7789^2* 8222^2 8414^3

Dancing Sands (IRE) *Charlie Appleby* a77 78
2 b f Dubawi(IRE) Past The Post (USA) (Danzig (USA))
5716^6 *6523^2* 6828^2 *7296^4 7874^4*

Dancing Shuffle (GER) *S Smrczek* 92
3 b f Big Shuffle(USA) Donatio (IRE) (Royal Academy (USA))
2910a^5

Dancing Welcome *Milton Bradley* a77 74
7 b m Kyllachy Highland Gait (Most Welcome)
86^6 271^6 1802^8 2096^7 2918^{11} 3269^5 3657^{10} *4148^6* 4709^4 5166^2 *5594^6* (5818) 6156^4 6324^5 *6752^4*

Dandana (IRE) *Clive Brittain* 72
2 b c Dandy Man(IRE) Miss Demure (Shy Groom (USA))
4958^3 ◆ 5727^9 7126^2 7529^5

Dandarrell *Julie Camacho* a75 69
6 b g Makbul Dress Design (IRE) (Brief Truce (USA))
1788^3 2889^3 *4169^4* 4953^6 6600^{13} *7378^6 7733^5 (8409)*

Dandeena (IRE) *Ronald Harris* 68
2 b f Dandy Man(IRE) Xena (IRE) (Mull Of Kintyre (USA))
2601^8 5646^2 6423^P

Dandino *Marco Botti* a113 117
6 br h Dansili Generous Diana (Generous (IRE))
2020^2 3556^2 (5550a) 7392a^2 7761a^5

Dandy (GER) *Andrew Balding* a41 81
4 b g Nayef(USA) Diacada (GER) (Cadeaux Genereux)
1673^{15} (2498) (2923) 3150^2 3791^5 4441^5 5006^6 6004^9 6428^2

Dandy Boy (ITY) *David Marnane* a92 117
7 b h Danetime(IRE) Fleet Of Light (Spectrum (IRE))
954a^9 2676a^{10} 3557^{14} 5320a^4 6414a^{10} 7025^4

Dandy Maid *Michael Appleby* 48
2 b f Dandy Man(IRE) Cut Back (Factual (USA))
2090^6 2625^{13}

Dandys Perier (IRE) *Ronald Harris* a55 48
2 br c Dandy Man(IRE) Casual Remark (IRE) (Trans Island)
4781^7 5811^6 6152^7 6487^3 *6979^5 7755^3 (7956) 8166^4 8317^6*

Dane Cottage *Richard Ford* a52 34
6 ch m Beat Hollow Lady Soleas (Be My Guest (USA))
22^6 458^8 1279^5

Daneglow (IRE) *Mike Murphy* a56 18
3 ch f Thousand Words Valluga (IRE) (Ashkalani (IRE))
1364^7 *1986^{10} 4176^5 6849^3 7203^5 7929^4 7969^4 8112^3 (8277)*

Danehill Brook (IRE) *David Wachman* 89
2 b c Danehill Dancer(IRE) River Flow (USA) (Affirmed (USA))
6021a^9

Danehill Dante (IRE) *Chris Gordon* a59 69
5 ch g Danehill Dancer(IRE) En Garde (USA) (Irish River (FR))
5403^7 *7447^9*

Danehill Flyer (IRE) *Philip Kirby* a74 76
3 b c Danehill Dancer(IRE) Zagreb Flyer (Old Vic)
1275^4 ◆ *2175^2* 2716^5 (3893) 4135^7 5786^3

Dan Emmett (USA) *John Quinn* a67
3 ch g Flower Alley(USA) Singing Dixie (USA) (Dixieland Band (USA))
8046^3 ◆ *8298^2*

Daneside (IRE) *P J O'Gorman* a45 72
6 b g Danehill Dancer(IRE) Sidecar (IRE) (Spectrum (IRE))
3534^5 3901^6 4373^6 4771^5 5426^7 5980^6 *6472^{11} 7850^9 8082^4 8258^6 8351^9*

Dane Street (USA) *Mrs John Harrington* 97
4 bb f Street Cry(IRE) Daneleta (IRE) (Danehill (USA))
4465a^3 4696a^7

Danetimeranger (IRE) *Ronald Harris* a45
2 b f Bushranger(IRE) Brave Cat (IRE) (Catrail (USA))
1924^6 2327^6 5351^4 5591^7 6511^{14}

Dan Excel (IRE) *J Moore* 119
5 b g Shamardal(USA) Love Excelling (FR) (Polish Precedent (USA))
(2066a) 2494a^2 8210a^8

Danfazi (IRE) *Kristin Stubbs* a69 74
2 ch g Dandy Man(IRE) Distant Shore (IRE) (Jareer (USA))
1573^4 1820^3 2161^2 2715^3 (3310) 4054^3 4528^{16} *8261^6 8442^5*

Dangerous Age *J W Hills* a84 68
3 br f Sleeping Indian Rye (IRE) (Charnwood Forest (IRE))
19^3 (356) (669) 894^3 2623^6 3134^{10} *3638^3 (4635)* 5060^6 *5673^3* (6040) *(6854)* (7112)

Dangerous Flower (USA) *Mick Channon* 45
2 b f Grand Slam(USA) Miss Sea Oats (USA) (Langfuhr (CAN))
5516^5 6112^9

Danglydontask *David Arbuthnot* 27
2 b g Lucky Story(USA) Strat's Quest (Nicholas (USA))
6184^{12}

Daniel Thomas (IRE) *Violet M Jordan* a66 51
11 b g Dansili Last Look (Rainbow Quest (USA))
73^8 200^3 320^7 508^7 722^{11} (993) 1161^2 1322^4 1617^7 3513^9 4355^6 4562^9 5126^9 5377^6 7963^4

Danisa *David Bridgwater* a57 86
4 b f Shamardal(USA) Divisa (GER) (Lomitas)
2360^3 2729^2 3271^4 4035^3 *5001^5*

Danjeu (IRE) *John Gosden* 68
2 b c Montjeu(IRE) Wanna (IRE) (Danehill Dancer (IRE))
7469^7

Dank *Sir Michael Stoute* a87 116
4 b f Dansili Masskana (IRE) (Darshaan)
(2045) ◆ 3456^3 (4567a) (5552a) (7708a)

Dansante *Richard Hannon Snr* a35
2 b f Champs Elysees Danseuse Du Soir (IRE) (Thatching)
8342^{11}

Dan's Heir *Wilf Storey* a56 54
11 b g Dansili Million Heiress (Auction Ring (USA))
5863^9 6177^{11} 7099^9 7375^9

Dansili Dutch (IRE) *David O'Meara* a69 73
4 gr f Dutch Art Joyful Leap (Dansili)
1017^9 1082^8 1610^7 3814^8 4161^{10} *6805^5 7350^4 (7931) (8038)* ◆ *8183^2 8295^{12}*

Danspi *B Grizzetti* 92
3 b f Singspiel(IRE) Dan Loose (IRE) (Danehill (USA))
3616a^6 7234a^5

Danvilla *Paul Webber* a63 88
6 b m Dansili Newtown Villa (Spectrum (IRE))
2269^4 2587^7 3065^3 5288^{10} *5895^{13}*

Danza Classica (GER) *W Hickst* 90
3 b f Peintre Celebre(USA) Dynamica (GER) (Dashing Blade)
7406a^6

Danz Choice (IRE) *Richard Hannon Snr* a77 75
3 b c Kheleyf(USA) Aphorism (Halling (USA))
2272^7 *2951^4* 3537^9 4710^5 5404^5 5668^5 6702^{11}

Danzeno *Michael Appleby* 86
2 b g Denounce Danzanora (Groom Dancer (USA))
6635^8 (7341) ◆

Danziger (IRE) *David Evans* a77 67
4 b f Modigliani(USA) Star On A Hill (IRE) (City On A Hill (USA))
404^2 (581) (719) (842) 924^7 1052^3 1807^8 2870^5 3042^{10} 4487^{10} 5094^4 *6310^8* 6850^7

Danzig In The Dark (IRE) *Tim Easterby* 51
2 b f Mastercraftsman(IRE) Cape Jasmine (IRE) (Danehill (USA))
3350^{10} 3760^{12}

Danzki (IRE) *Gay Kelleway* a54 59
2 b c Bushranger(IRE) Miniver (IRE) (Mujtahid (USA))
4724^5 *6169^9*

Danzoe (IRE) *Christine Dunnett* a76 77
6 br g Kheleyf(USA) Fiaba (Precocious)
186^5 360^2 (2132) 2550^{11} 2790^6 *3171^5* 4344^7 4866^4 5155^4 *6652^8* 7315^6 7772^{14} *(8034) 8352^6* 8457^6

Danz Star (IRE) *Malcolm Saunders* 58
2 ch g Ad Valorem(USA) Await (IRE) (Peintre Celebre (USA))
5811^5

Da Ponte *Michael Scudamore* a59 79
5 b g Librettist(USA) Naharnook (Fantastic Light (USA))
89^7

Da'Quonde (IRE) *Bryan Smart* a69 93
5 br f Pivotal Bobcat Greeley (USA) (Mr Greeley (USA))
164^9 1278^2 4992^3 5579^2 (6388) (7313)

Darakti (IRE) *Alan McCabe* a55 66
3 b g Rakti Mitawa (IRE) (Alhaarth (IRE))
(1332) 1469^6 2175^3 (2312) 2784^6 3809^{10} (4809) *5197^3* 7066^{11}

Daraybi (FR) *A De Royer-Dupre* 96
2 b c Street Cry(IRE) Daryaba (IRE) (Night Shift (USA))
6249a^4 6710a^3

Darbadar (FR) *M Delzangles* 109
3 b c Danehill Dancer(IRE) Darsha (FR) (Sakhee (USA))
7046a^4 7410a^5

D'Arcy Indiana *Amy Weaver* a41 49
2 b g Royal Applause Prowse (USA) (King Of Kings (IRE))
6724^6 7773^9 *8085^9*

Dare To Achieve *William Haggas* 100
3 b g Galileo(IRE) Mussoorie (FR) (Linamix (FR))
2442^2 ◆ (3606) ◆ 4211^5 5274^4 6186^{11}

Daring Damsel (IRE) *Brian Baugh* a68 59
4 b f Van Nistelrooy(USA) Serengeti Day (USA) (Alleged (USA))
53^4 198^3 430^3 671^3 755^4

Daring Dragon *Ed Walker* a74
3 gr g Intikhab(USA) The Manx Touch (IRE) (Petardia)
7037^2 (7484) 7880^2 8158^9

Daring Indian *Ian Williams* a79 79
5 ch g Zamindar(USA) Anasazi (IRE) (Sadler's Wells (USA))
1083^4 1733^8 2552^5

Daring Storm (GER) *J Hirschberger* 84
3 b g Big Shuffle(USA) Daring Action (Arazi (USA))
7968a^{11}

Dark Ages (IRE) *Paul Burgoyne* a73 77
4 ro f Dark Angel(IRE) Prosaic Star (IRE) (Common Grounds)
963a^0 2425^{10} *6135^{10} 6525^9 6937^{14}*

Dark Amber *Brendan Powell* a63 68
3 b f Sakhee(USA) Donna Vita (Vettori (IRE))
5959^2 6870^3 *7625^3*

Dark Castle *Micky Hammond* a89 89
4 b g Dark Angel(IRE) True Magic (Magic Ring (IRE))
1787^9 2007^{11} 2441^6 2834^9 3351^{11} (3811) (4138) 4778^4 5247^3 6331^8 7176^8

Dark Cove (USA) *Michael J Maker* a104 110
6 b h Medaglia d'Oro(USA) Crystal Cove (USA) (Kris S (USA))
(608a)

Dark Crusader (IRE) *A J Martin* a57 101
3 bb f Cape Cross(IRE) Monty's Girl (IRE) (High Chaparral (IRE))
(5764) ◆ 6991^6

Dark Crystal *John Gallagher* a58 58
2 b f Multiplex Glitz (IRE) (Hawk Wing (USA))
5646^8 6334^6 *7156^3* (7340)

Dark Dream (IRE) *Agostino Affe'* 96
3 rg c Dark Angel(IRE) Sparkling Ridge (Indian Ridge)
1865a^{10}

Dark Dune (IRE) *Tim Easterby* a83 85
5 b g Diamond Green(FR) Panpipes (USA) (Woodman (USA))
2277^{14} 3442^8 3808^3 ◆ 4202^6 4543^4 5086^4 5466^7

Dark Emerald (IRE) *Brendan Powell* a88 91
3 gr c Dark Angel(IRE) Xema (Danehill (USA))
(1912) 2604^5 3276^5 4769^5 *5134^2* 5534^8 *6694^9* 6867^3

Darkening (IRE) *Ismail Mohammed* a64 92
3 b g Shamardal(USA) Dama'A (IRE) (Green Desert (USA))
835a^6 *953a^9*

Darkest Night (IRE) *Jamie Osborne* a70 49
3 b g Dark Angel(IRE) Vadarousse (GER) (Numerous (USA))
55^3 (321) (506) 599^3 845^2 1064^7

Dark Flinch (FR) *G Martin* a66 66
3 b c Royal Assault(USA) Flinch (Zafonic (USA))
460a^3

Dark Justice (IRE) *Tim Pitt* a50 54
3 b f Lawman(FR) Dark Raider (IRE) (Definite Article)
1098^6 2233^4 2341^{10} *3578* 3925^5

Dark Lane *David Evans* a73 76
7 b g Namid Corps De Ballet (IRE) (Fasliyev (USA))
275 (92) 355^2 454^5 611^2 688^4 ◆ *727^5 (916) 946^3* (1324) 1475^3 1798^3 1888^3 (1952) 2268^3 2479^5 2825^5 3010^6 3315^7 3371^7 3733^6 3855^7 4303^7 4471^4 5388^2 5669^4 5841^6 7164^6 7445^5 5931^3 6096^2 (7729) 7937^5 8069^4

Dark Leopard *Roger Charlton* 77
2 b c Dubawi(IRE) Clouded Leopard (USA) (Danehill (USA))
6590^2 ◆ 7501^3

Dark Marvel (IRE) *Alan Berry*
3 b f Captain Marvelous(IRE) Starisa (IRE) (College Chapel)
2634^8

Dark Ocean (IRE) *Jedd O'Keeffe* a60 74
3 b g Dylan Thomas(IRE) Neutral (Beat Hollow)
1486^{11} 2041^3 2538^3 *4384^8* 4994^5 ◆ 5580^4 6587^2 7065^5

Dark Opal (IRE) *John Weymes* 75
3 b f Camacho Dark Albatross (USA) (Sheikh Albadou)
2544^8 2888^5 5141^5 5485^4 6287^4 6515^3 6728^7 (7150)

Dark Orchid (USA) *Saeed bin Suroor* 106
4 b f Dansili Pleione (FR) (Sadler's Wells (USA))
366a^4 743a^6 3409^3 3775^7 4705^8 5402^{10}

Dark Phantom (IRE) *Peter Makin* a42 42
2 b c Dark Angel(IRE) Stoneware (Bigstone (IRE))
2978^6 3175^7

Dark Ranger *Tim Pitt* a88 91
7 br g Where Or When(IRE) Dark Raider (IRE) (Definite Article)
2402^7 3118^2 *(3959)*

Dark Reality (IRE) *Ralph Beckett* 62
2 b f Intikhab(USA) Sunny Slope (Mujtahid (USA))
7102^8 7466^4

Dark Ruler (IRE) *Alan Swinbank* a66 83
4 b g Dark Angel(IRE) Gino Lady (IRE) (Perugino (USA))
5368^7 5918^8 6598^2 7425^3 (7498) *7849^7*

Dark Rumour (IRE) *John Bridger* 30
3 b f Azamour(IRE) Adjisa (IRE) (Doyoun)
2055^5 2389^{14} 3858^{11} 4345^6 *4522^5*

Darkside *Tracy Waggott* 70
3 b g Indesatchel(IRE) Romantic Destiny (Dubai Destination (USA))
1966^2 (2501) 3546^2 3730^5 4198^9 4890^P

Dark Spirit (IRE) *Evan Williams* a60 68
5 b f Whipper(USA) Dark Raider (IRE) (Definite Article)
3882^6 4938^2

Dark Templar *Ed Vaughan* a72 73
3 ch g Starcraft(NZ) Shuaily (PER) (Shuailaan (USA))
1928^4 2549^7 3011^3 *3438^4* 3793^7 4774^4

Dark Woman *H-A Pantall* a52 65
3 b f Manduro(GER) Sospel (Kendor (FR))
1866a^{20} *8441a^9*

Darling Boyz *John Quinn* 58
2 ch g Auction House(USA) Summertime Parkes (Silver Patriarch (IRE))
2883^3 3366^6 5338^{11} 7309^6

Darnathean *Paul D'Arcy* a67 79
4 b g Librettist(USA) Meddle (Diktat)
1717^8 (2534) (3052) 3575^5 3993^2 4237^5 4864^7 5621^7 *7307^{11} 7880^{11} 8059^3*

Darselect *Mme Pia Brandt* a89
2 b c Bertolini(USA) Pygmalion (IRE) (Dr Devious (IRE))
8143a^3

Darting *Andrew Balding* 15
2 b f Shamardal(USA) Dararita (IRE) (Halo (USA))
7244^6

Dartrix *Michael Dods* a44 77
4 b f Dutch Art Shrink (Mind Games)
(1388) 1465^4 (2217) 2835^7 3068^7 (4582) 4727^3 4993^2 5714^2

Darwin (USA) *A P O'Brien* a90 114
3 b c Big Brown(USA) Cool Ghoul (USA) (Silver Ghost (USA))
(4549a) ◆ 6440a^3

Darwinian *Dave Morris* a38 13
4 b f Three Valleys(USA) Force Of Nature (USA) (Sadler's Wells (USA))
633^8 888^9

Dashing David (IRE) *Richard Hannon Snr* a94 91
3 b c Lemon Drop Kid(USA) Nyarhini (Fantastic Light (USA))
2188^7 2857^7 3582^8 (4243) (4776) 5187^4 5721^7 6988^{10}

Dashing Star *David Elsworth* 104
3 b g Teofilo(IRE) Dashiba (Dashing Blade)
1847^5 2398^8 (2879) 3526^{11} 4211^6 5764^2 ◆

Dashwood *Anthony Carson* a74 77
6 b g Pivotal Most Charming (FR) (Darshaan)
(617) 1038^5 (1947) 2450^6 2929^6

Dastarhon (IRE) *Mme Pia Brandt* a95 114
3 gr c Dansili Top Toss (IRE) (Linamix (FR))
2298a^2 2907a^{19} 5808a^7 7047a^9

Daunt (IRE) *John Quinn* a59 74
4 ch g Namid Pearl Egg (IRE) (Mukaddamah (USA))
436^4 616^5

Dauphine Russe (FR) *F Doumen* 106
3 b f Russian Blue(IRE) Dauphine (SAF) (Rich Man's Gold (USA))
1561a^4 2299a^5 2906a^4

David Livingston (IRE) *M F De Kock* 115
4 b h Galileo(IRE) Mora Bai (IRE) (Indian Ridge)
838a^7 3458^5 ◆ 4027^4 (5270) 6253a^5

David's Folly (IRE) *Tim Vaughan* a47 57
4 b f Asian Heights Dolphin Stamp (IRE) (Dolphin Street (FR))
109^3 1369^3

Davids Park *John Joseph Murphy* 87
2 b c Lucky Story(USA) Dijital Power (Pivotal)
(6485) 7548a^6

David's Secret *Roy Brotherton* a67 57
3 ch g Sakhee's Secret Mozie Cat (IRE) (Mozart (IRE))
1977^7 2324^9 *4637^6 5393^6 8037^8 8275^7*

D'Avignon (USA) *John Gosden* a68
2 bb c Smart Strike(CAN) No Matter What (USA) (Nureyev (USA))
7461^5 7971^3

Dawn Approach (IRE) *J S Bolger* 128
3 ch c New Approach(IRE) Hymn Of The Dawn (USA) (Phone Trick (USA))
(2021) 2866^{12} (3421) 4875^2 5314a^5 7366^4

Dawn Beat *Jonathan Portman* a52 55
3 ch f Beat Hollow New Light (Generous (IRE))
1611^4 2157^6 3272^6 4222^7 4931^5 7104^6 *7440^{16}*

Dawn Calling (IRE) *Mark Johnston* a80 77
3 ch c Shamardal(USA) Miss Bellbird (IRE) (Danehill (USA))
5839^3 *6133^3* (6630) 6908^{15} 7374^6 *7603^5*

Dawn Catcher *Geoffrey Deacon* a61 67
3 ch f Bertolini(USA) First Dawn (Dr Fong (USA))
5447^8 6040^4 *7969^2*

Dawnfromthepast (IRE) *Luke Dace* a14 39
2 b g Tagula(IRE) Ball Cat (FR) (Cricket Ball (USA))
3009^5 3310^7 3659^7 *5066^{10}* 6111^{13}

Dawn Of Empire (USA) *Roger Charlton* a73 67
3 b f Empire Maker(USA) Didina (Nashwan (USA))
2455^2 3136^5 *4382^2*

Dawn Rock *Simon Dow* 55
3 b f Rock Of Gibraltar(IRE) Ommadawn (IRE) (Montjeu (IRE))
1769^7 3041^6 4170^3 (5126) 5980^4

Dayatthespa (USA) *Chad C Brown* 113
4 ch f City Zip(USA) M'Lady Doc (USA) (Doc's Leader (USA))
7043a^2

Daydreamer *William Haggas* 64
2 b c Duke Of Marmalade(IRE) Storyland (USA) (Menifee (USA))
7467^7

Day For Night (IRE) *H-A Pantall* a92 97
3 b f Desert Style(IRE) Nightdance Sun (GER) (Monsun (GER))
4468a^0 *8440a^{16}*

Day In Day Out *Seamus Mullins* a66 54
3 b g Notnowcato Cockatrice (Petong)
1177^4 1712^8 3376^{11} 4345^4 *7741^6 8149^{11}*

Daylight *Andrew Balding* 81
3 ch g Firebreak Dayville (USA) (Dayjur (USA))
2529^2 (3036) 3677^3 4413^5 6429^3 6900^4

Day Of Conquest *Richard Hannon Snr* a95 98
2 ch c Major Cadeaux Dayville (USA) (Dayjur (USA))
3979^3 (5299) *(6314)* 6866^2 7534^3

Day Of Destiny (IRE) *James Given* a73 76
8 gr g Clodovil(IRE) El Corazon (IRE) (Mujadil (USA))
165^6 520^2 624^2 1084^2 1279^4 *(1600)* 2886^3 3573^7 5264^2 6236^{14} 6730^{10}

Day Of The Eagle (IRE) *Michael Easterby* 81
7 b g Danehill Dancer(IRE) Puck's Castle (Shirley Heights)
1113^9 1569^5 (2884) 3300^4 3683^5 5026^8 5580^{15} 6727^7 7632^{10} 7824^{19}

Day Star Lad *Derek Shaw* a57
2 b g Footstepsinthesand Eurolink Mayfly (Night Shift (USA))
3640^8 4154^5 8005^7 8188^4 8317^4

Daytona Bay *Ferdinand J Leve* 102
3 b f Motivator Daytona (GER) (Lando (GER))
3604a^2 (4092a) 5044a^{14} 6887a^7

Dazeen *Richard Ford* a79 71
6 b g Zafeen(FR) Bond Finesse (IRE) (Danehill Dancer (IRE))
2911[4] 5564[9]

Dazinski *Mark H Tompkins* 93
7 ch g Sulamani(IRE) Shuheb (Nashwan (USA))
1841[4] 2402[14] 3099[12] 4782[7]

Dazza *Gary Moore* a42 68
2 ch f Bertolini(USA) Another Secret (Efisio)
5929[4] 7162[6] (7426)

Dazzlin Bluebell (IRE) *Tim Easterby* a58 53
4 b f Strategic Prince Sharamaine (IRE) (King Charlemagne (USA))
213[8]

Dazzling Valentine *Alan Bailey* a77 75
5 b f Oratorio(IRE) Bedazzling (IRE) (Darshaan)
82[7] 429[2] 614[4] 639[5] 753[4] 1831[6] 2136[2] 2311[5] 3258[3] 3635[9] 3755[5] (4172) 4663[3] 5672[8] 8343[6]

Deadly Approach *Charlie Appleby* 68
2 b c New Approach(IRE) Speirbhean (IRE) (Danehill (USA))
6570[5] 7332[7]

Deal Me In (IRE) *Ian Williams* a64
4 ch g Modigliani(USA) Lady Rapsody (USA) (Stravinsky (USA))
673[4] 1086[7] 1213[4] 3687[7]

Dean Iarracht (IRE) *Tracy Waggott* a60 64
7 b g Danetime(IRE) Sirdhana (Selkirk (USA))
1572[13] 3728[9] 4010[8] 4563[9] 4763[2] 5295[5] 5420[2] 6086[4] (6179) 6470[11] 6909[8]

Deano's Devil (IRE) *Richard Fahey* a49
2 b f Medicean Peninsula Girl (IRE) (Cape Cross (IRE))
8201[3]

Dear Ben *Brian Baugh* a50 35
4 b g Echo Of Light Miss Up N Go (Gorytus (USA))
551[13] 670[7]

Dear Demi (AUS) *Clarry Conners* 111
4 b f Dehere(USA) Shirley (AUS) (Zabeel (NZ))
7392a[3] 7702a[2] 7761a[19]

Dear Maurice *Tobias B P Coles* a69 76
9 b g Indian Ridge Shamaiel (IRE) (Lycius (USA))
1952[7] 1976[5] 3010[4] 7263[6] 7729[4] 7858[11] 8087[11] 8295[9]

Dear Nofa (IRE) *A Fabre* a67 92
3 b f Galileo(IRE) Classira (IRE) (Danehill (USA))
6962a[6]

Deauville Dancer (IRE) *Lady Herries* a48 65
2 b g Tamayuz Mathool (IRE) (Alhaarth (IRE))
6799[13] 7308[5] 7646[7]

Deauville Prince (FR) *Tom Dascombe* a96 104
3 b c Holy Roman Emperor(IRE) Queen Of Deauville (FR) (Diableneyev (USA))
658a[4] 835a[2] 953a[7]

Deavin *Nick Littmoden*
2 b c Mind Games So Discreet (Tragic Role (USA))
7853[9]

Debdebdeb *Andrew Balding* a70 91
3 b f Teofilo(IRE) Windmill (Ezzoud (IRE))
(814) 1487[3] 1923[3] 2641[2] (3243) 3982[2] (4681) 5764[5]

Debt Settler (IRE) *Luke Dace* a72 58
2 b c Art Connoisseur(IRE) Musical Dancer (Monsieur Bond (IRE))
3413[8] 3914[4] 4177[3] 4948[16] 5276[3] 5595[3] 6104[4] 7293[2] (7900) 7986[4] (8090) 8322[6]

Decaf Again (USA) *Barry Rose* a86 79
7 bb g Wised Up(USA) Pot Of Coffee (USA) (Kris S (USA))
608a[7]

Decana *Hughie Morrison* a73 62
5 ch f Doyen(IRE) Sahara Belle (USA) (Sanglamore (USA))
(1601) 2174[3] 5130[4] 5966[4] 7506[5]

Decathlete (USA) *A Fabre* 104
2 b c Medaglia d'Oro(USA) Rahiyah (USA) (Rahy (USA))
6249a[2]

Decent Fella (IRE) *Violet M Jordan* a88 97
7 b g Marju(IRE) Mac Melody (IRE) (Entrepreneur)
25[7] 78[U] 345[6] 586[10] 715[7] 880[8] 1092[8] 1309[5] 1746[9] 1952[6] 2837[4] 3087[3] (3661) 3926[3] 4496[5] 7319[6]

Deceptive *Paul Webber* a77 24
5 b f Red Ransom(USA) Fleeting Memory (Danehill (USA))
21[7] 3587[7]

Decimus Maximus *Richard Hannon Snr* 53
2 b c Elnadim(USA) Sempre Sorriso (Fleetwood (IRE))
5033[5] 5399[10]

Decision (FR) *Mme C Head-Maarek*
3 ch f Kentucky Dynamite(USA) Dame Blanche (USA) (Cherokee Run (USA))
2335a[0]

Decision By One *David Evans* a88 84
4 ch g Bahamian Bounty Intellibet One (Compton Place)
1984[2] 2150[12] 2663[8] 3371[8] 3802[5] 4165[8] 5183[2] 6526[7] 6850[6] (7730) 7959[6] 8122[8] 8304[9] 8431[11]

Declamation (IRE) *Mark Johnston* a73 76
3 ch g Shamardal(USA) Dignify (IRE) (Rainbow Quest (USA))
1570[8] 1908[6] (2340) 2763[3] 3062[6] 3464[3] (4586) 5291[5] 7076[7] 7487[6]

Declaration Of War (USA) *A P O'Brien* a124 124
4 b c War Front(USA) Tempo West (USA) (Rahy (USA))
(1556a) ◆ 2446[5] (3419) 4082[2] 4875[3] 5314a[4] (5654) 7715a[3]

Dee Aitch Dove *George Baker* a49 55
3 gr f Sakhee's Secret Fluttering Rose (Compton Place)
2226[7] ◆ 2934[6] 3679[9] 4916[2] 5499[11] 6436[13] 8151[12]

Deeds Not Words (IRE) *Mick Channon* 91
2 b c Royal Applause Wars (IRE) (Green Desert (USA))
2194[9] 2653[9] 3836[2] 4259[3] 4948[4] 5399[4] (6065) (6376) (6791) 7026[18]

Deepest Blue *Michael Wigham* a69 71
3 b g Sakhee's Secret Midnight Sky (Desert Prince (IRE))
1539[5] 1844[4] 2098[7] 2779[4] 2959[3] 3611[3] 3762[5] (4162) 4624[5] 5294[7] 5673[5] 5886[6] 7106[8]

Deep Pockets (NZ) *Cliff Brown* 107
6 b g Lucky Owners(NZ) Molly Singer (AUS) (El Moxie (USA))
2494a[10]

Deep Resolve (IRE) *Alan Swinbank* 6
2 b g Intense Focus(USA) I'Ll Be Waiting (Vettori (IRE))
6773[7]

Defence Council (IRE) *Mel Brittain* a84 88
5 b g Kheleyf(USA) Miss Gally (IRE) (Galileo (IRE))
1113[5] 1644[4] 2239[6] 2663[9] 3351[5] 3811[13] 4138[5] 4730[RR] 6774[3] 6908[RR]

Defendant *Sir Michael Stoute* a92 89
3 b c Medicean Razzle (USA) (Danzig (USA))
1881[4] 2306[3] (2765) ◆ 3342[6] ◆ 4014[3] 4295[3] 4743[11] (6925)

Defiant Spirit *Roger Charlton* 73
3 ch g Compton Place Muffled (USA) (Mizaaya)
5386[7] 5845[4] (6431) 6951[9]

Deficit (IRE) *Michael Bell* a84 90
3 gr g Dalakhani(IRE) Venturi (Danehill Dancer (IRE))
2500[3] 2784[2] 3257[3] (3916) 4681[5] 6202[2] 6793[2] 7242[2]

Definightly *Roger Charlton* 110
7 bb g Diktat Perfect Night (Danzig Connection (USA))
1672[8] 6391[16] 7010[14]

Definite Secret *James Tate* a60
2 ch f Sakhee's Secret Jasmick (IRE) (Definite Article)
7348[3] 7602[3] 7960[4] 8317[3]

Deflection (IRE) *S Botti* 94
3 ch f Dylan Thomas(IRE) Crumpetsfortea (IRE) (Henbit (USA))
1866a[14] 6890a[6]

Deglet Noor *Roger Varian* a82 89
3 br f New Approach(IRE) Almoutezah (USA) (Storm Cat (USA))
(6134) 6531[3] 7470[3] 7895[8]

Deia Sunrise (IRE) *Paul Webber* a74 102
4 gr g Clodovil(IRE) Hedera (USA) (Woodman (USA))
3559[15] 8428[6]

Deira Phantom (IRE) *Roger Varian* 82
3 b c Cape Cross(IRE) Ammo (IRE) (Sadler's Wells (USA))
(2055) 2602[5] 3783[2] 4286[5]

De Lesseps (USA) *James Moffatt* a55 37
5 ch g Selkirk(USA) Suez (Green Desert (USA))
5596[5] 6130[11]

Delft *Jeremy Noseda* a87 84
4 b f Dutch Art Plucky (Kyllachy)
345[7]

Deliberation (IRE) *John Quinn* a61 58
5 b g Antonius Pius(USA) Pursuit Of Truth (USA) (Irish River (FR))
3030[4] 3445[9] 5139[11] 5602[3] 5818[4] 6634[7] (6919) 7153[8]

Delicate Delight (IRE) *P Schiergen* 81
2 b f Kandahar Run Dawn Dew (GER) (Montjeu (IRE))
7967a[8]

Delicatezza *E Botti* 98
4 b f Danehill Dancer(IRE) Wickwing (In The Wings)
1709a[3]

Delicious Patrica *Tony Carroll* a33 36
4 b f Multiplex Cerulean Rose (Bluegrass Prince (IRE))
1821[7] 2437[7] 2824[8] 3433[11] 3954[7]

Delicious Poison *James Fanshawe* a68 53
3 ch c Pivotal Pediment (Desert Prince (IRE))
1881[9] 2340[5] 2952[6]

Delightful Sleep *David Evans* a67 66
5 b g Sulamani(IRE) Naemi (GER) (Tannenkonig (IRE))
33[4] 220[2] (381) 435[8] 737[7] 801[3] 883[2] 983[9] 1060[3] (1401) 1699[3] 1797[4] 2302a[4] 2594[6] 2875[6] 4171[5] 4357[8] 5002[3] 5172[2] 5596[6] 5816[4] 5948[9] 6153[7] 7246[3] 7515[6] (7733) 7930[7] 8038[3] 8183[3]

Dellapearl (FR) *F Sanchez* a66 74
4 b g Della Francesca(USA) Cat's Pearl (FR) (Enrique)
963a[5]

Dellbuoy *Pat Phelan* a83 83
4 b g Acclamation Ruthie (Pursuit Of Love)
3293[10] 3961[8] 4859[12] 6360[10] 7629[13] (8182) 8447[6]

Delores Rocket *Kevin Ryan* a68 72
3 b f Firebreak Artistic (IRE) (Noverre (USA))
1773[5] 2285[9] 2593[7] 3234[7] 3686[5] 4725[8] 5150[4] 6548[7] 7281[2] 7953[5] 8134[3]

Delphica (IRE) *Gary Moore* a35 47
3 b f Acclamation Expectation (IRE) (Night Shift (USA))
3316[7] 3922[10] 4170[9]

Delrock (GER) *S Bazzani* 97
6 ch h Rock Of Gibraltar(IRE) Delicia (GER) (Acatenango (GER))
7725a[4]

Demeteor (ITY) *R Menichetti* 97
3 b c Mujahid(USA) Eros Love (ITY) (Love The Groom (USA))
2490a[5] 6679a[7]

Democretes *Richard Hannon Snr* a98 100
4 ch g Cadeaux Genereux Petite Epaulette (Night Shift (USA))
1245[5] 1726[3] 2013[2] 2207[2] 3527[16] 4859[4] 5285[2] 5533[11] 6183[15] 7648[5] 7856[5]

Demoiselle Bond *Lydia Richards* a67 22
5 ch f Monsieur Bond(IRE) Baytown Flyer (Whittingham (IRE))
421[5] 790[8] 1063[8] 1196[8] 1304[6] 1717[10] 7850[3] 8082[10] 8393[4]

Demolition *Noel Wilson* a75 89
9 ch g Starborough Movie Star (IRE) (Barathea (IRE))
1824[7] 2478[3] 2766[5] 3477[3] 3685[12] (4559) 4888[2] 5367[3] 6239[13] (6468) 6758[13]

Demolition Blue (IRE) *Bill Turner* a2
4 b f Diamond Green(FR) Amoras (IRE) (Hamas (IRE))
7299[12]

Demon Express (FR) *Mme A-L Guildoux* 20
6 b g Fasliyev(USA) Singing Lark (FR) (Pampabird)
5464a[7]

Demonic *Lady Cecil* a72 92
3 b c Dansili Bionic (Zafonic (USA))
1624[3] 2384[4] 7131[6]

Demora *Michael Appleby* a90 103
4 b f Deportivo Danzanora (Groom Dancer (USA))
2173[2] (3135) 4263[5] 5651[4] 6639[8] (6830)

Denby Dale *Bill Turner* 28
2 b c Dubawi(IRE) With Fascination (USA) (Dayjur (USA))
2344[6] 2595[9] 4450[5]

Denim And Ruby (JPN) *Katsuhiko Sumii* 114
3 b f Deep Impact(JPN) Venenciador (JPN) (King Kamehameha (JPN))
8033a[2]

Denison Flyer *Lawrence Mullaney* a42 42
6 b g Tobougg(IRE) Bollin Victoria (Jalmood (USA))
7375[6]

Dennis *Tim Easterby* 71
3 b g Mind Games Hetti Lewis (Sir Harry Lewis (USA))
3593[3] 4050[5] 4400[2] (5089) 5581[7] 6291[10]

Denote *Paul Cole* a40
3 b c Motivator Darwinia (GER) (Acatenango (GER))
4356[7]

Denton Skyline (IRE) *Michael Dods* 49
3 b g Celtic Swing Fayr Sky (IRE) (Fayruz)
1487[6] 2508[7] 3463[10] 5334[9]

Denusa (IRE) *Laura Grizzetti* 91
2 b f Aussie Rules(USA) Ardent Lady (Alhaarth (IRE))
7415a[7]

Deodora (FR) *C Boutin* a69 70
3 b f Dai Jin Denissa (GER) (Second Set (IRE))
692a[4]

Departing (USA) *Albert M Stall Jr* a116
3 b g War Front(USA) Leave (USA) (Pulpit (USA))
2473a[6]

Depden (IRE) *Richard Price* a50 50
5 ch g Captain Rio Attribute (Warning)
2997[3] 3246[7] 3623[8] 4691[4] 5097[7] 5864[10] 6156[9]

Derbaas (USA) *A Al Raihe* a99 112
7 b h Seeking The Gold(USA) Sultana (USA) (Storm Cat (USA))
466a[8] 659a[9] 872a[7]

Der Blaue Reiter (IRE) *George Baker* 74
2 ch g Art Connoisseur(IRE) Kafayef (USA) (Secreto (USA))
(1749) 3424[24] 4528[24] 6279[2]

Derbyshire (IRE) *Kevin Ryan* 65
2 b g Green Tune(USA) Statia (FR) (Anabaa (USA))
5727[7] 6581[7] 7773[6]

Derby To Dubai *Kevin Ryan* a67 53
3 ch g Dubai Destination(USA) Bukhoor (IRE) (Danehill (USA))
525[6] 911[2] 1786[4]

De Repente (IRE) *Paul Green* 75
2 b f Captain Rio Suddenly (Puissance)
3044[6] 3624[5] 4477[3] (4802) 5226[3] 5366[2] 5773a[7] (6386) 6825[11] 7127[9]

Derfenna Art (IRE) *Seamus Durack* a72 74
4 b g Excellent Art Cordelia (Green Desert (USA))
1950[5] 2573[6] 2807[7] 3580[10] 7437[4] 7784[7] 8121[2] 8275[5]

De Rigueur *Marco Botti* a90 100
5 b g Montjeu(IRE) Exclusive (Polar Falcon (USA))
(52) 496[8] 1615[2] 2451[2] (3099)

Derwent (USA) *Roger Charlton* a83 88
3 b g Mizzen Mast(USA) Skiable (IRE) (Niniski (USA))
(2309) 2776[5] 3633[7] 6428[7]

Derwentwater (IRE) *John Gosden* a69 57
3 ch g Raven's Pass(USA) Waterways (IRE) (Alhaarth (IRE))
17[2] 122[2] 321[2] 414[2] (482)

Descaro (USA) *John O'Shea* a64 66
7 gr g Dr Fong(USA) Miarixa (FR) (Linamix (FR))
1949[9] 1979[4] 4713[4] 6492[2]

Desert Ace (IRE) *Clive Cox* 80
2 ch c Kheleyf(USA) Champion Place (Compton Place)
5949[5] (6354) ◆ 6958[3] 7333[7]

Desert Blanc *C Baillet* a101 112
5 b c Desert Style(IRE) Lumiere Rouge (FR) (Indian Ridge)
(6251a) 7047a[11] 7685a[16]

Desert Chicory (SWE) *Henrik Engblom*
2 ch f Proclamation(IRE) Richtee (IRE) (Desert Sun)
6452a[11]

Desert Colours *Kevin Ryan* 55
2 b g Exceed And Excel(AUS) Awwal Malika (USA) (Kingmambo (USA))
4199[6] 4724[11] 5145[5] 5610[7] 6111[7] 6755[12]

Desert Command *Andrew Balding* a89 80
3 b g Oasis Dream Speed Cop (Cadeaux Genereux)
4068[8] (4636) 5219[6] 5636[3] 5820[2] 7445[2] ◆

Desert Creek (IRE) *David Nicholls* a86 86
7 ch g Refuse To Bend(IRE) Flagship (Rainbow Quest (USA))
1599[8] 1840[9] 5546[9] 5861[4] 6720[9]

Desert Dawn (SWE) *Roy Arne Kvisla* a54
3 b g Desert Style(IRE) Gaelic's Fantasy (IRE) (Statoblest)
5326a[12]

Desert Donkey *Andrew Balding* a62 13
3 b g Acclamation Honky Tonk Sally (Dansili)
396[7] 667[2] 811[4] 879[3] 1180[3] 1361[5]

Deserted *Luca Cumani* a83 80
3 b f Oasis Dream Tentpole (USA) (Rainbow Quest (USA))
4013[3] ◆ 4978[4] (5802) 6743[6] 7765[3] ◆ 7976[11]

Desert Fairy *Trevor Wall* a54 46
7 b m Tobougg(IRE) Regal Fairy (IRE) (Desert King (IRE))
3954[8]

Desert Flute *Michael Blake* 23
2 b g Piccolo Hawait Al Barr (Green Desert (USA))
3631[9] 4414[16] 8414[5]

Desert Icon (IRE) *Alastair Lidderdale* a64 73
7 b g Desert Style(IRE) Gilded Vanity (IRE) (Indian Ridge)
1888[4] 2949[RR]

Desert Image *Charles Hills* 96
3 b f Beat Hollow Western Appeal (USA) (Gone West (USA))
1676[7] 3460[23] 5684[15]

Desert Island Dusk *John Bridger* a32
2 b g Superior Premium Desert Island Disc (Turtle Island (IRE))
7500[10] 7859[7] 8340[14]

Desert Law (IRE) *Saeed bin Suroor* a76 110
5 b g Oasis Dream Speed Cop (Cadeaux Genereux)
150a[13] 464a[9] 868a[8]

Desert Of Dreams *A Al Raihe* a81 84
3 b c Exceed And Excel(AUS) Majestic Desert (Fraam)
245a[12]

Desert Recluse (IRE) *Brendan Powell* a89 83
6 ch g Redback Desert Design (Desert King (IRE))
654[3] (1547) 2451[8] 3959[9] 4704[5] 5895[12] 6349[7] 7210[9] 7635[3]

Desert Red (IRE) *Phil McEntee* a52 50
4 b f Green Desert(USA) Penicuik (Hernando (FR))
136[4] 323[5] 349[11]

Desert Revolution *Mark Johnston* a79 86
3 ch g Pivotal Persian Secret (FR) (Persian Heights)
4152[2] ◆ (4481) 4859[6] 5335[4] 5838[9] 6288[14]

Desert Skies (IRE) *Saeed bin Suroor* a66 78
3 b f New Approach(IRE) Park Romance (IRE) (Dr Fong (USA))
6950[3] 7624[2] 7864[6]

Desert Skywalker (IRE) *Charlie Appleby* 48
2 ch g Raven's Pass(USA) Damiana (IRE) (Thatching)
5299[8] 5968[9]

Desert Society (IRE) *Richard Hannon Snr* a70 77
2 b c Kheleyf(USA) Sensasse (IRE) (Imperial Ballet (IRE))
6689[2] (7089) 7492[7]

Desert Strike *Conor Dore* a86 79
7 b g Bertolini(USA) Mary Jane (Tina's Pet)
(76) 187[7] 308[2] 481[7] 603[9] 754[8] 842[2] 1205[3] (1475) 1985[3] (2772) (3171) 4165[4] 5901[13] 6854[10] 7731[12] 7959[4] 8167[5] 8431[9]

Desert Vision *Michael Easterby* a91 71
9 b g Alhaarth(IRE) Fragrant Oasis (USA) (Rahy (USA))
23[2] (239) 519[U]

Desert Wings (IRE) *Charlie Appleby* a93 84
3 ch g Raven's Pass(USA) Rise And Fall (USA) (Quiet American (USA))
4978[3] 5484[7] 5845[2] (7154)

Deserving Honour *Charlie Appleby* 39
3 gr c Street Cry(IRE) Nahoodh (IRE) (Clodovil (IRE))
6950[9] 7253[11]

Designer Legs (USA) *Dallas Stewart* a102
2 ch f Graeme Hall(USA) Elegant Designer (USA) (Suave Prospect (USA))
7707a[7]

Desperado (JPN) *Akio Adachi* a107 113
5 b c Neo Universe(JPN) Meine Noel (JPN) (Tony Bin)
1868a[9]

Despot (IRE) *Charles Hills* 67
2 gr c Verglas(IRE) Ms Bossy Boots (USA) (Grand Slam (USA))
6277[9] 6975[4] 7271[3]

Destination Aim *Frederick Watson* 72
6 b g Dubai Destination(USA) Tessa Reef (IRE) (Mark Of Esteem (IRE))
2886[13] 3397[5] 3543[12] 4375[6] (4967) 6291[12]

Destiny Awaits (IRE) *Ian Semple* a61 37
4 b g Dubai Destination(USA) Mellow Jazz (Lycius (USA))
109[2] 2540[11] 2975[7] 3467[5]

Destiny Blue (IRE) *Brian Ellison* a39 78
6 b g Danehill Dancer(IRE) Arpege (IRE) (Sadler's Wells (USA))
1281[3] ◆ 1576[10] 7849[10]

Destiny Highway (FR) *Gay Kelleway* a73 72
3 b g Sir Percy Grace Bankes (Efisio)
605a[3] 692a[6] 818a[DSQ] 1756a[6] 2034a[4] 2434a[6] 3129a[11]

Destiny Of Dreams *Jo Crowley* a85 85
5 b f Dubai Destination(USA) Valjarv (IRE) (Bluebird (USA))
(190) 1327[3] 1663[4] 3022[9]

Destiny's Kitten (IRE) *Tom Dascombe* 69
2 b f Naaqoos Safqa (Singspiel (IRE))
6789[3]

Destor (GER) *U Stech* 98
3 rg c Sternkoenig(IRE) Desimona (GER) (Monsun (GER))
4042a[7] 6987a[2]

Destruct *A Fabre* a94 110
3 b c Rail Link Daring Miss (Sadler's Wells (USA))
(5463a)

Deux Saisons *D Guillemin* a87 93
3 gr f Chineur(FR) Joyeuse Entree (Kendor (FR))
1358a[9]

Deva Victrix *Lisa Williamson* 22
3 b g Kheleyf(USA) Danehill's Dream (IRE) (Danehill (USA))
2650[8] 2931[9] 3327[6] 4607[9]

Deveze (IRE) *Milton Bradley* a54 39
5 b f Kyllachy La Caprice (USA) (Housebuster (USA))
81[2] 111[10] 529[3] 670[6] 756[6] 997[12]

Devilment *Charlie Appleby* a79 81
2 b g Cape Cross(IRE) Mischief Making (USA) (Lemon Drop Kid (USA))
4926[4] 5811[2] (6688) 7471[2]

Devil's Cut (AUS) *S Burridge* 81
5 br g Exceed And Excel(AUS) Adorara (USA) (Silver Hawk (USA))
244a[10]

Devon Diva *John Gallagher* a40 54
7 b m Systematic General Jane (Be My Chief (USA))
2534[8] 3314[2] (3919) 4658[4] 5429[9] 6097[3] 6472[8] 7440[14]

Devon Drum *Paul Webber* a79
5 b g Beat Hollow West Devon (USA) (Gone West (USA))
7158[2]

Devout (IRE) *Jamie Osborne* a65 60
3 b f Holy Roman Emperor(IRE) Raphimix (FR) (Linamix (FR))
31[3] 310[4] 470[2] 598[2] (732) (977) (1008)

Dewala *Michael Appleby* a83 76
4 b f Deportivo Fuwala (Unfuwain (USA))
(601) (646) (914) ◆ 969[2] 1538[8] 2619[5] 7342[13]

Dewi Chinta (IRE) *Kevin Ryan* 59
3 b f Tagula(IRE) Damjanich (IRE) (Mull Of Kintyre (USA))
1935[9] 2756[10] 3082[10]

Dew Reward (IRE) *Bill Turner* a58 60
5 b g Aussie Rules(USA) Shariyfa (FR) (Zayyani)
1062[9] 1513[4] 8027[9] 8160[9] 8436[12]

Dha Chara (IRE) *Reg Hollinshead* a80 76
3 b g Ramonti(FR) Campiglia (IRE) (Fairy King (USA))
286a[6] 460a[2] 604a[2] 692a[3] 1829[3]

Dhaular Dhar (IRE) *Jim Goldie* a87 78
11 b g Indian Ridge Pescara (IRE) (Common Grounds)
3777[3] 4446[3] 4893[5] 5637[5]

Dhhamaan (IRE) *Ruth Carr* a59 63
8 b g Dilshaan Safe Care (IRE) (Caerleon (USA))
(42) 105[5] 409[7] 546[10] 976[7] 1394[7] 1734[10] 1995[7] 2125[8] (3030) 3444[3] 3770[2] 4161[2] 4339[9] 4966[10] (5471) 6367[8] 6634[F]

Diaccia (GER) *P Schiergen* 94
3 b f High Chaparral(IRE) Djidda (GER) (Lando (GER))
2910a[13]

Diaghan (FR) *M Delzangles* 103
2 gr c Lawman(FR) Diamilina (FR) (Linamix (FR))
7409a[2]

Dialogue *Geoffrey Harker* a89 72
7 b g Singspiel(IRE) Zonda (Fabulous Dancer (USA))
1693[3] 1932[9] 2707[4] 3546[9] 4160[2] 6634[8] 6907[13]

Diamant (GER) *Wido Neuroth* a55 103
3 b c Zamindar(USA) Diamantgottin (GER) (Fantastic Light (USA))
5326a[11]

Diaminda (IRE) *Alan Jarvis* 93
3 b f Diamond Green(FR) Lominda (IRE) (Lomond (USA))
2047[15]

Diamond Bachelor (USA) *Patrick L Biancone* a97 97
2 bb c War Front(USA) Seasoned (USA) (Pulpit (USA))
7711a[9]

Diamond Belle *Noel Quinlan* a83 86
4 b f Rock Of Gibraltar(IRE) Dixie Belle (Diktat)
4830[3] 5493[6] 6072[2] 6609[3] 7297[5] 7742[10] 8088[12]

Diamond Blue *Richard Fahey* a68 76
5 ch f Namid Petra Nova (First Trump)
1646[8] 1800[10] 2275[9] 2343[3] 2702[2] ◆ 2914[6] 3078[4] 3505[6] 4047[13] 4510[6] (5365) 5564[6] 6941[6] 7801[9]

Diamond Charlie (IRE) *Simon Dow* a94 88
5 br g Diamond Green(FR) Rosy Lydgate (Last Tycoon)
(113) (780) 1765[7] 2227[4] 3018[9] 4707[4] 6189[6] 7642[10] 7982[4] 8189[2]

Diamond Dove (GER) *Andreas Lowe* 104
2 ch f Dr Fong(USA) Dyveke (GER) (Lando (GER))
(7406a)

Diamond Dust (FR) *Mario Hofer* a62 54
2 b f Touch Down(GER) Diamond Fever (GER) (Orpen (USA))
5213a[14]

Diamondhead (IRE) *Ed de Giles* a73 80
4 b g Kyllachy Hammrah (Danehill (USA))
1798[4] 2286[8] 2929[7] 3393[2] (4338) 4837[8] 5798[2]

Diamond Lady *Jo Hughes* a59 84
2 b f Multiplex Ellen Mooney (Efisio)
1156[2] 1344[4] (2068) 2414[4] 3459[18] (4399) (4431) 4726[4] 5005[15] 7503[8]

Diamond Mine *Luca Cumani* a87 62
3 bg c Rock Of Gibraltar(IRE) Kassiyra (IRE) (Kendor (FR))
6062[7] 6402[3] (6926) (7739) ◆

Diamond Penny (IRE) *Seamus Durack* a76 77
5 b g Diamond Green(FR) Penny Fan (Nomination)
3573[3] 4167[3] 5185[3] 6173[8] 6358[8]

Diamond Pro (IRE) *Christopher Kellett* a17 59
4 b g Diamond Green(FR) Speedbird (USA) (Sky Classic (CAN))
5021a[10] 8229[10] 8373[7]

Diamonds A Dancing *Rebecca Curtis* 55
3 ch g Delta Dancer Zing (Zilzal (USA))
3606[4]

Diamondsinthesky (IRE) *Derek Shaw* a56
2 b f Dandy Man(IRE) Colourpoint (USA) (Forest Wildcat (USA))
7370[5] 7541[5] 7804[6] 8435[2]

Diamond Solitaire (IRE) *Alan Jarvis*
2 br f Diamond Green(FR) Eastern Blue (IRE) (Be My Guest (USA))
2625[14]

Diamond Stilettos (IRE) *Mrs A M O'Shea* 86
2 ch f Ad Valorem(USA) Vanitycase (IRE) (Editor's Note (USA))
6881a[6]

Diamond Vine (IRE) *Ronald Harris* a69 74
5 b g Diamond Green(FR) Glasnas Giant (Giant's Causeway (USA))
398[10] 494[7] 750[2] 898[6] 3010[7] 3623[5] 3949[9] 4148[8] 5097[6] 5817[9] 6156[2] ◆ 6732[6] 6901[5] 7323[5] 7599[7] 8023[6] 8412[5]

Dianora *Sir Michael Stoute* 74
2 b f New Approach(IRE) Nannina (Medicean)
6140[3] ◆

Diapenko *Brian Meehan* 75
2 b c Archipenko(USA) Diablerette (Green Desert (USA))
3291[2] ◆ 4026[P]

Dibajj (FR) *A De Royer-Dupre* a91 108
3 ch f Iffraaj Goleta (IRE) (Royal Applause)
(4274a) 5806a[3] (6445a) 7054a[10] 7941a[5]

Dibayani (IRE) *M Halford* 103
3 b g Shamardal(USA) Dibiya (IRE) (Caerleon (USA))
1555a[4]

Dice Flavor (USA) *Patrick Gallagher* a104 104
3 ch c Scat Daddy(USA) Afleet Summer (USA) (Afleet (CAN))
1264a[8]

Dicey Vows (USA) *Alan Jarvis* a64 55
5 b g Broken Vow(USA) Pretty Dicey (USA) (Cherokee Run (USA))
789[9] 883[11] 3662[5] 3977[11]

Dichoh *Michael Madgwick* a49 54
10 b g Diktat Hoh Dancer (Indian Ridge)
6554[11]

Dick Bos *David O'Meara* a93 98
4 ch g Dutch Art Cosmic Countess (IRE) (Lahib (USA))
1571[9] 2239[2] 2460[8] (2988) 3249[2] 3846a[4] 4780[7] 5545[16] 6621[21] 6850[2] 7171[15]

Dick Doughtywylie *John Gosden* a107 108
5 b g Oasis Dream Sugar Mill (FR) (Polar Falcon (USA))
1846[5] 2186[5] 3525[14] 4027[6] 4526[3] 6742[9] 7927[5] 8062[2] (8386)

Dickie Le Davoir *Richard Guest* a74 79
9 b g Kyllachy Downeaster Alexa (USA) (Red Ryder (USA))
27[9] 453[2] 526[3] (645) 760[10] 812[10] 885[13] 966[11] 1102[11] 1280[5] 1525[9] 1650[2] 1798[7] 1964[3] 2275[8]

Diddy Eric *Micky Hammond* 53
3 b g Oratorio(IRE) Amber Queen (IRE) (Cadeaux Genereux)
1759[10] 4113[4] 4449[3] 5143[2] 5343[3] 7027[9]

Didge (FR) *E Bergougnoux* a79
4 b f Solon(GER) Partie Majeure (FR) (Anabaa Blue)
(922a)

Diescentric (USA) *Julie Camacho* a97 111
6 b g Diesis Hawzah (Green Desert (USA))
2541[3] ◆ (2858) (3825) 5013[2]

Different *Bryan Smart* a74 71
3 ch f Bahamian Bounty Hill Welcome (Most Welcome)
(1911) 2626[6] 2888[7] 4976[6] 7937[2] 8319[7]

Different Scenario *Mel Brittain* a27 43
2 b f Araafa(IRE) Racina (Bluebird (USA))
1605[5] 2075[6] 6842[5] 7755[7]

Diffident Beats *Mick Channon* a59 59
2 ch g Assertive Princess Almora (Pivotal)
5646[7] 5891[8] 6079[4] 6494[5] (6654) 6924[11] 7156[5]

Diletta Tommasa (IRE) *John Stimpson* a69 64
3 ch f Dylan Thomas(IRE) Chronicle (Observatory (USA))
209[5] (613) 1119[4] 1487[10] 2331[5] 4523[5] (4755) 5204[5] 6109[5] (6218)

Dilgura *Stuart Kittow* a86 80
3 b f Ishiguru(USA) Dilys (Efisio)
1660[2] (2824) 6744[2] (7381)

Diman Waters (IRE) *Eric Alston* a78 87
6 br g Namid Phantom Waters (Pharly (FR))
1963[9] 3236[5] 3569[2] 3933[2] 4203[2] 4579[3] 4730[5] (5183) 6159[3]

Dimashq *Richard Guest* a33 49
11 b m Mtoto Agwaas (IRE) (Rainbow Quest (USA))
2721[5] 3595[6]

Dime Dancer (IRE) *Richard Hannon Snr* 72
2 b f Azamour(IRE) Happy Land (IRE) (Refuse To Bend (IRE))
5282[3] 6140[7] 6594[4] 6973[10]

Dimension *Conor Murphy* a107 111
5 bb g Medicean Palatial (Green Desert (USA))
6456a[5] 7710a[5]

Dimitar (USA) *Brendan Powell* a76 73
4 b g Mizzen Mast(USA) Peace And Love (IRE) (Fantastic Light (USA))
2573[7] 2920[3] 3617[7] 5479[10] 6080[10] (6855) 7306[8] 7487[4]

Dimity (IRE) *John Joseph Murphy* a64 85
2 b f Camacho Pretty Ballerina (USA) (Swain (IRE))
2944a[7] 6485[2]

Dingaan (IRE) *Peter Grayson* a53 30
10 b g Tagula(IRE) Boughtbyphone (Warning)
117[8] 327[7] 471[5] 655[11] 794[4] 819[5] 917[5] 1042[7] 4840[7] 5273[14]

Ding Ding *Mick Channon* a51 57
2 ch f Winker Watson Five Bells (IRE) (Rock Of Gibraltar (IRE))
1880[4] 2068[9] (2475) 2759[4] 4964[3] 5347[4] 5467[3] 6322[9] 6426[3] 6725[5] 7110[3]

Dingle View (IRE) *Bent Olsen* a83 87
5 b f Mujadil(USA) Livius Lady (IRE) (Titus Livius (FR))
2145a[6]

Dinkie *Geoffrey Oldroyd* a12 38
3 b f Misu Bond(IRE) Chez Cherie (Wolfhound (USA))
6289[9] 8054[5]

Dinkum Diamond (IRE) *Henry Candy* 108
5 b c Aussie Rules(USA) Moving Diamonds (Lomitas)
2396[11] 2865[3] 3558[3] 4986[10] 5726[16] 7010[5] 7821[6]

Diodoros (FR) *F Chappet* a95 100
7 ch g High Chaparral(IRE) Light Quest (USA) (Quest For Fame)
6060a[2]

Diplomatic (IRE) *Michael Squance* a79 58
8 b g Cape Cross(IRE) Embassy (Cadeaux Genereux)
13[7] 222[7] 272[2] (415) 650[7] 899[2] 984[7] 1292[5] 3434[9] 3993[7] 5135[7] 6315[10] 6933[4] (7437) (7629) 7836[2]

Diplomatic Force (USA) *Charlie Appleby* a61 75
2 b g Medaglia d'Oro(USA) Criticism (Machiavellian (USA))
3490[5] 4021[3] 5101[4] 6401[8] 6852[6]

Directorship *Patrick Chamings* a94 105
7 br g Diktat Away To Me (Exit To Nowhere (USA))
(1848) (2424) 3458[16] 4080[9] 5255[7] 7018[5]

Direct Times (IRE) *Peter Chapple-Hyam* 72
2 b c Acclamation Elegant Times (IRE) (Dansili)
7817[3]

Direct Trade *Mark Usher* a48 26
3 ch f Trade Fair Bold Love (Bold Edge)
2572[7] 3178[13] 3903[10] 4607[7] 4840[4] 5354[7] 6344[7] 7083[4] 7931[8]

Disa Leader (SAF) *M F De Kock* a107 104
8 b g Parade Leader(USA) Plumosa (SAF) (Sapieha (IRE))
154a[7] 367a[4] 836a[3] 957a[4]

Discay *Mark Johnston* a74 89
4 b g Distant Music(USA) Caysue (Cayman Kai (IRE))
(528) 969[3] 1993[6] 4435[5] 4889[3] (5384) 5712[3] (6086) 6280[3] 6668[2] (6846) 7239[9] 7496[7]

Discernable *H-A Pantall* a64 98
3 ch f Elusive Quality(USA) Louve Mysterieuse (USA) (Seeking The Gold (USA))
1636[8] 2024[3] 2367[6] 2844[12] 7993a[11]

Disclaimer *Lady Cecil* a102 108
3 b g Dansili Novellara (Sadler's Wells (USA))
(1803) (2086) ◆ (2620) 3526[12] 6638[5]

Disclosure *Bryan Smart* 74
2 b g Indesatchel(IRE) Gemini Gold (IRE) (King's Best (USA))
1989[6] 3391[2] 3680[2] (4470) 6493[9] 7170[7]

Disco Dale (IRE) *Richard Fahey* a71
2 gr g Verglas(IRE) Artisia (IRE) (Peintre Celebre (USA))
8346[10]

Disco Dave (IRE) *Daniel Mark Loughnane* a64 47
5 ch g Dalakhani(IRE) Amoureux (USA) (Deputy Minister (CAN))
8371[2]

Disco Inferno (IRE) *Brian Meehan* a67 81
3 b c Lawman(FR) Pink Sovietstaia (FR) (Soviet Star (USA))
3585[3] 4022[2] 4667[4] 5176[2] 5512[6] 5932[2] 6486[5] 7108[3] 7436[7]

Discovery Bay *Brian Ellison* a82 80
5 b g Dansili Rainbow's Edge (Rainbow Quest (USA))
(662) 691[3] ◆ 2369[7] ◆ 7369[7]

Discression *Kevin Ryan* a73 96
4 b g Indesatchel(IRE) Night Gypsy (Mind Games)
1485[9] 1675[9] 1992[2] 2592[11] ◆ 3207[7] 4540[8] 4879[12] 5481[5] 5824[4]

Discussiontofollow (IRE) *Mike Murphy* a83 71
3 b g Elusive City(USA) Tranquil Sky (Intikhab (USA))
5290[3] ◆ 5884[2] (8003) (8224) ◆

Dishy Guru *Michael Blanshard* a68 69
4 ch g Ishiguru(USA) Pick A Nice Name (Polar Falcon (USA))
582[6] 812[5] 1063[3] 1304[8] 1516[3] ◆ 2596[11] 3949[13] 7862[5]

Disko (IRE) *Daniel Kubler* 91
2 b f Kodiac Dissonance (IRE) (Rossini (USA))
2359[2] 2712[2] (3324) 3829[4] 5767[6]

Distant Past *Kevin Ryan* a77
2 b g Pastoral Pursuits Faraway Lass (Distant Relative)
(7804) 8203[7]

Distant Sun (USA) *Linda Perratt* a50 63
9 b g Distant View(USA) The Great Flora (USA) (Unaccounted For (USA))
2795[6] 3283[9] 3713[6] 3933[7] 4102[8] 4448[8] 4821[9] 5336[8] 5708[5] 5917[4] 6669[5] 7149[10] 7236[8]

Distant Sunrise *Ann Duffield* 18
3 b f Tobougg(IRE) Prairie Sun (GER) (Law Society (USA))
2885[7] 3545[10]

Di Stefano *Joseph Tuite* a25 67
6 b g Bahamian Bounty Marisa (GER) (Desert Sun)
822[9]

District Attorney (IRE) *Chris Fairhurst* a70 70
4 b g Lawman(FR) Mood Indigo (IRE) (Indian Ridge)
1567[11] 1788[11] 2537[12] 3081[2] 4119[10] 4824[7] 5427[4] 5882[9]

Diva Delight (IRE) *Robert Cowell* a45
3 b f Jeremy(USA) Wattrey (Royal Academy (USA))
6849[6] 7037[4] 7459[10]

Divea *Anthony Carson* a63 63
4 b f Dylan Thomas(IRE) Cumin (USA) (Fusaichi Pegasus (USA))
1836[11] 4126[7] 6479[3]

Divergence (IRE) *Michael Bell* a69 90
3 b f Teofilo(IRE) Min Alhawa (USA) (Riverman (USA))
1478[2] (2164) 2619[8] 3251[2] 3502[3] 4770[2] (5095) 5764[4] 6434[2] 7891a[14]

Divertimenti (IRE) *Roy Bowring* a60 69
9 b g Green Desert(USA) Ballet Shoes (IRE) (Ela-Mana-Mou)
88[7] (610) (1077) 1681[17] 1731[6] (2236) 2338[4] 2781[7] 3246[9] 4074[8] 4456[3] 4669[8] 7347[7] 7957[11] 8002[7] 8169[2] 8271[4] 8370[6]

Dividend Dan (IRE) *Mike Murphy* a51 55
3 ch g Danroad(AUS) Pip'n Judy (IRE) (Pips Pride)
1384[6] 1784[5] 3289[3]

Divina Comedia (FR) *N Clement* 95
2 gr f Footstepsinthesand Divine Promesse (FR) (Verglas (IRE))
7967a[2]

Divine Bay *Gary Moore* a41 36
2 b f Dutch Art Inchcoonan (Emperor Jones (USA))
6408[6] 6923[7] 7441[7]

Divine Call *Milton Bradley* a78 73
6 b g Pivotal Pious (Bishop Of Cashel)
1286[2] 2724[6] 2825[7] 3622[10] 5349[5] 6995[8] 7985[4] 8163[7] 8306[6]

Divine Force *M Ibrahim* a50 63
7 b g Bertolini(USA) Malcesine (IRE) (Auction Ring (USA))
394a[9]

Divine Pamina (IRE) *Jim Boyle* a74 62
4 br f Dark Angel(IRE) Greek Symphony (IRE) (Mozart (IRE))
(1303)

Divine Rule (IRE) *Laura Mongan* a67 54
5 br g Cacique(IRE) Island Destiny (Kris)
89[3] 223[6] 334[2] 510[3] 633[3] 883[6] 1056[3] (1100) 1303[6] 1925[8] 2225[10] 2747[4] 2954[3] 3330[6] 4169[6]

Divine Success (IRE) *Richard Fahey* a38 52
4 b g Amadeus Wolf Divine Pursuit (Kris)
5840[10] 6851[10]

Divin Leon (FR) *M Boutin* a86 90
5 b c Divine Light(JPN) Nera Zilzal (IRE) (Zilzal (USA))
(960a)

Divisional *John Gosden* 81
2 ch c Medicean Peppermint Green (Green Desert (USA))
6762[2]

Division Belle *William Muir* a64 63
2 gr f Dalakhani(IRE) Multiplication (Marju (IRE))
4702[18] 5352[7] 6063[6] 6749[3]

Dixie Gwalia *Michael Attwater* a62 39
5 b f Tobougg(IRE) Dixieanna (Night Shift (USA))
92[2] 233[0] 240[5] (323) 399[3] 1155[3] 8023[10]

Dixie's Dream (IRE) *William Jarvis* a92 88
4 b g Hawk Wing(USA) Hams (USA) (Dixie Union (USA))
6126[2] ◆ 6359[8] 6925[2] (7989) 8263[8]

Diyala (IRE) *Gordon Elliott* a72 80
4 b f Tiger Hill(IRE) Daliya (IRE) (Giant's Causeway (USA))
(6087) ◆

Diyalani (FR) *W Mongil* a69 67
5 gr c Cape Cross(IRE) Diasilixa (FR) (Linamix (FR))
5601a[2]

Diyamindar (FR) *J Boisnard* 108
3 b c Zamindar(USA) Diyawara (IRE) (Doyoun)
2355a[4] 3645a[6] 6250a[6]

Dizzy Miss Lizzy (IRE) *Richard Hannon Snr* a36 42
2 gr f Verglas(IRE) Maramba (USA) (Hussonet (USA))
3694[8] 5101[8] 5834[5]

Django James (IRE) *Robert Collet* a60 60
2 ch c Stormy River(FR) Abime (USA) (Woodman (USA))
6786a[10]

Djinni (IRE) *Richard Hannon Snr* a76 82
2 b f Invincible Spirit(IRE) La Persiana (Daylami (IRE))
3986[4] (4589) 5699[3] 7879[4]

Djolan (GER) *N Sauer* a83 85
3 b g Golan(IRE) Dunnella (IRE) (Brief Truce (USA))
960a[0]

Doc Hay (USA) *David O'Meara* a74 109
6 bb g Elusive Quality(USA) Coherent (USA) (Danzig (USA))
1704a[4] 2019[11] ◆ 2662[8] 3046[8] 3420[14] 5984[7] 6391[8] 6719[6] (6845) 7010[6] 7208[19] 7527[16]

Doc Hill *Michael Blanshard* a51 47
4 ch g Dr Fong(USA) Cultural Role (Night Shift (USA))
7371[2]

Doc Holliday (IRE) *Edward Lynam* a81 65
3 b g Lawman(FR) Miss Amadeus (IRE) (Mozart (IRE))
(8012a)

Docofthebay (IRE) *Scott Dixon* a95 92
9 ch g Docksider(USA) Baize (Efisio)
345[2] 443[6] (621) 944[5] 1148[2] 1233[11] 1571[4] 1830[8] 2310[6] 2657[2] 2988[7] 3096[12] 3684[13] 7648[10] 7949[7] 8094[5] 8269[7] 8350[9]

Docs Legacy (IRE) *Richard Fahey* a76 89
4 b g Ad Valorem(USA) Lunamixa (GER) (Linamix (FR))
(1238) 1391[2]

Doctor Hilary *Mark Hoad* a57 51
11 b g Mujahid(USA) Agony Aunt (Formidable (USA))
223[10] 440[8] 630[9] 794[5] 1042[2] 2170[6] 2997[2] 3325[2] 3897[5] 7905[9]

Doctor Parkes *Stuart Williams* a94 102
7 b g Diktat Lucky Parkes (Full Extent (USA))
2046[5] 2444[15] 2865[8] 3114[5] 3802[8] (4024) 4217[2] 5257[7] (5519) 5651[7] 5991[7] 6391[20] 6830[16] 7171[10] 7373[11] 8232[8]

Doctor's Gift *Pat Eddery* a47 50
3 b g Motivator Jocie May (USA) (Aljabr (USA))
2151[12] 3013[9] 6964[7] 7299[10] 7514[11]

Doctor Sim (IRE) *D De Waele* a91 77
4 b g King's Best(USA) Mas A Fuera (IRE) (Alzao (USA))
498a[3] 5042a[10]

Dodger Marley (IRE) *Stuart Williams* 64
2 b g Kodiac Shelini (Robellino (USA))
3035[4] 3883[2] 4347[5] 5509[5] 5842[5]

Dodina (IRE) *Brian Ellison* a74 74
3 b f Acclamation Etica (IRE) (Barathea (IRE))
2504[3] 2788[2] (4687) 5104[2] 5820[6] 6948[5] 7487[3] ◆ 8095[7]

Dogaressa (IRE) *Peter Chapple-Hyam* 75
2 ch f Mastercraftsman(IRE) Doregan (IRE) (Bahhare (USA))
7532[2]

Dogma Noir (IRE) *F Camici* 101
4 b c Iffraaj Patruel (Rainbow Quest (USA))
2489a[8] 7724a[3]

Dohasa (IRE) *Ismail Mohammed* a90 87
8 b g Bold Fact(USA) Zara's Birthday (IRE) (Waajib)
365a[12] 575a[5] 868a[12]

Do It All (USA) *Saeed bin Suroor* a108 110
6 b h Distorted Humor(USA) Stupendous Miss (USA) (Dynaformer (USA))
466a[10] 745a[10]

Do It Yourself (IRE) *Andreas Lowe* a64 69
5 b c Hurricane Run(IRE) Desert Classic (Green Desert (USA))
4467a[11]

Dolce La Hulpe *C Boutin* a33 57
2 b f Kodiac Soviet Terms (Soviet Star (USA))
5213a[7]

Dolce N Karama (IRE) *John Patrick Shanahan* a53 103
2 b c The Carbon Unit(USA) Janna's Jewel (IRE) (Traditionally (USA))
6807[4] 7528[4]

Doldrums (USA) *Mark Johnston* a78
3 b f Bernardini(USA) Appealing Storm (USA) (Valid Appeal (USA))
(7932) 8226[5]

Dolly Bantry *Alan McCabe* a22
3 ch f Pastoral Pursuits Seeker (Rainbow Quest (USA))
541[4] 708[9] 1429[10]

Dolly Colman (IRE) *Zoe Davison* a52 42
5 bg f Diamond Green(FR) Absolutely Cool (IRE) (Indian Ridge)
200[2] 508[8] 722[3] 896[14] 1090[9] 1183[3] 1498[4] 1779[6] 1909[4] 1987[3] 2533[9] 3213[4] 3580[3] 4350[7] 5002[9] 5311[5] 8335[8] 8448[9]

Dolly Diva *Paul Midgley* 62
4 b f Iffraaj Charlie Girl (Puissance)
1184[8] 1389[7] 2162[10] 2616[8] 3030[10] 3630[13] 4009[6] 4430[10] 6289[6]

Dolphin Club (IRE) *Richard Fahey* 56
2 ch c Duke Of Marmalade(IRE) Meon Mix (Kayf Tara)
3810[5]

Dolphin Rock *Brian Ellison* a77 84
6 b g Mark Of Esteem(IRE) Lark In The Park (IRE) (Grand Lodge (USA))
(1442) 1723[3] (2646) 4287[6] 5149[3] 5860[5] 6801[16] 7632[7]

Dolphin Village (IRE) *Richard Fahey* a61 85
3 b g Cape Cross(IRE) Reform Act (USA) (Lemon Drop Kid (USA))
1365[5] 1776[2] (2624) 2878[4] 4023[7] (5888) (6631) 6976[5]

Domeside *M Delcher Sanchez* 115
7 b h Domedriver(IRE) Buck's Fizz (Kris)
1871a[3] (2695a) (6447a)

Dominant (IRE) *J Moore* 119
5 bl c Cacique(IRE) Es Que (Inchinor)
(8208a)

Dominate *Richard Hannon Snr* 92
3 b c Assertive Blue Goddess (IRE) (Blues Traveller (IRE))
(1582) 2415[5] 3340[5] 3584[6] 4983[23] 6238[9]

Domination *C Byrnes* a82 97
6 b g Motivator Soliza (IRE) (Intikhab (USA))
7193[25]

Dominium (USA) *Jeremy Gask* a83 75
6 b g E Dubai(USA) Sudenlylastsummer (USA) (Rinka Das (USA))
95[2] 4837[7] 5697[2] (6135) 6525[4] 6744[6] (7264) 7436[3] 7742[6] 8088[6] 8181[10]

Do More Business (IRE) *Liam Corcoran* a59 55
6 b g Dubai Destination(USA) Tokyo Song (USA) (Stravinsky (USA))
77[5] 128[3] 223[5] 472[2] 975[6] 1087[6] 1194[2] 1657[2] 2303a[2] 2747[6] 4423[3] 4658[3] 6400[7] 7265[9] 8055[2] 8199[4] 8371[7] (8399)

Donard Lass *Jimmy Fox*
3 b f Assertive Veverka (King's Theatre (IRE))
5925[8] 6555[13] 7253[12]

Don Bosco (FR) *D Smaga* a113 113
6 ch h Barathea(IRE) Perfidie (IRE) (Monsun (GER))
1048a[2] 1420a[2] (1945a) 2694a[4] 4104a[3] 5040a[9] 7047a[10]

Don Caprice (FR) *E Leenders* a65
4 ch c Carlotamix(FR) Dame Caprice (IRE) (Bering)
922a[5]

Doncaster Belle (IRE) *Charles Smith* 54
2 b f Ad Valorem(USA) Gradetime (IRE) (Danetime (IRE))
1605[10] 1718[11] 1820[8] 2436[7] 2793[4] 3189[4] 3255[4] 7032[12] 7494[13] 7665[10] 7756[8]

Done Dreaming (IRE) *Richard Fahey* a64 70
3 b g Diamond Green(FR) Wishing Chair (USA) (Giant's Causeway (USA))
2581[3] 3221[7] 3929[3] 4371[7] 5054[3] 5485[5] 6760[5] 7149[11]

Don Eduardo *J S Moore* a54 58
3 b g Byron Angie And Liz (IRE) (Spectrum (IRE))
5[8] 2393[4] 2528[7] 2950[13]

Donibane (FR) *Mlle V Dissaux* a42 58
2 b f Dobby Road(FR) Dohibane (FR) (Danehill (USA))
4599a[8] 6059a[4]

Don Libre *Paul Cole* a93 69
4 b c Librettist(USA) Darwinia (GER) (Acatenango (GER))
2725[7] 3274[10] 3472[2]

Don Marco *Roger Charlton* 84
3 b g Choisir(AUS) Dolma (FR) (Marchand De Sable (USA))
7222[7]

Donna Prassede (ITY) *S Botti* 97
2 b f Manduro(GER) Everarda (GER) (Singspiel (IRE))
7415a[10]

Doncha (IRE) *Robert Eddery* a80 79
2 br c Captain Marvelous(IRE) Seasonal Style (IRE) (Generous (IRE))
5891[6] 7308[3] (7853)

Donn Halling (IRE) *V Luka Jr* 107
5 b g Halling(USA) Papering (IRE) (Shaadi (USA))
4571a[5] 5807a[7] 6678a[6] 7566a[11]

Donny Rover (IRE) *David C Griffiths* a39 80
2 b g Excellent Art My Lass (Elmaamul (USA))
1108[6] ◆ 1534[3] ◆ 1820[4] 3044[8] 3565[4] 3810[7] 4246[6] 4610[3] 5866[5] 6303[7] (6663) 7062[4] 7333[9] 7529[3] 7658[4] 7819[8]

Don Ottavio *David Lanigan* a52
2 b c Amadeus Wolf Lyric Art (USA) (Red Ransom (USA))
6340[9] 6689[B]

Don Padeja *Luca Cumani* a72 80
3 b g Dansili La Leuze (IRE) (Caerleon (USA))
2384[12] 4152[6] 5001[3] (5612) 5954[3] 7105[5]

Don'T *Luca Cumani* a74
2 b f Invincible Spirit(IRE) Frigid (Indian Ridge)
(7296)

Don't Be Scilly *Eric Wheeler* a37 13
5 ch f Reel Buddy(USA) Batchworth Breeze (Beveled (USA))
202[7] 438[4] 581[5] 1896[8] 2722[6]

Dont Bother Me (IRE) *Niall Moran* a101 103
3 br c Dark Angel(IRE) Faleh (USA) (Silver Hawk (USA))
1555a[2] 2021[8] 2290a[4] 3455[7] 5453a[5] 7051a[9]

Don't Call Me (IRE) *David Nicholls* a108 111
6 ch g Haafhd Just Call Me (NZ) (Blues Traveller (IRE))
154a[5] ◆ 367a[2] 557a[4] 745a[5] 872a[4] 1535[2] 1919[6] 2323[2] 2782[2] 3458[4] 4744[6] 6183[9]

Dont Have It Then *Willie Musson* a53 66
2 b g Myboycharlie(IRE) Mondovi (Kyllachy)
3017[8] 3836[6] 4379[6] 5371[6] 8166[6]

Dontpaytheferryman (USA) *Peter Hiatt* a62 34
8 ch g Wiseman's Ferry(USA) Expletive Deleted (USA) (Dr Blum (USA))
1795[3] 2509[3] 8047[9] 8349[7]

Don't Stare *James Fanshawe* a85 78
3 b g Zamindar(USA) Joshua's Princess (Danehill (USA))
2760[3] ◆ 4381[2] (5133)

Don't Tell *George Moore* 43
3 ch f Sakhee's Secret Starry Sky (Oasis Dream)
2121[4] 2386[6] 4161[6] 4585[5] 6687[8] 7343[12]

Dont Tell Nan *Derek Shaw* a40 37
2 b f Major Cadeaux Charlie Girl (Puissance)
6477[8] 6966[7] 7541[6] 7771[8] 7900[6]

Don'twait Toolong (USA) *Jane Cibelli* a89 77
9 b g War Chant(USA) Solvig (USA) (Caerleon (USA))
1001a[5]

Doodles *David Nicholls* a44 31
3 b f Pastoral Pursuits Burton Ash (Diktat)
5[7] 988[3]

Dorback *Tony Newcombe* a88 88
6 ch g Kyllachy Pink Supreme (Night Shift (USA))
3[2] ◆ 58[4] 196[4] 353[3] 457[4] 913[7] 1649[12] 1961[2] 2255[3] 2441[14] 2790[2] 3090[8] 3371[4] (3487) (3577) 3859[3] 4263[11] 4675[6] 4860[15] 5544[18] 6850[8] 8088[10] 8224[11]

Dorfman *Mark Johnston* a77 68
3 b g Halling(USA) Cercle D'Amour (USA) (Storm Cat (USA))
(712) ◆ 1470[U] 1834[4] 3336[U] (Dead)

Dorian Crown *Seth Benzel* a80 100
7 br h E Dubai(USA) Slow Jazz (USA) (Chief's Crown (USA))
552a[8]

Dorlesh Way (IRE) *Patrick Holmes* a39 9
6 ch g Rakti Patalavaca (GER) (Acatenango (GER))
708[8] 1282[12]

Dormello (IRE) *D Selvaratnam* a91 102
5 b h Dansili Field Of Hope (IRE) (Selkirk (USA))
661a[3] 873a[7]

Dorothy B (IRE) *John Gosden* a65 104
2 b f Fastnet Rock(AUS) Slow Sand (USA) (Dixieland Band (USA))
4409[4] ◆ (4924) 6142[2] 6836[5]

Dorothy's Dancing (IRE) *Gary Moore* a75 59
5 b f Acclamation Segoria (IRE) (Shinko Forest (IRE))
(322) 559[2] 728[2] (902) 1198[6]

Dorry K (IRE) *Brian Rothwell* a30 78
4 b f Ad Valorem(USA) Ashtaroute (USA) (Holy Bull (USA))
830[6] 989[5] 1445[14] 1789[11]

Dorset Cream *Lady Cecil* 68
2 b f Dansili Blend (Zafonic (USA))
6281[5] 7449[2]

Dos Amigos (IRE) *Michael Dods* 86
4 b g Clodovil(IRE) Ide Say (IRE) (Grand Lodge (USA))
1281[8] 3777[8]

Doshermanas (FR) *C Boutin* a52 45
2 ch f Carlotamix(FR) Love And Cry (FR) (Neverneyev (USA))
5213a[13]

Dotesy (IRE) *John Quinn* a31 61
2 b f Indian Haven Erreur (IRE) (Desert King (IRE))
1573[6] 1718[4] 2238[2] 2502[7] 3440[4] 4054[4] 4990[6] 5964[3]

Double Accord *Anthony Honeyball* a46 51
3 ch f Double Trigger(IRE) Got Tune (FR) (Green Tune (USA))
1671[13] 2198[8] 2713[9] 7331[8]

Double Bluff (IRE) *Mark Johnston* 90
2 b c Azamour(IRE) Damask Rose (IRE) (Dr Devious (IRE))
6330[2] (6740) 7409a[6]

Double Cee *Warren Greatrex* a46 80
4 ch g Haafhd Razzle (IRE) (Green Desert (USA))
1586[13] 2569[2] 3110[3] 3952[4] 4530[4] 5933[8]

Double Czech (IRE) *Amanda Perrett* 65
2 b c Bushranger(IRE) Night Of Joy (IRE) (King's Best (USA))
2847[5] 3238[8] 4439[4] 4948[19] 6322[4]

Double Discount (IRE) *Tom Dascombe* a74 93
3 b g Invincible Spirit(IRE) Bryanstown Girl (IRE) (Kalanisi (IRE))
1769[4] 2151[6] (3105) (4023) 4251[2] 4917[9] 6163[6]

Double Happiness *Brian Rothwell* 19
3 ch f Sakhee(USA) Fu Wa (USA) (Distant View (USA))
4008[13]

Double Mast (FR) *A Vetault* a69
5 b f Dano-Mast Double Melody (FR) (Double Bed (FR))
7573a[10]

Double Point (IRE) *Paul Cole* 95
2 ch g Iffraaj Up On Points (Royal Academy (USA))
2847[4] 3174[2] (3574) (5039a) 5628a[4]

Double Star *Jonathan Portman* a37 56
3 b f Elusive City(USA) Tease (IRE) (Green Desert (USA))
2392[13] (3040) 3919[5] 4170[10] 5615[11] 6321[10] 6698[6]

Double Your Money (IRE) *Mark Johnston* a81 78
3 b g Shamardal(USA) Zeiting (IRE) (Zieten (USA))
1444[5] ◆ 1806[9] (2160) 2495[6] 2987[4] (Dead)

Douce Vie (IRE) *S Botti* 106
7 b h Desert Prince(IRE) Ellendellendoo (IRE) (Ela-Mana-Mou)
2698a[3] 6889a[10]

Dougal Philps *W P Mullins* a73 84
4 b g Echo Of Light Bella Bertolini (Bertolini (USA))
1168a[13]

Douglas Pasha (IRE) *David Nicholls* a59 52
3 b g Compton Place Lake Nayasa (Nayef (USA))
636[5] 904[4] 1050[6] (1116) 1361[3] 1772[5] 2613[9]

Douman (USA) *Ed Dunlop* a50 58
2 bb g Giant's Causeway(USA) Totally Devoted (USA) (Seeking The Gold (USA))
5718[11] 5957[8] 6355[7] 7032[11] 7461[9]

Douneedahand *Seamus Mullins* a66 62
2 b f Royal Applause Our Sheila (Bahamian Bounty)
3310[4] 4749[3] (4937) 5595[2] 5842[3] 5976[5] 8322[4]

Dover The Moon (IRE) *Richard Hannon Snr* a59 60
2 b c Bushranger(IRE) Gold Script (FR) (Script Ohio (USA))
4026[8] 6168[11] 7119[11]

Dovil's Duel (IRE) *Rod Millman* a53 74
2 b g Clodovil(IRE) Duelling (Diesis)
1108[5] 1541[7] 2359[5] 4019[6] 4519[3] 5034[5] 5371[2] (5610) (6111) 6320[6] 7221[6]

Downhill Dancer (IRE) *Brian Meehan* a42 59
3 b f Montjeu(IRE) Wiener Wald (USA) (Woodman (USA))
3241[11] 4898[13] 5178[5] 5702[6]

Downhill Only *H-A Pantall* a81 69
2 b c Montjeu(IRE) Miss Emma May (IRE) (Hawk Wing (USA))
6961a[4]

Downright Dizzie *Alastair Lidderdale* a46 63
3 ch f Notnowcato Italian Goddess (Medicean)
1016[4] 1613[7] 1761[4]

Down Time (USA) *Jamie Osborne* 60
3 b g Harlan's Holiday(USA) Frappay (USA) (Deputy Minister (CAN))
2833[4]

Downtown Boy (IRE) *Ray Craggs* a61 49
5 br g Kheleyf(USA) Uptown (IRE) (Be My Guest (USA))
(1017) 1214[6] (1730) 2537[9] 3910[8]

Downturn *Richard Hannon Snr* 78
2 b c Invincible Spirit(IRE) Jouet (Reprimand)
2847[3] ◆ (3291) 5034[9]

Doyouknowwhoiam *John Quinn* a58 57
4 ch g Monsieur Bond(IRE) Tibesti (Machiavellian (USA))
600[3] 5239[8]

Dozy Joe *Joseph Tuite* a76 83
5 b g Sleeping Indian Surrey Down (USA) (Forest Wildcat (USA))
8157[9]

Dragon City *Harry Dunlop* a77 78
3 b g Elusive City(USA) Oulianovsk (IRE) (Peintre Celebre (USA))
1679[5] 2605[3] 3277[4] 3982[9] 5392[3] (6116) 6809[5] 7257[12]

Dragon Falls (IRE) *A Fabre* a96 105
4 b c Distorted Humor(USA) Tizdubai (USA) (Cee's Tizzy (USA))
5808a[6]

Dragoon Guard (IRE) *Marco Botti* a74 43
2 b c Jeremy(USA) Elouges (IRE) (Dalakhani (IRE))
7308[7] 8026[2] (8221)

Dragstair (FR) *C Boillot* a72 70
6 ch g Astair(FR) Yeninka (FR) (Neverneyev (USA))
3969a[8]

Drahem *James Fanshawe* a64 76
3 b f Teofilo(IRE) Carinae (USA) (Nureyev (USA))
(2504) (3254) 4180[4] 5181[3] 6080[9]

Dramatic Act *Arne O Karlsen* 79
5 b g Dansili Winter Solstice (Unfuwain (USA))
4095a[7]

Drawnfromthepast (IRE) *Luke Dace* a88 78
8 ch g Tagula(IRE) Ball Cat (FR) (Cricket Ball (USA))
(56) 379[6] 727[4] 3315[8] 3855[5] 4344[6] 5165[5] 5645[6] 8128[8] 8384[2]

Draw Two (USA) *Michelle Nihei* 99
3 rg c Macho Uno(USA) Belle Watling (USA) (Pulpit (USA))
5551a[4]

Dream About You (IRE) *Robert Mills* a65
3 br f Amadeus Wolf Peshawar (Persian Bold)
103[4] 321[5]

Dream Ally (IRE) *Jedd O'Keeffe* a75 73
3 b g Oasis Dream Alexander Alliance (IRE) (Danetime (IRE))
1647[3] 1935[6] 2408[9] 2959[5] 4069[6] 5878[11] (6219) 6653[3] 6995[5]

Dream And Hope *Clive Brittain* 46
2 b f Royal Applause Senta's Dream (Danehill (USA))
4921[12]

Dream And Search (GER) *Charles Hills* a66 74
2 b c Raven's Pass(USA) Diamond Eyes (GER) (Winged Love (IRE))
2401[9] 3044[4] 6174[5] 7626[8]

Dream Can True (IRE) *L Riccardi* 93
3 b f Marju(IRE) Giant Dream (Giant's Causeway (USA))
1866a[19] 7316a[8]

Dream Cast (IRE) *David Simcock* a40 78
3 b g Refuse To Bend(IRE) Star Studded (Cadeaux Genereux)
2719[3] (3086) 3866[2] 4057[6]

Dream Catcher (FR) *Henry Candy* a79 79
5 gr g Della Francesca(USA) Gallopade (FR) (Kendor (FR))
2128[4] 2441[12] 3622[8] 4440[3] 5537[10] 6135[2] 6652[9] 7743[5]

Dream Catcher (SWE) *Jonjo O'Neill* a69 61
10 b g Songline(SWE) Queen Ida (SWE) (Diligo (FR))
2563[10]

Dream Impossible (IRE) *Peter Makin* a38 52
2 b f Iffraaj Romea (Muhtarram (USA))
5442[11] 5949[6] 6589[4] 6923[9]

Dreaming Again *Jimmy Fox* a23 23
3 b g Young Ern Maedance (Groom Dancer (USA))
4774[6] 5444[8] 6133[10]

Dreaming Of Rubies *Ben Haslam* a53 79
4 b f Oasis Dream Rubies From Burma (USA) (Forty Niner (USA))
1431[7] 3078[2] 4017[10] 5985[13] 8321[7]

Dreamlim (FR) *Mme A-L Guildoux*
4 ch g Dream Well(FR) Lady Pauline (FR) (Hamas (IRE))
5464a[9]

Dream Maker (IRE) *Tim Easterby* 88
3 ch f Bahamian Bounty Pointed Arch (IRE) (Rock Of Gibraltar (IRE))
1690[5] 2371[6] 2666[6] 3734[6] 4260[9] 4757[3] 4993[3] 5511[4] 5769[9] 6212[5] 6564[3]

Dream Prospector *James Evans* a68 56
4 b g Oasis Dream Prospectress (USA) (Mining (USA))
13[9] 415[11] 896[2] 1239[11] 1949[6] 2328[5] 2828[7] 3473[10]

Dream'run (ITY) *Bettina Wilson*
2 b f Blu Air Force(IRE) Wishbird (ITY) (Bluebird (USA))
6452a[10]

Dream Scenario *Mel Brittain* a76 70
3 b f Araafa(IRE) Notjustaprettyface (USA) (Red Ransom (USA))
1112[9] 1647[6] 2593[13] 3025[2] 3445[7] 4725[7] 4967[10] 5184[4] 5581[4] 7964[3] (8052) 8134[4]

Dream Sika (IRE) *Clive Cox* a45 59
2 b g Elnadim(USA) Enchantment (Compton Place)
3631[7] 4259[6] 4680[2] ◆ 5814[7] 6778[8] 7127[8]

Dreams Of Glory *Ron Hodges* a64 73
5 ch c Resplendent Glory(IRE) Pip's Dream (Glint Of Gold)
842[6] (1902) 2074[7] 3341[5] 3667[3] (4369) 5060[7] 5669[2] 6096[4]

Dreamspeed (IRE) *C Von Der Recke* a97 103
6 b g Barathea(IRE) Kapria (FR) (Simon Du Desert (FR))
701a[11]

Dream Tune *Clive Cox* 101
4 b g Oasis Dream Play Bouzouki (Halling (USA))
1675[5] 2254[5] 3527[2] ◆ 4946[14]

Dream Vale (IRE) *Tim Easterby* a58 73
3 b f Moss Vale(IRE) Dream State (IRE) (Machiavellian (USA))
1771[4] 2542[9] 2959[4] 3475[3] 3639[2] 4149[7]

Dream Walker (FR) *Brian Ellison* a54 90
4 gr g Gold Away(IRE) Minnie's Mystery (FR) (Highest Honor (FR))
1271[6] 1752[4] 2536[2] 2889[8] 3083[7] 3329[6] (4807) (4826) (5138) 5947[4] (6550) 6801[13]

Dream Wild *Sir Michael Stoute* a79 79
3 b f Oasis Dream Wince (Selkirk (USA))
(1876) 2390[3] 4252[8] 5202[2] 5784[3]

Dream Win *Brian Ellison* a70 76
7 b h Oasis Dream Wince (Selkirk (USA))
49[6] 192[3] 593[9] 789[12]

Dreamy Ciara *David Brown* a56 72
3 b f Multiplex Billie Holiday (Fairy King (USA))
6547[10] 6948[9] 7381[7] 7443[2]

Dreese (IRE) *James Tate* a76
2 b c Dandy Man(IRE) Lucky Flirt (USA) (Gulch (USA))
7844[3] ◆

Dressed In Lace *Jo Crowley* a74 68
4 b f Dark Angel(IRE) Pure Speculation (Salse (USA))
535[4] 790[4] 1063[9]

Dr Faustus (IRE) *Doug Watson* a92 96
8 gr g Sadler's Wells(USA) Requesting (Rainbow Quest (USA))
871a[5]

Dr Finley (IRE) *Lydia Pearce* a71 70
6 ch g Dr Fong(USA) Farrfesheena (USA) (Rahy (USA))
351[4] 654[10] 1348[2] 1502[4] 2197[9] (2968) 4179[3] 4392[3] 4867[5] 5560[12] 6565[9] 6736[6] 7767[5] 8160[4]

Drinkuptrig (IRE) *Stuart Williams* a62 60
2 b c Bushranger(IRE) Maybe In May (USA) (Miswaki (USA))
3581[9] 4121[6] 4505[8] 6605[5] 7973[2]

Drinmoy Lad (IRE) *Michael McElhone* a56 65
4 b g Kheleyf(USA) Dafalia (IRE) (Mark Of Esteem (IRE))
7148[8]

Dr Irv *Philip Kirby* 81
4 ch g Dr Fong(USA) Grateful (Generous (IRE))
1464[5] 2242[3] 2720[6] 3301[4] (3771) (4159) 4782[5] (5972) 6466[3] 7210[8]

Drive Home (USA) *Noel Wilson* a54 64
6 bb g Mr Greeley(USA) Unique Pose (IRE) (Sadler's Wells (USA))
1757[4] 5471[14] 6464[9] 6919[12] 7886[14]

Drive On (IRE) *Eve Johnson Houghton* a78 53
2 b g Tagula(IRE) Thelma Louise (IRE) (Desert Style (IRE))
4680^{4} 4912^{5} 6110^{5} 6749^{5} (7978) (8126) (8426)

Dr Livingstone (IRE) *Charles Egerton* a85 72
8 b g Dr Fong(USA) Radhwa (FR) (Shining Steel)
823^{5} 1523^{2} 1884^{10} 5168^{14} 5535^{4} 6802^{5}

Dropping Zone *Des Donovan* a43 49
3 b g Duke Of Marmalade(IRE) Blue Azure (USA) (American Chance (USA))
2267^{7} 2499^{6} 4839^{9} 5407^{4} 6157^{6}

Dr Red Eye *Scott Dixon* a89 99
5 ch g Dr Fong(USA) Camp Fire (IRE) (Lahib (USA))
751^{3} 865^{6} 1148^{7} (1746) (2214) (2649) 2868^{5} 4284^{3} 4986^{16} 5545^{8} 5943^{10} 6352^{12} 6826^{5}

Dr Thibault (FR) *U Suter* a76 80
4 b g American Post Shashamene (FR) (Anabaa Blue)
963a^{3}

Drumadoon (IRE) *Liam Corcoran* a47 61
5 b g Hawk Wing(USA) Lady Taufan (IRE) (Taufan (USA))
342^{8}

Drummond *Bernard Llewellyn* a52 78
4 b g Zamindar(USA) Alrisha (IRE) (Persian Bold)
1069^{6} 1239^{8} 1716^{9} 2348^{4} 2923^{5} 3312^{7} 3954^{4} 4604^{9} 5813^{6} 6457^{3}

Drussell (IRE) *Martin Bosley* a66 35
7 b g Orpen(USA) Cahermee Queen (USA) (King Of Kings (IRE))
7433^{8}

Dr Victoria *John Norton* a35 35
4 ch f Three Valleys(USA) Spielbound (Singspiel (IRE))
602^{3} 1455^{9} 1962^{8} 2757^{13} 5487^{6}

Dry Summer (USA) *Jeff Mullins* a98 103
3 ch g Any Given Saturday(USA) Greenstreet (USA) (Street Cry (IRE))
8120a^{7}

Dry Your Eyes (IRE) *Mark Johnston* a61 70
2 b f Shamardal(USA) Kindling (Dr Fong (USA))
3753^{7} 4215^{4} 4505^{4} 5005^{10} 6206^{6} 6904^{4} 7979^{4}

Duaiseoir (IRE) *Venetia Williams* a64 77
7 b g Bachelor Duke(USA) Masnada (IRE) (Erins Isle)
2102^{2} 2939^{7} 3804^{7}

Dual Mac *Neville Bycroft* 75
6 br g Paris House Carol Again (Kind Of Hush)
3191^{3} 3592^{3} 4968^{3}

Dubaianswer *Tony Coyle* a91 36
5 b f Dubawi(IRE) Answered Prayer (Green Desert (USA))
644^{8} 1448^{13}

Dubai Applause *Charles Hills* a54
3 b f Royal Applause Maimoona (IRE) (Pivotal)
123^{4} 509^{3} 732^{8}

Dubai Celebration *Julie Camacho* a70 63
5 b g Dubai Destination(USA) Pretty Poppy (Song)
147^{2} 435^{3} 4119^{9} 4557^{2} 6598^{6} 7514^{3} ◆ (8006) ◆ 8116^{2} 8410^{5}

Dubai Deer *P D Deegan* a73 83
3 b c Manduro(GER) Dakhla Oasis (IRE) (Night Shift (USA))
1587a^{2}

Dubai Dynamo *Ruth Carr* a96 101
8 b g Kyllachy Miss Mercy (IRE) (Law Society (USA))
947^{4} ◆ 1036^{4} 1235^{20} (1688) 1840^{4} 2029^{7} 2210^{6} 2477^{4} 2592^{4} ◆ 2958^{3} 3207^{6} 3564^{2} 3725^{5} 4342^{4} 4758^{6} 4825^{5} 5546^{7} 5838^{4} 6274^{3} 6727^{3} 7337^{14}

Dubai Emerald (USA) *Chris Dwyer* a53 31
4 bb f Henny Hughes(USA) Zanoubia (USA) (Our Emblem (USA))
100^{9} 169^{5} 406^{7} 820^{9} 927^{7} 2966^{6} 3256^{7} 3637^{8}

Dubai Glory *Sheena West* a73 82
5 b f Dubai Destination(USA) Rosse (Kris)
3012^{4} 3150^{4}

Dubai Gold *John Best*
2 ch f Major Cadeaux Cheap N Chic (Primo Valentino (IRE))
5151^{6}

Dubai Hills *Bryan Smart* a106 96
7 b g Dubai Destination(USA) Hill Welcome (Most Welcome)
(889) (1148) 1233^{13} 1691^{5} 2310^{4} 2592^{2} 3207^{3} 3984^{3} 4733^{8} 6300^{5} 7028^{10} 7337^{12} (8231) 8428^{3}

Dubai Rythm *Michael Appleby* a51 43
4 b g Echo Of Light Slave To The Rythm (IRE) (Hamas (IRE))
1465^{12} 1525^{6} 1888^{6} 2169^{8}

Dubai Story *Alastair Lidderdale* a48
4 b f Dubai Destination(USA) Madrigale (Averti (IRE))
28^{6} 33^{5} 201^{4} 235^{4}

Dubara Reef (IRE) *Paul Green* a52 59
6 ch g Dubawi(IRE) Mamara Reef (Salse (USA))
970^{5} 1207^{4} 1279^{3} 1664^{9} (2328) 2721^{8} 3089^{12} 3910^{10} 5048^{9} 5592^{6} 5897^{5} 6853^{10} 7098^{3} 7375^{2} 7597^{2} 7847^{10} 8204^{9}

Dubawi Fun *Ismail Mohammed* a81 82
2 b c Dubawi(IRE) Arabian Treasure (USA) (Danzig (USA))
(2577) 3422^{11} 4747^{4}

Dubawi Island (FR) *James Tate* a94 84
4 b g Dubawi(IRE) Housa Dancer (FR) (Fabulous Dancer (USA))
239^{3} 644^{2} 751^{6} 889^{2} 1083^{5} 1500^{9} (1745) 1796^{5}

Dubawi Phantom *Alan McCabe* a84 82
6 ch g Dubawi(IRE) Anna Amalia (IRE) (In The Wings)
496^{11} 585^{5} ◆ 777^{9} 882^{7} 1831^{5} 3204^{10} 3906^{7}

Dubawi Sound *David Brown* a104 105
5 b g Dubawi(IRE) Hannah's Music (Music Boy)
467a^{3} 660a^{7} 834a^{3} 3527^{11} 4058^{3} 4744^{8} 4981^{4} 6352^{7} 6623^{14} 7368^{23}

Dubawi's Thunder *Richard Hannon Snr*
2 b c Dubawi(IRE) Eclaircie (IRE) (Thunder Gulch (USA))
5744^{10}

Dubaya *A Oliver* 90
3 b f Dubawi(IRE) Charlecote (IRE) (Caerleon (USA))
2108a^{6} 2689a^{14}

Dubday *A Trybuhl* a95 96
3 ch c Dubawi(IRE) Dayrose (Daylami (IRE))
5576a^{2} 6987a^{5}

Dubious Escapade (IRE) *Ann Duffield* a70 76
4 b f Dubawi(IRE) Brief Escapade (IRE) (Brief Truce (USA))
1823^{8} 2882^{10} (3395) 3895^{7} 4294^{5} 4994^{10} 7152^{4}

Dublin (GER) *M Nigge* a62 58
3 b c Azamour(IRE) Daisy Belle (GER) (Acatenango (GER))
6711a^{5}

Ducab (IRE) *Roger Varian* 88
3 b g Dansili Twyla Tharp (IRE) (Sadler's Wells (USA))
2547^{3} 3021^{2} ◆ 3417^{3} (3805) 4683^{6} 5258^{5} 5824^{8}

Duca Di Mantova *R Biondi* 97
4 ch g Manduro(GER) Vale Mantovani (Wolfhound (USA))
2489a^{7} 3147a^{6} 7414a^{6}

Ducal *Mike Murphy* a94 96
5 b g Iceman Noble Lady (Primo Dominie)
2424^{RR} 2665^{4} 3538^{4} 4062^{4} ◆ 4744^{23} 5285^{7}

Duc De Formigny (FR) *C Boutin* a38 67
2 ch c Gold Away(IRE) Udina (Unfuwain (USA))
5362a^{8} 7185a^{14}

Duchess Lemonade *P Harley* 97
3 ch f Duke Of Marmalade(IRE) Spirit Of South (AUS) (Giant's Causeway (USA))
(3604a)

Duchess Of Dreams *Richard Guest* a51 48
3 br f Royal Applause Wood Chorus (Singspiel (IRE))
106^{5} 195^{8} 328^{4} 482^{6} 1055^{5} 1320^{5} 1373^{2} 1966^{7} 2154^{4} 3653^{9} 3793^{4} 4049^{5} 4474^{4} 4849^{3} 5084^{4} 5432^{9} 6276^{15} 7034^{7}

Duchess Of Gazeley (IRE) *Dean Ivory* a74 94
3 ch f Halling(USA) Flying Finish (FR) (Priolo (USA))
2874^{4} (3820) (4634) (4961) 5743^{3} (7342) ◆ 7659^{2}

Duchess Of Hygrove *J W Hills* 14
3 b f Duke Of Marmalade(IRE) Elegant Pride (Beat Hollow)
3696^{6}

Duchess Of Seville *Marco Botti* a86
3 b f Duke Of Marmalade(IRE) Serrenia (IRE) (High Chaparral (IRE))
5071^{3} ◆ 5678^{3} (6366) ◆ 7330^{6} 7895^{7}

Dude Alert (IRE) *Peter Chapple-Hyam* a60 60
3 b g Windsor Knot(IRE) Policy (Nashwan (USA))
3432^{6}

Duke Cosimo *Sir Michael Stoute* a89 76
3 ch g Pivotal Nannina (Medicean)
2267^{2} (2556) (3212) 3803^{7} 5748^{6} 7123^{5}

Duke Jee Pee (IRE) *F Vermeulen* a50 47
3 b g Duke Of Marmalade(IRE) Graceful Bering (USA) (Bering)
818a^{10}

Duke Of Aricabeau (IRE) *Lydia Pearce* a71 76
4 ch g Modigliani(USA) Essential Fear (IRE) (Pivotal)
687^{9} 898^{10}

Duke Of Clarence (IRE) *Richard Hannon Snr* a74 100
4 gr c Verglas(IRE) Special Lady (FR) (Kaldoun (FR))
1290^{4} 1538^{4} (1883) 2520^{2} 2867^{2} (3531) 4857^{5} 5746^{7} 6741^{3} 7250^{3}

Duke Of Destiny (IRE) *Ed Walker* a81 76
4 br g Bachelor Duke(USA) Marghelan (FR) (Soviet Star (USA))
1426^{2} ◆ 2089^{4} 2773^{2} 3429^{2} 3946^{6} 5205^{5} (5622) 6794^{9} 7306^{2} 7785^{4} 8178^{6}

Duke Of Firenze *Sir Michael Stoute* 105
4 ch c Pivotal Nannina (Medicean)
1537^{10} (2014) ◆ 2669^{5} (2865) 3558^{8} 4079^{6} 4947^{10} 6623^{21}

Duke Of Grazeon (IRE) *Mrs Ilka Gansera-Leveque* a77 70
3 b g Duke Of Marmalade(IRE) Rambler (Selkirk (USA))
3479^{5} 4481^{4} 5110^{4} 6071^{8} (7067) 7505^{2} 8178^{4} 8345^{2} 8454^{3}

Duke Of Orange (IRE) *Mick Channon* 65
3 br g Duke Of Marmalade(IRE) High Society (IRE) (Key Of Luck (USA))
1291^{5} 1978^{2} 2135^{7} 2919^{7}

Duke Of Perth *Luca Cumani* a89 90
3 b g Danehill Dancer(IRE) Frangy (Sadler's Wells (USA))
1926^{6} 2600^{2} 3067^{2} (3917) 4476^{2} 4980^{2} 5953^{3} 7121^{5}

Duke Of Rainford *Michael Herrington* a41 46
6 gr g Bahamian Bounty Night Haven (Night Shift (USA))
326^{9}

Duke Of Yorkshire *Declan Carroll* 75
3 b g Duke Of Marmalade(IRE) Dame Edith (FR) (Top Ville)
1236^{5} 1487^{11} 2432^{11} 2743^{3} 3194^{4} ◆ 3809^{2} (4116) 4770^{4} 5343^{4} 5549^{4} 6290^{6} (6629) 6827^{2} 7210^{15}

Dukes Delight (IRE) *David Lanigan* a73 57
3 b f Duke Of Marmalade(IRE) Fashion Model (Rainbow Quest (USA))
2392^{7} 2804^{6} 4152^{4} 4755^{3} (5099) ◆

Dullahan (USA) *Dale Romans* a127 111
4 ch c Even The Score(USA) Mining My Own (USA) (Smart Strike (CAN))
957a^{11} 1269a^{11}

Dullingham *Charlie Appleby* 81
2 b g Dubawi(IRE) Dixey (Diktat)
3290^{7} 6378^{4} 6896^{2} (7061)

Duly Acclaimed (IRE) *J S Moore* a50 42
2 b f Acclamation Cloonkeary (In The Wings)
6079^{3} 6409^{5}

Dumbarton (IRE) *Philip Hobbs* a67 76
5 br c Danehill Dancer(IRE) Scottish Stage (IRE) (Selkirk (USA))
4305^{2} 4683^{3}

Dumbarton Rock *William Jarvis* a56 72
3 b g Kyllachy Ellablue (Bahamian Bounty)
4624^{2} 4956^{7} 5617^{5}

Dumbfounded (FR) *Lady Herries* a67 62
5 bb g Vettori(IRE) Take The Light (FR) (Take Risks (FR))
2321^{6} 4633^{6} 5100^{8} 6044^{2} 6899^{3} 7767^{3}

Dumfries House *Roger Charlton* a56
2 b c New Approach(IRE) Bonnie Doon (IRE) (Grand Lodge (USA))
7835^{11}

Dummy Traou Land (FR) *P Costes* a60 58
3 b f Apsis Peldrine (FR) (Pelder (IRE))
2335a^{5}

Dunaden (FR) *M Delzangles* a72 124
7 b h Nicobar La Marlia (FR) (Kaldounevees (FR))
1268a^{4} 1870a^{3} 2864^{2} 3615a^{2} 6449a^{8} 7761a^{11} 8033a^{5} 8208a^{3}

Dundonnell (USA) *Roger Charlton* 116
3 b g First Defence(USA) Family (USA) (Danzig (USA))
1638^{3} ◆ (2453) 3421^{6}

Dundrum (IRE) *Mrs John Harrington* 58
9 b g Marju(IRE) Tertia (IRE) (Polish Patriot (USA))
5021a^{9}

Dundrum Dancer (IRE) *Alex Hales* a69 70
6 b m Refuse To Bend(IRE) Sincere (IRE) (Bahhare (USA))
218^{2} 410^{5} 601^{3} 1479^{3}

Dungannon *Andrew Balding* a90 106
6 b g Monsieur Bond(IRE) May Light (Midyan (USA))
2396^{7} 2937^{10} 4024^{6} 5519^{9} 5998^{4} (6189) (6831) 7171^{11} (7527)

Dunhoy (IRE) *Tony Newcombe* a87 87
5 ch g Goodricke Belle Of The Blues (IRE) (Blues Traveller (IRE))
654^{9} 1670^{7} (2598) 3370^{2} 4029^{6}

Dunn'o (IRE) *David Nicholls* a65 87
8 b g Cape Cross(IRE) Indian Express (Indian Ridge)
23^{7} 206^{3} 452^{5} 650^{9}

Duntle (IRE) *David Wachman* a97 115
4 ch f Danehill Dancer(IRE) Lady Angola (USA) (Lord At War (ARG))
(2288a) (3456) ◆ 4817a^{2} 5552a^{7} 6837^{3}

Duponal (IRE) *C Gourdain* 112
3 b g Blackdoun(FR) Be Yourself (FR) (Marchand De Sable (USA))
7410a^{2}

Durham Express (IRE) *Tina Jackson* a40 54
6 b g Acclamation Edwina (IRE) (Caerleon (USA))
3934^{8} 4160^{12} 5139^{3} 6761^{10}

Durnford (AUS) *Pat Carey* 98
5 b g Helenus(AUS) Willow (AUS) (Woodman (USA))
7762a^{5}

Duroble Man *Alan King* a74 93
3 b g Manduro(GER) Jalousie (IRE) (Barathea (IRE))
2325^{3} (2786) 3294^{2} 3862^{3} 6172^{11}

Dursey Island (USA) *Richard Hannon Snr* a79
2 b c Elusive Quality(USA) Incircle Miss (USA) (Dayjur (USA))
6733^{2}

Dusky Lark *Hughie Morrison* a64 58
3 b g Nayef(USA) Snow Goose (Polar Falcon (USA))
1882^{7} 2599^{10} 4931^{4} 5432^{7}

Dusky Queen (IRE) *Richard Fahey* 93
3 b f Shamardal(USA) Sanna Bay (IRE) (Refuse To Bend (IRE))
1645^{3} 2309^{4} 3686^{2} 4725^{2} 5684^{11} 6665^{4} (7176) 7538^{5} 7820^{4}

Dustland Fairytale (IRE) *Ian Williams* a60 58
5 b f Noverre(USA) Subtle Affair (IRE) (Barathea (IRE))
1730^{3} 2072^{7} (7265) 7485^{5} 7806^{9}

Dusty In Memphis (USA) *David Wachman* a71 53
3 b f Broken Vow(USA) Crystal Downs (USA) (Alleged (USA))
8012a^{10}

Dusty Storm (IRE) *Ed McMahon* a79 86
3 ch f Kyllachy Halliwell House (Selkirk (USA))
2726^{4} 3160^{2} 4057^{3} 4734^{2} 5340^{4} 7112^{8}

Dutchartcollector *Gary Moore* a65 41
2 b g Dutch Art Censored (Pivotal)
7501^{5} 7860^{4} 7978^{7} (8262)

Dutch Art Dealer *Paul Cole* a79 74
2 b c Dutch Art Lawyers Choice (Namid)
4795^{3} ◆ (5584) 7782^{3} ◆

Dutch Barney *Mark Brisbourne*
3 b g Dutch Art Celeb Style (IRE) (Tagula (IRE))
6824^{9}

Dutch Breeze *Tim Easterby* 79
2 ch c Dutch Art Oasis Breeze (Oasis Dream)
4886^{2} 5330^{2} 5679^{18}

Dutch Courage *Richard Fahey* 92
2 b f Dutch Art Poldhu (Cape Cross (IRE))
1634^{10} ◆ 2419^{2} ◆ (3605) (4300)

Dutch Delight *Tony Coyle* a48 46
3 ch f Dutch Art Tetou (IRE) (Peintre Celebre (USA))
197^{6} 404^{6} 525^{8} 591^{2} 2341^{4} 2555^{8} 2794^{4}

Dutchessa *C Ferland* a80 99
4 b f Dutch Art Nippy (FR) (Anabaa (USA))
3969a^{6} 5360a^{7}

Dutch Gal *John Holt* 61
3 b f Dutch Art Spangle (Galileo (IRE))
1389^{3} 2308^{14} 3254^{9} 5784^{4} 6049^{4} 6083^{5}

Dutch Heritage *Richard Fahey* 78
4 b g Dutch Art Starstone (Diktat)
1286^{4} 1838^{7} 2797^{6}

Dutch Interior *Gary Moore* a81 30
2 ch g Dutch Art Rotunda (Pivotal)
6354^{4} (6746) 7329^{3} 7626^{7}

Dutch Lady *John Holt* a25 51
2 ch f Dutch Art Tattling (Warning)
4924^{8} 6342^{9} 6973^{8} 7789^{7}

Dutch Masterpiece *Gary Moore* a80 113
3 b g Dutch Art The Terrier (Foxhound (USA))
1625^{5} 2430^{7} (3097) ◆ (3584) ◆ (5772a) 7054a^{17}

Dutch Mistress *James Unett* a65 75
4 b f Dutch Art Royal Mistress (Fasliyev (USA))
(148) 2092^{3} 3098^{2} (3736) 3983^{5}

Dutch Old Master *Gary Moore* a80 84
4 b g Jeremy(USA) Wicken Wonder (IRE) (Distant Relative)
792^{8} 1092^{9} 1181^{4} 1599^{7} 2225^{7} 3172^{9}

Dutch Rifle *James Tate* a75
2 b f Dutch Art Vodka Shot (USA) (Holy Bull (USA))
(8415) ◆

Dutch Romance *Charles Hills* 94
2 ch f Dutch Art Endless Love (IRE) (Dubai Destination (USA))
6635^{4} (7245) 7537^{3}

Dutch Rose (IRE) *David O'Meara* a67 104
4 ch f Dutch Art Eloquent Rose (IRE) (Elnadim (USA))
1544^{10} 2476^{10} 3443^{3} 4137^{5} 4671^{2} (5684) 6300^{2} 7025^{6}

Dutch S *Clive Cox* 74
2 ch f Dutch Art Park Law (IRE) (Fasliyev (USA))
(6789) 7503^{3}

Dutiful Son (IRE) *Jeremy Noseda* a74 66
3 b c Invincible Spirit(IRE) Grecian Dancer (Dansili)
6289^{2} 7345^{5} (8146)

Dutyfree (TUR) *G Igdir* 101
5 b c Luxor(TUR) Freezone (TUR) (Wolf (CHI))
6254a^{8}

Dux Scholar *A Savujev* a101 115
5 b h Oasis Dream Alumni (Selkirk (USA))
467a^{2} (746a) 1265a^{7} 5940a^{5} 7059a^{4}

Dvinsky (USA) *Roger Ingram* a71 26
12 b g Stravinsky(USA) Festive Season (USA) (Lypheor)
76^{10} 130^{5} 274^{4} 471^{9} 655^{12} 900^{8} 1020^{7} 2125^{3} 3052^{7} 4424^{9} 6316^{13}

Dylan Boy (IRE) *E Lellouche* 100
2 b c Dylan Thomas(IRE) Stylish (Anshan)
7160a^{4} 7828a^{8}

Dylan's Centenary *Rod Millman* 10
2 b g Kyllachy Sheka (Ishiguru (USA))
2741^{11} 3245^{14}

Dylanson (AUS) *Phillip Stokes* 91
4 b g Dylan Thomas(IRE) Nena Candida (AUS) (Canny Lad (AUS))
7417a^{5}

Dynaglow (USA) *John Gosden* 79
2 b f Dynaformer(USA) Lantern Glow (USA) (Mineshaft (USA))
6298^{2} (6821)

Dynamic Idol (USA) *Gary Moore* a78 70
6 bb g Dynaformer(USA) El Nafis (USA) (Kingmambo (USA))
20^{7}

Dynamic Ranger (USA) *Gary Moore* a61
2 b c US Ranger(USA) Dynamous (USA) (Dynaformer (USA))
7647^{9} 7854^{7}

Dynamis (FR) *Mlle B Renk* a77 66
5 b g Gentlewave(IRE) Daisy Town (Doyoun)
5601a^{4}

Dynamoon (FR) *H-A Pantall* a71 71
3 b f Kentucky Dynamite(USA) Moon Gorge (Pursuit Of Love)
6713a^{8}

Dynamo Walt (IRE) *Derek Shaw* a63 48
2 b g Acclamation Cambara (Dancing Brave (USA))
5228^{4} 5590^{2} 6213^{5} 6967^{6} 7127^{7} 7293^{6} (7665) 7900^{4}

Dynastic *Tony Coyle* a73 76
4 b g Dynaformer(USA) Demure (Machiavellian (USA))
6758^{8} 7100^{6} (7881) 8299^{4}

Eager To Bow (IRE) *Patrick Chamings* a79 75
7 b g Acclamation Tullawadgeen (IRE) (Sinndar (IRE))
3172^{8} 3575^{4} 4496^{3} 5398^{7} 6316^{5} 7880^{8} 8158^{6}

Eagle Regiment (AUS) *K L Man* 119
6 b g El Moxie(USA) Fire Lake (AUS) (Bureaucracy (NZ))
1265a^{3} 8209a^{12}

Eagle Rock (IRE) *Tom Tate* 89
5 b g High Chaparral(IRE) Silk Fan (IRE) (Unfuwain (USA))
1536^{6} 1805^{4} 2402^{13} 3345^{6} 3609^{4} (4313) 5288^{3} 5655^{5} (6237) 6646^{13} 7193^{23}

Eagles Peak *Sir Michael Stoute* 106
5 b c Galileo(IRE) High Praise (USA) (Quest For Fame)
1846^{6}

Ealain Aibrean (IRE) *David Evans* a75 75
2 b f Excellent Art April (IRE) (Rock Of Gibraltar (IRE))
8113^{2} 8300^{3}

Eanans Bay (IRE) *Mark H Tompkins* a53 56
4 b g Tiger Hill(IRE) Gold Hush (USA) (Seeking The Gold (USA))
2563^{7} 3256^{3} 3744^{4} 5084^{5} 5897^{4} 6458^{7}

Earl Of Menteith (IRE) *Saeed bin Suroor* 57
2 b c Shamardal(USA) Inchmahome (Galileo (IRE))
3695^{3}

Earl Of Tinsdal (GER) *A Wohler* 116
5 b c Black Sam Bellamy(IRE) Earthly Paradise (GER) (Dashing Blade)
2492a^{3} 3483^{12} 5778a^{2} 6678a^{3} (7414a)

Earl Of Winds (GER) *P Schaerer* a88
8 b g Samum(GER) Earthly Paradise (GER) (Dashing Blade)
514a^{4} 701a^{7}

Earlsalsa (GER) *C Von Der Recke* 106
9 bb g Kingsalsa(USA) Earthly Paradise (GER) (Dashing Blade)
2492a^{10}

Earl's Bridge *Bill Turner* a8 55
2 b g Avonbridge Regal Quest (IRE) (Marju (IRE))
1833^{7} 2067^{3} 2474^{4} 6605^{10} 6897^{10} 7320^{10}

Early Applause *Nicky Richards* 78
5 b g Royal Applause Early Evening (Daylami (IRE))
5882^{10}

Early Morning (IRE) *Harry Dunlop* 77
2 gr c New Approach(IRE) Summer's Eve (Singspiel (IRE))
5188^{5} 5957^{2} 6528^{3}

Early One Morning *Hugo Palmer* a55 45
3 b f Medicean Still Small Voice (Polish Precedent (USA))
651^{7} 895^{5} 1057^{4} 1469^{7} 2341^{7} 2802^{8} 3405^{10}

Early Prime (FR) *Rod Collet* 98
2 b f Early March Valprime (FR) (Nombre Premier)
1894a^{3} 3875a^{4}

Earned Indulgence (USA) *Rowena Beck*
3 bb c Mecke(USA) Lady Francine (USA) (Quiet American (USA))
786a^{10}

Earnshaw (USA) *A Fabre* 112
2 gr c Medaglia d'Oro(USA) Emily Bronte (Machiavellian (USA))
(7160a) 7686a^{2}

Earth Amber *Nicky Henderson* 97
4 ch f Hurricane Run(IRE) Too Marvelous (FR) (Dansili)
1484^{2} ◆ 1920^{7} 7193^{32}

Earthflight *Philip McBride* a84 48
2 ch f Medicean Aliena (IRE) (Grand Lodge (USA))
5003^{11} 5488^{7} 5797^{10} 6924^{4} (7168) 7604^{3} (7846) (7944)

Easter Diva (IRE) *Gerard Butler* a74 81
4 b f Dansili Easter Fairy (USA) (Fusaichi Pegasus (USA))
(3635) 4348^{2} 4898^{14}

Eastern Belle *John Gosden* 81
2 b f Champs Elysees Fleche D'Or (Dubai Destination (USA))
7466^{3} 7693^{2}

Eastern Destiny *Richard Fahey* 94
4 gr f Dubai Destination(USA) Night Haven (Night Shift (USA))
(1237) 1933^{5} 2365^{3} 3775^{4} 4878^{12} 5683^{8}

Eastern Dragon (IRE) *Michael Scudamore* a78 72
3 b g Elnadim(USA) Shulammite Woman (IRE) (Desert Sun)
1064^{4} 1315^{3} (1695) 1759^{4} 3903^{3} 4378^{3} 4685^{6} (5644) (8095) 8345^{12}

Eastern Dynasty *Ben Haslam* 20
2 b g Exceed And Excel(AUS) Agooda (Rainbow Quest (USA))
6769^{10}

Eastern Impact (IRE) *Richard Fahey* 91
2 b g Bahamian Bounty Kate The Great (Xaar)
(1785) ◆ 2809^{3}

Eastern Magic *Andrew Hollinshead* a58 64
6 b g Observatory(USA) Inchtina (Inchinor)
2860^{8}

Eastlands Lad (IRE) *Micky Hammond* a61 67
4 bb g Strategic Prince Uisce Tine (IRE) (Bluebird (USA))
1757^{3} 2280^{5} 2616^{9} 3895^{9} 4400^{6} 7343^{11}

East Meets West (IRE) *Bent Olsen* a101 92
4 b c Dansili Minkova (IRE) (Sadler's Wells (USA))
2146a^{10} 3188a^{10} 5045a^{6}

Easton Arch (USA) *Brian Meehan* a54
2 b f Arch(USA) Shoofha (IRE) (Bluebird (USA))
7763^{10}

East Texas Red (IRE) *Mick Quinn* a56 69
3 ch c Danehill Dancer(IRE) Evangeline (Sadler's Wells (USA))
1365^{6} 1770^{6} 2094^{5} 2420^{6} 2549^{9} 3254^{6} 4170^{4} 4721^{7} 4881^{5} 5870^{5} 6406^{6} 7610^{10} 8339^{7}

Eastward Ho *Jason Ward* a67 78
5 ch g Resplendent Glory(IRE) Mofeyda (IRE) (Mtoto)
1932^{7} 2315^{2} 2753^{2} 3081^{5} 3506^{6} 4135^{6}

Easy De Glanville (FR) *C Baillet* a70 50
2 b f Librettist(USA) Facilita (IRE) (Fasliyev (USA))
4599a^{7} 7568a^{6}

Easydoesit (IRE) *Tony Carroll* a74 66
5 b g Iffraaj Fawaayid (USA) (Vaguely Noble)
(100) (169) 515^{2} 646^{2} 1084^{4} 1350^{2} 1744^{2} 2284^{4} 2739^{5} 7881^{10} 8115^{6}

Easy Life *Marcus Tregoning* a64
3 b f Sir Percy Eternelle (Green Desert (USA))
90^{2} 275^{2} 419^{7}

Easy Over (IRE) *Ed McMahon* a66 68
5 ch g Dr Fong(USA) Desert Alchemy (IRE) (Green Desert (USA))
1430^{7} 2286^{10} 2929^{9} 3946^{10}

Easy Risk (FR) *F Chappet* 85
2 b f My Risk(FR) Entre Deux Mers (FR) (Saint Estephe (FR))
5460a^{8} 7567a^{6} 7994a^{9}

Easy Terms *Edwin Tuer* 100
6 b m Trade Fair Effie (Royal Academy (USA))
1446^{4} 1689^{8} 2427^{9} 3345^{10} 6729^{4}

Eaton Oak *Lisa Williamson* a29 45
3 b g Assertive Not So Generous (IRE) (Fayruz)
3201^{7} 3950^{4} 5069^{9} 5856^{5}

Eba Chope (FR) *F Chappet* 84
2 b f Deportivo Easy Rocket (FR) (Indian Rocket)
5213a^{8}

Ebiyza (IRE) *A De Royer-Dupre* 110
3 ch f Rock Of Gibraltar(IRE) Ebalista (IRE) (Selkirk (USA))
6484a^{3} (7048a) 7566a^{5} 8208a^{6}

Ebn Arab (USA) *Charles Hills* 103
3 b g Dixie Union(USA) Daffaash (USA) (Mr Greeley (USA))
(2008) 2812^{3} 3484^{20} 5728^{11}

Ebony Clarets *Linda Perratt* a57 69
4 b f Kyllachy Pachanga (Inchinor)
7669^{8}

Ebony Express *Alan Swinbank* a40 93
4 bl g Superior Premium Coffee Ice (Primo Dominie)
1570^{3} 2041^{5} 2576^{6} 2886^{5} 3199^{3} ◆ (3768) 4293^{5} 5052^{3} 5712^{4} 6297^{3} (6758) (7433) (7778)

Ebony Roc (IRE) *Amanda Perrett* a71 62
3 br g Shirocco(GER) Chia Laguna (IRE) (Ela-Mana-Mou)
2802^{4} 3403^{2} 3675^{7} (5934) 6325^{4} (6522) 7258^{11} 7439^{6}

Ebony Song (USA) *Jo Crowley* a39 47
5 bb g Songandaprayer(USA) Thiscatsforcaryl (USA) (Storm Cat (USA))
1901^{9} 3433^{13}

Ebulli (FR) *J Van Handenhove* 84
3 b g Epalo(GER) Olanga (GER) (Shareef Dancer (USA))
191a^{0} 2434a^{0}

Eccleston *Richard Fahey* 85
2 b c Acclamation Miss Meggy (Pivotal)
(2436) 3481^{14} 4528^{6} ◆

Ececheira *Dean Ivory* a44 47
4 ch f Three Valleys(USA) Evening Guest (FR) (Be My Guest (USA))
120^{11}

Echion (IRE) *C Martinon* a80 77
3 b c Ishiguru(USA) Glittering Prize (UAE) (Cadeaux Genereux)
2034a^{10} 2557a^{13}

Echo Brava *Luke Dace* a74 73
3 gr g Proclamation(IRE) Snake Skin (Golden Snake (USA))
628^{9} 1014^{5} (1320) (1900) ◆ 2420^{4} 3294^{4} 3735^{4} 6360^{8} 6735^{5} 7447^{7} 7839^{2} 8159^{3} (8337)

Echoe Beach *Olivia Maylam*
3 b f Echo Of Light Pomponette (USA) (Rahy (USA))
2157^{11} 6557^{11}

Echoes Of War *Michael Attwater* a41 16
4 b g Echo Of Light Waraqa (USA) (Red Ransom (USA))
2224^{9} 3435^{7} 8154^{9} 8427^{10}

Echologic *Brian Baugh* a35
3 b g Echo Of Light Crown City (USA) (Coronado's Quest (USA))
8141^{5} 8313^{6}

Echo Of Footsteps *Michael Herrington* a45 67
4 b f Authorized(IRE) Opening Ceremony (USA) (Quest For Fame)
2555^{13} 3252^{5} 3728^{6} 4355^{4} 5143^{5} 5592^{9}

Echo Of Lightning *Noel Wilson* 50
3 b g Echo Of Light Classic Lass (Dr Fong (USA))
2634^{3} 3650^{4} 4400^{8} 5016^{13} 6587^{8}

Echo Of Silence (FR) *J-M Capitte* a78 75
3 b c Sandwaki(USA) Statia (FR) (Anabaa (USA))
8441a^{2}

Echua (IRE) *Emmet Michael Butterly* a64 73
7 b g King's Best(USA) Canouan (IRE) (Sadler's Wells (USA))
7767^{2} (7847)

Economic Crisis (IRE) *Alan Berry* a63 74
4 ch f Excellent Art Try The Air (IRE) (Foxhound (USA))
1278^{4} 1540^{10} 1596^{3} (2037) 2222^{4} 2797^{7} 3236^{13} 3933^{5} 4338^{3} 4579^{2} 4620^{4} 4993^{4} 5333^{8} 6469^{2} 6665^{9} 6908^{8} 7240^{13} 7845^{4} 8052^{9}

Economy *Sir Michael Stoute* a87
3 gr g Dalakhani(IRE) Quiff (Sadler's Wells (USA))
4632^{2}

Eco Warrior *J W Hills* a61 50
3 b g Echo Of Light Kryssa (Kris)
4978^{9} 5281^{5} 8141^{2}

Ectot *E Lellouche* 114
2 b c Hurricane Run(IRE) Tonnara (IRE) (Linamix (FR))
(5628a) (6710a) (7686a)

Edas *Thomas Cuthbert* a74 65
11 b g Celtic Swing Eden (IRE) (Polish Precedent (USA))
2315^{5} 2636^{7} 3397^{6} 5051^{8} 6297^{10}

Ed De Gas *Rae Guest* a92 101
4 b g Peintre Celebre(USA) Sambala (IRE) (Danehill Dancer (IRE))
1674^{8} 2407^{10} 3608^{6} 5006^{7} 6428^{4}

Eddie Jock (IRE) *S Seemar* a92 90
9 ch g Almutawakel Al Euro (FR) (Mujtahid (USA))
246a^{7} 362a^{7}

Eddiemaurice (IRE) *Richard Guest* 72
2 ch g Captain Rio Annals (Lujain (USA))
4724^{6} 5338^{2} 5969^{3} (6271) 6619^{7}

Ede's *Pat Phelan* a17
13 ch g Bijou D'Inde Ballagarrow Girl (North Stoke)
469^{8}

Ede's The Business *Pat Phelan* a58
2 ch f Halling(USA) My Amalie (IRE) (Galileo (IRE))
7779^{9} 8085^{5} 8328^{5}

Edge (IRE) *Richard Hannon Snr* a73 80
2 b c Acclamation Chanter (Lomitas)
3092^{3} ◆ 3350^{3} 4256^{6} (5995) 7326^{5}

Edge Closer *Tony Carroll* a111 100
9 b g Bold Edge Blue Goddess (IRE) (Blues Traveller (IRE))
2444^{16} 4024^{12} 4860^{13} 5998^{12} 6988^{16}

Edged Out *Christopher Mason* 76
3 b f Piccolo Edge Of Light (Xaar)
1661^{7} (1978) 2829^{9} 3160^{3} 3622^{4} 4244^{7} (4654) 4942^{2} 6045^{4} 6900^{3}

Edgewater (IRE) *Lee Carter* a77 83
6 b g Bahamian Bounty Esteemed Lady (IRE) (Mark Of Esteem (IRE))
3210^{3}

Edgeworth (IRE) *David Bridgwater* a73 77
7 b g Pyrus(USA) Credibility (Komaite (USA))
3410^{7} 4195^{6}

Edgware Road *Paul Morgan* a67 69
5 ch g Selkirk(USA) Bayswater (Caerleon (USA))
61^{9} 330^{2} 475^{10} 709^{9} 1100^{10} 1298^{2} (2130) 3106^{3} 3642^{4} 3954^{5} 8072^{11} 8314^{9}

Edin Burgher (FR) *Michael Murphy* a36 14
12 br g Hamas(IRE) Jaljuli (Jalmood (USA))
4691^{7} 5072^{13}

Edith Anne *Paul Midgley* a19 64
3 b f Sakhee's Secret Accusation (IRE) (Barathea (IRE))
(1284) 1566^{6} 2756^{11} 3025^{10} 4377^{4} (5054) 6604^{8}

Edna *Olivia Maylam*
3 ch f Papal Bull Walt Mc Don (IRE) (Tagula (IRE))
1089^{7}

Educate *Ismail Mohammed* 117
4 b g Echo Of Light Pasithea (IRE) (Celtic Swing)
(1233) ◆ 1675^{14} (2263) 3458^{15} 4310^{10} 5269^{3} ◆ 5739^{5} (6838)

Edward Elgar *Richard Whitaker* 51
2 ch g Avonbridge Scooby Dooby Do (Atraf)
6517^{7} 6842^{4}

Edwyn Ralph *David Simcock* a82 81
3 b c Sir Percy Edwardian Era (Bering)
184^{5} ◆ 373^{3} ◆ (663) 1053^{2} ◆ (1145) 4249^{3} 4914^{4} 5168^{3} 6827^{4} 7304^{8}

Eeny Mac (IRE) *Neville Bycroft* a47 79
6 ch g Redback Sally Green (IRE) (Common Grounds)
1603^{3} 2081^{4} 3192^{6} 3649^{11} 4005^{2} 4375^{4} (4893) 5291^{6} (5383) 5860^{2} 6211^{9} 7024^{13} 7498^{7}

Effie B *Mick Channon* a70 96
3 ch f Sixties Icon Blakeshall Rose (Tobougg (IRE))
1234^{7} 1690^{8} (2190) 2848^{10} 3584^{10} 4024^{8} 6990^{13} 7222^{11}

Efistorm *Conor Dore* a72 81
12 b g Efisio Abundance (Cadeaux Genereux)
115^{6} 354^{7} 536^{7}

Efteos (FR) *C Laffon-Parias* a79 84
3 b c Teofilo(IRE) Efesos (FR) (Kendor (FR))
1799a^{6}

Egotist (IRE) *Milton Bradley* a72 61
5 ch g Halling(USA) Devil's Imp (IRE) (Cadeaux Genereux)
6163^{8} 6489^{5} 6959^{11} 7319^{5} 7544^{4} 7961^{5} 8198^{5} 8360^{12}

Egyptian Warrior (IRE) *A P O'Brien* 79
4 bb g Galileo(IRE) Beltisaal (FR) (Belmez (USA))
7230a^{21}

Ehtedaam (USA) *Saeed bin Suroor* a107 102
4 b g Arch(USA) Bow River Gold (Rainbow Quest (USA))
(2422) 3113^{5} (4415) 4733^{6} (5894) 6199^{6} 7157^{2}

Ehtifaal (IRE) *William Haggas* 74
2 b g Teofilo(IRE) Kashoof (Green Desert (USA))
5472^{4} ◆ 6829^{8}

Eightfold *Seamus Durack* a58 67
4 b g Cadeaux Genereux Nirvana (Marju (IRE))
1948^{6} 5592^{4} 6325^{10}

Eijaaz (IRE) *Geoffrey Harker* a40 65
12 b g Green Desert(USA) Kismah (Machiavellian (USA))
1763^{2} 2118^{5} 2831^{4} 3625^{9} 3947^{8} 4888^{7} 7372^{6}

Eila Wheeler *Maurice Barnes* 30
6 b m Central Park(IRE) Only So Far (Teenoso (USA))
4445^{5} 5469^{5}

Eilean Mor *R Mike Smith* a45 55
5 ch g Ishiguru(USA) Cheviot Heights (Intikhab (USA))
2912^{6} 3197^{9} 4109^{2} 4339^{4} 4469^{5} 4824^{2} 5261^{2} 6083^{7} 6918^{4} 7153^{13}

Einsteins Folly (IRE) *J S Bolger* a73 94
3 b c Whipper(USA) Azra (IRE) (Danehill (USA))
2687a^{7} 7719a^{16}

Eishin Flash (JPN) *Hideaki Fujiwara* a112 124
6 bb h King's Best(USA) Moonlady (GER) (Platini (GER))
1872a^{3} 8033a^{10}

Eium Mac *Neville Bycroft* 57
4 b g Presidium Efipetite (Efisio)
2989^{7} 3542^{6} 4118^{5} 4966^{7} 5840^{9} 6276^{14}

Ejadah (IRE) *Roger Varian* 75
2 b f Clodovil(IRE) Bintalreef (USA) (Diesis)
4491^{6} 4921^{13} (7310)

Ektihaam (IRE) *Roger Varian* 121
4 b g Invincible Spirit(IRE) Liscune (IRE) (King's Best (USA))
1846^{3} (2252) 3556^{S} 4745^{8}

Elabela (IRE) *J E Hammond* a73 78
3 ch f Tamayuz Benalmadena (FR) (Nashwan (USA))
270a^{6}

Ela Goog La Mou *Peter Charalambous* a38 58
4 b f Tobougg(IRE) Real Flame (Cyrano De Bergerac)
1086^{11} 1300^{8} 1611^{9} 3496^{7} 5492^{4} 5803^{3} 6261^{2} 7608^{9}

Eland Ally *Tom Tate* 78
5 b g Striking Ambition Dream Rose (IRE) (Anabaa (USA))
2755^{5} 3487^{4} 4203^{7} 4930^{5} 5579^{7} 6757^{2} 7030^{7}

Elas Law *Jeremy Noseda* a61
3 gr f Lawman(FR) Ela Athena (Ezzoud (IRE))
2953^{8}

El Beau (IRE) *John Quinn* 77
2 ch g Camacho River Beau (IRE) (Galileo (IRE))
4053^{7} 4756^{3} 5083^{2} 5508^{8} 6271^{2} 6619^{2} (7146)

El Bravo *Shaun Harris* a63 74
7 ch g Falbrav(IRE) Alessandra (Generous (IRE))
9^{3} 361^{6} 458^{6} 671^{6} 888^{6} 1090^{3} 1270^{3} 1789^{13} (2332) 2435^{7} 3138^{3} 3467^{2} (3808) 3889^{2} 4287^{2} 5031^{4}

El Camino Real (IRE) *Barry Leavy* a48 47
5 b g Dansili Soviet Artic (FR) (Bering)
2709^{6} 3906^{5} 4163^{10}

El Cordobes (IRE) *Richard Fahey* 76
3 b c Montjeu(IRE) Mayano Sophia (IRE) (Rock Of Gibraltar (IRE))
6272^{6} 6498^{3}

Eldarion (IRE) *A Lyon* a63 65
5 ch c Aragorn(IRE) Madame Cerito (USA) (Diesis)
6060a^{6}

El Dececy (USA) *Charles Smith* a76 49
9 b g Seeking The Gold(USA) Ashraakat (USA) (Danzig (USA))
214^{10}

Elderly Paradise (AUS) *M C Tam* a107
6 ch g Danewin(AUS) Kali Smytzer (NZ) (Zabeel (NZ))
241a^{2} (364a) 659a^{7} 833a^{5}

El Dorado (FR) *K Borgel* 94
3 bl c Keltos(FR) Queen Douna (FR) (Kaldoun (FR))
4043a^{9}

El Duque *Bill Turner* a60 57
2 b g Byron Royal Tavira Girl (IRE) (Orpen (USA))
1156^{4} 1328^{4} 1659^{11} 2475^{3} (2759) 3189^{7} 7977^{5} 8025^{3} 8166^{7}

Eleanor Roosevelt (IRE) *Jamie Osborne* a39 53
3 b f Dalakhani(IRE) Shesasmartlady (IRE) (Dolphin Street (FR))
1653^{8} 1882^{8} 2093^{10} 4939^{7}

Electra Spectra *Luca Cumani* 81
3 b f Dansili Hyperspectra (Rainbow Quest (USA))
4495^{4} (5959) 6832^{4}

Electric Fusion (AUS) *Robert Smerdon* 100
4 b g Fastnet Rock(AUS) Silken Song (AUS) (Unbridled's Song (USA))
7417a^{13}

Electrician *Tim Pitt* a68 87
4 b g Echo Of Light Primrose Lane (JPN) (Sunday Silence (USA))
(15) 190^{9} 490^{2} 540^{6} 633^{5} 662^{4} 747^{2} (840) 1179^{4}

Electrickery *Mark Buckley* a24 11
4 b f Excellent Art Exultate Jubilate (USA) (With Approval (CAN))
3223^{7} 5515^{11} 6137^{12}

Electric Qatar *Tom Dascombe* a84 68
4 b g Pastoral Pursuits Valandraud (IRE) (College Chapel)
780^{5} 1121^{7} 6388^{5} 6995^{2} 7601^{6} 7985^{3} 8177^{3}

Elegant Ophelia *Dean Ivory* a72 66
4 ch f Osorio(GER) Ela's Giant (Giant's Causeway (USA))
165^{5} 1983^{6} 2348^{10}

Elenya (IRE) *M Cesandri* a100 100
4 b f Lawman(FR) Edwina (IRE) (Caerleon (USA))
1944a^{9} 6714a^{11}

Eleona (GER) *Frau E Mader* 89
6 b m Areion(GER) Evry (GER) (Torgos)
3852a^{11} 7233a^{6}

El Estruendoso (ARG) *M F De Kock* a84 106
4 ch g Giant's Causeway(USA) Estricta (ARG) (Roy (USA))
245a^{7} 553a^{2}

Elettrotreno (IRE) *A Giorgi* 101
3 b c Modigliani(USA) Alycus (USA) (Atticus (USA))
2491a^{6} 7416a^{4} 7830a^{2}

Eleuthera (FR) *P Demercastel* a87 110
3 ch f Spirit One(FR) Class A Fair (FR) (Shining Steel)
782a^{5} 1602a^{4} 2381a^{3} (2905a) 3614a^{10} 5629a^{3} 7057a^{7}

Elevato (TUR) *Z Guneli* 99
3 b f Kaneko(TUR) Zeynep Hanim (TUR) (Distant Relative)
6231a^{5}

Eleven Park (FR) *N Bertran De Balanda* a73 88
4 b g Walk In The Park(IRE) Lesothane (FR) (Lesotho (USA))
5601a^{12}

Eleventh Hour (IRE) *Charlie Appleby* 61
2 b f Invincible Spirit(IRE) Midnight Line (USA) (Kris S (USA))
4191^{4} 4723^{5} 5983^{4}

Elhaame (IRE) *Luca Cumani* a29 101
3 b g Acclamation Gold Hush (USA) (Seeking The Gold (USA))
1481^{2} 3105^{2} 3995^{3} (4929) (5302) ◆ 6186^{2} 7174^{13}

Elhathrah (IRE) *Ed Dunlop* a29 55
3 b f Nayef(USA) Arch Swing (USA) (Arch (USA))
2423^{7} 3469^{13}

Elidor *Mick Channon* 98
3 br g Cape Cross(IRE) Honorine (IRE) (Mark Of Esteem (IRE))
1443^{3} 1804^{2} 2262^{2} (3486) 4984^{5} 5764^{10} 6186^{8} 6793^{3}

Elijah Pepper (USA) *Conor Dore* a85 83
8 ch g Crafty Prospector(USA) Dovie Dee (USA) (Housebuster (USA))
2^{6} 219^{7} 410^{7} 1081^{9} 1797^{8}

Elik (IRE) *Sir Michael Stoute* a83 105
3 b f Dalakhani(IRE) Elopa (GER) (Tiger Hill (IRE))
1698^{2} 2148^{4} (2586) 3482^{3} 4920^{2}

Elite Army *Saeed bin Suroor* a83
2 b c Authorized(IRE) White Rose (GER) (Platini (GER))
(7835)

Elite Freedom (IRE) *Jo Hughes* a54 59
2 b f Acclamation Jebel Musa (IRE) (Rock Of Gibraltar (IRE))
4346^{4} 4963^{4} 5352^{6} 6663^{6} 7623^{5} 7973^{6}

Eliya *Jo Hughes* a37
3 b f Ishiguru(USA) Riff Raff (Daylami (IRE))
525^{11} 979^{4} 2154^{10}

Elizabeth Coffee (IRE) *John Weymes* a73 75
5 b f Byron Queens Wharf (IRE) (Ela-Mana-Mou)
82^{8} 429^{11} 2555^{10} 2974^{5} 3231^{9} 3728^{10} 3814^{2} 4099^{6} 4673^{3} 5143^{3} 5803^{5} 6339^{3} 6479^{6} 7201^{10} 7753^{13} 7963^{6} 8116^{12} 8183^{5}

Eljowzah (IRE) *Aidan Anthony Howard* a60 53
5 b m Acclamation Express Logic (Air Express (IRE))
975^{7} 993^{4}

Elkaayed (USA) *Roger Varian* 111
3 ch c Distorted Humor(USA) Habibti (USA) (Tabasco Cat (USA))
(2384) (2859) 3485^{5} 4874^{6}

Ellaal *Ruth Carr* a67 72
4 b g Oasis Dream Capistrano Day (USA) (Diesis)
1571^{10} 1963^{8} 2278^{11} 2551^{6} 2889^{13} 7283^{6} 7754^{8} 7931^{10} 8055^{11} 8142^{5} 8279^{3} (8371)

Ellalan *David Simcock* a49 74
2 b c Bahamian Bounty Frabjous (Pivotal)
3640^{6} 4414^{2} 4977^{3} 5819^{6} 7428^{7}

Ella Motiva (IRE) *Mark Brisbourne* a60 60
3 b f Motivator Stormy View (USA) (Cozzene (USA))
2274^{7} 3232^{12} 3650^{3} 4008^{7} 4391^{9} 4806^{4} 5126^{2} 5391^{7} 5942^{9} 6339^{5} 6518^{6} 7034^{6}

Ellell Duke (IRE) *Seamus Fahey* a29 82
4 b g Kheleyf(USA) Any Ellells (IRE) (Carrowkeel (IRE))
6089a^{10}

Ellen May *Gary Harrison* a58
3 b f Rock Of Gibraltar(IRE) Triskel (Hawk Wing (USA))
7459^{6} 7781^{4}

Elle Rebelle *Mark Brisbourne* a66 55
3 b f Cockney Rebel(IRE) Lille Ida (Hawk Wing (USA))
1697^{5} 2071^{S} 3396^{8} 3758^{7} 4113^{8} 5089^{5} 5391^{6} 5923^{6} 6260^{6} 7643^{4} 7966^{6} 8119^{4}

Elle Same *P Schiergen* 96
3 b f Samum(GER) Elle Danzig (GER) (Roi Danzig (USA))
7891a^{15}

Elleval (IRE) *David Marnane* a108 106
3 b g Kodiac Penny Rouge (IRE) (Pennekamp (USA))
(553a) ◆ 835a^{4} 953a^{4} 1264a^{2} 3844a^{5} 4696a^{5} 6225a^{2} 6440a^{7}

Elle West *Michael Easterby* 32
2 ch f Elnadim(USA) Leominda (Lion Cavern (USA))
7023^{12} 7209^{9} 7494^{12}

Elle Woods (IRE) *Michael Dods* 90
3 b f Lawman(FR) Lady Livius (IRE) (Titus Livius (FR))
2439^{3} 3066^{11} 3396^{2} (3686) (4056) 4671^{3} 5684^{7} 6625^{4} 6875^{3}

El Libertador (USA) *Eric Wheeler* a63 57
7 bb g Giant's Causeway(USA) Istikbal (USA) (Kingmambo (USA))
20^{8} 201^{3} 512^{2} 668^{3} 866^{4} 905^{2} 1031^{3} 1175^{9} 1877^{3} 2567^{10} 3180^{6} 3819^{3} 6737^{8} 7440^{2} 7899^{6} 8148^{10}

Ellie In The Pink (IRE) *Pat Phelan* a71 72
5 ch f Johannesburg(USA) Stravinia (USA) (Stravinsky (USA))
13^{3} ◆ 638^{2} 689^{7} 3111^{4} 3842^{5}

Ellies Image *Richard Ford* a27 49
6 b m Lucky Story(USA) Crown City (USA) (Coronado's Quest (USA))
2932^{15} 3511^{10} 8065^{8}

Ellingham (IRE) *Christine Dunnett* 11
2 b f Bushranger(IRE) No Way (IRE) (Rainbows For Life (CAN))
2419^{9} 3413^{10} 5199^{7}

Elliot Carver (FR) *M Munch* a80 65
2 ch c Linngari(IRE) Western Bowl (USA) (Gone West (USA))
7653a^{3} 8354a^{5}

Elliptique (IRE) *A Fabre* a90 105
2 br c New Approach(IRE) Uryale (FR) (Kendor (FR))
5628a^{3} 6710a^{2} (7409a)

Ellusivance (IRE) *E J O'Neill* a87 74
3 b c Elusive Quality(USA) Germance (USA) (Silver Hawk (USA))
72a^{2} 1495a^{6}

El Manati (IRE) *James Tate* 99
3 b f Iffraaj Limit (IRE) (Barathea (IRE))
1362^{5} 3562^{9} 6685^{2} 7010^{11}

El Massivo (IRE) *William Jarvis* a72 70
3 b g Authorized(IRE) Umthoulah (IRE) (Unfuwain (USA))
74^{5} 333^{2} (841) 1053^{4} 1729^{2} 2500^{7} 3055^{8} 4753^{8} 5234^{10} 5802^{6} 6109^{7} (6782) 7066^{10}

El McGlynn (IRE) *Eric Alston* a52 81
4 b f Elnadim(USA) Evelyn One (Alhaarth (IRE))
1649^{13} 2173^{9} 2550^{12} 4814^{9} 5227^{9} 5583^{4} 6287^{14} 7315^{14} 7728^{6} 7848^{11}

El Mirage (IRE) *Dean Ivory* a80 64
3 b f Elusive Quality(USA) Hucking Hot (Desert Prince (IRE))
(1616) 2010^{8} 2983^{9} 3212^{3} 3956^{9} 6535^{10} 6777^{7}

El Molino Blanco *Michael Easterby* 57
3 b f Royal Applause Forest Prize (Charnwood Forest (IRE))
3463^{5} 4008^{9} 4374^{7} 4982^{8}

Elna Bright *Peter Crate* a91 80
8 b g Elnadim(USA) Acicula (IRE) (Night Shift (USA))
584^{9} 723^{8} 880^{3} 1160^{9} 2196^{4} ◆ 3529^{5} 3816^{6} 4165^{9}

Elnadwa (USA) *Saeed bin Suroor* a83 84
3 b f Daaher(CAN) Magical Allure (USA) (General Meeting (USA))
3179^{2} 3777^{7} 4243^{4} 4776^{3} 5498^{9} 6780^{3} 7038^{2} 7297^{6}

El Najmm (IRE) *Roger Varian* 77
2 ch c Sea The Stars(IRE) My Dubai (IRE) (Dubai Millennium)
5811^{3} 6829^{2}

El Negrito (FR) *J-L Pelletan* a69 70
3 b c Hannouma(IRE) Dinger De L'Orme (FR) (Celtic Arms (FR))
191a^{9}

El Nino (FR) *M Nigge* a73
3 b c Layman(USA) Woven Silk (USA) (Danzig (USA))
191a^{6}

Elounta *John Best* a43 47
3 b f Dubawi(IRE) Santiburi Girl (Casteddu)
3699^{12} 4427^{6} 4654^{5} 5602^{7} 8146^{8}

Elpais (ITY) *G Botti* a71 43
6 ch g Altieri Lady Caribe (FR) (Kendor (FR))
127a^{6}

El Salvador (IRE) *A P O'Brien* a98 109
4 ch c Galileo(IRE) Balisada (Kris)
3073a^{3} 3483^{6} 3873a^{4}

Elsie Bay *J S Moore* a40 69
4 b f Sakhee(USA) Mary Sea (FR) (Selkirk (USA))
753^{3} 896^{13} 5479^{2} 5793^{7} 7605^{8}

Elsie Bond *Tim Easterby* 4
2 b f Monsieur Bond(IRE) Elsie Hart (IRE) (Revoque (IRE))
4199^{7} 4538^{9} 5289^{5}

Elsie Partridge (IRE) *Noel Quinlan* a60 67
2 b f Kodiac La Bataille (USA) (Out Of Place (USA))
5435^{3} 6174^{4} 6607^{5} 7261^{5}

Elsie's Orphan *Patrick Chamings* a66 76
6 br m Pastoral Pursuits Elsie Plunkett (Mind Games)
1426^{11}

Elsiniaar *Roger Varian* 77
3 bl g New Approach(IRE) Comic (IRE) (Be My Chief (USA))
3250^{2}

Elspeth's Boy (USA) *Philip Kirby* a78 81
6 bb g Tiznow(USA) Miss Waki Club (USA) (Miswaki (USA))
476^{3} 759^{8} 1442^{14} 2673^{8} 6856^{3} 7238^{10} (7669) 7849^{3}

Eltheeb *David O'Meara* a75 88
6 gr g Red Ransom(USA) Snowdrops (Gulch (USA))
2369^{5} 2718^{4} 3685^{7} 4264^{4}

Elualla (IRE) *Nigel Tinkler* 58
2 b f Elusive City(USA) Cote Quest (USA) (Green Desert (USA))
1574^{7} 2475^{8} 4115^{4} 4538^{2} 4847^{8} 5970^{5}

Elusive *Ann Stokell* a24
7 b m Reel Buddy(USA) Love Is All (IRE) (Second Empire (IRE))
28^{9} 197^{12} 230^{7} 324^{7} 541^{6} 602^{5} 712^{5}

Elusive Band (USA) *Bernard Llewellyn* a57 69
3 b g Elusive Quality(USA) Dancing Band (USA) (Dixieland Band (USA))
2456^{6} 2989^{9} 3250^{12} 5395^{10} 5813^{3} 6114^{2}

Elusive Bleu (IRE) *Tom Dascombe* 44
3 b g Elusive City(USA) Jamrah (IRE) (Danehill (USA))
1881^{12} 2548^{7}

Elusive Bonus (IRE) *David O'Meara* a49 79
4 b f Elusive City(USA) Over Rating (Desert King (IRE))
1649^{7} 2173^{8} 2755^{9} 3078^{6} 3505^{8} 4728^{7} 4852^{5} 5422^{8} 6547^{9} 7030^{5} 7315^{8} 7599^{4}

Elusive Flame *David Elsworth* a94 98
4 b f Elusive City(USA) Dimelight (Fantastic Light (USA))
1726^{10} 2254^{9} 3060^{8} 3720^{2} 4534^{3} (5247) 5561^{8} 6352^{13} 6768^{10} 7171^{18}

Elusive Gold (IRE) *J W Hills* a72 63
3 b f Elusive City(USA) Lady Angola (USA) (Lord At War (ARG))
(1874) 2572^{6} 3111^{6} 3699^{8} 4378^{2} 5104^{3} 5644^{4} 6856^{8} 7728^{3}

Elusive Guest (FR) *George Margarson* 68
2 b c Elusive City(USA) Mansoura (IRE) (Kalanisi (IRE))
7070^{4}

Elusive Hawk (IRE) *David Evans* a94 84
9 b g Noverre(USA) Two Clubs (First Trump)
548^{7} 650^{12} 795^{10} 971^{3} (1063) ◆ 1172^{3} (1205) (1309) 1451^{2} 1745^{7} 2214^{14} (2571) 3093^{8} 3754^{5} 4628^{3} 4908^{7} (5389) 5696^{5} 6215^{3} 6403^{7}

Elusive Kate (USA) *John Gosden* a80 118
4 b f Elusive Quality(USA) Gout De Terroir (USA) (Lemon Drop Kid (USA))
3419^{4} (4254) (4817a) 5314a^{7} 6837^{4} 7366^{5}

Elusive Pearl (FR) *F Rossi* 100
2 b f Elusive City(USA) Spirit Of Pearl (IRE) (Invincible Spirit (IRE))
5082a^{2}

Elusive Prince *T Hogan* a88 101
5 b g Storming Home Ewenny (Warrshan (USA))
679a^{7}

Elusive Ridge (IRE) *H Rogers* a101 96
7 b g Elusive City(USA) Woodwing (USA) (Indian Ridge)
2288a^{5}

Elusive Thought (IRE) *J S Moore* a59 48
3 b g Elusive City(USA) Thought Is Free (Cadeaux Genereux)
424^{3} 447^{2}

Elusive Time (IRE) *Takashi Kodama* a103 105
5 b g Elusive City(USA) Brosna Time (IRE) (Danetime (IRE))
3458^{28} 6883a^{9}

Elusive Warrior (USA) *Alan McCabe* a63 54
10 b g Elusive Quality(USA) Love To Fight (CAN) (Fit To Fight (USA))
537^{8} 620^{3} 831^{5} 965^{7} 2575^{8} 5198^{6} (5869) 7753^{2} 7886^{5} 8042^{8} 8235^{6}

Elusivity (IRE) *David O'Meara* a79 111
5 b g Elusive City(USA) Tough Chic (IRE) (Indian Ridge)
2019^{6} ◆ 2669^{4} 2909a^{4} 3558^{7} 4947^{12} ◆ 5375^{6} 6391^{11} 6830^{11} 7010^{12}

El Viento (FR) *Richard Fahey* a96 103
5 ch g Compton Place Blue Sirocco (Bluebird (USA))
1308^{3} ◆ 1672^{2} 2366^{8} 4285^{2} 4983^{7} 5545^{15} (5991) 6391^{10} 6845^{6} 7373^{9}

Elvin *Amanda Perrett* a48 46
3 br g Rock Of Gibraltar(IRE) Petite Nymphe (Golan (IRE))
2950^{11} 3428^{7} 3735^{7}

Elwaaryaa *F Head* a83 90
3 ch f Tamayuz Filfilah (Cadeaux Genereux)
5119a^{4}

El Wasmi *A Al Raihe* a80 83
5 b c Oasis Dream Wendylina (IRE) (In The Wings)
(412a)

Elysian *Sir Michael Stoute* a73 67
4 b f Galileo(IRE) Echelon (Danehill (USA))
(397)

Elysian Prince *Paul Cole* a79 61
2 b c Champs Elysees Trinkila (USA) (Cat Thief (USA))
5790^{9} (6079) 7979^{2}

Ely Valley *William Muir* a40
3 b f Haafhd Welsh Valley (USA) (Irish River (FR))
336^{7}

Emaad (USA) *Mark Johnston* 74
2 b c Arch(USA) Red Dot (USA) (Diesis)
3461^{6} 4470^{3} 5025^{2} 5745^{4} 6303^{11} 7309^{16}

Emaratiya Ana (IRE) *Roger Varian* a64
2 b f Excellent Art Tina Heights (Shirley Heights)
6523^{6}

Embankment *William Jarvis* a88 84
4 b g Zamindar(USA) Esplanade (Danehill (USA))
1848^{8} 2085^{7} 6167^{11} 6701^{12} 6925^{5} 7438^{9}

Embsay Crag *Philip Kirby* a58 80
7 b g Elmaamul(USA) Wigman Lady (IRE) (Tenby)
4376^{6} 4822^{3} (5560) 5879^{5} 6565^{4} (7280) 8130^{4}

Emef Diamond *Mick Channon* 79
2 b g Firebreak On The Brink (Mind Games)
5473^{3} (5969) 7336^{2}

Emell *Richard Hannon Snr* a94 106
3 ch c Medicean Londonnetdotcom (IRE) (Night Shift (USA))
1033 ^{2} 1621^{2} 2258^{5} 2843^{2} 3839^{2}

Emerahldz (IRE) *Richard Fahey* a69 62
2 b f Excellent Art Sancia (IRE) (Docksider (USA))
4756^{8} 5508^{10} 6206^{7} (6726) (7032)

Emerald Art (IRE) *J W Hills* a43 47
3 ch f Excellent Art Greenvera (USA) (Riverman (USA))
2447^{10} 2952^{8} 3858^{7} 5633^{9}

Emerald Breeze (IRE) *Charles Hills* 39
2 b f Tagula(IRE) Rebel Aclaim (IRE) (Acclamation)
4484^{13} 4877^{13} 5352^{11}

Emerald Gg (IRE) *J S Moore* a41 7
2 b g Diamond Green(FR) Florista Gg (URU) (Gulpha Gorge (USA))
7120^{13} 7568a^{10}

Emerald Girl (IRE) *Simon Hodgson* a39 75
6 b m Chineur(FR) Faypool (IRE) (Fayruz)
4034^{8}

Emerald Glade (IRE) *Jim Best* a59 70
6 b m Azamour(IRE) Woodland Glade (Mark Of Esteem (IRE))
5002^{4}

Emerald Sea *Chris Wall* a66 70
3 b f Green Desert(USA) Wind Surf (USA) (Lil's Lad (USA))
2006^{5} 2763^{4} 3699^{13} 5617^{2} 6135^{5} 6941^{4} 7861^{5}

Emerald Wilderness (IRE) *Mark Rimmer* a104 88
9 b g Green Desert(USA) Simla Bibi (Indian Ridge)
189^{5} 401^{3} (495) 585^{4} 777^{4} 7974^{8} 8263^{9} 8385^{2}

Emerging *David Elsworth* a76 90
3 b c Mount Nelson Pan Galactic (USA) (Lear Fan (USA))
(184) 1683^{3} 2054^{4} (2878) 3294^{3} (4980) 5274^{7} 6841^{6}

Emerging Artist (FR) *Evan Williams* a26 101
7 b g Dubai Destination(USA) Picture Princess (Sadler's Wells (USA))
747^{10}

Emilio Largo *James Fanshawe* a96 101
5 b g Cadeaux Genereux Gloved Hand (Royal Applause)
2207^{4} 3527^{19} 4297^{16} 5056^{7} 5894^{6} 6199^{8} 6989^{9}

Emily Davison (IRE) *David C Griffiths* a31 62
2 gr f Moss Vale(IRE) Carabine (USA) (Dehere (USA))
2856^{9} 3476^{3} 3681^{4} 4511^{3} 5029^{2} 5421^{7} 5857^{6} 6979^{11} 7199^{8}

Emily Hall *Bryan Smart* a14 56
4 ch f Paris House Raven (IRE) (Alzao (USA))
2170^{14} 4377^{3} 4892^{7} 5365^{6} 6761^{11}

Emiratesdotcom *Milton Bradley* a82 73
7 b g Pivotal Teggiano (IRE) (Mujtahid (USA))
1067^{6} 1346^{7} 1947^{5} 2364^{3} 2588^{3} 2918^{3} 3270^{2} 3511^{9} 4837^{6} 5522^{3} 5697^{7} 5816^{2} 6154^{3} 6316^{8} 7106^{10} 7444^{2} 7801^{5} 7964^{4}

Emirates Flyer *Saeed bin Suroor* 104
2 b c Acclamation Galapagar (USA) (Miswaki (USA))
(2823) 3481^{5} ◆ (4299) 4747^{2} 5999^{2} 7026^{2}

Emirates Galloper (IRE) *Saeed bin Suroor* 82
2 b g Dalakhani(IRE) Emmy Award (IRE) (Sadler's Wells (USA))
(4026) ◆ 4959^{5}

Emirates Queen *Luca Cumani* 113
4 b f Street Cry(IRE) Zomaradah (Deploy)
2397^{6} (4059) 5297a^{3} 5682^{7}

Emjayem *Ed McMahon* a44 76
3 ch g Needwood Blade Distant Stars (IRE) (Distant Music (USA))
1519^{4} (5345) (6100) ◆ 6900^{9}

Emkanaat *Amy Weaver* a91 85
5 b g Green Desert(USA) Miss Anabaa (Anabaa (USA))
2618^{14} 3060^{12} 3586^{10} 4014^{6} 4494^{5} 4746^{7} 5205^{2} 5522^{U} 6089a^{8} 7743^{2} (7880) 7896^{3} 8391^{6} 8455^{4}

Emman Bee (IRE) *Luke Dace* a71 79
4 gr f Dark Angel(IRE) Two Sets To Love (IRE) (Cadeaux Genereux)
1013^{6} 1585^{7} (2413) 3063^{5} 3899^{4} 4234^{9} 5001^{7} 6037^{2} 6405^{9} 6794^{11} 7437^{8} 7876^{10}

Emmuska *Clive Cox* a84 72
4 b f Sir Percy Tintac (Intikhab (USA))
(2573) 3269^{2} 3983^{4} 5978^{6} 6694^{13} 7438^{8}

Emollient (USA) *William Mott* a113 113
3 b f Empire Maker(USA) Soothing Touch (USA) (Touch Gold (USA))
7708a^{4}

Emotif (ARG) *M F De Kock* a99 95
4 br f Giant's Causeway(USA) Elisita (ARG) (Ride The Rails (USA))
554a^{5} 837a^{5} 953a^{5} 1264a^{12}

Emotionalblackmail (IRE) *Rod Collet* a79 53
3 b f Azamour(IRE) Uva Fragola (Nashwan (USA))
962a^{3}

Emperatriz *John Holt* a76 67
3 b f Holy Roman Emperor(IRE) Fairmont (IRE) (Kingmambo (USA))
1772^{6} ◆ 2387^{6} 3649^{12} 4885^{2} 5192^{2} 5870^{2} 6587^{7} 7754^{5} 7952^{2} 8316^{4} (8360)

Emperical *Lady Cecil* a82 83
3 b g Oasis Dream Kalima (Kahyasi)
1684^{3} 2568^{2} 7739^{4} ◆

Emperor Ferdinand (IRE) *Marcus Tregoning* a50
2 b g Holy Roman Emperor(IRE) Moon Flower (IRE) (Sadler's Wells (USA))
8333^{9} 8425^{12}

Emperor Julius (IRE) *Jo Crowley* a72
3 b g Antonius Pius(USA) Queen's Victory (Mujadil (USA))
(734) 1612^{11} 8345^{7}

Emperor's Hope (IRE) *Richard Hannon Snr* a68 75
2 b f Holy Roman Emperor(IRE) Nadwah (USA) (Shadeed (USA))
2978^{4} (3174) 3863^{3} 4239^{3} 6695^{17}

Empire Hurricane (GER) *A Wohler* 91
3 bb c Hurricane Run(IRE) Emy Coasting (USA) (El Gran Senor (USA))
1867a^{6}

Empire Storm (GER) *A Wohler* a106 109
6 b h Storming Home Emy Coasting (USA) (El Gran Senor (USA))
1564a^{4} 2146a^{8} 3612a^{2} 5940a^{3} 6451a^{5} 7053a^{5}

Empiricist (IRE) *Amanda Perrett* a58 81
3 b g Holy Roman Emperor(IRE) Charaig (Rainbow Quest (USA))
3276^{7} 4950^{11} 6115^{7} 6379^{6} 7429^{5}

Empoli (GER) *P Schiergen* 113
3 ch c Halling(USA) Estefania (GER) (Acatenango (GER))
3389a^{2} 4103a^{13} 5324a^{2} 6028a^{4} 6678a^{4}

Emporium *Gary Harrison* 35
2 b f Exceed And Excel(AUS) Australian Dreams (Magic Ring (IRE))
5797^{12}

Empowermentofwomen (IRE) *Michael Bell* a69 31
3 b f Manduro(GER) Miss Brown To You (IRE) (Fasliyev (USA))
184^{2} 377^{3} (590) 4715^{6}

Empreinte (USA) *C Laffon-Parias* 98
2 ch f Footstepsinthesand Zagzig (Selkirk (USA))
3875a^{3} 4816a^{5} 5628a^{6}

Empress Adelaide *William Haggas* 93
3 ch f Pivotal Emperice (USA) (Empire Maker (USA))
5495^{5} 5942^{2} ◆ (6532) 7223^{3}

Empress Ali (IRE) *Tom Tate* 70
2 b f Holy Roman Emperor(IRE) Almansa (IRE) (Dr Devious (IRE))
6125^{11} 6597^{2} 7277^{2}

Emulating (IRE) *James Fanshawe* a71 78
3 ch g Duke Of Marmalade(IRE) Ascendancy (Sadler's Wells (USA))
867^{3} (2324) 2600^{3} 3241^{8} 4593^{4} 5632^{2} 6003^{9} 7970^{13}

Enaitch (IRE) *Mick Channon* 78
3 gr f New Approach(IRE) Hotelgenie Dot Com (Selkirk (USA))
1636^{11} 1975^{3} 2261^{5} 2967^{2} 3272^{4} 3982^{6} 4417^{5} 5286^{6}

Encapsulated *Roger Ingram* a58 57
3 b g Zamindar(USA) Star Cluster (Observatory (USA))
2442^{15} 2746^{9} 3176^{6} 3903^{4} 4410^{5}

Enchanted Dream *David C Griffiths* a57 49
5 b f Halling(USA) Enchanted (Magic Ring (IRE))
4013^{9} 4727^{7} 5192^{9}

Enchanted Garden *Malcolm Jefferson* a45 71
5 ch g Sulamani(IRE) Calachuchi (Martinmas)
1653^{9} 1826^{6} 2462^{5} (2887) 3627^{4} ◆

Encore Encore (FR) *Harry Dunlop* a68
2 b f Royal Applause Angel Rose (IRE) (Definite Article)
5131^{9} 5891^{4} 6961a^{10} (7732)

Encore Merci (IRE) *F Rohaut* a68 79
3 ch f Danehill Dancer(IRE) Thanks Again (IRE) (Anabaa Blue)
7189a^{10}

Endeavor *Dianne Sayer* 54
8 ch g Selkirk(USA) Midnight Mambo (USA) (Kingmambo (USA))
3287^{4}

Endellion (USA) *A Fabre* 99
4 ch f Monsun(GER) Dunnes River (USA) (Danzig (USA))
5360a^{4}

Enderby Spirit (GR) *Bryan Smart* a82 88
7 gr g Invincible Spirit(IRE) Arctic Ice (IRE) (Zafonic (USA))
3367^{5} 5011^{14} 5537^{6} 7241^{10} 8088^{5} 8431^{6}

Endio (FR) *Mme L Audon* a68 88
3 b f Enrique Dionissima (FR) (Baillamont (USA))
3385a^{9} 4468a^{0}

Endless Applause *Richard Whitaker* 49
4 b f Royal Applause Petra Nova (First Trump)
2504^{7}

Endless Credit (IRE) *Luca Cumani* 86
3 bb g High Chaparral(IRE) Pay The Bank (High Top)
2456^{2} (3539) 4537^{3}

Endless Light *Jeremy Noseda* 80
3 ch f Pivotal Celeste (Green Desert (USA))
4125^{2} 5839^{2} 6486^{2} (7108)

End Of Line *Andrew Balding* 89
2 b c Pastoral Pursuits Just Devine (IRE) (Montjeu (IRE))
(7494)

Endorsing (IRE) *Richard Hannon Snr* a70 87
3 b c Dylan Thomas(IRE) Gently (IRE) (Darshaan)
(1086) 1829^{2} ◆ 3369^{5} ◆ 3756^{2} ◆ 4084^{3}

Endowing (IRE) *J Size* 117
4 b g Danehill Dancer(IRE) Brazilian Samba (IRE) (Sadler's Wells (USA))
8211a^{11}

Endura *Harry Dunlop* 31
3 b f Manduro(GER) Special Moment (IRE) (Sadler's Wells (USA))
1727^{10} 3272^{8} 4195^{7} 5433^{10}

Energia Colonial (BRZ) *Fabricio Borges* a102 85
6 bb g Giant Gentleman(USA) Karla Dora (BRZ) (Nugget Point (IRE))
2146a^{2}

Energia Davos (BRZ) *Marco Botti* a105 113
5 gr g Torrential(USA) Star Brisingamen (USA) (Maria's Mon (USA))
462a[7] 8386[4] ◆

Energia Dust (BRZ) *Fabricio Borges* a101 101
5 ch h Amigoni(IRE) Key Largo (BRZ) (Roi Normand (USA))
152a[6] 367a[10] 657a[12]

Energia El Gigante (BRZ) *Fabricio Borges* a62 84
4 br c Point Given(USA) Lira Da Guanabara (BRZ) (Pitu Da Guanabara (BRZ))
553a[8]

Enfijaar (IRE) *William Haggas* a64 59
3 b f Invincible Spirit(IRE) Harayir (USA) (Gulch (USA))
4911[3] 7624[3] (7946)

Enfys Hud *David Evans* a23 63
2 b f Multiplex Kyllachy Magic (Kyllachy)
5995[7] 6365[7] 6821[5] 7252[9]

English Deer (IRE) *P D Deegan* a94 92
3 b c Shamardal(USA) Ya Hajar (Lycius (USA))
6883a[2]

English Summer *David Simcock* a91 88
6 b g Montjeu(IRE) Hunt The Sun (Rainbow Quest (USA))
40[2] (208) (352) 496[2] 2385[4] 2775[7] 4020[4] 4643[7] 5129[8] 6217[6]

Enharmonic (USA) *John Gosden* 48
2 b f E Dubai(USA) Musicanti (USA) (Nijinsky (CAN))
4880[7]

Enide *P Schiergen* a73 76
4 ch f Shamardal(USA) Estefania (GER) (Acatenango (GER))
963a[7]

Enigma Code (UAE) *Damian Joseph English* a76 73
8 b g Elusive Quality(USA) Tempting Fate (IRE) (Persian Bold)
5775a[17] (6089a)

Ennistown *Charlie Appleby* 103
3 b g Authorized(IRE) Saoirse Abu (USA) (Mr Greeley (USA))
(3048) 3698[5] (6163) (6772) 7526[7]

Ennobled Friend (USA) *Charlie Appleby* a84
3 b c Malibu Moon(USA) Seek To Soar (USA) (Seeking The Gold (USA))
5133[2] ◆ 6134[4]

Enobled *Sir Michael Stoute* a79 92
3 b c Dansili Peeress (Pivotal)
(2192) 2666[5] 5958[9]

Enquiring *Mark Johnston* 38
2 b c Cape Cross(IRE) Questina (FR) (Rainbow Quest (USA))
5995[9] 6938[6] 7219[9]

Enraptured (IRE) *John Gosden* a64 81
2 b f Oasis Dream Arty Crafty (USA) (Arch (USA))
3471[6] 4491[2] (5716)

Enriching (USA) *Gary Harrison* a75 77
5 ch g Lemon Drop Kid(USA) Popozinha (USA) (Rahy (USA))
2966[5] 3788[3] (4504) 4752[2] 5124[6] 5491[5] 7447[5] 7629[6] 8060[4] 8323[4]

Enrol *Sir Michael Stoute* a99 100
4 b f Pivotal Constitute (USA) (Gone West (USA))
(2007) 3114[2] 3527[21] 4983[9] 5561[3] 5992[10] 6595[2] 7015[5] 7649[4] 7974[4]

Ensnare *Willie Musson* a68 71
8 b g Pivotal Entrap (USA) (Phone Trick (USA))
320[10] 665[10] 825[3] (1161)

Ensuring *James Fanshawe* 86
2 br c New Approach(IRE) Dynacam (USA) (Dynaformer (USA))
(5957) 7017[7]

Enter The Red (IRE) *Aidan Anthony Howard* a51 54
4 b g Red Clubs(IRE) Inter Madera (IRE) (Toca Madera)
997[4] 1042[12] 8034[3]

Entifaadha *M Al Muhairi* a98 95
4 b g Dansili Model Queen (USA) (Kingmambo (USA))
412a[2]

Entihaa *Alan Swinbank* 86
5 b g Tiger Hill(IRE) Magic Tree (UAE) (Timber Country (USA))
1689[2] ◆ 2040[10] 5706[8] 6729[5] 7596[7]

Entitlement *James Fanshawe* a66 58
4 b f Authorized(IRE) Applecross (Glint Of Gold)
(131) 542[6] 6404[6] 7767[4] 8160[7] 8331[12]

Entrance *Julia Feilden* a55 63
5 ch f Iceman Enrapture (USA) (Lear Fan (USA))
(3056) 4180[6] 5126[6] 5803[6] 7923[6]

Entrapping *John E Long* a61 61
3 b g Tiger Hill(IRE) Meddle (Diktat)
134[4] 414[3] 634[3] (804) 2154[7] 2802[5] 4688[8] 5528[4] 5935[8] 7035[4] (7610) 8121[8]

Entre Copas *J-M Osorio* 94
9 ch g Sakhee(USA) Priena (IRE) (Priolo (USA))
(6252a)

Entrenched (USA) *Charlie Appleby* a72 74
3 ch c Street Cry(IRE) Texas Tammy (USA) (Seeking The Gold (USA))
4152[5] 4454[5] 6036[3]

Entwined (IRE) *Clive Cox* a52 74
3 b f Elusive City(USA) Corryvreckan (IRE) (Night Shift (USA))
1832[3] 2439[2] 3242[5] 5187[6] 5896[9] 7531[7]

Enzaal (USA) *Philip Kirby* a82 83
3 b c Invasor(ARG) Ekleel (IRE) (Danehill (USA))
1387[2] (1735) 2193[3] 2651[7] 3105[3] 3756[5] (4251) 4765[8] 6514[4]

Epegard (IRE) *M Delzangles* a65
3 ch c Footstepsinthesand Essexford (IRE) (Spinning World (USA))
72a[9]

Epic Battle (IRE) *William Haggas* a88 76
3 b g Acclamation Wrong Key (IRE) (Key Of Luck (USA))
(7786) (8057) 8301[4] 8398[3]

Epic Charm *Mick Channon* a44 58
3 b f Kodiac Gayala (IRE) (Iron Mask (USA))
1678[10] 1907[9] 2308[7] 2528[6]

Epic Storm (IRE) *Paul Morgan* a81 68
5 b g Montjeu(IRE) Jaya (USA) (Ela-Mana-Mou)
39[4] 224[7] 562[3] 7758[6] 8204[4] 8309[4]

Epic Voyage (USA) *John Gosden* a85 77
2 b g Empire Maker(USA) Costume (Danehill (USA))
5405[2] 7925[2] 8067[4]

Epsom Hill (SWE) *Tobias B P Coles* 57
2 b c Homme D'Honneur(FR) Energiya Sacc (SWE) (Exceller (USA))
7502[8]

Epsom Salts *Pat Phelan* a68 79
8 b g Josr Algarhoud(IRE) Captive Heart (Conquistador Cielo (USA))
3328[6] 3662[9] 4437[4] 5854[5] 6404[7] 7767[7] 7984[4] (8160) 8331[5]

Equalizer *Tom Dascombe* a69 44
4 b g Authorized(IRE) Octaluna (Octagonal (NZ))
2465[6] 2995[8]

Equitania *Alan Bailey* a99 91
3 b f Pastoral Pursuits Clarice Orsini (Common Grounds)
85[4] (203) 337[2] 1234[8] 1625[3] 1808[11] 2213[4] 3220[9] 3584[9] 3786[5] 4797[8] 5103[3] 5769[10] (6647) (6920) 7803[7] (8189) 8232[2] 8334[8]

Equitissa (IRE) *Richard Hannon Snr* a72 75
3 b f Chevalier(IRE) Westcote (USA) (Gone West (USA))
2606[7] 2874[3] 3177[7] 3951[3] (4240) 5037[9] 7505[12]

Equity Risk (USA) *Kevin Ryan* a80 98
3 b g Henrythenavigator(USA) Moon's Tune (USA) (Dixieland Band (USA))
1892[2] (2708) (3234) 4255[18] 4922[9] 5728[2] 6208[4]

Erelight (IRE) *R P O'Keeffe* a39 35
5 bb f Erewhon(USA) Caradene (IRE) (Ballad Rock)
7082[9]

Eretara (IRE) *R P O'Keeffe* a49 58
4 b f Erewhon(USA) Hi Fasliyev (IRE) (Fasliyev (USA))
7083[5]

Erica Starprincess *George Moore* 40
3 b f Bollin Eric Presidium Star (Presidium)
2027[7] 2501[11] 3232[11] 4931[6] 7099[7]

Eric The Grey (IRE) *Richard Fahey* a56 86
3 gr g Verglas(IRE) Queens Wharf (IRE) (Ela-Mana-Mou)
1044[3] 1487[2] ◆ 1934[4] 2405[3] 3336[2] 4293[3] 5030[5] 6211[4] (6499) 6626[6] (7257) 7425[10]

Erin's Grace (IRE) *Gay Kelleway* a61 29
3 b f Tagula(IRE) Crystal Theatre (IRE) (King's Theatre (IRE))
3116[14]

Erlkonig (GER) *Markus Klug* 90
3 gr c Sternkoenig(IRE) Elora (GER) (Alkalde (GER))
1867a[5] 2696a[9] 4103a[10]

Ermyn Flyer *Pat Phelan* a57 64
4 b f Sakhee(USA) Famcred (Inchinor)
1781[6] 2534[7]

Ermyn Lodge *Pat Phelan* a41 89
7 br g Singspiel(IRE) Rosewood Belle (USA) (Woodman (USA))
2205[12] 3959[11] 4873[15]

Ermyntrude *Pat Phelan* a61 61
6 bb m Rock Of Gibraltar(IRE) Ruthie (Pursuit Of Love)
(334) 630[7] 3015[3] 3924[7] 4205[6] 5123[8] 8329[7]

Ernest Defarge *Michael Bell*
3 b g Cape Cross(IRE) Elizabethan Age (FR) (King's Best (USA))
4719[6]

Ernest Hemingway (IRE) *A P O'Brien* a98 116
4 br c Galileo(IRE) Cassydora (Darshaan)
1415a[4] (3873a) (5209a) 5776a[3] 6441a[6]

Ernest Speak (IRE) *David Evans* a49 41
4 b g Jeremy(USA) Mijouter (IRE) (Coquelin (USA))
1730[11] 1951[11] 4711[5] 5434[7] 5667[5]

Ernie *Geoffrey Deacon* a53 46
6 ch g Reset(AUS) Bonita Bee (King Of Spain)
1317[6] 1653[10] 1882[11] 2563[6] 6044[7]

Erodium *Richard Hannon Snr* a77 80
3 b g Kyllachy Alovera (IRE) (King's Best (USA))
(1035) 1471[3] 1977[3] 2584[3]

Errigal Lad *Garry Woodward* a57 64
8 ch g Bertolini(USA) La Belle Vie (Indian King (USA))
1681[7] 3246[8] 4074[3] 4456[7] 4669[5] 5373[6] 6568[6] 7101[2] 8082[2]

Erroneous (IRE) *David Simcock* 79
2 br g Footstepsinthesand Atir Love (USA) (Green Dancer (USA))
4731[2] (7023)

Ersaal *Roger Varian* a69 69
3 b g Dubawi(IRE) Makaaseb (USA) (Pulpit (USA))
2167[3] 2549[4]

Ertijaal (IRE) *William Haggas* 93
2 b c Oasis Dream Shabiba (USA) (Seeking The Gold (USA))
2741[2] (3737)

Ertikaan *Harry Whittington* a88 88
6 b g Oasis Dream Aunty Mary (Common Grounds)
127a[7] 340[5] 2571[3] 3108[3] 3886[6] 4207[6] 5735a[11] 7254[9]

Escape Artist *David Thompson* a54 44
6 gr g Act One Free At Last (Shirley Heights)
3085[7]

Escape To Glory (USA) *Michael Dods* a80 82
5 b g Bernstein(USA) Escape To Victory (Salse (USA))
1720[9] 2007[6] 2310[8] 3367[10] 3682[7] 4560[7] ◆ 5294[10] 5832[12] 5971[8] 6549[3] 7988[3] 8269[13]

Escarlata Rossa *J S Moore* a36 46
2 b f Multiplex Ella Y Rossa (Bertolini (USA))
4154[8] 4964[4] 5243[4] 5893[10] 6279[9]

Eseej (USA) *Geoffrey Deacon* a84 53
8 ch g Aljabr(USA) Jinaan (USA) (Mr Prospector (USA))
3012[3]

Eshtiaal (USA) *Brian Meehan* 100
3 b g Dynaformer(USA) Enfiraaj (USA) (Kingmambo (USA))
1624[4] ◆ (2198) (2641) 3486[12] 5746[6] 6186[3] 6793[7]

Eshtibaak (IRE) *John Gosden* a98 109
5 b c Dalakhani(IRE) Nanabanana (IRE) (Anabaa (USA))
1235[9] 2185[2] 2718[2]

Eshtyaaq *David Evans* a80 76
6 b g Mark Of Esteem(IRE) Fleet Hill (IRE) (Warrshan (USA))
1733[5] 2269[6] 3110[6] 3916[4] 4606[2] (4913) 5520[4] 5997[4] (6424) 7947[5] 8089[2]

Eskadi (FR) *J Heloury* a69 64
5 gr g Verglas(IRE) Partageuse (FR) (Green Tune (USA))
648a[3]

Esles (FR) *C Laffon-Parias* 104
5 b g Motivator Resquilleuse (USA) (Dehere (USA))
(4601a) 5465a[4]

Esoterique (IRE) *A Fabre* 114
3 b f Danehill Dancer(IRE) Dievotchka (Dancing Brave (USA))
(1869a) 2299a[2] ◆ 3385a[7]

Espero (FR) *J-C Rouget* a108 90
4 gr c Verglas(IRE) Queen's Conquer (King's Best (USA))
1048a[3] 7142a[11]

Espoir En Tete (FR) *P Adda* a57 53
2 b c Dr Fong(USA) Egypt Moon (Zieten (USA))
5296a[7]

Esprit De Midas *Dean Ivory* a92 98
7 b g Namid Spritzeria (Bigstone (IRE))
2937[13] 3538[7] 4879[16] 6215[11] 6702[16]

Es Que Love (IRE) *Mark Johnston* a105 110
4 br c Clodovil(IRE) Es Que (Inchinor)
244a[16] 660a[10] 834a[10] 868a[9] (1545) 1675[11] 1830[6] 2399[11] 2858[9] 3335[2] 3458[11] 3527[5] 4080[2] 4297[2] 4531[3] 4744[9] 4946[6] ◆ 5681[5] 5844[2] 5992[3] 7014[7]

Esquinade (FR) *A Bonin* a77 78
4 b f Archange D'Or(IRE) Estafilade (FR) (Gold Away (IRE))
963a[10]

Essanar *Andrew Hollinshead* 12
2 br g Notnowcato Spirito Libro (USA) (Lear Fan (USA))
7335[11]

Essell *Mick Channon* a57 62
4 ch f Singspiel(IRE) Londonnetdotcom (IRE) (Night Shift (USA))
105[6] 2966[2] 3222[4] 3728[7]

Esteaming *David Barron* 91
3 b g Sir Percy Night Over Day (Most Welcome)
1604[5] 1934[5] (2432) 2879[4] 5107[2] ◆ (5582)

Esteem *David Evans* a59 77
10 b g Mark Of Esteem(IRE) Please (Kris)
235[3] 458[3] 713[4] 1040[7]

Estemaala (IRE) *David O'Meara* 77
4 b f Cape Cross(IRE) Elutrah (Darshaan)
1825[6] 3321[6] (3627) ◆

Estibdaad (IRE) *Paddy Butler* a67 65
3 b g Haatef(USA) Star Of Siligo (USA) (Saratoga Six (USA))
2931[6] 4521[5] 4829[8] 6399[3] ◆ 7434[3] 7637[2] 7984[7] 8042[13] 8160[11]

Estifzaaz (IRE) *Charles Hills* a79 83
3 b g Invincible Spirit(IRE) Lulua (USA) (Bahri (USA))
1618[4] 2953[3] (3572) 4236[3] 4642[4]

Estimate (IRE) *Sir Michael Stoute* 113
4 b f Monsun(GER) Ebaziya (IRE) (Darshaan)
(1920) ◆ (3483) 7363[7]

Estinaad (USA) *Brian Ellison* a60 73
3 b f Street Sense(USA) Dawla (Alhaarth (IRE))
5065[8] 5791[2] 6629[3]

Estiqaama (USA) *William Haggas* 103
3 b f Nayef(USA) Ethaara (Green Desert (USA))
(2963) (3292) (5202) ◆ 6796[9]

Etaad (USA) *J W Hills* 58
2 b c Intidab(USA) Red's Lucky Lady (USA) (Lucky Lionel (USA))
4795[7] 6975[5] 7335[7]

Etalondes (FR) *J-C Rouget* a95 103
3 b c Royal Applause Fancy Dance (Rainbow Quest (USA))
1357a[4] 2298a[16] 4043a[5]

Etchy *Robin Bastiman*
2 rg c Paris House Solaris Dancer (Samim (USA))
3568[6] 7095[9]

Ethel *John Gosden* a73 73
3 b f Exceed And Excel(AUS) Agnus (IRE) (In The Wings)
2979[2] (4013) 4348[6] 6701[6]

Ethics Girl (IRE) *John Berry* a89 87
7 b m Hernando(FR) Palinisa (FR) (Night Shift (USA))
1673[3] 2385[2] 3685[10] 5168[8] 5514[7] 5879[4] 6377[7]

Ethiopia (AUS) *Pat Carey* 108
5 b g Helenus(AUS) Shona (AUS) (Spectrum (IRE))
7392a[13] 7700a[4] 7761a[7]

Etijaah (USA) *Brian Meehan* a53 78
3 b g Daaher(CAN) Hasheema (IRE) (Darshaan)
2209[9] 2603[4] 3235[5]

Eton Dorney (USA) *Mark Johnston* a77
4 b g Medaglia d'Oro(USA) Sweet And Firm (USA) (Peteski (CAN))
7422[8] 7734[2] 7894[6]

Eton Forever (IRE) *Roger Varian* a96 115
6 b g Oratorio(IRE) True Joy (IRE) (Zilzal (USA))
(2258) 3101[5]

Eton Miss (IRE) *Mike Murphy* a26
3 ch f Windsor Knot(IRE) Miss Barcelona (IRE) (Mac's Imp (USA))
729[6] 1906[10] 2963[6]

Eton Rambler (USA) *George Baker* a58 77
3 bb g Hard Spun(USA) Brightbraveandgood (USA) (Smart Strike (CAN))
2017[7] 3013[4] 3376[9] 5098[7] (5217) (6158) 6827[5]

Eton Rifles (IRE) *Stuart Williams* 111
8 b g Pivotal Maritsa (IRE) (Danehill (USA))
7010[2] 7821[7] (7995a)

Eugenic *Rod Millman* 54
2 br g Piccolo Craic Sa Ceili (IRE) (Danehill Dancer (IRE))
6430[6] 6975[7]

Euphrasia (IRE) *Joseph G Murphy* a47 108
4 b f Windsor Knot(IRE) Bishop's Lake (Lake Coniston (IRE))
1862a[5] (2375a) 6226a[5] 6441a[U] 7404a[4]

Eurato (FR) *C Laffon-Parias* 92
3 ch g Medicean Double Green (IRE) (Green Tune (USA))
2557a[2] (7412a)

Eurhythmic (IRE) *Jim Old* a55 55
6 b g Danehill Dancer(IRE) Russian Ballet (USA) (Nijinsky (CAN))
1586[P]

Euro Charline *Marco Botti* a78
2 b f Myboycharlie(IRE) Eurolink Artemis (Common Grounds)
(7934)

Euroquip Boy (IRE) *Michael Scudamore* a40 64
6 b g Antonius Pius(USA) La Shalak (IRE) (Shalford (IRE))
3270[12] 3910[9] 4714[11] 5434[6] 5818[2] (6156) 7079[5]

Eurystheus (IRE) *Michael Appleby* a85 77
4 b g Acclamation Dust Flicker (Suave Dancer (USA))
1583[6] 2256[6] 5974[7] 6562[3] 6701[5] 7632[2] 7961[3] (8314) 8416[3]

Euston Square *Alistair Whillans* a83 78
7 b g Oasis Dream Krisia (Kris)
1567[9] 2219[5] 3199[8] 4475[4] 5142[2] 5179[2] 5368[2] (5840) 6130[7] 6976[10] 7778[10]

Eutropius (IRE) *Alan Swinbank* a76 79
4 b g Ad Valorem(USA) Peps (IRE) (Val Royal (FR))
(1450) (1932) 2042[3] 2515[2] 3477[8] 4098[3] 4308[14] 5546[11] 6549[4] 6970[6]

Evacusafe Lady *John Ryan* a66 68
2 ch f Avonbridge Snow Shoes (Sri Pekan (USA))
1421[3] 1724[6] 3436[5] 4431[5] 4861[2] 5167[5] 5865[3] 7168[8] 7466[2] 7609[6] 7695[13] 7878[4] 8434[2]

Evan Elpus (IRE) *Tom Dascombe* a52 39
3 br g Footstepsinthesand Birthday (IRE) (Singspiel (IRE))
1078[4] 1660[9]

Evanescent (IRE) *John Quinn* a40 90
4 b g Elusive City(USA) Itsanothergirl (Reprimand)
3778[12] 4375[10] 4967[3] 5974[5] (6548) (6774) 7176[9]

Evangelist *Sir Michael Stoute* a93 91
3 b c Oasis Dream Hi Calypso (IRE) (In The Wings)
1713[3] 2495[3] ◆ 3235[2] (3899) 5030[4] (5649) (6380) ◆ 7304[3]

Evason *J S Bolger* 87
2 b c Galileo(IRE) Soneva (USA) (Cherokee Run (USA))
7050a[2]

Even Bolder *Eric Wheeler* a73 68
10 ch g Bold Edge Level Pegging (IRE) (Common Grounds)
719[7] 1902[10] (3154) 3667[7] 4369[6]

Evening Attire *David Brown* a88 81
2 b c Pastoral Pursuits Markova's Dance (Mark Of Esteem (IRE))
(4977) (6197)

Evens And Odds (IRE) *Peter Grayson* a63 74
9 ch g Johannesburg(USA) Coeur De La Mer (IRE) (Caerleon (USA))
2366[10] 3846a[29] 4800[18] 5636[8] 6162[8] 6653[7] 7728[13] 8035[8]

Even Stevens *Scott Dixon* a103 96
5 br g Ishiguru(USA) Promised (IRE) (Petardia)
319[2] 584[4] 5991[8] 6309[14] 6583[6] 7313[2] (7373) 7803[11] 7851[9] 8155[8] 8232[6]

Events Come (FR) *Mlle S Sine* a27 54
3 b g Country Reel(USA) Street Maya (FR) (Mtoto)
7187a[9]

Everest Hill *V Luka Jr* a43
3 b c Tiger Hill(IRE) Annapurna (IRE) (Brief Truce (USA))
460a[9]

Ever Fortune (USA) *Brian Ellison* 80
4 ch g El Corredor(USA) Beyond Price (USA) (King Of Kings (IRE))
3617[5] ◆ 4205[2] 4718[5] 7275[8] 8047[10]

Evergreen Forest (IRE) *Natalie Lloyd-Beavis* a71 73
5 ch g Haafhd Inaaq (Lammtarra (USA))
418[2] (653) 816[8] 1084[7] 1600[7] 1763[7] (2089) 5793[11] 6377[11]

Everlasting Dream *David Simcock* a52
3 b f Oasis Dream Magdalene (Act One)
1371[4]

Everlasting Light *Tim Walford* a71 65
3 b f Authorized(IRE) Blue Rocket (IRE) (Rock Of Gibraltar (IRE))
4454[4] 5478[8] 6398[5] 7033[3] 7439[3] 7961[6] 8299[8]

Everleigh *Richard Hannon Snr* a77 78
3 b f Bahamian Bounty Blur (Oasis Dream)
2195[5] 2622[3] 3251[7] 3666[4] 4898[10] 5758[6] 7462[7]

Evermore (IRE) *Mark Johnston* a64 62
3 b f Dansili Reunite (IRE) (Kingmambo (USA))
4381[7] 5495[4] 5942[8] 6491[8] 6933[11] 7847[2] ◆ 8004[3] 8129[3]

Everreadyneddy *J S Moore* a46 46
3 ch g Ad Valorem(USA) Maugwenna (Danehill (USA))
1903[7] 1982[3]

Ever Rider (ARG) *Maria Cristina Munoz* a107
5 rg h Rider Stripes(ARG) Alleg Dancer (ARG) (Il Corsaro (USA))
7687a[P]

Evervescent (IRE) *J S Moore* a66 88
4 b g Elnadim(USA) Purepleasureseeker (IRE) (Grand Lodge (USA))
2028[12] 3741[6] 4198[4] 4366[4] 5191[4] *5735a[12]* 5912a[4] 6720[12]

Everybody Knows *Jo Crowley* a66 96
8 b g King's Best(USA) Logic (Slip Anchor)
138[5]

Evident (IRE) *Jeremy Noseda* a82 78
3 b g Excellent Art Vestavia (IRE) (Alhaarth (IRE))
1881[7] 2306[17] (2872) 6642[5] *7076[2]* *7436[9]*

Evie Jay (IRE) *Paul Green* a10 66
2 ch f Windsor Knot(IRE) Carpet Lover (IRE) (Fayruz)
3045[5] 3942[6] 4053[2] 4399[3] 4511[6] 5225[4] 5773a[8] *7935[8]*

Ewell Place (IRE) *David Simcock* a80 94
4 br g Namid Miss Gibraltar (Rock Of Gibraltar (IRE))
3087[6] 3322[5] 3570[2] 3628[3] 4287[8] *5195[12]* *7076[11]* *7898[4]* *8227[4]*

Exactement (IRE) *Mrs K Burke* a96 97
3 ch f Speightstown(USA) Rakiza (IRE) (Elnadim (USA))
1000a[3] 1622[4] 2453[5] 2689a[9] 3734[2]

Examiner (IRE) *William Haggas* a77
2 ch g Excellent Art Therry Girl (IRE) (Lahib (USA))
7972[4] *(8214)* *8382[2]*

Excaper (USA) *Ian Black* a93 105
4 rg c Exchange Rate(USA) Ada Ruckus (CAN) (Bold Ruckus (USA))
6456a[6]

Excedo Praecedo *Amanda Perrett* a63 29
2 b g Exceed And Excel(AUS) Merle (Selkirk (USA))
6589[11] 6975[11] *7328[5]* *7893[9]*

Exceed And Exceed *George Margarson* a47 58
2 b c Exceed And Excel(AUS) Gandini (Night Shift (USA))
2401[12] 3044[7] 5344[6] *8126[5]*

Exceed Areeda (IRE) *James Tate* a60 39
2 b f Exceed And Excel(AUS) Areeda (IRE) (Refuse To Bend (IRE))
4497[5] *5352[4]* *6213[3]* *6605[8]* *7198[5]* *7352[10]*

Exceeder *Marco Botti* a78 73
2 b c Exceed And Excel(AUS) Norfolk Broads (IRE) (Noverre (USA))
3245[2] 3737[2] *4379[2]* 5186[4] 7127[6] *(7349)*

Exceedexpectations (IRE) *Conor Dore* a85 77
4 b g Intikhab(USA) Jazan (IRE) (Danehill (USA))
1874 *478[2]* *(791)* *1015[3]* *(1105)* *1220[2]* *(1354)* 1673[7] *1796[4]* 2278[3] 2929[2] 3192[3] 3472[8] 3926[2] 5124[15] 5928[11] 6204[10] 6476 [9] 7165[6] 7444[12] 7729[5] 7880[14] 8038[6] 8163[3] 8278[6] 8360[10]

Exceeding Power *Michael Bell* a75 62
2 b g Exceed And Excel(AUS) Extreme Beauty (USA) (Rahy (USA))
6569[8] 6790[10] *7200[4]* 7451[3] *(8222)*

Exceed Policy *David Dennis* 2
2 ch g Exceed And Excel(AUS) Policy Setter (USA) (Deputy Minister (CAN))
6641[11] 6739[14]

Excel Best *James Tate* a78
2 b c Exceed And Excel(AUS) Hannah's Dream (IRE) (King's Best (USA))
7901[6] *8067[8]* *8297[3]* *(8434)*

Excel Bolt *Bryan Smart* 94
5 ch g Exceed And Excel(AUS) Dearest Daisy (Forzando)
1248[9] 1807[7] 2031[10]

Excelette (IRE) *Bryan Smart* 106
4 b f Exceed And Excel(AUS) Madam Ninette (Mark Of Esteem (IRE))
1662[4] ◆ 3046[7] 3562[4] 4311[3] 5984[11] 6305[4] 6719[3]

Excellent Addition (IRE) *Declan Carroll* a65 70
3 ch g Excellent Art Race The Wild Wind (USA) (Sunny's Halo (CAN))
1577[6] 2340[2] 3629[4] ◆ 4045[6] 4544[10] 4722[4] 5644[7] *6655[7]* *6980[8]*

Excellent Aim *George Margarson* a65 74
6 b g Exceed And Excel(AUS) Snugfit Annie (Midyan (USA))
493[9] 3922[2] (4427) (5221) 5620[3] 6077[6] *8216[4]*

Excellent Guest *George Margarson* 104
6 b g Exceed And Excel(AUS) Princess Speedfit (FR) (Desert Prince (IRE))
(2254) 3458[9] 4297[15] 4744[12] 5738[15] 6183[8] 7364[10]

Excellentissime (IRE) *C Ferland* 99
3 b c Cape Cross(IRE) Luna Royale (IRE) (Royal Applause)
1799a[2]

Excellent Jem *Jane Chapple-Hyam* a77 74
4 b g Exceed And Excel(AUS) Polar Jem (Polar Falcon (USA))
2286[12] 2929[4] 3534[4] *4163[3]* *(5354)* *6317[8]* *(6652)* *7164[9]* 7661[8]

Excellent News (IRE) *Tony Forbes* a49 50
4 ch f Excellent Art Subito (Darshaan)
3133[5] 3231[6] 3721[7] *4355[3]* *4835[9]* 5377[9]

Excellent Puck (IRE) *Shaun Lycett* a85 77
3 b c Excellent Art Puck's Castle (Shirley Heights)
228[6] *740[2]* *994[2]* *1072[2]* *(1655)* 2153[7] 2827[4] 5802[10] 6306[2] *(6556)* 6898[3] 7505[3] 8416[2]

Excellent Result (IRE) *Saeed bin Suroor* 103
3 b c Shamardal(USA) Line Ahead (IRE) (Sadler's Wells (USA))
1679[9] (2605) 3486[7] (6186) 7206[4]

Excellent Royale (IRE) *Charles Hills* a76 66
2 b c Excellent Art Farbenspiel (IRE) (Desert Prince (IRE))
5344[8] 6581[9] 7019[7] *7892[5]*

Excellent Touch (IRE) *C Lerner* a73 53
3 b c Excellent Art Bold Bold (IRE) (Sadler's Wells (USA))
7188a[10]

Excellent View *Saeed bin Suroor* 60
2 gr f Shamardal(USA) Pearl Grey (Gone West (USA))
7692[6]

Excel's Beauty *James Tate* 98
2 b f Exceed And Excel(AUS) Continua (USA) (Elusive Quality (USA))
2740[2] ◆ (3132) (4451) 5005[11] 5476[2] 5767[4] 7011[5]

Excelsior Academy *Richard Phillips* a75 86
7 b g Montjeu(IRE) Birthday Suit (IRE) (Daylami (IRE))
224[P]

Exceptionelle *Roger Varian* a90 93
3 br f Exceed And Excel(AUS) Turning Leaf (IRE) (Last Tycoon)
3058[4] 4413[2] 6539[4] 6768[4] *7642[4]*

Excess Knowledge *John Gosden* 112
3 br c Monsun(GER) Quenched (Dansili)
4027[3] ◆ 4874[2] ◆ 6393[10]

Exchange *Frau M Muller* a70 73
5 b g Kheleyf(USA) Quantum Lady (Mujadil (USA))
514a[8] *700a[3]*

Exchequer (IRE) *Richard Hannon Snr* 80
2 ch c Exceed And Excel(AUS) Tara's Force (IRE) (Acclamation)
5957[4] 6641[2] 7251[2]

Exclusion (USA) *Noel Quinlan* a65 56
3 bb f Include(USA) Long Silence (USA) (Alleged (USA))
2095[4] *2566[8]* 3428[6] *(4144)* *5234[2]* *5966[3]* *7857[9]*

Exclusive Dancer *George Moore* 68
4 gr f Notnowcato Exclusive Approval (USA) (With Approval (CAN))
1610[6] 2280[11]

Exclusive Predator *Bryan Smart* a61 63
4 b g Misu Bond(IRE) Triple Tricks (IRE) (Royal Academy (USA))
59[3] *434[4]* 2507[5] 3572[5] *4144[11]* 7109[15]

Exclusive Waters (IRE) *Gary Moore* a78 64
3 b g Elusive City(USA) Pelican Waters (IRE) (Key Of Luck (USA))
2938[11] 3528[7] *3820[9]* *(5528)* 5615[7] *6315[2]* *(6398)* *6612[2]* *8339[5]*

Excuse To Linger *Jeremy Noseda* a84 89
3 ch c Compton Place Lady Le Quesne (IRE) (Alhaarth (IRE))
1714[4] 2100[2] 3153[5] 4288[4] (4864) 5489[11] *6403[6]* *7080[3]*

Exempt *Jeremy Noseda* 65
3 gr f Exceed And Excel(AUS) Miss University (USA) (Beau Genius (CAN))
2746[8] 3116[12] 3793[9]

Ex Ex *Nick Littmoden* a73
3 b g Exceed And Excel(AUS) Temple Of Thebes (IRE) (Bahri (USA))
8070[3] *8146[2]* *8303[2]*

Exit Clause *Mark Gillard* a58 38
3 b c Manipulator(IRE) Claws (Marju (IRE))
470[7] *732[6]* *824[14]* *1064[3]* *1373[5]* *1747[7]* 2095[8] 2919[8] 6902[16] 7249[7]

Exkaliber *Jeremy Gask* a58 30
4 b g Exceed And Excel(AUS) Kalindi (Efisio)
139[4] *327[2]* *551[4]* *5864[2]* *6651[9]* *7292[5]* *7850[2]* *8082[9]* *8271[10]*

Exning Halt *John Quinn* a74 80
4 b g Rail Link Phi Phi (IRE) (Fasliyev (USA))
(313) *614[7]* 2077[4] 3729[5] 4809[6] 5521[4]

Exogenesis (IRE) *G M Lyons* 107
2 b g Dark Angel(IRE) Secret Key (IRE) (Key Of Luck (USA))
(4694a) 5774a[3]

Exopuntia *Julia Feilden* a58 56
7 b m Sure Blade(USA) Opuntia (Rousillon (USA))
335[2] *631[8]* *907[3]* *5135[11]* 5622[4] *6554[6]* *6933[12]*

Ex Oriente (IRE) *Stuart Williams* a89 94
4 b g Azamour(IRE) Little Whisper (IRE) (Be My Guest (USA))
6868[9] 7431[8] 7823[14]

Exotic Guest *George Margarson* a46 78
3 ch g Bahamian Bounty Mamoura (IRE) (Lomond (USA))
1295[5] 4258[9] (5141) 5820[5] 6506[7] 7324[8] *7445[9]*

Exotic Isle *Ralph Beckett* a87 85
3 ch f Exceed And Excel(AUS) Paradise Isle (Bahamian Bounty)
1682[5] (2098) 2521[6] (3160) 4592[5] 5585[5] *6854[3]* *8021[4]*

Exotic Lady (IRE) *Sylvester Kirk* a47 51
3 bb f Excellent Art Princess Sabaah (IRE) (Desert King (IRE))
7253[9] *7490[5]*

Expect *Jeremy Noseda* a79 76
2 b f Invincible Spirit(IRE) Expressive (Falbrav (IRE))
6500[2] *(7078)* 7657[7] *8261[4]*

Expedition (IRE) *A P O'Brien* 97
2 b c Oasis Dream Littlefeather (IRE) (Indian Ridge)
5771a[6] 6021a[3]

Experimentalist *Tim Vaughan* a70 76
5 b g Monsieur Bond(IRE) Floppie (FR) (Law Society (USA))
131[2] *378[5]*

Expert (IRE) *Richard Hannon Snr* 101
2 gr c Mastercraftsman(IRE) Raphimix (FR) (Linamix (FR))
2358[4] 4256[2] (4764) 4876[5] 5530[4] 6065[2] 6304[3] 6958[5] (7658)

Expert Fighter (USA) *Saeed bin Suroor* a99 96
4 ch g Dubai Destination(USA) Porto Roca (AUS) (Barathea (IRE))
(2775) 4310[11] 4854[16] *6172[7]* *6927[3]* *7542[2]*

Exploratory (USA) *Charlie Appleby* a79
3 ch c New Approach(IRE) Arlette (IRE) (King Of Kings (IRE))
4632[3] *5678[5]*

Expose *Michael Appleby* a80 82
5 ch g Compton Place Show Off (Efisio)
(8384)

Express Himself (IRE) *Ed McMahon* 74
2 b c Dylan Thomas(IRE) Lightwood Lady (IRE) (Anabaa (USA))
6829[11] 7502[4]

Expressly (IRE) *Charlie Appleby* 91
3 ch f Street Cry(IRE) Express Way (ARG) (Ahmad (ARG))
(4799) 5271[6] 6796[8]

Extortionist (IRE) *Olly Stevens* 102
2 b c Dandy Man(IRE) Dream Date (IRE) (Oasis Dream)
(1680) 2370[4] (3424) 4572a[9] 6347[3] 7011[4]

Extra Noble *Ralph Beckett* a90 89
2 b c Sir Percy La Peinture (GER) (Peintre Celebre (USA))
2653[2] *(3689)* 6395[2] ◆ *(6935)* 7534[6]

Extrasolar *Amanda Perrett* a91 90
3 b g Exceed And Excel(AUS) Amicable Terms (Royal Applause)
1515[4] ◆ 2010[2] 2394[2] (2529) *2983[2]* (3279) 4989[6] 5303[3] ◆ 5538[13] 5721[3] *6204[3]* *6403[5]*

Extraterrestrial *Richard Fahey* a89 93
9 b g Mind Games Expectation (IRE) (Night Shift (USA))
1233[8] 1485[3] 1786[5] 2705[3] 2912[2] 3564[9] 4012[2] (4803) 5050[2] 5546[6] (5828) 6468[2] 7130[2]

Extremely Alert *Michael Bell* a53 23
4 ch g Nayef(USA) Megdale (IRE) (Waajib)
361[4] *456[3]*

Extreme Supreme *Derek Shaw* 71
2 b c Piccolo Kitty Kitty Cancan (Warrshan (USA))
3481[12] 4282[3]

Extremity (IRE) *Hugo Palmer* a73 81
2 ch c Exceed And Excel(AUS) Chanterelle (IRE) (Indian Ridge)
5924[6] (6635) 7017[10]

Extroverted *Doug Watson* a51 34
5 ch g Exceed And Excel(AUS) Star Profile (IRE) (Sadler's Wells (USA))
394a[4]

Exzachary *Jo Hughes* a84 76
3 b g Multiplex Icky Woo (Mark Of Esteem (IRE))
1725[10] *3438[2]* 3773[3] *4354[2]* 5477[6] 6664[6] 7452[10]

Eyebreak (FR) *B Goudot* a53 70
3 b g Sunday Break(JPN) Eye Witness (IRE) (Don't Forget Me)
2034a[7]

Eye Contact *Sir Michael Stoute* 65
2 br c Dansili Modern Look (Zamindar (USA))
5472[8]

Eyeline *Andrew Hollinshead* a56 58
3 b g Needwood Blade Waterline Twenty (IRE) (Indian Danehill (IRE))
207[3] *561[5]* *848[11]* *977[4]* 1289[3] *1747[9]* 2362[3] 3040[2] 3675[5] 3918[3] 5650[2] 5979[3] *6479[5]* 6895[5]

Eye Of The Storm (IRE) *A P O'Brien* 114
3 ch c Galileo(IRE) Mohican Princess (Shirley Heights)
1811[2] 7363[3]

Fabled City (USA) *Clive Cox* a84 84
4 ch g Johannesburg(USA) Fabulous Fairy (USA) (Alydar (USA))
759[9] 1849[10] 2232[12] 3780[4] 4718[6] 5310[4] 6037[5]

Fab Lolly (IRE) *James Bethell* a70 66
3 b f Rock Of Gibraltar(IRE) Violet Ballerina (IRE) (Namid)
2279[9] 2628[4] 3396[7] 3946[8] (5290) 5830[5] 6941[3] *(7841)* *8134[8]*

Fabriano (AUS) *Peter Donnelly* 95
7 b g Golan(IRE) Florete (NZ) (Volksraad)
7417a[3] 7760a[17]

Face East (USA) *Alan Berry* 51
5 b g Orientate(USA) Yes Honey (USA) (Royal Academy (USA))
2757[16]

Face Surface (GER) *F Rohaut* a90 100
3 ch c Turtle Bowl(IRE) Flower Bowl (FR) (Anabaa (USA))
(445a) 3645a[8]

Face The Problem (IRE) *Jamie Osborne* 111
5 b g Johannesburg(USA) Foofaraw (USA) (Cherokee Run (USA))
2152[4] 2368[13] 2768[6] 3334[7] ◆ 4275[14] 4800[6] 4986[25] 5651[3] (Dead)

Face Value *Adrian McGuinness* a73 83
5 b g Tobougg(IRE) Zia (GER) (Grand Lodge (USA))
5021a[14] 6585[8] 7723a[12]

Factory Time (IRE) *M Ibrahim* a91 107
4 b c Baltic King Mark One (Mark Of Esteem (IRE))
746a[10]

Faerie Reel (FR) *C Ferland* 79
3 b f Country Reel(USA) Final Whistle (IRE) (Rossini (USA))
(7569a)

Faffa *Tim Easterby* a61 57
3 ch g Araafa(IRE) Forever Fine (USA) (Sunshine Forever (USA))
328[3] ◆

Faintly (USA) *Amanda Perrett* 83
2 b c Kitten's Joy(USA) Tinge (USA) (Kingmambo (USA))
2194[8] 3426[3] (4518) 5524[4] 6139[2] 6865[7]

Fair Breeze *Richard Phillips* a49 33
6 b m Trade Fair Soft Touch (IRE) (Petorius)
788[5] *1080[5]* *3473[6]* 6099[4]

Fair Bunny *Alan Brown* a22 20
6 b m Trade Fair Coney Hills (Beverley Boy)
6603[9] *7958[U]* *8233[11]*

Fair Comment *Michael Blanshard* a67 65
3 b f Tamayuz Cliche (IRE) (Diktat)
2017[5] 2362[2] 3039[5] 3665[6] 3859[3] 4885[7] 5170[2] 5604[7] *5923[8]* 6321[5] 7071[4] *8121[7]* *8388[4]*

Fair Flutter (IRE) *Richard Fahey* 67
2 b g Manduro(GER) Polish Affair (IRE) (Polish Patriot (USA))
3461[8] 4218[5] 4756[9] 5424[8] 6085[3] (6275) 6844[2] (6946)

Fairlie Dinkum *Andrew Crook* a39 32
5 b f Tobougg(IRE) Fairlie (Halling (USA))
3195[14] 3592[7]

Fair Loch *K R Burke* a76 76
5 gr g Fair Mix(IRE) Ardentinny (Ardross)
2465[3] 3209[5] *8092[2]*

Fairly Fair (FR) *A De Royer-Dupre* 100
4 gr f Sinndar(IRE) Fairly Grey (FR) (Linamix (FR))
1895a[6] 2644a[9]

Fair Moon (FR) *D Smaga* a81 82
3 b f Gold Away(IRE) La Fee De Breizh (FR) (Verglas (IRE))
7188a[4]

Fair Ranger *Richard Hannon Snr* a74 85
2 b g Bushranger(IRE) Fairmont (IRE) (Kingmambo (USA))
2436[3] 3044[3] (3366) 3890[2] (4031) 5679[10] ◆ 6303[10] 7129[8] *7626[9]* *7879[6]*

Fair Share *Lady Cecil* a75
2 b c Rail Link Quota (Rainbow Quest (USA))
8067[2]

Fair Trade *Alan King* a22 85
6 ch g Trade Fair Ballet (Sharrood (USA))
3856[5]

Fair Value (IRE) *Simon Dow* a65 97
5 b f Compton Place Intriguing Glimpse (Piccolo)
2014[3] 2865[4] 3038[3] 4024[4] 4275[16] 4860[7] 5821[4] 6078[4] *7982[11]*

Fairwater (USA) *Mme C Head-Maarek* a78 48
2 b f Empire Maker(USA) Jazz Drummer (USA) (Dixieland Band (USA))
3752a[8] *5296a[3]*

Fairway To Heaven (IRE) *Michael Wigham* a75 93
4 b c Jeremy(USA) Luggala (IRE) (Kahyasi)
5183[5] ◆ 6331[2] 7013[9]

Fairyinthewind (IRE) *Alan King* a79 73
4 ch f Indian Haven Blue Daze (Danzero (AUS))
159[4] *222[2]* *421[3]* *7651[5]*

Fairy Mist (IRE) *John Bridger* a52 50
6 b g Oratorio(IRE) Prealpina (IRE) (Indian Ridge)
120[2] *334[7]* *510[9]* *(664)* *725[4]* *839[5]* *978[8]* *1162[6]* *1183[10]* 2057[10] 2873[5] 3430[2] 3926[4] 4517[4] 5170[5] 6019[2] 6261[7] 7266[5] 8244[6] 8450[8]

Fairy Nayef *B Grizzetti* 105
3 b g Nayef(USA) Fairy Sensazione (Fairy King (USA))
1865a[2] 2490a[9]

Fairy Wing (IRE) *Ann Stokell* a72 71
6 b g Hawk Wing(USA) Mintaka (IRE) (Fairy King (USA))
92[5] *399[10]* *493[7]* *652[7]* *688[8]* *805[3]* ◆ *863[11]* *(1147)* *(1186)* 1310[3] 1475[4] 1947[4] 2222[3] 2515[4] 4146[5] (5097) 5899[6] 6259[3] 7953[10] 8439[11]

Faisal Lion (IRE) *J S Moore*
2 ch c Camacho Premier Bird (IRE) (Bluebird (USA))
7128[12]

Faither *Keith Dalgleish* a54 41
3 b g Bertolini(USA) Hawait Al Barr (Green Desert (USA))
459[4] *623[3]* *717[4]* 1966[12] 5704[5] 5916[7]

Faithfilly (IRE) *F Rohaut* a72 96
3 b f Red Clubs(IRE) Bauci (IRE) (Desert King (IRE))
2334a[4] 4935a[0]

Faithful Ruler (USA) *Ronald Harris* a79 90
9 bb g Elusive Quality(USA) Fancy Ruler (USA) (Half A Year (USA))
311[3] *(433)* *(519)* *672[4]* *798[7]* *974[5]* *1104[5]*

Faith Jicaro (IRE) *James Unett* a68 40
6 b m One Cool Cat(USA) Wings To Soar (USA) (Woodman (USA))
3180[5] 4365[4]

Fa'iz (IRE) *E Charpy* a67 62
4 br g Dansili Carisolo (Dubai Millennium)
394a[11]

Fake Or Fortune (IRE) *Colin Teague* 32
3 b g Antonius Pius(USA) Fancy Theory (USA) (Quest For Fame)
2716[14] *2995[9]*

Falasteen (IRE) *Milton Bradley* a78 83
6 ch g Titus Livius(FR) Law Review (IRE) (Case Law)
946[6] *1058[5]* *1198[2]* *1516[2]* 1952[11] 2550[5] 2780[5] 2918[13] *7937[11]* *8216[2]* *8330[6]* 8457[9]

Falcon's Reign (FR) *Michael Appleby* a71 77
4 ch g Haafhd Al Badeya (IRE) (Pivotal)
1442[5] 1950[8] 2889[4] (7661) 7824[15]

Falcun *Nikki Evans* a30 63
6 b g Danehill Dancer(IRE) Fanofadiga (IRE) (Alzao (USA))
2165[8] 2922[7] 4035[10] 5432[10]

Falling Sky (USA) *John Terranova II* a106
3 b c Lion Heart(USA) Sea Dragoness (USA) (Sea Hero (USA))
2033a[19]

Falls Of Lora (IRE) *Charlie Appleby* a104 108
4 b f Street Cry(IRE) Firth Of Lorne (IRE) (Danehill (USA))
366a[3] 3775[6] 4705[6] 5271[4] 6000[5] 6796[6]

Falmouth Bay (USA) *Catharina Vang* a85 64
5 rg c Elusive Quality(USA) Halo America (USA) (Waquoit (USA))
2146a[5]

False Witness (IRE) *David Nicholls* 69
2 b g Amadeus Wolf Ten Commandments (IRE) (Key Of Luck (USA))
5338[15] 6206[5] 6627[5] 7147[8]

Faluka (IRE) *Paul Cole* 57
3 rg f Iffraaj Tortue (IRE) (Turtle Island (IRE))
1660[5] 1911[5]

Fama Mac *Neville Bycroft* a58 74
6 b g Fraam Umbrian Gold (IRE) (Perugino (USA))
2479[7] 5088[9] 6205[9] *6969[6]* 7281[9]

Fame Again *Michael Easterby* a78 76
5 b g Gentleman's Deal(IRE) Ballet Fame (USA) (Quest For Fame)
146[3] *443[5]* 3506[4] 4198[8] 4375[3] 4850[2] *7669[5]* *8008[6]* *8314[3]*

Familliarity *Roger Varian* a57 85
3 ch f Nayef(USA) Millistar (Galileo (IRE))
2989[4] 3764[3] (4404) 4898[6] (6098)

Family Album (USA) *Y Barberot* a73 73
3 b c Flower Alley(USA) Blush Damask (USA) (Green Dancer (USA))
(191a)

Famous Poet (IRE) *Saeed bin Suroor* a95 102
4 b c Exceed And Excel(AUS) Asfurah (USA) (Dayjur (USA))
3538^{2} 4276^{8} 5255^{2}

Famous Warrior (IRE) *Doug Watson* a101 91
6 b g Alhaarth(IRE) Oriental Fashion (IRE) (Marju (IRE))
363a^{6} ◆ 557a^{12} 744a^{6} 834a^{12}

Fancy Beat *Gianluca Bietolini* 98
6 b h Beat Hollow Fancy Shawl (Polish Precedent (USA))
7724a^{7}

Fancy Green (FR) *E Legrix* a89
3 ch f Muhtathir Fancy Stone (IRE) (Rainbow Quest (USA))
8440a^{10}

Fanny Squeers *Michael Bell* 56
3 b f New Approach(IRE) Whazzat (Daylami (IRE))
2384^{10} 3059^{8}

Fanoos *William Haggas* 83
4 b f Dutch Art Miss Otis (Danetime (IRE))
6940^{2} (7343) ◆

Fanoulpifer *B Grizzetti* 95
2 b c High Chaparral(IRE) Furbeseta (Danehill Dancer (IRE))
7235a^{4}

Fanrouge (IRE) *Rod Millman* a79 92
4 b f Red Clubs(IRE) Silk Fan (IRE) (Unfuwain (USA))
2265^{7} 2531^{2} (3407) 3720^{4} 3892^{6} 4746^{8} 5308^{7} 5896^{6} 6381^{7} 7123^{10}

Fantacise *Richard Fahey* 89
3 ch f Pivotal My First Romance (Danehill (USA))
1250^{8} 1444^{10} 1620^{7} 2371^{14} 3058^{11}

Fantastic Moon *Jeremy Noseda* 106
3 ch c Dalakhani(IRE) Rhadegunda (Pivotal)
1811^{5} 3523^{6} 4216^{4}

Fantastic Smartie *Richard Phillips* a22 60
4 b f Fantastic Spain(USA) Smart Cassie (Allied Forces (USA))
546^{8} 735^{9} 1088^{10}

Fantasy Fighter (IRE) *Ronald Harris* a61 50
8 b g Danetime(IRE) Lady Montekin (Montekin)
76^{9} 128^{7} 277^{7} 472^{4} 516^{3} 610^{8} 756^{5} 1043^{5}

Fantasy Gladiator *John Quinn* a85 76
7 b g Ishiguru(USA) Fancier Bit (Lion Cavern (USA))
25^{8} (3741) 4237^{8} 4864^{2} 5153^{5} 5799^{2} 6316^{2} ◆ 7130^{7} 7742^{5} ◆ (7964) 8053^{3}

Fantasy In Blue *Sir Michael Stoute* a66 78
3 b f Galileo(IRE) Blue Symphony (Darshaan)
1347^{2} ◆ 1653^{3} 2995^{4} 5854^{3} 6847^{3} 7488^{4}

Fantasy Invader (IRE) *John Quinn* a50 64
3 b g Captain Marvelous(IRE) Fields Of Joy (GER) (Waky Nao)
3509^{5} 5393^{7} 6074^{5} 6343^{6} 7079^{4} 7485^{6}

Fantasy Justifier (IRE) *Ronald Harris* 64
2 b c Arakan(USA) Grandel (Owington)
1659^{5} 2260^{4} 3035^{6} 6517^{10}

Fanunalter *M Hussain* a98 118
7 b g Falbrav(IRE) Step Danzer (IRE) (Desert Prince (IRE))
153a^{7} 466a^{9} 838a^{10} 957a^{7}

Fanzine *Hughie Morrison* 75
3 ch f Medicean Dash To The Front (Diktat)
1671^{3} 2389^{5} 3842^{6} 5125^{9}

Far Afield *A Fabre* a87 100
3 b c Rail Link Posteritas (USA) (Lear Fan (USA))
4043a^{8}

Faranadooney (USA) *S M Duffy* a51 49
6 bb g Sahm(USA) Sarina's Princess (USA) (Captain Bodgit (USA))
703^{3}

Faraway Land (USA) *Julia Feilden* a51 43
5 b f Empire Maker(USA) Out Of Reach (Warning)
157^{5} 469^{12} 1060^{6}

Far Gaze (IRE) *J S Moore* a72 81
2 b g Balmont(USA) Novosibirsk (USA) (Distant View (USA))
1208^{3} 1328^{2} (1344) 1917^{5} 2863^{8} 4703^{3}

Farhh *Saeed bin Suroor* 128
5 b c Pivotal Gonbarda (GER) (Lando (GER))
(2446) (7367)

Faridat (USA) *Shigeki Matsumoto* a100 97
8 br h Kingmambo(USA) Believe (JPN) (Sunday Silence (USA))
834a^{9} 955a^{9}

Farlow (IRE) *Richard Fahey* a82 94
5 ch g Exceed And Excel(AUS) Emly Express (IRE) (High Estate)
1232^{9} 1537^{9} 2366^{5} ◆ 4780^{14} 5437^{2} 6586^{5} ◆

Farmers Dream (IRE) *Derek Shaw* a40 50
6 b m Antonius Pius(USA) Beucaire (IRE) (Entrepreneur)
1887^{8} 2125^{5} 2998^{6} 3268^{2} 3623^{6} 4034^{7}

Farmleigh House (IRE) *W J Martin* a111 110
6 ch g Medecis Tabessa (USA) (Shahrastani (USA))
(78) 776^{2} 1032^{9} 2676a^{5} 5747^{5} 6414a^{3}

Farquhar (IRE) *Peter Chapple-Hyam* 83
2 ch c Archipenko(USA) Pointed Arch (IRE) (Rock Of Gibraltar (IRE))
(7631) ◆ 7967a^{9}

Farraaj (IRE) *Roger Varian* a107 100
4 b g Dubai Destination(USA) Pastorale (Nureyev (USA))
(1034) 1810^{5}

Farrier (USA) *S Seemar* a106 89
5 b g Tapit(USA) Wild Vision (USA) (Wild Again (USA))
151a^{6} 463a^{3}

Fashion Fund *Brian Meehan* 86
2 b f Oasis Dream So Silk (Rainbow Quest (USA))
4877^{11} 5529^{3} 6644^{3} 7016^{3}

Fashion Line (IRE) *Michael Bell* 71
3 b f Cape Cross(IRE) Shadow Roll (IRE) (Mark Of Esteem (IRE))
3116^{2} 3398^{2}

Fa'Side Castle (IRE) *Maurice Barnes* a13
4 b g Dylan Thomas(IRE) Keyaki (IRE) (Shinko Forest (IRE))
2118^{11}

Fast (IRE) *Richard Hannon Snr* 96
2 b f Kodiac Gypsy Royal (IRE) (Desert Prince (IRE))
(2344) 3459^{10} 3863^{6} (4653) 6347^{4} 7011^{7}

Fast Bullet (USA) *D Wayne Lukas* a119
5 ch c Speightstown(USA) Renfro Valley Star (USA) (Dayjur (USA))
7713a^{7}

Fast Delivery *Saeed bin Suroor* 75
2 b c Authorized(IRE) Rosenreihe (IRE) (Catcher In The Rye (IRE))
6330^{4} ◆

Fast Finian (IRE) *Paul D'Arcy* a92 95
4 gr g Clodovil(IRE) Delphie Queen (IRE) (Desert Sun)
121^{2} 400^{6} (1913) 2254^{18} 3060^{4}

Fast Freddie *Mrs A Corson* a76 49
9 b g Agnes World(USA) Bella Chica (IRE) (Bigstone (IRE))
1312a^{4} (1738a) 2303a^{3} 5328a^{2} 7143a^{2}

Fastidious *M D O'Callaghan* a83 90
4 b g Exceed And Excel(AUS) Felicitous (King's Best (USA))
679a^{3} 6883a^{24}

Fast In The Wind (IRE) *P D Deegan* a88 85
2 b c Footstepsinthesand Close Regards (IRE) (Danehill (USA))
2675a^{4} 7521a^{5}

Fast On (IRE) *Seamus Fahey* a56 49
4 gr g Verglas(IRE) Dream State (IRE) (Machiavellian (USA))
7886^{2} 8233^{6}

Fast Or Free *William Haggas* a85 103
4 ch g Notnowcato Ewenny (Warrshan (USA))
4854^{10}

Fast Pace *Amanda Perrett* a91 80
3 ch f Observatory(USA) Market Forces (Lomitas)
2389^{6} (3251) 4076^{3} (4523) 5132^{2} ◆ 6533^{6}

Fast Samurai (USA) *Tony Carroll* a47 54
5 ch c First Samurai(USA) Lady Blockbuster (USA) (Silent Screen (USA))
111^{7} 472^{8} 551^{10}

Fast Shot *Tim Easterby* a51 95
5 b g Fasliyev(USA) Final Pursuit (Pursuit Of Love)
1232^{14} 1688^{13} 2239^{3} 2460^{2} 2988^{2} 3823^{9} 4472^{2} 4780^{12} 5544^{8} 6621^{2} 6845^{8} 7495^{6}

Fast Stars Line (TUR) *N Kocken* 103
4 b c Ajmera Free Fighter (TUR) (Mujtahid (USA))
6254a^{6}

Fast Track *David Barron* 85
2 b g Rail Link Silca Boo (Efisio)
3295^{4} ◆ (3826) (5012) 6584^{9}

Fat Bottom Girl *Michael Easterby* a47 3
3 b f Pastoral Pursuits Answered Prayer (Green Desert (USA))
195^{9} 310^{8}

Fate (FR) *A De Royer-Dupre* 108
4 b f Teofilo(IRE) Specificity (USA) (Alleged (USA))
2644a^{2}

Fat Gary *Tom Dascombe* a93 89
3 ch g Dutch Art Suzuki (IRE) (Barathea (IRE))
2188^{8} 5182^{7} 6744^{8} (7164) (7593) (7959) 8189^{3}

Father Fred *Chris Dwyer* a77 59
3 br g Pastoral Pursuits Gramada (IRE) (Cape Cross (IRE))
2948^{5} 3494^{5} 4143^{6} 5275^{9} (6033) (6478) (6808) ◆

Father Shine (IRE) *Shaun Harris* a47 53
10 bb g Supreme Leader Shean Hill (IRE) (Bar Dexter (USA))
1^{4} 1189^{7} 1445^{8} 1721^{6} 7375^{3} 7612^{6}

Fathey (IRE) *Charles Smith* a43 39
7 ch g Fath(USA) Christoph's Girl (Efisio)
618^{9} 754^{6} 2998^{7} 3190^{9}

Fathom Five (IRE) *Shaun Harris* a70 61
9 b g Fath(USA) Ambria (ITY) (Final Straw)
124^{6} 3042^{9} 3667^{10} 6516^{7} 6760^{7} 6945^{3} 7598^{4} 7772^{4} 7957^{4} 8035^{5} (8048) 8152^{6} 8230^{5} 8352^{3} 8439^{9}

Fathsta (IRE) *Declan Carroll* a85 90
8 b g Fath(USA) Kilbride Lass (IRE) (Lahib (USA))
2663^{13} 3322^{8} 4398^{2} (4837) 5273^{8} 5523^{2} (5645) 5987^{3} 6215^{9} 6515^{6} 6995^{4} 7634^{4} 7885^{9}

Fatima's Gift *Stuart Williams* a68 76
3 b f Dalakhani(IRE) Heavenly Whisper (IRE) (Halling (USA))
2713^{4} 3975^{4} 5037^{2} 5411^{2} 6433^{5} 6997^{4} 7546^{6} 8036^{5}

Fattsota *David O'Meara* a104 111
5 b g Oasis Dream Gift Of The Night (USA) (Slewpy (USA))
661a^{7} 833a^{2} 1674^{7} 2839^{5} 3525^{9} (5822) 6636^{5} 7049a^{6} 7697^{3} 8062^{7}

Fault *Zoe Davison* a58 61
7 b g Bahamian Bounty Trundley Wood (Wassl)
1783^{13} 2954^{12} 3657^{12}

Faure Island *Henry Candy* 67
2 b c Myboycharlie(IRE) Free Offer (Generous (IRE))
5033^{10} 5744^{6} 7251^{4}

Faustinatheyounger (IRE) *David Elsworth* a54 62
3 b f Antonius Pius(USA) Tochar Ban (USA) (Assert)
2084^{14} 2392^{10} 3059^{6} 3821^{5} 4500^{7} 4961^{2} 5433^{8}

Favorite Girl (GER) *Michael Appleby* a70 76
5 b f Shirocco(GER) Favorite (GER) (Montjeu (IRE))
1076^{3}

Favourite Treat (USA) *Mark Johnston* a99 93
3 b g Hard Spun(USA) Truart (USA) (Yes It's True (USA))
6084^{4} (6486) 7648^{2} ◆ 7820^{19} 7991^{9} 8117^{11} 8264^{2} 8301^{7} 8445^{8}

Fawkner (AUS) *Robert Hickmott* 115
6 bb g Reset(AUS) Dane Belltar (AUS) (Danewin (AUS))
(7392a) 7761a^{6}

Faye Belle *Derek Shaw* a40 31
2 b f Lucky Story(USA) Vale Of Belvoir (IRE) (Mull Of Kintyre (USA))
1724^{10} 2778^{6} 3167^{4} 4141^{4} 5066^{12} 5351^{5} 5610^{13} 6364^{5}

Fayr Fall (IRE) *Tim Easterby* a78 78
4 b g Fayruz Keshena Falls (IRE) (Desert Prince (IRE))
2081^{9} 3087^{7} 3590^{4} 3945^{7} 4837^{4}

Fazza *Edwin Tuer* a74 89
6 ch g Sulamani(IRE) Markievicz (IRE) (Doyoun)
1576^{5} 4055^{9} 4540^{7} (5149) 5580^{7} 6126^{5} (6562) 7028^{6} 7499^{6}

Fearless Lad (IRE) *John Best* a70 24
3 b c Excellent Art Souffle (Zafonic (USA))
492^{4} 636^{2} 748^{3} 4416^{7} 5694^{7} 7446^{9} 8059^{8} 8443^{4}

Fear Or Favour (IRE) *Clive Cox* 80
2 b c Haatef(USA) Insaaf (Averti (IRE))
3836^{9} (5976) 6376^{2}

Feather Dancer *Jamie Poulton* 19
3 b f Norse Dancer(IRE) Featherlight (Fantastic Light (USA))
3278^{8} 3902^{6} 6312^{8} 8388^{12}

Febrayer Star (IRE) *Robert Cowell* a46
2 br c Majestic Missile(IRE) Ginger Not Blonde (USA) (Atticus (USA))
7162^{7} 7790^{7} 7978^{11} 8273^{6}

Fed Biz (USA) *Bob Baffert* a112 111
4 b c Giant's Causeway(USA) Spunoutacontrol (USA) (Wild Again (USA))
7689a^{6}

Federal (IRE) *Roger Teal* 62
3 b c Authorized(IRE) Yazmin (IRE) (Green Desert (USA))
1679^{10}

Federal Blue (USA) *Mark Johnston* a46 85
3 b c Elusive Quality(USA) Blue Duster (USA) (Danzig (USA))
333^{6} (3209) ◆ 3526^{13} 4279^{8} 4980^{6} 5258^{7} 5706^{5} 6202^{9} 6466^{8}

Feed Me Rainbow (FR) *R Pritchard-Gordon* a59 72
3 gr g Stormy River(FR) Dancing Rose (FR) (Dancing Spree (USA))
191a^{0} 5692a^{8}

Feedyah (USA) *Charlie Appleby* a83 92
2 b f Street Cry(IRE) Red Dune (IRE) (Red Ransom (USA))
(3471) 4682^{4} 5555a^{7} (6185)

Feeling (IRE) *Dai Burchell* a46 1
9 b g Sadler's Wells(USA) La Pitie (USA) (Devil's Bag (USA))
2350^{7}

Feeling Good *Brian Ellison* a77 62
4 b g Shamardal(USA) Lady Golan (IRE) (Golan (IRE))
1394^{8} 1603^{9} 1842^{6} 2514^{8} 2764^{12}

Feel Like Dancing *John Gosden* 101
3 b c Galileo(IRE) Maid Of Killeen (IRE) (Darshaan)
(1679) ◆ 2187^{4} 3061^{5} 3526^{2} (4211)

Feel The Heat *Bryan Smart* 76
6 ch g Firebreak Spindara (IRE) (Spinning World (USA))
1280^{7} (3026) 3197^{3} 4291^{2} 4669^{4} (6052)

Fehaydi *William Haggas* a62 99
3 b g Nayef(USA) Red Camellia (Polar Falcon (USA))
(1429) 1636^{5} 1809^{5} 3484^{7} ◆ 4242^{3} 4743^{7} 5792^{7}

Felice (IRE) *Scott Dixon* a37 27
3 b f Papal Bull Tarabaya (IRE) (Warning)
6319^{6} 7791^{7} 8046^{7}

Felician (GER) *Ferdinand J Leve* 109
5 b g Motivator Felicity (GER) (Inchinor)
(2202a) (4333a) 5940a^{2} 6451a^{8}

Felix Fabulla *Hughie Morrison* a76 79
3 b g Lucky Story(USA) Laser Crystal (IRE) (King's Theatre (IRE))
2054^{5} 2416^{8} 4150^{4}

Female Strategy (IRE) *Peter Chapple-Hyam* a52 25
2 b f Holy Roman Emperor(IRE) Strategy (Machiavellian (USA))
7533^{10} 8165^{3}

Fencing (USA) *John Gosden* 115
4 ch g Street Cry(IRE) Latice (IRE) (Inchinor)
(1919) 2446^{6} 4856^{6}

Fenella Foghorn *Jonathan Portman* a51 45
2 b f Elnadim(USA) Bundle Up (USA) (Miner's Mark (USA))
6409^{9} 6923^{6} 7243^{7}

Fenella Fudge *Derek Shaw* a72 74
5 b f Rock Hard Ten(USA) Rahcak (IRE) (Generous (IRE))
27^{7} 3489^{2} 3955^{2} 4163^{4} 4669^{2} 4884^{3}

Fen Flyer *John Berry* a50 35
4 ch g Piccolo Maraffi (IRE) (Halling (USA))
7873^{3} 8258^{10}

Fennann *Roger Varian* 11
2 b g Dutch Art Embraced (Pursuit Of Love)
7494^{11}

Fennell Bay (IRE) *Mark Johnston* a93 97
4 b g Dubawi(IRE) Woodrising (Nomination)
1159^{6} 1536^{4} (1774) 2044^{10} 2365^{4} 2775^{3} 3094^{9} (3442) 4060^{3} 4310^{12} 4501^{3} 4854^{5} 4979^{4} 5283^{10} (5559) 6001^{2} 6128^{3} 6638^{13} 7115^{2} 7312^{6}

Fenomeno (JPN) *Hirofumi Toda* 123
4 bb c Stay Gold(JPN) De Laroche (IRE) (Danehill (USA))
(1868a)

Fenton *Harry Dunlop* a45
3 b f Tiger Hill(IRE) Monteleone (IRE) (Montjeu (IRE))
1611^{5} 2157^{8} 2560^{10}

Feodora (GER) *Frau Agnieszka Klus* 97
2 ch f Lord Of England(GER) Forever Nice (GER) (Greinton)
7406a^{2}

Ferdy (IRE) *Paul Green* a64 74
4 b c Antonius Pius(USA) Trinity Fair (Polish Precedent (USA))
2707^{8} 3392^{3} 4051^{3} (4250) 4807^{7} 5183^{11} 5613^{7} 5947^{12} 7130^{15} 8095^{10}

Ferevia (IRE) *C Laffon-Parias* 110
3 b f Motivator Frynia (USA) (Cat Thief (USA))
(1602a) 2297a^{5} 2693a^{3} 3614a^{4} 5297a^{6}

Ferjaan *John Gosden* a73 75
3 b c Oasis Dream Bahja (USA) (Seeking The Gold (USA))
5103^{5}

Ferney Boy *Chris Fairhurst* a44 55
7 b g Courteous Jendorcet (Grey Ghost)
2120^{13} 2720^{4} 3363^{6} 5337^{5} 5863^{8} 7098^{7} 7376^{8}

Ferngrove (USA) *Jonathan Portman* 57
2 gr g Rockport Harbor(USA) Lucky Pipit (Key Of Luck (USA))
2411^{12} 4483^{10} 6485^{6}

Ferocious Fran (IRE) *Emmet Michael Butterly* a41 50
5 b f Footstepsinthesand Tipsy Lady (Intikhab (USA))
2074^{12} 3154^{10} 8050^{4} 8168^{5}

Ferro Sensation (GER) *D Klomp* 107
7 b g Paolini(GER) Fit To Ski (Niniski (USA))
1944a^{6} 3970a^{12} 5804a^{13}

Ferryview Place *Ian Williams* a72 62
4 b g Compton Place Songsheet (Dominion)
376^{3} 6475^{7} 6855^{7} 7163^{7} 7321^{10} 8399^{12}

Fersah (USA) *William Haggas* 91
3 b f Dynaformer(USA) Jaleela (USA) (Kingmambo (USA))
2206^{3} (2713) 3482^{8} 4015^{2} 4541^{4} 5496^{6}

Festival Dance *Ron Hodges* a51 71
5 b f Captain Rio Temple Dancer (Magic Ring (IRE))
399^{9} 558^{8}

Festival Theatre (IRE) *Sir Michael Stoute* a81 63
2 ch c Danehill Dancer(IRE) Scottish Stage (IRE) (Selkirk (USA))
4304^{4} (5101) ◆

Festive Cheer (FR) *A P O'Brien* a90 115
3 b c Montjeu(IRE) Bold Classic (USA) (Pembroke (USA))
2297a^{3} 2866^{10} 3849a^{3} ◆

Fetan Joa (FR) *J Heloury* 99
2 b f Enrique Grape Tree Hills (FR) (Grape Tree Road)
7184a^{4}

Feuerblitz (GER) *M Figge* 113
4 b c Big Shuffle(USA) Flamingo Island (GER) (Acatenango (GER))
5324a^{4} 6253a^{10} (7724a) 8208a^{8}

Fever Few *Jane Chapple-Hyam* a73 73
4 b f Pastoral Pursuits Prairie Oyster (Emperor Jones (USA))
5152^{6} 5830^{2} 6181^{12} 6535^{11} 7303^{4} 7880^{6}

Fiance Fiasco *Luke Dace* a41 22
3 b f Motivator Wise Little Girl (Singspiel (IRE))
374^{8}

Ficelle (IRE) *Nikki Evans* a53 68
4 b f Chineur(FR) Petite Boulangere (IRE) (Namid)
1802^{7} 1952^{8} 2596^{10} 2918^{15} 4884^{12} 5092^{6} 5817^{7} 6155^{3} 6436^{6} (7323) 7792^{9} 8418^{8}

Fidget *David Brown* 59
3 ch f Bertolini(USA) Record Time (Clantime)
2091^{7} 2703^{7} 3247^{10} 4430^{4} 4976^{10} 5156^{2} 5644^{8} 5788^{4}

Fiducia *Simon Dow* a69 69
3 b f Lawman(FR) Silca Key (Inchinor)
1319^{5} 1903^{4} (3216) 4385^{5} ◆ 5134^{6} 5853^{2}

Fieldgunner Kirkup (GER) *David Barron* a76 89
5 b g Acclamation Fire Finch (Halling (USA))
1113^{2} (1281) 2029^{10} 3335^{8} 4111^{3} ◆ 4340^{8} 5014^{9} 5481^{6} 6496^{7} 7949^{6} ◆ 8053^{5}

Field Of Dream *Jamie Osborne* a99 109
6 b g Oasis Dream Field Of Hope (IRE) (Selkirk (USA))
467a^{7} 744a^{5} 838a^{5} 1034^{6} 2585^{8} 3458^{6} (4297) 4744^{5} 4946^{9} 6183^{5} 6838^{15}

Field Of Fame *Andrew Balding* 81
2 b c Champs Elysees Aswaaq (IRE) (Peintre Celebre (USA))
(6953)

Fiesolana (IRE) *W McCreery* 116
4 b f Aussie Rules(USA) Tidal Reach (USA) (Kris S (USA))
(3263a) (3964a) 4567a^{6} (5688a) 6224a^{5} (7190)

Fife Jo *Jim Goldie* 59
3 b g Misu Bond(IRE) Musical Refrain (IRE) (Dancing Dissident (USA))
1829^{9} 2635^{4} 3392^{9} 5331^{8} 6083^{12} 6918^{8} 7150^{6}

Fiftyshadesdarker (IRE) *George Baker* a47
2 gr c Invincible Spirit(IRE) Poetry In Motion (IRE) (Ballad Rock)
8415^{7}

Fiftyshadesfreed (IRE) *George Baker* a69 56
2 gr g Verglas(IRE) Vasilia (Dansili)
3374^{15} 4379^{7} 5473^{9} 6111^{10} (6749) 7017^{16} 7878^{5} (7973) 8147^{3}

Fiftyshadesofgrey (IRE) *George Baker* a76 85
2 gr g Dark Angel(IRE) Wohaida (IRE) (Kheleyf (USA))
3035^{3} 3424^{13} 4858^{6} (6342)

Fighter Boy (IRE) *Michael Easterby* a73 69
6 b g Rock Of Gibraltar(IRE) In My Life (IRE) (Rainbow Quest (USA))
380^{4} (435) 545^{7}

Fighter Squadron (USA) *David Wachman* a80 102
3 bb c Medaglia d'Oro(USA) Whoopi Cat (USA) (Tale Of The Cat (USA))
2687a^{4}

Fig Roll *Richard Hannon Snr* a75 99
2 b f Bahamian Bounty Cake (IRE) (Acclamation)
1541^{2} (2053) 2944a^{3} 3459^{4} (3829) 4253^{4} 4742^{9} 7657^{6}

Figure Of Speech (IRE) *Charlie Appleby* a107 107
2 b g Invincible Spirit(IRE) Epic Similie (Lomitas)
(3536) 4212^{2} 4918^{4} 5573a^{8} 6201^{2} 6637^{4} 6958^{4} 7207^{8}

Filaga (FR) *M Figge* 94
2 b f Soldier Hollow Finessa (GER) (Law Society (USA))
7406a^{3}

Filament Of Gold (USA) *Mark Johnston* a67 60
2 b g Street Cry(IRE) Raw Silk (USA) (Malibu Moon (USA))
6256^{7} 6716^{7} 7120^{3} 7640^{5}

Filatore (IRE) *Bernard Llewellyn* a64 78
4 ch g Teofilo(IRE) Dragnet (IRE) (Rainbow Quest (USA))
(1979) 2990^{6} 3952^{2} 4913^{3} 5997^{6} 6424^{10} 7506^{2}

File And Paint (IRE) *Lawrence Mullaney* a68 65
5 b f Chevalier(IRE) Have A Heart (IRE) (Daggers Drawn (USA))
194^{6}

Filfil (USA) *Mahmood Al Zarooni* a66 61
3 b c Hard Spun(USA) Dixietwostepper (USA) (More Than Ready (USA))
245a^{6} 553a^{5} 658a^{5} 835a^{7}

Filia Regina *Ed Dunlop* a60 81
3 b f Galileo(IRE) Ouija Board (Cape Cross (IRE))
3764^{7} 4632^{7} 4978^{7} (5801) 6177^{7}

Fille D'Avril (FR) *E Leenders* a77 68
5 b f Zero Problemo(IRE) Taraison (FR) (The Quiet Bidder (IRE))
5042a^{9}

Filosofo (IRE) *Richard Hannon Snr* 43
2 b c Teofilo(IRE) Think (FR) (Marchand De Sable (USA))
4483^{13} 4987^{13}

Filou (SWI) *Th Von Ballmoos* 92
2 b c Lord Of England(GER) Fujairah (SWI) (Sri Pekan (USA))
7235a^{5}

Fils Anges (IRE) *Michael Bell* 97
3 gr c Dark Angel(IRE) La Piaf (FR) (Fabulous Dancer (USA))
1295^{2} 1482^{3} 2022^{10} 4014^{2} 4258^{2} 5439^{6} 6308^{6} 6993^{2} 7368^{22}

Filun *Anthony Middleton* a23 74
8 b g Montjeu(IRE) Sispre (FR) (Master Willie)
5168^{12} 7159^{12} 7440^{13}

Final Button (SAF) *M F De Kock* a84 98
5 ch g Tiger Ridge(USA) Red Buttons (SAF) (Shoe Danzig (USA))
149a^{13} 244a^{8} 467a^{6} 657a^{8} 869a^{5}

Final Countdown *Anthony Carson* a60 50
2 ch c Selkirk(USA) Culture Queen (King's Best (USA))
7655^{6} 8367^{2}

Final Delivery *Jim Boyle* a67 65
4 b g Three Valleys(USA) Bowled Out (GER) (Dansili)
883^{10} (1222) (1797) 2137^{6} 2532^{5} 3152^{2} 6970^{7} 7437^{7} 7923^{8}

Final Drive (IRE) *John Butler* a90 56
7 b g Viking Ruler(AUS) Forest Delight (IRE) (Shinko Forest (IRE))
49^{7} 219^{5} 439^{6} 603^{8} 813^{8}

Finalee *John Gallagher* a15 58
3 b f Cockney Rebel(IRE) Celtic Island (Celtic Swing)
1666^{11} 5695^{5} 6319^{8} 6895^{10} 7770^{8}

Final Folly (AUS) *Barbara Marshman* 89
7 gr g Desert Chief(AUS) Famous Folly (NZ) (Famous Star)
7417a^{12}

Finaz *Braem Horse Racing Sprl* a55 77
3 b c Bertolini(USA) Newkeylets (Diktat)
588^{2} (3454a)

Fin Bon (FR) *R Chotard* 24
3 ch g Falco(USA) Small Grey (FR) (Verglas (IRE))
3454a^{9}

Finch Flyer (IRE) *Aytach Sadik* a38 57
6 ch g Indian Ridge Imelda (USA) (Manila (USA))
3512^{6} 4036^{3} 4835^{4} 5671^{3} 5979^{4}

Findhornbay *Keith Dalgleish* a47 64
4 b f Ishiguru(USA) Sweet Cando (IRE) (Royal Applause)
59^{6}

Findhorn Magic *Peter Makin* 24
2 b f Kyllachy Enchanted Princess (Royal Applause)
7817^{10}

Findog *Linda Perratt* 74
3 b g Pastoral Pursuits Night Home (ITY) (Night Shift (USA))
2318^{7} 3283^{3} 3462^{5} 3714^{9} 4291^{3} 4613^{2} ◆ 4821^{5} 5878^{7} 6052^{12} 6471^{7}

Fine Altomis *Michael Dods* 74
4 b g Lomitas Mi Anna (GER) (Lake Coniston (IRE))
1568^{6} 2219^{8} 4100^{5} 4826^{8} 5143^{8} 5833^{9}

Fine Art Fair (IRE) *Gary Moore* a72 51
2 b g Kodiac Church Mice (IRE) (Petardia)
3288^{7} 4422^{3} (5000) (5595) ◆ 6104^{3} 7117^{7} 7349^{7}

Fine Kingdom *Brian Ellison* a59 59
4 b g King's Best(USA) Eurolink Sundance (Night Shift (USA))
1763^{10} 2174^{2} 2563^{9} 2887^{8} 3652^{7}

Fine 'n Dandy (IRE) *Tom Dascombe* a73 93
2 ch g Dandy Man(IRE) Pearly Brooks (Efisio)
1778^{2} (2189) 4025^{5}

Finesse *Ralph Beckett* a78 84
4 ch f Shamardal(USA) Clare Hills (IRE) (Orpen (USA))
1398^{3} (2286) 3098^{8} 4219^{4} 5125^{6} (6045) 7021^{13} 7699^{12}

Fine The World *Mrs A Corson*
9 b m Agnes World(USA) Fine Honor (FR) (Highest Honor (FR))
2301a^{P}

Fine Vintage (FR) *Mark Johnston* a71
2 b c Montjeu(IRE) Viking's Cove (USA) (Miswaki (USA))
8026^{3} 8389^{6}

Finflash (IRE) *Mick Channon* a63 80
2 b c Jeremy(USA) Sinegronto (IRE) (Kheleyf (USA))
2250^{2} 2595^{4} 2947^{2} 3424^{19} 5186^{6} (5428) 6328^{13} 7074^{3} 7503^{5}

Finidaprest (IRE) *B Grizzetti* 94
2 bb f Dylan Thomas(IRE) Sunsemperchi (Montjeu (IRE))
7415a^{3}

Finjaan *Doug Watson* a102 102
7 b h Royal Applause Alhufoof (USA) (Dayjur (USA))
241a^{7} 367a^{7} 657a^{9} 744a^{13}

Finlodex *Murty McGrath* a61 63
6 ch g Pastoral Pursuits Ela Aphrodite (Halling (USA))
320^{8} 631^{4} 2072^{3} 2533^{8} 3169^{7} 7321^{9}

Finn Class (IRE) *Michael Bell* a84 84
2 b c Exceed And Excel(AUS) Finnmark (Halling (USA))
2591^{5} 3245^{7} 3815^{4} (4246) (4717) 5400^{2} 5717^{3} (6076) 6303^{5} 6972^{2} (7122)

Finnegans Wake (USA) *Dale Romans* a109 109
4 b c Powerscourt Boat's Ghost (USA) (Silver Ghost (USA))
5553a^{4}

Finn Mac *John Norton* 57
3 ch g Norse Dancer(IRE) Strictly Elsie (IRE) (No Excuse Needed)
2279^{6} 2480^{6} 5016^{14} 5515^{12}

Fiorente (IRE) *Gai Waterhouse* 119
5 br c Monsun(GER) Desert Bloom (IRE) (Pilsudski (IRE))
7556a^{3} (7761a)

Fire (JPN) *Masaru Honda* 99
5 bb c Agnes Tachyon(JPN) Hoshino Kamikochi (USA) (Woodman (USA))
8033a^{16}

Firebeam *Charlie Appleby* a33 112
5 b g Cadeaux Genereux Firebelly (Nicolotte)
154a^{14} 869a^{9} 6129^{2} 6595^{3} 7025^{8} 7530^{5}

Fire Blaze (IRE) *Charlie Appleby* 81
2 gr f Dubawi(IRE) Nahoodh (IRE) (Clodovil (IRE))
(1634) 3459^{11} 4253^{7} 5994^{5}

Firecruise *David Barron* 80
2 b g Firebreak Catmint (Piccolo)
3624^{7} 4053^{9} 6546^{4} (7418) (7609)

Fire Eyes *David Brown* 101
3 b c Exceed And Excel(AUS) Wunders Dream (IRE) (Averti (IRE))
2019^{16}

Fire Fairy (USA) *Charles Hills* a54
3 bb f Henrythenavigator(USA) Fabulous Fairy (USA) (Alydar (USA))
197^{4} 492^{6} 817^{5} 1879^{10}

Fire Fighting (IRE) *Mark Johnston* a90 91
2 b g Soldier Of Fortune(IRE) Savoie (FR) (Anabaa (USA))
2553^{6} 3233^{4} 3689^{2} (4439) 4959^{4} (6207) 6395^{7} 6935^{3}

Firefly *John Weymes* a29 54
4 b g Firebreak Quick Flight (Polar Falcon (USA))
625^{9} 1603^{2} 2072^{6} 2764^{13} 3027^{7} 3081^{7} 3642^{13} 5200^{5} 5856^{4} 6518^{10}

Fire In Babylon (IRE) *Noel Quinlan* a55 52
5 b g Montjeu(IRE) Three Owls (IRE) (Warning)
226^{3} 820^{6} 1520^{11} 5633^{10} 8223^{2}

Fire King *Paul Burgoyne* a70 72
7 b g Falbrav(IRE) Dancing Fire (USA) (Dayjur (USA))
403^{3} 1585^{10} 1901^{6} 2413^{9} 3951^{6} 4411^{9}

Fire Ship *William Knight* a56 110
4 b g Firebreak Mays Dream (Josr Algarhoud (IRE))
1848^{5} 3339^{7} 3913a^{3} (4811) 4946^{5} (5808a) 7047a^{14}

Firestreak *M Al Muhairi* a96 96
8 b g Green Desert(USA) Flash Of Gold (Darshaan)
290a^{10}

Firey Sally (IRE) *Frank Sheridan* a33 6
3 b f Strategic Prince Serious Rock (IRE) (Rock Of Gibraltar (IRE))
310^{9} 482^{8} 591^{4}

Firmdecisions (IRE) *Brett Johnson* a89 79
3 b g Captain Rio Luna Crescente (IRE) (Danehill (USA))
581^{2} 686^{2} 1784^{2} (2016) 2844^{4} ◆ 3782^{5} 4413^{3} 4922^{7} (8345)

First Avenue *Laura Mongan* a85 91
8 b g Montjeu(IRE) Marciala (IRE) (Machiavellian (USA))
224^{9} 739^{4} 2867^{5} 3560^{4} 4407^{4} 4873^{9}

First Cat *S Arthur* a65 54
6 b g One Cool Cat(USA) Zina La Belle (Mark Of Esteem (IRE))
1312a^{5} 1739a^{4} 5327a^{3} 7143a^{6}

First City *A Al Raihe* a99 110
7 b m Diktat City Maiden (USA) (Carson City (USA))
366a^{2} 465a^{14}

First Class *Rae Guest* a70 68
5 b g Oasis Dream Break Point (Reference Point)
1801^{11} 2638^{10} 2964^{2} 3741^{4} 3993^{5} 4752^{3} ◆ (6317) 7263^{3} 7880^{3} 8158^{8}

First Class Favour (IRE) *Tim Easterby* a42 75
5 b f Exceed And Excel(AUS) Lamh Eile (IRE) (Lend A Hand)
3027^{10} 3506^{8} 3983^{8} 4807^{8} (5881) 6301^{3} 6634^{10} 6941^{5} 7489^{7}

First Commandment *Tim Easterby* 44
2 b g Major Cadeaux Golden Nun (Bishop Of Cashel)
4781^{8} 6842^{6} 7341^{9}

First Cornerstone (IRE) *A Oliver* 112
3 ch c Hurricane Run(IRE) Bintalreef (USA) (Diesis)
2677a^{5} ◆ 2907a^{15} 5551a^{8}

First Experience *Rae Guest* a64
2 b f Tamayuz Lolla's Spirit (IRE) (Montjeu (IRE))
6974^{11} (8005) 8382^{4}

First Flight (IRE) *Saeed bin Suroor* 93
2 b c Invincible Spirit(IRE) First Of Many (Darshaan)
(5033) ◆ 5652^{6}

First Glance *Michael Appleby* a46 52
4 br g Passing Glance Lady Santana (IRE) (Doyoun)
4504^{6} 5515^{7} 7981^{12} 8116^{6}

First In Command (IRE) *John Stimpson* a86 86
8 b g Captain Rio Queen Sigi (IRE) (Fairy King (USA))
2227^{5} 2461^{4} 3135^{8} 3796a^{12} 5036^{7} (5901) 6506^{3} 6539^{9} 7112^{12} 7777^{7}

Firstkissoflove *David C Griffiths* a58 67
3 br f Byron Jolies Dee (Diktat)
209^{7} 1330^{4} 1577^{8} 1772^{12}

Firstknight *Doug Watson* a69 55
5 b g Kyllachy Wedding Party (Groom Dancer (USA))
7683a^{4}

First Mohican *Lady Cecil* 113
5 ch g Tobougg(IRE) Mohican Girl (Dancing Brave (USA))
(2365) 5041a^{3} 5807a^{8} 6620^{5} 7206^{5}

First Peninsular *Chris Wall* a11 54
3 ch c Excellent Art Sarah's First (Cadeaux Genereux)
2548^{8} 2872^{7} 5932^{7} 7124^{14} 7454^{2} ◆

First Phase *Mel Brittain* 35
4 b f First Trump Melandre (Lujain (USA))
2280^{12}

First Post (IRE) *Derek Haydn Jones* a85 89
6 b g Celtic Swing Consignia (IRE) (Definite Article)
1583^{6} 1922^{18} 3019^{10} 3416^{4} 3864^{4} 4415^{5} 5759^{3} (6360) 7075^{6} (7224) 7632^{5} 8408^{5}

First Rebellion *Tony Carroll* a59 62
4 ch g Cockney Rebel(IRE) First Dawn (Dr Fong (USA))
128^{2} 339^{6} 471^{8} 551^{3} 754^{8} 997^{7} 1088^{2} (1396) 1734^{3} 2096^{2} 2364^{11}

First Sargeant *Geoffrey Harker* a70 65
3 gr c Dutch Art Princess Raya (Act One)
97^{3} 209^{3} 3418^{5} 3793^{5} (4122) 4995^{9}

First Secretary *Roger Charlton* a54 74
3 b f Nayef(USA) Spinning Queen (Spinning World (USA))
3278^{4} 3860^{6} (4939) 5762^{2} 6405^{6} 7066^{9}

First Serve (IRE) *Karen Tutty* a58 61
3 b f Bachelor Duke(USA) Mauresmo (IRE) (Marju (IRE))
197^{3} 356^{8} 1578^{4} 4144^{12} 4722^{7}

First Warning *Amanda Perrett* a80
3 b g Rail Link Tricked (Beat Hollow)
5100^{12} 6557^{2} (7158)

Fiscal *M Al Jahouri* a77 88
4 b h Cape Cross(IRE) Fibou (USA) (Seeking The Gold (USA))
154a^{12} 745a^{9}

Fisher Lane *Olly Stevens* a33 62
2 b c Captain Gerrard(IRE) Seren Teg (Timeless Times (USA))
5635^{8} 5950^{6} 6460^{5} 7126^{7}

Fishlake Rebel *Ruth Carr* 51
3 b g Cockney Rebel(IRE) Fishlake Flyer (IRE) (Desert Style (IRE))
1648^{11} 1967^{3} 2464^{10} 2742^{8} 3082^{11} 3281^{9} 4008^{12}

Fists And Stones *Simon Hodgson* a15 76
5 b g Distant Music(USA) Keeping The Faith (IRE) (Ajraas (USA))
788^{10} 1070^{11} 1194^{8}

Fit For A King (IRE) *John Best* a47 63
3 b g Royal Applause Sancia (IRE) (Docksider (USA))
4691^{9} 5818^{13} 7086^{13} 7323^{14}

Fitful Skies (IRE) *H-A Pantall* 108
4 b f Dubawi(IRE) Wajd (USA) (Northern Dancer (CAN))
2969a^{2} 6010a^{2} (6887a) 7562a^{2}

Fitrah (IRE) *W McCreery* a63 68
3 b f Tamayuz Almass (IRE) (Elnadim (USA))
7802^{4}

Fityaan *M Al Muhairi* a102 105
5 b g Haafhd Welsh Diva (Selkirk (USA))
(150a)

Fitz *Martin Bosley* a51 65
7 b g Mind Games Timoko (Dancing Spree (USA))
6399^{11} 6933^{14}

Fitz Flyer (IRE) *David Nicholls* a69 95
7 b g Acclamation Starry Night (Sheikh Albadou)
1537^{14} 2150^{5} 2396^{4} 2669^{17} 3776^{4} 4047^{4} ◆ 4263^{9} (4579) 4780^{16} 5056^{6} 6189^{3} 6699^{3} 6920^{2} 7171^{12} 7851^{10}

Fitzwilly *Mick Channon* a39 71
3 b g Sixties Icon Canadian Capers (Ballacashtal (CAN))
1678^{11} 1955^{9} 2192^{10} 2599^{12} 4931^{2} 5432^{3} (5630) 5702^{2} 6389^{3} (7395)

Five Avenue (IRE) *J-C Rouget* 104
3 ch c Tamayuz Luminata (IRE) (Indian Ridge)
5120a^{3}

Five Hearts *Mark H Tompkins* a59 57
5 b f Bertolini(USA) Light Hand (Star Appeal)
132^{4} 433^{3} 530^{5}

Fizzy Pink *Mrs K Burke* a75
3 b f Singspiel(IRE) Lady Hen (Efisio)
706^{2}

Flag Officer *Saeed bin Suroor* a87 96
5 b g Dubai Destination(USA) Dusty Answer (Zafonic (USA))
503a^{7}

Flag Of Glory *Peter Hiatt* a68 70
6 b g Trade Fair Rainbow Sky (Rainbow Quest (USA))
(98) 193^{9} (587) 896^{6} 1107^{4} 2875^{4} 3106^{11} 3889^{6} (4071) 4403^{4} 4853^{7} 5171^{2} 8308^{10}

Flag War (GER) *Saeed bin Suroor* 86
2 ch g Dubawi(IRE) Fantastic Flame (IRE) (Generous (IRE))
5957^{6} 6528^{2}

Flair For Fashion (IRE) *Ed McMahon* a34 41
2 b f Dark Angel(IRE) First Lady (IRE) (Indian Ridge)
3942^{7} 5229^{4}

Flamborough Breeze *Ed Vaughan* a82 74
4 ro f Ad Valorem(USA) Lothian Lass (IRE) (Daylami (IRE))
116^{9} 334^{3} (631) (737) ◆ (813) 840^{2} 1059^{2} 1500^{5} 3899^{5} 4523^{8} 5310^{5} 7307^{3} 7876^{5} 8178^{3}

Flameseeker (USA) *P J Prendergast* 78
3 ch g Heatseeker(IRE) Andtheliviniseasy (USA) (Gone West (USA))
7230a^{19}

Flaming Arrow (IRE) *Kevin Ryan* 54
5 b g Sadler's Wells(USA) Pescia (IRE) (Darshaan)
3364^{7}

Flamingo Beat *Rae Guest* a63 71
3 ch g Beat Hollow Flamingo Flower (USA) (Diesis)
748^{6} 1044^{5} 1450^{2} 1879^{6} (2341) 2769^{2} 3243^{7} 5702^{3} 6325^{2} 7273^{2}

Flamingo Fantasy (GER) *S Smrczek* 106
8 ch h Fantastic Light(USA) Flamingo Road (GER) (Acatenango (GER))
2492a^{8}

Flamingo Star (GER) *R Dzubasz* 98
3 b c Areion(GER) Flamingo Island (GER) (Acatenango (GER))
1867a^{9} 2696a^{2} 4103a^{18} 7053a^{9}

Flash City (ITY) *Bryan Smart* a76 87
5 b g Elusive City(USA) Furnish (Green Desert (USA))
1253^{8} 2880^{2} 3334^{13} 3561^{5} 4047^{2} 4507^{9} 5441^{4} 7314^{10} 7888^{9} 8319^{9}

Flash Crash *Anthony Carson* a78 71
4 b g Val Royal(FR) Tessara (GER) (Big Shuffle (USA))
2383^{11} 2966^{4} 3410^{4} 3997^{6} 4957^{8} 5377^{3} (5803) 6158^{6} 7132^{5} 7446^{5} 8270^{3}

Flash Dance (GER) *A Schennach* a93 100
6 b g Monsun(GER) Flashing Green (Green Desert (USA))
514a^{5} 609a^{5} 702a^{8}

Flashheart (IRE) *Marcus Tregoning* 82
3 b g Nayef(USA) Emerald Peace (IRE) (Green Desert (USA))
(1975) 2660^{5}

Flashlight (IRE) *Mark Johnston* a91 88
3 b c Shamardal(USA) Jazzy Jan (IRE) (Royal Academy (USA))
(796) 1091^{4} (1307) 1444^{2} ◆ 1809^{4} 2024^{5} 2188^{3} 2655^{3} 2844^{8} 4242^{4} 4540^{3} 4897^{6} 5439^{7} (5853)

Flashman *Richard Fahey* a61 88
4 ch g Doyen(IRE) Si Si Si (Lomitas)
1536^{3} 2009^{3} 2402^{9} 2973^{4} 3587^{2} (4782) 5655^{8} 6237^{2} 6585^{11} 7193^{18}

Flashy Approach *John M Oxx* 76
3 ch c New Approach(IRE) Flashy Wings (Zafonic (USA))
3844a^{7}

Flashy Queen (IRE) *Joseph Tuite* a61 67
2 ch f Bahamian Bounty Somersault (Pivotal)
5090^{2} ◆ 5593^{6} 6013^{2} 6778^{6} 7394^{2} (8017)

Flashy Star *Sheena West* 62
4 ch m Mr Greeley(USA) Galileo's Star (IRE) (Galileo (IRE))
4172^{5} 4655^{5}

Flat Out (USA) *William Mott* a122 87
7 b h Flatter(USA) Cresta Lil (USA) (Cresta Rider (USA))
7715a^{8}

Flavio Forte (GER) *U Stoltefuss* a84 90
4 b g Proclamation(IRE) Freixenet (GER) (Big Shuffle (USA))
5804a^{7}

Flavius Victor (IRE) *Patrick Charnings* a72 70
4 b g Holy Roman Emperor(IRE) Teslemi (USA) (Ogygian (USA))
80^{4} 749^{6} 878^{10} (1179) 1780^{10} 2571^{8} 3051^{2} 4517^{8} 5607^{7}

Flawless Beauty *Hugo Palmer* a91 97
3 b f Excellent Art Desert Classic (Green Desert (USA))
1000a^{5} 1383^{8} 2970a^{5} 3460^{19} 4700a^{5} 7316a^{10}

Flax (SAF) *David Hill* 111
7 b g Silvano(GER) Bejewelled Spring (SAF) (Elliodor (FR))
2494a^{13}

Flaxen Lake *Milton Bradley* a57 57
6 b g Sampower Star Cloudy Reef (Cragador)
649^{4} 754^{4} 819^{9} 1088^{8} 1395^{9} 1951^{15} 4660^{4} 5221^{3} 5670^{6} 5818^{6} 6033^{7} 7323^{13}

Fleckerl (IRE) *William Muir* a83
3 b g Danehill Dancer(IRE) Spinola (FR) (Spinning World (USA))
(8313) ◆ (8454)

Fledged *John Gosden* a93 102
3 b c Dansili Innocent Air (Galileo (IRE))
2384^{7} 3059^{2} 3989^{2} (4633) (5374) 5746^{9} 6793^{4}

Fleet Captain *Jane M Foley* a77 67
5 b g Compton Place Mrs Brown (Royal Applause)
8012a^{2}

Fleeting Fashion *Michael Appleby* a50 62
4 b f Alhaarth(IRE) Sempre Sorriso (Fleetwood (IRE))
4455^{4} 4809^{10} 5897^{10}

Fleeting Indian (IRE) *Linda Jewell* a49 31
4 b g Sleeping Indian Glebe Garden (Soviet Star (USA))
333^{9} 491^{6} 2125^{10} 7929^{3}

Fleeting Smile (USA) *Richard Hannon Snr* 98
3 b f Distorted Humor(USA) Fleet Indian (USA) (Indian Charlie (USA))
(2056) ◆ 3460^{13} 4307^{3}

Fleetwoodsands (IRE) *Milton Bradley* a77 62
6 b g Footstepsinthesand Litchfield Hills (USA) (Relaunch (USA))
7^{4} 110^{4} (440) 737^{4} 1021^{3}

Flemish School *Gerard Butler* a84 81
3 ch f Dutch Art Rosewood Belle (USA) (Woodman (USA))
5695^{3} 6136^{3} 6521^{3} 6847^{2} 7488^{2} 7894^{2} (7947)

Fletcher Christian *John Gallagher* a66 72
3 b g Bahamian Bounty Lady Dominatrix (IRE) (Danehill Dancer (IRE))
1582^{5} 2158^{7} 2521^{4} 3050^{5} 3159^{6} 6039^{6} 6560^{9} 6901^{12}

Fleur De Fortune *Eric Wheeler*
6 ch m Best Of The Bests(IRE) Fortuitious (IRE) (Polish Patriot (USA))
1876[12] 2389[13]

Fleur De Guerre (FR) *W Mongil* a68 55
3 ch f Gentlewave(IRE) Fleet Dancer (GER) (Platini (GER))
544a[9]

Fleur De La Vie (IRE) *Ralph Beckett* a89 76
4 ch f Primary(USA) Francophilia (Lomitas)
1302[5] (1733) 2402[10] 3344[10] 3959[7]

Fleur De Nuit (IRE) *John Bleahen* a72 90
8 b m Montjeu(IRE) Green Castle (IRE) (Indian Ridge)
3073a[5]

Fleurtille *Robert Johnson* a33 67
4 b f Tillerman Miss Fleurie (Alzao (USA))
706[8] 5715[5] 6180[4] 6634[11] 6945[5] (7101) (7598)

Flexible Flyer *Hughie Morrison* a86 77
4 b g Exceed And Excel(AUS) Windermere Island (Cadeaux Genereux)
1318[2] ◆ 2097[5] 2618[6] 3215[4] 3714[10] 4772[3]

Flic Flac (IRE) *D K Weld* a92 92
5 ch f Bahamian Bounty Polite Reply (IRE) (Be My Guest (USA))
3845a[21]

Flicksta (USA) *Ronald Harris* a69 70
2 b c Hard Spun(USA) Sindy Jacobson (USA) (More Than Ready (USA))
3914[2] 4175[3] 4937[3] 6320[3] 6778[4] 7317[3] 7393[2] 7978[6]

Flight Officer *Saeed bin Suroor* 79
2 b c New Approach(IRE) Danuta (USA) (Sunday Silence (USA))
7500[2]

Flighty Clarets (IRE) *Richard Fahey* a67 71
3 ch f Bahamian Bounty Flying Clarets (IRE) (Titus Livius (FR))
1307[6] 1608[9] 1935[2] 2703[9] 3396[6] 4114[4] (5333) 5836[3] 6052[9] 6568[7] 7282[6]

Flighty Peaches (IRE) *Rebecca Curtis* 58
2 b f Footstepsinthesand Miss Kittyhawk (IRE) (Hawk Wing (USA))
3605[4] 4191[2]

Flintshire *A Fabre* 121
3 b c Dansili Dance Routine (Sadler's Wells (USA))
(3386a) (4325a) 6446a[4] 7058a[8]

Flippant (IRE) *William Haggas* 79
2 ch f Pivotal Moon Dazzle (USA) (Kingmambo (USA))
3781[5] 4432[4] (6828) 7016[12]

Flipping *Nicky Richards* a61 61
6 br g Kheleyf(USA) Felona (Caerleon (USA))
1270[7] 2037[7] 2636[2] 3203[8] 4109[4] 4824[4] 5239[6] 6919[6] 8038[7]

Flirtinaskirt *Ed McMahon* a76 73
3 b f Avonbridge Talampaya (USA) (Elusive Quality (USA))
1539[3] (2169) 2994[3] 4203[11] 7634[13] 8096[11] 8319[8]

Floating Along (IRE) *William Haggas* a72 88
3 b f Oasis Dream Politesse (USA) (Barathea (IRE))
2006[2] (3109) ◆ 3773[2] (4219) (5125) 6143[3] 6768[6]

Floating Ballerino (IRE) *Olly Stevens* a69 75
2 gr c Aussie Rules(USA) Golden (FR) (Sanglamore (USA))
2653[5] 3238[5] 4631[2] 4926[2] (5347) ◆ 5717[5] 6865[4]

Floralys (USA) *Amy Weaver* a62 62
4 b f Flower Alley(USA) Search Mission (USA) (Red Ransom (USA))
651[4] 807[6] 1019[6] 1472[4] 1503[4] 2236[6] 2773[5] 3326[4] 3788[6] 4144[8]

Flora Medici *Sir Mark Prescott Bt* a56 75
2 b f Sir Percy Florentia (Medicean)
2751[10] 2947[3] 3282[4] (3992) 4277[6] (4618) (5424) 6770[3]

Florentino (JPN) *S Seemar* 89
7 b g Swept Overboard(USA) Must Be Loved (JPN) (Sunday Silence (USA))
242a[10]

Florida Beat *Andrew Balding* a62 40
3 br g Passing Glance Florida Heart (First Trump)
1086[8] 1213[3] 1741[4] 6521[14] 6971[6]

Florimund *Michael Butler* a24 31
10 b g Sadler's Wells(USA) Valentine Girl (Alzao (USA))
597[6]

Flotilla (FR) *M Delzangles* 115
3 b f Mizzen Mast(USA) Louvain (IRE) (Sinndar (IRE))
(2299a) ◆ 3385a[8] 6450a[6]

Flow (USA) *Lady Cecil* 92
3 bb c Medaglia d'Oro(USA) Enthused (USA) (Seeking The Gold (USA))
5436[3] 6596[5] 7211[2]

Flow Chart (IRE) *Peter Grayson* a60 43
6 b g Acclamation Free Flow (Mujahid (USA))
240[11] 349[2] (551) (1043) 1147[3] 1396[3] 1650[3] 2125[7] 2582[8] 4836[6] 5198[9] 5670[8] 6478[8] 6651[5] 6808[6] 6903[7] 7079[7] 7904[9] 8034[6] 8168[4]

Flower Arranger (IRE) *David Evans* a20 27
2 b f Bushranger(IRE) Flower Bowl (IRE) (Noverre (USA))
3753[8] 6279[6] 6983[8]

Fluctuate (USA) *John Gosden* a94 93
4 ch g Exchange Rate(USA) Cut Short (USA) (Diesis)
273[4]

Fluctuation (IRE) *Ian Williams* a72 64
5 b g Street Cry(IRE) Rise And Fall (USA) (Quiet American (USA))
13[12] 540[3] 620[2] (967) 1402[2] 4928[5] 5479[7] 5899[5] (6473) 6970[5] 7303[3] 7350[2]

Fluidity *Nigel Tinkler* a77 97
4 ch g Pastoral Pursuits Pip's Way (IRE) (Pips Pride)
1446[11] 2365[13] 3346[12]

Flumps *John Stimpson* a48
4 ch f Auction House(USA) Demolition Jo (Petong)
105[3]

Flycatcher (IRE) *Richard Fahey* 69
2 ro f Medicean Night Haven (Night Shift (USA))
3978[4] ◆ 4877[8] 5827[2] 6972[7]

Fly Haaf (IRE) *George Baker* a70 49
4 b g Haafhd Rose Indien (FR) (Crystal Glitters (USA))
108[4] 709[2] ◆ (3821) 5479[9] 5586[9]

Flying Applause *Roy Bowring* a65 72
8 b g Royal Applause Mrs Gray (Red Sunset)
83[6] 435[6] 1567[2] 1775[11] 3895[8] 4012[3] 4502[4] 4810[5] 4929[10] 5612[7] 7378[8] 7636[7] 7951[12] 8116[9] 8409[2]

Flying Author (IRE) *Phil McEntee* a45 49
2 b g Authorized(IRE) Fly Free (Halling (USA))
2250[9] 2382[6] 2863[11] 5524[6] 6322[15] 7936[7] 8274[4]

Flying Bear (IRE) *Jeremy Gask* a69 78
2 b c Kodiac Marinebird (IRE) (Bad As I Wanna Be (IRE))
2771[3] 3568[2] 3883[4] (4948) 5656[8] (6187)

Flying Cape (IRE) *Andrew Hollinshead* a67 67
2 b g Cape Cross(IRE) Reine Zao (FR) (Alzao (USA))
5299[7] 5843[6] 6340[4]

Flying Giant (IRE) *Jo Hughes* a58 39
3 ch g Danroad(AUS) Our Emmy Lou (Mark Of Esteem (IRE))
5133[11] 6630[6]

Flying Kitty *John Bridger* a53 37
4 b f One Cool Cat(USA) Flying Millie (IRE) (Flying Spur (AUS))
120[9] 277[6] 664[3] 721[5] 1161[5] 2125[9] 3700[8]

Flying Kyte *Pat Phelan* a40 41
2 bb g Pastoral Pursuits Red Kyte (Hawk Wing (USA))
1512[6] 1880[5] 2723[9] 3414[10] 5634[10] 6035[5]

Flying Officer (USA) *John Gosden* 105
3 b g Dynaformer(USA) Vignette (USA) (Diesis)
(3862) ◆

Flying Phoenix *Dai Burchell* a56 70
5 b f Phoenix Reach(IRE) Rasmalai (Sadler's Wells (USA))
626[10]

Flying Pickets (IRE) *Alan McCabe* a76 56
4 b g Piccolo Burn (Selkirk (USA))
540[2] 603[2] (620) 715[4] 912[5] 987[3] 1203[7] 3906[3] 4146[8] 5195[7] 5899[3]

Flying Power *John Norton* a96 81
5 b g Dubai Destination(USA) Rah Wa (USA) (Rahy (USA))
167[3] (563) 926[2] 2185[8] 2671[12] 3442[6] 4020[7] (4673) 5384[3] 5786[4] 6239[14]

Flying Tempo *Ed Dunlop* a78 66
3 b c Royal Applause Bel Tempo (Petong)
(55) 321[3] 803[2] (1016) (1098) 1604[6] 1959[5] 2564[5]

Flying The Flag (IRE) *A P O'Brien* 112
3 ch c Galileo(IRE) Halfway To Heaven (IRE) (Pivotal)
2298a[9] 2677a[6] 2866[8] (3798a)

Flying Trader (USA) *Jane Chapple-Hyam* a81 81
4 rg g Mizzen Mast(USA) Remediate (USA) (Miswaki (USA))
190[2] 1059[7] 1327[7] 1753[6] 3917[5]

Flyman *Richard Fahey* 97
3 b g Pastoral Pursuits Satin Bell (Midyan (USA))
2008[2] 2655[6] 3563[9] 6308[5] 6840[3] 6993[12] 7495[3]

Flynn's Boy *Rae Guest* a70 83
5 ch g Tobougg(IRE) Bukhoor (IRE) (Danehill (USA))
1963[6] 2425[2] 2964[3]

Fly Solo *Alan Swinbank* a77 82
4 b g Soviet Star(USA) Vino (Efisio)
1463[2] 1831[10] (2462) 2706[5] 7369[5] 7805[3] 8004[10]

Focail Maith *John Ryan* a90 77
5 b g Oratorio(IRE) Glittering Image (IRE) (Sadler's Wells (USA))
52[2] 318[2] 496[10] 882[6] 1464[6] 1728[6] 1884[2] (2136)

Focusofourthoughts (IRE) *Ann Duffield* 81
2 b g Intense Focus(USA) Inourthoughts (IRE) (Desert Style (IRE))
6286[3] (6681) (7062) 7268[2]

Focus On Venice (IRE) *J S Bolger* 84
2 b c Intense Focus(USA) Marina Of Venice (IRE) (Galileo (IRE))
3847a[5]

Focussed (IRE) *Brendan W Duke* 85
2 b g Intense Focus(USA) Tus Maith (IRE) (Entrepreneur)
5773a[5]

Foie Gras *Chris Dwyer* a66 51
3 b g Kyllachy Bint Zamayem (IRE) (Rainbow Quest (USA))
1710[12] 2345[11] 2791[2] 3316[2] 3679[4] 4607[6] 5128[9] 6930[7] 7265[4] 7643[7] 7924[4] (8258) (8338)

Foiled *Richard Hannon Snr* 38
3 b g Dutch Art Isengard (USA) (Cobra King (USA))
5176[6] 5588[12]

Fol Hollow (IRE) *Stuart Coltherd* a70 67
8 b g Monashee Mountain(USA) Constance Do (Risk Me (FR))
679a[8] 3505[4] 3714[6] 4992[7] 5047[8] 5336[10] 6088[6] 6878[8] (6903)

Folk Melody (IRE) *Saeed bin Suroor* 89
2 b f Street Cry(IRE) Folk Opera (IRE) (Singspiel (IRE))
(4491)

Followeveryrainbow *Richard Hannon Snr* a58 69
3 b f Oasis Dream Absolute Precision (USA) (Irish River (FR))
1518[4] 2071[3] 3039[8]

Follow The Flag (IRE) *Alan McCabe* a85 62
9 ch g Traditionally(USA) Iktidar (Green Desert (USA))
82[2] 314[5] 329[6] 528[5] 718[2] 798[6] 987[4] 1076[4] 1239[7] 1568[9] 2168[4] 2511[7] 2785[9] 2966[7] 4071[12] 7758[5] 7951[13] 8142[12]

Fonseca (IRE) *Andrew Balding* a47 20
3 bb f Red Clubs(IRE) Guajira (FR) (Mtoto)
2658[10] 2979[7] 3435[8]

Fontaine Margot (FR) *M Cesandri* 101
4 b f Ballingarry(IRE) Marie Jbeil (FR) (Double Bed (FR))
7408a[7]

Fonterutoli (IRE) *Roger Ingram* a65 61
6 gr g Verglas(IRE) Goldendale (IRE) (Ali-Royal (IRE))
158[5] (510) 805[6] 1303[5] 1498[3] 1716[5] 1779[3] 1987[4] 2534[3] 2787[2] 7458[8] 7622[8] 7981[2] (8449)

Foolbythepool *Keith Dalgleish* 64
3 b c Refuse To Bend(IRE) Rapsgate (IRE) (Mozart (IRE))
4339[8] 5240[8]

Footclass (IRE) *X Nakkachdji* a79
2 b c Footstepsinthesand Prime Classique (USA) (Elusive Quality (USA))
8143a[4]

Foot Patrol (USA) *Walter Bindner Jr* a31
3 bb g Badge Of Silver(USA) Foot Pick (USA) (Benny The Dip (USA))
786a[7]

Foot Perfect (IRE) *M Halford* a82 78
5 b f Footstepsinthesand Lupine (IRE) (Lake Coniston (IRE))
5775a[16]

Footsieonehundred (IRE) *Patrick Gilligan* a43
2 b f Footstepsinthesand Zapping (IRE) (Lycius (USA))
8328[11]

Footstepsintherain (IRE) *David Lanigan* a89 83
3 b g Footstepsinthesand Champagne Toni (IRE) (Second Empire (IRE))
3062[2] 3951[2] ◆ 4183[2] (6203) 6988[7] 7464[4]

Foot Tapper *Chris Wall* a67 70
4 b c Invincible Spirit(IRE) Jazz Princess (IRE) (Bahhare (USA))
354[3]

For Ayman *Seamus Durack* a65
2 b c Bertolini(USA) Saharan Song (IRE) (Singspiel (IRE))
7638[6]

Force Aliee (FR) *P Harley* 74
2 ch c Muhtathir Forces Sweetheart (Allied Forces (USA))
7726a[5]

Forced Family Fun *Michael Bell* a62 76
3 b g Refuse To Bend(IRE) Juniper Girl (IRE) (Revoque (IRE))
1614[7] 1923[8] 2602[6] 3394[5] (7151) 7338[6]

Forceful Appeal (USA) *Simon Dow* a92 86
5 bb g Successful Appeal(USA) Kinetic Force (USA) (Holy Bull (USA))
1061[6] 1500[6] (1878) 2618[5] 3060[3] 4281[4] 4677[2] 5190[6]

Forceful Flame *Robert Eddery* a66 69
3 ch g Assertive Noor El Houdah (IRE) (Fayruz)
628[6] 1427[U] 2324[12] 2791[6] 2962[14] 4666[6]

Foreign Princess (GER) *H J Groschel* 82
4 bb f Desert Prince(IRE) Foreign Affair (GER) (Goofalik (USA))
7233a[7]

Foreign Rhythm (IRE) *Ron Barr* a69 69
8 ch m Distant Music(USA) Happy Talk (IRE) (Hamas (IRE))
(1278) 1540[7] 2166[3] 3197[4] (4102) 4560[6] 5047[4] 5422[5] 6287[9] 6603[3] 7029[7] 7599[6]

Foreign Tune *C Laffon-Parias* a92 107
4 b f Invincible Spirit(IRE) Gwenseb (FR) (Green Tune (USA))
1456a[7] 1945a[9] 2897a[9] 3387a[4] 3913a[4] 5360a[3]

Forest Edge (IRE) *David Evans* a108 99
4 b g Amadeus Wolf Compass Light (USA) (Lear Fan (USA))
78[7] 405[8] 480[4] 586[3] 723[4] 880[5] 1160[11] 1385[7] (1652) (2150) 2214[7] 2461[6] 2647[4] 2868[11] (3038) 3249[5] 6699[13] 7527[14] (7642) (7803) (8155) 8334[6] 8395[4]

Forest Glen (IRE) *Sylvester Kirk* a33 55
2 b f Camacho Lisfannon (Bahamian Bounty)
5929[8] 6423[6] 6690[13]

Forest Philly (IRE) *John Wainwright*
3 b f Moss Vale(IRE) Red Beach (IRE) (Turtle Island (IRE))
2504[8] 2765[10]

Forest Row *Clive Cox* 89
4 b g Cockney Rebel(IRE) Forest Fire (SWE) (Never So Bold)
1922[14] 2813[8]

Foreteller *Chris Waller* 115
6 b g Dansili Prophecy (IRE) (Warning)
7556a[4] 7761a[17]

Forever Cinderella *Jimmy Fox* a74
2 b f High Chaparral(IRE) Tentpole (USA) (Rainbow Quest (USA))
(8083)

Forever Janey *Paul Green* a39 35
4 b f Indesatchel(IRE) Nee Lemon Left (Puissance)
105[7] 968[9] 1043[8] 2326[9] 4160[8] 5072[12] 5354[8] 6343[12]

Forever Now *John Gosden* a63
2 b c Galileo(IRE) All's Forgotten (USA) (Darshaan)
7834[8] ◆

Forever Snow (USA) *Fabricio Borges* a105 81
4 rg f Lion Heart(USA) Bullagio (USA) (Holy Bull (USA))
366a[7]

Forget Me Not Lane (IRE) *Kevin Ryan* a67 82
4 b g Holy Roman Emperor(IRE) Mrs Arkada (FR) (Akarad (FR))
2706[4] 3349[14] 4020[5] 5612[4] 6563[6] 7765[8]

Forgettable (JPN) *Yasutoshi Ikee* 112
7 bb h Dance In The Dark(JPN) Air Groove (JPN) (Tony Bin)
1868a[10]

Forging The Path (USA) *Richard Fahey* a66 81
3 b c Henrythenavigator(USA) Atitudeofgratitude (IRE) (Deputy Minister (CAN))
(2279) 2862[10] 3544[2]

Forgive *Richard Hannon Snr* a101 103
4 b f Pivotal Amira (Efisio)
3339[14] 3835[2] 4137[9] 4525[3] 4878[3] (5246) 6188[2] 6838[30] (7649)

Forgiving Light *John Berry* 68
4 b g Echo Of Light Redeem (IRE) (Doyoun)
7636[9]

Forgotten Hero (IRE) *Charles Hills* a91 97
4 bb g High Chaparral(IRE) Sundown (Polish Precedent (USA))
1848[4] 2424[3] 3094[2] 3832[9] 4310[13] 4798[4] 5768[6] (6394) 7823[19]

Forgotten Voice (IRE) *Nicky Henderson* a116 114
8 b g Danehill Dancer(IRE) Asnieres (USA) (Spend A Buck (USA))
(3525) (4944) 7483a[5] 7827a[4]

For Life (IRE) *John E Long* a66 79
11 b g Bachir(IRE) Zest (USA) (Zilzal (USA))
3738[9]

Formidable Guest *Jamie Poulton* a64 60
9 b m Dilshaan Fizzy Treat (Efisio)
15[4] 161[4] 343[6] 469[10]

For Posterity *Charlie Appleby* a80 76
3 b c Shamardal(USA) Past The Post (USA) (Danzig (USA))
4495[3] 4968[7] 5720[4] (6106) 6925[7]

Forrest Flyer (IRE) *Jim Goldie* a37 70
9 b g Daylami(IRE) Gerante (USA) (Private Account (USA))
1251[4] (2975) 4110[3] 4578[3] 5267[4] 6087[7] 6552[9] 6917[3] 7342[8] 7668[9]

For Shia And Lula (IRE) *Daniel Mark Loughnane* a74 66
4 b g Majestic Missile(IRE) Jack-N-Jilly (IRE) (Anita's Prince)
426[5] 452[4] 519[2] 749[4] 1015[7] (2073) 3030[7] 3513[8] 3885[2] 4193[2] 4521[3] (5166)

Forster Street (IRE) *Tim Easterby* a60 67
4 b g Acclamation Easy To Thrill (Soviet Star (USA))
709[12] 921[5]

Fort Bastion (IRE) *Richard Fahey* 109
4 b g Lawman(FR) French Fern (IRE) (Royal Applause)
2399[10] 5763[U] 6595[7] 7018[7] 7206[8]

Fort Belvedere *Keith Dalgleish* 94
5 ch g King's Best(USA) Sweet Folly (IRE) (Singspiel (IRE))
1843[7] 2339[2] 2976[3] 3346[14] 3725[7] 4825[3] 5335[2] 5706[9] 6551[9]

Forte Dei Marmi *Roger L Attfield* a64 114
7 b g Selkirk(USA) Frangy (Sadler's Wells (USA))
7563a[7]

Fortieth And Fifth (IRE) *Michael Bell* a89 87
4 b g Lemon Drop Kid(USA) Maugusta (USA) (Saint Ballado (CAN))
(1327)

Fortify (IRE) *A P O'Brien* 113
3 b c Danehill Dancer(IRE) Shaanara (IRE) (Darshaan)
3869a[2] 4465a[2] 4869a[6] 5317a[3]

Fortify (USA) *Mahmood Al Zarooni* a73 89
3 b c Distorted Humor(USA) Kotuku (A.P. Indy (USA))
658a[6]

Fortinbrass (IRE) *David O'Meara* a85 89
3 b g Baltic King Greta D'Argent (IRE) (Great Commotion (USA))
85[5] 982[2] 1112[5] 1477[9] 3320[2] 4478[4] (4905) 5303[6] 5851[7] 6382[10] 7507[3] (7792) 7949[5] (8365)

Fort Knox *J P Murtagh* a42 107
3 b c Dubawi(IRE) Savannah Belle (Green Desert (USA))
(1555a) 2677a[9] 6440a[6] 7051a[3]

Fort Larned (USA) *Ian Wilkes* a128 85
5 b c E Dubai(USA) Arlucea (USA) (Broad Brush (USA))
7715a[4]

Fortrose Academy (IRE) *Andrew Balding* a74 67
4 b g Iceman Auspicious (Shirley Heights)
11[3] 535[3] 812[6] 3841[6] 4494[9] 7427[3] 7958[7] 8128[10] 8330[9]

Fortunate Bid (IRE) *Linda Stubbs* a67 65
7 ch g Modigliani(USA) Mystery Bid (Auction Ring (USA))
24[4]

Fortune Hunter (FR) *F Rohaut* a81 98
4 b f High Chaparral(IRE) King's Folly (FR) (King's Best (USA))
3851a[8] 5804a[9]

Forty Winks *H-A Pantall* a65
3 b f Kheleyf(USA) Dilly Dally (AUS) (Rubiton (AUS))
3129a[9]

Forward March *Gary Harrison* a70 79
3 b g Beat Hollow Cantanta (Top Ville)
2938[2] 3539[3] 4384[6]

Forzarzi (IRE) *H A McWilliams* a59 44
9 b g Forzando Zarzi (IRE) (Suave Dancer (USA))
24[7]

Fossa *Dean Ivory* a79 69
3 b g Dubai Destination(USA) Gayanula (USA) (Yonaguska (USA))
1319[7] (1906) (2512) 3499[2] (3903) 4636[3] 5349[3] 6214[3] (6476) 6998[7]

Fossgate *James Bethell* a60 79
12 ch g Halling(USA) Peryllys (Warning)
2552[10] 3480[7] 3652[4] 4543[7]

Fossola (USA) *Charlie Appleby* a83 56
3 b f Elusive Quality(USA) Porto Roca (AUS) (Barathea (IRE))
4500[6] 5478[9] 6611[2] (7114)

Foster's Road *Mick Channon* a82 77
4 b g Imperial Dancer Search Party (Rainbow Quest (USA))
(1018) (1218) 1805[9] 2052[9] 2990[7] 3790[2] 4166[11] 4406[3]

Foundry (IRE) *A P O'Brien* 113
3 b c Galileo(IRE) Sharp Lisa (USA) (Dixieland Band (USA))
5653[2] 6393[5]

Fountain Girl *Edward Bevan*
4 b f Green Card(USA) Ballydoyle Counsel (IRE) (Leading Counsel (USA))
108[6]

Fountain Of Youth (IRE) *A P O'Brien* 98
2 b c Oasis Dream Attraction (Efisio)
3424[4]

Four Leaves (IRE) *Marco Botti* a87 80
4 ch f Singspiel(IRE) My Heart's Deelite (USA) (Afternoon Deelites (USA))
1544[11] 1825[3] 2750[2] 3158[6] 3742[4]

Four Maries (FR) *Mrs K Burke* 3
2 b f Whipper(USA) Maryqueenofscots (IRE) (Fantastic Light (USA))
5243[8]

Four Nations (USA) *George Baker* a77 81
5 ch g Langfuhr(CAN) Kiswahili (Selkirk (USA))
6787[2] 7217[4] 7863[2]

Four Winds *Tom Dascombe* a83 88
7 b g Red Ransom(USA) Fairy Godmother (Fairy King (USA))
3507[4] 4005[4] 4153[2] 4638[4] 5153[4] (6105) (7303) 7699[6] (7824) (8068)

Foxford *Patrick Chamings* a59
2 b f Clodovil(IRE) Pulau Pinang (IRE) (Dolphin Street (FR))
7780[5]

Foxhaven *Patrick Chamings* a79 78
11 ch g Unfuwain(USA) Dancing Mirage (IRE) (Machiavellian (USA))
475[7] 866[5] (1715) (2569) 3579[3] 7539[4]

Foxie Girl *John Best* a34
2 b f Virtual Santiburi Girl (Casteddu)
7301[10] 7780[8]

Foxtrot India (IRE) *Jeremy Gask* a59 66
4 b g Tagula(IRE) Mayfair (Green Desert (USA))
232[6] 448[6] 546[9]

Foxtrot Jubilee (IRE) *Ralph Beckett* a90 79
3 b g Captain Marvelous(IRE) Cool Cousin (IRE) (Distant Relative)
(337) 1806[6] 2158[2] 3104[10] 4033[5] 6854[11] 7633[4] 8088[2] 8430[6]

Foxtrot Pearl (IRE) *Olly Stevens* 56
2 b f Bahamian Bounty Nina Blini (Bertolini (USA))
6947[6] ◆ 7393[7]

Foxtrot Romeo (IRE) *J P Murtagh* 113
4 b c Danehill Dancer(IRE) Hawala (IRE) (Warning)
1413a[8] 3142a[9]

Foxy Clarets (IRE) *Richard Fahey* 87
2 ch g Camacho Muscari (Indian Ridge)
3724[3] ◆ 4528[9] (5140) 5679[8] 5955[3] 6328[9] 6582[6] 7026[19]

Foxy Dancer (IRE) *Richard Hannon Snr* a40 43
3 b f Jeremy(USA) Date Mate (USA) (Thorn Dance (USA))
1055[6] 1314[5]

Foxy Forever (IRE) *Michael Wigham* a76 93
3 b g Kodiac Northern Tara (IRE) (Fayruz)
(4734) ◆

Foxy Music *Eric Alston* a58 97
9 b g Foxhound(USA) Primum Tempus (Primo Dominie)
2150[13] 2614[9] 4018[6] 4992[8] 6547[6] 7029[4] (7634)

Frac Daddy (USA) *Kenneth McPeek* a102 102
3 rg c Scat Daddy(USA) Skipper's Mate (USA) (Skip Away (USA))
2033a[16] 3127a[14]

Fracking (IRE) *Olly Stevens* a79 87
2 ch g Intikhab(USA) Carson Dancer (USA) (Carson City (USA))
5924[4] 6184[5] (6739)

Fractal *David Simcock* a76
2 b c High Chaparral(IRE) Clincher Club (Polish Patriot (USA))
7835[9] 8340[10]

Fragonard *Lady Cecil* a72 85
4 ch f Teofilo(IRE) Delicieuse Lady (Trempolino (USA))
3469[5] 4633[8] 6236[2] 7738[4]

Framed Masterpiece *Paul Fitzsimons* a71 64
2 ch g Dutch Art Photographie (USA) (Trempolino (USA))
7335[5] 7655[5] (7955)

Frameit (IRE) *R Ducasteele* a65 48
6 b g Antonius Pius(USA) Delisha (Salse (USA))
3647a[8]

Francisca *James Given* 34
2 b f Byron Requiem (USA) (Royal Anthem (USA))
3064[6] 3760[P]

Franciscan *Luca Cumani* a56 95
5 b g Medicean Frangy (Sadler's Wells (USA))
1536[10] 2671[9] 3685[2] 4060[5]

Francis Of Assisi (IRE) *A P O'Brien* 109
3 b g Danehill Dancer(IRE) Queen Cleopatra (IRE) (Kingmambo (USA))
6025a[18] (7719a)

Francistown (IRE) *Charlie Appleby* a40
2 b c Cape Cross(IRE) Dove (IRE) (Sadler's Wells (USA))
7113[4]

Franco Is My Name *Peter Hedger* a91 82
7 b g Namid Veronica Franco (Darshaan)
7765[9] 7990[8]

Frangipanni (IRE) *Roger Charlton* a62
2 bb f Dansili Frizzante (Efisio)
7294[5] ◆ 7852[4] 8061[8]

Frankenstein *B Grizzetti* 108
6 b g Dubawi(IRE) Lifting (IRE) (Nordance (USA))
2489a[9] 3147a[5] 6679a[5]

Franklino (FR) *Chris Gordon* a42
6 ch g Gold Away(IRE) Amour Fatal (IRE) (Rainbows For Life (CAN))
2875[11]

Frank's Folly (IRE) *Tim Walford* 70
4 b g Tiger Hill(IRE) Pocket Book (IRE) (Reference Point)
4805[4] 4927[5] 7278[7]

Frankthetank (IRE) *Keith Dalgleish* a49
2 ch c Captain Gerrard(IRE) Mi Amor (IRE) (Alzao (USA))
7664[6] 7790[8] 8165[7]

Frankyfourfingers (FR) *C Delcher-Sanchez* 102
3 bb c Sunday Break(JPN) Texaloula (FR) (Kendor (FR))
5361a[12]

Frans Hals *Dominic Ffrench Davis* a52 61
3 b g Dutch Art Glory Oatway (IRE) (Desert Prince (IRE))
310[3] 442[4] 732[5]

Fraserburgh (IRE) *Mark Johnston* a74 77
3 b g Shamardal(USA) Nova Cyngi (USA) (Kris S (USA))
904[2] (990) 1250[9] 1645[9] 1912[3] 2309[5] 2776[7] 3434[10] 4119[6] 4515[4] (4806) 5355[5] 5815[7] 6297[5] 6730[2] 6951[8]

Frasers Hill *Roger Varian* a91 48
4 ch g Selkirk(USA) Shemriyna (IRE) (King Of Kings (IRE))
1423[2] ◆ 2041[6]

Fratellino *Alan McCabe* a103 83
6 ch h Auction House(USA) Vida (IRE) (Wolfhound (USA))
78[5] 319[4] 584[5] 776[3] 1032[4] 4217[9] 4507[10] 5009[8] 5247[8] 5998[8] 6647[7] 7928[8] 8064[8] 8231[9]

Fray *Roger Charlton* 72
2 b f Champs Elysees Short Dance (USA) (Hennessy (USA))
6643[7] (7466)

Fraygrance (IRE) *Paul Cole* a43
2 b f Azamour(IRE) Reside (IRE) (Montjeu (IRE))
5131[12]

Fred Archer (IRE) *Sue Smith* a89 2
5 b g Iffraaj Fairy Contessa (IRE) (Fairy King (USA))
2278[15] 3192[12] 6562[10]

Freddie Bolt *Frederick Watson* 43
7 b g Diktat Birjand (Green Desert (USA))
2885[9] 3201[5] 3947[11]

Freddie Kilroy *Ed Dunlop* a41 47
2 b c Pastoral Pursuits Pretty Davis (USA) (Trempolino (USA))
3536[8] 4716[5] 5105[6] 5893[9] 6322[12] 6897[7]

Freddy Q (IRE) *Roger Teal* a70 89
4 ch g Iffraaj Barnabas (ITY) (Slip Anchor)
3692[9] 4907[4] 6004[8] 6336[4] 6869[5] 7217[6]

Freddy With A Y (IRE) *Gary Moore* a76 93
3 b g Amadeus Wolf Mataji (IRE) (Desert Prince (IRE))
1582[7] (2394) 3279[2] ◆ 4210[2] 5303[7] 6692[9] 7507[7]

Frederic Chopin *Stuart Williams* a55 50
2 ch g Tamayuz Eliza Gilbert (Noverre (USA))
4764[8] 5490[6] 6277[11] 7855[4]

Frederick Alfred *Mark H Tompkins* a54 38
3 ch c Halling(USA) Trew Class (Inchinor)
663[5] 3403[3] 4931[9] 6257[7]

Frederick Engels *J Moore* a101 116
4 b g Iceman Colonel's Daughter (Colonel Collins (USA))
1266a[8] 8209a[3]

Frederick William *Stal Klaverhof* a73 48
5 b g Tobougg(IRE) Bisaat (USA) (Bahri (USA))
3647a[4]

Fred Lalloupet *D Smaga* 107
6 b h Elusive City(USA) Firm Friend (IRE) (Affirmed (USA))
5806a[7]

Fredricka *Garry Moss* 63
2 ch f Assertive Vintage Steps (IRE) (Bahamian Bounty)
2625[7] 2767[8] 4073[3] 4431[3] 4847[5] 5480[2] 5857[2] 6718[2] 7095[4]

Fred Willetts (IRE) *David Evans* a78 90
5 b g Noverre(USA) Intaglia (GER) (Lomitas)
86[8] 104[6] 1800[6] 1947[2] 2225[9] 2929[5] 4153[4]

Free Art *Geoffrey Harker* a83 73
5 b g Iffraaj Possessive Artiste (Shareef Dancer (USA))
1936[5]

Free Code (IRE) *James Tate* 90
2 b g Kodiac Gerobies Girl (USA) (Deposit Ticket (USA))
4199[2] (4724) (5226) 6021a[6] 6304[5]

Freedom Child (USA) *Thomas Albertrani* a114
3 ch r Malibu Moon(USA) Bandstand (USA) (Deputy Minister (CAN))
3127a[13]

Freedom's Light *John Gosden* a81
3 b f Galileo(IRE) Aricia (IRE) (Nashwan (USA))
6738[5] ◆ 7738[2] (7894)

Freedom Square (IRE) *J S Bolger* 83
2 b c Lawman(FR) Manger Square (IRE) (Danehill (USA))
3555[16] 5774a[5]

Free Eagle (IRE) *D K Weld* 100
2 b c High Chaparral(IRE) Polished Gem (IRE) (Danehill (USA))
6223a[2]

Free Island *James Tate* a67 66
3 b f Kheleyf(USA) Island Race (Common Grounds)
923[3] 1202[3] 1762[4] 1935[8] 2962[3]

Freemason *Sir Michael Stoute* 67
2 b c Cape Cross(IRE) Candy Mountain (Selkirk (USA))
6277[4]

Freeport *Brian Meehan* 83
3 b g Bahamian Bounty Perdicula (IRE) (Persian Heights)
(2727) 3369[2] 3995[4] 4508[5] 6379[4] 6951[5] 7275[4]

Free Port Lux *F Head* 80
2 b c Oasis Dream Royal Highness (GER) (Monsun (GER))
7828a[9]

Free Spin (IRE) *David Barron* a95 91
4 ch g Iffraaj Romea (Muhtarram (USA))
443[2] ◆ 723[2] 1160[5] 1542[10] 2834[2] 3096[7] 3811[9] 5705[2] (6609) 7540[6]

Freestyler (FR) *C Boutin* a74 85
3 b g Meshaheer(USA) Metaline (FR) (Dr Fong (USA))
647a[9]

Freetown (USA) *S Botti* 97
3 bb c Speightstown(USA) Fresnay (Rainbow Quest (USA))
1865a[13] 2491a[11]

Freewheel (IRE) *David Nicholls* a88 88
3 br c Galileo(IRE) La Chunga (USA) (More Than Ready (USA))
8156[5] 8385[7]

Free Wheeling (AUS) *Saeed bin Suroor* a108 107
5 b g Ad Valorem(USA) Miss Carefree (AUS) (Last Tycoon)
465a[3] 869a[2] 6595[4] 7013[5] 7530[4]

Free Winner (IRE) *M Tellini* 86
5 b c Oratorio(IRE) Freedom (GER) (Second Empire (IRE))
6889a[8]

Freezemaster (AUS) *S Burridge* a60 68
6 b g Reset(AUS) Her Grace (USA) (Northern Flagship (USA))
154a[15] 557a[13]

Free Zone *Bryan Smart* 109
4 b g Kyllachy Aldora (Magic Ring (IRE))
2019[10] 3046[6] 3822[7] 4986[18] 5375[7] (6539) 7010[4] 7527[17] 7821[16]

Fremont (IRE) *Hugo Palmer* a82 69
6 b g Marju(IRE) Snow Peak (Arazi (USA))
6802[2]

French Accent *John Best* a32
2 ch f Elnadim(USA) Saralea (FR) (Sillery (USA))
8328[12]

French Fifteen (FR) *N Clement* a111 120
4 ch c Turtle Bowl(IRE) Spring Morning (FR) (Ashkalani (IRE))
1267a[9]

French Navy *Charlie Appleby* 114
5 b c Shamardal(USA) First Fleet (USA) (Woodman (USA))
(3839) 6592[2] 7196[4] 7698[2]

French Press (IRE) *John Stimpson* a65 74
3 ch g Kheleyf(USA) Coffee Cream (Common Grounds)
(7079) 7347[4] 7729[6] 7885[12]

French Revolution *Jedd O'Keeffe* 49
3 gr g Paris House Hula Ballew (Weldnaas (USA))
1393[7] 2341[5] 2716[12]

Frequency *Keith Dalgleish* a86 84
6 br g Starcraft(NZ) Soundwave (Prince Sabo)
206[5] 217[12] 454[4] 611[5] 916[6]

Fresa *Sir Mark Prescott Bt* a76 79
4 b f Selkirk(USA) Flor Y Nata (USA) (Fusaichi Pegasus (USA))
6936[5] (7546) 7961[4] 8136[3] 8400[4]

Fridaynight Girl (IRE) *Alan Swinbank*
4 b f Red Ransom(USA) Miss Amanpuri (Alzao (USA))
2833[9]

Friendship (IRE) *A P O'Brien* 101
2 ch c Galileo(IRE) Squeak (Selkirk (USA))
3555[9] 5774a[4] 6442a[4] 7192[6]

Friendship Is Love *David Elsworth* a52 66
3 ch f Byron Silver Sail (Daylami (IRE))
(876) 4976[2] ◆ 5422[3] 5930[6]

Frine (IRE) *J-M Osorio* 108
3 b f High Chaparral(IRE) Castalia (Cardoun (FR))
7189a[4] (7843a)

Frog Hollow *David O'Meara* a93 96
4 gr g Intikhab(USA) The Manx Touch (IRE) (Petardia)
947[6] ◆ 1233[14] 1385[9] 1726[5] ◆ 1922[16] 3096[6] ◆ 3193[2] 4055[3] (4733) ◆ 5238[2] 5681[4]

Frognal (IRE) *Violet M Jordan* a79 78
7 b g Kheleyf(USA) Shannon Dore (IRE) (Turtle Island (IRE))
76[3] (399) (493) 582[8] 775[2] 1316[5] 1838[8] 1985[5] 3220[6] 3841[7] 5278[4] 6039[6] 6310[6] 6652[6] 7165[9] 7444[10] 7801[11]

Fromthestables Com (IRE) *Brendan Powell* a56 65
4 b g Strategic Prince Kathy Tolfa (IRE) (Sri Pekan (USA))
9[7] 131[4] 704[10]

Frontier Fighter *David O'Meara* a103 97
5 b g Invincible Spirit(IRE) Rawabi (Sadler's Wells (USA))
(108) 518[3] 603[3] (987) (1038) 1148[4] (1723) 1990[2] 2477[3] 2958[5] 6840[7] 7241[6] 7820[9] 7992[2] 8231[2] 8369[7]

Front Page News *Robert Eddery* 77
3 ch f Assertive Branston Berry (IRE) (Mukaddamah (USA))
2521[9] 3058[5] 3699[2] (3988) 5004[5] 5437[4] 5721[2] 6642[3] 7452[11] 7699[9]

Frosted Off *John Spearing* a53 58
3 gr g Verglas(IRE) Dispol Veleta (Makbul)
3621[5] 4916[6] 5499[9] 6154[9] 7354[7] 7753[4] 8293[10]

Frost Fire (USA) *Mark Johnston* a77 39
3 b f Medaglia d'Oro(USA) Alta Love (USA) (Gone West (USA))
7067[6] 7983[3] 8054[2] 8185[2] (8316) 8408[6]

Frost In May (IRE) *David O'Meara* 30
2 gr f Verglas(IRE) Venus Rising (Observatory (USA))
2793[8] 3588[7] 4065[5] 4617[4]

Frosty Berry *John Wainwright* a70 73
4 gr f Proclamation(IRE) Star Entry (In The Wings)
430[8] 1111[7] 2313[5] 2630[6] 4951[4] 5337[2] 5840[8] 7220[3]

Frosty Friday *J R Jenkins* a59 51
5 b f Storming Home Seasonal Blossom (IRE) (Fairy King (USA))
33[3] 342[5] 619[3] 1183[7] 2764[8] 3169[5] 3792[4] 4715[8] (7753) 8233[2]

Frosty Secret *Jane Chapple-Hyam* a58 66
4 b f Echo Of Light Raze (Halling (USA))
1987[8] 2764[10] 3151[3] (3792) 5216[7] 6137[11] 6457[5] 7090[7]

Frosty The Snowman (IRE) *Charles Hills* 45
2 gr g Mastercraftsman(IRE) Sleeveless (USA) (Fusaichi Pegasus (USA))
6184[11] 6528[7] 6954[12]

Frozen Over *Stuart Kittow* a75 81
5 b g Iceman Pearly River (Elegant Air)
1514[5] ◆ 1950[3] (2383) 3022[6] 3976[2] 4908[4] 5793[2] 6562[4]

Fruit Pastille *Hughie Morrison* a44
2 b f Pastoral Pursuits Classic Millennium (Midyan (USA))
8061[10] 8326[9]

Fudgeit (FR) *N Clement* 45
2 ch c Tertullian(USA) Hot Fudge (SWE) (Lomitas)
6786a[9]

Fuel Injection *Paul Midgley* 61
2 ch g Pastoral Pursuits Smart Hostess (Most Welcome)
1108[9] 1573[7] 4370[7] 4886[7] (5106) 5787[4] 6467[8]

Fugitive Motel (IRE) *Eric Wheeler* a71 66
4 b g Holy Roman Emperor(IRE) Zing Ping (IRE) (Thatching)
984[12] 1096[8]

Fujin Dancer (FR) *Brian Ellison* a86
8 ch g Storming Home Badaayer (USA) (Silver Hawk (USA))
(8308)

Fulbright *Charlie Appleby* a113 115
4 b h Exceed And Excel(AUS) Lindfield Belle (IRE) (Fairy King (USA))
153a[3] 659a[2] 872a[3] 1267a[13] 4433[3] 5446[5] 7775[5]

Fulgetta (ITY) *Gianluca Bietolini* 72
3 ch f Masterful(USA) Lodgetta (IRE) (Grand Lodge (USA))
1866a[12] 2697a[10]

Fulgora *Brendan Powell* a74 57
5 b f Desert King(IRE) Lightning Princess (Puissance)
637[2] 841[3] (1069) 1733[11] 2360[6] 2980[2] 3328[8] 4166[12]

Full Day *Ralph Beckett* a69 72
2 ch f Champs Elysees Capistrano Day (USA) (Diesis)
4026[3] ◆ 4702[12] 5394[6] ◆ 6852[5] 7310[3]

Full Pelt (USA) *Peggy Bastiaens-Vancauwenbergh* a63 67
5 bb g Orientate(USA) Class (USA) (Thunder Gulch (USA))
5735a[10]

Full Speed (GER) *Philip Kirby* a69 71
8 b g Sholokhov(IRE) Flagny (FR) (Kaldoun (FR))
(165) (1251) ◆ 2860[10] 3301[13] 3627[7] 4150[11] 7923[2] 8129[4]

Full Swing *Roger Varian* a74
4 br g Manduro(GER) Glorosia (FR) (Bering)
397[2] 612[2] 752[P]

Full Toss *Jim Goldie* a80 85
7 b g Nayef(USA) Spinning Top (Alzao (USA))
4098[9] (4888) 5335[5] 5860[8]

Fully Funded (USA) *Noel Meade* a81 63
8 b g Aptitude(USA) Fully Invested (USA) (Irish River (FR))
3073a[6]

Fulney *James Eustace* a78 85
4 b f Dr Fong(USA) Postage Stampe (Singspiel (IRE))
2253[10] 3158[4] 3742[2] 4642[8] 5125[8] 5896[7] 7307[5]

Funding Deficit (IRE) *David Barron* a52 71
3 ch g Rakti Bukat Timah (Inchinor)
3066[8] 3479[2] (4050) 4402[3] 6874[6] 7603[8] 8029[6]

Funinthesand (IRE) *Wido Neuroth* a90 87
4 b g Footstepsinthesand Funny Legend (NOR) (Funambule (USA))
2146a[6]

Funk Soul Brother *Charles Hills* 87
3 b g Cockney Rebel(IRE) Sweet Afton (IRE) (Mujadil (USA))
2453[9] 3117[6]

Funky Cold Medina *Charles Hills* a72 72
3 b f Cockney Rebel(IRE) Monica Campbell (Sakhee (USA))
1754[4] 6735[4] ◆ 7114[3]

Funky Munky *Alistair Whillans* a54 55
8 b g Talaash(IRE) Chilibang Bang (Chilibang)
4826[7] 5143[9] 6907[6] 7151[4] (7375) (8302)

Fun Mac (GER) *Hughie Morrison* 81
2 ch c Shirocco(GER) Favorite (GER) (Montjeu (IRE))
5790[6] 7061[3] (7332)

Furas (IRE) *Saeed bin Suroor* a85
2 br c Shamardal(USA) Albaraari (Green Desert (USA))
(7852) ◆

Furibondo *David Lanigan* a64 64
3 br g Monsun(GER) Geminiani (IRE) (King Of Kings (IRE))
1727[8] 3497[5]

Furnace (IRE) *E Charpy* a79 79
9 b g Green Desert(USA) Lyrical Dance (USA) (Lear Fan (USA))
412a[5]

Fury *William Haggas* 113
5 gr g Invincible Spirit(IRE) Courting (Pursuit Of Love)
2323[4] 3458[18] 6838[7] 7368[8]

Fushicho *Brendan Powell* a46 53
4 ch g Phoenix Reach(IRE) Rasmalai (Sadler's Wells (USA))
41[13] 2073[3] ◆ 3015[7] 3252[3] 4192[3] 5633[8]

Future Reference (IRE) *Saeed bin Suroor* a92 88
3 ch g Raven's Pass(USA) Mike's Wildcat (USA) (Forest Wildcat (USA))
1648[13] 2420[5] 2984[2] 3434[2] (4354) 4729[2] 5187[2] (6204) 6874[3] 7464[6]

Futurist *A bin Huzaim* a7 78
6 b h Halling(USA) Crystal Gazing (USA) (El Gran Senor (USA))
7679a[6]

Fuzzy Logic (IRE) *Bernard Llewellyn* a58 62
4 b g Dylan Thomas(IRE) Gates Of Eden (USA) (Kingmambo (USA))
1664[2] 1980[4] 2922[2] 3271[5] 3884[10] 4938[4]

Fyrecracker (IRE) *Marcus Tregoning* 57
2 ch g Kheleyf(USA) Spirit of Hope (IRE) (Danehill Dancer (IRE))
4858[10]

Gabbiano *Jeremy Gask* a83 96
4 b g Zafeen(FR) Hollybell (Beveled (USA))
11[6] ◆ 372[5] 583[8] (812) (2255) 2868[10] 3586[6] 4235[2] (4707) 5544[20] 6189[4] 6831[11]

Gabrial (IRE) *Richard Fahey* 113 4 b g Dark Angel(IRE) Guajira (FR) (Mtoto) (1535) 2186[3] 2840[3] 3419[13] 4276[5] 4811[2] 5725[3] 6191[3] 6742[4] 7196[6]

Gabrial's Gift (IRE) *Scott Dixon* a84 77 4 gr g Verglas(IRE) Sahara Lady (IRE) (Lomitas) 86[3] (2918) ◆ 3322[3] 3757[5] 4250[8] 5273[9] 5537[5] (6018) (6310) 6822[7] 7264[6] 8365[5]

Gabrial's Hope (FR) *David Simcock* a70 62 4 b g Teofilo(IRE) Wedding Night (FR) (Valanour (IRE)) 198[9] 671[7] 1084[6] 1342[2] (1700) (1983) 2136[5] 3085[4] 8226[7] 8335[9]

Gabrial's Kaka (IRE) *Richard Fahey* 102 3 b g Jeremy(USA) Love In May (IRE) (City On A Hill (USA)) 1767[3] 2211[5] 2661[10] 4769[4] 5182[3] (5562) 6208[2] 6823[5] 7205[2]

Gabrial's King (IRE) *David Simcock* a94 84 4 b g Hurricane Run(IRE) Danella (IRE) (Platini (GER)) (2418) 2648[2] 3118[3] 3807[2] 4313[3] 4913[6] 5997[2] 6424[7] (6809) 8202[2] 8429[3]

Gabrial's Star *Ian Williams* 88 4 b g Hernando(FR) Grain Only (Machiavellian (USA)) 1805[5] 2205[13] 2671[5] 3344[6] 3765[5] 4913[9] 5972[3] (6165) 6504[7]

Gabrial's Wawa *Roger Ingram* a81 81 3 b g Dubai Destination(USA) Celestial Welcome (Most Welcome) (815) (1119) ◆ 2216[4] 2651[4] 3756[4] 7661[5] 7970[9] 8178[8] 8453[9]

Gabrial The Boss (USA) *David Simcock* a78 63 3 ch g Street Boss(USA) Bacinella (USA) (El Gran Senor (USA)) (209) (231) 474[4] 666[6] 843[2] 949[5] 2763[8] 3758[6] 4710[3] 5527[2] 6998[3] 7325[4] 7544[8] 8339[2]

Gabrial The Duke (IRE) *David Simcock* a78 75 3 ch g Duke Of Marmalade(IRE) Literacy (USA) (Diesis) 103[7] 212[5] (634) (803) 867[2] 1103[2] (1177) 2784[7] 3497[2] 3756[6] (4401) 4714[2] 4961[6]

Gabrial The Great (IRE) *Luca Cumani* 101 4 b g Montjeu(IRE) Bayourida (USA) (Slew O'Gold (USA)) 2718[3] 3115[4] 3607[2] (4488) 5269[4] 6001[9] 6396[2] 6838[8]

Gabrial The Master (IRE) *Richard Fahey* a57 83 3 ch g Strategic Prince Kualke (IRE) (Celtic Swing) (1296) 1609[4] 1761[2] 2153[6] 3806[4] 4286[4] 5514[2] 6389[2] (6827) 7210[14]

Gabrial The Thug (FR) *Richard Fahey* a68 71 3 b g Azamour(IRE) Baliyna (USA) (Woodman (USA)) 814[3] 1719[3] 2624[4] 3573[4] 3809[5] 4251[4] 4515[2] 4806[5] 5975[5] 6387[2] 6810[3] 6824[3] 7169[12] 7786[12] 8047[4] 8223[7]

Gabriel's Lad (IRE) *Denis Coakley* a87 108 4 b g Dark Angel(IRE) Catherine Wheel (Primo Dominie) 2046[2] ◆ 3558[9] ◆ 3846a[18] (5285) 6183[2] 6623[9] 7190[5]

Gadobout Dancer *Julie Camacho* a45 59 6 b m Tobougg(IRE) Delta Tempo (IRE) (Bluebird (USA)) 3397[8] 3814[9] 4893[9] 6986[5] 7201[7] 7752[7]

Gadreel (IRE) *Anthony Middleton* a46 37 4 b g Dark Angel(IRE) Borsalino (USA) (Trempolino (USA)) 4503[6] 4658[8]

Gaelic Ice *Rod Millman* a58 60 4 b f Iceman Gaelic Lime (Lomitas) 2057[4] 2710[7] 3314[6] 3635[2] ◆ 3882[3] 4605[5] 5311[3] (5813) 7090[6]

Gaelic Silver (FR) *Gary Moore* a78 74 7 b g Lando(GER) Galatza (FR) (Johann Quatz (FR)) 273[6] 420[7] 639[2] ◆ 906[4] 1059[3] 1585[2] 2348[9] (7865) 8179[4] 8308[7]

Gaelic Space (FR) *J Bertran De Balanda* a80 80 4 gr g Enrique Gaelic Dream (FR) (Shining Steel) 963a[0]

Gaelic Wizard (IRE) *Dominic Ffrench Davis* a70 71 5 b g Fasliyev(USA) Fife (IRE) (Lomond (USA)) (37) 229[4] 645[6] 1694[9] 1793[2] 2588[5] 3042[8] 3511[6] 4155[9] (6344) 7068[5] 7347[5] 8306[8]

Gaga A (URU) *D Smaga* a100 106 4 rg f T. H. Approval(USA) Yin (BRZ) (Quinze Quilates (BRZ)) 7613a[2] 7843a[3] 8440a[4]

Galab (IRE) *Conrad Allen* 42 2 b c Danehill Dancer(IRE) Mount Klinovec (IRE) (Mujadil (USA)) 3581[13]

Gala Casino Star (IRE) *Geoffrey Harker* a88 93 8 ch g Dr Fong(USA) Abir (Soviet Star (USA)) 1281[5] 1643[3] 1990[3] 2478[4] 2976[6] 3651[5] 4929[4] 5521[6] 6239[9] 6563[8]

Galateia (IRE) *A De Royer-Dupre* 101 3 b f Dansili Gagnoa (IRE) (Sadler's Wells (USA)) 5806a[12]

Galatian *Rod Millman* a83 70 6 ch g Traditionally(USA) Easy To Imagine (USA) (Cozzene (USA)) 7224[13] 7629[10] 7836[3] ◆

Galaxy (IRE) *Alan McCabe* a70 43 2 b g Oratorio(IRE) Gravitation (Galileo (IRE)) 5785[5] 6513[10] 8067[7] 8382[3]

Galeb Warrior *William Haggas* 3 b g Duke Of Marmalade(IRE) Katrina (IRE) (Ela-Mana-Mou) 6926[12]

Gale Force Ten *A P O'Brien* a108 115 3 b c Oasis Dream Ronaldsay (Kirkwall) 2298a[4] 2677a[2] (3455) 4298[6] 5040a[11] 6450a[4]

Galeo Des Flandres (FR) *P Demercastel* a78 73 7 b h King's Theatre(IRE) Escouades (FR) (General Assembly (USA)) 315a[3]

Galician *Mark Johnston* a106 106 4 gr f Redoute's Choice(AUS) Gweneira (Machiavellian (USA)) 1061[4] 1252[3] 1385[8] 1720[2] 1913[11] 2265[2] 3590[3] 3725[10] (3931) 4062[10] 4297[10] (4525) (4744) 4946[4] 5561[5] 5738[10] 6183[6] 7025[5] 7233a[4] 7470[2] 7649[2] 7974[3] 8117[2] 8231[3] 8386[3] (8428)

Galilee Chapel (IRE) *Alistair Whillans* a60 56 4 b g Baltic King Triple Zero (IRE) (Raise A Grand (IRE)) 2536[11] 2972[9] 7153[12] 7752[4] 7963[2] (8055) 8199[5]

Galileo Rock (IRE) *David Wachman* 118 3 ch c Galileo(IRE) Grecian Bride (IRE) (Groom Dancer (USA)) 1811[3] ◆ 2866[3] 3849a[2] 6393[3]

Galinea (IRE) *M Boutin* a74 90 2 b f Excellent Art Galaktea (IRE) (Statue Of Liberty (USA)) 5363a[2] 7160a[7]

Galiotto (IRE) *Gary Moore* a65 66 7 b g Galileo(IRE) Welsh Motto (USA) (Mtoto) 469[3] 1664[10] 7899[4] 8160[8]

Galiway *A Fabre* 100 2 b c Galileo(IRE) Danzigaway (USA) (Danehill (USA)) 7534[2] ◆

Galizzi (USA) *Michael Bell* 61 2 b c Dansili Dancing Abbie (USA) (Theatrical (IRE)) 6953[6]

Gallant Leader (USA) *Tony Coyle* 4 b g Zamindar(USA) Real Trust (USA) (Danzig (USA)) 313[6] 434[7]

Gallantry *Paul Howling* a65 43 11 b g Green Desert(USA) Gay Gallanta (USA) (Woodman (USA)) 35[4] 205[8] 347[5] 630[5] 737[6] 900[4] 1093[9]

Gallena *William Haggas* a66 54 3 b f Invincible Spirit(IRE) Emily Blake (IRE) (Lend A Hand) 2098[9] 2959[6] 3903[9]

Galleon *Michael Bell* a88 89 4 b g Galileo(IRE) Tempting Prospect (Shirley Heights) 1733[10]

Galley Slave (IRE) *Michael Chapman* a62 42 8 b g Spartacus(IRE) Cimeterre (IRE) (Arazi (USA)) 1721[7]

Gallic Breeze (FR) *John Quinn* 78 2 b c Naaqoos Nateja (USA) (Diesis) 4610[2] (5025)

Gallipot *John Gosden* a103 106 4 b f Galileo(IRE) Spinning Queen (Spinning World (USA)) 2443[4] 3409[5] 4059[7] 5761[5]

Galuppi *Luca Cumani* a61 2 b c Galileo(IRE) La Leuze (IRE) (Caerleon (USA)) 8340[6]

Galvanize *Kevin Ryan* 85 2 b g Bahamian Bounty Xtrasensory (Royal Applause) 6234[11] 6790[2] 7173[3]

Galvaun (IRE) *A Fabre* 112 4 b f Galileo(IRE) Pharmacist (IRE) (Machiavellian (USA)) 3165a[4] 5297a[7] 6448a[5] 7048a[3] 7613a[5]

Galway Gem (IRE) *John Mackie* a43 5 b f Golan(IRE) Hasty Native (IRE) (Be My Native (USA)) 1069[8] 1187[6]

Gambino (IRE) *Alan Berry* a50 52 3 b c Red Clubs(IRE) Temptation Island (IRE) (Spectrum (IRE)) 5365[10] 5704[2] 6084[5] 6344[3] 6687[9] 7345[7]

Gamble *Michael Bell* a63 78 3 ch f Galileo(IRE) Pretty Face (Rainbow Quest (USA)) 3542[3] 4223[6] 4961[3] 6071[5] 6847[4] 7839[5]

Gambling Don (USA) *Daniel E Sanner* 4 ch c Forest Danger(USA) Flaming Mirage (USA) (Woodman (USA)) 413a[5]

Gambol (FR) *J W Hills* a71 3 ch g New Approach(IRE) Guardia (GER) (Monsun (GER)) 8427[2]

Gambolling Den (IRE) *David Simcock* a67 61 3 ch c Indian Haven Hidden Charm (IRE) (Big Shuffle (USA)) 491[5] (685) 1099[5] 1900[10] 3528[6]

Game All (IRE) *Hugo Palmer* a65 58 4 b f Acclamation Love Thirty (Mister Baileys) 5522[4] 6323[10] (6752) 7197[6]

Game Ball (USA) *Donna Green* a93 98 6 ch h Sky Mesa(USA) Balldo (USA) (Saint Ballado (CAN)) 773a[6]

Game Mascot *C Ferland* a100 72 3 ch g Kheleyf(USA) Tolzey (USA) (Rahy (USA)) 999a[8]

Game On Dude (USA) *Bob Baffert* a128 6 bb g Awesome Again(CAN) Worldly Pleasure (USA) (Devil His Due (USA)) (4106a) 7715a[9]

Gamesome (FR) *Olly Stevens* 95 2 b c Rock Of Gibraltar(IRE) Hot Coal (USA) (Red Ransom (USA)) 4987[11] (5494)

Gamgoom *Harry Dunlop* a73 73 2 b c Exceed And Excel(AUS) Danidh Dubai (IRE) (Noverre (USA)) 3948[6] 5399[3] ◆ 6342[2] 6790[8]

Gammarth (FR) *H-A Pantall* a98 109 5 ch c Layman(USA) Emouna Queen (IRE) (Indian Ridge) 2300a[9] 2909a[3] 3557[10] 4935a[2] 5804a[2] 7054a[18]

Ganas (IRE) *Ernst Oertel* a107 87 5 b g Oasis Dream Hollow Dynasty (USA) (Deputy Commander (USA)) 365a[3] 660a[11] 955a[5] 1265a[16]

Gandalak (FR) *David O'Meara* a85 98 4 b g Oasis Dream Grand Vadla (FR) (Grand Lodge (USA)) 1248[3] ◆ 1652[3] (1787) ◆ (1992) 2210[4] 2868[16] 3335[7] 6621[22] 7241[5]

Ganges (IRE) *James Toller* a56 71 2 b c Shamardal(USA) Quantum (IRE) (Alhaarth (IRE)) 6799[5] 7647[5]

Gangsterbanksters (FR) *Mrs K Burke* a50 65 4 b g High Chaparral(IRE) Pantelleria (GER) (Monsun (GER)) 100[6] 238[7] 1916[10]

Gannicus *Brendan Powell* 66 2 b g Phoenix Reach(IRE) Rasmani (Medicean) 6378[6] 6953[10] 7467[5]

Ganymede *Eve Johnson Houghton* a62 2 b c Oasis Dream Gaze (Galileo (IRE)) 8425[5] ◆

Garbah (IRE) *A Al Raihe* a106 94 5 b f Kodiac Baraloti (IRE) (Barathea (IRE)) 365a[9]

Garde Cotiere (USA) *Richard Fahey* a94 93 5 b g Giant's Causeway(USA) Amonita (Anabaa (USA)) 1233[17] (2766) 4310[17] 4778[10] 5768[11]

Garden Party *T J Bougourd* a79 72 9 b g Green Desert(USA) Tempting Prospect (Shirley Heights) 4846a[2] (5329a) 7144a[2]

Garfunkel (IRE) *Tony Coyle* 49 2 b c Excellent Art Intricate Dance (USA) (Aptitude (USA)) 6286[8] 6627[9] 7023[15]

Garraun (IRE) *Jeremy Noseda* a68 2 b f Tamayuz French Fern (IRE) (Royal Applause) 8145[2]

Garrisson (IRE) *Charles Hills* a70 66 4 b g Cape Cross(IRE) Desertion (IRE) (Danehill (USA)) 1585[12] 2413[11] 3106[7] 3244[7] 3676[5]

Garrogorille (FR) *Y Durepaire* 106 3 gr c Rock Of Gibraltar(IRE) From This Day On (USA) (El Prado (IRE)) 1737a[5] 3386a[5]

Garswood *Richard Fahey* 113 3 b c Dutch Art Penchant (Kyllachy) (1621) ◆ 2021[7] 3455[4] (4856) 6193[6] 7059a[3]

Garud (IRE) *Michael Moroney* 98 5 b g High Chaparral(IRE) Global Pearl (GER) (Acatenango (GER)) 7700a[5] 7827a[6]

Garzoni *Tim Easterby* a51 61 4 ch f Medicean Rainbow Queen (Rainbow Quest (USA)) 1111[16] 2162[6] 2537[11]

Gaspard *David O'Meara* a38 74 3 b g Sakhee(USA) Photogenic (Midyan (USA)) 2507[4] 5563[3] 6084[6] 6810[5]

Gassin Golf *Richard Lee* a78 98 4 b g Montjeu(IRE) Miss Riviera Golf (Hernando (FR)) 6192[11]

Gatepost (IRE) *Richard Fahey* a88 99 4 br g Footstepsinthesand Mandama (IRE) (Warning) 2150[9] 2647[3] ◆ 3114[10] 3825[4] 4758[5] 6384[6] 6822[11] (7255) 7452[6]

Gaterie (USA) *A Fabre* 104 4 b f Dubai Destination(USA) Galatee (FR) (Galileo (IRE)) 6447a[5] 7890a[4]

Gatewood *John Gosden* a106 112 5 b c Galileo(IRE) Felicity (IRE) (Selkirk (USA)) 6307[2] 7012[3] 7768[2] 8386[2]

Gathering Power (IRE) *Edward Lynam* a73 91 3 b f Kyllachy Nutkin (Act One) (2374a) 3845a[11] 6883a[15]

Gauchita *Michael Bell* a51 50 2 b f Invincible Spirit(IRE) Rex Regina (IRE) (King's Best (USA)) 6947[9] 7766[13] 7852[11] ◆ 8090[3]

Gaul Wood (IRE) *Tom Dascombe* a92 99 4 b g Amadeus Wolf Emly Express (IRE) (High Estate) 1233[7] 1905[5] 2191[6] 2813[3] 3339[3] (3864) 4080[14]

Gavlar *William Knight* 55 2 b g Gentlewave(IRE) Shawhill (Dr Fong (USA)) 4896[6] 6355[6] 7070[9]

Gay Gallivanter *Mick Quinn* a55 45 5 b f Iceman Gallivant (Danehill (USA)) 15[5] 441[11] 536[4] 601[4] 886[3] 1600[9] 1916[11]

Gay Marriage (IRE) *John Gosden* a73 2 b f New Approach(IRE) Doctrine (Barathea (IRE)) 7435[6] ◆ 7763[2] (8175)

Geanie Mac (IRE) *Linda Perratt* a50 66 4 ch f Needwood Blade Dixie Evans (Efisio) 2316[12] 2798[5] 2975[5] 3467[3] 3771[5] 4343[3] 4614[5] 5240[2] 5267[6] 5643[3] 5920[2] 6087[3] 6470[2] 6909[5] 7239[5] 7668[6]

Gebayl *Olivia Maylam* a63 3 b f Compton Place Glimpse (Night Shift (USA)) 148[3] 470[3] 623[2] 845[5] 990[2] 1190[2] (2992) 6367[9] 7263[10] 7652[12]

Geeaitch *Peter Hiatt* a73 60 4 ch g Cockney Rebel(IRE) Grand Rebecca (IRE) (Namid) 2383[7] 4591[6] 5234[7] 5980[5] 6218[9] 7093[3] 7515[10] 8006[5] 8148[3] 8373[4] 8417[3]

Gee Sharp *Julie Camacho* a58 2 b g Captain Gerrard(IRE) Cumbrian Concerto (Petong) 7341[13] 7732[6] 8005[5] 8346[5]

Gee Wizz (IRE) *Robert Collet* a74 72 3 b f Whipper(USA) Midnight Mystique (IRE) (Noverre (USA)) 962a[10]

Gemara (USA) *Gary Brown* a48 74 5 b g War Chant(USA) Top Tier (USA) (King Of Kings (IRE)) 750[11] 983[10] 1070[10]

Genax (IRE) *Richard Guest* a32 49 2 b f Green Desert(USA) Steam Cuisine (Mark Of Esteem (IRE)) 4924[9] 5877[8] 6174[7] 8317[8]

Gender Agenda *Michael Bell* a73 81 2 b f Holy Roman Emperor(IRE) Friendlier (Zafonic (USA)) 2419[6] 3471[3] 4408[3] 5536[4] (5699) 6572[2] 7221[4]

General Tufto *Charles Smith* a59 52 8 b g Fantastic Light(USA) Miss Pinkerton (Danehill (USA)) 522[8] 597[4] 886[7] 908[5] 1311[7] 1603[13] 3195[11] 8199[2] 8233[5] 8399[2]

Generalyse *Ben De Haan* a82 82 4 b g Cadeaux Genereux Dance To The Blues (IRE) (Danehill Dancer (IRE)) 1814[10] 2196[3] 2736[5] 4220[4] 4669[6] 5349[2] 5697[4] 6929[2] (7106) 7888[4] 8088[9]

Generous Dream *Mel Brittain* 70 5 ch f Generous(IRE) First Harmony (First Trump) 1390[11] 5137[6] 5862[3] 7280[3] 7597[11] 8268[8]

Generous George (IRE) *Mel Brittain* a27 58 4 b g Generous(IRE) Bolino Swing (IRE) (Celtic Swing) 5902[7] 6498[11] 7279[5] 8268[5]

Generous Heart *Harry Dunlop* 2 ch f Sakhee's Secret Lonely Heart (Midyan (USA)) 4827[P]

Gengis (FR) *G Doleuze* 111 3 gr c King's Best(USA) Ashiyna (IRE) (Green Desert (USA)) (1562a) 2298a[8] 3128a[3] 3851a[10] 6251a[9] 7685a[15]

Geniusinrhyme *Nigel Tinkler* 46 2 b g Amadeus Wolf Ardessie (Bahamian Bounty) 1565[7] 4820[6] 7125[7] 7419[9]

Gentildonna (JPN) *Sei Ishizaka* 126 4 b f Deep Impact(JPN) Donna Blini (Bertolini (USA)) 1268a[2] (8033a)

Gentle Breeze (IRE) *Charlie Appleby* a75 65 2 b f Dubawi(IRE) Laureldean Gale (USA) (Grand Slam (USA)) 3781[7] 4409[2] 4828[6] 5421[5] 7078[5]

Gentle Maine (IRE) *J-M Beguigne* a70 73 3 ch c Muhtathir Maine Rose (Red Ransom (USA)) 2557a[9]

Gentleman Is Back (USA) *Ed de Giles* a32 47 5 bb g Johannesburg(USA) Torros Straits (USA) (Boundary (USA)) 1397[9]

Gentleman Jackson (USA) *Mark Casse* 90 6 b g Alert(USA) Somethingquiet (USA) (Quiet American (USA)) 773a[2] 1001a[3]

Gentleman Only (IRE) *S Botti* 105 2 b c Holy Roman Emperor(IRE) Goldendale (IRE) (Ali-Royal (IRE)) (7678a)

Gentlemax (FR) *Jim Boyle* a49 61 3 b c Gentlewave(IRE) Marcela Howard (IRE) (Fasliyev (USA)) 5064[9] 5892[9] 6402[12] 6824[5] 8443[8]

Gentlemen *P J O'Gorman* a49 2 ch c Ad Valorem(USA) Stoney Cove (IRE) (Needwood Blade) 7852[9]

Gentlemen's Bet (USA) *Ronald Moquett* a114 4 bb c Half Ours(USA) Lady Of Sun (USA) (Gentlemen (ARG)) 7713a[3]

Gentle Storm (FR) *Y Barberot* 108 4 b c Gentlewave(IRE) Aznavour (GER) (Lagunas) 1048a[4] 1658a[2] 2184a[7] 7410a[4] 7590a[3]

Gentry (IRE) *John M Oxx* 68 2 ch c Nayef(USA) Elegant Way (IRE) (Cape Cross (IRE)) 7050a[5]

Genuine Quality (USA) *Ed Vaughan* a83 86 2 b f Elusive Quality(USA) Genuine Devotion (IRE) (Rock Of Gibraltar (IRE)) 2856[3] 3318[2] 4539[2] 6034[2] 6477[2] (6967) 7657[3]

Genzy (FR) *Ian Williams* a105 108 5 b g Gentlewave(IRE) Zycia (IRE) (Bishop Of Cashel) 1241[3] 2656[2] 3525[15] 4796[2] 5531[4] 5766[2] ◆ 6447a[10] 6766[P]

Geoffrey Chaucer (USA) *A P O'Brien* 108 2 b c Montjeu(IRE) Helsinki (Machiavellian (USA)) (6884a)

George Baker (IRE) *George Baker* a77 81 6 b g Camacho Petite Maxine (Sharpo) 2286[3] ◆ 2920[5] 4685[3] ◆ 5621[4] 7462[14]

George Benjamin *Michael Appleby* a77 79 6 b g Trade Fair Unchain My Heart (Pursuit Of Love) 986[8] 1115[7] 1366[4] 1947[6] 2395[7] 2932[3] 3511[8] 4155[7] 4357[9] 6324[8] 7485[3] 7753[14] 7885[2] (8293)

Georgebernardshaw (IRE) *Richard Guest* a72 67 8 b g Danehill Dancer(IRE) Khamseh (Thatching) 504[4] 1101[2] 3348[8] 4083[3]

George Cinq *Michael Bell* a88 92 3 b g Pastoral Pursuits Fairnilee (Selkirk (USA)) 1912[4] 2209[2] 2776[2] 3633[5] (4897) 5958[6] 6356[4] 6801[17] 7337[8]

George Fenton *Conor Dore* a82 78 4 ch g Piccolo Mashmoum (Lycius (USA)) 77[7] 115[5] 426[7] (559) 640[2] 831[4] 971[6] 1102[6] 1351[5] 1525[5] 1800[4] 1994[7] 4884[4] 5139[8] 5486[4] (5583) 5971[2] 6053[4] (6367) (6634) 6855[4] (6995) 7633[12] 7792[3] 7896[10] 7965[2] 8095[3] (8198) 8304[6] 8401[5]

George Guru *Michael Attwater* a101 101 6 b g Ishiguru(USA) Waraqa (USA) (Red Ransom (USA)) 495[4] 690[2] 897[5] 1036[6] 1545[6] (2013) 2585[2] 3339[4] 4297[17] 6767[5] 7368[13] 7641[3] 7991[3] 8263[3]

George Rooke (IRE) *Kevin Ryan* a55 85
3 b g Rock Of Gibraltar(IRE) Double Fantasy (GER) (Indian Ridge)
2371^{7} 2666^{4} 3028^{3} 4265^{5} 5440^{5} 7531^{4} 8127^{14}

George The First *Alan Swinbank* a26 68
2 gr g Aqlaam Mrs Gray (Red Sunset)
3588^{2} 4044^{3} 6271^{5} 6852^{8} 7451^{6}

George Vancouver (USA) *A P O'Brien* a92 117
3 b c Henrythenavigator(USA) Versailles Treaty (USA) (Danzig (USA))
2021^{10} 2677a^{7} 3421^{7}

Georgian Bay (IRE) *Mrs K Burke* a100 95
3 b g Oratorio(IRE) Jazzie (FR) (Zilzal (USA))
1543^{3} 2208^{4} 2661^{8} 4265^{6}

Gerdani *Michael Easterby* 33
2 ch f Captain Gerrard(IRE) Danifah (IRE) (Perugino (USA))
2337^{8} 2830^{5} 4583^{6}

Gereon (GER) *C Zschache* 108
5 b g Next Desert(IRE) Golden Time (GER) (Surumu (GER))
4333a^{3} (5940a) 7047a^{16}

German Rules *H-W Hiller* 48
2 gr c Aussie Rules(USA) Bonnie Belle (Imperial Ballet (IRE))
5939a^{9}

Geronimo Chief (IRE) *Andrew Crook* a57 50
5 b g Sleeping Indian Portorosa (USA) (Irish River (FR))
61^{6} 1079^{9}

Gerrards Cross (IRE) *Richard Hannon Snr* 67
3 b c Cape Cross(IRE) Shin Feign (USA) (El Prado (IRE))
1635^{9} 1826^{5} 2055^{4} 7396^{8}

Gertrude Gray (IRE) *Lady Cecil* a67 78
3 b f Hurricane Run(IRE) Canterbury Lace (USA) (Danehill (USA))
2321^{5} 2713^{5} 3272^{2} 3975^{5} 5392^{5}

Gertrude Versed *John Gosden* a79 100
3 b f Manduro(GER) Sugar Mill (FR) (Polar Falcon (USA))
74^{2} (275) 2148^{2} 2842^{8} 3482^{6} 4532^{2} 5402^{4} 7020^{7}

Gervinho (USA) *Carla Gaines* a94 108
3 b c Unusual Heat(USA) Foreverinthegame (USA) (Out Of Place (USA))
8120a^{4}

Getabuzz *Tim Easterby* 87
5 b g Beat Hollow Ailincala (IRE) (Pursuit Of Love)
1273^{9} 1689^{11} 2552^{2} 2855^{9} 4929^{6} 5559^{3} 5823^{3} 6237^{7} 6668^{4}

Getaway Car *Gerard Butler* a88 71
3 ch g Medicean Lomapamar (Nashwan (USA))
1885^{8} (2599) 2878^{8} 3783^{4} 3908^{3} 4961^{4} (6658) 6869^{6} (7166) ◆

Get Going *Hughie Morrison* a28 32
3 b g Motivator Good Girl (IRE) (College Chapel)
3176^{8} 4382^{11} 5962^{4}

G Force (IRE) *Richard Hannon Snr* 84
2 b c Tamayuz Flanders (IRE) (Common Grounds)
7501^{2}

Ghaamer (USA) *D K Weld* a39 88
3 b g Hard Spun(USA) Teeba (USA) (Seeking The Gold (USA))
6883a^{22}

Ghaawy *Sir Michael Stoute* 90
2 b c Teofilo(IRE) Asawer (IRE) (Darshaan)
4483^{11} 5188^{3} (5811) (6501)

Ghanaian (FR) *Charlie Appleby* 102
3 b f Shamardal(USA) Ghanaj (Caerleon (USA))
(3179) ◆ 3835^{3} 5493^{2} 6143^{2} 7015^{2}

Ghasabah *William Haggas* a73 93
3 b f Dansili Muwakleh (Machiavellian (USA))
2979^{3} (3787) (4453) 4766^{2} 5684^{3} ◆

Ghasaq (IRE) *Brian Meehan* 40
2 b c Invincible Spirit(IRE) Manuka Magic (IRE) (Key Of Luck (USA))
2194^{10} 3374^{13}

Ghazi (IRE) *Saeed bin Suroor* 81
2 b g Exceed And Excel(AUS) Concordia (Pivotal)
(5744) ◆

Ghetto Diva *Daniel Kubler* a13 40
3 b f Compton Place Like A Virgin (IRE) (Iron Mask (USA))
3327^{4} 7490^{9}

Ghibli *R Bouresly* a23 9
3 b f Shirocco(GER) Portodora (USA) (Kingmambo (USA))
243a^{9}

Ghinia (IRE) *Pam Sly* 69
2 b f Mastercraftsman(IRE) Jorghinia (FR) (Seattle Slew (USA))
5282^{9} 6281^{3} 6828^{5}

Ghor (FR) *M Boutin* a75 100
5 ch g Gold Away(IRE) Pragmatica (Inchinor)
3187a^{3} 7085a^{7} 7995a^{6}

Ghost Army (IRE) *A Fabre* a89 97
4 b g Elusive Quality(USA) Pure Illusion (IRE) (Danehill (USA))
3187a^{8}

Ghosting (IRE) *Tom Dascombe* a72
2 ro c Invincible Spirit(IRE) Exclusive Approval (USA) (With Approval (CAN))
7119^{3}

Ghost Opera *Philip McBride* a25
5 b f Librettist(USA) Materialize (USA) (Chester House (USA))
1890^{7}

Ghost Runner (IRE) *Lady Cecil* 82
3 b g Tagula(IRE) Ball Cat (FR) (Cricket Ball (USA))
1769^{3} (2099) 3117^{8} 4908^{8}

Ghost Train (IRE) *Tim McCarthy* a75 72
4 b g Holy Roman Emperor(IRE) Adrastea (IRE) (Monsun (GER))
3499^{3} 4520^{2} 8220^{8} 8330^{10}

Ghostwing *Luke Dace* a73 75
6 gr g Kheleyf(USA) Someone's Angel (USA) (Runaway Groom (CAN))
1516^{5} ◆ 1780^{6} 2225^{3} 2918^{4} 5931^{4} 6039^{8} 6937^{13} 7437^{12}

Ghufa (IRE) *Lydia Pearce* a45 41
9 b g Sakhee(USA) Hawriyah (USA) (Dayjur (USA))
7379^{7} 7612^{7}

Ghurair (USA) *John Gosden* 108
3 bb c Elusive Quality(USA) Alta Moda (Sadler's Wells (USA))
1636^{3} 2398^{4}

Gianni (FR) *C Ferland* 99
3 b c Kentucky Dynamite(USA) Loretta Gianni (FR) (Classic Account (USA))
5463a^{8}

Giant Finish (USA) *Anthony Dutrow* a101
3 ch c Frost Giant(USA) Apocalyptic (USA) (Hickman Creek (USA))
2033a^{10} 3127a^{11}

Giant Samurai (USA) *John Quinn* a71 54
2 ch g First Samurai(USA) Willow Point (USA) (Fusaichi Pegasus (USA))
4731^{6} 7371^{8} (7902)

Giant Sandman (IRE) *Rune Haugen* a87 109
6 b h Footstepsinthesand Sharamana (IRE) (Darshaan)
4936a^{2} (5804a) 7941a^{6}

Giant's Legend (USA) *J S Moore* 71
2 b c Giant's Causeway(USA) Kissed By A Star (USA) (Kingmambo (USA))
5167^{2}

Giant's Quest (AUS) *H Rogers* 81
7 b g Giant's Causeway(USA) Rushing Wind (IRE) (Danehill (USA))
7230a^{6}

Giantstepsahead (IRE) *Michael Wigham* a62 53
4 br g Footstepsinthesand Salty Air (IRE) (Singspiel (IRE))
800^{3} 1735^{5} 5072^{4} 5492^{3} 6216^{2}

Gifted Girl (IRE) *Paul Cole* a97 110
4 b f Azamour(IRE) Hoodwink (IRE) (Selkirk (USA))
(2253) ◆ 2838^{2} (4137) 5552a^{2} 6636^{2} 7057a^{5} ◆

Gifted Heir (IRE) *Ray Peacock* a30 20
9 b g Princely Heir(IRE) Inzar Lady (IRE) (Inzar (USA))
5429^{10} 7962^{10} 8116^{11}

Gift Of Music (IRE) *James Eustace* a70 67
3 b f Cadeaux Genereux Loch Verdi (Green Desert (USA))
1682^{4} 2329^{3} 2806^{9} 4033^{2} 4830^{5}

Gift Of Rain (IRE) *Ed Dunlop* a61 64
2 b f Galileo(IRE) La Sylvia (IRE) (Oasis Dream)
7296^{11} 7606^{2} 7874^{7}

Gift Of Silence *John Berry* a66 72
4 gr f Cadeaux Genereux Not A Word (Batshoof)
821^{5} 1086^{3} 1323^{6} 1914^{2} 2640^{2} 2963^{3} 3686^{8} (5617) 6535^{5} 6941^{10}

Giftorm (USA) *Fredrik Reuterskiold* a81
3 b c War Pass(USA) High Cholesterol (USA) (Until Sundown (USA))
5326a^{4}

Gigawatt *Jim Boyle* a55 76
3 b g Piccolo Concubine (IRE) (Danehill (USA))
1582^{9} 2285^{10} 2844^{10} 2984^{8}

Gilbey's Mate *John Gosden* 78
2 b g Medicean Al Joudha (FR) (Green Desert (USA))
3581^{5} ◆ 4218^{3} 6799^{10} (7371)

Gilded Age *Chris Gordon* a72 75
7 b g Cape Cross(IRE) Sweet Folly (IRE) (Singspiel (IRE))
1670^{10} 3473^{12}

Gilded Frame *Marcus Tregoning* a62 70
3 b g I Was Framed(USA) Glint (Pivotal)
1486^{13} 1900^{7} 5960^{5} 6522^{6} 6898^{5}

Gilmer (IRE) *Charlie Appleby* a78 76
2 b g Exceed And Excel(AUS) Cherokee Rose (IRE) (Dancing Brave (USA))
3737^{3} 4676^{2} 6169^{3} 7349^{4}

Gimli (FR) *G Collet* a58 42
3 ch c Ballingarry(IRE) Geisha Lady (IRE) (Raise A Grand (IRE))
445a^{0} 647a^{11}

Gimme Five *Alan King* a50 47
2 b g Champs Elysees Waitingonacloud (In The Wings)
6733^{9} 7069^{8} 7308^{8}

Ginger Beer (FR) *J Helouiry* a68
3 gr g Irish Wells(FR) Rose Of Tralee (FR) (Kendor (FR))
331a^{0} 818a^{4}

Ginger Fizz *Ben Case* a75 70
6 ch m Haafhd Valagalore (Generous (IRE))
351^{5} 1927^{4} 2570^{5} 3110^{7} 6736^{8}

Ginger Jack *Geoffrey Harker* a88 95
6 ch g Refuse To Bend(IRE) Coretta (IRE) (Caerleon (USA))
1840^{5} 3346^{4} (3503) 4342^{5} 5335^{6} 6164^{8} 6792^{7} 7172^{18}

Gingka (FR) *Mme P Butel* a51 67
3 b g One Cool Cat(USA) Top Sauce (Hector Protector (USA))
4575a^{5}

Ginjo *Nigel Twiston-Davies* a54
3 b f Sakhee(USA) Gulshan (Batshoof)
5925^{6} 6312^{9} 7734^{7}

Gin Time (IRE) *David Evans* a49 54
2 b f Kalanisi(IRE) Littleton Liberty (Royal Applause)
1285^{2} 1432^{2} 1574^{2} 2068^{3} 2189^{4} 3992^{4}

Giny Queen (FR) *Mlle V Dissaux* a53 59
2 bb f King's Best(USA) Lady Weasley (FR) (Zieten (USA))
6961a^{13}

Ginzan *Malcolm Saunders* a56 82
5 b f Desert Style(IRE) Zyzania (Zafonic (USA))
2266^{8} 2825^{3} 3018^{7} (4368) 4830^{4} 5219^{4} 5308^{3} 6045^{5} 6381^{4}

Giofra *A De Royer-Dupre* 118
5 b f Dansili Gracefully (IRE) (Orpen (USA))
1267a^{3} 1870a^{4} 4254^{3} 4817a^{12}

Gioia Di Vita *David Thompson* a76 81
3 b c Sakhee(USA) Dhuyoof (IRE) (Sinndar (IRE))
1934^{2} 2651^{3} 3470^{5} 4672^{2} 5483^{7} 5835^{3} 6701^{8} 7028^{2} ◆ 7596^{3} 8139^{4}

Giorgio's Dragon (IRE) *Robert Stephens* 73
4 b g Le Vie Dei Colori Broadways Millie (IRE) (Imperial Ballet (IRE))
3788^{8} 5097^{8} 5816^{14}

Giovanni Boldini (USA) *A P O'Brien* a111 115
2 bb c War Front(USA) Dancing Trieste (USA) (Old Trieste (USA))
6442a^{3} 7688a^{2}

Girl At The Sands (IRE) *Edward Creighton* a69 71
3 gr f Clodovil(IRE) Invincible Woman (IRE) (Invincible Spirit (IRE))
225^{5} (643) 1075^{4} 7743^{12} 7841^{7} 8177^{4}

Girl Of Cadiz *Richard Hannon Snr* a71 68
3 br f Byron Gennie Bond (Pivotal)
(1907) 2387^{12} 2919^{2} 3178^{2} 3861^{7}

Girl On Fire (IRE) *P Schiergen* 47
2 b f Desert Style(IRE) Patrimony (Cadeaux Genereux)
7406a^{12}

Girolamo (GER) *P Schiergen* 114
4 ch c Dai Jin Golden Time (GER) (Surumu (GER))
1268a^{8} 2294a^{4} (2822a) 3879a^{2} 4571a^{4} 5324a^{3}

Giulietta (GER) *W Hickst* 92
3 ch f Sternkoenig(IRE) Gillenia (GER) (Greinton)
3146a^{9}

Give Me High Five *Richard Hannon Snr* a63 58
3 b f Dubawi(IRE) Mountain Holly (Shirley Heights)
17^{5} 845^{4} 1289^{4} 1712^{13}

Give Us A Belle (IRE) *Christine Dunnett* a72 54
4 b g Kheleyf(USA) Bajan Belle (IRE) (Efisio)
441^{6} 2134^{3} 2788^{5} 3644^{10} 5200^{6} 5499^{8} 5930^{10} (7068) 7197^{8} 7454^{4} 7850^{8} (8035) 8051^{2} (8168) (8411) ◆

Give Us A Reason *James Toller* a41
3 b f Motivator Ela's Giant (Giant's Causeway (USA))
7298^{10}

Give Way Nelson (IRE) *Brian Meehan* a72 86
3 b f Mount Nelson Give A Whistle (IRE) (Mujadil (USA))
2783^{6} 6993^{13} 7297^{10}

Glacial Age (IRE) *Jo Hughes* a84 104
3 gr c Verglas(IRE) Lady's Secret (IRE) (Alzao (USA))
1046a^{7} (1595) 1812^{2} 2211^{3} 2907a^{13} 3645a^{2} 4573a^{6}

Gladiatrix *Rod Millman* a88 96
4 b f Compton Place Lady Dominatrix (IRE) (Danehill Dancer (IRE))
(1308) ◆ 1726^{9} 2088^{3} 3018^{3} 3371^{9} 3786^{2} 4024^{7} 4707^{2} 5036^{4} 5561^{12} 6189^{12}

Gladsome *Jason Ward* 69
5 b f Resplendent Glory(IRE) Christening (IRE) (Lahib (USA))
1271^{5} 1788^{12} 2280^{2} 2616^{6} 3946^{12}

Gladstone (IRE) *Polly Gundry* a58 38
5 b g Dansili Rockerlong (Deploy)
1877^{2} (2333) 2777^{2} 3037^{8} 3406^{11} 4380^{9} 7984^{9}

Gladys' Gal *Roger Varian* a91 96
5 b f Tobougg(IRE) Charming Lotte (Nicolotte)
1235^{P}

Glamour Star (GER) *Mme P Butel* a81 81
4 b g Shirocco(GER) Grouper (USA) (Gone West (USA))
4467a^{2} 5042a^{3} 5601a^{7}

Glance Of Doon (IRE) *David Harry Kelly* 32
2 b f Tagula(IRE) Five Star Maria (IRE) (Carrowkeel (IRE))
7050a^{14}

Glanely (IRE) *Martyn Meade* a85 78
3 b g Exceed And Excel(AUS) Bon Ton Roulet (Hawk Wing (USA))
2448^{6} 2934^{4} 4667^{6} (6214) 6642^{4} ◆ 7123^{6} 7531^{8} 8455^{5}

Glan Lady (IRE) *Michael Appleby* a45 51
7 b m Court Cave(IRE) Vanished (IRE) (Fayruz)
2578^{3} 3029^{3} 3431^{4} 4145^{9} 5198^{10} 5426^{5} 5840^{6} 6283^{5} 6518^{13}

Glasgon *Declan Carroll* 50
3 gr g Verglas(IRE) Miss St Tropez (Danehill Dancer (IRE))
5484^{8} 5839^{6} 6497^{9}

Glasgow Central *Charles Hills* 69
2 b c Rail Link Musical Key (Key Of Luck (USA))
4987^{8} 6430^{5} 7070^{3}

Glassatura (IRE) *M Halford* a74 86
2 gr f Verglas(IRE) Dunbrody (FR) (Jeune Homme (USA))
2944a^{4} 5318a^{6}

Glassenbury Lass *Mark Hoad* a23 20
3 b f Haafhd Skirt Around (Deploy)
3435^{6} 4404^{7}

Glass Mountain (IRE) *John Mackie* a72 79
5 gr g Verglas(IRE) Exotic Mix (FR) (Linamix (FR))
83^{9} 1836^{12}

Glass Office *David Simcock* a107 110
3 bg c Verglas(IRE) Oval Office (Pursuit Of Love)
245a^{5} 658a^{7} 2415^{6} 3103^{2} 3558^{5} 4947^{4} ◆

Glastonberry *Geoffrey Deacon* a81 55
5 gr f Piccolo Elderberry (Bin Ajwaad (IRE))
116^{2} 271^{5} 2596^{6} 3691^{3} 4385^{4} 5104^{5} 6135^{3} (6653) 6982^{2} 7897^{2} 8181^{3} 8430^{7}

Glean *Richard Hannon Snr* a99 107
3 ch c Raven's Pass(USA) Harvest Queen (IRE) (Spinning World (USA))
1543^{2} (2024)

Glebe Spirit (IRE) *Richard Hannon Snr* a64 66
2 b c Invincible Spirit(IRE) Starry Messenger (Galileo (IRE))
4773^{3} 5473^{5} 6168^{6} 6487^{4}

Glee Club *Noel Quinlan* a51
3 b f Kyllachy Penmayne (Inchinor)
8313^{5}

Glenard *Charles Hills* 98
3 b g Arch(USA) Olaya (USA) (Theatrical (IRE))
1641^{6} 3899^{3} 4349^{2} 4748^{2} (5274) 6186^{4} 6793^{6}

Glencadam Gold (IRE) *Gai Waterhouse* 113
5 b g Refuse To Bend(IRE) Sandrella (IRE) (Darshaan)
7392a^{14}

Glen Moss (IRE) *Charles Hills* a98 105
4 b c Moss Vale(IRE) Sail With The Wind (Saddlers' Hall (IRE))
1542^{2} 2254^{12} 2858^{4} (4014) 4744^{4} (5533) 5738^{7} 6183^{16} 7014^{11}

Glennten *Sylvester Kirk* a60 55
4 b g Ishiguru(USA) Uplifting (Magic Ring (IRE))
(87) 276^{6} 422^{2} 449^{3} 560^{2} 655^{6}

Glenreef *Mark Johnston* a69 54
3 ch f Three Valleys(USA) Grand Coral (Grand Lodge (USA))
(1187) 1453^{3} 2079^{5} 2586^{10} 3232^{10}

Glenridding *James Given* a68 66
9 b g Averti(IRE) Appelone (Emperor Jones (USA))
976^{8} 1460^{6} 1693^{10} 1887^{3} 2836^{9} 3643^{9} 3909^{6} 4155^{2} 4357^{7} (4966) 5354^{3} 6218^{10} 6634^{6} 6855^{2} 7669^{7} 7953^{9} 8163^{5}

Glen's Diamond *Richard Fahey* 114
5 b g Intikhab(USA) Posta Vecchia (USA) (Rainbow Quest (USA))
(2428) 3873a^{5} 4919^{13} 5724^{5} 6453a^{11}

Glens Wobbly *Jonathan Geake* a52 51
5 ch g Kier Park(IRE) Wobbly (Atraf)
1716^{3} 1794^{4} 1877^{6} 2567^{3} 3037^{3} 3312^{4} 4192^{2} 4365^{5} 5433^{3} 6099^{3} 6853^{5} 6895^{2}

Global Bang (GER) *Mario Hofer* 107
3 bb c Manduro(GER) Goonda (Darshaan)
1708a^{2} 2526a^{2} 4103a^{5} 4819a^{5}

Global City (IRE) *Saeed bin Suroor* a57 75
7 b h Exceed And Excel(AUS) Victory Peak (Shirley Heights)
660a^{14} 834a^{11}

Global Explorer (USA) *Stuart Williams* a61 46
2 b g Henrythenavigator(USA) Trulips (USA) (Elusive Quality (USA))
2778^{4} 3640^{7} 3815^{6}

Global Icon *Michael Dods* a69 87
3 b g Green Desert(USA) Maganda (IRE) (Sadler's Wells (USA))
6630^{3} 7269^{3}

Global Leader (IRE) *Paul D'Arcy* a51
3 b c Dark Angel(IRE) Headborough Lass (IRE) (Invincible Spirit (IRE))
7802^{6} 7932^{5} 8063^{5}

Global Recovery (IRE) *David Evans* a61 46
6 b g El Corredor(USA) Altarejos (IRE) (Vettori (IRE))
2764^{4} 5434^{10} 5671^{6} 6984^{5}

Global Thrill *J Hirschberger* a58 107
4 b c Big Shuffle(USA) Goonda (Darshaan)
(1564a) 2202a^{8} 3612a^{3} 4333a^{2} 5940a^{9} 7053a^{6}

Global Village (IRE) *Brian Ellison* a96 104
8 b g Dubai Destination(USA) Zelding (IRE) (Warning)
945^{6} ◆ 1235^{2} ◆ 1675^{4} 4869a^{10} 6025a^{19} 6396^{6}

Gloomy Sunday (FR) *C Ferland* 110
4 b f Singspiel(IRE) Fine And Mellow (FR) (Lando (GER))
(2810) 5575a^{4} 7060a^{4}

Gloriam (USA) *Ruth Carr* a89 85
4 b g War Chant(USA) Amandas Bandit (USA) (Royal Academy (USA))
1115^{10} 1281^{2} 1485^{12} 2078^{5}

Glorious Days (AUS) *J Size* 122
6 br g Hussonet(USA) San Century (NZ) (Centaine (AUS))
2066a^{4} (8210a)

Glorious Empire (IRE) *Ed Walker* a79
2 br g Holy Roman Emperor(IRE) Humble And Proud (IRE) (Pivotal)
(8061)

Glorious Protector (IRE) *Ed Walker* a92 95
3 b c Azamour(IRE) Hasaiyda (IRE) (Hector Protector (USA))
1678^{4} (2321) ◆ 3214^{3} 6936^{2} 7223^{2}

Glorious Sinndar (FR) *George Margarson* a74 43
2 b g Sinndar(IRE) Aloisi (Kalanisi (IRE))
7089^{6} 7513^{5} 7854^{2}

Glory Awaits (IRE) *Kevin Ryan* 115
3 ch c Choisir(AUS) Sandbox Two (IRE) (Foxhound (USA))
1623^{3} 2021^{2} 3421^{5} 4945^{4} 6797^{6}

Glory Traou Land (FR) *P Sogorb*
2 b f Della Francesca(USA) Risk Of Traou Land (FR) (Take Risks (FR))
7653a^{11}

Gloss (IRE) *Richard Hannon Snr* a65 64
2 b c Acclamation Glitter Baby (IRE) (Danehill Dancer (IRE))
4231^{8} 4896^{7} 5843^{8} 6749^{4}

Glossy Posse *Richard Hannon Snr* a66 77
3 b f Dubawi(IRE) Nouvelle Lune (Fantastic Light (USA))
2308^{8} 2806^{6} (3375) (3699)

Glowing Cloud *C Ferland* a99 103
4 ch f Dylan Thomas(IRE) Power Girl (GER) (Dashing Blade)
(6714a) 7142a^{3} 7843a^{2}

G Man (IRE) *Olly Stevens* a53 67
2 b g Intense Focus(USA) Saoodah (IRE) (Green Desert (USA))
3148^{4} 3659^{3} 3972^{2} 5634^{7} 7087^{5}

Gm Hopkins *John Gosden* 81
2 b c Dubawi(IRE) Varsity (Lomitas)
2411^{4} 3112^{12}

Goadby *John Holt* a57 57
2 gr f Kodiac Gone Sailing (Mizzen Mast (USA))
3009^{3} 3476^{5} 4616^{3} 5215^{3} 6073^{8} 7094^{2} 7788^{4}

Goal (IRE) *Charles Smith* a76 68
5 b g Mujadil(USA) Classic Lin (FR) (Linamix (FR))
(6083) 6803^{4} (6851) 7383^{6} 8408^{8}

Go Amwell *J R Jenkins* a34 33
10 b g Kayf Tara Daarat Alayaam (IRE) (Reference Point)
1721^{11} 4173^{4}

Go Angellica (IRE) *David Simcock* a72 100
3 ch f Kheleyf(USA) Areyaam (USA) (Elusive Quality (USA))
554a^{10} 837a^{9} 3460^{22}

Go Baby Go (AUS) *C H Yip* 114
6 b g Medal Of Honor(AUS) Miss Whirl (AUS) (Pricelessly (USA))
8209a^{9}

Gobertier *Richard Hannon Snr* a64
2 b c Avonbridge Barnezet (GR) (Invincible Spirit (IRE))
7852^{10} 8066^{10} 8326^{2} 8383^{7}

Go Charlie *Ronald Harris*
2 b c Myboycharlie(IRE) Branston Gem (So Factual (USA))
2823^{7} 3948^{8}

God's County (FR) *Sophie Leech* a90 35
8 gr g Verglas(IRE) Toujours Elle (USA) (Lyphard (USA))
5586^{8}

Gods Gift (IRE) *Rae Guest* a68 67
3 ch g Dalakhani(IRE) Guilia (Galileo (IRE))
712^{2} 1009^{3} 4851^{6} 5196^{4} 6996^{6} 7395^{5}

God's Speed (IRE) *Rae Guest* a46
2 b c Oratorio(IRE) Guilia (Galileo (IRE))
8201^{5}

God Willing *Ed Dunlop* 102
2 b c Arch(USA) Bourbon Ball (USA) (Peintre Celebre (USA))
(5472) 6765^{5} 7195^{4}

Go Far *Alan Bailey* a75 71
3 b g Dutch Art Carranita (IRE) (Anita's Prince)
129^{3} ◆ 425^{3} 468^{2} 1433^{4} 1760^{2} 2308^{10} 3253^{3} 8224^{3} 8345^{3} (8407)

Go For Broke *Richard Hannon Snr* a71 70
2 ch c Assertive Level Pegging (IRE) (Common Grounds)
5307^{4} ◆ (5950) 7837^{9} 8126^{2}

Gogeo (IRE) *Alan Swinbank* a74 87
6 b g Val Royal(FR) Steal 'Em (Efisio)
8299^{3}

Go Glamorous (IRE) *Ronald Harris* a77 77
2 b f Elnadim(USA) Glamorous Air (IRE) (Air Express (IRE))
1240^{2} ◆ 1399^{2} 1924^{2} 3459^{23} 4828^{5} (5929) 6432^{4}

Go Go Green (IRE) *Jim Goldie* a82 79
7 b g Acclamation Preponderance (IRE) (Cyrano De Bergerac)
1248^{4} (1280) 2276^{3} 5333^{6} 5579^{6} 6469^{4} 6547^{2} 6920^{5} 7777^{3}

Going French (IRE) *Dai Burchell* a76 72
6 ch g Frenchmans Bay(FR) Easy Going (Hamas (IRE))
1694^{3} 2664^{12} 4837^{3} 6652^{5} 7164^{8}

Going Grey (IRE) *Richard Fahey* a64 64
4 ro g Diamond Green(FR) Incendio (Siberian Express (USA))
145^{3} 548^{4} 996^{5} (1568) 1836^{10} 3083^{8} 3977^{6}

Going Somewhere (BRZ) *D Smaga* 116
4 ch c Sulamani(IRE) Angel Star (BRZ) (Special Nash (IRE))
6449a^{4} 7058a^{9} 7566a^{2}

Go Jamesway *Richard Fahey* 65
2 b c Royal Applause Tatbeeq (IRE) (Invincible Spirit (IRE))
3766^{3} 4107^{5}

Golan Heights (IRE) *Adrian McGuinness* a56 51
7 br g Golan(IRE) Lady Abigail (IRE) (Royal Academy (USA))
41^{2} 62^{2}

Golbahar (IRE) *X Thomas-Demeaulte* a80 96
3 b f Holy Roman Emperor(IRE) Grosgrain (USA) (Diesis)
7993a^{2}

Goldan Jess (IRE) *Philip Kirby* a60 74
9 b g Golan(IRE) Bendis (GER) (Danehill (USA))
22^{3} (458) 2328^{4} 4614^{2} (5267)

Gold Approach *William Haggas* 73
2 ch f New Approach(IRE) Samira Gold (FR) (Gold Away (IRE))
6643^{6} 7449^{4}

Gold Beau (FR) *Kristin Stubbs* a71 78
3 b g Gold Away(IRE) Theorie (FR) (Anabaa (USA))
1301^{3} 2719^{2} 2916^{2} (3593) 4198^{5} 4962^{5} 5393^{3} (5704) (5878) 6382^{4} 6774^{7}

Gold Chain (IRE) *Clive Cox* 70
3 b f Authorized(IRE) Mountain Chain (USA) (Royal Academy (USA))
1666^{4} 2519^{5} (6407)

Gold Class *Ed McMahon* 59
2 ch g Firebreak Silken Dalliance (Rambo Dancer (CAN))
5338^{6} 6152^{8} 6513^{3} 7309^{12}

Gold Club *Ed McMahon* a54 73
2 b g Multiplex Oceana Blue (Reel Buddy (USA))
4351^{5} 5225^{2} 6127^{3} 6718^{4}

Golden Beau (FR) *J-P Delaporte* a77 78
5 gr c Gold Away(IRE) Dinner Bell (FR) (Highest Honor (FR))
648a^{0} 6421a^{5}

Golden Bowl (FR) *J Bertran De Balanda* 106
3 b c Turtle Bowl(IRE) Maid Of Dawkins (IRE) (Kendor (FR))
2297a^{6} 3386a^{7} 5463a^{5}

Golden Buck (FR) *P Van De Poele* a86 82
3 ch c Gold Away(IRE) Khaylama (IRE) (Dr Devious (IRE))
3166a^{3} 6713a^{4}

Golden Causeway *Charles Hills* a67 69
3 ch f Giant's Causeway(USA) Cast In Gold (USA) (Elusive Quality (USA))
(532) 3983^{9} 4715^{7}

Goldencents (USA) *Doug O'Neill* a123
3 b c Into Mischief(USA) Golden Works (CAN) (Banker's Gold (USA))
2033a^{17} 2473a^{5} (7689a)

Golden Compass *Giles Bravery* a70 77
5 ch f Sakhee(USA) Northern Bows (Bertolini (USA))
4120^{12}

Golden Desert (IRE) *Simon Dow* a75 77
9 b g Desert Prince(IRE) Jules (IRE) (Danehill (USA))
(130) 650^{8} 3274^{5} 3974^{11} 4637^{7} 4998^{3} 6039^{3} 6317^{3} 7303^{7} 7880^{4} 8019^{7} 8158^{11}

Golden Flower *David O'Meara* a79 63
3 b f Royal Applause Silver Kestrel (USA) (Silver Hawk (USA))
4^{2} (75) 203^{3}

Golden Future *Peter Niven* a55 72
10 b g Muhtarram(USA) Nazca (Zilzal (USA))
2242^{7} 2720^{3} 4563^{3} 4951^{2} (5241) 5786^{8}

Golden Games (IRE) *Daniel O'Brien* a19 32
7 b m Montjeu(IRE) Ski For Gold (Shirley Heights)
2922^{8}

Golden Groom *Patrick Holmes* 50
10 b g Groom Dancer(USA) Reine De Thebes (FR) (Darshaan)
6917^{7} 7098^{9}

Golden Jason (USA) *Gennadi Dorochenko* a71 94
3 b c Kitten's Joy(USA) On The Bus (USA) (Ghazi (USA))
5551a^{12}

Golden Journey (IRE) *Clive Cox* 67
2 ch c Nayef(USA) Beatrix Potter (IRE) (Cadeaux Genereux)
5399^{7} 6184^{7} 7070^{6}

Golden Jubilee (USA) *Nigel Twiston-Davies* a79 67
4 bb g Zavata(USA) Love Play (USA) (Friendly Lover (USA))
2350^{4} 2828^{3} (3213) 3985^{3} (4604) 5099^{6} 5966^{2} 7000^{2} 7169^{2} ◆ (7857) 8047^{2}

Golden Secret *Clive Cox* a60 68
3 ch f Sakhee's Secret Tahara (IRE) (Caerleon (USA))
3837^{7} 4627^{2} 6397^{5}

Golden Shaheen (IRE) *M bin Shafya* a83 89
6 b g Invincible Spirit(IRE) Cheeky Weeky (Cadeaux Genereux)
290a^{3}

Golden Share (USA) *Marco Botti* a47
4 bb c Medaglia d'Oro(USA) Siempre Asi (USA) (Silver Hawk (USA))
215^{7} 434^{6}

Golden Shoe (IRE) *J T Gorman* a82 81
5 br g Footstepsinthesand Goldilocks (IRE) (Caerleon (USA))
4869a^{16} 6025a^{14}

Golden Soul (USA) *Dallas Stewart* a116
3 ch c Perfect Soul(IRE) Hollywood Gold (USA) (Mr Prospector (USA))
2033a^{2} 3127a^{9}

Golden Spear *Noel Quinlan* 78
2 ch c Kyllachy Penmayne (Inchinor)
2497^{4} 4602^{2} 5646^{4} (6487) ◆ 7062^{9}

Golden Steps (FR) *Marco Botti* a60
2 b c Footstepsinthesand Kocooning (IRE) (King's Best (USA))
8165^{2}

Golden Surprise (FR) *D Windrif* a69 72
2 ch f Deportivo Plasence Surprise (FR) (Marathon (USA))
6786a^{2} 7568a^{8}

Golden Ticket (USA) *Kenneth McPeek* a118 91
4 bb c Speightstown(USA) Business Plan (USA) (Deputy Minister (CAN))
7689a^{2}

Golden Town (IRE) *Saeed bin Suroor* 90
2 b c Invincible Spirit(IRE) Princesse Dansante (IRE) (King's Best (USA))
4987^{4} (5727)

Gold For Tina (FR) *J Van Handenhove* a93 98
4 b f Lando(GER) Mascara (GER) (Monsun (GER))
5298a^{7}

Gold-Fun (IRE) *R Gibson* 120
4 ch g Le Vie Dei Colori Goodwood March (Foxhound (USA))
2066a^{5} 8210a^{2}

Gold Hunter (IRE) *Saeed bin Suroor* 100
3 b g Invincible Spirit(IRE) Goldthroat (IRE) (Zafonic (USA))
(4011) 4767^{4} 5439^{5} 6308^{3} 6993^{3} 7337^{13}

Goldie Horn *Nigel Twiston-Davies* a54 53
5 ch f Where Or When(IRE) Gulshan (Batshoof)
3989^{7} 5071^{7} 5386^{5} 5967^{3} 6102^{5} 6783^{3} 7951^{7}

Goldmadchen (GER) *James Given* a73 62
5 b f Ivan Denisovich(IRE) Goldkatze (GER) (Czaravich (USA))
198^{6} 528^{2} ◆ (624) 886^{2} 908^{2} 989^{4} 1207^{3} 1600^{6} 2511^{10} 8270^{12} 8410^{6}

Gold Medal (IRE) *Richard Hannon Snr* a74 67
3 b g Dylan Thomas(IRE) Sogno Verde (IRE) (Green Desert (USA))
1300^{2} 2442^{12} 4257^{8} 5132^{7} 6787^{4}

Gold Mine *Andrew Balding* a82 51
5 b g Diktat Memsahib (Alzao (USA))
2418^{10} 2982^{2} 3180^{7} 4208^{7} 4832^{8}

Gold Nugget (IRE) *Richard Hannon Snr* 31
3 b c Elusive City(USA) Glamadour (IRE) (Sanglamore (USA))
2442^{13}

Goldoni (IRE) *David Hayes* a93 105
4 ch g Dylan Thomas(IRE) Lasso (Indian Ridge)
7483a^{9}

Goldream *Robert Cowell* a87 102
4 br g Oasis Dream Clizia (IRE) (Machiavellian (USA))
2046^{8} ◆ 2396^{2} ◆ 4275^{6} 4536^{4} 4983^{17} 5651^{2} 6539^{6} 7085a^{9} 7642^{8}

Gold Roll (IRE) *Ruth Carr* a60 67
3 b g Intikhab(USA) Sopran Marida (IRE) (Darshaan)
1190^{6} 1608^{4} 2274^{12} 2464^{5} 2743^{7} 2916^{7} 3281^{8} 3762^{10} 3903^{12}

Gold Save The King (IRE) *F Doumen* a70 86
6 ch g King's Best(USA) Beringold (Bering)
5601a^{15}

Gold Ship (JPN) *Naosuke Sugai* 128
4 gr c Stay Gold(JPN) Point Flag (JPN) (Mejiro McQueen (JPN))
1868a^{5} 8033a^{15}

Gold Show *Edwin Tuer* 82
4 gr f Sir Percy Pearl Bright (FR) (Kaldoun (FR))
(1448) ◆ 1936^{4} 2277^{12} 3477^{7} 3827^{3} 4373^{4} 4889^{7} 6599^{6} 7346^{3}

Goldstorm *Brian Baugh* a82 86
5 ch f Storming Home Antonia Bertolini (Bertolini (USA))
(218) 478^{4} (758) (1081) 1823^{6} 2498^{3} 3349^{8} (3983) ◆ 5613^{4}

Goldtara (FR) *A Lyon* a89 111
5 ch f Gold Away(IRE) Diatara (FR) (Sillery (USA))
4324a^{3} 5575a^{7} 6447a^{3} 7566a^{4}

Gold Top (IRE) *Richard Hannon Snr* 81
2 ch f Teofilo(IRE) Top Row (Observatory (USA))
2740^{4} (3664) 4524^{3} 5536^{14} 6763^{4} 7107^{2}

Gold Trader (USA) *Joe Woodard*
5 bb g Johannesburg(USA) Educated Risk (USA) (Mr Prospector (USA))
(413a)

Gold Trail (IRE) *Charlie Appleby* 91
2 ch c Teofilo(IRE) Goldthroat (IRE) (Zafonic (USA))
5188^{7} (6125) 7129^{2}

Gold Weight *Michael Madgwick* a42
3 ch g Denounce Jewel (IRE) (Cyrano De Bergerac)
123^{6} 7154^{7} 7443^{6} 8339^{8}

Goleador (USA) *Marco Botti* a65 61
2 b c English Channel(USA) Stormin' Home (USA) (Storm Cat (USA))
4518^{2} 5922^{6} 6689^{5} 7935^{7}

Golly Miss Molly *Jeremy Gask* a50 45
2 b f Exceed And Excel(AUS) Amicable Terms (Royal Applause)
4409^{8} 5385^{6} 6342^{7} 7293^{7}

Go Nani Go *Ed de Giles* a82 86
7 b g Kyllachy Go Between (Daggers Drawn (USA))
1198^{5} 1467^{2} (1976) 3331^{5} (3855) 4675^{7}

Gone Dutch *James Fanshawe* a88 81
3 ch g Dutch Art Ice Palace (Polar Falcon (USA))
2224^{7} 2765^{3} 3176^{7} (5395) ◆ 6106^{5} 6335^{8} (6802) (7330)

Gonetrio (USA) *N Caullery* a71 67
6 b g Gone West(USA) Balletomaine (IRE) (Sadler's Wells (USA))
648a^{6}

Gone Viral (IRE) *Ms Sheila Lavery* 70
2 ch g Virtual Dorinda Gray (IRE) (Docksider (USA))
4694a^{DSQ}

Gone With The Wind (FR) *Y Barberot* a82 15
2 ch c Mr Greeley(USA) Tremuntana (IRE) (Danehill (USA))
7570a^{4} 7889a^{6}

Gone With The Wind (GER) *Jeremy Noseda* a64
2 b c Dutch Art Gallivant (Danehill (USA))
7972^{5}

Goninodaethat *Jim Goldie* 62
5 b g Proclamation(IRE) Big Mystery (IRE) (Grand Lodge (USA))
1271^{7} 1995^{3} 2319^{7} 2977^{8} 3286^{4} 3770^{4} (4339) 5331^{10} 6083^{10} 6549^{7} 6919^{7} 7153^{6}

Good As New *Denis Quinn* a52 4
3 b f Araafa(IRE) New Design (IRE) (Bluebird (USA))
2762^{12} 8373^{8}

Good Authority (IRE) *Karen George* a91 95
6 b g Chineur(FR) Lady Alexander (IRE) (Night Shift (USA))
1745^{4} 1922^{3} 2618^{2} (3274) ◆ 4067^{6} 4879^{7} 7992^{11} 8127^{10}

Good Boy Jackson *R Mike Smith* a23 84
5 b g Firebreak Fisher Island (IRE) (Sri Pekan (USA))
4643^{8} 6550^{7} 6906^{6}

Good Evans *Tom Dascombe* a70 85
3 ch g Mount Nelson Alexia Reveuse (IRE) (Dr Devious (IRE))
211^{2} 473^{4} (591) 2153^{2} 2216^{3} 2784^{4} (3206) (4029) 4286^{3} 5288^{5}

Good Game (IRE) *Y De Nicolay* a65 65
3 b c Excellent Art Numbers Game (Rainbow Quest (USA))
1756a^{0} 7187a^{3}

Good Hope *Michael Bell* 51
2 b f Cape Cross(IRE) Fairy Godmother (Fairy King (USA))
7103^{7} 7532^{9}

Good Luck Charm *Gary Moore* a83 90
4 b g Doyen(IRE) Lucky Dice (Perugino (USA))
1739a^{5} 2266^{4} (3153) 3974^{2} 4124^{2} 5759^{7}

Goodlukin Lucy *Keith Dalgleish* a59 56
6 ch m Supreme Sound Suka Ramai (Nashwan (USA))
2313^{6} (2630) 2975^{2} 3467^{4} 7099^{6} 7239^{11} 7612^{2} 7735^{2} 7951^{5} (8349)

Good Morning Lady *Mick Channon* 57
2 b f Compton Place Baldemosa (FR) (Lead On Time (USA))
3978^{5} 4505^{11} 4937^{6}

Good Morning Star (IRE) *Mark Johnston* a76 99
4 bb f Shirocco(GER) Hollow Ridge (Beat Hollow)
1841^{8} 2149^{6} 2407^{8} 3333^{5} 3824^{18} 4873^{13} 5256^{10}

Good Old Boy Lukey *Richard Fahey* 104
2 ch c Selkirk(USA) Pivotting (Pivotal)
(2404) (3723) (4296)

Good On Numbers (IRE) *A Oliver* 74
3 b g Celtic Swing Gitchee Gumee Rose (IRE) (Paris House)
1587a^{5}

Good Speech (IRE) *Tom Tate* a66 80
3 ch f Haatef(USA) Privileged Speech (USA) (General Assembly (USA))
428^{2} (1579) 2079^{2} 2878^{5} 5223^{3} 5549^{2} ◆ 6302^{5} 6846^{4}

Good Things (FR) *N Bertran De Balanda* a46 47
2 b f Martaline Songbird (FR) (Starborough)
5213a^{5}

Good Value *Sir Michael Stoute* 57
2 ch g Champs Elysees Change Course (Sadler's Wells (USA))
4256^{9} 5968^{5}

Goodwood Mirage (IRE) *William Knight* 103
3 b c Jeremy(USA) Phantom Waters (Pharly (FR))
2438^{4} (3276) ◆ 4214^{4} ◆ 4950^{2} 6186^{14} 6591^{2} 6991^{4}

Goodwood Storm *William Knight* a68 56
2 ch f Shamardal(USA) Artifice (Green Desert (USA))
5061^{10} 6318^{6} 7294^{3}

Go On (FR) *C Boillot* a41 60
3 ch g Kentucky Dynamite(USA) Golden Sea (FR) (Saint Cyrien (FR))
7569a^{6}

Gordol Du Mes (USA) *Gianluca Bietolini* 100
3 ch c Exchange Rate(USA) Twinkle Twinkle (USA) (Arazi (USA))
1865a^{12} 5806a^{15}

Gordon Lord Byron (IRE) *T Hogan* a110 121
5 b g Byron Boa Estrela (IRE) (Intikhab (USA))
1266a^{7} 2368^{3} 3557^{4} ◆ 4549a^{2} 5040a^{3} (5453a) (6193) 7059a^{2} ◆ 7366^{7} 8210a^{4}

Gorgeous Goblin (IRE) *David C Griffiths* a95 70
6 b m Lujain(USA) Tama (IRE) (Indian Ridge)
353^{8} 586^{5} 776^{5} 913^{5} 1160^{10}

Gorki Park (FR) *Mme G Rarick* a70 72
3 b g Sageburg(IRE) Lears Ly (USA) (Lear Fan (USA))
72a^{10} 445a^{0} 647a^{7} 7188a^{9}

Go Sakhee *Roger Varian* a67 68
2 br g Sakhee's Secret Bling Bling (IRE) (Indian Ridge)
6534^{5} 7162^{3} 7818^{11}

Gosforth Park *Mel Brittain* a57 70
7 ch g Generous(IRE) Love And Kisses (Salse (USA))
4809^{5} 5059^{5} 5786^{6} 7278^{3} 8004^{7}

Gosh (IRE) *Mme Pia Brandt* a76 103
3 ch f Peintre Celebre(USA) Ragazza Mio (IRE) (Generous (IRE))
5315a^{3} 6294a^{3}

Gospel Choir *Sir Michael Stoute* 106
4 ch g Galileo(IRE) Chorist (Pivotal)
5723^{7} (6741) 7012^{5}

Got Bird (FR) *C Ferland* a70
3 b f Oratorio(IRE) Byre Bird (USA) (Diesis)
461a^{3}

Gotham News (USA) *J-C Rouget* a94
3 ch c Awesome Again(CAN) Teammate (USA) (A.P. Indy (USA))
(692a)

Gothic *Sir Michael Stoute* 82
2 b c Danehill Dancer(IRE) Riberac (Efisio)
6799^{6} (7274)

Gothic Dance (IRE) *B Grizzetti* 92
4 ch f Dalakhani(IRE) Future Flight (Polar Falcon (USA))
6890a^{8}

Got Shades (USA) *Danny Pish* 98
2 bb c Pollard's Vision(USA) Melancholy (USA) (Run Softly (USA))
7688a^{5}

Got Slick (FR) *P Monfort* a82 53
6 gr m Slickly(FR) Fancy Yellow (FR) (Anabaa (USA))
5042a^{2} 5601a^{14}

Gottcher *Keith Dalgleish* a76 79
5 b g Fasliyev(USA) Danalia (IRE) (Danehill (USA))
4613^{3} ◆ 5085^{3} (5641) (5708) 5889^{10} 6583^{24} 7240^{2}

Got To Dance *Ralph Beckett* a68 72
2 b f Selkirk(USA) Mullein (Oasis Dream)
2053^{5} 2625^{12} 4164^{2} 5850^{5} (6695)

Gouray Girl (IRE) *Brian Ellison* a58 94
6 b m Redback Brillano (FR) (Desert King (IRE))
621^{7} (1113) ◆ 1675^{25} 2476^{7} 2541^{7} 3684^{14} 5544^{15} 5783^{3} 6274^{8} 6496^{10}

Govenor Charlie (USA) *Bob Baffert* a114
3 bb c Midnight Lute(USA) Silverbulletway (USA) (Storm Cat (USA))
2473a^{8}

Govinda (USA) *Vanja Sandrup* a98 104
6 bb g Pulpit(USA) Garden In The Rain (FR) (Dolphin Street (FR))
150a^{16} 365a^{6} 660a^{9} 834a^{6} 2145a^{5} 3970a^{4} 4936a^{3} 5325a^{4}

Gowanharry (IRE) *Michael Dods* 83
4 ch f Choisir(AUS) Aahgowangowan (IRE) (Tagula (IRE))
(1681) (2542) 3078^{5} 4821^{2} 5266^{5} 6583^{4} 7314^{4}

Gower Princess *Ronald Harris* a66 58
2 ch f Footstepsinthesand Hollow Quaill (IRE) (Entrepreneur)
4491^{16} 5385^{5} 6095^{3} (7293) (7623) 7837^{12}

Gower Rules (IRE) *John Bridger* a63 67
5 gr g Aussie Rules(USA) Holy Norma (Nashwan (USA))
94^{12} 132^{5} 512^{5} 724^{3} 820^{7} 901^{4}

Gown (IRE) *Charles Hills* 77
2 b f Excellent Art Chehalis Sunset (Danehill Dancer (IRE))
3107^{2} 3710^{2} 5508^{6} (6002) 6326^{4} ◆ 6795^{9} 7537^{9}

Gracchus (USA) *Tony Carroll* a63 70
7 b g Black Minnaloushe(USA) Montessa (USA) (Montbrook (USA))
439^{7} 626^{5} 921^{6}

Grace And Beauty (IRE) *Paul Henderson* a43 62
5 b f Diamond Green(FR) Balliamo (IRE) (Royal Academy (USA))
1466^{8} 3180^{8}

Gracefilly *Ed Walker* a12
2 b f Invincible Spirit(IRE) Marula (IRE) (Sadler's Wells (USA))
7435^{13}

Graceful Act *Ron Barr* a60 59
5 b f Royal Applause Minnina (IRE) (In The Wings)
2754^{3} 3397^{9} 3774^{2} 4400^{3} 4561^{4} 5139^{7} 5427^{6} 6180^{2} 6289^{4} 6634^{3} 6941^{7} 7345^{8}

Graceful Descent (FR) *Karen Tutty* a74 74
8 b m Hawk Wing(USA) Itab (USA) (Dayjur (USA))
1390^{3} 1993^{10} 2615^{7} 3133^{8}

Graceful Willow *John E Long*
3 b f Phoenix Reach(IRE) Opera Belle (Dr Fong (USA))
5444^9

Grace Hull *Garry Moss* a67 46
3 gr f Piccolo Smart Hostess (Most Welcome)
2572^9 2829^{10} 3903^7 4378^5 6075^4 7904^2 8048^2 ◆ 8235^4

Grace Lady (FR) *Mlle T Puitg* 115
4 b f Muhtathir Parcelle De Sou (FR) (Ajdayt (USA))
1895a^9 (2644a) 4817a^6 5574a^6 6618a^5

Gracesome (IRE) *Stuart Williams* 49
2 b f Shirocco(GER) Simonda (Singspiel (IRE))
7693^8

Gracia Directa (GER) *D Moser* 106
5 b f Kyllachy Glyceria (IRE) (Common Grounds)
1944a^2 3102^2 4260^2 7021^{10} 7821^{18}

Gracie Hart *Jo Hughes* 67
2 b f Sakhee's Secret Dictatrix (Diktat)
7070^{10} 7449^3

Gracie's Games *John Spearing* a44 66
7 b m Mind Games Little Kenny (Warning)
2170^8 2918^{14} 4163^7 4836^5 5097^4 5499^2 6219^{10} 6436^5 6994^9 7086^{10} 7454^{13}

Gracious George (IRE) *Jimmy Fox* a74 82
3 b c Oratorio(IRE) Little Miss Gracie (Efisio)
2394^3 3242^4 4306^4 4776^2 (5187) 5958^5 6642^{11} 7988^9 8345^6

Gracious Lady *Andrew Balding* a63
2 b f Royal Applause Succinct (Hector Protector (USA))
7296^9

Gramercy (IRE) *David Simcock* a82 102
6 b g Whipper(USA) Topiary (IRE) (Selkirk (USA))
3114^{11} 3823^4 ◆ 4297^{13} 4780^{10} 5026^3 (5696) 6352^6 6621^{24} 7368^3 7495^{11}

Grammar *David Thompson* 73
4 b g Rail Link Comma (USA) (Kingmambo (USA))
3727^{10} (4010) 4403^{10} 4809^8 5420^3 5863^4 6290^9 6717^7

Grams And Ounces *John Flint* a62 36
6 b g Royal Applause Ashdown Princess (IRE) (King's Theatre (IRE))
3110^9

Gran Canaria Queen *Tim Easterby* a65 78
4 bb f Compton Place Ex Mill Lady (Bishop Of Cashel)
(4291) 4762^5 (4970) (5227) (5714) 6052^{11} 6547^4 6916^4

Grandad Bill (IRE) *Jim Goldie* a47 30
10 ch g Intikhab(USA) Matikanehanafubuki (IRE) (Caerleon (USA))
2313^{10} 2630^8 3771^7

Grandad Chunk (IRE) *Noel Quinlan* 54
2 rg c Acclamation Silverdreammachine (IRE) (Marju (IRE))
3132^5

Grandad Mac *Alan Coogan* a59 71
5 b g Invincible Spirit(IRE) No Rehearsal (FR) (Baillamont (USA))
8160^{13} 8295^7 8410^8

Grand Archer (IRE) *J D Hillis* a68 89
9 b g Grand Lodge(USA) Asnieres (USA) (Spend A Buck (USA))
127a^4

Grand Art (IRE) *Noel Wilson* a63 62
9 b g Raise A Grand(IRE) Mulberry River (IRE) (Bluebird (USA))
1464^{10} 2120^{12} 2313^8

Grand Denial (IRE) *Clive Cox* a72 82
3 b g Thousand Words The Oldladysays No (IRE) (Perugino (USA))
1582^3 ◆ 2016^2 (2437) (3159) 4797^4 5477^3 6382^9 6959^4

Grand Diamond (IRE) *Jim Goldie* a68 66
9 b g Grand Lodge(USA) Winona (IRE) (Alzao (USA))
2630^3 2972^6 (3287) 3768^4 (4343) (4578) 5240^3 5643^4 6086^6 6552^6 (6917) 7239^7

Grande Mago (IRE) *Robert Cowell* a62 56
2 b g Dandy Man(IRE) On Thin Ice (IRE) (Verglas (IRE))
3295^9 6477^{10} 6966^5 7789^9 8017^2 8113^4

Grandest *John Gosden* a82 67
2 b c Dansili Angara (Alzao (USA))
4764^5 (8346)

Grandeur (IRE) *Jeremy Noseda* 118
4 rg g Verglas(IRE) Misskinta (IRE) (Desert Sun)
4213^4 4779^2 5553a^7 (6742) 8211a^7

Grande Vision (FR) *T Larriviere*
5 b f Bernebeau(FR) True Vision (USA) (Lear Fan (USA))
(6680a)

Grandezza (GER) *W Mongil* a82 69
3 b f Samum(GER) Grouper (USA) (Gone West (USA))
(5119a)

Grandiloquent *Kevin Ryan* a70 66
4 b g Rail Link High Praise (USA) (Quest For Fame)
691^9 948^7 3930^7 4455^2 5222^5 5384^4 5854^4 6598^{15} 6909^4 7305^2 7767^{11} 8027^6

Grand Jipeck (IRE) *Ian McInnes* a56 55
3 b g Soviet Star(USA) Inourthoughts (IRE) (Desert Style (IRE))
923^4 1066^4

Grand Liaison *John Berry* 75
4 b f Sir Percy Dancinginthedark (IRE) (Fasliyev (USA))
1849^9 3063^6

Grand Meister *Michael Bell* 74
2 gr c Mastercraftsman(IRE) Wait It Out (USA) (Swain (IRE))
6570^4 7089^2

Grandorio (IRE) *David O'Meara* a70 97
3 b g Oratorio(IRE) Grand Splendour (Shirley Heights)
(2167) ◆ 2309^3 2879^9 (3296) 4063^3 6551^3

Grand Piano (IRE) *Andrew Balding* a32 47
6 b g Arakan(USA) Stately Princess (Robellino (USA))
2395^8 2773^{13} 8446^{10}

Grand Reality (ARG) *Elizabeth Gray* 61
6 b g Grand Slam(USA) Firm Reality (USA) (Roy (USA))
773a^9

Grand Theft Equine *Jim Boyle* a72 34
5 b g Piccolo Red Storm (Dancing Spree (USA))
33^2 1925^4 2417^{11} 3580^6

Grand Treasure (IRE) *G Colella* 100
3 b f Aussie Rules(USA) Lizzey Letti (Grand Lodge (USA))
1866a^2 4700a^8 6890a^4

Grand Vintage (FR) *W Mongil* 105
4 b c Marchand De Sable(USA) Fifty Niner (FR) (Fijar Tango (FR))
7186a^6 7685a^{10}

Granell (IRE) *Brian Meehan* a72 83
3 ch g Excellent Art Granny Kelly (USA) (Irish River (FR))
(2455) 3117^4 4897^9 6596^{12} 7330^9 7765^6

Gran Maestro (USA) *Ruth Carr* a75 82
4 ch g Medicean Red Slippers (USA) (Nureyev (USA))
1238^9 1448^5 ◆ 1568^4 2077^6 2594^5 2886^2 (3043) ◆ 3204^3 3301^7 3808^2 4543^9 4810^6 5087^2 5367^2 5466^3 5823^4 6239^8 6631^3 6758^4 7100^4

Granny Mc's Kitten (USA) *Chad C Brown* 98
2 b f Kitten's Joy(USA) Granny Franny (USA) (Grand Slam (USA))
7690a^{12} ◆

Granule *Peter Chapple-Hyam* a39 54
3 b f Hernando(FR) Grain Only (Machiavellian (USA))
2206^{11} 7490^8 8148^{13}

Grapes Hill *Mark Rimmer* 52
3 b f Kingsalsa(USA) Red Blossom (Green Desert (USA))
2760^{14} 3116^{11} 3740^8 4391^{10} 5156^6 5407^{12}

Graphene *Rod Millman* 19
2 b c Nayef(USA) Annapurna (IRE) (Brief Truce (USA))
2741^9

Graphic (IRE) *William Haggas* a101 112
4 ch g Excellent Art Follow My Lead (Night Shift (USA))
2444^9 2647^7 ◆ 3693^4 4237^3 4746^4 (5268) (6199) 6838^4 (7172) (7775) 7974^5

Graphic Guest *Mick Channon* 95
3 ch f Dutch Art Makara (Lion Cavern (USA))
1620^3 1921^5 2843^7

Grasped *Lady Cecil* a78
3 ch f Zamindar(USA) Imroz (USA) (Nureyev (USA))
(8154) ◆

Grass Green *William Haggas* a50 47
2 b f Dubawi(IRE) Grasshoppergreen (IRE) (Barathea (IRE))
4121^{10} 4680^3 5000^5 5480^6

Gratzie *Mick Channon* a72 74
2 b f Three Valleys(USA) La Gazzetta (IRE) (Rossini (USA))
4702^3 5394^4 5812^2 6140^{10}

Gravitate *Paul Webber* a76 61
4 ch g Pivotal Spacecraft (USA) (Distant View (USA))
1653^2 5356^5 7169^6 7840^6

Gravitational (IRE) *Chris Wall* a73 85
3 b g Invincible Spirit(IRE) Flower Of Kent (USA) (Diesis)
1832^2 2593^2 5303^2 5611^6 (6502) 7255^6

Gravy Dipper (IRE) *John Quinn*
2 ch c Champs Elysees Aldburgh (Bluebird (USA))
4351^{12} 6174^{10} 7339^{10}

Graylyn Ruby (FR) *Robin Dickin* a25 74
8 b g Limnos(JPN) Nandi (IRE) (Mujadil (USA))
7159^{10}

Graylyn Valentino *Robert Eddery* a70 68
4 b g Primo Valentino(IRE) Rhuby River (IRE) (Bahhare (USA))
1950^6 2413^{12} 3246^3 3700^2

Grayswood *William Muir* a77 67
3 gr g Dalakhani(IRE) Argent Du Bois (USA) (Silver Hawk (USA))
2564^3 3214^8 3809^7 4753^2 5343^5 6071^7 6693^2 (6899) 7439^2 ◆

Great Attack (USA) *Wesley A Ward* 113
6 b h Greatness(USA) Cat Attack (USA) (Storm Cat (USA))
1265a^{11}

Great Conquest (USA) *Jamie Osborne* a61
3 b c First Samurai(USA) Conquestress (USA) (Cherokee Run (USA))
8063^3 8313^4 8427^8

Great Crested (IRE) *Gary Moore* a75
3 bg g Clodovil(IRE) Roskeen (IRE) (Grand Lodge (USA))
2566^2 (3405) 3495^2

Great Demeanour (USA) *David Elsworth* a79 33
3 b g Bernstein(USA) Hangin Withmy Buds (USA) (Roar (USA))
350^2 (492) 666^3 738^3 (1612) 2309^6

Greatest (FR) *Mme G Rarick* a69 68
4 b g Anabaa(USA) Golden Life (USA) (Coronado's Quest (USA))
6421a^{13}

Great Expectations *J R Jenkins* a71 82
5 b g Storming Home Fresh Fruit Daily (Reprimand)
1751^4 (2266) 2761^6 3693^9 6360^7 6571^9 7130^8 7318^2 7699^{10}

Great Fighter *Saeed bin Suroor* a91 60
3 b g Street Cry(IRE) Evil Empire (GER) (Acatenango (GER))
6696^6 (7488) ◆

Great Hall *Brian Meehan* a93 101
3 b c Halling(USA) L'Affaire Monique (Machiavellian (USA))
2384^6 (3059) (3982) ◆ 6393^9 7768^5

Great Hot (BRZ) *A C Avila* a107 98
5 bb m Orientate(USA) That's Hot (USA) (Seeking The Gold (USA))
7709a^7

Great Minds (IRE) *T Stack* 77
3 ch g Bahamian Bounty Raja (IRE) (Pivotal)
7345^2

Great Ormond (IRE) *David Simcock* a61
3 b g Zamindar(USA) Paint The Town (IRE) (Sadler's Wells (USA))
103^8 212^2 (237) 419^3

Great Timing (USA) *Charlie Appleby* 101
3 ch f Raven's Pass(USA) Rumors Are Flying (USA) (Kris S (USA))
3292^2 ◆ (3835) 4878^8 5246^3 6188^4 7020^{10}

Great Wave (IRE) *David Simcock* 67
2 b f Duke Of Marmalade(IRE) Rosamixa (FR) (Linamix (FR))
5282^8 6973^3 7277^6

Great White Eagle (USA) *A P O'Brien* 107
2 b c Elusive Quality(USA) Gender Dance (USA) (Miesque's Son (USA))
(6021a) 7191^8

Greatwood *Luca Cumani* a81 110
3 b g Manduro(GER) Gaze (Galileo (IRE))
1636^2 ◆ 2398^7 3523^7 6394^2 ◆ 6991^2

Grecian (IRE) *Paul Cole* a76 81
2 gr c Dark Angel(IRE) Law Review (IRE) (Case Law)
(3211) 4232^2 ◆ 4948^{10}

Greeb *Charles Hills* 77
2 bb c Oasis Dream Shamtari (IRE) (Alhaarth (IRE))
4958^4 (5646)

Greed Is Good *K R Burke* a82 91
2 b c Myboycharlie(IRE) Merch Rhyd-Y-Grug (Sabrehill (USA))
3350^8 4218^4 4640^2 5539^2 (5968) 6314^4 (6844) 7421^5

Greek Canyon (IRE) *G M Lyons* a84 97
4 gr g Moss Vale(IRE) Lazaretta (IRE) (Dalakhani (IRE))
6883a^8

Greek Goddess (IRE) *A P O'Brien* 84
3 b f Galileo(IRE) Beauty Bright (IRE) (Danehill (USA))
1557a^8

Greek Islands (IRE) *Ed de Giles* a63 63
5 b g Oasis Dream Serisia (FR) (Exit To Nowhere (USA))
117^{12} 339^7 523^8 (733) 794^2 1056^4 ◆ 1497^3

Greek Spirit (IRE) *Jeremy Noseda* a69 54
3 b f Invincible Spirit(IRE) Greek Symphony (IRE) (Mozart (IRE))
1986^5 2650^5 3401^5 (7197)

Greek War (IRE) *Charlie Appleby* 104
4 ch g Monsun(GER) Gonfilia (GER) (Big Shuffle (USA))
4765^2 (5749) 6332^{10}

Greeleys Love (USA) *Mark Johnston* 89
3 ch c Mr Greeley(USA) Aunt Winnie (IRE) (Deputy Minister (CAN))
1250^5 2322^2 ◆ 2554^3 2862^2 ◆ 3094^6 3296^5 3486^{15} ◆ 4214^8 4537^6

Green And White (ITY) *Frank Sheridan* a47 4
3 b g Denon(USA) Sequita (GER) (Lomitas)
3641^{10} 3907^8 4356^6 5407^{11}

Greenbury (IRE) *Ann Duffield* 50
2 b g Jeremy(USA) Truly Genuine (IRE) (Hernando (FR))
2883^{14} 3461^7 7146^6 7340^4

Green Byron (FR) *J-M Lefebvre* a68 108
3 b c Green Tune(USA) Heritiere (AUS) (Anabaa (USA))
191a^5 3386a^6 5463a^3 6250a^7 7046a^5 7566a^9

Green Door (IRE) *Olly Stevens* a91 108
2 b c Camacho Inourhearts (IRE) (Pips Pride)
1669^4 ◆ (2048) 3481^7 4299^3 (5228) 5679^{11} (6347) 7191^{10}

Green Earth (IRE) *Pat Phelan* a69 67
6 b g Cape Cross(IRE) Inchyre (Shirley Heights)
813^6 1196^9 1617^4 (2533) (3152) (3412) (3656) 4904^4 5168^7 6037^3 6458^3

Greenery (IRE) *Roger Charlton* a74 68
3 b f Green Desert(USA) Go Between (Daggers Drawn (USA))
5585^3 5956^8

Greenfordgirl (IRE) *John Weymes* a22
3 b f Diamond Green(FR) Cappadoce (IRE) (General Monash (USA))
1897^{10}

Greenhead High *David Nicholls* a80 69
5 b g Statue Of Liberty(USA) Artistry (Night Shift (USA))
27^4 214^9 448^4 640^5 (831) (890) (998) (1276) 1388^5 1758^3 2037^2 2222^2 2409^8 8365^4

Green Howard *Robin Bastiman* 92
5 ch g Bahamian Bounty Dash Of Lime (Bold Edge)
1723^4 2463^{11} 2958^7 3684^{12} 4733^7 (5481) 6164^7 6586^2 7176^4 7452^7

Green Light *Peter Chapple-Hyam* 35
2 b c Authorized(IRE) May Light (Midyan (USA))
7175^{15}

Green Medi (FR) *Y Durepaire* a85 90
3 b c Medecis Greenside (FR) (King Charlemagne (USA))
461a^6

Green Millionaire *Jeremy Gask* a63 33
3 b g Green Desert(USA) Millyant (Primo Dominie)
356^7 549^2 1660^{17} 5388^6 6732^8

Green Mitas (ITY) *Frank Sheridan* a69 63
4 ch g Denon(USA) Sequita (GER) (Lomitas)
27^{10} 380^7 1657^9 3326^{14} 7167^6

Green Monkey *James Fanshawe* a23 83
3 b g Green Desert(USA) Firenze (Efisio)
2267^6 2499^4 2962^{10} 3221^4 (3789) 4390^2 (4976) ◆ (5620)

Green Moon (IRE) *Robert Hickmott* 117
6 b h Montjeu(IRE) Green Noon (FR) (Green Tune (USA))
7556a^9 7761a^{21}

Green Music *James Eustace* a62 61
2 b f Oratorio(IRE) Loch Verdi (Green Desert (USA))
3324^7 3986^5 5435^7 7451^{12} 7878^6 8061^3 (8273) 8322^5

Green Park (IRE) *Declan Carroll* a48 86
10 b g Shinko Forest(IRE) Danccini (IRE) (Dancing Dissident (USA))
1115^9 1459^5 2239^8 2834^7 3088^6 (3628) 4250^7 5026^{10} 5051^5 5481^8 6215^8 6496^2 6727^6 6822^8 7374^7 7595^9

Green Run *Richard Hannon Snr* 73
2 b f Compton Place Gee Kel (IRE) (Danehill Dancer (IRE))
2601^7 (2869) 4019^4

Green Special (ITY) *Frank Sheridan* a67 52
3 ch g Denon(USA) Groove (ITY) (Dashing Blade)
561^3 849^2 1213^2 1424^3 1928^2 2094^6 3621^4

Greensward *Conor Dore* a81 89
7 b g Green Desert(USA) Frizzante (Efisio)
792^{11} 1363^8 2450^{12} 3322^{10} 4864^6 5406^4 6316^4 (6606) (6856) 7076^4 7436^5 8068^5 8178^5 8401^9

Green To Gold (IRE) *Don Cantillon* a68 75
8 gr g Daylami(IRE) Alonsa (IRE) (Trempolino (USA))
1084^3 2721^6 3744^2 (4204) 5409^2 5954^7

Green Zone (IRE) *Nigel Tinkler* 67
2 b g Bushranger(IRE) Incense (Unfuwain (USA))
6939^8 7175^5 7494^8

Gregori (IRE) *Brian Meehan* a81 56
3 b c Invincible Spirit(IRE) Three Wrens (IRE) (Second Empire (IRE))
2447^6 4382^8 4968^8 5431^4 5674^5 5981^3 (6980) 7862^2 (8022) (8216) 8431^4

Gregorian (IRE) *John Gosden* 118
4 gr c Clodovil(IRE) Three Days In May (Cadeaux Genereux)
2258^2 (2840) 3419^3 4875^5 (5532) 6392^3 7047a^8 7366^6

Grendisar (IRE) *Marco Botti* a95 59
3 b c Invincible Spirit(IRE) Remarkable Story (Mark Of Esteem (IRE))
(141) 1614^2 (2564) 3206^4 6136^2 6693^3 (7267) 7542^8 7976^2 8387^2

Grethel (IRE) *Alan Berry* a35 35
9 b m Fruits Of Love(USA) Stay Sharpe (USA) (Sharpen Up)
2974^8 4376^{10} 5052^6

Grevillea (IRE) *Mick Channon* 77
2 b f Admiralofthefleet(USA) Louve Heureuse (IRE) (Peintre Celebre (USA))
3664^3 ◆ 4215^6 (4906) 5530^7

Grey Blue (IRE) *Mark Johnston* a70 83
3 gr g Verglas(IRE) Zut Alors (IRE) (Pivotal)
1934^7 5582^4 6071^3 6470^{10} 7091^2

Grey Command (USA) *Philip Kirby* a39 73
8 gr g Daylami(IRE) Shmoose (IRE) (Caerleon (USA))
406^6

Grey Destiny *Mel Brittain* 53
3 gr g Desideratum Mother Corrigan (IRE) (Paris House)
1687^6 2274^{10}

Greyemkay *Richard Price* a57 59
5 gr g Fair Mix(IRE) Magic Orb (Primo Dominie)
1665^{13} 3138^4 3513^3 ◆ (3885) 4604^4 5091^3 5387^2 5694^2 6492^7 6851^3 7201^4 7733^4 7962^5 8148^5

Greyfriarschorista *Tom Keddy* a93 78
6 ch g King's Best(USA) Misty Heights (Fasliyev (USA))
217^{10} 415^6 (984) 1583^{12} 1849^{11} 2225^2 ◆ 2450^5 2964^4 3780^{10} 4496^2 4718^8 5153^2 6608^5 (6970) 7661^4 7989^7 8350^5 (8408)

Grey Gazelle *Mick Channon* 73
3 gr f Verglas(IRE) Hampton Lucy (IRE) (Anabaa (USA))
1666^3 2672^6 2850^{10} 3149^3 3488^6 4193^5 6074^{10}

Grey Greezly (FR) *B Grizzetti* 101
2 b c Red Rocks(IRE) Dan Grey (IRE) (Danehill (USA))
3880a^4 7235a^2

Grey Hawk (FR) *X Thomas-Demeaulte* a81 84
3 gr c Teofilo(IRE) Magical Hawk (USA) (Silver Hawk (USA))
3166a^2

Greyhope *Lucinda Russell* 55
4 gr g Pastoral Pursuits Espana (Hernando (FR))
1572^{11}

Greylami (IRE) *Clive Cox* a93 82
8 gr g Daylami(IRE) Silent Crystal (USA) (Diesis)
273^2 1242^6 1883^3 2498^7 3157^5 4126^2 5436^6 6559^5 7765^5

Grey Mirage *Marco Botti* a105 101
4 b g Oasis Dream Grey Way (USA) (Cozzene (USA))
495^2 1036^3 (1542) 2649^8 6411^3 7540^3 (7856) 8344^2

Grey Odyssey *Dean Ivory* a8
2 gr g Verglas(IRE) Reading Habit (USA) (Half A Year (USA))
8312^6

Grey Panel (FR) *T Le Brocq*
5 gr g Largesse Minnie's Mystery (FR) (Highest Honor (FR))
1313a^4 (1740a)

Grey Poppett *Chris Dwyer*
3 gr f Paris House Maraffi (IRE) (Halling (USA))
3253^8 3787^6 4687^4

Grey Street *Richard Fahey* 74
3 rg f Royal Applause Good Enough (FR) (Mukaddamah (USA))
2167^2 2876^3

Griffin Point (IRE) *William Muir* a71 68
6 b m Tagula(IRE) Lady Corduff (IRE) (Titus Livius (FR))
2736^9 3317^9 3623^2 3888^2 4344^4 5036^8 5094^3 (5670) 6018^4 6040^2 6463^U 6745^3 7068^2 7324^6

Grilletto (USA) *James Tate* a85 67
3 b g Exchange Rate(USA) Casuarina (USA) (Menifee (USA))
674^2 1033^9 (1400) 1958^3 2285^5 2984^7 5195^{10} 5676^8 6476^3 (7076)

Griraz (FR) *P Sogorb* a78 111
8 gr g Nombre Premier Niraz (FR) (Nikos)
(315a) 3362a^4 7590a^4

Gris Caro *Jake Stephens* 107
4 ch c With Approval(CAN) Aviane (GER) (Winged Love (IRE))
7762a[8]

Gris De Reve (FR) *A Lyon* a97 102
4 gr g Slickly(FR) Oa Chereve (FR) (Kaldounevees (FR))
7685a[8] 7968a[5]

Grissom (IRE) *Tim Easterby* 98
7 b g Desert Prince(IRE) Misty Peak (IRE) (Sri Pekan (USA))
4285[8]

Grivola (GER) *Conrad Allen* a20
3 b f Ransom O'War(USA) Ginza (GER) (Acatenango (GER))
2172[6] 3907[9]

Groovejet *Peter Chapple-Hyam* a76 72
2 b f Cockney Rebel(IRE) Vino Veritas (USA) (Chief's Crown (USA))
6643[9] 7310[4] *(7854) (8164)*

Groove On (IRE) *Marco Botti* a74
3 ch c Iffraaj Dance On (Caerleon (USA))
(106) 730[5] 1041[2]

Groundbreaking *Charlie Appleby* 92
3 b c New Approach(IRE) Ladeena (IRE) (Dubai Millennium)
(4978) ◆ 5792[5] ◆ 7497[8]

Ground Ginger *James Bethell* a46 50
3 ch g Byron Hoh Hedsor (Singspiel (IRE))
1760[8] 2279[11] 2556[5] *3405[9]* 4008[11] 4849[2] 5500[7] *6216[3] 6782[5] 7034[2] 7923[5]*

Groundworker (IRE) *Sylvester Kirk* a65 21
2 b c Tagula(IRE) Notepad (King's Best (USA))
5033[12] *6746[4] 7261[5] 7804[3]*

Groupie Doll (USA) *William Bradley* a123 101
5 ch f Bowman's Band(USA) Deputy Doll (USA) (Silver Deputy (CAN))
(7709a)

Guagliona *Patrizia Giorgi* 78
4 b f Elusive City(USA) Bride Of The Sea (Cape Cross (IRE))
7416a[5] 7830a[11]

Guajaraz (FR) *J-C Rouget* 108
3 b c Rashbag Rahyna (USA) (Rahy (USA))
3128a[5] 4093a[5]

Guaracha *Clive Brittain* a52
2 ch g Halling(USA) Pachanga (Inchinor)
8333[7]

Guarantee *William Haggas* 110
4 b g Authorized(IRE) Zuleika Dobson (Cadeaux Genereux)
1674[6] 2428[7] 4309[4] 4857[7] 5766[7] 5993[P] (Dead)

Guardi (IRE) *Dean Ivory* a50 60
4 gr g Dalakhani(IRE) Grizel (Lion Cavern (USA))
1317[3] 1716[8] 2057[6] *3433[10] 3909[10]*

Guards Chapel *Gary Moore* a74 70
5 b g Motivator Intaaj (IRE) (Machiavellian (USA))
(724) 851[2] 1158[2] 1348[3] 4754[4] 5954[5] 7217[10] *7863[6]*

Guava *Shaun Harris* a69 19
4 b f Kyllachy Spunger (Fraam)
238[6]

Gucci D'Oro (USA) *David Simcock* a63 73
4 bb g Medaglia d'Oro(USA) Ninette (USA) (Alleged (USA))
2159[5] 2642[6] *2991[4]* (4403) (4951) 5241[2] *5672[5]*

Guest Book (IRE) *Alan Jones* a76 69
6 b g Green Desert(USA) Your Welcome (Darshaan)
11[11] 850[9] 1105[3] 1434[8] 2126[4] (5091)

Guest Of Honour (IRE) *Marco Botti* a102 116
4 b c Cape Cross(IRE) Risera (IRE) (Royal Academy (USA))
792[2] 945[2] ◆ 1675[2] ◆ (2323) 4276[3] ◆ 5553a[9] 6797[7]

Guilded Spirit *Stuart Kittow* a59 75
3 b g Ishiguru(USA) Soft Touch (IRE) (Petorius)
1288[3] 1977[5] 3418[10] *4384[7]* (5694) 6358[4] 7275[7]

Guilla (FR) *P Van De Poele* a81 76
3 gr f Blackdoun(FR) Simple Dreams (USA) (Dixieland Band (USA))
1756a[7]

Guinnes Will (IRE) *Agostino Affe'* 80
3 b c Refuse To Bend(IRE) Siphon Melody (USA) (Siphon (BRZ))
7830a[12]

Guishan *Michael Appleby* a50 61
3 b f Ishiguru(USA) Fareham (Komaite (USA))
1305[2] 1595[4] 2231[5] 2544[6] 3179[5] 4068[4] *8235[8]*

Guising *David Brown* a81 92
4 ch g Manduro(GER) Trick Or Treat (Lomitas)
994[3] (1274) (1728) 2369[16] 6128[2] 6394[9] 6876[7] *7805[4]*

Gulland Rock *William Muir* a54 59
2 b g Exceed And Excel(AUS) Sacre Coeur (Compton Place)
4346[6] 4808[8] *6477[6] (6872) 7623[6]*

Gumnd (IRE) *Chris Grant* a5 50
6 b g Selkirk(USA) Surval (IRE) (Sadler's Wells (USA))
801[10] 1080[11]

Gunboat (IRE) *Ed Dunlop* a54 50
5 b g Danehill Dancer(IRE) Ramruma (USA) (Diesis)
3625[4] *4380[3]*

Gung Ho (FR) *Tony Newcombe* a54 63
4 bb c Marju(IRE) Moonlit Water (Rainbow Quest (USA))
6895[3] 7375[7] *8121[9] 8399[13]*

Gung Ho Jack *John Best* a75 76
4 b g Moss Vale(IRE) Bijan (IRE) (Mukaddamah (USA))
11[7] 187[3] 372[4] 2227[8] 2530[5] 3090[7] 3841[5] 4120[4] 5278[3] 5522[6] *(6929) 7263[7]*

Gunner Lindley (IRE) *Reginald Roberts* 89
6 ch g Medicean Lasso (Indian Ridge)
1168a[14]

Gunner Will (IRE) *Paul Midgley* a76 70
4 b g Le Vie Dei Colori Ros The Boss (IRE) (Danehill (USA))
51[2] 508[4] (633) 791[7] 886[6] 1111[15] 1603[12] 1842[7] 3649[13]

Gunning For Glory *Martin Bosley* a59
3 b g Indesatchel(IRE) Today's The Day (Alhaarth (IRE))
685[6] 877[4] 3665[10]

Guru Baby *John E Long* a53 13
3 b f Ishiguru(USA) Lefty's Dollbaby (USA) (Brocco (USA))
734[4] 876[3] 2123[5] 3325[11]

Gut Instinct (FR) *Mme R-W Allen* a64 67
3 gr f Slickly(FR) Frundin (Anshan)
5119a[10]

Gwael (USA) *James Tate* a67 52
3 b f A.P. Indy(USA) Maskunah (IRE) (Sadler's Wells (USA))
2995[3] ◆ 3711[2] *8046[2] 8200[3]*

Gwenelda *Andrew Balding* 65
4 b f Rock Of Gibraltar(IRE) Cherokee Stream (IRE) (Indian Ridge)
3530[6]

Gwen Lady Byron (IRE) *Michael Mulvany* a68 47
2 ch f Dandy Man(IRE) Silent Secret (IRE) (Dubai Destination (USA))
3868a[7] 5773a[13]

Gworn *Ed Dunlop* a86 97
3 b c Aussie Rules(USA) Crochet (IRE) (Mark Of Esteem (IRE))
2438[2] 2655[8] (3492) 5182[4] 6163[2] 6989[3] (7337)

Gym Shoes *Richard Fahey* a12 70
2 b c Pastoral Pursuits Slave To The Rythm (IRE) (Hamas (IRE))
4289[4] 4528[23] 5364[7] 6187[4] 6582[11] 6904[2] *7300[9]*

Gypsy Jazz (IRE) *Ann Stokell* a17 47
6 b m Antonius Pius(USA) Dawn's Folly (IRE) (Bluebird (USA))
1596[4] 7508[11]

Gypsy Rider *Roger Curtis* a61 63
4 b g Ishiguru(USA) Spaniola (IRE) (Desert King (IRE))
143[3] (4424) 4752[5] 7092[13] *7643[3] 7981[3] 8073[3] 8341[6]*

Gyrella (IRE) *A De Royer-Dupre* a82 90
3 b f Oasis Dream Ysoldina (FR) (Kendor (FR))
1495a[5] 7993a[3]

Haadeeth *David Evans* a76 81
6 b g Oasis Dream Musical Key (Key Of Luck (USA))
187[5] 399[7] 493[2] 688[7] 898[2] 998[2] 1102[2] 1286[6] *(1516) 1793[4]* (2303a) 2657[7] 2873[2] 3181[5] 3431[3] 3716[2] 3888[12] 4149[4] 6761[5] 6929[5] 6995[3] 7444[6] (7728) 8384[7] ◆

Haafaguinea *Clive Cox* a86 106
3 ch c Haafhd Ha'Penny Beacon (Erhaab (USA))
(1809) ◆ 4946[12] 5838[5] (6638)

Haaf A Sixpence *Ralph Beckett* a98 100
4 b g Haafhd Melody Maker (Diktat)
(121) 443[4] 1233[3] (1675) ◆ 2254[20] 6625[12] (7696) *8117[3]*

Haaffa Sovereign *George Margarson* a37
2 ch g Haafhd Royal Nashkova (Mujahid (USA))
8451[12]

Haajes *Paul Midgley* a76 85
9 ch g Indian Ridge Imelda (USA) (Manila (USA))
885[8] 1649[4] (1961) 2479[2] (3069) 3713[3] 3769[3] 4930[2] 6309[5] 6388[3] 6848[9]

Haarmonic *Richard Whitaker* 17
3 ch g Haafhd Abundant (Zafonic (USA))
2960[10]

Haatefina *Mark Usher* 70
3 b f Haatef(USA) Felona (Caerleon (USA))
2324[8] 3241[5] 3861[5] 4485[6] 4885[6] 6260[4]

Haatheq (USA) *A Al Raihe* a114 101
6 b h Seeking The Gold(USA) Alshadiyah (USA) (Danzig (USA))
659a[4] 958a[7] 1262a[2]

Haayil *John Gosden* a67 73
2 b c Halling(USA) Early Morning Rain (IRE) (Rock Of Gibraltar (IRE))
3044[5] 3581[8] 5941[3] *6401[4]* 6946[2]

Habdab *Richard Hannon Snr* a66 69
2 ch f Halling(USA) Dawnus (IRE) (Night Shift (USA))
3958[9] 5122[5] 5812[3] 6426[4] 7309[8] *7979[5]*

Habeshia *John Best* a79 75
3 ch g Muhtathir Lumiere Rouge (FR) (Indian Ridge)
72a[5] 1799a[7] 2557a[14] 3166a[7] 5245[7] *6521[13] 6748[5] 7187a[2] 7740[7]*

Hab Reeh *Ruth Carr* a71 65
5 gr g Diktat Asian Love (Petong)
(81) 142[6] 213[2] (326) (422) 645[5] 760[3] 971[6] 1351[9] 1757[11] 2162[4] 2319[3] 3026[5] (3197) 3630[2] 3934[5] 4051[4] 4582[6] 5139[12] 5583[7] 5876[10] 6053[7]

Hadaj *Ruth Carr* a92 92
4 b g Green Desert(USA) My Amalie (IRE) (Galileo (IRE))
2813[7] 4014[5] 4730[6] 5183[4] (5489) 6162[3] (6273) 6586[18] 6977[12]

Hadya (IRE) *James Tate* a70
2 b f Teofilo(IRE) Lafleur (IRE) (Grand Lodge (USA))
6999[2] 7779[4]

Haftohaf *Marco Botti* a83 76
4 b g Haafhd Piper's Ash (USA) (Royal Academy (USA))
133[3] 272[4] 518[2] 1363[3] 1720[12] *1878[3]*

Hagree (IRE) *Marco Botti* a74
2 b c Haatef(USA) Zuniga's Date (USA) (Diesis)
6807[2] ◆

Haikbidiac (IRE) *William Haggas* 102
2 b c Kodiac Silk Fan (IRE) (Unfuwain (USA))
(1820) 2370[3] 2863[3] 3424[11] 4528[4] (5679) 6293a[3] 7207[7]

Hail Bold Chief (USA) *Alan Swinbank* a19 59
6 b g Dynaformer(USA) Yanaseeni (USA) (Trempolino (USA))
1460[9] 2753[11] 5920[5] 6296[10] 6723[3] *8006[13]*

Hail Promenader (IRE) *Anthony Carson* a69 67
7 b g Acclamation Tribal Rite (Be My Native (USA))
376[4] 758[4] 1081[7] 1354[8] 1950[2] 2273[6] 2640[5] 3788[7] 4623[5] 5204[7] 6038[2] 6153[3] *6554[3]* 7124[6] (7511) 7639[6] 8042[6] (8199)

Hail Shower (IRE) *James Evans* a64 75
3 b f Red Clubs(IRE) Beat The Rain (Beat Hollow)
7993a[8] *8316[8]*

Hail To Princess *Patrick Chamings* a48 31
3 ch f Dr Fong(USA) Bob's Princess (Bob's Return (IRE))
2748[2] 3918[5]

Hail To The Chief (FR) *L Viel* a76 84
5 b c Shirocco(GER) Basse Besogne (IRE) (Pursuit Of Love)
125a[7]

Haines *Brett Johnson* 44
2 ch g Shirocco(GER) Spring Dream (IRE) (Kalanisi (IRE))
3290[10] 4439[7] 6460[7]

Hairy Rocket *William Haggas* a98 95
3 b f Pivotal Asaawir (Royal Applause)
1662[9] 2039[6] 2928[4] 3348[11]

Hajoum (IRE) *A Al Raihe* a94 91
7 b h Exceed And Excel(AUS) Blue Iris (Petong)
290a[9]

Hajras (IRE) *Mark Johnston* a73 109
4 b g Dubai Destination(USA) Nufoos (Zafonic (USA))
6620[6] 7012[7]

Hakuna Matata *Michael Dods* a81 83
6 b g Dubai Destination(USA) Green Song (FR) (Green Tune (USA))
1576[9] 2163[6] (2551) 2889[5] (3506) 3683[7] 4540[6] 5291[3] 5546[5] 6288[7] 6562[5] 7024[3]

Hala Hala (IRE) *Michael Bell* 78
2 b f Invincible Spirit(IRE) Galistic (IRE) (Galileo (IRE))
3664[14] (5330) (6041) 6839[10]

Haleo *William Muir* a38
2 ch g Halling(USA) Oatey (Master Willie)
8312[5]

Half A Billion (IRE) *Michael Dods* a85 87
4 b g Acclamation Amankila (IRE) (Revoque (IRE))
1599[4] 2239[9] (2441) 3441[7] 4812[3] 6586[27] *7080[4]*

Half A Crown (IRE) *Nick Kent* a74 74
8 b g Compton Place Penny Ha'Penny (Bishop Of Cashel)
2275[14] 2781[9] 5974[12] *7754[9]*

Halfsin (IRE) *Marco Botti* a94 88
5 b g Haafhd Firesteed (IRE) (Common Grounds)
2185[9] 3113[8] *3692[LFT]* 4435[4] 5008[5] *8007[2] (8150) 8327[10]*

Half To You *Kevin Ryan* a24
3 b f Haafhd After You (Pursuit Of Love)
590[6]

Half Turn *Luke Dace* a60 57
3 b c Pivotal Half Glance (Danehill (USA))
1012[3] 1199[3] 1384[4] 1712[14] 1874[4] 2129[7] 2919[4] *3495[10]*

Half Way *Henry Candy* a64 50
2 b g Haafhd Amhooj (Green Desert (USA))
3836[10] 4218[8] *5675[2]*

Halfwaytocootehill (IRE) *Ollie Pears* a51 55
3 b g Duke Of Marmalade(IRE) May Kiersey (IRE) (Sadler's Wells (USA))
1966[10] 2341[3] 2716[3] 3653[4] 3893[9] 4849[4] *6361[8]* 6717[2] *6964[3]* 7375[10]

Hallaga *William Jarvis* a56
2 ch f Halling(USA) Gayanula (USA) (Yonaguska (USA))
8175[9] 8328[7]

Hallbeck *Henry Candy* 53
2 ch f Halling(USA) Goslar (In The Wings)
5812[7]

Hallelujah *James Fanshawe* a83 107
5 b f Avonbridge My Golly (Mozart (IRE))
(2444) ◆ 3373[4] 3784[3] (6235) 7208[3] 7821[10]

Halling Dancer *Lee Carter* a78 81
4 b g Halling(USA) Ballet Ballon (USA) (Rahy (USA))
1673[14] *2085[3] 2580[6] 2981[7]* (3575) 3974[8] 4908[11] 5825[7] 7071[8]

Hallingham *Jonathan Portman* 68
3 b g Halling(USA) In Luck (In The Wings)
2938[12] 3618[6] 3989[6] 4961[11] 6491[5] 7248[6]

Halling River (IRE) *M Weiss* a57 87
6 ch g Halling(USA) Cunas (USA) (Irish River (FR))
514a[6] 701a[8]

Halling's Quest *Hughie Morrison* a96 82
4 b g Halling(USA) Capriolla (In The Wings)
3960[8] 5895[6] ◆

Halling's Treasure *Andrew Balding* a81 75
3 ch g Halling(USA) Perfect Treasure (IRE) (Night Shift (USA))
2321[13] 2605[6] 3021[7] 3618[2] 4305[4] *5392[2]* ◆ 5514[8] *(6557)*

Halling's Wish *John Best* a57 54
3 br g Halling(USA) Fair View (GER) (Dashing Blade)
2017[8] 2800[5] *3497[3]* 4417[6] 5500[5]

Halljoy (IRE) *Clive Brittain* 93
2 b f Halling(USA) Tithcar (Cadeaux Genereux)
4432[3] 5003[3] 5737[3] 6350[5] 6645[7]

Hallouella *James Tate* a59
2 ch f Halling(USA) Louella (USA) (El Gran Senor (USA))
7513[6]

Halloween Chope (FR) *D Prod'Homme* a75 80
3 ch f Soave(GER) Halloween Star (FR) (Wagon Master (FR))
647a[2]

Halloween Moon *James Bethell* 25
2 b g Halling(USA) Mamounia (IRE) (Green Desert (USA))
3724[12] 5577[12] 6206[11]

Hallstatt (IRE) *John Mackie* a73 74
7 ch g Halling(USA) Last Resort (Lahib (USA))
1045[3] 1218[7] 1434[7] (1794) (2269) 2648[4] 3133[3] 3807[4] 4512[5] *4838[5]*

Hal Of A Lover *Lisa Williamson* a53 32
5 b g Halling(USA) Latent Lover (IRE) (In The Wings)
3595[12] 6899[12]

Hamble *Julia Feilden* a40 65
4 b g Librettist(USA) Time For Tea (IRE) (Imperial Frontier (USA))
2134[4] 2640[6] (3534) 5204[6] 5622[3] 6702[4] 7455[6] *7981[11]*

Hamelin (IRE) *Lady Cecil* a83 100
3 b c Cape Cross(IRE) Love Divine (Diesis)
1679[7] ◆ 2198[5] *(6402)* (7105) ◆

Hamilton Hill *Bernard Llewellyn* a51 76
6 b g Groom Dancer(USA) Loriner's Lass (Saddlers' Hall (IRE))
6490[7]

Hamis Al Bin (IRE) *Milton Bradley* a71 66
4 b g Acclamation Paimpolaise (IRE) (Priolo (USA))
1950[10] 2780[9] 3246[11] 3325[4] (3660) 4197[3] 4517[5] *4840[6]* 5373[10] 6156[5] *6753[4] 6980[6]* 7323[6] *7905[5] 8413[2]*

Hamish McGonagall *Tim Easterby* 116
8 b g Namid Anatase (Danehill (USA))
1249[5] 2909a[DSQ] 3334[15] 5726[4]

Hamla *Mark Johnston* a64 39
3 b f Cape Cross(IRE) High Days (IRE) (Hennessy (USA))
590[2] 685[8] 1177[2] 3313[4] 4116[3]

Hammerfest *J E Hammond* a88 110
6 b g Fantastic Light(USA) Bathilde (IRE) (Generous (IRE))
3559[8] 5575a[5]

Hammer Shaft (IRE) *Amy Weaver* a45
3 b g Excellent Art Delicacy (IRE) (Danehill Dancer (IRE))
228[9] 491[7]

Hamoody (USA) *David Nicholls* a91 86
9 ch g Johannesburg(USA) Northern Gulch (USA) (Gulch (USA))
(379) 586[2] 727[2] 880[4] (1065) (1451) 1964[4] 2914[7] (3713) (4619) 4860[14] 5917[2] 6205[5] 6583[9] *(8177)*

Hamza (IRE) *Kevin Ryan* 113
4 b g Amadeus Wolf Lady Shanghai (IRE) (Alhaarth (IRE))
1537[4] (2046) ◆ (2768) 4298[8] 4527[2] 5320a[2] 5772a[2] 6193[7] 6623[15] 7054a[3]

Hanalei Bay (IRE) *Keith Dalgleish* a71 67
3 b c Tamayuz Genial Jenny (IRE) (Danehill (USA))
4200[7] 4991[4] 5581[5] 5919[2] 6084[2] 6464[6] 6587[3] 6905[2] 6921[6] *7515[2] 7669[2] (8185)*

Handazan (IRE) *Alan King* a56 101
4 b g Nayef(USA) Handaza (IRE) (Be My Guest (USA))
1484[3] 1920[6]

Hand Grenade (IRE) *Eve Johnson Houghton* 67
3 b f Majestic Missile(IRE) Felin Gruvy (IRE) (Tagula (IRE))
3508[2] 3915[2] 4627[3] 4911[2] 5647[P]

Handheld *Julia Feilden* a74 80
6 ch g Observatory(USA) Kid Gloves (In The Wings)
73[4] 161[5] 1292[3] *1466[4]* (2273) 3534[8] (7132) 7661[2]

Hand In Glove *Robert Cowell* a67 56
3 ch f Kyllachy Cape Trafalgar (IRE) (Cape Cross (IRE))
(549) 710[9] 2965[2] 4390[6] *6397[7]*

Handiwork *Michael Bell* a64 69
3 ch g Motivator Spinning Top (Alzao (USA))
814[5] 1326[2] 1425[2] 2312[4] 2716[2] 7278[4]

Hands Of Time *Richard Hannon Snr* a70 72
3 b c Pivotal Virtuous (Exit To Nowhere (USA))
1423[7] 1928[7]

Handsome King *J R Jenkins* a67 65
6 ch g Lucky Story(USA) Samar Qand (Selkirk (USA))
1184[7]

Handsome Man (IRE) *Saeed bin Suroor* 104
4 ch g Nayef(USA) Danceabout (Shareef Dancer (USA))
1689[2] 3115[2] 3824[17] 5993[3]

Handsome Mike (USA) *Doug O'Neill* a111 104
4 bb c Scat Daddy(USA) Classic Strike (USA) (Smart Strike (CAN))
7710a[8]

Handsome Molly *David Elsworth* a55
4 b f Halling(USA) However (IRE) (Hector Protector (USA))
140[4] 343[3] 579[10] 722[9]

Handsome Ransom *David O'Meara* a80 88
4 b g Red Ransom(USA) Maid For The Hills (Indian Ridge)
1753[9] 2923[6] 4810[12] (5712) 6165[4]

Handsome Stranger (IRE) *Alan Bailey* a66 66
3 ch g Tamayuz Just Special (Cadeaux Genereux)
122[6] 134[5] 427[4] 1982[2] 2528[3] 2737[7] 3014[5] (3219) *3497[7]* 3785[3] 4171[3] 4405[3] *5072[6] 5961[4]* (6260) 6533[4] 6612[4] 6971[5] 7169[10]

Hands Up (IRE) *William Knight* a58 74
2 b c Bushranger(IRE) Christa Maria (Alhaarth (IRE))
5718[4] 6954[9] *7302[9]* 7606[4]

Handwoven (IRE) *Mark Johnston* a74 72
2 b g Shamardal(USA) Seamstress (IRE) (Barathea (IRE))
2645[7] 2925[4] 3565[6] 4232[4] 4703[6] 5175[2] 5703[2] 6628[9] *7300[3] 7626[3]*

Hanga Roa (IRE) *Gary Moore* a55 13
3 b g Hannouma(IRE) Fine And Mellow (FR) (Lando (GER))
114[3] 350[7] 527[8] 1879[8] 7331[9]

Hank Schrader *John Davies* 49
2 b g Avonbridge Swift Baba (USA) (Deerhound (USA))
7818[7]

Hanky Panky (IRE) *A P O'Brien* 100
3 ch f Galileo(IRE) Mariah's Storm (USA) (Rahy (USA))
2689a[7] 3263a[3] 3845a[8] 3964a[6] 4647a[4] 5688a[5] 6023a[6]

Hannaford (AUS) *Robbie Laing* 88
4 ch g Trotamondo(CHI) Best Offer (AUS) (Marscay (AUS))
7417a[4]

Hannah Louise (IRE) *Olivia Maylam* a41
2 b f Iffraaj Answer Do (Groom Dancer (USA))
4630[3] 5229[3] 5891[13] 8016[6]

Hannahs Turn *Chris Dwyer* a93 48
3 b f Dubai Destination(USA) Fontaine House (Pyramus (USA))
(598) 848[3] (985) (1073) (1204) ◆ 1892[9] 2521[10] 4145[8] 6969[5] 7164[4] 7381[6] 7663[3] (7958) 8052[4] 8319[3]

Hannibal Hayes (USA) *M Al Muhairi* a65 59
4 ch c Elusive Quality(USA) Top Ten List (CAN) (Bold Executive (CAN))
394a[5]

Hanno (USA) *Ed Dunlop* a68 67
2 b c Henrythenavigator(USA) Archstone (USA) (Arch (USA))
5718[8] 7971[3]

Hanoverian Baron *Tony Newcombe* a93 99
8 b g Green Desert(USA) Josh's Pearl (IRE) (Sadler's Wells (USA))
189[2] (926) 1242[8] 2427[2] 3559[14] 4060[7] ◆ 5766[12] 6394[7] 7174[3]

Hanseatic *John Gosden* a79 97
4 b c Galileo(IRE) Insinuate (USA) (Mr Prospector (USA))
1883[2] (2256)

Hansinger (IRE) *Cathrine Erichsen* a72 96
8 b g Namid Whistfilly (First Trump)
4936a[5]

Hanzada (USA) *Ed Dunlop* a81 83
3 bb f Arch(USA) Chocolate Mauk (USA) (Cozzene (USA))
1908[3] 2429[6] 2850[8] 6134[2] 6611[3]

Happy Clappy (IRE) *Michael Bell* 30
2 b c Art Connoisseur(IRE) Narmeen (Royal Applause)
4347[8]

Happy Dubai (IRE) *A Al Raihe* a108 107
6 ch h Indian Ridge Gentle Wind (USA) (Gentlemen (ARG))
150a[5] 244a[11]

Happy Families *Heather Main* a70 72
3 b f Singspiel(IRE) One Of The Family (Alzao (USA))
3237[10] 4223[5] 4940[2] 5606[6] 6557[5] 7305[3] 8089[8]

Happy Few *R H Huayas* 45
5 b g Ballingarry(IRE) Ventolera (FR) (Gulch (USA))
2380a[7]

Happy Monster (FR) *M Boutin* a82 77
5 b g Xaar Armama (Linamix (FR))
960a[0] 6421a[11]

Happy Trails (AUS) *Byron Cozamanis* 117
6 ch g Good Journey(USA) Madame Flurry (AUS) (Perugino (USA))
7556a[2]

Happy Valley (ARG) *Mlle H Mennessier* a70 76
7 gr g Alphabet Soup(USA) Perfect Valley (BRZ) (Clackson (BRZ))
4467a[13]

Harare *Karen Tutty* a60 68
12 b g Bahhare(USA) Springs Eternal (Salse (USA))
1572[10] 2785[6] 2977[9] 3287[5]

Harasiya (IRE) *John M Oxx* 108
3 br f Pivotal Hazariya (IRE) (Xaar)
2689a[12] 3870a[4]

Harbin (IRE) *Adrian McGuinness* 44
3 gr g Verglas(IRE) Rainbow City (IRE) (Rainbow Quest (USA))
7151[9]

Harbinger Lass *Mick Channon* a64 77
3 b f Thousand Words Penang Cry (Barathea (IRE))
1671[2] 1845[3] 2148[9] 2586[11] 3821[2] 4157[8] (5010) 5694[6] 6357[2] 6657[7] 7027[6]

Harbour Captain (IRE) *Jo Hughes* a43 75
3 ch g Captain Rio English Harbour (Sabrehill (USA))
1072[8] 1450[3] 1750[3] (2363) 2994[5] 3678[3] (4193) (4771) 5096[5] 6548[11] 6664[9]

Harbour Light (DEN) *Soren Jensen*
2 gr f Academy Award(IRE) Lady Clementine (DEN) (Richard Of York)
(6452a)

Harbour Of Hope (GER) *H-A Pantall* 95
3 b f Monsun(GER) Hanami (Hernando (FR))
7891a[6]

Hard Core Debt *Brian Ellison* 81
3 b g Muhtathir Al Durrah (USA) (Darshaan)
2374a[18] 4586[2] 4729[6]

Hard Divorce (USA) *David Brown* a72 58
2 b c Hard Spun(USA) Divorce Settlement (USA) (Stormin Fever (USA))
6330[7] (6656)

Hard Walnut (IRE) *Olly Stevens* a80 69
3 b f Cape Cross(IRE) Yaria (IRE) (Danehill (USA))
185[2] (509) 730[4] 879[2] (1345) 2264[8] 2983[5] 3691[7]

Hard Work (IRE) *Adam Wyrzyk*
4 b c Refuse To Bend(IRE) Blue Banner (IRE) (Grand Lodge (USA))
1564a[9]

Hardy Blue (IRE) *Danielle McCormick* a68 67
3 b f Red Clubs(IRE) Alexander Wonder (IRE) (Redback)
3025[1] 3762[1] 3900[6] 4070[6] 5007[10] 5990[8]

Hardy Plume *Denis Coakley* a33 56
4 ch g Manduro(GER) Macleya (GER) (Winged Love (IRE))
6986[10]

Hardy Red (IRE) *Jamie Osborne* a71 75
3 b g Mujadil(USA) Salonga (IRE) (Shinko Forest (IRE))
38[4] 216[4] 468[4]

Harem Lady (FR) *D Smaga* a92 108
4 b f Teofilo(IRE) Luminosity (Sillery (USA))
1895a[2] 2644a[8] 3165a[3] 4421a[9] 5574a[4]

Hares Grove (IRE) *Richard Price* 23
4 ch g Kheleyf(USA) Attribute (Warning)
1078[7] 1291[8]

Harlestone Wood *Peter Hedger* a73 84
4 b g Olden Times Harlestone Lady (Shaamit (IRE))
157[2] 397[3] 637[3]

Harmonic Note *F-H Graffard* a93 85
3 b f Nayef(USA) Musical Key (Key Of Luck (USA))
1557a[6] 2586[3] 3460[11] 3845a[13] 8440a[7]

Harpers Ruby *Simon Griffiths* a23
3 b f Byron La Belle Katherine (USA) (Lyphard (USA))
6940[9] 7884[5] 8070[6]

Harrison George (IRE) *P J O'Gorman* a95 105
8 b g Danetime(IRE) Dry Lightning (Shareef Dancer (USA))
947[5] 1245[3] 1537[8] 1726[4] ◆ 2266[2] 2444[5] 2618[4] 2937[6] 3096[11] (3249) (3720) 6190[2] 6621[17] 7208[13] 7527[3] 7856[4]

Harrison's Cave *Chris Grant* a66 100
5 b g Galileo(IRE) Sitara (Salse (USA))
2402[11] 2855[8] 3726[9] 4759[5] 5640[4] 7280[10] 7597[7]

Harris Tweed *William Haggas* a106 118
6 b g Hernando(FR) Frog (Akarad (FR))
2443[2] 3830[3] (4857) (5741) 7363[2]

Harrogate Fair *Michael Squance* a70 61
3 b g Trade Fair Starbeck (IRE) (Spectrum (IRE))
1433[5] 1742[2] 2129[8] 2623[4] 2779[3] ◆ 6138[4] 6527[5] 6753[2] (7263) 7432[12]

Harry Bosch *Brian Meehan* a67 81
3 b g Kyllachy Fen Guest (Woodborough (USA))
1612[10] 1900[5] 2324[3] (2935) 3633[2] 5004[8]

Harry Buckle *Philip McBride* a92 87
4 ch g Byron Native Ring (FR) (Bering)
(32) (318) 496[4] (691) 777[8] 4301[10] 5008[3] 5542[4] 6211[7] 6537[4] 7131[8]

Harry Hunt *Graeme McPherson* a85 91
6 b g Bertolini(USA) Qasirah (IRE) (Machiavellian (USA))
40[3] (7217)

Harry's Summer (USA) *Nick Littmoden* a57
2 bb c Roman Ruler(USA) Magnificent Lady (USA) (Cherokee Run (USA))
8213[7] 8451[6]

Harry Trotter (IRE) *David Marnane* a90 94
4 b g Kodiac Defined Feature (IRE) (Nabeel Dancer (USA))
679a[4] 3846a[15]

Hartford Starts (IRE) *Ian McInnes* 25
3 b g Chineur(FR) Desert Design (Desert King (IRE))
1044[9] 1272[7] 1575[5] 2341[11]

Hartforth *Donald Whillans* a48 46
5 ch g Haafhd St Edith (IRE) (Desert King (IRE))
53[10] 3727[12] 4614[6]

Harting Hill *Violet M Jordan* a72 24
8 b g Mujahid(USA) Mossy Rose (King Of Spain)
4623[13]

Hartlebury *James Bethell* a44 51
3 ch g Sakhee's Secret Marakabei (Hernando (FR))
4118[7] 4667[8] 7201[11] 7922[7] 8149[10]

Hartnell *Mark Johnston* 102
2 b c Authorized(IRE) Debonnaire (Anabaa (USA))
4731[9] 5968[2] (6430) 6955[2] (7492) (7694) 7828a[3]

Hartwright *Michael Bell* a74 81
3 b g Exceed And Excel(AUS) All For Laura (Cadeaux Genereux)
(1524) 1935[7] (2544) 2756[3] 4529[5] 5477[5] 6410[2] 6867[6] (7443)

Harvard N Yale (USA) *Jeremy Noseda* a89 93
4 ch c Smart Strike(CAN) Compete (USA) (El Prado (IRE))
2251[3] ◆ 2648[8] 3960[6]

Harvest (GER) *K Klein*
6 br m Sholokhov(IRE) Holita (GER) (Lomitas)
609a[6]

Harvest Mist (IRE) *Shaun Lycett* a63 53
5 ch f Captain Rio Thaw (Cadeaux Genereux)
108[3] 312[4] (409) 655[5] 1020[2] 1214[5] 2345[4] (7353) 7808[6] 8163[2] 8278[4]

Harvey's Hope *Keith Reveley* 71
7 b g Sinndar(IRE) Ancara (Dancing Brave (USA))
1279[2] 5137[8] 5560[2]

Harwoods Star (IRE) *Amanda Perrett* a71 74
3 b g Danehill Dancer(IRE) Showbiz (IRE) (Sadler's Wells (USA))
2192[8] 3062[9] 6521[6] 6743[11] 7249[4] 8072[8]

Harwoods Volante (IRE) *Amanda Perrett* a83 77
2 ch g Kheleyf(USA) Semiquaver (IRE) (Mark Of Esteem (IRE))
3695[2] (4773) 5372[4] 6640[7] (8261) 8442[4]

Hasanan *Clive Brittain* a77 81
3 b f Rail Link Dance Solo (Sadler's Wells (USA))
1091[5]

Hasbah (IRE) *Peter Chapple-Hyam* a47 68
3 b f Cape Cross(IRE) Gimasha (Cadeaux Genereux)
1122[4] 2226[2] 3508[4]

Hashanar (IRE) *M Weiss*
5 b c Oratorio(IRE) Third Dimension (FR) (Suave Dancer (USA))
609a[7]

Hasheem *Roger Varian* 93
3 ch g New Approach(IRE) Masaafat (Act One)
2151[8] (2538) 2878[3] 3526[7]

Hasna (FR) *P Bary* a83 100
4 ch f American Post Harriet (FR) (Mizoram (USA))
2969a[4] 6714a[12]

Hasopop (IRE) *Marco Botti* a94 109
3 b g Haatef(USA) Convenience (IRE) (Ela-Mana-Mou)
1033[5] 1668[3] ◆ 1921[3] (2452) 2843[3] 3348[6] 5538[9] 6183[3] 6623[18] (7247)

Hassle (IRE) *Clive Cox* 87
4 b g Montjeu(IRE) Canterbury Lace (USA) (Danehill (USA))
3417[4] 4590[2] 5190[4] 6280[2] (6696) 7072[3]

Hasta La Vista *Mark Johnston* a41 47
2 b f Hernando(FR) Sterling Sound (USA) (Street Cry (IRE))
5516[7] 6949[9] 7332[8] 7755[12] 7944[5] 8274[5] 8434[7]

Haswell (SPA) *M Delcher Sanchez* 55
2 b f Caradak(IRE) Malinche (Hernando (FR))
2558a[7] 5213a[2]

Hatch Hall *Joseph G Murphy* 62
2 b g Sleeping Indian Speech (Red Ransom (USA))
7050a[9]

Hatha Hooh *Richard Hannon Snr* 81
2 b c Exceed And Excel(AUS) Mystery Ocean (Dr Fong (USA))
2194[6] 2925[3] (3035) 5028[5] 5438[2]

Hats Off *John Best* a54 36
3 b g Royal Applause Miriam (Forzando)
31[8] 207[9] 2962[12] 3495[11] 4405[10]

Hatta Stream (IRE) *Lydia Pearce* a83 70
7 b g Oasis Dream Rubies From Burma (USA) (Forty Niner (USA))
582[9] 740[2] 822[7] 1748[7] 2596[8] 3172[10] 4636[9]

Hatti (IRE) *Micky Hammond* 65
2 gr f Haatef(USA) Common Charisma (IRE) (Highest Honor (FR))
3217[3] 3324[5] 4177[2] 4422[2] 4847[7] (5243) 5717[6] 5829[3] 6233[6] (6755)

Hattie Jacques *Mick Channon* a22 66
3 b f Sixties Icon Funny Girl (IRE) (Darshaan)
3278[6] 3641[7] 4404[5] 4939[5] (5500) 6363[8] 7395[3]

Havana (USA) *Todd Pletcher* a115
2 rg c Dunkirk(USA) Missy Turtle (USA) (Kyle's Our Man (USA))
7711a[2]

Havana Beat (IRE) *Andrew Balding* 103
3 b g Teofilo(IRE) Sweet Home Alabama (IRE) (Desert Prince (IRE))
1636[4] 2187[3] 3523[5] 4211[3] 4874[7] 6393[8]

Havana Cooler (IRE) *Luca Cumani* 102
3 ch c Hurricane Run(IRE) Unquenchable (USA) (Kingmambo (USA))
(1845) (4301) ◆ 4984[3] 5764[3]

Havana Gold (IRE) *Richard Hannon Snr* 113
3 b c Teofilo(IRE) Jessica's Dream (IRE) (Desert Style (IRE))
1638[2] 2298a[5] 2677a[4] (3876a) 5462a[5]

Have A Great Day (IRE) *A Oliver* a77 71
2 b c Kodiac Collada (IRE) (Desert Prince (IRE))
8368[3]

Havelock (USA) *Darrin Miller* a112 112
6 b g Great Notion(USA) Piconeach (NZ) (Spectacular Love (USA))
3557[11] 4298[11] 7710a[10]

Havelovewilltravel (IRE) *Jeremy Noseda* a83
3 b f Holy Roman Emperor(IRE) Strategy (Machiavellian (USA))
(6748) 7437[2] ◆ (7741) ◆ 7876[4]

Haverstock *Mark Johnston* a62 63
3 b g New Approach(IRE) Endorsement (Warning)
803[3] 1064[6]

Having A Ball *Geoffrey Deacon* a66 54
9 b g Mark Of Esteem(IRE) All Smiles (Halling (USA))
112[4] 789[5] 896[4] 978[2] 1298[5] 2159[7] 2533[5] 3399[5] 3656[5] 6283[3] 6952[5] 8121[13]

Hawaiian Dream (IRE) *Roger Teal* a59 53
3 b f Catcher In The Rye(IRE) Polynesian Goddess (IRE) (Salmon Leap (USA))
332[5] 651[3] 904[3] 1321[2] 4209[4] 4442[6] 5135[12] 6406[5]

Hawaiian Freeze *John Stimpson* a45 51
4 b f Avonbridge Autumn Affair (Lugana Beach)
725[3] 825[10] 900[6] 1149[6] 1951[14] 3138[7] (3314) 3656[6] 4195[4] 5002[8] 5633[5] 6044[4] 6782[6] 7351[6] 7440[9] 8448[8]

Hawdyerwheesht *Jim Goldie* a76 85
5 b g Librettist(USA) Rapsgate (IRE) (Mozart (IRE))
1251[5] 2316[2] 2973[6] 3287[2] (4110) (4447) 5237[5] 5706[14] 6626[4] ◆ 6876[3] 7239[2]

Hawker *Charlie Appleby* a88
3 ch g Street Cry(IRE) Dunnes River (USA) (Danzig (USA))
6366[3] ◆ 6738[2] (7864)

Hawkeyethenoo (IRE) *Jim Goldie* a108 116
7 b g Hawk Wing(USA) Stardance (USA) (Rahy (USA))
1637[4] 2368[4] 3557[6] ◆ 3831[5] 4744[15] 4986[8] 6193[4] 6623[17] 7364[8] 7527[2] 7928[4] 8334[2]

Hawk High (IRE) *Tim Easterby* 88
3 b g High Chaparral(IRE) Septembers Hawk (IRE) (Machiavellian (USA))
(2833) 3502[4] 3982[3] ◆ (4480) 5223[2] 5764[7] 6793[5]

Hawk Moth (IRE) *John Spearing* a72 67
5 b g Hawk Wing(USA) Sasimoto (USA) (Saratoga Six (USA))
218[4] 1303[13] 3052[8] 3429[4] 3656[9] 4424[2] (4752) 5177[11] 5607[4] 7092[5] 7321[11]

Hawk Mountain (UAE) *John Quinn* a22 84
8 b g Halling(USA) Friendly (USA) (Lear Fan (USA))
2118[7] ◆ 3085[6] (4969) 5640[2] 6237[5] 6585[6] 7210[11] 7947[8]

Hawkspur (AUS) *Chris Waller* 116
4 ch g Purrealist(AUS) Mollyhawk (AUS) (Catbird (AUS))
7392a[7] 7761a[20]

Hawsies Dream *Tracy Waggott* a55 33
3 ch f Dubawi(IRE) Petong's Pet (Petong)
1050[5] 1073[4] 1349[8] 1427[4] 1888[5] 1906[6] 2756[13]

Haya Kan (FR) *Mme L Audon* 77
3 b c American Post Haya Samma (IRE) (Pivotal)
1756a[5] 2434a[4] 2907a[18]

Haya Landa (FR) *Mme L Audon* a100 112
5 b f Lando(GER) Haya Samma (IRE) (Pivotal)
1420a[5] 1870a[7] 2184a[2] 2908a[2] 3615a[3] 5807a[6] 6449a[6] 7058a[17]

Hay Chewed (IRE) *Peter Chapple-Hyam* 94
2 b f Camacho Titian Saga (IRE) (Titus Livius (FR))
2712[3] ◆ 3217[2] (4177) (4965) 7011[9]

Hay Dude *K R Burke* a91 108
3 ch c Dubawi(IRE) Inaminute (IRE) (Spectrum (IRE))
1246[2] 1668[6] (2259) 2857[4] 3563[3] (5182) 5728[5] 6191[2] 7116a[3] 7685a[6]

Hayek *Tim Easterby* a75 81
6 b g Royal Applause Salagama (IRE) (Alzao (USA))
1442[7] 1723[7] 2081[8] 3193[7] 3683[13] 4245[11] 4482[6] 5427[7] 6600[11]

Haylaman (IRE) *David Simcock* a88 97
5 b g Diamond Green(FR) Schonbein (IRE) (Persian Heights)
1751[3] ◆ 2191[2] 2422[5] 3094[3] (3607) 3838[4] 4060[12] 4798[2] 5259[5] 6741[4]

Hayley *Jim Goldie* 28
3 b f Halling(USA) Gargoyle Girl (Be My Chief (USA))
1274[5] 2799[8] 3281[11] 4474[6] 4824[8] 5334[11] 6049[10]

Haymarket *Michael Bell* a70 77
4 b g Singspiel(IRE) Quickstyx (Night Shift (USA))
5337[8] 5793[4] (6722)

Haywain *Kevin Ryan* a75 68
4 b g Peintre Celebre(USA) Shall We Dance (Rambo Dancer (CAN))
219[8] 410[4] 546[2] ◆ 812[4] 1209[3] 1800[9] 2757[4] 2949[4]

Hayyona *Mick Channon* 59
3 b f Multiplex Shemriyna (IRE) (King Of Kings (IRE))
1821[4]

Hazard Warning (IRE) *Tim Easterby* a67 29
3 b c Haatef(USA) Hazardous (Night Shift (USA))
(207) ◆ 598[3] (848) (923) 1433[6] 1935[10] 2329[6]

Hazariban (IRE) *Seamus Fahey* a62 62
4 b g Kahyasi Hazarista (IRE) (Barathea (IRE))
8229[3]

Hazaz (IRE) *M Al Muhairi* a71 59
4 b c Dubawi(IRE) Treble Seven (USA) (Fusaichi Pegasus (USA))
290a[15] 7679a[5]

Hazelrigg (IRE) *Tim Easterby* a68 95
8 b g Namid Emma's Star (ITY) (Darshaan)
2007[15] 2396[13] 2461[9] 4263[13] 5011[11] 5108[13] 5901[8] 6309[7] (6583) 6920[9] 7313[10]

Hazy Glow (IRE) *D K Weld* a89 69
3 b f Invincible Spirit(IRE) Genuine Charm (IRE) (Sadler's Wells (USA))
2374a[15]

Hazzaat (IRE) *Gary Harrison* a65 72
3 ch g Iffraaj Hurricane Irene (IRE) (Green Desert (USA))
1829[6] 2874[9] 5855[8] 6522[12] 7899[2] 8331[13]

Hazza The Jazza *Richard Guest* a62 67
3 br g Jeremy(USA) Zagaleta (Sri Pekan (USA))
(8) 325[3] 550[5] 2308[13] 3630[3] 3949[6] 4113[3] 4499[5] 4967[2] 5150[2] 5487[3] 5878[4] 6181[7] 6368[6] 6921[9] 7886[9] 8042[14]

Heading North *Richard Hannon Snr* a76 96
3 b f Teofilo(IRE) Round The Cape (Cape Cross (IRE))
1641[3] 1933[2] 2586[2] 3240[8] 3834[3]

Heading To First *Paddy Butler* a47 51
6 b g Sulamani(IRE) Bahirah (Ashkalani (IRE))
522[11] 2332[4] 2875[8] 3151[5] 3637[6]

Headline News (IRE) *Rae Guest* a71 93
4 ch f Peintre Celebre(USA) Donnelly's Hollow (IRE) (Docksider (USA))
(6358) 7424[4] 7659[5]

Headlong (IRE) *Brian Meehan* a47 67
2 gr g Aussie Rules(USA) Trois Graces (USA) (Alysheba (USA))
3536[5] 4379[9] 4716[3] 7467[4]

Head Of Steam (USA) *Amanda Perrett* a96 96
6 ch g Mizzen Mast(USA) Summer Mist (USA) (Miswaki (USA))
1542[4] 2013[9] (2585) 3697[4] 4744[17] 4859[9] 5285[4] 5738[16] 6164[4] 6840[9] 7464[2]

Head Space (IRE) *Ruth Carr* a82 100
5 b g Invincible Spirit(IRE) Danzelline (Danzero (AUS))
1607[3] 1720[8] 2150[11] 2460[11] 2834[6] 3249[4] 3561[6] 3811[3] 3981[2] 4138[3] (4560) 5009[6] (5294) 5544[7] 5851[3] 6273[6] 6831[14]

Headstight (IRE) *Paul Midgley* a47 54
4 b f Holy Roman Emperor(IRE) Regal Star (Sadler's Wells (USA))
1276[6] 1578[3] 2276[2] 3026[4] 4009[4] 4371[6] 5139[9] 5989[4] 6469[8] 6878[4] 7101[8]

Heart Beat Song *James Moffatt* a48 42
5 b g Cape Cross(IRE) Polly Perkins (IRE) (Pivotal)
1887[5] 2977[4] 5864[11] 6339[10]

Heart Focus (IRE) *J S Bolger* 99
2 br f Intense Focus(USA) Have A Heart (IRE) (Daggers Drawn (USA))
2944a[2] 3522[4] 3868a[2] 4462a[4]

Heartily (IRE) *Charlie Appleby* 44
2 b f Dubawi(IRE) Heart's Content (IRE) (Daylami (IRE))
5516[6] 6281[11]

Heart Of Dubai (USA) *Micky Hammond* a69 52
8 b g Outofthebox(USA) Diablo's Blend (USA) (Diablo (USA))
2120[8] 3363[5]

Hearts And Minds (IRE) *Braem Horse Racing Sprl* a66 72
4 b g Clodovil(IRE) Heart's Desire (IRE) (Royal Applause)
5735a[8]

Heartsong (IRE) *John Gallagher* a66 88
4 b f Kheleyf(USA) Semiquaver (IRE) (Mark Of Esteem (IRE))
1287[6] 2561[6] 2848[9] 3371[12] 4165[10] 6381[6] 7432[7]

Heartstrings *Mick Channon* 73
2 b f Invincible Spirit(IRE) Strings (Unfuwain (USA))
3986[2] 4702[16]

Heavenly *Jeremy Noseda* 54
2 ch f Pivotal Celeste (Green Desert (USA))
5003[9] 6974[10]

Heavenly Prospect *William Muir* 43
3 b f Authorized(IRE) Bread Of Heaven (Machiavellian (USA))
2389[10] 3272[P]

Heavenly Sound *Marco Botti* a78 68
3 b f Street Cry(IRE) Helena Molony (IRE) (Sadler's Wells (USA))
(1371) 6832[5]

Heavens Edge *Christopher Mason* 81
2 b f Royal Applause Elidore (Danetime (IRE))
1946[8] 2411[8] (5174)

Heavens Eyes (IRE) *Pat Murphy* a39
2 b f Oasis Dream Snowtime (IRE) (Galileo (IRE))
7934[7]

Heaven's Guest (IRE) *Richard Fahey* 109
3 b g Dark Angel(IRE) Bakewell Tart (IRE) (Tagula (IRE))
1112[2] ◆ 1625[7] (2408) (2844) 3348[4] (4255) 4986[11] 5738[14] 6623[4] (7014) 7364[7]

Heavy Metal *Mark Johnston* 110
3 b g Exceed And Excel(AUS) Rock Opera (SAF) (Lecture (USA))
1621[9] 2415[8] 3114[9] 3348[19] 3803[9] 4285[10] 4767[10] 5260[5] 5510[6] 6650[16]

He Be Fire N Ice (USA) *John W Sadler* a81 112
5 rg c Unusual Heat(USA) Deputy Tombe (USA) (Deputy Commander (USA))
7714a[8]

Hebridean Princess (IRE) *Paul Midgley* 14
2 b f Rock Of Gibraltar(IRE) Jacaranda Ridge (Indian Ridge)
1565[5] 2474[8]

Hecate (IRE) *J E Pease* a77 81
6 b m Act One Turn To Black (USA) (Alleged (USA))
6421a[9]

Hectomare (IRE) *J-C Rouget* 96
4 b g Hurricane Run(IRE) Overruled (IRE) (Last Tycoon)
7142a[10]

Hector's Chance *Heather Main* a79 72
4 ch g Byron Fleur A Lay (USA) (Mr Greeley (USA))
2982[3] (3580) 3854[4] 4831[3] (5479) 5793[3] 6359[2] 7132[11] 7651[3] 7840[4]

Hector Spectre (IRE) *Nikki Evans* a15 64
7 gr g Verglas(IRE) Halicardia (Halling (USA))
99[10]

Heddwyn (IRE) *Marcus Tregoning* a96 66
6 b g Bahri(USA) Penny Rouge (IRE) (Pennekamp (USA))
4854[11] 5742[9] ◆

Hedge End (IRE) *Richard Hannon Snr* a79 64
2 gr f Verglas(IRE) Trilemma (Slip Anchor)
1421[6] (1946) 2414[5] 5951[6] 6322[5] (6924) (7110) 7782[8] (8147)

Hedy *Mick Channon* a58 64
2 ch f Winker Watson Jollyhockeysticks (Fantastic Light (USA))
1156[3] 1680[7] 2067[2] 2344[2]

Heeraat (IRE) *William Haggas* a86 116
4 b c Dark Angel(IRE) Thawrah (IRE) (Green Desert (USA))
(1672) ◆ 2019[4] 2768[2] 3420[6] 4311[2] (4527) 6193[12] 7013[4]

Heezararity *Jonathan Geake* a71 74
5 b g Librettist(USA) Extremely Rare (IRE) (Mark Of Esteem (IRE))
4591[2] 6080[4] 6358[10] (8141) 8314[8]

Hefner (IRE) *William Jarvis* a89 95
4 b g Tagula(IRE) Classic Style (IRE) (Desert Style (IRE))
2210[3] 2841[6] 3538[5] 4744[20] 6004[5] 6801[7] 7211[4] (7499)

Heho *Sir Michael Stoute* a54
2 b f Dansili Nitya (FR) (Indian Ridge)
6690[8]

Heidi's Delight (IRE) *Ann Duffield* a49 34
4 b f Red Clubs(IRE) Alexander Confranc (IRE) (Magical Wonder (USA))
1147[6] 1395[10] 2575[6] 8235[3]

Heintassin (FR) *Mlle B Renk* a76
3 b c Turtle Bowl(IRE) Champagnepouryoyo (USA) (Bering)
72a[0]

Heirgold *Milton Bradley*
6 b h Son And Heir(IRE) Seagold (Shahrastani (USA))
1522[P]

Hekaayaat (USA) *Roger Varian* a73 82
3 ch f Mr Greeley(USA) Mostaqeleh (USA) (Rahy (USA))
(3619)

Helamis *Alison Hutchinson* a53 55
3 b f Shirocco(GER) Alnoor (USA) (Danzig (USA))
2800[7] 3257[4] 3578 (4178) 4688[2] 5633[7] 6361[3] 6964[5] 7382[7]

Helene Spirit (IRE) *C Fownes* a89 119
6 ch g Footstepsinthesand Arazena (USA) (Woodman (USA))
2066a[2] 8210a[7]

Hellbender (IRE) *Shaun Harris* a78 50
7 ch g Exceed And Excel(AUS) Desert Rose (Green Desert (USA))
96[10] (523) 715[2] 831[3] 986[2] 1334[2] 1599[3] 2515[5] 2884[8] 3657[7] 5921[9] 6919[4] 7153[9] (7754) 7953[3] 8037[3] 8198[3] 8401[3]

Hell Hath No Fury *Michael Appleby* a45 54
4 b f Oratorio(IRE) Sagamartha (Rainbow Quest (USA))
1274[4] 1522[7] 1826[4] 2828[6] 5196[3]

Hello Beautiful (IRE) *Ann Duffield* 67
2 ch f Captain Rio Tekhania (IRE) (Dalakhani (IRE))
1718[2] 1839[10] 2830[3] (3476) 4261[4] 4783[3] 5468[4] 6295[9]

Hello Gorgeous *Keith Dalgleish* a24 55
3 b f Phoenix Reach(IRE) Roman Fun (IRE) (Peintre Celebre (USA))
2409[6] 2796[3] 3203[9] 4449[4] 5334[4] 5920[6]

Hellolini *Robin Bastiman* a12 59
3 b f Bertolini(USA) Smiddy Hill (Factual (USA))
3789[4] 4558[7] 7101[14] 7236[11]

Hello Pump Pump (FR) *M Pimbonnet* a68
3 b c Della Francesca(USA) Pump Pump Girl (FR) (Kendor (FR))
605a[5]

Hello Sailor *Ralph Beckett* a57 64
3 b g Mount Nelson Fairy Queen (IRE) (Fairy King (USA))
1481[3] ◆ 1885[2] 2784[8] 3820[14]

Hello Stranger (IRE) *Tim Easterby* a71 73
4 ch g Redback Bobbydazzle (Rock Hopper)
1283[4] 1692[15] 2703[5] 3068[13] 3778[10] 4669[7]

Hello Sweetness *Jason Ward* a41 36
2 b f Aqlaam Atnab (USA) (Riverman (USA))
6597[10] 6938[8] 7419[7] 7954[4]

Helmsley Flyer (IRE) *David O'Meara* a52 59
3 b g Baltic King Dorn Hill (Lujain (USA))
1044[4] 1185[3] 1429[9] 2342[6] 2508[4] 2716[4] 8366[5]

Helterskelter Girl *Ann Duffield* 42
3 b f Firebreak Eloquent Isle (IRE) (Mull Of Kintyre (USA))
3479[3] 4118[9] 4400[7] 5916[8]

Hendry Trigger *Bernard Llewellyn* 59
4 ch g Double Trigger(IRE) Denise Best (IRE) (Goldmark (USA))
5813[5] 6046[3] 6457[2]

Henke (IRE) *Nigel Tinkler* 63
2 b g Elnadim(USA) Miss Frangipane (IRE) (Acclamation)
2883[2] 3624[6] 4731[5] 6295[4] 6904[6]

Henpecked *Alistair Whillans* 62
3 b f Footstepsinthesand Poule De Luxe (IRE) (Cadeaux Genereux)
3774[6] 4805[6] 5110[3] 6686[3]

Henry Bee *Richard Fahey* a74 81
4 b g Cadeaux Genereux Emerald Fire (Pivotal)
2239[11] 2663[10] 3090[12] 3628[9] 4956[6] 5365[13]

Henry Grace (IRE) *Jimmy Fox* a58
2 b c Oratorio(IRE) Little Miss Gracie (Efisio)
6931[10] 7501[11] 7766[14] 8342[7]

Henry Morgan *Bryan Smart* 58
6 ch g Bahamian Bounty Hill Welcome (Most Welcome)
7772[8]

Henry The Aviator (USA) *Mark Johnston* a80 93
3 b c Henrythenavigator(USA) Fashion Star (USA) (Chief's Crown (USA))
(425) 666[2] 3028[2] (3235) 3492[3] 4258[3] (4508) 4743[13]

Hepworth *John Gosden* a81 87
4 b f Singspiel(IRE) Annalina (USA) (Cozzene (USA))
215[2] (429) 2619[4] 3258[2] 4015[7] 4720[6] 6302[2]

Heraclius *J-M Beguigne* a82 89
5 b g Lemon Drop Kid(USA) Hermance (Enrique)
4467a[5]

Herbah *Roger Varian* a60 61
2 b f Dansili Khulood (USA) (Storm Cat (USA))
2625[4] 3318[6] 4409[5] 6311[4] 6695[6]

Herbalist *Ben Pauling* a59 82
3 ch g Haafhd Puya (Kris)
2934[7] 6971[3] 8129[7] 8335[3]

Here Comes Jeanie *Michael Madgwick* a51 42
4 b f Act One Full English (Perugino (USA))
9[4] 579[6] 724[11] 983[11] 1877[9]

Here Comes When (IRE) *Andrew Balding* 102
3 b g Danehill Dancer(IRE) Quad's Melody (IRE) (Spinning World (USA))
1668[2] (2188) ◆ 2843[4] 3455[12]

Hereford Boy *Dean Ivory* a70 74
9 ch g Tomba Grown At Rowan (Gabitat)
451[4] (665)

Here For Good (IRE) *Richard Hannon Snr* a64
2 b c Aqlaam North East Bay (USA) (Prospect Bay (CAN))
8333[4] 8415[6]

Here Now And Why (IRE) *Iain Jardine* a66 68
6 br g Pastoral Pursuits Why Now (Dansili)
1465[7] 2043[3] 2409[7] 2632[2] 3196[2] 3283[6] 3778[5] 4102[5] 4448[7] 4615[6] 4761[6] 5336[6] 5641[2] 6088[2] 6471[3] 6879[3] 7236[3] 7728[7]

Hereselllie (IRE) *Michael Chapman* a64 15
5 b f Clodovil(IRE) Special Dissident (Dancing Dissident (USA))
3716[9]

Here's Johnny (USA) *Wesley A Ward* 96
2 b g Colonel John(USA) Bon Caro (USA) (Bon Point)
5460a[4]

Her Honour (IRE) *John Gosden* a56
2 b f Shamardal(USA) Hazarayna (Polish Precedent (USA))
7645[9] 8083[7]

Herminia (IRE) *A Fabre* a80 80
3 b f Hernando(FR) Danseuse Indienne (IRE) (Danehill (USA))
6031a[9]

Hermosa Vaquera (IRE) *Anna Newton-Smith* a53 65
3 b f High Chaparral(IRE) Sundown (Polish Precedent (USA))
2392[8] 2742[2] 3014[3] 4688[4] 5099[11] 5216[4] 5650[4] 7091[11] 7628[14]

Hernan Cortez (FR) *G Botti* a85 82
3 b c Elusive City(USA) Madame Anne Peters (Selkirk (USA))
7188a[8] 7736a[9]

Hernando Torres *Michael Easterby* a62 69
5 b g Iffraaj Espana (Hernando (FR))
2875[5] 3504[5] 4071[2] 4376[2] (4853) 6051[4] 6667[7] 6721[4] 7132[7]

Her Nibbs *Micky Hammond* a32 62
4 b f Lucky Story(USA) The Pen (Lake Coniston (IRE))
2237[2] 2956[P]

Herod The Great *Alan King* 81
3 ch g Sakhee's Secret Pella (Hector Protector (USA))
2547[2] 3343[6] 5032[2] ◆ 5847[4]

Heroes Welcome (IRE) *Deborah Sanderson* 37
3 b f Ramonti(FR) Sagaing (Machiavellian (USA))
14[5] 4927[10] 5867[4]

Heroine Required (FR) *William Haggas* 74
3 ch f Muhtathir Tiger Mist (IRE) (Galileo (IRE))
1845[2] ◆ 2261[6] 5707[4] 6498[4] 7114[4]

Heroique (IRE) *Tim Easterby* 68
2 b f Acclamation Gay Heroine (Caerleon (USA))
3023[5] 4073[4] 4505[2] 4963[6] 5543[3] 5877[4] 6295[3] 6628[7] (7096) 7503[2]

Hero's Story *Amanda Perrett* a63 65
3 b c Mount Nelson Red Roses Story (FR) (Pink (FR))
2442[14] 3021[11] 3343[5] 4753[9] 5762[3] ◆ 6109[4] 6435[4] 6895[8] 7248[2] 7434[2]

Herostatus *Jason Ward* a94 91
6 ch g Dalakhani(IRE) Desired (Rainbow Quest (USA))
2369[8] (3609) 4313[9] 4873[16]

Her Royal Empress *James Unett* a39 44
3 b f Holy Roman Emperor(IRE) Aurelia (Rainbow Quest (USA))
36[5] 207[5]

Herschel (IRE) *Gary Moore* a59 65
7 br g Dr Fong(USA) Rafting (IRE) (Darshaan)
94[14] 820[11]

Her Star (USA) *P Bary* 96
3 b f Harlan's Holiday(USA) Silver Comic (USA) (Silver Hawk (USA))
2970a[7] 4700a[3] 6124a[8]

Herve (IRE) *T Castanheira* a84 84
3 b c Excellent Art Dance Idol (Groom Dancer (USA))
2557a[15] 3007a[4]

He's A Striker (IRE) *Michael Blake* a65 78
3 br g Footstepsinthesand Aiming Upwards (Blushing Flame (USA))
673[2] 799[3] 1072[3] 1584[3] (2322) 6358[11] 6743[10]

Hesbaan (IRE) *Marcus Tregoning* a75 76
2 b c Acclamation Celestial Dream (IRE) (Oasis Dream)
6169[4] ◆ 6589[2] 7120[4]

He's Had Enough (USA) *Doug O'Neill* a114 91
3 gr c Tapit(USA) Amelia (USA) (Dixieland Band (USA))
1264a[11]

Heska (IRE) *Mick Channon* a72 60
2 b c Rock Of Gibraltar(IRE) Sweet Sioux (Halling (USA))
5033[9] 5584[4] 5811[9] 6656[4] 7113[2] 7326[4] 7945[2] 8016[3]

Heskin (IRE) *Richard Fahey* 76
2 b f Acclamation Carpet Lady (IRE) (Night Shift (USA))
1718[3] 2426[10] 2856[4] (3753) 4246[4] 5136[2] 5536[3] 6395[6] 6839[5]

He's My Boy (IRE) *James Fanshawe* a69 58
2 gr g Dark Angel(IRE) Rose Of Battle (Averti (IRE))
6569[7] 7638[4] 7978[9]

He's No Angel (IRE) *Clive Cox* a78 63
4 ch g Excellent Art Gentle Night (Zafonic (USA))
108[5] (708) 3273[7] 4150[8]

Hes Our Music (IRE) *Patrick J Flynn* a80 78
4 b g Oratorio(IRE) Matibibi (ITY) (Barathea (IRE))
3869a[4]

Hester Street *Rae Guest* a10
3 b f Kyllachy Fascination Street (IRE) (Mujadil (USA))
185[7] 424[7] 664[5]

Heuston (IRE) *Reginald Roberts* a72 89
4 b g Acclamation On The Razz (USA) (With Approval (CAN))
5775a[3]

Hey Little Gorl (GER) *Markus Klug* 101
3 ch f Sternkoenig(IRE) Homing Instinct (Arctic Tern (USA))
2905a[5] 3604a[10] (6248a)

Heyward Boy (IRE) *Robert Eddery* 29
3 ch g Intikhab(USA) Kashoof (Green Desert (USA))
1361[4]

Hi Candy (IRE) *Ben Haslam* a22 41
3 b f Diamond Green(FR) Dancing Steps (Zafonic (USA))
1743[7]

Hickster (IRE) *Tom Dascombe* a69 39
2 br g Intense Focus(USA) Surrender To Me (USA) (Royal Anthem (USA))
1605[7] 1930[9] 4021[7] 5175[6] 6131[2] 6654[3] (6983)

Hi Dancer *Ben Haslam* a55 61
10 b g Medicean Sea Music (Inchinor)
2120[11] 2887[7] 3771[6]

Hidden Asset *Michael Appleby* a54 52
3 ch c Sakhee's Secret Petite Epaulette (Night Shift (USA))
2512[3] 4144[5] 5869[8]

Hidden Belief (IRE) *Ralph Beckett* a82 78
3 b f Holy Roman Emperor(IRE) Crossanza (IRE) (Cape Cross (IRE))
2084[4] 3116[7] (3950) 4671[6] 5398[3] ◆ 5896[2] 6524[2] 6780[2]

Hidden Justice (IRE) *John Quinn* a70 85
4 b g Lawman(FR) Uncharted Haven (Turtle Island (IRE))
(1445) ◆ 2402[8]

Hidden Link *Ronald Harris* a72 71
3 b g Rail Link Gloved Hand (Royal Applause)
37[4] (212) ◆ 419[2] 632[5] 1103[4] (1171) 1320[3] 1900[3] 3528[4] 4193[4] 6810[7]

Hidden Oasis (IRE) *David Wachman* 104
2 b g Lawman(FR) Spesialta (Indian Ridge)
7939a[6]

Hidden Talent *David Brown* a47 83
3 b g Kyllachy Creative Mind (IRE) (Danehill Dancer (IRE))
1645[6] 3582[11] 5195[9] 5527[7] 7344[3] 7608[11]

Hiddon Coin (IRE) *David O'Meara* a82 82
3 b g Red Clubs(IRE) Dianella (IRE) (Gold Away (IRE))
(38) (424) 643[3] (827) (1041) 1250[3] 1677[5]

Hide The Evidence (IRE) *Michael McElhone* a43 68
12 ch g Carroll House Andarta (Ballymore)
7151[5]

Hierarch (IRE) *David Simcock* a72 73
6 b g Dansili Danse Classique (IRE) (Night Shift (USA))
89[2] 452[2] 546[3] 791[4] 1901[2] 2163[5] 3087[5] 3534[7] 5135[9] (6316) 8198[4]

Hi Filwah (USA) *Jeremy Noseda* a91 73
3 b c Medaglia d'Oro(USA) Star Landing (USA) (Caller I.D. (USA))
3109[2] 3759[3] 4839[2] 5345[2] 5618[2] 5989[2] (6176) 6777[2] (7165) ◆ 7888[3]

High Accolade *Roger Varian* 68
2 ch f Medicean Hightime Heroine (IRE) (Danetime (IRE))
5950[2] 6789[10]

High Duty *P Schiergen* 104
2 b c Oratorio(IRE) Heart Of Ice (IRE) (Montjeu (IRE))
5911a[5] 7184a[2] 7939a[5]

Higher Court (USA) *David Nicholls* 59
5 b g Shamardal(USA) Nawaiet (USA) (Zilzal (USA))
7171[17]

High Five Prince (IRE) *Milton Bradley* a23 57
4 br g Strategic Prince Lady Georgina (Linamix (FR))
630[10] 737[13] 820[10] 993[8]

High Five Society *Roy Bowring* a22 79
9 b g Compton Admiral Sarah Madeline (Pelder (IRE))
62[P]

High Flame (IRE) *Tim Easterby* 25
3 b f High Chaparral(IRE) Noble Flame (IRE) (Doyoun)
2121[7] 6847[10]

High Jinx (IRE) *James Fanshawe* 113
5 b g High Chaparral(IRE) Leonara (GER) (Surumu (GER))
2810[4] 6349[2] 7060a[5] 7363[10]

Highland Acclaim (IRE) *Andrew Balding* a74 88
2 b g Acclamation Emma's Star (ITY) (Darshaan)
2250[7] 6169[5] 6645[5] 7125[3]

Highland Castle *David Elsworth* 100
5 b g Halling(USA) Reciprocal (IRE) (Night Shift (USA))
1843[4] 2252[5] (3115) 3559[12] 4060[4] 4704[3] 5256[4] 5766[14] 7526[3] 7823[15]

Highland Colori (IRE) *Andrew Balding* a81 116
5 b g Le Vie Dei Colori Emma's Star (ITY) (Darshaan)
1830[4] 2254[10] (3060) 3527[22] 4297[6] 5285[3] (5844) (6623) 7190[4] (7530) 7821[2]

Highland Duke (IRE) *Clive Cox* 95
4 b g Dansili House In Wood (FR) (Woodman (USA))
2101[2] ◆ 2532[2] 3022[5] 4207[3] (4923)

Highland Knight (IRE) *Andrew Balding* a101 114
6 b g Night Shift(USA) Highland Shot (Selkirk (USA))
1535[5] 1810[2] 2186[2] 5446[4] 6191[6] 6427[5] (7196) 7927[7]

Highland Princess (IRE) *Paul Midgley* a41 41
2 b f Amadeus Wolf Ten Spot (IRE) (Intikhab (USA))
1642[12] 2337[6] 2715[9] 3461[9] 4538[4] 5289[3] 5900[3] 6511[12]

Highland River *Dave Roberts* a28 55
7 b g Indian Creek Bee One (IRE) (Catrail (USA))
7668[8]

Highland Stardust *Clive Cox* 43
2 b f Sakhee(USA) Highland Starlight (USA) (Dixieland Band (USA))
5529[12] 6140[9]

Highlife Dancer *Mick Channon* a66 74
5 br g Imperial Dancer Wrong Bride (Reprimand)
1909[8] 2137[7] 2533[11] (3037) (3151) (3312) 3412[8] 3662[4] 3985[6] 4832[7] 5312[7] 6158[9] 6492[9]

High Lightning *Mrs K Burke* a17
3 b f High Chaparral(IRE) Kyle Akin (Vettori (IRE))
184[9]

Highly Likely (IRE) *Steve Woodman* a64 56
4 b g Elnadim(USA) Height Of Fantasy (IRE) (Shirley Heights)
132[2] 653[13] 788[2] (1877) 2569[3] 2777[7] 3168[3] 3688[7] 5216[8] 5934[9]

Highly Toxic (IRE) *Patrick J Flynn* 68
2 gr c Dalakhani(IRE) Chiang Mai (IRE) (Sadler's Wells (USA))
7050a[8]

High Master (IRE) *Richard Hannon Snr* a64 67
2 b c High Chaparral(IRE) Enchant (Lion Cavern (USA))
6739[6] 6954[5] 7646[5]

High Meadow Prince *Robert Johnson*
4 b g Boogie Street High Meadow Girl (Pursuit Of Love)
5715[9]

High 'n Dry (IRE) *Roger Curtis* a59 66
9 ch m Halling(USA) Sisal (IRE) (Danehill (USA))
158[7] 579[4]

High Net Worth *Gordon Elliott* a76 78
4 b g Oasis Dream Return (USA) (Sadler's Wells (USA))
8301[9]

High Octane *John Joseph Murphy* 101
3 b c Motivator Las Beatas (Green Desert (USA))
1555a[3] 2023[5]

High Office *Richard Fahey* a45 95
7 b g High Chaparral(IRE) White House (Pursuit Of Love)
1774[3] 2369[9] 2671[2] 3297[7] 4262[4] 4873[6] 5655[13] 6239[4] 6626[7] 7193[13] 7496[4] ◆ 7805[8]

High On A Hill (IRE) *Iain Jardine* a68 61
6 b g Val Royal(FR) Blue Kestrel (IRE) (Bluebird (USA))
4543[10] 4822[8] 5712[8] 6177[5] 6470[5] 7668[2] 8031[7] (8204) 8229[5]

High On Life *Jamie Osborne* a72 69
2 b g Invincible Spirit(IRE) Lovely Thought (Dubai Destination (USA))
4912[4] 5646[6] 6477[3]

High On The Hog (IRE) *Mark Brisbourne* a63 76
5 b g Clodovil(IRE) Maraami (Selkirk (USA))
1734[2] 2130[2] 2773[11] 3210[5] 3644[3] 4155[11] 4357[11] 5594[7] 6610[7] 7354[10]

High Resolution *Linda Perratt* a59 78
6 ch g Haafhd Individual Talents (USA) (Distant View (USA))
2220^5 2406^8 4098^5 4446^6 4475^6 4994^3 5051^6 5918^7 6048^8 6667^3 6907^2 6921^2 7152^5

High Secret (IRE) *Sir Mark Prescott Bt* a43 46
2 b g High Chaparral(IRE) Secret Question (USA) (Rahy (USA))
7494^9 *7646^8* 7774^8

High Spirit (IRE) *Mme Pia Brandt* 105
3 b c Danehill Dancer(IRE) Sina Cova (IRE) (Barathea (IRE))
5808a^5

High Stand *Sir Michael Stoute* a52 52
2 b c Kyllachy Maugwenna (Danehill (USA))
7448^5

High Star (FR) *J-C Rouget* a93 91
6 ch g High Yield(USA) Etoile D'Or (FR) (Midyan (USA))
5735a^3

High Time Too (IRE) *Hugo Palmer* a82 69
3 b f High Chaparral(IRE) Dane Thyme (IRE) (Danetime (IRE))
1468^2 2127^3 2586^9 3251^5 4509^8 *(5070) 5395^2 6115^4 8219^5*

High Tone *Dean Ivory* a37 53
3 b f Bertolini(USA) High Finale (Sure Blade (USA))
1875^5 3837^{10} *4176^4* 5128^2

High Troja (IRE) *Ed Dunlop* a83 92
3 b g High Chaparral(IRE) Theben (GER) (Monsun (GER))
1219^2 (1365) 2050^3 (2445) 2862^4

High Twelve (IRE) *S Seemar* a94 110
6 b g Montjeu(IRE) Much Faster (IRE) (Fasliyev (USA))
364a^3

Highway Code (USA) *Richard Lee* 76
7 b g Street Cry(IRE) Fairy Heights (IRE) (Fairy King (USA))
(6325) 6788^3 6960^3 7539^2

Highway Pursuit *George Moore* 39
2 b g Pastoral Pursuits Extreme Pleasure (IRE) (High Chaparral (IRE))
5969^7 7276^7

Highway United (IRE) *John Weymes* a22 8
3 ch f Arakan(USA) Luscinia (Bluebird (USA))
686^6

Highway Warrior *Sean Curran* a49 54
4 b f Ishiguru(USA) Blue Topaz (IRE) (Bluebird (USA))
1090^8 1520^9

Hija *Bill Turner* a46 38
2 b f Avonbridge Pantita (Polish Precedent (USA))
3211^7 3753^6 4065^4 4583^7 *7509^5 7945^4*

Hikari (IRE) *D K Weld* 93
3 b f Galileo(IRE) Something Mon (USA) (Maria's Mon (USA))
7891a^8

Hiking (USA) *Roger Charlton* a85 84
2 b f First Defence(USA) Trekking (USA) (Gone West (USA))
(3631) (5524) *7326^2*

Hilali (IRE) *Gary Brown* a85 82
4 b g Sakhee(USA) Mufradat (IRE) (Desert Prince (IRE))
(810) 5824^3 6336^8 7075^{14}

Hilda Ogden (IRE) *David Nicholls* 34
3 ch f Peintre Celebre(USA) Shellin (IRE) (Sinndar (IRE))
6497^{13} 6759^6 7027^7

Hilden *William Muir* 54
4 b f Dansili Singleton (Singspiel (IRE))
3417^{13} 4171^2 4345^5 5123^5 5667^6

Hillbilly Boy (IRE) *Bill Turner* a70 83
3 b g Haafhd Erreur (IRE) (Desert King (IRE))
188^5 424^4 (588) (684) 827^2 918^4 8450^3

Hillbilly Girl *Bill Turner* 3
2 b f Champs Elysees Drastic Measure (Pivotal)
5578^6

Hill Of Dreams (IRE) *Dean Ivory* a83 72
4 b f Indian Danehill(IRE) Shaunas Vision (IRE) (Dolphin Street (FR))
418^{13} 825^2 1017^3 (1498) 1617^2 2534^4 (2787) *(3434) 3961^7* 5124^9 5589^5 7256^7 *7989^6* 8178^{10} 8314^7

Hills Of Dakota *Keith Dalgleish* 74
5 b g Sleeping Indian Pontressina (USA) (St Jovite (USA))
4582^8 5261^7 6687^2 6903^6 7149^{13}

Hillstar *Sir Michael Stoute* 119
3 b c Danehill Dancer(IRE) Crystal Star (Mark Of Esteem (IRE))
1641^2 2445^2 (3523) ◆ 4745^3 5654^4 7367^6

Hillview Boy (IRE) *Jim Goldie* a49 96
9 bb g Bishop Of Cashel Arandora Star (USA) (Sagace (FR))
1238^3 1538^{12} 2040^7

Himalaya Dream (FR) *E Libaud* a79 105
3 b c Stormy River(FR) Orange Blossom (FR) (Vettori (IRE))
3386a^8 5361a^4

Himalayan Peak *James Eustace* a61 57
3 b g Tiger Hill(IRE) Rosy Outlook (USA) (Trempolino (USA))
1684^{10} *2157^5 3497^9* 6458^8 *7298^8*

Hi Note *Sheena West* a68 88
5 b f Acclamation Top Tune (Victory Note (USA))
1062^4 1158^3 3512^3 (4173) 4406^2 4530^3 (4938) (5535) *5895^{11}* 6573^4

Hint Of A Tint (IRE) *David Wachman* 102
3 b f Danehill Dancer(IRE) Mine Excavation (FR) (Galileo (IRE))
1557a^7 2289a^2 3460^5 3964a^5 5688a^7

Hinton Admiral *Pat Eddery* a64 62
9 b g Spectrum(IRE) Shawanni (Shareef Dancer (USA))
50^7 143^{10} 2236^9 *3643^5 4836^4 5230^2 7511^6 7643^2 8022^6 8151^7* 8446^4

Hiorne Tower (FR) *John Best* a21
2 b c Poliglote Hierarchie (FR) (Sillery (USA))
8213^9

Hip Hip Hooray *Luke Dace* a70 70
7 ch m Monsieur Bond(IRE) Birthday Belle (Lycius (USA))
13^6 348^3 652^5 3635^7 4350^5

Hippolyte (FR) *T Clout* a84 106
4 b g Gold Away(IRE) Standout (FR) (Robellino (USA))
2559a^6 5912a^3 7968a^6

Hippy (FR) *E Libaud* a81 102
5 b f Muhtathir Peace And Love (FR) (Highest Honor (FR))
5360a^5

Hippy Hippy Shake *Luca Cumani* a77 107
4 b f Danehill Dancer(IRE) Hyperspectra (Rainbow Quest (USA))
2015^6 4137^4 (4732) 5402^2 6536^{11}

Hipster *Ralph Beckett* a88 75
3 b g Kingsalsa(USA) Hip (Pivotal)
(359) 2100^3 2844^{11} 3633^8 4124^8 4908^3 5825^8 5853^5 6335^4 6956^2 7505^8

Hipz (IRE) *George Baker* a71 71
2 br f Intense Focus(USA) Radha (Bishop Of Cashel)
5929^2 (6408) 6695^4 *(7117) 7782^{11} 8126^3 8383^3*

Hisaabaat (IRE) *D K Weld* 81
5 b g Dubawi(IRE) Phariseek (IRE) (Rainbow Quest (USA))
7230a^{14}

Hispania (IRE) *Michael Bell* a27 51
3 b f Teofilo(IRE) Badalona (Cape Cross (IRE))
2456^8 4404^6 5495^8 *7034^4*

History Book (IRE) *Charlie Appleby* a84
3 b f Raven's Pass(USA) Pure Illusion (IRE) (Danehill (USA))
(7791)

Hitchens (IRE) *David Barron* a104 115
8 b g Acclamation Royal Fizz (IRE) (Royal Academy (USA))
365a^8 660a^8 834a^4 955a^6 1234^4 1537^3 2046^7 (2676a) 3558^{19} (5027) 6235^5 6414a^7 7013^7 *7928^6*

Hi There (IRE) *Richard Fahey* a51 104
4 b g Dark Angel(IRE) Ornellaia (IRE) (Mujadil (USA))
(1252) ◆ 1830^7 2477^2 2841^8 3725^4 4342^6 4854^9 5768^3 (6551) (7536) 7823^{10}

Hit The Jackpot (IRE) *David O'Meara* a59 100
4 ch g Pivotal Token Gesture (IRE) (Alzao (USA))
1235^{12} 1446^7 2477^7 3207^8 4435^6 *5195^6* 5580^{13} 6237^4 6466^4 6942^3 7210^5

Hit The Lights (IRE) *Ollie Pears* a61 76
3 b g Lawman(FR) Dawn Chorus (IRE) (Mukaddamah (USA))
1190^4 (1461) (1935) 2408^4 2888^2 3540^5 5088^6 5985^4 *6362^9* 6771^7

Hit The Target (JPN) *Keiji Kato* 112
5 ch c King Kamehameha(JPN) Latir (JPN) (Tamamo Cross (JPN))
8033a^{11}

Hittin'The Skids (IRE) *Mandy Rowland* a58 60
5 ch f Fruits Of Love(USA) Hush Deal (Tipsy Creek (USA))
42^4 537^4 1021^6 1452^{10} 1734^4 1886^5 2345^3 3513^{12} *6986^9 7353^{11}*

Hi Ya Pal (USA) *N Clement* a83 70
4 b g Pulpit(USA) Cloon (USA) (Lure (USA))
5735a^6

Hoarding (USA) *John Gosden* a95 101
3 b c Elusive Quality(USA) What A Treasure (IRE) (Cadeaux Genereux)
1033 ^{3} 1383^7 1767^5 2023^3 (2454) 3485^{10}

Hoist The Colours (IRE) *David Lanigan* a55
2 b c Sea The Stars(IRE) Multicolour Wave (IRE) (Rainbow Quest (USA))
8124^{13} 8340^{12}

Hokko Brave (JPN) *Yasutoshi Matsunaga* 111
5 b c Marvelous Sunday(JPN) Hokko Memory (JPN) (Dancing Brave (USA))
8033a^{12}

Hoku (IRE) *Olly Stevens* a56 98
2 b f Holy Roman Emperor(IRE) Scylla Cadeaux (IRE) (Cadeaux Genereux)
1724^3 2426^2 3829^8 *4408^7* 4924^2 (5061) 5837^4 6622^2 7055a^8 7194^6

Holding Fast (IRE) *Tobias B P Coles* a56 48
3 b g Balmont(USA) Eschasse (USA) (Zilzal (USA))
137^2 207^2 357^2 442^6 527^7 848^7

Hold On Tight (IRE) *Ralph Beckett* a66 87
3 ch f Hernando(FR) Wait It Out (USA) (Swain (IRE))
2157^3 (3989) 4594^3 5542^2 7659^4

Hold The Line (IRE) *John Patrick Shanahan* a86 97
3 b c Ivan Denisovich(IRE) Janna's Jewel (IRE) (Traditionally (USA))
4473^5 5760^5

Hold The Star *Ann Stokell* a64 49
7 b m Red Ransom(USA) Sydney Star (Machiavellian (USA))
88^6 240^3 408^5 565^9 733^8 1052^6 1173^6 1474^9

Holley Shiftwell *Stuart Williams* a70 82
3 ch f Bahamian Bounty Persario (Bishop Of Cashel)
581^U (686) 1682^2 (3540) 4057^2 (4674) 4989^4

Holli Deya *Andi Brown* a51 28
3 b f Halling(USA) Never Say Deya (Dansili)
3764^{10} *4632^9 5100^9* 5979^7 *6804^3 7034^8 7753^6 8055^3*

Hollow Beat *Tim Walford* 38
3 b f Beat Hollow Sing For Fame (USA) (Quest For Fame)
1236^6 1684^{11} 5010^4

Hollowina *David Brown* 87
3 ch f Beat Hollow Trick Or Treat (Lomitas)
2148^5 2367^5 3482^9 6196^7 7223^5 7596^5

Holly Filly (IRE) *D Guillemin* a77 88
3 b f Holy Roman Emperor(IRE) Casmine (FR) (Tot Ou Tard (IRE))
4274a^7 7993a^6

Holly Polly (GER) *H-A Pantall* 97
4 b f Dylan Thomas(IRE) Hanami (Hernando (FR))
6447a^{13} 7189a^6

Hollywood All Star (IRE) *William Muir* a54 55
4 b g Kheleyf(USA) Camassina (IRE) (Taufan (USA))
226^4 579^5 852^5 983^6 1183^6 2237^5

Holy Angel (IRE) *Tim Easterby* a79 79
4 b g Dark Angel(IRE) Bakewell Tart (IRE) (Tagula (IRE))
27^2 214^6 (453) (558) 795^2 885^{10} 1067^5 1351^3 1694^{11} 2239^5 2663^{12} 3087^4 3444^4 4051^2 4510^2 4728^6 4852^6 5273^3 5971^{15} (6516) 6771^4 7594^3

Holy Dazzle *J E Pease* a85 107
3 b f Sunday Break(JPN) Belle Alicia (FR) (Smadoun (FR))
1358a^2 2970a^3

Holy Lute (USA) *James Cassidy* a107
3 rg c Midnight Lute(USA) Holy Christmas (USA) (Holy Bull (USA))
7689a^{10}

Holystones (IRE) *Marco Botti* a49 60
2 b c Holy Roman Emperor(IRE) Cappagh Strand (USA) (Grand Slam (USA))
3493^5 4497^7 5405^5

Holy Warrior (IRE) *Gay Kelleway* a95 97
3 b g Holy Roman Emperor(IRE) If Dubai (USA) (Stephen Got Even (USA))
(350) (782a) 1419a^7 2454^5 3007a^5

Holy Water (IRE) *Jonathan Portman* 29
2 b g Holy Roman Emperor(IRE) Gambling Spirit (Mister Baileys)
5443^9 6152^{10}

Homage (IRE) *Jeremy Noseda* a78 92
3 b g Acclamation Night Sphere (IRE) (Night Shift (USA))
(2593) 3020^2 ◆ 4922^{10} 6308^{10}

Homeboy (IRE) *Marcus Tregoning* a71 48
5 b g Camacho Berenica (IRE) (College Chapel)
(317) (355) 898^3 1155^2 (1195) 1516^8 1780^8 1954^2 2949^5 7652^3 7862^3 8022^4 8244^8

Homeric (IRE) *Ed Dunlop* a86 96
4 b g Montjeu(IRE) Al Saqiya (USA) (Woodman (USA))
1501^5 (2205) 3423^7 4704^2 (5256) 5655^{10}

Homeric Hymn (FR) *Mrs John Harrington* 76
2 b f Acclamation Mary Arnold (IRE) (Hernando (FR))
2944a^{10}

Home School (IRE) *Doug O'Neill* 104
2 b c Intense Focus(USA) Lavender Blue (Galileo (IRE))
4547a^5 4694a^2 7688a^{12}

Homestretch *Mick Channon* 79
2 b c Holy Roman Emperor(IRE) Sharp Mode (USA) (Diesis)
(3155) 4108^2 4988^3

Hometown Glory *Brian Meehan* a88 79
4 b g Compton Place Pomponette (USA) (Rahy (USA))
133^5 2450^{15} 3974^6 4426^3

Homeward Strut *Laura Mongan* a71 45
4 ch g Needwood Blade Piccante (Wolfhound (USA))
878^5 1304^3 1516^6 1717^2 2228^8 2565^7 2773^8 3051^8

Honest Deal *Alan Swinbank* a85 76
5 b g Trade Fair Sincerely (Singspiel (IRE))
1443 642^2 (830) 1083^6 (1523) 3791^3

Honest Strike (USA) *Daniel Mark Loughnane* a65 40
6 b g Smart Strike(CAN) Honest Lady (USA) (Seattle Slew (USA))
20^5 539^5 714^2 1146^2 (1325) 1520^6 (1953) 2570^8 *8331^6* ◆

Honey Haven (IRE) *Mark Brisbourne* a47 58
3 b f Indian Haven Condilessa (IRE) (Key Of Luck (USA))
237^4 3578 4352^4 4931^3 5432^2 5846^6 6389^5

Honey Meadow *Robert Eddery* a69 67
2 ch f Avonbridge All The Nines (IRE) (Elusive City (USA))
1421^5 1724^4 (3017) 4431^6 5842^7 6035^3 6320^4 6695^{11} 7451^{11} *7623^2 7878^8 (8166)*

Honeymoon Cocktail (FR) *J-C Rouget* 91
2 gr c Martaline Caipirinia (FR) (Hawk Wing (USA))
5039a^2 (5875a)

Honeymoon Express (IRE) *Julia Feilden* 78
3 br f Mujadil(USA) Royal Jelly (King's Best (USA))
3253^4 3787^2 4390^3 5200^4 ◆ (5616) (5800)

Honey Of A Kitten (USA) *David Evans* a77 55
5 b g Kitten's Joy(USA) Sweet Baby Jane (USA) (Kingmambo (USA))
(183) 314^{10} 403^7 476^4 614^6 638^3 672^3 (747) 906^3 (974) 984^6 1220^6 (1402) (1890) 2646^7 2923^7 3156^2 3617^3 3917^6 3951^4 4475^7 4904^6 6473^2 6759^5 7350^3 (8028) 8093^2 8308^2 8335^2 8450^6

Honeysuckle Rose (FR) *P Bary* a79 80
2 ch f Turtle Bowl(IRE) Valleyrose (IRE) (Royal Academy (USA))
7567a^5

Honiton Lace *J W Hills* a43
2 ch f Tobougg(IRE) Mellifluous (IRE) (Noverre (USA))
8138^6 8451^{11}

Honor Bound *Ralph Beckett* 60
2 b f Authorized(IRE) Honorine (IRE) (Mark Of Esteem (IRE))
6063^7 7069^3

Honor Chop (FR) *C Martinon* a57
3 b g Indian Rocket Sospelle (Highest Honor (FR))
818a^6 2034a^0

Honourable Knight (IRE) *Mark Usher* a75 69
5 b g Celtic Swing Deemeh (IRE) (Brief Truce (USA))
(119) 351^{10} 1502^7 1670^{12} (2570) 3110^8 3971^3 *4754^2 5231^7* 5954^2 *(6173)* 6424^{13}

Honoured (IRE) *Michael Appleby* a88 72
6 ch g Mark Of Esteem(IRE) Traou Mad (IRE) (Barathea (IRE))
107^4 338^{13} 2511^3 2961^2 (3138) 3651^9 5059^8 *(7758) (8047) 8353^2*

Hooded (USA) *Roger Charlton* a78
2 b c Empire Maker(USA) Yashmak (USA) (Danzig (USA))
7834^7 ◆ *(8066)*

Hoodna (IRE) *Saeed bin Suroor* a102 90
3 b f Invincible Spirit(IRE) Heaven's Cause (USA) (Giant's Causeway (USA))
2476^{11} *(6692)* 6990^{12} *7928^7*

Hoofalong *Michael Easterby* a40 92
3 b g Pastoral Pursuits Baymist (Mind Games)
(2010) (2521) 3066^5 5769^2 6238^U

Hoof It *Michael Easterby* a108 108
6 b g Monsieur Bond(IRE) Forever Bond (Danetime (IRE))
4311^7 4986^{15} 5545^{13} 6193^3 6623^8 7013^3 7364^4 7821^4 *8334^5*

Hoofs (IRE) *Gary Harrison* 3
2 ch f Camacho Laylati (IRE) (Green Desert (USA))
4073^{11}

Hoof's So Lucky *Michael Easterby* 48
2 ch f Compton Place Lucky Dip (Tirol)
4046^8 4505^{12} 5053^{11} 7096^6

Hooligan Sean *Mark Usher* a21 57
6 ch g Ishiguru(USA) Sheesha (USA) (Shadeed (USA))
7246^7 *7808^8 7930^{10} 8329^8*

Hoon (IRE) *Rae Guest* 72
2 b g Camacho Luggala (IRE) (Kahyasi)
5843^4 6277^6 7218^6

Hoonose *Pat Eddery* a63 48
4 ch g Cadeaux Genereux Roodeye (Inchinor)
(469) (851) 1348^5 4380^{11} 4754^{10}

Hopefilly (IRE) *Ed Walker* 80
2 b f Compton Place Kondakova (IRE) (Soviet Star (USA))
2869^5 (4073) ◆ 4528^8 5082a^7 6791^7 (7127) 7771^6

Hope For Glory *Jason Ward* a40
4 b g Proclamation(IRE) Aissa (Dr Devious (IRE))
8046^4

Hopeigetlucky *Stuart Kittow* 46
2 b g Lucky Story(USA) Maxilla (IRE) (Lahib (USA))
7270^7

Hopes N Dreams (IRE) *Kevin Ryan* a85 102
5 b f Elusive City(USA) Hope Of Pekan (IRE) (Sri Pekan (USA))
1370^7 1765^6 2007^7 2476^6 2914^3 (3200) 3714^7 (4444) 4860^{18} (4993) 5544^{13} (5851) (6685) 7021^{12}

Hope's Wishes *Andrew Balding* a59
3 b f Kayf Tara Otarie (FR) (Lute Antique (FR))
6926^7 7298^9

Hoppy's Flyer (FR) *Mark Brisbourne* a66 68
5 b f Country Reel(USA) Madeleine's Blush (USA) (Rahy (USA))
1271^{11} 1757^{13} 2280^6 3029^4 3098^3 ◆ 3445^2 4245^3 4709^5 4967^8 5471^3 *6368^4 6610^2 6980^4 7353^8*

Hornblower (FR) *Mme C Head-Maarek* a55
2 b c Mr. Sidney(USA) Riziere (FR) (Groom Dancer (USA))
7568a^{15}

Hornboy *Jeremy Noseda* a67 74
3 b g Medicean Soar (Danzero (AUS))
1086^2 1384^2 2934^5 (3327) *4354^8* 5853^6 *7303^{11}*

Hors De Combat *James Fanshawe* a87 87
2 ch c Mount Nelson Maid For Winning (USA) (Gone West (USA))
(5488) *6197^2*

Horse No Name (FR) *H-A Pantall* 79
3 b g Librettist(USA) Zulbis (TUR) (Down The Flag (USA))
3166a^4

Horsted Keynes (FR) *Roger Varian* a94
3 ch g Giant's Causeway(USA) Viking's Cove (USA) (Miswaki (USA))
(6608) ◆ *(7648)* ◆ *7769^3*

Hostile Fire (IRE) *Ed de Giles* a50 65
2 b g Iffraaj Royal Esteem (Mark Of Esteem (IRE))
5924^{11} 6340^6 6635^6 *7119^{10}*

Hostile Takeover (IRE) *Jo Crowley* a43 53
2 ch g Iffraaj Theroseofloughrea (IRE) (Lake Coniston (IRE))
2771^5 4631^9 4925^9 *8262^9*

Hot Amber (USA) *Robert Cowell* a41 55
2 ch f Langfuhr(CAN) Tres Chaud (USA) (French Deputy (USA))
4206^2 4686^4 *7348^5 8273^8*

Hot Bed (IRE) *David Wachman* a92 107
4 b g Dashing Blade Mer De Corail (IRE) (Sadler's Wells (USA))
5681^3 ◆

Hot Chili Peper (FR) *F Seguin* a78
7 b g Cardoun(FR) Hot Favourite (FR) (Fast Topaze (USA))
6680a^6

Hot Coffee (IRE) *Tom Dascombe* 88
2 b f Haatef(USA) Cafe Creme (IRE) (Catrail (USA))
(3978) ◆ 5555a^8 6185^4

Hot Mustard *Michael Bell* a53 65
3 b g Pastoral Pursuits Lihou Island (Beveled (USA))
1712^{11} 2308^5 2501^2 2762^3 *7784^9 8151^9*

Hototo *Fawzi Abdulla Nass* 103
3 ch g Sleeping Indian Harlem Dancer (Dr Devious (IRE))
553a^{13}

Hot Prospect *J J Lambe* a51 87
6 b g Motivator Model Queen (USA) (Kingmambo (USA))
3599a^{13} 3844a^9

Hot Reply *Sir Mark Prescott Bt*
2 br f Notnowcato Cool Question (Polar Falcon (USA))
4833^6 5193^6

Hot Right Now *Mrs K Burke* a59 6
3 ch f Sleeping Indian American Rouge (IRE) (Grand Lodge (USA))
1019[4] (1329) 2156[9] 3232[13]

Hot Rod Mamma (IRE) *Dianne Sayer* a42 90
6 ch m Traditionally(USA) Try The Air (IRE) (Foxhound (USA))
1463[10] 1819[11] 2240[6] 2753[5] 2915[3] 3443[2] 3683[2] 3712[4] 4055[6] (5051) 5548[2] 5880[5] 6210[2] 6300[3] 6875[7] 7374[9] 7595[4]

Hot Secret *Andrew Balding* a73 74
3 b f Sakhee's Secret Harryana (Efisio)
1661[4] 2083[2] 2363[3] 3058[6] 3678[2] 4069[5] 5796[3] 6100[2] 6338[4] 6745[9]

Hot Snap *Lady Cecil* a80 113
3 ch f Pivotal Midsummer (Kingmambo (USA))
(1622) ◆ 2047[9] 4985[3] 6416a[2] 7365[5]

Hot Spice *Michael Easterby* 76
5 b g Kodiac Harlestone Lady (Shaamit (IRE))
5612[3] 6051[6] 6775[6] 7132[8] 7635[8]

Hot Stock (FR) *Jo Hughes* a64 47
2 b g Elusive City(USA) Hermance (Enrique)
1606[4] 2082[4] 4412[3] 5898[5] 8317[2] 8363[4]

Hot Streak (IRE) *Kevin Ryan* a91 115
2 ch c Iffraaj Ashirah (USA) (Housebuster (USA))
(4781) (5767) 6201[5] 6637[3] (7011) ◆ 7191[2]

Hot Sugar (USA) *Michael Appleby* a72 70
4 b g Lemon Drop Kid(USA) Plaisir Des Yeux (FR) (Funambule (USA))
29[6] 453[4] 627[4] 885[5] 998[7] 6948[6] 7347[3] 7728[4] 8135[4] 8384[6]

Houdini Bright (USA) *James Given* a55 52
5 rg g Tapit(USA) Scootie Utie (USA) (Fappiano (USA))
455[10] 714[6] 888[3] 908[4]

Houghton Hill (FR) *J Rossi* a59
3 ch g Green Tune(USA) Hierarchie (FR) (Sillery (USA))
331a[4]

House Of Orange (IRE) *Mark Johnston* a58 58
3 b g Kheleyf(USA) Cox Orange (USA) (Trempolino (USA))
800[2] 1372[3] 2156[8] 2325[9]

Houston Dynimo (IRE) *Nicky Richards* a76 76
8 b g Rock Of Gibraltar(IRE) Quiet Mouse (USA) (Quiet American (USA))
2633[7]

How Fortunate *Tim Etherington* a63 51
5 b f Haafhd However (IRE) (Hector Protector (USA))
6497[4] 7100[9] 7283[10] 7622[4] 7857[8]

How Rude *Mel Brittain*
2 b f Virtual My Golly (Mozart (IRE))
3350[15] 4731[10]

How's Life *Tim Easterby* a72 93
3 b f Layman(USA) Get The Ring (FR) (Linamix (FR))
(1772) 2429[8] 3734[5] 4949[12] 5561[11] 6875[4] 7172[17]

Howyadoingnotsobad (IRE) *Karen George* a83 79
5 b g Kodiac Beau Petite (Kyllachy)
1984[5] 3577[6] 4123[7] 4344[2] 4675[2] 5036[5] 5669[3] 7080[11] 7445[6]

How You Fixed (IRE) *Denis Quinn* a39
3 b g Antonius Pius(USA) Untimely (Inchinor)
211[12] 468[5] 712[8]

Howz The Family (IRE) *Tom Dascombe* a67 68
2 b c Myboycharlie(IRE) Lady Raj (USA) (El Prado (IRE))
2307[3] (2985) 7252[10] 7945[3] (8137) 8311[3]

Hoyam *Michael Bell* 105
3 b f Royal Applause Christmas Tart (IRE) (Danetime (IRE))
2019[8] 2270[2] 3102[3] 3420[13] 4079[5] 5772a[10] 6305[6] 6719[8]

Huascaran (FR) *F Chappet* a83 71
3 b g Turtle Bowl(IRE) Multimedia (FR) (Exit To Nowhere (USA))
1511a[9]

Hubood *Zoe Davison* a58 55
5 b f Refuse To Bend(IRE) Shuheb (Nashwan (USA))
3656[7]

Hubris (FR) *J-L Pelletan* a80
3 b g Desert Style(IRE) Codicille (FR) (Mendocino (USA))
126a[6]

Huffoof (IRE) *Roger Varian* a64 82
3 b f Dalakhani(IRE) Albahja (Sinndar (IRE))
580[2] ◆ 2164[3] 2803[5] (3610) 3891[3] 4678[3]

Hujaylea (IRE) *M Halford* a102 93
10 b g Almutawakel Red Eagle (IRE) (Eagle Eyed (USA))
1168a[7] 3869a[12]

Hulcolt (IRE) *Garry Moss* 74
2 b c Acclamation Fusili (IRE) (Silvano (GER))
3648[6] 4861[3] 5338[4] 5945[5] 6285[4] (6513) 6972[9]

Humidor (IRE) *George Baker* a91 109
6 b g Camacho Miss Indigo (Indian Ridge)
464a[6] 868a[4] 1483[2] 2300a[7] 3187a[4] 4986[19] 6282[3] 6623[11] 7208[8] 7364[14]

Humour (IRE) *Roger Varian* 57
2 b c Invincible Spirit(IRE) Hucking Hot (Desert Prince (IRE))
2401[10]

Humungosaur *Richard Ford* a55 84
4 b c Red Ransom(USA) Fabulously Fast (USA) (Deputy Minister (CAN))
2629[10] 2972[11]

Hundred Acre Wood *Olivia Maylam* a53
3 b g Modigliani(USA) Bom Chicka Wah Wah (USA) (Dynaformer (USA))
1086[9] 1423[12] 1904[10] 6137[9] 6558[12]

Hunger (AUS) *Mick Price* 87
4 ch g Snitzel(AUS) Hollaback (AUS) (Fusaichi Pegasus (USA))
7417a[10]

Hungry Island (USA) *Claude McGaughey III* 112
5 b f More Than Ready(USA) Flying Passage (USA) (A.P. Indy (USA))
7043a[5]

Hunters Belt (IRE) *George Bewley* a75 64
9 b g Intikhab(USA) Three Stars (Star Appeal)
6552[3] 6942[8]

Hunters Creek (IRE) *John Gosden* a79 94
2 b c Cape Cross(IRE) Cinnamon Rose (USA) (Trempolino (USA))
4925[2] (5279) 6002[4] 7017[4]

Hunter's Light (IRE) *Saeed bin Suroor* a116 117
5 ch c Dubawi(IRE) Portmanteau (Barathea (IRE))
(556a) ◆ (958a) 1269a[7] 2494a[6] 4819a[3] 5553a[10] 7367[4]

Hunting Ground (USA) *Mark Johnston* a92 82
3 b g Street Cry(IRE) Panty Raid (USA) (Include (USA))
2953[6] 3364[5] (5902) 6302[8] 6729[8] 7022[3] 7211[20]

Hunting Rights (USA) *Mark Johnston* a75 86
3 ch g E Dubai(USA) Possession (USA) (Belong To Me (USA))
1822[7] 2432[13] 3571[3] 3828[6] 4168[3] (4442) ◆ 4769[7] 4908[6] 5440[7] (6258) 6596[8] 7312[12] 7611[13]

Hunting Tower *Tim Vaughan* a61 76
9 b g Sadler's Wells(USA) Fictitious (Machiavellian (USA))
5933[6]

Huntsmans Close *Michael Bell* 88
3 b g Elusive Quality(USA) Badminton (Zieten (USA))
2208[6] 3104[8] 3634[4] 4670[2] 5340[3] 5769[8] 6575[3] 7531[11]

Hurakan (IRE) *Richard Price* a75 77
7 gr g Daylami(IRE) Gothic Dream (IRE) (Nashwan (USA))
1699[4] 1973[4] 2569[4] 3157[6] 3985[4] 4775[3] 5666[2] 6377[8]

Hurricane Harry *William Knight*
2 b g Royal Applause Stormy Weather (Nashwan (USA))
5744[9]

Hurricane Hymnbook (USA) *Willie Musson* a76 69
8 b g Pulpit(USA) April Squall (USA) (Summer Squall (USA))
112[6] 403[10] 1699[P]

Hurricane John (IRE) *David Nicholls* a57 52
3 b g Hurricane Run(IRE) Top Lady (IRE) (Shirley Heights)
1685[10] 2341[6] 3653[8] 5143[6] 6964[2] (7204) 7376[6]

Hurricane Lady (IRE) *Mike Murphy* a43 84
5 b f Hurricane Run(IRE) Yaria (IRE) (Danehill (USA))
1922[11] 2639[5]

Hurricane Red (IRE) *Lennart Reuterskiold Jr* a97 97
3 ch c Hurricane Run(IRE) Bounce (FR) (Trempolino (USA))
(5326a) 6453a[3]

Hurricane Spear *Ricardo Lanfranco* a40 41
5 ch g Hurricane Run(IRE) Sarissa (USA) (Diesis)
98[12]

Hurricane Spirit (IRE) *Joseph Tuite* a83 81
9 b g Invincible Spirit(IRE) Gale Warning (IRE) (Last Tycoon)
(221) 415[3] (476) (721) (1094) 1316[2] 1890[4]

Hurrican Source (IRE) *M Delzangles* a63 50
3 b f Hurricane Run(IRE) Source Of Life (IRE) (Fasliyev (USA))
5805a[6]

Hurry Home Poppa (IRE) *John Mackie* a60 70
3 b g Holy Roman Emperor(IRE) My Renee (USA) (Kris S (USA))
6272[3] 7066[8]

Hurry Up George *Ralph Beckett* a91 99
4 b g Intikhab(USA) Digamist Girl (IRE) (Digamist (USA))
8064[6]

Hurryupharriet (IRE) *W McCreery* 98
2 b f Camacho Nova Tor (IRE) (Trans Island)
5771a[2] (6584)

Hussar Ballad (USA) *Mel Brittain* a61 63
4 bb g Hard Spun(USA) Country Melody (USA) (Gone West (USA))
2279[5] 2753[9] 2961[12] 3649[10] 6598[16] (7951) 8233[7]

Hustle Bustle (IRE) *David Brown* 50
2 b f Elusive City(USA) Coachhouse Lady (USA) (Rahy (USA))
2230[6] 2856[6] 3245[12]

Huzzah (IRE) *Michael Appleby* a56 32
8 b g Acclamation Borders Belle (IRE) (Pursuit Of Love)
240[8] 8056[10] 8371[5]

Hvasstan (AUS) *Peter Gelagotis* 102
4 b c Fastnet Rock(AUS) Snow Hero (AUS) (True Hero (USA))
7702a[8]

Hyde Lea Flyer *Barry Leavy* a48 53
8 b g Hernando(FR) Sea Ridge (Slip Anchor)
455[11] 852[10]

Hydrant *Richard Guest* a72 86
7 b g Haafhd Spring (Sadler's Wells (USA))
2785[2] (3397) (3651) (3996) 4798[6] 5382[3] 5860[3] 6288[11] 6976[7] 7131[10] 7424[2]

Hymenaios (IRE) *Richard Hannon Snr* 81
2 ch c Danehill Dancer(IRE) Wedding Morn (IRE) (Sadler's Wells (USA))
5180[2] ◆ 5698[3]

Hymn Book (USA) *Claude McGaughey III* a118 104
7 bb g Arch(USA) Vespers (USA) (Known Fact (USA))
7689a[5]

Hypatia (IRE) *John Joseph Murphy* a49 63
3 b f Holy Roman Emperor(IRE) Kahira (IRE) (King's Best (USA))
6491[10]

Hyper (USA) *Chad C Brown* 113
6 b h Victory Gallop(CAN) Raw Nerve (USA) (Nureyev (USA))
7563a[2]

Hyperlink (IRE) *Michael Bell* a76 76
4 b g Cape Cross(IRE) Surf The Web (IRE) (Ela-Mana-Mou)
5065[5] 5466[5] 6130[6] 7433[2] 7778[11]

Hypnotism *Ronald Harris* a39 41
3 ch g Pivotal Hypnotize (Machiavellian (USA))
1660[10] 1896[6] 2547[10] 8056[3] 8186[4]

I Am That (IRE) *Braem Horse Racing Sprl* a76 78
6 b g Statue Of Liberty(USA) Victory Again (IRE) (Victory Note (USA))
127a[0]

I Am Who I Am *Iain Jardine* a41
3 b f Notnowcato Elusive Kitty (USA) (Elusive Quality (USA))
8200[4]

Ian's Dream (USA) *Jeremy Noseda* a74 101
3 ch g Speightstown(USA) She's Loaded (USA) (Deputy Minister (CAN))
2499[2] 2861[3] (3170) 3455[19]

Ian's Memory (USA) *Jeremy Noseda* a73
2 bb c Smart Strike(CAN) Rite Moment (USA) (Vicar (USA))
6733[4] 7461[4]

Iave Con (FR) *I Endaltsev* a67 75
3 b g Country Reel(USA) Lapol Di San Jore (IRE) (Pursuit Of Love)
1495a[9]

Ibecke *Mark Johnston* a7 41
2 b f Exceed And Excel(AUS) Granted (FR) (Cadeaux Genereux)
4107[6] 4443[3] 5988[10] 6725[4] 7199[9]

Iberis *Lady Cecil* a68 75
3 b f Nayef(USA) Isis (USA) (Royal Academy (USA))
1683[9] 2622[5] 3062[10] 4354[7] 6214[10]

Ibicenco (GER) *Peter G Moody* 113
5 b c Shirocco(GER) Iberi (GER) (Rainbow Quest (USA))
(7483a) 7761a[16]

Ibiza Sunset (IRE) *Brendan Powell* a40 76
5 b g Chineur(FR) Romanylei (IRE) (Blues Traveller (IRE))
8308[9] 8447[11]

Ibn Hiyyan (USA) *Conor Dore* a23 53
6 rg g El Prado(IRE) Lovely Later (USA) (Green Dancer (USA))
4692[3] 5231[10] 5409[5]

Icanboogie *Anthony Middleton* a49 44
3 b g Tobougg(IRE) Dubai Marina (Polish Precedent (USA))
59[5] 212[6] 336[2] 506[4] 910[5] 1098[9] 1289[6] 8388[9] 8417[7]

Ican'Tknow *Gary Moore*
2 ch g Compton Place Oomph (Shareef Dancer (USA))
6079[P]

Ice Apple *John E Long* a55 52
5 b f Iceman Star Apple (Barathea (IRE))
132[3] 653[11] 983[8] 1325[5] 1953[6] 2563[2] 2921[P] 6558[7] 7159[3] (7612) 8027[4] 8268[3]

Iceblast *Michael Easterby* a72 65
5 b g Iceman Medici Princess (Medicean)
1351[7] 1994[5] 2536[13] (3630) 7076[10] 7801[4] (8029)

Icebreaker Two *John E Long* a52 53
4 b g Iceman Mintlaw (Mujahid (USA))
1877[5] 2642[8] 3688[8]

Icebuster *Rod Millman* a92 92
5 ch g Iceman Radiate (Sadler's Wells (USA))
1302[2] 1501[2] (1831) 2018[4] 2520[4] 3208[2] 4060[11] 4488[7] 5259[3] 6172[6] 6801[5] 7976[5] 8150[3] 8327[3] 8429[5]

Ice Cool (FR) *W Hefter* 103
4 b c Lateral Indianapolis (GER) (Tiger Hill (IRE))
5912a[5]

Ice Falcon (IRE) *James Tate* a38
2 gr f Verglas(IRE) Katimont (IRE) (Montjeu (IRE))
6365[5]

Ice Love (FR) *T Castanheira* a86 81
2 b f Three Valleys(USA) Xcape To Victory (IRE) (Cape Cross (IRE))
5555a[11]

Iceman George *Alison Hutchinson* a66 67
9 b g Beat Hollow Diebiedale (Dominion)
(2714) 3037[4] 3721[6] 4179[2] 4455[3] 5833[6] 6290[15] 6632[11]

Ice Mayden *Bryan Smart* a48 55
2 b f Major Cadeaux Reel Cool (Reel Buddy (USA))
5338[5] 6299[6] 7237[7] 7755[4] 7955[7]

Ice Nelly (IRE) *Stuart Kittow* a56 73
5 b f Iceman Dancing Nelly (Shareef Dancer (USA))
3854[3] 4832[6] 7628[9]

Ice Pie *Tom Dascombe* a74 83
3 b f Mount Nelson Statua (IRE) (Statoblest)
2026[3] ◆ 2387[8] 6743[3] 7105[2] 7659[10]

Ice Slice (IRE) *Richard Hannon Snr* a76 76
2 b g Dark Angel(IRE) Ice Rock (IRE) (Rock Of Gibraltar (IRE))
3155[3] 3836[11] 4716[2] 5033[2] 5693[3] 6731[2]

Ice Tres *Rod Millman* a59 59
4 br f Iceman Tup Tim (Emperor Jones (USA))
215[4] 397[5] 651[9] 925[8] 1654[3] 1949[4] 2714[5] 3037[5] 3854[6] 8148[4] 8373[2]

Ice Trooper *Kristin Stubbs* a78 74
5 b g Iceman Out Like Magic (Magic Ring (IRE))
398[11] 558[9] 750[10] 1397[3]

Ichimoku *Bryan Smart* a53 60
3 b g Indesatchel(IRE) Mythicism (Oasis Dream)
1762[5] 1988[3] (2535) 2756[12] 4290[5] 5141[4] 6604[10] 8272[9] 8351[10]

Icon Dance *Ben De Haan* a56 74
3 b f Sixties Icon Dance To The Blues (IRE) (Danehill Dancer (IRE))
2658[3] 3375[4] 4219[3] 4750[2] 7167[4]

Iconic Artist (USA) *Andrew Balding* 45
2 br c Arch(USA) Seeking Silence (USA) (Seeking The Gold (USA))
3581[12] 5188[8]

Icy Blue *Richard Whitaker* a66 56
5 b g Iceman Bridal Path (Groom Dancer (USA))
1788[15] 2911[2] 3889[5] 4119[8] 4823[4] 5341[4] 5783[5] 6276[4] 6667[5] (7082) 7383[2] 7515[5] 7952[7] 8162[2]

Icy Quiet *David O'Meara* a55 22
5 b f Shirocco(GER) Winter Silence (Dansili)
100[3] 169[7] 646[3]

Idamante *Kristin Stubbs* 55
2 b g Amadeus Wolf Gower Valentine (Primo Valentino (IRE))
1606[6] 1960[3] 6175[9]

Idarose (IRE) *Alan Berry* a15 24
4 b f Scorpion(IRE) Garra Princess (IRE) (Golan (IRE))
28[8] 5370[8] 6177[13] 6759[8]

Idder (IRE) *Roger Varian* 79
2 br c Authorized(IRE) Epiphany (Zafonic (USA))
7308[4] ◆ (7655)

Idea (USA) *Sir Michael Stoute* 80
2 gr c Mizzen Mast(USA) Discuss (USA) (Danzig (USA))
6739[U] (7251)

Ideal (GER) *Ferdinand J Leve* 103
3 b c Areion(GER) Intschu Tschuna (GER) (Lando (GER))
1708a[3] 3485[11] 7968a[7]

Idle Curiosity (IRE) *Jim Boyle* a64 64
3 b f Red Clubs(IRE) Idle Fancy (Mujtahid (USA))
1180[4] (1319) 1710[5] 3216[10] 3405[3] 4410[11] (4607) 5349[8] 5602[2] 6017[5] 6560[6]

Idle Warrior *Richard Fahey* 60
3 b g Indesatchel(IRE) Amused (Prince Sabo)
2861[2] 3593[4] 5989[7]

Idol Deputy (FR) *James Bennett* a88
7 gr g Silver Deputy(CAN) Runaway Venus (USA) (Runaway Groom (CAN))
82[4] (219) (478) 614[9] 1081[4] 1327[8] (1699) 1796[2] 2085[5] 6167[12]

Idolise (IRE) *John Spearing* a14 50
4 b g Elusive Quality(USA) Victoria Star (IRE) (Danehill (USA))
990[8] 3319[7] 5092[8] 6473[9]

Idyllic Star (IRE) *Keith Dalgleish* a69 75
4 ch f Choisir(AUS) Idolize (Polish Precedent (USA))
1842[2] (4469) (4615)

If (GER) *Andrew Balding* 79
2 b c Rock Of Gibraltar(IRE) Ianapourna (GER) (Dai Jin)
4231[11] 4906[2] (5167) 6041[3] 6501[4] 7129[5]

Ifan (IRE) *Tim Vaughan* a70 72
5 b g Ivan Denisovich(IRE) Montana Miss (IRE) (Earl Of Barking (IRE))
619[2] (849) 2395[2] 2920[2] 3676[2] 5263[2]

Iffley Fields *Michael Squance* a39 55
3 b g Indesatchel(IRE) Happy Omen (Warning)
3405[8] 4391[8] 5935[12] 6138[5] 6462[6] 6849[7]

Iffraaj Pink (IRE) *Roger Varian* a69 82
3 b f Iffraaj Red Vale (IRE) (Halling (USA))
1828[2] ◆ (2231) 3177[4] 4878[13]

Iffranesia (FR) *Robert Cowell* a72 18
3 ch f Iffraaj Farnesina (FR) (Anabaa (USA))
7454[10] (7850) (8051) 8411[2] ◆

If I Had Him (IRE) *George Baker* a63 66
9 b g City Honours(USA) Our Valentine (IRE) (Be My Native (USA))
12[3] 973[2] 2301a[2] 3256[2] (3647a) 3884[9]

If I Were A Boy (IRE) *Dominic Ffrench Davis* a70 73
6 b m Invincible Spirit(IRE) Attymon Lill (IRE) (Marju (IRE))
906[7] 1200[3] (1480) 1956[3] 2939[3] 3244[9] 3635[6] ◆ 3900[5] 5762[6] 8447[7]

Ifrika *Clive Brittain* a69 69
2 ch f Iffraaj Poyle Caitlin (IRE) (Bachir (IRE))
3574[4] 6799[4] 8018[3] 8332[5]

If So *James Fanshawe* a98 95
4 b f Iffraaj Persario (Bishop Of Cashel)
(1957) ◆ (2745) 3472[3] 5009[10] (5636) 6331[7] ◆ 6831[3] 7642[2] 7982[2]

Iftaar (IRE) *Charles Hills* 75
2 b c Bushranger(IRE) Kheleyf's Silver (IRE) (Kheleyf (USA))
2411[6] 2778[2] 6799[8] 7170[9]

Iftikaar (IRE) *F Rohaut* a61
3 b c Cape Cross(IRE) Anbella (FR) (Common Grounds)
460a[5]

Ifwecan *Mark Johnston* 88
2 b g Exceed And Excel(AUS) Kirk (Selkirk (USA))
1930[5] ◆ (2250) 2863[4] 3481[13] 4248[3] 4948[5] 5656[11] 6187[5]

If What And Maybe *John Ryan* a55 54
5 ch g Needwood Blade Pink Champagne (Cosmonaut)
579[13] 635[8] 724[5] 973[6] 1601[5] 1953[4] 2435[15] 2642[12] 3473[7] 3688[9] 4380[10]

If You Whisper (IRE) *Mike Murphy* a73 46
5 b g Iffraaj Little Whisper (IRE) (Be My Guest (USA))
417[4] 653[8] 747[7]

Iggy *Michael Easterby* a62 53
3 ch g Lucarno(USA) Fujakka (IRE) (Vettori (IRE))
59[2] (236) 2308[11] 4725[9] 5016[9] 5471[6]

Ighraa (IRE) *F-H Graffard* a73 108
3 b f Tamayuz Frond (Alzao (USA))
126a[8] 1869a[5] 2838[4] 3877a[6]

Ignight *Mark Usher* a41 46
2 ch c Compton Place Time Clash (Timeless Times (USA))
4827[10] 6590[9] 8061[9]

I Got You Babe (IRE) *Doug Watson* a66 65
5 gr f Clodovil(IRE) Duck Over (Warning)
394a[3]

Iguacu *Richard Price* a58 61
9 b g Desert Prince(IRE) Gay Gallanta (USA) (Woodman (USA))
1434[6] 1700[2] 1948[7] 2567[2] 3133[7] 3406[4] 4071[11] 5377[4] 6895[7]

Iguazu Falls (USA) *M bin Shafya* a83 110
8 ch g Pivotal Anna Palariva (IRE) (Caerleon (USA))
367a[3] 745a[3] 959a[8]

Igugu (AUS) *M F De Kock* 111
6 b m Galileo(IRE) Zarinia (IRE) (Intikhab (USA))
743a[3] 959a[6] 1267a[5] 1872a[8] 6796[2] 7365[8]

Ihtikar (USA) *Ed Dunlop* a69
3 b g Invasor(ARG) Ranin (Unfuwain (USA))
1178^{5} 1468^{5}

Ihtimal (IRE) *Saeed bin Suroor* 107
2 b f Shamardal(USA) Eastern Joy (Dubai Destination (USA))
2583^{2} 3057^{2} 3555^{3} ◆ (5284) (6350) ◆ 6798^{3}

Ikc Dragon Heart (USA) *Johan Reuterskiold* a65 50
3 b c Lion Heart(USA) Champaigne Amelia (USA) (Cure The Blues (USA))
5326a^{7}

Ikhtisas (USA) *Saeed bin Suroor* a80 81
3 b c Street Sense(USA) Any For Love (ARG) (Southern Halo (USA))
4223^{7} (4672) 5189^{6} 6108^{5} 6559^{8}

Iktiview *Philip Kirby* 62
5 ch g Iktibas Eastview Princess (J B Quick)
1282^{11} 2462^{3} 7372^{9}

Ile De Re (FR) *Donald McCain* 107
7 gr g Linamix(FR) Ile Mamou (IRE) (Ela-Mana-Mou)
2149^{13} 2668^{4} 3824^{12} 6385^{8}

Ilena (GER) *Dr A Bolte* 99
4 b f Areion(GER) Incita (GER) (Royal Solo (IRE))
3852a^{10}

Ilewin Dundee *Gary Brown* a46
7 b g Loup Sauvage(USA) Ilewin Janine (IRE) (Soughaan (USA))
886^{9}

Il Grande Maurizio (IRE) *A Al Raihe* a96 102
9 b h King Charlemagne(USA) Ciubanga (IRE) (Arazi (USA))
149a^{14} 367a^{14}

Illawalla *Alan Berry* a14 42
5 b g Indesatchel(IRE) Adorable Cherub (USA) (Halo (USA))
6297^{11} 6806^{7}

I'll Be Good *Alan Berry* a62 47
4 b g Red Clubs(IRE) Willisa (Polar Falcon (USA))
3778^{13} 4203^{9} 4613^{6} 5051^{12} 5138^{9} 8035^{3} ◆ 8135^{2} 8439^{5}

I'Ll Be Your Man *M Figge* a46
3 b g High Chaparral(IRE) If You Ever (IRE) (Singspiel (IRE))
460a^{10}

I'Lldoit *Michael Scudamore* a47 16
6 br g Tamayaz(CAN) Club Oasis (Forzando)
755^{8} 1080^{8}

Illegal Action (USA) *Olly Stevens* a54 51
2 b c Smart Strike(CAN) Polar Circle (USA) (Royal Academy (USA))
5399^{8} 6110^{8} 8061^{7} 8452^{5}

Illegale (IRE) *Nikki Evans* 40
7 b m Poliglote Pinkai (IRE) (Caerleon (USA))
6895^{11} 7636^{8}

Illshowya (IRE) *Michael McElhone*
4 b g Antonius Pius(USA) Rajani (IRE) (Johannesburg (USA))
1735^{7}

Illuminating Dream (IRE) *David Brown* 78
2 b f High Chaparral(IRE) Massada (Most Welcome)
4668^{3} ◆ (5983) 6545^{2}

Illustrate (IRE) *A P O'Brien* 89
3 b c Oasis Dream Kassiopeia (IRE) (Galileo (IRE))
3796a^{11}

Illustrious Forest *John Mackie* a87 50
5 ch g Shinko Forest(IRE) Illustre Inconnue (USA) (Septieme Ciel (USA))
(39) 563^{2} 1083^{2} (1212)

Illustrious Lad (IRE) *Jim Boyle* a64 44
4 ch g Bertolini(USA) Squeak (Selkirk (USA))
156^{8} 354^{9} 610^{5} 736^{3} 819^{4} 909^{9}

Illustrious Prince (IRE) *Declan Carroll* a80 85
6 b g Acclamation Sacred Love (IRE) (Barathea (IRE))
1366^{5} 1430^{6} 1686^{7} 1819^{9} 2096^{3} 2275^{6} 2580^{5} 3068^{3} 3445^{8} 3546^{4} 4198^{2} (4496) (4628) 5292^{7} 5564^{2} 5711^{5} 6072^{7} (6291) 6475^{4} 6774^{6} 6988^{13} 7885^{4} (7948)

Il Paparazzi *Daniel Kubler* 100
2 b g Royal Applause Birdie (Alhaarth (IRE))
3291^{6} (4731) 5652^{3}

I'm A Dreamer (IRE) *David Simcock* 114
6 b m Noverre(USA) Summer Dreams (IRE) (Sadler's Wells (USA))
1267a^{7}

Imaginary Diva *George Margarson* a61 65
7 b m Lend A Hand Distant Diva (Distant Relative)
30^{4} 139^{7} 322^{4} 862^{7} 2643^{2} ◆ 2870^{2} ◆ 3425^{3} 3994^{6} (5408) 5608^{6} 8457^{8}

Imaginary World (IRE) *John Balding* a73 75
5 b f Exceed And Excel(AUS) Plutonia (Sadler's Wells (USA))
218^{6} 330^{3} 1521^{2} 2155^{3} 2514^{2} 2956^{7} 3814^{5} 4928^{3} (5192) 5515^{2} (5830) 6341^{3} 6941^{8} 8134^{6} 8316^{5}

I'm Back (IRE) *Saeed bin Suroor* a95 97
3 b c Exceed And Excel(AUS) Paracel (USA) (Gone West (USA))
245a^{2} 553a^{6} 953a^{6} 7247^{4}

I'm Fraam Govan *George Baker* a99 88
5 ch g Fraam Urban Dancer (IRE) (Generous (IRE))
2989^{3} 4382^{3} (5100) ◆ 6004^{4} (7121) (8327) ◆

I'm Harry *George Baker* a63 68
4 b g Haafhd First Approval (Royal Applause)
7^{6} 375^{8} (1313a) 1739a^{3} (2302a) 2764^{2} 4605^{7} 5329a^{2} (7145a) 6553^{3} 6985^{6} (7458)

Imjin River (IRE) *William Stone* a62 57
6 b g Namid Lady Nasrana (FR) (Al Nasr (FR))
143^{5} 516^{2} 750^{8} 968^{2} 1783^{9} 2096^{5} 6343^{9} 7850^{5} 8082^{5} 8393^{9} 8457^{4}

I'm Lucy (IRE) *Linda Jewell* a7
2 b f Papal Bull Melaaya (USA) (Aljabr (USA))
8084^{9}

Immediately *Robert Cowell* a45 21
3 b f Notnowcato Two Step (Mujtahid (USA))
2637^{5} 3401^{7} 4176^{7} 7353^{12}

Immigrand Child (FR) *Mlle S-V Tarrou* a62 70
4 b c Celtic Swing Indanehill (IRE) (Indian Danehill (IRE))
922a^{10}

Impeccability *John Mackie* a53 46
3 b f Lucky Story(USA) Impeccable Guest (IRE) (Orpen (USA))
590^{3} 757^{4} 972^{4} 1685^{6} 3137^{5} 3910^{11} 6851^{4} 7035^{5} 7847^{7} 8417^{2}

Imperator Augustus (IRE) *Patrick Holmes* a79 73
5 b g Holy Roman Emperor(IRE) Coralita (IRE) (Night Shift (USA))
3441^{5} 3981^{6} 4198^{7} 4956^{5} 5273^{11} (5614) 6702^{7} 8012a^{8} 8219^{7} 8323^{9}

Imperial Bond *Jason Ward* a40 55
4 b g Misu Bond(IRE) Liability (IRE) (Bluebird (USA))
59^{7} 4762^{8} 5139^{5} 5903^{7} 6630^{2} 7153^{7} 7345^{4}

Imperial Concorde (IRE) *D K Weld* 102
3 bb c High Chaparral(IRE) Irish Style (IRE) (Mujadil (USA))
1558a^{3}

Imperial Djay (IRE) *Ruth Carr* a66 102
8 b g Dilshaan Slayjay (IRE) (Mujtahid (USA))
1232^{11} ◆ 1485^{6} 1830^{11} 2028^{8} 2463^{10} 2665^{9}

Imperial Elegance *Sheena West* a32 40
4 b f Imperial Dancer Canadian Capers (Ballacashtal (CAN))
417^{10} 469^{6}

Imperial Glance *Andrew Balding* a56 72
3 br g Passing Glance Juno Mint (Sula Bula)
1011^{5} 1900^{8} 2495^{5} (3376) 3665^{5}

Imperial Guest *George Margarson* 109
7 ch g Imperial Dancer Princess Speedfit (FR) (Desert Prince (IRE))
10^{P}

Imperial Ike *Lisa Williamson*
2 b g Imperial Dancer Betws Y Coed (IRE) (Indian Haven)
8415^{9}

Imperial Legend (IRE) *David Nicholls* 93
4 b g Mujadil(USA) Titian Saga (IRE) (Titus Livius (FR))
2122^{7} 3069^{6} 3283^{2} 3505^{5} (3933) 4479^{2} 4613^{4} 5639^{3} 5971^{9} (6159) 6583^{2} 7171^{6} 7373^{8}

Imperial Monarch (IRE) *A P O'Brien* 118
4 b c Galileo(IRE) Ionian Sea (Slip Anchor)
1263a^{6}

Imperial Spirit *Mick Channon* a64 75
3 b g Imperial Dancer Country Spirit (Sayf El Arab (USA))
1896^{5} 2363^{4} 2616^{10} 2962^{6} 3316^{4} 3789^{3} 3994^{5} 4176^{2} 4244^{6} 4544^{2} 4607^{4} 4916^{5} 5431^{3} 5890^{3} 5981^{4} 6157^{4} (6651) 6902^{2} 7292^{8} 7772^{16}

Imperial Stargazer *Sheena West* a47 54
4 gr g Imperial Dancer Sky Light Dreams (Dreams To Reality (USA))
4173^{5}

Imperiator *P Decouz* a97 97
2 b g Footstepsinthesand Jarhes (IRE) (Green Desert (USA))
5911a^{4} (7570a)

Impertinent *Jonathan Portman* a53 51
3 b f Halling(USA) Incarnation (IRE) (Samum (GER))
90^{5} 1897^{9} 6996^{7} (7440)

Imprimis Tagula (IRE) *Alan Bailey* a83 77
9 b g Tagula(IRE) Strelitzia (IRE) (Bluebird (USA))
155^{3} 311^{4} 540^{5} 715^{9} 912^{8}

Improvisation (IRE) *Mahmood Al Zarooni* 94
3 b c Teofilo(IRE) Dance Troupe (Rainbow Quest (USA))
(1624)

Improvized *William Muir* a52 63
2 b f Authorized(IRE) Rhapsodize (Halling (USA))
(6460) 7110^{4}

Impulsive Moment (IRE) *Andrew Balding* a76 65
2 ch c Galileo(IRE) Luas Line (IRE) (Danehill (USA))
7500^{5} (8382) ◆

Imshivalla (IRE) *Richard Fahey* 72
2 b f Acclamation Subtle Affair (IRE) (Barathea (IRE))
2670^{8} 3826^{7} 4115^{3} 4726^{3} 5235^{5} (5850) 6233^{3}

I'm So Glad *Mick Channon* a78 101
4 b f Clodovil(IRE) Dilag (IRE) (Almutawakel)
1544^{8} 2013^{13} 2858^{13} 3102^{6} 3562^{3} 4297^{3} 4534^{7} 5285^{6} 6143^{5} 6411^{5} 7015^{8}

I'm Super Too (IRE) *Alan Swinbank* a70 82
6 b g Fasliyev(USA) Congress (IRE) (Dancing Brave (USA))
2163^{3} 2539^{4} 3349^{15} 3715^{5} 6048^{7} 6730^{4} 6906^{5} 6943^{9}

Imtithal (IRE) *John Weymes* a71 68
4 b f Invincible Spirit(IRE) Dream Time (Rainbow Quest (USA))
1015^{4} 1184^{6} 1389^{6} 1736^{7} 2155^{8} 2794^{5} 2974^{2} 3203^{10} 3644^{7} 3910^{13} 5200^{7}

I'm Your Man (FR) *A De Royer-Dupre* 114
4 bb c Cape Cross(IRE) Via Saleria (IRE) (Arazi (USA))
2908a^{6} 3830^{2} 5531^{5}

Inaad (IRE) *Saeed bin Suroor* a77 81
3 b c New Approach(IRE) Athreyaa (Singspiel (IRE))
2885^{3} 4151^{3} (4813)

Inaugural *Roger Charlton* a60 74
3 b g Invincible Spirit(IRE) Anasazi (IRE) (Sadler's Wells (USA))
1471^{7} 2420^{10}

Inca Chief *Ann Duffield* a30 43
5 b g Sleeping Indian Queen Of Havana (USA) (King Of Kings (IRE))
3030^{6} 3466^{7}

Incendo *Ian Williams* a102 88
7 ch g King's Best(USA) Kindle (Selkirk (USA))
496^{9} 1037^{5} 2590^{3} 5237^{8} 6128^{4} 6421a^{3} 6984^{3} 7758^{4} 7950^{2} 8057^{4} 8202^{4}

Inchelle (IRE) *E Lellouche* 72
3 b f Zamindar(USA) Inchiri (Sadler's Wells (USA))
3166a^{8} 5913a^{2}

Inchila *Peter Chapple-Hyam* 74
2 b f Dylan Thomas(IRE) Inchiri (Sadler's Wells (USA))
4921^{2} 5488^{3}

Inciting Incident (IRE) *Ed McMahon* 72
2 b g Camacho Halliwell House (Selkirk (USA))
1605^{2} 2189^{2} 3017^{5} 4289^{5}

Incognita *Chris Down* 14
3 ch f Sakhee's Secret Angel Sprints (Piccolo)
6319^{7} 7073^{11} 7459^{11}

Incognito (USA) *Kiaran McLaughlin* a112
3 rg c A.P. Indy(USA) Octave (USA) (Unbridled's Song (USA))
3127a^{4}

Incorporate *Pat Eddery* a73 86
3 ch c Beat Hollow Five Fields (USA) (Chester House (USA))
663^{3} 895^{2} (1236) 1667^{4} 2416^{9}

Incroyable (USA) *C Laffon-Parias* a87 100
4 b f Singspiel(IRE) Soft Pleasure (USA) (Diesis)
7189a^{5} 7843a^{8}

Indastar *John Weymes* 42
3 b g Indesatchel(IRE) Charcoal (Primo Valentino (IRE))
3479^{8}

Indego Blues *David Nicholls* 83
4 b g Indesatchel(IRE) Yanomami (USA) (Slew O'Gold (USA))
1692^{7} 2239^{7} ◆ 2781^{4} (3393) 3945^{14} 5011^{5} 5832^{4} (6209) 6586^{14} 6908^{6} 7374^{5} 7594^{5}

Indepub *Kevin Ryan* 86
4 b g Indesatchel(IRE) Champenoise (Forzando)
1238^{10} 1831^{11} 3827^{9} 4293^{6} 5087^{3}

Index Waiter *Brian Meehan* a59 61
3 ch g Exceed And Excel(AUS) Snowy Indian (Indian Ridge)
2154^{8} 2393^{8} 2926^{4}

Indian Affair *Milton Bradley* a72 75
3 b c Sleeping Indian Rare Fling (USA) (Kris S (USA))
(628) 879^{4} 1014^{4} 1433^{2} 1524^{3} 2329^{2} 2544^{3} (3050) 3733^{5} 4354^{10} 4710^{4} 5820^{4} 6362^{4} 7432^{10} 8029^{2} 8128^{11} 8456^{10}

Indian Billionaire (IRE) *Paul Fitzsimons*
3 b g Red Clubs(IRE) Tabrina (IRE) (Fasliyev (USA))
2938^{15}

Indian Chief (IRE) *A P O'Brien* 110
3 b g Montjeu(IRE) Buck Aspen (USA) (Seeking The Gold (USA))
(1587a) ◆ 2398^{3} 3485^{9} 6440a^{10}

Indian Giver *Alan Berry* a29 68
5 b f Indesatchel(IRE) Bint Baddi (FR) (Shareef Dancer (USA))
5369^{7} 6301^{8} 6600^{9} 6730^{6} 7379^{9}

Indian Jack (IRE) *Ed Walker* a95 93
5 ch g Indian Haven Almaviva (IRE) (Grand Lodge (USA))
7648^{3} ◆ 7989^{8}

Indian Jones (USA) *Philip T Aristone* a105
6 ch g Smarty Jones(USA) Native Wind Dancer (USA) (Incinderator (USA))
7687a^{5}

Indian Rainbow (IRE) *Andreas Lowe* 90
2 ch f Indian Haven Pent House (IRE) (Titus Livius (FR))
7406a^{5}

Indian Scout *Anabel K Murphy* a49 52
5 b g Indesatchel(IRE) Manderina (Mind Games)
7847^{9} 8270^{13}

Indian Sly (FR) *P Capelle* 84
8 b h Indian Rocket Slyders (IRE) (Hector Protector (USA))
3851a^{12} 5040a^{12} 5314a^{13}

Indian Tinker *Robert Cowell* a55 73
4 b g Sleeping Indian Breakfast Creek (Hallgate)
2736^{4} 3317^{2} 3816^{3} 4675^{8} 5620^{4} 6412^{2} 7432^{2} 7634^{9}

Indian Trail *David Nicholls* a74 76
13 ch g Indian Ridge Take Heart (Electric)
1692^{6} 2343^{2} 3569^{9} 4047^{8} 4588^{3} 4728^{5} 4852^{2} 5381^{9} 5985^{6}

Indian Trifone (IRE) *Ed Walker* 69
3 ch c Indian Haven Almaviva (IRE) (Grand Lodge (USA))
2507^{2}

Indian Violet (IRE) *Zoe Davison* a61 38
7 b g Indian Ridge Violet Spring (IRE) (Exactly Sharp (USA))
510^{11} (805) 907^{5} 1056^{7} 1473^{2} 1873^{7} 1981^{3} 2534^{9} 2954^{4} 3329^{3}

Indian Walk (FR) *M Gentile* a73
3 gr c Literato(FR) Brilliantly (FR) (Priolo (USA))
460a^{6} 604a^{4}

India's Song *David Simcock* a67
3 b f Zamindar(USA) Sea Chorus (Singspiel (IRE))
685^{3} 1185^{4} 7038^{5} 8182^{4} 8417^{4}

Indie Banned *Ben Haslam* 24
3 b g Indesatchel(IRE) Day By Day (Kyllachy)
4400^{10}

Indie Star *Harry Dunlop* a33 49
2 b f Indesatchel(IRE) Flying Highest (Spectrum (IRE))
3574^{6} 4154^{7} 5812^{8} 6322^{11} 7301^{7}

Indignant *Richard Hannon Snr* a83 102
3 ch f Gold Away(IRE) Moiava (FR) (Bering)
2449^{2} 3342^{2} (4252) 4949^{13} 5684^{2} 7649^{9}

Indigo (FR) *C Ferland* 104
3 b f Falco(USA) Blanche (FR) (Loup Solitaire (USA))
(1972a) 5461a^{10} 6962a^{12}

Indigo Lady *Peter Chapple-Hyam* 103
3 b f Sir Percy Seal Indigo (IRE) (Glenstal (USA))
2367^{4} 3482^{7} 6962a^{10}

Indigo Moon *Denis Coakley* a54 48
3 b f Sleeping Indian Ewenny (Warrshan (USA))
2824^{5} 3405^{6}

Indikova (IRE) *A Wohler* a80 83
2 b f Bushranger(IRE) Interim Payment (USA) (Red Ransom (USA))
5911a^{6}

Indira *John Berry* a60
2 ch f Sleeping Indian Forever Loved (Deploy)
8259^{2}

Indomito (GER) *A Wohler* a96 104
7 b h Areion(GER) Insola (GER) (Royal Solo (IRE))
2202a^{6}

Indonesienne (IRE) *C Ferland* 111
2 b f Muhtathir Mydarshaan (Darshaan)
(7055a)

Indriya (FR) *F Rohaut* 103
4 ch f Stormy River(FR) Killgra (IRE) (Grand Lodge (USA))
5940a^{6}

Induna (AUS) *Saeed bin Suroor* a69 113
5 b g Elusive Quality(USA) Camarena (NZ) (Danehill (USA))
661a^{12} 833a^{10}

Indus River (IRE) *Charlie Appleby* 59
2 b c New Approach(IRE) Tarbela (IRE) (Grand Lodge (USA))
7019^{10} 7339^{8}

Indy (IRE) *David Barron* 87
2 b c Indian Haven Maddie's Pearl (IRE) (Clodovil (IRE))
(7818)

Indy Point (ARG) *Richard E Mandella* a113 119
4 ch c Indygo Shiner(USA) Red Point (ARG) (Parade Marshal (USA))
5553a^{13} 7712a^{3}

Indy Spirit (IRE) *Laura Mongan* a53
3 gr f Indian Haven Madame Moonshine (Machiavellian (USA))
1095^{7} 1499^{8} 2803^{8} 3403^{9}

I Need A Dollar *J R Jenkins* a49 1
3 b g Phoenix Reach(IRE) Lady Starlight (IRE) (Almutawakel)
114^{8} 1904^{9} 2566^{12} 3495^{12}

Inessa Armand (IRE) *J S Moore* a67 58
3 ch f Shamardal(USA) Shakti (Indian Ridge)
141^{4} 231^{2} 419^{3} 1428^{3} (1613) 1885^{7} 3578 3675^{4} 4122^{4} 4755^{2}

Inevitable *Mark Johnston* 73
2 b g Dubawi(IRE) Come What May (Selkirk (USA))
5827^{6} 6125^{9} 6666^{4} 7252^{4}

Infanta Branca (USA) *A P O'Brien* a89 96
3 b f Henrythenavigator(USA) Totemic (USA) (Vanlandingham (USA))
2108a^{8} 2676a^{11}

Inffiraaj (IRE) *Mick Channon* a61 64
4 b f Iffraaj Incense (Unfuwain (USA))
1214^{9} 1502^{6} 4365^{6} 4754^{9} 5337^{10} 5671^{7} 5977^{5}

Infinite Hope (USA) *Luca Cumani* a86 82
4 b f Dynaformer(USA) Shared Dreams (Seeking The Gold (USA))
5445^{5} 6108^{4}

Infinite Magic (USA) *Richard C Mettee* a91 104
3 b c More Than Ready(USA) Truly Enchanting (IRE) (Danehill Dancer (IRE))
(474) 3360a^{6} 8120a^{7}

Infinity One (SPA) *Barbara Valenti* 99
4 ch f Green Tune(USA) Tropical Chic (USA) (Thunder Gulch (USA))
7891a^{12}

In Focus (IRE) *Alan Swinbank* 67
2 ch c Intense Focus(USA) Reine De Neige (Kris)
2701^{2} 3350^{11}

Infolinia (USA) *C Lerner* a53 56
2 b f Royal Applause Infon Line (IRE) (High Chaparral (IRE))
5213a^{4} 6059a^{5}

Ingenti *Christopher Wilson* 75
5 ch f Blue Dakota(IRE) Kungfu Kerry (Celtic Swing)
2338^{6} 2542^{3} 2702^{5} 3630^{4} 4009^{2} 4371^{4} (4448) 4761^{2} (5422) 5470^{5} 5985^{5} 6516^{3} 7029^{5}

Ingleby Angel (IRE) *David O'Meara* a57 99
4 br g Dark Angel(IRE) Mistress Twister (Pivotal)
2406^{6} (2753) (3027) 3544^{3} 3684^{10} 4540^{4} 5014^{6} (5291) (6792) (7024) 7152^{8}

Ingleby Royale *Richard Fahey* 70
3 b f Royal Applause Lay A Whisper (Night Shift (USA))
2737^{9} 3611^{8}

Ingleby Spirit *Richard Fahey* a79 97
6 b g Avonbridge Encore Du Cristal (USA) (Quiet American (USA))
(1536) 2149^{2} 3824^{16}

Ingleby Star (IRE) *John Stimpson* a56 77
8 b g Fath(USA) Rosy Scintilla (IRE) (Thatching)
558^{10} 795^{9} 1101^{6} 1253^{5} 1758^{4} 2338^{8} 2632^{8} 3888^{6} 4430^{3} 4608^{5} 4943^{4} 5701^{6} 6033^{6} 6471^{6}

Ingleby Symphony (IRE) *Richard Fahey* a59 76
3 b f Oratorio(IRE) Alizaya (IRE) (Highest Honor (FR))
(1486) ◆ 1822^{3} 2342^{3} 3610^{6} 4994^{8} 6587^{5} 7038^{6} (7152) 7499^{8}

Ingot Of Gold *Ralph Beckett* a65 71
3 b f Dubawi(IRE) Cresta Gold (Halling (USA))
3858^{4} 4590^{4} 5403^{6}

Inheritance *Sir Michael Stoute* 59
2 b f Oasis Dream Peeress (Pivotal)
7693^{6} ◆

Inherited *Sir Mark Prescott Bt* a64 62
3 b g Selkirk(USA) Akdariya (IRE) (Shirley Heights)
2874^{5} 3497^{4} 5203^{3} 5801^{3} 6686^{2} 7081^{3} 7331^{5}

Inigo Montoya *Alan McCabe* a44 52
3 ch g Compton Place Cugina (Distant Relative)
800^{4} 1236^{8} 1481^{7} 2770^{9} 6700^{9} 7514^{6} 7666^{9}

Inis Meain (USA) *Denis Gerard Hogan* a40 107
6 b g Bernstein(USA) Runaway Fields (USA) (Runaway Groom (CAN))
1168a^{4} 1415a^{2} 3525^{13} 7890a^{2}

Injaz *Kevin Ryan* a45 61
2 ch g Compton Place Belle's Edge (Danehill Dancer (IRE))
5494^{9} 6681^{5} 7348^{6} 7789^{4}

Inka Express *Mike Sowersby* 5
3 b f Rail Link Coolberry (USA) (Rahy (USA))
4559^{5} 6498^{10} 6717^{8}

Inka Surprise (IRE) *Ralph Beckett* a83 81
3 b g Intikhab(USA) Sweet Surprise (IRE) (Danetime (IRE))
2726[5] *3474[5]*

In Love Kelty (FR) *T Larriviere* 63
2 b f Green Tune(USA) Kelty In Love (FR) (Keltos (FR))
7185a[5]

Inniscastle Boy *Jim Goldie* a67 57
4 b g Sir Percy Galapagar (USA) (Miswaki (USA))
3727[9] 4951[6] 5833[10] 6907[8] 7238[9]

Innocently (IRE) *David O'Meara* 77
2 ch c Kheleyf(USA) Innocency (USA) (Diesis)
(1960) 2370[6] 3439[3] (4054) 4261[3] 4511[2] (4783) 5272[3] 5787[6] 5859[4]

Innocent Touch (IRE) *Richard Fahey* 67
2 bl g Intense Focus(USA) Guajira (FR) (Mtoto)
5379[4] 5968[4] 6299[5]

Innoko (FR) *Tony Carroll* a76 67
3 gr g Carlotamix(FR) Chalana (Ashkalani (IRE))
4349[5]

Innsbruck *John Quinn* 87
3 b g Tiger Hill(IRE) Lille Hammer (Sadler's Wells (USA))
(6566)

Inovate (IRE) *Tim Easterby* 59
3 ch g Intikhab(USA) Julianne (IRE) (Persian Bold)
1772[10] 2508[5] 2716[8] 3809[8] 4509[3] 4955[3] 5789[7]

Insaany *Mark Johnston* 67
2 b c Shamardal(USA) Mother Of Pearl (IRE) (Sadler's Wells (USA))
6581[11] 7237[5]

In Salutem *K J Condon* a85 93
3 ch g Sakhee's Secret Irish Light (USA) (Irish River (FR))
5320a[6]

Inside Knowledge (USA) *Garry Woodward* a54 55
7 rg g Mizzen Mast(USA) Kithira (Danehill (USA))
622[3] 888[8] 1601[6] 6565[8] *8436[8]*

Insight (IRE) *David Wachman* 46
2 b f Bushranger(IRE) Ribbon Glade (UAE) (Zafonic (USA))
5773a[12]

Insolenceofoffice (IRE) *Richard Ford* a66 58
5 b g Kodiac Sharp Diversion (USA) (Diesis)
2281[8] *(2997)* 3285[2] 3934[3] *8049[4] 8271[3]*

Inspiriter *Charlie Appleby* a76 77
2 b f Invincible Spirit(IRE) Floristry (Fasliyev (USA))
3049[5] 3510[4] *(4409)* 5005[5] *6170[3]* 6695[2]

Instance *Jeremy Noseda* a98 106
5 b f Invincible Spirit(IRE) Hannda (IRE) (Dr Devious (IRE))
3831[6] 4949[3]

Instant Attraction (IRE) *Jedd O'Keeffe* a78 77
2 b g Tagula(IRE) Coup De Coeur (IRE) (Kahyasi)
3350[5] 3826[2] 4289[3] *(4630)* 5656[10] 6295[2] 7062[3] 7819[3]

Instinctual *Brendan Powell* a43 54
3 ch g Observatory(USA) Be Glad (Selkirk (USA))
(1897) *3403[5]* 5178[6] *8148[11]*

Instruction (IRE) *C Boutin* a75 51
3 b c Danehill Dancer(IRE) Chenchikova (IRE) (Sadler's Wells (USA))
2434a[0]

Integral *Sir Michael Stoute* 116
3 b f Dalakhani(IRE) Echelon (Danehill (USA))
(2850) ◆ (4081) ◆ 4985[7] (6000) ◆ 6837[2] ◆

Intello (GER) *A Fabre* 125
3 b c Galileo(IRE) Impressionnante (Danehill (USA))
(1623) ◆ 2298a[3] ◆ (2907a) (4104a) 5314a[3] (6712a) 7058a[3]

Intense Debate (IRE) *J S Bolger* a55 82
2 b f Intense Focus(USA) Bronntanas (IRE) (Spectrum (IRE))
6881a[5]

Intense Effort (IRE) *Charlie Appleby* 42
2 b g Acclamation Pretty Demanding (IRE) (Night Shift (USA))
6277[12] 6954[10]

Intense Feeling (IRE) *David Evans* a68 75
2 br f Intense Focus(USA) Titania (Fairy King (USA))
1156[6] 1247[3] (1285) 2053[6] 2147[3] 2553[4] 2767[11] 3424[21] 4519[5] 5029[4] (5693) 6386[4] 6432[3] 7609[2] *7782[7] 7846[4] 7977[4]* 8325[3]

Intense Pink *Chris Wall* 107
4 b f Pivotal Clincher Club (Polish Patriot (USA))
2264[3] 3557[12] 6193[10] 7059a[10]

Intense Tango *Alan Jarvis* 54
2 b f Mastercraftsman(IRE) Cover Look (SAF) (Fort Wood (USA))
7274[4]

Intensical (IRE) *J S Bolger* 88
2 b c Intense Focus(USA) Christinas Letter (IRE) (Galileo (IRE))
5771a[10] 6021a[7] 7548a[5]

Interakt *Joseph Tuite* a55 59
6 b m Rakti Amelie Pouliche (FR) (Desert Prince (IRE))
1814[15] 2196[10] 2657[9] 3010[9] 6255[5] 6535[9] *7652[11] 7985[10] 8121[5] 8449[5]*

Interception (IRE) *David Lanigan* a92 70
3 ch f Raven's Pass(USA) Badee'A (IRE) (Marju (IRE))
7108[2] ◆ *(7600) (7845)* ◆ *(8088)* ◆

Interchoice Star *Ray Peacock* a55 48
8 b g Josr Algarhoud(IRE) Blakeshall Girl (Piccolo)
6156[13] *7485[4] 7905[8] 8118[4] 8413[3]*

Interconnection *Ed Vaughan* 60
2 ch g Mount Nelson Lacework (Pivotal)
5488[5]

Interesting (IRE) *H-A Pantall* a95 94
3 b f Raven's Pass(USA) With Fascination (USA) (Dayjur (USA))
1000a[4]

Interior Minister *Jo Hughes* a86 88
3 b g Nayef(USA) Sister Maria (USA) (Kingmambo (USA))
1754[3] ◆ 2827[2] *(3214)* 3806[5] 4447[2] 4980[5] 5448[6]

Interject (USA) *Charles Hills* a55
2 bb f Empire Maker(USA) Introducing (USA) (Deputy Minister (CAN))
7764[9]

Intermath (IRE) *David Evans* 84
2 br g Camacho Royal Interlude (IRE) (King's Theatre (IRE))
(3374) 3857[U] 4212[9] 5028[2] 5524[3] 5945[4] 6697[3] 6865[3] 7097[4]

Intermedium *Charlie Appleby* a80 71
2 ro c Exceed And Excel(AUS) Gweneira (Machiavellian (USA))
5101[2] ◆ 5718[6] *5924[3] 7835[2]*

Intermix (IRE) *Paul Cole* a90
3 b g Intikhab(USA) Bermuxa (FR) (Linamix (FR))
1471[2]

International Love (IRE) *Andrew Balding* a79 80
3 ch f Manduro(GER) Marika (Marju (IRE))
2084[3] ◆ 3239[5] 3619[2] 4799[4]

In The Crowd (IRE) *Richard Price* 65
4 ch g Haafhd Eliza Gilbert (Noverre (USA))
6435[11]

In The Spotlight (IND) *S Padmanabhan* a100 99
5 ch f Alnasr Alwasheek Radiate (IND) (Placerville (USA))
246a[4] 555a[6] *833a[3]*

Intiba (USA) *Saeed bin Suroor* a75 75
3 b f Street Cry(IRE) Danelagh (AUS) (Danehill (USA))
5847[7] *6925[11]*

Intibaah *Brian Meehan* a87 113
3 b g Elnadim(USA) Mawaared (Machiavellian (USA))
1921[2] ◆ 5027[10] 6411[2] (6990)

Intimhir (IRE) *F Head* 105
3 ch f Muhtathir Sahel (GER) (Monsun (GER))
3877a[5] 7116a[7]

Intimidate *Jeremy Noseda* a88 87
3 b g Royal Applause Crystal Power (USA) (Pleasant Colony (USA))
1112[7] *(1477)* 2439[7] 3342[11] 6571[8] 6871[2]

Intomist (IRE) *Jim Boyle* a79 79
4 ch g Strategic Prince Fast Temper (USA) (In The Wings)
1193[9] 1717[5] (1783) (2395) *(2565)* 3181[2] *3404[2] 5928[6]* 6337[3] 7075[13] *7436[8] 8069[7]* 8430[5] 8455[6]

Into The Wind *Rod Millman* a45 72
6 ch m Piccolo In The Stocks (Reprimand)
1586[3] 3180[4] 4035[5] 4643[2] 5586[5]

Intransigent *Andrew Balding* a106 109
4 b g Trans Island Mara River (Efisio)
947[2] ◆ *1032[7]* 2207[9] 2647[2] 3114[6] 3840[6] 4285[3] 5027[2] 5738[2] (6129) 7013[8]

Intrepid (IRE) *Jeremy Noseda* a81 78
3 b g Invincible Spirit(IRE) Imiloa (USA) (Kingmambo (USA))
2984[3] 4908[5] 6488[7]

Intrigo *Richard Hannon Snr* a79 103
3 b g Medicean A Thousand Smiles (IRE) (Sadler's Wells (USA))
(1476) ◆ *1714[2]* (1832) 2209[7] 2844[2] (3763) 4743[3] 5287[7] 7018[6] 7368[2]

Intrinsic *Sir Michael Stoute* a61 83
3 b c Oasis Dream Infallible (Pivotal)
5678[8] 6133[6] 6502[3] (6940)

Invasor Luck (USA) *James Fanshawe* a77
2 b c Invasor(ARG) Lonely Ahead (USA) (Rahy (USA))
7442[2] ◆

Investissement *David Pipe* 91
7 b g Singspiel(IRE) Underwater (USA) (Theatrical (IRE))
2149[9] 3423[12] 4233[10]

Investment Expert (IRE) *Brian Ellison* a75 88
3 b g Tamayuz Kindling (Dr Fong (USA))
1713[10] 2456[7] (4495) 4957[2] 6126[7] (7075) *8416[6]*

Invigilator *Derek Shaw* a71 59
5 b g Motivator Midpoint (USA) (Point Given (USA))
86[4] 1102[7] 1304[7] 1525[3] (1650) 6777[6] 7165[7] 7432[9] 7729[3] 8029[5] 8220[5] 8306[4] ◆ 8432[11]

Invincible Ash (IRE) *M Halford* a102 110
8 b m Invincible Spirit(IRE) Fully Fashioned (IRE) (Brief Truce (USA))
150a[8] 244a[5] 746a[7] 868a[3] 954a[11] 1265a[10]

Invincible Beauty (IRE) *Seamus Durack* a53 44
4 b f Invincible Spirit(IRE) Beautiful Note (USA) (Red Ransom (USA))
117[2] 349[5] 733[6]

Invincible Cara (IRE) *Ed Dunlop* a63 84
3 b f Invincible Spirit(IRE) Cara Fantasy (IRE) (Sadler's Wells (USA))
1640[7] *2229[5]* 2727[4] 3365[2] (4076) 4485[4] 4878[11] 6387[3] 6976[14]

Invincible Force (IRE) *Paul Green* a70 38
9 b g Invincible Spirit(IRE) Highly Respected (IRE) (High Estate)
1758[11] 2281[10]

Invincible Hero (IRE) *Declan Carroll* a58 89
6 b g Invincible Spirit(IRE) Bridelina (FR) (Linamix (FR))
1113[3] 1840[10] (2232) 2463[4] 3368[5] 3812[8] 4825[7] 5014[4] 5268[3] 5580[6] 6236[8] 7131[4] (7632)

Invincible Lad (IRE) *Ed McMahon* a72 80
9 b g Invincible Spirit(IRE) Lady Ellen (Horage)
6161[11] 6745[13] 7633[10]

Invincible Magic (IRE) *Charlie Appleby* 66
3 b f Invincible Spirit(IRE) Lady Circe (USA) (Spinning World (USA))
5038[5] 5695[2] *6611[6]*

Invincible Ridge (IRE) *D J Bunyan* a83 82
5 b g Invincible Spirit(IRE) Dani Ridge (IRE) (Indian Ridge)
6883a[4]

Invincible Strike (IRE) *James Tate* a97 95
2 gr c Invincible Spirit(IRE) Lazaretta (IRE) (Dalakhani (IRE))
(5915) 6697[2] 7534[8] *7933[2]*

Invincibull (IRE) *Linda Jewell*
3 b g Papal Bull Wishfully Tropical (IRE) (Desert Prince (IRE))
5100[13]

In Vino Veritas (IRE) *Ann Duffield* 61
2 b c Art Connoisseur(IRE) Robin (Slip Anchor)
5915[3] 6299[4]

Invisible Hunter (USA) *Saeed bin Suroor* a93 98
4 ch g Rahy(USA) Madeline P (USA) (Theatrical (IRE))
1675[20] 3113[7] 3503[4] *5355[3] 6403[2] 6608[2]*

Invoke (IRE) *Michael Bell* 72
2 b f Kodiac Tides (Bahamian Bounty)
6354[2] (7095)

Inxile (IRE) *David Nicholls* a107 113
8 b g Fayruz Grandel (Owington)
150a[6] 244a[3] 464a[4] 746a[6] 1255a[8] 2768[7] 5375[2] 5984[13]

Inyordreams *James Given* a58 76
2 b f Teofilo(IRE) Wunders Dream (IRE) (Averti (IRE))
3295[5] ◆ 3760[3] 4723[2] (5577) 6326[9] 6695[5] *7662[2]*

Ioannou *Ian Williams* a64
4 b c Excellent Art Sandtime (IRE) (Green Desert (USA))
194[5] 6610[8] 7958[11] 8329[11]

Ioya Bigtime (USA) *Chris Block* a115 115
6 b h Dynaformer(USA) Ioya Two (USA) (Lord At War (ARG))
5550a[6]

Iphigeneia (TUR) *E Sengel* 99
4 b f Okawango(USA) Mihrisah (TUR) (Mountain Cat (USA))
6231a[6]

Iptisam *James Tate* a99 88
4 ch g Rahy(USA) Grain Of Truth (Gulch (USA))
4118[2] 4968[2] (5512) (6871) ◆ 7241[8] *8053[2] 8231[4] 8369[2]*

Irene Hull (IRE) *Garry Moss* 52
2 b f Excellent Art Wing Diva (IRE) (Hawk Wing (USA))
6513[7] 6938[4] 7310[6]

Irene Kennet *Paul Burgoyne* a68 74
6 b m Kayf Tara Evaporate (Insan (USA))
(9) (417) 653[2] 883[3] (1175) 1654[5] (2360) *3437[5] 5231[11]*

Irian (GER) *J Moore* 114
7 br g Tertullian(USA) Iberi (GER) (Rainbow Quest (USA))
1872a[9]

Iridescence *Jeremy Noseda* a77 82
3 b f Dutch Art Radiate (Sadler's Wells (USA))
(377) (1754)

Irish Boy (IRE) *Christine Dunnett* a51 73
5 b g Desert Millennium(IRE) Shone Island (IRE) (Desert Sun)
2132[8] 2338[2] 3196[7] *4148[5]* (4430) 4707[8] 5620[2] 5956[9] 6527[12] *6732[9]* 7106[14]

Irish Dream (IRE) *Mark Johnston* a64 34
3 bb f Oasis Dream Royal Blue (Machiavellian (USA))
185[6] 341[2] 1299[4] 1874[6] 2635[8]

Irish Girls Spirit (IRE) *Paul Midgley* 64
4 b f Desert Millennium(IRE) Shone Island (IRE) (Desert Sun)
1283[8] 1681[14] 2074[11] 2611[7] 6088[4] ◆ 6471[4] (6878) 7101[9]

Irish Heartbeat (IRE) *Barry Leavy* a83 96
8 b g Celtic Swing She's All Class (USA) (Rahy (USA))
58[6] 217[5] 317[5] 1598[3]

Irish Jugger (USA) *Michael Appleby* a64 58
6 ch g Johannesburg(USA) Jinny's Gold (USA) (Gold Fever (USA))
4147[7]

Irish Mission (CAN) *Mark Frostad* a97 101
4 ch f Giant's Causeway(USA) Misty Mission (CAN) (Miswaki (USA))
7562a[7]

Irish Star (IRE) *Paul Midgley*
2 ch f Thousand Words Zimushka (IRE) (Soviet Star (USA))
3500[7]

Irish Surf (USA) *Dan L Hendricks* 107
3 b c Giant's Causeway(USA) Surfside (USA) (Seattle Slew (USA))
8120a[9]

Irish Tears *John Gosden* a72 70
2 b c Compton Place Deora De (Night Shift (USA))
5488[8] 5957[3] *7302[10] 8147[2] 8389[2] 8452[11]*

Iron Butterfly *James Eustace* a45 64
4 b f Shirocco(GER) Coh Sho No (Old Vic)
(7098) 7597[4]

Irondale Express *Tony Coyle* 66
2 b f Myboycharlie(IRE) Olindera (GER) (Lomitas)
2502[3] 3588[5] 3761[4] 5136[4] 5829[6]

Iron Duke *Liam Corcoran* a49 27
7 gr g Refuse To Bend(IRE) Arinaga (Warning)
109[5] 2301a[3]

Irons On Fire (USA) *Gay Kelleway* a70 50
5 ch g Tale Of The Cat(USA) One And Twenty (USA) (Honour And Glory (USA))
1325[8] 1513[3] 1700[3] 1877[8] 2533[4] 2794[6] 4467a[15] 5464a[4] 6058a[7] 6680a[10]

Ironstein (AUS) *Gerald Ryan* 108
8 br g Zabeel(NZ) Gentle Genius (AUS) (Danehill (USA))
7700a[6] 7827a[5]

Irradiance (IRE) *Charlie Appleby* a46
2 b f Raven's Pass(USA) Pure Illusion (IRE) (Danehill (USA))
6691[7]

Isabella Beeton *Pat Phelan* a71
2 b f Archipenko(USA) Famcred (Inchinor)
6922[2] (8259)

Isabella Bird *Mick Channon* a61 76
2 b f Invincible Spirit(IRE) Meetyouthere (IRE) (Sadler's Wells (USA))
4484[4] *7155[5]*

Isabella Liberty (FR) *Robert Eddery* a70 65
2 b f Soldier Of Fortune(IRE) Samsa (FR) (Zafonic (USA))
4921[14] 7532[5] ◆ *7875[5]*

I Say (IRE) *William Haggas* 81
3 b f Oratorio(IRE) Lisieux Orchid (IRE) (Sadler's Wells (USA))
(4805) 5548[4] 6574[4]

Isdaal *Kevin Morgan* a69 71
6 ch m Dubawi(IRE) Faydah (USA) (Bahri (USA))
2555[6] 3095[7] *6346[9]* 7278[6]

Iseemist (IRE) *John Gallagher* a65 71
2 gr f Verglas(IRE) Krasivaya (IRE) (Soviet Star (USA))
1421[7] 1659[4] (2011) 2767[4] 3522[16] 4025[6] 7074[4] 7451[4] *7837[4]*

Ishetoo *Peter Grayson* a65 70
9 b g Ishiguru(USA) Ticcatoo (IRE) (Dolphin Street (FR))
88[5] 163[11] 339[2] 1043[7] 1087[12] 1149[4] 2170[9] 2578[9] 4635[7] 4836[7] 5408[6] 5982[5] 8050[6] 8169[9]

Ishi *Rod Millman* a49 46
4 b f Ishiguru(USA) Chorus (Bandmaster (USA))
357[2] 128[8] 440[7] 537[3] 655[13] 909[7]

Ishiamiracle *Phil McEntee* a59 55
4 ch f Ishiguru(USA) Sukuma (IRE) (Highest Honor (FR))
159[7] 271[7] 523[11] 778[6] 884[9] 1294[9] 1748[6] *2578[2] 2998[3] 3496[4]* 4623[6] 5192[6] 6323[3] 7323[2] 7455[11] 7957[9] 8048[9] 8293[7]

Ishigunnaeatit *Mrs K Burke* a63 71
3 b f Ishiguru(USA) It's Toast (IRE) (Diktat)
18[4] 216[2] 414[5] 1008[4]

Ishi Honest *Mark Usher* a64 72
3 b f Ishiguru(USA) Honesty Pays (Dr Fong (USA))
2329[5] 3050[4] 3407[7] *3903[6]* 4624[3] 5184[7] *6560[3]* 7086[6] 7315[7]

Ishikawa (IRE) *K R Burke* a84 79
5 b g Chineur(FR) Nautical Light (Slip Anchor)
(21) 850[2] (1220) 1883[7] *3468[6]* 4638[2] (4894) 5191[2] 6360[4] *7849[4] 8057[2] 8117[5] 8336[3]*

Ishisoba *Ronald Harris* a60 50
3 ch f Ishiguru(USA) Bundle Up (USA) (Miner's Mark (USA))
1424[5] 1712[7] 2528[2] 2802[6] 3661[5] 4240[3] 5275[7] 6038[12] *7380[8] 7508[6] 8320[2] 8437[3]*

Isioma *Mario Hofer* 88
3 b f Shamardal(USA) Russian Dance (USA) (Nureyev (USA))
2065a[10] 2910a[14]

Isis Blue *Rod Millman* a75 77
3 b g Cockney Rebel(IRE) Bramaputra (IRE) (Choisir (AUS))
1091[2] 1307[3] 1714[8] 2094[3] (2600) 3294[5] 3698[6] *4384[3]*

Island Express (IRE) *Ann Stokell* a58 53
6 b g Chineur(FR) Cayman Expresso (IRE) (Fayruz)
123[3] 136[3] 356[4] 404[7] 581[3] 667[3] 807[11] 863[10] 1077[6] 1150[4] 1451[3] 1539[6] 2169[4] 5864[12] 6145[5] 8438[5]

Island Kingdom (IRE) *J S Moore* a69 64
2 ch g Duke Of Marmalade(IRE) Tohama (In The Wings)
2344[5] 2617[4] *2978[2]* 4662[3] *5848a[9]* 6271[4] 6724[3] 7218[10] *8259[3]*

Island Legend (IRE) *Milton Bradley* a85 64
7 b g Trans Island Legand Of Tara (USA) (Gold Legend (USA))
113[8] 457[9] 1121[10] 1370[8] 8324[5]

Island Remede *Ed Dunlop* a69 91
2 b f Medicean Island Odyssey (Dansili)
3991[7] *4409[9]* 4880[3] 5424[5] *6924[2]* 7309[2] (7471) 7695[3]

Isle Of Beauty *Tom Dascombe* a32 51
3 b f Refuse To Bend(IRE) Munaawashat (IRE) (Marju (IRE))
2754[9] 3463[2] 4049[8] 4656[4] 6321[11]

Isle Of Ellis (IRE) *Ron Barr* a39 54
6 b g Statue Of Liberty(USA) Fable (Absalom)
2757[9] 3547[3] 4377[11] 5139[15]

Ismaali *James Given* a17 6
3 b f Acclamation Dream Vision (USA) (Distant View (USA))
3136[11] *6611[8]* 7108[9] *7787[6]*

Ismene (USA) *Bill Spawr* a102 97
4 bb f Tribal Rule(USA) Never To Excess (USA) (In Excess)
7709a[11]

Isola Bella *Jonathan Portman* a47 42
4 ch f Sleeping Indian Tetravella (IRE) (Groom Dancer (USA))
597[3] 704[7] 908[7] 5586[7]

Isola Verde *James Fanshawe* a70 71
4 b f Oasis Dream Firenze (Efisio)
3223[5] 3738[10]

Is This Love (IRE) *Jamie Osborne* a60 48
3 b f Danehill Dancer(IRE) Glamour (IRE) (Sadler's Wells (USA))
197[9] 1019[2] 2226[6] 3016[4] *5072[8]*

Istikshaf (IRE) *Saeed bin Suroor* 81
2 b c Exceed And Excel(AUS) Shinko Hermes (IRE) (Sadler's Wells (USA))
5718[5] 6570[2] 7308[2] 7606[3]

Istimraar (IRE) *Saeed bin Suroor* a77 77
2 b c Dansili Manayer (IRE) (Sadler's Wells (USA))
3490[3] 4304[2] 5299[4] 6572[6] *(7113)*

It Ain't To Grand *Roger Ingram* a42
4 ch g Auction House(USA) Charlottevalentina (IRE) (Perugino (USA))
19[6] 123[7] 350[9] 5645[9]

Italian Riviera *Sir Mark Prescott Bt* a86 73
4 b g Galileo(IRE) Miss Corniche (Hernando (FR))
2749[3] (3328) 3512[2] 4873[11] 5423[5] *5895[10]* 6565[5] *6809[9]*

Italian Tom (IRE) *Ronald Harris* a80 82
6 b h Le Vie Dei Colori Brave Cat (IRE) (Catrail (USA))
1726[12] 2255[23] 2441[9] 2825[2] 3315[13] 5183[6] 5775a[17] 6382[7] 6527[3] 7452[2] 7593[4] *8069[10] 8321[10]*

I Thank You (FR) *Y Barberot* a74 78
3 b f Poliglote Folie Gaillarde (FR) (Valanour (IRE))
(2434a)

Ithoughtitwasover (IRE) *Mark Johnston* a99 107
5 b c Hurricane Run(IRE) Green Castle (IRE) (Indian Ridge)
246a[8] 555a[10] 4262[3]
Itlaaq *Michael Easterby* a89 97
7 b g Alhaarth(IRE) Hathrah (IRE) (Linamix (FR))
(1689) 2365[8] 3297[3] ◆ 4313[11] 4796[6] 5723[9] 6192[13] 6394[6] 7174[7] 7526[12] 7823[20]
It Must Be Faith *Michael Appleby* a78 78
3 b g Mount Nelson Purple Rain (IRE) (Celtic Swing)
4667[7] 5715[2] 6502[2] 7787[3] (7802)
Itoobeboss (IRE) *Rod Collet* 91
2 gr c Lawman(FR) Dookus (IRE) (Linamix (FR))
7967a[7]
It's A Dundeel (NZ) *Murray Baker* 116
4 b c High Chaparral(IRE) Stareel (NZ) (Zabeel (NZ))
7556a[8]
It's A Girl Thing (IRE) *Gary Moore* a63 65
4 ch f Hurricane Run(IRE) Princess Magdalena (Pennekamp (USA))
5171[3] 5605[6] 6457[8] 7305[4] 7628[13]
It's All A Game *Richard Guest* a57 56
2 ch g Sleeping Indian St Edith (IRE) (Desert King (IRE))
2436[11] 2883[7] 3298[9] 4108[5] (4990) 5175[3] 5424[7] 5898[3] 6085[6] 6284[5] 6494[8] 6755[10] 7032[3] 7604[5]
It's A Mans World *Brian Ellison* a71 87
7 b g Kyllachy Exhibitor (USA) (Royal Academy (USA))
1459[3] 1786[3] 2278[10] (2463) 2881[5] 3683[9] 3777[6] 5051[9] 5580[11]
It's Just George *Keith Dalgleish* 30
2 b g Cockney Rebel(IRE) Dead Womans Pass (IRE) (High Chaparral (IRE))
6299[11] 6666[5]
Its My Life (FR) *J Reynier*
2 ch f Green Tune(USA) She's All Class (USA) (Rahy (USA))
7568a[16]
Itsmyluckyday (USA) *Edward Plesa Jr* a115 116
3 bb c Lawyer Ron(USA) Viva La Slew (USA) (Doneraile Court (USA))
2033a[15] 2473a[2]
It's My Time *Richard Fahey* a74 74
4 b f Green Desert(USA) Soviet Terms (Soviet Star (USA))
1800[2] ◆ 2286[6] 2711[6] (3098) 3583[4] 4098[7] 4542[2] 5006[4] 7169[3] 7546[3] 7974[9] 8162[3] 8453[6]
Itsnowcato *Ed Walker* a77 49
2 b c Notnowcato Blaenavon (Cadeaux Genereux)
7607[6] 7853[2] ◆ 8221[3]
It's Only Business *Bill Turner* a72 64
3 ch g Haafhd Noble Plum (IRE) (King's Best (USA))
195[4] (371) (468) (547) (726)
It's Taboo *Mark Usher* a51 74
3 b f Tobougg(IRE) Faraway Moon (Distant Relative)
2226[3] 2597[2] 3111[2] 4685[5] 5444[2] 5896[10] (6043) 6564[8]
Ittijah (USA) *Mark Johnston* 52
3 ch f Pivotal Rahiyah (USA) (Rahy (USA))
7253[8]
Itum *Christine Dunnett* a55 41
6 ch g Bahamian Bounty Petomi (Presidium)
2169[7]
Ivan B *Mick Channon* 30
2 ch c Winker Watson Blakeshall Rose (Tobougg (IRE))
2947[7] 3311[5] 3631[8] 3992[3] 4450[6]
Ivan Grozny (FR) *D Rabhi* a91 103
3 b g Turtle Bowl(IRE) Behnesa (IRE) (Suave Dancer (USA))
1419a[3] 2035a[5]
Ivanhoe *Michael Blanshard* a70 73
3 b c Haafhd Marysienka (Primo Dominie)
1900[9] 2325[2] ◆ 3243[4] 3636[3] 4882[3] 5612[5] 6435[3] 6743[8]
Ivanhowe (GER) *W Giedt* 103
3 b c Soldier Hollow Indigo Girl (GER) (Sternkoenig (IRE))
(3389a) 4103a[8]
Ivan The Engine *Paul Fitzsimons* a47
5 b g Ivan Denisovich(IRE) Silk Daisy (Barathea (IRE))
99[8] 226[9]
Ivan Vasilevich (IRE) *John Quinn* a90 85
5 b g Ivan Denisovich(IRE) Delisha (Salse (USA))
2590[7]
Iver Bridge Lad *John Ryan* a109 114
6 b h Avonbridge Fittonia (FR) (Ashkalani (IRE))
149a[6] ◆ 241a[9] 465a[4] 660a[5]
Ivestar (IRE) *Michael Easterby* a69 63
8 b g Fraam Hazardous (Night Shift (USA))
(143) 399[8] 558[5] 760[7] 2550[9] 2835[10] 3197[8] 3446[8] 4009[7] 4371[9] 4619[5] 5047[10] 5470[10] 6343[4] 7101[7] 7729[2] 8152[2]
Ivor's Princess *Rod Millman* a68 67
4 b f Atraf Rosina May (IRE) (Danehill Dancer (IRE))
4603[5] 5404[3] 5816[5] 7429[8] 7836[12] (8151) 8316[7]
Ivory *Garry Moss* a19 43
2 ch f Three Valleys(USA) Sweetypie (IRE) (Golan (IRE))
6654[6] 7340[5] 7630[5]
Ivory Land (FR) *A De Royer-Dupre* 118
6 ch h Lando(GER) Ivory Coast (FR) (Peintre Celebre (USA))
1871a[4]
Ivy Port *Michael Appleby* a68 48
3 b f Deportivo Ivy Bridge (IRE) (Namid)
197[11] 479[4] 706[6] 1071[2] (1190) ◆ 1486[9] 7636[11] 8042[4] 8234[2] 8316[2]
Ivy Trump *Michael Appleby* 68
2 b f First Trump Ivy Bridge (IRE) (Namid)
3760[5] 4497[6] 5053[8]
Iwilsayzisonlyonce *Joseph Tuite* a61 61
3 ch g Kyllachy Resistance Heroine (Dr Fong (USA))
374[7] 531[7] 811[6] 2393[7] 2791[7]
Ixelles Diamond (IRE) *Richard Fahey* 69
2 br f Diamond Green(FR) Silk Point (IRE) (Barathea (IRE))
2282[3] 2715[4] 3391[3] 4053[4] 4948[7] 5468[6] 6070[3]
Izaaj (USA) *M bin Shafya* a92 92
6 ch g Giant's Causeway(USA) Miss Coronado (USA) (Coronado's Quest (USA))
412a[11]
Izbushka (IRE) *Ian Williams* a58
2 b g Bushranger(IRE) Zaynaba (IRE) (Traditionally (USA))
8333[12] 8425[13]
Izola *F Head* 99
3 ch f Beat Hollow Pivka (Pivotal)
2693a[8]
Izzy Boy (USA) *Mark Johnston* a63 57
3 b g Elusive Quality(USA) Michele Royale (USA) (Groovy (USA))
1772[8] 2624[7] 6969[8] 7197[7] (7508) ◆ (8235) 8409[3]
Izzy Too *Alison Hutchinson* a37
3 b f Oratorio(IRE) Quiet Counsel (IRE) (Law Society (USA))
7377[4]
Jaaryah (IRE) *Mick Channon* a91 85
5 ch f Halling(USA) Albahja (Sindar (IRE))
1484[7] 1825[4]
Jaasoos (IRE) *D Selvaratnam* a88 105
9 ch g Noverre(USA) Nymphs Echo (IRE) (Mujtahid (USA))
154a[9] 467a[8] 838a[2] 955a[7]
Jabhaat (USA) *Ed Dunlop* 97
3 b f Hard Spun(USA) Ishraak (USA) (Sahm (USA))
(1608) 4278[3] 4878[4] 5534[2] 6536[2] 7822[8]
Jacbequick *Karen Tutty* 52
2 b g Calcutta Toking N' Joken (IRE) (Mukaddamah (USA))
3648[7] 4505[13] 5338[14] 6513[5]
Jackaddock *James Bethell* a56 56
3 b g Motivator Selkirk Sky (Selkirk (USA))
1648[5] 2306[15] 2957[9] 7066[4] 7847[8] 8148[12]
Jack Barker *Robin Bastiman* 59
4 b g Danbird(AUS) Smiddy Hill (Factual (USA))
1951[5] 2133[5] 3738[7] 5341[12] 7455[13]
Jack Beauregard (IRE) *Gianluca Bietolini* 68
2 b c Observatory(USA) Baciami Stupida (Diktat)
6059a[3] 6786a[6] 7568a[7]
Jack Daddy *Joseph G Murphy* 85
4 b g Monsun(GER) Snow Princess (IRE) (Ela-Mana-Mou)
7230a[20] 7723a[15]
Jack Dawkins (USA) *David Nicholls* a80 49
8 b g Fantastic Light(USA) Do The Mambo (USA) (Kingmambo (USA))
524[3] (886) (908) 1074[2] 1201[2]
Jack Dexter *Jim Goldie* 119
4 bb g Orientor Glenhurich (IRE) (Sri Pekan (USA))
(1234) 1537[12] 2368[6] 3420[4] (3822) 6623[3] 7364[2] (7821)
Jack Firefly *Michael Murphy* a3 33
4 b g Echo Of Light Charlottebutterfly (Millkom)
1296[6] 2172[9] 2568[8] 3213[11]
Jackie Love (IRE) *Olivia Maylam* a57 58
5 b f Tobougg(IRE) Gutter Press (IRE) (Raise A Grand (IRE))
117[7] 274[8] 497[4] 665[9] 1783[5] 1951[3] 2575[11] 3054[8] 3430[4] 5525[5] 5817[5] 6019[8] 6462[3] 6871[12] 7511[4] ◆
Jack Luey *Lawrence Mullaney* a63 91
6 b g Danbird(AUS) Icenaslice (IRE) (Fayruz)
2459[4] (2505) 3776[3] 5108[12] 6190[8] 6331[4] 7507[6]
Jack Milton (USA) *Todd Pletcher* 109
3 bb c War Front(USA) Preserver (USA) (Forty Niner (USA))
5551a[3] 8120a[6]
Jack My Boy (IRE) *David Evans* a85 83
6 b g Tagula(IRE) Bobanlyn (IRE) (Dance Of Life (USA))
194[2] 398[2] (452) 583[2] 687[3] (775) 1287[4] 1726[11] 2441[8] 2871[8] (3622) 3887[3] 5489[10] 6388[7] 6854[8] 7031[6] 7254[4] 7427[10]
Jack Of Diamonds (IRE) *Roger Teal* a95 86
4 b g Red Clubs(IRE) Sakkara Star (IRE) (Mozart (IRE))
1385[2] 1878[2] 2265[3] 3274[6] 4281[7] 6647[8]
Jackpot *Mrs A Malzard* a12 34
3 b f Avonbridge Strat's Quest (Nicholas (USA))
3134[12] 3657[8] 4424[7] 4666[5] (5328a) 7145a[7]
Jack's Revenge (IRE) *George Baker* a77 100
5 br g Footstepsinthesand Spirit Of Age (IRE) (Indian Ridge)
1235[5] 3527[8] 4488[6] 4859[2] 5255[3] 5738[4] 6838[21] 7172[2] 7368[15]
Jack Who's He (IRE) *William Muir* a86 91
4 b g Red Clubs(IRE) Annus Iucundus (IRE) (Desert King (IRE))
133[7] 311[2] 4593[5] 5063[2] 5825[4] 6280[4] 6869[7] 7071[6]
Jacob Black *Clive Cox* 67
2 b c Amadeus Wolf First Eclipse (IRE) (Fayruz)
4937[2] 5307[10]
Jacob Cats *Olly Stevens* a83 100
4 b g Dutch Art Ballet (Sharrood (USA))
2029[14] 3697[10] 5255[9] 5894[11]
Jacobella *Jonathan Portman* a66 66
3 b f Rob Roy(USA) Veni Bidi Vici (Horse Chestnut (SAF))
1499[4] 2092[7] 2606[6] 3437[4] 3820[11] (5178) 6109[9] 7258[4]
Jacob McCandles *Shaun Lycett* a69 66
6 br g Trade Fair Feather Circle (IRE) (Indian Ridge)
6404[9]
Jacob's Pillow *William Haggas* a75 76
2 b c Oasis Dream Enticing (IRE) (Pivotal)
5186[2] 6842[3] 7638[2]
Jacobs Son *Michael Appleby* a81 64
5 ch g Refuse To Bend(IRE) Woodwin (IRE) (Woodman (USA))
20[2] (161) (969) 1188[3] 1597[2] 1884[11] 2418[8] 4810[8] 5560[10] 5868[6]
Jacqueline Jouliac *John Gosden* a61
2 b f Oasis Dream Sugar Mill (FR) (Polar Falcon (USA))
3958[4] ◆
Jacquotte Delahaye *Bryan Smart* a72 73
2 ch f Kyllachy Mary Read (Bahamian Bounty)
2337[2] 2877[3] 3565[7] 5380[5] 7817[11] (7960)
Jadanna (IRE) *James Given* a90 99
3 b f Mujadil(USA) Savannah Poppy (IRE) (Statue Of Liberty (USA))
1000a[6] 1622[8] 1921[11] 3103[6] 3562[6] 4117[2] 4989[11] 5260[9] 6238[11]
Jadesnumberone (IRE) *Michael Bell* a62 75
3 b f Authorized(IRE) Gabriella (Cape Cross (IRE))
2423[8] 3201[2] 4182[3] (5695) 6210[10] 6556[8] 7325[8]
Jaeger Connoisseur (IRE) *K R Burke* a48 45
2 b f Art Connoisseur(IRE) Nilassiba (Daylami (IRE))
4886[10] 6160[6] 6983[3] 7788[6] 8137[2]
Jaeger Train (IRE) *K R Burke* a71
2 b g Captain Rio Marigold (FR) (Marju (IRE))
8414[2] ◆
Jaga Time *Richard Fahey* a52 55
2 ch c Compton Place Tender (IRE) (Zieten (USA))
1449[4] 1749[5] 2161[4] 2475[2] 3298[8] 4964[6] 5289[4] 5366[7]
Jaguar Mail (JPN) *Noriyuki Hori* 123
9 b h Jungle Pocket(JPN) Haya Beni Komachi (JPN) (Sunday Silence (USA))
1868a[6]
Jake's Destiny (IRE) *George Baker* a62 98
4 b g Desert Style(IRE) Skehana (IRE) (Mukaddamah (USA))
1848[6] 4028[9] 4488[9] 4923[17] 6538[9] 6805[2]
Jake The Snake (IRE) *Tony Carroll* a82 73
12 ch g Intikhab(USA) Tilbrook (IRE) (Don't Forget Me)
11[9] 535[2] 650[3] 740[4] (1793) 3210[2] 5697[5]
Jakey (IRE) *Pat Phelan* a56 78
3 b g Cape Cross(IRE) Off Message (IRE) (In The Wings)
(6870) ◆ 7257[7]
Jakeys Girl *Pat Phelan* a31 4
6 b m Dubai Destination(USA) Rosewood Belle (USA) (Woodman (USA))
226[13] 475[9] 522[10] 2332[10] 4437[5]
Jakkalberry (IRE) *Marco Botti* 119
7 b h Storming Home Claba Di San Jore (IRE) (Barathea (IRE))
(956a)
Jalaa (IRE) *Richard Hannon Snr* 97
3 b g Street Cry(IRE) Daneleta (IRE) (Danehill (USA))
1812[4] 2438[6] (3080) 3484[25] 3987[2] 4529[3]
Jaladee *Roger Varian* a78
3 b g Cape Cross(IRE) Atamana (IRE) (Lahib (USA))
7738[6] (8054) 8227[3]
Jalebi *Jim Boyle* a60
2 ch f Sleeping Indian Sweet Pickle (Piccolo)
2771[4] 4164[9]
Jalingo (IRE) *Mark Johnston* a74
2 b c Cape Cross(IRE) Just Special (Cadeaux Genereux)
7860[3] 8067[9] 8346[2] (8425)
Jallota *Mick Channon* 111
2 b c Rock Of Gibraltar(IRE) Lady Lahar (Fraam)
2411[5] 2670[3] (3112) 3422[5] ◆ 4212[3] 4547a[4] 4918[5] 5573a[4] 6645[2] 7017[5] 7191[7]
Jally (IRE) *J-C Rouget* 102
3 ch c Tamayuz Miss Beatrix (IRE) (Danehill Dancer (IRE))
4816a[3] 5628a[11]
Jamaica Grande *Dave Morris* a64 57
5 ch g Doyen(IRE) Mary Sea (FR) (Selkirk (USA))
2637[3] (3222) 4718[9] (6102) 6398[3] 6787[3] 7857[4] (8148) 8410[7]
Jamaican Bolt (IRE) *Geoffrey Oldroyd* a81 102
5 b g Pivotal Chiming (IRE) (Danehill (USA))
1232[5] ◆ 6539[3] 7171[7] 7527[6]
Jambobo *Chris Down* a37
4 b g Acclamation Hovering (IRE) (In The Wings)
3957[11]
Jamboree Girl *Tim Easterby* 73
2 b f Bahamian Bounty Danehurst (Danehill (USA))
3942[2] 4370[3] (5638) 6791[3] 7333[6]
Jameela's Dream *Robert Cowell* a51
3 ch f Nayef(USA) Doors To Manual (USA) (Royal Academy (USA))
2979[11] 6554[10]
Jamesbo's Girl *Philip Kirby* 88
3 ch f Refuse To Bend(IRE) Donna Anna (Be My Chief (USA))
2022[9] 5303[9] 5518[8] 6208[8]
Jamesie (IRE) *David Marnane* a100 99
5 b g Kodiac Pretty Woman (IRE) (Night Shift (USA))
2254[7] 3527[17]
James Pollard (IRE) *Bernard Llewellyn* a68 75
8 ch g Indian Ridge Manuetti (IRE) (Sadler's Wells (USA))
1239[4] 1466[5] 1948[3] 2348[6] 4714[8] 4915[3] 5171[5] 5434[5] 6068[3]
Jammy Guest (IRE) *George Margarson* 94
3 b g Duke Of Marmalade(IRE) Ardbrae Lady (Overbury (IRE))
1618[5] (2224) 2454[3] 3455[9] 4295[8]
Jamr *M bin Shafya* a107 28
5 br g Singspiel(IRE) Never Enough (GER) (Monsun (GER))
153a[6] 364a[2] 556a[7] 656a[6] 958a[5]
Jana *Sylvester Kirk* a48 54
2 ch f Compton Place Hasten (USA) (Lear Fan (USA))
2282[8] 2562[6] 3107[6] 3414[6] 5034[8] 5893[7] 6131[6] 7032[5] 8039[6]
Janaab (IRE) *J E Hammond* a60 77
3 ch g Nayef(USA) Mood Indigo (IRE) (Indian Ridge)
460a[4]
Jan De Heem *Ralph Beckett* a54 72
3 ch g Dutch Art Shasta (Shareef Dancer (USA))
1347[5] (2017) 2600[6] 3636[6] 4714[5] 5216[2] (6015) 6898[8]
Janet's Legacy *Harry Dunlop* 6
2 b f Bahamian Bounty Spunger (Fraam)
7243[8] 7859[9]
Janie Runaway (IRE) *Brian Meehan* a56 65
3 b f Antonius Pius(USA) Await (IRE) (Peintre Celebre (USA))
2206[8] 2786[3] 3243[15] 3900[8]
Janna's Jingle (IRE) *John Patrick Shanahan* a53 85
3 b f Oratorio(IRE) Bonnie Bluebell (IRE) (Montjeu (IRE))
4475[2] (5758)
Janoub Nibras (IRE) *Ismail Mohammed* a98 95
3 b g Acclamation Wildsplash (USA) (Deputy Minister (CAN))
5533[12] 5958[8] 6356[12] 7464[8]
Jan Smuts (IRE) *Wilf Storey* a27 69
5 b g Johannesburg(USA) Choice House (USA) (Chester House (USA))
1789[6] (2120) (2313) 2540[5] 2887[3] 3504[6] 3709[4] 3944[5] 5048[12] 5862[2] 6087[2] 6290[2] 6466[5]
Jardim (BRZ) *M F De Kock* a61 90
7 gr h Ski Champ(USA) Copacabana Beach (BRZ) (Midnight Tiger (USA))
241a[10] 362a[10] 552a[4] 656a[5] 873a[9]
Jareeda (USA) *Sir Michael Stoute* a66 40
3 bb f First Samurai(USA) Manaal (USA) (Bahri (USA))
2084[7] 2560[7] 3995[6]
Jarlath *Seamus Mullins* a58 48
2 b c Norse Dancer(IRE) Blue Lullaby (IRE) (Fasliyev (USA))
2653[8] 5279[7] 5811[7] 6924[3] 7855[3]
Jarrow (IRE) *Milton Bradley* a67 88
6 ch g Shamardal(USA) Wolf Cleugh (IRE) (Last Tycoon)
947[11] 1245[11] 1581[11] 1976[4] 3341[6] 3577[5] 4220[5] 4712[6] 5060[8] 5376[4] 5645[4] 5841[7] 6033[2] 6156[10] 6323[5] 6928[7] 7109[6] 7303[10]
Jathabah (IRE) *Clive Brittain* a81 104
3 b f Singspiel(IRE) Zibet (Kris)
1099[3] (1321) 1614[4] 2148[3] 3240[4] 4211[2] 4920[5] 5683[3] 6329[4] 7020[9]
Java Rose *Henry Candy* 79
4 b f Ishiguru(USA) Mighty Splash (Cape Cross (IRE))
(3618) 4506[2] 5445[2] 5795[6] 6405[5]
Java's War (IRE) *Kenneth McPeek* a114 101
3 b c War Pass(USA) Java (Rainbow Quest (USA))
2033a[13]
Jawaab (IRE) *Philip Kirby* a64 71
9 ch g King's Best(USA) Canis Star (Wolfhound (USA))
2673[9] 4512[7] 4969[9] 5712[7] 6086[7] 6470[8] 6909[6] 7668[4] (8027)
Jawhar (IRE) *Doug Watson* a91 97
5 ch g Halling(USA) Kawn (Cadeaux Genereux)
871a[6]
Jawim *Malcolm Saunders* a50 54
4 br f Piccolo Craic Sa Ceili (IRE) (Danehill Dancer (IRE))
1665[15] 3268[8] 3425[5]
Jawinski (IRE) *David Evans* a58 61
3 b g Jeremy(USA) Karinski (USA) (Palace Music (USA))
1373[4] 1743[4] 1897[6] 2312[5] 2924[8] 4352[10]
Jawking *Frank Sheridan* a66 22
4 b g Compton Place Just Down The Road (IRE) (Night Shift (USA))
560[8] 998[3] 1397[2] 1525[2] 1650[4]
Jawmiener (IRE) *David Evans*
2 b f Bushranger(IRE) Nice One Clare (IRE) (Mukaddamah (USA))
1240[10] (Dead)
Jay Bee Blue *Sean Curran* a86 72
4 b g Kyllachy Czarna Roza (Polish Precedent (USA))
2565[4] 2773[4] (3841) 5346[3] 5931[2] 6306[5] 6929[4] 7262[2] (7444) (7743) ◆ 7896[5] (7965) 8181[8] 8305[2]
Jayeff Herring (IRE) *Michael Bell* a57
2 b g Excellent Art Biasca (Erhaab (USA))
6999[4] 7960[5] 8138[4]
Jay Kay *Danielle McCormick* a59 57
4 b g Librettist(USA) Turn Back (Pivotal)
2089[10] 3030[9] 4621[11]
Jazri *Milton Bradley* a58 50
2 b c Myboycharlie(IRE) Read Federica (Fusaichi Pegasus (USA))
3175[8] 3640[9] 4031[4] 5068[4] (5893)
Jazz (IRE) *Charles Hills* a87 88
2 b c Danehill Dancer(IRE) Jazz Baby (IRE) (Fasliyev (USA))
1669[5] 2250[6] 2847[2] 3424[16] 4948[3] 5656[6] 6303[3] 6747[3] (7817)
Jazz Master *Luca Cumani* a92 82
3 b c Singspiel(IRE) Turn Of A Century (Halling (USA))
1882[4] 2321[3] 3059[5] 4076[5] 4490[2] 5132[4] 5743[2] ◆ (6200) ◆ 6559[2] 6936[7] (7627) 8327[6]
Jazz Poem (FR) *Mlle B Renk* a58 63
2 b c Pomellato(GER) Jaragua (FR) (Medaaly)
6961a[12]
Jazzy Lady (IRE) *David Evans* a72 54
2 b f Intikhab(USA) Lock's Heath (CAN) (Topsider (USA))
1573[10] 1718[9] 2474[6] 4065[10] 4387[2] 5893[6] 6322[2] 6520[7] 6755[6] (7604) (7855) ◆ 7935[3] 7944[3] (8132) 8164[2] 8311[2] 8397[4]
Jd Rockefeller *Paul D'Arcy* a55 43
3 ch g Sakhee(USA) Perle D'Or (IRE) (Entrepreneur)
507[4] 1098[5] 1469[4] 2156[7] 2743[6] 5127[5] 5217[4] 5801[5] 6717[5]
Jean De Medicis (FR) *J Heloury* a65 63
3 bb c Medecis Turn To Black (USA) (Alleged (USA))
331a[9]

Jeanie Johnston (IRE) *P Harley* a91 82
6 b m One Cool Cat(USA) Bahamamia (Vettori (IRE))
960a^{10} 8062^{6}
Jeannie Galloway (IRE) *Keith Dalgleish* a70 78
6 b m Bahamian Bounty Housekeeper (IRE) (Common Grounds)
2166^{6} 3200^{7} 4097^{2} 4956^{2} 5637^{7} 6210^{12} 6549^{10}
Jebel Tara *Alan Brown* a72 79
8 b g Diktat Chantilly (FR) (Sanglamore (USA))
(1995) (2319) (2575) (2636) 3770^{7} (4100) 4341^{6} 4807^{4} 4994^{4} 5382^{7} 6048^{5} 6468^{5} 7953^{6} 8187^{8}
Jebril (FR) *Jonathan Portman* 75
3 b g Astronomer Royal(USA) Happy Clapper (Royal Applause)
1365^{4} 1729^{3} 2846^{6} 6435^{5}
Jebulani *Barry Murtagh* a39 60
3 b g Jelani(IRE) Susan's Dowry (Efisio)
3653^{6} 4401^{4} 4587^{2} (4849) 5084^{2} 5343^{2} 5885^{3} 6629^{4}
Jedward (IRE) *Kevin Ryan* a84 93
6 ch m Namid Input (Primo Dominie)
1253^{6} 2459^{7} 3331^{2} 3561^{2} 4860^{20} 4954^{9} 5821^{3} 6190^{9} 6583^{23}
Jee Pee And Jeremy (FR) *Mme Pia Brandt* a67 73
3 b c Shirocco(GER) Selective (FR) (Linamix (FR))
818a^{7} 5914a^{6} 6713a^{17}
Jeer (IRE) *Michael Easterby* a70 73
9 ch g Selkirk(USA) Purring (USA) (Mountain Cat (USA))
107^{6} 3947^{12} 5420^{10} 5833^{12} 8031^{12}
Jeeraan (USA) *Ed Dunlop* a81 91
3 b g Distorted Humor(USA) Jaish (USA) (Seeking The Gold (USA))
4978^{6} (5484) 6172^{10} 6767^{4} 7205^{5}
Jefferson City (IRE) *John Gosden* 71
2 b c Montjeu(IRE) Reina Blanca (Darshaan)
7502^{5} 7774^{3}
Jehannedarc (IRE) *Ed Dunlop* a88 105
5 b f Montjeu(IRE) Lucky Rainbow (USA) (Rainbow Quest (USA))
2012^{2} 2443^{3} 3100^{7} 4920^{6} 5741^{6} 6329^{5} 7414a^{4} 7768^{7}
Jelly Fish *Amanda Perrett* a78 75
2 ch g Observatory(USA) Grand Coral (Grand Lodge (USA))
4997^{3} (5785) (6520) 7471^{5}
Jembatt (IRE) *Michael Mulvany* a75 89
6 ch g Captain Rio Silly Imp (IRE) (Imperial Frontier (USA))
679a^{9} 6089a^{4} 6883a^{16}
Jemimaville (IRE) *Giles Bravery* a52 42
6 b m Fasliyev(USA) Sparkling Isle (Inchinor)
6310^{9} 6930^{9} 8082^{8} 8413^{8}
Jenna Lee Kuma (USA) *Larry Lay*
3 bb g Kuma(USA) Miss Jenna Lee (USA) (Lee's Badger (USA))
786a^{8}
Jenny Twigg *Chris Fairhurst* a11
3 b f Paris House Yorke's Folly (USA) (Stravinsky (USA))
8003^{6}
Jeranimo (USA) *Michael Pender* a105 117
7 b h Congaree(USA) Jera (USA) (Jeblar (USA))
7710a^{7}
Jeremos (IRE) *Richard Hannon Snr* a65 69
2 b c Jeremy(USA) Bon Ton Roulet (Hawk Wing (USA))
3833^{9} 4483^{5} 5279^{5} 7892^{4}
Jericho (IRE) *Jamie Osborne* a62 61
4 br g Manduro(GER) Jinsiyah (USA) (Housebuster (USA))
218^{12} 617^{7} 825^{9}
Jermatt *J R Jenkins* a63 51
4 b g Kyllachy Miss Ippolita (Diktat)
19^{4} 136^{2} 356^{5}
Jersey Brown (IRE) *Mick Channon* a54 68
2 br f Marju(IRE) Daniysha (IRE) (Doyoun)
4302^{4} 4921^{3} 5443^{6} 5926^{7}
Jersey Cream (IRE) *Gary Moore* a56 60
2 ch f Iffraaj Unicamp (Royal Academy (USA))
3631^{3} 4206^{3} 5003^{10} 5634^{6} 6111^{6} 6749^{10}
Jersey Royal *Richard Hannon Snr* 62
2 b g Royal Applause Rolexa (Pursuit Of Love)
4483^{14} 4773^{4} 6641^{5} 7069^{4} 7252^{8}
Jessica's Gold *Christine Dunnett* a45 9
4 b f Iceman Capstick (JPN) (Machiavellian (USA))
1876^{11} 2746^{16} 3788^{9} 4178^{5}
Jessie's Spirit (IRE) *Ann Duffield* 69
4 gr f Clodovil(IRE) Alexander Anapolis (IRE) (Spectrum (IRE))
1963^{10} (2613) 3501^{4} 4005^{3} 4823^{2} 5263^{5}
Jessy Mae *Derek Haydn Jones*
2 b f Oratorio(IRE) Welsh Valley (USA) (Irish River (FR))
6409^{11}
Jet Away *David Hayes* 116
6 b h Cape Cross(IRE) Kalima (Kahyasi)
7392a^{4} 7702a^{6}
Jet Legend (SAF) *M F De Kock* 98
6 ch h Jet Master(SAF) Majestic Guest (SAF) (Northern Guest (USA))
367a^{8} 557a^{P}
Jeu De Roseau (IRE) *Chris Grant* a57 64
9 b g Montjeu(IRE) Roseau (Nashwan (USA))
1721^{5} 2887^{6} 3089^{9} 3771^{2} 4204^{10}
Jewelled *Lady Herries* a79 78
7 b m Fantastic Light(USA) Danemere (IRE) (Danehill (USA))
810^{3} 906^{2} 1327^{4} 1753^{5} 2070^{3} 4126^{3} 5190^{5} (5605) 5948^{2} 6258^{6} 6898^{6}
Jewelled Dagger (IRE) *Sharon Watt* a31 61
9 b g Daggers Drawn(USA) Cappadoce (IRE) (General Monash (USA))
(1949) 2714^{3} 3406^{2} 3625^{12} 4343^{7} 4714^{13} 6895^{9}
Jezlay (FR) *W Hickst* a2
3 ch f Layman(USA) Jezebel (Owington)
126a^{0}
Jezza *Karen George* a72 72
7 br g Pentire Lara (GER) (Sharpo)
208^{5} 458^{4} (671) (928) 1117^{2} 1350^{3} 1744^{3} 3271^{2} 3952^{5} 5535^{2} 6173^{2} 6996^{8} 7159^{2} 7863^{11}
Jigsaw (FR) *S Wattel* a77 77
4 b g Gentlewave(IRE) Grove Daffodil (IRE) (Salt Dome (USA))
5601a^{10}
Jillnextdoor (IRE) *Mick Channon* 101
3 b f Henrythenavigator(USA) Royal Shyness (Royal Academy (USA))
1362^{3} 1662^{10} 1808^{8} 2213^{6} 3097^{7} 3478^{6} 3562^{5} 4247^{6} 4367^{2} 4734^{7} 4989^{2} 5769^{6} 6189^{14}
Jillywinks *Scott Dixon* a64 60
3 b f Milk It Mick Thunderous Days (Diktat)
1114^{5} 1329^{4} 6316^{6} 6556^{7} 6941^{11} 7263^{8} 8320^{6} 8437^{8}
Jiminy *Scott Dixon* a58 27
3 b g Acclamation Grasshoppergreen (IRE) (Barathea (IRE))
5884^{6} 6965^{2} 7759^{4} 8034^{8} 8272^{3} 8351^{7} 8406^{8}
Jimmy Chop (FR) *C Boutin* a57 84
3 b g Indian Rocket Free Track (FR) (Solid Illusion (USA))
2335a^{0}
Jimmy Crackle (IRE) *Brian Ellison* a30 17
2 b g Intense Focus(USA) Slieve (Selkirk (USA))
2404^{5} 2577^{6}
Jimmy Elder *Richard Hannon Snr* a69 75
3 b g Invincible Spirit(IRE) Hijab (King's Best (USA))
667^{7} (811) 1345^{6} 2983^{6} 3621^{2} (4244) 4772^{4} 7319^{7}
Jimmy Mack (SWE) *Patrick Wahl* 50
4 ch c Eishin Dunkirk(USA) Delta Downs (Deputy Minister (CAN))
3188a^{11}
Jimmy Sewell (IRE) *Michael Appleby* a75 61
4 b g Catcher In The Rye(IRE) Starway To Heaven (ITY) (Nordance (USA))
2093^{9} 2885^{6} (2995) 7635^{9}
Jimmy Styles *Clive Cox* a105 111
9 ch g Inchinor Inya Lake (Whittingham (IRE))
1637^{2} 2676a^{14} 7013^{13} 7208^{4} ◆
Jimmy The Snooze (IRE) *Stuart Williams* a72
3 b c Moss Vale(IRE) Mrs Kepple (King's Best (USA))
228^{2} (636) 843^{3}
Jimsneverright *Geoffrey Harker* 37
5 b g Iktibas Lady Lexie (Cape Cross (IRE))
4118^{11} 4667^{9} 5469^{8}
Jim Tango (FR) *Karen McLintock* 63
9 bb g Jimble(FR) Fitanga (FR) (Fijar Tango (FR))
3625^{8}
Jinker Noble *Ed de Giles* a80 82
4 b g Green Desert(USA) Depressed (Most Welcome)
(5349) 6018^{2} 6848^{3} 7601^{2}
Jinky *Linda Perratt* a77 82
5 b g Noverre(USA) Aries (GER) (Big Shuffle (USA))
2410^{9} 2797^{8} 3331^{6} 3714^{2} 4111^{2} 4340^{4} (4821) 5266^{6} 5705^{7} 6052^{7} 6586^{12} 6908^{5} 7240^{8}
Jiroft (ITY) *Robert Cowell* a86 106
6 b g Blu Air Force(IRE) Dexia (ITY) (Indian Ridge)
2865^{5} ◆ 3046^{5} 3776^{7} 4275^{18} 5821^{6} 6539^{2} 6830^{15} 8155^{9}
Jive *Richard Hannon Snr* a69 72
2 b f Major Cadeaux Lindy Hop (IRE) (Danehill Dancer (IRE))
1724^{5} 2189^{5} 2625^{11} (2805) 4061^{5} 4498^{3} 5005^{13} 5634^{2} 6401^{6} 7088^{2} 7418^{11}
Joan's Legacy *Dave Roberts* a32 51
6 b m Piccolo CC Canova (Millkom)
6781^{5}
Jo Bob (USA) *Colleen Patterson*
5 bb g Johannesburg(USA) Pure Energy (USA) (Sefapiano (USA))
413a^{4}
Jo'Burg (USA) *David O'Meara* a75 96
9 b g Johannesburg(USA) La Martina (Atraf)
2718^{10} 3544^{5} (4012) 4542^{7} 4733^{3} 5291^{7} 5828^{5} 6300^{4} 6756^{3} 7024^{7} 7211^{19}
Jocasta Dawn *Henry Candy* a58 81
4 b f Kyllachy Jubilee Dawn (Mark Of Esteem (IRE))
2724^{10} 4165^{11}
Jo De Vati (FR) *S Wattel* a101 93
3 b c Vatori(FR) Etoile De Vati (FR) (Kingsalsa (USA))
72a^{0} (2335a)
Jodies Jem *William Jarvis* a85 92
3 br g Kheleyf(USA) First Approval (Royal Applause)
188^{2} 2603^{2} 3763^{8} 6356^{3} ◆ 6989^{7} 7696^{5}
Jody Bear *Jonathan Portman* a49 45
5 b f Joe Bear(IRE) Colins Lady (FR) (Colonel Collins (USA))
7090^{9} 7440^{4} 7899^{8} 8225^{7}
Joe Eile (IRE) *G M Lyons* a94 99
5 b g Iffraaj Encouragement (Royal Applause)
3846a^{3} 6623^{16} 6883a^{19} 7227a^{9}
Joeluke *Philip Kirby* a44 44
3 br g Cockney Rebel(IRE) Enthralled (Zafonic (USA))
4045^{9} 4436^{6} 4763^{4} 5869^{10}
Joe Packet *Jonathan Portman* a89 106
6 ch g Joe Bear(IRE) Costa Packet (IRE) (Hussonet (USA))
2444^{14} 2937^{9} 3249^{3} 3527^{18} 4024^{2} ◆ 4275^{9} 4800^{10} 5247^{4} 5998^{7} 6352^{5} 6831^{2} 7222^{3}
Joe Sugden *Mrs Ilka Gansera-Leveque* 88
4 ch g Araafa(IRE) Mountain Law (USA) (Mountain Cat (USA))
(5720) 6538^{3} 7337^{10}
Joe The Coat *Mark H Tompkins* a71 71
4 ch g Act One Torcross (Vettori (IRE))
2545^{6} ◆ 3328^{3} 4166^{10} 5863^{7} 6736^{9} 7372^{3} 7612^{10}
Joey's Destiny (IRE) *George Baker* 86
3 ch g Kheleyf(USA) Maid Of Ailsa (USA) (Pivotal)
2708^{7} 3279^{6} 4283^{6} (5611) (6744) 7255^{3}
Jofranka *David Barron* a53 82
3 b f Paris House Gypsy Fair (Compton Place)
4045^{5} 5814^{4} 1122^{3} 1458^{2} (1566) 2542^{2} ◆ (2779) (4136) 4734^{3} 5057^{2} 6212^{6}
Joha (USA) *Thomas Albertrani* a103 104
3 bb c Johar(USA) Mujado (IRE) (Mujadil (USA))
3360a^{10}
Johann Bach (IRE) *Patrick G Harney* a82 79
4 b g Oratorio(IRE) Belleinga (IRE) (Orpen (USA))
5021a^{16}
Johannes (IRE) *Richard Fahey* a92 101
10 b g Mozart(IRE) Blue Sirocco (Bluebird (USA))
1537^{16} 2046^{10} 2621^{7} 3114^{7} 3823^{16} 4472^{6} ◆ 4879^{11} 5971^{11}
Johann Strauss *A P O'Brien* 110
2 b c High Chaparral(IRE) Inchmina (Cape Cross (IRE))
7019^{4} ◆ 7528^{2}
Johara (IRE) *Chris Wall* a55 69
2 b f Iffraaj Hurricane Irene (IRE) (Green Desert (USA))
4164^{7} 5577^{4} 6644^{5} 7218^{4}
John Biscuit (IRE) *Andrew Balding* a88 94
5 ch g Hawk Wing(USA) Princess Magdalena (Pennekamp (USA))
1159^{7} 1242^{P} 1768^{7} 2365^{5} 2867^{4} 3370^{5} 7765^{10} 7976^{8}
John Coffey (IRE) *Michael Appleby* a57 71
4 b g Acclamation Appleblossom Pearl (IRE) (Peintre Celebre (USA))
873 2136 4494 3446^{2} 4220^{3} ◆ 4377^{7} (5709) 5965^{6} 6568^{2} 7283^{11}
John Lea (IRE) *Derek Shaw* a31 36
2 b c Bahamian Bounty Eastern Appeal (IRE) (Shinko Forest (IRE))
2778^{5} 3211^{9} 4142^{9} 5066^{8}
John Lightbody *Mark Johnston* a69 79
4 b g Teofilo(IRE) Patacake Patacake (USA) (Bahri (USA))
32^{5} 190^{8}
Johnno *J W Hills* a85 89
4 br g Excellent Art Vert Val (USA) (Septieme Ciel (USA))
1782^{6} 2424^{10} 3293^{8} 4798^{8} 6596^{15} (7307)
Johnny Castle *Amanda Perrett* a81 92
5 b g Shamardal(USA) Photogenic (Midyan (USA))
2665^{12} 3060^{10} 3586^{3} 4879^{14} 5722^{4} 6067^{9} 6489^{6} 6744^{9}
Johnny Cavagin *Richard Guest* a66 85
4 b g Superior Premium Beyond The Rainbow (Mind Games)
(1644) 1787^{5} 2441^{5} 3351^{12} 4812^{6} 6774^{4} 7731^{8} 8350^{8}
Johnnys Legacy (IRE) *Conor Dore* a80 67
6 b g Ecton Park(USA) Lexy May (USA) (Lear Fan (USA))
6004^{14} 6346^{12}
Johnny Splash (IRE) *Roger Teal* a60 58
4 b g Dark Angel(IRE) Ja Ganhou (Midyan (USA))
(30) 135^{3} 316^{2} 369^{3} (750) 902^{5} 1196^{3} 1516^{11} 3051^{7} 3425^{4} 3660^{5} (3921) 4427^{4} 4943^{3} 5608^{4} 6732^{3} 7985^{9}
John Potts *Brian Baugh* a63 48
8 b g Josr Algarhoud(IRE) Crown City (USA) (Coronado's Quest (USA))
82^{6} 330^{9} 587^{2} 801^{2} 1017^{2} 1214^{8} 3642^{7} 4357^{13}
Johnson's Cat (IRE) *Mandy Rowland* a23 19
4 b g One Cool Cat(USA) Takanewa (IRE) (Danetime (IRE))
88^{10} 312^{7} 618^{11} 8035^{7} 8051^{8}
Johns Porridge *Peter Hiatt*
4 ch f Needwood Blade Obsessive Secret (IRE) (Grand Lodge (USA))
63^{5}
Johnstown Lad (IRE) *Daniel Mark Loughnane* a74 70
9 b g Invincible Spirit(IRE) Pretext (Polish Precedent (USA))
449^{6}
Jolaine *Ralph Beckett* a64 45
4 b f Medicean Fancy Rose (USA) (Joyeux Danseur (USA))
492^{3} 1035^{4}
Jolie Blonde *Sir Mark Prescott Bt* a54
2 ch f Sir Percy Affaire D'Amour (Hernando (FR))
7442^{10} 7763^{11} 7853^{10}
Jolie Demoiselle (FR) *C Boutin* 45
2 ch f Redback Honolua (GER) (Singspiel (IRE))
2558a^{3}
Jollification (IRE) *George Baker* a82 91
3 b f Acclamation Improvise (Lend A Hand)
1000a^{10} 1477^{10}
Jolly Old Chap (FR) *M Nigge* a88 84
3 b c Acclamation Compulsive Quality (USA) (Elusive Quality (USA))
(8441a)
Jolly Ranch *Tony Newcombe* a57 28
7 gr m Compton Place How Do I Know (Petong)
516^{11} 1902^{7}
Jolly Red Jeanz (IRE) *J W Hills* a61 57
2 ch f Intense Focus(USA) Sovienne (IRE) (Soviet Star (USA))
6789^{6} 7200^{2} 7790^{4}
Jolly Roger (IRE) *Tony Carroll* 68
6 b g Oratorio(IRE) Chalice Wells (Sadler's Wells (USA))
1586^{6} ◆ 1899^{4} 2418^{7}
Jomari (IRE) *Declan Carroll* a16 52
3 ch g Ad Valorem(USA) Love Valentine (IRE) (Fruits Of Love (USA))
1764^{14} 2237^{8} 2716^{7} 4030^{3} 4222^{6} 4587^{5} 4849^{7}
Jonnie Skull (IRE) *Phil McEntee* a68 79
7 b g Pyrus(USA) Sovereign Touch (IRE) (Pennine Walk)
76^{6} 87^{7} 156^{3} 277^{5} 398^{9} 560^{6} 728^{6} 917^{2} (1021) 1042^{6} 1657^{5} (1752) (2134) 3052^{4} 3153^{6} 3430^{3} 3700^{6} (3788) 4183^{3} 4496^{10} 4865^{4} (5153) 5406^{2} 5621^{5} (5799) 6072^{10} 6809^{8} 7699^{14}
Jonny Delta *Jim Goldie* 86
6 ch g Sulamani(IRE) Send Me An Angel (IRE) (Lycius (USA))
(2973) 3333^{3} ◆ 4313^{7} 5237^{4} 5655^{15} 6626^{2} 6833^{3} 7193^{7} 7496^{8}
Jonny Lesters Hair (IRE) *Tim Easterby* a71 83
8 b g Danetime(IRE) Jupiter Inlet (IRE) (Jupiter Island)
1448^{11} 1775^{7} 2753^{7} 4889^{2} 4953^{5} 5144^{6} 5861^{8} 6297^{7} 7024^{15} 7238^{14}
Jonny Wombat *Richard Ford* a40 28
3 b g Avonbridge Moonlight Angel (Kyllachy)
207^{8} 310^{6} 459^{5} 598^{5} 1759^{14}
Jontleman (IRE) *Mick Channon* a67 83
3 b g Whipper(USA) Gandia (IRE) (Danehill (USA))
1213^{6} (1519) 1832^{8} 2544^{14} 3279^{11} (3494) (3818) 4162^{4} 4592^{2} 4751^{2} 4966^{4} (5477) 5996^{7} 6648^{9} 6977^{16}
Joohaina (IRE) *Marco Botti* a75 72
2 b f New Approach(IRE) Rouge Noir (USA) (Saint Ballado (CAN))
3471^{4} 7245^{3} 7875^{7} (8201)
Jordan Princess *Luca Cumani* a63 76
2 b f Cape Cross(IRE) Princess Nada (Barathea (IRE))
6523^{8} (7277)
Jordanstown *Kevin Ryan* a59 49
3 ch g Piccolo Pigment (Zamindar (USA))
357^{4} 598^{4} 848^{U} 1066^{2} (1349) 1695^{5} 2080^{11}
Jordaura *Alan Berry* a67 79
7 br g Primo Valentino(IRE) Christina's Dream (Spectrum (IRE))
23^{5} 84^{4} 672^{6} 798^{2} 987^{6} 1104^{6} 1270^{5} 1730^{7} (2221) (2594) 2976^{7} 3231^{5} 3889^{5} 4609^{5} 4810^{7} 5050^{4} 6296^{2} 6598^{3} (6667) 7425^{7} 7498^{6} 8006^{7} 8136^{5} 8436^{10}
Josefa Goya *Hughie Morrison* a71 53
3 b f Sakhee's Secret Maria Theresa (Primo Dominie)
3170^{4} (4839) 5422^{4} 5930^{9} 6655^{3}
Joshua The First *Ian Semple* a74 65
4 br g Kheleyf(USA) Newkeylets (Diktat)
2042^{8} 2539^{7} 3285^{3} 3466^{4} 3715^{2} 4100^{6} 4823^{7} 5368^{6} 5637^{6} 6083^{3} 6297^{9} 6548^{10} 7733^{6} 8006^{3}
Joshua Tree (IRE) *Ed Dunlop* a100 116
6 b h Montjeu(IRE) Madeira Mist (IRE) (Grand Lodge (USA))
2428^{6} 2864^{3} 3615a^{10} 5575a^{2} 7058a^{13} (7563a) 8033a^{17}
Josie's Dream (IRE) *Jo Hughes* a39 60
5 b g Tau Ceti Gallery Breeze (Zamindar (USA))
1664^{12} 3312^{5} (3406) 3792^{6} 4204^{12} 7984^{12}
Journalistic (USA) *M Ibrahim* a79 79
4 b c Street Sense(USA) Cajun Two Step (USA) (Tabasco Cat (USA))
7683a^{2}
Jowhara *Gerard Butler* a50 17
3 ch f Mount Nelson Call Account (USA) (Private Account (USA))
6696^{12} 6997^{5} 7488^{8}
Joy And Fun (NZ) *D Cruz* 120
10 b g Cullen(AUS) Gin Player (NZ) (Defensive Play (USA))
1265a^{2} 8209a^{13}
Joybringer (IRE) *Richard Hannon Snr* 34
2 b f Acclamation Pina Colada (Sabrehill (USA))
3288^{8} 5061^{11}
Joyeuse *Lady Cecil* 105
2 b f Oasis Dream Kind (IRE) (Danehill (USA))
(2744) ◆ 3522^{3} (6142) 6836^{6}
Joy For Life *Tobias B P Coles* a57 67
4 b f Pivotal Gallivant (Danehill (USA))
218^{11}
Joyful Friend *John Gosden* a75
2 b f Dubawi(IRE) Cheerleader (Singspiel (IRE))
8332^{6}
Joyful Motive *Tom Tate* 55
4 ch g Motivator Triple Joy (Most Welcome)
3589^{8} 4204^{2} 4969^{8} 5337^{4} 7597^{8}
Joyful Risk (IRE) *Martin Bosley* a31
3 ch f Kheleyf(USA) Joyfullness (USA) (Dixieland Band (USA))
8427^{12}
Joyful Sound (IRE) *Brian Ellison* 63
5 b g Acclamation Eman's Joy (Lion Cavern (USA))
(3081) 3649^{4} 4052^{9}
Joyous *Dean Ivory* a69 67
3 b f Assertive Ivory's Joy (Tina's Pet)
3837^{9} 5345^{4} 5647^{4} 7073^{3} 8330^{2} ◆
Joyously *Violet M Jordan* a51 78
5 ch f Needwood Blade Lambadora (Suave Dancer (USA))
820^{4} 1022^{10}
Joys Of Spring (IRE) *Luca Cumani* 58
2 b f Invincible Spirit(IRE) Sonachan (IRE) (Darshaan)
7102^{4} 7493^{10}
Juan Alonso (IRE) *Richard Hannon Snr* 81
2 ch g Rock Of Gibraltar(IRE) Izzy Lou (IRE) (Spinning World (USA))
5244^{6} 5442^{3} 5790^{2} (6256) (6865)
Jubilance (IRE) *Bent Olsen* a87 96
4 b c Oratorio(IRE) Literacy (USA) (Diesis)
5045a^{4} 5809a^{5} 6453a^{5}
Jubilante *Hughie Morrison* 93
3 b f Royal Applause Lavinia's Grace (USA) (Green Desert (USA))
(1821) 2452^{2} 3058^{3} 4252^{5} (6564) 7021^{11} 7538^{2}
Jubilant Queen *Clive Cox* a51 80
3 b f Kyllachy Hector's Girl (Hector Protector (USA))
1616^{6} 2738^{8} (3246) 3841^{2} 4962^{2} (5308) 6564^{6}
Jubilee Brig *Gary Moore* a81 81
3 b g Kheleyf(USA) Voile (IRE) (Barathea (IRE))
5124^{14} 6067^{4} 6525^{5} 7964^{2} ◆ 8127^{6} 8455^{8}
Jubilee Dancer *Geoffrey Oldroyd* 80
3 b f Misu Bond(IRE) Bond Babe (Forzando)
(2719) (3762) (4558) 5611^{4}
Jubilee Games *Richard Fahey* 78
3 b g Pastoral Pursuits Jane Jubilee (IRE) (Mister Baileys)
3207^{9} 3571^{5} 5293^{2}

Jubilini *Brett Johnson* a22 38
3 ch f Bertolini(USA) Days Of Grace (Wolfhound (USA))
137[4]

Judd Street *Eve Johnson Houghton* a82 69
11 b g Compton Place Pudding Lane (IRE) (College Chapel)
3181[4] 4120[11]

Judge 'n Jury *Ronald Harris* a85 108
9 ch g Pivotal Cyclone Connie (Dr Devious (IRE))
2396[3] 2669[18] 2865[14] 3848a[6] 4800[5] 5257[8]
5772a[11] 6190[3] 6305[3] 6639[12] 7010[13] 7527[19]

Judicious *Geoffrey Harker* 86
6 ch g Pivotal Virtuous (Exit To Nowhere (USA))
2383[12] 3545[7] 5179[4] (5882) 6730[5] 7369[11]

Judy The Beauty (CAN) *Wesley A Ward* a115 98
4 ch f Ghostzapper(USA) Holy Blitz (USA) (Holy Bull (USA))
7709a[2]

Julienas (IRE) *Gai Waterhouse* a99 106
6 b g Cape Cross(IRE) Dora Carrington (IRE) (Sri Pekan (USA))
7392a[18] 7700a[11]

Julissima *P Schiergen* 97
3 b f Beat Hollow Skimmia (Mark Of Esteem (IRE))
3852a[5] 7233a[5]

Julius Geezer (IRE) *Amy Weaver* a88 92
5 b g Antonius Pius(USA) Victoria's Secret (IRE) (Law Society (USA))
608a[5] (773a) 1001a[4]

Julius Quercus (IRE) *F Chappet* a85 84
3 b c Holy Roman Emperor(IRE) Gifts Galore (IRE) (Darshaan)
(270a) 782a[0] 4274a[10]

Jullundar (IRE) *Mick Channon* a70 70
3 b g Refuse To Bend(IRE) Announcing Peace (Danehill (USA))
1057[6] 1741[3] 1898[4] 3242[9] 3861[2] 4209[2] 4515[6]
5016[U] 5839[4]

July Days (IRE) *Brian Baugh* a66 83
7 b m Exceed And Excel(AUS) Tocade (IRE) (Kenmare (FR))
426[9] 616[9]

Jumbo Prado (USA) *John Stimpson* a69 75
4 rg g El Prado(IRE) Sant Elena (Efisio)
(147) 410[2] 478[7] 758[3] 896[11] 2417[12] 3054[4]
3642[11]

Jumbo Steps (IRE) *J F Levins* a53 72
6 b g Footstepsinthesand Night Delight (IRE) (Night Shift (USA))
5677[7]

Jumeirah (DEN) *Lone Bager* 89
5 b g Black Sam Bellamy(IRE) Sypha (FR) (Saumarez)
4095a[4]

Jungle Bay *Jane Chapple-Hyam* a83 82
6 b g Oasis Dream Dominica (Alhaarth (IRE))
1782[8] 2266[3] 3215[6] 4281[10] 4960[6] (5798)
6461[5] 6744[12] 7601[3] 7896[4] (8069) 8391[3]
8431[5] ◆

Junior *David Pipe* a93 98
10 ch g Singspiel(IRE) For More (FR) (Sanglamore (USA))
3560[15]

Junket *Dr Jon Scargill* a84 84
6 b m Medicean Gallivant (Danehill (USA))
5149[2] ◆ 5491[2]

Junoob *Chris Waller* a102 92
5 ch g Haafhd Faydah (USA) (Bahri (USA))
7760a[9]

Jupiter (FR) *E Leenders* a70 84
3 b c Astronomer Royal(USA) Frissonante (Sri Pekan (USA))
7736a[8]

Jupiter Fidius *Karen Tutty* 72
6 b g Haafhd Kyda (USA) (Gulch (USA))
1394[5] 1995[5] (2537) 3286[8] 4160[5] 5341[2] 5471[10]
(6181) 6943[12]

Jupiter Storm *Gary Moore* a81 88
4 ch g Galileo(IRE) Exciting Times (FR) (Jeune Homme (USA))
(1973) (2939) 3838[6] 5259[8] 5823[8] 6559[6] 7072[8]

Just A Pound (IRE) *Jo Hughes* a62 63
3 b g Ad Valorem(USA) Gallery Breeze (Zamindar (USA))
1885[8] (3041) 3313[3] 3376[2] 3772[7] 6588[9] 7511[2]
7966[7] 8308[8]

Justbookies Dotnet *Louise Best* a69 57
4 b g Kheleyf(USA) Moly (Inchinor)
115[7] 274[10]

Just Breathe (IRE) *Olivia Maylam* a67
4 b f Choisir(AUS) Opium Creek (IRE) (Darshaan)
335[9]

Justcallmehandsome *Dominic Ffrench Davis* a54 32
11 ch g Handsome Ridge Pearl Dawn (IRE) (Jareer (USA))
7[2] 41[10] 312[5] 587[3] 737[9] 927[3] 1017[6] 1222[7]
1797[9] 5032[9] 6339[6] 6472[4] 6985[5] 7083[6] 8055[9]
8399[9]

Just Darcy *Sir Michael Stoute* a71 75
3 b f Danehill Dancer(IRE) Jane Austen (IRE) (Galileo (IRE))
1837[5] 2462[2] 3243[5] 3900[2] 4523[7] 5410[3] 6997[3]

Just Divine (FR) *J Helouri* 33
2 f Dylan Thomas(IRE) Whitby (FR) (Gold Away (IRE))
7567a[7]

Just Fabulous *George Moore* 84
4 b f Sakhee(USA) Tipsy Me (Selkirk (USA))
2042[5]

Just Five (IRE) *John Weymes* a57 52
7 b g Olmodavor(USA) Wildsplash (USA) (Deputy Minister (CAN))
1222[2] 1730[5] (2171) 2575[4] 3642[12] 4834[11]
5426[8] 6472[7] 7752[5] 7963[7]

Just For Mary *Daniel Mark Loughnane* a40 69
9 b g Groom Dancer(USA) Summer Dance (Sadler's Wells (USA))
3197[13]

Just Gets Better (IRE) *Sean Curran*
4 gr g Bertolini(USA) Fun Loving (IRE) (Selkirk (USA))
4590[12] 5233[9]

Just Gwen *Brian Baugh* a20
4 b f Young Ern Grandads Dream (Never So Bold)
590[8] 796[7] 1019[8]

Just Hurricane (FR) *F Chappet* a73 74
3 bb f Hurricane Run(IRE) Just Aerdee (FR) (Kahyasi)
6713a[18]

Justice Day (IRE) *David Elsworth* 110
2 b c Acclamation Rock Exhibition (Rock Of Gibraltar (IRE))
(1669) 1917[2] ◆ (2421) 2877[2] 3424[9] 5765[5]
6304[2] (6958) 7191[3]

Justification *A P O'Brien* a82 93
5 b g Montjeu(IRE) Colorspin (FR) (High Top)
2149[7] 3423[13]

Justineo *Roger Varian* a93 110
4 b c Oasis Dream Loulwa (IRE) (Montjeu (IRE))
154a[11] 467a[5] 834a[5] 1287[2] 2013[11] 2768[3] 3373[2]
3822[5] (4493) 4947[3] (6305) 7054a[11]

Justine Time (IRE) *Julie Camacho* a50 59
4 b f Kodiac Sinn Time (IRE) (Key Of Luck (USA))
98[5] 375[5] 600[6] 886[4]

Justin Phillip (USA) *Steven Asmussen* a118
5 bb c First Samurai(USA) Ava Knowsthecode (USA) (Cryptoclearance (USA))
7713a[5]

Just In Time (SLO) *M Weiss* a55
5 br c Desert Track Just Me (IRE) (Lake Coniston (IRE))
700a[5]

Just Isla *Peter Makin* a42 64
3 ch f Halling(USA) Island Rapture (Royal Applause)
815[7] 1095[5] 2093[12] 3040[3] 3859[4] (4423) (4666)
5407[6] 6019[7] (6323) 7093[7] 7354[8]

Just Jimmy (IRE) *George Jones* a45 65
8 b g Ashkalani(IRE) Berkeley Hall (Saddlers' Hall (IRE))
1350[9] 1893[6]

Just Like Heaven (IRE) *Tim Easterby* a74 72
4 b g Kodiac Night Beauty (King Of Kings (IRE))
2122[5] (2914) ◆ 3236[11] 3682[10] 4588[9] 6469[10]
7029[3]

Just Lille (IRE) *Ann Duffield* a71 88
10 b m Mull Of Kintyre(USA) Tamasriya (IRE) (Doyoun)
1795[2] (2118) 3085[5] 5087[4] 6217[4]

Justonefortheroad *Richard Fahey* a18 101
7 b g Domedriver(IRE) Lavinia's Grace (USA) (Green Desert (USA))
1235[4] 1675[23] 2399[7] 3725[9] 4744[26] 5838[11]
6625[6] 7172[10] 7696[7] 7885[11]

Just One Kiss *Lady Cecil* a83 78
3 b f Cape Cross(IRE) Kissing (Grand Lodge (USA))
1671[12] ◆ 2206[5] 4594[4] 6566[7] 8178[2] 8454[4]

Just One Wish (IRE) *H De Nicolay* a80 77
3 b f Araafa(IRE) Three Wishes (Sadler's Wells (USA))
7188a[12]

Just Past Andover (IRE) *Lee Carter* a36 79
3 b g Amadeus Wolf Fancy Feathers (IRE) (Redback)
368[4] 828[7] 4378[7]

Just Paul (IRE) *Philip Kirby* 80
3 b g Clodovil(IRE) Tatamagouche (IRE) (Sadler's Wells (USA))
1759[5] 1966[9] (2837) (3445) (4045) 4158[5] (4956)
5642[2] (6874) 7374[13]

Just Poppy (IRE) *Stuart Coltherd* 49
4 ch f Ad Valorem(USA) Nebulae (IRE) (Unfuwain (USA))
3774[4]

Just Pretending (USA) *A P O'Brien* a75 112
3 b f Giant's Causeway(USA) Moon Safari (USA) (Mr Prospector (USA))
(2289a) 2689a[3] 3482[2] 4550a[3] 4985[6] 6224a[8]

Just River *Seamus Mullins* a46
4 ch g Medicean Just Wood (FR) (Highest Honor (FR))
1035[5] 5429[14]

Just Rubie *Michael Blanshard* a63 24
2 b f Refuse To Bend(IRE) Island Rapture (Royal Applause)
3853[11] 7244[5] (7664) 7878[13] 8222[5] 8325[4]

Just The Judge (IRE) *Charles Hills* 111
3 br f Lawman(FR) Faraday Light (IRE) (Rainbow Quest (USA))
2047[2] ◆ (2689a) 3524[3] 4985[12] 6837[6]

Just The Tonic *Marjorie Fife* a66 81
6 ch m Medicean Goodwood Blizzard (Inchinor)
1995[2] 2636[5] 3027[9] (4160) 4375[9] (5049) 5711[10]
6728[2] 6908[9] (7594) 7964[9]

Jutland *Doug Watson* a107 109
6 b g Halling(USA) Dramatique (Darshaan)
661a[4] 873a[2] 1263a[4]

Juvenal (IRE) *Richard Hannon Snr* a68 87
4 b g Holy Roman Emperor(IRE) Final Opinion (IRE) (King's Theatre (IRE))
4859[5] ◆ 5063[5] 5436[5] 5759[6] 6215[6] 6700[2]
7071[3] 7306[7]

Juvenile Lead (IRE) *Sir Michael Stoute* 59
2 ch c Sea The Stars(IRE) Drama Class (IRE) (Caerleon (USA))
2925[6] (Dead)

Jwala *Robert Cowell* a84 115
4 b f Oasis Dream Kangra Valley (Indian Ridge)
1662[5] 2152[7] 3046[2] ◆ 3562[2] (4311) 4947[17]
(5726) 7054a[4] 8209a[F]

J Wonder (USA) *Brian Meehan* 97
2 b f Footstepsinthesand Canterbury Lace (USA) (Danehill (USA))
(4484) ◆ (5005) ◆ 5680[7]

Kaab (IRE) *Ed Dunlop* 82
2 b c Kheleyf(USA) Ms Victoria (IRE) (Fasliyev (USA))
2712[7] (7448)

Kaabamix (FR) *D Windrif* a69 78
3 gr f Carlotamix(FR) Sindella (IRE) (Sendawar (IRE))
5913a[6]

Kaafel (IRE) *Peter Hedger* a87 86
4 b g Nayef(USA) Tafaani (IRE) (Green Desert (USA))
189[6] 897[6] 1422[4] 1922[13] 6004[13] 6694[14]

Kaahen (USA) *Pat Eddery* a41 21
3 bb g Jazil(USA) Khassah (Green Desert (USA))
1296[8] 2529[4] 2934[8] 3679[11] 4193[6] 6043[5] 6965[6]
7154[5] 7459[9] 7929[6]

Kabbaas (IRE) *Roger Varian* a79 68
3 ch g Pivotal Dorrati (USA) (Dubai Millennium)
492[2] ◆ (602) 826[2] 2160[3] 2951[5] 3289[4] 3571[6]

Kadabra (IRE) *E Botti* 96
6 b m Dubawi(IRE) Windy Britain (Mark Of Esteem (IRE))
6890a[2] 7558a[6]

Kadison (GER) *H Blume* a63 71
5 bb g Lomitas Kaleica (GER) (Cricket Ball (USA))
5042a[11]

Kadou (FR) *P Monfort* a83 94
5 b g High Yield(USA) Kadouville I (FR) (Kaldoun (FR))
5735a[7]

Kafeel (USA) *Roger Varian* a78 72
2 b g First Samurai(USA) Ishraak (USA) (Sahm (USA))
7209[4] (7647)

Kahdian (IRE) *M Delzangles* 77
3 br c Rock Of Gibraltar(IRE) Katiykha (IRE) (Darshaan)
7412a[6]

Kaheyll *William Haggas* a59 59
2 br c Pastoral Pursuits Dansa Queen (Dansili)
6790[7] 7162[5] 7348[4]

Kai *Alan McCabe* a64 42
4 b g Kyllachy Belle Ile (USA) (Diesis)
87[2] (162) 380[6] 559[6] 616[8] 890[8] 1656[10]
6634[13] 7905[12] 8023[8] 8118[11]

Kaiss (USA) *S Seemar* a99 94
6 ch g Seeking The Gold(USA) November Snow (USA) (Storm Cat (USA))
290a[11]

Kaiulani (IRE) *Mick Channon* 94
2 b f Danehill Dancer(IRE) Royal Shyness (Royal Academy (USA))
(2740) ◆ 3459[9] 5680[8]

Kaizen Factor *Rod Millman* a54 64
2 b g Azamour(IRE) Best Side (IRE) (King's Best (USA))
4926[9] 5309[8] 6152[4] 6520[9] 6897[9]

Kakapuka *Anabel K Murphy* a83 81
6 br g Shinko Forest(IRE) No Rehearsal (FR) (Baillamont (USA))
1925[2] 2807[4] 3511[2] 4245[4] (4677) 5187[7] 5621[3]
6096[7] 7898[8] 8157[4]

Kakatosi *Mike Murphy* a89 91
6 br g Pastoral Pursuits Ladywell Blaise (IRE) (Turtle Island (IRE))
164[8] 353[5] 880[6] 1061[3] 2013[4] 3060[2] 3812[2]
4960[5] 7464[9] 8181[5] 8455[2]

Kalahari Breeze (IRE) *William Muir* a47 57
3 b f Jeremy(USA) Staceymac (IRE) (Elnadim (USA))
31[9] 350[8] 588[4] 651[6] 804[6]

Kalahari Kingdom (IRE) *Richard Fahey* 59
2 b g Footstepsinthesand Visite Royale (USA) (Danehill Dancer (IRE))
4731[7] 6754[6] 7371[5]

Kala Kanta (IRE) *M Ramadan* a70 64
7 gr g Verglas(IRE) Rappide (IRE) (Fayruz)
7679a[P]

Kalamill (IRE) *Shaun Lycett* a75 54
6 b g Kalanisi(IRE) Desert Pageant (IRE) (Desert King (IRE))
823[3] 1018[3] 1721[8] 2087[3]

Kalani's Diamond *Bryan Smart* 26
3 ch f Kalani Bay(IRE) Cryptonite Diamond (USA) (Hennessy (USA))
6289[13]

Kalevala (FR) *R Pritchard-Gordon* a65 72
3 gr f Big Shuffle(USA) Gute Zeit (GER) (Platini (GER))
126a[0]

Kalicamix *Paul Cole* a94 94
3 b c Bahamian Bounty Heather Mix (Linamix (FR))
961a[5] 999a[9] 1668[8] (3708a)

Kalifi (USA) *Amanda Perrett* a54
2 bb f First Defence(USA) Out Of Reach (Warning)
7435[7]

Kalily *Rae Guest* a66 67
4 b c Dubawi(IRE) Mail Express (IRE) (Cape Cross (IRE))
1837[4] 2383[6] 2981[4] 3719[6]

Kalispell (IRE) *Charlie Appleby* 92
3 b f Singspiel(IRE) Genovefa (USA) (Woodman (USA))
6532[5] (7504)

Kalithea *Julie Camacho* a60 48
3 b f Kheleyf(USA) Baralinka (IRE) (Barathea (IRE))
4887[4] 6497[7] 8119[2]

Kalk Bay (IRE) *Michael Easterby* a94 92
6 b g Hawk Wing(USA) Politesse (USA) (Barathea (IRE))
1576[7] 2028[10] 2310[13] 2882[3] ◆ 3349[4] 3684[4]
4373[7] 7176[3] 7499[2] 7661[6]

Kalon Brama (IRE) *Peter Charalambous* a63 58
2 b f Kodiac Gilded Truffle (IRE) (Peintre Celebre (USA))
6807[5] (7111) 7468[4] 7771[11]

Kambis *Gary Moore* a13 46
5 b g Tobougg(IRE) Queen Tomyra (IRE) (Montjeu (IRE))
132[11]

Kamchatka *Philip Hide* a59 83
3 ch g Sakhee's Secret Queensgate (Compton Place)
1612[9] 2394[5] 3661[2] 4207[7] 4492[6] 4998[U] 5280[7]
(5607) (6259)

Kamellata (FR) *H-A Pantall* 80
2 b f Pomellato(GER) Kamakura (GER) (Exit To Nowhere (USA))
5419a[6]

Kames Park (IRE) *Richard Guest* a79 51
11 b g Desert Sun Persian Sally (IRE) (Persian Bold)
(53) 167[2] (198) 273[5] 420[6] 563[9]

Kanaf (IRE) *M Al Muhairi* a102 87
6 b g Elnadim(USA) Catcher Applause (Royal Applause)
746a[9] 868a[10]

Kandari (FR) *Jonjo O'Neill* 61
9 b g Kahyasi Nee Brune (FR) (Akarad (FR))
2552[8]

Kangaroo Court (IRE) *Emma Lavelle* a77 84
9 b g Lahib(USA) Tombazaan (IRE) (Good Thyne (USA))
3118[7] 3856[6]

Kano's Ghirl (IRE) *Keith Dalgleish* a46 62
2 b f Kodiac Southern Barfly (USA) (Southern Halo (USA))
4107[4] 4963[2] 5638[5] (6082) 6364[3] 6467[7]

Kantara Castle (IRE) *Richard Hannon Snr* a70 32
2 b c Baltic King Arbitration (IRE) (Bigstone (IRE))
6279[6] 7766[8] 7853[3] 8131[3] (8311)

Kanz *Mick Channon* 76
2 ch f Kyllachy Frambroise (Diesis)
4484[7] 4877[6] 5174[2] (5609) 6293a[7] 6839[11] 7503[7]

Kaolak (USA) *Jim Goldie* a95 69
7 bb h Action This Day(USA) Cerita (USA) (Magesterial (USA))
2221[4]

Kapour (IRE) *F Rohaut* 108
3 b c Toylsome Kitcat (GER) (Monsun (GER))
(1046a) 1737a[2] 5807a[11] 7142a[4]

Kapstadt (FR) *F Doumen* a94 103
3 b c Country Reel(USA) King's Parody (IRE) (King's Best (USA))
3007a[3] 4043a[2] 5120a[4]

Kapunda *Sean Curran* a6 53
5 b g Pastoral Pursuits Kiss Me Again (IRE) (Cyrano De Bergerac)
5127[6] 6103[8]

Karaka Jack *David Nicholls* a91 91
6 ch g Pivotal Mauri Moon (Green Desert (USA))
(1819) 1922[2] (2220) 2881[2] 3684[7] 4746[2] 5014[2]
5291[4] 6550[5] 6624[5] 6792[13] 7211[7] ◆ 7499[5]

Karakontie (JPN) *J E Pease* 117
2 b c Bernstein(USA) Sun Is Up (JPN) (Sunday Silence (USA))
5313a[2] (6249a) (7056a)

Karam Albaari (IRE) *J R Jenkins* a91 89
5 b c King's Best(USA) Lilakiya (IRE) (Dr Fong (USA))
1913[6] 2841[9] 3812[4] 4435[3] 5302[4] 7765[2] (8218)

Karamaya (IRE) *John M Oxx* 94
3 b f Invincible Spirit(IRE) Karawana (IRE) (King's Best (USA))
6025a[20]

Karate (IRE) *Hans Adielsson* a67 52
5 ch g Exceed And Excel(AUS) La Belle Katherine (USA) (Lyphard (USA))
813[7] 1107[5] 1617[9] 1981[2] 2954[9] 3433[12]
3687[6] 4169[10]

Karate Queen *Ron Barr* a25 52
8 b m King's Best(USA) Black Belt Shopper (IRE) (Desert Prince (IRE))
1962[4] 2276[4] 2757[5] 3393[9] 4161[7] 4398[3] 4727[5]
4891[3]

Kareman (FR) *T Lemer* a69 93
3 b c Zamindar(USA) Sterope (FR) (Hernando (FR))
445a[7] 1046a[4]

Karitza (FR) *Jeremy Gask* a53 57
3 b f Barathea(IRE) Kritzia (Daylami (IRE))
4152[9] 5281[8] 5925[6] 7569a[8]

Karl Marx (IRE) *Mark Gillard* a44 53
3 b g Red Clubs(IRE) Brillano (FR) (Desert King (IRE))
1314[6] 1897[3] 2599[6] 2924[3]

Karluv Most (FR) *J L Maroto* 77
7 b g Della Francesca(USA) La Vltava (IRE) (Grand Lodge (USA))
(2380a)

Kasbah Bliss (FR) *F Doumen* a78 114
11 b g Kahyasi Marital Bliss (FR) (Double Bed (FR))
1658a[4] 6447a[6]

Kasbhom *Anthony Carson* a61 52
3 b g Refuse To Bend(IRE) Summerstrand (IRE) (Cape Cross (IRE))
1086[10] ◆ 1908[9] 2456[9] 4520[5] 5406[6] 6752[9]
7508[7] 7904[7] 8338[5] (8393)

Kashgar *Bernard Llewellyn* a67 80
4 b g Hernando(FR) Miss Katmandu (IRE) (Rainbow Quest (USA))
2350[6] (2828) (2921) ◆ (3807) 4913[11] 5946[4]
6377[5] 7396[10]

Kashmiri Star *Mick Quinn* a68 64
4 b f Barathea(IRE) Biriyani (IRE) (Danehill (USA))
523[2]

Kashmiri Sunset *Ed de Giles* 53
2 b c Tiger Hill(IRE) Sagamartha (Rainbow Quest (USA))
7631[6] 7773[7]

Kashmir Peak (IRE) *John Quinn* a89 94
4 b g Tiger Hill(IRE) Elhareer (IRE) (Selkirk (USA))
5031[2] ◆ 5335[3] 7174[8] 7526[2]

Kashstaree *David Barron* 47
2 b f Sakhee(USA) Celestial Welcome (Most Welcome)
4723[8] 5379[9] 6298[8] 7418[4]

Kassiano (GER) *Saeed bin Suroor* a113 107
4 b g Soldier Hollow Kastila (GER) (Sternkoenig (IRE))
151a[2] ◆ (463a) ◆ (656a) (833a) 958a[2]
1269a[9] (5540) 6636[6] 7196[7]

Kastini *Denis Coakley* a73 76
3 b g Halling(USA) Toucantini (Inchinor)
1879[4] 3055[2] 3243[3] (4405) 5001[4] 6313[3]
7249[2] 7447[2]

Katawi *Peter Chapple-Hyam* 50
2 b f Dubawi(IRE) Purring (USA) (Mountain Cat (USA))
5797[9] 7692[9]

Katchy Lady *P J Prendergast* 83
3 ch f Kyllachy Star Approval (IRE) (Hawk Wing (USA))
2374a[16]

Kateeva (IRE) *J P Fogarty* a66 72
6 br m Statue Of Liberty(USA) Time Limit (IRE) (Alzao (USA))
1255a[7]

Kathinka (GER) *M Munch* a94 91
3 b f Speedmaster(GER) Karsawina (GER) (Lando (GER))
2910a[12] 4468a[9]

Kathlatino *Micky Hammond* 64
6 b m Danbird(AUS) Silver Rhythm (Silver Patriarch (IRE))
2555[9] 2961[10] 3814[7] 5050[3] 7372[5]

Katie Gale *Tim Pitt* a60 39
3 b f Shirocco(GER) Karla June (Unfuwain (USA))
2157[9] 4753[6] 5197[2] 6404[2] ◆ (6558)

Katie Galore (IRE) *David Evans*
4 ch f Bahamian Bounty Silicon Star (FR) (Starborough)
2529[P] 2746[15]

Katja *J W Hills* 56
2 b f Sleeping Indian Toffee Vodka (IRE) (Danehill Dancer (IRE))
4827[6] 5949[7] 6423[5] 6972[10]

Katla (IRE) *J F Grogan* a98 105
5 b f Majestic Missile(IRE) Bratislava (Dr Fong (USA))
2676a[16] 3263a[11]

Katmai River (IRE) *Mark Usher* a65 72
6 b g Choisir(AUS) Katavi (USA) (Stravinsky (USA))
50[6] 274[2] 616[7] 899[5] 1100[8] 1426[8] 2126[3] 2578[10] 2932[4] 3909[5] 5177[7] 6261[4] 6472[2] 6803[7] 8065[4] 8279[6] 8329[3]

Kat Moon *Tim Easterby* a40 52
3 b f Cockney Rebel(IRE) Damelza (IRE) (Orpen (USA))
3910[7] 4140[6] 4557[6]

Kattaf (IRE) *Marco Botti* 58
3 ch g Hernando(FR) Decision Maid (USA) (Diesis)
1931[6] 2384[11] 3059[7] 5801[4]

Katy Spirit (IRE) *Michael Blanshard* a65 58
3 b f Invincible Spirit(IRE) Katy Guest (IRE) (Be My Guest (USA))
31[2] 357[3] (628) 811[3] 923[5] 1616[7] 1978[6] 2528[4] 2951[8] 4836[8] (5397) 7729[12] 7897[8]

Katy's Secret *William Jarvis* a79 49
6 b m Mind Games Katy O'Hara (Komaite (USA))
317[4] 2134[5] 3993[6] 5166[5]

Kavanagh (SAF) *M F De Kock* a113 119
6 b g Tiger Ridge(USA) Quaestio (USA) (Seeking The Gold (USA))
365a[5] ◆ 467a[13] 660a[2] (868a) 1266a[6] 5747[6] 6193[8] 7013[10]

Kawa Blanc (FR) *P Khozian* a64
3 b c Della Francesca(USA) Senteur Cafe (USA) (Zavata (USA))
331a[5]

Kayaan *Pam Sly* a67 70
6 br g Marju(IRE) Raheefa (USA) (Riverman (USA))
2435[12]

Kayalar (IRE) *Evan Williams* a76 74
5 b g Noverre(USA) Katiykha (IRE) (Darshaan)
1973[6] 4914[8] 6435[8]

Kayef (GER) *Michael Scudamore* a71 74
6 ch g Nayef(USA) Kassna (IRE) (Ashkalani (IRE))
1670[13] 2197[4] 2570[3] 3328[4] 3609[8] 4530[5] 5862[9] 6336[11] 6853[4] 7382[6]

Kay Gee Be (IRE) *Alan Berry* a89 88
9 b g Fasliyev(USA) Pursuit Of Truth (USA) (Irish River (FR))
2646[8] 3094[11] 4101[7] 5149[9]

Kaylee *Brett Johnson* a57 50
4 b f Selkirk(USA) Mrs Brown (Royal Applause)
128[4] 649[12] 733[5] 819[3] 1087[8] 1195[5] 7508[10] 7983[5] 8180[4] 8393[10]

Kazak *Roger Charlton* 72
3 b c Royal Applause Kazeem (Darshaan)
1678[13] 2306[7] 3021[12] 3585[7] 7505[11]

Kazbow (IRE) *Richard Ford* a82 91
7 b g Rainbow Quest(USA) Kasota (IRE) (Alzao (USA))
(622) (713) (1721) 4873[18]

Kazlian (FR) *Johnny Farrelly* a71 99
5 b g Sinndar(IRE) Quiet Splendor (USA) (Unbridled (USA))
8202[6]

Keckerrockernixes (IRE) *Paul Burgoyne*
7 ch g Tomba Dromhall Lady (IRE) (Imperial Frontier (USA))
7738[12]

Keegsquaw (IRE) *Mme A Fabre* a99 102
4 ch f Street Cry(IRE) Kentucky Rose (FR) (Hernando (FR))
2969a[3] 5360a[2] 6714a[7] 7843a[7]

Keene *Philip McBride* a72 62
3 b g Cockney Rebel(IRE) Lumpini Park (Halling (USA))
1891[7] 2760[11] 3149[4] 3665[4] 6339[2] ◆ 6737[2] (8162) 8337[3]

Keene's Pointe *J W Hills* a78 78
3 br g Avonbridge Belle's Edge (Danehill Dancer (IRE))
(341) 550[4] 2160[2] 2844[6] 3438[6] 4288[5] 5280[4] 6214[8]

Keen Glance (IRE) *Y Gourraud* a71 90
3 ch f Sakhee(USA) Glint Of Green (USA) (Jade Hunter (USA))
7736a[14]

Keep Calm *Richard Hannon Snr* a68 67
3 b c War Chant(USA) Mayaar (USA) (Grand Slam (USA))
2322[3] 2564[6]

Keep Close *Mick Channon* 52
2 b f Cape Cross(IRE) Kelucia (IRE) (Grand Lodge (USA))
6641[8] 6973[7]

Keep Cool *Mme C Janssen* a99 87
6 b h Starcraft(NZ) Kirov (Darshaan)
125a[2]

Keeping (IRE) *G M Lyons* a80 82
3 b f Teofilo(IRE) My (King's Best (USA))
2148[8]

Keep It Cool (IRE) *David O'Meara* a64 76
9 ch g Spinning World(USA) Sudden Stir (USA) (Woodman (USA))
3442[7] 3944[3] 4159[5] 4673[2] 4759[4] 5466[11]

Keep It Dark *Tony Coyle* a70 74
4 b g Invincible Spirit(IRE) Tarneem (USA) (Zilzal (USA))
1184[4] 1271[2] (1394) 1801[5] 2037[5] 2884[4] 3445[6] 3895[4] 4669[3] 4970[2] 5139[6] 5564[5] 6181[4] 6944[2] 7029[2] (7281) 7634[3]

Keep Kicking (IRE) *Simon Dow* a73 71
6 b g Tiger Hill(IRE) Dalannda (IRE) (Hernando (FR))
752[2] 1069[4] 1300[5] 1889[4] 2284[2] 2749[5] 5619[2] 6404[8] 7738[11] 7899[5] 8160[3] 8331[3]

Keep The Dream *Paul Cole* a69 69
3 b g Oasis Dream Mimisel (Selkirk (USA))
1784[7] 3159[5]

Keep The Secret *William Knight* a74 64
3 ch f Sakhee's Secret Starfleet (Inchinor)
3583[6] 4383[13] 5152[5] 6734[10]

Keep To The Beat *Kevin Ryan* a46 37
2 b f Beat Hollow Cadeau Speciale (Cadeaux Genereux)
4880[10] 8138[5] 8362[6]

Keiai Leone (JPN) *Katsuichi Nishiura* a108
3 gr c Henny Hughes(USA) Most Remarkable (USA) (Marquetry (USA))
1264a[10]

Keladiva *David Simcock* a16
3 b f Dixie Union(USA) Keladora (USA) (Crafty Prospector (USA))
590[7]

Kelamita (IRE) *Hughie Morrison* 48
2 ch f Pivotal Keladora (USA) (Crafty Prospector (USA))
6739[12] 7103[9] 7501[9]

Kel Away (FR) *Mlle M Henry* a67 79
6 gr m Keltos(FR) Flamaway (FR) (Gold Away (IRE))
648a[0]

Kelinni (IRE) *Chris Waller* a75 113
5 b g Refuse To Bend(IRE) Orinoco (IRE) (Darshaan)
7392a[9] 7700a[10] 7827a[9]

Kellys Eye (IRE) *Zoe Davison* a75 79
6 b g Noverre(USA) Limit (IRE) (Barathea (IRE))
1286[3] 1814[14] 2128[3] 2871[7] 3415[7] 3955[6]

Kelpie Blitz (IRE) *Seamus Durack* a82 82
4 gr g Verglas(IRE) Summer Spice (IRE) (Key Of Luck (USA))
2498[10] 3022[2] 3976[5] 4280[7] 5847[5] 6358[12] 6898[4] 7651[4] 7840[12] 8179[3]

Kelvingrove (IRE) *Ed Vaughan* a73 91
3 b g Hurricane Run(IRE) Silversword (FR) (Highest Honor (FR))
1754[6] 2589[5] (5619) (6540) 7210[12]

Kenasie (FR) *J-M Capitte* a76 79
3 b c Kendargent(FR) Maille Asie (FR) (Kahyasi)
445a[6] 543a[2]

Kenbella (FR) *H-A Pantall* 105
3 gr f Kendargent(FR) Nebela (FR) (Bernebeau (FR))
782a[0] 5361a[3] 6124a[4] 6714a[5] 7843a[5]

Kendal Mint *Clive Cox* 81
2 b f Kyllachy Windermere Island (Cadeaux Genereux)
3107[3] (3663)

Kendam (FR) *H-A Pantall* 112
4 b f Kendargent(FR) Damdam Freeze (FR) (Indian Rocket)
2264[2] 2897a[7] 4093a[8] 6251a[11]

Kenhope (FR) *H-A Pantall* 110
3 b f Kendargent(FR) Bedford Hope (GER) (Chato (USA))
(1561a) 2299a[15] 2906a[3] 3524[2] 4817a[3] 6224a[4]

Kenny Powers *Tom Dascombe* a106 106
4 b g Vital Equine(IRE) Alexander Ballet (Mind Games)
154a[6] 467a[4] 838a[3] 944[2]

Kenny's Girl (IRE) *William Muir* a58 68
3 b f Manduro(GER) Tanz (IRE) (Sadler's Wells (USA))
2231[7] 2803[2] 3237[7] 3666[7] 6116[3] 6809[7]

Kenny The Captain (IRE) *Tim Easterby* 88
2 ch c Captain Rio Kelso Magic (USA) (Distant View (USA))
4053[10] 4801[3] 5105[2] 5508[9] (6175) 6582[4] (7147) (7819)

Kensea (FR) *H-A Pantall* a98 102
3 ch f Kendargent(FR) Sea Island (FR) (Gold Away (IRE))
1000a[2] 1358a[6] 2299a[20]

Kensington Gardens *Michael Bell* 61
3 b f Oasis Dream Wendylina (IRE) (In The Wings)
2760[8] 3136[10] 4170[2] 4436[4]

Kent Ragstone (USA) *William Haggas* a79 22
4 ch g Stonesider(USA) Sweet Charity (USA) (A.P. Indy (USA))
(752) 1200[2] 6504[8] 7840[13]

Kentucky Winner (FR) *A Lyon* a64 70
4 ch c Kentucky Dynamite(USA) Olanga (GER) (Shareef Dancer (USA))
6060a[5]

Kenzadargent (FR) *J-C Rouget* 104
2 bl f Kendargent(FR) Quiza Bere (FR) (Epistolaire (IRE))
6292a[5] 7571a[2]

Kept *Ronald Harris* a64 73
4 ch g Pivotal Possessed (Desert Prince (IRE))
1243[5] 1801[7] 1901[8] 2710[11] 2920[10] 5177[8] 6518[9] 8065[5] (8361)

Keravnos (FR) *C Gourdain* a101 98
3 b c Elusive City(USA) Kypriano's Angel (FR) (Kendor (FR))
999a[5]

Kerbaaj (USA) *Charles Hills* 81
3 bb g Dixie Union(USA) Mabaahej (USA) (Belong To Me (USA))
1623[7] 2438[7] 5721[8]

Kerfuffle (IRE) *Simon Dow* a53
4 b f Kheleyf(USA) Chiosina (IRE) (Danehill Dancer (IRE))
649[5] 863[9] 7380[5] (7929)

Kerosin (GER) *W Giedt* 97
2 b c Tertullian(USA) Karavel (GER) (Monsun (GER))
5911a[3]

Kersivay *Mrs A Malzard* a76 66
7 b g Royal Applause Lochmaddy (Selkirk (USA))
1738a[3] 2303a[4] 7143a[4]

Kerstenia (FR) *D Sepulchre* a55 49
2 b f Desert Style(IRE) Krestena (FR) (Kendor (FR))
5323a[8]

Ketchikan (IRE) *J-P Carvalho* a83 98
3 b c Dansili Bayberry (UAE) (Bering)
1419a[6] 4815a[4] 5779a[5]

Kettle Corn (USA) *John W Sadler* a112 109
6 b h Candy Ride(ARG) Somethingbeautiful (USA) (Lil E.Tee (USA))
4106a[2]

Key Ambition *Garry Moss* a77 72
4 ch g Auction House(USA) Love Thing (Phountzi (USA))
86[9] 345[3] 426[4] 582[4] 715[5] 1038[6] 2781[3] (3247) 4884[6]

Key Appointment *Paul Cole* a80 80
4 b g Pivotal Appointed One (USA) (Danzig (USA))
1423[4] 1849[5] 4684[2]

Key Gold *Richard Fahey* a68 80
4 b f Cape Cross(IRE) Key Academy (Royal Academy (USA))
1083[7] 2860[11] 5137[5] 6552[7] 6917[6] 7280[8]

Keyhole Kate *Polly Gundry* 39
4 b f Kheleyf(USA) Striking Pose (IRE) (Darshaan)
1579[9] 2030[10] 3657[6] 3924[8] 4658[9] 5126[10]

Keys Of Cyprus *David Nicholls* a57 65
11 ch g Deploy Krisia (Kris)
24[10]

Key To Fun (GER) *Frau E Mader* 84
2 bb c Dashing Blade Key To Win (Lead On Time (USA))
5939a[4]

Key To Peace (IRE) *A Fabre* 105
3 b f Kheleyf(USA) African Peace (USA) (Roberto (USA))
7316a[2] 7993a[12]

Key To Your Heart *Hughie Morrison* 23
2 b f Sakhee(USA) You Too (Monsun (GER))
6949[11] 7310[8]

Khabi *E J O'Neill* 63
2 b c Intikhab(USA) Ticklestone (IRE) (Mark Of Esteem (IRE))
5323a[5]

Khajaaly (IRE) *Michael Appleby* a78 56
6 b g Kheleyf(USA) Joyfulness (USA) (Dixieland Band (USA))
370[5] 517[5] 1294[3] 2134[10] 3015[4] 3700[4] 5713[5] 6475[3] 6606[2] 7754[4] 7880[10] 8038[4]

Khalice *Richard Fahey* 81
2 b f Bahamian Bounty Siena Gold (Key Of Luck (USA))
3064[2] 3710[5] 4528[13] (5053) (5858) 6328[12]

Khawatim *Richard Guest* a95 92
5 b g Intikhab(USA) Don't Tell Mum (IRE) (Dansili)
(86) 372[2] (679a) (1245) 2444[12] 2868[13] 3590[5] 4138[9] 8232[13]

Khee Society *David Evans* 68
2 b g Sakhee(USA) Society Rose (Saddlers' Hall (IRE))
2925[5] 3245[3] 3555[18] 4997[5] 5347[6] 5951[8]

Khefyn (IRE) *J Reynier* a59 64
3 br g Kheleyf(USA) Highly Respected (IRE) (High Estate)
1482[10] 1661[8] 2544[4] 4244[5] 4797[5] 5300[6] 6900[7] 7150[3] 8441a[8]

Khelac *Philip Hide* a71 71
3 b g Kheleyf(USA) Miss Lacey (IRE) (Diktat)
1725[9] 2549[10] 3434[11] 4008[3] (4170) 4411[3] 4442[4] 5032[4] 5953[7] 6276[8] 7322[2]

Kheleyf Diamond (IRE) *Tony Coyle* a40 45
2 ch f Kheleyf(USA) Luceball (IRE) (Bluebird (USA))
6561[7] 6966[6]

Khelman (IRE) *Richard Fahey* 77
3 b g Kheleyf(USA) Mandolin (IRE) (Sabrehill (USA))
1114[2] 1250[7] (1750) 2371[13] 2987[5] 3894[3] 5011[7] 5836[4] 6664[2] 6916[2] 7594[7] 7824[6]

Kheskianto (IRE) *Michael Chapman* a38 54
7 b m Kheleyf(USA) Gently (IRE) (Darshaan)
456[9] 646[9] 1610[5] 2273[11] 6518[11] (6723) 8116[8]

Khione *Luca Cumani* 104
4 b f Dalakhani(IRE) Sularina (IRE) (Alhaarth (IRE))
(2012) ◆

Khloe *Michael Blanshard* 40
2 gr f Clodovil(IRE) Owdbetts (IRE) (High Estate)
3986[13] 5442[8] 5950[8] 7218[12]

Khobaraa *John Gosden* a82 55
3 bb f Invincible Spirit(IRE) Deyaar (USA) (Storm Cat (USA))
1958[2] 2495[10] 2983[4]

Khotan *Sir Mark Prescott Bt* a70 78
3 b g Hernando(FR) Miss Katmandu (IRE) (Rainbow Quest (USA))
2312[2] 2971[4] 5157[2]

Khubala (IRE) *Hugo Palmer* a72 105
4 b g Acclamation Raghida (IRE) (Nordico (USA))
1913[2] 2254[16] 2444[6] (2937) 3558[4] 4780[3] 5027[4] ◆ 5804a[6] 6623[24] 7208[9]

Khudoua *John Gosden* a79 79
3 b g Nayef(USA) Danehill Dreamer (USA) (Danehill (USA))
1119[2] 1317[2] 1804[5] 2952[3] 3805[2]

Kiama Bay (IRE) *Richard Fahey* a92 97
7 b g Fraam La Panthere (USA) (Pine Bluff (USA))
2149[14] 2648[5] 3099[13] 3804[6] 4512[3] (5147) (5513) 5723[3] 6192[5] 6833[8] 7174[14] 7542[3] 7823[12] 8202[3]

Kian's Delight *Peter Bowen* a77 80
5 b g Whipper(USA) Desert Royalty (IRE) (Alhaarth (IRE))
823[7]

Kian's Joy *Jedd O'Keeffe* a47 53
4 b g Mind Games Lunasa (IRE) (Don't Forget Me)
1700[4] 2721[7]

Kia Royale *Ralph Beckett* a40
3 b f Tobougg(IRE) Hilarious (IRE) (Petorius)
74[8]

Kickboxer (IRE) *Mick Channon* 92
2 gr g Clodovil(IRE) Ajig Dancer (Niniski (USA))
4121[9] 4412[2] 4781[3] (4912) 5468[2] 5693[4] (6194) 6582[7] 7011[3] 7170[10] 7534[7]

Kickingthelilly *Rae Guest* a90 84
4 ch f Byron Teller (ARG) (Southern Halo (USA))
79[3] 621[6] (865) 944[9] 1363[4] 1883[5] 2639[2] 3477[4] 4957[3] 5825[3] 6360[9] 6875[8]

Kidmenot (IRE) *J S Moore* a49 69
2 b f Ad Valorem(USA) Monsusu (IRE) (Montjeu (IRE))
1512[3] ◆ 1724[2] 2053[4] (2282) 3522[17] 3857[6] 4277[P]

Kidnapped (AUS) *S Seemar* a78 86
7 br g Viscount(AUS) Youthful Presence (AUS) (Dehere (USA))
246a[16] 555a[9]

Kid Wizzard (USA) *David Flood* 23
4 b g Lemon Drop Kid(USA) Dear Daughter (Polish Precedent (USA))
3819[7] 4193[7]

Kielty's Folly *Brian Baugh* a61 65
9 gr g Weet-A-Minute(IRE) Three Sweeties (Cruise Missile)
24[3] 105[2] 408[2] 617[2] 801[8] 1079[10] 3644[4] 4834[5] 5232[9] 5596[9] (6553) 6932[4] 7639[9] 8118[8]

Kijivu *Alastair Lidderdale* a49 53
8 gr m Erhaab(USA) Alsiba (Northfields (USA))
458[5] 579[8] 1080[4]

Kikonga *Luca Cumani* a90 98
3 b f Danehill Dancer(IRE) Kibara (Sadler's Wells (USA))
(2546) 3610[2] (4234) ◆ 5035[5] 6764[5] 7650[6]

Kilburn *Alastair Lidderdale* a45 68
9 b g Grand Lodge(USA) Lady Lahar (Fraam)
2225[4] 2981[8] 5346[10] 5948[6] 6612[9] 7784[10]

Killachy Loose *B Grizzetti* 101
4 br f Kyllachy Vettori Loose (IRE) (Vettori (IRE))
1563a[7] (6890a) 7413a[3] 7706a[4]

Killing Time (IRE) *Ralph Beckett* a80 78
2 b g Oratorio(IRE) Enchanting Muse (USA) (Fusaichi Pegasus (USA))
2723[4] 3174[4] 3836[3] 6401[2] (7252) (7640)

Killusty Fancy (IRE) *S Smrczek* a67 70
6 b g Refuse To Bend(IRE) Crafty Fancy (IRE) (Intikhab (USA))
3647a[3]

Kilt Rock (IRE) *Doug Watson* a106 77
6 ch g Giant's Causeway(USA) Eliza (USA) (Mt. Livermore (USA))
(575a)

Kimbali (IRE) *David Evans* a80 75
4 b g Clodovil(IRE) Winnifred (Green Desert (USA))
4803[3] 5378[5] 5899[7] 6606[3] 7303[2] (8037) ◆

Kimberella *Michael Attwater* a84 88
3 b g Kyllachy Gleam Of Light (IRE) (Danehill (USA))
1112[8] 1714[3] 2844[7] 3279[4] 3974[7] 5748[2] 6586[10]

Kindanyce (IRE) *Richard Fahey* a46 49
2 b f Bushranger(IRE) Rublevka Star (USA) (Elusive Quality (USA))
1240[8] 2701[8] 3298[6] 4156[4] 4583[2]

Kindergarden Kid (USA) *M Nigge* 113
6 b g Dynaformer(USA) Amelia (USA) (Dixieland Band (USA))
3362a[9]

Kindia (IRE) *Michael Attwater* a78 29
5 b f Cape Cross(IRE) Susu (Machiavellian (USA))
415[2] ◆ 792[9] 984[9] 1176[10] 1386[5] 2155[5] 2773[9] 4169[8] 6399[10] 6932[8] 7429[9] 7458[5] 7922[8] 8149[9]

Kind Invitation *Charlie Appleby* a79
2 b f New Approach(IRE) French Bid (AUS) (Anabaa (USA))
(7875)

Kindlelight Storm (USA) *Nick Littmoden* a60 49
3 b g Stormy Atlantic(USA) Rose Of Zollern (IRE) (Seattle Dancer (USA))
4839[11] 5932[5] 6555[9] (7266) 7458[9] 7966[3] 8341[7] 8449[3] ◆

Kindu *Luca Cumani* a87
3 b f Pivotal Kithanga (IRE) (Darshaan)
(7738) ◆

Kinema (IRE) *Ed Dunlop* 67
2 b c Galileo(IRE) Bon Nuit (IRE) (Night Shift (USA))
3581[11] 4640[5]

Kinesthetic (AUS) *Leon Corstens* 85
6 b g Niello(AUS) Fresh Feeling (AUS) (Spectacular Spy (USA))
7417a[8]

King Air (FR) *R Pritchard-Gordon* a97 109
6 b g Kingsalsa(USA) Haine Amour (FR) (Mtoto)
1945a[12] 2897a[10] 4104a[6]

Kingaroo (IRE) *Garry Woodward* a65 58
7 b g King Charlemagne(USA) Lady Naomi (USA) (Distant View (USA))
624[3] 714[4] 1600[8] 2174[7] 2860[9] 8270[11]

Kingarrick *Noel Wilson* a69 64
5 ch g Selkirk(USA) Rosacara (Green Desert (USA))
646[8] 1603[8] 1789[5] (1993) 2642[2] 3467[8] 4343[8] 5084[7] 6552[11] 7098[8]

King Bertie (IRE) *Michael Wigham* a86 69
3 b g Clodovil(IRE) Jouel (FR) (Machiavellian (USA))
491[2] ◆ (748) 1476[3] 2549[5] 3289[7] 4146[2] 5398[11] 6362[2] ◆ (6969) 7452[9]

King Calypso *Denis Coakley* 27
2 ch g Sir Percy Rosa De Mi Corazon (USA) (Cozzene (USA))
4827[9] 5307[9] 5757[7]

Kingdoms (NZ) *J O'Shea* 101
4 b g High Chaparral(IRE) A Real Princess (NZ) (O'Reilly (NZ))
7700a[7]

Kingdom's Call (USA) *Charlie Appleby* a72
2 bb c Smart Strike(CAN) Wile Cat (USA) (Storm Cat (USA))
6168[4] ◆ 6656[2] (Dead)

King Drok (TUR) *T Turkmen* a103
4 b c West By West(USA) Ms Hero (TUR) (Sea Hero (USA))
6232a[2]

King Fingal (IRE) *John Quinn* a70 65
8 b g King's Best(USA) Llia (Shirley Heights)
1[3] 3410[9]

Kingfisher (IRE) *A P O'Brien* 102
2 b c Galileo(IRE) Mystical Lady (IRE) (Halling (USA))
6223a[3] 6835[5]

King George River (IRE) *Alan Bailey* a99 105
3 b c Danehill Dancer(IRE) Butterfly Blue (IRE) (Sadler's Wells (USA))
359[2] 474[2] (666) (920) ◆ 1623[2] 4779[6] 4917[13] 5728[3] 6838[22] 7205[10]

King Kenny *Mrs A Corson* a78 44
8 ch g Lomitas Salanka (IRE) (Persian Heights)
1739a[6] 5329a[5] 7144a[7]

King Kreesa (USA) *Jeremiah C Englehart* 113
4 bb g King Cugat(USA) Storm's Advance (USA) (Storm Creek (USA))
8210a[12]

King Kurt (IRE) *Kevin Ryan* 84
5 b g Holy Roman Emperor(IRE) Rutledge (IRE) (Entrepreneur)
1568[2] 1763[6] 2594[7] 3195[5] (3977) 4995[4] 5384[2] 5786[2] 7210[16]

Kinglami *Brian Gubby* a85 85
4 b g Kingsalsa(USA) Red Japonica (Daylami (IRE))
(1386) 1878[5] 2573[3] 3864[3] 4237[2] (5062) 5928[4] 6067[3] 7368[5] 7856[3] 8088[4]

Kinglet (USA) *Saeed bin Suroor* a106 40
4 bb g Kingmambo(USA) Karen's Caper (USA) (War Chant (USA))
557a[7] 836a[6] 4531[7]

King Lollipop (FR) *T Lemer* a71 75
3 b c King's Best(USA) Rowat Arazi (Arazi (USA))
445a[9]

Kingman *John Gosden* 112
2 b c Invincible Spirit(IRE) Zenda (Zamindar (USA))
(3833) ◆ (5999) ◆

King Mufhasa (NZ) *Bruce Wallace* 118
9 br g Pentire Sheila Cheval (NZ) (Mi Preferido (USA))
2066a[9]

King Muro *Andrew Balding* a79 79
3 b g Halling(USA) Ushindi (IRE) (Montjeu (IRE))
(1468) 2153[9] 2862[3] 3276[6] 3908[5] 4950[10] 6693[7] 7304[7]

King Of Dixie (USA) *Ruth Carr* a106 45
9 ch g Kingmambo(USA) Dixie Accent (USA) (Dixieland Band (USA))
3592[6]

King Of Eden (IRE) *Eric Alston* a69 96
7 b g Royal Applause Moonlight Paradise (USA) (Irish River (FR))
944[10] 1233[16] (1571) 1787[2] 2254[17] 2665[11] 3825[8] 4067[8] 5481[3] 5943[9] 6164[10] 7176[6]

King Of Forces *Denis Quinn* a55
4 b g Halling(USA) Group Force (IRE) (Montjeu (IRE))
637[8] 712[6] 5002[13]

King Of Jazz (IRE) *Peter Bowen* a86 104
5 b g Acclamation Grand Slam Maria (FR) (Anabaa (USA))
1232[3] 1537[7] ◆ 1913[3] 2310[5] 2725[2] 3590[7] 5247[13] 5696[8] 6278[7] 7131[11]

King Of Kudos (IRE) *Scott Dixon* a71 72
3 b g Acclamation Perugina (FR) (Highest Honor (FR))
1958[10] 3289[8] 6367[5] 6587[11] 7083[8] 7465[7]

King Of Macedon (IRE) *Mark Johnston* a82 82
2 b g Invincible Spirit(IRE) Allexina (Barathea (IRE))
(6842) 7097[2] 7463[3]

King Of Paradise (IRE) *Eric Alston* 80
4 b g Hurricane Run(IRE) Silly Game (IRE) (Bigstone (IRE))
1442[15] 2042[6] 2753[8] (3199) 4135[3] 4612[5] 4995[5] 5222[2] 6051[3] (6668)

King Of The Celts (IRE) *Tim Easterby* 80
5 b g Celtic Swing Flamands (IRE) (Sadler's Wells (USA))
6236[19] 6721[5] 7656[9]

King Of The Danes *Mark Johnston* a70 96
3 b c Dansili Our Queen Of Kings (Arazi (USA))
1991[2] (2209) (2584) ◆ 6823[4] 7205[9]

King Of The Moors (USA) *Dai Burchell* a12 53
10 b g King Of Kings(IRE) Araza (USA) (Arazi (USA))
530[10] 801[12]

King Of Windsor (IRE) *John Wainwright* a78 51
6 b g Intikhab(USA) Kismah (Machiavellian (USA))
192[8] 410[9] 921[12] 2845[11] 8006[8] 8129[9]

King Of Wing (IRE) *Phil McEntee* a53 60
4 b g Hawk Wing(USA) Miss Shivvy (IRE) (Montjeu (IRE))
1915[5] 2875[13] 3406[8] 3909[3] 3997[5] 4403[11] 4623[11] (5525) 5622[5] 6038[9] 6803[3] 7082[7] 7266[12]

King Olav (UAE) *Tony Carroll* a80 93
8 ch g Halling(USA) Karamzin (USA) (Nureyev (USA))
93[8] 420[9] 720[6] 1097[2] (1716) 1983[2] 3468[2] 4167[8] 5129[4] 6173[3] 6750[13] 7976[12] 8323[8]

King Pin *Tracy Waggott* a65 74
8 b g Pivotal Danehurst (Danehill (USA))
1569[6] (1786) 2163[4] 2884[9] 5138[8] 5828[2] 6600[3]

King Rubi *Matthieu Palussiere* a84 100
2 ch c Green Tune(USA) King's Doll (IRE) (King's Best (USA))
5628a[5] 7828a[5]

Kingsbarns (IRE) *A P O'Brien* 120
3 b c Galileo(IRE) Beltisaal (FR) (Belmez (USA))
6226a[6] 7366[3]

King's Ciel *Sean Curran* a21 68
4 ch g Septieme Ciel(USA) King's Jewel (King's Signet (USA))
8169[8] 8272[10]

Kingscombe (USA) *Linda Jewell* a67 54
4 rg g Mizzen Mast(USA) Gombeen (USA) (Private Account (USA))
1466[7] 1716[7] (2168) 2801[10] 3326[6] 5614[8] 5899[8] 7083[3] 7622[7] 7847[5]

Kingscroft (IRE) *Richard Ford* a96 92
5 b g Antonius Pius(USA) Handsome Anna (IRE) (Bigstone (IRE))
6[3] 1745[6] 2214[10] 2463[2] 2541[2] 3096[5] 3335[6] 3757[2] 3984[2] 4111[4] 6161[8]

Kingsdesire (IRE) *Marco Botti* a79 106
4 b g King's Best(USA) Lucky Clio (IRE) (Key Of Luck (USA))
463a[13] 1446[2]

King's Future *Lee Carter* a62 47
4 b g King's Best(USA) Las Beatas (Green Desert (USA))
160[5] 497[8] 667[4]

Kingsgate Choice (IRE) *Ed de Giles* a92 113
6 b g Choisir(AUS) Kenema (IRE) (Petardia)
1249[2] 1672[3] 2150[3] (2669) (3334) 4311[4] 5772a[4] 7054a[14]

Kingsgate Native (IRE) *Robert Cowell* a85 117
8 b g Mujadil(USA) Native Force (IRE) (Indian Ridge)
2019[2] (2662) 3420[16] 4079[2] 4947[15] 5726[5] 6639[3] 7054a[16]

King's Hall *A Wohler* 106
5 ch g Halling(USA) Konigin Turf (GER) (Turfkonig (GER))
1456a[9] 2202a[11]

Kingship Spirit (IRE) *M Ramadan* a50 82
7 b g Invincible Spirit(IRE) Jupiter Inlet (IRE) (Jupiter Island)
412a[9]

King's Land *Saeed bin Suroor* 76
2 bb c New Approach(IRE) Kazzia (GER) (Zinaad)
6762[3] ◆

Kings 'n Dreams *Dean Ivory* a59 70
6 b g Royal Applause Last Dream (IRE) (Alzao (USA))
35[10] 1665[6] 2516[7] 2781[2] 3841[11] 5373[7] 5869[9] 6462[7] 7427[8]

King's Realm (IRE) *Tina Jackson* a70 48
6 ch g King's Best(USA) Sweet Home Alabama (IRE) (Desert Prince (IRE))
3248[5]

King's Request (IRE) *Laura Mongan* a71 59
3 ch g New Approach(IRE) Palace Weekend (USA) (Seattle Dancer (USA))
1727[6] 2833[6] 7258[7] 7839[4] 8159[6] 8331[7] 8447[5]

King's Road *Anabel K Murphy* a62 62
8 ch g King's Best(USA) Saphire (College Chapel)
120[8] 2801[3] 3213[8]

Kingston Eucalypt *David Elsworth* a76 73
3 b f Halling(USA) Derartu (AUS) (Last Tycoon)
748[5] 1009[5] 2231[4] 3535[4] 4172[2] 4656[3] 5492[5] 7298[3] 7894[3] 8260[2]

Kingston Hill *Roger Varian* 119
2 rg c Mastercraftsman(IRE) Audacieuse (Rainbow Quest (USA))
(6641) (7195) (7528) ◆

Kingston Jamaica (IRE) *A P O'Brien* 103
3 b c Galileo(IRE) Aleagueoftheirown (IRE) (Danehill Dancer (IRE))
3142a[3]

Kingston Tiger *Jo Davis* a52 48
5 b g Tiger Hill(IRE) Gretna (Groom Dancer (USA))
978[7]

King's Warrior (FR) *Peter Chapple-Hyam* 106
6 b g King's Best(USA) Save Me The Waltz (FR) (Halling (USA))
1768[4] ◆ 2427[11] 4310[16] 6957[RR] 7536[6]

Kingsway Lad (IRE) *Derek Shaw* a28 49
2 b g New Approach(IRE) Obsessive (USA) (Seeking The Gold (USA))
6197[4] 6570[8] 7126[8]

Kingswinford (IRE) *Alastair Lidderdale* a75 85
7 b g Noverre(USA) Berenica (IRE) (College Chapel)
1015[6] 1179[3] 1252[5] (1514)

King Torus (IRE) *Ruth Carr* a107 98
5 b g Oratorio(IRE) Dipterous (IRE) (Mujadil (USA))
3754[8] 4280[9] (4521) 5238[8] 5546[15] (5880) 6300[6] 6625[5] 7176[10]

King Vahe (IRE) *Olivia Maylam* a68 34
4 b g One Cool Cat(USA) Tethkar (Machiavellian (USA))
791[6] 1181[6] 1827[5] 2234[10] 5232[12] 5523[6] 8230[10]

King Wood (TUR) *Charles Hills* a18
3 ch c Dilum(USA) Dancinginthoclouds (IRE) (Rainbow Quest (USA))
425[6] 814[9]

Kingzar (FR) *Mme C Barande-Barbe* a90 90
3 b c King's Best(USA) Zarkiyna (FR) (Sendawar (IRE))
(711a) 782a[4]

King Zeal (IRE) *Barry Leavy* a66 77
9 b g King's Best(USA) Manureva (USA) (Nureyev (USA))
144[8] 7275[14]

Kinkohyo *Bryan Smart* a58
2 b f Indesatchel(IRE) Mythicism (Oasis Dream)
7756[6] 8113[6] (8188)

Kinloss *Richard Hannon Snr* a64 67
2 ch f Kheleyf(USA) Celtic Cross (Selkirk (USA))
5529[10] 6112[4] 6821[3] 7296[7] 7837[10]

Kiram (FR) *J-C Rouget* 112
2 b c Elusive City(USA) King Luna (FR) (King's Best (USA))
(7184a) (7939a)

Kirkman (IRE) *James Bethell* a51
2 ch g Virtual Validate (Alhaarth (IRE))
7971[8] 8340[13]

Kirkstall Abbey (IRE) *Tony Coyle* 57
2 b f Bushranger(IRE) Spanish Falls (Belmez (USA))
2985[3] 3391[5] 5083[7]

Kirtling Belle *Keith Dalgleish* 66
2 br f Pastoral Pursuits Twenty Seven (IRE) (Efisio)
1960[2] 2751[5] 3280[9] 4952[2] (5710)

Kisanji *Mick Channon* 65
2 b c Teofilo(IRE) Al Kamah (USA) (Kingmambo (USA))
6953[5] ◆

Kiss And Kill (FR) *J-M Capitte* a2
3 gr f Country Reel(USA) Kavusakan (FR) (Sagamix (FR))
604a[5]

Kissavos *Y Barberot* a82 77
7 b g Montjeu(IRE) Loxandra (Last Tycoon)
(6421a)

Kiss From A Rose *Rae Guest* a68 60
2 ch f Compton Place Dayrose (Daylami (IRE))
4686[3] 6013[4] (6776) 7837[5]

Kiss Goodnight (IRE) *John Joseph Murphy* a56 95
3 b f Papal Bull Hugs 'n Kisses (IRE) (Noverre (USA))
5115a[4]

Kiss My Heart *Eric Wheeler* a14
4 br f Byron Kisses (Sakhee (USA))
335[10] 852[12]

Kiss The Stars (IRE) *T G McCourt* 80
3 b f Thousand Words Lady Piste (IRE) (Ali-Royal (IRE))
5775a[5] 6883a[14]

Kitco (GER) *A Kleinkorres* 103
4 b c Shirocco(GER) Kittiwake (Barathea (IRE))
4819a[4]

Kitten Kaboodle (USA) *Chad C Brown* 96
2 ch f Kitten's Joy(USA) Easy Slam (USA) (Grand Slam (USA))
7690a[11]

Kitten On The Run (USA) *Luca Cumani* 106
3 ch c Kitten's Joy(USA) Personal Odyssey (USA) (Lemon Drop Kid (USA))
2445[4] 3485[8] 4531[5]

Kitten Rock (FR) *K Borgel* 71
3 b g Laverock(IRE) The Cat Eater (FR) (Tagel (USA))
711a[10]

Kittens *William Muir* a73 73
4 b f Marju(IRE) Purring (USA) (Mountain Cat (USA))
1983[5] 2360[7] 3321[4] (3721) 4172[4] 4626[2] 4832[2] 6377[RR] 6574[5] 7033[2]

Kitten's Dumplings (USA) *Michael J Maker* a90 105
3 b f Kitten's Joy(USA) Granny Franny (USA) (Grand Slam (USA))
7708a[9]

Kitty Brown (IRE) *David Evans* a56 56
2 b f Bushranger(IRE) Daanaat (IRE) (Kheleyf (USA))
1240[9] 1449[2] 3414[8] 4141[7] 4387[5] 5893[12] 6520[11] 7604[8] 7630[7] 7755[11] 8131[8]

Kiwayu *Philip Kirby* a89 93
4 b g Medicean Kibara (Sadler's Wells (USA))
2385[6] 2648[6] 3208[5] (3804) (4262) ◆ 6729[3] 7174[9] 7496[12]

Kiwi Bay *Michael Dods* a88 89
8 b g Mujahid(USA) Bay Of Plenty (FR) (Octagonal (NZ))
1238[6] 1538[6] 1831[4] 2232[3] 2673[10] 3368[2] 4055[10] 5291[2] 6288[10] 6567[7] 7024[8] 7824[5]

Kiyoshi *Charles Hills* 111
2 b f Dubawi(IRE) Mocca (IRE) (Sri Pekan (USA))
1634[4] (2583) (3522) ◆ 6024a[3] 6836[3]

Kizuna (JPN) *Shozo Sasaki* 121
3 bb c Deep Impact(JPN) Catequil (CAN) (Storm Cat (USA))
(6446a) 7058a[4]

Kleitomachos (IRE) *Stuart Kittow* 86
5 b g Barathea(IRE) Theben (GER) (Monsun (GER))
1670[5]

K Lightning (IRE) *J W Hills* 38
3 ch g Danehill Dancer(IRE) Arosa (IRE) (Sadler's Wells (USA))
3176[12] 4032[5]

Klynch *Ruth Carr* a85 99
7 b g Kyllachy Inchcoonan (Emperor Jones (USA))
966[3] 1252[8] 1644[7] 1838[3] 2007[4] (2239) ◆ (2460) 2649[6] 2988[8] 3367[9] 3823[14] 4138[7] 5056[10] 6161[10] 6496[8] 6908[11]

Knight Charm *Gay Kelleway* a70 43
3 b g Haafhd Enchanted Princess (Royal Applause)
1582[8] 2158[5] 3050[7] 4661[3] 5098[5] 5395[7] 6400[2] 6932[3] 7248[7] 7437[10] 8042[9] 8441a[5]

Knight In Purple *John Mackie*
9 b g Sir Harry Lewis(USA) Cerise Bleue (FR) (Port Lyautey (FR))
612[5]

Knightly Escapade *Brian Ellison* a82 84
5 ch g Sakhee(USA) Queen Of Iceni (Erhaab (USA))
1212[5] 1464[4] 2009[2] 2633[5] 3345[8] 6942[6] 7342[11]

Knight Owl *James Fanshawe* a67 83
3 b g Rock Of Gibraltar(IRE) Miss Ivanhoe (IRE) (Selkirk (USA))
1928[3] 2308[2] 2770[3] ◆ 3365[3] 4068[3] (4928) (6701)

Knight's Parade (IRE) *Amanda Perrett* a76 74
3 b g Dark Angel(IRE) Toy Show (IRE) (Danehill (USA))
1469[3] 1879[2] 2017[2] 2124[4] 2599[3] (2924) (3313) 3636[5] 4679[6] 4748[4] 5526[2] 5606[5] 6158[4] 6405[8] 6743[9] 7118[2]

Knockamany Bends (IRE) *John Wainwright* a52 46
3 b g Majestic Missile(IRE) Sweet Compliance (Safawan)
2076[11] 2719[6] 7759[6] 8119[6] 8320[3] 8407[3]

Knockgraffon Lad (USA) *Brendan Powell* a85 18
6 b g Forestry(USA) Miss Dahlia (USA) (Strawberry Road (AUS))
(7950) 8159[2] 8276[4]

Knockroon *Andrew Balding* 53
2 b c Royal Applause Spring Touch (USA) (Elusive Quality (USA))
4795[6]

Knock Stars (IRE) *Patrick Martin* a85 85
5 b f Soviet Star(USA) Knockatotaun (Spectrum (IRE))
3796a[5]

Knowe Head (NZ) *James Unett* a84 74
6 b g High Chaparral(IRE) Royal Errant (NZ) (Royal Academy (USA))
146[2] 239[2] 614[2] 759[4] 1831[7] 2646[9] 3349[12] 4287[7] 7605[6]

Know No Fear *Alastair Lidderdale* a66 76
8 b g Primo Valentino(IRE) Alustar (Emarati (USA))
6316[11] 7092[6] 7429[6]

Know Your Name *David Evans* a68 76
2 ch g Halling(USA) Lady Agnes (Singspiel (IRE))
2391[4] 2741[6] (3245) 3555[17] 4246[5] 5029[6] 5945[7] 6041[2] 6401[7] 6852[4] (7088) 7819[6]

Knox Overstreet *Mick Channon* a60 73
5 b g Indesatchel(IRE) Charlie Girl (Puissance)
1670[11] (1980) 2087[7] 2629[5] 2860[4] 2968[2] 3284[7] 3637[2] 3952[3]

Kodafine (IRE) *David Evans* a69 53
2 br f Kodiac Zafine (Zafonic (USA))
1240[3] ◆ (1432) 2147[12] 2426[9] 3267[3] 4174[U] 6654[5] 7036[2] 7349[5] (7509) 7900[2] 8024[3] 8215[3] 8322[3] 8383[2] 8442[3]

Kodatish (IRE) *Ronald Harris* a69 70
3 b g Kodiac Atishoo (IRE) (Revoque (IRE))
3212[9] 3678[6] 4149[10]

Kodicil (IRE) *Tim Walford* 72
5 b g Kodiac Miss Caoimhe (IRE) (Barathea (IRE))
1448[7] 1789[8] 2120[2] 2540[2] 2990[2] 3363[3] 4204[5] (5863) 6565[2] 7280[7]

Koffi Angel (GER) *H J Groschel* 95
4 b f Soldier Hollow Koffibini (IRE) (Platini (GER))
(7233a)

Koharu *Peter Makin* a58 72
3 rg f Ishiguru(USA) Vellena (Lucky Story (USA))
2829[8] 3316[3] 3817[3] 4424[3] (5128) 5607[5] 6560[5] (7086) 7318[4] 7861[6]

Kohlaan (IRE) *Roger Varian* a71 93
3 b g Elusive City(USA) Rock Salt (Selkirk (USA))
1086[4] 1323[4] (2094) (2627) (3369) 4306[3] (6274) 6650[6]

Kokaltash (FR) *M Delzangles* 100
3 ch c Haafhd Kozaka (FR) (Mark Of Esteem (IRE))
7116a[2] 7685a[9]

Kokoumin (FR) *M Boutin* 78
2 b f Slickly(FR) Orzie (FR) (Solicitor I (FR))
7653a[12]

Kolonel (GER) *Mario Hofer* a91 109
4 b g Manduro(GER) Kristin's Charm (USA) (Swain (IRE))
3970a[5] 5804a[10] (7941a)

Kolonel Kirkup *Michael Dods* 74
3 b g Dr Fong(USA) Strawberry Lolly (Lomitas)
2235[4] 3730[6] 4140[4] 4806[6] 5016[5] 5342[7] 5581[6] 6587[4]

Kommander Kirkup *Michael Dods* 87
2 ch g Assertive Bikini (Trans Island)
2670[2] 6546[2] 7341[2]

Komreyev Star *Ray Peacock* a18 7
11 b g Komaite(USA) L'Ancressaan (Dalsaan)
3513[13] 5429[11]

Konig Concorde (GER) *C Sprengel* a105 106
8 b g Big Shuffle(USA) Kaiserin (GER) (Ile De Bourbon (USA))
1564a[6] 1944a[4] 3970a[10]

Konkan (IRE) *L Riccardi* 97
2 gr f Aussie Rules(USA) Cheloca (Selkirk (USA))
6293a[6] 7571a[8]

Konzert (ITY) *Ian Williams* a66 66
3 b g Hurricane Cat(USA) Known Alibi (USA) (Known Fact (USA))
2151[11] 2628[5] 3047[5] 5030[7] 5668[4] 6657[2] 6906[8] 7383[9] 7733[10]

Koo And The Gang (IRE) *Brian Ellison* a61 71
6 b g Le Vie Dei Colori Entertain (Royal Applause)
98[6] 1788[8] 2042[4] 2511[2] 2764[7] 2991[7] 3728[4] 5198[3]

Koolgreycat (IRE) *Noel Wilson* 64
4 gr f One Cool Cat(USA) Brooks Masquerade (Absalom)
2832[12] 3026[13]

Koos (GER) *Marco Botti* a53 69
5 b f Konigstiger(GER) Kiss Me (GER) (Alwasmi (USA))
7907[3] 8148[6]

Kopenhagen (IRE) *Ed de Giles* a54 26
2 ch c Captain Rio Quizzical Lady (Mind Games)
4937[10] 6169[11] 7155[8] 7956[5]

Kopkap *Ed McMahon* a33 53
2 ch c Captain Gerrard(IRE) Sharoura (Inchinor)
2282[7] 3044[12] 3681[5] 5066[9] 5814[4] 6511[11] 6979[8]

Korba (FR) *Y Gourraud* 71
2 b f Exceed And Excel(AUS) Sirene Doloise (FR) (Marchand De Sable (USA))
7994a[8]

Korngold *Tracy Waggott* a43 69
5 b g Dansili Eve (Rainbow Quest (USA))
3195[9] 3727[14] 4835[5] 5370[5] 5833[5] 6290[3] 6598[7] 6909[2] 7342[6]

Kosika (USA) *Mahmood Al Zarooni* a56 70
3 b f Hard Spun(USA) Song Of Africa (USA) (Alzao (USA))
243a[8]

Kourdo (FR) *J Parize* a78 99
5 b g Double Heart(FR) Sea Launch (FR) (Neverneyev (USA))
(648a)

Kozmina Bay *Bernard Llewellyn* a52 60
4 b f Notnowcato Kozmina (IRE) (Sadler's Wells (USA))
2828[10]
Krackerjill (IRE) *Mark Usher* a61 39
2 b f Kheleyf(USA) Knockenduff (Oratorio (IRE))
4175[2] 4708[6] 5000[7] 5610[9]
Kraka Gym (IRE) *Michael Easterby* a44 58
2 b g Clodovil(IRE) Accounting (Sillery (USA))
1108[8] 2075[2] 2337[5] 4618[7] 5068[8]
Kramulkie (IRE) *A Marcialis* 96
3 b g Aussie Rules(USA) Intricate Design (Zafonic (USA))
7416a[2]
Kristallo (GER) *Dai Burchell* a37 54
8 ch g Lando(GER) Key West (GER) (In The Wings)
3637[5] 3952[6] 4380[8] 4714[12] 5093[10]
Krupskaya (FR) *K R Burke* a50 73
3 b f Dubai Destination(USA) Willows World (Agnes World (USA))
827[3] 1393[5] 2274[2] (2464) 3718[4] 4803[5] 5293[5] 6410[4] 6587[10]
Krymka (IRE) *C Laffon-Parias* 57
3 ch f Medicean La Seine (USA) (Rahy (USA))
6711a[13]
Krypton Factor *Fawzi Abdulla Nass* a123 116
5 bb g Kyllachy Cool Question (Polar Falcon (USA))
660a[3] 955a[2] 1266a[3] 3557[3] 4527[3] 4856[9]
Kuala Queen (IRE) *Denis Coakley* 70
2 b f Kodiac See Nuala (IRE) (Kyllachy)
5609[3] 5929[3] 6697[4]
Kuantan One (IRE) *Paul Cole* a76 84
3 b g Strategic Prince Starfish (IRE) (Galileo (IRE))
1604[4] 1934[8] 2322[8] (2846) 3783[5] (4543)
Kuanyao (IRE) *David Nicholls* a77 88
7 b g American Post Nullarbor (Green Desert (USA))
2031[13] 2459[9] 3090[9] ◆ 3628[12] 5011[12] 5876[2] 6916[8] 7593[5] (7985) (8158) 8430[4]
Kuda Huraa (IRE) *Alan King* a93 93
5 b g Montjeu(IRE) Healing Music (FR) (Bering)
1766[2] 2205[9] 2648[10]
Kukurun (FR) *Mme M Bollack-Badel* a86 88
3 gr c Kouroun(FR) Knout (FR) (Kendor (FR))
126a[3] 1594a[7]
Kung Hei Fat Choy (USA) *James Given* a89 80
4 b g Elusive Quality(USA) Lady Succeed (JPN) (Brian's Time (USA))
(25) 407[4] 443[10] 621[5] 810[8] 1115[3] 1203[4] 1692[11] 3416[10] 3945[2] 5238[9] 6291[2] 6609[6] 7123[12] 7374[4] 7608[12] 7824[17] 8008[3] 8178[9] 8269[2] 8408[2]
Kuraanda *John Wainwright* a44 19
4 b f Kyllachy Palm Cove (UAE) (Jade Robbery (USA))
28[4] 313[5] 375[9] 1222[9]
Kuwait Star *Jason Ward* a53 78
4 ch g Resplendent Glory(IRE) Mofeyda (IRE) (Mtoto)
1936[5] 2278[9] 2889[6] 3628[2] 3945[12] 5580[9]
Kwanto *Ken Wingrove* a51 62
3 b f Piccolo Craic Sa Ceili (IRE) (Danehill Dancer (IRE))
1519[6] 2528[8] 4499[7] 5192[8] 5864[4] 6343[3] 6651[7] 7508[9]
Kyleakin Lass *Jonathan Portman* a87 102
4 b f Kyllachy Local Fancy (Bahamian Bounty)
1662[7] 2014[2] 2461[5] 2768[4] 4024[14] 5247[11] 6190[4] 6699[2] 7171[2] 7527[10]
Kyle Of Bute *Richard Ford* a66 55
7 ch g Kyllachy Blinding Mission (IRE) (Marju (IRE))
219[6] 587[8] 1082[5] 1214[2] 1401[4] 2089[6] 3043[9] 5921[6] (6339) 6851[5] 7201[2] 7733[2] 7963[5] 8275[6]
Kyllachykov (IRE) *Robin Bastiman* a62 57
5 ch g Kyllachy Dance On (Caerleon (USA))
(41) ◆ (110) 435[13] 1949[P]
Kyllachy Rise *Richard Hannon Snr* a94 96
3 b c Kyllachy Up And About (Barathea (IRE))
1678[2] ◆ 2021[13] 2672[3] (3176) 3484[15] 4078[5] 4922[4] 5759[2] (6488) 6871[3] 7495[21] 7820[20] 8264[8]
Kyllachy Star *Richard Fahey* a76 92
7 b g Kyllachy Jaljuli (Jalmood (USA))
4245[7] 4859[8] 5947[11] 6567[2] ◆ 7307[6] 7608[8] 8227[7]
Kyllachy Storm *Ron Hodges* a62 64
9 b g Kyllachy Social Storm (USA) (Future Storm (USA))
1397[4] 1665[7] 1902[2] 2364[6] 3622[6] 3841[8] 4197[7]
Kylladdie *Steve Gollings* a78 81
6 ch g Kyllachy Chance For Romance (Entrepreneur)
6648[4] 6928[3] (7262) 7634[6]
Kytano (FR) *D Prod'Homme* 57
3 b c Le Fou(IRE) Magic Fairy (FR) (Ski Chief (USA))
191a[0]
Kyurem (IRE) *T Clout* 100
3 gr f Verglas(IRE) Epistoliere (IRE) (Alzao (USA))
7613a[4]
Kyzer Chief *Tina Jackson* 69
8 b g Rouvres(FR) Payvashooz (Ballacashtal (CAN))
5579[11] 5889[8] 6757[15] 6878[5] 7029[13]
Laajooj (IRE) *Mahmood Al Zarooni* a78 111
5 b g Azamour(IRE) Flanders (IRE) (Common Grounds)
(242a) 956a[5]
La Amistad (AUS) *Michael, Wayne & John Hawkes* 95
4 b f Redoute's Choice(AUS) Tugela (USA) (Riverman (USA))
7827a[8]
Laa Rayb (USA) *D Selvaratnam* a84 100
9 b g Storm Cat(USA) Society Lady (USA) (Mr Prospector (USA))
149a[11]
La Arenosa (IRE) *Saeed bin Suroor* 106
4 b f Exceed And Excel(AUS) Baranquilla (Acatenango (GER))
(3409) 4532[6]

La Bacouetteuse (FR) *Iain Jardine* a28 78
8 b g Miesque's Son(USA) Toryka (Vettori (IRE))
1390[6] 1993[3] 2860[12] 3089[3] 3627[8] 3726[12] 4343[6] ◆ (4614) 5241[3] 5640[3] 6086[5]
La Banderilla (FR) *F Rohaut* a90 103
3 b f Muhtathir La Bandera (Bahhare (USA))
1602a[3] 3614a[6] 7234a[2]
La Barbacane (FR) *Y Barberot* a69
3 ro f Excellent Art Venize (IRE) (Kaldoun (FR))
962a[0]
Labarinto *Sir Michael Stoute* 107
5 b g Dansili Tarocchi (USA) (Affirmed (USA))
3525[12] 4854[3] 5269[11] 6001[14]
La Belle Doyenne *Alan King* a69
5 ch f Doyen(IRE) Tarabela (CHI) (Hussonet (USA))
20[3]
La Belle Epoque (USA) *Gerard Butler* a70
3 b f Tapit(USA) Catlike Dancer (USA) (Tale Of The Cat (USA))
6133[5] 6611[5] 7663[7] 8087[13]
La Best (FR) *M Figge*
3 gr f King's Best(USA) Lady Time (FR) (Orpen (USA))
461a[0]
Labienus *David Lanigan* a97 94
3 b g Compton Place Guermantes (Distant Relative)
1958[5] ◆ 2506[2] (2984) (3472) (4281)
Lacalifornie (FR) *E Leenders* 66
2 b f Hold That Tiger(USA) Septieme Face (USA) (Lit De Justice (USA))
5323a[4]
Lacarolina (FR) *J-C Rouget* 102
2 ch f Charge D'Affaires Malinday (FR) (Lord Of Men)
5555a[U] 6292a[4] (7940a)
Lacateno *W Hickst* 107
6 b g Green Tune(USA) Lacatena (GER) (Acatenango (GER))
2492a[7]
Lacey *Andrew Hollinshead* a66 56
4 b g Rail Link Shamana (USA) (Woodman (USA))
215[5] 521[3] 925[6] 3410[6] 4010[7] 4355[7] 5432[6] 5897[3] (7899) 8027[3] (8223) 8331[8]
Lacock *Henry Candy* 72
2 b c Compton Place Puya (Kris)
6589[6] ◆ 6790[4] 7271[2]
La Collina (IRE) *Kevin Prendergast* 111
4 ch f Strategic Prince Starfish (IRE) (Galileo (IRE))
1413a[3] 2375a[2] 2678a[2] 3870a[6] 4696a[6] (6224a) 6837[5]
Laconicos (IRE) *William Stone* a63 68
11 ch g Foxhound(USA) Thermopylae (Tenby)
2383[5] 3106[4] 3504[12] 4071[9] 4490[3] 5245[3] 5492[2] 6137[6]
Lac Sacre (FR) *Tony Carroll* a66 66
4 b g Bering Lady Glorieuse (FR) (Le Glorieux)
1700[6] 6853[6]
La Cumbia (IRE) *X Thomas-Demeaulte* 80
2 b f Clodovil(IRE) Green Empire (IRE) (Second Empire (IRE))
5082a[5] (6786a)
Ladies Are Forever *Geoffrey Oldroyd* a111 111
5 b f Monsieur Bond(IRE) Forever Bond (Danetime (IRE))
(776) (1032) 2368[12] 3102[5] (4260) 4947[5] 5726[7] 6235[2] 7054a[7]
Ladies In Waiting *Richard Fahey* 45
2 b f Piccolo Rose Siog (Bahamian Bounty)
4115[6] 4847[6] 5380[11]
Ladweb *John Gallagher* a60 74
3 ch g Bertolini(USA) Adweb (Muhtarram (USA))
3509[4] (5060) 5499[4] 6412[5] 7324[2]
Lady Alaska (IRE) *John Quinn* 43
2 b f Kodiac Lady Justice (Compton Place)
3476[7] 4156[5]
Lady Amakhala *George Moore* 81
5 b f Val Royal(FR) Isla Negra (IRE) (Last Tycoon)
2040[9]
Lady Artiste (IRE) *Alan Swinbank* 71
3 ch f Excellent Art Elauyun (IRE) (Muhtarram (USA))
(1389) 1991[3] 2390[4] 3202[3]
Lady Barastar (IRE) *Amanda Perrett* a57 57
5 b f Barathea(IRE) Stariya (IRE) (Soviet Star (USA))
579[9] 3169[2] 3580[U] 3924[3] 5126[4] 6137[10] 7091[13] 7923[11]
Lady Bayside *Malcolm Saunders* a73 79
5 ch f Ishiguru(USA) Seldemosa (Selkirk (USA))
1947[3] 2395[6] 2792[2] (3269) 3617[2] 5430[4] 7256[4] 7489[4] 7785[5] 7970[14]
Lady Bentinck (IRE) *Alan Berry* 43
4 b f Mujadil(USA) Lady Graigie (IRE) (Fruits Of Love (USA))
2613[6] 2912[7] 3946[13]
Lady Bonanova (IRE) *Pat Phelan* 50
3 b f Haatef(USA) Lady Express (IRE) (Soviet Star (USA))
2345[13]
Lady Bridget *Mark Gillard* a58 51
5 b f Hawk Wing(USA) Change Partners (IRE) (Hernando (FR))
2801[5] 3271[10]
Lady Bubbles *Michael Easterby* a40 48
2 b f Distant Peak(IRE) Mount Hillaby (IRE) (Mujadil (USA))
6298[6] 6821[10] 7664[7]
Lady By Red (IRE) *Ann Duffield* a31 50
5 ch f Redback Antonia's Dream (Clantime)
327[9]
Lady Calantha *Alan Berry* a44 49
3 b f Byron Brooklyn's Sky (Septieme Ciel (USA))
36[6] 549[3] 669[7] 829[5] 985[5] 1458[10] 2241[3] 3932[3] 4290[6] 4611[5] 4991[7] 5089[3] 5919[4] 6630[10] 7484[6]
Lady Captain (IRE) *Kevin Ryan* a64 61
2 ch f Captain Rio Alexander Goldmine (Dansili)
1718[6] 1960[6] 3189[3] 3440[3] 4065[2] (4538) 4964[5] (5289) 5591[2] 7202[10] 7340[10]

Lady Cavallo *J R Jenkins* 25
3 b f Tiger Hill(IRE) Cavallo Da Corsa (Galileo (IRE))
1640[15] 2016[8] 2637[9]
Lady Chantilly (IRE) *Jo Hughes* 93
2 b f Kodiac Flashy Life (Averti (IRE))
(3510) 3829[7] 4572a[8] 5476[4] 6584[5] 6622[7] 7011[11]
Lady Chaparral *Michael Dods* 89
6 b m High Chaparral(IRE) La Sylphide (Rudimentary (USA))
2463[7] 4055[2] 5051[7] 6353[8]
Lady Cliche *Roger Curtis* 38
4 b f Kirkwall Madam Cliche (Classic Cliche (IRE))
3858[9] 4633[12] 6696[15]
Lady Cricketer *Michael Squance* a25 31
4 b f Compton Place Hickleton Lady (IRE) (Kala Shikari)
4353[6] 4839[12] 5373[12] 5614[12] 5800[4] 6219[9] 6502[8] 6965[9]
Lady Crossmar (IRE) *Richard Hannon Snr* a73
2 b f Duke Of Marmalade(IRE) Rekindled Cross (IRE) (Cape Cross (IRE))
6691[10] 7763[3] (8145) 8442[9]
Lady Dancer (IRE) *George Moore* 26
2 b f Captain Rio Anesthesia (Fantastic Light (USA))
5053[6] 5339[7] 5883[6] 6284[9] 6494[11] 7096[10] 7370[4]
Lady Dapper *David Thompson*
3 b f Dapper Russian Velvet (IRE) (Soviet Lad (USA))
4813[9]
Lady Del Sol *Jo Hughes* 73
5 b f Monsieur Bond(IRE) Villa Del Sol (Tagula (IRE))
1692[17] 2409[13] 2837[9] 3654[10] (3929) 4292[7] 4893[17]
Ladydolly *Roy Brotherton* a63 46
5 b f Kyllachy Lady Pekan (Sri Pekan (USA))
4427[9]
Lady Emmuska *Richard Hannon Snr* a51 4
2 b f Sir Percy Medicea Sidera (Medicean)
4484[15] 5131[10] 6690[9] 7293[9]
Lady Farah *Robert Cowell* a52
3 b f Exceed And Excel(AUS) Bint Makbul (Makbul)
197[8] 509[4] 1732[8] 2330[10]
Lady Faye *Andrew Hollinshead* a7 29
4 b f Multiplex Rebel County (IRE) (Maelstrom Lake)
6824[7] 7488[9] 8303[5]
Lady Frances *Mark Johnston* a86 77
2 b f Exceed And Excel(AUS) Lady Catherine (Bering)
(1792) 2053[8] 2370[7] 3761[2] 4277[4] 5005[6] (5396) 5927[2] 8426[4]
Lady Gargoyle *Jim Goldie* 52
5 br f Lucky Story(USA) Gargoyle Girl (Be My Chief (USA))
3728[13] 4614[3] (5643) 6177[12] 7151[7]
Lady Gibraltar *Alan Jarvis* a76 97
4 b f Rock Of Gibraltar(IRE) Lady Adnil (IRE) (Stravinsky (USA))
1765[8] 2014[6] 2207[6] 2669[3] 3776[6] 4263[3] 5651[14] 6189[2] 6830[6] 7010[7] 7171[19]
Lady Guinevere *Stuart Williams* a66 69
3 b f Pivotal Birdie (Alhaarth (IRE))
685[2] ◆ 864[3] 7311[2] 8154[3]
Lady Heidi *Philip Kirby* 97
2 b f High Chaparral(IRE) Water Feature (Dansili)
6206[4] 6597[3] (7421)
Lady Horatia *William Muir* a61
2 gr f Mount Nelson Lady Xara (IRE) (Xaar)
7435[3] 7732[3]
Lady Ibrox *Alan Brown* 91
3 b f Ishiguru(USA) Last Impression (Imp Society (USA))
2039[4] 2430[8] 3340[7] 3802[10] 5057[5]
Lady In Blue (IRE) *William Haggas* a69 74
2 ch f Iffraaj Compton Girl (Compton Place)
2204[6] 4073[5] (4686) 5536[7] 6326[11] 6731[4] 7300[4]
Lady Jacamira (GER) *R Dzubasz* 103
4 ch f Lord Of England(GER) Latley (GER) (Sillery (USA))
2698a[7] (3852a) 6231a[4]
Lady Jean *Reg Hollinshead* a40
3 b f Striking Ambition Parkside Prospect (Piccolo)
588[5] 977[8]
Lady Kashaan (IRE) *Alan Swinbank* a42 96
4 b f Manduro(GER) Lady's Secret (IRE) (Alzao (USA))
(1273) 1841[2] 2451[9] 3333[6]
Lady Kathian (IRE) *Joseph Tuite* a64
2 gr f Verglas(IRE) Nurama (Daylami (IRE))
8259[4]
Lady Kildare (IRE) *Jedd O'Keeffe* a42 62
5 br f Bachelor Duke(USA) Teodora (IRE) (Fairy King (USA))
2835[2] 3026[15] 4009[13] 4621[9] 4891[11] 5422[9] 6343[7]
Lady Knight (IRE) *J S Moore* a66
2 b f Champs Elysees Knight's Place (IRE) (Hamas (IRE))
7441[5] 7780[3] 8085[8] 8296[2]
Lady Lara (IRE) *Alan Jarvis* 96
2 b f Excellent Art Shanty (Selkirk (USA))
3522[8] ◆ 3978[2] 4742[6] 5652[4] 6350[3] (6594)
Lady Layla *Lady Herries* a79 79
4 b f Excellent Art Tartouche (Pursuit Of Love)
1752[9]
Lady Liberty (IRE) *Andreas Lowe* 98
3 b f Shirocco(GER) Love And Laughter (IRE) (Theatrical (IRE))
4092a[5] 5044a[11]
Lady Liz *George Moore* 60
2 b f Byron Sister Rose (FR) (One Cool Cat (USA))
1718[13] 2458[11] 2955[7] 3624[4] 5468[9] 7097[6]
Lady Loch *Richard Fahey* 92
4 b f Dutch Art Locharia (Wolfhound (USA))
(1446) ◆ 1768[9] 7822[7]
Lady Love (GER) *M Angermann*
2 bb f Toylsome Lady Estamerra (IRE) (Be My Guest (USA))
7232a[10]

Lady Lunchalot (USA) *Laura Mongan* a75 60
3 b f More Than Ready(USA) Betty Johanne (USA) (Johannesburg (USA))
16[2] 230[3] 684[2] 962a[7] 1008[3] 1177[3] (1343) 1685[4] 1897[5] 6737[5] (6971) 7637[5] (7923) (8072) 8323[2]
Lady Lydia (IRE) *Michael Wigham* 75
2 b f Kheleyf(USA) Piece Unique (Barathea (IRE))
1634[12] ◆ (1910) 2421[2] 3829[10] 4682[7]
Lady Lyrath (IRE) *S M Duffy* a54 62
6 b m Whipper(USA) Poly Dancer (Suave Dancer (USA))
522[12]
Lady Macduff (IRE) *Mark Johnston* a82 91
4 b f Iffraaj Tamora (Dr Fong (USA))
1092[12] 1281[9] 1753[7] 2078[4] 2339[5] 3083[6] 3468[3] 3567[5] (3755) 3827[8] 4075[6]
Lady Mai (IRE) *William Kinsey* 51
2 b f Camacho Evelyn One (Alhaarth (IRE))
1573[5] 3298[5] 3724[8]
Lady Malet *William Haggas* a68
3 b f Azamour(IRE) Miss Rochester (IRE) (Montjeu (IRE))
324[4] 525[9]
Lady Mango (IRE) *Ronald Harris* a73 65
5 ch f Bahamian Bounty Opera (Forzando)
35[8] 139[5] 323[4] 449[7] 5097[11] 5818[7] 6478[10]
Lady Margaeux (IRE) *Alan Brown* a1 72
3 b f Redback Storm Lady (IRE) (Alhaarth (IRE))
2027[6] 2506[7] 3202[5] 3809[9] 7204[8]
Lady Marl *Gary Moore* a61 62
2 b f Duke Of Marmalade(IRE) Empress Anna (IRE) (Imperial Ballet (IRE))
2583[6] 3275[4] 3663[9] (5068) 5951[4] 6311[5]
Lady Marmelo (IRE) *Mick Channon* a64 69
3 b f Duke Of Marmalade(IRE) Mooretown Lady (IRE) (Montjeu (IRE))
1119[5] 1487[7] 2094[7]
Lady Montenegro *Ann Duffield* a44 49
2 b f Milk It Mick Floral Spark (Forzando)
1839[11] (3189) 7094[3] 7340[6] 7788[7]
Lady Montjeu (IRE) *Alan Jarvis* 28
3 b f Montjeu(IRE) Edabiya (IRE) (Rainbow Quest (USA))
3237[13]
Lady Niramax *David Nicholls* 45
3 b f Indesatchel(IRE) Just A Gem (Superlative)
977[9]
Lady Nouf *William Haggas* 103
3 b f Teofilo(IRE) Majestic Sakeena (IRE) (King's Best (USA))
1622[11] 2049[2] 3240[3] 4732[2] 5683[5]
Lady Of Budysin (GER) *Markus Klug* 98
4 b f Soldier Hollow Lots Of Love (GER) (Java Gold (USA))
6887a[4] 7407a[6] 7891a[13]
Lady of Burgundy *Mark Usher* a75 74
7 b m Montjeu(IRE) Helena's Paris (IRE) (Peintre Celebre (USA))
417[5] 653[7] 724[9] 929[4] 1068[2] ◆ 1217[4]
Lady Of Shamrock (USA) *John W Sadler* a95 111
4 bb f Scat Daddy(USA) Blushing Issue (USA) (Blushing John (USA))
7708a[8]
Lady Of The House (IRE) *Kevin Ryan* a73 87
3 b f Holy Roman Emperor(IRE) Miss Delila (USA) (Malibu Moon (USA))
1822[5] 2026[4] 2783[3] 3235[6] 3734[7] 4201[2] 5004[6] 5684[13] 7769[10]
Lady Of Yue *Eugene Stanford* a63 70
3 b f Manduro(GER) Desert Royalty (IRE) (Alhaarth (IRE))
2802[2] 3735[5] (7066) 8089[7]
Lady Penko (ITY) *M Guarnieri* 94
2 ch f Archipenko(USA) Lady Rangali (IRE) (Danehill Dancer (IRE))
7415a[4]
Lady Petrus *S Arthur* a53 54
8 b m Oasis Dream Odalisque (IRE) (Machiavellian (USA))
4846a[3] 5328a[4] 7145a[8]
Lady Phill *Bill Turner* a71 84
3 ch f Avonbridge Lady Filly (Atraf)
1662[8] 1921[9] 3340[8] 3803[8] 4413[6]
Lady Pimpernel *Henry Candy* 93
3 ch f Sir Percy Angeleno (IRE) (Belong To Me (USA))
2054[3] 3277[5] 3990[2] 4681[2] ◆ 5448[5] 5953[2] (6533) 7223[7]
Lady Platinum Club *Linda Stubbs* a55 57
5 ch f Monsieur Bond(IRE) Bond Platinum Club (Pivotal)
423[9]
Lady Poppy *George Moore* a39 80
3 b f Kyllachy Poppets Sweetlove (Foxhound (USA))
1690[6] 3299[16] 3591[7] 3813[6] 4136[6] 4402[5] 4558[6] 5470[4] 5889[6] 6757[4] 7030[2] ◆ 7236[5]
Lady Prodee *Bill Turner* a65 56
5 b f Proclamation(IRE) Dee-Lady (Deploy)
124[8] 354[5] 535[6] 611[7] 805[8] 1665[5] 1951[7]
Lady Raffa *Michael Dods* a37 37
3 ch f Araafa(IRE) Locharia (Wolfhound (USA))
1071[5] 1759[12]
Lady Rain *Milton Bradley* a39 39
4 b f Resplendent Glory(IRE) Devils Desire (Superior Premium)
4627[5] 4839[10] 6145[6]
Lady Red Oak *Tom Dascombe* 69
2 ch f Medicean Nuit Sans Fin (FR) (Lead On Time (USA))
3205[2] 4218[6] 5812[4]
Lady Rosamunde *Marcus Tregoning* a74 89
5 gr f Maria's Mon(USA) String Quartet (IRE) (Sadler's Wells (USA))
2052[10] 2654[4] 3344[7] 4234[4] 8387[7]
Lady Royale *Geoffrey Oldroyd* a71 71
5 ch f Monsieur Bond(IRE) Bond Royale (Piccolo)
58[9] 431[6] 795[11] 1802[12] 3190[5] 4203[6] 4727[6] 5305[3]

Ladys First *Richard Fahey* 110
4 b f Dutch Art Like A Dame (Danehill (USA))
2397[3] 2838[3] 3347[6] 3456[2] 4137[2] 4732[3] (6000) 6454a[5]
Ladyship *Sir Michael Stoute* 105
4 b f Oasis Dream Peeress (Pivotal)
2046[9] 3558[13] (4284) 4949[6] 5651[9] (6768) 7013[12]
Lady Silvy (IRE) *A Marcialis* 72
3 ch f Bahamian Bounty Beacon Of Hope (IRE) (Barathea (IRE))
1866a[17]
Lady Sledmere (IRE) *Paul Midgley* 62
5 b f Barathea(IRE) Helena's Paris (IRE) (Peintre Celebre (USA))
1239[6] 1579[7] 2162[5]
Lady Sparkler (IRE) *Roger Varian* 68
2 b f Tamayuz Capote West (USA) (Capote (USA))
4702[8]
Lady Stella *Rae Guest* a56 69
2 b f Dylan Thomas(IRE) Maseera (USA) (Seeking The Gold (USA))
4880[6] (5603) 6070[8] 6779[2]
Lady Sylvia *Joseph Tuite* a76 74
4 ch f Haafhd Abide (FR) (Pivotal)
511[3] 749[7] 2845[3] 3269[4] 3676[6] 5346[2] 5793[10] (6146) 6315[4] 6898[10] 7629[2] 7876[9]
Lady Tabitha (IRE) *Jo Crowley*
3 b f Tamayuz Kimola (IRE) (King's Theatre (IRE))
3401[10]
Lady Tee *Bill Turner*
2 b f Proclamation(IRE) Wavet (Pursuit Of Love)
5279[8]
Lady Theodora *Alan Jarvis* a54 54
3 b f Sleeping Indian Silent Waters (Polish Precedent (USA))
5478[7] 5925[4] 6557[10]
Lady Tiana *Lucy Wadham* a72 70
2 b f Sir Percy Cartoon (Danehill Dancer (IRE))
3760[4] 4409[3] 5435[5] 6070[6]
Lady Tycoon *Mark Brisbourne* a50 46
4 b f Indesatchel(IRE) Tycoon's Last (Nalchik (USA))
1401[9] 2073[9] 2974[4] 3642[9] 4036[7] 5377[10] 6518[17]
Lady Tyne *Roger Charlton* a57 84
2 ch f Halling(USA) Susun Kelapa (USA) (St Jovite (USA))
5922[5] (7533)
Lady Valtas *Martin Bosley* a32 30
5 b f Val Royal(FR) Phantasmagoria (Fraam)
4423[9] 4660[6] 5166[6]
Lady Vermeer *Ralph Beckett* a51 72
3 b f Dutch Art Classic Vision (Classic Cliche (IRE))
2051[9] 2597[8] 3216[7] 3699[9] 4442[7]
Lady Who *William Muir* a68
3 b f Sir Percy Herminoe (Rainbow Quest (USA))
184[3] 580[4] 1499[3] 7786[9] 8443[10]
Lady Wingshot (IRE) *J S Bolger* 108
4 b f Lawman(FR) Nassma (IRE) (Sadler's Wells (USA))
1413a[9] 7051a[8]
Lady Yeats *George Moore* 65
2 b f Yeats(IRE) Oblique (IRE) (Giant's Causeway (USA))
5224[3] 6597[5] 7277[4]
La Estrella (USA) *Don Cantillon* a93 58
10 b g Theatrical(IRE) Princess Ellen (Tirol)
(1) 227[2] 2579[3] 3423[18] (8318)
La Faisan Blanche (USA) *Luca Cumani* a43 46
2 gr f Exchange Rate(USA) Tjinouska (USA) (Cozzene (USA))
5003[14] 6281[9] 6690[11] 7168[5]
La Ferruja (IRE) *David Barron* 32
2 b f Camacho Lorena (IRE) (Bishop Of Cashel)
1574[3]
Laffan (IRE) *Tim Easterby* a96 96
4 b g Dark Angel(IRE) Lady Corduff (IRE) (Titus Livius (FR))
945[8] 1252[2] 1675[10] 2649[3] 3060[15] 4062[12] 4758[3] 5238[5] (5943) 6625[3] 6826[6] 7540[4] 7820[3] 8117[4] 8231[8]
La Fortunata *Mike Murphy* a79 99
6 b m Lucky Story(USA) Phantasmagoria (Fraam)
1765[2] 2865[6] 3973[2] 4493[6] (5700) 5821[2] 6078[3] 6768[8] 7021[7] 8064[9]
Lagan Honey *Bill Turner* 22
3 b f Avonbridge Sally's Dilemma (Primo Valentino (IRE))
5444[7]
Lager Time (IRE) *David Evans* a68 74
3 b g Tagula(IRE) Polish Belle (Polish Precedent (USA))
(31) (137) 195[3] 402[2] 710[2] 730[3] 982[4] 1661[9] 1892[12] 3638[4] 4069[2] 4244[2] 4608[2] (4712) 4905[4] 5477[7] 6214[9] 6900[6] 7324[7] 7634[10] 7848[4] ◆
La Giaconda *Olivia Maylam* a38 47
4 ch f Excellent Art Always On My Mind (Distant Relative)
714[8] 900[11] 1149[5] 1474[10]
Lagonda Blue (FR) *C Baillet* a50
3 b f Turtle Bowl(IRE) Fasliyeva (FR) (Fasliyev (USA))
543a[10]
La Goutte D'Or (FR) *M Boutin* a66 79
2 ch f Soave(GER) Vocatine (IRE) (Royal Applause)
5363a[11]
La Grassetta (GER) *Tobias B P Coles* a60
2 b f Nayef(USA) La Reine Noir (GER) (Rainbow Quest (USA))
5819[7] 7260[9] 7875[10]
Lahaag *John Gosden* 106
4 b g Marju(IRE) Chater (Alhaarth (IRE))
1235[17] 2365[2] 3559[5] 4979[5] (7174) 7823[21]
La Havrese (FR) *Ann Duffield* 61
2 ch f Le Havre(IRE) La Buena (IRE) (Big Shuffle (USA))
5983[5] 6512[4]
La Hoguette (FR) *J-C Rouget* 99
2 b f Le Havre(IRE) Isanous (FR) (Zamindar (USA))
(7084a)

Laia Chope (FR) *X Nakkachdji* 86
2 b f Soave(GER) Chopinette (FR) (Sin Kiang (FR))
(2558a) 7567a[2]
Lake George (IRE) *James M Barrett* a68 77
5 b g Alkaadhem Ballyronan Girl (IRE) (Elbio)
8012a[5]
Lakeman (IRE) *Brian Ellison* a65 60
7 b g Tillerman Bishop's Lake (Lake Coniston (IRE))
539[6]
Lakota Ghost (USA) *Seamus Durack* a72 19
5 b g Rockport Harbor(USA) Political Alert (USA) (Giant's Causeway (USA))
(539) 1189[8] 1664[13] 1948[11]
Lalandia (IRE) *P Schiergen* a86 96
4 ch f Medicean Landia (Acatenango (GER))
6887a[6] 7650[10]
Lalinde *Daniel Kubler* a50 17
3 b f Tiger Hill(IRE) Ciboure (Norwick (USA))
877[5] 3989[8] 7490[4] 7806[8] 8031[10]
La Luz Del Sol *Richard Fahey* a57 64
3 b f Misu Bond(IRE) Villa Del Sol (Tagula (IRE))
1319[4] (1764) 2318[3] 2756[9] 8352[8]
Lamar (IRE) *James Tate* 92
2 b f Cape Cross(IRE) Deveron (USA) (Cozzene (USA))
3057[5] (3781) 4682[3] 5284[6] 6142[5]
Lambert Pen (USA) *Mick Channon* a56 62
3 ch g Johannesburg(USA) Whiletheiron'shot (USA) (Smart Strike (CAN))
2935[7] 3281[6] 3636[7] 4170[7] 5429[5] 6146[2] 6260[5] 6321[3] 6986[7] 7124[3] 8142[9]
Lambeth Palace *Ronald Harris* a27 24
2 ch g Pastoral Pursuits Palais Polaire (Polar Falcon (USA))
3695[6] 4708[7] 6279[12] 6779[4]
La Messalina (FR) *Alex Fracas* a79 75
3 b f Apsis Mariyati (FR) (Marignan (USA))
4575a[4] 6713a[9]
L'Ami Fernand (FR) *D De Waele* a74 73
2 ch c Layman(USA) Baby Chope (FR) (Indian Rocket)
5214a[3]
L'Ami Louis (IRE) *Henry Candy* 96
5 b g Elusive City(USA) Princess Electra (IRE) (Lake Coniston (IRE))
2207[13] 2937[8] 3720[6] 5009[5] 5489[4] 5991[4]
L'Amour De Ma Vie (USA) *Mme Pia Brandt* a106 98
4 gr f Dansili Cuaba (USA) (Smoke Glacken (USA))
(8440a)
Lamusawama *Ed Dunlop* a84 71
3 b g Acclamation Intrepid Queen (USA) (Theatrical (IRE))
(1923) ◆ 2584[8] 3214[5] 4384[2] 4929[8]
Lanansaak (IRE) *Roger Varian* 103
3 ch f Zamindar(USA) Bunood (IRE) (Sadler's Wells (USA))
(6188) 6796[3] 7698[6]
Lanark (IRE) *Mark Johnston* 94
2 b c Cape Cross(IRE) Amenixa (FR) (Linamix (FR))
2194[2] ◆ (2653) 3422[12] 4314[2] (4524) 4876[6] 6645[14] 7017[14]
Lancelot Du Lac (ITY) *Dean Ivory* a109 102
3 b c Shamardal(USA) Dodie Mae (USA) (Capote (USA))
(2371) 2844[9] 3342[12] 5004[4] (5748) ◆ (6238) ◆ 7495[7] 7928[3] (8064) 8334[3]
Landaho *Alan Berry* a38 44
4 b f Tobougg(IRE) Ellovamul (Elmaamul (USA))
6730[8] 7081[10]
Landau (IRE) *Sylvester Kirk* a79 69
3 gr g Aussie Rules(USA) Before The Storm (Sadler's Wells (USA))
580[5] 748[4] 5386[4] 5816[6] 6521[2] 6743[4] 7258[6] (7446) (7605)
Landesherr (GER) *Thomas Cuthbert* a72 72
6 b g Black Sam Bellamy(IRE) Lutte Marie (GER) (Frontal (FR))
9[5] 626[3] 978[9] 1916[2] 2137[4] 2630[7] 3287[8] 4052[8] 4376[9] 5050[8]
Land Hawk (IRE) *Lydia Pearce* a65 53
7 br g Trans Island Heike (Glenstal (USA))
2764[6] 3996[4] 5073[10]
Landown Littlerock *Reg Hollinshead* a62 66
4 b g Sakhee(USA) Maraha (Lammtarra (USA))
99[3] 375[4] 545[5]
Landym (FR) *H-A Pantall* 96
2 b c Lando(GER) Ymlaen (IRE) (Desert Prince (IRE))
7409a[4]
Langavat (IRE) *Richard Hannon Snr* 97
2 b c Bushranger(IRE) Bishop's Lake (Lake Coniston (IRE))
2250[3] 2653[U] (3079) 4025[2] ◆
Langham Lily (USA) *Chris Wall* a69 65
4 bb f Badge Of Silver(USA) Silver Frau (USA) (Silver Charm (USA))
338[8] 668[7] 3330[2] 3635[3] 4172[6]
Langley *Tim Vaughan* a70 54
6 b g Trempolino(USA) Late Night (GER) (Groom Dancer (USA))
(4355) 4605[4]
Langley Vale *Roger Teal* a76 85
4 b g Piccolo Running Glimpse (IRE) (Runnett)
(1985) 2790[3] (3010) 4210[3] 4707[7] 5219[7]
Langridge Street (AUS) *Michael Hibbs* 83
6 br g Elvstroem(AUS) Fleur De L'Orient (NZ) (Thunder Gulch (USA))
7762a[9]
Lang Shining (IRE) *Mrs A Malzard* a86 91
9 ch g Dr Fong(USA) Dragnet (IRE) (Rainbow Quest (USA))
2302a[5]
Lanyard (USA) *D K Weld* 81
2 gr f Mizzen Mast(USA) Geographic (USA) (Empire Maker (USA))
7548a[7]
La Oliva (IRE) *Paul W Flynn* a66 63
4 bb f Strategic Prince Banba (IRE) (Docksider (USA))
7378[4]

La Paiva (FR) *Scott Dixon* a38
2 b f Milk It Mick Cora Pearl (IRE) (Montjeu (IRE))
8044[3] 8266[7]
Lapis Blue (IRE) *David Evans* a77 63
3 b f Invincible Spirit(IRE) Triple Try (IRE) (Sadler's Wells (USA))
8427[9]
La Pomme D'Amour *A Fabre* 113
5 ch f Peintre Celebre(USA) Winnebago (Kris)
1895a[10] 2644a[6] 4324a[2] (5297a) 6448a[9]
Laquiella (FR) *A Wohler* a82
3 b f Soldier Hollow Lakme (GER) (Surumu (GER))
7736a[2]
Laraaj (IRE) *David Barron* 45
2 b f Iffraaj Lamh Eile (IRE) (Lend A Hand)
3023[10] 4046[10]
Lara Lipton (IRE) *Jane Chapple-Hyam* a45
2 b f Excellent Art Dyness (USA) (Dynaformer (USA))
8176[6]
Larga Charla (IRE) *G Botti* a96 70
4 b c Elusive City(USA) Tinareena (IRE) (Barathea (IRE))
5735a[4]
Larghetto (USA) *Daniel Mark Loughnane* a67 55
5 b f Giant's Causeway(USA) Marquetessa (USA) (Marquetry (USA))
758[8] 919[6] (1657) 1734[6] 7383[11] 7733[8] 8073[2] (8329) 8432[6]
La Rosiere (USA) *Pat Murphy* a62 63
4 b f Mr Greeley(USA) Snowtime (IRE) (Galileo (IRE))
1926[10] 2392[6] 3530[5] 4167[9] 5434[8] 6553[4] 7299[3] 7458[3] 7930[P]
Larra Chope (FR) *C Boutin* a61 67
2 b f Deportivo Deauville Royale (Royal Applause)
2558a[5] 5213a[10]
Larsen Bay (IRE) *Tom Dascombe* a58 58
2 b c Kodiac Teem (IRE) (Xaar)
1833[2] 2011[3] 6999[3] 7309[11] 8039[5]
Lars Krister (IRE) *Hans Adielsson* a63
3 b g Clodovil(IRE) Ann's Annie (IRE) (Alzao (USA))
4176[6] 4839[7] 5393[8] 5923[7] 6553[9]
L'Artiste (IRE) *John Quinn* 70
2 gr f Mastercraftsman(IRE) Sepia (Dansili)
3605[8] 4668[5] (5379)
La Sabara *A Wohler* 91
3 ch f Sabiango(GER) La Hermana (Hernando (FR))
3604a[6]
La Sage (FR) *J Heloury* 86
3 b f Sageburg(IRE) Last Trip (FR) (Anabaa (USA))
2335a[3]
Lasaraleen (IRE) *Richard Fahey* a43 33
3 b f Amadeus Wolf Rosy Dudley (IRE) (Grand Lodge (USA))
202[6] 509[7] 3091[6]
Lascaux *Luke Dace* a78 75
4 ch f Pivotal Tora Bora (Grand Lodge (USA))
275[3] 809[5]
Las Encinas *Adrian McGuinness* a38 52
3 b f Pastoral Pursuits Hot Tin Roof (IRE) (Thatching)
5334[3]
Laser Blazer *Jeremy Gask* a75 78
5 b g Zafeen(FR) Sashay (Bishop Of Cashel)
2417[10] 3012[2] 3971[9] 4673[4] 5168[9] (5954) 6424[8] 7396[4] 7840[7] 8159[7]
Lasilia (IRE) *Kevin Ryan* 88
3 b f Acclamation Vasilia (Dansili)
1808[10] 2270[4] 3340[9] 6665[10] 7776[2]
Last Bid *Tim Easterby* 91
4 b f Vital Equine(IRE) Manderina (Mind Games)
1607[8] 2396[15] 3299[14] 4138[8] 4560[10]
Last Born (FR) *A Fabre* 105
4 ch f Monsun(GER) America (IRE) (Arazi (USA))
2695a[4] 3362a[6] 6294a[9]
Lastchancelucas *Declan Carroll* 88
3 b g Ishiguru(USA) Light Of Aragon (Aragon)
2430[10] 3066[6] 5511[2] ◆ 6238[6] 6496[6] 6822[13] 7420[9]
Last Chance Ranch *Derek Shaw* a41
3 b g Manduro(GER) Rakata (USA) (Quiet American (USA))
55[7] 212[7] 7666[8]
Last Destination (IRE) *Nigel Tinkler* a51 64
5 b g Dubai Destination(USA) Maimana (IRE) (Desert King (IRE))
1801[10] 2911[3] 3081[4] 3649[5] 4070[9] 4375[8] 4469[6]
Last Echo (IRE) *Ralph Beckett* a40
2 b f Whipper(USA) Priory Rock (IRE) (Rock Of Gibraltar (IRE))
3958[10]
Last Gunfighter (USA) *Chad C Brown* a115
4 bb c First Samurai(USA) Saratoga Cat (USA) (Sir Cat (USA))
7715a[5]
Last Hooray *David Elsworth* a59 70
3 b f Royal Applause Dodo (IRE) (Alzao (USA))
1364[2] 2084[11] 2448[11] 2597[10]
Lastkingofscotland (IRE) *Conor Dore* a85 81
7 b g Danehill Dancer(IRE) Arcade (Rousillon (USA))
11[2] (95) 353[7] 1878[11] 2128[7] 3215[11] 5636[10] 6203[12] 6475[8] 7307[10] 7486[9] 7652[10] 7728[8] 7858[10] 8037[6] 8152[3] 8278[3]
Last Minute Lisa (IRE) *S Donohoe* a70 63
3 b f Strategic Prince Bradwell (IRE) (Taufan (USA))
923[2] 5331[6] 8134[7]
Last Shadow *Jonjo O'Neill* 96
4 b g Notnowcato Fairy Queen (IRE) (Fairy King (USA))
6729[7]
Last Sovereign *Ollie Pears* a95 99
9 b g Pivotal Zayala (Royal Applause)
1607[2] 1807[2] 2150[8] 2505[2] 3135[5] (3501) (4217) 4536[3] (5917)

Last Supper *James Bethell* a52 71
4 b f Echo Of Light Scotland The Brave (Zilzal (USA))
2219[7] 2836[7] 4145[4] 5899[4] 7153[10] 7639[12]
Last Train *A Fabre* a100 117
4 b c Rail Link Rainbow Lake (Rainbow Quest (USA))
(1871a) 2695a[3] 3483[11] 4324a[4]
Las Verglas Star (IRE) *Richard Fahey* a85 95
5 gr g Verglas(IRE) Magnificent Bell (IRE) (Octagonal (NZ))
810[6] 1233[12] 1446[3] 1824[5] 2191[7] 2718[6] 3204[2] 3503[3] 6353[3] 6772[4] 7312[2] 7656[8]
La Sylphe *Derek Shaw* a77 57
3 b f Refuse To Bend(IRE) Naayla (IRE) (Invincible Spirit (IRE))
531[6] 643[2] 828[4] 1041[4] (1216) 1361[2] (1771) 2779[5] 3134[9] 6653[8] 6994[8] 7730[7] 7903[10] 8051[5]
Lataradud (IRE) *Roy Arne Kvisla* 90
6 br g Marju(IRE) Abington Angel (Machiavellian (USA))
6453a[8]
Latenightrequest *Richard Fahey* 78
2 b f Major Cadeaux Love Quest (Pursuit Of Love)
2913[6] 3298[4] ◆ 3648[3] (4108) 4988[8] 6303[6] (6619) (7336)
Lateral Thinking (IRE) *James Evans* a31 72
3 b g Excellent Art Sumingasefa (Danehill (USA))
8043[5] 8260[8]
Lateran Accord (IRE) *W Hickst* a89 92
4 ch c Rock Of Gibraltar(IRE) La Ina (GER) (Monsun (GER))
2492a[9] 3615a[11]
Later In Life *Christine Dunnett*
4 ch f Notnowcato Life's A Whirl (Machiavellian (USA))
2224[10] 2746[17]
Late Shipment *Mark Johnston* a62
2 b g Authorized(IRE) Time Over (Mark Of Esteem (IRE))
7461[6] 7779[7] 7936[6]
Lat Hawill (IRE) *Marco Botti* 92
2 b c Invincible Spirit(IRE) Arbella (Primo Dominie)
(6939) ◆
La Tia (USA) *Armando de la Cerda* a107 104
4 bb f City Place(USA) La Adelita (USA) (Sky Classic (CAN))
5552a[5] 6454a[4]
Latin Charm (IRE) *Marco Botti* 74
2 b c Cape Cross(IRE) Di Moi Oui (Warning)
6570[3] ◆ (7339)
Latino (SWI) *H-A Pantall* 64
4 b c Meshaheer(USA) Sun Godess (FR) (Starborough)
5912a[6]
Latin Rebel (IRE) *Jim Goldie* 64
6 b g Spartacus(IRE) Dance To The Beat (Batshoof)
1570[5] 4012[6] 4887[8] 5264[4] 6179[5] 6552[2] 7151[3]
La Tinta Bay *Richard Hannon Snr* a45 83
2 b f Compton Place Cumana Bay (Dansili)
(3896) 4717[5] (6035) 6825[7] 7300[8]
Latkhaf (USA) *A Al Raihe* a89 63
5 ch c Pivotal Nasmatt (Danehill (USA))
(7683a)
Laudate Dominum (IRE) *Richard Fahey* a71 77
3 b f Oratorio(IRE) Feeling Wonderful (IRE) (Fruits Of Love (USA))
8057[7] 8408[7]
Laudation *Danielle McCormick* a65 68
3 b g Royal Applause Calamanco (Clantime)
185[4] ◆ 341[4] 807[5] 1014[7] 2135[2] 2544[13] 3634[5] 5016[15] 5784[7] 6664[7] 7077[5] 7353[6]
Laugharne *Roger Charlton* a72 86
2 b c Authorized(IRE) Corsican Sunset (USA) (Thunder Gulch (USA))
6168[2] (7219) 7828a[6]
Laughing (IRE) *Alan E Goldberg* a73 110
5 b f Dansili Comic (IRE) (Be My Chief (USA))
7708a[7]
Laughing Dove (IRE) *William Haggas* 54
2 b f Tamayuz Asfurah (USA) (Dayjur (USA))
5797[8] 6034[3]
Laughing Jack *Tony Carroll* a80 84
5 b g Beat Hollow Bronzewing (Beldale Flutter (USA))
1176[9] 1915[2] (3719) (3985) 4126[4] 4923[14] 6236[15] 6869[11]
Laughing Musketeer (IRE) *Paul Cole* a51 34
2 b g Azamour(IRE) Sweet Clover (Rainbow Quest (USA))
3238[10] 3905[7] 6365[8]
Laughing Rock (IRE) *Michael Appleby* a61 68
3 b f Rock Of Gibraltar(IRE) The Last Laugh (Kyllachy)
2095[9] 2996[2] (4064) 4453[5] 5300[4] 5611[3]
Laugh Or Cry *Dean Ivory* a69 40
5 br g Firebreak Turkish Delight (Prince Sabo)
1752[6] 2096[9] 2345[14]
Laugh Out Loud *J-C Rouget* a92 113
4 rg f Clodovil(IRE) Funny Girl (IRE) (Darshaan)
1945a[11]
Laugh Track (USA) *Mark Casse* a118
4 b c Distorted Humor(USA) Flaming Heart (USA) (Touch Gold (USA))
7713a[2]
Laura's Bairn *J R Jenkins* a69 73
4 ch g Piccolo Primula Bairn (Bairn (USA))
885[12] 4866[6] 5930[11] 7068[8]
Laura Secord (CAN) *Heather Main* a74
3 b f Henny Hughes(USA) Heart Lake (CAN) (Unbridled (USA))
1499[7] (3435) 6735[9]
Laurelita (IRE) *George Baker* 79
2 b f High Chaparral(IRE) Chervil (Dansili)
5061[2] (6318)
Lava Flow (IRE) *A Fabre* 101
3 ch f Dalakhani(IRE) Mount Elbrus (Barathea (IRE))
2905a[7]
L'Avenue (IRE) *James Tate* a70
2 b f Champs Elysees Mrs Seek (Unfuwain (USA))
8312[2]

La Verte Rue (USA) *Mrs A Malzard* a48 65
7 b m Johannesburg(USA) Settling In (USA) (Green Desert (USA))
1313a[2] 1740a[5] 5328a[7]

Lavilla (FR) *D Allard* 60
3 b f Sholokhov(IRE) Wildlife (GER) (Waky Nao)
5913a[5]

Lavistahermosa (FR) *B De Montzey* 12
2 b f Deportivo Cruelle (USA) (Irish River (FR))
6786a[12]

Laviva *Ferdinand J Leve* 96
5 bb f High Chaparral(IRE) Lavorna (GER) (Acatenango (GER))
6887a[10]

Law Enforcement (IRE) *Richard Hannon Snr* a98 110
3 b g Lawman(FR) Broken Spectre (Rainbow Quest (USA))
1264a[5] 2526a[9] 3484[17] (4295)

Law Hill *Michael Murphy* a45
4 b g Zamindar(USA) Absoluta (IRE) (Royal Academy (USA))
814[8] 8437[10]

Lawman's Lady (IRE) *Mark Johnston* a54
2 b f Lawman(FR) Hasanat (Night Shift (USA))
1240[5] 6776[7] 7301[5]

Lawmans Thunder *Charlie Appleby* a54 67
3 b g Lawman(FR) Rhapsodize (Halling (USA))
5069[4]

Lawyer (IRE) *Luca Cumani* a81 64
2 b c Acclamation Charaig (Rainbow Quest (USA))
4231[7] 4958[6] 5744[8] (6778) (7202) ◆

Layali Al Andalus *S Seemar* a95 90
6 b g Halling(USA) Lafite (Robellino (USA))
362a[2] 552a[7] 871a[7]

Laygirl (FR) *J-M Capitte* a86 108
5 ch f Layman(USA) Freak Out (FR) (Bering)
3387a[2] 4817a[8]

Layl (USA) *Mark Johnston* a96 77
3 bb c Street Cry(IRE) Cymbal (IRE) (Singspiel (IRE))
7298[5] (7794) 7990[10] 8327[7]

Layla's Boy *Simon West* a69 41
6 ch g Sakhee(USA) Gay Romance (Singspiel (IRE))
53[6] 198[5] 597[2] 646[4] 970[3] 1217[3] 1520[8] 1763[11] 7951[8] 8302[3]

Layla's Dancer *Michael Appleby* a62 49
6 b g Danehill Dancer(IRE) Crumpetsfortea (IRE) (Henbit (USA))
1794[6] 1889[6] 4673[5]

Layla's Hero (IRE) *David Nicholls* a49 93
6 b g One Cool Cat(USA) Capua (USA) (Private Terms (USA))
2707[9] 3090[11] 3630[6] ◆ 4146[4] 4621[4] 4892[2] 4970[11] 7148[U]

Layla's King *David C Griffiths* a66 66
5 b g Dubawi(IRE) Top Jem (Damister (USA))
2582[7] 3946[9] 4380[6]

Layla's Oasis *Richard Fahey* a74 73
3 b f Oasis Dream Kirk (Selkirk (USA))
75[2] 3097[12] 3569[6] 4018[8] 4283[5] 4976[3] 5184[8] 5996[4] 6547[15] (7240) 7432[4] 8096[8] 8216[5]

Layla's Red Devil (IRE) *Richard Fahey* 66
2 b f Dalakhani(IRE) Brazilian Samba (IRE) (Sadler's Wells (USA))
6821[6] 7237[3] 7493[6]

Layline (IRE) *Gay Kelleway* a92 78
6 b g King's Best(USA) Belle Reine (King Of Kings (IRE))
1037[8] 1586[11] 2383[9] 2775[6] 3480[5] 3791[4] 5129[3] 6108[8] (6435) 6552[4] 7453[8] (8041) 8353[3]

Lazarus Bell *Alan Brown* a61 87
3 ch g Bahamian Bounty Snake's Head (Golden Snake (USA))
1991[5] 2371[2] 2666[3] 2876[7] 6495[7] 6874[4] 7531[2] 7849[9]

Lazy Sioux *Richard Guest* a45 60
2 b f Sleeping Indian Aimee's Delight (Robellino (USA))
3605[10] 4781[4] 5339[5] 5858[4] 6295[10] 6778[7]

Lazzaz (FR) *D De Watrigant* a87 88
4 b g Bahri(USA) Rosalita (FR) (Nashamaa)
7085a[10]

Leadenhall Lass (IRE) *Pat Phelan* a75 66
7 ch m Monsieur Bond(IRE) Zest (USA) (Zilzal (USA))
2196[13] 3052[6]

Leaderene *Mark Johnston* 44
2 b f Selkirk(USA) La Felicita (Shareef Dancer (USA))
3291[8] 3810[6] 5379[6]

Leading Light (IRE) *A P O'Brien* 118
3 b c Montjeu(IRE) Dance Parade (USA) (Gone West (USA))
(2687a) (3526) (6393) ◆ 7058a[12]

Lead Role *James Tate* a66
3 b f Exceed And Excel(AUS) Fanny's Fancy (Groom Dancer (USA))
(197) 710[8]

Leafcutter (IRE) *D K Weld* 83
2 b g Shamardal(USA) Bee Eater (IRE) (Green Desert (USA))
7720a[5]

League Champion (USA) *M Ramadan* a90 35
10 b g Rahy(USA) Meiosis (USA) (Danzig (USA))
290a[16]

Lean On Pete (IRE) *Ollie Pears* a82 56
4 b g Oasis Dream Superfonic (FR) (Zafonic (USA))
(82) ◆ 314[4] 759[3] 850[3] 995[2] 1796[3] 5304[12] 6346[3] 7000[4] 7544[3] 7805[6] (7961) 8057[6] 8226[4]

Learaig (IRE) *Lady Cecil* 88
2 b c Diamond Green(FR) Sweet Kristeen (USA) (Candy Stripes (USA))
(5718)

Lear Oile Oile (IRE) *S Cannavo'* 94
3 ch f Bachelor Duke(USA) Waiting For John (IRE) (Traditionally (USA))
1866a[5]

Lea Valley *Julia Feilden* a46 49
4 b f Araafa(IRE) Guaranda (Acatenango (GER))
14[4] 275[7] 418[9] 641[2] 5377[11] 5619[4] 7376[12]

Le Baron Rouge (FR) *J Heloury* a80 75
2 ch c Vatori(FR) Billette (FR) (Thunder Gulch (USA))
7889a[2]

Le Bernardin (USA) *Mahmood Al Zarooni* a99
4 bb c Bernardini(USA) La Rosa (USA) (Wild Again (USA))
836a[13]

Le Big (GER) *P Schaerer* a98 104
9 b g Big Shuffle(USA) La Luganese (IRE) (Surumu (GER))
700a[2]

Lebresem *James Tate* a45
3 b c Elusive City(USA) Laheen (IRE) (Bluebird (USA))
3401[11]

Le Chat D'Or *Michael Dods* 87
5 b g One Cool Cat(USA) Oh So Well (IRE) (Sadler's Wells (USA))
1569[2] 2220[4] 3570[4] ◆ (4825) 5546[16] 6550[6] ◆ 7632[3]

Le Deluge (FR) *John Best* a91 85
3 b g Oratorio(IRE) Princess Sofia (UAE) (Pennekamp (USA))
(1495a) 3028[6] 3484[16] 4214[15] 5534[4] 5805a[5] 7188a[7]

Le Drakkar (AUS) *A bin Huzaim* a104 108
8 gr g Anabaa(USA) My Mo Rally (NZ) (Mi Preferido (USA))
(154a) 745a[7] 872a[8]

Leelu *David Arbuthnot* a65 63
7 b m Largesse Strat's Quest (Nicholas (USA))
116[8] 446[4]

Lees Anthem *Mel Brittain* a50 60
6 b g Mujahid(USA) Lady Rock (Mistertopogigo (IRE))
2043[6] 3024[6] 3286[2] 3630[11] 4160[3] 4615[8] 4891[8] 6180[3] 6603[2] (6761) 7344[11] 7958[4] 8049[7]

Le Feu Du Ciel (FR) *G Arizkorreta Elosegui* a91 79
7 ch g Johann Quatz(FR) Gialla (FR) (Le Nain Jaune (FR))
6252a[7]

Left Defender (IRE) *Jo Hughes* a73 79
2 b c Camacho Consultant Stylist (IRE) (Desert Style (IRE))
1208[5] 2359[4] 2723[3] (2993) 3267[4] 4434[3] 4717[3] 5347[3] 6582[12] 6663[4] 7428[6]

Legal Bond *David O'Meara* a37 61
4 b g Misu Bond(IRE) Lawless Bridget (Alnasr Alwasheek)
2036[5] 2613[4] 3475[2] 3946[3] 4891[9] 5139[10] 6568[3] 6633[8] 6980[11] 8048[10]

Legal Eagle (IRE) *Noel Williams* a62 85
8 b g Invincible Spirit(IRE) Lupulina (CAN) (Saratoga Six (USA))
1021[8] 1396[7] 7905[3] 8118[9] 8418[6]

Legal Legacy *Lee Carter* a66 84
7 ch g Beat Hollow Dans Delight (Machiavellian (USA))
73[7] 403[8] 626[8] 789[4] 883[8] 1175[11] 1474[5] 1617[11] 7458[2] 7639[2] 7980[5] 8072[10]

Legal Lyric (IRE) *W P Mullins* a58 83
4 b f Lawman(FR) Flaming Song (IRE) (Darshaan)
4647a[8] 5019a[11]

Legal Pursuit *Edward Bevan*
4 b g Proclamation(IRE) Trysting Grove (IRE) (Cape Cross (IRE))
1497[9] 8116[10] 8233[12]

Legal Waves (IRE) *Brian Meehan* 88
3 b g Lawman(FR) Surf The Web (IRE) (Ela-Mana-Mou)
1769[2] 2321[2] 2717[3] 5649[3] 7075[2]

Le Gamin (FR) *N Leenders* a44
6 gr g Charming Groom(FR) God's Counsel (FR) (Leading Counsel (USA))
127a[0]

Legenda Aurea (GER) *P Schiergen* 88
3 bb f Shamardal(USA) Lazeyma (Fantastic Light (USA))
2065a[8] 2910a[15]

Legendary *Ed Vaughan* a90 82
4 b g Exceed And Excel(AUS) Red Carnation (IRE) (Polar Falcon (USA))
2232[10] (2981) 3218[2] 3812[7] 7989[4] 8219[2]

Legend Rising (IRE) *Richard Hannon Snr* a72 90
2 ch c Tamayuz Encouragement (Royal Applause)
2307[2] (2778) (3267) 3481[10] 5396[3] 5837[5]

Legends (IRE) *Sir Michael Stoute* a95 72
3 b c Medaglia d'Oro(USA) Elusive Legend (USA) (Elusive Quality (USA))
2605[4] ◆ 3059[9] 5133[3] 5960[6] (6810) ◆

Leggy Lass (FR) *S Wattel* a55 63
3 bb f Green Tune(USA) Shocking Pink (FR) (Diktat)
2434a[0] 3129a[14]

Le Grande Cheval (IRE) *Harry Dunlop* a71
3 b g Jeremy(USA) Theory Of Law (Generous (IRE))
4356[2] 5100[3] 5678[4]

Leiloken (FR) *Christina Bucher* a90 91
6 ch h Lando(GER) Leila (FR) (Lahint (USA))
514a[11]

Leisure Cruise (USA) *Richard Hannon Snr* 14
2 b c Henrythenavigator(USA) Snowfield (USA) (Tale Of The Cat (USA))
6330[10]

Leitir Mor (IRE) *J S Bolger* a81 116
3 b c Holy Roman Emperor(IRE) Christinas Letter (IRE) (Galileo (IRE))
1704a[6] 2021[9] 2676a[8] (3262a) 3421[8] 4549a[3] 4875[6] 5314a[6] 5453a[3] 7227a[11] 7366[9]

Leitrim King (IRE) *Murty McGrath* a60 62
4 b g High Chaparral(IRE) Therry Girl (IRE) (Lahib (USA))
335[5] 455[3] 653[12] 1080[7] 2332[9]

Leitrim Pass (USA) *William Haggas* a80 83
3 ch g Raven's Pass(USA) Santolina (USA) (Boundary (USA))
1612[4] ◆ 3369[3] 4416[2] 5146[3] 8453[8]

Le King Beau (USA) *John Bridger* a71 71
4 b g Leroidesanimaux(BRZ) Berine (IRE) (Bering)
139[9] 472[6] 649[8] 747[8]

Le Laitier (FR) *Scott Dixon* a61 66
2 b g Milk It Mick La Brigitte (Tobougg (IRE))
3288[6] 4046[4] 4497[3] 5215[2] 5787[3] 7837[6] 8091[3] 8261[3]

Lelouch (JPN) *Kazuo Fujisawa* 115
5 bb c Zenno Rob Roy(JPN) Danseuse D'Etoile (FR) (Highest Honor (FR))
8033a[6]

Le Magellan (FR) *H De Nicolay* a53 78
2 ch c Medecis La Perousa (GER) (Perugino (USA))
5848a[11]

Le Meltem (FR) *Laura Grizzetti* a48
3 b c Orpen(USA) Mona Des Sables (IRE) (Marchand De Sable (USA))
460a[8]

Lemon Pearl *Ralph Beckett* a85 89
3 ch f Singspiel(IRE) Basemah (FR) (Lemon Drop Kid (USA))
1684[7] 2392[2] 3021[3] (4500) (5514) ◆ 6196[5] 7650[11]

Lemon River (FR) *N Leenders* a85
5 b f Mister Sacha(FR) Riviere Citron (FR) (Epervier Bleu)
960a[8]

Lena Player (SWE) *Linda Jewell*
2 ch f Honeysuckle Player(SWE) Russian Rhapsody (SWE) (Sonnen Gold)
7860[8]

Lendal Bridge *Tony Coyle* 59
2 ch g Avonbridge Dunloe (IRE) (Shaadi (USA))
1573[8] 2314[3] 2553[5] 6285[5] 7371[2]

Lenderking (IRE) *Michael Chapman* 16
5 b g Sleeping Indian Roses From Ridey (IRE) (Petorius)
2926[5] 5586[13] 6756[8]

Lenny Bee *Garry Moss* a75 86
7 rg g Kyllachy Smart Hostess (Most Welcome)
586[9] 1652[5] 2275[2] 2441[2] 2914[8] 3441[12] 4047[5] 4507[4] 4863[6] 5381[4] 5901[5]

Leo El Toro (GER) *A Wohler* a79
3 b c Paolini(GER) La Belle Blue (GER) (Law Society (USA))
(7736a)

Leo Luna *Gary Moore* a61 80
4 b g Galileo(IRE) Eva Luna (USA) (Alleged (USA))
6926[8]

Leonard Thomas *David Lanigan* a79
3 b g Singspiel(IRE) Monawara (IRE) (Namaqualand (USA))
(7625) 7898[2]

Leopardin (GER) *H J Groschel* 100
5 b f Areion(GER) Lolli Pop (GER) (Cagliostro (GER))
2492a[5] 6887a[13]

Le Ring (FR) *F Rossi* a86 110
3 b c Slickly(FR) Joha (FR) (Johann Quatz (FR))
286a[4] 782a[0]

Le Roi Mage (IRE) *P Monfort* a81 88
8 ch g City On A Hill(USA) Lycius Girl (ITY) (Lycius (USA))
315a[2]

Leroy Parker (IRE) *Barry Murtagh* 74
5 ch g Titus Livius(FR) Jameela (IRE) (Danehill (USA))
2706[6]

Les Affres (FR) *C Boutin* 59
3 gr g Slickly(FR) Morna (FR) (Spectrum (IRE))
6711a[6]

Les Andelys *Michael Murphy* a2
7 b g Zieten(USA) Oasis Song (IRE) (Selkirk (USA))
8437[9]

Les Beaufs (FR) *Mme V Seignoux* 118
4 b g Apsis Yeomanry (FR) (Saumarez)
1871a[5] 2695a[2] 4324a[5] 6447a[2] 7060a[8] 7566a[10]

L'Es Fremantle (FR) *Michael Chapman*
2 b g Orpen(USA) Grand Design (Danzero (AUS))
4848[6] 7883[7] 8265[6]

Les Gar Gan (IRE) *Keith Dalgleish* 75
2 b f Iffraaj Story (Observatory (USA))
(4820) 5656[4] 6047[3] 6326[8] 6619[5] 7695[10]

Lesha (IRE) *Kevin Ryan* a70
2 b g Amadeus Wolf Dane Blue (IRE) (Danehill Dancer (IRE))
7955[2] 8123[7] (8297)

Lesley's Choice *Sean Curran* a86 24
7 b g Lucky Story(USA) Wathbat Mtoto (Mtoto)
56[7] 379[5] 1186[6] 1465[11] 1731[10] 2326[5]

L'Espagna (FR) *P Khozian* 95
4 b f Rock Of Gibraltar(IRE) Luanda (IRE) (Bigstone (IRE))
6714a[8]

Lesstalk In Paris (IRE) *J-C Rouget* 109
2 b f Cape Cross(IRE) Top Toss (IRE) (Linamix (FR))
(6292a) 7055a[2]

Les Troyens *Saeed bin Suroor* a94 98
5 b c Librettist(USA) Native Blue (Seeking The Gold (USA))
290a[2] 503a[2] 4062[6] 4778[6] 5268[11] 6183[13] 6571[4]

Lethal Force (IRE) *Clive Cox* 124
4 gr c Dark Angel(IRE) Land Army (IRE) (Desert Style (IRE))
2368[2] (3557) (4298) 5040a[2] 6193[9]

Le Tholoney (FR) *F Rohaut* a63 63
3 b c Great Journey(JPN) Reinamixa (FR) (Linamix (FR))
605a[6]

Le Tigre De Bronze *Hughie Morrison* a50 65
3 b g Tiger Hill(IRE) Papillon De Bronze (IRE) (Marju (IRE))
2938[8] 3957[8] 5281[6] 5967[8]

Let It Song (FR) *E Libaud* a68 33
3 ch c Muhtathir Song Of Kintyre (FR) (Mull Of Kintyre (USA))
5692a[10]

Let Me In (IRE) *Patrick Chamings* a71 57
3 ch g Pivotal I Hearyou Knocking (IRE) (Danehill Dancer (IRE))
1282[13] 1759[7] 2613[5] 3475[5] (6321) (6985) 7378[5] (7666)

Le Toreador *Kevin Ryan* a94 96
8 ch g Piccolo Peggy Spencer (Formidable (USA))
3[5] 56[2] 379[4] 780[7]

Let'sgoforit (IRE) *Bodil Hallencreutz* a92 78
5 gr g Verglas(IRE) Slewcie (USA) (Seattle Slew (USA))
2145a[4] 5325a[7]

Let's Go Live *Paul Midgley* 57
3 b g Firebreak Enchantment (USA) (Cozzene (USA))
5839[5] 6178[6] 6497[8]

Let's Make Adeal (AUS) *Nigel Blackiston* 104
4 b f Red Ransom(USA) Let's Get Famous (AUS) (Danehill (USA))
7700a[2] 7827a[3]

Let's Rhumba *Rae Guest*
3 b f Medicean Rhumba Rage (USA) (Nureyev (USA))
1711[10]

Lets Rock Malcolm (FR) *H Billot*
3 bl f High Rock(IRE) Tashifiya (FR) (Sendawar (IRE))
7569a[10]

Letterfromamerica (USA) *John Patrick Shanahan* 79
2 b f Ghostzapper(USA) Kindness (Indian Ridge)
2645[9]

Letthemusictakeus (IRE) *Ralph Beckett* a47
2 b f Holy Roman Emperor(IRE) Side Of Paradise (IRE) (Sadler's Wells (USA))
4408[9]

Letty *A Klimscha Jr* a63 87
6 ch m Trade Fair Love Is All (IRE) (Second Empire (IRE))
514a[13]

Le Valentino (FR) *T Doumen* a49 43
2 bb c Early March Lune D'Amour (Invincible Spirit (IRE))
6961a[16]

Levanto (IRE) *W P Mullins* a76 102
3 b f Lawman(FR) Crossbreeze (USA) (Red Ransom (USA))
4465a[10] 7005a[8]

Level Best *Mark Johnston*
3 b g Oasis Dream Utmost (IRE) (Most Welcome)
2241[8]

Levi Draper *James Fanshawe* a85 83
4 b g Rock Of Gibraltar(IRE) Splice (Sharpo)
(2596) ◆ (3404) (3993) 4960[3] 5928[3] 6403[4] 6988[4]

Le Vie Infinite (IRE) *R Brogi* 85
6 b h Le Vie Dei Colori Looking Back (IRE) (Stravinsky (USA))
2491a[10]

Levitate *John Quinn* a87 110
5 ch g Pivotal Soar (Danzero (AUS))
(1235) 1675[21] 2841[4] 6396[3] (6624) 7368[4] (7820)

Lewamy (IRE) *John Best* a79 79
3 b c Amadeus Wolf Thai Dye (UAE) (Jade Robbery (USA))
126a[2] 1594a[4] 2335a[10] 3454a[7] 4354[11] 5154[6] 5564[11]

Lewisham *Ralph Beckett* a82 104
3 b g Sleeping Indian Almunia (IRE) (Mujadil (USA))
1539[2] (2123) 3348[15] 5748[4] 6692[7]

Lexington Abbey *Kevin Ryan* 81
2 b g Sleeping Indian Silvereine (FR) (Bering)
5364[4] 6546[5] (7125)

Lexington Bay (IRE) *Richard Fahey* a86 85
5 b g High Chaparral(IRE) Schust Madame (IRE) (Second Set (IRE))
926[4] (1188) 1547[3] 1841[3] 7990[11] 8276[3]

Lexington Blue *David O'Meara* a69 71
3 b g Bertolini(USA) Jasmine Breeze (Saddlers' Hall (IRE))
1966[5] (2581) (3082) 3463[8] 4008[5] 4449[5] (4955) 5072[2] 5642[4] 5835[6]

Lexington Place *David O'Meara* a66 87
3 ch g Compton Place Eldore (Danetime (IRE))
1275[9] (1392) 2010[5] 2544[7] 2888[6] (3594) (4069) ◆ (4290) (4402) 4674[2] 4989[3] 5769[4] 6583[13]

Lexington Rose *Bryan Smart* a69 80
2 b f Captain Gerrard(IRE) Silca Destination (Dubai Destination (USA))
1565[3] (1839) 2426[4] 2767[2] ◆ (3332) 4528[22] 6791[6] 7026[16] 7349[3] 7545[5]

Lexington Spirit (IRE) *Richard Fahey* a64 54
4 b f Iffraaj Festivite (IRE) (Fasliyev (USA))
206[9]

Lexi's Beauty (IRE) *Brian Baugh* a47 2
3 br f Kheleyf(USA) Voyage Of Dreams (USA) (Riverman (USA))
36[3] 669[2] 828[6] 1116[2] 1651[5] 3134[13] 8050[8] 8277[5]

Lexi's Dancer *Ian Williams* a50 56
3 ch f Danehill Dancer(IRE) Ravine (Indian Ridge)
1828[9] 2215[5] 2504[4] 3194[7] 4374[6] 4715[5] 5072[7] 5605[4] 5961[6]

Lexi's Hero (IRE) *Richard Fahey* a80 67
5 b g Invincible Spirit(IRE) Christel Flame (Darshaan)
1726[14] 2097[6] 2459[12] 3093[9] 4619[2] 5088[11] 5183[12] 7801[3] 8224[2] ◆ 8321[2]

Ley Hunter (USA) *Saeed bin Suroor* 77
6 b g Kingmambo(USA) Lailani (Unfuwain (USA))
2810[10]

L Frank Baum (IRE) *Bernard Llewellyn* a69 84
6 b g Sinndar(IRE) Rainbow City (IRE) (Rainbow Quest (USA))
3807[5] 4606[5] 4913[7] 5997[9]

L Ge R *Peter Charalambous* a56 55
2 b f Pastoral Pursuits Cashbar (Bishop Of Cashel)
6500[6] 8085[4] 8259[5]

L'Hirondelle (IRE) *Michael Attwater* a76 61
9 b g Anabaa(USA) Auratum (USA) (Carson City (USA))
112[7] 403[13] 450[7] 813[14]

Lhotse Sherpa *John Holt* a49
4 b g Byron Soyalang (FR) (Alydeed (CAN))
979[3] 1193[6] 1394[11] 2932[16]

Libano (IRE) *L Polito* 102
7 b h Indian Ridge Daniela Grassi (Bound For Honour (USA))
2698a[2] 6889a[9] 7725a[2]
Libeccio (FR) *Andrew Balding* 70
2 b g Shirocco(GER) Francais (Mark Of Esteem (IRE))
5698[9] 6528[5] 6896[3]
Liberal Lady *Ralph Smith* a66 61
5 b f Statue Of Liberty(USA) Noble Story (Last Tycoon)
30[2] 156[6] 399[11] 448[7] 493[11] 1467[7]
Liberating *Mrs John Harrington* a94 94
3 b f Iffraaj Ros The Boss (IRE) (Danehill (USA))
1557a[4] 1921[6] 3263a[8] 3845a[2] 7227a[5] 7993a[4]
Liberation (IRE) *Ismail Mohammed* a65 100
7 b h Refuse To Bend(IRE) Mosaique Bleue (Shirley Heights)
394a[8]
Liberator (AUS) *D E Ferraris* 116
6 b g Encosta De Lago(AUS) Miss Helga (IRE) (Alzao (USA))
8208a[10]
Liber Nauticus (IRE) *Sir Michael Stoute* 102
3 b f Azamour(IRE) Serres (IRE) (Daylami (IRE))
(2367) 2842[5]
Libertarian *Charlie Appleby* 118
3 b c New Approach(IRE) Intrum Morshaan (IRE) (Darshaan)
(1443) 1811[4] (2398) 2866[2] ◆ 3849a[8] 6393[4]
Liberty Island (IRE) *Ian Semple* a84 84
8 b g Statue Of Liberty(USA) Birthday (IRE) (Singspiel (IRE))
2880[5] 3331[7]
Liberty Jack (IRE) *Jim Boyle* a82 82
3 b g Sakhee(USA) Azeema (IRE) (Averti (IRE))
1904[3] ◆ 2346[3] 3582[4] 4068[2] (4750) 5676[3] 6072[3] 8127[11] 8391[8]
Liberty Love (IRE) *Niall Moran* a60 57
8 b g Statue Of Liberty(USA) Alserna (IRE) (Alhaarth (IRE))
100[2] 361[3] 406[2] 3882[8]
Liberty Red (GER) *Ed Dunlop* 75
2 b c Dubawi(IRE) Late Night (GER) (Groom Dancer (USA))
4896[4] 5379[2] 7061[2]
Liberty Ship *Mark Buckley* a67 63
8 b g Statue Of Liberty(USA) Flag (Selkirk (USA))
26[3] (142) 213[5] 2132[7] 3317[7] 4018[7]
Libranno *Richard Hannon Snr* 117
5 b c Librettist(USA) Annabelle Ja (FR) (Singspiel (IRE))
1810[4] 2446[11] 3101[4] 3419[6] 3831[7] 4856[4] 5532[5] 5794[9] 6254a[5] 7190[3]
Libra Romana (IRE) *Sir Mark Prescott Bt* a46
2 b f Holy Roman Emperor(IRE) Sliding Scale (Sadler's Wells (USA))
8165[4] 8300[4] 8368[4]
Licence To Till (USA) *Mark Johnston* a101 99
6 b g War Chant(USA) With A Wink (USA) (Clever Trick (USA))
1446[5] 2018[9]
Lichen Angel *Richard Whitaker* a47 42
3 gr f Dark Angel(IRE) Moss Likely (IRE) (Clodovil (IRE))
4050[6] 4619[6] 5265[5] 6289[12] 6944[5] 7443[4]
Lichtlein (FR) *D Barone* a55 36
6 b m Mull Of Kintyre(USA) Airlight (IRE) (Trempolino (USA))
6058a[3]
Licia (ITY) *S Botti* 99
3 b f Singspiel(IRE) Love Money (IRE) (Intikhab (USA))
2697a[4] (3616a) 7234a[4] 7558a[8]
Lictus (FR) *F Rohaut* a84 83
3 b c Literato(FR) Lunaba (FR) (Anabaa (USA))
1511a[4] (5805a)
Lidar (FR) *Alan King* a18 86
8 ch g Take Risks(FR) Light Wave (FR) (Marignan (USA))
157[8]
Liddle Dwiggs *Denis Coakley* 24
2 b f Bertolini(USA) Slims Lady (Theatrical Charmer)
6974[9] 7245[9] 7854[9]
Liebling *Niels Petersen*
2 b f Touch Down(GER) Lupinie (GER) (Platini (GER))
6452a[7]
Liefie *Jo Hughes* a34 27
2 b f Tobougg(IRE) Take The Plunge (Benny The Dip (USA))
1724[12] 5350[6]
Lieutenant Dan (IRE) *Michael Appleby* a73 57
6 b g Danroad(AUS) Dakhira (Emperor Jones (USA))
193[4] 223[3] (408) 546[6] 805[2] (1056) 1214[4] 1599[2] 1746[7] 2515[8] 8157[8]
Lieutenant Miller *Nicky Henderson* 98
7 b g Beat All(USA) Still Runs Deep (Karinga Bay)
1670[2] (1805) 3423[3] 4873[2] 7193[3]
Lieutenant Nelson *Kevin Tork*
3 ch g Mount Nelson Franglais (GER) (Lion Cavern (USA))
7380[0] 7781[11]
Life And Soul (IRE) *Donald McCain* a78 99
6 b g Azamour(IRE) Way For Life (GER) (Platini (GER))
1242[12]
Life And Times (USA) *Mark Johnston* 74
5 bb g Medaglia d'Oro(USA) Sur Ma Vie (USA) (Fusaichi Pegasus (USA))
6178[3] 6431[4] 7075[7] 7424[10]
Lifejacket (IRE) *Ed Dunlop* a54
2 ch g Notnowcato My American Beauty (Wolfhound (USA))
7301[4]
Life Of Laughter (USA) *Willie Musson* a54
5 b g Elusive Quality(USA) Country Garden (Selkirk (USA))
458[2] 724[7] 1022[3] 1369[7]

Life Partner (IRE) *Charlie Appleby* 96
3 b g Cape Cross(IRE) Miss Intimate (USA) (War Chant (USA))
4011[3] (4667) (5721) 6308[15] 6993[7]
Lifetime (IRE) *Brian Ellison* a73 80
5 b g Shamardal(USA) La Vita E Bella (IRE) (Definite Article)
40[4] 622[5] 3807[6]
Ligeia *Richard Hannon Snr* a85 82
2 b f Rail Link Elegant Beauty (Olden Times)
2617[2] ◆ (3107) (3690) ◆ 4682[6] 7537[5]
Light Burst (USA) *Ismail Mohammed* a90 85
4 b c Hard Spun(USA) Kew Garden (USA) (Seattle Slew (USA))
(715) 1782[4] 2266[5] 3411[5] 4181[3] ◆ 5195[3] 6204[4] 6609[2]
Light Catcher *Andrew Balding* 14
3 b f Sakhee(USA) Exorcet (FR) (Selkirk (USA))
2051[13]
Light From Mars *Ronald Harris* a91 88
8 gr g Fantastic Light(USA) Hylandra (USA) (Bering)
217[2] 272[3] (443) (629) 944[6] 1061[10] 1542[13] 3096[15] 3507[3] (3906) 5537[2] 6162[6] 6648[8] 7031[4] 7792[2] 8127[4] 8350[6]
Light Heavy (IRE) *J S Bolger* a100 114
4 ch c Teofilo(IRE) Siamsa (USA) (Quest For Fame)
466a[7] 741a[7]
Lightning Cloud (IRE) *Kevin Ryan* a79 106
5 gr g Sleeping Indian Spree (IRE) (Dansili)
1688[3] 2254[14] 2858[7] (3527) 4744[18] 5763[5] 6235[4] 6623[22]
Lightning Launch (IRE) *Mick Channon* 83
3 b g Kheleyf(USA) Launch Time (USA) (Relaunch (USA))
(1272) 1645[2] 2056[2] 2439[4] 3234[8] 3758[2] 4056[6]
Lightning Shower (USA) *Marco Botti* a65
2 b c Mr Greeley(USA) Lightning Show (USA) (Storm Cat (USA))
5675[3] 6168[8] 6688[5]
Lightning Spear *Ralph Beckett* a85
2 ch c Pivotal Atlantic Destiny (IRE) (Royal Academy (USA))
(5924)
Lightning Spirit *Gary Moore* a56 63
5 b f Storming Home Lucky Dice (Perugino (USA))
1740a[7] 2534[5] 2747[13] 3169[6] (3657) 3924[6] 5170[3] 6261[8] 6553[7] 7639[11]
Lightning Thunder *Olly Stevens* 109
2 b f Dutch Art Sweet Coincidence (Mujahid (USA))
(5529) ◆ (6304) 6795[2] 7194[4]
Lightnin Hopkins (IRE) *G M Lyons* a82 94
3 b g Kodiac Bundle Of Joy (IRE) (Golan (IRE))
2374a[13] 5775a[14]
Light Of Asia (IRE) *Ed Dunlop* a64
2 b c Oratorio(IRE) Lucy Cavendish (USA) (Elusive Quality (USA))
8066[8]
Light Rose (IRE) *Mark Johnston* a77 79
3 b f Cape Cross(IRE) Laureldean Lady (IRE) (Statue Of Liberty (USA))
1321[4] 3666[3] ◆ 4101[6] 4502[3] 4890[7] 5398[5] 5830[9] 6475[2] 6875[2] 7256[3] 7438[5]
Light The City (IRE) *Ruth Carr* a53 72
6 b g Fantastic Light(USA) Marine City (JPN) (Carnegie (IRE))
914[6] 1188[5] 1390[8] 2165[6] 2629[9] 2961[3] 3231[8] 3595[4] 3947[5] 4403[12] 5196[2] 5420[5] 5897[6] 6479[4] 6909[7] 7151[6]
Light Up My Life (IRE) *Richard Hannon Snr* 101
3 b f Zamindar(USA) Shine Like A Star (Fantastic Light (USA))
1622[13] 3460[6] 4081[2] 4705[10] 5402[9] 6183[12]
Light Weight (IRE) *Kevin Ryan* 75
2 b f Danehill Dancer(IRE) Foofaraw (USA) (Cherokee Run (USA))
5330[8] (5827) 6619[9]
Lignum Vitae *Richard Fahey* a51
3 b g Vita Rosa(JPN) Pat Or Else (Alzao (USA))
564[2] 925[7]
Like A Carousel (AUS) *Ken Keys* 106
4 ch g Helike(USA) Carnival Ride (AUS) (Spinning World (USA))
7760a[2] 7938a[2]
Like A Diamond (IRE) *Evan Williams* a80 64
3 b g Antonius Pius(USA) Silk Law (IRE) (Barathea (IRE))
7932[2]
Like A Prayer *Ralph Beckett* a57 50
2 b c Compton Place Floating (Oasis Dream)
6534[8] 7120[9] 8061[5]
Like Clockwork *Mark H Tompkins* a54 59
4 b g Rail Link Tenpence (Bob Back (USA))
2642[4] 5370[4] 5934[7] 6558[8] 7090[2] 7376[4] 7951[11]
Likelihood (USA) *John Gosden* a75 77
2 gr f Mizzen Mast(USA) Light Jig (Danehill (USA))
4702[10] 5394[2] ◆ (5812)
Likelikelikelikeit *Mark H Tompkins* a51 57
3 b f Avonbridge Rutland Water (IRE) (Hawk Wing (USA))
5497[5] 6479[8] 6717[3] 7331[3]
Lilac Lace (IRE) *Tim Easterby* a73 90
3 b f Captain Marvelous(IRE) Lilac Mist (Spectrum (IRE))
(1577) ◆ (2026) (2704) 3296[2] 3443[5] 6210[6] 6495[4] 7024[4] (7538) 7820[10]
Lilac Tree *Mark Johnston* a78 79
3 b c Dubawi(IRE) Kalidasa (USA) (Nureyev (USA))
1683[4] 7257[6] 7531[9] 7849[6]
Lilbourne Lass *Richard Hannon Snr* 93
2 ch f Pastoral Pursuits Talampaya (USA) (Elusive Quality (USA))
(2359) 2933[2] (3311) 4528[2] ◆ (5306) 5476[3] 5994[2] 6142[6]
L'Ile Rousse *Chris Dwyer*
4 ch f Muhtathir Felucca (Green Desert (USA))
3787[7] 4687[5]
Liliana (IRE) *Peter Chapple-Hyam* a63
3 b f Haatef(USA) Stop Out (Rudimentary (USA))
90[3] 228[8]

Liliargh (IRE) *Ben Haslam* 74
4 b f Acclamation Discover Roma (IRE) (Rock Of Gibraltar (IRE))
1578[5] 2889[9] 2974[6] 4893[8] 6179[7] 6599[7] 7344[10]
Lili Moon (GER) *Werner Glanz* 96
4 bb f Desert Prince(IRE) Lisibila (GER) (Acatenango (GER))
2969a[8] 6887a[11]
Lillebonne (FR) *David O'Meara* a68 88
3 b f Danehill Dancer(IRE) Lidana (IRE) (King's Best (USA))
7205[6] ◆ 7822[12] 8020[9]
Lilly May (IRE) *Phil McEntee* a45 42
3 b f Haatef(USA) Love Of Silver (USA) (Arctic Tern (USA))
1982[4] 4030[5] 4400[11]
Lilly White (USA) *John Butler* a53 53
3 b f Speightstown(USA) Unrestrained (USA) (Unbridled (USA))
5407[3] 5869[4] 7265[11]
Lilo Lil *David C Griffiths* a66 66
2 b f Captain Gerrard(IRE) Rebel County (IRE) (Maelstrom Lake)
1247[6] 1573[2] 1792[2] 1910[2] 2147[7] 4370[5] (4749) (5066) 5509[3] 5842[2] 6386[5] 6967[3] 7545[9]
Lil Rockerfeller (USA) *Richard Hannon Snr* a61
2 ch c Hard Spun(USA) Layounne (USA) (Mt. Livermore (USA))
7835[8]
Lil Sophella (IRE) *Patrick Holmes* a40 63
4 ch f Indian Haven Discotheque (USA) (Not For Love (USA))
28[5] 168[5] 1804[10] 2237[3] 2537[3] 2972[5] 3337[2] 4005[7] 4469[4] 4623[3] 5331[2] 5614[2] (6633) 6918[2] 7153[3]
Lily Edge *John Bridger* a76 69
4 b f Byron Flaming Spirt (Blushing Flame (USA))
230[2] (651) (899) 1181[7] 1500[10] 2155[7] 2395[13] 3106[5] 3635[8] 4126[11] 4755[12] 4894[9]
Lilyfire (USA) *Roger Charlton* 85
2 b f First Defence(USA) Didina (Nashwan (USA))
(4702) 6002[2] ◆
Lily In Pink *Jonathan Portman* a77 102
5 b f Sakhee(USA) In Luck (In The Wings)
1484[8] 2012[7] 6649[7]
Lily Merrill *J-M Lefebvre* a78 84
3 b f Lawman(FR) Tonic Star (FR) (Enrique)
(461a)
Lily Of Kenmare (IRE) *M Halford* a69 73
5 b f Exceed And Excel(AUS) Zoudie (Ezzoud (IRE))
3845a[18]
Lilyofthevalley *John Weymes*
3 b f Avonbridge Linden's Lady (Compton Place)
2503[10] 3774[10]
Lily Potts *Chris Down* a56 66
4 gr f Proclamation(IRE) Jucinda (Midyan (USA))
3953[2] 4775[4] 5130[5]
Lily Rules (IRE) *Tony Coyle* 92
2 br f Aussie Rules(USA) Causeway Charm (USA) (Giant's Causeway (USA))
1606[2] 1785[2] 2075[5] (3724) 4061[2] (5136) 5536[2] 6195[3]
Lily's Angel (IRE) *G M Lyons* a110 110
4 b f Dark Angel(IRE) Noyelles (IRE) (Docksider (USA))
(149a) 743a[4] 1413a[7] (1544) (2264) 2678a[3] 3262a[2] 3964a[4] 6224a[2]
Lily's Star (IRE) *H Rogers* a69 87
6 b m Chineur(FR) Voodoo Lily (IRE) (Petardia)
6089a[5]
Lily The Dragon (IRE) *Mick Quinn* a28 39
3 b f Moss Vale(IRE) Noble Rocket (Reprimand)
1911[7] 2637[8] 3494[6] 5156[3] 6965[8] 7969[5]
Limario (GER) *R Dzubasz* 104
3 bb c Areion(GER) Limaga (Lagunas)
1708a[5] 2526a[8] 4103a[7] (5576a) 6987a[10]
Limegrove *David Evans* a78 78
2 b f Captain Gerrard(IRE) Cherry Belle (IRE) (Red Ransom (USA))
1399[3] ◆ 1634[7] (1778) 2053[2] 2147[4] 2767[7] 3801[6] 4019[9] 4630[2] 5121[4] 5351[6] (5591) 5963[3] (6364) 6778[5] 7117[6] 7199[7] 7665[8]
Limit Up *Mark Johnston* a83 80
3 b g Shamardal(USA) Love Me Tender (Green Desert (USA))
1012[2] (1174) 1620[13] 2022[11] 2984[4] 3320[7] (3715) 4101[5]
Limoges *Luke Dace* a48 42
3 b f Bertolini(USA) China Cherub (Inchinor)
341[5] 509[5] 824[11] 1171[5] 1781[7] 2095[7]
Limon Squeezy *Mike Murphy* a44
4 b f Royal Applause Limonia (GER) (Perugino (USA))
8063[7] 8437[4]
L'Importante *Marco Botti* 73
2 b c New Approach(IRE) L'Indiscreta (Desert Prince (IRE))
3112[6] ◆
Linarda (DEN) *M Rulec* 94
3 bb f Rock Of Gibraltar(IRE) Miss Skycat (USA) (Tale Of The Cat (USA))
2970a[8] 7234a[6]
Lincoln (IRE) *Mick Channon* 80
2 b c Clodovil(IRE) Gilt Linked (Compton Place)
3295[7] 4231[5] 4808[4] 5508[2] 5819[2] 5995[2] 6206[2] (6581) 7026[9]
Lincolnrose (IRE) *Michael Appleby* a57 57
3 gr f Verglas(IRE) Imelda (USA) (Manila (USA))
122[4] 482[7] 2084[13] (2528) 3016[7] 3316[6] 5128[8] 6655[11] 7104[3] 7637[4] 7907[6] 8293[11]
Linda Radlett (IRE) *A Fabre* a93 101
4 b f Manduro(GER) Portmanteau (Barathea (IRE))
4601a[2] 6294a[5]
Lindenhurst (IRE) *John C McConnell* a42 77
3 b g Captain Marvelous(IRE) Royal Jubilee (IRE) (King's Theatre (IRE))
(6051) 6086[2]
Lindenthaler (GER) *Fredrik Reuterskiold* a91 108
5 b c Azamour(IRE) Lasira (GER) (Vettori (IRE))
242a[6] 661a[10] 873a[4] 2146a[3] 3188a[5] 6453a[9]

Lindoro *Sean Curran* a70 77
8 b g Marju(IRE) Floppie (FR) (Law Society (USA))
50[5] 223[7] 370[7] 735[8]
Lindsay's Dream *Zoe Davison* a61 50
7 b m Montjeu(IRE) Lady Lindsay (IRE) (Danehill Dancer (IRE))
2567[4] 2801[11] 3655[4]
Line Drummer (FR) *A P O'Brien* 103
3 b c Galileo(IRE) Miss Bio (FR) (River Mist (USA))
6025a[17] 7388a[5]
Line Et Bleu (FR) *F Vermeulen* a76 81
5 gr f Anabaa Blue La Josselinaise (FR) (Balleroy (USA))
7573a[9]
Lineman *Andrew Hollinshead* a73 63
3 b g Rail Link Shamana (USA) (Woodman (USA))
6166[4] (6781) 7105[7] 7510[8]
Line Of Reason (IRE) *Paul Midgley* a91 92
3 br g Kheleyf(USA) Miss Party Line (USA) (Phone Trick (USA))
793[2] (879) 1806[2] 2371[15] (3066) 3367[4] 4117[5] 4780[15] 6331[9] 6831[12]
Lines Of Battle (USA) *A P O'Brien* a111 110
3 b g War Front(USA) Black Speck (USA) (Arch (USA))
(1264a) 2033a[7] 3142a[2] 3876a[8]
Lingfield Lupus (IRE) *John Best* a40 11
2 b g Amadeus Wolf Clytha (Mark Of Esteem (IRE))
4997[8] 6688[7] 7301[9]
Linguine (FR) *Seamus Durack* 96
3 ch c Linngari(IRE) Amerissage (USA) (Rahy (USA))
1847[6] 2416[6] 3277[2] 4279[7] 5086[2] (5879) 6992[9] 7496[5]
Linkable *Brendan Powell* a72 73
4 b c Rail Link Fashionable (Nashwan (USA))
161[2] 342[3] 475[5] (668) (905) 1445[13] 2939[4] 3412[5] 3865[6] 6960[7] 7735[7] (7984)
Links Drive Lady *Dean Ivory* a86 93
5 br f Striking Ambition Miskina (Mark Of Esteem (IRE))
1726[8] 2097[7] (2848) 4138[2] 4534[2] 4983[21] 5700[2] 6621[14] 7021[14] 7222[10]
Linngara (FR) *Mario Hofer* a79 87
3 b f Linngari(IRE) Loa Loa (GER) (Anabaa Blue)
1495a[7]
Linngaro (FR) *Mario Hofer* a100 101
3 ch c Linngari(IRE) Indochine (BRZ) (Special Nash (IRE))
286a[8] 999a[6]
Linroyale Boy (USA) *Alan Swinbank* a79 54
5 ch g Giant's Causeway(USA) Welcometotheworld (USA) (Woodman (USA))
888[2] 989[3] (1146) (1333) 1601[3] (2511)
Linton (AUS) *John D Sadler* 115
7 gr g Galileo(IRE) Our Heather (NZ) (Centaine (AUS))
8210a[13]
Lion Beacon *Amanda Perrett* a79 89
3 ch g Beat Hollow Second Of May (Lion Cavern (USA))
1614[3] (2079) (2602) 3982[7] 5448[2] 6302[3] 6978[4]
Lion D'Anvers (FR) *J Van Handenhove* 107
3 b c Kentucky Dynamite(USA) Alcestes Selection (Selkirk (USA))
2298a[13] 2907a[16] 3911a[4] 6712a[4]
Lionel (FR) *Carmen Bocskai* a24
3 b g Sunday Break(JPN) Land Bridge (FR) (Bering)
8441a[13]
Lionheart *Luca Cumani* a79 89
3 ch g Zamindar(USA) Victoire Celebre (USA) (Stravinsky (USA))
1476[2] 1770[8] 2593[12] (3927) 4354[4] (4863) 5219[11] 6161[7] ◆ 6692[6]
Lions Arch (IRE) *Richard Hannon Snr* a89 85
3 b c Rock Of Gibraltar(IRE) Swynford Lady (IRE) (Invincible Spirit (IRE))
(1012) (1822) 2259[7] 8219[6] 8455[3]
Lion's Maid *Michael Attwater* a46
4 b f Iceman Steppin Out (First Trump)
157[7] 841[5]
Lions Park (IRE) *Mark Johnston* a76 81
3 b c Dubawi(IRE) Gold's Dance (FR) (Goldneyev (USA))
4022[3] 4257[6] 4632[4]
Lipocco *J D Hillis* a68 96
9 b g Piccolo Magical Dancer (IRE) (Magical Wonder (USA))
(700a) 1944a[8]
Lips Dancer (IRE) *Andreas Lowe*
4 ch c Big Shuffle(USA) Lips Plane (IRE) (Ashkalani (IRE))
963a[0]
Lisahane Bog *Peter Hedger* a52 24
6 b g Royal Applause Veronica Franco (Darshaan)
896[12] 1054[7] 8448[5]
Lisamour (IRE) *Paul Cole* a70
2 b f Azamour(IRE) Lisa De La Condra (IRE) (Galileo (IRE))
7780[9] 7874[2]
Lisa's Legacy *Daniel Kubler* a85 85
3 b g Kyllachy Lisathedaddy (Darnay)
3861[4] 4169[3] 4503[4] 5234[6] (5403) 5789[3] 6071[2] (6313) 6693[4]
Lisiere (IRE) *K R Burke* a66 86
4 b f Excellent Art Sahara Sky (IRE) (Danehill (USA))
1823[5] 3300[3] 3988[4] 5051[3] 5684[12] 6341[7] 6586[21]
Lisselan Pleasure (USA) *Bernard Llewellyn* a59 61
6 gr m Macho Uno(USA) Cute Connie (USA) (Struggler)
3314[7] 3882[2]
Lisselton Cross *Martin Bosley* a58 47
5 ch g Compton Place Sweet Myrtle (USA) (Mutakddim (USA))
87[5] 111[8] 649[6]
Litian Rocket (FR) *M Boutin* a80 86
3 b c Indian Rocket Lit (IRE) (Danehill (USA))
544a[5] 647a[3] 2557a[7] 4575a[6]

Litigant *Seamus Durack* a101 90
5 b g Sinndar(IRE) Jomana (IRE) (Darshaan)
7990[2] ◆ (8202)

Litmus (USA) *Simon Dow* a60 48
4 ch f Latent Heat(USA) Fairy Glade (USA) (Gone West (USA))
120[4] 320[4] (441) 510[6] 630[3] 6038[11] 6553[11] 7930[2] 7981[4] (8142) 8341[5]

Little Alice *Stuart Williams* a57 28
3 ch f Haafhd Allespagne (USA) (Trempolino (USA))
1086[5] 2016[7] 2519[13] 2748[5] 3319[4] 3820[12]

Little Arrows (IRE) *K J Condon* a70 70
7 b g Danehill Dancer(IRE) Lovers Walk (USA) (Diesis)
6089a[3]

Little Big Man *Sylvester Kirk* a71 41
2 b g Sleeping Indian Doris Souter (IRE) (Desert Story (IRE))
1580[8] 3631[11] 4412[4] 5595[5] 5850[7] 6364[2] 7036[3] 7293[5] 7893[4] (8025) 8166[3] 8364[2]

Little Big Shot (IRE) *F-H Graffard* 91
2 b c Whipper(USA) Gravieres (FR) (Saint Estephe (FR))
6249a[6] 7994a[4]

Little Briar Rose *John Spearing* 55
2 ch f Sleeping Indian Penrice Castle (Averti (IRE))
4847[10] 5307[8] 5929[5] 7426[3]

Little Bruv *Tim Easterby* 48
2 b g Observatory(USA) Ailincala (IRE) (Pursuit Of Love)
5969[6] 6513[6] 6938[7]

Little Buxted (USA) *Robert Mills* a83
3 bb g Mr Greeley(USA) Mo Cheoil Thu (IRE) (In The Wings)
(74) 7267[3] 7840[8] 7970[2]

Little China *William Muir* a70 66
4 b f Kyllachy China Beads (Medicean)
101[7] 431[3] 535[9] 971[8] 1398[8] 1802[5] 2074[10] 2870[3] 3154[9] 3921[4] (4353) 4999[8] 5982[3] 6157[2] 6652[3] 6901[10] (7077)

Little Choosey *Anabel K Murphy* a64 68
3 ch f Cadeaux Genereux Little Nymph (Emperor Fountain)
1875[3] 2394[11] 2829[3] 3268[6] 3678[4] 4654[2] 5349[4] 6154[8] (6849) 7164[5] 7381[9]

Littlecote Lady *Mark Usher* a60 56
4 b f Byron Barefooted Flyer (USA) (Fly So Free (USA))
223[9] 409[4] 655[2] (735) 1088[5] 1395[2] 1734[5] 1929[4] 2125[6] 8413[5]

Little Cupcake *E J O'Neill* a73 79
2 b f Myboycharlie(IRE) Imco Cracking (IRE) (Piccolo)
5419a[4] 7653a[4]

Little Dolly *Alan McCabe* a61 28
3 b f Nayef(USA) Tahirah (Green Desert (USA))
(102) 538[4] 1486[12] 2331[9]

Little Dutch Girl *Nicky Henderson* 87
4 ch f Dutch Art Photographie (USA) (Trempolino (USA))
4015[8]

Little Eli *Eric Alston* a63 61
3 b g Green Desert(USA) Princess Ellis (Compton Place)
1539[8] 2091[3] (2861) 3198[7] 4114[10] (5067) 5485[7] 6345[2]

Little Garcon (USA) *Robert Cowell* a86 80
6 b g Bernstein(USA) Demure (Machiavellian (USA))
58[8] 1067[7] 1346[9] 1692[12]

Little Herbert *Michael Attwater*
2 ch g Avonbridge Filemot (Largesse)
8017[8]

Little Indian *J R Jenkins* a67 66
3 b c Sleeping Indian Once Removed (Distant Relative)
31[4] (1180) 1928[8] 2802[7] (3739) (5275) 7841[3]

Little Jimmy Odsox (IRE) *Tim Easterby* a67 81
5 b g Namid September Tide (IRE) (Thatching)
1801[13] 2707[6] 3393[5] 4009[9] 4148[2] (4892) 5333[4] 6287[6] 6760[10] 7149[2]

Little Mike (USA) *Dale Romans* a102 121
6 b g Spanish Steps(USA) Hay Jude (USA) (Wavering Monarch (USA))
958a[8] 1267a[11] 5553a[6] 7712a[7] 8211a[9]

Little Miss Becky *Giles Bravery* a3
2 b f Piccolo Boojum (Mujtahid (USA))
8058[6] 8326[11]

Little Miss Zuri (IRE) *Sylvester Kirk* a50 44
3 ch f Choisir(AUS) Miss Kinabalu (Shirley Heights)
31[7] 5981[5] 6033[5] 6902[8]

Little Power (FR) *J-P Carvalho* a66 83
4 b g Lord Of England(GER) Little Memories (IRE) (Montjeu (IRE))
127a[0]

Little Pudding *Mary Hambro* a24
5 b f Sleeping Indian Neptunalia (Slip Anchor)
7625[8]

Little Red Nell (IRE) *Martin Bosley* a42
4 b f Red Clubs(IRE) Naughty Nell (Danehill Dancer (IRE))
7987[6] 8140[7]

Little Tinka *Mark H Tompkins* a42 56
2 b f Three Valleys(USA) Tenpence (Bob Back (USA))
6500[5] 6974[8] 7954[5] 8215[6]

Little White Cloud (IRE) *John M Oxx* a82 106
3 gr c Dalakhani(IRE) Quest For Eternity (IRE) (Sadler's Wells (USA))
2290a[3] 2687a[2] 3849a[6]

Little Windsor *Peter Hiatt*
4 b f Central Park(IRE) Sonderborg (Great Dane (IRE))
7298[13]

Live Dangerously *Keith Dalgleish* a68 79
3 b g Zamindar(USA) Desert Lynx (IRE) (Green Desert (USA))
2687a[8] 5705[8] 6181[11] 6549[2] 7165[3]

Lively Little Lady *Mrs A Corson* a57 38
3 b f Beat All(USA) Ever So Lonely (Headin' Up)
492[5] 667[8] 2129[10] 3221[5] 3789[6] 5327a[6]

Livento (FR) *A Bonin* a76 76
3 b g Falco(USA) Estafilade (FR) (Gold Away (IRE))
1850a[7] 5914a[4]

Livia Drusilla (IRE) *Brian Ellison* a56
2 b f Holy Roman Emperor(IRE) Shaiyadima (IRE) (Zamindar (USA))
1449[3]

Livia's Dream (IRE) *Ed Walker* a93 88
4 b f Teofilo(IRE) Brindisi (Dr Fong (USA))
2855[6] 3573[2] 4287[3] (4760) 5436[2] 6280[5] 6764[6] 7650[2] 8062[5]

Living Desert *James Toller* a80 73
3 gr g Oasis Dream Sell Out (Act One)
1908[4] 2776[4] 3117[5] 3961[5] 5069[2] 6502[4]

Living Leader *Nick Littmoden* a85 74
4 b g Oasis Dream Royal Jade (Last Tycoon)
844[7] 1318[3] ◆ 2046[15] 3586[11] 4165[7] 4718[4] 5489[6] 6609[10] 6943[P] 7785[9] 8037[7] 8447[3] ◆

Living The Life (IRE) *Jamie Osborne* a85 83
3 b f Footstepsinthesand Colour And Spice (IRE) (Machiavellian (USA))
1246[4] 1683[6] 2223[5] 6003[8] (6702) 6856[2] (6998) 7603[3] 7949[2] 8053[4]

Lizarre (SAF) *Patrick Shaw* 109
7 b g Jet Master(SAF) Leading Dame (SAF) (Jallad (USA))
2494a[4]

Lizzie Tudor *Andrew Balding* a83 89
3 ch f Tamayuz Silca Destination (Dubai Destination (USA))
2253[4] 3460[18] 4252[4] 4897[7]

Lizzy's Dream *Robin Bastiman* a64 68
5 ch g Choisir(AUS) Flyingit (USA) (Lear Fan (USA))
2832[10] 3505[7] 5336[3] ◆ 5639[6] 6944[9] 7236[6]

Llamadas *Olivia Maylam* a72 66
11 b g Josr Algarhoud(IRE) Primulette (Mummy's Pet)
131[3] (351) 905[4] (1062) 1158[6] 1502[3] 1927[2] 2980[6]

Llanarmon Lad (IRE) *Brian Ellison* 80
4 b g Red Clubs(IRE) Blue Crystal (IRE) (Lure (USA))
5484[2] (6178)

Llandanwg *Jamie Osborne* a37
2 b f Lawman(FR) New Light (Generous (IRE))
7301[6] 7779[8]

Llaregyb (IRE) *David Elsworth* 94
3 br g Dylan Thomas(IRE) Tango Tonic (IRE) (Trans Island)
1678[9] (2420) ◆ (2876) 3484[18]

Llewellyn *David Nicholls* a77 80
5 b g Shamardal(USA) Ffestiniog (IRE) (Efisio)
1459[2] 1693[2] 2028[2] 2119[6] 3945[6] 4956[U] 5138[4] 5378[3] 5783[2] 5973[3] (6549) 7374[3] 7595[3] 7885[5]

Llyrical *Derek Haydn Jones* 68
2 b g Firebreak One Of The Family (Alzao (USA))
2344[3] 2723[2] 3290[8] 4347[6] 6487[2] 7125[9]

Loafer *Olivia Maylam* a6
3 b g Beat Hollow Cartuccia (IRE) (Doyoun)
3821[8]

Lobster Pot *Hugo Palmer* 58
2 b f Dylan Thomas(IRE) Classical Flair (Distant Music (USA))
7244[3]

Local Flier *Brian Ellison* 63
2 b f Byron Local Fancy (Bahamian Bounty)
3084[6] 3324[9] (4847) 5468[3] 5710[6] 6872[8]

Local Lover (FR) *H-A Pantall* a83 100
3 ch c Choisir(AUS) La Victoria (IRE) (Brief Truce (USA))
999a[10] 1357a[8]

Local Singer (IRE) *Frank Sheridan* a65 87
5 b g Elusive City(USA) Alinga (IRE) (King's Theatre (IRE))
1221[2]

Lochalsh (IRE) *William Knight* 49
2 ch g Duke Of Marmalade(IRE) Kylemore (IRE) (Sadler's Wells (USA))
6355[8] 7069[11]

Loch Garman (IRE) *J S Bolger* 112
3 b c Teofilo(IRE) Irish Question (IRE) (Giant's Causeway (USA))
2290a[2] 2907a[10]

Lochiel *Ian Semple* a64 68
9 b g Mind Games Summerhill Special (IRE) (Roi Danzig (USA))
3199[5] 3930[5] (5137) (5592) 6087[5] 6552[12] 7735[4]

Lochluichart (IRE) *Ian Semple*
4 gr g Verglas(IRE) Hetty (IRE) (In The Wings)
2221[5]

Loch Ma Naire (IRE) *Ed Dunlop* a63 72
2 gr f Galileo(IRE) Hotelgenie Dot Com (Selkirk (USA))
7260[5] 7693[3] 7936[4]

Loch Moy *Richard Fahey* 69
3 b g Kyllachy Dixielake (IRE) (Lake Coniston (IRE))
1683[8] 3398[6] 4805[7] 5564[7] 6664[10]

Lockwood *Saeed bin Suroor* a94 116
4 gr g Invincible Spirit(IRE) Emily Bronte (Machiavellian (USA))
154a[4] 465a[10] ◆ 869a[4] 3839[3] (5013) (5794) 6392[2] 7190[9]

Locky Taylor (IRE) *Kevin Ryan* a52 25
2 b g Bushranger(IRE) Hawk Eyed Lady (IRE) (Hawk Wing (USA))
7341[8] 7978[8]

Locum *Mark H Tompkins* a65 63
8 ch g Dr Fong(USA) Exhibitor (USA) (Royal Academy (USA))
662[5]

Lodovico Il Moro (IRE) *L Riccardi* 100
3 b c Shamardal(USA) Kykuit (IRE) (Green Desert (USA))
1865a[3] 2490a[4] 7724a[5]

Logans Lad (IRE) *John Stimpson* a67 61
3 b g Baltic King Lulu Island (Zafonic (USA))
673[7] 1323[5] 3950[3] 6368[9] 7197[2] 7354[6]

Logans Legend (IRE) *Lawrence Mullaney* a68 62
5 b g Johannesburg(USA) Almost Blue (USA) (Mr Greeley (USA))
3286[9] 3946[4] 4160[4] 4891[10] 5471[9] 6633[6]

Loki's Revenge *William Jarvis* a92 79
5 b g Kyllachy Amira (Efisio)
2007[12]

Loki's Strike *Mrs K Burke* a57 65
3 ch g Firebreak Citron (Reel Buddy (USA))
1071[3] 1206[4]

Lolita Lebron (IRE) *Lawrence Mullaney* a71 80
4 b f Royal Applause Alsharq (IRE) (Machiavellian (USA))
3098[5] 3628[11]

Loma Mor *Alan McCabe* a64 67
2 b f Auction House(USA) Dancing Loma (FR) (Danehill Dancer (IRE))
(2510) 2758[3] 2993[3] 3439[5] 4498[4] 5595[8] 6493[8]

Lombok *Gary Moore* a71 66
7 b g Hernando(FR) Miss Rinjani (Shirley Heights)
3473[5] 3688[2] 5099[10]

Lomond Lassie *Keith Dalgleish* 48
2 ch f Sakhee's Secret Numanthia (IRE) (Barathea (IRE))
3280[7] 3724[6] 5877[6]

London Bridge (USA) *Jo Hughes* a108 104
3 b c Arch(USA) Kindness (Indian Ridge)
994[6] 2093[7] (3013) (3294) ◆ (3502) 4279[3] 5463a[4] (7687a)

London Citizen (USA) *K R Burke* a92 98
3 ch c Proud Citizen(USA) Sally Bowles (SAF) (London News (SAF))
1645[3] 1991[4] 2862[5] 3862[4] 4541[2] 5326a[2] (5986)

London Silver *Ben De Haan* 60
4 b g Zafeen(FR) Princess Londis (Interrex (CAN))
2417[13]

London Skolar *James Eustace* a59 27
3 b g Tobougg(IRE) Coh Sho No (Old Vic)
895[6] 1089[4] 1296[7] 8182[7]

Lone Rider (FR) *S Cerulis* a77 79
7 ch g American Post Treasure Hunt (FR) (Bold Arrangement)
5042a[5]

Lone Warrior (IRE) *David Evans* a81 97
2 b g Oratorio(IRE) Warrior Wings (Indian Ridge)
(3175) 3555[5] 4747[3] 5530[6] 6314[5] 6866[3] 6955[5]

Long Awaited (IRE) *David Barron* 98
5 b g Pivotal Desertion (IRE) (Danehill (USA))
2865[12] 3334[4] 4275[4] 4800[12]

Long John (AUS) *Peter Snowden* 113
3 b g Street Cry(IRE) Hosiery (AUS) (Night Shift (USA))
7556a[9]

Long Journey Home (IRE) *Daniel William O'Sullivan* a82 87
5 b g Dansili Quest For Eternity (IRE) (Sadler's Wells (USA))
4465a[11]

Longton *Richard Fahey* 75
2 b c Myboycharlie(IRE) Lauren Louise (Tagula (IRE))
4096[3] 4576[2] (5482)

Lookbeforeyouleap *David O'Meara* a75 69
3 ch f Teofilo(IRE) One Giant Leap (IRE) (Pivotal)
6780[5] 7066[3] 7791[3] 7881[2] 8115[5]

Look Here's Al *Ed McMahon* a72 60
2 gr g Alhaarth(IRE) Look Here's Dee (Dansili)
5494[4] 6342[3] (7200)

Look Left *Nikki Evans* 76
5 ch g Observatory(USA) Stage Left (Nashwan (USA))
1973[9] 2563[11]

Look On By *Ruth Carr* a63 63
3 gr g Byron Where's Carol (Anfield I)
964[7] 1349[7] 1762[8] 2501[4] 3082[7] 3463[4] 3772[2] 4008[4] 4824[6] (5016) 5642[5] 6083[8]

Looks Like Rain *Brian Ellison* a71 74
4 ch f Medicean Hippogator (USA) (Dixieland Band (USA))
1579[4] 2165[3] ◆ 2721[2] (3301) 4015[6] 4506[5] 5885[5]

Looks Like Slim *Ben De Haan* a46 56
6 b g Passing Glance Slims Lady (Theatrical Charmer)
6554[8]

Loot *Richard Fahey*
2 b c Bahamian Bounty Amira (Efisio)
6754[14]

Loraine *Jamie Osborne* a68 63
3 b f Sir Percy Emirates First (IRE) (In The Wings)
1300[6] 1712[4] 2095[5] 3040[6] 3859[2] 4170[5] 5596[4] 6019[4] (6400) 7093[5] 7622[3]

Lord Aeryn (IRE) *Richard Fahey* 95
6 b g Antonius Pius(USA) White Paper (IRE) (Marignan (USA))
1840[2] 2029[5] 2958[2] 3346[5] 4308[4] 4733[9] 5546[3] 6792[11] 7172[11]

Lord Ashley (IRE) *Tom Dascombe* 88
3 ch g Iffraaj Mrs Dalloway (IRE) (Key Of Luck (USA))
(1687) (2626) 3234[4] 3803[5] 4265[3] 5004[3] 5268[6]

Lord Avonbrook *Andrew Crook* a66 69
3 b g Avonbridge Miss Brookie (The West (USA))
1844[6]

Lord Brantwood *Mick Channon* 13
2 b c Sir Percy Diddymu (IRE) (Revoque (IRE))
7219[10]

Lord Buffhead *Richard Guest* a62 62
4 br g Iceman Royal Pardon (Royal Applause)
76[8] 276[2] (423) 558[11] 640[7] 760[11] 831[8] 968[8] 1395[12] 1731[3] 1929[9] 2043[4] 2217[7] 2611[3] 2835[8] 2998[8] 3654[5] 3994[3] 4102[7] 4840[11] (5470) 5864[5] 5965[2] 6219[2] 6344[9] 6478[12] 6994[6] 8002[9] 6604[5] 6687[3] 6944[13] 8169[7]

Lord Clyde *Richard Fahey* 74
2 ch g Sakhee's Secret Sabina (Prince Sabo)
1108[3] 2830[2] 3077[3]

Lord Emery (GER) *M Figge* 85
5 b c Mamool(IRE) Latley (GER) (Sillery (USA))
315a[5] 6421a[2]

Lord Franklin *Eric Alston* a59 75
4 ch g Iceman Zell (IRE) (Lend A Hand)
1401[10] 2089[8] 2536[3] 2972[3] (3203) 3895[2] (4070) 4446[4] 4953[3] 5304[2] 6667[2]

Lord Golan *Violet M Jordan* a60 53
5 b g Singspiel(IRE) Lady Golan (IRE) (Golan (IRE))
752[3] 789[10] 1217[8] 1916[6] 7440[3] 7951[9]

Lord Kanaloa (JPN) *Takayuki Yasuda* 129
5 b c King Kamehameha(JPN) Lady Blossom (JPN) (Storm Cat (USA))
(8209a)

Lord Lexington *Richard Hannon Snr* 48
2 ch c Dutch Art Spiralling (Pivotal)
4640[10] 5811[8] 6896[7] 8133[7]

Lord Of The Dance (IRE) *Michael Mullineaux* a77 96
7 ch g Indian Haven Maine Lobster (USA) (Woodman (USA))
192[5] 218[8] 410[6] (426) 518[5] 705[9] 758[5] 987[7] 1038[3] (1172) 1303[3] 1514[3] 1746[6] (1827) 2232[5] 2646[6] (3207) 3349[10] (3683) 3984[6] (4746) 5026[7] 5681[15] 6164[3] 6792[9] 7337[15]

Lord Ofthe Shadows (IRE) *Richard Hannon Snr* a98 93
4 ch g Kyllachy Golden Shadow (IRE) (Selkirk (USA))
690[10] 865[4] 1327[2] 2841[2] ◆ 3108[4] 3697[3] 4258[4] 4488[5] 4923[7] 6956[3]

Lord Paget *Reg Hollinshead* a66 49
4 b g Three Valleys(USA) Appelone (Emperor Jones (USA))
42[5] 110[5] 240[4] 381[7] 927[2] 1893[10]

Lordship (IRE) *Tom Gretton* a21 51
9 b g King's Best(USA) Rahika Rose (Unfuwain (USA))
4070[12] 4623[10] 5091[5] 7636[4]

Lord Unfuwain *M Sardelli* 86
3 br c Byron Larousse (Unfuwain (USA))
1865a[8]

Loredana (FR) *M Delzangles* 103
3 b f Azamour(IRE) Luna Caerla (IRE) (Caerleon (USA))
5297a[9]

Lorimer's Lot (IRE) *Tim Walford* 74
2 ch f Camacho Alwiyda (USA) (Trempolino (USA))
1573[3] 1839[5] (2117) 2767[3] 3459[16] 4965[5] 5468[8]

Los Nadis (GER) *Jim Goldie* 86
9 ch g Hernando(FR) La Estrella (GER) (Desert King (IRE))
1273[8] 6585[5] 7193[24]

Lost In Paris (IRE) *Tim Easterby* a76 84
7 b g Elusive City(USA) Brazilia (Forzando)
1308[8] 1649[14] 2031[12] 2614[2] (2832) 3331[4] 4047[12] (4620) 4860[12] 5639[5] 6273[8] 6848[14] 6920[12]

Lost In The Moment (IRE) *Saeed bin Suroor* a103 113
6 b h Danehill Dancer(IRE) Streetcar (IRE) (In The Wings)
(3830) 4944[2] 5531[3] (6253a)

Lothair (IRE) *Alan Swinbank* a41 74
4 b g Holy Roman Emperor(IRE) Crafty Example (USA) (Crafty Prospector (USA))
1994[4] 2409[10] 4292[2] 5341[5] (5876) (6053) (6180) 6728[3] 6908[3] 7030[12]

Lothian Countess *Ian Semple* a36 64
3 ch f Auction House(USA) Immortelle (Arazi (USA))
2888[9] 3929[5] 4292[6] 8351[11]

Louarn (IRE) *J Heloury* 82
2 b f Elusive City(USA) Lil's Jessy (IRE) (Kris)
7939a[12]

L'Oublieuse (FR) *J Bertran De Balanda* 15
2 b f Namid Luteine (FR) (Sabrehill (USA))
6059a[14]

Loucal *Noel Quinlan* a59 64
3 b c Lucky Story(USA) Penny Ha'Penny (Bishop Of Cashel)
(1759) 2129[5] 2501[5] 3041[2] 3739[2] 4045[3] 4721[6] 5650[6]

Loud *Mark Johnston* a74 79
3 ch g Dutch Art Applauding (IRE) (Royal Applause)
(7073) 7436[4] 7742[8]

Louis The Pious *David O'Meara* 106
5 bb g Holy Roman Emperor(IRE) Whole Grain (Polish Precedent (USA))
2366[6] 3558[12] (4058) 4986[7] 5545[12] 6623[2] 7208[10] 7495[9]

Louis Vee (IRE) *Roy Brotherton* a20 20
5 bb g Captain Rio Mrs Evans (IRE) (College Chapel)
8054[6] 8142[10]

Loukoumi *Tim Easterby* a42 65
5 b f Iffraaj Odalisque (IRE) (Machiavellian (USA))
1802[11] 2280[9] 2536[5] 2956[8] 5198[5] 5426[6] 5709[4] 6918[5]

Loulou Vuitton *Steph Hollinshead* a61 54
3 ch f Needwood Blade Shepherds Warning (IRE) (Vettori (IRE))
106[6] 561[2] 796[2] 923[7] 3327[3] 3699[6] 4064[5] 5353[7] 5818[5] 8418[9]

Love And Cherish (IRE) *David Wachman* a93 96
3 b f Excellent Art Party Feet (IRE) (Noverre (USA))
7361a[5]

Love Club *Brian Baugh* a50 54
5 ch g Kheleyf(USA) Avondale Girl (IRE) (Case Law)
326[4] 610[7] 754[5] 997[5] 1356[7]

Loved One *James Fanshawe* a61 82
3 b f Medicean Embraced (Pursuit Of Love)
1891[6] 2560[6] 3136[4] 4013[6] (4927) 5758[2] 6951[7]

Lovedose *F-H Graffard* a60 47
3 b f Duke Of Marmalade(IRE) Angel Rose (IRE) (Definite Article)
7187a[7]

Love Excel *Charles Hills* a84
3 b c Exceed And Excel(AUS) Navajo Love Song (IRE) (Dancing Brave (USA))
1713[5] (8303)

Love In The Desert *Noel Quinlan* 94
2 b f Lemon Drop Kid(USA) Jenny Lake (USA) (Danzig (USA))
2601^3 (3023) 3829^3 4742^4

Love Island *Richard Whitaker* a98 98
4 b f Acclamation Sally Traffic (River Falls)
(1807) 2031^8 2476^3 2988^3 3367^12 (3892) 4263^2 5544^12 6564^2 6845^4 *7642^9 7851^2* ◆ *8064^5*

Lovelocks (IRE) *Charles Hills* 70
2 b f High Chaparral(IRE) Civility Cat (USA) (Tale Of The Cat (USA))
4702^6 ◆ 5330^4 7277^5

Lovely Lily *Bill Turner* a7 47
2 ch f Dutch Art Amelie Pouliche (FR) (Desert Prince (IRE))
4937^8 *5351^7* 6279^11

Lovely Pass (IRE) *Saeed bin Suroor* a102 95
3 b f Raven's Pass(USA) Macadamia (IRE) (Classic Cliche (IRE))
(554a) 837a^2 3524^14 4081^7

Love Magic *Sir Michael Stoute* a77 85
3 b f Dansili Magical Romance (IRE) (Barathea (IRE))
1822^2 2844^5 4278^4 5169^2

Love Marmalade (IRE) *Mark Johnston* a74 89
3 ch c Duke Of Marmalade(IRE) Green Castle (IRE) (Indian Ridge)
(1685) *1923^2* (2235) ◆ 2457^4 2879^6 3607^5 (4280) 4441^2 4798^3 5006^5 5768^10 6163^7 6514^5 7028^9

Love Pegasus (USA) *Paddy Butler* a58 52
7 bb g Fusaichi Pegasus(USA) Take Charge Lady (USA) (Dehere (USA))
158^10 475^8 579^11 703^7 820^8 2333^7

Lover Man (IRE) *Keith Dalgleish* a81 104
4 b g Lawman(FR) Seltitude (IRE) (Fairy King (USA))
(3187a) 6623^26

Love's Last Adieu *J S Moore* 34
2 b f Byron Last Romance (IRE) (Last Tycoon)
1574^4 2068^6 2475^7 3255^6

Lovesome *Michael Bell* a74 81
3 b f Kheleyf(USA) Heavenly Bay (USA) (Rahy (USA))
1371^2 1698^5 2546^3 3537^4 (4068) 4453^4 5152^2 5406^7 *6341^9 7487^5*

Love Tangle (IRE) *Brian Meehan* 73
2 b g Azamour(IRE) Dragnet (IRE) (Rainbow Quest (USA))
6762^10 (7773)

Love You Louis *J R Jenkins* a78 76
7 b g Mark Of Esteem(IRE) Maddie's A Jem (Emperor Jones (USA))
(135) 1058^4 1331^3 2132^2 *2772^3* 3317^5 4866^5

Love Your Looks *Mike Murphy* a98 95
5 b f Iffraaj Play Around (IRE) (Niniski (USA))
1544^3

Loving Home *John Gosden* 55
2 b c Shamardal(USA) Fallen In Love (Galileo (IRE))
7654^3 ◆

Loving Spirit *James Toller* a103 106
5 b g Azamour(IRE) Lolla's Spirit (IRE) (Montjeu (IRE))
1545^2 2254^8 ◆ 3527^6 4744^3 5738^11 *6199^3* 7014^3

Loving Your Work *George Baker* a63 62
2 b g Royal Applause Time Crystal (IRE) (Sadler's Wells (USA))
3155^7 3853^6 4773^5 5472^9 6322^13 *7935^4 7944^4*

Lowenstein (GER) *Frau J Mayer* a86 91
3 bb c Doyen(IRE) La Lyra (Slip Anchor)
2696a^7

Low Key (IRE) *John Butler* a70 93
6 b h Pentire La Capilla (Machiavellian (USA))
119^7 542^7

Lowther *Lee Carter* a97 83
8 b g Beat All(USA) Ever So Lonely (Headin' Up)
79^2 (133) 495^5 1061^8 1500^4 (1796) 1905^3 2265^5 3339^12 3974^12 4895^4 5348^8 (5855) 6336^13 (6927) 7542^5 7926^8 7990^2 8071^2 8301^12 8387^6

Lowtherwood *William Muir* a30 59
4 b g Green Desert(USA) Imperial Bailiwick (IRE) (Imperial Frontier (USA))
326^8 529^9

Loyal N Trusted *Karen Tutty* a70 63
5 b g Motivator Baby Don't Cry (USA) (Street Cry (IRE))
1950^11 2781^8 (3700) 4771^6 5177^5 *5594^4 6343^2 6777^4 7511^3* ◆ *7808^4*

Loyal Royal (IRE) *Milton Bradley* a66 25
10 b g King Charlemagne(USA) Supportive (IRE) (Nashamaa)
142^2 399^5 494^5 1101^7 1196^6 (1355) 1902^13 *2582^5 3498^8 4148^7*

Loyalty *Derek Shaw* a99 53
6 b g Medicean Ecoutila (USA) (Rahy (USA))
(79) (189) 400^10 495^3 644^3 (792) 865^2 945^9 1036^9 5894^12 6199^9 7648^9 7926^3 (7991) 8264^5 8391^2 8428^2

Luca Brasi (FR) *Francisco Castro* a94 97
9 b g Singspiel(IRE) Diamond Field (USA) (Mr Prospector (USA))
2146a^9

Lucanin *Sir Michael Stoute* a78 79
4 b g Galileo(IRE) Teggiano (IRE) (Mujtahid (USA))
1926^3 3692^8 5006^8

Lucarelli (GER) *Ferdinand J Leve* 104
7 b h High Chaparral(IRE) Lavorna (GER) (Acatenango (GER))
2492a^4 7566a^14

Lucarvey *Chris Dwyer*
2 b f Lucarno(USA) Split Briefs (IRE) (Mull Of Kintyre (USA))
5229^6 5490^8

Lucax (FR) *Mlle V Dissaux* a49 30
3 b f Lugny(FR) Calyx (FR) (Irish River (FR))
6713a^19 7188a^17 *7573a^16*

Lucayan (FR) *Neil Drysdale* a86 112
4 b c Turtle Bowl(IRE) La Vltava (IRE) (Grand Lodge (USA))
7563a^9

Lucies Diamond (IRE) *Michael Dods* a62 67
3 ch f Iffraaj Lucies Pride (IRE) (Noverre (USA))
828^2 3779^4 4727^10

Lucifers Shadow (IRE) *Mrs C Gilbert* a62 50
4 gr g Dark Angel(IRE) Marianne's Dancer (IRE) (Bold Fact (USA))
1312a^3 5328a^6 7145a^4

Lucilla *Stuart Williams* a60 48
3 b f Holy Roman Emperor(IRE) Lady In Waiting (Kylian (USA))
90^6 4830^6 *5923^9* 6260^7 6406^4

Lucio Silla *H-A Pantall* a82 82
3 ch c Osorio(GER) Serpina (IRE) (Grand Lodge (USA))
445a^3 (543a) 711a^4

Luck (IRE) *Stuart Williams* 80
3 b g Red Clubs(IRE) Pure Fiction (Zilzal (USA))
1293^3 1912^6

Luckster *David Evans* a57 60
3 b g Lucky Story(USA) Bisaat (USA) (Bahri (USA))
5630^4 *6363^2* ◆ *(7331)* 7395^2 *7668^5*

Lucky Beggar (IRE) *Charles Hills* 108
3 gr c Verglas(IRE) Lucky Clio (IRE) (Key Of Luck (USA))
1621^3 2039^2 2400^2 3103^4 3348^9 (4767) 5538^5 6990^11

Lucky Black Star (IRE) *George Baker* a62 58
3 b g Lawman(FR) Silver Bandana (USA) (Silver Buck (USA))
3418^11 4629^4 5497^4 *6137^2 6361^7 6996^4 7770^4*

Lucky Dan (IRE) *Paul Green* a83 80
7 b g Danetime(IRE) Katherine Gorge (USA) (Hansel (USA))
58^3 196^5 481^5 593^8 (795) 1067^3 1308^6 (1431) 1646^4 2755^10 2914^10 3093^13 3980^8 4018^4 4245^10 5049^8 6516^4 6850^5 7633^11

Lucky Di *Peter Hedger* a82 78
3 br f Araafa(IRE) Lucky Date (IRE) (Halling (USA))
225^2 674^6 1033^8 1477^7 2387^10 *2806^5* 3159^4 *3956^3 5280^3* (5697) 6338^5 6959^9 *7861^4* 8345^9

Lucky Diva *Bill Turner* a61 65
6 ch m Lucky Story(USA) Cosmic Countess (IRE) (Lahib (USA))
1664^7 1980^5 2921^7 3884^6 4655^4 5977^3

Lucky Dottie *Pat Phelan* a36
2 bb f Lucky Story(USA) Auntie Dot Com (Tagula (IRE))
5635^10 6079^8 6923^8

Lucky Henry *Clive Cox* a88 92
4 br g Lucky Story(USA) Seldemosa (Selkirk (USA))
1824^2 2193^4 (2728) 5348^6 6004^11

Lucky Jim *Chris Wall* a63 66
2 b g Lucky Story(USA) Lateralle (IRE) (Unfuwain (USA))
7469^9 *7854^5 8123^8*

Lucky Kristale *George Margarson* 110
2 b f Lucky Story(USA) Pikaboo (Pivotal)
(2382) (2758) ◆ 3522^6 (4253) (5680)

Lucky Lodge *Mel Brittain* a43 68
3 b g Lucky Story(USA) Melandre (Lujain (USA))
1791^7 1844^8 3134^3 3446^7 4970^5 (5485) 5788^2 6287^3 6771^10 6916^3 7282^2 *8037^9*

Lucky Look (FR) *D Smaga* 107
3 b f Teofilo(IRE) Victoria College (FR) (Rock Of Gibraltar (IRE))
5297a^4 6250a^2 7046a^3 7890a^11

Lucky Mark (IRE) *Garry Moss* a70 48
4 b g Moss Vale(IRE) Vracca (Vettori (IRE))
96^6 162^5 (354) 535^8 831^9 1063^6 1465^8 2280^8 *2949^6 7862^9* 8168^6 8272^2 8413^6

Lucky Mellor *Barry Murtagh* a27 62
6 b g Lucky Story(USA) Lady Natilda (First Trump)
8035^6 8272^8

Lucky Mountain *Scott Dixon* a67 51
3 ch c Mount Nelson Wild Clover (Lomitas)
428^3 867^5 1145^3 1453^2 1743^8 2175^5 3629^6 3859^5 4391^2 4722^6 5217^5 *6472^10* 7082^6 7514^10 7752^13

Lucky Nine (IRE) *C Fownes* a109 121
6 b g Dubawi(IRE) Birjand (Green Desert (USA))
8209a^7

Lucky North *Mel Brittain* 12
3 ch g Lucky Story(USA) Eurolink Cafe (Grand Lodge (USA))
6272^7

Lucky Numbers (IRE) *David O'Meara* a80 94
7 b g Key Of Luck(USA) Pure Folly (IRE) (Machiavellian (USA))
(2614) 2834^5 (3093) 3776^8 4812^8 5108^7 6273^7 6920^8

Lucky Prize *Mel Brittain* 35
3 b f Lucky Story(USA) Mana Pools (IRE) (Brief Truce (USA))
1389^5 3137^11 4049^9

Lucky Rebel *Lisa Williamson*
3 ch g Cockney Rebel(IRE) Para Siempre (Mujahid (USA))
2960^11

Luckys Connoisseur *Mark Johnston* 60
2 b c Art Connoisseur(IRE) Luck Will Come (IRE) (Desert Style (IRE))
2404^4 2712^5 2913^4 4054^2

Lucky Serena (IRE) *Agostino Affe'* 94
3 b f Bertolini(USA) Singora Lady (IRE) (Intikhab (USA))
3616a^4 7558a^7

Lucky Speed (IRE) *P Schiergen* 108
3 b c Silvano(GER) Lysuna (GER) (Monsun (GER))
1867a^2 (2696a) (4103a)

Lucky Suit (IRE) *Ronald Harris* a44 58
3 b f Red Clubs(IRE) Alexander Family (IRE) (Danetime (IRE))
3316^8

Lucky Surprise *Gay Kelleway* 64
2 b f Lucky Story(USA) Bella Bertolini (Bertolini (USA))
4215^9 4808^7 5609^4

Lucky Visione *Gay Kelleway* a70 70
2 b g Lucky Story(USA) Maid For Running (Namaqualand (USA))
1534^4 *1778^3 3436^3 4154^2* (4861) 6275^4 *6852^2* 7252^7

Lucky Windmill *Alan Swinbank* 81
6 b g Lucky Story(USA) Windmill Princess (Gorytus (USA))
1538^15

Lucky You (SWE) *Sandra Brolin*
2 ch f Heart Of Oak(USA) Quite Lucky (SWE) (Sharp Matt)
6452a^13

Lucrece *F Rohaut* a72 84
4 ch f Pivotal Sun Bittern (USA) (Seeking The Gold (USA))
7995a^13

Luctor Emergo (IRE) *Keith Dalgleish* a66 75
4 b g Amadeus Wolf Batilde (IRE) (Victory Piper (USA))
2540^10

Lucy Bee *Michael Appleby* a59 65
3 ch f Haafhd Procession (Zafonic (USA))
2770^5 3281^5 4826^6 (5331) *5594^10* 6588^7 6907^10 7150^9 *8186^3 8372^5*

Lucy Minaj *Bryan Smart* a47 60
3 b f Dylan Thomas(IRE) Keyaki (IRE) (Shinko Forest (IRE))
2635^2 3082^12 4114^U 4544^13 4891^12 6760^13 *7512^3 7966^10 8361^7*

Lucy Parsons (IRE) *David Barron* 72
2 ch f Thousand Words Consensus (IRE) (Common Grounds)
4539^4 (4963)

Luggers Hall (IRE) *Tony Carroll* a70 83
5 b g Cape Cross(IRE) Saabga (USA) (Woodman (USA))
333^3 637^3 (1239) 1290^3 1673^6 2385^5 2849^3 5065^2 6992^11

Luhaif *Mick Channon* a102 106
3 b g Cape Cross(IRE) Hot And Spicy (Grand Lodge (USA))
245a^10 553a^3 835a^5 *1383^2* 1623^5 2857^8 3235^3 3563^7 3987^5

Lui Rei (ITY) *Fawzi Abdulla Nass* a95 107
7 b g Reinaldo(FR) My Luigia (IRE) (High Estate)
150a^4 244a^6 746a^5

Lujeanie *Peter Crate* a88 84
7 br g Lujain(USA) Ivory's Joy (Tina's Pet)
353^4 443^7 780^6 ◆ *1096^7 1694^4 1984^7* 4707^10 *6928^4 7783^2 7897^7* 8128^6 ◆ 8384^5

Lulu's Gift (IRE) *Michael Mullineaux* 20
7 gr m Lahib(USA) She's A Gift (Bob's Return (IRE))
3272^11

Lulu The Zulu (IRE) *Michael Appleby* 80
5 ch f Danroad(AUS) Timbervati (USA) (Woodman (USA))
3191^5 3759^2 4200^3 4982^2 (5498) 6205^2 6977^5 7452^5

Lumiere Rose *H-A Pantall* 95
4 ch f Motivator La Dangeville (Danehill (USA))
2969a^6

Lunar Deity *Eve Johnson Houghton* a71 89
4 b g Medicean Luminda (IRE) (Danehill (USA))
1838^9 2255^9 2964^10 3733^9 3973^5 (4426) 5124^4 (5825) 6274^2 6871^4 *7464^12*

Lunar Spirit *Ralph Beckett* a67 55
2 b f Invincible Spirit(IRE) Kitty O'Shea (Sadler's Wells (USA))
3986^8 *6168^5 7260^3*

Luna Sunrise *Alan Jarvis* a19 33
2 b f Virtual Moon Crystal (Fasliyev (USA))
5922^11 6355^9

Lunesdale Buddy *Alan Berry*
2 b c Indesatchel(IRE) Darling Buds (Reel Buddy (USA))
5364^11 5970^9

Lunette (IRE) *Ralph Beckett* a77 75
3 b f Teofilo(IRE) Princess Luna (GER) (Grand Lodge (USA))
(3696) *4385^2* (4709) *7297^3 7785^8*

Lupara *Paul Fitzsimons* a20
2 ch f Double Trigger(IRE) Pooka's Daughter (IRE) (Eagle Eyed (USA))
4631^10

Lupin Pooter *David Barron* 83
4 b g Bertolini(USA) Carrie Pooter (Tragic Role (USA))
1248^5 ◆ 2031^14 2410^5 3331^10 4338^8

Lupo D'Oro (IRE) *John Best* a74 91
4 b g Amadeus Wolf Vital Laser (USA) (Seeking The Gold (USA))
1814^5 2388^4 2725^3 (3341) 4024^10 4800^3 5533^7 5998^14 6331^12 7313^6

Lustrous *Richard Hannon Snr* 94
2 b f Champs Elysees Tamzin (Hernando (FR))
(6141) 6350^4 7194^8

Luthien (IRE) *Alex Hales* a66 31
7 b m Polish Precedent(USA) Triplemoon (USA) (Trempolino (USA))
2212^6

Lutine Bell *Mike Murphy* a79 100
6 ch g Starcraft(NZ) Satin Bell (Midyan (USA))
1542^6 2265^6 2858^3 4642^3 5518^6 *6608^7* 6988^2 *7123^7 7436^6*

Lutine Charlie (IRE) *Pat Eddery* a70 69
6 b g Kheleyf(USA) Silvery Halo (USA) (Silver Ghost (USA))
899^3 1426^5 3676^3 4070^3 4194^4 4894^2 5622^6 5948^5 *7740^3 7858^9 8087^9 8125^8* 8329^10

Lutra *Paul Cole* 13
2 ch f Halling(USA) Tarkamara (IRE) (Medicean)
6973^11

Luv U Honey *Jo Hughes* a59 59
2 b f Captain Gerrard(IRE) Lady Suesanne (IRE) (Cape Cross (IRE))
1421^8

Luv U Whatever *Jo Hughes* a81 50
3 b g Needwood Blade Lady Suesanne (IRE) (Cape Cross (IRE))
(717) 824^5 (1071) 1206^2 1685^9 *(2175) (8372)*

Lybica (IRE) *Gary Moore* a76 66
3 b f Galileo(IRE) Tingling (USA) (Storm Cat (USA))
1640^6 2192^9 2850^5 4898^5 *6109^2* ◆ *(6521)* 7431^4 *7786^7*

Lykea (IRE) *C Laffon-Parias* 93
3 b f Oasis Dream Alyzea (IRE) (King Charlemagne (USA))
7085a^3 7995a^12

Lynngale *Jo Hughes* a59 51
2 b f Myboycharlie(IRE) Belle Annie (USA) (Aptitude (USA))
5727^10 *7955^3*

Lyn Valley *Mark Johnston* 97
2 b c Shamardal(USA) Demisemiquaver (Singspiel (IRE))
1989^4 4096^2 4858^2 (5539) (6064) 6645^15 7534^10

Lyric Ace (IRE) *Paul D'Arcy* a92 93
3 b g Thousand Words Aces Dancing (GER) (Big Shuffle (USA))
1033^11 2213^8

Lyric Ballad *Hughie Morrison* a65 83
3 b f Byron Skies Are Blue (Unfuwain (USA))
(2606) (3177) 4066^3 6533^3 6976^9

Lyric Piece *Sir Mark Prescott Bt* a82 84
3 ch f Dutch Art Humouresque (Pivotal)
5392^4 (5835) 6098^3 *7000^3 7330^5 7491^4*

Lyric Poet (USA) *David Thompson* a77 69
6 bb g Distorted Humor(USA) Baltic Nations (USA) (Seattle Slew (USA))
145^7 542^4 1789^9 2313^12

Lyric Street (IRE) *Jeremy Noseda* a80 99
5 b g Hurricane Run(IRE) Elle Danzig (GER) (Roi Danzig (USA))
2671^8 3531^4 6573^3 *7115^6*

Lytham (IRE) *Tony Carroll* a61 62
12 b g Spectrum(IRE) Nousaiyra (IRE) (Be My Guest (USA))
(530) 625^4 (725) 852^2 978^4 1090^2 1298^10 1987^7 3213^3

Maakirr (IRE) *Roy Bowring* a73 31
4 b g Street Cry(IRE) Zayn Zen (Singspiel (IRE))
1202^2 1522^2 2576^3 3719^5 4070^10 *5677^5* 6760^11 7109^8 *7354^2 7512^2* ◆ *7952^4* 8270^4 8407^2

Maarek *B Lalor* a61 118
6 b g Pivotal Ruby Rocket (IRE) (Indian Rocket)
(1704a) 2368^5 3557^9 6414a^11 (6639) (7054a) 7364^12

Maath Gool *M Al Muhairi* a76 87
6 b g Dubawi(IRE) My First Romance (Danehill (USA))
412a^13

Mabait *David Simcock* a93 103
7 b g Kyllachy Czarna Roza (Polish Precedent (USA))
1542^7 2013^12 2254^11 2649^5 3300^5 3697^9 4062^2 5474^3 5738^5 5992^4 (6767) (7018)

Mabdhool (IRE) *Marcus Tregoning* 71
2 b g Mount Nelson Berry Baby (IRE) (Rainbow Quest (USA))
3290^6 3853^4 4640^7

Ma Bella Paola (FR) *Paul Cole* a27
2 b f Naaqoos Dilag (IRE) (Almutawakel)
7893^10

Macaabra (IRE) *James Tate* a63 83
3 b f Exceed And Excel(AUS) Al Cobra (IRE) (Sadler's Wells (USA))
1447^8 (1760) *2329^7* (2836) (3016) 3153^4

Macau (FR) *Matthieu Palussiere* 88
2 b f Dashing Blade Macarena (GER) (Platini (GER))
5555a^10

Macbeth (IRE) *K J Condon* 99
4 b g Acclamation Filandre (Cadeaux Genereux)
1168a^5 2105a^4 3142a^10 3599a^11

Maccabees *Roger Curtis* a55 59
4 b g Motivator Takarna (IRE) (Mark Of Esteem (IRE))
704^9 1949^10 2714^8 2801^8

Macchiara *Rae Guest* a75 84
4 ch f Medicean Castaway Queen (IRE) (Selkirk (USA))
1751^7 3111^5 3583^3 (4183) 4642^7 5310^8 6538^7

Macdillon *Stuart Kittow* a81 78
7 b g Acclamation Dilys (Efisio)
1814^7 2388^5 2657^5 3371^5 3855^8 4487^4 5060^2 5441^3 5956^3 6745^4

Macdonald Mor (IRE) *Michael Wigham* a76 52
4 b g Dansili Imperial Beauty (USA) (Imperial Ballet (IRE))
740^3 1947^7 2640^7

Macevil (USA) *Kellyn Gorder* a68
3 b g Doneraile Court(USA) Lucretia (USA) (Bertrando (USA))
786a^2

Machete Mark (IRE) *G M Lyons* a80 98
3 b g Indian Haven Beziers (IRE) (Fasliyev (USA))
3484^6 4743^2 5728^7 6883a^12

Mack's Sister *Dean Ivory* a68 30
6 ch m Pastoral Pursuits Linda's Schoolgirl (IRE) (Grand Lodge (USA))
354^4 559^3 806^6 1063^4

Mack The Knife (FR) *C Lerner* 59
3 b c Enrique Iputaspellonyou (Highest Honor (FR))
3454a^6

Mac Moneysac (GER) *A Wohler* 87
2 ch c Sholokhov(IRE) Manipura (GER) (Dansili)
7232a^6

Macnamara *Harry Dunlop* a20
2 ch f Dylan Thomas(IRE) Portrait Of A Lady (IRE) (Peintre Celebre (USA))
6409^12 *6922^11*

Mac's Power (IRE) *Willie Musson* a102 104
7 b g Exceed And Excel(AUS) Easter Girl (Efisio)
3840^13 4986^23 6352^14 7427^7

Mac's Superstar (FR) *James Fanshawe* a77 50
3 b g Elusive City(USA) Diamond Light (USA) (Fantastic Light (USA))
1908[5]

Mac Tiernan (IRE) *Philip Kirby* a64 72
6 b g Minashki(IRE) Softly Softly (IRE) (Lucky Guest)
(2977) (3252)

Mad About Harry (IRE) *John Best* a71 36
3 b g Mujadil(USA) Caro Mio (IRE) (Danehill Dancer (IRE))
685[5] 877[3] 1423[9] 2156[2] 2432[12] 3243[13] 6810[9]

Madagascar Moll (IRE) *David O'Meara* a69 68
2 bb f Captain Gerrard(IRE) Fontanally Springs (IRE) (Namid)
(3942) 4965[8] 5710[8] 6778[2] 6967[2]

Madame Blavatsky (FR) *Simon West* a32 54
5 gr f Super Celebre(FR) Lovarisk (FR) (Take Risks (FR))
1790[8] 2316[9] 2536[7] 2796[6] 3727[2] 4052[7] 4763[3] 7372[7] 7963[10]

Madame Chiang *David Simcock* 77
2 b f Archipenko(USA) Robe Chinoise (Robellino (USA))
(7449) ◆

Madame Defarge (IRE) *Michael Bell* 93
3 b f Motivator Friendlier (Zafonic (USA))
2049[3] ◆ 2842[11]

Madame Elizabeth *Andrew Hollinshead* a75 81
3 b f Multiplex Madame Jones (IRE) (Lycius (USA))
4515[3] 4941[6] 5181[2] 5942[6] (6379) 7256[5] 7491[7]

Madame Giry (IRE) *David O'Meara* 29
2 b f Intense Focus(USA) Edouna (FR) (Doyoun)
4156[8] 4538[11]

Madame Katie (IRE) *Nigel Tinkler* 42
2 ch f Kheleyf(USA) Diamond Katie (IRE) (Night Shift (USA))
5053[10] 5578[3]

Madame Kintyre *Rod Millman* a49 54
5 b f Trade Fair Chorus (Bandmaster (USA))
2096[12] 3375[9] 4603[4] 5094[5] 5388[3] 5670[9] 6436[2] 7068[2] 7957[7] 8338[9]

Madame Mere (IRE) *Roger Varian* 78
2 b f Dalakhani(IRE) Napoleon's Sister (IRE) (Alzao (USA))
7450 [2]

Madame Mime Artist *Alastair Lidderdale* a49
2 b f Dutch Art Silent Waters (Polish Precedent (USA))
8332[10]

Madame Mirasol (IRE) *Kevin Ryan* a72 70
2 b f Sleeping Indian Confidentiality (IRE) (Desert Style (IRE))
1718[7] 2625[8] 3605[5] (5865) 7252[5] 7418[14] 7782[2] 7892[2] 8267[2]

Madame Vestris (IRE) *Sir Michael Stoute* a81 87
3 ch f Galileo(IRE) Mrs Lindsay (USA) (Theatrical (IRE))
2389[8] (3491) 4417[3] 5514[3] 6693[5] 7497[2]

Madam Fifi *Alan McCabe* a29 49
3 b f Firebreak Reel Cool (Reel Buddy (USA))
706[7] 1291[7] 1648[6] 2080[12]

Madam Lilibet (IRE) *Sharon Watt* 68
4 b f Authorized(IRE) Foxilla (IRE) (Foxhound (USA))
(6177) (7423)

Madam Mojito (USA) *John Quinn* a68 85
3 b f Smart Strike(CAN) Asuncion (USA) (Powerscourt)
2430[11] 3058[8]

Madam Tessa (IRE) *Tim Vaughan* a37 51
5 br f Hawk Wing(USA) Anita's Contessa (IRE) (Anita's Prince)
1342[6] 1949[7] 2828[11] 3314[3] 3954[6] 4355[8] 4604[6]

Madeed *Brian Meehan* 84
2 b c Nayef(USA) Danehill Dreamer (USA) (Danehill (USA))
4764[2] (5698)

Madeira Girl (IRE) *Jonjo O'Neill* a72 80
4 b f Bachelor Duke(USA) Last Cry (FR) (Peintre Celebre (USA))
2948[3] 3375[5] 3817[6] 4145[3] 5070[7] (5967) 7038[4] 7881[14]

Made It (IRE) *Anthony Carson* a43 31
3 b f Oratorio(IRE) Theebah (Bahamian Bounty)
509[6] 1986[8]

Made Of More *Roger Ingram* a59 63
4 ch c Auction House(USA) Dam Certain (IRE) (Damister (USA))
132[9]

Maderienne (FR) *L Baudron* a68 53
3 ch f King's Best(USA) Sometime (FR) (Anabaa (USA))
461a[7]

Mad For Fun (IRE) *Paul Midgley* a50 56
4 b f Ivan Denisovich(IRE) Franny (Selkirk (USA))
884[6] 1104[7] 1842[8] 2073[6] 2752[8]

Mad Jazz *Tony Coyle* a59 76
3 b f Sir Percy Gwen John (USA) (Peintre Celebre (USA))
1365[3] (2555) 2769[4] 3067[5]

Mad Moose (IRE) *Nigel Twiston-Davies* 98
9 ch g Presenting Sheshollystar (IRE) (Fourstars Allstar (USA))
(1804) 2212[2] 2668[RR] 3560[18]

Madoka (FR) *L A Urbano-Grajales* 67
2 b f Lucky Story(USA) Regal Step (Royal Applause)
7568a[3]

Madrasa (IRE) *Keith Reveley* a63 75
5 b g High Chaparral(IRE) Shir Dar (FR) (Lead On Time (USA))
1993[7] 2316[3] 2720[5] 2860[3] 3589[2] (4563) 4809[3] 4969[5] 5831[6]

Madurai (GER) *W Hickst* 99
2 b c Marju(IRE) Moonlight Danceuse (IRE) (Bering)
7232a[3] 7726a[2]

Mafeteng *Roger Charlton* a70 77
5 b f Nayef(USA) Marakabei (Hernando (FR))
1728[9]

Mafi (IRE) *Mark Hoad* a72 75
5 b g Modigliani(USA) Yulara (IRE) (Night Shift (USA))
205[2] 320[6] (638) (749) 984[3] 1181[5] 1514[7] 1780[3] 2228[3] 2807[6] 3642[10] 8453[11]

Magali (GER) *W Giedt* 85
3 ch f Monsun(GER) Montfleur (Sadler's Wells (USA))
3604a[8] 6887a[14]

Maggie Dalton (IRE) *J S Bolger* 94
4 b f Mr Greeley(USA) Bowstring (IRE) (Sadler's Wells (USA))
3599a[2] 3869a[10]

Maggie Mey (IRE) *Lawrence Mullaney* a48 63
5 b f Kodiac Christmas Kiss (Taufan (USA))
2537[5] 3029[2] 3444[5] 4562[3] 4893[7] 5198[4] 5903[5]

Maggie Pink *Michael Appleby* a79 73
4 b f Beat All(USA) Top Notch (Alderbrook)
437[5] 617[4] 801[4] 919[3] (1079) 1151[2] (1503) 2092[2] 2884[6] 7595[10] 7824[2] 7861[3] (8134)

Maggie's Diamond *Richard Fahey* 59
2 b f Authorized(IRE) Parsonagehotelyork (IRE) (Danehill (USA))
5727[8]

Maghaanem (IRE) *Ed Dunlop* a68
2 b c Acclamation Shishangaan (IRE) (Mujadil (USA))
7119[6]

Magical Dream (IRE) *A P O'Brien* 106
3 b f Galileo(IRE) Red Evie (IRE) (Intikhab (USA))
3381a[2] 4550a[6] 4985[8] 6224a[11] 6416a[3]

Magical Empress (IRE) *Mme Pia Brandt* a76 72
3 b f Alhaarth(IRE) Testa Unica (ITY) (Nordance (USA))
6711a[7]

Magical Kingdom (IRE) *Marco Botti* a79 70
3 b c Danehill Dancer(IRE) Al Saqiya (USA) (Woodman (USA))
(333) 1470[4] 2416[7]

Magical Macey (USA) *David Barron* a86 107
6 ch g Rossini(USA) Spring's Glory (USA) (Honour And Glory (USA))
2396[5] 2669[10] (3776) 6305[8] 6391[5]

Magical Mischief *Chris Fairhurst*
3 b f Rob Roy(USA) Magical Flute (Piccolo)
7067[9] 7311[7]

Magicalmysterytour (IRE) *Willie Musson* a30 85
10 b g Sadler's Wells(USA) Jude (Darshaan)
8447[9]

Magical Rose (IRE) *Paul D'Arcy* a76 75
3 b f Elusive City(USA) Xarzee (IRE) (Xaar)
1471[5] 1770[7] 2223[6] 3289[2] 3611[7] 4453[3] 4865[3] 5799[5] 6317[10] 6734[7] 8019[3] 8432[4]

Magical Speedfit (IRE) *George Margarson* a77 70
8 ch g Bold Fact(USA) Magical Peace (IRE) (Magical Wonder (USA))
(1694) 2225[11] 2790[7] 4746[15]

Magic Art (IRE) *W Figge* 88
3 b f Nayef(USA) Artisti (Cape Cross (IRE))
6031a[7]

Magic Artist (IRE) *W Figge* 102
2 br c Iffraaj Artisti (Cape Cross (IRE))
5911a[2] 7232a[4]

Magic City (IRE) *Richard Hannon Snr* a89 107
4 b g Elusive City(USA) Annmarie's Magic (IRE) (Flying Spur (AUS))
1363[6] (2618) 3757[3] (4440) (4879) (5738) ◆ 6595[5] 7014[9] 7247[7] 7856[2]

Magic Destiny *K R Burke* 93
4 b f Dubai Destination(USA) Magic Music (IRE) (Magic Ring (IRE))
3684[5] (4097) 4514[2] 5246[4] 5684[8] 6625[2] 7538[4]

Magic Hurricane (IRE) *James Fanshawe* a87 78
3 b g Hurricane Run(IRE) Close Regards (IRE) (Danehill (USA))
5720[3] 6133[2]

Magician (IRE) *A P O'Brien* a83 123
3 b c Galileo(IRE) Absolutelyfabulous (IRE) (Mozart (IRE))
(2211) ◆ (2677a) ◆ 3421[9] (7712a)

Magic Ice *Brian Ellison* a56 57
3 b f Royal Applause Winter Ice (Wolfhound (USA))
356[3] 669[6] 1349[2] 1458[3] 1962[10] 2643[8] 5708[7] 6219[8] 6345[8]

Magic Lando (FR) *Ismail Mohammed* a58 70
3 b g Lando(GER) Blackberry Pie (USA) (Gulch (USA))
1481[6] 2548[4] 3250[7] 5204[4] 5833[11] 6612[8] 7082[3] 7322[7]

Magic Mirage (FR) *Y Barberot* 58
3 b c Observatory(USA) Magic Sun (GER) (Speedmaster (GER))
6711a[10]

Magic Music Man *K R Burke* 9
2 b c Authorized(IRE) Magic Music (IRE) (Magic Ring (IRE))
6581[12]

Magic Of Reality (FR) *Lady Cecil* 96
3 ch f Galileo(IRE) Breathe (FR) (Ocean Of Wisdom (USA))
1671[6] ◆ 2049[4] 2850[2] ◆ (3372) (4307) 5246[2] 6792[12]

Magic Secret *William Muir* 96
5 b g Trade Fair Just Devine (IRE) (Montjeu (IRE))
3840[8] 4812[9] 6647[11] (6959)

Magic Shoes (IRE) *Roger Charlton* a56
2 b f Manduro(GER) Ammo (IRE) (Sadler's Wells (USA))
7645[10]

Magic Skyline (IRE) *Brian Ellison* 66
3 b f Refuse To Bend(IRE) Grecian Air (FR) (King's Best (USA))
3775[8] 4157[5] 4805[2] 5707[3] 6296[4] 6601[6]

Magika *Marco Botti* a84 77
3 b f Dubawi(IRE) Aline's Wings (ITY) (In The Wings)
1923[4] 2555[3] 3055[4] 3535[3] 4417[4] 5130[2] (7258) (8276) ◆

Magique (IRE) *Jeremy Noseda* a81 81
3 b f Jeremy(USA) Misskinta (IRE) (Desert Sun)
2127[4] 2606[4] 3173[9] 4383[2] 4721[2] 5245[4] 6531[7] (7256) 7608[7]

Magistral *John Gosden* 93
3 b g Manduro(GER) Tamalain (USA) (Royal Academy (USA))
3250[3] (3902) 4765[6] 5562[3] 6951[2] 7696[2] 7820[12]

Maglietta Fina (IRE) *Robert Cowell* a67 92
4 gr f Verglas(IRE) Whipped Queen (USA) (Kingmambo (USA))
1563a[6] 4389[4] 4863[3] 5537[12] (6381) 7085a[8] 7373[7] 7776[4] 8232[10]

Magma *Andrew Balding* a82 80
4 b f Singspiel(IRE) Rakata (USA) (Quiet American (USA))
1663[8] (2085)

Magnolia Ridge (IRE) *Kristin Stubbs* a92 80
3 b g Galileo(IRE) Treasure The Lady (IRE) (Indian Ridge)
5021a[11] 7361a[9] 8159[5] 8400[5]

Magnus Maximus *Richard Hannon Snr* a84 72
2 b c Holy Roman Emperor(IRE) Chanrossa (IRE) (Galileo (IRE))
6635[3] 6953[12] (7155)

Magnus Romeo *Marco Botti* a55 41
2 b c Manduro(GER) Chili Dip (Alhaarth (IRE))
5488[9] 6365[3]

Magog *Roger Charlton* 96
3 br g Dansili Margarula (IRE) (Doyoun)
2271[2] ◆ (5743) ◆

Mahadee (IRE) *Ed de Giles* a85 80
8 br g Cape Cross(IRE) Rafiya (Halling (USA))
2571[4] 2920[7] 3901[4] 4593[7] 5387[3] (5948) 8219[9] 8450[7]

Mahajanga (FR) *C Boutin* a70 77
3 b f Amadeus Wolf Kota Kinabalu (Ashkalani (IRE))
(962a) 7573a[14]

Mahatta (IRE) *Charles Hills* a64 59
2 b f Halling(USA) Tafaani (IRE) (Green Desert (USA))
5394[10] 6141[5] 7296[8]

Mahdiyah *Saeed bin Suroor* a77
3 ch f Halling(USA) Malakaat (USA) (Danzig (USA))
5100[2] ◆ 5892[3] 7158[3] (7490)

Mahendranagar (FR) *J Boisnard* a83 81
3 b f Rail Link Maria Candela (Spectrum (IRE))
1602a[8]

Mahican (IRE) *Mark Johnston* a96 96
3 b g Cape Cross(IRE) Dark Indian (IRE) (Indian Ridge)
5563[2] ◆ (6050) (6387) 6537[2] 7022[7] 7304[4]

Mahlah (IRE) *Richard Hannon Snr* 79
2 b f Acclamation Somerset Falls (UAE) (Red Ransom (USA))
3049[6] (3760) 4742[8] 5272[4] 5955[4]

Mahnaz *A Fabre* a82 99
4 b f Dansili Minaccia (GER) (Platini (GER))
6294a[7] 7891a[2]

Mahon Falls *David Evans* a51 64
2 ch f Dandy Man(IRE) Saphire (College Chapel)
8026[8] 8114[3] 8368[6]

Mahyar Glaz (FR) *C Boutin* a81 66
3 b g Desert Style(IRE) Mahyara (FR) (Lomitas)
(331a) 544a[3]

Maid A Million *David Elsworth* a72 97
3 b f Kyllachy Poldhu (Cape Cross (IRE))
2229[3] (2763) ◆ 3039[7] 3718[2] 4492[3] 5125[2] 5439[2] 5538[3] 7015[3] 7470[7] 7538[3]

Maidana (IRE) *Tim Easterby* a32 36
2 ch f Intikhab(USA) Tofana (IRE) (Bold Fact (USA))
5543[8] 5900[5] 6286[10] 6726[9]

Maiden Approach *Richard Fahey* a68 60
2 b f New Approach(IRE) Ivowen (USA) (Theatrical (IRE))
6298[4] 6973[5] (7541) ◆

Maid In Rio (IRE) *Mark Johnston* 71
2 ch f Captain Rio Silver Whale (FR) (Highest Honor (FR))
4820[5] 5380[12] 5773a[15] (6465) 7221[8]

Maid Of Meft *Paul Midgley* a68 71
6 b m Auction House(USA) Lady Margaret (Sir Harry Lewis (USA))
1111[10] 1445[11] 1721[9] 2120[5] 3065[8] 4204[8]

Maid Of Tuscany (IRE) *Mark Usher* a49 58
2 b f Manduro(GER) Tuscania (USA) (Woodman (USA))
4640[8] 5922[7] 6739[13]

Maillot Jaune (IRE) *Patrick Holmes* a48 52
3 b f Ramonti(FR) Roclette (USA) (Rock Of Gibraltar (IRE))
3774[9] 4013[11] 5290[4] 6083[9] 6919[2] 8180[3]

Mainsail *P Bary* 112
4 b c Oasis Dream Docklands (USA) (Theatrical (IRE))
2559a[3] (3387a) 4104a[2] 5808a[9] 7047a[12]

Main Sequence (USA) *David Lanigan* a113 116
4 ch g Aldebaran(USA) Ikat (IRE) (Pivotal)
2252[3] 2811[2] 3608[4] 6198[3] 6636[3] 7367[8]

Mairise *Sir Michael Stoute* a67
2 b g Authorized(IRE) Maigold Lass (Mark Of Esteem (IRE))
7835[7] 8124[5] 8214[6]

Maisie's Moon (USA) *Hughie Morrison* a52 58
3 b f Curlin(USA) Reverently (CAN) (Pulpit (USA))
1747[8] 3178[3] 3885[7] 5198[8] 5395[8] 5923[11]

Maison Brillet (IRE) *Clive Drew* a69 63
6 b g Pyrus(USA) Stormchaser (IRE) (Titus Livius (FR))
53[8] (512) 816[5] 1097[5] 2136[4] 2570[4] 3328[7] 8182[6]

Majeed *David Simcock* a86 84
3 b g Mount Nelson Clever Millie (USA) (Cape Canaveral (USA))
(799) 2153[4] ◆ 3277[3] ◆ 7330[3]

Majenta (IRE) *Kevin Prendergast* a96 99
3 b f Marju(IRE) What A Picture (FR) (Peintre Celebre (USA))
7230a[4] 7723a[9]

Majestic Alexander (IRE) *David Evans* a82 91
2 b f Bushranger(IRE) Tshusick (Dancing Brave (USA))
(1399) ◆ 2426[8] 3311[2] (3863) 4025[3] 4855[7] 5476[8]

Majestic Angel (IRE) *Brian Rothwell* 43
4 b f Majestic Missile(IRE) Free Angel (USA) (Mystery Storm (USA))
3026[16] 3196[9] 4544[11]

Majestic Dream (IRE) *Michael Easterby* a85 80
5 b g Exceed And Excel(AUS) Tallassee (Indian Ridge)
1460[2] 2081[2] 2659[5] 3087[8] 3462[2] 4051[6] 4956[8] 5481[10] 6720[2] 7595[11] 7824[20]

Majestic Jasmine (IRE) *John M Oxx* a94 93
3 ch f New Approach(IRE) Majestic Roi (USA) (Street Cry (IRE))
7361a[8]

Majestic Jess (IRE) *Luke Dace* a85 58
3 b g Majestic Missile(IRE) Ginger Not Blonde (USA) (Atticus (USA))
1345[4] (1784) 2393[3] 3494[2]

Majestic Manannan (IRE) *David Nicholls* a72 80
4 b g Majestic Missile(IRE) Miraculous (IRE) (Marju (IRE))
1681[4] 2268[8] 2702[7] (3738) 4074[6] 4814[2] 5088[8] 5887[2] 6515[13] 7593[9] 8319[6]

Majestic Moon (IRE) *Richard Fahey* 97
3 b g Majestic Missile(IRE) Gala Style (IRE) (Elnadim (USA))
2285[3] ◆ 2738[2] 3234[3] 3758[3] (4265) ◆ (4492) (4922) 5728[6] 6840[4] 7368[7]

Majestic Mount *R Pritchard-Gordon* a95 84
3 b c Exceed And Excel(AUS) Our Poppet (IRE) (Warning)
3454a[5]

Majestic Myles (IRE) *Richard Fahey* a85 114
5 b g Majestic Missile(IRE) Gala Style (IRE) (Elnadim (USA))
1235[7] 1691[2] 1835[4] 3822[4] 4284[6] 5651[17] 6623[20]

Majestic Oasis *Robert Cowell* a77 93
4 b f Oasis Dream Mycenae (Inchinor)
963a[2] 2264[7] 3835[5] 4181[5]

Majestic Power (GER) *M Rulec* a91 85
3 ch c Silvano(GER) Milana (GER) (Highest Honor (FR))
1511a[6] 7706a[5]

Majestic Queen (IRE) *Tracey Collins* a86 91
3 b f Kheleyf(USA) Night Fairy (IRE) (Danehill (USA))
(3845a)

Majestic Red (IRE) *Malcolm Saunders* 62
3 b f Red Clubs(IRE) Majestic Eviction (IRE) (King's Theatre (IRE))
2363[5] 2791[4] 3178[11] 3679[5] 4244[8] 4369[7]

Majestic Song *James Toller* a65
2 b f Royal Applause Sakhee's Song (IRE) (Sakhee (USA))
7737[3]

Majestic Stride (USA) *Jeff Bonde* a118
4 b g Trippi(USA) Great Looking Miss (USA) (Great Above (USA))
7713a[4]

Majestic Sun (IRE) *Peter Chapple-Hyam* a31 62
2 b c King's Best(USA) Shining Vale (USA) (Twilight Agenda (USA))
6184[8] 6931[9] 7271[4]

Majestic Timeline (IRE) *Adrian Brendan Joyce* a78 61
4 ch f Majestic Missile(IRE) Brooklands Time (IRE) (Danetime (IRE))
670[2] (997) (1356) ◆

Majestic Zafeen *Alastair Lidderdale* a83 61
4 b f Zafeen(FR) Arasong (Aragon)
3215[10] 4593[11] 7038[7] 7462[9]

Majesty (IRE) *Richard Hannon Snr* 87
3 gr c Shamardal(USA) Princess Serena (USA) (Unbridled's Song (USA))
3278[5] 3619[3] (4032) 5537[9]

Majeyda (USA) *Charlie Appleby* 101
2 bb f Street Cry(IRE) Alzerra (UAE) (Pivotal)
(3318) 3829[5] (4682) 6350[2] 7055a[9] (7695)

Majnon Fajer (IRE) *Roger Ingram* a36 33
3 b g Captain Marvelous(IRE) Noble View (USA) (Distant View (USA))
5133[13] 5588[11] 6036[6] 7265[13]

Major Buckley (IRE) *David Evans* a37
4 ch g Haafhd Woodwin (IRE) (Woodman (USA))
1072[6] 1987[6] 2533[P]

Major Crispies *James Eustace* 78
2 b g Pastoral Pursuits Nellie Melba (Hurricane Sky (AUS))
2741[3] 3374[3] 3991[3] 4948[8] 6233[4] 6972[8]

Major Domo (FR) *Alan Swinbank* a68 74
5 ch g Domedriver(IRE) Raphaela (FR) (Octagonal (NZ))
2277[11] 2552[3] 2990[13] 4159[4] ◆ (4759) 5640[9] 5972[6]

Major Eradicator (USA) *Alastair Lidderdale* a16 5
6 b g Purge(USA) Pontook (USA) (French Deputy (USA))
1120[6] 1251[8] 1270[10]

Majorities *Brian Meehan* 70
2 b g Major Cadeaux Mania (IRE) (Danehill (USA))
7270[3] 7818[4]

Major Jack *Roger Charlton* 72
2 b c Kheleyf(USA) Azeema (IRE) (Averti (IRE))
3374[11] 5399[5]

Major Maximus *Mrs C Gilbert* a69 31
6 br g Domedriver(IRE) Madame Maxine (USA) (Dayjur (USA))
(1739a) 7144a[4]

Major Muscari (IRE) *Shaun Harris* a61 52
5 ch g Exceed And Excel(AUS) Muscari (Indian Ridge)
997[11] 1042[8] 1396[9] 1748[9] 7347[12] 7508[3] 7903[3] 8050[2] 8271[2] 8338[2] (8413)

Major Rowan *Bryan Smart* 20
2 b g Captain Gerrard(IRE) Julie's Gift (Presidium)
7341[12] 7818[12]

Major Surprise (USA) *K R Burke* a68 70
2 b c Hard Spun(USA) Abiding (USA) (Dynaformer (USA))
5180[3] 5969[4] 6340[3] 6873[4]

Majuro (IRE) *Violet M Jordan* a91 89
9 b g Danetime(IRE) First Fling (IRE) (Last Tycoon)
56[4] 155[2] 353[6] 443[9] 446[2]

Makafeh *Luca Cumani* 96
3 br g Elusive Quality(USA) Demisemiquaver (Singspiel (IRE))
2050[4] 2862[8] 3763[2] 4743[6] 6308[7]

Makbullet *Michael Smith* 60
6 gr g Makbul Gold Belt (IRE) (Bellypha)
1932[5]

Make It Reel (FR) *P Bary* 98
2 b c Country Reel(USA) Maka (FR) (Slickly (FR))
(3752a) 4816a[6] 6293a[4]

Ma Kellys (IRE) *Micky Hammond* a57 61
4 ch g Compton Place Western Sal (Salse (USA))
1567[5] 2273[10] 2536[14] 4071[7] 4763[6]

Makhfar (IRE) *John Gosden* 83
2 b g Bushranger(IRE) Let Me Shine (USA) (Dixie Union (USA))
4795[2] ◆ 5494[3]

Makin (IRE) *Marco Botti* a74 70
3 b c Shirocco(GER) Cuca Vela (USA) (Devil's Bag (USA))
1803[7] 2420[9] 4829[3] 5070[5]

Making Eyes (IRE) *Hugo Palmer* a90 104
5 b f Dansili Lady's View (USA) (Distant View (USA))
2015[7] 2838[8] (3775) 4421a[5] 6742[3] 7822[13]

Makinson Lane (IRE) *Richard Fahey* a68 66
3 b g Acclamation Subtle Affair (IRE) (Barathea (IRE))
129[4] (619) 826[4] 1206[5] 6548[3] ◆ 7163[5]

Makin The Rules (IRE) *John Quinn* 79
2 b g Lawman(FR) Shinto Duchess (IRE) (Bachelor Duke (USA))
4977[4] (5364) 6233[2] ◆ 6582[2] ◆ 7170[13]

Makruma *J W Hills* 77
2 b f Dubawi(IRE) Qelaan (USA) (Dynaformer (USA))
4491[3] 5003[5] 7692[2]

Malachim Mist (IRE) *Richard Hannon Snr* 88
2 gr g Dark Angel(IRE) Sixfields Flyer (IRE) (Desert Style (IRE))
1669[8] (2194) 2553[2] (3761) 4300[2] 6328[8] 6640[5] 7129[3] 7529[4]

Malaysian Boleh *Simon Dow* a79 63
3 ch c Compton Place Orlena (USA) (Gone West (USA))
(470) 1345[3] 2098[6] 2394[14] 4636[5] 5397[3] 5697[6] (6368) 6560[4] 6998[2] 7462[3]

Malekat Jamal (IRE) *David Simcock* a65 87
4 b f Dutch Art Haretha (IRE) (Alhaarth (IRE))
1914[5] 2711[2] (3158) 3532[5] (4561) (4766) 5493[3] 5684[9] ◆

Malih *Jamie Osborne* a67 76
4 b g Echo Of Light Sultry Lass (USA) (Private Account (USA))
3736[2] 4591[3] 5479[4] 6612[6] 7741[3] 7923[7] 8329[6]

Malilla (IRE) *Clive Cox* a63 89
3 b f Red Clubs(IRE) Maleha (IRE) (Cape Cross (IRE))
6768[7] 7821[12] 7974[10]

Malindi *James Given* a53 67
4 b f Compton Place Mana Pools (IRE) (Brief Truce (USA))
(28) 439[9] 476[6]

Malka (FR) *Matthieu Palussiere* 96
2 ch f Green Tune(USA) Quadrupa (GER) (Big Shuffle (USA))
5555a[5] 6292a[6]

Malki D'Aze (FR) *N Leenders* a77
3 b g Loup Solitaire(USA) Malnight (FR) (April Night (FR))
191a[2]

Mallory Heights (IRE) *Luca Cumani* a84 73
3 gr g Dalakhani(IRE) My Dark Rosaleen (Sadler's Wells (USA))
1885[5] 2564[4] 3243[10] (5356) 6202[5] 7840[2] (8159)

Malory Towers *Richard Hannon Snr* 58
2 b f Giant's Causeway(USA) Dalisay (IRE) (Sadler's Wells (USA))
6643[12]

Malossol (USA) *G Botti* a101 100
4 b c Rahy(USA) Mambo Queen (USA) (Kingmambo (USA))
367a[5] 659a[12] 2698a[4]

Malraaj *Richard Fahey* 48
2 b g Iffraaj Lafontaine Bleu (Piccolo)
4337[3]

Maltease Ah *Andrew Reid* a66 63
4 br f Librettist(USA) Manic (Polar Falcon (USA))
4148[3] 4635[2] 5305[5]

Malthouse (GER) *S Seemar* a85 99
5 b g Green Desert(USA) Maltage (USA) (Affirmed (USA))
462a[10]

Mama Quilla (USA) *William Haggas* 82
4 ch f Smart Strike(CAN) Myth To Reality (FR) (Sadler's Wells (USA))
(2729) 3301[3] 3834[5] 4914[5]

Mambo Rhythm *Mark Johnston* 69
2 b f Authorized(IRE) Mambo Halo (USA) (Southern Halo (USA))
7061[5] 7237[2] 7774[5]

Mambo Spirit (IRE) *Tony Newcombe* a68 73
9 b g Invincible Spirit(IRE) Mambodorga (USA) (Kingmambo (USA))
30[9] 274[6] 408[6] (1088) (1304) 1929[3] 2281[6] 2871[5] 3315[2] (4303) 4746[12] 5669[6] 6856[6] 8224[13]

Mamlook (IRE) *David Pipe* 83
9 br g Key Of Luck(USA) Cradle Brief (IRE) (Brief Truce (USA))
7635[5]

Mamy Way (FR) *J Heloury* 58
2 ch f Kentucky Dynamite(USA) Mary Way (FR) (Grape Tree Road)
5213a[6]

Manalapan (IRE) *P J Prendergast* a107 105
3 b c Six Sense(JPN) Mia Mambo (USA) (Affirmed (USA))
6225a[7] 7005a[2] 7361a[2]

Manamerican (FR) *J Heloury* a70 86
3 b f American Post Manadouna (FR) (Kaldounevees (FR))
7188a[6]

Man Amongst Men (IRE) *Brian Meehan* a84 81
2 b g Holy Roman Emperor(IRE) Bankeress (IRE) (Barathea (IRE))
2411[2] 3833[7] 6799[11] 7463[2] 7859[2]

Manatee Bay *David Nicholls* 62
3 b g Royal Applause Dash Of Lime (Bold Edge)
3479[7] ◆ 3759[5] 4887[6] 5486[5] (6682) 6903[3]

Manchestar *Richard Fahey* a52 78
3 b g Elusive City(USA) Grande Terre (IRE) (Grand Lodge (USA))
1777[2] 2628[6] 3281[4] 4076[4] (4953) 5562[2] 6976[4]

Manchester (FR) *Niels Petersen* 79
5 ch g Domedriver(IRE) Metaline (FR) (Dr Fong (USA))
5809a[9] 6453a[13]

Manchu (FR) *F Chappet* a74 77
2 bb g Great Journey(JPN) Marishaan (IRE) (Darshaan)
4599a[10]

Mandaean *Mahmood Al Zarooni* 113
4 b g Manduro(GER) Summertime Legacy (Darshaan)
(367a) ◆ 745a[6]

Mandalay King (IRE) *Marjorie Fife* a49 82
8 b g King's Best(USA) Mahamuni (IRE) (Sadler's Wells (USA))
2036[2] 2217[2] ◆ 2409[4] 3068[8] (3934) 4291[5] 4970[3] 5294[4] 6052[8]

Mandarin Bar *David O'Meara* a26
3 b f Kyllachy Lady Donatella (Last Tycoon)
8052[10] 8295[13]

Mandatario *J S Bolger* a98 85
2 br c Manduro(GER) Crystal Mountain (USA) (Monashee Mountain (USA))
7720a[3]

Manderley (IRE) *Richard Hannon Snr* a73 90
2 gr f Clodovil(IRE) Three Days In May (Cadeaux Genereux)
2774[4] 4215[7] 5394[3] 6644[11] 7016[2]

Mandeville (IRE) *Michael Dods* 73
3 b f Kodiac Olympia Theatre (Galileo (IRE))
2167[5] 3251[8]

Mandistana (FR) *M Delzangles* 105
4 gr f Azamour(IRE) Minatlya (FR) (Linamix (FR))
1870a[9]

Mandour (USA) *A De Royer-Dupre* 118
4 ch c Smart Strike(CAN) Mandesha (FR) (Desert Style (IRE))
2694a[3] ◆ (4027) 5298a[4] 6449a[9] 7049a[2]

Mandy Layla (IRE) *Bryan Smart* a63 81
3 ch f Excellent Art Chervil (Dansili)
3283[8] 4558[4] 5485[6] 6088[9] 6757[7]

Mandy Lexi (IRE) *Ian Williams* a67 75
3 gr f Dark Angel(IRE) Petite Arvine (USA) (Gulch (USA))
1892[11] 3920[6] 4712[4] 5067[4]

Mandy's Boy (IRE) *Ian Williams* a63 75
3 b g Kyllachy African Queen (IRE) (Cadeaux Genereux)
1293[5] 1829[8] 2549[6] 3241[3] 3571[4] 4957[5] (5293) 5632[3] 5975[2] 6357[4] 6734[6]

Mandy's Choice *Richard Fahey* 52
2 b f Tiger Hill(IRE) Quest For Freedom (Falbrav (IRE))
2645[6]

Mandy's Hero *Olivia Maylam* a58 55
5 b g Compton Place Bandanna (Bandmaster (USA))
1731[11] 1902[14]

Mandy The Nag (USA) *Ian Williams* a82 78
3 bb f Proud Citizen(USA) Storm To Glory (USA) (Storm Bird (CAN))
2127[6] 2606[8] 3137[4] 3756[7] (4143) 4383[3] (4711) 5181[8] 6700[7]

Man From Seville *Sir Mark Prescott Bt* a83 66
3 ch g Duke Of Marmalade(IRE) Basanti (USA) (Galileo (IRE))
2500[6] (2716) 4931[12] 6290[10] (6736) (6853)

Mange All *William Haggas* 80
2 b g Zamindar(USA) Blancmange (Montjeu (IRE))
7469[3]

Mangiapregaama (ITY) *B Grizzetti* 94
3 b f Dubawi(IRE) Lapistanera (IRE) (Cape Cross (IRE))
1866a[8] 2697a[5] 3616a[3]

Mango Diva *Sir Michael Stoute* a91 104
3 b f Holy Roman Emperor(IRE) Mango Mischief (IRE) (Desert King (IRE))
(2084) ◆ 2812[2] 3460[9] (5402) (6674a)

Mango Music *David Thompson* a52 70
10 ch m Distant Music(USA) Eurolink Sundance (Night Shift (USA))
423[5] 618[4] 884[5]

Manighar (FR) *Peter G Moody* 120
7 gr g Linamix(FR) Mintly Fresh (USA) (Rubiano (USA))
7392a[15]

Maningrey (GER) *W Hickst* a101 98
4 b g Soldier Hollow Mandrella (GER) (Surumu (GER))
7968a[4]

Man In The Arena *Dr Jon Scargill* a57 61
3 b g Bertolini(USA) Torver (Lake Coniston (IRE))
17[4] 414[6] 3405[11] 5407[7] 5890[7] 7266[6]

Manipulation (IRE) *David Simcock* a58 74
2 b g Elnadim(USA) Intriguing (IRE) (Fasliyev (USA))
6132[3] (7087)

Mankini (IRE) *Luca Cumani* 89
4 b g Dansili Fashion Statement (Rainbow Quest (USA))
(3063) 3719[2] (4016) (4626) 6128[5]

Mannaro (IRE) *Marco Botti* 81
2 b g Manduro(GER) Donoma (IRE) (Beat Hollow) (7607)

Manndawi (FR) *A De Royer-Dupre* 116
3 gr c Dalakhani(IRE) Mintly Fresh (USA) (Rubiano (USA))
3386a[4] 4325a[2]

Mannerist *Daniel Mark Loughnane*
2 br c Excellent Art Atienza (USA) (Chief's Crown (USA))
2344[7] 3255[8]

Mano Diao *Mario Hofer* a46 99
4 br g Authorized(IRE) Messina (GER) (Dashing Blade)
5042a[15]

Man Of Erin (IRE) *W T Farrell* a56 83
5 b g Invincible Spirit(IRE) Dark Rosaleen (IRE) (Darshaan)
1168a[11] 5775a[23]

Man Of Harlech *Andrew Balding* 76
2 b c Dansili Ffestiniog (IRE) (Efisio)
6773[2]

Man Of Law (USA) *Ralph Beckett* a44 39
2 br c Proud Citizen(USA) Spring Tale (USA) (Stravinsky (USA))
4304[6] 4827[8] 6981[4]

Man Of My Word *Scott Dixon* a71 55
4 b g Milk It Mick Promised (IRE) (Petardia)
991[2] 1147[9] 1951[12] 2582[10]

Man Of Plenty *Ed Dunlop* 89
4 ch g Manduro(GER) Credit-A-Plenty (Generous (IRE))
1536[7] 1728[8] 2587[12] (3248) 5109[6] (6466) 6992[2] 7338[7] 7660[9]

Manomine *Clive Brittain* a69 73
4 b g Manduro(GER) Fascinating Hill (FR) (Danehill (USA))
638[4] 978[3] 1466[2] (2137) 4435[2] 5129[6] 5855[5]

Manor Way (IRE) *Richard Hannon Snr* a62 60
2 b c Holy Roman Emperor(IRE) Cannikin (IRE) (Lahib (USA))
6485[4] 6953[9] 7302[11] 7623[4]

Manshoor (IRE) *Lucy Wadham* a66 56
8 gr g Linamix(FR) Lady Wells (IRE) (Sadler's Wells (USA))
475[4] 5409[4] 5977[2] ◆ 6899[5]

Mansion House (IRE) *David Wachman* 105
2 b c Galileo(IRE) Coralita (IRE) (Night Shift (USA))
4547a[3]

Mansoreen *Saeed bin Suroor* a14 68
3 ch g Monsun(GER) Mandellicht (IRE) (Be My Guest (USA))
4139[4] 4633[9] 6870[4]

Mantonize (USA) *Brian Meehan* 51
2 ch c Smart Strike(CAN) L'Ile Aux Loups (IRE) (Rock Of Gibraltar (IRE))
4256[7]

Many Elements *Lee Carter* a54 51
3 b g Multiplex Park's Girl (Averti (IRE))
2154[6]

Many Levels *John Quinn* a37 37
3 br g Nayef(USA) Polygueza (FR) (Be My Guest (USA))
4352[9] 4763[5]

Manyriverstocross (IRE) *Alan King* 92
8 b g Cape Cross(IRE) Alexandra S (IRE) (Sadler's Wells (USA))
1841[7]

Manzanita (IRE) *D J Bunyan* a30 24
3 b f Barathea(IRE) Somerset Falls (UAE) (Red Ransom (USA))
5818[8]

Maoi Chinn Tire (IRE) *Jennie Candlish* a63 73
6 b g Mull Of Kintyre(USA) Primrose And Rose (Primo Dominie)
5099[7] 5666[4] 6658[4] 7382[4] 7735[6]

Map Of Love (IRE) *Jeremy Gask*
3 b f Dylan Thomas(IRE) Maramba (Rainbow Quest (USA))
1666[12] 2392[14]

Mappa Mundi (USA) *Eve Johnson Houghton* 88
2 b c Henrythenavigator(USA) Princess Desire (IRE) (Danehill (USA))
2595[7] 3991[2] (4231) 4486[2] (Dead)

Mappin Time (IRE) *Tim Easterby* a83 86
5 b g Orientate(USA) Different Story (USA) (Stravinsky (USA))
1248[6] 1644[6] 2007[10] 2664[3] 2834[4] 3300[7] 3811[4] 3981[4] ◆ 4479[5] 4730[11] 6822[9] 6977[10] 7731[9] (8321)

Maputo *Mark Johnston* 116
3 b c Cape Cross(IRE) Insijaam (USA) (Secretariat (USA))
(2041) (2717) ◆ (3061) 3484[23] (4214) ◆ (4473) (5317a) ◆ 7049a[10]

Maqaraat (IRE) *Doug Watson* a88 82
5 gr g Dalakhani(IRE) Raghida (IRE) (Nordico (USA))
503a[11]

Maraayill (IRE) *Marco Botti* a76 78
2 b c Sea The Stars(IRE) Navajo Moon (IRE) (Danehill (USA))
5957[7] 6975[2] 7647[2]

Marabout (IRE) *Mel Brittain* a44 60
3 b g Haafhd Nirvana (Marju (IRE))
6757[3] 7030[9] 7904[11]

Maracuja *Mark Johnston* 52
2 b f Medicean Blinking (Marju (IRE))
6873[5] 7466[6]

Mar Adentro (FR) *R Chotard* a68 113
7 b g Marju(IRE) Guermantes (Distant Relative)
961a[8]

Maraweh (IRE) *J W Hills* 69
3 b g Muhtathir Itqaan (USA) (Danzig (USA))
1635[10] 2151[10] 2605[7] 3618[4] 6696[2] 7422[10]

Marble Silver (IRE) *Tim Easterby* 52
3 gr f Notnowcato Serena's Storm (IRE) (Statue Of Liberty (USA))
1776[7] 2274[8]

Marble Statuette (USA) *Richard Fahey* a73
3 gr f Mizzen Mast(USA) Offbeat Fashion (IRE) (Rock Of Gibraltar (IRE))
8180[2] 8348[2] 8444[6]

Mar Bravo (USA) *Braulio Lopez Jr* 1
5 b c Marciano(USA) Jazz Gal (USA) (Lord Avie (USA))
1001a[11]

Marbre Rose (IRE) *F Head* 99
2 b f Smart Strike(CAN) Manerbe (USA) (Unbridled's Song (USA))
6292a[3] 7160a[3]

March *Marco Botti* a72 103
3 b f Dutch Art Royal Pardon (Royal Applause)
(2726) 3340[2] ◆ 4260[3] ◆ 5561[7]

Marchese Marconi (IRE) *A P O'Brien* a72 92
4 b c Galileo(IRE) Charroux (IRE) (Darshaan)
3423[9] 7230a[2]

Marching Time *Doug Watson* a88 93
7 b g Sadler's Wells(USA) Marching West (USA) (Gone West (USA))
151a[11] 364a[7]

Marchwood *Amy Weaver* a69 69
3 b g Assertive Reeli Silli (Dansili)
(786a)

Marciano (IRE) *Alan Brown* a82 71
3 b g Pivotal Kitty Matcham (IRE) (Rock Of Gibraltar (IRE))
5541[7] 8095[4] 8224[6]

Marcret (ITY) *David O'Meara* a95 110
6 b g Martino Alonso(IRE) Love Secret (USA) (Secreto (USA))
777[6] 1241[7] 2399[14] 3335[9] (3754) 5992[5] 6838[28] 7906[4] 8094[6]

Marcus Antonius *Jim Boyle* a71 70
6 b g Mark Of Esteem(IRE) Star Of The Course (USA) (Theatrical (IRE))
866[2] 1018[5] 3971[6] 4679[8]

Marcus Caesar (IRE) *Ruth Carr* a31 69
3 b g Antonius Pius(USA) Skyscape (Zafonic (USA))
990[6] 1764[4] 2274[3] 2501[9] 4113[2] (4722) 5581[3] 5975[7]

Maremmadiavola (IRE) *J Heloury* a74 95
2 b f Kheleyf(USA) Naked Poser (IRE) (Night Shift (USA))
5363a[4]

Marengo *Ed de Giles* a60 59
2 gr c Verglas(IRE) Cloudchaser (IRE) (Red Ransom (USA))
4883[5] 6168[10] 6641[6]

Marford Missile (IRE) *Amy Weaver* a82 86
4 b g Majestic Missile(IRE) Khawafi (Kris)
413a[7]

Margo Channing *Micky Hammond* 60
4 ch f Three Valleys(USA) Charlotte Vale (Pivotal)
2956[9] 3814[4] 4509[5] 7376[11]

Margot Machance *F Doumen* a86 80
2 b f Creachadoir(IRE) Margot Mine (IRE) (Choisir (AUS))
5419a[2]

Margrets Gift *Tim Easterby* 68
2 ch f Major Cadeaux Its Another Gift (Primo Dominie)
3476[2] 5053[3] 5380[6] 7126[6]

Marguerite St Just *Olivia Maylam* a57 26
3 b f Sir Percy Ships Watch (IRE) (Night Shift (USA))
2874[8] 3495[8] 3910[5] 4752[7] 5527[4] 5935[4]

Marhaba Malayeen (IRE) *Kevin Ryan* a62 74
3 b c Dutch Art Poyle Caitlin (IRE) (Bachir (IRE))
1829[12] 1991[6] (2342) 2717[4] 3067[6] 3502[5] 4023[4]

Maria Bella (IRE) *Charlie Appleby* a76 73
2 ch f Raven's Pass(USA) Infinite Spirit (USA) (Maria's Mon (USA))
6690[3] 7102[3] (7763)

Mariage Tardif (FR) *Mme Pia Brandt* a92 96
5 b c Slickly(FR) Joha (FR) (Johann Quatz (FR))
125a[4]

Maria Kristina (FR) *S Wattel* a66 65
3 b f Footstepsinthesand Maria De La Luz (Machiavellian (USA))
2034a[0]

Maria Lombardi *Jeremy Noseda* 69
3 b f Medicean Fabulously Fast (USA) (Deputy Minister (CAN))
(3253) 3818[3] 4830[7]

Maria Montez *J W Hills* a61 73
4 b f Piccolo Easy Feeling (IRE) (Night Shift (USA))
2096[4] 3010[2] (3181) (3325) 3431[7] 4368[2] 4830[2] 5165[3] 5697[8] 7106[3]

Maria's Choice (IRE) *Alan McCabe* a84 88
4 b g Oratorio(IRE) Amathusia (Selkirk (USA))
2251[4] 3118[8] 3960[7] 5987[6] 6288[6] 6562[7] 7115[5] 7785[2] (7970) 8269[8]

Marie D'o (FR) *K Borgel* 92
2 b f Librettist(USA) Suave Marie (IRE) (Suave Dancer (USA))
5628a[7] 6292a[7] 7994a[6]

Mariella *John Wainwright* a46 51
3 ch f Piccolo Viva Maria (Hernando (FR))
5989[11] 6759[11]

Marie's Fantasy *Zoe Davison* a60 48
4 b f Whipper(USA) My American Beauty (Wolfhound (USA))
1196[10] 1710[10] 1951[10]

Mariet *Suzy Smith* a61 62
4 ch f Dr Fong(USA) Medway (IRE) (Shernazar)
12[10] 2567[6] 3412[4] 4035[11] 5123[3] 5934[12] 7090[5]

Marilyn Marquessa *Jo Hughes* a64 58
2 ch f Captain Gerrard(IRE) Elusive Deal (USA) (Elusive Quality (USA))
1156[7] 1240[4] 1399[5] 1749[3] 2147[5] 3092[7] 4965[9] 5351[3] 5591[5] 6364[8] 6511[4]

Marina Ballerina *Roy Bowring* a62 37
5 bb f Ballet Master(USA) Marinaite (Komaite (USA))
927[10] 2168[6] 2995[5] 3721[10] 5192[5] 5961[2] 7379[10] 8006[2] 8116[3]

Marine Commando *Ruth Carr* 86
5 b g Pastoral Pursuits Carollan (IRE) (Marju (IRE))
1646[6] 5011[13] 5376[6] 5985[11] 6287[12]

Mariner's Cross (IRE) *Mahmood Al Zarooni* a109 106
4 b c Dubawi(IRE) Trilemma (Slip Anchor)
241a[12] 557a[3]

Mariners Moon (IRE) *Mark Johnston* 62
2 ch g Mount Nelson Dusty Moon (Dr Fong (USA))
4218[9] 5790[10] 7237[8]

Marino Prince (FR) *Joanne Foster* a57 20
8 b g Dr Fong(USA) Hula Queen (USA) (Irish River (FR))
6723[8]

Mariol (FR) *Robert Collet* a106 109
10 b g Munir La Bastoche (IRE) (Kaldoun (FR))
3187a[6] 3851a[9]

Marishi Ten (IRE) *Andrew Balding* 65
3 b f Invincible Spirit(IRE) Scripture (IRE) (Sadler's Wells (USA))
1896[7] 7108[4]

Maritimer (CAN) *Seth Benzel* a100 88
4 b c Stormy Atlantic(USA) Highland Mood (CAN) (Highland Ruckus (USA))
463a[6] 744a[14]

Marjong *Simon Dow* 79
3 b f Mount Nelson Vermilliann (IRE) (Mujadil (USA))
1666[6] 2051[2] 2597[5] 3375[3] 4774[2] (5647) 6338[2] 6977[11]

Marju's Quest (IRE) *David Simcock* a59 81
3 b g Marju(IRE) Queen's Quest (Rainbow Quest (USA))
3254[5] 3739[5] (4665) (5204) ◆ (5606) 6841[5]

Markami (FR) *A De Royer-Dupre* a70 71
3 ch g Medicean Marque Royale (Royal Academy (USA))
3129a[6]

Marketing Mix (CAN) *Thomas F Proctor* a99 116
5 bb f Medaglia d'Oro(USA) Instant Thought (USA) (Kris S (USA))
5552a[4] 7708a[5]

Market Puzzle (IRE) *Mark Brisbourne* a59 54
6 ch g Bahamian Bounty Trempjane (Lujain (USA))
852[9] 1090[11] 1730[8] 3043[2] 3314[12] 4071[15] 4904[3] 5127[3] 5377[8] 5803[7] 6794[12]

Market Share *P Bary* 111
3 b c Zamindar(USA) Winter Solstice (Unfuwain (USA))
5120a[2] 6251a[12]

Market Storm (FR) *Michael Mullineaux* a68
2 b c After Market(USA) Minted (USA) (Mineshaft (USA))
8026[6] 8221[2] 8415[4]

Market Town (USA) *Charles Hills* a88 93
3 b g Mizzen Mast(USA) Geographic (USA) (Empire Maker (USA))
(1387) 1809[2] 3484[8]

Mark To Market (IRE) *Doug Watson* a77 67
6 b g Clodovil(IRE) Genetta (Green Desert (USA))
7679a[3]

Markttag *Luca Cumani* a76 79
3 b g Manduro(GER) Makhsusah (IRE) (Darshaan)
2938[7] 3417[6] 5286[5] 5847[3] 6738[3] 6976[2] 7275[6]

Marlborough House *James Given* a59 62
3 b g Dylan Thomas(IRE) Eurolink Raindance (IRE) (Alzao (USA))
1926[9] 3232[4] 4076[6] 4629[5] 5099[12]

Marlismamma (FR) *David O'Meara* a40 55
2 ch f Turtle Bowl(IRE) Karawan (Kris)
5883[7] 6213[6] 6477[12] (6914) 7096[5]

Marmalade Moon *Robert Cowell* a38 56
4 ch f Shamardal(USA) Frascati (Emarati (USA))
2870[6] 3547[5] 3994[8] 4866[7]

Marmalady (IRE) *Gary Moore* a82 83
3 ch f Duke Of Marmalade(IRE) Grecian Glory (IRE) (Zafonic (USA))
2658[8] 3372[7] 4125[4] 4658[5] 5393[2] (5890) (6138) (6900)

Mar Mar (IRE) *Saeed bin Suroor* a98 100
3 b f Invincible Spirit(IRE) Queen Of Tara (IRE) (Sadler's Wells (USA))
243a[4] 554a[4] 837a[6] 3103[3] 3784[4] 4766[3] 6411[4] 7247[2] 7658[2]

Marmaris (FR) *C Lerner* a82 80
4 b f Divine Light(JPN) Margaret (TUR) (Octagonal (NZ))
7573a[6]

Marmarus *Clive Cox* 67
2 b g Duke Of Marmalade(IRE) Polly Perkins (IRE) (Pivotal)
5950[3] ◆ 7243[4]

Marmas *John Mackie* a72 70
4 ch g Sir Percy Kitabaat (IRE) (Halling (USA))
1218[6] 1445[5] 1805[8]

Marmoom *Charles Hills* 72
2 ch c Dutch Art Cosmic Song (Cosmonaut)
5473[4]

Marmot Bay (IRE) *Philip Kirby* a63
3 b f Kodiac Tides (Bahamian Bounty)
368[2] 424[5] 470[6] 1050[3] 1157[2] 1171[6] 1651[6] 1695[7] 5397[6] 6400[11] 6651[10] 8002[2] ◆

Marphilly (IRE) *John Best* a59
2 b f Amadeus Wolf Pilda (IRE) (Princely Heir (IRE))
8328[4]

Marquesa Naranja (IRE) *David O'Meara* 14
2 ch f Duke Of Marmalade(IRE) Renashaan (FR) (Darshaan)
6512[8]

Mars (IRE) *A P O'Brien* a93 121
3 ch c Galileo(IRE) Massarra (Danehill (USA))
2021[6] 2866[6] 3421[3] 4082[4] 4696a[2]

Marsden Cuckoo (IRE) *David O'Meara*
2 b f Bushranger(IRE) Telesina (ITY) (Marju (IRE))
4156[9] 4538[10]

Marshall Art *Ken Wingrove* a67
4 b g Lawman(FR) Portrait Of A Lady (IRE) (Peintre Celebre (USA))
50[2] 77[10] 162[3] 497[6] (537) 687[8] 831[10] 976[10] 1186[7] 1452[7] 1886[4] 3643[8] 4834[4] 5594[9] 6478[6] 6808[8] 7485[8]

Marsh Dragon *Mark H Tompkins* a51 71
3 b f Beat Hollow Qilin (IRE) (Second Set (IRE))
1931[5] 2387[9] 2763[9] 5200[2] 6502[5] (6698) 7455[10]

Marshgate Lane (USA) *Mark Johnston* a109 100
4 b c Medaglia d'Oro(USA) Louvain (IRE) (Sinndar (IRE))
7641[5] 7926[2] ◆ 8071[3] (8156) (8301)

Marshland *Mark Johnston* a79 71
3 b g Kheleyf(USA) Neptune's Bride (USA) (Bering)
(1305) 1773[4] 2056[5] 2708[10] 3289[9] 3649[6] 4075[7]

Martagon Lily *John Gosden* a61 79
3 ch f Manduro(GER) Mezzogiorno (Unfuwain (USA))
4632[6] 5892[7] 6532[3] 7504[12]

Martial Art (IRE) *Andrew Balding* a81 80
3 ch g Compton Place Brush Strokes (Cadeaux Genereux)
2650[2] 3950[2] 5512[4] 5845[3] 7307[8] (7459)

Martian (IRE) *William Haggas* 93
3 b g Duke Of Marmalade(IRE) Starship (IRE) (Galileo (IRE))
4978[5] (6062) (7611)

Martinas Delight (USA) *Alan Jarvis* a72 78
3 b f Johannesburg(USA) Lerici (USA) (Woodman (USA))
2449[3] ◆ 3136[U] 4485[5] 5037[6] 7257[13] 7462[10] 8060[6] 8343[4]

Martin Chuzzlewit (IRE) *David Simcock* 98
4 ch g Galileo(IRE) Alta Anna (FR) (Anabaa (USA))
2427[4] 3297[6] 5655[7] 6066[5] 7174[12]

Marti's Boy *J S Moore* a15
2 ch g Bertolini(USA) Rock Art (IRE) (Rock Of Gibraltar (IRE))
8451[13]

Marti's Girl *J S Moore* a53 53
2 b f Sakhee's Secret Forest Girl (IRE) (Shinko Forest (IRE))
2068[4] 2327[3] 3414[3] 3767[3]

Marvelino *Pat Eddery* a74 67
3 b c Captain Marvelous(IRE) Aimee's Delight (Robellino (USA))
106[4] (202) 531[3] 894[4] 1616[4] 2098[10] 2600[5] 3243[11] 3658[4] 3921[5] 5890[11] 6345[9] 7068[7]

Marvelous James (IRE) *Paul W Flynn* a61 62
3 b g Captain Marvelous(IRE) Answer Do (Groom Dancer (USA))
7351[8]

Marvelous Miss (IRE) *Christine Dunnett* a18 37
3 b f Captain Marvelous(IRE) Abbeyleix Lady (IRE) (Montjeu (IRE))
2133[6] 2643[9] 3789[5] 4390[5] 5156[5]

Marvo *Dai Burchell* a71 64
9 b g Bahamian Bounty Mega (IRE) (Petardia)
5172[7] 5816[13]

Marygold *Lee Carter* a42 70
4 b f Cockney Rebel(IRE) Contrary Mary (Mujadil (USA))
6745[14] 7086[11]

Mary Le Bow *Lucy Wadham* a59 57
2 b f Sir Percy Bermondsey Girl (Bertolini (USA))
6974[7] 7450 [8] 8213[4]

Mary's Daughter *Richard Fahey* 95
3 b f Royal Applause Aunty Mary (Common Grounds)
1249[3] 2400[5] 3348[17] 4255[12] 5769[11] 6238[4] 6586[23] 7314[8]

Mary's Pet *Lee Carter* a67 67
6 b m Where Or When(IRE) Contrary Mary (Mujadil (USA))
115[9] 472[3] 863[7] 1087[5] (1193) 1452[2] 1783[11] 2582[9] 2745[2]

Marzocco (USA) *John Gosden* a81
2 bb c Kitten's Joy(USA) Dynamia (USA) (Dynaformer (USA))
(7460)

Masaadr *James Tate* a71 51
3 br c Manduro(GER) Masandra (IRE) (Desert Prince (IRE))
211[4] 534[2] (1009) 1719[4]

Masaalek *Doug Watson* a77 63
8 b g Green Desert(USA) Hammiya (IRE) (Darshaan)
394a[10]

Masai King (IRE) *Robin Bastiman* a8 53
3 b g Kheleyf(USA) Masai Queen (IRE) (Mujadil (USA))
2959[9]

Masai Moon *Rod Millman* a79 79
9 b g Lujain(USA) Easy To Imagine (USA) (Cozzene (USA))
34[6] 415[5] 645[2] 721[3] 912[4]

Masamah (IRE) *Marco Botti* a108 111
7 gr g Exceed And Excel(AUS) Bethesda (Distant Relative)
2152[2] 2662[7] 4058[2] (4275) 4947[8] 5984[4] 6305[2] 6830[7] 7010[8] 8395[2]

Masarah (IRE) *Clive Brittain* a99 99
3 b f Cape Cross(IRE) Fragrancy (IRE) (Singspiel (IRE))
1383[5] (1918) 2047[8] 2689a[15] 3524[12] 4081[9] 5728[12] 6308[14] 7649[3]

Mashaari (IRE) *Brian Ellison* a78 93
4 b g Monsun(GER) Thakafaat (IRE) (Unfuwain (USA))
2402[4] 3560[9] 3824[14]

Mash Potato (IRE) *Michael Dods* 76
3 b g Whipper(USA) Salva (Grand Lodge (USA))
(1393) 2464[3] 3418[3] 5334[2] (5483) 6588[2] 7275[3]

Masiyann (FR) *A De Royer-Dupre* a78 99
3 b c Anabaa(USA) Marasima (IRE) (Barathea (IRE))
(1850a)

Maska Pony (IRE) *George Moore* 62
9 gr g Celtic Swing Clotted Cream (USA) (Eagle Eyed (USA))
1789[7] 2540[4] 2887[2] (3589) 4204[11]

Masked Dance (IRE) *Scott Dixon* a65 81
6 gr g Captain Rio Brooks Masquerade (Absalom)
426[6] 526[8] (716) 890[3] 986[4] 1309[4] 7886[4] 8042[11] 8234[10]

Masked Marvel *Robert Hickmott* 113
5 b c Montjeu(IRE) Waldmark (GER) (Mark Of Esteem (IRE))
7556a[13] 7761a[18]

Maslak (IRE) *Peter Hiatt* a67 69
9 b g In The Wings Jeed (IRE) (Mujtahid (USA))
198[11] 475[2] (597) 668[8] 888[10] (1207)

Mason Hindmarsh *Karen McLintock* a73 73
6 ch g Dr Fong(USA) Sierra Virgen (USA) (Stack (USA))
830[5] 1464[9] (2242) 2540[8] 2990[8] 3627[3] 4759[6] 5640[8]

Masquerading (IRE) *David Lanigan* a95 91
3 b g Singspiel(IRE) Moonlight Dance (USA) (Alysheba (USA))
1713[8] (2157) ◆ 3214[2] 3470[3] 4202[3] 5475[7] 6751[3]

Massena (IRE) *Venetia Williams* 64
6 b g Marju(IRE) Mayara (IRE) (Ashkalani (IRE))
3209[4]

Mass Rally (IRE) *Michael Dods* a82 113
6 b g Kheleyf(USA) Reunion (IRE) (Be My Guest (USA))
1232[8] (2366) 3558[11] 3822[2] 5320a[5] 6235[10] 6623[11] (7208) 7364[6] 7821[13]

Master Bond *David O'Meara* a82 87
4 b g Misu Bond(IRE) Bond Royale (Piccolo)
2459[8] 2755[U] 4930[4] (6515) 6908[13] 7313[5] 7887[5] 8305[7] 8439[4]

Master Carpenter (IRE) *Rod Millman* 91
2 ch c Mastercraftsman(IRE) Fringe (In The Wings)
(1360) ◆ 1917[3] (2553) 3555[15] 4212[8] 6303[2] 6640[3]

Master Clockmaker (IRE) *Ann Duffield* 28
2 gr c Mastercraftsman(IRE) Mairead Anne (USA) (Elusive Quality (USA))
6754[13]

Master Dan *James Given* a65
2 b c Mastercraftsman(IRE) Danella (IRE) (Platini (GER))
7774[11] 7955[6] 8297[2]

Master Dancer *Philip Hide* 74
2 gr c Mastercraftsman(IRE) Isabella Glyn (IRE) (Sadler's Wells (USA))
3972[4] 5122[4] (7069)

Mastered (IRE) *John Best* a53
3 ch g Refuse To Bend(IRE) Woodmaven (USA) (Woodman (USA))
184[6] 350[4] 2566[9] 3432[7] 5217[6]

Masterful Act (USA) *Alan McCabe* a100 80
6 ch g Pleasantly Perfect(USA) Catnip (USA) (Flying Paster (USA))
642[3] (887) ◆ (989) 1110[5] 1547[6] 2648[9] 3765[8] 7542[7] (7757) 7975[8]

Master Hamilton *Tobias B P Coles* a61 47
3 ch g Mount Nelson Oomph (Shareef Dancer (USA))
211[6] 3194[10]

Master Ming (IRE) *Brian Meehan* a81 84
3 b g Excellent Art China Pink (Oasis Dream)
1641[7] 2259[4] 2651[5] 3338[5] 4384[4] 4683[5] 7224[6]

Master Mylo (IRE) *Martin Bosley* a80 86
6 ch g Bertolini(USA) Sheboygan (IRE) (Grand Lodge (USA))
415[7] 740[6]

Master Of Alkmaar *Roger Varian* a48 60
2 ch c Dutch Art Lalina (GER) (Trempolino (USA))
5334[5] 7302[12] 7860[7]

Master Of Disguise *Brian Baugh* a69 78
7 b g Kyllachy St James's Antigua (IRE) (Law Society (USA))
27[6] 214[4] 308[7] 760[2] 946[4] 1039[4] 1801[6] 2281[2] 2918[10] 8351[3]

Master Of Finance (IRE) *Mark Johnston* a79 82
2 ch c Mastercraftsman(IRE) Cheal Rose (IRE) (Dr Devious (IRE))
4731[4] (5508) 6207[4] 7846[2]

Master Of Gold (FR) *E J O'Neill* 81
2 b c Gold Away(IRE) Margalita (FR) (Green Tune (USA))
7939a[11]

Master Of Hounds (USA) *M F De Kock* a113 115
5 b c Kingmambo(USA) Silk And Scarlet (Sadler's Wells (USA))
745a[2] 959a[5] 1262a[15]

Master Of Song *Roy Bowring* a71 67
6 ch g Ballet Master(USA) Ocean Song (Savahra Sound)
98[9] 2089[11] 2575[5] 3546[10] 4070[4] 4928[2] 5198[2] 5614[5] (5903) 6963[6] 7130[16] 7515[11] 8360[9]

Master Of Suspense *Peter Chapple-Hyam* 70
2 ch c Exceed And Excel(AUS) Ridotto (Salse (USA))
3536[3] 7501[4]

Masteroftherolls (IRE) *Saeed bin Suroor* a104 103
5 b g Refuse To Bend(IRE) Miss Sally (IRE) (Danetime (IRE))
(363a) 675a[5] 836a[10] 3825[11] (Dead)

Master Of War *Richard Hannon Snr* 108
3 ch c Compton Place Mamma Morton (IRE) (Elnadim (USA))
5747[3] 6505[3] 6990[10]

Masterpaver *Alan Bailey* a63 49
2 gr g Mastercraftsman(IRE) Most-Saucy (Most Welcome)
6762[14] 7308[10] 7607[12] 8262[4] 8363[2]

Master Rocket (USA) *Kris Nemann*
5 b g Part The Waters(USA) Kara's Rockin Role (USA) (Broad Brush (USA))
413a[3]

Master Rooney (IRE) *Geoffrey Harker* 92
7 bb g Cape Cross(IRE) Wimple (USA) (Kingmambo (USA))
1253[4] 2614[10] 3351[16] 4588[8] 4852[11] 6516[9] 7030[11] 7240[10] 7598[10]

Masters Blazing *John Ryan* a68 78
4 ch g Iceman Loquacity (Diktat)
668[6] 1290[7] 5492[9]

Master's Spirit (IRE) *P Demercastel* 76
2 gr c Mastercraftsman(IRE) Lavayssiere (FR) (Sicyos (USA))
5039a[4]

Masterstroke (USA) *Charlie Appleby* a92 114
4 b c Monsun(GER) Melikah (IRE) (Lammtarra (USA))
4944[5] 6198[8] 7535[7]

Master The World (IRE) *Gerard Butler* 86
2 gr c Mastercraftsman(IRE) Zadalla (Zaha (CAN))
4987[2] 5727[5] (6762)

Master Wizard *David C Griffiths* a70
3 b c Motivator Enchanted (Magic Ring (IRE))
6965[3] 7459[5]

Mataajir (USA) *Derek Shaw* a69 30
5 b g Redoute's Choice(AUS) Hamasah (USA) (Irish River (FR))
96[3] 163[2] 223[8] 618[6] 794[6] 1063[5] (1149) 1310[2] 1521[9] 2273[13] 2514[12] 3210[7] 3977[13] 7512[7] 7643[10] 7886[6] 8118[5] 8233[4] 8409[4]

Matador Yasar (TUR) *H Derinsu* 104
4 b c Native Procida(TUR) Freezone (TUR) (Wolf (CHI))
6253a[6]

Mata Hari Blue *Michael Appleby* a93 83
7 ch m Monsieur Bond(IRE) Feeling Blue (Missed Flight)
1309[2] 1540[6] (1596) 2173[3] (2513) 2657[4] 3299[10] 4536[7] 4860[11]

Matauri Pearl (IRE) *Mme Pia Brandt* 97
4 b f Hurricane Run(IRE) Moonrise (GER) (Grand Lodge (USA))
6714a[6]

Matchday *Frau E Mader* 87
4 b f Acclamation Midnight Sky (Desert Prince (IRE))
4935a[0]

Match Point (FR) *Niels Petersen* a90 70
7 gr m Verglas(IRE) Danira (IRE) (Danehill (USA))
2145a[3] 5325a[6]

Mathematics *Charlie Appleby* a24 60
2 b g Exceed And Excel(AUS) Mindsharp (USA) (Gone West (USA))
3991[6] 4958[7] 6807[9]

Matorico (IRE) *M Delzangles* a50 75
2 b c Mastercraftsman(IRE) Hashbrown (GER) (Big Shuffle (USA))
6961a[15]

Matraash (USA) *Daniel Mark Loughnane* a83 62
7 b h Elusive Quality(USA) Min Alhawa (USA) (Riverman (USA))
593[7] 896[10] 1107[6] 1368[2] 1797[3] (1987) 2413[7] 3043[8] 3545[3] (4171) (4522) (8309)

Matravers *Sir Michael Stoute* 56
2 b c Oasis Dream Maakrah (Dubai Destination (USA))
6739[9]

Matrooh (USA) *William Haggas* 93
3 b g Distorted Humor(USA) Rockcide (USA) (Personal Flag (USA))
1635[4] (2306) 2857[3] 4214[5] ◆ 7497[4]

Maughami *Marco Botti* a61 56
3 gb f Manduro(GER) Grey Way (USA) (Cozzene (USA))
1178[4] 1518[6] 1876[10] 2762[5] 4180[5]

Maupiti Express (FR) *David O'Meara* a58 54
2 b g Chineur(FR) Azucar (FR) (Marathon (USA))
2883[10] 3298[11] 3541[3] 8131[4] 8265[2] 8347[4]

Maureen (IRE) *Richard Hannon Snr* 107
3 b f Holy Roman Emperor(IRE) Exotic Mix (FR) (Linamix (FR))
(1676) 2047[6] 2689a[6] 3524[4] 4817a[7] 6327[5] 6796[4]

Maurice (GER) *S Smrczek* a77 88
3 b c Big Shuffle(USA) Moyenne (IRE) (Trans Island)
1708a[7]

Maven *Tim Easterby* a78 92
5 b f Doyen(IRE) Bollin Jeannie (Royal Applause)
1237[7] 1538[11] 2431[2] 2673[2] 3346[3] (3567) 4264[11] 4777[5] 5269[9] (5860) 6551[6] 7337[11]

Maverick Wave (USA) *John Gosden* 82
2 ch c Elusive Quality(USA) Misty Ocean (USA) (Stormy Atlantic (USA))
(6277)

Maverik *William Knight* a95 76
5 ch g Iceman Nouvelle Lune (Fantastic Light (USA))
400[2] 701a[10] (1485) 1848[3] 2841[10] 3527[20] 4923[12] 5894[3] 6199[13] 7641[11] (7988) 8263[4] 8445[4]

Mavree (IRE) *Tim Easterby* a24 38
2 b f Captain Marvelous(IRE) Hemasree (IRE) (Exceed And Excel (AUS))
4963[12] 6286[9] 6546[8] 7340[11] 8317[7]

Mawaakef (IRE) *J R Jenkins* a95 97
5 b g Azamour(IRE) Al Euro (FR) (Mujtahid (USA))
189[4] 401[5] 585[3] 739[2] 1766[10] 2520[3] 4028[7] 4280[6] 5348[5] 6504[2] 6992[12] 7757[6] 8387[3]

Mawaqeet (USA) *Sir Michael Stoute* 99
4 b g Dynaformer(USA) Lady Ilsley (USA) (Trempolino (USA))
2052[6] 3423[15] 4313[2] 4704[6] 5655[2] 6066[7]

Mawfoor (IRE) *Brian Meehan* 91
2 b g Iffraaj Miss Odlum (IRE) (Mtoto)
2543[2] (3044) ◆ 3422[8] 6328[3] 6765[7]

Mawingo (GER) *M Freedman* 118
5 b c Tertullian(USA) Montfleur (Sadler's Wells (USA))
2494a[3]

Mawj Tamy (USA) *Charles Hills* a69 59
3 b c Invasor(ARG) Plenty Of Sugar (CAN) (Ascot Knight (CAN))
1904[2] 2547[7] 6738[7]

Mawson *Roger Charlton* a60 56
3 b g Starcraft(NZ) No Fear No Favour (AUS) (Carnegie (IRE))
2447[8]

Mawzoona *Mick Channon* a65 67
2 b f Authorized(IRE) Umniya (IRE) (Bluebird (USA))
3471[5] 4439[5] 4997[2] 5400[6] 5951[9] 6311[3] 6520[8]

Max Dynamite (FR) *J Van Handenhove* a77 109
3 b c Great Journey(JPN) Mascara (GER) (Monsun (GER))
1737a[4] 2297a[7] 2907a[8] 4325a[8] 6446a[7]

Maxentius (IRE) *Peter Chapple-Hyam* a99 105
3 b g Holy Roman Emperor(IRE) Guantanamera (IRE) (Sadler's Wells (USA))
1033 [6] 1383[4] 2023[6] 3080[2]

Maxi Dress (IRE) *John Gosden* a69
3 b f Shamardal(USA) Fashion Trade (Dansili)
(230)

Maxie T *Mark Johnston* a60 73
2 b c Dalakhani(IRE) Ballet Ballon (USA) (Rahy (USA))
3581[7] 4756[5] 6635[2] 7017[P] 7935[5]

Maxim Gorky (IRE) *Noel Meade* 84
6 b g Montjeu(IRE) Altruiste (USA) (Diesis)
7230a[11]

Maximilianthefirst *Mark Rimmer* a42 39
2 b g Holy Roman Emperor(IRE) Deep Bleu (Kyllachy)
2510[4] 3717[7] 4175[9] 4412[5] 5066[4] 5276[4] 5494[8] 8215[7] 8363[7]

Maximito *Marco Botti* 29
3 b c Motivator Lorien Hill (IRE) (Danehill (USA))
4030[4]

Maximum Velocity (FR) *J E Hammond* a80 82
3 b g Muhtathir Ratukidul (FR) (Danehill (USA))
3454a[2] 6713a[2]

Maxios *J E Pease* 122
5 b c Monsun(GER) Moonlight's Box (USA) (Nureyev (USA))
(1420a) 1870a[2] (2694a) 3457[6] (6450a) 7366[8]

Max The Machine *Derek Shaw* a69 67
3 b g Intikhab(USA) Digamist Girl (IRE) (Digamist (USA))
3400[5] 3638[5] 6397[8] 6519[3] (6965) 7848[5] 8271[11] 8351[2]

Mayaasem *Charles Hills* 90
3 b g Royal Applause Rolexa (Pursuit Of Love)
(1722) 2190[2] 3066[9] 5009[3] 5722[2] 6331[15]

Maya De Ventura *Alison Hutchinson*
3 b f Tiger Hill(IRE) Sharp Dresser (USA) (Diesis)
7311[8]

Mayan Flight (IRE) *Tony Carroll* a56 61
5 b g Hawk Wing(USA) Balimaya (IRE) (Barathea (IRE))
9[12] 625[10] 846[5] 1070[3] 1949[8] 2333[4] 3168[6]

Maybeagrey *Tim Easterby* a72 78
4 b f Shamardal(USA) Grey Again (Unfuwain (USA))
1391[7] 1774[8] 2555[11] 3477[2] 3814[3] 4506[4] 4760[3] 5015[4] 5548[6] 6470[7] 6599[3] 7132[10]

Maybeme *Neville Bycroft* a39 71
7 b m Lujain(USA) Malvadilla (IRE) (Doyoun)
(2956) 3195[7] 3504[3] (3652) 4403[7] (4584) 5059[2] 5337[7] 5786[7] 6130[8]

May Be Some Time *Stuart Kittow* a69 79
5 ch g Iceman Let Alone (Warning)
2228[6] 2498[8] 3273[2] 4679[3] 5390[5] 6869[9] 7778[7]

May Boy *Ron Hodges* a52 33
7 br g Bandmaster(USA) Kathies Pet (Tina's Pet)
41[4] 226[10] 522[5] 625[3]

Mayfield Boy *Mel Brittain* 75
2 b c Authorized(IRE) Big Pink (IRE) (Bigstone (IRE))
6513[4] 6938[2] (7175) 7492[9]

Mayfield Girl (IRE) *Mel Brittain* 87
3 br f One Cool Cat(USA) Rose Of Mooncoin (IRE) (Brief Truce (USA))
(1482) (1690) 2430[16] 3478[5] 4263[8] 4734[11] 5340[5] 5769[13] 6212[8]

Mayforde Jack *Simon Hodgson* a49
4 b g Septieme Ciel(USA) Jessinca (Minshaanshu Amad (USA))
564[5] 1093[7] 1221[6] 1474[8] 5166[9] 5667[8]

Maygo's Joy *Ralph Smith* a46 42
3 b g Josr Algarhoud(IRE) Nikki Bea (IRE) (Titus Livius (FR))
5281[7] 6062[9] 8245[5] 8427[11]

Maymyo (IRE) *Sylvester Kirk*
2 b c Invincible Spirit(IRE) Lady Windermere (IRE) (Lake Coniston (IRE))
6110[9]

Mayoman (IRE) *David O'Meara* a64 94
8 b g Namid America Lontana (FR) (King's Theatre (IRE))
3299[11] 3776[5] 4954[10] 6159[12]

Maypole Joe (IRE) *Raymond York* a60 48
3 b g Iffraaj Spanish Needle (Green Desert (USA))
(310) 321[6] 482[5] 588[3] 684[4] 7303[12]

Maypole Lass *Sir Michael Stoute* a66 71
3 ch f Halling(USA) Maigold Lass (Mark Of Esteem (IRE))
2804[3] 4633[3]

May's Boy *James Moffatt* a77 63
5 gr c Proclamation(IRE) Sweet Portia (IRE) (Pennekamp (USA))
13[2] 89[6] 813[12] 1100[6] 1303[4] 1466[3] 5882[3] 6598[11]

Maysville (IRE) *Charles Hills* a56 56
2 bb f Lawman(FR) Morality (Elusive Quality (USA))
3664[13] 4164[6] 5352[9] 6035[4] 6426[6] 6897[6]

May Whi (IRE) *John Quinn* a61 45
2 b f Whipper(USA) May (Montjeu (IRE))
2517[5] 2751[11] 3905[5] 4990[4] 5893[4] (6779) 7604[6] 7954[6] 8137[5]

Mayyadah (IRE) *F Head* 109
3 b f Invincible Spirit(IRE) Seralia (Royal Academy (USA))
4817a[10] 5461a[5] 6251a[2]

Maz *Alan Bailey* a70 68
5 ch f Needwood Blade Lady Mytton (Lake Coniston (IRE))
83[3] 633[7] 747[9] 927[5] 1017[7] (1221) 1498[7] 1730[9]

Mazaaher *J W Hills* a62 82
3 b c Elnadim(USA) Elutrah (Darshaan)
2093[2] 3011[4] (4721) ◆ 5004[2] 6003[6] 6358[6] 7275[11]

Mazameer (IRE) *F Head* 108
3 b c Green Desert(USA) Straight Miss (IRE) (In The Wings)
1357a[7] (2334a) 2909a[8] 5806a[11]

Mazeydd *D Selvaratnam* a90 72
4 b g Motivator Jathaabeh (Nashwan (USA))
412a[12]

Mazij *Peter Hiatt* a83 74
5 b f Haafhd Salim Toto (Mtoto)
39[6] 429[7] 528[7] 816[4] 929[2] (1217) 1434[4] 1654[2] 2234[5] 2826[3] 3244[4]

Mazovian (USA) *Michael Chapman* a79 63
5 b g E Dubai(USA) Polish Style (USA) (Danzig (USA))
453[3] 526[7] 603[4] 715[8] 832[6] 1309[6] 6969[7] 7886[13]

Mbhali (IRE) *Mark Johnston* a67
2 b c Cape Cross(IRE) Ma Paloma (FR) (Highest Honor (FR))
8415[5]

Mcbirney (USA) *Paul D'Arcy* a79 79
6 b g Danehill Dancer(IRE) Dear Girl (IRE) (Fairy King (USA))
22[11] (338) 528[6] (1097) 1218[5] 1523[5] 2385[3] 3063[3] 3780[6] 4490[5] 5492[8] 7132[2] 7865[4] 8337[6]

McCarthy Mor (IRE) *Richard Fahey* 54
2 b g Bushranger(IRE) Alexander Anapolis (IRE) (Spectrum (IRE))
2670[10] 6581[8] 7335[10]

Mcconnell (USA) *Violet M Jordan* a67 58
8 ch g Petionville(USA) Warsaw Girl (IRE) (Polish Precedent (USA))
49[8] 340[6] 511[10] 718[6] 1151[3] 1311[2] 1455[5] 2168[2] 2514[11] 3687[10] 5123[9] (5961) 6261[3] (6457) 6804[5] 6907[9] 7321[8] (8042)

McCool Bannanas *James Unett* a71 69
5 b g Firebreak Dances With Angels (IRE) (Mukaddamah (USA))
850[6] 996[3] 1827[3] 3780[3] 4482[3] 6042[4] 6943[6]

Mcdelta *Geoffrey Deacon* a77 79
3 b g Delta Dancer Mcnairobi (Josr Algarhoud (IRE))
3632[4] 4032[3] 5277[7] (6042) ◆ (6335) 6556[2]

Mcmonagle (USA) *Alan Brown* a76 74
5 ch g Mizzen Mast(USA) Dippers (USA) (Polish Numbers (USA))
2162[3] 2835[3] 3068[10] 3630[8] 4119[2] 4503[3] (4557) 5383[5] 8162[5] 8227[6] 8454[10]

Mcvicar *Alan King* a69 73
4 b g Tobougg(IRE) Aries (GER) (Big Shuffle (USA))
639[6] 7506[7]

Meadway *Bryan Smart* a88 85
2 b g Captain Gerrard(IRE) Tibesti (Machiavellian (USA))
2314[2] 6517[6] (6966) 7333[4]

Meandmyshadow *Alan Brown* a62 88
5 ch f Tobougg(IRE) Queen Jean (Pivotal)
1819[2] 2166[2] 2664[2] (2834) 3093[14] (3441) 3811[7] 4138[11] 4730[8] 4993[5] 5498[3] 5832[14] 6516[8] 6871[11] 7282[4] ◆ 7593[8]

Meandre (FR) *A Savujev* a98 122
5 gr c Slickly(FR) Penne (FR) (Sevres Rose (IRE))
1269a[6] 2494a[9] 4571a[3] 6028a[3] (6678a) 7058a[10]

Meaning Of Life (IRE) *Marco Botti* a70 79
2 b c Exceed And Excel(AUS) Emirates Hills (Dubawi (IRE))
2778[3] 3211[3] 3991[5] (5371)

Mean It (IRE) *David Simcock* 88
4 b g Danehill Dancer(IRE) Lilissa (IRE) (Doyoun)
1583[2] 2539[3] 4923[15]

Mecca's Angel (IRE) *Michael Dods* a97 95
2 gr f Dark Angel(IRE) Folga (Atraf)
2458[4] (3568) (4141) 5767[2] ◆ 6584[2] 7026[4]

Meconopsis *Tim Easterby* a19 42
2 b c Indesatchel(IRE) High Lady (Pivotal)
3391[6] 4154[10] 4616[7] 5379[7] 6494[6]

Medal Count (USA) *Dale Romans* a95
2 b c Dynaformer(USA) Brisquette (USA) (Unbridled's Song (USA))
7711a[11]

Medam *Shaun Harris* a62 49
4 b f Medicean Mamounia (IRE) (Green Desert (USA))
863[5] 1020[6] 1088[4] 1271[4] 1452[9] 1540[13] 3738[6] 4893[16] 4982[6] 7643[8] 7904[3] 8119[3] 8258[2] 8446[6]

Medburn Singer *George Baker* 25
3 b g Superior Premium Menina (Alflora (IRE))
3278[7]

Meddling *Sir Michael Stoute* 67
3 ch f Halling(USA) Piffling (Pivotal)
2231[6] 3176[3] 3906[4] 5617[3] 6535[7]

Medecis Mountain *John Wainwright* a48 48
4 b g Medecis Moon Cat (IRE) (Desert Story (IRE))
1578[8] 1893[7] 2757[7] 5290[5] 5876[6] 6803[11] 7787[4] 8054[4]

Medecriss (FR) *Y Durepaire* a67 82
3 ch c Medecis Excellent Sun (GER) (Monsun (GER))
5805a[7]

Medeleck (FR) *Mme C De La Soudiere-Niault* a82 81
3 b c Medecis Electricity (Elusive City (USA))
126a[5] 1594a[2]

Media Hype *K R Burke* a104 104
6 b h Tiger Hill(IRE) Hyperspectra (Rainbow Quest (USA))
6620[7]

Media Jury *John Wainwright* a56 58
6 b g Lucky Owners(NZ) Landofheartsdesire (IRE) (Up And At 'Em)
87[6] ◆ (240) 408[4] 565[3] 655[4] 733[2] 917[6] 1193[4] 1459[9] 1657[4] 2125[4]

Medicean Man *Jeremy Gask* a108 113
7 ch g Medicean Kalindi (Efisio)
(464a) 746a[3] 954a[6] 1265a[9] (3046) 3420[11] 3848a[5] 4947[9] 6305[9] 7010[3]

Medici Dancer *Tim Easterby* 74
3 ch f Medicean Dance Away (Pivotal)
1647[8] 2308[4] 2770[4] 3365[6] 5342[3] 5975[3] 6588[5] 7130[12] 7350[5]

Medicine Hat *George Moore* 54
2 b g Multiplex Blushing Heart (Observatory (USA))
7276[4]

Medici Time *Tim Easterby* 86
8 gr g Medicean Pendulum (Pursuit Of Love)
1807[15] 2505[7] 3351[17] 3586[12] 4560[2] 4730[15] 5537[13] 5985[9] 6515[7] 6948[7]

Medieval Bishop (IRE) *Tim Walford* a56 69
4 b g Bachelor Duke(USA) On The Backfoot (IRE) (Bob Back (USA))
1916[4] 2328[2] 2991[9] (3625) (5831) 6237[12]

Medipearl (FR) *F Chappet* a73 69
3 b c Medecis Cat's Pearl (FR) (Enrique)
647a[4]

Mediska *Henry Candy* 56
3 b f Medicean Silca Boo (Efisio)
2051[6] 2597[7]

Mediterranean Sea (IRE) *J R Jenkins* a81 79
7 b m Medecis High Glider (High Top)
57[4] 429[10] (642) 887[3] 969[4] 1306[3] 2349[5] (3744) 4692[4] 7217[8] 8047[3] 8299[7] 8433[3]

Meebo (IRE) *J R Jenkins* a51 64
2 b f Captain Rio Abbeyleix Lady (IRE) (Montjeu (IRE))
8405[2]

Meetha Achar *Jim Boyle* a44
3 b f Sakhee(USA) Sweet Pickle (Piccolo)
821[8] 1051[5] 1711[5] 8390[10]

Meeting In Paris (IRE) *Richard Fahey* a51 63
3 b f Dutch Art Sharplaw Star (Xaar)
4050[2] 4991[5] 5486[2] 5830[6]

Meetings Man (IRE) *Ali Brewer* a82 74
6 gr g Footstepsinthesand Missella (IRE) (Danehill (USA))
1775[5] (2234) 2673[7] 3085[3] (4179) (5231) 5895[9] 6750[8] 7510[3] 8004[8]

Meeting Waters *William Haggas* 83
2 ch f Aqlaam Paradise Isle (Bahamian Bounty)
3288[2] ◆ 3694[5] 4827[3] (6572) ◆ 6839[7]

Meet Marhaba (IRE) *J W Hills* a62 27
3 b f Marju(IRE) Tadris (USA) (Red Ransom (USA))
4495[5] 5071[5] 7791[4]

Meet Me Halfway *Chris Wall* a71 58
3 b f Exceed And Excel(AUS) Pivotal Drive (IRE) (Pivotal)
2544[12] 6362[6] 6998[5]

Megalala (IRE) *John Bridger* a83 84
12 b g Petardia Avionne (Derrylin)
1327[9] 1586[12] 2532[6] 2845[10] 3330[5] 3580[2] 3925[2] 4205[3] 4665[4] 5528[6] 5762[8] 7090[4] 7321[7]

Megaleka *Alan Bailey* a58 68
3 b f Misu Bond(IRE) Peyto Princess (Bold Arrangement)
985[6] 1284[2] 1566[7] 1962[13] 2962[9] 3594[2] 3994[10] 4427[7] 4611[3] 5067[3] (5499) 5800[2] 5889[5] 6345[3] 7236[12] (7772) 7937[8] 7958[8] 8135[5] 8352[5]

Megamunch (IRE) *Kristin Stubbs* a78 74
3 b g Camacho Liscoa (IRE) (Foxhound (USA))
1295[4] 2329[4] 2544[5] 4354[5] 5016[2] 5342[5] (5870)

Meganisi (IRE) *Rebecca Curtis* 106
6 b g Galileo(IRE) Cland Di San Jore (IRE) (Lando (GER))
1674[9]

Megastar *Gary Moore* a73
8 b g Kayf Tara Megalex (Karinga Bay)
(157)

Meglio Ancora *Richard Ford* a66 60
6 ch g Best Of The Bests(IRE) May Fox (Zilzal (USA))
193[2] 312[3] 3203[5] 3909[9] 4099[2] 4376[4] 4853[10] 5426[3] 6472[9] 7238[8] 7753[10] 7962[10] 8065[3] (8279) 8390[6]

Mehdi (IRE) *David Nicholls* a104 98
4 b g Holy Roman Emperor(IRE) College Fund Girl (IRE) (Kahyasi)
1688[8] 4285[9] 4778[7] 5292[2] 5544[2] ◆ 6384[12]

Mehen (FR) *H-A Pantall* a82 56
3 b g Country Reel(USA) Ridja Queen (FR) (Highest Honor (FR))
1594a[8] 2335a[0]

Mehitabel (FR) *N Sauer* a80 92
4 b f Authorized(IRE) Kresna (FR) (Distant Relative)
963a[9]

Meiner Kitz (JPN) *Sakae Kunieda* 111
10 ch h Chief Bearhart(CAN) Takara Kanna (JPN) (Soccer Boy (JPN))
1868a[7]

Meisho Kampaku (JPN) *Yoshiyuki Arakawa* 114
6 bb h Grass Wonder(USA) Dancing Happiness (JPN) (Dance In The Dark (JPN))
1868a[14]

Mekong River (IRE) *A P O'Brien* 104
2 b c Galileo(IRE) Simply Perfect (Danehill (USA))
(7720a) ◆ 7828a[4]

Melbourne Memories *Clive Cox* 99
3 b f Sleeping Indian Three Decades (IRE) (Invincible Spirit (IRE))
1676[3] 2299a[7] 2910a[9] 5271[5] 7015[9]

Meleagros (IRE) *F Couetil* a88 114
4 b c King's Best(USA) Viola Royale (IRE) (Royal Academy (USA))
2184a[6] 3615a[4]

Melivea (FR) *C Laffon-Parias* a75 75
3 b f Green Tune(USA) Cerita (IRE) (Wolfhound (USA))
962a[2]

Melodique (FR) *C Laffon-Parias* 104
3 b f Falco(USA) Elodie Des Charmes (FR) (Diesis)
2381a[4] 4792a[4] 5629a[6]

Melody Of Love *Ann Duffield* 99
3 b f Haafhd Tamzin (Hernando (FR))
2452[14]

Melrose Abbey (IRE) *Ralph Beckett* 61
2 ch f Selkirk(USA) Villa Carlotta (Rainbow Quest (USA))
7128[3]

Melvin The Grate (IRE) *Andrew Balding* a86 89
3 b g Danehill Dancer(IRE) Hawala (IRE) (Warning)
(1091) 1477[3] 2554[5] 4922[6] 6867[2] 7075[3] 7499[3]

Memorize (IRE) *Ed Walker* 28
3 b g Dark Angel(IRE) Cape Cod (IRE) (Unfuwain (USA))
2093[13]

Memory Cloth *Brian Ellison* a92 104
6 b g Cape Cross(IRE) Gossamer (Sadler's Wells (USA))
945[12] 1235[13] 1675[7] 2018[12] 2477[8] 3725[8] 3825[10] 4979[9] 5367[5] 6626[9] 7131[9]

Memory Styx *Mick Channon* a69 79
2 gr f Clodovil(IRE) Quickstyx (Night Shift (USA))
1208[2] 1421[2] 1605[6] 1839[2] 2090[2] 2583[3] 2774[5] 3092[2] 3280[2] 4073[2] (4289) 4528[15] 5012[2] 5306[2] 5699[4] 6065[3] 6386[2] 6825[8]

Memphis Magic (GER) *Ed Walker* a67
3 b g Tertullian(USA) Maltage (USA) (Affirmed (USA))
7167[2] 7490[2] 7987[5]

Memphis Man *Milton Bradley* a63 60
10 b g Bertolini(USA) Something Blue (Petong)
2578[11] 3052[10] 3270[9] 3623[7] 4712[8] 5177[14]

Memphis Tennessee (IRE) *A P O'Brien* a81 110
5 b c Hurricane Run(IRE) Hit The Sky (IRE) (Cozzene (USA))
2212[4]

Menadati (USA) *Peter Hiatt* a72 67
5 b g More Than Ready(USA) Ramatuelle (CHI) (Jeune Homme (USA))
94[7] 348[6] 626[7] 805[7] 2273[7] 2533[7] 2787[7]

Menardais (FR) *P Bary* a100 113
4 b c Canyon Creek(IRE) Madeleine's Blush (USA) (Rahy (USA))
1456a[2] 1945a[5] 7186a[8] 7968a[13]

Mendacious Harpy (IRE) *George Baker* a66 73
2 b f Dark Angel(IRE) Idesia (IRE) (Green Desert (USA))
3986[6] ◆ 4484[6] 5635[3] 6452a[6] 7657[5]

Mendip (USA) *Saeed bin Suroor* a114 38
6 bb h Harlan's Holiday(USA) Well Spring (USA) (Coronado's Quest (USA))
556a[5] 958a[12] 4027[11]

Men Don't Cry (IRE) *Ed de Giles* a70 60
4 b g Street Cry(IRE) Naissance Royale (IRE) (Giant's Causeway (USA))
1710[8] 2514[5] 2954[7] 3169[4] 3909[2] 4071[6] (4605) 5633[3] 6044[3] 6479[2] 6895[6] 7379[3] 7628[2] 7857[2] 8031[2]

Meneas (FR) *C Laffon-Parias* 107
3 b g American Post Okalea (IRE) (Dalakhani (IRE))
3645a[7] 4573a[4]

Menelik (IRE) *Tom Dascombe* a73 56
4 b g Oasis Dream Chica Roca (USA) (Woodman (USA))
2807[5] (4155) 4340[7] (4637) 8304[7] 8453[10]

Mental (AUS) *Mahmood Al Zarooni* a121 126
5 b g Lonhro(AUS) Intrigues (AUS) (Night Shift (USA))
(660a) 1266a[10]

Menyllos (GR) *C Laffon-Parias* a85 67
4 b g Kavafi(IRE) Ipeiros (GR) (Pivotal)
(963a)

Mercers Row *Karen Tutty* a63 80
6 b g Bahamian Bounty Invincible (Slip Anchor)
1692[5] 2275[7] 2832[2] 3283[4] 3713[4] 4074[2] 4203[10] 4852[3] 5381[10] 5985[12] 6287[11] (6760) 7344[9]

Merchant Of Dubai *Jim Goldie* a79 82
8 b g Dubai Destination(USA) Chameleon (Green Desert (USA))
1536[9] 2040[14] 2633[2] (3284) 4512[2] 5185[2] 5640[6] 6466[6] 6876[6] 7193[30]

Merchant Of Medici *Micky Hammond* a91 79
6 b g Medicean Regal Rose (Danehill (USA))
1442[13] 2478[2] 2673[3] 3349[7] 3889[9] 4376[8] 5245[8]

Merchants Return *Lydia Pearce* a57 40
4 b g Byron Molly Pitcher (IRE) (Halling (USA))
62[6] 1916[12]

Mercury Magic *Ralph Beckett* a57
2 b g Oratorio(IRE) Lochridge (Indian Ridge)
8326[7]

Merevale *Michael Appleby* a23 40
4 b g Selkirk(USA) A Thousand Smiles (IRE) (Sadler's Wells (USA))
406[8] 458[13]

Meridius (IRE) *Gary Harrison* a74 74
3 b g Invincible Spirit(IRE) Eliza Acton (Shirley Heights)
3170[2] 3837[5] 4499[2] 4636[7] 6476[8] 7444[5]

Meri Shika (FR) *Roger L Attfield* 104
3 bl f Spirit One(FR) Folle Biche (FR) (Take Risks (FR))
2299a[14] 2970a[2] 6454a[9]

Meritocracy (IRE) *Paul Cole* a90 95
2 br g Kheleyf(USA) Chiosina (IRE) (Danehill Dancer (IRE))
1541[3] 1669[3] 1930[3] (2082) 2433a[2] (4239) 4528[21] 4855[8] (7329)

Merletta *Jeremy Noseda* a78 100
2 b f Raven's Pass(USA) Light Hearted (Green Desert (USA))
3760[6] 5344[4] 5680[4] 6160[2] (7328)

Merrjanah *John Wainwright* a54 53
5 b f Diktat Aberdovey (Mister Baileys)
28[2] 434[5] 587[5] 703[5] 3106[10] 3244[6] 4204[9] 7984[8] 8148[8]

Merry Me (IRE) *Andrew Balding* a70 61
2 b f Invincible Spirit(IRE) Thought Is Free (Cadeaux Genereux)
3690[4] 4877[12] 8175[2]

Mersad (IRE) *James Tate* a71 61
2 ch g Shamardal(USA) Fortress (Generous (IRE))
3493[6] 3948[4] 7646[6] 7973[3] 8147[5] (8452)

Mesharc (FR) *Mme C Barande-Barbe* a43 62
3 b g Meshaheer(USA) Arcole (FR) (River Bay (USA))
270a[9] 647a[5]

Meshardal (GER) *Ruth Carr* 68
3 b g Shamardal(USA) Melody Fair (IRE) (Montjeu (IRE))
2746[3] 3021[14] 3977[10] 5580[14] 6075[6] 6634[4] 6916[5]

Mesmerized (IRE) *Marco Botti* a73 69
3 b f Duke Of Marmalade(IRE) Margot (Sadler's Wells (USA))
1828[6] 2850[3] 4523[2] 4898[8] 5192[3] 5395[6] 6521[5] 7249[5]

Mespone (FR) *Alan Bailey* a81 85
4 b g Vespone(IRE) Manon (Alzao (USA))
3094[12] 3503[5] 7611[12] 7865[10] 8183[6]

Messageinabottle (USA) *James Bethell* a53 64
3 bb f Grand Slam(USA) Devine (USA) (Seattle Slew (USA))
4887[2] 5517[5] 6291[4] 7037[5] 7455[14]

Messila Star *Jeremy Noseda* a84 62
3 ch c Pivotal Jamboretta (IRE) (Danehill (USA))
1618[6] (1908) 3633[10] 6204[11] 7224[10]

Mestizo *Declan Carroll* a28 49
2 b f Oratorio(IRE) Sarah's First (Cadeaux Genereux)
6206[8] 6724[7] 7175[11] 7944[8]

Meteoroid (USA) *Lady Cecil* 79
2 bb c Dynaformer(USA) Enthused (USA) (Seeking The Gold (USA))
4764[4] (5843) 6640[2]

Methaaly (IRE) *Michael Mullineaux* a69 59
10 b g Red Ransom(USA) Santorini (USA) (Spinning World (USA))
54[4] 214[8] 516[4] (560) 688[3] 924[6] 971[10] 1351[7] 1516[9] 1694[6] (2096) 3317[3] 3569[3] 3716[5] 4102[6] 4245[9] 5049[5] 5273[7] 6219[3] 6344[6] 7106[7] 7512[5] 7905[7] 8002[6] 8370[3] 8412[4]

Metropolis (IRE) *Adrian Brendan Joyce* a27 64
8 b g Fasliyev(USA) Arcade (Rousillon (USA))
1779[8]

Metropolitan Chief *Paul Burgoyne* a59 56
9 b g Compton Place Miss Up N Go (Gorytus (USA))
471[4] 649[9] 819[6] (917) 1088[7] 1396[6] (6930) 7292[2] 7644[5] 8022[2]

Mexicali (IRE) *Dean Ivory* a84 87
5 b f Tiger Hill(IRE) Guadalajara (GER) (Acatenango (GER))
2251[6] 2939[12] 3765[9] (4166) 4873[8] 5895[7]

Mexikoma (USA) *Richard C Mettee* a109
2 bb c Birdstone(USA) Toccet Over (USA) (Toccet (USA))
7711a[6]

Mey Blossom *Richard Whitaker* a67 69
8 ch m Captain Rio Petra Nova (First Trump)
101[9] 1802[13] (2338) 2703[2] 3069[7] 4017[5] 4203[8] 4588[2] 4852[10] 5422[2] 5985[10] 6771[9] 7381[8]

Meydan Style (USA) *Richard Ford* a52 14
7 b g Essence Of Dubai(USA) Polish Ruby (USA) (Polish Pro (USA))
41[6] 220[6] 348[4] 440[9] 523[5] 884[4]

Mezel *Sir Michael Stoute* a55 75
2 b g Tamayuz Mumayeza (Indian Ridge)
3689[9] (4199) 4988[5]

Mezmaar *Charles Hills* 95
4 b g Teofilo(IRE) Bay Tree (IRE) (Daylami (IRE))
2257[5]

Mezzotint (IRE) *Marco Botti* a97 104
4 b g Diamond Green(FR) Aquatint (Dansili)
78[8] (2310) 2858[11] 3114[3] 3527[12] 4297[11] 5247[12] (6278) 6840[2]

Mezzotinto (FR) *P Le Gal* a63 49
6 b g Fairly Ransom(USA) Montgarri (FR) (Johann Quatz (FR))
5464a[3]

Mfiftythreedotcom (IRE) *Richard Fahey* 65
2 ch g Tamayuz Pearl Trader (IRE) (Dubai Destination (USA))
2985[8] 3680[5] 4046[6] 5025[5] 5995[6]

Miako (USA) *Michael Appleby* a74
3 ch g Speightstown(USA) Bond Queen (USA) (Stormy Atlantic (USA))
628[7] 710[6] (828) 1075[3] 1204[3] 2994[4] 3638[9] 8096[10] 8351[8]

Miakora *Mick Quinn* a57 61
5 ch f Compton Place Hickleton Lady (IRE) (Kala Shikari)
346[3] 440[13] 903[7] 1748[8] 1914[8] 2133[4] 3922[8] (4691)

Miami Gator (IRE) *K R Burke* a72 46
6 ch g Titus Livius(FR) Lovere (St Jovite (USA))
118[2] 478[3] 536[2] 718[3] 1786[8] 2219[9] 8136[6] 8294[2]

Miaplacidus (IRE) *Richard Fahey* 66
2 b f Shamardal(USA) Nandy's Cavern (Lion Cavern (USA))
2625[6] 3205[3] 4723[3] 6002[7]

Mia San Triple *Peter Chapple-Hyam* a75 75
2 b f Invincible Spirit(IRE) Atlantide (USA) (Southern Halo (USA))
6171[3] 6691[2] 6974[3]

Mia's Boy *Chris Dwyer* a101 87
9 b g Pivotal Bint Zamayem (IRE) (Rainbow Quest (USA))
401[4] 585[2] 690[4] 945[4] 1036[7] 1159[3] 1745[3] (1905) 2592[8] 7648[8] 7926[7] 8071[9] 8156[3] 8385[4]

Miblish *Clive Brittain* a106 113
4 b c Teofilo(IRE) Triton Dance (IRE) (Hector Protector (USA))
777[2] (1241) 2186[4] 2811[3] 3457[5] 4082[5]

Mica Mika (IRE) *Richard Fahey* a87 90
5 ch g Needwood Blade Happy Talk (IRE) (Hamas (IRE))
(167) 496[6] 1273[4] 1689[6] 2040[3] 2402[6] 3118[6] 3685[4] 4313[12] 8276[7]

Michaelmas (USA) *A P O'Brien* 101
2 b c Elusive Quality(USA) Christmas Kid (USA) (Lemon Drop Kid (USA))
7548a[2]

Michael's Nook *Alastair Lidderdale* a65 47
6 b g Intikhab(USA) Mysterious Plans (IRE) (Last Tycoon)
274[5] (349) 422[4] 440[5] 967[4] 1020[4] 1149[3] 1271[12] 1452[5]

Michael With Us (USA) *Stephen DiMauro* a95 95
3 b c Bluegrass Cat(USA) Unbridled Melody (USA) (Unbridled's Song (USA))
3360a[8]

Mick Duggan *Simon Hodgson* a76 70
3 ch g Pivotal Poppy Carew (IRE) (Danehill (USA))
2827[5] 3173[6] 4383[12] 5099[3] ◆ 5954[4] 7950[3] 8115[2] 8337[7]

Mick Dundee (IRE) *John Ryan* a67 43
3 b g Aussie Rules(USA) Lucky Oakwood (USA) (Elmaamul (USA))
210[2] (427) (447) 615[3] 5870[6] 6317[12] 6968[6] 7322[5] 7808[7] (8446)

Mickelson (IRE) *Jonjo O'Neill* 78
7 b g Old Vic Life Support (IRE) (High Estate)
1069[9] 4223[12]

Mick Slates (IRE) *Declan Carroll* a53 78
4 b g Moss Vale(IRE) Sonic Night (IRE) (Night Shift (USA))
1286[7] 1462[7] 2406[7] 2836[5]

Mick's Yer Man *Bill Turner* 86
2 b g Bahamian Bounty Sheer Indulgence (FR) (Pivotal)
(1108) ◆ (1247) 5236[4] 5372[3] 6386[7]

Micquus (IRE) *Jonathan Geake* a52 56
4 b g High Chaparral(IRE) My Potters (USA) (Irish River (FR))
1979[5]

Micras *Andrew Balding* 66
2 b f Medicean Purple Heather (USA) (Rahy (USA))
7493[5]

Microlight *John E Long* a51 52
5 b g Sleeping Indian Skytrial (USA) (Sky Classic (CAN))
736[4] 1087[3] 1954[4] 3325[9] 7323[9] 8393[3]

Microtheos (FR) *M Boutin* a50 60
3 b g Layman(USA) Lady Nora (FR) (Warrshan (USA))
460a[7]

Midaz *Hughie Morrison* a76
3 br g Zamindar(USA) Schlague (FR) (Pulpit (USA))
1713[7] 2576[5] 3957[5] 5392[7]

Midnight Bahia (IRE) *Dean Ivory* a58 27
4 b f Refuse To Bend(IRE) Midnight Partner (IRE) (Marju (IRE))
169[2] (455) 653[5] 1090[12] 6479[11]

Midnight Dancer (FR) *F Chappet* a75 41
3 ch g Choisir(AUS) Miss Madisyn Rose (USA) (Storm Bird (CAN))
1594a[6] 2335a[7]

Midnight Dream (FR) *Kristin Stubbs* a80 49
3 bb g Country Reel(USA) Tatante (IRE) (Highest Honor (FR))
85[2] 550[2] 730[6] 1482[11] 1892[5] 2983[7] 7601[10] 8096[12]

Midnight Dynamo *Jim Goldie* 83
6 b m Lujain(USA) Miss Hermione (Bahamian Bounty)
2882[8] 3331[3] ◆ (3561) 3892[4] 4579[4] 4954[3] 5639[7] 6161[9] 6583[16] 6665[12]

Midnight Feast *Lee Carter* a74 80
5 b g Ishiguru(USA) Prince's Feather (IRE) (Cadeaux Genereux)
878[3] 1426[3] (1717) (2228) 2807[8] (3210) 4067[U] 4281[8] 5522[9] 5931[8] 6167[6] 7306[4] 7629[11] 8158[7]

Midnight Flower (IRE) *David Simcock* a75 100
3 b f Haafhd Takawiri (IRE) (Danehill (USA))
2160[5] (3058) (4534) ◆ 4767[2] 5538[4] 5700[3] 7021[6]

Midnight Game *W P Mullins* 98
6 b g Montjeu(IRE) Midnight Angel (GER) (Acatenango (GER))
3599a[7]

Midnight Muscida (IRE) *Tim Easterby* 62
2 b f Kodiac Nose One's Way (IRE) (Revoque (IRE))
2751[9] 3084[2] ◆ 3710[4] 4134[7] 4847[11] 5289[2] 5467[4] 6494[4]

Midnight Oil *W P Mullins* 93
5 b g Motivator One So Marvellous (Nashwan (USA))
3423[10] (Dead)

Midnight Pearl (USA) *John Gallagher* 34
10 bb m Woodman(USA) Elegant Ridge (IRE) (Indian Ridge)
7465[12]

Midnight Rambler (IRE) *Richard Hannon Snr* a56 60
2 ch c Compton Place Crowd Pleaser (IRE) (Royal Applause)
5584[8] 6110[6] 6342[5] 6749[7] 7428[2]

Midnight Rider (IRE) *Chris Wall* a86 91
5 b g Red Ransom(USA) Foreplay (IRE) (Lujain (USA))
4217[10] 5009[7] 5489[2] 6647[3] 6977[6] 7464[11]

Midnight Sequel *Michael Blake* a57 59
4 b f Midnight Legend Silver Sequel (Silver Patriarch (IRE))
169[6] 343[8] (820) (983) 1342[4] 2828[4] 3312[6] 4380[7] 5123[7] 7081[9]

Midnight Soprano (IRE) *P D Deegan* 108
6 b m Celtic Swing Midnight Glimmer (IRE) (Dr Devious (IRE))
(3381a) 4059[6] 5115a[3]

Midnight Taboo (USA) *Todd Pletcher* a98
3 ch c Langfuhr(CAN) Hot Red (USA) (Thunder Gulch (USA))
3127a[12]

Midnight Warrior *Ron Barr* a65 71
3 b g Teofilo(IRE) Mauri Moon (Green Desert (USA))
2027[3] 2506[6] 3828[4] 4436[5] 4887[7] 5342[6] 5975[6] 6518[3]

Midnite Angel (IRE) *Richard Hannon Snr* 97
2 gr f Dark Angel(IRE) Two Sets To Love (IRE) (Cadeaux Genereux)
2283[2] (2517) 3522[10] 3857[3] 5005[2] ◆ 5284[2] 5737[4] 6795[6]

Midnite Silver (USA) *Giuseppe Iadisernia* 89
7 bb h Silver Deputy(CAN) Fastria (USA) (Fast Play (USA))
773a[3] (1001a)

Midsummer Sun *Sam Kavanagh* a104 102
5 b g Monsun(GER) Midsummer (Kingmambo (USA))
7762a[2]

Mid Yorkshire Golf *Peter Grayson* a53
4 b f Doyen(IRE) Jodeeka (Fraam)
1519[5] 2169[10] 7203[4] 7380[4] 7929[5] 8003[2] 8140[4] 8277[2] 8338[3]

Mighty Ambition (USA) *Charlie Appleby* a95 86
4 b c Street Cry(IRE) New Morning (IRE) (Sadler's Wells (USA))
7641[9] 7926[5]

Mighty Clarets (IRE) *Peter Bowen* a76 69
6 br g Whipper(USA) Collected (IRE) (Taufan (USA))
4208[3]

Mighty Force (IRE) *Nick Littmoden* a55 40
2 b c Acclamation Ikan (IRE) (Sri Pekan (USA))
6769[8] 7308[11] 8333[6]

Mighty Mata *Mark Usher* a52 52
3 b c Lucky Story(USA) Dudleys Delight (Makbul)
341[6] 729[4] 3898[3] 5397[7] 6138[7] 6553[12]

Mighty Missile (IRE) *Tom Tate* 62
2 ch g Majestic Missile(IRE) Magdalene (FR) (College Chapel)
6754[5] 7023[9] 7494[10]

Mighty Thor *Lydia Richards* a65
3 b g Norse Dancer(IRE) Leyaaly (Night Shift (USA))
373[7] 774[5] 1009[4] 1425[5] 5102[6]

Mighty Whitey (IRE) *Noel C Kelly* a56 64
7 b g Sesaro(USA) Deeco Valley (IRE) (Satco (FR))
597[5]

Mighty Yar (IRE) *Lady Cecil* a75 91
3 gr c Teofilo(IRE) Karaliyfa (IRE) (Kahyasi)
(4416) ◆

Mignonne *Hans Adielsson* a54
3 ch f With Approval(CAN) Miss Rinjani (Shirley Heights)
3469[9] 3957[7] 6134[10] 7299[6] 7770[3]

Miguela McGuire *Eric Alston* a43 50
2 b f Sir Percy Miss McGuire (Averti (IRE))
2025[5] 2625[10] 6383[4] 7352[8]

Miguel Grau (USA) *Roger Varian* a82
3 b g City Zip(USA) Zuri Ridge (USA) (Cox's Ridge (USA))
(7167) 7446[3] 8008[2] (8323) ◆

Mihrimahal (TUR) *S Altundag* 75
4 ch f Medya(TUR) Gulbin Sultan (TUR) (Asakir)
6231a[9]

Mijhaar *Roger Varian* a109 113
5 b g Shirocco(GER) Jathaabeh (Nashwan (USA))
(2407) 3873a[7] 4944[6] 7012[6]

Mikelino *G Botti* 71
2 ch c Dubawi(IRE) Oulianovsk (IRE) (Peintre Celebre (USA))
7185a[3]

Mikhail Glinka (IRE) *Seth Benzel* a100 115
6 b h Galileo(IRE) Lady Karr (Mark Of Esteem (IRE))
657a[3] 741a[5]

Mila (FR) *A De Royer-Dupre* 101
3 b f Cape Cross(IRE) Minatlya (FR) (Linamix (FR))
5315a[4] 7048a[8]

Milano Blues (FR) *B De Montzey* a77 87
3 b c Anabaa Blue Milanaise (FR) (Marignan (USA))
1046a[5] 2907a[17]

Mil Azul (SPA) *E Leon Penate* a95 93
5 b c Russian Blue(IRE) Cuittled (USA) (Charismatic (USA))
2897a[13]

Mildenhall *Richard Hannon Snr* a36 54
2 ch f Compton Place Night Kiss (FR) (Night Shift (USA))
2583[8] 3374[14] 3663[8] 5034[4] 5347[5] 5893[11]

Miles Of Sunshine *Ron Hodges* a57 58
8 b g Thowra(FR) Rainbow Nation (Rainbow Quest (USA))
7668[10]

Miliika *Rae Guest* 88
4 b f Green Desert(USA) Miss Anabaa (Anabaa (USA))
5009[9] 5308[2] 6382[8] 6959[10]

Military Attack (IRE) *J Moore* a56 123
5 b g Oratorio(IRE) Almaaseh (IRE) (Dancing Brave (USA))
(1872a) (2494a) 8211a[4]

Military Call *R Mike Smith* a36 64
6 b g Royal Applause Trump Street (First Trump)
2636[8] 2977[5] 4339[6] 4469[8] 6083[11] 7149[9]

Millers Wharf (IRE) *Richard Hannon Snr* a74 79
3 b c Acclamation Applaud (USA) (Rahy (USA))
1612[3] 2394[8] 3062[3] 3242[8] 3576[2] 3837[3]

Mill I Am (USA) *Stuart Williams* a55 51
3 b f Henny Hughes(USA) Courageous (USA) (Kingmambo (USA))
3116[13] 7108[6] 7770[6] 7962[6] 8055[4] 8371[8]

Millie N Aire *Danielle McCormick* a59 65
3 b f Multiplex Hillside Girl (IRE) (Tagula (IRE))
2091[4] 2512[5] 5878[12]

Millies Quest *Martin Smith* a54 67
4 b f Generous(IRE) Alexander Star (IRE) (Inzar (USA))
5071[6] 5720[7] 6134[9] 6612[10] 7346[12]

Million Faces *Rae Guest* 79
4 ch f Exceed And Excel(AUS) Millyant (Primo Dominie)
5620[5] 6077[5] 7240[11]

Millkwood *John Davies* a59 81
3 b g Millkom Wedgewood Star (Bishop Of Cashel)
2672[4] 3025[8] 5150[5] 5485[2] 6212[2] ◆ 6516[2] 6940[3] 7314[3] 7633[3] 7759[2]

Mill Marin (IRE) *Wido Neuroth* a53 91
3 b f Pivotal Mill Guineas (USA) (Salse (USA))
5326a[10]

Milly's Gift *Clive Cox* a91 95
3 b f Trade Fair Milly's Lass (Mind Games)
(979) 2449[11] (2983) 4252[7] 4983[14] (6382) 6768[5]

Milly's Secret (IRE) *Ann Duffield* 79
2 ch f Sakhee's Secret Swan Sea (USA) (Sea Hero (USA))
2612[2] (3064) 3723[3] 4134[2] 4618[5] 5547[2] 5858[8] (6904)

Milo D'Acampo *Tim Etherington*
2 ch g Firebreak Karminskey Park (Sabrehill (USA))
7901[8]

Mimbleberry *Tom Dascombe* a55 59
2 b f Winker Watson Baldovina (Tale Of The Cat (USA))
3318[5] 4164[11] 5225[3] 6322[7] 6726[4] 7032[4] 7168[P]

Mime Dance *Andrew Balding* a72 77
2 b c Notnowcato Encore My Love (Royal Applause)
2391[3] 4439[3] 4987[5] (6334) 6865[2] 7122[4]

Mimi Luke (USA) *Alan Bailey* a67 67
2 b f US Ranger(USA) Hard As Nails (USA) (Holy Bull (USA))
1634[15] 1880[3] 2131[3] 3753[3] 4277[7] 6607[2]

Minakshi (FR) *Michael Matz* a81 105
5 bb f Footstepsinthesand Maria De La Luz (Machiavellian (USA))
(6454a) 7562a[4]

Minalisa *Rae Guest* a69 102
4 b f Oasis Dream Mina (Selkirk (USA))
2513[4] 2988[6] (3733) ◆ 4017[2] (4389) 4647a[2] 5561[2] 5984[5] 7021[4]

Mince *Roger Charlton* 116
4 ch f Medicean Strut (Danehill Dancer (IRE))
2368[10] 2936[3] 3557[16] 4079[3] 6235[3] (7021)

Mind *Henry Candy* a60 48
2 b g Zamindar(USA) Danae (Dansili)
5957[10] 7302[8]

Mindblowing *Kevin Ryan* 78
2 b g Mind Games Musical Day (Singspiel (IRE))
6754[11] 7023[3] (7237)

Mindsforgemanacles (IRE) *C Boutin* a62 63
2 b f Oratorio(IRE) Medicean Star (IRE) (Galileo (IRE))
5213a[11]

Mind That Girl (IRE) *Y Durepaire*
2 b f Ad Valorem(USA) Pegase Hurry (USA) (Fusaichi Pegasus (USA))
7084a[9]

Miner's Lamp (IRE) *Charlie Appleby* 89
2 b c Shamardal(USA) Truly Mine (IRE) (Rock Of Gibraltar (IRE))
5405[4] (6528) (7107)

Mingun Bell (USA) *Ed de Giles* a93 88
6 b g Mingun(USA) Miss Tippins (USA) (Squadron Leader (USA))
1878[7] 3019[5] 3693[7] 4502[5] 5195[2] 5802[8] 6167[4] 6963[5]

Ming Zhi Cosmos (FR) *N Clement* 95
2 b f Duke Of Marmalade(IRE) The Wise Lady (FR) (Ganges (USA))
7084a[6]

Mini Light *Mick Channon* 23
2 b f Royal Applause Kind Of Light (Primo Dominie)
5529[14] 6013[6]

Minimee *Phil McEntee* a70 72
3 b g Dubai Destination(USA) Malaaq (Green Desert (USA))
663[4] 793[4] (918) 1293[4] 1486[2] 1655[5] 1912[7] 3537[12] 4143[3] 6109[12] 6522[11] 6968[3] 7322[3] (7455) 7610[4] 7639[8] 7931[5] 8042[10] 8409[5]

Minionette (IRE) *Alan Swinbank* 28
2 b f Manduro(GER) La Vita E Bella (IRE) (Definite Article)
7493[12]

Miniskirt *Rae Guest* 81
2 b f Naaqoos Minnola (Royal Applause)
7245[2]

Ministerofinterior *Richard Ford* a60 74
8 b g Nayef(USA) Maureen's Hope (USA) (Northern Baby (CAN))
2545[9] 5048[10]

Ministry *Gary Moore* a71 56
5 b g Iceman Choirgirl (Unfuwain (USA))
131[5]

Minley *Rae Guest* a74 75
2 b g Acclamation Fatal Attraction (Oasis Dream)
2955[6] 3413[4] 3815[3] 4498[2] (5215) 5848a[6] 6376[7]

Minnaloushe (IRE) *John Gosden* a74 62
2 b f Lawman(FR) Traou Mad (IRE) (Barathea (IRE))
6112[3] 6828[6] 7294[2] 7844[2] 8084[3]

Minneapolis *Alison Batchelor* a102 58
8 b g Sadler's Wells(USA) Teggiano (IRE) (Mujtahid (USA))
7217[11]

Minnie Miracle *Mark Usher*
2 ch f Compton Place Splicing (Sharpo)
8326[12]

Minnie Punt (USA) *J David Braddy* 108
7 b g Gold Fever(USA) Let's Punt (USA) (Rubiano (USA))
608a[6]

Minnyvinny *Dave Roberts* a19
2 b f Multiplex Bounty Reef (Bahamian Bounty)
7200[8] 7541[8] 7844[5]

Minorette (USA) *A P O'Brien* 96
2 ch f Smart Strike(CAN) Silk And Scarlet (Sadler's Wells (USA))
5318a[4] 6881a[8]

Minority Interest *Brett Johnson* a74 74
4 ch g Galileo(IRE) Minority (Generous (IRE))
140[5] 397[6] 637[6] 816[10] 1176[11] (1779) 2567[8] 3110[5] 3819[5] (4350) 5032[3] (5377) (5650) 6068[4]

Minor Swing (FR) *R Houthoofd* a71 88
5 gr g Kouroun(FR) Group One (FR) (Poliglote)
6060a[7]

Minortransgression (USA) *Sean Curran* a74 59
6 ch g Yes It's True(USA) Casting Pearls (USA) (Fusaichi Pegasus (USA))
218[7] 221[5] 536[3] 967[3]

Minot Street (CAN) *John C McConnell* a29 54
3 b g Van Nistelrooy(USA) Just Outta Here (USA) (Rahy (USA))
4449[2] 6049[2] 6083[13]

Minsky Mine (IRE) *Michael Appleby* a70 75
6 b g Montjeu(IRE) Summer Trysting (USA) (Alleged (USA))
39[5]

Minstrel Lad *Lydia Pearce* a62 62
5 ch g Where Or When(IRE) Teal Flower (Pivotal)
1949[3] 2801[4] 3399[2] 3953[7] 7299[7] 7639[3] (7907) 8121[3]

Mintaka (FR) *A De Royer-Dupre* 74
2 gr f Zamindar(USA) Minatlya (FR) (Linamix (FR))
5419a[3]

Mint Crisp *Hughie Morrison* 61
3 gr f Dalakhani(IRE) Peppermint Green (Green Desert (USA))
2850[9] 3372[8]

Minty Fox *Noel Williams* a60 62
4 gr f Dalakhani(IRE) Quantum (IRE) (Alhaarth (IRE))
6068[5] *7159[6]* 7539[12]

Minty Jones *Michael Mullineaux* a43 55
4 b c Primo Valentino(IRE) Reveur (Rossini (USA))
42[11] 409[9] 819[8] 1042[11] 1305[5] 2236[3] 3268[7] 3754[6] 5614[2] *8146[6]*

Miracle Cure (IRE) *J S Bolger* a84 96
4 b g Whipper(USA) Bring Back Matron (IRE) (Rock Of Gibraltar (IRE))
1168a[17]

Miracle Of Medinah *Mark Usher* a79 105
2 ch c Milk It Mick Smart Ass (IRE) (Shinko Forest (IRE))
2617[6] 3017[4] *(3493)* (3857) (4486) 4918[9] 5679[7] (6765)

Mironica (IRE) *David Wachman* 89
3 ch f Excellent Art Lisfannon (Bahamian Bounty)
4647a[9]

Mirror (IRE) *Ed Dunlop* a26
2 b f Dandy Man(IRE) Fields Of Joy (GER) (Waky Nao)
8145[7] 8396[5]

Mirror Image *S Wattel* a71 71
3 b f Acclamation Mystic Spirit (IRE) (Invincible Spirit (IRE))
126a[4]

Mirsaale *James Tate* 109
3 ch c Sir Percy String Quartet (IRE) (Sadler's Wells (USA))
(1767) 2866[9] 4027[7]

Mirth *Mark Johnston* a59 63
3 ch f Teofilo(IRE) Birthstone (Machiavellian (USA))
541[2] 841[2] 1009[6] 1613[4] 2769[6] 3194[3] *3497[8] 4150[6]*

Mirza *Rae Guest* a68 110
6 b g Oasis Dream Millyant (Primo Dominie)
1672[7] 2909a[7] 3822[3] 4935a[5] 6235[7] (6445a) 7054a[19]

Miserere Mei (IRE) *Richard Guest* a58 52
4 b f Moss Vale(IRE) Flying Clouds (Batshoof)
111[2] 213[3] 326[3] 422[5] 529[2] 610[2] 756[7] 997[10] 1276[5] *1356[5]* 1961[5]

Misfer *Lady Cecil* a74 66
3 ch c Byron Diliza (Dilum (USA))
1735[3] 2322[5] *3641[3]*

Mishaal (IRE) *Michael Herrington* a76 76
3 ch g Kheleyf(USA) My Dubai (IRE) (Dubai Millennium)
3773[4] 4400[4] 4887[3] 5290[2] *5676[5]* (6084) *6367[2]* 6874[2]

Mishhar (IRE) *Tony Coyle* a59 68
4 b f Authorized(IRE) Jakarta (IRE) (Machiavellian (USA))
1282[8] 1389[4] 1610[4] 1757[5] 2273[4] 2616[2] 2837[7] 3193[5] 3946[5] 4557[5] 5142[6] 5828[6]

Mishko (IRE) *Clive Cox* 67
2 b c Amadeus Wolf Miss Shangri La (Rainbow Quest (USA))
4896[5] 5698[5] 6954[7]

Mishnah *John Holt* a35 53
2 b f Orpen(USA) Minshar (Noverre (USA))
5950[7] 6546[6] *7790[6] 7954[7]*

Mishrif (USA) *J R Jenkins* a77 69
7 bb g Arch(USA) Peppy Priscilla (USA) (Latin American (USA))
1717[4] 1925[3] 2565[12] 3054[5] 3656[8] *4411[2]* 5205[3] 5622[2] *6315[8] 7858[4] (8295)* 8360[4]

Misleading Promise (IRE) *John Butler* a69
3 b g Refuse To Bend(IRE) Farthing (IRE) (Mujadil (USA))
237[7] 419[6] (538) 726[2] 804[3] 918[3] (988)

Misplaced Fortune *Nigel Tinkler* a46 99
8 b m Compton Place Tide Of Fortune (Soviet Star (USA))
1720[6] 2476[4] 2988[4] 3249[7] 3892[2] 4472[7] 5056[5] 6564[4] 6768[2] 7241[9] 7495[3] 7820[17]

Miss Acclaimed (IRE) *Brian Ellison* a24 66
2 gr f Acclamation Miss Shaan (FR) (Darshaan)
4351[11] 4756[2] 5419a[7] 6330[6] 7125[5]

Miss Atomic Bomb *Marco Botti* a77 73
2 b f Intikhab(USA) Green Bonnet (IRE) (Green Desert (USA))
6423[2] *(6981) 7662[3]*

Miss Avonbridge (IRE) *Tom Dascombe* a79 64
3 b f Avonbridge Red Planet (Pivotal)
(2806) 3216[2] 4145[5] 5353[2] 8134[2] 8401[6]

Miss Blakeney *Marcus Tregoning* a84 63
4 b f Sir Percy Misplace (IRE) (Green Desert (USA))
2939[11] *8150[6] 8336[7]*

Miss Blink *Robin Bastiman* a71 73
6 ch m Compton Place Tawny Way (Polar Falcon (USA))
1579[8] 2137[5] 4099[5] 5377[2] 6794[7]

Miss Bossy Boots *Tracy Waggott* 34
4 b f Ishiguru(USA) Mighty Flyer (IRE) (Mujtahid (USA))
1389[8] 1842[11] 2503[5] 2613[7] 4887[11] 5641[7]

Miss Brazil (IRE) *Richard Hannon Snr* a71 73
2 ch f Exceed And Excel(AUS) Amazon Beauty (IRE) (Wolfhound (USA))
6318[5] 6789[4] 7103[2] *7295[3] 7737[2]*

Miss Buckshot (IRE) *Rae Guest* a81 79
2 b f Tamayuz Miss Bellbird (IRE) (Danehill (USA))
4924[6] *6107[4]* ◆ (6973) *7626[4]*

Miss Bunter *David O'Meara* a78 58
4 b f Bahamian Bounty The Terrier (Foxhound (USA))
(26) (54) 234[3] 885[3] 924[2] 1102[3] 4588[6] 4728[9] 5227[8]

Miss Cap Estel *Andrew Balding* 103
4 b f Hernando(FR) Miss Cap Ferrat (Darshaan)
3158[2] ◆ 3610[3] 3755[4] 4234[2] 4920[7] 5795[7] (6434) 7590a[9] (7822)

Miss Chardonay *Mandy Rowland* a43 40
6 b m Helissio(FR) Up The Creek (IRE) (Supreme Leader)
313[4] 541[5] 590[5] 1093[11] 1730[10] 2764[9] 3252[8] 4504[7] *5073[8]*

Miss Chuckles *Tim Easterby* 38
3 ch f Medicean Heckle (In The Wings)
2306[13] 2989[10]

Miss Dashwood *James Fanshawe* a85 97
4 b f Dylan Thomas(IRE) Dash To The Front (Diktat)
1544[9] 2639[4] 3177[3] (5008) (5795) 6764[9] 7822[14]

Miss Diva *Richard Hannon Snr* 87
3 b f Acclamation Mina (Selkirk (USA))
1808[13] 2270[7] 3058[10] 3279[3] 3634[3] 4413[4] 4989[7] 7254[10]

Missed Call (IRE) *Lady Cecil* a67 91
3 b f Authorized(IRE) Incoming Call (USA) (Red Ransom (USA))
2953[7] (3764) 4929[2] 5496[2]

Miss Ella Jade *Richard Whitaker* a55 59
4 b f Danbird(AUS) Keen Melody (USA) (Sharpen Up)
2316[11] 2956[6] 3195[2] 3543[8] 4853[4] 5144[8] *5967[2]* 6598[5] *7081[5] 7951[3] 8229[7] 8436[3]*

Missfire *Brian Baugh*
3 b f Firebreak Gary's Indian (IRE) (Indian Danehill (IRE))
8348[8]

Miss Fortywinks *Joseph Tuite* a45 73
4 gr f Act One Andromache (Hector Protector (USA))
2349[3] *2982[11]*

Miss France (IRE) *A Fabre* 112
2 b f Dansili Miss Tahiti (IRE) (Tirol)
(6795) ◆

Miss Glorioso *Alexandra Dunn* a9
4 b m Helissio(FR) Miss Glory Be (Glory Of Dancer)
752[8] 8068[10]

Missie Snaffles *Alan Swinbank* a16 19
3 b f Compton Place Mrs Snaffles (IRE) (Indian Danehill (IRE))
972[7] 2538[7] *8437[11]*

Missing Ones (FR) *P Chatelain* a65 94
3 b c Lawman(FR) Vassileva (FR) (Lomitas)
1756a[4]

Missionaire (USA) *Tony Carroll* a59 51
6 bb g El Corredor(USA) Fapindy (USA) (A.P. Indy (USA))
943[5] 510[10] 1111[13] *1779[4] 3169[10]* 5065[7] 6325[16]

Mission Approved *Sir Michael Stoute* a89 86
3 b g Dansili Moon Search (Rainbow Quest (USA))
(1958) 2554[4] 4641[3] 5998[5] *6525[2]* 6977[3]

Mission Impossible *Tracy Waggott* a28 79
8 gr g Kyllachy Eastern Lyric (Petong)
1283[3] (1692) 2275[11] 2614[8] 3778[8] 5294[11] 5832[10] 6547[11] 7029[10] 7282[7] 7315[3] 7599[5]

Mississippi *David Barron* a88 94
4 b g Exceed And Excel(AUS) Ruby Rocket (IRE) (Indian Rocket)
1571[7] 2007[2] ◆ 3367[2] 3846a[6] 4472[5] 4780[19]

Miss Lahar *Mick Channon* 102
4 b f Clodovil(IRE) Brigadiers Bird (IRE) (Mujadil (USA))
2152[5] 2621[4] 3046[4] 3373[3] 3784[2] 4275[7] (4647a) 6639[7] 7021[8]

Miss Lawlass (IRE) *James Given* a39 44
2 b f Lawman(FR) Corryvreckan (IRE) (Night Shift (USA))
5609[9] *6213[11] 6607[10]* 7340[7] 7630[4] *7883[4] 8040[5]*

Miss Lillie *Roger Teal* a72 82
2 b f Exceed And Excel(AUS) Never Lose (Diktat)
2601[5] 3049[2] *5131[2]* 5737[7] (7693)

Miss Lucy Jane *Richard Fahey* 64
2 ch f Aqlaam Ocean View (USA) (Gone West (USA))
5482[7] 6069[3]

Miss Macnamara (IRE) *Martin Todhunter* a56 67
4 b f Dylan Thomas(IRE) Kincob (USA) (Kingmambo (USA))
(3089) 3944[4] 5048[5] 5831[12]

Miss Marjurie (IRE) *Denis Coakley* a75 84
3 b f Marju(IRE) Kazatzka (Groom Dancer (USA))
2195[4] 3292[8] 4769[6] (5632) ◆ 7022[4]

Miss Massucco (FR) *B Vidovic* a64 51
3 b f Medecis Royal Song (FR) (Royal Academy (USA))
3616a[9]

Miss Matiz *Alan Kirtley* 46
6 b m Rock City Doodle Wood (Nomination)
2503[8] 3398[7] 3727[11] 4005[8] 4557[8] 5515[6] 5830[8]

Miss Meticulous *Ed McMahon*
3 ch f Bahamian Bounty Umniya (IRE) (Bluebird (USA))
1660[14]

Miss Mitigate *Andrew Balding* a49 57
3 b f Sir Percy Oblige (Robellino (USA))
2346[4] 2938[9] 3858[5] *4634[6]* 7258[12]

Miss Mocca *Jonathan Portman* a63 62
3 b f Bahamian Bounty Mocca (IRE) (Sri Pekan (USA))
1928[9] 2324[5] 2770[10] 6321[8]

Miss Mohawk (IRE) *Alan Brown* a46 44
4 ch f Hawk Wing(USA) Karmafair (IRE) (Always Fair (USA))
2164[6] 2887[9] 3589[9] *4147[3]* 5137[U] 5560[11] *8229[6]*

Miss Mysterious (FR) *Philip Kirby* 47
5 b f Dubai Destination(USA) Torrealta (In The Wings)
2721[3] 3595[8]

Missouri Spirit *Kevin Ryan* a71 75
2 b g Sleeping Indian Sahariri (IRE) (Red Ransom (USA))
4820[3] 5577[5] 6174[3] 6627[4] 6915[2] *7261[2]*

Miss Polly Plum *Chris Dwyer* a57 73
6 b m Doyen(IRE) Mrs Plum (Emarati (USA))
862[8]

Miss Rebero *Tim Fitzgerald* 41
3 b f Cockney Rebel(IRE) One Zero (USA) (Theatrical (IRE))
6178[7] 6630[8] 7108[11]

Miss Sophisticated *David Barron* 67
2 b f Bahamian Bounty Miss Sophisticat (Alhaarth (IRE))
4668[7] 5338[9] 6271[3]

Miss Tallulah (IRE) *Mel Brittain* 55
2 ch f Iffraaj Taalluf (USA) (Hansel (USA))
3023[11] 6286[11] 6947[7]

Misstemper (IRE) *Sean Curran* a57
2 b f Diamond Green(FR) Legnani (Fasliyev (USA))
7756[2]

Miss Tiger Lily *Harry Dunlop* a78 78
3 b f Tiger Hill(IRE) Waitingonacloud (In The Wings)
1347[4] 1613[2] (2124) 2924[7] 4035[2] (4406) *(4753)* ◆ *5102[4]* 5972[4] 6646[11] 7395[4]

Miss Tilly Oscar (IRE) *David Evans* a42
7 b m Oscar(IRE) Whisky Chaser (Never So Bold)
8092[5]

Miss Tweedy *Rod Millman* 59
2 b f Sleeping Indian Ile Royale (Royal Applause)
3664[11] 4218[11]

Missunited (IRE) *Michael Winters* 109
6 bb m Golan(IRE) Lets Clic Together (IRE) (Don't Forget Me)
3073a[2] 7566a[3]

Miss Verdoyante *Sir Mark Prescott Bt* a35
2 b f Montjeu(IRE) Miss Provence (Hernando (FR))
3689[12] 8415[8]

Miss You Too *David Simcock* 103
3 b f Montjeu(IRE) Portrait Of A Lady (IRE) (Peintre Celebre (USA))
2261[2] 2842[6] 4468a[3] 5044a[15] (6536) 7613a[6]

Missy Wells *Tim Walford* a40
3 b f Misu Bond(IRE) Aqua (Mister Baileys)
8348[4]

Misteray *Bill Turner* a40 47
3 ch g Singspiel(IRE) Hannda (IRE) (Dr Devious (IRE))
6899[11] *7440[12]*

Mister Big Shuffle (GER) *Niels Petersen* 98
3 br c Big Shuffle(USA) Marmorea (IRE) (Tiger Hill (IRE))
553a[9] 835a[8]

Mister Black (FR) *F-X De Chevigny* a63 67
3 bl c Country Reel(USA) Miss Anelia (FR) (Majorien)
331a[6] 544a[7]

Mister Bob (GER) *James Bethell* a63 33
4 ch g Black Sam Bellamy(IRE) Mosquera (GER) (Acatenango (GER))
397[4] ◆ *(641) 1097[3]* 1390[9]

Mister Carter (IRE) *Ian Williams* a52 84
6 b g Antonius Pius(USA) Kotdiji (Mtoto)
3512[5] 4882[6] 5337[3] 5863[3] 5885[7] *6736[7]*

Mister Fantastic *Dai Burchell* a7 53
7 ch g Green Tune(USA) Lomapamar (Nashwan (USA))
6102[8]

Mister Fizz *Miss Imogen Pickard* a85 80
5 b g Sulamani(IRE) Court Champagne (Batshoof)
4489[4] 4915[2] 5312[4] (6068) 6239[5] (6787) *(7033) 7739[5]*

Mister Frosty (IRE) *Christine Dunnett* a56 54
7 gr g Verglas(IRE) La Chinampina (FR) (Darshaan)
7951[4] 8149[12] 8270[6]

Mister Green (FR) *David Flood* a75 85
7 b g Green Desert(USA) Summertime Legacy (Darshaan)
1303[11] 1386[3] 1715[4] 1846[7] *(1925) 2228[7] 3906[8]*

Mister Impatience *Mark Johnston* 105
3 b c Hernando(FR) Katy Nowaitee (Komaite (USA))
(1109) ◆ 1767[4] 2187[2] 2454[4] 3526[4] 4473[3] 4919[11] 5764[8] 6394[8] 6741[2] 6957[5] 7496[3]

Mister Manannan (IRE) *David Nicholls* a7 96
6 b g Desert Style(IRE) Cover Girl (IRE) (Common Grounds)
(1607) 2150[6] ◆ 2396[12] 2865[16] 3334[14] 3776[10] 4860[10] 5056[8] 6273[4] 6583[21] 6848[11]

Mister Marcasite *Mel Brittain* a70 76
3 gr g Verglas(IRE) No Rehearsal (FR) (Baillamont (USA))
1109[4] 1486[3] 1604[8] (2549) 5342[8] 6495[8] 6602[4] 6951[10] 7632[6] *8008[4] 8227[10]*

Mister Massagot (FR) *C Baillet* a83
3 ch c Hurricane Cat(USA) In Memory (FR) (Chimes Band (USA))
782a[10]

Mister Mayday (IRE) *George Baker* 67
2 br g Kheleyf(USA) Soxy Doxy (IRE) (Hawk Wing (USA))
2067[6] 3238[7] 5033[7] 5610[11]

Mister Music *Richard Hannon Snr* a105 108
4 b g Singspiel(IRE) Sierra (Dr Fong (USA))
1545[5] 1848[7] 2841[14] 5007[5] (5742) 6001[6] *6199[2]* (6427) 6742[8] 7018[3] 7536[12]

Mister Musicmaster *Ron Hodges* a86 55
4 b g Amadeus Wolf Misty Eyed (IRE) (Paris House)
(400) (511) 865[5] 1092[4] 1385[6] 1583[13] 6959[8] 7318[5] *7769[5] 7989[10] 8454[5]*

Mister Pagan *Jim Goldie* 87
5 b g Sulamani(IRE) Gunnor Marc (Gunnor B)
2465[4] (2971) 3726[4] 4782[12] 5831[2] (6585)

Mister Ryan (FR) *H-A Pantall* a98 104
4 b c Acclamation Irish Flower (IRE) (Zieten (USA))
3187a[2] 4935a[10] 7085a[4]

Mister Sandro (ITY) *S Botti* 99
4 b c Dane Friendly Diega (USA) (Diesis)
1709a[5] 2489a[6]

Mister Six (FR) *A Lamotte D'Argy* a83 73
4 b c Apsis Miss Godiva (FR) (Bahamian Bounty)
5735a[9]

Mister Uno (IRE) *Ann Duffield* a26 51
2 b c Tamayuz Starlight Smile (USA) (Green Dancer (USA))
4053[12] 5083[6] 5379[5] 6285[6] 6726[5] *7032[9]*

Mister Vellucci (IRE) *A Di Dio* 86
5 b g Namid Edwina (IRE) (Caerleon (USA))
2491a[12]

Mister Worldwide (FR) *Y Gourraud* a80 91
2 bb c Librettist(USA) Elsie Wagg (USA) (Mt. Livermore (USA))
7939a[10] *8143a[6]*

Mistral Wind (IRE) *Ed Dunlop* a72 69
3 b f Hurricane Run(IRE) Grable (IRE) (Sadler's Wells (USA))
230[4] 2503[4] 3251[4] *6081[2]* ◆ *6363[4] 7033[4]* 7258[2] 7453[4]

Mistress And Maid *Joseph Tuite* a33 22
2 ch f Dutch Art Passing Fancy (Grand Lodge (USA))
3663[13] *4175[8]*

Mistress Shy *Peter Hiatt* a55 36
6 b m Zafeen(FR) Nicholas Mistress (Beveled (USA))
41[12] 2575[7] 2992[2] 4146[7] 5097[9] 5645[5] *6804[10]*

Mists Of Time (IRE) *Pat Eddery* 60
3 b f Excellent Art Capriole (Noverre (USA))
1364[5]

Misty Eyes *Geoffrey Harker* a54 36
4 b f Byron Wax Eloquent (Zaha (CAN))
1802[14] 6518[7] 7269[6] *7807[4] 8258[4] 8438[6]*

Misty Pearl *Michael Appleby* 28
3 b f Royal Applause Pearl Valley (Indian Rocket)
1447[5] ◆ 1828[12] 2547[12]

Misty Sparkler *Brian Meehan* a73 65
2 ch f Mount Nelson Statua (IRE) (Statoblest)
2230[3] *2774[3]* 3760[8] *6170[2]* ◆ 6695[16] *7463[11]*

Misu Mac *Neville Bycroft* 17
3 b f Misu Bond(IRE) Umbrian Gold (IRE) (Perugino (USA))
4050[7] 6518[15]

Misu's Maite *Roy Bowring* a37 46
2 b f Misu Bond(IRE) Magical Flute (Piccolo)
5494[7] *5866[4]*

Mitcd (IRE) *Richard Fahey* 61
2 gr f Mastercraftsman(IRE) Halicardia (Halling (USA))
2436[6] 2793[2] 3391[4] 4061[7] 6755[11]

Mitchell *David Thompson* a60 73
3 ch g Haafhd Maid To Matter (Pivotal)
2593[8] 3234[5] 3591[3] 4291[4] 4670[8] 5878[5] 6287[10] 6469[7] 6757[8] *7881[9] 8360[3]*

Mitchelton (FR) *Mark Johnston* 79
2 b f High Chaparral(IRE) Fortunately (Forzando)
3366[3] ◆ (3710) 7503[6]

Mitch Rapp (USA) *Jamie Osborne* a61 24
4 b g Yankee Gentleman(USA) Foolish Party (USA) (Party Manners (USA))
2954[10] 3657[9]

Mitchum *Ron Barr* a84 73
4 b g Elnadim(USA) Maid To Matter (Pivotal)
1819[4] 2707[10] 2884[3] 3444[8] (3778) 4540[9] 5583[11] 6181[10] 6515[11] 7283[9]

Mitico (TUR) *Z Guneli* 91
5 b c Red Bishop(USA) Princess Galina (IRE) (Spectrum (IRE))
6253a[11]

Mitlaa (FR) *F Rohaut* a61
2 b f Naaqoos Djayapura (FR) (Fabulous Dancer (USA))
5296a[4]

Mitraad (IRE) *William Haggas* 90
2 ch g Aqlaam Badweia (USA) (Kingmambo (USA))
(6799)

Mixed Message (IRE) *Brian Ellison* a76 75
3 b f Kodiac Berenica (IRE) (College Chapel)
(826) 1486[8] 1965[2] 2235[5] 3137[7] *4143[2]* 5368[3] 6297[4]

Mizdirection (USA) *Mike Puype* a104 111
5 rg f Mizzen Mast(USA) Deceptive (USA) (Clever Trick (USA))
(7710a)

Miz Ida (USA) *Steve Margolis* 106
4 b f Proud Citizen(USA) May Gator (USA) (Green Alligator (USA))
7043a[4]

Mizyen (IRE) *James Tate* a74 77
3 b g Teofilo(IRE) Housekeeper (IRE) (Common Grounds)
1064[2] (1372) 1655[2] 2235[3] *2874[6]* 4665[2] 5218[2] 5606[2] (6037) 6258[3] *6810[2] 7169[5]*

Mizzava (IRE) *M Halford* a65 104
3 bb f Cape Cross(IRE) Flamanda (Niniski (USA))
2289a[3] 2689a[5] 3524[5] 4567a[5] 7404a[2] 7719a[4]

Mizzeni (FR) *Gay Kelleway* a35 26
2 gr c Verglas(IRE) Bashful (IRE) (Brief Truce (USA))
5323a[9] *6656[5]*

M J Woodward *Paul Green* a74 65
4 b c Needwood Blade Canina (Foxhound (USA))
26[4] (213) (481) (640) 795[8] 885[2] 1283[5] *1694[12]* 1758[8] 5047[9] 5365[8] *5673[6]* 5887[6] 6515[4] 6855[6]

M'Lady Ermyn *Pat Phelan* a55 49
2 b f Pastoral Pursuits Penelope Tree (IRE) (Desert Prince (IRE))
4175[7] 4630[4] 5524[5] 5850[3] *6401[3] 6520[6] 8262[11] 8452[7]*

Mme Sans Gene *Ralph Beckett* a14 46
3 gr f Verglas(IRE) Diablerette (Green Desert (USA))
3417[10] *4151[11]*

Moaning Butcher *Mark Johnston* a36 60
3 b g Lucarno(USA) Musical Chimes (Josr Algarhoud (IRE))
1103[5] 2233[2] 2716[16] 3916[5] *4352[8]* 4587[4] 4931[13] 5560[4] 5846[4]

Mobaco (FR) *Luca Cumani* a105 109
4 b c Slickly(FR) Lunaa (FR) (Anabaa (USA))
2652[5] 3525[11] 4526[6]

Mobley Chaos *Ronald Harris* a37 27
3 b g Darnay Emmarander (Bob's Return (IRE))
5813[8] 6155[5] *8437[5]*

Mocacha (IRE) *William Haggas* 73
2 b g Camacho Mama Angela (IRE) (Titus Livius (FR))
5584[2] 6069[2] 6546[7]

Moccasin (FR) *Geoffrey Harker* 98
4 b g Green Tune(USA) Museum Piece (Rainbow Quest (USA))
1446[12] 1643[5] 2431[8] 2766[3] 3204[5] 3477[5] 5086[5] 5382[8] 6563[2] ◆ 7028[7] 7425[2]

Mocenigo (IRE) *Peter Chapple-Hyam* a82 104
3 ch g Refuse To Bend(IRE) Doregan (IRE) (Bahhare (USA))
1667[5] 2661[3]

Model Pupil *Charles Hills* 109
4 b c Sinndar(IRE) Modesta (IRE) (Sadler's Wells (USA))
(1110) ◆ 1674[4] 2810[3] 3483[7] 4083[5] 5531[9] 5741[5] 6766[4] 7535[6]

Modem *Rod Millman* a74 69
3 b g Motivator Alashaan (Darshaan)
6431[3] 7253[5] 7781[7] 8182[2] (8388)

Moderator *Gary Moore* a85 91
4 b g Motivator Alessandra (Generous (IRE))
93[7]

Modern Art *Mark Johnston* a28 37
2 b f New Approach(IRE) Galipette (Green Desert (USA))
7113[5] 7332[9] 7533[12]

Modern Eagle (GER) *A De Royer-Dupre* a85 102
3 b f Montjeu(IRE) Millionaia (IRE) (Peintre Celebre (USA))
7189a[12] (7891a)

Modern History (IRE) *Mahmood Al Zarooni* a103 107
5 b g Shamardal(USA) Fatefully (USA) (Private Account (USA))
241a[16] 552a[5] 836a[4]

Modernism *David Simcock* a87 89
4 b g Monsun(GER) La Nuit Rose (FR) (Rainbow Quest (USA))
2191[12] 2646[10] 3301[14] 6080[3] 6750[5] (7651) (8226) 8301[10]

Modern Lady *Richard Guest* a67 73
3 b f Bertolini(USA) Lady Natilda (First Trump)
75[3] 374[2] 531[2] 710[4] 847[2] 894[2] 992[3] 1315[2] 2832[7] 5265[3] 5639[2] 6515[2] 7030[4]

Modern Romance (IRE) *Marco Botti* 83
4 ch f Muhtathir Khulan (USA) (Bahri (USA))
1823[3] 2253[7] 2711[4]

Modern Society *Andrew Reid* a27
3 sk c I Was Framed(USA) Artzola (IRE) (Alzao (USA))
3403[8] 4151[12]

Modernstone *William Knight* a99 77
3 b f Duke Of Marmalade(IRE) Post Modern (USA) (Nureyev (USA))
(7253) 7661[3] 7895[2] 8062[4] (8387)

Modern Tutor *Sir Michael Stoute* 101
4 b g Selkirk(USA) Magical Romance (IRE) (Barathea (IRE))
2444[11] 3096[8] (5759) 6650[5] 6989[2] 7337[2]

Modify *Bryan Smart* a44 56
2 ch f New Approach(IRE) Hill Welcome (Most Welcome)
4723[7] 5577[6] 6716[6] 7016[13] 7756[4] 7956[4]

Modun (IRE) *Saeed bin Suroor* a110 110
6 br g King's Best(USA) Olympienne (IRE) (Sadler's Wells (USA))
656a[3] 833a[7] (Dead)

Moe's Place (IRE) *Kristin Stubbs* a71 55
3 b g Acclamation Sahara Sky (IRE) (Danehill (USA))
525[2] 964[2] 1190[3] 1760[7] 2276[7] 2737[6] 3903[5] 4722[3] 5594[2] 5961[3]

Mohair *Luke Dace* a70 59
4 b f Motivator Cashmere (Barathea (IRE))
6737[9] 7159[8] 7440[7]

Mohanad (IRE) *Philip Hide* a77 82
7 b g Invincible Spirit(IRE) Irish Design (IRE) (Alhaarth (IRE))
1182[3] 2749[4] 3587[10]

Mohawk Ridge *Michael Dods* a35 80
7 b g Storming Home Ipsa Loquitur (Unfuwain (USA))
(1390) (2316) 2615[4] 3726[10] 4804[8] 5466[6] 5966[6] 7100[2] 7372[2] 7596[6]

Moheebb (IRE) *Robert Johnson* a72 78
9 b g Machiavellian(USA) Rockerlong (Deploy)
61[4] 98[3] 347[6] 831[13] 1569[9] 2163[7] 2889[7] 3466[6] 3827[4] 4559[3] 4759[3] 5137[9] 5828[7] 6177[10] 6598[12]

Mohicane (FR) *W Walton* a78 105
3 b f Samum(GER) Suborneuse (USA) (Diesis)
5463a[2] 6250a[5]

Moidore *John Quinn* a77 98
4 b g Galileo(IRE) Flash Of Gold (Darshaan)
1273[2] 1841[9] 2402[2] 3824[6] 4782[6] 5946[2] 6585[4] 7193[10] ◆

Moi Lolita *Markus Klug* a70 94
4 b f Lawman(FR) Mahamuni (IRE) (Sadler's Wells (USA))
7649[12]

Moissanite *Sean Regan* 4
4 b f Danbird(AUS) Nikita Sunrise (IRE) (Namid)
5563[8] 6178[10] 6630[9]

Mojave Desert (IRE) *Mark Johnston* a45 72
3 b f Shamardal(USA) Innclassic (IRE) (Stravinsky (USA))
1272[8] 1713[12] 1931[2] 2405[8]

Mojo Bear *Sylvester Kirk* a65 63
3 b f Indesatchel(IRE) Four Legs Good (IRE) (Be My Guest (USA))
1907[6] 2331[3] 2935[5] 3376[8] 4385[8] 7740[4] 7930[5] 8186[2] 8275[4] 8399[7]

Mojolika *Tim Easterby* a67 81
5 ch g Motivator Kalandika (Diesis)
3065[5] 4372[5] 5109[5] 5423[4] 5879[6]

Moldowney *Luca Cumani* a93 93
4 ch g Dalakhani(IRE) Danehill's Dream (IRE) (Danehill (USA))
1766[5] 2654[8] 3208[7]

Molesne Chop (FR) *Mlle C Cardenne* a40 66
2 ch c Deportivo Amour Parfait (IRE) (Spinning World (USA))
5214a[4] 7185a[11] 7653a[6]

Mollasses *Jonathan Portman* 64
2 b f Authorized(IRE) Muscovado (USA) (Mr Greeley (USA))
4702[13] 5716[8] 6643[10]

Molly Ahoy *Alan McCabe* a6
2 b f Captain Gerrard(IRE) Demolition Molly (Rudimentary (USA))
7162[9]

Molly Amour (GER) *M Rulec* 92
4 b f Ransom O'War(USA) Molly Art (GER) (Big Shuffle (USA))
6010a[9] 7233a[3]

Molly Hayes *David Simcock* a59
3 ch f Teofilo(IRE) Miss Marvellous (USA) (Diesis)
7894[5]

Molly Jones *Derek Haydn Jones* a56 54
4 b f Three Valleys(USA) And Toto Too (Averti (IRE))
124[3] 213[9] 728[7] 968[6] 1195[4] 1665[3] 2074[2] 3042[4] 6344[8]

Molly Mara (GER) *J Hirschberger* a77 96
3 b f Big Shuffle(USA) Molly Dancer (GER) (Shareef Dancer (USA))
2065a[5] 2910a[6] 3852a[7]

Molly Molone *David Brown* a12
2 b f Byron Dress Design (IRE) (Brief Truce (USA))
7023[16] 7341[14] 7756[7] 7882[11]

Mollyvator (IRE) *Mrs K Burke* 78
3 ch f Motivator Gazebo (Cadeaux Genereux)
1620[8]

Moma Lee *John Gosden* a75 73
3 b f Duke Of Marmalade(IRE) Comeraincomeshine (IRE) (Night Shift (USA))
972[3] 1640[8] 1876[6] (2330) 2806[4] (3817) 4385[7] 5395[3] 6106[4] 7297[8]

Momaris *D Selvaratnam* a79 66
5 b g Dubai Destination(USA) Anaamil (IRE) (Darshaan)
394a[2]

Mombasa *Ralph Beckett* 81
3 b g Dubawi(IRE) Limuru (Salse (USA))
1365[2] 2432[9] 3277[6] 6389[6] 7275[12]

Moment In The Sun *David Flood* a67 23
4 ch f Dubai Destination(USA) Special Moment (IRE) (Sadler's Wells (USA))
1298[4] 1381[3] 1794[5] 1983[3] 2159[4] 2571[2] 2948[2] 3156[5] 3496[2] 3910[2] 4149[6] 4521[4] 4754[7] 6218[7] 6399[6] 6554[2] (6805) 7124[10]

Moment In Time (IRE) *David Simcock* a78 110
4 b f Tiger Hill(IRE) Horatia (IRE) (Machiavellian (USA))
1663[2] ◆ (2004) 2656[3] (3100) 4059[2] 4985[10] 5682[6] 7562a[3]

Moment Of Majesty (CAN) *Roger L Attfield* a103 105
6 b m Saint Liam(USA) Lady Indy (USA) (A.P. Indy (USA))
6454a[3] 7562a[8]

Momentus (IRE) *David Simcock* 68
2 b f Montjeu(IRE) Race For The Stars (USA) (Fusaichi Pegasus (USA))
7227[3]

Momo No Sekku (FR) *S Kobayashi* 81
2 b f Leroidesanimaux(BRZ) Academic Angel (USA) (Royal Academy (USA))
7940a[6]

Monakova (IRE) *David O'Meara* a73 96
3 b f Diamond Green(FR) Koukalova (IRE) (Desert Prince (IRE))
4544[4] (5139) (5486) (5836) 6665[8] 7176[2] 7595[8]

Monarch Maid *Peter Hiatt* a56 64
2 b f Captain Gerrard(IRE) Orange Lily (Royal Applause)
4880[8] 5558[3] 6947[5] 7623[8]

Monashka Bay (IRE) *Michael Blanshard* a1
2 b g Kodiac River Style (IRE) (Desert Style (IRE))
3436[7]

Monastrella (FR) *A Wohler* 75
3 b f Sinndar(IRE) Mandalay (GER) (Celtic Swing)
(6711a)

Mon Brav *Brian Ellison* a81 88
6 b g Sampower Star Danehill Princess (IRE) (Danehill (USA))
2275[5] 2441[3] (2657) 3351[3] 4730[2] 5355[4] 6161[5] 7176[12] 7420[8] 7777[9]

Mon Cadeaux *A bin Huzaim* a79 102
6 b g Cadeaux Genereux Ushindi (IRE) (Montjeu (IRE))
290a[13] 503a[12]

Mon Chic *Geoffrey Oldroyd* a35 40
3 b f Monsieur Bond(IRE) Chicago Bond (USA) (Real Quiet (USA))
5290[6] 5989[5] 6289[8] 7354[5] 8119[11] 8293[8]

Mon Choix (FR) *Y Barberot* a98 94
4 b f Choisir(AUS) Macina (IRE) (Platini (GER))
961a[4] 3969a[3] 8440a[5]

Moncofar (IRE) *D Prod'Homme* a86 93
5 b c Refuse To Bend(IRE) Moonbaby (FR) (Le Balafre (FR))
960a[5]

Mondialiste (IRE) *F Head* a84 109
3 b c Galileo(IRE) Occupandiste (IRE) (Kaldoun (FR))
3876a[3] 5120a[6]

Monel *Jim Goldie* 60
5 ch g Cadeaux Genereux Kelucia (IRE) (Grand Lodge (USA))
2884[10] 3778[3] 3934[4] (4823) 5263[7] 6180[5] 6600[6] 6918[3] 7148[9]

Money In Motion (USA) *Philip M Serpe* 90
4 bb g Rainmaker(USA) Napili Bay (CAN) (Katahaula County (CAN))
773a[5] (3361a)

Moneypennie *Marcus Tregoning* a56
2 b f Captain Gerrard(IRE) Snoozy (Cadeaux Genereux)
7972[8] 8123[10] 8328[8]

Money Talks *Michael Madgwick* a52 59
3 b g Motivator Movie Mogul (Sakhee (USA))
1955[7] 2560[9] 3674[3] 4634[8]

Money Team (IRE) *Philip Kirby* a70 80
2 b c Kodiac Coral Dawn (IRE) (Trempolino (USA))
2358[2] (2631) 2863[6] 3801[5] (4156) 5468[5] 5859[3] 6493[6] 7062[8] 7545[6] 7846[5]

Money Time (IRE) *S Wattel* a82
3 b f Arch(USA) Green Girl (FR) (Lord Of Men)
7573a[3]

Mon Fleur (DEN) *Bodil Hallencreutz*
2 b f Academy Award(IRE) Fleur En Fleur (FR) (Hernando (FR))
6452a[5]

Monnoyer *Scott Dixon* a73 46
4 ch g Dutch Art Ellebanna (Tina's Pet)
(1331) 1952[4] 2550[2] 2832[9] 4930[12] 5901[7] 6547[18] 6969[2] 7315[10] 7957[8] 8048[3] 8406[2] 8439[6]

Monopoli *John O'Shea* a72 75
4 ch f Cadeaux Genereux Jump Ship (Night Shift (USA))
810[7] 1076[5] 1715[6] 2417[6] (2709) 3721[9] 6491[2]

Mon Petit Secret *Kevin Ryan* a39
2 b f Sakhee's Secret Crab Apple (Alhaarth (IRE))
7960[3]

Monsea (IRE) *Richard Hannon Snr* a92 86
2 gr c Manduro(GER) Sea Drift (FR) (Warning)
6184[4] 6430[2] (6829) (7626)

Monsieur Bachir (FR) *C Lerner* a81 67
2 b c Bachir(IRE) Hirasah (IRE) (Lahib (USA))
4599a[4]

Monsieur Blanc (IRE) *Denis Coakley* a33 54
2 ch c Kheleyf(USA) Sley (FR) (Lomitas)
2723[8] 3310[8] 4937[7] 5814[6] 6073[9] 6983[9] 7117[10]

Monsieur Chevalier (IRE) *P J O'Gorman* a106 108
6 b h Chevalier(IRE) Blue Holly (IRE) (Blues Traveller (IRE))
690[9] 944[4] ◆ (1385) 1919[4] 2323[5] 3101[6] 3419[12] 3840[5] 4856[5] 5738[18] 6183[10] 6391[15] 6826[3] 7172[6] 7641[7] 7820[14]

Monsieur Jamie *J R Jenkins* a86 83
5 b g Monsieur Bond(IRE) Primula Bairn (Bairn (USA))
95[6] 2364[5] (2550) 3341[4] 4930[6] (6412) 7313[3] 7452[3] ◆ 7777[5] 7887[2] 8232[5]

Monsieur Joe (IRE) *Robert Cowell* a101 114
6 b g Choisir(AUS) Pascali (Compton Place)
954a[8] 1265a[12] 2300a[8] 3187a[7] 6282[5] 6719[5] 7521a[2]

Monsieur Lavene (IRE) *Robert Mills* a66
2 b g Kodiac Sign Of Luck (IRE) (Daylami (IRE))
7328[4] 7638[10] 7893[3]

Monsieur Playboy (GER) *Mme Pia Brandt* a84 104
4 b g Muhtathir Minar Salam (IRE) (Danehill Dancer (IRE))
6251a[5] 7186a[2]

Monsieur Pontaven *Robin Bastiman* a61 55
6 b g Avonbridge Take Heart (Electric)
42[3] 381[3] 565[8] 927[4] 1120[3] 1222[4] (1893) 2537[6] 3029[5] 3788[5] 4109[5] 5341[6] 6324[2] 7153[5] 7455[4]

Monsieur Rieussec *Jonathan Portman* 86
3 bl g Halling(USA) Muscovado (USA) (Mr Greeley (USA))
2322[4] (3117) (4306) 5401[4] 6356[10]

Monsieur Royale *Geoffrey Oldroyd* a73 61
3 ch g Monsieur Bond(IRE) Bond Royale (Piccolo)
2076[7] 3025[5] 3649[9] 4499[8] 7165[5] 7801[7] (8030) 8384[8]

Monsoon (IRE) *P Bary* a68 88
3 b f Cape Cross(IRE) Mirina (FR) (Pursuit Of Love)
5119a[7]

Montaff *Mick Channon* a87 96
7 b g Montjeu(IRE) Meshhed (USA) (Gulch (USA))
1841[5] 2205[7] 2587[11] 3333[4] 3807[3] 4407[3] 4913[4] 5520[6]

Montaigne *Ralph Beckett* a82 82
2 b c Exceed And Excel(AUS) Autumn Pearl (Orpen (USA))
(1541) 1917[4] ◆ 6791[4] 7329[5] 7771[2]

Montalban (FR) *D De Waele* a93 87
6 b g Elusive City(USA) Realy Queen (USA) (Thunder Gulch (USA))
5735a[2]

Montaly *Andrew Balding* a73 82
2 b c Yeats(IRE) Le Badie (IRE) (Spectrum (IRE))
6733[5] (7308) 7694[2]

Montaser (IRE) *David Simcock* 103
4 b g Rail Link For Example (USA) (Northern Baby (CAN))
(3297) 4309[5] 4944[4] 5993[7] 6385[7]

Mont Athos (FR) *R Chotard* a84 66
4 ch c My Risk(FR) Sea Goddess (FR) (Crystal Glitters (USA))
5042a[8]

Mont Blanc *Jane Chapple-Hyam* a39 76
4 b f Singspiel(IRE) Ushindi (IRE) (Montjeu (IRE))
5312[2] 5831[9] 6346[8]

Montclair (IRE) *A Fabre* 112
3 b c Montjeu(IRE) Minaccia (GER) (Platini (GER))
5041a[2] 6250a[3] 7046a[2]

Montebell (IRE) *K J Condon* 95
4 b f Dylan Thomas(IRE) Megec Blis (IRE) (Soviet Star (USA))
1415a[6]

Monte Cassino (IRE) *Bryan Smart* a64 64
8 ch g Choisir(AUS) Saucy Maid (IRE) (Sure Blade (USA))
2171[4] (7354) 7807[2] 8235[9]

Monte Cavallo (SAF) *Rebecca Curtis* a75 86
8 b g Saumarez Mufski (SAF) (Al Mufti (USA))
563[8]

Montefeltro *Brian Ellison* 95
5 ch g Medicean Bustling (Danehill (USA))
5563[5] (6239) ◆ (6573) (7230a)

Monterosso *Mahmood Al Zarooni* a126 116
6 b h Dubawi(IRE) Porto Roca (AUS) (Barathea (IRE))
958a[10]

Montesquieu (FR) *C Boutin* a75 72
3 b g Silvano(GER) Beiramar (IRE) (Monsun (GER))
3129a[5] 7569a[2]

Montevideo (GER) *S Botti* 92
3 b f Desert Prince(IRE) Moricana (GER) (Konigsstuhl (GER))
3616a[11]

Monte Viso *Stuart Kittow* a69 64
2 b g Piccolo Mrs Snaffles (IRE) (Indian Danehill (IRE))
4937[5] 5950[4] 6776[2] 7202[11]

Monthly Medal *Wilf Storey* a61 70
10 b g Danehill Dancer(IRE) Sovereign Abbey (IRE) (Royal Academy (USA))
2886[12] 3543[11] 4052[6] 5713[7] 5840[3] 6053[9] 6598[8] 7238[5] 7498[14]

Montiridge (IRE) *Richard Hannon Snr* 117
3 b c Ramonti(FR) Elegant Ridge (IRE) (Indian Ridge)
2323[3] (2812) 3455[2] (4216) (4945) ◆ 6191[5] 6797[2]

Montjess (IRE) *Tom Dascombe* a79 79
3 b f Montjeu(IRE) Wing Stealth (IRE) (Hawk Wing (USA))
1329[3] 2206[7] 3900[4] 4417[2] ◆ 5374[4] 6389[4] 6629[6] 8004[2] 8041[2] 8310[4]

Montmorency (IRE) *S Seemar* a99 103
7 ch h Pivotal Clear Spring (USA) (Irish River (FR))
149a[5] 467a[16] 836a[9]

Mont Pelato (USA) *M Weiss* a63
5 rg c Forest Danger(USA) Zada Rae (USA) (Unbridled's Song (USA))
513a[4] 702a[2]

Mont Ras (IRE) *David O'Meara* a104 107
6 ch g Indian Ridge Khayrat (IRE) (Polar Falcon (USA))
(1963) 2028[6] (2592) 3527[14] (3984) 4811[6] (5681) 6834[6] (8344)

Mont Ventoux (FR) *Philip Mitchell* a49
3 bb g Elusive City(USA) Recreation (Dansili)
8361[4]

Monty Fay (IRE) *Derek Haydn Jones* a45 60
4 bb g Iffraaj Blast (USA) (Roar (USA))
4836[11] 5817[2] 6156[6] 6478[5] 7079[9] 7512[4] 7729[11] 8146[4]

Monumental Man *James Unett* a81 85
4 b g Vital Equine(IRE) Spark Up (Lahib (USA))
(156) 795[4] (1984) 3171[3] 3658[6] 4203[3] (4675) 6189[8]

Monzino (USA) *Michael Chapman* a73 50
5 bb g More Than Ready(USA) Tasso's Magic Roo (USA) (Tasso (USA))
(312) (410) 455[5] 548[2] 758[6] 832[4] 1076[6] 2081[10] 3195[13] 3412[9] 4718[10] (6612) 6963[7] 8049[5] 8183[4] 8270[2] (8373) 8433[4]

Moohaajim (IRE) *Marco Botti* 116
3 b c Cape Cross(IRE) Thiella (USA) (Kingmambo (USA))
1677[3] 2021[12]

Moonday Sun (USA) *Amanda Perrett* a92 106
4 gr c Mizzen Mast(USA) Storm Dove (USA) (Storm Bird (CAN))
2559a[7] 8263[6]

Moonfaarid *M F De Kock* a75 77
2 b c Dubawi(IRE) Manoeuvre (IRE) (Galileo (IRE))
5744[2] ◆ 7460[3]

Moonlight Cloud *F Head* a94 125
5 b f Invincible Spirit(IRE) Ventura (IRE) (Spectrum (IRE))
(4093a) (5040a) (5314a) (7059a) 8210a[6]

Moonlight Dreamer *David C Griffiths* 23
4 ch f Doyen(IRE) Cos I Do (IRE) (Double Schwartz)
1777[6] 2172[8] 2279[14]

Moon Over Rio (IRE) *Ben Haslam* 53
2 b f Captain Rio Moonchild (GER) (Acatenango (GER))
6298[5] 6597[9]

Moonspring (IRE) *Tobias B P Coles* a64 58
2 gr f Aussie Rules(USA) Unintentional (Dr Devious (IRE))
4631[6] 5488[4] 6409[6] 6923[2] 7327[6]

Moonstone Magic *Ralph Beckett* 109
4 b f Trade Fair Woodcock Moon (Kyllachy)
2108a[3] (2782)

Moontime *Charlie Appleby* 80
2 b g Sea The Stars(IRE) Time On (Sadler's Wells (USA))
(7469)

Moontown *Charles Hills* a58
2 ch c Sea The Stars(IRE) Eva's Request (IRE) (Soviet Star (USA))
7460[9]

Moonvale (IRE) *Tony Carroll* 29
3 gr f Verglas(IRE) Artistry (Night Shift (USA))
1821[5] 2437[6]

Moonwalk In Paris (FR) *Mahmood Al Zarooni* a115 115
5 b g Oratorio(IRE) Shining Glory (Singspiel (IRE))
(659a) ◆ 957a[3] 1262a[3]

Moorhouse Lad *Garry Moss* a91 91
10 b g Bertolini(USA) Record Time (Clantime)
3[3] 319[6] 586[8] 1807[3] 2031[3] 2388[11] 4954[2] 5519[5] 6159[5] ◆ 6699[7] 6920[11] 7887[3] 8167[7]

Moortahan *Richard Hannon Snr* a70 62
3 b c Dutch Art Rotunda (Pivotal)
1243[3] 1908[8] 5444[4] 6146[3] 6702[13] 7430[8] 7807[8] 8073[9] 8341[9] 8446[11]

Moorway (IRE) *Andrew Hollinshead* a60 58
3 b g Dylan Thomas(IRE) Cordelia (Green Desert (USA))
270a[7] 445a[0] 543a[7] 647a[10] 711a[11] 4008[10] 4625[6]

Moose Moran (USA) *Mrs J L Le Brocq* a23 71
6 rg g Lemon Drop Kid(USA) After All (IRE) (Desert Story (IRE))
7144a[6]

Mops Angel *Michael Appleby* 72
2 b f Piccolo Tanning (Atraf)
1108[4] (1718) 2767[10] 6070[4] 7221[7]

Morache Music *Peter Makin* 110
5 b g Sleeping Indian Enchanted Princess (Royal Applause)
2667[2] 3373[6] 3851a[3] 5806a[13] 6505[2] 7013[14] (7495) 7821[9]

Moral Issue *Alan Swinbank* a73 73
5 b g Ishiguru(USA) Morale (Bluebird (USA))
147^{7} 218^{9} 976^{4} 1079^{3} 1401^{8} 3192^{7} 3546^{6} 5369^{2} 5713^{2} (6276) 6600^{4}

Morally Bankrupt *Richard Hannon Snr* a76 70
2 b c Holy Roman Emperor(IRE) Lyra's Daemon (Singspiel (IRE))
4858^{11} 5188^{6} 5819^{4} (6131) (6401)

Morandi (FR) *J-C Rouget* 117
3 gr c Holy Roman Emperor(IRE) Vezina (FR) (Bering)
1562a^{2} 2298a^{6} 2907a^{2} 5462a^{7} 6712a^{2} 7367^{7}

Moran Gra (USA) *Ms Joanna Morgan* a103 103
6 ch g Rahy(USA) Super Supreme (IND) (Zafonic (USA))
2399^{6} 3458^{19} 3869a^{3} (6025a)

Morawij *Roger Varian* 111
3 ch c Exceed And Excel(AUS) Sister Moonshine (FR) (Piccolo)
2662^{6} (3340) 3848a^{3}

Mordanmijobsworth (IRE) *G M Lyons* a78 85
3 b g Clodovil(IRE) Alta Petens (Mujadil (USA))
6025a^{6}

Moreamore (IRE) *Alan Jarvis* 18
3 b f Lemon Drop Kid(USA) Final Legacy (USA) (Boston Harbor (USA))
3764^{11} 5064^{10}

More Aspen (USA) *Marco Botti* a79 62
2 ch f More Than Ready(USA) Jade Aspen (USA) (Jade Hunter (USA))
4164^{5} 4924^{5} 5797^{5} (6605) 7202^{2} 7640^{3}

Moreno (USA) *Eric J Guillot* a117
3 b g Ghostzapper(USA) Danceinthesunlight (CAN) (A.P. Indy (USA))
7715a^{10}

More Than Sotka (FR) *Matthieu Palussiere* a92 101
3 ch f Dutch Art King's Doll (IRE) (King's Best (USA))
243a^{3} 554a^{6} 837a^{7} 1166a^{4} 4700a^{4} 5461a^{7} 6962a^{4}

Morgans Bluff *Pat Phelan* a40 42
2 ch f Bahamian Bounty River Cara (USA) (Irish River (FR))
3663^{11} 4206^{4} 5891^{10}

Moriarty (IRE) *Chris Waller* 112
5 b g Clodovil(IRE) Justice System (USA) (Criminal Type (USA))
7392a^{10} 7702a^{3}

Morning Frost (IRE) *C Ferland* a100 106
3 gr f Duke Of Marmalade(IRE) Evening Time (IRE) (Keltos (FR))
(1000a) 2299a^{16} 4935a^{7} 5806a^{4} 7316a^{6}

Morning Post *Kevin Ryan* 103
2 b c Acclamation Thankful (Diesis)
3295^{3} ◆ 3928^{2} 4528^{10} 4886^{5} 5679^{14} 6194^{6} (6328) 7026^{3} 7534^{9}

Morning Watch (IRE) *Lady Cecil* a68
2 b c Azamour(IRE) Lady Of Kildare (IRE) (Mujadil (USA))
7854^{3}

Mornin Mr Norris *John Quinn* a47 49
2 b g Byron Fractured Foxy (Foxhound (USA))
3084^{7} 3826^{9} 4724^{10} (5898) 6725^{2}

Morny's Place (IRE) *G Collet* 79
3 b f Clodovil(IRE) Baileys Cream (Mister Baileys)
5913a^{8}

Morocco *David O'Meara* a69 88
4 b g Rock Of Gibraltar(IRE) Shanghai Lily (IRE) (King's Best (USA))
1282^{5} 1569^{11} 2081^{7} 2539^{5} ◆ 2798^{8} 3543^{2} ◆ 4016^{5} (4889) (5179) 6236^{6} 6353^{4} 7028^{4}

Morpheus *Lady Cecil* 95
3 b c Oasis Dream Kind (IRE) (Danehill (USA))
1624^{6} 2192^{2} (3250) (4236) 4897^{4} (5440) 6801^{4}

Moscato *Sir Mark Prescott Bt* a54 26
2 gr g Hernando(FR) Alba Stella (Nashwan (USA))
7070^{11} 7308^{12} 7460^{10}

Mosconi (GER) *M Keller* a33
3 gr g Lateral Miss Eden (FR) (Sagamix (FR))
818a^{8}

Moscow Circus (IRE) *Mark Johnston* a60 15
3 b c Hurricane Run(IRE) Zalama (FR) (Red Ransom (USA))
211^{7} ◆ 373^{5} 4139^{6}

Moshe (IRE) *Hughie Morrison* 63
2 b c Dansili Rosinka (IRE) (Soviet Star (USA))
7502^{6}

Mosman *Dean Ivory* a69 21
3 b g Haafhd Last Dream (IRE) (Alzao (USA))
168^{3} 6735^{10} 7073^{9} 7437^{9} 7784^{8} (8116) 8275^{2}

Mossgo (IRE) *John Best* a68 73
3 b g Moss Vale(IRE) Perovskia (USA) (Stravinsky (USA))
531^{5} 2779^{6} 3816^{5} 4390^{4} 4608^{3} 5376^{5} 5930^{8} 6397^{3} 6732^{2} 6901^{2} 8457^{2}

Moss Hill *Charles Hills* a58 58
4 b g Moss Vale(IRE) Borders Belle (IRE) (Pursuit Of Love)
1202^{4} 1656^{2} 1887^{2} 2932^{5} 3326^{3} 4834^{9} 5232^{6} 6113^{2}

Moss Quito (IRE) *David O'Meara* a65 61
3 b g Moss Vale(IRE) Gold Majesty (Josr Algarhoud (IRE))
8277^{3}

Moss The Boss (IRE) *Paul Midgley* a12 49
3 b g Moss Vale(IRE) Lady Of Bilston (IRE) (Bin Ajwaad (IRE))
985^{7} 1458^{9} 1742^{11} 1988^{10} 3134^{6} 3594^{6} 4430^{12} 5054^{5} 5965^{7} 6176^{3} 6879^{6}

Mossy Lea *Richard Fahey* 45
2 ch f Bahamian Bounty Dea Caelestis (FR) (Dream Well (FR))
5609^{7}

Most Improved (IRE) *A P O'Brien* 118
4 b c Lawman(FR) Tonnara (IRE) (Linamix (FR))
3798a^{3} 7051a^{10}

Motamayezah *Ismail Mohammed* a33 8
2 ch f Tamayuz Classical Dancer (Dr Fong (USA))
3833^{10} 7756^{5} 8368^{7}

Moth (IRE) *A P O'Brien* 108
3 b f Galileo(IRE) Pieds De Plume (FR) (Seattle Slew (USA))
2047^{3} ◆ 2842^{4}

Mother Jones *David Brown* a78 73
5 b f Sleeping Indian Bella Chica (IRE) (Bigstone (IRE))
29^{4} 56^{3} 234^{4} 611^{4} 716^{3} 861^{3} 1052^{2} 6757^{13} 6982^{6}

Motion Lass *Ralph Beckett* 66
3 b f Motivator Tarneem (USA) (Zilzal (USA))
1671^{9} 2390^{5} 6325^{9}

Motivado *David Hayes* a81 109
5 b g Motivator Tamise (USA) (Time For A Change (USA))
7700a^{9}

Moudre (AUS) *Ciaron Maher* 111
8 bb g Blevic(AUS) Tolkaami (AUS) (Raami I)
7483a^{3} 7700a^{8} 7827a^{7} 7938a^{5}

Mount Abora (IRE) *Laura Mongan* a73 69
6 br m Rock Of Gibraltar(IRE) Ragtime Blues (IRE) (Grand Lodge (USA))
662^{2} 1060^{2} 1175^{10} 1716^{2}

Mountain Fighter *Saeed bin Suroor* 73
2 b g Dubawi(IRE) River Pearl (GER) (Turfkonig (GER))
6829^{10} 7774^{2}

Mountain Kingdom (IRE) *Sir Mark Prescott Bt* 61
2 b g Montjeu(IRE) Althea Rose (IRE) (Green Desert (USA))
7089^{5}

Mountain Lion (IRE) *Saeed bin Suroor* a72 72
2 b c Invincible Spirit(IRE) Tuzla (FR) (Panoramic)
5941^{5} 7019^{5} 7834^{5}

Mountain Range (IRE) *Willie Musson* a80 68
5 b g High Chaparral(IRE) Tuscany Lady (IRE) (Danetime (IRE))
614^{8} 850^{8} 1220^{10} 1585^{8} 2808^{3} (2982) 3692^{6} 7611^{9} 8059^{9}

Mountain View (GER) *Frau Nina Bach* a67 84
3 b g Tertullian(USA) Mutige (Warning)
1495a^{10}

Mount Athos (IRE) *Luca Cumani* a102 120
6 b g Montjeu(IRE) Ionian Sea (Slip Anchor)
(2212) 3556^{5} 4919^{8} 5741^{2} ◆ 7761a^{3} 8208a^{9}

Mount Cheiron (USA) *Dianne Sayer* a62 60
2 b g Henrythenavigator(USA) Chalamont (IRE) (Kris)
2382^{8} 3436^{6} 4631^{5} 4964^{7} (5467) 6284^{2} 7097^{7} 7340^{8}

Mount Hollow *Andrew Hollinshead* a85 85
8 b g Beat Hollow Lady Lindsay (IRE) (Danehill Dancer (IRE))
3093^{11} 3733^{7} (4220) 4730^{18} 5183^{8} 6161^{4} 6977^{15} 7742^{9} 8096^{6} 8224^{8} 8321^{6}

Mount Logan (IRE) *Luca Cumani* 84
2 ch c New Approach(IRE) Vistaria (USA) (Distant View (USA))
4483^{4} ◆ (6570) ◆ 7195^{7}

Mount Macedon *Luca Cumani* a73 70
3 b g Hernando(FR) White Palace (Shirley Heights)
4257^{7} 4719^{3} 5892^{5} 7279^{4} 7894^{4}

Mount McLeod (IRE) *Patrick J Flynn* a61 59
4 b f Holy Roman Emperor(IRE) Northern Gulch (USA) (Gulch (USA))
4647a^{5}

Mount Tiger *James Tate* a89 77
3 b c Tiger Hill(IRE) Fly Me To The Moon (GER) (Galileo (IRE))
(3641) 4416^{6} (5355) 6495^{5} 6936^{8}

Mourani (IRE) *John M Oxx* 91
3 b c Dalakhani(IRE) Mouramara (IRE) (Kahyasi)
7230a^{10}

Mourayan (IRE) *Robert Hickmott* 112
7 bb h Alhaarth(IRE) Mouramara (IRE) (Kahyasi)
7702a^{7} 7761a^{15}

Mourinho (AUS) *Peter Gelagotis* 104
6 b g Oratorio(IRE) Benevolent (NZ) (Generous (IRE))
7827a^{11}

Mousie *Alan McCabe* a36 44
4 b f Auction House(USA) Goes A Treat (IRE) (Common Grounds)
754^{9} 917^{9} 3154^{5} 3660^{10} 4377^{5} 5709^{7} 8234^{11}

Mousquetaire (JPN) *Yasuo Tomomichi* 112
5 bb c Mayano Top Gun(JPN) Cherir (JPN) (Sunday Silence (USA))
1868a^{16}

Mouth Piece *A Oliver* a18 53
3 ch g Singspiel(IRE) Misleading Lady (Warning)
1587a^{7}

Move In Time *David O'Meara* a75 107
5 ch g Monsieur Bond(IRE) Tibesti (Machiavellian (USA))
(1253) ◆ (1537) 1637^{3} 2300a^{2} 3420^{7} 3848a^{4} 4275^{12}

Movementneverlies *Charles Hills* a76 74
3 ch f Medicean Frabjous (Pivotal)
332^{2} (706) 2449^{4} 2935^{4} 4523^{6} 5037^{8} 6642^{6} 8020^{8}

Moves Like Jagger (IRE) *Phil McEntee* a30 23
3 b g Danehill Dancer(IRE) Lucky Spin (Pivotal)
1236^{7} 7932^{7} 8140^{6}

Move To Strike (IRE) *J S Bolger* 96
3 b c Lawman(FR) Alamanta (IRE) (Ali-Royal (IRE))
1555a^{7}

Movie Magic *John Bridger* 33
2 b f Multiplex Alucica (Celtic Swing)
2260^{6} 2583^{7} 3815^{7} 4304^{8} 5061^{13}

Moviesta (USA) *Bryan Smart* a85 115
3 b g Hard Spun(USA) Miss Brickyard (USA) (A.P. Indy (USA))
1482^{8} ◆ (1806) (2430) 3348^{2} 4255^{2} (4947) ◆ 5726^{17}

Moving Waves (IRE) *Ollie Pears* a48 52
2 b f Intense Focus(USA) Kimola (IRE) (King's Theatre (IRE))
3605^{6} 4505^{6} 5053^{9} 5893^{5}

Mowhoob *Jim Goldie* a71 76
3 b g Medicean Pappas Ruby (USA) (Red Ransom (USA))
1822^{6} 2279^{2} 2318^{2} 2876^{4} 3566^{5} 4340^{9} 4956^{3} 5642^{6} 6084^{3} 6464^{5} 6588^{10}

Moxey *Henry Candy* 49
2 ch g Nayef(USA) Emily Blake (IRE) (Lend A Hand)
6277^{13} 6762^{16} 7467^{11}

Mr Big (AUS) *M Freedman* a111 111
5 b g Elusive Quality(USA) Basamaat (IRE) (Danehill (USA))
1265a^{5}

Mr Blue Nose *Karen George* a47 38
3 b g Tobougg(IRE) Cape Siren (Warning)
1429^{8} 1741^{7} 2568^{5} 3916^{6}

Mr Burbidge *Neil Mulholland* a88 43
5 b g Midnight Legend Twin Time (Syrtos)
6046^{4} 6402^{11} 6781^{3} 7382^{3} (7668) ◆ (7767) ◆ (8130) (8433) ◆

Mr Carbonfootprint *Richard Fahey* a26 72
2 ch c Footstepsinthesand Diamond Lass (IRE) (Rock Of Gibraltar (IRE))
(2474) 4988^{9} 5963^{4} 6303^{8} 6791^{10} 7340^{2}

Mr Childrey (IRE) *J S Moore* 43
2 b g Art Connoisseur(IRE) Tomanivi (Caerleon (USA))
1580^{7} 3174^{9} 4617^{2} 5243^{5} 6131^{9} 6279^{10}

Mr Chocolate Drop (IRE) *Mandy Rowland* a66 59
9 b g Danetime(IRE) Forest Blade (IRE) (Charnwood Forest (IRE))
83^{4} ◆ 218^{10} 801^{5} 921^{7} 1100^{5} 7930^{9} 8055^{7} 8409^{8}

Mr Churchill (IRE) *Ismail Mohammed* a53 53
4 b c Invincible Spirit(IRE) Mayoress (Machiavellian (USA))
7679a^{4}

Mr Crystal (FR) *Micky Hammond* a41 65
9 ch g Trempolino(USA) Iyrbila (FR) (Lashkari)
1445^{12} 2242^{8} 3065^{9} 4759^{7} 5560^{6} 6565^{3} 7423^{7}

Mr Dandy Man (IRE) *Ronald Harris* 74
2 ch c Dandy Man(IRE) Boudica (IRE) (Alhaarth (IRE))
1534^{2} 1946^{5} 2358^{6} 2823^{4} (2917) 3311^{4} 4783^{2} 5121^{3} 5648^{4}

Mr David (USA) *Jamie Osborne* a94 89
6 b g Sky Mesa(USA) Dancewiththebride (USA) (Belong To Me (USA))
1542^{12} 1782^{5} 2214^{12} 3153^{2} 3472^{4} 3906^{2} 5799^{7} (6215) 6609^{8} 7031^{3} (7123) 7464^{13} 7992^{8} 8122^{3} 8217^{3} (8391)

Mr Dream Maker (IRE) *Noel Wilson* a26 50
5 b g Araafa(IRE) Paola Maria (Daylami (IRE))
3314^{11} 4109^{11} (4622) 5897^{7} 6086^{P} 7099^{P}

Mr Edge (USA) *Lennart Reuterskiold Jr* a62
3 bb g Added Edge(USA) Beauty Times (USA) (Salt Lake (USA))
5326a^{9}

Mr Fickle (IRE) *Gary Moore* a67 74
4 b g Jeremy(USA) Mamara Reef (Salse (USA))
2596^{P} 3010^{8} 3416^{11} 4411^{6} 5091^{2} (5429) 6458^{2} 7091^{6}

Mr Fitzroy (IRE) *Andrew Balding* a77 77
3 ch g Kyllachy Reputable (Medicean)
2455^{3} 3061^{6} 4168^{2} 5792^{9} 6734^{8} 7257^{5}

Mr Gallivanter (IRE) *John Quinn* 80
2 ch g Heliostatic(IRE) Purepleasureseeker (IRE) (Grand Lodge (USA))
5785^{4} (6666) 7492^{3}

Mr Greenspan (USA) *Richard Hannon Snr* a72 30
2 b c Mr Greeley(USA) In Escrow (USA) (Vindication (USA))
7654^{9} 7972^{2}

Mr Hadif (USA) *Christopher Van Culin* 71
6 bb g Hadif(USA) Rain Dancing (USA) (Lost Mountain (USA))
1001a^{7}

Mr Khan *Linda Perratt* 47
5 ch g Rambling Bear Frabrofen (Mind Games)
1995^{8} 3932^{11}

Mr Knightley (IRE) *Jim Boyle* a81 71
4 b g Strategic Prince Emma's Surprise (Tobougg (IRE))
104^{7} 370^{4} 1094^{3} (1316) 1496^{2}

Mr Lando *Tony Carroll* a71 69
4 b g Shirocco(GER) Capitana (GER) (Lando (GER))
788^{3} (2567) (2801) 3410^{2} 5694^{4} 7622^{2} 7881^{7} 8060^{7}

Mr Lover Lover (IRE) *John Butler*
4 b g Catcher In The Rye(IRE) Lovingit (IRE) (Fasliyev (USA))
3319^{6}

Mr Lucas (FR) *M Le Forestier* 90
2 ch c Anabaa Blue Anna Conda (Bijou D'Inde)
(7889a)

Mr Majeika (IRE) *F Vermeulen* a89 91
4 b c Oasis Dream Before The Storm (Sadler's Wells (USA))
963a^{0}

Mr Mallo *John Stimpson* a28 39
4 b g Bertolini(USA) Londonnet (IRE) (Catrail (USA))
2172^{7} 2576^{12} 3657^{5} 4996^{9} 5615^{8} 6102^{9}

Mr Man In The Moon (IRE) *Alan Swinbank* a33 61
5 gr g Verglas(IRE) Dancing Drop (Green Desert (USA))
1681^{12} 3068^{6} 3317^{6} 4836^{10} 5408^{3} 6180^{12} 6604^{7}

Mr Matthews (IRE) *K R Burke* 82
2 b g Diamond Green(FR) Five Sisters (Mujahid (USA))
2282^{2} (3391) 3723^{2} 4314^{3} 4703^{5} 6582^{U} 7170^{16}

Mr Maynard *Sir Michael Stoute* a74 72
4 ch g Notnowcato Crystal Cavern (USA) (Be My Guest (USA))
1956^{5}

Mr Moet (AUS) *Adam Durrant* 112
6 b g Mosayter(USA) Marlock Miss (AUS) (Karioi Star (AUS))
7392a^{6} 7702a^{4}

Mr Mo Jo *Lawrence Mullaney* a47 75
5 b g Danbird(AUS) Nampara Bay (Emarati (USA))
(1758) 2122^{2} 2614^{6} 5148^{6} 6469^{3} 6757^{6} 7029^{8} 7937^{10}

Mr Moondance (IRE) *Timothy Doyle* a66 66
2 ch c Windsor Knot(IRE) Miss Sundance (IRE) (Desert Sun)
7050a^{11}

Mr Muzzare (USA) *M Massimi Jr* 97
4 b c Langfuhr(CAN) Clefairy (IRE) (Sri Pekan (USA))
7706a^{3}

Mr O'Ceirin (NZ) *Ciaron Maher* 109
6 b g Postponed(USA) Cadell (NZ) (Yachtie (AUS))
7392a^{11}

Mr Optimistic *Paul Howling* a62 89
5 b g Kyllachy Noble Desert (FR) (Green Desert (USA))
111^{5} (339) (736) ◆ 898^{8} 1304^{9}

Mr Opulence *T Le Brocq* a48 59
4 ch g Generous(IRE) Miss Opulence (IRE) (Kylian (USA))
1696^{4} 5327a^{5} 7145a^{3}

Mr Plod *J R Jenkins* a65 52
8 ch g Silver Patriarch(IRE) Emily-Mou (IRE) (Cadeaux Genereux)
755^{3} 1040^{2} 1520^{2} 1794^{2}

Mr Pommeroy (FR) *Mario Hofer* a78 84
2 ch c Linngari(IRE) Amerissage (USA) (Rahy (USA))
5939a^{5}

Mr Red Clubs (IRE) *Michael Appleby* a93 98
4 b g Red Clubs(IRE) Queen Cobra (IRE) (Indian Rocket)
495^{10} 585^{6} 1036^{8} 3346^{11} 4012^{5} 4929^{7} 6384^{7} 6609^{4} 7224^{8} 7629^{7}

Mrs Bannock (IRE) *Charlie Appleby* a75
3 b f Shamardal(USA) Laoub (USA) (Red Ransom (USA))
6341^{5} 6780^{8}

Mrs Dubawi (IRE) *F Rohaut* a78
4 b f Dubawi(IRE) Lucky Lune (FR) (Priolo (USA))
(7573a)

Mrs Gorsky *Patrick Holmes* a37
3 b f Duke Of Marmalade(IRE) Dowager (Groom Dancer (USA))
7067^{10} 8070^{5}

Mrs J (IRE) *Tim Easterby* 6
2 br f Bushranger(IRE) Keepers Dawn (IRE) (Alzao (USA))
3680^{7} 4756^{12}

Mrs Mann (USA) *Willie Musson* a54 44
3 rg f Mizzen Mast(USA) Dixiana Delight (USA) (Gone West (USA))
1926^{8} 2560^{11} 3957^{10} 6783^{6} 7610^{5}

Mrs Medley *Ann Stokell* a18 21
7 b m Rambling Bear Animal Cracker (Primo Dominie)
6176^{6} 6611^{10} 6994^{7} 7203^{8} 7759^{9} 8407^{6}

Mrs Micawber *Michael Bell* a78 38
3 gr f Nayef(USA) Under The Rainbow (Fantastic Light (USA))
6532^{8} 6926^{4} 7488^{6} 7857^{3} (8183) 8416^{8}

Mrs Miller (GER) *S Smrczek* 91
5 ch f Lord Of England(GER) Moreau (IRE) (Kornado)
4467a^{8} 6060a^{3}

Mr Smith *John Gosden* a34
2 gr c Galileo(IRE) Intrigued (Darshaan)
7835^{13}

Mr Snooks *David Nicholls* a36 51
3 b g Bertolini(USA) Meadow Floss (Cyrano De Bergerac)
1450^{4} 1687^{8} 2241^{7} 3246^{6} ◆ 3739^{9} 5614^{15} 6088^{3} ◆ 6345^{6} 6879^{7} 6945^{6}

Mr Snoozy *Tim Walford* 85
4 b g Pursuit Of Love Hard To Follow (Dilum (USA))
1790^{2} ◆ 2277^{6} (2435) (2860) (3765)

Mrs Pat *Richard Fahey* 47
2 b f With Approval(CAN) Miss Prism (Niniski (USA))
6281^{7} 6828^{12} 7277^{7}

Mr Spiggott (IRE) *Gary Moore* a20 86
4 b g Intikhab(USA) Green Green Grass (Green Desert (USA))
1233^{18} 1673^{16} 2981^{9} 6306^{6} 7130^{5} 7433^{3}

Mrs Sands *J S Moore* a10
2 ch f Firebreak Smooth As Silk (IRE) (Danehill Dancer (IRE))
5591^{8} 6779^{6}

Mrs Warren *George Baker* a62 64
3 b f Kyllachy Bold Bunny (Piccolo)
1608^{6} 2226^{4} 2872^{5} (3946) 6937^{4} 7269^{5} 8330^{11}

Mr Udagawa *Bernard Llewellyn* a70 56
7 b g Bahamian Bounty Untold Riches (USA) (Red Ransom (USA))
2072^{2} 3314^{10} 3885^{8}

Mr Vendman (IRE) *Ian Williams* a44 52
3 b g Whipper(USA) So Precious (IRE) (Batshoof)
2599^{7} 2924^{9} 3432^{4} 5500^{2} 5846^{3} 6177^{9} 6853^{7} 7770^{5}

Mr Wickfield *John Best* a67
2 b c Champs Elysees First Approval (Royal Applause)
7441^{2} 7779^{5} 8085^{2} 8328^{10}

Mr Win (IRE) *Chris Wall* a56 59
2 b c Intikhab(USA) Midnight Oasis (Oasis Dream)
6569^{6} 7155^{6}

M'Selle (IRE) *Ronald Harris* a69 74
2 b f Elnadim(USA) Key Rose (IRE) (Key Of Luck (USA))
(1156) 1619^{2} 1785^{3} 2147^{11} 2933^{4} 4174^{4} 4239^{2} 4783^{6} (4910) 5771a^{8} 6731^{9}

Mshawish (USA) *M Delzangles* a74 117
3 bb c Medaglia d'Oro(USA) Thunder Bayou (USA) (Thunder Gulch (USA))
2355a^{2} 2907a^{4} 3421^{4} (5120a) 7047a^{7}

Mu'Ajiza *Mark Johnston* a49 79
3 ch f Pivotal Siyasa (USA) (Rahy (USA))
4382^{7} 4799^{2} ◆ 4968^{4} 5332^{3} 5546^{4} 5855^{3} 6016^{3}

Mubaraza (IRE) *Ed Dunlop* a92 102
4 ch g Dalakhani(IRE) Mokaraba (Unfuwain (USA))
1547^7 2044^5 2451^3 3423^4 3824^3

Mubrook (USA) *Brian Ellison* a82 68
8 b g Alhaarth(IRE) Zomaradah (Deploy)
2706^8 3609^5

Mubtadi *Ismail Mohammed* a86 81
5 b g Dr Fong(USA) Noble Peregrine (Lomond (USA))
(205) (320) (709) (1176) (1901) 2234^4 (3468)

Mucho Macho Man (USA) *Kathy Ritvo* a128
5 b c Macho Uno(USA) Ponche De Leona (USA) (Ponche (CAN))
(7715a)

Much Promise *John Gosden* a79 68
2 b f Invincible Spirit(IRE) Prowess (IRE) (Peintre Celebre (USA))
4408^2 ◆ 4877^9 7155^2 (7737)

Muck 'N' Brass (IRE) *J Larkin* a98 78
4 bb c Aussie Rules(USA) Crystal Springs (IRE) (Kahyasi)
151a^{15} 364a^5 552a^9 742a^7 3599a^{12}

Mucky Molly *Alison Hutchinson* a62 60
5 ch f Bahamian Bounty Indian Flag (IRE) (Indian Ridge)
128^9 537^9 (884) ◆ 965^5 1149^2 1455^3 1656^6 2170^2 2575^2 3643^3 4145^{11} 6610^{11} 7455^8 7753^9 8293^5

Mudaawem (USA) *Mark Johnston* a61 62
3 ch g Exchange Rate(USA) Raajiya (USA) (Gulch (USA))
414^4 613^3 1171^2 1330^3 1966^8 6049^6 6667^9 7083^2 7238^{13} 7514^{12}

Mud Hilah (FR) *A De Mieulle* 96
4 b f Kingsalsa(USA) Arionella (Bluebird (USA))
2969a^0 6447a^8

Mudhish (IRE) *Clive Brittain* a66 25
8 b g Lujain(USA) Silver Satire (Dr Fong (USA))
806^3 1294^{10} 1783^6 5205^6

Mufarrh (IRE) *A Al Raihe* a113 105
6 b g Marju(IRE) What A Picture (FR) (Peintre Celebre (USA))
153a^5 ◆ 556a^8 (836a) 1262a^{12}

Muffin McLeay (IRE) *David Barron* 96
5 b g Hawk Wing(USA) Youngus (USA) (Atticus (USA))
1235^{19} 1485^{10} 1840^8 2240^2 4280^8

Muftarres (IRE) *Frank Sheridan* a69 82
8 b g Green Desert(USA) Ghazal (USA) (Gone West (USA))
971^9 1102^9 1351^6 1650^7 1757^{12} (1887) 2089^3 3192^2 4007^3 4250^4 4685^4 (5406) (5621)

Muhamee (IRE) *A bin Huzaim* a60 57
4 ch g Proud Citizen(USA) Santolina (USA) (Boundary (USA))
7679a^2

Muhandis (IRE) *Nick Littmoden* a75 60
5 b g Muhtathir Ahdaaf (USA) (Bahri (USA))
34^2 199^2 344^3 358^3 511^7

Muharaaj (IRE) *Matthieu Palussiere* 103
2 b c Iffraaj Desert Sprite (IRE) (Tagula (IRE))
(2433a) 4572a^4 5460a^3 5573a^6 6249a^7

Muharrer *Michael Dods* a84 90
4 b g Shamardal(USA) Shawahid (USA) (A.P. Indy (USA))
1538^{14} 2256^2 2706^2 3442^5 4110^2 4810^2 5147^4 6353^7 6750^7

Muharrib (IRE) *Saeed bin Suroor* a88 98
3 b c Oasis Dream Manhattan Dream (USA) (Statue Of Liberty (USA))
3763^3 4295^2 4922^{12} 5728^{14} 6772^8

Muhawalah (IRE) *Roger Varian* 64
2 ch f Nayef(USA) Al Ishq (FR) (Nureyev (USA))
6973^6

Muhdiq (USA) *Mike Murphy* a85 82
4 b g Hard Spun(USA) Enfiraaj (USA) (Kingmambo (USA))
2255^{11} 3018^{12} 4675^4 6948^4

Muhtaris (IRE) *Saeed bin Suroor* a89 84
3 b g Teofilo(IRE) Fann (USA) (Diesis)
7257^8 7498^3 (7805)

Muir Lodge *Andrew Balding* a84 92
2 ch g Exceed And Excel(AUS) Miss Chaussini (IRE) (Rossini (USA))
4858^8 ◆ 5558^2 (6213) 6645^3 7017^{13}

Mujaadel (USA) *David Nicholls* a72 73
8 ch g Street Cry(IRE) Quiet Rumour (USA) (Alleged (USA))
878^6 (976) 1462^4 1686^4 (2081) 2339^6 3027^8 3445^{10} 4007^8 4375^7 4967^{11} 5341^8 6720^3

Mujadale (AUS) *Paul A Jones* 100
6 b g Mujahid(USA) Newdale (AUS) (New Regent (CAN))
(7760a) 7938a^7

Mujarrad (USA) *Ian Semple* 73
3 b g Street Sense(USA) Sayedah (IRE) (Darshaan)
1624^7 2279^4 3191^4 4068^7 6588^8 7238^{11}

Mujazif (IRE) *Brian Meehan* 100
3 br c Shamardal(USA) Red Bandanna (IRE) (Montjeu (IRE))
1812^2 5540^5 6163^4 6592^4 7223^8

Mukaynis (IRE) *Lady Cecil* 79
2 b c Tamayuz Wild Ways (Green Desert (USA))
5405^3 5941^2

Mukhabarat (IRE) *Saeed bin Suroor* a68 73
3 b c Exceed And Excel(AUS) Counterclaim (Pivotal)
5176^3 (5517) ◆ 6338^6 6653^{DSQ}

Mukhadram *William Haggas* 123
4 b c Shamardal(USA) Magic Tree (UAE) (Timber Country (USA))
(2811) 3457^2 4082^3 (4779) 7367^5

Mukhtazel (IRE) *Mark Johnston* 47
2 ch c Nayef(USA) Tomoohat (USA) (Danzig (USA))
4926^8 5826^7 7128^9

Mulakim *Saeed bin Suroor* 93
3 b g Pivotal Tamarillo (Daylami (IRE))
(4022) 4452^2 5944^6

Mullins Way (USA) *Jo Hughes* a89 87
5 ch g Mr Greeley(USA) Aljawza (USA) (Riverman (USA))
13^{11} 1303^{10} 3138^9 3727^3 4195^3 4294^4

Mull Of Killough (IRE) *Jane Chapple-Hyam* a101 117
7 b g Mull Of Kintyre(USA) Sun Shower (IRE) (Indian Ridge)
(1639) 2494a^5 4276^2 5553a^8 7556a^{11} 7762a^3 7826a^4

Multi Bene *Ed McMahon* a88 93
4 b g Multiplex Attlongglast (Groom Dancer (USA))
4124^3 4850^5 (6126)

Multifact *Michael Dods* 56
3 b g Multiplex Subtle Move (USA) (Known Fact (USA))
1393^4 1967^8 4806^7 5856^3 6759^7

Multi Fours *Daniel Kubler* a50
3 ch f Medicean Spiralling (Pivotal)
336^8 591^3 717^7

Multilicious *Tim Easterby* a40 57
3 b f Multiplex Ryan's Quest (IRE) (Mukaddamah (USA))
2504^5 3463^3 4008^6 4401^6 5903^{11} 6049^7

Multisure *Ruth Carr* a58 63
3 b g Multiplex Sharoura (Inchinor)
1210^3 1393^2 1772^4 2080^{10} 2501^{13} 3629^{12} 4070^5 4585^3 4722^8 5016^{10} 5334^6 5903^8 5961^7

Multitask *Michael Madgwick* a70 59
3 b g Multiplex Attlongglast (Groom Dancer (USA))
203^4 2394^{13} 2727^{10} 3577^7 4751^4 4999^2 6732^4 7086^{14} (7465) 8151^6 8443^2

Mumeyez *John Gosden* a81 72
3 ch g Motivator Twelfth Night (IRE) (Namid)
(800) 1293^7 1770^5 2776^3

Mumtaza *Richard Hannon Snr* a45 23
2 b f Nayef(USA) Natagora (FR) (Divine Light (JPN))
3978^{10} 6340^5

Munaaser *Sir Michael Stoute* 82
2 b c New Approach(IRE) Safwa (IRE) (Green Desert (USA))
6534^3 ◆

Munaawib *David C Griffiths* a66 62
5 b g Haafhd Mouwadh (USA) (Nureyev (USA))
716^4 911^4 990^4 1221^7 1355^5 1539^{11} 2170^{11} 2435^{13} (2578) 2954^5 3203^3 3513^2 3657^4 3909^8 7498^{16} 7806^{11} 7903^4 (8119) 8293^2

Mundahesh (IRE) *William Haggas* a84 89
3 ch g Tamayuz Kawn (Cadeaux Genereux)
2371^{11} 2862^{11} 3338^8 4084^2 ◆ 4917^{12}

Munfallet (IRE) *Richard Hannon Snr* a74 79
2 b g Royal Applause Princess Mood (GER) (Muhtarram (USA))
2653^3 3211^2 4858^4

Mungo Park *Sophie Leech* a82 70
5 b g Selkirk(USA) Key Academy (Royal Academy (USA))
(5586) (6217)

Munhamer (IRE) *John Gosden* a61 75
3 ch c Iffraaj Khibraat (Alhaarth (IRE))
1114^3 1291^4 5133^6 6358^7 7248^3

Munjally *Richard Hannon Snr* 79
2 b g Acclamation Parabola (Galileo (IRE))
2670^4 3112^3 4026^4 4988^6

Munjaz *John Gosden* 80
2 ch c Sea The Stars(IRE) Qurrah (IRE) (Zafonic (USA))
5490^3 ◆ 7469^2

Munro Bagger (IRE) *John Quinn* 56
4 b g Whipper(USA) Prashock (IRE) (Traditionally (USA))
1842^3 2237^4 2831^5 4893^{15}

Munsarim (IRE) *Lee Carter* a88 44
6 b g Shamardal(USA) Etizaaz (USA) (Diesis)
7438^{10} 7989^{11} 8068^4 8179^{12} 8226^6 8454^2

Muntasir (IRE) *Saeed bin Suroor* a92 98
4 b g Distorted Humor(USA) Mansfield Park (Green Desert (USA))
2451^{13} 3099^{14} 5374^2 6876^5

Muraafiq (USA) *Simon West* 28
4 bb g Jazil(USA) Reem Al Barari (USA) (Storm Cat (USA))
6166^7 6566^{10}

Murasil (USA) *Saeed bin Suroor* a84
3 ch g Elusive Quality(USA) Show Me The Roses (USA) (Storm Cat (USA))
6926^2 7298^7

Muraweg (IRE) *Fawzi Abdulla Nass* a89 94
7 b g Kheleyf(USA) Lady Moranbon (USA) (Trempolino (USA))
153a^{10} 744a^9

Murbeh (IRE) *A Al Raihe* a99 100
5 b g Elusive City(USA) My Funny Valentine (IRE) (Mukaddamah (USA))
575a^2

Murcar *Liam Corcoran* a87 75
8 ch g Medicean In Luck (In The Wings)
(40) 378^2 654^2 1218^4 2587^6 8041^5

Murcielago (GER) *M Keller* a85 96
6 ch g Areion(GER) My Angel (GER) (Luigi (GER))
7995a^8

Murfreesboro *Raymond York* a59 90
10 b g Bahamian Bounty Merry Rous (Rousillon (USA))
475^{11} 630^{11}

Murillo (FR) *J-M Beguigne* a77 72
3 b c Anabaa Blue Materialiste (IRE) (Zafonic (USA))
1850a^3 5805a^2 6713a^5

Murphy (IRE) *Nick Gifford* a59
11 b g Lord Americo Kyle Cailin (IRE) (Over The River (FR))
512^8

Musaafer (IRE) *M Al Muhairi* a81 89
6 b g Marju(IRE) Alexander Icequeen (IRE) (Soviet Star (USA))
412a^3

Musaddas *Saeed bin Suroor* a78 88
3 b g Exceed And Excel(AUS) Zuleika Dobson (Cadeaux Genereux)
6738^4 6950^2 7253^2 7787^2

Musa D'Oriente *B Grizzetti* 85
2 b f Nayef(USA) Musa Golosa (Mujahid (USA))
7415a^9

Musalaha (IRE) *Ed Dunlop* 55
2 b f Nayef(USA) Gilded (IRE) (Redback)
4215^{11} 4723^6 5435^8

Muscle Beach (USA) *Charles O'Brien* a61 81
2 ch c Langfuhr(CAN) Sky Fraulein (USA) (Sky Mesa (USA))
3847a^4

Mushaakis (IRE) *Mark Johnston* a70 93
3 b g Shamardal(USA) Shamayel (Pivotal)
1712^3 2770^2 (3281) 3537^3 4028^2 (4542) 4917^6 5562^4 6300^9

Mushir *Roger Varian* a92 103
2 b c Oasis Dream Shimah (USA) (Storm Cat (USA))
(6747) (7207) ◆

Mushreq (AUS) *M F De Kock* a101 116
5 b g Flying Spur(AUS) Alharir (AUS) (Jeune)
151a^{10} 363a^4 ◆ (462a) ◆ 556a^6 (745a) 1267a^{10}

Musical Bridge *Lisa Williamson* a62 37
7 b g Night Shift(USA) Carrie Pooter (Tragic Role (USA))
2736^7 3236^{12}

Musical Comedy *Richard Hannon Snr* 105
2 b g Royal Applause Spinning Top (Alzao (USA))
3112^8 (5757) 6194^2 7170^2 (7334) (7503)

Musical Express (IRE) *W A Murphy* a13 8
10 br g Black Minnaloushe(USA) Illustre Inconnue (USA) (Septieme Ciel (USA))
1017^{11} 4824^9

Musical Molly (IRE) *Brian Ellison* 63
2 gr f Mastercraftsman(IRE) Park Approach (IRE) (Indian Ridge)
2005^2 ◆ 2401^{11} (3084) 4431^4 7418^9

Musical Strike *Shaun Harris* a10 31
4 b g Striking Ambition Musical Fair (Piccolo)
5166^{10} 5622^9 6344^{11} 6878^7 6903^8

Music Chart (USA) *Saeed bin Suroor* a102 86
3 b f Exchange Rate(USA) Conchita (USA) (Cozzene (USA))
(243a) 554a^3 837a^3 3240^6

Music Festival (USA) *Jim Goldie* a64 62
6 b g Storm Cat(USA) Musical Chimes (USA) (In Excess)
2636^3 2889^2 2977^3 3337^6 3770^5 4109^3 4953^8 5515^4 6760^3 7149^8

Music In The Rain (IRE) *David O'Meara* 91
5 b g Invincible Spirit(IRE) Greek Symphony (IRE) (Mozart (IRE))
1115^5 ◆ (1363) 1830^5 2463^3 3684^6

Music Man (IRE) *Jo Crowley* a79
3 b g Oratorio(IRE) Chanter (Lomitas)
8245^4 (8444)

Music Master *Henry Candy* 106
3 b c Piccolo Twilight Mistress (Bin Ajwaad (IRE))
(1618) 2453^2 ◆ 3455^5 4529^2 5738^8 ◆ 7013^2 ◆

Musicora *Richard Hannon Snr* a91 87
2 b f Acclamation Belladera (IRE) (Alzao (USA))
2856^5 3760^2 (4164) 5005^8 (6070) 7329^2 7657^8

Music Stop *Phil McEntee* a52 55
2 b f Iffraaj Tan Tan (King's Best (USA))
2117^5 2510^3 4676^3 (4862) 5229^7 5964^5 6320^{10}

Music Theory (IRE) *Charlie Appleby* 103
2 b g Acclamation Key Girl (IRE) (Key Of Luck (USA))
4497^2 ◆ (4958) (5438) ◆ 5999^3

Musikhani *Andrew Balding* 77
3 b f Dalakhani(IRE) Musicanna (Cape Cross (IRE))
1636^6 1975^2 3177^6 3990^5 6158^2

Musir (AUS) *M F De Kock* a122 120
7 b h Redoute's Choice(AUS) Dizzy De Lago (AUS) (Encosta De Lago (AUS))
745a^4 872a^2

Muskat Link *Henry Candy* a66 66
3 b g Rail Link Muskat Rose (IRE) (One Cool Cat (USA))
1900^6 2324^{10} 3173^4 3821^3 4633^7 5099^5 6325^3

Musnad (USA) *Brian Ellison* a73 81
5 ch g Mr Greeley(USA) Jadarah (USA) (Red Ransom (USA))
329^5 540^7 1237^8 7424^3

Muspelheim *Ann Duffield* 75
2 b c Firebreak Ticcatoo (IRE) (Dolphin Street (FR))
1642^2 1989^5 (2913) 4726^6 5859^2 6791^8 7026^{14}

Mustadaam (IRE) *Brian Meehan* 73
2 br c Dansili Sundus (USA) (Sadler's Wells (USA))
6762^5

Mustadrik (USA) *J W Hills* a60 62
2 b c Jazil(USA) Uroobah (USA) (Dynaformer (USA))
6762^{11} 7128^6 7902^7

Mustaheel (IRE) *A Al Raihe* a100 108
4 b g Lawman(FR) Lidanski (IRE) (Soviet Star (USA))
463a^9 552a^6 ◆ 657a^6 872a^6

Mustajeeb *D K Weld* 107
2 ch c Nayef(USA) Rifqah (USA) (Elusive Quality (USA))
5774a^2

Mustamir (IRE) *James Tate* 75
2 b c Medicean Perfect Plum (IRE) (Darshaan)
5969^2 6528^4

Must Be Me *D Grilli* a59 84
3 b f Trade Fair Roodeye (Inchinor)
1866a^{11}

Mutabaser *F Rohaut* 97
3 b c Muhtathir Tuiga (FR) (Commands (AUS))
5361a^7

Mutafaakir (IRE) *Ruth Carr* a69 80
4 b g Oasis Dream Moon's Whisper (USA) (Storm Cat (USA))
1203^8 1462^3 1686^3 1801^2 2450^4 2884^5 (3090) 3778^2 3980^3 4510^5 5011^4 5088^5 5711^2 5974^4 (6205) 6586^{15}

Mutajally *Sir Michael Stoute* 86
3 b c Teofilo(IRE) Dhelaal (Green Desert (USA))
1635^5 2306^4 2960^2

Mutajare (IRE) *A Al Raihe* a91 80
5 b g Cadeaux Genereux Bona Dea (IRE) (Danehill (USA))
503a^9

Mutakayyef *William Haggas* 78
2 ch c Sea The Stars(IRE) Infallible (Pivotal)
7467^2

Mutamakkin (IRE) *Richard Hannon Snr* a29
2 b g Shamardal(USA) Princess Speedfit (FR) (Desert Prince (IRE))
7460^{11}

Mutanaker *Ed de Giles* a58 42
6 b g Cape Cross(IRE) Purple Haze (IRE) (Spectrum (IRE))
158^{12}

Mutanaweb (IRE) *John Gosden* a74 80
3 b c Tamayuz Diary (IRE) (Green Desert (USA))
1926^4 2456^5 5484^4 6108^9 6504^4 7369^4

Mutaraadif (USA) *Roger Varian* 66
2 b c Dynaformer(USA) Dawla (Alhaarth (IRE))
7469^8

Mutashabek (USA) *Brian Meehan*
3 b g Arch(USA) Siyadah (USA) (Mr Prospector (USA))
7311^{10}

Mutashaded (USA) *Roger Varian* 110
3 b c Raven's Pass(USA) Sortita (GER) (Monsun (GER))
(2604) 3523^3 ◆

Mutatis Mutandis (IRE) *Ed Walker* 77
2 gr f Mastercraftsman(IRE) Amathia (IRE) (Darshaan)
4702^{11} (5516) 6770^2 7695^5

Mutawathea *Richard Hannon Snr* a65 58
2 b c Exceed And Excel(AUS) Esteemed Lady (IRE) (Mark Of Esteem (IRE))
3833^6 6931^4 ◆

Mutazamen *Richard Hannon Snr* a57 88
3 ch g Sakhee's Secret Disco Lights (Spectrum (IRE))
1668^9 3020^6 3763^7 4255^{16}

Mu Tazz (FR) *Y Fouin* 93
3 b c Singspiel(IRE) Across (ARG) (Roy (USA))
(2403a)

Muteela *Mark Johnston* a75
2 b f Dansili Nufoos (Zafonic (USA))
(7645) ◆

Muthafar (IRE) *William Haggas* a78 75
3 b g Tamayuz Etizaaz (USA) (Diesis)
4535^3 6366^2 7491^3

Mutheeb (USA) *M Al Muhairi* a89 94
8 b h Danzig(USA) Magicalmysterykate (USA) (Woodman (USA))
290a^7

Muthmera (USA) *Roger Varian* 86
3 b f Dynaformer(USA) Burooz (IRE) (King's Best (USA))
1813^4 3237^2 (3806) 4234^7

Muthmir (IRE) *William Haggas* 94
3 b g Invincible Spirit(IRE) Fairy Of The Night (IRE) (Danehill (USA))
3176^4 ◆ 3731^2 (4200) 5748^5

Mutin (FR) *J-C Rouget* 104
3 b c Kentucky Dynamite(USA) Mytographie (FR) (Anabaa (USA))
3455^{18} 4573a^9

Muttley *Mark Brisbourne*
5 gr g Iceman Amarella (FR) (Balleroy (USA))
1522^{11}

Mutual Regard (IRE) *Sir Mark Prescott Bt* a100 100
4 b g Hernando(FR) Hidden Charm (IRE) (Big Shuffle (USA))
2973^2 3284^3 3959^4 (4606) 5256^2 6066^2 7064^2

Muwaary *John Gosden* 81
2 bb c Oasis Dream Wissal (USA) (Woodman (USA))
(4483) ◆

Muzhil (IRE) *Clive Brittain* a66 63
4 b f Manduro(GER) Mazuna (IRE) (Cape Cross (IRE))
1544^{14} 1986^4 2511^{14} 3222^2 4016^2

My Anchor *Sylvester Kirk* a37 63
2 b g Mount Nelson War Shanty (Warrshan (USA))
3853^9 4154^{11} 4631^8 6152^2 6460^3 6897^5 7309^4

My Approach (IRE) *Robert Collet* a90 102
3 b c New Approach(IRE) Zelding (IRE) (Warning)
1357a^5 2298a^{15}

My Arch *Ollie Pears* 83
11 b g Silver Patriarch(IRE) My Desire (Grey Desire)
1445^9 1721^4

Myasun (FR) *C Baillet* a107 113
6 ch g Panis(USA) Spain (FR) (Bering)
(961a) 2909a^6 3851a^7 (5806a) 7054a^8 7941a^3

My Best Man *Tony Carroll* a41 23
7 b g Forzando Victoria Sioux (Ron's Victory (USA))
6101^7 6478^{13}

Myboyalfie (USA) *J R Jenkins* a83 93
6 b g Johannesburg(USA) Scotchbonnetpepper (USA) (El Gran Senor (USA))
1233^{10} 2541^9 6650^8 6988^5 7224^2 7696^8 7820^6

My Boy Bill *Michael Easterby* a52 68
3 b g Dutch Art Pious (Bishop Of Cashel)
4670^3 6362^5 7149^3

My Boy Bob *Richard Fahey* 36
2 b g Myboycharlie(IRE) Empress Jain (Lujain (USA))
3350^{14} 4259^8

My Catch (IRE) *David Brown* 103
2 b c Camacho Catch The Sea (IRE) (Barathea (IRE))
3079^2 ◆ 3424^5 ◆ (4651a) (4816a) 5765^7

My Claire *Nigel Tinkler* a55 51
3 b f Piccolo Aymara (Darshaan)
1760^6 2501^7 2762^6 3082^3 3418^8 4045^5 4391^7 7035^2 7351^2 7666^6 7962^7

My Conquestadory (USA) *Mark Casse* a104 107
2 bb f Artie Schiller(USA) Golden Artemis (USA) (Malibu Moon (USA))
7690a^4 ◆

My Dear Watson *Matthieu Palussiere* a77 78
2 ch c Winker Watson Begonia (IRE) (Selkirk (USA))
4651a[5] 5214a[7]

My Destination (IRE) *Declan Carroll* a68 71
4 b g Dubai Destination(USA) Gossamer (Sadler's Wells (USA))
2860[6] 3363[7] 3627[6] 4822[4] 4969[2] 5514[6] 5972[5] 6237[11] *6658[2] 6996[3]* 7342[3] *7881[3]*

My Direction *Mark Johnston* a77
3 ch g Singspiel(IRE) Ejlaal (IRE) (Caerleon (USA))
6116[2] 6402[2]

My Freedom (IRE) *Saeed bin Suroor* a110 103
5 b g Invincible Spirit(IRE) Priere (Machiavellian (USA))
503a[4] *744a[10]* (3725) 4297[12] *(7540)*

My Gigi *Gary Moore* a65 67
3 b f Medicean Choirgirl (Unfuwain (USA))
2616[3] 3178[6] *4144[3] 5098[3] (7873) 8087[10] 8330[8]*

My Girl Anna (IRE) *Muredach Kelly* a82 104
6 b m Orpen(USA) Kooyong (IRE) (College Chapel)
1704a[8]

My Girl Rio (IRE) *Geoffrey Harker* a25
2 ch f Captain Rio Pinewoods Lily (IRE) (Indian Ridge)
8058[5]

My Good Brother (IRE) *T G McCourt* a93 97
4 b g Elusive City(USA) Final Favour (IRE) (Unblest)
6883a[23]

My Grand Duke (USA) *R Schoof* a52 52
6 b g Johannesburg(USA) Hit It Here Cafe (USA) (Grand Slam (USA))
4467a[12]

My Guardian Angel *Mark H Tompkins* a29 77
4 b g Araafa(IRE) Angels Guard You (Bahamian Bounty)
1753[8] 2552[6] (2966) 3218[3] 6306[11] 6721[9]

My History (IRE) *Mark Johnston* a72 79
3 b c Dubawi(IRE) Reine Zao (FR) (Alzao (USA))
6036[2] (6272) 7105[8] *7627[5] 7947[7] 8159[8] 8353[7]*

My Inspiration (IRE) *William Haggas* 78
2 b f Invincible Spirit(IRE) Lulua (USA) (Bahri (USA))
6234[5] 6789[2] 7173[4]

Myjestic Melody (IRE) *Brian Ellison* a47 49
5 b f Majestic Missile(IRE) Bucaramanga (IRE) (Distinctly North (USA))
3024[11] 3286[6] 3932[6] 4102[12] 4398[5] 6944[3] 7236[7] *7905[6] 8051[4]*

Mykia *Ollie Pears*
5 b g Iktibas My Desire (Grey Desire)
7422[11]

My Kingdom (IRE) *Stuart Williams* a82 91
7 b g King's Best(USA) Nebraas (Green Desert (USA))
1726[13] 2255[17] 2725[5] *3172[3]* (3586) 3974[4] 4067[7] 4812[2] 4879[10] 5247[10] 5722[3] 6337[2] 6871[6] 6977[7] 7699[8] *8127[7] 8304[3]*

My Learned Friend (IRE) *Andrew Balding* a58 63
9 b g Marju(IRE) Stately Princess (Robellino (USA))
3181[8] 3575[6] 3926[5] 4237[9] 6154[4] 7109[13] *8073[6] 8157[6] 8446[7]*

Mylington Light *Roger Varian* 48
3 ch f Mount Nelson Atlantic Light (Linamix (FR))
4182[5]

My Little Friend *Mark H Tompkins* 57
2 ch g Pastoral Pursuits Sosumi (Be My Chief (USA))
2131[4] 2543[6] 3298[12] 3992[2] 4862[4] 5243[6]

My Lord *Luke Dace* a68 78
5 br g Ishiguru(USA) Lady Smith (Greensmith)
2808[5] 6004[7] 6787[10]

Mylute (USA) *Thomas Amoss* a114
3 rg c Midnight Lute(USA) Stage Stop (USA) (Valid Expectations (USA))
2033a[5] 2473a[3]

My Manekineko *J R Jenkins* a65 60
4 b g Authorized(IRE) Echo River (USA) (Irish River (FR))
4411[10] 5099[4] 5312[3] 5615[4] *6398[6] 6558[2] 7628[5]*

My Mary (GER) *M Weiss* 79
6 br m Denon(USA) Masaya (SWI) (In The Wings)
514a[10]

My Mate Jake (IRE) *James Given* a76 80
5 ch g Captain Rio Jam (IRE) (Arazi (USA))
3349[18] 5050[6]

My Meteor *Tony Newcombe* a59 72
6 b g Bahamian Bounty Emerald Peace (IRE) (Green Desert (USA))
6040[7]

My Mum Mo *Simon West* a53 49
5 b f Statue Of Liberty(USA) Come To The Point (Pursuit Of Love)
3398[5] 3542[5] 5370[6]

My My My Diliza *J S Moore* a57 53
2 br f Sakhee's Secret Diliza (Dilum (USA))
2805[8] 3107[7] 4668[6] 5951[7] 6322[8] *7117[4] 7878[3] 8039[4] 8262[6] 8383[6]*

My Name Is Rio (IRE) *Michael Dods* a68 76
3 ch g Captain Rio Walk In My Shadow (IRE) (Orpen (USA))
(829) 1482[4] ◆ 2430[14] 3104[4] 3611[5] *4354[6]*

My New Angel (IRE) *Jason Ward* a54 68
4 gr f Dark Angel(IRE) Mynu Girl (IRE) (Charnwood Forest (IRE))
646[5] 890[7] 3592[2] 3946[2] 4557[3] 4966[2] *5192[4]* 5881[5] 6633[7] 6941[9] 7283[13]

My Own Way Home *David Evans* a67 72
5 b f Danbird(AUS) Wenden Belle (IRE) (Brave Act)
76[2] ◆ 186[4] ◆ 398[5] 494[8] 687[7] 775[6] 1063[11] 1802[4] 2596[3] 3111[3] 3223[3] 3660[3] 3920[3] (4517) (4603) (4998) 5447[3] 6045[P]

My Painter (IRE) *Charles Hills* 72
2 b f Jeremy(USA) Last Cry (FR) (Peintre Celebre (USA))
5282[4] ◆ 5995[3] 6281[8]

My Peggy Sue *Tom Keddy* 39
3 b f Cockney Rebel(IRE) Groom Landing (PR) (Runaway Groom (CAN))
3860[8] 4719[5]

My Propeller (IRE) *Peter Chapple-Hyam* a81 106
4 b m Holy Roman Emperor(IRE) Incise (Dr Fong (USA))
1662[2] 2019[13] 3046[3] (3562) 4311[5] 5772a[7]

My Quest For Peace (IRE) *Peter G Moody* 115
5 b c Galileo(IRE) Play Misty For Me (IRE) (Danehill Dancer (IRE))
7392a[16] 7700a[14]

My Red Devil (IRE) *Richard Fahey* a48
2 b f Duke Of Marmalade(IRE) Square Pants (USA) (King Of Kings (IRE))
8214[8]

My Renaissance *Ben Case* a32 55
3 bb g Medicean Lebenstanz (Singspiel (IRE))
2448[9] 3585[10] 4885[9]

Myrtlewood (IRE) *F-H Graffard* 101
4 gr f Montjeu(IRE) Walkamia (FR) (Linamix (FR))
6294a[6]

My Sapphire (IRE) *R Pritchard-Gordon* 91
2 b f Haatef(USA) Sapphire Spray (IRE) (Viking Ruler (AUS))
3875a[6]

My Scat Daddy (USA) *Brett Johnson* a56 54
4 b g Scat Daddy(USA) Will Be A Bates (USA) (Bates Motel (USA))
205[4] 471[2] 510[7]

My Secret Dream (FR) *Ron Hodges* a40 40
2 b f Stormy River(FR) Aventure Secrete (FR) (Polish Precedent (USA))
2917[7] 3853[10] 5061[8] *7293[10]*

My Single Malt (IRE) *Julie Camacho* a79 79
5 b g Danehill Dancer(IRE) Slip Dance (IRE) (Celtic Swing)
1963[5] 2761[4] 4245[2] 4628[2] 5138[5] 5947[5] 6291[6] *8269[5]*

My Son Max *Michael Blake* a92 87
5 b g Avonbridge Pendulum (Pursuit Of Love)
780[4] ◆ 1121[2] ◆ (1370) 1581[3] 2388[10] 2663[4] 3586[9] 3980[4] 4217[5] *8189[6] 8324[3]*

My Special J'S (USA) *John Patrick Shanahan* a94 105
3 b f Harlan's Holiday(USA) Shadow On The Moon (USA) (Deputy Minister (CAN))
243a[5] 554a[7] 837a[4] 954a[16]

Mysterial *Richard Hannon Snr* a75 82
3 b g Invincible Spirit(IRE) Diamond Dilemma (IRE) (Sinndar (IRE))
1174[2] (1288) 2584[7] (3507)

Mysterieux (FR) *F Foresi* a32
3 ch g Tamayuz Sister Trouble (FR) (Spectrum (IRE))
818a[9]

Mysterious Man (IRE) *Andrew Balding* 99
4 b g Manduro(GER) Edabiya (IRE) (Rainbow Quest (USA))
2052[2] 2648[3] 3423[5] 4704[4] (5746) 6144[3]

Mysterious Wonder *Philip Kirby* a60 64
3 b g Oasis Dream Raskutani (Dansili)
1180[6] 2464[14] 4430[6] 4762[6] 4976[4] 5709[5] 6180[6] (6687) 7149[5] *7966[8] 8162[4] 8361[5]*

Mystery Bet (IRE) *Richard Fahey* a83 86
3 b f Kheleyf(USA) Dancing Prize (IRE) (Sadler's Wells (USA))
1641[5] 3048[4] 4777[7] 7275[2] 7611[2] *7786[2] 7895[5] 8218[6]*

Mystery Drama *Alan King* a81 56
3 b f Hernando(FR) Mystery Lot (IRE) (Revoque (IRE))
3239[9] *4632[8]* 5038[6] *(6964) (7543)* ◆

Mystery Woman (IRE) *Peter Chapple-Hyam* a57
3 b f Holy Roman Emperor(IRE) Parvenue (FR) (Ezzoud (IRE))
184[4] 336[3] 507[3]

Mystical King *Linda Perratt*
3 b g Notnowcato Mystical Ayr (IRE) (Namid)
6684[4]

Mystical Man *James Tate* a76 89
3 br c Sakhee's Secret Dancing Nelly (Shareef Dancer (USA))
1109[6] 2554[2] 3067[3] (3758)

Mystical Maze *Mark Brisbourne* 44
2 b f Multiplex Musical Maze (Distant Music (USA))
6318[10] 6789[9]

Mystical Moment *Richard Hannon Snr* a80 86
3 ch f Dutch Art Tinnarinka (Observatory (USA))
2195[8] 2738[5] 3242[6] 3817[5] 5173[2] 6433[8] 7505[6]

Mystical Rock (FR) *D Windrif* 71
2 ch f High Rock(IRE) Miss Maguilove (FR) (Dyhim Diamond (IRE))
4599a[5]

Mystical Sapphire *Jo Crowley* a95 78
3 b f Sakhee's Secret Nadyma (IRE) (Daylami (IRE))
(129) 1091[3] 1676[9] *(7297) 7649[5]*

Mystical Witch *Christine Dunnett* a50 30
4 b f Kyllachy Shifty Night (IRE) (Night Shift (USA))
536[6] 600[8] 4388[5] *4840[10]* 5085[10] 5499[10]

Mystic Angellina *Mrs Ilka Gansera-Leveque* 35
2 ch f Medicean World's Heroine (IRE) (Spinning World (USA))
2993[5] 3648[10] 3896[7] 5151[7] *8045[4] 8214[10]*

Mysticism (USA) *Saeed bin Suroor* 58
5 b g A. P. Warrior(USA) Wild Catseye (USA) (Forest Wildcat (USA))
290a[14] *744a[15]*

Mystified (IRE) *Alan Berry* a59 35
10 b g Raise A Grand(IRE) Sunrise (IRE) (Sri Pekan (USA))
3467[7] 3709[8]

Mystique Rider *Olly Stevens* a84 85
2 b c Kyllachy Greenmeadow (Sure Blade (USA))
2595[3] ◆ 4858[3] *(6169)*

My Stroppy Poppy *David Evans* a42 44
4 b f Multiplex Aspen Ridge (IRE) (Namid)
2346[6] *2578[12]* 5429[8] 5667[7]

My Sweet Lord *Mark Usher* a60 59
3 b g Byron Sweetest Revenge (IRE) (Daggers Drawn (USA))
2347[3] (2791) 3533[4] *4410[10]* 5373[4] *6752[7]* 7086[9] *8022[9] 8151[11] 8306[2] 8412[7]*

My Target (IRE) *Saeed bin Suroor* a78 47
2 b c Cape Cross(IRE) Chercheuse (USA) (Seeking The Gold (USA))
6769[6] *7302[3] (7646)*

My Time *Michael Mullineaux* a58 58
4 b g Mind Games Tick Tock (Timeless Times (USA))
1355[7] 1681[4] ◆ 2757[11] 4074[9] *8112[4] (8370)*

My Titania (IRE) *John M Oxx* 105
2 b f Sea The Stars(IRE) Fairy Of The Night (IRE) (Danehill (USA))
(6881a)

My Trust (IRE) *Saeed bin Suroor* a63
3 b f Exceed And Excel(AUS) Alizes (NZ) (Rory's Jester (AUS))
7600[3]

Myzamour *Michael Wigham* a56 47
3 b f Azamour(IRE) Lady Ragazza (IRE) (Bering)
5[2] 988[4]

Naabegha *Ed de Giles* a96 92
6 ch g Muhtathir Hawafiz (Nashwan (USA))
2014[7] 2461[7] 3135[6] 4024[13] 4536[6] 6822[2] ◆ 7222[2] 7373[10] *7648[4]* ◆ *7803[6] 7982[3] (8217)*

Naadirr (IRE) *Marco Botti* a79 59
2 b c Oasis Dream Beach Bunny (IRE) (High Chaparral (IRE))
7467[9] *(7972)*

Naafetha (IRE) *Ian Semple* 59
5 b f Alhaarth(IRE) Doctrine (Barathea (IRE))
2537[10] 2972[10]

Naalatt (IRE) *Roger Varian* a79 80
3 b f Dansili Vine Street (IRE) (Singspiel (IRE))
(541) 1307[2] 1725[2] 2195[7]

Naaz (IRE) *Ed Dunlop* a90 87
3 ch c Tamayuz Naazeq (Nashwan (USA))
1291[3] *1713[11]* 2041[7] (2506) *3173[3]* 5483[3] 5835[4] (6359) 6642[2] 7224[5] 7499[9] *7988[5] 8218[5]*

Nabah *A Al Raihe* a67 45
5 b f Motivator Kiss And Fly (IRE) (Priolo (USA))
412a[14]

Nabatean (IRE) *Andrew Balding* 47
2 b g Rock Of Gibraltar(IRE) Landinium (ITY) (Lando (GER))
7502[10]

Nabat Seif (USA) *Ed Dunlop* 47
3 b f Street Sense(USA) Sierra Madre (FR) (Baillamont (USA))
1640[9]

Nabbaash *J-C Rouget* a81
2 b c Aqlaam Poppo's Song (CAN) (Polish Navy (USA))
(8354a)

Nabeel (IRE) *Saeed bin Suroor* 48
2 b g Invincible Spirit(IRE) Screen Star (IRE) (Tobougg (IRE))
6939[7]

Nabstarlini *Ed Vaughan*
2 ch g Bertolini(USA) Welcome Star (IRE) (Most Welcome)
4386[5] 5299[10] 5785[8]

Nabucco *John Gosden* 113
4 b c Dansili Cape Verdi (IRE) (Caerleon (USA))
2422[3] 3113[2] (3832) 4854[2] (6957) (7697)

Nabucco (GER) *R Rohne* 101
3 b c Areion(GER) Numero Uno (GER) (Lavirco (GER))
1865a[5] 4043a[7] 6889a[3] (7413a) 7725a[5]

Naburn *Alan Swinbank* a57 75
5 b g Cape Cross(IRE) Allespagne (USA) (Trempolino (USA))
1572[3] (1789) 2165[5] 2540[3] 3790[3] 5862[7] 6290[5] (6632) 6909[9] 7597[10]

Nadelwald *P Schiergen* 97
2 b c Shamardal(USA) Nobilissima (GER) (Bluebird (USA))
7232a[2]

Nadema Rose (IRE) *Keith Dalgleish* a60 80
4 b f Elnadim(USA) Noctilucent (JPN) (Lammtarra (USA))
1068[3] 1567[8] 1993[8]

Nadia Naes (IRE) *Roger Ingram* a46 17
4 b f Strategic Prince Tread The Boards (Reprimand)
12[9] 342[7] 635[9]

Nadmah *Roger Varian* a37
3 ch f Sakhee(USA) Hamsat Elqamar (Nayef (USA))
373[8]

Nafa (IRE) *Daniel Mark Loughnane* a89 88
5 br f Shamardal(USA) Champs Elysees (USA) (Distant Relative)
81[4] 142[7] 326[6] 610[3] 968[5] (1731) 2074[4] *(2326) (2873) (3498)* (3888) ◆ 4203[4] 4866[3] 8324[2]

Naggers (IRE) *Paul Midgley* 38
2 ch g Excellent Art Trika (First Trump)
6769[9]

Nahthen Alice *Shaun Harris* a9
2 b f Phoenix Reach(IRE) Shosolosa (IRE) (Dansili)
5193[5]

Naivasha *Robert Cowell* a40
2 b f Captain Gerrard(IRE) Netta (IRE) (Barathea (IRE))
6607[7]

Najinska (GER) *Z Koplik* 80
2 b f Areion(GER) Najinskaja (GER) (Tannenkonig (IRE))
7084a[8]

Najjaar (USA) *Daniel Peitz* a102 103
4 b c Jazil(USA) Hasheema (IRE) (Darshaan)
5550a[3]

Nakayama Knight (JPN) *Yoshitaka Ninomiya* 118
5 ch c Stay Gold(JPN) Fiji Girl (JPN) (Cacoethes (USA))
8033a[9]

Nakeeta *Mick Channon* 70
2 b g Sixties Icon Easy Red (IRE) (Hunting Lion (IRE))
4925[5] 5309[5] 5785[2] 6014[4] 7320[7]

Nakuru Breeze (IRE) *Suzzanne France* a44 47
4 b f King's Best(USA) Tropical Breeze (IRE) (Kris)
5515[13] 6497[10] 6759[9] *6986[4] 7484[4]*

Nakuti (IRE) *Sylvester Kirk* 71
2 b f Mastercraftsman(IRE) Sheba Five (USA) (Five Star Day (USA))
3986[12] 4921[7] 5443[2] 6326[7] 7218[2] ◆

Naledi *Richard Price* a50 52
9 b g Indian Ridge Red Carnation (IRE) (Polar Falcon (USA))
852[7] 2714[6]

Naloudia (IRE) *H-A Pantall* a75 58
2 ch f Piccolo Fanciful Dancer (Groom Dancer (USA))
8354a[2]

Nameitwhatyoulike *Michael Easterby* 97
4 b g Trade Fair Emma Peel (Emarati (USA))
1233[15] 1688[12] 3300[2] 4308[11] 4778[5] 5056[3] 5544[11] 6621[26] 7172[8]

Namely (IRE) *Sir Mark Prescott Bt* a48 48
2 b f Rock Of Gibraltar(IRE) Viz (IRE) (Darshaan)
6690[10] 7102[9] 7371[3]

Namera (GER) *W Haustein* 95
4 b f Areion(GER) Najinskaja (GER) (Tannenkonig (IRE))
5804a[3]

Nam June Paik (FR) *S Wattel* a85 76
3 b g Orpen(USA) Marisa Merz (IRE) (Lend A Hand)
2434a[10] *7736a[7]*

Nam Ma Prow *Simon West* 48
2 ch g Bahamian Bounty Charlotte Vale (Pivotal)
5364[10] 5968[7]

Nancy O (IRE) *Carolyn M Costigan* 98
3 b f Pivotal Arravale (USA) (Arch (USA))
7562a[10]

Nandura *Harry Dunlop* a34 33
3 b f Motivator Nando's Dream (Hernando (FR))
2938[14] 5176[7] 5816[11] *7440[10]*

Nanton (USA) *Jim Goldie* a81 90
11 rg g Spinning World(USA) Grab The Green (USA) (Cozzene (USA))
1273[6] 1689[9] 2369[10] 2633[3] (3345) 4262[6] 6192[14] 6646[14] 7193[22] *7976[10] 7990[12]*

Nant Saeson (IRE) *John Quinn* a66 68
4 b g Elusive City(USA) Lady Power (IRE) (Almutawakel)
147[4] (380) 705[4] 831[6] 1271[3] 2037[4]

Napinda *Philip McBride* a63 63
3 b f Sleeping Indian Aptina (USA) (Aptitude (USA))
321[4] 371[3] 527[2] (599) 684[3] 824[10] 1071[6] 1781[3] 2762[4] 3537[6] (3740) 4585[6] 5152[7] 5527[3] 5923[4] (6038) 6804[2] 7378[9]

Naqshabban (USA) *Mahmood Al Zarooni* 111
5 b g Street Cry(IRE) Reem Three (Mark Of Esteem (IRE))
242a[2] (Dead)

Narborough *Mick Channon* a58 61
2 b g Winker Watson Solmorin (Fraam)
1344[3] 3413[5] 3815[5] 4363[6] 4910[4] 5610[2] 5814[3] 6320[7] 6511[2]

Narcissist (IRE) *Michael Easterby* a71 84
4 b g Dylan Thomas(IRE) Gabare (FR) (Galileo (IRE))
2040[13] 2431[9] 5086[6] 7498[18]

Nardin *Ed Dunlop* a90 91
3 b f Royal Applause Third Party (Terimon)
3058[2] 3586[2] 4252[3] 4757[2] 5247[6] 5700[5] *6524[3]*

Nargys (IRE) *Luca Cumani* 110
3 b f Lawman(FR) Spesialta (Indian Ridge)
1622[14] 3460[4] 4081[8] 4949[9] 5561[9] (6327) 7015[6]

Narla *Clive Cox* a54 19
4 b f Nayef(USA) Polygueza (FR) (Be My Guest (USA))
275[6] 3272[12]

Narmin (IRE) *John Gosden* 89
3 b f Pivotal Ulfah (USA) (Danzig (USA))
2448[4] ◆ 3116[3] (4535) (5173) 6531[4] 7470[8]

Narniyn (IRE) *A De Royer-Dupre* 111
3 b f Dubawi(IRE) Narmina (IRE) (Alhaarth (IRE))
(6962a) (7613a)

Naru (IRE) *James Tate* a91 88
3 b c Authorized(IRE) Jabbara (IRE) (Kingmambo (USA))
(211) (428) ◆ *613[2] (1453)* 1609[2] 2050[6] 2660[3] 2879[2] 3526[15] 3990[3]

Naseem Alyasmeen (IRE) *A Al Raihe* a71 96
4 gr f Clodovil(IRE) Phillippa (IRE) (Galileo (IRE))
152a[5] 366a[5]

Nasharra (IRE) *Kevin Ryan* a21 89
5 ch g Iffraaj There With Me (USA) (Distant View (USA))
1692[10] (2036) (2222) (3980) 5011[9] 5544[19] 6586[25] 7595[6]

Nashmi *Fawzi Abdulla Nass* a58 64
2 b c Compton Place Black Tribal (IRE) (Mukaddamah (USA))
5244[7] 5488[6] *5924[8]*

Nashrah (USA) *J W Hills* 49
3 bb f Jazil(USA) Taleef (Sakhee (USA))
1640[11] 2231[10]

Nashville (IRE) *Richard Fahey* a74 81
4 b g Galileo(IRE) Brown Eyes (Danehill (USA))
2277[13] 3089[4] 3609[2] 4372[3] *4754[3]* 5423[3] (5885) (5997) 6237[15] 6646[15] 7338[12]

Nashville (NZ) *Adrian Bull* 108
5 br g Darci Brahma(NZ) Royal Kiss (IRE) (Royal Academy (USA))
7826a[10]

Nasri *Milton Bradley* a67 92
7 b g Kyllachy Triple Sharp (Selkirk (USA))
2097[9] 2725[8] 3038[4] 3415[10] 4067[9] 4628[8] 5841[8] *6135[7]*

Nassau Storm *William Knight* a97 96
4 b g Bahamian Bounty Got To Go (Shareef Dancer (USA))
2207[5] 3249[6] 3527[23] 4389[3] 4983[13] 5533[5] 6278[6] 6831[8] *7464[7] 8127[5]* ◆ *8391[7] 8455[10]*

Natalia *Andrew Hollinshead* a45 60
4 ch f Dutch Art Pintle (Pivotal)
2437[3] 2824[7] 5512[3] 7741[8] 8063[9]

Nateeja (IRE) *J W Hills* a77 88
3 b f Shamardal(USA) Merayaat (IRE) (Darshaan)
2095[2] 2599[5] 3257[2] 3916[3] (4352) 4899[4] 5997[3] 6540[2] (6978) 7338[10]

Nates Mineshaft (USA) *Anne P Smith* a122 110
6 b r Mineshaft(USA) Angel's Tearlet (CAN) (Silver Deputy (CAN))
5553a[12]

Nathr (USA) *Charles Hills* 76
2 bb c Dixie Union(USA) Sweet Rider (USA) (Seeking The Gold (USA))
2048[3] ◆ 2591[2]

Nationalism *S Seemar* a96 103
6 b g Pivotal Las Flores (IRE) (Sadler's Wells (USA))
873a[5]

National Poet (IRE) *Saeed bin Suroor* a68 78
3 ch g Nayef(USA) Reve D'Iman (FR) (Highest Honor (FR))
4223[3] 4632[5]

National Service (USA) *Stuart Williams* a72
2 b g War Chant(USA) Cotton Club Ballet (USA) (Street Cry (IRE))
(8058)

Native Colony *Neil King* a66 68
5 b g St Jovite(USA) Self Esteem (Suave Dancer (USA))
351[7] 1502[9] 4179[7]

Native Falls (IRE) *Alan Swinbank* 65
2 ch g Elnadim(USA) Sagrada (GER) (Primo Dominie)
1930[12] 2631[4] 6716[4] 7418[7]

Natural Choice *Saeed bin Suroor* a80 69
2 b f Teofilo(IRE) Oiseau Rare (FR) (King's Best (USA))
7493[4] ◆ (7764) ◆

Natural High (IRE) *Sean Curran* a67 85
8 b g Sadler's Wells(USA) Cool Clarity (IRE) (Indian Ridge)
948[6] 1464[11] 6173[7] 7863[9] 8129[10]

Natures Law (IRE) *Keith Dalgleish* a43 66
3 b f Lawman(FR) Misaayef (USA) (Swain (IRE))
1570[7] (1962) 5365[11] 5642[8] 6588[3] (6918) 7489[8]

Naughtybychoice *Ollie Pears* a52 57
3 gr g Dubai Destination(USA) Gracia (Linamix (FR))
527[3] 717[3] 910[3] 8436[5]

Naughty Spice *Rod Millman* 54
2 b f Three Valleys(USA) Milldown Story (Lucky Story (USA))
4827[5]

Nausica Time (GER) *S Smrczek* 105
3 bb f Dubawi(IRE) Namat (IRE) (Daylami (IRE))
5361a[5]

Nautical Twilight *Malcolm Jefferson* a26
3 gr f Proclamation(IRE) Anabranch (Kind Of Hush)
5071[10] 5484[12] 6566[9]

Nautilus *John Gosden* a100 99
3 b g Medicean Fickle (Danehill (USA))
1178[3] 1468[6] 1735[4] 5245[2] (5492) 5719[2] (6280) 7304[5] 8150[5] 8387[5]

Navajo Charm *Alan Jarvis* a62 65
4 b f Authorized(IRE) Navajo Love Song (IRE) (Dancing Brave (USA))
722[10] 813[9]

Navajo Chief *Alan Jarvis* a95 111
6 b g King's Best(USA) Navajo Rainbow (Rainbow Quest (USA))
(2399) 3458[27] 4284[5] 5269[12] 5681[14] 6592[6] 6834[8]

Navajo Nights *E Leon Penate* 63
3 b c Sleeping Indian Nuit Sans Fin (FR) (Lead On Time (USA))
7995a[14]

Nave (USA) *David Simcock* a85 85
6 b g Pulpit(USA) Lakabi (USA) (Nureyev (USA))
161[3] 420[5] 2532[3] 3180[2] (3865) (4208) 5008[6] 6559[4] 6750[4] 7174[16] 7765[7] 7975[7] 8392[5]

Nawwaar (USA) *A Al Raihe* a97 99
4 ch h Distorted Humor(USA) Mostaqeleh (USA) (Rahy (USA))
(503a) 957a[9]

Nazreef *Hughie Morrison* a108 78
6 b g Zafeen(FR) Roofer (IRE) (Barathea (IRE))
401[8] 621[2] 945[5] 1545[7] 3108[9] 5894[13] 6199[15] 6428[6]

Neamour *David Simcock* a74 72
3 b f Oasis Dream Ever Rigg (Dubai Destination (USA))
2127[2] ◆ 2846[4] 4305[3] 5392[6]

Nearly Caught (IRE) *Hughie Morrison* a92 104
3 b c New Approach(IRE) Katch Me Katie (Danehill (USA))
(1584) ◆ 4815a[3] (5132) (6196) 7046a[6] 7823[22]

Near Time *Andrew Balding* a77 77
3 ch f New Approach(IRE) Time Away (IRE) (Darshaan)
1813[6] 3021[5] ◆ 3606[5] 5245[5] 6312[3] 6926[3] 7659[8]

Neatico (GER) *P Schiergen* 113
6 b h Medicean Nicola Bella (IRE) (Sadler's Wells (USA))
1564a[2] 2202a[2] (3612a) (4042a) (4819a) 5778a[6] (6987a) 8211a[8]

Neckara (GER) *A Wohler* a83 80
3 b f Shirocco(GER) Narooma (GER) (Silver Hawk (USA))
6887a[12]

Needless Shouting (IRE) *Mick Channon* 68
2 b c Footstepsinthesand Ring The Relatives (Bering)
3857[5] 4414[3] 4756[4] 5790[3] 6002[3] 6334[3] 6628[4] 6972[6] 7218[5] 7393[3]

Need To Be Bold *Derek Haydn Jones* a42 18
4 b f Needwood Blade Bold Loch (Never So Bold)
1891[8] 2746[13] 3469[14]

Needwood Park *Ray Craggs* a59 56
5 br g Needwood Blade Waterpark (Namaqualand (USA))
704[4] 1022[2] 1217[5] 3625[14] 4052[11]

Needwood Ridge *Frank Sheridan* a73 51
6 ch g Needwood Blade Aspen Ridge (IRE) (Namid)
206[6] 426[10] 546[7] 1038[7] (1734)

Needy McCredie *James Turner* 66
7 ch m Needwood Blade Vocation (IRE) (Royal Academy (USA))
2479[3] 2703[10] (2835) 3078[9] 3393[8] 4160[6]

Negotiate *Ms Joanna Morgan* 93
5 b f Red Ransom(USA) Poised (USA) (Rahy (USA))
2105a[5] 2397[8] 2688a[4] 3869a[14] 6440a[9]

Neige D'Antan *Sir Mark Prescott Bt* a71 58
4 gr f Aussie Rules(USA) Ninotchka (USA) (Nijinsky (CAN))
145[2] 450[6] 753[6]

Neighbother *Richard Fahey* 72
2 b g Invincible Spirit(IRE) Aravonian (Night Shift (USA))
1669[7] (2283) 2863[9] 4314[5] 4783[7] 6233[8] 7147[2] 7170[6]

Neighbourhood (USA) *James Evans* a73 63
5 bb g Street Cry(IRE) Miznah (IRE) (Sadler's Wells (USA))
(970) 1189[2] 1601[2] 1979[3] (2174) 2922[3] 6404[4] 7159[4] 8229[4] 8268[2]

Neil's Pride *Richard Fahey* a58 61
4 b f Dubai Destination(USA) Collette's Choice (Royal Applause)
201[2] 542[2] 973[4] 1189[5]

Nelina *Robert Cowell* a65 31
3 b f Mount Nelson Naralina (FR) (Linamix (FR))
6368[5] 6855[3] 7455[12] 8037[5] 8125[12]

Nellie Bly *Mark Johnston* a69 22
3 b f Exceed And Excel(AUS) La Presse (USA) (Gone West (USA))
706[4] (808) 1014[3] 1345[8] 1647[13] 1907[5] 2329[8] 2919[6] 3622[11]

Nellie Forbush *Andrew Balding* a68 65
3 b f Phoenix Reach(IRE) Santa Isobel (Nashwan (USA))
1611[3] 2423[5] 3402[5] 4899[7] 5432[5]

Nelson Quay (IRE) *Jeremy Gask* a72 64
3 b g Holy Roman Emperor(IRE) Frippet (IRE) (Ela-Mana-Mou)
1711[2] 2306[11] 2916[8] 4383[7] 4885[3] 5391[8]

Nelson's Bay *Wilf Storey* a66 63
4 b g Needwood Blade In Good Faith (USA) (Dynaformer (USA))
759[10] 3368[8] 6291[7] 6758[12] 7952[12]

Nelson's Muse *Tobias B P Coles* a27
3 b f Mount Nelson French Quartet (IRE) (Lycius (USA))
8302[9]

Nelson's Pride *Kevin Ryan* a22 61
2 b f Mount Nelson Bandanna (Bandmaster (USA))
2751[6] 3461[3] 4046[5] 5194[5] 6085[7]

Nemushka *Richard Fahey* 85
4 ch f Sakhee(USA) Dame De Noche (Lion Cavern (USA))
1990[5] 2704[5] 3443[4] (4066) 4777[3] (5548) 6001[10] 6236[16]

Nenge Mboko *George Baker* a75 87
3 b g Compton Place Floppie (FR) (Law Society (USA))
1714[5] 2303a[5] 2738[6] (3897) (4072) (4592) 4879[5] 6647[10]

Nepalese Pearl *Pat Eddery* a58 30
3 b f Tiger Hill(IRE) Grey Pearl (Ali-Royal (IRE))
1671[16] 2123[2] 2597[12] 3405[12] 4385[13] 5935[2] 6102[2] 7770[10]

Nephrite *A P O'Brien* 110
4 ch c Pivotal Cape Merino (Clantime)
1413a[2] ◆

Nero Emperor (IRE) *T Stack* a98 103
4 b g Holy Roman Emperor(IRE) Blue Iris (Petong)
1704a[9] 3334[17] 5775a[4] (6883a)

Nervi (FR) *P Bary* 95
3 b c Orpen(USA) O'Keefe (IRE) (Be My Guest (USA))
1799a[5] 7116a[10]

Nesso (USA) *Vann Belvoir* 97
2 ch f Roman Ruler(USA) Devotedness (USA) (Anet (USA))
7690a[10]

Net Whizz (USA) *Jeremy Noseda* a93 75
4 bb c Mr Greeley(USA) Reboot (USA) (Rubiano (USA))
1878[4] 3108[7] 3693[2] 3961[4]

Network Perfection *Michael Easterby* 50
2 ch c Distant Peak(IRE) Word Perfect (Diktat)
2591[9] 3233[6] 4312[9]

Neuf Des Coeurs *Keith Dalgleish* 65
2 b f Champs Elysees Intervene (Zafonic (USA))
3896[5] 5364[6] (6873)

Neuf Histoire (FR) *R Le Gal* a56 47
2 b g Maresca Sorrento(FR) Semterra (FR) (Charge D'Affaires)
7653a[7]

Neuilly *Mrs A Malzard* a72
6 b m Nayef(USA) Narasimha (USA) (Nureyev (USA))
7144a[3]

Nevada (GER) *P Harley* 94
4 b f Dubai Destination(USA) Norwegian Pride (FR) (Diktat)
7233a[2]

Nevada Blue *Tony Coyle* 64
2 ch g Pastoral Pursuits Nevada Princess (IRE) (Desert Prince (IRE))
2701[3] 3079[6] 4756[10] 6285[10]

Never A Quarrel (IRE) *Jeremy Gask* a72 61
3 b f Acclamation Welsh Mist (Damister (USA))
1896[9] 4839[5] 5345[3] (6345) 6745[10] 7937[5] 8216[7] 8384[3] 8457[7]

Never Forever *George Moore* 77
4 ch g Sir Percy Codename (Sadler's Wells (USA))
(2162) 2406[2] (2889) 3477[6] 4929[9] 6563[4] 7028[11]

Nevermindapete *David Evans* a43
5 b g Mutamarkiz(IRE) Lavender Della (IRE) (Shernazar)
712[4] 752[6]

Never Perfect (IRE) *Peter Chapple-Hyam* 70
4 b g Galileo(IRE) Dapprima (GER) (Shareef Dancer (USA))
1673[12]

Never Say Never (ITY) *S Botti* 102
3 b c Colossus(IRE) Do Diesis (ITY) (Barathea (IRE))
1865a[9]

Never To Be (USA) *John Gosden* a82 72
2 b c Thewayyouare(USA) Kitty Foille (USA) (Black Minnaloushe (USA))
4764[6] (4997) 7221[5] (7463) 7626[2]

Never Too Much (IRE) *Chris Wall* a37 48
3 b g Johannesburg(USA) Muskoka Dawn (USA) (Miswaki (USA))
3417[11] 4152[8]

Nevis (IRE) *A P O'Brien* 108
3 b c Dansili Moonstone (Dalakhani (IRE))
(2262)

New Bidder *Jedd O'Keeffe* 79
2 bb g Auction House(USA) Noble Nova (Fraam)
1930[6] 2670[5] (5145) 5858[3] 6233[7] 7062[7]

Newbury Street *Patrick Holmes* a65 69
6 b g Namid Cautious Joe (First Trump)
7148[12]

New Colours *Marcus Tregoning* a70
2 gr g Verglas(IRE) Briery (IRE) (Salse (USA))
7955[4] 8124[8] (8328)

New Decade *Milton Bradley* a73 72
4 ch g Pivotal Irresistible (Cadeaux Genereux)
187[8] 831[12] (1351) 1800[14] 2364[4] 2588[9] 3246[5] 6368[11] 7315[2] 7598[5] 7772[6] (8306)

New Elite (FR) *C Boutin* a55 72
2 ch f Panis(USA) Elite Super (USA) (Shadeed (USA))
1894a[7] 2433a[6] 7567a[8]

New Falcon (IRE) *James Tate* a77 78
3 b f New Approach(IRE) Wimple (USA) (Kingmambo (USA))
2026[7] 3039[2] 3712[5] 4442[3] 5125[3] 5978[2] 6379[3] 6780[4]

New Fforest *Andrew Balding* a72 100
3 b f Oasis Dream Ffestiniog (IRE) (Efisio)
1808[9] 2213[3] 2521[7] 3097[9] (4221) 5991[2] (6699) 7010[10]

Newgate Queen *Tony Coyle* 56
2 gr f Phoenix Reach(IRE) Arctic Queen (Linamix (FR))
4556[3] 5180[5] 6330[8]

Newington *Lydia Pearce* a50 51
4 b f Iceman Almunia (IRE) (Mujadil (USA))
7[9] 455[6] 579[12] 1369[5]

New Leyf (IRE) *David Thompson* a61 86
7 bb g Kheleyf(USA) Society Fair (FR) (Always Fair (USA))
1787[3] 2007[9] 2460[12] 2834[12] 3628[7] 5711[3] 6549[8] 7595[12] 8365[3]

Newmarket Warrior (IRE) *Michael Bell* a68 81
2 b c Dalakhani(IRE) Heavens Peak (Pivotal)
3490[6] 4764[3] 5309[6] 6501[2] ◆ 6763[2] 7332[5] 7835[5]

Newnton Lodge *Ian Williams* a62 82
4 b g Rail Link Widescreen (USA) (Distant View (USA))
1745[8] 2463[13] 2929[11] 3319[2] 3507[2] 3719[4] 4153[5] 4193[3]

New Rich *Eve Johnson Houghton* a70 55
3 b g Bahamian Bounty Bling Bling (IRE) (Indian Ridge)
2919[5] 3927[6] 4654[3] 4916[4] 5404[6] 5981[2] 6145[4] (6753) 7841[6] 8023[7] (8152)

New Row *William Jarvis* a73 51
2 b f Teofilo(IRE) Memo (Groom Dancer (USA))
6500[7] (7327) 7626[5]

Newsreader (USA) *Mark Johnston* a52 75
3 b g New Approach(IRE) Headline (Machiavellian (USA))
7422[6] 7738[7] 8298[4]

Newstead Abbey *David Barron* a89 101
3 b g Byron Oatcake (Selkirk (USA))
(561) (949) ◆ (1250) ◆ 2661[2] 3484[22]

New Street (IRE) *Richard Fahey* 73
2 gr c Acclamation New Deal (Rainbow Quest (USA))
3282[2] (4556) 5829[4]

Newton's Law (IRE) *Brian Meehan* 71
2 b c Lawman(FR) Royal Alchemist (Kingsinger (IRE))
6645[10] 7017[15]

Newtown Cross (IRE) *Jimmy Fox* 59
3 ch c Kheleyf(USA) Sacred Pearl (IRE) (Daylami (IRE))
5191[8] 5762[9] 7248[4]

New Year's Day (USA) *Bob Baffert* a118
2 b c Street Cry(IRE) Justwhistledixie (USA) (Dixie Union (USA))
(7711a)

New Youmzain (FR) *Mick Channon* 88
4 b g Sinndar(IRE) Luna Sacra (FR) (Sadler's Wells (USA))
6585[7] 6846[7] 7338[8]

Next Door (IRE) *David Barron* a59 74
3 b f Elusive City(USA) Lamh Eile (IRE) (Lend A Hand)
404[3] (1447) 2010[4] 3740[7] (4114)

Next Dream (FR) *P Monfort* a84 86
6 b m Dream Well(FR) Neriella (Darshaan)
6421a[6]

Next Edition (IRE) *Philip Kirby* a68 88
5 b g Antonius Pius(USA) Starfish (IRE) (Galileo (IRE))
(1990) 2240[3] 3345[14] 5031[3] 5712[6] 6239[2] 6499[5] 7906[8] 8276[6] 8416[10]

Next Green (GER) *P Schiergen* 97
3 b f Green Desert(USA) Night Petticoat (GER) (Petoski)
3612a[5] 5044a[16]

Next Stop *Lee Carter* a54
2 b f Rail Link Reaching Ahead (USA) (Mizzen Mast (USA))
7764[11] 8340[8]

Next Time (FR) *Mlle S Sine* 74
3 b g Next Desert(IRE) Veendam (FR) (Victory Note (USA))
5914a[8]

Nezami (IRE) *Patrick Clinton* a60 73
8 b g Elnadim(USA) Stands To Reason (USA) (Gulch (USA))
4250[9] 4807[6] 5304[8] 5521[5] 6153[10] 6723[2] 6803[5] 7346[6] 7733[7] 8042[3]

Nezar (IRE) *William Haggas* 97
2 ch g Mastercraftsman(IRE) Teddy Bears Picnic (Oasis Dream)
(4121) 5034[2] ◆ 5679[3] ◆ (5945) 6765[3] 7195[8]

Nibani (IRE) *John Butler* a73 71
6 ch g Dalakhani(IRE) Dance Of The Sea (IRE) (Sinndar (IRE))
1076[7] 1333[6] 1779[10]

Nibbling (IRE) *Paul Cole* a66 55
2 b f Invincible Spirit(IRE) Albarouche (Sadler's Wells (USA))
6523[4] 7103[6]

Nice Arty (IRE) *Jamie Osborne* a63 66
2 b c Amadeus Wolf Fritillary (Vettori (IRE))
4414[13] 5167[3] 5675[7] 6460[2] 6922[5] 6999[5] 7630[2] 7944[6] (8131) 8274[7]

Nice Life (IRE) *Saeed bin Suroor* a72
2 b f Invincible Spirit(IRE) Rosa Parks (Sadler's Wells (USA))
7645[4] ◆ 7934[3]

Niceofyoutotellme *Ralph Beckett* a96 97
4 b g Hernando(FR) Swain's Gold (USA) (Swain (IRE))
(1501) (3113) ◆ 4310[14] 5269[8] 6801[21]

Niceonemyson *Christopher Wilson* 65
4 b g Misu Bond(IRE) Kungfu Kerry (Celtic Swing)
3247[7] 3547[2] 4050[3] (4377) 4762[4] 5381[6] 5470[13] 6761[3]

Nice Story (IRE) *Mick Channon* 80
3 ch f Suave(USA) Royal Aly (USA) (Royal Academy (USA))
1604[2] 2054[8] 2651[6]

Nicholascopernicus (IRE) *Ed Walker* a79 101
4 ch g Medicean Ascendancy (Sadler's Wells (USA))
1658a[5] 2407[7] 7174[2] 7526[6] 7823[7]

Nichols Canyon *John Gosden* 113
3 b c Authorized(IRE) Zam Zoom (IRE) (Dalakhani (IRE))
1847[3] 2416[2] 3526[6] 5653[7] (6991) 7535[2] (7890a)

Nickels And Dimes (IRE) *Richard Fahey* a78 83
3 b f Teofilo(IRE) Neat Shilling (IRE) (Bob Back (USA))
4151[2] 4594[5] 5720[5] 6062[2] 7257[3] (8036)

Nick The Odds (IRE) *Jo Hughes* a47 65
2 b g Diamond Green(FR) Impressive Act (IRE) (Brave Act)
3836[13] 4351[7] 6485[3] 7451[10] 8325[5]

Nicky Nutjob (GER) *John O'Shea* a21 44
7 b g Fasliyev(USA) Natalie Too (USA) (Irish River (FR))
4192[4] 4365[3] 5432[8]

Nicolosio (IRE) *W Hickst* 113
3 b c Peintre Celebre(USA) Nicolaia (GER) (Alkalde (GER))
4103a[14] 5576a[5] (7705a)

Nidoran (ITY) *L Riccardi* 29
2 b c Blu Air Force(IRE) Stoxx (IRE) (Desert Style (IRE))
6059a[12]

Niente Paura (IRE) *C Lerner* a68 75
3 ch c Tot Ou Tard(IRE) Your Wife Never (TUR) (Palace Pageant (USA))
1737a[7] 2557a[4] 7412a[5]

Nifty Kier *Martin Bosley* a64 57
4 b g Kier Park(IRE) Yeldham Lady (Mujahid (USA))
3417[14] 4032[4] 5277[3] 5697[10] 7784[4] 8140[2] 8329[5]

Nigel's Destiny (USA) *Jeremy Noseda* a74
2 b c Giant's Causeway(USA) Ticket To Seattle (USA) (Capote (USA))
7302[4]

Nightdance Dream (GER) *P Schiergen* 85
2 ch c Desert Prince(IRE) Nightdance Forest (IRE) (Charnwood Forest (IRE))
7726a[3]

Nightdance Paolo (GER) *A Schaerer* 102
6 b h Paolini(GER) Nightdance (GER) (Shareef Dancer (USA))
514a[2] 701a[3]

Night Of Light (IRE) *F Camici* 91
3 b f Tenby Polvere Di Luna (ITY) (Hunting Hawk (IRE))
1866a[10] 2697a[11] 3616a[7]

Night Of Thunder (IRE) *Richard Hannon Snr* 108
2 ch c Dubawi(IRE) Forest Storm (Galileo (IRE))
(7218) (7525) ◆

Night Party (IRE) *Saeed bin Suroor* 83
2 b f Dansili La Salina (GER) (Singspiel (IRE))
5003[2] ◆ 5716[4]

Night Power (FR) *W Hickst* 102
3 b f Poliglote Night Green (GER) (Green Forest (USA))
6887a[2] 7891a[7]

Night Song *John Gosden* a87 81
2 b f Oasis Dream All For Laura (Cadeaux Genereux)
(5282) ◆ 6171[2] 7016[9]

Nightster (IRE) *Mark Johnston* 82
3 ch c Raven's Pass(USA) Ama (USA) (Storm Cat (USA))
(5707) 6048[2] 6335[7] 6721[8] (Dead)

Night's Watch *William Jarvis* a68 55
3 b c Authorized(IRE) Nachtigall (GER) (Danehill (USA))
6696[9] 7248[8] 7622[6] 8125[11]

Night Trade (IRE) *Ronald Harris* a73 73
6 b m Trade Fair Compton Girl (Compton Place)
431[2] 582[11] 812[8] 1102[10] 1952[10] (2588) 2745[5] 3622[5] 3920[4] 4368[6] 4830[8] 4884[8] 5931[6] 6777[3] 6982[4] 7148[10] 7862[8] 7958[9] 8152[8]

Night Wish (GER) *W Figge* 92
3 b c Sholokhov(IRE) Night Woman (GER) (Monsun (GER))
$2696a^{4}$ $3389a^{9}$

Niknad *Brian Ellison* a54 59
3 b f Zafeen(FR) Eau Rouge (Grand Lodge (USA))
1210^{4} (1747) 2124^{3} 2799^{2} 3194^{6} 3653^{10} 4809^{12}

Nile Knight *Marcus Tregoning* 76
3 b c Sir Percy Sahara Belle (USA) (Sanglamore (USA))
2927^{6} 3338^{9} 4209^{5} (4679) 4950^{13} 5606^{3} 7066^{5}

Nimble Kimble *James Eustace* a68 70
2 ch f Kirkwall Lovely Lyca (Night Shift (USA))
3663^{7} 4880^{2} 5593^{2} 6695^{7}

Nimiety *Mark Johnston* a81 85
4 b f Stormy Atlantic(USA) Nadeszhda (Nashwan (USA))
1990^{6} (2361) 2761^{5} 3506^{3} 3742^{3} 4100^{3} 4850^{3} (5245) 5706^{2} 6200^{5} 7976^{7} 8336^{6}

Nina Nosei (IRE) *M Oppo* 50
3 b f Red Clubs(IRE) Extra Time (Shadeed (USA))
$1866a^{18}$

Nine Bean Rows (IRE) *Niall Moran* a53 49
4 b g Red Clubs(IRE) Faleh (USA) (Silver Hawk (USA))
7082^{11}

Nine Before Ten (IRE) *Charles Smith* a61
5 ch f Captain Rio Sagaing (Machiavellian (USA))
1636^{6} 968^{4} 1356^{8} 1540^{5} 1734^{8} 2611^{11} 2926^{2} 3026^{17}

Nineinthenine (USA) *Humberto Toledo* 102
7 b g Brushing Up(USA) Strawberry Custard (USA) (First And Only (USA))
$608a^{2}$

Nine Iron (IRE) *Mick Channon* a68 73
3 gr g Verglas(IRE) Sevi's Choice (USA) (Sir Ivor (USA))
(1743) 1776^{3} 2233^{5}

Ninepointsixthree *John O'Shea* 42
3 b g Bertolini(USA) Armada Grove (Fleetwood (IRE))
5176^{4} 6486^{6}

Nine Realms *William Haggas* a90 103
4 b g Green Desert(USA) Bourbonella (Rainbow Quest (USA))
4308^{10} (5255) 6191^{7} 6838^{16}

Ninety Minutes (IRE) *John Best* a73 70
2 b c Oratorio(IRE) Fleeting Mirage (USA) (Afleet Alex (USA))
4414^{5} 5443^{4} (6689) 7326^{6} 7782^{10}

Ninfea (IRE) *Sylvester Kirk* a68 72
5 b f Le Vie Dei Colori Attymon Lill (IRE) (Marju (IRE))
7091^{7} 7622^{10}

Ningaloo Reef (IRE) *Garvan Donnelly* a74 76
5 b g Acclamation Madanisa (IRE) (Zayyani)
$8012a^{3}$

Ningara *Andrew Balding* a98 96
3 b g Singspiel(IRE) Garanciere (FR) (Anabaa (USA))
91^{2} 666^{5} (3338) 4084^{5} (4683) 5283^{2} 5944^{2} 6751^{2}

Ningbo Express (IRE) *Rae Guest* a22 78
3 b f Jeremy(USA) Sunlit Skies (Selkirk (USA))
1711^{9} 3116^{9} 4927^{4} 5386^{3} (5990)

Nini Ok (IRE) *John Joseph Murphy* a74 90
4 b f Acclamation Charmed Forest (IRE) (Shinko Forest (IRE))
$3845a^{17}$ $7995a^{15}$

Ninjago *Richard Hannon Snr* a92 107
3 b c Mount Nelson Fidelio's Miracle (USA) (Mountain Cat (USA))
(1921) ◆ 2415^{3} 3455^{8} 4255^{4} 4986^{5} ◆ 5538^{7} 6990^{9}

Ninja Lady *James Fanshawe* a41 47
3 b f Nayef(USA) Galaxy Highflyer (Galileo (IRE))
3469^{11} 3975^{6}

Nip A Bear *John Holt* 37
2 b c Rail Link Nippy (FR) (Anabaa (USA))
2382^{10} 4505^{10} 4883^{6}

Nippy Nikki *John Norton* a55 38
5 b f Needwood Blade Spielbound (Singspiel (IRE))
1207^{8} 2986^{7} 3589^{10}

Nirva (IRE) *Lady Cecil* a43
2 gr f Verglas(IRE) Nirvana (Marju (IRE))
6689^{9}

Nissaki Kasta *Hughie Morrison* a41 63
2 ch f Sakhee's Secret Casterossa (Rossini (USA))
6590^{3} 7244^{4} 8138^{7}

Nixyba *Tim Vaughan* a44
2 b f Cockney Rebel(IRE) Hisaronu (IRE) (Stravinsky (USA))
8312^{3}

Niya (FR) *P Schaerer* a31
6 ch m High Yield(USA) Flyer (FR) (Highest Honor (FR))
$513a^{3}$ $702a^{7}$

Noble Alan (GER) *Nicky Richards* a88 95
10 gr g King's Theatre(IRE) Nirvavita (FR) (Highest Honor (FR))
2251^{2} 3824^{7} 5237^{3} 5706^{6} 6626^{12} 7805^{5} 8041^{3}

Noble Asset *John Quinn* 70
2 ch g Compton Place Chance For Romance (Entrepreneur)
4259^{7} 5883^{2} 6175^{6} 6467^{5}

Noble Bacchus (IRE) *Tom Dascombe* a52 56
3 b g Acclamation Vintage Tipple (IRE) (Entrepreneur)
2124^{6} 2716^{11} 3232^{6}

Noble Bull (IRE) *Charles Hills* 78
3 b g Papal Bull Fernlawn Hope (IRE) (Danehill Dancer (IRE))
1719^{2} 2153^{8} 2604^{2} 2957^{5} 3294^{6} 4124^{4}

Noble Citizen (USA) *David Simcock* a88 83
8 b g Proud Citizen(USA) Serene Nobility (USA) (His Majesty (USA))
1913^{8} 2585^{6} 3339^{8} 4879^{13} 5799^{3} 5928^{2} 7648^{7} 7988^{8}

Noble Deed *Michael Attwater* a92 94
3 ch g Kyllachy Noble One (Primo Dominie)
(2934) 3634^{2} (3894) ◆ 4265^{4} (4757) 5260^{2} 8391^{5}

Noble Galileo (GER) *Mario Hofer* 98
3 b c Galileo(IRE) Nordtanzerin (GER) (Danehill Dancer (IRE))
$1867a^{3}$ $3389a^{7}$ $4103a^{17}$

Noble Gift *William Knight* a84 90
3 ch g Cadeaux Genereux Noble Penny (Pennekamp (USA))
(2272) 3338^{6} (4168) 4917^{4} 5742^{3} ◆ 6537^{6} 6957^{3}

Noble Hachy *L Riccardi* 92
4 b f Kyllachy Noble Hero (IRE) (Daggers Drawn (USA))
$1563a^{5}$ $7830a^{5}$

Noble Inn (FR) *M Delzangles* a75 54
3 b g Sinndar(IRE) Nataliana (Surumu (GER))
$3129a^{2}$

Noble Jack (IRE) *Jo Hughes* a84 67
7 b g Elusive City(USA) Begine (IRE) (Germany (USA))
(23) (314)

Noble Maximus *Alan Berry*
3 b g Oratorio(IRE) Perfect Peach (Lycius (USA))
6940^{8} 7345^{12} 7787^{7}

Noble Metal *Peter Chapple-Hyam* 83
2 gr c With Approval(CAN) Grain Only (Machiavellian (USA))
(3490) 4296^{7} 5530^{5} 7468^{2}

Noble Mission *Lady Cecil* 116
4 b c Galileo(IRE) Kind (IRE) (Danehill (USA))
1674^{3} 2020^{4} (2656) 3556^{4} 5270^{3} $7049a^{4}$

Noble Protector *Stuart Kittow* a87 77
3 b f Haafhd All Glory (Alzao (USA))
3372^{2} (4381) 6359^{6} 7627^{2}

Noble Reach *Geoffrey Harker* 52
2 b f Phoenix Reach(IRE) Comtesse Noire (CAN) (Woodman (USA))
2025^{6} 2502^{5} 3476^{4} 3942^{5} 5610^{3} 6295^{5}

Noble Silk *Lucy Wadham* a94 97
4 gr g Sir Percy Tussah (Daylami (IRE))
(93) 273^{3} (496) 1689^{7} 3531^{2} 4233^{3} 5147^{6} 5655^{14}

Noble Storm (USA) *Ed McMahon* a112 104
7 b h Yankee Gentleman(USA) Changed Tune (USA) (Tunerup (USA))
2150^{4} 2461^{3} 2669^{13} (6282) 6830^{3} 7010^{15}

No Compromise *Richard Phillips* a59 82
4 b f Avonbridge Highly Liquid (Entrepreneur)
4126^{12} 5526^{4}

Nocturn *Jeremy Noseda* a87 107
4 b g Oasis Dream Pizzicato (Statoblest)
1346^{2} (1726) (2097) 2366^{2} (3114) 3558^{23} 5747^{2} 6235^{8} 6623^{25}

Nocturnal Affair (SAF) *David Marnane* a107 112
7 bb g Victory Moon(SAF) Aretha (SAF) (Centenary (USA))
$2676a^{7}$ 3046^{9} $5772a^{8}$ $6414a^{9}$ $7521a^{7}$

Nocturnal Secret *J E Pease* 105
3 b g Beat Hollow Midnight Ransom (Red Ransom (USA))
$(7116a)$

No Diamond *Michael Appleby* a57
6 b g Helissio(FR) Diamond Swan (Colonel Collins (USA))
455^{12}

No Dominion (IRE) *James Given* a83 82
4 b g Dylan Thomas(IRE) Boast (Most Welcome)
1827^{2} (2278) 2580^{3} 3193^{3} 3683^{10} 4075^{5} 4540^{2} 5304^{7} 6288^{2} 6567^{3} 7024^{6} 7632^{8} (8008)

No Easy Day *Kevin Ryan* 24
2 b g Kheleyf(USA) Komena (Komaite (USA))
3275^{8} 6383^{7}

No Explaining (IRE) *Roger L Attfield* 94
6 b m Azamour(IRE) Claustra (FR) (Green Desert (USA))
$6454a^{6}$ $7562a^{6}$

Noguchi (IRE) *Michael Murphy* a84 79
8 ch g Pivotal Tuscania (USA) (Woodman (USA))
93^{3} 420^{2} 810^{4} 1237^{5} (1597) (1795) 2579^{2} 3370^{7}

No Heretic *David Simcock* 102
5 b g Galileo(IRE) Intrigued (Darshaan)
(2044) 3115^{3} 3560^{6} 4919^{5} 6144^{6}

No Jet Lag (USA) *Simon Callaghan* a85 114
3 b g Johar(USA) Desert Sky (IRE) (Green Desert (USA))
1668^{10} 3348^{18} $7714a^{6}$

No Leaf Clover (IRE) *Ollie Pears* 103
2 b c Kodiac Rajmahal (UAE) (Indian Ridge)
5140^{2} (5877) 6582^{3} ◆ 7207^{2} $7939a^{7}$

Nolecce *Tony Forbes* a66 62
6 ch g Reset(AUS) Ghassanah (Pas De Seul)
9^{9} 100^{4} 169^{4} (226) 338^{10} 418^{3} 3719^{3} (4838) 5356^{7} 6658^{5} 6996^{2} 7166^{3} 7510^{5}

Nomathemba (IRE) *David Evans* a36 43
2 b f Mujadil(USA) Rorkes Drift (IRE) (Royal Abjar (USA))
1399^{7} 1512^{7} 1833^{6} 2759^{3}

No Mean Trick (USA) *Paul Midgley* a74 40
7 b g Grand Slam(USA) Ruby's Reception (USA) (Rubiano (USA))
308^{6} 516^{5}

Nomoreblondes *Paul Midgley* a66 81
9 ch m Ishiguru(USA) Statuette (Statoblest)
1649^{9} 1758^{12}

No More Tears (FR) *E Lellouche* a74
4 b f Enrique Doucelisa (FR) (Cardoun (FR))
$7573a^{15}$

Nonagon *Noel Quinlan* 43
2 b c Pastoral Pursuits Nine Red (Royal Applause)
1833^{4}

Nonaynever *Ruth Carr* a62 55
5 ch g Nayef(USA) Qirmazi (USA) (Riverman (USA))
950^{6} 1082^{4} 1567^{10} 1836^{9} 2130^{8} 2536^{6} 2757^{3} 2884^{13} 3286^{5} 3445^{5} 3910^{12} 4109^{6} 4509^{6} 4893^{12} 4967^{5} (5198) 5869^{6} 6276^{7} 6600^{15} 6919^{3}

No Nay Never (USA) *Wesley A Ward* 117
2 bb c Scat Daddy(USA) Cat's Eye Witness (USA) (Elusive Quality (USA))
(3481) ◆ $(5573a)$

Non Dom (IRE) *Wilf Storey* a58 60
7 b g Hawk Wing(USA) Kafayef (USA) (Secreto (USA))
4804^{9} 5337^{11} 5643^{6} 6086^{9}

Nonotnow *Tim Easterby* 70
3 ch g Notnowcato Get Jealous (IRE) (Intikhab (USA))
(3191) 4048^{5} ◆ 4672^{4} ◆ 5107^{3} 7066^{7}

Noodles Blue Boy *Ollie Pears* a65 91
7 b g Makbul Dee Dee Girl (IRE) (Primo Dominie)
1807^{13} 2031^{16} 2441^{16} (3716) 4047^{10} 4507^{7} (4954) 5519^{6} 6309^{11} 6699^{8} 7314^{5} 7593^{10}

Noor Al Haya (IRE) *Mark Usher* a58 62
3 b f Tamayuz Hariya (IRE) (Shernazar)
1727^{9} (2362) 2566^{6} 3040^{5} 3418^{4} 3820^{5} 4222^{2} (4713) 5500^{3} 5630^{2} 5846^{5} 7331^{7} 7767^{8}

Noor Zabeel (USA) *A Al Raihe* a98 97
4 b c Elusive Quality(USA) Brave The Storm (USA) (Storm Cat (USA))
$290a^{12}$ $503a^{13}$

Noosa Boy *Luke Dace* a55 34
4 b g Pivotal Maroochydore (IRE) (Danehill (USA))
7071^{9}

Noosa Sound *John Davies* 60
3 ch f Halling(USA) Crimson Topaz (Hernando (FR))
2274^{13} 3194^{8} 3893^{11} 4587^{7} 5789^{2} 6598^{4} 7636^{6}

Noozhoh Canarias (SPA) *E Leon Penate* 115
2 b c Caradak(IRE) Noozhah (Singspiel (IRE))
$(5082a)$ $7056a^{2}$

No Poppy (IRE) *Tim Easterby* 97
5 b f Chineur(FR) Capetown Girl (Danzero (AUS))
1688^{14} 2029^{13} 2440^{2} 2718^{9} 3503^{6} 3984^{7} 4308^{5} 4733^{4} 5014^{7} 5546^{2} ◆ 5838^{8} 6210^{8} 6550^{2} 7172^{16}

No Quarter (IRE) *Tracy Waggott* 70
6 b g Refuse To Bend(IRE) Moonlight Wish (IRE) (Peintre Celebre (USA))
1459^{6} 1757^{14} 2162^{7} (2280) 2837^{3} 4966^{4} 5861^{2} 6291^{8} 6633^{9}

Norab (GER) *Marco Botti* 65
2 b c Galileo(IRE) Night Woman (GER) (Monsun (GER))
7773^{4}

Nordic Affair *S Arthur* a86 54
9 b g Halling(USA) Affair Of State (IRE) (Tate Gallery (USA))
$4846a^{4}$

Nordic Light (USA) *Mrs A Malzard* a47 39
9 bb g Belong To Me(USA) Midriff (USA) (Naevus (USA))
$1738a^{4}$ $7143a^{7}$

Nordico (GER) *Mario Hofer* 101
2 ch c Medicean Norwegian Pride (FR) (Diktat)
$(7726a)$

Nordic Quest (IRE) *Gerard Butler* a87 80
4 b g Montjeu(IRE) Nordtanzerin (GER) (Danehill Dancer (IRE))
2044^{12} 2598^{5} 2939^{5} 3692^{5} 3976^{3} 6758^{7} 7220^{7}

Nordic Truce (USA) *P Schiergen* a96 95
6 b h Yes It's True(USA) Nyramba (Night Shift (USA))
$241a^{13}$ $465a^{9}$ $836a^{12}$ $1944a^{5}$

Nordikhab (IRE) *Kevin Ryan* a80 81
3 b g Intikhab(USA) Pourquoi Pas (IRE) (Nordico (USA))
1687^{3} 2172^{2} 2719^{5} 3369^{7} 4048^{6} 4625^{5} 5232^{3} (5594) 6214^{7} 6856^{4}

Nordvulkan (GER) *R Dzubasz* 107
3 bb c Kallisto(GER) Nur Bani (GER) (Artan (IRE))
$2696a^{8}$ $4103a^{3}$ $4571a^{6}$ $6253a^{8}$

Norfolk Sky *Laura Mongan* a79 75
4 ch m Haafhd Cayman Sound (Turtle Island (IRE))
(450) 779^{3} 1182^{5} 1585^{3} 2004^{2} 2418^{6} 3971^{2} 4205^{4} 5312^{9} 5855^{6} 6736^{2} (8089) 8392^{4}

Normal Equilibrium *Robert Cowell* 96
3 b g Elnadim(USA) Acicula (IRE) (Night Shift (USA))
1808^{4} (2213) 3340^{6} 3584^{4} 4112^{3} 4989^{5} 5769^{3} 6190^{7} 6539^{5} 6990^{4} 7222^{8}

Normandy Invasion (USA) *Chad C Brown* a114
3 b c Tapit(USA) Boston Lady (USA) (Boston Harbor (USA))
$2033a^{4}$

Normanna (IRE) *Marco Botti* a59
2 b f Elusive City(USA) Nantes (GER) (Night Shift (USA))
8342^{3}

Norphin *Denis Coakley* a58 59
3 b c Norse Dancer(IRE) Orphina (IRE) (Orpen (USA))
4591^{7} 5346^{6} 6321^{9} 7322^{4} 7981^{10}

Norse Blues *David Barron* a92 101
5 ch g Norse Dancer(IRE) Indiana Blues (Indian Ridge)
1675^{12} (2029) 3339^{13} 3564^{6} 4308^{9} (5014) 5681^{7} 6352^{10} 6624^{8}

Norse King (FR) *Mme M Bollack-Badel* a74 116
4 ch g Norse Dancer(IRE) Angel Wing (Barathea (IRE))
$(7410a)$

Norse Legend *Daniel Kubler* 47
2 b c Norse Dancer(IRE) Methodical (Lujain (USA))
7243^{9} 7500^{8} 7774^{9}

Norse Light *Ralph Beckett* 51
2 ch g Norse Dancer(IRE) Dimelight (Fantastic Light (USA))
7774^{6}

Norse Song *David Elsworth* a52 39
4 b f Norse Dancer(IRE) Blue Lullaby (IRE) (Fasliyev (USA))
1617^{6} 2134^{6} 2764^{11} 3213^{9}

Norse Star (IRE) *Sylvester Kirk* 59
2 b c Norse Dancer(IRE) Spot Prize (USA) (Seattle Dancer (USA))
6762^{12} 7219^{8}

Nors The Panic *Richard Guest* a47 36
3 ch g Bahamian Bounty Croeso Bach (Bertolini (USA))
847^{3} 915^{4} 1216^{2} 1349^{9} 1651^{4} 1742^{9} 1988^{5} 2336^{5} 2997^{6} 3198^{9} 3475^{7}

North Central (USA) *Ruth Carr* a62 62
6 bb g Forest Camp(USA) Brittan Lee (USA) (Forty Niner (USA))
50^{3} 194^{8} 1994^{6} 2319^{6} 3029^{9} 3285^{7}

Northern Acres *N W Alexander* 42
7 b g Mtoto Bunting (Shaadi (USA))
7098^{5}

Northern Meeting (IRE) *Sir Michael Stoute* a79 80
3 b f Dylan Thomas(IRE) Scottish Stage (IRE) (Selkirk (USA))
2321^{4} ◆ (4157) 4950^{7} 5496^{4} 7038^{3}

Northern Reach *Geoffrey Harker*
2 b f Phoenix Reach(IRE) Rasmalai (Sadler's Wells (USA))
3648^{8} 5969^{9}

Northern Rocked (IRE) *D K Weld* a79 96
7 b g Refuse To Bend(IRE) Gifts Galore (IRE) (Darshaan)
$(5019a)$ $6025a^{15}$ $7719a^{12}$

Northern Spy (USA) *Simon Dow* a69 68
9 b g War Chant(USA) Sunray Superstar (Nashwan (USA))
117^{5} 220^{12}

Northern Star (IRE) *Tom Dascombe* 91
3 b f Montjeu(IRE) Slow Sand (USA) (Dixieland Band (USA))
2261^{7} (2827) 4777^{4}

Northern Surprise (IRE) *Timothy Doyle* 60
2 b c Azamour(IRE) Surprise Treat (IRE) (Shalford (IRE))
$7050a^{10}$

Northern Water *K R Burke* a82 85
2 b c Pastoral Pursuits Musical Twist (USA) (Woodman (USA))
4539^{3} 4808^{2} (5380) 5787^{2} (5859) 6201^{7} 7207^{6}

Northgate Lodge (USA) *Mel Brittain* a28 32
8 ch g Hold That Tiger(USA) Sabaah Elfull (Kris)
5897^{11} 8006^{10}

North Lodge (AUS) *John Blacker* 90
8 b g Festival Hall(IRE) Kita Ryokan (AUS) (Grand Lodge (USA))
$7760a^{6}$

North Pole *Sir Mark Prescott Bt* a67 76
3 b g Compton Place Cool Question (Polar Falcon (USA))
3438^{3} 4068^{6} 4400^{5} 4751^{3} 5204^{2} 5386^{2} (5604) 5668^{2} 6667^{8}

Northside Prince (IRE) *Alan Swinbank* a92 92
7 b g Desert Prince(IRE) Spartan Girl (IRE) (Ela-Mana-Mou)
830^{2} 1188^{2} 1536^{5} 1843^{2} 2369^{2} 2633^{4} 3685^{16} 5147^{8} 5868^{7} 8047^{5} 8353^{6}

North Star Boy (IRE) *Amy Weaver* a83 91
4 b g Acclamation Isla Azul (IRE) (Machiavellian (USA))
1346^{5} 1838^{5} (1954) (2516) $3361a^{2}$

North Weald (IRE) *J W Hills* a52 59
3 b f Hurricane Run(IRE) Foreign Relation (IRE) (Distant Relative)
2599^{13}

Norville (IRE) *Lee Smyth* a96 83
6 b g Elusive City(USA) Saraposa (IRE) (Ahonoora)
$5775a^{8}$

Norway Cross *Luca Cumani* 85
3 b f Cape Cross(IRE) Queen Of Norway (USA) (Woodman (USA))
6532^{2} (7422)

Norwegian Reward (IRE) *Michael Wigham* a63 50
5 ch g Hernando(FR) Stay Behind (Elmaamul (USA))
200^{7} 545^{2} 626^{9} 1297^{8} 3780^{7} 4357^{5} 5002^{6} 5170^{4}

Nos Da *Bryan Smart* 22
3 b f Cape Cross(IRE) Nantyglo (Mark Of Esteem (IRE))
2041^{8} 4887^{12}

No Second Thoughts (IRE) *Michael Blanshard* a22 5
2 b f Oratorio(IRE) Margot (Sadler's Wells (USA))
4997^{10} 5443^{8} 6079^{10} 6922^{10}

Nos Galan (IRE) *Richard Hannon Snr* 48
2 b c Dylan Thomas(IRE) Chalice Wells (Sadler's Wells (USA))
6378^{3} 7219^{7}

Nostro Amico (GER) *Mario Hofer* 102
4 b g Martillo(GER) Narola (GER) (Nebos (GER))
$6421a^{8}$

No Such Number *Julia Feilden* a69 76
5 b g King's Best(USA) Return (USA) (Sadler's Wells (USA))
2009^{5} 3150^{3} 3971^{5} 4437^{3} 5065^{3} 5823^{5} 6377^{4} 7220^{4} 7506^{4}

Notabadgirl *Simon Dow* a53 32
4 ch f Denounce Lady Jo (Phountzi (USA))
1317^{4} 1877^{7} 2567^{11} 7093^{9} 7752^{14}

Notacatbutallama (USA) *Todd Pletchera* 104 105
3 b c Harlan's Holiday(USA) Self Rising (USA) (Hansel (USA))
$(3360a)$

Not A Given (USA) *Mahmood Al Zarooni* a102
4 b c Any Given Saturday(USA) Any For Love (ARG) (Southern Halo (USA))
$241a^{5}$ $463a^{5}$ $742a^{6}$

Notaire (IRE) *P Bary* 100
3 b c Nayef(USA) Aiglonne (USA) (Silver Hawk (USA))
$5779a^{4}$

Notarised *Mark Johnston* 76
2 b c Authorized(IRE) Caribbean Dancer (USA) (Theatrical (IRE))
5969^{5} 6528^{8} (6896) 7471^{3}

Notebook *William Haggas* a56
2 b c Invincible Spirit(IRE) Love Everlasting (Pursuit Of Love)
8333^{8} 8425^{8}

Not Expected (GER) *A Trybuhl* 89
3 b f Dubawi(IRE) Nonette (Marju (IRE))
$7233a^{10}$

Notion (IRE) *F Chappet* a85 85
5 gr c Sadler's Wells(USA) Reina Blanca (Darshaan)
648a[10]

Not My Choice (IRE) *Paul Howling* a70 73
8 ch g Choisir(AUS) Northgate Raver (Absalom)
317[3] 440[10] 565[6] 664[4] 1021[5]

Not Now Blondie *Chris Dwyer* a60 60
3 ch f Notnowcato Gretel (Hansel (USA))
1349[4] 1907[7]

Notnow Penny *Milton Bradley* a17 45
2 ch f Notnowcato Tuppenny (Salse (USA))
2917[6] 3914[8] 4937[9] (5814) 6311[9] 6511[13]

Not Rigg (USA) *Gary Harrison* a70 75
3 b g Henrythenavigator(USA) St Helens Shadow (USA) (Septieme Ciel (USA))
341[3] 3137[2] 3537[11] (4077) 4928[7] 6379[5] 6735[8] 7544[2] 7924[7] 8187[5] 8339[6]

No Truth (IRE) *Charles Hills* a66 45
3 b f Galileo(IRE) State Crystal (IRE) (High Estate)
(1352) 1743[6]

Not Til Monday (IRE) *J R Jenkins* a71 75
7 b g Spartacus(IRE) Halomix (Linamix (FR))
5312[5] 5862[6]

Notti Magiche (FR) *B Grizzetti* 88
3 b c Montjeu(IRE) Sea Sex Sun (Desert Prince (IRE))
2490a[10]

Not To Yield (USA) *D K Weld* 82
2 gr c English Channel(USA) Miarixa (FR) (Linamix (FR))
6884a[5]

Notts So Blue *Shaun Harris* 27
2 b f Pastoral Pursuits Blue Nile (IRE) (Bluebird (USA))
3064[10] 3605[9] 6513[11]

Nouailhas *Reg Hollinshead* a45 53
7 b g Mark Of Esteem(IRE) Barachois Princess (USA) (Barachois (CAN))
109[4]

Nougaboo (USA) *F Head* 74
2 bb f King's Best(USA) Top Order (USA) (Dayjur (USA))
7653a[10]

Novabridge *Neil Mulholland* a76 70
5 ch g Avonbridge Petrovna (IRE) (Petardia)
124[4] 627[2] 924[3] 3042[11] 3887[4] (7143a) 6412[10] 7730[4] 8216[3] 8457[5]

Nova Champ (IRE) *Stuart Williams* a71 72
2 ch c Intikhab(USA) Baby Bunting (Wolfhound (USA))
2925[7] 4883[2] 5428[2] 7221[2] 7817[8] 8061[2] (8165)

Novalist *Robin Bastiman* a64 66
5 ch g Avonbridge Malelane (IRE) (Prince Sabo)
1758[5] 3026[9] 3630[9] 4840[8] 5408[7] 6180[8]

Nova Neyev (FR) *P Capelle* a71 95
5 b c Diableneyev(USA) Gioiosa Marea (IRE) (Highest Honor (FR))
4093a[10] 5040a[13] 5314a[10]

Nova Nimph *Mark Brisbourne* a39
4 ch f Avonbridge Nimphida (Acatenango (GER))
63[7]

Nova Princesse (GER) *Marco Botti* a77 53
2 b f Desert Prince(IRE) Nova Scotia (GER) (Sholokhov (IRE))
4997[6] 6334[5] (6607) (7879) 8261[8]

Nova Valorem (IRE) *Bent Olsen* a95 101
5 ch c Ad Valorem(USA) Utr (USA) (Mr Prospector (USA))
2146a[12] 4936a[6]

Novel Approach (IRE) *J S Bolger* 65
2 b f New Approach(IRE) Altarejos (IRE) (Vettori (IRE))
7050a[12]

Novel Dancer *Lydia Richards* a57 50
5 b g Dansili Fictitious (Machiavellian (USA))
417[9] 4429[3] 5126[7]

Novellen Lad (IRE) *Willie Musson* a90 93
8 b g Noverre(USA) Lady Ellen (Horage)
2724[8] 3415[11] 5636[5] 6203[7] 6648[2] (7897) (8181)

Novellist (IRE) *A Wohler* 128
4 b c Monsun(GER) Night Lagoon (GER) (Lagunas)
(2294a) (3615a) (4745) ◆ (6028a)

Novelty Seeker (USA) *Mahmood Al Zarooni* a94 101
4 b g Street Sense(USA) Nawaiet (USA) (Zilzal (USA))
364a[4] 555a[7]

Noverre To Go (IRE) *Ronald Harris* a93 91
7 ch g Noverre(USA) Ukraine Venture (Slip Anchor)
379[2] 584[6] 776[9] (1155) 1245[9] 1581[4] 1787[12] 2097[10] 2516[2] 2789[2] 3093[6] (3351) 3720[7] 4494[3] 4983[12] (5219) 5544[9] 5851[5] 6647[6]

Novirak (IRE) *James Fanshawe* a48 92
5 gr g Noverre(USA) Manchaca (FR) (Highest Honor (FR))
1766[3] 2369[3] 2855[2] 3531[3] ◆

Nowcando *K R Burke* 40
3 ch f Notnowcato Sienna Sunset (IRE) (Spectrum (IRE))
5839[8] 6847[8] 7279[7]

Nowdoro *Julie Camacho* a49 36
4 ch g Notnowcato Salydora (FR) (Peintre Celebre (USA))
94[13] 7899[7]

Nowinaminute (IRE) *James Given* a27 60
2 b f Bushranger(IRE) Hapipi (Bertolini (USA))
4583[3] 5364[5] 5983[6] 6605[9] 6939[9]

No Win No Fee *Michael Appleby* a72 66
3 b g Firebreak Milliscent (Primo Dominie)
1481[4] 1845[6] 2198[7] 2624[6] 7353[3] 7605[5] 7987[2] (8233)

Now My Sun *K R Burke* 83
4 ch g Notnowcato Sienna Sunset (IRE) (Spectrum (IRE))
1538[7] 1831[3] 2256[5] (3204) 4098[4] 5302[3] 6211[5] ◆ 6729[6] 7369[9]

Now Spun (USA) *Charlie Appleby* a84 106
3 b c Hard Spun(USA) Campionessa (USA) (A.P. Indy (USA))
(835a) ◆ 1264a[9] 6427[6]

Now We Can *N Clement* a102 112
4 b c Martillo(GER) Notre Dame (GER) (Acatenango (GER))
(1658a) (2908a) 5807a[9] 6449a[7] 7563a[4]

Now What *Jonathan Portman* a64 67
6 ch m Where Or When(IRE) Vallauris (Faustus (USA))
131[7] 2777[4] 3662[3] 4238[4]

Nubar Boy *Ian Williams* a61 63
6 ch g Compton Place Out Like Magic (Magic Ring (IRE))
2596[7] 2918[9] 3661[6] 8157[5] 8456[12]

Nu Form Fire (IRE) *Nigel Tinkler* 51
2 b g Footstepsinthesand Maimana (IRE) (Desert King (IRE))
4539[10] 5105[8] 5380[7] 6286[6] 6517[8] 7209[8]

Nuit D'Amour (FR) *Mme Pia Brandt* a88 103
3 b f Azamour(IRE) Banyu Dewi (GER) (Poliglote)
4700a[2] 6124a[5] 6962a[2]

Nulera (FR) *C Ferland* a46
3 b f Poliglote Loup The Loup (FR) (Loup Solitaire (USA))
461a[10]

Nullarbor Sky (IRE) *Lucy Wadham* a62 73
3 gr f Aussie Rules(USA) Grenouillere (USA) (Alysheba (USA))
2555[5] 3243[6] 4405[2] (4688) (5411) 6574[3]

Number One London (IRE) *Brian Meehan* a79 91
3 b g Invincible Spirit(IRE) Vadorga (Grand Lodge (USA))
1678[3] 2151[3] 2605[2] 3061[2] 3486[16] 4084[6] 4542[6] 7337[8] 7864[4]

Number Theory *John Holt* 113
5 b g Halling(USA) Numanthia (IRE) (Barathea (IRE))
2252[4] 2810[2] 3483[9] 4309[3] 4919[4] 5766[3] ◆

Number Winner (FR) *M Gentile* a70 80
3 b c Orpen(USA) Amonita (GER) (Medaaly)
286a[7]

Numen (IRE) *Barry Brennan* a57 37
9 b g Fath(USA) Hawala (IRE) (Warning)
724[6] 788[7] 2333[8] 3213[12] 4192[5]

Nunkie Bill *James Unett*
2 b g Multiplex Lady Castanea (Superlative)
4676[4]

Nuntius (GER) *A Wohler* 87
3 rg c Dalakhani(IRE) Night Lagoon (GER) (Lagunas)
3389a[6]

Nuracale *Marco Gasparini* 72
3 ch c Compton Place Nevada Princess (IRE) (Desert Prince (IRE))
7830a[8]

Nur Jahan (IRE) *David Lanigan* a58 72
3 b f Selkirk(USA) Have Faith (IRE) (Machiavellian (USA))
4013[2] 4687[3] 6319[5]

Nurpur (IRE) *David O'Meara* a79 88
3 b f Dark Angel(IRE) The Good Life (IRE) (Rainbow Quest (USA))
1429[3] 1570[6] 1760[3] 2672[2] (3091) 3478[2] 3894[2] (4515) (4729) ◆ 5684[5] 6495[3] 6796[7]

Nurse Dominatrix (IRE) *Richard Guest* a52 43
4 br f Whipper(USA) Medica Boba (Dr Fong (USA))
375[10] 456[8] 545[4] 625[8] 1022[6]

Nutello (USA) *C Laffon-Parias* a78 105
4 b c Lemon Drop Kid(USA) Nutcase (USA) (Forest Wildcat (USA))
1048a[6] 4421a[7]

Nyanza (GER) *Alan King* 62
2 b f Dai Jin Nouvelle Fortune (IRE) (Alzao (USA))
3664[9] 4491[11] 6063[8] 7309[5]

Nymphea (IRE) *P Schiergen* 116
4 ch f Dylan Thomas(IRE) Neele (IRE) (Peintre Celebre (USA))
3100[2] (4571a) 6253a[3] 7365[6] 8208a[12]

Oak Bluffs (IRE) *Richard Fahey* 55
2 b g Royal Applause Key Stage (IRE) (King's Best (USA))
5494[5] 6234[10]

Oakley Dancer *Tony Carroll* a35 21
2 ch f Assertive My Dancer (IRE) (Alhaarth (IRE))
2283[5] 2723[10] 3167[3] 5350[7] 6322[14]

Oakwell (IRE) *Sally Hall* a9 51
5 b g Antonius Pius(USA) Cindy's Star (IRE) (Dancing Dissident (USA))
2168[9]

Oasis Dancer *Kevin Ryan* a101 91
6 b g Oasis Dream Good Enough (FR) (Mukaddamah (USA))
149a[9] 365a[11]

Oasis Fantasy (IRE) *Ed Dunlop* 71
2 br c Oasis Dream Cara Fantasy (IRE) (Sadler's Wells (USA))
4925[4] (7070)

Oasis Knight (IRE) *C Von Der Recke* a46 101
7 b g Oasis Dream Generous Lady (Generous (IRE))
513a[6]

Oasis Spirit *Andrew Balding* a77 75
3 b f Oasis Dream Fearless Spirit (USA) (Spinning World (USA))
3401[4] (3837) 4453[6] 5280[5] 6135[4] 7297[2] 7841[2] 8020[7]

Oasis Town *Kevin Ryan* 87
2 br f Sleeping Indian Town And Gown (Oasis Dream)
3280[6] (3681) 4528[3] 5679[15] 6584[4] 7011[6]

Obaha (USA) *J W Hills* 53
3 b f Lemon Drop Kid(USA) Tayibah (IRE) (Sadler's Wells (USA))
3239[7] 3674[4]

Obboorr *Brian Rothwell* 69
4 b g Cape Cross(IRE) Felawnah (USA) (Mr Prospector (USA))
3398[4] 4118[4] 4810[3] 5368[4] 5580[3] ◆ 6296[9] 6567[4] 6943[7] 7346[5]

Obliterelight (IRE) *William Knight* a92 92
4 ch g Bertolini(USA) Doctrine (Barathea (IRE))
(8455)

Observational *Roger Charlton* 78
2 ch c Galileo(IRE) Party (IRE) (Cadeaux Genereux)
7502[2]

Obstacle *John Gosden* 84
3 ch c Observatory(USA) Stage Left (Nashwan (USA))
3539[2] 6696[5] 7279[3]

Obviously (IRE) *Mike Mitchell* a95 121
5 b g Choisir(AUS) Leala (IRE) (Montjeu (IRE))
7714a[5]

Oceana Dreamer (IRE) *Ed McMahon* a49 42
4 b g Oasis Dream Arbella (Primo Dominie)
1395[6]

Ocean Applause *John Ryan* a87 83
3 b g Royal Applause Aldora (Magic Ring (IRE))
1293[9] 1383[9] 1767[8] 2866[11] 3537[2] (4182) 4383[10] 4957[4] 5218[3] 5440[4] 5540[4] 6356[7] 6538[6] 6823[2] 7257[11] 7531[5] 7661[7] 7841[4] 8136[4] 8339[3] (8450)

Ocean Club *Brian Ellison* a15 55
6 ch g Storming Home Strictly Cool (USA) (Bering)
5196[5]

Ocean Legend (IRE) *Tony Carroll* a85 69
8 b g Night Shift(USA) Rose Of Mooncoin (IRE) (Brief Truce (USA))
629[6] 822[8] (1096) 1782[2] 1901[5] 2657[10] 3215[2] 3472[5] 4165[5] 4685[8] 5062[4] (5928) 6403[8] 7436[2] 7769[6] 7992[6] 8122[2]

Ocean Park (NZ) *Gary Hennessy* 122
5 b h Thorn Park(AUS) Sayyida (NZ) (Zabeel (NZ))
1267a[12]

Ocean Power (IRE) *Richard Phillips* a49 51
3 b g Papal Bull Petticoat Power (IRE) (Tomba)
122[7] 4070[11] 5178[2] 6899[7] 7770[2] 7963[11] 8388[7]

Ocean Secret (IRE) *Jeremy Noseda* a67
3 ch c Shirocco(GER) Shell Garland (USA) (Sadler's Wells (USA))
3907[5] 5100[5]

Ocean's Minstrel *John Ryan* a96 96
7 b g Pivotal Minstrel's Dance (CAN) (Pleasant Colony (USA))
3560[P]

Ocean Storm (IRE) *James Tate* a70 84
2 b c Royal Applause Cedar Sea (IRE) (Persian Bold)
1820[5] 2194[4] 2577[2] 3290[3] 3905[3] (4848) 5424[2] 5951[3] 6275[2]

Ocean Tempest *John Ryan* a93 109
4 gr g Act One Ipsa Loquitur (Unfuwain (USA))
1233[5] 2018[7] 2841[3] 3693[3] 4960[2] 5355[2] 6167[2] (6384) (6571) (6826)

Ocean War *Charlie Appleby* 108
5 gr g Dalakhani(IRE) Atlantic Destiny (IRE) (Royal Academy (USA))
3525[8] ◆ 4526[5] 6307[3]

Ocovango *A Fabre* 117
3 br c Monsun(GER) Crystal Maze (Gone West (USA))
(2035a) 2866[5] ◆ 4325a[3] 6446a[3] 7058a[14]

Odd Ball (IRE) *Lisa Williamson* a55 34
6 b g Redback Luceball (IRE) (Bluebird (USA))
4834[12] 5072[11] 5596[11]

Oddsmaker (IRE) *Maurice Barnes* a42 66
12 b g Barathea(IRE) Archipova (IRE) (Ela-Mana-Mou)
2972[8]

Oddysey (IRE) *Michael Dods* 92
4 b f Acclamation Darling Smile (IRE) (Darshaan)
(1576) 1823[4] 2440[3] (3443) (4201) 4525[6] 5014[11] 6875[6]

Odeliz (IRE) *K R Burke* 104
3 ch f Falco(USA) Acatama (USA) (Efisio)
1828[4] (3136) 3995[2] (5496) (6031a) 6714a[3] 7843a[4]

Odeon *James Given* 54
2 b c Galileo(IRE) Kite Mark (Mark Of Esteem (IRE))
7339[5]

Odin (IRE) *Don Cantillon* a89 82
5 b g Norse Dancer(IRE) Dimelight (Fantastic Light (USA))
93[4] 378[4] 3785[6] 7970[4] 8089[3] (8310) (8400)

Odooj (IRE) *William Haggas* a84 103
3 b g Pivotal Shabiba (USA) (Seeking The Gold (USA))
2453[7] 3348[8]

Odyssee (FR) *C Lerner* a88 83
3 ch f Teofilo(IRE) Uruk (Efisio)
5361a[9]

Oeil De Tigre (FR) *H-A Pantall* a69 96
2 b c Footstepsinthesand Suerte (Halling (USA))
3875a[7] 5848a[7] 7939a[9]

Oetzi *Alan Jarvis* a60 77
5 ch g Iceman Mad Annie (USA) (Anabaa (USA))
2594[8] 3022[7] (3729) 4264[8] 6200[8] 6596[14]

Of Course Darling *Ed Dunlop* a74 83
3 ch f Dalakhani(IRE) Whazzis (Desert Prince (IRE))
(1697) 2223[2] 2586[6] 3610[5] 5169[5] 5548[7]

Ofcoursewecan (USA) *Mark Johnston* a68 73
3 b g Elusive Quality(USA) Valid Warning (USA) (Valid Appeal (USA))
211[5] 473[3] 615[5] (1776) 2079[4] 2786[6] 3365[7] 4098[8] 4672[8]

Ofelia (IRE) *Brian Ellison* 42
2 b f Teofilo(IRE) Rose Bourbon (USA) (Woodman (USA))
3723[4] 4610[5]

Off Art *Tim Easterby* 99
3 ch c Dutch Art Off Camera (Efisio)
(2027) (2439) (3563)

Offbeat Safaris (IRE) *Ronald Harris* a63 75
5 b g Le Vie Dei Colori Baywood (Emarati (USA))
1800[5] 2395[10] 2709[3] 3270[3] 3919[2] 4241[2] 4604[3] 4711[3] 5177[3] 5387[9] 5816[12] 6153[11] 7923[4] 8073[12]

Officer Drivel (IRE) *Luke Dace* a71 71
2 b g Captain Rio Spiritville (IRE) (Invincible Spirit (IRE))
4175[4] 5101[5] 5635[2] 6002[6] 6401[5]

Officer In Command (USA) *John Butler* a79 40
7 bb g Officer(USA) Luv To Stay N Chat (USA) (Candi's Gold (USA))
73[6] 403[6] 490[5] ◆ (652) 791[2] (1010) 1094[2] (1496) 1699[5] 1890[2] 6215[10] 7544[6] (8093)

Offshore Bond *Jedd O'Keeffe* 66
2 b g Bahamian Bounty Miss Rimex (IRE) (Ezzoud (IRE))
2955[5] 4282[5] 4808[11] 7126[5]

Off The Pulse *John Mackie* a89 79
3 b g Araafa(IRE) Off By Heart (Royal Applause)
757[2] 1044[2] 1429[5] (1891) 2627[4] 3369[6] 6495[6] 7491[2] (8007) 8416[4]

Ogaritmo *Seamus Durack* a72 68
4 ch f Manduro(GER) Querida (Rainbow Quest (USA))
190[6] 753[2] 1176[8] 2360[5] 3138[6] 3635[5] 4350[3] 4711[6] 7836[13] 8072[7]

Ogbourne Downs *Charles Hills* 86
3 b c Royal Applause Helen Sharp (Pivotal)
(1881) 2603[P] (3633) 4280[5] 4897[5] 7224[3] 7696[11]

Ogermeister (USA) *Wesley A Ward* a89 83
2 b g Silver Train(USA) To The Good Times (USA) (Polish Numbers (USA))
3424[15]

O'Gorman *Gary Brown* a86 90
4 b g Sleeping Indian Harryana (Efisio)
1370[2] 1517[3] 2097[4] (3415) 5998[13] 6525[3]

Oh Boy Oh Boy *James Moffatt* 47
3 b g Misu Bond(IRE) Mitchelland (Namaqualand (USA))
2799[5] 3394[7] 4449[7]

Ohio (IRE) *Gary Harrison* a43 53
2 b f Teofilo(IRE) Royals Special (IRE) (Caerleon (USA))
3905[8] 4491[14] 5151[3]

Oh Marcius (IRE) *Kieran P Cotter* 42
5 bb g Green Desert(USA) Daniysha (IRE) (Doyoun)
2611[8]

Oh So Sassy *Chris Wall* a88 61
3 b f Pastoral Pursuits Almasi (IRE) (Petorius)
1750[4] 2437[2] 3221[3] (6397) ◆ (7445) ◆

Oh So Spicy *Chris Wall* 80
6 ch m Pastoral Pursuits Almasi (IRE) (Petorius)
2441[10] 3223[4] 4120[9] 5154[3] (6535) 7254[11]

Oh Star (USA) *John Gosden* a76
2 bb f Tale Of The Cat(USA) Sleepytime (IRE) (Royal Academy (USA))
6690[2]

Oilinda *Michael Bell* a71 74
3 b f Nayef(USA) Loyal Love (USA) (Danzig (USA))
1697[2] 2387[7] 3202[4] 4240[2] 5430[5] 7669[3]

Oilisblackgold (USA) *Craig Dollase* a108
6 ch g Tapit(USA) Dancing Tempest (USA) (Seeking The Gold (USA))
4106a[5]

Oil Of England (GER) *M Figge* 92
2 bb c Lord Of England(GER) Oligarchica (GER) (Desert King (IRE))
7232a[5]

Oil Strike *Michael Easterby* a71 67
6 b g Lucky Story(USA) Willisa (Polar Falcon (USA))
3392[7] 3945[15] (4588) (4728) 4954[7] 5639[8] 6496[13] 7420[12] 7776[10] 7949[8] 8167[6] 8321[11]

Ojibway Signal (CAN) *David R Bell* a75 84
5 bb g Niigon(CAN) Apache Signal (CAN) (Announce (USA))
608a[8]

Ojos De Hielo (USA) *Larry Rivelli* 97
4 ch c Songandaprayer(USA) Passionate Dancer (USA) (Cat Thief (USA))
5550a[7]

Okavango *James Fanshawe* a79 76
3 ch f Nayef(USA) Ivory Gala (FR) (Galileo (IRE))
2206[6] 2713[2] ◆ (7298)

Okhtay (FR) *P Olsanik* a20
5 b c Black Sam Bellamy(IRE) Oh So Lovely (Bering)
498a[10]

Oklahoma City *A P O'Brien* 106
2 b c Oasis Dream Galaxy Highflyer (Galileo (IRE))
4547a[2] 6884a[2] (7017) 7195[2]

Oldjoesaid *Paul Midgley* a77 89
9 b g Royal Applause Border Minstral (IRE) (Sri Pekan (USA))
885[4] (1248) 1649[2] 2459[5] 2669[15] 4047[14] 4507[3] 4954[8] 5108[9] 6159[9] (6771) 7420[2]

Old Man Clegg *Michael Easterby* 73
3 b g Pastoral Pursuits Stolen Melody (Robellino (USA))
1577[3] 1934[9] 2371[3] 2593[9] 4048[7] 4890[5] 5342[9] 5784[6] 6549[6] 6588[6]

Old Peg *Dai Burchell* a31 53
8 b m Mujahid(USA) Giggleswick Girl (Full Extent (USA))
529[8] 649[11]

Old Time Hockey (USA) *Thomas F Proctor* a96 109
4 ch g Smarty Jones(USA) Grat (USA) (A.P. Indy (USA))
7687a[6]

Old Town Boy *Philip McBride* a62
2 b c Myboycharlie(IRE) Native Ring (FR) (Bering)
7902[6] ◆ 8214[4]

Olimamu (IRE) *Lydia Pearce* a57 41
6 b m Barathea(IRE) La Galeisa (IRE) (Warning)
2642[11] 3256[5]

Oliver's Gold *Tim Walford* a58 56
5 b g Danehill Dancer(IRE) Gemini Gold (IRE) (King's Best (USA))
3727[7]

Olivers Mount *Ed Vaughan* a60 37
3 ch g Mount Nelson Phoebe Woodstock (IRE) (Grand Lodge (USA))
2456[10] 2746[11] 3250[11] 6146[6] 6399[7] (7378) 7667[3] 8065[2]

Ollie Olga (USA) *Mick Channon* 104
3 bb f Stormy Atlantic(USA) Card Shop (USA) (Chester House (USA))
2047[12] 3524[10] 4081[5] 4949[8]
Olney Lass *Lydia Pearce* a58 76
6 b m Lucky Story(USA) Zalebe (Bahamian Bounty)
145[5] 335[6] (1294) 1914[4] 2638[5] 3741[9] 4864[8] (6019) 6324[4] (6461) 6871[8] 7318[3] 7699[11]
Olymnia *Robert Eddery* 43
2 b f Teofilo(IRE) Diotima (High Estate)
4668[8] 7533[9] ◆
Olympiad (IRE) *D K Weld* 98
5 b g Galileo(IRE) Caumshinaun (IRE) (Indian Ridge)
2149[17] 7230a[28]
Olympic Glory (IRE) *Richard Hannon Snr* 127
3 b c Choisir(AUS) Acidanthera (Alzao (USA))
(1677) 2298a[11] 5314a[2] 6450a[2] (7366) 7714a[9]
Olympic Jule *Harry Dunlop* a71 68
3 b f Shamardal(USA) Jules (IRE) (Danehill (USA))
2806[3] 3216[4] 4637[11] 6080[11] 7303[8]
Olynard (IRE) *Michael Mullineaux* a50 52
7 b g Exceed And Excel(AUS) Reddening (Blushing Flame (USA))
117[10] 423[6] 565[7] 754[10] 825[5] 900[7] 1021[4] 1043[2] 1147[5] 1310[7] 2037[9] 3270[8] 3513[11] 3687[8] 3754[7] 8413[7]
Oly'Roccs (IRE) *David Nicholls*
2 b c Tagula(IRE) Orpendonna (IRE) (Orpen (USA))
7335[12] 7853[11]
Omaha Gold (IRE) *Bryan Smart* 73
2 b f Kodiac Naraina (IRE) (Desert Story (IRE))
4847[2] 5364[2] 5638[3] (6561) 7026[20]
O Ma Lad (IRE) *John Quinn* a90 97
5 ch g Redback Raydaniya (IRE) (In The Wings)
(1463) (2040) 5237[6] 6302[6] 6631[9] 7526[8]
Omana (FR) *H-A Pantall* 107
4 b f Speedmaster(GER) Orion Girl (GER) (Law Society (USA))
1895a[8]
Omanome (IRE) *David O'Meara* 70
2 b f Acclamation Dance Set (Selkirk (USA))
3500[6] 3978[6] 4470[2] 5053[4] (5703) 6047[5] 6663[8]
Omar Khayyam *Andrew Balding* a75 92
4 b c Pivotal Kithanga (IRE) (Darshaan)
2385[9] (6869) ◆ 8150[7]
Omaticaya (IRE) *Manila Illuminati* 105
2 br f Bernstein(USA) Pronghorn (USA) (Gulch (USA))
3880a[2] 4572a[2] 7830a[9]
Ombrage (FR) *B Grizzetti* 105
2 b f Orpen(USA) Hideaway Heroine (IRE) (Hernando (FR))
(7415a)
Omega Omega *Julia Feilden* a49 50
4 b f Halling(USA) In Luck (In The Wings)
1916[7] 2332[8] 3792[5] 4178[2] 5123[6] 6097[4] 7612[3] 7838[4] 8349[5]
Omid *Nicky Vaughan* a65 58
5 b g Dubawi(IRE) Mille Couleurs (FR) (Spectrum (IRE))
713[3] 887[6] 2991[8]
Ominous *Nigel Blackiston* 98
4 b c Oasis Dream Merle (Selkirk (USA))
7417a[15]
Omnipresent *Sir Michael Stoute* a84 78
3 b g Rail Link Protectress (Hector Protector (USA))
2938[3] 5469[2] (5892) 6514[3]
Omokoroa (IRE) *Braem Horse Racing Sprl* a62 43
7 b g Hawkeye(IRE) Alycus (USA) (Atticus (USA))
3647a[5]
Omotesando *Mark Johnston* a35
3 b g Street Cry(IRE) Punctilious (Danehill (USA))
708[7]
Omy *D Smaga* a80 76
3 b c Zamindar(USA) Galipette (Green Desert (USA))
3454a[3]
Onceaponatime (IRE) *Michael Squance* a57 73
8 b g Invincible Spirit(IRE) Lake Nyasa (IRE) (Lake Coniston (IRE))
88[3] 163[10] 409[6] 551[12] 735[4] 909[6] 1396[5] 1525[8]
Ondeafears (IRE) *M Halford* a41 96
6 b m Chineur(FR) Irma La Douce (IRE) (Elbio)
3845a[16] 5688a[9] 7719a[9]
On Demand *Andrew Balding* 71
2 ch f Teofilo(IRE) Mimisel (Selkirk (USA))
6140[6]
One And Only (FR) *P Decouz* a67 74
3 ch f Muhtathir Alaskan Way (USA) (Giant's Causeway (USA))
8441a[3]
One Boy (IRE) *Michael Dods* 73
2 ch g Captain Gerrard(IRE) Paris Song (IRE) (Peintre Celebre (USA))
(1573) 2370[5] 4726[5] 5710[5] (6467) 6791[5] 7026[13]
One Chance (IRE) *Tim Pitt* 95
2 b f Invincible Spirit(IRE) Towards (USA) (Fusaichi Pegasus (USA))
1634[6] (2090) 3459[3] 4253[8]
Onedargent (FR) *J-P Gallorini* 102
3 gr g Kendargent(FR) One Day (FR) (Act One)
1419a[4] 3007a[2]
One Dark Night *Gary Moore* a44
3 b g Proclamation(IRE) Night Storm (Night Shift (USA))
492[7] 1199[4] 1769[8] 5127[8] 6103[9]
One For Joules (IRE) *John Flint* a72 70
6 b m Choisir(AUS) Stuttgart (Groom Dancer (USA))
20[6] 6492[8]
One For The Girls *Nicky Vaughan* a49 46
4 b g Primo Valentino(IRE) Countrywide Girl (IRE) (Catrail (USA))
215[8] 713[5]
One In A Thousand (IRE) *Chris Dwyer* 45
3 b f Thousand Words Noora (IRE) (Bahhare (USA))
4182[8] 4625[7] 5277[4] 5616[4] 5869[11] 6074[6]

One Kool Dude *Neville Bycroft* a25 69
4 ch g Iceman Hiraeth (Petong)
1294[11] 1748[5] 2132[9] 2643[5] 4009[11] 5085[6] ◆ 5487[2] 5709[2] 6603[4] 7347[10]
Oneladyowner *David O'Meara* a84 91
5 b g Auction House(USA) Inya Lake (Whittingham (IRE))
1160[6] 1787[6] 2664[9] 2725[11] 4338[9]
One Last Dream *Ron Hodges* a64 62
4 ch g Resplendent Glory(IRE) Pip's Dream (Glint Of Gold)
1395[7] 2057[5] 2596[2] 2918[6] 3529[3] 6156[11] 6980[5] 7197[11] (7643) 7858[3] 8151[2]
One Lord (FR) *T Castanheira* a54 58
2 ch c Spirit One(FR) Dust In The Wing (FR) (Highest Honor (FR))
5214a[9]
One Man Band (IRE) *Charlie Appleby* a65 28
2 b c Pivotal Musicanna (Cape Cross (IRE))
5718[12] 6733[7]
One Million *Rose Dobbin* 34
4 b g Dubai Destination(USA) Talwin (IRE) (Alhaarth (IRE))
1270[6] 2986[9]
Oneofapear (IRE) *Ian McInnes* a63 86
7 b g Pyrus(USA) Whitegate Way (Greensmith)
562[4] 1239[16] 1790[12] 3195[15]
One Of Twins *Michael Easterby* a67 43
5 b g Gentleman's Deal(IRE) Miss Twiddles (IRE) (Desert King (IRE))
1521[10] 1797[5] 2273[9] 4052[10]
One Pekan (IRE) *Roger Varian* a87 91
3 b g Hard Spun(USA) Stormy Blessing (USA) (Storm Cat (USA))
1429[2] (1769) 3899[2] 4214[6] ◆ 4765[7] 7330[7]
One Penny Piece *Philip McBride* a69 74
2 b f Archipenko(USA) Silken Promise (USA) (Pulpit (USA))
(3255) 3761[3] (4134) 5005[12] 5536[8] 5926[4] (7977) (8086)
One Picture *Richard Hannon Snr* a26 13
2 ch c Bertolini(USA) Marannatha (IRE) (Pursuit Of Love)
7155[12] 7320[9] 7647[10] 8016[7]
One Pursuit (IRE) *Brendan Powell* a49 85
5 br g Pastoral Pursuits Karinski (USA) (Palace Music (USA))
6898[11] (7396) (7539) 7757[3] 7976[13]
Onertother *Joseph Tuite* a54 57
4 br g Nomadic Way(USA) Ceilidh Band (Celtic Swing)
7266[14] 7894[8]
One Scoop Or Two *Andrew Hollinshead* a81 77
7 b g Needwood Blade Rebel County (IRE) (Maelstrom Lake)
82[3] 219[2] 329[2] (593) 759[2] 995[6] 1354[7] 1827[7] 2659[7] 4250[2] 5026[9] 5947[10] 6126[3] 6384[8] 7965[6] 8227[2] 8314[4]
One Spirit (IRE) *F Dunne* 104
5 b f Invincible Spirit(IRE) Recite (JPN) (Forty Niner (USA))
5453a[6] 5688a[8] 6023a[5] 6224a[9]
One Way Or Another (AUS) *David Evans* a73 62
10 b g Carnegie(IRE) True Blonde (AUS) (Naturalism (NZ))
15[3] (97) (118) 376[2] 490[6] 672[7] 832[8] 971[2] 1101[3] 1286[5] 1521[4] 6476[7] 6856[7] 7092[4] (7652) (7808) 7964[6] 8187[7] 8314[6]
One Word More (IRE) *Charles Hills* a100 104
3 b c Thousand Words Somoushe (IRE) (Black Minnaloushe (USA))
(1543) 2526a[10] 3455[20] 5728[8] 6308[2] ◆ 7368[17]
Ongoodform (IRE) *David Nicholls* a85 73
6 b g Invincible Spirit(IRE) Elfin Queen (IRE) (Fairy King (USA))
3506[10]
Onkenbayasowaka (FR) *S Kobayashi* a72 81
3 ch f Excellent Art Eglesia (GER) (Lavirco (GER))
2403a[3]
Online *Tracy Waggott*
3 b g Rail Link Fairy Steps (Rainbow Quest (USA))
1282[14] 3398[11]
Online Alexander (IRE) *Kevin Ryan* 82
2 b f Acclamation Dance Club (IRE) (Fasliyev (USA))
4924[3] (5421) 7207[9]
Only A Pleasure (IRE) *A Fabre* 108
4 b c Montjeu(IRE) Sense Of Style (USA) (Thunder Gulch (USA))
2908a[7] 5575a[9] 6447a[14]
Only For You *Alan Brown* a54 56
3 b f Elusive City(USA) Enlisted (IRE) (Sadler's Wells (USA))
2512[6] 2650[4] 3091[2] 3594[10] 3946[7] 4499[6] 4621[6]
Only Orsenfoolsies *Micky Hammond* 76
4 b g Trade Fair Desert Gold (IRE) (Desert Prince (IRE))
1391[6]
Only Ten Per Cent (IRE) *J R Jenkins* a82 49
5 b g Kheleyf(USA) Cory Everson (IRE) (Brief Truce (USA))
34[3] 344[4] 511[8] 721[2] 912[7] 6317[4] 6928[6] 7263[9] 7953[11]
Onlyyouknowme (IRE) *E Botti* a100 97
5 b f Martino Alonso(IRE) Sopran New (USA) (Cozzene (USA))
961a[2] 1563a[3] 2491a[3] 7830a[10]
Only You Maggie (IRE) *Gary Harrison* a62 68
6 b m Atraf First Kiss (GER) (Night Shift (USA))
4403[6] 7132[12]
On My Own (TUR) *J W Hills* a75 83
4 b c Rock Of Gibraltar(IRE) Dancingintheclouds (IRE) (Rainbow Quest (USA))
1926[5] 2574[4] 3063[4] (4718) 6288[13] 6801[11]
On Stage *Stuart Kittow* 65
4 ch f Act One In The Stocks (Reprimand)
2350[2] (4036) 4915[5] 6325[14] 7433[5]
On The Cusp (IRE) *Ann Stokell* a67 56
6 b g Footstepsinthesand Roman Love (IRE) (Perugino (USA))
439[8] 718[7] 883[12] 1184[5] 2171[2] 2514[13] 5091[10] 6803[6] (7752) 8042[5] 8436[2]

On The Feather *Jim Best* a67 76
7 br m Josr Algarhoud(IRE) Fotheringhay (Loup Sauvage (USA))
469[2] 635[4]
On The High Tops (IRE) *Colin Teague* a43 66
5 b g Kheleyf(USA) Diplomats Daughter (Unfuwain (USA))
6604[11] 6757[14] 6945[11] 7101[13]
On The Hoof *Michael Easterby* a83 76
4 gr g Monsieur Bond(IRE) Smart Hostess (Most Welcome)
49[4] 217[6] 314[2] 439[3] 563[5]
Ontology (USA) *Simon Callaghan* a88 91
2 ch c Tapit(USA) Shytoe Lafeet (USA) (King Of Kings (IRE))
7688a[10]
Onwards'N'Upwards *Christine Dunnett* a25 26
5 b g Diktat Lunar Goddess (Royal Applause)
2568[7]
On With The Dance (IRE) *Ed Vaughan* a74 73
3 ch g Byron Caldy Dancer (IRE) (Soviet Star (USA))
807[3] 911[3] (1213) 2935[2] 3901[3] 4383[4] 5395[4] 6214[5] 7605[4]
Oojooba *Roger Varian* 100
4 b f Monsun(GER) Ameerat (Mark Of Esteem (IRE))
2015[3] 2440[4] 4137[7]
Oor Jock (IRE) *John Patrick Shanahan* a88 88
5 ch g Shamardal(USA) Katdogawn (Bahhare (USA))
4444[3]
Open Eagle (IRE) *David O'Meara* a93 100
4 b g Montjeu(IRE) Princesse De Viane (FR) (Kaldoun (FR))
(6729) 7823[3] 7990[9] 8327[11]
Open Letter (IRE) *Mark Johnston* a68 64
3 b f New Approach(IRE) Deveron (USA) (Cozzene (USA))
1219[5] 1579[6] 2127[7] 2878[7] 3900[7]
Open Water (FR) *Andrew Balding* 93
4 b g Orpen(USA) So Stream (ITY) (Elmaamul (USA))
2101[5] 6957[2] 7312[4]
Opera Box *Marcus Tregoning* a95 92
5 b f Singspiel(IRE) Annex (Anabaa (USA))
(1518) 1825[2] 2369[15] 4488[2] 4878[9] (6004) 6649[9] 7768[4]
Opera Buff *Sean Curran* a73 87
4 b g Oratorio(IRE) Opera Glass (Barathea (IRE))
2640[4] 3580[4] 4755[4] 5099[2] 6080[5] 6200[4] (6960) 7217[2] 7635[6]
Opera Duke (IRE) *Andrew Balding*
2 ch g Duke Of Marmalade(IRE) Opera Glass (Barathea (IRE))
7274[6]
Opera Fan (FR) *Mark Johnston* a62 64
2 b f Cape Cross(IRE) Persian Belle (Machiavellian (USA))
4432[7] 5122[2] 5852[4] 6605[4]
Opera Gloves (IRE) *M Halford* a89 102
3 b f Dalakhani(IRE) Chan Tong (BRZ) (Hampstead (URU))
4465a[6] 7005a[7] 7361a[7]
Opera Moon (GER) *W Hickst* a67 59
6 ch g Big Shuffle(USA) Opera Nova (IRE) (Perugino (USA))
127a[5]
Operateur (IRE) *Ben Haslam* a52 63
5 b g Oratorio(IRE) Kassariya (IRE) (Be My Guest (USA))
1572[5] 1789[3] 2120[9] 2986[4] 3625[3] 7375[8]
Operation Chariot (IRE) *Andrew Balding* a92 100
3 b g Refuse To Bend(IRE) Dona Royale (IRE) (Darshaan)
1383[6] 1767[6] 2857[10] 4078[6] 5510[10] 6871[7] 7325[5]
Opera Vert (FR) *D Sepulchre* a83 101
5 b g Green Tune(USA) Caramba Kelly (IRE) (Mtoto)
7590a[5]
Operettist *Tony Carroll* a60 50
4 b f Singspiel(IRE) Demi Voix (Halling (USA))
1948[9] 2729[7] 3169[12] 5091[4] 7201[9] 7643[14] 7907[10]
Opinion (IRE) *Chris Waller* 109
4 b g Oasis Dream Kiltubber (IRE) (Sadler's Wells (USA))
2044[3] (3559) 4060[5] 5766[10] 7760a[18]
Opposite (IRE) *A Fabre* a104 111
4 b g Dansili Silver Rain (FR) (Rainbow Quest (USA))
4819a[2]
Optical *Sir Henry Cecil* a69 74
3 ch f Observatory(USA) Blueberry (USA) (Bertrando (USA))
1955[4]
Opt Out *Alistair Whillans* a76 81
3 ch g Pivotal Easy Option (IRE) (Prince Sabo)
982[3] 1075[6] 2190[9] 3234[6] 3566[8] 3769[5] 4338[11] 5333[7] 5878[6] 6052[14] (6471) 7150[5] 7240[1] ◆
Opus (IRE) *Lucy Wadham* a54 50
4 br g Danehill Dancer(IRE) Mixed Blessing (Lujain (USA))
2764[3] 7440[6] 7735[5] 7984[5]
Opus Dei *Alan McCabe* a76 47
6 b g Oasis Dream Grail (USA) (Quest For Fame)
1334[5] 1650[6] 1964[5]
Opus Maximus (IRE) *Jennie Candlish* a55 51
8 ch g Titus Livius(FR) Law Review (IRE) (Case Law)
2932[10] 3642[2] 3909[4] 5179[6] 5596[7]
Oracle Boy *William Muir* a42 40
2 b c Mount Nelson Snow Princess (IRE) (Ela-Mana-Mou)
6762[15] 7780[7]
O'Raghallaigh (IRE) *Richard Fahey* a18
2 b f Papal Bull Kahyasi Moll (IRE) (Brief Truce (USA))
8091[6] 8346[9]

Orangefield (FR) *J-C Rouget* 80
2 b c Soave(GER) Moon Serenade (Key Of Luck (USA))
(7653a)
Orange Grove *Tobias B P Coles* a80 19
2 ch c Hernando(FR) Ryella (USA) (Cozzene (USA))
6430[7] (7901)
Oratorio's Joy (IRE) *Jamie Osborne* a82 75
3 b f Oratorio(IRE) Seeking The Fun (USA) (Alhaarth (IRE))
651[2] ◆ 895[3] (972) 1321[3] 4348[4] (4941) 5304[11] 7546[2] 7970[6] (8136) 8336[4]
Oratory (IRE) *Mrs K Burke* a66 86
7 b g Danehill Dancer(IRE) Gentle Night (Zafonic (USA))
984[10] 1699[10] 2929[10] 4341[2] 4540[5] 5304[3]
Orb (USA) *Claude McGaughey III* a122
3 b c Malibu Moon(USA) Lady Liberty (USA) (Unbridled (USA))
(2033a) 2473a[4] 3127a[3]
Orbison (IRE) *Roger Varian* 77
3 b g Azamour(IRE) Glenmara (USA) (Known Fact (USA))
1881[6] 2306[12] 2765[6] (3861) 4593[9] 6003[12] 7319[8]
Orbit The Moon (IRE) *Michael Dods* a78 86
5 b g Oratorio(IRE) Catch The Moon (IRE) (Peintre Celebre (USA))
2028[13] 3087[11] 3590[2] 3741[2] 4111[6] 4560[9] 4812[5] 5292[10] 5711[4] 7824[7]
Ordensritter (GER) *Chris Down* a74 97
5 ch g Samum(GER) Dramraire Mist (Darshaan)
1062[3] (1502)
Order Of Service *David Brown* a82 74
3 ch g Medicean Choir Gallery (Pivotal)
(1712) 2094[2] 2624[U] 2957[7] (3438) 4056[4] 6204[9] 7075[8]
Orders From Rome (IRE) *Eve Johnson Houghton* a71 87
4 b g Holy Roman Emperor(IRE) Fatat Alarab (USA) (Capote (USA))
2196[5] 2724[4] 3108[6] 3404[10] 3661[8] 6306[10] 6937[11] 7303[9]
Orfevre (JPN) *Yasutoshi Ikee* 130
5 ch c Stay Gold(JPN) Oriental Art (JPN) (Mejiro McQueen (JPN))
(6449a) 7058a[2]
Oriel *Richard Hannon Snr* 81
2 b f Fastnet Rock(AUS) Labisa (IRE) (High Chaparral (IRE))
2204[2] 2414[3] 3459[17] 4215[3] (4828) 5536[9] 6644[8]
Oriental Cavalier *Mark Buckley* a40 47
7 ch g Ishiguru(USA) Gurleigh (IRE) (Pivotal)
3977[12] 5204[8] 7962[8]
Oriental Dream (IRE) *Nigel Tinkler* 11
2 b c Shamardal(USA) Oriental Melody (IRE) (Sakhee (USA))
5145[11] 6790[11] 7023[14]
Oriental Fox (GER) *Mark Johnston* 111
5 ch g Lomitas Oriental Pearl (GER) (Big Shuffle (USA))
1689[5] ◆ 2427[6] 2654[2] 3099[11] 3824[2] 4857[10] 5256[3] 5766[5] 6192[12] (6646) 7193[6]
Oriental Lady (GER) *J Hirschberger* 97
3 b f Doyen(IRE) Oriental World (GER) (Platini (GER))
3146a[2] 4092a[6] 5044a[9] 6010a[5]
Oriental Magic (GER) *J Hirschberger* 91
2 bb f Doyen(IRE) Oriental Pearl (GER) (Big Shuffle (USA))
5939a[6]
Oriental Relation (IRE) *James Given* a81 80
2 gr g Tagula(IRE) Rofan (USA) (Cozzene (USA))
2497[3] 3481[9] 3943[2] 4987[17] 6493[3] 7609[3] 7853[4] 8091[2] (8300) (8404)
Oriental Wind *Rod Collet* 101
3 b f Zamindar(USA) Orion Girl (GER) (Law Society (USA))
5315a[6] 6484a[5] 7189a[2]
Orient Class *Paul Midgley* 50
2 ch g Orientor Killer Class (Kyllachy)
6383[5] 6627[7] 7095[6]
Orient Sky *Paul Midgley* 41
2 b g Orientor Sister Eugenie (IRE) (Indian Lodge (IRE))
2005[6] 2337[7]
Orion Love *H-A Pantall* 109
3 ch f Zamindar(USA) Okocha (GER) (Platini (GER))
1602a[5] 2905a[2] 3614a[3] 5044a[8] 6448a[4] 7048a[9] 7613a[7]
Orion's Bow *John Gosden* 21
2 ch c Pivotal Heavenly Ray (USA) (Rahy (USA))
6953[13]
Orions Hero (IRE) *Richard Fahey* a65 73
3 b g Oasis Dream La Reine Mambo (USA) (High Yield (USA))
1803[2] 2538[6] 3067[9] 4048[2] 4341[8] 5383[6] 6296[11]
Orla (IRE) *John Gallagher* a47 38
5 b f Hawk Wing(USA) Irish Ensign (SAF) (National Emblem (SAF))
1095[4] 1981[7] 2345[7] 3513[10]
Orlando Star (CAN) *Roger Teal* a69 67
2 b c Henrythenavigator(USA) Clayton's Lass (USA) (Forest Camp (USA))
5306[3] 5635[4] 6013[5] 6731[8]
Orla's Rainbow (IRE) *Gary Moore* a38 57
3 b g Oratorio(IRE) Red Ray (Pivotal)
5123[2] 5630[5] 6257[6]
Ormer *David Evans* a9 40
2 b f Kyllachy Authoritative (Diktat)
4518[4] 5385[7] 6318[9] 6656[6]
Oromo (FR) *J Heloury* a81 88
2 b c Elusive City(USA) Hamida (USA) (Johannesburg (USA))
5362a[3]
Orpello (IRE) *S Botti* 107
4 b c Orpen(USA) Princess Angelina (IRE) (Almutawakel)
(1709a) 2295a[2] 3881a[3]
Orpen Bid (IRE) *Michael Mullineaux* a34 51
8 b m Orpen(USA) Glorious Bid (IRE) (Horage)
973[8] 1146[7] 1207[9] 2333[9] 3199[10]

Orpen Wide (IRE) *Michael Chapman* a50 26
11 b g Orpen(USA) Melba (IRE) (Namaqualand (USA))
6756[9] 6952[10]

Orpha *Mick Channon* 91
3 b f New Approach(IRE) Garah (Ajdal (USA))
2429[4]

Orpsie Boy (IRE) *Ruth Carr* a85 92
10 b g Orpen(USA) Nordicolini (IRE) (Nordico (USA))
2119[4] 2573[8] 3087[9] 3628[6] 4111[5] 4340[5] 5138[7] 5677[4] 6368[2] 6633[4] 6855[5] 7163[3] 7486[2] (7807) 8037[4] 8163[4]

Orsello (GER) *N Sauer* 96
3 bb c Mount Nelson Ogmore Vale (GER) (Silvano (GER))
1867a[7] 3389a[3]

Orsino (GER) *R Rohne* 109
6 b h Mamool(IRE) Orosole (GER) (Platini (GER))
6679a[2] 7414a[3] 7724a[6]

Orsippus (USA) *Michael Smith* a78 86
7 bb g Sunday Break(JPN) Mirror Dancing (USA) (Caveat (USA))
3609[6]

Ortac Rock (IRE) *Richard Fahey* a89 81
4 b g Aussie Rules(USA) Fashion Guide (IRE) (Bluebird (USA))
1061[9] 1385[10] 1782[3] ◆ 2266[11] 3108[10] 3274[8] (4438) 4758[4] 5026[6] 6072[4] 7031[2] 7427[2]

Ortea *Ian Williams* a70 78
4 b g Vital Equine(IRE) Artistic (IRE) (Noverre (USA))
219[4] 548[5] 1081[10]

Orton Park (IRE) *Tobias B P Coles* a69 79
2 b f Moss Vale(IRE) Notley Park (Wolfhound (USA))
(1240) 1619[4] 1894a[4] 3332[4] 3801[3] 4528[11] 5029[5] 7545[8]

Orwellian *Bryan Smart* a52 59
4 b g Bahamian Bounty Trinny (Rainbow Quest (USA))
640[8] 1686[6] 6181[9] 6761[6] 7344[6] 7958[5] 8234[6] 8315[4]

Oscars Journey *J R Jenkins* a64 74
3 ch g Dubai Destination(USA) Fruit Of Glory (Glory Of Dancer)
1661[5] 3866[4] 3956[5]

Oscilate Wildly (IRE) *Peter Chapple-Hyam* a72 74
3 b f Mount Nelson Marisa (GER) (Desert Sun)
2389[7] 2713[6] 6312[4] 6788[4] 7166[6]

Oscuro *Tim Easterby*
2 b g Manduro(GER) Jabbara (IRE) (Kingmambo (USA))
2401[14]

Ossie's Dancer *Martin Smith* a54 35
4 ch g Osorio(GER) Nina Ballerina (Kahyasi)
7490[6] 7894[7]

Ostaad (IRE) *Saeed bin Suroor* a85 85
3 b c Marju(IRE) Almansoora (USA) (Bahri (USA))
(5678) 6356[9]

Ostentation *Alastair Lidderdale* a73 70
6 ch g Dubawi(IRE) Oshiponga (Barathea (IRE))
1031[6] 1251[7]

Osteopathic Remedy (IRE) *Michael Dods* a87 100
9 ch g Inchinor Dolce Vita (IRE) (Ela-Mana-Mou)
1485[8] 1688[7] 2029[6] 2477[5] 2958[4] 4101[2] 5014[13] (5838) 6624[7] 7172[12] 7337[7]

Ostinato (GER) *Sandor Kovacs* a105 107
5 b c Ransom O'War(USA) Oxotica (GER) (Subotica (FR))
364a[6] 656a[4] 870a[6] 6987a[4] 7831a[8]

Ostourah (USA) *A De Royer-Dupre* a90 85
3 b f Teuflesberg(USA) Bella Dorato (USA) (Goldminers Gold (CAN))
8440a[9]

Ostralegus *John Gallagher* a63 65
3 b g Choisir(AUS) Midnight Pearl (USA) (Woodman (USA))
7459[4] 8070[4] 8146[3]

Ottavino (IRE) *Jane Chapple-Hyam* a50 41
4 b g Piccolo Indian's Feather (IRE) (Indian Ridge)
3906[4] 6400[10] 8390[11]

Ottoman Empire (FR) *John Butler* a105 107
7 ch g Pivotal Chesnut Bird (IRE) (Storm Bird (CAN))
151a[8] 362a[5] (552a) 3525[4] ◆ 4465a[16] 6772[7]

Otto The First *John Best* a53 55
3 b g Holy Roman Emperor(IRE) Paquita (IRE) (Sadler's Wells (USA))
442[8] 1066[3] 1320[4] 1710[3] 2129[9] 2950[8] 4423[6] 4658[7] 5275[5] 7266[10]

Otto The Great *Richard Fahey* a74 91
4 b g Holy Roman Emperor(IRE) Vayavaig (Damister (USA))
2592[13] 3322[2] 4014[4]

Our Boy Jack (IRE) *Richard Fahey* a79 92
4 b g Camacho Jina (IRE) (Petardia)
1168a[19] 1385[11] 1992[3] 2463[8] 3411[2] 3945[3] 4340[2] 5014[5] 5481[7] 5974[2] (6496) 7176[14]

Our Channel (USA) *William Haggas* 87
2 ch c English Channel(USA) Raw Gold (USA) (Rahy (USA))
5877[3] 6256[2] (6716)

Our Diane (IRE) *Richard Fahey* 74
3 b f Exceed And Excel(AUS) Medalha Milagrosa (USA) (Miner's Mark (USA))
1791[4] 2076[5] 2888[8] 3779[2] 6469[5] 6547[3] 7150[7] 7315[11]

Our Duchess (IRE) *Richard Hannon Snr* 75
2 ch f Duke Of Marmalade(IRE) Honey Gold (IRE) (Indian Ridge)
5443[7] 5949[2] (6409)

Our Folly *Stuart Kittow* a46 79
5 b g Sakhee(USA) Regent's Folly (IRE) (Touching Wood (USA))
(1664) (2197) 3065[2] 4530[2] 5231[9] 6424[4] 7217[5] 7660[4]

Our Gabrial (IRE) *Richard Fahey* a74 74
2 b g Rock Of Gibraltar(IRE) Jojeema (Barathea (IRE))
3461[5] 4021[5] 4282[2] 4802[2] 5945[3] 7492[2] 7902[4] 8153[2] 8267[3]

Our Generation (IRE) *Marco Botti* a83
2 br g Footstepsinthesand Almost Blue (USA) (Mr Greeley (USA))
(6931)

Our Golden Girl *Shaun Lycett* a61 51
3 ch f Dutch Art Nemorosa (Pivotal)
821[3] 1928[11] 2129[4] 2742[6] 3619[4] 3919[7] 5346[8] 6137[5] 6361[2] 7204[2] 7543[5] 8225[3] 8302[4] 8373[5]

Our Ivor *Michael Appleby* a87 81
4 gr g Cape Town(IRE) Caprice (Mystiko (USA))
(536) (600) (718) 832[5] 1203[5] 1723[6] (2515) 2580[2] 3027[2]

Our Jonathan *David Simcock* a103 112
6 b g Invincible Spirit(IRE) Sheik'n Swing (Celtic Swing)
1234[3] 1537[15] 2667[4] 3558[26] 5696[6] 6391[12] 6623[7] 7368[11] 7495[8]

Our Manekineko *J A Nash* a75 56
3 b g Kyllachy Gallivant (Danehill (USA))
824[6]

Our Obsession (IRE) *William Haggas* 108
3 ch f Shamardal(USA) Hidden Hope (Daylami (IRE))
(4777) (5683)

Our Old Fella *Daniel Mark Loughnane*
2 gr g Misu Bond(IRE) Kilmovee (Inchinor)
4833[5]

Our Phylli Vera (IRE) *Alan King* a58 80
4 b f Motivator With Colour (Rainbow Quest (USA))
(1974) 3095[5] 7504[9]

Our Play (IRE) *Lydia Richards* a64 66
5 b g Oratorio(IRE) Red Shoe (Selkirk (USA))
418[14] 788[9] 1062[8] 1175[14]

Our Queenie (IRE) *Richard Hannon Snr* 85
2 ch f Strategic Prince Matibibi (ITY) (Barathea (IRE))
1634[14] 2382[2] (2617) (4302) 4988[4]

Our Red Devil (IRE) *David Nicholls*
2 ch g Dandy Man(IRE) Candela Bay (IRE) (Captain Rio)
6127[4]

Our Sherona *Gary Harrison* a60 53
2 b f Rock Of Gibraltar(IRE) Spia (USA) (Diesis)
2869[6] 5000[3] 5584[11] 6408[5] 7541[9]

Our Sweet Art *John Best* a62 62
3 ch f Dutch Art Break Of Dawn (USA) (Mt. Livermore (USA))
2962[8] 4607[2] ◆ 5373[11] 6752[10] 7465[8]

Our Three Graces (IRE) *Andre Hermans* a62 45
3 b f Red Clubs(IRE) Villa Nova (IRE) (Petardia)
2528[9] 2950[2] ◆ 4424[5] 5128[7] 6038[13] 8441a[14]

Outback (IRE) *Neil King* a76 69
4 b g Kodiac Florida City (IRE) (Pennekamp (USA))
1586[7] 4179[4] 4392[2] 4692[2] 4867[3] 5619[3]

Outbacker (IRE) *Mark Johnston* a71
2 b f Aussie Rules(USA) Naomh Geileis (USA) (Grand Slam (USA))
8332[2] 8451[2]

Outback Lover (IRE) *J S Moore* a67 66
2 b f Bushranger(IRE) Lady Thyne (IRE) (Mujadil (USA))
1156[5] (1208) 2053[7] 2147[8] 3863[5] 4639[4] 4910[2] 5591[3] 6364[7] 7036[4] 7771[9] 8024[5]

Outback Traveller (IRE) *Jeremy Noseda* a81 76
2 b c Bushranger(IRE) Blue Holly (IRE) (Blues Traveller (IRE))
5744[4] (6110) (7300)

Outback Warrior (IRE) *Kevin Ryan* a63 51
2 b c Bushranger(IRE) Choice House (USA) (Chester House (USA))
5482[6] 8266[3]

Outbid *Tony Carroll* a64 58
3 ch f Auction House(USA) Thicket (Wolfhound (USA))
(19) 374[5] 669[8] 2996[3] 3323[6] 3679[6] 5067[9] 5818[9] 6397[2] 6753[6] 6980[10] 7292[4]

Out Do *Luca Cumani* a80 100
4 ch g Exceed And Excel(AUS) Ludynosa (USA) (Cadeaux Genereux)
(3220) 3840[3] 4472[10] 4983[5]

Outer Space *Richard Hannon Snr* 94
2 b c Acclamation Venoge (IRE) (Green Desert (USA))
(5186) 7011[2] 7207[10]

Outlawed *Ed Walker* a80
2 b c Kyllachy Regent's Park (Green Desert (USA))
8201[2]

Outlaw Torn (IRE) *Richard Guest* a69 66
4 ch g Iffraaj Touch And Love (IRE) (Green Desert (USA))
61[5] 410[8] 478[6] 593[6] 705[10] 903[4] (975) 1271[10] 1462[8] 1788[4] 2273[3] 2753[6] 2889[12] 3728[2] 4052[4] 4109[8] (4763) 4853[8] 4953[4] 5261[5] 5383[3] 5840[2] 6296[6] 6794[10] 6952[3] 7169[7] 7383[7] 7605[3] 7733[3] 7930[4] 8006[9] 8233[8]

Out Of Bounds (USA) *Saeed bin Suroor* a110 110
4 ch c Discreet Cat(USA) Unbridled Elaine (USA) (Unbridled's Song (USA))
153a[2] 659a[10] ◆ 871a[3] (6307) 7206[13]

Out Of The Blocks *Ruth Carr* a32 64
3 b g Firebreak Suzie Fong (Dr Fong (USA))
1206[6] 1764[5] 2318[6] 3082[9] 3629[8] 4113[10]

Outpost (IRE) *Alan Bailey* a94 63
5 ch g Giant's Causeway(USA) Southern Migration (USA) (Kingmambo (USA))
60[4] 1796[9] 3590[8]

Outrageous Request *William Stone* a77 78
7 ch g Rainbow Quest(USA) La Sorrela (IRE) (Cadeaux Genereux)
(8331)

Outset (USA) *Mark Johnston*
3 ch c Street Boss(USA) Now It Begins (USA) (Two Punch (USA))
4118[12]

Outstrip *Charlie Appleby* 116
2 gr c Exceed And Excel(AUS) Asi Siempre (USA) (El Prado (IRE))
(3581) 4876[2] (6390) 7192[3] (7688a)

Ouzinkie (IRE) *A Al Raihe* a39 72
3 b g Kodiac Sleeponit (IRE) (Marju (IRE))
553a[11]

Ovatory *Amanda Perrett* a61 61
3 b g Acclamation Millsini (Rossini (USA))
1660[6] 2051[8] 7781[6] 8019[8] 8152[10]

Overanalyze (USA) *Todd Pletcher* a115
3 b c Dixie Union(USA) Unacloud (USA) (Unaccounted For (USA))
2033a[11] 3127a[7]

Overrider *Alastair Lidderdale* a75 77
3 b g Cockney Rebel(IRE) Fustaan (IRE) (Royal Applause)
533[4] 793[3] 1008[5] 4707[11] 5477[9] 5931[9] 6362[8] 8443[9]

Overrule (USA) *Chris Bealby* a70 67
9 b g Diesis Her Own Way (USA) (Danzig (USA))
430[7] 6130[9] 6783[4] 7951[10]

Overstep (IRE) *Mark Johnston* 75
2 b c Exceed And Excel(AUS) Crossover (Cape Cross (IRE))
3245[15] 3568[5] (3928) 4768[4] 5468[7] 5787[7] 6663[7] 7074[7]

Over The Ocean (USA) *Niels Petersen* a79 91
3 rg c Rockport Harbor(USA) Endless Sea (CAN) (Mt. Livermore (USA))
5326a[5]

Owlam *Mme M Bollack-Badel* a71 78
2 b f Astronomer Royal(USA) October Winds (USA) (Irish River (FR))
5419a[5]

Owner Occupier *Chris Gordon* a13 54
8 ch g Foxhound(USA) Miss Beverley (Beveled (USA))
2875[12]

Oxanueva (FR) *H-A Pantall* 87
2 b f Country Reel(USA) Swandor (USA) (Swain (IRE))
3752a[4] 4651a[3] 5939a[3]

Oxbow (USA) *D Wayne Lukas* a119
3 b c Awesome Again(CAN) Tizamazing (USA) (Cee's Tizzy (USA))
2033a[6] (2473a) 3127a[2]

Oxbow Lake (USA) *Roger Varian* 18
2 bb f Dynaformer(USA) Shelly River (USA) (Irish River (FR))
7277[9]

Oxlip *Richard Hannon Snr* a51 57
2 b f Three Valleys(USA) Age Of Chivalry (IRE) (Invincible Spirit (IRE))
2805[5] 3324[8] 3414[5] 4363[4] (5276) 5610[4] 6111[4]

Oxsana *William Haggas* 94
2 b f Dubawi(IRE) Turning Leaf (IRE) (Last Tycoon)
5797[7] (6534) 6644[2] 7016[4] 7537[2]

Oyster (IRE) *Gary Harrison* 61
2 br f Diamond Green(FR) Lost Icon (IRE) (Intikhab (USA))
3663[5] (4115) 4948[13] 5536[12]

Ozeta (FR) *Niall Madden* a83 90
5 gr f Martaline Ozehy (USA) (Rahy (USA))
1168a[6]

Ozz *Frank Sheridan* a54 67
4 gr f Aussie Rules(USA) Spicey (Mizoram (USA))
1211[6] 1430[8] 5841[4] 6154[6] 6368[7] 6753[5]

Paan (IRE) *A Fabre* 85
3 b c Dalakhani(IRE) Wingspan (USA) (Silver Hawk (USA))
6712a[6]

Pabusar *Jamie Osborne* a91 109
5 b g Oasis Dream Autumn Pearl (Orpen (USA))
150a[9] 464a[10] 746a[11] 2868[15] 3299[3] ◆ 4024[11] 4275[17] 4536[5] 4986[26] 7171[14] 7642[6] 8177[2] 8324[4]

Pacarama *Jason Ward* 42
2 b f Avonbridge Skirt Around (Deploy)
2474[5] 2793[7] 6512[6] 7168[9]

Pacific Heights (IRE) *Brian Ellison* a73 99
4 b g Galileo(IRE) Song To Remember (USA) (Storm Cat (USA))
2041[2] 2405[2] (2705) 3684[3] (4758) (6300) 6838[13] 7014[8]

Pacific Ridge (USA) *Amy Weaver* a76 71
4 bb c Gone West(USA) National Pastime (USA) (Polish Numbers (USA))
434[3]

Pacific Rim (IRE) *M Delzangles* 114
3 b f Singspiel(IRE) Prairie Runner (IRE) (Arazi (USA))
(3614a)

Pacific Trip *Andrew Balding* a40
2 b c Tagula(IRE) Marajuana (Robellino (USA))
5646[10] 6689[10]

Packet Station *Alan McCabe* a19
2 ch f Compton Place Jump Ship (Night Shift (USA))
1924[7] 2856[10]

Packing Whiz (IRE) *C Fownes* 119
5 ch g Trade Fair Swizzle (Efisio)
2066a[3] 8210a[3]

Pack Leader (IRE) *Amanda Perrett* 87
2 b g Hurricane Run(IRE) Bright Enough (Fantastic Light (USA))
4987[12] 5698[2] 6740[2]

Pacquiao (IRE) *John Quinn* a50 38
3 b g Teofilo(IRE) Woodland Chant (USA) (War Chant (USA))
237[5]

Pacquita *Mark Johnston* 50
2 b f Dubawi(IRE) Pryka (ARG) (Southern Halo (USA))
5053[12] 6112[5] 6821[11] 7096[8]

Pactolus (IRE) *Stuart Williams* a44
2 b g Footstepsinthesand Gold Marie (IRE) (Green Desert (USA))
8342[9]

Paddy Burke *Stuart Kittow* 50
3 b g Bertolini(USA) Feathergrass (IRE) (Fasliyev (USA))
3950[5] 4881[7]

Paddyfrommenlo (IRE) *Gary Harrison* a3 84
4 ch g Hurricane Run(IRE) Dolce Dovo (Medicean)
7611[11]

Paddy Partridge *Tim Vaughan* a23 58
7 b g Pivotal Treble Heights (IRE) (Unfuwain (USA))
1080[12]

Paddy's Bay *Kevin Ryan* a52 52
2 b g Sleeping Indian Plausabelle (Royal Applause)
3282[5] 3724[9] 6299[7] 6725[3] 7032[6] 7168[4] 8265[5]

Paddy's Rock (IRE) *Ann Duffield* 57
2 b c Whipper(USA) Hedera (USA) (Woodman (USA))
5145[6] 5482[4] 5826[6]

Paddy's Saltantes (IRE) *J S Moore* a73 65
3 b g Redback Shall We Tell (Intikhab (USA))
1729[6] 3908[7] 4634[7] 6325[6] 7736a[5] 7922[4] 8072[3] 8388[5]

Paddy The Celeb (IRE) *M Halford* a92 96
7 ch g Peintre Celebre(USA) On The Razz (USA) (With Approval (CAN))
3599a[9] 7230a[16] 7723a[14]

Paene Magnus (IRE) *J S Bolger* a106 95
4 ch c Teofilo(IRE) Luminaria (IRE) (Danehill (USA))
363a[8] 462a[15] 1556a[5] (7361a)

Pageant Belle *Roger Charlton* a64
2 ch f Bahamian Bounty Procession (Zafonic (USA))
6107[5] 6607[4]

Pagera (FR) *H-A Pantall* 111
5 ch f Gentlewave(IRE) Panthesilea (FR) (Kendor (FR))
1048a[5] 1420a[7] 2644a[7] 3165a[6] 3615a[7] 5298a[6] 6294a[2]

Pahente *Tony Carroll* a71 58
5 bg g Silver Patriarch(IRE) Miss Tehente (FR) (Tehente (FR))
(132) 779[5] 1097[4]

Paige Flyer *Mick Quinn* a50 52
3 b f Multiplex Captain Margaret (Royal Applause)
321[8] 447[4] 3219[7] 5630[6]

Paintball (IRE) *Charlie Longsdon* a73 61
6 b g Le Vie Dei Colori Camassina (IRE) (Taufan (USA))
2849[5] 3512[4] 4166[14]

Painted Tail (IRE) *Alan Swinbank* a72 75
6 b m Mark Of Esteem(IRE) Bronwen (IRE) (King's Best (USA))
2220[9] 2555[12] 2974[3]

Painters Easel (IRE) *Maria Sandh* 83
5 b g Modigliani(USA) Stands With A Fist (JPN) (Giant's Causeway (USA))
6453a[10]

Paint It Red (IRE) *Richard Guest* a6 41
2 ch f Papal Bull Skerries (IRE) (Dr Fong (USA))
2436[9] 2883[9] 6999[6]

Pairumani Prince (IRE) *Ed Dunlop* a75
3 b c Choisir(AUS) Pairumani Princess (IRE) (Pairumani Star (IRE))
(204) 920[4] 1119[3]

Pakal (GER) *Mick Price* 111
4 b g Lord Of England(GER) Perima (GER) (Kornado)
7702a[5]

Palace Dragon (IRE) *Sir Mark Prescott Bt* a31 63
2 b g Lawman(FR) Mayonga (IRE) (Dr Fong (USA))
6733[10] 7113[6] 7274[5] 7631[5]

Palace Malice (USA) *Todd Pletcher* a122
3 b c Curlin(USA) Palace Rumor (USA) (Royal Anthem (USA))
2033a[12] (3127a) 7715a[6]

Palace Moon *William Knight* a87 110
8 b g Fantastic Light(USA) Palace Street (USA) (Secreto (USA))
2936[5] 3558[25] 3840[12] 4744[27] 5247[5] 5696[4] 7464[10] 7769[8] 8088[7] 8430[2] ◆

Palace Princess (FR) *Ed Dunlop* a61 56
2 ch f Dubawi(IRE) Queen Of Norway (USA) (Woodman (USA))
3958[6] 4702[14] 5352[2] 7609[7]

Palazzo Bianco *Brian Ellison* a94 91
5 b g Shirocco(GER) White Palace (Shirley Heights)
1774[4] 2269[5] (2587) 3099[10] 3560[10]

Pale Mimosa (IRE) *D K Weld* 110
4 b f Singspiel(IRE) Katch Me Katie (Danehill (USA))
(3073a) 6441a[7] 7363[4]

Palio Square (USA) *John Flint* a81 76
6 bb g Harlan's Holiday(USA) Teewee's Hope (CAN) (Defrere (USA))
691[8]

Palkin *William Haggas* 73
3 b f Singspiel(IRE) Winds Of Time (IRE) (Danehill (USA))
3764[5] 4500[8] 5038[8]

Pallasator *Sir Mark Prescott Bt* a96 107
4 b g Motivator Ela Athena (Ezzoud (IRE))
6192[3] ◆ 7193[5] ◆

Palmyra (IRE) *Martin Hill* a63 59
4 ch f Haafhd Tasjeel (USA) (Aljabr (USA))
403[12]

Palo Dancer (FR) *T Roumazeilles*
5 b g Epalo(GER) Petite Emilie (FR) (Mtoto)
6680a[5]

Pal Of The Cat *Brian Gubby* a69 82
3 ch g Choisir(AUS) Evenstorm (USA) (Stephen Got Even (USA))
3400[4] 3866[3] 4487[5] (4989)

Paloma's Prince (IRE) *Jim Boyle* a82 82
4 ch g Nayef(USA) Ma Paloma (FR) (Highest Honor (FR))
(1302) 1884[5] 2849[2] 4208[4] 5008[7] 5823[6] 7396[6] 7840[11]

Palomita (GER) *Frau Nina Bach* 97
5 bb f High Chaparral(IRE) Perima (GER) (Kornado)
3852a[8]

Palus San Marco (IRE) *Graeme McPherson* a81 83
4 b g Holy Roman Emperor(IRE) Kylemore (IRE) (Sadler's Wells (USA))
2418[2]

Panama Cat (USA) *Kevin Ryan* a58 60
3 b f Tale Of The Cat(USA) Oceans Apart (Desert Prince (IRE))
977[3] 1118[4] 1393[10] 1759[8] 1966[6] 2501[8] 4722[9]
Pandar *Robert Cowell* a91 104
4 b g Zamindar(USA) Pagnottella (IRE) (Dansili)
1637[5] ◆ 2257[4] 2936[7] 3373[8] 4493[5] 5257[6] 5998[9] 6699[12]
Pandorica *Bernard Llewellyn* a73 74
5 b f Indesatchel(IRE) Hope Chest (Kris)
1111[12] 1663[3] 1974[4] 2349[2] 2826[2] 3095[2] 3985[5] 5390[7] 6435[6]
Panettone (IRE) *Roger Varian* a63 72
4 b f Montjeu(IRE) Tea Break (Daylami (IRE))
2729[5] 3655[3] 4179[6] (6458) 6782[4] 7132[9] 7611[7]
Panther Patrol (IRE) *Eve Johnson Houghton* a81 78
3 b g Tagula(IRE) Quivala (USA) (Thunder Gulch (USA))
202[3] (438) (730) 1625[11] 2190[12] 5278[2] 5477[2] 5853[3] 6692[5] 7264[3] 8127[8] 8430[8]
Pantoloni *Charlie Appleby*
2 b c Dansili Short Skirt (Diktat)
7655[10]
Pants On Fire (USA) *Kelly Breen* a114
5 bb c Jump Start(USA) Cabo De Noche (USA) (Cape Town (USA))
7689a[7]
Panzi Potter Too *Michael Dods*
2 gr f Winker Watson Toy Top (USA) (Tactical Cat (USA))
3681[8]
Paparima (IRE) *Paul Green*
2 b f Elnadim(USA) Daily Double (FR) (Unfuwain (USA))
2025[8] 3624[10] 4513[7] 5225[6]
Paperetto *Robert Mills* a70 70
5 b g Selkirk(USA) Song Of Hope (Chief Singer)
80[2] 358[9]
Paphos *David Evans* a79 76
6 b g Oasis Dream Tychy (Suave Dancer (USA))
15[2] (199) (229) (340) 700a[8] 839[2] 1746[10] 2395[17] 3015[2] (3429) 3736[5] 3993[3] 4366[P]
Papriformer (USA) *J-C Rouget* a75
3 b c Dynaformer(USA) Louve Royale (IRE) (Peintre Celebre (USA))
(818a)
Paradise Child *Bill Turner* a48 53
2 ch f Compton Place Halfwaytoparadise (Observatory (USA))
2320[4] 2823[6] 3694[6] 4174[5] 4910[5] 5066[3] 7198[9] 7665[12] 8017[7]
Paradise Expected *Mark Gillard* a63 47
10 ch m North Briton Phenomenon (Unfuwain (USA))
1664[14]
Paradise Sea (USA) *Jo Hughes* a24
4 b f Stormy Atlantic(USA) Paradise River (USA) (Irish River (FR))
8036[8] 8298[6] 8449[9]
Paradise Spectre *Mrs K Burke* a77 78
6 b g Firebreak Amber's Bluff (Mind Games)
878[2] 981[2] 1316[4] 2038[2] 2276[10] 3897[4] 4970[9] 5523[4] 5645[3]
Paradise Watch *Luca Cumani* 85
3 b g Royal Applause Ocean View (USA) (Gone West (USA))
2872[3] ◆ 4011[2] (5444) 6126[6]
Paraggi *Mme Pia Brandt* a91 88
4 ch g Iffraaj Topkamp (Pennekamp (USA))
7968a[9]
Paramour *David O'Meara* a69 91
6 b g Selkirk(USA) Embraced (Pursuit Of Love)
1693[4] ◆ 1827[4] 2515[3] 2911[5] 3628[4] 4341[3] 5149[8] 5378[8] 5828[8]
Paramythi (IRE) *Marjorie Fife* a55 67
4 ch g Peintre Celebre(USA) The Spirit Of Pace (IRE) (In The Wings)
1763[14]
Parbold (IRE) *Richard Fahey* 109
2 b c Dandy Man(IRE) Gala Style (IRE) (Elnadim (USA))
(2401) 3422[2] 4876[3] 5765[3]
Parhelion *John Flint* a64 48
6 b g Fantastic Light(USA) Shamaiel (IRE) (Lycius (USA))
15[6]
Parigino (FR) *Nick Gifford* a82 87
5 b g Panis(USA) Loretta Gianni (FR) (Classic Account (USA))
190[4] 352[4]
Parish Hall (IRE) *J S Bolger* a108 112
4 b c Teofilo(IRE) Halla Siamsa (IRE) (Montjeu (IRE))
(1415a) 2105a[3] 6226a[4] (7005a) 7367[9]
Parisian Melody *Mel Brittain* 23
2 b f Paris House Melandre (Lujain (USA))
1839[12]
Parisian Pyramid (IRE) *Richard Fahey* a77 96
7 gr g Verglas(IRE) Sharadja (IRE) (Doyoun)
2425[9] 2781[5] 3392[6] 4149[11] 8306[3]
Parisian Queen *Nikki Evans*
2 b f Paris House Queen Lucia (IRE) (Pursuit Of Love)
7078[9] 7509[9]
Paris Rose *William Haggas* a91 89
3 b f Cape Cross(IRE) Samira Gold (FR) (Gold Away (IRE))
2093[3] ◆ 2989[2] (3542) (3785) 4066[4] 6649[6] (7895)
Paris Snow *F Head* 88
3 b c Montjeu(IRE) Snow Key (USA) (Cozzene (USA))
4815a[5]
Parivash *W Hickst* 98
4 b f Singspiel(IRE) Passata (FR) (Polar Falcon (USA))
(7591a)
Parker Ridge (FR) *Luca Cumani* a67 83
3 ch c Green Tune(USA) Peinture Bleue (USA) (Alydar (USA))
2560[4] 3364[4] ◆

Park Lane *Noel Quinlan* a66 55
7 b g Royal Applause Kazeem (Darshaan)
5065[10] 5245[9] 5672[3]
Park Reel (FR) *E Lellouche* 110
3 b c Country Reel(USA) Adeje Park (IRE) (Night Shift (USA))
1046a[2] 2297a[2] 3386a[2] 4325a[6] 5463a[6]
Parle Moi (IRE) *P Bary* 109
3 b f Montjeu(IRE) Di Moi Oui (Warning)
1869a[4] 2693a[6] 3614a[7]
Parliament Square (IRE) *A P O'Brien* 112
3 b c Acclamation Bold Desire (Cadeaux Genereux)
2676a[9] 3455[16] 3848a[8]
Parlour Games *Charlie Appleby* a103 102
5 ch g Monsun(GER) Petrushka (IRE) (Unfuwain (USA))
3115[6] 3838[7] 5746[12]
Parsons Green *Michael Attwater* a44
4 b f Sakhee(USA) Anastasia Venture (Lion Cavern (USA))
1057[8] 1317[7] 1611[6] 4632[10] 5233[6] 6404[10] 7305[9] 8260[5]
Partner (IRE) *Noel Wilson* a86 96
7 b g Indian Ridge Oregon Trail (USA) (Gone West (USA))
1787[11] 2505[8] 2914[9] 4338[6] 4970[8] 5088[10] 5378[4] 5973[4] 6464[11] 6547[19]
Partner's Gold (IRE) *Alan Berry* a49 52
3 b c Red Clubs(IRE) Unfortunate (Komaite (USA))
3086[6] 3479[9] 4976[7] 5517[7] 5884[5] 6682[4] 7966[9] 8438[4]
Party Doctor *Martin Todhunter* a71 71
6 ch g Dr Fong(USA) Wedding Party (Groom Dancer (USA))
2118[8] 2706[7]
Party Line *Mark Johnston* 98
4 b f Montjeu(IRE) Party (IRE) (Cadeaux Genereux)
1841[6] 2451[11] 2867[12] 3345[5] 3824[13] 4234[5] 4804[3] 5086[3] (5237) 5655[3]
Party Palace *Stuart Howe* a55 57
9 b m Auction House(USA) Lady-Love (Pursuit Of Love)
165[3] 458[7] (515) 671[2] 755[7] 1040[5] 2828[2] 3953[6]
Party Royal *Mark Johnston* a85 93
3 b g Royal Applause Voliere (Zafonic (USA))
2876[5] 3207[2] 3464[2] 3563[2] 3763[6] 4214[9] 4581[3] (5124) 5728[10] 6208[3] 6767[8] (7063) 7696[15] 7793[7]
Party Ruler (IRE) *Tom Dascombe* a75 83
2 b g Holy Roman Emperor(IRE) Calypso Dancer (FR) (Celtic Swing)
1669[13] 2005[3] 2645[3] 4061[4] 4246[2] (5029) 5679[16] 5945[2] 6628[3] 7117[3]
Pasaka Boy *Jonathan Portman* 93
3 ch g Haafhd Shesha Bear (Tobougg (IRE))
1847[4] 2262[3] (2862) 3486[14] 4214[12] 5189[4] 5792[8] (6596)
Pasalsa (FR) *Carmen Bocskai* a52 100
5 b f Kingsalsa(USA) Pasupata (IRE) (Barathea (IRE))
513a[5] 702a[10]
Pas D'Action *Mrs A Malzard* 60
5 ch g Noverre(USA) Bright Vision (Indian Ridge)
(1312a) (2305a) (5327a) 7145a[2]
Pashan Garh *Pat Eddery* a71 80
4 b g Anabaa(USA) Mimisel (Selkirk (USA))
1115[2] 2450[9] 3961[9] 6486[4] 7073[7] 7699[2] 7824[12] 7964[10]
Passage Du Caire (FR) *H-A Pantall* a65 64
3 b f Linngari(IRE) Festive Style (SAF) (Fort Wood (USA))
126a[0]
Passaggio (ITY) *A Cascio* 100
5 b c Exceed And Excel(AUS) Copious (IRE) (Generous (IRE))
7413a[4] 7725a[7]
Passato (GER) *Jo Davis* a52 69
9 b g Lando(GER) Passata (FR) (Polar Falcon (USA))
22[8]
Passing Burg (FR) *L A Urbano-Grajales* 104
2 b f Sageburg(IRE) Passing Lady (FR) (Anabaa (USA))
(7567a) 7939a[3]
Passing By *Richard Hannon Snr* a69
2 b f Raven's Pass(USA) Miss Anabaa (Anabaa (USA))
8175[3] 8332[3]
Passionada *Ed McMahon* a73 70
4 bb f Avonbridge Lark In The Park (IRE) (Grand Lodge (USA))
308[5] 2550[4] 3078[7] 4017[7] 5227[4] 7315[4] (7937) 8135[7]
Passionate Affair (IRE) *Tom Dascombe* a70
2 ch c Broken Vow(USA) Charmgoer (USA) (Nureyev (USA))
7111[2] ◆
Passionate Diva (USA) *Ed Vaughan* a74
3 bb f Street Cry(IRE) Roshani (USA) (Fantastic Light (USA))
211[3] ◆ 377[2]
Passion Planet (IRE) *John C McConnell* a69 68
5 b f Medicean Katch Me Katie (Danehill (USA))
1068[5] 6087[4]
Passion Play *William Knight* a70 78
5 gr f Act One Addicted To Love (Touching Wood (USA))
2360[2] 3110[2] 3587[9]
Passover *Andrew Balding* a59 55
2 b g Passing Glance Floriana (Selkirk (USA))
6197[3] 6689[7] 6975[6]
Pass The Time *Neil Mulholland* a46 57
4 b f Passing Glance Twin Time (Syrtos)
100[8] 226[7] (2301a) 2921[5] 3271[3] 3884[2] 4713[3]
Pastoral *Tony Coyle* 48
4 b f Rail Link Cut Corn (King's Theatre (IRE))
6498[5] 6847[7]
Pastoral Dancer *Richard Rowe* a46 17
4 b g Pastoral Pursuits Dancing Flame (Groom Dancer (USA))
6113[6] 6748[8] 7624[7] 7873[5] 8065[10] 8456[11]

Pastoral Jet *Richard Rowe* a66 42
5 bb c Pastoral Pursuits Genteel (IRE) (Titus Livius (FR))
348[2] 813[4] 1100[3] 1426[10] 8125[7]
Pastoral Player *Hughie Morrison* a67 116
6 b g Pastoral Pursuits Copy-Cat (Lion Cavern (USA))
1919[7] 2258[4] 3101[2] 3831[3] 4276[11] 4856[8] 5794[4] 6392[6] 7014[13] 7208[11] 7540[9]
Pastoral Prey *Ian Semple* 67
3 b g Pastoral Pursuits Bird Of Prey (IRE) (Last Tycoon)
2218[3] 2634[2] 3198[5] 3932[7] 4290[4] 4991[8] 5336[12] 6084[7]
Pastoral Symphony *John Best* a18 1
3 br f Pastoral Pursuits Hucking Harmony (IRE) (Spartacus (IRE))
1875[6]
Pastoral Witness *Clive Brittain* a54 72
2 b f Pastoral Pursuits Witness (Efisio)
1669[9] 3958[7] 4686[2]
Pastorius (GER) *Mario Hofer* 122
4 b c Soldier Hollow Princess Li (GER) (Monsun (GER))
(1870a) 2494a[12] 4082[6]
Pastureyes *Scott Dixon* a26 69
3 ch f Milk It Mick Veils Of Salome (Arkadian Hero (USA))
1122[5] 3626[2] (5220) 6075[9] 7315[13]
Patavium (IRE) *Edwin Tuer* a55 77
10 b g Titus Livius(FR) Arcevia (IRE) (Archway (IRE))
1463[7] 2165[7] 2615[6] 3287[7] 3504[9] 4563[7] 4969[7]
Patavium Prince (IRE) *Jo Crowley* a65 74
10 ch g Titus Livius(FR) Hoyland Common (IRE) (Common Grounds)
665[5] 1194[4] 5232[4] 5607[3] 6039[4]
Pateese (FR) *Philip Hobbs* 79
8 b g Priolo(USA) Flyer (FR) (Highest Honor (FR))
1670[3] 7506[6]
Pategonia *John Gosden* a83
4 b c Oasis Dream Cozy Maria (USA) (Cozzene (USA))
160[2] 434[2] 906[8] (3172) 3693[5]
Patentar (FR) *Marco Botti* 81
2 b c Teofilo(IRE) Poppets Sweetlove (Foxhound (USA))
(7209)
Patently (IRE) *Brian Meehan* a62 72
3 b c Moss Vale(IRE) Trader Secret (IRE) (Montjeu (IRE))
2448[5] 2931[5] 3537[5] 4721[4] 5055[5] 5527[5] 6756[7]
Path Wind (FR) *A Wohler* 104
4 b f Anabaa(USA) Wild Queen (GER) (Sternkoenig (IRE))
6010a[6] 6887a[9] 7558a[2]
Patino Kash *Richard Rowe*
3 ch f Monsieur Bond(IRE) Parri Vii (Damsire Unregistered)
4404[9]
Patisserie *Ann Duffield* a39 62
2 b f Myboycharlie(IRE) Khafayif (USA) (Swain (IRE))
2458[6] 3023[9] 3943[4] 4156[7] 4538[7] 5066[5] 5467[6] 6511[7]
Patrickswell (IRE) *Marcus Callaghan* a75 78
9 gr g Iron Mask(USA) Gladstone Street (IRE) (Waajib)
5775a[11]
Patriotic (IRE) *Chris Dwyer* a87 82
5 b g Pivotal Pescara (IRE) (Common Grounds)
121[3] 400[4] ◆ (614) 995[3] 1233[4] 1538[3] 2018[8] 2431[4] 2761[2] 3785[7] 6236[13]
Patrona Ciana (FR) *David O'Meara* a69 80
3 b f Falco(USA) Bavaria Patrona (FR) (Kahyasi)
5684[10] 6208[7] 6410[3] 6874[8] 7603[6]
Pat's Legacy (USA) *Pat Phelan* a71 69
7 ch g Yankee Gentleman(USA) Sugars For Nanny (USA) (Brocco (USA))
1752[2] ◆ 2514[4] 4755[10] 5762[10] 6315[9] (7092) 7515[4]
Pattaya (ITY) *S Botti* 107
5 b c Philomatheia(USA) Tirsa (Benny The Dip (USA))
1709a[6] 2295a[3] (3881a)
Patterning *Chris Grant* 55
6 b g Pivotal Historian (IRE) (Pennekamp (USA))
3442[9]
Patuca *A Wohler* 74
3 br f Teofilo(IRE) Praia (GER) (Big Shuffle (USA))
7233a[8]
Pavers Bounty *Noel Wilson* 59
2 ch g Bahamian Bounty Pride Of Kinloch (Dr Devious (IRE))
1820[7] 3023[7] 3766[6]
Pavers Star *Noel Wilson* a61 64
4 ch g Pastoral Pursuits Pride Of Kinloch (Dr Devious (IRE))
1388[8] 1465[9] 2343[9] (2632) 3769[6] 4009[15] 4430[2] 4762[7] 5085[12] 6088[8] 6878[6] 7728[11] 8035[9]
Pavlosk (USA) *Sir Michael Stoute* 103
3 b f Arch(USA) Tsar's Pride (Sadler's Wells (USA))
(1666) (2429) 3524[9] 4949[5] ◆ 5725[4] 7196[11]
Pay Freeze (IRE) *Mick Channon* 100
3 b c Baltic King Banco Solo (Distant Relative)
2208[3] 2655[4] ◆
Paynter (USA) *Bob Baffert* a123
4 b c Awesome Again(CAN) Tizso (USA) (Cee's Tizzy (USA))
7715a[7]
Pay The Greek *Noel Quinlan* 38
2 b c Sleeping Indian To Grace (IRE) (Barathea (IRE))
3624[9] 4716[7] 5539[6]
Peace At Last (IRE) *H-A Pantall* a93 110
3 b c Oasis Dream National Day (IRE) (Barathea (IRE))
(2526a) 3876a[11] 5314a[9] 5940a[8] 7047a[17] 7685a[12]
Peace Burg (FR) *J-C Rouget* 111
3 b f Sageburg(IRE) Peace Talk (FR) (Sadler's Wells (USA))
1358a[4] (2906a) 4817a[5] 7047a[6] 7685a[5]

Peaceful Mind (GER) *P Schiergen* 70
3 bb f Sinndar(IRE) Pats Martini (USA) (Red Ransom (USA))
6711a[4]
Peace In Our Time *Anthony Carson* a64 65
4 b g Echo Of Light Deira (USA) (Green Desert (USA))
169[3] 226[2] ◆ 406[4] (522) 1207[7] 1909[2] 2533[2] 2875[3] 3792[2]
Peacemaker (IRE) *Eve Johnson Houghton* a54 69
2 b f High Chaparral(IRE) Sauterne (Rainbow Quest (USA))
3664[6] 5394[9] (6069) 6529[3]
Peace Seeker *Anthony Carson* a94 87
5 b g Oasis Dream Mina (Selkirk (USA))
1067[4] 1430[2] 1985[2] 2286[4] 2724[2] 4494[4] 5489[9] (5750) (6506) 7642[3] 7803[2] 7982[5] 8064[3] 8189[4] 8369[4]
Peachez *Seamus Durack* a82 61
5 ch m Observatory(USA) Streccia (Old Vic)
1670[9] 7739[8] 8004[5] 8139[5] 8331[4] ◆
Peak Royale *Richard Hannon Snr* 78
2 b g Royal Applause Mountain Law (USA) (Mountain Cat (USA))
3536[4] 4021[2] 4439[2] (6014) 6972[4]
Peaks Of Fire (IRE) *Joanne Foster* 17
6 b g High Chaparral(IRE) Crimson Glory (Lycius (USA))
7100[11]
Peak Storm *John O'Shea* a62 79
4 b g Sleeping Indian Jitterbug (IRE) (Marju (IRE))
59[4] 324[3] 436[7] 611[6] 1951[4] (2345) (2920) 3534[3] 3886[5] 3951[5] 4241[5] 4711[2] 5172[4] (6155) (6489) 6720[8]
Pearl (IRE) *Ron Hodges* a33 71
9 b m Daylami(IRE) Briery (IRE) (Salse (USA))
7668[7]
Pearla *Robert Stephens* a67 39
3 gr f Dalakhani(IRE) Propaganda (IRE) (Sadler's Wells (USA))
4500[9] 5434[9] 6783[5]
Pearl Acclaim (IRE) *Robert Cowell* a90 103
3 b c Acclamation With Colour (Rainbow Quest (USA))
1921[8] 3103[5] 5375[5]
Pearl Angel (IRE) *Olly Stevens* 71
3 b f Dark Angel(IRE) Serious Delight (Lomond (USA))
5277[2] ◆ 5647[3] 7073[2]
Pearl Blue (IRE) *Chris Wall* 100
5 b f Exceed And Excel(AUS) Sanfrancullinan (IRE) (Bluebird (USA))
2461[8] 2848[11] 6699[4] 7171[3] 7527[4]
Pearl Bridge *Ralph Beckett* a72 83
3 b g Avonbridge Our Little Secret (IRE) (Rossini (USA))
1299[2] (2672) 3400[6]
Pearl Castle (IRE) *Andrew Balding* 90
3 b g Montjeu(IRE) Ghurra (USA) (War Chant (USA))
1725[5] (5189) 6741[7]
Pearl Earing (IRE) *David Wachman* 82
2 b f Excellent Art Triple Axel (IRE) (Danehill Dancer (IRE))
3868a[6]
Pearl Flute (IRE) *F-H Graffard* 111
3 b c Piccolo Secret Melody (FR) (Inchinor)
2298a[14] (2897a) 3455[6] 3876a[5] 7706a[2]
Pearl Frost *Laura Mongan* a56 5
4 gr g Verglas(IRE) Eternelle (Green Desert (USA))
5123[10] 5586[12]
Pearl Goddess *M Delzangles* 79
3 gr f Dubawi(IRE) Grey Again (Unfuwain (USA))
6713a[10]
Pearl Ice *David Barron* a88 102
5 b g Iffraaj Jezebel (Owington)
2046[12] 2647[6] 3823[6] 5056[2] 5545[11] (6331) 6621[19] 7368[21] 7495[15]
Pearl Nation (USA) *Brian Baugh* a83 84
4 b g Speightstown(USA) Happy Nation (USA) (Lear Fan (USA))
792[5] 1318[5] 1819[8] 2659[8] 8401[2]
Pearl Noir *Scott Dixon* a62 57
3 b g Milk It Mick Cora Pearl (IRE) (Montjeu (IRE))
2962[13] 3533[7] 5788[3] 6138[6] 6944[12] 6965[10] 7759[5] 7886[3] 7958[6] 8043[2] 8233[10] (8320) 8438[2]
Pearl Of Africa (IRE) *Edward Lynam* a99 104
3 b f Jeremy(USA) Kournikova (SAF) (Sportsworld (USA))
6023a[3] 6416a[4]
Pearlofthequarter *Marco Botti* a64 27
2 b f Rock Of Gibraltar(IRE) Run For Lassie (USA) (Fappiano (USA))
6523[7] 7449[9] 7934[4]
Pearl Queen (USA) *Chris Wall* 75
3 bb f Street Sense(USA) Island Queen (USA) (Ogygian (USA))
4125[5] 4813[7] 5588[5] (6074) 6702[3]
Pearl Ransom (IRE) *Lady Herries* a65 67
3 b g Intikhab(USA) Massada (Most Welcome)
7741[2] 8125[4]
Pearl Sea (IRE) *David Brown* 95
3 b f Elusive City(USA) Catch The Sea (IRE) (Barathea (IRE))
1918[2] 2429[3] 3455[17] 4529[4] 5561[4] 5984[10] 6665[2] 6990[5]
Pearl Secret *David Barron* 114
4 ch c Compton Place Our Little Secret (IRE) (Rossini (USA))
3420[3]
Pearlside (FR) *M Delcher Sanchez* 109
3 b f Alhaarth(IRE) Prickly Pearl (IRE) (Lahib (USA))
1869a[3] 3385a[5] 3877a[2]
Pearls Or Passion (FR) *F Rohaut* 101
4 b f Monsun(GER) Pearly Shells (Efisio)
1895a[5] 6010a[4] (7189a)
Pearl Spectre (USA) *Andrew Balding* a80 79
2 ch c Street Cry(IRE) Dark Sky (USA) (Storm Cat (USA))
3238[2] 4640[3] (7119) (8153)

Pearl Spice (IRE) *Tim Pitt* a81 83
3 ch g Dalakhani(IRE) Cinnamon Rose (USA) (Trempolino (USA))
815^5 1053^6 4222^4 (4931) (5102) 5240^4 6237^{10} 6540^4

Pearl Street (USA) *Henry Candy* a68 69
3 b f Street Sense(USA) Pretty Meadow (USA) (Meadowlake (USA))
3237^6 3975^7 4898^7 5534^5 6521^{11} 7622^{13}

Pearl Style (FR) *Olly Stevens* a66 59
3 b g Desert Style(IRE) Back The Winner (IRE) (Entrepreneur)
5517^6 6043^2 6555^5

Pearl War (USA) *John Mackie* a62 65
4 b f War Front(USA) B W Chargit (USA) (Meadowlake (USA))
758^7 5515^8

Pea Shooter *Kevin Ryan* a81 87
4 b g Piccolo Sparkling Eyes (Lujain (USA))
1807^{11} 2031^5 2664^7 3351^8 (3981) 4730^{14} 5183^7 5971^{12} 6159^4 ◆ 6822^{12}

Pegasus Bridge (FR) *K Borgel* a53 60
3 gr c Slickly(FR) Tarkwa (Doyoun)
543a^{11}

Peintre Du Roi (USA) *Natalie Lloyd-Beavis* a19
9 ch g El Prado(IRE) Peinture Bleue (USA) (Alydar (USA))
704^8

Peintre Francais (FR) *F-X De Chevigny* a70 79
3 b g Della Francesca(USA) Peinture Celeste (IRE) (Peintre Celebre (USA))
331a^7

Pelagian (USA) *Dean Ivory* a52
2 b g Henrythenavigator(USA) Japon (Alzao (USA))
3690^5 5635^6 6776^5

Pelerin (IRE) *Marco Botti* a82
2 ch f Shamardal(USA) Fragrancy (IRE) (Singspiel (IRE))
(7295)

Pelicano (AUS) *Tony McEvoy* 105
5 b g Court Of Jewels(NZ) Musk (NZ) (Kaapstad (NZ))
7762a^6

Pelican Rock (IRE) *David Thompson* a42 61
4 b g Amadeus Wolf Darby Shaw (IRE) (Kris)
1788^{13} 2168^{11} 8294^5

Pelmanism *Brian Ellison* a83 76
6 b g Piccolo Card Games (First Trump)
1525^{10} 1800^{11} 2036^3 2280^7 2536^9 2797^2 2884^2 3529^6 3981^8 (4149) (4357) 5070^2 6306^2 6801^{10} 7608^4

Pembroke (IRE) *William Haggas* 50
3 b c Excellent Art Mrs Marsh (Marju (IRE))
1881^{11}

Penang Cinta *Mrs A Malzard* a62 66
10 b g Halling(USA) Penang Pearl (FR) (Bering)
2304a^2

Penang Pegasus *Roger Teal* a56 59
4 ch g Zamindar(USA) Pulau Pinang (IRE) (Dolphin Street (FR))
1909^3 2801^7 3213^{13}

Penang Power *Michael Bell* a50 52
3 b f Manduro(GER) Penang Pearl (FR) (Bering)
1813^8 2455^6 ◆ 3428^8 3859^{12} 5092^4 5650^5 6361^5 7035^3 7667^7

Penara *Philip Hide* a53 38
2 b f Archipenko(USA) Takegawa (Giant's Causeway (USA))
3836^{12} 5435^9 6523^{12} 7755^8 8016^2 8131^6 8332^{14}

Penbryn (USA) *Nick Littmoden* a65 24
6 b g Pivotal Brocatelle (Green Desert (USA))
21^8 205^6 361^9 508^5 626^2 896^9 (1214) 1401^3 1797^7 2773^3 3054^9 3643^2 4155^6 4840^9 7807^7 (8002) 8306^{10} 8456^7

Penchesco (IRE) *Amanda Perrett* a63 33
8 b g Orpen(USA) Francesca (IRE) (Perugino (USA))
6068^{10}

Pencil Hill (IRE) *Tracey Collins* a87 70
8 b g Acclamation Como (USA) (Cozzene (USA))
679a^{11} 3796a^8

Pencombe (FR) *David Simcock* a72 61
3 b g Teofilo(IRE) Barbuda (Rainbow Quest (USA))
211^8 473^5 731^2 5702^5 7033^5 7434^6 7637^6 7877^6

Penderyn *Charles Smith* a20 37
6 b m Sakhee(USA) Brecon (Unfuwain (USA))
597^7 1603^{11} 2785^8 3191^7 6723^{11} 7422^9 8046^8

Pendle Lady (IRE) *Mark Brisbourne* a45 63
4 b f Chineur(FR) Rose Of Battle (Averti (IRE))
3029^{10} 3395^6 4109^{13} 8118^6 8279^9 8371^{12}

Pendo *Alastair Lidderdale* a67 47
2 b g Denounce Abundant (Zafonic (USA))
6589^8 7111^U

Penelopa *M G Mintchev* 102
3 b f Giant's Causeway(USA) Lady Linda (USA) (Torrential (USA))
2910a^8 3604a^3 (5044a) 6448a^{10}

Pengabelot (FR) *C Boutin* a64 82
2 b g Chineur(FR) Sheaks In Love (FR) (Neverneyev (USA))
2433a^5 7568a^9

Penglai Pavilion (USA) *A Fabre* 118
3 bb c Monsun(GER) Maiden Tower (Groom Dancer (USA))
(4815a) 5807a^2 7058a^5

Penhill *James Bethell* 67
2 b g Mount Nelson Serrenia (IRE) (High Chaparral (IRE))
4756^6 5508^5 7175^{12}

Peniaphobia (IRE) *Richard Fahey* 100
2 b c Dandy Man(IRE) Umlani (IRE) (Great Commotion (USA))
(1930) 2370^2 (3439) (4528)

Penina (IRE) *Brian Ellison* a27 68
2 b f Lawman(FR) Poussiere d'Or (IRE) (Grape Tree Road)
1399^8 (1605) 7170^4 7819^{12}

Peninsula *Tobias B P Coles* 59
4 b f Rock Of Gibraltar(IRE) Kayah (Kahyasi)
2093^{11} 2628^{14} 2991^{10}

Penitent *David O'Meara* a100 117
7 b g Kyllachy Pious (Bishop Of Cashel)
1262a^8 2066a^7 2446^7 2840^2 3419^8 5794^6 (6530) 6797^4 7047a^{15} (7698)

Penmaen (IRE) *J E Hammond* 99
3 b f Pivotal Lady Grace (IRE) (Orpen (USA))
7316a^5

Pennine Warrior *Scott Dixon* a71 62
2 b c Lucky Story(USA) Discoed (Distinctly North (USA))
1580^5 5194^2 5577^3 7147^5 (7756)

Penniston Line (IRE) *D Selvaratnam* a55 48
4 b g Holy Roman Emperor(IRE) Willowbridge (IRE) (Entrepreneur)
7683a^6

Penny Drops *William Haggas* 87
2 b f Invincible Spirit(IRE) Penny Cross (Efisio)
7218^3 7657^2 7818^2

Penny Garcia *Tim Easterby* 85
3 b f Indesatchel(IRE) Katie Boo (IRE) (Namid)
1806^{10} 2408^7 3104^5 (3396) 3803^4 4265^2 4725^3 5510^5 5886^4 6564^7

Penny Pursuits *Alan Berry* 57
2 b f Pastoral Pursuits Sattelight (Fraam)
5558^7 6160^4 6718^7 6915^3

Penny Rose *Mark Johnston* 86
3 b f Danehill Dancer(IRE) Love Everlasting (Pursuit Of Love)
1250^6 5169^3 5496^3 6188^3 6533^4 6976^8

Penny's Boy *Sylvester Kirk* a70 71
2 ch c Firebreak Sunderland Echo (IRE) (Tagula (IRE))
4937^4 5399^6 (6013) 6640^4 6825^5 7300^6 7892^3

Penny Serenade (IRE) *Edward Lynam* a57 70
3 b f Lawman(FR) Michikabu (IRE) (Grand Lodge (USA))
8012a^7

Penny Sixpence (FR) *John Gosden* a61 37
2 bb f Kheleyf(USA) Zerky (USA) (Kingmambo (USA))
4716^6 7435^5 7978^3

Penny's Picnic (IRE) *D Guillemin* 112
3 b c Kheleyf(USA) Zerky (USA) (Kingmambo (USA))
1357a^3 2298a^{18}

Penny Stock (IRE) *Mark Johnston* 51
3 b f Dansili Beta (Selkirk (USA))
5919^3 6289^7 6611^7

Pensax Lad (IRE) *Ronald Harris* a75 70
2 gr c Verglas(IRE) Betelgeuse (Kalaglow)
3132^3 3413^7 4781^2 5186^5 (5543) 6376^4 7147^4 7837^2 (8228) 8364^4

Pepito Grillo *L A Urbano-Grajales* a96 94
5 b g Kheleyf(USA) Dena (Deploy)
5465a^6

Perci French *David O'Meara* a23 35
3 b g Tiger Hill(IRE) Annabelle Ja (FR) (Singspiel (IRE))
5715^7 5989^8 6806^5

Percybelle *William Knight* a61 62
2 ch f Sir Percy Chelsea (USA) (Miswaki (USA))
5716^9 7780^4 8085^3

Percy's Gal *Karen Tutty* 72
2 ch f Sir Percy Galette (Caerleon (USA))
5988^6 6754^2 7419^2 7817^4

Percys Princess *Ed Vaughan* 26
2 b f Sir Percy Enford Princess (Pivotal)
4491^{15}

Percythepinto (IRE) *George Baker* a65 59
4 b g Tiger Hill(IRE) Tullawadgeen (IRE) (Sinndar (IRE))
120^7 5622^7 6261^9 7109^7 7458^{12} 7639^{10}

Pereira *David Simcock* a65 74
3 b f Tiger Hill(IRE) Manoeuvre (IRE) (Galileo (IRE))
564^4 925^3 1089^3 (7278)

Perennial *Philip Kirby* a91 101
4 ch g Motivator Arum Lily (USA) (Woodman (USA))
1766^5 2451^{10} 3959^6 5706^{12} 6217^2 (6984) 7975^3

Perfect Alchemy (IRE) *Ralph Beckett* a71 69
2 b f Clodovil(IRE) Desert Alchemy (IRE) (Green Desert (USA))
5061^3 5435^2 (6107)

Perfect Blossom *Alan Berry* a58 77
6 b m One Cool Cat(USA) Perfect Peach (Lycius (USA))
3562^8 3892^5 4507^6 4580^3 5027^7 5561^{10} 6159^7 6309^4 6848^6 6920^3 7420^{13} 7959^7

Perfect Calm (USA) *Julie Camacho* a49 71
3 b f Discreet Cat(USA) Rima (USA) (Jade Hunter (USA))
1711^3 2979^6 4240^5 6601^5 7258^{10}

Perfect Ch'I (IRE) *Paul Fitzsimons* a71 34
6 b m Choisir(AUS) Agouti (Pennekamp (USA))
980^2 1426^6 1717^9 2134^{11} 2578^8

Perfect Cracker *Clive Cox* a81 82
5 ch g Dubai Destination(USA) Perfect Story (IRE) (Desert Story (IRE))
792^4 1092^7 1422^3 2417^3 (2826) 3492^4 3917^3 4194^3 7970^{11} ◆ 8179^2

Perfect Delight *Ralph Beckett* a80 73
4 b f Dubai Destination(USA) Perfect Spirit (IRE) (Invincible Spirit (IRE))
1884^6 2619^6 3427^4 4882^4 5587^4 6405^4 7611^5 8182^3

Perfect Haven *Clive Cox* a73 77
3 gr f Singspiel(IRE) Night Haven (Night Shift (USA))
(1640) 2449^8 3179^4 4485^7 4957^7 5493^4 6106^7 6556^9 8019^4 (8432)

Perfect Heart *Roger Varian* a77 90
4 gr g Dalakhani(IRE) Maid To Perfection (Sadler's Wells (USA))
6498^2 6992^6 (7338)

Perfect Mission *Andrew Balding* a83 78
5 b g Bertolini(USA) Sharp Secret (IRE) (College Chapel)
344^6 822^6 1096^3 1318^4 1514^4 (5404) 5607^2 7306^6 8127^{13}

Perfect Mood (IRE) *W Hickst* 79
2 b f High Chaparral(IRE) Pillars Of Society (IRE) (Caerleon (USA))
7406a^{10}

Perfect Muse *Clive Cox* a54 64
3 b f Oasis Dream Perfect Echo (Lycius (USA))
123^2 5444^5 6145^2 7634^2 ◆

Perfect Outlook *Charlie Longsdon* a49 53
5 b f Doyen(IRE) Cautiously (USA) (Distant View (USA))
2073^2 3037^7 3314^4 3919^8

Perfect Pastime *Jim Boyle* a76 70
5 ch g Pastoral Pursuits Puritanical (IRE) (Desert King (IRE))
1160^7 1814^{12} 2255^{24} 2725^{10} 3172^6 3404^4 4210^7 4637^4 5398^9 6259^4 6459^7 7086^7 7262^5 7862^6 (8073) 8151^4 8456^6

Perfect Pasture *Michael Easterby* a105 97
3 b g Pastoral Pursuits Word Perfect (Diktat)
1522^9 3730^3 4114^3 4544^5 (4992) (6728) (6948) (7029) ◆ (7851) ◆

Perfect Persuasion *William Haggas* a75
2 b f Myboycharlie(IRE) Just Dreams (Salse (USA))
8083^2 ◆ (8451)

Perfect Pose (IRE) *Michael Dods* 56
3 b f Amadeus Wolf Interpose (Indian Ridge)
3398^3 4049^7

Perfect Pursuit *Clive Cox* a68 70
2 b f Pastoral Pursuits Perfect Cover (IRE) (Royal Applause)
6423^3 ◆ 7294^6 8083^3 8326^5

Perfect Queen (FR) *F Head* a93 100
3 b f Mount Nelson Chic Retreat (USA) (Elusive Quality (USA))
6484a^4 7705a^4

Perfect Shot (IRE) *Frank Sheridan* a61 94
7 b g High Chaparral(IRE) Zoom Lens (IRE) (Caerleon (USA))
12^4 469^5 515^7 1080^2 1189^4

Perfect Son *C Zeitz* a90 100
6 ch h Sabiango(GER) Pacific Blue (GER) (Bluebird (USA))
4601a^4

Perfect Spell *Andrew Balding* 69
3 ch c Singspiel(IRE) Flamjica (USA) (Real Quiet (USA))
2605^8 3491^4 4223^8 4961^5 5954^6

Perfect Summer (IRE) *Lady Cecil* a65 75
3 b f High Chaparral(IRE) Power Of Future (GER) (Definite Article)
4151^6 5100^4 5942^7 6788^2 7342^2 ◆

Perfect Timber (CAN) *Roger L Attfield* 105
4 bb c Perfect Soul(IRE) Timber Ice (USA) (Woodman (USA))
7563a^{10}

Perfect Venture *Clive Cox* a74 69
3 b f Bahamian Bounty Perfect Cover (IRE) (Royal Applause)
3988^6 (4410) ◆ 4636^2 5300^3 6341^8 7263^5 7897^5 8330^4 (8456)

Perfect Words (IRE) *Marjorie Fife* a61 65
3 ch g Thousand Words Zilayah (USA) (Zilzal (USA))
1762^6 2076^6 3025^3 3198^3 3594^4 4162^2 4891^6 5470^8 5887^3 6464^4 6633^3 7343^7

Perforce *Lucy Wadham* a43 10
4 b g Sir Percy Enforce (USA) (Kalanisi (IRE))
5100^{10}

Performance (IRE) *D Grilli* a70 76
3 b c Danehill Dancer(IRE) Ahdaab (USA) (Rahy (USA))
543a^5

Perhaps (IRE) *A P O'Brien* 104
2 b f Galileo(IRE) Anna Karenina (IRE) (Green Desert (USA))
4462a^2 5318a^2 6024a^5

Perivale (USA) *Mark Johnston* a57 47
3 b f Street Cry(IRE) Windsharp (USA) (Lear Fan (USA))
3764^8 7311^4 8036^3 8227^9 8388^8

Perlachy *Ronald Harris* a72 72
9 b g Kyllachy Perfect Dream (Emperor Jones (USA))
95^5 453^6 558^6 760^{12} 946^5 1087^9 1665^{14} 5982^8 6808^9

Permeate *Charles Hills* a73 70
3 b f Rail Link Quota (Rainbow Quest (USA))
1371^3 1611^2

Permission Slip (IRE) *A Fabre* 97
3 b f Authorized(IRE) Najmati (Green Desert (USA))
6962a^3

Permsiri (IRE) *Malcolm Saunders* a15 26
2 b f Ad Valorem(USA) Swiss Roll (IRE) (Entrepreneur)
5891^{12} 6152^9

Pernica *Lucy Wadham* a68 78
3 b f Sir Percy Nicola Bella (IRE) (Sadler's Wells (USA))
2952^5 3764^4 (4454) 5015^3 5743^7

Perpetual Ambition *Paul D'Arcy* a63 68
3 b g Avonbridge Never Enough (GER) (Monsun (GER))
1931^4 3739^3 5098^6 5204^9 6109^{10} 6612^7

Perrecalla (FR) *J Van Handenhove* a85 90
3 ch f Anabaa Blue Pomposa (IRE) (Barathea (IRE))
3708a^2 8441a^6

Perrydot (IRE) *Jo Crowley* a50
2 b f Footstepsinthesand Titoli Di Coda (IRE) (Bertolini (USA))
8326^8

Persepolis (IRE) *Brett Johnson* a92 91
3 gr g Dansili La Persiana (Daylami (IRE))
1727^2 2457^5 3276^2 ◆ (4684) 5824^6 8071^7 8218^3

Perseverent Pete (USA) *Christine Dunnett* a46 53
3 bb g Johannesburg(USA) Indian Halloween (USA) (Sunday Break (JPN))
2099^5 2508^8 2762^9 5618^3 6804^4 7322^9

Pershing *Brian Meehan* 64
2 rg c Mount Nelson La Gandilie (FR) (Highest Honor (FR))
6184^9 6829^9

Persian Bolt (USA) *Eve Johnson Houghton* a66 72
2 b f US Ranger(USA) Silent Cat (USA) (Rahy (USA))
6140^5 ◆ 6594^5 7296^6

Persian Herald *Neil King* a54 69
5 gr g Proclamation(IRE) Persian Fortune (Forzando)
361^{10}

Persian Marvel (IRE) *Jim Boyle* a51 53
3 b g Captain Marvelous(IRE) Jezyah (USA) (Chief's Crown (USA))
207^7 2791^5 3178^{12} 3405^{14}

Persian Patriot *William Jarvis* a72 68
3 ch f Bahamian Bounty Persian Lass (IRE) (Grand Lodge (USA))
1986^7 2456^3 3116^5 3537^8 5932^4 7108^5 7786^6 8072^2 8343^2

Persian Peril *Alan Swinbank* a75 91
9 br g Erhaab(USA) Brush Away (Ahonoora)
2040^{12} 2552^7 5055^4 5831^{11} 6302^9 7342^{14}

Personable *Charlie Appleby* 86
3 b g Cape Cross(IRE) Likeable (Dalakhani (IRE))
6566^2 7131^{12}

Personal Opinion *Charlie Appleby* a76 76
2 ch c New Approach(IRE) Sentimental Value (USA) (Diesis)
6829^5 7332^2 (7936)

Personal Touch *Richard Fahey* 85
4 ch g Pivotal Validate (Alhaarth (IRE))
(1115) ◆ 2214^5 3300^9 4983^{24} 6586^{13} 6988^9 7374^2 7699^5 7949^9

Perspicacity *J R Jenkins* 24
2 ch f Sir Percy Sakhacity (Sakhee (USA))
6500^8

Pertemps Networks *Michael Easterby* a82 67
9 b g Golden Snake(USA) Society Girl (Shavian)
4995^7

Pertuis (IRE) *Micky Hammond* a81 72
7 gr g Verglas(IRE) Lady Killeen (IRE) (Marju (IRE))
1464^{12} 1936^3 2615^5 3195^6 (3504) 3930^4 4543^5 4853^6 5144^3 5466^{10} 6775^2 7346^4

Petale Noir *Jonathan Portman*
2 b f Mount Nelson Apple Blossom (IRE) (Danehill Dancer (IRE))
6141^8 7310^9

Petaluma *Mick Channon* a41 79
4 b f Teofilo(IRE) Poppo's Song (CAN) (Polish Navy (USA))
1670^6 2069^5 6173^{10}

Petella *George Moore* 68
7 b m Tamure(IRE) Miss Petronella (Petoski)
1789^{12} 2242^6 2990^5 (3363) 3595^2 4563^6 4759^2 4969^3 5560^8 5863^2 6565^7 6942^9

Petergate *Brian Rothwell* 62
2 b g Alhaarth(IRE) Shamayel (Pivotal)
2883^{13} 3350^9 4781^6 5424^6 5829^7 6755^9 7175^7 7494^7

Peter Island (FR) *John Gallagher* a62 77
10 b g Dansili Catania (USA) (Aloma's Ruler (USA))
232^5 535^{10}

Peterkin (IRE) *Mark Johnston* a85 85
2 b c Invincible Spirit(IRE) Alizes (NZ) (Rory's Jester (AUS))
1360^7 (1534) 2933^3 3424^{22} 7545^4 ◆ 7771^{10}

Peter Mac (IRE) *Richard Fahey* 92
2 b c Kodiac Open Verse (USA) (Black Minnaloushe (USA))
(3217) (4006) ◆

Petersboden *Michael Blanshard* a55 52
4 b g Iceman Bowden Rose (Dashing Blade)
98^4 512^4 820^2 973^3 1175^3 1520^7 1877^{10} 3213^5 3473^9 3688^5 4365^2 5127^2 5615^6 5980^7 (6097) 6491^3 7922^3 8448^4

Peter's Friend *Michael Herrington* a75 60
4 b g Gentleman's Deal(IRE) Giffoine (Timeless Times (USA))
994^5 1522^3 1777^3 2514^3 3642^3 4509^7 5098^4 5677^3 6218^3 (6963) 7952^5

Pether's Moon (IRE) *Richard Hannon Snr* a112 106
3 b c Dylan Thomas(IRE) Softly Tread (IRE) (Tirol)
(1713) 2054^2 ◆ 3486^{11} ◆ 4301^2 (4984) ◆ 6348^3 (7768)

Petit Arc En Ciel *E J O'Neill* a55 71
2 br c Footstepsinthesand Billie Jean (Bertolini (USA))
5848a^{10}

Petit Chevalier (FR) *W Mongil* a103 111
5 bb g High Chaparral(IRE) Pivoline (FR) (Pivotal)
4042a^2 (5298a) 5778a^3 7049a^3 7831a^2

Petite Cadeaux (IRE) *Tom Tate*
2 ch f Bahamian Bounty Travel On (USA) (Joyeux Danseur (USA))
6298^{11}

Petite Georgia (IRE) *George Baker* a62 55
3 b f Camacho Petite Maxine (Sharpo)
31^5 482^3 848^2 977^5 1695^2

Petite Madame (IRE) *Ann Duffield*
2 b f Champs Elysees Seeking The Fun (USA) (Alhaarth (IRE))
7061^7

Petits Potins (IRE) *Rod Collet* 94
2 b f Verglas(IRE) Babacora (IRE) (Indian Ridge)
4651a^7 7084a^2 7940a^7

Petra *Michael Appleby* a43
3 b f Arkadian Hero(USA) Moody Style (IRE) (Desert Style (IRE))
102^4 332^7

Petrarchan *Milton Bradley* a46 57
5 ch g Pivotal Summer Sonnet (Baillamont (USA))
559^9 617^8

Petrify *Luca Cumani* a63 61
3 b g Rock Of Gibraltar(IRE) Frigid (Indian Ridge)
2760^{13} 3731^5 4182^4 4629^3 5492^6 6400^9 7383^4

Petrol *David O'Meara* a62 67
4 ch g Danehill Dancer(IRE) Pongee (Barathea (IRE))
(852) ◆ 927[8] 1146[6] 1572[2] 1789[4] 2986[2] 3625[7] 3947[2]

Pettochside *Stuart Williams* a78 70
4 b g Refuse To Bend(IRE) Clear Impression (IRE) (Danehill (USA))
2255[13] 2918[8] (6928) ◆ 7264[7]

Phaenomena (IRE) *Lady Cecil* a89 97
3 ch f Galileo(IRE) Caumshinaun (IRE) (Indian Ridge)
2804[5] 3237[8] 4257[5] (5038) 5944[3] (6649) 7650[7]

Phangio (USA) *P J Rothwell* a69 72
4 ch g Invasor(ARG) Muneera (USA) (Green Dancer (USA))
5021a[4]

Phantom Brew (NZ) *Colin Little* 94
6 b g Elusive City(USA) Pina Colada (NZ) (Dahar (USA))
7417a[9]

Phantom Ranch *Alastair Lidderdale* a48 61
4 b g Act One Highbrook (USA) (Alphabatim (USA))
2545[11] 3473[11] 4835[10]

Pharoh Jake *John Bridger* a64 58
5 ch g Piccolo Rose Amber (Double Trigger (IRE))
77[3] 156[5] 354[10] 750[3] 902[3] 981[7] 1196[2] 1324[4] 1467[8] 3052[5] 3325[5] 3529[4] 3816[4] 4635[4] 5060[3] 5522[5] (6017) 6732[5] 7086[4] 8023[2] 8152[7] (8457)

Phase Shift *Brian Ellison* a53 64
5 b f Iceman Silent Waters (Polish Precedent (USA))
2435[10]

Phils Wish (IRE) *John C McConnell* a60 44
4 b g Dark Angel(IRE) Red Titian (IRE) (Titus Livius (FR))
409[2] 4155[5] 4840[5] 7351[5]

Phiz (GER) *John Gosden* a93 104
3 b f Galileo(IRE) Peace Time (GER) (Surumu (GER))
2392[5] 3957[6] (5233) 6329[2] 6764[7] 7650[3] 7891a[4]

Phoenix Angel *Derek Shaw* a19
2 b g Footstepsinthesand Ruthie (Pursuit Of Love)
3436[9] 4142[7] 5591[9]

Phoenix Clubs (IRE) *Paul Midgley* a56 79
4 b f Red Clubs(IRE) Hollow Haze (USA) (Woodman (USA))
885[9] 1278[3] 1807[5] 2268[2] 2410[4] 3069[4] 3505[3] 4017[6] 4852[4] 5148[2] 5422[6]

Phoenix Flight (IRE) *James Evans* a84 41
8 b g Hawk Wing(USA) Firecrest (IRE) (Darshaan)
224[6] 654[4] 1188[4] 1454[5] 6490[8]

Phoenix Joy *Simon Griffiths*
5 b f Presidium Miss Ceylon (Brief Truce (USA))
2504[10]

Phosphorescence (IRE) *Lady Cecil* a65 65
3 b g Sakhee(USA) Eccentricity (USA) (Kingmambo (USA))
2384[13] (8260)

Photography (IRE) *Hugo Palmer* 75
2 b g Haatef(USA) Sierva (GER) (Darshaan)
4414[7] 4997[4] 5307[5] (6395) 6763[6] 7129[4] 7471[6]

Phuket (SPA) *A Remolina Diaz* 74
4 ch c Multazem(USA) New Vert (SPA) (Vert Amande (FR))
5465a[7]

Piana (FR) *A Bonin* 104
3 gr f Doyen(IRE) Gaudera (GER) (Big Shuffle (USA))
2381a[6] 4792a[6] 6031a[2] 6962a[11]

Pianoro (FR) *F Pedrono* a71 68
4 b g Intikhab(USA) Perilla (GER) (Dulcero (USA))
5042a[16]

Piazon *Michael Bell* 73
2 br g Striking Ambition Colonel's Daughter (Colonel Collins (USA))
2048[7] (2502) 3267[2]

Piazza San Pietro *Zoe Davison* a77 95
7 ch g Compton Place Rainbow Spectrum (FR) (Spectrum (IRE))
1517[5] 2097[8] 3220[2] 3270[5] 4235[9] 4389[5] 4863[4] 5219[5] 5489[5] 5722[5] 7743[9]

Picabo (IRE) *Henry Candy* a72 98
5 b f Elusive City(USA) Gi La High (Rich Charlie)
2270[5] 2848[2] 3367[3] 3840[7]

Picador (IRE) *Carmen Bocskai* 37
2 b c Shirocco(GER) Rahada (GER) (Peintre Celebre (USA))
5039a[5]

Picalily *Brendan Powell* a89 84
4 b f Piccolo Kaylianni (Kalanisi (IRE))
3406[8] 3953[5] (5196) 5868[P] (5966) 6499[2]

Picanight *Eve Johnson Houghton* a32 31
2 b f Piccolo Midnight Fling (Groom Dancer (USA))
4379[10] 4828[8] 7393[6]

Picansort *Peter Crate* a91 70
6 b g Piccolo Running Glimpse (IRE) (Runnett)
186[2] (232) (360) 583[5] (627) 780[2] (1517) 1902[4] 2561[4] 5701[2] 5956[10] 6850[3] (8021) 8155[6]

Piccolo Express *Brian Baugh* a64 60
7 b g Piccolo Ashfield (Zilzal (USA))
96[4] 437[4] 617[6] 5072[9] 6354[2] 6307[4] 6610[4] 7353[7] 7807[3] 8163[6] 8278[7]

Piccolo Mondo *Philip Hide* a68 61
7 b g Piccolo Oriel Girl (Beveled (USA))
1498[2] 1873[2] 2228[4] 2845[5] 3687[2] 4070[6] 5135[5] 5594[5]

Piceno (IRE) *Scott Dixon* a83 81
5 b g Camacho Ascoli (Skyliner)
511[2] 644[7] 715[3] 832[3] 889[5] 1113[7] 1334[4] 1442[4] 1723[8] 5398[10] 5580[5] 5899[2] (5947) 6306[7] 6963[9] 7076[6] 7595[2] (7699) 7824[10] 7898[4] 8095[11] 8269[10] 8350[2] 8408[9]

Pick A Little *Michael Blake* a81 80
5 b g Piccolo Little Caroline (IRE) (Great Commotion (USA))
(981) 1346[9] 2128[5] 2255[20] 2825[9] 3315[10] 4303[11] 4837[11] 5673[9] 6135[11] 6928[12] 7729[10] (8412)

Picks Pinta *Jo Hughes* 66
2 b g Piccolo Past 'N' Present (Cadeaux Genereux)
1108[7] (3659) 6628[8]

Picture Dealer *Lydia Pearce* a99 96
4 b g Royal Applause Tychy (Suave Dancer (USA))
2255[16] 2871[2] 3093[3] 3733[2] (4494) (4730) ◆ 4983[11] 5851[4] 6621[4] 8064[2]

Piddie's Power *Kevin Frost* a85 85
6 ch m Starcraft(NZ) Telori (Muhtarram (USA))
4067[4] 4671[5] 5437[5] 7080[6] 7949[4] 8053[7] 8431[10]

Pied A Terre (AUS) *Saeed bin Suroor* a84 105
5 b g Ad Valorem(USA) Masonette (AUS) (Grand Lodge (USA))
465a[7] ◆ 838a[8] 4062[13] 5518[2] 6396[4] 7014[15]

Pieman's Girl *Anthony Carson* a57 65
2 b f Henrythenavigator(USA) Aromatherapy (Oasis Dream)
2744[3] 5797[11] 8084[6] 8396[3]

Piers Gaveston (IRE) *George Baker* 69
4 b g Amadeus Wolf Dancing Tempo (Vettori (IRE))
3106[8] 3997[4] 4714[3]

Pigeon Pie *Mark Johnston* 68
2 b f Bahamian Bounty Pixie Ring (Pivotal)
(1565) 2877[7] 3890[4] 6047[4] 6663[3]

Pilates (IRE) *Mark Johnston* a64 79
3 b f Shamardal(USA) Caribbean Escape (Pivotal)
4200[4] 4535[4] 4991[2] 5373[3] (5668) (6039) 6337[8] 6720[10] 7486[6]

Pilgrims Rest (IRE) *Richard Hannon Snr* a88 95
4 ch g Rock Of Gibraltar(IRE) Holly Blue (Bluebird (USA))
945[11] 2193[2] 2839[8] 4028[8]

Pillow (IRE) *J P Murtagh* 81
2 b f Bushranger(IRE) Silk Feather (USA) (Silver Hawk (USA))
5773a[6]

Pilote (IRE) *A Fabre* 115
3 ch c Pivotal Legerete (USA) (Rahy (USA))
1562a[4] (3007a) 3911a[2] 4573a[2] 5462a[2] 6618a[4]

Pim Street (USA) *David O'Meara* a68 63
3 b f Street Sense(USA) Crown Of Jewels (USA) (Half A Year (USA))
5478[6] (7930) 8006[12] 8372[8]

Pindar (GER) *Neil Mulholland* a64 57
9 b g Tertullian(USA) Pierrette (GER) (Local Suitor (USA))
4604[7]

Pingit *Alan McCabe* a35
3 b f Multiplex Sharayif (IRE) (Green Desert (USA))
2979[12] 3641[8]

Pink And Black (IRE) *William Muir* a65
2 b f Yeats(IRE) Raysiza (IRE) (Alzao (USA))
7763[4]

Pink Cadillac (IRE) *Ben Haslam* a36 43
3 b f Clodovil(IRE) Green Life (Green Desert (USA))
1447[3] 1764[10] 2501[15] 7806[10]

Pink Lips *J R Jenkins* a22 64
5 b f Noverre(USA) Primrose Queen (Lear Fan (USA))
2134[2] (2747) 3788[2] 4689[2]

Pink Mirage (IRE) *Jonathan Portman* 58
2 gr f Verglas(IRE) Deira (USA) (Green Desert (USA))
3986[9] 4589[5] 5061[5]

Pink Mischief *Harry Dunlop* a53 53
3 gr f Holy Roman Emperor(IRE) Feather (USA) (Unbridled's Song (USA))
1897[4] 3013[8] 4170[6] 4424[8] 5404[8] 6103[2] 6522[8] 7331[6] 7637[7]

Pinotage *Peter Niven* a67 65
5 br g Danbird(AUS) Keen Melody (USA) (Sharpen Up)
7100[10]

Pintrada *James Bethell* 81
5 b g Tiger Hill(IRE) Ballymore Celebre (IRE) (Peintre Celebre (USA))
2369[12] ◆ 2671[7] 3442[2] 3804[5] 4301[9]

Pintura *Kevin Ryan* a39 110
6 ch g Efisio Picolette (Piccolo)
1691[7] 2258[6] (2667) 3347[8] 4869a[5] 5019a[2] 5681[16] 6624[6] 7540[12]

Pinturicchio (IRE) *E Lellouche* 114
5 b g Holy Roman Emperor(IRE) Precious Pearl (IRE) (Peintre Celebre (USA))
(3913a) 5808a[4] 7047a[2] 7685a[4]

Pinzolo *Charlie Appleby* 97
2 b c Monsun(GER) Pongee (Barathea (IRE))
(5490) (6593) ◆ 7528[10]

Pipe Dream *Brian Meehan* 62
2 ch g Piccolo Bold Love (Bold Edge)
6590[4] 7270[9]

Pipers Note *Richard Whitaker* 96
3 ch g Piccolo Madam Valentine (Primo Valentino (IRE))
2614[7] 3066[2] (3478) (4117)

Pipers Piping (IRE) *John Butler* a76 67
7 b g Noverre(USA) Monarchy (IRE) (Common Grounds)
98[11] 348[8] 523[10]

Piping Rock *Richard Hannon Snr* 107
2 ch c Dubawi(IRE) Anna Oleanda (IRE) (Old Vic)
(4795) (6955) (7534) ◆

Pippy *Tom Dascombe* a67 63
3 b g Exceed And Excel(AUS) Gandini (Night Shift (USA))
1400[3] 1829[7] 2308[6] 3016[2] 3178[7] 4160[11] 4666[3] 6803[9]

Piracicaba (IRE) *A De Royer-Dupre* a92 95
4 b f Dansili Montaria (GER) (Dashing Blade)
2969a[10]

Pira Palace (IRE) *William Knight* a81 78
3 b f Acclamation Takrice (Cadeaux Genereux)
2983[10]

Pirate Chest (IRE) *Patrick Holmes* a57 67
5 b g Montjeu(IRE) Cash Run (USA) (Seeking The Gold (USA))
23[6] 166[5] 455[8] 704[3] 1279[9]

Pirate Du Bresil (FR) *J Rossi*
3 b c Librettist(USA) Trip To Fame (FR) (Lordmare (FR))
5805a[8]

Pirika (IRE) *A Fabre* 110
5 b f Monsun(GER) Paita (Intikhab (USA))
1658a[3] (2184a) ◆ 2908a[4] 3615a[6] 5297a[5] 6449a[3] 7058a[15]

Piscean (USA) *Tom Keddy* a107 93
8 bb g Stravinsky(USA) Navasha (USA) (Woodman (USA))
78[3] 407[2] (480) 584[2] 776[7] 1542[9] 2013[10] 2254[23] (2621) 2937[7] 3367[6] 4983[20] 5533[10] 6078[7] 6648[10] 7540[10]

Pisco Sour (USA) *Saeed bin Suroor* a98 91
5 bb g Lemon Drop Kid(USA) Lynnwood Chase (USA) (Horse Chestnut (SAF))
362a[3] 555a[12] 833a[6]

Piste *Tina Jackson* a68 60
7 b m Falbrav(IRE) Arctic Char (Polar Falcon (USA))
4009[16] 4430[9] 4761[7] 5085[5] 5470[9] 6761[13] 6879[5] 6945[7] 7101[11]

Pistol (IRE) *Philip Hobbs* a77 82
4 b g High Chaparral(IRE) Alinea (USA) (Kingmambo (USA))
7660[7]

Pitchoun (IRE) *Mark Johnston* 90
3 ch g Street Cry(IRE) Altesse Imperiale (IRE) (Rock Of Gibraltar (IRE))
(3674) ◆ 4249[2] 4501[4] 4984[9] 5944[9] 6434[4] 7072[6]

Piton *Mark Johnston* a57 47
2 b g Archipenko(USA) Scandalette (Niniski (USA))
7271[5] 7494[14] 7936[5]

Pitt Rivers *Linda Perratt* 58
4 br g Vital Equine(IRE) Silca Boo (Efisio)
2038[4] 5333[9] 5705[9] 6547[17] 6903[9] 7148[4]

Pivotal Movement *Richard Hannon Snr* a85 85
3 ch c Pivotal Selinka (Selkirk (USA))
2738[4] 3472[9] (5280) 5928[14] 6642[7] ◆ 6959[2] 7264[2]

Pivotal Prospect *Tracy Waggott* a13 72
5 b f Nayef(USA) Buon Amici (Pivotal)
1278[8] 1540[8] 2409[15] 2542[5] 5138[10] 5830[7] 6603[6] 7343[6] 7598[6]

Pivotal Silence *Amanda Perrett* a78 78
3 ch f Vita Rosa(JPN) Tara Moon (Pivotal)
(1469) 1885[3] 2432[7] 3243[2] (3497) 4770[3] 5445[7]

Pivotman *Michael Easterby* 91
5 ch g Pivotal Grandalea (Grand Lodge (USA))
1442[8] ◆ 3081[6] ◆ 3729[7] 4994[6] (5144) 5383[2] 6906[4] 7778[8]

Pixie Cut (IRE) *Alistair Whillans* a76 70
3 b f Chineur(FR) Fantastic Cee (IRE) (Noverre (USA))
(3488) 3900[6] 4122[3] 4753[2] 5692a[5] (5913a) 7573a[8] 8184[2]

Pixie Hollow (IRE) *Kevin Prendergast* 80
2 gr f Verglas(IRE) High Fun (FR) (Kahyasi)
5773a[9]

Pixilated *Gay Kelleway* a69 84
3 b g Phoenix Reach(IRE) Chocolada (Namid)
75[4] 2135[3] 2623[2] (2965) 3677[4] (4413) 4989[12] 6506[4]

Pixmiester *James Unett* a9 16
2 b g Piccolo Rare Cross (IRE) (Cape Cross (IRE))
1792[4] 2712[9]

Place In My Heart *Clive Cox* a85 106
4 ch f Compton Place Lonely Heart (Midyan (USA))
(1662) 2300a[3] 3263a[4] 4260[5] 5806a[9] 6639[13]

Placidia (IRE) *David Lanigan* a72 75
2 b f Sea The Stars(IRE) Palmeraie (USA) (Lear Fan (USA))
4702[17] 5394[8] 6141[2] 6691[4]

Plaine Monceau (FR) *D Henderson* a46 88
3 gr f One Cool Cat(USA) Luroya (FR) (Daylami (IRE))
5462a[9]

Planchette *Jane Chapple-Hyam* a34 50
3 b f Mount Nelson Cruinn A Bhord (Inchinor)
2762[13] 3219[3] 4170[8] 4688[6] 6103[5] 6518[12] 7907[8]

Planete Bleue (IRE) *F-H Graffard* 97
3 b f Dansili Poughkeepsie (IRE) (Sadler's Wells (USA))
2905a[4]

Planetex (IRE) *John Quinn* 79
4 b g Majestic Missile(IRE) Xena (IRE) (Mull Of Kintyre (USA))
1692[14] 2239[9] (3475) 4072[2] 5049[6] 5148[4] 5841[5] 6287[8] 6547[8] (6604)

Planetoid (IRE) *Jim Best* a75 92
5 b g Galileo(IRE) Palmeraie (USA) (Lear Fan (USA))
7739[6] 7970[8]

Planet Purple (AUS) *Kerry Parker* 96
7 ch g Universal Prince(AUS) Jewel Of Atlantis (AUS) (Sea Road (AUS))
7760a[4] 7938a[8]

Plantagenet (SPA) *Niels Petersen* a105 105
6 ch h Trade Fair Crafty Buzz (USA) (Crafty Prospector (USA))
151a[4] 463a[8] 742a[2] (871a) 956a[6] (2146a) 3188a[9] 4095a[6] 5809a[11]

Planteur (IRE) *Marco Botti* a110 119
6 b h Danehill Dancer(IRE) Plante Rare (IRE) (Giant's Causeway (USA))
(777) 1260a[3] 2094a[2] (5760) 7049a[12] 7715a[11]

Plastiki *T J O'Mara* 71
4 b g Oasis Dream Dayrose (Daylami (IRE))
5021a[15]

Platinum (IRE) *Philip Kirby* a71 100
6 b g Azamour(IRE) Dazzling Park (IRE) (Warning)
476[7] 672[5] 798[4] 1464[2] (2633) 3284[5] 4372[2] (5086) (5640) (6192) 7193[28]

Platinum Pearl *Peter Chapple-Hyam* a55
2 b f Shamardal(USA) Gimasha (Cadeaux Genereux)
8332[7] ◆

Platinum Proof (USA) *David O'Meara* a64 36
3 bb g Smart Strike(CAN) Keeper Hill (USA) (Deputy Minister (CAN))
2017[10] 2874[10] 6657[8] 6964[8] 7351[4] 7543[7] 7666[2] 7770[7] 7907[7]

Plauseabella *Stuart Kittow* 36
2 b f Royal Applause Ellablue (Bahamian Bounty)
7218[9]

Playbill *Sir Michael Stoute* a73 80
3 b f Medicean Set The Scene (IRE) (Sadler's Wells (USA))
1955[2] ◆ 2713[3] 4023[3] 4506[3] (5281) 5589[2] 6531[6]

Playful Promises (IRE) *W P Browne* 49
3 ch f Elnadim(USA) Playful (Piccolo)
4050[9] 5989[9]

Play It Loud (USA) *Michelle Nihei* 96
3 bb c Unbridled's Song(USA) Bsharpsonata (USA) (Pulpit (USA))
3360a[2]

Play Street *Jonathan Portman* a60 82
4 ch f Tobougg(IRE) Zoena (Emarati (USA))
1663[7] 1974[2] 2349[4] (3273) 4678[2] 6433[4]

Play The Blues (IRE) *Dominic Ffrench Davis* a52 59
6 gr m Refuse To Bend(IRE) Paldouna (IRE) (Kaldoun (FR))
117[4] 8082[6] 8393[8]

Play Tiger (FR) *Peter Hiatt* a49 49
4 b g Tiger Hill(IRE) Shagadellic (USA) (Devil's Bag (USA))
3402[7] 3819[4] 4152[7] 4521[9]

Playtothewhistle *Bryan Smart* a42
2 b g Sakhee's Secret Prima Ballerina (Pivotal)
8346[3]

Pleasant Bay (IRE) *David Wachman* a79 94
2 b c Bushranger(IRE) Alexander Confranc (IRE) (Magical Wonder (USA))
5771a[4]

Please Let Me Go *Julie Camacho* 58
2 ch f Sleeping Indian Elhida (IRE) (Mujtahid (USA))
2793[6] 3391[9] 3826[4] ◆ 4990[5] 6285[2] 6755[4]

Pleasure Bent *Luca Cumani* a87 78
3 b c Dansili Nitya (FR) (Indian Ridge)
(2093) (3241) 4416[4] 6694[3] 7438[4]

Pleats (FR) *Matthieu Palussiere* a48 39
2 b f Turtle Bowl(IRE) Sky Spark (USA) (Septieme Ciel (USA))
5213a[12] 6059a[13]

Pleine Forme (USA) *Marco Botti* a96 99
5 b f Grand Slam(USA) Why Worry (FR) (Cadeaux Genereux)
2264[5] 3102[8]

Plenum (GER) *David Lanigan* a77 72
3 b g Shamardal(USA) Prima Luce (IRE) (Galileo (IRE))
2324[6] 2549[2] ◆ 2874[2] 6080[8]

Plough Boy (IRE) *Willie Musson* a60 12
2 b c Dandy Man(IRE) Ribald (Alhaarth (IRE))
4958[12] 5243[7] 6131[4] 7878[2] 8262[3]

Plover *Sir Michael Stoute* a89 87
3 b f Oasis Dream Short Dance (USA) (Hennessy (USA))
2447[2] ◆ (2979) 4078[4] 4766[5] 6188[6]

Plucky Dip *John Ryan* a55 46
2 b g Nayef(USA) Plucky (Kyllachy)
2382[5] 2562[4] 3574[9] 7471[8]

Plunder *Richard Ford* a80 72
3 ch g Zamindar(USA) Reaching Ahead (USA) (Mizzen Mast (USA))
1714[7] 2374a[17] 2737[4] 5828[4] 6296[5] (6657) 6877[5]

Plus Fours (USA) *Michael Appleby* a68 19
4 rg g Mizzen Mast(USA) Quick To Please (USA) (Danzig (USA))
2171[8] 3429[7]

Plutocracy (IRE) *David Lanigan* a68 99
3 b c Dansili Private Life (FR) (Bering)
(2325) ◆ (2500) (5953) ◆ 6380[2]

Pobs Trophy *Richard Guest* a51 54
6 b g Umistim Admonish (Warning)
63[3] 226[11] 455[9]

Poco De Oro (FR) *M Gentile*
3 b c Nombre Premier Poca De Gracia (IRE) (Royal Applause)
331a[0]

Poco Piccolo *Deborah Sanderson* 37
2 b g Piccolo Angel Maid (Forzando)
4046[13] 5083[8] 6175[8] 7096[9]

Poetic Belle *Shaun Harris* a57 48
3 b f Byron Sahariri (IRE) (Red Ransom (USA))
1710[6] 1906[3] 3494[4] 5198[13] 5617[4] 5869[7] 6074[9] 6362[3] 6918[10] 7353[2] 7465[6] 7806[7] 7886[8] 8055[10] 8361[6]

Poetic Choice *Nick Littmoden* a76 60
2 b f Byron Ennobling (Mark Of Esteem (IRE))
5282[14] 6607[6] 6939[2] 7309[7] (7788) 7879[2]

Poetic Dancer *Clive Cox* a91 96
4 ch f Byron Crozon (Peintre Celebre (USA))
2310[2] 2858[8] 4534[6] 5533[6] 6143[4] 6988[11]

Poetic Lord *Sylvester Kirk* a81 80
4 b g Byron Jumairah Sun (IRE) (Scenic)
1514[2] (1780) 2101[6] 2573[2] 3019[12] 3693[10] 4124[5] 4771[8] 4831[5] 5479[8] 6459[2] 7130[11] 7306[5] 7462[8] 7970[10]

Poetic Power (IRE) *Ian Williams* a70 79
4 b g Dylan Thomas(IRE) Chalice Wells (Sadler's Wells (USA))
83[8]

Poetic Verse *Rod Millman* a76 82
3 gr f Byron Nina Fontenail (FR) (Kaldounevees (FR))
103[6] 336[4] (527) 634[2] 803[4] (1053) (1425) (1729) ◆ 2602[4] 3698[3] 4234[6] 4914[6] 6136[4] 7118[3]

Poetry Writer *Michael Blanshard* a61 61
4 ch g Byron Away To Me (Exit To Nowhere (USA))
(1781) 2954[6] 3399[7] 3919[10] 6103[6] 6985[12]

Poet's Prospect (IRE) *Marco Botti* a82
3 b f Byron Shbakni (USA) (Mr Prospector (USA))
148[4] (332) (793)

Point Blank (GER) *Mario Hofer* 105
5 b g Royal Dragon(USA) Princess Li (GER) (Monsun (GER))
1564a[3] 1870a[8] 2202a[5] 6451a[3] 7053a[8]

Point North (IRE) *John Balding* a80 81
6 b g Danehill Dancer(IRE) Briolette (IRE) (Sadler's Wells (USA))
206[7] 454[3] 645[4] 987[8] (1525) 1798[5] (2780) 3811[10] 4837[2] 6653[5] 7776[6] 7888[7] 8321[8]

Point Of Control *Michael Bell* a63 63
3 b f Pivotal Finlaggan (Be My Chief (USA))
1876[5] 2713[7] 3820[10] 5037[4] 5411[3] 6015[4] 6964[4] 7331[4] 7847[3]

Point Of Entry (USA) *Claude McGaughey III* 124
5 b c Dynaformer(USA) Matlacha Pass (USA) (Seeking The Gold (USA))
7712a[4]

Poisson D'Or *Rae Guest* a72 84
4 b f Cape Cross(IRE) Lille Hammer (Sadler's Wells (USA))
1922[9] 2450[3] (3259) 4181[2] 4766[7] 5437[10]

Poitin *Harry Dunlop* a92 66
3 b f Kheleyf(USA) Port Providence (Red Ransom (USA))
2049[7] 2951[6] 3576[3] 4410[3] 5393[4] (6113) (7325) 7924[3] 8386[8]

Poker Gold (FR) *Heather Main* a68
2 b c Gold Away(IRE) Becquarette (FR) (Nombre Premier)
8066[5] (8213)

Poker Player (USA) *Wayne Catalano* a100 93
2 rg c Harlan's Holiday(USA) Revel In The Win (USA) (Red Bullet (USA))
7688a[8]

Polar Annie *Tim Vaughan* a59 74
8 b m Fraam Willisa (Polar Falcon (USA))
2792[5]

Polar Chief *Kristin Stubbs* 89
3 b g Motivator Polar Storm (IRE) (Law Society (USA))
1293[10] 3571[2] 4890[8] (5784) 6550[14] 7063[P]

Polar Express *Jonathan Portman* a47 55
2 ch g Sakhee's Secret Polar Dawn (Polar Falcon (USA))
4414[11] 5151[4] 5790[11] 6979[10] 7878[10] 8325[6]

Polar Eyes *Peter Chapple-Hyam* 48
2 b f Dubawi(IRE) Everlasting Love (Pursuit Of Love)
4484[9]

Polar Forest *Richard Guest* a64 63
3 br g Kyllachy Woodbeck (Terimon)
324[6] 538[5] 2274[11] 3629[2] 4076[2] 4140[2] 4449[6] 4806[2] 5178[3] 5500[8] 6049[3] 6297[2] 7066[6] 7378[2] 7666[4]

Polaris (USA) *Richard Budge* a45
3 b c Henrythenavigator(USA) Rushen Heat (USA) (Unusual Heat (USA))
786a[6]

Polarity *Gerry Enright* a59
7 b m Hamas(IRE) Snowy Mantle (Siberian Express (USA))
157[3] 417[6] 635[10] 983[5] 1175[12]

Polarix *H-A Pantall* a88 96
7 gr h Linamix(FR) Freezing (USA) (Bering)
3913a[5] 5735a[5]

Polar Kite (IRE) *Paul Morgan* a86 87
5 b g Marju(IRE) Irina (IRE) (Polar Falcon (USA))
25[6] (206) (370) 629[2] (1459) 2214[2] 2618[13] 3754[4] 4438[2] 5474[6] 8068[6] 8217[4]

Polar Legend (FR) *L A Urbano-Grajales* a67
3 b f Falco(USA) Legendary (FR) (Fabulous Dancer (USA))
5119a[8]

Polar Venture *William Haggas* a80 67
4 b g Invincible Spirit(IRE) Sharplaw Venture (Polar Falcon (USA))
(187) ◆ (372) ◆ 881[2] 2663[5] 3351[15] 5636[7]

Polish Crown *Mark Johnston* a74 72
3 b f Royal Applause Czarna Roza (Polish Precedent (USA))
(1122) 1315[4] 1616[3] 1978[4] 2331[2] 2635[3] 2916[3] 3082[2] 3279[10] 4111[7]

Polish Knight (NZ) *Michael, Wayne & John Hawkes* 109
5 ch g Encosta De Lago(AUS) Polish Princess (Polish Precedent (USA))
7483a[8]

Polish Rider *Richard Hannon Snr* a46 45
3 b g Dutch Art Lady Darayna (Polish Precedent (USA))
3176[11] 4381[8] 4684[3] 5275[4] 5615[12] 6038[5] 6321[7] 7092[10]

Polish Vulcano (GER) *H J Groschel* 106
5 ch c Lomitas Polska Infa (GER) (Trempolino (USA))
(5778a) 6987a[8] 7831a[3]

Polish World (USA) *Paul Midgley* a34 91
9 b g Danzig(USA) Welcometotheworld (USA) (Woodman (USA))
4007[10] 5138[11] 5564[3] 5987[5] 6720[4] 6969[11] 7344[13]

Politbureau *Michael Easterby* a47 57
6 b g Red Ransom(USA) Tereshkova (USA) (Mr Prospector (USA))
1790[3] 2332[2] 2720[9] 3504[2] 3652[6] 4853[2] 5420[9] 6907[5] 7376[5]

Political Courage (USA) *Michael Matz* 101
4 b g Elusive Quality(USA) Ladina (USA) (Wild Again (USA))
608a[4]

Pollyana (IRE) *D Prod'Homme* 112
4 b f Whipper(USA) Shamah (Unfuwain (USA))
2559a[2] 2897a[3] (7047a)

Polly's Love (IRE) *Clive Cox* a52 70
3 b f Antonius Pius(USA) Kotdiji (Mtoto)
2390[6] 2935[9] 3861[8]

Polo (GER) *D Smaga* a78 91
3 ch g Sholokhov(IRE) Poule D'Essai (GER) (Dashing Blade)
(1756a) 2557a[5]

Polski Max *Richard Fahey* a86 102
3 b g Kyllachy Quadrophenia (College Chapel)
(1444) (2039) 2400[4] 3348[16] 4986[22] 5545[9] 6621[15] 7171[13]

Polvere D'Oro *Michael Mullineaux* a27 28
3 b g Revoque(IRE) Dusty Anne (IRE) (Dushyantor (USA))
5069[11] 6366[10] 6824[8]

Polydamos *Tony Carroll* a54 49
4 b g Nayef(USA) Spotlight (Dr Fong (USA))
6103[7] 6492[4] 6933[7] 8149[4] 8390[2]

Pomodoro *John Gosden* a65
3 ch g Pivotal Foodbroker Fancy (IRE) (Halling (USA))
6134[7] 6566[8]

Pomology (USA) *John Gosden* a91 108
3 bb f Arch(USA) Sharp Apple (USA) (Diesis)
(3417) (4384) (5315a) ◆

Pompeia *Ralph Beckett* a83 84
3 ch f Singspiel(IRE) Caesarea (GER) (Generous (IRE))
1725[3] ◆ 2546[2] 3177[5] 3834[2] 6559[3] 7105[4] 7659[6]

Poncho *Mark Rimell* a50
4 b f Cape Cross(IRE) Pixie Ring (Pivotal)
6783[2] 7379[4] 8047[6] 8149[8]

Ponte Di Rosa *Simon Hodgson* a35 66
5 b f Avonbridge Ridgewood Ruby (IRE) (Indian Ridge)
5846[9] 6736[10]

Ponthieu (FR) *Matthieu Palussiere* 67
2 b c Palace Episode(USA) Piste Sauvage (IRE) (Brief Truce (USA))
5362a[7]

Pont Marie (FR) *F Chappet* a89 91
3 b c Great Journey(JPN) Cite Fleurie (IRE) (Mark Of Esteem (IRE))
1419a[9]

Pont Neuilly (FR) *Y De Nicolay* a100 100
3 ch c Medecis Panzella (FR) (Kahyasi)
3128a[6] 4043a[4] 5120a[5]

Ponty Acclaim (IRE) *Tim Easterby* 104
4 b f Acclamation Leopard Creek (Weldnaas (USA))
2396[10] 2669[14] 3299[2] ◆ 3562[7] 4263[12]

Ponty Pursuit *Tim Easterby*
2 b f Pastoral Pursuits Spring Clean (FR) (Danehill (USA))
5053[13]

Poole Harbour (IRE) *Richard Hannon Snr* a95 104
4 b g Elusive City(USA) Free Lance (IRE) (Grand Lodge (USA))
1726[2] 2046[3] 2444[2] 2937[3] 3558[15] 3840[4]

Pool House *Andrew Balding* a76 74
2 b c Sakhee's Secret Gitane (FR) (Grand Lodge (USA))
5186[3] 5744[3] 6333[2] 6931[2] 7893[2]

Pool Play (CAN) *Mark Casse* a112 104
8 bb h Silver Deputy(CAN) Zuri Ridge (USA) (Cox's Ridge (USA))
7687a[7]

Poor Duke (IRE) *Jamie Osborne* a65 76
3 b g Bachelor Duke(USA) Graze On Too (IRE) (Rainbow Quest (USA))
1900[2] 2324[2] 2549[8] (3901) 4593[8] 5491[6] 5978[3] 6735[6] 7629[9] 8454[8]

Pop Art (IRE) *Charles O'Brien* 94
3 b f Excellent Art Doctrine (Barathea (IRE))
7051a[7] 7388a[6] 7719a[3]

Poppanella (IRE) *Lawrence Mullaney*
4 b f Namid Bobanlyn (IRE) (Dance Of Life (USA))
2172[10]

Poppapp (SWE) *Jaana Alvesparr*
2 b f Academy Award(IRE) Safe Trip (Hector Protector (USA))
6452a[12]

Popping Candy *Roger Varian* a62
2 br f Oasis Dream Blessing (Dubai Millennium)
7645[8]

Poppy Bond *Alan Bailey* a62 63
3 b f Misu Bond(IRE) Matilda Peace (Namaqualand (USA))
1073[5] 1458[12] 3779[5] 4290[7] 5054[7] 5869[2] 6803[2] (7351) 7667[2] (7963) 8116[5] 8184[4]

Poppy Gregg *Dr Jeremy Naylor* a42 45
8 b m Tamure(IRE) Opalette (Sharrood (USA))
12[6] 458[9]

Porcini *Philip McBride* a82 89
4 b f Azamour(IRE) Portal (Hernando (FR))
1615[4] 2598[3] 3118[5] (3587) (4643) 5520[5] 6646[18]

Porgy *Brian Ellison* a93 79
8 b g Dansili Light Ballet (Sadler's Wells (USA))
948[2] 1273[5] 1733[2] 2654[9] 3685[14]

Porsenna (IRE) *S Botti* 100
3 b c Dylan Thomas(IRE) Miss Mariduff (USA) (Hussonet (USA))
1865a[4] 7413a[2] 7725a[3]

Porsh Herrik *John Quinn* 55
2 ch c Sakhee's Secret Clansinge (Clantime)
2117[4] 2436[8] 3189[5] 4156[2] 4583[5]

Port Alfred *Charlie Appleby* a86 87
3 b g Oasis Dream Cape Merino (Clantime)
3837[2] 4200[2] (4627) 5303[4] 5585[2] 6189[9] 7112[4]

Port Charlotte *Hughie Morrison* a72 72
4 b f Oasis Dream Maria Theresa (Primo Dominie)
338[14]

Porte Dauphine (IRE) *C Boutin* a50 53
3 b f Hurricane Run(IRE) Lady From Limerick (IRE) (Rainbows For Life (CAN))
3129a[13]

Porteous *Mick Channon* a80 64
2 b f Sixties Icon Fading Away (Fraam)
3049[8] 3298[7] 3414[2] 4061[6] (4387) 4948[15] 6233[5] (7986) (8024) 8203[2] 8261[2]

Porthos Du Vallon *Keith Dalgleish* 69
2 b g Jeremy(USA) Princess Caraboo (IRE) (Alzao (USA))
3282[6] 5262[2] 6299[3] 6873[2] 7237[6]

Port Lairge *Jonjo O'Neill* a65 20
3 b g Pastoral Pursuits Stylish Clare (IRE) (Desert Style (IRE))
7108[7] 7625[4] 7787[5]

Portland River (FR) *A De Royer-Dupre* a58 98
3 b f Stormy River(FR) Porza (FR) (Septieme Ciel (USA))
6711a[3]

Portland Stone *O Auchere* a69 30
9 b g Lear Fan(USA) Porta Marzia (CHI) (Roy (USA))
5464a[6]

Portmonarch (IRE) *David Lanigan* a87 87
3 b g Galileo(IRE) Egyptian Queen (USA) (Storm Cat (USA))
1584[6] 1959[3] 2564[2] (3908) 4681[3] 6108[3] 6693[8]

Portrait *Sir Mark Prescott Bt* a81 86
3 ch f Peintre Celebre(USA) Annalina (USA) (Cozzene (USA))
(3918) (4196) (4656) 5448[3] 5888[5] 6693[6]

Portrush Storm *Ray Peacock* a44 61
8 ch m Observatory(USA) Overcast (IRE) (Caerleon (USA))
3098[7] 3622[3] 4064[9] 6075[7] 6606[6] 6995[9]

Pose (IRE) *Roger Ingram* a60 65
6 b m Acclamation Lyca Ballerina (Marju (IRE))
120[12]

Posh Bounty *Bill Turner* 29
2 ch f Bahamian Bounty Fission (Efisio)
1360[6] 2068[7]

Posh Boy (IRE) *Chris Wall* a69 65
3 b g Duke Of Marmalade(IRE) Sauvage (FR) (Sri Pekan (USA))
2094[4] 3254[7] 4755[8] (5234) 6521[12] 7091[12] (7434)

Positive Parenting (IRE) *Stuart Williams* a30 34
3 b f Malibu Moon(USA) Real Cat (USA) (Storm Cat (USA))
103[9] 685[9] 1332[4]

Postal Order *James Eustace* 49
2 b f Medicean Postage Stampe (Singspiel (IRE))
7466[7]

Poste Restante *David Simcock* a56
3 b f Halling(USA) Postage Stampe (Singspiel (IRE))
1828[13] 6361[10]

Postmaster *Tim Vaughan* a32 53
11 b g Dansili Post Modern (USA) (Nureyev (USA))
458[10]

Postponed (IRE) *Luca Cumani* 96
2 b c Dubawi(IRE) Ever Rigg (Dubai Destination (USA))
4256[5] (5405) ◆ 7017[2]

Postscript (IRE) *David Simcock* a87 97
5 ch g Pivotal Persian Secret (FR) (Persian Heights)
1745[5] 2210[10] 2592[12] 3088[3] 3411[3] (3570) 4080[10] (4242) 5268[4] 6199[14] 6650[9] 6834[4]

Potentate (IRE) *Richard Hannon Snr* a81
2 b c Acclamation Wish List (IRE) (Mujadil (USA))
7120[2] 7328[2]

Potentiale (IRE) *Alastair Lidderdale* a75 69
9 ch g Singspiel(IRE) No Frills (IRE) (Darshaan)
2798[3] 2968[6]

Pound Piece (IRE) *J S Moore* a85 83
2 b g Ad Valorem(USA) Peps (IRE) (Val Royal (FR))
2436[5] 2805[2] (3009) 7300[2] 7567a[3] (7933) 8203[5]

Poupee Flash (USA) *P Bary* 103
4 b f Elusive Quality(USA) Modesty Blaise (USA) (A.P. Indy (USA))
3387a[3] 4104a[5] 4817a[11]

Pour La Victoire (IRE) *Tony Carroll* a56 60
3 b g Antonius Pius(USA) Lady Lucia (IRE) (Royal Applause)
1966[4] 2330[2] 4885[5] (5170) 5604[2] 5816[3] 6260[2] 6985[3] 7034[5]

Powder Hound *Andrew Balding* a89 95
3 b g Lucarno(USA) Balnaha (Lomond (USA))
(1727) 2086[2] ◆ 6533[5] (6823)

Powerful Pierre *Ollie Pears* a80 67
6 ch g Compton Place Alzianah (Alzao (USA))
214[7] 559[8] 750[4] 1079[7] (1397) 2836[4] 3068[14] 3192[5] 3649[8] 4456[5] 4836[2] 5354[4] 6980[3] (7347) (7512) (7801) 7896[2] 8224[7] (8401)

Powerful Presence (IRE) *David O'Meara* a91 97
7 ch g Refuse To Bend(IRE) Miss A Note (USA) (Miswaki (USA))
1688[5] 1992[4] 2665[6] (2882) (3088) 3527[25] 3823[12] 4235[7] 5238[4] 5544[10] 6164[6] 6608[9] 7176[7]

Powerful Wind (IRE) *Ronald Harris* a90 81
4 ch g Titus Livius(FR) Queen Of Fools (IRE) (Xaar)
2268[9] 2561[5] (3042) 3371[11] 3796a[3] 4364[5] 5669[8] 8021[3] (8319) 8439[2]

Power Of Good News (FR) *Kevin Ryan*
2 b f Kyllachy Big Day Today (FR) (Linamix (FR))
4723[10]

Power Up *Mark Johnston* a73 66
2 b f Rail Link Melpomene (Peintre Celebre (USA))
4925[3] 5330[6] 5785[6] 6520[4] 6897[4] 7110[2] (8312)

Poyle Thomas *Ralph Beckett* a81 87
4 b g Rail Link Lost In Lucca (Inchinor)
2605[5] (3402) 4301[5] (4832) (5475) 6192[10] 7193[11]

Poyle Todream *Roy Brotherton* a57 52
5 b g Oasis Dream Lost In Lucca (Inchinor)
440[12] 733[9] 915[3] 1215[5] 1356[4] 1665[16]

Poyle Vinnie *George Margarson* a71 67
3 b g Piccolo Poyle Dee Dee (Oasis Dream)
7073[4] 7459[2] 7802[3] (7969) 8384[4] ◆

Practising *Ralph Beckett* 74
2 b f Rail Link Beautiful Lady (IRE) (Peintre Celebre (USA))
4026[2] ◆ 4668[2]

Prairie Prince (IRE) *Gay Kelleway* a52 31
3 b g High Chaparral(IRE) Palatine Dancer (IRE) (Namid)
5233[5] 6406[7] 6657[6] 7035[6]

Prairie Prize *David Elsworth* 66
2 b c High Chaparral(IRE) Premier Prize (Selkirk (USA))
5244[8] 5718[9] 6762[13]

Prairie Ranger *Andrew Balding* 97
3 b g Montjeu(IRE) No Frills (IRE) (Darshaan)
1826[2] (2416) 4279[4] 5258[4]

Prairie Sunset (FR) *S Wattel* a75 74
3 b f Silvano(GER) Prairie Scilla (GER) (Dashing Blade)
5913a[3] 7736a[16]

Pravda Street *Brian Ellison* a79 77
8 ch g Soviet Star(USA) Sari (Faustus (USA))
1460[7] 1693[8] 2042[2] 2496[2] 2673[5] 3349[3] (4153) 7369[6] 7611[10] 7948[2] (8187) (8294)

Precariously Good *David Barron* 20
2 b f Oasis Dream Danceabout (Shareef Dancer (USA))
4963[7]

Precedence (NZ) *Bart & James Cummings* 110
8 b g Zabeel(NZ) Kowtow (USA) (Shadeed (USA))
(7827a)

Precious Stone (IRE) *David Wachman* a93 89
4 b f Galileo(IRE) Anna Karenina (IRE) (Green Desert (USA))
2678a[6] 5688a[10]

Precision Five *Jeremy Gask* a74 76
4 b f Proclamation(IRE) Sashay (Bishop Of Cashel)
(158) 330[4] 3676[4] (4411) 5002[2] (5667) 5980[3] 6398[4] (6898) 7447[6] 7970[7] 8179[9]

Precision Strike *Richard Guest* a66 63
3 b g Multiplex Dockside Strike (Docksider (USA))
55[6] 103[3] 212[4] 336[5] (411) ◆ (507) 2274[4] 3653[7] 4401[3] 4688[7] 5107[4] 5433[4] 5990[6] (6361) 6787[5] 7543[6] 7778[6] 7881[4]

Preempt *P Bary* 81
3 b c Dansili Perfect Hand (Barathea (IRE))
3454a[4] 6446a[10]

Premio Loco (USA) *Chris Wall* a115 117
9 ch g Prized(USA) Crazee Mental (Magic Ring (IRE))
1034[5] 1639[6] 3101[7] 3458[2] 4276[10] (5007) 5739[4] 6797[3] 7196[13]

Premium *Charles Hills* a72 86
3 b f Dansili Arum Lily (USA) (Woodman (USA))
(994) 2148[6] ◆ 3990[6] 7659[11]

Premium Pressure (USA) *David Barron* 74
2 bb c War Front(USA) Judy's Magic (USA) (Wavering Monarch (USA))
7209[3]

Presburg (IRE) *Joseph Tuite* a89 86
4 b g Balmont(USA) Eschasse (USA) (Zilzal (USA))
112[2] 329[4] 585[9] 1585[6] (2532) 3022[3] 3293[6] 5168[4] 5723[10] 6596[2] 7028[8] 7431[5] 7739[3] (7976) 8150[4] 8327[4]

Present Day *Clive Cox* a11 58
4 gr f Cadeaux Genereux Crackle (Anshan)
1948[5] 3252[7] 5434[4] 6492[3]

Presidente *Ed Walker* 57
2 b c Myboycharlie(IRE) Madam President (Royal Applause)
5344[7] 6334[7]

President Lincoln (USA) *Declan Carroll* a51 83
5 bb g First Samurai(USA) Preach (USA) (Mr Prospector (USA))
1363[2] 1485[7] 5974[9] 6236[11] 6701[7] 7076[9]

Press Room (USA) *Saeed bin Suroor* a87 67
3 ch g Street Cry(IRE) Causeway Lass (AUS) (Giant's Causeway (USA))
(3173) ◆

Pressure Point *Sir Michael Stoute* 79
3 b c Oasis Dream Arrive (Kahyasi)
2628[2] 3047[2]

Prestige Roses (IRE) *Marco Botti* a41 73
2 gr f Dalakhani(IRE) Leopoldine (Desert Prince (IRE))
7450 [4] 8114[4] 8362[7]

Prestige Vendome (FR) *N Clement* 112
2 gr c Orpen(USA) Place Vendome (FR) (Dr Fong (USA))
7686a[3]

Presto Volante (IRE) *Amanda Perrett* a84 85
5 b g Oratorio(IRE) Very Racy (USA) (Sri Pekan (USA))
2102[6] (2749) 3959[2] 4913[2] 5895[4] 6424[3] 6992[7] 7660[6]

Presumido (IRE) *Simon Dow* a74 41
3 b g Iffraaj Miss Megs (IRE) (Croco Rouge (IRE))
4382[12] 5277[5] 5932[6] 6519[2] 7079[2] ◆ 7459[3] (7862)

Pretend (IRE) *Charlie Appleby* a90
2 b c Invincible Spirit(IRE) Fafinta (IRE) (Indian Ridge)
7461[3] (7766) ◆

Pretty Bubbles *J R Jenkins* a73 51
4 b m Sleeping Indian Willmar (IRE) (Zafonic (USA))
4927[6] 5962[3] 6748[4] 7299[2] 7458[4] (7987) (8125)

Pretty Flemingo (IRE) *Richard Hannon Snr* a68 89
2 b f Danehill Dancer(IRE) Kicking Bird (FR) (Darshaan)
5529[6] ◆ 6107[3] 6408[2] (7221) 7537[7]

Pretty Pearl (FR) *N Caullery* 41
2 b f Kingsalsa(USA) Perle Rare (IRE) (Dansili)
7653a[8]

Pretty Prisca *J R Jenkins*
4 ch f Layman(USA) Subtle One (IRE) (Polish Patriot (USA))
1595[P]

Pretzel (IRE) *Roger Varian* 82
2 ch c New Approach(IRE) Foodbroker Fancy (IRE) (Halling (USA))
(7467)

Previous Acclaim (IRE) *Julia Feilden* a51 64
2 b f Acclamation Erstwhile (FR) (Desert Prince (IRE))
5740[3] 7294[10] 7852[7] 8017[5] 8383[8]

Pride And Joy (IRE) *Riccardo Santini* a82 95
4 b c Dark Angel(IRE) Fey Rouge (IRE) (Fayruz)
7830a[3]

Priestley's Reward (IRE) *Mrs K Burke* a69 75
4 b g Whipper(USA) Prima Figlia (IRE) (Inchinor)
235[2] 922a[6] 1010[4] 3319[3]

Prigsnov Dancer (IRE) *Deborah Sanderson* a63 53
8 ch g Namid Brave Dance (IRE) (Kris)
81[3] 422[6] 610[9] 1395[3] 2236[2] 2611[5] 3026[8] 3196[6] 5085[2] 5470[3] 6808[2] 7101[3] (7485) 7808[9] 8002[3] 8278[9] 8411[7]

Primacy (IRE) *Neil Mulholland* a57 53
4 br f Primary(USA) Seaborne (Slip Anchor)
3272[7] 3618[7] 8027[8] 8149[6] 8436[11]

Primadonna Girl (IRE) *C Boutin* a67 64
3 b f King's Best(USA) Winners Chant (IRE) (Dalakhani (IRE))
126a^{10} 270a^{10} 2034a^{9}

Prim And Proper *Brendan Powell* a58 41
2 b f Sleeping Indian Quite Fantastic (IRE) (Fantastic Light (USA))
5529^{11} 6107^{7} 6607^{8} 7293^{8} 7855^{6}

Primary Route (IRE) *David Barron* a27 59
3 ch f Primary(USA) Ashtaroute (USA) (Holy Bull (USA))
2754^{2} 3465^{3} 4118^{3} 5789^{6}

Primatist (GER) *M Weber*
4 ch g Manduro(GER) Patineuse (IRE) (Peintre Celebre (USA))
514a^{9}

Prime Exhibit *Daniel Mark Loughnane* a89 79
8 b g Selkirk(USA) First Exhibit (Machiavellian (USA))
1368^{3} 1796^{7} (2496) 2659^{4} 3349^{11} 3886^{3} 5070^{3} 5815^{6} 6215^{5} 6468^{3} 7000^{7} 7429^{3} 7629^{4} 7824^{9} 8187^{3} 8450^{2}

Primera Vista *Mario Hofer* a85 95
7 b g Haafhd Colorvista (Shirley Heights)
1564a^{8} 4467a^{6} (5042a)

Primitorio (IRE) *Ralph Beckett* a64 82
2 b g Oratorio(IRE) Primissima (GER) (Second Set (IRE))
1580^{4} 2082^{2} 2595^{6} 4232^{8} (4519) 4948^{11} (5842) 6035^{2} 6825^{4}

Primo Blanca *Michael Mullineaux* a41 47
4 b g Primo Valentino(IRE) Quay Four (IRE) (Barathea (IRE))
1826^{7} 2785^{11}

Primo D'Oro (USA) *Richard Hannon Snr* a66 51
3 b g Medaglia d'Oro(USA) First Glimmer (USA) (Glitterman (USA))
4684^{4} 5133^{7} 5588^{7} 6407^{4} 6752^{3} 6932^{11} 7427^{11}

Primrose Posy *Julia Feilden*
2 b f Byron Manuka Too (IRE) (First Trump)
3112^{15} 3255^{7}

Prince Alzain (USA) *Gerard Butler* a114 102
4 b c Street Sense(USA) Monaassabaat (USA) (Zilzal (USA))
5822^{3} 6198^{4} 7005a^{6} (7793) (7927) ◆

Prince Bishop (IRE) *Saeed bin Suroor* a114 101
6 ch g Dubawi(IRE) North East Bay (USA) (Prospect Bay (CAN))
556a^{3} 958a^{3} 1268a^{10} (6198) 7535^{8}

Prince Caracallo (FR) *Carmen Bocskai* a89 64
5 b g Russian Blue(IRE) Lovigna (GER) (Komtur (USA))
702a^{4}

Prince D'Alienor (IRE) *A Fabre* a100 112
5 gr c Verglas(IRE) Vassiana (FR) (Anabaa (USA))
4104a^{4} 5314a^{12}

Princedargent (FR) *H-A Pantall* 109
3 ch c Kendargent(FR) Norwegian Princess (IRE) (Fairy King (USA))
1562a^{5} 2298a^{12} 3851a^{2} 5040a^{14} 5806a^{14} 6251a^{8}

Prince Freddie *Roy Brotherton* a65 74
5 b g Red Ransom(USA) Pitcroy (Unfuwain (USA))
100^{11}

Prince Gerard (FR) *Mlle S-V Tarrou* a69
3 ch c Anabaa Blue Capillano Smile (BEL) (River Smile (USA))
191a^{8}

Prince Gibraltar (FR) *J-C Rouget* 114
2 ch c Rock Of Gibraltar(IRE) Princess Sofia (UAE) (Pennekamp (USA))
(7828a)

Prince James *Michael Easterby* a69 65
6 b g Danroad(AUS) Lawless Bridget (Alnasr Alwasheek)
27^{11} (436) 976^{2} 1038^{8} 1351^{10} 1757^{10} 2611^{12} 5674^{12}

Prince Jock (USA) *John Patrick Shanahan* a82 84
6 b g Repent(USA) My Special K'S (USA) (Tabasco Cat (USA))
(4446)

Prince Khurram *J-P Carvalho* 102
3 b c Nayef(USA) Saree (Barathea (IRE))
5779a^{2}

Princely Sum (IRE) *Stuart Williams* a44 71
4 b g Refuse To Bend(IRE) Green Dollar (IRE) (Kingmambo (USA))
1294^{13} 1710^{9}

Prince Of Arabia (IRE) *Alan Jarvis* 80
3 b c Baltic King Umlaut (Zafonic (USA))
(2447) ◆

Prince Of Burma (IRE) *David Evans* a82 72
5 b h Mujadil(USA) Spinning Ruby (Pivotal)
164^{6} 345^{5} 792^{10} 1170^{2} 1901^{3} 2574^{2} 2728^{3} 3157^{8} 4237^{6} 4521^{2} 5389^{4} 5928^{10} 6388^{8} 6744^{10} 7165^{8} 7601^{8} 7937^{9} (8019) 8162^{6} 8432^{5}

Prince Of Johanne (IRE) *Tom Tate* a42 110
7 gr g Johannesburg(USA) Paiute Princess (FR) (Darshaan)
1235^{11} 2399^{2} 3458^{13} (4080) 4744^{14} 5681^{13} 6838^{26} 7206^{10}

Prince Of Passion (CAN) *Derek Shaw* a71 64
5 ch g Roman Ruler(USA) Rare Passion (CAN) (Out Of Place (USA))
115^{4} (437) 652^{8} 1038^{9} 1397^{6} 1656^{8} 1886^{3} 2280^{10} (2582) 2932^{9} 3247^{4} 3955^{3} 4146^{9} 7068^{4} 7315^{9} 7728^{9} 7957^{3} 8049^{3} 8135^{8} 8235^{7}

Prince Of Prophets (IRE) *Stuart Williams* a57 40
3 b g Antonius Pius(USA) Chifney Rush (IRE) (Grand Lodge (USA))
(36) 374^{6}

Prince Of Thebes (IRE) *Michael Attwater* a59 56
12 b g Desert Prince(IRE) Persian Walk (FR) (Persian Bold)
94^{10}

Princeofthedesert *Garry Woodward* a56 56
7 b g Nayef(USA) Twilight Sonnet (Exit To Nowhere (USA))
2462^{6} 2860^{7} 4809^{4} 6498^{7} 7099^{4} 7951^{2}

Prince Of Vasa (IRE) *Michael Smith* a72 50
6 b g Kheleyf(USA) Suzy Street (IRE) (Dancing Dissident (USA))
3462^{7} 4161^{8} 4615^{9}

Prince Regal *Alan Jarvis* 84
3 ch g Cockney Rebel(IRE) Wachiwi (IRE) (Namid)
2285^{4} 2626^{7} 3289^{5} (6338) 6871^{5} (7254)

Princess Bavaroise (FR) *H-A Pantall* 99
2 b f Desert Prince(IRE) Sascilaria (Fasliyev (USA))
7055a^{12}

Princess Bounty *Phil McEntee* a48 34
3 b f Bahamian Bounty Regal Magic (IRE) (Sadler's Wells (USA))
5069^{6} 5277^{6} 5616^{5} 6651^{6} 6965^{11} 7079^{12} 8003^{4}

Princess Caetani (IRE) *David Dennis* a75 93
4 b f Dylan Thomas(IRE) Caladira (IRE) (Darshaan)
2619^{3} ◆ 3095^{3} 3834^{4} 5095^{2} 5795^{4} (6490) 6832^{7} 7250^{9}

Princess Cammie (IRE) *John Bridger* a56 58
3 b f Camacho Hawattef (IRE) (Mujtahid (USA))
202^{2} 368^{3} 470^{4} 686^{3} 1041^{5} 1180^{2} 1345^{5} 1695^{6} 1903^{2} (2393) 2870^{4} 3178^{4} 3699^{4} 4378^{6} 4666^{4} 5128^{6} 5397^{4} 6745^{12} 7266^{11} 7443^{7}

Princess Cayan (IRE) *Linda Perratt* 17
3 b f Kodiac Silk Point (IRE) (Barathea (IRE))
2218^{7} 3566^{9} 3772^{9} 4113^{9} 4582^{9} 4991^{10}

Princesse Fiona (FR) *J-P Gallorini* 89
3 b f Malinas(GER) Princesse Turgeon (FR) (Turgeon (USA))
4468a^{7}

Princesse Fleur *Michael Scudamore* 56
5 b f Grape Tree Road Princesse Grec (FR) (Grand Tresor (FR))
(5432) 5977^{4}

Princess Florentia *John Gallagher* a8
2 b f Misu Bond(IRE) Medici Princess (Medicean)
2856^{11} 7301^{11}

Princess Gail *Mark Brisbourne* a45 40
5 b f Ad Valorem(USA) First Musical (First Trump)
4109^{10} 5387^{7} 6261^{10}

Princess Highway (USA) *D K Weld* 110
4 b f Street Cry(IRE) Irresistible Jewel (IRE) (Danehill (USA))
2375a^{3} 3870a^{7} 6416a^{6}

Princess Hollow *Tony Coyle* a3 46
3 ch f Beat Hollow Lothian Lass (IRE) (Daylami (IRE))
2341^{8} 2716^{10}

Princess Icicle *Jo Crowley* a73 47
5 b f Iceman Sarabah (IRE) (Ela-Mana-Mou)
1059^{6} 2155^{2} 4898^{12}

Princess In Exile *Ian Semple* 62
3 ch f Bertolini(USA) Music In Exile (USA) (Diesis)
2635^{7} 3626^{5} 4992^{9} 5485^{9}

Princess Kaiulani (GER) *A Wohler* 87
3 rg f King's Best(USA) Pivoline (FR) (Pivotal)
3146a^{7}

Princess Kheleyf *Geoffrey Oldroyd*
4 b f Kheleyf(USA) Jugendliebe (IRE) (Persian Bold)
28^{10} 641^{4}

Princess Kiara (FR) *N Caullery* a70 78
2 b f Spirit One(FR) Lizzy's Cat (FR) (Sir Cat (USA))
5296a^{5}

Princess Loulou (IRE) *Roger Varian* 96
3 ch f Pivotal Aiming (Highest Honor (FR))
3759^{4} 4799^{5} (6497) (7272) 7822^{4}

Princess Myla (IRE) *Paul Midgley* 56
2 b f Intense Focus(USA) Romany Princess (IRE) (Viking Ruler (AUS))
1606^{8} 1930^{8} 4199^{5} 4847^{4} 5366^{4} 5883^{4} 6561^{4} 6872^{4}

Princess Noor (IRE) *Roger Varian* a72 110
2 b f Holy Roman Emperor(IRE) Gentle Night (Zafonic (USA))
(2774) ◆ 3522^{9} 4253^{5} (4742) 6836^{2}

Princess Of Orange *Rae Guest* a63 96
4 ch f Dutch Art Radiate (Sadler's Wells (USA))
1913^{7} 2253^{3} 3060^{14} 4278^{2} 5246^{5} 6989^{8} 7272^{4}

Princess Of Sylmar (USA) *Todd Pletcher* a122
3 ch f Majestic Warrior(USA) Storm Dixie (USA) (Catienus (USA))
7691a^{6}

Princess Palmer *Lydia Pearce* a48 41
4 b f Iceman Tapas En Bal (FR) (Mille Balles (FR))
3015^{6} 3326^{12} 3792^{7}

Princess Patsky (USA) *Michael Bell* a65 54
3 bb f Mr Greeley(USA) Kamarinskaya (USA) (Storm Cat (USA))
1476^{4} 1907^{4} 2763^{10} 6655^{9} 8158^{12}

Princess Pheeny (IRE) *Richard Fahey* 67
2 b f Tagula(IRE) Carmona (Rainbow Quest (USA))
1565^{2} ◆ 1960^{4} 2558a^{8}

Princess Quest *Mick Channon* 41
4 gr f Clodovil(IRE) Corniche Quest (IRE) (Salt Dome (USA))
3731^{4} 4072^{4}

Princess Rose *William Haggas* a66 73
2 b f Royal Applause Mystical Spirit (IRE) (Xaar)
2090^{3} 2458^{5} 3673^{2} 4232^{3} 4431^{2} 5005^{4} 5508^{7} 6070^{5} 7117^{2}

Princess Sheila (IRE) *J S Moore* a55 50
3 b f Jeremy(USA) Princess Atoosa (USA) (Gone West (USA))
1458^{7} 2345^{15} 6849^{4} 6902^{5} 7265^{5} 7600^{4} 8073^{13}

Princess Spirit *Edward Creighton* a66 50
4 b f Invincible Spirit(IRE) Habariya (IRE) (Perugino (USA))
1876^{9} 2519^{9} 3169^{11} 3433^{5} 4350^{10} 5135^{3} 6102^{3} 6400^{3} (6554) (7299) 8125^{2} 8151^{3}

Princess Tamay (IRE) *Mark Johnston* a59 60
2 ch f Tamayuz Fearn Royal (IRE) (Ali-Royal (IRE))
1421^{4} 1642^{6} 2793^{3} 3084^{4} 3436^{4} 3710^{3} 5773a^{11} 6465^{3} 6779^{5} 6983^{4} 7156^{4}

Princess Tilly *Bill Turner* a18
2 ch f Proclamation(IRE) Dusty Dazzler (IRE) (Titus Livius (FR))
3853^{12} 7882^{7} 8016^{8}

Princess Willow *John E Long* a63 46
5 b f Phoenix Reach(IRE) Highland Hannah (IRE) (Persian Heights)
1090^{5} 1468^{7} 2159^{2} 2801^{6} 3213^{2} 4411^{4} 6137^{3} 7628^{4} 8148^{2}

Prince's Trust *Richard Hannon Snr* 89
3 b g Invincible Spirit(IRE) Lost In Wonder (USA) (Galileo (IRE))
1678^{5} 2192^{3} ◆ (2456) 4295^{7}

Principe Adepto (USA) *E Botti* a66 107
5 bb c Dubawi(IRE) Aischa (Giant's Causeway (USA))
2295a^{6} (2698a) 6889a^{7} 7725a^{10}

Prinsessen *Bent Olsen*
2 ch f Dutch Art Sallysaysso (IRE) (Danehill Dancer (IRE))
6452a^{2}

Printmaker (IRE) *Tim Easterby* a82 56
5 b g Shamardal(USA) Marie Laurencin (Peintre Celebre (USA))
7176^{16} 7499^{10} 7824^{18}

Priore Philip (ITY) *S Botti* 108
2 ch c Dane Friendly Lan Force (ITY) (Blu Air Force (IRE))
(7235a)

Priors Gold *Laura Mongan* a81 77
6 ch g Sakhee(USA) Complimentary Pass (Danehill (USA))
166^{2} 309^{5} 1201^{5} 1586^{10} 2197^{2} 4029^{7} 5231^{4} 6336^{12}

Prisca *Richard Hannon Snr* 66
2 b f Holy Roman Emperor(IRE) Ainia (Alhaarth (IRE))
2419^{4} 2744^{4} 3318^{3} 3896^{2} 5121^{5} 6320^{8}

Private Alexander (IRE) *David O'Meara* 100
3 b f Footstepsinthesand Private Seductress (USA) (Private Account (USA))
2687a^{6} 4081^{3} 4236^{6} 4732^{4} 6000^{9} 6796^{10}

Private Dancer *Alan Swinbank* 54
2 b g Halling(USA) Anamilina (IRE) (Anabaa (USA))
6754^{8}

Private Equity (FR) *Nicky Henderson* a87 86
5 b g High Yield(USA) Annette Girl (IRE) (Mtoto)
224^{5}

Private Jones *Miss Imogen Pickard*
4 br g Trade Fair Dafne (Nashwan (USA))
6926^{13}

Private Zone (CAN) *Doug O'Neill* a119 109
4 b g Macho Uno(USA) Auburn Beauty (USA) (Siphon (BRZ))
1266a^{9} 7713a^{10}

Prize *Richard Hannon Snr* a36 52
2 b f Exceed And Excel(AUS) Holamo (IRE) (Montjeu (IRE))
2204^{8} 6589^{5} 7874^{11}

Probably (IRE) *Rune Haugen* 105
3 b c Danehill Dancer(IRE) Wedding Morn (IRE) (Sadler's Wells (USA))
4103a^{19}

Procks Girl *Clive Cox* a47
2 gr f Proclamation(IRE) Sashay (Bishop Of Cashel)
8175^{7}

Proclamationofwar *Kevin Ryan* 74
2 b g Proclamation(IRE) Rockburst (Xaar)
2591^{4} ◆ 2913^{2} 3332^{2} 4528^{20} 6791^{11}

Prodigality *Ronald Harris* a101 107
5 ch g Pivotal Lady Bountiful (Spectrum (IRE))
(1287) ◆ 1537^{11} 2366^{3} 2621^{2} 3558^{10} 3846a^{16} 4780^{4} 4986^{13} 5545^{10} 6391^{13} 7013^{11} 7495^{5} 7982^{12}

Producer *Richard Hannon Snr* a112 114
4 ch c Dutch Art River Saint (USA) (Irish River (FR))
557a^{2} 836a^{11} (1835) 2840^{4} (3831) 4856^{10} (6254a)

Professor *Richard Hannon Snr* 114
3 ch c Byron Jubilee (Selkirk (USA))
1625^{4} (2208) (3103) ◆ (3373) 4856^{7} 5446^{3} 5794^{3}

Profile Star (IRE) *David Barron* a93 86
4 b g Kodiac Fingal Nights (IRE) (Night Shift (USA))
(58) 353^{2} 405^{3} 584^{3} 947^{7} 1644^{10} 2459^{6} 2755^{7} 3299^{15} 6159^{11} 6309^{9} 6583^{20} 8324^{7}

Progenitor (IRE) *David Lanigan* a76 80
3 b g Mujadil(USA) Bradamante (Sadler's Wells (USA))
(4383) ◆ 4629^{2}

Prohibit *Robert Cowell* a92 102
8 b g Oasis Dream Well Warned (Warning)
3187a^{5} 3420^{15} 4275^{19} 5375^{3} 6190^{10} 6539^{10} 7851^{4} 8155^{10}

Prohibition (IRE) *John Butler* a65 62
7 b g Danehill Dancer(IRE) Crumpetsfortea (IRE) (Henbit (USA))
884^{10}

Prokeel (IRE) *Tim Easterby* 59
3 gr g Proclamation(IRE) Kayf Keel (Kayf Tara)
3650^{6}

Prom Dress *J R Jenkins* a56 38
3 b f Mount Nelson Dress Code (IRE) (Barathea (IRE))
332^{3} 817^{6} 1906^{9} 7610^{7} 7759^{8} 8258^{11}

Promise You *Saeed bin Suroor* 68
2 b f Teofilo(IRE) Eilean Ban (USA) (Silver Hawk (USA))
7450 ^{5}

Prompter *Jonjo O'Neill* a83 93
6 b g Motivator Penny Cross (Efisio)
2365^{7} 3094^{7} 4488^{4} 5894^{10} 7312^{9} 7696^{14} 7849^{5} ◆

Proofreader *John Gosden* 93
4 b g Authorized(IRE) Blixen (USA) (Gone West (USA))
2191^{3} ◆ 2520^{6}

Proper Charlie *Lee Carter* a77 46
5 b g Cadeaux Genereux Ring Of Love (Magic Ring (IRE))
372^{7} 454^{2} 688^{5} 861^{4} 916^{2} 4520^{3} 4996^{6} 5930^{3} 6928^{9} 8023^{3} 8073^{10} 8306^{12}

Prophesy (IRE) *Declan Carroll* 92
4 ch g Excellent Art Race The Wild Wind (USA) (Sunny's Halo (CAN))
1237^{4} 2431^{10} 3544^{6} 3812^{5} 4264^{3} 4804^{5} 5612^{2} 6239^{6} 6758^{2} 7211^{15}

Prophet In A Dream *Paddy Butler* a45 18
5 b g Fath(USA) Princess Dariyba (IRE) (Victory Note (USA))
220^{9} 355^{4} 423^{7} 903^{9} 1162^{9} 2057^{13}

Prophets Pride *Jeremy Noseda* a91 63
3 b c Sakhee(USA) Winner's Call (Indian Ridge)
(444) (1246) (2776) 3484^{21}

Proposal (FR) *Mme J Bidgood* a88 61
3 b g Orpen(USA) Note To Cathy (USA) (Notebook (USA))
72a^{0}

Propulsion (IRE) *F Head* 106
4 b c Pulpit(USA) Brooklyn's Storm (USA) (Storm Cat (USA))
3362a^{7} 4601a^{5}

Prospera (IRE) *Ralph Beckett* a90 76
3 b f Cape Cross(IRE) Opera (Forzando)
1486^{6} 1959^{4} 2874^{11} 3900^{3} (4436) (5130) 5445^{4} (6081) (6693) 7650^{13}

Prostate Awareness (IRE) *Patrick Holmes* 65
2 b c Camacho Genuinely (IRE) (Entrepreneur)
4977^{5} 5482^{9} 5827^{4} 7309^{14}

Protected *Richard Hannon Snr* 42
2 b c Exceed And Excel(AUS) Pink Stone (FR) (Bigstone (IRE))
7019^{12}

Protestant (IRE) *Mrs John Harrington* a76 80
3 b g Papal Bull Vintage Escape (IRE) (Cyrano De Bergerac)
1587a^{3}

Proud Chieftain *Clifford Lines* a103 104
5 b g Sleeping Indian Skimra (Hernando (FR))
1639^{5} 2018^{3} 2811^{4} 3832^{6} 5007^{4} 5283^{4} 6001^{3} ◆ 6332^{5} ◆ 6838^{9} 7196^{12} 7697^{2} 8071^{8} 8386^{6}

Proud Times (USA) *Ali Brewer* a70 42
7 bb g Proud Citizen(USA) Laura's Pistolette (USA) (Big Pistol (USA))
3579^{8} 3819^{2} (4147) 4380^{5} 5868^{4} 6736^{5} 7159^{7} 7628^{6}

Proventi *Alan McCabe* a57 44
3 b g Auction House(USA) Miss Poppy (Averti (IRE))
136^{5} 404^{8}

Proximate *Sir Michael Stoute* a82 82
3 b g Nayef(USA) Contiguous (USA) (Danzig (USA))
5588^{3} 6134^{3} 6684^{2} 7311^{3}

Prussian *Charlie Appleby* a80 107
4 b f Dubai Destination(USA) Russian Snows (IRE) (Sadler's Wells (USA))
743a^{2} 3100^{5} 3775^{5} 7822^{17}

Psiloveyou *John Gosden* 51
2 ch f Sea The Stars(IRE) Soinlovewithyou (USA) (Sadler's Wells (USA))
5516^{4}

Psychometry (FR) *Sir Michael Stoute* a80 78
2 b f Danehill Dancer(IRE) Seven Magicians (USA) (Silver Hawk (USA))
4702^{2} ◆ 5716^{2} (6523)

Ptolemy *David Barron* 68
4 b g Royal Applause Rydal Mount (IRE) (Cape Cross (IRE))
1801^{12} 2319^{2} (3029) 3337^{8} 4198^{11} 4823^{6} 5471^{11} 6464^{10}

Ptolomeos *Sean Regan* a13 60
10 b g Kayf Tara Lucy Tufty (Vin St Benet)
2536^{12} 3252^{2} 5142^{5}

Pucker Up *David Brown* a64 49
3 b f Royal Applause Smooch (Inchinor)
6425^{2} 7073^{6} 7625^{2} 8432^{12}

Pucon *Roger Teal* a68 76
4 b f Kyllachy The Fugative (Nicholas (USA))
3171^{6} (3498) 4635^{3} (5522) 6077^{2} 6412^{7} 7445^{3}

Puissance De Lune (IRE) *Darren Weir* 115
5 gr c Shamardal(USA) Princess Serena (USA) (Unbridled's Song (USA))
7556a^{12}

Puligny (IRE) *Charles Hills* a62 81
3 b f Holy Roman Emperor(IRE) Le Montrachet (Nashwan (USA))
2519^{2} 2930^{2} 6824^{2} 7504^{6}

Pullmen *J R Jenkins* a59
5 gr g Silver Patriarch(IRE) Moon Spinner (Elmaamul (USA))
313^{3} 521^{2} 752^{4} 905^{7} 1080^{10}

Pull The Pin (IRE) *Ann Stokell* a73 69
4 b g Kheleyf(USA) Inscribed (IRE) (Fasliyev (USA))
829^{4} 909^{2} ◆ (991) 1276^{3} 1388^{4} (1452) 1757^{8} 2281^{4} 2319^{8} 2611^{4} 3026^{3} 3190^{3} 3654^{2} 4009^{3} (4146) 5273^{4} 5305^{2} 5674^{4} 5901^{3} (6669) 7101^{6} (7599) 7772^{7} (8096) 8431^{12}

Pull The Plug (IRE) *Declan Carroll* a66 82
2 b f Sleeping Indian Babylonian (Shamardal (USA))
(4351) (5366)

Pulpitarian (USA) *Lucinda Russell* 81
5 b g Pulpit(USA) Bedanken (USA) (Geri (USA))
2427^{12} 3345^{11}

Pulpit Point (USA) *S Seemar* a49 71
7 br g Pulpit(USA) Point Gained (USA) (Hennessy (USA))
394a^{7}

Pump Pump Boy (FR) *M Pimbonnet* a104 108
5 b c Kingsalsa(USA) Pump Pump Girl (FR) (Kendor (FR))
3362a^{5} 4421a^{4}

Punching *Conor Dore* a77 58
9 b g Kyllachy Candescent (Machiavellian (USA))
323^{6} 1452^{8} 2170^{5}

Punditry *James Toller* a74 74
3 b g Medicean Las Flores (IRE) (Sadler's Wells (USA))
895^{4} 1057^{3} 1296^{3} 1584^{2} 1955^{5} 2952^{4} 3923^{4} 5440^{8} 6080^{13} 6521^{8} (7515)

Punk *Fawzi Abdulla Nass* a72 66
2 b g Bahamian Bounty Maysarah (IRE) (Green Desert (USA))
4256[8] 5101[3] 5539[4] (5926) 6170[5]

Punta Stella (IRE) *S Kobayashi* 103
3 b f Elusive City(USA) Eroica (GER) (Highest Honor (FR))
1561a[5] 1866a[7] 6124a[3]

Pupil (IRE) *Richard Hannon Snr* 92
2 b c Mastercraftsman(IRE) Blue Iris (Petong)
5472[10] (6330) ◆ 6593[3] 7195[6]

Purcell (IRE) *Andrew Balding* a94 91
3 b g Acclamation Lyca Ballerina (Marju (IRE))
1345[2] (1515) 2022[3] 2452[6] 3474[2] 4255[13] 4797[3] (5511) 6692[3] 6993[4]

Pure Amber (IRE) *Mark Johnston* a76 70
2 b c Shamardal(USA) Ile Rousse (Danehill (USA))
4616[8] 6681[4] 7023[5] 7329[4] 7647[3]

Pure Blue Sky (USA) *Sam Di Pasquale* a94 92
4 b f Purim(USA) Sky Nine (USA) (Sky Classic (CAN))
6454a[7]

Pure Champion (IRE) *A S Cruz* a100 118
6 b h Footstepsinthesand Castara Beach (IRE) (Danehill (USA))
2066a[8] 8210a[10]

Pure Excellence *Mark Johnston* a73 99
3 b f Exceed And Excel(AUS) Albavilla (Spectrum (IRE))
554a[9] 658a[8] 837a[8] 1250[10] 1645[4] 2050[7] 2661[6]

Pure Flight (IRE) *Anthony Honeyball* a8 56
3 b f Papal Bull Wings To Soar (USA) (Woodman (USA))
2519[12] 2713[8] 3272[13] 4405[7] 5197[4]

Pure Impressions *K R Burke* 57
2 b g Footstepsinthesand Like A Virgin (IRE) (Iron Mask (USA))
5577[7] 6175[4] 6754[12] 7340[3]

Pure Mischief (IRE) *David Lanigan* a55 37
3 ch f Rock Of Gibraltar(IRE) Fig Tree Drive (USA) (Miswaki (USA))
2389[12] 2938[13] 3469[8] 4835[8]

Pure Sovereignty (USA) *Tanya Boulmetis*
5 rg g Pure Prize(USA) Princess Butterfly (USA) (Open Forum (USA))
413a[6]

Purettan (AUS) *John Leek Jr* 59
7 gr g Pure Theatre(AUS) Rattan (AUS) (Jade Hunter (USA))
7417a[16]

Purford Green *Michael Attwater* a50 30
4 ch f Kyllachy Mo Stopher (Sharpo)
667[6] 1086[12] ◆ 1660[15] 5230[9] 5796[6] 6519[4]

Purley Queen (IRE) *Sylvester Kirk* a63 70
4 b f Piccolo Queenie (Indian Ridge)
116[6] 617[3] 665[7] 806[5] ◆ 1013[3] 1194[3] 1503[5] 5522[8] 7644[7] 7807[6] 7980[4] 8073[7] 8119[5]

Purple American (FR) *E Lellouche* 88
3 bb c American Post March Violet (IRE) (Rainbow Quest (USA))
3166a[6]

Purple Lane (IRE) *David Simcock* a65 59
2 ch c Danehill Dancer(IRE) Big Heart (Mr Greeley (USA))
7469[11] 8124[6]

Purple 'n Gold (IRE) *David Pipe* a83 83
4 b g Strategic Prince Golden Dew (IRE) (Montjeu (IRE))
(112) ◆ 352[3] 439[2] 3468[7] 4075[4] 5348[4] 6004[3] 7121[10]

Purple Spectrum *William Haggas* a67
2 gr g Verglas(IRE) Rainbow's Edge (Rainbow Quest (USA))
8123[3]

Purr Along *William Muir* a80 111
3 b f Mount Nelson Purring (USA) (Mountain Cat (USA))
3524[8] 4254[4] 5629a[4] 6416a[5] 6796[5]

Pursivere *Hughie Morrison* a58 59
3 b g Pastoral Pursuits Fealeview Lady (USA) (Red Ransom (USA))
1882[5] 2321[9] 2560[8] 3636[8] 4931[14]

Pusey Street Vale *John Gallagher* 29
2 b f Moss Vale(IRE) Pusey Street Girl (Gildoran)
3408[5]

Pushkar *Lady Cecil* 60
2 b f Danehill Dancer(IRE) Mail The Desert (IRE) (Desert Prince (IRE))
3664[10]

Pushkin Museum (IRE) *Gary Moore* a80
2 gr g Soviet Star(USA) Chaste (Groom Dancer (USA))
6747[4] 7155[4] (7893) (8322) ◆ 8404[2]

Push Me (IRE) *Iain Jardine* a78 77
6 gr m Verglas(IRE) Gilda Lilly (USA) (War Chant (USA))
159[5] 511[3] 689[2] 1480[2] 4953[2] 5239[7] 5830[3] 6048[4] 7876[12]

Puteri Kash *Gary Moore*
3 b f Bertolini(USA) Puteri Sas (IRE) (Fasliyev (USA))
7154[8] 7864[7]

Puteri Nur Laila (IRE) *Paul Cole* a66 62
3 b f Strategic Prince Asian Lady (Kyllachy)
1384[3] 1784[4] 2169[5] 2806[8] 4544[8] 7644[11]

Putin (IRE) *Phil McEntee* a68 69
5 b g Fasliyev(USA) Consignia (IRE) (Definite Article)
(77) 88[2] 117[14] 187[10] 399[4] 448[3] 494[4] 640[4] 775[12] 1077[7] 1087[7] (1151) 1294[6] 1497[6] 1748[2] 2171[3] 2425[8] 2530[2] 2790[4] 2871[4] 3431[5] 3738[2] (3816) 3921[3] 4210[4] 4494[11] 4675[5] 4860[17] 5965[3] 6368[3] 5522[2] 5798[6] 6653[4] 6963[8]

Pyjama Day *Hugo Palmer* a72 73
2 b f Royal Applause Miss Otis (Danetime (IRE))
3064[11] 5199[3] (5593) 6076[2] 6572[4] 7202[5]

Pythagorean *Roger Charlton* 98
3 b g Oasis Dream Hypoteneuse (IRE) (Sadler's Wells (USA))
(2495) (2738) 3342[4] 4078[3] ◆ 4922[2] 5738[6] 6183[7]

Pytheas (USA) *Alastair Lidderdale* a64 71
6 b g Seeking The Gold(USA) Neptune's Bride (USA) (Bering)
316[4] 381[4] 441[13]

Qanan *Chris Wall* a80 79
4 b g Green Desert(USA) Strings (Unfuwain (USA))
2232[9] (2640) 3780[5] 4865[2] 5802[2] (6080) 6750[6] 7121[6]

Qareenah (USA) *Sir Michael Stoute* a62 60
3 b f Arch(USA) Princess Kris (Kris)
4404[4]

Qasima (FR) *Mme L Audon*
2 bb f Diableneyev(USA) Queen Aida (FR) (Ganges (USA))
6059a[15]

Qatar Princess (IRE) *Olly Stevens* a43 71
2 b f Marju(IRE) Bridal Dance (IRE) (Danehill Dancer (IRE))
5344[3] ◆ 6107[11] 6947[2]

Qawaafy (USA) *Roger Varian* 92
3 b f Street Cry(IRE) Eswarah (Unfuwain (USA))
2885[4] 3572[2] (4180) 5649[2] 6016[2]

Qawaasem (IRE) *Charles Hills* 100
2 b f Shamardal(USA) Misdaqeya (Red Ransom (USA))
3781[3] (4215) 4682[2] 5737[2] 6350[7]

Qeethaara (USA) *Mark Brisbourne* a76 59
9 gr m Aljabr(USA) Aghsaan (USA) (Wild Again (USA))
89[9] 410[10] 737[3] 825[7] 1100[7] 1221[3] 1401[2] (1474) ◆ 1736[5] 2073[8]

Qewy (IRE) *John M Oxx* 97
3 b c Street Cry(IRE) Princess Nada (Barathea (IRE))
5317a[5]

Qibtee (FR) *Mick Channon* a59 63
3 b c Antonius Pius(USA) Embers Of Fame (IRE) (Sadler's Wells (USA))
3021[10] 3402[4] 3907[6] 4509[2] 5391[4] 5789[4] 6870[5]

Quadriga (IRE) *Robert Eddery* a85 65
3 b g Acclamation Turning Light (GER) (Fantastic Light (USA))
2455[4] 2763[6] 3117[7] 3434[8] 6702[12] 7434[5] 7628[11] (7806) 7907[4] 7980[3] 8142[2] 8361[3] 8448[6]

Quaduna *A Wohler* 102
3 b f Duke Of Marmalade(IRE) Quelle Amore (GER) (Monsun (GER))
4092a[10] (7234a)

Quality Alliance *James Fanshawe* a60
3 ch f Dubai Destination(USA) Allied Cause (Giant's Causeway (USA))
5925[3] 6926[6] 7488[7]

Quality Art (USA) *Richard Guest* a71 69
5 b g Elusive Quality(USA) Katherine Seymour (Green Desert (USA))
113[5] 627[5] 719[5] 795[5] 902[2] 1101[8] 1324[7] 1650[8] 2268[4] 2550[7] 3024[5] 3246[12] 3446[6] 3716[7] 4930[3] 5085[7] (5305) 5499[3] 5641[4] 6088[10] 7598[7] 7772[3] 7937[4] 8135[6] 8271[6] (8351) 8406[3]

Quan (IRE) *Milton Bradley* a56 57
4 b g Shamardal(USA) Assumption (IRE) (Beckett (IRE))
24[6] 147[8] 1951[9] 2582[12] 3326[11] 3623[9] 5177[13]

Quantify (USA) *Luca Cumani* a72 82
3 b f Giant's Causeway(USA) Measure (USA) (Seeking The Gold (USA))
3696[5] (5071) 6098[2] ◆

Quantum Dot (IRE) *Tom Dascombe* a70 66
2 ch c Exceed And Excel(AUS) Jeed (IRE) (Mujtahid (USA))
3092[4] ◆ 6477[5] 6931[3]

Quaroma *Paul Midgley* a81 78
8 ch m Pivotal Quiz Time (Efisio)
1278[7] 1540[12] 2632[4] 5336[11]

Quasi Congaree (GER) *Paul Fitzsimons* a77 87
7 ch g Congaree(USA) Queens Wild (USA) (Spectacular Bid (USA))
650[13] 812[7] 1286[9] 2196[7] 2781[12]

Quatorze (FR) *F Rohaut* a99 95
3 b g Elusive City(USA) Queseraisjesanstoi (FR) (Rainbow Quest (USA))
782a[3]

Quatuor (IRE) *Tom Dascombe* a59 85
2 b f Kodiac Infinitely (Fantastic Light (USA))
1344[2] (1724) (2147) 2426[5] 3459[19] 4248[2] 5460a[7] 5994[4] 6825[6]

Queen Aggie (IRE) *David Evans* a87 81
3 b f Elnadim(USA) Catfoot Lane (Batshoof)
1033[10] 1444[8] 1662[11] 2190[6] 2655[9] 3097[4] 3803[3] 4288[2] 4453[7] 5125[4] 5676[6] 6045[3] 7123[8] 7603[7] 8020[4] ◆ 8227[5] 8454[9]

Queen Bubble (IRE) *Y De Nicolay* a96 96
4 b f Layman(USA) Bubble Back (FR) (Grand Lodge (USA))
5360a[6] 6294a[8]

Queen Cassiopeia *J R Jenkins* a63 19
4 b f Echo Of Light Fresh Fruit Daily (Reprimand)
1450[6] 2133[8] 4503[8]

Queen Catrine (IRE) *Charles Hills* 106
2 b f Acclamation Kahira (IRE) (King's Best (USA))
3057[3] (3565) 4253[3] 4742[2] 5680[2] 7055a[3]

Queen Cee *Simon Hodgson* a45
2 b f Royal Applause Tee Cee (Lion Cavern (USA))
7860[6]

Queen Flush (IRE) *David Nicholls* a37 64
3 b f Red Clubs(IRE) Alexander Nitelady (IRE) (Night Shift (USA))
1539[4] 1844[9] 2317[7] 2861[4] 3086[3] 3594[9] 4136[2] 4558[5] 5054[9] 5869[12]

Queen Hermione (IRE) *Derek Shaw* a39 69
5 b f Camacho Almeida (IRE) (Sadler's Wells (USA))
2997[4] (3268) 4148[9] ◆ (4982) 5498[6]

Queenie's Home *James Given* a71 64
2 gr f Shamardal(USA) Nolas Lolly (IRE) (Lomitas)
1718[10] 2856[7] 5394[5] 6076[5] 6326[14] 6755[3] 7782[4] 8266[2] (8368)

Queenie's Star (IRE) *Michael Attwater* a53 44
6 b m Arakan(USA) Starway To Heaven (ITY) (Nordance (USA))
1093[14] 1473[4] 1779[2] 1987[5] 3056[5] 3399[12] 5528[7] 5934[10]

Queen Of Alba (IRE) *John Patrick Shanahan* a77 64
4 b m Rock Of Gibraltar(IRE) Mad Madam Mym (Hernando (FR))
4447[8]

Queen Of Arts *Richard Fahey* 29
2 ch f Dutch Art Grande Terre (IRE) (Grand Lodge (USA))
5380[8] 6769[11] 7818[13]

Queen Of Epirus *Brian Rothwell* a48 55
5 ch f Kirkwall Andromache (Hector Protector (USA))
3625[5] 4010[5] 5084[3] 5420[11]

Queen Of Ice *William Haggas* 78
2 ch f Selkirk(USA) Ice Palace (Polar Falcon (USA))
(7692) ◆

Queen Of Norway (IRE) *John Joseph Murphy* a65 71
2 b f Papal Bull Fanacanta (IRE) (Olden Times)
7994a[10]

Queen Of Skies (IRE) *Michael Appleby* a64 41
4 b f Shamardal(USA) Attractive Crown (USA) (Chief's Crown (USA))
429[9] 7278[8] 7922[5] 8121[6] 8270[9]

Queen Of The Sand (IRE) *G M Lyons* a85 84
3 ch f Footstepsinthesand Lough Mewin (IRE) (Woodman (USA))
3845a[6]

Queen Of The Tarts *Olly Stevens* a61 63
2 b f Royal Applause Tart And A Half (Distant Relative)
1240[6] 1580[3] 2090[4] 2985[2] 3275[5] 4174[3] 5175[4] 6111[12] 6749[13]

Queensberry Rules (IRE) *William Haggas* a88 104
3 b g Teofilo(IRE) Fantastic Spring (USA) (Fantastic Light (USA))
(1423) ◆ (1812) 2859[3] 3484[3] ◆ 4744[22] 5681[6] 6838[20]

Queen's Daughter (FR) *N Clement* 101
3 b f American Post Queen's Conquer (King's Best (USA))
(7993a)

Queen's Estate (GER) *Patrick Gilligan* a62 81
4 b g Hurricane Run(IRE) Questabelle (Rainbow Quest (USA))
3204[12] 3791[7] 4135[8] 5048[11]

Queen's Princess *John Wainwright* a43 43
5 b f Danbird(AUS) Queen's Lodge (IRE) (Grand Lodge (USA))
2503[3] 2757[14] 3593[7] 3654[7] 7791[9] 7946[5] 8140[5] 8320[7]

Queen's Prize *Sir Michael Stoute* a78
2 b f Dansili Daring Aim (Daylami (IRE))
(6691)

Queens Revenge *Tim Easterby* 84
4 b f Multiplex Retaliator (Rudimentary (USA))
1646[5] 2214[8] 2463[14] 2988[10] 3686[6] 4135[4] 4609[6] 4891[7] 5471[7]

Queen's Star *Andrew Balding* a65 68
4 ch f With Approval(CAN) Memsahib (Alzao (USA))
2197[6] 2545[8] (2922) 3790[4] 4166[8]

Quelle Affaire *Brendan Powell* a44
3 b f Bahamian Bounty Qui Moi (CAN) (Swain (IRE))
332[8] 416[4] 1050[4]

Querido (GER) *Paddy Butler* a61 64
9 b g Acatenango(GER) Quest Of Fire (FR) (Rainbow Quest (USA))
220[10] 587[7] 625[7] 825[6] 1161[3] 1474[3] 1779[5] 2130[7] 2747[5]

Quest For More (IRE) *Roger Charlton* a85 86
3 b g Teofilo(IRE) No Quest (IRE) (Rainbow Quest (USA))
3902[4] (4593) 5134[7] (6071) 6380[3] 7627[3]

Questioning (IRE) *John Gosden* a80 115
5 b g Elusive Quality(USA) Am I (USA) (Thunder Gulch (USA))
2782[3] 3347[7] 3839[4] 5822[4] 6592[5]

Quest Of Colour (IRE) *Richard Fahey* 53
2 b f Iffraaj With Colour (Rainbow Quest (USA))
6271[8] 6828[9]

Questor (FR) *M Boutin* a78 67
4 b g High Cotton(USA) Equestria (USA) (Red Ransom (USA))
963a[4]

Quickaswecan *Mark Johnston* a79 87
2 b c Shamardal(USA) Arctic Air (Polar Falcon (USA))
5915[2] ◆ 6645[6] 7017[8] (7317) 7933[3]

Quick Decision *Bill Turner*
2 b c Moss Vale(IRE) Clodova (IRE) (Clodovil (IRE))
5963[5]

Quick Jack (IRE) *A J Martin* a67 89
4 ch g Footstepsinthesand Miss Polaris (Polar Falcon (USA))
5021a[2] (5719) 7723a[2] ◆

Quick Wit *Saeed bin Suroor* a111 112
6 b h Oasis Dream Roo (Rudimentary (USA))
367a[6] 657a[7] (873a) 3347[2] 3931[2] (4433) 5270[7] 6254a[7] 6742[2]

Quidamo *Frau J Mayer* 110
6 b g Monsun(GER) Qelle Amie (CAN) (Beau Genius (CAN))
2822a[5] 3362a[2] 5324a[6] 7890a[5]

Quiet Diplomacy *A Fabre* a85 88
3 b c New Approach(IRE) Coy (IRE) (Danehill (USA))
1972a[2] 2557a[11]

Quiet Warrior (IRE) *Marco Botti* a81
2 b g Kodiac Pretty Woman (IRE) (Night Shift (USA))
7971[2] ◆ (8326)

Quilita (GER) *P Schiergen* 100
3 ch f Lomitas Quirigua (Intikhab (USA))
3146a[6] 4092a[2] 5044a[5] 6010a[8]

Quincel *Tom Dascombe* a66 66
2 b g Exceed And Excel(AUS) Quinzey's Best (IRE) (King's Best (USA))
2189[6] 2591[7] 3568[3] 5068[2]

Quinindo (GER) *Elfie Schnakenberg* a75 101
5 bb c Monsun(GER) Quebrada (IRE) (Devil's Bag (USA))
701a[13] 4042a[4] 5778a[5]

Quinta Feira (IRE) *Ed de Giles* a50
2 gr g Medicean Bunditten (IRE) (Soviet Star (USA))
1778[4] 7766[9]

Quintain (IRE) *Tim Easterby* a61 56
5 b g Olden Times Seek Supremacy (IRE) (Supreme Leader)
602[2] 708[3] 1282[7] 1775[8] 2273[8] 2986[8] 3543[10]

Quintet (IRE) *Ralph Beckett* a74 66
3 ch f Pivotal Possessed (Desert Prince (IRE))
2447[9] 3176[5] 4535[5] (5677) 6316[9]

Quinzieme Monarque (USA) *J Hirschberger* a92 106
3 bb c Rock Hard Ten(USA) Quintela (Giant's Causeway (USA))
3389a[5] 4103a[4] 6028a[5] 7566a[12]

Quite A Catch (IRE) *Jonathan Portman* a65 45
5 b g Camacho Dear Catch (IRE) (Bluebird (USA))
3736[4]

Quite A Mission (SWE) *Niels Petersen* a64 88
3 ch c Eishin Dunkirk(USA) Theatre Antique (USA) (Theatrical (IRE))
5326a[8]

Quite Sparky *Mike Sowersby* 60
6 b g Lucky Story(USA) Imperialistic (IRE) (Imperial Ballet (IRE))
2615[8]

Quixote *Clive Brittain* a92 95
4 ch g Singspiel(IRE) Rainbow Queen (FR) (Spectrum (IRE))
1382[5] 1547[4] 2205[2] 3297[2] 4060[13] 5723[13] 6573[5]

Quixote (GER) *P Schiergen* 103
3 b c Pivotal Quebrada (IRE) (Devil's Bag (USA))
4333a[5] 5940a[12]

Quiz Evolution (ITY) *B Grizzetti* 96
2 b g Mujahid(USA) Marie Camargo (Kyllachy)
3880a[3] 5460a[5]

Quiz Mistress *Hughie Morrison* a82 109
5 ch f Doyen(IRE) Seren Quest (Rainbow Quest (USA))
1674[2] 2428[5] 3100[6] 5297a[8] (6294a) 7535[4]

Quoth *Charlie Appleby* a13
2 ch f Raven's Pass(USA) Hearsay (Dubai Destination (USA))
7295[9]

Qurqul *Pierrick Le Geay* a69 49
7 b g Mujahid(USA) Paris Dreamer (Paris House)
6058a[2]

Qushchi *H Graham Motion* a83 102
5 bb f Encosta De Lago(AUS) La Persiana (Daylami (IRE))
7708a[10]

Raafa's Jigsaw *Michael Appleby* a40 54
4 ch f Araafa(IRE) Puzzling (Peintre Celebre (USA))
5071[9] 5563[6] 5845[7]

Raajis (IRE) *Richard Hannon Snr* 78
2 gr f Dark Angel(IRE) Rumline (Royal Applause)
3986[7] 4702[7] 5174[3] (6426)

Raamz (IRE) *Kevin Morgan* a61 73
6 ch m Haafhd Tarbiyah (Singspiel (IRE))
2219[3] ◆ 3496[5] 4638[3] 7132[15] 7453[7] 8087[6]

Rabdaan *James Fanshawe* a77 43
3 ch c Sakhee(USA) Maghya (IRE) (Mujahid (USA))
2507[7] 3641[2]

Race And Status (IRE) *Andrew Balding* 98
3 b g Raven's Pass(USA) Love Excelling (FR) (Polish Precedent (USA))
1623[6]

Race For Fame (IRE) *H-A Pantall* 79
2 b c Meshaheer(USA) Rocky Mixa (FR) (Rock Of Gibraltar (IRE))
5323a[2]

Race Hunter (USA) *David Barron* 80
2 bb f Dixie Union(USA) Shriek (USA) (Street Cry (IRE))
(2830) 3522[18] 4965[2]

Rachael's Ruby *Roger Teal* a38 33
6 b m Joe Bear(IRE) Fajjoura (IRE) (Fairy King (USA))
201[8] 1480[6]

Racing Mate (IRE) *Paul D'Arcy* 84
2 b c Art Connoisseur(IRE) A L'Aube (IRE) (Selkirk (USA))
(5339)

Racing's Dream *Brian Meehan* a63 65
2 b c Iffraaj There's Two (IRE) (Ashkalani (IRE))
7494[5] ◆ 8213[6]

Racy *Brian Ellison* a85 105
6 b g Medicean Soar (Danzero (AUS))
1765[13] (2789) 3334[2] 3846a[25] 4275[2] 4986[4] 5257[5] 6190[5] 6391[4] 6830[2] 7364[9]

Radiator *Sir Michael Stoute* 99
2 b f Dubawi(IRE) Heat Haze (Green Desert (USA))
4921[5] (6112) 6795[4]

Radio Gaga *Ed McMahon* a55 100
4 b f Multiplex Gagajulu (Al Hareb (USA))
1544[13] 2585[10] 6625[13] 7538[6]

Raeburn (AUS) *Brian Smith* 100
9 ch g Danehill Dancer(IRE) Portrait (AUS) (Octagonal (NZ))
7760a[12]

Rafaaf (IRE) *Richard Phillips* a66 84
5 b g Royal Applause Sciunfona (IRE) (Danehill (USA))
214[5] 831[11] 968[7] (8118)

Ragazzo (FR) *Mario Hofer* 93
2 b c Footstepsinthesand Rosa Di Brema (ITY) (Lomitas)
7939a[8]

Ragazzo (NOR) *Annike Bye Hansen* a105 102
4 b g Academy Award(IRE) Private Property (IRE) (Pips Pride)
(4936a) 5325a[2]

Ragged Robbin (FR) *David Lanigan* a59 49
2 ch c Speightstown(USA) Ikat (IRE) (Pivotal)
7461[11] 7655[7] 7859[4] 8132[5]

Raging Bear (USA) *James Evans* a78 76
3 b g Leroidesanimaux(BRZ) Gliding Light (USA) (Always A Classic (CAN))
(1011) 1365[7] 2737[3] 4438[3] 5124[7] 5632[4] (6410) 6489[2] 7824[3]

Raging Bob (IRE) *Ralph Beckett* a64
2 br g Big Bad Bob(IRE) Lanasara (Generous (IRE))
8340[5]

Rahy's Promise (USA) *David O'Meara* a57
4 ch g Rahy(USA) Promise Me This (Fusaichi Pegasus (USA))
397[9] 637[7] 1060[7] 7375[11]

Rahystrada (USA) *Byron G Hughes* 114
9 ch g Rahy(USA) Ministrada (USA) (Deputy Minister (CAN))
5553a[11]

Rail Star *Roger Charlton* a69 59
3 b f Rail Link Widescreen (USA) (Distant View (USA))
2084[6] ◆ 2850[11]

Rainbow Beauty *Gerard Butler* a82 82
3 ch f Manduro(GER) Just Like A Woman (Observatory (USA))
(6003) 6701[3] 7256[2] 7470[6] 7786[3] ◆ 7895[4]

Rainbow Chic (IRE) *C Fownes* 113
4 ch g Peintre Celebre(USA) Doohulla (USA) (Stravinsky (USA))
8211a[12]

Rainbow Knight *J-M Capitte* a76
5 b g Rainbow Quest(USA) Poli Knight (Polish Precedent (USA))
648a[2]

Rainbow Riches (IRE) *Roger Curtis* a47 49
4 b f Princely Heir(IRE) Another Rainbow (IRE) (Rainbows For Life (CAN))
120[10] 220[7] 497[7] 736[9] 2305a[3]

Rainbow Rock (IRE) *Mark Johnston* 69
2 b c Rock Of Gibraltar(IRE) Celtic Fling (Lion Cavern (USA))
3581[6] 6762[9] 7146[5]

Rainbows And Roses *Chris Wall* a50 51
3 ch f Beat Hollow Rainbow Sky (Rainbow Quest (USA))
2519[8] 5281[4] 5678[7]

Rain Drum (AUS) *Gai Waterhouse* 110
6 b g Fastnet Rock(AUS) Gifted Spirit (AUS) (Thunder Gulch (USA))
7762a[4]

Raineon (FR) *Mme C Barande-Barbe* a66 53
3 gr g Turgeon(USA) Rainbow Pointe (ITY) (Linamix (FR))
331a[P]

Rainford Glory (IRE) *David Simcock* a65 55
3 ch g Rock Of Gibraltar(IRE) My Dolly Madison (In The Wings)
209[4] 411[5] 632[4] 824[3] 910[4] 1064[5] (1326) 1613[6] 1743[5] 2095[6] 2709[4] (8225) 8388[3]

Rain Mac *Donald McCain* a52 67
5 b g Beat Hollow Quenched (Dansili)
4407[5]

Rain Of Melody (IRE) *Y Gourraud* a65 82
7 b g Night Shift(USA) Hit The Sky (IRE) (Cozzene (USA))
6447a[12]

Raise A Billion *Alan Berry* 39
2 b c Major Cadeaux Romantic Destiny (Dubai Destination (USA))
5262[4] 5638[6] 6681[8] 7094[5]

Raise The Rafters (IRE) *John Butler* a62 76
8 ch g Monashee Mountain(USA) Zolube (IRE) (Titus Livius (FR))
193[6]

Raise Your Gaze *Clive Cox* 79
2 gr g Mastercraftsman(IRE) Regal Magic (IRE) (Sadler's Wells (USA))
4640[4] 5472[2] 6277[10]

Rajang (FR) *F Chappet* a67 74
2 b g Yeats(IRE) Rockabout (IRE) (Rock Of Gibraltar (IRE))
5296a[6]

Rajaratna (IRE) *Lady Cecil* 18
3 b f Galileo(IRE) Coup De Genie (USA) (Mr Prospector (USA))
3239[11]

Rajeh (IRE) *Peter Grayson* a55 92
10 b g Key Of Luck(USA) Saramacca (IRE) (Kahyasi)
579[7] 714[7] 5592[8]

Rakaan (IRE) *Jamie Osborne* a94 90
6 ch g Bahamian Bounty Petite Spectre (Spectrum (IRE))
6[4] 206[2] 495[6] 690[6] 844[2] 1092[6] (1353) 1796[6] 2571[5] 3019[8] 3416[3] (8336) 8445[5]

Raki (AUS) *Tony McEvoy* 89
6 br g Rakti Marks Gain (AUS) (Biscay (AUS))
7760a[8]

Rakticate (IRE) *J S Moore* a65 61
3 b f Rakti Authenticate (Dansili)
141[2] 237[2] 1332[3]

Raleigh Quay (IRE) *Micky Hammond* 74
6 b g Bachelor Duke(USA) Speedbird (USA) (Sky Classic (CAN))
1463[9] 1993[4] 2633[8] 2961[9] 3709[5] 4204[4] 4614[7] 5337[6] 5863[6]

Ralphy Boy (IRE) *Alistair Whillans* a56 76
4 b g Acclamation Silcasue (Selkirk (USA))
3683[8] 4294[3] 4446[7] (5239) 5637[3] 5947[2] 6562[2] 6906[3] 7152[9]

Ralphy Lad (IRE) *Alan Swinbank* 68
2 b g Iffraaj Hawattef (IRE) (Mujtahid (USA))
5482[3] 6125[6] 6299[10]

Ralston Road (IRE) *John Patrick Shanahan* 109
3 b c Dylan Thomas(IRE) Advertising Space (IRE) (Galileo (IRE))
(2651) 3526[8] 3849a[7] 5531[10] 6393[7]

Ramata *James Unett* 39
3 b f Milk It Mick Lamarita (Emarati (USA))
2597[9] 3641[9] 6940[10]

Rambo Will *J R Jenkins* a77 76
5 b g Danbird(AUS) Opera Belle (Dr Fong (USA))
11[8] 535[5] 719[6] 898[5] 1186[2] 1452[4] 4691[3] 4999[3] (5931) 6929[7] (7432) 7776[8] 7888[2] 8319[4]

Ramone (IRE) *W T Farrell* 75
3 b f Marju(IRE) Hayworth (IRE) (Night Shift (USA))
5775a[15] 6883a[20]

Rampoldi (TUR) *S Keresteci* a98 99
4 ch c Bosporus(IRE) Deep Sea (TUR) (Distant Relative)
6232a[5]

Ramsa (FR) *John Francis Egan* 80
3 b f Shamardal(USA) Value Of Time (IRE) (Xaar)
2289a[8]

Rancher (IRE) *Tony Carroll* a55 55
3 b g High Chaparral(IRE) Shot Of Redemption (Shirley Heights)
2599[9] (2748) 4931[8] 5813[7]

Rancho Montoya (IRE) *Andrew Balding* a72 48
3 b f High Chaparral(IRE) Congress (IRE) (Dancing Brave (USA))
3469[4] 5100[6] 5892[8] 6435[7] 7422[4] 8031[3] 8223[3]

Random *John Stimpson* a58
2 b f Shamardal(USA) Paracel (USA) (Gone West (USA))
7541[4] 8017[6]

Random Success (IRE) *Roger Charlton* a67 42
3 b f Shamardal(USA) Foreplay (IRE) (Lujain (USA))
4627[4] 7802[2] 8003[3] 8456[2]

Rangali *H-A Pantall* 94
2 ch c Namid Tejaara (USA) (Kingmambo (USA))
5875a[3] 7084a[5] 7994a[2]

Rangi *Tony Coyle* a76 79
3 ch g New Approach(IRE) Miss Queen (USA) (Miswaki (USA))
(16) 474[5] 1444[3] 1935[4] 2318[4] 2756[2] 2836[3]

Rangi Chase (IRE) *Richard Fahey* 76
2 b c Lawman(FR) Tirunesh (USA) (More Than Ready (USA))
6125[3] ◆ 6666[3] 7175[2]

Rangooned *Ann Duffield* a58 74
3 gr f Bahamian Bounty Dansa Queen (Dansili)
(1762) 1988[8] 4136[7] 4402[4] 4734[8] 5422[7] 5985[3] 6516[6]

Rano Pano (USA) *Brian Ellison* a55 53
4 b f Proud Citizen(USA) Princess Aries (USA) (Royal Anthem (USA))
(63)

Raphinae *Charlie Appleby* a38
2 b f Dubawi(IRE) Dodo (IRE) (Alzao (USA))
7875[11]

Rapid Advance *Roger Varian* a77 40
2 b c Medicean Snow Gretel (IRE) (Green Desert (USA))
7271[7] 7834[2] ◆

Rapideur (FR) *S Smrczek* a89 103
3 b c Elusive City(USA) Perelada (FR) (Montjeu (IRE))
4274a[3]

Rapid Heat Lad (IRE) *Andrew Hollinshead* a81 68
4 b g Aussie Rules(USA) Alwiyda (USA) (Trempolino (USA))
(309) 5631[1] 2990[9] 4406[4] 8004[4]

Rapido (GER) *Andreas Lowe* 47
2 b c Rock Of Gibraltar(IRE) Rondinay (FR) (Cadeaux Genereux)
7828a[12]

Rapid Rabbit Foot *John Holt* a37 31
3 ch f Three Valleys(USA) Rabshih (IRE) (Green Desert (USA))
1777[5] 2231[14] 2800[10]

Rapid Water *Pat Eddery* a61 51
7 b g Anabaa(USA) Lochsong (Song)
147[6] 335[7] 631[5] 721[4] (825) 1100[4] 1497[8] 1617[8] 2130[3] 2747[9] 3433[8] 4195[8] 5032[10] 5172[5] 5948[10] 6489[4] 7741[7] 8122[6] 8315[5] 8436[7]

Rapscallion Deep (IRE) *Kevin Ryan* a66 66
3 b g Danehill Dancer(IRE) Lucina (Machiavellian (USA))
102[2] (2241) 3025[7] 5878[8] 6874[11]

Rapunzal *Henry Candy* 52
2 b f Mount Nelson Cinnas Ransom (Red Ransom (USA))
7243[5]

Rare Coincidence *Alan Berry* a17 41
12 ch g Atraf Green Seed (IRE) (Lead On Time (USA))
2313[11] 4343[10] 5267[7]

Rasaman (IRE) *Jim Goldie* a84 86
9 b g Namid Rasana (Royal Academy (USA))
1252[6] 1819[6] 2914[5] 3200[3] 3367[7] (4111) 4472[3] 4780[8] 5238[7] 5832[9] 6648[3] 6920[4] 7731[6]

Rasameel (USA) *J W Hills* 76
2 ch c Jazil(USA) Positioning (USA) (Boundary (USA))
5244[5] 5941[7] 7019[2]

Rasheeda *Marco Botti* 86
2 ro f Mastercraftsman(IRE) Violette (Observatory (USA))
(2856) 3522[14] 4682[5] 5699[2]

Raskova (USA) *William Jarvis* 81
3 b f Henrythenavigator(USA) Diamond Necklace (USA) (Unbridled's Song (USA))
4125[3] 4500[4] (5037) 5743[0] 7257[2] 7504[3] 7656[2]

Rasmeyaa (IRE) *D K Weld* a48 99
3 ch f New Approach(IRE) Posterity (IRE) (Indian Ridge)
2047[14] 5688a[3] ◆ 7404a[5]

Rassam (IRE) *Saeed bin Suroor* a102 77
4 bb g Dansili Vantive (USA) (Mr Prospector (USA))
367a[13]

Rasselas (IRE) *David Nicholls* a62 68
6 b g Danehill Dancer(IRE) Regal Darcey (IRE) (Darshaan)
993[5] 1151[5] 1788[7] 2537[2] 2889[14] (4005) 4160[10] 4893[11] 5341[9] 6634[5] (6921) 7153[4] 7283[5]

Rasteau (IRE) *Tom Keddy* a45 43
5 b g Barathea(IRE) Mistra (IRE) (Rainbow Quest (USA))
200[6] 406[9] 703[12] 3399[10] 3997[7]

Ratana (GER) *Andreas Lowe* a87 87
3 ch f Big Shuffle(USA) Rakayeb (USA) (Gone West (USA))
2910a[10]

Rat Catcher (IRE) *Andrew Crook* 72
3 b g One Cool Cat(USA) Molly Marie (IRE) (Fasliyev (USA))
1647[12] 2832[5] 3134[7] 3630[7] 4162[6] 4621[2] 5265[7]

Rathealy (IRE) *Alan Bailey* a66 65
2 b g Baltic King Baltic Belle (IRE) (Redback)
5718[13] 6256[6] 6569[4] 6972[3] 7168[2] ◆

Ratmansky (ITY) *F Camici* 89
2 gr c Mastercraftsman(IRE) Sharafanya (IRE) (Zafonic (USA))
7678a[4]

Raushan (IRE) *Sir Michael Stoute* 86
3 gr f Dalakhani(IRE) Chiang Mai (IRE) (Sadler's Wells (USA))
(2392) 3177[2] 4015[3]

Ravenous *Ralph Beckett* 76
2 b g Raven's Pass(USA) Supereva (IRE) (Sadler's Wells (USA))
2194[7] 6799[15] 7500[3]

Raven Ridge (IRE) *Michael Bell* 79
2 b c High Chaparral(IRE) Green Castle (IRE) (Indian Ridge)
6330[3] (6938)

Ravensburg *Chris Wall* 66
3 ch f Raven's Pass(USA) Generous Lady (Generous (IRE))
2760[6] 3572[4]

Ravens Nest *Ben Pauling* a58 39
3 b g Piccolo Emouna (Cadeaux Genereux)
1367[6] 7839[6] 8229[11]

Raven's Rock (IRE) *Roger Varian* a63 64
3 b g Raven's Pass(USA) Delphinus (Soviet Star (USA))
1928[6] 2763[5] 3438[7]

Raven's Tower (USA) *Mark Johnston* a68 70
3 b g Raven's Pass(USA) Tizdubai (USA) (Cee's Tizzy (USA))
731[5] 1053[5] 1614[8]

Ravi River (IRE) *Alistair Whillans* a70 69
9 ch g Barathea(IRE) Echo River (USA) (Irish River (FR))
4803[6] 5370[2] 6632[13] 7278[5]

Rawaafed (IRE) *Keith Dalgleish* a76 72
4 b g Invasor(ARG) Holly's Kid (USA) (Pulpit (USA))
797[3] 950[3] 1081[6] 1272[6] 1459[8] 1801[4] 2162[2] 2219[4] 2752[DSQ] (2794) 3337[3] 3397[2] 3683[11] 3827[7] 4341[7] 4612[2]

Rawaaq *D K Weld* 104
3 b f Invincible Spirit(IRE) Zaqrah (USA) (Silver Hawk (USA))
(1557a) 2289a[7] 6414a[12]

Rawaki (IRE) *Andrew Balding* a92 103
5 b g Phoenix Reach(IRE) Averami (Averti (IRE))
2407[3] 3115[9] (3838) 4796[3] 5256[5] 7407a[7]

Rawnaq (IRE) *Matthew J Smith* a71 85
6 b g Azamour(IRE) Sharemata (IRE) (Doyoun)
7723a[5]

Rawoof (IRE) *Ed Dunlop* 74
2 b f Nayef(USA) Tanaghum (Darshaan)
5003[7] 5516[2] 6716[2]

Rayadour (IRE) *Micky Hammond* a77 77
4 b g Azamour(IRE) Rayyana (IRE) (Rainbow Quest (USA))
333[5] 612[3] 1111[4] 1448[8] 2009[7] 2435[2] 2630[5] 3504[8] 5052[2]

Rayaheen *Richard Hannon Snr* 82
3 b f Nayef(USA) Natagora (FR) (Divine Light (JPN))
3020[8] 5125[5]

Raymond's Dream *J R Jenkins*
3 bb f Lightning Lad Spirit Of Song (IRE) (Selkirk (USA))
2226[10] 4687[6]

Ray Of Joy *J R Jenkins* a78 72
7 b m Tobougg(IRE) Once Removed (Distant Relative)
2088[4] 2657[8] 3259[3] 3691[4] 3892[7] 5498[4] 6535[3] 6969[4] 7164[3] 7381[4] 7663[6] 8052[7] 8128[3] ◆ 8321[9]

Rayoumti (IRE) *Marco Botti* a72 65
2 b f Lawman(FR) Sveva (IRE) (Danehill Dancer (IRE))
3205[9] 3958[3] 6512[3] (7352)

Ray Ward (IRE) *David Simcock* a74 96
3 b g Galileo(IRE) Kentucky Warbler (IRE) (Spinning World (USA))
(373) (2223) 2445[5] 3048[2] 3526[5] 4211[7] 6066[8]

Razera (IRE) *John Quinn* 58
3 b g Dylan Thomas(IRE) Rahila (IRE) (Kalanisi (IRE))
5469[4] 6272[5] 6847[9]

Razin' Hell *Alan McCabe* a56
2 b g Byron Loose Caboose (IRE) (Tagula (IRE))
5827[8] 6340[8] 7155[10] 7956[2] 8044[2] (8317) 8404[3]

Razor Quest *Philip McBride* a77 79
2 b c Virtual Takarna (IRE) (Mark Of Esteem (IRE))
2382[4] (2978) 3690[2] 4300[3]

Razzle Dazzle 'Em *Shaun Harris* a11 42
4 b g Phoenix Reach(IRE) Rasmani (Medicean)
4927[11] 7984[16]

Reach The Beach *Brendan Powell* a52 59
4 ch f Phoenix Reach(IRE) Comtesse Noire (CAN) (Woodman (USA))
1317[5] 1468[8] 1837[6] 3744[5] 5093[5] 7612[4]

Reaction *Michael Appleby* a67 66
7 ch g Alhaarth(IRE) Hawas (Mujtahid (USA))
57[3] 351[F]

Ready (IRE) *Garry Moss* a89 85
3 ch g Elnadim(USA) Fusili (IRE) (Silvano (GER))
1246[5] 1571[3] 1958[9] 2439[5] 2951[3] (3571) 4007[5] 4508[2] 5676[2] 6164[9] 6608[4]

Ready To Act (USA) *Chad C Brown* 103
2 rg f More Than Ready(USA) Always Auditioning (USA) (Mizzen Mast (USA))
7690a[6]

Ready To Strike (NZ) *Laurie Laxon* 109
6 b g Colombia(NZ) Bankers Tonic (NZ) (British Banker (CAN))
2494a[11]

Reaffirmed (IRE) *Ed Vaughan* a59 59
2 ch g Pivotal Quiet Protest (USA) (Kingmambo (USA))
4795[5] 7155[7] 7817[15]

Reale Silenzio *John Weymes* a20 37
2 b f Royal Applause Silent Miracle (IRE) (Night Shift (USA))
4046[11] 4556[6] 4886[9] 5480[3] 5898[7] 6295[6] 6511[6] 7096[11] 7198[8] 8090[9]

Realistic *David Brown* 35
2 b f Virtual Ile Deserte (Green Desert (USA))
3978[7]

Realistically (IRE) *Tony Coyle*
2 b c Bushranger(IRE) River Fairy (USA) (Irish River (FR))
1574[6]

Reality Show (IRE) *Shaun Harris* a52 8
6 b g Cape Cross(IRE) Really (IRE) (Entrepreneur)
8373[6] 8449[6]

Realize *Hughie Morrison* a69 78
3 b g Zafeen(FR) Relkida (Bertolini (USA))
1732[3] 2224[3] 2934[2] (3898) 4592[3] 4962[3]

Real Jazz (IRE) *Sir Mark Prescott Bt* a56
2 b f Marju(IRE) Sedna (IRE) (Priolo (USA))
7934[4] 8091[5] 8346[4]

Real Solution (USA) *Chad C Brown* 114
4 b c Kitten's Joy(USA) Reachfortheheavens (USA) (Pulpit (USA))
(5553a) 7712a[9]

Real Specialist (NZ) *J Size* 116
6 b g Storming Home There's No Doubt (NZ) (Pompeii Court (USA))
8210a[5]

Reasons Unknown (IRE) *Thomas McLaughlin* a67 67
5 ch g Camacho Locorotondo (IRE) (Broken Hearted)
158[3] 198[2] (630) 662[3] 996[6]

Rebecca Romero *Denis Coakley* a78 88
6 b m Exceed And Excel(AUS) Cloud Dancer (Bishop Of Cashel)
1814[3] 2388[2] 3018[6] (3371) 4217[4] 4800[14] 5750[2] 6189[15] 6699[6]

Rebel Code (USA) *James Given* a53 47
2 b c City Zip(USA) Confederate Lady (USA) (Dixie Union (USA))
5000[6] 5236[3] 5590[3] 7665[7]

Rebel Force (IRE) *Mark Johnston* a77 80
3 b f Dalakhani(IRE) Rebelline (IRE) (Robellino (USA))
7950[6] (8184)

Rebellious Guest *George Margarson* 101
4 b g Cockney Rebel(IRE) Marisa (GER) (Desert Sun)
2254[15] 3558[17] 4744[24] 6571[5] 6988[6] 7368[24]

Rebel Magic *Richard Hannon Snr* a81 87
3 b f Cockney Rebel(IRE) Aastral Magic (Magic Ring (IRE))
2848[8] 3292[9] 4168[6]

Rebel Woman *Mrs A Corson* a58 52
7 b m Royal Applause Wild Woman (Polar Falcon (USA))
1313a[8] 1740a[6] 5328a[5] 7145a[9]

Recanted (USA) *Brian Meehan* 87
2 b c Empire Maker(USA) Deaconess Bonnie (USA) (Pulpit (USA))
(3238) 4296[8] 4876[7] 7107[3]

Recession Proof (FR) *John Quinn* a80 67
7 ch g Rock Of Gibraltar(IRE) Elevate (Ela-Mana-Mou)
6237[9] 7193[27]

Reckless Abandon *Clive Cox* 117
3 b c Exchange Rate(USA) Sant Elena (Efisio)
2662[3] ◆ 3420[5] 7054a[5]

Reckoning (IRE) *Jeremy Noseda* 104
4 b f Danehill Dancer(IRE) Great Hope (IRE) (Halling (USA))
2012[5] 2652[3] 3775[2] 4732[5] 7822[9]

Reconsider Baby (IRE) *Mrs K Burke* a19 72
3 ch f Refuse To Bend(IRE) Rockahoolababy (IRE) (Kalanisi (IRE))
2010[3] 2593[5] 3396[9] 4143[7] 4625[2]

Rectory Lane *Eve Johnson Houghton* a39 40
3 ch f Compton Place Pudding Lane (IRE) (College Chapel)
16[4] 2447[11] 3036[4] 4911[4]

Redact (IRE) *Richard Hannon Snr* a89 103
4 b g Strategic Prince Rainbow Java (IRE) (Fairy King (USA))
1244[7] 2667[3] 3458[25] 3697[7] 3987[3] 5255[4] 6772[5]

Red Aggressor (IRE) *Clive Brittain* a91 71
4 b g Red Clubs(IRE) Snap Crackle Pop (IRE) (Statoblest)
621[9] 1160[2] 1245[6] 1720[14] 3220[10] 5750[4]

Redalani (IRE) *Alan Brown* a29 58
3 b f Redback Zafaraya (IRE) (Ashkalani (IRE))
6178[8] 6497[12] 6940[4] 7203[7]

Red Army Blues (IRE) *John C McConnell* a44 40
5 b g Soviet Star(USA) Liscoa (IRE) (Foxhound (USA))
997[9]

Red Art (IRE) *Tony Newcombe* a84 86
4 b c Excellent Art All Began (IRE) (Fasliyev (USA))
3411[6] 3757[8] (5301) 6203[5] 7075[4] 7269[2] 7964[7] 8127[12] 8321[5]

Red Avenger (USA) *Ed Dunlop* 104
3 bb c War Front(USA) Emotional Rescue (USA) (Smart Strike (CAN))
1809[7] 2024[2] ◆ 2661[7] 3484[13] (4063) 4214[2] 4917[2] 5725[5] 6838[25]

Red Baron (IRE) *Eric Alston* a65 87
4 b c Moss Vale(IRE) Twinberry (IRE) (Tagula (IRE))
1215[3] 1687[2] 2317[2] 2757[2] 2914[2] (3283) (3769) 4479[9] (4613) 4954[12] 6583[22]

Red Bay *Jane Chapple-Hyam* a34 50
4 b g Haafhd Red Zinnia (Pivotal)
5154[7] 6259[6] 7197[12]

Red Biba (IRE) *Alan McCabe* a48 48
2 ch f Intense Focus(USA) Vital Laser (USA) (Seeking The Gold (USA))
1108[11] 1432[6] 5866[3] 6286[5] 6517[5] 6967[7] 7755[10]

Red Cadeaux *Ed Dunlop* a119 119
7 ch g Cadeaux Genereux Artisia (IRE) (Peintre Celebre (USA))
1269a[2] 1868a[3] 2494a[8] 3457[9] 4745[6] 5531[2] 6441a[4] 7761a[2] 8208a[4]

Red Cape (FR) *Ruth Carr* a76 79
10 b g Cape Cross(IRE) Muirfield (FR) (Crystal Glitters (USA))
2276[5] 2703[3] 2914[4] 3069[5] 3501[5] 3713[2] (3904) 4149[5] (4398) 4619[3] 4970[7] 5583[10] 5887[4] 5973[5] 6995[6]

Red Catkin *George Margarson* a53 66
3 b f Notnowcato Red Salvia (Selkirk (USA))
7321[6] 7610[2] 8121[14] 8388[10]

Red Charmer (IRE) *Ann Duffield* 82
3 b g Red Clubs(IRE) Golden Charm (IRE) (Common Grounds)
1776[5] 2342[5] 2616[7] 3546[12] (4449) 4474[2] 5425[2] (6048) 6296[7] 6846[5]

Red Cobra (IRE) *Tim Easterby* a59 70
3 b g Redback Queen Cobra (IRE) (Indian Rocket)
1647[11] 3025[6] 3758[9] 4976[8] 5704[8] 6633[2] 7148[3] 7343[2] 7807[5]

Red Cossack (CAN) *Paul Webber* a75 62
2 ch g Rebellion Locata (USA) (Stravinsky (USA))
6069[7] 6689[4] 7327[2]

Red Current *Michael Scudamore* a67 53
9 b m Soviet Star(USA) Fleet Amour (USA) (Afleet (CAN))
12[11] 1664[5] 2360[4] 3953[3] 4192[6] 4605[6] 5433[5]

Red Dakota (IRE) *Claes Bjorling* a51 55
2 gr f Clodovil(IRE) Dom Pennion (Dominion)
1718[12] 2577[4] 3023[8] 4387[3] 4862[2] 6452a[9]

Red Davis (JPN) *Hidetaka Otonashi* 120
5 b g Agnes Tachyon(JPN) Dixie Jazz (JPN) (Tony Bin)
1868a[12]

Red Dragon (IRE) *Michael Blanshard* a79 74
3 b g Acclamation Delphie Queen (IRE) (Desert Sun)
(195) 444[2] (738) 1400[2] 1725[8] 2420[3] 3241[13] 7505[4] 7989[3] 8226[3]

Red Dubawi (IRE) *David Marnane* a98 109
5 ch h Dubawi(IRE) Maredsous (FR) (Homme De Loi (IRE))
242a[8] 467a[9] 557a[10] 834a[7] 954a[12] 1255a[3] 1704a[3] 3848a[10] 6623[13] 7227a[3] 7719a[10]

Red Duke (USA) *David Simcock* a107 111
4 ch g Hard Spun(USA) Saudia (USA) (Gone West (USA))
152a[9] 557a[6] 869a[3] 1810[7] 2323[6] 3101[8]

Red Eight (USA) *John Butler* a73 57
3 bb g Gone West(USA) Katherine Seymour (Green Desert (USA))
1965[7] 2549[11] 2949[7] 5098[10]

Redemptor *E Charpy* a81 96
5 gr c Elusive City(USA) Restless Rixa (FR) (Linamix (FR))
503a[5]

Red Explorer (USA) *Jamie Osborne* a75 88
3 b c Henrythenavigator(USA) Remote (USA) (Seattle Slew (USA))
3474[4] (4033) 4283[2] 4592[4] 5247[9] 5987[9] 7985[5] 8068[8]

Red Eyes *Chris Grant* a83 58
5 b g Beat Hollow Kardelle (Kalaglow)
3930[6] 4435[7] 7098[6]

Red Fighter (AZE) *Anar Balahuseynov* a17
3 bb c Scat Daddy(USA) Red Tulle (USA) (A.P. Indy (USA))
6232a[6]

Red Forever *Alan Berry* a19 55
2 ch c Major Cadeaux Spindara (IRE) (Spinning World (USA))
2189[7] 2645[8] 3092[8] 3568[4] 4511[5] 5029[7] 5226[5] 6286[4] 6904[5] 7095[5] 7789[8]

Red Four *George Baker* a45 68
3 ch f Singspiel(IRE) Protectorate (Hector Protector (USA))
1486[14] 2331[6] 7258[5] (7636)

Red Galileo *Ed Dunlop* a82 91
2 b c Dubawi(IRE) Ivory Gala (FR) (Galileo (IRE))
5244[2] ◆ 5727[2] 6593[2] (6934)

Red Gift (IRE) *Brian Ellison* a72 75
3 b g Chineur(FR) Kiva (Indian Ridge)
202[8] 325[2] ◆ 538[2] 738[4] (964) 1275[2] 1647[7] 3533[2] 3730[9] 6575[6] 7282[8]

Red Highlites (IRE) *Ann Duffield* 67
3 br f Red Clubs(IRE) High Lite (Observatory (USA))
2861[5] 3091[5]

Red House *David C Griffiths* a56 53
2 b g Auction House(USA) Highest Dream (IRE) (Highest Honor (FR))
1328[5] 2715[5] 3167[2] 3766[4]

Red Inca *Brian Ellison* a75 84
5 ch g Pivotal Magicalmysterykate (USA) (Woodman (USA))
239[6] 2976[4]

Redinha *Clive Cox* 70
2 b f Dansili So Squally (GER) (Monsun (GER))
3664[5] 5003[4]

Red Invader (IRE) *Charles Hills* a53 40
3 b c Red Clubs(IRE) Tifariti (USA) (Elusive Quality (USA))
6806[2] 7253[10]

Red Jazz (USA) *Charles Hills* a108 114
6 b h Johannesburg(USA) Now That's Jazz (USA) (Sword Dance)
957a[10] 1262a[16] 2258[3] 3101[3] 3831[2] 4276[9] 6392[9]

Red Joker (IRE) *Alan Swinbank* 78
3 br g Red Clubs(IRE) Lady Singspiel (IRE) (Singspiel (IRE))
1645[7] 2408[10] 4100[8] 8294[7]

Red Lady (IRE) *Brian Meehan* a73 83
2 ch f Dutch Art Felucca (Green Desert (USA))
2204[9] (2625) 3522[11] 7329[7]

Red Lago (IRE) *S Arthur* a70 68
5 b g Encosta De Lago(AUS) Speciale (USA) (War Chant (USA))
1740a[3]

Red Larkspur (IRE) *Roger Teal* a85 80
4 b f Red Clubs(IRE) Holda (IRE) (Docksider (USA))
(1173) 2128[8] 2531[3] 3691[5] 5308[6] 6018[7]

Red Lips (GER) *Andreas Lowe* 112
3 b f Areion(GER) Rosarium (GER) (Zinaad)
2065a[2] 2910a[7] 3852a[4] 5044a[4] 7057a[4] 7558a[3]

Redlorryyellowlorry (IRE) *George Baker* 43
2 b g Bushranger(IRE) Bronze Baby (USA) (Silver Charm (USA))
2011[4] 2778[7] 5584[9]

Red Mystique (IRE) *Philip Hide* a61 40
4 b g Red Clubs(IRE) Sacred Love (IRE) (Barathea (IRE))
12[13] 469[4] 579[2] 703[2] 905[6] 1175[7] 7090[10] 7440[15]

Red Oasis *Robert Eddery* a45 22
2 b g Captain Gerrard(IRE) Sahara Silk (IRE) (Desert Style (IRE))
2260[5] 2562[8] 3112[11] 6778[9] 7352[11]

Redondelle (FR) *M Maillard* a70 72
6 b m Indian Rocket Revolera (FR) (Bering)
7573a[2]

Red Orator *Mark Johnston* a88 93
4 ch g Osorio(GER) Red Roses Story (FR) (Pink (FR))
1733[3] 2069[2] 2451[7] 3531[8] 4159[3]

Redoute Star (AUS) *Paul D'Arcy* a63 61
7 br g Redoute's Choice(AUS) Significant Moment (AUS) (Bletchingly (AUS))
1434[5] 1520[5] 1915[3] 2137[2] 2533[6]

Red Paladin (IRE) *Kevin Ryan* 73
3 b g Red Clubs(IRE) Alexander Goldmine (Dansili)
(1575) 2308[3] 2916[5] 3546[3] 4045[4] 4628[5] (5515) 6181[3] 6702[5]

Red Passiflora *Sir Mark Prescott Bt* a63 63
2 b f Danehill Dancer(IRE) Red Peony (Montjeu (IRE))
6949[8] 7450[7] 7875[8]

Red Pike (IRE) *Bryan Smart* 73
2 ch g Kheleyf(USA) Fancy Feathers (IRE) (Redback)
1680[2] ◆ 6174[6] 6681[2] 7026[15]

Red Pilgrim (IRE) *James Toller* a61 78
3 b g Authorized(IRE) Plenty Of Action (USA) (Hennessy (USA))
4382[6] ◆ 5132[6] 6696[3] 7453[3]

Red Ramesses (IRE) *John Best* a74 25
4 br g Red Clubs(IRE) Marasem (Cadeaux Genereux)
163[7] 369[8] 529[5] (649) (863) 1063[7] 6753[7]

Red Red Wine *Alan McCabe* 66
3 b g Dutch Art Atnab (USA) (Riverman (USA))
2547[5] 3047[4] 3632[5] 5030[8] 5884[7] 6291[11]

Red Refraction (IRE) *Richard Hannon Snr* a76 87
3 b c Red Clubs(IRE) Dreamalot (Falbrav (IRE))
(904) 1246[6] 1582[2] 2190[4] ◆ 2626[2] 3320[4] 3658[3] 4283[3] (4797) 5303[5] 5748[3] 6238[8]

Red Rifle (USA) *Todd Pletcher* 91
3 ch c Giant's Causeway(USA) May Night (USA) (Gulch (USA))
3360a[4]

Red Roar (IRE) *Alan Berry* a10 74
6 ch m Chineur(FR) Unfortunate (Komaite (USA))
2343[6] 5049[7] 6603[10] 6903[4] 7599[10]

Red Rocker (IRE) *Brian Meehan* 86
3 ch c Redback Feet Of Flame (USA) (Theatrical (IRE))
1618[2] ◆ 3360a[12]

Red Runaway *Ed Dunlop* a80 86
3 ch g Medicean Gretna (Groom Dancer (USA))
1470[3] (1834) (2216) 2660[4] 3486[9] 4349[4] 6196[6] 6503[5] 7121[9]

Red Seventy *Harry Dunlop* a83 92
4 b g Sakhee(USA) Dimakya (USA) (Dayjur (USA))
1849[6] (2450) 2858[15] 4124[7] 4746[10]

Red Shadow *Alan Brown* a63 58
4 b f Royal Applause Just A Glimmer (Bishop Of Cashel)
162[8] 537[2] 618[6] 890[4] 1079[8] 1147[7] 7197[5] 7508[4] 7808[3] (7904) 8119[9] 8412[3]

Red Shot (FR) *H-A Pantall* a90 86
3 b f Gentlewave(IRE) Red Kiss (IRE) (Fasliyev (USA))
4468a[8]

Red Shuttle *Andi Brown* a73 77
6 b g Starcraft(NZ) Red Azalea (Shirley Heights)
4183[4] 4665[3] 5403[2] 6258[4] 6898[7]

Red Somerset (USA) *Mike Murphy* a83 68
10 b g Red Ransom(USA) Bielska (USA) (Deposit Ticket (USA))
133[6] (311) 340[2]

Red Stargazer (IRE) *David Barron* 87
2 b g Intikhab(USA) Autumn Star (IRE) (Mujadil (USA))
(6546) 7334[3]

Red Star Lady (IRE) *Shaun Harris* a45 42
3 b f Redback Vigorous (IRE) (Danetime (IRE))
985[3] 1197[3] 1367[5] 2996[5] 3325[8] 3739[8] 4353[5] 5864[9] 7150[8] 7347[11] 7752[9] 8234[5] 8438[3]

Red Style (IRE) *Paul Midgley* a32 67
3 b g Red Clubs(IRE) In The Fashion (IRE) (In The Wings)
1204[4] 1461[4] 1764[6] 2336[7]

Red Tide (IRE) *Alan McCabe* a58 70
2 gr g Tamayuz Rectify (IRE) (Mujadil (USA))
3366[4] 3810[3] 5379[3] 6284[10] 7782[9]

Red Tiger Lily *Nigel Tinkler* a48 32
2 ch f Piccolo Juncea (Elnadim (USA))
1534[6] 1839[13] 4583[4] 4847[9] 5578[5] 5964[2] 6511[8] 7036[8]

Red To Amber (IRE) *Clive Cox* a71 71
3 b c Redback Amber's Bluff (Mind Games)
685[7] ◆ (815) 1471[4] 2209[8] 2549[3] 3241[6] 5191[6]

Red Tulip *James Fanshawe* a67 59
3 br f Kheleyf(USA) Red Carnation (IRE) (Polar Falcon (USA))
1712[6] 2330[3] 2528[5] 3495[3] 4885[4] (5923) 6315[7] 6937[8]

Red Turban *Jeremy Noseda* 74
3 b f Kyllachy Red Tiara (USA) (Mr Prospector (USA))
2983[11]

Red Tyke (IRE) *John Quinn* a39 69
4 b g Red Clubs(IRE) Teutonic (IRE) (Revoque (IRE))
1111[5] 3199[2]

Red Valerian (IRE) *Charles Hills* a75 25
3 b c Royal Applause Hidden Heart (USA) (Kingmambo (USA))
(123)

Redvers (IRE) *Ed Vaughan* a87 105
5 br g Ishiguru(USA) Cradle Brief (IRE) (Brief Truce (USA))
2254[4] (2665) ◆ 3527[7] ◆ 4297[5] 4744[11] (6183) 7014[5]

Red Warrior (IRE) *Ismail Mohammed* a83 78
3 ch c Iffraaj Wiolante (GER) (Lagunas)
3585[8] 4968[5] 5495[2] 6178[4] 6630[7] 7651[2] 7864[3]

Red Wifey (IRE) *Alan McCabe* 16
2 b f High Chaparral(IRE) Raspberry Beret (IRE) (Danehill Dancer (IRE))
6512[7]

Red Willow *John E Long* a51 43
7 ch m Noverre(USA) Chelsea Blue (ITY) (Barathea (IRE))
5234[8] 5528[10] 7458[7] 8031[9] 8449[8]

Redwood Blade *Jim Goldie*
4 ch f Needwood Blade Red Typhoon (Belfort (FR))
3465[5] 4888[10]

Redy To Rumble *Michael Attwater* a20
2 ch g Three Valleys(USA) Sorara (Aragon)
3436[8] 4175[11]

Reedcutter *James Toller* 74
2 b c Passing Glance Violet's Walk (Dr Fong (USA))
7469[4]

Ree's Rascal (IRE) *Jim Boyle* a87 92
5 gr g Verglas(IRE) Night Scent (IRE) (Scenic)
(1092) 1583[3] 2085[4] (3108) 3864[2] 4923[3] 5742[6] 6925[4] 7989[5]

Reet Thicknstrong *Bryan Smart* 54
2 b f Captain Gerrard(IRE) Dazzling Quintet (Superlative)
2631[3] 2913[5] 3942[8]

Refectory (IRE) *Andrew Balding* 103
3 b c Danehill Dancer(IRE) Akuna Bay (USA) (Mr Prospector (USA))
4257[2] ◆ 5286[3] (6166) 6991[3]

Refer *Charles Hills* 74
3 b g Rail Link Trellis Bay (Sadler's Wells (USA))
1584[5] (1898) 2325[7]

Reflect (IRE) *Derek Shaw* a80 83
5 b g Hurricane Run(IRE) Raphimix (FR) (Linamix (FR))
39[2] 144[5] (420) 882[2] 1037[7] 2277[2] 2590[2] 3960[10] 6694[12] 6936[10] 7970[12] 8159[9]

Reflected Love (IRE) *Mick Channon* 59
2 b f Mujadil(USA) Cant Hurry Love (Desert Prince (IRE))
3986[11] (4206)

Reflection *Brian Baugh* a34 53
2 ch f Major Cadeaux River Song (USA) (Siphon (BRZ))
5915[5] 6546[10] 6983[5] 7732[7]

Refractor (IRE) *Michael Bell* a89 82
5 ch g Refuse To Bend(IRE) Fancy Intense (Peintre Celebre (USA))
1501[9] 1884[12] 3545[9]

Refreshestheparts (USA) *George Baker* a80 54
4 ch f Proud Citizen(USA) St Francis Wood (USA) (Irish River (FR))
(192) 338[9] (672) (1479) 4348[7]

Refuse Colette (IRE) *Paul Green* a49 56
4 ch f Refuse To Bend(IRE) Roclette (USA) (Rock Of Gibraltar (IRE))
4161[11] 5073[9] 5615[13] 7083[7]

Refuse To Bobbin (IRE) *A Giorgi* 98
3 ch c Refuse To Bend(IRE) Super Bobbina (IRE) (Daggers Drawn (USA))
7724a[8]

Refuse To Mambo *Andrew Hollinshead* a51 48
3 ch g Refuse To Bend(IRE) Sovereign's Honour (USA) (Kingmambo (USA))
2742[7] 3488[5] 3722[5]

Regal Acclaim (IRE) *Ian McInnes* a62 65
4 b g Acclamation Certain Charm (USA) (Thunder Gulch (USA))
1021[7] 1734[9] 2537[13] 3029[8] 3192[11]

Regal Dan (IRE) *Charles Hills* a85 94
3 b c Dark Angel(IRE) Charlene Lacy (IRE) (Pips Pride)
1625[2] 2208[5] 4255[8] 4922[3] 6308[4] 6840[6] ◆ 7769[4]

Regal Hawk *James Tate* a84 93
3 br f Singspiel(IRE) Elegant Hawk (Generous (IRE))
(1219) (2915) (5190) 6031a[6] 6764[4]

Regal Parade *Milton Bradley* a88 113
9 ch g Pivotal Model Queen (USA) (Kingmambo (USA))
944[7] 1234[6] 1691[6] (2257) 2936[6] 3373[5] 3558[14] 4780[11] 4986[17] 5545[4] 5992[6] 6623[6] 7368[12]

Regal Power *J P Murtagh* a68 79
4 b g Royal Applause Be My Charm (Polish Precedent (USA))
5775a[20] 8012a[6]

Regal Silk *Jeremy Noseda* a76 88
3 b f Pivotal Regal Velvet (Halling (USA))
1518[2] 1813[7] (4590) 5348[2] 5958[7] 6951[4]

Regal Swain (IRE) *Alan Swinbank* a5 79
5 b g Ivan Denisovich(IRE) Targhyb (IRE) (Unfuwain (USA))
1282[2] 1448[3] 1568[5] 5051[11] 6498[8]

Regarde Moi *S Botti* 106
5 b g King's Best(USA) Life At Night (IRE) (Night Shift (USA))
2698a[6] (7706a)

Regardez *Ralph Beckett* 84
2 b f Champs Elysees Look So (Efisio)
4921[8] 6318[2] 6949[2] (7493)

Reggae Star *Mark Johnston* a73 76
3 b f Cape Cross(IRE) Caribbean Dancer (USA) (Theatrical (IRE))
(2071) 2387[11] 2915[6] 3322[7] (3620) 4168[4]

Reggie Bond *Geoffrey Oldroyd* a60 57
3 ch g Monsieur Bond(IRE) Triple Tricks (IRE) (Royal Academy (USA))
2080[3] 2950[3] 4008[8] 7806[2] 8142[3]

Reggie Perrin *Pat Phelan* a69 70
5 ch g Storming Home Tecktal (FR) (Pivotal)
3971[7] 4754[5]

Reggie Rabbit *Richard Ford*
4 br g Iceman School Days (Slip Anchor)
63[6] 564[6]

Regiment *Richard Fahey* 81
2 ch c Major Cadeaux My First Romance (Danehill (USA))
3366[5] (3943) 4399[2] 4948[20] 6328[U] 6645[8] 7017[11] 7529[8]

Reginald Claude *Mark Usher* a69 62
5 b g Monsieur Bond(IRE) Miller's Melody (Chief Singer)
(139) 399[6] 728[3] 971[4] 1102[5] 1798[6] 2096[8] 2781[6] 3247[6] 3499[6] 3841[4] (4836) 5230[7] 5674[7] 6040[5] 6343[5] 8152[9]

Regina Mundi (IRE) *Ottavio Di Paolo* 99
6 b m Montjeu(IRE) Delauncy (Machiavellian (USA))
5297a[10]

Regulation (IRE) *M Halford* a99 99
4 br g Danehill Dancer(IRE) Source Of Life (IRE) (Fasliyev (USA))
3869a[8] 6025a[2]

Regy From Sedgy *Frederick Watson* 27
6 ch g Beckett(IRE) Deekazz (IRE) (Definite Article)
2030[9] 3542[8] 5469[7] 5783[8]

Rehanaat (USA) *Ed Dunlop* a57
2 b f Daaher(CAN) Sultana (USA) (Storm Cat (USA))
5131[8] 5924[9] 7295[6]

Rehn's Nest (IRE) *J S Bolger* 108
3 bb f Authorized(IRE) Solas Na Greine (IRE) (Galileo (IRE))
(1166a) 2375a[4] 2689a[2] 3524[15] 3870a[8]

Reillys Daughter *Richard Mitchell* a66 67
5 b f Diktat Compose (Anabaa (USA))
7506[9] 7767[13]

Reimpose (USA) *Pat Eddery* a65 46
2 b f First Defence(USA) Rougeur (USA) (Blushing Groom (FR))
3673[4] (8342)

Reina Cross (ITY) *S Botti* 94
3 b f Reinaldo(FR) Starry Cross (IRE) (Cape Cross (IRE))
1866a[16]

Reinvigorate (IRE) *Emmet Michael Butterly* a53 53
3 b f Invincible Spirit(IRE) Miss Serendipity (IRE) (Key Of Luck (USA))
8119[7] 8169[5]

Reiterate *Milton Bradley* a44 83
4 b f Three Valleys(USA) Rive (USA) (Riverman (USA))
972[5] 1193[7] 1948[12]

Rekindled Interest (AUS) *Jim Conlan* 115
6 b g Redoute's Choice(AUS) Rekindled Affair (IRE) (Rainbow Quest (USA))
7556a[14]

Related *Clive Cox* a84 90
3 b g Kheleyf(USA) Balladonia (Primo Dominie)
245a[11] 553a[14] 4078[2] 4642[2] 5401[5] 6488[2] 6993[10]

Relation Alexander (IRE) *Paul D'Arcy* a70 60
2 ch f Dandy Man(IRE) Elshamms (Zafonic (USA))
3132[4] 3781[9] 5435[6] (6311) 6474[5]

Relentless (IRE) *John Gosden* a76 68
3 b g Dylan Thomas(IRE) Karamiyna (IRE) (Shernazar)
1187[2] 1729[3] (1959)

Relentless Harry (IRE) *George Baker* a75 78
4 gr g Excellent Art Les Alizes (IRE) (Cadeaux Genereux)
1801[8] (2638) 2884[12] 4998[5]

Relight My Fire *Tim Easterby* a81 80
3 ch g Firebreak Making Music (Makbul)
1647[5] 2616[5] 3082[4] 3629[9] 4045[2] (4113) (4375) (4585) 5292[8] 5784[5] 5987[7] 6602[2] 6720[11] 7487[2] 7965[8]

Relizane *A De Royer-Dupre* a74 85
4 b f Zamindar(USA) Reine Zao (FR) (Alzao (USA))
5912a[2]

Remember *Richard Hannon Snr* 90
2 b f Selkirk(USA) Forgotten Dreams (IRE) (Olden Times)
4921[10] (5435) (6233) ◆ 6839[4] 7695[14]

Remember Rocky *Lucy Normile* a47 56
4 ch g Haafhd Flower Market (Cadeaux Genereux)
1270[4] 1790[9] 2537[3] 4469[3] 4826[3] 5921[8] 6083[6] 6921[3]

Remember Salsa (FR) *R Le Gal* a76 76
4 b f Green Tune(USA) Sweet Salsa (FR) (Highest Honor (FR))
7573a[11]

Remember You (IRE) *David Wachman* 95
2 b f Invincible Spirit(IRE) Miss Dela (IRE) (King's Best (USA))
6021a[2] 6622[5]

Reminisce (IRE) *Marco Botti* a78 37
3 b g Oasis Dream Sedna (IRE) (Priolo (USA))
1926[2] ◆ 2547[11] 3253[6] 5867[3] 6998[6]

Remix (IRE) *Ian Williams* a61 72
4 b f Oratorio(IRE) Miss Lopez (IRE) (Key Of Luck (USA))
1886[9] 2092[5] 2711[3] 3098[9] 4996[3] (5521) (5631) 5882[4] 7546[7] 7865[6]

Remote *John Gosden* 116
3 b c Dansili Zenda (Zamindar (USA))
1931[3] (2442) ◆ (2857) ◆ (3485)

Remus De La Tour (FR) *K Borgel* a97 112
4 b c Stormy River(FR) Calithea (IRE) (Marju (IRE))
2184a^{3} 2908a^{3}

Renaione (IRE) *F Chappet* a89 91
7 ch h Storming Home Renilde (FR) (Bigstone (IRE))
(498a)

Renaissance Rio (IRE) *Ed McMahon* a52
2 b f Captain Rio Danish Gem (Danehill (USA))
7294^{9}

Reneesgotzip (USA) *Peter Miller* a110 110
4 ch f City Zip(USA) No Dress Code (USA) (Distorted Humor (USA))
7710a^{2}

Renee's Titan (USA) *Doug O'Neill* a102 77
3 b f Bernstein(USA) Titan Queen (USA) (Tiznow (USA))
7709a^{10}

Renegotiate *Dr Richard Newland* a76 70
4 ch g Trade Fair L'Extra Honor (USA) (Hero's Honor (USA))
1^{2} (107) 167^{5} 5356^{9}

Rene Mathis (GER) *Richard Fahey* a84 92
3 ch g Monsieur Bond(IRE) Remina (GER) (Erminius (GER))
(85) 2190^{7} 2708^{3} ◆ 3066^{3} 3803^{2} 4255^{3} 4767^{5} 5510^{2} 6826^{2}

Renew (IRE) *Marco Botti* 108
3 b c Dansili Hold Me Love Me (IRE) (Sadler's Wells (USA))
(2030) 2457^{2} (4202) 5274^{2} 6196^{3} (6800)

Renny Storm (CZE) *J Michal* a79 90
3 b c Stormy Jail(IRE) Renaissance (CZE) (High Extreme (IRE))
3708a^{3}

Renoir's Lady *Joseph Tuite* a61 61
5 b f Peintre Celebre(USA) Marie De Blois (IRE) (Barathea (IRE))
162^{7} 655^{3} 903^{3} 3015^{5} (3922) 4424^{4} 4909^{5} 5447^{2} 6017^{6}

Rento (FR) *D Prod'Homme* a81 62
10 gr g Medaaly Rosalita (FR) (Nashamaa)
498a^{2}

Repeater *David O'Meara* a68 112
4 b g Montjeu(IRE) Time Over (Mark Of Esteem (IRE))
3483^{10} 4083^{4} 4919^{14} 6349^{3} 6766^{6} 7012^{4}

Repetition *Kristin Stubbs* a76 68
3 b g Royal Applause Uno (Efisio)
(525) 1832^{6} 2408^{8} *2951^{2}* 3566^{3} *4354^{9}* 6291^{9} *6969^{9} 8158^{4} 8345^{5}*

Replicator *Patrick Gilligan* a56 41
8 b g Mujahid(USA) Valldemosa (Music Boy)
143^{9} 327^{8}

Reply (IRE) *A P O'Brien* a58 112
4 b c Oasis Dream Cap Coz (IRE) (Indian Ridge)
1266a^{13} 2446^{9} 2676a^{2} 3262a^{5} 3557^{18} 3846a^{22} 4875^{7}

Reponds Moi (USA) *F Head* 95
3 b f More Than Ready(USA) Pas De Reponse (USA) (Danzig (USA))
6124a^{10}

Reposer (IRE) *Muredach Kelly* a81 86
5 br g Kheleyf(USA) Tragic Point (IRE) (Tragic Role (USA))
194^{7} 2882^{6}

Reqaaba *Robert Cowell* a80 91
3 b f Exceed And Excel(AUS) Something Blue (Petong)
(1875) 2449^{12} (5585) 6768^{3} 7021^{9}

Requested *Mahmood Al Zarooni* a82 77
3 b g Dubawi(IRE) Dream Quest (Rainbow Quest (USA))
(1653)

Reroute (IRE) *Ed Walker* 93
2 b f Acclamation Divert (IRE) (Averti (IRE))
(3295) ◆ 3459^{5} 4855^{6} 5680^{9}

Rerouted (USA) *M F De Kock* a113 111
5 ch h Stormy Atlantic(USA) Rouwaki (USA) (Miswaki (USA))
152a^{3} *(465a)* 657a^{4} *(869a)* *1262a^{6}*

Reset City *Mark Johnston* a70 83
7 ch m Reset(AUS) City Of Angels (Woodman (USA))
2555^{2} 2710^{5} 2956^{2} (3195) ◆ 3427^{2} ◆ 3651^{6} 4098^{2} 4287^{5} (4455) 4663^{2} 4854^{7}

Resist *Tobias B P Coles* a56 56
2 b f Rock Of Gibraltar(IRE) Cecily (Oasis Dream)
3426^{5} *3640^{5}* 3942^{4} 4363^{3} 4910^{3} *7665^{9}*

Resolute *William Haggas* a86 79
2 b g Pivotal Coy (IRE) (Danehill (USA))
7448^{2} ◆ 7817^{2} *(8044) 8397^{2}*

Resonare *Stuart Williams* a52 64
4 b g Echo Of Light Pretty Kool (Inchinor)
(2133) (3326) 4996^{4} 7454^{3}

Resourceful Miss *Paul Webber* a57
4 b f Dubai Destination(USA) Resourceful (IRE) (Entrepreneur)
7838^{3} 8092^{3}

Respect Me *Saeed bin Suroor* a94 83
3 b g Street Cry(IRE) Secret Charm (IRE) (Green Desert (USA))
1635^{8} 3021^{4} ◆ 3542^{4} *3957^{2}*

Resplendent Alpha *Alastair Lidderdale* a70 71
9 ch g Best Of The Bests(IRE) Sunley Scent (Wolfhound (USA))
2^{4} 73^{2} 192^{7} 376^{5} 477^{5} 976^{12} 1015^{5} 1054^{2}

Response *William Haggas* 77
3 ch g New Approach(IRE) Spotlight (Dr Fong (USA))
2746^{2} 3572^{3} 3923^{3} 4404^{2} 5110^{2} 6272^{2}

Restaurateur (IRE) *Andrew Balding* a87 83
4 b g Excellent Art Velvet Appeal (IRE) (Petorius)
1849^{3} 2659^{3} *(3215)* 3684^{11} 3757^{7} 4440^{7} *5928^{5} 6608^{8} 7123^{3}*

Restiadargent (FR) *William Haggas* 117
4 b f Kendargent(FR) Restia (FR) (Montjeu (IRE))
2270^{3} 4260^{4} 4981^{6}

Restless Bay (IRE) *Conor Dore* a81 84
5 br g Elusive City(USA) Argus Gal (IRE) (Alzao (USA))
(186) 229^{2} 426^{3} 452^{6} 583^{7} 688^{6} 971^{5} 1038^{4} 1205^{5} 1351^{2} 1525^{4} 1694^{2} ◆ 1798^{8} 2515^{6} 3171^{7} 3499^{5}

Resurge (IRE) *Stuart Kittow* a92 102
8 b g Danehill Dancer(IRE) Resurgence (Polar Falcon (USA))
(2839) 3832^{11} 6001^{11} 6332^{7} 6957^{6} 7536^{7}

Retirement Plan *Lady Cecil* 96
3 bb c Monsun(GER) Passage Of Time (Dansili)
2442^{10} (3364) (4950)

Retrofit *William Muir* 70
2 b c Exceed And Excel(AUS) Passe Passe (USA) (Lear Fan (USA))
4347^{3} ◆ 4858^{12}

Returntobrecongill *James Given* a89 75
3 ch g Pastoral Pursuits Turn Back (Pivotal)
(3398) 6758^{5} 7028^{12} *7952^{9} 8299^{2} (8366)*

Reve De Nuit (USA) *Mrs K Burke* a99 90
7 ch g Giant's Causeway(USA) My Dream Castles (USA) (Woodman (USA))
1990^{7} *(2579)* 3085^{2} 3345^{3} 4202^{4} 5008^{2} 5513^{3}

Reverberate *Andrew Crook*
4 b f Echo Of Light Niseem (USA) (Hennessy (USA))
1570^{9}

Revert (USA) *Gerry Enright* a55 33
4 b f Rail Link Chaminade (USA) (Danzig (USA))
473^{6} 752^{7} 1089^{5} 3151^{6} 3655^{6}

Revise (IRE) *David Elsworth* a74 74
3 b g Dansili Niner's Home (USA) (Forty Niner (USA))
2151^{7} *3908^{6} 8154^{6}*

Revolutionary (USA) *Todd Pletcher* a114
3 bb c War Pass(USA) Runup The Colors (USA) (A.P. Indy (USA))
2033a^{3} 3127a^{5}

Revolving World (IRE) *Lee James* a49 15
10 b g Spinning World(USA) Mannakea (USA) (Fairy King (USA))
169^{8} 522^{4} 714^{5} 3085^{8}

Rewarded *James Toller* a102 110
4 b g Motivator Granted (FR) (Cadeaux Genereux)
2186^{6} (2652) 3525^{10} 5654^{5} *6198^{5}* 6742^{6}

Rex Imperator *William Haggas* 116
4 b g Royal Applause Elidore (Danetime (IRE))
367a^{12} 2858^{2} 3558^{6} 3840^{2} (4986) 5763^{2} 6193^{11}

Rex Romanorum (IRE) *Patrick Holmes* 72
5 b g Holy Roman Emperor(IRE) Willowbridge (IRE) (Entrepreneur)
2315^{3} 2753^{3} 3649^{2} 4007^{6} 6301^{9} 7772^{17}

Rex Whistler (IRE) *Julie Camacho* a69 75
3 b g Tamayuz Dangle (IRE) (Desert Style (IRE))
1570^{4} 2506^{3} 3232^{3} 3809^{3} 6794^{2} *7734^{3}*

Reyaadah *Charles Hills* 102
3 b f Tamayuz Tafaani (IRE) (Green Desert (USA))
1622^{6} 2148^{10} 5271^{2} 6000^{6} 7020^{3}

Reynaldothewizard (USA) *S Seemar* a116 96
7 b g Speightstown(USA) Holiday Runner (USA) (Meadowlake (USA))
(365a) (955a) (1266a)

Rezia (FR) *A Mesnil*
5 b f Sunshack Rezha (FR) (Ramouncho (FR))
6680a^{7}

Rezwaan *Murty McGrath* a81 51
6 b g Alhaarth(IRE) Nasij (USA) (Elusive Quality (USA))
403^{4} 652^{9} 813^{11} (1497) (1617) 1780^{2} 2808^{9} 3780^{11} 7318^{7} *7438^{11} 7785^{12}* 8178^{12}

Rhagori *Ralph Beckett* a92 93
4 b f Exceed And Excel(AUS) Cresta Gold (Halling (USA))
1768^{8} *(2750)* 3409^{8} 4878^{2} 5402^{8} *7649^{7}*

Rhagori Aur *Bryan Smart* a85 80
3 ch f Exceed And Excel(AUS) Aberdovey (Mister Baileys)
1690^{4} 2039^{9} 3478^{3} 3813^{7} 4117^{4} 4478^{2} 5057^{4} *7731^{7}*

Rhamnus *Richard Hannon Snr* a89 86
3 b c Sakhee's Secret Happy Lady (FR) (Cadeaux Genereux)
7820^{8} *8071^{6} 8218^{7} 8385^{3}*

Rhinestone Rebel (IRE) *Peter Hiatt* a57
7 ch g Rashar(USA) Flute Opera (IRE) (Sharifabad (IRE))
6402^{7} 7422^{7} *7734^{4} 8149^{13}*

Rhombus (IRE) *Ismail Mohammed* 95
3 b g Authorized(IRE) Mathool (IRE) (Alhaarth (IRE))
2386^{3} (3528) 5030^{2} 5792^{4} (6211) ◆ 7072^{7} 7823^{18}

Rhossili Bay *Alastair Lidderdale* a57 50
4 b f Beat Hollow Welsh Dawn (Zafonic (USA))
2533^{10} 2801^{9} *5002^{10}*

Rhyolite (IRE) *Marco Botti* a69 55
3 b c Rock Of Gibraltar(IRE) Ghenwah (FR) (Selkirk (USA))
195^{2} 371^{2}

Rhythm Lake (USA) *William R Edwards* a62
3 bb g Friends Lake(USA) Royal Rhythm (USA) (Rhythm (USA))
786a^{3}

Rhythm To Spare (NZ) *Michael Moroney* 100
4 b g Pins(AUS) Stanica (NZ) (Zabeel (NZ))
7826a^{7}

Ria Antonia (USA) *Jeremiah C Englehart* a110
2 b f Rockport Harbor(USA) Beer Baroness (USA) (Mr Greeley (USA))
(7707a)

Ribaat (IRE) *Roger Varian* 99
3 b g Invincible Spirit(IRE) Fonda (USA) (Quiet American (USA))
1668^{4} ◆ 2188^{5}

Ribbleton *Richard Fahey* 75
2 b g Bushranger(IRE) Bayleaf (Efisio)
4801^{2} ◆ 5338^{3} 6546^{3} (7419)

Ribbons *James Fanshawe* a72 99
3 ch f Manduro(GER) Sister Act (Marju (IRE))
(2195) (3583) (4878) 6536^{3}

Rich Again (IRE) *James Bethell* a73 72
4 b g Amadeus Wolf Fully Fashioned (IRE) (Brief Truce (USA))
399^{2} 493^{4} 775^{10} 3981^{3} 4338^{5} 4560^{8} 5273^{2} 5985^{2} 6603^{5}

Rich Coast *J P Murtagh* a96 109
5 b g King's Best(USA) Costa Rica (IRE) (Sadler's Wells (USA))
3599a^{14} (7388a)

Rich Forever (IRE) *James Bethell* a53 74
3 b g Camacho Sixfields Flyer (IRE) (Desert Style (IRE))
3062^{8} 4007^{4} 4158^{2} 4725^{6} 6274^{6} 6720^{6} 7065^{3}

Richies Party Girl (USA) *Wesley A Ward* 99
2 bb f Any Given Saturday(USA) Very Special Lite (USA) (Majestic Light (USA))
5555a^{4}

Richo *Shaun Harris* a49 46
7 ch g Bertolini(USA) Noble Water (FR) (Noblequest (FR))
406^{5} 515^{5} 703^{8} 3882^{7} 4429^{4} 5093^{4} 5433^{7} 6518^{14}

Rich Pickings (FR) *P Peltier* a66 68
4 b g Muhtathir Last Harvest (FR) (Kahyasi)
922a^{2}

Rich Tapestry (IRE) *C W Chang* a82 114
5 b g Holy Roman Emperor(IRE) Genuine Charm (IRE) (Sadler's Wells (USA))
8209a^{6}

Ridasiyna (FR) *M Delzangles* 121
4 b f Motivator Ridafa (IRE) (Darshaan)
1870a^{6}

Ridgeblade *Noel Wilson* 48
3 ch f Bahamian Bounty Verasina (USA) (Woodman (USA))
1458^{4} 1762^{9} 5265^{8}

Ridgeway Hawk *Mark Usher* a59 36
5 ch g Monsieur Bond(IRE) Barefooted Flyer (USA) (Fly So Free (USA))
1621^{0} 618^{2} 890^{5} 1087^{10} 1452^{3} 1734^{7} 2170^{3} 2582^{2}

Ridgeway Sapphire *Mark Usher* a24 52
6 b m Zafeen(FR) Barefooted Flyer (USA) (Fly So Free (USA))
3247^{11} 3660^{2} 3922^{4} 4423^{4} 4659^{9} 5602^{5} 6101^{2}

Ridgeway Storm (IRE) *Lady Cecil* 83
3 b g Hurricane Run(IRE) Hesperia (Slip Anchor)
5286^{4}

Riding The River (USA) *David Cotey* a94 113
6 b g Wiseman's Ferry(USA) Glow Ruby Go (USA) (Rubiano (USA))
6456a^{4}

Rievaulx Ranger (IRE) *Kevin Ryan* a19 34
2 b g Bushranger(IRE) Geht Fasteur (IRE) (Chineur (FR))
5970^{7} *7882^{8}*

Right Behind You *Tom Dascombe* a18
2 b c Royal Applause Aegean Shadow (Sakhee (USA))
5941^{9} *7113^{7}*

Rightcar *Peter Grayson* a54 43
6 b g Bertolini(USA) Loblolly Bay (Halling (USA))
128^{5} 326^{5} 339^{3} 670^{5} 756^{2} (819) 997^{3} 1042^{3} 1088^{6} 1356^{3} 1395^{5} 6930^{8} 8051^{7} 8168^{7}

Right Divine (IRE) *Peter Fahey* a59 67
4 gr g Verglas(IRE) Yellow Trumpet (Petong)
679a^{12}

Right Of Appeal *Mark Johnston* 54
2 b g Dubawi(IRE) Easy To Love (USA) (Diesis)
3350^{7} 7448^{8} 7817^{14}

Right Step *Alan Jarvis* a85 102
6 b g Xaar Maid To Dance (Pyramus (USA))
882^{4} 1766^{9} 2590^{4} 2867^{10} 3827^{10} 4923^{16} 6358^{13}

Right Stuff (FR) *Gary Moore* a97 63
10 bb g Dansili Specificity (USA) (Alleged (USA))
(227) 901^{2} 1201^{4} 1513^{2} (3819)

Right Touch *Richard Fahey* 88
3 b g Royal Applause Amira (Efisio)
1288^{2} (1647) 2371^{9} 2626^{3} 3566^{6} 5056^{4} (5832) 6238^{3} 6586^{17}

Rigid *Tony Carroll* a59 48
6 ch g Refuse To Bend(IRE) Supersonic (Shirley Heights)
110^{9} 441^{8} 630^{6} 725^{7} (900) 1093^{10} 1617^{3} 2072^{5} *3433^{7}* 3736^{3}

Rigid Rock (IRE) *J T Gorman* a74 72
6 b g Refuse To Bend(IRE) Delia (IRE) (Darshaan)
3796a^{6}

Rigolleto (IRE) *Anabel K Murphy* a72 82
5 b g Ad Valorem(USA) Jallaissine (IRE) (College Chapel)
1286^{10} *1694^{10}* 2225^{5} *3172^{4}* 3511^{7} *4636^{6}* 5049^{2} 5583^{2} (5841) 6463^{3} 7282^{5} *7897^{4} 8128^{5}*

Riley's Missile (IRE) *Charles Smith* a35 47
2 ch g Majestic Missile(IRE) Cockaleekie (USA) (Alphabet Soup (USA))
1285^{5} 1574^{5} 1820^{6} 2005^{5} 2475^{6} *2947^{6}* 3541^{5} *7036^{9} 7755^{13}*

Rime A Rien *F Rohaut* a89 93
3 b f Amadeus Wolf Rainbow Crossing (Cape Cross (IRE))
1000a^{7}

Ri Na Si *Michael Appleby* a48 61
3 b g Green Horizon Luisa Miller (IRE) (Entrepreneur)
5517^{3} 6074^{8} 7345^{6} *7643^{12}*

Ring Of Fire *John Spearing* a49
6 b g Firebreak Sweet Patoopie (Indian Ridge)
909^{10}

Rio Cato *Alex Hales* a26 41
3 ch f Notnowcato Brazilian Terrace (Zilzal (USA))
2924^{10}

Rio Cobolo (IRE) *David Nicholls* a70 73
7 b g Captain Rio Sofistication (IRE) (Dayjur (USA))
912^{3} 976^{5} (986) 1205^{4} 1271^{8} 1460^{8} 2663^{7} 3068^{15} 3090^{6} 3715^{4} 4482^{7} 4623^{2} 4893^{2} 5427^{5} 6181^{2} 6464^{7}

Rioja Day (IRE) *J W Hills* a50 69
3 b c Red Clubs(IRE) Dai E Dai (USA) (Seattle Dancer (USA))
1900^{13} *4521^{10}* 4829^{2} 5346^{4} *6748^{6}* 7093^{4} (7429)

Rio Ranger (IRE) *Bryan Smart* a24
2 b f Bushranger(IRE) Desert D'Argent (IRE) (Desert Story (IRE))
8266^{5}

Rio Royale (IRE) *Amanda Perrett* a70 45
7 b g Captain Rio Lady Nasrana (FR) (Al Nasr (FR))
3326^{13} 3660^{11} 4424^{6}

Rio Sands *Richard Whitaker* a47 48
8 b g Captain Rio Sally Traffic (River Falls)
1961^{DSQ} 2611^{9} 3654^{12}

Rio's Girl *Tony Coyle* a49 64
6 br m Captain Rio African Breeze (Atraf)
1077^{8} 1278^{6} 2702^{8} 2795^{3} 3024^{8} 3392^{8} 4009^{14} 4761^{5} 5708^{8}

Rio's Pearl *Ralph Beckett* a80 82
3 b f Captain Rio Agony Aunt (Formidable (USA))
3279^{12} *5103^{2}* 6162^{5} ◆ 6583^{10} *7731^{4}*

Rio's Rosanna (IRE) *Richard Whitaker* a91 95
6 b m Captain Rio Ling Lane (Slip Anchor)
2240^{7} 2427^{7} 2855^{5} 3345^{4} 5147^{2} 5723^{2} 6302^{4} 6729^{2} 7174^{10} 7526^{9} 7823^{2} *7990^{6}*

Riot Of Colour *Ralph Beckett* a76 92
4 b f Excellent Art Riotous Applause (Royal Applause)
2444^{10}

Rio Yuma (ITY) *Kristin Stubbs* a43
2 b f Gold Sphinx(USA) Selsey (Selkirk (USA))
7260^{10}

Riponian *Susan Corbett* 42
3 ch g Trade Fair Dispol Katie (Komaite (USA))
1272^{4} 1648^{10} 1967^{10} 3463^{11} 3772^{8} 4374^{8} 5139^{14}

Riposte *Lady Cecil* 111
3 b f Dansili Rainbow Lake (Rainbow Quest (USA))
1813^{2} ◆ (2423) ◆ (3482) ◆ 4550a^{5} 5682^{5} 7048a^{7}

Riptide *Michael Scudamore* 87
7 b g Val Royal(FR) Glittering Image (IRE) (Sadler's Wells (USA))
1721^{3} 2205^{10} (3065) 3560^{12} 4913^{10} (6565) 7064^{4}

Rise To Glory (IRE) *Shaun Harris* a71 67
5 b c King's Best(USA) Lady At War (Warning)
35^{6} 240^{9} 349^{9} 409^{5} (565) 733^{3} 917^{4} (1042) (1271) 1394^{4} *1657^{6}* 1995^{6} 6219^{6} 6478^{9} 6808^{4} 6980^{7} (6994) (7148) 7346^{9} 7455^{9} 7728^{2} 7848^{3} 8030^{5} 8217^{5} 8456^{5}

Rising Breeze (FR) *K R Burke* 85
2 b c Shirocco(GER) Moon Tree (FR) (Groom Dancer (USA))
(4926) 5875a^{2} 6710a^{5} 7409a^{7}

Rising Dawn (IRE) *Richard Hannon Snr* a55 73
2 gr c Dark Angel(IRE) Irish Design (IRE) (Alhaarth (IRE))
3017^{9} *3689^{8}* 4414^{6} ◆ 5347^{2} ◆ 5951^{5} (6322) 6897^{2}

Rising Rainbow *Mel Brittain*
2 b g Rainbow High Lord Conyers (IRE) (Inzar (USA))
5180^{8} 5785^{7}

Riskit Fora Biskit (IRE) *Michael Bell* a80 105
3 b f Kodiac Miss Brief (IRE) (Brief Truce (USA))
(729) (894) 992^{2} (1808) ◆ 2521^{2} 3562^{11} (4247) (4935a) 6445a^{4}

Risk 'N' Reward (IRE) *Amy Weaver* a49
2 ch g Dandy Man(IRE) Sharp Diversion (USA) (Diesis)
5000^{9} 8326^{10} 8451^{10}

Risky Rizkova *Jonathan Portman* 64
3 b g Sleeping Indian Tri Pac (IRE) (Fairy King (USA))
2098^{8} 6412^{8} 6527^{8} 7772^{11}

Risquillo (FR) *M Boutin* a85 79
7 b h Ballingarry(IRE) Alexia Fedorovna (USA) (Steinlen)
960a^{2}

Ritaach (IRE) *Clive Brittain* 42
3 b f Compton Place Golubitsa (IRE) (Bluebird (USA))
2548^{10}

Rite To Reign *Philip McBride* a74
2 b g Tiger Hill(IRE) Magical Cliche (USA) (Affirmed (USA))
7513^{7} 7854^{8} (8026)

Rivas Rhapsody (IRE) *Rae Guest* a83 94
5 b f Hawk Wing(USA) Riva Royale (Royal Applause)
2928^{5} 3407^{2} 3892^{2} 4284^{2}

Rivellino *K R Burke* a100 96
3 b g Invincible Spirit(IRE) Brazilian Bride (IRE) (Pivotal)
1806^{4} ◆ *(2158)* 2452^{11} 3348^{5} 4255^{10} *6692^{8} 7982^{6} (8305)*

River Ardeche *Tracy Waggott* a71 65
8 b g Elnadim(USA) Overcome (Belmez (USA))
718^{4} 965^{4} 1394^{9} 2912^{4} 3395^{7}

Riverboat Springs (IRE) *Mick Channon* 94
2 b c Bushranger(IRE) Mashie (Selkirk (USA))
(2358) 2863^{2} ◆ 3422^{13} 5837^{2} 6195^{4} 6866^{5} 7421^{3}

River Dreamer (IRE) *Robert Stephens* a44
2 ch f Intense Focus(USA) Guard Hill (USA) (Rahy (USA))
8188^{6}

River Du Nord (FR) *Susan Gardner* a42
6 b m Voix Du Nord(FR) Palala River (Colmore Row)
(4846a) 5329a^{3} (7144a) *7382^{5} 8204^{6}*

River Goddess (IRE) *Charles Hills* a60 63
2 b f Marju(IRE) Talwin (IRE) (Alhaarth (IRE))
3760^{13} *4409^{6}* 5435^{4}

Riverkaye (FR) *J-C Rouget* a85 92
4 b f Orpen(USA) River Ballade (USA) (Irish River (FR))
(5912a)

River Pageant *Brendan Powell* 59
4 ch f Primo Valentino(IRE) Belly Dancer (IRE) (Danehill Dancer (IRE))
4996[10]

River Prince (FR) *P Adda* a68 79
3 b g Stormy River(FR) Princess Liu (IRE) (Desert Style (IRE))
3129a[12] 7569a[9]

Rizal Park (IRE) *Andrew Balding* 77
2 b g Amadeus Wolf Imelda (USA) (Manila (USA))
2382[3] 2645[2] (3836) 4703[4] 4988[7]

Rizeena (IRE) *Clive Brittain* 113
2 b f Iffraaj Serena's Storm (IRE) (Statue Of Liberty (USA))
1634[5] ◆ (2204) (2809) (3459) ◆ 4253[2] 5573a[3] (6024a) 6798[2]

Roachdale House (IRE) *Richard Fahey* 93
2 b c Mastercraftsman(IRE) Golden Legacy (IRE) (Rossini (USA))
4886[3] (5826) 6545[3] (7529)

Road Tosky (IRE) *E Botti* 94
3 b f Elusive City(USA) Victory Peak (Shirley Heights)
2697a[9] 3616a[5]

Roanne (USA) *Clive Cox* 68
3 b f Lemon Drop Kid(USA) Chalamont (IRE) (Kris)
1900[4] 2495[7] 2824[4] 3699[7] 4069[4] 4659[2] 5431[2]

Roaring Rocks (FR) *Heather Main* a49
3 gr g Stormy River(FR) Saulace (FR) (Saumarez)
1848 6926[11] 7299[5] 7923[10]

Roatan *Mlle A Imaz-Ceca* a90 97
8 gr g Daylami(IRE) Celestial Lagoon (JPN) (Sunday Silence (USA))
5465a[9] 6252a[8]

Robbmaa (FR) *Mrs J L Le Brocq* a30 43
8 bl g Cape Cross(IRE) Native Twine (Be My Native (USA))
1313a[7] 4846a[6] 5329a[9]

Robert Le Diable (FR) *D Prod'Homme* a86 99
4 ch c Dutch Art Red Begonia (Pivotal)
961a[7]

Roberto Pegasus (USA) *Alan King* a86 89
7 bb g Fusaichi Pegasus(USA) Louju (USA) (Silver Hawk (USA))
93[6]

Robertson (IRE) *James Fanshawe* a61
3 b g Duke Of Marmalade(IRE) Mythologie (FR) (Bering)
6402[6]

Robert The Painter (IRE) *David O'Meara* 102
5 b g Whipper(USA) Lidanna (Nicholas (USA))
2450[16] 3087[2] 3349[2] 3777[5] (4373) (4850) (5546) 5838[2] 6624[3] 6838[27] 7172[7]

Robin Du Nord (FR) *J-P Gauvin* a101 100
6 b h Voix Du Nord(FR) La Romagne (FR) (Art Francais (USA))
3969a[7]

Robin Hood (IRE) *Philip Mitchell* a85 101
5 b g Galileo(IRE) Banquise (IRE) (Last Tycoon)
1034[9] 1382[7] 1673[5] 2251[7] 2728[5] 3273[4] 4166[7] 5793[8]

Robin Hoods Bay *Ed Vaughan* a106 112
5 b g Motivator Bijou A Moi (Rainbow Quest (USA))
189[3] (401) (897) 1034[2] 1241[4] (5269) 5725[7] 6198[6]

Robot Boy (IRE) *David Barron* 96
3 ch g Shamardal(USA) Pivotal's Princess (IRE) (Pivotal)
(1539) 2022[7] 2371[10] 3104[2] (3634) 4255[7] 4767[7] 6238[7] 6990[6]

Robyn *Scott Dixon* a53 46
3 b f Byron Discoed (Distinctly North (USA))
1458[8] 2169[6] 3654[8] 3994[9] 5085[9] 5788[5] 7459[8] 7759[3] (8112) 8271[7] 8352[4] 8406[6]

Robynelle *Keith Dalgleish* 69
2 b f Royal Applause Chicita Banana (Danehill Dancer (IRE))
1565[4] 1820[2] 2404[3] (2701) 3332[5] 3459[15] 5703[6] 6082[5]

Rocaille (FR) *Mme C Head-Maarek* a96 80
3 b f Anabaa(USA) Rose Rose (USA) (Cozzene (USA))
8440a[11]

Roca Tumu (IRE) *Ms Joanna Morgan* 107
3 br c Footstepsinthesand Lucy Diamonds (IRE) (Orpen (USA))
(3484)

Roccarina (FR) *H-A Pantall* a85 71
3 gr f Shirocco(GER) Carinamix (FR) (Linamix (FR))
5805a[4]

Rocco Breeze (IRE) *James Unett* a52 30
4 b g Shirocco(GER) Crossbreeze (USA) (Red Ransom (USA))
5650[7]

Roc De Prince *David O'Meara* a74 77
4 b g Shirocco(GER) Louella (USA) (El Gran Senor (USA))
712[3] 969[6] 1390[2] 1763[3] 2118[9]

Roc Fort *James Moffatt* 50
4 b g Rock Of Gibraltar(IRE) Frangy (Sadler's Wells (USA))
2462[9] 2833[7] 3595[11] 4343[9] 4562[8] 4822[7] 5295[9] 7099[10] 7372[8]

Rochambeau (IRE) *Sir Michael Stoute* a61
2 b g Sir Percy Tableau Vivant (IRE) (Pivotal)
6168[7]

Rochdale *A Al Raihe* a81 86
10 ch g Bertolini(USA) Owdbetts (IRE) (High Estate)
151a[12] 362a[9] 657a[11]

Rochelle (IRE) *William Muir* a44 46
2 b f Duke Of Marmalade(IRE) Emilion (Fantastic Light (USA))
7335[9] 7764[14]

Rochester *Saeed bin Suroor* a63
2 ch c Exceed And Excel(AUS) Bahamian Babe (Bahamian Bounty)
7638[11] 7893[5]

Rock A Doodle Doo (IRE) *Sally Hall* a103 90
6 b g Oratorio(IRE) Nousaiyra (IRE) (Be My Guest (USA))
1536[8] 2040[8] 2590[6] 4512[8]

Rockalong (IRE) *Luca Cumani* a89 100
4 b c Rock Of Gibraltar(IRE) High Spot (Shirley Heights)
(1500) (1922) ◆ 2424[7] 3697[2] 4080[13] 4765[3] 5768[7] 6650[2] 7172[3]

Rock Anthem (IRE) *Mike Murphy* a69 68
9 ch g Rock Of Gibraltar(IRE) Regal Portrait (IRE) (Royal Academy (USA))
13[4] 1873[5] 4865[5] 5346[9] 6400[6] 6933[10] 7639[4]

Rockawango (FR) *James Ewart* 75
7 b g Okawango(USA) Janou La Belle (FR) (Shining Steel)
7423[6]

Rock Band *Emmet Michael Butterly* a71 71
4 b g Rock Of Gibraltar(IRE) Decision Maid (USA) (Diesis)
6218[8] 6283[10]

Rock Canyon (IRE) *Linda Perratt* a56 66
4 b g Rock Of Gibraltar(IRE) Tuesday Morning (Sadler's Wells (USA))
2217[5] 2409[3] 2795[9] 3197[7] 3713[5] 3934[7] 4292[4] 4448[6] 4992[6] 5047[3] 5336[5] 5708[2] 6053[8] 6471[9] 6669[2] 6687[5] 6903[5] 7149[4]

Rock Charm *Stuart Williams* 41
2 b g Araafa(IRE) Evening Charm (IRE) (Bering)
7467[12] 7654[6]

Rock Choir *William Haggas* 101
3 b f Pivotal Choir Mistress (Chief Singer)
1666[7] ◆ 2960[3] (3530) (4485) ◆ 5402[3] 6536[4] 7020[5]

Rock Diamond (IRE) *Brendan Powell* a50 54
3 b f Rock Of Gibraltar(IRE) Yaky Romani (IRE) (Victory Note (USA))
1671[11] 1879[5] 2566[3] 2950[7] 3041[3] 3428[3] 3578 3820[8] (4345) 7907[9] 8225[6] 8371[9] 8448[10]

Rocked The Boat *Tobias B P Coles* a63
2 b c Mizzen Mast(USA) Jazz Jam (Pivotal)
7901[3] 8044[4] 8201[7]

Rocket Rob (IRE) *Willie Musson* a84 87
7 b g Danetime(IRE) Queen Of Fibres (IRE) (Scenic)
113[6] 457[5] 1346[6] 1814[2] 2255[7] 2725[6] 3341[2] 3786[7] 4217[6] 5673[2] (5956) 6331[5] 8021[9] 8181[12] 8431[7]

Rocket Ronnie (IRE) *David Nicholls* 88
3 b g Antonius Pius(USA) Ctesiphon (USA) (Arch (USA))
1759[3] 1966[3] 2080[8] 2770[6] (3463) (4008) 4374[2] 5016[3] (5342) (5425) 5944[7] 6874[9] 7211[14]

Rockfella *Denis Coakley* a59 86
7 ch g Rock Of Gibraltar(IRE) Afreeta (USA) (Afleet (CAN))
2587[3] 3344[9] 5746[13]

Rockgoat (IRE) *Daniel Mark Loughnane* a70 62
4 b g Rock Of Gibraltar(IRE) Queveda (IRE) (Mark Of Esteem (IRE))
545[3] 801[9] 886[8] 993[7] 1017[10] 2168[3] 2514[7] 2986[10] 3252[4] 8360[13]

Rock God (IRE) *Eve Johnson Houghton* a75 83
3 br g Shirocco(GER) Melatonina (IRE) (King Charlemagne (USA))
1678[14] 3214[7] 3907[4] 4899[6] 5743[5] 5854[2] 6081[7] 6743[12] 7071[5]

Rockie Road (IRE) *Paul Green* a45 55
2 b c Footstepsinthesand Roclette (USA) (Rock Of Gibraltar (IRE))
4351[10] 4513[5] 5025[6] 5610[5] 6663[2] 6726[3] 7032[10] 7935[6]

Rock Me Baby (USA) *Craig Dollase* a94 105
4 bb g Rock Hard Ten(USA) Barbara Orr (USA) (Tale Of The Cat (USA))
7710a[6]

Rock 'N' Roll Star *Charles Hills* 74
2 b c Cockney Rebel(IRE) Sweet Afton (IRE) (Mujadil (USA))
4256[4] 5490[4] 5968[3] 7492[6]

Rock N Rouge (IRE) *David Brown* a65 76
2 ch f Rock Of Gibraltar(IRE) Samorra (IRE) (In The Wings)
5339[4] 6234[3] 6746[3] 7095[3]

Rock Of Ages *Michael Murphy* a65 38
4 ch g Pivotal Magic Peak (IRE) (Danehill (USA))
1352[3] 1804[11] 2568[6] 2991[2] 7159[11] 7612[11] 8129[2] (8229)

Rock Of Cashel (GER) *R Dzubasz* 72
2 b c Areion(GER) Rocket Light (GER) (Lando (GER))
7232a[8]

Rock Of Dreams (IRE) *Charles Hills* 75
2 b g Rock Of Gibraltar(IRE) Manhattan Dream (USA) (Statue Of Liberty (USA))
3155[2] ◆ 3836[7] 6739[3] (7270)

Rock Of Leon *Michael Bell* 41
2 b g Rock Of Gibraltar(IRE) Leonica (Lion Cavern (USA))
7607[9] 7773[8]

Rock Of Romance (IRE) *A Wohler* 103
3 br c Rock Of Gibraltar(IRE) Romantic Venture (IRE) (Indian Ridge)
7591a[2]

Rock On Candy *John Spearing* a56 77
4 b f Excellent Art Rock Candy (IRE) (Rock Of Gibraltar (IRE))
(2870) 4930[9] (5094) 7633[6] 7777[8]

Rock Peak (IRE) *Bernard Llewellyn* a67 49
8 b g Dalakhani(IRE) Convenience (IRE) (Ela-Mana-Mou)
3271[11] 3884[3] 5433[6]

Rock Relief (IRE) *Chris Grant* a56 73
7 gr g Daylami(IRE) Sheer Bliss (IRE) (Sadler's Wells (USA))
(2540) 3726[8]

Rock Rose (SWE) *R Hirschfeld* 4
7 b m Bal Du Seigneur(USA) Rutger Wolga (SWE) (Valiyar)
4333a[7]

Rocksee (IRE) *Tom Dascombe* a66
2 ch f Rock Of Gibraltar(IRE) Sightseer (USA) (Distant View (USA))
5352[3] 6607[3]

Rocksilla *Chris Wall* a70 90
3 b f Rock Of Gibraltar(IRE) Hope Island (IRE) (Titus Livius (FR))
(2637) 3489[4] (5150) (6575)

Rocks Off *Fawzi Abdulla Nass* a95 94
5 b c Motivator Chambray (IRE) (Barathea (IRE))
151a[7]

Rock Song *John Mackie* a74 79
4 b g Rock Of Gibraltar(IRE) Jackie's Opera (FR) (Indian Ridge)
(1434) 1889[3] 2383[4] 2710[2] 3204[8] 4135[2]

Rock Supreme (IRE) *Michael Dods* 76
4 b g Rock Of Gibraltar(IRE) Love And Affection (USA) (Exclusive Era (USA))
2705[7] 3729[3] 4889[5] 5332[7] 6758[11] 7130[9] 7369[8]

Rocktherunway (IRE) *Michael Dods* 89
4 ch g Nayef(USA) Femme Fatale (Fairy King (USA))
1391[8] 1536[11] (2009) 2633[6] 3765[6] 4782[2] 5109[8] 6237[3] 6585[3] 7338[11]

Rock Up (IRE) *David Elsworth* a76 76
3 b g Kheleyf(USA) Kissing Time (Lugana Beach)
1618[9] 2394[6] 2722[3] 3171[2] 4499[3] 5616[2] (6425) 6929[3] 7445[4]

Rockweiller *Steve Gollings* a70 62
6 b h Rock Of Gibraltar(IRE) Ballerina Suprema (IRE) (Sadler's Wells (USA))
896[7] 1111[9] 1239[3] 1775[4] 3081[3] 3195[10] 4071[3] 4853[3] 5427[3] 5840[4] 6722[8] 7458[11]

Rockwood *Jane Chapple-Hyam* 49
2 b c Rock Of Gibraltar(IRE) Hannah Frank (IRE) (High Chaparral (IRE))
3366[7] 6570[6]

Rocky Couloir *Michael Easterby* a37 50
3 ch g Rock Of Gibraltar(IRE) Framboise (Diesis)
2306[16] 2516[8] 2989[8] 6074[11] 6986[8]

Rocky Ground (IRE) *Roger Varian* 104
3 b c Acclamation Keriyka (IRE) (Indian Ridge)
5538[8] 6282[2] (6719)

Rocky Hill Ridge *Alan McCabe* a5 13
2 b g Auction House(USA) Amwell Star (USA) (Silver Buck (USA))
4142[10] 5826[10] 6773[6]

Rocky Rebel *Michael Blake* a66 76
5 b g Norse Dancer(IRE) Gulchina (USA) (Gulch (USA))
131[6] 351[6] 5672[9]

Rocky Reef *Philip Hide* a73 86
4 b g Danbird(AUS) Leah's Pride (Atraf)
1583[10] 1922[15] 2618[10] 3274[4] 4237[4] 4440[6] 5398[4] 5815[5] 6360[2] ◆ 6959[3] ◆ (7319)

Rocky Ride (IRE) *Andrew Balding* a39 64
3 b f Rock Of Gibraltar(IRE) Sidecar (IRE) (Spectrum (IRE))
3923[5] 4381[9] 5064[6]

Rocky Two (IRE) *David O'Meara* a52 75
3 ch g Rock Of Gibraltar(IRE) Toorah Laura La (USA) (Black Minnaloushe (USA))
1829[10] 3394[6] 4931[10] 5497[7] 7543[4] ◆ 7667[5]

Rocquaine (IRE) *Mrs A Malzard* 46
4 b f Oratorio(IRE) Watch The Clock (Mtoto)
1313a[6] 1740a[4] 2302a[3] 5329a[8]

Rodion Raskolnikov (FR) *C Lerner* a71 73
3 b g Russian Blue(IRE) Mikalia (FR) (Kaldoun (FR))
1850a[5] 2434a[2]

Rodrigo De Freitas (IRE) *Jim Boyle* a64 62
6 b g Captain Rio Brazilian Sun (IRE) (Barathea (IRE))
9[8] 6531[0] 883[9] 1175[4] 1877[4] 2284[6] 5099[9] 5934[2]

Rodrigo De Torres *David Nicholls* a104 101
6 ch g Bahamian Bounty Leonica (Lion Cavern (USA))
1691[3] 2029[12] 2667[6] 3300[6] 3823[3] (4472) 4780[9] 5545[3] 6621[23] 6845[11] 7495[19]

Roedean (IRE) *William Stone* a72 77
4 b f Oratorio(IRE) Exotic Mix (FR) (Linamix (FR))
116[4] 601[5]

Roe Valley (IRE) *Linda Jewell* a33 36
6 ch g Arakan(USA) Waaedah (USA) (Halling (USA))
118[5]

Roger Thorpe *Deborah Sanderson* a65 29
4 b g Firebreak Nunthorpe (Mystiko (USA))
5962[2] 8294[4]

Rogue Agent (IRE) *A Fabre* 91
2 b c Montjeu(IRE) Rolly Polly (IRE) (Mukaddamah (USA))
5039a[3]

Rogue Reporter (IRE) *Stuart Williams* a70 66
4 b g Sir Percy Princess Nala (IRE) (In The Wings)
61[7] 274[9] 408[7]

Rogue Wave (IRE) *Alan Jarvis* 83
2 b c Iffraaj Lady Naomi (USA) (Distant View (USA))
3422[10] 3979[2] 5727[12] 6127[2] 6829[6] 7335[2]

Rokeby *George Moore* 52
2 b g Byron Scarlet Royal (Red Ransom (USA))
1642[9] 1930[13] 5105[5] 5577[10] 6842[9]

Roker Park (IRE) *David O'Meara* 91
8 b g Choisir(AUS) Joyful (IRE) (Green Desert (USA))
1787[14] 2460[5] ◆ 3093[5] 3200[6] 3981[9] 5011[3] 5088[4] 5333[2] 5832[5] 5971[14] 6728[9] 7281[7]

Roland *Kevin Ryan* a63 74
3 ch g Byron Muja Farewell (Mujtahid (USA))
5[5] (328) 623[5] 811[2] 3082[13] (3509) 4033[4] 4881[8] 5973[6] 6547[20] 7269[7] 7443[8]

Rolen Sly *Brian Rothwell* 39
4 b g Tillerman Feiticeira (USA) (Deposit Ticket (USA))
1282[10] 1777[7] 2030[8] 2986[6] 3595[9] 3947[10] 4376[11] 5378[7]

Rollex Borget (FR) *J Bertran De Balanda* 106
6 b g Khalkevi(IRE) Jasmine Des Bordes (FR) (Epervier Bleu)
2184a[9] 7890a[10]

Rolling Dice *Dominic Ffrench Davis* 75
2 b c Rail Link Breathing Space (USA) (Expelled (USA))
2723[6] 6790[5] 7243[2]

Rollin 'n Tumblin *Michael Attwater* a57
9 ch g Zaha(CAN) Steppin Out (First Trump)
12[5] (635) 820[5] 1175[2] 1325[2]

Roma Eria (FR) *P Monfort* a75 76
4 ch f Gold Away(IRE) Gallia Eria (Night Shift (USA))
922a[4]

Roman Dream (IRE) *Giada Ligas* 95
3 b f Holy Roman Emperor(IRE) Quick Thinking (IRE) (Daylami (IRE))
1866a[15]

Roman Flight (IRE) *David O'Meara* a82 93
5 b g Antonius Pius(USA) Flight Sequence (Polar Falcon (USA))
563[3] (2277) 2671[3] 3423[16] 4060[14]

Roman Legend (IRE) *Jeremy Noseda* a70 35
2 b c Holy Roman Emperor(IRE) Taking Liberties (IRE) (Royal Academy (USA))
2670[12] 3211[4]

Roman Order (IRE) *Brian Meehan* a69 70
3 b c Holy Roman Emperor(IRE) Web Of Intrigue (Machiavellian (USA))
129[5]

Roman Royal *Richard Hannon Snr* 43
2 b f Holy Roman Emperor(IRE) Favourita (Diktat)
4828[7] 7817[12]

Roman Senate (IRE) *Martin Bosley* a58 51
4 b g Holy Roman Emperor(IRE) Indian Fun (Poliglote)
94[4] 417[11] 983[7] 1183[5] 1298[7]

Romantica *A Fabre* 114
4 b f Galileo(IRE) Banks Hill (Danehill (USA))
(1895a) 2644a[3] (5574a) 6448a[7] 7708a[2]

Romantic Bliss (IRE) *K R Burke* 45
2 b f Holy Roman Emperor(IRE) Thea Di Bisanzio (IRE) (Dr Fong (USA))
3978[9] 4616[6] 5225[5] 6073[3] 6725[8] 7094[9]

Romanticize *Jason Ward* a63 58
7 b m Kyllachy Romancing (Dr Devious (IRE))
(163) 560[3] 640[3] 890[6] 976[3] 1079[5] 1211[3] (1656) 1886[6] 5486[7]

Romantic Settings *Richard Fahey* 99
3 ch f Mount Nelson Lacework (Pivotal)
(1991) 2367[2] 3240[5] 6186[12] 6620[4] 6823[3] 7205[4] 7822[5]

Romantic Stroll (IRE) *T Stack* a89 92
4 b f Oratorio(IRE) Home You Stroll (IRE) (Selkirk (USA))
2678a[8] 7404a[6] 7719a[7]

Romantic Wave (IRE) *S Botti* 105
4 br c Rock Of Gibraltar(IRE) Eurirs (FR) (Indian Ridge)
(2489a) 3147a[3] 6679a[4]

Romeo Montague *Ed Dunlop* a95 99
5 b g Montjeu(IRE) Issa (Pursuit Of Love)
2775[5]

Romeo Saint Cyr (FR) *C Martinon* a71 77
7 b h Lord Of Men La Romagne (FR) (Art Francais (USA))
648a[9]

Romeo's On Fire (IRE) *Adrian McGuinness* a77 67
9 b g Danehill(USA) Fighting Countess (USA) (Ringside (USA))
7[10] 24[8]

Ronaldinho (IRE) *Richard Hannon Snr* a80 89
3 b g Jeremy(USA) Spring Glory (Dr Fong (USA))
1109[5] 2086[5] 3276[8] 5534[6] 5953[6] 6358[9] (7248)

Rondeau (GR) *Patrick Chamings* a70 66
8 ch g Harmonic Way Areti (GR) (Wadood (USA))
2571[7] 3215[5] 3974[10] 4998[4] 5474[6] 6135[6] 6310[7] 6937[5] 7652[6] 8019[10]

Roninski (IRE) *Garry Moss* a92 91
5 b g Cadeaux Genereux Ruby Affair (IRE) (Night Shift (USA))
1061[11] 1148[6] (1782) 2028[4] 2310[11] 2882[5]

Ronya (IRE) *K R Burke* 64
2 b f Bushranger(IRE) Beenablaw (IRE) (Alzao (USA))
5915[6] 6581[3] 7371[4]

Roodee Lady *Lisa Williamson*
2 ch f Three Valleys(USA) Poly Blue (IRE) (Thatching)
2283[6]

Rookery (IRE) *Mark Johnston* 42
2 b c Raven's Pass(USA) Zacheta (Polish Precedent (USA))
7089[7]

Rookie Sensation (USA) *John Shirreffs* 107
3 rg c Unbridled's Song(USA) My Marchesa (USA) (Stately Don (USA))
8120a[5]

Rooknrasbryripple *Ralph Smith* a58 53
4 b f Piccolo Here To Me (Muhtarram (USA))
472[5] 529[6] 819[7] 1052[4] 1173[5] 1783[8] 2133[3] 2787[6] 3052[3] 4072[5] 5166[8]

Roomie *Tim Easterby* 43
2 b f Pastoral Pursuits Pomponette (USA) (Rahy (USA))
7818[8]

Ropehanger *Lee Carter* a46 45
3 b f Cockney Rebel(IRE) Robanna (Robellino (USA))
1319[8] 1476[7] 3376[12]

Roring Samson (IRE) *George Baker* 63
2 b c Art Connoisseur(IRE) Marju Guest (IRE) (Marju (IRE))
6333[4] 7251[6]

Rosaceous *Daniel Kubler* a80 88
3 ch f Duke Of Marmalade(IRE) Briery (IRE) (Salse (USA))
2930[3] ◆ (3237) 4748[3] 5402[7] 6433[2] 6936[6] 7504[7] 7891a[9]

Rosairlie (IRE) *Micky Hammond* a69 80
5 ch f Halling(USA) Mrs Mason (IRE) (Turtle Island (IRE))
1454[6] 2242[9] 5109[2] 5972[2] 6237[14] 7280[2] 7596[8]

Rosalind (USA) *Kenneth McPeek* a109
2 ch f Broken Vow(USA) Critics Acclaim (USA) (Theatrical (IRE))
7707a[3]
Rosa Lockwood *Ed McMahon* a57 46
4 b f Needwood Blade Star Of Flanders (Puissance)
2231[1] 530[11] 5817[4] 7792[8] 8082[3] 8418[5]
Rosarina *Jo Crowley* a53
2 ch f Rock Of Gibraltar(IRE) Spring Fashion (IRE) (Galileo (IRE))
8340[9]
Rosaspera (IRE) *A De Royer-Dupre* a51 67
3 b f Azamour(IRE) Rose Story (FR) (Observatory (USA))
7187a[6]
Ros Cuire (IRE) *W A Murphy* a24 51
8 br h Expelled(USA) Haven Island (IRE) (Revoque (IRE))
1020[9] 4826[9]
Rosdhu Queen (IRE) *William Haggas* 108
3 b f Invincible Spirit(IRE) Green Minstrel (FR) (Green Tune (USA))
1676[4] 3557[5] ◆ 4260[11] 5726[11]
Rosebay Coral (IRE) *Tony Coyle* 67
2 b f Kodiac Red Fanfare (First Trump)
1839[9] (2238) 2767[6] 3298[3] 3801[4] 4261[5] 5710[3] 6695[13]
Rose Boeuf (FR) *David O'Meara* a7
2 ch f Layman(USA) Dream Rose (IRE) (Anabaa (USA))
7664[9] 7902[11] 8221[5]
Rose Buck *Lee Carter* a62
2 b f Acclamation Housekeeper (IRE) (Common Grounds)
6107[10] 7790[5] 7977[3] 8086[3] 8262[5] 8382[5]
Roseburg (IRE) *Luca Cumani* 82
2 ch c Tamayuz Raydaniya (IRE) (In The Wings)
4477[7] 4977[2]
Rose Garnet (IRE) *Tony Carroll* a68 54
5 b f Invincible Spirit(IRE) Chanterelle (IRE) (Indian Ridge)
142[3] 497[2] 640[6] 790[3] 1304[2] 1472[2] 1731[2] 1929[7] 2281[7] 2773[7]
Rose Gloria (IRE) *Mick Channon* a55 66
2 ch f Haatef(USA) Western Sky (Barathea (IRE))
1580[2] 2625[5] 2805[4] 3724[4]
Rosehill Artist (IRE) *Charles Hills* 84
2 b f Excellent Art Conference (IRE) (Montjeu (IRE))
5003[6] ◆ 5488[2] (6140) 6594[2] 7695[4]
Rose Madder *Roger Curtis* a35 46
4 b f Singspiel(IRE) Crimson Year (USA) (Dubai Millennium)
7331[0] 7266[13] 7752[11]
Rosendhal (IRE) *G Botti* 109
6 ch h Indian Ridge Kathy College (IRE) (College Chapel)
244a[9] 467a[12] 868a[6] 2491a[2] (7830a)
Rose Of May (IRE) *David O'Meara* a22 47
3 b f Chineur(FR) Flower Bowl (IRE) (Noverre (USA))
1578[6] 1962[5] 2241[5] 2997[7] 4114[6] 4621[7] 5089[6]
Roseraie (IRE) *Kevin Prendergast* a67 95
3 b f Lawman(FR) Red Feather (IRE) (Marju (IRE))
1704a[4] 2108a[5] 2374a[7] 4647a[7]
Rose Ransom (IRE) *Mark Johnston* a76 68
3 b f Oasis Dream Rapid Ransom (USA) (Red Ransom (USA))
231[3] (419) ◆ 534[3]
Roserrow *Andrew Balding* a92 103
4 ch g Beat Hollow Sabah (Nashwan (USA))
1905[4] 2592[6] (3019) (3339) 4080[11] 5255[5] 7926[12] 8263[5]
Rose Vista (FR) *J-L Guillochon* a92 98
4 ch f Vatori(FR) Rose Ciel (FR) (Septieme Ciel (USA))
2969a[9]
Rosewood Lad *J S Moore* a78 63
6 ch g Needwood Blade Meandering Rose (USA) (Irish River (FR))
809[4]
Rosia Bay *Tom Dascombe* a40 36
3 ch f Rock Of Gibraltar(IRE) Penny Cross (Efisio)
2462[7] 2799[7]
Rosie Future (IRE) *Rae Guest* a55 46
3 b f Azamour(IRE) Auspicious (Shirley Heights)
103[5] 237[3] 717[5] 804[5]
Rosie Hall (IRE) *Bryan Smart* 52
3 ch f Lion Heart(USA) Baltic Dip (IRE) (Benny The Dip (USA))
2340[4] 2507[8] 3629[13] 5425[4]
Rosie Probert *Nicky Henderson* 80
4 b f Dylan Thomas(IRE) Corsican Sunset (USA) (Thunder Gulch (USA))
(3975)
Rosie Prospects *Roger Ingram* a62
2 b f Byron Sea Jade (IRE) (Mujadil (USA))
8145[3] 8326[2]
Rosie Rebel *Rae Guest* a60 80
3 ch f Cockney Rebel(IRE) Meandering Rose (USA) (Irish River (FR))
148[2] (2346) 3276[3] 5037[7] 6405[2] 7100[3] 7504[8]
Rosie's Lady (IRE) *Paul Green* a71 61
4 b f Elusive City(USA) Blushing Libra (Perugino (USA))
(7) (99) 110[8] 429[3] 675[2] 4929[11] 5514[9] 7636[10] 8399[10]
Rosina Bella (IRE) *P L Giannotti* 99
4 b f Oratorio(IRE) La Bella Grande (IRE) (Giant's Causeway (USA))
6890a[7]
Rosina Jay (IRE) *Clive Cox* a47 61
2 b f Art Connoisseur(IRE) Noora (IRE) (Bahhare (USA))
4408[10] 5061[9] 6069[6]
Rosita *Jonathan Portman* a36 54
2 br f Firebreak Muskat Rose (IRE) (One Cool Cat (USA))
4073[6] 4708[5] 5174[4] 7837[8]
Roskilly (IRE) *Andrew Balding* a77 67
2 ch c Hurricane Run(IRE) Party Feet (IRE) (Noverre (USA))
5473[8] 6762[8] 7460[2] 8124[3]
Rosselli (IRE) *K R Burke* a61 74
4 b g Iffraaj Special Ellie (FR) (Celtic Swing)
1059[8] 1239[10] 2594[3] 5052[9] 5856[2] 6283[8] 6683[3]
Rossetti *Gary Moore* a81 81
5 gr g Dansili Snowdrops (Gulch (USA))
104[9] 1354[2] 1723[5] 2232[13] 3925[4] 4679[2] 5168[5] 5762[5] (6336)
Rosslyn Castle *Gary Brown* 98
4 ch g Selkirk(USA) Margarula (IRE) (Doyoun)
2052[13]
Rosso Corsa *Mick Channon* a82 97
2 b c Footstepsinthesand Lady Scarlett (Woodman (USA))
1669[10] 2194[3] (2645) 3422[9] 4296[5] 4524[2] 4876[4] 5999[4] 6064[2] 6328[5] 6955[4] 7329[6]
Rossvoss *T M Walsh* 81
5 b g Medicean Dixielake (IRE) (Lake Coniston (IRE))
7230a[9]
Rostrum (FR) *Mahmood Al Zarooni* a107 107
6 b g Shamardal(USA) En Public (FR) (Rainbow Quest (USA))
363a[10] 744a[3] 836a[5]
Rostrum Farewell *David Brown* a33 61
2 b g Royal Applause Acicula (IRE) (Night Shift (USA))
4883[3] 5558[6] 7901[7]
Rosy Ryan (IRE) *Tina Jackson* 39
3 b f Tagula(IRE) Khaydariya (IRE) (Akarad (FR))
3759[6] 4813[5] 5715[6] 6276[10]
Rothera (AUS) *Brian Smith* 110
8 ch g Tobougg(IRE) Nova Serrure (AUS) (Celestial Dancer (IRE))
7827a[13]
Rothesay Chancer *Jim Goldie* a67 79
5 ch g Monsieur Bond(IRE) Rhinefield Beauty (IRE) (Shalford (IRE))
1253[3] 2031[5] 2410[2] (2880) 3334[8] 3561[10] 3769[8] 4472[14] 4954[13] 5639[9] 6583[7] 7240[3] 7730[2] 7985[11]
Rottingdean *John Gosden* a73 78
3 gr g Oasis Dream Misk (FR) (Linamix (FR))
1683[5] 2209[5]
Rottmayer (IRE) *G Botti* 87
3 b c Hurricane Run(IRE) Regina Aldi (IRE) (Dowsing (USA))
1511a[5] 1799a[4] 2490a[11]
Rouge Carmen (FR) *D Allard* 71
4 b f Early March A Ma Maniere (FR) (Johann Quatz (FR))
5601a[16]
Rouge Nuage (IRE) *Conrad Allen* a77 77
3 ch g Indian Haven Nom Francais (First Trump)
(479) 666[4] 1246[3] 2223[3] 2604[4] 3338[3] 4214[11]
Rouge Sang (FR) *J Bertran De Balanda* a52 60
2 b c Redback Castagne (FR) (Cardoun (FR))
5214a[8]
Rough Courte (IRE) *Mick Channon* a63 85
2 b f Clodovil(IRE) Straight Sets (IRE) (Pivotal)
1541[6] 1634[11] 1839[7] 2458[2] 3829[6] 4053[6] 4248[6] 4747[5] 5053[2] 5994[3] 6234[2] 6423[4] 6821[2] 7175[13]
Roughlyn *Lisa Williamson* a57 56
4 ch g Haafhd Dime Bag (High Line)
22[5]
Rough Rock (IRE) *Chris Dwyer* a54 77
8 ch g Rock Of Gibraltar(IRE) Amitie Fatale (IRE) (Night Shift (USA))
1800[8] 2638[2] 2964[6] 3534[11] 4183[5] 4865[6] 5154[2] 5406[8] 5798[4] 6259[5] 6702[8] 7109[12] 7454[9]
Rousseau (FR) *Carmen Bocskai* a78 48
7 b g Where Or When(IRE) Illumination (Saddlers' Hall (IRE))
648a[7]
Roving Bunny *James Given* 68
2 b f Aqlaam Weqaar (USA) (Red Ransom (USA))
4977[9] 5338[12] 5988[8] (6725) 7309[10]
Rowan Spirit (IRE) *Mark Brisbourne* a82 76
5 gr g Captain Rio Secret Justice (USA) (Lit De Justice (USA))
214[11]
Rowayton *Gary Brown* a44 56
7 gr m Lujain(USA) Bandanna (Bandmaster (USA))
997[8]
Rowe Park *Linda Jewell* a90 85
10 b g Dancing Spree(USA) Magic Legs (Reprimand)
586[6] 881[3] 1245[4] 1984[6] 3018[5] 4707[12] 6854[7] 7601[4] 7897[6] 8069[8]
Rowland (AUS) *Robbie Laing* 90
8 b g Lonhro(AUS) Paris In The Fall (IRE) (Sadler's Wells (USA))
7760a[6] 7938a[10]
Rowlestone Express *Tony Carroll* 37
2 b f Rail Link Charmante Femme (Bin Ajwaad (IRE))
7500[9]
Rowlestone Lad *John Flint* a56 62
6 b g Sulamani(IRE) Charmante Femme (Bin Ajwaad (IRE))
1209[4] 1423[13] 1522[4] 1715[7] 2130[9] 3248[2] 3406[5] 3884[4] 4838[6] 6325[7]
Rowlestone Lass *Richard Price* a48 42
3 b f Hernando(FR) Charmante Femme (Bin Ajwaad (IRE))
4927[9] 5386[9] 6950[10] 7738[10] 8260[4]
Roxanne (FR) *H-A Pantall* a84 96
3 b f Falco(USA) Super Vite (USA) (Septieme Ciel (USA))
7993a[5] 8440a[13]
Roxy Beat *David Evans*
5 b f Beat All(USA) Roxy River (Ardross)
8092[8]
Roxy De Vindecy (FR) *J Phelippon* a87 83
8 b g Spadoun(FR) High Light (FR) (Zino)
5601a[13] 6421a[4]
Roxy Flyer (IRE) *Amanda Perrett* a103 98
6 b m Rock Of Gibraltar(IRE) Dyna Flyer (USA) (Marquetry (USA))
2520[5] (Dead)
Roxy Lane *Peter Hiatt* 52
4 b f Byron Comme Ca (Cyrano De Bergerac)
3250[10] 3860[4] 4590[11] 5429[6]
Royaaty (IRE) *M bin Shafya* a93 93
7 b g Singspiel(IRE) Whisper To Dream (USA) (Gone West (USA))
246a[10] 555a[14]
Royal Acclamation (IRE) *Michael Scudamore* a55 58
8 b g Acclamation Lady Abigail (IRE) (Royal Academy (USA))
117[13] 1193[5] 1396[10] 2126[8]
Royal Acquisition *Robert Cowell* a74 61
3 b c Royal Applause Flavian (Catrail (USA))
1844[7] (3400) 4221[4] 5673[10]
Royal Alcor (IRE) *Gay Kelleway* a87 75
6 b g Chevalier(IRE) Arundhati (IRE) (Royal Academy (USA))
5171[7] 5377[5] 5633[2] (5897) (6216) 6405[3] 6809[2] 7115[3] 7539[11] 7758[2] 8139[3]
Royal Award *Jonathan Portman* a41 64
4 b f Cadeaux Genereux Red Sovereign (Danzig Connection (USA))
2173[10] 3407[5] 4123[9] 5060[4] 6527[6] 7315[15] 8177[5]
Royal Bajan (USA) *James Given* a89 81
5 rg g Speightstown(USA) Crown You (USA) (Two Punch (USA))
3[6] 113[7] 405[9] (457) 780[9] 913[2] 1121[5] 1308[2] 1652[7] 2122[8] 2550[3] 3569[5] 4074[4] 4728[8] 4930[10] (5336) (5608) (6077) 6506[9] 6854[9] 7112[6] 7887[4] 8021[10] (8167) 8232[3] 8324[8]
Royal Banker *Jedd O'Keeffe* 94
2 b c Medicean Regal Rose (Danehill (USA))
4312[4] (6174)
Royal Barge (IRE) *Eve Johnson Houghton* a51 18
3 b f Shirocco(GER) Sahara Lady (IRE) (Lomitas)
373[6] 774[6] 1098[8]
Royal Betty *Lee Carter* a35 46
3 b f Royal Applause Peryllys (Warning)
1906[7]
Royal Birth *Stuart Williams* a84 62
2 b c Exceed And Excel(AUS) Princess Georgina (Royal Applause)
6234[7] 8300[2] (8396)
Royal Blue Star (IRE) *Mrs John Harrington* a95 98
5 b f Dalakhani(IRE) Etizaan (IRE) (Unfuwain (USA))
3845a[15] 5453a[7]
Royal Brave (IRE) *William Muir* a61 61
2 b c Acclamation Daqtora (Dr Devious (IRE))
6947[4] 7394[4] 7893[6] 8322[2] 8442[8]
Royal Bushida *Derek Shaw* a49
2 b g Royal Applause Moonmaiden (Selkirk (USA))
5590[5] 5900[4] 6169[10] 7789[5] 7878[7] 7973[5] 8133[6] 8317[5]
Royal Caper *John Ryan* a63 59
3 b g Royal Applause Ukraine (IRE) (Cape Cross (IRE))
1928[10] 2229[6] 3405[7] 3772[3] 4615[5] 4721[5] 5128[4] 5275[6] 5407[5] 6553[8] 6930[5]
Royal Challis *Richard Hannon Snr* a78 79
3 b g Royal Applause Oh Hebe (IRE) (Night Shift (USA))
2051[3] 2447[4] (2722) 3159[3] 3400[2] 3866[6] 4494[8]
Royal Connection *Richard Hannon Snr* 70
2 b f Bahamian Bounty Fisadara (Nayef (USA))
2583[5] 3275[3] 3753[2] 4277[3] 4948[12] 5242[3] 6076[3] 7175[3] 7533[6]
Royal Connoisseur (IRE) *Richard Fahey* 76
2 b g Art Connoisseur(IRE) Valferno (IRE) (Val Royal (FR))
5877[9] 6627[2] 7173[5]
Royal Defence (IRE) *Mick Quinn* a52 58
7 b g Refuse To Bend(IRE) Alessia (GER) (Warning)
515[3] 1601[7] 2801[2] 3151[4] 6458[4] 7612[5]
Royal Delta (USA) *William Mott* a123
5 bb f Empire Maker(USA) Delta Princess (USA) (A.P. Indy (USA))
1269a[10] 7691a[4]
Royal Derby (FR) *C Plisson*
2 gr c Fairly Ransom(USA) Royalrique (FR) (Enrique)
5323a[11]
Royal Descent (AUS) *Chris Waller* 112
4 br f Redoute's Choice(AUS) Mulan Princess (NZ) (Kaapstad (NZ))
7392a[5]
Royal Destination (IRE) *Fawzi Abdulla Nass* a97 82
8 b g Dubai Destination(USA) Royale (IRE) (Royal Academy (USA))
463a[10]
Royal Diamond (IRE) *J P Murtagh* a85 115
7 b g King's Best(USA) Irresistible Jewel (IRE) (Danehill (USA))
870a[7] 1268a[7] 2428[3] 3873a[2] 5209a[2] (5776a) 6441a[5] (7363)
Royal Duchess *Lucy Normile* 55
3 b f Dutch Art Royal Citadel (IRE) (City On A Hill (USA))
1272[3] 1570[10] 2634[5] 3932[2] 4448[9] 4991[6] 5708[9] 6088[12] 7148[2]
Royal Dutch *Denis Coakley* a79 81
4 ch g Nayef(USA) Shersha (IRE) (Priolo (USA))
1673[10] 2383[2] 4720[5] (5542) 6108[7] 6750[3]
Royale Du Buisson (IRE) *F Head* 93
2 b f Invincible Spirit(IRE) Biswa (USA) (Kafwain (USA))
3752a[3] 4651a[2] 7185a[8]
Royal Empire (IRE) *Saeed bin Suroor* a117 114
4 b c Teofilo(IRE) Zeiting (IRE) (Zieten (USA))
(151a) ◆ 462a[2] ◆ 656a[2] 873a[11] (4526) (5531) 6198[2] 7012[2] 7761a[14]
Royal Empress (IRE) *David Wachman* 90
3 br f Holy Roman Emperor(IRE) Weekend Fling (USA) (Forest Wildcat (USA))
3846a[24]
Royal Encounter *Ed Vaughan* a54
2 b c Royal Applause Alhufoof (USA) (Dayjur (USA))
8425[9]
Royal Envoy (IRE) *Paul Howling* a58 18
10 b g Royal Applause Seven Notes (Zafonic (USA))
649[10] 917[8]
Royal Etiquette (IRE) *Lawney Hill* a70 70
6 b g Royal Applause Alpine Gold (IRE) (Montjeu (IRE))
633[2] 747[4] 3156[3] 3865[2] 5065[6] 6068[7] 7081[4] 7439[4] 7628[10] 8449[4]
Royal Flag *Saeed bin Suroor* 91
3 b c New Approach(IRE) Gonbarda (GER) (Lando (GER))
2384[3]
Royal Fox *P Schiergen* 97
3 ch c Manduro(GER) Rahada (GER) (Peintre Celebre (USA))
2526a[7] 4333a[6] 5940a[10] 6451a[7]
Royal Gig *Tim Etherington* 19
4 br f Val Royal(FR) Sainte Gig (FR) (Saint Cyrien (FR))
515[11]
Royal Guinevere *Dean Ivory* a64 82
3 b f Invincible Spirit(IRE) Elegant Beauty (Olden Times)
1427[5] (1682) 2098[2] 2623[3] 3762[2] (4670) (4830) 6067[8]
Royal Holiday (IRE) *Marjorie Fife* a73 75
6 ch g Captain Rio Sunny Slope (Mujtahid (USA))
194[4] 603[6] 1076[2] (1184) (2536) 3395[3] 5195[11] 6600[2] 6963[3] (7283) 7824[4]
Royal Intruder *Violet M Jordan* a36 23
8 b g Royal Applause Surprise Visitor (IRE) (Be My Guest (USA))
5373[9] 7265[8]
Royalitta (FR) *M Boutin* a73 78
3 ch f Royal Assault(USA) Minervitta (Warrshan (USA))
544a[2] 1756a[0]
Royal Jenray *Jedd O'Keeffe* a6 50
3 gr g Royal Applause In The Highlands (Petong)
1566[9] 1764[15]
Royal Law (IRE) *A Couetil* 107
3 b c Lawman(FR) Queen Of The Game (IRE) (Montjeu (IRE))
5361a[2] 6712a[5]
Royalmania *F Head* 105
2 ch f Elusive Quality(USA) Safari Queen (ARG) (Lode (USA))
7055a[4]
Royal Marskell *K F Clutterbuck* a69 68
4 b g Multiplex Socialise (Groom Dancer (USA))
2321[11] 3250[5] 4151[7] 5346[7] 7455[5] 7778[3] 7984[2] 8337[4]
Royal Mezyan (IRE) *William Haggas* 93
2 b g Royal Applause Rice Mother (IRE) (Indian Ridge)
2250[4] 3295[2] 3481[6] (4259) 7011[8]
Royal Opera *Brian Ellison* a70 78
5 b g Acclamation Desert Gold (IRE) (Desert Prince (IRE))
1111[6] (1464) 1774[7] 2118[2] 2794[3]
Royal Peculiar *Michael Appleby* a87 95
5 b c Galileo(IRE) Distinctive Look (IRE) (Danehill (USA))
1083[3] 1273[10] 1501[6] 3442[4] 3685[5] 4202[5] 4512[6] 5712[5] 6071[6] (6346) 6809[4]
Royal Preserve *Andrew Balding* a72 60
2 ch g Duke Of Marmalade(IRE) Castaway Queen (IRE) (Selkirk (USA))
6799[12] 7270[8] (7859)
Royal Prize *Ralph Beckett* a95 92
3 ch g Nayef(USA) Spot Prize (USA) (Seattle Dancer (USA))
(1471) 2054[7] 3117[2] 3563[5] 4214[14] 4769[2] 5401[6] 6203[6] 6694[2] 6801[18]
Royal Rascal *Tim Easterby* 99
3 b f Lucky Story(USA) Royal Punch (Royal Applause)
2368[14] 7025[9]
Royal Reyah *Stuart Kittow* 80
4 b g Royal Applause Dilys (Efisio)
(1286) 2618[7] 3411[8] 6461[4] 6959[6] 7427[6]
Royal Ridge (SAF) *M F De Kock* a109 108
5 ch g Tiger Ridge(USA) Princess Faberge (SAF) (Jallad (USA))
290a[5] (557a) 872a[5] 957a[8]
Royal River *J S Moore* a63 37
2 b c Royal Applause Rivermead (USA) (Irish River (FR))
4175[5] ◆ 4302[5] 6923[4] 7300[7] 7568a[11] 8215[4]
Royal Rock *Chris Wall* a89 113
9 b g Sakhee(USA) Vanishing Point (USA) (Caller I.D. (USA))
2257[2] 3558[24] 4981[3] 6235[9] (6505) 7014[10] 7495[13]
Royal Sea (IRE) *Michael Mullineaux* a67 66
4 b g Refuse To Bend(IRE) Janayen (USA) (Zafonic (USA))
53[7] (145) 477[6] 1948[10] 2328[3] 2615[2] 3248[4] 3977[7] 4287[4] 4516[3] 4755[7] 5052[5] (5222) 5466[9] 6658[3] 6787[9] 7379[6]
Royal Signaller *Amanda Perrett* a76 87
3 b g Dylan Thomas(IRE) Whirly Bird (Nashwan (USA))
1468[3] 2157[2] 2589[3] (3277) 3698[2] 4984[8] 5953[4] (6377)
Royal Skies (IRE) *Mark Johnston* a85 104
3 b g Dubawi(IRE) Kalana (FR) (Rainbow Quest (USA))
1145[2] 1847[7] 2416[5] 2878[2] (3067) (3336) 3526[10] ◆ 4984[6] (5258) 6186[9] 6503[3] 6841[4]
Royal Straight *Linda Perratt* a48 81
8 ch g Halling(USA) High Straits (Bering)
1990[9] 2315[7] 3466[2] 3715[3] 4293[4] 4609[2] 5239[5] 5882[8] 5918[5] 6468[4] 6877[3] 7238[3] 7669[6]
Royal Style (IRE) *David Barron* 58
3 ch f Windsor Knot(IRE) Christeningpresent (IRE) (Cadeaux Genereux)
1389[2] 1828[11] 2754[5] 3629[7] 4144[13]
Royal Trix *Marcus Tregoning* 63
4 b f Royal Applause Apple Town (Warning)
4774[5] 5220[4] 5608[5]

Royal Trooper (IRE) *Mark Brisbourne* a65 80
7 b g Hawk Wing(USA) Strawberry Roan (IRE) (Sadler's Wells (USA))
7220[11] *7628[12] (8129)*

Royal Warranty *Andrew Balding* a59
2 ch f Sir Percy Royal Patron (Royal Academy (USA))
8213[3]

Royal Warrior *Alan McCabe* a72
2 b g Royal Applause Tiana (Diktat)
(1328)

Roycano *Michael Easterby* a30 33
3 ch g Lucarno(USA) Royal Distant (USA) (Distant View (USA))
5110[8] 5469[6] *5678[10]*

Roy Rocket (FR) *John Berry* a25 50
3 gr g Layman(USA) Minnie's Mystery (FR) (Highest Honor (FR))
4688[5] 5630[3]

Roy's Legacy *Shaun Harris* a79 63
4 b c Phoenix Reach(IRE) Chocolada (Namid)
(29) 113[3] 232[3] 627[7] 1121[6] 1276[2] 1388[7] 1681[15] 4430[11] 4761[8] 5221[4] 5708[11] *6135[8] 6475[9]* 8135[3] 8220[6] 8411[5] 8457[3]

Roy The Boy (USA) *Alan Bailey* a82 78
5 b g Pomeroy(USA) Mrs. M (USA) (Mecke (USA))
25[3] 723[5]

Roz *Harry Dunlop* a81 102
3 b f Teofilo(IRE) Debonnaire (Anabaa (USA))
2047[10] 2842[9] 3524[16]

Rozene (IRE) *David Barron* 70
2 b f Sleeping Indian Few Words (Fraam)
(6517) 7170[12]

Rubbamaa *Clive Brittain* a71 58
4 b f Singspiel(IRE) Lady Hen (Efisio)
1035[3] 1518[3] 2519[7] 3996[5]

Rubenstar (IRE) *Daniel Mark Loughnane* a20 53
10 b g Soviet Star(USA) Ansariya (USA) (Shahrastani (USA))
194[9]

Rubi Dia *Sean Curran* a63 69
6 ch g Hernando(FR) Oblique (IRE) (Giant's Causeway (USA))
888[5] 1217[9] 1520[4] 1700[7]

Rub Of The Relic (IRE) *Paul Midgley* a63 73
8 b g Chevalier(IRE) Bayletta (IRE) (Woodborough (USA))
2836[8] 3106[6] 3504[4] 3889[3] 4071[4] 4403[5] 5426[4] 5840[5] 6179[3] 6723[9]

Ruby Glass (IRE) *Ruth Carr* a60 41
4 b g Red Clubs(IRE) Gold Bar (IRE) (Barathea (IRE))
3625[11] 4010[10]

Ruby Hull (IRE) *Garry Moss* 12
2 b f Bushranger(IRE) Zuzu (IRE) (Acclamation)
6517[13]

Rubylicious (IRE) *J S Moore* 13
2 b f Bushranger(IRE) Dreamalot (Falbrav (IRE))
3767[6] 4065[7] 4450[4]

Ruby's Day *David Brown* a69 95
4 ch f Vital Equine(IRE) Isabella's Best (IRE) (King's Best (USA))
4935a[0] 6848[4] 7313[9] *7731[11] 7803[9] 7887[8]*

Ruby Wedding (FR) *C Baillet* a72 82
3 ch f Panis(USA) Loda (FR) (Zieten (USA))
2335a[8]

Rudi Five One (FR) *Robert Eddery* a71 71
2 b c American Post Dansia (GER) (Lavirco (GER))
4533[2] 5309[3] *5922[4]* 6763[5] *7780[2]*

Ruffled *John Gosden* a65 77
3 b f Harlan's Holiday(USA) Mirabilis (USA) (Lear Fan (USA))
3116[4] ◆ *4381[4]* 4927[3] 5410[2] *7786[11]*

Ruff Luck *Seamus Mullins* a57 31
3 b f Lucarno(USA) Ruffie (IRE) (Medicean)
864[6] 1095[6] 3014[7] 6899[10] *7299[11]*

Rufford (IRE) *Richard Fahey* 109
2 b c Invincible Spirit(IRE) Speedy Sonata (USA) (Stravinsky (USA))
(3350) 3890[3] 5679[5] ◆ 6637[2] 7207[5] 7525[4]

Rufoof *Charles Hills* a54 82
3 ch f Zamindar(USA) Tahrir (IRE) (Linamix (FR))
1666[5] 3372[3] 3774[5] 4544[3] 5512[2] (5932) (6941) *7297[9]*

Ruggero *A Fabre* 101
3 b g Tiger Hill(IRE) Bergamask (USA) (Kingmambo (USA))
5463a[7]

Rugosa *Charles Hills* a83 80
4 b f Oasis Dream Zathonia (Zafonic (USA))
79[7] 5310[7] *7898[7] 8037[10] 8401[11]*

Rulbin Realta *Pat Phelan* a56 47
6 b m Jendali(USA) Paulines Gem (IRE) (Petorius)
512[6]

Ruler Of The World (IRE) *A P O'Brien* 126
3 ch c Galileo(IRE) Love Me True (USA) (Kingmambo (USA))
(2187) (2866) ◆ 3849a[5] 6446a[2] 7058a[7] 7367[3]

Rulesn'regulations *Alastair Lidderdale* a93 79
7 b g Forzando Al Awaalah (Mukaddamah (USA))
2225[6] 2530[3] 2797[4] 2964[5]

Ruling Pole (IRE) *N Leenders* a72
4 gr g Aussie Rules(USA) Queen Of Poland (FR) (Polish Precedent (USA))
922a[7]

Rumble Of Thunder (IRE) *Philip Kirby* a83 75
7 b g Fath(USA) Honey Storm (IRE) (Mujadil (USA))
2860[2]

Rum Point (USA) *Doug O'Neill* a97
2 b c Malibu Moon(USA) Quiet Weekend (USA) (Quiet American (USA))
7711a[12]

Runaway (GER) *A Trybuhl* 107
6 b h Slickly(FR) Rain Lily (IRE) (Red Ransom (USA))
2822a[2] (3879a)

Rundell *Richard Hannon Snr* a92 90
3 b c Notnowcato Shardette (IRE) (Darshaan)
2432[2] ◆ 2927[2] *(3470)*

Run It Twice (IRE) *David Evans* a75 60
3 b g Dark Angel(IRE) Alinda (IRE) (Revoque (IRE))
18[3] 141[6] (210) 547[2] (615) 949[4] 1400[4] 2209[11] *6777[8] 7118[4]* 7439[8] 7754[7] 8030[6] (8163) 8295[8] (8443)

Running Bull (IRE) *Linda Jewell* a45
3 b g Papal Bull Miss Barbados (IRE) (Hawk Wing (USA))
184[7] 2566[11] 2748[3] 3403[7] 3819[6]

Running Deer (IRE) *Lady Cecil* a79 84
4 b f Hurricane Run(IRE) Sweet Sioux (Halling (USA))
1663[5] 2729[3] 3321[2] 3765[7] 4898[2] 5802[4] *6611[4]* (7211) 7504[4]

Runninglikethewind (IRE) *Chris Wall* a73 71
3 b g Hurricane Run(IRE) Virgin Hawk (USA) (Silver Hawk (USA))
3793[3] 4436[3] 5203[2] 5606[4] *(6109)*

Running Mate (IRE) *Jo Crowley* a67 68
6 b g Acclamation It Takes Two (IRE) (Alzao (USA))
115[8] 728[10] 3325[12]

Running On Faith *Garry Woodward* 15
5 b g Phoenix Reach(IRE) Amazing Grace Mary (Dancing Spree (USA))
911[8] 1187[7] 6497[11]

Running Reef (IRE) *Tracy Waggott* 73
4 b g Hurricane Run(IRE) Half-Hitch (USA) (Diesis)
1567[7] 1788[5] 2406[5] (2616) (3286) 3628[8] 5861[9] 6181[5] 6720[5]

Running Water *Alan Berry* a46 56
5 ch f Blue Dakota(IRE) Floral Spark (Forzando)
5917[3] *6345[5]* 6669[9]

Running Wolf (IRE) *Michael Dods* 71
2 b g Amadeus Wolf Monet's Lady (IRE) (Daylami (IRE))
3624[8] 5538[10] (6724) 7418[13]

Run Of The Day *Eve Johnson Houghton* a59 41
4 b f Three Valleys(USA) Shall We Run (Hotfoot I)
2511[13] 5196[7]

Run The Show (FR) *P Schaerer* a74 77
5 bl c Dano-Mast Money Bag (FR) (Badayoun)
609a[2]

Rupeetoups *Jim Boyle* a30 37
5 b g Deportivo Rock Flower (Rock City)
2722[7] *3170[5]* 3731[9]

Rural Affair *Michael Appleby* a67 56
2 b f Pastoral Pursuits Torcross (Vettori (IRE))
3174[8] 3663[10] *4512[4] 5635[5]* 6460[9] *6983[2] 7156[2] (7630) (8040) 8132[2]*

Rural Celebration *David O'Meara* a73 71
2 b f Pastoral Pursuits Queens Jubilee (Cayman Kai (IRE))
2327[2] 2631[2] 3064[4] (5857)

Ruscello (IRE) *Ed Walker* a100 103
4 b g Cape Cross(IRE) Sea Picture (IRE) (Royal Academy (USA))
1501[3] 2365[9] *3960[4]* 4488[3] 4979[3] *6172[3]* 7417a[2] (7700a) 7761a[23]

Rush *Paul Cole* a62 51
2 ch f Compton Place Dorelia (IRE) (Efisio)
1659[7] *7852[3] 8083[8]*

Russian Bullet *Jamie Osborne* a50 53
4 b g Royal Applause Gandini (Night Shift (USA))
30[3] 163[8] 233[0] 369[2] 516[7] 558[3] 719[3] 1356[6] 2074[8] *2326[4]* 3154[3] (3425) 3660[12] 3888[7]

Russianduke (IRE) *S Botti* 88
3 b c Duke Of Marmalade(IRE) Russian Roubles (IRE) (Sadler's Wells (USA))
2490a[6]

Russian George (IRE) *Steve Gollings* a80 58
7 ch g Sendawar(IRE) Mannsara (IRE) (Royal Academy (USA))
928[3] 1158[7] 2087[4] 5831[13] 6565[12]

Russian Ice *Dean Ivory* a83 56
5 ch f Iceman Dark Eyed Lady (IRE) (Exhibitioner)
34[5] 421[2] (650) 822[3] 1092[5] 1318[9] 7462[11] 7876[11] 8158[10]

Russian Link *John Berry* a44 62
3 b f Rail Link Zathonia (Zafonic (USA))
2392[9] 2938[6] *3402[6]* 6978[8] *7838[5] 8268[7]*

Russian Realm *Sir Michael Stoute* 90
3 b c Dansili Russian Rhythm (USA) (Kingmambo (USA))
2151[9] 2442[3] (5401) ◆ 6356[2]

Russian Reel (FR) *J Heloury* a88 87
3 b c Country Reel(USA) Russian Beauty (USA) (Diesis)
(544a) 711a[2] *782a[9]*

Russian Rock (IRE) *M Al Muhairi* a114 107
6 b h Rock Of Gibraltar(IRE) Mala Mala (IRE) (Brief Truce (USA))
244a[4] 954a[4] 1265a[13]

Russian Royale *Stuart Kittow* a68 76
3 b f Royal Applause Russian Ruby (FR) (Vettori (IRE))
(2597) 3179[6] 5037[5] 5815[2] *6780[6]* 7256[9]

Russian Soul (IRE) *M Halford* a101 110
5 b g Invincible Spirit(IRE) Russian Hill (Indian Ridge)
244a[2] 464a[2] 746a[2] 954a[3] 1265a[15] 2676a[4] ◆ 3848a[2] 5772a[3] (6414a)

Russian Storm *Pat Phelan* a65 68
5 b f Hurricane Run(IRE) Yesteryear (Green Desert (USA))
3330[7] 3580[11] 4411[11]

Russian Tango (GER) *A Wohler* 108
6 ch h Tertullian(USA) Russian Samba (IRE) (Laroche (GER))
(701a) 4042a[3]

Rust (IRE) *Ann Duffield* a63 70
3 b c Elnadim(USA) Reddening (Blushing Flame (USA))
2506[5] 3068[4] 6728[8] 7067[4] *7741[4]*

Rustic Deacon *Willie Musson* a92 89
6 ch g Pastoral Pursuits Anne-Lise (Inchinor)
3411[7] 4281[9] 5580[12] *6694[10]*

Rusty Rocket (IRE) *Paul Green* a83 93
4 ch c Majestic Missile(IRE) Sweet Compliance (Safawan)
966[7] 1308[4] 1644[5] 2031[11] 2460[4] (3236) 3682[3] (3802) 4285[11] 5943[8] 5991[10] 6159[2] 6586[20] 6826[10] 7314[9] (7777)

Rutherglen *George Baker* 82
3 b g Tiger Hill(IRE) Hanella (IRE) (Galileo (IRE))
1684[9] (2743) 3365[4] (5762) 6490[4] 7338[3]

Rutland Boy *A Al Raihe* a109 81
5 ch g Bertolini(USA) Israar (Machiavellian (USA))
153a[3] 557a[11]

Rutterkin (USA) *James Moffatt* a54 53
5 gr g Maria's Mon(USA) Chilukki Cat (USA) (Storm Cat (USA))
1656[4] 1951[6] 2884[7] 3236[10] 3393[6] 4034[6] 5047[5] 5470[6] 5887[5] *6219[4]* 6471[10] *8293[4] 8393[6]*

Ruwaiyan (USA) *James Tate* a90 59
4 bb c Cape Cross(IRE) Maskunah (IRE) (Sadler's Wells (USA))
5902[5] 6497[3] *7000[5] (7603) 7949[3] 8117[8]*

Ruwasi *James Tate* a56 69
2 b c Authorized(IRE) Circle Of Love (Sakhee (USA))
7339[4] *7732[4]*

R Woody *Robert Cowell* a77 66
6 ch g Ishiguru(USA) Yarrita (Tragic Role (USA))
5062[6] *5901[9]* 6506[5] *(6850)* 7314[11] *7985[7] 8096[5]*

Ryan Style (IRE) *Lisa Williamson* a75 67
7 b g Desert Style(IRE) Westlife (IRE) (Mind Games)
2588[7] 3667[2] 3716[6] 4344[5] 4608[4] 5154[4] 6040[6] *7262[10] 8022[7] 8151[10]*

Rydan (IRE) *Robert Mills* a70
2 ch c Intense Focus(USA) Lough Mewin (IRE) (Woodman (USA))
7834[6]

Rydilluc (USA) *Gary Contessa* a107 107
3 b c Medaglia d'Oro(USA) Swift And Classy (USA) (Clever Trick (USA))
5551a[11]

Ryedale Dancer (IRE) *Richard Guest* a63 66
5 ch f Refuse To Bend(IRE) Saik (USA) (Riverman (USA))
26[2] 163[4] 213[4] 277[4] 560[7] 735[7] 909[3] 991[5] 1147[4]

Ryedale Lass *Geoffrey Deacon* a62 67
5 b f Val Royal(FR) First Dawn (Dr Fong (USA))
5002[11] 5528[5] 6102[4] 8258[5] *8371[11]*

Ryedale Valley *Mlle M Henry* a52 46
3 ch g Three Valleys(USA) Phi Phi (IRE) (Fasliyev (USA))
3762[8] 4114[9] 4722[11] *8441a[11]*

Ryedane (IRE) *Tim Easterby* a78 68
11 b g Danetime(IRE) Miss Valediction (IRE) (Petardia)
2276[8] 2835[9] 3446[5] 4102[2] 4430[7] 4892[6] 4970[6]

Rye House (IRE) *Sir Michael Stoute* 101
4 b g Dansili Threefold (USA) (Gulch (USA))
(2431)

Ryeolliean *David O'Meara* 76
2 ch g Haafhd Brave Mave (Daylami (IRE))
7023[6] (7276)

Rylee Mooch *Richard Guest* a83 87
5 gr g Choisir(AUS) Negligee (Night Shift (USA))
457[7] 881[4] 913[3] 1198[3] 1431[5] 2388[2] 2505[3] 3090[2] 3341[8] 3682[2] 4024[9] 4707[5] 5108[3] 5266[2] 5537[4] 6189[7] 6309[6] 6583[11] 7112[3] 7420[5]

Rysbrack (USA) *Paul Webber* a78 80
7 ch g Selkirk(USA) Super Tassa (IRE) (Lahib (USA))
654[6]

Saab Almanal *James Fanshawe* 72
2 b c Dubawi(IRE) Caribbean Pearl (USA) (Silver Hawk (USA))
7128[2]

Saamidd *Saeed bin Suroor* a116 104
5 b c Street Cry(IRE) Aryaamm (IRE) (Galileo (IRE))
467a[10] *659a[5] 957a[5] 1262a[9]*

Saayerr *William Haggas* 108
2 b c Acclamation Adorn (Kyllachy)
(2595) (2933) 3481[8] (4918) 5765[6]

Sabianga (FR) *P Prunet-Foch* 25
6 b m Sabiango(GER) Ninazeyra (FR) (Sheyrann (IRE))
6680a[9]

Sab Le Beau (FR) *Alan Brown* 28
4 b g Sabiango(GER) La Peliniere (FR) (Mansonnien (FR))
3542[7]

Sabor A Triunfo (CHI) *Ed Dunlop* a109 97
4 ch f Dance Brightly(CAN) Sally Mash (CHI) (Mash One (CHI))
6198[7] 6766[8]

Saborido (USA) *Amanda Perrett* a88 89
7 gr g Dixie Union(USA) Alexine (ARG) (Runaway Groom (CAN))
3344[3] ◆ 4029[10] *5895[3]* 6646[16]

Sabre Rock *John Best* a78 78
3 b g Dubawi(IRE) Retainage (USA) (Polish Numbers (USA))
1495a[4] 1972a[7] 2624[3] 3294[10] 5632[6]

Sabrina's Secret *Tom Tate* a57 31
3 b f Sakhee's Secret Sabrina Brown (Polar Falcon (USA))
3774[8] 4200[6] *4839[3]* ◆ 5485[8] *6345[7] 6777[5]*

Sacco D'Oro *Michael Mullineaux* a51 51
7 b m Rainbow High Speedy Native (IRE) (Be My Native (USA))
1001[0] 1146[4] 1207[5] 1369[4]

Sacha Park (IRE) *Richard Hannon Snr* 95
2 ch c Iffraaj Silicon Star (FR) (Starborough)
2595[2] 2943a[2] 3424[6] ◆ 4299[2] 4858[5] 6234[4]

Sacred Aspect (IRE) *K J Condon* 96
2 gr f Haatef(USA) Again Royale (IRE) (Royal Academy (USA))
3522[12] 5318a[5]

Sacred Dream (AUS) *Robbie Griffiths* 65
5 b m God's Own(AUS) Dream The Dream (AUS) (Encosta De Lago (AUS))
7760a[16]

Sacre Del Myre (FR) *J-M Jouteau* a83 84
7 b g Until Sundown(USA) Spelunca (FR) (Kaldoun (FR))
960a[0]

Sacred Falls (NZ) *Chris Waller* 114
4 b c O'Reilly(NZ) Iguazu's Girl (NZ) (Redoute's Choice (AUS))
7826a[5]

Sacred Square (GER) *William Haggas* 74
3 ch g Peintre Celebre(USA) Square The Circle (Second Empire (IRE))
1624[10] 2538[5] 3250[4] 4070[2] ◆ 4241[3] 5218[4]

Sacrilege *Daniel O'Brien* a62 72
8 ch g Sakhee(USA) Idolize (Polish Precedent (USA))
2383[P]

Sacrosanctus *Scott Dixon* a86 96
5 ch g Sakhee(USA) Catalonia (IRE) (Catrail (USA))
1765[12] 4744[28] 4983[18]

Saddaqa (USA) *Saeed bin Suroor* a87 86
3 b f Raven's Pass(USA) Sky Song (IRE) (Sadler's Wells (USA))
3975[3] *4633[2]* 5038[2] 5478[2] *5902[2]* 6696[10] *7298[4] 7738[3]*

Saddler's Rock (IRE) *John M Oxx* 117
5 b c Sadler's Wells(USA) Grecian Bride (IRE) (Groom Dancer (USA))
870a[5] ◆ 1263a[7] 3483[8] 4919[12] 6441a[3] 7363[5]

Sadeek's Song (USA) *Mahmood Al Zarooni* a65 104
5 ch c Kingmambo(USA) New Morning (IRE) (Sadler's Wells (USA))
246a[9]

Sadiigah *Clive Brittain* a64 44
3 b f Medicean Regal Riband (Fantastic Light (USA))
1515[5]

Sadiq *Saeed bin Suroor* 92
3 b g Invincible Spirit(IRE) Miss Particular (IRE) (Sadler's Wells (USA))
3343[3] (3923) (4425) 4683[2] 5944[5] 7312[13]

Sadler's Risk (IRE) *Mark Johnston* 97
5 b g Sadler's Wells(USA) Riskaverse (USA) (Dynaformer (USA))
4233[6] 4720[2] 4914[7] 5259[2] 5746[11] 6591[9] *7542[10]*

Safety Check (IRE) *Charlie Appleby* a91 100
2 ch c Dubawi(IRE) Doors To Manual (USA) (Royal Academy (USA))
3044[2] ◆ (4533) 4747[5] 5224[2] (5745) *6314[2]* (6763) 7195[5] 7421[2]

Saffire Song *Alan Bailey* a53 58
2 ch f Firebreak Saffwah (IRE) (King's Best (USA))
3781[8] 4215[13] 5003[12] 5610[6] 6872[3] *7986[5] 8090[8]*

Saffron Park *John Best* a43 49
4 ch g Compton Place Beacon Silver (Belmez (USA))
418[11] 530[8]

Saffron Town (IRE) *Alan Swinbank* 71
4 ch g Saffron Walden(FR) Magic Feeling (IRE) (Magical Wonder (USA))
4157[2] 4805[3] 5469[3] 5920[4]

Safrana (FR) *D Prod'Homme* a36 64
3 b f Oratorio(IRE) Alyousufeya (IRE) (Kingmambo (USA))
461a[0] 647a[8]

Safwaan *Michael Squance* a67 70
6 b g Selkirk(USA) Kawn (Cadeaux Genereux)
158[2] 508[2] 639[10] 978[6] 1909[5] (3909) 4755[6] 5073[6] 7378[7] 8125[10] 8341[3]

Saga Dream (FR) *F Lemercier* 117
7 gr g Sagacity(FR) Manixa (FR) (Manninamix)
(1048a) 1420a[3] 2908a[9] 3165a[5] (4421a)

Saga Lout *Ray Peacock* a75 58
3 b g Assertive Intellibet One (Compton Place)
2521[8] *3212[6] 3638[2] 3904[2]* 7633[13]

Sage Melody (FR) *M Delzangles* a80 97
3 b f Sageburg(IRE) Desert Melody (FR) (Green Desert (USA))
2299a[18] 3385a[11] 6450a[7]

Sagesse *Sir Mark Prescott Bt* a56
3 ch f Smart Strike(CAN) Summer Night (Nashwan (USA))
5071[4]

Sagredo (USA) *Jonjo O'Neill* a76 70
9 b g Diesis Eternity (Suave Dancer (USA))
2498[9] 2860[5] 3271[7]

Sagua La Grande (IRE) *Lady Cecil* 81
3 b c Teofilo(IRE) Water Fountain (Mark Of Esteem (IRE))
3343[4]

Sahara Desert (IRE) *Sir Michael Stoute* a57 67
2 b g Montjeu(IRE) Festoso (IRE) (Diesis)
7120[6] 7461[8] 7773[5]

Saharia (IRE) *Jo Hughes* a86 78
6 b g Oratorio(IRE) Inchiri (Sadler's Wells (USA))
221[2] 517[3] (707) (839) (1322) (1696) 2571[6] 2912[3] *8179[10]*

Sahawar (FR) *C Ferland* 113
3 bl c Dark Angel(IRE) Saaryeh (Royal Academy (USA))
7058a[11]

Sahra Al Khadra *Charles Hills* 72
2 b c Green Desert(USA) Maimoona (IRE) (Pivotal)
4958[5] 5494[6] 6014[2] (6972)

Saigon City *Luca Cumani* 86
3 b g Mount Nelson Hoh Chi Min (Efisio)
3176[2] 3731[6] 4182[6] (4865) (6951) 7611[4]

Sail Home *Julia Feilden* a74 74
6 b m Mizzen Mast(USA) Bristol Channel (Generous (IRE))
21[3] 429[4] (753) 919[4] 1176[7]

Sailorman (IRE) *Ismail Mohammed* a86 79
6 ch h Dubawi(IRE) Squaw Dance (Indian Ridge)
412a[7]

Sainglend *Sean Curran* a62 72
8 b g Galileo(IRE) Verbal Intrigue (USA) (Dahar (USA))
4035[8]

Saint And Sinner (GER) *A Wohler* 80
3 b c Authorized(IRE) Sworn Mum (GER) (Samum (GER))
3389a[8]

Saint Baudolino (IRE) *Saeed bin Suroor* a105 119
4 b c Pivotal Alessandria (Sunday Silence (USA))
556a[4] 3457[10]

Saint Bernard *D Camuffo* a71 105
4 b c Three Valleys(USA) Savignano (Polish Precedent (USA))
465a[11] 744a[11] 6889a[2] 7413a[6] (7725a)

Saint Boniface *Peter Makin* a51 60
4 ch g Bahamian Bounty Nursling (IRE) (Kahyasi)
3326[5] 5232[5] 5667[2] 6097[2] 6553[10] 7351[9]

Saint Clement (FR) *N Clement* a77
2 b c Mount Nelson Scarley Secret (IRE) (Royal Applause)
6961a[8]

Saint Helena (IRE) *Harry Dunlop* a74 82
5 b f Holy Roman Emperor(IRE) Tafseer (IRE) (Grand Lodge (USA))
1302[3] 2004[3] (2102) 2750[3] 2939[2] 3579[4] 4234[8] 5130[7] 5535[3] 6336[6] 6869[3] 7220[6]

Saint Hilary *William Muir* 93
4 b f Authorized(IRE) Bright Halo (IRE) (Bigstone (IRE))
2443[6] 3409[4] 4234[3] 5761[4] 6329[7] 6766[9]

Saint Irene *Michael Blanshard* a60 70
4 ch f Halling(USA) Santorini (USA) (Spinning World (USA))
896[8] 1298[12] 1950[9] 2534[2] 3111[7] 3926[6] 4894[4] 5191[7] 5948[7] 6261[6] 6459[8] 7093[8]

Saint Jerome (IRE) *Jamie Osborne* a71 86
3 b g Jeremy(USA) Eminence Gift (Cadeaux Genereux)
1477[6] 1977[4] 2603[3] 3241[10] (3951) 4729[4] 5218[5] 6379[2]

Saint Louet (FR) *F Chappet* a94 86
4 b g Panis(USA) Byanozza (Mtoto)
963a[8]

Saint's Victory *Sir Michael Stoute* a50
2 b f Oasis Dream Hi Calypso (IRE) (In The Wings)
7874[8]

Saint Thomas (FR) *P Bary* 106
3 b c Dansili Metisse (USA) (Kingmambo (USA))
3128a[4] 3911a[3] 4573a[8]

Saint Thomas (IRE) *John Mackie* a69 78
6 b g Alhaarth(IRE) Aguilas Perla (IRE) (Indian Ridge)
1220[5] 1523[6] 1775[2] (2077) 2498[2] 3083[3] 3651[2] 4584[4] 5382[4]

Sairaam (IRE) *Charles Smith* a58 71
7 b m Marju(IRE) Sayedati Eljamilah (USA) (Mr Prospector (USA))
7[5] 42[7] 1757[15] 2134[12] 3246[13] 4005[12] 4456[4] 4623[9]

Sajjhaa *Saeed bin Suroor* 117
6 b m King's Best(USA) Anaamil (IRE) (Darshaan)
(366a) (743a) (959a) (1267a) 1872a[4] 4985[4]

Sakash *J R Jenkins* a77 61
3 b c Sakhee(USA) Ashwell Rose (Anabaa (USA))
2637[6] 3253[5] 3740[2] 4391[3] (5407) 7966[2] (8234)

Sakhalin Star (IRE) *Richard Guest* a44 63
2 ch g Footstepsinthesand Quela (GER) (Acatenango (GER))
3077[6] 3500[4] 4199[3] 4618[2] 5136[8] 5467[5] 6914[2] 7168[6]

Sakhee's Alround *K F Clutterbuck* a52 54
3 ch f Sakhee's Secret Regal Run (USA) (Deputy Minister (CAN))
1640[13] 1955[8] 2384[14] 2931[7] 3325[14] 3922[RR] 4535[6] 5128[3] 5407[2] 6038[4] 6400[4] 7266[4] 7644[12] 7885[10] 7980[RR]

Sakhees Romance *Philip Kirby* a22 53
3 b f Sakhee(USA) Chance For Romance (Entrepreneur)
2635[5] 3463[6] 3772[4] 5016[12] 7667[8]

Sakhee's Rose *Ed McMahon* a70 68
3 b f Sakhee's Secret Isobel Rose (IRE) (Royal Applause)
3489[3] 4064[2] 4962[7] 5841[9] 6560[2] 6982[5]

Sakhee'Ssquirrel *David Evans* a44 61
2 ch f Sakhee's Secret China Cherub (Inchinor)
3107[8] 3413[6] 3659[2] 3914[6]

Sakina (FR) *G Brillet* a61 62
3 b f Spirit One(FR) Talena (Zafonic (USA))
1756a[10]

Sakuramachi *Nikki Evans* 61
2 b f Sixties Icon Queen Of Narnia (Hunting Lion (IRE))
2612[3] (4065) 4519[8] 5175[7] 5976[4] 8039[8]

Salai (FR) *J-C Rouget* 102
2 b c Myboycharlie(IRE) Mabadi (USA) (Sahm (USA))
5082a[4] 7409a[3]

Salam Alaykum (IRE) *John Francis Egan* a90 90
5 b c Galileo(IRE) Alicia (IRE) (Darshaan)
3142a[7] 4869a[7]

Salar Art *B Grizzetti* 94
2 b f Dutch Art Salar Violet (IRE) (Orpen (USA))
7415a[F]

Salford Excel *Marco Botti* a63
3 b f Exceed And Excel(AUS) Steeple (Selkirk (USA))
2084[8] 2953[P]

Salford Prince (IRE) *David Elsworth* a40
5 b g Invincible Spirit(IRE) Bring Plenty (USA) (Southern Halo (USA))
7292[9] 7465[9] 7644[6]

Salford Red Devil *Richard Fahey* 97
2 b c Pastoral Pursuits Tittle (Tobougg (IRE))
2189[3] (3092) ◆ 3801[2] (4248) 4918[7]

Salford Secret (IRE) *Marco Botti* a81 93
2 b c Sakhee's Secret Dhuyoof (IRE) (Sinndar (IRE))
3275[2] ◆ 3717[4] 4351[3] 5926[2] 6513[8] (7162)

Salhooda (IRE) *D K Weld* a88 93
3 b f Nayef(USA) Alshakr (Bahri (USA))
2148[7] 7404a[9]

Salient *Michael Attwater* a60 71
9 b g Fasliyev(USA) Savannah Belle (Green Desert (USA))
205[7] 320[9] 631[7] 907[6] (1183) (1909) 3169[3] 3580[9] 4411[12] 6737[12] 7321[13] 8449[2]

Salinas Road (FR) *M Figge* a81 84
3 b c Elusive City(USA) Mamounia (GER) (Platini (GER))
2335a[9]

Sally Bruce *Edward Creighton* a52 56
3 b f Byron Show Trial (IRE) (Jade Robbery (USA))
442[2] 821[7] 876[2] 1906[8] 2123[3] 5220[2] 5602[4] 5890[5] 7265[6] 7323[8] 8338[5] 8393[7]

Sally Friday (IRE) *Edwin Tuer* a78 68
5 b f Footstepsinthesand Salee (IRE) (Caerleon (USA))
1464[8] 2118[3] (2721) 3589[5] 4563[2] 5295[2] 5831[5] 6632[4]

Sally's Swansong *Eric Alston* a62 56
7 b m Mind Games Sister Sal (Bairn (USA))
142[4] 946[7] 1355[8] 2043[7] 3026[14]

Salmon Sushi *David Lanigan* a55 66
2 ch g Dalakhani(IRE) Salsa Steps (USA) (Giant's Causeway (USA))
6799[9] 7766[5]

Salon Soldier (GER) *Kris Lees* 106
4 b c Soldier Hollow Salonblue (IRE) (Bluebird (USA))
462a[14] 741a[3] 2294a[6] (7762a)

Saloomy *John Butler* a88 91
4 ch c Shamardal(USA) Oystermouth (Averti (IRE))
2255[6] ◆ 2663[2] 2871[3] (5722) 6526[3]

Saltanat (IRE) *Artut Resulov* 83
3 ch f Duke Of Marmalade(IRE) Perihelion (IRE) (Galileo (IRE))
7407a[5]

Saltas (GER) *P Schaerer* a78 110
5 b c Lomitas Salde (GER) (Alkalde (GER))
125a[6] 701a[4]

Saltwater Creek (IRE) *Michael Bell* 39
2 b f Marju(IRE) Crossing (Cape Cross (IRE))
7466[9]

Saluberlin (FR) *J-C Rouget* a47
3 bb g Layman(USA) Sohaila (GER) (Owington)
270a[8]

Salut (GER) *P Schiergen* 107
5 b c Lomitas Saldentigerin (GER) (Tiger Hill (IRE))
7407a[4]

Salutation (IRE) *Mark Johnston* a38 99
3 b g Iffraaj Totally Yours (IRE) (Desert Sun)
2050[2] (2271) 2641[4] 2862[7] 3338[2] 3486[6] ◆ 4023[5] 4194[2] (4541) 4984[2] 5274[3] 5513[5] 5749[6] 6638[11] 7223[6] 7536[9]

Salute To Seville (IRE) *J S Moore* a61
3 b f Duke Of Marmalade(IRE) Vingt Et Une (FR) (Sadler's Wells (USA))
(103) 411[3] 428[5]

Salut Gabriel (FR) *S Jesus* a74 65
3 gr g Ange Gabriel(FR) Salut Bebs (FR) (Kendor (FR))
2403a[6]

Salvatore Fury (IRE) *Keith Dalgleish* a62 74
3 b g Strategic Prince Nocturnal (FR) (Night Shift (USA))
1566[3] 1988[6] 2218[5] 2336[2] 2703[4] (2795) 3198[2] (3392) 3933[6] 4290[2] (4471) 4611[2] 5333[3] 5705[3] 5878[2] 6547[16] 6728[4]

Samana Cay (USA) *A Fabre* a98 97
4 b f Authorized(IRE) Tessa Reef (IRE) (Mark Of Esteem (IRE))
7968a[3]

Samara Jazz (IRE) *Patrick Carey* a38 55
3 b f Camacho Jina (IRE) (Petardia)
669[4] 1050[7] (Dead)

Samawi (IRE) *Saeed bin Suroor* 62
3 b g Street Cry(IRE) Hi Dubai (Rahy (USA))
1624[9]

Samba Brazil (GER) *J Hirschberger* 104
4 ch f Teofilo(IRE) Sasuela (GER) (Dashing Blade)
2202a[10] 3165a[8] 3612a[6] 5940a[4] (6451a) 6889a[4] 7562a[5]

Samba King *Charlie Appleby* 99
4 b g Dubai Destination(USA) Dance Of Leaves (Sadler's Wells (USA))
6591[8] 7250[11]

Samba Night (IRE) *Jeremy Gask* a59 65
4 b g Dark Angel(IRE) Brazilia (Forzando)
2596[12] 3154[6] 3499[9] 3888[4] 4197[4]

Same World *J Moore* 108
5 b g Hawk Wing(USA) Spinamix (Spinning World (USA))
8211a[10]

Samhain *David Brown* 45
2 b g Compton Place Athboy Nights (IRE) (Night Shift (USA))
4801[6] 6975[10] 7271[6]

Sammyman *Michael Blanshard* 60
6 b g Tamure(IRE) Bajan Rose (Dashing Blade)
1804[8] 2568[4] 3209[7] 5954[9]

Sam Nombulist *Ian Semple* a39 86
5 ch g Sleeping Indian Owdbetts (IRE) (High Estate)
2310[9] 2541[4] 2958[8] 3096[13] 3300[8] 5014[14] 6164[2] 6550[13] 6625[10] 7820[18] 8028[5] 8350[10]

Samoan (IRE) *Alan Berry* 69
4 b g Danehill Dancer(IRE) Rain Flower (IRE) (Indian Ridge)
2628[13] 3417[8] 3858[3] 5032[5] 5823[9] 6315[12] 7238[12] 7346[14]

Samos (GER) *W Hickst* 98
3 b c Doyen(IRE) Sea Road (GER) (Dashing Blade)
2696a[6] 4103a[9]

Samoset *Alan Swinbank* a37 61
3 b g Sir Percy Great Quest (IRE) (Montjeu (IRE))
1648[3] 2885[5] 3201[4] 6629[7] 8046[5] 8270[8]

Sam Run *Christopher Kellett*
4 b g Samraan(USA) Misty Cay (IRE) (Mujadil (USA))
2995[7]

Sam Sharp (USA) *Ian Williams* a81 102
7 bb g Johannesburg(USA) Caffe (USA) (Mr Prospector (USA))
2592[3] (3346) 4531[2] 5255[6] (5768) 6838[12] 7206[7] 7536[10]

Sam Spade (IRE) *Derek Shaw* a69 70
3 gr g Clodovil(IRE) Red Empress (Nashwan (USA))
1057[5] 1320[2] (1424) 2324[4] 2727[5] 3289[6] 8030[7]

Samtu (IRE) *Clive Brittain* a58 68
2 b c Teofilo(IRE) Samdaniya (Machiavellian (USA))
5438[4] 5941[6] 6314[6] 6897[3] 7694[4]

Samurai Sword *Mahmood Al Zarooni* 100
5 b h Motivator Japanese Whisper (UAE) (Machiavellian (USA))
363a[7]

San Benedeto (FR) *C Lerner* a83 83
2 ch c Layman(USA) Cinco Baidy (FR) (Lure (USA))
6961a[2]

San Cassiano (IRE) *Ruth Carr* a75 87
6 b g Bertolini(USA) Celtic Silhouette (FR) (Celtic Swing)
1824[6] 2277[8] 2590[5] 2855[7] 3204[4] (3477) 3729[8] 4098[6] 4542[4] 5055[3] 5860[4] 6211[10] 6563[10] 6846[8] (7028) 7211[13] 7424[7]

Sancho Panza *Julia Feilden* a52 66
6 b g Zafeen(FR) Malvadilla (IRE) (Doyoun)
(2642) 3587[6]

Sanctioned *Robert Stephens* a82 64
4 b g Authorized(IRE) Kazeem (Darshaan)
8298[8]

Sandagiyr (FR) *Saeed bin Suroor* a111 112
5 b c Dr Fong(USA) Sanariya (IRE) (Darshaan)
241a[3] ◆ 463a[7] 744a[2] 836a[7] 3458[17] 4946[3] 5681[10] 6396[5] 6834[3]

Sand And Deliver *Peter Crate* a45 67
3 b f Royal Applause Alhufoof (USA) (Dayjur (USA))
1051[4] 2091[9]

Sand Boy (IRE) *Charles Hills* a76 82
3 b c Footstepsinthesand Farbenspiel (IRE) (Desert Prince (IRE))
185[3] (416) ◆ 628[5] 1582[4] 1935[5] 2394[9] 2959[2] (3566) 3887[2]

Sanderiana *Mel Brittain* 14
3 b f Lucky Story(USA) Guadaloup (Loup Sauvage (USA))
2765[9] 2960[9]

Sandfield (IRE) *Paul Midgley* 52
2 b g Kodiac Red Rabbit (Suave Dancer (USA))
4731[8] 5543[7] 6206[10]

Sandfrankskipsgo *Peter Crate* a87 88
4 ch g Piccolo Alhufoof (USA) (Dayjur (USA))
586[4] ◆ (1121) 1765[15] 2227[3] 3341[9] (3658) 4123[4] 4675[3] 4800[17] 5821[5] 6854[6] 8021[6] 8430[10]

Sand Grouse *Marco Botti* a60 56
3 b f Mr Greeley(USA) Gentle On My Mind (IRE) (Sadler's Wells (USA))
411[4] 634[5] 977[2] 1055[2] 1367[4] 1427[3]

Sandiva (IRE) *Richard Fahey* 106
2 ch f Footstepsinthesand Miss Corinne (Mark Of Esteem (IRE))
(2230) (2944a) ◆ 3522[2] (5555a) 7055a[7]

Sandoka (FR) *J-P Delaporte* a76 79
4 b g Sagacity(FR) Ninazeyra (FR) (Sheyrann (IRE))
6060a[8]

Sandra's Diamond (IRE) *Keith Dalgleish* 77
2 b f Footstepsinthesand Lucky Us (IRE) (Fayruz)
5638[2] 6174[2] 6622[11] (6915) (7370)

Sandreamer (IRE) *Mick Channon* 99
3 b f Oasis Dream Alsharq (IRE) (Machiavellian (USA))
1921[10] 3340[3] 4260[10]

Sands Legends *James Given* a33 33
2 b f Avonbridge T G's Girl (Selkirk (USA))
2436[10] 3413[9] 4073[10] 7036[6] 7882[10]

Sandsman's Girl (IRE) *James Given* a57 75
2 b f Kodiac Inter Madera (IRE) (Toca Madera)
2327[4] (2715) 3459[20] 4141[3] 4965[3] (5235) 5536[10] 6070[7] 7097[5] 7463[9] 7837[11] 8018[5] 8273[3]

Sand Stormer (IRE) *William Muir* a55
2 b g Footstepsinthesand Claustra (FR) (Green Desert (USA))
8451[7]

Sandwith *Ian Semple* a63 76
10 ch g Perryston View Bodfari Times (Clantime)
2410[13] 2880[6] 3933[9]

Sandy Cove *Roger Charlton* a54 63
2 br g Oasis Dream Maganda (IRE) (Sadler's Wells (USA))
4347[9] 5033[3] 5584[6] 6170[4] 6605[7]

Sandy Lane (IRE) *David O'Meara* a77 92
4 b g Elusive City(USA) Ipanema Beach (Lion Cavern (USA))
54[2] (1460) (1646) 2665[5]

Sandy Smile (IRE) *M Halford* a64 68
2 b f Footstepsinthesand Shy Smile (IRE) (Peintre Celebre (USA))
5773a[10]

Sandy's Row (USA) *Mark Johnston* a18 69
3 b f Street Cry(IRE) Carry On Katie (USA) (Fasliyev (USA))
2992[5] 3254[4] 3629[5] 3917[RR] (4049)

San Gabriel (IRE) *Ed Walker* a71 24
3 b c Soviet Star(USA) Rancho Cucamonga (IRE) (Raphane (USA))
1595[2] 1891[3] 2346[5]

Sango (IRE) *H-A Pantall* a71 76
3 gr c Dalakhani(IRE) Home You Stroll (IRE) (Selkirk (USA))
445a[5] 2434a[7]

Sangrail *William Muir* a50 63
4 b f Singspiel(IRE) Wars (IRE) (Green Desert (USA))
158[11] 510[12] 662[6] 3429[5]

San Jose City (IRE) *Gary Brown* a49 54
8 b g Clodovil(IRE) Allspice (Alzao (USA))
1093[6] 1149[7]

San Juan (FR) *C Lerner* a80 96
3 b c Librettist(USA) Milonga (IRE) (Barathea (IRE))
286a[5]

Sanjuro (IRE) *Mick Channon* 81
3 br g Manduro(GER) Kind Regards (IRE) (Unfuwain (USA))
1444[6] 1806[8]

San Marino Grey (FR) *A Fabre* a97 113
3 gr c Clodovil(IRE) Montagne Magique (IRE) (King's Best (USA))
3128a[2] 3876a[2]

San Martin *P Monfort* a80 103
6 b g Oasis Dream Suedoise (Kris)
4467a[9]

Sannibel *Graeme McPherson* a69 60
5 ch f Needwood Blade Socialise (Groom Dancer (USA))
139[6] 560[5] 665[2] 903[2] ◆ 991[9] 1172[6] 1656[7] 1886[7] 2130[5]

San Remo Rose (IRE) *Nigel Tinkler* 44
2 b f Tagula(IRE) Satin Rose (Lujain (USA))
2075[9] 2715[7] 7818[14]

Sans Loi (IRE) *Brian Ellison* a81 86
4 b g Lawman(FR) Lady Elysees (USA) (Royal Academy (USA))
526[4] 966[2] ◆ 1249[7] 1644[3] 2007[14] 2882[11] 4494[12]

Santadelacruze *Gary Moore* a69 66
4 b g Pastoral Pursuits Jupiters Princess (Jupiter Island)
4195[5] (5002) 5528[P] 6737[3] 6933[3] 7858[4] 8072[4]

Santa Fe Stinger *Tim Easterby* 45
3 b f Rail Link Highly Liquid (Entrepreneur)
3809[6] 4587[6] 4849[6] 6964[10]

Santa Ponsa (FR) *F Rossi* 106
3 b f Slickly(FR) Tounsi (FR) (Sendawar (IRE))
2381a[2] 3614a[8]

Santayana (GER) *David Evans* a37 15
4 ch f Manduro(GER) Saderlina (IRE) (Sadler's Wells (USA))
6696[13] 6996[5]

Santefisio *Keith Dalgleish* a104 109
7 b g Efisio Impulsive Decision (IRE) (Nomination)
290a[8] 503a[6] 659a[6] 744a[8] 1720[3] 2029[9] 3458[14] 3527[4] 3825[7] 4744[21]

Santo Prince (USA) *Michael Bell* 75
3 bb g Henrythenavigator(USA) Sally Wood (CAN) (Woodman (USA))
1293[8] 1832[7] 2495[9] 3818[4] 4829[9] 6459[3] 7091[3] ◆ 7346[8]

Santorini Sunset *J R Jenkins*
4 ch f Haafhd Fantasy Ridge (Indian Ridge)
275[8] 641[3] 911[10]

Sanzatu (TUR) *S Aydogdi* 99
4 b c Bin Ajwaad(IRE) Red Fact (TUR) (Asakir)
6253a[7]

Saoi (USA) *William Knight* a93 83
6 ch g Wiseman's Ferry(USA) Careyes (IRE) (Sadler's Wells (USA))
(146) 691[2] ◆ 926[5] 7121[2]

Saonois (FR) *J-P Gauvin* a80 118
4 b c Chichicastenango(FR) Saonoise (FR) (Homme De Loi (IRE))
1870a[5] 2908a[8] 4421a[6]

Saphir Nonantais (FR) *W Walton* a54 68
3 ch c Medecis Royale Vettorie (FR) (Vettori (IRE))
711a[3] 2034a[0]

Sapphire Sky *Jim Goldie*
4 ch f Zafeen(FR) Miss Hermione (Bahamian Bounty)
6084[9]

Saptapadi (IRE) *Brian Ellison* a106 98
7 ch g Indian Ridge Olympienne (IRE) (Sadler's Wells (USA))
2427[5] ◆ 3608[5] 4310[7] 4857[9] 5256[8] 5766[8] 6394[4] ◆ 6833[7] 7174[4] 7723a[4]

Sara Francesca (FR) *S-R Simon* 76
3 b f Le Fou(IRE) Avenza (FR) (Zayyani)
711a[8]

Sarah Berry *Chris Dwyer* a64 64
4 b f First Trump Dolly Coughdrop (IRE) (Titus Livius (FR))
2643[3] 3223[6] 3498[7] 3738[8] 4752[9] 5230[3] 5864[3] 6345[4] 6752[5] 7079[3] (7292) 8022[5] 8135[11] 8272[7] 8457[10]

Sarahs Pal *Mandy Rowland* a23
3 b f No Time(IRE) Danum Diva (IRE) (Danehill Dancer (IRE))
102[8] 377[7]

Sara Lucille *F Head* a88 100
3 b f Dansili Magic America (USA) (High Yield (USA))
1358a[8] 6445a[9]

Sarando *Alex Hales* a63 45
8 b g Hernando(FR) Dansara (Dancing Brave (USA))
7767[9]

Sarangoo *Malcolm Saunders* a72 84
5 b f Piccolo Craic Sa Ceili (IRE) (Danehill Dancer (IRE))
1521[5] 2070[2] 2361[3] (3270) 3988[2] 4243[2] (4909) 5589[3] 6337[10] 7254[3]

Saranta *Richard Fahey* 68
2 b f Mount Nelson Oh Hebe (IRE) (Night Shift (USA))
7023[4] ◆

Sara Taylor (SER) *B Vidovic* 59
2 b f Just A Miner(USA) Sahaadi (Dansili)
7185a[7]

Saratino (GER) *Mario Hofer* 104
3 ch c Lord Of England(GER) Saratina (IRE) (Monsun (GER))
2696a[5] 3612a[7] 4103a[6] 6248a[2] 7046a[7]

Saratoga Baby (IRE) *Peter Fahey* a82 82
5 b f High Chaparral(IRE) Miss Moses (USA) (Gulch (USA))
3845a[10]

Saratoga Black (IRE) *B Grizzetti* 95
6 b g Pyrus(USA) Mary Martins (IRE) (Orpen (USA))
7591a[3]

Sardanapalus *Kevin Ryan* 82
4 b g Byron Crinkle (IRE) (Distant Relative)
1460[5] 1686[5] 1963[2] 2278[5] 2551[3] 3193[6] 4055[11] 4245[8] 4966[9] 5491[3] 5861[5] 6306[14] (6720)

Sareeah (IRE) *David O'Meara* a68 66
4 b f Cadeaux Genereux Jules (IRE) (Danehill (USA))
2026[5] ◆ 2551[7] 2796[5] 3649[7] 3895[12] 4673[6]

Sargasses (FR) *Mlle V Dissaux* a100 100
7 b m Kingsalsa(USA) Sarabande (Nashwan (USA))
1895a[7] *8440a[6]*

Sarina (GER) *J-P Carvalho* 62
2 b f Lord Of England(GER) Sovereign Baby (IRE) (Cadeaux Genereux)
5323a[7]

Sarjinsky (IRE) *Peter Chapple-Hyam* 62
3 ch g Raven's Pass(USA) Dinka Raja (USA) (Woodman (USA))
1722[5]

Sarkiyla (FR) *A De Royer-Dupre* a104 111
4 b f Oasis Dream Sarlisa (FR) (Rainbow Quest (USA))
1262a[4] 1945a[2] 3456[5] 5574a[2] 7057a[8] 7685a[3]

Sarlat *Mark Brisbourne* a44 13
2 b f Champs Elysees Midnight Sky (Desert Prince (IRE))
2067[7] 3391[11] *8114[6]* *8274[2]*

Sarpech (IRE) *Sir Mark Prescott Bt* 50
2 b c Sea The Stars(IRE) Sadima (IRE) (Sadler's Wells (USA))
7128[8]

Sarrebourg (FR) *J-P Gauvin*
3 bl c
8441a[15]

Sartingo (IRE) *Alan Swinbank* a64 72
6 b g Encosta De Lago(AUS) Alicia (IRE) (Darshaan)
(1270)

Sartori *Marjorie Fife* 73
2 b c Elnadim(USA) Little Caroline (IRE) (Great Commotion (USA))
1659[6] 1930[2] 2260[3] 3017[7] 4218[7] 5834[2] 6233[9] 7096[2]

Sartorialist (IRE) *J S Moore* 72
2 b g Oratorio(IRE) Personal Design (IRE) (Traditionally (USA))
2917[4] 3310[2] ◆ 3624[3] (4232)

Saskatchewan *Luca Cumani* 70
3 ch c Peintre Celebre(USA) Sarabande (USA) (Woodman (USA))
1635[6] 2442[8]

Saskia's Dream *Jane Chapple-Hyam* a77 68
5 b f Oasis Dream Swynford Pleasure (Reprimand)
1915[4] 2638[7] 3534[6] 3817[4] 4496[4] 6039[2] (6255) 6744[13] *7743[6]* *8019[9]* *8052[5]* *8330[3]* *8456[8]*

Sassaway (IRE) *Eamonn O'Connell* a90 89
6 ch m Bertolini(USA) Sassari (IRE) (Darshaan)
5775a[2] 6883a[5]

Sassi Sioux *Tom Keddy* a40 27
4 b f Sleeping Indian Dhurwah (IRE) (Green Desert (USA))
333[7] *1082[6]* *1700[8]* 2567[9] *3056[6]*

Sassy Brown (IRE) *Tim Easterby* 43
2 b f Bushranger(IRE) Tip the Scale (USA) (Valiant Nature (USA))
3681[6] 4115[8] 4505[7] 4990[8]

Satanic Beat (IRE) *Jedd O'Keeffe* a53 91
4 br g Dark Angel(IRE) Slow Jazz (USA) (Chief's Crown (USA))
1233[9] 1538[5] 1990[4] 2478[8] 3204[9] 4994[2] *5195[5]* 6288[4] (6567)

Satin Waters *Eve Johnson Houghton* 41
2 b f Halling(USA) Velvet Waters (Unfuwain (USA))
4921[16] 5812[9] 6281[12]

Satono Shuren (JPN) *Akira Murayama* 102
5 bb c Stay Gold(JPN) Red Diamond (JPN) (Erhaab (USA))
1868a[18]

Satsuma *David Brown* a57 90
3 ch f Compton Place Jodrell Bank (IRE) (Observatory (USA))
1690[3] 2039[8] 2213[5] 2430[17] 3104[6] 4402[2] 4734[6] 6309[12] 6848[10] *7112[11]*

Satwa Laird *Ann Stokell* a77 80
7 b g Johannesburg(USA) Policy Setter (USA) (Deputy Minister (CAN))
971[12] *1172[7]* *1426[12]* *1600[4]* *1696[2]* *1956[4]* *2511[8]* *2875[10]* *3329[8]* 6479[7] 6804[9] 7752[10]

Satwa's Sister *Robert Cowell* a30
3 b f Elusive City(USA) Black Tribal (IRE) (Mukaddamah (USA))
796[6] *1078[6]* *1215[6]* 2762[14]

Satwa Story *Charlie Appleby* a88 85
3 ch c Street Cry(IRE) Satwa Queen (FR) (Muhtathir)
1727[5] 4535[2] *(5069)* 5799[6] *6203[9]*

Saucy Minx (IRE) *Amanda Perrett* a85 86
3 b f Dylan Thomas(IRE) Market Day (Tobougg (IRE))
1640[2] *2084[5]* (2658) (3532) 4307[2] 4878[5] 5589[4] 6188[7] *6524[4]*

Savanna Days (IRE) *Mick Channon* a83 83
4 ch f Danehill Dancer(IRE) Dominante (GER) (Monsun (GER))
1159[8] *1500[3]* 1823[2] 2266[10] 2964[9] 3532[2] 3842[2] 4278[5] 5014[8] *6167[9]* *7462[5]*

Savannah Blue (GER) *Markus Klug* 91
5 b f Lando(GER) Sonia (GER) (Robellino (USA))
7233a[9]

Savanna La Mar (USA) *Sir Mark Prescott Bt* a93 100
3 ch f Curlin(USA) Soft Morning (Pivotal)
3604a[5] 4468a[5] 5035[4] 5993[6] *6751[6]*

Savanna Spring (IRE) *Alan Jarvis* 57
2 b f Bushranger(IRE) Brogan's Well (IRE) (Caerleon (USA))
3760[9] 7175[8]

Save The Bees *Declan Carroll* a83 82
5 b g Royal Applause Rock Concert (Bishop Of Cashel)
1932[8] 2551[8] 3081[8] *4357[2]* (4824) (5142) (5368) 6236[4] *(7000)* 7130[4] 7425[6]

Saxo Jack (FR) *G M Lyons* a95 106
3 b g King's Best(USA) Gamma (FR) (Sadler's Wells (USA))
6638[4] ◆

Saxonette *Linda Perratt* a61 60
5 b f Piccolo Solmorin (Fraam)
2632[5] 4102[3] (4292) 4471[3] 4582[2] 5336[2] 5708[6] 6053[5] 6469[6] 6547[12] 6669[3] 6916[6] 7149[6]

Saxon Princess (IRE) *Roger Charlton* 41
2 b f Dalakhani(IRE) Rhadegunda (Pivotal)
4484[10]

Saxon Soldier *Ed Dunlop* a67 72
3 br c Kyllachy Gwyneth (Zafonic (USA))
1881[5] 2746[5] *3434[6]*

Saxony *Mark Usher* 32
2 b f Bertolini(USA) Just Down The Road (IRE) (Night Shift (USA))
3408[4] 6423[11] *6746[11]*

Say (IRE) *A P O'Brien* 109
3 b f Galileo(IRE) Riskaverse (USA) (Dynaformer (USA))
2842[10] 3381a[5] 3870a[5] 4567a[2] 5683[2] (6023a) 6224a[3] 7043a[6]

Sayaad (USA) *Kiaran McLaughlin* 104
3 b c Street Sense(USA) Time For A Crown (USA) (Time For A Change (USA))
3360a[5]

Sayed Youmzain *Marco Botti* 66
2 b c Dalakhani(IRE) Silver Touch (IRE) (Dansili)
7774[4]

Saytara (IRE) *Saeed bin Suroor* a89 98
4 b f Nayef(USA) Celtic Silhouette (FR) (Celtic Swing)
4796[5] *6172[9]* 6649[10] 7250[10]

Saythatagain (IRE) *Tim Easterby* 60
2 b f Echo Of Light The Oldladysays No (IRE) (Perugino (USA))
7209[6] 7493[8]

Sbraase *James Tate* a78 71
2 ch c Sir Percy Hermanita (Hernando (FR))
3291[4] 3810[4] *(7513)*

Scala Romana (IRE) *Sir Mark Prescott Bt* a63 65
3 b f Holy Roman Emperor(IRE) Sliding Scale (Sadler's Wells (USA))
2437[4] 2637[7] *2979[5]* *3956[6]* 4158[4] (4625) (5201)

Scala Santa *Martin Bosley* 38
4 b f Kentucky Dynamite(USA) Maid In England (Mujadil (USA))
4223[11] 5586[11] *6116[7]*

Scamperdale *Brian Baugh* a69 67
11 br g Compton Place Miss Up N Go (Gorytus (USA))
83[2] *314[6]* *709[7]* *(1054)* *1402[3]* *1956[7]* 2710[8] *3580[5]* *5234[5]* *7622[12]* *8072[9]* 8399[8]

Scandalous Act (USA) *Kathleen O'Connell* a94
2 bb f Act Of Duty(USA) Seductive Lady (USA) (Langfuhr (CAN))
7707a[6]

Scarborough (IRE) *Paul Midgley* a52 50
2 ch f Dandy Man(IRE) Alchimie (IRE) (Sri Pekan (USA))
2458[10] 2701[7] 3350[12] 5480[4] *(5964)* *6967[5]*

Scargill *Brian Ellison* 76
2 ro c Sixties Icon Rose Cheval (USA) (Johannesburg (USA))
1247[4] 1360[5] (1574) 2068[2] 2553[3] 3555[11] (3767) 4134[3]

Scarlet Sonnet (IRE) *S Wattel* a89 96
3 b f Invincible Spirit(IRE) Sahara Sonnet (USA) (Stravinsky (USA))
6484a[11]

Scarlet Strand *Andrew Hollinshead* a51 54
3 b f Pastoral Pursuits Vermilion Creek (Makbul)
37[3] *197[10]* *669[5]* *848[12]* *923[11]* 4371[10] 5227[7] (5981) *6362[12]* 6902[3]

Scarlette D'Or *Alastair Lidderdale* a57 31
4 ch f Iceman Double Stake (USA) (Kokand (USA))
479[3] *5133[10]* 5588[10]

Scarlet Whispers *Pam Sly* 83
4 b f Sir Percy Hieroglyph (Green Desert (USA))
2277[9] 2939[10]

Scary Movie (IRE) *Emmet Michael Butterly* a74 62
8 b g Daggers Drawn(USA) Grinning (IRE) (Bellypha)
361[7] *789[8]* *(883)* *(896)* *921[4]* *7865[12]*

Scatt Cirio (ITY) *P Riccioni* 88
4 b c Blu Air Force(IRE) Scintillosa (Compton Place)
2491a[7]

Scatter Dice (IRE) *Mark Johnston* a69 99
4 ch f Manduro(GER) Sensation (Soviet Star (USA))
1766[4] 2052[3] 2251[11] 2867[11] 3208[3] 3599a[3] 3824[5] 4060[15] 4796[7] 5259[7] 5513[2] 5723[5] 6192[6] 6585[13] 6876[4] (7193)

Scatty Cat (IRE) *Peter McCreery* a69 88
3 b f One Cool Cat(USA) Shinko Dancer (IRE) (Shinko Forest (IRE))
3796a[10] 5775a[19] 6583[15]

Scent Of Roses (IRE) *Clive Cox* a61 75
3 b f Invincible Spirit(IRE) Moy Water (IRE) (Tirol)
706[3] *821[2]* 1682[6] *7759[10]*

Scentpastparadise *Ann Duffield* 78
3 b f Pastoral Pursuits Centenerola (USA) (Century City (IRE))
2987[8] 3611[6] 3929[2] (4891) 5141[2] 5836[5] 6515[9]

Scepticism (USA) *Charlie Mann* a63 58
3 b g Elusive Quality(USA) Never Is A Promise (USA) (Capote (USA))
632[6] *845[7]* *1071[4]* *1428[2]* *1747[2]* *1879[7]* *(7035)* *7201[8]* *7667[9]*

Schachspieler (GER) *W Figge* a94 61
7 ch g Samum(GER) English Rose (FR) (Caerleon (USA))
5601a[3]

Schelm (GER) *Ronald O'Leary* a69 60
11 b g Alwuhush(USA) Shoba (GER) (Local Suitor (USA))
3884[5]

Schiaman Force (ITY) *G Botti* 63
2 b c Blu Air Force(IRE) Kiri's Fantasy (ITY) (Scenic)
5214a[6]

Schmooze (IRE) *Linda Perratt* a63 71
4 b f One Cool Cat(USA) If Dubai (USA) (Stephen Got Even (USA))
2316[5] 2798[2] 3199[4] (3467) 3709[2] 3930[2] 4447[4] ◆ 4578[2] 4822[6]

Schoolboy Champ *Lisa Williamson* a51 41
6 ch g Trade Fair Aswhatilldois (IRE) (Blues Traveller (IRE))
408[9] *436[5]* *725[6]* 5816[8] 6154[10] 6687[10] 6921[4] *7512[9]*

School Fees *Olly Stevens* a64 90
4 b f Royal Applause Cankara (IRE) (Daggers Drawn (USA))
880[7] (1540) 2255[4] 3532[7] (4210) 5062[5] 5247[7]

Schottische *Derek Haydn Jones* a66 48
3 ch f Pastoral Pursuits Calligraphy (Kris)
55[5] *(216)* *482[4]* *732[7]* 3040[10] 6698[4] *(6986)* *7784[3]* *7953[4]* *8295[6]*

Schulz (GER) *Markus Klug* 99
3 b c Rail Link Simply Red (GER) (Dashing Blade)
3389a[4] 4103a[12]

Schwarzweiss (IRE) *W Hickst* a50 68
3 b f Rock Of Gibraltar(IRE) Silver Mitzva (IRE) (Almutawakel)
7187a[8]

Scintillula (IRE) *J S Bolger* 113
3 b f Galileo(IRE) Scribonia (IRE) (Danehill (USA))
3844a[2] 4550a[4] ◆ (4696a) 5209a[3] 5317a[4] 5682[4] 6224a[6] 6674a[3]

Sciolina (IRE) *Cristiana Signorelli* 102
4 b f Oratorio(IRE) Grigora (USA) (Carson City (USA))
3881a[4] 7234a[7] 7725a[6]

Scoglio *Dave Roberts* a63 62
5 b g Monsieur Bond(IRE) Ex Mill Lady (Bishop Of Cashel)
2977[2]

Scommettitrice (IRE) *Nigel Twiston-Davies* a61 67
5 b f Le Vie Dei Colori Hard To Lay (IRE) (Dolphin Street (FR))
30[5] *559[7]* *736[2]* *862[2]* *1087[11]* 1665[8] 2074[9] 2596[4] 3154[7] 3325[6] 3425[2] 3623[4] 6033[4] 6156[12] 6901[11] 8119[10] 8412[6]

Scoobys Girl (IRE) *Daniel Mark Loughnane* a41 39
3 b f Holy Roman Emperor(IRE) Mystiara (IRE) (Orpen (USA))
36[4] *207[10]* *424[6]*

Scooping (IRE) *Richard Hannon Snr* 30
2 b f Dylan Thomas(IRE) Meseta (Lion Cavern (USA))
2382[9] 3310[6]

Scoppio Del Carro *Andrew Balding* a64 61
2 b g Medicean Sadie Thompson (IRE) (King's Best (USA))
7175[9] *7780[6]*

Scoreline *David O'Meara* 62
2 b g Captain Gerrard(IRE) Waterline Twenty (IRE) (Indian Danehill (IRE))
2075[7] 6286[2] 6561[6] 7094[8]

Scotland (GER) *Andrew Balding* 95
2 b c Monsun(GER) Sqillo (IRE) (Bachelor Duke (USA))
6355[3] (6866) ◆

Scotland Forever (IRE) *John Patrick Shanahan* a84 72
3 b c Rock Of Gibraltar(IRE) Wee Mad Snout (IRE) (Soviet Star (USA))
2374a[3] 3846a[19] 4472[13] 6414a[13]

Scots Gaelic (IRE) *John Quinn* a64 89
6 ch g Tomba Harmonic (USA) (Shadeed (USA))
7210[10]

Scots Law (IRE) *Keith Dalgleish* 70
2 b f Lawman(FR) Misaayef (USA) (Swain (IRE))
5330[5] 5827[5] 6160[3] 6582[5]

Scottish Academy *Mark Johnston* 58
2 ch f Mount Nelson Key Academy (Royal Academy (USA))
4723[9] 5812[6] 6271[6] 6946[7]

Scottish Boogie (IRE) *Seamus Durack* a91 87
6 b g Tobougg(IRE) Scottish Spice (Selkirk (USA))
318[4] *691[5]* *(779)* *1302[6]* *4167[11]* *(8004)* *8392[3]*

Scottish Glen *Patrick Chamings* a88 77
7 ch g Kyllachy Dance For Fun (Anabaa (USA))
2286[5] 3108[8] 3416[8] 4685[7] *7123[4]* *(7785)* *(8219)*

Scottish Lake *Olivia Maylam* a81 69
5 b g Bertolini(USA) Diabaig (Precocious)
345[4] *443[8]* *650[10]* *984[5]* *1096[6]* *6316[3]* *7306[11]* *8157[12]*

Scottish Star *James Eustace* a86 83
5 gr g Kirkwall Child Star (FR) (Bellypha)
(759) *995[4]* *1242[9]* 1922[12] 3022[4] 4683[4] 5190[2] *6200[2]* *6750[2]* 6801[19] *7739[2]* *7976[9]* *8336[5]*

Scottish Strand *Ed Walker* 46
2 b c Selkirk(USA) Starlit Sands (Oasis Dream)
3245[8]

Scoville (GER) *H Hesse* 100
4 bb f Sholokhov(IRE) Stravina (GER) (Platini (GER))
3852a[3] 6451a[10]

Scrafton *James Bethell* 36
2 b g Leporello(IRE) Some Diva (Dr Fong (USA))
6271[9] 7175[14]

Scrapper Smith (IRE) *Alistair Whillans* a65 98
7 b g Choisir(AUS) Lady Ounavarra (IRE) (Simply Great (FR))
2407[4] 3685[6]

Scream Blue Murder (IRE) *T Stack* 106
3 b f Oratorio(IRE) Holly Blue (Bluebird (USA))
1704a[2] (2270) 3263a[10] 5772a[6] 6414a[4] 7227a[10]

Screenshot (IRE) *W McCreery* a78 76
2 b g Kheleyf(USA) Lear's Crown (USA) (Lear Fan (USA))
7050a[6]

Scribe (IRE) *David Evans* a77 65
5 b g Montjeu(IRE) Crafty Example (USA) (Crafty Prospector (USA))
100[7] *165[2]* *515[4]* *(542)* *724[2]* *851[3]* *887[2]* *1189[3]* *(1369)* (1520) 2087[5] 2509[2] 2749[2] 3065[7] 7166[7] 7757[5] 8130[2] 8204[3] 8310[2] 8433[5]

Script *Alan Berry* a51 62
4 b f Firebreak Signs And Wonders (Danehill (USA))
37[5] *327[5]* *423[2]* *525[7]* *991[8]* *1209[2]* 1461[3] *1732[6]* 1962[3] (2218) 2409[5] 3197[5] 3462[4] (3569) 3929[4] 4018[5] 4448[3] 4582[3] 4814[3] 4992[4] 5227[3] 5564[10]

Scruffy Tramp (IRE) *Alan Bailey* a89 89
2 br g Kheleyf(USA) Reem One (IRE) (Rainbow Quest (USA))
(3408) *(4174)* 4653[2] *5228[2]* 6304[4] *8203[6]*

Scrutiny *William Haggas* a13 87
2 b g Aqlaam Aunty Mary (Common Grounds)
7119[12] (7501)

Scurr Mist (IRE) *Keith Dalgleish* 67
2 gr g Aussie Rules(USA) Stratospheric (Slip Anchor)
6724[4] 6939[3] 7146[3]

Seabougg *James Eustace* a60 57
5 ch g Tobougg(IRE) Sea Jade (IRE) (Mujadil (USA))
6036[5] 6696[11] *7158[5]*

Seachantach (USA) *Marco Botti* a96 103
7 b g Elusive Quality(USA) Subtle Breeze (USA) (Storm Cat (USA))
868a[4] 954a[7] 3840[9] 4981[7]

Sea Claria (FR) *T Doumen* 83
3 b f Sinndar(IRE) Triclaria (GER) (Surumu (GER))
6484a[12]

Sea Cliff (IRE) *Andrew Crook* a33 46
9 b g Golan(IRE) Prosaic Star (IRE) (Common Grounds)
2120[10]

Sea Defence (USA) *Roger Charlton* a72 84
2 rg c Mizzen Mast(USA) Palisade (USA) (Gone West (USA))
7119[5] (7654)

Sea Fire Salt (FR) *D Prod'Homme* a75 89
6 b h Trempolino(USA) La Juriste (FR) (Homme De Loi (IRE))
960a[9]

Sea Goddess (IRE) *Ralph Beckett* 56
2 ch f Galileo(IRE) Castara Beach (IRE) (Danehill (USA))
6954[6] 7533[11]

Seagull Star *William Haggas* 79
2 b c Sea The Stars(IRE) Dash To The Top (Montjeu (IRE))
(7019) ◆

Seaham *Rod Millman* a72 72
2 b g Myboycharlie(IRE) Be Decisive (Diesis)
1669[11] 2283[3] 2595[5] 3174[3] *3689[4]* 4708[8] 5443[5]

Sea Here *Ralph Beckett* a71 45
2 ch c Sea The Stars(IRE) Look Here (Hernando (FR))
7308[6] *8067[6]*

Sealed With A Kiss *James Fanshawe* a41
2 b f Authorized(IRE) Always On My Mind (Distant Relative)
8067[10]

Seal Of Approval *James Fanshawe* a102 118
4 b f Authorized(IRE) Hannda (IRE) (Dr Devious (IRE))
(3960) (5035) 6329[F] (7365)

Seal Rock *A Oliver* 104
5 b g Ishiguru(USA) Satin Doll (Diktat)
3846a[11] 5775a[13] 6883a[17]

Sea Meets Sky (FR) *Sir Henry Cecil* 100
3 b f Dansili Sacred Song (USA) (Diesis)
(2206) 2859[2]

Seamless *Charles Hills* a75 91
3 b c Beat Hollow Fashionable (Nashwan (USA))
1468[4] 1804[3] 2198[2] 3059[3] (3743) 4084[4]

Sea Monkey *Nicky Vaughan* 2
2 ch c Sakhee(USA) Northern Bows (Bertolini (USA))
6125[12]

Sea Moon *Robert Hickmott* 125
5 b c Beat Hollow Eva Luna (USA) (Alleged (USA))
7761a[13]

Seamster *Richard Ford* a65 49
6 ch g Pivotal Needles And Pins (IRE) (Fasliyev (USA))
(618) *890[2]* *991[3]* *1310[5]* *3329[7]* *3643[6]* 5365[7] *6610[6]* *7347[9]* *7752[12]* *8293[9]* 8418[2]

Seanie (IRE) *David Marnane* a92 99
4 b g Kodiac Cakestown Lady (IRE) (Petorius)
2210[8] 3846a[7] 4869a[4] 5019a[10]

Seaquel *Tony Carroll* a50 35
7 b m Kyllachy Broughton Singer (IRE) (Common Grounds)
99[4] *530[7]* *724[8]* *820[3]* *1022[5]*

Searchlight *Kevin Ryan* a76 76
2 b g Kyllachy Baralinka (IRE) (Barathea (IRE))
2474[2] 2955[2] 3680[3] 4314[4] 6493[2] 7127[5] *8442[2]*

Sea Shanty (USA) *Richard Hannon Snr* a94 97
3 b g Elusive Quality(USA) Medley (Danehill Dancer (IRE))
(1725) ◆ (2100) (2603) 3484[11] 4214[7] 4897[2] 7337[4] *7641[4]*

Seaside Rock (IRE) *Keith Dalgleish* a72 67
3 b g Oratorio(IRE) Miss Sacha (IRE) (Last Tycoon)
3241[9] *7491[8]*

Seaside Runner (IRE) *R Brogi* 58
2 b c Excellent Art Beyond The Sea (IRE) (Fasliyev (USA))
3880a[5]

Seaside Sizzler *Ralph Beckett* a91 93
6 ch g Rahy(USA) Via Borghese (USA) (Seattle Dancer (USA))
(1615) 2052[4] 3560[3] 4873[3] 6252a[3] 7193[33]

Sea Siren (AUS) *A P O'Brien* 120
5 b m Fastnet Rock(AUS) Express A Smile (AUS) (Success Express (USA))
3557[8] 5320a[3] 5688a[2]

Sea Soldier (IRE) *Andrew Balding* a86 64
5 b g Red Ransom(USA) Placement (Kris)
1746[8] 2450[10] 2920[8] *6317[9]* *6937[7]*

Sea Spear *David Barron* a63
2 ch g Virtual Fred's Dream (Cadeaux Genereux)
8328[6]

Sea The Bloom *Sir Michael Stoute* 68
2 b f Sea The Stars(IRE) Red Bloom (Selkirk (USA))
7692[4] ◆

Sea The Flames (IRE) *David O'Meara* a59 62
5 b g Chineur(FR) Flames (Blushing Flame (USA))
5337[9] *6783[P]*

Sea The Skies *Gerard Butler* 79
2 b c Sea The Stars(IRE) Model Queen (USA) (Kingmambo (USA))
3833[3] (4640) 5242[2]

Seattle Drive (IRE) *Brian Ellison* a75 83
5 b g Motivator Seattle Ribbon (USA) (Seattle Dancer (USA))
889[9] 1238[5] 1571[5] 2078[6] 2551[2] (3777) 4746[13] (5050) 6468[6]

Seawood *Roy Bowring* a52 36
7 b g Needwood Blade Ocean Song (Savahra Sound)
99[2] 455[7] 927[9] 1120[7] 2171[6]

Sebastian Beach (IRE) *Richard Hannon Snr* 77
2 b c Yeats(IRE) Night Club (Mozart (IRE))
5244[4] 6139[3] 6740[4]

Sebs Sensei (IRE) *Richard Hannon Snr* a74 73
2 ch c Art Connoisseur(IRE) Capetown Girl (Danzero (AUS))
3238[4] 3631[2] 4906[4] *5926[5] 8383[4] 8452[2]*

Secondo (FR) *Roger Charlton* 98
3 b g Sakhee's Secret Royal Jade (Last Tycoon)
(2051) ◆ 2708[4] (4478) ◆ 4767[8] 6238[2] ◆

Second Step (IRE) *Luca Cumani* 80
2 b g Dalakhani(IRE) My Dark Rosaleen (Sadler's Wells (USA))
7607[2]

Secret Advice *Keith Dalgleish* a51 72
3 ch f Sakhee's Secret Flylowflylong (IRE) (Danetime (IRE))
236[4] 673[5] 1078[3] 1458[5] 1988[9] (2702) 2962[5] (3198) 4291[6] 4558[2] (4611) 4976[5] 6052[10]

Secret Applause *Michael Dods* 63
2 b f Sakhee's Secret Royal Pardon (Royal Applause)
2025[3] (2883) 4019[8] 4802[4] 5106[3] 5710[7] 6082[2] 7096[7]

Secret Archive (USA) *Ralph Beckett* a73
2 rg g Arch(USA) Mystic Miracle (Dalakhani (IRE))
7766[10] (7971)

Secret Art (IRE) *Ralph Beckett* a81 93
3 ch g Excellent Art Ivy Queen (IRE) (Green Desert (USA))
1387[3] 1977[2] (2548) (3342) 4236[4] 4743[4] 5439[3] 5728[4] ◆ 6308[9]

Secret Asset (IRE) *Jane Chapple-Hyam* a96 107
8 gr g Clodovil(IRE) Skerray (Soviet Star (USA))
868a[11] 954a[13] 2152[3] 3046[10] (4263) *5325a[10]* 5651[12] 6830[14]

Secret Beau *David Evans* a87 78
3 gr g Sakhee's Secret Belle Reine (King Of Kings (IRE))
1612[2] 3782[3] 4710[2] (5277) *6215[2]* 6488[3] *7123[2] 7438[2]* 7507[2] *7742[7] 8127[3] 8219[4] 8350[11]* 8455[9]

Secret Circle (USA) *Bob Baffert* a119
4 b c Eddington(USA) Ragtime Hope (USA) (Dixieland Band (USA))
(7713a)

Secret City (IRE) *Robin Bastiman* 77
7 b g City On A Hill(USA) Secret Combe (IRE) (Mujadil (USA))
1757[2] (2275) 3441[4] 3741[5] 4510[7] 4970[10] 6916[10] 7343[9]

Secret Compass (USA) *Bob Baffert* a106
2 bb f Discreet Cat(USA) Maria's Pride (USA) (Maria's Mon (USA))
7707a[F]

Secret Dancer (IRE) *Alan Jones* 76
8 b g Sadler's Wells(USA) Discreet Brief (IRE) (Darshaan)
2348[5] 5031[8]

Secret Edge *Alan King* a64 76
5 b g Tobougg(IRE) Burton Ash (Diktat)
(7506) 7660[5] *8130[3]*

Secret Empress *Bryan Smart* a40 50
3 b f Sakhee's Secret Empress Jain (Lujain (USA))
1305[3] 2556[4] 3762[7] 4585[2] 5369[6] 6518[8]

Secret Gesture *Ralph Beckett* 110
3 b f Galileo(IRE) Shastye (IRE) (Danehill (USA))
(2261) 2842[2] 5044a[2] 5682[3] 7057a[9]

Secret Hint *Andrew Balding* a69
2 b f Oasis Dream Teeky (Daylami (IRE))
7155[3]

Secretinthepark *Ed McMahon* a84 100
3 ch g Sakhee's Secret Lark In The Park (IRE) (Grand Lodge (USA))
(2022) 2452[10] 4255[5] 4767[3] 5538[2] 6308[8] 6990[8]

Secret Keeper *Sir Mark Prescott Bt* a40
2 ch f New Approach(IRE) Confidante (USA) (Dayjur (USA))
7645[11] 7874[10] 8026[9]

Secret Kode (IRE) *Brendan Powell* a56 74
2 b f Kodiac Finty (IRE) (Entrepreneur)
3663[2] 4302[2] 4880[5] 5603[2] 6695[8] *7261[8]*

Secret Lodge *Garry Woodward* a5 44
5 ch f Needwood Blade Obsessive Secret (IRE) (Grand Lodge (USA))
4013[12] 4504[4] 4982[9] *7753[11]*

Secret Look *Ed McMahon* a77 98
3 ch g Sakhee's Secret Look Here's Carol (IRE) (Safawan)
1482[5] 2430[4] 3097[8] 3802[3] (5009) 5943[6] 6685[4] 7495[16] *7851[8]*

Secretly *Henry Candy* 80
3 ch f Sakhee's Secret The Cat's Whiskers (NZ) (Tale Of The Cat (USA))
2051[4] 2658[4] 3179[7] 3696[3]

Secret Millionaire (IRE) *Tony Carroll* a71 93
6 b g Kyllachy Mithl Al Hawa (Salse (USA))
(369) 448[2]

Secret Missile *William Muir* a84 84
3 b g Sakhee's Secret Malelane (IRE) (Prince Sabo)
1482[7] 1808[5] 2022[12] 2521[5] (4942) 5477[8] (6429) *7112[10]*

Secret Number *Saeed bin Suroor* a110 115
3 b c Raven's Pass(USA) Mysterial (USA) (Alleged (USA))
(953a) ◆ *1264a[3]* 2398[6] 3485[4] 4874[5] 5653[3] 6393[6] (7012)

Secret Oasis *Bryan Smart* 57
2 b f Captain Gerrard(IRE) Annellis (UAE) (Diesis)
4886[6]

Secret Ocean (IRE) *J S Moore* a22 51
2 b c Bahamian Bounty Tropical Moment (IRE) (Cape Cross (IRE))
4154[9] 5243[3] *6131[10]* 6279[4] 6726[8]

Secret Of Success *Rae Guest* a66 65
3 ch f Johannesburg(USA) Live Life (FR) (Linamix (FR))
(667) (1315) ◆ *1784[6]* 3540[3]

Secretori *Jo Hughes* a60 65
3 b g Sakhee's Secret Ticki Tori (IRE) (Vettori (IRE))
1712[9] 2464[11] 3040[9] 4939[6] *5903[6]*

Secret Pursuit (IRE) *Marcus Tregoning* a49
2 b f Lawman(FR) Secret Melody (FR) (Inchinor)
8332[9]

Secret Rebel *Sylvester Kirk* a73 84
3 ch g Sakhee's Secret Indiana Blues (Indian Ridge)
2708[9] 3242[2] (3621) 4641[2]

Secret Romance *Tom Dascombe* 80
2 ch f Sakhee's Secret Our Little Secret (IRE) (Rossini (USA))
(5665) 6825[2]

Secret Run (FR) *V Luka Jr* a66 74
2 b f Hurricane Run(IRE) Sydney's Secret (USA) (Fusaichi Pegasus (USA))
5213a[9]

Secret Session (USA) *Marco Botti* a70 70
3 b g Mizzen Mast(USA) Lynnwood Chase (USA) (Horse Chestnut (SAF))
1323[3] ◆ 1678[15] 2006[4]

Secret Seven (USA) *J L Hassett* a37 66
3 b f Lemon Drop Kid(USA) Dalisay (IRE) (Sadler's Wells (USA))
6942[2] ◆

Secret Song *Sir Mark Prescott Bt* a61
3 b g Singspiel(IRE) Confidante (USA) (Dayjur (USA))
2576[10] 2953[9] 3435[5] 8275[3] ◆ *8399[5]*

Secret Success *Paul Cole* a68 56
3 b g Exceed And Excel(AUS) Magic Music (IRE) (Magic Ring (IRE))
1660[16] 2788[4] 3679[3] *6138[3] (6399)* 7092[9]

Secret Suspect *Ed Walker* a73
2 b f Invincible Spirit(IRE) Madura (GER) (Dashing Blade)
7200[7] 7532[11]

Secret Taboo (FR) *A Lyon* a71 75
3 b c Miesque's Son(USA) Taboo (GER) (Pivotal)
6713a[14] 7188a[16]

Secret Talent *Hughie Morrison* a91 93
3 b g Sakhee's Secret Aqaba (Lake Coniston (IRE))
(1711) 2208[2] 3484[26] 5533[14]

Secret Weapon *William Muir* 87
3 b g Choisir(AUS) Just Devine (IRE) (Montjeu (IRE))
3837[4] ◆ (4774)

Secret Witness *Ronald Harris* a105 110
7 ch g Pivotal It's A Secret (Polish Precedent (USA))
2366[13] 2396[6] 3114[14] 3558[20] 3848a[7] 4780[18] 4986[9] 5247[2] 5545[19] 6352[9] 6391[3] 6830[10] 7013[15] 7208[16] 7495[12] 7527[12]

Secret Woman (IRE) *Alan Jarvis* a43 11
3 b f Manduro(GER) Coveted (Sinndar (IRE))
3239[12] *6555[11]*

Secular Society *Brian Meehan* a77 74
3 b g Royal Applause Fantastic Santanyi (Fantastic Light (USA))
8154[2] ◆ *8427[3]*

Secure Cloud (IRE) *J W Hills*
2 b g High Chaparral(IRE) Cabo (FR) (Sagamix (FR))
6954[11]

Sedenoo *Marco Botti* a72 92
3 b g Cape Cross(IRE) Eternity Ring (Alzao (USA))
1423[6] 1713[4] 2306[6] 3062[7] 3731[3] (4499) (4624) 5836[2] 6575[4]

Sedgwick *Shaun Harris* a72 71
11 b g Nashwan(USA) Imperial Bailiwick (IRE) (Imperial Frontier (USA))
3133[6] 3808[4] *4838[3]*

Sediciosa (IRE) *Y Barberot* 110
4 b f Rail Link Seditieuse (IRE) (Night Shift (USA))
1895a[4] 2644a[4] 3615a[8]

See And Be Seen *Sylvester Kirk* a64 62
3 b g Sakhee's Secret Anthea (Tobougg (IRE))
2742[5] 3243[14] *3432[3] 3820[7]* 4196[4] (4664) 4939[2] 5702[4] (5979) *(6363)* 6629[5] 6899[4] *7204[3]*

See Clearly *Tim Easterby* a65 76
4 b f Bertolini(USA) True Vision (IRE) (Pulpit (USA))
1278[5] 1540[4] 1802[10] 3090[3] 3407[4] 4727[2] 4982[5] 5583[9] 5947[9] 6287[13] 6728[6] 7772[12]

Seek Again (USA) *John Gosden* a104 113
3 ch c Speightstown(USA) Light Jig (Danehill (USA))
(5439) *5894[2] 6199[4]* ◆ 6838[5] (7205) ◆ (8120a)

Seek A Star (USA) *Luca Cumani* a54 70
2 ch f Smart Strike(CAN) Queen Of The Night (Sadler's Wells (USA))
7274[3] *7764[10]*

Seeking Magic *Clive Cox* a90 104
5 b g Haafhd Atnab (USA) (Riverman (USA))
1644 (1838) 2444[3] 2868[3] (4983) 6845[3] 7208[2] ◆

Seek The Fair Land *Lee Carter* a93 90
7 b g Noverre(USA) Duchcov (Caerleon (USA))
(164) 405[4] 947[10] 1061[5] 1245[8] 1782[9] 2266[9] 4438[4] *6215[7] 6995[7] 7436[11]* 7896[8] 8069[2] 8304[4]

Seemenomore *Michael Bell* a73 47
3 b g Bahamian Bounty Rise (Polar Falcon (USA))
8[2] 225[4]

See Me Sometime *Mark H Tompkins* 49
2 ch c Observatory(USA) Nice Time (IRE) (Tagula (IRE))
2502[9] 2759[2] 3255[3] 4065[6]

See No Ships *Mark Usher* 38
2 b f Compton Place Queen Of Havana (USA) (King Of Kings (IRE))
6589[9]

See The Rock (IRE) *A Wohler* 95
3 b c Shirocco(GER) Samara (IRE) (Polish Patriot (USA))
4103a[11] 6678a[7] 7407a[9]

See The Storm *Ian Williams* a68 76
5 bb g Statue Of Liberty(USA) Khafayif (USA) (Swain (IRE))
(2425) 2638[4] (3511) 4250[3] 4746[14] 5841[10]

See The Sun *Tim Easterby* 87
2 ch g Assertive Cocabana (Captain Rio)
4539[5] 5105[3] (5558) (6493) 7026[23] 7334[2]

See Vermont *Robin Bastiman* a33 52
5 b g Kyllachy Orange Lily (Royal Applause)
1731[9] 3024[4] 3654[3] 4371[3] 4762[2] 6088[11]

Sefaat *Brian Meehan* 77
2 bb f Haatef(USA) Thamara (USA) (Street Cry (IRE))
2625[3] 3057[6] 3424[18] 4046[2] 4639[2] (5090) 5693[2] 6695[3]

Sefri (USA) *J-C Rouget* a98 104
3 b g Jazil(USA) Taseel (USA) (Danzig (USA))
1419a[2] 3911a[5]

Sehnsucht (IRE) *John Quinn* a79 79
4 b g Amadeus Wolf Kirk Wynd (Selkirk (USA))
1297[6] 1932[3] (2710) 5144[2]

Seismos (IRE) *A Wohler* 112
5 ch g Dalakhani(IRE) Sasuela (GER) (Dashing Blade)
1263a[10] 2294a[5] 3879a[6] (5324a) 6028a[2] 7060a[6] 7563a[3] 8208a[11]

Sejalaat (IRE) *Ed Dunlop* 87
3 br g Kheleyf(USA) Laqataat (IRE) (Alhaarth (IRE))
1806[5] 2285[7] 2708[2] 3279[8] 3813[5]

Seldom (IRE) *Mel Brittain* a71 71
7 b g Sesaro(USA) Daisy Dancer (IRE) (Distinctly North (USA))
1568[3] 3138[5]

Self Employed *Garry Woodward* a71 87
6 b g Sakhee(USA) Twilight Sonnet (Exit To Nowhere (USA))
2232[6] 2463[9] 6306[4] 6952[8] 7283[7] *8087[3]*

Selim (RUS) *S Arslangirej* a69 81
5 b c Caitano Stilistika (RUS) (Triple Buck (USA))
2492a[11]

Selkie's Friend *Stuart Williams* a61 82
4 b g Elnadim(USA) T G's Girl (Selkirk (USA))
2266[7] 3987[4]

Sellingallthetime (IRE) *Philip Kirby* a61 67
2 ch c Tamayuz Anthyllis (GER) (Lycius (USA))
4987[7] *5924[7]* 6256[5] 7088[3] 7819[9]

Semai (IRE) *Marco Botti* a69 49
3 gr c Exceed And Excel(AUS) Mango Lady (Dalakhani (IRE))
5839[7] *6133[7] 6555[3]*

Semayyel (IRE) *Clive Brittain* a78 107
4 b f Green Desert(USA) Lii Najma (Medicean)
2045[7] 2397[7] 4137[8] 4985[11] 5402[6] 6536[8]

Semeen *Luca Cumani* a72 92
4 b g Dubawi(IRE) Zeeba (IRE) (Barathea (IRE))
(2417) (3321) ◆ 4020[3] (4720)

Sempre Medici (FR) *Mme M Bollack-Badel* 101
3 b c Medicean Sambala (IRE) (Danehill Dancer (IRE))
5361a[6]

Senafe *Marco Botti* a92 98
3 b f Byron Kiruna (Northern Park (USA))
1546[2] 2429[2] 2910a[3] 3460[20] 3734[8]

Senator Bong *David Elsworth* a77 75
3 ch c Dutch Art Sunley Gift (Cadeaux Genereux)
6159[8] 6527[7] 7313[4] *7897[3] 8021[5]*

Send For Me *F Chappet* a80 83
4 b g Dalakhani(IRE) Salutare (IRE) (Sadler's Wells (USA))
922a[9]

Sendiym (FR) *Dianne Sayer* 56
6 b g Rainbow Quest(USA) Seraya (FR) (Danehill (USA))
4110[7] 5052[8] 6290[11]

Sendmylovetorose *A Oliver* 104
3 b f Bahamian Bounty Windy Gulch (USA) (Gulch (USA))
5320a[7]

Sennockian Star *Mark Johnston* a85 107
3 ch g Rock Of Gibraltar(IRE) Chorist (Pivotal)
920[2] ◆ *1011[2]* 1770[2] (1977) 3276[4] *(3693)* 3862[2] (4055) (4342) 4537[2] (4706) 5269[2] 5768[2] 6001[4] 6332[9] 6638[7] 7174[15]

Senora Lobo (IRE) *Lisa Williamson* a43 57
3 b f Amadeus Wolf Valencia (FR) (Croco Rouge (IRE))
2347[2] 2643[4] 3323[7] 3789[7] 4607[5] 5089[4] 5916[4] 6902[14] *7354[9]* 7598[9]

Senorita Guest (IRE) *Mick Channon* a62 67
2 b f Kheleyf(USA) Atishoo (IRE) (Revoque (IRE))
2320[3] 2869[3] 3148[3] 3324[6] 4277[2] 4618[4] 5242[4] *5634[4]* 6076[6] 6487[7] *6979[4]*

Sensiz (IRE) *Roger Varian* 85
3 b f Marju(IRE) Much Faster (IRE) (Fasliyev (USA))
(6950)

Sentaril *William Haggas* a102 108
4 b f Danehill Dancer(IRE) Superstar Leo (IRE) (College Chapel)
2015[2] 2838[7] 3964a[9]

Sentimentodarcadia (ITY) *B Grizzetti* 83
2 gr c Red Rocks(IRE) Pauletta Jodler (Danehill (USA))
7235a[6]

Sequester *David Lanigan* a57 66
2 ch f Selkirk(USA) Al Theraab (USA) (Roberto (USA))
7103[3] ◆ *7435[8] 7763[8]*

Sequined (USA) *Charlie Appleby* a80
2 bb f Street Cry(IRE) Sunspangled (IRE) (Caerleon (USA))
6523[3] ◆ *(7260)*

Seraphiel *Chris Down* a52 34
4 b c Royal Applause Angel Sprints (Piccolo)
3325[10] 3949[11] 6324[7] *7459[7]*

Seraphima *James Unett* a52 67
3 b f Fusaichi Pegasus(USA) Millestan (IRE) (Invincible Spirit (IRE))
817[7] 7733[11] 7946[3] 8278[10]

Serapi Cat (USA) *Eduardo Mondol Jr* 77
8 bb g Wind Whipper(CAN) Ms Fancy Pants (USA) (Huckster (USA))
773a[8]

Serata Di Gala (FR) *Marco Botti* 65
2 b f Footstepsinthesand Sea Sex Sun (Desert Prince (IRE))
4880[4]

Serena Grae *Marcus Tregoning* a69 60
2 gr f Arakan(USA) Success Story (Sharrood (USA))
5740[5] *6690[5] 8332[4]*

Serenata (IRE) *Paul Cole* a49 66
3 b f Oratorio(IRE) Seren Devious (Dr Devious (IRE))
1575[3] *1907[8]* 2528[11]

Serendippidy *James Unett* a43 52
3 b f Indesatchel(IRE) Dipple (Komaite (USA))
1986[9] 2650[7] *2979[9] 7966[P]*

Serenissime (USA) *C Ferland* a72
3 b f Fairbanks(USA) First Class Donna (USA) (Taylor's Special (USA))
270a[3]

Serenity Spa *Roger Charlton* a68 80
3 gr f Excellent Art Molly Mello (GER) (Big Shuffle (USA))
2449[5] 3375[2] (3842) ◆ 4348[3] 5037[3] 5825[6]

Serez (IRE) *N Clement* a91 83
3 b c Shamardal(USA) Afya (Oasis Dream)
1594a[5]

Sergeant Ablett (IRE) *Luke Dace* 80
5 b g Danehill Dancer(IRE) Dolydille (IRE) (Dolphin Street (FR))
3019[13] 4029[4] 5288[9] 6646[17]

Sergeant Pink (IRE) *Dianne Sayer* a63 56
7 b g Fasliyev(USA) Ring Pink (USA) (Bering)
2630[2] 5048[6] *8027[2]*

Serjeant Buzfuz *Michael Appleby* a52 60
4 b g Halling(USA) Anastasia Storm (Mozart (IRE))
1981[0] 967[6]

Sermoneta (IRE) *G Botti* a79 82
3 ch f Danehill Dancer(IRE) Sara Moon (IRE) (Barathea (IRE))
6713a[7]

Sertorius (AUS) *Jamie Edwards & Bruce Elkington* 106
6 b g Galileo(IRE) Pretty Penny (AUS) (Encosta De Lago (AUS))
7827a[2]

Setai *Brian Meehan* a59 35
2 b f Dubawi(IRE) Zietory (Zieten (USA))
3978[8] *4408[5] 7294[8]*

Set The Trend *David O'Meara* a100 109
7 bb g Reset(AUS) Masrora (USA) (Woodman (USA))
1691[4] 2399[12] 3335[4] 3564[5] (4514) 4946[15] 5763[4] 6129[6] (6411)

Seussical (IRE) *Luca Cumani* a92 116
3 bb c Galileo(IRE) Danehill Music (IRE) (Danehill Dancer (IRE))
(7206) ◆

Seven Des Aigles (FR) *F Chappet* a55
2 b c Mr. Sidney(USA) Fille Des Aigles (FR) (Jeune Homme (USA))
8143a[8]

Seven Lucky Seven *Gary Harrison* a40 50
2 b c Avonbridge Moon Bird (Primo Dominie)
3369[9] 6460[6] 7218[8] *8058[4] 8188[7]*

Seven Of Clubs (IRE) *Noel Quinlan* a76 78
3 b c Red Clubs(IRE) Solo Symphony (IRE) (Fayruz)
1515[3] 2229[2] 2544[2] 2779[2] 3540[2]

Seven Seas (FR) *M Delzangles* a83 77
3 ch f Astronomer Royal(USA) Hot Property (USA) (Thunder Gulch (USA))
7573a[12]

Seven Summits (IRE) *Sophie Leech* a8 14
6 b g Danehill Dancer(IRE) Mandavilla (IRE) (Sadler's Wells (USA))
2234[9] *2511[11]*

Seventh Sense (GER) *P Van De Poele* a90 96
3 ch f Samum(GER) Salcita (GER) (Zieten (USA))
(7188a) *8440a[15]*

Severiano (USA) *Roger Varian* a72
3 b g Danehill Dancer(IRE) Time Control (Sadler's Wells (USA))
1199[2] 1570[11] *4381[3] 8313[3] 8437[2]*

Severn Crossing *William Muir*
2 b g Authorized(IRE) Croeso Cariad (Most Welcome)
6430[8] 6954[13]

Severnwind (IRE) *Ronald Harris* a56 40
2 b g Diamond Green(FR) Zeena (Unfuwain (USA))
2344[4] *2562[5] 3211[6] 4833[3] 6474[9] 6983[6] 7509[4] 7855[11] 7954[3] 8045[5]*

Seville (GER) *Robert Hickmott* 112
5 b c Galileo(IRE) Silverskaya (USA) (Silver Hawk (USA))
7556a[7] 7761a[12]

Sevros (FR) *C Laffon-Parias* a83 83
3 b g Falco(USA) Betwixt (IRE) (Sinndar (IRE))
7412a[4]

Sewn Up *Andrew Hollinshead* a78 52
3 ch c Compton Place Broughton Bounty (Bahamian Bounty)
106[3] 236[2] 328[2] (404) (550) 710[5] 949[3] 992[4] (1075) 1204[2] 1307[5] 1892[6] 2158[6] 5303[8] 5511[5] 5928[8] 6653[6] 7164[7] 7444[3] 7487[7] 7743[8] 7888[8] 8029[3] 8230[4] 8319[5]

Sextons House (IRE) *Alan McCabe* a60 55
5 b g King's Best(USA) Lolita's Gold (USA) (Royal Academy (USA))
223[4] 736[6] 863[4] 991[6] 1043[4] 1149[8] 1355[3] 1395[4] 1681[11] 1748[4] 2236[8] 2948[6] 3507[5] 3904[6]

Sexy Secret *Noel Quinlan* a57 27
2 b c Sakhee's Secret Orange Walk (IRE) (Alzao (USA))
4958[11] 5488[11] 6365[6] 8016[4] 8045[3] 8265[4] 8347[2]

Seymour Place *Roger Charlton* a52
3 b f Compton Place Perfect Night (Danzig Connection (USA))
821[4]

Shabaka (FR) *F Foresi* a82 71
3 bl c Hurricane Cat(USA) River Trebor (USA) (Myrakalu (FR))
445a[10] 543a[3] 711a[6] (2034a)

Shada (IRE) *F-H Graffard* a75 91
4 ch f Galileo(IRE) Banquise (IRE) (Last Tycoon)
7891a[5]

Shadarpour (IRE) *Gary Moore* a61 71
4 b g Dr Fong(USA) Shamadara (IRE) (Kahyasi)
7863[12]

Shades Of Grey *Clive Cox* a70 86
6 gr m Dr Fong(USA) Twosixtythreewest (FR) (Kris)
1663[6] 2619[7] 5535[7] 6377[10] 6960[4] 7539[5]

Shades Of Silver *Sir Michael Stoute* 75
3 b g Dansili Silver Pivotal (IRE) (Pivotal)
1684[6] 3250[8]

Shadowtime *Tracy Waggott* a73 84
8 b g Singspiel(IRE) Massomah (USA) (Seeking The Gold (USA))
1723[2] 2078[3] 2339[3] 2705[2] 3193[4] 4007[11] 4373[5] 4850[7] 5880[7] 5987[2] 6274[5] 6567[8] 6721[6]

Shady McCoy (USA) *David Barron* 87
3 b g English Channel(USA) Raw Gold (USA) (Rahy (USA))
2448[8] 2719[4] (3932) (4725) 5541[2] 6586[7]

Shafaani *Clive Brittain* a98 91
3 b f Green Desert(USA) Amalie (IRE) (Fasliyev (USA))
1033[4] (1384) 1620[10] (4690) 4922[14] 5538[10] 6564[5] (7080) 8334[11]

Shafrah (IRE) *Richard Hannon Snr* a76 77
2 b c Acclamation Rosy Dudley (IRE) (Grand Lodge (USA))
5299[2] 5924[5]

Shaft Of Light *Sir Mark Prescott Bt* a62
2 b c Exceed And Excel(AUS) Injaaz (Sheikh Albadou)
7638[7] 7893[8]

Shagwa (IRE) *Mark Johnston* a58 36
3 b f Clodovil(IRE) Hedera (USA) (Woodman (USA))
4927[12] 5425[5] 5789[9]

Shahad (IRE) *F Head* 103
3 b f Galileo(IRE) Dapprima (GER) (Shareef Dancer (USA))
2381a[5] 2905a[6] 4700a[6] 6714a[9]

Shahdaroba (IRE) *Rod Millman* a97 97
3 b g Haatef(USA) Gold Script (FR) (Script Ohio (USA))
1112[4] (1625) 2022[4] 2452[13] 3342[5] 4242[2] 5260[7] 5894[5] 6308[13] 6989[4] 7368[20]

Shaheen Shah (GER) *Conrad Allen* a53 10
2 b c Soldier Hollow Sunshine Story (IRE) (Desert Story (IRE))
4959[6] 5193[4] 5922[10]

Shahrazad (IRE) *Patrick Gilligan* a72 61
4 b f Cape Cross(IRE) Khulasah (IRE) (Darshaan)
980[5] (1710) 2638[9] (2773) 3404[6] 3700[9] (5032) 5311[2] 5672[2] 6130[4] 7439[7]

Shahwardi (FR) *A De Royer-Dupre* 107
7 b g Lando(GER) Shamdara (IRE) (Dr Devious (IRE))
2695a[6] 3560[2]

Shahzan (IRE) *Roger Varian* a91 92
5 br g Dansili Femme Fatale (Fairy King (USA))
621[4]

Shaishee (USA) *Charles Hills* a81 82
3 br g Indian Charlie(USA) Hatpin (USA) (Smart Strike (CAN))
1908[2] 3585[2] 4032[2] 4481[2]

Shakedown *Kevin Frost*
8 b g Domedriver(IRE) Stormy Weather (Nashwan (USA))
7962[13]

Shaken Not Stirred *Milton Bradley* a48
3 b f Monsieur Bond(IRE) Kanisfluh (Pivotal)
532[5] 673[6] 821[6] 1066[7]

Shaker Style (USA) *Barry Murtagh* a55 62
7 ch g Gulch(USA) Carr Shaker (USA) (Carr De Naskra (USA))
330[5] 515[10]

Shakespeare Dancer *James Evans* a40 27
4 b f Norse Dancer(IRE) Sharbasia (IRE) (King's Best (USA))
2714[9]

Shalambar (IRE) *Tony Carroll* a73 64
7 gr g Dalakhani(IRE) Shalama (IRE) (Kahyasi)
20[4] 338[7] (816) 2284[5] 2982[6] 4166[13] 8059[7] 8323[11]

Shalianzi (IRE) *Gary Moore* a63 76
3 b g Azamour(IRE) Shalama (IRE) (Kahyasi)
7298[6]

Shallow Lake (USA) *Charlie Appleby* a53 51
2 bb f Bernardini(USA) Scarlet Ibis (Machiavellian (USA))
6949[7] 7260[7]

Shalwa *Marco Botti* a66 86
3 ch f Galileo(IRE) Kite Mark (Mark Of Esteem (IRE))
1347[3] 2164[2] 3975[2] 4594[2] 5445[3] 6574[2] 6978[7]

Shama (IRE) *Sir Michael Stoute* a72
2 b f Danehill Dancer(IRE) Shamadara (IRE) (Kahyasi)
7875[3]

Shamaal Nibras (USA) *Ismail Mohammed* a100 104
4 b h First Samurai(USA) Sashay Away (USA) (Farma Way (USA))
1244[4] 1542[5] 2013[5] 2813[2] 3527[3] 4527[5] 4744[10] 7014[6] 7247[3]

Shamahan *Gary Moore* a72 83
4 b g Shamardal(USA) Hanella (IRE) (Galileo (IRE))
1838[4] 2618[9] 3322[6] 3741[7] (5669) 6526[5]

Shamaheart (IRE) *Richard Hannon Snr* a71 78
3 b c Shamardal(USA) Encouragement (Royal Applause)
1923[6] 3989[3] (4209) 4950[9] 7105[6]

Shamalad *Lydia Pearce* 59
3 b c Shamardal(USA) Steam Cuisine (Mark Of Esteem (IRE))
3585[6]

Shamalgan (FR) *X Thomas-Demeaulte* a97 110
6 ch h Footstepsinthesand Genevale (FR) (Unfuwain (USA))
4421a[3] 5739[7] (6889a) 7724a[2] 8210a[11]

Shamardyh (IRE) *David Evans* a60 59
2 b f Shamardal(USA) State Secret (Green Desert (USA))
3318[4] 4215[12] 4801[5] 6035[6] 8166[U] 8396[2]

Shamassiba (IRE) *Andrew Balding* a67
3 b f Shamardal(USA) Nilassiba (Daylami (IRE))
7884[2]

Shama's Song (IRE) *Sir Michael Stoute* a66
2 b f Teofilo(IRE) Green Dollar (IRE) (Kingmambo (USA))
7645[6]

Shamdarley (IRE) *Marco Botti* a93 89
5 b g Shamardal(USA) Siphon Melody (USA) (Siphon (BRZ))
1751[5] 2813[6] 3416[2] (3961) 5285[10]

Shameless Man (IRE) *Anthony Middleton* 46
6 b g Atraf Fleetfoot (IRE) (Bravefoot)
2093[14] 3156[6] 3417[12] 3865[7]

Shamexpress (NZ) *Danny O'Brien* 118
4 b c O'Reilly(NZ) Volkrose (NZ) (Volksraad)
3420[9] 4298[7]

Shamglas Queen *J Larkin* a51
3 b f Shamardal(USA) Green Silk (IRE) (Namid)
923[9]

Shamiana *Daniel Kubler* a55 57
3 bb f Manduro(GER) Camp Riverside (USA) (Forest Camp (USA))
2215[6] 2962[4] 3740[6] 4064[8] 7806[4] 7962[3] 8056[8] 8348[3]

Shamir *Jo Crowley* a93 80
6 b g Dubai Destination(USA) Lake Nyasa (IRE) (Lake Coniston (IRE))
897[3] 1585[11] 5894[9] 7157[4] 7988[4]

Shamiran (IRE) *Rodger Sweeney* a54 79
8 br g Polish Precedent(USA) Sharemata (IRE) (Doyoun)
7230a[22]

Shamo Hill Theatre *Lawrence Mullaney* a51 54
6 b g Millkom Hannalou (FR) (Shareef Dancer (USA))
703[10]

Shamouti (IRE) *Kevin Ryan* a30 49
2 ch f Duke Of Marmalade(IRE) Pitrizza (IRE) (Machiavellian (USA))
1839[8] 3064[13] 5352[10]

Shamrocked (IRE) *Ollie Pears* a63 64
4 b g Rock Of Gibraltar(IRE) Hallowed Park (IRE) (Barathea (IRE))
1686[9] 1819[3] 2395[12] 2613[3] 3475[4] 4005[5] 4893[3] 5301[4] 5614[7] (6843) 7077[2] 7729[9] 8048[8] 8234[7]

Sham Sheer *Fawzi Abdulla Nass* a82 102
7 br g Cape Cross(IRE) Viola Da Braccio (IRE) (Vettori (IRE))
152a[4] 246a[14]

Shamshon (IRE) *Richard Hannon Snr* 105
2 b c Invincible Spirit(IRE) Greenisland (IRE) (Fasliyev (USA))
(4680) (5460a) 6637[5] 7688a[11]

Shamus Award (AUS) *Danny O'Brien* 112
3 b c Snitzel(AUS) Sunset Express (AUS) (Success Express (USA))
(7556a)

Shan Dun na nGall (IRE) *John Joseph Murphy* 70
2 b c Shantou(USA) Omanah (USA) (Kayrawan (USA))
7050a[15]

Shanjia (GER) *Frau C Brandstatter* a73 101
4 b f Soldier Hollow Shivara (GER) (Monsun (GER))
(5360a) 6714a[10]

Shankly *Clive Cox* 80
2 br c Monsun(GER) Miracle Seeker (Rainbow Quest (USA))
(6139) ◆ 7828a[11]

Shannon Haven (IRE) *Daniel Mark Loughnane* a50
2 b g Oratorio(IRE) Red Shoe (Selkirk (USA))
8333[10]

Shanti *Michael Bell* a71
3 b g Dansili Maycocks Bay (Muhtarram (USA))
6402[4] 6781[2]

Shaolin (IRE) *Seamus Durack* a74 73
3 b g Footstepsinthesand Baboosh (IRE) (Marju (IRE))
228[3] (491) 731[3] 3665[3] 5515[3] 6075[2] 6702[15]

Sharaar (IRE) *Gerard Butler* a63
3 ch g Choisir(AUS) Oriane (Nashwan (USA))
636[4] ◆ 1044[7] 1305[6]

Sharaarah (IRE) *David O'Meara* a94 89
3 b f Oasis Dream Nidhaal (IRE) (Observatory (USA))
1892[8] 2408[3] (2994) 3320[8] 5340[2] (5639) 5996[3] 6212[4] 7776[11] (7888) 8232[14] 8305[8]

Sharareh *Luca Cumani* a77 75
3 b f Sir Percy You Too (Monsun (GER))
3116[8] 5064[2] 5942[10] 7298[2] (7838)

Shared Account *P Bary* 99
3 br f Dansili Imbabala (Zafonic (USA))
6031a[3]

Shared Equity *Jedd O'Keeffe* 62
2 b g Elnadim(USA) Pelican Key (IRE) (Mujadil (USA))
4808[5] 6561[2]

Shared Moment (IRE) *Luke Dace* a72 61
7 ch m Tagula(IRE) Good Thought (IRE) (Mukaddamah (USA))
138[6] 334[6] 1783[7] 2089[9] (3054) (3329)

Shareel (FR) *N Clement* a75
3 b f Country Reel(USA) Shaking (Linamix (FR))
461a[4]

Share Option *Tony Carroll* a37 55
11 b g Polish Precedent(USA) Quota (Rainbow Quest (USA))
132[7] 458[11] 1022[8]

Sharestan (IRE) *Saeed bin Suroor* 118
5 b g Shamardal(USA) Sharesha (IRE) (Ashkalani (IRE))
(152a) 466a[3] 959a[7] 1268a[9] (6620)

Shareta (IRE) *A De Royer-Dupre* 119
5 b f Sinndar(IRE) Shawara (IRE) (Barathea (IRE))
1268a[6]

Share The Dosh *J R Jenkins* a42
5 ch f Doyen(IRE) Lady Starlight (IRE) (Almutawakel)
7158[6] 8260[6]

Sharin (GER) *Markus Klug* 79
2 b f Areion(GER) Sisika (IRE) (King's Theatre (IRE))
5939a[8]

Sharp And Smart (IRE) *Hughie Morrison* a72 83
4 b f Dark Angel(IRE) Church Road (IRE) (Danehill Dancer (IRE))
(1950) (2070) 2253[6] 3532[4] 3845a[4] 4278[6] 6337[7] 6963[10] 7489[6]

Sharp Anna (FR) *P Vidotto* a74 62
3 b f Anabaa(USA) Sharp Acting (USA) (Diesis)
543a[8]

Sharp Lookout *Roger Charlton* a74
2 b c Shamardal(USA) Tempting Prospect (Shirley Heights)
7120[11] 7766[7] 8067[3]

Sharp Shoes *Christopher Wilson* a73 63
6 br g Needwood Blade Mary Jane (Tina's Pet)
2343[8] 2611[10] 5085[11] 6603[8] 6944[10]

Sharqawiyah *Luca Cumani* a49 87
3 b f Dubawi(IRE) Pompey Girl (Rainbow Quest (USA))
1640[3] 2206[4] (2783) 3835[4] 4485[3] 5202[6] 6210[3] 6531[8]

Shasta Daisy *Lady Cecil* a75
2 ch f Champs Elysees Bouvardia (Oasis Dream)
7645[3] ◆

Shatin Secret *Noel Wilson* a65 48
3 b g Sakhee's Secret Al Corniche (IRE) (Bluebird (USA))
1647[9] 3025[12] 5067[8] 5788[7] 6655[10]

Shaunas Spirit (IRE) *Dean Ivory* a79 45
5 b f Antonius Pius(USA) Shaunas Vision (IRE) (Dolphin Street (FR))
(116) 415[8] 589[4] 1096[5] 1503[3] 6105[4] 6316[10] 7109[11] (7740) (8157)

Shavansky *Rod Millman* a94 90
9 b g Rock Of Gibraltar(IRE) Limelighting (USA) (Alleged (USA))
1485[4] 2085[2] 2592[9] ◆ 3293[7] 3697[8] 4502[6] (5129) 6199[10] 6801[8] (7990) 8327[8]

Shawkantango *Derek Shaw* a77 73
6 b g Piccolo Kitty Kitty Cancan (Warrshan (USA))
86[11] 308[4] 481[6] 558[7] 760[4] 924[4] (968) 1101[10] 1331[2] 2550[10] 2736[3] 5673[8] 5901[6] 6516[10] 7432[6] 7633[8] 7772[5] (8135) 8220[11] (8406)

Shea *Ralph Beckett* a69
4 b f Dubai Destination(USA) Shasta (Shareef Dancer (USA))
1654[7]

Sheacheval (IRE) *J S Moore* a64 55
2 b f Excellent Art Colour And Spice (IRE) (Machiavellian (USA))
3107[10] 3857[7] 5593[3] 6605[6] 7352[5] 7977[2] (8016)

Shearian *Tracy Waggott* a68 68
3 b g Royal Applause Regal Asset (USA) (Regal Classic (CAN))
55[4] 482[2] 527[4] 599[2] (824) 918[2] 1428[5] 1712[2] (1842) 2342[4] 2957[6] 3281[2] 3629[11] 4140[3] 4508[6] 5293[3] 5425[6]

Shea Shea (SAF) *M F De Kock* 123
6 b g National Emblem(SAF) Yankee Clipper (SAF) (Jallad (USA))
464a[7] (954a) ◆ (1265a) 3420[2] 4298[4] 5726[2]

Shebebi (USA) *Mark Johnston* 106
3 bb g Mr Greeley(USA) Tashawak (IRE) (Night Shift (USA))
(1773) 2208[7] (2661) 3484[9] 4062[3] 4531[4] 5026[4] (5518) 5738[12] 6183[17]

She Can Jig *Kevin Ryan* a54 60
2 b f Dutch Art Dance Card (Cape Cross (IRE))
2701[4] 3510[5] 4142[4] 4965[4] (5480) 5898[4] 6295[8]

Sheema *James Tate* a32
3 ch f Teofilo(IRE) Shimna (Mr Prospector (USA))
1009[7]

Sheer Poetry (IRE) *Mike Murphy* a52
2 b f Yeats(IRE) Sassari (IRE) (Darshaan)
6922[7]

Sheer Talent (AUS) *Mark Kavanagh* 105
4 b c Redoute's Choice(AUS) St. Katherine (AUS) (Barathea (IRE))
7762a[7]

Sheikh The Reins (IRE) *John Best* a77 81
4 b g Iffraaj Wychwood Wanderer (IRE) (Barathea (IRE))
2964[11] 3511[3] (4163) 4685[10] 5398[8] 6317[2] 7436[10] 7743[3] 8453[7]

Sheikhzayedroad *David Simcock* 108
4 b g Dubawi(IRE) Royal Secrets (IRE) (Highest Honor (FR))
(1824) 2263[2] (2867) ◆ 3525[2] 4944[3] 5766[9]

Sheila's Buddy *J S Moore* a82 82
4 ch g Reel Buddy(USA) Loreto Rose (Lahib (USA))
32[3] 1673[2] 2101[3] 2728[6] 4923[6] 5348[7] 6358[3] ◆ 6801[2] ◆ 7211[11]

Sheila's Castle *Sean Regan* a34 64
9 b m Karinga Bay Candarela (Damister (USA))
3089[6] 3589[3]

Sheila's Footsteps *J S Moore* a72
2 b g Footstepsinthesand Marmaga (IRE) (Shernazar)
4154[6] 4631[3] 8214[2] (8389)

Sheila's Heart *Julia Feilden* 32
3 ch g Dubai Destination(USA) Sefemm (Alhaarth (IRE))
3539[6]

Shelford (IRE) *Michael Appleby* a95 91
4 b g Galileo(IRE) Lyrical (Shirley Heights)
1615[9] (6504) 7660[3] 7975[4]

Shelley's Choice (IRE) *Tom Dascombe* a62 61
2 b f Lawman(FR) Fantastic Opinion (IRE) (Fantastic Light (USA))
1399[4] 1718[5] 3605[7] 4511[4] 5595[6] 6073[7]

Shelling Peas *Derek Shaw* a49 18
4 b f Val Royal(FR) Meditation (Inchinor)
2746[14] 5071[8] 5678[11] 6399[13] 6554[12] 7037[3] 7485[7] 7886[10] 8003[5]

Shelovestobougie *Mark Brisbourne* a68 71
5 b f Tobougg(IRE) Bowled Out (GER) (Dansili)
145[4] 330[8] 375[6] 626[11]

Shemaal (IRE) *Roger Varian* a70 69
3 b c Monsun(GER) Zahrat Dubai (Unfuwain (USA))
2198[6] 5902[3]

Shena's Dream (IRE) *Stuart Williams* 85
4 gr f Oasis Dream Sallanches (USA) (Gone West (USA))
2253[11]

Shenliyka (FR) *A De Royer-Dupre* a80 76
3 b f Danehill Dancer(IRE) Shemissa (IRE) (Fairy King (USA))
4700a[9] 5461a[12]

Shenval *Noel Quinlan* a58 52
3 b c Celtic Swing Cape Finisterre (IRE) (Cape Cross (IRE))
350[5] 4927[8] 5495[7]

Shepherd Gate (USA) *J S Moore* a80 73
2 ch c Kitten's Joy(USA) Keeping Watch (IRE) (Danehill (USA))
3555[10] 3833[5] 4524[4] 4948[14] 5362a[2] 5508[3] 5848a[2] 7568a[13]

Sherinn *Roger Varian* a69 76
3 b f Refuse To Bend(IRE) Hall Hee (IRE) (Invincible Spirit (IRE))
359[5] 533[5]

Sherjawy (IRE) *Zoe Davison* a58 54
9 b g Diktat Arruhan (IRE) (Mujtahid (USA))
124[2] 156[4] 277[3] 369[4] 448[5] 735[5] 1088[3] 1196[7] 1304[5] 1467[5] 1929[5] 2170[12] 3325[13] 8338[4]

Sherman McCoy *Brian Ellison* a79 83
7 ch g Reset(AUS) Naomi Wildman (USA) (Kingmambo (USA))
57[2] 351[9] 3180[3] 6984[2] (7372) 7635[2] ◆ 8353[5]

Sherry For Nanny (IRE) *Marjorie Fife* 50
2 b f Amadeus Wolf Sugars For Nanny (USA) (Brocco (USA))
1285[3] 1946[3] 2475[4] 3440[2] 3541[7] 6494[9] 6725[9]

Sherston *Mark Johnston* 75
2 b g Shamardal(USA) Shersha (IRE) (Priolo (USA))
5995[5] 6277[3] 6790[3] 7170[3] 7451[9]

Sherzam *Michael Dods* a77 83
3 b f Exceed And Excel(AUS) Shersha (IRE) (Priolo (USA))
(5715) 6495[2] 6874[7] 7374[14]

Shesadanser *Ann Duffield*
2 b f Dutch Art Broughton Bounty (Bahamian Bounty)
3624[11]

She's A Honey *Kevin Morgan* 46
3 ch f Firebreak Manuka Too (IRE) (First Trump)
3743[3] 7838[6]

She's A Lucky Lady *Bill Turner* 2
2 ch f Avonbridge Lady Killer (IRE) (Daggers Drawn (USA))
1718[8] 3414[13]

Shesastar *David Barron* 93
5 b f Bahamian Bounty Celestial Welcome (Most Welcome)
1252[7] 2026[6] 2310[14] 3259[2] 3686[3] 4097[4] (4671) 5684[6] 6210[4] 6571[2] 7176[11]

She's A Tiger (USA) *Jeff Bonde* a110
2 b f Tale Of The Cat(USA) Shandra Smiles (USA) (Cahill Road (USA))
7707a[2] ◆

Shes Ellie *Jo Hughes* a39 55
3 ch f Lucky Story(USA) Shes Minnie (Bertolini (USA))
1695[8] 3679[10] 5092[7] 5397[5]

She's Gorgeous (IRE) *Lady Cecil* 77
2 b f Acclamation Acquiesced (IRE) (Refuse To Bend (IRE))
7450[3] ◆

She's Late *John Gosden* a92 95
3 ch g Pivotal Courting (Pursuit Of Love)
1635[7] 2442[4] 2953[4] 3470[4] 3957[4] (5286) 6172[5] 6591[4] (7072)

Shesnotforturning (IRE) *Ben Haslam* 36
3 b f Refuse To Bend(IRE) Diplomats Daughter (Unfuwain (USA))
1962[6] 4727[8]

Shes Rosie *Ed de Giles* a66 77
5 b f Trade Fair Wintzig (Piccolo)
3375[8] 4145[6]

She's Some Girl (IRE) *Richard Fahey* a45
3 ch f Camacho Tea Service (IRE) (Roi Danzig (USA))
507[5]

She Wont Tell *John Bridger* a26
4 b f Doyen(IRE) Who Goes There (Wolfhound (USA))
7624[8] 7873[7]

Shifting (IRE) *W McCreery* a63 89
4 b f Oratorio(IRE) Shifting Place (Compton Place)
1168a[18]

Shifting Power *Richard Hannon Snr* 104
2 ch c Compton Place Profit Alert (IRE) (Alzao (USA))
(4414) (4959) ◆

Shifting Star (IRE) *John Bridger* a87 75
8 ch g Night Shift(USA) Ahshado (Bin Ajwaad (IRE))
2266^{6} 2618^{12} 2657^{12} 3215^{7} 3575^{3} 3901^{2} 4124^{6} 4637^{8} 5346^{5} 5948^{11} 6937^{3} 7262^{6} 7740^{8} 8019^{2}

Shikamoo *Dr Jeremy Naylor* 48
3 b f Beat Hollow Shangazi (USA) (Miswaki (USA))
2051^{12} 2746^{6} 3401^{9} 4240^{6} 7322^{8}

Shikari *Robin Bastiman* 57
2 ch g Sakhee's Secret Hickleton Lady (IRE) (Kala Shikari)
4370^{8} 7173^{7} 7419^{8}

Shikarpour (IRE) *A De Royer-Dupre* 114
3 ch c Dr Fong(USA) Shibina (IRE) (Kalanisi (IRE))
$2907a^{5}$ 3485^{2} $4573a^{5}$ $6446a^{5}$

Shilla (IRE) *Henry Candy* 71
2 b f Kodiac Shimla (IRE) (Rudimentary (USA))
5307^{2} ◆ 5609^{2} ◆ (6095) 6695^{15}

Shillito *Tony Coyle* a40 74
3 b g Kyllachy Kiss Me Kate (Aragon)
3626^{3} 3894^{4} 4624^{4} 4976^{9} 5884^{3} 6176^{2} 6843^{2} 6965^{7} 7345^{11}

Shimba Hills *Mick Channon* 73
2 b g Sixties Icon Search Party (Rainbow Quest (USA))
2653^{6} 2985^{5} 3282^{3} 4246^{7} 6844^{4} 7252^{3} (7774)

Shimraan (FR) *Mahmood Al Zarooni* 118
6 b g Rainbow Quest(USA) Shemriyna (IRE) (King Of Kings (IRE))
$661a^{6}$ ◆

Shindigger (IRE) *J Merienne* a75 84
5 b f Whipper(USA) Shigeru Summit (Be My Chief (USA))
$7189a^{8}$

Shingueti (FR) *C Baillet* a81 89
3 b f Desert Style(IRE) Spain (FR) (Bering)
$3708a^{5}$

Shining Copper (USA) *Oussama Aboughazale* 93
3 ch g Aragorn(IRE) La Minuta (CHI) (Winged Victory (USA))
$3360a^{7}$

Shining Cross (IRE) *Jo Hughes* a63 21
3 b g Cape Cross(IRE) Shining Debut (IRE) (In The Wings)
525^{3} ◆

Shining Emerald *P D Deegan* 107
2 b c Clodovil(IRE) Janayen (USA) (Zafonic (USA))
$7548a^{3}$

Shining Glitter (IRE) *James Fanshawe* a66
2 b f Shamardal(USA) Lune Rose (High Chaparral (IRE))
8066^{4}

Shirataki (IRE) *Peter Hiatt* a73 73
5 b g Cape Cross(IRE) Noodle Soup (USA) (Alphabet Soup (USA))
9^{6} 417^{3} 653^{4} 789^{3} 883^{7} (1342) 1715^{2} 1983^{4} 2777^{8} 3662^{2} (4489) 4832^{5} 5168^{11} 6068^{9} 6775^{7} 7446^{2} 7865^{9} 8060^{5}

Shirazz *Seamus Durack* a61 38
4 b f Shirocco(GER) Streccia (Old Vic)
215^{6} 342^{6} 1178^{7} 3635^{12} 4714^{9} (7962) 8149^{7} 8302^{2}

Shirley's Kitten (USA) *Gianluca Bietolini* 95
3 b f Kitten's Joy(USA) La Cat (USA) (Mr Greeley (USA))
$1866a^{6}$ $3616a^{2}$ $7558a^{9}$

Shirley's Pride *Michael Appleby* a42 71
3 b f Byron Feeling Blue (Missed Flight)
(1458) 1762^{2} (2091) (2623) 2829^{6} 4069^{3} 4221^{2} 5094^{2}

Shirley Vanessa (IRE) *Luke Dace* a47 48
2 b f Camacho Mas A Fuera (IRE) (Alzao (USA))
5929^{6} 6408^{4} 6689^{8} 7199^{6}

Shirls Son Sam *Chris Fairhurst* a44 54
5 b g Rambling Bear Shirl (Shirley Heights)
2030^{7} 2511^{8} 2887^{4} 3595^{10} 4204^{7} 5137^{4} 5560^{9} 5833^{4}

Shirocco Passion *Tony Coyle* 74
2 b f Shirocco(GER) Pete's Passion (Rock Of Gibraltar (IRE))
4432^{8} 4848^{2} 5180^{7} (6284) 6770^{3}

Shirocco Star *Hughie Morrison* 114
4 b f Shirocco(GER) Spectral Star (Unfuwain (USA))
2045^{5} $3870a^{3}$ 5761^{2} $6416a^{8}$

Shisun (IRE) *M Weiss* 95
4 ch c Shirocco(GER) Oblique (IRE) (Giant's Causeway (USA))
$7591a^{4}$

Shock *Daniel Kubler* 29
2 b g Kheleyf(USA) Montcalm (IRE) (Montjeu (IRE))
4773^{7} 5399^{12}

Shockingdancer (IRE) *Marco Botti* a58 28
3 b c Danehill Dancer(IRE) Jalys (IRE) (Sri Pekan (USA))
211^{10} 708^{2} 994^{7} 1487^{12}

Sho Girl (IRE) *P J Prendergast* 77
4 b f Lawman(FR) Shizao (IRE) (Alzao (USA))
$7723a^{16}$

Sholaan (IRE) *D Selvaratnam* a104 99
4 b g Invincible Spirit(IRE) Jazz Up (Cadeaux Genereux)
$464a^{5}$

Shomberg *Dai Burchell* a57 61
4 b g Bahamian Bounty Qilin (IRE) (Second Set (IRE))
1696^{3} 2345^{5} 3270^{10} 3643^{4} 4153^{6} 5172^{8}

Shore Patrol (IRE) *Richard Fahey* a61 61
2 br c Footstepsinthesand Fatwa (IRE) (Lahib (USA))
5915^{4} 7209^{14} 7901^{4} 8147^{8}

Shore Step (IRE) *Mick Channon* 92
3 br g Footstepsinthesand Chatham Islands (USA) (Elusive Quality (USA))
(1660) 2285^{2} 2626^{4} (3104) 4989^{8} 6382^{3}

Short Shrift (IRE) *Richard Fahey* a70 65
3 ch f Nayef(USA) Dusty Answer (Zafonic (USA))
377^{4} 2760^{4} 3116^{10} 7923^{3} 8054^{3} 8372^{4}

Short Squeeze (IRE) *Hugo Palmer* a78 111
3 b g Cape Cross(IRE) Sunsetter (USA) (Diesis)
1803^{5} 2235^{2} 2846^{5} 3633^{3} (4642) ◆ (5728) (6834) ◆ 7196^{5}

Shotgun Start *Michael Wigham* a54 64
3 b g Kyllachy Fly In Style (Hernando (FR))
5069^{5} 5989^{3} 6502^{6}

Shot In The Dark (IRE) *Jonathan Geake* a46 71
4 ch g Dr Fong(USA) Highland Shot (Selkirk (USA))
5954^{8} 7305^{10}

Shotinthefog (USA) *Danny Gargan* 80
4 b g Saint Anddan(USA) Brewmatic (USA) (Charismatic (USA))
$3361a^{6}$

Shot In The Sun (IRE) *Richard Fahey* 75
2 b f Kodiac Summer Sunshine (Dubai Destination (USA))
1833^{5} 2282^{5} 3255^{2} 3648^{2} (4044) 4988^{2} 5536^{6} 6207^{2}

Showboating (IRE) *Alan McCabe* a84 92
5 b g Shamardal(USA) Sadinga (IRE) (Sadler's Wells (USA))
164^{5} 518^{4} 582^{2} (751) 846^{6} 1571^{2} 1751^{2} 1963^{4} 2450^{7} 3060^{9} 3351^{9} 3586^{4} 3811^{8} 4014^{8} (5564) 5832^{6} 6162^{2} 6496^{5} 6774^{2} (7374) (7595) 7820^{7} 7992^{10}

Show Gorb (SPA) *P Sogorb* a100 102
3 b f Caradak(IRE) Triple Two (Pivotal)
$1358a^{5}$ $2299a^{12}$

Show More Faith *Sylvester Kirk* a54
3 b g Pastoral Pursuits Lalina (GER) (Trempolino (USA))
5^{4} 977^{7} 1098^{10}

Showpiece *Richard Hannon Snr* 83
2 b c Kyllachy Striving (IRE) (Danehill Dancer (IRE))
3238^{3} 3581^{3} 4958^{9} (5399) 6395^{5}

Showtime Girl (IRE) *Tim Easterby* a65 62
3 b f Tamayuz Zuccini Wind (IRE) (Revoque (IRE))
2241^{6} 2650^{6} 3190^{6} 4149^{9} 4611^{4}

Shrewd *Michael Bell* 98
3 b g Street Sense(USA) Cala (FR) (Desert Prince (IRE))
3486^{17} (4249) 4541^{3} 5274^{6} 6186^{10} 6503^{4} 7823^{23}

Shrewd Bob (IRE) *Robert Eddery* 48
2 b c Whipper(USA) Cheyenne Spirit (Indian Ridge)
4749^{4} 5539^{5} 6069^{8}

Shrimper Roo *Tim Easterby* 87
3 b g Byron Piper's Ash (USA) (Royal Academy (USA))
2430^{3} 2987^{2} 3478^{7} (3813) 4112^{4} 4734^{10} 5292^{5} 5728^{13} 7374^{12} 7531^{10}

Shrimpton *Mick Channon* 78
3 b f Cadeaux Genereux Feather Boa (IRE) (Sri Pekan (USA))
1661^{3} ◆

Shropshire (IRE) *Charles Hills* a96 107
5 gr g Shamardal(USA) Shawanni (Shareef Dancer (USA))
1232^{4} 1537^{2} 2046^{4} 3558^{2} 4986^{14} 6352^{4}

Shukhov (IRE) *J F Levins* a82 60
4 b g Ivan Denisovich(IRE) Just One Smile (IRE) (Desert Prince (IRE))
4516^{5} 5671^{4}

Shu Lewis (IRE) *Ms M Dowdall Blake* a95 100
7 b m Pyrus(USA) Poppy Lewis (IRE) (Paris House)
$5776a^{5}$

Shuruq (USA) *Saeed bin Suroor* a110 109
3 b f Elusive Quality(USA) Miss Lucifer (FR) (Noverre (USA))
$243a^{2}$ $554a^{2}$ (837a) $1264a^{7}$ 4949^{7} 6000^{3} 6536^{10}

Shushu Sugartown (IRE) *Ian Williams* a60
2 b f Invincible Spirit(IRE) Landela (Alhaarth (IRE))
7971^{5} 8145^{4}

Shut Up Chris (USA) *Larry Demeritte* a56
3 b c Storm's Eye(USA) Haunted Hotel (USA) (Silver Ghost (USA))
$786a^{5}$

Shwaiman (IRE) *James Fanshawe* a92 99
3 br c Authorized(IRE) Blue Lightning (Machiavellian (USA))
1679^{3} 2198^{3} 3364^{2} 3957^{3} (5520) 6348^{2} 6991^{5}

Shy Bride (IRE) *Alan Jarvis* a74 38
3 b f Excellent Art Blushing Away (USA) (Blushing Groom (FR))
1612^{8} 2593^{11} 5395^{9}

Shyron *George Margarson* a73 59
2 b g Byron Coconut Shy (Bahamian Bounty)
4121^{7} 4716^{4} 5140^{5} (6979) (7199) 7352^{3} 7609^{4}

Shy Rosa (USA) *Marcus Tregoning* a64 44
4 bb f Dixie Union(USA) Lethal Temper (USA) (Seattle Slew (USA))
7600^{2}

Sian Gwalia *David Simcock* a57
3 b f Echo Of Light House Maiden (IRE) (Rudimentary (USA))
925^{4} 1187^{3} 1741^{5}

Sian Kaan (FR) *J-C Rouget* a85 79
3 ch c Literato(FR) Birdy Namnam (USA) (Langfuhr (CAN))
$3708a^{7}$

Sibaya *Roger Charlton* a65 54
3 b f Exceed And Excel(AUS) Abunai (Pivotal)
808^{4} 1078^{2} 2051^{7} 2829^{7}

Sibling Honour *Charlie Appleby* a70
2 b f Bernardini(USA) Porto Roca (AUS) (Barathea (IRE))
7764^{2} ◆

Sicilian Bay (IRE) *Paul Midgley*
2 b f Jeremy(USA) Taormina (IRE) (Ela-Mana-Mou)
3298^{14}

Sid *Zoe Davison* a41
5 ch g Needwood Blade Easter Moon (FR) (Easter Sun)
734^{5}

Side Glance *Andrew Balding* a109 116
6 br g Passing Glance Averami (Averti (IRE))
$959a^{4}$ ◆ $1269a^{4}$ 3457^{7} $5553a^{3}$ $7556a^{6}$ (7702a) $8211a^{5}$

Sidonia (IRE) *F-X De Chevigny* a40 48
3 b f Shirocco(GER) Selinea (FR) (Keltos (FR))
$7187a^{10}$

Sighora (IRE) *Richard Hannon Snr* 56
2 b f Royal Applause Singitta (Singspiel (IRE))
5003^{8}

Signature Dish (IRE) *Andrew Balding* a70 65
3 b f Galileo(IRE) Magic Carpet (IRE) (Danehill (USA))
3292^{7} 4523^{4} 5181^{7} 6153^{6} 6612^{3} 7000^{6} 7249^{3}

Signed Up *Amanda Perrett* 97
4 b c Rail Link Sing For Fame (USA) (Quest For Fame)
3531^{5} ◆ 5746^{10} 6591^{5} 7250^{7}

Sign From Heaven (IRE) *David Wachman* a96 95
2 b f Raven's Pass(USA) Sahara Sky (IRE) (Danehill (USA))
$6021a^{8}$

Significant Move *Stuart Kittow* a73 81
6 b g Motivator Strike Lightly (Rainbow Quest (USA))
(1585) 2256^{3} 2808^{8} 3573^{5} (4126) 4831^{4} 5847^{9} 6336^{10}

Sign Manual *Michael Bell* a63 86
4 b g Motivator New Assembly (IRE) (Machiavellian (USA))
(1670) 2205^{11} 3765^{4} 4913^{5} 6504^{5} 7193^{12}

Signora Frasi (IRE) *Tony Newcombe* a65 88
8 b m Indian Ridge Sheba (IRE) (Lycius (USA))
158^{9} 655^{9} 794^{8} 1093^{2} 1497^{4} 2875^{9} 3409^{6} 4411^{7} 5667^{4}

Signorellina (FR) *J Rossi* 50
3 gr f Desert Style(IRE) Signorinella (FR) (Kendor (FR))
$5913a^{7}$

Signore Piccolo *Eric Alston* 69
2 b g Piccolo Piccolo Cativo (Komaite (USA))
4282^{4} 4539^{7} 6383^{3} (7094)

Signor Sassi *William Knight* a89 91
4 b g Acclamation Fairy Contessa (IRE) (Fairy King (USA))
2444^{8} 4235^{3} ◆ 4863^{5} 6203^{4} 6525^{8} 7080^{12}

Signposted (IRE) *Andrew Balding* 88
2 b c Rock Of Gibraltar(IRE) Portentous (Selkirk (USA))
5472^{5} (5819) (6529) 7017^{9}

Silaah *M Ramadan* a72 90
9 b g Mind Games Ocean Grove (IRE) (Fairy King (USA))
$290a^{4}$ $575a^{9}$ $954a^{15}$

Silas Marner (FR) *J-C Rouget* a113 113
6 b h Muhtathir Street Kendra (FR) (Kendor (FR))
(1456a) $2897a^{5}$ $4093a^{9}$ $5040a^{6}$ $5808a^{8}$

Silasol (IRE) *C Laffon-Parias* 111
3 b f Monsun(GER) Stormina (USA) (Gulch (USA))
$1869a^{2}$ (2693a) $3385a^{3}$ $5462a^{4}$ $6448a^{6}$ $7057a^{6}$

Silca's Dream *Mick Channon* a72 72
3 b g Oasis Dream Silca-Cisa (Hallgate)
808^{3} 1051^{2} (1215) 1524^{4} 1844^{3} 2098^{5} 2623^{5} 2959^{11} 3400^{3} (3638) 3732^{2} 3888^{10} 4221^{5}

Silent Achiever (NZ) *Roger James* 112
5 br m O'Reilly(NZ) Winning Spree (NZ) (Zabeel (NZ))
$7392a^{8}$

Silent Bullet (IRE) *Saeed bin Suroor* 90
2 b g Exceed And Excel(AUS) Veil Of Silence (IRE) (Elusive Quality (USA))
(4513) (5224) 6765^{8}

Silentio (USA) *Gary Mandella* 118
4 bb c Silent Name(JPN) Listen A P (USA) (A.P. Indy (USA))
$7714a^{3}$

Silent Movie (IRE) *Mark Johnston* a82 85
3 gr c Cape Cross(IRE) Screen Star (IRE) (Tobougg (IRE))
(6997) 7242^{5} 7660^{10}

Silent Sam *Michael Appleby*
5 b g Elusive City(USA) Luisa Miller (IRE) (Entrepreneur)
8200^{7} 8313^{7}

Siljan's Saga (FR) *J-P Gauvin* 109
3 bl f Sagamix(FR) Humoriste (FR) (Saint Cyrien (FR))
$2381a^{8}$ (4468a) $5629a^{5}$ (6484a) $7048a^{5}$

Silkee Supreme *Richard Hannon Snr* a70 67
4 b c Primo Valentino(IRE) Sodelk (Interrex (CAN))
21^{4} 132^{6} 508^{6} (626) 789^{6} 4904^{5}

Silkelly *David O'Meara* a59 78
3 b f Medicean Sleave Silk (IRE) (Unfuwain (USA))
(2635) ◆ 3396^{5} 4158^{3} 4586^{4} 5150^{3} 5353^{6} 5714^{3} 6338^{3} 6728^{10}

Silken Express (IRE) *Robert Cowell* a95 84
4 ch f Speightstown(USA) Laureldean Express (Inchinor)
(2173) ◆ 2848^{6} 3561^{7} 7851^{3} 8232^{4}

Silk Route *Henry Candy* a66 69
3 ch f Dubai Destination(USA) Crinolette (IRE) (Sadler's Wells (USA))
3239^{6} 3989^{5} 4719^{4} 5403^{3} 6158^{8} 6557^{4} 7258^{3}

Silk Sari *Luca Cumani* a67 93
3 b f Dalakhani(IRE) So Silk (Rainbow Quest (USA))
3469^{7} (4139) 6649^{4} 7659^{3}

Silk Scarf (IRE) *Mark H Tompkins* a48 50
3 br f Windsor Knot(IRE) Tarziyma (IRE) (Kalanisi (IRE))
1346 427^{3} 534^{4}

Silk Train *David Simcock* a68 68
3 b f Rail Link Monsoon Wedding (Monsun (GER))
2423^{4} ◆ 3618^{5} (5925) 7659^{12}

Silky (IRE) *David Wachman* 99
3 b f Montjeu(IRE) Tree Chopper (USA) (Woodman (USA))
$3381a^{4}$

Silly Billy (IRE) *Brian Ellison* a76 66
5 b g Noverre(USA) Rock Dove (IRE) (Danehill (USA))
205^{3} 348^{5} 1021^{2} 1195^{6} 1455^{2} 1783^{3} 1887^{3} 4155^{8} 4660^{3} 5047^{7} (5427) 5876^{3} 6276^{3} 6610^{3} (7083) 7238^{2} 7754^{3} (7885) 8136^{2} 8295^{10} 8350^{3}

Silly Gilly (IRE) *Ron Barr* a40 69
9 b m Mull Of Kintyre(USA) Richly Deserved (IRE) (Kings Lake (USA))
2956^{10}

Si Luna (GER) *W Mongil* a88 108
4 ch f Kallisto(GER) Signorita (GER) (Generous (IRE))
$7053a^{4}$

Silvala Dance *Chris Wall* a53 44
3 b f Kyllachy Bride Of The Sea (Cape Cross (IRE))
3405^{2}

Silvaner (GER) *P Schiergen* 112
5 bb c Lomitas Suisun (GER) (Monsun (GER))
$661a^{8}$ $956a^{4}$ $2294a^{8}$ $2822a^{4}$ $3879a^{3}$ $7407a^{8}$

Silvanus (IRE) *Paul Midgley* a72 94
8 b g Danehill Dancer(IRE) Mala Mala (IRE) (Brief Truce (USA))
1249^{4} 1483^{4} 1765^{3} 2150^{7} 2669^{8} 3299^{12} 3802^{9} 4507^{5} 4620^{3} 5108^{5} 5639^{4} 5971^{4} 6309^{3} 6848^{5} 7314^{13}

Silvas Romana (IRE) *Mark Brisbourne* a72 80
4 b f Holy Roman Emperor(IRE) Triple Wood (USA) (Woodman (USA))
2070^{4} 3098^{6} 3269^{3} 3983^{7} 4482^{2} 4894^{3} 5172^{6} 5430^{2} 5947^{6} 6780^{9} 7515^{12}

Silvee *John Bridger* a66 69
6 gr m Avonbridge Silver Louie (IRE) (Titus Livius (FR))
3817^{8} 4303^{10} 4909^{6} 5404^{4} 6462^{2} 7092^{12} 7265^{10} 7643^{13}

Silver Alliance *Julia Feilden* a78 81
5 gr g Proclamation(IRE) Aimee Vibert (Zilzal (USA))
(477) 798^{5} 1292^{4} (1915) 2532^{4} (3218) 4923^{8} 5587^{6} 6898^{9} 7130^{3} 7608^{5}

Silver Axe (FR) *Mme P Butel* a67 70
3 bb g Silver Cross(FR) Maraxa (FR) (Marathon (USA))
$6711a^{9}$

Silvercombe *Sylvester Kirk* a52 32
2 gr c Archipenko(USA) Cherrycombe-Row (Classic Cliche (IRE))
4827^{7} 5145^{9} 6689^{F}

Silver Dixie (USA) *Peter Hedger* a87 88
3 br c Dixie Union(USA) More Silver (USA) (Silver Hawk (USA))
396^{2} ◆ (731) 1053^{3} 4126^{5} ◆ (4490) 4950^{3} 5440^{2} 6003^{3} 6801^{14} 7976^{6} 8336^{2}

Silver Fawn (IRE) *John Weymes* a54 44
3 gr g Clodovil(IRE) Tinareena (IRE) (Barathea (IRE))
459^{3} 634^{6} 757^{3} 1016^{3} (1314) 1428^{4} 1747^{3} 2156^{11} 3463^{9} 3735^{8} 3909^{11} 7514^{7} 7666^{7} 7962^{4} 8142^{8} 8186^{5}

Silver Forest (IRE) *John Weymes* a41 26
3 b f Mujadil(USA) Forest Storm (USA) (Woodman (USA))
1735^{6} 2027^{8} 2340^{7} 2613^{8}

Silver Gilt *D De Waele* a49 48
13 b g Silver Hawk(USA) Memory's Gold (USA) (Java Gold (USA))
$3647a^{0}$

Silverheels (IRE) *Paul Cole* a94 95
4 gr g Verglas(IRE) Vasilia (Dansili)
2013^{7} 2585^{5} 3411^{4} 3961^{2} (4540) 4859^{14} 5894^{8} 6767^{6} 7368^{27} 8385^{6}

Silver Lace (IRE) *Chris Wall* a75 58
4 bg f Clodovil(IRE) Rockahoolababy (IRE) (Kalanisi (IRE))
4385^{12} 4894^{5} 5491^{8} (6315) 7446^{4} 7865^{7}

Silver Lime (USA) *Roger Charlton* 101
4 b c Mizzen Mast(USA) Red Dot (USA) (Diesis)
2044^{4} 2718^{7} 3559^{9} (4233) 4857^{4}

Silver Marizah (IRE) *Roger Ingram* a53 21
4 b f Manduro(GER) Maharani (USA) (Red Ransom (USA))
1107^{10} 522^{2} 704^{11} 886^{5} 1207^{6} 1342^{7} 2159^{10} 3637^{3} 4071^{16} 5586^{4} 5948^{12} 6457^{6} 8065^{7} 8318^{3}

Silver Max (USA) *Dale Romans* a120 117
4 b c Badge Of Silver(USA) Kissin Rene (USA) (Kissin Kris (USA))
$7714a^{4}$

Silver Mirage *Michael Bell* a66 52
2 b f Oasis Dream Phantom Gold (Machiavellian (USA))
6789^{8} 7295^{4}

Silver Ocean (USA) *Niels Petersen* a108 103
5 br g Silver Train(USA) Endless Sea (CAN) (Mt. Livermore (USA))
$465a^{12}$ $659a^{14}$ $838a^{12}$ $4936a^{7}$

Silver Panther *Aytach Sadik* a36
5 gr g Proclamation(IRE) Sydney Star (Machiavellian (USA))
1^{5} 51^{4} 950^{7} 1082^{7}

Silverrica (IRE) *Malcolm Saunders* 73
3 gr f Ad Valorem(USA) Allegorica (IRE) (Alzao (USA))
1896^{2} 2363^{2} 2829^{2} 3036^{2} (3678)

Silver Rime (FR) *Linda Perratt* a60 93
8 gr g Verglas(IRE) Severina (Darshaan)
1992^{5} 2315^{6} 3285^{5} (3770) (4294) 4807^{2} 5238^{3} (5332) 5880^{2} 6550^{10} (6625) 7152^{10} 7241^{2}

Silver Samba *Andrew Balding* a70 87
4 gr f Dalakhani(IRE) Fancy Dance (Rainbow Quest (USA))
1899^{2} 2205^{3} 2587^{8} 3587^{4} (4238) (5185) 5879^{3} 6646^{7} 7250^{5}

Silver Six *Sheena West* a61 49
4 gr g Aussie Rules(USA) Bahara (Barathea (IRE))
724^{10} 1175^{13} 1342^{8}

Silver Starlet (IRE) *Alastair Lidderdale* a41 49
2 ch f Verglas(IRE) Whatagoodcatch (IRE) (Bachelor Duke (USA))
3155^{5} 3659^{6} 4164^{10} 5610^{14}

Silver Tigress *George Moore* 67
5 gr f Tiger Hill(IRE) Cinnamon Tree (IRE) (Barathea (IRE))
1763^{8} 2165^{2} 2435^{8} 3231^{4} 3808^{7} 4622^{4} 5222^{3} 5833^{15} 6632^{9} 7372^{4}

Silver Trail *M Delzangles* 96
3 ch c Indian Haven Sureyya (GER) (Monsun (GER))
3645a^{5}

Silver Treasure (FR) *Amy Weaver* 93
2 gr c Clodovil(IRE) Ardesia Si (FR) (Treasure Kay)
5744^{7} 6569^{2} 7185a^{2} 7653a^{2} 7994a^{3}

Silver Valny (FR) *Mlle M-L Mortier* a69 106
7 ch g Vertical Speed(FR) Mendoreva (FR) (Mendocino (USA))
1871a^{6} 3362a^{8} 7566a^{13}

Silverware (USA) *Kristin Stubbs* a85 81
5 bb g Eurosilver(USA) Playing Footsie (USA) (Valiant Nature (USA))
217^{9} 400^{3} 629^{3} 751^{5} 1318^{10} 1746^{2} 1963^{7} 2659^{10} 4100^{7} 4577^{7} (5378) 5978^{4} 6721^{2} (7849) 8094^{3} 8416^{5}

Silver Wind *Alan McCabe* a72 79
8 b g Ishiguru(USA) My Bonus (Cyrano De Bergerac)
143^{8} 437^{6}

Silvery Moon (IRE) *Tim Easterby* 94
6 gr g Verglas(IRE) Starry Night (Sheikh Albadou)
1446^{8} 2365^{12} 3346^{2} (3684) 4979^{10}

Silvio Dante (USA) *David O'Meara* a55 49
3 ch g Street Boss(USA) Merit (USA) (Meadowlake (USA))
1764^{11} 2330^{6} 4144^{7}

Silvy Du Normandy (IRE) *J Heloury* a72 79
3 b f Orpen(USA) Sorpresa (FR) (Octagonal (NZ))
692a^{5}

Simayill *John Berry* a87 66
5 b f Oasis Dream Triennial (IRE) (Giant's Causeway (USA))
338^{4} 675^{5} 905^{8}

Simba *A Wohler* 83
2 ch c Teofilo(IRE) Sarabia (GER) (One Cool Cat (USA))
7232a^{7} 7726a^{4}

Simenon (IRE) *W P Mullins* 116
6 b g Marju(IRE) Epistoliere (IRE) (Alzao (USA))
2149^{4} 3483^{2} 5724^{2} 7761a^{4} 8033a^{13} 8208a^{5}

Simple Jim (FR) *David O'Meara* a51 58
9 b g Jimble(FR) Stop The Wedding (USA) (Stop The Music (USA))
1369^{2}

Simple Joys *Andrew Balding* a54 61
3 b f Singspiel(IRE) Chance Dance (IRE) (Danehill Dancer (IRE))
3632^{2} 6015^{3} 6325^{13}

Simple Love (USA) *D K Weld* 96
2 b f Proud Citizen(USA) Offbeat Fashion (IRE) (Rock Of Gibraltar (IRE))
4462a^{5} 4694a^{4}

Simple Magic (IRE) *John Gosden* a91 76
2 b f Invincible Spirit(IRE) Cephalonie (USA) (Kris S (USA))
2204^{7} 4828^{3} (5352) 6201^{3} 6622^{12}

Simply Black (IRE) *David O'Meara* a62 71
3 br f Kheleyf(USA) Tashyra (IRE) (Tagula (IRE))
3280^{4} 3681^{2} 4289^{2} 4783^{5} 5857^{3} 6966^{2} 7349^{6} 7541^{2} 7804^{5}

Simply Dreaming *Michael Squance* a43 33
3 b f Pastoral Pursuits Tilly's Dream (Arkadian Hero (USA))
2965^{4} 3405^{13}

Simply Elegant (IRE) *Amanda Perrett* a77 71
3 b f Tamayuz Femme Fatale (Fairy King (USA))
2084^{10} 2519^{6} (2746) 3292^{5} 4898^{9} 5130^{3}

Simply Ozzy (IRE) *V Luka Jr* a76
2 b c Aussie Rules(USA) Stroppy (IRE) (Xaar)
5362a^{9} 5848a^{3}

Simply Shining (IRE) *Richard Fahey* a73 79
3 ch f Rock Of Gibraltar(IRE) Bright Smile (IRE) (Caerleon (USA))
2438^{5} 3369^{4} 3712^{2} 4201^{3} 4729^{3} 5784^{2} 6210^{7} 6875^{5} 7785^{6}

Simpson Millar *Zoe Davison* a22 48
4 b g Librettist(USA) Scented Garden (Zamindar (USA))
1170^{5}

Sinaadi (IRE) *Clive Brittain* a89 82
3 b f Kyllachy Quantum (IRE) (Alhaarth (IRE))
1499^{2} 1958^{7} 2231^{13} 3242^{7} 4689^{3} (5311) 6198^{9} 6387^{4} 7121^{4}

Sinai (IRE) *Geoffrey Harker* 64
4 b f Moss Vale(IRE) Ten Commandments (IRE) (Key Of Luck (USA))
2835^{6} 3630^{5} 3934^{6} 4621^{5}

Sinatramania *Tracy Waggott* 60
6 b g Dansili Come Fly With Me (Bluebird (USA))
2118^{4} 2886^{6} 3195^{8} 3543^{6} 3727^{5} 4562^{5} 5882^{5} 6723^{7}

Sinbad The Sailor *George Baker* a69 64
8 b g Cape Cross(IRE) Sinead (USA) (Irish River (FR))
3647a^{7} 4754^{6} 6736^{3}

Sinchiroka (FR) *Ralph Smith* a62 38
7 b g Della Francesca(USA) Great Care (USA) (El Gran Senor (USA))
(62) 201^{6} 330^{6} 907^{2} (1015) 2413^{8} 3056^{P}

Sindjara (USA) *John M Oxx* a100 95
4 br f Include(USA) Sindirana (IRE) (Kalanisi (IRE))
2678a^{7} 4465a^{15}

Sing Alana Sing *Bill Turner* a46 40
5 b f Singspiel(IRE) Choralist (Danehill (USA))
343^{5} 432^{4} 635^{6}

Singapore Secret (IRE) *James Given* a42 66
2 b f Bushranger(IRE) Capessa (IRE) (Perugino (USA))
4668^{4} 5338^{8} 5675^{6}

Singersongwriter *Ed Dunlop* a77 83
3 ch f Raven's Pass(USA) Independence (Selkirk (USA))
1486^{4} ◆ 2160^{4} (6433) 7627^{6}

Singeur (IRE) *Robin Bastiman* a97 100
6 b g Chineur(FR) Singitta (Singspiel (IRE))
1720^{5} 2366^{15} 4507^{2} 5108^{6} 5544^{6} 6273^{2} 6621^{16} 7171^{8} 7373^{4}

Singing (FR) *C Laffon-Parias* a88 114
3 b c Singspiel(IRE) Ring Beaune (USA) (Bering)
4325a^{4} 5807a^{10}

Singing Star (IRE) *Mel Brittain* a44 41
2 b f Iffraaj Seven Sing (USA) (Machiavellian (USA))
7817^{5} 8005^{6}

Single (FR) *C Laffon-Parias* 106
3 ch f Singspiel(IRE) Tender Morn (USA) (Dayjur (USA))
2970a^{6} 7316a^{7}

Single Mast (USA) *Charles Hills* a53
3 ch f Mizzen Mast(USA) Single Market (USA) (Dynaformer (USA))
1178^{6} 1653^{5} (Dead)

Sing Out Sister *Mick Channon* a33 41
2 ch f Compton Place Sister Moonshine (Averti (IRE))
3896^{6} 4589^{9} 5590^{4} 6364^{6}

Sings Poet *Peter Hiatt* a40
3 ch g Singspiel(IRE) Royale Rose (FR) (Bering)
333^{8} 5233^{8} 6363^{6} 6853^{9} 7637^{8} 7770^{9} 8268^{9}

Singzak *Michael Easterby* a79 80
5 ch g Singspiel(IRE) Zakuska (Zafonic (USA))
(1889) 2671^{6} 3301^{2} 3726^{13} 4313^{13} 7498^{13} 7950^{4} 8139^{2} 8400^{2}

Sinister (IRE) *Roger Varian*
3 b g Sinndar(IRE) Shamsada (IRE) (Kahyasi)
4978^{11}

Sinndar Perfection (FR) *M Delzangles* a78 92
3 b c Sinndar(IRE) Tall Perfection (USA) (Distorted Humor (USA))
1511a^{7}

Sinnderelle (FR) *Mme M Bollack-Badel* a80 74
3 b f Sinndar(IRE) Summer Wave (IRE) (King's Best (USA))
5119a^{2}

Sioux Chieftain (IRE) *Michael Appleby* a58 84
3 b g Mount Nelson Lady Gin (USA) (Saint Ballado (CAN))
(1487) 2432^{3} 3783^{3} 7596^{2}

Siouxperhero (IRE) *William Muir* a69 74
4 b g Sleeping Indian Tintern (Diktat)
1514^{8} 1901^{7} 2728^{7} 4070^{13} 4593^{3} 4894^{7} (5304) (5978) 6360^{5} 6701^{9} 7306^{12}

Sir Bedivere (IRE) *Brian Meehan* 92
4 b g Dansili Miss Ivanhoe (IRE) (Selkirk (USA))
(1882) 2385^{8} 4914^{3} 5475^{3} 5946^{7} 6591^{3}

Sir Boss (IRE) *Michael Mullineaux* a86 87
8 b g Tagula(IRE) Good Thought (IRE) (Mukaddamah (USA))
(2) 52^{3} 144^{2} 563^{4} 691^{4} 882^{5} 1774^{5} 2102^{4} 2552^{9} 2739^{3} 3345^{16} (3692) 3804^{2} 4202^{7} 5031^{7} 5129^{5} 6750^{12} 7115^{4} 7950^{5} 8159^{4}

Sir Bruno (FR) *Tim Vaughan* a73 67
6 ch g Hernando(FR) Moon Tree (FR) (Groom Dancer (USA))
96^{7} 5261^{3}

Sir Charlie Kunz *Mark Johnston* 54
2 ch c Dalakhani(IRE) Darrfonah (IRE) (Singspiel (IRE))
4987^{14} 5727^{11}

Sir Don (IRE) *Michael Mullineaux* a37 25
14 b g Lake Coniston(IRE) New Sensitive (Wattlefield)
1304^{11} 1902^{12}

Sir Dylan *Ronald Harris* a64 57
4 b g Dylan Thomas(IRE) Monteleone (IRE) (Montjeu (IRE))
9^{11} 132^{12} 418^{6} (455) 626^{12} 789^{7} 2828^{9} 8436^{13}

Sir Ector (USA) *J J Lambe* 107
6 br g Dynaformer(USA) Beyond The Waves (USA) (Ocean Crest (USA))
(3599a) 5776a^{4} (7723a)

Sir Freddie (USA) *Fredrik Reuterskiold* a52
4 gr g Unbridled's Song(USA) Judy Soda (USA) (Personal Flag (USA))
2146a^{7}

Sir Geoffrey (IRE) *Scott Dixon* a71 63
7 b g Captain Rio Disarm (IRE) (Bahamian Bounty)
481^{8} 986^{7} 3529^{8} (3994) 4377^{2} 4814^{7} 5085^{4} 5499^{5} 5701^{5} 6603^{7} 8168^{2} (8271) 8439^{3}

Sir George (IRE) *Suzzanne France* a78 74
8 b g Mujadil(USA) Torrmana (IRE) (Ela-Mana-Mou)
23^{4} 587^{9} 967^{5} 1603^{6} 3081^{9} 4893^{10} 5840^{11} 6723^{10}

Sir Graham Wade (IRE) *Mark Johnston* 109
4 gr g Dalakhani(IRE) Needwood Epic (Midyan (USA))
1484^{5} 1920^{3} 2428^{8} 2810^{8} 3559^{6} 4060^{10} 4309^{7} 4857^{8}

Sir Guy Porteous (IRE) *Mark Johnston* 73
2 ch g Shamardal(USA) Ermine And Velvet (Nayef (USA))
6645^{11} 7017^{12} 7270^{6}

Sirius Prospect (USA) *Dean Ivory* a107 115
5 bb g Gone West(USA) Stella Blue (FR) (Anabaa (USA))
2368^{11} 2936^{4} 3557^{13} (4778) 4946^{11} (5763) 6392^{5} 7014^{12} 7364^{5} (7974)

Sir Jack Layden *David Brown* 109
2 b c Sir Percy Barawin (IRE) (Hawk Wing (USA))
2670^{7} 3233^{2} 3555^{7} (4096) 6395^{4} 6835^{3}

Sir John Hawkins (USA) *A P O'Brien* 104
2 b c Henrythenavigator(USA) Peeping Fawn (USA) (Danehill (USA))
3422^{3} 4212^{4} 4694a^{3}

Sir John Hawkwood (IRE) *Sir Michael Stoute* 113
4 b g Sir Percy Athene (IRE) (Rousillon (USA))
(2185) ◆ (2427) 3556^{7}

Sir Lando *Wido Neuroth* 115
6 b h Lando(GER) Burqa (Nashwan (USA))
2294a^{7} 3188a^{6} 3879a^{4} 6453a^{4}

Sir Maximilian (IRE) *Nicky Vaughan* a91 94
4 b g Royal Applause Nebraska Lady (IRE) (Lujain (USA))
(2388) 2669^{7} 3135^{4} 3802^{2} 4285^{5} 5519^{8} 5998^{3}

Sir Mike *Amanda Perrett* a90 85
4 ch g Haafhd Tara Moon (Pivotal)
1583^{7} 2193^{5} (2574) 3019^{7} 3274^{7} 4718^{2} 4923^{2} (5191) 5742^{7} 6203^{3} (6403) 6694^{5} 7224^{4} 7464^{3}

Sir Nod *Julie Camacho* a68 71
11 b g Tagula(IRE) Nordan Raider (Domynsky)
143^{6} 4891^{2} 5583^{5}

Sir Oscar (GER) *Christina Bucher* 108
6 b g Mark Of Esteem(IRE) Sintenis (GER) (Polish Precedent (USA))
1945a^{8}

Sir Patrick Moore (FR) *Harry Dunlop* 106
3 gr c Astronomer Royal(USA) America Nova (FR) (Verglas (IRE))
1677^{2} 3347^{4} 4093a^{4}

Sir Pedro *Robert Cowell* a81 85
4 b g Acclamation Milly-M (Cadeaux Genereux)
2255^{10} 2724^{9} 3351^{2} 3714^{3} 4235^{10} 4730^{19} 5971^{5} (6309) 8021^{7} 8167^{3} 8324^{6}

Sir Percy Blakeney *Marcus Tregoning* a25 44
2 b g Sir Percy Sulitelma (USA) (The Minstrel (CAN))
5891^{11} 6256^{8} 6460^{8}

Sirpertan *Tim Walford* 44
2 b g Sir Percy Tanwir (Unfuwain (USA))
1930^{11} 2502^{6} 4926^{5} 6275^{8}

Sir Rabbit (USA) *Jessica J Campitelli* 94
10 ch g Marquetry(USA) Fancy Verse (USA) (Opening Verse (USA))
1001a^{6}

Sir Reginald *Richard Fahey* a90 99
5 b g Compton Place Clincher Club (Polish Patriot (USA))
1720^{10} 2665^{7} 5943^{2} ◆ (6352) 6621^{6} ◆ 7368^{26} 7991^{6}

Sir Robert Cheval *Marco Botti* a89 70
2 b c Green Desert(USA) Aunt Ruby (USA) (Rubiano (USA))
7448^{3} (7860) 8018^{2}

Sir Tyto (IRE) *Peter Makin* a60
5 b g Fruits Of Love(USA) Sophie May (Glint Of Gold)
6402^{8} 6926^{10} 7738^{5} 8092^{4} 8225^{4}

Sirvino *David Barron* a99 105
8 b g Vettori(IRE) Zenita (IRE) (Zieten (USA))
1446^{9} ◆ 1824^{4} 2369^{11} (2671) 2867^{9} 3345^{7} 5147^{5} 5706^{7} (6302) 6626^{10} 7496^{10}

Si Senor (IRE) *Ed Vaughan* a65
2 b g Dansili Kotsi (IRE) (Nayef (USA))
5924^{10} 7120^{5} 7647^{4}

Sissi Guihen (FR) *Mrs A Malzard*
7 ch m Lord Of Men Assermara (FR) (Assert)
5329a^{4} 7144a^{5}

Sister Guru *Peter Hedger* a74 30
4 b f Ishiguru(USA) Ulysses Daughter (IRE) (College Chapel)
(398) 1472^{5} 2588^{8}

Sisyphe (FR) *P Demercastel* a74 74
4 b c Slickly(FR) European Style (FR) (Ezzoud (IRE))
5601a^{8}

Sitting Pritty (IRE) *Tom Dascombe* 47
2 b f Compton Place Queen Bodicea (IRE) (Revoque (IRE))
6160^{5}

Situational Ethics (USA) *Mark Hennig* 82
4 b g Broken Vow(USA) Ayla Bella (USA) (Touch Gold (USA))
3361a^{4}

Si Violente (FR) *J Parize* a62 67
3 b f Solon(GER) Secret Gold (GER) (Lemhi Gold (USA))
543a^{4}

Six Of Clubs *Bill Turner* a75 62
7 ch g Bertolini(USA) Windmill Princess (Gorytus (USA))
119^{4}

Six Of Hearts *Cecil Ross* a81 100
9 b g Pivotal Additive (USA) (Devil's Bag (USA))
6883a^{7}

Six Silver Lane *Derek Shaw* a82 41
5 gr g Aussie Rules(USA) Aurelia (Rainbow Quest (USA))
112^{8} 850^{5} 1239^{14} 1448^{10} 2348^{7} 2982^{10} 8142^{4} 8275^{8} 8399^{11}

Sixties Queen *Alan Bailey* a65 64
3 b f Sixties Icon Lily Of Tagula (IRE) (Tagula (IRE))
864^{5} 1122^{2} 2092^{6} 2215^{3} 3537^{10} 3641^{5} 4144^{6} 4356^{3} 4689^{4} 5497^{2} 5615^{3} 5967^{6} 6321^{2} 6730^{9}

Sixtine's Lucky *N Bertran De Balanda* a74 76
2 b f Naaqoos Chopassing (FR) (Indian Rocket)
8354a^{7}

Sixty Minutes *David Brown* 71
3 b c Compton Place Passing Hour (USA) (Red Ransom (USA))
1911^{3} 2722^{5} 3086^{2} (3626)

Six Wives *Scott Dixon* a88 86
6 b m Kingsalsa(USA) Regina (Green Desert (USA))
319^{8} 457^{8} 913^{4} 1121^{4} 1308^{5} 1649^{3} 1807^{12} 2173^{6} 3682^{4} 3855^{2} 4479^{8} 4588^{5} 4860^{2} 5701^{4}

Siyenica (FR) *A De Royer-Dupre* 109
3 b f Azamour(IRE) Sichilla (IRE) (Danehill (USA))
2693a^{7} 3524^{11} (4700a) 5461a^{3} 7047a^{3}

Size (IRE) *Richard Fahey* 76
4 b g Oratorio(IRE) Primissima (GER) (Second Set (IRE))
1570^{2} ◆ 2121^{3} (2634) (3337) 3506^{5} (3543) 4264^{7} 5918^{3} 6667^{4} 7453^{5}

Sizzler *Ralph Beckett* a85 100
3 ch g Hernando(FR) Gino's Spirits (Perugino (USA))
(1317) ◆ 2086^{4} 3206^{3} 4233^{8} 4681^{4} (5448) (7250)

Skaters Waltz (IRE) *Paul Cole* 63
2 gr g Verglas(IRE) Xarzee (IRE) (Xaar)
5790^{8}

Skating Over (USA) *Jane Chapple-Hyam* a63 63
3 ch f Giant's Causeway(USA) Annie Skates (USA) (Mr Greeley (USA))
2423^{6} 3403^{4}

Sketch Map (IRE) *Jedd O'Keeffe* 61
2 b g Excellent Art Atlas Silk (Dansili)
5482^{5} 6175^{3} 6627^{6}

Skidby Mill (IRE) *Laura Mongan* a60 64
3 b f Ramonti(FR) Glasnas Giant (Giant's Causeway (USA))
2464^{9} 3137^{9} 3630^{14} 6752^{6} 7086^{5} 7465^{4} (7980) 8125^{5}

Skiddaw View *John Weymes* a40 33
5 b f Goodricke Skiddaw Wolf (Wolfhound (USA))
537^{12}

Skilled *Roger Charlton* 76
2 b g Mastercraftsman(IRE) Treacle (USA) (Seeking The Gold (USA))
6953^{3} ◆

Skimming Stone (IRE) *John Joseph Murphy* a47 62
3 b f Refuse To Bend(IRE) Chartres (IRE) (Danehill (USA))
5021a^{5}

Skinny Latte *Micky Hammond*
2 ch c Piccolo Coffee Ice (Primo Dominie)
7348^{8} 8266^{9} 8346^{8}

Skinny Love *Robert Cowell* a64 64
2 b f Holy Roman Emperor(IRE) Lady Mickataine (USA) (Speightstown (USA))
3896^{4} 4346^{5} 5421^{3} 6170^{6} 6731^{5} (7036) 7900^{3} 8090^{2} 8228^{2}

Skiperia (FR) *H-A Pantall* a78 81
2 ch f Gold Away(IRE) Lerina (FR) (Priolo (USA))
1894a^{6} 5082a^{6}

Skyblue *Tobias B P Coles* a42 37
4 b f Royal Applause Fiina (Most Welcome)
120^{6} 522^{7}

Sky Crossing *Tom Tate* a80 57
4 b g Cape Cross(IRE) Sky Wonder (Observatory (USA))
1827^{6} 2580^{8} 3192^{9} 7486^{8} 8269^{12}

Skye's The Limit *Richard Fahey* a70 70
2 ch g Pastoral Pursuits Sound Of Sleat (Primo Dominie)
1247^{2} 1541^{5} (5883) 6386^{6} 7333^{11}

Skyfall (IRE) *Mlle B Renk* a62 68
3 ch c Rock Of Gibraltar(IRE) Queen Of Fire (Dr Fong (USA))
7736a^{13}

Skyfire *Nick Kent* a48 74
6 ch g Storm Cat(USA) Sunray Superstar (Nashwan (USA))
1366^{2} 2273^{2} 2889^{10} 3573^{6} 4928^{4} 5144^{4} (5861) 6600^{10} 7498^{5}

Sky Garden *William Haggas* a65 74
3 b f Acclamation Superstar Leo (IRE) (College Chapel)
2824^{3} 4068^{5} 5345^{5} (5884)

Sky Hunter *A Fabre* 117
3 b c Motivator Pearl Kite (USA) (Silver Hawk (USA))
(1799a) 2907a^{3}

Sky Khan *Philip Kirby* a79 88
4 b g Cape Cross(IRE) Starlit Sky (Galileo (IRE))
4437^{2}

Sky Kingdom (USA) *Bob Baffert* a113 86
4 b c Empire Maker(USA) Sky Beam (USA) (Kingmambo (USA))
4106a^{3}

Sky Lantern (IRE) *Richard Hannon Snr* 120
3 gr f Red Clubs(IRE) Shawanni (Shareef Dancer (USA))
1622^{2} (2047) (3524) ◆ 4254^{2} 4985^{5} (6837) 8210a^{14}

Sky Painter (USA) *Kiaran McLaughlin* 104
2 bb f Street Cry(IRE) Skylighter (USA) (Sky Mesa (USA))
7690a^{9}

Sky Ranger (IRE) *James Tate* a63
2 b f Bushranger(IRE) Cassava (IRE) (Vettori (IRE))
6607^{9} 7111^{3} 7883^{3}

Skyring (USA) *Jose Fernandez* a101 110
4 b c English Channel(USA) Violet Lady (USA) (Seattle Slew (USA))
7712a^{10}

Sky Skipper (IRE) *G Doleuze* a67 70
6 ch h Golan(IRE) Sky Gift (USA) (Stravinsky (USA))
127a^{2}

Skytrain *Mark Johnston* a75 88
3 ch g Exceed And Excel(AUS) Viola Da Braccio (IRE) (Vettori (IRE))
(843) 949^{2} (1275) 1608^{3} 1958^{4} (2318) 2738^{7} 3342^{9} (3782) 4078^{7} (4181) 4628^{7} 5004^{7} (5437) (5886) 6274^{4} 6727^{5} 7241^{12}

Slade Power (IRE) *Edward Lynam* a107 119
4 b c Dutch Art Girl Power (IRE) (Key Of Luck (USA))
2676a^{3} 3557^{7} (3848a) 4298^{3} (5320a) 5726^{15} 6193^{2} (7364) 8209a^{10}

Slanderous *Scott Dixon* 48
2 b f Sleeping Indian Honesty Pays (Dr Fong (USA))
3318^{7} 3680^{6} 6383^{6}

Slatey Hen (IRE) *Violet M Jordan* a59 59
5 b f Acclamation Silver Arrow (USA) (Shadeed (USA))
30^{6} 76^{5} ◆ 111^{3} 277^{8} 670^{3} 736^{5} 819^{2} 863^{3} 997^{6} 1087^{2} 1355^{2} 1396^{2} 1731^{4} 2326^{2} 3154^{2} 3922^{7} 4427^{2}

Sleaford *Mel Brittain*
2 ch g Three Valleys(USA) Niseem (USA) (Hennessy (USA))
1108^{11} 1606^{10} 3648^{9}

Sleek *Marco Botti* a68 55
3 b f Oasis Dream Slink (Selkirk (USA))
4013^{7} 4382^{10} 5069^{3} 5674^{6} (6610) ◆

Sleeper Class *Jim Goldie* 53
2 b f Sleeping Indian Class Wan (Safawan)
6842[8] 7341[3]
Sleeper King (IRE) *Kevin Ryan* 101
2 b c Holy Roman Emperor(IRE) Catherine Palace (Grand Lodge (USA))
2401[4] (2877) 3424[8] 4855[4] ◆ 5679[4] 6347[6]
Sleeping Angel *Milton Bradley* a32 10
2 ch f Sleeping Indian Ellopassoff (Librate)
1344[6] 1659[13]
Sleeping Beauty (IRE) *D K Weld* a62 91
3 b f Oasis Dream Nightime (IRE) (Galileo (IRE))
5115a[6] 6674a[5]
Sleeping Giant (GER) *Luca Cumani* 79
3 gr c Dalakhani(IRE) Special Delivery (IRE) (Danehill (USA))
1975[4] 2589[4] 3209[3]
Sleeping Princess (IRE) *Clive Brittain* a60 45
2 ch f Dalakhani(IRE) Savignano (Polish Precedent (USA))
2090[7] 3958[5]
Sleeping Shadow *Keith Dalgleish* 65
2 ch f Sleeping Indian Short Shadow (USA) (Out Of Place (USA))
(2161)
Sleeping Star *Mel Brittain* 18
2 ch f Sleeping Indian Silver Purse (Interrex (CAN))
5577[13] 5827[7]
Sleeping Venus (IRE) *George Baker* 57
2 ch f Excellent Art Sun Moon And Stars (IRE) (Galileo (IRE))
3107[5] 3631[4] 4861[4]
Sleeping Wan *Mlle A Imaz-Ceca* 64
3 ch c Sleeping Indian Vivre Sa Vie (Nashwan (USA))
5465a[8]
Sleepy Blue Ocean *John Balding* a81 84
7 b g Oasis Dream Esteemed Lady (IRE) (Mark Of Esteem (IRE))
196[12] 885[6] 2275[10] 2550[6] 2832[8] 3811[11] (4074) (4203) (4479) 5155[2] 5519[3] 6309[16] 8232[7]
Sleepy Haven (IRE) *David Barron* a45 62
3 b g Indian Haven High Society Girl (IRE) (Key Of Luck (USA))
988[2] (2237)
Sleepy Joe (IRE) *Mick Channon* a60 62
2 b g Jeremy(USA) Rocking (Oasis Dream)
(1833) 2147[10] 2553[8] 3267[5] 4451[3] 5034[3] 5243[2] 5591[6] 6279[5] 7117[5]
Sleepy Lucy *Richard Guest* a49 46
4 b f Multiplex Millie The Filly (Erhaab (USA))
35[9] 105[4] 193[7] 335[3] 409[8] 421[6]
Sleepy Sioux *David Elsworth* 84
2 b f Sleeping Indian Bella Chica (IRE) (Bigstone (IRE))
3057[8] 3522[13] 5421[2] ◆ 5797[3] (6423) 6795[8] 7127[3] ◆ (7333)
Sleet (IRE) *Michael Appleby* a37
2 b c Amadeus Wolf Secret Justice (USA) (Lit De Justice (USA))
8405[5] 8435[6]
Slewpy's Image (USA) *Edward Harrison Frederick* a58
3 bb c Ready's Image(USA) Slewpy's Storm (USA) (Storm Creek (USA))
786a[4]
Slewtoo *James Given* a51 42
4 b f Three Valleys(USA) Red Slew (Red Ransom (USA))
1311[10] 3026[7] 7905[2] 8412[8]
Slice Of Life (FR) *Mme M Bollack-Badel* a69 68
3 gr f Nombre Premier Cortiguera (Oasis Dream)
962a[4] 8441a[7]
Slick Pardoned Me (USA) *Vernon Obermeier* a73
7 bb g Skip Away(USA) Golden Antigua (USA) (Hansel (USA))
413a[2]
Slide Show *David Nicholls* a33 63
5 b f Galileo(IRE) First Exhibit (Machiavellian (USA))
3467[6] 3625[2] ◆ (3947) 4403[2] 4612[4]
Slim Chance (IRE) *Simon West* a77 73
4 b f Clodovil(IRE) Valluga (IRE) (Ashkalani (IRE))
5124[11] 5881[3] 6855[8]
Slingsby *Michael Easterby* a37 36
2 b g Dutch Art Ballet Fame (USA) (Quest For Fame)
7023[13] 7209[11] 7341[10] 7662[4]
Slinky McVelvet *Garry Moss* a75 54
2 ch f Refuse To Bend(IRE) Rania (GER) (Paolini (GER))
2751[12] 3245[10] 4848[4] 7061[4] 7630[3] ◆ (7945) 8040[4] (8265)
Slip Of A Girl (IRE) *Patrick Holmes* a40 47
3 b f Strategic Prince Fig Leaf (FR) (Distant Relative)
4118[6] 5484[10] 6178[11] 8180[5]
Slip Of The Tongue *Sir Mark Prescott Bt* a85 86
3 ch g Zamindar(USA) Kiswahili (Selkirk (USA))
3432[5] 4634[4] (5001) (5197) (5526) 5868[3] 7242[3]
Slipper Orchid (IRE) *M Halford* a75 95
4 ro f Verglas(IRE) Lahiba (IRE) (Lahib (USA))
3845a[3]
Slipper Satin (IRE) *Noel Quinlan* a66 67
3 b f Excellent Art In The Ribbons (In The Wings)
8184[5] 8366[4]
Slip Sliding Away (IRE) *Peter Hedger* a87 88
6 b g Whipper(USA) Sandy Lady (IRE) (Desert King (IRE))
5009[14] 5636[9] (6067) 6744[4] 8088[3] 8264[9]
Slope *David O'Meara* a82 88
3 gr f Acclamation Bandanna (Bandmaster (USA))
8303[4] 8407[5]
Slowfoot (GER) *Markus Klug* 106
5 b c Hernando(FR) Simply Red (GER) (Dashing Blade)
2492a[6] 6248a[6] 7407a[2]
Slow Pace (USA) *F Head* a99 114
5 b g Distorted Humor(USA) Slow Down (USA) (Seattle Slew (USA))
2184a[4] (3165a) 5041a[4] 5807a[3]

Slumber *William Mott* 114
5 b c Cacique(IRE) Sound Asleep (USA) (Woodman (USA))
7563a[6]
Smalib Monterg (FR) *Dr Richard Newland* a72 77
7 b g Smadoun(FR) Liberty'S (FR) (Chamberlin (FR))
1069[3] 1653[4] 1837[3] 2968[3] 3248[3]
Small Fury (IRE) *Jo Hughes* a78 78
3 b f Windsor Knot(IRE) Sisal (IRE) (Danehill (USA))
1661[2] 2083[4] 2825[10] 3407[6] 4772[2] 4942[5] 6341[2] 6549[9] 6665[14]
Smalljohn *Bryan Smart* a80 76
7 ch g Needwood Blade My Bonus (Cyrano De Bergerac)
104[4] 217[11] 518[6] 2119[3] (2707) 3087[10] 3945[5] 7076[5] 7486[5] 7965[5] 8095[5] 8304[8]
Smart Alec (IRE) *Alan Swinbank* 63
2 br g Dandy Man(IRE) Art Critic (USA) (Fusaichi Pegasus (USA))
6769[3] 7023[8]
Smart Alice *Chris Wall* a44 42
3 b f Soviet Star(USA) Ailincala (IRE) (Pursuit Of Love)
1904[8] 3014[6] 3428[5] 4391[5] 5275[8]
Smart Casual (FR) *R Laplanche* a67 42
3 b g Kentucky Dynamite(USA) Sindibad (USA) (Rock Of Gibraltar (IRE))
711a[12]
Smart Daisy K *Andrew Hollinshead* a68 89
3 b f Pastoral Pursuits Katy-Q (IRE) (Taufan (USA))
3097[3] 3677[2] (4057) 4247[3] 5511[3] 5991[3]
Smart Eighteen *Paul D'Arcy* a70 66
3 b g Exceed And Excel(AUS) Papabile (USA) (Chief's Crown (USA))
5517[4] 5715[4] 6134[6] 6998[8]
Smart Gear (JPN) *Masaru Sayama* a86 109
8 ch h Marvelous Sunday(JPN) Squarehead Line (JPN) (Pas De Seul)
8033a[14]
Smart Payer *Jo Hughes* 68
2 b c Captain Gerrard(IRE) Goes A Treat (IRE) (Common Grounds)
4422[4] (4617) 5850[2]
Smart Salute *Ed Walker* 78
2 b c Royal Applause Naizak (Medicean)
4121[2] (4886) 6002[5] 7170[15]
Smart Spender (IRE) *Jo Hughes* a82 87
3 b g Chineur(FR) Smart Starprincess (IRE) (Soviet Star (USA))
1112[3] ◆ 1295[3] 2521[3] 2726[3]
Smarty's Echo (USA) *Anne P Smith* a106
2 ch c Smarty Jones(USA) Silver Echo (USA) (Eastern Echo (USA))
7711a[10]
Smarty Socks (IRE) *David O'Meara* a80 105
9 ch g Elnadim(USA) Unicamp (Royal Academy (USA))
1830[10] 2254[24] (3300) 3527[13] 4308[2] 4778[2] 5518[5] 5681[12] 6129[5]
Smidgen (IRE) *Ed de Giles* 67
2 b c Bahamian Bounty Brazilian Style (Exit To Nowhere (USA))
5949[8] 6769[2] 7251[3]
Smileswithhiseyes (IRE) *Gay Kelleway* a76 82
3 b g Marju(IRE) Amoureux (USA) (Deputy Minister (CAN))
(91) 1812[5] 3528[2]
Smirfys Blackcat (IRE) *Michael Mullineaux*
4 b f One Cool Cat(USA) Smirfys Dance Hall (IRE) (Halling (USA))
3572[6]
Smirfy's Silver *Michael Mullineaux* a55 40
9 b g Desert Prince(IRE) Goodwood Blizzard (Inchinor)
1101[3] 625[6] (846) 1040[6] 1342[3] 5179[7] 5615[9] 6216[9] 7514[8] 7963[12]
Smoke On The Water (GER) *Mario Hofer* 95
2 b c Areion(GER) Salzgitter (Salse (USA))
5911a[8]
Smokethatthunders (IRE) *James Toller* a80 78
3 gr g Elusive City(USA) Zinstar (IRE) (Sinndar (IRE))
(1732) 2708[5] 3212[2] 3956[8] (4866) 5441[5] 6506[6] 8069[3] 8431[2]
Smokey Oakey (IRE) *Mark H Tompkins* a79 71
9 b g Tendulkar(USA) Veronica (Persian Bold)
639[7] 906[9] 1297[4] 1752[7] 5903[10] 7091[4] (7321)
Smoking Sun (USA) *P Bary* a104 111
4 b c Smart Strike(CAN) Burning Sunset (Caerleon (USA))
3165a[2] 5298a[3] 6618a[3] 7049a[5]
Smokin' Joey (AUS) *Wez Hunter* 109
6 b g Encosta De Lago(AUS) Dalzing (AUS) (Blazing Sword (AUS))
7826a[2]
Smoky Cloud (IRE) *Terry Clement* a70 81
6 ch g Refuse To Bend(IRE) Pirie (USA) (Green Dancer (USA))
339[4]
Smoky Hill (IRE) *M Delzangles* 99
4 gr g Galileo(IRE) Danaskaya (IRE) (Danehill (USA))
6447a[4] 7193[17] 7890a[7]
Smooth Handle *Danielle McCormick* a40 50
3 ch g Dutch Art Naomi Wildman (USA) (Kingmambo (USA))
4374[5] 4672[7] 5334[10]
Smooth Operator (GER) *Mario Hofer* a100 110
7 b g Big Shuffle(USA) Salzgitter (Salse (USA))
150a[7] ◆ 365a[4] 465a[5] 744a[12] 869a[8] 1944a[3] 3970a[2] 5804a[8]
Smoothtalkinrascal (IRE) *David O'Meara* 107
3 b g Kodiac Cool Tarifa (IRE) (One Cool Cat (USA))
(1362) 1808[2] ◆ 2039[3] (2400) 2865[2] ◆ 4947[16] 6235[6]

Smugglers Gold (IRE) *David Evans* a73 72
2 ch g Majestic Missile(IRE) Stravinskaya (USA) (Stravinsky (USA))
1156[8] 1360[3] (1512) 2147[6] 2518[3] 2758[4] (3414)
Snap Call *J-C Rouget* a92
3 ch c Tamayuz Sister Agnes (IRE) (Dr Fong (USA))
(605a) 782a[2]
Snap Crackle (IRE) *Mrs K Burke*
3 b f Whipper(USA) Glasheen (USA) (Take Me Out (USA))
2279[15]
Snap Music (USA) *Mark Johnston* a53 65
3 ch f Mutakddim(USA) Rapper (ARG) (Southern Halo (USA))
4011[6] (4400) 4824[5] 5342[4] 5642[7] 6276[5] 6932[7] 7378[11]
Sniper *G M Lyons* a45 95
2 b c Dubawi(IRE) Anayid (A.P. Indy (USA))
5319a[5] 6442a[5]
Snooky *Richard Fahey* a73 85
4 b g Exceed And Excel(AUS) Quintrell (Royal Applause)
1442[3] ◆ (1751) 2240[5] 3777[2] 4308[12] 4859[11] 6126[10] 7024[9]
Snoqualmie Chief *David Elsworth* a64 70
3 b g Montjeu(IRE) Seattle Ribbon (USA) (Seattle Dancer (USA))
2071[2] 2600[7] 3820[13] 4664[3]
Snow Bay *Paul Midgley* a80 92
7 ch g Bahamian Bounty Goodwood Blizzard (Inchinor)
1462[2] (1686) 2119[2] 2882[7] (3757) 5014[12] 5518[4] 5943[13] 6496[9] 7176[19]
Snow Bell (FR) *N Clement* a92 106
3 b f Kendargent(FR) Makisarde (FR) (Xaar)
(2970a) 3877a[4] 6124a[9] 7316a[9]
Snowboarder (USA) *Charlie Appleby* a103 111
3 ch c Raven's Pass(USA) Gaudete (USA) (Distorted Humor (USA))
245a[3] 658a[2] 953a[3] 1264a[4] (4531) 4945[3] ◆ 5446[6] 7157[3]
Snow Conditions *Philip Hide* a30 51
2 b f Aussie Rules(USA) Snow Gonal (FR) (Octagonal (NZ))
5131[14] 6281[10] 7070[7]
Snowday (FR) *C Laffon-Parias* 104
3 b c Falco(USA) Oceanique (USA) (Forest Wildcat (USA))
1357a[2]
Snow Hill *Chris Wall* a78 79
5 gr g Halling(USA) Swift Dispersal (Shareef Dancer (USA))
1673[8] ◆ 3977[2] 4882[7] 5356[3] 6346[4] 6809[6]
Snow King (USA) *Ted Powell* a85 88
3 ch g Elusive Quality(USA) Cloudspin (USA) (Storm Cat (USA))
1921[13] 8445[9]
Snow Pine *A Fabre* 84
3 rg f Dalakhani(IRE) Shinko Hermes (IRE) (Sadler's Wells (USA))
6484a[10]
Snow Powder (IRE) *John Gosden* a71 80
3 ch f Raven's Pass(USA) Multicolour Wave (IRE) (Rainbow Quest (USA))
4125[6] 4799[3] 5478[3] 5942[4] 6312[5]
Snow Queen (IRE) *A P O'Brien* 106
3 b f Danehill Dancer(IRE) Bonheur (IRE) (Royal Academy (USA))
1557a[3] 2047[5] ◆ 2689a[10] 3524[17] 3964a[3] 4647a[11]
Snow Rose (USA) *Charlie Appleby* a61 77
3 b f Elusive Quality(USA) Ascutney (USA) (Lord At War (ARG))
3583[5] 4941[5]
Snow Sky *Sir Michael Stoute* 93
2 b c Nayef(USA) Winter Silence (Dansili)
5244[3] 6125[4] (6954) 7528[8]
Snow Squall *Charlie Appleby* 85
2 b g Dansili Snow Ballerina (Sadler's Wells (USA))
(4021) 4959[3] 5524[2] 6207[3] 6572[3]
Snow Train *James Given* 44
3 b f Rail Link Weqaar (USA) (Red Ransom (USA))
3364[9] 3764[9] 4157[6] 4931[7]
Snow Trooper *Dean Ivory* a82 91
5 ch g Iceman Snow Shoes (Sri Pekan (USA))
1237[2] (1583) 1840[7] 6537[8] 7312[7]
Snow Trouble (USA) *Marcus Tregoning* a75 82
2 gr c Tapit(USA) Smara (USA) (Storm Cat (USA))
3689[3] ◆ (4987)
Snowy Dawn *Andrew Hollinshead* a69 86
3 gr g Notnowcato Tereyna (Terimon)
270a[4] 445a[8] 605a[4] 711a[7] 2153[3] 2651[2] 3698[4] (4286) 5764[9] 6978[2]
Snowy Valley *Simon Earle* a58
4 ch g Three Valleys(USA) Rasseem (IRE) (Fasliyev (USA))
7371[0] 8464 1022[4] 1090[7]
Snugfit Sam *John Quinn* 52
2 b g Acclamation Swanky Lady (Cape Cross (IRE))
4046[9] 4808[6] 5646[9]
Soaring Spirits (IRE) *Dean Ivory* a86 86
3 ch g Tamayuz Follow My Lead (Night Shift (USA))
2272[4] 3537[7] 4168[5] (4829) 5632[5] 6701[2] 6963[4] (7531) 7988[7] 8219[3]
So Beautiful (FR) *Doug Watson* a96 112
4 ch c Zamindar(USA) Silver Tulip (USA) (Silver Hawk (USA))
152a[2] 466a[6] 556a[11] 741a[2] 959a[9]
So Beloved *Roger Charlton* 95
3 b g Dansili Valencia (Kenmare (FR))
1668[7] ◆ (2666) 3484[12] ◆ 4897[3]
Soccer Mom (GER) *X Nakkachdji* 93
3 ch f Monsun(GER) Sasuela (GER) (Dashing Blade)
6484a[7] 6962a[5]
So Cheeky *Richard Guest* a33 53
4 ch f Fantastic View(USA) Fallujah (Dr Fong (USA))
4835[6] 5196[6] 6216[8]

Social Rhythm *Alistair Whillans* a62 72
9 b m Beat All(USA) Highly Sociable (Puissance)
1569[12] 2220[10] 2974[7]
Society Diva (IRE) *George Baker* a41 54
2 b f Kheleyf(USA) Mistle Thrush (USA) (Storm Bird (CAN))
2978[8] 4175[6] 4997[7] 5757[4] 6979[13]
Society Pearl (IRE) *Charles Hills* 76
3 b f Kheleyf(USA) Mamonta (Fantastic Light (USA))
2389[4] 3239[4] 3674[2] 4157[4] 4941[3] 5403[4] 5959[3]
Society Rock (IRE) *James Fanshawe* 122
6 b h Rock Of Gibraltar(IRE) High Society (IRE) (Key Of Luck (USA))
(2368) ◆ 3557[2] 4298[2]
Sofast (FR) *F Head* 112
4 ch c Rock Of Gibraltar(IRE) Beautifix (GER) (Bering)
1945a[3] 2694a[7]
Sofias Number One (USA) *Roy Bowring* a86 53
5 bb g Silver Deputy(CAN) Storidawn (USA) (Hennessy (USA))
909[5] 1070[4] ◆ (1120) (1311) (1455) (2514) 2929[8] (5195) 5615[10] 8007[7] 8269[4]
Sofi's Spirit (IRE) *J S Moore* a61
3 bb f Captain Marvelous(IRE) Sofistication (IRE) (Dayjur (USA))
8[3]
Soft Falling Rain (SAF) *M F De Kock* a116 125
4 b c National Assembly(CAN) Gardener's Delight (USA) (Giant's Causeway (USA))
(245a) (658a) (1262a) 5532[2] (6797) 7366[11]
Softly She Treads (IRE) *Pat Phelan* a58 63
2 b f Azamour(IRE) Lady Lucre (IRE) (Last Tycoon)
5790[4] 7327[5]
Softsong (FR) *Philip Hobbs* 105
5 b g Singspiel(IRE) Soft Gold (USA) (Gulch (USA))
2149[8] 3423[19] 4233[5] 5256[9] 5946[5]
Sognando La Cometa (IRE) *P L Giannotti* 89
2 gr f Clodovil(IRE) Shamaness (USA) (Darshaan)
7415a[5]
So Grateful (FR) *F Pedrono* a1 50
4 b f Sandwaki(USA) Val Ramier (FR) (Westheimer (USA))
127a[0]
Sohar *James Toller* a81 91
5 b f Iceman Desert Joy (Daylami (IRE))
2654[5] 3560[7] 4873[12] 5895[8] 7193[26] (7660)
Sohcahtoa (IRE) *Andrew Crook* a76 78
7 b g Val Royal(FR) Stroke Of Six (IRE) (Woodborough (USA))
(57) 309[4] 2242[10] 2990[11] 3287[6] 3771[3] 4563[10] 5267[2] 5643[5] 6087[8]
Soho Dancer *James Toller* 90
3 b f Galileo(IRE) River Belle (Lahib (USA))
2384[8] 3240[7] 4532[3] 6800[5]
So In Love *A Fabre* 97
2 b f Smart Strike(CAN) Soft Morning (Pivotal)
7571a[5]
Soiree D'Ete *Sir Mark Prescott Bt* a54
2 b f Selkirk(USA) Souvenance (Hernando (FR))
3471[7] 3958[8] 5131[13]
Solace (USA) *John Gosden* a65 68
3 ch f Langfuhr(CAN) Songerie (Hernando (FR))
168[2] 373[4]
Solaras Exhibition (IRE) *Tim Vaughan* a89 85
5 b g Great Exhibition(USA) Solara (GER) (Danehill (USA))
691[6] 1037[2] 1273[7] 3115[7] 6434[3]
Solar Deity (IRE) *Marco Botti* a115 87
4 b c Exceed And Excel(AUS) Dawn Raid (IRE) (Docksider (USA))
60[3] (690) (944) 1545[3] 2254[25] 6199[5] 7540[2] 7926[5] (8117) 8301[2]
Solarmaite *Roy Bowring* a67 65
4 b f Needwood Blade Marinaite (Komaite (USA))
911[5] 1072[4] 1329[2] 1595[3] 2172[4] 2511[4] 2992[U] 3247[3] 3546[13] 4144[4] 5674[2] (5965) ◆ 7106[15] 8006[11] 8163[9] 8406[4]
Solar Sky *David Elsworth* a94 111
5 ch g Galileo(IRE) La Sky (IRE) (Law Society (USA))
1920[8]
Solar Spirit (IRE) *Tracy Waggott* a89 89
8 b g Invincible Spirit(IRE) Misaayef (USA) (Swain (IRE))
1281[4] 1787[10] 2028[5] 2119[5] 2705[9] 2834[3] 3088[4] ◆ 3945[11] 4138[10] (5088) 5564[8] 6205[8] 6496[12] 6774[8]
Sole Danser (IRE) *Milton Bradley* a82 77
5 b g Dansili Plymsole (USA) (Diesis)
164[2] 481[3] 582[5] 1952[5] 2196[8] 2825[6] 3667[4] (4034) 4303[3] 5349[10]
Solemn *Milton Bradley* a76 70
8 b g Pivotal Pious (Bishop Of Cashel)
1581[12] 3018[10] 5673[4] 6527[4] 6745[8] 7432[5] 7937[3] 8096[2] 8439[8]
Solent Lad (USA) *Robert Eddery* a52 44
2 ch c English Channel(USA) Ting A Folie (ARG) (Careafolie)
5151[5] 6079[5] 6923[11] 7973[7] 8133[5] 8363[3]
Sole Power *Edward Lynam* a101 120
6 b g Kyllachy Demerger (USA) (Distant View (USA))
954a[2] 1265a[4] (2019) 2662[4] (3420) 4298[5] 5726[3] 7054a[6] 8209a[2]
Sole Reign (FR) *T Clout* a79 78
3 b f Desert Style(IRE) Hokey Pokey (FR) (Lead On Time (USA))
2905a[8] 6713a[3]
Solfilia *Hughie Morrison* a86 83
4 ch f Teofilo(IRE) Suntory (IRE) (Royal Applause)
93[5] 318[3]
Solicitation (IRE) *Ralph Beckett* 22
2 b g Lawman(FR) Make Me Blush (USA) (Blushing John (USA))
4708[9] 5194[6] 5757[6]
Solid Appeal (USA) *Reade Baker* a86 109
4 bb f Successful Appeal(USA) Star Of The Woods (USA) (Woodman (USA))
5552a[6] 6454a[8]

Solidarity *Charlie Appleby* 75
2 b g Dubawi(IRE) Assabiyya (IRE) (Cape Cross (IRE))
3291[7] (5852) 6501[3] 7418[2]

Solid Justice (IRE) *Charles Hills* 43
2 b g Rock Of Gibraltar(IRE) Burnin' Memories (USA) (Lit De Justice (USA))
7069[10]

Solis (GER) *Dianne Sayer* 30
10 ch g In The Wings Seringa (GER) (Acatenango (GER))
4614[8]

Solo Hunter *David Evans* 71
2 b g Sleeping Indian Night Owl (Night Shift (USA))
3174[7] 3853[3] 4304[3] 5025[3] 5442[2] 5693[5] 6865[8] 6954[3] 7243[3]

Solomar (ITY) *S Botti* 99
5 b g Martino Alonso(IRE) Love Secret (USA) (Secreto (USA))
2489a[2] 3147a[P]

Solonder (FR) *M Le Forestier* 89
2 b g Solon(GER) Schlenderana (FR) (Monsun (GER))
5323a[3]

So Long Malpic (FR) *T Lemer* a94 109
6 b m Fairly Ransom(USA) Poussiere D'Or (FR) (Marchand De Sable (USA))
4093a[3] 6251a[7]

Solow *F Head* 85
3 gr c Singspiel(IRE) High Maintenance (FR) (Highest Honor (FR))
(3166a)

Solvanna *Heather Main* a70 44
3 b f Haafhd Solva (Singspiel (IRE))
864[4] 1095[2] 1314[2] 2017[9] 2560[3] 3040[8] 5135[4] 6315[11] 6521[9] (6737) 7434[4] 7622[5] 7786[5]

So Lyrical *Pat Murphy* a47 37
3 b f Pivotal Caro George (USA) (Distant View (USA))
1210[5] 1781[5] 2950[12] 3859[8]

Solzhenitsyn (NZ) *Robert Heathcote* 117
7 b g St Petersburg(AUS) Tri Victory (NZ) (Victory Dance)
7702a[9] 7826a[13]

Someone's Darling *Jim Goldie* a41 77
3 b f Jeremy(USA) Green Sensazione (Green Desert (USA))
1275[5] 1566[4] 1988[2] (2756) 3566[2] (4580) 5184[3] (5581) 6665[7] 6874[10] 7240[12]

Somerton Star *Pat Eddery* a42
3 b c Avonbridge Leaping Flame (USA) (Trempolino (USA))
3641[6] 7037[6]

Some Site (IRE) *David Simcock* 67
2 b f Nayef(USA) Horatia (IRE) (Machiavellian (USA))
7450[6]

Somethingboutmary *Neville Bycroft* a69 59
3 ch f Sleeping Indian Loch Leven (Selkirk (USA))
3509[6] 3866[5] 4674[3] 4982[7] 6397[6] 8048[7] 8234[8] 8372[7]

Something Magic *Sylvester Kirk* a65 67
3 gb f Proud Citizen(USA) Comeback Queen (Nayef (USA))
1907[10] 2874[7] 3428[9]

Somewhat (USA) *Mark Johnston* 111
2 b c Dynaformer(USA) Sometime (IRE) (Royal Academy (USA))
(3282) 3555[4] 4296[2] (5530) ◆ 6835[2] 7528[9]

Sommerabend *M Rulec* a110 114
6 b h Shamardal(USA) Sommernacht (GER) (Monsun (GER))
1564a[5] 2202a[7] 3913a[6] 6251a[3] 7059a[9] 7685a[2]

Sommersturm (GER) *David Evans* a70 69
9 b g Tiger Hill(IRE) Sommernacht (GER) (Monsun (GER))
61[8] 193[5] 343[7] 530[3] (579) 722[6] (755) 846[7] (973) 1158[5] 1306[4] 1733[7] 1927[3] 2069[3] 2328[6] 3012[5] 3473[3] 3688[6] 4150[7] 4714[10] 7950[8] 8115[4] 8160[2] 8331[11]

Somoud (IRE) *J R Jenkins* 73
3 ch c Kheleyf(USA) Harmonist (USA) (Hennessy (USA))
4942[4] 5585[4] 6077[4] 6900[8] 7106[9]

So Much *B Dutruel* a74 84
3 b c Green Tune(USA) Arbalette (IRE) (Anabaa (USA))
7188a[15]

Sonara (IRE) *David Evans* a57 39
9 b g Peintre Celebre(USA) Fay (IRE) (Polish Precedent (USA))
22[9] 227[6]

Son Cesio (FR) *H-A Pantall* 85
2 b c Zafeen(FR) Slitana (FR) (Dansili)
(7185a) 7994a[11]

Sondeduro *Jamie Osborne* a82 82
4 br g Manduro(GER) Madame Cerito (USA) (Diesis)
1422[6] 1884[13] 3321[5] 3854[7] 6658[10] 7733[9]

Son Du Silence (IRE) *James Ewart* 92
4 bb g Elusive City(USA) Fez (Mujtahid (USA))
3823[10] 6583[8] 7593[6] 7777[12]

Song And Dance Man *William Haggas* 78
3 b g Danehill Dancer(IRE) Song (IRE) (Sadler's Wells (USA))
2456[4] 2885[2] 6870[2]

Song Beam *Michael Bell* a60 22
2 ch f Shamardal(USA) Basanti (USA) (Galileo (IRE))
7102[10] 7763[6]

Songbird (IRE) *Lady Cecil* 103
4 ch f Danehill Dancer(IRE) Mine Excavation (FR) (Galileo (IRE))
(2389) (3258) 5035[2] 5683[7] 6764[2] 7891a[17]

Songbird Blues *Mark Usher* a61 46
4 b f Beat All(USA) Billie Holiday (Fairy King (USA))
1926 3487

Songcraft (IRE) *Saeed bin Suroor* 112
5 b g Singspiel(IRE) Baya (USA) (Nureyev (USA))
(2668) 3556[6] 4309[2] 5741[7] 6348[5]

Song Light *David Elsworth* a68 76
3 b g Echo Of Light Blue Lullaby (IRE) (Fasliyev (USA))
1684[8] (2386) 3105[4] 3783[6] 7765[11]

Song Of Norway *Peter Makin* a75 75
2 b f Halling(USA) Amarullah (FR) (Daylami (IRE))
6974[2] 7645[2]

Song Of Parkes *Peter Grayson* a83 74
6 b m Fantastic Light(USA) My Melody Parkes (Teenoso (USA))
58[10] 431[5] 583[3] 1102[4] 1398[2] 1540[9] 1984[3] 2173[5] 3171[4] 3236[8] 3569[8] 3816[2] (4520) 5227[6] 5498[7] 5931[5] 6310[4] 6905[4] 7845[7] 8052[2]

Song Of Pride (GER) *Mandy Rowland* a7 79
9 ch g Platini(GER) Song Of Peace (GER) (Zampano (GER))
6479[9]

Song Of Rowland (IRE) *David O'Meara* a49 67
2 b g Holy Roman Emperor(IRE) Makarova (IRE) (Sadler's Wells (USA))
2758[6] 3298[2] 4312[6] 4616[5] 5106[5] 5834[3] (5970) 6194[5] 6386[3] 6654[4]

Song Of Snowdon *William Muir* a50 67
3 b f Singspiel(IRE) Portmeirion (Polish Precedent (USA))
(5386) 6042[3] 6810[4]

Song Of The Siren *David O'Meara* a55 78
5 ch f With Approval(CAN) Sulitelma (USA) (The Minstrel (CAN))
3301[9] 7369[10] 7597[5] 7881[13] 8130[6] 8223[4] 8309[5]

Song Of Victory (GER) *M Weiss* a70 64
9 bb g Silvano(GER) Song Of Hope (GER) (Monsun (GER))
513a[2] 701a[12]

Sonnetation (IRE) *Jim Boyle* a67 59
3 b f Dylan Thomas(IRE) Southern Migration (USA) (Kingmambo (USA))
1881[8] 2224[6] 2802[9] 3428[4] 3919[4] (4658) 5204[3] 6399[2] 6553[2] (7639) (7784)

Sonny Jim *John Mackie* a45
5 b g Needwood Blade Sonderborg (Great Dane (IRE))
7734[5] 8036[6] 8200[5]

Son Of Feyan (IRE) *Roger Teal* a64 66
2 ch g Nayef(USA) Miss Penton (Primo Dominie)
4640[6] 5188[9] 6733[8]

Son Of May *Jo Hughes* a52 53
4 b g Royal Applause Second Of May (Lion Cavern (USA))
105[8] 522[9] 725[8]

Son Of Neptune *Nigel Tinkler*
3 gr g Monsieur Bond(IRE) Not A Word (Batshoof)
2237[9] 2752[9] 4050[8]

Son Vida (IRE) *Alan Bailey* a78 57
5 b g Titus Livius(FR) Sombreffe (Polish Precedent (USA))
1797[10] 2332[6]

So Oops (IRE) *S Wattel* a88 85
3 b f Whipper(USA) Hasanat (Night Shift (USA))
(126a) 1000a[8] 1972a[6]

Sooqaan *Mel Brittain* 43
2 bl c Naaqoos Dream Day (FR) (Spectrum (IRE))
6286[7] 7209[12]

Sophie's Beau (USA) *Michael Chapman* a43 57
6 b g Stormy Atlantic(USA) Lady Buttercup (USA) (Meadowlake (USA))
81[5] 756[3] 1465[5] 1758[7] 2997[9] (3190) 3654[9] 3716[8] 4344[8] 4456[8] (5085) 7101[12] 8272[11]

Soprana (GER) *Markus Klug* 96
4 ch f Cadeaux Genereux Sopran Gallow (IRE) (Galileo (IRE))
3852a[9]

Sorcellerie *Mel Brittain* 66
3 ch f Sir Percy Souvenance (Hernando (FR))
1447[4] 1967[6] 2508[11]

Sorella Bella (IRE) *Mick Channon* a74 103
3 ro f Clodovil(IRE) Anazah (USA) (Diesis)
1622[9] 2188[4] 2655[10] 3460[7] 3734[4] 4252[10] 4525[5] 6188[5] 6993[9] 7470[9]

Soresca (IRE) *X Nakkachdji* a80 90
2 b f Elusive City(USA) Aubonne (GER) (Monsun (GER))
7160a[6]

Sorn (IRE) *James Fanshawe* 53
3 ch g Galileo(IRE) Dame Again (AUS) (Danehill (USA))
2589[6]

Sorry Woman (FR) *H-A Pantall* 104
3 b f Ivan Denisovich(IRE) Oppamattox (FR) (Munir)
7941a[7]

Soryah (IRE) *Luca Cumani* a94 95
3 b f Shamardal(USA) Dirtybirdie (Diktat)
2979[4] 3764[2] (4678) ◆ 5095[3] (6016) 7330[4]

Sotise (IRE) *Marco Botti* a69
2 br f Shamardal(USA) Tropical Glamour (IRE) (Rock Of Gibraltar (IRE))
7874[5] 8175[4]

Soubrette *George Margarson* a45 37
3 ch f Zafeen(FR) Nihal (IRE) (Singspiel (IRE))
3837[11] 4657[3] 5127[7] 6038[6]

Soul (AUS) *Saeed bin Suroor* a68 120
6 b g Commands(AUS) Marvilha (AUS) (Night Shift (USA))
3557[17] 5027[5] 6193[5] 7013[6]

Soul Artist (IRE) *Tim Easterby* 47
2 b f Bushranger(IRE) Itsanothergirl (Reprimand)
5577[8] 5983[8]

Soul Brother (IRE) *Tim Easterby* 67
2 b c Captain Rio Goodwood March (Foxhound (USA))
3295[8]

Soul Instinct *Kevin Ryan* a63 70
2 b g Myboycharlie(IRE) However (IRE) (Hector Protector (USA))
3023[6] 3500[5] 4443[2] (4801) 5366[6] 5858[9] 6904[3] 7451[8] 7819[11] 7882[2]

Soul Intent (IRE) *J W Hills* a86 40
3 b c Galileo(IRE) Flamingo Guitar (USA) (Storm Cat (USA))
1387[4] (2874) 3294[9] (7491) ◆ 8007[4] 8218[4]

Soul Of Motion *Gay Kelleway* a37 77
2 b g Phoenix Reach(IRE) Chocolada (Namid)
2863[7] 3288[5] 5635[7]

Soul Sacrifice *A De Mieulle* a29 74
3 ch c Indian Haven Dream Dance (Diesis)
4575a[3]

Sound Advice *Keith Dalgleish* a78 89
4 b g Echo Of Light Flylowflylong (IRE) (Danetime (IRE))
1569[3] (2163) 2705[4] 2964[7] 4825[4] (5580) 6288[9] 6550[3] 7024[2] 7241[7] 7499[4] 7793[3] 8416[7]

Sound Affects *Alan Brown* a36 38
3 ch f Compton Place Rare Cross (IRE) (Cape Cross (IRE))
1962[12] 2535[6] 2996[8]

Sound Amigo (IRE) *Declan Carroll* a84 88
5 b g Iceman Holly Hayes (IRE) (Alzao (USA))
526[9] 715[6] 966[9] 1746[4] 4730[12] 5183[10]

Sound Hearts (USA) *Roger Varian* a81 104
4 bb f Sir Percy Crystal Seas (Zamindar (USA))
2399[9] 3409[2] 3775[3] 4532[7] (7020)

Sound Of Guns *Ed Walker* 102
3 b f Acclamation Eastern Lily (USA) (Eastern Echo (USA))
1622[7] 2415[4] 3340[4] 4260[8]

Sound Of Summer (IRE) *Charles Hills* a61 73
2 b f Excellent Art Ibtikar (USA) (Private Account (USA))
5529[4] ◆ 5988[3] 6318[4] 7202[8]

Sound Reflection (USA) *Charlie Appleby* a92 100
2 b f Street Cry(IRE) Echoes In Eternity (IRE) (Spinning World (USA))
(5003) ◆ (6171) 6798[6]

Souter Point (USA) *William Kinsey* a63 63
7 bb g Giant's Causeway(USA) Wires Crossed (USA) (Caller I.D. (USA))
3721[8] 4147[6] 4835[3] 5420[8] 5592[5] 6216[5]

South Cape *Gary Moore* a69 73
10 b g Cape Cross(IRE) Aunt Ruby (USA) (Rubiano (USA))
(348) 813[3] 1717[3] 2395[5] 4169[2] 4996[2] 6146[4] 6459[6]

Southern Sapphire *Kristin Stubbs* a49 44
3 ch g Compton Place Brecon (Unfuwain (USA))
374[4] 848[8] 1771[5] 5067[7] 5864[8]

South Kenter (USA) *Heather Main* a52
4 ch g Silver Deputy(CAN) Crystal Downs (USA) (Alleged (USA))
350[6] 1711[8] 2582[13] 3433[6] 3955[4] 5230[8] 6317[6] 7292[10] 7980[9]

Souviens Toi *Marco Botti* 106
4 b f Dalakhani(IRE) Diavla (USA) (Bahri (USA))
2012[3] ◆ 3100[4] 3608[2] 4920[4] 5761[3] 6764[10]

Souville *Chris Wall* a79 69
2 b f Dalakhani(IRE) Royale Danehill (IRE) (Danehill (USA))
3978[3] ◆ 5145[8] 6500[4] 7119[9] (7837)

So Vain (IRE) *David Brown* a44
3 b g Elusive City(USA) Vanitycase (IRE) (Editor's Note (USA))
102[5]

Sovento (GER) *Alan McCabe* a68 26
9 ch g Kornado Second Game (GER) (Second Set (IRE))
418[4]

Sovereign Debt (IRE) *Michael Bell* 117
4 gr g Dark Angel(IRE) Kelsey Rose (Most Welcome)
1535[4] 1919[2] 2446[2] 3419[9] 4298[9] 5007[2] 6392[8] 7530[2]

Sovereign Power *Paul Cole* a63 65
3 b g Royal Applause Tafiya (Bahri (USA))
2154[3] 3041[5] (3428) 4196[3] 5604[4] 6803[12]

Soviet Courage (IRE) *William Haggas* a71 56
2 ch g Dutch Art Place De Moscou (IRE) (Rock Of Gibraltar (IRE))
6769[5] 7209[5] 7646[2] ◆

Soviet Rock (IRE) *Andrew Balding* 97
3 b g Rock Of Gibraltar(IRE) Anna Karenina (USA) (Atticus (USA))
(1641) ◆ (2050) ◆ 3486[8] 4214[13] 7536[5]

Soweto Star (IRE) *John Best* a71 73
5 ch g Johannesburg(USA) Lady Of Talent (USA) (Siphon (BRZ))
338[5] 724[4] 1062[5] 1325[7] 3256[6] 4147[2] 5897[9] 6558[5] 7612[8]

Space Artist (IRE) *Bryan Smart* a82 86
3 b g Captain Marvelous(IRE) Dame Laura (IRE) (Royal Academy (USA))
1075[2] (1661) 2430[13] 3097[10] (5996) 6429[4] 7731[3]

Space Ship *John Gosden* a95 98
3 ch g Galileo(IRE) Angara (Alzao (USA))
1236[2] 1624[2] (2151) 2862[6] 3486[2] 4214[10] 7304[6]

Space Walker (IRE) *Harry Dunlop* a68
2 b c Astronomer Royal(USA) Hot Property (USA) (Thunder Gulch (USA))
6689[3] 7162[4]

Space War *Michael Easterby* a75 75
6 b g Elusive City(USA) Princess Luna (GER) (Grand Lodge (USA))
1220[8] 1354[6] 1819[5] (2225) 2845[9] 4245[5] 4746[5] 5051[10] 5948[4] 6720[7] 7343[4]

Spacious Sky (USA) *A J Martin* a85 85
4 b g North Light(IRE) Ratings (USA) (Caveat (USA))
7230a[8] ◆

Spanish Art *Mlle M Henry* a76 68
3 b g Byron Spanish Gold (Vettori (IRE))
2786[4] 3219[5] 3488[3] 3859[9] 4178[3] 5692a[6] 6711a[11]

Spanish Artist *Harry Dunlop* 63
2 gr c Archipenko(USA) Alicante (Pivotal)
7631[4] 8085[P]

Spanish Bounty *Mrs A Malzard* a87 79
8 b g Bahamian Bounty Spanish Gold (Vettori (IRE))
1312a[8] 1739a[2] 5327a[2] 7143a[5]

Spanish Duke (IRE) *Brian Ellison* a83 103
6 b g Big Bad Bob(IRE) Spanish Lady (IRE) (Bering)
1446[6] ◆ 1768[10] 2427[10] 3685[17] 6551[8]

Spanish Legacy *Julie Camacho* 53
4 b f Dr Fong(USA) Spanish Lace (Hernando (FR))
5143[4] 5833[7] 6290[8] 7382[9]

Spanish Plume *Andrew Hollinshead* a82 74
5 b g Ishiguru(USA) Miss Up N Go (Gorytus (USA))
146[6] 314[8] 758[2] 878[12] 996[4] 1104[3] 1353[4] 1402[4] 2435[5] 2714[2] 3037[2] 3410[3] 3721[4] 4376[5] 4655[3] 5179[3] (5671) 6130[5] 6377[3]

Spanish Trail *Christopher Kellett* a54 14
4 b f Rail Link La Coruna (Deploy)
2714[10] 3687[9] 4503[7]

Spanish Wedding *D Selvaratnam* a79 25
4 ch g Hernando(FR) I Do (Selkirk (USA))
7679a[8]

Spark (GER) *C Von Der Recke* 52
4 b g Nicaron(GER) Song Of Night (GER) (Tiger Hill (IRE))
3647a[10]

Sparkaway *Ross O'Sullivan* a46 56
7 ch g Gold Away(IRE) West River (USA) (Gone West (USA))
22[7]

Sparkel D'Hermeray (FR) *Mme C De La Soudiere-Niault* a65 51
2 b f Tomorrows Cat(USA) Illumination (Saddlers' Hall (IRE))
6961a[9]

Sparkling Beam (IRE) *J E Pease* 114
3 b f Nayef(USA) Pearl Dance (USA) (Nureyev (USA))
2906a[7] (3877a) 4792a[2] 5629a[2]

Spark Of Genius *Alan McCabe* a77 48
4 b f Oratorio(IRE) Lolla's Spirit (IRE) (Montjeu (IRE))
(96) 194[3] 589[3] 919[5] 986[3] 1211[2] 1386[2] 1540[11] 2513[3] 2949[2] 4145[7]

Spark Plug (IRE) *Brian Meehan* 79
2 b c Dylan Thomas(IRE) Kournikova (SAF) (Sportsworld (USA))
(6378) ◆

Sparks Fly (FR) *S Kobayashi* a65 60
3 b g Astronomer Royal(USA) Creme De Cuvee (USA) (Cuvee (USA))
72a[0]

Spartic *Alan McCabe* a66 47
5 gr g Needwood Blade Celtic Spa (IRE) (Celtic Swing)
35[3] 139[3] 233[2] 346[5] 1681[9] 2932[13] 3644[8]

Spa's Dancer (IRE) *James Eustace* a86 103
6 b g Danehill Dancer(IRE) Spa (Sadler's Wells (USA))
1848[2] (2813) 3458[23]

Spats Colombo *Micky Hammond* a43 62
3 ch g Notnowcato Charlotte Vale (Pivotal)
1393[8] 2716[6] (3394) 3893[4] 4474[5] (5295) 6290[P]

Spavento (IRE) *Eric Alston* a61 76
7 gr m Verglas(IRE) Lanasara (Generous (IRE))
(1788) 2796[8] (2974) 3712[6] 3983[6] 4201[4] 4561[2] 4994[7]

Speak The Truth (IRE) *Jim Boyle* a76 68
7 br g Statue Of Liberty(USA) Brave Truth (IRE) (Brief Truce (USA))
76[7] ◆ 187[6] 398[3] (494) 775[8] 981[4]

Special Meaning *Mark Johnston* a63 97
3 b f Mount Nelson Specifically (USA) (Sky Classic (CAN))
332[6] (2742) ◆ 2957[2] (3535) (4293) (4506) ◆ (5706) ◆ 6186[6] 6764[3]

Special Miss *Marco Botti* a68
2 b f Authorized(IRE) Whatamiss (USA) (Miswaki (USA))
7874[3] 8213[8]

Special Mix *Martin Smith* a71 75
5 b g Proclamation(IRE) Flaming Spirt (Blushing Flame (USA))
(1936) 3043[5] 3573[8] 5861[10] 6217[7] 8072[5] 8337[2]

Special Report (IRE) *Peter Hiatt* a54 57
3 b g Mujadil(USA) Elistown Lady (IRE) (Red Sunset)
1210[6] 1764[7] 2080[13] 2330[8] 3319[5] 4503[2] 4657[2] 5016[7] 5217[2] 5667[3] 5990[3] 6257[2] 6457[4]

Special Request (FR) *M Gentile* a89 77
6 gr g Kaldounevees(FR) Radio Mesnil (FR) (Nashamaa)
5042a[7]

Special Reward *H-A Pantall* a79 89
3 b f Bahamian Bounty Nellie Gwyn (King's Best (USA))
1000a[9]

Special Skills (USA) *Alan E Goldberg* 93
3 bb c Bernstein(USA) Kentucky Whisper (USA) (Southern Halo (USA))
3360a[9]

Specialty (IRE) *Pam Sly* a40 69
3 b f Oasis Dream Speciosa (IRE) (Danehill Dancer (IRE))
7861[8] 8157[11]

Specific Gravity (FR) *M F De Kock* a91 103
5 b g Dansili Colza (USA) (Alleged (USA))
503a[3] 742a[3]

Speckled (USA) *Charlie Appleby* a96
3 b f Street Cry(IRE) Painted Lady (USA) (Broad Brush (USA))
1698[3] (6312) (7650)

Speckled Hill *Ed Dunlop*
3 b g Oasis Dream World's Heroine (IRE) (Spinning World (USA))
2548[9]

Spectator *Andrew Balding* a62 66
2 br c Passing Glance Averami (Averti (IRE))
7320[4] 7854[6] 8214[5]

Speculative Bid (IRE) *Gerard Butler* 73
2 b c Excellent Art Barzah (IRE) (Darshaan)
2411[7] 3112[5]

Speechday (IRE) *Marco Botti* a54
2 b f Kodiac Privileged Speech (USA) (General Assembly (USA))
8342[6]

Speedbird One *Peter Chapple-Hyam* 67
2 ch f Mount Nelson Good Girl (IRE) (College Chapel)
4491[12] 5819[3]

Speed Boogie *Marco Botti* a74 78
3 b c Oasis Dream Wickwing (In The Wings)
814[7] 950[2] (1300) 1754[2] 2386[5]

Speed Date *Tobias B P Coles* a63 24
3 b f Sakhee's Secret See You Later (Emarati (USA))
2226[8] 2992[4]

Speed Dream (IRE) *James M Barrett* a82 82
9 ch g Pivotal Copper Creek (Habitat)
3796a[2] 5775a[12]

Speedfiend *Noel Quinlan* a92 106
2 b c Bahamian Bounty Vive Les Rouges (Acclamation)
3112[7] 3991[4] 5494[2] 6747[2] 7191[4]

Speedfit Boy (IRE) *George Margarson* a55 68
3 b g Red Clubs(IRE) Princess Speedfit (FR) (Desert Prince (IRE))
1750[5] 3221[8] 4666[2] 5220[3] 5604[3] 6462[8] 7086[3] 7484[3]

Speed Hawk (USA) *Robert Cowell* a82
2 bb c Henny Hughes(USA) Cosmic Wing (USA) (Halo (USA))
7638[3] (7844)

Speediness (AUS) *Colin Scott* 114
6 b g Testa Rossa(AUS) Fine Glass (AUS) (Flying Spur (AUS))
7826a[3]

Speed Society *Jim Boyle* a48 57
2 b g Bertolini(USA) Tamara (Marju (IRE))
2805[6] 3275[6] 5603[5] 6311[6]

Speed Steed (IRE) *Tim Vaughan* a59 65
6 b g One Cool Cat(USA) Dhakhirah (IRE) (Sadler's Wells (USA))
(406) 671[5] (4192) 4655[2]

Speed The Plough *Richard Hannon Snr* 74
2 b g Kyllachy Danceatdusk (Desert Prince (IRE))
2823[DSQ] 3132[2] 3413[2] (4346) 4948[9] 5656[12] 6645[12]

Speedy Approach *Michael Bell* 91
2 ch c New Approach(IRE) Height Of Vanity (IRE) (Erhaab (USA))
3238[6] (3810) 5530[3] 6866[4]

Speedyfix *Christine Dunnett* a63 68
6 b g Chineur(FR) Zonnebeke (Orpen (USA))
369[5] 398[8] 493[5] 618[7] 735[6] (862) 1101[2] 1324[2] 1681[2] 2132[3] (2643) 3498[9] 7783[8] 7848[8] 8034[5] 8135[10] 8271[5] 8351[5]

Speedy Glaz (FR) *A Clement* 66
2 b c Literato(FR) South Island (IRE) (Sadler's Wells (USA))
5323a[6]

Speedy Star (IRE) *Tina Jackson* 31
4 b g Authorized(IRE) North Sea (IRE) (Selkirk (USA))
3252[11] 5295[7] 7376[9]

Speedy Utmost Meg *William Kinsey* 43
3 b f Medicean Al Joudha (FR) (Green Desert (USA))
1828[10] 2628[11] 3047[6] 3805[4]

Speedy Writer *Henry Candy* a62 78
3 b g Byron Merch Rhyd-Y-Grug (Sabrehill (USA))
5133[5] 5588[4] 6134[8]

Speightowns Kid (USA) *Alan Berry* a78 56
5 rg g Speightstown(USA) Seize The Wind (USA) (Maria's Mon (USA))
164[7] 405[6] 583[11] 842[4] 924[5] 1058[7] 1351[11] 1681[16] 5901[12] 6652[7] 6980[2] 7353[9] (7848) 8029[7] 8096[4] 8224[9]

Spellbind *Saeed bin Suroor* 69
2 b f Shamardal(USA) Bedazzle (USA) (Dixieland Band (USA))
3781[6]

Spellbound (FR) *M Munch* a59 42
3 ro f Tertullian(USA) Sky News (GER) (Highest Honor (FR))
2334a[8]

Spellmaker *Tony Newcombe* a60 51
4 b g Kheleyf(USA) Midnight Spell (Night Shift (USA))
(472) ◆ 649[2] 1087[4] 1665[9] 3433[14] 4999[4] 7644[8] (8082)

Spellwork (USA) *Saeed bin Suroor* a85 104
4 b f Hard Spun(USA) Satin Kiss (USA) (Seeking The Gold (USA))
366a[6] 743a[5] 5271[7]

Speronella *Hughie Morrison* a62 50
3 ch f Raven's Pass(USA) Rosinka (IRE) (Soviet Star (USA))
1875[4] 2499[3] 3268[5] 5890[4] 6753[8] 7754[6]

Spes Nostra *David Barron* a53 78
5 b g Ad Valorem(USA) Millagros (IRE) (Pennekamp (USA))
2220[2] 2881[6] 4889[6] 5882[6] 5918[2] 6548[8] (6906)

Spessartine (IRE) *Robert Eddery* a31
3 b g Duke Of Marmalade(IRE) Lasting Chance (USA) (American Chance (USA))
7311[11] 7983[6] 8154[8]

Spice Fair *Mark Usher* a85 91
6 ch g Trade Fair Focosa (ITY) (In The Wings)
2052[7] 2598[7] 3344[2] ◆ 3959[5] 4643[4] 5185[4] 5895[5] 6992[8] 7217[3]

Spice Souk *A bin Huzaim* a20 33
6 b h Tiger Hill(IRE) Zanzibar (IRE) (In The Wings)
394a[12]

Spiceupyourlife (IRE) *Richard Fahey* 73
2 b f Sakhee's Secret Tiger Spice (Royal Applause)
2075[4] 2751[3] (3500) 7170[8]

Spic 'n Span *Ronald Harris* a66 59
8 b g Piccolo Sally Slade (Dowsing (USA))
861[2] 946[2] 1101[5] 1186[8] 1731[7] 1888[2] 2074[5] 2326[3] 2873[6] 3888[9] 4427[U] (4608) 4943[8] 5388[5] 5670[7] 5982[6] 6436[11] 8411[10]

Spicy (IRE) *Marco Botti* a74 42
3 ch f Footstepsinthesand Shivaree (Rahy (USA))
2135[5] 2572[5] 3216[5]

Spicy Dal *Hughie Morrison* a91 93
3 ch f Dalakhani(IRE) Salsa Steps (USA) (Giant's Causeway (USA))
1666[2] 1986[3] (2519) 3240[2] 5035[7] 6536[9] 7649[6]

Spider House *David O'Meara* a55 63
3 bb g Araafa(IRE) Golden Flyer (FR) (Machiavellian (USA))
757[5] 990[3] 1106[4] 1373[3] 2080[4] 2501[3] 2756[8] 3772[5] 4144[9]

Spider Lily *Peter Makin* a42 45
2 b f Sleeping Indian Scarlett Ribbon (Most Welcome)
3694[7] 5929[7] 6776[4]

Spiekeroog *David O'Meara* a57 70
7 ch g Lomitas Special (Polar Falcon (USA))
1993[5] 2831[2] 3089[5] (3595) 4016[7] 4563[8] 5295[3] 6179[6] 6632[3] 8004[6]

Spieta (IRE) *Luca Cumani* a76 72
3 gr f Shirocco(GER) Zarawa (IRE) (Kahyasi)
3013[2] 3437[2] 3925[3] 5130[6] 6313[7] 7169[9]

Spifer (IRE) *Marco Botti* a100 94
5 gr g Motivator Zarawa (IRE) (Kahyasi)
(273) 897[2] 1242[4] 1768[5] ◆ 2775[2] 3094[8] 3832[7] 6772[3] 7990[5] 8327[12] 8398[5]

Spillway *Eve Johnson Houghton* a88 110
3 b c Rail Link Flower Market (Cadeaux Genereux)
(1057) (1614) ◆ (1847) 2445[3] 3486[10] 4874[3] 5653[4] 6636[4]

Spinacre (IRE) *Roger Varian* a90 106
3 gr f Verglas(IRE) Spinamix (Spinning World (USA))
1358a[3] 2299a[9] 2897a[4] 5461a[8] 7404a[8] 7649[8]

Spin Again (IRE) *John Ryan* a77 71
8 b g Intikhab(USA) Queen Of The May (IRE) (Nicolotte)
490[2] 652[4] 749[3] 806[2] 1294[5] 1426[9] 2134[7] 2571[9] 3054[3] 3329[2] 3788[4] 4637[12]

Spin Artist (USA) *Mark Johnston* 92
3 b g Hard Spun(USA) Miss Cap (USA) (Capote (USA))
(5176) (5705) ◆ 6078[5] 6384[11] 6840[10] 7176[17]

Spinatrix *Michael Dods* 112
5 b f Diktat Shrink (Mind Games)
1232[2] 1537[13] (2476) 3823[15] (5056) 5545[2] 6623[10] 6845[2] 7208[5] 7495[2] 7821[3]

Spin A Wish *Richard Whitaker* a47 55
5 b f Captain Rio Be My Wish (Be My Chief (USA))
98[10]

Spin Cast *Philip Kirby* a76 77
5 b g Marju(IRE) Some Diva (Dr Fong (USA))
2886[8] (5052) 7539[8]

Spinner Lane *Richard Whitaker* 24
2 ch f Three Valleys(USA) Petra Nova (First Trump)
6718[6]

Spinning Ridge (IRE) *Ronald Harris* a73 72
8 ch g Spinning World(USA) Summer Style (IRE) (Indian Ridge)
61[10] 118[4] 274[3] 320[3] 436[2] (497) 616[4] 801[11] 903[6] 1039[6] 1194[5] 1401[7] 1786[6] (2072) 2954[11] 3513[7] 3885[4] 4153[7] 4834[3] 5091[7] 5429[12] 6323[6] 6985[11]

Spinning Waters *Dai Burchell* a44 49
7 b g Vettori(IRE) Secret Waters (Pharly (FR))
1980[3] 3271[12]

Spiraea *Mark Rimell* 71
3 ch f Bahamian Bounty Salvia (Pivotal)
2597[3] 3837[8] 6145[3] 7106[13]

Spirited Silver *John Bridger*
2 gr f Proclamation(IRE) Real Emotion (USA) (El Prado (IRE))
5698[11] 6141[9] 6408[7]

Spiritjim (FR) *P Bary* 110
3 b c Galileo(IRE) Hidden Silver (Anabaa (USA))
2355a[5] 6446a[6]

Spirit Man *Derek Shaw* a52
3 b g Manduro(GER) World Spirit (Agnes World (USA))
211[9] 6133[12] 6968[5] 7204[6]

Spirit Of Adjisa (IRE) *David C Griffiths* a84 71
9 br g Invincible Spirit(IRE) Adjisa (IRE) (Doyoun)
6346[10] 6942[10] 7342[10]

Spirit Of Alsace (IRE) *Roger Varian* a56 61
2 b f Invincible Spirit(IRE) Alsace (King's Best (USA))
4215[10] 4924[7] 6746[5]

Spirit Of Battle (USA) *A bin Huzaim* a105 98
5 b h Elusive Quality(USA) Victoria Star (IRE) (Danehill (USA))
149a[4] ◆ 241a[8] 575a[8] 838a[4]

Spirit Of Dixie *Alan McCabe* a46 46
6 ch m Kheleyf(USA) Decatur (Deploy)
754[3] 1042[10] 5709[3] 6343[11]

Spirit Of Gondree (IRE) *Milton Bradley* a68 61
5 b g Invincible Spirit(IRE) Kristal's Paradise (IRE) (Bluebird (USA))
7[3] (193) 435[5] 626[3] 722[4] 896[5] 1082[3] 1214[7] 1950[12] 3329[5] 3909[7] 4357[4] 4755[9] (8341)

Spirit Of Parkes *Eric Alston* 50
3 gr g Fair Mix(IRE) Lucky Parkes (Full Extent (USA))
1519[7] 2535[2] 5989[12] 6176[7]

Spirit Of Rio (IRE) *David Barron* 79
3 b g Footstepsinthesand Batilde (IRE) (Victory Piper (USA))
4667[5] ◆ (5110) 5860[9] 7497[6]

Spirit Of Sharjah (IRE) *Julia Feilden* a99 91
8 b g Invincible Spirit(IRE) Rathbawn Realm (Doulab (USA))
(10) 495[9] 1061[7] 1244[5] 1385[5] 1913[9] 2424[9] 2937[11] 3974[3] 4440[5] 4879[8]

Spiritofsixtynine (IRE) *Jamie Poulton* a28
5 b g Tagula(IRE) Alouchier (FR) (Kendor (FR))
5133[14] 5586[U]

Spirit Of Success *Michael Bell* a53 59
3 b f Invincible Spirit(IRE) Isabella Glyn (IRE) (Sadler's Wells (USA))
419[5] 824[12]

Spirit Of The Law (IRE) *Richard Fahey* a93 93
4 b g Lawman(FR) Passion Bleue (In The Wings)
1463[6] (1753) 2191[9] 3827[2] 4854[4] ◆ (5335) ◆ 5768[5] 6551[5] 6801[25] 7906[3] (8071) 8301[8]

Spiritoftheunion *Michael Bell* a43
2 b f Authorized(IRE) Kahlua Kiss (Mister Baileys)
7442[9]

Spiritoftomintoul *Tony Carroll* a93 86
4 gr g Authorized(IRE) Diamond Line (FR) (Linamix (FR))
3364[3] 5008[4] (5895) ◆ 8392[6]

Spirit Of Winning *John Gosden* a55
2 b f Invincible Spirit(IRE) Crossmolina (IRE) (Halling (USA))
8425[7]

Spirit Of Xaar (IRE) *Linda Jewell* a74 59
7 b g Xaar Jet Cat (IRE) (Catrail (USA))
320[2] 665[3] 813[2] 984[4] 1925[6] 2417[5] 2954[8]

Spirit O Goodchild *Alan McCabe* a16 19
2 b g Sleeping Indian Well Of Echoes (Diktat)
1642[10] 3640[12] 4142[8] 4964[8]

Spirit Or Soul (FR) *Marco Botti* a67
2 b c Soldier Of Fortune(IRE) Far Across (Common Grounds)
8005[3] 8328[2]

Spirit Quartz (IRE) *Robert Cowell* a103 118
5 b g Invincible Spirit(IRE) Crystal Gaze (IRE) (Rainbow Quest (USA))
954a[5] 1265a[8] (1483) 2019[5] 2662[5] (2909a) 3420[18] 4079[7] 4947[6] 5726[13] 7054a[13]

Spirit Raiser (IRE) *James Fanshawe* a61
2 b f Invincible Spirit(IRE) Macadamia (IRE) (Classic Cliche (IRE))
7296[10]

Spirit Rider (USA) *John Gosden* a78 75
3 b g Candy Ride(ARG) Teenage Queen (USA) (Regal Classic (CAN))
2306[5] 2760[5] 3250[6] (4152) 5070[6]

Spirit's Revench (FR) *P Demercastel* a81 99
3 ch c Spirit One(FR) European Style (FR) (Ezzoud (IRE))
2557a[3]

Spiritual Art *Luke Dace* a74 67
7 b m Invincible Spirit(IRE) Oatey (Master Willie)
4591[5] (5633) 6068[2]

Spiritual Flame *William Haggas* a79 66
2 b f Invincible Spirit(IRE) Secret Flame (Machiavellian (USA))
4409[7] 5646[3] (6690) (7326) 7640[2] 8153[4]

Spiritual Girl *Michael Bell* a55 73
3 gr f Invincible Spirit(IRE) Clizia (IRE) (Machiavellian (USA))
1019[5] 3111[P]

Spiritual Star (IRE) *Anthony Carson* 104
4 b g Soviet Star(USA) Million Spirits (IRE) (Invincible Spirit (IRE))
2667[5] 3373[7] 5518[3] 6129[4] 6352[11] 6840[11]

Spitfire *J R Jenkins* a74 78
8 b g Mujahid(USA) Fresh Fruit Daily (Reprimand)
199[4] 1205[6] 3210[6] 5965[5] 7958[2] (8049) 8230[2]

Spithead *Ian McInnes* a61 65
3 b g Tiger Hill(IRE) Cyclone Connie (Dr Devious (IRE))
2635[6] 2957[8]

Spivey Cove *Karen Tutty* 55
3 b g Royal Applause Cherokee Stream (IRE) (Indian Ridge)
1967[9] 2464[6]

Splendid Light *A Oliver* a84 78
5 gr g Selkirk(USA) Light Of Morn (Daylami (IRE))
7230a[30]

Split Rock *Mark Johnston* a69 78
2 ch c Shamardal(USA) Adonesque (IRE) (Sadler's Wells (USA))
(1449) 1619[3] 2421[3] 2518[2] 3332[3] 4006[3] 5235[2] 5945[6]

Spoil The Fun (FR) *C Ferland* a102 112
4 ch c Rock Of Gibraltar(IRE) Avezia (FR) (Night Shift (USA))
(2559a) 3387a[6] 4093a[6] 5808a[3] 7186a[3]

Spoken To Me (IRE) *Mme Pia Brandt* 87
2 b f Dylan Thomas(IRE) Well Spoken (IRE) (Sadler's Wells (USA))
7967a[5]

Spoken Words *Alan Berry* a45 43
4 b f Fruits Of Love(USA) Jerre Jo Glanville (USA) (Skywalker (USA))
87[8] 5921[11] 6760[8] 6806[4] 7083[9] 7380[3]

Spokesperson (USA) *Frederick Watson* 19
5 b g Henny Hughes(USA) Verbal (USA) (Kingmambo (USA))
6759[10] 7027[10]

Spokeswoman (IRE) *Saeed bin Suroor* a85 22
3 b f Invincible Spirit(IRE) Devil's Imp (IRE) (Cadeaux Genereux)
5896[8] 6692[11] 7314[15]

Spoof Master (IRE) *Lydia Pearce* a48 61
9 b g Invincible Spirit(IRE) Talbiya (IRE) (Mujtahid (USA))
30[8] 143[7] 471[10] 735[3] 863[8]

Sporting Club Girl *Jim Best* a20 4
3 b f Kyllachy Validate (Alhaarth (IRE))
3116[15] 3657[11] 4405[9] 4664[6] 5528[8] 7637[9]

Sporting Gold (IRE) *Roger Varian* a83 78
4 b g Shirocco(GER) Pink Stone (FR) (Bigstone (IRE))
(33) (6788) 7342[9] 7840[3]

Spray Tan *Tony Carroll* 66
3 b f Assertive Even Hotter (Desert Style (IRE))
(2829) 3699[10] 4654[4] 5796[7] 6901[3]

Spreadable (IRE) *Nick Littmoden* a54 33
2 br g Duke Of Marmalade(IRE) Spring View (Fantastic Light (USA))
4716[8] 4958[10] 5488[10] 8039[2] 8133[3]

Spread Boy (IRE) *Alan Berry* a41 56
6 b g Tagula(IRE) Marinka (Pivotal)
422[7] 523[9] 2038[3] 2319[4] 2636[6] 2911[7] 2977[11] 4444[4] 5049[4] 5261[8] 6053[6] 6687[7]

Spreading *Michael Blanshard* a56 48
3 b f Ad Valorem(USA) Churn Dat Butter (USA) (Unbridled (USA))
228[5] 470[5] 732[4] 824[7] 1055[4] 2950[6]

Spring Bird *David Nicholls* 44
4 b f Danbird(AUS) Dolphin Dancer (Dolphin Street (FR))
5290[7] 5563[7] 6630[4] 6940[6]

Spring Carnival (USA) *Charlie Appleby* 68
2 b f Bernardini(USA) Shesabullwinkle (USA) (Hesabull (USA))
3664[8] 5516[3] 5988[4]

Spring Fling *Henry Candy* a50
2 b f Assertive Twilight Mistress (Bin Ajwaad (IRE))
8061[6]

Springheel Jake *Ann Duffield* a55 89
4 b g Lawman(FR) Rye (IRE) (Charnwood Forest (IRE))
1599[6] (2912) (3464) 3684[9]

Springinmystep (IRE) *Ed de Giles* a72 93
4 b g Footstepsinthesand Joyful (IRE) (Green Desert (USA))
1745[9] 2664[8] 3096[2] 3846a[27]

Spring Lady *Alan Jarvis* a43 43
2 b f Refuse To Bend(IRE) Spring Goddess (IRE) (Daggers Drawn (USA))
6318[8] 6691[8] 7102[7]

Spring Secret *Bryn Palling* a53 70
7 b g Reset(AUS) Miss Brooks (Bishop Of Cashel)
99[5]

Spring Tonic *Simon Dow* a79 72
4 b g Fantastic View(USA) Nukhbah (USA) (Bahri (USA))
814[2] 1035[2] 1106[2] 1849[7] 2574[5] 2981[5] 6080[2] 6869[4] 7651[7] 7840[9] 8060[3] 8323[5]

Spring To The Sky (USA) *Bruce R Brown* a52 105
4 bb c Langfuhr(CAN) Seek To Soar (USA) (Seeking The Gold (USA))
7710a[11]

Spring Willow (IRE) *Eric Alston* 8
2 b g Camacho Twinberry (IRE) (Tagula (IRE))
1565[6] 3928[5]

Spurned Girl *Michael Appleby*
3 b f Passing Glance Highlight Girl (Forzando)
5495[12]

Spurtonic (AUS) *Gai Waterhouse* 106
4 ch g Flying Spur(AUS) Platonic (AUS) (Nassipour (USA))
7826a[9]

Spykes Bay (USA) *Mrs K Burke* a82 75
4 ch g Speightstown(USA) She's A Rich Girl (USA) (Affirmed (USA))
1038[2] 1801[9] 2275[3] (2703) 3069[3] 3441[9] 4018[3]

Spymistress *Zoe Davison* a49
3 ch f Sakhee's Secret Martha (IRE) (Alhaarth (IRE))
1197[2] 1299[5] 6932[13]

Squad *Simon Dow* a77 67
7 ch g Choisir(AUS) Widescreen (USA) (Distant View (USA))
119[6] 224[4] 5933[5]

Square Lamartine (FR) *M Boutin* a67 72
2 b c Great Journey(JPN) Cite Fleurie (IRE) (Mark Of Esteem (IRE))
7653a[5]

Squawk *Bill Turner* a47
3 ch f Sleeping Indian Easy Mover (IRE) (Bluebird (USA))
5[6]

Squaw King *Eve Johnson Houghton* a50 53
2 b g Sleeping Indian Change Partners (IRE) (Hernando (FR))
6641[7] 6975[8] 7442[8]

Squeeze My Brain (IRE) *Ralph Beckett* a73 75
3 b f Lawman(FR) Arctic Hunt (IRE) (Bering)
2606[3] 3666[6] 5356[6] 6313[8] 7248[5]

Squire *Saeed bin Suroor* 42
2 b g Teofilo(IRE) Most Charming (FR) (Darshaan)
3833[8]

Squire Osbaldeston (IRE) *Lady Cecil* a86 92
3 b c Mr Greeley(USA) Kushnarenkovo (Sadler's Wells (USA))
1679[4] ◆ 2198[4] (6738) ◆ 7656[5]

Squirrel Wood (IRE) *George Baker* a64 62
5 b f Sadler's Wells(USA) Didbrook (Alzao (USA))
4423[2] 4658[6] 5525[4] 6399[12] 7465[2] 7644[2] (7981) 8329[4]

Srinagar Girl *Clive Cox* a78 72
4 b f Shamardal(USA) Adees Dancer (Danehill Dancer (IRE))
(140) 2750[4] 3106[12] 4715[4]

Sri Putra *Roger Varian* a116 118
7 b h Oasis Dream Wendylina (IRE) (In The Wings)
2840[7] 4027[9] 4779[5] 5270[5]

Sr Swing *Philip Kirby* 45
2 b f Passing Glance Wigman Lady (IRE) (Tenby)
7339[7]

Srucahan (IRE) *P D Deegan* a80 92
4 b g Kheleyf(USA) Giveupyeraulsins (IRE) (Mark Of Esteem (IRE))
1255a[5] 3846a[20] 6883a[11]

Sruthan (IRE) *P D Deegan* a83 112
3 b g Arakan(USA) Giveupyeraulsins (IRE) (Mark Of Esteem (IRE))
2687a[5] 3262a[6] 6440a[4] (7051a)

Ssafa *Alastair Lidderdale* a76 71
5 b f Motivator Orange Sunset (IRE) (Roanoke (USA))
1211[4] 1610[2] (1736) 1933[4] 2361[4] 2417[4] 2796[2] 2963[2] 6609[9] 7307[7] 7629[12] (8059)

Stableford *Brian Meehan* 90
3 ch c Smart Strike(CAN) Paris Winds (IRE) (Galileo (IRE))
2306[2] (2760) ◆ 3338[4] 4236[2] 5721[4]

Stadium Of Light (IRE) *Shaun Harris* a48 36
6 b g Fantastic Light(USA) Treble Seven (USA) (Fusaichi Pegasus (USA))
5521[10] 7440[5] 7498[9] 7984[11]

Staffhoss *Mark Johnston* a83
3 b g Lucky Story(USA) Jerre Jo Glanville (USA) (Skywalker (USA))
18[2] 188[3] 674[4]

Stafford Charlie *John O'Shea* a29 17
7 ch g Silver Patriarch(IRE) Miss Roberto (IRE) (Don Roberto (USA))
3953[8]

Staff Sergeant *Michael Appleby* a74 58
6 b g Dubawi(IRE) Miss Particular (IRE) (Sadler's Wells (USA))
(2315) 2705[5] 5149[10] 5637[8] 6756[5] 7281[6] 7605[7] 8294[3] (8410)

Stage Girl *Chris Dwyer*
2 b f Tiger Hill(IRE) Primavera (Anshan)
7294[11] 7844[7]

Stagemanship (USA) *Charlie Appleby* a68 73
2 b c Pivotal Vacare (USA) (Lear Fan (USA))
(4925) 5717[4] 6520[5]

Stage Trip (CAN) *Roger Laurin* 75
5 ch f Trippi(USA) At A Stage (USA) (Atticus (USA))
773a[7]

Stagewise (IRE) *Jonathan Portman* a36 48
2 gr f Mastercraftsman(IRE) Second Act (Sadler's Wells (USA))
4589[10] 5442[6] 6152[6] 6924[8]

Stag Hill (IRE) *Bernard Llewellyn* a61 65
4 ch g Redback Counting Blessings (Compton Place)
1070[2] (1466) 1716[4] 1948[2] 2348[6] 3314[8] (3882) 4604[2] 4915[4] 5671[5] 5813[2] 6283[4] 6700[6]

Stagweekend (IRE) *John Quinn* 65
3 b g Footstepsinthesand Basin Street Blues (IRE) (Dolphin Street (FR))
1577[4] 2080[9] 2508[9]

Staines Massive *Brett Johnson* 46
3 b g Delta Dancer Russian Silk (Fasliyev (USA))
7073[8]

Stake Winning (FR) *S Wattel* 69
2 b f Da Stoops(USA) Rudi's Leslie (USA) (Struggler)
5363a[10] 6059a[8]

Stalactite (IRE) *Charlie Appleby* a20 39
2 b g Teofilo(IRE) Stairway To Glory (IRE) (Kalanisi (IRE))
3112[10] 4764[7] 5279[6]

Stamp Duty (IRE) *Suzzanne France* a51 58
5 b g Ad Valorem(USA) Lothian Lass (IRE) (Daylami (IRE))
41[7] 381[5] 733[7] 1221[4] 1893[3] 6985[8] 8056[9] 8399[6]

Stampede (IRE) *Sir Michael Stoute* 43
2 b c High Chaparral(IRE) Summerhill Parkes (Zafonic (USA))
5957[13]

Stanarley Pic *Alan Swinbank* 61
2 b g Piccolo Harlestone Lady (Shaamit (IRE))
6939[6] 7276[3]

Stand Guard *John Butler* a91 70
9 b g Danehill(USA) Protectress (Hector Protector (USA))
(166) (235) (432) (524) 713[2] (901) (1074) (1513)

Standing Bear (IRE) *Paul Cole* a47 62
3 b g Excellent Art Sweet Sioux (Halling (USA))
1487[4] 1685[5] 2156[10]

Standing Strong (IRE) *Zoe Davison* a67 71
5 b g Green Desert(USA) Alexander Three D (IRE) (Pennekamp (USA))
130[6] 652[6] 1298[3] 1716[6] 1950[4] 2966[3] 3218[5] 3656[4] 4205[5] 5099[13] 8125[13]

Stand My Ground (IRE) *David O'Meara* a91 107
6 b g Cape Cross(IRE) Perfect Hedge (Unfuwain (USA))
1535[3] 1810[6] 2559a[8] 6396[9] 7530[3] 7775[4]

Stand N Applaude *David Nicholls* a37 61
3 b g Royal Applause Neardown Beauty (IRE) (Bahhare (USA))
2308[15] 2992[3] 3629[10] 5704[7]

Standpoint *Conor Dore* a84 83
7 b g Oasis Dream Waki Music (USA) (Miswaki (USA))
39[3] 190[7] 314[9] 1081[8] 1220[3] 1333[4] 1699[6] 1827[10] 2574[10] 3195[4] ◆ (3330) (3579) (3662) 3854[5] 5129[7] 6108[11] 7306[9] 7651[10] 7961[8] 8136[7]

Stanley Rigby *Richard Fahey* a72 59
7 b g Dr Fong(USA) Crystal (IRE) (Danehill (USA))
2[2] 144[7] 528[3] 914[2] 969[5] 1333[5]

Stanlow *John Stimpson* a58 45
3 b g Invincible Spirit(IRE) Ghazal (USA) (Gone West (USA))
5069[7] 6950[7] 7624[6]

Stan Nineteen (IRE) *George Baker* a66 64
2 b c Kodiac Redwood Forest (IRE) (Barathea (IRE))
6590[8] 7218[7] 7893[7] 8342[2] 8426[7]

Stanwell *H Edward Haynes*
5 ch g Kier Park(IRE) Magical Dancer (IRE) (Magical Wonder (USA))
6114[4]

Stapleford Lad *Stuart Williams* a54 18
2 b c Shirocco(GER) World Spirit (Agnes World (USA))
7655[9] 8342[8]

Star Alliance (IRE) *Ian Williams* a66 62
5 ch g Dalakhani(IRE) Kalagold (IRE) (Magical Strike (USA))
1040[3] 2642[5] 3688[3] (4380) 5084[6] 5933[3]

Star Anise (FR) *Harry Dunlop* a66
2 b f Astronomer Royal(USA) Sasicha (IRE) (Montjeu (IRE))
3958[11] 4880[12] 6523[9] 7664[3] 7944[2] 8132[3]

Starboard *T Clout* 111
4 b c Zamindar(USA) Summer Shower (Sadler's Wells (USA))
741a[6] 873a[10] 5298a[5]

Starbotton *James Bethell* a47 46
3 b f Kyllachy Bonne Etoile (Diesis)
3281[10] 3762[9] 4807[9] 7953[7] 8142[7] 8390[3]

Starbright (IRE) *Kevin Prendergast* 97
3 b f Duke Of Marmalade(IRE) Starry Messenger (Galileo (IRE))
1166a[3] 1862a[7] 7404a[12]

Star Chart (IRE) *John Gosden* 54
2 b f Dubawi(IRE) Star Express (Sadler's Wells (USA))
6949[6]

Star Chope (FR) *C Boutin* a56 61
2 b f Deportivo Via Appia (FR) (Exit To Nowhere (USA))
2558a[2]

Star City (IRE) *Michael Dods* a68 67
4 b g Elusive City(USA) Teacher Preacher (IRE) (Taufan (USA))
1693[5] 2278[14] 3778[11] 4161[4] 4357[12] 5471[4]

Star Code (IRE) *Richard Hannon Snr* a80 75
2 b c Kodiac Mira (IRE) (Turtle Island (IRE))
5757[3] (6333) 7640[4]

Star Date (IRE) *Michael Attwater* a82 86
4 b g Galileo(IRE) Play Misty For Me (IRE) (Danehill Dancer (IRE))
1884[9] 2982[4] 3865[3] 4679[9] 5967[4] 6658[7] 7220[8] 7430[7] 7636[3] ◆

Star Dolois (FR) *A Bonin* 77
2 ch c Naaqoos Bee Bee (FR) (Barathea (IRE))
7889a[5]

Star Empire (SAF) *M F De Kock* a99 109
7 b g Second Empire(IRE) Lady Maroof (NZ) (Maroof (USA))
246a[3] (555a) 870a[3] 1263a[5]

Starfield *John Gosden* a92 87
4 b g Marju(IRE) Sister Moonshine (FR) (Piccolo)
2424[12] 3157[7]

Starformer (USA) *William Mott* a100 110
5 b f Dynaformer(USA) Etoile Montante (USA) (Miswaki (USA))
5552a[9]

Star Hill *Alan King* a69 47
6 b m Starcraft(NZ) Mistress Bankes (IRE) (Petardia)
3406[7] 4035[9]

Stark Danon (FR) *W Hickst* a93 100
5 b g Marchand De Sable(USA) Sue Generoos (IRE) (Spectrum (IRE))
7085a[12]

Star Kingdom (IRE) *Brian Ellison* a51 65
4 b g Marju(IRE) Appetina (Perugino (USA))
24[11]

Star Lahib (IRE) *Mark Johnston* 103
4 b f Cape Cross(IRE) Cannikin (IRE) (Lahib (USA))
1238[2] ◆ 1933[6] 2646[3] (3095) 3567[2] (4060) 4310[8] (5259) 5683[4] 5993[5] 6385[4]

Starlight Angel (IRE) *Ronald Harris* a68 71
3 b f Dark Angel(IRE) King Of All (IRE) (King Of Clubs)
1482[9] 2098[4] 2572[4] 2829[4] 3216[9] 3699[5] 4244[3] 5184[6] 5644[2] 7150[2] 8128[12] 8352[7]

Starlight Princess (IRE) *J S Moore* a65 53
2 b f Mastercraftsman(IRE) Definitely Royal (IRE) (Desert Prince (IRE))
3664[15] 4484[14] 6132[4] 6749[2] 6924[7] 7789[3] (7878) 8039[3] 8262[2] 8296[4] 8426[8]

Starlight Serenade *Ralph Beckett* a59 64
2 ch f Three Valleys(USA) Melody Maker (Diktat)
3175[2] (5442) 6474[4]

Starlight Symphony (IRE) *Eve Johnson Houghton* a48 82
3 b f Oratorio(IRE) Phillippa (IRE) (Galileo (IRE))
1822[4] 2387[5] 2586[8] 3666[5] 4048[3] (4348) 4941[2] 5202[5] 6003[2] 6188[8] 7075[5]

Star Links (USA) *S Donohoe* a89 83
7 b g Bernstein(USA) Startarette (USA) (Dixieland Band (USA))
2191[10] 5332[2] (8094) 8301[5]

Starlit Cantata *Eve Johnson Houghton* a62 65
2 b f Oratorio(IRE) Starlit Sky (Galileo (IRE))
4164[4] 4924[4] 5716[10] 6275[9] 7435[4]

Starlite Jewel *Ollie Pears* 36
2 b f Virtual Celestial Empire (USA) (Empire Maker (USA))
6769[7]

Starluck (IRE) *David Arbuthnot* a99 55
8 gr g Key Of Luck(USA) Sarifa (IRE) (Kahyasi)
585[7]

Star Of Mayfair (USA) *Alan Jarvis* a43 68
3 ch g Tale Of The Cat(USA) Kinsale Lass (USA) (Royal Academy (USA))
1829[4] 2017[6] 3137[3] ◆ 3665[9] 5391[5] 6325[17] 7446[8]

Star Of Missouri *Mark H Tompkins* a51 65
3 ch g Namid Missouri (Charnwood Forest (IRE))
3055[6] 3893[8]

Star Of Namibia (IRE) *Michael Mullineaux* a66 68
3 b g Cape Cross(IRE) Sparkle Of Stones (FR) (Sadler's Wells (USA))
1481[5] 1584[4] 2599[8] 2924[2] 4150[9] 4753[7] 5010[2] 5692a[3] 5914a[2] 6711a[8] 7569a[3] 7877[3] 8373[3]

Star Of Rohm *Michael Bell* a75 81
3 ch g Exceed And Excel(AUS) Noble Desert (FR) (Green Desert (USA))
808[2] 964[3] 1345[7] (2267) 3053[4] 3813[4] 4303[8] 4962[8] 6362[11]

Star Of Tralee (NZ) *David Hayes* 83
5 b m Zabeel(NZ) Rose Of Tralee (AUS) (Sadler's Wells (USA))
7938a[9]

Star Pearl (USA) *Roger Varian* a90 84
3 b f Tapit(USA) Lexi Star (USA) (Crypto Star (USA))
3136[2] (3632) 4769[3] ◆ (6341)

Star Prince (FR) *J-C Rouget* 101
3 b c Green Tune(USA) Princess Love (FR) (Verglas (IRE))
4043a[3]

Star Request *Frederick Watson* 61
3 b f Urgent Request(IRE) Carahill (AUS) (Danehill (USA))
2409[9] 3463[14] 3932[4] 4113[5] 5714[4]

Starry Night (FR) *S Wattel* 87
3 b f Marchand De Sable(USA) Seracina (Nashwan (USA))
2403a[4]

Stars Above Me *Roger Charlton* 87
2 b f Exceed And Excel(AUS) Kalinova (IRE) (Red Ransom (USA))
4877[2] ◆ (6697)

Stars Aligned (IRE) *Richard Hannon Snr* a20
2 b f Sea The Stars(IRE) Senora Galilei (IRE) (Galileo (IRE))
7295[8]

Starscope *John Gosden* 110
4 ch f Selkirk(USA) Moon Goddess (Rainbow Quest (USA))
2397[4] 2838[6]

Star Sequence (IRE) *Hugo Palmer* a45
3 b f Tagula(IRE) Sonic Night (IRE) (Night Shift (USA))
230[6]

Starship Truffles (USA) *Martin D Wolfson* a116
4 b f Ghostzapper(USA) Bobbie Use (USA) (Not For Love (USA))
7709a[12]

Stars Legacy *George Moore*
4 b f Presidium Pagan Star (Carlitin)
2504[9]

Stars Over The Sea (USA) *Mark Johnston* 92
2 b c Sea The Stars(IRE) Exciting Times (FR) (Jeune Homme (USA))
3490[4] ◆ 4021[6] (4576) (5829) 6195[5]

Starspangledbanner (AUS) *A P O'Brien* a103 111
7 ch h Choisir(AUS) Gold Anthem (AUS) (Made Of Gold (USA))
1265a[14]

Start Right *Saeed bin Suroor* a102 107
6 b g Footstepsinthesand Time Crystal (IRE) (Sadler's Wells (USA))
151a[3] 462a[3]

Star Up In The Sky (USA) *Kevin Ryan* a71 77
3 rg f Speightstown(USA) Prenuptial Plans (USA) (Runaway Groom (CAN))
1690[7] 3160[4] 3894[5] 4670[7] 5487[7] 6367[6]

Starwatch *John Bridger* a89 94
6 b g Observatory(USA) Trinity Reef (Bustino)
1583[5] 1883[8] 2193[7] 3108[2] 3274[9] 3974[5] 4207[5] 4908[9] 5124[13] 5587[3] 5855[2] 6359[3] 6596[10] 7072[9] 7431[7]

Stasio (USA) *David Simcock* a89 81
3 b g Street Boss(USA) Believe (USA) (Chimes Band (USA))
553a[7] 953a[10] 7926[10] ◆ 8263[10]

State Anthem *Mick Channon* 73
2 b f Royal Applause Arctic Song (Charnwood Forest (IRE))
3035[5] 3565[3] 4191[3] 4828[4] 5536[13] 6070[2] 6326[10] (6627)

State Law (IRE) *Charlie Appleby* 61
2 b g Invincible Spirit(IRE) Mayoress (Machiavellian (USA))
5244[12] 5969[8] 6773[5] 7219[5]

State Senator (USA) *Richard Ford* a59 73
5 bb g Mr Greeley(USA) Summer Night (Nashwan (USA))
53[9] 361[5] 539[8] 703[9]

Statue Of Dreams (IRE) *Noel Lawlor* a63 85
7 b g Statue Of Liberty(USA) Phyliel (USA) (Lyphard (USA))
3796a[13]

Status Symbol (IRE) *Anthony Carson* a86 90
8 ch g Polish Precedent(USA) Desired (Rainbow Quest (USA))
1824[3] 2422[6] 3113[9]

Statutory (IRE) *Mark Johnston* 107
3 b g Authorized(IRE) Mialuna (Zafonic (USA))
4139[2] ◆ (4445) 4950[5] 5258[3] ◆ 5475[4] (5946) ◆ 6196[4] 6766[2] (7064)

Stay Tuned (ITY) *Jessica Lari* 93
2 b f Blu Air Force(IRE) Raganella (IRE) (Fasliyev (USA))
5460a[9]

Stealth Missile (IRE) *Clive Brittain* 86
2 b f Invincible Spirit(IRE) Wing Stealth (IRE) (Hawk Wing (USA))
4702[15] (6184) 6795[5] 7695[11]

Steel City Boy (IRE) *Ann Stokell* a60 52
10 b g Bold Fact(USA) Balgren (IRE) (Ballad Rock)
26[6] 124[7] 233[0] (327) 516[6] 618[3] 735[2] 831[7] 968[3] 1186[3] 1331[5] 1452[6] 6478[11] 6808[3] 7079[6] 7197[9] 7485[9]

Steelcut *Mark Buckley* a70 48
9 b g Iron Mask(USA) Apple Sauce (Prince Sabo)
115[3] 1058[2] 1101[4] 1304[4] 1467[6] 2268[7] 2772[2] 3024[10] 3904[4] 4852[8] 5674[3] 6752[11] 7197[10] 7985[8] 8035[2] 8306[9] 8411[3]

Steeler (SPA) *R Martin* 49
4 b g Caradak(IRE) Corfu (IRE) (Daylami (IRE))
2380a[6]

Steele Ranger *Peter Chapple-Hyam* a70 68
2 b c Bushranger(IRE) Tatora (Selkirk (USA))
2741[4] 4379[3] 4963[3]

Steel Rain *Nikki Evans* a48 81
5 b g Striking Ambition Concentration (IRE) (Mind Games)
1665[11] (3623) 3888[3] (4930) 5097[2] 5389[3] (7633) 7776[7]

Steelriver (IRE) *James Bethell* a87 86
3 b g Iffraaj Numerus Clausus (FR) (Numerous (USA))
2371[5] ◆ 2857[5] 3563[8] 4295[5] 4890[6] 6308[16] 6694[6] 7024[16]

Steel Stockholder *Mel Brittain* a49 82
7 b g Mark Of Esteem(IRE) Pompey Blue (Abou Zouz (USA))
1115[6] (1462) 1571[8] 3628[5] 3945[4] 4733[5] 5149[5] 5481[9] 5974[8] 7824[8] 7965[7]

Steely *Gary Moore* a65 75
5 b g Librettist(USA) No Comebacks (Last Tycoon)
1899[8] 2569[5] 3168[4] 3655[2] 4380[2] 5093[2] 5433[2] 6404[3] 6736[4]

Steer By The Stars (IRE) *Mark Johnston* 90
3 b f Pivotal Mundus Novus (USA) (Unbridled's Song (USA))
3028[5] 3443[6] 3563[10] 4342[8] 4825[8] 6210[5] 6433[3] 6906[7] 7275[5]

Stella Clavisque (IRE) *Brian Meehan* a70 69
2 ch c Camacho Grand Baie (IRE) (Grand Lodge (USA))
4379[4] 4977[6] 5296a[2] 5675[4] 6328[20] 6786a[4] 7087[3]

Stella Indiana (FR) *J Heloury* 68
2 b f Blu Air Force(IRE) Brave Indian (IRE) (Indian Ridge)
5363a[6] 6059a[10]

Stellar Express (IRE) *Michael Appleby* a72 91
4 b f Royal Applause Aitch (IRE) (Alhaarth (IRE))
2232[4] 2646[2] 3098[4] (4287) 4502[2] 4929[3] 6353[5] 7131[5] 7651[9]

Stellar Path (FR) *X Thomas-Demeaulte* 106
2 gr f Astronomer Royal(USA) America Nova (FR) (Verglas (IRE))
(7571a)

Stellarta *Michael Blanshard* a63 71
2 b f Sakhee's Secret Torgau (IRE) (Zieten (USA))
2562[2] 2978[3] 3694[2] 4346[3] 5648[2] 6320[2] (6718)

Stellar Wind (JPN) *Tomohito Ozeki* 112
4 bb c Zenno Rob Roy(JPN) Be Wind (JPN) (Spinning World (USA))
6449a[5] 7049a[7]

Stellato *A Wohler* 90
3 ch c Dalakhani(IRE) Sky Dancing (IRE) (Exit To Nowhere (USA))
1867a[4]

St Elmo's Fire *Peter Chapple-Hyam* 48
3 b g Bahamian Bounty Firebelly (Nicolotte)
3585[9] 5290[8]

Stelway (FR) *P Bary* a96 102
4 ch c Gold Away(IRE) Hill Tiger (IRE) (Indian Ridge)
(6060a)

Stencive *William Haggas* 110
4 b c Dansili Madeira Mist (IRE) (Grand Lodge (USA))
2044[6] 3559[2] ◆ 4310[2]

Stenka Razine (FR) *C Boutin* a65 64
3 bl c Country Reel(USA) Lady Nasrana (FR) (Al Nasr (FR))
331a[8] 543a[9] 605a[9]

Stentorian (IRE) *Gary Moore* a89 86
5 ch g Street Cry(IRE) Nomistakeaboutit (CAN) (Affirmed (USA))
(20) (475) ◆ 779[2] 1031[2] (1306) 1454[3]

Step Away *Charles Hills* 53
2 b f Dansili Because (IRE) (Sadler's Wells (USA))
5282[12] 6112[7] 6974[U] 7532[10]

Step By Step (TUR) *M Kaya* a91 101
5 b c Mountain Cat(USA) Committal (USA) (Chief's Crown (USA))
6232a[4]

Steppe Daughter (IRE) *Denis Coakley* a61
2 b f Steppe Dancer(IRE) Carmencita (Rock Of Gibraltar (IRE))
6922[4]

Stepper Point *William Muir* 109
4 b g Kyllachy Sacre Coeur (Compton Place)
1483[5] 2019[9] 2300a[4] 2909a[5] 3420[12] 4311[8] 4493[3] 4935a[3] (5375) (5984) 6639[4] 7054a[20]

Stepping Ahead (FR) *K R Burke* a68 98
3 ch g Footstepsinthesand Zghorta (USA) (Gone West (USA))
(1481) (2554) 3296[4] 4295[4] 6396[8] (7497)

Stepping Out (IRE) *Tom Dascombe* 80
2 b f Tagula(IRE) Teodora (IRE) (Fairy King (USA))
2230[2] 2625[2] (3148)

Steps (IRE) *Roger Varian* a84 111
5 br g Verglas(IRE) Killinallan (Vettori (IRE))
2014[5] (2461) 2937[4] 4024[3] ◆ 4275[8] 4800[2] ◆ 5257[2] 6391[2] ◆ 6639[10] (7010) 7527[7]

Steps To Freedom (IRE) *Mrs John Harrington* a109 112
7 b g Statue Of Liberty(USA) Dhakhirah (IRE) (Sadler's Wells (USA))
1415a[3] 1920[5]

Stepturn *Michael Wigham* a70 65
4 b g Invincible Spirit(IRE) Gay Gallanta (USA) (Woodman (USA))
80[6] 494[9]

Stereo Love (FR) *Clive Cox* a57 75
2 b f Champs Elysees My Heart's Deelite (USA) (Afternoon Deelites (USA))
6523[11] 7310[2]

Stereotypical *Ralph Beckett* 75
4 ch g Notnowcato Delightful Rhythm (USA) (Diesis)
5484[3]

Sterling City (AUS) *J Moore* 116
5 br g Nadeem(AUS) So Gorgeous (AUS) (Brief Truce (USA))
8209a[5]

Sternrubin (GER) *Peter Chapple-Hyam* 68
2 b g Authorized(IRE) Sworn Mum (GER) (Samum (GER))
7607[4]

Stetchworth (IRE) *Mark Johnston* 77
2 ch c New Approach(IRE) Hallowed Park (IRE) (Barathea (IRE))
7467[3] 7655[3]

Stetson *Ian Williams* a64 63
7 b g Groom Dancer(USA) Mindomica (Dominion)
165[4]

Steventon Star *Alan Bailey* a97 91
2 b g Pastoral Pursuits Premiere Dance (IRE) (Loup Solitaire (USA))
1669[2] (1880) (2370) 2809[4] 3424[23] 4248[5] 6187[6] 6328[4] 7925[3] (8203)

Steve Rogers (IRE) *Sir Michael Stoute* a60 49
2 b c Montjeu(IRE) Three Owls (IRE) (Warning)
7460[8] 7774[7]

Stevie Thunder *Ian Williams* a87 97
8 ch g Storming Home Social Storm (USA) (Future Storm (USA))
2424[4] 2858[10] 5546[10] 6801[20] 7211[16] 7656[3] (7765) 7906[6] 8150[2]

St Georges Hill (IRE) *Michael Wigham* a69 61
3 b g Marju(IRE) Lyrical Dance (USA) (Lear Fan (USA))
396[3] 5932[3] 6555[8] 7093[6]

Stickleback *Micky Hammond* a44 63
4 ch f Manduro(GER) The Stick (Singspiel (IRE))
1445[3] 1721[2] 7597[6]

Stiff Upper Lip (IRE) *Richard Hannon Snr* a69 80
3 b c Sakhee's Secret Just In Love (FR) (Highest Honor (FR))
3535[5] 3917[2] (4591) 5132[8] 6200[9] 6743[7] 7071[2] 7257[9] 7839[7]

St Ignatius *Alan Bailey* a85 80
6 b g Ishiguru(USA) Branston Berry (IRE) (Mukaddamah (USA))
112^5 420^8 718^8 866^8 1350^7 1585^{13} 3656^3 4099^3 4195^2 (4429) 4612^3 5168^2 5666^3 (5920) *6346^2* 6552^{13} 7239^{13} (8115) (8353)

Stilla Afton *Marcus Tregoning* a51
2 bb f Nayef(USA) Sourire (Domedriver (IRE))
7971^9 8124^{12}

Stillman (FR) *Mario Hofer* a80 108
2 b c Vespone(IRE) Kikinda (FR) (Daliapour (IRE))
6249a^3 7160a^2 7686a^4

Stipulate *David Hayes* 114
4 b g Dansili Indication (Sadler's Wells (USA))
1639^2 1919^3 2652^2 3347^3 5739^2 7826a^{12}

Stirring Ballad *Andrew Balding* a101 104
4 ch f Compton Place Balnaha (Lomond (USA))
1244^3 1544^2 ◆ 2015^4 3458^{22}

Stir Trader (IRE) *Philip Hide* a83 80
4 b g Titus Livius(FR) Changari (USA) (Gulch (USA))
133^2 792^3 1318^8 2085^6

St Jean (IRE) *Kevin Prendergast* a49 106
3 b c Teofilo(IRE) Oriental Fashion (IRE) (Marju (IRE))
5209a^4

St Moritz (IRE) *David O'Meara* a94 104
7 b g Medicean Statua (IRE) (Statoblest)
(1643) 2029^{15} 2399^{15} 2958^6 4080^7 4308^7 4946^{17} 5860^{10} 7211^{10}

St Nicholas Abbey (IRE) *A P O'Brien* 126
6 b h Montjeu(IRE) Leaping Water (Sure Blade (USA))
(1268a) (2864)

Stockhill Diva *Brendan Powell* 66
3 ch f Haafhd April Stock (Beveled (USA))
2850^6 3372^5 4799^7 6491^6

Stock Hill Fair *Brendan Powell* 91
5 b g Sakhee(USA) April Stock (Beveled (USA))
2269^3 (2849) 4914^2

Stomachion (IRE) *Sir Michael Stoute* a61 89
3 b g Duke Of Marmalade(IRE) Insight (FR) (Sadler's Wells (USA))
2760^7 3278^3 *6366^5* (7249) (7453) ◆

Stomp *Roger Charlton* a75 72
2 b g Nayef(USA) Strut (Danehill Dancer (IRE))
4231^{10} 5646^5 6589^3 7062^6 *7879^3*

Stoneacre Brigitte (IRE) *Peter Grayson*
4 b c Refuse To Bend(IRE) Kaveri (USA) (War Chant (USA))
6806^9

Stoneacre Hull (IRE) *Peter Grayson* a53 42
4 b f Bachelor Duke(USA) Amount (Salse (USA))
236^5 472^7 670^8 1078^5 5884^4 *7077^6 7380^6 7730^3 7946^4 8338^8*

Stoneacre Oskar *Peter Grayson* a52 62
4 b f Echo Of Light Keidas (FR) (Lomitas)
849^8 1215^7 2172^5 2576^8 (4991) 5273^{10} 5515^5 *6368^8* 6687^U 6918^6 7149^{12} *7639^5 8056^6* 8279^8 8371^{13}

Stoneacre Thirsk (IRE) *Peter Grayson* a34
4 br f Red Clubs(IRE) Alexander Eliott (IRE) (Night Shift (USA))
7203^6 7484^5

Stonecrabstomorrow (IRE) *Roy Brotherton* a71 71
10 b g Fasliyev(USA) Tordasia (IRE) (Dr Devious (IRE))
1976^2 2364^8 2530^7 3317^8 3949^3 4428^2 4712^7 5177^9 5816^{10} *6343^{10}* 7772^{10}

Stonefield Flyer *Keith Dalgleish* a92 95
4 b c Kheleyf(USA) Majestic Diva (IRE) (Royal Applause)
244a^{14} 464a^{11} 746a^{12} 5984^9 6621^{27} 6920^7 *7642^5 7803^4 7982^7*

Stone Me (FR) *J-C Rouget* 61
2 ch f Muhaymin(USA) Jennhill (FR) (Sabrehill (USA))
5363a^9

Stone Of Folca *John Best* 102
5 b g Kodiac Soyalang (FR) (Alydeed (CAN))
3334^6 3776^{13} 4263^{10} 5519^{10} 6189^{13}

Stones Peak (IRE) *Patrick Martin* a48 83
5 b m Rock Of Gibraltar(IRE) Slupia (IRE) (Indian Ridge)
3796a^7

Stoney Quine (IRE) *Keith Dalgleish* a65 61
2 b f Royal Applause Shauna's Honey (IRE) (Danehill (USA))
2458^9 3461^2 3681^3 4399^4 4952^3 6582^{13} *7199^2 7509^2 (7755)* 7788^8 *7882^4 (8045)* 8296^3 (8347)

Stony Grey (IRE) *A Oliver* 96
3 gr g Winged Love(IRE) Grand Lili (Linamix (FR))
7723a^{13}

Stopped Out *Philip Kirby* 86
8 gr g Montjoy(USA) Kiomi (Niniski (USA))
2465^2 3560^{16} 6847^5 7338^2

Storey Hill (USA) *Richard Guest* a60 27
8 bb g Richter Scale(USA) Crafty Nan (USA) (Crafty Prospector (USA))
2280^{13} 3196^8 4892^{10} *7266^8 8056^4 8293^3 (8418)*

Storm (IRE) *Charles Hills* a78 74
3 b f Excellent Art Bali Breeze (IRE) (Common Grounds)
807^2 (1095) 7504^5 ◆ *8060^2*

Storma Norma *Tim Easterby* a28 68
3 b f Royal Applause Icing (Polar Falcon (USA))
3546^7 3730^4 4162^7 *5677^{10}* 6289^{16}

Stormardal (IRE) *Ismail Mohammed* 100
2 b c Shamardal(USA) Dievotchkina (IRE) (Bluebird (USA))
5199^4 5826^2 (6299) 6763^3 7192^5

Stormbound (IRE) *Paul Cole* a76 63
4 b g Galileo(IRE) A Footstep Away (USA) (Giant's Causeway (USA))
138^2 (434) 963a^0 1901^4 *2574^9* 3429^3 4623^7 *(8087)*

Storm Fall (FR) *D Prod'Homme* a54 82
3 b f Vatori(FR) Les Trois Rivieres (FR) (Grape Tree Road)
8441a^{12}

Storm Force Ten *Andrew Balding* a71 67
2 b c Shirocco(GER) Stravinsky Dance (Stravinsky (USA))
4896^8 *6168^3 6688^3* 7428^5

Storming (IRE) *Andrew Balding* a80 80
3 b g Stormy Atlantic(USA) French Lady (NZ) (Entrepreneur)
1219^3 1769^5 2627^2 3294^8 3886^2 ◆ *4383^5* (5310) 6126^4 7130^6

Storming Loose *B Grizzetti* 103
6 bb g Storming Home Dan Loose (IRE) (Danehill (USA))
1709a^4 2295a^7 3881a^2 6889a^6 7413a^5

Storm King *Jane Chapple-Hyam* a101 104
4 b c Shamardal(USA) Tarandot (IRE) (Singspiel (IRE))
2424^{13} 3347^5 (3812) 4811^7 5268^5 *6199^7* 6650^{10}

Storm Lightning *Mark Brisbourne* a80 80
4 b g Exceed And Excel(AUS) All For Laura (Cadeaux Genereux)
2275^{13} *3215^8* 3716^3 4034^2 4487^6 *4837^9 (5673)* 6388^4 6527^{10} 7634^8

Storm Moon (USA) *Mark Johnston* a93 94
3 b g Invincible Spirit(IRE) Storm Lily (USA) (Storm Cat (USA))
1625^9 *(2083)* 2213^7 3348^7 3584^8 3802^4 (4112) 4472^{11} 4800^9 5108^{15} 5260^6 5538^{11} 5769^{12} 5996^5 (6212) 6539^7 6990^{17}

Storm Of Choice *Michael Attwater* 5
2 b g Shirocco(GER) New Choice (IRE) (Barathea (IRE))
3291^9 *4631^{13}*

Stormont Bridge *Maurice Barnes* a28 58
5 b g Avonbridge Stormont Castle (USA) (Irish River (FR))
2121^6 2636^4 2977^{10}

Storm Quest *Robin Dickin* a28
6 ch m Storming Home Recherchee (Rainbow Quest (USA))
4632^{11} 5233^7

Storm Rider (IRE) *Richard Hannon Snr* 40
2 b c Fastnet Rock(AUS) On The Nile (IRE) (Sadler's Wells (USA))
6635^{11}

Storm Runner (IRE) *George Margarson* a77 54
5 b g Rakti Saibhreas (IRE) (Last Tycoon)
138^3 272^6 (344) 451^2 511^6 2057^{11} *7785^{10} 8323^6*

Storm Trooper (IRE) *Richard Hannon Snr* 83
2 b c Acclamation Maid To Order (IRE) (Zafonic (USA))
3948^3 (4412) 6697^5 7170^{14}

Storm Ultralight (ARG) *S Seemar* a82 79
7 b g Bernstein(USA) Ultrasexy (ARG) (Equalize (USA))
241a^{15} 834a^{13}

Stormy Coast (FR) *N Clement* a67
3 b c Stormy River(FR) Coastline (Night Shift (USA))
1850a^6

Stormy Len (USA) *David Donk* a77 110
3 bb c Harlan's Holiday(USA) Rietondale (USA) (Dynaformer (USA))
5551a^2 7563a^8

Stormy Morning *Philip Kirby* a69 66
7 ch g Nayef(USA) Sokoa (USA) (Peintre Celebre (USA))
(22) 430^2

Stormy Paradise (IRE) *Brian Meehan* 94
2 br c Excellent Art Stormy Larissa (IRE) (Royal Applause)
2250^8 (3275) 4031^3 (4703) 5313a^4 6328^6 7084a^4

Stormyra (FR) *J-P Gallorini* 105
2 gr f Stormy River(FR) One Day (FR) (Act One)
3752a^2 5555a^3 6249a^5 7055a^5 7571a^6

Stormy Weather (FR) *Brian Ellison* 92
7 gr g Highest Honor(FR) Stormy Moud (USA) (Storm Bird (CAN))
5147^7

Storyline (IRE) *Tim Easterby* 49
2 b f Kodiac Petite Histoire (IRE) (Desert Story (IRE))
6947^{10}

Story Of Dubai *M Weiss*
6 b m Dubai Destination(USA) Briery (IRE) (Salse (USA))
702a^5

Story Writer *William Knight* a83 67
4 b g Sakhee(USA) Celestial Princess (Observatory (USA))
63^2 342^2 637^5 925^2 1352^2 1899^7 2418^3 *3328^2 4166^2 5233^2* (5933)

Stosur (IRE) *Gay Kelleway* 88
2 b f Mount Nelson Jules (IRE) (Danehill (USA))
6409^3 ◆ 7320^3 7537^4 7695^9

Stout Cortez *Mark Johnston* a41 71
2 b g Hernando(FR) Zooming (IRE) (Indian Ridge)
7607^5 7773^2 *7955^5*

St Paul De Vence (IRE) *Paul Cole* a82 75
3 b g Oratorio(IRE) Ring The Relatives (Bering)
1725^7 2862^9 *3214^6*

St Paul'S (IRE) *David C Griffiths*
2 b c Bushranger(IRE) Regina Ballerina (IRE) (High Chaparral (IRE))
8346^7

Straight Gin *Alan Berry* 52
2 b g Major Cadeaux Nee Lemon Left (Puissance)
3767^5 4337^4 5578^4 6082^6 6467^6 6872^7

Straight Shot (IRE) *John Butler* a67 70
4 ch g Manduro(GER) Forest Express (AUS) (Kaaptive Edition (NZ))
6612^{11} 6932^{12}

Straight Thinking (USA) *A Fabre* 103
2 gr f Mizzen Mast(USA) Hachita (USA) (Gone West (USA))
5555a^2 6292a^2

Strait Of Zanzibar (USA) *K J Condon* a89 87
4 b g Arch(USA) Royal Opportunity (USA) (Kingmambo (USA))
3846a^{14} 4869a^{14}

Strait Run (IRE) *Richard Hannon Snr* 80
2 ch c Rock Of Gibraltar(IRE) Gentlemen's Guest (USA) (Gentlemen (ARG))
6953^7 (7500)

Straits Of Malacca *Kevin Ryan* 71
2 ch g Compton Place Cultural Role (Night Shift (USA))
3565^5 (4107) 5012^3 6187^7 7147^3

Strandfield Bay (IRE) *Sharon Watt* a68
7 b m Wizard King Stylish Chic (IRE) (Arazi (USA))
7885^6 8036^2 8200^2

Strandfield Lady (IRE) *H Rogers* a75 92
8 ch m Pairumani Star(IRE) Stylish Chic (IRE) (Arazi (USA))
4465a^5

Strangelittlegirl *Patrick Gilligan* a5
5 b f Shirocco(GER) Cephalonia (Slip Anchor)
1189^9

Strange Magic (IRE) *Richard Fahey* 92
3 b f Diamond Green(FR) Blue Daze (Danzero (AUS))
2669^{19} 3097^6 3562^{10} 4993^7 6212^7 6583^{18} 7313^{12}

Strassman *Mark Johnston* a51 45
2 b c Halling(USA) Jomana (IRE) (Darshaan)
4513^6 5262^3 *5922^8 6401^9* 6946^8

Strategic Action (IRE) *Linda Jewell* a63 62
4 ch g Strategic Prince Ruby Cairo (IRE) (Nashwan (USA))
158^4 (335) 805^5 1873^3 2533^{12} 2747^2 *3433^3* 3901^7 *6933^8* 7246^6 *7784^5 7980^7* 8073^{11} 8293^{12}

Strategical (USA) *Charlie Appleby* a93 100
2 b c More Than Ready(USA) Mary Ellise (USA) (In Excess)
4477^2 (5199) *(5590)* (5955)

Strategic Force (IRE) *Clive Cox* a51 16
2 b g Strategic Prince Mooching Along (IRE) (Mujahid (USA))
6589^{12} *7155^9*

Strategic Strike (IRE) *Paul Cole* a72 74
3 b g Strategic Prince Puteri Wentworth (Sadler's Wells (USA))
1300^4 1478^3 (1741) 2325^4 *3055^7* 3636^9 *3908^8* 4591^4 *6521^4* ◆ 7258^8

Strawberry Jam *Paul Cole* a76 67
3 b g Duke Of Marmalade(IRE) Farfala (FR) (Linamix (FR))
1679^{13} 1882^3 2442^{11} 3067^8 *5132^5 (5392)* 5719^4 *6136^5 6559^7*

Streak *David Lanigan* a66 59
3 b f Marju(IRE) Eliza Gilbert (Noverre (USA))
2156^4 3014^4

Stream Of Light *John Mackie* 39
2 b f Multiplex Flawspar (Montjoy (USA))
6949^{10} 7371^9

Street Act (USA) *A Al Raihe* a82 14
6 br g Street Cry(IRE) Cannons Crown (USA) (Best Of Luck (USA))
(7679a)

Street Artist (IRE) *Mark Johnston* a73 81
3 ch c Street Cry(IRE) Portrayal (USA) (Saint Ballado (CAN))
1069^2 2030^2 *2995^2* 3806^3 3982^5 4447^6

Street Band (IRE) *Johan Reuterskiold* 95
5 b g Desert Style(IRE) Savoy Street (Vettori (IRE))
3188a^7

Street Battle (USA) *Tony Coyle* a77 48
3 b g Street Boss(USA) J J's Kitty (USA) (Storm Cat (USA))
(324) 674^5 1307^4 1647^{10} *5676^{10}*

Street Boss (IRE) *Tim Easterby* 61
2 gr g Verglas(IRE) Gladstone Street (IRE) (Waajib)
2670^{11} 3588^3 3943^3 4618^8 5136^5 5858^5

Street Entertainer (IRE) *David Pipe* a83 78
6 br g Danehill Dancer(IRE) Opera Ridge (FR) (Indian Ridge)
(3133) 3284^4

Street Fight (CAN) *Gary Contessa* 83
4 b g Street Sense(USA) Reportedly (CAN) (Silver Deputy (CAN))
3361a^3

Street Force (USA) *Clive Brittain* 91
2 b c Street Cry(IRE) Maskunah (IRE) (Sadler's Wells (USA))
3290^4 3555^{13} 4296^4 4747^7 5400^3 5745^6 6303^9 6865^5

Street Girl (USA) *Manuel J Azpurua* a106
3 b f Street Hero(USA) Kristy Beethoven (USA) (Kris S (USA))
7691a^5

Streethowlingmama (USA) *William Jarvis* a3 39
2 bb f Street Cry(IRE) Mama Nadine (USA) (A.P. Indy (USA))
3049^9 5995^8 *6654^8*

Street Power (USA) *Jeremy Gask* a78 79
8 bb g Street Cry(IRE) Javana (USA) (Sandpit (BRZ))
881^6 1318^6 2128^6 2825^4 *5636^6 6526^8 7262^{11} 7880^5 8220^2 8456^4*

Street Runner *Karl Thornton* a59 63
7 b g Rainbow Quest(USA) Dansara (Dancing Brave (USA))
7382^2

Street Sailing (USA) *Richard C Mettee* 92
2 rg f Street Boss(USA) Sailing Free (USA) (Mizzen Mast (USA))
7690a^{13}

Strength And Honor (IRE) *Sir Michael Stoute* 16
3 b c Galileo(IRE) Kasora (IRE) (Darshaan)
1584^7

Stresa *John Gosden* a86 76
3 b f Pivotal Bay Tree (IRE) (Daylami (IRE))
2084^2 (2628) 3460^{16} *5134^4 6115^6*

Strictly Ballroom (IRE) *Mark Johnston* a75 78
3 b f Choisir(AUS) Desert Alchemy (IRE) (Green Desert (USA))
2158^4 2622^2 3053^3 4577^5 5125^{10} 6003^{10}

Strictly Glitz (IRE) *John Quinn* 55
2 b f Kodiac Dancing Steps (Zafonic (USA))
1605^9 3064^5 (3541) 6285^9 6494^3 6914^7

Strictly Silca *Mick Channon* a85 81
3 ch f Danehill Dancer(IRE) Silca Chiave (Pivotal)
1243^2 (3479) 4905^3 5308^5 5700^4 6642^{10} *7255^7 (8020)* ◆ *8391^4*

Strictly Silver (IRE) *Alan Bailey* a104 108
4 gr g Dalakhani(IRE) Miss Chaussini (IRE) (Rossini (USA))
401^2 (945) 1235^8 3564^7 3832^2 4060^8 4854^6 (5283) 5768^4 6838^{14} 7206^3 *7793^6*

Strike A Light *Rae Guest* 45
2 gr f Dutch Art Bridal Path (Groom Dancer (USA))
7125^6 7448^6

Strike Force *Alison Hutchinson* a82 65
9 b g Dansili Miswaki Belle (USA) (Miswaki (USA))
107^3 219^3 (329) (548) 691^7 759^6 2383^8 3106^{13} 3996^3 4584^3 4851^2 5384^6 5802^7 6071^4 6346^7

Strikemaster (IRE) *Lee James* a47 64
7 b g Xaar Mas A Fuera (IRE) (Alzao (USA))
3089^8 4204^3 4622^3 (5337) 5885^4

Striker Torres (IRE) *Daniel Mark Loughnane* a69 73
7 ch g Danehill Dancer(IRE) Silver Skates (IRE) (Slip Anchor)
1886^8 2551^{10} 2753^{10} 3543^9 *8341^8*

Strike The Stars (NZ) *Anthony Cummings* 104
5 bb g Savabeel(AUS) Ambitious (NZ) (Last Tycoon)
7826a^8

Striking Echo *Andrew Hollinshead* a69 22
3 b g Striking Ambition Sunderland Echo (IRE) (Tagula (IRE))
(673) 1832^{12} 2094^8 *7898^{10} 8401^{10}*

String Theory (IRE) *Marco Botti* a105 88
3 b c Medicean Shebelia (GER) (Black Sam Bellamy (IRE))
1635^3 ◆ *(1926)* ◆ 2526a^4 3484^{27} *(8263) (8398)*

Striving (GER) *H-A Pantall* 13
2 b c Konigstiger(GER) Stravina (GER) (Platini (GER))
4599a^9

Stroll On (IRE) *Rae Guest* 63
2 ch f Exceed And Excel(AUS) Violet (IRE) (Mukaddamah (USA))
5797^4 6517^4

Strong Conviction *Mick Channon* 79
3 ch g Piccolo Keeping The Faith (IRE) (Ajraas (USA))
(1293) 1683^2 1977^6 2584^4 3633^4 4306^2 4890^3 5440^6 6003^5 6335^2 6867^5

Stronger Than Me (IRE) *W T Farrell* a69 82
5 b g Marju(IRE) Easter Song (USA) (Rubiano (USA))
4465a^7

Strong Man *Michael Easterby* a76 76
5 b g Gentleman's Deal(IRE) Strong Hand (First Trump)
86^2 308^3 453^7 3068^9 3778^9 (4161) 4339^2 (4456) 5138^2 5711^8 6548^5 7824^{14} *8095^{12} 8198^2 8401^7*

Strong Mandate (USA) *D Wayne Lukas* a114
2 b c Tiznow(USA) Clear Mandate (USA) (Deputy Minister (CAN))
7711a^3

Strove For Gold (IRE) *Thomas McLaughlin* a53 58
8 b g Goldmark(USA) My Name's Not Bin (IRE) (Good Thyne (USA))
672^8 6985^7

Stubbs (IRE) *A P O'Brien* 101
2 b c Danehill Dancer(IRE) Moonstone (Dalakhani (IRE))
(2943a) 3422^6 7525^3

Stuccodor (IRE) *D K Weld* 106
4 b g Modigliani(USA) Armilina (FR) (Linamix (FR))
5019a^3 6025a^{16} 6440a^5

Studfarmer *John Panvert* a68 69
3 b g Multiplex Samadilla (IRE) (Mujadil (USA))
628^3 ◆ *843^4 982^5 1041^3* (1361) 1578^2 2393^5 2737^8 *7783^{10}*

Stun Gun *Derek Shaw* a66
3 b g Medicean Tapas En Bal (FR) (Mille Balles (FR))
8043^3 (8437)

St Vincent (IRE) *David Lanigan* a62 33
2 b g Danehill Dancer(IRE) Lace (IRE) (Sadler's Wells (USA))
2925^8 3245^{11} *3905^4 6605^{11} 6924^{10}*

Stybba *Andrew Balding* 52
2 b f Medicean Time Saved (Green Desert (USA))
6141^7 6821^7 7466^5

Style Vendome (FR) *N Clement* a107 115
3 gr c Anabaa(USA) Place Vendome (FR) (Dr Fong (USA))
(999a) (1357a) (2298a) 3876a^4 6450a^5 7059a^{11}

Stylistickhill (IRE) *Scott Dixon* a70 59
5 gr f Desert Style(IRE) Anemone (Arkadian Hero (USA))
410^3 548^3 753^5 866^6 1111^{14} *1736^4*

Sublimation (IRE) *David Barron* a78 89
3 ch g Manduro(GER) Meon Mix (Kayf Tara)
1008^2 1429^4 1684^2 (2960) ◆ 3563^6

Sublime Talent (IRE) *Evan Williams* a57 21
7 b g Sadler's Wells(USA) Summer Trysting (USA) (Alleged (USA))
6435^9

Submariner (USA) *A bin Huzaim* a102 95
7 ch g Singspiel(IRE) Neptune's Bride (USA) (Bering)
246a^{15}

Substantivo (IRE) *Alan Jarvis* a55 65
3 b g Duke Of Marmalade(IRE) Damson (IRE) (Entrepreneur)
2624^5 3241^{12} *5923^5 6400^{12} 8341^P*

Subtle Difference *Andrew Balding* a62
3 b f Vita Rosa(JPN) Sulitelma (USA) (The Minstrel (CAN))
14^2 134^2 411^2

Subtle Knife *Giles Bravery* a87 89
4 ch f Needwood Blade Northern Bows (Bertolini (USA))
5014[10]

Successful Year *Mark Johnston* a72
3 b c Distorted Humor(USA) Emotion Parade (ARG) (Parade Marshal (USA))
4151[5] ◆

Sudden Wish (IRE) *Gary Moore* a61 60
4 b f Jeremy(USA) Fun Time (Fraam)
89[8] 320[5] 375[3] 5092[2] ◆ (6103) 6554[5] 7090[3]

Sudden Wonder (IRE) *Charlie Appleby* 96
2 ch c New Approach(IRE) Dubai Surprise (IRE) (King's Best (USA))
3581[4] 5490[2] (7468)

Sudirman (USA) *David Wachman* 114
2 b c Henrythenavigator(USA) Shermeen (IRE) (Desert Style (IRE))
(3847a) (5319a) 6442a[2] 7191[5]

Suegioo (FR) *Marco Botti* a89 98
4 ch g Manduro(GER) Mantesera (IRE) (In The Wings)
1689[4] 2044[2] 3115[8] 4233[4] ◆ 5746[2] 6144[5] 6833[2]

Suehail *Robert Cowell* a87 69
4 b g Cadeaux Genereux Why Dubai (USA) (Kris S (USA))
7769[9] 8053[6] (8227) 8416[11]

Suffice (IRE) *Richard Fahey* a79 77
4 b g Iffraaj Shallat (IRE) (Pennekamp (USA))
140[2] (612) 1242[10] 1689[10] 2256[4] 2431[5] 3301[5] 3827[5]

Sufranel (IRE) *Marco Botti* a71
2 b c Galileo(IRE) Noelani (IRE) (Indian Ridge)
8123[2]

Sugar Blaze *Jim Goldie* 50
3 ch f Orientor Harrken Heights (IRE) (Belmez (USA))
1821[6] 2795[4] 3198[4]

Sugar Boy (IRE) *Marco Botti* a98 111
3 b c Authorized(IRE) Steel Princess (IRE) (Danehill (USA))
1558a[2] (1811) 3849a[9] 6742[7] 7535[5] 7927[8]

Sugar Coated (IRE) *Michael Bell* 56
3 b f Duke Of Marmalade(IRE) Crystal Curling (IRE) (Peintre Celebre (USA))
2231[12] 2455[8] 3194[5] 4405[4] 5979[5]

Sugarcraft (USA) *Charlie Appleby* 59
3 b f Bernardini(USA) Sugar Shake (USA) (Awesome Again (CAN))
3774[3] 5695[4]

Sugarformyhoney (IRE) *Brendan Powell* a79 70
4 ch f Dutch Art Sweetsformysweet (USA) (Forest Wildcat (USA))
421[4] (7836) 8134[5]

Sugar Hiccup (IRE) *Jim Best* a19 80
5 b f Refuse To Bend(IRE) Raysiza (IRE) (Alzao (USA))
8447[12]

Sugar House (USA) *Charlie Appleby* a79 77
3 ch f Distorted Humor(USA) Malibu Mint (USA) (Malibu Moon (USA))
4941[4] 5896[5]

Sugar Love (GER) *P Schiergen* 85
2 b f Elusive City(USA) Sugar Baby Love (GER) (Second Empire (IRE))
5939a[2]

Sugar Town *Peter Niven* a56
3 b f Elusive City(USA) Sweetsformysweet (USA) (Forest Wildcat (USA))
7884[3] 8043[4] 8348[5]

Suhailah *Michael Attwater* a45 32
7 ch m Sulamani(IRE) Vrennan (Suave Dancer (USA))
2159[11] 2777[9] 3473[8]

Suite (IRE) *Richard Hannon Snr* a80 88
2 b f Invincible Spirit(IRE) Rakiza (IRE) (Elnadim (USA))
(1924) 2414[2] 3522[15] 4948[6] 6326[6] 6795[7]

Suited And Booted (IRE) *M Al Muhairi* a85 77
6 ch h Tagula(IRE) Carpet Lady (IRE) (Night Shift (USA))
(394a)

Suits Me *David Barron* a106 99
10 ch g Bertolini(USA) Fancier Bit (Lion Cavern (USA))
(2958) 3346[6] 4342[3] 4825[2] 5838[6] 6300[8] 6792[5]

Suitsus *Peter Makin* a67 21
2 b g Virtual Point Perfect (Dansili)
7251[8] 7647[6] 7978[2]

Sujet Bellagio *Damian Joseph English* a70 78
4 b g Acclamation Markova's Dance (Mark Of Esteem (IRE))
8002[10]

Sukari Gold (IRE) *Tom Dascombe* a41 57
2 b f Kodiac Storm Lady (IRE) (Alhaarth (IRE))
3077[7] 4616[2] 5053[5] 6047[7] 6279[3] 6494[2] 7198[7] 7604[7]

Sula Two *Ron Hodges* a71 90
6 b m Sulamani(IRE) There's Two (IRE) (Ashkalani (IRE))
1884[3] 2520[7] 2939[8] 3856[2] (4530) 4873[7] 6237[8] (6591) 6992[5]

Sulis Minerva (IRE) *Jeremy Gask* a92 80
6 b m Arakan(USA) Lacinia (Groom Dancer (USA))
78[4] 405[5] 586[7] 723[3] 1160[3] 1370[5] 1581[6] 1878[9] 2441[15] 2745[3] 3236[2] 4017[3] 4368[4] 8324[9]

Sullivan Park *Ian McInnes* 21
2 b f Haatef(USA) Fee Faw Fum (IRE) (Great Commotion (USA))
1605[8] 1960[7]

Sullivan Street (IRE) *Charlie Appleby* a72 69
2 ch c Street Cry(IRE) Utrecht (Rock Of Gibraltar (IRE))
5279[4] 6014[3] 6256[3] 7088[9] 7202[3]

Sultanah Heyam *William Haggas* a69 68
3 br f Manduro(GER) Royal Secrets (IRE) (Highest Honor (FR))
1876[4] ◆ 2938[4] 3618[3] 4634[5] 5130[8]

Sultanty *Kevin Ryan* a56
2 b f Shamardal(USA) Caught On Camera (Red Ransom (USA))
7294[7] 7493[13]

Sultry Lady *Jamie Poulton*
3 b f Pastoral Pursuits Naemi (GER) (Tannenkonig (IRE))
5959[4]

Sumaro (GER) *W Hickst* a91 82
6 b h Big Shuffle(USA) Sarir (GER) (Platini (GER))
127a[9]

Sumatra Tiger (GER) *P Vovcenko* a77 77
8 b g Tiger Hill(IRE) Sohaila (GER) (Owington)
514a[12] 701a[P]

Summer Applause (USA) *Chad C Brown* a109
4 b f Harlan's Holiday(USA) Summer Exhibition (USA) (Royal Academy (USA))
7709a[4]

Summer Dancer (IRE) *Paul Midgley* a67 74
9 br g Fasliyev(USA) Summer Style (IRE) (Indian Ridge)
1462[6] 2081[5] 2565[9] 3192[8] 4375[5] 4967[7] 5341[3] 6083[2] (6464) 6721[7]

Summer Dream (IRE) *Marco Botti* a78 75
3 b f Oasis Dream Star On Stage (Sadler's Wells (USA))
1612[5] 2010[7] 2806[2] 4354[3] 5353[3] 6341[4] 6734[9] 7486[7]

Summer Fall (USA) *B Grizzetti* 94
4 rg f Mizzen Mast(USA) Momix (Selkirk (USA))
7234a[3] 7414a[5]

Summerfree (USA) *Mark Johnston* a69 59
3 bb g Medaglia d'Oro(USA) Summer Flash (USA) (Belong To Me (USA))
6696[8] 7311[5] 7488[3]

Summer In February *Nikki Evans* a23 40
3 b f Sixties Icon Endless Love (IRE) (Dubai Destination (USA))
5386[8] 7154[9] 7791[8]

Summerinthecity (IRE) *David Nicholls* a81 98
6 ch g Indian Ridge Miss Assertive (Zafonic (USA))
104[2] 217[7] 1830[2] 1963[3] (2647) 3114[12] 3823[11] 4285[4] 4780[2] 5545[5] ◆ 6183[11] 6608[10] 6845[5]

Summerlea (IRE) *Patrick Holmes* a65 60
7 ch g Alhaarth(IRE) Verbania (IRE) (In The Wings)
2313[4] 2831[3] 3625[6] 6290[13] 6470[6]

Summerling (IRE) *Jonathan Portman* 13
2 br f Excellent Art Sun Seasons (IRE) (Salse (USA))
6641[10]

Summer School (IRE) *Mark Johnston* a86
3 b f Street Cry(IRE) Measured Tempo (Sadler's Wells (USA))
(8200)

Summer Sun *Phil McEntee* a54 50
4 b f Oratorio(IRE) Woodland Glade (Mark Of Esteem (IRE))
19[2] 114[4] 276[7] 471[7]

Sum Of The Parts (USA) *Thomas Amoss* a113 100
4 bb c Speightstown(USA) Enjoy The Moment (USA) (Slew's Royalty (USA))
7713a[12]

Sun And Stars *Brendan Powell* a35 38
5 ch g Haafhd Leading Role (Cadeaux Genereux)
2321[10] 2746[10] 3011[6] 8065[6]

Sunblazer (IRE) *William Muir* a84 83
3 gr g Dark Angel(IRE) Damask Rose (IRE) (Dr Devious (IRE))
2500[5] 3055[5] 3653[2] (4349) 4899[3] 5390[4] 5888[4] 6363[3] 6629[2] 7105[3] (7510)

Sunbula (USA) *Charles Hills* a78 77
3 ch f Singspiel(IRE) Uroobah (USA) (Dynaformer (USA))
1876[2] 3530[2] (4223) 4634[3] 5483[8]

Sun Central (IRE) *William Haggas* 117
4 ch c Galileo(IRE) Bordighera (USA) (Alysheba (USA))
(2052) 3099[2] (4309) (5993)

Sunday Dream (FR) *M Gentile* a88
3 b c Sunday Break(JPN) Lyphard's Dream (IRE) (Lyphard (USA))
782a[8]

Sunday Meadow (IRE) *William Knight* 56
4 b f Dylan Thomas(IRE) Angel Rose (IRE) (Definite Article)
3272[5] 4633[10] 5093[8]

Sun Dream *Tony Carroll* a46 64
6 b m Desert Sun I Have A Dream (SWE) (Mango Express)
41[8] 220[5] 456[5] 631[10]

Sundream (GER) *G Macaire* 96
5 b g Lomitas Salista (GER) (Heraldiste (USA))
(5464a)

Suni Dancer *Paul Green* a28 49
2 b f Captain Gerrard(IRE) Sunisa (IRE) (Daggers Drawn (USA))
5025[9] 5299[9] 5364[8] 5898[8] 6725[7] 6755[2] 7032[8] 7944[7]

Sunnandaeg *Keith Dalgleish* 80
6 ch g Haafhd Come Away With Me (IRE) (Machiavellian (USA))
1994[10]

Sunningdale Rose (IRE) *Gay Kelleway* a53 59
2 b f Art Connoisseur(IRE) Eloquent Rose (IRE) (Elnadim (USA))
1910[3] 2230[4] 7448[7] 7844[4] 8228[6]

Sunny Bank *Alan Coogan* a58 58
4 b g Notnowcato Sweet Mandolin (Soviet Star (USA))
1161[7] 1333[7] 1916[13]

Sunnybridge Boy (IRE) *K R Burke* 84
4 br g Strategic Prince Reem One (IRE) (Rainbow Quest (USA))
1448[9] 1936[2] 2673[4] 3349[19] 5050[7] 5802[9] 6759[2] 7027[2]

Sunny Cat (FR) *C Gourdain* a66 43
5 b g Until Sundown(USA) Heat Storm (USA) (Storm Cat (USA))
6058a[4]

Sunny Future (IRE) *Malcolm Saunders* a26 81
7 b g Masterful(USA) Be Magic (Persian Bold)
1899[3] 2587[9] (3180) 3856[3] (4305) (4775) 5475[5] 6424[6] 6992[10] 7217[9] 7396[7]

Sunny Harbor (IRE) *David O'Meara* 80
2 b f Indian Haven Kathy Sun (IRE) (Intikhab (USA))
(2751) ◆ 3829[9]

Sunny Hollow *James Toller* a58 57
3 b f Beat Hollow Corndavon (USA) (Sheikh Albadou)
2528[10] 3016[3] 3679[2] 4654[6] 5981[6] 6849[2] 7124[9] 7508[8]

Sunny Reagh *Tim Etherington*
8 ch m Presidium Owenreagh (IRE) (Glacial Storm (USA))
2833[10]

Sunny Side Up (IRE) *Richard Fahey* a66 83
4 b f Refuse To Bend(IRE) Feeling Wonderful (IRE) (Fruits Of Love (USA))
2755[4] 3299[9] 4017[8] 4580[4] 6848[7] 7281[3] 7593[2]

Sunraider (IRE) *Paul Midgley* a47 86
6 b g Namid Doctrine (Barathea (IRE))
966[8] 1460[3] 2663[11] 3068[5] (3462) (3714) 4138[4] 4444[2] 4730[10] 5705[5] 5971[13] 6908[7]

Sunrise Dance *Robert Johnson* a78 83
4 ch f Monsieur Bond(IRE) Wachiwi (IRE) (Namid)
214[3] 558[2] (760) 2166[5] 2542[4] 3090[4] (3446) 3778[4] 4620[2] (5011) 5294[9] 5971[3] 6209[6] 6665[11] 7594[9]

Sunrise Star *Lady Cecil* 80
2 b f Shamardal(USA) Tudor Court (IRE) (Cape Cross (IRE))
3057[4] 3605[3] 5797[2]

Sunset Shore *Sir Mark Prescott Bt* a79 73
2 b f Oasis Dream Summer Night (Nashwan (USA))
2740[7] 3049[3] 3510[2] (3673) 4134[6] 4363[2] 5396[2] 5976[3] 7349[2] 7626[6] 8261[5]

Sunshine Always (IRE) *Michael Attwater* a76 26
7 gr g Verglas(IRE) Easy Sunshine (IRE) (Sadler's Wells (USA))
80[3]

Sunshine Superman *Bill Turner* a45 39
2 ch c Captain Gerrard(IRE) Miss Dunwoody (Classic Cliche (IRE))
1208[4] 1285[4]

Suns Out Guns Out (USA) *Dale Romans* a101
4 b c Empire Maker(USA) Angel Arch (USA) (Smart Strike (CAN))
7687a[4]

Suntracer (USA) *Chris Block* a100 104
5 ch c Kitten's Joy(USA) Taxable Deduction (USA) (Prized (USA))
5550a[2]

Sun Valley *Anthony Carson* 44
3 ch f Three Valleys(USA) Tanasie (Cadeaux Genereux)
2746[7] 5201[3]

Supachap *Hughie Morrison* a57 70
2 br g High Chaparral(IRE) Supamova (USA) (Seattle Slew (USA))
7070[8] 7461[7] 7773[3]

Supa Seeker (USA) *Tony Carroll* a53 56
7 bb g Petionville(USA) Supamova (USA) (Seattle Slew (USA))
456[7] 522[3] 703[6] 900[3] 975[2] 1093[8] 3244[3] (3513) 3700[3] 5172[3] 6102[7] 6472[3] 7636[5]

Supastarqueen (USA) *Brian Baugh* a22
5 bb f El Corredor(USA) Supamova (USA) (Seattle Slew (USA))
28[7] 377[6] 911[9]

Supa U *Tim Easterby* a65 66
2 b f Authorized(IRE) Supa Sal (King's Best (USA))
2502[2] 3064[3] 4044[5] 4756[7] 6047[2] 6724[2] 7418[6] 7883[2] 8005[4]

Super Blue Cat (USA) *J Heloury* a55
3 b c Bluegrass Cat(USA) Supergirl (USA) (Woodman (USA))
605a[8]

Superboot (IRE) *Michael Wigham* 91
3 b g Holy Roman Emperor(IRE) Balting Lass (IRE) (Orpen (USA))
2650[3] 3109[3] 4058[5] 4981[5] 5616[3] 6235[12]

Superciliary *Chris Gordon* a67 69
4 b g Dansili Supereva (IRE) (Sadler's Wells (USA))
4679[5] 5403[5] (6404) 7305[6] 7539[10]

Super Collider *Susan Corbett* a68 79
6 b g Montjeu(IRE) Astorg (USA) (Lear Fan (USA))
5828[9]

Super Cookie *Philip McBride* a68 70
3 b f Dylan Thomas(IRE) Dance Lesson (In The Wings)
2156[5] 2743[10] 3666[2] (3995) 4508[7] 5492[7] 7437[6]

Super Cool (AUS) *Mark Kavanagh* 116
4 b g Fastnet Rock(AUS) Queen Mother (USA) (Kingmambo (USA))
7556a[5] 7761a[9]

Supercruiser (IRE) *Nigel Tinkler* a4 39
3 b g Majestic Missile(IRE) Balance The Books (Elmaamul (USA))
1539[10] 1762[11]

Super Duplex *Roger Teal* a71 71
6 b g Footstepsinthesand Penelope Tree (IRE) (Desert Prince (IRE))
344[2] 639[4] 1059[5] 1304[10] 1985[8] 2395[11] (2954) 4126[8] 4441[4] 4679[7] 7439[5] 7858[6] 7984[6]

Superior Duchess *Michael Blanshard* a29 57
8 b m Superior Premium Downclose Duchess (King's Signet (USA))
6986[11] 7728[12]

Superior Edge *Christopher Mason* a53 68
6 b m Exceed And Excel(AUS) Beveled Edge (Beveled (USA))
1952[2] 2364[10] 2918[12] 3667[9] 5094[6] 6156[7] 6436[8]

Super Moment (IRE) *Saeed bin Suroor* 64
2 b f Oasis Dream Philae (USA) (Seeking The Gold (USA))
6974[6] 7533[5]

Supernova Heights (IRE) *Brian Meehan* a71 97
3 b f Oasis Dream Athene (IRE) (Rousillon (USA))
2453[10] 2928[2] 3784[7] 4252[11] 4671[9] 6524[8]

Superoo (IRE) *Mark Johnston* a35 40
3 ch g Bahamian Bounty Roo (Rudimentary (USA))
1759[13] 2095[10]

Superplex (FR) *M Figge* 110
3 b c Multiplex Salute The Sun (FR) (Fly To The Stars)
2035a[4] 2907a[11] (3911a) 5462a[8] 6451a[11] 7049a[11]

Super Say (IRE) *Michael Appleby* a95 86
7 ch g Intikhab(USA) Again Royale (IRE) (Royal Academy (USA))
897[7] 1159[9] 1501[8] 1728[5] 3204[7] 3607[7] (5847) 6236[12] 6976[6] 7793[4] 7990[4] 8387[4]

Supersonic Flight (GER) *M Rulec* a95 103
6 ch h Lomitas So Royal (GER) (Royal Solo (IRE))
2492a[2]

Supersta *Ronald Harris* 74
2 ch c Pivotal Resort (Oasis Dream)
4795[4] 5122[3] 5727[6] 6303[4] 7209[2] 7451[14]

Superstition *Michael Madgwick* a52
4 b f Red Ransom(USA) Go Supersonic (Zafonic (USA))
417[14] 579[14] 1953[7]

Super Test (ITY) *M Oppo* 97
4 b g Altieri Mien Toujours (IRE) (Intikhab (USA))
2698a[5] 7725a[9]

Super Winnie (FR) *P Cottier* a73 71
3 b c Super Celebre(FR) Scarborough (FR) (Starborough)
818a[2]

Supplicant *Richard Fahey* 111
2 b c Kyllachy Pious (Bishop Of Cashel)
(2337) 3079[3] ◆ 3424[2] 4855[5] (5547) (5837) (6637) 7191[6]

Supreme Luxury (IRE) *Kevin Ryan* a71 74
4 b f Iffraaj Stay Hernanda (Hernando (FR))
2220[8] 2704[6] 3977[3]

Supreme Warrior (NZ) *Leon Corstens* 91
5 bb g Golan(IRE) Paierau Princess (NZ) (Wallenda (USA))
7417a[6]

Suprise Vendor (IRE) *Stuart Coltherd* a76 43
7 ch g Fath(USA) Dispol Jazz (Alhijaz)
3504[10] 3709[7]

Suraj *Michael Bell* 103
4 ch g Galileo(IRE) Maid Of Killeen (IRE) (Darshaan)
2149[10] 3423[11] 4857[3] 5655[11] 6192[8]

Surcingle (USA) *Sir Michael Stoute* 78
2 b f Empire Maker(USA) Promising Lead (Danehill (USA))
(6281) ◆ 7695[7]

Sure Fire (GER) *David Evans* a49 24
8 b g Monsun(GER) Suivez (FR) (Fioravanti (USA))
5093[7] 5592[3] 5672[7] 6696[14]

Sureness (IRE) *Marco Botti* 80
3 ch f Hurricane Run(IRE) Silk Dress (IRE) (Gulch (USA))
2389[9] 2803[7] 3764[6] 4436[2] (4715) (5410) 6832[6]

Surety (IRE) *Clive Brittain* 58
2 b c Cape Cross(IRE) Guarantia (Selkirk (USA))
2758[5]

Surfer (USA) *S Seemar* a109 109
4 ch g Distorted Humor(USA) Surf Club (USA) (Ocean Crest (USA))
556a[2] 958a[4] 1262a[7]

Surge Ahead (IRE) *Ed Walker* a80 80
3 b g Danehill Dancer(IRE) Croisiere (USA) (Capote (USA))
1477[4] 2056[4] 2408[5] 3472[10] 3956[2] 5511[7]

Surrey Dream (IRE) *John Bridger* a47 64
4 b g Oasis Dream Trois Graces (USA) (Alysheba (USA))
441[12] 530[12] 655[8] 1162[8] 2051[11] 2529[3] 2588[6] 3051[4] 3326[10] 3657[3] 3922[5] 4517[6] (4660) 5166[4] 5525[6] 6033[3] 6462[5] 7068[6] 7323[11] 7644[9] 8393[5]

Surround Sound *Tim Easterby* 72
3 b g Multiplex Tintera (IRE) (King's Theatre (IRE))
1764[2] (1966) 2627[5] 3067[7] 3730[2] 7024[14]

Surspenders (FR) *S Wattel* 79
2 b c Whipper(USA) Lanciana (IRE) (Acatenango (GER))
7828a[10]

Survived *William Haggas* 90
2 b f Kyllachy Regina (Green Desert (USA))
2601[2] (3049) 3459[6] 4025[4] 4486[3]

Sushi Tuna *F Rohaut* 95
3 ch f Halling(USA) Sleeping Storm (IRE) (Danehill Dancer (IRE))
1602a[7]

Susiescot (IRE) *W McCreery* a62 83
4 gr f Verglas(IRE) Princess Susie (IRE) (Spectrum (IRE))
1168a[9] 5775a[21]

Suspension *Hughie Morrison* a61 56
3 b f Avonbridge Summertime Parkes (Silver Patriarch (IRE))
717[2] 1190[5] 2330[4] 2802[3] 3376[6] 4625[3] 5791[3] 6700[4]

Suspicieuse (FR) *W Walton* a94 103
3 b f Elusive City(USA) Seditieuse (IRE) (Night Shift (USA))
782a[6]

Susukino (FR) *S Kobayashi* a68 71
4 gr f Great Journey(JPN) Sapporo (FR) (Smadoun (FR))
7573a[7]

Sutton Sid *Chris Gordon* a63 63
3 ch g Dutch Art Drastic Measure (Pivotal)
1312a[6] 1712[12] (1982) 2709[5] 3040[4] 3495[9] 4345[3] 4664[4] 5002[5] (6406) 7091[5] 7321[2] 7922[2] 8121[11]

Sutton Sioux *Jeremy Gask* a42 35
2 b f Sleeping Indian Once Removed (Distant Relative)
6423[9] 6746[9] 7261[10]

Suzi's A Class Act *Paul D'Arcy* a68 87
5 gr f Act One Latour (Sri Pekan (USA))
4920[8] 5288[11] 5868[8]

Suzi's Connoisseur *Mark Johnston* 96
2 b g Art Connoisseur(IRE) Suzi Spends (IRE) (Royal Applause)
(2314) 2877[4] 3079[5] (3801) 5272[2] 5656[7] (5939a) 6328[16] 7333[8]

Swale Star *Seamus Mullins* a50
2 b f Three Valleys(USA) Salim Toto (Mtoto)
2774[6] 8328[9]

Swan Lakes (IRE) *David Simcock* a77
2 gr f Dalakhani(IRE) Rock Salt (Selkirk (USA))
7260[2]

Swan Song *Andrew Balding* 97
4 br f Green Desert(USA) Lochsong (Song)
1662[6] 2019[7] 3046[11] 4800[13] 5257[3] (5821) 6305[10]

Swanwick Shore (IRE) *Richard Hannon Snr* 48
2 b c Tagula(IRE) Cinzia Vegas (IRE) (Dr Fong (USA))
7500[7]

Sweeney Todd *John Best*
2 b g Refuse To Bend(IRE) Ashantiana (Ashkalani (IRE))
3972[7]

Sweeping Rock (IRE) *Marcus Tregoning* a60 59
3 b g Rock Of Gibraltar(IRE) Sweeping Story (USA) (End Sweep (USA))
5743[8] *6081[5] 6558[4] 7331[12]*

Sweeping Up *Hughie Morrison* 73
2 b f Sea The Stars(IRE) Farfala (FR) (Linamix (FR))
6281[2] ◆ 6949[3]

Sweet Acclaim (IRE) *Noel Quinlan* 96
2 b f Acclamation Wildsplash (USA) (Deputy Minister (CAN))
(5797) 6795[3]

Sweet Alabama *Rod Millman* a52 45
3 gr f Johannesburg(USA) Alybgood (CAN) (Alydeed (CAN))
1095[3] 1423[11] 1747[5] 2124[5] 2743[4] 3041[9] 3376[7] 4604[8]

Sweet Alibi (IRE) *J S Moore* a61 62
2 b f Lawman(FR) Zingari (Groom Dancer (USA))
2283[4] 2382[7] 3107[4] 3829[11] 4277[5] (5213a) 5773a[16] *8452[8]*

Sweet Amaalie (IRE) *William Haggas* a54 40
2 b f Royal Applause Amalie (IRE) (Fasliyev (USA))
4484[11] *6107[9]* 6517[9] *6979[3] 7199[5]*

Sweet Angelica *James Given* a54 65
2 ch f Pastoral Pursuits Glencal (Compton Place)
6607[11] 7126[3] 7419[4] *7986[10] 8188[3] 8317[9] 8405[4]*

Sweet Annathea (IRE) *Thomas Cleary* a61 61
4 b m Barathea(IRE) On The Horizon (IRE) (Definite Article)
679a[13] 6089a[7]

Sweet Charlie *Mike Murphy* a31
2 b f Myboycharlie(IRE) Play Around (IRE) (Niniski (USA))
8175[8]

Sweet Cherry (IRE) *Pat Murphy* a59
2 b f Mastercraftsman(IRE) Dear Gracie (IRE) (In The Wings)
7501[10] *8145[5]*

Sweet Deal (IRE) *Jeremy Noseda* a89 88
3 gr g Verglas(IRE) Compromise (FR) (Fasliyev (USA))
5743[4] ◆ (6743) *7330[2]*

Sweet Emma Rose (USA) *Wesley A Ward* 99
2 b f City Zip(USA) Miss Moneypenny (USA) (Deputy Minister (CAN))
3459[2]

Sweet Force *Marco Botti* a60
3 b c Beat Hollow Sweet Power (Pivotal)
(122)

Sweetheart Abbey *William Knight* a55 49
2 b f Dancing Spree(USA) Hinton Pearl (Loch Pearl)
6378[7] *7119[8] 7764[13]*

Sweetie Royale (IRE) *John Wainwright* 14
4 b f King's Best(USA) Halomix (Linamix (FR))
6415 2164[8]

Sweet Lavender (IRE) *Michael Wigham* a71 19
5 b f Dalakhani(IRE) Dievotchkina (IRE) (Bluebird (USA))
107[7]

Sweet Liberta (IRE) *Andrew Balding* a72 58
4 b f Cape Cross(IRE) Hendrina (IRE) (Daylami (IRE))
(94) (201) 338[3] 528[4]

Sweet Lightning *David O'Meara* a101 112
8 b g Fantastic Light(USA) Sweetness Herself (Unfuwain (USA))
(1168a) ◆ 1556a[4] 2288a[3] 3458[20] 4696a[4] 6025a[7] *7361a[4] 8301[11]*

Sweet Lily Pea (USA) *Olly Stevens* a43 55
2 ch f Hard Spun(USA) Tree Pipit (USA) (Woodman (USA))
6690[12] 7069[5] *7461[10]*

Sweet Louise (IRE) *Barry Brennan* a44 50
3 b f Azamour(IRE) Maria Luisa (IRE) (King's Best (USA))
3530[7] 4590[10] *6522[10] 6964[9] 8302[8]*

Sweet Lulu (USA) *Jerry Hollendorfer* a110
3 ch f Mr Greeley(USA) Successful Outlook (USA) (Orientate (USA))
7709a[5]

Sweet Martoni *William Knight* a74 74
3 b f Dubawi(IRE) Sweetness Herself (Unfuwain (USA))
2192[4] 2606[11] 3251[3] *4150[5] 5001[2]* 5795[5] *6081[3]* 6978[6] *7439[9]*

Sweet Marwell (IRE) *Jo Crowley* a62
3 b f Excellent Art Bee Eater (IRE) (Green Desert (USA))
3435[9] 4382[5] 8427[4]

Sweetnessandlight *Jason Ward* a67 100
4 b f Aussie Rules(USA) Taschlynn (IRE) (Second Empire (IRE))
2928[3] 3456[7] 4137[6] 4433[2] 4705[7] 5255[8] 5684[4]

Sweetness Lady *Olly Stevens* a60
2 ch f Sleeping Indian Eforetta (GER) (Dr Fong (USA))
8084[7] 8326[4] 8451[4]

Sweet Ovation *Mark Usher* a68 56
4 b f Royal Applause Sweetest Revenge (IRE) (Daggers Drawn (USA))
560[4] 750[7] 998[5] (1196) ◆ *1472[6]* 3181[6] *3499[7] 4148[11]*

Sweet P *Marcus Tregoning* a68 63
2 b f Sir Percy Desert Run (IRE) (Desert Prince (IRE))
6141[6] 6460[4] 7087[2] *(7441) 7892[7]*

Sweet Reason (USA) *Leah Gyarmati* a112
2 b f Street Sense(USA) Livermore Leslie (USA) (Mt. Livermore (USA))
7707a[4]

Sweet Summer *John Holt*
2 ch f Sakhee(USA) Sweet Reply (Opening Verse (USA))
8297[5]

Sweet Talking Guy (IRE) *Lydia Pearce* a61 57
3 b g Oratorio(IRE) Sweet Namibia (IRE) (Namid)
2455[7] 2931[8] 3922[3] (4388) 5128[10] *6138[2]* 7109[13]

Sweet Vintage (IRE) *Mark Brisbourne* a61 49
3 b f Singspiel(IRE) Sauterne (Rainbow Quest (USA))
1225[5] 1747[4] 2274[5] 3137[12] *5923[10]* 6319[3] 6630[5] *(7644) 7966[4] 8278[2]*

Swehan (IRE) *Kevin Ryan* a75 65
3 b g Diamond Green(FR) Golden (FR) (Sanglamore (USA))
6050[2] 6498[9] *7781[3] (7983) 8453[5]*

Sweltering (FR) *P Monfort* a84 88
2 b f Zambezi Sun Pragmatica (Inchinor)
7940a[5]

Swendab (IRE) *John O'Shea* a69 92
5 b g Trans Island Lavish Spirit (USA) (Southern Halo (USA))
95[4] 354[6] 616[6] 1952[3] 2736[6] 3042[5] 3270[5] (3887) ◆ 3949[2] 4120[2] 4487[2] (5036) (5155) 5696[9] 5998[6] 6719[7]

Sweni Hill (IRE) *Y De Nicolay* a71 69
3 b f Danehill Dancer(IRE) Nancy Spain (IRE) (Sadler's Wells (USA))
1756a[9] 2434a[8] 3166a[5]

Swift Blade (IRE) *Lady Herries* a75 76
5 ch g Exceed And Excel(AUS) Gold Strike (IRE) (Rainbow Quest (USA))
4832[3] 6068[6] *7863[3] 8331[10] (8447)*

Swift Bounty *Alan Jarvis* a81 84
3 ch c Bahamian Bounty Famcred (Inchinor)
2209[4] 2584[5] 3763[4] 4416[3] (5218) 5534[7]

Swift Cedar (IRE) *Alan Jarvis* a76 85
3 ch c Excellent Art Ravish (Efisio)
1612[7] ◆ 1770[4] (3242) (3828) 4641[4] 5268[9] 6337[4] *7988[10] 8339[4]*

Swift Code (IRE) *Nigel Tinkler* 10
3 br g Elnadim(USA) Gradetime (IRE) (Danetime (IRE))
1392[10] 4627[6] 5054[8] 6289[14]

Swift Encounter (IRE) *Ann Duffield* 62
4 bb g Antonius Pius(USA) Eucalyptus Hill (USA) (Peaks And Valleys (USA))
2961[5] 3595[5] 4010[6] 4995[8] 7151[8]

Swiftly Done (IRE) *Declan Carroll* a74 100
6 b g Whipper(USA) Ziffany (Taufan (USA))
1235[14] 3346[8] 3869a[5] 4869a[15] 5268[7] 5546[13] *6167[10]* (6288) 6550[4] 7172[14] 7337[6] 7696[4] 7820[15]

Swilken *Mark H Tompkins* a74
2 ch c Halling(USA) Azure Mist (Bahamian Bounty)
7606[6] *7860[2]*

Swilly Ferry (USA) *David Nicholls* a82 65
6 b g Wiseman's Ferry(USA) Keepers Hill (IRE) (Danehill (USA))
1644[9] 2275[15]

Swindy *Sue Smith* a87 33
5 b g Hurricane Run(IRE) Red Passion (USA) (Seeking The Gold (USA))
6563[13]

Swing Alone (IRE) *Gay Kelleway* a96 96
4 b g Celtic Swing Groupetime (USA) (Gilded Time (USA))
1036[2] (1159) 2191[4] 2813[4] 3503[2] 4601a[3] *8218[2] 8398[4]*

Swing Easy *Robert Mills* a92 95
3 b c Zamindar(USA) Shahmina (IRE) (Danehill (USA))
(867) (2054) ◆

Swinging Hawk (GER) *Ian Williams* a82 86
7 ch g Hawk Wing(USA) Saldenschwinge (GER) (In The Wings)
(2648) 4233[9] 5514[4] 6668[3] (6833) 7193[15] *8202[5] 8429[7]*

Swinging Song *M Delzangles* a73 90
2 b f Mr. Sidney(USA) Singing Machine (USA) (Rossini (USA))
5628a[8]

Swinging Sultan *Keith Reveley* 94
6 b g Sulamani(IRE) Nobratinetta (FR) (Celtic Swing)
1282[6] 1804[4] (2590) ◆ (2855) 3208[4]

Swiss Cross *Phil McEntee* a103 99
6 b g Cape Cross(IRE) Swiss Lake (USA) (Indian Ridge)
78[6] 319[7] 480[5] 584[10] 776[8] 1607[6] 1765[4] ◆ 1913[5] 2046[6]

Swiss Kiss *John Gosden* 64
2 br f Dansili Swiss Lake (USA) (Indian Ridge)
3057[10]

Swiss Spirit *John Gosden* 116
4 b c Invincible Spirit(IRE) Swiss Lake (USA) (Indian Ridge)
2368[7] 2662[2] ◆ 3420[8] 4947[2] 5726[12] 6193[13]

Switcharooney (IRE) *Tom Dascombe* a44 66
3 b g Bahamian Bounty Amazon Beauty (IRE) (Wolfhound (USA))
1678[8] 2306[10] 3901[9] 4515[5] *5073[7]*

Switcher (IRE) *Richard Fahey* a80 105
4 b f Whipper(USA) Bahamamia (Vettori (IRE))
1255a[4] *1544[7]* 3822[6] 5763[3] 6327[2] 6796[11] 7015[10]

Switch On *Chris Wall* a46 39
3 b g Oasis Dream Noodle Soup (USA) (Alphabet Soup (USA))
1481[8] 2547[8] *2952[10] 6361[4] 7034[3]*

Swnymor (IRE) *Rebecca Curtis* 93
4 b g Dylan Thomas(IRE) Propaganda (IRE) (Sadler's Wells (USA))
7823[6]

Swooning (IRE) *H-A Pantall* a91 98
3 ch f Raven's Pass(USA) Rosa Parks (Sadler's Wells (USA))
7085a[14]

Swordbearer *James Fanshawe* a61
2 ch g Selkirk(USA) Isis (USA) (Royal Academy (USA))
6922[6]

Swordhalf *A Wohler* a88 94
3 b f Haafhd Sword Roche (GER) (Laroche (GER))
3146a[10] 7831a[5]

Sword In Hand *Alan Jarvis* a76 81
4 b g Exceed And Excel(AUS) Valhalla Moon (USA) (Sadler's Wells (USA))
1500[7] 2232[7] 2659[9] 5474[4] 6306[9] 7319[2]

Sword Of Light (IRE) *David Marnane* a72 82
3 b g Kodiac Bird In Blue (IRE) (Bluebird (USA))
2374a[12]

Sword Of The Lord *Michael Bell* a68 76
3 b g Kheleyf(USA) Blue Echo (Kyllachy)
5275[2] *5923[2]* 6153[5] (7093) (7322)

Swords *Ray Peacock* a47 47
11 b g Vettori(IRE) Pomorie (IRE) (Be My Guest (USA))
6130[10]

Sworn Vow (IRE) *John Gosden* 51
2 b c Yeats(IRE) Aitch (IRE) (Alhaarth (IRE))
7128[7] *7513[P]* (Dead)

Sybilicious *Stuart Williams* 32
2 b f Royal Applause Tora Bora (Grand Lodge (USA))
7448[9]

Sydney James (IRE) *Lee Carter* a62 14
2 b g Thousand Words Blue Bamboo (Green Desert (USA))
5307[11] *6132[5] 6747[6] (7156) 7352[6] 8086[2] 8311[4]*

Sygnature *Alan Swinbank* a54 66
4 b g Authorized(IRE) Perfect Story (IRE) (Desert Story (IRE))
145[6] 646[6] 5897[8]

Sylvan Spirit (IRE) *Roger Teal* a19
2 gr f Camacho Spree (IRE) (Dansili)
7737[5]

Sylvia Pankhurst (IRE) *David C Griffiths* a84 80
3 b f Antonius Pius(USA) Spinning Gold (Spinning World (USA))
550[7] 828[3] 1073[2] (1433) 1892[4] (2329) (2572) 3058[9] 4162[3] (4283) 4670[5] 5027[6] 5511[6] 7080[7] 7593[3]

Sylvia's Diamond *Richard Guest* a35 26
3 br f Cockney Rebel(IRE) Korolieva (IRE) (Xaar)
122[9] 195[10] 550[9] 717[8]

Symboline *Mick Channon* 67
3 b f Royal Applause Ashes (IRE) (General Monash (USA))
2091[8] 2393[6] 2791[3]

Symphony Break (IRE) *N Caullery* a66 63
3 b f King's Best(USA) Melody Break (USA) (Sunday Break (JPN))
544a[6] 962a[9]

Symphony Of Dreams *Dai Burchell* a33 20
3 b f Primo Valentino(IRE) Flying Lion (Hunting Lion (IRE))
915[6] 1349[10]

Symphony Of Pearls *Dai Burchell*
2 b f Lucarno(USA) Echostar (Observatory (USA))
4379[11]

Synaesthesia (FR) *Lady Cecil* a36
2 bb f High Chaparral(IRE) I'm Sensational (Selkirk (USA))
7435[10]

Syncopate *Pam Sly* a78 75
4 b g Oratorio(IRE) Millistar (Galileo (IRE))
1200[4] 1448[6] *1699[2] 1956[2]* 2808[4] 3218[4] *7462[4] 7629[3] 7952[6] (8179) 8336[DSQ]*

Synonym (ITY) *J W Hills* a47
2 ch f Haatef(USA) Shatarah (Gulch (USA))
6689[B] 7162[8]

Synphonic Air (IRE) *John Weymes* a18 45
3 b f Amadeus Wolf Summer Crush (USA) (Summer Squall (USA))
2121[5] 2501[14]

Syrenka *Marcus Tregoning* a62 70
3 ch f Sir Percy Sirena (GER) (Tejano (USA))
4799[8] 6015[2] *6658[8]* 7091[8] *7434[7] (7637) 7877[2]*

Syrian *Thomas McLaughlin* a78 82
6 b g Hawk Wing(USA) Lady Lahar (Fraam)
206[4] 238[4] 633[4] 974[6]

Syrian Pearl *Chris Wall* a61 42
2 gr f Clodovil(IRE) Syrian Queen (Slip Anchor)
4175[10] 4977[8] *5593[7] 6749[8]* 7609[5]

Syrina (FR) *F-X De Chevigny* 59
2 b f Canyon Creek(IRE) Semire (FR) (Mizoram (USA))
6059a[7]

Syros (IRE) *Brian Meehan* a77 72
2 ch g Kheleyf(USA) Starring (FR) (Ashkalani (IRE))
6277[8] 6754[3] *7302[2]*

Szabo's Art *Sir Mark Prescott Bt* a56 58
3 br f Excellent Art Violette (Observatory (USA))
4152[11] 4382[9] (5143) 5334[8] *5935[5]* 7321[14]

Szoff (GER) *W Giedt* 81
3 b c Shirocco(GER) Slawomira (GER) (Dashing Blade)
4042a[6]

Taajub (IRE) *Peter Crate* a95 109
6 b g Exceed And Excel(AUS) Purple Tiger (IRE) (Rainbow Quest (USA))
1032[10] 1672[5] 2865[10] 4024[5] ◆ 4275[11] 4800[15] 6699[10]

Taaresh (IRE) *Kevin Morgan* a78 38
8 b g Sakhee(USA) Tanaghum (Darshaan)
6280[6]

Taayel (IRE) *John Gosden* 108
3 b c Tamayuz Sakhee's Song (IRE) (Sakhee (USA))
(4981) 5747[7] 7025[7]

Tabaayun (IRE) *David O'Meara* a82 70
3 b g Nayef(USA) Garden City (FR) (Majorien)
6357[5] (6683) 7425[5] *(7924) 8028[2] 8318[4]*

Tableaux (USA) *A Fabre* 110
3 ch c Giant's Causeway(USA) Golden Antigua (USA) (Hansel (USA))
(1737a) (2297a)

Tableforten *J S Moore* a71 76
2 ch g Pastoral Pursuits Twitch Hill (Piccolo)
2436[2] (2723) 3424[17] *3690[3]* 4300[4] *5848a[8]* 6065[4] 6187[2] 6825[10] 7333[5] 7771[5] 7819[7]

Table Forty Six (IRE) *Jarlath P Fahey* a52 60
7 b m Refuse To Bend(IRE) Tashreefat (IRE) (Danehill (USA))
515[6]

Table Ronde (IRE) *J-C Rouget* a98 107
3 b f Astronomer Royal(USA) Tanzania (IRE) (Alzao (USA))
3877a[3] 5461a[2] 6714a[4]

Taboule *G Martin* a72 75
3 b c Mount Nelson Zia (GER) (Grand Lodge (USA))
543a[6] 605a[7] 1850a[2] 7736a[15]

Tac De Boistron (FR) *Marco Botti* 119
6 gr g Take Risks(FR) Pondiki (FR) (Sicyos (USA))
5741[3] (6385) 7060a[2] (7566a)

Tactical Strike *Hugo Palmer* 48
2 ch c Pivotal Alvee (IRE) (Key Of Luck (USA))
7607[8]

Tacticus (USA) *Lady Cecil* a72
2 b c A.P. Indy(USA) Visions Of Clarity (IRE) (Sadler's Wells (USA))
8066[3]

Tadabeer *Ian Williams* a91 77
5 b g Green Desert(USA) Perfect Plum (IRE) (Darshaan)
400[9] (1059) (1422) 1501[4]

Tadalavil *Linda Perratt* a76 61
8 gr g Clodovil(IRE) Blandish (USA) (Wild Again (USA))
2037[8] 2409[12] 6879[4] 7148[11] (7236)

Tafaaseel (USA) *Sir Michael Stoute* 66
3 b f Mr Greeley(USA) Wasseema (USA) (Danzig (USA))
2658[5] 3136[7]

Tafadhali (SPA) *J A Lopez* 62
5 b f Dyhim Diamond(IRE) Laida (FR) (Slip Anchor)
2380a[4]

Tafawuk (USA) *Roger Varian* a58 79
4 b g Nayef(USA) Yaqeen (Green Desert (USA))
(1836) 1973[7] 2808[6]

Tagalaka (IRE) *Eve Johnson Houghton* a66 56
3 b g Tagula(IRE) Queeny's Princess (IRE) (Daggers Drawn (USA))
1424[4] 1900[11] *(2154)* 2727[6] 3665[8] *4168[7] 5135[6] 6315[6] 6805[4] 6933[9] 7325[7]*

Tagar Bere (FR) *M Pimbonnet* a101 106
6 ch h High Yield(USA) Arrondie (FR) (Inchinor)
2559a[5]

Taghrooda *John Gosden* 85
2 b f Sea The Stars(IRE) Ezima (IRE) (Sadler's Wells (USA))
(6643)

Taglietelle *Andrew Balding* a83 90
4 b g Tagula(IRE) Averami (Averti (IRE))
(1089) 1523[4] 2451[6] (3118) 3531[6] 4233[7] 4606[4] 7193[16]

Tag's Book (IRE) *U Suter* a68 65
6 ch g Tagula(IRE) First Book (Ashkalani (IRE))
127a[8]

Tagula Night (IRE) *Dean Ivory* a86 89
7 ch g Tagula(IRE) Carpet Lady (IRE) (Night Shift (USA))
(1814) 2255[15] 2657[6] 3341[3] *4165[2]* 5036[3] 5750[3] *6525[6]* 7255[2] *8088[11] 8455[7]*

Tahaamah *Saeed bin Suroor* a98 100
5 ch g King's Best(USA) Russian Snows (IRE) (Sadler's Wells (USA))
2251[5] ◆ 2718[5] 5269[6] 5749[3] (7312)

Tahadee (IRE) *Mick Channon* 78
2 b c Teofilo(IRE) Queen Of Lyons (USA) (Dubai Destination (USA))
4987[3] 5727[4] 6125[2] 6740[3]

Tahaf (IRE) *Clive Brittain* 63
3 b g Authorized(IRE) Lady Zonda (Lion Cavern (USA))
2508[3] 2743[5] 3194[11]

Tahchee *James Fanshawe* a58 31
2 ch g Sleeping Indian Neyraan (Lujain (USA))
7251[7] *7664[5] 8061[4]*

Tahlia Ree (IRE) *Michael Bell* a59 77
4 b f Acclamation Dora Carrington (IRE) (Sri Pekan (USA))
1802[2] 1914[3] 2639[3]

Taiga Dream (FR) *D Rabhi* a73
3 b c Vespone(IRE) Katka (GER) (Law Society (USA))
818a[3]

Taisei Legend (JPN) *Yoshito Yahagi* a115 89
6 ch h King Kamehameha(JPN) Sharp Kick (JPN) (Mejiro McQueen (JPN))
1266a[12]

Tai She (SWE) *Soren Jensen*
2 b f Academy Award(IRE) Taiwan (Most Welcome)
6452a[4]

Tajaaweed (USA) *Doug Watson* a93 107
8 br h Dynaformer(USA) Uforia (USA) (Zilzal (USA))
153a[8] 363a[5] *656a[7]*

Tajheez (IRE) *Roger Varian* a94 89
3 b g Raven's Pass(USA) Ghaidaa (IRE) (Cape Cross (IRE))
(2156) ◆ (3232) 3785[4] 4516[2] 5189[2] *(6136)* 6823[8]

Tajneed (IRE) *David Nicholls* a83 89
10 b g Alhaarth(IRE) Indian Express (Indian Ridge)
(1280) 1598^{2} (2276) 2516^{4} 3501^{2} 5088^{3} 5832^{2} 6908^{10} (7282) 7594^{8}

Takaathur (USA) *Saeed bin Suroor* a68
3 ch c Hard Spun(USA) Vague (USA) (Elusive Quality (USA))
6366^{4} 7154^{3}

Takajan (IRE) *Mark Brisbourne* a61 48
6 b g Barathea(IRE) Takaliya (IRE) (Darshaan)
87^{9} 276^{8}

Takar (IRE) *Rod Collet* 109
4 b c Oratorio(IRE) Takarouna (USA) (Green Dancer (USA))
1456a^{8} 2897a^{8}

Take A Break *Robert Johnson*
2 b f Josr Algarhoud(IRE) Waterpark (Namaqualand (USA))
5826^{9} 6627^{10} 6939^{11}

Takealookatmenow (IRE) *David Nicholls* a59 77
4 b f Moss Vale(IRE) Batool (USA) (Bahri (USA))
454^{6} 1205^{7} (1578) 1802^{9} (2038)

Take A Note *Patrick Chamings* a85 81
4 b g Singspiel(IRE) Ela Paparouna (Vettori (IRE))
3153^{3} 3693^{6} 4366^{2} 5191^{3} 6080^{6} (6475)

Take Cover *David C Griffiths* a107 105
6 b g Singspiel(IRE) Enchanted (Magic Ring (IRE))
4983^{2} 6621^{7} (7171) 7527^{15} 7928^{2}

Takeitfromalady (IRE) *Lee Carter* a91 94
4 b g Intikhab(USA) Pinheiros (IRE) (Rock Of Gibraltar (IRE))
865^{7} 1159^{4} 1242^{5} 1501^{10} 1883^{6} 2841^{12} 3692^{4} 5129^{2} 6108^{6} 6490^{3} 6868^{7} 7072^{10} 7431^{9}

Takemybreathaway *Brian Rothwell*
2 b f Court Masterpiece Corblets (Timeless Times (USA))
7419^{10}

Take Ten *S Seemar* a101 95
6 b g Bahamian Bounty See You Later (Emarati (USA))
(290a) 575a^{6}

Take The Lead *Richard Hannon Snr* a68 67
3 ch f Assertive My Dancer (IRE) (Alhaarth (IRE))
2544^{11} 5697^{11} 6255^{2} 6928^{2} 7262^{4}

Take Two *Alex Hales* a40 88
4 b g Act One Lac Marmot (FR) (Marju (IRE))
415^{10} (1290) (1673) 2431^{6} 3208^{6} (4075) 4798^{7}

Takitwo *Geoffrey Deacon* a51 68
10 b g Delta Dancer Tiama (IRE) (Last Tycoon)
2057^{3} 3052^{2} 4517^{3} 4771^{4} 4996^{5} 5525^{3} 5948^{3}

Takreym (IRE) *Roger Varian* 72
2 b g Clodovil(IRE) Somoushe (IRE) (Black Minnaloushe (USA))
7270^{2}

Talent *Ralph Beckett* a82 115
3 ch f New Approach(IRE) Prowess (IRE) (Peintre Celebre (USA))
(2049) ◆ (2842) 4550a^{7} 6393^{2} 7365^{3}

Talented Kid *Mark Johnston* 97
4 b g Teofilo(IRE) See You Later (Emarati (USA))
(5588) 6278^{2} 6792^{4}

Talent Scout (IRE) *Karen Tutty* a62 90
7 b g Exceed And Excel(AUS) Taalluf (USA) (Hansel (USA))
1442^{6} 1932^{10} (2911) (3192) (3895) 4308^{6} 4850^{4} 5880^{3} 6727^{2}

Talent Spotter *Charlie Appleby* a54 63
2 b f Exceed And Excel(AUS) Sophie's Girl (Bahamian Bounty)
3049^{4} 3760^{10} 4408^{8} 7078^{4}

Tale Of A Champion (USA) *Kristin Mulhall* 103
5 b c Tale Of The Cat(USA) If Angels Sang (USA) (Seattle Slew (USA))
7712a^{12}

Tales Of Grimm (USA) *Richard Fahey* a101 113
4 b g Distorted Humor(USA) Stupendous Miss (USA) (Dynaformer (USA))
2840^{5} (6592) 7196^{2} ◆ 7927^{4} 8386^{7}

Taleteller (USA) *Charlie Appleby* a70 58
2 b f Bernardini(USA) Taletobetold (USA) (Tale Of The Cat (USA))
3205^{7} 3958^{2} 4432^{5} 5068^{6}

Talip Han (IRE) *B Dag* 109
3 b c Oratorio(IRE) Idle Rich (USA) (Sky Classic (CAN))
6253a^{4}

Talitha Kum (IRE) *P D Deegan* 90
3 b f Chineur(FR) Belle Of The Blues (IRE) (Blues Traveller (IRE))
2289a^{6} 3845a^{5}

Talk Of Saafend (IRE) *Dianne Sayer* a31 61
8 b m Barathea(IRE) Sopran Marida (IRE) (Darshaan)
2313^{3} 3287^{9} 3709^{3} 4612^{6}

Talksalot (IRE) *J S Moore* a84 80
2 b g Thousand Words Lady Piste (IRE) (Ali-Royal (IRE))
2238^{4} 2617^{5} (3436) 4302^{3} (5362a) 7570a^{6}

Tallaay (IRE) *Mark Johnston* 53
3 b c Cape Cross(IRE) Ghizlaan (USA) (Seeking The Gold (USA))
1837^{8} 3653^{11}

Tallevu (IRE) *Noel Chance* a61 67
4 ch g Stormy River(FR) Pascarina (FR) (Exit To Nowhere (USA))
626^{6}

Tall Ship (IRE) *Sir Michael Stoute* 70
2 b c Sea The Stars(IRE) Magical Romance (IRE) (Barathea (IRE))
6799^{7} ◆ 7335^{6}

Tallulah Mai *Matthew Salaman* a57 56
6 b m Kayf Tara Al Awaalah (Mukaddamah (USA))
4605^{8}

Talmada (USA) *Roger Varian* a55
2 b f Cape Cross(IRE) Aryaamm (IRE) (Galileo (IRE))
7763^{9}

Talqaa *Mick Channon* a55 79
3 b f Exceed And Excel(AUS) Poppo's Song (CAN) (Polish Navy (USA))
1773^{3} 2051^{10} 2722^{4} 3109^{6} 3533^{6} 5447^{5} 6425^{3} 6901^{9} (7203)

Talusstern (GER) *P Sogorb* a70 68
4 b c Konigstiger(GER) Tala (FR) (Lomitas)
5601a^{5}

Tamaathul *A Al Raihe* a113 117
6 gr g Tiger Hill(IRE) Tahrir (IRE) (Linamix (FR))
154a^{2} (244a) 660a^{6} 868a^{7} 1266a^{4}

Tamaletta (IRE) *Paul Burgoyne* a45 54
3 ch f Tamayuz Annaletta (Belmez (USA))
2804^{4} 7738^{8} 7894^{9} 8229^{8}

Tamara Bay *John Davies* a61 66
5 b f Selkirk(USA) Tamalain (USA) (Royal Academy (USA))
1800^{7} 4967^{9} 5331^{7} 5830^{RR}

Tamara Quest (SWE) *Maria Johansson*
2 ch f Special Quest(FR) Tamara Red (IRE) (Mukaddamah (USA))
6452a^{8}

Tamarasha *Clive Cox* 8
2 b f Holy Roman Emperor(IRE) Catch Us (FR) (Selkirk (USA))
4589^{11}

Tamarkuz (USA) *Saeed bin Suroor* a107 80
3 ch c Speightstown(USA) Without You Babe (USA) (Lemon Drop Kid (USA))
6650^{17} (7157)

Tamayuz Dream (IRE) *Mark Johnston* 59
2 ch c Tamayuz Cradle Brief (IRE) (Brief Truce (USA))
2497^{5} 3077^{4} 3972^{5} 4990^{9}

Tamayuz Magic (IRE) *Mark Johnston* a62 65
2 b g Tamayuz Anne Tudor (IRE) (Anabaa (USA))
2337^{3} 2577^{3} 2985^{7} 4399^{5} 6487^{6}

Tamayuz Star (IRE) *George Margarson* 103
3 ch c Tamayuz Magical Peace (IRE) (Magical Wonder (USA))
1620^{5} 2453^{8} 2655^{2} 3455^{10} (3987) 4743^{8} 5439^{4} 5728^{9} 6990^{7}

Taming The Tweet *J R Jenkins* a55
3 b f Act One Pants (Pivotal)
275^{5} 541^{3} 1098^{7} 1343^{3}

Tammis *Ron Hodges* 42
3 b f Whipper(USA) Tamise (USA) (Time For A Change (USA))
3239^{13} 3674^{6}

Tammuz (IRE) *Tony Carroll* a69 56
3 ch f Tamayuz Favourita (Diktat)
3508^{3} 5096^{4} 6074^{4} 6655^{4} (6932) 7437^{5} 7876^{13} 8125^{9}

Tanawar (IRE) *Tim Etherington* a72 69
3 b g Elusive City(USA) Parakopi (IRE) (Green Desert (USA))
16^{3} 160^{3} 615^{2} 814^{4} 3327^{2} 4048^{4} 5975^{9} 6272^{4} 6758^{14} 7067^{5}

Tancred (IRE) *Tony Coyle* 73
2 b g Oratorio(IRE) Mythologie (FR) (Bering)
2670^{6} 5145^{3} 5843^{7} 7170^{5} 7529^{2}

Tandem *D K Weld* 104
4 b g Dansili Light Ballet (Sadler's Wells (USA))
1168a^{12} (4465a) 4869a^{8} 6225a^{3} 7388a^{7}

Tanfeeth *M Al Muhairi* a102 101
5 ch h Singspiel(IRE) Nasij (USA) (Elusive Quality (USA))
151a^{9} ◆ 242a^{3} 462a^{4}

Tanforan *Brian Baugh* a61 66
11 b g Mujahid(USA) Florentynna Bay (Aragon)
3513^{5} 4070^{7} (5172) 5429^{2} 6153^{8} 6803^{13}

Tangerine Trees *Bryan Smart* a103 109
8 b g Mind Games Easy To Imagine (USA) (Cozzene (USA))
(1249) 2019^{3} 2662^{9} 4311^{9} 5984^{6} 6305^{7} 7527^{5} 7928^{9} 8155^{3}

Tanghan (IRE) *Richard Fahey* a60 78
3 b g Invincible Spirit(IRE) Rose De France (IRE) (Diktat)
(136) 550^{8} 1806^{12}

Tango Sky (IRE) *David Nicholls* a87 86
4 b g Namid Sky Galaxy (USA) (Sky Classic (CAN))
3^{4} 196^{6} 1692^{8} (1888) (2410) 2664^{4} 3093^{7} 4620^{8} 5011^{10} 6209^{7}

Tannery (IRE) *Alan E Goldberg* a90 109
4 b f Dylan Thomas(IRE) Danse Grecque (IRE) (Sadler's Wells (USA))
(7562a)

Tannhauser Gate (IRE) *Jamie Osborne* 21
3 b g Shamardal(USA) Twiggy's Sister (IRE) (Flying Spur (AUS))
2872^{10} 3011^{8} 3176^{14} 6783^{7}

Tanojin (IRE) *Mick Channon* a61 61
2 ch f Thousand Words Indiannie Moon (Fraam)
5949^{4} 6318^{7} 6746^{6} 7198^{2}

Tanqeya (IRE) *Richard Hannon Snr* a78
2 b c Intense Focus(USA) Spinning Well (IRE) (Pivotal)
(7442) ◆

Tanseeb *Mark Johnston* 90
2 b c Royal Applause Perfect Story (IRE) (Desert Story (IRE))
1989^{2} ◆ 2401^{8} 3023^{2} 3565^{2} 4061^{3} (4498) 4948^{2} 6328^{18}

Tantalising (IRE) *P J Prendergast* a65 90
5 b f Sadler's Wells(USA) Bluffing (IRE) (Darshaan)
3423^{17} 7723a^{U}

Tantshi (IRE) *Roger Varian* 104
3 b f Invincible Spirit(IRE) Qasirah (IRE) (Machiavellian (USA))
2056^{3} 2848^{7} (3718) 4252^{2} 4766^{6} (6143) (7015)

Tanzeel (IRE) *Charles Hills* 85
2 b c Elusive City(USA) Royal Fizz (IRE) (Royal Academy (USA))
4231^{2} ◆ (4716) 6328^{19}

Tapestry (IRE) *A P O'Brien* 111
2 b f Galileo(IRE) Rumplestiltskin (IRE) (Danehill (USA))
(5318a) 6024a^{2}

Tapis Libre *Michael Easterby* a72 83
5 b g Librettist(USA) Stella Manuela (FR) (Galileo (IRE))
(2629) (3889) (4437) 6563^{12} 6729^{9} 7131^{14} 7539^{6}

Tap It Rich (USA) *Bob Baffert* a110
2 rg r Tapit(USA) Gold Canyon (USA) (Mr Prospector (USA))
7711a^{5}

Tappanappa (IRE) *Brian Ellison* a95 89
6 b g High Chaparral(IRE) Itsibitsi (IRE) (Brief Truce (USA))
739^{3} 1615^{3} 1805^{3} 2205^{5} 3099^{7} 3685^{11}

Taquka (IRE) *Ralph Beckett* 73
2 b c Kodiac Dubai Princess (IRE) (Dubai Destination (USA))
2917^{3} 3408^{2} 3815^{2} 4346^{2}

Tarantella Lady *George Moore* 68
5 b f Noverre(USA) Shortfall (Last Tycoon)
1572^{8} 2242^{5}

Tara's Treasure (IRE) *Gary Moore* a49 48
2 b c Amadeus Wolf Bean Island (USA) (Afleet (CAN))
7654^{4} 7853^{7} ◆ 8367^{4}

Tarbawi (IRE) *M bin Shafya* a68 100
3 b g Anabaa(USA) Born Something (IRE) (Caerleon (USA))
245a^{9} 553a^{4} 835a^{3} 953a^{8}

Tarfasha (IRE) *D K Weld* 93
2 ch f Teofilo(IRE) Grecian Bride (IRE) (Groom Dancer (USA))
6881a^{3}

Target Acquired (IRE) *A Oliver* 82
3 ch g Majestic Missile(IRE) Brioney (IRE) (Barathea (IRE))
6025a^{9}

Tarikhi (USA) *Saeed bin Suroor* 102
3 b g Bernardini(USA) Caffe Latte (IRE) (Seattle Dancer (USA))
2445^{7} 3484^{2} 4214^{3} ◆ 4743^{9}

Tariq Too *Amy Weaver* a63 106
6 ch g Kyllachy Tatora (Selkirk (USA))
2621^{5} ◆ 5533^{9} 6625^{7} 6840^{5} ◆ 7408a^{3} (7507) 7820^{2} 7995a^{9}

Tarmo (IRE) *Marco Botti* a30
3 b c Rakti Mamlakah (IRE) (Unfuwain (USA))
4632^{13} 5281^{9} 5962^{5} 7299^{9}

Tarn *T Stack* 87
2 b f Royal Applause Starry Sky (Oasis Dream)
4547a^{7}

Tarooq (USA) *David Barron* a110 88
7 b g War Chant(USA) Rose Of Zollern (IRE) (Seattle Dancer (USA))
(155) (405) (584) (947) 1032^{3} 3220^{7} 3823^{8} 4281^{5} 4730^{7} 4780^{5} 5696^{2} 5974^{6} 6331^{10} 6831^{4} 7222^{5} 7540^{5} 7991^{5} (8334)

Taro Tywod (IRE) *Mark Brisbourne* a64 69
4 br f Footstepsinthesand Run To Jane (IRE) (Doyoun)
3043^{7} 3814^{6} (4195) 4562^{2} 5144^{9} 5479^{5} 5980^{2} 6283^{2}

Tarquin (IRE) *Kristin Stubbs* a66 56
4 b g Excellent Art Umlani (IRE) (Great Commotion (USA))
6940^{5} 7624^{4} 8063^{2}

Tarrsille (IRE) *Paul Midgley* a86 84
7 b g Dansili Tara Gold (IRE) (Royal Academy (USA))
3846a^{28} 5544^{14} 5974^{11} 6209^{4}

Tartan Blue *Robert Cowell* a56
3 b f Kyllachy Poly Blue (IRE) (Thatching)
137^{3} 985^{4}

Tartan Gigha (IRE) *Geoffrey Harker* a73 90
8 b g Green Desert(USA) High Standard (Kris)
1774^{6} 2077^{3} 2766^{6} 3651^{8} 7805^{9} 8059^{6} 8335^{4}

Tartan Jura *Mark Johnston* a84 80
5 b g Green Desert(USA) On A Soapbox (USA) (Mi Cielo (USA))
622^{2} 823^{2} 1018^{4} 1454^{2} 1615^{5} 2009^{8} 2587^{4} 2990^{3} 3609^{7} (3944) 4372^{4} 5109^{7} 5423^{2} 5831^{10} 6237^{13} 6942^{7}

Tartan Trip *Michael Appleby* a77 51
6 b g Selkirk(USA) Marajuana (Robellino (USA))
2450^{18} 2724^{7} 3210^{4} 3736^{6} 4522^{2} 5099^{14} 5793^{13} 8125^{6} (8278) ◆

Tartaria *Edward Creighton* a47 16
7 b m Oasis Dream Habariya (IRE) (Perugino (USA))
753^{7} 840^{7} 1100^{11} 1472^{7} 1710^{7} 2130^{6} 5171^{9}

Tartarin (IRE) *Mme C Head-Maarek* a70 81
6 b g Statue Of Liberty(USA) Tigresse Africaine (FR) (Tiger Hill (IRE))
6421a^{10}

Tartary (IRE) *Roger Charlton* a79 81
3 b c Oasis Dream Tamso (USA) (Seeking The Gold (USA))
1625^{12} 2158^{3} 2983^{8} (4367) 4797^{9}

Tartiflette *Ed McMahon* 101
4 b f Dr Fong(USA) Bright Moll (Mind Games)
(1830) 2254^{6} 2858^{5} 4062^{8} 4766^{8} 5684^{14} 6665^{6} 7368^{9} 7820^{4}

Tasaday (USA) *A Fabre* 116
3 rg f Nayef(USA) Tashelka (FR) (Mujahid (USA))
1561a^{2} 2299a^{3} 3385a^{4} (4792a) (5629a) 6448a^{3} 7057a^{2}

Tashtu *Bill Turner* a21
2 b f Tobougg(IRE) Tashkiyla (FR) (Alzao (USA))
6807^{8}

Tasrih (USA) *Alan McCabe* a90
4 b g Hard Spun(USA) Rare Gift (USA) (Unbridled's Song (USA))
6289^{15} 7154^{2} (7781) 7989^{2} (8127) 8385^{8}

Tassel *Richard Hannon Snr* 91
3 b f Kyllachy Xtrasensory (Royal Applause)
1921^{7} 2264^{6} 2848^{4} 3784^{5} 4534^{5} 5260^{8} 5700^{8}

Taste The Wine (IRE) *Bernard Llewellyn* a67 74
7 gr g Verglas(IRE) Azia (IRE) (Desert Story (IRE))
1111^{8} 1973^{5} 3133^{2} ◆ 4238^{3} 4714^{6} 4915^{6}

Tatlisu (IRE) *Richard Fahey* 89
3 b g Red Clubs(IRE) Zwadi (IRE) (Docksider (USA))
1771^{2} 2190^{10} 2987^{6} (3320) 4056^{2} 4725^{4} (5474) 6278^{3} 6586^{3} 7531^{3}

Tattenham (USA) *William Mott* 103
3 bb c Rock Hard Ten(USA) Proud Fact (USA) (Known Fact (USA))
5551a^{9}

Tatting *Chris Dwyer* a85 51
4 ch g Street Cry(IRE) Needlecraft (IRE) (Mark Of Esteem (IRE))
801^{7} 1294^{14} 1521^{7} 2514^{10} 3642^{6} 3924^{5} 5073^{2} 5596^{2} ◆ 6103^{3} (6472) 6554^{7} (6804) ◆ (7169) ◆ 7383^{5} 7605^{2} 8057^{3} (8269)

Taurus Twins *Richard Price* a75 91
7 b g Deportivo Intellibet One (Compton Place)
1431^{2} 1581^{8} 1765^{11} 2663^{3} ◆ 3135^{7} 3415^{6} 3855^{12} 6382^{11} 6850^{9} 6948^{8} 7427^{9} 7743^{11}

Tautira (IRE) *Michael Bell* a68 66
2 b f Kheleyf(USA) Ballantrae (IRE) (Diktat)
2751^{7} 3324^{2} 3724^{5} 4191^{5} 5693^{6} (7198) 7837^{7} 8228^{3}

Tavistock Fair *Michael Squance* a32
3 b g Proclamation(IRE) Music Maid (IRE) (Inzar (USA))
663^{6} 815^{9} 876^{4} 1118^{6}

Tawan *Brian Rothwell* 22
2 b g Tiger Hill(IRE) Lady Netbetsports (IRE) (In The Wings)
7023^{17} 7339^{9}

Tawhid *Saeed bin Suroor* 114
3 gr c Invincible Spirit(IRE) Snowdrops (Gulch (USA))
1638^{4} 2526a^{3} 3455^{3} 4945^{2} 5532^{3} 6191^{4} (6595)

Taws *Rod Millman*
2 b f Hernando(FR) Reaf (In The Wings)
6740^{7}

Tawseef (IRE) *Roy Brotherton* a50 76
5 b g Monsun(GER) Sahool (Unfuwain (USA))
1836^{8} (2348) 2923^{3} 3273^{6} 5311^{6} 6788^{5} 7433^{6}

Tawtheeq (IRE) *Richard Hannon Snr* 74
3 b c Acclamation Grand Slam Maria (FR) (Anabaa (USA))
1618^{7} 2447^{3} ◆ 4011^{4} 4628^{6} 5815^{8}

Tax Enough (USA) *Brian Meehan* 52
2 bb c Awesome Again(CAN) Unbridled Ambiance (USA) (Unbridled Time (USA))
2391^{6} 3490^{7}

Tax Free (IRE) *David Nicholls* a92 100
11 b g Tagula(IRE) Grandel (Owington)
1537^{20} 2007^{8} 2366^{11} 2880^{4} 3135^{2} 3561^{9} (3786) 4263^{4} 4536^{2} 4983^{16} 5519^{12} 5651^{16} 6920^{6} 7851^{7} 8181^{7} (8324)

Taxiformissbyron *Michael Herrington* a69 60
3 b f Byron Miss Respect (Mark Of Esteem (IRE))
(134) (336) (459) 506^{2} 615^{4} 2770^{8} 3730^{7} 4045^{7} 5016^{6} 5334^{5} 5921^{2} (6049) 6723^{5} 6907^{3} 7325^{3} 7489^{5} 7924^{5} 8187^{6} 8372^{2} 8399^{4}

Tax Reform (IRE) *Mark Hoad* a67 73
3 b g Namid Happy Flight (IRE) (Titus Livius (FR))
8245^{3} 8427^{5}

Tcharmeddotorg *Phil McEntee*
3 b f Authorized(IRE) Tidie France (USA) (Cape Town (USA))
1986^{11}

Tchekhov (FR) *J-C Rouget* a80 80
2 b c King's Best(USA) From This Day On (USA) (El Prado (IRE))
(5296a)

Tea And Sympathy *Michael Appleby*
5 b f Avonbridge Merch Rhyd-Y-Grug (Sabrehill (USA))
6611^{9}

Tea In Transvaal (IRE) *Richard Hannon Snr* 80
2 b f Teofilo(IRE) Mpumalanga (Observatory (USA))
4702^{4} ◆ 5529^{2} 6063^{2} 6643^{3} (7244)

Teak (IRE) *Ian Williams* a76 83
6 b g Barathea(IRE) Szabo (IRE) (Anabaa (USA))
3118^{4} 4407^{2} 4782^{4} 6646^{9}

Teaks North (USA) *Eric J Guillot* a93 109
6 bb g Northern Afleet(USA) Teaksberry Road (USA) (High Honors (USA))
7712a^{11}

Tea Leaf (IRE) *Ralph Beckett* a72
2 b f Bushranger(IRE) Boston Ivy (USA) (Mark Of Esteem (IRE))
(5635) ◆

Team Challenge *Tim Easterby* 66
3 b g Araafa(IRE) Passionforfashion (IRE) (Fasliyev (USA))
2464^{12} 3546^{11}

Teardrops (FR) *R Chotard* a74
2 bb c Naaqoos Fair West (USA) (Gone West (USA))
8143a^{7} 8354a^{8}

Tears And Rain (IRE) *Tim Easterby* 54
2 b f Iffraaj Massalia (IRE) (Montjeu (IRE))
2238^{3} ◆ 7023^{11}

Tears Of The Sun *Roger Varian* a73 70
2 b f Mastercraftsman(IRE) Perfect Star (Act One)
5131^{3} 6298^{3} 6644^{14} 8176^{2} (8362)

Tebbit (USA) *Philip Hide* a67
3 rg g Tapit(USA) Baroness Thatcher (USA) (Johannesburg (USA))
726^{3} 1171^{4} 1425^{6} 1879^{8}

Tebee's Oasis *John Gosden* a72
3 b f Oasis Dream Tebee (Selkirk (USA))
774^{3} (1103)

Technokrat (IRE) *W Hickst* a91 111
5 b c Oratorio(IRE) Tech Engine (GER) (Enrique)
2294a^{3} 2822a^{6} 4042a^{5}

Techtycoon *Michael Easterby* a49
2 b g Echo Of Light Appelone (Emperor Jones (USA))
7882^{5} 8091^{4} 8131^{5}

Tecla (IRE) *Mme C Head-Maarek* 90
3 b f Whipper(USA) Mahalia (IRE) (Danehill (USA))
7116a^{6}

Tectonic (IRE) *Keith Dalgleish* a60 76
4 b g Dylan Thomas(IRE) Pine Chip (USA) (Nureyev (USA))
2219^{2} 2536^{8} 2972^{2} 3203^{2} (3466) 4052^{2} (4109) 4475^{3} 4609^{4} 4953^{9} 5332^{5} 5882^{2} 6048^{6} (6296) 6730^{3} 6877^{2} 6906^{2} 7152^{7}

Teddy's Promise (USA) *Ronald W Ellis* a110 98
5 bb f Salt Lake(USA) Braids And Beads (USA) (Capote (USA))
7709a^{8}

Ted's Brother (IRE) *Richard Guest* a66 77
5 b g Fath(USA) Estertide (IRE) (Tagula (IRE))
650[6] 740[5] 878[9] 1394[2] 1569[10] 1801[3] (2219) 2707[7] 2884[14] 3444[2] (3649) 4055[7] 4807[3] (4994) 5263[6] 5711[7] 6048[3] 6291[3] 6548[6] 6943[4] 7152[6] 7608[2] 7824[16]

Ted Veale (IRE) *A J Martin* 102
6 b g Revoque(IRE) Rose Tanner (IRE) (Roselier (FR))
5766[4]

Tee It Up Tommo (IRE) *Michael Wigham* a69 59
4 gr g Clodovil(IRE) Lamh Eile (IRE) (Lend A Hand)
2576[4] 4632[12] 5100[11] 7109[3] 7784[2] (7858) 8087[4]

Teeline (IRE) *Charlie Appleby* 66
3 b f Exceed And Excel(AUS) Journalist (IRE) (Night Shift (USA))
4687[2] 5647[2] 6425[4]

Teenage Idol (IRE) *Dianne Sayer* 66
9 bb g Sadler's Wells(USA) Kaaba (Darshaan)
2628[12] 2833[5] 2971[2] 3442[10] 4110[6] 5048[8] 5560[13]

Teen Ager (FR) *Paul Burgoyne* a67 52
9 b g Invincible Spirit(IRE) Tarwiya (IRE) (Dominion)
(117) 349[3] 440[2] 631[9] 903[5] 1056[5] (1194) (1426) 2954[2] 3404[3] 4163[9]

Teetotal (IRE) *Nigel Tinkler* 80
3 ch g Footstepsinthesand Tea Service (USA) (Atticus (USA))
1284[3] 1687[7] 1771[3] 2076[4] 2535[3] (3323) (3611) 3813[3] 4136[3] 4478[5] 5150[8] 5878[3] 6287[7] (6568) 6682[2] 7531[6]

Tefflah *Roger Varian* a57 69
3 b f Teofilo(IRE) Anaamil (IRE) (Darshaan)
1518[5] 2055[3] 2465[P]

Teide Peak (IRE) *Paul D'Arcy* a66 70
4 b g Cape Cross(IRE) Teide Lady (Nashwan (USA))
475[3] (2629) 3504[11] 5065[9] 5672[6] 7984[15] 8308[5]

Teixidor (ITY) *Ottavio Di Paolo* 97
4 ch c St Paul House Rosetta Stone (ITY) (Tisserand (ITY))
2295a[8] 6679a[6]

Telamon (IRE) *Milton Bradley*
3 b g Rock Of Gibraltar(IRE) Laureldean Express (Inchinor)
3109[8] 3639[5] 4153[9]

Telegraph (IRE) *Andrew Balding* 67
2 b g Bushranger(IRE) Vampire Queen (IRE) (General Monash (USA))
5033[8] 5995[4] 6383[2] 6825[3]

Telegraphy (USA) *Ed Dunlop* 58
2 gr f Giant's Causeway(USA) Cable (USA) (Dynaformer (USA))
7493[9]

Telescope (IRE) *Sir Michael Stoute* 116
3 b c Galileo(IRE) Velouette (Darshaan)
(4452) 5270[2] (5653)

Tell Me When *Brian Rothwell* 50
2 b f Monsieur Bond(IRE) Giffoine (Timeless Times (USA))
5053[7] 5543[4] 5988[9] 7094[7]

Tellovoi (IRE) *Ian Williams* a89 89
5 b c Indian Haven Kloonlara (IRE) (Green Desert (USA))
2185[6] 2592[14] 3096[14] (5026) 5880[4] 6840[8] 7699[4] 7820[13] 8117[9] 8231[5]

Temeraine (USA) *Thomas F Proctor* 107
4 bb g Arch(USA) Lonely Fact (USA) (Known Fact (USA))
5553a[5] 7563a[5]

Temida (IRE) *M G Mintchev* 113
5 b f Oratorio(IRE) Interim Payment (USA) (Red Ransom (USA))
4571a[2] 5324a[5]

Tempelfeuer (GER) *Conrad Allen* 39
2 b f Soldier Hollow Tempelsonne (GER) (Acatenango (GER))
2419[8] 5003[13]

Tempest Fugit (IRE) *John Gosden* a99 93
4 b f High Chaparral(IRE) Diary (IRE) (Green Desert (USA))
5993[4] 7650[9] 7891a[10]

Tempete En Mer (FR) *F Chappet* a68 73
3 gr f Della Francesca(USA) Avis De Tempete (FR) (Baroud D'Honneur (FR))
461a[5]

Templar Boy *J R Jenkins* 24
2 br g Myboycharlie(IRE) Zagala (Polar Falcon (USA))
6569[9]

Template (IRE) *Richard Hannon Snr* a72 70
2 ch g Iffraaj Sagaing (Machiavellian (USA))
5472[7] ◆ 5922[3] 6689[6] 6896[4]

Temple Bar (FR) *F Rossi* 105
4 b c Rock Of Gibraltar(IRE) Ozone Bere (FR) (Verglas (IRE))
3362a[3]

Temple Meads *David Brown* a49 105
5 ch c Avonbridge Harryana (Efisio)
150a[2] 464a[12] 746a[13]

Temple Road (IRE) *Milton Bradley* a81 67
5 b g Street Cry(IRE) Sugarhoneybaby (IRE) (Docksider (USA))
186[3] (583) ◆ 775[11] 1346[4] 1814[11] 2196[6]

Tempo Royale (FR) *S Wattel* a81 76
2 b f Boris De Deauville(IRE) Macho Tempo (USA) (Macho Uno (USA))
(6961a)

Tempuran *David Bridgwater* a68 71
4 rg g Unbridled's Song(USA) Tenderly (IRE) (Danehill (USA))
3273[3] 3865[4]

Temuco (IRE) *David Evans* a63 71
4 b g Bachelor Duke(USA) La Chinampina (FR) (Darshaan)
(120) 433[6] 633[6] 866[7] 888[7]

Tenacity *Karen Tutty* 58
4 b g Passing Glance Wigman Lady (IRE) (Tenby)
2537[7] 3589[7] 4204[6] 4622[5]

Tenancy (IRE) *Shaun Harris* a55 58
9 b g Rock Of Gibraltar(IRE) Brush Strokes (Cadeaux Genereux)
618[12] 884[7] 1077[5] 1311[8] 2043[8] 2575[12]

Tenbridge *Derek Haydn Jones* a66 71
4 b f Avonbridge Tenebrae (IRE) (In The Wings)
116[10] 778[7] 965[6] 1079[2] 1193[3] 1521[6] 1887[10] 2345[2] 2773[10] 5177[2] (5430) (5816) 6702[6] 7130[14] 7952[11]

Tender Emotion *Charlie Appleby* a76 87
2 ch f Pivotal Silca's Sister (Inchinor)
4921[9] (5394) (6770)

Tenenbaum *Charlie Appleby* 109
4 b g Authorized(IRE) Al Hasnaa (Zafonic (USA))
870a[4] 1263a[8] 4309[6] 6348[6]

Tenessee *Jamie Osborne* a71 67
6 b g Nayef(USA) Shukran (Hamas (IRE))
1780[4] 2417[8] 3642[5] 4169[7] 6218[5] 6932[6]

Tenhoo *Eric Alston* a59 76
7 b g Reset(AUS) Bella Bambina (Turtle Island (IRE))
1111[11] 1448[4] 1836[6] 2629[3] (3231) 3889[4] 4447[3] 5514[5] 5706[11]

Tennessee Wildcat (IRE) *G M Lyons* a97 92
3 b g Kheleyf(USA) Windbeneathmywings (IRE) (In The Wings)
4255[11]

Tenor (IRE) *Roger Varian* a73 75
3 b g Oratorio(IRE) Cedar Sea (IRE) (Persian Bold)
1678[12] 2093[4] ◆ (3793) 4075[3] 6313[5]

Tenure *Amy Weaver* a77 80
4 b g Dansili Alumni (Selkirk (USA))
396[4] (978) ◆ 1054[3] 1753[2] ◆ 4706[4]

Teolagi (IRE) *J S Moore* a90 74
3 ch g Teofilo(IRE) Satulagi (USA) (Officer (USA))
1486[10] 3418[2] (4575a) 4950[8] (5914a) 6713a[20] 7736a[6] 8301[3] 8398[2]

Teophilip (IRE) *Marco Botti* a97 83
3 bb c Teofilo(IRE) Triomphale (USA) (Nureyev (USA))
(674) (1033)

Tepmokea (IRE) *Mrs K Burke* a101 97
7 ch g Noverre(USA) Eroica (GER) (Highest Honor (FR))
125a[3] 514a[3] 701a[6] 777[3] 1242[3] 1382[2] 2263[3] 2867[6] 4060[2] 4854[14] 5269[7] 5723[11]

Tequila Sunrise *J W Hills* a46 59
3 gr f Dansili Kenmist (Kenmare (FR))
8154[7]

Terdaad (IRE) *Saeed bin Suroor* a96 97
5 ch g Shamardal(USA) Akrmina (Zafonic (USA))
503a[14]

Terenzium (IRE) *Micky Hammond* a52 53
11 br g Cape Cross(IRE) Tatanka (ITY) (Luge)
2313[9] 5048[13]

Terhaab (USA) *John Gosden* a74 52
2 b f Elusive Quality(USA) Star Of Paris (USA) (Dayjur (USA))
4484[8] 6690[6] (7638)

Terntheothercheek *Jennie Candlish*
4 b f Multiplex My Tern (IRE) (Glacial Storm (USA))
641[6]

Terpsichore *Sylvester Kirk* a49 33
3 ch f Beat Hollow Effie (Royal Academy (USA))
2800[9] 3243[12] 3859[7] 5604[8] 5935[10] 6257[5] 7035[7]

Tertio Bloom (SWE) *Fabricio Borges* a102 98
8 ch g Tertullian(USA) Yankee Bloom (USA) (El Gran Senor (USA))
149a[7] 467a[15]

Teshali (IRE) *Anthony Middleton* a62 97
7 bg g Anabaa(USA) Tashiriya (IRE) (Kenmare (FR))
401[9]

Testamatta *Marco Botti* a71 76
3 b f Motivator Rummage (Zamindar (USA))
(2172) 2738[9]

Testa Rossa (IRE) *J W Hills* a68 63
3 b c Oratorio(IRE) Red Rita (IRE) (Kefaah (USA))
(59) 2420[8] 3241[7] 4928[8] 6218[4] 6612[5] 7515[3]

Testa Rossi (FR) *Chad C Brown* 108
2 ch f Dr Fong(USA) Peggy Lane (FR) (Dancing Spree (USA))
7690a[2]

Testina (IRE) *J-M Beguigne* 82
2 b f Lawman(FR) Avventura (USA) (Johannesburg (USA))
7055a[11]

Testing (FR) *Mark Johnston* a51 69
2 gr f New Approach(IRE) Testama (FR) (Testa Rossa (AUS))
6512[5] 6828[3] 7260[8]

Testosterone (IRE) *Ed Dunlop* 107
5 br f Dansili Epopee (IRE) (Sadler's Wells (USA))
(1484) ◆ 2184a[8] 3381a[7] (Dead)

Testudo (IRE) *Brian Meehan* 106
3 gr c Duke Of Marmalade(IRE) Santa Sophia (IRE) (Linamix (FR))
2442[6] (3021) ◆ 4211[4] 4874[4] 5531[8] 6800[3]

Tetbury (USA) *David O'Meara* a84 90
4 b g Giant's Causeway(USA) Fanzine (USA) (Cozzene (USA))
1522[10] 2030[4] 2478[5] 2855[4] (3480) 3808[5] 4447[5] 5185[7] (5786) 6239[12] 6846[2]

Tete Orange *Stuart Williams* 32
2 ch f Pastoral Pursuits Imperialistic (IRE) (Imperial Ballet (IRE))
7466[14] 7692[8]

Teth *Anthony Carson* a59 41
4 br f Dansili Beta (Selkirk (USA))
7[7] 510[2] 1162[4] 1473[6] 2747[10]

Tevez *Des Donovan* a84 87
8 b g Sakhee(USA) Sosumi (Be My Chief (USA))
995[8] 2450[17] 3172[11] 3719[7] (5135) (5205) ◆ 5799[4] 6167[8]

Tez *Marco Botti* a48 61
2 b c Exceed And Excel(AUS) Gwyneth (Zafonic (USA))
4199[4] 4883[7] 5194[4] 7198[10]

Thackeray *Chris Fairhurst* a55 47
6 b g Fasliyev(USA) Chinon (IRE) (Entrepreneur)
987[5] 6600[14] 7778[9]

Tha'ir (IRE) *Saeed bin Suroor* 109
3 b c New Approach(IRE) Flashing Green (Green Desert (USA))
2454[2] 3523[8] (4537) 4917[11] 5822[2] 6332[2] 6838[11]

Thakana *J W Hills* a76 72
3 br f Cape Cross(IRE) Shohrah (IRE) (Giant's Causeway (USA))
1986[2] ◆ 2448[2] 3242[10]

Thalie De La Vis (FR) *Mme C Barande-Barbe* a63 68
2 b f Sandwaki(USA) Milady De La Vis (FR) (Lost World (IRE))
4599a[6]

Thalweg (CAN) *Mahmood Al Zarooni* 53
3 bb g Hard Spun(USA) Meandering Stream (CAN) (Gone West (USA))
1648[7]

Thane Of Cawdor (IRE) *Joseph Tuite* a62 59
4 b g Danehill Dancer(IRE) Holy Nola (USA) (Silver Deputy (CAN))
631[3] 921[2] (1090) 1434[3] 1715[3] 2828[8] 3168[7] 7628[7] 8447[8]

Thank You Joy *J R Jenkins* a54 62
5 b f Iceman Once Removed (Distant Relative)
62[4]

Thankyou Very Much *James Bethell* a71 67
3 b f Lucky Story(USA) Maid Of Perth (Mark Of Esteem (IRE))
2503[2] (3191) 3983[3] ◆ 6154[2] 6588[4] 7786[4] (8060)

Tharsis (IRE) *C Laffon-Parias* a86 98
3 ch f Gold Away(IRE) Highphar (FR) (Highest Honor (FR))
7142a[8]

Thataboy (IRE) *Tom Dascombe* a70 40
2 b g Green Desert(USA) Hawas (Mujtahid (USA))
3044[11] 4477[6] 7978[5] 8166[2] (8442)

That Be Grand *Shaun Harris* 20
2 b f Firebreak Manila Selection (USA) (Manila (USA))
4432[9] 4926[7] 6271[10]

Thatchereen (IRE) *Michael Bell* 66
2 b f Mastercraftsman(IRE) Roof Fiddle (USA) (Cat Thief (USA))
5282[13] 5983[7] 6334[2]

Thatcherite (IRE) *Tony Coyle* a78 75
5 gr g Verglas(IRE) Damiana (IRE) (Thatching)
3027[4] 3337[7] 3977[9] 4119[12] 4562[4] 5471[2] 5713[6] 6760[4] (6945) ◆ (7030)

Thatchit (IRE) *Paul Cole* a68 69
2 b f Invincible Spirit(IRE) Security Interest (USA) (Belong To Me (USA))
3863[4] 4164[3] 4589[2]

Thatchmaster (USA) *Mark Johnston* a84 57
3 bb g Street Cry(IRE) Michita (USA) (Dynaformer (USA))
1713[2] 7067[3] 7425[8]

Thats A Fret (IRE) *Liam McAteer* a73 66
7 b g Choisir(AUS) Reality Check (IRE) (Sri Pekan (USA))
679a[10]

That's Plenty (IRE) *John Patrick Shanahan* a88 71
4 b g Dr Fong(USA) Tyranny (Machiavellian (USA))
(6806) (7350) 8094[4]

The Absent Mare *Robin Dickin* a74 46
5 gr f Fair Mix(IRE) Precious Lucy (FR) (Kadrou (FR))
351[3] 654[8] 1218[3] 1502[5]

The Alamo (IRE) *Richard Hannon Snr* 79
2 b c High Chaparral(IRE) Inner Strength (FR) (Take Risks (FR))
3290[5] 3972[3] (5309) 6002[8] 6763[7] 7252[2] (7428)

The Apache (SAF) *M F De Kock* 118
6 b h Mogok(USA) Apache Rose (SAF) (Dolpour (IRE))
(466a) ◆ 959a[2] 1267a[2] 4779[4] 5553a[2]

The Art Of Racing (IRE) *Alan McCabe* a72 89
3 b g Acclamation Divert (IRE) (Averti (IRE))
1482[2] (1844) 2726[2] 4057[5] 4367[3] 4989[9] 6429[2] 6848[13] 7887[7]

Theatrical Dancer *Jim Goldie*
6 ch m Theatrical Charmer Red Freesia (Timeless Times (USA))
1392[8] 1828[14]

The Bay Bandit *Neil Mulholland* a60 44
6 b g Highest Honor(FR) Pescara (IRE) (Common Grounds)
2305a[2] 3919[6]

The Bay Tigress *Lisa Williamson* a41 22
3 b f Tiger Hill(IRE) Singasongosixpence (Singspiel (IRE))
3774[7] 4356[8] 7167[3] 7667[6] 8200[6]

The Bells O Peover *Mark Johnston* a76 84
5 b g Selkirk(USA) Bay Tree (IRE) (Daylami (IRE))
5854[6] 6211[13] 6658[6]

The Bendy Fella (IRE) *Mark Usher* a53 42
5 ch g Choisir(AUS) Missish (Mummy's Pet)
276[5] 655[10] 736[7] 1093[12] 4456[6] 5177[12]

The Best Doctor (IRE) *Jeremy Noseda* a40 73
3 ch c Pivotal Strawberry Fledge (USA) (Kingmambo (USA))
5720[6] 6133[8] 7253[4]

The Betchworth Kid *Michael Bell* a83 97
8 b g Tobougg(IRE) Runelia (Runnett)
2052[11] 2654[10] 4873[14] 5374[3] 6165[3] 6336[5] 6960[5]

The Black Jacobin *J S Moore* a67 78
3 b g Piccolo Greenfly (Green Desert (USA))
160[4] 204[4] (402) 468[3] 2394[10] (2919) 3533[3] 3927[5] 4244[4]

The Blue Banana (IRE) *Edwin Tuer* a60 70
4 b g Red Clubs(IRE) Rinneen (IRE) (Bien Bien (USA))
1462[9] 1790[10] 2280[3] 2537[8] 3027[5] 4119[4] 4893[6] 6276[6] (6518) 6943[2] 7346[10]

The Blue Dog (IRE) *Phil McEntee* a76 66
6 b m High Chaparral(IRE) Jules (IRE) (Danehill (USA))
338[11] 653[6] 755[2] (1040) 1350[4] (1654) 1889[2] 2004[4] 2729[4] 3301[12] 8004[9] 8159[11] 8343[7] 8447[2]

The Body (USA) *Mlle S Sine* 38
3 b g Speightstown(USA) Vikki Slew (USA) (Slew O'Gold (USA))
3454a[8]

The Boss Of Me *Kevin Ryan* a49 41
2 ch g Bahamian Bounty Orange Pip (Bold Edge)
3044[10] 5558[8] 6213[4]

The Brockster *Richard Ford*
2 ch g Proclamation(IRE) Synergie (IRE) (Exit To Nowhere (USA))
8188[8]

The Brothers War (USA) *J-C Rouget* a102 109
3 b c War Front(USA) Moon Queen (IRE) (Sadler's Wells (USA))
999a[3] 3455[11]

The Bull Hayes (IRE) *Michael Appleby* 94
7 b g Sadler's Wells(USA) No Review (USA) (Nodouble (USA))
1110[2] 1273[3] 1484[6] 1643[4] 1843[6] 2040[5] 3344[5] 5008[8]

The Bunny Catcher *Sharon Watt* a21 30
2 b f Jeremy(USA) Passionforfashion (IRE) (Fasliyev (USA))
1432[5] 2025[7] 8044[6]

The Call (FR) *J Hirschberger* 99
4 b g Call Me Big(GER) Tennessee Waltz (Caerleon (USA))
3970a[8]

The Cat *Nigel Twiston-Davies* a22 18
2 gr f Josr Algarhoud(IRE) Animal Cracker (Primo Dominie)
6681[9] 7662[6] 8123[13]

The Cayterers *Ronald Harris* a60 85
11 b g Cayman Kai(IRE) Silky Smooth (IRE) (Thatching)
4242[5] 5124[10] 5847[2] 6353[6] 6428[3] 7849[8]

The Champagne Boy *Jim Boyle* 8
2 ch g Sleeping Indian Desert Cristal (IRE) (Desert King (IRE))
4997[9]

The Cheka (IRE) *Eve Johnson Houghton* a104 113
7 b g Xaar Veiled Beauty (USA) (Royal Academy (USA))
1637[8] 2368[15] 5013[3] 5844[3] 6411[6] 7247[6]

The Codger *David O'Meara* a48 66
3 bl g Observatory(USA) Berry Baby (IRE) (Rainbow Quest (USA))
964[6] 1150[3] 1392[5] (1967) 5483[5] 6598[13]

The Confessor *Henry Candy* a96 98
6 b g Piccolo Twilight Mistress (Bin Ajwaad (IRE))
2013[3] 2585[3] (3538) 4744[25] 5533[8] 5943[4] 6621[9] 7222[4]

Thecornishcockney *John Ryan* a103 71
4 bl g Cockney Rebel(IRE) Glittering Image (IRE) (Sadler's Wells (USA))
496[7] (654) ◆ (823)

Thecornishcowboy *John Ryan* a83 78
4 b g Haafhd Oriental Dance (Fantastic Light (USA))
810[5] 1031[7] (1200) 1390[7] 1753[4] 2101[4] 2383[10] 2939[6] (3150) 3412[7] 3587[3] 3971[4] 4490[4] 5491[7] (6775) 6794[4] 6976[12] 7453[6] 8159[10] 8400[6]

Thecornishwren (IRE) *John Ryan* a36
4 ch f Medecis Coulisse (IRE) (In The Wings)
3907[10] 4867[6] 5493[8] 5622[8] 5803[8] 6700[8] 7167[5] 7484[7]

The Dancing Lord *Bill Turner* a70 75
4 br g Imperial Dancer Miss Brookie (The West (USA))
806[7] 916[5] (8169) (8244)

The Dandy Yank (IRE) *Jamie Osborne* a66 69
2 b g Dandy Man(IRE) Bronze Queen (IRE) (Invincible Spirit (IRE))
2595[8] 3017[10] 3413[3] 3883[3] 4141[2] 4451[4]

The Dark Wizard (IRE) *Roger Charlton* a80 80
3 gr g Dark Angel(IRE) Knapton Hill (Zamindar (USA))
1660[11] 1896[3] 2267[3] 2722[2] 3401[2] 4303[5] (4911) 5389[5] (6075) 6526[4] 7255[4]

The Doyle Machine (IRE) *Noel Quinlan* a57 65
2 b g Camacho Berenica (IRE) (College Chapel)
3310[5] 5140[3] 6069[4] 6776[3] 8414[4]

The Ducking Stool *Julia Feilden* a65 75
6 ch m Where Or When(IRE) Dance Sequel (Selkirk (USA))
53[5] 1031[4] (1297) 1600[10] 2137[3] 2785[5] (3997) 5144[5] 5802[5] (6574) 7453[2] 7611[3]

The Dukkerer (IRE) *David O'Meara* a62 58
2 bb f Footstepsinthesand Saffron Crocus (Shareef Dancer (USA))
3280[5] 3766[2] 4115[5] 4820[4] 5898[2] 6474[3] 6778[3] 7198[4]

The Fugue *John Gosden* 123
4 bb f Dansili Twyla Tharp (IRE) (Sadler's Wells (USA))
3457[3] ◆ 4082[7] (5682) (6226a) 7712a[2] 8208a[2]

The Fun Crusher *Tim Easterby* 88
5 ch g Halling(USA) South Rock (Rock City)
1238[4] 1463[4] 2402[12] 2648[7]

The Gatling Boy (IRE) *Richard Hannon Snr* a80 82
3 ch g Tamayuz Miniver (IRE) (Mujtahid (USA))
1636[9] 2604[7] 2984[5] 3633[6] 5401[7] 6106[6] 6642[8]

The Ginger Berry *Dr Jon Scargill* a56 48
3 ch g First Trump Dolly Coughdrop (IRE) (Titus Livius (FR))
1711[6] 3137[8] 4391[6] 4961[8] 7104[7] (8448)

The Gold Cheongsam (IRE) *Jeremy Noseda* 105
3 b f Red Clubs(IRE) Fuerta Ventura (IRE) (Desert Sun)
1676[10] 3460[15] (4529) 4949[4] 7021[3]

The Great Gabrial *Alan McCabe* a84 72
4 b g Oasis Dream Quiff (Sadler's Wells (USA))
521[4] 708[4] 1106[3] 1297[10] 3410[8] 3919[3] (4148) 4430[5] 4520[6] (5232) ◆ 5471[12] (6154) 6476 [5] 6856[5] 7076[3] (7306) 7437[3] 7742[4] (7898) 8350[4]

The Green Ogre *Gary Moore* 63
3 b g Dubai Destination(USA) Takegawa (Giant's Causeway (USA))
2605[10] 2938[10] 3632[3]

The Grey Gatsby (IRE) *Kevin Ryan* 107
2 ch c Mastercraftsman(IRE) Marie Vison (IRE) (Entrepreneur)
(4312) 5652^{2} 6390^{2} 7528^{7}

The Grumpy Gnome (IRE) *Richard Fahey* a66 66
2 b g Dandy Man(IRE) Certain Charm (USA) (Thunder Gulch (USA))
4312^{8} 4781^{5} 5339^{6} 6605^{3} 7146^{4} 7782^{13}

The Guru Of Gloom (IRE) *William Muir* a82 85
5 b g Dubai Destination(USA) Gabriella (Cape Cross (IRE))
34^{7} 358^{6} (518) 740^{7} 751^{4} 1096^{4} 1430^{3} 1746^{5} 2286^{7} 2929^{12} 3430^{5} 4163^{8} 5631^{2} 6473^{3}

The Happy Hammer (IRE) *Eugene Stanford* a76 59
7 b g Acclamation Emma's Star (ITY) (Darshaan)
79^{6} 344^{5} (822) 981^{6} 1172^{U} 1514^{10} 1800^{3} 2286^{9} 2573^{4} 6317^{7} 7880^{7}

The Holyman (IRE) *Jo Crowley* a82 80
5 ch g Footstepsinthesand Sunset (IRE) (Polish Precedent (USA))
779^{4} 1973^{3} (3012) 3856^{4} 5168^{6}

The Hooded Claw (IRE) *Tim Easterby* 91
2 ch g Dandy Man(IRE) Changari (USA) (Gulch (USA))
2238^{5} 4963^{5} 5577^{2} 6234^{6} 6842^{2} 7026^{5} ◆ 7170^{11} (7592)

The Jailer *John O'Shea* a60 58
10 b m Mujahid(USA) Once Removed (Distant Relative)
81^{7} 92^{6} 408^{10}

The Kernigal (IRE) *Paul Howling* a68 58
4 b g Red Clubs(IRE) Ellens Princess (IRE) (Desert Prince (IRE))
517^{7}

The Kicking Lord *Noel Wilson* a63 41
4 b g Avonbridge Lady Killer (IRE) (Daggers Drawn (USA))
6180^{U} 6761^{9}

The Kid *Tom Dascombe* 63
2 b g High Chaparral(IRE) Shine Like A Star (Fantastic Light (USA))
3233^{5} 4021^{4}

The Lark *Michael Bell* 108
3 ch f Pivotal Gull Wing (IRE) (In The Wings)
2412^{3} 2842^{3} 3614a^{5} (6329) 7566a^{7}

The Lock Master (IRE) *Michael Appleby* a89 86
6 b g Key Of Luck(USA) Pitrizza (IRE) (Machiavellian (USA))
167^{6} (644) 830^{3} 889^{4} 1148^{5} 1237^{3} 1536^{12} 1831^{12} (2580) 2766^{2} 3293^{9} 5195^{4} 5559^{5} 5613^{9} 7906^{5} 8007^{6} 8269^{6} 8408^{4}

The Lodge Road (IRE) *Martin Todhunter* a69 73
5 b g Holy Roman Emperor(IRE) Golden Coral (USA) (Slew O'Gold (USA))
2961^{6} 3625^{10} 3727^{4} 4016^{4} 5052^{10} 5713^{9}

The Lumber Guy (USA) *Michael Hushion* a112
4 rg c Grand Slam(USA) Boltono (USA) (Unbridled's Song (USA))
7713a^{11}

The Manx Missile *Michael Bell* a60 53
3 ch g Sakhee's Secret Careless Freedom (Bertolini (USA))
1050^{DSQ} 1349^{3} 1742^{4} 2962^{7} 3739^{6}

The Monarck (FR) *T Lallie* a71 73
3 ch g Zamindar(USA) Rock Harmonie (FR) (Rock Of Gibraltar (IRE))
1495a^{0}

The Mongoose *David Evans* a72 75
5 b g Montjeu(IRE) Angara (Alzao (USA))
130^{4} 340^{3} 446^{3} (490) 519^{3} 652^{10} 899^{4} 1039^{5} 1322^{3} 1656^{9} 1950^{7} (2057) 2281^{5} 2395^{14} 2918^{5} 3051^{3} 3270^{11} (3430) 3661^{4} 3949^{7} 4250^{5} (4996) (5177) 5387^{8} 5815^{4} 6039^{5} 6475^{6} 7303^{5} 8068^{3} 8157^{3} 8244^{2}

The Name Is Frank *Mark Gillard* a63 67
8 b g Lujain(USA) Zaragossa (Paris House)
1902^{6} 2395^{4} 3181^{3} 3326^{8} 3700^{5} 4197^{2} 4427^{5} 4659^{7} 5404^{9} 5817^{3} 6101^{4} 6323^{7}

The Nifty Blaze *Tim Easterby* 54
3 ch g Firebreak Nifty Alice (First Trump)
1687^{9} 2535^{4} 2719^{7}

The Nifty Fox *Tim Easterby* a87 86
9 b g Foxhound(USA) Nifty Alice (First Trump)
2031^{18} 2410^{12} 2797^{5} 3283^{4} (3331) 3769^{4} 4340^{6} 4613^{5} 4954^{6} 5266^{3} 6052^{5} 6583^{17} 6908^{14} 7240^{7} 7593^{7}

The Noble Ord *Sylvester Kirk* a70 77
4 b g Indesatchel(IRE) Four Legs Good (IRE) (Be My Guest (USA))
120^{5} 221^{3} 801^{6} 975^{5} 1020^{5} 1170^{4} 1294^{4} 1474^{2} 1893^{8} 2073^{5}

Theo Danon (GER) *Mario Hofer* a98 99
5 ch g Lord Of England(GER) Ticinella (GER) (Hernando (FR))
152a^{7} 363a^{9} 552a^{10}

Theodore Gericault (IRE) *Sir Michael Stoute* a89 89
3 b g Sir Percy Tableau Vivant (IRE) (Pivotal)
(1323) (1934) ◆ 2604^{3} 3338^{7} 5436^{4} 6976^{3} 7330^{8}

Theology *Steve Gollings* a99 92
6 b g Galileo(IRE) Biographie (Mtoto)
1547^{5} 2149^{15} 3099^{9} 3959^{3} 6833^{4} 7210^{2} 7660^{8} 7975^{2} (8429)

The Osteopath (IRE) *John Davies* 86
10 ch g Danehill Dancer(IRE) Miss Margate (IRE) (Don't Forget Me)
1115^{4} (1569) 2463^{6} 3570^{7} 5149^{7} 5580^{2} 5861^{6} 6288^{5}

The Ploughman *John Bridger* a47 47
4 gr g Tillerman Kilmovee (Inchinor)
1877^{11}

The Power Of One (IRE) *James Given* 21
3 b g Duke Of Marmalade(IRE) Mustique Dream (Don't Forget Me)
2547^{9} 2885^{8} 3250^{14}

The Quarterjack *Ron Hodges* a45 80
4 b g Haafhd Caressed (Medicean)
2102^{7} 2598^{2} 3344^{8} 4720^{4} 5312^{8} 6158^{7} 7220^{5}

Therapeutic *Scott Dixon* a48 64
3 b f Milk It Mick Theoretical (Marju (IRE))
3247^{9} 4930^{11}

Thereabouts (USA) *Michael Appleby* a71 72
4 b g Singspiel(IRE) Around (Danehill (USA))
104^{5} 478^{5} 593^{3} ◆ 709^{4} 816^{6} 987^{2} 1184^{3} 1333^{2} 1600^{3} 6700^{3} 6952^{4} 7275^{10} 7758^{3}

The Reaper (IRE) *G M Lyons* a110 108
5 b g Footstepsinthesand Lady Gregory (IRE) (In The Wings)
244a^{15}

The Rectifier (USA) *Seamus Durack* a99 103
6 bb g Langfuhr(CAN) Western Vision (USA) (Gone West (USA))
3207^{4} (3544) (4308) 5838^{13} 6650^{4} 6838^{19}

The Red Arctic *Lisa Williamson*
3 b g Vitus Danehill Princess (IRE) (Danehill (USA))
2833^{11}

There's No Rules *Richard Guest* a48 46
4 br g Authorized(IRE) Excellent (Grand Lodge (USA))
820^{13} 846^{6} 908^{6} 1022^{7} 1146^{5} 1369^{8}

The Scuttler (IRE) *Mick Channon* a72 73
3 b g Rakti Common Rumpus (IRE) (Common Grounds)
807^{4} (1014) 1275^{6} 1608^{5} 1900^{12} 2727^{8} 3254^{2} (3859) 4077^{2} (4140) 4241^{6} 4829^{6} 4940^{3} 5668^{3} 5975^{8} (6587) 6794^{13} 7429^{2} 7505^{10}

The Silver Kebaya (FR) *Jeremy Noseda* a22
2 b f Rock Of Gibraltar(IRE) Music House (IRE) (Singspiel (IRE))
7295^{7}

The Smart One (IRE) *Mick Channon* 70
2 b c Exceed And Excel(AUS) Bareilly (USA) (Lyphard (USA))
1669^{6} 2048^{6} 3045^{2} 3311^{3} 4019^{5}

The Strig *Stuart Williams* a79 81
6 b g Mujahid(USA) Pretty Kool (Inchinor)
232^{2} 360^{3} 650^{5} 812^{3} 981^{5} 1198^{4} 2450^{11} 3431^{6} 3841^{9} 3921^{DSQ} 4494^{10} 4884^{5} 5165^{4} 5608^{2} 5701^{3} 5956^{2} (6463) (6527) 7254^{5} 7452^{8}

The Taj (USA) *Richard Hannon Snr* a76 88
3 ch g Street Cry(IRE) India (USA) (Hennessy (USA))
1625^{6} 1808^{12} 3831^{8} 4284^{7}

The Third Man *John Gosden* a77
2 b c Dalakhani(IRE) Spinning Queen (Spinning World (USA))
(8333) ◆

The Tichborne (IRE) *Roger Teal* a85 78
5 b g Shinko Forest(IRE) Brunswick (Warning)
(1346) 2255^{21} 2724^{5} 4165^{3} 6203^{10} 7255^{5} 7507^{4} 8181^{6} (8453)

The Tiddly Tadpole *Simon West* 72
8 b g Tipsy Creek(USA) Froglet (Shaamit (IRE))
2465^{7} 2855^{10}

The Tiger *Ed Dunlop* a97 99
5 b g Tiger Hill(IRE) Rafiya (Halling (USA))
926^{3} 1037^{4} 1547^{10} 2040^{2}

The Troyster *Brian Ellison* a19 21
3 b g Indesatchel(IRE) Spindara (IRE) (Spinning World (USA))
2027^{9} 2507^{9} 8407^{4}

The United States (IRE) *A P O'Brien* 107
3 ch c Galileo(IRE) Beauty Is Truth (IRE) (Pivotal)
1555a^{6} (6225a)

The Wallace Line (IRE) *Mick Channon* a59 63
2 b g Mastercraftsman(IRE) Surval (IRE) (Sadler's Wells (USA))
3291^{5} 3972^{6} 4518^{3} 6520^{3} 6946^{4} 7418^{3} 7855^{9} 8131^{2}

Thewandaofu (IRE) *Jamie Osborne* a86 96
2 ro f Clodovil(IRE) Sweet Times (Riverman (USA))
2282^{4} (2562) 2993^{2} 6426^{2} 6839^{2} 7194^{5} (7925)

The Wee Chief (IRE) *Jimmy Fox* a63 68
7 ch g King Charlemagne(USA) La Belle Clare (IRE) (Paris House)
2657^{11} 3855^{4} 4303^{6} 5349^{6} 5956^{11} 6929^{8} 7652^{9} 7862^{4} 8023^{11}

The Welsh Wizard (IRE) *Charles Hills* a78 79
3 b g Dylan Thomas(IRE) Golden Dew (IRE) (Montjeu (IRE))
799^{2} ◆ 1236^{3} ◆ 1443^{2} 3606^{3} 5058^{4} 6202^{3} 6557^{3} 6978^{5}

Thewestwalian (USA) *Peter Hiatt* a57 53
5 bb g Stormy Atlantic(USA) Skies Of Blue (USA) (Ogygian (USA))
1795^{4} 2198^{9} 2496^{6} 6154^{5} 6323^{8} 7299^{8} 7485^{2}

The Which Doctor *Violet M Jordan* a52 53
8 b g Medicean Oomph (Shareef Dancer (USA))
441^{10} 825^{4} 1093^{4} 1474^{7} 1951^{8} 2787^{5} 7511^{7}

The Winged Assasin (USA) *Shaun Lycett* a64 69
7 b g Fusaichi Pegasus(USA) Gran Dama (USA) (Rahy (USA))
2328^{7} 6658^{9}

Thewinningmachine *Jo Hughes* a51 59
4 b f Kheleyf(USA) Spinning Reel (Spinning World (USA))
2155^{6} 4357^{10} (5127) 5596^{10} 6283^{9} 7091^{14} 7980^{8}

The Wizard Of Aus (IRE) *Andrew Balding* a74 69
3 b g Aussie Rules(USA) Dyness (USA) (Dynaformer (USA))
3821^{7} 4590^{6} 5281^{3} ◆ 5960^{4} 6522^{2} ◆ 6775^{4}

The Wonga Coup (IRE) *Pat Phelan* a67 59
6 b g Northern Afleet(USA) Quichesterbahn (USA) (Broad Brush (USA))
3499^{8} 3976^{7} 4591^{8} 5216^{5} 7740^{5} 8072^{6} 8448^{7}

The Yank *Tony Carroll* a59 53
4 b g Trade Fair Silver Gyre (IRE) (Silver Hawk (USA))
983^{3} ◆ 1730^{4} 2777^{6} 5093^{11} 6137^{8} 8148^{7}

The Young Master *Neil Mulholland* a59
4 b g Echo Of Light Fine Frenzy (IRE) (Great Commotion (USA))
(8268)

Thiang (IRE) *Tim Easterby* 33
2 b f Tamayuz Bryanstown Girl (IRE) (Kalanisi (IRE))
6842^{7}

Thimaar (USA) *Donald McCain* a106 108
5 bb g Dynaformer(USA) Jinaan (USA) (Mr Prospector (USA))
2149^{16}

Think *Clive Mulhall* a48 51
6 ch g Sulamani(IRE) Natalie Jay (Ballacashtal (CAN))
7376^{3}

Think Again *Kevin Ryan* 48
2 b f Dubawi(IRE) Maziona (Dansili)
2830^{4} 3049^{7} 7780^{10}

Think Ahead *Saeed bin Suroor* 80
2 b c Shamardal(USA) Moonshadow (Diesis)
6938^{3} 7654^{2}

Third Strike *Gary Moore* a63
2 b c Tertullian(USA) Shaabra (IRE) (Rainbow Quest (USA))
7302^{7}

Thirteen Shivers *Michael Easterby* a78 87
5 b g Iceman Thirteen Tricks (USA) (Grand Slam (USA))
1067^{9} 1248^{7} 1644^{11}

This Charming Man (IRE) *Keith Dalgleish* a50
2 b g Diamond Green(FR) Incendio (Siberian Express (USA))
8346^{6}

This Is Me *Don Cantillon* a69 52
5 b g Presenting Shayzara (IRE) (Turtle Island (IRE))
2157^{7} 2321^{8} 2754^{6} 3222^{6} 3909^{12} 7951^{6} (8149) 8349^{6} (8417) ◆

This Is Nice (IRE) *Tom Dascombe* a73 74
3 ch f Exceed And Excel(AUS) Spanish Quest (Rainbow Quest (USA))
(2788) 3179^{3} 3620^{2} 3927^{2}

This Is The Day *William Haggas* a72 56
2 b f Footstepsinthesand Miss Pinkerton (Danehill (USA))
6974^{4} 7645^{5} 8176^{3}

This Ones For Eddy *John Balding* a68 59
8 b g Kyllachy Skirt Around (Deploy)
193^{3} 312^{2} 435^{10} 600^{4} 1222^{3}

Thisonesmine (IRE) *David C Griffiths*
2 ch g Haatef(USA) Jersey Lillie (IRE) (Hector Protector (USA))
4886^{11}

This Time (FR) *H-A Pantall* 104
2 b f Zafeen(FR) Scalotta (GER) (Winged Love (IRE))
(6293a) 7939a^{2}

Thistleandtworoses (USA) *David O'Meara* a77 69
3 ch g Lion Heart(USA) Country Again (USA) (Awesome Again (CAN))
(877) 1543^{6} 5030^{6} 6970^{9} 7438^{6} ◆ 7989^{9}

Thistle Bird *Roger Charlton* a56 115
5 b f Selkirk(USA) Dolma (FR) (Marchand De Sable (USA))
2045^{3} (2838) 3456^{9} 4985^{2} 5739^{6} 7057a^{3}

Thomaraz (FR) *P Sogorb* a87 75
6 ch h Nombre Premier Niraz (FR) (Nikos)
498a^{4} 5464a^{2}

Thomas Blossom (IRE) *Nigel Tinkler* a37 32
3 b g Dylan Thomas(IRE) Woman Secret (IRE) (Sadler's Wells (USA))
6748^{9} 7311^{6} 7932^{6}

Thomas Chippendale (IRE) *Lady Cecil* 119
4 br c Dansili All My Loving (IRE) (Sadler's Wells (USA))
1846^{2} 2252^{2} (3556) (Dead)

Thomas Hobson *John Gosden* a68 106
3 b c Halling(USA) La Spezia (IRE) (Danehill Dancer (IRE))
1727^{3} 3021^{8} ◆ (4882) (5534) 6503^{2} (7223) (7526)

Thomasina *Denis Coakley* a48 48
3 b f One Cool Cat(USA) Jemiliah (Dubai Destination (USA))
1710^{4} 2362^{5} 3013^{6} 3859^{11} 5166^{3} 5604^{5} 6260^{3} 7269^{4}

Thornaby Nash *David O'Meara* 77
2 br g Kheleyf(USA) Mistress Twister (Pivotal)
2404^{2} 2701^{5} 4886^{4} 5656^{13} (6285)

Thornaby Princess *Marjorie Fife* 59
2 b f Camacho Ingleby Princess (Bold Edge)
4724^{3} 5140^{6} 5883^{3}

Thorntoun Care *Jim Goldie* 67
2 b g Rail Link Thorntoun Piccolo (Groom Dancer (USA))
6545^{5} 7146^{2}

Thorntoun Lady (USA) *Jim Goldie* 67
3 b f Henrythenavigator(USA) Valery Lady (ARG) (Roy (USA))
4013^{4} ◆ 4887^{5} 5517^{2} 5878^{10}

Thorpe (IRE) *Ralph Beckett* a81 81
3 b g Danehill Dancer(IRE) Minkova (IRE) (Sadler's Wells (USA))
1443^{4} ◆ 2386^{2} 4150^{2} 4899^{5} 5390^{3} 6202^{4} (7311)

Thorpe Bay *Michael Appleby* a78 61
4 b g Piccolo My Valentina (Royal Academy (USA))
30^{7} 142^{8} 1077^{2} 1147^{2} 1186^{4} 1681^{4} (2170) 2236^{7} 2582^{3} 3196^{5} 7848^{2} 7862^{7} 8049^{2} (8272) (8439)

Thought And Memory (IRE) *Mick Channon* a54 46
3 ch c Raven's Pass(USA) Sadinga (IRE) (Sadler's Wells (USA))
74^{7}

Thouwra (IRE) *Saeed bin Suroor* a86 101
3 b c Pivotal Cape Verdi (IRE) (Caerleon (USA))
1684^{4} 2480^{2} 2953^{2} 3858^{2} 4454^{2} (5495) 5958^{2} (6538) (6867) 7205^{P} (Dead)

Thrasos (IRE) *Jo Crowley* a54 27
4 b g Invincible Spirit(IRE) Plymsole (USA) (Diesis)
123^{5} 1660^{12} 6753^{10}

Threat Resolved (IRE) *A Oliver* a42 56
3 ch g Nayef(USA) Palanca (Inchinor)
1587a^{6}

Threave *Violet M Jordan* a26 78
5 b f Diktat Bianca Sforza (Anabaa (USA))
2576^{9} (6145) 6463^{2} (6745) 6982^{7} 7324^{4} 7633^{9}

Three Choirs (IRE) *William Stone* a72 74
3 br f Rock Of Gibraltar(IRE) Three Owls (IRE) (Warning)
2606^{2} 3277^{7} 3785^{5} 4416^{5} 4865^{7} 5491^{11} 6402^{10}

Three Cliffs *Roger Varian* a71
2 b c Exceed And Excel(AUS) Gower Song (Singspiel (IRE))
7119^{4} 7646^{4}

Three Crowns *Jonathan Portman* a69 79
3 b f Three Valleys(USA) Red Sovereign (Danzig Connection (USA))
3988^{3} 5173^{4} 6105^{5}

Three D Alexander (IRE) *David Wachman* 87
2 ch f Aqlaam Pivotal's Princess (IRE) (Pivotal)
5771a^{5}

Three Glasses (IRE) *Tim Easterby* 64
3 br c Excellent Art Sinamay (USA) (Saint Ballado (CAN))
2279^{8} 2765^{5} ◆ 3232^{5} 3711^{4}

Three Heart's *Hugo Palmer* a40 57
2 b f Three Valleys(USA) Heart's Harmony (Blushing Groom (FR))
5282^{11} 6597^{6} 7310^{5} 8434^{6}

Three Peaks *Charles Hills* 77
2 ch c Three Valleys(USA) Coming Back (Fantastic Light (USA))
3695^{5} 7335^{3}

Threepence *Richard Whitaker* 47
3 b g Three Valleys(USA) The Jotter (Night Shift (USA))
1966^{11} 2342^{8} 4140^{8} 4849^{5} 5010^{3} 6717^{6}

Three Pips *Ed McMahon* a70 18
2 b c Captain Gerrard(IRE) Samadilla (IRE) (Mujadil (USA))
7341^{11} 7790^{2} 8138^{3} (8414)

Three Quid (IRE) *Gary Harrison* 36
2 b f Clodovil(IRE) Justice System (USA) (Criminal Type (USA))
7466^{12}

Threes Grand *Scott Dixon* a82 91
3 b f Milk It Mick Ginger Cookie (Bold Edge)
1112^{6} 1806^{3} 2430^{15} 3097^{11} 3367^{8} 4255^{9} 5519^{4} (5769) 6309^{13} 6583^{14} 7314^{6} 7777^{11} 8167^{2} 8232^{11}

Threetimesalady *Sir Mark Prescott Bt* a64 84
2 b f Royal Applause Triple Joy (Most Welcome)
4164^{8} 4408^{6} (4708) (5175) 5366^{3} 5927^{5} 6628^{2}

Three White Socks (IRE) *Brian Ellison* a71 59
6 b g Whipper(USA) Halesia (USA) (Chief's Crown (USA))
1454^{4} 2313^{7} 8047^{11}

Thrilled To Bits (IRE) *A Oliver* 72
2 b f Tagula(IRE) Daunting Lady (IRE) (Mujadil (USA))
2675a^{5} 2944a^{9}

Throne Room *John Gosden* 70
2 b c Oasis Dream Magnificient Style (USA) (Silver Hawk (USA))
6534^{4} 7070^{2} (Dead)

Throwing Roses *Lawrence Mullaney* a53 63
3 b f Clodovil(IRE) Mizooka (Tobougg (IRE))
1284^{7} 1759^{9} 2507^{6} 4005^{6} (5341) 5903^{4} 6600^{5}

Thrtypointstothree (IRE) *Nikki Evans* 65
2 b g Kodiac Miss Taken (IRE) (Dubai Destination (USA))
2823^{3} 3422^{15} 3883^{6} 5842^{6} 6487^{5} 7393^{5}

Thrust Control (IRE) *Tracy Waggott* a51 64
6 ch g Fath(USA) Anazah (USA) (Diesis)
1394^{10} 1459^{7} (1603) (1757) 2081^{3} 2551^{11} 2911^{8} 3192^{10} 3649^{14} 4160^{9} 4967^{12} 5341^{11} 6276^{12}

Thubiaan (USA) *Chris Waller* 94
5 b g Dynaformer(USA) Barzah (IRE) (Darshaan)
7760a^{5}

Thumbs Up (NZ) *C Fownes* 120
9 b g Shinko King(IRE) Regelle (NZ) (Exploding Prospect (USA))
1872a^{7}

Thunderball *Scott Dixon* a92 99
7 ch g Haafhd Trustthunder (Selkirk (USA))
405^{2} 584^{8} 621^{8} (1232) 1537^{19} 1720^{13} 2868^{9} 3527^{27} 5545^{6} 5992^{9} 6331^{3} 6621^{20} 6845^{9} 7222^{P}

Thundering Cloud (IRE) *Brendan Powell* a63 53
2 b f Clodovil(IRE) Porky Pie (IRE) (Grand Lodge (USA))
6423^{7} 7261^{4} 7638^{5} 7892^{6}

Thundering Home *Richard Mitchell* a73 60
6 gr g Storming Home Citrine Spirit (IRE) (Soviet Star (USA))
309^{3} 2284^{3} 3412^{3}

Thunder Pass (IRE) *Hughie Morrison* 63
2 b c High Chaparral(IRE) Hadarama (IRE) (Sinndar (IRE))
5309^{7} 5698^{10} 7069^{6}

Thunder Strike *Richard Hannon Snr* 100
2 ch c Sakhee's Secret Trump Street (First Trump)
(2005) ◆ (2518) (2863) ◆ 3422^{4} 4486^{5} 4918^{3} 5679^{2} 6347^{5}

Thunderstruck (GER) *R Dzubasz* 95
3 b f Silvano(GER) Trikolore (GER) (Konigsstuhl (GER))
4092a^{7} 5044a^{12} 6887a^{8}

Thurayaat *Roger Varian* 70
2 b f Tamayuz Ghaidaa (IRE) (Cape Cross (IRE))
4432^{6} 5983^{2}

Thwart *Ralph Beckett* a78 80
3 ch f Refuse To Bend(IRE) Jump Ship (Night Shift (USA))
1685^{2} ◆ (2127) (3437) 4349^{3} 7267^{4}

Thyan (FR) *P Capelle* a71 50
6 b h Indian Rocket Slyders (IRE) (Hector Protector (USA))
2559a^{10} 5806a^{16}

Thylyer (IRE) *Peter Makin*
2 b c Alhaarth(IRE) Wassendale (Erhaab (USA))
7243^{10}

Tianjin City (FR) *N Clement* a82 82
3 gr g Holy Roman Emperor(IRE) Tenepia (FR) (Keltos (FR))
72a^{4}

Tiberio (SPA) *M Delzangles* a71 76
3 ch c Panis(USA) Peinture D'Or (IRE) (Peintre Celebre (USA))
72a^{0} 460a^{0} 2335a^{2}

Ticking Katie (IRE) *K R Burke* 89
2 b f Baltic King Danccalli (IRE) (Traditionally (USA))
3044^9 3624^2 (4337) 5226^2 5745^2 ◆ 6326^2 6839^3

Tickled Pink (IRE) *Lady Cecil* 114
4 gr f Invincible Spirit(IRE) Cassandra Go (IRE) (Indian Ridge)
(1637) 2368^9 3263a^5 (4079) 4947^7 5726^6 6639^6 7054a^{12}

Ticoz (USA) *Marco Botti* a93 15
8 bb h Cozzene(USA) Transition Time (USA) (Dynaformer (USA))
7612^9

Tidal Beauty *Tony Carroll* a34 18
2 gr f Verglas(IRE) Tidal (Bin Ajwaad (IRE))
2978^7 3631^{10} 4164^{12}

Tidal's Baby *Tony Carroll* a75 85
4 b g Dutch Art Tidal (Bin Ajwaad (IRE))
96^5 494^2 687^5 878^7 3315^{12} 3622^7 (4120) 4220^2 (4860) 5998^2 ◆ 6586^{26} 6744^3 7254^6

Tiddliwinks *Kevin Ryan* a97 116
7 b g Piccolo Card Games (First Trump)
1637^9 2368^{17} 2676a^{12} 4986^{27} 5726^9 6719^9 7928^5 8064^7 8344^7

Tidentime (USA) *Mick Channon* a84 86
4 bb g Speightstown(USA) Casting Call (USA) (Dynaformer (USA))
(2871) 3274^3 4281^2 4879^9 6067^2 6337^9 7992^5

Tides Reach (IRE) *Roger Charlton* a69 75
2 ch f Mastercraftsman(IRE) Oystermouth (Averti (IRE))
5385^2 ◆ 5949^3 (6923)

Tidy Affair (IRE) *Gary Moore* a79 83
4 b g Amadeus Wolf Pride Of My Heart (Lion Cavern (USA))
(704) (788) (1084)

Tiffany Bay (IRE) *John Patrick Shanahan* a64 73
2 b f The Carbon Unit(USA) Crackling Rosie (IRE) (Dr Fong (USA))
6821^4

Tiger Cliff (IRE) *Lady Cecil* a86 107
4 b g Tiger Hill(IRE) Verbania (IRE) (In The Wings)
(2451) 3423^2 ◆ (5766) 7193^8

Tigerino (IRE) *Chris Fairhurst* a54 45
5 b g Tiger Hill(IRE) Golden Shadow (IRE) (Selkirk (USA))
4614^9 6853^3

Tigerish *Amanda Perrett* a64 19
3 b g Tiger Hill(IRE) Dimakya (USA) (Dayjur (USA))
1729^5 6106^8 6459^9 6932^{10}

Tiger Jim *Chris Wall* a63
3 b g Tiger Hill(IRE) Quintrell (Royal Applause)
3435^4 7484^2

Tiger Reigns *John Butler* a61 88
7 b g Tiger Hill(IRE) Showery (Rainbow Quest (USA))
2463^{12} 3827^6 5149^4 5580^{10} 6236^{18} 7880^{12}

Tiger's Home *Julia Feilden* a59 59
3 b f Tiger Hill(IRE) Homeward (IRE) (Kris)
817^2 1424^6 2331^7 3740^4 4881^3 6502^7 (6902) 7845^2 8052^6

Tigers Tale (IRE) *Roger Teal* a88 95
4 b g Tiger Hill(IRE) Vayenga (FR) (Highest Honor (FR))
1092^3 1922^6 2424^2 3019^2 4080^{12} 6801^3 7536^{11} 7926^9

Tiger Twenty Two *Richard Fahey* 87
2 b g Authorized(IRE) Collette's Choice (Royal Applause)
2401^3 2670^9 3233^3 (4314) 5656^{14} 6619^3

Tightend Touchdown (USA) *Jason Servis* 116
4 ch g Pure Precision(USA) Starry Mark (USA) (Marquetry (USA))
7710a^2

Tight Fit *Henry Candy* a64 89
3 ch f Assertive Bikini (Trans Island)
1907^2 2387^4 (3178) 3718^3 (4685) (5541) 6488^4 6959^7

Tight Knit (USA) *John Weymes* a79 11
3 b g Hard Spun(USA) Tamdiid (USA) (Horse Chestnut (SAF))
209^2 359^3 538^3 867^4 1206^3 1725^{12} 8139^7 8366^2

Tight Lipped (IRE) *James Eustace* a79 85
4 gr g Dark Angel(IRE) Kayoko (IRE) (Shalford (IRE))
(168) 832^2 912^6 1292^2 1442^{10} 2383^3 (2808) 3293^2 4028^6

Tigre D'Or (FR) *A Couetil* 103
7 gr g Tiger Hill(IRE) Sporades (USA) (Vaguely Noble)
7590a^7

Tijori (IRE) *Bernard Llewellyn* a74 71
5 b g Kyllachy Polish Belle (Polish Precedent (USA))
1664^8 2350^3 (3271) (3952) 5997^5 6424^{12} 7506^8

Tijuca (IRE) *Ed de Giles* a55 42
4 b f Captain Rio Some Forest (IRE) (Charnwood Forest (IRE))
28^3 335^4

Tilly T (IRE) *J S Moore* a18 48
3 b f Thousand Words Pippi (IRE) (City On A Hill (USA))
1289^5 1685^8 1897^7 3014^8

Tilstarr (IRE) *Roger Teal* a68 75
3 b f Shamardal(USA) Vampire Queen (IRE) (General Monash (USA))
(17) 204^3 2387^2 3241^2 3842^4 4898^3 6734^{11} 7505^9

Timbergold (FR) *J-V Toux* a67 15
2 b f Full Of Gold(FR) Theoricienne (FR) (Kendor (FR))
4651a^9

Time After Time (AUS) *W Y So* 119
6 bb g Danehill Dancer(IRE) Recurring (NZ) (Pentire)
8209a^8

Time And Place *Richard Fahey* 83
3 ch g Compton Place Forthefirstime (Dr Fong (USA))
(1295) 1625^{13} 3813^2 4734^4

Time For Action (IRE) *David Wachman* a90 101
3 ch c Dylan Thomas(IRE) Celtic Heroine (IRE) (Hernando (FR))
7230a^7

Time For Crabbies (IRE) *Lisa Williamson* a57 28
3 b g Moss Vale(IRE) Westlife (IRE) (Mind Games)
3593^5 3932^8 4839^4 5788^8 6519^5

Time For Lambrini (IRE) *Lisa Williamson* a71
3 b f Amadeus Wolf Princess Madaen (IRE) (Elusive Quality (USA))
3212^8 3638^8

Time For Mabel (FR) *F-H Graffard* a81 81
2 ch c Soldier Of Fortune(IRE) Athens Two O Four (USA) (Distant View (USA))
6961a^5

Timeless *Tobias B P Coles* a44 66
3 b f Tamayuz Sandtime (IRE) (Green Desert (USA))
2006^3 ◆ 2979^8 3860^5 4624^6

Timeless Appeal (IRE) *Peter Chapple-Hyam* a53 53
3 br f Kheleyf(USA) Elegant Times (IRE) (Dansili)
2556^2 4839^6

Timeless Call (IRE) *Reginald Roberts* a101 101
5 b f Sakhee(USA) Pourquoi Pas (IRE) (Nordico (USA))
1032^2 5772a^{12} (7521a)

Timeless Stride (IRE) *Madeleine Smith* a84 84
6 b g Kyllachy Trois Heures Apres (Soviet Star (USA))
2145a^7 5325a^8

Timeless War (USA) *William Haggas* a67
2 b c Bernardini(USA) The Best Day Ever (USA) (Brahms (USA))
8333^{11} 8389^3

Time Medicean *Tony Carroll* a65 82
7 gr g Medicean Ribbons And Bows (IRE) (Dr Devious (IRE))
11^{10} 196^{10} 494^{11} 728^9 4635^8 5594^{11} 6067^{11} 6527^2 7633^7

Time Of My Life (IRE) *Patrick Holmes* a36 76
4 b g Galileo(IRE) In My Life (IRE) (Rainbow Quest (USA))
3729^4 4851^5 5185^6

Time Prisoner (USA) *Mahmood Al Zarooni* a98 114
6 gr g Elusive Quality(USA) Zelanda (IRE) (Night Shift (USA))
(467a) 955a^4 1262a^{14}

Time Square (FR) *Tony Carroll* a68 68
6 b g Westerner Sainte Parfaite (FR) (Septieme Ciel (USA))
9^{10} 238^5 (625) (722) 883^4 1090^3 1342^5 2159^3 2845^2 (3399) 3865^5 8060^{10}

Times Up *Ed Dunlop* 115
7 b g Olden Times Princess Genista (Ile De Bourbon (USA))
2810^6 3483^{13} 5724^3 (6349) 7060a^3 7363^8

Time To Begin (IRE) *Alan McCabe* a71 56
3 b g Exceed And Excel(AUS) Zahour Al Yasmeen (Cadeaux Genereux)
796^3 1539^7 1742^7 5354^6 5965^4 6344^4 6698^9

Time To Dance *Joseph Tuite* a71
4 b g Silent Times(IRE) Bravo Dancer (Acatenango (GER))
1354^4 1699^8 1983^7

Time To Work (IRE) *Gordon Elliott* 79
5 b g Hurricane Run(IRE) Viscoumtess Brave (IRE) (Law Society (USA))
5021a^6

Timoneer (USA) *Mahmood Al Zarooni* a71 101
3 bb c Elusive Quality(USA) Gentle Gale (USA) (Storm Cat (USA))
245a^{13}

Timothy T *Philip Hide* a69 53
5 bl g Pastoral Pursuits Point Perfect (Dansili)
7075^{12} 7611^8 7898^6 8336^8

Tim Twister (GER) *B Vidovic* 68
2 b c Lando(GER) Timbalada (GER) (Big Shuffle (USA))
7185a^4

Tinchy Ryder *Bryan Smart* 48
2 b g Dylan Thomas(IRE) Keyaki (IRE) (Shinko Forest (IRE))
6513^{12} 6754^{10} 7419^6

Tinctoria *Kevin Ryan* 55
3 b f Oratorio(IRE) Blue Indigo (FR) (Pistolet Bleu (IRE))
1648^2 2405^6 2754^{10} 3463^{12} 3893^7 5293^4

Tinga (IRE) *Mick Channon* 84
2 ch f Galileo(IRE) Tingling (USA) (Storm Cat (USA))
2856^3 ◆ 3555^6 ◆ 4432^2 5284^5 6063^3

Tinghir (IRE) *David Lanigan* a94 101
3 b c Dansili Palmeraie (USA) (Lear Fan (USA))
1624^5 (2480) 2927^4 (6115) 6537^5 (6989) 7696^6

Tingle Tangle (USA) *Tony Carroll* a60 74
3 bb g Mizzen Mast(USA) Tinge (USA) (Kingmambo (USA))
5133^8 6113^3

Tingo In The Tale (IRE) *David Arbuthnot* a78 76
4 b g Oratorio(IRE) Sunlit Skies (Selkirk (USA))
144^4 352^2 562^2 948^5 1200^6 3370^4 4208^2 5231^5 6108^{10} 6960^9

Tinkerbell Will *John E Long* a57 54
6 ch m Where Or When(IRE) Highland Hannah (IRE) (Persian Heights)
94^2 722^7 1909^7

Tinseltown *Brian Rothwell* a41 74
7 b g Sadler's Wells(USA) Peony (Lion Cavern (USA))
1763^5 2277^4 2615^3 3543^7 3808^6 4853^9 5059^7 5222^4 (5466) 6239^{15} 6631^2

Tinshu (IRE) *Derek Haydn Jones* a100 91
7 ch m Fantastic Light(USA) Ring Of Esteem (Mark Of Esteem (IRE))
401^6 777^5 897^4 1034^4 1241^6 2251^8 2728^4 3293^3 3899^6 6004^2 6596^{13} 7072^4 7927^6 8071^5 8386^5

Tinsill *Nigel Tinkler* a9 72
2 ch g Firebreak Concentration (IRE) (Mind Games)
4046^{12} 4450^3 4724^7 5066^{11} 6073^2 (6511) 6872^5 7127^4

Tin Town Boy (IRE) *H Rogers* a75 60
12 b g Danehill Dancer(IRE) Sushari (IRE) (Shardari)
(5021a)

Tiny Thompson *Lydia Pearce* a39 28
4 b f Tobougg(IRE) Mon Petit Diamant (Hector Protector (USA))
215^{11}

Tioga Pass *Paul Cole* a66 66
2 b f High Chaparral(IRE) Seren Devious (Dr Devious (IRE))
6523^5 6896^5 7533^2

Tioman Legend *Roger Charlton* 97
4 b g Kyllachy Elegant Times (IRE) (Dansili)
2207^8 2937^{12} 3840^{10} 4860^{19} 6078^6

Tioman Pearl *Roger Varian* a45 87
4 b c Royal Applause Mazarine Blue (Bellypha)
723^9

Tipping Over (IRE) *Hugo Palmer* 89
3 gr f Aussie Rules(USA) Precipice (Observatory (USA))
1668^5 2253^5 4766^4 5493^7 6993^8

Tipsy Star *Daniel Kubler* a56 33
2 b f Tobougg(IRE) Extremely Rare (IRE) (Mark Of Esteem (IRE))
7466^{13} 7853^6 8085^6

Tiptree Lace *William Knight* 22
2 b f Duke Of Marmalade(IRE) Crinolette (IRE) (Sadler's Wells (USA))
4921^{17}

Titan Diamond (IRE) *Mark Usher* a52 53
5 b g Diamond Green(FR) Ditton Dancer (Danehill Dancer (IRE))
41^{11} 110^3 456^4 565^2 806^4 1473^9 1981^6 2073^7 3314^{13}

Titan Triumph *Michael Attwater* a72 31
9 b g Zamindar(USA) Triple Green (Green Desert (USA))
344^7 749^5 844^5 1386^4 1514^{11} 2807^3 3172^7 4637^{13} 8454^6

Titletown Five (USA) *D Wayne Lukas* a98
3 bb c Tiznow(USA) D'Wildcat Speed (USA) (Forest Wildcat (USA))
2473a^9

Tittle Tattle *E J O'Neill* a65 68
3 br f Elnadim(USA) Salagama (IRE) (Alzao (USA))
3708a^8

Titus Bolt (IRE) *Jim Goldie* a59 72
4 b g Titus Livius(FR) Megan's Bay (Muhtarram (USA))
1270^2 1567^3 (1790) 2277^7 2630^4 3768^3 4264^9 6877^7 7239^{12}

Titus Gent *Jeremy Gask* a87 93
8 ch g Tumbleweed Ridge Genteel (IRE) (Titus Livius (FR))
1121^9 1814^4 2227^2 2868^2 3220^4 3973^6 4860^6 5441^2 6189^5 6850^4 7792^{10}

Tiz Flirtatious (USA) *Martin F Jones* a100 111
5 bb f Tizbud(USA) Masquerade Belle (USA) (Victory Gallop (CAN))
7708a^6

Tizlove Regardless (USA) *Mark Johnston* a60 55
2 b c Tiznow(USA) Dianehill (IRE) (Danehill (USA))
6299^{12} 6773^4 7276^5 7604^4 7855^{14}

Toast Of New York (USA) *Jamie Osborne* a99 66
2 b c Thewayyouare(USA) Claire Soleil (USA) (Syncline (USA))
5299^5 ◆ 5922^2 (6365) ◆ (7662)

Toast Of The Town (IRE) *John Gosden* 86
3 b f Duke Of Marmalade(IRE) Boast (Most Welcome)
1671^7 ◆ 2206^2 3237^9 4257^3

Tobacco *Tim Easterby* 54
3 b g Manduro(GER) Wonderful Desert (Green Desert (USA))
2716^9 3893^5 ◆ (4222) 4931^{11} 6565^{13}

Tobacco Road (IRE) *Richard Hannon Snr* a78 89
3 b g Westerner Virginias Best (King's Best (USA))
2209^{10} 5721^6 5958^3 (6356) 6867^4 7224^9

Tobann (IRE) *J S Bolger* a88 104
3 b f Teofilo(IRE) Precipitous (IRE) (Indian Ridge)
3263a^7 5688a^4 6025a^5 ◆ 7404a^7

Toberogan (IRE) *W A Murphy* a17 55
12 b g Docksider(USA) Beltisaal (FR) (Belmez (USA))
1022^{11}

Toboggan Star *Ann Duffield* a65 68
2 b g Lucky Story(USA) Toboggan Lady (Tobougg (IRE))
4053^8 4820^2 (5193)

Tobougg Happy *James Tate* 84
2 b f Tobougg(IRE) Happy Lady (FR) (Cadeaux Genereux)
3948^2 (4422) 5029^3 5679^6 6328^{11}

Tobrata *Mel Brittain* a65 60
7 ch g Tobougg(IRE) Sabrata (IRE) (Zino)
2991^3 5137^7 7342^4 8229^2 8349^2

Toccata Blue (IRE) *G M Lyons* a86 83
3 gr g Verglas(IRE) Jinxy Jill (Royal Applause)
2374a^6 5775a^9

Toepaz *Alan Kirtley*
4 b g Boogie Street Tribal Mischief (Be My Chief (USA))
4805^8 5469^{10}

Toffee Nose *Ron Barr* 51
6 b g Ishiguru(USA) The Synergist (Botanic (USA))
2757^6

Toffee Shot *J W Hills* a21 50
3 ch f Dutch Art Toffee Vodka (IRE) (Danehill Dancer (IRE))
2226^9 2658^7 3372^6 3859^6 5198^{12} 6019^9 6319^4 6698^8

Toga Tiger (IRE) *Jeremy Gask* a84 82
6 b g Antonius Pius(USA) Minerwa (GER) (Protektor (GER))
(104) (272) (689) 1922^8 3961^3 4642^6 5124^5 5580^8

Toggle *Mrs A Corson* a51 48
9 b g Tobougg(IRE) Niggle (Night Shift (USA))
1312a^2 1738a^2 4846a^5 5329a^6

Togiak (IRE) *David Pipe* a64 68
6 b g Azamour(IRE) Hawksbill Special (IRE) (Taufan (USA))
3838^8 4488^8 6004^{10} 6750^9

Tohono *Kevin Ryan* 51
2 b c Sleeping Indian Bijan (IRE) (Mukaddamah (USA))
2985^6 (Dead)

Toh's Grey Cat (USA) *Manuel J Wayar* a60 57
6 rg g D'Wildcat(USA) Cryptophyllis (USA) (Cryptoclearance (USA))
1001a^9

Tohugo (IRE) *Michael Mulvany* a53 61
4 ch g Notnowcato Avicia (Vettori (IRE))
5021a^{12}

Tokai Paradise (JPN) *Hidetaka Tadokoro* 114
6 bb h Gold Allure(JPN) Tokai Miyabi (JPN) (Maruzensky (JPN))
1868a^8

Tokai Trick (JPN) *Kenji Nonaka* 110
11 b h El Condor Pasa(USA) Zoonaqua (USA) (Silver Hawk (USA))
1868a^{11}

Tokei Halo (JPN) *Hisashi Shimizu* 121
4 b c Gold Halo(JPN) Dance Queen (JPN) (Mill George (USA))
8211a^2

Token Of Love *William Haggas* 79
2 b f Cape Cross(IRE) Nyarhini (Fantastic Light (USA))
(7103) ◆

Tokum (FR) *N Bertran De Balanda* a83 88
3 ch c Rock Of Gibraltar(IRE) Headdress (IRE) (Halling (USA))
191a^3 (1511a) 7705a^6

Tokyo Brown (USA) *Heather Main* a61 57
4 b g Marquetry(USA) Miasma (USA) (Lear Fan (USA))
8027^5 8204^2 8331^9

Tolly McGuiness *Julia Feilden* 31
2 ch c Araafa(IRE) Golden Flyer (FR) (Machiavellian (USA))
4862^5

Tolmias (GR) *Luca Cumani* 61
2 br c Ialysos(GR) Shikasta (IRE) (Kris)
5244^{10}

Tomasini *John Weymes* 32
4 b g Misu Bond(IRE) Bond Stasia (IRE) (Mukaddamah (USA))
2121^8 2611^{13} 2795^{11}

Tom Dooley (IRE) *Michael Mulvany* 77
2 b g Dylan Thomas(IRE) Shizao (IRE) (Alzao (USA))
5773a^{14}

Tominator *Jonjo O'Neill* a95 110
6 gr g Generous(IRE) Jucinda (Midyan (USA))
2149^3 (3824)

Tomintoul Magic (IRE) *Lady Cecil* a71 71
3 b f Holy Roman Emperor(IRE) Trois Graces (USA) (Alysheba (USA))
1821^2 2437^5 3086^4 3817^7

Tom Kitten (USA) *Marcus J Vitali* 88
6 bb g Kitten's Joy(USA) Coax Classic (USA) (Caveat (USA))
773a^4 1001a^2

Tom Mix (FR) *F-X De Chevigny* a73 74
3 b g Sunday Break(JPN) Tangshan (CAN) (Zilzal (USA))
1756a^8

Tommy's Secret *Jane Chapple-Hyam* a87 88
3 gr g Sakhee's Secret La Gessa (Largesse)
1806^7 3020^7 ◆ 5004^9 5537^8

Tom's Anna (IRE) *Tim Easterby* 67
3 b f Antonius Pius(USA) Vanilla Delight (IRE) (Orpen (USA))
1760^4 (2121) 2506^9 2959^8 3396^{11} 4561^5

Tom Sawyer *Julie Camacho* a81 77
5 b g Dansili Cayman Sunset (IRE) (Night Shift (USA))
1798^9 2132^4 2832^{11} 3569^{10} 4992^2 (5930) 6471^2 7240^5 (7887)

Tonabrocky (IRE) *J S Bolger* 79
3 ch c Pivotal Abigail Pett (Medicean)
1587a^4

Tongalooma *James Moffatt* a56 59
7 ch m Shinko Forest(IRE) Schatzi (Chilibang)
1758^{10} 2542^6 4471^2 4892^5 5365^9 5889^7 6669^8 7599^2 7903^9

Toni Fortebracci (FR) *G Botti* a71 77
3 b c Muhtathir Fosool (IRE) (Pivotal)
445a^0 2557a^8 7188a^5

Tony Hollis *Michael Appleby* a54 57
5 b g Antonius Pius(USA) Seasons Parks (Desert Prince (IRE))
1311^9 1603^5 1994^2 2536^{10} 2578^4 2752^6 2912^5 (3285) 4005^9 4161^3 4557^4 5198^{11} 5471^5 6180^{14} 8279^5 8371^3 8418^3

Too Ambitious *Andrew Hollinshead* a45 45
4 b f Striking Ambition Ticcatoo (IRE) (Dolphin Street (FR))
4377^9 4659^8 4943^7 5227^{11}

Too Difficult (IRE) *Andrew Balding* a63 63
3 ch f Rock Of Gibraltar(IRE) Etizaan (IRE) (Unfuwain (USA))
74^4 275^4

Too Elusive *Kristin Stubbs* a59 66
2 b g Major Cadeaux Elusive Kitty (USA) (Elusive Quality (USA))
2913^3 5877^7 6718^3 7261^7

Toofi (FR) *Roger Varian* 97
2 b c Henrythenavigator(USA) Silver Bark (Royal Applause)
4231^3 ◆ 4958^2 (6645) 7017^6

Toogoodtobegood (FR) *Kevin Ryan*
2 gr g Virtual Get The Ring (FR) (Linamix (FR))
4470[5]

Tooley Woods (IRE) *Tony Carroll* a64 61
4 b f Cape Cross(IRE) Kondakova (IRE) (Soviet Star (USA))
921[10] 1221[8] (1951) 2073[4] 2747[12] 3623[3] 3922[6] 4709[2] 5177[10] 5301[5]

Toormore (IRE) *Richard Hannon Snr* 121
2 b c Arakan(USA) Danetime Out (IRE) (Danetime (IRE))
(2741) ◆ (4876) (6442a)

Toothache *Garry Woodward* a14 48
5 gr f Proclamation(IRE) Zilkha (Petong)
2170[13] 5614[16]

Topadee (IRE) *Patrick J Flynn* a75 77
6 b m Golan(IRE) Sundown (Polish Precedent (USA))
3845a[14]

Topamichi *Mark H Tompkins* 86
3 b g Beat Hollow Topatori (IRE) (Topanoora)
1754[5] 2508[2] (2802) (5030) 5944[8] 6358[2] 6533[2] 7632[9]

Topaze Blanche (IRE) *C Laffon-Parias* a78 110
3 b f Zamindar(USA) Pearl Earrine (FR) (Kaldounevees (FR))
1561a[3] 2299a[13] 2906a[2] 4817a[4] 6714a[2] 7047a[5] 7685a[14]

Topaze Du Paon (FR) *J-L Dubord* a57
6 gr m Fairly Ransom(USA) Liza Du Paon (FR) (Nombre Premier)
648a[5]

Top Banana *Stuart Williams* 10
3 b g Tiger Hill(IRE) Special Green (FR) (Sadler's Wells (USA))
1635[12] 2321[15]

Top Boy *Derek Shaw* a72 99
3 b g Exceed And Excel(AUS) Injaaz (Sheikh Albadou)
(915) 1808[6] 2039[5] 2430[5] 3097[5] 3584[7] 4255[15] 5996[6] 6539[8] *7112[9]* 7420[10]

Top Chill (FR) *N Clement* 81
3 b c Falco(USA) Top Order (USA) (Dayjur (USA))
3876a[12]

Topclas (FR) *M bin Shafya* a103 103
7 b h Kutub(IRE) Noble Presence (FR) (Fasliyev (USA))
151a[14] 362a[8] 661a[2] 870a[9]

Top Cop *Andrew Balding* a71 96
4 b g Acclamation Speed Cop (Cadeaux Genereux)
2014[4] 2444[7] 2865[15] 3038[2] 3371[10] 4677[3] 5187[3] 5696[7] *6204[7]* 6337[5]

Top Diktat *Gary Moore* a61 74
5 b g Diktat Top Romance (IRE) (Entrepreneur)
2728[8] 3416[9] *4167[7] 5928[12]* 7346[2] *8047[8]*

Top Dollar *James Tate* a81 66
2 ch f Elusive Quality(USA) Elrehaan (Sadler's Wells (USA))
5891[3] (6152) *(6852)* 7695[6]

Top Joker *Saeed bin Suroor* 83
3 b g Raven's Pass(USA) French Bid (AUS) (Anabaa (USA))
(3585)

Top Line Banker *Michael Mullineaux* 47
3 b g Top Line Dancer(IRE) Ice Pack (Mukaddamah (USA))
4813[U] 5517[9] 6178[9] 7067[7] *8418[10]*

Top Notch Tonto (IRE) *Brian Ellison* 120
3 ch g Thousand Words Elite Hope (USA) (Moment Of Hope (USA))
1250[4] 1809[6] 2259[5] 3080[4] 3296[3] (4769) 5287[2] (6191) (7025) 7366[2]

Top Offer *Peter Crate* a72 78
4 b g Dansili Zante (Zafonic (USA))
3060[11] 3697[11] 5009[15] 6988[12] 7254[7] *7988[11] 8178[11]*

Topofthedrops (IRE) *Philip Hide* a38 26
2 b g High Chaparral(IRE) Basin Street Blues (IRE) (Dolphin Street (FR))
6460[11] *6923[12] 7156[6]*

Top Of The Glas (IRE) *Alan Jarvis* a61 80
2 gr c Verglas(IRE) Fury Dance (USA) (Cryptoclearance (USA))
2562[3] 4414[4] (5180) 7129[6]

Topolski (IRE) *David Arbuthnot* a81 70
7 b g Peintre Celebre(USA) Witching Hour (IRE) (Alzao (USA))
496[12] 823[4] 1547[9] 3531[7] *6173[5]*

Top Set (IRE) *Marco Botti* a73 74
3 ch c Tamayuz Pray (IRE) (Priolo (USA))
2760[9] 3585[4] *4151[4]* ◆

Toptempo *Mark H Tompkins* a74 85
4 ch f Halling(USA) Topatoo (Bahamian Bounty)
2205[8] 2990[12] 5542[3] (5854) 6336[2]

Top Trail (USA) *Roger Charlton* a69 62
3 bb f Exchange Rate(USA) Trekking (USA) (Gone West (USA))
(1209) 1433[3] 2394[7]

Top Trip *F Doumen* a89 115
4 b c Dubai Destination(USA) Topka (FR) (Kahyasi)
1420a[6] 2428[2] 3483[3] 5575a[5]

Top Tug (IRE) *Sir Michael Stoute* a85 71
2 ch c Halling(USA) Top Romance (IRE) (Entrepreneur)
4896[3] *(5922) 6935[2]* ◆

Torchlighter (IRE) *Mark Johnston* 89
2 ch c Shamardal(USA) Ever Love (BRZ) (Nedawi)
6110[7] 6534[2] (6769) 7529[6] 7819[2]

Torero *Kevin Ryan* a61 73
4 b g Hernando(FR) After You (Pursuit Of Love)
397[7] 520[5] 624[4] 2316[10] 2642[10] 2721[4] 2986[5] 3721[3] 4010[3] *4835[7]* (5084) 5643[2] *5897[2]* 6177[6] *6853[2]* (7099)

Tornado Battle *Phil McEntee* a55 45
3 b g War Chant(USA) Child Bride (USA) (Coronado's Quest (USA))
729[5] 4182[7] 4625[4] 4750[3] *5527[6] 5935[3]* 6257[3] *6361[9] 6804[8] 7930[3] 8043[6] 8279[10]* 8388[2]

Tornado Force (IRE) *Alan McCabe* a77 65
5 ch g Shamardal(USA) Pharma West (USA) (Gone West (USA))
340[4] 689[6] 906[6] (1201) ◆ *1353[2] 1597[3] 1956[6]* 3808[8] *4150[10] 5967[5]*

Tornesel *John Gosden* 77
2 b c Teofilo(IRE) Bezant (IRE) (Zamindar (USA))
4896[2] ◆

Toronado (IRE) *Richard Hannon Snr* 129
3 b c High Chaparral(IRE) Wana Doo (USA) (Grand Slam (USA))
(1638) 2021[4] 3421[2] (4875) 5654[6]

Torran Sound *James Eustace* a49 48
6 b g Tobougg(IRE) Velvet Waters (Unfuwain (USA))
2197[8]

Torres Del Paine *Brett Johnson* a76 38
6 b g Compton Place Noble Story (Last Tycoon)
4998[6] *5398[12] 5928[13] 6310[3]* 6527[11] *6929[10] 7985[6] 8152[4] 8446[5]*

Torrid *Amanda Perrett* 90
2 ch c Three Valleys(USA) Western Appeal (USA) (Gone West (USA))
4483[2] ◆ 5299[3] (7128)

Tortoise *Richard Guest* a41
2 b f Multiplex Wonderful Island (GER) (Turtle Island (IRE))
5968[10] *7602[4] 7732[5] 8132[4] 8363[6]*

Tosca (GER) *Mrs Ilka Gansera-Leveque* a61 89
3 b f Amadeus Wolf Tamarita (GER) (Acatenango (GER))
1358a[10] 2783[2] 3835[6] *7927[10]*

Tosen Jordan (JPN) *Yasutoshi Ikee* 120
7 b h Jungle Pocket(JPN) Every Whisper (JPN) (Northern Taste (CAN))
8033a[3]

Tosen Ra (JPN) *Hideaki Fujiwara* 117
5 bb c Deep Impact(JPN) Princess Olivia (USA) (Lycius (USA))
1868a[2]

Totalize *Brian Ellison* a84 93
4 b g Authorized(IRE) You Too (Monsun (GER))
7174[18] (7425) 7723a[6]

Total Obsession *Mark Hoad* a58 43
6 b m Mujahid(USA) Buon Amici (Pivotal)
343[12] 662[7] 805[9] (907) 1013[4] 1162[3] 1381[4] 1480[3] 1781[2] 1981[5] 2747[7] 3169[8] 3579[6] 3655[5]

Toto Skyllachy *David O'Meara* a72 99
8 b g Kyllachy Little Tramp (Trempolino (USA))
1688[9] (2078) (2339) 2841[11] 3094[5] 3458[24] 3754[3] 4310[18] 4803[2] 5050[5] (5367) 5783[4] 6288[3] 6550[9] 7024[11] 7424[8]

Touche De Rouge (IRE) *Peter Makin* a50 28
2 b f Sholokhov(IRE) Chaguaramas (IRE) (Mujadil (USA))
4302[6] 5812[10] *6922[8] 7855[8] 8274[6]*

Touching History (IRE) *Tim Etherington* a38 48
4 b g Titus Livius(FR) Lady Naryana (IRE) (Val Royal (FR))
3728[8] 4339[10] 4667[10]

Touch Of Fire (IRE) *C Lerner* 31
3 ch c Lando(GER) Touch Of Class (GER) (Be My Guest (USA))
6711a[12]

Touch Of Hawk (FR) *Wido Neuroth* a83 97
7 bl g Hawk Wing(USA) Touch Of Class (GER) (Be My Guest (USA))
3188a[8] 4095a[2] 5045a[3] 5809a[10] 6453a[12]

Touch Of Snow (IRE) *John Joseph Murphy* 73
2 b f Camacho In The Ribbons (In The Wings)
6024a[7]

Touch Paper (IRE) *Richard Hannon Snr* a59 54
2 b f Acclamation Light It Up (IRE) (Elusive City (USA))
1924[5] 2082[3] 5131[6] 5699[7] 6111[3]

Touch The Clouds *Kevin Ryan* a74 79
2 b g Sleeping Indian Aptina (USA) (Aptitude (USA))
2404[6] 2715[8] 3298[10] (4450) (4952) (5272) 5679[13] 6582[10] 7074[5] (7771) *7933[4] (8383) (8405)*

Touch The Dream (FR) *T Doumen* 24
2 ch f Dunkerque(FR) Touchee D'Amour (GER) (Neshad (USA))
7185a[12]

Touch The Sky *Lady Cecil* 75
2 br c Sea The Stars(IRE) Love Divine (Diesis)
6762[4] ◆ 7469[5]

Toufan Express *Adrian McGuinness* a74 75
11 ch g Fraam Clan Scotia (Clantime)
5332[6] 7152[3]

Toughness Danon *Ian Williams* a71 82
7 b g Tiger Hill(IRE) Templerin (GER) (Acatenango (GER))
592[4] 914[7] 2710[9] *3473[2] 4838[2] 7166[5]* (7597) *8041[6]*

Tourtiere *George Moore* 48
5 b g Act One Kindle (Selkirk (USA))
2462[8] 2961[11] 6598[14]

Tous Les Deux *Dr Jeremy Naylor* a50 70
10 b g Efisio Caerosa (Caerleon (USA))
456[11]

Touz Price (FR) *Rune Haugen* a81 103
5 b c Priolo(USA) Touz De Saint Cyr (FR) (Saint Cyrien (FR))
(4095a) 5809a[6]

Touzr *Richard Hannon Snr* 22
2 b c Invincible Spirit(IRE) Carrig Girl (Nayef (USA))
6354[5]

Towbee *Michael Easterby* a81 87
4 b g Doyen(IRE) Bow Bridge (Bertolini (USA))
1370[6] 1646[10] (2459) 2988[9] 3441[11] 3682[8] 4047[15] 4620[7] 5088[2] 5832[13] 6908[2] 7314[12]

Tower Power *Ismail Mohammed* a60
2 b c Nayef(USA) Voile (IRE) (Barathea (IRE))
7859[5] 8123[9]

Town Mouse *Neil King* a69 73
3 ch g Sakhee(USA) Megdale (IRE) (Waajib)
1469[2] 1613[3] 2500[2] 2784[3] (3319) 5087[5] *5966[7]*

Toydini (AUS) *Guy Walter* 112
4 b g Bernardini(USA) Johan's Toy (AUS) (Johan Cruyff)
7826a[6]

Toymaker *James Given* a81 81
6 b g Starcraft(NZ) Eurolink Raindance (IRE) (Alzao (USA))
(376)

Tracks Of My Tears *Giles Bravery* a64 32
3 b f Rail Link Policy Setter (USA) (Deputy Minister (CAN))
4691[8] *5393[5] (7034) 7543[2] (8031) 8225[2]*

Trade Commissioner (IRE) *John Gosden* a77 109
5 b g Montjeu(IRE) Spinning Queen (Spinning World (USA))
3458[7] ◆ 4811[5] 5540[2] 6001[5] ◆ 6638[6]

Trader Jack *David Flood* a97 98
4 b g Trade Fair Azeema (IRE) (Averti (IRE))
2813[5] 3339[5] ◆ 4080[4] 4501[2] 5742[2] 6638[8] *7982[8] 8117[12] 8385[9]*

Trade Secret *Mel Brittain* a78 92
6 b g Trade Fair Kastaway (Distant Relative)
1232[12] 2665[8] 3300[11] 3441[10] 4730[17] 5183[9] 6774[5]

Trade Storm *David Simcock* a100 118
5 b c Trade Fair Frisson (Slip Anchor)
367a[11] (657a) ◆ (872a) 1267a[4] 3419[5] 4276[4] 4875[4] 5739[3] 6456a[3]

Trading Leather (IRE) *J S Bolger* 121
3 b c Teofilo(IRE) Night Visit (Sinndar (IRE))
2398[2] 2677a[3] (3142a) (3849a) 4745[2] 5654[2] 6226a[3]

Trading Profit *Andrew Balding* 103
2 br c Kheleyf(USA) Avessia (Averti (IRE))
3374[12] (4347) ◆ 6637[7] 7026[8] (7268) 7534[5]

Traditional Chic (IRE) *L Riccardi* 101
5 ch c Ad Valorem(USA) Minimal Chic (IRE) (King's Best (USA))
2491a[5] 7830a[4]

Traditionelle *Tim Easterby* 36
2 b f Indesatchel(IRE) Mookhlesa (Marju (IRE))
5883[5] 6517[12]

Trail Blaze (IRE) *Kevin Ryan* 102
4 b g Tagula(IRE) Kingpin Delight (Emarati (USA))
2029[8] 3564[4] 3825[3] 4531[6] 4744[2] 5014[3] 5838[7] 6183[4] 6621[18] 7018[4] 7368[10]

Trailblazer (JPN) *Yasutoshi Ikee* a85 117
6 b h Zenno Rob Roy(JPN) Lirio (USA) (Forty Niner (USA))
958a[11] 1268a[11]

Train Hard *Mark Johnston* a63 60
3 b g Rail Link Melpomene (Peintre Celebre (USA))
1103[3] 1326[3] 6899[2] *7081[2] 7543[3] 7668[3]*

Trajet (AUS) *Liam Birchley* 94
8 bb g Good Journey(USA) Tres Belle (NZ) (Honor Grades (USA))
7760a[14]

Tram Express (FR) *Shaun Lycett* a63 53
9 ch g Trempolino(USA) Molly Dance (FR) (Groom Dancer (USA))
576 671[4] 846[3] 2563[3] 3248[7] 4036[4]

Tranquility Cove (USA) *David Barron* a52
3 bb f Rock Hard Ten(USA) South Bay Cove (CAN) (Fusaichi Pegasus (USA))
580[7]

Transfer *Richard Price* a59 67
8 br g Trans Island Sankaty Light (USA) (Summer Squall (USA))
1297[3] 2828[13] 3231[3] 3662[7] 3882[5] 6283[7]

Transluscent (IRE) *Andrew Balding* a47 55
3 b g Trans Island Little Miss Diva (IRE) (Diktat)
1323[7] 2016[6] 2637[4] 3178[8] *3903[11]*

Trapeze *John Gosden* a86 84
3 ch f Pivotal Miss Penton (Primo Dominie)
1612[6] 2195[2] 2586[5] 3460[26] 7272[3] 7504[10] *7895[3]*

Travel (USA) *Mark Johnston* a59 60
3 ch f Street Cry(IRE) Away (USA) (Dixieland Band (USA))
3136[9] 6566[4] 6907[11] *7379[5]*

Travelling *Tony Carroll* a81 71
4 b f Dubai Destination(USA) Attune (Singspiel (IRE))
(89) 511[5] 720[2] (798) (919) 4898[11] 5491[9] *6167[13]*

Travis Bickle (IRE) *Sylvester Kirk* a66 71
2 b g Sky Mesa(USA) Out Of Woods (USA) (Woodman (USA))
5000[2] 6110[2] 6739[4] *7972[9]*

Travis County (IRE) *Brian Ellison* a70 69
4 b g Jeremy(USA) Manchaca (FR) (Highest Honor (FR))
7498[12]

Treason Trial *Jason Ward* a36 29
12 b g Peintre Celebre(USA) Pampabella (IRE) (High Estate)
1369[6]

Treasure Beach *M F De Kock* a107 119
5 bb c Galileo(IRE) Honorine (IRE) (Mark Of Esteem (IRE))
958a[6] ◆ *1269a[8]* 1872a[11]

Treasure Cay (IRE) *Paul Cole* a68 30
2 ch c Bahamian Bounty Expedience (USA) (With Approval (CAN))
7501[8] *7779[6] 8425[2]*

Treaty Of Paris (IRE) *Henry Candy* 104
2 b c Haatef(USA) Symbol Of Peace (IRE) (Desert Sun)
3374[7] 3857[2] (4505) 4959[2] (5652) 6390[4]

Treble Jig (USA) *M Al Muhairi* a113 99
6 b h Gone West(USA) Light Jig (Danehill (USA))
659a[11] 742a[5] 956a[8]

Tree Of Grace (FR) *Richard Hannon Snr* a78
2 ch c Gold Away(IRE) Three Times (SWE) (Domynsky)
(7302)

Trefnant (IRE) *Chris Dwyer* a27
2 ch f Bahamian Bounty Miss Trish (IRE) (Danetime (IRE))
7078[7] 7261[11]

Tregereth (IRE) *Jonathan Portman* a60 65
3 b f Footstepsinthesand Ringmoor Down (Pivotal)
374[3] 811[5] 2091[6] 3134[8] 3699[3] 4064[3] 4368[5] 4916[3] (5447)

Trending (IRE) *Jeremy Gask* a72 64
4 gr g Dark Angel(IRE) Call Later (USA) (Gone West (USA))
1902[11] 3317[4] 3949[10] 4377[8] 5602[6] (6157) 6771[8] *7347[2] 7801[2] 8030[3] 8216[6]*

Trendsetter (IRE) *David Simcock* 42
2 b c Mastercraftsman(IRE) Fashion Trade (Dansili)
6430[4]

Tres Blue (IRE) *Gai Waterhouse* a92 117
3 b c Anabaa Blue Tres Ravi (GER) (Monsun (GER))
1046a[6] 3386a[3] 4103a[2] (5041a) (5807a) 7761a[22]

Tres Coronas (IRE) *David Barron* a86 101
6 b g Key Of Luck(USA) Almansa (IRE) (Dr Devious (IRE))
1391[4] 1538[2] 1831[2] (2191) 2839[3] ◆ 4310[3] 6838[3]

Tres Rock Danon (FR) *Gerald Geisler* 111
7 b h Rock Of Gibraltar(IRE) Tres Ravi (GER) (Monsun (GER))
1920[10] 6248a[4] 7566a[6] 7890a[3]

Treve (FR) *Mme C Head-Maarek* 131
3 b f Motivator Trevise (FR) (Anabaa (USA))
(3385a) (6448a) (7058a)

Trevose (IRE) *Roy Brotherton* a28 54
4 b g Barathea(IRE) Cape Jasmine (IRE) (Danehill (USA))
169[10]

Tribal Myth (IRE) *Kevin Ryan* 70
6 b g Johannesburg(USA) Shadow Play (USA) (Theatrical (IRE))
1775[10] 2739[7] 3083[4] 3652[8]

Tribal Path (IRE) *Mark Johnston* a79 60
3 b c Giant's Causeway(USA) Navajo Moon (IRE) (Danehill (USA))
(396) 1577[7] 1829[13] *6115[5] 6556[6] 6970[4] 7491[6]*

Tricksome (IRE) *Ann Duffield* a54 53
2 b f Jeremy(USA) Travel Tricks (IRE) (Presidium)
2612[4] 3280[8] 3943[7] 4990[7] 5710[4] 6073[5] 6511[5]

Trigger Park (IRE) *Ronald Harris* a50 61
2 ch c Tagula(IRE) Raazi (My Generation)
5811[10] 6152[5] 6485[5] *7623[9] 7855[10] 8262[10]*

Trillian Astra (IRE) *Clive Cox* a57 39
2 b f Bahamian Bounty Ms Sophie Eleanor (USA) (Grand Slam (USA))
6691[11] 7245[7] *7859[3]*

Tri Nations (UAE) *Anthony Middleton* a72 42
8 ch g Halling(USA) Six Nations (USA) (Danzig (USA))
5168[10]

Trinity Boy *Clive Cox* 63
2 b c Footstepsinthesand Maybe I Will (IRE) (Hawk Wing (USA))
1833[3] 2723[5] 3175[3]

Trinityelitedotcom (IRE) *Tom Dascombe* a96 88
3 b g Elusive City(USA) Beal Ban (IRE) (Daggers Drawn (USA))
3320[6] (3915) 4487[3] ◆ 5340[6] 5996[2] *(6525) 6854[2]* (6977) *(8369)*

Trinity Lorraine (IRE) *Alan Bailey* a53 45
2 b f Dark Angel(IRE) Known Class (USA) (Known Fact (USA))
4491[13] 5061[12] 6112[6] 6914[6] *7788[3] 7973[8] (8133) 8274[3]*

Trinity River *Daniel Kubler* a76 78
2 b f Three Valleys(USA) Blane Water (USA) (Lomond (USA))
3694[3] 4259[4] ◆ 4828[2] *(5350)* 5476[7] 6376[5] *6731[3]* 7074[2]

Trinity Star (IRE) *Michael Dods* 48
2 gr g Kheleyf(USA) Zamiyla (IRE) (Daylami (IRE))
3391[7] 5338[13] 6175[5]

Trinniberg (USA) *Shivananda Parbhoo* a123 40
4 bb c Teuflesberg(USA) Bella Dorato (USA) (Goldminers Gold (CAN))
1266a[11] 7713a[9]

Triple Aitch (USA) *Giles Bravery* a67 64
3 b g Harlan's Holiday(USA) Hadley (USA) (Kingmambo (USA))
211[11] 425[4] 2548[5] 3137[6] 3582[10] 3740[3] *4378[4] 4410[7]* 4721[10] *7808[2] 7966[5] 8073[5]*

Triple Chocolate *Roger Ingram* a77
3 b g Danehill Dancer(IRE) Enticing (IRE) (Pivotal)
(7624) 8345[4]

Triple Dream *Milton Bradley* a88 82
8 ch g Vision Of Night Triple Joy (Most Welcome)
113[2] 196[3] 457[2] (586) 780[3] 1121[3] 1370[4] 1517[4] 1652[4] 2561[2] 2825[11] 3315[5] 3855[6] 4344[3] (4487) 6159[13] 7112[2] 8021[2] 8167[4]

Triple Eight (IRE) *Philip Kirby* a75 82
5 b g Royal Applause Hidden Charm (IRE) (Big Shuffle (USA))
2539[2] 3083[5] 3545[2] 4119[3] 4542[3] (5055) 5382[2] 5860[6] 6563[9] 7211[8] 7498[15] *8299[5] 8400[3]*

Triple O Seven (IRE) *John Best* a39
2 b c Kodiac Triple Zero (IRE) (Raise A Grand (IRE))
2591[8] *3493[7]*

Triple Threat (FR) *A Fabre* 115
3 b c Monsun(GER) Drei (USA) (Lyphard (USA))
(1419a) 2355a[3] (4573a) 6446a[8] 7367[10]

Trip Switch *John Butler* a75 58
7 b g Reset(AUS) Caribbean Star (Soviet Star (USA))
107[8] 338[12] 600[10] 805[10] 1060[P]

Trip To Paris (IRE) *Ed Dunlop* a76 89
2 b c Champs Elysees La Grande Zoa (IRE) (Fantastic Light (USA))
4414[14] *(4631)* 5717[2]

Trip To Rhodos (FR) *Pavel Tuma* 107
4 b c Rail Link Tropical Mark (Mark Of Esteem (IRE))
5575a[8]

Trisara *Harry Dunlop* a43 54
3 b f Exceed And Excel(AUS) Hiddendale (IRE) (Indian Ridge)
2979[10] 3898[2] 5345[7] *6752[12]*

Triskaidekaphobia *Wilf Storey* a62 42
10 b g Bertolini(USA) Seren Teg (Timeless Times (USA))
1961^6 3030^8 4469^2 5583^8 5876^4

Tristessa *Derek Haydn Jones* a57 52
3 b f Amadeus Wolf On Point (Kris)
1742^{10} 4607^{10} 6436^{12}

Triumphant (IRE) *A P O'Brien* 103
4 b g Danehill Dancer(IRE) Meek Appeal (USA) (Woodman (USA))
2105a^2

Trixie Malone *K R Burke* 68
3 b f Ishiguru(USA) Lady-Love (Pursuit Of Love)
1392^9 1722^6 2613^2 (6588) 7283^2

Trois Rois (FR) *Ismail Mohammed* a90 102
8 b g Hernando(FR) Trevise (FR) (Anabaa (USA))
151a^{16} 555a^{11}

Trois Vallees (USA) *James Tate* a84 73
4 bb g Elusive Quality(USA) Chamrousse (USA) (Peaks And Valleys (USA))
6^6 *7926* *(1203)*

Trois Voeux (FR) *P Monfort* a68 68
3 b c Orpen(USA) Trois Rivieres (IRE) (Dr Fong (USA))
2335a^0

Trojan Nights (USA) *M Al Muhairi* a93 90
5 ch g Street Cry(IRE) Dabaweyaa (Shareef Dancer (USA))
503a^8

Trojan Rocket (IRE) *Michael Wigham* a74 87
5 b g Elusive City(USA) Tagula Bay (IRE) (Tagula (IRE))
(2725) 3586^5 3823^5 5009^{13} 5489^7

Troopingthecolour *Steve Gollings* a96 101
7 b g Nayef(USA) Hyperspectra (Rainbow Quest (USA))
(6936) *8327*^{5}

Tropenfeuer (FR) *James Moffatt* a73 54
6 b m Banyumanik(IRE) Tropensonne (GER) (Konigsstuhl (GER))
1568^7 2540^7 3709^6

Trophee (FR) *Mme C Head-Maarek* a90 72
2 b f Mr. Sidney(USA) Trevise (FR) (Anabaa (USA))
7570a^2

Tropical Bachelor (IRE) *Nicky Vaughan* a67 41
7 b g Bachelor Duke(USA) Tropical Coral (IRE) (Pennekamp (USA))
4835^{12} 6632^{12}

Tropical Beat *David O'Meara* a95 103
5 b g Beat Hollow Tropical Heights (FR) (Shirley Heights)
5237^2 6348^4 6766^5

Tropical Duke (IRE) *Ron Barr* a62 49
7 ch g Bachelor Duke(USA) Tropical Dance (USA) (Thorn Dance (USA))
1786^7 3285^6 3545^4 3947^9 4562^7

Tropical Mist (IRE) *George J Kent* 83
3 b f Marju(IRE) Tropical Lady (IRE) (Sri Pekan (USA))
3845a^{19}

Tropics (USA) *Dean Ivory* a88 117
5 ch g Speightstown(USA) Taj Aire (USA) (Taj Alriyadh (USA))
2207^7 (2724) 2937^2 (3840) (4780) 4986^6 (5747) 6623^{23} (7013)

Trove (IRE) *Michael Attwater* a54 31
4 b g Rock Of Gibraltar(IRE) Cache Creek (IRE) (Marju (IRE))
1056^8 *1474*^{6} *1781*^{9}

Troy Boy *Robin Bastiman* 47
3 b g Choisir(AUS) Love Thing (Phountzi (USA))
3739^4 4585^4 5407^{10} 6919^{10}

Truancy (IRE) *K R Burke* a71
2 b c Intense Focus(USA) Date Mate (USA) (Thorn Dance (USA))
6174^9 *7972*^{3} *(8138)* *8426*^{5}

Trucanini *Chris Wall* a92 84
3 b f Mount Nelson Jalissa (Mister Baileys)
3062^3 3983^2 (5152) *(5896)* *(6524)* 6993^{11}

True Comment *Ed Walker* 90
2 ch g Dutch Art Stravie (IRE) (Stravinsky (USA))
(6790)

True Match (IRE) *Saeed bin Suroor* 67
2 b f Cape Cross(IRE) West Wind (Machiavellian (USA))
7693^4 ◆

True Pleasure (IRE) *James Bethell* a72 72
6 b m Choisir(AUS) Absolute Pleasure (Polar Falcon (USA))
3307 *921*^{9} *3399*^{3} 3728^5 (4052) (4341) 4609^3 (5369) 5881^4 7152^2 7344^{12} *7836*^{4}

True Prince (USA) *Alastair Lidderdale* a61 59
4 ch g Yes It's True(USA) Whenthedoveflies (USA) (Dove Hunt (USA))
559^{10} *1617*^{5} *2125*^{2} 2911^6 3026^{11} *3644*^{6} *6367*^{7} *7353*^{4} *7465*^{10}

True Spirit *Paul D'Arcy* a64 54
3 b g Shamardal(USA) Petonellajill (Petong)
746 *396*^{5} 3740^5 4962^4 6702^{14} 7109^5

True Story *Saeed bin Suroor* 90
2 bb c Manduro(GER) Tanzania (USA) (Darshaan)
3581^2 (4256)

True That (IRE) *David Nicholls* 29
3 b g Captain Marvelous(IRE) Bratislava (Dr Fong (USA))
3479^6 3932^5 4887^{10} 6878^9

True To Form (IRE) *Alan McCabe* a103 83
6 b g Rock Of Gibraltar(IRE) Truly Yours (IRE) (Barathea (IRE))
3812^9 5283^6 5749^4 *7641*^{10} *8071*^{4} *8386*^{9}

True Verdict (IRE) *David Wachman* a72 100
3 b f Danehill Dancer(IRE) Foolish Act (IRE) (Sadler's Wells (USA))
3263a^6 3964a^7 4549a^5

Trulee Scrumptious *Peter Charalambous* a57 74
4 b f Strategic Prince Morning Rise (GER) (Acatenango (GER))
1480^5 4496^6 4715^2 5622^{10} *6805*^{3} 7470^5 *7987*^{3} *8148*^{9}

Truly Madly (IRE) *Hans Adielsson* a73 71
3 bb f Royal Applause Triennial (IRE) (Giant's Causeway (USA))
4942^3 *(5104)* 5430^3 5820^3 *5896*^{3} 6100^3 *6341*^{10} 6698^5

Trumpet Major (IRE) *Richard Hannon Snr* 117
4 b c Arakan(USA) Ashford Cross (Cape Cross (IRE))
(1810) 2446^{10} 3419^{10} 4276^6 7190^6

Trumpet Voluntary (IRE) *Nicky Vaughan* a61 77
4 b g Red Clubs(IRE) Woodmaven (USA) (Woodman (USA))
755^9

Trust Fund Babe (IRE) *Tim Easterby* a56 64
4 b f Captain Rio Perfect Order (USA) (Red Ransom (USA))
1278^9 1800^{12}

Trust Me Boy *John E Long* a24 51
5 gr g Avonbridge Eastern Lyric (Petong)
903^{12} 2534^{11}

Trust The Wind *John Gosden* a64
2 b f Dansili Hypnology (USA) (Gone West (USA))
7645^7

Truth Hurts *Violet M Jordan*
3 br g Cockney Rebel(IRE) Vino Veritas (USA) (Chief's Crown (USA))
5962^6 *7167*^{8}

Truth Or Dare *Richard Hannon Snr* 104
2 b c Invincible Spirit(IRE) Unreachable Star (Halling (USA))
3374^6 3853^2 (4304) (5400) 7195^3

Truthwillsetufree (IRE) *D K Weld* 91
4 b f Dalakhani(IRE) Truly Mine (IRE) (Rock Of Gibraltar (IRE))
7230a^5 7723a^{17}

Trymyluck *Pam Sly* a45 57
3 b f Royal Applause Borders Belle (IRE) (Pursuit Of Love)
1906^4 ◆ *2566*^{10} 3221^6

Tubeanie (IRE) *Clive Cox* 64
2 ch f Intense Focus(USA) Ryalahna (IRE) (High Chaparral (IRE))
1634^{16} 3717^3 5442^4 6426^5

Tucci (ITY) *M Guarnieri* 95
2 b f Azamour(IRE) Terynka (GER) (Exit To Nowhere (USA))
7415a^6

Tucson Arizona *Anthony Carson* a74 65
2 b c High Chaparral(IRE) Kasakiya (IRE) (Zafonic (USA))
7128^4 *(8085)* *8397*^{3}

Tuddenham (USA) *Charles Hills* a35 47
2 bb g Latent Heat(USA) Storming On (USA) (Storm Cat (USA))
7209^7 *7646*^{9}

Tuffan (USA) *Clive Brittain* a66 66
3 b g Bernardini(USA) Love Of Dubai (USA) (More Than Ready (USA))
1293^{11} 3254^8

Tuibama (IRE) *Tracy Waggott* a54 68
4 ch g Bertolini(USA) Supportive (IRE) (Nashamaa)
1283^7 1465^3 1758^2 2122^3 2611^6 4009^5 (4762) 5889^4 6088^7 6604^4 6757^9 6903^2 6945^4 7315^{12}

Tukitinyasok (IRE) *Clive Mulhall* a57 60
6 b g Fath(USA) Mevlana (IRE) (Red Sunset)
711 2537^{14} 5369^5 5713^4 5921^3 7344^8 *7930*^{6} *8116*^{4} *(8275)* *8399*^{3}

Tulips (IRE) *A Fabre* a79 111
4 b f Pivotal Hint Of Spring (Seeking The Gold (USA))
2300a^6 2897a^2 3851a^4 5040a^4 5806a^2 6251a^6

Tullia (IRE) *William Knight* a70 75
2 b f Footstepsinthesand Whipped Queen (USA) (Kingmambo (USA))
5716^7 6409^2 *6922*^{3} (7243)

Tullius (IRE) *Andrew Balding* a90 116
5 ch g Le Vie Dei Colori Whipped Queen (USA) (Kingmambo (USA))
7196^{10} 7698^3 *7974*^{7}

Tumaini (IRE) *U Suter* 39
2 b f Lawman(FR) La Gioconda (SWI) (King Of Kings (IRE))
4651a^8

Tumblecloud (IRE) *W A Murphy* a45 43
8 b m Mujadil(USA) Sudden Interest (FR) (Highest Honor (FR))
1021^9

Tumbledown (USA) *Ed Walker* a63 30
3 b f Bernardini(USA) Freeroll (USA) (Touch Gold (USA))
7983^4 *8154*^{5}

Tumbleweed Finale *Rae Guest* a20 37
3 ch f Tumbleweed Ridge Poyle Kiera (Diktat)
3253^7 4013^{10} 6036^7 *6985*^{9} *7465*^{11}

Tumblewind *Richard Whitaker* 90
3 ch f Captain Rio African Breeze (Atraf)
1647^2 1791^3 (2076) 2987^3 (3591) 4057^4 4247^2 4734^4 5836^6 6212^3 6848^2

Tuna Papita (USA) *F Rohaut* 99
3 bb f Henrythenavigator(USA) Viapervita (IRE) (Spectrum (IRE))
2299a^{19}

Tunkwa (FR) *D Sepulchre* 106
3 b f Gold Away(IRE) Tigresse Africaine (FR) (Tiger Hill (IRE))
5315a^7 6484a^9 (7590a)

Tunnel Tiger (IRE) *William Knight* a36 55
2 b f Dylan Thomas(IRE) Nakiska (Darshaan)
3414^7 3541^4 4065^3 4964^2 *7352*^{9}

Turfmaid (GER) *J Hirschberger* 48
2 ch f Call Me Big(GER) Turfblume (GER) (Lando (GER))
7406a^{11}

Turin (IRE) *Charlie Appleby* a77 68
2 b f Raven's Pass(USA) Veronica Cooper (IRE) (Kahyasi)
4491^{10} *(5131)* 5699^6

Turjuman (USA) *Simon West* a68 51
8 ch g Swain(IRE) Hachiyah (IRE) (Generous (IRE))
84^2 *198*^{8} *417*^{8} *539*^{7} *(703)* *846*^{8} *1080*^{6} 1279^6 1763^9 2242^{11} *2332*^{5} 2509^5 2720^7

Turkey Jackson (FR) *F Sanchez* a55 63
3 b g Sakhee(USA) Winding Road (FR) (Barathea (IRE))
2557a^{12}

Turmalina (GER) *J Hirschberger* 92
2 b f Doyen(IRE) Trinidad (GER) (Big Shuffle (USA))
7406a^4

Turnbury *Robert Mills* a64
2 b g Azamour(IRE) Scottish Heights (IRE) (Selkirk (USA))
3689^{11} *7854*^{4} *8213*^{5}

Turned To Gold (IRE) *Robert Johnson* a52 22
4 ch g Teofilo(IRE) Silver Bracelet (Machiavellian (USA))
1059^{10} 1568^{10} 1790^{11} 2162^9

Tuscan Fire (AUS) *Dan O'Sullivan* 104
7 bb g Tuscanos(AUS) Jetfire Lass (NZ) (Jetball (AUS))
7392a^{12}

Tuscan Fun *Roger Varian* a68 82
3 ch g Medicean Elfin Laughter (Alzao (USA))
2957^3 (3573) *4167*^{6} 4810^9 6428^5

Tuscan Gold *Laura Mongan* a66 87
6 ch g Medicean Louella (USA) (El Gran Senor (USA))
1670^8 *8392*^{7}

Tuscania *Lucy Wadham* a87 92
5 b f King's Best(USA) Contiguous (USA) (Danzig (USA))
(3742) 4066^2 ◆ 4777^2 5742^4 (6537) 7020^6

Tussie Mussie *Mark Johnston* a65 78
3 b f Royal Applause Loveleaves (Polar Falcon (USA))
2026^2 2704^3 3396^4 3712^3 *4145*^{10} 4671^7 5548^5 5835^2 6210^{11} 6877^4

Tuxedo *Peter Hiatt* a36 43
8 ch g Cadeaux Genereux Serengeti Bride (USA) (Lion Cavern (USA))
7857^{10} *8335*^{10}

Twary (USA) *Roger Varian* a61 83
3 b g Indian Charlie(USA) Street Sounds (CAN) (Street Cry (IRE))
2628^8 *3173*^{8}

Tweed *William Haggas* a91 94
3 b f Sakhee(USA) Frog (Akarad (FR))
(7279) (7659) *7794*^{2}

Tweedle Dee *Noel Quinlan* 49
4 b f Araafa(IRE) Sismique (Warning)
1292^7 1914^6 2932^6 3727^7 5429^4

Tweety Pie (IRE) *Declan Carroll* 72
2 ch f Rock Of Gibraltar(IRE) Princesse Sonia (FR) (Ashkalani (IRE))
3064^8 (4046) 4726^2 5272^5 6295^7

Twelve Bore *Willie Musson* a41
2 b g Medicean Lifetime Romance (IRE) (Mozart (IRE))
6342^8 *7155*^{11}

Twelve Strings (IRE) *Brian Ellison* a61 90
4 b g Iffraaj Favoritely (USA) (Favorite Trick (USA))
2269^2 3333^2 3765^3 5946^3 6585^{10} 7210^7 7496^9 (7635) 7823^9

Twentyfourseven *Ed Dunlop* a60 58
2 br c Sleeping Indian Anytime Baby (Bairn (USA))
2502^4 *2805*^{3} 3245^6

Twenty One Choice (IRE) *Ed de Giles* a90 89
4 ch g Choisir(AUS) Midnight Lace (Tomba)
(1318) ◆ 1922^5 4340^3 *6203*^{2} *6526*^{2} 6883a^6

Twenty Roses (IRE) *Ed Walker* a59 43
2 b f Mastercraftsman(IRE) Stunning Rose (IRE) (Sadler's Wells (USA))
5716^{11} 7023^{10} *7934*^{6} *8133*^{4}

Twilight Angel *Pat Eddery* a52
5 ch f Compton Place Leaping Flame (USA) (Trempolino (USA))
7929^2

Twilight Eclipse (USA) *Thomas Albertrani* a110 117
4 b g Purim(USA) My Twilight Dancer (USA) (Twilight Agenda (USA))
7712a^6

Twilight Legend (IRE) *Seamus Mullins* a29
4 b f Chevalier(IRE) Almost Twilight (USA) (Silver Hawk (USA))
332^9

Twilight Pearl *Tim Easterby* a30 60
3 b f Pastoral Pursuits Branston Gem (So Factual (USA))
1284^6 *3638*^{7} 5054^4

Twin Appeal (IRE) *David Barron* a56 68
2 b g Oratorio(IRE) Velvet Appeal (IRE) (Petorius)
7126^4 *7664*^{4}

Twin Point *John Gosden* a66
2 br c Invincible Spirit(IRE) Gemini Joan (Montjeu (IRE))
7766^3 *8123*^{4}

Twinwood Star (IRE) *John Weymes* a49 44
3 b f Moss Vale(IRE) Bonkers (Efisio)
36^2 *686*^{5} *848*^{10} 1762^{10} 2336^6 3316^5

Twist And Shout *Bill Turner* a69 76
2 b f Acclamation Sheik'n Swing (Celtic Swing)
1634^3 *1924*^{4} 2517^2

Twist And Twirl *Derek Shaw* a52
3 b f Cockney Rebel(IRE) Silent Miracle (IRE) (Night Shift (USA))
236^7 *356*^{2} *7969*^{3} *8112*^{5} *8277*^{6}

Twistedlittlestar (IRE) *Niels Petersen*
3 b f Aussie Rules(USA) Miss Asia Quest (Rainbow Quest (USA))
5326a^{14}

Two Days In Paris (FR) *J-C Rouget* 99
4 bl f Authorized(IRE) Isalou (FR) (Unfuwain (USA))
7189a^{11} 7891a^{16}

Two For Two (IRE) *David O'Meara* 106
5 b g Danehill Dancer(IRE) D'Articleshore (IRE) (Definite Article)
1576^2 ◆ (1840) 2029^3 ◆ 2399^4 3458^{12} 3525^6 4946^8 5768^9 6624^4 7172^5

Two In The Pink (IRE) *Ralph Smith* a64 23
3 b f Clodovil(IRE) Secret Circle (Magic Ring (IRE))
(114) 2544^{15} *4385*^{6} *8330*^{5}

Twombly (SPA) *C Boutin* a79 73
2 b c Pyrus(USA) Topita (IRE) (Daggers Drawn (USA))
5214a^2

Two Minds (FR) *Eugene Stanford* a69 62
6 ch g Choisir(AUS) Dynamic Dream (USA) (Dynaformer (USA))
(3433) *(4169)* 5191^5

Two Moons *Tony Coyle* 73
3 b g Echo Of Light Forever Loved (Deploy)
5563^4 6566^5

Two No Bids (IRE) *Phil McEntee* a85 59
3 bb g Footstepsinthesand Milwaukee (FR) (Desert King (IRE))
228^7 *491*^{3} *729*^{3} *849*^{3} *(1044)* 1487^8 3793^8 4077^6 4721^9 5156^4 5373^5 6074^2 6324^3 6970^3 7454^5 7953^2 8095^2 (8304) (8350) 8401^4

Two Shades Of Grey (IRE) *Richard Fahey* 63
2 gr g Oratorio(IRE) Elitista (FR) (Linamix (FR))
3565^8 4046^7 4539^9 5371^4 6663^5 6914^3

Two Smart (IRE) *K R Burke* 79
2 b f Cape Cross(IRE) Smartest (IRE) (Exceed And Excel (AUS))
5797^6 6644^7 7016^{11}

Two Sugars *Laura Mongan* a56 62
5 b g Val Royal(FR) Princess Galadriel (Magic Ring (IRE))
5234^9 5633^6 6899^6

Two Turtle Doves (IRE) *Michael Mullineaux* a67 66
7 b m Night Shift(USA) Purple Rain (IRE) (Celtic Swing)
1681^{10} (2043) 2281^3 2425^3 2780^3 3197^6

Two Tykes *Michael Easterby* 8
2 b g Piccolo Whitby (IRE) (Dubawi (IRE))
2401^{13} *7882*^{9}

Tychaios *Stuart Williams* a55 63
3 b g Green Desert(USA) Tychy (Suave Dancer (USA))
2224^5 (3866) 4962^6 7106^5 7432^3

Ty Cobb (IRE) *John Quinn* 52
2 b g Dandy Man(IRE) Mrs Moonlight (Ajdal (USA))
6174^8 7341^5

Tycoon Rob (NZ) *Doug Harrison* 63
6 ch g Undoubtedly(AUS) La Luciole (AUS) (Last Tycoon)
7417a^{14}

Tyfos *Brian Baugh* a89 89
8 b g Bertolini(USA) Warminghamsharpish (Nalchik (USA))
457^3 ◆ *780*^{8} *1067*^{2} *1370*^{3} *1652*^{2} 2388^9 3093^{10} 3981^5 ◆ 4479^7 4852^7

Ty Gwr *Brian Ellison* a74 90
4 b g Echo Of Light House Maiden (IRE) (Rudimentary (USA))
5356^2 *6200*^{6} 6721^3 (7275) 7498^2

Tylery Wonder (IRE) *W McCreery* a75 92
3 ch g Choisir(AUS) Over The Tylery (IRE) (Swallow Flight (IRE))
6883a^3

Tymismoni (IRE) *Michael Attwater* a42 56
5 ch f Choisir(AUS) Berenice (ITY) (Marouble)
336

Typhon (USA) *David Lanigan* a75 76
3 b g Proud Citizen(USA) Seven Moons (JPN) (Sunday Silence (USA))
1655^3 *1923*^{9} (3365) 4209^3 4672^5 5304^{13} *6521*^{7} *(7447)*

Typhoon Lily (USA) *M D O'Callaghan* a89 92
3 gr f Unbridled's Song(USA) River Drive (USA) (Belong To Me (USA))
1918^4 3460^{12}

Typography *Alastair Lidderdale* a72 72
4 br g Byron Bold Byzantium (Bold Arrangement)
3901^8

Tyrana (GER) *Ian Williams* a44 57
10 ch m Acatenango(GER) Tascalina (GER) (Big Shuffle (USA))
1068^6

Tyrsal (IRE) *Robert Eddery* a63 56
2 b g Jeremy(USA) Blanchelande (IRE) (Subotica (FR))
1328^3 1606^9 1910^4 4519^4 *5068*^{5} *5634*^{9} *5893*^{3} 6322^3 *6749*^{12} *7352*^{2} *7855*^{5} *(8039)* 8133^2

Tyrur Ted *Frank Sheridan* a69 66
8 b g Val Royal(FR) Spanish Serenade (Nashwan (USA))
375^2 *455*^{4} *477*^{3} *(545)* *1105*^{2} *1220*^{9} 2348^3 (2785) 3617^4 *4355*^{9} *6339*^{7}

Ubetterbegood (ARG) *Robert Cowell* a103 94
5 b g Distorted Humor(USA) Movie Star (BRZ) (Royal Academy (USA))
2150^{10} 2669^9 3334^{10} 3776^{14} 4263^{15} *7851*^{5} *8155*^{4} *8334*^{12}

Ubiquitous Mantle (IRE) *G M Lyons* a31 85
2 b f Alhaarth(IRE) Za Aamah (USA) (Mr Prospector (USA))
7720a^4

Ucanchoose (IRE) *Andrew Slattery* a74 77
7 b g Choisir(AUS) Ruacana Falls (USA) (Storm Bird (CAN))
5775a^7 *6089a*^{2}

Uchenna (IRE) *David Simcock* a64 93
2 b f Fastnet Rock(AUS) Uriah (GER) (Acatenango (GER))
5394^7 (6063) 6798^7

Udana (IRE) *M Delzangles* a78 69
3 b f Dubawi(IRE) Ganar El Cielo (Ashkalani (IRE))
5119a^3

Uganda Glory (USA) *George Baker* a44 68
3 bb f Hat Trick(JPN) Febrile (USA) (Trempolino (USA))
1174^4 *1698*^{7} 3428^2 ◆ 3675^6 4664^2 5500^4 (6257)

Ujagar (IRE) *Tom Dascombe* a74 58
2 gr g Dalakhani(IRE) No Secrets (USA) (El Corredor (USA))
6829^{12} *7301*^{2} *7732*^{2}

Ukrainian (IRE) *A Al Raihe* a92 91
4 b g Teofilo(IRE) Livadiya (IRE) (Shernazar)
412a^{10}

Uldiko (FR) *Mme C Barande-Barbe* a89 89
5 b g Enrique Nakamti (FR) (Lahint (USA))
7408a6

Uleavemebreathless *A Oliver* 100
3 b f Tiger Hill(IRE) Sovereign Abbey (IRE) (Royal Academy (USA))
2289a4 2689a11 346010 3798a4 6225a5 6674a2 7404a3

Ultimate *Brian Ellison* a78 82
7 b g Anabaa(USA) Nirvana (Marju (IRE))
20406 25794 71159 (7369)

Ultimate Act *Seamus Mullins* 66
2 ro c Act One Ruffie (IRE) (Medicean)
64303 69542 73326

Ultimate Warrior (IRE) *Richard Hannon Snr* a72 67
2 ch c Winker Watson Sakaka (Tobougg (IRE))
32757 55397 60695 65202 68527 69465

Ultradargent (FR) *H-A Pantall* a91 93
2 b f Kendargent(FR) Dulce De Leche (FR) (Victory Note (USA))
3875a5 7084a7 7940a8

Ultrasonic (USA) *Sir Michael Stoute* 105
4 b f Mizzen Mast(USA) Quickfire (Dubai Millennium)
22644 28385 38314 41373 47052 52713

Ultra Special *Iain Jardine*
6 b m Reset(AUS) Exclusive Davis (USA) (Our Native (USA))
21510

Ultraviolet (IRE) *David Simcock* 70
2 b f Tamayuz Aphorism (Halling (USA))
366412 44915 59885 6426P (Dead)

Uma Mia (IRE) *T Lemer* 72
2 b f Whipper(USA) Princesse Bleue (FR) (Anabaa Blue)
6786a3

Umneyati *James Tate* a74 95
2 b f Iffraaj Honky Tonk Sally (Dansili)
27124 (3167) 41742 (5121) (5648) 65843 701112

Una Bella Cosa *Alan McCabe* a54 39
3 b f Dubai Destination(USA) Blinding Mission (IRE) (Marju (IRE))
552 2123 5279 8456 11852 21723 25124 46895 51927 59026 83486 83464

Unassailable *Kevin Ryan* a57 59
3 ch g Bahamian Bounty Reeling N' Rocking (IRE) (Mr Greeley (USA))
20106 250112 29504 50897 54079 62197

Unbreak My Heart (IRE) *Violet M Jordan* a84 93
8 ch g Bahamian Bounty Golden Heart (Salse (USA))
31524

Unbridled Ocean (USA) *S Seemar* a103 103
5 gr c Unbridled's Song(USA) Ocean Drive (USA) (Belong To Me (USA))
(744a) ◆ 957a6

Unbridled's Note (USA) *Steven Asmussen* a112 112
4 b c Unbridled's Song(USA) Siberian Fur (USA) (Siberian Express (USA))
7710a4

Uncle Bernie (IRE) *Andrew Hollinshead* a60 59
3 gr g Aussie Rules(USA) Alwiyda (USA) (Trempolino (USA))
29896 37353 44055 49394 55922 59978 63637 68276 73798 76665 81167

Uncle Bobby *Michael Easterby* 57
2 ch g Avonbridge Aunt Hilda (Distant Relative)
23374 28835 335013 60476

Uncle Brit *Malcolm Jefferson* a68 67
7 b g Efisio Tarneem (USA) (Zilzal (USA))
20427 59033 (6600) 72834 77784 79523 82953

Uncle Dermot (IRE) *Brendan Powell* a63 81
5 b g Arakan(USA) Cappadoce (IRE) (General Monash (USA))
15833 223211 29209 34167 475511 50634 59488 70932 73193 74302 (7608) 836011

Uncle Fred *Patrick Chamings* a71 78
8 b g Royal Applause Karla June (Unfuwain (USA))
192510 22289 31523 390110 69336 77846 79817

Uncle Roger (IRE) *Eve Johnson Houghton* a65 72
4 b g Camacho Felin Gruvy (IRE) (Tagula (IRE))
5123 25675 30563

Uncoiled (FR) *Yoshito Yahagi* 113
4 b c Giant's Causeway(USA) Tanzania (IRE) (Alzao (USA))
8033a8

Uncomplicated *Jim Boyle* a60 76
3 b f Bahamian Bounty Complication (Compton Place)
15156 20924 33757 41498

Uncut Stone (IRE) *Peter Niven* a67 58
5 b g Awesome Again(CAN) Suitably Discreet (USA) (Mr Prospector (USA))
7555 29754 35957 50484 55605 58635 61773

Under Ambition *Frederick Watson* 33
5 b f Striking Ambition Understudy (In The Wings)
21647 275411

Under Approval *David O'Meara* a65 18
2 b g Captain Gerrard(IRE) Dockside Strike (Docksider (USA))
295510 372410 44434 (8435)

Under My Wing (IRE) *Richard Hannon Snr* 67
2 ch c Raven's Pass(USA) Ra Hydee (USA) (Rahy (USA))
265310 49876 58525

Under Par *Michael Easterby* a56 52
5 b f Gentleman's Deal(IRE) Fun To Ride (Desert Prince (IRE))
242 1639 2402 3812 9177 10429 12228

Understory (USA) *Tim McCarthy* a75 74
6 b g Forestry(USA) Sha Tha (USA) (Mr Prospector (USA))
212 1905 4505 (639) 9065 11766 (1956) 33304 53114 74466 78652 83233

Under The Moon (IRE) *Charles Hills* 31
2 b g Exceed And Excel(AUS) Strawberry Moon (IRE) (Alhaarth (IRE))
485813 694712

Under The Radar (FR) *F Doumen* 98
2 b c Footstepsinthesand Fast Lane Lili (Fasliyev (USA))
6710a4 (7967a)

Underwhelm *Andrew Reid* a43
3 ch f Bahamian Bounty Depressed (Most Welcome)
802210 82589

Underwritten *John Weymes* a66 75
4 b g Authorized(IRE) Grain Of Gold (Mr Prospector (USA))
25094 (2831) 328710 (3637) 41475 43924 (4692) 48674 556014 67755 710012 759712 82048 84178

Under Your Thumb (IRE) *David Evans* 23
2 b f Dylan Thomas(IRE) On My Kness (FR) (Fasliyev (USA))
165910 19469 20688

Une Des Bieffes (FR) *Michael Scudamore* a32
5 b f Le Fou(IRE) Belle D'Ecajeul (FR) (Le Nain Jaune (FR))
13524

Unex Michelangelo (IRE) *Michael Easterby* a91 94
4 b g Dansili Chenchikova (IRE) (Sadler's Wells (USA))
148513 22409 243112 334515 362810 40517 54272 (5596) 56772 67589 71324 81627 83083

Unex Modigliani (IRE) *Michael Bell* a49 76
4 ch g Hurricane Run(IRE) Chronicle (Observatory (USA))
12912 15228 18046

Unfashionable (IRE) *Stuart Kittow* 34
2 b f Iffraaj Fashion Guide (IRE) (Bluebird (USA))
20675 42065 544212 632210

Unfinishedbusiness *Richard Fahey* 61
2 b g Selkirk(USA) Alizadora (Zilzal (USA))
66817 70237

Unidexter (IRE) *Mick Channon* a51 57
3 br g Footstepsinthesand Run To Jane (IRE) (Doyoun)
28008 32194

Unique Indygo (USA) *Claire Reece*
3 b f Indygo Shiner(USA) Unique Monique (USA) (Northern Park (USA))
786a9

Unison (IRE) *Peter Makin* a67 76
3 b c Jeremy(USA) Easter Song (USA) (Rubiano (USA))
43838 50962 ◆ (5391) 63797 75055 76566

United Color (USA) *D Selvaratnam* a112 102
4 b c Ghostzapper(USA) Silk Candy (CAN) (Langfuhr (CAN))
575a3 (834a) 1266a5

Universal (IRE) *Mark Johnston* a109 117
4 ch c Dubawi(IRE) Winesong (IRE) (Giant's Causeway (USA))
151a13 462a9 552a3 871a9 12422 (1382) (1674) (2020) 35563 (4213) 47455

Universal Bank (JPN) *Hiroyoshi Matsuda* 108
5 bb c Neo Universe(JPN) Victory Bank (JPN) (Dr Devious (IRE))
1868a13

Unknown Villain (IRE) *Tom Dascombe* a74 79
3 gr g Verglas(IRE) Ragtime Blues (IRE) (Grand Lodge (USA))
23714 334213 (3773) 38287 487915 64885 70652 74878

Unlimited *Tony Carroll* a71 63
11 b g Bold Edge Cabcharge Blue (Midyan (USA))
968 4268 6162 7052 9933 10794 13038 16563 18876 25658 35114 415510

Unlimited Budget (USA) *Todd Pletcher* a111
3 b f Street Sense(USA) Unlimited Pleasure (USA) (Valid Appeal (USA))
3127a6

Unmoothaj *Pam Sly* a74 76
3 b g Green Desert(USA) Sundus (USA) (Sadler's Wells (USA))
(1837) 29275 65337 76518 805910

Unsinkable (IRE) *Richard Fahey* a100 98
3 gr g Verglas(IRE) Heart's Desire (IRE) (Royal Applause)
13833 20234

Untapable (USA) *Steven Asmussen* a105
2 b f Tapit(USA) Fun House (USA) (Prized (USA))
7707a8

Until Midnight (IRE) *Alexandra Dunn* 58
3 b g Moss Vale(IRE) Emma's Star (ITY) (Darshaan)
685111

Until The Man (IRE) *Natalie Lloyd-Beavis*
6 b g Tillerman Canoe Cove (IRE) (Grand Lodge (USA))
802711

Upavon *David Elsworth* a93 67
3 b g Avonbridge Blaina (Compton Place)
(185) 7302 (982) ◆ 162515 237116 669210 72548 (7992) 82646

Updated (FR) *Ismail Mohammed* a37 44
2 ch f New Approach(IRE) Dance Treat (USA) (Nureyev (USA))
62989 66919

Up Hill Battle'S *Daniel Mark Loughnane* a45
2 b f Tiger Hill(IRE) Nasij (USA) (Elusive Quality (USA))
833213

Uphold *Gay Kelleway* a89 85
6 b g Oasis Dream Allegro Viva (USA) (Distant View (USA))
315a6 498a6 648a4 960a6 (5601a) 6060a4 (6750) 71217 76567 78057

Upholland *Richard Fahey* 69
2 b c Dutch Art Never Away (Royal Applause)
48589 66813 69394 78195

Up In Flames (IRE) *Martin Keighley* a57 57
4 b g Red Clubs(IRE) Flames (Blushing Flame (USA))
40365 54339 58169 72663

Uplifted (IRE) *Kevin Ryan* a15 41
2 b g Jeremy(USA) Misty Peak (IRE) (Sri Pekan (USA))
658113 69385 77328

Uppercut *Stuart Kittow* a93 92
5 ch g Needwood Blade Uplifting (Magic Ring (IRE))
148511 19224 259215 42072 48597 57425 (6167) 67672 76418

Upper Echelon *Mark Johnston* a23 53
3 ch f Danehill Dancer(IRE) Lady High Havens (IRE) (Bluebird (USA))
749 2379

Upper Grosvenor *Roger Varian* a64 62
4 b g Notnowcato Nsx (Roi Danzig (USA))
(6519) ◆ 696910 734310

Upper Lambourn (IRE) *Christopher Kellett* a62 43
5 b g Exceed And Excel(AUS) In The Fashion (IRE) (In The Wings)
969 5237 6185 (909) 9914 114710 195116 25759 29982 788611 80498 82349 84065

Uprise *George Margarson* a76 76
4 b g Pivotal Soar (Danzero (AUS))
22558 27259 384110 44283 466910 56076 72633 82204

Up Ten Down Two (IRE) *Michael Easterby* a79 74
4 b g Hurricane Run(IRE) Darabela (IRE) (Desert King (IRE))
20096 34808 43726 68776

Up Tipp *Mike Murphy* a62 22
3 ch g Medicean Jetbeeah (IRE) (Lomond (USA))
438110 549511 613413 69269 72994 77402 ◆ 83412

Uradel (GER) *H Blume* a77
2 b c Kallisto(GER) Unavita (GER) (Vettori (IRE))
6961a6

Uramazin (IRE) *Philip Hide* a102
7 ch g Danehill Dancer(IRE) Uriah (GER) (Acatenango (GER))
79273 81562

Urban Dance (IRE) *Charlie Appleby* a85 106
3 b g Street Cry(IRE) Melikah (IRE) (Lammtarra (USA))
(4257) (5006) ◆ 68412 77686

Urban Dreamer (IRE) *Rod Millman* 80
2 gr c Intense Focus(USA) Sioduil (IRE) (Oasis Dream)
165915 19462 22602 28095 30173 30352 42827 452812 49122 54283 55583 59552 64322 67912 702610 73333 75034

Urban Sanctuary *Ed Walker* 43
2 ch c Mount Nelson White Dress (IRE) (Pivotal)
663510 71258 76065

Urban Space *Tony Carroll* a58 78
7 ch g Sulamani(IRE) Rasmalai (Sadler's Wells (USA))
459110 506511 55863 665811 74339

Urban Tiger (GER) *Ecurie'T Heyveld* a23 70
10 b g Marju(IRE) Ukraine Venture (Slip Anchor)
3647a0

Urbonite (IRE) *Alan Swinbank* 29
4 b g Proud Citizen(USA) Bronze Baby (USA) (Silver Charm (USA))
18268

Uriah Heep (FR) *Alan King* a81 91
4 b g Danehill Dancer(IRE) Canasita (Zafonic (USA))
54756 62003 ◆ 675011

Ursus *Christopher Wilson* a52 59
8 ch g Rambling Bear Adar Jane (Ardar)
363015 49668 618013

Us Law (IRE) *P Bary* 110
3 gr g Lawman(FR) Dookus (IRE) (Linamix (FR))
1562a3 2298a17 3876a6 5040a10 6251a10

Usquaebach *Paddy Butler* a62
6 b m Trade Fair Mashmoum (Lycius (USA))
25097

Ustura (USA) *Saeed bin Suroor* a97 100
4 b g Nayef(USA) Calando (USA) (Storm Cat (USA))
(2520) ◆ 35593 39605 52596 57464

Usuelo (FR) *J-L Guillochon* 115
5 b g Epalo(GER) Gezabelle (FR) (Garde Royale)
7590a2 7890a13

Utterance *John Gosden* a74 81
4 b g Dansili Valentine Waltz (IRE) (Be My Guest (USA))
34726

Uxia Du Lin (FR) *J-P Trinquier* 50
5 b f Until Sundown(USA) Xena Du Lin (FR) (Goldneyev (USA))
6421a12

Vacoas (IRE) *F Head* a48
3 b g Kentucky Dynamite(USA) Rosinda (FR) (Danehill (USA))
2034a0

Vadamar (FR) *M Delzangles* 119
5 b g Dalakhani(IRE) Vadawina (IRE) (Unfuwain (USA))
348314

Vadara *Michael Easterby* a39 8
2 b g Aqlaam Hufflepuff (IRE) (Desert King (IRE))
549410 62138 675415 694713

Vagabond Shoes (IRE) *John W Sadler* a107 117
6 ch g Beat Hollow Atiza (IRE) (Singspiel (IRE))
7712a5

Vaguely Spanish *Tony Carroll* 58
2 b g Oratorio(IRE) Spanish Quest (Rainbow Quest (USA))
66419 712810 75027

Vague Nouvelle (IRE) *R Biondi* 95
2 ch f Mastercraftsman(IRE) Zona (ITY) (Mr Greeley (USA))
7415a2

Vahiney (FR) *Mme Pia Brandt* a77 81
3 b f American Post Nostalchia (FR) (Genereux Genie)
3708a4

Vainglory (USA) *David Simcock* a94 97
9 ch g Swain(IRE) Infinite Spirit (USA) (Maria's Mon (USA))
24245 26465 (2841) 333911

Valais Girl *Marcus Tregoning* a82 96
3 b f Holy Roman Emperor(IRE) Ellen (IRE) (Machiavellian (USA))
16765 31037 70154 764910

Valamar (FR) *J-Y Artu* a89 99
4 ch c Pivotal Vadapolina (FR) (Trempolino (USA))
922a3

Valantino Oyster (IRE) *Tracy Waggott* a62 65
6 b g Pearl Of Love(IRE) Mishor (Slip Anchor)
178910 (2961) 319512 35455 36525 45433 48885 (5420) 60863 64704

Valbchek (IRE) *Jeremy Noseda* a108 106
4 b g Acclamation Spectacular Show (IRE) (Spectrum (IRE))
49812 57474 671910 72086 752713 (7928)

Valcy Great (FR) *E Lecoiffier*
2 b c Great Journey(JPN) Valicyose (FR) (Sicyos (USA))
5323a10

Valdaw *Mike Murphy* a80 68
5 b g Val Royal(FR) Delight Of Dawn (Never So Bold)
(276) (449) 7285 (898) 11724 (1798) 19854 29648 44968 54065 710612 774213 83045

Valdemar *John Weymes* a46 50
7 ch g Tobougg(IRE) Stealthy Times (Timeless Times (USA))
8710

Vale Mentor (IRE) *Tim Easterby* a18 45
2 b c Moss Vale(IRE) Sinamay (USA) (Saint Ballado (CAN))
75925 78176 80917

Valen (IRE) *Michael Bell* 85
2 gr f Acclamation Ardea Brave (IRE) (Chester House (USA))
48775 ◆ (5385) 57376 76574

Valentine's Gift *Neville Bycroft* 67
5 b g Presidium Efipetite (Efisio)
298611 372811 40104 43767 48513 52406 53845 54207 57865 58624 61778 67222 (6952) (7346)

Vale Of Clara (IRE) *Peter Niven* a61 42
5 b f Iffraaj Luggala (IRE) (Kahyasi)
17366 28378 788612 82343

Vale Of Lingfield (IRE) *John Best* a70
4 b g Moss Vale(IRE) Celtic Guest (IRE) (Be My Guest (USA))
1176 3494 4404 ◆

Validor (FR) *S Labate* a84 79
7 ch g American Post Panthesilea (FR) (Kendor (FR))
315a4

Valid Reason *Dean Ivory* a62 87
6 b g Observatory(USA) Real Trust (USA) (Danzig (USA))
3786 50089 55207 61739 66468 72103

Validus *Luca Cumani* a107 107
4 b g Zamindar(USA) Victoire Finale (Peintre Celebre (USA))
17686 37252 431015 56819 65304 70182

Valirann (FR) *A De Royer-Dupre* 111
3 b c Nayef(USA) Valima (FR) (Linamix (FR))
(6250a) (7046a)

Valkov *Tony Carroll* a46 29
6 b m Val Royal(FR) Petrikov (IRE) (In The Wings)
3349 9754 110012 17799 19796

Vallado (IRE) *Edward Lynam* 90
2 gr f Clodovil(IRE) Knapton Hill (Zamindar (USA))
(5773a)

Vallarta (IRE) *Mick Channon* 85
3 b c Footstepsinthesand Mexican Miss (IRE) (Tagula (IRE))
20226 24529 30209 37826 44783 66472 69002

Vallecupa (ITY) *D Zarroli* 93
2 b f Mujahid(USA) My Meltemi (IRE) (Hawk Wing (USA))
7678a3

Valley Dreamer *Robert Stephens* a39 42
3 b f Sleeping Indian Blaenavon (Cadeaux Genereux)
581710 680310 71187

Valley Fire *Ed McMahon* a31 47
3 ch f Three Valleys(USA) Fireburst (Spectrum (IRE))
40138 506912 68063

Valley Girl (FR) *H-A Pantall* a56 81
3 ch f Motivator Nanty (IRE) (Nashwan (USA))
6713a11

Valley Stream (USA) *Kelly Breen* 74
4 bb c Gone West(USA) Endless Parade (USA) (Williamstown (USA))
1001a8

Vallila *Roger Charlton* a67 59
2 b f Dunkerque(FR) Villabella (FR) (Hernando (FR))
29475 34144 57572 61112 (6474)

Vally Jem (FR) *D Sepulchre* a85 107
4 b f Dylan Thomas(IRE) Ballymena Lassie (Giant's Causeway (USA))
(2969a) 4421a2 5574a5 6618a2 7613a3

Valmina *Tony Carroll* a74 82
6 b g Val Royal(FR) Minnina (IRE) (In The Wings)
33159 38553 60677 63826 65869 67452 77835 80699

Valonia *Henry Candy* 97
2 ch f Three Valleys(USA) Descriptive (IRE) (Desert King (IRE))
42152 (4877) 66224 71943

Val's Diamond (IRE) *Ann Duffield* a15 39
3 b f Mujadil(USA) More Respect (IRE) (Spectrum (IRE))
168711

Valtina (IRE) *William Haggas* 89
3 b f Teofilo(IRE) Vassiana (FR) (Anabaa (USA))
(1828) 24126 25867 346014

Value (IRE) *Richard Hannon Snr* a42 73
2 br f Clodovil(IRE) Shalev (GER) (Java Gold (USA))
23914 398610 (4880) 59276

Valued Opinion (IRE) *Tim Pitt* a49 40
2 b g Art Connoisseur(IRE) Paix Royale (Royal Academy (USA))
25627 40659 59703 677810

Valvibrata (ITY) *C Felaco* 101
4 b f Mujahid(USA) Victorian Girl (GER) (Lomitas)
7558a5

Vamos (IRE) *Mrs A Malzard* a65 61
7 b g Royal Applause Feather Boa (IRE) (Sri Pekan (USA))
1313a[3] 1740a[2] 5328a[3]

Vamosalaplaya (FR) *F Doumen* a68 66
2 ch c Footstepsinthesand Marital Bliss (FR) (Double Bed (FR))
6961a[11]

Vancouverite *A Fabre* 118
3 b c Dansili Villarrica (USA) (Selkirk (USA))
(5462a) 6446a[9]

Van Der Neer *Richard Hannon Snr* a104 116
3 b c Dutch Art Lalectra (King Charlemagne (USA))
(1383) 2021[3] 2677a[8] 3485[3] 4027[5]

Vandross (IRE) *Chris Wall* a32 67
3 b g Iffraaj Mrs Kanning (Distant View (USA))
2800[3] 3257[6] *4352[5]* 7098[2]

Van Ellis *Mahmood Al Zarooni* a106 111
4 b c Shamardal(USA) Jalousie (IRE) (Barathea (IRE))
465a[2]

Vanessa *Ian Semple* a21 60
3 ch f Sixties Icon Fly Butterfly (Bahamian Bounty)
3566[10] 3772[10] 3929[6]

Vanishing Cupid (SWI) *H-A Pantall* 107
3 b c Galileo(IRE) Vanishing Prairie (USA) (Alysheba (USA))
3645a[3] (5361a) 6987a[3] 7705a[2]

Vanistas (FR) *S Wattel*
3 b c Manduro(GER) Viane (FR) (Cardoun (FR))
191a[0]

Vanity Rules *John Gosden* a85 83
3 b f New Approach(IRE) Miss Pinkerton (Danehill (USA))
2049[6] 3292[4] 5588[2] *(6611)*

Van Mildert (IRE) *Dianne Sayer* 39
4 b f Observatory(USA) Vanilla Delight (IRE) (Orpen (USA))
2754[8]

Van Percy *Andrew Balding* 95
3 b g Sir Percy Enforce (USA) (Kalanisi (IRE))
1641[4] 2216[2] (2660) 2879[3] 4984[4] ◆ 5764[6] 6841[3] 7174[5] 7526[5]

Vanvidd (FR) *C Boutin* a56 58
2 gr c Verglas(IRE) Magic Spin (USA) (Lord Avie (USA))
3167[5] 6169[8] 7570a[9]

Vanvitelli *James Fanshawe* 73
3 b g Shamardal(USA) Treble Seven (USA) (Fusaichi Pegasus (USA))
1635[11] 2192[5] 2628[9] 4961[9]

Vaquera (NZ) *Gai Waterhouse* 96
4 b f High Chaparral(IRE) The Mighty Lions (NZ) (Grosvenor (NZ))
7700a[13]

Varing (FR) *P Chatelain* a76 76
3 b c Vadasin(IRE) Noverings (Noverre (USA))
331a[2] 711a[DSQ] 1756a[2] *2034a[3]*

Varsity (USA) *Christophe Clement* 113
6 b g Indian Charlie(USA) Tears Of Joy (USA) (Mt. Livermore (USA))
1265a[6]

Vasias (FR) *C Lotoux* 100
5 b g Motivator Vivacity (Trempolino (USA))
7590a[6]

Vasily *Robert Eddery* a2 105
5 b c Sadler's Wells(USA) Red Bloom (Selkirk (USA))
1242[13] 1768[3] 3115[5] 3838[2] (4501) 4706[2] 5269[5] (6001)

Vastly (USA) *Julia Feilden* a74 69
4 rg g Mizzen Mast(USA) Valentine Band (USA) (Dixieland Band (USA))
815[3] ◆ *1057[2]* 1296[4] 2234[8] *2807[2]* 3222[3] 6283[6] *6748[7]*

Vastonea (IRE) *Kevin Prendergast* 97
5 gr g Verglas(IRE) Roystonea (Polish Precedent (USA))
3869a[7] 4465a[12] 4869a[3] 6025a[10]

Vaunoise (IRE) *J-C Rouget* a105 100
3 b f Teofilo(IRE) Tipperary Honor (FR) (Highest Honor (FR))
2299a[8] 7993a[10] *8440a[2]*

Vayakhan (FR) *A De Royer-Dupre* a89 95
3 gr c Dalakhani(IRE) Vadaza (FR) (Zafonic (USA))
1511a[2]

Veda (FR) *A De Royer-Dupre* 89
2 b f Dansili Vadapolina (FR) (Trempolino (USA))
7055a[10]

Vedelago (IRE) *S Botti* 109
4 b c Red Clubs(IRE) Queen Shy (Marju (IRE))
(2295a) 6889a[5] 7724a[4]

Vedeux (IRE) *C Lerner* 106
2 b c Elusive City(USA) Qahatika (FR) (Polish Precedent (USA))
(3875a) 4572a[3] 5573a[10]

Veeraya *Julia Feilden* a88 94
3 b g Rail Link Follow Flanders (Pursuit Of Love)
3582[2] 4492[2] 5287[3] 5510[8] 7063[3] *8445[3]*

Vega Dance (IRE) *Clive Cox* 50
3 b f Danehill Dancer(IRE) Young And Daring (USA) (Woodman (USA))
2231[11] 5478[10]

Vegas Belle *Geoffrey Oldroyd* a47 56
3 b f Misu Bond(IRE) Bond Casino (Kyllachy)
7204[7] 8142[6] 8279[4]

Veiled Intrigue *Henry Candy* 94
2 b f Pastoral Pursuits Verbal Intrigue (USA) (Dahar (USA))
5061[4] ◆ (5740) 6622[6] 7537[6]

Veligandu (GER) *R Dzubasz* 83
2 ch f Hurricane Run(IRE) Venia Legendi (GER) (Zinaad)
7406a[9]

Velox *Luca Cumani* 94
3 b g Zamindar(USA) Victoire Finale (Peintre Celebre (USA))
2093[5] ◆ (2930) 4023[2] 5006[2] 5944[4]

Velvetina (IRE) *Harry Dunlop* a84 57
3 b f Barathea(IRE) Pershaan (IRE) (Darshaan)
1955[3] (2560) (4150) ◆

Velvety (USA) *Charlie Appleby* 78
3 b f Bernardini(USA) Caress (USA) (Storm Cat (USA))
(4125) 4777[8] 5202[4]

Venetias Dream (IRE) *Stuart Williams* a57
4 b f Librettist(USA) Machaera (Machiavellian (USA))
62[7] 276[3] 440[6]

Venezia (IRE) *Lady Cecil* 75
2 gr c Galileo(IRE) St Roch (IRE) (Danehill (USA))
6355[4] 7019[3]

Venir Rouge *Harry Whittington* a39 58
9 ch g Dancing Spree(USA) Al Awaalah (Mukaddamah (USA))
3110[4] 3884[8] 5846[7] *6558[10]*

Vent De Force *Hughie Morrison* 64
2 b c Hurricane Run(IRE) Capriolla (In The Wings)
6740[5] 7219[3]

Ventura Ice (IRE) *Richard Hannon Snr* a60 56
2 gr f Oratorio(IRE) Tipperary Honor (FR) (Highest Honor (FR))
5922[9] 6690[7] 6974[5]

Ventura Mist *Tim Easterby* 97
2 ch f Pastoral Pursuits Kerry's Dream (Tobougg (IRE))
1642[3] 1839[3] (2458) (2767) 3459[8] 3829[2] 5679[12] 5837[3] 6622[3] (7026) 7194[7]

Ventura Quest (USA) *Richard Fahey* 85
2 b g Henrythenavigator(USA) Ing Ing (FR) (Bering)
4312[3] (5105) 5656[9] (7097)

Ventura Reef (IRE) *Richard Fahey* a54
2 b c Excellent Art Run To Jane (IRE) (Doyoun)
8266[4] 8451[8]

Ventura Spirit *Richard Fahey* 71
4 b g Royal Applause Jalissa (Mister Baileys)
2881[4]

Venturous Spirit (FR) *M Delzangles* 103
3 b f Arch(USA) Vatrouchka (USA) (Kingmambo (USA))
3877a[9] 4468a[2] 6962a[8]

Venue *Lady Cecil* a51 101
3 b c Beat Hollow Shirley Valentine (Shirley Heights)
(3858) (4476) (6128) ◆

Venus De Milo (IRE) *A P O'Brien* 115
3 br f Duke Of Marmalade(IRE) Inchmahome (Galileo (IRE))
4550a[2] ◆ (5115a) 5682[2] ◆ 6448a[8]

Venus Grace *Ralph Beckett* a73
2 b f Royal Applause Basque Beauty (Nayef (USA))
7766[4] ◆ *8084[2]*

Venus Marina *Chris Wall* 52
2 b f Tiger Hill(IRE) Danvers (Cape Cross (IRE))
7693[7]

Venutius *Philip Kirby* a88 93
6 b g Doyen(IRE) Boadicea's Chariot (Commanche Run)
2958[9] 4435[8] 5149[6] 6550[11] 7424[5] *7950[10]*

Vera Lou (IRE) *Pat Eddery* a47 44
2 ch f Manduro(GER) Baltica (IRE) (Sadler's Wells (USA))
7245[6] 7692[7] *8362[5]*

Ver Coquin (FR) *J-P Carvalho* a76 78
3 gr g Verglas(IRE) Afra Tsitsi (FR) (Belong To Me (USA))
1511a[10] 7188a[13]

Verdant *Robert Smerdon* a82 108
6 b g Singspiel(IRE) Orford Ness (Selkirk (USA))
7483a[2] 7827a[10]

Verde-Mar (BRZ) *Fabricio Borges* a106 95
6 b h Gilded Time(USA) Jolie Marcia (BRZ) (Spend A Buck (USA))
(5325a)

Verema (FR) *A De Royer-Dupre* 115
4 b f Barathea(IRE) Vermentina (IRE) (Darshaan)
1263a[3] 1871a[2] 2695a[5] (4324a) (5575a) 7761a[P]

Veremeroad (FR) *G Martin* a69 72
3 b c Dobby Road(FR) Golden Ebene (FR) (Double Heart (FR))
7995a[11]

Vergality Ridge (IRE) *Ronald Harris* a64 49
3 gr g Verglas(IRE) Phoenix Factor (IRE) (Indian Ridge)
122[8] 321[7] 357[6] 2347[4] 3268[4] 3679[7] *4353[4]*

Vergrigio (IRE) *David Pipe* a65 49
4 gr g Verglas(IRE) Roystonea (Polish Precedent (USA))
929[5]

Verinco *Bryan Smart* a68 86
7 b g Bahamian Bounty Dark Eyed Lady (IRE) (Exhibitioner)
1968 457[10] 2505[5] 3331[11] 7776[12]

Vermeyen *Geoffrey Deacon* a47 36
4 b g Dutch Art Madame Maxine (USA) (Dayjur (USA))
117[11] 349[7] 456[10] 3326[9] *3687[5] 4522[4]* 5091[6] *7167[7]*

Vermont (IRE) *Luca Cumani* a92 87
3 b g Muhtathir Venetian Beauty (USA) (Lear Fan (USA))
3343[2] 4257[4] 6566[3] 6950[4] *7864[2] (8245)*

Vermuyden *Pam Sly* a56
4 b g Oasis Dream Speciosa (IRE) (Danehill Dancer (IRE))
7625[6] 8146[7]

Veronica's Pursuit *Peter Hedger* a45
3 b f Pastoral Pursuits Veronica Franco (Darshaan)
8444[7]

Verrazano (USA) *Todd Pletcher* a124
3 b c More Than Ready(USA) Enchanted Rock (USA) (Giant's Causeway (USA))
2033a[14] 7689a[4]

Verse Of Love *David Evans* a96 92
4 b g Byron Lovellian (Machiavellian (USA))
(60) 407[5] 495[12] 690[8] 944[3] 1252[4] *1542[8] 1745[2] 1905[6]* 2210[7] 2254[22] 2649[4] 3096[9] 3757[6] (4245) 4778[9] 5026[5] 5348[3] 5943[5] 6427[4] 6868[8] 7641[13] 8094[2] 8117[6] (8264) 8344[3] 8428[4] 8445[6]

Versilia Gal (IRE) *Patrick Martin* a74 82
3 b f Footstepsinthesand Tuscany Lady (IRE) (Danetime (IRE))
2374a[9]

Vertueux (FR) *Tony Carroll* a65 62
8 gr g Verglas(IRE) Shahrazad (FR) (Bering)
973[5] 1217[6] 1980[2] 2570[7] 2921[3] 3271[13] 5216[6] (5846) (6099)

Verus Delicia (IRE) *John Stimpson* a54 70
4 b f Chineur(FR) Ribbon Glade (UAE) (Zafonic (USA))
1101[9] 2043[9] *2997[8]* 3026[2] 3660[7] (3949) 4456[2] 4603[2] 5097[3] 6156[3] 6535[4] 6761[2] *7728[5]*

Verxina (JPN) *Yasuo Tomomichi* 112
4 bl f Deep Impact(JPN) Halwa Sweet (JPN) (Machiavellian (USA))
8033a[7]

Very First Blade *Mark Brisbourne* a61 22
4 b g Needwood Blade Dispol Verity (Averti (IRE))
42[10] 240[7] 440[11] 551[9] 716[2] (754) 909[4] 1043[6] 1395[8] 2170[4] 2582[4] (2998) 3644[2] 4834[8] 5198[7] 5818[12] 6478[4] 6808[5]

Very Good Day (FR) *Mick Channon* 97
6 b g Sinndar(IRE) Picture Princess (Sadler's Wells (USA))
2149[11]

Very Nice Name (FR) *A De Mieulle* a83 116
4 b c Whipper(USA) Namona (IRE) (Halling (USA))
1268a[3] 4745[7] 5807a[4] 6449a[2] 7058a[16]

Vesper (GER) *M Munch* a68 79
3 b f Sholokhov(IRE) Vera Longa (GER) (Lando (GER))
8441a[4]

Vexillum (IRE) *Simon Hodgson* a73 70
4 br g Mujadil(USA) Common Cause (Polish Patriot (USA))
7273[3] 8223[6]

Veya (USA) *Ed Walker* 74
2 ch c Giant's Causeway(USA) Gossamer (USA) (Seattle Slew (USA))
2741[7] 4026[6] 4513[2]

Veyepea *Sylvester Kirk* a49 49
4 ch f Dutch Art Endear (Pivotal)
7[8] 41[5] 226[12]

Vhujon (IRE) *Peter Grayson* a50 48
8 b g Mujadil(USA) Livius Lady (IRE) (Titus Livius (FR))
87[4] 111[6] 327[6] 349[6] 7905[10] 8051[3] 8169[4]

Via Ballycroy (IRE) *M Halford* a96 90
4 b f Lawman(FR) Via Milano (FR) (Singspiel (IRE))
3846a[10] 4647a[6]

Via Chope (FR) *C Boutin* 97
3 b f Indian Rocket Via Appia (FR) (Exit To Nowhere (USA))
2334a[3]

Via Garibaldi (ITY) *L Riccardi* 97
4 b c Byron Surela (IRE) (Dolphin Street (FR))
2491a[15] 4935a[0]

Vicksburg *Andrew Balding* 86
3 b f Cape Cross(IRE) Totality (Dancing Brave (USA))
1671[10] 2389[3] (5942) 6832[3]

Vicky Valentine *Alistair Whillans* 69
3 b f Rock Of Gibraltar(IRE) Silcasue (Selkirk (USA))
2915[7] 5107[5] 6296[3] (6601) 6827[3] 7100[5] *7757[7]*

Victoire De Lyphar (IRE) *Ruth Carr* a34 93
6 b g Bertolini(USA) Victory Peak (Shirley Heights)
966[10] 1646[7] 1787[4] 2007[5] 3441[8] 3811[6] (4198) 4758[7] 5292[4] 5481[2] 6288[8] 7024[10] 7374[10]

Victorian Bounty *Tony Newcombe* a77 76
8 b g Bahamian Bounty Baby Bunting (Wolfhound (USA))
186[6] 603[10] 976[11]

Victorian Number (FR) *Geoffrey Deacon* a69 77
5 ch g Numerous(USA) Malaisia (FR) (Anabaa (USA))
(1087) (2126) 3433[2] (5230) ◆ *6315[5] 6928[5] 8019[U] 8158[5] 8432[3]*

Victorianvalentine (FR) *Matthieu Palussiere* a75 78
2 ch f Dyhim Diamond(IRE) Victorian Dancer (IRE) (Groom Dancer (USA))
3875a[8] 5363a[7] 6059a[2]

Victorinna (FR) *C Laffon-Parias* a88 105
5 ch f Gentlewave(IRE) Marcela Howard (IRE) (Fasliyev (USA))
1895a[3] 2644a[10] 5041a[6]

Victory Danz (IRE) *David O'Meara* 56
2 b c Bushranger(IRE) Victoria Lodge (IRE) (Grand Lodge (USA))
4886[8] 6175[7] 6716[5] 7418[8]

Victory De Rebecq (USA) *D Prod'Homme* a56 86
3 ch c Any Given Saturday(USA) Fanny Cerrito (USA) (Gulch (USA))
286a[9] 6713a[12]

Victory Laurel (IRE) *Robert Cowell* 98
3 b c Holy Roman Emperor(IRE) Special Cause (IRE) (Fasliyev (USA))
(2491a) 6445a[8]

Victory Song (IRE) *A P O'Brien* a91 82
3 b c Dansili All Too Beautiful (IRE) (Sadler's Wells (USA))
7230a[18]

Victory Tiger (GER) *W Hefter* 78
2 b c Konigstiger(GER) Velocity (FR) (Galileo (IRE))
5911a[7]

Victrix Ludorum (IRE) *Richard Hannon Snr* 97
3 b f Invincible Spirit(IRE) Matikanehamatidori (JPN) (Sunday Silence (USA))
1620[6] 2452[4] 2936[2] 3734[3] 4949[13] 6768[9]

Vied (USA) *Robert Cowell* a60
2 b f Elusive Quality(USA) Unacloud (USA) (Unaccounted For (USA))
7120[12] 7763[12] 7902[5]

Viennese Verse *Henry Candy* a71 63
3 b g Byron Teller (ARG) (Southern Halo (USA))
2099[4] 2930[5] *3821[6] 5135[10] 5869[3]* (6324) *(6655) (7163)*

Viewpoint (IRE) *Richard Hannon Snr* a98 102
4 b g Exceed And Excel(AUS) Lady's View (USA) (Distant View (USA))
3832[4] 4706[3] (4854) 5540[3] 6332[6] 6638[12] 6957[4] *8071[10] 8263[7]*

Vif Monsieur (GER) *S Smrczek* 108
3 b c Doyen(IRE) Vive Madame (GER) (Big Shuffle (USA))
(1867a) 2696a[10] 4103a[15] 5576a[4] 6678a[2] (7407a)

Vigor (IRE) *David Simcock* a81 89
2 b c Iffraaj Miss Gibraltar (Rock Of Gibraltar (IRE))
2758[2] ◆ (3426) ◆ 4296[6] 4768[3]

Viking Hall (IRE) *Rae Guest*
2 ch g Halling(USA) Magdalene (Act One)
6279[13]

Viking Storm *Harry Dunlop* a103 106
5 b g Hurricane Run(IRE) Danehill's Dream (IRE) (Danehill (USA))
1034[7] 2443[7] 4796[8] 5655[12] (6144) 6833[5]

Viking Warrior (IRE) *Shaun Harris* a61 62
6 ch g Halling(USA) Powder Paint (Mark Of Esteem (IRE))
1462[5] 1757[6] 2273[5] 2837[5] 3286[7] 5471[8] 6634[12] 6919[9] 7153[2] *8042[12] 8341[11]*

Viletta (GER) *J Hirschberger* a75 95
3 b f Doyen(IRE) Vallauris (GER) (Surumu (GER))
3604a[4] 5044a[6]

Village Cricket *Pam Sly* a21 47
2 br g Pastoral Pursuits Black Salix (USA) (More Than Ready (USA))
3245[13] 3737[4] 3991[9] *5893[13]*

Village Green *Ollie Pears* a60 50
4 b g Green Desert(USA) Avessia (Averti (IRE))
324[2] 525[10] 1079[11] 2236[10]

Villa Royale *David O'Meara* a66 87
4 b f Val Royal(FR) Villa Carlotta (Rainbow Quest (USA))
2277[10] (2615) 2973[5] 3791[2] 5031[5] 5997[7] 6631[5] 6846[9] 7369[3] 7596[4]

Villequier (FR) *J-C Rouget* a88
3 b c Footstepsinthesand Interior (USA) (Fusaichi Pegasus (USA))
(460a)

Villoresi (IRE) *James Fanshawe* a88 91
4 b g Clodovil(IRE) Villafranca (IRE) (In The Wings)
2498[4] ◆ 3370[3] *3692[2]* ◆ 4720[3] 5746[5] *6172[8]* 7131[3]

Vim (FR) *C Boutin* a72 74
2 ch c Zafeen(FR) Version Originale I (FR) (Poliglote)
5214a[5]

Vimiero (USA) *Jonjo O'Neill* a81 68
6 bb g Dynaformer(USA) Merrymaker (ARG) (Rainbow Corner)
224[8] 823[8] 2087[2] 3065[10]

Vincentti (IRE) *Ronald Harris* 93
3 b g Invincible Spirit(IRE) Bint Al Balad (IRE) (Ahonoora)
2430[2] 3348[14] 4989[10] 5260[10] 6990[16] 7777[10]

Vin Chaud *Bill Turner*
5 b f Fair Mix(IRE) Bayrouge (IRE) (Gorytus (USA))
713[6]

Vine De Nada *Mark Johnston* 74
2 b c Bahamian Bounty Hip (Pivotal)
1247[5] (1606) 1785[4] 2877[5] 4019[7] 6645[13] 6844[6] 7062[11]

Vinson Massif (USA) *A P O'Brien* a84 88
3 ch c Giant's Causeway(USA) Swan Nebula (USA) (Seeking The Gold (USA))
2374a[14]

Vintage Red (FR) *C Baillet* 91
2 b f Turtle Bowl(IRE) Irish Vintage (FR) (Loup Solitaire (USA))
4816a[7]

Viola Da Gamba (IRE) *William Knight* a65 68
4 b f Alhaarth(IRE) Addaya (IRE) (Persian Bold)
53[3] 342[4]

Violent Velocity (IRE) *John Quinn* a75 79
10 b g Namid Lear's Crown (USA) (Lear Fan (USA))
97[2] 376[7] 1239[15] 1693[7] 2551[9] 3506[9] 5426[2] (5637) 6276[2] 6600[12] 7152[11] 7238[4]

Violet Dancer *Gary Moore* a80 46
3 b g Bertolini(USA) Another Secret (Efisio)
1881[10] *2560[5] 3402[2]*

Violetgrace *Michael Madgwick*
3 ch f Bertolini(USA) Magical Dancer (IRE) (Magical Wonder (USA))
4176[8] 4750[4]

Violet Plum *Laura Mongan* 47
3 br f Araafa(IRE) Raphaela (FR) (Octagonal (NZ))
2953[10] 6407[3] 7071[7]

Virgin Queen (IRE) *S Botti* a73 96
3 ch f Iffraaj Glencoe Solas (IRE) (Night Shift (USA))
7416a[6]

Vision Of Judgment *Ollie Pears* 45
3 b g Byron Glorious Colours (Spectrum (IRE))
1967[4] 2799[4]

Vision Of Rome *Mick Channon* a50
2 b f Holy Roman Emperor(IRE) Purple Vision (Rainbow Quest (USA))
7852[8] 8025[5] 8137[7]

Visions Of Johanna (USA) *Charles Smith* a64 30
8 b g Johannesburg(USA) Belle Turquoise (FR) (Tel Quel (FR))
1597[5] 2435[14] *2575[10] 3637[7]*

Visit Copenhagen (USA) *Mrs K Burke* a72 80
3 ch f Speightstown(USA) Nomistakeaboutit (CAN) (Affirmed (USA))
1546[6] 3047[3] 3722[2] ◆ 4180[2] 4561[3] (5181)

Visiyani (FR) *A De Royer-Dupre* 104
3 gr c Rock Of Gibraltar(IRE) Visionnaire (FR) (Linamix (FR))
5551a[5]

Visual Aspect *Dean Ivory* a60
3 b g Assertive Enclave (USA) (Woodman (USA))
114[5] 1086[6] 1323[8] 1874[5] 2347[7]

Vital Edition (IRE) *David O'Meara* a17
3 b g Pivotal Triple Edition (USA) (Lear Fan (USA))
2576[11] 3201[6]

Vital Evidence (USA) *Sir Michael Stoute* a85 95
3 b g Empire Maker(USA) Promising Lead (Danehill (USA))
(3343) 4476[3] 5189[5] 6751[4] (7431)

Vital Spirit (FR) *E J O'Neill* 102
4 b g Vital Equine(IRE) Reel Twister (Reel Buddy (USA))
4935a[8] 7085a[13]

Vitruvian Lady *Noel Quinlan* 73
3 b f Manduro(GER) Vas Y Carla (USA) (Gone West (USA))
(2547)

Vittachi *Alistair Whillans* a56 69
6 b g Bertolini(USA) Miss Lorilaw (FR) (Homme De Loi (IRE))
2316[6] 2975[6] 4343[5] 4614[4] (5240) 5833[2] 6179[4] 6552[10] (6909) 7239[4] 7376[2] 8270[5]

Vitznau (IRE) *K F Clutterbuck* a66 78
9 b g Val Royal(FR) Neat Dish (CAN) (Stalwart (USA))
(223) 334[4] 517[6] 652[U] 813[10] 965[3] 1310[4] 7353[10] 7886[7] 8118[12]

Viva Colonia (IRE) *Brian Ellison* 63
8 ch g Traditionally(USA) Ansariya (USA) (Shahrastani (USA))
3729[6] 4343[4]

Viva Diva *John C McConnell* a74 67
5 ch f Hurricane Run(IRE) Vas Y Carla (USA) (Gone West (USA))
5267[3]

Viva L'Inghilterra (IRE) *Robert Cowell* a56 43
3 b f Refuse To Bend(IRE) Whipped Queen (USA) (Kingmambo (USA))
532[4] 734[3] 979[5] 2512[7] 2996[7] 3323[4] 3789[8]

Viva Ronaldo (IRE) *Richard Fahey* a83 94
7 b g Xaar Papaha (FR) (Green Desert (USA))
1113[10] 1693[6] 2882[9] 3464[5] 5947[8] 6464[3] 6634[9]

Viva Valaria *A Fabre* a50 51
2 b f Oasis Dream On A Soapbox (USA) (Mi Cielo (USA))
6961a[14]

Viva Verglas (IRE) *David Barron* a97 96
2 gr g Verglas(IRE) Yellow Trumpet (Petong)
2670[14] 3023[4] (3766) (4261) (5236) 5679[9] 7026[21] 7333[2] (7545)

Viva Vettori *Brian Forsey* a59 93
9 ch g Vettori(IRE) Cruinn A Bhord (Inchinor)
1890[6]

Vivere (IRE) *David O'Meara* 87
2 b f Montjeu(IRE) Valdara (Darshaan)
5330[3] ◆ 6350[6] 6666[2]

Viztoria (IRE) *Edward Lynam* 114
3 b f Oratorio(IRE) Viz (IRE) (Darshaan)
(2108a) 3524[6] ◆ (6392) 7059a[6] 7364[3]

Vocational (USA) *A Al Raihe* a79 77
4 b f Exceed And Excel(AUS) Carry On Katie (USA) (Fasliyev (USA))
954a[14]

Voce Della Note (FR) *Mme A Soulat*
3 ch f Royal Assault(USA) Verte Rive (FR) (Green Tune (USA))
7569a[11]

Vodka Chaser (IRE) *J S Moore* a54 64
2 b f Baltic King Suffer Her (IRE) (Whipper (USA))
1432[4] 1724[8] 3857[8] 4363[5] 4749[2] 5363a[5] 6111[8] 6474[7] 7036[5] 7986[6] 8025[2] 8137[4] 8383[5]

Vodka Time (IRE) *David Evans* a75 82
2 b c Indian Haven Cappuccino (IRE) (Mujadil (USA))
1108[2] ◆ 1541[4] (1619)

Vogarth *Michael Chapman* a37 44
9 ch g Arkadian Hero(USA) Skara Brae (Inchinor)
1310[6] 1455[7] 2168[10] 3501[7] 5378[6] 6606[9] 6952[9]

Voice From Above (IRE) *Patrick Holmes* a58 70
4 b f Strategic Prince Basin Street Blues (IRE) (Dolphin Street (FR))
3977[4] 4853[U] 5179[8] 5521[7] 5615[2] 6297[8] 6700[5] 8329[9]

Voice Of A Leader (IRE) *Peter Chapple-Hyam* 93
2 b c Danehill Dancer(IRE) Thewaytosanjose (IRE) (Fasliyev (USA))
4256[3] (4896) 6351[3]

Voix Des Aigles (FR) *E Daure* a37 50
5 b g Victory Note(USA) Udina (Unfuwain (USA))
5464a[8]

Vola E Va *B Grizzetti* 103
4 b g Oratorio(IRE) Veronica Franco (ITY) (Lomitas)
1709a[2] 2295a[4] 2489a[5] 3147a[4] 3881a[5]

Volcanic Dust (IRE) *Milton Bradley* a66 69
5 b m Ivan Denisovich(IRE) Top Of The Form (IRE) (Masterclass (USA))
77[8] 369[7] 1731[5] 1902[5] 3154[4] 3498[3] 4197[5] 4427[8] 4943[5] 5670[3] 5982[4] 6930[2] 7292[3] 7903[5]

Volcanic Jack (IRE) *Philip Kirby* a66 68
5 b g Kodiac Rosaria Panatta (IRE) (Mujtahid (USA))
198[7] 309[6] 432[3] 4622[2] ◆ 4951[3] 5420[4]

Volcanic Wind (USA) *Saeed bin Suroor* a94 86
4 b g Distorted Humor(USA) Sundrop (JPN) (Sunday Silence (USA))
2592[5] 3019[4]

Voleuse De Coeurs (IRE) *Michael Moroney* a75 118
4 b f Teofilo(IRE) Vadorga (Grand Lodge (USA))
3873a[3] 5776a[2] (6441a) 7761a[10]

Vol Freak *Willie Musson* a49
3 b g Kyllachy Sister Moonshine (Averti (IRE))
5069[10] 5133[12] 6134[11]

Volito *Anabel K Murphy* a60 62
7 ch g Bertolini(USA) Vax Rapide (Sharpo)
1929[6] 2281[9] 4034[3] 4369[3] 4659[5] 5165[2] 5522[7] 5608[3] 6017[2] 7086[2]

Volkovkha *J-C Rouget* 78
2 b f Holy Roman Emperor(IRE) Armanda (GER) (Acatenango (GER))
7571a[9]

Volochope (FR) *M Delaplace* 43
10 b g Volochine(IRE) Nicotera (IRE) (Baby Turk)
(6058a)

Volodina (IRE) *Alan McCabe* a57 36
2 ch f Soviet Star(USA) Why Now (Dansili)
2856[8] 3245[9] 3978[11] 5068[9] 5193[2] 5865[8] 8362[3] 8434[8]

Volume *Luca Cumani* 89
2 b f Mount Nelson Victoire Finale (Peintre Celebre (USA))
5716[3] (6597) (7129)

Vonn (IRE) *Tim Easterby* 37
3 b f Desert Millennium(IRE) Shone Island (IRE) (Desert Sun)
2719[8] 3086[5]

Voodoo Prince *Ed Dunlop* a97 102
5 b g Kingmambo(USA) Ouija Board (Cape Cross (IRE))
(1843) 2407[9] 3838[5] 6172[4] 6394[3] ◆ 6638[3] 7526[4]

Vorda (FR) *P Sogorb* 113
2 b f Orpen(USA) Velda (Observatory (USA))
(1894a) (4572a) 5573a[2] (6836) 7690a[7]

Vosne Romanee *Keith Dalgleish* a35 40
2 ch g Arakan(USA) Vento Del Oreno (FR) (Lando (GER))
4756[11] 6681[6] 7371[7] 7755[5]

Voyager (FR) *Mme C Head-Maarek* 56
2 b c Mr. Sidney(USA) Villadolide (FR) (Anabaa (USA))
7185a[9]

Vyjack (USA) *Rudy Rodriguez* a112
3 b g Into Mischief(USA) Life Happened (USA) (Stravinsky (USA))
2033a[18] 3127a[8]

Waabel *Violet M Jordan* a77 74
6 bb g Green Desert(USA) Najah (IRE) (Nashwan (USA))
77[2] 186[7] 398[4] 494[6] 583[9] 775[3]

Waahej *Peter Hiatt* a66 18
7 b g Haafhd Madam Ninette (Mark Of Esteem (IRE))
2939[9] 3637[4] 4522[3] 4835[2] 5356[4] 5672[4] 6216[4] (6783)

Wadaa (USA) *James Tate* a85 94
3 b f Dynaformer(USA) Cloud Castle (In The Wings)
2392[3] 3272[3] 3891[4] (4804) 5868[2] 6329[6] 7338[4]

Wadacre Sarko *Mark Johnston* a65 83
3 b c Oratorio(IRE) Saxon Maid (Sadler's Wells (USA))
1429[6] 1595[5] 2405[4] 2799[3] 3394[3] (3653) (3930) 4543[2]

Wadi Alamardi *Michael Bell* a56 51
2 ch c Lucky Story(USA) Thicket (Wolfhound (USA))
5665[4] 6342[6] 6561[5] 7094[6]

Wadi Al Hattawi (IRE) *Saeed bin Suroor* a77 93
3 b g Dalakhani(IRE) Carisolo (Dubai Millennium)
4202[2] 4980[3] 5258[8] 6186[7]

Wafer Ice (IRE) *Ms Joanna Morgan* 55
2 gr f Dalakhani(IRE) Dream Time (Rainbow Quest (USA))
4462a[6]

Waffle (IRE) *David Barron* a72 113
7 ch g Kheleyf(USA) Saphire (College Chapel)
365a[10]

Waha (IRE) *Saeed bin Suroor* a63
3 b f Oasis Dream Hazarayna (Polish Precedent (USA))
5902[4] 6402[9]

Wahaab (IRE) *Richard Hannon Snr* 86
2 ch g Tamayuz Indian Ink (IRE) (Indian Ridge)
(2847) ◆ 3422[7] 6064[3]

Wahgah (USA) *Saeed bin Suroor* 68
2 b f Distorted Humor(USA) Basaata (USA) (Dixieland Band (USA))
5282[5] ◆

Wahib (FR) *M Delzangles* 97
3 b c Invincible Spirit(IRE) Wardat Allayl (IRE) (Mtoto)
7186a[9]

Waikika (FR) *Y Barberot* 103
2 b f Whipper(USA) Fruhling Feuer (FR) (Green Tune (USA))
7571a[3]

Waila *Sir Michael Stoute* 110
3 ch f Notnowcato Crystal Cavern (USA) (Be My Guest (USA))
(1813) 3482[5] (4532) 7365[7]

Wake Forest (GER) *A Wohler* 102
3 b c Sir Percy Wurfspiel (GER) (Lomitas)
1708a[4]

Wakeup Little Suzy (IRE) *Marco Botti* a78 76
3 ch f Peintre Celebre(USA) Maramba (USA) (Hussonet (USA))
230[5] 532[2] (1019) 2195[3] 6524[6] 7489[2] ◆ 7876[7] 8020[5] (8339)

Waking Warrior *Kevin Ryan* a87 82
5 b g Sleeping Indian Scented Garden (Zamindar (USA))
58[5] (196) 405[7] 526[6] 2255[2] 2664[5] 3351[7] 4047[3] ◆ 5579[9] 6205[6] 6583[12] 7080[2]

Waldpark (GER) *Anthony Freedman* 115
5 b c Dubawi(IRE) Wurftaube (GER) (Acatenango (GER))
2294a[2] 7392a[17]

Waldsee (GER) *Paul Morgan* a53 55
8 b g Xaar Wurftaube (GER) (Acatenango (GER))
99[6] 703[4] 1080[3] 8204[7]

Walero (GER) *J Hirschberger* 105
7 br h Big Shuffle(USA) Waterbor (GER) (Lagunas)
1944a[7]

Waletta (GER) *H J Groschel* 85
3 ch f Saddex Walinka (GER) (Platini (GER))
3146a[8]

Walk Like A Giant *Tom Tate*
2 b g Sir Percy Temple Of Thebes (IRE) (Bahri (USA))
7061[8]

Walks In Dark (TUR) *Sab Arslan*
3 c Always A Classic(CAN) Ozenkiz (TUR) (Mountain Cat (USA))
6232a[7]

Walk With An Angel *Philip McBride* a59
2 b f Myboycharlie(IRE) Broughtons Revival (Pivotal)
8084[5]

Wall Of Sound *Tom Dascombe* 94
3 b f Singspiel(IRE) Veiled Beauty (USA) (Royal Academy (USA))
1828[3] 2231[2] (3465) 4485[2] 5361a[11] (6832)

Wall Street Boss (USA) *James Fanshawe* a74
3 b g Street Boss(USA) Pad The Wallet (USA) (Skip Away (USA))
5678[6] 6116[4] 7490[3] (7839)

Walta (IRE) *Ronald Harris* a23 6
2 b g Tagula(IRE) Hi Katriona (IRE) (Second Empire (IRE))
4631[11] 5215[4]

Walter De La Mare (IRE) *Anabel K Murphy* a47 59
6 b g Barathea(IRE) Banutan (IRE) (Charnwood Forest (IRE))
520[3] 921[8] 3169[13] 5171[6] 5650[3] 5979[6] 6099[2] 6723[4] 6895[4] 7767[10] 8129[8] 8302[6]

Walter White (IRE) *Andrew Balding* a68 68
3 b g Dark Angel(IRE) Fun Time (Fraam)
(5) 204[2] 428[4]

Waltz Darling (IRE) *Keith Reveley* 75
5 b g Iffraaj Aljafliyah (Halling (USA))
1111[2] 1567[6] 3545[8] 6306[15] 6756[6] 7027[5] 7342[12]

Wandering Heart (IRE) *Liam P Cusack* a36 34
5 ch f Iffraaj Inourhearts (IRE) (Pips Pride)
5775a[22] 6089a[9]

Wandsworth (IRE) *Roger Varian* a85 67
3 bb g Authorized(IRE) Henties Bay (IRE) (Cape Cross (IRE))
6366[6] 6824[4] 7253[6] (8063) (8178) 8445[7]

Wannabe Better (IRE) *T Stack* a63 109
3 b f Duke Of Marmalade(IRE) Wannabe (Shirley Heights)
2289a[5] 6224a[12] 7051a[4] (7404a)

Wannabe King *Geoffrey Harker* 96
7 b g King's Best(USA) Wannabe Grand (IRE) (Danehill (USA))
1688[4] 2029[4] 3207[5] (3590) 5238[6] 6300[7] 6826[7] 7241[3] 7696[13]

Wannabe Loved *John Gosden* a87 106
4 b f Pivotal Wannabe Posh (IRE) (Grand Lodge (USA))
(2619) 4059[4]

Wannabe Magic *Jedd O'Keeffe* 48
2 bb f Authorized(IRE) Wannabe Free (Red Ransom (USA))
6298[7] 7277[8]

Wannabe Your Man *Roger Varian* 60
3 b c Halling(USA) Wannabe Posh (IRE) (Grand Lodge (USA))
6696[7] 7422[3]

Wannabe Yours (IRE) *John Gosden* 68
2 b c Dubawi(IRE) Wannabe Posh (IRE) (Grand Lodge (USA))
7019[6] 7494[3]

Warbond *Michael Madgwick* a67 57
5 ch g Monsieur Bond(IRE) Pick A Nice Name (Polar Falcon (USA))
222[4] 451[3] 652[3] 984[8] 1497[2] 1925[12] 2565[5] 2747[8] 3575[8] 4894[6] 5170[6] 6105[3] 6932[2] 8125[3]

Warbrook (IRE) *John Gosden* a63 74
2 ch c Tamayuz Squander (Dr Fong (USA))
7655[4] 8124[10] 8425[4]

War Command (USA) *A P O'Brien* 118
2 b c War Front(USA) Wandering Star (USA) (Red Ransom (USA))
(3422) ◆ 5319a[3] (5774a) (7192) ◆

Warcrown (IRE) *Richard Fahey* 79
4 b g Azamour(IRE) Alikhlas (Lahib (USA))
1448[14] 2077[5] 2431[11] 3301[8] 3729[2]

Warden Bond *William Stone* a69 48
5 ch g Monsieur Bond(IRE) Warden Rose (Compton Place)
3063[7] 3534[9] 3780[9] 4357[3] (5073) 6218[6] 7515[7] 7857[11] 8121[4]

Warfare *Kevin Ryan* a83 86
4 b g Soviet Star(USA) Fluffy (Efisio)
1115[8] 2028[7]

Waris (FR) *R Chotard* a79 86
2 gr f Verglas(IRE) Encircle (USA) (Spinning World (USA))
7571a[7]

Waris Magic (FR) *J Parize* a52
3 b f Next Desert(IRE) Magic Giulia (FR) (Mille Balles (FR))
544a[10]

War Lord (IRE) *David O'Meara* 72
3 b g Aussie Rules(USA) Carn Lady (IRE) (Woodman (USA))
(2274) 2464[7] 3281[3] 4140[5] 5016[4] 5497[3] 5789[5]

Warlu Way *Michael Easterby* 95
6 b h Sakhee(USA) Conspiracy (Rudimentary (USA))
1446[10] ◆ 2718[8] 3345[2] (3685) 4262[8] 5723[12] 7174[17] 7526[10]

War Monger (USA) *Doug Watson* a65 96
9 b h War Chant(USA) Carnival Delight (USA) (Half A Year (USA))
242a[9]

Warm Order *Tony Carroll* a38 52
2 b f Assertive Even Hotter (Desert Style (IRE))
3694[9] 6947[8] 7393[9] 7978[12]

Warned (FR) *Mme A Blanchard*
4 b f High Chaparral(IRE) Joonayh (Warning)
127a[0]

War Of Art (IRE) *Tom Dascombe* a62
2 b c Tamayuz Lucky Clio (IRE) (Key Of Luck (USA))
8425[6]

War Poet *Brian Ellison* 98
6 b g Singspiel(IRE) Summer Sonnet (Baillamont (USA))
2431[7] 2718[11] 3442[3] 3685[9] 4929[5] 6211[2] 6499[3] 7211[3] 7499[7]

Warrant Officer *Mick Channon* a57 60
3 gr g Misu Bond(IRE) Kilmovee (Inchinor)
804[4] 1016[7] 1171[3]

Warrendale *Henry Candy* 66
2 b f Three Valleys(USA) Swynford Pleasure (Reprimand)
3663[4] 5443[3]

Warrigal (IRE) *Jeremy Noseda* a71 58
3 ch c Mount Nelson Waldblume (GER) (Halling (USA))
(1178) 1803[6] 7121[8]

Warrior Of Light (IRE) *David Lanigan* a79
2 b c High Chaparral(IRE) Strawberry Fledge (USA) (Kingmambo (USA))
7460[6] (7834)

War Singer (USA) *David Pipe* a93 91
6 b g War Chant(USA) Sister Marilyn (USA) (Saint Ballado (CAN))
3345[17]

War Spirit *Richard Hannon Snr* 69
2 b c Exceed And Excel(AUS) Alybgood (CAN) (Alydeed (CAN))
4987[9] 5744[5]

Warwarick (AUS) *David Hayes* 99
7 b m High Chaparral(IRE) Simply Aloof (FR) (Spectrum (IRE))
7483a[6]

Was (IRE) *A P O'Brien* 115
4 b f Galileo(IRE) Alluring Park (IRE) (Green Desert (USA))
2678a[4] 3870a[2]

Wasabi (IRE) *John Berry* 58
4 b f Tiger Hill(IRE) Quinzey (JPN) (Carnegie (IRE))
1916[3] 2642[3]

Waseem Faris (IRE) *Mick Channon* a84 88
4 b g Exceed And Excel(AUS) Kissing Time (Lugana Beach)
1581[9] 2031[4] ◆ 2388[7] 2459[3] 2614[4] 3018[4] 3299[6] 3786[4] 4123[6] 4364[4] 4860[4] 5108[4] 5579[4] 5971[6] 6189[11] 6388[2] 6745[6] (7324) 7420[4]

Washaar (IRE) *Richard Hannon Snr* 108
2 b c Kodiac Dabtiyra (IRE) (Dr Devious (IRE))
(3233) 4296[3] (4747) ◆ (5952) 6835[4]

Wasimah (GER) *H J Groschel* 101
4 bb f Desert Prince(IRE) Waleria (GER) (Artan (IRE))
3612a[4] 5778a[7]

Waspy *Dr Jeremy Naylor* a57 62
4 ch f King's Best(USA) Gib (IRE) (Rock Of Gibraltar (IRE))
3052[9] 3700[10] 4350[11] 5528[9] 7092[11]

Watchable *Tobias B P Coles* 63
3 ch g Pivotal Irresistible (Cadeaux Genereux)
7345[3]

Watcheroftheskies *J W Hills* a76 66
3 b g Dutch Art Red Heaven (Benny The Dip (USA))
2788[3] 3620[3] 4383[14] 5387[5] 6080[12] 6492[10] 7091[9]

Watch The Birdie (IRE) *Ronald Harris* a62 69
5 b f Kodiac Silk Point (IRE) (Barathea (IRE))
227[4] 469[9] 515[8]

Waterclock (IRE) *Roger Charlton* a83 96
4 ch g Notnowcato Waterfall One (Nashwan (USA))
3692[7] 4606[3] 5288[2] 6066[4] 7193[2] ◆

Watered Silk *Lucy Wadham* a73 88
5 gr g Encosta De Lago(AUS) Tussah (Daylami (IRE))
6504[3]

Water For Life *Dave Morris* a52 55
2 ch f Mount Nelson Echo River (USA) (Irish River (FR))
5151[2] 5891[7] 6643[14] 7855[12]

Watergate (IRE) *Richard Rowe* a67 89
7 gr g Verglas(IRE) Moy Water (IRE) (Tirol)
119[8] 1927[6]

Water Hole (IRE) *John Gosden* a79
2 b f Oasis Dream Arosa (IRE) (Sadler's Wells (USA))
7875[2] (8176)

Waterloo Dock *Mick Quinn* a64
8 b g Hunting Lion(IRE) Scenic Air (Hadeer)
76[11] 322[2] 449[2] ◆ 750[9] 1195[2] 1516[9] 1793[3] 3499[10] 8446[12]

Waterloo Sunrise (IRE) *S M Duffy* a65 64
8 b g Craigsteel Waterloo Sunset (Deep Run)
539[3]

Water Queen *William Haggas* 77
2 b f Shamardal(USA) Central Force (Pivotal)
6594[3]

Waterway Run (USA) *Ralph Beckett* 102
3 b f Arch(USA) Princess Consort (USA) (Dixieland Band (USA))
1622[5] 2299a[6] 3460[21]

Watouka (FR) *F Rohaut* 65
2 b f Orpen(USA) Zoriana (FR) (Danehill Dancer (IRE))
7994a[7]

Watson Sama *Amy Weaver* a54
3 ch g Pivotal Precocious Star (IRE) (Bold Fact (USA))
4521[8]

Watt Broderick (IRE) *Ian Williams* a69 70
4 ch g Hawk Wing(USA) Kingsridge (IRE) (King's Theatre (IRE))
1176[3] ◆ 1220[4] 6907[4] 7169[11]

Watts Up Son *Declan Carroll* a48 84
5 b g Diktat Local Fancy (Bahamian Bounty)
2552[4] 3804[4] 5031[6] 6239[11] 6346[6] 6562[6] 6970[8] 7275[13]

Waveguide (IRE) *David Simcock* a73 75
4 b f Dubawi(IRE) Million Waves (IRE) (Mull Of Kintyre (USA))
1736[2] 2361[2] 3427[3] 4180[3] 6599[4] 7876[6]

Waverunner *Mark Johnston* a77 80
3 ch f Raven's Pass(USA) Danuta (USA) (Sunday Silence (USA))
1698[4] (3039) 3443[7] 6499[7] 6936[4] 7267[6] 7785[7] 8314[5] 8366[3]

Waving *Tony Carroll* a77 63
4 b g High Chaparral(IRE) Pretty Davis (USA) (Trempolino (USA))
(342) (592) ◆ 797[4] 1117[4] 3617[8] 4126[10] 4591[9] 5093[6] 5846[2] 6044[5] 7950[9] 8115[7] 8302[7] 8417[6]

Wayne Manor (IRE) *Lucinda Russell* a75 77
4 br g Cape Cross(IRE) Inchmahome (Galileo (IRE))
5831[14]

Wayward Glance *Keith Dalgleish* a49 79
5 b g Sadler's Wells(USA) Daring Aim (Daylami (IRE))
7280[5] 7423[3] 7757[4]

Weald *Hans-Inge Larsen* a25 93
8 b g Bering New Abbey (Sadler's Wells (USA))
2146a[11]

Wealth (IRE) *Richard Fahey* a66 69
2 b c Invincible Spirit(IRE) Whisp (GER) (Rainbow Quest (USA))
5508[4] ◆ 6873[3] 7766[6] 8164[4]

Wealthy (IRE) *Saeed bin Suroor* a103 93
6 b g Refuse To Bend(IRE) Enrich (USA) (Dynaformer (USA))
242a[P] (Dead)

Weapon Of Choice (IRE) *Stuart Kittow* a91 95
5 b g Iffraaj Tullawadgeen (IRE) (Sinndar (IRE))
1485[2] 2210[5] 3339[10] 3984[8] 6167[7] 6596[9] (6868) 7312[10]

We Are City *Bryan Smart* a64 62
3 b f Elusive City(USA) Musique Magique (IRE) (Mozart (IRE))
106[7] 357[5] 1566[8] 3247[13]

Weather Watch (IRE) *Mrs John Harrington* 99
3 b c Hurricane Run(IRE) Caravan Of Dreams (IRE) (Anabaa (USA))
7230a[15]

Webbow (IRE) *Julie Camacho* a102 100
11 b g Dr Devious(IRE) Ower (IRE) (Lomond (USA))
495[7] 690[7] 4062[9] 4778[8] 5738[17] 6278[4] 6925[8]

Webby's Boy *Dai Burchell*
5 b g Ad Valorem(USA) Zambezi (USA) (Rahy (USA))
4381[13]

Wedding Ring (IRE) *Charlie Appleby* 96
2 b f Oasis Dream Cast In Gold (USA) (Elusive Quality (USA))
(3057) 3522[5] 5284[3] 6142[3] (6644) (7016)

Wedding Speech (IRE) *James Fanshawe* a58 60
3 b f Acclamation Wedding Cake (IRE) (Groom Dancer (USA))
3860[7] 4590[8] 5935[6] 6522[7]

Wedding Wish (IRE) *Michael Bell* 85
2 b f Acclamation Have Faith (IRE) (Machiavellian (USA))
5282[7] 6140[4] 7016[5]

Wedge Trust (IRE) *J-C Rouget* 102
3 ch f Zamindar(USA) Wedge (USA) (Storm Cat (USA))
2334a[2] 5806a[6] (7085a) 7941a[2]

Wedgewood Estates *Tony Carroll* a56 13
2 ch f Assertive Heaven (Reel Buddy (USA))
7393[8] 7852[6] 8083[9]

Wedgwood (IRE) *Richard Hannon Snr* a23
2 br g Mastercraftsman(IRE) Vingt Et Une (FR) (Sadler's Wells (USA))
6378[9] 6688[8]

Wednaan *M F De Kock* 79
2 b c Dubawi(IRE) Marine Bleue (IRE) (Desert Prince (IRE))
(6569)

Wee Giant (USA) *Tony Coyle* a64 62
7 ch g Giant's Causeway(USA) Christmas In Aiken (USA) (Affirmed (USA))
2887[5] 3627[9] 6177[2] 6290[7] (7376) 7597[3]

Wee Jean *Mick Channon* a94 92
2 b f Captain Gerrard(IRE) Reeli Silli (Dansili)
(3948) 4742[7] 5372[2] 5737[5] 8203[3] 8426[3]

Weekendatbernies (IRE) *Ed de Giles* 59
2 b g War Chant(USA) Morena Park (Pivotal)
6277[7]

Weekend Getaway (IRE) *Clive Brittain* 68
2 b f Acclamation Week End (Selkirk (USA))
6500[3] 7102[5]

Weetentherty *Keith Dalgleish* a45 62
6 b g Bertolini(USA) Binaa (IRE) (Marju (IRE))
2217[6] 2632[11] 3197[2] 3770[8]

Wee Willy Wilfords (IRE) *John Patrick Shanahan* 71
3 b g Whipper(USA) Last Spin (Unfuwain (USA))
4445[3]

We Have A Dream *Violet M Jordan* a81 74
8 bb g Oasis Dream Final Shot (Dalsaan)
2128[2] 2657[13] 2871[9] 3415[9] 3897[2] 4220[6] 4884[11] (5523) 5645[2] 5901[10] 6018[6] 6077[3] 6310[5] 6606[8] 6905[5] 7263[11] 7601[5] 7848[9]

Weisse Girl *Noel Quinlan* a57 54
2 b f Halling(USA) White Turf (GER) (Tiger Hill (IRE))
1512[2] ?117[3] 2947[4] 6924[9] 7293[11]

Weisse Socken (IRE) *Ralph Beckett* a74 73
2 b f Acclamation Playful (Piccolo)
2320[2] 3023[3] 3694[4] (4282) 4528[19] 5121[2] 5509[4] 6104[2] 6731[7]

Welcome Sir (FR) *E Lellouche* 87
3 b c Zamindar(USA) Chandi Dasa (IRE) (Sadler's Wells (USA))
445a[0]

Welease Bwian (IRE) *Stuart Williams* a73 72
4 b g Kheleyf(USA) Urbanize (USA) (Chester House (USA))
29[5] 187[2] 583[6] 687[2] 775[5] 1694[7] 2425[5] 3341[7] 3577[2] 3716[4] 4120[7] 4866[2] 5060[5] 5221[2] 6412[3] (6732) (8330)

Well Acquainted (IRE) *Clive Cox* a95 107
3 b c Orientate(USA) Stunning Rose (IRE) (Sadler's Wells (USA))
1621[7] 2453[4] (2843) 3455[13] 4945[6] 5794[5] 6595[9]

Well Bank (IRE) *David Nicholls* a32 55
4 ch g Iffraaj Latin Lace (Dansili)
2757[12]

We'll Deal Again *Michael Easterby* a89 80
6 b g Gentleman's Deal(IRE) Emma Amour (Emarati (USA))
1807[10]

Wellesbourne *Charlie Appleby* a65
2 b c Dubawi(IRE) Charlecote (IRE) (Caerleon (USA))
6807[3] 7120[8]

We'll Go Walking (IRE) *J S Bolger* 105
3 b f Authorized(IRE) Senora Galilei (IRE) (Galileo (IRE))
1862a[2] ◆ 2289a[9] 3381a[6]

Welliesinthewater (IRE) *Derek Shaw* a72 65
3 b g Footstepsinthesand Shadow Ash (IRE) (Ashkalani (IRE))
1075[5] 8096[9] 8430[9]

Wellingrove (IRE) *Mark Johnston* a67 79
3 b g Cape Cross(IRE) Isla Azul (IRE) (Machiavellian (USA))
2342[2] 2600[4] 3466[3] 3722[3] 4100[4] (4475) 4994[11] 5383[4] (5918) 6126[8] 6563[7]

Well Owd Mon *Andrew Hollinshead* a57 62
3 b g Vitus Farina (IRE) (Golan (IRE))
4881[2] 5301[3] 6473[4] 6971[4] 7104[5] 7907[5] 8031[4] 8225[5]

Well Painted (IRE) *William Haggas* a93 96
4 ch g Excellent Art Aoife (IRE) (Thatching)
2254[26] 2541[6] 5894[4] 6551[10] (7071) 7988[6] 8219[8] 8445[2]

We'Ll Shake Hands (FR) *K R Burke* 73
2 b g Excellent Art Amou Daria (FR) (Kendor (FR))
(5225) ◆ 5858[7] 6285[7]

Well Sharp *Jonjo O'Neill* 107
5 b g Selkirk(USA) Saphila (IRE) (Sadler's Wells (USA))
(2402) (3423)

Wells Lyrical (IRE) *Bryan Smart* a41 84
8 b g Sadler's Wells(USA) Lyrical (Shirley Heights)
887[7]

Welsh Inlet (IRE) *John Bridger* a67 72
5 br f Kheleyf(USA) Ervedya (IRE) (Doyoun)
35[5] (274) 452[3] 665[6] 778[3] 980[4] 1717[7] 2196[11] 4163[2] 4909[3] 5349[7] 5758[5] 6553[6] 6933[5] 7124[2] 7643[9]

Welsh Moonlight *Stuart Williams* a70 67
3 ch f Vita Rosa(JPN) Moonlight Applause (Royal Applause)
1640[10] 1904[7] 2872[9] 3789[2] (5156) 5611[5] 6397[4] (8220)

Welsh Sunrise *Ed Walker* a71 45
3 b f Vita Rosa(JPN) Chapel Corner (IRE) (Alhaarth (IRE))
(564) 6735[7] 7430[6] 7876[2] 8087[5] 8432[2]

Weltklasse (GER) *Markus Klug* 85
2 bb f Kallisto(GER) Well American (USA) (Bertrando (USA))
7406a[8]

We Miss Artie (CAN) *Todd Pletcher* a112 84
2 bb c Artie Schiller(USA) Athena's Gift (USA) (Fusaichi Pegasus (USA))
7711a[7]

Wentworth (IRE) *Richard Hannon Snr* 110
3 b c Acclamation Miss Corinne (Mark Of Esteem (IRE))
2621[3] ◆ 3484[4] ◆ 4080[3] (4946) 6530[5]

We'Re In The Red (IRE) *Mark Hoad* 38
3 br g Daaher(CAN) Elaflaak (USA) (Gulch (USA))
1904[11] 2560[12] 3327[5] 5393[9]

Wesleydale (IRE) *Simon West* a17 39
6 b g Westerner Fully Focused (IRE) (Rudimentary (USA))
215[9] 2118[10] 2628[10] 3203[6] 3589[11]

West Beat *David O'Meara* 45
3 b f Singspiel(IRE) West Lorne (USA) (Gone West (USA))
2306[14] 2960[6] 4113[6] 4629[6] 5142[8]

West Brit (IRE) *Charlie Longsdon* a62 76
5 b g High Chaparral(IRE) Aldburgh (Bluebird (USA))
2234[3] 4167[10]

West Coast Dream *Roy Brotherton* a83 93
6 b g Oasis Dream Californie (IRE) (Rainbow Quest (USA))
1483[6] 1765[10] 2561[3] 3371[3] 4123[8] 5036[6] 6854[5] 7634[7] 7776[9]

West End Lad *Roy Bowring* a71 88
10 b g Tomba Cliburnel News (IRE) (Horage)
82[9] (238) 433[2] 709[11] (1366) 1569[8] 2234[7] 2496[3] 2710[4] 3545[6] 4077[4] (4503) 4928[6] 6567[5] 6701[11] 7132[13] 7881[12] 8093[3] 8360[6] 8410[4]

Western Hymn *John Gosden* a87
2 b c High Chaparral(IRE) Blue Rhapsody (Cape Cross (IRE))
(8124) ◆

Western Sands (IRE) *Richard Fahey* 67
2 ch f Footstepsinthesand West One (Gone West (USA))
3760[7] 5330[7] 6597[4]

West Leake (IRE) *Paul Burgoyne* a70 60
7 b g Acclamation Kilshanny (Groom Dancer (USA))
130[2] ◆ 347[2] (806) 1172[2] 1426[3] 1717[6] 1925[7] 2228[5] 2565[6] 3054[2] 3404[7] 4163[6] 8019[6] 8151[8] 8456[9]

West Leake Diman (IRE) *Keith Dalgleish* a51 86
4 b g Namid Roselyn (Efisio)
1232[17] 4285[7] 5009[12] 6331[11] 7313[8] 7792[11]

West Leake Hare (IRE) *David Nicholls* a66 83
4 b g Choisir(AUS) March Hare (Groom Dancer (USA))
1757[9] 1994[3] 2278[8] 2836[2] (3087) 3337[5] (3444) (3945) 4577[2] 5292[6] 5974[10] 6496[3] 6586[11] 7374[8] 7595[7]

Westminster (IRE) *John Gosden* a84
2 b c Exceed And Excel(AUS) Pivka (Pivotal)
7647[7] 7972[6] (8266)

West Of The Moon *Sir Michael Stoute* a41 58
3 ch f Pivotal Canda (USA) (Storm Cat (USA))
2760[10] 3469[12]

West Riding (IRE) *Charlie Appleby*
3 b g Cape Cross(IRE) West Wind (Machiavellian (USA))
6133[P] (Dead)

West Side (IRE) *Mick Quinn* a53 55
5 b g Oratorio(IRE) Castelletto (Komaite (USA))
220[8]

Westwiththenight (IRE) *William Haggas* a84 97
4 b f Cape Cross(IRE) Hidden Hope (Daylami (IRE))
(1823) 2253[2] 3346[7] 4705[5] 6530[6] 7020[8]

Wexford Opera (IRE) *J S Bolger* a85 93
3 bb c New Approach(IRE) Sister Angelina (USA) (Saint Ballado (CAN))
2374a[8] 6883a[18]

Wexford Town (IRE) *J S Bolger* 82
2 b c Teofilo(IRE) Night Visit (Sinndar (IRE))
6223a[4]

Weybridge Light *David Thompson* a58 59
8 b g Fantastic Light(USA) Nuryana (Nureyev (USA))
(4835) 5240[5] 5370[3] 6216[7]

Whaileyy (IRE) *Marco Botti* a110 100
5 b g Holy Roman Emperor(IRE) Alshoowg (USA) (Riverman (USA))
78[2] 365a[U] 834a[8] 2046[11] 3135[9]

Whaleweigh Station *Tom Dascombe* 101
2 b g Zamindar(USA) Looby Loo (Kyllachy)
2925[2] 3536[2] 4212[5] 4816a[4]

What About Carlo (FR) *Eve Johnson Houghton* 85
2 b c Creachadoir(IRE) Boccatenera (GER) (Artan (IRE))
4483[7] 5472[3] (5790) 6593[4]

What A Dandy (IRE) *Jim Boyle* a65
2 b c Dandy Man(IRE) Ibtihal (IRE) (Hamas (IRE))
2723[11] 8333[5] 8451[3]

What A Name (IRE) *M Delzangles* 110
3 ch f Mr Greeley(USA) Bonnie Byerly (USA) (Dayjur (USA))
(1358a) 2047[7] 2906a[6] 5461a[6] 6251a[4]

What A Scorcher *Clive Cox* 44
2 b f Authorized(IRE) Street Fire (IRE) (Street Cry (IRE))
7533[8]

Whatever You Do (IRE) *Richard Hannon Snr* a63 63
3 ch f Barathea(IRE) Petite Spectre (Spectrum (IRE))
1499[5] 1874[3] 2092[8]

Whats For Pudding (IRE) *Richard Whitaker* a55 55
5 ch f Kheleyf(USA) Margaret's Dream (IRE) (Muhtarram (USA))
1455[10]

What Style (IRE) *John M Oxx* 100
3 ch f Teofilo(IRE) Out Of Time (IRE) (Anabaa (USA))
1557a[2] 2689a[13] 4567a[8]

What's Up Doc (IRE) *Lawney Hill* a35 79
12 b g Dr Massini(IRE) Surprise Treat (IRE) (Shalford (IRE))
7984[14] 8129[11]

Whatwehavewehold *Alan McCabe* a56 58
3 b g Avonbridge Dancing Loma (FR) (Danehill Dancer (IRE))
796[4] 1461[5] 3446[10] 3762[3] 4410[6] 5200[3] 5499[6] 5617[6]

Where's Reiley (USA) *Michael Attwater* a79 71
7 bb g Doneraile Court(USA) Plateau (USA) (Seeking The Gold (USA))
92[4] (316) 582[10] (727) (861) (946) 1065[3] 1467[3] 1665[2] 1902[3] 2196[2] 2772[4] (3529) 3921[2] 4210[8] 4707[9] 5697[9] 6018[3] 6652[2] 6745[7] 8384[9]

Where's Susie *Michael Madgwick* a77 76
8 ch m Where Or When(IRE) Linda's Schoolgirl (IRE) (Grand Lodge (USA))
119[2] 224[3] 779[6] 1200[5] 1502[2] 1927[7] 2749[6] 6173[6] 7267[2] 7863[5] 8089[6] 8343[3]

Where's Tiger *Jedd O'Keeffe* 53
2 b g Tiger Hill(IRE) Where's Broughton (Cadeaux Genereux)
6299[8] 6754[9] 6939[10]

Where The Boys Are (IRE) *Ed McMahon* a57 66
2 b f Dylan Thomas(IRE) Promise Of Love (Royal Applause)
3205[8] 4115[2] 4880[9] 5609[5] 6695[12] 7199[4] 7665[2] 8090[5]

While You Wait (IRE) *Gary Moore* a81 77
4 b g Whipper(USA) Azra (IRE) (Danehill (USA))
318[7] 5586[2] 5933[2] 7220[9] 7840[10]

Whimsical (IRE) *Richard Hannon Snr* a88 98
4 b f Strategic Prince Sweet Namibia (IRE) (Namid)
1544[6] 2015[5]

Whinging Willie (IRE) *Gary Moore* a71 72
4 b g Cape Cross(IRE) Pacific Grove (Persian Bold)
450[4] 1303[12] 1925[9] 2533[3] 2787[3] 3106[2] 3656[2] (5171) 5793[14] 7132[3] 8059[5]

Whipcrackaway (IRE) *Peter Hedger* a66 80
4 b g Whipper(USA) Former Drama (USA) (Dynaformer (USA))
639[8] 7396[5]

Whip My Heart (IRE) *U Suter* a83 88
4 b g Whipper(USA) Capetown Girl (Danzero (AUS))
(5735a)

Whipper's Boy (IRE) *Brian Meehan* 103
3 b g Whipper(USA) Glympse (IRE) (Spectrum (IRE))
4945[5] 5822[5] 6307[4] 6650[14]

Whipper Snapper (FR) *E J O'Neill* a63 81
3 b g Whipper(USA) Margot Mine (IRE) (Choisir (AUS))
8441a[10]

Whipper Snapper (IRE) *William Knight* a74 84
3 b g Whipper(USA) Topiary (IRE) (Selkirk (USA))
2394[4] (3053) 3582[7] 4494[2] 4864[3] 5541[10] 5853[4] (6642) 6993[6] 7507[5]

Whipphound *Mark Brisbourne* a67 67
5 b g Whipper(USA) Golden Symbol (Wolfhound (USA))
143[3] (277) 559[4] 760[9] 898[7] 2582[6] 2997[10] 3247[2] (3643) 4148[4] 4840[2] 4966[3] 5273[6] 5674[9] 6344[2] 7197[3]

Whippy Cream (IRE) *Marco Botti* a78 98
3 b f Dansili Diavla (USA) (Bahri (USA))
1671[4] 2261[3] 2697a[3] 4532[5] 5035[8] 6312[2] 6532[4]

Whiskey Junction *Mick Quinn* a61 61
9 b g Bold Edge Victoria Mill (Free State)
163[3] 423[8] 516[8] 916[3] 1396[8] 2132[6] 3154[8] 3994[7] 4691[6] 5408[4]

Whiskeymack *Mick Channon* a39 58
3 b g Mount Nelson Dream Day (Oasis Dream)
2154[9] 2345[16]

Whiskey N Stout (IRE) *Jamie Osborne* a50 39
3 b g Amadeus Wolf Yasmin Satine (IRE) (Key Of Luck (USA))
824[8] 1016[6] 1424[7]

Whisky Bravo *David C Griffiths* a72 63
4 b g Byron Dress Design (IRE) (Brief Truce (USA))
(1598) (1748) 2036[6] 2780[7] 4146[6] 5523[3] 6568[9] 8230[6] 8315[7]

Whispered Times (USA) *Tracy Waggott* a41 69
6 bb g More Than Ready(USA) Lightning Show (USA) (Storm Cat (USA))
(1693) 3192[4] 3445[4] 4615[7] 5341[10] 5711[9] 5828[3] 6181[6] 6943[11]

Whispering Lady (IRE) *David Simcock* a76 71
3 b f Pivotal Bon Nuit (IRE) (Night Shift (USA))
(864) 1546[5] 2622[6] 5181[5] 7489[3] 7895[6]

Whispering Star (USA) *David Simcock* a44
2 b f War Front(USA) Eclisse (FR) (Ski Chief (USA))
5352[8] 8145[6]

Whispering Warrior (IRE) *David Simcock* a85 96
4 b g Oasis Dream Varenka (IRE) (Fasliyev (USA))
(222) (451) ◆ 2018[6] (2673) (3827) 4854[13] 6001[8]

Whistler (DEN) *Niels Petersen* a67 82
3 b f Academy Award(IRE) Wings Of A Dove (Hernando (FR))
5326a[6]

Whistle We Go (GER) *Nick Kent* a12 40
5 ch f Kalatos(GER) Whoopie (GER) (Neshad (USA))
2279[12] 2833[8] 3250[13] 4161[9] 5967[7]

Whitby High Light *Andrew Hollinshead* 68
2 b g Halling(USA) Ballroom Dancer (IRE) (Danehill Dancer (IRE))
6125[7] 6829[14]

Whitby Jet (IRE) *Ed Vaughan* a78 79
5 b g Mujadil(USA) Anazah (USA) (Diesis)
112[3] 439[5] 720[3] 1585[9] 3976[4] 4489[2] 5245[10] 5825[5] 6398[7] 7447[4] 7865[5] 8323[10]

Whitechapel *Keith Goldsworthy* a74 70
6 gr g Oasis Dream Barathiki (Barathea (IRE))
206[8]

White Coppice *Richard Fahey* 77
3 ch g Pivotal Finchley (Machiavellian (USA))
1236[4] 1636[15]

Whitecrest *John Spearing* a66 85
5 ch f Ishiguru(USA) Risky Valentine (Risk Me (FR))
1814[16] (2268) 2614[5] (2790) 3018[11] 3371[6] 3658[2] 4123[5] 4364[2] 4707[6] 4860[8] 5308[4] 5498[8] 6159[6] 6381[5] 7324[5]

White Deer (USA) *Geoffrey Harker* a64 67
9 b g Stravinsky(USA) Brookshield Baby (IRE) (Sadler's Wells (USA))
671[8]

White Diamond *Michael Appleby* a66 66
6 b m Bertolini(USA) Diamond White (Robellino (USA))
52[4] 439[4] 477[4] 1239[9] 1836[5] 2311[8] 7081[7]

Whitefall (USA) *David Evans* a47 63
3 b f Street Cry(IRE) Nalani (IRE) (Sadler's Wells (USA))
1624[8] 1698[6] 1837[7] 2599[4] 2800[2] ◆ 3735[2] 3918[4] 4474[3] 5391[3] (5434) ◆ 6158[5] 6406[3]

White Flag *Tim Easterby* a32 59
2 b f Sakhee's Secret Rainbow Spectrum (FR) (Spectrum (IRE))
1606[5] 5857[5] (6286) 6872[9] 7094[10] 7755[9] 7956[9]

Whiteflats *Derek Shaw* a53 50
3 b g Mind Games Chertsey (IRE) (Medaaly)
37[6] 185[5] 669[3] (1651) 2996[4] 3323[3]

White Fusion *David O'Meara* a78 59
5 gr g Oratorio(IRE) Divine Grace (IRE) (Definite Article)
215[3] 542[3]

White Month *Andrew Balding* a78 78
3 b g Tiger Hill(IRE) Purple Heather (USA) (Rahy (USA))
1679[8] 1959[2] 3055[3] 3907[2] 5390[2] 6389[7]

White Nile (IRE) *David Simcock* 92
4 b c Galileo(IRE) Super Gift (IRE) (Darshaan)
5723[4] ◆ 6499[4] (7496)

White Peak (USA) *Mark Johnston* a58 36
3 rg g Bernardini(USA) Dyna Peak (USA) (Dynaformer (USA))
6555[10] 6870[6] 7625[5]

White Ram (TUR) *Hakan El* 110
5 b c Sri Pekan(USA) Endless Freedom (TUR) (Zilzal (USA))
6254a[3]

White Rose Runner *Mel Brittain* 45
2 b f Virtual Entrap (USA) (Phone Trick (USA))
7818[6]

White Russian *Henry Candy* 65
2 ch f Sir Percy Danse Russe (Pivotal)
6635[7] 7244[2]

White Waves (USA) *A Fabre* 105
3 ch f Any Given Saturday(USA) Surf Club (USA) (Ocean Crest (USA))
2906a[5]

Whitey O' Gwaun (IRE) *D K Weld* 86
2 gr g Dalakhani(IRE) Angel Of The Gwaun (IRE) (Sadler's Wells (USA))
7050a[4]

Whitford (IRE) *Chris Dwyer* a62 56
3 b g Jeremy(USA) Linette (GER) (In The Wings)
204[5] 623[4] 2951[9] 3495[7] 5407[8] 5890[9] 6368[10] 7443[5] 7644[10] 7924[8]

Whitstable Native *Joseph Tuite* a58 64
5 b g Bertolini(USA) Break Of Dawn (USA) (Mt. Livermore (USA))
1925^{13} 2130^{4} 2932^{12} 5404^{7} 5614^{13}

Who Followed Who *Nigel Tinkler* 42
2 b g Footstepsinthesand Glorious Dreams (USA) (Honour And Glory (USA))
2670^{13} 3084^{8} 3826^{10}

Who Splashed Me *J R Jenkins* a35 33
2 ch f Medicean Cavallo Da Corsa (Galileo (IRE))
2744^{8} 6947^{11} 7348^{7} 8405^{3}

Who's Shirl *Chris Fairhurst* a80 77
7 b m Shinko Forest(IRE) Shirl (Shirley Heights)
2278^{12} (3068) 3393^{4} 3686^{7} 4198^{6} 4510^{4} 5292^{3} (5711) 6567^{6}

Who's That Chick (IRE) *Ralph Smith* a58 61
4 ch f Footstepsinthesand Poule De Luxe (IRE) (Cadeaux Genereux)
140^{3} 2606^{5} 2792^{3} 3496^{6} 4071^{10} 6038^{3} (6261) 6737^{13} 7246^{2}

Whozthecat (IRE) *Declan Carroll* a93 101
6 b g One Cool Cat(USA) Intaglia (GER) (Lomitas)
2031^{17} 2459^{2} 2663^{6} 3114^{4} (3367) 3846a^{2} 4986^{24} 5651^{10}

Why Not (GER) *David Hayes* 107
5 b g Konigstiger(GER) Win For Us (GER) (Surumu (GER))
7760a^{10}

Why Not Now *Roger Charlton* a54
2 ch f Notnowcato Perfect Night (Danzig Connection (USA))
8342^{4} 8451^{9}

Wicked Spirit (IRE) *Keith Dalgleish* a73 75
5 b f Bahri(USA) The Spirit Of Pace (IRE) (In The Wings)
49^{9}

Wicked Tara *Frank Sheridan*
3 b f Assertive Tara King (Deploy)
2215^{8} 2581^{4}

Wicked Wench *Jeremy Gask* a83 83
4 b f Kyllachy Effervescent (Efisio)
316^{3} 795^{3} 924^{8} 2173^{4} 2736^{2} 3236^{3} 3407^{3} 3796a^{4} 4149^{3}

Wicked Wilma (IRE) *Alan Berry* a13 72
9 b m Tagula(IRE) Wicked (Common Grounds)
1276^{4} 1465^{6} 1758^{6} 2043^{5} 2217^{3} 2410^{6} 2632^{9} 2795^{8} 3654^{6} 4102^{4} 4377^{10} 4762^{3} 5047^{5} 5085^{8} 5336^{4} 5470^{12} 5708^{10} 6669^{6} 6878^{3} 6945^{10} 8034^{9}

Wickhambrook (IRE) *Ismail Mohammed* a77 81
2 ch c Dubawi(IRE) Beautiful Filly (Oasis Dream)
1680^{5} 3350^{4} 3640^{2} 5339^{3} 6747^{5} (6975) 7428^{4}

Wiggins (IRE) *Ralph Beckett* a35
2 b g High Chaparral(IRE) Al Ihsas (IRE) (Danehill (USA))
7835^{12} 8123^{12}

Wight Is Wight (IRE) *J-C Rouget* a92 97
3 b g Peintre Celebre(USA) Alenteja (IRE) (Danehill (USA))
1419a^{8}

Wigmore Hall (IRE) *Michael Bell* a89 114
6 b g High Chaparral(IRE) Love And Laughter (IRE) (Theatrical (IRE))
1267a^{8} 2020^{3} 4213^{5} 4779^{3} 5550a^{5} 6198^{10} 6800^{2}

Wiki Tiki *Stuart Williams* a32 66
2 br f Dixie Union(USA) Witten (USA) (Fusaichi Pegasus (USA))
2048^{10} 2517^{4} 3017^{2} 3295^{10} 4073^{7} 8322^{8}

Wilberfoss (IRE) *Mel Brittain* a32 56
2 b c Amadeus Wolf Pietra Dura (Cadeaux Genereux)
5900^{6} 7419^{3} 7883^{5} 8040^{6}

Wild Anthem *Hughie Morrison* a21 63
3 b f Manduro(GER) Wild Gardenia (Alhaarth (IRE))
2803^{4} 5892^{10}

Wildcat Lass (USA) *David O'Meara* a64
2 bb f Street Cry(IRE) Lexington Girl (USA) (Storm Cat (USA))
8362^{2}

Wild Coco (GER) *Lady Cecil* 114
5 ch f Shirocco(GER) Wild Side (GER) (Sternkoenig (IRE))
(4920) 6448a^{2}

Wildcrafting *Michael Bell* a58 25
3 ch f Exceed And Excel(AUS) Local Spirit (USA) (Lion Cavern (USA))
1384^{5} 1695^{4} 2135^{6} 3198^{8}

Wild Desert (FR) *Tony Carroll* a89 88
8 bb g Desert Prince(IRE) Sallivera (IRE) (Sillery (USA))
166^{3} 378^{7} 562^{5} (3512) 3744^{3}

Wilddrossel (GER) *Markus Klug* 102
4 rg f Dalakhani(IRE) Wild Side (GER) (Sternkoenig (IRE))
2822a^{3} 3879a^{8} 6887a^{3} 7407a^{3} 7891a^{3}

Wilde Inspiration (IRE) *Ralph Beckett* a49 73
2 ch g Dandy Man(IRE) Wishing Chair (USA) (Giant's Causeway (USA))
4231^{9} 6739^{2} 7120^{7}

Wildling *Jim Boyle* a15
2 b f Piccolo Concubine (IRE) (Danehill (USA))
5924^{13} 6528^{9} 7320^{11} 7435^{12}

Wildomar *Tony Carroll* a91 73
4 b g Kyllachy Murrieta (Docksider (USA))
93^{2} 224^{2} 420^{4} 496^{3} (739) 1382^{8} 2044^{11} 8392^{8}

Wild Perfection (USA) *Jena M Antonucci* 66
3 ch g D'Wildcat(USA) Perfect Marriage (USA) (Lexicon (USA))
3361a^{7}

Wild Sauce *Bryan Smart* a83 83
4 b f Exceed And Excel(AUS) Salsa Brava (IRE) (Almutawakel)
1807^{14} 2173^{7} 4018^{2} 4479^{3} 5381^{3} (5887) 6205^{4} 7420^{6} 7777^{4} 7959^{5} 8096^{3}

Wild Silva *Markus Klug* 97
3 gr f Silvano(GER) Wild Side (GER) (Sternkoenig (IRE))
4092a^{4} 5044a^{10}

Wild Step (GER) *Markus Klug* 85
2 b f Footstepsinthesand Zaynaat (Unfuwain (USA))
7406a^{7}

Wild Wolf (IRE) *S Botti* 107
4 b g Rail Link Mary Rose (ITY) (Royal Academy (USA))
3147a^{2} 3881a^{7} 6679a^{3} 7414a^{7}

Wilfred Pickles (IRE) *Jo Crowley* a77 75
7 ch g Cadeaux Genereux Living Daylights (IRE) (Night Shift (USA))
32^{4} 1878^{6} 2981^{2} 3917^{4} 4718^{3} 5245^{6} 6080^{6} 7307^{2} 7836^{5} 8453^{3}

Wilhana (IRE) *Pam Sly* a74
3 b f Singspiel(IRE) Jathaabeh (Nashwan (USA))
7114^{2} ◆ 7377^{2} 7791^{2} 7983^{2} 8260^{3} 8444^{4}

Wilholden (FR) *P Nador* 51
3 b c Hannouma(IRE) Sinueuse (FR) (Fabulous Dancer (USA))
2034a^{0}

Willbeme *Neville Bycroft* 83
5 b f Kyllachy Befriend (USA) (Allied Forces (USA))
2755^{8} 3441^{6} 6515^{8} 6948^{2} 7029^{6}

William Hogarth *Keith Goldsworthy* a53 48
8 b g High Chaparral(IRE) Mountain Holly (Shirley Heights)
1973^{8} 2328^{8} 2922^{6} 3271^{6}

William Van Gogh *Michael Easterby* a70 82
6 b g Dansili Flower Girl (Pharly (FR))
435^{4} ◆ 1017^{4} (1107) 1434^{2} 1788^{14} 3642^{8}

Willie The Whipper *Ann Duffield* 109
3 b c Whipper(USA) Anna Simona (GER) (Slip Anchor)
2211^{4} 2907a^{6} 5653^{5} 6620^{2} 7049a^{8}

Willie Wag Tail (USA) *Ed Walker* a95 99
4 b g Theatrical(IRE) Night Risk (USA) (Wild Again (USA))
2044^{7} 4301^{6} 5259^{4} 5655^{9}

Willing Foe (USA) *Saeed bin Suroor* a62 116
6 bb g Dynaformer(USA) Thunder Kitten (USA) (Storm Cat (USA))
(2443)

Will O'The Wisp (FR) *Mme A-C Trouve* 45
3 ch f Vatori(FR) White And Blue (FR) (Mansonnien (FR))
5913a^{9}

Willow Beauty *J R Jenkins* a51 53
4 br f Val Royal(FR) Opera Belle (Dr Fong (USA))
530^{9} 651^{8}

Willow Beck *John Gosden* a66 96
4 b f Shamardal(USA) Woodbeck (Terimon)
(3996) (4898) (5436) 5749^{2} 6649^{3} 7659^{7}

Willowing (USA) *Saeed bin Suroor* a77 74
3 b f Hard Spun(USA) Sweet Arizona (USA) (Gone West (USA))
4678^{4}

Willow Island (IRE) *David Evans* a44 44
4 b g Dark Angel(IRE) Cidaris (IRE) (Persian Bold)
6046^{2} 6217^{8} 6366^{9} 7201^{12} 7440^{8} 7612^{12} 8417^{5}

Willpower (TUR) *Z Bektas* 104
3 b f Victory Gallop(CAN) Free Trade (TUR) (Shareef Dancer (USA))
6231a^{3}

Will Take Charge (USA) *D Wayne Lukas* a128
3 ch c Unbridled's Song(USA) Take Charge Lady (USA) (Dehere (USA))
2033a^{8} 2473a^{7} 3127a^{10} 7715a^{2}

Will To Survive (IRE) *Richard Guest* a10 67
2 ch g Camacho Night Eyes (IRE) (Night Shift (USA))
1792^{3} 2436^{4} 2715^{6} 3084^{3} 3476^{6}

Willy Brennan (IRE) *Andrew Balding* 37
2 br g Bushranger(IRE) Miss Assertive (Zafonic (USA))
7501^{7}

Wilshire Boulevard (IRE) *A P O'Brien* 110
2 b c Holy Roman Emperor(IRE) Tyranny (Machiavellian (USA))
3424^{10} (4547a) 5765^{2} 7056a^{4} 7688a^{9}

Wily Fox *James Eustace* a63 66
6 ch g Observatory(USA) Kamkova (USA) (Northern Dancer (CAN))
1445^{2} 2545^{7} 6325^{8}

Windfast (IRE) *Brian Meehan* 83
2 b c Exceed And Excel(AUS) Fair Sailing (IRE) (Docksider (USA))
2048^{2} ◆ (2543)

Windfinder *M Guarnieri* 97
2 b c Shirocco(GER) Clarita Dear (CHI) (Hussonet (USA))
7678a^{5}

Wind Fire (USA) *David Brown* 102
2 b f Distorted Humor(USA) A P Dream (USA) (A.P. Indy (USA))
2048^{4} ◆ (2601) 3481^{3} 4742^{5} (5476) 5680^{3} 6347^{2}

Windforpower (IRE) *Tracy Waggott* a70 65
3 b g Red Clubs(IRE) Dubai Princess (IRE) (Dubai Destination (USA))
38^{2} 106^{2} (368) 424^{2} (531) 628^{4} 710^{3} (847) 1844^{5} 2076^{10} 3283^{11} 3594^{7} 4136^{4} 4162^{5} 4621^{10} 5470^{7} 5889^{3} ◆ (6469) (6944)

Windhoek *Mark Johnston* 111
3 b c Cape Cross(IRE) Kahlua Kiss (Mister Baileys)
(1636) (2023) 2398^{5} 3485^{6} 4080^{8} 4946^{7} 5681^{2} 5986^{2}

Winding Way (USA) *Carla Gaines* a95 98
4 bb f Malibu Moon(USA) More Than Pretty (USA) (More Than Ready (USA))
7043a^{7}

Windlass (IRE) *John Gosden* a70
2 b f Teofilo(IRE) Emerald Peace (IRE) (Green Desert (USA))
7875^{4}

Windpfeil (IRE) *Dominic Ffrench Davis* a43 29
7 bl g Indian Ridge Flying Kiss (IRE) (Sadler's Wells (USA))
2333^{6}

Windshear *Richard Hannon Snr* 78
2 b c Hurricane Run(IRE) Portal (Hernando (FR))
(6355) ◆

Windshield *Sir Mark Prescott Bt* a54
2 b f Montjeu(IRE) Westerly Air (USA) (Gone West (USA))
8362^{4}

Wind Shuffle (GER) *Lucinda Russell* 57
10 b g Big Shuffle(USA) Wiesensturmerin (GER) (Lagunas)
5370^{9} 5921^{10}

Windsor (GER) *Markus Klug* 89
3 bb c Soldier Hollow Well American (USA) (Bertrando (USA))
5576a^{6} 7831a^{7}

Windsor Palace (IRE) *A P O'Brien* a81 107
8 br h Danehill Dancer(IRE) Simaat (USA) (Mr Prospector (USA))
1556a^{3} 2688a^{3} 3457^{11}

Windsor Rose (IRE) *Mark Brisbourne* a53 57
3 ch f Windsor Knot(IRE) Rose Of Battle (Averti (IRE))
1842^{10} 3219^{6} 4143^{8}

Windsor Secret *Keith Dalgleish* a53 38
3 ch f Sakhee's Secret Lady Of Windsor (IRE) (Woods Of Windsor (USA))
5261^{6} 5916^{6} 6049^{9} 6921^{7} 7514^{2} 7667^{4} 8418^{4}

Windy Citi *Chris Wall* 44
2 ch f Zamindar(USA) Windy Britain (Mark Of Esteem (IRE))
7466^{8}

Windygoul Lad *Michael Smith* a46 64
4 br g Kheleyf(USA) Millymix (FR) (Linamix (FR))
1686^{10} 2036^{4} 2582^{14}

Windy King *J Bertran De Balanda* a79 82
4 b g Hurricane Run(IRE) Vanishing Prairie (USA) (Alysheba (USA))
922a^{8}

Wine Police (USA) *Henry Dominguez* a105
5 ch g Speightstown(USA) Deputy Cures Blues (CAN) (War Deputy (USA))
7713a^{8}

Wingate *H-A Pantall* a85 102
3 b g Zamindar(USA) Sirene Doloise (FR) (Marchand De Sable (USA))
7408a^{2}

Winged Farasi *Joanne Foster* a58 35
9 b g Desert Style(IRE) Clara Vale (IRE) (In The Wings)
3889^{10}

Winged Icarus (USA) *Brian Ellison* a82 58
3 b g Speightstown(USA) Daedal (USA) (Orientate (USA))
2876^{6} 3828^{5} 5195^{8} 6587^{9} 6970^{2}

Wingland (FR) *Mme M Bollack-Badel* 72
3 b f Lando(GER) Angel Wing (Barathea (IRE))
2434a^{0} 5692a^{4}

Wing N Prayer (IRE) *Neville Bycroft* a50 36
6 b m Xaar Jazmeer (Sabrehill (USA))
4623^{14}

Winnie Perry *Rod Millman* a64 64
3 ch g Assertive Hayley's Flower (IRE) (Night Shift (USA))
1400^{5} 1900^{14} 2495^{8} 3178^{9} 3376^{10} 3732^{3} 3888^{8} 4410^{2} 4836^{9} 5644^{3} 6043^{3} 6902^{10}

Winning Dream (FR) *J-P Carvalho* a83 63
4 b f Green Desert(USA) Wings Of Glory (GER) (Monsun (GER))
5042a^{13}

Winning Express (IRE) *Ed McMahon* 108
3 gr f Camacho Lady Fabiola (USA) (Open Forum (USA))
1622^{3} 2047^{4} (3734) 4949^{2} 6327^{3} 7021^{2}

Winning Spark (USA) *Gary Moore* a79 81
6 b g Theatrical(IRE) Spark Sept (FR) (Septieme Ciel (USA))
905^{5}

Winshine (FR) *J-M Capitte* 83
2 b f Chineur(FR) Fusee Francaise (FR) (Anabaa (USA))
5460a^{6} 6293a^{8} 7567a^{4}

Winsili *John Gosden* 116
3 b f Dansili Winter Sunrise (Pivotal)
(2412) 3482^{4} (4985)

Winslow Arizona (IRE) *Michael Bell* a76 63
3 b g Danehill Dancer(IRE) Buffalo Berry (IRE) (Sri Pekan (USA))
(2566) 2950^{5} (3665) 5073^{4} (5935) 6306^{13} 7447^{3}

Winterlude (IRE) *Charlie Appleby* a108 100
3 b c Street Cry(IRE) New Morning (IRE) (Sadler's Wells (USA))
(4151) (4979) 5723^{14} (7304)

Winter Music (IRE) *Andrew Balding* a60 63
3 b g Oratorio(IRE) Alpine Park (IRE) (Barathea (IRE))
1072^{7} 1343^{2} 1897^{2} 2924^{6} 3488^{4} 4122^{5}

Winter Picnic (IRE) *Tobias B P Coles* a49 55
2 b f Oratorio(IRE) Salpiglossis I (GER) (Monsun (GER))
5603^{4} 6079^{6} 7111^{4}

Winter's Night (IRE) *Clive Cox* 101
5 b f Night Shift(USA) Woodland Glade (Mark Of Esteem (IRE))
3458^{10} 4705^{3} 6000^{7} 7015^{7}

Winter Song (IRE) *Charles Hills* a66 66
3 b f Pivotal Speed Song (Fasliyev (USA))
2572^{3} 4636^{10} 8019^{11}

Winter Spice (IRE) *Clive Cox* 63
2 gr g Verglas(IRE) Summer Spice (IRE) (Key Of Luck (USA))
4414^{9} 5473^{7} 6953^{8}

Winterwell (USA) *David O'Meara* a79 76
3 b f First Defence(USA) Kinetic Force (USA) (Holy Bull (USA))
7946^{2} 8348^{7}

Winterwind (IRE) *Carmen Bocskai* a89 90
8 b g Orpen(USA) Brickey Beech (IRE) (Precocious)
701a^{2}

Wintour Leap *Roger Charlton* a55 44
2 b f Nayef(USA) Mountain Leap (IRE) (Sadler's Wells (USA))
7102^{6} 7764^{8} 8066^{9}

Wire To Wire (FR) *J-C Rouget* 106
3 b c Observatory(USA) Sachet (USA) (Royal Academy (USA))
2035a^{3} 3128a^{7}

Wise Dan (USA) *Charles LoPresti* a128 130
6 ch g Wiseman's Ferry(USA) Lisa Danielle (USA) (Wolf Power (SAF))
(6456a) (7714a)

Wise Venture (IRE) *Alan Jarvis* a55 77
4 b g Kheleyf(USA) Chia Laguna (IRE) (Ela-Mana-Mou)
2286^{2} 2565^{10} 4517^{7}

Wish Come True (IRE) *S Botti* 105
3 b c Aussie Rules(USA) Tibouchina (IRE) (Daylami (IRE))
2490a^{2}

Wishformore (IRE) *Zoe Davison* a56 60
6 b m Chevalier(IRE) Terra Nova (Polar Falcon (USA))
1093^{5} 1497^{7} (3051) 3326^{2} 3661^{3} 3817^{2} 4752^{6} 4999^{6} 6462^{4} 7265^{12} 7643^{5} 8073^{4} 8151^{5}

Wishful (SWE) *Erik Svensson*
2 b f Philomatheia(USA) Raise The Rhythm (IRE) (Raise A Grand (IRE))
6452a^{14}

Wishing Bridge *Pat Eddery* a64 12
3 ch g Pastoral Pursuits Dunloe (IRE) (Shaadi (USA))
2672^{8} 3401^{8}

Wishing Gate (IRE) *David Barron*
3 b c Kyllachy Rydal Mount (IRE) (Cape Cross (IRE))
4200^{8}

Witch From Rome *Ralph Beckett* a60
2 b c Holy Roman Emperor(IRE) Spangle (Galileo (IRE))
8340^{7}

Witchry *Tony Newcombe* a65 54
11 gr g Green Desert(USA) Indian Skimmer (USA) (Storm Bird (CAN))
884^{8}

Witch Way Went *Brian Ellison* a24 62
3 b f Royal Applause Celestial Princess (Observatory (USA))
6178^{5} 6497^{5} 7132^{14} 7952^{10}

Witchy Woman *K R Burke* 56
2 b f Intikhab(USA) Lady McBeth (IRE) (Avonbridge)
3217^{5} 4115^{7} 4538^{3} (4964) 6914^{9}

With A Twist *Andrew Balding* 32
2 b f Excellent Art Bint Zamayem (IRE) (Rainbow Quest (USA))
6590^{11} 7069^{12}

Withernsea (IRE) *Richard Fahey* 79
2 b g Dark Angel(IRE) Charlene Lacy (IRE) (Pips Pride)
1642^{4} (1989) 2877^{6}

With Hindsight (IRE) *Peter Grayson* a70 79
5 ch g Ad Valorem(USA) Lady From Limerick (IRE) (Rainbows For Life (CAN))
1045^{4} 1716^{10}

Without Fear (FR) *Niels Petersen* a87 101
5 b g Refuse To Bend(IRE) Kansas (Kahyasi)
463a^{11} 741a^{4} 873a^{8} (3188a) 4095a^{5} 5809a^{7} (6453a)

Without Truth (IRE) *David Brown* a46
2 b g Excellent Art Miss Informed (IRE) (Danehill (USA))
3640^{11} 4142^{6} 7509^{6}

Wizara (IRE) *Saeed bin Suroor* a76 80
3 b f Teofilo(IRE) Princesse Dansante (IRE) (King's Best (USA))
5478^{4} ◆ 6062^{5} (6847) 7267^{5} 7659^{9}

Wognan (IRE) *J Heloury* a52 89
4 b g One Cool Cat(USA) Wigman (USA) (Rahy (USA))
5735a^{15}

Wolf Heart (IRE) *Lucy Normile* a76 53
5 b g Dalakhani(IRE) Lisieux Orchid (IRE) (Sadler's Wells (USA))
1274^{3} 1572^{12} 2536^{4}

Wolfs Breath (TUR) *Charles Hills* a50 66
3 b f Montjeu(IRE) Uva (TUR) (The Best (TUR))
2206^{9} 3469^{10} 6036^{4} 6788^{7}

Wolfwood *John Davies* a30 43
2 b g Ferrule(IRE) Wedgewood Star (Bishop Of Cashel)
2161^{6} 2985^{10} 5482^{10} 7341^{6} 7755^{6}

Wolverine (FR) *H Billot* 81
6 b g Take Risks(FR) Sevres (USA) (Lyphard's Wish (FR))
5601a^{11}

Wom *Neil King* a66 63
5 b g Tiger Hill(IRE) Vayavaig (Damister (USA))
(361) 816^{7} 1084^{5}

Wonderfully (IRE) *A P O'Brien* 105
2 b f Galileo(IRE) Massarra (Danehill (USA))
3522^{7} ◆ (4462a) 6024a^{6} ◆ 6798^{4} 7055a^{6}

Won Diamond *M Halford* a83 95
3 b g Mount Nelson Read Federica (Fusaichi Pegasus (USA))
3484^{19}

Woodacre *Richard Whitaker* 67
6 b g Pyrus(USA) Fairy Ring (IRE) (Fairy King (USA))
1804^{7} 2030^{6} 2989^{5} 3651^{3} ◆ (5264) 6297^{6} 7346^{7}

Woodbridge *Richard Fahey* 47
2 ch g Exceed And Excel(AUS) Kristal Bridge (Kris)
3928^{4}

Wooden King (IRE) *Malcolm Saunders* a70 79
8 b g Danetime(IRE) Olympic Rock (IRE) (Ballad Rock)
1976^{6} 2530^{4} 2790^{5} 3042^{3} 3315^{11} 3855^{11} 4369^{2} 4659^{4} (5388) 5796^{2} 5956^{4} 6382^{2} 7783^{7} 8029^{8}

Woodland Aria *John Gosden* a86 101
3 b f Singspiel(IRE) Magic Tree (UAE) (Timber Country (USA))
(1698) ◆ 2367^{3} (2928) ◆ 3460^{3} 4081^{6} 4949^{11}

Woodland Fleur *Tony Carroll* a55
3 b f Astronomer Royal(USA) Ultimate Court (IRE) (Kendor (FR))
19^{5} 207^{11} 442^{9} 3036^{5}

Woodland Girl *Richard Fahey* 69
2 ch f Kyllachy Locharia (Wolfhound (USA))
1839^{6} 2458^{7} 3205^{6} (4019)

Woodley Wonder (IRE) *Ben Haslam* a22 45
3 b g Byron City Maiden (USA) (Carson City (USA))
911[7] 1305[4] 2960[7] 4722[10]

Woodstock (IRE) *Brian Ellison* a73 71
3 b g High Chaparral(IRE) Woodwin (IRE) (Woodman (USA))
(1347) 1811[7] 2325[6] 2935[8] 3365[5] 4729[5] ◆ 4995[3] ◆ (5789) 6552[14]

Woody Bay *James Given* a82 83
3 b g New Approach(IRE) Dublino (USA) (Lear Fan (USA))
1829[5] 2272[6] 2616[4] (3137) (3722) 4077[3] (4890) 5182[5] 6208[6] 6563[14] 6951[6] *7438[3] 8007[3]*

Woolfall Sovereign (IRE) *George Margarson* a105 69
7 b g Noverre(USA) Mandragore (USA) (Slew O'Gold (USA))
(3) (319) 584[7] 1032[8] 1581[10] 2227[6] 3220[8] 3741[8] *7803[8]*

Woolfall Treasure *Gary Moore* a94 94
8 gr g Daylami(IRE) Treasure Trove (USA) (The Minstrel (CAN))
(224) 1547[P]

Woolston Ferry (IRE) *Henry Candy* a76 80
7 b g Fath(USA) Cathy Garcia (IRE) (Be My Guest (USA))
2232[8] 3780[8] 4593[6] 5304[6] 5855[4] *6398[2]* ◆ 6898[12] *7462[6] 7836[7] 8059[4]*

Wooly Bully *Alan King* 60
3 b g Sixties Icon Baycliffe Rose (Karinga Bay)
3858[6] *4633[11]*

Worcharlie'Slass *Michael Herrington* a31 6
2 b f Myboycharlie(IRE) Angry Bark (USA) (Woodman (USA))
6938[9] *7955[8] 8131[7] 8265[3] 8434[9]*

Wordiness *Brendan Powell* a87 76
5 br g Dansili Verbose (USA) (Storm Bird (CAN))
338[2] (520) (797) (1031) 1182[2] 1733[9] 3370[6] 4489[5] 6787[6] 7433[7]

Wordismybond *Peter Makin* a69 73
4 b g Monsieur Bond(IRE) La Gessa (Largesse)
807 2845[14] 3511[5] 3885[6] 4771[2] (5346) 6042[2] 6459[5] *6937[2] 7652[7] 8087[12]*

Word Of Warning *Philip Kirby* a42 46
9 gr g War Chant(USA) Frosty Welcome (USA) (With Approval (CAN))
5295[6] *8092[6]*

Work Ethic (IRE) *Gerard Butler* a74 70
3 ch g Camacho Foret Noire (IRE) (Barathea (IRE))
3639[3] 4136[5] 4499[4] *5395[5] 6214[6]*

World Domination (USA) *Lady Cecil* a98 73
5 b c Empire Maker(USA) Reams Of Verse (USA) (Nureyev (USA))
4027[10] 4979[11]

World Freight Girl *Dean Ivory* a53 39
3 ch f Tumbleweed Ridge Bens Georgie (IRE) (Opening Verse (USA))
336[6] 632[3] 824[9] 5126[8] *5935[9]* 6698[7] *7265[7] 8056[11]*

World Heritage *Robert Eddery* 85
7 b g Kahyasi Imbabala (Zafonic (USA))
6004[6]

Worldly (USA) *Brendan P Walsh* a108
6 b h A.P. Indy(USA) Urbane (USA) (Citidancer (USA))
7687a[3]

World Map (IRE) *Mark Johnston* a61 64
3 b f Pivotal Danse Arabe (IRE) (Seeking The Gold (USA))
807[8] 950[4] 1743[3] 1959[6] 2500[4] *3055[9]* (3675) 3893[6] 4035[6]

World Record (IRE) *Paul Green* a79 77
3 b c Choisir(AUS) Dancing Debut (Polar Falcon (USA))
1423[3] (1904) 2322[7] 3235[4] 3683[14] 3758[5] 4055[12] 7065[4]

Worth A King'S *Philip Kirby* a62 64
7 b g Red Ransom(USA) Top Romance (IRE) (Entrepreneur)
430[6] 6917[4] 7239[10]

Worthy Spirit (GER) *Andrew Balding*
2 b g Shirocco(GER) Wakytara (GER) (Danehill (USA))
7019[U]

Wotabooty *Hugo Palmer* a61
3 b f Black Sam Bellamy(IRE) Exexel (Dansili)
228[4] 532[3] 807[7]

Wotalad *Richard Whitaker* a59 58
3 b g Bertolini(USA) Cosmic Song (Cosmonaut)
2006[6] 2317[3] 2672[7] 3196[4] 3547[4] 6633[10] *6849[5] 7512[6] 7644[4] 7904[10] 8235[2]*

Woza Moya (USA) *Gay Kelleway* a66 64
3 b c Mizzen Mast(USA) Mrs Marcos (USA) (Private Account (USA))
331a[0] 461a[8] 544a[8]

Wrangler *William Haggas* 76
2 b c High Chaparral(IRE) Tipsy Me (Selkirk (USA))
7607[3]

Wrath of Fire (NZ) *D Cruz* 111
6 b g Bahhare(USA) Pesky (NZ) (Paris Opera (AUS))
1872a[10]

Wrecking Ball (IRE) *Amy Weaver* a65 63
3 b g Royal Applause Shatarah (Gulch (USA))
7637[3] 7877[5]

Wreningham *Pat Eddery* a70 64
8 br g Diktat Slave To The Rythm (IRE) (Hamas (IRE))
26[5] 213[7]

Wulfthryth *Tobias B P Coles* a56 36
2 b f Champs Elysees Bolsena (USA) (Red Ransom (USA))
7449[8] 7693[9] *7874[6]*

Wunderbar (GER) *J-C Rouget* a74 55
3 b c Silvano(GER) Wonderful World (GER) (Dashing Blade)
604a[3]

Wunderkind (USA) *Sir Mark Prescott Bt* a37 39
2 b f Langfuhr(CAN) Traum (USA) (Elusive Quality (USA))
6807[6] 7466[10] *7859[8]*

Wyatt Earp (IRE) *Richard Guest* a38 47
12 b g Piccolo Tribal Lady (Absalom)
6760[12] *8002[8] 8168[8] 8338[7]*

Wyborne *Brian Ellison* a86 88
4 ch g Halling(USA) Coraline (Sadler's Wells (USA))
(521) 926[6] 1536[14] 3726[3] 4313[5] 5655[17] 6192[4] 6626[3] *7115[7]*

Wyldfire (IRE) *Richard Fahey* 74
3 ch g Raven's Pass(USA) Miss Sally (IRE) (Danetime (IRE))
(1282) 1604[3] 2432[8] 3756[3] 4809[11] 5368[5] 6758[10]

Wylye *Andrew Balding* 75
2 gr f Dalakhani(IRE) Tavy (Pivotal)
(7532)

Wyndham Wave *Rod Millman* a63 61
4 gr g Dr Fong(USA) Atlantic Light (Linamix (FR))
1948[8] *3433[4] (3687)* 3885[5] *4169[11]*

Wynyard Boy *Tim Easterby* 56
3 ch g Pastoral Pursuits Woodcock Moon (Kyllachy)
2480[4] 4157[7]

Xanders Secret *Brett Johnson* a6
3 br f Sakhee's Secret Point Perfect (Dansili)
2722[8] *2979[13] 3494[7]*

Xanim Qiz (IRE) *Y Musayev* 90
4 b f Antonius Pius(USA) Claudia Of Nowhere (FR) (Exit To Nowhere (USA))
6231a[8]

Xanthos *Ed Walker* a69 82
2 ch g Medicean My Girl Jode (Haafhd)
4347[4] (4756) 5679[19] 6529[2] 6844[3] *7326[7]*

Xcellence (FR) *F Doumen* 100
2 b f Champs Elysees Xanadu Bliss (FR) (Xaar)
7940a[2]

Xclusive *Ronald Harris* a51 68
3 b g Pivotal Dance A Daydream (Daylami (IRE))
1584[8] 1975[5] 2548[6] 3137[10] 6321[6] *6782[7] 7753[5] 8149[5]*

Xenophanes (IRE) *P Schiergen* a89 88
3 b c Shamardal(USA) Nipping (IRE) (Night Shift (USA))
1594a[3] 3970a[11] 7085a[11]

Xenophon *Michael Chapman* a42 49
5 b g Phoenix Reach(IRE) Comtesse Noire (CAN) (Woodman (USA))
6722[7]

Xilerator (IRE) *David Nicholls* a72 94
6 b g Arakan(USA) Grandel (Owington)
1537[17] 1688[2] ◆ 1840[11] 2541[8] 3335[10] 5546[14] 5943[12] 6162[7] 7176[15]

Xinbama (IRE) *J W Hills* a81 83
4 b c Baltic King Persian Empress (IRE) (Persian Bold)
1181[3] 1827[12] *2981[3] 3468[4]* (4205) (4441) 4923[9] 5824[5] 6869[8] *7651[6] 7970[5] 8179[11]*

Xotic (FR) *D Prod'Homme* a93 103
4 b g Holy Roman Emperor(IRE) Xstase (SWE) (Trempolino (USA))
2559a[4]

Xpres Maite *Roy Bowring* a69 50
10 b g Komaite(USA) Antonias Melody (Rambo Dancer (CAN))
707[2] 908[3] 1074[3] 1201[3] 1333[3] 1600[2] 2174[6] 2785[10] *7514[4] 7881[8]* 8233[3] 8409[7]

Xtension (IRE) *J Moore* 117
6 br h Xaar Great Joy (IRE) (Grand Lodge (USA))
2066a[6] 8210a[9]

Yaakooum (IRE) *Richard Hannon Snr* 70
2 b c Cape Cross(IRE) Anna's Rock (IRE) (Rock Of Gibraltar (IRE))
5033[4] 6355[5]

Yaa Wayl (IRE) *Saeed bin Suroor* a108 114
6 b g Whipper(USA) Lidanna (Nicholas (USA))
149a[3] 557a[8] 742a[8]

Yadelarumbadanlair (FR) *G Pannier* a67 58
3 ch f Sandwaki(USA) Winter Delice (FR) (Marignan (USA))
7187a[5] 7573a[4]

Yagheer (IRE) *Roger Varian* a73 74
2 b c Lawman(FR) Dawn Raid (IRE) (Docksider (USA))
7494[2] ◆ *8018[4]*

Ya Hafed *Sheena West* a74 76
5 ch g Haafhd Rule Britannia (Night Shift (USA))
119[5]

Yahilwa (USA) *James Tate* a83 79
3 br f Medaglia d'Oro(USA) Verbanella (USA) (Smart Strike (CAN))
1291[9] *1784[3] 1907[3] 2129[3] (2576)* 2837[2] 3375[6] *(4145) 5676[9] 6609[7]*

Yair Hill (IRE) *Noel Wilson* 96
5 b g Selkirk(USA) Conspiracy (Rudimentary (USA))
(2028) 2647[5] 3527[26] 4758[8] 5518[7] 5943[11] 6586[24] 7176[18]

Yajamila *James Tate* a72 69
2 b f Royal Applause Yatir (FR) (Red Ransom (USA))
3673[3] 4708[3] *(5194)* 5858[6] 6284[6] *7202[7]*

Yajber (USA) *Jamie Poulton* a63
4 rg g Aljabr(USA) Futuh (USA) (Diesis)
2807[9] 5234[11]

Yalding Dancer *John Best* a48
4 b f Zafeen(FR) Daughters World (Agnes World (USA))
655[7] 794[7] 1183[8] 1781[11] 5525[8]

Yangoon (FR) *J Bertran De Balanda* a65
3 gr g Enrique Ikra (FR) (Simon Du Desert (FR))
818a[5]

Yankee Red *John Best* a17 54
2 b g Pastoral Pursuits Miriam (Forzando)
3752a[7] 5307[12] *5635[9]*

Yankee Storm *Michael Wigham* a77 63
8 b g Yankee Gentleman(USA) Yes Virginia (USA) (Roanoke (USA))
199[5] (705) 1172[5] 1521[3]

Yarn *William Haggas* a65 62
3 ch f Dutch Art Spinneret (Pivotal)
4991[3] 5715[3] 6289[3] *6752[2]*

Yarroom (IRE) *Roger Varian* a61 102
3 b g Cape Cross(IRE) Aryaamm (IRE) (Galileo (IRE))
1809[3] 4743[10] 5182[2] (5944)

Yasir (USA) *Conor Dore* a83 76
5 b g Dynaformer(USA) Khazayin (USA) (Bahri (USA))
4521[7] (5087) *5868[5] 6346[5]* 6631[8] *7169[4]* (7273) 7539[3] *7863[8] 8115[3] 8129[5] (8270) 8349[3]* 8433[2]

Yazdi (IRE) *Charlie Mann* a41 92
4 b g Galileo(IRE) Lucky Spin (Pivotal)
3560[17]

Yeager (USA) *Jeremy Noseda* a63 97
3 bb g Medaglia d'Oro(USA) Lucky Flyer (USA) (Fusaichi Pegasus (USA))
1423[8] 1881[2] ◆ (2931) (4743) ◆ 5551a[10] 6650[15]

Yeah Baby (IRE) *Charles Hills* 71
2 b f Danehill Dancer(IRE) Street Shaana (FR) (Darshaan)
5061[6] 6643[8] 6973[4] 7533[4]

Year Of Glory (IRE) *Marco Botti* a61 67
2 b c Kheleyf(USA) Baila Salsa (IRE) (Barathea (IRE))
5180[4] ◆ 6829[7]

Yeeoow (IRE) *K R Burke* a94 99
4 b g Holy Roman Emperor(IRE) Taraya (IRE) (Doyoun)
(881) 1245[2] 1537[5] (2207) 2988[11] 3846a[13] 4472[9] 4983[6] ◆ 6352[3] ◆ 6621[8] 7495[10]

Yellow And Green *N Clement* 112
4 b f Monsun(GER) Green Swallow (FR) (Green Tune (USA))
2644a[5] 7048a[6]

Yellow Emperor (IRE) *Jeremy Noseda* a54 63
2 b g Holy Roman Emperor(IRE) Valentine Hill (IRE) (Mujadil (USA))
4631[12] 6534[6]

Yellow Lady (IRE) *Olly Stevens* a41 49
2 b f Lawman(FR) Gamble In Gold (IRE) (Monashee Mountain (USA))
2517[3] 3408[3] *4142[5] 5066[7]* 6073[10]

Yellow Mountain (IRE) *Marco Botti* a65 75
3 b c Danehill Dancer(IRE) Singing Diva (IRE) (Royal Academy (USA))
(757)

Yellow Rosebud (IRE) *D K Weld* 110
4 b f Jeremy(USA) Nebraas (Green Desert (USA))
1166a[2] 1413a[6] 3262a[3] 7047a[4] 7685a[7]

Yemaya (FR) *U Suter* 77
2 b f Teofilo(IRE) Sparkling Star (FR) (Art Sebal (USA))
1894a[8]

Yenhaab (IRE) *William Haggas* 70
2 b c Cape Cross(IRE) Skiphall (Halling (USA))
5941[4]

Yeoman (USA) *C Ferland* a76
3 gr c Raven's Pass(USA) Trust Your Heart (USA) (Relaunch (USA))
445a[4] 3129a[4]

Yeomanoftheguard *Richard Fahey* a71 69
4 b g Librettist(USA) Red Blooded Woman (USA) (Red Ransom (USA))
49[5] 218[5] 709[6] 929[6] (1111) 1523[7] 2165[4] 2798[7] 3248[6]

Yes Chef *Chris Gordon* a64 81
6 ch g Best Of The Bests(IRE) Lady Chef (Double Trigger (IRE))
7628[3] 7863[7] 8089[9] 8182[5] 8447[10]

Yes Daddy (IRE) *Kevin Ryan* 59
5 b g Golan(IRE) Hollygrove Samba (IRE) (Accordion (IRE))
3209[6]

Yes I Do (FR) *S Wattel* a92 89
6 b m Kingsalsa(USA) Yes My Love (FR) (Anabaa (USA))
2559a[9]

Yojimbo (IRE) *Mick Channon* a75 91
5 gr g Aussie Rules(USA) Mythie (FR) (Octagonal (NZ))
1233[6] 1675[17] 1922[17] 2592[10] 3108[5] 3886[4] 4207[4] 4908[10] 5310[3] 5613[2] (5815) 5978[5] 6360[6] 6792[2]

Yojojo (IRE) *Gay Kelleway* a84 91
4 ch f Windsor Knot(IRE) Belle Of The Blues (IRE) (Blues Traveller (IRE))
313[2] (996) 1479[2] 1736[3] (2155) (2792) (3427) 5360a[9] 6599[5] *(7038)* (7470) *8440a[14]*

York Glory (USA) *Kevin Ryan* a107 114
5 rg c Five Star Day(USA) Minicolony (USA) (Pleasant Colony (USA))
480[2] 776[4] 1032[5] 1537[6] (1720) 2366[4] 2669[2] (3558) 4986[20] 5726[8] 5984[2] ◆ 6639[2]

Yorkshire Lass (IRE) *H-A Pantall* a85 92
5 b f Pivotal White Rose (GER) (Platini (GER))
7189a[7] 7890a[9]

Yorkshireman (IRE) *David Brown* a69 74
3 b g Red Clubs(IRE) Ossiana (IRE) (Polish Precedent (USA))
1275[3] 1608[8] 4135[5] *4753[5]* 5791[5]

Yorkshire Relish (IRE) *Kevin Ryan* 76
2 b g Amadeus Wolf Patroller (USA) (Grand Slam (USA))
2883[4] (3298) 4528[7] ◆ 4948[17] 5679[17] 6582[9]

Yorksters Prince (IRE) *Marjorie Fife* a73 63
6 b g Beat Hollow Odalisque (IRE) (Machiavellian (USA))
1070[5] 1222[6] (3545) 3728[3] (4562) 6468[8] 6877[8] 7346[11]

You Da One (IRE) *Andrew Balding* a79 98
3 b g Footstepsinthesand Shenkara (IRE) (Night Shift (USA))
979[2] (1197) 2190[3] (2655) 2844[3] ◆ 3484[14] 4236[5] 6384[3] 7025[3]

Youhavecontrol (IRE) *Nicky Vaughan* a65 65
5 b g Hawk Wing(USA) Chameleon (Green Desert (USA))
705[8] 1800[13] 2707[3] 2918[16] 3392[10] *4155[3]*

You Look So Good *Roger Varian* a66 51
3 gr f Excellent Art Divine Grace (IRE) (Definite Article)
2760[12] *6748[3] (7037) 7489[9]*

Youmaysee *Mick Channon* 36
3 b f Authorized(IRE) Purple Vision (Rainbow Quest (USA))
2803[6] 3239[10] 3530[9] 4030[U] 4171[4] 4664[5]

Youm Jamil (USA) *Tony Carroll* a62 56
6 rg g Mizzen Mast(USA) Millie's Choice (IRE) (Taufan (USA))
193[8] 417[2] 653[9] 3037[6] 4036[2]

Youm Mutamiez (USA) *M Al Muhairi* a109 78
6 br h Seeking The Gold(USA) Shy Lady (FR) (Kaldoun (FR))
575a[7]

Young Dottie *Pat Phelan* a73 73
7 b m Desert Sun Auntie Dot Com (Tagula (IRE))
2745[8] (4908) 5587[2] 6869[10] *7785[11] 8020[6]*

Young Jackie *George Margarson* a60 60
5 b f Doyen(IRE) Just Warning (Warning)
120[3] (375) (456) 579[3] 907[4] 1183[2] 1297[5] *2333[3] 2875[7] 3056[2]* (3169) (3924) 4071[8] 5002[7]

Young Jay *Mark Johnston* 65
3 b g Josr Algarhoud(IRE) Young Sue (Local Suitor (USA))
4118[8] 4813[6] 5110[5] 5612[6] 6179[2] 6389[8] 6601[3] 7066[12]

Young Lisa *George Margarson* a19 48
4 b f Echo Of Light Just Warning (Warning)
1296[5] *1611[7]*

Yourartisonfire *K R Burke* 89
3 ch c Dutch Art Queens Jubilee (Cayman Kai (IRE))
1912[2] 2438[3] 3028[4] (4641) 4922[5] 5510[4] 6356[11] 6988[17]

You're A Rich Girl *Dr Jon Scargill* a24
3 b f Proclamation(IRE) Ribh (Zafonic (USA))
5527[8]

You're Fired (IRE) *Alan Jarvis* a75 60
2 b c Firebreak My Sweet Georgia (IRE) (Royal Applause)
5307[7] *(7261)*

You're Golden (IRE) *E Legrix* a85 94
3 bb c Lawman(FR) Golden Shadow (IRE) (Selkirk (USA))
1495a[3] 1972a[3] *4274a[8]*

You'relikemefrank *Richard Ford* a64 66
7 ch g Bahamian Bounty Proudfoot (IRE) (Shareef Dancer (USA))
308[9] 560[9] 1324[6] 1396[4] 2326[7] 2632[10] 3030[5] 3197[10] 3325[3] 4371[5] 4659[10]

You're The Boss *Ed Walker* a90 86
3 b g Royal Applause Trinny (Rainbow Quest (USA))
1618[3] 2027[2] 2448[7] (4887) *5928[7]* 6575[7] *7165[2] (7601)*

Your Gifted (IRE) *Lisa Williamson* a59 64
6 b m Trans Island Dame Laura (IRE) (Royal Academy (USA))
5519[15] 6159[14] 6388[6] 7029[11] 7240[9] 7599[9] *7848[6] 8034[4] 8271[8] 8370[2]*

Yourholidayisover (IRE) *Patrick Holmes* 53
6 ch g Sulamani(IRE) Whitehaven (Top Ville)
2971[6] 3364[8] 4445[4] 5295[8] 5921[5] 6518[5] 6722[3]

Yourinthewill (USA) *Daniel Mark Loughnane* a75 66
5 ch g Aragorn(IRE) Lenarue (USA) (Gone West (USA))
84[3] 238[2] (330) 476[2] 672[2] 747[6] 974[4] (1104) 1353[3] 1699[7] 2417[9] 2709[2] 3138[10]

Your Pal Tal *T Stack* a78 77
3 b g Dark Angel(IRE) Good Health (Magic Ring (IRE))
2190[5]

You Will See (FR) *Mario Hofer* a87 87
3 b f Librettist(USA) Suvretta Queen (IRE) (Polish Precedent (USA))
2065a[9]

Ypres *Jason Ward* a66 81
4 b g Byron Esligier (IRE) (Sabrehill (USA))
2832[3] (3505) 5381[2] 5583[3] 6516[5] 6771[2] *7887[9]*

Ysper (FR) *M Nigge* a64 73
3 b f Orpen(USA) Velda (Observatory (USA))
2335a[0]

Yuften *William Haggas* 91
2 b c Invincible Spirit(IRE) Majestic Sakeena (IRE) (King's Best (USA))
5473[2] ◆ 6799[3]

Yuki (IRE) *B Goudot* 78
2 b f Lawman(FR) High Limits (IRE) (High Chaparral (IRE))
4651a[4] 7185a[10]

Yul Finegold (IRE) *George Baker* a67 77
3 b g Invincible Spirit(IRE) Mascara (Mtoto)
1114[4] 1725[6] 2603[5] 3636[2] 4672[6] *7950[7]*

Yulong Baoju (IRE) *Edward Lynam* a101 99
3 gr f Acclamation Masaader (USA) (Wild Again (USA))
2374a[10] (3796a) 5772a[9] *7521a[6]*

Yungaburra (IRE) *David C Griffiths* a64 63
9 b g Fath(USA) Nordic Living (IRE) (Nordico (USA))
326[2] 398[7] 516[9] 750[5]

Yurituni *Eve Johnson Houghton* a70 82
6 b m Bahamian Bounty Vax Star (Petong)
116[7]

Zaafran (FR) *N Bertran De Balanda* a73 83
3 b f Medecis Zython (FR) (Kabool)
7188a[14]

Za Approval (USA) *Christophe Clement* 119
5 rg g Ghostzapper(USA) Win Approval (USA) (With Approval (CAN))
6456a[2] 7714a[2]

Zac Brown (IRE) *David Barron* 86
2 b c Kodiac Mildmay (USA) (Elusive Quality (USA))
2401[7] 2955[4] 7173[2]

Zack Hall (FR) *F Rohaut* a93 109
6 b g Muhtathir Halawa (IRE) (Dancing Brave (USA))
(3362a)

Zack Hope *N Caullery* 106
5 b g Araafa(IRE) Afaf (FR) (Spectrum (IRE))
1456a[5] 1945a[7] 7685a[13]

Zack Tiger (IRE) *P Schaerer* a69 79
4 ch g Hold That Tiger(USA) Energetic Star (Anabaa (USA))
700a[4]

Zac's Princess *Milton Bradley* a40 44
2 ch f Zahran(IRE) Royal Supremacy (IRE) (Desert Prince (IRE))
1724[7] 2327[5] 2917[5] 3914[7] 5066[6] 5814[5] 6073[11] 6511[9]

Zacynthus (IRE) *Kevin Ryan* a89 97
5 ch g Iffraaj Ziria (IRE) (Danehill Dancer (IRE))
1688[6] 2310[3] 2665[2] 3538[3] 5545[18] 5943[7] 6826[12] 7241[11]

Zaeem *Dean Ivory* a75 87
4 b g Echo Of Light Across (ARG) (Roy (USA))
6925[10] 7438[12] 7865[3] 8179[7]

Zafaraban (IRE) *Tony Carroll* a57 53
6 gr g Dalakhani(IRE) Zafaraniya (IRE) (Doyoun)
397[8] 612[4] 708[6] 1175[8] 1916[5] 3884[7] 4173[3]

Zafarqand (IRE) *Patrick O Brady* 83
5 b g Halling(USA) Zafaraniya (IRE) (Doyoun)
2212[5] 3073a[4] 3873a[6]

Zafeen Speed *M Al Muhairi* a90 69
6 ch g Zafeen(FR) Dakhla Oasis (IRE) (Night Shift (USA))
869a[6] 957a[14]

Zafeen Style (FR) *H-A Pantall*
2 b c Zafeen(FR) Silver Swain (FR) (Swain (IRE))
7653a[13]

Zafisio (IRE) *Jo Hughes* 84
7 b g Efisio Goldthroat (IRE) (Zafonic (USA))
3339[15] 4923[5] 6336[9] 6596[4] 7312[11]

Zafraaj *Ronald Harris* a17 65
2 b c Iffraaj Woodbury (Woodborough (USA))
2359[7] 3009[2] 3659[5] 4602[3] 5814[2] 6111[11] 7394[5] 7986[9]

Zafranagar (IRE) *Tony Carroll* a73 80
8 b g Cape Cross(IRE) Zafaraniya (IRE) (Doyoun)
52[5] 403[11] 1836[7]

Zaftual *K F Clutterbuck* 21
2 b f Virtual Zaffrani (IRE) (Danehill (USA))
4215[14] 4828[9] 6034[4]

Zagros (FR) *J Heloury* a88 106
4 b g Slickly(FR) Jalapegnas (FR) (Hamas (IRE))
7142a[9] 7590a[8]

Zahee (NZ) *M F De Kock* a104 98
4 b c Dylan Thomas(IRE) Zaheeya (AUS) (Encosta De Lago (AUS))
245a[4] 658a[3] 953a[2] 1264a[6]

Zaheeb *Dave Morris* a71 70
5 b g Haafhd Gay Music (FR) (Gay Mecene (USA))
13[8] 130[3] 638[6] 1294[2] 1752[5] 2638[8] 3329[9] 4637[9] 4752[4] 5931[7] 6317[11] 6400[5] 6933[13] 7124[13]

Zaidan (USA) *A S Cruz* 114
5 bb g Street Cry(IRE) Element Of Truth (USA) (Atticus (USA))
1872a[12]

Zaidiyn (FR) *M Delzangles* 104
3 b c Zamindar(USA) Zainta (IRE) (Kahyasi)
2297a[8]

Zainda (IRE) *John Wainwright* a66 56
3 b f Dr Fong(USA) Zafayra (IRE) (Nayef (USA))
849[6] 2008[4] 2501[6] 2765[8] 5144[7] 7498[8] 7962[9] 8298[3]

Zain Eagle *Gerard Butler* a101 100
3 b c Dylan Thomas(IRE) Pearl City (USA) (Carson City (USA))
(5839) (6353) ◆ 6823[6] 7497[7] 7906[2] ◆

Zain Heart (IRE) *Gerard Butler* a31
3 b f Shamardal(USA) Antillia (Red Ransom (USA))
994[8]

Zain Joy (CAN) *Gerard Butler* a47
3 b f Survivalist(USA) Zawaahy (USA) (El Gran Senor (USA))
1243[6] 1732[5] 1962[14]

Zain Shamardal (IRE) *A Al Raihe* a105 104
5 b c Shamardal(USA) Novelina (IRE) (Fusaichi Pegasus (USA))
556a[10] 742a[4] 959a[10]

Zain Spirit (USA) *Gerard Butler* a75 39
3 b g Tapit(USA) American Jewel (USA) (Quiet American (USA))
6106[3] 6335[9] 6556[4] 6998[4] 7325[9]

Zain Zone (IRE) *Gerard Butler* a75 75
2 ch c Pastoral Pursuits Right After Moyne (IRE) (Imperial Ballet (IRE))
2048[9] 2391[2] 3092[5] (3972) 4833[2]

Zaitsev (IRE) *Ollie Pears* a63 78
3 ch g Refuse To Bend(IRE) Zuniga's Date (USA) (Diesis)
1185[5] 1429[7] 1648[12] 2464[4] (2957) 3232[9] (4048) 4586[3] 5304[10]

Za'Lan (USA) *Chris Gordon* a70 64
4 b g Street Sense(USA) Calista (Caerleon (USA))
131[8] 469[7] 522[13]

Zalty (FR) *David Marnane* a89 88
3 b g Elusive City(USA) Dubai's Gazal (Fraam)
4743[12]

Zalzilah *James Tate* a90 90
2 br g Kheleyf(USA) Tarneem (USA) (Zilzal (USA))
1680[6] (2075) 2863[10] 3079[4] 3424[20] (4363) (4511) 5012[5] 6187[3] 6791[9] 7545[3] 8203[8]

Zal Zilhom (IRE) *Kevin Ryan* a64 66
2 gr c Verglas(IRE) Intaglia (GER) (Lomitas)
4848[3] 5543[2] (5866) 6628[10]

Zamaam *F Rohaut* 100
3 bb c Muhtathir Nasheed (USA) (Riverman (USA))
7116a[5]

Zamaya (ITY) *M Grassi* 49
3 b f Colossus(IRE) King Tracks (USA) (King Cugat (USA))
3616a[10]

Zambeasy *Philip Hide* a54 16
2 b c Zamindar(USA) Hanella (IRE) (Galileo (IRE))
3574[7] 5101[6]

Zamfara *H-A Pantall* a32 83
3 br f Azamour(IRE) Zayraba (IRE) (Doyoun)
6711a[2] 7189a[9]

Zaminate *Patrick Chamings* a53 46
4 b f Zamindar(USA) Whitgift Rose (Polar Falcon (USA))
5038[7] 5631[4] 6899[8] 7118[5]

Zamiro (IRE) *Sebastiano Latina* 91
3 ch c Zamindar(USA) Euroceleb (IRE) (Peintre Celebre (USA))
1865a[7]

Zammy *Michael Wigham* a51 40
4 ch g Zamindar(USA) Barbs Pink Diamond (USA) (Johannesburg (USA))
1873[6] 2168[7] 2578[6]

Zamoyski *Steve Gollings* a92 86
3 ch g Dutch Art Speech (Red Ransom (USA))
1725[4] 2259[3] 2584[2] 2927[3] (4167) 8327[9]

Zampa Manos (USA) *Andrew Balding* a86 80
2 b g Arch(USA) Doryphar (USA) (Gone West (USA))
3695[4] (5344) 5745[5] 6314[3] 6935[6]

Zand (IRE) *John M Oxx* 91
3 b g Zamindar(USA) Zanara (IRE) (Kahyasi)
3142a[6] 6225a[6]

Zanetto *Andrew Balding* a96 111
3 b g Medicean Play Bouzouki (Halling (USA))
1362[2] (1620) 1921[4] (2415) 3557[15] 4298[10] 5804a[12] 7928[10]

Zanouska (USA) *Mark Johnston* a25 59
2 b f Bernardini(USA) Zanoubia (USA) (Our Emblem (USA))
7103[5] 7435[11]

Zanthalia (FR) *S Wattel* a75 68
2 b c Chineur(FR) Athalia (FR) (Desert King (IRE))
5848a[5]

Zapata Rebel (FR) *J-M Lefebvre* a71 55
3 ch g Cockney Rebel(IRE) Zurs (GER) (Lando (GER))
331a[10] 544a[4]

Zaplamation (IRE) *John Quinn* a40 74
8 b g Acclamation Zapatista (Rainbow Quest (USA))
1239[2] (1279) 1445[4] ◆ 1805[6] 2242[2] 3089[2] 3363[4] 3944[7] 6565[6] 7342[5]

Zaraee (IRE) *William Haggas* 86
2 b c Dubawi(IRE) Camaret (IRE) (Danehill (USA))
(3979) 4434[2] (5028) 6328[17]

Zara's Boy (IRE) *Evan Williams* 40
5 b g Soviet Star(USA) Zara's Birthday (IRE) (Waajib)
6431[5]

Zaria *John Butler* a17
2 b f Tomba Princess Zara (Reprimand)
7078[6]

Zarla *Tom Dascombe* a53 32
3 b f Zamindar(USA) Ikhteyaar (USA) (Mr Prospector (USA))
2215[7] 5495[9] 5923[12]

Zarosa (IRE) *John Berry* a44 71
4 b f Barathea(IRE) Shantalla Peak (IRE) (Darshaan)
(1572) 2545[2] 3627[5] 4913[8] 5831[3] 6632[6] 7280[11]

Zaroud (IRE) *Emmet Michael Butterly* a47
4 b g Zamindar(USA) Zarwala (IRE) (Polish Precedent (USA))
900[9] 917[10] 7806[5]

Zarras (GER) *J Hirschberger* a93 92
4 b g Big Shuffle(USA) Zanana (Zafonic (USA))
3969a[4]

Zarwaan *Ed Dunlop* 89
2 b c Dutch Art Develyn (Pivotal)
3112[4] (4477)

Zaungast (IRE) *W Hickst* a103 79
9 b g Alkalde(GER) Zauberwelt (Polar Falcon (USA))
4467a[3]

Zavier (FR) *Gary Brown* a48 42
4 b g Shamardal(USA) Zarkiyna (FR) (Sendawar (IRE))
8279[11]

Zawiyah *Luca Cumani* 80
2 b f Invincible Spirit(IRE) Marika (Marju (IRE))
4589[6] 5344[2] ◆ 6112[2] 6644[4] 7016[10]

Zayade (FR) *J Boisnard* a97 102
4 b f Country Reel(USA) Hallen (FR) (Midyan (USA))
2969a[5] 3913a[2] 7995a[5] 8440a[8]

Zazou (GER) *W Hickst* a116 112
6 b h Shamardal(USA) Zaza Top (GER) (Lomitas)
1262a[13] 2202a[9] (7053a) 7831a[4]

Zealand (IRE) *John Best* a31
2 b c Baltic King Zafaraya (IRE) (Ashkalani (IRE))
8328[13]

Zed Candy Girl *John Stimpson* a47 46
3 ch f Sakhee's Secret Musical Twist (USA) (Woodman (USA))
5069[8] 5517[8] 7323[10] 7806[6] 7963[9]

Zee Zeely *William Haggas* a73 79
2 ch c Champs Elysees Zee Zee Gee (Galileo (IRE))
7302[5] 7655[2] ◆

Zefooha (FR) *Tim Walford* a64 73
9 ch m Lomitas Bezzaaf (Machiavellian (USA))
542[5]

Zejel *C Ferland* a87 106
3 b f Gold Away(IRE) Dinaha (FR) (Octagonal (NZ))
4274a[2] 7316a[3]

Ze King *Chris Wall* a73 59
4 b g Manduro(GER) Top Flight Queen (Mark Of Esteem (IRE))
450[2] 4831[6]

Zelia Chope (FR) *C Boutin* 53
2 b f Deportivo Selam (GER) (Tertullian (USA))
2558a[4]

Zelos Diktator *Sean Curran* a58 63
7 br g Diktat Chanterelle (IRE) (Indian Ridge)
418[5] 704[6]

Zenafire *Andrew Hollinshead* a64 82
4 b c Firebreak Zen Garden (Alzao (USA))
1797[2] 2089[5] 2594[4] 3231[2] 3916[2] (4512) (5031) 5946[6] 6833[6] 7338[5]

Zenarinda *Mark H Tompkins* a73 71
6 b m Zamindar(USA) Tenpence (Bob Back (USA))
6802[6] 7453[9] 8335[7]

Zenji (USA) *G Henrot* a80 100
3 b c Hat Trick(JPN) Zinziberine (USA) (Zieten (USA))
3876a[9] 7408a[5]

Zephyr *John Gosden* 48
2 ch c Shirocco(GER) Pelagia (IRE) (Lycius (USA))
6528[6] 6740[6]

Zerdabi (FR) *A De Royer-Dupre* 79
3 b c Tiger Hill(IRE) Zewara (IRE) (Alhaarth (IRE))
5361a[13]

Zerfaal *John Gosden* 66
2 br c Dubawi(IRE) Dhelaal (Green Desert (USA))
5473[6]

Zero Game (IRE) *Michael Bell* a70 70
3 b f High Chaparral(IRE) Freezing Love (USA) (Danzig (USA))
(1428) 1655[6] (2331) 2783[4] 3418[6] 3861[6] 4721[8] (5527) ◆

Zero Money (IRE) *Hugo Palmer* a77 106
7 ch g Bachelor Duke(USA) Dawn Chorus (IRE) (Mukaddamah (USA))
3114[8] 3558[22] 4275[3] 4800[7] 5257[4] 5651[15] (6078) 6391[21]

Zeshov (IRE) *Jeremy Noseda* 79
2 b c Acclamation Fathoming (USA) (Gulch (USA))
2591[3] (3290) 6233[10]

Zeteah *David Lanigan* a45 40
3 b f Passing Glance Ajeebah (IRE) (Mujtahid (USA))
6366[7] 6950[8] 7873[4]

Zeus Magic *David Elsworth* a82 82
3 b g Zamindar(USA) Milly Of The Vally (Caerleon (USA))
1614[5] 2086[3] 3470[6]

Zeva *David Simcock* a71 60
3 b f Zamindar(USA) Mennetou (IRE) (Entrepreneur)
2164[4] 2952[7]

Zeyran (IRE) *Lady Cecil* a56 88
4 ch f Galileo(IRE) Chervil (Dansili)
2392[4] (2761) ◆ 3583[2] 4348[5]

Zhiggy's Stardust *Henry Candy* a92 71
4 b g Zafeen(FR) Lady Natilda (First Trump)
1660[4] 1985[7] (3401) (3955) 5636[2] (6526)

Zhiyi (USA) *P Bary* 114
3 b g Henrythenavigator(USA) Burning Sunset (Caerleon (USA))
(4043a) 5462a[3] 6712a[3]

Zhuba (IRE) *John Best* a64 66
3 b c Elusive Quality(USA) Lilium (Nashwan (USA))
685[4] 845[3] 3254[3] 3793[2] 4688[3] 5497[6] 6522[9] 6788[9] 7331[11]

Zibelina (IRE) *Charlie Appleby* 109
3 b f Dansili Zaeema (Zafonic (USA))
(3774) (4705) (5461a) 6000[4]

Ziefhd *Tim McCarthy* a68 75
4 b f Haafhd Zietory (Zieten (USA))
116[11] 130[7] 535[11] 1783[14] 5930[7] 7086[12] 8082[12]

Ziekhani *Hughie Morrison* a90 84
3 gr c Dalakhani(IRE) Zietory (Zieten (USA))
2547[4] 2930[4] (3731) 4492[5] (5676)

Ziggy Lee *Geoffrey Harker* a91 90
7 b g Lujain(USA) Mary O'Grady (USA) (Swain (IRE))
(4047)

Ziggy's Secret *Lucy Wadham* 75
3 b f Sakhee's Secret Ziggy Zaggy (Diktat)
4033[U] 5441[6]

Zigzag (FR) *J E Hammond* a76 80
3 ch f Dylan Thomas(IRE) Gabare (FR) (Galileo (IRE))
6713a[13]

Zigzag Hill *Bill Turner*
2 b f Compton Place Ziggy Zaggy (Diktat)
7630[8]

Ziking (FR) *A Schaerer* a74 77
8 gr g Kingsalsa(USA) Zizoune (FR) (Kadrou (FR))
609a[3] 702a[6]

Zilber (GER) *Ed Dunlop* 64
2 b c High Chaparral(IRE) Zephyrine (IRE) (Highest Honor (FR))
7494[6]

Zillion Dollar Cup (FR) *F Cheyer* 80
5 ch g Anabaa Blue State Of Mind (FR) (Priolo (USA))
6421a[7]

Zimbali (FR) *A Fabre* a79 77
3 b c Hurricane Run(IRE) Zaltana (USA) (Cherokee Run (USA))
2434a[5] 3129a[3]

Zinabaa (FR) *Mlle T Puitg* 119
8 gr g Anabaa Blue Zigrala (FR) (Linamix (FR))
1456a[6] 1945a[4] 2694a[5] 7186a[5] 7685a[11]

Zing Wing *David Evans* a77 73
5 ch f Hawk Wing(USA) Zietory (Zieten (USA))
431[4] ◆ 517[4] (589) 689[4] 980[3] 1039[3] 1368[4] 1398[7]

Zinnobar *Jonathan Portman* 55
3 gr f Ishiguru(USA) Demolition Jo (Petong)
3530[8] 5586[6] 5791[4] 6971[2] 7104[2] 7636[2]

Zipp (IRE) *Charles Hills* 90
3 b f Excellent Art Subito (Darshaan)
1671[14] 3417[2] (5064) 6649[5] 7496[2] 7890a[8]

Zlatan Dream (FR) *P Van De Poele* a76 82
2 b c Oasis Dream Serandine (IRE) (Hernando (FR))
8354a[4]

Zlatan In Paris (FR) *J-C Rouget* a82
2 gr c Slickly(FR) Tossup (USA) (Gone West (USA))
6961a[3]

Zoom In *Lee James* 42
5 b g Indesatchel(IRE) Korolieva (IRE) (Xaar)
2757[15] 4544[12]

Zor (FR) *T Larriviere* a83 83
3 ch c Tot Ou Tard(IRE) Kirklandi (TUR) (Majorien)
4274a[6]

Zorro's Blade *Michael Mullineaux*
5 b g Needwood Blade Beechy Bank (IRE) (Shareef Dancer (USA))
5469[9] 5892[12]

Zugzwang (IRE) *Ed de Giles* a73 69
2 b c Kodiac Kris's Bank (Inchinor)
6169[7] 6590[6] 6923[3] 7252[6] (7782)

Zuhd (IRE) *William Haggas* a67
3 b g Cape Cross(IRE) Street Star (USA) (Street Cry (IRE))
6555[4] 7154[4]

Zumurudah (FR) *Mark Johnston* a71 80
2 b f Dubawi(IRE) Brianza (USA) (Thunder Gulch (USA))
4848[5] (6298) ◆ 6934[3] 7336[3]

Zurbriggen *Charlie Appleby* a62 81
3 ch c Raven's Pass(USA) Zanzibar (IRE) (In The Wings)
5720[2] 6555[7]

Zurigha (IRE) *Richard Hannon Snr* a100 108
3 b f Cape Cross(IRE) Noyelles (IRE) (Docksider (USA))
(1546) 2299a[4] 3460[24] 6327[6] (6796)

Zvarov (IRE) *J-C Rouget* a93
2 b c Elusive City(USA) Marie Rossa (Testa Rossa (AUS))
8143a[2]

Zygmunt (FR) *Mme M Bollack-Badel* 96
2 ch c Vespone(IRE) Zython (FR) (Kabool)
(7994a)

Zylpha (IRE) *H-A Pantall* a44 90
2 b f Elusive City(USA) Zaltana (USA) (Cherokee Run (USA))
5628a[10] 7570a[8]

INDEX TO MEETINGS FLAT 2013

† Abandoned
* All-Weather
(M) Mixed meeting

Leading Turf Flat Trainers 2013

(22nd March – 9th November 2013)

TRAINER	WINS–RUNS		2NDS	3RDS	4THS	WIN PRIZE	TOTAL PRIZE	£1 STAKE
Richard Hannon Snr	187–1130	17%	146	139	128	£2,923,741	£4,233,900	-276.75
A P O'Brien	13–80	16%	11	9	9	£2,700,650	£3,819,986	-9.06
Saeed bin Suroor	80–430	19%	68	54	43	£1,802,479	£2,492,082	-77.91
Mark Johnston	166–1176	14%	140	129	122	£1,619,887	£2,406,327	-278.13
Richard Fahey	147–1110	13%	142	126	127	£1,527,548	£2,344,899	-131.91
John Gosden	69–355	19%	60	47	38	£1,133,475	£1,817,076	-6.94
William Haggas	88–408	22%	69	60	45	£1,045,040	£1,775,610	-3.19
Sir Michael Stoute	68–326	21%	45	56	31	£1,112,280	£1,612,949	-70.35
Kevin Ryan	74–611	12%	52	62	56	£1,018,988	£1,500,222	-14.73
Andrew Balding	72–511	14%	60	71	54	£780,208	£1,200,157	+20.15
Roger Varian	66–301	22%	44	38	27	£796,347	£1,182,139	+32.95
Charles Hills	53–439	12%	66	54	59	£532,886	£1,171,545	-43.86
Roger Charlton	36–190	19%	24	27	20	£782,628	£1,073,759	-25.73
David O'Meara	105–701	15%	58	80	68	£693,826	£1,032,967	-57.45
J S Bolger	2–19	11%	4	0	3	£425,325	£995,906	-14.38
Ralph Beckett	46–286	16%	40	33	30	£545,621	£982,807	+11.33
Clive Cox	27–264	10%	31	32	35	£792,554	£971,457	-62.84
Luca Cumani	52–266	20%	51	32	30	£525,082	£937,366	-63.07
Charlie Appleby	38–209	18%	29	22	27	£587,527	£836,319	-23.11
James Fanshawe	26–130	20%	13	23	14	£502,037	£799,711	+37.46
Lady Cecil	29–128	23%	27	13	14	£581,316	£781,903	+32.30
Mick Channon	60–739	8%	98	99	93	£325,926	£752,219	-349.43
Tim Easterby	59–794	7%	67	68	79	£450,285	£748,955	-354.13
David Simcock	51–299	17%	39	41	33	£404,079	£744,559	+55.78
Brian Ellison	43–383	11%	47	42	33	£275,783	£708,819	-27.44
Edward Lynam	4–14	29%	1	3	1	£497,077	£696,811	+12.00
Marco Botti	33–270	12%	38	38	29	£345,702	£656,610	-73.26
Mrs K Burke	29–205	14%	34	31	24	£213,960	£644,864	-53.03
Ed Dunlop	35–256	14%	41	21	28	£325,943	£641,305	-40.44
David Barron	55–300	18%	38	26	20	£368,919	£626,037	+31.51
A Wohler	1–6	17%	0	1	0	£603,962	£624,137	+1.50
Michael Bell	32–349	9%	46	42	39	£191,300	£484,296	-163.06
Jim Goldie	34–350	10%	31	45	45	£210,353	£444,211	-86.41
Tom Dascombe	34–263	13%	33	38	27	£245,171	£386,144	-109.44
Brian Meehan	29–258	11%	31	32	30	£179,247	£381,614	-74.15
Robert Cowell	7–154	5%	15	13	20	£261,333	£381,531	-47.80
Clive Brittain	15–158	9%	17	20	18	£186,377	£370,456	-13.05
Michael Dods	39–345	11%	40	32	41	£208,258	£365,465	-10.97
David Wachman	1–10	10%	0	5	1	£77,375	£343,410	-5.67
Mme C Barande-Barbe	0–2	—	1	0	1	£0	£336,584	-2.00
David Nicholls	38–419	9%	51	37	37	£168,632	£331,009	-128.88
Jeremy Noseda	29–156	19%	25	17	15	£197,364	£328,855	+0.76
Ian Williams	29–195	15%	22	22	24	£180,246	£315,142	+38.67
Henry Candy	20–171	12%	20	20	27	£133,300	£311,256	-37.92
Michael Easterby	36–371	10%	33	25	22	£181,165	£310,380	-66.88
M F De Kock	3–18	17%	5	0	3	£87,900	£291,714	-4.50
Bryan Smart	20–232	9%	26	22	28	£165,792	£277,356	-98.2
Sir Henry Cecil	15–70	21%	14	8	9	£181,118	£275,558	+13.81
Ed McMahon	14–139	10%	18	18	20	£153,825	£275,344	-20.22
David Elsworth	17–113	15%	16	19	6	£157,233	£271,796	-2.41

Flat Jockeys Championship 2013

(22nd March – 9th November 2013)

JOCKEY	WINS–RUNS		2NDS	3RDS	4THS	WIN PRIZE	TOTAL PRIZE	£1 STAKE
Richard Hughes	203–995	20%	169	130	90	£3,104,247	£4,106,563	-168.32
Ryan Moore	186–879	21%	133	132	100	£2,938,246	£4,476,063	-100.86
Silvestre De Sousa	153–789	19%	105	80	74	£2,115,791	£2,686,877	+74.33
William Buick	115–647	18%	94	73	60	£1,407,236	£2,544,817	-53.93
Luke Morris	109–925	12%	101	108	110	£437,249	£746,840	-274.95
Joe Fanning	109–852	13%	113	104	90	£896,864	£1,406,303	-242.68
Paul Hanagan	107–719	15%	91	81	86	£970,237	£1,866,071	-131.78
Neil Callan	105–647	16%	83	84	62	£884,948	£1,212,208	-43.02
Graham Lee	99–896	11%	94	103	105	£719,562	£1,293,093	-280.69
Jim Crowley	99–673	15%	85	72	56	£625,088	£1,226,068	-24.13
Adam Kirby	88–644	14%	79	91	75	£1,001,490	£1,302,298	-25.97
Andrea Atzeni	86–624	14%	92	68	79	£920,021	£1,375,221	+23.66
Jamie Spencer	84–561	15%	83	69	62	£806,521	£1,922,296	-158.75
Daniel Tudhope	84–498	17%	50	70	56	£483,080	£787,152	-52.58
James Doyle	82–602	14%	79	78	69	£1,201,137	£1,761,236	-106.40
Dane O'Neill	76–515	15%	62	65	68	£401,239	£685,275	-35.11
George Baker	74–489	15%	66	49	52	£660,617	£891,634	-14.25
Mickael Barzalona	74–358	21%	55	47	34	£638,506	£1,146,170	-22.49
Tom Queally	72–637	11%	62	73	75	£967,321	£1,402,555	-165.90
Graham Gibbons	71–509	14%	62	49	42	£429,197	£662,748	-73.16
Franny Norton	70–466	15%	66	58	63	£452,021	£702,214	-42.33
Martin Harley	68–604	11%	80	80	67	£448,507	£855,551	-157.42
Paul Mulrennan	65–524	12%	63	56	57	£496,274	£721,368	-14.83
Kieren Fallon	61–537	11%	73	56	60	£564,351	£1,163,293	-131.99
P J McDonald	59–542	11%	65	59	52	£231,202	£363,111	-39.32
Robert Winston	59–510	12%	58	48	68	£480,591	£709,661	-128.47
Shane Kelly	55–456	12%	48	55	50	£197,775	£418,730	-40.49
Seb Sanders	54–416	13%	53	57	38	£304,033	£467,351	-40.52
Richard Kingscote	54–401	13%	52	51	52	£484,653	£741,813	-106.18
Tom Eaves	53–764	7%	86	71	73	£269,667	£483,599	-268.88
Tony Hamilton	52–461	11%	55	64	50	£447,543	£697,299	-144.64
David Probert	51–417	12%	55	51	41	£298,155	£585,597	+40.40
Jason Hart	51–369	14%	44	33	44	£194,610	£308,134	+30.94
Frederik Tylicki	50–441	11%	36	62	42	£219,807	£363,304	-58.65
Liam Keniry	47–579	8%	50	66	61	£351,152	£506,811	-204.04
Pat Dobbs	47–424	11%	50	32	60	£282,438	£455,593	-171.75
Sean Levey	44–410	11%	49	41	40	£189,812	£382,835	-98.37
Martin Lane	42–429	10%	43	39	46	£375,330	£518,247	-75.43
Cathy Gannon	41–499	8%	47	58	60	£153,414	£295,951	-181.17
Hayley Turner	41–304	13%	43	35	33	£216,621	£326,614	-77.86
Ted Durcan	40–399	10%	39	42	55	£161,143	£301,449	-157.11
Thomas Brown	40–240	17%	26	25	33	£177,126	£244,046	-2.97
Jimmy Quinn	39–445	9%	27	38	48	£150,847	£272,387	+0.00
Pat Cosgrave	39–360	11%	38	30	39	£144,438	£280,855	+15.44
Robert Havlin	39–357	11%	50	49	39	£303,340	£440,756	-145.62
Oisin Murphy	38–226	17%	22	28	21	£304,385	£376,309	+38.67
Liam Jones	37–331	11%	37	39	40	£329,455	£451,864	-109.54
Martin Dwyer	35–422	8%	43	40	49	£183,598	£327,243	-152.92
Andrew Mullen	35–389	9%	34	42	42	£170,621	£246,286	-40.27
Robert Tart	35–343	10%	43	52	33	£183,534	£306,941	-86.68

Leading Flat Owners 2013

(22nd March – 9th November 2013)

OWNER	WINS–RUNS		2NDS	3RDS	4THS	WIN PRIZE	TOTAL PRIZE
Godolphin	122–652	19%	99	77	72	£2,825,358	£3,888,299
Hamdan Al Maktoum	93–538	17%	93	63	60	£786,508	£1,588,137
Mrs John Magnier/Michael Tabor /Derrick Smith	4–28	14%	3	5	4	£932,785	£1,442,706
Sheikh Hamdan Bin Mohammed Al Maktoum	79–524	15%	60	59	50	£830,537	£1,118,739
HE Sh Joaan Bin Hamad Al Thani	8–25	32%	4	1	5	£919,823	£1,095,658
Derrick Smith & Mrs John Magnier /Michael Tabor	5–31	16%	5	2	3	£855,709	£1,046,541
K Abdullah	63–284	22%	36	44	34	£711,065	£1,043,519
Dr Marwan Koukash	42–400	11%	52	48	46	£481,669	£826,662
Mrs J Magnier/Michael Tabor /Derrick Smith/Joseph Allen	2–5	40%	1	1	0	£623,810	£752,690
D J Deer	6–43	14%	6	9	3	£570,019	£673,940
B Keswick	3–6	50%	2	0	0	£568,064	£625,044
Cheveley Park Stud	37–172	22%	28	24	16	£391,765	£614,211
Dr Christoph Berglar	1–1	100%	0	0	0	£603,962	£603,962
Alan G Craddock	4–13	31%	3	2	2	£572,599	£599,892
Mrs S Power	3–10	30%	1	2	1	£440,367	£595,512
Qatar Racing Limited	25–191	13%	22	23	25	£258,899	£585,949
Sheikh Mohammed Obaid Al Maktoum	18–70	26%	11	8	6	£285,811	£480,680
J L Rowsell & M H Dixon	2–4	50%	1	1	0	£264,410	£450,438
Saleh Al Homaizi & Imad Al Sagar	19–81	23%	13	11	7	£266,438	£437,905
Mrs J S Bolger	0–10	—	3	0	1	£0	£430,277
Saeed Manana	29–213	14%	27	30	28	£198,834	£407,306
HRH Princess Haya Of Jordan	14–62	23%	11	12	7	£238,570	£403,244
Hubert John Strecker	2–7	29%	1	1	2	£90,240	£390,866
Michael Tabor/Derrick Smith/Mrs John Magnier	2–23	9%	3	3	4	£76,559	£376,728
The Queen	16–76	21%	7	10	9	£337,541	£364,499
Sir Robert Ogden	16–72	22%	11	5	6	£273,023	£353,695
Sheikh Juma Dalmook Al Maktoum	16–84	19%	14	12	11	£230,116	£350,537
Jean-Claude-Alain Dupouy	0–2	—	1	0	1	£0	£336,584
Andrew Tinkler	10–82	12%	12	12	5	£149,913	£334,894
Lady Rothschild	13–80	16%	19	12	6	£154,787	£334,567
T R G Vestey	2–5	40%	1	0	0	£323,247	£324,595
Keith Brown	8–35	23%	3	2	4	£83,618	£322,837
Sir Evelyn De Rothschild	3–11	27%	2	2	1	£128,396	£312,532
J Allen/Mrs J Magnier/M Tabor/D Smith	2–2	100%	0	0	0	£296,593	£296,593
Mrs Angie Bailey	6–21	29%	0	1	1	£281,369	£283,963
W H Ponsonby	7–60	12%	7	10	6	£212,629	£276,726
Simon Gibson	1–11	9%	2	0	2	£60,481	£275,842
Johnnie Delta Racing	7–100	7%	8	17	11	£88,050	£263,626
Lord Lloyd-Webber	1–3	33%	0	1	0	£200,895	£254,695
Sultan Ali	9–40	23%	4	5	4	£166,944	£247,290
Sheikh Ahmed Al Maktoum	16–66	24%	7	10	4	£192,619	£234,251
Matt & Lauren Morgan	1–48	2%	7	4	4	£175,130	£232,618
Abdulla Al Mansoori	7–43	16%	2	3	6	£161,770	£229,805
Michael O'Flynn	0–6	—	0	3	0	£0	£224,830
Charles Wentworth	9–44	20%	7	5	6	£112,260	£206,240
J C Smith	6–88	7%	15	6	6	£102,910	£205,872
Manor Farm Stud & Miss S Hoare	2–7	29%	2	0	0	£177,219	£194,850
J K Shannon & M A Scaife	4–17	24%	1	1	3	£177,657	£192,282
Mrs Fitri Hay	9–93	10%	16	15	9	£89,264	£188,084
Sheikh Rashid Dalmook Al Maktoum	11–40	28%	6	5	3	£112,120	£188,057

Leading Flat Sires 2013

(22nd March – 9th November 2013)

STALLION	WINNERS–RUNNERS		WINS	RUNS	2ND	3RD	4TH	WIN PRIZE	TOTALPRIZE
Galileo	92–206	45%	135	698	99	102	77	£2,530,874	£4,569,210
Dubawi	39–106	37%	63	376	47	48	42	£1,493,090	£2,418,871
Dansili	49–123	40%	73	448	74	53	41	£1,595,408	£2,126,385
Teofilo	44–116	38%	66	437	64	62	52	£1,217,638	£2,122,962
Oasis Dream	68–148	46%	98	632	90	68	47	£1,531,571	£2,100,408
New Approach	28–79	35%	38	255	38	38	29	£1,041,577	£1,869,910
Pivotal	48–138	35%	65	580	59	52	66	£1,418,241	£1,788,688
Dark Angel	34–79	43%	56	440	67	49	47	£1,120,828	£1,583,775
Montjeu	30–97	31%	38	315	30	39	43	£1,174,344	£1,581,748
Acclamation	68–175	39%	86	778	87	108	79	£778,866	£1,317,842
Danehill Dancer	45–140	32%	54	540	79	70	48	£672,089	£1,306,418
Cape Cross	59–143	41%	95	575	69	62	58	£932,486	£1,264,260
Dutch Art	40–108	37%	66	418	41	48	39	£810,983	£1,253,981
Invincible Spirit	62–190	33%	81	688	76	74	74	£633,218	£1,237,727
Shamardal	49–121	40%	73	544	74	59	76	£713,155	£1,226,137
War Front	4–9	44%	9	27	6	4	0	£1,025,848	£1,223,675
Authorized	32–92	35%	45	305	36	29	34	£817,858	£1,056,948
Kyllachy	45–122	37%	64	635	77	75	64	£632,682	£1,056,622
Choisir	19–65	29%	32	334	33	27	44	£815,717	£1,009,428
Monsun	10–27	37%	13	75	8	6	7	£895,725	£991,804
Exceed And Excel	53–155	34%	72	655	67	64	84	£617,579	£935,516
Rock Of Gibraltar	34–117	29%	53	489	46	58	52	£383,284	£926,465
Holy Roman Emperor	48–118	41%	59	541	69	56	61	£522,002	£924,601
Iffraaj	27–97	28%	40	427	47	41	38	£519,870	£816,724
Red Clubs	21–68	31%	28	339	35	42	33	£669,190	£809,392
High Chaparral	20–96	21%	26	310	32	34	37	£355,538	£725,952
Clodovil	29–79	37%	40	376	52	43	32	£367,985	£724,311
Footstepsinthesand	42–103	41%	58	454	59	64	44	£442,433	£713,423
Kodiac	36–94	38%	50	419	59	48	37	£430,719	£664,796
Bahamian Bounty	39–133	29%	55	611	64	66	65	£388,238	£664,457
Lawman	25–76	33%	37	301	29	41	37	£416,375	£663,132
Royal Applause	51–139	37%	68	656	80	79	60	£360,838	£626,789
Medicean	33–97	34%	48	440	57	44	40	£381,001	£620,398
Verglas	38–111	34%	53	482	48	52	55	£339,053	£582,698
Oratorio	37–101	37%	51	436	36	60	58	£389,840	£569,096
Dalakhani	24–109	22%	33	357	44	42	42	£248,567	£568,037
Manduro	25–75	33%	31	240	37	26	24	£326,825	£535,460
Byron	24–84	29%	33	354	32	42	41	£370,169	£525,106
Duke Of Marmalade	23–74	31%	33	268	25	31	38	£272,213	£505,079
Kheleyf	41–138	30%	52	601	57	53	79	£289,374	£500,902
Pastoral Pursuits	32–105	30%	45	447	48	54	41	£272,852	£499,062
King's Best	14–43	33%	22	213	21	19	32	£357,103	£483,859
Mastercraftsman	17–53	32%	25	166	26	22	18	£346,109	£479,654
Excellent Art	35–102	34%	44	394	34	41	48	£269,320	£456,405
Azamour	15–48	31%	25	179	19	14	15	£261,261	£455,159
Henrythenavigator	13–35	37%	19	145	23	18	14	£286,699	£443,051
Elusive Quality	16–43	37%	19	188	19	21	18	£265,417	£442,491
Intense Focus	12–48	25%	18	176	27	19	24	£325,412	£427,913
Street Cry	26–64	41%	34	233	20	36	25	£312,898	£425,482
Selkirk	19–50	38%	24	166	13	16	13	£296,453	£412,274

European Top Peformers

2yo RP Ratings

Horse	Trainer	RPR
Toormore	*Richard Hannon*	121
Kingston Hill	*Roger Varian*	119
War Command	*A P O'Brien*	118
Karakontie	*J E Pease*	117
Astaire	*Kevin Ryan*	116
Outstrip	*Charlie Appleby*	116
Cable Bay	*Charles Hills*	115
Giovanni Boldini	*A P O'Brien*	115
Hot Streak	*Kevin Ryan*	115
Chriselliam	*Charles Hills*	114
Ectot	*E Lellouche*	114
Sudirman	*David Wachman*	114
Australia	*A P O'Brien*	113
Rizeena	*Clive Brittain*	113
Vorda	*P Sogorb*	113
Big Time	*John Joseph Murphy*	112
Charm Spirit	*F Head*	112
Earnshaw	*A Fabre*	112
Kingman	*John Gosden*	112
Miss France	*A Fabre*	112
Prestige Vendome	*N Clement*	112
Berkshire	*Paul Cole*	111
Indonesienne	*C Ferland*	111
Jallota	*Mick Channon*	111
Kiyoshi	*Charles Hills*	111
Supplicant	*Richard Fahey*	111
Tapestry	*A P O'Brien*	111
Al Thakhira	*Marco Botti*	110
Anjaal	*Richard Hannon*	110
Brown Sugar	*Richard Hannon*	110
Johann Strauss	*A P O'Brien*	110
Justice Day	*David Elsworth*	110

3yo RP Ratings

Horse	Trainer	RPR
Treve	*Mme C Head-Maarek*	131
Toronado	*Richard Hannon*	129
Dawn Approach	*J S Bolger*	128
Olympic Glory	*Richard Hannon*	127
Ruler Of The World	*A P O'Brien*	126
Intello	*A Fabre*	125
Magician	*A P O'Brien*	123
Flintshire	*A Fabre*	121
Mars	*A P O'Brien*	121
Trading Leather	*J S Bolger*	121
Sky Lantern	*Richard Hannon*	120
Top Notch Tonto	*Brian Ellison*	120
Hillstar	*Sir Michael Stoute*	119
Battle Of Marengo	*A P O'Brien*	118
Galileo Rock	*David Wachman*	118
Kingsbarns	*A P O'Brien*	118
Leading Light	*A P O'Brien*	118
Libertarian	*Mrs K Burke*	118
Penglai Pavilion	*A Fabre*	118
Vancouverite	*A Fabre*	118
Montiridge	*Richard Hannon*	117
Morandi	*J-C Rouget*	117
Mshawish	*M Delzangles*	117
Ocovango	*A Fabre*	117
Sky Hunter	*A Fabre*	117
Tres Blue	*H-A Pantall*	117
Chopin	*A Wohler*	116
Dundonnell	*Roger Charlton*	116
Integral	*Sir Michael Stoute*	116
Manndawi	*A De Royer-Dupre*	116
Maputo	*Mark Johnston*	116
Reckless Abandon	*Clive Cox*	116

4yo+ RP Ratings

Horse	Trainer	RPR
Farhh	*Saeed bin Suroor*	126
St Nicholas Abbey	*A P O'Brien*	126
Al Kazeem	*Roger Charlton*	124
Mukhadram	*William Haggas*	123
Declaration Of War	*A P O'Brien*	122
Dunaden	*M Delzangles*	121
Ektihaam	*Roger Varian*	121
Novellist	*A Wohler*	121
Pastorius	*Mario Hofer*	121
Camelot	*A P O'Brien*	120
Maxios	*J E Pease*	120
Aljamaaheer	*Roger Varian*	119
Planteur	*Marco Botti*	119
Thomas Chippendale	*Lady Cecil*	119
Gregorian	*John Gosden*	118
Les Beaufs	*Mme V Seignoux*	118
Trade Storm	*David Simcock*	118
Amaron	*Andreas Lowe*	117
Dandino	*Marco Botti*	117
Mandour	*A De Royer-Dupre*	117
Mull Of Killough	*Jane Chapple-Hyam*	117
Saga Dream	*F Lemercier*	117
Sovereign Debt	*Michael Bell*	117
Trumpet Major	*Richard Hannon*	117
Altano	*A Wohler*	116
Guest Of Honour	*Marco Botti*	116
Willing Foe	*Saeed bin Suroor*	116
Zinabaa	*Mlle T Puitg*	116
Domeside	*M Delcher Sanchez*	115
Fencing	*John Gosden*	115
Grace Lady	*Mlle T Puitg*	115
Red Cadeaux	*Ed Dunlop*	115

2yo Speed Ratings

Horse	Trainer	Rating
Indonesienne	*C Ferland*	116
Hot Streak	*Kevin Ryan*	115
Lesstalk In Paris	*J-C Rouget*	115
Queen Catrine	*Charles Hills*	113
Royalmania	*F Head*	113
Stormyra	*J-P Gallorini*	113
War Command	*A P O'Brien*	113
Wonderfully	*A P O'Brien*	113
Toast Of New York	*Jamie Osborne*	112
Miss France	*A Fabre*	111
Sandiva	*Richard Fahey*	111
Tapestry	*A P O'Brien*	111
Al Thakhira	*Marco Botti*	110
Astaire	*Kevin Ryan*	110
Cable Bay	*Charles Hills*	110
Lightning Thunder	*Olly Stevens*	110
Perhaps	*A P O'Brien*	109
Piping Rock	*Richard Hannon*	109
Sudirman	*David Wachman*	109
Toormore	*Richard Hannon*	109
Anjaal	*Richard Hannon*	108
Australia	*A P O'Brien*	108
Avenue Gabriel	*P D Deegan*	108
Big Time	*John Joseph Murphy*	108
Coach House	*A P O'Brien*	108
Extortionist	*Olly Stevens*	108
Flying Jib	*D K Weld*	108
Kingston Hill	*Roger Varian*	108
Outstrip	*Charlie Appleby*	108
Reroute	*Ed Walker*	108
Steventon Star	*Richard Hannon*	108
Anticipated	*Richard Hannon*	107

3yo Speed Ratings

Horse	Trainer	Rating
Toronado	*Richard Hannon*	122
Trading Leather	*J S Bolger*	122
Dawn Approach	*J S Bolger*	121
Hillstar	*Sir Michael Stoute*	119
Treve	*Mme C Head-Maarek*	119
Zurigha	*Richard Hannon*	117
Olympic Glory	*Richard Hannon*	116
Ruler Of The World	*A P O'Brien*	116
Telescope	*Sir Michael Stoute*	116
Al Waab	*Lady Cecil*	115
Hot Snap	*Lady Cecil*	115
Intello	*A Fabre*	115
Leading Light	*A P O'Brien*	115
Libertarian	*Mrs K Burke*	115
Magician	*A P O'Brien*	115
Ninjago	*Richard Hannon*	115
Thouwra	*Saeed bin Suroor*	115
Van Der Neer	*Richard Hannon*	115
Bin Singspiel	*James Tate*	114
Feel Like Dancing	*John Gosden*	114
Intibaah	*Brian Meehan*	114
Lanansaak	*Roger Varian*	114
Luhaif	*Mick Channon*	114
Magical Dream	*A P O'Brien*	114
Maputo	*Mark Johnston*	114
Say	*A P O'Brien*	114
The United States	*A P O'Brien*	114
Battle Of Marengo	*A P O'Brien*	113
Boite	*Peter Chapple-Hyam*	113
Brigh	*David Simcock*	113
Elleval	*David Marnane*	113
Flotilla	*M Delzangles*	113

4yo+ Speed Ratings

Horse	Trainer	Rating
Planteur	*Marco Botti*	124
Miblish	*Clive Brittain*	123
Farhh	*Saeed bin Suroor*	121
Tepmokea	*Mrs K Burke*	121
Farraaj	*Roger Varian*	120
Cai Shen	*Richard Hannon*	119
Robin Hoods Bay	*Ed Vaughan*	119
Tinshu	*Derek Haydn Jones*	118
Emerald Wilderness	*Mark Rimmer*	117
Maxios	*J E Pease*	117
Novellist	*A Wohler*	117
Sovereign Debt	*Michael Bell*	117
Aljamaaheer	*Roger Varian*	116
Dunaden	*M Delzangles*	116
Field Of Dream	*Jamie Osborne*	116
Lily's Angel	*G M Lyons*	116
Marcret	*Marco Botti*	116
Premio Loco	*Chris Wall*	116
Swing Alone	*Gay Kelleway*	116
Al Kazeem	*Roger Charlton*	115
Aquilonius	*Stuart Williams*	115
Arsaadi	*William Haggas*	115
Grey Mirage	*Marco Botti*	115
Haya Landa	*Mme L Audon*	115
Ladies Are Forever	*Geoffrey Oldroyd*	115
Mandour	*A De Royer-Dupre*	115
Piscean	*Tom Keddy*	115
Cirrus Des Aigles	*Mme C Barande-Barbe*	114
Declaration Of War	*A P O'Brien*	114
Domeside	*M Delcher Sanchez*	114
Don Bosco	*D Smaga*	114
George Guru	*Michael Attwater*	114

Raceform Median Times 2013

ASCOT	
5f	1m 0.5
5f 110y	1m 08.3
6f	1m 14.5
6f 110y	1m 21.0
7f	1m 27.6
1m Str	1m 40.8
1m Rnd	1m 40.7
1m 2f	2m 7.4
1m 4f	2m 32.5
2m	3m 29.0
2m 4f	4m 24.8
2m 5f 159y	4m 49.4

AYR	
5f	59.4s
6f	1m 12.4
7f 50y	1m 33.4
1m	1m 43.8
1m 1f 20y	1m 57.5
1m 2f	2m 12.0
1m 5f 13y	2m 54.0
1m 7f	3m 20.4
2m 1f 105y	3m 59.7

BATH	
5f 11y	1m 2.5
5f 161y	1m 11.2
1m 5y	1m 40.8
1m 2f 46y	2m 11.0
1m 3f 144y	2m 30.6
1m 5f 22y	2m 52.0
2m 1f 34y	3m 51.9

BEVERLEY	
5f	1m 3.5
7f 100y	1m 33.8
1m 100y	1m 47.6
1m 1f 207y	2m 7.0
1m 4f 16y	2m 39.8
2m 35y	3m 39.8

BRIGHTON	
5f 59y	1m 2.3
5f 213y	1m 10.2
6f 209y	1m 23.1
7f 214y	1m 36.0
1m 1f 209y	2m 3.6
1m 3f 196y	2m 32.7

CARLISLE	
5f	1m 0.8
5f 193y	1m 13.7
6f 192y	1m 27.1
7f 200y	1m 40.0
1m 1f 61y	1m 57.6
1m 3f 107y	2m 23.1
1m 6f 32y	3m 7.5
2m 1f 52y	3m 53.0

CATTERICK	
5f	59.8s
5f 212y	1m 13.6
7f	1m 27.0
1m 3f 214y	2m 38.9
1m 5f 175y	3m 3.6
1m 7f 177y	3m 32.0

CHEPSTOW	
5f 16y	59.3s
6f 16y	1m 12.0
7f 16y	1m 23.2
1m 14y	1m 36.2
1m 2f 36y	2m 10.6
1m 4f 23y	2m 39.0
2m 49y	3m 38.9
2m 2f	4m 3.6

CHESTER	
5f 16y	1m 1.0
5f 110y	1m 6.2
6f 18y	1m 13.8
7f 2y	1m 26.5
7f 122y	1m 33.8
1m 2f 75y	2m 11.2
1m 3f 79y	2m 24.8
1m 4f 66y	2m 38.5
1m 5f 89y	2m 52.7
1m 7f 195y	3m 28.0
2m 2f 147y	4m 4.8

DONCASTER	
5f	1m 0.5
5f 140y	1m 8.8
6f	1m 13.6
6f 110y	1m 19.9
7f	1m 26.3
1m Str	1m 39.3
1m Rnd	1m 39.7
1m 2f 60y	2m 9.4
1m 4f	2m 34.9
1m 6f 132y	3m 7.4
2m 110y	3m 40.4
2m 2f	3m 55.0

EPSOM	
5f	55.7s
6f	1m 9.4
7f	1m 23.3
1m 114y	1m 46.1
1m 2f 18y	2m 9.7
1m 4f 10y	2m 38.9

FFOS LAS	
5f	58.3s
6f	1m 10.0
1m	1m 41.0
1m 2f	2m 9.4
1m 4f	2m 37.4
1m 6f	3m 3.8
2m	3m 30.0

GOODWOOD	
5f	1m 0.2
6f	1m 12.2
7f	1m 27.0
1m	1m 39.9
1m 1f	1m 56.3
1m 1f 192y	2m 8.1
1m 3f	2m 26.5
1m 4f	2m 38.4
1m 6f	3m 3.6
2m	3m 29.0
2m 5f	4m 31.0

HAMILTON	
5f 4y	1m
6f 5y	1m 12.2
1m 65y	1m 48.4
1m 1f 36y	1m 59.7
1m 3f 16y	2m 25.6
1m 4f 17y	2m 38.6
1m 5f 9y	2m 53.9

HAYDOCK	
5f (inner)	1m 0.8
5f (outer)	1m 0.8
6f (inner)	1m 13.8
6f (outer)	1m 13.8
7f	1m 30.7
1m	1m 43.7
1m 2f 95y	2m 15.5
1m 3f 200y	2m 33.8
1m 6f	3m 2.0
2m 45y	3m 34.3

KEMPTON AW	
5f	1m 0.5
6f	1m 13.1
7f	1m 26.0
1m	1m 39.8
1m 2f	2m 8.0
1m 3f	2m 21.9
1m 4f	2m 34.5
2m	3m 30.1

LEICESTER	
5f 2y	1m
5f 218y	1m 13.0
7f 9y	1m 26.2
1m 60y	1m 45.1
1m 1f 218y	2m 7.9
1m 3f 183y	2m 33.9

LINGFIELD TURF	
5f	58.2s
6f	1m 11.2
7f	1m 23.3
7f 140y	1m 32.3
1m 1f	1m 56.6
1m 2f	2m 10.5
1m 3f 106y	2m 31.5
1m 6f	3m 10.0
2m	3m 34.8

LINGFIELD AW	
5f	58.8s
6f	1m 11.9
7f	1m 24.8
1m	1m 38.2
1m 2f	2m 6.6
1m 4f	2m 33.0
1m 5f	2m 46.0
2m	3m 25.7

MUSSELBURGH	
5f	1m 0.4
7f 30y	1m 29.0
1m	1m 41.2
1m 1f	1m 53.9
1m 4f	2m 39.7
1m 4f 100y	2m 42.0
1m 5f	2m 52.0
1m 6f	3m 5.3
2m	3m 33.5

NEWBURY	
5f 34y	1m 1.4
6f 8y	1m 13.0
6f 110y	1m 19.3
7f	1m 25.7
1m (str)	1m 39.7
1m 7y (rnd)	1m 38.7
1m 1f	1m 55.5
1m 2f 6y	2m 8.8
1m 3f 5y	2m 21.2
1m 4f 5y	2m 35.5
1m 5f 61y	2m 52.0
2m	3m 32.0

NEWCASTLE	
5f	1m 1.1
6f	1m 14.6
7f	1m 27.8
1m Rnd	1m 45.3
1m 3y Str	1m 43.4
1m 1f 9y	1m 58.1
1m 2f 32y	2m 11.9
1m 4f 93y	2m 45.6
1m 6f 97y	3m 11.3
2m 19y	3m 39.4

NEWMARKET ROWLEY	
5f	59.1s
6f	1m 12.2
7f	1m 25.4
1m	1m 38.6
1m 1f	1m 51.7
1m 2f	2m 5.8
1m 4f	2m 32.0
1m 6f	2m 57.0
2m	3m 30.5
2m 2f	3m 56.8

NEWMARKET JULY	
5f	59.1s
6f	1m 12.5
7f	1m 25.7
1m	1m 40.0
1m 2f	2m 5.5
1m 4f	2m 32.9
1m5f	2m 44.0
1m 6f 175y	3m 8.4
2m 24y	3m 27.0

NOTTINGHAM	
5f 13y	1m 1.5
6f 15y	1m 14.7
1m 75y	1m 49.0
1m 2f 50y	2m 14.3
1m 6f 15y	3m 7.0
2m 9y	3m 34.5

PONTEFRACT	
5f	1m 3.3
6f	1m 16.9
1m 4y	1m 45.9
1m 2f 6y	2m 13.7
1m 4f 8y	2m 40.8
2m 1f 22y	3m 44.6
2m 1f 216y	3m 56.2
2m 5f 122y	4m 51.0

REDCAR	
5f	58.6s
6f	1m 11.8
7f	1m 24.5
1m	1m 38.0
1m 1f	1m 53.0
1m 2f	2m 7.1
1m 3f	2m 21.7
1m 6f 19y	3m 4.7
2m 4y	3m 31.4

RIPON	
5f	1m 0.7
6f	1m 13.0
1m	1m 41.4
1m 1f	1m 54.7
1m 1f 170y	2m 5.4
1m 4f 10y	2m 36.7
2m	3m 31.8

SALISBURY	
5f	1m 1.0
6f	1m 14.8
6f 212y	1m 28.6
1m	1m 43.5
1m 1f 198y	2m 9.9
1m 4f	2m 38.0
1m 6f 21y	3m 7.4

SANDOWN	
5f 6y	1m 1.6
7f 16y	1m 29.5
1m 14y	1m 43.3
1m 1f	1m 55.7
1m 2f 7y	2m 10.5
1m 6f	3m 4.5
2m 78y	3m 38.7

SOUTHWELL AW	
5f	59.7s
6f	1m 16.5
7f	1m 30.3
1m	1m 43.7
1m 3f	2m 28.0
1m 4f	2m 41.0
1m 6f	3m 8.3
2m	3m 45.5

THIRSK	
5f	59.6s
6f	1m 12.7
7f	1m 27.2
1m	1m 40.1
1m 4f	2m 36.2
2m	3m 28.3

WARWICK	
5f	59.6s
5f 110y	1m 5.9
6f	1m 11.8
7f 26y	1m 24.6
1m 22y	1m 41.0
1m 2f 188y	2m 21.1
1m 4f 134y	2m 44.6
1m 6f 213y	3m 19.0
2m 39y	3m 33.8

WINDSOR	
5f 10y	1m 0.3
6f	1m 13.0
1m 67y	1m 44.7
1m 2f 7y	2m 8.7
1m 3f 135y	2m 29.5

WOLVERHAMPTON AW	
5f 20y	1m 2.3
5f 216y	1m 15.0
7f 32y	1m 29.6
1m 141y	1m 50.5
1m 1f 103y	2m 1.7
1m 4f 50y	2m 41.1
1m 5f 194y	3m 6.0
2m 119y	3m 41.8

YARMOUTH	
5f 43y	1m 2.7
6f 3y	1m 14.4
7f 3y	1m 26.6
1m 3y	1m 40.6
1m 1f	1m 55.8
1m 2f 21y	2m 10.5
1m 3f 101y	2m 28.7
1m 6f 17y	3m 7.6
2m	3m 32.4

YORK	
5f	59.3s
5f 89y	1m 4.1
6f	1m 11.9
7f	1m 25.3
1m	1m 39.8
1m 208y	1m 52.0
1m 2f 88y	2m 12.5
1m 4f	2m 33.2
1m 6f	3m 0.2
2m 88y	3m 34.5
2m 2f	3m 55.4

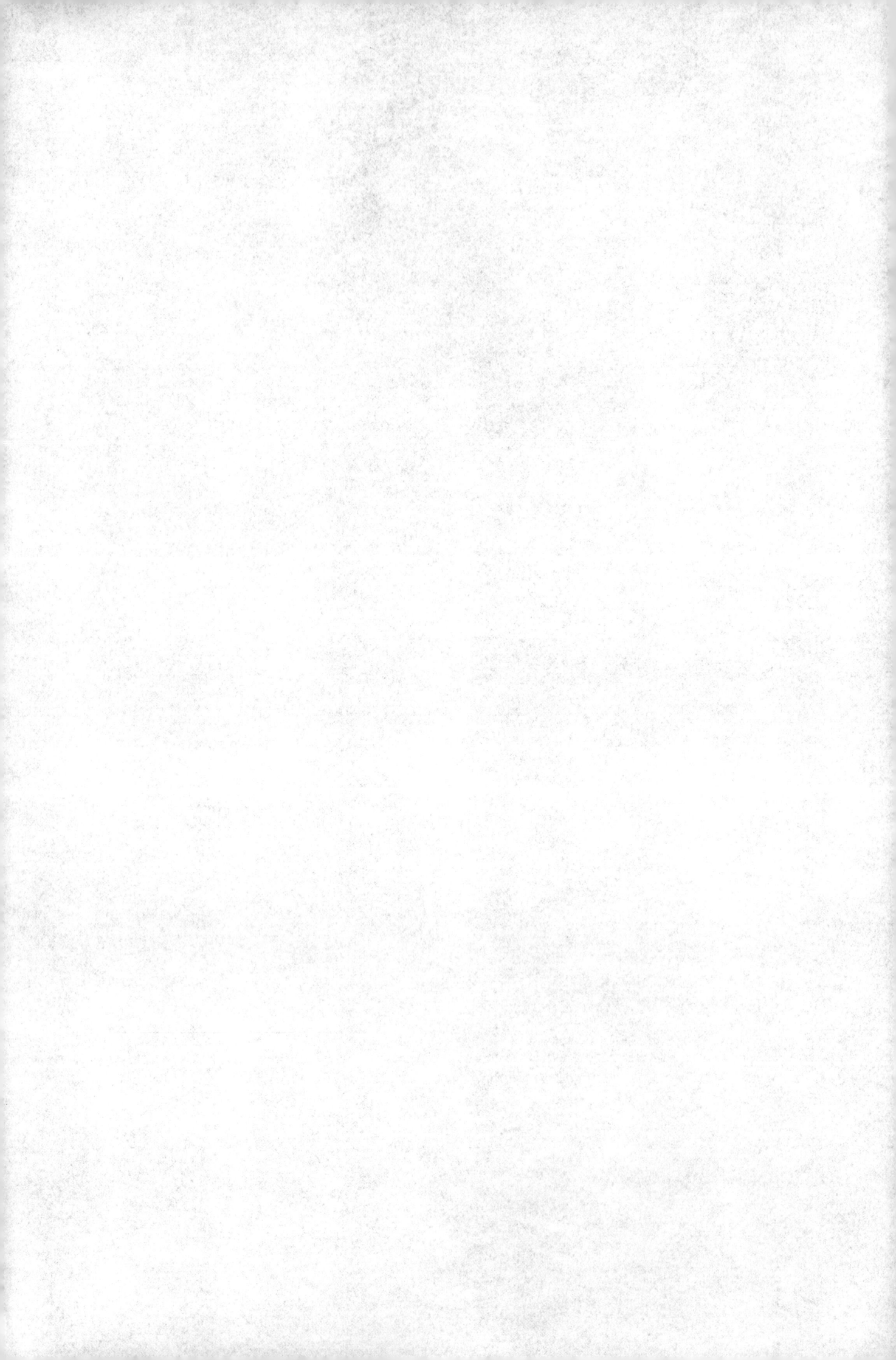